The Oxford Russian Dictionary

The Oxford Russian Dictionary

Third edition

Russian–English

Edited by
Marcus Wheeler and Boris Unbegaun

English–Russian

Edited by
Paul Falla

Revised and updated by
Della Thompson

OXFORD
UNIVERSITY PRESS

OXFORD
UNIVERSITY PRESS
Great Clarendon Street, Oxford OX2 6DP
Oxford University Press is a department of the University of Oxford.
It furthers the University's objective of excellence in research, scholarship,
and education by publishing worldwide in
Oxford New York
Auckland Bangkok Buenos Aires Cape Town Chennai
Dar es Salaam Delhi Hong Kong Istanbul Karachi Kolkata
Kuala Lumpur Madrid Melbourne Mexico City Mumbai Nairobi
São Paulo Shanghai Singapore Taipei Tokyo Toronto
and an associated company in Berlin
Oxford is a registered trade mark of Oxford University Press
in the UK and in certain other countries
Published in the United States
by Oxford University Press Inc., New York

First edition Russian/English 1972
First edition English/Russian 1984
Second edition published in one volume 1993
Revised with corrections 1997
Third edition 2000

British Library Cataloguing in Publication Data
Data available
Library of Congress Cataloging in Publication Data
Data available
ISBN 0-19-860160-3
10 9 8 7 6 5 4
Typeset in Nimrod and Arial
by Tradespools Ltd., Frome
Printed in Italy
by La Tipografica Varese S.p.A.

Contents

Project Team

Managing Editor Della Thompson

Data Capture Manager Chris Cowley

Keyboarding Assistants Vivian Thiele, Lida Birch, Janet Phillips

Critical Readers Albina Ozieva, Olga Stott, Vera Konnova, Elena Cook

Assistant Editor Andrew Hodgson

Proofreaders George Tulloch, Maree Airlie, Sandra Harper, Simon Beattie

Other Contributors Alexander Levtov, Vladimir Raivitch, Ilona Stole, Alexander Stoliarchuk, James Davie, Lucy Popova, Kevin Windle

Technical Support Sid Siddle, Ken Moore

Preface

This third edition of the *Oxford Russian Dictionary* is based on the text of the earlier editions, but it has been enhanced in several important ways.

Firstly, while the earlier editions were aimed particularly at the English native speaker, this one has been made much more useful to the Russian native speaker, chiefly by greatly expanding the provision of sense indicators in the Russian-English half of the dictionary, and by providing inflectional information for English headwords in the English-Russian half of the dictionary.

Secondly, much more information is now given about American spelling and usage with the labels *US* and *Br.* employed extensively throughout the text. This makes the dictionary more user-friendly to its American audience as well as benefiting the Russian native speaker who wishes to use or understand American English.

Thirdly, the text has been updated to reflect the changes that have taken place in the Russian language in recent years, resulting from the demise of the Communist regime, the introduction of Western institutions and terminology, and the influx of Western goods and ideas.

Finally, the entire text has been critically read by Russian native speakers in order to improve the quality of the word list and translations as a whole.

DELLA THOMPSON

December 1999

Guide to the use of the Dictionary

Russian-English Section

Presentation

1. The following devices are used to save space:

(i) The first letter of the headword, followed by a full point, represents the whole headword. Thus:

това́рный ... **т. соста́в** (= **това́рный соста́в**)

(ii) The swung dash, in conjunction with a vertical stroke, represents that part of the headword which is to the left of the vertical stroke. Thus:

роди́м|ый ... **~ое пятно́** (= **роди́мое пятно́**)

exceptions: the swung dash is not used in indicating the genitive singular of nouns or the 1st and 2nd persons singular of the present tense of verbs with unchanged stress (for examples, see below: *Grammatical Information: Nouns and Verbs*); and, in cross-references from the imperfective to the perfective verbal aspect, it may, when preceded by a prefix, represent the entire headword. Thus:

ста́|рить, ю, ишь *impf.* (of **со~**) ... (= of **соста́рить**)

Pronunciation

2. With the general exception of monosyllables, stress is indicated for every Russian word. A stress mark above the swung dash, where this sign represents two or more syllables, indicates shift of stress to the syllable immediately preceding the vertical stroke dividing the headword. Thus:

запи|са́ть, шу́, ~́шешь ... (= **запишу́, запи́шешь**)

3. Conversely, a stress mark above a syllable to the right of the swung dash indicates shift of stress away from the syllable(s) represented by the swung dash. Thus:

а́дрес, а, *pl.* **~а́** ... (= **адреса́**)

4. Where a variant stress is permissible, both variants are shown. Thus:

скобл|и́ть, ю́, ~́ишь (= **ско́блишь** *or* **скобли́шь**)

Meaning

5. Separate meanings of a word are indicated by means of Arabic numerals. Thus:

безда́рность ... **1** lack of talent. **2** person without talent.

6. Shades of meaning, represented by translations not considered strictly synonymous, are indicated by means of a semicolon, whereas translations considered synonymous are indicated by a comma. Thus:

боля́чка ... sore; scab.

газо́н ... grassed area, lawn.

7. Homonyms are indicated by repetition of the headword as a separate entry, followed by a superscript Arabic numeral. Thus:

газ¹, а *m.* gas.

газ², а *m.* gauze.

It should be noted that there is no accepted all-embracing criterion for differentiating homonymy from polysemy (plurality of meanings of a single word) or 'meaning' from 'shade of meaning'.

Explanation

8. Where necessary for the avoidance of ambiguity, explanatory glosses are given in brackets in italic type. Thus:

интерпрета́тор, а *m.* interpreter (*expounder*). [i.e. *not* translator]

9. This device is used in particular in the case of words denoting specifically Russian or Soviet concepts (e.g. **ка́ша, микрорайо́н, толка́ч**) and makes it possible to use one-word transliterations rather than clumsy paraphrases as a substitute for translation.

10. Indications of style or usage are given, where appropriate, in brackets. Thus:

(*coll.*), (*dial.*); (*fig.*), (*joc.*); (*agric.*), (*pol.*), etc.

Grammatical Information

11. The following grammatical information is given:

Nouns

The genitive singular ending and gender of all nouns are shown. Thus:

мо́лот, а *m.* hammer.

мо́лни|я, и *f.* lightning.

молок|о́, а́ *nt.* milk.

пья́ниц|а, ы *c.g.* drunkard.

Other case endings are shown where declension or stress is, in relation to generally accepted systems of classification, irregular.

Thus:

англича́н|ин, ина, *pl.* **~е, ~** *m.* Englishman.

бор|ода́, оды́, *a.* **~́оду,** *pl.* **~́оды, ~о́д,** *d.* **~ода́м** *f.* beard.

(But the inserted vowel in the genitive plural ending of numerous feminine nouns with nominative singular ending **-ка** is not regarded as irregular, e.g. **англича́нка,** *g. pl.* **англича́нок.**)

Nouns ending **-ость** derived from adjectives have not always been included where an appropriate English rendering can be obtained by adding *-ness* to the corresponding adjective (e.g. **зо́ркий** ... sharp-sighted ... **зо́ркость** ... sharp-sightedness ...).

Where an abbreviation is marked (*indecl.*) this indicates that, although not usually declined, it may be declined in order to avoid ambiguity. Thus:

переда́ча информа́ции ТАССом (*opp.* **ТАССа** *or* **ТАССу**)

Adjectives

Only the masculine nominative singular of the full form of the adjective is shown. Endings of the short forms, where these are found, are shown in brackets. Thus:

глу́п|ый (~, ~а́, ~о) ...

The neuter short form ending is omitted where stress is as for the feminine. Thus:

нау́ч|ный (~ен, ~на)

Verbs

Endings are shown of the 1st and 2nd persons singular of the present tense (or of the 1st person only of verbs with infinitive ending **-ать, -ова́ть, -ять, -еть** which retain stem and stress unchanged throughout the present tense). Thus:

говор|и́ть, ю́, и́шь ...

чита́|ть, ю ...

Other endings of the present tense and endings of the past tense are shown where formation or stress is irregular. Thus:

ид|ти́, у́, ёшь, *past* **шёл, шла, шло** ...

стере́|чь, гу́, жёшь, гут, *past* **~̈г, ~гла́, ~гло́** ...

Participles and gerunds, and forms of the passive voice, are not shown unless they have special semantic or syntactical features. Verbal aspects: the imperfective aspect is normally treated as the basic form of the simple verb, a cross-reference to the relevant form being shown in brackets. Thus:

чита́|ть, ю *impf.* (*of* **про~**) ...

The corresponding entry is:

прочита́|ть, ю *pf. of* **чита́ть**

In the case, however, of compound verbs formed by means of a prefix, the perfective aspect is treated as the basic form. Thus:

зачит|а́ть, а́ю *pf.* (*of* **~́ывать**) ...

Since, in a number of cases, a correspondence cannot, for semantic or other reasons, be firmly established (e.g. **иска́ть-сыска́ть**), the absence of a corresponding aspect is not necessarily noted.

Meanings and phraseology are shown under the basic form in each case unless peculiar to the other aspect.

Prefixes and Combining Forms

A number of prefixes and combining forms are shown as separate entries.

Thus:

до...[1] *vbl. pref.*

гидро... *comb. form* hydro-

сов... *comb form, abbr. of* **~е́тский**

Numerous compounded words, the meaning of which is judged sufficiently clear from a knowledge of the meaning of the prefix and the root word, have, to save space, been excluded from the dictionary.

English-Russian Section

Orthography

1. The English spelling follows British usage, with American variations also noted, e.g. **honour**... (*US* **honor**).

2. Russian cardinal numbers, given without 'tags' denoting inflection, are to be read in the nominative form. (This does not apply to year-dates.)

3. Secondary stress is not indicated in Russian words unless they are hyphenated (or unless the syllable in question contains the letter ё). If stress is optional, as between two vowels, an accent is placed on both. When prepositions attract the accent from a noun, or не from a verb, the fact is shown by a stress mark; otherwise monosyllables are not generally shown as stressed. A form such as брази́л|ец (*fem.* -ья́нка) means that the feminine noun is stressed on the penultimate only (cf. Paragraph 36 (iii)).

Pronunciation

4. For the convenience of users whose native language is not English, all headwords are transcribed into the International Phonetic Alphabet. An exception is made for those abbreviations, such as BBC, whose component letters are pronounced individually.

Transcriptions are supplied, however, where an abbreviation is pronounced in the same way as its expansion, e.g. **c.** meaning 'century'. In compound words where the second element is listed elsewhere, only the first element is generally transcribed.

A key to the phonetic symbols used is supplied below, immediately before the list of abbreviations used in the Dictionary.

Arrangement and presentation of entries: principal rules

5. These matters are explained in detail in paragraphs 10–40 below. Attention is drawn to the nesting principle (paragraph 21) and to the fact that compounds, whether hyphenated or written as one word, are listed under the first element and not the second: e.g. **pen-knife** under **pen**, not **knife**. As regards the placing of idioms see paragraph 22; and for the placing of labels such as *(coll.)* and *(sl.)* see paragraph 25.

Paragraphs 35–39 deal with the presentation of Russian grammatical information, including verb aspects.

6. Attention is also drawn to paragraphs 24–25 on the subject of usage labels and their position; and to the fact that the oblique stroke / signifies an alternative affecting *one* word on either side of it (paragraphs 30–32).

7. For the use of the vertical stroke and swung dash (~) see paragraphs 16–17; for the approximate sign (≈) see paragraph 25.

8. The gender of nouns in ь is marked only when they are masculine (paragraph 35 (*a*)).

9. Many Russian nouns have an adjectival form (e.g. го́род – городско́й) corresponding to the attributive use of their English equivalent. Such adjectives are frequently given under the English noun entry, preceded by the abbreviation '*attr.*'.

Presentation: detailed rules

10. Headwords are printed in bold roman type except for non-naturalized foreign words and expressions, for which bold italic is used. Alternative spellings (including American variants) are presented alongside the preferred spelling in full or abbreviated form, or shown in brackets: these variants appear again in alphabetical sequence (unless adjacent to the main entry), as cross-references. Thus:

cosy (*US* **cozy**) **cozy** = **cosy**
hicc|up, -ough
curts(e)y

11. Similar treatment is applied to words in which an alternative termination can be used without affecting the sense. Thus:

cumb|ersome, -rous; submer|gence, -sion

Here as elsewhere (paragraphs 16–17), a vertical stroke (divider) is placed after those letters which are common to both forms and which, in the alternative form as shown, are replaced by a hyphen.

12. Also presented as headwords are a few two-word expressions of which the first element does not qualify for an individual entry, e.g. **Boxing Day**, **Parkinson's disease**.

13. Separate headword entries with superscript numerals are made for words which, though identical in spelling, differ in basic meaning and origin (**fine** as noun and verb; **fine** as adjective and adverb), or in pronunciation and/or stress (**house** and **supplement** as nouns and as verbs), or both (**tear** meaning 'tear-drop' and **tear** meaning 'rip').

14. Separate entries for adverbs in '-ly' are made only when they have meanings or usage (idiom, compounds, etc.) which cannot conveniently be treated under the corresponding adjective. Examples are **hardly**, **really**, and **surely**. When there is no separate entry, and no instance of the adverb in the adjectival entry, it can be assumed that the corresponding Russian adverb is also formed regularly from the adjective. Thus **clumsy** неуклю́жий, нело́вкий implies that the Russian for 'clumsily' is неуклю́же and нело́вко; **critical** крити́ческий implies that 'critically' can be translated крити́чески, and so on.

15. Gerundial and participial forms of English verbs, used as nouns or adjectives, are often accommodated within the verb entry (transitive or intransitive as appropriate). Thus:

revolving doors is found under **revolve** *v.i.*

a retarded child is found under **retard** *v.t.*

but in certain cases, for the sake of clarity, such forms have been treated as independent headwords, e.g.

packing *n.*; **flying** *n.* and *adj.*; **barbed** *adj.*

16. Some headwords are divided by a vertical stroke in order that the unchanging letters preceding the stroke may subsequently be replaced, in inflected forms, by a swung dash. Where there is no divider, the swung dash represents the headword *in toto*, e.g.

house ... **keep ~** ... **~hold** ... **~hold word** ... **~-painter**

17. The vertical divider is also used in both English and Russian to separate the main part of a word from its termination when it is necessary to show modifications or alternative forms of the latter: e.g. paragraphs 10, 35 (*c*), and 36.

18. Within the headword entry each grammatical function has its own paragraph, introduced by a part-of-speech indicator (in this order); *n.*, *pron.*, *adj.*, *adv.*, *v.t.*, *v.i.*, *prep.*, *conj.*, *int.* A combined heading, e.g. **adagio** *n., adj., & adv.*, may sometimes be used for convenience; the most common instance is *v.t. & i.* when the two moods are not clearly distinguishable, or when the Russian intransitive is expressed by means of the suffix -ся.

19. Verb-adverb combinations forming phrasal verbs normally appear in a separate paragraph headed '*with advs.*', immediately following simple verb usage; they are given in alphabetical order of the adverb, transitive and intransitive usage within each phrasal verb being separated. Only when the possible combinations are very few and uncomplicated are they contained within the *v.t.* or *v.i.* paragraph.

20. There are also a few verbs (e.g. **go**) where idiomatic usage with prepositions is extensive and complex enough to call for a separate paragraph headed '*with preps.*'.

21. Hyphenated or single-word compounds in which the headword forms the first element are brought together or 'nested' under the headword in a final paragraph headed '*cpds.*'. Here the headword is represented by a swung dash, and the second element, in bold type, determines the alphabetical sequence. An exception is made to the 'nesting' principle in some cases where compounds are particularly numerous, e.g. those beginning with such elements as '**back**', '**by**', '**out**', '**over**', etc. Forms like '**bull's eye**' and '**Englishman**' (despite the reduced 'a') are treated as compounds.

Phrases such as '**labour exchange**' will generally be found in the main paragraph of the entry for the first noun, in some cases preceded by '*attr.*' (for 'attributive').

22. Adjective-noun expressions generally appear under the adjective unless this has relatively little weight, as in '**good riddance**'; but some may also be repeated under the noun, e.g. '**French bean**' and '**French horn**'. Idioms of a more complex nature, and proverbs, are generally entered under the first noun, but here too the rule is not inflexible and some duplication may be found.

23. Within an entry, differences of meaning or application are defined by synonym, context, or other means. Major differences may be distinguished by numerals in bold type. Thus:

gag *n.* **1** (*to prevent speech etc.*) ... (*parl.*) ... (*fig.*) ... **2** (*joke*) ...

24. A second type of label indicates status or level of usage: e.g. *arch*(aic), *liter*(ary), *coll*(oquial), *sl*(ang), *vulg*(ar). It may apply to the headword as a whole, to one of its functions or meanings, or to a single phrase or sentence, and is placed accordingly. Thus:

pep (*coll.*) *n.* ... *v.t.* (*usu.* **~ up**)

tart *n.* **1** (*flat pie*) ... **2** (*sl., prostitute*) ... *v.t.* **~ up** (*Br. coll., embellish*) ...

bell *n.* ... **that rings a ~** (*fig., coll.*)

25. In cases where Russian has an expression corresponding closely in level of usage to a given colloquialism, vulgarism, or slang term in English, the status label (*coll.*), (*sl.*), etc. is placed *after* the Russian, and should be understood to apply equally to the preceding English equivalent. In other cases a 'literary' (non-colloquial) Russian translation is given, and the status label is placed immediately after the English. Russian expressions, especially idioms or proverbs, which parallel rather than translate English ones are preceded by the symbol ≈.

26. The use of the comma or the semicolon to separate Russian words offered as translations of the same English word reflects a greater or lesser degree of equivalence; in the latter case an auxiliary English gloss is often used to express the nuance of difference. Thus:

inexhaustible *adj.* (*unfailing*) неистощи́мый, неисчерпа́емый; ... (*untiring*) неутоми́мый.

27. When shades of meaning of an adjective or verb have been defined in this way, and similar distinctions exist between derivative abstract nouns, the glosses are not usually repeated. Thus:

bookish *adj.* (*literary, studious*) кни́жный; (*pedantic*) педанти́чный.

bookishness *n.* кни́жность; педанти́чность.

28. To avoid ambiguity the semicolon is used when the alternatives are complete phrases or sentences, and also in most cases between synonymous verbs.

Thus:

what is he getting at? что он хо́чет сказа́ть?; куда́ он гнёт?

allow *v.t.* позв|оля́ть, -о́лить; разреш|а́ть, -и́ть.

Idiom and illustration

29. The examples of characteristic and idiomatic usage in both languages, which illustrate and supplement the standard Russian equivalents, may consist of phrases or finite sentences.

30. In both English and Russian there are many instances when one word in a phrase or sentence may be replaced by a synonymous alternative. This is shown by means of a comma or oblique stroke in English, and an oblique stroke in Russian.

Thus:

have, get one's hair cut стри́чься, по-.

my better half моя́ дража́йшая/лу́чшая полови́на.

lose one s hair (*lit.*) лысе́ть, об-/по- (either prefix may be used to form the perfective).

31. Non-synonymous alternatives are linked by the oblique stroke in *both* languages. Thus:

high/low tension высо́кое/ни́зкое напряже́ние.

32. In most cases the oblique stroke expresses an alternative on only one word on either side of it. Other alternatives are generally shown in the form (*or* ...). Thus:

the estate came (*or* was brought) under the hammer.

I could do with a drink я охо́тно (*or* с удово́льствием) вы́пил бы.

33. Optional extensions of words, phrases, or sentences, which may be included at discretion, e.g. for greater clarity, are shown within brackets, and in ordinary roman or Cyrillic type.

34. Italics within brackets are used for such matters as labels of meaning and usage (paragraphs 24–25) and in connection with Russian grammatical information (paragraph 35). Russian italics (without stress marks) are used for brief definitions or explanations of English terms which have no counterpart in Russian: see e.g. at **commuter**: also to specify noun-objects of certain verbs in order to limit their application to that implicit in the English, e.g.

wall up *v.t.* заде́л|ывать, -ать (*дверь, окно*).

Grammatical Information

35. The following grammatical information is given in respect of words offered as translations of headwords:

(a) the gender of *masculine* nouns ending in -ь, except when this is made clear by an accompanying adjective (e.g. **polar bear** бéлый медвéдь) or by the existence of a corresponding female form (see (*e*) below).

(b) the gender of nouns (e.g. neuters in -мя, masculines in -а and -я, foreign borrowings in -и and -у) whose final letter does not serve as an indicator of gender. Nouns of common gender are designated (*c.g.*). Indeclinable nouns are designated (*indecl.*), preceded by a gender indicator if required. The many adjectives used as nouns (e.g. портнóй) are not specially marked.

(c) the gender (or, for *pluralia tantum*, the genitive plural termination) and number (*pl.*) of all plural nouns which translate a headword or compound.

Thus:

timpani *n.* литáвры (*f. pl.*).

pliers *n.* щипц|ы́ (*pl.*, *g.* -óв); клéщ|и (*pl.*, *g.* -éй).

This information, however, is not given if the singular form has already appeared in the same entry, nor in the case of neuter plurals with an accompanying adjective, where the number and gender are self-evident from the terminations. Plurals of adjectives used substantivally are shown as (*pl.*).

(d) the nominative plural termination (-á or -я́) of certain masculine nouns when this form denotes a meaning different from that of the plural in -ы or -и, e.g.

icon ... óбраз (*pl.* -á).

(e) the forms of nouns used where Russian differs from English in making a verbal distinction between male and female. Thus:

teacher учи́тель (*fem.* -ница)

(f) aspectual information: see paragraphs 36–39 below.

(g) case usage with prepositions, e.g. **before** до+*g*.

(h) the case, with or without preposition, required to provide an equivalent to an English transitive verb. Thus:

attack *v.t.* нап|адáть, -áсть на+*a*.

If no case is thus indicated, it is to be taken that the Russian verb is transitive.

(i) When English and Russian terms are equivalent as they stand, but both may be regularly extended e.g. by a prepositional phrase, the Russian idiom may be made explicit as in (*h*), but in brackets. Thus:

conduce *v.i.* способствовать (*impf.*) (+*d.*)

(j) Use is also made of oblique cases of the Russian pronouns кто and что (in brackets and italics) to indicate case/preposition usage after a verb. Thus:

suit (*adapt*) *v.t.* приспос|áбливать, -óбить (*что к чему*); соглаcóв|ывать, -áть (*что с кем*)

Aspects

36. Aspectual information is given on all verbs (except быть, *impf.*) offered as renderings in infinitive form (except when they are subordinate to the finite verb in a sentence). If the verb is mono-aspectual, or used in a phrase to which only one aspect applies, it is designated either imperfective (*impf.*) or perfective (*pf.*) as the case may be.

With verbs of motion a distinction is made between determinate (*det.*) and indeterminate (*indet.*) forms, the imperfective aspect being assumed unless otherwise stated. Bi-aspectual infinitives are shown as (*impf.*, *pf.*). In all other cases both aspects are indicated (the imperfective always preceding the perfective) as in the following examples:

(i) получ|áть, -и́ть; возра|жáть, -зи́ть; сн|оси́ть, -ести́.

(ii) позв|оля́ть, -óлить; встр|ечáть, -éтить.

(iii) покáз|ывать, -áть: (i.e. *pf.* показáть); очарóв|ывать, -áть.

(iv) гоня́ть, гнать; брать, взять; вынуждáть, вы́нудить.

(v) смотрéть, по-; греть, по- (i.e. *pf.* погрéть); мости́ть, вы́- (i.e. *pf.* вы́мостить); лысéть, об-/по-.

(vi) и|мпровизи́ровать, сы-.

37. It will be seen from the above that

(i) when the first two or more letters of both aspects are identical, a vertical divider in the imperfective separates these letters from those which undergo change in the perfective. The perfective is then represented by the changed letters, preceded by a hyphen.

(ii) a 'change' includes change of stress only if the stress shifts *back* in the perfective to the previous vowel: the divider then precedes this vowel in the imperfective.

(iii) if it shifts forward, only the stressed syllable of the perfective is shown.

(iv) when the two aspects have only their first letter in common, or are in fact different verbs, or both begin with вы- (which is always accented in the perfective), both are given in full.

(v) perfectives of the type prefix+imperfective are shown by giving the prefix only, followed by a hyphen. Prefixes are unstressed except for вы́-.

Alternative prefixes are separated by an oblique stroke.

38. Where a verb has two possible imperfective or perfective forms, the alternative form is shown in brackets. Thus:

разв|орáчивать (*or* -ёртывать), -ерну́ть.

возвра|щáться, -ти́ться (*or* верну́ться).

пали́ть (*or* опáливать), о-.

39. When two or three verbs separated by an oblique stroke are followed by the indication (*pf.*) or (*impf.*) this applies to both or all of them.

40. The following grammatical information is given in respect of English headwords.

(a) Irregular or difficult plural forms of nouns. Thus:

child ... (*pl.* **children**).

leaf ... (*pl.* **leaves**).

monkey ... (*pl.* ~**s**).

solo ... (*pl.* ~**s**; *sense 1: pl.* ~**s** *or* **soli**).

(b) The comparative and superlative forms of adjectives which take **-er**, **-est**. Thus:

chic ... (**chic-er, chic-est**).
glib ... (**glibber, glibbest**).
tatty ... (**tattier, tattiest**).

(c) Irregular or difficult forms of verbs. Thus:

eat ... (*past* **ate**; *pp* **eaten**).
go ... (*3rd pers. sing. pres.* **goes**; *past* **went**; *p.p.* **gone**).
hold ... (*past and p.p.* **held**).
run ... (**running**; *past* **ran**; *p.p.* **run**).
tattoo ... (**tattoos, tattooed**).
taxi ... (**taxies, taxied, taxiing** *or* **taxying**).
tip ... (**tipped, tipping**).

Phonetic symbols used in the Dictionary

Consonants		Vowels	
b	*b*ut	æ	c*a*t
d	*d*og	ɑ:	*a*rm
f	*f*ew	e	b*e*d
g	*g*et	ɜ:	h*er*
h	*h*e	ɪ	s*i*t
j	*y*es	i:	s*ee*
k	*c*at	ɒ	h*o*t
l	*l*eg	ɔ:	s*aw*
m	*m*an	ʌ	r*u*n
n	*n*o	ʊ	p*u*t
p	*p*en	u:	t*oo*
r	*r*ed	ə	*a*go
s	*s*it	aɪ	m*y*
t	*t*op	aʊ	h*ow*
v	*v*oice	eɪ	d*ay*
w	*w*e	əʊ	n*o*
z	*z*oo	eə	h*air*
ʃ	*sh*e	ɪə	n*ear*
ʒ	deci*s*ion	ɔɪ	b*oy*
θ	*th*in	ʊə	p*oor*
ð	*th*is	aɪə	f*ire*
ŋ	ri*ng*	aʊə	s*our*
x	lo*ch*		
ʧ	*ch*ip		
ʤ	*j*ar		

(ə) signifies the indeterminate sound as in gard*e*n, carn*a*l, and rhyth*m*.

(r) at the end of a word indicates an r that is sounded when a word beginning with a vowel follows, as in *clutter up* and *an acre of land*.

The mark ˜ indicates a nasalized sound, as in the following sounds that are not natural in English: æ̃ (t*im*bre), ɑ̃ (el*an*), ɔ̃ (b*on* vivant).

The main or primary stress of a word is shown by ˈ preceding the relevant syllable; any secondary stress in words of three or more syllables is shown by ˌ preceding the relevant syllable.

Abbreviations used in the Dictionary

a	accusative (case)	винительный падеж
abbr.	abbreviat|ion, -ed (to)	сокращение, сокращённо
abs.	absolute	абсолютный
abstr.	abstract	абстрактный
acad.	academic	академический термин
acc.	according	согласно
act.	active (voice)	действительный (залог)
adj., adjs.	adjectiv|e, -al, -es	имя прилагательное, адъективное, имена прилагательные
admin.	administration	администрация
adv., advs.	adverb, -ial, -s	наречие, наречное, наречия
aeron.	aeronautics	авиация
agric.	agriculture	сельское хозяйство
alg.	algebra	алгебра
anat.	anatomy	анатомия
anc.	ancient	древний
anthrop.	anthropology	антропология
approx.	approximate(ly)	приблизительн|ый, -о
arch.	archaic	устаревшее слово/выражение
archaeol.	archaeology	археология
archit.	architecture	архитектура
astrol.	astrology	астрология
astron.	astronomy	астрономия
attr.	attributive	определительное, атрибутивное
Austral.	Austral(as)ian	австралийский
aux.	auxiliary	вспомогательный глагол
bibl.	biblical	библейский термин
biol.	biology	биология
bot.	botany	ботаника
Br.	British; British usage	британский английский; употребительно в Великобритании
c.g.	common gender	общий род
chem.	chemistry	химия
cin.	cinema(tography)	кинематография
coll.	colloquial	разговорное
collect.	collective	собирательное (существительное)
comb.	combin|ation, -ing	сочетание
comm.	commerc|e, -ial	коммерческий термин
comp.	comparative	сравнительная степень
comput.	computing	вычислительная техника
concr.	concrete	конкретный
conj., conjs.	conjunction, -s	союз, -ы
cpd., cpds.	compound, -s	сложн|ое слов|о, -ые -а
cul.	culinary	кулинария
d.	dative (case)	дательный падеж
decl.	decl|ined, -ension	склоняется, склонение
def. art.	definite article	определённый артикль

<table>
<tr><td>det.</td><td>determinate</td><td>определённый</td></tr>
<tr><td>dial.</td><td>dialect(al)</td><td>диалектизм</td></tr>
<tr><td>dim.</td><td>diminutive</td><td>уменьшительное</td></tr>
<tr><td>dipl.</td><td>diploma|cy, -tic</td><td>дипломатический термин</td></tr>
<tr><td>disp.</td><td>disputed</td><td>спорное</td></tr>
<tr><td>eccl.</td><td>ecclesiastical</td><td>церковный термин</td></tr>
<tr><td>econ.</td><td>economics</td><td>экономика</td></tr>
<tr><td>educ.</td><td>education, -al</td><td>образование</td></tr>
<tr><td>elec.</td><td>electric|al, -ity</td><td>электротехника</td></tr>
<tr><td>ellipt.</td><td>elliptical</td><td>эллиптический</td></tr>
<tr><td>emph.</td><td>empha|size(s), -sizing; -tic</td><td>подчёркива|ть, -ет, -ющее; усилительное</td></tr>
<tr><td>eng.</td><td>engineering</td><td>машиностроение</td></tr>
<tr><td>Eng.</td><td>English</td><td>английский (язык)</td></tr>
<tr><td>entom.</td><td>entomology</td><td>энтомология</td></tr>
<tr><td>esp.</td><td>especially</td><td>особенно</td></tr>
<tr><td>ethnol.</td><td>ethnology</td><td>этнология</td></tr>
<tr><td>euph.</td><td>euphemis|m, -tic</td><td>эвфеми|зм, -стическое</td></tr>
<tr><td>exc.</td><td>except</td><td>исключая</td></tr>
<tr><td>excl.</td><td>exclamation</td><td>междометие</td></tr>
<tr><td>expr.</td><td>express|ed, -es, -ing; -ion</td><td>выраж|енный, -ает, -ающее; выражение</td></tr>
<tr><td>f.</td><td>feminine</td><td>женский род</td></tr>
<tr><td>fem.</td><td>female</td><td>форма женского рода</td></tr>
<tr><td>fig.</td><td>figurative</td><td>переносно</td></tr>
<tr><td>fin.</td><td>financ|e, -ial</td><td>финансы, финансовый термин</td></tr>
<tr><td>Fr.</td><td>French</td><td>французский (язык)</td></tr>
<tr><td>freq.</td><td>frequentative</td><td>многократный (глагол)</td></tr>
<tr><td>fut.</td><td>future (tense)</td><td>будущее время</td></tr>
<tr><td>g.</td><td>genitive (case)</td><td>родительный падеж</td></tr>
<tr><td>geod.</td><td>geodesy</td><td>геодезия</td></tr>
<tr><td>geog.</td><td>geography</td><td>география</td></tr>
<tr><td>geol.</td><td>geology</td><td>геология</td></tr>
<tr><td>geom.</td><td>geometry</td><td>геометрия</td></tr>
<tr><td>ger.</td><td>gerund</td><td>герундий</td></tr>
<tr><td>Ger.</td><td>German</td><td>немецкий (язык)</td></tr>
<tr><td>Gk.</td><td>Greek</td><td>греческий (язык)</td></tr>
<tr><td>gram.</td><td>grammar</td><td>грамматика</td></tr>
<tr><td>her.</td><td>heraldry</td><td>геральдика</td></tr>
<tr><td>hist.</td><td>histor|y, -ical</td><td>история</td></tr>
<tr><td>hort.</td><td>horticulture</td><td>садоводство</td></tr>
<tr><td>i.</td><td>instrumental (case);
intransitive in ‘v.i.’</td><td>творительный падеж;
непереходный глагол</td></tr>
<tr><td>imper.</td><td>imperative</td><td>повелительное наклонение</td></tr>
<tr><td>impers.</td><td>impersonal</td><td>безличное</td></tr>
<tr><td>impf.</td><td>imperfective</td><td>несовершенный вид</td></tr>
<tr><td>ind.</td><td>indirect</td><td>косвенный</td></tr>
<tr><td>indecl.</td><td>indeclinable</td><td>несклоняемое</td></tr>
<tr><td>indef. art.</td><td>indefinite article</td><td>неопределённый артикль</td></tr>
<tr><td>indet.</td><td>indeterminate</td><td>неопределённый</td></tr>
<tr><td>inf.</td><td>infinitive</td><td>инфинитив</td></tr>
<tr><td>inst.</td><td>instantaneous</td><td>мгновенный</td></tr>
<tr><td>int.</td><td>interjection</td><td>междометие</td></tr>
<tr><td>interrog.</td><td>interrogative</td><td>вопросительный</td></tr>
</table>

intrans.	intransitive	непереходный глагол
iron.	ironical	в ироническом смысле
Ital.	Italian	итальянский (язык)
joc.	jocular	шутливое
journ.	journalism	журналистика
Lat.	Latin	латинский (язык)
leg.	legal	юридический термин
ling.	linguistics	лингвистика
lit.	literal	буквально
liter.	literary	книжное
log.	logic	логика
m.	masculine	мужской род
math.	mathematics	математика
mech.	mechanics	механика
med.	medic|ine, -al	медицин|а, -ский термин
metall.	metallurgy	металлургия
meteor.	meteorology	метеорология
mil.	military	военное дело
min.	mineralogy	минералогия
mod.	modern	современный
mus.	music(al)	музыка, -льный термин
myth.	mythology	мифология
n.	noun	имя существительное
naut.	nautical	морское дело
nav.	naval	военно-морской термин
neg.	negative	отрицательный
nn.	nouns	имсна существительные
nom.	nominative (case)	именительный падеж
nom.-a.	nominative-accusative	именительный-винительный
nt.	neuter	средний род
num., nums.	numer|al, -ical, -als	числительное, числовой, числительные
obj.	object	дополнение
obs.	obsolete	устаревшее слово/выражение
offens.	offensive	оскорбительное
oft.	often	часто
onomat.	onomatopeia	звукоподражание, звукоподражательное слово
opp.	opposite (to); as opposed to	противоположное
opt.	optics	оптика
o.s.	oneself	себя
p.	prepositional (case). See also *p.p.* and *p.p.p.*	предложный падеж
palaeog.	palaeography	палеография
parl.	parliamentary	парламентский термин
part.	participle	причастие
pass.	passive (voice)	страдательный (залог)
path.	pathology	патология
pej.	pejorative	пренебрежительное
pers.	person(s); personal	лицо; личный
pert.	pertaining	относительно
pf.	perfective	совершенный вид
pharm.	pharmaceutical	фармакология, фармация
phil.	philosophy	философия

philol.	philology	языкознание
phon.	phonetic(s)	фонетика
phot.	photography	фотография
phr., phrr.	phrase, -s	фраз|а, -ы
phys.	physic|s, -al	физика
physiol.	physiology	физиология
pl.	plural	множественное число
poet.	poet|ical, -ry	поэтическое, поэзия
pol.	political	политический термин
poss.	possessive	притяжательное
p.p.	past participle	причастие второе
p.p.p.	past participle passive	страдательное причастие прошедшего времени
pr.	pronounce(d); pronunciation	произносить; произношение
pred.	predicate; predicative	сказуемое; предикативный
pref.	prefix	префикс
prep., preps.	preposition, -s	предлог, -и
pres.	present (tense)	настоящее время, настоящего времени
pres. part.	present participle	причастие первое
pret.	preterite	претерит, прошедшее время
pron., prons.	pronoun, -s	местоимени|е, -я
pronunc.	pronunciation	произношение
propr.	proprietary term	фирменное название
pros.	prosody	просодия
prov., provs.	proverb, -s	пословиц|а, -ы
psych.	psychology	психология
radiol.	radiology	рентгенология
rail.	railway	железнодорожный термин
refl.	reflexive (verb)	возвратный (глагол)
rel.	relative (pronoun)	относительное (местоимение)
relig.	religion	религия
rhet.	rhetorical	высокого стиля
Rom.	Roman	римский
Ru.	Russian	русский (язык)
Sc.	Scottish	шотландский (язык)
sc.	scilicet	а именно
sg.	singular	единственное число
sl.	slang	сленг
s.o.	someone	кто-нибудь
soc.	social	общественный
stat.	statistics	статистика
sth.	something	что-нибудь
subj.	subject	подлежащее
suff.	suffix	суффикс
superl.	superlative	превосходная степень
surv.	surveying	топография
t.	transitive in *v.t.*	переходный глагол
tech.	technical	техника
teleg.	telegraphy	телеграфия
teleph.	telephony	телефония
text.	textiles	текстильный термин
theatr.	theatr|e, -ical	театр, театральный термин
theol.	theology	богословие
trans.	transitive	переходный глагол

trig.	trigonometry	тригонометрия
TV	television	телевидение
typ.	typography	типографский термин
univ.	university	университетский жаргон
US	United States; United States usage	американский английский; употребительно в Америке
usu.	usually	обычно
v.	verb	глагол
var.	variant	вариант
v. aux.	auxiliary verb	вспомогательный глагол
vbl.	verbal	отглагольное
vet.	veterinary	ветеринария
v.i.	intransitive verb	непереходный глагол
voc.	vocative (case)	звательный (падеж)
v.t.	transitive verb	переходный глагол
vulg.	vulgar(ism)	грубое
vv.	verbs	глаголы
zool.	zoology	зоология

The Russian -н. or -л. in illustrative phrases within entries stands for the enclitic нибудь or либо (in the words кто-нибудь, что-нибудь, что-либо, etc.).

This dictionary includes some words which are, or are asserted to be, proprietary names or trademarks. These words are labelled (*propr.*). The presence or absence of this label should not be regarded as affecting the legal status of any proprietary name or trademark.

Aa

А (*abbr. of* **ампе́р**) amp, ampere.

а¹ *conj.* **1** (*и*) and; **вот ма́рки, а вот три рубля́ сда́чи** here are the stamps and here is three roubles change; **иди́те напра́во, пото́м нале́во, а пото́м ещё раз напра́во** turn right, then left, (and) then right again; **а и́менно** namely; to be exact.
2 (*но*) but (*or not translated*); **моя́ жена́ лю́бит о́перу, а я предпочита́ю кино́** my wife likes opera, but I prefer the cinema; **я иду́ не в кино́, а в теа́тр** I am not going to the cinema, but to the theatre (*Br.*), theater (*US*); **пиши́ карандашо́м, а не ру́чкой** write in pencil, not pen.
3: **а как же!** (*coll.*) of course!; **а то** or (else), otherwise; **спеши́, а то мы опозда́ем** hurry up or (else) we'll be late.

а² *interrog. particle* (*coll.*) eh?; what('s that)?; huh?

а³ *int.* (*coll.*) ah, oh; **а ну его́!** oh, to hell with him!

абажу́р, а *m.* lampshade.

абба́т, а *m.* (*в монастыре*) abbot.

аббати́с|а, ы *f.* abbess.

абба́тств|о, а *nt.* abbey.

аббревиату́р|а, ы *f.* abbreviation; acronym.

аберра́ци|я, и *f.* (*opt. and fig.*) aberration.

абза́ц, а *m.* **1** (*typ.*) indention; **сде́лать а.** to indent; **нача́ть с но́вого ~а** to begin a new line, new paragraph.
2 (*часть текста*) paragraph.

абитурие́нт, а *m.* **1** (*university, college*) entrant. **2** (*obs.*) (*выпускник средней школы*) (school-)leaver.

абитурие́нт|ка, ки *f. of* ⇨~

аблати́в, а *m.* (*gram.*) ablative; **а. абсолю́тный** ablative absolute.

абонеме́нт, а *m.* (*право пользования чем-н.*) subscription; (*многоразовый билет*) season ticket; **сверх ~а** extra.

абонеме́нтн|ый *adj.*: **~ая ка́рточка** reader's *or* borrower's card; **~ая пла́та** (*TV, radio*) licence fee; **а. я́щик** PO (*abbr. of* Post Office) Box.

абоне́нт, а *m.* (*телефона*) subscriber; (*библиотеки*) borrower, reader; (*театра*) season-ticket holder.

абоне́нтск|ий *adj.* subscription; **~ое телеви́дение** subscription television, pay TV; **~ая пла́та** rental fee.

аборда́ж, а *m.* (*naut.*) boarding; **взять на а.** to board.

абориге́н, а *m.* aboriginal.

абориге́нный *adj.* aboriginal; native.

або́рт, а *m.* (*искусственный*) abortion; (*самопроизвольный*) miscarriage; **подпо́льный а.** backstreet abortion; **сде́лать а.** to have an abortion.

абрази́вный *adj.* abrasive.

абракада́бр|а, ы *f.* gibberish, gobbledygook.

абрико́с, а *m.* **1** (*плод*) apricot.
2 (*дерево*) apricot-tree.

абрико́с|овый *adj. of* ⇨~

а́брис, а *m.* contour(s); outline.

абсе́нт, а *m.* absinthe.

абсентеи́зм, а *m.* absenteeism.

абсентеи́ст, а *m.* absentee.

абсолю́т, а *m.* (*phil.*) the absolute.

абсолюти́зм, а *m.* (*pol.*) absolutism.

абсолюти́ст, а *m.* (*pol.*) absolutist.

абсолю́т|ный (~ен, ~на) *adj.* absolute; **а. слух** (*mus.*) perfect pitch.

абсорби́р|овать, ую *impf. and pf.* to absorb.

абсо́рбци|я, и *f.* absorption.

абстине́нт, а *m.* abstainer.

абстине́нтный *adj.*: **а. синдро́м** (*med.*) withdrawal symptoms.

абстине́нци|я, и *f.* (*med.*) withdrawal symptoms; **наркоти́ческая а.** drug withdrawal symptoms.

абстраги́р|овать, ую *impf. and pf.* to abstract.

абстраги́р|оваться, уюсь *impf. and pf.* to abstract oneself.

абстра́кт|ный (~ен, ~на) *adj.* abstract.

абстракциони́зм, а *m.* abstractionism.

абстракциони́ст, а *m.* abstractionist.

абстра́кци|я, и *f.* abstraction.

абсу́рд, а *m.* absurdity; **довести́ до ~а** to carry to the point of absurdity.

абсу́рдност|ь, и *f.* absurdity.

абсу́рд|ный (~ен, ~на) *adj.* absurd.

абсце́сс, а *m.* abscess.

абха́з|ец, ца *m.* Abkhazian.

абха́з|ка, ки *f. of* ⇨~ец

абха́зский *adj.* Abkhazian.

аванга́рд, а *m.* **1** vanguard (*also fig.*).
2 (*fig.*) avant-garde.

авангарди́зм, а *m.* avant-gardism.

авангарди́ст, а *m.* avant-gardist.

авангард|и́стский *adj. of* ⇨~ 2

аванга́рд|ный *adj. of* ⇨~ 1

аванза́л, а *m.* ante-room.

аванпо́ст, а *m.* (*mil.*) outpost; forward position (*also fig.*).

ава́нс, а *m.* **1** (*деньги*) advance; **получи́ть а.** to receive an advance.
2 (*pl. only; fig.*) advances, overtures.

аванси́р|овать, ую *impf. and pf.* to advance (*money*).

ава́нс|овый *adj. of* ⇨~; **а. отчёт** expense account, expense claim.

ава́нсом *adv.* in advance, on account.

авансце́н|а, ы *f.* (*theatr.*) proscenium.

аванта́ж|ный (~ен, ~на) *adj.* (*obs., coll.*) fine.

аванто́р|а, ы *f.* **1** (*приключение*) adventure; escapade; **пусти́ться в ~ы** to embark on adventures. **2** (*coll.*) shady enterprise.

авантюри́зм, а *m.* adventurism.

авантюри́ст, а *m.* adventurist.

авантюр|исти́ческий *adj. of* ⇨~и́зм

авантюри́стк|а, и *f.* adventuress.

авантю́рно-плутовско́й *adj.* picaresque.

авантю́рност|ь, и *f.* adventurousness.

авантю́р|ный (~ен, ~на) *adj.* adventurous; **а. рома́н** adventure story.

авари́йно-спаса́тельный *adj.* (emergency-)rescue, life-saving.

аварийност|ь, и *f.* accidents, accident rate.

аварийн|ый *adj.* **1** *adj. of* ⇨**авария; а. комплект** survival kit; **~ая машина** breakdown van; **~ая посадка** crash landing; **а. сигнал** distress signal. **2** (*запасной*) emergency, spare.

авари|я, и *f.* **1** (*несчастный случай*) crash, accident. **2** (*поломка*) breakdown; **цепная а.** (*vehicle*) pile-up; **потерпеть ~ю** to crash, have an accident.

авгур, а *m.* augur.

август, а *m.* August.

август|овский *adj. of* ⇨~

Авди|й, я *m.* (*bibl.*) Obadiah.

авиа (*abbr. of* ***авиапочтой***) '(by) airmail'.

авиа... *comb. form, abbr. of* ***авиационный***

авиабаз|а, ы *f.* air base.

авиабилет, а *m.* airline ticket.

авиадесант, а *m.* **1** (*высадка*) airborne assault landing. **2** (*войска*) airborne assault force.

авиадесантник, а *m.* paratrooper.

авиадесантн|ый *adj.* airborne assault; **~ые войска** airborne assault troops.

авиадиспетчер, а *m.* air-traffic controller.

авиадиспетчерск|ий *adj.*: **~ая служба** (air) flight control.

авиакаскадёр, а *m.* stunt flyer.

авиакасс|а, ы *f.* air tickets booking office.

авиакатастроф|а, ы *f.* air crash.

авиакомпани|я, и *f.* airline, air carrier.

авиаконструктор, а *m.* aircraft designer.

авиакосмический = **авиационно-космический**

авиалайнер, а *m.* airliner.

авиалини|я, и *f.* airway, air route.

авиамеханик, а *m.* aircraft mechanic.

авиамоделизм, а *m.* aeromodelling (*Br.*), aeromodeling (*US*).

авиамоделист, а *m.* aeromodeller (*Br.*), aeromodeler (*US*).

авиамодел|ь, и *f.* model aircraft.

авиамодель|ный *adj. of* ⇨~

авианос|ец, ца *m.* aircraft carrier.

авиапассажир, а *m.* airline passenger.

авиапереброск|а, и *f.* airlift.

авиаписьм|о, а, *pl.* **~а, авиаписем, ~ам** *nt.* air(mail) letter; aerogramme (*Br.*), aerogram (*US*).

авиапочт|а, ы *f.* air mail.

авиасалон, а *m.* air show.

авиасмотр, а *m.* = **авиасалон**

авиаспорт, а *m.* aerial sports.

авиасъёмк|а, и *f.* air photography, aerial surveying.

авиатор, а *m.* aviator.

авиатор|ский *adj. of* ⇨~

авиатранспортн|ый *adj.*: **~ая компания** airline, air carrier.

авиатрасс|а, ы *f.* air route, air lane, airway.

авиационно-космическ|ий *adj.* aerospace; **~ая промышленность** the aerospace industry.

авиационный *adj. of* ⇨**авиация**

авиаци|я, и *f.* **1** aviation. **2** (*collect.*) aircraft; **бомбардировочная а.** bomber force.

авиачаст|ь, и *f.* air force unit.

авиашкол|а, ы *f.* flying school.

авизо *nt. indecl.* (*comm.*) advice (note).

авокадо *nt. indecl.* **1** (*плод*) avocado. **2** (*дерево*) avocado(-tree).

авось *particle* (*coll.*) perhaps; **на а.** on the off-chance.

авоськ|а, и *f.* (*coll.*) string bag.

аврал, а *m.* **1** (*naut.*) all-hands evolution; (*as int.*) all hands on deck! **2** (*coll.*) rush job.

аврал|ьный *adj.*: **~ьная работа** = **аврал**

авpop|а, ы *f.* (*poet.*) aurora, dawn.

австрали|ец, йца *m.* Australian.

австрали|йка, йки *f. of* ⇨**~ец**

австралийский *adj.* Australian.

Австрали|я, и *f.* Australia.

австри|ец, йца *m.* Austrian.

австри|йка, йки *f. of* ⇨**~ец**

австрийский *adj.* Austrian.

Австри|я, и *f.* Austria.

австро-венгерский *adj.* (*hist.*) Austro-Hungarian.

Австро-Венгри|я, и *f.* (*hist.*) Austria-Hungary.

авто *nt. indecl.* (*coll.*) (motor-)car.

авто... *comb. form* **1** self-, auto-. **2** *abbr. of* (*i*) ***автоматический*** *and* (*ii*) ***автомобильный***

автоавари|я, и *f.* road accident.

автоантизапотевател|ь, я *m.* demister.

автоатлас, а *m.* road atlas.

автобаз|а, ы *f.* motor-transport depot.

автобиографический *adj.* autobiographical.

автобиографичност|ь, и *f.* autobiographical nature, character.

автобиографи|я, и *f.* **1** (*описание своей жизни*) autobiography. **2** (*описание своей карьеры*) curriculum vitae, CV.

автобус, а *m.* bus; (*междугородный*) coach (*Br.*), bus (*US*).

автобусн|ый *adj.* bus; **~ая остановка** bus stop; **~ая станция** bus station.

автоветеран, а *m.* vintage car.

автовладел|ец, ьца *m.* car owner.

автовокзал, а *m.* bus terminal; coach station (*Br.*).

автовор, а *m.* (*coll.*) car thief.

автогенный *adj.* (*tech.*) autogenous.

автогонк|а, и *f.* car-race; (*pl.*) motor racing (*Br.*), automobile racing (*US*).

автогонщик, а *m.* racing-driver.

автограф, а *m.* (*in var. senses*) autograph.

автогужевой *adj.* vehicular.

автодорог|а, и *f.* road; highway.

автодорожник, а *m.* highway engineer.

автодорожн|ый *adj.* road-transport; highway; **~ая катастрофа** road *or* traffic accident.

автодрезин|а, ы *f.* (*tech.*) motor trolley.

автодром, а *m.* **1** (*для испытания автомобилей*) vehicle testing point. **2** (*для автогонок*) motor-racing circuit.

автожир, а *m.* autogyro.

автозавод, а *m.* motor-car factory.

автозаправочн|ый *adj.* filling, refuelling (*Br.*), refueling (*US*); **~ая (станция)** petrol- *or* filling-station.

автозаправщик, а *m.* petrol tanker.

автоинспектор, а *m.* traffic inspector.

автоинспекци|я, и *f.* traffic inspectorate.

автокар, а *m.* motor trolley.

автокарандаш, а *m.* propelling pencil.

автокаскадёр, а *m.* stunt driver.

автокатастроф|а, ы *f.* road accident.

автокефальный *adj.* (*eccl.*) autocephalous.

автоклав, а *m.* (*tech.*) autoclave.

автоколонк|а, и *f.* petrol pump (*Br.*), gas(oline) pump (*US*).

автоколонн|а, ы *f.* motorcade; (*mil.*) convoy.

автокоррид|а, ы *f.* stock-car race; stock-car racing.

автокосметик|а, и *f.* car care products.

автокран, а *m.* mobile crane, crane truck.

автократ, а *m.* autocrat.

автократический *adj.* autocratic.

автократи|я, и *f.* autocracy.

автокросс, а *m.* autocross.

автокухн|я, и *f.* mobile kitchen.

автол, а *m.* motor oil.

автолавк|а, и *f.* mobile shop.

автолихач, а *m.* reckless driver.

автолюбител|ь, я *m.* (private) motorist.

автомагазин, а *m.* **1** (*автолавка*) mobile shop. **2** (*магазин по продаже автомобилей*) motor-car showroom, car dealer's.

автомагистрал|ь, и *f.* motorway (*Br.*), interstate (highway) (*US*).

автомастерск|ая, ой *f.* car repair garage.

автомат, а *m.* **1** automatic machine, slot-machine; **билетный а.** ticket machine; **бильярдный а.** pinball machine; **денежный а.** cash dispenser; **игровой а.** one-armed bandit; **телефон-а.** pay phone; (*fig.*) automaton, robot. **2** (*mil.*) sub-machine-gun.

автоматизаци|я, и *f.* automation.

автоматизированн|ый *adj.*

computer-aided; **~ое проекти́рование** CAD, computer-aided design.

автоматизи́р|овать, ую *impf. and pf.* to automate.

автома́тик|а, и *f.* **1** (*отрасль науки*) automation. **2** (*автоматические механизмы*) automatic equipment.

автомати́ческ|ий *adj.* **1** (*tech.*) automatic; **~ая винто́вка** automatic (rifle); **а. то́рмоз** automatic brake. **2** (*fig.*) automatic, involuntary; **~ое движе́ние** involuntary movement.

автомати́ч|ный (~ен, ~на) = **~еский** 2

автома́т|ный *adj. of* ⇒**~** 2

автома́тчик, а *m.* (*mil.*) sub-machine-gunner.

автомаши́н|а, ы *f.* motor vehicle.

автомеха́ник, а *m.* car mechanic.

автомобилево́з, а *m.* (*vehicle*) transporter.

автомобили́зм, а *m.* motoring.

автомобили́ст, а *m.* motorist.

автомоби́л|ь, я *m.* motor vehicle; (motor-)car; **легково́й а.** car; **грузово́й а.** lorry; **води́ть а.** to drive a car.

автомоби́л|ь-бо́мба, ~я-бо́мбы *m.* car bomb.

автомоби́ль|ный *adj. of* ⇒**~**

автомодели́зм, а *m.* car modelling (*Br.*), modeling (*US*).

автомодели́ст, а *m.* car modeller (*Br.*), modeler (*US*).

автомоде́л|ь, и *f.* model car.

автомо́йк|а, и *f.* car wash.

автомотодро́м, а *m.* race-track.

автоно́ми|я, и *f.* autonomy.

автоно́м|ный (~ен, ~на) *adj.* autonomous; (*comput.*) stand-alone

автоотве́тчик, а *m.* answering machine.

автопавильо́н, а *m.* bus shelter.

автопа́рк, а *m.* car fleet.

автопаро́м, а *m.* car ferry.

автопило́т, а *m.* autopilot.

автопогру́зчик, а *m.* fork-lift truck.

автопо́езд, а, *pl.* **~а́** *m.* articulated lorry (*Br.*), juggernaut (*Br.*), tractor trailer (*US*).

автопортре́т, а *m.* self-portrait.

автоприёмник, а *m.* car radio.

автоприце́п, а *m.* trailer; **жило́й а.** caravan (*Br.*), mobile home; **тури́стский а.** caravan (*Br.*), camper.

автопроисше́стви|е, я *nt.* road accident.

автопрока́т|ный *adj.*: **~ая компания** car hire company.

а́втор, а *m.* author; (*mus.*) composer; (*fig.*) architect.

авторазмора́живател|ь, я *m.* (*windscreen*) de-icer.

автора́лли *nt. indecl.* (car) rally.

автора́лли́ст, а *m.* rallyist, rally driver.

авторефера́т, а *m.* abstract (*of dissertation, etc.*).

авториза́ци|я, и *f.* authorization.

авториз|о́ванный *p.p.p. of* ⇒**~ова́ть** *and adj.* authorized.

авториз|ова́ть, у́ю *impf. and pf.* to authorize.

авторитари́зм, а *m.* authoritarianism.

авторита́р|ный (~ен, ~на) *adj.* authoritarian.

авторите́т, а *m.* authority; **по́льзоваться ~ом** to enjoy authority, have prestige, command respect; **счита́ться ~ом** to be considered an authority; (*sl.*) boss, big shot.

авторите́тност|ь, и *f.* authoritativeness; trustworthiness.

авторите́т|ный (~ен, ~на) *adj.* authoritative; trustworthy; **а. исто́чник** an authoritative source (of information).

а́втор|ский *adj. of* ⇒**~**; **а. гонора́р** royalty, royalties; **а. лист** (*typ.*) unit of 40,000 ens (*used in calculating author's royalties*); **~ское пра́во** copyright; *as n. pl.* **~ские, ~ских** royalties.

а́вторско-правово́й *adj.* copyright.

а́вторств|о, а *nt.* authorship.

авто́ру́чк|а, и *f.* fountain-pen.

автосало́н, а *m.* **1** (*магазин*) motorcar showroom. **2** (*выставка*) motor show.

автоса́н|и, е́й *no sg.* sledge car, motor sleigh.

автосе́рвис, а *m.* service station.

автосмо́тр, а *m.* = **автосало́н** 2

автоспо́рт, а *m.* motor sports.

автоста́нци|я, и *f.* bus station; coach station.

автосто́п, а *m.* **1** (*в поезде*) communication cord (*Br.*), emergency brake (*US*). **2** (*способ путешествия*) hitch-hiking; **путеше́ствовать** (*impf.*) **~ом** to hitch-hike.

автосто́рож, а *m.* anti-theft device (*for car*).

автостоя́нк|а, и *f.* car park.

автостра́д|а, ы *f.* motorway (*Br.*), interstate (highway) (*US*).

автосуфлёр, а *m.* Autocue (*propr.*), teleprompter.

автосце́пк|а, и *f.* (*rail.*) automatic coupling.

автотелефо́н, а *m.* car phone.

автотра́нспорт, а *m.* motor transport.

автотра́сс|а, ы *f.* highway.

автотрюка́ч, а́ *m.* stunt driver.

автотури́зм, а *m.* motor touring.

автотури́ст, а *m.* motor tourer.

автоуго́нщик = **автово́р**

автофурго́н, а *m.* van

автохто́нный *adj.* autochthonous.

автоцисте́рн|а, ы *f.* tanker.

автошко́л|а, ы *f.* driving school; **преподава́тель** (*m.*) **~ы** driving instructor.

авуа́р|ы, ~ *no sg.* (*fin.*) holdings; foreign assets.

ага́ *int.* (*coll.*) (*expr.* (*i*) *comprehension,* (*ii*) *malicious pleasure*) ah!; aha!

ага́в|а, ы *f.* (*bot.*) agave.

ага́т, а *m.* (*min.*) agate.

ага́т|овый *adj. of* ⇒**~**

агглютинати́вный *adj.* (*ling.*) agglutinative.

а́генс, а *m.* (*ling.*) agent (noun).

аге́нт, а *m.* (*in var. senses*) agent.

аге́нтств|о, а *nt.* agency; **а. печа́ти** news agency, press agency; **а. (для) по́мощи** aid agency; **информац-ио́нное/телегра́фное а.** news agency.

агенту́р|а, ы *f.* **1** (*служба*) secret service. **2** (*collect.*) agents.

агиогра́фи|я, и *f.* hagiography.

агит... *comb. form, abbr. of* ***агитацио́нный***

агита́тор, а *m.* (*pol.*) agitator; campaigner.

агитацио́нн|ый *adj.* (*pol.*) agitation; **~ая речь** campaign speech.

агита́ци|я, и *f.* (*pol.*) agitation; campaign; **вести́ ~ю** to campaign; **предвы́борная а.** electioneering.

агити́р|овать, ую *impf.* **1** (*impf. only*) (*pol.*) (**за** + *a.*) to agitate, campaign (for). **2** (*pf.* **с~**) (*coll.*) to (try to) persuade.

аги́тк|а, и *f.* (*pol.*) propaganda piece (*plays, posters, etc.*).

агитпро́п, а *m.* (*abbr. of* ***отде́л агита́ции и пропага́нды***) (*hist.*) agitation and propaganda section (*of central and local committees of the CPSU*).

агитпу́нкт, а *m.* agitation centre (*Br.*), center (*US*).

а́гн|ец, ца *m.* **1** (*eccl.*) lamb (*Agnus Dei*). **2** *fig. of a meek person*: **прики́нуться ~цем** to play the innocent.

агно́стик, а *m.* agnostic.

агностици́зм, а *m.* agnosticism.

агности́ческий *adj.* agnostic.

агонизи́р|овать, ую *impf.* to be in one's death-throes.

аго́ни|я, и *f.* (*med. and fig.*) death-throes.

агорафо́би|я, и *f.* agoraphobia.

аго́рновый *adj.*: **а. сиро́п** maple syrup.

агра́рный *adj.* agrarian.

агрега́т, а *m.* **1** (*часть машины*) unit. **2** (*соединение несколько машин*) assembly.

агрега́тный *adj.* modular.

агресси́вност|ь, и *f.* aggression.

агресси́в|ный (~ен, ~на) *adj.* aggressive.

агре́сси|я, и *f.* (*pol.*) aggression.

агре́ссор, а *m.* aggressor.

агро... *comb. form* agro-, agricultural, farm.

агроно́м, а *m.* agronomist.

агроно́ми|я, и *f.* agronomics; agricultural science.

агроте́хник, а *m.* agricultural technician.

агроте́хник|а, и *f.* agricultural technology.

агрохимика́т|ы, ов *pl.* (*sg.* **~, ~а** *m.*) agrochemicals.

агрохими́ческий *adj.* agrochemical.

ад, а *m.* hell; (*fig.*) bedlam; **душе́вный а.** mental torment, anguish.

ада́жио (*mus.*) **1** *adv.* adagio. **2** *n.*; *nt. indecl.* adagio.

ада́мов *adj.*: **~о я́блоко** Adam's apple.
адапта́ци|я, и *f.* (*in var. senses*) adaptation.
ада́птер, а *m.* **1** (*tech.*) adapter. **2** (*mus.*) pick-up.
адапти́р|овать, ую *impf. and pf.* to adapt.
адапти́р|оваться, уюсь *impf. and pf.* to adapt; to get used to sth.
адвенти́ст, а *m.* (*relig.*) (Seventh-day) Adventist.
адвока́т, а *m.* (*поверенный*) solicitor, lawyer; (*выступающий в суде*) barrister (*Br.*), attorney (*US*); (*fig.*) advocate.
адвокату́р|а, ы *f.* **1** (*деятельность адвоката*) the legal profession; practising law. **2** (*collect.*) lawyers; the Bar (*Br.*).
Адди́с-Абе́б|а, ы *f.* Addis Ababa.
адеква́т|ный (~ен, ~на) *adj.* identical, coincident; adequate.
адено́ид, а *m.* (*usu. pl.*) (*med.*) adenoid.
аде́пт, а *m.* adherent, disciple.
аджа́р|ец, ца *m.* Adzharian.
аджа́р|ка, ки *f. of* ⇒**~ец**
аджа́рский *adj.* Adzharian.
администрати́вн|ый *adj.* administrative; **в ~ом поря́дке** by administrative order.
администра́тор, а *m.* administrator; manager (*of hotel, theatre, etc.*).
администра́ци|я, и *f.* administration; management.
администри́р|овать, ую *impf.* to administrate.
адмира́л, а *m.* **1** admiral. **2** (*zool.*) red admiral.
адмиралте́й|ский *adj. of* ⇒**~ство**
адмиралте́йств|о, а *nt.* the Admiralty.
адмира́л|ьский *adj. of* ⇒**~**; **а. кора́бль** flagship; **а. чин, ~ьское зва́ние** flag rank.
а́дов *adj.* (*relig. and fig., coll.*) *of* ⇒**ад**
Адони́с, а *m.* Adonis.
адренали́н, а *m.* adrenalin.
а́дрес, а, *pl.* **~а́, ~о́в** *m.* (*in var. senses*) address; **в а.** (+*g.*) addressed to; (*fig.*) directed at; **не по ~у** (*fig.*) to the wrong quarter.
адреса́нт, а *m.* sender (*of mail*).
адреса́т, а *m.* addressee; **в слу́чае ненахожде́ния ~а** 'if undelivered'; **за ненахожде́нием ~а** 'not known' (*on letters*).
а́дрес|ный *adj. of* ⇒**~**; **~ная кни́га** directory; **а. стол** address bureau.
адрес|ова́ть, у́ю *impf. and pf.* (*письмо*) to address; (*критику, вопрос*) to direct.
адрес|ова́ться, у́юсь *impf. and pf.* (**к**+*d.*) to address o.s. (to).
Адриати́ческ|ое мо́р|е, ~ого ~я *nt.* the Adriatic (Sea).
а́дски *adv.* (*coll.*) terribly, fearfully.
а́дский *adj.* infernal, diabolical; (*fig.*) hellish, intolerable.
адсо́рбци|я, и *f.* (*chem.*) adsorption.
адъю́нкт, а *m.* **1** (*obs.*) (*помощник профессора*) junior scientific assistant. **2** (*аспирант*) graduate student in military academy.
адъюта́нт, а *m.* (*mil.*) aide-de-camp; **ста́рший а.** adjutant.
адюльте́р, а *m.* adultery.
адюльте́р|ный *adj. of* ⇒**~**
аж *particle and conj.* (*coll.*) **1** (*particle*) (*даже*) even; **аж до** right up to; **аж на** (+*a.*) right on to. **2** (*conj.*) (*так что*) so that, until.
а́жио *nt. indecl.* (*comm.*) agio.
ажиота́ж, а *m.* **1** (*comm.*) speculation in stocks. **2** (*fig.*) stir, excitement.
ажита́ци|я, и *f.* (*obs.*) agitation.
ажу́р[1], а *m.* open-work.
ажу́р[2], а *m.* (*comm.*): **учёт в ~е** the accounts are up to date; **всё в (по́лном) ~е** (*fig., coll.*) everything's fine.
ажу́рн|ый *adj.* open-work; (*fig.*) delicate, fine; **~ая рабо́та** open-work; (*archit.*) tracery.
аз, а́ *m.* **1** az (*Slavonic name of the letter A*). **2** (*usu. pl.; coll.*) basics, rudiments; **начина́ть с ~о́в** to begin at the beginning; **ни ~а́ не знать (о**+*p.*) not to know the first thing (about).
аза́ли|я, и *f.* (*bot.*) azalea.
аза́рт, а *m.* excitement; fervour (*Br.*), fervor (*US*); **войти́ в а.** to grow excited.
аза́рт|ный (~ен, ~на) *adj.* excited, ardent; **~ная игра́** game of chance.
а́збук|а, и *f.* alphabet; the ABC (*also fig.*); **а. Мо́рзе** Morse code; **дакти́льная а.** sign language; **но́тная а.** musical notation.
а́збучн|ый *adj.* alphabetical; **~ая и́стина** truism.
Азербайджа́н, а *m.* Azerbaijan.
азербайджа́н|ец, ца *m.* Azerbaijani(an).
азербайджа́н|ка, ки *f. of* ⇒**~ец**
азербайджа́нский *adj.* Azerbaijani.
азиа́т, а *m.* Asian.
азиа́т|ка, ки *f. of* ⇒**~**
азиа́тский *adj.* **1** Asian. **2** (*geog., geol.*) Asiatic.
а́зимут, а *m.* azimuth.
А́зи|я, и *f.* Asia; **Ма́лая А.** Asia Minor.
Азо́вск|ое мо́р|е, ~ого ~я *nt.* the Sea of Azov.
Азо́рск|ие острова́, ~их ~о́в *no sg.* the Azores (*islands*).
азо́т, а *m.* (*chem.*) nitrogen; **о́кись ~а** nitric oxide.
азотистоки́слый *adj.* (*chem.*) nitrite.
азо́тистый *adj.* (*chem.*) nitrous.
азотноки́слый *adj.* (*chem.*) nitrate.
азо́тн|ый *adj.* (*chem.*) nitric; **~ая кислота́** nitric acid.
а́ир, а *m.* (*bot.*) sweet flag.
а́ист, а *m.* (*zool.*) stork.
ай *int.* (*expr.* (*i*) *fear,* (*ii*) *surprise and/or pleasure*) oh!; ow!, ouch!; **ай, бо́льно!** ow, that hurts!; **ай да** (*expr. approval*) what a ...!; **ай да моло́де́ц!** well done!
айв|а́, ы́ *f.* **1** (*плод*) quince. **2** (*дерево*) quince-tree.
айво́вый *adj.* quince.
айда́ *int.* (*coll.*) come along!; let's go!
а́йе-а́йе *m. indecl.* (*zool.*) aye-aye.
айкидо́ *nt. indecl.* aikido.
а́йсберг, а *m.* iceberg.
академи́зм, а *m.* academic manner.
акаде́мик, а *m.* academician (*member of a specific academy*).
академи́ческий *adj.* academic; **а. о́тпуск** sabbatical (leave) (*for undergraduates or postgraduates*).
академи́ч|ный (~ен, ~на) *adj.* academic, theoretical.
акаде́ми|я, и *f.* academy.
акаде́мк|а, и *f.* (*sl.*) (officially authorized) year out.
а́канье|е, я *nt.* 'akanie' (*pronunciation of unstressed Russian 'o' as 'a'*).
а́ка|ть, ю *impf.* to pronounce unstressed Russian 'o' as 'a'.
ака́ци|я, и *f.* (*bot.*) acacia.
аквала́нг, а *m.* aqualung.
акваланги́ст, а *m.* (skin *or* scuba) diver.
аквалангист|ка, ки *f. of* ⇒**~**
аквамари́н, а *m.* (*min.*) aquamarine.
аквамари́н|овый *adj. of* ⇒**~**
аквапла́н, а *m.* aquaplane; **ката́ться на ~е** to aquaplane.
акварели́ст, а *m.* watercolourist (*Br.*), watercolorist (*US*).
акваре́л|ь, и *f.* (*краски*) watercolours (*Br.*), watercolors (*US*); **писа́ть ~ью** to paint in watercolours; (*картина*) watercolour (*Br.*), watercolor (*US*).
акваре́льный *adj.* watercolour (*Br.*), watercolor (*US*).
аква́риум, а *m.* aquarium, fish-tank.
аквариуми́ст, а *m.* aquarist.
аквато́ри|я, и *f.* (*defined*) waters.
акведу́к, а *m.* aqueduct.
акклиматиза́ци|я, и *f.* acclimatization.
акклиматизи́р|овать, ую *impf. and pf.* to acclimatize.
акклиматизи́р|оваться, уюсь *impf. and pf.* to become acclimatized; to acclimatize.
акколя́д|а, ы *f.* accolade.
аккомпанеме́нт, а *m.* (*mus.*) accompaniment (*also fig.*); **под а.** (+*g.*) to the accompaniment of.
аккомпаниа́тор, а *m.* (*mus.*) accompanist.
аккомпани́р|овать, ую *impf.* (+*d.*, **на**+*p.*; *mus.*) to accompany; **а. певцу́ на роя́ле** to accompany a singer on the piano.
акко́рд, а *m.* (*mus.*) chord; **заключи́тельный а.** (*fig.*) finale; **взять а.** to strike a chord (*on the piano*).
аккордео́н, а *m.* accordion.
аккордеони́ст, а *m.* accordionist.
акко́рдн|ый *adj.*: **~ая пла́та** payment by the job; **~ая рабо́та** piecework.
аккредити́в, а *m.* (*fin.*) letter of credit.
аккредит|ова́ть, у́ю *impf. and pf.* to accredit.

аккумули́р|овать, ую *impf. and pf.* to accumulate.

аккумуля́тор, а *m.* (*tech.*) accumulator; (*elec.*) accumulator (*Br.*), storage battery (*US*).

аккумуля́ци|я, и *f.* accumulation.

аккура́тност|ь, и *f.* **1** exactness, thoroughness. **2** tidiness, neatness.

аккура́т|ный (~ен, ~на) *adj.* **1** (*тщательный*) exact, thorough. **2** (*опрятный*) tidy, neat. **3** (*студент*) thorough, orderly. **4** (*регулярный*) regular, punctual.

акмеи́зм, а *m.* (*liter.*) acmeism.

акмеи́ст, а *m.* (*liter.*) acmeist.

акри́л, а *m.* acrylic.

акри́л|овый *adj. of* ⇨**~**

акроба́т, а *m.* acrobat.

акроба́тик|а, и *f.* acrobatics.

акробати́ческий *adj.* acrobatic.

акро́ним, а *m.* acronym.

акро́пол|ь, я *m.* (*hist.*) acropolis.

акрости́х, а *m.* acrostic.

акселера́т, а *m.* (*med.*) early developer, maturer.

акселера́тор, а *m.* accelerator.

акселера́ци|я, и *f.* (*med.*) early development, maturation; **а. ро́ста** accelerated growth.

аксельба́нт, а *m.* aiguillette.

аксессуа́р, а *m.* **1** accessory. **2** *pl.* (*theatr.*) props.

аксио́м|а, ы *f.* axiom.

акт, а *m.* **1** act; **полово́й а.** sexual intercourse. **2** (*theatr.*) act. **3** (*leg.*) deed, document; **обвини́тельный а.** indictment.

актёр, а *m.* actor.

актёр|ский *adj. of* ⇨**~**

актёрств|о, а *nt.* acting; (*fig.*) affectation, posing.

акти́в[1]**, а** *m.* (*fin.*) assets; (*fig.*) asset.

акти́в[2]**, а** *m.* (*pol.*) most active members; **парти́йный а.** party activists.

актива́ци|я, и *f.* (*chem., biol.*) activation.

активиза́ци|я, и *f.* activation; stimulation.

активизи́р|овать, ую *impf. and pf.* (*приводить в действие*) to activate; (*оживлять*) to stimulate, enliven.

активи́р|овать, ую *impf. and pf.* (*chem., biol.*) to activate.

активи́ст, а *m.* (*pol.*) activist.

акти́в|ный (~ен, ~на) *adj.* active, energetic.

акти́ни|я, и *f.* sea anemone.

а́ктовый *adj.*: **а. зал** assembly hall.

актри́с|а, ы *f.* actress.

актуа́льност|ь, и *f.* topicality.

актуа́л|ьный (~ен, ~ьна) *adj.* topical, current.

аку́л|а, ы *f.* (*zool.*) shark (*also fig.*).

акупункту́р|а, ы *f.* acupuncture.

аку́стик, а *m.* sound-man, sound technician.

аку́стик|а, и *f.* acoustics.

акусти́ческий *adj.* acoustic.

аку́т, а *m.* (*ling.*) acute accent.

акуше́р, а *m.* obstetrician.

акуше́рк|а, и *f.* midwife.

акуше́рский *adj.* obstetric(al).

акуше́рств|о, а *nt.* obstetrics; midwifery.

акце́нт, а *m.* accent.

акценти́р|овать, ую *impf. and pf.* to accentuate.

акце́пт, а *m.* (*comm.*) acceptance.

акцепт|ова́ть, у́ю *impf. and pf.* (*comm.*) to accept.

акци́з, а *m.* (excise-)duty; **обложи́ть ~ом** to excise.

акци́зный *adj.* excise (*attr.*).

акционе́р, а *m.* shareholder, stockholder.

акционе́р|ный *adj. of* ⇨**~**; **~ное о́бщество** joint-stock company.

а́кци|я[1]**, и** *f.* (*fin.*) share; **обыкнове́нная а.** ordinary share; **привилегиро́ванная а.** preference share.

а́кци|я[2]**, и** *f.* (*действие*) action.

алба́н|ец, ца *m.* Albanian.

Алба́ни|я, и *f.* Albania.

алба́н|ка, ки *f. of* ⇨**~ец**

алба́нский *adj.* Albanian.

а́лгебр|а, ы *f.* algebra.

алгебраи́ческий *adj.* algebraic(al).

алгори́тм, а *m.* algorithm.

алгоритми́ческий *adj.* algorithmic.

алеба́рд|а, ы *f.* (*hist.*) halberd.

алеба́стр, а *m.* alabaster.

александри́т, а *m.* (*min.*) alexandrite.

Александри́|я, и *f.* Alexandria.

але́|ть, ю *impf.* **1** (*становиться алым*) to redden, flush. **2** (*видне́ться*) to show red.

Алеу́тск|ие острова́, ~их ~о́в *no sg.* the Aleutians (*islands*).

Алжи́р, а *m.* **1** (*страна*) Algeria. **2** (*столица*) Algiers.

алжи́р|ец, ца *m.* Algerian.

алжи́р|ка, ки *f. of* ⇨**~ец**

алжи́рский *adj.* Algerian.

а́ли (*coll.*) = **и́ли**

а́либи *nt. indecl.* (*leg.*) alibi; **установи́ть а.** to establish an alibi.

алиме́нтщик, а *m.* (*coll.*) person paying alimony.

алиме́нтщиц|а, ы *f.* (*coll.*) woman in receipt of alimony.

алиме́нт|ы, ов *no sg.* (*leg.*) alimony, maintenance.

ал|ка́ть, ~чу́, ~чешь *impf.* (+*g.*; *obs. poet.*) to hunger (for), crave (for).

алка́ш, а́ *m.* (*coll., pej.*) boozer, dipso.

алкоголи́зм, а *m.* alcoholism.

алкого́лик, а *m.* alcoholic; (*coll.*) drunkard.

алкоголи́ческий *adj.* alcoholic.

алкого́л|ь, я *m.* alcohol; **прове́рить на а.** to breathalyse (*Br.*), breathalyze (*US*).

алкого́льный *adj.* alcoholic.

алкоме́тр, а *m.* breathalyser (*Br.*), Breathalyzer (*US, propr.*).

алкоте́ст = **алкоме́тр**

Алла́х, а *m.* Allah; **А. его́ ве́дает** God knows; **одному́ ~у изве́стно** God alone knows.

аллегори́ческий *adj.* allegorical.

аллегори́ч|ный (~ен, ~на) = **~еский**

аллего́ри|я, и *f.* allegory.

алле́гро (*mus.*) **1** *adv.* allegro. **2** *n.*; *nt. indecl.* allegro.

аллерге́н, а *m.* allergen.

алле́ргик, а *m.* allergy sufferer.

аллерги́ческий *adj.* allergic.

аллерги́|я, и *f.* allergy; **а. на клубни́ку** an allergy to strawberries.

алле́|я, и *f.* tree-lined path, avenue.

аллига́тор, а *m.* alligator.

аллилу́йя *nt. indecl. and as int.* alleluia, hallelujah.

аллитера́ци|я, и *f.* alliteration.

алло́ *int.* hello!

аллювиа́льный *adj.* (*geol.*) alluvial.

аллю́ви|й, я *m.* (*geol.*) alluvium.

аллю́р, а *m.* pace, gait (*of horses*).

Алма́-Ат|а́, ы́ *f.* Alma-Ata.

алма́з, а *m.* (uncut) diamond.

алма́з|ный *adj. of* ⇨**~**

Алма́ты *m. indecl.* Almaty.

ало́э *nt. indecl.* (*bot.*) aloe; (*med.*) aloes.

алта́р|ь, я́ *m.* **1** (*жертвенник*) altar; **возложи́ть, принести́ на а.** (+*g.*) to sacrifice (to). **2** (*восточная часть церкви*) chancel.

алты́н, а *m.* (*obs.*) three-kopeck piece.

алфави́т, а *m.* alphabet; (*comput., typ.*) character set.

алфави́тно-цифрово́й *adj.* alphanumeric.

алфави́тный *adj.* alphabetical; **а. указа́тель** index.

алхи́мик, а *m.* alchemist.

алхи́ми|я, и *f.* alchemy.

а́лчност|ь, и *f.* greed, avidity, cupidity.

а́лч|ный (~ен, ~на) *adj.* greedy, grasping.

а́лчущий *pres. part. of* ⇨**алка́ть**

а́л|ый (~, ~а) *adj.* scarlet.

алыч|а́, и́ *f.* cherry-plum (*Prunus cerasifera*).

аль (*coll.*) = **и́ли**

альбатро́с, а *m.* albatross.

альбино́с, а *m.* (*med.*) albino.

альбо́м, а *m.* (*книга; грампластинка*) album.

альвеоля́рный *adj.* (*ling.*) alveolar.

алько́в, а *m.* alcove.

а́льма-ма́тер *f. indecl.* Alma Mater.

альмана́х, а *m.* anthology.

альпака́ *c.g. indecl. and nt. indecl.* **1** *c.g.* (*животное*) alpaca. **2** *nt.* (*шерсть*) alpaca.

альпи́йский *adj.* alpine.

альпина́ри|й, я *m.* rock garden.

альпини́зм, а *m.* mountaineering.

альпини́ст, а *m.* mountain-climber, mountaineer.

альпини́ст|ка, ки *f. of* ⇨**~**

Альп|ы, ~ *no sg.* the Alps.
альт, а́ *m.* (*mus.*) **1** (*певец, голос*) alto. **2** (*инструмент*) viola.
альтера́ци|я, и *f.* (*mus.*) change in pitch of notes (*by a tone or semitone*); **зна́ки ~и** accidentals.
альтернати́в|а, ы *f.* alternative.
альтернати́в|ный (~ен, ~на) *adj.* alternative.
альти́ст, а *m.* viola-player.
альт|о́вый *adj. of* ⇒~; **~о́вая па́ртия** alto part.
альтруи́зм, а *m.* altruism.
альтруи́ст, а *m.* altruist.
альтруисти́ческий *adj.* altruistic.
а́льф|а, ы *f.* alpha; **от ~ы до оме́ги** from A to Z.
альфо́нс, а *m.* (*pej.*) gigolo.
алья́нс, а *m.* alliance.
алюми́ниевый *adj.* aluminium (*Br.*), aluminum (*US*).
алюми́ни|й, я *m.* aluminium (*Br.*), aluminum (*US*).
а-ля́ *prep.* à la.
аляпова́т|ый (~, ~а) *adj.* garish, cheap-looking; crude(ly fashioned).
Аля́ск|а, и *f.* Alaska.
а-ля фурше́т, а *m.* buffet; fork lunch *or* supper.
Амазо́нк|а, и *f.* the Amazon (*river*).
амазо́нк|а, и *f.* **1** (*myth.*) Amazon. **2** (*всадница*) horsewoman. **3** (*платье*) riding-habit.
амальга́м|а, ы *f.* (*chem. and fig.*) amalgam.
амальгами́р|овать, ую *impf. and pf.* (*chem. and fig.*) to amalgamate.
амана́т, а *m.* (*obs.*) hostage.
амба́р, а *m.* (*для зерна*) barn, granary; (*для товаров*) warehouse, storehouse.
амба́р|ный *adj. of* ⇒~
амбицио́з|ный (~ен, ~на) *adj.* arrogant, conceited.
амби́ци|я, и *f.* **1** arrogance; **вломи́ться в ~ю** (*coll.*) to take offence (*Br.*), offense (*US*). **2** *pl.* claims (to) (**на**+*a.*).
а́мбр|а, ы *f.* ambergris.
амбразу́р|а, ы *f.* (*mil., archit.*) embrasure.
амбре́ *nt. indecl.* scent, smell, fragrance (*now usu. iron.*).
амбро́зи|я, и *f.* ambrosia.
амбулато́ри|я, и *f.* (*med.*) (*в больнице*) out-patient department; (*кабинет врача*) doctor's surgery (*Br.*), doctor's office (*US*).
амбулато́р|ный *adj. of* ⇒**~ия; а. больно́й** out-patient; **а. приём** out-patient reception hours; surgery hours.
амбушю́р, а *m.* (*mus.*) mouthpiece.
амво́н, а *m.* (*eccl.*) ambo, pulpit.
амёб|а, ы *f.* (*zool.*) amoeba (*Br.*), ameba (*US*).
Аме́рик|а, и *f.* America.
америка́н|ец, ца *m.* American.
американиза́ци|я, и *f.* Americanization.
американизи́р|овать, ую *impf. and pf.* to Americanize.
американи́зм, а *m.* (*ling.*) Americanism.
американи́стик|а, и *f.* American studies.
америка́н|ка, ки *f. of* ⇒**~ец**
америка́нск|ий *adj.* American; **~ие го́ры** Big Dipper, switchback; **а. дя́дюшка** 'rich uncle'; **а. замо́к** Yale (*propr.*) lock; **а. оре́х** Brazil nut.
амети́ст, а *m.* (*min.*) amethyst.
амети́ст|овый *adj. of* ⇒~
аминокислот|а́, ы́ *f.* (*chem.*) amino acid.
ами́нь *particle* (*eccl.*) amen.
аммиа́к, а *m.* (*chem.*) ammonia.
аммиа́чный *adj.* (*chem.*) ammoniac.
аммо́ни|й, я *m.* (*chem.*) ammonium.
амнисти́р|овать, ую *impf. and pf.* to amnesty.
амни́сти|я, и *f.* amnesty.
амора́лк|а, и *f.* (*sl.*) immoral behaviour (*Br.*), behavior (*US*).
амора́льност|ь, и *f.* amorality; immorality.
амора́л|ьный (~ен, ~ьна) *adj.* (*нейтральный в отношении морали*) amoral; (*безнравственный*) immoral.
амортиза́тор, а *m.* (*tech.*) shock-absorber.
амортиза́ци|я, и *f.* **1** (*econ.*) amortization, depreciation. **2** (*tech.*) shock-absorption.
амортизи́р|овать, ую *impf. and pf.* (*econ.*) to amortize.
амо́рф|ный (~ен, ~на) *adj.* amorphous.
Амо́с, а *m.* (*bibl.*) Amos.
ампе́р, а, *g. pl.* **а.** *m.* (*phys.*) ampere.
ампи́р, а *m.* Empire style (*of furniture, etc.*).
ампи́р|ный *adj. of* ⇒~
амплиту́д|а, ы *f.* amplitude.
амплуа́ *nt. indecl.* (*theatr.*) type; (*fig.*) role.
а́мпул|а, ы *f.* ampoule (*Br.*), ampule (*US*).
ампута́ци|я, и *f.* (*med.*) amputation.
ампути́р|овать, ую *impf. and pf.* (*med.*) to amputate.
Амстерда́м, а *m.* Amsterdam.
амуле́т, а *m.* amulet.
амуни́ци|я, и *f.* (*collect.*) (*mil., hist.*) accoutrements (*Br.*), accouterments (*US*).
Аму́р, а *m.* **1** (*myth.*) Cupid. **2**: **аму́ры** (*pl. only*) (*coll.*) intrigues, love affairs.
аму́рнич|ать, аю *impf.* (**с**+*i.*; *coll.*) to flirt (with), have an affair (with).
аму́рн|ый *adj.* (*coll.*) love; amorous; **~ые дела́** love affairs; **~ые пи́сьма** love letters.
амфетами́н, а *m.* (*pharm.*) amphetamine.
амфи́би|я, и *f.* (*zool., bot.*) amphibian.
амфитеа́тр, а *m.* (*hist.*) amphitheatre (*Br.*), amphitheater (*US*); (*theatr.*) circle.
АН *f. indecl.* (*abbr. of* ***Акаде́мия нау́к***) Academy of Sciences.
ан *conj.* (*coll.*) on the contrary; but in fact.
анабо́лик, а *m.* (*coll.*) anabolic steroid.
анаболи́ческий *adj.*: **а. стеро́ид** anabolic steroid.
анагра́мм|а, ы *f.* anagram.
ана́лиз, а *m.* analysis; **а. кро́ви** blood test; **(радио)углеро́дный а.** carbon-dating.
анализи́р|овать, ую *impf.* to analyse (*Br.*), analyze (*US*).
анали́тик, а *m.* analyst.
аналити́ческий *adj.* analytic(al).
аналити́чный *adj.* = **аналити́ческий**
ана́лог, а *m.* analogue.
аналоги́ческ|ий *adj.* analogical.
аналоги́ч|ный (~ен, ~на) *adj.* analogous; **~ные слу́чаи** analogous cases.
анало́ги|я, и *f.* analogy; **по ~и (с**+*i.*) by analogy (with), on the analogy (of); **проводи́ть ~ю** to draw an analogy.
ана́лого-цифрово́й *adj.*: **а. преобразова́тель** analogue to digital converter.
анало́|й, я *m.* (*eccl.*) lectern.
ана́льный *adj.* anal.
анамне́з, а *m.* case history.
анана́с, а *m.* pineapple.
анана́с|ный *adj. of* ⇒~
анана́с|овый *adj. of* ⇒**~; а. сок** pineapple juice.
ана́пест, а *m.* (*liter.*) anapaest (*Br.*), anapest (*US*).
анархи́зм, а *m.* (*pol.*) anarchism.
анархи́ст, а *m.* (*pol.*) anarchist.
анархи́ческий *adj.* anarchic(al).
ана́рхи|я, и *f.* anarchy.
ана́том, а *m.* anatomist.
анатоми́р|овать, ую *impf. and pf.* (*med.*) to dissect.
анатоми́ческий *adj.* anatomical; **а. теа́тр** dissecting room.
анатоми́чк|а, и *f.* (*coll.*) dissecting room.
анато́ми|я, и *f.* anatomy.
ана́фем|а, ы *f.* (*eccl.*) anathema; excommunication; **преда́ть ~е** to excommunicate; (*fig.*) to denounce.
анафема́тств|овать, ую *impf.* (*eccl.*) to excommunicate; (*fig.*) to denounce.
ана́фемский *adj.* (*coll.*) accursed.
анахоре́т, а *m.* hermit, anchorite; (*fig.*) recluse.
анахрони́зм, а *m.* anachronism.
анахрони́ческий *adj.* anachronistic.
анаш|а́, и́ *f.* (*sl.*) pot, hash; **закру́тка ~и́** joint (= *marijuana cigarette*).
анаши́ст, а *m.* (*sl.*) pot smoker; pot-head.
ангажеме́нт, а *m.* (*obs., theatr.*) engagement.
ангажи́р|овать, ую *impf. and pf.* (*obs., theatr.*) to engage.
анга́р, а *m.* (*aeron.*) hangar.
а́нгел, а *m.* angel; **а.-храни́тель (*m.*)** guardian angel; **а. во плоти́ (*coll.*)** (an absolute) angel; **день (*m.*) ~а** name-day.

áнгельский *adj.* angelic (*also fig.*).

ангидри́д, а *m.* (*chem.*) anhydride.

анги́н|а, ы *f.* (*med.*) quinsy; tonsillitis.

англизи́р|овать, ую *impf. and pf.* to anglicize.

англи́йск|ий *adj.* **1** English; **~ая болéзнь** rickets; **~ая була́вка** safety-pin; **а. рожóк** (*mus.*) cor anglais; **~ая соль** Epsom salts. **2** (*британский*) British.

англика́н|ец, ца *m.* Anglican.

англика́н|ка, ки *f. of* ⇨**~ец**

англика́нский *adj.* (*eccl.*) Anglican.

англици́зм, а *m.* Anglicism.

англича́н|ин, ина, *pl.* **~е, ~** *m.* Englishman.

англича́нк|а, и *f.* Englishwoman.

А́нгли|я, и *f.* **1** England. **2** (*Британия*) Britain.

áнгло-бу́рск|ий *adj.*: **~ая войнá** (*hist.*) Boer War.

англоговоря́щий = **англоязы́чный** 1

англомáн, а *m.* Anglomaniac.

англомáни|я, и *f.* Anglomania.

англомáн|ка, ки *f. of* ⇨**~**

англосáкс, а *m.* Anglo-Saxon.

англосаксóнский *adj.* Anglo-Saxon.

англофи́л, а *m.* Anglophile.

англофили́|я, и *f.* Anglophilia.

англофóб, а *m.* Anglophobe.

англофóби|я, и *f.* Anglophobia.

англоязы́чный *adj.* **1** (*англоговорящий*) English-speaking, anglophone. **2** (*на английском языке*) English-language.

Ангóл|а, ы *f.* Angola.

ангóл|ец, ца *m.* Angolan.

ангóл|ка, ки *f. of* ⇨**~ец**

ангóльский *adj.* Angolan.

ангóрск|ий *adj.* Angora; **~ая шерсть** Angora (wool).

Андалу́зи|я, и *f.* Andalusia.

андáнте *adv.* (*mus.*) andante.

андергрáунд, а *m.* (*sl.*) underground (activity against the State).

андрóид, а *m.* android.

А́нд|ы, ~ *no sg.* the Andes.

анекдóт, а *m.* **1** (*рассказ*) anecdote, story. **2** (*шутка*) joke.

анекдоти́ческий *adj.* anecdotal.

анекдоти́чност|ь, и *f.* humorousness.

анекдоти́ч|ный (~ен, ~на) *adj.* humorous.

анекдóтчик, а *m.* raconteur.

анеми́ческий *adj.* anaemic (*Br.*), anemic (*US*).

анеми́ч|ный (~ен, ~на) *adj.* anaemic (*Br.*), anemic (*US*), pale.

анеми́|я, и *f.* anaemia (*Br.*), anemia (*US*).

анемóн, а *m.* (*bot.*) anemone.

анерóид, а *m.* aneroid (barometer).

анестезиóлог, а *m.* anaesthetist (*Br.*), anesthesiologist (*US*).

анестези́р|овать, ую *impf. and pf.* (*med.*) to anaesthetize (*Br.*), anesthetize (*US*); **~ующее срéдство** anaesthetic (*Br.*), anesthetic (*US*).

анестези́|я, и *f.* (*med.*) anaesthesia (*Br.*), anesthesia (*US*).

анимали́ст, а *m.* animal painter.

ани́с, а *m.* **1** (*растение*) anise. **2** (*семя*) aniseed.

ани́с|овый *adj. of* ⇨**~**; **~овое сéмя** aniseed; **~овая вóдка** anisette.

АНК *m. indecl.* (*abbr. of* ***Африкáнский национáльный конгрéсс***) ANC (*African National Congress*).

Анкар|á, ы *m.* Ankara.

анкéт|а, ы *f.* (*опросный лист*) questionnaire; (*бланк*) form; (*сбор сведений*) poll, survey.

анкéт|ный *adj. of* ⇨**~а; ~ные дáнные** biographical details.

анклáв, а *m.* enclave.

аннáл|ы, ов *no sg.* annals.

аннекси́р|овать, ую *impf. and pf.* (*pol.*) to annex.

аннéкси|я, и *f.* (*pol.*) annexation.

аннотáци|я, и *f.* abstract, précis.

аннoти́р|овать, ую *impf. and pf.* to summarize.

аннули́р|овать, ую *impf. and pf.* (*договор*) to annul, nullify; (*долг*) to cancel; (*закон*) to abrogate.

аннуля́ци|я, и *f.* annulment; cancellation; abrogation.

анóд, а *m.* (*phys.*) anode.

аномáли|я, и *f.* anomaly.

аномáл|ьный (~ен, ~ьна) *adj.* anomalous.

анони́м, а *m.* anonymous author.

анони́мк|а, и *f.* (*coll.*) **1** (*письмо*) poison-pen letter. **2** (*звонок*) anonymous telephone call.

анони́мност|ь, и *f.* anonymity.

анони́м|ный (~ен, ~на) *adj.* anonymous.

анóнс, а *m.* announcement, notice; (*cin.*) trailer.

анонси́р|овать, ую *impf. and pf.* (+*a. or* **o**+*p.*) to announce.

анорáк, а *m.* anorak.

анорéкси|я, и *f.* anorexia.

анормáл|ьный (~ен, ~ьна) *adj.* abnormal.

ансáмбл|ь, я *m.* ensemble.

антагони́зм, а *m.* antagonism.

антагони́ст, а *m.* antagonist.

Антаркти́д|а, ы *f.* Antarctica.

Антáрктик|а, и *f.* the Antarctic.

антаркти́ческий *adj.* Antarctic.

антéнн|а, ы *f.* **1** (*zool.*) antenna. **2** (*tech.*) aerial, antenna.

антéнн|ый *adj. of* ⇨**~а**

анти... *pref.* anti-.

антиалкогóльный *adj.* anti-alcohol.

антиáтомный *adj.*: **а. марш** antinuclear march.

антибиóтик, а *m.* (*med.*) antibiotic.

антивеществ|ó, á *nt.* antimatter.

антивоéнный *adj.* anti-war.

антигерó|й, я *m.* anti-hero.

антигистами́н, а *m.* (*med.*) antihistamine.

антидемократи́ческий *adj.* antidemocratic.

антидепрессáнт, а *m.* (*med.*) antidepressant.

антидóпинговый *adj.*: **а. контрóль** dope testing.

антизапотевáтел|ь, я *m.* demister.

антиквáр, а *m.* (*любитель антикварных предметов*) antiquary; (*дилер*) antique dealer.

антиквариáт, а *m.* **1** (*collect.*) antiques. **2** (*obs.*) antique-shop.

антиквáрный *adj.* (*книга*) antiquarian; (*ваза; магазин*) antique.

антилóп|а, ы *f.* (*zool.*) antelope.

Анти́льск|ие острова́, ~их ~óв *no sg.* the Antilles (*islands*).

антиобледени́тел|ь, я *m.* anti-icer; de-icer.

антипати́ч|ный (~ен, ~на) *adj.* antipathetic, unpleasant.

антипáти|я, и *f.* antipathy.

антипóд, а *m.* antipode, opposite.

антипригáрный *adj.* non-stick.

антиракéт|а, ы *f.* anti-missile missile, antimissile.

антиракéтчик, а *m.* ban-the-bomb campaigner.

антисанитари́|я, и *f.* insanitary conditions.

антисанитáрный *adj.* insanitary.

антисеми́т, а *m.* anti-Semite.

антисемити́зм, а *m.* anti-Semitism.

антисеми́т|ка, ки *f. of* ⇨**~**

антисеми́тский *adj.* anti-Semitic.

антисéптик, а *m.* antiseptic.

антисéптик|а, и *f.* **1** antisepsis. **2** (*collect.*) antiseptics.

антисепти́ческий *adj.* antiseptic.

антисовéтский *adj.* anti-Soviet.

антитéз|а, ы *f.* antithesis.

антитéзис, а *m.* (*phil.*) antithesis.

антитéл|о, а *nt.* antibody.

антитети́ческий *adj.* antithetical.

антифри́з, а *m.* antifreeze.

анти́христ, а *m.* Antichrist.

антициклóн, а *m.* (*meteor.*) anticyclone.

античеловéческий *adj.* inhuman.

анти́чност|ь, и *f.* antiquity; (*hist.*) classical antiquity.

анти́чный *adj.* ancient; classical; **а. мир** the ancient world.

антолóги|я, и *f.* (*liter.*) anthology.

антóновк|а, и *f.* Antonovka (*variety of winter apple*).

антóновск|ий *adj.*: **~ое я́блоко** = **антóновка**

антрáкт, а *m.* **1** (*theatr.*) interval. **2** (*mus.*) entr'acte.

антраци́т, а *m.* (*min.*) anthracite.

антрашá *nt. indecl.* entrechat; **вы́дéлывать а.** (*coll.*) to cut capers.

антрекóт, а *m.* entrecôte, steak.

антрепренёр, а *m.* impresario.

антрепри́з|а, ы *f.* (*theatr.*) private theatrical concern.

антресо́л|ь, и *f.* (*usu. pl.*) **1** (*полуэтаж*) mezzanine. **2** (*полка*) shelf.

антропо́ид, а *m.* anthropoid.

антропо́лог, а *m.* anthropologist.

антропологи́ческий *adj.* anthropological.

антрополо́ги|я, и *f.* anthropology.

антропоморфи́зм, а *m.* anthropomorphism.

антропоморфи́ческий *adj.* anthropomorphic.

антропомо́рфный *adj.* anthropoid.

антропофа́ги|я, и *f.* cannibalism.

антура́ж, а *m.* environment; (*collect.*) entourage, associates.

анфа́с *adv.* full face.

анфила́д|а, ы *f.* suite (of rooms).

анча́р, а *m.* (*bot.*) upas-tree (*Antiaris toxicaria*).

анчо́ус, а *m.* anchovy.

аншла́г, а *m.* **1** (*theatr.*) sell-out notice; **спекта́кль идёт с ~ом** the show is sold out, the house is full. **2** (*в газете*) banner headline.

а́ншлюс(с), а *m.* anschluss.

аню́тины: а. гла́зки (*bot.*) pansy.

ао́рт|а, ы *f.* (*anat.*) aorta.

апартаме́нт|ы, ов *pl.* (*sg.* **~, ~а** *m.*) large apartment.

апартеи́д, а *m.* apartheid.

апати́т, а *m.* (*min.*) apatite.

апати́ч|ный (~ен, ~на) *adj.* apathetic.

апа́ти|я, и *f.* apathy.

апа́ч, а *m.* Apache.

апа́ш *adj. indecl.*: **руба́шка а.** (man's) open-necked shirt.

апелли́р|овать, ую *impf. and pf.* (**к**+*d.*) to appeal (to).

апелля́нт, а *m.* (*leg.*) appellant.

апелл|яцио́нный *adj. of* ⇒**~я́ция; а. суд** Court of Appeal.

апелля́ци|я, и *f.* (**к**+*d.*) appeal (to).

апельси́н, а *m.* **1** (*плод*) orange. **2** (*дерево*) orange-tree.

апельси́н|ный *adj. of* ⇒**~**

апельси́нов|ый *adj.* orange; **~ое варе́нье** orange marmalade.

Апенни́н|ы, ~ *no sg.* the Apennines.

аперити́в, а *m.* apéritif.

аплоди́р|овать, ую *impf.* (+*d.*) to applaud.

аплодисме́нт|ы, ов *m. pl.* applause.

апло́мб, а *m.* aplomb, assurance.

АПН *nt. indecl.* (*abbr. of* ***Аге́нтство печа́ти «Но́вости»***) APN, Novosti Press Agency.

апоге́|й, я *m.* (*astron.*) apogee; (*fig.*) climax.

Апока́липсис, а *m.* (*bibl.*) (the Book of) Revelation, the Apocalypse.

апокалипти́ческий *adj.* apocalyptic.

апо́криф, а *m.* apocryphal work, story.

апокрифи́ческий *adj. of* ⇒**апо́криф**

апокрифи́ч|ный (~ен, ~на) *adj.* (*coll.*) apocryphal.

апо́криф|ы, ов *pl.* Apocrypha.

аполити́чност|ь, и *f.* political indifference.

аполити́ч|ный (~ен, ~на) *adj.* apolitical; politically indifferent.

апологе́т, а *m.* apologist.

апологе́тик|а, и *f.* apologetics.

аполо́ги|я, и *f.* apologia.

апоплекси́ческий *adj.* (*med.*) apoplectic.

апопле́кси|я, и *f.* (*med.*) apoplexy.

апо́рт *int.* fetch! (*command to dog*).

апостерио́ри *adv.* (*phil.*) a posteriori.

апостерио́рный *adj.* (*phil.*) a posteriori.

апо́стол, а *m.* **1** apostle (*also fig.*). **2** (*bibl.*) Books of the Apostles (*the Acts of the Apostles and the Epistles*).

апо́стольник, а *m.* wimple.

апо́стольский *adj.* apostolic.

апостро́ф, а *m.* apostrophe.

апофео́з, а *m.* apotheosis.

Аппала́ч|и, ей *no sg.* the Appalachians.

аппара́т, а *m.* **1** (*прибор*) apparatus; appliance; **копирова́льный а.** photocopier; **косми́ческий лета́тельный а.** spacecraft; **ка́ссовый а.** cash register; **слухово́й а.** hearing aid; **телефо́нный а.** telephone; **факсими́льный а.** fax (machine); **фотографи́ческий а.** camera; **а. «иску́сственная по́чка»** kidney machine. **2** (*physiol.*): **пищевари́тельный а.** digestive system. **3** (*admin.*): **госуда́рственный а.** machinery of State; **суде́бный а.** judicial system. **4** (*штат*) staff, personnel.

аппара́тно-програ́ммн|ый *adj.* (*comput.*) firmware; **~ые сре́дства** firmware.

аппара́тн|ый *adj.* (*comput.*) hardware; **~ые сре́дства** hardware.

аппарату́р|а, ы *f.* (*tech., collect.*) apparatus, equipment; (*comput.*) hardware.

аппара́тчик, а *m.* **1** (machine) operative. **2** (*pol.*) apparatchik.

аппе́ндикс, а *m.* appendix.

аппендици́т, а *m.* appendicitis.

апперко́т, а *m.* uppercut.

аппети́т, а *m.* appetite; **прия́тного ~а!** bon appétit!

аппети́т|ный (~ен, ~на) *adj.* **1** appetizing, mouth-watering. **2** (*coll.*) (*привлекательный*) fetching, dishy.

аппликату́р|а, ы *f.* (*mus.*) fingering.

апплика́ци|я, и *f.* appliqué.

апплике́ *adj. indecl.* plated.

аппрету́р|а, ы *f.* (*tech.*) dressing.

апре́л|ь, я *m.* April; **с пе́рвым ~я!** April Fool!

апре́ль|ский *adj. of* ⇒**~**

априо́ри *adv.* a priori.

априо́р|ный (~ен, ~на) *adj.* a priori.

апроба́ци|я, и *f.* approbation.

апроби́р|овать, ую *impf. and pf.* to approve (*having tested*).

апси́д|а, ы *f.* (*archit.*) apse.

апте́к|а, и *f.* chemist's (shop) (*Br.*), pharmacy; **как в ~е** (*coll., joc.*) just so, exactly right.

апте́карский *adj.* chemist's (*Br.*); pharmaceutical.

апте́кар|ь, я *m.* chemist (*Br.*); pharmacist.

апте́чк|а, и *f.* (*первой помощи*) first-aid kit; (*коробка*) medicine chest; **а. для ремо́нта шин** tyre (*Br.*), tire (*US*) repair kit.

апчхи́ *int.* atishoo.

ар, а *m.* are (*unit of land measurement*).

а́ра *m. indecl.* macaw.

ара́б, а *m.* Arab, Arabian.

арабе́ск, а *m.* = **арабе́ска**

арабе́ск|а, и *f.* arabesque.

араби́ст, а *m.* Arabic scholar, Arabist.

ара́б|ка, ки *f. of* ⇒**~**

ара́бск|ий *adj.* Arab; Arabian; Arabic; **~ие ци́фры** arabic numerals; **а. язы́к** Arabic.

арави́йский *adj.* Arabian, of Arabia.

Ара́ви|я, и *f.* Arabia.

ара́к, а *m.* arrack.

араме́йский *adj.* Aramaic.

аранжи́р|овать, ую *impf. and pf.* to arrange.

аранжиро́вк|а, и *f.* arrangement.

ара́п, а *m.* (*obs., sl.*) cheat, swindler; **на ~а** by bluffing.

ара́пник, а *m.* riding crop.

арauка́ри|я, и *f.* araucaria, monkey-puzzle tree.

ара́хис, а *m.* peanut, groundnut.

ара́хисов|ый *adj.*: **~ая па́ста** peanut butter; **~ое ма́сло** groundnut oil.

арб|а́, ы́, *pl.* **~ы** *f.* bullock-cart.

арбале́т, а *m.* arbalest, crossbow.

арби́тр, а *m.* (*в споре*) arbiter, arbitrator; (*в спорте*) umpire, referee.

арбитра́ж, а *m.* arbitration.

арбу́з, а *m.* water-melon.

Аргенти́н|а, ы *f.* Argentina.

аргенти́н|ец, ца *m.* Argentinian.

аргенти́н|ка, ки *f. of* ⇒**~ец**

аргенти́нский *adj.* Argentine.

арго́ *nt. indecl.* argot, slang.

арго́н, а *m.* (*chem.*) argon.

арготи́зм, а *m.* slang expression.

арготи́ческий *adj. of* ⇒**арго́**

аргуме́нт, а *m.* argument.

аргумента́ци|я, и *f.* reasoning, argumentation.

аргументи́р|овать, ую *impf. and pf.* to argue; (*pf. only*) to prove.

ареа́л, а *m.* (*bot. and zool.*) natural habitat; (*fig.*) region.

аре́н|а, ы *f.* arena, ring; (*fig.*) arena.

аре́нд|а, ы *f.* lease; **сдать в ~у** to rent,

lease (*of owner, landlord*); **взять в ~у** to rent, lease (*of tenant*).
арендáтор, а *m.* tenant, lessee.
арéнд|ный *adj. of* ⇨**~а; ~ная плáта** rent; **а. подря́д** contract for lease (*of land*).
аренд|овáть, у́ю *impf. and pf.* to rent, lease (*of tenant*).
арéст, а *m.* (*человека*) arrest; (*имущества*) seizure, sequestration; **взять под а.** to place under arrest; **сидéть, находи́ться под ~ом** to be under arrest, in custody; **наложи́ть а. на** (+*a.*) to sequestrate; **казáрменный а.** confinement to barracks.
арестáнт, а *m.* prisoner.
арестáнтск|ая, ой *f.* lock-up, cells.
арест|овáть, у́ю *pf.* (*of* ⇨**~óвывать**) (*человека*) to arrest; (*имущество*) to sequestrate.
арестóвыва|ть, ю *impf. of* ⇨**арестовáть**
ари́|ец, йца *m.* Aryan.
ари́|йка, йки *f. of* ⇨**~ец**
ари́йский *adj.* Aryan.
аристокрáт, а *m.* aristocrat.
аристократи́ческий *adj.* aristocratic.
аристокрáти|я, и *f.* aristocracy.
аритми́ч|ный (~ен, ~на) *adj.* arrhythmic.
арифмéтик|а, и *f.* arithmetic.
арифмети́ческий *adj.* arithmetical.
арифмóметр, а *m.* calculating machine; calculator.
áри|я, и *f.* aria.
áрк|а, и *f.* arch.
аркáд|а, ы *f.* arcade.
аркáдский *adj.* Arcadian.
аркáн, а *m.* lasso.
аркáн|ить, ю, ишь *impf.* (*pf.* **за~**) to lasso.
Áрктик|а, и *f.* the Arctic.
аркти́ческий *adj.* arctic.
арлеки́н, а *m.* harlequin.
армáд|а, ы *f.* armada.
армади́л, а *m.* armadillo.
армату́р|а, ы *f.* (*collect.*) fittings; (*tech.*) steel framework.
армату́р|ный *adj. of* ⇨**~а**
армату́рщик, а *m.* (*tech.*) fitter.
армé|ец, йца *m.* soldier.
армéйский *adj. of* ⇨**áрмия**
Армéни|я, и *f.* Armenia.
áрми|я, и *f.* army; **А. Спасéния** Salvation Army; **дéйствующая а.** front-line forces.
армя́к, á *m.* (*hist.*) armyak (*peasant's coat of heavy cloth*).
армян|и́н, и́на, *pl.* **~е, ~** *m.* Armenian.
армя́н|ка, ки *f. of* ⇨**~и́н**
армя́нский *adj.* Armenian.
áрник|а, и *f.* (*bot., med.*) arnica.
аромáт, а *m.* (*цветов*) scent, fragrance; (*пищи*) aroma; (*молодости*) spirit.
ароматерапи́|я, и *f.* aromatherapy.
ароматизáтор, а *m.* (*cul.*) flavouring (*Br.*), flavoring (*US*).
аромати́ческий = **аромáтный**
аромати́ч|ный (~ен, ~на) = **аромáтный**
аромáт|ный (~ен, ~на) *adj.* aromatic, fragrant.
áрочный *adj.* arched, vaulted.
арпéджио *nt. indecl.* arpeggio.
арсенáл, а *m.* arsenal.
арт. *abbr. of* **артиллéрия**
арт... *comb. form* **1** *abbr. of* **артиллери́йский. 2** (*искусство*) art-.
артáч|иться, усь, ишься *impf.* (*coll.*) to jib, balk.
артезиáнский *adj.*: **а. кóлодец** artesian well.
артéл|ь, и *f.* artel (*workers' or peasants' co-operative*).
артéль|ный *adj.* **1** *adj. of* ⇨**~.** **2** (*coll.*) (*коллективный*) collective; **на ~ных начáлах** on collective principles. **3** (*coll.*) (*общительный*) chummy, sociable.
артéльщик, а *m.* member of an artel.
артериáльный *adj.* (*anat.*) arterial.
артериосклерóз, а *m.* arteriosclerosis.
артéри|я, и *f.* artery.
арти́кл|ь, я *m.* (*gram.*) article.
арти́кул, а *m.* **1** (*род изделия*) type of manufactured article. **2** (*его обозначение*) code (*of manufactured article, in numbers or letters*).
артикули́р|овать, ую *impf.* (*ling.*) to articulate.
артикуля́ци|я, и *f.* (*ling.*) articulation.
артиллери́йский *adj.* (*mil.*) artillery; **а. обстрéл** bombardment, shelling; **а. склад** ordnance depot.
артиллéри|я, и *f.* artillery.
арти́ст, а *m.* **1** artist(e); **óперный а.** opera singer; **а. балéта** ballet dancer; **а. кинó** film actor. **2** (*fig.*) artist, expert.
артисти́зм, а *m.* artistry, virtuosity.
артисти́ческ|ий *adj.* artistic; *as n.* **~ая, ~ой** *f.* (*theatr.*) green-room, dressing-room.
артисти́чност|ь, и *f.* = **артисти́зм**
арти́ст|ка, ки *f. of* ⇨**~**
артишóк, а *m.* artichoke.
артри́т, а *m.* arthritis; **больнóй** (*fem.* **больнáя**) **~ом** arthritic (*person*).
áрф|а, ы *f.* harp.
арфи́ст, а *m.* harpist.
арфи́ст|ка, ки *f. of* ⇨**~**
архаи́зм, а *m.* archaism.
архаи́ческий *adj.* archaic.
архаи́ч|ный (~ен, ~на) *adj.* archaic.
арх́ангел, а *m.* archangel.
архáнгельский *adj.* archangelic.
архáр, а *m.* (*zool.*) argali.
археóлог, а *m.* archaeologist (*Br.*), archeologist (*US*).
археологи́ческий *adj.* archaeological (*Br.*), archeological (*US*).
археолóги|я, и *f.* archaeology (*Br.*), archeology (*US*).
архи... *comb. form* arch-.
архи́в, а *m.* archive; (*collect.*) archives; **сдать в а.** (*coll., fig.*) to shelve, throw out, leave out of account.
архивáриус, а *m.* archivist.
архи́в|ный *adj. of* ⇨**~**
архидья́кон, а *m.* archdeacon.
архиепи́скоп, а *m.* archbishop.
архиерé|й, я *m.* member of higher orders of clergy (*bishop, archbishop or metropolitan*).
архимандри́т, а *m.* (*eccl.*) archimandrite.
архипелáг, а *m.* archipelago.
архитектóник|а, и *f.* architectonics.
архитектони́ческий *adj.* architectonic.
архитéктор, а *m.* architect.
архитекту́р|а, ы *f.* architecture.
архитекту́рный *adj.* architectural.
архитрáв, а *m.* (*archit.*) architrave.
арши́н, а *m.* **1** (*мера*) arshin (*old Russian measure, equivalent to 71 cm*). **2** (*линейка*) rule one arshin in length; **мéрить на свой а.** to measure by one's own yardstick.
арши́нн|ый *adj.* (*coll.*) great big; whopping great; **~ая бородá** great long beard; **~ые заголóвки** banner headlines.
ары́к, а *m.* irrigation canal (*in Central Asia*).
арьергáрд, а *m.* (*mil.*) rearguard.
арьергáрдный *adj.* (*mil.*) rearguard.
ас, а *m.* (*air*) ace; (*fig.*) expert.
асбéст, а *m.* asbestos.
асбéстовый *adj.* asbestos.
асимметри́ческий *adj.* asymmetrical.
асимметри́ч|ный (~ен, ~на) *adj.* asymmetrical.
асимметри́|я, и *f.* asymmetry.
аскéт, а *m.* ascetic.
аскети́зм, а *m.* asceticism.
аскети́ческий *adj.* ascetic.
асоциáльный *adj.* anti-social.
аспéкт, а *m.* (*сторона*) aspect; (*точка зрения*) viewpoint, perspective; **в ~е** (+*g.*) in the light of.
áспид[1], а *m.* (*zool.*) asp; (*fig.*) viper.
áспид[2], а *m.* (*obs., min.*) slate.
áспид|ный *adj. of* ⇨**~[2]**; **~ная доскá** slate (*for writing on*).
аспирáнт, а *m.* post-graduate student.
аспирáнт|ка, ки *f. of* ⇨**~**
аспиранту́р|а, ы *f.* post-graduate study.
аспири́н, а *m.* (*med.*) aspirin; **таблéтка ~а** an aspirin.
ассамблé|я, и *f.* **1** assembly. **2** (*hist.*) ball.
ассенизáци|я, и *f.* sewage disposal.
ассигнáци|я, и *f.* (*hist.*) assignat (*a form of paper money in use 1769–c.1840*).

ассигнова́ни|е, я *nt.* (*fin.*) assignation, allocation.
ассигн|ова́ть, у́ю *impf. and pf.* (*fin.*) to assign, allocate.
ассигно́вк|а, и *f.* (*fin.*) assignment; grant (*of funds*).
ассимили́р|овать, ую *impf. and pf.* to assimilate.
ассимиля́ци|я, и *f.* assimilation.
ассири́йский *adj.* Assyrian.
Асси́ри|я, и *f.* Assyria.
ассисте́нт, а *m.* **1** (*помощник*) assistant. **2** (*в вузе*) junior member of teaching or research staff.
ассисти́р|овать, ую *impf.* (*med.*) (+*d.*) to assist.
ассона́нс, а *m.* assonance.
ассорти́ *nt. indecl.*: **шокола́дное а.** chocolate assortment.
ассортиме́нт, а *m.* assortment; range (*of goods*).
ассоциа́ци|я, и *f.* association.
ассоции́р|овать, ую *impf. and pf.* (**с**+*i.*) to associate (with).
АССР *f. indecl.* (*abbr. of* ***Автоно́мная Сове́тская Социалисти́ческая Респу́блика***) ASSR (*Autonomous Soviet Socialist Republic*).
астеро́ид, а *m.* asteroid.
астигмати́зм, а *m.* astigmatism.
а́стм|а, ы *f.* asthma.
астма́тик, а *m.* asthmatic.
астмати́ческий *adj.* asthmatic.
а́стр|а, ы *f.* aster.
астра́льный *adj.* astral.
астро́лог, а *m.* astrologer.
астрологи́ческий *adj.* astrological.
астроло́ги|я, и *f.* astrology.
астроля́би|я, и *f.* astrolabe.
астрона́вт, а *m.* astronaut.
астроно́м, а *m.* astronomer.
астрономи́ческий *adj.* astronomic-(al).
астроно́ми|я, и *f.* astronomy.
астрофи́зик|а, и *f.* astrophysics.
асфа́льт, а *m.* asphalt.
асфальти́р|овать, ую *impf. and pf.* (*pf. also* **за~**) (*tech.*) to asphalt.
асфа́льтовый *adj.* asphalt.
асфи́кси|я, и *f.* asphyxia.
ась *int.* (*coll.*) what?; eh?; huh?
атави́зм, а *m.* atavism.
атависти́ческий *adj.* atavistic.
ата́к|а, и *f.* attack.
атак|ова́ть, у́ю *impf. and pf.* to attack, charge, assault; **а. с ты́ла** to take in rear; **а. с фла́нга** to take in flank.
ата́ман, а *m.* **1** ataman (*Cossack chieftain*). **2** (*coll.*) (gang-)leader, (robber) chief.
ата́с (*sl.*): **стоя́ть на ~е** to keep lookout; *int.* watch out!
атеи́зм, а *m.* atheism.
атеи́ст, а *m.* atheist.
атеисти́ческий *adj.* atheistic.
атеи́ст|ка, ки *f. of* ⇨**~**
ателье́ *nt. indecl.* studio; **портно́вское а.** tailor's shop; **телевизио́нное а.** TV repair shop; **а. мод** dressmaking and tailoring establishment; dressmaker's shop, tailor's shop.
атеросклеро́з, а *m.* atherosclerosis.
Атланти́ческ|ий океа́н, ~ого ~а *m.* the Atlantic Ocean; the Atlantic.
а́тлас, а *m.* atlas.
атла́с, а *m.* satin.
атла́сный *adj.* satin; (*гладкий*) satiny.
Атла́сск|ие го́р|ы, ~их ~ *no sg.* the Atlas Mountains.
атле́т, а *m.* (*спортсмен*) athlete; (*в цирке*) strongman.
атлети́зм, а *m.* **1** (*телосложение*) athleticism. **2** (*культуризм*) body-building.
атле́тик|а, и *f.* athletics; **лёгкая а.** (track-and-field) athletics; **тяжёлая а.** weightlifting.
атлети́ческий *adj.* athletic.
атмосфе́р|а, ы *f.* atmosphere.
атмосфери́ческий *adj.* atmospheric.
атмосфе́рн|ый *adj.* atmospheric; **~ые оса́дки** atmospheric precipitation, rainfall.
ато́лл, а *m.* atoll.
а́том, а *m.* atom.
а́томн|ый *adj.* atomic; nuclear; **~ая бо́мба** atomic bomb; **а. вес** (*chem.*) atomic weight; **~ая электроста́нция** nuclear power station.
атомохо́д, а *m.* nuclear-powered vessel.
атона́льный *adj.* atonal.
атрибу́т, а *m.* attribute.
атрибути́вный *adj.* (*ling.*) attributive.
а́триум, а *m.* (*archit.*) atrium.
атропи́н, а *m.* (*med.*) atropine.
атрофи́р|оваться, уюсь *impf. and pf.* to atrophy.
атрофи́|я, и *f.* atrophy.
АТС *f. indecl.* (*abbr. of* ***автомат-и́ческая телефо́нная ста́нция***) automatic telephone exchange.
атташе́ *m. indecl.* (*dipl.*) attaché.
аттеста́т, а *m.* testimonial; certificate; pedigree; **а. зре́лости** school-leaving certificate.
аттестацио́нн|ый *adj.*: **~ая коми́ссия** examination board.
аттеста́ци|я, и *f.* **1** (*действие*) attestation. **2** (*отзыв*) testimonial.
аттест|ова́ть, у́ю *impf. and pf.* (*дать отзыв*) to recommend; (*присвоить звание*) to confer a rank on; (*оценить знания*) to grade.
аттракцио́н, а *m.* (*theatr.*) attraction; (*fairground*) sideshow, ride; **парк ~ов** amusement park.
ату́ *int.* (*hunting*) tally-ho!; halloo!
ать-два *int.* (*mil.*) hep, two!
ау́ *int.* **1** hi!, halloo! (*used to attract attention*). **2** (*coll.*) (*пропало*) it's all up!; it's done for!
аудие́нци|я, и *f.* audience.
аудиовизуа́льный *adj.* audiovisual.
аудиокассе́т|а, ы *f.* audio cassette.
аудиопла́т|а, ы *f.* (*comput.*) sound card.
аудиоплёнк|а, и *f.* audiotape.
ауди́т, а *m.* audit.
ауди́тор, а *m.* auditor.
аудито́ри|я, и *f.* **1** auditorium; lecture-hall. **2** (*collect.*) audience.
ау́ка|ть, ю *impf.* (*pf.* **ау́кнуть**) to shout 'hi!'; to halloo.
ау́к|аться, аюсь *impf.* (*of* ⇨**~нуться**) to halloo to one another.
ау́к|нуть, ну, нешь *pf. of* ⇨**~ать**
ау́к|нуться, нусь, нешься *pf. of* ⇨**~аться; как ~нется, так и откли́кнется** serves you, *etc.*, right; do as you would be done by.
аукцио́н, а *m.* auction, auction sale; **продава́ть с ~а** to auction.
аукциони́ст, а *m.* auctioneer.
аукцио́н|ный *adj. of* ⇨**~; а. зал** auction room.
ау́л, а *m.* aul (*mountain village in Caucasus or Central Asia*).
а́ур|а, ы *f.* aura.
а́ут, а *m.* (*sport*) out (*also as int.*).
аутенти́ч|ный (~ен, ~на) *adj.* authentic.
аути́зм, а *m.* autism.
аутодафе́ *nt. indecl.* auto-da-fé.
аутоиммýнный *adj.* autoimmune.
ауто́пси|я, и *f.* autopsy, post-mortem.
аутса́йдер, а *m.* outsider.
афа́зи|я, и *f.* (*med.*) aphasia.
афга́н|ец, ца *m.* Afghan; **«а.»** Afghan war vet(eran).
Афганиста́н, а *m.* Afghanistan.
афга́н|ка, ки *f. of* ⇨**~ец**
афга́нский *adj.* Afghan.
афе́р|а, ы *f.* swindle, trickery.
афери́ст, а *m.* swindler; trickster.
Афи́н|ы, ~ *no sg.* Athens.
афи́ш|а, и *f.* poster, placard; **театра́льная а.** playbill; **раскле́йщик ~** billsticker.
афиши́р|овать, ую *impf.* to parade, advertise.
афори́зм, а *m.* aphorism.
афористи́ческий *adj.* aphoristic.
афористи́ч|ный (~ен, ~на) *adj.* aphoristic.
А́фрик|а, и *f.* Africa.
африка́анс, а *m.* Afrikaans.
африка́нер, а *m.* Afrikaner.
африка́н|ец, ца *m.* African.
африка́н|ка, ки *f. of* ⇨**~ец**
африка́нский *adj.* African.
а́фро-америка́н|ец, ца *m.* African American.
а́фро-америка́н|ка, ки *f. of* ⇨**~ец**
а́фро-америка́нский *adj.* African American.
а́фро-кари́бский *adj.* Afro-Caribbean.
аффе́кт, а *m.* (*psych., leg.*) fit of passion; temporary insanity.
аффекта́ци|я, и *f.* affectation.

аффекти́рованный *adj.* affected.
а́ффикс, а *m.* (*ling.*) affix.
ах *int.* ah! oh!
а́хань|е, я *nt.* (*coll.*) sighing.
а́ха|ть, ю *impf.* (*coll.*) to sigh; to exclaim 'ah!', 'oh!'.
ахилле́сов *adj.*: **~а пята́** Achilles heel; **~о сухожи́лие** (*anat.*) Achilles tendon.
ахине́|я, и *f.* (*coll.*) nonsense; **нести́ ~ю** to talk nonsense.
а́х|нуть, ну, нешь *pf.* **1** *pf. of* **⇒~ать; он и а. не успе́л** before he knew where he was. **2** (*coll.*) (*издать громкий звук*) to bang.
а́ховый *adj.* (*coll.*) **1** (*удивительный*) breath-taking; **он па́рень а.** he is a great bloke. **2** (*плохой*) rotten.
ахромати́ческий *adj.* achromatic.
ахтерште́в|ень, ня *m.* (*naut.*) stern-post.
ахти́ *int.* (*coll.*) alas!; **а. мне!** woe is me!; **не а. как** not particularly; **не а. како́й** not particularly good; **он был не а. каки́м студе́нтом** he was not the brightest of students.
ацетиле́н, а *m.* (*chem.*) acetylene.
ацето́н, а *m.* (*chem.*) acetone.
АЦП *m. indecl.* (*abbr. of* ***ана́лого-цифрово́й преобразова́тель***) ADC (*analogue to digital converter*).
ацте́к, а *m.* Aztec.
ашу́г, а *m.* ashug (*folk poet and singer in the Caucasus*).
Ашхаба́д, а *n.* Ashgabat, Ashkhabad.
аэра́ри|й, я *m.* sun terrace.
аэро... *comb. form* aero-; air-, aerial.
аэро́бик|а, и *f.* aerobics.
аэро́бн|ый *adj.* aerobic; **~ая гимна́стика** aerobics, aerobic exercises.
аэро́бус, а *m.* air bus.
аэровокза́л, а *m.* air terminal.
аэрогра́мм|а, ы *f.* aerogramme (*Br.*), aerogram (*US*); air letter.
аэро́граф, а *m.* air brush.
аэродина́мик|а, и *f.* aerodynamics.
аэродинами́ческ|ий *adj.* aerodynamic; **~ая труба́** wind tunnel.
аэродро́м, а *m.* aerodrome.
аэрозо́л|ь, я *m.* aerosol, spray; **а. для воло́с** hair spray.
аэрозо́льный *adj.*: **а. балло́н** spray can.
аэрокатастро́ф|а, ы *f.* = **авиакатастро́фа**
аэрокосми́ческий *adj.* aerospace.
аэро́н, а *m.* travel sickness pill.
аэрона́вт, а *m.* aeronaut; balloonist.
аэрона́втик|а, и *f.* aeronautics.
аэропла́н, а *m.* (*obs.*) aeroplane (*Br.*), airplane (*US*).
аэропо́рт, а, об ~е, в ~у́ *m.* airport.
аэроса́н|и, е́й *no sg.* aero-sleigh (*sleigh with a propeller*).
аэросни́м|ок, ка *m.* aerial photograph.
аэроста́т, а *m.* balloon; **а. загражде́ния** barrage balloon.
аэроста́тик|а, и *f.* aerostatics.
аэрофотосъёмк|а, и *f.* aerial survey; aerial photography.
аэрохо́д, а *m.* hovercraft, air cushion vehicle (*abbr.* ACV).
АЭС *f. indecl.* (*abbr. of* ***а́томная электроста́нция***) atomic power station.
аятолл|а́, ы *m.* ayatollah.
а/я *m. indecl.* (*abbr. of* ***абонеме́нтный я́щик***) PO (*abbr. of* Post Office) Box.

Бб

б *particle* = **бы** (*after words ending in vowel*).

б. (*abbr. of* **бы́вший**) former, ex-; **Санкт-Петербу́рг (б. Ленингра́д)** St Petersburg (formerly Leningrad).

ба *int.* (*coll.*) well! (*expr. surprise*).

ба́б|а¹, ы *f.* **1** (*замужняя крестьянка*) married peasant woman. **2** (*coll.*) (*женщина*) woman; **сне́жная б.** snowman. **3** (*coll.*) (*мужчина*) 'old woman', sissy.

ба́б|а², ы *f.* (*tech.*) ram (*of pile-driver*).

ба́ба³, ы *f.*: **ро́мовая б.** rum-baba.

бабá хн|уть, у, ешь *pf.* (*coll.*) to bang.

ба́ба-яга́, ба́бы-яги́ *f.* Baba-Yaga (*witch in Russian folk-tales*).

бабёнк|а и *f.* (*coll.*) bimbo, bit of skirt.

ба́б|ий *adj.* (*coll.*) women's; **~ье ле́то** Indian summer; **~ьи ска́зки** old wives' tales.

ба́бк|а¹, и *f.* = **ба́бушка**

ба́бк|а², и *f.* **1** (*anat.*) (*у животных*) pastern. **2** (*кость*) knuckle-bone; **~и** (*pl.*) babki (*Russian children's game*). **3**: **~и** (*pl., coll.*) (*деньги*) money.

ба́бник, а *m.* (*coll.*) womanizer.

ба́бочк|а, и *f.* butterfly; **ночна́я б.** moth.

бабуи́н, а *m.* baboon.

ба́бушк|а, и *f.* grandmother; (*coll.*) old woman; gran(nie) (*as mode of address*); **б. на́двое сказа́ла** we shall see!

ба́бушкин *adj.* grandmother's; **~ы ска́зки** old wives' tales.

бабь|ё, я́ *nt.* (*collect., coll.*) womenfolk.

Бава́ри|я, и *f.* Bavaria.

бава́рский *adj.* Bavarian.

бага́ж, а́ *m.* luggage; **сдать свои́ ве́щи в б.** to register one's luggage.

бага́жник, а *m.* (*в автомобиле*) boot (*Br.*), trunk (*US*); (*на крыше*) roof rack; (*на велосипеде*) carrier.

бага́жнич|ек, ка *m.* glove compartment (*in car*).

бага́ж|ный *adj. of* ⇒**~**; **б. ваго́н** luggage van (*Br.*), baggage car (*US*).

Бага́мск|ие о́стров|а́, ~их ~о́в *no sg.* the Bahamas.

ба́гги *m. indecl.* (*автомобиль*) (*beach, dune etc.*) buggy.

Багда́д, а *m.* Baghdad.

баг|о́р, ра́ *m.* boat-hook.

багре́ц, а́ *m.* crimson.

багрове́|ть, ю *impf.* (*of* ⇒**по~**) to turn crimson.

багро́в|ый (~, ~а) *adj.* crimson, purple.

багря́н|ец, ца *m.* crimson, purple.

багряни́ц|а, ы *f.* (*hist.*) purple (mantle).

багря́нник, а *m.* (*bot.*) Judas-tree.

багря́н|ый (~, ~а) *adj.* (*poet.*) crimson.

багу́льник, а *m.* (*bot.*) Labrador tea (*Ledum*).

бадминто́н, а *m.* badminton.

бадминтони́ст, а *m.* badminton-player.

бад|ья́, ьи́, *g. pl.* **~е́й** *f.* tub.

ба́з|а, ы *f.* **1** (*mil., archit.*) base; (*склад*) depot; (*туристов*) centre (*Br.*), center (*US*); **б. да́нных** database; **плаву́чая б.** factory ship. **2** (*основание*) basis; **на ~е** (*+g.*) on the basis (of); **подвести́ ~у** (**под**+*a.*) to give good grounds (for).

база́льт, а *m.* basalt.

база́льтовый *adj.* basaltic.

база́р, а *m.* market; bazaar; **пти́чий б.** bird-colony; (*fig., coll.*) din, racket.

база́р|ить, ю, ишь (*impf.*) (*coll.*) to wrangle, squabble.

база́рнича|ть, ю (*impf.*) to make a racket *or* din.

база́р|ный *adj. of* ⇒**~**; (*coll.*) of the market-place, rough, crude; **~ная ба́ба** noisy woman, fishwife; **б. день** market-day.

базе́дов *adj.* (*med.*): **~а боле́знь** exophthalmic goitre (*Br.*), goiter (*US*), Graves' disease.

Ба́зел|ь, я *m.* Basle.

базили́к, а *m.* (*bot.*) basil; **б. души́стый** sweet basil.

базили́к|а, и *f.* (*archit.*) basilica.

базиро́вани|е, я *nt.*: **ракéта назе́много/морско́го ~я** ground-based/sea-launched missile.

бази́р|овать, ую *impf.* (**на**+*p.*) to base (on).

бази́р|оваться, уюсь *impf.* **1** (**на**+*p.*) to be based (on); to rest (on); **все его́ мне́ния ~уются на газе́тах** all his opinions are based on what he reads in the newspapers. **2** (**на**+*a.*) (*mil.*) to be based (at).

ба́зис, а *m.* (*archit.*) base; (*основание*) basis.

ба́зовый *adj.* **1** basic; **б. курс** foundation course. **2**: **б. ла́герь** base camp.

базу́к|а, и *f.* bazooka.

ба́иньки = **бай-ба́й**

ба|й, я *m.* bai (*rich landowner in Central Asia*).

бай-ба́й *int.* bye-byes; **пора́ б.!** time for bye-byes!

байба́к, а́ *m.* (*zool.*) steppe marmot; (*fig.*) lazybones.

байда́рк|а, и *f.* kayak; canoe.

байда́рочник, а *m.* canoeist.

байда́рочни|ца, цы *f. of* ⇒**~к**

байда́р|очный *adj. of* ⇒**~ка**

ба́йк|а¹, и *f.* (*ткань*) flannelette.

ба́йк|а², и *f.* (*coll.*) (*сказка*) fairy story, cock-and-bull story.

ба́йковый *adj.* flannelette.

ба́йт, а *m.* (*comput.*) byte.

бак¹, а *m.* cistern; tank; **му́сорный б.** dustbin (*Br.*), garbage can (*US*).

бак², а *m.* (*naut.*) forecastle.

бакала́вр, а *m.* bachelor (*holder of bachelor's degree*).

бакале́йный *adj.* grocery; **б. магази́н** grocer's shop (*Br.*), grocery store (*US*).

бакале́йщик, а *m.* grocer.

бакале́|я, и *f.* **1** (*collect.*) groceries. **2** (*в магазине*) grocery section.

бака́ут, а *m.* (*bot.*) lignum vitae, guaiacum.

ба́кен, а *m.* buoy.

бакенба́рд|ы, ~ *pl.* (*sg.* **~а, ~ы** *f.*) side-whiskers.

ба́кенщик, а *m.* buoy-keeper.

Б

бáкен|ы, ов *pl.* (*sg.* **~, ~а** *m.*) (*obs.*) side-whiskers.

бáк|и, ~ *no sg.* = **бакенбáрды**

баккарá *nt. indecl.* baccarat (card-game).

баклáг|а, и *f.* flask, water-bottle.

баклажáн, а *m.* aubergine (*Br.*), egg-plant (*US*).

баклáн, а *m.* cormorant.

баклýши *now only in phr.* **бить б.** (*coll.*) to idle, fritter away one's time.

бáк|овый *adj. of* ⇒**~**²; bow.

бáкс|ы, ов *pl.* (*sl.*) bucks, American dollars.

бактериáльный *adj.* bacterial.

бактерúйный *adj.* bacterial.

бактериóлог, а *m.* bacteriologist.

бактериологúческ|ий *adj.* bacteriological; **~ая войнá** germ warfare.

бактериолóги|я, и *f.* bacteriology.

бактерицúдный *adj.* germicidal.

бактéри|я, и *f.* bacterium.

Бакý *m. indecl.* Baku.

бал, а, о ~е, на ~ý, *pl.* **~ы́** *m.* ball, dance; **кóнчен б.!** it's all over; the show is over; **прáвить б.** (*coll.*) to run the show.

балабóл|ить, ю, ишь *impf.* (*coll.*) to chatter idly, gas.

балабóлк|а, и *c.g.* (*coll.*) (*болтун*) chatterbox, gasbag.

балагáн, а *m.* **1** (*постройка*) booth (*at fairs*). **2** (*theatr.*) low farce; (*fig.*) farce, tomfoolery.

балагáн|ить, ю, ишь *impf.* (*coll.*) to play the fool.

балагáн|ный *adj. of* ⇒**~**; farcical.

балагýр, а *m.* joker, clown.

балагýр|ить, ю, ишь *impf.* to jest, joke.

балагýрств|о, а *nt.* foolery, buffoonery.

балáка|ть, ю *impf.* (*dial.*) to chatter, natter.

балалáечник, а *m.* balalaika-player.

балалáечни|ца, цы *f. of* ⇒**~к**

балалá|ечный *adj. of* ⇒**~йка**

балалáйк|а, и *f.* balalaika.

баламýт, а *m.* (*coll.*) trouble-maker.

баламý|тить, чу, тишь *impf.* (*of* ⇒**вз~**) (*coll.*) to stir up, trouble (*water*); (*fig.*) to upset.

баламýт|ка, ки *f. of* ⇒**~**

балáнд|а, ы *f.* (*sl.*) thin broth (*in prison or labour camp*).

балáнс, а *m.* (*econ., tech.*) balance; **платёжный б.** balance of payment; **торгóвый б.** balance of trade.

балансёр, а *m.* tightrope-walker.

балансúр, а *m.* (*tech.*) **1** (*рычаг*) (balance) beam. **2** (*в часах*) balance-wheel.

балансúр|овать, ую *impf.* **1** (*impf. only*) (*сохранять равновесие*) to balance. **2** (*pf.* **за~, с~**) (*в бухгалтерии*) to balance.

балахóн, а *m.* (*coll.*) shapeless garment, sack.

балбéс, а *m.* (*coll.*) booby, nitwit.

балбéснича|ть, ю *impf.* (*coll.*) to idle away one's time.

балд|á, ы́ *f. and c.g.* **1** *f.* (*tech.*) heavy hammer, sledge-hammer. **2** *c.g.* (*coll.*) (*дурак*) blockhead.

балдахúн, а *m.* canopy.

балдёж, á *m.* (*sl.*) good time; party; *int.* great!; brill!

балдёжный *adj.* (*sl.*) great, ace, brill.

балдé|ть, ю *impf.* (*sl.*) to be high, be stoned; **б. от** (+*g.*) to 'dig', get a kick *or* buzz out of; **я от неё ~ю** she really turns me on.

балерúн|а, ы *f.* ballerina.

балéт, а *m.* ballet; **б. на льдý** ice review *or* show.

балетмéйстер, а *m.* ballet-master.

балéт|ный *adj. of* ⇒**~**

балетомáн, а *m.* balletomane.

балетомáни|я, и *f.* balletomania.

бáлк|а[1]**, и** *f.* (*брус*) beam, girder.

бáлк|а[2]**, и** *f.* (*лощина*) gully; ravine.

балкáнский *adj.* Balkan.

Балкáн|ы, ~ *no sg.* the Balkans.

балкóн, а *m.* balcony.

балл, а *m.* **1** (*meteor.*) number; **вéтер в пять ~ов** wind force 5. **2** (*в школе*) mark; **вы́сший б.** an 'A'; **проходнóй б.** pass mark; (*sport*) point; score.

баллáд|а, ы *f.* **1** (*стихотворение*) ballad. **2** (*mus.*) ballade.

балласт, а *m.* ballast (*also fig.*).

баллúстик, а *m.* ballistics expert.

баллúстик|а, и *f.* ballistics.

баллистúческий *adj.* ballistic.

бáлл|овый *adj. of* ⇒**~ 1**

баллóн, а *m.* **1** (*сосуд*) container (*of glass, metal, or rubber*); carboy; **аэрозóльный б.** spray can; **б. с кислорóдом** oxygen cylinder. **2** (*шина*) balloon tyre (*Br.*), tire (*US*).

баллотúр|овать, ую *impf.* to ballot (for), vote (for).

баллотúр|оваться, уюсь *impf.* (**в**+*a.*, **на**+*a.*) to stand (*Br.*), run (*US*) (for), be a candidate (for); **б. на дóлжность секретаря пáртии** to stand for secretary of the party.

баллотирóвк|а, и *f.* **1** vote, ballot, poll. **2** (*процесс*) voting, balloting, polling.

баллотирóв|очный *adj. of* ⇒**~ка; б. бюллетéнь** ballot paper.

балóв|анный *p.p.p. of* ⇒**~áть** *and adj.* (*coll.*) spoiled.

бал|овáть, ýю *impf.* (*of* ⇒**из~**) **1** (*детей*) to spoil; to pamper. **2** (**с**+*i.*; *coll.*) to play (with), amuse o.s. (with).

бал|овáться, ýюсь *impf.* **1** (*шалить*) to get up to mischief. **2** (**с**+*i.*; *coll.*) (*со спичками*) to play, fool about (with). **3** (+*i.*; *coll.*) (*живописью*) to dabble (in).

бáлов|ень, ня *m.* (*coll.*) **1** spoilt child; pet, favourite (*Br.*), favorite (*US*); **б. судьбы́** favourite of fortune. **2** (*шалун*) naughty child.

баловнúк, á *m.* (*coll.*) naughty child.

баловств|ó, á *nt.* (*coll.*) **1** spoiling; pampering. **2** (*шалости*) mischief.

балтúйский *adj.* Baltic.

балы́к, á *m.* balyk (*cured fillet of sturgeon, etc.*).

бáльза, ы *f.* balsa(wood).

бальзáм, а *m.* balsam; (*fig.*) balm; **б. для волóс** hair conditioner; **оттéночный б.** (hair) rinse.

бальзамúровани|е, я *nt.* embalming, embalmment.

бальзамúр|овать, ую *impf. and pf.* (*pf. also* **за-, на~**) to embalm.

бальзамúческ|ий *adj.* (*bot.*) balsam, balsamic; (*fig.*) balmy; **~ая пúхта** fir; **б. вóздух** balmy air.

бáл|ьный *adj. of* ⇒**~; ~ьные тáнцы** ballroom dancing.

бáльс|а, ы *f.* = **бáльза**

балюстрáд|а, ы *f.* balustrade.

балясин|а, ы *f.* baluster.

БАМ *m.* (*indecl.*) (*abbr. of* ***Байкáло-Амýрская (железнодорóжная) магистрáль***) Baikal–Amur railway.

бамбýк, а *m.* bamboo.

бамбýк|овый *adj. of* ⇒**~**

бáмпер, а *m.* bumper.

банáльност|ь, и *f.* **1** (*свойство*) banality. **2** (*замечание*) banal remark; platitude.

банáл|ьный (~ен, ~ьна) *adj.* banal, trite.

банáн, а *m.* banana.

бананов́оз, а *m.* banana boat.

банáн|овый *adj. of* ⇒**~**

Бангкóк, а *m.* Bangkok.

Бангладéш, а *m.* Bangladesh.

бангладéш|ец, ца *m.* Bangladeshi.

бангладéш|ка, ки *f. of* ⇒**~ец**

бангладéшский *adj.* Bangladeshi.

бáнд|а, ы *f.* band, gang.

бандáж, á *m.* **1** support bandage; **грыжевóй б.** truss. **2**; **спортúвный б.** athletic supporter; jockstrap. **3** (*tech.*) tyre (*Br.*), tire (*US*), band (*of metal*).

бандерóл|ь, и *f.* **1** (*обёртка*) wrapper (*for dispatching newspapers, etc., by post*). **2** (*почтовое отправление*) small package; **отправлять ~ью** to send as a small package.

бандúт, а *m.* bandit; thug; **вооружённый б.** armed robber.

бандитúзм, а *m.* banditry; thuggery; **вооружённый б.** armed robbery.

бандúт|ский *adj. of* ⇒**~**

бандúтств|овать, ую *impf.* to rampage.

бандýр|а, ы *f.* (*mus.*) bandura (*Ukrainian string instrument similar to large mandolin*).

бандурúст, а *m.* (*mus.*) bandura-player.

банк, а *m.* **1** bank (*also fig.*); **б. дáнных** databank; **Всемúрный б.** World Bank. **2** (*игра*) faro.

бáнк|а[1]**, и** *f.* (*стеклянная*) jar; (*жестяная*) tin (*Br.*), can (*US*).

бáнк|а[2]**, и** *f.* (*отмель*) sandbank.

банкéт, а *m.* banquet.

банкúр, а *m.* banker.

банки́р|ский *adj. of* ⇨~; **б. дом** banking-house.

банкно́т, а *m.* bank-note.

банкно́т|а, ы *f.* = ~

ба́нк|овский *adj. of* ⇨~; **б. биле́т** bank-note; **~овская кни́жка** passbook, bank-book.

ба́нк|овый *adj. of* ⇨~

банкома́т, а *m.* cash machine.

банкомёт, а *m.* banker (*at cards*); (*крупье*) croupier.

банкро́т, а *m.* bankrupt; **объявля́ть ~ом** to declare bankrupt.

банкро́|титься, чусь, тишься *impf.* (*of* ⇨**о~**) to become bankrupt (*also fig.*).

банкро́тств|о, а *nt.* bankruptcy.

ба́н|ный *adj. of* ⇨**~я**

бант, а *m.* bow; **завяза́ть ~ом** to tie in a bow.

ба́нтик, а *m. dim. of* ⇨**бант**

ба́нщик, а *m.* bath-house attendant.

ба́н|я, и *f.* (Russian) baths; bath-house; **крова́вая б.** blood-bath; **фи́нская б.** sauna; **зада́ть ~ю** (+*d.*; *coll.*) to give (s.o.) what for.

бапти́зм, а *m.* the doctrine of Baptists.

бапти́ст, а *m.* Baptist.

баптисте́ри|й, я *m.* baptist(e)ry.

бапти́ст|ка, ки *f. of* ⇨~

бапти́стский *adj.* Baptist.

бар[1], а *m.* bar; **пивно́й б.** pub.

бар[2], а *m.* (*phys.*) bar (*unit of atmospheric pressure*).

бараба́н, а *m.* drum (*also tech.*).

бараба́н|ить, ю, ишь *impf.* to drum.

бараба́н|ный *adj. of* ⇨~; **~ная дробь** drum-roll; **~ная перепо́нка** (*anat.*) ear-drum, tympanum.

бараба́нщик, а *m.* drummer.

бараба́нщи|ца, цы *f. of* ⇨**~к**

бара́к, а *m.* hut.

бара́н, а *m.* ram; (wild) sheep.

бара́н|ий *adj.* **1** sheep's; ram's; **согну́ть в б. рог** (*coll.*) to make (s.o.) knuckle under. **2** (*из кожи барана*) sheepskin. **3** (*о еде*) mutton; **~ья котле́та** mutton chop.

бара́нин|а, ы *f.* mutton; (*молодая*) lamb.

бара́нк|а, и *f.* **1** (*булочка*) baranka (*ring-shaped roll*). **2** (*coll.*) (steering-) wheel.

бара́|ть, ю *impf.* (*vulg.*) to screw, hump.

барахл|и́ть, ю́, и́шь *impf.* (*coll.*) **1** (*о моторе*) to pink (*Br.*), rattle. **2** (*о телевизоре. часах*) to be unreliable; to be on the blink.

барахл|о́, а́ *nt.* (*collect.*; *coll.*) trash, junk.

бараxо́лк|а, и *f.* (*coll.*) flea market.

барах|о́льный *adj. of* ⇨**~ло́**

барахо́льщик, а *m.* (*coll.*) dealer in second-hand goods.

бара́хта|ться, юсь *impf.* (*coll.*) to flounder; (*валяться*) to wallow.

бара́|чный *adj. of* ⇨**~к**

бара́ш|ек, ка *m.* **1** young ram; lamb; **б. в бума́жке** (*coll.*) bribe. **2** (*шкурка*) lambskin. **3** (*pl.*) (*волны*) 'white horses'. **4** (*pl.*) (*облака*) fleecy clouds. **5** (*гайка*) wing nut, thumbscrew. **6** (*bot.*) catkin.

бара́шковый *adj.* lambskin.

Барба́дос, а *m.* Barbados.

барбари́с, а *m.* (*bot.*) barberry.

барбитура́т, а *m.* barbiturate.

барбо́с, а *m.* watch-dog.

барви́н|ок, ка *m.* (*bot.*) periwinkle (*Vinca minor*).

бард, а *m.* bard.

барда́к, а́ *m.* (*coll.*) brothel; (*fig.*) chaos.

бардач|о́к, ка́ *m.* (*coll.*) glove compartment (*in car*).

барелье́ф, а *m.* bas-relief.

Ба́ренцев|о мо́р|е, ~а ~я *nt.* the Barents Sea.

ба́рж|а, и *f.* barge.

барж|а́, и́, *g. pl.* **~е́й** = **ба́ржа**

ба́ри|й, я *m.* (*chem.*) barium.

ба́р|ин, а, *pl.* **~е** *and* **~ы, ~** *m.* landowner; gentleman; (*as mode of address*) sir, master; **жить ~ином** to live like a lord.

бари́т, а *m.* (*min.*) barytes.

барито́н, а *m.* baritone.

ба́рич, а *m.* landowner's son; (*coll., pej.*) = **ба́рин**

барк, а *m.* barque.

ба́рк|а, и *f.* wooden barge.

баркаро́л|а, ы *f.* (*mus.*) barcarole.

барка́с, а *m.* launch; long boat.

ба́рмен, а *m.* barman, bartender.

ба́рменш|а, и *f.* (*coll.*) barmaid.

баро́граф, а *m.* barograph.

баро́кко *nt. indecl.* baroque.

баро́метр, а *m.* barometer.

барометри́ческий *adj.* barometric.

баро́н, а *m.* baron.

бароне́сс|а, ы *f.* baroness.

баро́нский *adj.* baronial.

баро́нств|о, а *nt.* barony.

ба́рочник, а *m.* bargee.

ба́р|очный *adj of* ⇨**~ка**

баро́чный *adj.* baroque.

ба́ррел|ь, я *m.* (*мера*) barrel.

баррика́д|а, ы *f.* barricade.

баррикади́р|овать, ую *impf.* (*of* ⇨**за~**) to barricade.

барс, а *m.* (*zool.*) snow leopard (*Uncia uncia*).

ба́рск|ий *adj. of* ⇨**ба́рин; б. дом** manor-house; **жить на ~ую но́гу** to live like a lord.

ба́рствен|ный (~, ~на) *adj.* lordly, grand.

ба́рств|о, а *nt.* **1** (*высокомерие*) lordliness. **2** (*collect., obs.*) (*помещики*) gentry.

ба́рств|овать, ую *impf.* to live in idleness and plenty.

барсу́к, а́ *m.* badger.

барсу́чий *adj.* **1** *adj. of* ⇨**барсу́к. 2** (*сделанный из меха барсука*) badger-skin.

ба́ртер, а *m.* barter.

бару́ха, и *f.* (*sl.*) girlfriend.

барха́н, а *m.* (sand-)dune.

ба́рхат, а *m.* velvet.

бархати́ст|ый (~, ~а) *adj.* velvety.

ба́рхатк|а, и *f.* (*кусочек бархата*) piece of velvet; (*ленточка бархата*) velvet ribbon.

ба́рхатный *adj.* **1** velvet; **б. сезо́н** autumn season, autumn months (*in the south of Russia*). **2** (*fig.*) velvety.

ба́рхат|цы, цев *pl.* (*sg.* **~ец, ~ца** *m.*) (African) marigold (*Tagetes*).

бархо́тк|а, и *f.* = **ба́рхатка**

барч|о́нок, о́нка, *pl.* **~а́та, ~а́т** *m.* landowner's son.

барчу́к, а́ *m.* (*coll.*) landowner's son.

ба́рщин|а, ы *f.* (*hist.*) corvée.

барыг|а, и *c.g.* (*sl.*) spiv, dealer, speculator.

ба́рын|я, и *f.* landowner's wife; lady; (*as term of address*) mistress, madam.

бары́ш, а́ *m.* profit.

бары́шник, а *m.* **1** (*перекупщик*) profiteer; (ticket) tout (*Br.*), scalper (*US*). **2** (*торговец лошадьми*) horse-dealer.

бары́шнича|ть, ю *impf.* to profiteer; (+*i.*) to speculate (in).

бары́шничеств|о, а *nt.* profiteering; speculation.

ба́рыш|ня, ни, *g. pl.* **~ень** *f.* **1** (*девушка из барской семьи*) girl of gentry family; (*as term of address*) miss. **2** (*coll.*) (*девушка*) girl, young lady.

барье́р, а *m.* barrier (*also fig.*); **звуково́й б.** sound barrier; **языково́й б.** language barrier; (*sport*) hurdle; **взять б.** to clear a hurdle; **поста́вить кого́-н. к ~у** to make s.o. fight a duel.

барьери́ст, а *m.* hurdler.

барьери́ст|ка, ки *f. of* ⇨~

бас, а, *pl.* **~ы** *m.* (*mus.*) bass.

бас-гита́р|а, ы *f.* bass guitar.

ба́с|енный *adj. of* ⇨**~ня**

баси́ст|ый (~, ~а) *adj.* (*coll.*) bass.

ба|си́ть, шу́, си́шь *impf.* (*coll.*) to speak (*or* sing) in a deep voice.

баск, а *m.* Basque.

баске́т, а *m.* (*coll.*) basketball (*sport*).

баскетбо́л, а *m.* basketball (*sport*).

баскетболи́ст, а *m.* basketball player.

баскетболи́ст|ка, ки *f. of* ⇨~

баске́т|ки, ок *pl.* (*sg.* **~ка, ~ки** *f.*) basketball boots.

баск|о́нка, о́нки *f. of* ⇨~

ба́скский *adj.* Basque.

баснопи́с|ец, ца *m.* (*liter.*) fabulist.

баснослóви|е, я *nt.* (*obs.*) **1** mythology. **2** (*collect.*) fabulous stories, fabrications.

баснoсло́в|ный (~ен, ~на) *adj.* **1** mythical, legendary. **2** (*fig., coll.*) fabulous.

ба́с|ня, ни, *g. pl.* **~ен** *f.* **1** fable. **2** (*fig., coll.*) fable, fabrication.

бас|о́вый *adj. of* ⇨~; **б. ключ** (*mus.*) bass clef.

бас|óк, кá *m.* **1** (*coll.*) (*голос*) weak bass (voice). **2** (*mus.*) (*струна*) bass-string.
бассéйн, а *m.* **1** (*man-made*) pool; **б. для плáвания** swimming-pool. **2** (*geog.*) basin; **каменноугóльный б.** coalfield.
бáста *int.* (*coll.*) that's enough!; that'll do!
бастиóн, а *m.* (*mil. and fig.*) bastion.
баст|овáть, ýю *impf.* to strike, go on strike; to be on strike.
баст|ýющий *pres. part. of* ⇒**~овáть** *and adj.* striking; *as n.* **б., ~ýющего** *m.* striker.
баталúст, а *m.* painter of battle scenes.
батáли|я, и *f.* (*coll.*) fight; row, squabble.
батáл|ьный *adj. of* ⇒**~ия; ~ьная сцéна** (*art*) battle scene.
батальóн, а *m.* battalion.
батальóн|ный *adj. of* ⇒**~**
батарé|ец, йца *m.* (*mil.*; *coll.*) gunner.
батарéйк|а, и *f.* (*electric*) battery.
батарé|йный *adj. of* ⇒**~я**
батарé|я, и *f.* (*mil. and tech.*) battery; (*отопительная*) radiator.
бáтеньк|а, и *m.* (*coll.*) (*mode of address*) old chap!
батúст, а *m.* cambric, lawn.
батúст|овый *adj. of* ⇒**~**
батóн, а *m.* **1** (*хлеб*) (*long*) white loaf. **2** (*шоколадный*) stick (*of confectionery*).
батрáк, á *m.* farm-labourer (*Br.*), -laborer (*US*).
батрá|цкий *adj. of* ⇒**~к**
батрáчеств|о, а *nt.* **1** (*занятие*) farm work. **2** (*collect.*) farm-labourers (*Br.*), -laborers (*US*).
батрáч|ить, у, ишь *impf.* to work as a farm-labourer (*Br.*), -laborer (*US*).
баттерфля́|й, я *m.* butterfly (*swimming stroke*).
батýд = **батýт**
батýт, а *m.* trampoline.
батутúст, а *m.* trampolinist.
батутúст|ка, ки *f. of* ⇒**~**
батýт|ный *adj. of* ⇒**~; б. спорт** trampolining.
бáтьк|а, и *m.* (*coll. or dial.*) = **бáтюшка** 1
бáтюшк|а, и *m.* **1** (*coll.*) (*отец*) father; **как вас по ~е?** what is your patronymic? **2** (*священник*) father. **3** (*coll.*) (*обращение*) old chap!; my dear fellow!
бáтюшки *int.*: **б. (мой)!** good gracious!
баýл, а *m.* small trunk; large sturdy suitcase.
бах *int.* bang!
бахвáл, а *m.* (*coll.*) braggart, boaster.
бахвáл|иться, юсь, ишься *impf.* (*coll.*; +*i.*) to brag (of).
бахвáльств|о, а *nt.* (*coll.*) bragging.
бáхн|уть, у, ешь *pf.* (*coll.*) **1** (*издать резкий звук*) to bang. **2** (*ударить*) to bang, slap; **б. когó-н. по спинé** to slap s.o. on the back.
бáхн|уться, усь, ешься *pf.* (*coll.*) (+*i.*) to bang, bump (o.s.); **б. головóй о стол** to bang one's head on the table.
Бахрéйн, а *m.* Bahrain
бахром|á, ы́ *f.* fringe.
бахрóмчатый *adj.* fringed.
бахч|á, и́ *f.* melon *or* pumpkin field.
бахчéвник, а *m.* melon-grower.
бахчевóдств|о, а *nt.* melon-growing.
бахч|евóй *adj. of* ⇒**~á; ~евы́е культýры** melons and gourds.
бац *int.* = **бах**
бацúлл|а, ы *f.* bacillus.
бациллоносúтел|ь, я *m.* (bacillus-) carrier.
бáцн|уть, у, ешь *pf.* (*coll.*) = **бáхнуть**
бáшенк|а, и *f.* turret.
бáш|енный *adj. of* ⇒**~ня; ~енные часы́** tower clock.
башк|á, ú *no g. pl., f.* (*coll.*) head; **глýпая б.** blockhead.
башкúр, а *m.* Bashkir.
башкúр|ка, ки *f. of* ⇒**~**
башкúрский *adj.* Bashkir.
башковúт|ый (~, ~а) *adj.* (*coll.*) brainy.
бáшл|и, ей *no sg.* (*sl.*) bread, dosh (*Br.*).
башлы́к, á *m.* hood.
башмáк, á *m.* **1** (*ботинок*) boot; (*туфель*) shoe; **быть под ~óм у когó-н.** to be under s.o.'s thumb. **2** (*тормозной*) brake-shoe, brake-block.
башмáчник, а *m.* shoemaker, cobbler.
башмá|чный *adj. of* ⇒**~к**
башма|чóк, чкá *m. dim. of* ⇒**~к; вя́заный б.** bootee.
бáш|ня, ни, *g. pl.* **~ен** *f.* tower; turret; **пизáнская б.** the Leaning Tower of Pisa.
ба|шý, сúшь *see* ⇒**~сúть**
баюкá|ть, ю *impf.* to sing lullabies (to).
бáюшки-баю́ *int.* lullaby.
бая́н, а *m.* (*mus.*) bayan (*kind of accordion*).
баянúст, а *m.* (*mus.*) bayan-player.
баянúст|ка, ки *f. of* ⇒**~**
бдéни|е, я *nt.* vigil; **всéнощное б.** (*eccl.*) all-night vigil.
бд|еть, *1st person sg. not used,* **~ишь** *impf.* (*obs.*) to keep watch, keep vigil; **б.** (**о**+*p.*) to watch (over).
бдúтельност|ь, и *f.* vigilance, watchfulness.
бдúтел|ьный (~ен, ~ьна) *adj.* vigilant, watchful.
бег, а, о, ~е, на ~ý, *pl.* **~á, ~óв** *m.* **1** run, running; **~óм, на ~ý** at the double; **на всём ~ý** at full speed; **б. на мéсте** running on the spot; marking time (*also fig.*); **оздоровúтельный б.** jogging, **б. трусцóй** (*sport*) jogging. **2** (*sport*) (*состязание*) race. **3** (*pl.*) (*гонки упряжных лошадей*) harness races; trotting races; **быть на ~áх** to be at the races. **4**: **быть в ~áх** to be on the run.
бéга|ть, ю *impf.* (*indet. of* ⇒**бежáть**) **1** to run (about); (**за**+*i.*; *coll.*) to run (after), chase (after). **2** (*о глазах*) to rove, roam.
бегемóт, а *m.* hippopotamus.
беглéц, á *m.* fugitive.
бéглост|ь, и *f.* fluency; dexterity.
бéглый *adj.* **1** (*убежавший*) fugitive, runaway. **2** (*свободный*) fluent, quick. **3** (*поверхностный*) superficial; cursory; **б. взгляд** fleeting glance. **4**: **б. глáсный** (*gram.*) mobile vowel.
бег|овóй *adj. of* ⇒**~; ~овáя дорóжка** racetrack, running-track; **~овáя лóшадь** racehorse.
бегóм *adv.* running; at the double.
бегóни|я, и *f.* (*bot.*) begonia.
беготн|я́, ú *f.* (*coll.*) running about; bustle.
бéгств|о, а *nt.* flight; escape; **обратúть в б.** to put to flight; **обратúться в б., спасáться ~ом** to take to flight.
бе|гý, ~жúшь *see* ⇒**~жáть**
бегýн, á *m.* runner.
бегун|óк, кá *m.* (*tech.*) runner.
бед|á, ы́, *pl.* **~ы** *f.* **1** (*несчастье*) misfortune; calamity; **на ~ý** unfortunately; **на свою́ ~ý** to one's cost; **быть ~é!** there's trouble brewing; **пришлá б. — отворя́й воротá** (*prov.*) it never rains but it pours; **семь ~ — одúн отвéт** (*prov.*) in for a penny, in for a pound. **2** *as pred.* it is awful!; it is a trouble; **б. в том, что** the trouble is (that); **прóсто б.!** it's simply awful!; **б. мне с ним** (*coll.*) he's nothing but trouble; **не б.!** it doesn't matter; **что за б.!** what does it matter?; so what? **3** (*coll.*) (*много*) an awful lot.
бедлáм, а *m.* bedlam.
беднé|ть, ю *impf.* (*of* ⇒**о~**) (+*i.*) to grow poor (in).
бéдност|ь, и *f.* poverty (*also fig.*).
беднот|á, ы́ *f.* **1** (*collect.*) the poor. **2** (*coll.*) poverty.
бéд|ный (~ен, ~нá) *adj.* poor; meagre (*Br.*), meager (*US*); (*fig.*) barren.
бедня́г|а, и *m.* (*coll.*) poor devil, poor thing.
бедня́жк|а, и *c.g. and f.* (*coll.*) **1** *c.g. dim. of* ⇒**бедня́га. 2** *f. of* ⇒**бедня́га**
бедня́к, á *m.* pauper.
бедня́|цкий *adj of* ⇒**~к**
бедóв|ый (~, ~а) *adj.* (*coll.*) mischievous; daredevil.
бедокýр, а *m.* (*coll.*) mischief-maker.
бедокýр|ить, ю, ишь *impf.* (*of* ⇒**на~**) (*coll.*) to get up to mischief.
бедолáг|а, и *c.g.* poor devil.
бéдренный *adj.* (*anat.*) femoral.
бед|рó, рá, *pl.* **~ра, ~ер, ~рам** *nt.* **1** (*верхняя часть ноги*) thigh; (*таз*) hip. **2** (*кусок мяса*) leg.
бéдствен|ный (~, ~на) *adj.* disastrous, calamitous.
бéдстви|е, я *nt.* calamity, disaster; **райóн ~я** disaster area; **сигнáл ~я** distress signal.
бéдств|овать, ую *impf.* to live in poverty.
бедуúн, а *m.* bedouin.
бедуúн|ский *adj. of* ⇒**~**
беж *adj. indecl.* beige.
бе|жáть, гý, жúшь, гýт *impf.* (*det. of* ⇒**бéгать**) **1** to run; (*fig.*) (*о воде*) to

run; (*о крови*) to flow; (*при кипении*) to boil over; **вре́мя ~жи́т** time flies. **2** (*impf. and pf.*) (*спасаться*) to escape.

бе́жевый *adj.* beige.

бе́жен|ец, ца *m.* refugee.

бе́жен|ка, ки *f. of* ⇒**~ец**

бе́женский *adj.* refugee.

без *prep.+g.* without; in the absence of; minus, less; **не б.** not without, not devoid (of); **б. вас** in your absence; **б. пяти́ (мину́т) три** five (minutes) to three; **б. четверти час** a quarter to one; **б. ма́лого** (*coll.*) almost, all but; **быть б. ума́** (**от**+*g.*) to be crazy (about).

без... *pref.* in-, un-, -less.

безала́берност|ь, и *f.* disorder; lack of system.

безала́бер|ный (~ен, ~на) *adj.* disorderly; slovenly.

безала́берщин|а, ы *f.* (*coll.*) muddle; slovenliness.

безалкого́льный *adj.* non-alcoholic; **б. напи́ток** non-alcoholic drink, soft drink.

безапелляцио́н|ный (~ен, ~на) *adj.* peremptory, categorical.

безбе́д|ный (~ен, ~на) *adj.* well-to-do, comfortable.

безбиле́тник, а *m.* fare dodger.

безбиле́тный *adj.* ticketless; **б. пассажи́р** fare dodger; (*на корабле*) stowaway.

безбо́жи|е, я *nt.* atheism.

безбо́жник, а *m.* atheist.

безбо́жно *adv.* (*coll.*) shamelessly, outrageously.

безбо́жный *adj.* **1** irreligious, anti-religious. **2** (*coll.*) (*бессовестный*) outrageous.

безболе́знен|ный (~, ~на) *adj.* painless.

безборо́дый *adj.* beardless (*also fig.*).

безбоя́знен|ный (~, ~на) *adj.* fearless.

безбра́чи|е, я *nt.* celibacy.

безбра́чный *adj.* celibate.

безбре́ж|ный (~ен, ~на) *adj.* boundless.

безбу́р|ный (~ен, ~на) *adj.* calm, peaceful.

безве́ри|е, я *nt.* unbelief.

безве́стност|ь, и *f.* obscurity.

безве́ст|ный (~ен, ~на) *adj.* unknown; obscure.

безве́трен|ный (~, ~на) *adj.* calm, windless.

безве́три|е, я *nt.* calm.

безви́н|ный (~ен, ~на) *adj.* guiltless.

безвку́си|е, я *nt.* lack of taste.

безвку́сиц|а, ы *f.* lack of taste; **что за б.!** what bad taste!

безвку́с|ный (~ен, ~на) *adj.* tasteless.

безвла́сти|е, я *nt.* anarchy.

безвла́ст|ный (~ен, ~на) *adj.* powerless.

безво́д|ный (~ен, ~на) *adj.* arid; waterless.

безво́дь|е, я *nt.* aridity.

безвозвра́т|ный (~ен, ~на) *adj.* irrevocable; irretrievable; **~ная ссу́да** permanent loan.

безвозду́шный *adj.* airless.

безвозме́здный *adj.* free (of charge); **б. труд** unpaid work.

безво́ли|е, я *nt.* lack of will; weak will.

безволо́сый *adj.* hairless, bald.

безво́л|ьный (~ен, ~ьна) *adj.* weak-willed.

безвре́д|ный (~ен, ~на) *adj.* harmless.

безвре́менник, а *m.* (*bot.*) autumn crocus.

безвре́менн|ый *adj.* untimely, premature; **~ая кончи́на** untimely decease.

безвре́мень|е, я *nt.* (*obs.*) **1** (*тяжёлое время*) hard times. **2** (*время застоя*) period of (social) stagnation.

безвы́ездно *adv.* uninterruptedly, without a break.

безвы́ездн|ый *adj.* uninterrupted; **~ое пребыва́ние** continuous residence.

безвы́ход|ный (~ен, ~на) *adj.* hopeless, desperate.

безгла́с|ный (~ен, ~на) *adj.* (*fig.*) silent, dumb.

безголо́в|ый (~, ~а) *adj.* **1** headless; (*iron.*) brainless. **2** (*fig., coll.*) forgetful, scatter-brained.

безголо́сный *adj.* (*ling.*) unvoiced.

безголо́с|ый (~, ~а) *adj.* (*певец*) with a weak voice.

безгра́мотност|ь, и *f.* illiteracy.

безгра́мот|ный (~ен, ~на) *adj.* illiterate (*also fig.*); ignorant.

безграни́ч|ный (~ен, ~на) *adj.* infinite, limitless, boundless.

безгре́шност|ь, и *f.* innocence.

безгре́ш|ный (~ен, ~на) *adj.* innocent, sinless.

безда́рност|ь, и *f.* **1** (*свойство*) lack of talent. **2** (*человек*) person without talent.

безда́р|ный (~ен, ~на) *adj.* (*человек*) talentless, undistinguished; (*произведение*) third-rate.

бе́здар|ь, и *f.* (*coll.*) person without talent; third-rater.

безде́йствен|ный (~, ~на) *adj.* inactive.

безде́йстви|е, я *nt.* inaction, idleness; (*leg.*) (criminal) negligence.

безде́йств|овать, ую *impf.* (*о человеке*) to be inactive; (*о машине*) to lie idle; to not work.

безде́лиц|а, ы *f.* trifle, bagatelle.

безделу́шк|а, и *f.* knick-knack.

безде́ль|е, я *nt.* idleness.

безде́льник, а *m.* idler, loafer.

безде́льни|ца, цы *f. of* ⇒**~к**

безде́льнича|ть, ю *impf.* to idle, loaf about.

безде́л|ьный (~ен, ~ьна) *adj.* (*coll.*) idle.

безде́нежный *adj.* **1** impecunious. **2** (*econ.*) non-monetary.

безде́нежь|е, я *nt.* lack of money, impecuniousness.

безде́тност|ь, и *f.* childlessness.

безде́т|ный (~ен, ~на) *adj.* childless.

безде́ятельност|ь, и *f.* inactivity, inertia.

безде́ятел|ьный (~ен, ~ьна) *adj.* inactive; sluggish.

бе́здн|а, ы *f.* **1** abyss, chasm. **2** (*coll.*) a huge number.

бездо́ждь|е, я *nt.* dry weather, drought.

бездоказа́тел|ьный (~ен, ~ьна) *adj.* unsubstantiated.

бездо́м|ный (~ен, ~на) *adj.* homeless; **~ная ко́шка** stray cat.

бездо́нный *adj.* bottomless; (*fig., poet.*) fathomless.

бездоро́жь|е, я *nt.* **1** (*отсутствие дорог*) absence of roads. **2** (*распутица*) bad condition of roads; season when roads are impassable.

безду́м|ный (~ен, ~на) *adj.* unthinking; feckless.

безду́ши|е, я *nt.* heartlessness, callousness.

безду́ш|ный (~ен, ~на) *adj.* **1** (*человек*) heartless, callous. **2** (*fig.*) soulless.

бездыха́н|ный (~ен, ~на) *adj.* lifeless.

безе́ *nt. indecl.* meringue.

безжа́лост|ный (~ен, ~на) *adj.* ruthless, pitiless.

безжи́знен|ный (~, ~на) *adj.* lifeless, inanimate; (*fig.*) spiritless.

беззабо́т|ный (~ен, ~на) *adj.* carefree, light-hearted; (*бездумный*) careless.

беззаве́т|ный (~ен, ~на) *adj.* selfless, wholehearted; **~ная хра́брость** selfless courage.

беззако́ни|е, я *nt.* **1** (*отсутствие законности*) lawlessness. **2** (*поступок*) unlawful act.

беззако́ннича|ть, ю *impf.* (*coll.*) to transgress, break the law.

беззако́н|ный (~ен, ~на) *adj.* **1** illegal, unlawful. **2** (*poet.*) lawless, wayward.

беззасте́нчив|ый (~, ~а) *adj.* shameless; **б. лгун** brazen liar; **~ая ложь** barefaced lie.

беззащи́т|ный (~ен, ~на) *adj.* defenceless (*Br.*), defenseless (*US*), unprotected.

беззвёзд|ный (~ен, ~на) *adj.* starless.

беззву́ч|ный (~ен, ~на) *adj.* soundless, noiseless.

безземе́ль|е, я *nt.* lack of land.

безземе́льный *adj.* landless.

беззло́би|е, я *nt.* good nature.

беззло́б|ный (~ен, ~на) *adj.* good-natured.

беззу́б|ый (~, ~а) *adj.* toothless; (*fig.*) weak, impotent.

безле́с|ный (~ен, ~на) *adj.* woodless; treeless.
безле́сь|е, я *nt.* **1** (*пространство*) woodless tract. **2** (*отсутствие лесов*) absence of forest.
безли́кий *adj.* featureless; faceless, impersonal.
безли́ственный *adj.* leafless.
безли́ч|ие, ия *nt.* = **~ность**
безли́чност|ь, и *f.* lack of personality; impersonality.
безли́ч|ный (~ен, ~на) *adj.* **1** without personality, characterless, impersonal. **2** (*gram.*) impersonal.
безлу́н|ный (~ен, ~на) *adj.* moonless.
безлю́д|ный (~ен, ~на) *adj.* (*малонаселённый*) uninhabited; sparsely populated; (*улица*) empty, deserted.
безлю́дь|е, я *nt.* absence of human life; **на б. и Фома́ дворяни́н** (*prov.*) in the land of the blind the one-eyed is king.
безме́н, а *m.* steelyard.
безме́р|ный (~ен, ~на) *adj.* (*счастье*) boundless; (*требования*) excessive.
безмо́згл|ый (~, ~а) *adj.* (*coll.*) brainless.
безмо́лви|е, я *nt.* silence; **цари́т б.** silence reigns.
безмо́лв|ный (~ен, ~на) *adj.* silent, mute; **~ное согла́сие** tacit consent.
безмо́лвств|овать, ую *impf.* to keep silent.
безмоло́чный *adj.* dairy-free.
безмяте́жност|ь, и *f.* serenity, placidity.
безмяте́ж|ный (~ен, ~на) *adj.* serene, placid.
безнадёжност|ь, и *f.* hopelessness, despair.
безнадёж|ный (~ен, ~на) *adj.* hopeless; despairing; **больно́й ~ен** the patient's case is hopeless.
безнадзо́рност|ь, и *f.* neglect.
безнадзо́р|ный (~ен, ~на) *adj.* neglected.
безнака́занно *adv.* with impunity; **э́то ему́ не пройдёт б.** he won't get away with this.
безнака́занност|ь, и *f.* impunity.
безнака́зан|ный (~, ~на) *adj.* unpunished.
безнали́чный *adj.* without cash transfer; **б. расчёт** (*fin.*) clearing.
безнало́говый *adj.* tax-free.
безнача́ли|е, я *nt.* anarchy.
безно́г|ий (~, ~а) *adj.* (*без ног*) legless; (*без ноги*) one-legged.
безнра́вственност|ь, и *f.* immorality.
безнра́вствен|ный (~, ~на) *adj.* immoral.
безо *prep.* (*before g. of* ⇒**весь** *and* **вся́кий**) = **без**
безоби́д|ный (~ен, ~на) *adj.* inoffensive.
безо́блачност|ь, и *f.* cloudlessness; (*fig.*) serenity.
безо́блач|ный (~ен, ~на) *adj.* cloudless; (*fig.*) serene, unclouded.
безобра́зи|е, я *nt.* **1** (*уродство*) ugliness. **2** (*поступок*) outrage. **3** (*as pred., coll.*) it is disgraceful; **э́то про́сто б.!** it's simply disgraceful, scandalous.
безобра́|зить, жу, зишь *impf.* (*of* ⇒**о~**) **1** to disfigure, mutilate. **2** (*coll.*) to behave disgracefully; to make a nuisance of o.s.
безобра́зник, а *m.* (*coll.*) **1** (*хулиган*) hooligan. **2** (*озорник*) naughty child.
безобра́знича|ть, ю *impf.* (*coll.*) to behave disgracefully; to make a nuisance of o.s.
безо́браз|ный (~ен, ~на) *adj.* vague, featureless.
безобра́з|ный (~ен, ~на) *adj.* **1** (*уродливый*) ugly. **2** (*поступок*) disgraceful, outrageous.
безогля́д|ный (~ен, ~на) *adj.* reckless, impetuous.
безоговоро́оч|ный (~ен, ~на) *adj.* unconditional, unreserved, absolute.
безопа́сност|ь, и *f.* safety, security; **по́яс/реме́нь ~и** seat belt; **Сове́т Безопа́сности** Security Council.
безопа́с|ный (~ен, ~на) *adj.* safe, secure; **~ная бри́тва** safety razor.
безору́ж|ный (~ен, ~на) *adj.* unarmed; (*fig.*) defenceless (*Br.*), defenseless (*US*).
безоснова́тел|ьный (~ен, ~ьна) *adj.* groundless.
безостано́вочный *adj.* unceasing; non-stop.
безотве́т|ный (~ен, ~на) *adj.* **1** (*любовь*) unrequited. **2** (*существо*) meek, dumb.
безотве́тственност|ь, и *f.* irresponsibility.
безотве́тствен|ный (~, ~на) *adj.* irresponsible.
безотка́з|ный (~ен, ~на) *adj.* **1** (*человек*) dependable. **2** (*работа машины*) trouble-free.
безотлага́тел|ьный (~ен, ~ьна) *adj.* urgent.
безотлу́чно *adv.* continually; **она́ нахо́дится б. до́ма** she is tied to the home, she never gets out.
безотлу́ч|ный (~ен, ~на) *adj.* ever-present; continuous.
безотноси́тельно *adv.* (**к**+*d.*) irrespective (of); **б. к его́ пла́нам я пое́ду за́втра в Ло́ндон** irrespective of his plans I shall go to London tomorrow.
безотноси́тел|ьный (~ен, ~ьна) *adj.* absolute.
безотра́д|ный (~ен, ~на) *adj.* cheerless, bleak.
безотчётност|ь, и *f.* **1** (*отсутствие контроля*) absence of control. **2** (*бессознательность*) instinctiveness.
безотчёт|ный (~ен, ~на) *adj.* **1** (*бесконтрольный*) not subject to control. **2** (*бессознательный*) unconscious, instinctive.
безоши́боч|ный (~ен, ~на) *adj.* (*решение*) correct; (*судья*) faultless, infallible.
безрабо́тиц|а, ы *f.* unemployment.
безрабо́т|ный *adj.* unemployed; *as n.* **~ые, ~ых** *pl.* the unemployed; **постоя́нно ~ые** the long-term unemployed.
безра́дост|ный (~ен, ~на) *adj.* joyless; dismal.
безразде́л|ьный (~ен, ~ьна) *adj.* (*внимание*) undivided; **~ьная власть** complete sway; **~ьное иму́щество** indivisible property.
безразли́чи|е, я *nt.* indifference.
безразли́чно *adv.* indifferently; **относи́ться б.** (**к**+*d.*) to be indifferent (to); **б. кто, где** no matter who, where.
безразли́ч|ный (~ен, ~на) *adj.* indifferent; **мне ~но** it's all the same to me.
безразме́р|ный (~ен, ~на) *adj.* one-size (*nylon, etc.*); **~ные носки́** stretch socks.
безрассу́д|ный (~ен, ~на) *adj.* reckless; foolhardy.
безрассу́дств|о, а *nt.* recklessness, foolhardiness.
безрасчёт|ный (~ен, ~на) *adj.* uneconomical.
безрезульта́тност|ь, и *f.* futility; failure.
безрезульта́т|ный (~ен, ~на) *adj.* futile; unsuccessful.
безро́г|ий *adj.* hornless; **~ое живо́тное** pollard.
безро́д|ный (~ен, ~на) *adj.* **1** without kith or kin. **2** (*obs.*) (*незнатного рода*) of humble origin. **3** (*fig.*) homeless, stateless.
безро́пот|ный (~ен, ~на) *adj.* uncomplaining.
безрука́вк|а, и *f.* (*кофта*) sleeveless top; (*куртка*) sleeveless jacket.
безру́к|ий (~, ~а) *adj.* **1** (*без рук*) armless. **2** (*без руки*) one-armed. **3** (*fig.*) clumsy.
безры́бь|е, я *nt.* absence of fish; **на б. и рак ры́ба** (*prov.*) in the land of the blind the one-eyed is king.
безубы́точ|ный (~ен, ~на) *adj.* (*comm.*) break-even.
безуда́р|ный (~ен, ~на) *adj.* (*ling.*) unstressed.
безу́держ|ный (~ен, ~на) *adj.* unrestrained; impetuous.
безукори́знен|ный (~, ~на) *adj.* irreproachable; impeccable.
безу́м|ец, ца *m.* madman.
безу́ми|е, я *nt.* madness; **довести́ до ~я** to drive crazy; **люби́ть до ~я** to love to distraction.
безу́мно *adv.* madly, terribly, dreadfully.
безу́м|ный (~ен, ~на) *adj.* **1** (*план*) mad, crazy. **2** (*fig., coll.*) (*страсть*) wild; **~ные це́ны** absurd, crazy prices.
безумо́лч|ный (~ен, ~на) *adj.* incessant (*of noise*).
безу́мств|о, а *nt.* madness; foolhardiness.
безу́мств|овать, ую *impf.* to behave like a madman; to rave.

безупре́ч|ный (~ен, ~на) *adj.* (*человек*) irreproachable; (*работа*) flawless.

безуса́дочный *adj.* pre-shrunk, shrinkproof.

безусло́вно *adv.* **1** (*повиноваться, доверять*) unconditionally, absolutely. **2** (*coll.*) (*несомненно*) of course, it goes without saying, undoubtedly.

безусло́вност|ь, и *f.* certainty.

безусло́в|ный (~ен, ~на) *adj.* **1** (*повиновение, доверие*) unconditional, absolute. **2** (*успех*) undoubted, indisputable.

безуспе́ш|ный (~ен, ~на) *adj.* unsuccessful.

безуста́н|ный (~ен, ~на) *adj.* tireless, indefatigable.

безу́сый *adj.* having no moustache (*Br.*), mustache (*US*); (*fig.*) callow.

безуте́ш|ный (~ен, ~на) *adj.* inconsolable.

безу́хий *adj.* **1** (*без ушей*) earless. **2** (*без уха*) one-eared.

безуча́сти|е, я *nt.* apathy, unconcern.

безуча́стност|ь, и *f.* = **безуча́стие**

безуча́ст|ный (~ен, ~на) *adj.* apathetic, indifferent.

безъя́дерный *adj.* nuclear-free.

безыде́йност|ь, и *f.* lack of principle(s); lack of ideological content.

безыде́|йный (~ен, ~йна) *adj.* unprincipled; lacking ideals; lacking ideological content.

безызве́стност|ь, и *f.* obscurity.

безызве́ст|ный (~ен, ~на) *adj.* unknown, obscure.

безымя́нн|ый *adj.* (*не имеющий названия*) nameless; (*анонимный*) anonymous; **б. па́лец** third finger, ring-finger; **~ая неде́ля** the third week in Lent.

безынициати́в|ный (~ен, ~на) *adj.* lacking initiative.

безынтере́с|ный (~ен, ~на) *adj.* uninteresting.

безыску́ствен|ный (~ен, ~на) *adj.* artless, ingenuous.

безысхо́д|ный (~ен, ~на) *adj.* (*положение*) hopeless; (*горе*) interminable.

бе́й(те) *imper. of* ⇒**бить**

Бейру́т, а *m.* Beirut.

бейсбо́л, а *m.* baseball.

бейсболи́ст, а *m.* baseball player.

Бе́йсик *m.* (*comput.*) BASIC.

бека́р, а *m.* (*also as indecl. adj.*) (*mus.*) natural; **до б.** C natural.

бека́с, а *m.* (*zool.*) snipe.

беко́н, а *m.* bacon.

Белару́с|ь, и *f.* Belarus.

Белгра́д, а *m.* Belgrade.

белен|а́, ы́ *f.* (*bot.*) henbane; **что ты, ~ы объе́лся?** have you gone crazy?

беле́ни|е, я *nt.* bleaching.

белёный *adj.* bleached.

белесова́т|ый (~, ~а) *adj.* whitish.

белёс|ый (~, ~а) *adj.* whitish.

беле́|ть, ю *impf.* (*of* ⇒**по~**) **1** (*становиться белым*) to grow white. **2** (*no pf.*) (*виднеться*) to show up white.

беле́|ться, юсь *impf.* to show up white.

белиберд|а́, ы́ *f.* (*coll.*) nonsense, rubbish.

белизн|а́, ы́ *f.* whiteness.

бели́л|а, ~ *no sg.* **1** (*краска*) whitewash; **свинцо́вые б.** white lead; **ци́нковые б.** zinc white. **2** (*косметические*) ceruse.

бели́льный *adj.* bleaching.

бел|и́ть, ю́, ~́ишь *impf.* **1** (*pf.* **по~**) (*стены*) to whitewash. **2** (*pf.* **на~**) (*лицо*) to white(n). **3** (*pf.* **вы́~**) (*полотна*) to bleach.

бел|и́ться, ю́сь, ~́ишься *impf.* **1** *pass. of* ⇒**~и́ть**. **2** (*pf.* **на~**) to whiten one's face.

бе́л|ичий *adj. of* ⇒**~ка[1]**; **б. мех** squirrel (fur).

бе́лк|а[1], и *f.* squirrel; **верте́ться, кружи́ться как б. в колесе́** to run round in circles.

бе́лк|а[2], и *f.* (*coll.*) bleaching.

белкови́н|а, ы *f.* (*chem.*) albumen.

белко́вый *adj.* (*chem.*) albuminous.

белладо́нн|а, ы *f.* (*bot.*) belladonna.

беллетриза́ци|я, и *f.* fictionalization.

беллетризи́р|овать, ую *impf. and pf.* to fictionalize.

беллетри́ст, а *m.* fiction writer.

беллетри́стик|а, и *f.* (*liter.*) fiction.

беллетристи́ческий *adj.* (*liter.*) fictional.

бело... *comb. form* white-

белобры́с|ый (~, ~а) *adj.* (*coll.*) tow-haired.

белова́т|ый (~, ~а) *adj.* whitish.

белови́к, а́ *m.* fair copy.

белово́й *adj.* clean, fair; **б. экземпля́р** fair copy.

белогварде́|ец, йца *m.* (*pol.*) White Guard.

белогварде́|йский *adj. of* ⇒**~ец**

белоголо́в|ый (~, ~а) *adj.* **1** (*с седыми волосами*) white-haired. **2** (*со светлыми волосами*) fair(-haired).

белодере́в|ец, ца *m.* carpenter (*making simple unvarnished articles*).

бел|о́к[1], ка́ *m.* (*biol., chem.*) albumen; protein.

бел|о́к[2], ка́ *m.* (*яйца*) white (of egg).

бел|о́к[3], ка́ *m.* (*глаза*) white (of the eye).

белокро́ви|е, я *nt.* (*med.*) leukaemia (*Br.*), lukemia (*US*).

белоку́р|ый (~, ~а) *adj.* blond(e), fair(-haired).

белоли́ц|ый (~, ~а) *adj.* pale, white-faced.

белору́с, а *m.* Byelorussian.

белору́с|ка, ки *f. of* ⇒**~**

Белору́сси|я, и *f.* Byelorussia.

белору́сский *adj.* Byelorussian.

белору́чк|а, и *c.g.* (*coll., pej.*) person shirking rough *or* dirty (physical) work; shirker.

Белосне́жк|а, и *f.* Snow-White.

белосне́ж|ный (~ен, ~на) *adj.* snow-white.

белошве́йк|а, и *f.* seamstress.

белошве́йн|ый *adj.* linen; **~ая мастерска́я** seamstress's workshop.

белоэмигра́нт, а *m.* (*pol.*) White Russian émigré.

белу́г|а, и *f.* beluga, white sturgeon (*Huso huso*); **реве́ть ~ой** to bellow.

белу́|жий *adj. of* ⇒**~га**

белу́жин|а, ы *f.* (*meat of*) white sturgeon.

белу́х|а, и *f.* white whale (*Delphinapterus leucus*).

бе́л|ый (~, ~а́, ~о) *adj* **1** white; **~ая берёза** silver birch; **Б. дом** White House; (*Russian*) Parliament Building; **~ая кни́га** White Paper; **б. медве́дь** polar bear; **~ая сова́** snowy owl. **2** (*светлый*) white; fair; **б. биле́т** 'white chit' (*certificate of exemption from mil. service*); **~ое вино́** white wine; **~ое духове́нство** secular clergy; **~ое зо́лото** 'white gold' (= *cotton*); **~ое кале́ние** white heat, incandescence; **~ые кровяны́е ша́рики** white blood corpuscles; **~ое мя́со** white meat; **~ые но́чи** 'white nights', 'midnight sun'; **б. у́голь** 'white coal' (= *water power*); **б. хлеб** white bread, wheatmeal bread; **на ~ом све́те** in all the world; **средь ~а дня** in broad daylight; **э́то ши́то ~ыми ни́тками** it is all too obvious; it is quite transparent; *as n.* **~ые, ~ых** *pl.* white-skinned people, white men. **3** (*чистый*) clean; blank; **б. лист** clean sheet (*of paper*); **~ая страни́ца** blank page (*in book*); **~ые стихи́** blank verse. **4** (= *of superior quality*): **б. гриб** cep (*Boletus edulis*). **5**: **~ая горя́чка** delirium tremens. **6** (*pol.*) White (*also as n.*).

бельведе́р, а *m.* belvedere.

бельги́|ец, йца *m.* Belgian.

бельги́|йка, йки *f. of* ⇒**~ец**

бельги́йский *adj.* Belgian.

Бе́льги|я, и *f.* Belgium.

бель|ё, я́ *nt.* (*collect.*) linen; **да́мское б.** lingerie; **ни́жнее б.** underclothes; **посте́льное б.** bed-linen.

бель|ево́й *adj. of* ⇒**~ё**; **б. шкаф** linen cupboard.

бельме́с, а *m.*: **ни ~а** (*coll.*) nothing; **он ни ~а не понима́ет** he hasn't a clue.

бельм|о́, а́, *pl.* **~́а** *nt.* (*med.*) wall-eye; **как б. на глазу́** (*fig.*) a thorn in the flesh; bête noire.

бельэта́ж, а *m.* **1** (*второй этаж*) first floor (*Br.*), second floor (*US*). **2** (*theatr.*) dress circle.

беля́к, а́ *m.* white hare.

бемо́л|ь, я *m.* (*also as indecl. adj.*) (*mus.*) flat; **ре б.** D flat.

бенга́льский *adj.* Bengali; Bengal; **б. ого́нь** sparkler.

бенедикти́н, а *m.* benedictine (*liqueur*).

бенедикти́н|ец, ца *m.* (*eccl.*) Benedictine.

бенедикти́нский *adj.* (*eccl.*) Benedictine.

бенефи́с, а *m.* (*theatr.*) benefit performance.

бенефи́с|ный *adj. of* ⇨**~; б. спектáкль** benefit performance.

бенефициáри|й, я *m.* (*leg.*) beneficiary.

бенефициáнт, а *m.* (*theatr.*) artist for whom benefit performance is given.

бенефи́ци|я, и *f.* (*eccl.*) living, benefice.

бензи́н, а *m.* benzine; (*для автомобиля*) petrol (*Br.*), gas (*US*); **неэтили́рованный б.** unleaded petrol.

бензи́н|овый *adj. of* ⇨**~**; petrol (*Br.*), gas (*US*); **~овая коло́нка** petrol pump (*Br.*), gas(oline) pump (*US*).

бензоме́р, а *m.* petrol gauge (*Br.*), gasoline gauge (*US*), fuel gauge.

бензопрово́д, а *m.* petrol pipe (*Br.*), gasoline pipe (*US*).

бензо... *comb. form, abbr. of* ***бензи́новый***

бензобáк, а *m.* petrol tank (*Br.*), gas tank (*US*).

бензово́з, а *m.* petrol tanker (*Br.*), gasoline truck (*US*).

бензоколо́нк|а, и *f.* petrol pump (*Br.*), gas(oline) pump (*US*).

бензо́л, а *m.* (*chem.*) benzol, benzene.

бензохрани́лищ|е, а *nt.* petrol tank (*Br.*), gas tank (*US*).

бенуáр, а *m.* (*theatr.*) boxes (*on level of the stalls*).

бе́рег, а, о ~е, на ~у́, *pl.* **~á** *m.* (*реки*) bank; (*моря, озера*) shore; (*суша*) land (*opp.* sea); **на ~у́ мо́ря** at the seaside; **вы́броситься нá берег** to run aground; **вы́йти из ~о́в** to burst its banks; **сойти́ на б.** to go ashore.

бер|ёг, ~глá *see* ⇨**бере́чь**

берегов|о́й *adj.* coastal; waterside; **б. ве́тер** offshore wind, land-wind; **~áя оборо́на** coastal defence (*Br.*), defense (*US*); **~о́е прáво** (*leg.*) right of salvage; **~о́е судохо́дство** coastal shipping; **~áя лáсточка** sand-martin.

бере|гу́, ~жёшь, ~гу́т *see* ⇨**бере́чь**

бере|ди́ть, жу́, ди́шь *impf.* (*of* ⇨**раз~**) (*coll.*) to irritate; **б. стáрые рáны** (*fig.*) to re-open old wounds.

бережли́вост|ь, и *f.* thrift, economy.

бережли́в|ый (~, ~а) *adj.* thrifty, economical.

бе́режност|ь, и *f.* care; caution; solicitude.

бе́реж|ный (~ен, ~на) *adj.* (*осторожный*) careful; cautious; (*заботливый*) solicitous.

берёз|а, ы *f.* birch.

Берёзк|а, и *f.* Beryozka (*hard-currency shop*).

бере́зник, а *no pl., m.* birch grove.

березня́к, á *no pl., m.* **1** (*роща*) birch grove. **2** (*лес*) birch-wood.

берёз|овый *adj. of* ⇨**~а; ~овая кáша** (*coll.*) the birch; a flogging.

бере́йтор, а *m.* riding-master.

бере́мене|ть, ю, ешь *impf.* (*of* ⇨**за~**) (*coll.*) to become pregnant.

бере́ме|нная (~нна) *adj.* (+*i.*) pregnant (with).

бере́менност|ь, и *f.* (*состояние*) pregnancy; (*процесс*) gestation.

берёст|а, ы *f., no pl.* birch-bark.

берёст|овый *adj. of* ⇨**~а**

берестяно́й = **берёстовый**

бере́т, а *m.* beret.

бер|е́чь, егу́, ежёшь, егу́т, *past* **~ёг, ~еглá** *impf.* **1** (*человека, здоровье, предмет*) to take care (of), look after. **2** (*не тратить*) to be careful with; **б. кáждую копе́йку** to count every penny; **б. тáйну** to keep a secret.

бер|е́чься, егу́сь, ежёшься, егу́тся, *past* **~ёгся, ~еглáсь** *impf.* **1** (*быть осторожным*) to be careful, take care. **2** (+*g. or* +*inf.*) (*остерегаться*) to beware (of); **~еги́тесь воро́в** beware of pickpockets!; **~еги́тесь переедáть!** mind you don't eat too much! **3** *pass. of* ⇨**~е́чь**

бери́лл, а *m.* (*min.*) beryl.

бери́лли|й, я *m.* (*chem.*) beryllium.

Бе́рингов|о мо́р|е, ~а ~я *nt.* the Bering Sea.

бе́ркут, а *m.* golden eagle.

Берли́н, а *m.* Berlin.

берли́нск|ий *adj.* Berlin; **~ая лазу́рь** Prussian blue.

берло́г|а, и *f.* den, lair.

Берму́дск|ие острова́, ~их ~о́в *no sg.* the Bermudas (*islands*), Bermuda.

берму́д|ы, ов *no sg.* Bermuda shorts.

бер|у́, ёшь *see* ⇨**брать**

берцо́в|ый *adj.* (*anat.*): **больша́я ~ая кость** shin-bone, tibia; **мáлая ~ая кость** fibula.

бес, а *m.* demon, evil spirit; **рассыпáться ме́лким ~ом (пе́ред**+*i.*; *coll.*) to fawn (on), ingratiate o.s. (with).

бесе́д|а, ы *f.* **1** talk, conversation; **б. по душáм** heart-to-heart (talk). **2** (*дискуссия*) discussion; **провести́ ~у** to give a talk.

бесе́дк|а, и *f.* summer-house.

бесе́д|овать, ую *impf.* (**с**+*i.*) to talk, converse (with).

бесён|ок, ка, *pl.* **~я́та, ~я́т** *m.* imp, little devil (*also fig.*).

бе|си́ть, шу́, ~сишь *impf.* (*of* ⇨**вз~**) (*coll.*) to enrage, madden, infuriate.

бе|си́ться, шу́сь, ~сишься *impf.* (*of* ⇨**вз~**) **1** to go mad (*of animals*). **2** (*fig.*) to rage, be furious; **с жи́ру б.** (*coll.*) to grow fastidious, fussy; to be too well off.

беска́мерн|ый *adj.*: **~ая ши́на** tubeless tyre (*Br.*), tire (*US*).

бесклáссовый *adj.* classless.

бескозы́рк|а, и *f.* peakless cap.

бескозы́рный *adj.* (*о карточной игре*) without trumps.

бескомпроми́сс|ный (~ен, ~на) *adj.* uncompromising.

бесконе́чно *adv.* infinitely, endlessly; (*coll.*) extremely.

бесконе́чност|ь, и *f.* endlessness; infinity; **до ~и** endlessly.

бесконе́ч|ный (~ен, ~на) *adj.* (*дорога*) endless; (*время, удовольствие*) infinite; (*слишком длинный*) interminable; **~ная дробь** (*math.*) recurring decimal.

бесконтро́л|ьный (~ен, ~ьна) *adj.* uncontrolled.

бес738ко́рмиц|а, ы *f.* fodder shortage.

бескоры́сти|е, я *nt.* disinterestedness.

бескоры́ст|ный (~ен, ~на) *adj.* disinterested; (*альтруистичный*) unselfish.

беско́стный *adj.* boneless.

бескофеи́новый *adj.*: **б. ко́фе** decaffeinated coffee.

бескрáйний *adj.* boundless.

бескро́в|ный (~ен, ~на) *adj.* **1** (*бледный*) anaemic (*Br.*), anemic (*US*), pale. **2** (*без кровопролития*) bloodless; **~ная револю́ция** bloodless revolution.

бескры́л|ый (~, ~а) *adj.* wingless; (*fig.*) uninspired, pedestrian.

бескульту́рь|е, я *nt.* lack of culture.

бесновáтый *adj.* raging, raving.

бесн|овáться, у́юсь *impf.* to rage, rave.

бесо́вский *adj.* devilish, diabolical.

беспáлый *adj.* lacking one *or* more fingers *or* toes.

беспáмят|ный (~ен, ~на) *adj.* (*coll.*) forgetful.

беспáмятств|о, а *nt.* **1** (*обморочное состояние*) unconsciousness; **впасть в б.** to lose consciousness. **2** (*исступление*) frenzy, delirium; **быть в ~е** to be beside o.s.; to be delirious.

беспардо́н|ный (~ен, ~на) *adj.* shameless, brazen.

беспарти́|йный (~ен, ~йна) *adj.* non-party; *as n.* **б., ~йного** *m., and* **~йная, ~йной** *f.* non-party man, woman.

беспáспортный *adj.* not having a passport.

беспате́нтный *adj.* unlicensed.

бесперебо́йный *adj.* uninterrupted; (*регулярный*) regular.

беспересáдочный *adj.* direct; **б. по́езд** through train.

бесперспекти́в|ный (~ен, ~на) *adj.* having no prospects; (*безнадёжный*) hopeless.

беспечáл|ьный (~ен, ~ьна) *adj.* carefree.

беспе́чност|ь, и *f.* carelessness, unconcern.

беспе́ч|ный (~ен, ~на) *adj.* carefree.

беспило́тный *adj.* unmanned.

беспи́сьменный *adj.* having no written language.

бесплáновост|ь, и *f.* absence of plan.

бесплáновый *adj.* planless, having no plan.

бесплáтно *adv.* free of charge, gratis.

бесплáт|ный (~ен, ~на) *adj.* free, gratuitous; **б. билéт** free ticket, complimentary ticket.

бесплóди|е, я *nt.* (*почвы*) barrenness; (*женщины*) infertility.

бесплó**дност|ь, и** *f.* fruitlessness, futility.

бесплó**д|ный (~ен, ~на)** *adj.* **1** (*почва*) barren; (*женщина*) infertile; (*брак*) childless. **2** (*fig.*) fruitless, futile.

бесплóт|ный (~ен, ~на) *adj.* (*relig.*; *poet.*) incorporeal.

бесповорóтност|ь, и *f.* irrevocability, finality.

бесповорóт|ный (~ен, ~на) *adj.* irrevocable, final; **~ное решéние** final decision.

бесподóб|ный (~ен, ~на) *adj.* matchless; incomparable; **~но!** *int.* superb!; splendid!

беспозвонóчн|ый *adj.* (*zool.*) invertebrate; *as n.* **~ое, ~ого** *nt.* invertebrate.

беспокó|ить, ю, ишь *impf.* **1** (*волновать*) to concern, worry. **2** (*pf.* **по~**) (*мешать*) to disturb, worry.

беспокó|иться, юсь, ишься *impf.* **1** (**о** + *p.*) to worry, be worried *or* anxious (about). **2** (*pf.* **по~**) (*coll.*) to trouble o.s., put o.s. out; **не ~йтесь!** don't trouble!; don't worry!

беспокó|йный (~ен, ~йна) *adj.* **1** (*человек, вид, состояние*) agitated, disturbed; anxious; uneasy; (*ребёнок*) fidgety. **2** (*ночлег, сон*) restless, disturbed; (*поездка*) uncomfortable; (*море*) choppy.

беспокóйств|о, а *nt.* **1** (*волнение*) agitation; anxiety; unrest; **с ~ом** anxiously. **2** (*нарушение покоя*) disturbance.

бесполéз|ный (~ен, ~на) *adj.* useless.

беспóл|ый *adj.* sexless; **~ое размножéние** asexual reproduction.

беспóмощ|ный (~ен, ~на) *adj.* helpless, powerless; (*fig.*) feeble; **б. ум** feeble intellect.

беспорóд|ный (~ен, ~на) *adj.* not thoroughbred, not pedigree; **~ная собáка** mongrel.

беспорóч|ный (~ен, ~на) *adj.* blameless, irreproachable; **~ная слýжба** irreproachable service.

беспоря́д|ок, ка *m.* disorder, confusion; (*pl. only*; *pol.*) disturbances, riots.

беспоря́доч|ный (~ен, ~на) *adj.* disorderly; untidy.

беспосáдочный *adj.*: **б. перелёт** non-stop flight.

беспóчвен|ный (~, ~на) *adj.* groundless; unfounded.

беспóшлинн|ый *adj.* (*econ.*) duty-free; **~ая торгóвля** free trade.

беспощáд|ный (~ен, ~на) *adj.* merciless, relentless.

бесправи|е, я *nt.* **1** (*отсутствие законности*) lawlessness; arbitrariness. **2** (*отсутствие прав*) lack of rights.

бесправност|ь, и *f.* = **бесправие** 2

бесправ|ный (~ен, ~на) *adj.* without rights.

беспредéл, а *m.* (*coll.*) lawlessness, scandalous practices; chaos, mayhem; **ценовóй б.** outrageous prices.

беспредéл|ьный (~ен, ~ьна) *adj.* boundless, infinite.

беспредмéтный *adj.* pointless; aimless.

беспрекослóв|ный (~ен, ~на) *adj.* unquestioning, absolute.

беспрепя́тствен|ный (~, ~на) *adj.* free, clear, unimpeded.

беспреры́вно *adv.* continuously; uninterruptedly; non-stop.

беспреры́в|ный (~ен, ~на) *adj.* continuous; uninterrupted.

беспрестáнно *adv.* continually, incessantly.

беспрестáн|ный (~ен, ~на) *adj.* continual; incessant.

беспрецедéнт|ный (~ен, ~на) *adj.* unprecedented.

бесприбыл|ьный (~ен, ~ьна) *adj.* unprofitable.

беспризóрник, а *m.* waif, street urchin.

беспризóрн|ый *adj.* **1** (*заброшенный*) neglected. **2** (*бездомный*) homeless; *as n.* **б., ~ого** *m.* waif, street urchin.

беспримéр|ный (~ен, ~на) *adj.* unparalleled.

беспримесный *adj.* unalloyed.

беспринцип|ный (~ен, ~на) *adj.* unscrupulous, unprincipled.

беспристрáсти|е, я *nt.* impartiality.

беспристрáстност|ь, и *f.* impartiality.

беспристрáст|ный (~ен, ~на) *adj.* impartial, unbias(s)ed.

беспричин|ный (~ен, ~на) *adj.* groundless.

бесприют|ный (~ен, ~на) *adj.* homeless.

беспробýд|ный (~ен, ~на) *adj.* **1** (*сон*) deep, heavy. **2** (*пьянство*) unrestrained.

беспрóволочный *adj.* wireless; **б. телегрáф** wireless.

беспрóигрышный *adj.* safe; risk-free.

беспросвéт|ный (~ен, ~на) *adj.* **1** pitch-dark; **~ная тьма** thick darkness. **2** (*fig.*) hopeless; unrelieved.

беспроцéнтный *adj.* (*fin.*) interest-free.

беспýтиц|а, ы *f.* = **бездорóжье**

беспýтник, а *m.* (*coll.*) debauchee.

беспýтнича|ть, ю *impf.* (*coll.*) to lead a dissipated life.

беспýт|ный (~ен, ~на) *adj.* dissipated, dissolute.

беспýтств|о, а *nt.* dissipation, debauchery.

Бессарáби|я, и *f.* Bessarabia.

бессвя́зност|ь, и *f.* incoherence.

бессвя́з|ный (~ен, ~на) *adj.* incoherent.

бессемéйный *adj.* having no family.

бессемя́нный *adj.* seedless.

бессердéч|ие, ия *nt.* = **~ность**

бессердéчност|ь, и *f.* heartlessness; callousness.

бессердéч|ный (~ен, ~на) *adj.* heartless; callous.

бесси́ли|е, я *nt.* (*слабость*) weakness; debility; (*fig.*) impotence.

бесси́л|ьный (~ен, ~ьна) *adj.* (*слабый*) weak; (*fig.*) impotent, powerless.

бессистéмност|ь, и *f.* lack of system.

бессистéм|ный (~ен, ~на) *adj.* unsystematic.

бесслáви|е, я *nt.* infamy.

бесслáв|ить, лю, ишь *impf.* (*of* ⇒**о~**) to defame.

бесслáв|ный (~ен, ~на) *adj.* ignominious; inglorious.

бесслéдно *adv.* without leaving a trace; completely.

бесслéд|ный (~ен, ~на) *adj.* without leaving a trace; **~ное исчезновéние** complete disappearance.

бессловéс|ный (~ен, ~на) *adj.* dumb, speechless; (*fig.*) silent; **~ные живóтные** dumb animals; **~ная роль** (*theatr.*) non-speaking part.

бессмéн|ный (~ен, ~на) *adj.* permanent; continuous.

бессмéрти|е, я *nt.* immortality.

бессмéртник, а *m.* (*bot.*) immortelle.

бессмéрт|ный (~ен, ~на) *adj.* immortal; undying.

бессмы́слен|ный (~, ~на) *adj.* (*поступок*) senseless; foolish; (*слова*) meaningless, nonsensical; (*взгляд*) vacant, inane.

бессмы́слиц|а, ы *f.* nonsense.

бесснéжный *adj.* snowless.

бессóвест|ный (~ен, ~на) *adj.* **1** (*нечестный*) unscrupulous, dishonest. **2** (*бесстыдный*) shameless, brazen.

бессодержáтел|ьный (~ен, ~ьна) *adj.* (*жизнь*) empty; (*слова*) tame; dull.

бессознáтел|ьный (~ен, ~ьна) *adj.* **1** unconscious. **2** (*непроизвольный*) involuntary.

бессóнниц|а, ы *f.* insomnia, sleeplessness.

бессóнный *adj.* sleepless.

бесспóрно *adv.* indisputably; undoubtedly.

бесспóр|ный (~ен, ~на) *adj.* indisputable, incontrovertible.

бессрéбреник, а *m.* person who is not interested in personal gain.

бессрóчн|ый *adj.* without time-limit; **б. óтпуск** indefinite leave; **~ое тюрéмное заключéние** life imprisonment.

бесстрáсти|е, я *nt.* impassiveness, impassivity.

бесстрáст|ный (~ен, ~на) *adj.* impassive.

Б

бесстра́ши|е, я *nt.* fearlessness, intrepidity.

бесстра́ш|ный (~ен, ~на) *adj.* fearless, intrepid.

бессты́дник, а *m.* shameless person.

бессты́дниц|а, ы *f.* shameless woman, hussy.

бессты́д|ный (~ен, ~на) *adj.* shameless.

бессты́дств|о, а *nt.* shamelessness.

бесстыж|ий (~, ~а) *adj.* (*coll.*) shameless, brazen.

бессу́дный *adj.* (*obs.*) arbitrary, summary.

бессчётный *adj.* innumerable.

беста́ктност|ь, и *f.* **1** (*свойство*) tactlessness. **2** (*поступок*) tactless action, faux pas.

беста́кт|ный (~ен, ~на) *adj.* tactless.

бесталá́н|ный (~ен, ~на) *adj.* **1** (*бездарный*) untalented. **2** (*folk poet.*) (*несчастный*) ill-starred, luckless; **~ная голо́вушка** poor devil.

бестеле́с|ный (~ен, ~на) *adj.* incorporeal.

бе́сти|я, и *f.* (*coll.*) rogue; **то́нкая б.** sly rogue.

бестолко́вщин|а, ы *f.* (*coll.*) disorder, confusion.

бестолко́в|ый (~, ~а) *adj.* **1** (*человек*) slow-witted, muddle-headed. **2** (*рассказ*) disconnected, incoherent.

бе́столоч|ь, и *f.* (*coll.*) **1** (*беспорядок*) confusion. **2** (*человек*) muddle-headed person (*also collect.*).

бестре́пет|ный (~ен, ~на) *adj.* (*poet.*) dauntless.

бестсе́ллер, а *m.* best-seller (*book*).

бесфо́рмен|ный (~, ~на) *adj.* shapeless, formless.

бесхара́ктер|ный (~ен, ~на) *adj.* weak-willed; spineless.

бесхво́ст|ый *adj.* tailless; *as n.* **~ое, ~ого** *nt.* (*zool.*) ecaudate.

бесхи́трост|ный (~ен, ~на) *adj.* (*человек*) artless; (*слова*) ingenuous.

бесхо́зн|ый *adj.* ownerless; **~ое иму́щество** property in abeyance.

бесхозя́йственност|ь, и *f.* thriftlessness; bad management.

бесхозя́йствен|ный (~, ~на) *adj.* thriftless; improvident.

бесхребе́т|ный (~ен, ~на) *adj.* (*fig.*) spineless, weak.

бесцве́т|ный (~ен, ~на) *adj.* colourless (*Br.*), colorless (*US*).

бесце́л|ьный (~ен, ~ьна) *adj.* aimless; idle.

бесце́н|ный (~ен, ~на) *adj.* **1** (*сокровище*) priceless. **2** (*друг*) dear. **3** (*obs.*) (*малоценный*) valueless.

бесце́н|ок, ка *m.* (*coll.*): **купи́ть за б.** to buy for a song.

бесцеремо́н|ный (~ен, ~на) *adj.* unceremonious; familiar; cavalier.

бесчелове́чност|ь, и *f.* inhumanity.

бесчелове́ч|ный (~ен, ~на) *adj.* inhuman.

бесче́|стить, щу, стишь *impf.* (*of* **⇨о~**) **1** (*позорить*) to dishonour (*Br.*), dishonor (*US*), disgrace. **2** (*девушку*) to violate.

бесче́ст|ный (~ен, ~на) *adj.* dishonourable (*Br.*), dishonorable (*US*); disgraceful.

бесче́сть|е, я *nt.* dishonour (*Br.*), dishonor (*US*); disgrace.

бесчи́нный *adj.* (*obs.*) unseemly.

бесчи́нств|о, а *nt.* excess; enormity.

бесчи́нств|овать, ую *impf.* to commit excesses.

бесчи́сленност|ь, и *f.* innumerable quantity.

бесчи́слен|ный, ,и ~на) *adj.* innumerable.

бесчу́вственност|ь, и *f.* **1** (*отсутствие сознания*) insensibility. **2** (*равнодушие*) insensitivity.

бесчу́встве|ный (~, ~на) *adj.* **1** (*лишённый сознания*) insensible. **2** (*равнодушный*) insensitive, unfeeling.

бесчу́встви|е, я *nt.* **1** (*потеря сознания*) loss of consciousness; **пья́ный до ~я** dead drunk; **бить до ~я** to knock senseless. **2** (*равнодушие*) insensitivity.

бесшаба́ш|ный (~ен, ~на) *adj.* (*coll.*) reckless.

бесшо́вный *adj.* (*tech.*) seamless.

бесшу́м|ный (~ен, ~на) *adj.* noiseless.

бето́н, а *m.* (*tech.*) concrete.

бетони́р|овать, ую *impf.* (*tech.*) to concrete.

бето́нный *adj.* (*tech.*) concrete.

бетоново́з, а *m.* concrete-delivery truck.

бетономеша́лк|а, и *f.* (*tech.*) cement mixer.

бетоносмеси́тел|ь, я *m.* = **бетономеша́лка**

бето́нщик, а *m.* concrete worker.

бефстро́ганов *m. indecl.* (*cul.*) beef Stroganoff.

бехевиори́зм, а *m.* behaviourism (*Br.*), behaviorism (*US*).

бечев|а́, ы́ *no pl., f.* tow-rope.

бечёвк|а, и *f.* string, twine.

бече́вник, а́ *or* **а** *m.* tow-path.

бечев|о́й *adj. of* **⇨~а́; ~а́я тя́га** towing; *as n.* **~а́я, ~о́й** *f.* tow-path.

бешаме́л|ь, и *f.* (*cul.*) béchamel sauce.

бе́шенств|о, а *nt.* **1** (*med.*) hydrophobia; rabies. **2** (*fig.*) fury, rage; **довести́ до ~а** to enrage.

бе́шен|ый *adj.* **1** (*med.*) rabid, mad; **~ая соба́ка** mad dog. **2** (*fig.*) furious; violent; **~ая ско́рость** furious pace; **~ые це́ны** (*coll.*) exorbitant prices.

бешме́т, а *m.* beshmet (*kind of quilted coat*).

бз|деть, (д)жу, дишь *impf.* (*of* **⇨набзде́ть**) (*vulg.*) **1** (*пердеть*) to fart (*silently*). **2** (*говорить вздор*) to bullshit. **3** (*бояться*) to be shit scared.

бздун, а́ *m.* (*vulg.*) **1** farter, fart-arse (*Br.*), -ass (*US*). **2** (*брехун*) bullshitter. **3** (*трус*) chicken.

бзик, а *m.* (*coll.*) quirk, oddity; **он с ~ом** he's loopy.

биатло́н, а *m.* biathlon.

биатлони́ст, а *m.* biathlete, biathlon competitor.

биатлони́ст|ка, ки *f. of* **⇨~**

бибабо́ *nt. indecl.* glove puppet.

библеи́зм, а *m.* biblical expression.

библе́йский *adj.* biblical.

библио́граф, а *m.* bibliographer.

библиографи́ческий *adj.* bibliographical.

библиогра́фи|я, и *f.* bibliography.

библиоте́к|а, и *f.* library.

библиоте́кар|ша, ши *f. of* **⇨~ь**

библиоте́кар|ь, я *m.* librarian.

библиотекове́дени|е, я *nt.* library science.

библиоте́|чный *adj. of* **⇨~ка**

библиофи́л, а *m.* bibliophile.

би́бли|я, и *f.* bible; **(Б.)** the Bible.

би́бльдрук, а *m.* India paper.

бива́к, а *m.* (*mil.*) bivouac, camp; **стоя́ть ~ом, на ~ах** to bivouac, camp.

бива́|чный *adj. of* **⇨~к**

би́в|ень, ня, *pl.* **~ни, ~ней** *m.* tusk.

бивуа́к = **бива́к**

бигл|ь, я *m.* beagle (*dog*).

бигуд|и́, е́й *no sg.* (*also indecl.*) (hair) curlers.

биде́ *nt. indecl.* bidet.

бидо́н, а *m.* can, churn; **б. для молока́** milk-can.

бие́ни|е, я *nt.* beating; throb; **б. се́рдца** heartbeat; **б. пу́льса** pulse.

бижуте́ри|я, и *f.* costume jewellery.

биза́н|ь, и *f.* (*naut.*) mizzen; **б.-ма́чта** mizzen-mast.

би́знес, а *m.* business; **рекла́мный б.** advertising.

бизнесме́н, а *m.* businessman.

бизнесме́нк|а, и *f.* (*coll.*) businesswoman.

бизо́н, а *m.* (*zool.*) bison.

бикарбона́т, а *m.* (*chem.*) bicarbonate.

бики́ни *nt. indecl.* bikini.

би́кс|а, ы *f.* (*sl.*) tart.

бикфо́рдов *adj.*: **б. шнур** (*tech.*) Bickford (safety) fuse.

билабиа́льный *adj.* (*ling.*) bilabial.

биле́т, а *m.* ticket; (*удостоверение*) card; **входно́й б.** entrance ticket, permit; **еди́ный б.** rover ticket; **креди́тный б.** banknote; **обра́тный б.** return ticket; **экзаменацио́нный б.** examination question(-paper) (*at oral examination*).

билетёр, а *m.* ticket-collector.

билетёр|ша, ши *f. of* **⇨~;** (*in cinema, etc.*) usherette.

биллио́н, а *m.* billion (*one thousand million*).

билл|ь, я *m.* (*pol.*) bill.

би́л|о, а *nt.* **1** (*tech.*) beater. **2** (*для подачи сигналов*) gong.

билья́рд, а *m.* **1** (*стол*) billiard-table. **2** (*игра*) billiards.

бильярди́ст, а *m.* billiards player.

билья́рд|ный *adj. of* **⇨~; б. шар**

billiard ball; *as n.* **~ная, ~ной** *f.* billiard-room.

биметалли́ческий *adj.* bimetallic.

бимс, а *m.* (*naut.*) beam, transom.

бина́рный *adj.* binary.

бино́кл|ь, я *m.* binoculars; **полево́й б.** field glasses; **театра́льный б.** opera glasses.

бинокуля́рный *adj.* binocular.

бино́м, а *m.* (*math.*) binomial.

бинт, а́ *m.* bandage.

бинт|ова́ть, у́ю *impf.* to bandage.

бинто́вк|а, и *f.* bandaging.

био... *comb. form* bio-.

биоге́нный *adj.* biogenic.

био́граф, а *m.* biographer.

биографи́ческий *adj.* biographical.

биогра́фи|я, и *f.* biography; (*жизнь*) life story.

биоинженери́|я, и *f.* bioengineering.

биокре́м, а *m.* skin cream.

био́лог, а *m.* biologist.

биологи́ческий *adj.* biological.

биоло́ги|я, и *f.* biology.

биомедици́нский *adj.* biomedical.

биони́ческий *adj.* bionic.

биопси́|я, и *f.* biopsy.

биоресу́рс|ы, ов *no sg.* bioresources.

биори́тм|ы, ов *no sg.* biorhythms.

биоста́нци|я, и *f.* biological research station.

биосфе́р|а, ы *f.* biosphere.

биотехноло́ги|я, и *f.* biotechnology.

биофи́зик, а *m.* biophysicist.

биофи́зик|а, и *f.* biophysics.

биофизи́ческий *adj.* biophysical.

биохи́мик, а *m.* biochemist.

биохими́ческий *adj.* biochemical.

биохи́ми|я, и *f.* biochemistry.

биоци́д, а *m.* biocide.

бипла́н, а *m.* biplane.

биполя́рност|ь, и *f.* (*phys.*) bipolarity.

биполя́рный *adj.* (*phys.*) bipolar.

би́рж|а, и *f.* exchange; **фо́ндовая б.** stock-exchange; **б. труда́** (*Br.*) labour exchange.

биржеви́к, а́ *m.* stockbroker.

бирж|ево́й *adj. of* ⇒**~а; б. ма́клер** stockbroker.

би́рк|а, и *f.* tag, label.

Би́рм|а, ы *f.* Burma.

бирма́н|ец, ца *m.* Burmese, Burman.

бирма́н|ка, ки *f. of* ⇒**~ец**

бирма́нский *adj.* Burmese.

бирюз|а́, ы́ *no pl., f.* turquoise.

бирюзо́вый *adj.* turquoise.

бирю́к, а́ *m.* (*dial.*) lone wolf; (*fig.*) lone wolf, unsociable person; **смотре́ть ~о́м** (*coll.*) to look morose.

бирю́льк|а, и *f.* spillikin; **игра́ть в ~и** to play at spillikins; (*fig.*) to occupy o.s. with trifles.

бис *int.* encore; **сыгра́ть, спеть на б.** to play, sing an encore.

бисексуа́льный *adj.* bisexual.

би́сер, а *no pl., m.* beads; **мета́ть б. пе́ред сви́ньями** (*fig.*) to cast pearls before swine.

би́серин|а, ы *f.* bead.

би́сер|ный *adj. of* ⇒**~**; (*fig.*) minute.

биси́р|овать, ую *impf. and pf.* to repeat, give an encore.

Биска́йск|ий зали́в, ~ого ~а *m.* the Bay of Biscay.

бискви́т, а *m.* sponge-cake.

бискви́т|ный *adj. of* ⇒**~; б. руле́т** Swiss roll.

биссектри́с|а, ы *f.* (*math.*) bisector.

бит, а *m.* (*comput.*) bit.

бит|а́, ы́ *f.* (*sport*) bat.

би́тв|а, ы *f.* battle; **б. под Полта́вой, при Трафа́льгаре** Battle of Poltava, of Trafalgar.

битко́м *adv. only in phr.* **б. наби́ть** (*coll.*) to pack, crowd; **авто́бус был б. наби́т** the bus was packed, crammed.

бит-му́зык|а, и *f.* beat music.

би́тник, а *m.* beatnik.

би́товый[1] *adj.* (*mus.*) beat.

би́товый[2] *adj.* (*comput.*) bit-mapped.

бит|о́к, ка́ *m.* (*round*) rissole.

би́тум, а *m.* (*min.*) bitumen.

битумино́зный *adj.* (*min.*) bituminous.

би́т|ый (~, ~а) *p.p.p. of* ⇒**~ь** *and adj.*: **б. час** (*coll.*) a full hour, a good hour; **~ое стекло́** broken glass.

бить, бью, бьёшь *impf.* **1** (*pf.* **по~**) (*избивать*) to beat (*a person, an animal, etc.*).
2 (*pf.* **по~**) (*побеждать*) to beat, defeat (*in war, sports or games*).
3 (**уда́рить** *used in place of pf.*) (*ударять*) **to strike, hit**; **б. кнуто́м** to whip, flog; **б. в лицо́** to strike, hit in the face (*also fig.*).
4 (*impf. only*) (*производить звуки*) to strike, hit; to beat, thump, bang; **б. в бараба́н** to beat a drum; **б. в ладо́ши** to clap one's hands; **б. по столу́** to bang on the table; **б. за́дом** to kick (*of a horse*).
5 (*impf. only*) (*убивать*) to kill, slaughter (*animals*); **б. гарпуно́м** to harpoon.
6 (*pf.* **с~**): **б. ма́сло** to churn butter.
7 (*pf.* **раз~**) (*ломать*) to break, smash (*crockery, etc.*).
8 (**уда́рить** *used in place of pf.*) (*бороться*) to combat, fight (against), wage war (on); **б. по хулига́нству** to combat hooliganism; **б. по карма́ну** to cost one a pretty penny.
9 (*pf.* **про~**) (*издавать звуки*) to strike, sound; **б. (в) наба́т** to sound the alarm; **б. отбо́й** to beat a retreat (*also fig.*); **часы́ бьют пять** the clock is striking five; (*impers.*): **бьёт пять** it is striking five.
10 (*impf. only*) (*вытекать*) to spurt, gush; **б. ключо́м** to gush out, well up; (*fig.*) to be in full swing.
11 (*impf. only*) (*стрелять*) to shoot, fire; (*with fire-arms; also fig.*) to hit; to have a range (of); **б. из духово́го ружья́** to fire an air-gun; **б. в цель** to hit the target (*also fig.*); **б. наверняка́** (*fig.*) to take no chances; **б. на́ два киломе́тра** to have a range of two kilometres.
12 (*impf. only*; **на** + *a.*) (*стремиться*) to strive (for, after); **б. на эффе́кт** to strive after effect.

бить|ё, я́ *nt.* (*coll.*) beating, flogging; smashing.

би́ться, бьюсь, бьёшься *impf.* **1** (**с** + *i.*) (*драться*) to fight (with, against); **б. на поеди́нке** to fight a duel. **2** (*о сердце*) to beat; **се́рдце его́ переста́ло б.** his heart stopped beating. **3** (**о** + *a.*) (*ударяться*) to knock (against), hit (against), strike; **б. голово́й об сте́ну** to bang one's head against a brick wall. **4** (*метаться*) to writhe, struggle; **б. в исте́рике** to writhe in hysterics. **5** (**над** + *i.*; *fig.*) (*бороться*) to struggle (with), exercise o.s. (over); **б. над зада́чей** to rack one's brains over a problem; **как бы он ни би́лся** however hard he tried. **6** (*о стекле*) to break, smash; **легко́ б.** to be very fragile. **7**: **б. об закла́д** to bet, wager.

битю́г, а́ *m.* bityug (*Russian breed of cart-horse*); (*fig.*) strong man; **он настоя́щий б.** he is strong as a horse.

бифште́кс, а *m.* beefsteak.

бифште́ксн|ая, ой *f.* steakhouse.

би́цепс, а *m.* (*anat.*) biceps.

бич[1]**, а́** *m.* whip; (*fig.*) scourge.

бич[2]**, а́** *m.* (*sl.*) homeless person, vagrant.

бичева́ = **бечева́**

бичева́ни|е, я *nt.* flogging; flagellation.

бич|ева́ть, у́ю *impf.* to flog; (*fig.*) to lash, castigate.

бичёвка = **бечёвка**

бичу́ющ|ий *adj.*: **~ая сати́ра** scathing satire.

бишь *particle* (*expr. effort to recall name, etc.*; *coll.*) now (*or not translated*); **как б. его́ зову́т?** what was the name now?; **то б.** that is to say.

бла́г|о[1]**, а** *nt.* good, the good; blessing; **о́бщее б.** the common weal; **жела́ю вам всех благ!** I wish you every happiness; **всех благ!** (*coll.*) all the best! **ни за каки́е ~а** not for the world.

бла́го[2] *conj.* (*coll.*) since; seeing that; **скажи́те ему́ сейча́с, б. он здесь** tell him now since he is here.

благове́рн|ый *now used only facetiously as n.*; **б., ~ого** *m.* husband; **~ая, ~ой** *f.* wife.

бла́говест, а *m.* ringing of church bell.

бла́гове|стить, щу, стишь *impf.* **1** (*pf.* **от~**) to ring for church. **2** (*pf.* **раз~**) (*coll., iron.*) to publish, spread news.

Благове́щени|е, я *nt.* (*eccl.*) the Annunciation.

благове́щен|ский *adj. of* ⇒**~ие**

благови́д|ный (~ен, ~на) *adj.* plausible.

благоволе́ни|е, я *nt.* goodwill, kindness; favour; **по́льзоваться чьим-н. ~ем** to be in favour with s.o.

благовол|и́ть, ю́, и́шь *impf.* (**к** + *d.*) to be favourably (*Br.*), favorably (*US*) disposed (toward); to favour (*Br.*), favor (*US*); **~и́те** (+ *inf.*) (*obs.*) have the kindness (to); **~и́те отве́тить на э́то письмо́** kindly answer this letter.

благово́ни|е, я *nt.* fragrance, aroma.

благово́н|ный (~ен, ~на) *adj.* fragrant.

благовоспи́танност|ь, и *f.* good manners; good breeding.

благовоспи́тан|ный (~, ~на) *adj.* well-mannered; well brought up.

благовре́мени|е, я *nt. only in phr.* **во ~и** (*obs. or joc.*) at the appropriate time, opportunely.

благовре́менный *adj.* (*obs.*) timely.

благогове́|йный (~ен, ~йна) *adj.* reverential.

благогове́ни|е, я *nt.* reverence; veneration.

благогове́|ть, ю *impf.* (**пе́ред** + *i.*) to revere, venerate.

благодар|и́ть, ю́, и́шь *impf.* (*of* ⇒**по~**) to thank; **~ю́ вас** (**за** + *a.*) thank you (for).

благода́рност|ь, и *f.* **1** gratitude; **не сто́ит ~и** don't mention it. **2** (*usu. pl.*) (*выражение благодарности*) thanks. **3** (*mil.*) citation, commendation.

благода́р|ный (~ен, ~на) *adj.* **1** grateful. **2** (*стоящий*) rewarding; worthwhile.

благода́рственн|ый *adj.* expressing thanks; **б. моле́бен** thanksgiving service; **~ое письмо́** letter of thanks.

благодаря́ *prep.* + *d.* thanks to, owing to, because of; **б. тому́, что** owing to the fact that.

благода́т|ный (~ен, ~на) *adj.* beneficial; (*изобильный*) abundant; **б. край** land of plenty.

благода́т|ь, и *f.* **1** (*изобилие*) abundance. **2** (*relig.*) grace. **3** *as pred.* (*coll.*) paradise.

благоде́нстви|е, я *nt.* prosperity.

благоде́нств|овать, ую *impf.* to prosper, flourish.

благоде́тел|ь, я *m.* benefactor.

благоде́тельниц|а, ы *f.* benefactress.

благоде́тел|ьный (~ен, ~ьна) *adj.* beneficial.

благоде́тельств|овать, ую *impf.* (+ *d.*) to be a benefactor (to).

благодея́ни|е, я *nt.* (*доброе дело*) good deed; (*одолжение*) blessing, boon.

благоду́шеств|овать, ую *impf.* (*coll.*) to take life easily.

благоду́ши|е, я *nt.* (*спокойствие*) placidity, equability; (*доброта*) good humour (*Br.*), humor (*US*).

благоду́ш|ный (~ен, ~на) *adj.* (*спокойный*) placid, equable; (*добродуш -ный*) good-humoured (*Br.*), humored (*US*).

благожела́тел|ь, я *m.* well-wisher.

благожела́тельност|ь, и *f.* goodwill; benevolence.

благожела́тел|ьный (~ен, ~ьна) *adj.* (*человек*) kind; well-disposed; (*приём, улыбка*) friendly, cordial; (*рецензия*) favourable (*Br.*), favorable (*US*).

благозву́чи|е, я *nt.* euphony.

благозву́чност|ь, и *f.* euphony.

благозву́ч|ный (~ен, ~на) *adj.* euphonious; (*голос*) melodious.

благ|о́й[1] *adj.* good; **~а́я мысль** a happy thought; **~и́е наме́рения** good intentions.

благ|о́й[2] *adj.*: **~и́м ма́том** (*coll.*) at the top of one's voice.

благоле́пи|е, я *nt.* (*obs.*) grandeur.

благомы́слящий *adj.* (*obs.*) right-thinking.

благонадёжност|ь, и *f.* reliability, trustworthiness.

благонадёж|ный (~ен, ~на) *adj.* reliable, trustworthy.

благонаме́ренност|ь, и *f.* (*obs.*) loyalty.

благонаме́рен|ный (~, ~на) *adj.* (*obs.*) loyal.

благонра́ви|е, я *nt.* (*obs.*) good behaviour (*Br.*), behavior (*US*).

благонра́в|ный (~ен, ~на) *adj.* (*obs.*) well-behaved.

благообра́з|ный (~ен, ~на) *adj.* fine-looking, noble-looking.

благополу́чи|е, я *nt.* well-being; prosperity.

благополу́чно *adv.* well, all right; happily; (*в целости и сохранности*) safely; **всё ко́нчилось б.** everything turned out happily.

благополу́ч|ный (~ен, ~на) *adj.* (*удачный*) successful; (*прибытие*) safe; **б. коне́ц** happy ending.

благоприобре́тенный *adj.* acquired oneself, not inherited.

благопристо́йност|ь, и *f.* decency, decorum.

благопристо́|йный (~ен, ~йна) *adj.* decent, decorous.

благоприя́т|ный (~ен, ~на) *adj.* favourable (*Br.*), favorable (*US*); **~ные ве́сти** good news.

благоприя́тствовани|е, я *nt.*: **поли́тика/режи́м наибо́льшего ~я** the most favourable (*Br.*), favorable (*US*) policy/regime.

благоприя́тств|овать, ую *impf.* (+ *d.*) to favour (*Br.*), favor (*US*).

благоразу́ми|е, я *nt.* prudence; sense.

благоразу́м|ный (~ен, ~на) *adj.* prudent; sensible.

благорасположе́ни|е, я *nt.* (*obs.*) favour (*Br.*), favor (*US*).

благорасполо́жен|ный (~, ~на) *adj.* (*obs.*) favourably disposed (*Br.*), favorably disposed (*US*).

благоро́ди|е, я *nt.* (*obs.*): **ва́ше б.** (*term of address to officers of rank up to and including that of captain*) your Honour (*Br.*), Honor (*US*).

благоро́д|ный (~ен, ~на) *adj.* noble; **б. мета́лл** precious metal; **на ~ном расстоя́нии** (*coll., joc.*) at a decent distance.

благоро́дств|о, а *nt.* nobleness; nobility.

благоскло́нност|ь, и *f.* favour (*Br.*), favor (*US*); **по́льзоваться чьей-н. ~ью** to be in s.o.'s good graces.

благоскло́н|ный (~ен, ~на) *adj.* favourable (*Br.*), favorable (*US*); gracious.

благослове́ни|е, я *nt.* (*eccl. and fig.*) blessing; **с ~я** (+ *g.*) with the blessing (of).

благослове́н|ный (~, ~на) *adj.* (*eccl., poet.*) blessed, blest.

благослов|и́ть, лю́, и́шь *pf.* (*of* ⇒**~ля́ть**) **1** (*перекрестить*) to bless; (*выразить одобрение*) to give one's blessing (to). **2** (*воздать благодарность*) to be grateful to; **б. свою́ судьбу́** to thank one's stars.

благослов|и́ться, лю́сь, и́шься *pf.* (*of* ⇒**~ля́ться**) (*coll.*) **1** (**у** + *g.*) (*получить благословение*) to receive the blessing (of). **2** (*перекреститься*) to cross o.s.

благослов|ля́ть(ся), ля́ю(сь) *impf. of* ⇒**~и́ть(ся)**

благосостоя́ни|е, я *nt.* well-being, welfare.

благотвори́тел|ь, я *m.* philanthropist.

благотвори́тельност|ь, и *f.* charity, philanthropy.

благотвори́тельный *adj.* charitable, philanthropic; **б. спекта́кль** charity performance.

благотво́р|ный (~ен, ~на) *adj.* beneficial; wholesome, salutary.

благоусмотре́ни|е, я *nt.* (*obs.*) consideration.

благоустра́ива|ть, ю *impf. of* ⇒**благоустро́ить**

благоустро́ен|ный (~, ~на) *p.p.p. of* ⇒**благоустро́ить** *and adj.* well-equipped; comfortable; **б. дом** house with all modern conveniences.

благоустро́|ить, ю, ишь *pf.* (*of* ⇒**благоустра́ивать**) to equip with services and utilities.

благоустро́йств|о, а *nt.* equipping with services and utilities.

благоуха́ни|е, я *nt.* fragrance.

благоуха́н|ный (~ен, ~на) *adj.* fragrant, sweet-smelling.

благоуха́|ть, ю *impf.* to be fragrant; to smell sweet.

благочести́в|ый (~, ~а) *adj.* pious, devout.

благоче́сти|е, я *nt.* piety.

благочи́ни|е, я *nt.* (*obs.*) decency, decorum.

благочи́н|ный (~ен, ~на) *adj.* (*obs.*) decent, decorous.

блаже́н|ный (~, ~на) *adj.* blissful; (*eccl.*) the Blessed.

блаже́нств|о, а *nt.* bliss.

блаже́нств|овать, ую *impf.* to be in a state of bliss.

блаж|и́ть, у́, и́шь *impf.* (*coll.*) to be capricious.

блажно́й *adj.* (*coll.*) capricious.

блаж|ь, и *f.* (*coll.*) whim, caprice.

бланк, а *m.* form; **анке́тный б.** questionnaire; **фи́рменный б.** sheet of headed notepaper; **запо́лнить б.** to fill in a form.

бланманже́ *nt. indecl.* blancmange.

блат, а *m.* (*sl.*) **1** pull, string-pulling; **получи́ть по ~у** to obtain through connections. **2** thieves' cant.

блатме́йстер, а *m.* (*sl.*) racketeer.

блатни́к, а́ *m.* (*sl.*) wangler, fixer.

блатн|о́й *adj.* (*sl.*) criminal; **~а́я му́зыка** thieves' cant.

бл|ева́ть, юю́, юёшь *impf.* (*vulg.*) to puke.

блево́тин|а, ы *f.* (*vulg.*) **1** vomit. **2** (*fig.*) filth.

бледне́|ть, ю, ешь *impf.* (*of* ⇒**по~**) to grow pale; to pale.

бледноли́ц|ый (~, ~а) *adj.* pale.

бле́дност|ь, и *f.* paleness, pallor; (*fig.*) dullness.

бле́д|ный (~ен, ~на́, ~но) *adj.* pale, pallid; **б. как полотно́** white as a sheet; (*fig.*) colourless (*Br.*), colorless (*US*), insipid, dull.

бле́йзер, а *m.* blazer.

блёкл|ый (~, ~а) *adj.* faded; wan.

блёк|нуть, ну, нушь, *past* **~, ~ла** *impf.* (*of* ⇒**по~**) to fade; to wither.

блеск, а *m.* brightness, brilliance, shine; (*fig.*) splendour (*Br.*), splendor (*US*), magnificence; (*as int., sl.*) **б.!** brilliant!; great!; super!; **во всём ~е** in all (one's) glory; **прида́ть б.** to add lustre (*Br.*), luster (*US*) (to); **игра́ть с ~ом на роя́ле** to play the piano brilliantly.

блесн|а́, ы́, *pl.* **~ы** *f.* spoon-bait.

блесн|у́ть, у́, ёшь *pf.* to flash; **у меня́ ~у́ла мысль** a thought flashed across my mind; **у нас ~у́ла наде́жда** we saw a ray of hope.

бле|сте́ть, щу́, сти́шь *and* **~щешь** *impf.* to shine; to glitter; to sparkle; **её глаза́ ~сте́ли ра́достью** her eyes shone with joy; **он не ~щет умо́м** he's no genius.

блёстк|а, и *f.* **1** (*яркое проявление*) sparkle; **~и остроу́мия** flashes of wit. **2** (*блестящая пластинка*) spangle, sequin; **усе́янный ~ами** spangled.

блестя́щ|ий (~, ~а, ~е) *pres. part. of* ⇒**блесте́ть** *and adj.* shining, bright; (*fig.*) brilliant.

блеф, а *m.* bluff.

блеф|ова́ть, у́ю *impf.* (*coll.*) to bluff.

бле|щу́, ~щешь *see* ⇒**~сте́ть**

бле́яни|е, я *nt.* bleat(ing).

бле́|ять, ю, ешь *impf.* to bleat.

ближа́йш|ий *superl. of* ⇒**бли́зкий**; (*город, почта*) nearest; (*день, год*) next; (*задача*) immediate; **в ~ем бу́дущем** in the near future; **б. друг** closest friend; **б. нача́льник** immediate superior; **б. ро́дственник** next of kin; **при ~ем рассмотре́нии** on closer examination.

бли́|же *comp. of* ⇒**~зкий, ~зко** nearer; (*fig.*) closer.

ближневосто́чный *adj.* Middle East; Middle Eastern.

бли́жн|ий *adj.* **1** (*близкий*) near; (*соседний*) neighbouring (*Br.*), neighboring (*US*); **Б. Восто́к** Middle East. **2** (*mil.*) short range, close range, close; **б. ого́нь** close (range) fire. **3** (*родственник*) close; *as n.* **б., ~его** *m.* (*fig.*) one's neighbour (*Br.*), neighbor (*US*). **4** (*путь*) shortest.

близ *prep.* + *g.* near, close to, by.

бли|зиться, жусь, зишься *impf.* to approach, draw near.

бли́з|кий (~ок, ~ка́, ~ко) *adj.* **1** (*место*) nearby, close; **на ~ком расстоя́нии** a short way off; at close range. **2** (*конец*) near; imminent; **~кое бу́дущее** the near future. **3** (*в тесных отношениях*) intimate, close; **б. друг** close friend; **быть ~ким с кем-н.** to be on intimate terms with s.o.; **быть ~ким** (+*d.*) to be dear (to); *as n.* **~кие, ~ких** one's nearest and dearest. **4** (*похожий*) (**к**+*d.*) like; similar (to); close (to); **б. нам по ду́ху челове́к** kindred spirit.

бли́зко *adv.* **1** (**от**+*g.*) near close (to); close by. **2** *as pred.* it is not far; **ему́ б. ходи́ть** he has not far to go.

близлежа́щий *adj.* neighbouring (*Br.*), neighboring (*US*), nearby.

близне́ц, а́ *m.* twin (*also triplet, etc.*); **Б~ы́** (*созвездие*) Gemini.

близору́к|ий (~, ~а) *adj.* short-sighted (*Br.*), nearsighted (*US*) (*also fig.*).

близору́кост|ь, и *f.* short-sightedness (*Br.*), nearsightedness (*US*); (*med.*) myopia (*also fig.*).

бли́зост|ь, и *f.* nearness, proximity; (*близкие отношения*) intimacy.

блик, а *m.* speck, patch of light.

блин, а́ *m.* pancake; **пе́рвый б. ко́мом** (*prov.*) practice makes perfect.

блинда́ж, а́ *m.* (*mil.*) dug-out.

бли́нн|ая, ой *f.* pancake parlour (*Br.*), parlor (*US*).

бли́нчик, а *m.* pancake.

блиста́тельност|ь, и *f.* brilliance, splendour (*Br.*), splendor (*US*).

блиста́тел|ьный (~ен, ~ьна) *adj.* brilliant, splendid.

блиста́|ть, ю *impf.* to shine; **б. отсу́тствием** (*iron.*) to be conspicuous by one's absence.

блиц, а *m.* (*phot.*) flash (attachment).

блиц(-) *comb. form* lightning ..., whirlwind ...; **~визи́т** flying visit.

бли́цкриг, а *m.* blitzkrieg.

блок¹, а *m.* (*tech.*) block, pulley.

блок², а *m.* (*pol.*) bloc.

блок³, а *m.* carton (of cigarettes); unit; **б. пита́ния** power supply (unit).

блока́д|а, ы *f.* blockade; **снять ~у** to raise the blockade.

блока́дник, а *m.* victim of siege of Leningrad (1941–44).

блока́дни|ца, цы *f. of* ⇒**~к**

блокга́уз, а *m.* (*mil.*) blockhouse.

блоки́р|овать, ую *impf. and pf.* **1** to blockade. **2** (*sport*) to block.

блоки́р|оваться, уюсь *impf. and pf.* **1** *pass. of* ⇒**~овать**. **2** (**с**+*i.*; *pol.*) to form a bloc with.

блокиро́вк|а, и *f.* (*mech., elec.*) interlock.

блокно́т, а *m.* notebook, notepad.

блокпо́ст, а́, о ~е́, на ~у́ *m.* checkpoint.

блок-схе́м|а, ы *f.* (*tech.*) flow chart.

блонди́н, а *m.* fair-haired man.

блонди́нк|а, и *f.* blonde (woman).

блох|а́, и́, *pl.* **~и, ~а́м** *and* **~ам** *f.* flea; **иска́ть ~** to nitpick (*fig.*).

бло́чный *adj.* modular.

блошело́вк|а, и *f.* flea collar.

бло|ши́ный *adj. of* ⇒**~ха́**; **б. уку́с** flea-bite.

бло́ш|ки, ек *f. pl.* tiddlywinks.

блуд, а *m.* (*obs.*) debauchery, fornication.

блу|ди́ть¹, жу́, ди́шь *impf.* (*распутничать*) to lecher, fornicate.

блу|ди́ть², жу́, ~дишь *impf.* (*coll.*) (*блуждать*) to wander, roam.

блудли́в|ый (~, ~а) *adj.* **1** (*распутный*) lascivious, lecherous. **2** (*проказливый*) mischievous, roguish; (*вороватый*) thievish.

блудни́к, а́ *m.* (*obs.*) lecher, fornicator.

блудни́ц|а, ы *f.* (*obs.*) **1** (*распутница*) fornicatress, loose woman. **2** (*шлюха*) whore.

блу́д|ный *adj. of* ⇒**~**; **б. сын** (*eccl. and fig.*) prodigal son.

блужда́ни|е, я *nt.* wandering, roaming.

блужда́|ть, ю *impf.* to roam, wander; to rove; **б. по у́лицам** to roam the streets.

блужда́|ющий *pres. part. of* ⇒**~ть**; **б. огонёк** will-o'-the-wisp; **~ющая по́чка** (*med.*) floating kidney.

блу́з|а, ы *f.* (working) blouse; smock.

блу́зк|а, и *f.* blouse.

блю́деч|ко, ка, *pl.* **~ки, ~ек, ~кам** *nt.* (*блюдце*) saucer; (*тарелка*) small dish; **б. для варе́нья** jam dish.

блю́д|о, а *nt.* dish; **обе́д из трёх ~** three-course dinner; **вку́сное б.** a tasty dish.

блюдоли́з, а *m.* (*coll.*) toady.

блю|ду́, дёшь *see* ⇒**~сти́**

блю́д|це, ца, *g. pl.* **~ец** *nt.* saucer.

блюз, а *m.* (*mus.*) the blues.

блю́зовый *adj.* (*mus.*) blues.

блю́минг, а *m.* (*tech.*) blooming (mill).

блю|сти́, ду́, дёшь, *past* **~л, ~ла́** *impf.* to guard, watch over; **б. зако́ны** to abide by the law; **б. поря́док** to keep order.

блюсти́тел|ь, я *m.* keeper, guardian; **б. поря́дка** (*coll., iron.*) arm of the law.

блю|ю́, ёшь *see* ⇒**блева́ть**

бля́д|ский *adj.* (*vulg.*) *of* ⇒**~ь**; fucking.

бляд|ь, и *f.* (*vulg.*) (*проститутка*) whore; (*женщина*) bitch; (*мужчина*) bastard; *as int.* fuck!

блядю́г|а, и *f.* (*vulg.*) tart, scrubber.

бля́х|а, и *f.* (*на форме*) badge; (*на сбруе*) horse brass; (*на мебели*) plate.

боа́ *m. indecl. and nt. indecl.* **1** *m.* (*zool.*) boa, boa-constrictor. **2** *nt.* (*шарф*) boa; **мехово́е б.** fur boa.

боб, а́ *m.* bean; **туре́цкий б.** kidney bean, haricot; **~ы́ разводи́ть** (*coll.*) to talk nonsense; **оста́ться, сиде́ть на ~а́х** (*coll.*) to get nothing for one's pains.

боб|ёр, ра́ *m.* **1** (*мех*) beaver (fur). **2** (*pl. only*) (*воротник*) beaver collar.

боби́н|а, ы *f.* (*tech.*) bobbin.
бобк|и́, о́в *no sg.* (*bot.*) bayberries.
боб|о́вый 1 *adj. of* ⇒~; **б. стручо́к** bean-pod. **2** *as n.* **~о́вые, ~о́вых** leguminous plants.
бобр, а́ *m.* beaver; **уби́ть ~а́** to be in luck; (*often iron.*) to get a bad deal.
бо́брик, а *m.*: **во́лосы ~ом** (*coll.*) crew cut; **постри́чься ~ом** to have a crew cut.
бобр|о́вый *adj. of* ⇒~; beaver; beaver-fur.
бобслеи́ст, а *m.* bobsleigher.
бо́бсле|й, я *m.* (*сани*) bobsleigh; (*вид спорта*) bobsleighing.
бобы́л|ь, я́ *m.* **1** (*obs.*) (*крестьянин*) poor, landless peasant. **2** (*одинокий человек*) solitary, lonely man; **жить ~ём** to lead a solitary, lonely existence.
Бог, а, *voc. sg.* **Бо́же** *m.* God; god; **Бо́же мой!** good God!, my God!; **Б. зна́ет!, Б. весть!** God knows!; **Б. его́ зна́ет!** who knows!; **не дай Б.!** God forbid!; **ра́ди ~а!** for God's sake!; **Б. с ним!** blow it; **сла́ва ~у** thank God!; **как Б. на́ душу поло́жит** anyhow; **Б. с ним** let it pass; good luck to him (*iron.*).
богаде́л|ьня, ьни, *g. pl.* **~ен** *f.* almshouse, workhouse.
богате́|й, я *m.* (*coll.*) rich man.
богате́|ть, ю, ешь *impf.* (*of* ⇒**раз~**) to grow rich.
бога́тств|о, а *nt.* **1** riches, wealth; **есте́ственные ~а** natural resources. **2** (*fig.*) richness, wealth.
бога́т|ый (~, ~а) *adj.* (+*i.*) rich (in), wealthy; **~ая расти́тельность** luxuriant vegetation; **б. о́пыт** wide experience; **чем ~ы, тем и ра́ды** you are welcome to whatever we have; *as n.* **б., ~ого** *m.* rich man.
богаты́р|ский *adj. of* ⇒**~ь;** heroic; (*fig.*) powerful, mighty; **б. э́пос** the Russian folk-epic; **~ское сложе́ние** powerful physique; **б. сон** profound sleep.
богаты́рств|о, а *nt.* heroic qualities.
богаты́р|ь, я́ *m.* **1** bogatyr (*hero in Russian folklore*). **2** (*fig.*) Hercules; hero.
бога́ч, а́ *m.* rich man; **~и́** (*collect.*) the rich.
боге́м|а, ы *f.* (*collect.*) bohemians; (*образ жизни*) bohemianism.
боге́мистый *adj.* bohemian; arty-farty (*coll.*).
Боге́ми|я, и *f.* Bohemia.
боге́м|ный *adj. of* ⇒**~а**
боги́н|я, и *f.* goddess (*also fig.*).
богобоя́знен|ный (~, ~на) *adj.* god-fearing.
богоизбранный *adj.* (*rel.*): **б. наро́д** the Chosen people.
Богома́тер|ь, и *f.* Mother of God.
богомо́л, а *m.* (*zool.*) praying mantis.
богомо́л|ец, ьца *m.* **1** (*богомольный человек*) devout person. **2** (*паломник*) pilgrim.
богомо́л|ка, ки *f. of* ⇒**~ец**
богомо́ль|е, я *nt.* pilgrimage.
богомо́л|ьный (~ен, ~ьна) *adj.* religious, devout.
богоотсту́пник, а *m.* apostate.
богоотсту́пничеств|о, а *nt.* apostasy.
богоподо́б|ный (~ен, ~на) *adj.* god-like.
богопроти́в|ный (~ен, ~на) *adj.* **1** (*obs.*) impious. **2** (*coll.*) hideous, repulsive.
Богоро́диц|а, ы *f.* the Virgin, Our Lady.
богосло́в, а *m.* theologian.
богосло́ви|е, я *nt.* theology.
богосло́вский *adj.* theological.
богослуже́|бный *adj. of* ⇒**~ние;** liturgical; **~бная кни́га** prayer-book.
богослуже́ни|е, я *nt.* divine service, worship; liturgy.
боготвор|и́ть, ю́, и́шь *impf.* to worship, idolize.
богоуго́д|ный (~ен, ~на) *adj.* (*obs.*) pleasing to God; **~ное заведе́ние** charitable institution.
богоху́льник, а *m.* blasphemer.
богоху́льный *adj.* blasphemous.
богоху́льств|о, а *nt.* blasphemy.
богоху́льств|овать, ую *impf.* to blaspheme.
богочелове́к, а *m.* (*theol.*) 'God-Man', God incarnate.
Богоявле́ни|е, я *nt.* (*eccl.*) (*в православной церкви*) the Baptism of Christ.
бод, а *m.* (*comput.*) baud.
бода́|ть, ю *impf.* (*of* ⇒**за~**) to butt.
бода́|ться, юсь *impf.* to butt (*intrans.*).
бодн|у́ть, у́, ёшь *pf.* to butt, give a butt.
бодр|и́ть, ю́, и́шь *impf.* to stimulate, invigorate.
бодр|и́ться, ю́сь, и́шься *impf.* to try to keep one's spirits up, try to be cheerful.
бо́дрост|ь, и *f.* cheerfulness; good spirits; (*мужество*) courage.
бо́дрствовани|е, я *nt.* keeping awake; vigilance.
бо́дрств|овать, ую *impf.* to stay awake, to keep vigil.
бо́др|ый (~, ~а́, ~о) *adj.* cheerful, bright; (*старик*) hale and hearty.
бодр|я́щий *pres. part. of* ⇒**~и́ть** *and adj.* invigorating, bracing.
бодя́г|а, и *f.* fresh-water sponge; **разводи́ть ~у** to talk through one's hat.
боеви́к, а́ *m.* **1** (*солдат*) fighter; militant. **2** (*coll.*) (*остросюжетный фильм*) action movie, thriller.
боеви́тост|ь, и *f.* fighting spirit.
боев|о́й *adj.* **1** military, fighting, battle; **~ы́е де́йствия** operations; **б. дух** fighting spirit; **~о́е креще́ние** baptism of fire; **б. патро́н** live cartridge; **б. поря́док** battle formation; **~ы́е припа́сы** (live) ammunition. **2** (*неотложный*) urgent; **~а́я зада́ча** urgent task. **3** (*coll.*) (*воинственный*) militant; energetic. **4**: **б. механи́зм** striking mechanism (*of clock*).
боеголо́вк|а, и *f.* (*mil.*) warhead.
боеготóвност|ь, и *f.* combat readiness.
бо|ёк, йка́ *m.* (*tech.*) firing-pin.
боеприпа́с|ы, ов *no sg.* ammunition.
боеспосо́бност|ь, и *f.* (*mil.*) fighting efficiency.
боеспосо́б|ный (~ен, ~на) *adj.* (*mil.*) battle-worthy.
бо|е́ц, йца́ *m.* **1** (*участник боя*) fighter; (*солдат*) private soldier; **пету́х-б.** fighting-cock. **2** (*на скотобойне*) butcher, slaughterman.
божб|а́, ы *f.* swearing.
Бо́же *see* ⇒**Бог**
бо́жеск|ий *adj.* (*coll.*) (*приемлемый*) fair; **~ая цена́** a fair price.
боже́ственност|ь, и *f.* divinity; divine nature.
боже́ствен|ный (~, ~на) *adj.* divine (*also fig.*).
божеств|о́, а́ *nt.* deity, divine being.
бо́ж|ий, ья, ье *adj.* God's; **я́сно, как б. день** it is as clear as could be; **~ья коро́вка** (*zool.*) ladybird.
бож|и́ться, у́сь, ~и́шься *impf.* (*of* ⇒**по~**) to swear.
бож|о́к, ка́ *m.* idol (*also fig.*).
бо|й, я, *pl.* **~и́, ~ёв** *m.* **1** (*сражение*) battle, fight, action, combat; **~и́** fighting; **в ~ю́** in action; **взять с ~я** to take by force; **б. быко́в** bullfight. **2** beating; **бить сме́ртным ~ем** to thrash within an inch of one's life. **3** (*часов*) striking, strike; **часы́ с ~ем** striking clock; **бараба́нный б.** drum-beat. **4** (*убой*) killing, slaughtering; **б. кито́в** whaling. **5** (*посуды*) breakage; **бы́ло мно́го ~я** there were many breakages.
бо́|йкий (~ек, ~йка́, ~йко) *adj.* **1** (*дерзкий*) bold, spry, smart; **б. ум** ready wit; **б. язы́к** glib tongue. **2** (*живой*) lively, animated; **~йкая торго́вля** brisk trade; **~йкая у́лица** busy street.
бо́йкост|ь, и *f.* (*coll.*) **1** (*языка*) smartness; glibness. **2** (*живость*) liveliness, animation.
бойко́т, а *m.* boycott; **объяви́ть б.** (+*d.*) to declare a boycott (of).
бойкоти́р|овать, ую *impf.* to boycott.
бо́йлер, а *m.* boiler.
бойни́ц|а, ы *f.* embrasure.
бо́йн|я, и, *g. pl.* **бо́ен** *f.* slaughter-house, abattoir; (*fig.*) slaughter, butchery, carnage.
бойска́ут, а *m.* Boy Scout.
бойскаути́зм, а *m.* scouting; the Boy Scout movement.
бо́йфре́нд, а *m.* boyfriend.
бойцо́вый *adj.* fighting; **б. пету́х** fighting-cock.
бо́йче *comp. of* ⇒**бо́йкий, бо́йко**
бок, а, о ~е, на ~у́, *pl.* **~а́** *m.* side; flank; **в б.** sideways; **схвати́ться за ~а́ (от сме́ха)** to split one's sides (with laughter); **на́ б.** sideways, to the side; **на ~у́** on one side; **б. о́ б.** side by side; **по́ ~у** away with...!; **по́д ~ом** nearby, close at hand; **с ~у** from the side, from the flank; **с ~ на́ б.** from side to side.
бока́л, а *m.* (wine)glass, goblet; **подня́ть б. (за**+*a.*) to drink the health (of), raise one's glass (to).

боковин|а, ы *f.* wall (*of tyre etc.*).

боков|ой *adj.* side, flank, lateral, sidelong; **~ая улица** side-street; **отправиться на ~ую** (*coll.*) to go to bed, turn in.

боком *adv.* **1** sideways; **ходить б.** to sidle. **2**: **выйти б.** (*coll.*) to turn out badly.

бокс[1], **а** *m.* (*sport*) boxing.

бокс[2], **а** *m.* (*причёска*) short back and sides.

бокс[3], **а** *m.* (*в больнице*) cubicle.

боксёр, а *m.* (*спортсмен*; *собака*) boxer.

боксир|овать, ую *impf.* (*sport*) to box.

боксит, а *m.* (*min.*) bauxite.

болван, а *m.* (*coll.*) **1** (*человек*) twit (*Br.*), jerk (*US*). **2** (*для расправления шляп*) block. **3** (*в карточных играх*) dummy.

болванк|а, и *f.* **1** (*tech.*) pig (*of iron, etc.*); **железо в ~ах** pig-iron. **2** (*для расправления шляп*) block.

болгар|ин, ина, *pl.* **~ы, ~** *m.* Bulgarian.

Болгари|я, и *f.* Bulgaria.

болгар|ка, ки *f. of* ⇒**~ин**

болгарский *adj.* Bulgarian.

боле (*obs.*) = **более**

болев|ой *adj. of* ⇒**боль; ~ое ощущение** sensation of pain.

более *adv.* more; **б. толстый** thicker; **б. и б.** more and more; **б. или менее** more or less; **не б. и не менее, как** neither more nor less than; **б. всего** most of all; **тем б., что** especially as.

болезненност|ь, и *f.* **1** sickliness; (*fig.*) abnormality, morbidity. **2** painfulness.

болезнен|ный (~, ~на) *adj.* **1** (*нездоровый*) sickly; unhealthy; (*fig.*) abnormal, morbid; **~ное любопытство** morbid curiosity. **2** (*вызывающий боль*) painful.

болезнетворный *adj.* (*med.*) pathogenic.

болезный *adj.* (*dial.*) piteous; **мой б.!** poor thing!; my dear one!

болезн|ь, и *f.* illness; disease; (*fig.*) abnormality; **б. Альцгеймера** Alzheimer's disease; **б. «бешеной коровы»** mad cow disease; **б. Дауна** Down's syndrome; **б. Паркинсона** Parkinson's disease; **б. роста** growing pains; **морская б.** sea-sickness.

болельщик, а *m.* (*coll.*) fan, supporter.

болельщи|ца, цы *f. of* **~к**

болеро *nt. indecl.* (*танец*; *кофта*) bolero.

боле|ть[1], **ю, ешь** *impf.* **1** (+*i.*) to be ill, be down (with); (*intrans.*) to ail; **она с детства ~ет астмой** she has suffered from asthma ever since she was a child; **б. душой (за**+*a.*) to be worried (about). **2** (**за**+*a.*; *coll.*) to be a fan (of), support.

бол|еть[2] *1st and 2nd persons not used,* **~ит** *impf.* to ache, hurt; **у меня зубы ~ят** I have toothache; **у меня душа ~ит (о**+*p.*) I'm very worried (about).

болеутоляющ|ий *adj.* soothing, analgesic; **~ее средство** (*med.*) pain-killer, analgesic.

боливи|ец, йца *m.* Bolivian.

боливи|йка, йки *f. of* ⇒**~ец**

боливийский *adj.* Bolivian.

Боливи|я, и *f.* Bolivia.

болиголов, а *m.* (*bot.*) hemlock.

болид, а *m.* (*astron.*) fireball.

болонк|а, и *f.* lap-dog.

болонь|я, и *f.* plastic mackintosh.

болотист|ый (~, ~а) *adj.* marshy, boggy, swampy.

болотн|ый *adj.* marsh; **~ая вода** stagnant water; **б. газ** marsh gas; **~ая лихорадка** marsh fever, malaria.

болот|о, а *nt.* marsh, bog, swamp; **торфяное б.** peatbog; (*fig.*) mire, slough.

болт, а *m.* (*tech.*) bolt.

болтанк|а, и *f.* (*aeron.*; *coll.*) turbulence.

болта|ть[1], **ю** *impf.* **1** (*мешать*) to stir; (*взбалтывать*) to shake. **2** (+*i.*) to dangle.

болта|ть[2], **ю** *impf.* (*coll.*) (*говорить*) to chatter, jabber (away); **б. глупости** to talk nonsense; **б. по-французски** to jabber away in French.

болта|ться[1], **юсь** *impf.* (*coll.*) **1** (*качаться*) to dangle, swing; to hang loosely. **2** (*слоняться*) to hang about, loaf.

болта|ться[2], **ется** *impf.* (*coll.*) *pass. of* ⇒**~ть**[2]; **здесь ~ется много вздору** a lot of nonsense is being talked here.

болтливост|ь, и *f.* garrulity, talkativeness.

болтлив|ый (~, ~а) *adj.* garrulous, talkative; (*бестактный*) indiscreet.

болтн|уть, у, ёшь, *pf.* to blurt out.

болтн|уться, ~ётся *pf.* to work loose; to come off.

болтовн|я, и *f.* (*coll.*) chatter; (*сплетня*) gossip.

болтун, а *m.* (*coll.*) **1** (*пустослов*) chatterbox; gas-bag. **2** (*сплетник*) gossip.

болтунь|я, ьи *f. of* ⇒**~; яичница-б.** scrambled eggs.

болтушк|а[1], **и** *c.g.* (*coll.*) = **болтун**

болтушк|а[2], **и** *f.* **1** (*пойло*) swill, mash. **2** (*орудие*) whisk.

бол|ь, и *f.* pain; ache; **б. в боку** stitch; **зубная б.** toothache; **душевная б.** mental anguish.

больниц|а, ы *f.* hospital; **лечь в ~у** to go to hospital; **лежать в ~е** to be in hospital.

больни|чный *adj. of* ⇒**~ца; б. листок** medical certificate.

больно[1] *adv.* **1** painfully, badly; **б. ушибиться** to be badly bruised. **2** *as pred.* it is painful (*also fig.*); **мне б. дышать** it hurts me to breathe.

больно[2] *adv.* (*coll.*) (*очень*) very, exceedingly, badly; **он б. хитёр** he is too cunning by half.

бол|ьной (~ен, ~ьна) *adj.* (*человек*) ill, sick; (*орган*) diseased; (*часть тела*) sore (*also fig.*); **~ьные дёсны** sore gums; **б. зуб** bad tooth; **он тяжело ~ен** he is seriously ill; **б. вопрос** sore subject; **~ьное место** sore spot; *as n.* **б., ~ьного** *m.*, **~ьная, ~ьной** *f.* patient, invalid; **амбулаторный б.** out-patient; **стационарный б.** in-patient; **б. анорексией** anorexic (*person*); **б. артритом** arthritic (*person*); **б. гемофилией** haemophiliac (*person*).

большак, а *m.* (*dial.*) **1** (*глава семьи*) head of the family. **2** (*дорога*) high road.

больше 1 (*comp. of* ⇒**большой** *and* **великий**) bigger, larger; (*об отвлечённых понятиях*) greater; **Лондон б. Парижа** London is larger than Paris. **2** (*comp. of* ⇒**много**) more; **чем б.... тем б.** the more ... the more; **б. того** and what is more; **б. не** no more, no longer; **он б. не живёт на той улице** he does not live in that street any longer; **б. не буду!** I won't do it again!; **б. нет вопросов?** any more questions?; **б. у** (+*g.*) (*tennis*) advantage. **3** *adv.* (*coll.*) (*главным образом*) for the most part.

большевизм, а *m.* Bolshevism.

большевик, а *m.* Bolshevik.

большевистский *adj.* Bolshevik, Bolshevist.

больш|ий *comp. of* ⇒**~ой** *and* **великий**; greater, larger; **~ей частью, по ~ей части** for the most part; **самое ~ее** at most; **съезд будет продолжаться самое ~ее три дня** the congress will last at most three days.

большинств|о, а *nt.* majority; most (of); **в ~е случаев** in most cases; **б. голосов** a majority vote.

больш|ой *adj.* (*по величине*) big, large; (*значительный*; *важный*) great; (*coll.*) (*взрослый*) grown-up; **~ая буква** capital (letter); **~ая дорога** high road; **~ое знакомство** wide range of acquaintance; **б. палец** thumb; **б. палец ноги** big toe; **б. свет** haut monde, society; **когда я буду б.** when I grow up.

большух|а, и *f.* (*dial.*) mistress (of the house).

большущий *adj.* (*coll.*) huge.

болячк|а, и *f.* sore; scab; (*fig.*) defect.

бол|ящий *pres. part. of* ⇒**~еть**[2]; *as n.* **б., ~ящего** *m.* (*usu. joc.*) the patient.

бомб|а, ы *f.* bomb; **зажигательная б.** incendiary (device), petrol bomb; **кассетная б.** cluster bomb; **б.-посылка** letter bomb.

бомбардир, а *m.* **1** (*mil., hist.*) bombardier. **2** (*aeron.*) bomb-aimer. **3** (*sport*) striker.

бомбардир|овать, ую *impf.* to bombard; (*сбрасывать бомбы на*) to bomb; **б. просьбами** (*fig.*) to bombard with requests.

бомбардировк|а, и *f.* bombardment; bombing; **ковровая б.** carpet bombing.

бомбардировочный *adj.* bombing.

бомбардировщик, а *m.* **1** (*самолёт*) bomber; **пикирующий б.** dive-bomber. **2** (*coll.*) (*лётчик*) bomber pilot.

бомбёжк|а, и *f.* (*coll.*) bombing.

бомб|ить, лю, ишь *impf.* to bomb.

бомб|овый *adj. of* ⇒**~а**

бомбодержател|ь, я *m.* bomb-rack.

бомбометани|е, я *nt.* bomb-dropping, bomb-release.

бомбоубежищ|е, а *nt.* air-raid shelter, bomb shelter.

бом-бра́мсел|ь, я *m.* (*naut.*) royal (sail).

бом-брам-сте́ньг|а, и *f.* (*naut.*) royal mast.

бомж, а *m.* (*abbr. of* ***без определённого ме́ста жи́тельства***) homeless person, vagrant.

бомо́нд, а *m.* beau monde, society.

бон, а *m.* (*naut.*) boom (*floating barrier*).

бонвива́н, а *m.* (*человек, любящий хорошо жить*) bon vivant.

бо́нда́р|ь, я *or* **я́** *m.* cooper.

бо́нз|а, ы, *g. pl.* **~** *m.* (*fig.*) superior, distant person; bigwig; **парти́йный б.** Party boss.

бонмо́ *nt. indecl.* (*obs.*) bon mot, witticism.

бо́нн|а, ы *f.* nursery-governess.

бо́н|ы, ~ *pl.* (*sg.* **~а, ~ы** *f.*) **1** (*временные деньги*) vouchers, tokens. **2** (*кредитные документы*) bonds.

бор[1], а, о ~е, на ~у́, *pl.* **~ы́, ~о́в** *m.* (*лес*) coniferous forest; **с ~у да с со́сенки, с ~у по со́сенке** chosen at random; **(я ви́жу,) отку́да сыр б. загоре́лся** (I see) how it all started.

бор[2], а *m.* (*chem.*) boron.

борде́л|ь, я *m.* (*coll.*) brothel.

бордо́ 1 *nt. indecl.* claret. **2** *as adj.* claret-coloured (*Br.*), -colored (*US*).

бордо́вый *adj.* claret-coloured (*Br.*), -colored (*US*).

бордю́р, а *m.* border.

боре́ни|е, я *nt.* (*rhet.*) struggle, fight.

бор|е́ц, ца́ *m.* **1** (**за**+*a.*) fighter (for); campaigner; activist; **б. за мир** peace campaigner; **б. за права́ же́нщин** women's liberationist. **2** (*sport*) wrestler.

боржо́м, а *m.* (*and* **~и,** *nt. indecl.*) Borzhomi (*variety of mineral water*).

борз|а́я, о́й *f.*: **англи́йская б.** greyhound; **афга́нская б.** Afghan (hound); **ру́сская б.** borzoi, Russian wolfhound.

борзопи́с|ец, ца *m.* (*iron.*) hack writer.

бо́рз|ый (~, ~а́, ~о) *adj.* (*obs. or poet.*) swift, fleet.

бормаши́н|а, ы *f.* (dentist's) drill.

бормота́ни|е, я *nt.* muttering.

бормо|та́ть, чу́, ~чешь *impf.* to mutter.

бормоту́н, а́ *m.* (*coll.*) mutterer.

бормоту́х|а, и *f.* (*coll.*) plonk (*cheap wine*).

борм|очу́, о́чешь *see* ⇨**~ота́ть**

Борне́о *nt. indecl.* Borneo.

бо́рн|ый *adj.* (*chem.*) boric, boracic, **~ая кислота́** boric, boracic acid.

бо́ров[1], а *m.* hog; (*fig.*) obese man.

бо́ров[2], а, *pl.* **~а́** *m.* (*tech.*) horizontal flue.

борови́к, а́ *m.* (*coll.*) cep (*kind of mushroom*).

бор|ово́й *adj. of* ⇨**~[1]**

бор|ода́, оды́, *a.* **~оду,** *pl.* **~оды, ~о́д, ~ода́м** *f.* **1** beard. **2** (*у птицы*) wattle.

борода́вк|а, и *f.* wart.

борода́вчатый *adj.* warty.

борода́ст|ый (~, ~а) *adj.* (*coll.*) long-bearded, heavily bearded.

борода́т|ый (~, ~а) *adj.* bearded.

борода́ч, а́ *m.* **1** (*coll.*) bearded man. **2** (*bot.*) beard grass. **3** (*zool.*) bearded vulture, lammergeyer.

боро́дк|а[1], и *f.* small beard, tuft.

боро́дк|а[2], и *f.* (*tech.*) key-bit; barb (*of hook*).

бор|озда́, озды́, *a.* **~озду** *and* **~озду́,** *pl.* **~озды, ~о́зд, ~оздам** *f.* furrow; (*anat.*) fissure.

бороз|ди́ть, жу́, ди́шь *impf.* (*of* ⇨**из~**) to furrow; **морщи́ны ~ди́ли его́ лоб** (*fig.*) wrinkles furrowed his brow; **б. океа́ны** (*poet.*) to plough, furrow the seas.

боро́здк|а, и *f.* furrow; groove.

боро́здчатый *adj.* furrowed; grooved.

бор|она́, оны́, *a.* **~ону,** *pl.* **~оны, ~о́н, ~она́м** *f.* (*agric.*) harrow.

борон|и́ть, ю́, и́шь *impf.* (*of* ⇨**вз~**) (*agric.*) to harrow.

борон|ова́ть, у́ю *impf.* (*of* ⇨**вз~**) = **~и́ть**

бороньб|а́, ы́ *f.* (*agric.*) harrowing.

бор|о́ться, ю́сь, ~ешься *impf.* (**с**+*i.*; **за**+*a.*; **про́тив**+*g.*) to wrestle; (*fig.*) to struggle, fight (with; for; against); **б. со свое́й со́вестью** to wrestle with one's conscience.

борт, а, о ~е, на ~у́, *pl.* **~а́, ~о́в** *m.* **1** (*судна, грузовика*) side; **пра́вый б.** starboard side; **ле́вый б.** port side; **на ~у́** on board (*ship* or *aircraft*); **вы́бросить за́ б.** to throw overboard (*also fig.*). **2** (*пальто*) coat-breast. **3** (*бильярда*) cushion.

бортмеха́ник, а *m.* (*aeron.*) flight engineer.

борт|ово́й *adj. of* ⇨**~**; **б. журна́л** (ship's) log-book; **~ова́я ка́чка** (*naut.*) rolling.

бортпроводни́к, а́ *m.* air steward.

бортпроводни́ц|а, ы *f.* stewardess; air hostess (*Br.*).

борщ, а́ *m.* (*cul.*) bor(t)sch.

борьб|а́, ы́ *f.* **1** (*sport*) wrestling; **америка́нская б.** all-in wrestling; **спорти́вная б.** martial arts. **2** (*fig.*) (**с**+*i.*; **за**+*a.*; **про́тив**+*g.*) struggle, fight (with; for; against); conflict; **душе́вная б.** mental strife; **кампа́ния по ~е́ с престу́пностью** crime-prevention campaign.

босано́в|а, ы *f.* bossa nova.

босико́м *adv.* barefoot; **ходи́ть б.** to go barefoot.

Бо́сни|я и Герцегови́н|а, ~и и ~ы *f.* Bosnia-Herzegovina, Bosnia and Herzegovina.

бос|о́й (~, ~а́, ~о) *adj.* barefooted; **на ~у но́гу** with bare feet, barefoot.

босоно́г|ий (~, ~а) *adj.* barefooted.

босоно́ж|ки, ек *pl.* (*sg.* **~а, ~и** *f.*) sandals; (*без задников*) mules.

босс, а *m.* boss.

босто́н, а *m.* Boston (**1** *card-game.* **2** *kind of wool cloth.* **3** *name of dance*).

Босфо́р, а *m.* the Bosp(h)orus.

턉ся́к, а́ *m.* tramp; down-and-out.

обся́|цкий *adj. of* ⇨**~к**

ося́|чка, чки *f. of* ⇨**~к**

бот, а *m.* boat.

ботанизи́рк|а, и *f.* (*coll.*) plant-collecting box.

ботанизи́р|овать, ую *impf.* to collect plants (*for study*).

бота́ник, а *m.* **1** botanist. **2** (*sl.*) swot (*Br.*), nerd (*US*).

бота́ник|а, и *f.* botany.

ботани́ческий *adj.* botanical; **б. сад** botanical gardens.

ботв|а́, ы́ *f.* leafy tops of root vegetables (*esp. beet leaves*).

ботви́нь|я, и *f.* botvinia (*cold soup of fish, pot-herbs, and kvass*).

бо́тик, а *m.* (*obs.*) small boat.

бо́тик|и, ов *pl.* (*sg.* **~, ~а** *m.*) high (women's) over-shoes.

боти́н|ок, ка, *g. pl.* **б.** *m.* (*ankle-high*) boot.

ботфо́рт|ы, ов *pl.* (*sg.* **~, ~а** *m.*) (*hist.*) jackboots, Hessian boots.

бо́т|ы, ов *pl.* (*sg.* **~, ~а** *m.*) high overshoes.

бо́цман, а *m.* (*naut.*) boatswain.

боча́р, а́, *pl.* **~ы́** *m.* cooper.

бо́чк|а, и *f.* barrel, cask; (*fig.*): **плати́ть де́ньги на ~у** to pay on the nail.

бочко́м *adv.* sideways.

бочо́н|ок, ка *m.* small barrel, keg.

боязли́в|ец, ца *m.* wimp.

боязли́вост|ь, и *f.* timidity, timorousness.

боязли́в|ый (~, ~а) *adj.* timid, timorous.

бо́язно *adv. as pred.* (+*d.*; *coll.*) to be afraid, frightened; **ей б. остава́ться одно́й по вечера́м** she is frightened of being left alone in the evening.

боя́зн|ь, и *f.* (+*g. or* **пе́ред**+*i.*) fear (of), dread of; **б. темноты́** fear of the dark; **б. простра́нства** (*med.*) agoraphobia; **из ~и** for fear of, lest; **он перемени́л фами́лию из ~и, что над ним бу́дут смея́ться** he changed his name for fear of being laughed at.

боя́р|ин, ина, *pl.* **~е, ~** *m.* (*hist.*) boyar.

боя́р|ский *adj. of* ⇨**~ин**

боя́рств|о, а *nt.* (*collect.*; *hist.*) the boyars, the nobility.

боя́рын|я, и *f.* (*hist.*) boyar's wife.

боя́рышник, а *m.* (*bot.*) hawthorn.

бо|я́ться, ю́сь, и́шься *impf.* (+*g.*) **1** (*испытывать страх*) to fear, be afraid (of); **она́ ~и́тся темноты́** she is afraid of the dark; **он ~и́тся пойти́ к врачу́** he is afraid to go to the doctor; **~ю́сь, что он (не) прие́дет** I am afraid that he will (not) come; **~ю́сь, как бы (что́бы) он не прие́хал** I am afraid that he may come; **~ю́сь сказа́ть** I would not like to say. **2** (*не переносить*) to be afraid of, suffer from; **э́ти расте́ния ~я́тся хо́лода** these plants do not like the cold.

бра *nt. indecl.* (*подсвечник*) sconce; (*держатель для лампы*) lamp-bracket.
брава́д|а, ы *f.* bravado.
брави́р|овать, ую *impf.* (+*i.*) (*опасностью*) to defy; (*щеголять*) to flaunt.
бра́во *int.* bravo!
браву́р|ный (~ен, ~на) *adj.* (*mus.*) bravura.
бра́вый *adj.* gallant; manly.
бра́г|а, и *f.* home-brewed beer.
бра́жник, а *m.* (*obs.*) reveller.
бра́жнича|ть, ю *impf.* (*obs.*) to revel, carouse.
бразд|а́, ы́ *f.* (*poet., obs.*) furrow.
бразд|ы́, ~ *now only in phr.* **б. правле́ния** the reins of government.
брази́л|ец, ьца *m.* Brazilian.
Брази́ли|я, и *f.* **1** (*страна*) Brazil. **2** (*город*) Brasilia.
брази́льский *adj.* Brazilian.
бразил|ья́нка, ья́нки *f. of* ⇒**~ец**
бра́йлевский *adj.*: **б. шрифт** Braille.
Брайл|ь, я *m.*: **шрифт ~я** Braille.
брак[1]**, а** *m.* (*супружество*) marriage; matrimony; **свиде́тельство о ~е** marriage certificate; **рождённый вне ~а** born out of wedlock.
брак[2]**, а** *m.* (*продукция*) rejects; (*изъян*) defect.
брако́ван|ный (~, ~а) *p.p.p. of* ⇒**бракова́ть** *and adj.* rejected; defective.
брак|ова́ть, у́ю *impf.* (*of* ⇒**за~**) to reject.
брако́вщик, а *m.* sorter (*of manufactured articles*).
брако́вщиц|а, ы *f. of* ⇒**брако́вщик**
бракоде́л, а *m.* (*coll.*) bad workman.
браконье́р, а *m.* poacher.
браконье́рств|о, а *nt.* poaching.
бракопосре́дническ|ий *adj.*: **~ое аге́нтство** marriage bureau.
бракоразво́дный *adj.* divorce; **б. проце́сс** divorce suit.
бракосочета́ни|е, я *nt.* wedding, wedding ceremony.
брам-... *comb. form* (*naut.*) top-.
брами́н, а *m.* Brahmin.
брам-ре́|й, я *m.* (*naut.*) topgallant yard.
бра́мсел|ь, я *m.* (*naut.*) topgallant sail.
брам-сте́ньг|а, и *f.* (*naut.*) topgallant (mast).
брандахлы́ст, а *m.* (*coll.*) **1** slops. **2** (*fig.*) worthless person.
брандва́хт|а, ы *f.* guard-ship.
брандма́уэр, а *m.* fire-proof wall.
брандспо́йт, а *m.* **1** (*насос*) fire-pump. **2** (*наконечник*) nozzle.
бран|и́ть, ю́, и́шь *impf.* (*of* ⇒**вы~**) (*выговаривать*) to reprove; to scold; (*ругать*) to abuse, curse (*coll.*).
бран|и́ться, ю́сь, и́шься *impf.* **1** (*of* ⇒**по~**) (**с**+*i.*) (*ссориться*) to quarrel (with). **2** (*ругаться*) to swear, curse (*intrans.*).
бра́нн|ый[1] *adj.* abusive; **~ое сло́во** swearword.
бра́нный[2] *adj.* (*obs., poet.*) martial.
бранч(л)и́в|ый (~, ~а) *adj.* (*coll.*) quarrelsome.
бран|ь[1]**, и** *f.* swearing; abuse; bad language.
бран|ь[2]**, и** *f.* (*obs., poet.*): **по́ле ~и** field of battle.
брас, а *m.* (*naut.*) brace.
брасле́т, а *m.* bracelet.
брасс, а *m.* (*sport*) breast stroke.
брат, а, *pl.* **~ья, ~ьев** *m.* **1** brother; **сво́дный б.** stepbrother; **единокро́вный б.** half-brother (*by father*); **единоутро́бный б.** half-brother (*by mother*); **двою́родный б.** cousin. **2** (*fig.*) brother; comrade; **~ья-писа́тели** fellow-writers; **наш б.** (*coll.*) we, the likes of us; **ваш б.** (*coll.*) you, you and your sort.
брата́ни|е, я *nt.* fraternization.
брата́|ться, юсь *impf.* (*of* ⇒**по~**) (**с**+*i.*) to fraternize (with).
братв|а́, ы́ *f.* (*collect.; coll.*) comrades; chaps, lads.
бра́т|ец, ца *m. affectionate or patronizing dim. of* ⇒**~**; (*as term of address*) old man, old chap; boy.
братиш|ка, ки, *g. pl.* **~ек** *m.* (*coll.*) **1** little brother. **2** = **брат** 2
бра́ти|я, и, *g. pl.* **~й** *f.* (*collect.*) brotherhood, fraternity (*also fig.*); **актёрская б.** the acting fraternity.
бра́тнин *adj.* (*coll.*) brother's, belonging to one's brother.
брат|о́к, ка́ *m.* (*coll.*) = **брат** 2
братоуби́йственный *adj.* fratricidal (*also fig.*).
братоуби́йств|о, а *nt.* fratricide (*act*).
братоуби́йц|а, ы *c.g.* fratricide (*agent*).
бра́тск|ий *adj.* brotherly, fraternal; **~ая моги́ла** communal grave (*esp. of war dead*).
бра́тств|о, а *nt.* (*abstr. and concr.*) brotherhood, fraternity.
бра|ть, беру́, берёшь, *past* **~л, ~ла́, ~ло** *impf.* (*of* ⇒**взять**). **1** (*in var. senses*) to take; **б. наза́д, б. обра́тно** to take back; **б. курс (на**+*a.*) to make (for), head (for); **б. нача́ло (в**+*p.*) to originate (in); **б. но́ту** to sing, play a note; **б. поруче́ние** to undertake a commission; **б. приме́р (с**+*g.*) to follow the example (of); **б. сло́во** to take the floor; **б. в ско́бки** to place in brackets; **б. в плен** to take prisoner; **б. на пору́ки** (*leg.*) to go bail (for); **б. на себя́** to take upon o.s.; **б. под аре́ст** to put under arrest; **б. кого́-н. по́д руку** to take s.o.'s arm. **2** (*получить*) to get, obtain; (*принимать*) to take on; **б. биле́ты** to book tickets; **б. верх** to get the upper hand; **б. такси́** to take a taxi; **б. своё** to get one's way; to make itself felt; **го́ды беру́т своё** age tells; **б. взаймы́** to borrow; **б. в аре́нду** to rent; **б. напрока́т** to hire. **3** (**в**+*nom.-a.*) to take (as); **б. в жёны** to take to wife; **б. в свиде́тели** to call to witness. **4** (*захватить*) to seize; to grip; **б. власть** to seize power; **б. за се́рдце** to move deeply. **5** (*требовать*) to exact; to take (= *to demand, require*); **б. штраф** to exact a fine; **б. вре́мя** to take time. **6** (*преодолевать*) to take; to surmount; **б. барье́р** to clear a hurdle. **7** (+*i.*) (*добиваться своей цели*) to succeed (by means of, by dint of); **она́ берёт такти́чностью** the secret of her success is tact. **8** (*usu.*+*neg.; coll.*) (*действовать*) to work, operate; to be effective; (**на**+*a.; of a fire-arm*) to have a range (of); **э́ти но́жницы не беру́т** these scissors don't cut; **э́та винто́вка берёт на пятьсо́т ме́тров** this rifle has a range of, is effective at, five hundred metres. **9** (+*adv. of place; coll.*) to bear; **б. вле́во** to bear left.
бра́|ться, беру́сь, берёшься, *past* **~лся, ~ла́сь, ~ло́сь** *impf.* (*of* ⇒**взя́ться**). **1** *pass. of* ⇒**~ть.** **2** (**за**+*a.*) (*трогать*) to touch, lay hands (upon); **не бери́сь за то́рмоз!** don't touch the brake!; **б. за́ руки** to link arms. **3** (**за**+*a.*) (*приниматься*) to take up; to get down (to); **б. за де́ло** to get down to business, get down to brass tacks; **б. за перо́** to take up the pen; **б. за чте́ние** to get down to reading. **4** (**за**+*a. or* +*inf.*) (*принимать на себя*) to undertake; to take upon o.s.; **б. за поруче́ние** to undertake a commission; **б. вы́полнить рабо́ту** to undertake a job; **не беру́сь суди́ть** I do not presume to judge. **5** (*3rd person only*) (*coll.*) (*появляться*) to appear, arise; **не зна́ю, отку́да у них де́ньги беру́тся** I don't know where they get their money from. **6**: **б. за ум** (*coll.*) to come to one's senses.
бра́т|ья[1] *see* ⇒**~**
бра́ть|я[2]**, и** *f.* = **бра́тия**
бра́унинг, а *m.* Browning (*automatic pistol*).
брахма́н, а *m.* = **брами́н**
бра́чн|ый *adj.* marriage; conjugal; **б. во́зраст** marriageable age; **~ая жизнь** married life; **~ая конто́ра** marriage bureau; **~ое свиде́тельство** marriage certificate; **~ое опере́ние** (*zool.*) breeding plumage.
бра́чующ|иеся, ихся *no sg.* the bride and groom; the happy couple; **дороги́е б.!** dearly beloved!
бра́шпил|ь, я *m.* (*naut.*) windlass, capstan.
бреве́нчатый *adj.* log, made of logs.
брев|но́, на́, *pl.* **~на, ~ен, ~нам** *nt.* log, beam; (*sport*) caber; **мета́ние ~на́** (*sport*) tossing the caber; (*fig.*) (*тупой человек*) dullard, insensitive person.
брег, а *pl.* **~а́** *m.* (*poet., arch.*) = **бе́рег**
бред, а, о ~е, в ~у́, *m.* delirium; ravings; (*fig.*) gibberish; **быть в ~у́** to be delirious.
бре́д|ень, ня *m.* drag-net.
бре́|дить, жу, дишь *impf.* to be delirious, rave; (+*i.; fig.*) to be mad about; **он ~дит джа́зом** he is crazy about jazz.
бре́|диться, дится *impf.* (*impers.*+*d.; coll.*) to dream (of); **ему́ всё ~дилось,**

что он па́дает в про́пасть he was always dreaming that he was falling down a precipice.

бре́дн|и, ей *no sg.* ravings; fantasies.

бредово́й *adj.* **1** delirious. **2** (*fig.*) fantastic, nonsensical.

бредо́вый *adj.* crackpot, crazy.

бре|ду́, дёшь *see* ⇒**~сти́**

бре́|жу, дишь *see* ⇒**~дить**

бре́зг|ать, аю, аешь *impf.* (*of* ⇒**по~**) (+*i.*) to be squeamish, fastidious (about); **он ~ает есть немы́тые фру́кты** he is squeamish about eating unwashed fruit.

брезгли́вост|ь, и *f.* squeamishness, fastidiousness; (*отвращение*) disgust.

брезгли́в|ый (~, ~а) *adj.* squeamish, fastidious; **~ое чу́вство** feeling of disgust.

бре́зг|овать, ую *impf.* (*of* ⇒**по~**) (+*i.*) = **бре́згать**

брезе́нт, а *m.* tarpaulin.

брезе́нтовый *adj.* tarpaulin, canvas.

бре́зж|ить(ся), ~ит(ся) *impf.* to dawn; to glimmer; **~ила заря́** dawn was breaking.

брейк, а *m.* break-dancing.

бре́йкер, а *m.* break-dancer.

брёл, а́ *see* ⇒**брести́**

брело́к, а *m.* (*bracelet*) charm; **б. для ключе́й** key ring.

бремен|и́ть, ю́, и́шь *impf.* (*obs.*) to burden.

бре́м|я, ~ени, ~енем, ~ени *nt.* burden; load; **разреши́ться от ~ени** (*obs.*) to give birth.

бре́нди *m. and nt. indecl.* brandy.

бре́нн|ый (~а, ~о) *adj.* perishable; **~ые оста́нки** mortal remains.

бренч|а́ть, у́, и́шь *impf.* **1** (+*i.*) to jingle; **он всё ~а́л моне́тами в карма́не** he kept jingling coins in his pocket. **2** (*coll.*) (*играть*) to strum; **б. на роя́ле** to strum on the piano.

бр|ести́, еду́, едёшь, *past* **~ёл, ~ела́** *impf.* (*идти с трудом*) to trudge (along); to drag o.s. along.

Брета́н|ь, и *f.* Brittany.

брете́льк|а, и *f.* shoulder-strap.

бретёр, а *m.* (*obs.*) duellist, swashbuckler.

бре|ха́ть, шу́, ~́шешь *impf.* (*coll.*) **1** (*лаять*) to yelp, bark. **2** (*fig.*) (*врать*) to tell lies.

брехн|я́, и́ *no pl., f.* (*coll.*) lies; nonsense.

бреху́н, а́ *m.* (*coll.*) liar.

брехýн|ья, ьи *f. of* ⇒**~**

бреш|у́, ~ешь *see* ⇒**бреха́ть**

бреш|ь, и *f.* breach; **проби́ть б.** (**в**+*p.*) to breach; (*fig.*) (*недостача*) gap, deficit.

бре́|ю, ешь *see* ⇒**бри́ть**

бре́ющий *pres. part. of* ⇒**бри́ть; б. полёт** hedge-hopping flight.

бриг, а *m.* brig.

брига́д|а, ы *f.* **1** (*mil.*) brigade; (*naut.*) subdivision. **2** (*группа рабочих*) brigade, (work-)team; **поездна́я б.** train crew.

бригади́р, а *m.* **1** (*mil.*; *obs.*) brigadier. **2** (*руководитель*) team-leader; foreman.

бригади́рш|а, и *f.* (*obs.*) brigadier's wife.

брига́дник, а *m.* member of a brigade, team.

брига́д|ный *adj. of* ⇒**~а**

бриганти́н|а, ы *f.* brigantine.

бри́дер, а *m.* (*phys.*) breeder reactor.

бридж, а *m.* bridge (*card-game*).

бри́дж|и, ей *no sg.* breeches.

бриз, а *m.* sea breeze.

briза́нтн|ый *adj.* high-explosive; **~ые вещества́** high explosives; **б. снаря́д** high-explosive shell.

брике́т, а *m.* briquette.

брил|лиа́нт, а *and* **~ья́нт, а** *m.* (cut) diamond.

бриллиа́нт|овый *adj. of* ⇒**~**

брил|ья́нт = **~лиа́нт**

брил|ья́нтовый = **~лиа́нтовый**

брита́н|ец, ца *m.* Briton; **~цы** the British.

Брита́ни|я, и *f.* Britain.

брита́н|ка, ки *f. of* ⇒**~ец**

Брита́нск|ие острова́|а, ~их ~о́в *no sg.* the British Isles.

брита́нский *adj.* British.

бри́тв|а, ы *f.* razor; **безопа́сная б.** safety razor.

бри́твенн|ый *adj.* shaving; **~ые принадле́жности** shaving things; **б. реме́нь** (razor-)strop.

бритоголо́вый *adj.* shaven-headed; **б. подро́сток** skinhead; *as n.* **бритоголо́в|ый, ого** *m.* skinhead.

бритт, а *m.* (ancient) Briton.

бри́т|ый (~, ~а) *p.p.p. of* ⇒**~ь** *and adj.* clean-shaven.

бр|ить, е́ю, е́ешь *impf.* (*of* ⇒**по~**) to shave.

брить|ё, я́ *nt.* shave; (*процесс*) shaving; **лосьо́н по́сле ~я́** aftershave.

бр|и́ться, е́юсь, е́ешься *impf.* (*of* ⇒**по~**) to shave, have a shave.

бри́финг, а *m.* (press) briefing.

бри́чк|а, и *f.* (*obs.*) britzka (*light carriage*).

бро́вк|а, и *f.* **1** *dim. of* ⇒**бровь. 2** edge (*of running track*).

бров|ь, и, *pl.* **~́и, ~е́й** *f.* eyebrow; brow; **~́и дуго́й** arched eyebrows; **хму́рить ~́и** to knit one's brows, frown; **он и ~́ью не повёл** he did not turn a hair; **попа́сть не в б., а (пря́мо) в глаз** (*prov.*) to hit the nail on the head.

брод, а *m.* ford; **не зна́я ~́у, не су́йся в во́ду** (*prov.*) look before you leap.

броди́льный *adj.* (*tech.*) fermenting.

бро|ди́ть[1]**, жу́, ~́дишь** *impf.* (*гулять*) to wander, roam; **б. по магази́ну** to browse round a shop; **б. по у́лицам** to roam the streets; **б. в потёмках** (*fig.*) to be in the dark.

бро|ди́ть[2]**, ~́дит** *impf.* (*о пиве*) to ferment.

бродя́г|а, и *c.g.* tramp, vagrant; down-and-out.

бродя́жнича|ть, ю *impf.* to be a tramp, be on the road.

бродя́жничеств|о, а *nt.* vagrancy.

бродя́ч|ий *adj.* vagrant; wandering, roving; (*fig.*) restless; **~ие племена́** nomadic tribes; **~ая соба́ка** stray dog.

броже́ни|е, я *nt.* fermentation; **б. умо́в** (*fig.*) intellectual ferment.

бро|жу́, ~́дишь *see* ⇒**~ди́ть**

бро́кер, а *m.* broker; **биржево́й б.** stockbroker.

бро́кер|ский *adj. of* ⇒**~**

бро́кколи *f. indecl.* broccoli.

бром, а *m.* (*chem.*) bromine; (*med.*) bromide.

бро́мистый *adj.* (*chem.*) bromide; **б. на́трий** sodium bromide.

бро́м|овый *adj. of* ⇒**~**

броне... *comb. form* (*mil.*) armoured- (*Br.*), armored- (*US*).

бронеавтомоби́л|ь, я *m.* armoured car (*Br.*), armored car (*US*).

бронебо́йный *adj.* armour-piercing (*Br.*), armor-piercing (*US*).

бронебо́йщик, а *m.* anti-tank rifleman.

броневи́к, а́ *m.* armoured car (*Br.*), armored car (*US*).

бронев|о́й *adj.* armoured (*Br.*), armored (*US*); **~ы́е пли́ты** (*mil.*) armour plating (*Br.*), armor plating (*US*).

бронежиле́т, а *m.* bulletproof vest.

брононо́с|ец[1]**, ца** *m.* (*naut.*) battleship.

брононо́с|ец[2]**, ца** *m.* (*zool.*) armadillo.

брононо́сный *adj.* armoured (*Br.*), armored (*US*).

бронепо́езд, а, *pl.* **~а́** *m.* armoured train (*Br.*), armored train (*US*).

бронеси́л|ы, ~ *no sg.* armoured forces (*Br.*), armored forces (*US*).

бронета́нковый *adj.* (*mil.*) armoured (*Br.*), armored (*US*).

бронетранспортёр, а *m.* armoured (*Br.*), armored (*US*) personnel carrier.

бро́нз|а, ы *f.* bronze.

бронзир|ова́ть, у́ю *impf. and pf.* to bronze.

бронзиро́вк|а, и *f.* bronzing.

бронзо́вщик, а́ *m.* worker in bronze.

бро́нзов|ый *adj.* bronze; (*загорелый*) tanned; **~ая боле́знь** Addison's disease; **б. век** the Bronze Age; **б. зага́р** sunburn, sun-tan.

брони́рова|нный *p.p.p. of* ⇒**~ть** *and adj.* reserved.

брониро́в|анный *p.p.p. of* ⇒**~а́ть** *and adj.* armoured (*Br.*), armored (*US*).

брони́р|овать, ую *impf.* (*of* ⇒**за~**) to reserve, book.

бронир|ова́ть, у́ю *impf. and pf.* to armour (*Br.*), armor (*US*).

бронх, а *m.* (*anat.*) bronchial tube.

бронхиа́льный *adj.* bronchial.

бронхи́т, а *m.* bronchitis.

брон|ь, и *f.* (*coll.*) reservation.

бро́н|я, и *f.* reservation.

брон|я́, и́ *f.* armour (*Br.*), armor (*US*); armour-plating (*Br.*), armor-plating (*US*).

броса́|ть, ю *impf.* (*of* ⇨**бро́сить**). **1** (*метать*) to throw, cast, fling; **б. взгляд** to dart a glance; **б. обвине́ния** to hurl accusations; **б. тень** to cast a shadow; (**на**+*a.*; *fig.*) to cast aspersions (on); **б. я́корь** to drop anchor; **б. на ве́тер** to throw away, waste. **2** (*покинуть*) to leave, abandon, desert; **б. му́жа** to desert one's husband; **б. ору́жие** to lay down one's arms; **б. рабо́ту** to give up, throw up one's work. **3** (+*inf.*) (*переставать*) to give up, leave off; **он бро́сил кури́ть** he gave up smoking.

брос|а́ться, а́юсь *impf.* **1** (*impf. only*) (+*i.*) to throw at one another, pelt one another (with); **мы ~а́лись снежка́ми** we used to pelt one another with snowballs. **2** (*impf. only*) (+*i.*) to throw away; **б. деньга́ми** to throw away, squander one's money. **3** (*pf.* **~иться**) (**на, в**+*a.*) to throw o.s. (on, upon), rush (to); **б. на еду́** to fall upon one's food; **б. на коле́ни** to fall on one's knees; **б. в объя́тия** (+*d.*) to fall into the arms (of); **б. на по́мощь** to rush to assistance; **б. на ше́ю** (+*d.*) to fall on the neck (of). **4** (*pf.* **~иться**): **б. в глаза́** to be striking, arrest attention. **5** (*pf.* **~иться**) (+*inf.*) to begin, start.

бро́|сить, шу, сишь *pf. of* ⇨**~са́ть; ~сь(те)!** stop it!; **хоть ~сь** (*coll.*) it is no good.

бро́|ситься, шусь, сишься *pf. of* ⇨**~са́ться**

бро́с|кий (~ок, ~ка́, ~ко) *adj.* (*coll.*) bright, loud, garish.

бро́совый *adj.* **1** worthless; trashy. **2**: **б. э́кспорт** (*econ.*) dumping.

брос|о́к, ка́ *m.* **1** throw; **штрафно́й б.** (*sport*) free throw. **2** bound; spurt; **благодаря́ после́днему ~ку́** thanks to a final spurt.

бро́узер, а *m.* (*comput.*) browser.

брошир... (~ова́ть, *etc.*) = **брошюр...**

бро́шк|а, и *f.* brooch.

бро́|шу, сишь *see* ⇨**~сить**

брош|ь, и *f.* brooch.

брошю́р|а, ы *f.* pamphlet; (*рекламный*) brochure.

брошюр|ова́ть, у́ю *impf.* (*of* ⇨**с~**) (*tech.*) to stitch.

Бруне́|й, я *m.* Brunei.

брус, а, *pl.* **~ья, ~ьев** *m.* beam; **паралле́льные ~ья** (*sport*) parallel bars.

бруско́вый *adj.* bar, bar-shaped.

брусни́к|а, и *f.* cowberry (*Vaccinium vitis-idaea*).

брусни́|чный *adj. of* ⇨**~ка**

брус|о́к, ка́ *m.* bar; ingot; **б. мы́ла** bar of soap; **точи́льный б.** whetstone.

бру́ствер, а *m.* (*mil.*) breastwork, parapet.

бру́тто *adj. indecl.* gross; **вес б.** gross weight.

бры́ж|и, ей *no sg.* (*obs.*) ruff, frill.

бры́згалк|а, и *f.* (*coll.*) **1** (*разбрызгиватель*) sprinkler, sprayer. **2** (*водяной пистолет*) water-pistol.

бры́з|гать, жу, жешь *impf.* (*of* ⇨**~нуть**) (+*i.*) **1** to splash, spatter; (*забить струёй*) to gush, spurt; **б. гря́зью** (**на**+*a.*) to splash mud (on to), spatter with mud. **2** (*pres.* **~жу** *or* **~гаю**) (*окроплять*) to sprinkle.

бры́зга|ться, юсь *impf.* (*coll.*) to splash; to splash o.s., one another; **соба́ки лю́бят б. в лу́жах** the dogs enjoy splashing in the puddles; **б. духа́ми** to spray o.s. with scent.

бры́зг|и, ~ *no sg.* **1** (*капли*) spray, splashes. **2** (*частицы*) fragments, splinters.

бры́з|жу, жешь *see* ⇨**~гать**

бры́з|нуть, ну, нешь *pf. of* ⇨**~гать**

брык|а́ть, а́ю *impf.* (*of* ⇨**~ну́ть**) to kick.

брыка́|ться, юсь *impf.* (*ребёнок*) to kick; (*лошадь*) to buck; (*fig.*) to kick, rebel.

брык|ну́ть, ну́, нёшь *pf. of* ⇨**~а́ть**

бры́нз|а, ы *f.* brynza (*sheep's milk cheese*).

брысь *int.* shoo! (*to a cat*).

Брю́гге *m. indecl.* Bruges.

брюзг|а́, и́ *c.g.* grumbler.

брюзгли́в|ый (~, ~а) *adj.* grumbling, peevish.

брюзж|а́ть, у́, и́шь *impf.* to grumble.

брю́кв|а, ы *f.* (*bot.*) swede (*Br.*), rutabaga (*US*).

брю́кв|енный *adj. of* ⇨**~а**

брю́к|и, ~ *no sg.* trousers; **б.-ю́бка** culottes.

брюне́т, а *m.* dark-haired man.

брюне́тк|а, и *f.* brunette.

Брюссе́л|ь, я *m.* Brussels.

брюссе́льск|ий *adj.* Brussels; **~ая капу́ста** Brussels sprouts.

брюха́ст|ый (~, ~а) *adj.* (*coll.*) big-bellied.

брюха́т|ый (~, ~а) *adj.* (*coll.*) = **брюха́стый; ~ая** big with child.

брю́х|о, а, *pl.* **~и** *nt.* (*coll.*) belly; (*большой живот*) paunch.

брюхоно́г|ие, их (*zool.*) gasteropods.

брю́чный *adj. of* ⇨**брю́ки; б. костю́м** trouser suit.

брюши́н|а, ы *f.* (*anat.*) peritoneum; **воспале́ние ~ы** (*med.*) peritonitis.

брюшк|о́, а́, *pl.* **~и́, ~о́в** *nt.* abdomen; (*coll.*) paunch.

брюшно́й *adj.* abdominal; **б. тиф** typhoid (fever).

бряк *int.* bang!; crash!

бря́кань|е, я *nt.* (*coll.*) clatter.

бря́к|ать, аю *impf.* (*of* ⇨**~нуть**) (*coll.*) **1** (+*i.*) to clatter; **б. посу́дой** to clatter crockery. **2** (*уронить*) to let fall with a bang; (*fig.*) to drop a clanger. **3** (*сказать*) to blurt out.

бря́к|аться, аюсь *impf.* (*of* ⇨**~нуться**) (*coll.*) to crash, fall heavily.

бря́к|нуть(ся), ну(сь), нешь(ся) *pf. of* ⇨**~ать(ся)**

бряца́ни|е, я *nt.* rattle; clang; clank; **б. шпор** the rattle of spurs; **б. ору́жием** sabre-rattling.

бряца́|ть, ю *impf.* (+*i. or* **на**+*p.*) to rattle; to clang; to clank; **б. цимба́лами** to clash cymbals; **б. ору́жием** (*fig.*) to indulge in sabre-rattling.

БТР *m. indecl.* (*abbr. of* ***бронетранспортёр***) APC (*armoured personnel carrier*).

бу́б|ен, на *m.* tambourine.

бубен|е́ц, ца́ *m.* little bell.

бубе́нчик, а *m.* **1** *dim. of* ⇨**бубене́ц. 2** (*bot.*) harebell, campanula.

бу́блик, а *m.* boublik (*thick, ring-shaped bread roll*).

бубн|и́ть, ю́, и́шь *impf.* (*of* ⇨**про~**) (*coll.*) (*бормотать*) to grumble; to mutter; (*монотонно твердить*) to drone on (*of a speaker*).

бубно́вый *adj.* (*cards*) diamond; **б. туз** ace of diamonds.

бу́б|ны[1] *pl. of* ⇨**~ен**

бу́б|ны[2], ён *pl.* (*sg. coll.* **~на, ~ны** *f.*) (*в картах*) **1** diamonds; **дво́йка ~ён** the two of diamonds. **2** (*sg.*) a diamond.

бубо́н, а *m.* (*med.*) bubo.

бубо́н|ный *adj. of* ⇨**~; ~ная чума́** (*med.*) bubonic plague.

буга́|й, я *m.* (*dial.*) bull (*also fig.*).

буги-вуги *nt. indecl.* boogie-woogie.

буг|о́р, ра́ *m.* (*холм*) mound, knoll; (*на коже*) bump, lump; **за ~ро́м** (*coll.*) abroad.

бугор|о́к, ка́ *m.* **1** *dim. of* ⇨**~** knob, protuberance. **2** (*med.*) tubercle.

бугорча́тый *adj.* **1** lumpy. **2** (*bot.*) tuberous.

бугри́ст|ый (~, ~а) *adj.* (*земля*) hilly; (*поверхность*) bumpy.

Будапе́шт, а *m.* Budapest.

будди́зм, а *m.* Buddhism.

будди́йский *adj.* Buddhist.

будди́ст, а *m.* Buddhist.

будди́ст|ка, ки *f. of* ⇨**~**

бу́де *conj.* (*obs.*) if, provided that.

бу́дет 1 *3rd person sg. fut. of* ⇨**быть; б. ему́ за э́то!** he'll catch it. **2** *as pred.* (*coll.*) that's enough; that'll do; **б. с вас э́того?** will that do?; **б. вам писа́ть** it's time you stopped writing.

буди́льник, а *m.* alarm clock.

бу|ди́ть, жу́, ~дишь *impf.* **1** (*pf.* **раз~**) to wake, awaken, call. **2** (*pf.* **про~**) (*fig.*) (*возбуждать*) to rouse, arouse; to stir up; **б. мысль** to set (one) thinking.

бу́дк|а, и *f.* (*сторожа*) box, booth; (*ларёк*) stall; **карау́льная б.** sentry-box; **соба́чья б.** dog kennel; **телефо́нная б.** telephone booth.

бу́д|ни, ней *pl.* (*sg. obs. or coll.* **~ень, ~ня** *m.*) **1** weekdays; working days, workdays; **по ~ням** on weekdays. **2** (*однообразная жизнь*) humdrum life; colourless existence.

бу́дний *adj.*: **б. день** weekday.

бу́дничн|ый *adj.* **1**: **б. день** weekday; **~ое расписа́ние** weekday timetable.

2 (*для будней*) everyday; (*скучный*) dull, humdrum.

бу́днишний *adj.* = **бу́дничный**

будора́ж|ить, у, ишь *impf.* (*of* ⇨**вз~**) (*coll.*) (*беспокоить*) to disturb; (*возбуждать*) to excite.

бу́дочник, а *m.* **1** (*obs.*) policeman on duty. **2** (*rail.*) trackman; crossing-keeper.

бу́дто 1 *conj.* as if, as though; **он верну́лся с таки́м ви́дом, б. его́ изби́ли** he came back looking as if he had been beaten up. **2** *conj.* that (*implying doubt as to the truth of a statement*); **он утвержда́ет, б. говори́т свобо́дно на десяти́ языка́х** he claims that he speaks ten languages fluently. **3** (*also* **б. бы, как б.**) *particle* (*coll.*) (*кажется*) apparently; **она́ б. должна́ уха́живать за отцо́м** apparently she has to look after her father. **4** *interrog. particle* (*coll.*) (*разве*) really?; **уж б. он так умён?** is he really all that clever?

бу́д|у, ешь *fut. of* ⇨**быть**

будуа́р, а *m.* boudoir.

будуа́р|ный *adj. of* ⇨**~**

бу́дучи *pres. ger. of* ⇨**быть** being.

бу́дущ|ий *adj.* future; next; . . . to be; **~ее вре́мя** (*gram.*) future tense; **в ~ем году́** next year; **~ая мать** expectant mother; **в б. раз** next time; *as n.* **~ее, ~его** *nt.* (*i*) the future; **в ближа́йшем ~ем** in the near future, (*ii*) (*gram.*) future tense.

бу́дущност|ь, и *f.* future; **ему́ предстои́т блестя́щая б.** a brilliant future lies before him.

бу́дь(те) *imper. of* ⇨**быть** (*sg. also used in place of* **е́сли** + *main v. to form protasis of conditional sentences*): **бу́дьте добры́, б. любе́зны** (+ *inf. or imper.*) please; would you be good enough (to), kind enough (to); **будь, что бу́дет** come what may; **не будь вас, всё бы пропа́ло** but for you all would have been lost; **будь он бога́т, будь он бе́ден, мне всё равно́** be he rich or be he poor, it is all one to me.

бу|ёк, йка́ *m.* (*naut.*) anchor-buoy, lifebuoy.

бу́ер, а, *pl.* **~а́** *m.* iceboat.

буера́к, а *m.* (*dial.*) gully; coomb.

бу́ерный *adj.*: **б. спорт** ice-yachting.

буж, а́ *m.* (*med.*) probe.

бужени́н|а, ы *f.* boiled salted pork.

бу|жу́, ~дишь *see* ⇨**~ди́ть**

буз|а́[1], ы́ *f.* (*dial.*) bouza (*fermented beverage*).

буз|а́[2], ы́ *f.* (*coll.*) row; **подня́ть ~у́** to kick up a row.

бузи́л|а, ы *c.g.* (*coll.*) = **бузотёр**

бузин|а́, ы́ *f.* (*bot.*) elder.

бузи́нник, а *m.* (*dial.*) elder grove.

бузи́н|ный *adj. of* ⇨**~а́**

бузи́|ть (*1st person not used*), **~шь** *impf.* (*coll.*) to kick up a row.

бузотёр, а *m.* (*coll.*) troublemaker, hell-raiser.

бу|й, я, *pl.* **~и́, ~ёв** *m.* buoy.

бу́йвол, а *m.* (*zool.*) buffalo.

бу́йвол|овый *adj. of* ⇨**~; ~овая ко́жа** buff.

бу́|йный (~ен, ~йна́, ~йно) *adj.* **1** (*непокорный*) wild; tempestuous; **б. сумасше́дший** violent, dangerous lunatic. **2** (*обильный*) luxuriant, lush; **б. рост** luxuriant growth.

бу́йств|о, а *nt.* unruly conduct.

бу́йств|овать, ую *impf.* (*coll.*) to create uproar; to run riot.

бук, а *m.* beech.

бу́к|а, и *c.g.* (*coll.*) **1** bogy(man), bugbear. **2** (*угрюмый человек*) unsociable, surly person; **смотре́ть ~ой** to look surly.

бука́шк|а, и *f.* small insect.

бу́кв|а, ы, *g. pl.* **~** *f.* letter (*of the alphabet*); **б. в ~у** literally; **б. зако́на** (*fig.*) the letter of the law.

буква́льно *adv.* literally; (*дословно*) word for word.

буква́льн|ый *adj.* literal; **~ое значе́ние** literal meaning; **б. перево́д** word-for-word translation.

буква́р|ь, я́ *m.* ABC; primer.

бу́квенно-цифрово́й *adj.* alphanumeric.

бу́квенный *adj.* in letters.

бу́квиц|а, ы *f.* (*bot.*) betony.

буквое́д, а *m.* pedant.

буквое́дств|о, а *nt.* pedantry.

буке́т, а *m.* **1** bouquet; bunch of flowers. **2** (*аромат*) bouquet; aroma.

букини́ст, а *m.* second-hand bookseller.

букинисти́ческий *adj.*: **б. магази́н** second-hand bookshop.

букле́т, а *m.* (fold-out) leaflet.

бу́кл|я, и *f.* (*obs.*) curl; ringlet.

букме́кер, а *m.* bookmaker; bookie.

бу́ковый *adj.* beech(en); **б. жёлудь** beechnut.

буколи́ческий *adj.* bucolic, pastoral.

букс, а *m.* (*bot.*) box.

бу́кс|а, ы *f.* (*tech.*) axle-box.

букси́р, а *m.* **1** (*судно*) tug, tugboat. **2** (*канат*) tow-rope; **взять на б.** to take in tow; (*fig.*) to give a helping hand; **тяну́ть на ~е** to have in tow.

букси́р|ный *adj. of* ⇨**~; б. парохо́д** steam tug.

букси́р|овать, ую *impf.* to tow, have in tow.

буксиро́вк|а, и *f.* towing.

буксова́ни|е, я *nt.* skidding, wheelspin.

букс|ова́ть, у́ю *impf.* to skid; to go into wheelspin.

бу́кс|овый *adj. of* ⇨**~**

булав|а́, ы́ *f.* mace.

була́вк|а, и *f.* pin; **англи́йская б.** safety-pin.

була́в|очный *adj. of* ⇨**~ка**

була́ный *adj.* dun (*colour of horse*).

була́т, а *m.* (*hist.*) damask steel; (*fig.*) sword.

булга́ч|ить, у, ишь *impf.* (*coll.*) to stir up, excite.

бу́лев *adj.* (*comput.*) Boolean; **~а а́лгебра** Boolean algebra; **~о выраже́ние** Boolean expression.

булими́|я, и *f.* bulimia.

бу́лк|а, и *f.* (*булочка*) roll; (*белый хлеб*) white bread; **сдо́бная б.** bun.

бу́лл|а, ы *f.* (*Papal*) bull.

бу́лочн|ая, ой *f.* bakery; baker's shop.

бу́лочник, а *m.* baker.

булты́х *int.* plop!; splosh!

булты́х|аться, а́юсь *impf.* (*coll.*) **1** (*pf.* **~ну́ться**) (*с шумом падать*) to (fall) plop. **2** (*impf. only*) (*барахтаться*) to splash *or* thrash (about).

булты́х|ну́ться, ~ну́сь, ~нёшься *pf. of* ⇨**~а́ться**

булы́жник, а *m.* cobble-stone (*also collect.*).

бульва́р, а *m.* avenue; boulevard.

бульва́р|ный *adj. of* ⇨**~; ~ная литерату́ра** pulp fiction; **~ная пре́сса** the tabloids; gutter press; **б. рома́н** pulp novel.

бульва́рщин|а, ы *f.* (*pej.*) pulp literature.

бульдо́г, а *m.* bulldog.

бульдо́зер, а *m.* bulldozer.

бульдозери́ст, а *m.* bulldozer driver.

бу́лькань|е, я *nt.* gurgling.

бу́лька|ть, ю *impf.* to gurgle.

бульо́н, а *m.* broth; stock.

бульо́нный *adj.*: **б. ку́бик** stock cube.

бультерье́р, а *m.* bull terrier.

бум[1], а *m.* **1** (*econ.*) boom. **2** (*газетный*) newspaper sensation.

бум[2], а *m.* (*sport*) beam.

бум[3] *int.* boom!; **ни ~-~** (*coll., joc.*) (*to know, understand, etc.*) bugger all.

бума́г|а[1], и *f.* **1** (*материал*) paper; **газе́тная б.** newsprint; **б. в кле́тку** squared paper; **почто́вая б.** notepaper. **2** (*документ*) document; (*pl.*) (official) papers; **це́нные ~и** (*fin.*) securities.

бума́г|а[2], и *f.* (*in full* **хлопча́тая б.**) cotton.

бумагодержа́тел|ь[1], я *m.* (*fin.*) holder of securities, bondholder.

бумагодержа́тел|ь[2], я *m.* paper-clip.

бумагомара́ни|е, я *nt.* (*coll.*) scrawl.

бумагомара́тел|ь, я *m.* (*coll.*) scribbler.

бумагопряди́льн|ый *adj.* cotton-spinning; **~ая фа́брика** cotton mill.

бумагопряди́л|ьня, ьни, *g. pl.* **~ен** *f.* cotton mill.

бумагоре́зк|а, и *f.* shredder.

бума́жк|а, и *f.* **1** *dim. of* ⇨**бума́га;** (*листок бумаги*) scrap of paper. **2** (*деньги*) note; (paper) money.

бума́жник, а *m.* wallet.

бума́|жный[1] *adj. of* ⇨**~га[1]**; (*fig.*) (existing only on) paper; **~жная волоки́та** red tape; **~жные де́ньги** paper money; **б. змей** kite; **~жная фа́брика** paper-mill.

бума́|жный[2] *adj. of* ⇨**~га[2]**; **~жная пря́жа** cotton yarn; **~жная ткань** cotton fabric.

бумажо́нк|а, и *f.* (*coll.*) scrap of paper.

бумазе́|я, и *f.* fustian.

бумазе́йный *adj.* fustian.

бумера́нг, а *m.* boomerang.

бу́нгало *nt. indecl.* bungalow (*in tropical countries*).
бу́нкер, а *m.* (*tech.*) bunker.
бунт¹, а *m.* revolt; riot; mutiny.
бунт², а́ *m.* bale; packet; bundle.
бунта́рский *adj.* **1** seditious; mutinous. **2** (*fig.*) rebellious; turbulent; **б. дух** rebellious spirit.
бунта́рств|о, а *nt.* rebelliousness.
бунта́р|ь, я́ *m.* rebel (*also fig.*); insurgent; mutineer; rioter; **он б. в душе́** he is a rebel at heart.
бунт|ова́ть, у́ю *impf.* **1** (*pf.* **взбунтова́ться**) to revolt, rebel; to mutiny; to riot; (*fig.*) to rage, go berserk. **2** (*pf.* **вз~**) (*obs.*) to incite to revolt, mutiny.
бунт|ова́ться, у́юсь *impf.* = **~ова́ть** 1
бунт|ово́й *adj. of* ⇒**~²**
бунтовско́й *adj.* rebellious, mutinous.
бунтовщи́к, а́ *m.* rebel, insurgent; mutineer; rioter.
бур¹, а *m.* (*tech.*) auger.
бур², а *m.* Boer.
бур|а́, ы́ *f.* (*chem.*) borax.
бура́в, а́, *pl.* **~а́** *m.* (*tech.*) auger; gimlet.
бура́в|ить, лю, ишь *impf.* (*of* ⇒**про~**) to bore, drill.
бура́вчик, а *m.* gimlet.
бура́к, а́ *m.* (*dial.*) beetroot.
бура́н, а *m.* snow-storm (*in steppes*).
бурбо́н, а *m.* bourbon.
бургоми́стр, а *m.* **1** burgomaster. **2** (*zool.*) glaucous gull.
бургу́ндск|ий *adj.* Burgundian; *as n.* **~ое, ~ого** *nt.* burgundy (*wine*).
бурд|а́, ы́ *f.* (*coll.*) slops.
бурдю́к, а́ *m.* (*для вина*) wineskin; (*для воды*) water-skin.
буреве́стник, а *m.* stormy petrel.
бур|ево́й *adj. of* ⇒**~́я;** stormy.
буре́ло́м, а *m.* wind-fallen trees.
буре́ни|е, я *nt.* (*tech.*) boring, drilling.
буре́|ть, ю, ешь *impf.* (*of* ⇒**по~**) to grow brown.
буржуа́ *m. indecl.* bourgeois.
буржуази́|я, и *f.* bourgeoisie; **ме́лкая б.** petty bourgeoisie.
буржуа́з|ный (~ен, ~на) *adj.* bourgeois.
буржу́|й, я *m.* (*coll.*) bourgeois.
буржу́й|ка, ки *f.* **1** *f. of* ⇒**~.** **2** (*coll.*) (*печка*) small stove.
буржу́йский *adj.* (*coll.*) bourgeois.
бури́льный *adj.* (*tech.*) boring.
бури́льщик, а *m.* borer; driller, drill-operator.
бур|и́ть, ю́, и́шь *impf.* (*of* ⇒**про~**) (*tech.*) to bore; to drill.
бу́рк|а, и *f.* felt cloak (*worn in Caucasus*).
бу́рк|ать, аю *impf.* (*of* ⇒**~нуть**) (*coll.*) to mutter, growl.
бу́рк|нуть, ну, нешь *pf. of* ⇒**~ать**
бурла́к, а́ *m.* barge hauler.
бурла́|цкий *adj. of* ⇒**~к**
бурла́честв|о, а *nt.* trade of barge hauler.
бурли́в|ый (~, ~а) *adj.* turbulent; seething.
бурл|и́ть, ю, и́шь *impf.* to seethe, boil up (*also fig.*).
бурну́с, а *m.* burnous.
бу́р|ный (~ен, ~на́) *adj.* **1** (*погода, море*) stormy, rough; (*спор*) heated; (*жизнь, восторг, аплодисменты*) wild. **2** (*рост*) rapid.
burови́к, а́ *m.* (*tech.*) boring, drilling technician.
буров|о́й *adj.* boring; **~а́я вы́шка** derrick; **~а́я сква́жина** bore, bore-hole, well.
бу́рский *adj.* Boer.
буру́н, а́ *m.* breaker; (*под носом корабля*) bow-wave.
бурунду́к, а́ *m.* (*zool.*) chipmunk.
бурча́ни|е, я *nt.* (*coll.*) grumbling; (*в животе*) (stomach-)rumbling.
бурч|а́ть, у́, и́шь *impf.* (*of* ⇒**про~**) (*coll.*) **1** (*бормотать*) to mutter; to grumble. **2** (*impf. only*) (*в животе*) to rumble; (*в котле*) to bubble; (*impers.*): **у меня́ ~и́т в животе́** my stomach is rumbling.
бу́р|ый (~, ~а́, ~о) *adj.* brown; **б. медве́дь** brown bear; **~ая лиси́ца** red fox.
бурья́н, а *m.* tall weeds.
бу́р|я, и *f.* storm (*also fig.*); **б. в стака́не воды́** storm in a teacup.
буря́т, а, *g. pl.* **б.** *m.* Buryat.
буря́т|ка, ки *f. of* ⇒**~**
буря́тский *adj.* Buryat.
бу́син|а, ы *f.* bead.
буссо́л|ь, и *f.* surveying compass.
бу́с|ы, ~ *no sg.* beads.
бутафо́р, а *m.* (*theatr.*) property-man.
бутафо́ри|я, и *f.* (*theatr.*) properties; (*в витрине*) dummies; (*fig.*) window-dressing, sham.
бутафо́р|ский *adj. of* ⇒**~ия;** (*fig.*) sham, mock-; illusory.
бутербро́д, а *m.* slice of bread and butter; sandwich; **зако́н ~а** Sod's Law, Murphy's Law.
бутербро́дн|ая, ой *f.* sandwich bar.
бути́к, а *m.* boutique.
бути́л, а *m.* (*chem.*) butyl.
бутиле́н, а *m.* (*chem.*) butylene.
буто́н, а *m.* **1** bud. **2** (*coll.*) (*прыщ*) pimple.
бутонье́рк|а, и *f.* buttonhole, posy.
бу́тс|ы, ~ *pl.* (*sg.* **~а, ~ы** *f.*) football boots.
буту́з, а *m.* (*coll.*) chubby lad.
буты́лк|а, и *f.* bottle.
буты́лочк|а, и *f.* small bottle; (*пузырёк*) vial, phial.
буты́л|очный *adj. of* ⇒**~ка;** **~очного цве́та** bottle-green.
буты́л|ь, и *f.* large bottle; carboy.
бу́фер, а, *pl.* **~а́** *m.* **1** (*rail.*; *comput.*; *fig.*) buffer. **2** (*у автомобиля*) bumper.
бу́фер|ный *adj. of* ⇒**~;** **~ное госуда́рство** (*pol.*) buffer state.
буфе́т, а *m.* **1** (*шкаф*) sideboard. **2** (*закусочная*) buffet, snack bar; (*стойка*) (refreshment) bar, counter.
буфе́тн|ая, ой *f.* pantry.
буфе́т|ный *adj. of* ⇒**~**
буфе́тчик, а *m.* assistant (in snack bar).
буфе́тчи|ца, цы *f. of* ⇒**~к**
буфф *adj. indecl.* comic, buffo; **о́пера-б.** comic opera; **теа́тр-б.** comedy.
буффо́н, а *m.* buffoon.
буффона́д|а, ы *f.* buffoonery.
бу́ф|ы, ~ *no sg.* gathers, puffs; **б. на рукава́х** puff sleeves.
бух *int.* bang!; plonk!; *as pred.*: **он б. на зе́млю** he fell to the ground with a thud.
буха́нк|а, и *f.* loaf.
Бухаре́ст, а *m.* Bucharest.
бу́х|ать, аю *impf.* (*of* ⇒**~нуть**) **1** (*ударять*) to thump, bang; **б. кулако́м в дверь** to bang on the door with one's fist. **2** (*о выстреле*) to thud, thunder; **слы́шно бы́ло, как вдали́ ~али пу́шки** the thunder of cannon could be heard in the distance. **3** (*fig.*, *coll.*) (*необдуманно сказать*) to blurt out.
бух|а́ть, а́ю *impf.* (*of* **~ну́ть**) (*coll.*) (*пить*) to drink.
бу́х|аться, аюсь *impf.* (*of* ⇒**~нуться**) (*coll.*) (*упасть*) to fall heavily; (*броситься*) to plonk o.s. down.
бухга́лтер, а, *pl.* **~ы** *m.* book-keeper, accountant.
бухгалте́ри|я, и *f.* **1** book-keeping, accountancy. **2** (*отдел*) counting-house.
бухга́лтерск|ий *adj.* book-keeping, account; **~ая кни́га** account book.
бу́х|нуть¹, ну, нешь, *past* **~нул** *pf. of* ⇒**~ать**
бу́х|нуть², ну, нешь, *past* **~, ~ла** *impf.* (*расширяться*) to swell, expand.
бух|ну́ть, ну́, нёшь, *past* **~ну́л** *pf. of* ⇒**буха́ть**
бу́х|нуться, нусь, нешься *pf. of* ⇒**~аться**
бу́хт|а¹, ы *f.* (*geog.*) bay.
бу́хт|а², ы *f.* coil (*of rope*).
бу́хточк|а, и *f.* creek, cove, inlet.
бу́хты-бара́хты *only in phr.* (*coll.*) **с б.-б.** (*необдуманно*) offhand; off the cuff; (*внезапно*) suddenly.
бу́ч|а, и *f.* (*coll.*) row.
буш|ева́ть, у́ю *impf.* to rage; (*fig.*) to rage, storm.
бу́шел|ь, я *m.* bushel.
бушла́т, а *m.* (*naut.*) pea-jacket.
бушпри́т, а *m.* (*naut.*) bowsprit.
Буэ́нос-А́йрес, а *m.* Buenos Aires.
буя́н, а *m.* (*coll.*) rowdy, brawler.
буя́н|ить, ю, ишь *impf.* (*coll.*) to make a row; to brawl.
буя́нств|о, а *nt.* (*coll.*) rowdyism, brawling.
БЦЖ *f. indecl.* (*representation of French pronunciation of BCG*) BCG (*Bacillus Calmette-Guérin*).
бы (*abbr.* **б)** *particle* **1** (*выражает предположительную возможность*) (*see also* ⇒**е́сли**): **я мог бы об э́том**

Б

догадáться I might have guessed it; **бы́ло бы óчень прия́тно вас ви́деть** it would be very nice to see you. **2** (+**ни**) *forms indef. prons.*: **кто бы ни** whoever; **что бы ни** whatever; **как бы ни** however; **кто бы ни пришёл** whoever comes; **что бы ни случи́лось** whatever happens; **как бы то ни́ бы́ло** however that may be, be that as it may.
3 (*выражает пожелание*): **я бы вы́пил пи́ва** I should like a drink of beer.
4 (*выражает предложение*): **вы бы отдохну́ли** you should take a rest.

быва́|ло 1 *see* ⇨**~ть. 2** *particle indicating repetition of an action in past time*: **моя́ мать, б., чáсто пéла э́ту пéсню** my mother would often sing this song.

быва́л|ый *adj.* **1** (*опытный*) experienced; worldly-wise. **2** (*coll.*) (*привычный*) familiar; **э́то дéло ~ое** this is nothing new. **3** (*obs.*) (*прежний*) former.

быва́|ть, ю *impf.* **1** (*случаться*) to happen; (*происходить*) to take place; **заседáния горсовéта ~ют раз в недéлю** the town council meets once a week; **~ет, что поездá с сéвера опáздывают** trains from the north are sometimes late.
2 (*быть*) to be; (*находиться*) to be present; (*посещать*) to frequent; **он ~ет кáждый день в кабинéте** he is in his office every day; **они́ рéдко ~ют в теáтре** they seldom go to the theatre (*Br.*), theater (*US*).
3 (*быть склонным*) to be inclined to be, tend to be; **он ~ет раздражи́телен** he is inclined to be irritable.
4: **как ни в чём не ~ло** (*coll.*) as if nothing had happened; **как не ~ло** (+*g.*) to have completely disappeared; **головно́й бо́ли у меня́ как не ~ло** my headache has completely gone.

бы́вший *p.p. of* ⇨**быть** *and adj.* former, ex-; one-time; **б. президéнт** former president, ex-president; **гóрод Санкт-Петербу́рг, б. Ленингрáд** St. Petersburg, formerly Leningrad.

бы́дл|о, а *nt.* (*collect.; dial.; also fig.*) cattle.

бык[1], á *m.* **1** bull; ox; **рабо́чий б.** draught ox; **бой ~óв** bullfight; **взять ~á за рогá** (*fig.*) to take the bull by the horns; **здорóв, как б.** as strong as an ox. **2** male (*of certain horned animals*); **олéний б.** stag.

бык[2], á *m.* pier (*of a bridge*).

был|евóй *adj. of* ⇨**~и́на**

были́н|а, ы *f.* (*liter.*) bylina (*Russian traditional heroic poem*).

были́нк|а, и *f.* blade of grass.

были́н|ный *adj. of* ⇨**~а**; epic.

бы́ло *particle* (*indicates that an action was impending or had just begun, but was not completed*): **он поéхал б. с ни́ми, но заболéл** he would have gone with them, but he fell ill; **он отпрáвился б. с ни́ми, но верну́лся** he started out with them but turned back; **чуть б.** very nearly; **я чуть б. не забы́л** I very nearly forgot; **они́ чуть б. не уби́ли егó** they all but killed him.

был|óй *adj.* former, past, bygone; **в ~ы́е временá** in days of old; *as n.* **~óе, ~óго** *nt.* (*poet.*) the past, olden time.

был|ь, и *f.* **1** (*obs.*) (*то, что было*) past event, fact. **2** (*рассказ о действительном происшествии*) true story.

быль|ё, я́ *nt.* (*obs.*) grass; *now only in phr.* **~ём поросло́** long forgotten.

быстрин|á, ы́, *pl.* **~́ы** *f.* (*geog.*) rapid(s).

быстроглáз|ый (~, ~а) *adj.* sharp-eyed; lively.

быстродéйстви|е, я *nt.* (*tech.*) speed, response time.

быстродéйствующий *adj.* high-speed; quick-acting.

быстрозаморо́женный *adj.* (quick-)frozen.

быстроно́гий *adj.* (*poet.*) fleet of foot.

быстросбо́рный *adj.* quick-assembly.

быстросо́хнущий *adj.* quick-dry(ing).

быстросхвáтывающийся *adj.* quick-setting.

быстрот|á, ы́ *f.* rapidity, quickness; (*скорость*) speed.

быстротеку́щий *adj.* (*poet., obs.*) swift-flowing.

быстротéч|ный (~ен, ~на) *adj.* fleeting, transient.

быстрохо́д|ный (~ен, ~на) *adj.* fast, high-speed.

бы́стр|ый (~, ~á, ~о) *adj.* rapid, fast, quick; (*немедленный*) prompt.

быт, а, о ~́е, б ~у́, *no pl., m.* way of life; life; **домáшний б.** family life; **солдáтский б.** army life; **слу́жба ~́а** consumer services.

быти|é, я́ *nt.* (*phil.*) being, existence, objective reality; **кни́га Б~я́** (*bibl.*) Genesis.

бы́тност|ь, и *f. only in phr.* **в б.** during a given period; **в б. мою́ студéнтом** in my student days; **в б. егó в Ри́ме** during his stay in Rome.

быт|овáть, у́ет *impf.* to occur, be current.

бытóвк|а, и *f.* (*coll.*) site hut; rest-room.

быт|овóй *adj. of* ⇨**~**; social; **~овáя жи́вопись** genre painting; **~овы́е прибо́ры** domestic appliances; **~овáя ЭВМ** home computer; **~овóе обслу́живание населéния** consumer services; **~овóе явлéние** everyday occurrence.

бытописáни|е, я *nt.* (*obs.*) annals, chronicles.

бытописáтел|ь, я *m.* **1** (*obs.*) (*историк*) historian. **2** (*автор бытовых произведений*) writer on social themes.

быть *pres. not used exc. 3rd person sg.* **есть** *and* (*obs.*) *3rd person pl.* **суть,** *fut.* **бу́ду, бу́дешь,** *past* **был, былá, бы́ло (нé был, не былá, нé было)** *imper.* **бу́дь(те)** (*see also* ⇨**бу́дет, бу́дь(те), бы́ло, есть**).
● **I.** (*существовать*) to be; **есть таки́е лю́ди** there are such people, such people do exist. **1**: **б. у** (*see also* ⇨**есть**) (*иметь*) to be in the possession of (of); **у них былá прекрáсная дáча** they had a lovely dacha.
2 (*находиться*) to be; (**к**+*d.*) to come (to), be present (at); **здесь был тракти́р** there used to be an inn here; **где вы бы́ли вчерá?** where were you yesterday?; **он тут был ни при чём** he had nothing to do with it; **они́ бу́дут к нам зáвтра** they are coming (to see us) tomorrow; **на ней былá рóзовая ко́фточка** she had on a pink blouse.
3 (*случаться*) to be, happen, take place; **э́того не мо́жет б.!** it cannot be!; **что с ним бы́ло?** what happened to him?; **как б.?** what is to be done?; **так и б.** so be it, all right, very well, have it your own way.
● **II.** *as v. aux.* to be.

быть|ё, я́ *nt.* (*obs.*) way of life.

бычá|чий *adj. of* ⇨**бык[1]**; **~ья ко́жа** oxhide.

бы́чий *adj.* = **бычáчий**

быч|óк[1], кá *m.* (*бык*) steer.

быч|óк[2], кá *m.* (*рыба*) goby.

быч|óк[3], кá *m.* (*coll.*) cigarette butt.

бьеф, а *m.* reach; **вéрхний б.** head water.

бью, бьёшь *see* ⇨**бить**

бювáр, а *m.* writing-case (with blotting paper).

бювéт, а *m.* pump-room.

бюджéт, а *m.* budget.

бюджéтник, а *m.* (*sl.*) person who is paid from the State budget (*e.g. a teacher*).

бюджéтный *adj.* budgetary; **б. год** fiscal year.

бюллетéн|ить, ю, ишь *impf.* (*coll.*) to be off sick.

бюллетéн|ь, я *m.* **1** bulletin; **информаци́онный б.** newsletter.
2 (избирáтельный) б. voting-paper.
3 (больни́чный) б. medical certificate; **быть на ~е** (*coll.*) to be on sick-leave.

бю́ргер, а *m.* burgher.

бюрéтк|а, и *f.* (*tech.*) burette.

бюрó *nt. indecl.* **1** (*контора*) bureau, office; **б. нахóдок** lost-property office; **б. по трудоустро́йству** employment agency; **спрáвочное б.** inquiry office, information office; **туристи́ческое б.** travel agency. **2** (*стол*) bureau, writing-desk.

бюрокрáт, а *m.* bureaucrat.

бюрократи́зм, а *m.* bureaucracy; red tape.

бюрократи́ческий *adj.* bureaucratic.

бюрокрáти|я, и *f.* bureaucracy (*also collect.*).

бюст, а *m.* (*скульптура*) bust; (*женский*) bust, bosom.

бюстгáльтер, а *m.* bra(ssière).

бя́з|евый *adj. of* ⇨**~ь**

бяз|ь, и *f.* coarse calico.

бя́к|а, и *f.* (*in children's speech*) (*дело, предмет*) nasty thing; (*человек*) nasty man.

Вв

В (*abbr. of* ***восто́к***) E, East.

в *prep.*

● **I.** + *a. and p.* **1** (+ *a., denoting direction*) into, to; (+ *p., denoting position*) in, at; **поéхать в Москвý** to go to Moscow; **роди́ться в Москвé** to be born in Moscow; **сесть в вагóн** to get into the carriage; **сидéть в вагóне** to be in the carriage; **разорвáть в клóчья** to tear to pieces; **привести́ в востóрг** to delight, enrapture; **быть в востóрге** to be delighted, be in raptures.
2 *in reference to external attributes*: **рубáшка в клéтку** check(ed) shirt; **лицó в веснýшках** freckled face; **лекáрство в порошкáх** medicine in powder form; **ходи́ть в шýбе** to wear a fur coat.
3 (+ *nom.-a. pl. and p. pl.*) *in reference to occupation*: **пойти́ в учителя́** to become a teacher.
4 *in reference to calendar units and periods of time*: **в понедéльник** on Monday; **в январé** in January; **в 1899-ом годý** in 1899; **в двадцáтом вéке** in the twentieth century; **в четы́ре часá** at four o'clock; **в четвёртом часý** between three and four; **в нáши дни** in our day; **в течéние** (+ *g.*) during, in the course (of).

● **II.** + *a.* **1** *in reference to objects through which vision is directed*: **смотрéть в окнó** to look out of the window; **смотрéть в бинóкль** to look through binoculars.
2 *in attribution of resemblance*: **быть в когó-н.** to take after s.o.; to be like s.o.; **онá вся в тётю** she is just like her aunt.
3 *indicating aim or purpose*: for, as; **сказáть в шýтку** to say for a joke.
4 *in specification of quantitative attributes*: **морóз в дéсять грáдусов** ten degrees of frost; **высотóй в три мéтра** three metres high; **вéсом в пять килогрáммов** weighing five kilograms.
5 (+ **раз** *and comp. adv.*) *indicates comparison in numerical terms*: **в два рáза бóльше** twice as big, twice the size; **в два рáза мéньше** half as big, half the size.
6 *of time*: in, within; **надéюсь кóнчить черновик в мéсяц** I hope to finish the rough draft in a month.
7 *indicates game or sport played*: **игрáть в кáрты, шáхматы, футбóл** to play cards, chess, football.

● **III.** + *p.* **1** at a distance of; **в трёх киломéтрах от гóрода** three kilometres from the town; **они́ живýт в десяти́ минýтах ходьбы́ отсю́да** they live ten minutes' walk from here.
2 in; of (= *consisting of, amounting to*); **пьéса в трёх дéйствиях** play in three acts; **рáзница в двух копéйках** a difference of two kopecks.

в. (*abbr. of* ***век***) c., century.

ва-бáнк *adv.* (*cards*) **игрáть, идти́ ва-б.** to stake everything; (*fig.*) to stake one's all.

Вавилóн, а *m.* Babylon.

вавилóнск|ий *adj.* Babylonian; **~ое столпотворéние** babel; **~ая бáшня** the tower of Babel.

вагóн, а *m.* **1** carriage (*Br.*), coach (*Br.*), car (*US*); **мя́гкий, жёсткий в.** soft-seated, hard-seated carriage (*Br.*), car (*US*); **багáжный в.** luggage van; **в.-ресторáн** dining-car, restaurant car; **служéбный в.** guard's van; **спáльный в.** sleeping-car; **трамвáйный в.** tram-car; **в.-цистéрна** tank truck. **2** (*груз*) wagon-load; (*fig., coll.*) loads, lots; **врéмени у нас в.** we have masses of time.

вагонéтк|а, и *f.* truck; trolley; **подвеснáя в.** cable car.

вагóн|ный *adj. of* ⇒**~**; **в. парк** (*подвижной состав*) rolling-stock; (*депо*) train depot.

вагоновожáт|ая, ой *f. of* ⇒**~ый**

вагоновожáт|ый, ого *m.* tram-driver.

вагоноремóнтный *adj.*: **в. завóд** carriage repair shop (*Br.*), car repair shop (*US*).

вагоностроéни|е, я *nt.* carriage-building (*Br.*), car-building (*US*).

вагоностроúтельный *adj.* carriage-building (*Br.*), car-building (*US*); **в. завóд** carriage(-building) works.

важнéцкий *adj.* (*coll.*) good, good-quality.

вáжничани|е, я *nt.* airs and graces.

вáжнича|ть, ю *impf.* (*coll.*) to give o.s. airs, get a swelled head; (+ *i.*) to plume o.s. (on).

вáжност|ь, и *f.* **1** importance; significance; **не великá в.** (*coll.*) it's of no consequence. **2** (*надменность*) pomposity, pretentiousness.

вáж|ный (~ен, ~нá, ~но) *adj.* **1** important; weighty, consequential; **сáмое ~ное узнáть, откýда они́ приéхали** the (important) thing is to discover where they have come from; **~ная пти́ца/ши́шка** (*coll.*) bigwig, big knob. **2** (*гордый*) pompous, pretentious.

вáз|а, ы *f.* vase, bowl.

вазели́н, а *m.* Vaseline (*propr.*).

вазóн, а *m.* (flower-)pot.

вáй|я, и, *g. pl.* **вáий** *f.* **1** (*bot.*) (*лист папоротника*) fern-branch. **2** (*лист пальмы*) palm(-branch); **недéля вáий** (*eccl.*) Palm Sunday.

вакáнси|я, и *f.* vacancy.

вакáнт|ный (~ен, ~на) *adj.* vacant, unfilled; **~ная дóлжность** vacancy.

вакáци|я, и *f.* (*obs.*) vacation.

вáкс|а, ы *f.* black (shoe) polish.

вáк|сить, шу, сишь *impf.* (*of* ⇒**на~**) (*coll.*) to black, polish.

вáкуум, а *m.* vacuum.

вáкуум|ный *adj. of* ⇒**~**

вакханáли|я, и *f.* (*usu. pl.*) bacchanalia.

вакхáнк|а, и *f.* Bacchante, maenad.

вакхи́ческий *adj.* Bacchic.

вакци́н|а, ы *f.* vaccine.

вакцинáци|я, и *f.* vaccination.

вакцини́р|овать, ую *impf. and pf.* to vaccinate.

вáк|шу, сишь *see* ⇒**~сить**

вал¹, а, *pl.* **~ы́** *m.* billow, roller.

вал², а, *pl.* **~ы́** *m.* bank, earthen wall; (*mil.*) rampart.

вал³, а, *pl.* **~ы́** *m.* (*tech.*) shaft.

вал⁴, а *m.* (*econ.*) gross output.

валáнда|ться, юсь *impf.* (*coll.*) **1** (*слоняться*) to loiter, hang about. **2** (**с** + *i.*) (*возиться*) to dawdle (over), mess about (with).

В

вале́жник, а *no pl., m.* (*collect.*) windfallen trees, branches.

вал|ёк, ька́ *m.* (*tech.*) **1** (*бельевой*) battledore. **2** (*экипажа*) swingle-tree.

ва́лен|ки, ок *pl.* (*sg.* **~ок, ~ка** *m.*) valenki (*felt boots*).

вале́нтност|ь, и *f.* (*chem.*) valency (*Br.*), valence.

валерья́н|а, ы *f.* (*bot.*) valerian.

валерья́нк|а, и *f.* (*coll.*) tincture of valerian.

валерья́нов|ый *adj.* (*med.*): **~ые ка́пли** tincture of valerian.

вале́т, а *m.* (*cards*) jack; **спать ~ом** to sleep top to tail.

ва́лик, а *m.* **1** (*tech.*) (*в машине*) roller, cylinder. **2** (*подушка*) bolster.

вал|и́ть[1], ю́, ~́ишь *impf.* **1** (*pf.* **по~** *and* **с~**) (*свергать*) to throw down, bring down, send toppling; to overthrow; **в. кого́-н. с ног** to knock s.o. off his feet; **в. дере́вья** to fell trees; **нас всех ~и́л грипп** we were all being laid low by the flu. **2** (*pf.* **с~**) (*в кучу*) to heap up, pile up; **в. вину́ (на+*a.*)** to lump the blame (on).

вал|и́ть[2], и́т *impf.* (*coll.*) **1** (*двигаться массой*) to flock, throng, pour; **вало́м в.** to throng, go en masse; **лю́ди ~и́ли на стадио́н** people were flocking to the stadium; **снег ~и́т кру́пными хло́пьями** the snow is coming down in large flakes; **дым ~и́л из трубы** smoke was belching from the chimney. **2**: **~и́(те)!** go on!; have a go!; **~и́, беги́!** be off with you!

вал|и́ться, ю́сь, ~́ишься *impf.* (*of* ⇒**по~** *and* **с~**) to fall, collapse; to topple over; **в. от уста́лости** to drop from tiredness; **у него́ всё из рук ~́ится** (*coll.*) he is all fingers and thumbs; **де́ло у него́ ~́ится из рук** his heart is not in the matter, he cannot put his mind to the matter.

ва́лк|а, и *f.* felling.

ва́л|кий (~ок, ~ка́, ~ко) *adj.* unsteady, shaky; **ни ша́тко, ни ~ко** middling; neither good nor bad.

валли́|ец, йца *m.* Welshman.

валли́йк|а, и *f.* Welshwoman.

валли́йский *adj.* Welsh.

валова́н, а *m.* vol-au-vent.

валово́й *adj.* (*econ.*) gross; wholesale; **в. вну́тренний проду́кт** gross domestic product; **в. дохо́д** gross revenue; **в. национа́льный проду́кт** gross national product; **в. сбор** gross yield.

вало́м *see* ⇒**вали́ть[2]**

валто́рн|а, ы *f.* (*mus.*) French horn.

валторни́ст, а *m.* (*mus.*) French horn player.

валу́н, а́ *m.* boulder.

ва́льдшнеп, а *m.* (*zool.*) woodcock.

вальс, а *m.* waltz.

вальси́р|овать, ую *impf.* to waltz.

вальц|ева́ть, у́ю *impf.* (*tech.*) to roll.

вальцо́вк|а, и *f.* (*tech.*) **1** (*действие*) rolling. **2** (*инструмент*) rolling press.

вальцо́в|ый *adj.* (*tech.*): **~ая ме́льница** rolling-mill.

вальц|ы́, о́в *no sg.* (*tech.*) rolling press.

валья́жный *adj.* (*obs., iron.*) noble, virtuous.

валю́т|а, ы *f.* (*fin., econ.*) **1** (*денежная система*) currency; **курс ~ы** rate of exchange. **2** (*collect.*) (*иностранные деньги*) foreign currency; **свобо́дно конверти́руемая в.** freely convertible currency; **твёрдая в.** hard currency.

валю́тно-фина́нсов|ый *adj.*: **~ая би́ржа** foreign exchange market.

валю́т|ный *adj. of* ⇒**~а;** currency; **в. фонд** monetary fund.

валю́тчик, а *m.* (*coll.*) currency speculator.

валя́льный *adj.* fulling.

валя́л|ьня, ьни, *g. pl.* **~ен** *f.* fulling-mill.

валя́льщик, а *m.* fuller.

валя́ни|е, я *nt.* (*tech.*) fulling, milling.

ва́ляный *adj.* felt.

валя́|ть, ю *impf.* **1** (*impf. only*) (*катать*) to drag; **в. по́ полу** to drag along the floor. **2** (*pf.* **вы́~**) (*валяя, покрыть чем-н.*) to roll, drag; **в. в грязи́** to drag in the mire. **3** (*pf.* **с~**) (*хлеб*) to knead. **4** (*pf.* **с~**) (*валенки*) to full; to felt. **5** (*pf.* **на~**) (*coll.*) (*делать небрежно*) to botch, bungle; to muck about. **6**: **в. дурака́** (*coll.*) to play the fool. **7** **~й(те)!** (*coll.*) go ahead!, carry on!

валя́|ться, юсь *impf.* **1** (*кататься*) to roll. **2** (*coll.*) (*бездельничать*) to lie about; **он весь день ~ется в хала́те** he lies about in his dressing-gown all day; **её оде́жда ~лась по ко́мнате** her clothes lay scattered all over the room; **таки́е специали́сты на доро́ге/земле́ не ~ются** you don't come across such experts that often.

вам *d. of* ⇒**вы**

ва́ми *i. of* ⇒**вы**

вампи́р, а *m.* **1** vampire. **2** (*zool.*) vampire-bat.

вана́ди|й, я *m.* (*chem.*) vanadium.

ванда́л, а *m.* (*hist.*) Vandal; (*fig.*) vandal.

вандали́зм, а *m.* vandalism.

ванили́н, а *m.* vanillin.

вани́л|ь, и *f.* vanilla.

вани́ль|ный *adj. of* ⇒**~**

ва́нн|а, ы *f.* bath; **грязева́я в.** mud bath; **сидя́чая в.** hip-bath; **приня́ть ~у** to take a bath.

ва́нн|ая, ой *f.* bathroom.

ва́нночк|а, и *f. dim. of* ⇒**ва́нна;** (*phot.*) developing tray; **глазна́я в.** eye-bath.

ва́нн|ый *adj. of* ⇒**~а**

ва́нт|а, ы *f.* (*naut.*) shroud.

ва́нька-вста́нька, ва́ньки-вста́ньки *m.* tumbler (*doll with weighted base*).

вар, а *m.* **1** (*смола*) pitch; (*сапожный*) cobbler's wax. **2** (*dial.*) (*кипяток*) boiling water.

вара́н, а *m.* (*zool.*) monitor lizard.

ва́рвар, а *m.* barbarian.

варвари́зм, а *m.* (*ling., liter.*) barbarism.

ва́рварский *adj.* barbarian; (*fig.*) barbaric.

ва́рварств|о, а *nt.* barbarity.

варга́н|ить, ю, ишь *impf.* (*of* ⇒**с~**) (*coll.*) to botch, bungle.

ва́рев|о, а *nt.* (*coll., pej.*) broth; slop.

ва́режк|а, и *f.* **1** (*рукавица*) mitten. **2** (*sl.*) (*рот*) mouth, kisser (*sl.*).

варен|е́ц, ца́ *m.* fermented boiled milk.

варе́ние = **ва́рка**

варе́ник, а *m.* varenik (*curd or fruit dumpling*).

варёный *adj.* boiled.

варе́нь|е, я *nt.* preserve(s) (*containing whole fruit*), jam (*Br.*).

вариа́нт, а *m.* (*разновидность*) variant; version; (*возможность*) option; (*сценарий*) scenario; model; **нулево́й в.** (*pol.*) zero option.

вариа́ци|я, и *f.* variation.

варико́зн|ый *adj.* (*anat.*) varicose; **~ые ве́ны** varicose veins.

вар|и́ть, ю́, ~́ишь *impf.* (*of* ⇒**с~**) **1** to boil; to cook; **в. карто́фель** to boil potatoes; **в. обе́д** to cook dinner; **в. глинтве́йн** to mull wine; **в. пи́во** to brew beer. **2** (*3rd pers. sg.* **вари́т**) (*о желудке*) to digest; (*о голове*): **у него́ голова́/котело́к вари́т** (*coll.*) he's quick on the uptake. **3** (*сталь*) to found. **4** (*металл*) to weld.

вар|и́ться, ю́сь, ~́ишься *impf.* (*of* ⇒**с~**) **1** (*в кипятке*) to boil (*intrans.*); (*приготовляться на огне*) to cook (*intrans.*); **карто́фель уже́ полчаса́ ~́ится** the potatoes have been on for half an hour already. **2** *pass. of* ⇒**~и́ть**

ва́рк|а, и *f.* boiling; cooking; **в. варе́нья** preserve-making; **в. желе́за** iron-founding; **в. пи́ва** brewing.

Варша́в|а, ы *f.* Warsaw.

варша́вский *adj.* (of) Warsaw.

варьете́ *nt. indecl.* variety (show); **теа́тр-в.** music-hall.

варьи́р|овать, ую *impf.* to vary, modify.

варя́г, а *m.* (*hist.*) Varangian.

варя́жский *adj.* (*hist.*) Varangian.

вас *g., a., and p. of* ⇒**вы**

васил|ёк, ька́ *m.* (*bot.*) cornflower.

васили́ск, а *m.* basilisk.

васил|ько́вый *adj. of* ⇒**~ёк;** cornflower blue.

васса́л, а *m.* vassal, liege(-man).

васса́льн|ый *adj.* vassal; **~ая зави́симость** vassalage.

ва́т|а, ы *f.* cotton wool (*Br.*), absorbent cotton (*US*); (*для подкладки*) wadding; **са́харная в.** candyfloss; **пальто́ на ~е** wadded coat.

вата́г|а, и *f.* band, gang.

ватерклозе́т, а *m.* water-closet.

ватерли́ни|я, и *f.* (*naut.*) water-line.

Ватерло́о *nt. indecl.* Waterloo.

ватерпа́с, а *m.* spirit-level.

ватерполи́ст, а *m.* water polo player.

ватерпо́ло *nt. indecl.* water polo.

Ватика́н, а *m.* the Vatican; **(госуда́рство-го́род) В.** Vatican City.

ватика́нский *adj.* Vatican.

вати́н, а *m.* batting, wadding.

ва́тк|а, и *f.* small piece of cotton wool (*Br.*), absorbent cotton (*US*).

ва́тман, а *m.* Whatman paper.

ва́тник, а *m.* quilted jacket.

ва́тн|ый *adj.* wadded, quilted; **~ое одея́ло** quilt; **от испу́га но́ги ста́ли ~ые** my legs turned to jelly.

ватру́шк|а, и *f.* curd tart; cheese-cake.

ватт, а, *g. pl.* **в.** *m.* watt.

ва́ттност|ь, и *f.* wattage.

ва́учер, а *m.* voucher.

ва́фельниц|а, ы *f.* waffle-iron.

ва́ф|ельный *adj. of* **⇒~ля;** (*о ткани*) made of a lightweight cellular material.

ва́ф|ля, ли, *g. pl.* **~ель** *f.* waffle; wafer.

вахла́к, а́ *m.* (*coll.*) lout.

ва́хмистр, а *m.* (*obs.*) cavalry sergeant-major.

ва́хт|а, ы *f.* (*сменная работа*) shift; **нести́ ~у** to be on duty; (*naut.*) watch; **стоя́ть на ~е** to keep watch.

ва́хт|енный *adj. of* **⇒~а** (*naut.*); **в. журна́л** log(-book); **в. команди́р** officer of the watch; *as n.* **в., ~енного** *m.* watch.

вахтёр, а *m.* janitor, porter.

ва́хтовый *adj.* shift-based.

ваш, ~его; *f.* **~а, ~ей;** *nt.* **~е, ~его;** *pl.* **~и, ~их** *possessive pron.* (*при существительном*) your; (*без существительного*) yours; **э́то в. каранда́ш** this is your pencil; **э́тот каранда́ш в.** this pencil is yours; **не ~е де́ло** it is none of your business; **с ~е** (*coll.*) as much/as long as you have; *as n.* **~и, ~их** your people, your folk; **и на́шим и ~им** (*coll. pej.*) all things to all people.

Вашингто́н, а *m.* Washington.

ва́яни|е, я *nt.* (*obs.*) sculpture.

ва́ятел|ь, я *m.* (*obs.*) sculptor.

ва́я|ть, ю *impf.* (*of* **⇒из~**) to sculpt; (*из камня, дерева*) to carve, chisel.

вбега́|ть, ю *impf.* (**в** + *a.*) to run (into).

вбе|жа́ть, гу́, жи́шь, гу́т *pf. of* **⇒~га́ть**

вбер|у́, ёшь *see* **⇒вобра́ть**

вбива́|ть, ю *impf. of* **⇒вбить**

вбира́|ть, ю *impf. of* **⇒вобра́ть**

вбить, вобью́, вобьёшь *pf.* (*of* **⇒вбива́ть**) to drive in, hammer in; (*sport*) **в. мяч в воро́та** to score a goal; (*coll.*) **в. в го́лову** (+*d.*; *fig.*) to knock into s.o.'s head; **в. себе́ в го́лову** to get into one's head.

вблизи́ *adv.* (**от** + *g.*) close by; not far (from); **они́ живу́т где́-то в.** they live somewhere near here; **в. от библиоте́ки** not far from the library; **рассма́тривать в.** to examine closely.

вбок *adv.* sideways, to one side.

вбра́сывани|е, я *nt.* **в. (мяча́)** throw-in (*in football*); **в. (ша́йбы)** face-off (*in ice-hockey*).

вбра́сыва|ть, ю *impf. of* **⇒вбро́сить**

вброд *adv.*: **переходи́ть в.** to wade; to ford.

вбро́|сить, шу, сишь *pf.* (*of* **⇒вбра́сывать**) to throw in(to).

вбу́ха|ть, ю *pf.* (*coll.*) to chuck in (*in large amounts*).

вв. (*abbr. of* ***века́***) cc., centuries.

вва́лива|ть, ю *impf. of* **⇒ввали́ть**

вва́лива|ться, юсь *impf. of* **⇒ввали́ться**

ввал|и́ть, ю́, ~ишь *pf.* to hurl, heave into.

ввал|и́ться, ю́сь, ~ишься *pf.* **1** (*coll.*) (*упасть внутрь*) to tumble into, sink into. **2** (*fig., coll.*) (*входить*) to burst into. **3** (*стать впалым*) to become hollow, sunken; **с ~ившимися щека́ми** hollow-cheeked.

введе́ни|е, я *nt.* **1** (*действие*) leading in(to). **2** (*вводная часть*) introduction. **3** (*comput.*) input.

вве|ду́, дёшь *see* **⇒~сти́**

ввез|ти́, у́, ёшь, *past* **~, ~ла́** *pf.* (*of* **⇒ввози́ть**) to import.

ввек *adv.* (*now only used before neg.*) ever; **я э́того в. не забу́ду** I shall not forget it as long as I live.

вверг|а́ть, а́ю *impf. of* **⇒~нуть**

вве́рг|нуть, ну, нешь, *past* **~** *and* **~нул, ла** *pf.* (*of* **⇒~а́ть**) (**в** + *a.*) (*поместить*) to cause to fall (into); (*привести в какое-либо состояние*) to reduce (to); **в. в тюрьму́** to cast into prison; **в. в нищету́** to bring to ruin; **в. в отча́яние** to drive to despair.

вве́р|ить, ю, ишь *pf.* (*of* **⇒~я́ть**) to entrust; **в. та́йну кому́-н.** to entrust s.o. with a secret.

вве́р|иться, юсь, ишься *pf.* (*of* **⇒~я́ться**) (+*d.*) to trust (in), put one's faith (in), put o.s. in the hands of.

вверн|у́ть, у́, ёшь *pf.* (*of* **⇒ввёртывать**) **1** to screw in, insert. **2** (*fig., coll.*) to insert, put in; **ему́ не удало́сь в. ни сло́ва** he could not get a word in.

ввер|те́ть, чу́, ~тишь *pf.* (*of* **⇒~тывать**) (*coll.*) to screw in.

ввёртыва|ть, ю *impf. of* **⇒вверну́ть** *and* **вверте́ть**

вверх *adv.* up, upward(s); **идти́ в. по ле́стнице** to go upstairs; **в. по тече́нию** upstream; **в. дном** upside down; **в. нога́ми** head over heels.

вверху́ *adv. and prep.* +*g.* above, overhead; **в. страни́цы** at the top of the page.

ввер|чу́, ~тишь *see* **⇒~те́ть**

вверя́|ть(ся), ю(сь) *impf. of* **⇒вве́рить(ся)**

вве|сти́, ду́, дёшь, *past* **~л, ~ла́** *pf.* (*of* **⇒вводи́ть**) (*человека, животного*) to lead in, bring in, take in; (*закон, пошлины*) to introduce, bring in; (*поместить внутрь*) to introduce, put into; (*данные*) to enter, key in; **в. мо́ду** to introduce a fashion; **в. в заблужде́ние** to mislead; **в. в искуше́ние** to lead into temptation; **в. в курс чего́-н.** to acquaint with (the facts of) sth.

ввива́|ть, ю *impf. of* **⇒ввить**

ввиду́ *prep.* +*g.* in view (of); **в. того́, что** as; **в. того́, что вы прие́хали** as you have come.

ввин|ти́ть, чу́, ти́шь *pf.* (*of* **⇒~чивать**) (**в** + *a.*) to screw (in); **в. што́пор в про́бку** to insert a corkscrew into a cork.

вви́нчива|ть, ю *impf. of* **⇒ввинти́ть**

ввить, вовью́, вовьёшь *pf.* (*of* **⇒ввива́ть**) to weave in.

ввод, а *m.* **1** bringing in. **2** (*elec.*) lead-in. **3** (*comput.*) input; **в. да́нных** data input.

вво|ди́ть, жу́, ~дишь *impf. of* **⇒ввести́**

вво́дн|ый *adj.* introductory; (*gram.*) **~ое сло́во** parenthetic word, parenthesis; **в. тон** (*mus.*) leading note.

вво|жу́[1]**, ~дишь** *see* **⇒вводи́ть**

вво|жу́[2]**, ~зишь** *see* **⇒ввози́ть**

ввоз, а *no pl., m.* **1** (*действие*) importation. **2** (*импорт*) import; (*collect.*) imports.

вво|зи́ть, жу́, ~зишь *impf. of* **⇒ввезти́**

вво́зн|ый *adj.* (*товар*) imported; (*attr.*) import; **~ая по́шлина** import duty.

вола́кива|ть, ю *impf. of* **⇒вволо́чь**

вволо́|чь, ку́, чёшь, ку́т, *past* **~к, ~кла́** *pf.* (*coll.*) to drag in.

вво́лю *adv.* (*coll.*) = **вдо́воль**

вво́сьмеро *adv.* eight times; **в. бо́льше** eight times as much.

ввосьмеро́м *adv.* eight together; **они́ в. сде́лали рабо́ту** eight of them did the job together.

ВВП *m. indecl.* (*abbr. of* ***валово́й вну́тренний проду́кт***) GDP (*gross domestic product*).

ВВС *no sg., indecl.* (*abbr. of* ***вое́нно-возду́шные си́лы***) Air Force.

ввысь *adv.* up, upward(s).

ввя|за́ть, жу́, ~жешь *pf.* (*of* **⇒~зывать**) to knit in; (*fig., coll.*) to involve, mix up.

ввя|за́ться, жу́сь, ~жешься *pf.* (**в** + *a.*; *coll.*) (*вмешаться*) to meddle (in); (*впутаться*) to get involved (in); mixed up (in); **в. в неприя́тную исто́рию** to get mixed up in a nasty business.

ввя́зыва|ть(ся), ю(сь) *impf. of* **⇒ввяза́ть(ся)**

вгиб, а *m.* fold.

вгиба́|ть, ю *impf. of* **⇒вогну́ть**

вглубь *adv. and prep.* +*g.* deep down; deep into, into the depths.

вгля|де́ться, жу́сь, ди́шься *pf.* (*of* **⇒~дываться**) (**в** + *a.*) to peer (at).

вгля́дыва|ться, юсь *impf. of* **⇒вгляде́ться**

вгоня́|ть, ю *impf. of* **⇒вогна́ть**

вгрыз|ться, у́сь, ёшься *pf.* (*coll.*) to get one's teeth into (*of animals*).

вда|ва́ться, ю́сь, ёшься *impf. of* **⇒~ться**

вдав|и́ть, лю́, ~ишь *pf.* (*of* **⇒~ливать**) to press in(to).

вда́влива|ть, ю *impf. of* **⇒вдави́ть**

вда́лблива|ть, ю *impf. of* **⇒вдолби́ть**

вдалеке́ *adv.* in the distance; **в. от** (+*g.*) a long way from.

вдали́ *adv.* in the distance, far off; **в. от го́рода** a long way from the city; **исчеза́ть в.** to vanish into the distance.

вдаль *adv.* afar, at a distance; **гляде́ть в.** to look into the distance.

вд|а́ться, а́мся, а́шься, а́стся, ади́мся, ади́тесь, аду́тся *pf.* (*of* ⇒**вдава́ться**) (**в**+*a.*) to jut out (into); (*fig.*) to give oneself up to; to get immersed in; **в. в подро́бности** to go into details.

вдвига́|ть(ся), ю(сь) *impf. of* ⇒**вдви́нуть(ся)**

вдвижно́й *adj.* insertable.

вдви́|нуть, ну, нешь *pf.* (*of* ⇒**~га́ть**) to push in(to).

вдви́|нуться, нусь, нешься *pf.* (*of* ⇒**~га́ться**) to push in, squeeze in.

вдво́е *adv.* twice; double; **в. лу́чше** twice as good; **сложи́ть в.** to fold double.

вдвоём *adv.* the two together; **они́ написа́ли статью́ в.** the two of them together wrote the article.

вдвойне́ *adv.* twice, double; doubly (*also fig.*); **плати́ть в.** to pay double; **он в. винова́т** he is doubly to blame.

вдева́|ть, ю *impf. of* ⇒**вдеть**

вде́л|ать, аю *pf.* (*of* ⇒**~ывать**) (**в**+*a.*) to fit (into), set (into).

вде́лыва|ть, ю *impf. of* ⇒**вде́лать**

вде́н|у, ешь *see* ⇒**вдеть**

вдёргива|ть, ю *impf. of* ⇒**вдёрнуть**

вдёрн|уть, у, ешь *pf.* (*of* ⇒**вдёргивать**) to pull through; to thread; **в. ни́тку в иглу́** to thread a needle.

вде́сятеро *adv.* ten times; **в. бо́льше** ten times as much.

вдесятеро́м *adv.* ten together; **мы в.** ten of us.

вде|ть, ~ну, ~нешь *pf.* (*of* ⇒**~ва́ть**) (**в**+*a.*) to put in(to); **в. ни́тку в иглу́** to thread a needle.

ВДНХ *f. indecl.* (*abbr. of* ***Вы́ставка достиже́ний наро́дного хозя́йства СССР***) (*hist.*) Exhibition of National Economic Achievements (*in Moscow*).

вдоба́вок *adv.* in addition; moreover; into the bargain; **в. к** (+*d.*) in addition to.

вдов|а́, ы́, *pl.* **~ы** *f.* widow; **соло́менная в.** (*coll.*) grass widow.

вдове́|ть, ю *impf.* (*о женщине*) to be a widow; (*о мужчине*) to be a widower.

вдов|е́ц, ца́ *m.* widower; **соло́менный в.** grass widower.

вдо́в|ий *adj. of* ⇒**~а́**

вдови́ц|а, ы *f.* (*obs.*) widow.

вдо́воль *adv.* (*coll.*) **1** (*в изобилии*) in abundance; **у нас фру́ктов в.** we have an abundance of fruit. **2** (*вполне достаточно*) enough; **он нае́лся в.** he ate his fill.

вдовств|о́, а́ *nt.* widowhood; widowerhood.

вдо́вств|овать, ую *impf.* (*obs.*) = **вдове́ть**

вдо́в|ый (~) *adj.* widowed.

вдого́нку *adv.* after, in pursuit of; **бро́ситься в.** (**за**+*i.*) to rush (after).

вдолб|и́ть, лю́, и́шь *pf.* (*of* ⇒**вда́лбливать**) (*coll.*) **в. что-н. кому́-н. в го́лову** to drum, din sth. into s.o.'s head.

вдоль 1 *prep.* (+*g. or* **по**+*d.*) along; **в. бе́рега** along the bank; **в. по доро́ге** along the road; **я поплы́л в. по реке́** I sailed down the river. **2** *adv.* lengthwise, longways; **разре́зать мате́рию в.** to cut material lengthwise; **в. и попере́к** (*повсюду*) in all directions, far and wide; (*подробно*) inside out.

вдо́сталь *adv.* **1** (*coll.*) in plenty. **2** (*obs.*) completely.

вдох, а *m.* breath; **сде́лать глубо́кий в.** to take a deep breath.

вдохнове́ни|е, я *nt.* inspiration.

вдохнове́нный *adj.* inspired.

вдохнови́тел|ь, я *m.* inspirer; inspiration (*of persons*); **он — наш в.** he is an inspiration to us.

вдохнов|и́ть, лю́, и́шь *pf.* (*of* ⇒**~ля́ть**) (+*a. or* **на**+*a.*) to inspire (to).

вдохновля́|ть, ю *impf. of* ⇒**вдохнови́ть**

вдохн|у́ть, у́, ёшь *pf.* (*of* ⇒**вдыха́ть**) (**в**+*a.*) **1** (*воздух*) to breathe in; (*дым*) inhale. **2** (*настроение*) to inspire (with), instil (into); **в. му́жество в кого́-н.** to instil courage into s.o.; **в. жизнь в кого́-н.** to stimulate into action.

вдре́безги *adv.* (*на мелкие части*) to pieces, to smithereens; **разби́ть в.** to smash to smithereens; (*полностью*) completely; **в. пьян** (*coll.*) dead drunk.

вдруг *adv.* **1** (*неожиданно*) suddenly, all of a sudden; (*одновременно*) simultaneously, at once; **все в.** all together. **2** *as interrog. particle* (*coll.*) (*а что если*) what if, suppose; **(а) в. они́ узна́ют?** but suppose they find out?

вдрызг, *adv.* (*coll.*) completely; **в. пьян** dead drunk.

вдува́|ть, ю *impf. of* ⇒**вдуть**

вду́м|аться, аюсь *pf.* (*of* ⇒**~ываться**) (**в**+*a.*) to think over, ponder, meditate (on).

вду́мчив|ый (~, ~а) *adj.* pensive, meditative; thoughtful.

вду́мыва|ться, юсь *impf. of* ⇒**вду́маться**

вду́н|уть, у, ешь *pf.* = **вдуть**

вду|ть, ~ю, ~ешь *pf.* (*of* ⇒**~ва́ть**) to blow into; **в. во́здух в ши́ну** to inflate, blow up a tyre.

вдыха́ни|е, я *nt.* inhalation.

вдыха́тельный *adj.* (*med.*) respiratory.

вдыха́|ть, ю *impf. of* ⇒**вдохну́ть**

веб, а *m.* (*comput.*) the Web.

вебса́йт, а *m.* (*comput.*) website.

вегетариа́н|ец, ца *m.* vegetarian.

вегетариа́н|ка, ки *f. of* ⇒**~ец**

вегетариа́нский *adj.* vegetarian.

вегетариа́нств|о, а *nt.* vegetarianism.

вегетати́вный *adj.* (*biol.*) vegetative.

вегетацио́н|ный *adj.* (*biol.*) vegetation; **~ное размноже́ние** vegetative propagation/reproduction.

вегета́ци|я, и *f.* vegetation.

ве́да|ть, ю *impf.* **1** (*знать*) to know. **2** (+*i.*) (*заведовать*) to manage, be in charge of.

ве́дени|е, я *nt.* authority; jurisdiction; **э́ти дела́ в моём ~и** I am in charge of these things.

веде́ни|е, я *nt.* conducting, conduct; **в. де́ла** the conduct of an affair; **в. журна́ла** the keeping of a diary; **в. протоко́ла** the taking of minutes; **в. хозя́йства** the running of a household.

ве́дома *only in phrr.*: **без в., с в.; без моего́ в.** unknown to me; **с моего́ в.** with my knowledge, with my consent.

ве́домост|ь, и, *pl.* **~и, ~е́й** *f.* **1** (*список*) list, register; **платёжная в.** pay-roll; **в. расхо́дов** expense-sheet. **2** (*pl. only*) Gazette (*as name of newspaper*); **Моско́вские ~и** Moscow Gazette.

ве́домственный *adj.* departmental; **в. подхо́д к де́лу** narrow-minded approach.

ве́домств|о, а *nt.* department.

ве́дом|ый (~, ~а) *adj.* known; **ему́ не ~ страх** he doesn't know fear.

ведо́м|ый (~, ~а) *pres. part. pass. of* ⇒**вести́** led; **~ самолёт** supporting aircraft.

вед|ро́, ра́, *pl.* **~ра, ~ер** *nt.* **1** (*сосуд*) bucket, pail; **по́лное в.** a pailful. **2** (*мера*) vedro (*Old Russian liquid measure, equivalent to approx. 12 litres*).

вед|у́, ёшь *see* ⇒**вести́**

веду́щ|ий *pres. part. act. of* ⇒**вести́** *and adj.* leading; (*tech.*) **~ее колесо́** driving-wheel; *as n.* **в., ~его** *m.* presenter; compère.

ведь *conj.* **1** (*дело в том, что*) you see, you know (*but oft. requires no translation*); **она́ всё вре́мя покупа́ет но́вые пла́тья — в. она́ о́чень бога́та** she is always buying new dresses — she is very rich, you know. **2** (*particle*) (*не правда ли?*) is it not?; is it?; **в. э́то пра́вда?** it's the truth, isn't it?

ве́дьм|а, ы *f.* witch.

ведьм|овско́й *adj. of* ⇒**~а**

ве́ер, а, *pl.* **~а́** *m.* fan (*also fig.*); **обма́хиваться ~ом** to fan o.s.

веерообра́зный *adj.* fan-shaped.

ве́жливост|ь, и *f.* politeness, courtesy.

ве́жлив|ый (~, ~а) *adj.* polite, courteous.

везде́ *adv.* everywhere; **в. и всю́ду** here, there, and everywhere.

вездесу́щ|ий (~, ~а) *adj.* (*человек*) ubiquitous; (*Бог*) omnipresent.

вездехо́д, а *m.* four-wheel drive vehicle; all-terrain vehicle (*abbr.* ATV).

везе́ни|е, я *nt.* luck.

вез|ти́, у́, ёшь, *past* **~, ~ла́** *impf.* (*of* ⇒**по~**) (*det. of* ⇒**вози́ть**) **1** (*перемещать*) to take, convey, carry (*of beasts of burden, mechanical transport, or people when on transport*). **2** (*coll.*)

(*impers.* + *d.*) (*об удаче*) to have luck; **ему́ не ~ёт в ка́рты** he has no luck at cards.

Везу́ви|й, я *m.* (Mt.) Vesuvius.

везу́чий *adj.* (*coll.*) lucky.

вей[1] *imper. of* ⇨**вить**

вей[2] *imper. of* ⇨**ве́ять**

век, а, о ~е, на ~у́, *pl.* **~а́** (*obs.* **~и**) *m.* **1** (*столетие*) century. **2** (*эпоха*) age; **ка́менный в.** Stone Age; **сре́дние ~а́** the Middle Ages; **испоко́н ~о́в** from time immemorial; **отжи́ть свой в.** to have had one's day; **в кои-то ~и** once in a blue moon; **во ~и ~о́в** for all time; **на ~и ве́чные** for ever; **в. живи — в. учи́сь!** (*prov.*) live and learn! **3** (*жизнь*) life, lifetime; **на моём ~у́** in my lifetime. **4** *as adv.* (*очень долго*) for ages; **мы с ва́ми в. не вида́лись** we have not seen each other for ages.

ве́к|о, а, *pl.* **~и, ~** *nt.* eyelid.

векове́чный *adj.* eternal, everlasting.

веково́й *adj.* ancient, age-old.

векселеда́тел|ь, я *m.* (*comm.*) drawer (*of a bill*).

векселедержа́тел|ь, я *m.* (*comm.*) payee, holder (*of a bill*).

ве́ксел|ь, я, *pl.* **~я́** *m.* promissory note; bill of exchange.

ве́ктор, а *m.* (*math.*) vector.

вёл, ~а́ *see* ⇨**вести́**

веле́ни|е, я *nt.* command, behest; **по ~ю со́вести** as dictated by one's conscience; **в. вре́мени** the dictates of the present time.

велеречи́в|ый (~, ~а) *adj.* (*obs. or iron.*) bombastic.

вел|е́ть, ю́, и́шь *impf. and pf.* (+*d. and inf. or* **что́бы**) **1** to order; **я ~е́л ему́ сде́лать э́то** *or* **что́бы он сде́лал э́то** I ordered him to do this; **де́лайте, как вам ~ено** do as you are told. **2**: **не в.** to forbid.

ве́лик, а *m.* (*coll.*) bike.

велика́н, а *m.* giant.

велика́нский *adj.* gigantic.

вели́к|ий (~, ~а́, ~о́) *adj.* **1** (*short form* **~а, ~о**) (*выдающийся*) great; **~ие держа́вы** the Great Powers; **Екатери́на Вели́кая** Catherine the Great; **В. князь** grand prince, grand duke; **~ое мно́жество** a lot, a great deal; **~ая седми́ца** Passion Week; **В. четве́рг** Maundy Thursday. **2** (*short form* **~а́, ~о́,** *pl.* **~и́**) (*большой*) big, large; **от ма́ла до ~а** (*coll.*) young and old. **3** (*short form only*; **~а́, ~о́,** *pl.* **~и́**) (+*d. or* **для**+*g.*) (*слишком большой*) too big; **э́ти брю́ки мне ~и́** these trousers are too big for me.

Великобрита́ни|я, и *f.* Great Britain.

великова́т|ый (~, ~а) *adj.* (*coll.*) rather large, big; **э́ти боти́нки мне ~ы** these boots are rather big for me.

великодержа́вный *adj.* great-power.

великоду́ши|е, я *nt.* magnanimity, generosity.

великоду́шнича|ть, ю *impf.* (*coll.*) to be unnecessarily magnanimous, generous.

великоду́ш|ный (~ен, ~на) *adj.* magnanimous, generous.

великоле́пи|е, я *nt.* splendour (*Br.*), splendor (*US*), magnificence.

великоле́п|ный (~ен, ~на) *adj.* **1** (*роскошный*) splendid, magnificent. **2** (*отличный*) excellent; **~но!** (*int.*) splendid!; excellent!

великому́ченик, а *m.* great martyr.

великопо́стный *adj.* (*eccl.*) Lenten.

велико|ро́сс, а *m.* (*obs.*) = **~ру́с**

великору́с, а *m.* Russian.

великору́сский *adj.* Russian.

великосве́тский *adj.* high-society.

велича́вост|ь, и *f.* stateliness, majesty.

велича́в|ый (~, ~а) *adj.* stately, majestic.

велича́йш|ий *adj.* (*superl. of* ⇨**вели́кий**) greatest, extreme, supreme; **де́ло ~ей ва́жности** a matter of extreme importance; **с ~им удово́льствием** with the greatest pleasure.

велича́|ть, ю *impf.* **1** (+*a. and i. or nom.*; *coll.*) (*звать*) to call; **как вас ~ют?** what is your name?; **его́ ~ют Ива́ном/Ива́н** he's called Ivan. **2** (+*a. and i.*; *obs. and iron.*) (*называть*) to hail as. **3** (*folk poet.*) (*чествовать*) to honour with songs.

велича́|ться, юсь *impf.* **1** *pass. of* ⇨**~ть. 2** (+*i.*; *coll.*) to glory (in), plume o.s. (on).

вели́чественност|ь, и *f.* majesty, grandeur.

вели́чествен|ный (~, ~на) *adj.* majestic, grand.

вели́честв|о, а *nt.* majesty; **Ва́ше в.** Your Majesty.

вели́чи|е, я *nt.* greatness; grandeur; **ма́ния ~я** megalomania.

величин|а́, ы́, *pl.* **~ы, ~ам** *f.* **1** size; **дом сре́дней ~ы́** a house of average size. **2** (*math.*) quantity, magnitude; (*значение*) value; **постоя́нная в.** constant. **3** (*о человеке*) great figure; **литерату́рная в.** an eminent literary figure.

вело... *comb. form* bicycle-, cycle-.

велого́нк|а, и *f.* cycle race.

велого́нщик, а *m.* racing cyclist.

велодро́м, а *m.* cycle track; velodrome.

велокро́сс, а *m.* cyclo-cross.

велопробе́г, а *m.* cycle race.

велосипе́д, а *m.* bicycle; cycle; **во́дный в.** pedalo; **па́рный в.** tandem; **в.-пау́к** penny-farthing; **изобрета́ть в.** (*coll.*) to reinvent the wheel.

велосипеди́ст, а *m.* bicyclist; cyclist.

велосипе́д|ный *adj. of* ⇨**~**

велоспо́рт, а *m.* cycling.

велотре́к, а *m.* cycle track.

велотренажёр, а *m.* exercise bicycle.

велофигури́ст, а *m.* trick cyclist.

вельбо́т, а *m.* whale-boat, whaler.

вельве́т, а *m.* corduroy.

вельве́товый *adj.* corduroy.

вельмо́ж|а, и *m.* grandee.

вельмо́ж|ный *adj. of* ⇨**~а**

велю́р, а *m.* velour.

веля́рный *adj.* (*ling.*) velar.

Ве́н|а, ы *f.* Vienna.

ве́н|а, ы *f.* (*anat.*) vein; **расшире́ние ~** varicose veins.

венге́р|ка, ки *f.* **1** *f. of* ⇨**венгр. 2** (*танец*) Hungarian dance. **3** (*куртка*) dolman (*jacket*).

венге́рский *adj.* Hungarian.

венгр, а *m.* Hungarian.

Ве́нгри|я, и *f.* Hungary.

венери́ческий *adj.* (*med.*) venereal; **в. диспансе́р** VD clinic.

венеро́лог, а *m.* specialist in venereal diseases.

венероло́ги|я, и *f.* science of venereal diseases.

Венесуэ́л|а, ы *f.* Venezuela.

венесуэ́л|ец, ьца *m.* Venezuelan.

венесуэ́л|ка, ки *f. of* ⇨**~ец**

венесуэ́льский *adj.* Venezuelan.

вен|е́ц, ца́ *m.* **1** (*корона*) crown; **терно́вый в.** crown of thorns; (*fig.*) completion, consummation. **2** (*при венчании*): **пойти́ под в. с кем-н.** to marry; **под ~цо́м** during the wedding. **3** (*poet.*) (*венок*) wreath, garland. **4** (*astron.*) corona.

венециа́нск|ий *adj.* Venetian; **~ая ярь** verdigris.

Вене́ци|я, и *f.* Venice.

вене́чный *adj.* **1** (*anat.*) coronal, coronary. **2** *adj. of* ⇨**вене́ц**

ве́нзел|ь, я, *pl.* **~я́, ~е́й** *m.* monogram; **~я́ писа́ть** (*coll.*) to walk unsteadily (*of a drunken person*).

ве́ник, а *m.* **1** (*из прутьев*) besom, broom. **2** (*в бане*) birch twigs (*used in Russian baths*).

ве́нич|ек, ка *m.* (*cul.*) whisk.

вен|о́зный *adj. of* ⇨**~а;** venous.

вен|о́к, ка́ *m.* wreath, garland.

ве́нский *adj.* Viennese; **в. стул** bentwood chair.

вентили́р|овать, ую *impf.* (*of* ⇨**про~**) to ventilate (*also fig.*).

ве́нтил|ь, я *m.* valve.

вентиля́тор, а *m.* ventilator; extractor (fan).

вентиля́ци|я, и *f.* ventilation.

венцено́с|ец, ца *m.* (*epithet of monarch*; *rhet.*) wearer of crown, crowned head.

венча́|льный *adj. of* ⇨**~ние; ~льное кольцо́** wedding ring; **в. наря́д** wedding dress.

венча́ни|е, я *nt.* **1**: **в. (на ца́рство)** coronation. **2** (*бракосочетание*) wedding ceremony.

венча́|ть, ю *impf.* **1** (*pf.* **в.** *and* **у~**) (*находиться наверху*) to crown. **2** (*pf.* **у~**) (*fig.*) to crown; **коне́ц ~ет де́ло** all's well that ends well. **3** (*pf.* **об~** *and* **по~**) (*соединять браком*) to marry (*of officiating priest*).

венча́|ться, юсь *impf.* **1** (*pf.* **об~** *and* **по~**) to be married, marry. **2** *pass. of* ⇨**~ть**

ве́нчик, а *m.* **1** halo, nimbus. **2** (*bot.*) corolla.

вепр|ь, я *m.* wild boar.

ве́р|а, ы *f.* (**в**+*a.*) faith, belief (in); (*уверенность*) trust, confidence; **приня́ть на ~у** to take on trust; **~ой и пра́вдой служи́ть** (*coll.*) to serve faithfully.

вера́нд|а, ы *f.* veranda.

ве́рб|а, ы *f.* willow; (*ветка*) willow branch.

верба́льный *adj.* verbal.

вербе́н|а, ы *f.* (*bot.*) verbena.

верблю́д, а *m.* camel; **одного́рбый в.** Arabian camel, dromedary; **двуго́рбый в.** Bactrian camel.

верблю́|жий *adj. of* ⇒**~д**; **~жья шерсть** camel's hair; **~жье сукно́** camel-hair cloth.

верблюж|о́нок, о́нка, *pl.* **~а́та, ~а́т** *m.* camel foal.

ве́рб|ный *adj. of* ⇒**~а**; **~ное воскресе́нье** (*eccl.*) Palm Sunday; **~ная неде́ля** Holy Week.

верб|ова́ть, у́ю *impf.* (*of* **за~** *and* **на~**) to recruit, enlist; (*fig.*) to win over.

вербо́вк|а, и *f.* recruiting.

вербо́вщик, а *m.* recruiter.

ве́рбов|ый *adj.* willow; osier; **~ая корзи́на** wicker basket.

верди́кт, а *m.* verdict.

верёвк|а, и *f.* cord, rope; string; (*fig.*) noose; **в. для белья́** clothes-line; **свя́зывать ~ой** to tie up.

верёв|очный *adj. of* ⇒**~ка**

вере|ди́ть, жу́, ди́шь *impf.* (*of* ⇒**раз~**) (*coll.*) to knock, irritate (*a sore place*; *also fig.*).

верезж|а́ть, у́, и́шь *impf.* (*coll.*) to squeal.

верени́ц|а, ы *f.* file, line; **в. лошаде́й** a string of horses; (*fig.*): **в. иде́й** a series of ideas.

ве́реск, а *m.* (*bot.*) heather.

веретён|ный *adj. of* ⇒**~о́**

веретен|о́, а́, *pl.* **веретёна, веретён** *nt.* spindle.

верещ|а́ть, у́, и́шь *impf.* (*coll.*) (*говорить пискливо*) to squeal; (*говорить много*) to chatter; (*стрекотать*) to chirp (*of a cricket, etc.*).

верзи́л|а, ы *c.g.* (*coll.*) lanky person.

вери́г|и, ~ *pl.* (*sg.* **~а, ~и** *f.*) chains, fetters (*worn by ascetics*; *also fig.*).

вери́тельн|ый *adj.*: **~ая гра́мота** (*dipl.*) credentials.

ве́р|ить, ю, ишь *impf.* (*of* ⇒**по~**) (+*d. or* **в**+*a.*) to believe, have faith (in); (+*d.*) (*доверять*) to trust (in), rely (upon); **в. в Бо́га** to believe in God; **в. в прогре́сс** to believe in progress; **э́тому челове́ку никто́ не ~ит** no one believes that man; **он не ~ит свое́й жене́** he does not trust his wife; **в. на́ слово** to take on trust; **я не ~ил свои́м уша́м, свои́м глаза́м** I could not believe my ears, eyes.

ве́р|иться, ится *impf.* (*impers.*+*d.*): **мне ~ится с трудо́м** I find it hard to believe; **мне не ~ится, что э́то так** I can't believe it's true.

вермише́л|ь, и *f.* vermicelli.

ве́рмут, а *m.* vermouth.

верн|е́е *adv.* (*comp. of* ⇒**~о**) rather; **в. всего́** most probably; **а в. (сказа́ть)** to be more exact.

вернисаж, а *m.* (*art*) **1** (*закрытый просмотр*) private viewing. **2** (*день открытия*) opening-day (*of an exhibition*).

ве́рн|о *adv. of* ⇒**~ый**; *as particle* (*coll.*) probably, I suppose; **вы, в., уже́ слы́шали но́вости** you have probably already heard the news.

верноподданнически|й *adj.*: **~е чу́вства** loyalty.

вернопо́дданн|ый *adj.* (*obs.*) loyal, faithful; *as n.* **в., ~ого** *m.* loyal subject.

ве́рност|ь, и *f.* **1** (*преданность*) faithfulness, loyalty. **2** (*правильность*) truth, correctness; **для ~и** (*coll.*) to be on the safe side.

верн|у́ть, у́, ёшь *pf.* (*of* ⇒**возвраща́ть**) **1** (*отдать обратно*) to give back, return; **в. кому́-н. наде́жду** to give s.o. back hope. **2** (*получить обратно*) to get back, recover, retrieve; **в. поте́рянное** to recover what one has lost.

верн|у́ться, у́сь, ёшься *pf.* (*of* ⇒**возвраща́ться**) to return (*also fig.*); **в. домо́й** to return home.

ве́р|ный (~ен, ~на́, ~но) *adj.* **1** (*правильный*) true, correct; **~ны ли ва́ши часы́?** is your watch right?; **~но ли, что вы уезжа́ете?** is it true that you are going away? **2** (*преданный*) faithful, loyal, true; **в. свои́м убежде́ниям** true to one's convictions. **3** (*надёжный*) sure, reliable; **в. исто́чник** reliable source; **~ная ко́пия** faithful copy; **в. при́знак** sure sign. **4** (*несомненный*) certain, sure; **~ная смерть** certain death.

верня́к, а́ *m.* (*coll.*) certain success, winner.

ве́ровани|е, я *nt.* belief, creed.

ве́р|овать, ую *impf.* (**в**+*a.*) to believe (in).

вероиспове́дани|е, я *nt.* creed, denomination; **свобо́да ~я** freedom of religion.

вероло́м|ный (~ен, ~на) *adj.* treacherous, perfidious.

вероло́мств|о, а *nt.* treachery, perfidy.

верони́к|а, и *f.* (*bot.*) speedwell, veronica.

вероотсту́пник, а *m.* apostate.

вероотсту́пничеств|о, а *nt.* apostasy.

вероподо́б|ный (~ен, ~на) *adj.* (*obs.*) likely.

веротерпи́мост|ь, и *f.* (*relig.*) toleration

веротерпи́м|ый (~, ~а) *adj.* (*relig.*) tolerant.

вероуче́ни|е, я *nt.* (*relig.*) dogma.

вероучи́тел|ь, я *m.* religious teacher, apologist.

веро́яти|е, я *nt.* probability, likelihood; **по всему́ ~ю** in all probability.

веро́ятно *adv.* probably.

веро́ятност|ь, и *f.* probability; **по всей ~и** in all probability; **тео́рия ~ей** (*math.*) theory of probability.

вероя́т|ный (~ен, ~на) *adj.* probable, likely; **э́то вполне́ ~но** it is highly probable; **~нее всего́** most probably; **в. насле́дник** heir presumptive.

Верса́л|ь, и *f.* Versailles.

верса́льский *f.*: **в. догово́р** Treaty of Versailles.

версифика́ци|я, и *f.* versification.

ве́рси|я, и *f.* version.

верст|а́, ы́, *a.* **~у́** *pl.* **~ы, ~** *f.* (*мера*) verst (*old Russian measurement, equivalent to approx. 1.06 kilometres*); (*столб*) verst-post; **за́ ~у** (*coll.*) from far off; **ме́рить ~ы** (*coll.*) to travel a long way; **коло́менская в.** (*coll.*) beanpole, lanky person.

верста́к, а́ *m.* (*tech.*) (work)bench.

верста́|ть, ю *impf.* (*of* ⇒**с~**) (*typ.*) to impose, make up into pages.

вёрстк|а, и *f.* (*typ.*) **1** (*действие*) page make-up. **2** (*для корректуры*) page proofs.

верст|ово́й *adj. of* ⇒**~а́**; **в. столб** milestone.

ве́ртел, а, *pl.* **~а́** *m.* spit; skewer.

верте́п, а *m.* **1** den (*of thieves, etc.*). **2** (*theatr.*) puppet-show.

вер|те́ть, чу́, ~тишь *impf.* (+*a. or i.*) (*рукоятку, колесо*) to turn; (*быстро*) to twirl; **в. голово́й** to shake one's head; **в. тро́стью** to twirl a cane; **в. что-н. в рука́х** to fiddle with sth.; **она́ ~тит им, как хо́чет** she can twist him round her little finger; **как ни ~ти́, нам приде́тся заплати́ть** there is nothing for it, we shall have to pay.

вер|те́ться, чу́сь, ~тишься *impf.* **1** (*вращаться*) to rotate, turn (round), revolve (*also fig.*); **разгово́р у них всё ~тится о́коло войны** conversation with them always revolves around the war; **в. в голове́** to go round and round in one's head; **его́ фами́лия весь день ~те́лась у меня на языке́** his name was on the tip of my tongue all day; **в. под нога́ми, пе́ред глаза́ми** (*coll.*) to be under one's feet, in the way. **2** (*coll.*) (*общаться*) to move (among), hang around (with); **он бо́льшей ча́стью ~тится среди́ иностра́нцев** he hangs around mainly with foreigners. **3** (*coll.*) (*ёрзать*) to fidget. **4** (*coll.*) (*увиливать*) to prevaricate; **отве́ть на вопро́с пря́мо, не ~ти́сь** answer the question directly and don't prevaricate.

вертика́л, а *m.* (*astron.*) vertical.

вертика́л|ь, и *f.* (*линия*) vertical line; (*на шахматной доске*) file; (*в кроссворде*) down.

вертика́льный *adj.* vertical.

вертихво́стк|а, и *f.* (*coll.*) flirt.

вёрт|кий (~ок, ~ка́, ~ко) *adj.* (*coll.*) nimble, agile.

вертлу́г, а́ *m.* (*anat.*) head of the femur.

вертлю́г, а́ *m.* (*tech.*) swivel.

вертлю́|жный *adj. of* ⇒**~г**

вертля́в|ый (~, ~а) *adj.* (*coll.*)

1 (*подвижный*) restless, fidgety. **2** (*легкомысленный*) frivolous.

вертогра́д, а *m.* (*obs.*) garden.

вертодро́м, а *m.* heliport.

вертолёт, а *m.* helicopter; **боево́й в.** helicopter gunship.

вертолётчик, а *m.* helicopter pilot.

вертолётчи|ца, цы *f. of* ⇨**~к**

вертопра́х, а *m.* (*coll.*) frivolous person.

вертуха́|й, я *m.* (*sl.*) screw (*prison warder*).

верту́шк|а, и *f.* (*coll.*) **1** revolving object (*e.g. door, bookcase*). **2** (*игрушка*) whirligig, teetotum. **3** (*c.g.*) (*человек*) flighty person. **4** (*проигрывателя*) turntable.

ве́рующ|ий *adj.* religious; *as n.* **в., ~его** *m.* believer.

верф|ь, и *f.* dockyard; shipyard.

верх, а, *pl.* **~и́** *m.* **1** (*верхняя часть*) top, (*горы*) summit (*also fig.*); **совеща́ние в ~а́х** (*pol.*) summit conference; (*крайняя степень*) height; **в. глу́пости** the height of folly. **2** (*экипажа, автомашины*) hood (*Br.*), folding top (*US*); **«верх!»** (*sign*) 'this side up'; (*fig.*) (*общества*) **~и́** (*pl. only*) upper crust; (*mus.*) high notes; **взять, одержа́ть в.** (**над**+*i.*) to gain the upper hand (over). **3** (*лицевая сторона*) outside, top; right side (*of material*); **хвата́ть ~и́, нахвата́ться ~о́в** (*fig., coll.*) to get a smattering (of), acquire a superficial knowledge (of).

ве́рхн|ий *adj.* upper; **~яя оде́жда** outer clothing; **~яя пала́та** (*pol.*) upper chamber; **~ее тече́ние (реки́)** upper reaches (of river); **в. я́щик** top drawer.

верхове́нств|о, а *nt.* supremacy.

верхо́вн|ый *adj.* supreme; **~ое кома́ндование** high command; **В. Сове́т** (*hist.*) Supreme Soviet; **В. суд** Supreme Court.

верхово́д, а *m.* (*coll.*) boss, leader.

верхово́|дить, жу, дишь *impf.* (+*i.*; *coll.*) to lord it over, boss around.

верх|ово́й[1] *adj.*: **~ова́я езда́** riding (*Br.*), horseback riding (*US*); **~ова́я ло́шадь** saddle-horse; **~ова́я тропа́** bridle path; *as n.* **в., ~ово́го** *m.* rider.

верхово́й[2] *adj.* up-river.

верхо́вь|е, я, *g. pl.* **~ев** *nt.* upper reaches.

верхогля́д, а *m.* (*coll.*) superficial person.

верхогля́дств|о, а *nt.* (*coll.*) superficiality.

верхола́з, а *m.* steeplejack.

ве́рхом *adv.* **1** on high ground. **2** (*выше краёв*) brim-full; **нали́ть стака́н в.** to pour out a full glass.

верхо́м *adv.* astride; on horseback; **е́здить в.** to ride.

верхоту́р|а, ы *f.* (*coll.*) top.

верху́шк|а, и *f.* **1** top; **~ а́йсберга** tip of the iceberg. **2** (*fig., coll.*) (*организации*) elite, top.

ве́рченый *adj.* (*coll., pej.*) flighty, frivolous.

вер|чу́, ~́тишь *see* ⇨**~те́ть**

ве́рш|а, и *f.* fish-trap (*made of osiers*).

верши́н|а, ы *f.* **1** (*дерева, холма*) top; (*горы*) summit, peak; (*fig.*) peak, acme. **2** (*math.*) vertex; apex.

верши́тел|ь, я *m.*: **в. су́деб** controller of fate; **он ведёт себя́ как в. су́деб** he behaves as if he were God.

верш|и́ть у́, и́шь *impf.* (+*a. or i.*) (*управлять*) to manage, control, decide; **в. суд и распра́ву** to administer justice and mete out punishment; **в. все́ми дела́ми** to run the whole show.

вершк|и́, о́в *pl.* (*coll.*) top part.

вершко́вый *adj.* one vershok long.

верш|о́к, ка́ *m.* vershok (*old Russian measure of length, equivalent to 4.4 cm*); (*fig.*) smattering.

вес, а, *pl.* **~а́** *m.* **1** weight; **ли́шний в.** excess baggage; (*fig.*) (*значение*) weight, authority; **на в.** by weight; **~́ом в сто фу́нтов** weighing a hundred pounds; **на ~у́** balanced, hanging, suspended; **держа́ться на ~у́** to be balanced; **приба́вить, уба́вить в ~́е** to put on, lose weight; **быть на в. зо́лота** to be worth one's weight in gold; **име́ть в ~́е** to carry weight. **2** (*система мер*) system of weights; **апте́карский в.** apothecaries' weight. **3**: **уде́льный в.** specific gravity.

веселе́|ть, ю *impf.* (*of* ⇨**по~**) to cheer up.

весел|и́ть, ю́, и́шь *impf.* (*of* ⇨**раз~**) to amuse.

весел|и́ться, ю́сь, и́шься *impf.* to enjoy o.s.; to have fun.

ве́село *adv.* gaily, merrily; *as pred.* (+*d.*) to enjoy o.s.; **нам тут о́чень в.** we are having fun here; **бы́ло в.** it was fun.

весёлост|ь, и *f.* gaiety; cheerfulness.

весёл|ый (ве́сел, ~а́, ве́село) *adj.* **1** cheerful, merry; **у него́ ~ое настрое́ние сего́дня** he is in good spirits today. **2** (*no short form*) (*фильм, рассказ*) cheerful, feel-good; (*краски, обои*) bright, cheerful.

весе́л|ье, ья, *g. pl.* **~ий** *nt.* gaiety, merriment.

вес|е́льный *adj. of* ⇨**~ло́; ~е́льная ло́дка** rowing-boat.

весельча́к, а́ *m.* (*coll.*) convivial fellow.

веселя́щий *adj.*: **в. газ** laughing gas.

вес|е́нний *adj. of* ⇨**~на́; ~е́ннее равноде́нствие** vernal equinox.

ве́|сить, шу, сишь *impf.* **1** (*иметь тот или иной вес*) to weigh; **груз ~сит три то́нны** the cargo weighs three tons. **2** (*взвешивать*) (*coll.*) to weigh.

ве́с|кий (~ок, ~ка) *adj.* weighty.

ве́скост|ь, и *f.* weightiness.

вес|ло́, ла́, *pl.* **~́ла, ~́ел, ~́лам** *nt.* oar; (*гребок*) paddle; **подня́ть ~́ла** to rest on one's oars.

вес|на́, ны́, *pl.* **~́ны, ~́ен, ~́нам** *f.* spring (*season*).

весно́й *adv.* in the spring.

весну́ш|ки, ек *pl.* (*sg.* **~ка, ~ки** *f.*) freckles.

весну́шчатый *adj.* freckled.

вес|ово́й 1 *adj. of* ⇨**~; ~ова́я катего́рия** (*sport*) weight category. **2** (*продаваемый на вес*) sold by weight.

весо́м|ый (~, ~а) *adj.* (*phys.*) ponderable; (*fig.*) weighty; substantial.

вест, а *m.* (*naut.*) **1** (*запад*) west. **2** (*западный ветер*) west wind.

веста́лк|а, и *f.* vestal (virgin).

ве́стерн, а *m.* western (*film*).

ве|сти́, ду́, дёшь, *past* **~́л, ~ла́** *impf.* (*det. of* ⇨**води́ть**) **1** (*pf.* **по~**) (*сопровождать*) to lead; to take; (*войска*) to lead. **2** (*pf.* **про~**) (+*i.* **по**+*d.*) to run (over), pass (over, across); **в. смычко́м по стру́нам** to run one's bow over the strings. **3** (*pf.* **про~**) (*осуществлять, делать*) to conduct; to carry on; **в. войну́** to wage war; **в. ого́нь (по**+*d.*) to fire (on); **в. перегово́ры** to carry on negotiations; **в. перепи́ску (с**+*i.*) to correspond (with); **в. проце́сс** to carry on a lawsuit. **1** (*impf. only*) (*машину*) to drive; **в. кора́бль** to navigate a ship; **в. самолёт** to pilot an aircraft. **2** (*impf. only*) (*руководить*) to conduct, direct, run; (*передачу*) to present; (*собрание*) to chair; **в. де́ло** to run a business; **в. по́иск** (*comput.*) to run a search; **в. хозя́йство** to keep house. **3** (*impf. only*) (*учёт*) to keep; **в. дневни́к** to keep a diary; **в. кни́ги** to keep books, keep accounts; **в. протоко́л** to keep minutes. **4** (*impf. only*): **в. себя́** to behave. **5** (*impf. only*) (*служить путём куда-нибудь*) to lead (*also fig.*); **куда́ ~дёт э́та доро́га?** where does this road lead (to)?; **э́то ни к чему́ не ~дёт** this is leading nowhere. **6** (*impf. only*): **в. своё нача́ло (от**+*g.*) to originate (in).

вестибуля́рный *adj.*: **в. аппара́т** (*anat.*) vestibular apparatus.

вестибю́л|ь, я *m.* entrance hall, lobby.

вести́мо *adv.* (*dial.*) of course, certainly.

вест-и́нд|ец, ца *m.* West Indian.

Вест-И́нди|я, и *f.* the West Indies.

вест-и́нд|ка, ки *f. of* ⇨**~ец**

вест-и́ндский *adj.* West Indian.

ве|сти́сь, ду́сь, дёшься, *past* **вёлся, ~ла́сь** *impf.* (*of* ⇨**по~**) **1** *pass. of* ⇨**~сти́**. **2** (*usu. impers.*; *coll.*) (*быть принятым*) to be observed (*of customs, etc.*); **так ~дётся уже́ три́ста лет** this has been the custom for three hundred years. **3** (*происходить*) to take place.

ве́стник, а *m.* **1** (*человек*) messenger, herald. **2** (*название издания*) Bulletin.

ве́стни|ца, цы *f. of* ⇨**~к 1**

вестов|о́й *adj.* (*obs.*) signal; *as n.* **в., ~о́го** *m.* orderly.

ве́сточк|а, и *f.* (*coll.*) news; **пришли́те мне ~у, как то́лько прие́дете** drop me a line as soon as you arrive.

вест|ь[1]**, и,** *pl.* **~́и, ~е́й** *f.* news; piece of news; **пропа́сть бе́з ~и** (*mil.*) to be missing.

весть[2] *only in coll. phrr.*: **Бог в.** God knows; **не в. что** goodness knows, heaven knows what; **не Бог в. когда́** recently; **не/Бог в. како́й** trifling, insignificant.

вес|ы́, о́в *no sg.* **1** scales, balance; **мостовы́е в.** weighbridge; **пружи́нные в.** spring balance. **2**: **В.** (*созвездие*) the Scales, Libra.

весь[1]**, вся, всё,** *g.* **всего́, всей,**

В

всего́, *pl.* **все, всех** *pron.* all; **весь день** all day; **вся страна́** the whole country; **вся Фра́нция** the whole of France; **по всему́ го́роду** all over the town; **он весь в отца́** he is the (very) image of his father; **весь в лохмо́тьях** all in rags; **вы́йти весь** to be used up; **бума́га вся вы́шла** the paper is all used up; **во весь го́лос** at the top of one's voice; **во всю мочь** with all one's might; **от всего́ се́рдца** from the bottom of one's heart, with all one's heart; **пре́жде всего́** before all, first and foremost; **при всём том** for all that, moreover; **вот и всё** that's all; there's nothing more to it; **всего́ (хоро́шего)!** good-bye!, all the best!; **всё и вся** all and everything; **по всему́** (*coll.*) all the signs indicate; *as n.* **всё, всего́** *nt.* everything; **все, всех** *no sg.* all, everyone.

вес|ь², **и** *f.* village.

весьма́ *adv.* very, highly; **в. успе́шный о́пыт** highly successful experiment.

ветви́ст|ый (~, ~а) *adj.* branchy, spreading.

ветвра́ч, а́ *m.* vet.

ветв|ь, и, *pl.* **~и, ~е́й** *f.* branch, bough; (*fig.*) branch.

ве́т|ер, ра *m.* wind; (*fig.*) **броса́ть слова́ на в.** to talk idly; **броса́ть де́ньги на в.** to waste money; **у него́ в. в голове́** he is a thoughtless fellow; **подби́тый ~ром** (*coll.*) (*i*) empty-headed, (*ii*) light, flimsy.

ветера́н, а *m.* veteran.

ветерина́р, а *m.* veterinary surgeon (*Br.*), veterinarian (*US*).

ветерина́ри|я, и *f.* veterinary science.

ветерина́рный *adj.* veterinary.

ветер|о́к, ка́ *m.* breeze; **с ~ко́м** fast.

ве́тк|а, и *f.* branch; (*мелкая*) twig; **железнодоро́жная в.** branch-line.

вет|ла́, лы́, *pl.* **~лы, ~ел** *f.* (*bot.*) white willow.

ве́то *nt. indecl.* veto; **наложи́ть в.** (**на** + *a.*) to veto.

ве́точк|а, и *f.* twig, sprig, shoot.

ве́тош|ь, и *f.* old clothes, rags.

ве́треник, а *m.* (*coll.*) empty-headed, frivolous person.

ве́треница¹, цы *f. of* ⇒**~к**

ве́трениц|а², ы *f.* (*bot.*) anemone.

ве́треност|ь, и *f.* empty-headedness.

ве́трен|ый (~, ~а) *adj.* **1** windy; **за́втра бу́дет ~о** it will be windy tomorrow. **2** (*fig.*) (*человек*) empty-headed.

ветри́л|о, а *nt.* (*poet.*) sail.

ветро|во́й *adj. of* ⇒**ве́тер; ~во́е стекло́** windscreen (*Br.*), windshield (*US*).

ветроме́р, а *m.* (*phys.*) anemometer.

ветроуказа́тел|ь, я *m.* (*aeron.*) wind sock.

ветря́к, а́ *m.* **1** (*tech.*) wind turbine. **2** (*coll.*) windmill.

ветря́нк|а, и *f.* (*coll.*) **1** (*мельница*) windmill. **2** (*med.*) chicken-pox.

ветрян|о́й *adj.* wind(-powered); **~а́я ме́льница** windmill.

ве́трян|ый *adj.*: **~ая о́спа** chicken-pox.

ве́тх|ий (~, ~а́, ~о) *adj.* (*очень старый*) old, ancient; (*здание*) dilapidated, tumbledown; (*здание, человек*) decrepit; **В. Заве́т** the Old Testament.

ветхозаве́тный *adj.* Old Testament; (*fig.*) antiquated.

ве́тхост|ь, и *f.* decrepitude; dilapidation.

ветчин|а́, ы *no pl., f.* ham.

ветчи́н|ный *adj. of* ⇒**~а́**

ветша́|ть, ю *impf.* (*of* ⇒**об~**) (*здание*) to decay; to become dilapidated; (*человек*) to become decrepit.

ве́х|а, и *f.* landmark (*also fig.*); milestone.

ве́ч|е, а *nt.* (*hist.*) veche (*popular assembly in medieval Russian towns*).

вечево́й *adj. of* ⇒**ве́че**

ве́чер, а, *pl.* **~а́** *m.* **1** (*время*) evening; **по ~а́м** in the evenings; **под в., к ~у** towards evening. **2** (*собрание*) party; evening, soirée; **музыка́льный в.** musical evening.

вечере́|ть, ет *impf.* (*impers.*) to grow dark; **~ет** night is falling.

вечери́нк|а, и *f.* party.

вечерко́м *adv.* (*coll.*) in the evening.

вече́рн|ий *adj. of* ⇒**ве́чер; ~яя заря́** twilight, dusk; **~ие ку́рсы** evening classes; **~ее пла́тье** evening dress; **~яя шко́ла** night-school.

вече́рник, а *m.* (*coll.*) night-school student.

вече́р|ня, ни, *g. pl.* **~ен** *f.* (*eccl.*) vespers.

ве́чером *adv.* in the evening.

ве́чер|я, и *f.*: **Та́йная в.** (*bibl.*) the Last Supper.

ве́чник, а *m.* (*sl.*) lifer (*convict serving life sentence*).

ве́чно *adv.* (*всегда*) for ever, eternally; (*coll.*) (*постоянно*) always; **они́ в. ссо́рятся** they are always quarrelling.

вечнозелёный *adj.* (*bot.*) evergreen.

ве́чност|ь, и *f.* eternity; **ка́нуть в в.** to sink into oblivion; **це́лую в.** (*coll.*) for ages, for an age.

ве́ч|ный (~ен, ~на) *adj.* **1** (*льды, слава*) eternal, everlasting; **~ная мерзлота́** permafrost. **2** (*бессрочный*) indefinite, perpetual; **~ное владе́ние** possession in perpetuity; **~ное перо́** fountain-pen. **3** (*coll.*) (*постоянный*) perpetual, continual.

вечо́р *adv.* (*coll., obs.*) yesterday evening.

вечо́рк|а, и *f.* (*coll.*) evening paper.

ве́шалк|а, и *f.* **1** (*крючок*) peg, (*планка*) rack, (*стойка*) stand. **2** (*петля*) tab (*on clothes for hanging on pegs*). **3** (*гардероб*) cloak-room. **4** (*плечики*) (coat-)hanger.

ве́ша|ть¹, ю *impf.* (*of* ⇒**пове́сить**) to hang; **в. бельё на верёвку** to hang washing on a line; **в. уби́йцу** to hang a murderer; **в. го́лову** (*coll.*) to despair.

ве́ша|ть², ю *impf.* (*of* ⇒**взве́сить**) to weigh, weigh out; **в. фунт ко́фе** to weigh out a pound of coffee.

ве́ша|ться¹, юсь *impf.* (*of* ⇒**пове́ситься**) **1** *pass. of* ⇒**~ть¹**; (*картина*) to be hung; (*убийца*) to be hanged; **хоть ~йся!** it's enough to make you hang yourself! **2** (*кончать свою жизнь*) to hang o.s. **3**: **в. на ше́ю кому́-н.** (*coll.*) to run after.

ве́ша|ться², юсь *impf.* (*of* ⇒**с~**) (*определять свой вес*) to weigh o.s.

ве́шний *adj.* (*poet.*) vernal.

ве́|шу, сишь *see* ⇒**~сить**

веща́ни|е, я *nt.* **1** (*предсказание*) prophesying. **2** (*по радио, телевидению*) broadcasting.

веща́|ть, ю *impf.* **1** (*предсказывать*) to prophesy. **2** (*говорить догматически*) to pontificate, lay down the law. **3** (*по радио, телевидению*) to broadcast.

вещ|ево́й *adj. of* ⇒**~ь; ~ево́е дово́льствие** (*mil.*) clothing, kit; **в. мешо́к** hold-all; kit-bag; **в. склад** storage warehouse, store; (*mil.*) stores.

веще́ственност|ь, и *f.* substantiality, materiality.

веще́ственн|ый *adj.* substantial, material; **~ые доказа́тельства** material evidence.

веществ|о́, а́ *nt.* substance; matter; **взры́вчатое в.** explosive; **пита́тельное в.** nutrient; **се́рое в.** grey matter; **хими́ческое в.** chemical substance.

вещи́зм, а *m.* materialism.

ве́щий *adj.* prophetic.

вещ|и́ца, и́цы *f. dim. of* ⇒**~ь;** little thing; bagatelle.

вещу́н, а́ *m.* (*obs.*) soothsayer.

вещ|ь, и, *pl.* **~и, ~е́й** *f.* **1** (*in var. senses*) thing; **э́то в.!** (*expr. approval; coll.*) that's quite sth.! **2** (*pl.*) things (= (*i*) *belongings; baggage;* (*ii*) *clothes*); **э́то ва́ши ~и?** are these things yours? **3** (*произведение*) work; piece, thing.

ве́ялк|а, и *f.* (*agric.*) winnowing-fan; winnowing-machine.

ве́яни|е, я *nt.* **1** (*agric.*) winnowing. **2** (*ветра*) blowing. **3** (*fig.*) (*тенденция*) current, tendency, trend; **в. вре́мени** spirit of the times.

ве́|ять, ю, ешь *impf.* **1** (*agric.*) to winnow. **2** (*о ветре*) to blow; **~ял прохла́дный ветеро́к** a cool breeze was blowing; (*impers.,* + *i.*): **~ет весно́й** spring is in the air; **~ет но́выми иде́ями** new ideas are in the air. **3** (*o флаге*) to wave, flutter.

в|жать, ожму́, ожмёшь *pf.* (*of* ⇒**вжима́ть**) to press (into).

в|жа́ться, ожму́сь, ожмёшься *pf.* (*of* ⇒**вжима́ться**) to press o.s. (into).

вжива́|ться, юсь *impf. of* ⇒**вжи́ться**

вжив|и́ть, лю́, и́шь *pf.* (*of* ⇒**~ля́ть**) (*med.*) to implant.

вживл|я́ть, я́ю, я́ешь *impf. of* ⇒**вживи́ть**

вжима́|ть(ся), ю(сь) *impf. of* ⇒**вжа́ть(ся)**

вжи́|ться, ву́сь, вёшься *pf.* (**в** + *a.*; *coll.*) to get used (to), grow accustomed (to); **он с трудо́м ~вётся в вое́нную жизнь** he will find it hard to get used to army life; **в. в роль** to get into a role.

взад *adv.* (*coll.*) back; **в. и вперёд**

backwards and forwards, to and fro; **ни в. ни вперёд** motionless, not moving.

взаи́мност|ь, и *f.* reciprocity; return (*of affection*); **отвеча́ть кому́-н. ~ью** to reciprocate s.o.'s feelings, return s.o.'s love; **любо́вь без ~и** unrequited love.

взаи́м|ный (~ен, ~на) *adj.* mutual, reciprocal.

взаимовы́год|ный (~ен, ~на) *adj.* mutually beneficial.

взаимовы́ручк|а, и *f.* mutual help.

взаимоде́йстви|е, я *nt.* (*связь*) interaction; (*mil.*) co-operation, co-ordination.

взаимоде́йств|овать, ую *impf.* to interact; (*mil.*) to co-operate.

взаимоотноше́ни|е, я *nt.* interrelation; (*pl.*) relationship(s), relation(s).

взаимопо́мощ|ь, и *f.* mutual aid; mutual assistance; **ка́сса ~и** credit union.

взаимопонима́ни|е, я *nt.* mutual understanding.

взаимосвя́з|ь, и *f.* interrelationship.

взаймы́ *adv.*: **взять в.** to borrow; **дать в.** to lend, loan.

взалка́|ть, ю *pf.* (*obs.*) to hunger (for) (*+g. or +inf.; fig., now usu. iron.*).

взаме́н *prep.+g.* (*вместо*) instead (of); (*в обмен на что-то*) in return (for), in exchange (for).

взаперти́ *adv.* **1** (*под замком*) under lock and key. **2** (*в уединении*) in seclusion.

взапра́вду *adv.* (*coll.*) in truth, indeed.

вза́пуски *adv.*: **бе́гать в.** to chase one another.

взасо́с *adv.*: **целова́ться в.** (*coll.*) to exchange long-drawn-out kisses.

взатя́жку *adv.* **кури́ть в.** (*coll.*) to inhale (*in smoking*).

взахлёб *adv.* (*coll.*) eagerly, with gusto.

взаше́й *adv.* (*coll.*): **вы́гнать в.** to chuck out.

взба́дрива|ть, ю *impf. of* ⇒**взбодри́ть**

взбаламу́|тить, чу, тишь *pf. of* ⇒**баламу́тить**

взба́лмошный *adj.* (*coll.*) unbalanced, eccentric.

взба́лтывани|е, я *nt.* shaking (up).

взба́лтыва|ть, ю *impf. of* ⇒**взболта́ть**

взбега́|ть, ю *impf.* (*of* ⇒**взбежа́ть**) to run up; **в. на́ гору** to run up a hill; **в. по ле́стнице** to run upstairs.

взбе|жа́ть, гу́, жи́шь, гу́т *pf. of* ⇒**~га́ть**

взбелен|и́ться, ю́сь и́шься *pf.* (**на**+*a.*; *coll.*) to become enraged (with).

взбе|си́ть(ся), шу́(сь), ~сишь(ся) *pf. of* ⇒**беси́ть(ся)**

взбива́|ть, ю *impf. of* ⇒**взбить**

взбира́|ться, юсь *impf. of* ⇒**взобра́ться**

взби́т|ый (~, ~а) *p.p.p. of* ⇒**~ь**; **~ые сли́вки** whipped cream.

вз|бить, обью́, обьёшь *pf.* (*of* ⇒**~бива́ть**) **1** (*яйца*) to beat (up); **в. сли́вки** to whip cream. **2** (*подушку*) to fluff up.

взбодр|и́ть, ю *pf.* (*of* ⇒**взба́дривать**) to cheer up; to encourage.

взболта́|ть, ю *pf.* (*of* ⇒**взба́лтывать**) to shake (up) (*liquids*).

взбороз|ди́ть, жу́, ди́шь *pf.* to furrow.

взборон|и́ть, ю́, и́шь *pf. of* ⇒**борони́ть**

взборон|ова́ть, у́ю *pf. of* ⇒**боронова́ть**

взбра́сыва|ть, ю *impf. of* ⇒**взбро́сить**

взбреда́|ть, ю *impf. of* ⇒**взбрести́**

взбре|сти́, ду́, дёшь, *past* **взбрёл, ~ла́** *pf.* (*of* ⇒**~да́ть**) (**на**+*a.*; *coll.*) to trudge (up); **в. в го́лову, на ум** to come into one's head; **ему́ ~ло́ на ум, что все его́ ненави́дят** he got it into his head that everyone hated him.

взбро́|сить, шу, сишь *pf.* (*of* ⇒**взбра́сывать**) (*coll.*) to throw up, toss up.

взбудора́ж|ить, у, ишь *pf. of* ⇒**будора́жить**

взбунт|ова́ть(ся), у́ю(сь) *pf. of* ⇒**бунтова́ть(ся)**

взбух|а́ть, а́ет *impf. of* ⇒**~нуть**

взбу́х|нуть, нет *past* **~, ~ла** *pf.* (*of* ⇒**~а́ть**) to swell out.

взбу́чк|а, и *f.* (*coll.*) **1** (*побои*) thrashing, beating. **2** (*выговор*) dressing-down.

взва́лива|ть, ю *impf. of* ⇒**взвали́ть**

взвал|и́ть, ю́ ~ишь *pf.* (*of* ⇒**~ивать**) to load, lift (onto); **в. мешо́к на́ спину** to hoist a pack onto one's back; **всю рабо́ту ~или на но́вого учи́теля** (*coll.*) the new teacher was loaded with all the work; **всю вину́ ~или на него́** he was made to shoulder all the blame.

взве́|сить, шу, сишь *pf.* (*of* ⇒**~шивать** *and* **ве́шать**) (*груз*) to weigh; (*fig.*) (*варианты*) to weigh, consider.

взве|сти́, ду́, дёшь, *past* **~л, ~ла́** *pf.* (*of* ⇒**взводи́ть**) **1** (*глаза, взгляд*) to raise; (*помочь подняться наверх*) to lead up, take up; **в. куро́к** to cock a gun. **2** (**на**+*a.*) to level (at, against); **на генера́ла ~ли́ обвине́ние в пораже́нии** blame for the defeat was laid on the general.

взвес|ь, и *f.* (*chem.*) suspension.

взве́шен|ный (~, ~а) *adj.* carefully thought out; **во ~ном состоя́нии** (*fig.*) in suspense.

взве́шивани|е, я *nt.* weighing.

взве́шива|ть, ю *impf. of* ⇒**взве́сить**

взвива́|ть(ся), ю(сь) *impf. of* ⇒**взви́ть(ся)**

взви́|деть, жу, дишь *pf. only in phr.* **све́та не в.** (*coll.*) to see stars.

взвизг, а *m.* (*coll.*) scream; yelp (*of a dog*).

взви́згива|ть, ю *impf. and freq. of* ⇒**взви́згнуть**

взви́згн|уть, у, ешь *pf.* to scream, cry out; (*собака*) to yelp.

взвин|ти́ть, чу́, ти́шь *pf.* (*of* ⇒**взви́нчивать**) (*coll.*) (*нервы*) to excite, work up; **в. це́ны** to inflate prices.

взви́нчен|ный (~, ~а) *p.p.p. of* ⇒**взвинти́ть** *and adj.* excited, worked up; **не́рвы у него́ ~ы** he is on edge; **~ные це́ны** inflated prices.

взви́нчива|ть, ю *impf. of* ⇒**взвинти́ть**

взвить, взовью́, взовьёшь *pf.* (*of* ⇒**взвива́ть**) to raise.

взви́ться, взовью́сь, взовьёшься *pf.* (*of* ⇒**взвива́ться**) **1** (*взлететь*) to fly up, soar; (*о флагах*) to be raised, go up; **за́навес взви́лся ро́вно в во́семь часо́в** the curtain went up at eight o'clock exactly. **2** (*coll.*) (*рассердиться*) to fly into a temper.

взвод[1], а *m.* (*mil.*) platoon.

взвод[2], а *m.* (cocking) notch (*of guns*); **на боево́м ~е** cocked; **на ~е** (*coll.*) (*слегка пьян*) tipsy; (*в состоянии нервного возбуждения*) worked up, on edge.

взво|ди́ть, жу́, ~дишь *impf. of* ⇒**взвести́**

взво́дн|ый, ого *m.* platoon commander.

взволно́ван|ный (~, ~на) *adj.* anxious, worried; (*от счастья*) excited.

взволн|ова́ть, у́ю *pf. of* ⇒**волнова́ть**

взволн|ова́ться, у́юсь *pf. of* ⇒**волнова́ться**

взво́|ю, ешь *see* ⇒**взвыть**

взвыва́|ть, ю *impf. of* ⇒**взвыть**

взв|ыть, о́ю, о́ешь *pf.* (*of* ⇒**~ыва́ть**) to howl.

взгляд, а *m.* **1** (*выражение глаз*) look; (*быстрый*) glance; (*пристальный*) gaze, stare; **бро́сить в.** (**на**+*a.*) to glance (at); **останови́ть в.** (**на**+*p.*) to rest one's gaze (on); **на в.** to judge from appearances; **на пе́рвый в., с пе́рвого ~а** at first sight. **2** (*мнение*) view; opinion; **на мой в.** in my opinion, as I see it.

взгля́дыва|ть, ю *impf. of* ⇒**взгляну́ть**

взгльян|у́ть, у́, ~ешь *pf.* (*of* ⇒**взгля́дывать**) (**на**+*a.*) to look (at); (*быстро*) to cast a glance (at); **в. на что-н. серьёзно** (*fig.*) to take a serious view of sth.

взго́рь|е, я *nt.* hillock.

взгре́|ть, ю, ешь *pf.* (*coll.*) (*побить*) to thrash; (*fig.*) (*выругать*) to give it hot.

взгроможда́|ть, ю *impf. of* ⇒**взгромозди́ть**

взгроможда́|ться, юсь *impf. of* ⇒**взгромозди́ться**

взгромоз|ди́ть, жу́, ди́шь *pf.* (*of* ⇒**взгроможда́ть**) (*coll.*) to pile up.

взгромоз|ди́ться, жу́сь, ди́шься *pf.* (*of* ⇒**взгроможда́ться**) (*coll.*) to clamber up.

взгрустн|у́ть, у́, ёшь *pf.* (*coll.*) to feel sad.

взгрустн|у́ться, ётся *pf.* (*impers.*,

+*d.*; *coll.*) to feel sad; **ему́ ~у́лось** he feels sad.

вздёргива|ть, ю *impf. of* ⇒**вздёрнуть**

вздёрнут|ый (~, ~а) *p.p.p. of* ⇒**~ь; в. нос** snub nose.

вздёрн|уть, у, ешь *pf.* (*coll.*) **1** (*поднять*) to hitch up; to jerk up. **2** (*coll.*) (*вешать*) to string up.

вздор, а *no pl., m.* (*coll.*) nonsense; **городи́ть, моло́ть в.** to talk nonsense.

вздо́р|ить, ю, ишь *impf.* (*of* ⇒**по~**) (*coll.*) to squabble.

вздо́р|ный (~ен, ~на) *adj.* (*coll.*) **1** (*глупый*) foolish, stupid **2** (*сварливый*) cantankerous, quarrelsome.

вздорожа́ни|е, я *nt.* rise in price.

вздорожа́|ть, ю *pf. of* ⇒**дорожа́ть**

вздох, а *m.* sigh; deep breath; **испусти́ть после́дний в.** to breathe one's last.

вздохн|у́ть, у́, ёшь *pf.* (*of* ⇒**вздыха́ть**) **1** to sigh. **2** (*coll.*) (*отдохнуть*) to take a breather. **3**: **в. свобо́дно** to breathe freely; to relax (*after having been frightened*).

вздра́гива|ть, ю *impf.* (*of* ⇒**вздро́гнуть**) to shudder, quiver.

вздремн|у́ть, у́, ёшь *pf.* (*coll.*) to have a nap, doze.

вздремн|у́ться, ётся *pf.* (*impers.*, +*d.*; *coll.*): **по́сле еды́ ему́ ~у́лось** after the meal he dozed off.

вздро́гн|уть, у, ешь *pf.* (*of* ⇒**вздра́гивать**) to start; to wince, flinch.

вздува́|ть, ю *impf. of* ⇒**вздуть**[1]

взду́ма|ть, ю *pf.* (+*inf.*; *coll.*) to take it into one's head; **не ~й(те)** don't even think of it; don't you dare; **не ~йте ныря́ть здесь!** don't even think of diving in here!

взду́ма|ться, ется *pf.* (*impers.*, +*d.*; *coll.*) to take it into one's head; **ему́ ~лось пое́хать в Аме́рику** he took it into his head to go to America.

взду́ти|е, я *nt.* (*med.*) swelling.

взду́т|ый (~, ~а) *p.p.p. of* ⇒**~ь**[1] *and adj.* swollen; (*цены*) inflated.

взду́|ть[1]**, ю, ешь** *pf.* (*of* ⇒**вздува́ть**) **1** (*мяч*) to blow up, inflate. **2** (*цены*) to inflate.

взду́|ть[2]**, ю, ешь** *pf.* (*coll.*) to thrash, give a thrashing (to).

взду́|ться, ется, ются *pf.* **1** (*о щеке, парусах*) to swell. **2** (*coll.*) (*о ценах*) to shoot up.

вздыб|ить, лю, ишь *pf.* (*of* ⇒**взды́бливать**) **1** (*волосы*) to make stand on end. **2** (*коня*) to make rear.

взды́б|иться, ится, ятся *pf.* (*of* ⇒**взды́бливаться**) **1** (*о волосах*) to stand on end. **2** (*о коне*) to rear.

взды́блива|ть(ся), ю, ет(ся) *impf. of* ⇒**взды́бить(ся)**

вздыма́|ть, ю *impf.* to raise.

вздыма́|ться, ется *impf.* to rise; **~лась мгла над о́зером** mist was rising over the lake.

вздыха́|ть, ю *impf.* (*of* ⇒**вздохну́ть**) **1** to breathe; to sigh. **2** (**о**+*p.*, **по**+*d.*) (*тосковать*) to pine (for); to long, sigh (for); (*по девушке*) to be in love (with).

взима́ни|е, я *nt.* levy, collection, raising.

взима́|ть, ю *impf.* (*налог, штраф*) to levy, collect, raise.

взира́|ть, ю *impf.* (**на**+*a.*) **1** (*obs.*) to look (at), gaze (at). **2**: **не ~я на** in spite of, notwithstanding; **не ~я на ли́ца** without respect of persons; objectively.

взла́мыва|ть, ю *impf. of* ⇒**взлома́ть**

взлеза́|ть, ю *impf. of* ⇒**взлезть**

взлез|ть, у, ешь, *past* **~, ~ла** *pf.* (*of* ⇒**~а́ть**) to climb up.

взлеле́|ять, ю, ешь *pf. of* ⇒**леле́ять**

взлёт, а *m.* (*птицы*) (upward) flight (*also fig.*); (*самолёта*) take-off; **в. фанта́зии** flight of fancy.

взлета́|ть, ю *impf. of* ⇒**взлете́ть**

взле|те́ть, чу́, ти́шь *pf.* (*of* ⇒**~та́ть**) (*птица*) to fly up; (*самолёт*) to take off; **в. по ле́стнице** to fly upstairs; **в. на во́здух** to explode, blow up.

взлёт|ный *adj. of* ⇒**~**; (*aeron.*): **~ная доро́жка** runway; **~но-поса́дочная полоса́** landing strip.

взли́з|а, ы (*coll.*) bald patch (*above the temples*).

взлом, а *m.* (*сейфа*) breaking (into); (*двери*) forcing; **кра́жа со ~ом** house-breaking.

взлома́|ть, ю *pf.* (*of* ⇒**взла́мывать**) to break open, force; (*разворотить*) to smash; **в. замо́к** to force a lock; (*comput.*) to hack into.

взло́мщик, а *m.* burglar, house-breaker; **компью́терный в.** hacker.

взлохма́|тить, чу, тишь *pf. of* ⇒**лохма́тить**

взлохма́|ченный (~чен, ~чена) *p.p.p. of* ⇒**~тить** *and adj.* tousled; dishevelled.

взлюб|и́ть, лю́, ~ишь *pf., only with neg.*; **не в. с пе́рвого взгля́да** to take an instant dislike (to).

взман|и́ть, ю́, и́шь *pf. of* ⇒**мани́ть** 2

взмах, а *m.* (*руки*) wave; (*крыльев*) flap, flapping; (*весла*) stroke; **одни́м ~ом** at one stroke.

взма́хива|ть, ю *impf. of* ⇒**взмахну́ть**

взмахн|у́ть, у́, ёшь *pf.* (+*i.*) (*рукой*) to wave; (*крылом*) flap.

взметн|у́ть, у́, ёшь *pf.* (*of* ⇒**взмётывать**) (+*i.*) to throw up, fling up; **в. рука́ми** to throw up one's hands.

взметн|у́ться, у́сь ёшься *pf.* to leap up, fly up.

взмётыва|ть, ю *impf. of* ⇒**взметну́ть**

взмётыва|ться, юсь *impf. of* ⇒**взметну́ться**

взмол|и́ться, ю́сь, ~ишься *pf.* (**о**+*p.*) to beg (for).

взмо́рь|е, я *nt.* sea-shore; seaside.

взмо|сти́ться, щу́сь, сти́шься *pf.* (*coll.*) (**на**+*a.*) to clamber (onto); (**на**+*p.*) to perch (on).

взму|ти́ть, чу́, ти́шь *pf. of* ⇒**мути́ть**

взмыва́|ть, ю *impf. of* ⇒**взмыть**

взмы́лива|ть(ся), ю(сь) *impf. of* ⇒**взмы́лить(ся)**

взмы́л|ить, ю, ишь *pf.* to cause to foam, lather.

взмы́л|иться, юсь, ишься *pf.* to foam (*intrans.*), froth.

взмы|ть, о́ю, о́ешь *pf.* (*of* ⇒**~ыва́ть**) to soar (up).

взнос, а *m.* (*платёж*) payment; (*членский*) fee, dues; **вступи́тельный в.** membership fee; **очередно́й в.** instalment.

взнузда́|ть, ю *pf.* to bridle.

взну́здыва|ть, ю *impf. of* ⇒**взнузда́ть**

взобра́|ться, взберу́сь, взберёшься, *past* **~лся, ~ла́сь** *pf.* (*of* ⇒**взбира́ться**) (**на**+*a.*) to climb (up), clamber (up).

взобь|ю́, ёшь *see* ⇒**взбить**

взовь|ю́, ёшь *see* ⇒**взвить**

взо|йти́, йду́, йдёшь, *past* **~шёл, ~шла́,** *p.p.* **~ше́дший** *pf.* (*of* ⇒**всходи́ть** *and* **восходи́ть**) **1** (**на**+*a.*) to ascend, mount. **2** (*солнце; тесто*) to rise. **3** (*семена*) to come up.

взор, а *m.* look; glance.

взорв|а́ть, у́, ёшь *pf.* (*of* ⇒**взрыва́ть**) **1** (*здание*) to blow up; (*бомбу*) to detonate. **2** (*fig.*) (*рассердить*) to exasperate, madden; (*impers.*): **его́ ~а́ло, когда́ они́ сообщи́ли о свое́й помо́лвке** he exploded when they announced their engagement.

взорв|а́ться, у́сь, ёшься *pf.* (*of* ⇒**взрыва́ться**) (*о бомбе, газе*) to explode; (*о здании*) to blow up; (*fig.*) (*о человеке*) to blow up, explode.

взо|шёл, шла́ *see* ⇒**~йти́**

взра|сти́ть, щу́, сти́шь *pf.* (*растения*) to grow, cultivate; (*воспитывать*) to bring up, nurture.

взра́щива|ть, ю *impf. of* ⇒**взрасти́ть**

взра|щу́, сти́шь *see* ⇒**~сти́ть**

взрев|е́ть, у́, ёшь *pf.* to let out a roar.

взре́ж|у, ешь *see* ⇒**взре́зать**

взре́|зать, жу, жешь *pf.* to cut open.

взреза́|ть, ю *impf. of* ⇒**взре́зать**

взре́зыва|ть, ю *impf.* = **взреза́ть**

взро́сл|ый *adj.* grown-up, adult; *as n.* **в., ~ого** *m.*; **~ая, ~ой** *f.*

взрыв, а *m.* explosion; (*fig.*) burst, outburst; **в. аплодисме́нтов** burst of applause; **«Большо́й в.»** the Big Bang.

взрыва́тел|ь, я *m.* detonator.

взрыва́|ть[1]**, ю** *impf. of* ⇒**взорва́ть**

взрыва́|ть[2] *impf. of* ⇒**взрыть**

взрыва́|ться, юсь *impf. of* ⇒**взорва́ться**

взрывни́к, а́ *m.* explosives expert; shotfirer.

взрывн|о́й *adj.* **1** explosive; **~а́я волна́** blast. **2** (*ling.*) plosive.

взрывоопа́сн|ый *adj.*: **~ая ситуа́ция** explosive situation.

взрывча́тк|а, и *f.* (*coll.*) explosive.

взры́вчат|ый *adj.* explosive; **~ое веществó** explosive.

взр|ы́ть, óю, óешь *pf.* (*of* ⇒**~ыва́ть²**) to plough up, turn up.

взрыхл|и́ть, ю́, и́шь *pf. of* ⇒**рыхли́ть**

взрыхля́|ть, ю *impf. of* ⇒**взрыхли́ть**

взъёбк|а, и *f.* (*vulg.*) bollocking.

взъеда́|ться, юсь *impf. of* ⇒**взъе́сться**

взъезжа́|ть, ю *impf. of* ⇒**взъе́хать**

взъерепе́н|иться, юсь ишься *pf. of* ⇒**ерепе́ниться**

взъеро́шен|ный (~, ~а) *p.p.p. of* ⇒**взъеро́шить** *and adj.* tousled, dishevelled.

взъеро́шива|ть(ся), ю(сь) *impf. of* ⇒**взъеро́шить(ся)**

взъеро́ш|ить, у, ишь *pf.* (*of* ⇒**~ивать**) (*coll.*) to tousle, rumple.

взъеро́ш|иться, усь, ишься *pf.* (*of* ⇒**~иваться**) (*coll.*) to rumple one's hair; to become dishevelled.

взъ|е́сться, е́мся, е́шься, е́стся, еди́мся, еди́тесь, едя́тся, *past* **~е́лся** *pf.* (*of* ⇒**~еда́ться**) (**на** + *a.*; *coll.*) to pitch into, go for (*fig.*).

взъе́|хать, ду, дешь *pf.* (*of* ⇒**~зжа́ть**) to mount, ascend (*in a vehicle or on an animal*).

взыва́|ть, ю *impf. of* ⇒**воззва́ть**

взыгра́|ть, ю *pf.* **1** (*прийти в весёлое состояние*) to leap (for joy); **се́рдце во мне ~ло** my heart leapt. **2** (*прийти в бурное состояние*) to become disturbed; **мо́ре ~ло** the sea grew rough.

взыска́ни|е, я *nt.* **1** (*выговор*) reprimand; (*наказание*) penalty; punishment; **наложи́ть в. на** (+*a.*) to penalize; **подве́ргнуться ~ю** to incur a penalty. **2** (*штрафа*) exaction; (*долга*) recovery; **пода́ть на кого́-н. ко ~ю** (*leg.*) to proceed against s.o. (*for recovery of debt, etc.*).

взыска́тел|ьный (~ен, ~ьна) *adj.* (*требовательный*) exacting; (*публика*) demanding; (*строгий*) severe.

взы|ска́ть, щу́, ~щешь *pf.* (*of* ⇒**~скивать**) **1** (*штраф*) to exact; (*долг*) to recover. **2** (**с** + *g.*) to call to account; **не ~щи́(те)!** (*coll.*) please forgive (me)!; don't be hard on (me)!

взы́скива|ть, ю *impf. of* ⇒**взыска́ть**

взыску́ющий *adj.*: **~ ум** questioning mind.

взы|щу́, ~щешь *see* ⇒**~ска́ть**

взя́ти|е, я *nt.* taking; (*крепости*) capture; (*власти*) seizure.

взя́тк|а, и *f.* **1** bribe; backhander. **2** (*cards*) trick; **с него́ ~и гла́дки** (*coll.*) he isn't going to take responsibility.

взя́точник, а *m.* bribe-taker.

взя́точни|ца, цы *f. of* ⇒**~к**

взя́точничеств|о, а *nt.* bribery, bribe-taking.

взя|ть, возьму́, возьмёшь, *past* **~л, ~ла́, ~ло** *pf.* (*of* ⇒**брать**) **1** *see* ⇒**брать. 2** (*coll.*) (*думать*): **с чего́/отку́да ты взял?** what makes you think so? **3**: **в. да, в. и, в. да и...** (*coll.*) to do sth. suddenly; **он ~л да убежа́л** he up and ran; **он возьми́ да скажи́** he up and spoke. **4**: **чёрт возьми́!** (*coll.*) devil, deuce take it! **5**: **ни дать ни в.** (*coll.*) exactly, neither more nor less. **6**: **взять/возьми́те студе́нтов: их фина́нсовое положе́ние незави́дное** take students, their financial situation is unenviable.

взя́|ться, возьму́сь, возьмёшься, *past* **взя́лся, ~ла́сь, взя́ло́сь** *pf.* (*of* ⇒**бра́ться**): **отку́да ни возьми́сь** (*coll.*) from nowhere, out of the blue.

виаду́к, а *m.* viaduct.

вибра́тор, а *m.* vibrator.

вибрафо́н, а *m.* (*mus.*) vibraphone.

вибра́ци|я, и *f.* vibration.

вибри́р|овать, ую *impf.* to vibrate.

вива́ри|й, я *m.* vivarium.

виве́рр|а, ы *f.* (*zool.*) civet.

вивисе́кци|я, и *f.* vivisection.

вигва́м, а *m.* wigwam.

вид¹, а *m.* **1** (*внешность*) air, look; appearance; aspect; **у вас хоро́ший в.** you look well; **у него́ был мра́чный в.** he looked gloomy; **сде́лать в., бу́дто** to make it appear that, pretend that; **не показа́ть/пода́ть ~у** to not show; **не показа́л ~у, что оби́жен** he didn't show that he was offended; **для ~у** for the sake of appearances; **на в., с ~у** in appearance; **знать по ~у** to know by sight; **под ~ом** (+*g.*) under the guise (of); **ни под каки́м ~ом** on no account. **2** (*состояние*) shape, form; condition; **в хоро́шем ~е** in good condition/shape. **3** (*панорама*) view; **ко́мната с ~ом на го́ры** room with a view of the mountains; **в. сбо́ку** side-view; **откры́тка с ~ом** picture postcard. **4** (*pl.*) (*перспективы*) prospect; **~ы на бу́дущее** prospects for the future; **име́ть ~ы на** (+*a.*) to have designs on. **5** (*поле зрения*) sight; **потеря́ть и́з ~у** to lose sight (of); **упусти́ть и́з ~у** (*fig.*) to lose sight (of), fail to take into account; **на ~у́ у** (+*g.*) within sight of; **быть на ~у́** to be in the public eye; **при ~е** (+*g.*) at the sight (of); **в ~у́** (+*g.*) in sight (of); **в ~у́ того́, что** as, since, seeing that; **име́ть в ~у́** (*i*) to plan, intend, (*ii*) to mean; **что вы име́ли в ~у́, говоря́ э́то?** what did you mean when you said that?, (*iii*) to bear in mind; **име́й(те) в ~у́** bear in mind, don't forget; **име́ться в ~у́** (*i*) to be intended, be envisaged, (*ii*) to be meant.

вид², а *m.* **1** (*biol.*) species; **исчеза́ющий в.** endangered *or* threatened species. **2** (*тип*) type, kind. **3** (*gram.*) aspect; **соверше́нный, несоверше́нный в.** perfective, imperfective aspect.

вида́к, а́ *m.* (*coll.*) video recorder, VCR.

ви́дан|ный (~, ~а) *p.p.p. of* ⇒**вида́ть; ~ное ли э́то де́ло?** have you ever heard of such a thing?; **где э́то ~о?** can that be possible?; whatever next!

вида́|ть, ю *impf.* (*of* ⇒**у~**) (*coll.*) to see; **их не в.** they are nowhere to be seen; **ничего́ подо́бного я не ~л** I have never seen such a thing; **в., она́ у́мная** she must be clever.

вида́|ться, юсь *impf.* (*of* ⇒**по~**) (**с** + *i.*; *coll.*) to meet; to see one another.

ви́дени|е, я *nt.* vision, outlook.

виде́ни|е, я *nt.* vision, apparition.

ви́део *nt. indecl.* video (recorder, film, cassette).

видео... *comb. form* video-.

видеоза́пис|ь, и *f.* video recording.

видеоигр|а́, ы́, *pl.* **~ы** *f.* video game.

видеока́мер|а, ы *f.* video camera, camcorder.

видеокассе́т|а, ы *f.* video cassette.

видеокли́п, а *m.* advertising video.

видеоконфере́нци|я, и *f.* videoconference.

видеоле́нт|а, ы *f.* videotape.

видеомагнитофо́н, а *m.* video recorder.

видеоплёнк|а, и *f.* videotape.

видеопрока́т, а *m.* video rental.

видеоте́к|а, и *f.* video library.

видеотелефо́н, а *m.* videophone.

видеофи́льм, а *m.* video film.

ви́|деть, жу, дишь *impf.* (*of* ⇒**у~**) to see; **в. кого́-н. наскво́зь** to see through s.o.; **в. во сне** to dream (of); **его́ то́лько и ~дели** (*coll.*) he was gone in a flash; **~дишь (ли); ~дите (ли)** you see; **вот уви́дишь** (*coll.*) you'll see; **там уви́дим** we'll see.

ви́|деться, жусь, дишься *impf.* **1** (*встречаться*) to see one another; (**с** + *i.*) to meet with. **2** (*осознаваться*): **вы́ход ~дится в рефо́рмах** reforms are viewed as the solution. **3** (*pf.* **при~**) to appear; **ему́ ~делся стра́шный сон** he had a terrifying dream.

ви́дик, а *m.* (*coll.*) video (recorder).

ви́димо *adv.* evidently, apparently.

ви́димо-неви́димо *adv.* (*coll.*) in immense quantity; **наро́ду бы́ло в.-н** there was an immense crowd.

ви́димост|ь, и *f.* **1** (*различаемость*) visibility. **2** (*внешность*) outward appearance; **для ~и** (*coll.*) for show. **3**: **по (всей) ~и** to all appearances.

ви́дим|ый (~, ~а) *pres. part. pass. of* ⇒**ви́деть** *and adj.* **1** visible. **2** (*очевидный*) apparent, evident; **без ~ой причи́ны** for no apparent reason. **3** (*кажущийся*) apparent, seeming.

видне́|ться, ется, ются *impf.* to be visible.

ви́дно 1 *adv.* obviously, evidently; **она́, в., уста́ла** obviously she is tired; *as pred.* it is obvious, it is apparent; **в. бы́ло, как она́ расстро́илась** you could see how upset she was; **всем бы́ло в., что он лжёт** it was obvious to everyone, everyone could see that he was lying; **там в. бу́дет** (*coll.*) we'll see. **2** *adv. as pred.* visible; in sight; **берега́ ещё не́ было в.** the coast was not yet visible; **бы́ло хорошо́ в.** visibility was good.

ви́д|ный *adj.* **1** (**~ен, ~на́, ~но**) (*заметный*) visible; conspicuous. **2** (*важный*) distinguished, prominent. **3** (*coll.*) (*статный*) well-built, strapping; **в. мужчи́на** fine figure of a man.

видово́й[1] *adj. of* ⇒**вид**[1]; **в. фильм** travel film, travelogue.

видово́й[2] *adj.* (*of* ⇒**вид**[2]) **1** (*biol.*) species. **2** (*gram.*) aspectual.

видоизмене́ни|е, я *nt.* **1** (*действие*) modification, alteration. **2** (*разновидность*) type, variety.

видоизмен|и́ть, ю́, и́шь *pf.* (*of* ⇒**~я́ть**) to modify, alter.

видоизмен|и́ться, ю́сь, и́шься *pf.* (*of* ⇒**~я́ться**) to alter (*intrans.*).

видоизмен|я́ть(ся), я́ю(сь) *impf. of* ⇒**~и́ть(ся)**

видоиска́тел|ь, я *m.* view finder.

видообразова́ни|е, я *nt.* (*biol.*) formation of species.

ви́з|а, ы *f.* **1** visa. **2** (*пометка*) official signature.

визави́ 1 *adv.* opposite; **они́ сиде́ли в.** they sat opposite one another. **2** *n.*; *c.g. indecl.* the person opposite; **мы с мои́м в. завяза́ли разгово́р** I struck up a conversation with the person opposite.

Византи́|й, я *m.* (*hist.*) Byzantium.

византи́йский *adj.* Byzantine.

Византи́|я, и *f.* (*hist.*) Byzantine Empire.

визг, а *m.* (*человека*) scream, (*поросёнка*) squeal, (*собаки*) yelp, (*тормозов*) screech.

визгли́в|ый (~, ~а) *adj.* **1** (*голос*) shrill. **2** (*крикливый*) given to screaming, squealing, yelping.

визж|а́ть, у́, и́шь *impf.* to scream; to squeal; to yelp.

визи́р, а *m.* **1** (*mil.*) sight. **2** (*phot.*) view-finder.

визи́р|овать[1]**, ую** *impf. and pf.* (*pf. also* **за~**) to stamp.

визи́р|овать[2]**, ую** *impf. and pf.* to sight; to take a sight (on).

визи́р|ь, я *m.* vizier.

визи́т, а *m.* visit; call; **нанести́ в.** to make an (*official*) visit; **прийти́ с ~ом к кому́-н.** to visit s.o., pay s.o. a call.

визи́тк|а, и *f.* **1** (*сюртук*) morning coat. **2** (*карточка*) business card. **3** (*мужская сумочка*) men's handbag.

визи́т|ный *adj. of* ⇒**~**; **~ная ка́рточка** visiting card (*Br.*), calling card (*US*); (business) card.

визуа́л|ьный (~ен, ~ьна) *adj.* visual.

ви́к|а, и *no pl., f.* vetch.

вика́ри|й, я *m.* (*eccl.*) vicar.

ви́кинг, а *m.* Viking.

вико́нт, а *m.* viscount.

викториа́нский *adj.* Victorian.

виктори́н|а, ы *f.* quiz.

ви́лк|а, и *f.* **1** fork. **2** (*elec.*) plug.

ви́лл|а, ы *f.* villa.

вилообра́з|ный (~ен, ~на) *adj.* forked.

ви́л|ы, ~ *no sg.* pitchfork; **э́то ещё ~ами на воде́ пи́сано** (*coll.*) there is little probability of that.

вильн|у́ть, у́, ёшь *pf. of* ⇒**виля́ть** 1, 2

Ви́льнюс, а *m.* Vilnius.

виля́ни|е, я *nt.* **1** wagging. **2** (*fig.*) (*уклонение от прямого ответа*) prevarication; evasions.

виля́|ть, ю *impf.* **1** (*pf.* ⇒**вильну́ть**) to wag; **в. хвосто́м** to wag one's tail; **хвост у соба́ки всё вре́мя ~л** the dog's tail was wagging the whole time. **2** (*pf.* ⇒**вильну́ть**) (*coll.*) (*дорога*) to wind, turn sharply. **3** (*coll.*) (*уклоняться от прямого ответа*) to prevaricate; to be evasive.

вин|а́, ы́, *pl.* **~́ы** *f.* fault, guilt; (*причина*) blame; **моя́ в.** it is my fault; **не по их ~е́** through no fault of theirs; **поста́вить кому́-н. в ~у́** to accuse s.o. of, blame s.o. for; **свали́ть ~у́ (на** + *a.*) to lay the blame (on); **по ~е́** + *g.* because of.

виндсерфинг, а *m.* **1** (*спорт*) windsurfing. **2** (*доска*) windsurfer.

виндсерфинги́ст, а *m.* windsurfer.

винегре́т, а *m.* beetroot salad; (*fig.*) (*смесь*) mishmash.

вини́л, а *m.* vinyl.

вини́ловый *adj.* vinyl.

вини́тельный *adj.* (*gram.*): **в. паде́ж** accusative case.

вин|и́ть, ю́ и́шь *impf.* (**в** + *p.*) (*обвинять*) to accuse (of); (*считать виноватым*) to blame; **я ~ю́ его́ за наш прова́л** I blame him for our failure.

вин|и́ться, ю́сь, и́шься *impf.* (*of* ⇒**по~**) (**в** + *p.*; *coll.*) to confess (to).

ви́нкел|ь, я, *pl.* **~я́** *m.* (*tech.*) set-square.

виннока́менн|ый *adj.* (*chem.*) **~ая кислота́** tartaric acid.

ви́нн|ый *adj.* wine; winy; vinous; **в. ка́мень** (*chem.*) tartar; **~ая кислота́** tartaric acid; **в. спирт** alcohol.

вин|о́, а́, *pl.* **~́а** *nt.* wine.

винова́т|ый (~, ~а) *adj.* **1** (*взгляд*) guilty; (*человек*) guilty; to blame; **мы все ~ы в э́том** we are all to blame for this. **2**: **~!** sorry!

вино́вник, а *m.* culprit; **в. преступле́ния** perpetrator of a crime; **в. пожа́ра** arsonist; (*торжества, праздника*) cause, reason.

вино́вност|ь, и *f.* guilt.

вино́в|ный (~ен, ~на) *adj.* (**в** + *p.*) guilty (of); **призна́ть себя́ ~ным** to plead guilty.

виногра́д, а (у) *m.* **1** (*растение*) vine. **2** (*collect.*) (*ягоды*) grapes.

виногра́дарств|о, а *nt.* viticulture; wine-growing.

виногра́дар|ь, я *m.* wine-grower.

виногра́дин|а, ы *f.* (*coll.*) grape.

виногра́дник, а *m.* vineyard.

виногра́д|ный *adj. of* ⇒**~**; **~ная лоза́** vine; **в. сезо́н** vintage; **~ное су́сло** must.

виноде́л, а *m.* wine-maker.

виноде́ли|е, я *nt.* wine-making.

винoку́р, а *m.* distiller.

винокуре́ни|е, я *nt.* distillation.

виноку́р|енный *adj. of* ⇒**~е́ние; в. заво́д** distillery.

виноторго́в|ец, ца *m.* wine-merchant.

виноторго́вл|я, и *f.* wine-trade.

винт[1]**, а́** *m.* **1** (*стержень*) screw; **подъёмный в.** jack-screw; **упо́рный в.** stop screw; **установо́чный в.** adjusting set screw. **2** (*самолёта*) propeller. **3** (*спираль*) spiral; **ле́стница ~о́м** spiral staircase.

винт[2]**, а́** *m.* (*игра*) vint (*card-game*).

ви́нт|ик, а *m. dim. of* ⇒**~**[1]; **у него́ ~а не хвата́ет** (*coll.*) he has a screw loose somewhere.

вин|ти́ть, чу́, ти́шь *impf.* to screw up.

винто́вк|а, и *f.* rifle.

винт|ово́й *adj. of* ⇒**~**[1]; spiral; **~ова́я ле́стница** spiral staircase; **~ова́я наре́зка** spiral thread (*of screw*).

винтообра́з|ный (~ен, на) *adj.* spiral.

винторе́зный *adj.* (*tech.*) screw-cutting.

винче́стер, а *m.* (*comput.*) Winchester disk.

вин|чу́, ти́шь *see* ⇒**~ти́ть**

винье́тк|а, и *f.* vignette.

вио́л|а, ы *f.* viol; viola.

виолончели́ст, а *m.* cellist.

виолончели́ст|ка, ки *f. of* ⇒**~**

виолонче́л|ь, и *f.* cello.

ви́ра *int.* (*dockers' sl.*) lift!

вира́ж[1]**, а** *m.* (*phot.*) intensifier; **в.-фикса́ж** tone-fixing bath.

вира́ж[2]**, а́** *m.* **1** (*поворот*) turn; **круто́й в.** steep turn. **2** (*на треке*) bend, curve.

виртуа́л|ьный (~ен, ~ьна) *adj.* virtual; **~ьная реа́льность** (*comput.*) virtual reality.

виртуо́з, а *m.* virtuoso.

виртуо́зност|ь, и *f.* virtuosity.

виртуо́з|ный (~ен, на) *adj.* masterly, virtuosic.

вируле́нт|ный (~ен, ~на) *adj.* (*med.*) virulent.

ви́рус, а *m.* (*med.*) virus; bug, (*comput.*) virus.

ви́рус|ный *adj. of* ⇒**~**

вирусоло́ги|я, и *f.* virology.

вирусоноси́тел|ь, я *m.* (*med.*) carrier.

ви́рш|и, ей *no sg.* **1** (*liter.*) (Russian or Ukrainian) syllabic verses. **2** (*coll.*) (*плохие стихи*) doggerel.

ви́селиц|а, ы *f.* gallows, gibbet.

ви|се́ть, шу́, си́шь *impf.* to hang; to be suspended; **в. над** (+ *i.*) (*fig.*) to hang over; **в. на волоске́** to hang by a thread; **в. на ше́е у** (+ *g.*) (*coll.*) to be a burden on; **в. на телефо́не** (*coll.*) to talk a lot on the phone; **в. в во́здухе** to be up in the air.

ви́ски *nt. indecl.* whisky (*Br.*), whiskey (*US*).

виско́з|а, ы *f.* **1** (*tech.*) viscose. **2** (*искусственный шёлк*) rayon.

Ви́сл|а, ы *f.* the Vistula (*river*).

ви́смут, а *m.* (*chem.*) bismuth.

ви́сн|уть, у, ешь *impf.* (на+*p.*) to hang; to droop; **в. на ше́е у** (+*g.*) (*coll.*) to be a burden on; **в. на ком-н.** (*coll.*) to chase.

вис|о́к, ка́ *m.* (*anat.*) temple.

високо́сный *adj.*: **в. год** leap-year.

висо́чный *adj.* (*anat.*) temporal.

вист, а *m.* whist (*card-game*).

висю́льк|а, и *f.* (*coll.*) pendant.

вися́чий *adj.* hanging, pendent; **в. замо́к** padlock; **в. мост** suspension bridge.

витами́н, а *m.* vitamin.

витаминизи́р|овать, ую *impf. and pf.* to add vitamins to.

витами́н|ный *adj.* **1** *adj. of* ⇨**~**; **~ная недоста́точность** vitamin deficiency. **2** vitamin-rich *or* -packed.

витамин|о́зный = **~́ный**

вита́|ть, ю *impf.* (*obs.*) to be; (*носиться в вышине*) to hover; **он ~ет в ми́ре фанта́зий** he lives in a fantasy world; **в. в облака́х** to be up in the clouds; **смерть ~ла над ней** death was hovering over her.

витиева́т|ый (~, ~а) *adj.* flowery, ornate.

вит|о́й *adj.* twisted; spiral; **~а́я ле́стница** spiral staircase.

вит|о́к, ка́ *m.* **1** (*спирали*) turn, twist. **2** (*проволоки*) coil. **3** (*при полёте*) orbit. **4** (*fig.*) (*цикл*) round.

витра́ж, а *m.* stained-glass window.

витри́н|а, ы *f.* **1** (*в магазине*) (shop-) window. **2** (*в музее*) show-case.

ви|ть, вью, вьёшь, *past* **~л, ~ла́, ~́ло** *impf.* (*of* ⇨**с~**) to weave; **в. гнездо́** to build a nest; **в. верёвки из кого́-н.** (*coll.*) to twist round one's little finger.

ви́|ться, вьюсь, вьёшься, *past* **~лся, ~ла́сь, ~ло́сь** *impf.* (*of* ⇨**с~**) **1** (*растение*) to wind, twine. **2** (*волосы*) to curl, wave. **3** (*птица*) to hover, circle. **4** (*змея*) to writhe, twist. **5** (*пыль, дым*) to spiral up.

ви́тяз|ь, я *m.* (*poet., arch.*) knight; hero.

вихля́|ть, ю *impf.* (*coll.*) to reel.

вихля́|ться, юсь *impf.* (*coll.*) to wobble.

вих|о́р, ра́ *m.* forelock.

вихра́ст|ый (~, ~а) *adj.* (*coll.*) shaggy; shock-headed.

вихрево́й *adj.* (*phys.*) vortical.

вихр|ь, я *m.* **1** whirlwind; **сне́жный в.** blizzard. **2** (*fig.*) whirlwind, maelstrom.

ви́це-... *comb. form* vice-.

вице-адмира́л, а *m.* vice-admiral.

вице-коро́л|ь я́ *m.* viceroy.

вице-президе́нт, а *m.* vice-president.

вицмунди́р, а *m.* (*hist.*) uniform (*of civil-servants*).

ВИЧ *m. indecl.* (*abbr. of* ***ви́рус иммунодефици́та челове́ка***) (*med.*) HIV (*human immunodeficiency virus*); **вич-инфици́рованный** HIV-positive.

вишнёвк|а, и *f.* cherry brandy.

вишнёвый *adj.* **1** cherry; **в. сад** cherry orchard. **2** (*о цвете*) cherry-coloured (*Br.*), -colored (*US*), burgundy.

ви́ш|ня, ни, *g. pl.* **~ен** *f.* **1** (*дерево*) cherry-tree. **2** (*плод*) cherry; (*collect.*) cherries.

вишь (*contraction of* **ви́дишь**; *coll.*) look!; just look!; **в., что сде́лал!** look what he's done!

вка́лыва|ть, ю *impf.* **1** *impf. of* ⇨**вколо́ть**. **2** *impf. only* (*sl.*) to slave; to slog away.

вка́пыва|ть, ю *impf. of* ⇨**вкопа́ть**

вка|ти́ть, чу́, ~́тишь *pf.* (*of* ⇨**~́тывать**) **1** to roll into, onto; (*на колёсах*) to wheel in, into; **в. бо́чку в подва́л** to roll a barrel into a cellar. **2** (*fig., coll.*) (*укол*) to administer; (*выговор, двойку*) to give; **в. пощёчину** (+*d.*) to slap in the face.

вка|ти́ться, чу́сь, ~тишься *pf.* (*of* ⇨**~́тываться**) to roll in (*intrans.*); (*coll.*) (*вбежать*) to run in.

вка́тыва|ть(ся), ю(сь) *impf. of* ⇨**вкати́ть(ся)**

вкл. (*abbr. of* ***включи́тельно***) incl., including.

вклад, а *m.* **1** (*в банк*) deposit. **2** (*действие*) investment. **3** (*fig.*) contribution.

вкла́дк|а, и *f.* supplementary sheet, insert.

вклад|но́й 1 *adj. of* ⇨**~.** **2** supplementary, inserted; **в. лист** = **вкла́дка.**

вкла́дчик, а *m.* depositor, investor.

вкла́дчи|ца, цы *f. of* ⇨**~к**

вкла́дыва|ть, ю *impf. of* ⇨**вложи́ть**

вкла́д|ыш, а *m.* = **~ка**

вкле́ива|ть, ю *impf. of* ⇨**вкле́ить**

вкле́|ить, ю, ишь *pf.* (*of* ⇨**~ивать**) to paste in.

вкле́йк|а, и *f.* **1** (*действие*) sticking in. **2** (*вклеенный лист*) inset.

вкли́нива|ть(ся), ю(сь) *impf. of* ⇨**вклини́ть(ся)**

вкли́н|ить, ~ю́, ~и́шь *pf.* (*of* ⇨**вкли́нивать**) to wedge in; **в. сло́во** (*fig., coll.*) to put a word in.

вкли́н|иться, ~ю́сь, ~и́шься *pf.* (*of* ⇨ **вкли́ниваться**) (в+*a.*) to force one's way into; (*mil.*) to drive a wedge (into).

включ|а́ть(ся), а́ю(сь) *impf. of* ⇨**~и́ть(ся)**

включа́|я *pres. ger. of* ⇨**~ть;** *as prep.*+*a.* including.

включе́ни|е, я *nt.* **1** (в+*a.*) inclusion (in); **со ~ем** (+*g.*) including, with the inclusion of. **2** (*лампы, станка*) switching on, turning on.

включи́тельно *adv.* inclusive; **с пя́того по девя́тое в.** from the 5th to the 9th inclusive.

включ|и́ть, у́, и́шь *pf.* (*of* ⇨**~а́ть**) **1** (в+*a.*) to include (in); **в. в себя́** to include, comprise, take in; **в. в пове́стку дня** to enter on the agenda; **в. в спи́сок** to enter on a list. **2** (*tech.*) to switch on, turn on; (*в розетку*) to plug in; **в. ра́дио** to switch on the radio; **в. ско́рость** to engage a gear.

включ|и́ться, у́сь, и́шься *pf.* (*of* ⇨**~а́ться**) **1** (в+*a.*) to join (in), enter (into). **2** (*о свете, радио*) to come on.

вкола́чива|ть, ю *impf. of* ⇨**вколоти́ть**

вкол|оти́ть, очу́, ~о́тишь *pf.* (*of* ⇨**~а́чивать**) to knock in, hammer in (*also fig.*); **в. в го́лову** (+*d.*; *coll.*) to knock into s.o.'s head.

вкол|о́ть, ю́, ~́ешь *pf.* (*of* ⇨**вка́лывать**) (в+*a.*) to stick (in, into).

вкол|очу́, ~о́тишь *see* ⇨**~оти́ть**

вконе́ц *adv.* (*coll.*) completely, absolutely.

вко́пан|ный (~, ~а) *p.p.p. of* ⇨**вкопа́ть;** как **в.** rooted to the ground.

вкопа́|ть, ю *pf.* (*of* ⇨**вка́пывать**) to dig in.

вкорен|и́ть, ю́, и́шь *pf.* (*of* ⇨**~я́ть**) to inculcate.

вкорен|и́ться, и́тся, я́тся *pf.* (*of* ⇨**~я́ться**) to be inculcated; to take root.

вкореня́|ть(ся), ю, ет(ся) *impf. of* ⇨**вкорени́ть(ся)**

вкось *adv.* obliquely; slantwise; **вкривь и в.**, *see* ⇨**вкривь**

вкрад|у́сь, ёшься *see* ⇨**вкра́сться**

вкра́дчив|ый (~, ~а) *adj.* insinuating, ingratiating.

вкра́дыва|ться, юсь *impf. of* ⇨**вкра́сться**

вкра́п|ить, лю, ишь *pf.* (*of* ⇨**~ливать**) to sprinkle (with); (*fig.*) to intersperse (with); **он ~ил в речь цита́ты** he interspersed his speech with quotations.

вкра́плива|ть, ю *impf. of* ⇨**вкра́пить**

вкрапл|я́ть, я́ю *impf.* = **~ивать**

вкра́|сться, ду́сь, дёшься, *past* **~лся** *pf.* (*of* ⇨**~дываться**) to steal in, creep in; **в текст ~лось мно́го оши́бок** many mistakes have crept into the text; **в. в дове́рие к кому́-н.** to worm o.s., insinuate o.s. into s.o.'s confidence.

вкра́тце *adv.* briefly; succinctly.

вкривь *adv.* (*не прямо*) aslant; (*fig.*) wrongly, in a distorted manner; **в. и вкось** all over the place; (*fig., coll.*) indiscriminately.

вкруг = **вокру́г**

вкругову́ю *adv.* (*coll.*) round; **пусти́ть ча́шу в.** to send the cup round (*at banquets*).

вкру|ти́ть, чу́, ~́тишь *pf.* (*of* ⇨**~́чивать**) to screw in.

вкруту́ю *adv.* (*coll.*): **яйцо́ в.** hard-boiled egg; **свари́ть яйцо́ в.** to hard-boil an egg.

вкру́чива|ть, ю *impf. of* ⇨**вкрути́ть**

вкру|чу́, ~́тишь *see* ⇨**~ти́ть**

вку́пе *adv.* (с+*i.*) together (with).

вкус, а *m.* **1** taste (*also fig.*); **на чей-н. в., в чьём-н. ~́е** to s.o.'s taste; **э́то мне не по ~у** I don't like it; it's not to my taste; **кому́ как по ~у** each to his own; **о**

∼ах не спорят (*prov.*) tastes differ; **это дело ∼а** it is a matter of taste; **человек со ∼ом** a man of taste; **одеваться со ∼ом** to dress tastefully. **2** (*стиль*) manner, style; **во ∼е Ренессанса** in the Renaissance style.

вку|сить, шу, ∼сишь *pf.* (*of* ⇒**∼шать**) (*fig., poet.*) to taste, savour.

вкус|ный (∼ен, ∼на, ∼но) *adj.* tasty, delicious, good.

вкусов|ой *adj.* taste; gustatory; **∼ые вещества** flavouring substances.

вкуша|ть, ю *impf. of* ⇒**вкусить**

вку|шу, ∼сишь *see* ⇒**∼сить**

влаг|а, и *no pl., f.* moisture, liquid.

влагалищ|е, а *nt.* vagina.

влага|ть, ю *impf. of* ⇒**вложить**

владел|ец, ьца *m.* (*магазина*) owner, proprietor; (*предмета*) owner.

владел|ица, ицы *f. of* ⇒**∼ец**

владени|е, я *nt.* **1** ownership; possession; **в. имуществом** possession of property. **2** (*поместье*) estate; (*pl.*) possessions; **колониальные ∼я** colonies.

владе|ть, ю, ешь *impf.* (+*i.*) **1** (*иметь*) to own, possess. **2** (*подчинять себе*) to control; to be in possession (of); **в. собой** to control o.s.; **им ∼ют страсти** he is at the mercy of his passions. **3** (*fig.*) (*уметь пользоваться*) to have (a) command (of); to have the use (of); **в. пером** to wield a skilful pen; **она ∼ет шестью языками** she has a command of six languages; **он не ∼ет правой рукой** he has not the use of his right arm.

владык|а, и *m.* master, sovereign; (*eccl.*) member of higher orders of clergy (*bishop, archbishop or metropolitan*).

владычеств|о, а *nt.* dominion, sway.

владычеств|овать, ую *impf.* (**над**+*i.*) to hold sway, exercise dominion (over).

владычиц|а, ы *f.* **1** mistress, sovereign. **2**: **В.** (*eccl.*) Our Lady.

влажне|ть, ю, ешь *impf.* (*of* ⇒**по∼**) (*погода, воздух*) to become damp, humid; (*почва*) to become damp.

влажност|ь, и *f.* (*воздуха*) humidity; (*почвы*) dampness.

влаж|ный (∼ен, ∼на, ∼но) *adj.* (*воздух, климат*) humid, damp; (*простыня*) damp; (*глаза, лоб*) moist.

взламыва|ться, юсь *impf. of* ⇒**вломиться**

властв|овать, ую *impf.* (**над**+*i.*) to rule, hold sway (over).

властелин, а *m.* (*usu. fig.*) (*правитель*) ruler; (*хозяин*) lord, master.

властител|ь, я *m.* = **властелин**; (*fig.*): **в. дум** dominant influence.

власт|ный (∼ен, ∼на) *adj.* **1** (*характер, жест*) imperious, commanding; masterful; **∼ные структуры** authorities. **2** (**в**+*p.*; *leg.*) authoritative, competent; **я не ∼ен в этом деле** I have no competence to deal with this matter; **он не ∼ен изменить что-нибудь** he is powerless to change anything; **он не ∼ен над собой** he can't control his feelings, actions.

властолюб|ец, ца *m.* power-seeker.

властолюбив|ый (∼, ∼а) *adj.* power-loving; (*стремящийся к власти*) power-seeking.

властолюби|е, я *nt.* love of power; (*стремление к власти*) lust for power.

власт|ь, и, *pl.* **∼и, ∼ей** *f.* **1** (*политическая*) power; **прийти к ∼и** to come to power; **у ∼и** in power. **2** (*родительская*) power, authority; **во ∼и** (+*g.*) at the mercy (of), in the power (of); (*над чувствами*) control; (*pl.*) authorities; **местная в., в. на местах** local authority; **советская в.** (*hist.*) Soviet rule. **3**: **ваша в.** (*coll.*) as you like, it's up to you.

власяниц|а, ы *f.* hair shirt.

влач|ить, у, ишь *impf.* (*obs., poet.*) to drag; **в. жалкое существование** to lead/drag out a miserable existence.

влач|иться, усь, ишься *impf.* (*obs., poet.*) to drag o.s. along.

влево *adv.* to the left (*also fig., pol.*).

влеза|ть, ю *impf. of* ⇒**влезть**

влез|ть, у, ешь, *past* **∼, ∼ла** *pf.* (*of* ⇒**∼ать**) **1** (*в окно*) to climb in(to); (*на дерево*) to climb (up); (*на крышу*) to climb onto; **в. в долги** (*fig.*) to get into debt; **в. в душу** (+*g.*) to worm o.s. into s.o.'s confidence. **2** (*coll.*) (*сесть*) to get on, board; **в. в автобус** to get on the bus. **3** (*coll.*) (*уместиться*) to fit in, go in, go on; **все эти вещи не ∼ут в мою сумку** these things will not all go into my bag.

влеп|ить, лю, ∼ишь *pf.* to stick in, fasten in; (*coll.*): **в. пощёчину кому-н.** to slap s.o.'s face.

влепля|ть, ю *impf. of* ⇒**влепить**

влет|ать, аю *impf. of* ⇒**∼еть**

вле|теть, чу, тишь *pf.* (*of* ⇒**∼тать**) to fly in, into; (*fig., coll.*) to rush in, into; **в. в историю** to get into trouble; (*impers.*): **ему опять ∼тело** he is in trouble again.

влечени|е, я *nt.* (**к**+*d.*) attraction (to).

вле|чь, ку, чёшь, кут, *past* **влёк, ∼кла** *impf.* (*тащить*) to draw, drag; (*привлекать*) to attract; **в. за собой** to involve, entail.

вливани|е, я *nt.* (*med.*) infusion, injection.

влива|ть, ю *impf. of* ⇒**влить**

влипа|ть, ю *impf. of* ⇒**влипнуть**

влип|нуть, ну, нешь, *past* **∼, ∼ла** *pf.* (*coll.*) to get into a mess; to put one's foot in it; **в. в историю** to get into trouble.

вли|ть, волью, вольёшь, *past* **∼л, ∼ла, ∼ло** *pf.* (*of* ⇒**∼вать**) **1** to pour in; (*med.*) to infuse; (*fig.*) to instil; **в. силы/уверенность в кого-н.** to give s.o. strength/confidence. **2** (*добавить*) to bring in.

влияни|е, я *nt.* influence; **под ∼ем** (+*g.*) under the influence of; **оказать в. на** (+*a.*) to influence; **пользоваться ∼ем** to have influence, be influential.

влиятел|ьный (∼ен, ∼ьна) *adj.* influential.

влия|ть, ю *impf.* (*of* ⇒**по∼**) (**на**+*a.*) to influence, have an influence on; (*действовать*) to affect.

вложени|е, я *nt.* **1** enclosure. **2** (*fin.*) investment.

влож|ить, у, ∼ишь *pf.* (*of* ⇒**вкладывать** *and* **влагать**) **1** to put in, insert; (*в письмо*) to enclose (*with a letter*); **он ∼ил всю свою душу в работу** (*fig.*) he put his whole soul into his work. **2** (*fin.*) to invest.

влом|иться, люсь, ∼ишься *pf.* (*of* ⇒**вламываться**) to break in, into.

влопа|ться, юсь *pf.* (*coll.*) **1** (*влипнуть*) to get into a mess. **2** (*влюбиться*) to fall in love. **3** (*в лужу, грязь*) to tread in.

влюб|ить, лю, ∼ишь *pf.* (*of* ⇒**∼лять**) (**в**+*a.*) to make fall in love (with).

влюб|иться, люсь, ∼ишься *pf.* (*of* ⇒**∼ляться**) (**в**+*a.*) to fall in love (with).

влюблённост|ь, и *f.* love; being in love.

влюблён|ный (∼, ∼а) *p.p.p. of* ⇒**влюбить** *and adj.* **1** (*p.p.p.*) (*человек*) in love; **в. по уши** head over heels in love. **2** (*adj.*) (*взгляд*) loving; tender.

влюбля|ть, ю *impf. of* ⇒**влюбить**

влюбля|ться, юсь *impf. of* ⇒**влюбиться**

влюбчив|ый (∼, ∼а) *adj.* (*coll.*) amorous, susceptible.

вляпа|ться, юсь *pf.* (*coll.*) to plunge into; (*fig.*) **в. в историю** to get into a mess.

вм. (*abbr. of* ***вместо***) instead of; in place of.

вма|зать, жу, жешь *pf.* (*of* ⇒**вмазывать**) (*sl.*) (+*d.*) to hit.

вма|заться, жусь, жешься *pf.* (*of* ⇒**вмазываться**) (*sl.*) to inject drugs, shoot up.

вмазыва|ть(ся), ю(сь) *impf. of* ⇒**вмазать(ся)**

вмен|ить, ю, ишь *pf.* (*of* ⇒**∼ять**): **в. (что-н.) в вину** (+*d.*) to blame (sth.) on (s.o.); **в. в обязанность кому-н.** to impose as a duty on; **он ∼ил себе в обязанность чтение всех газет** he imposed on himself the duty of reading all the newspapers.

вменяемост|ь, и *f.* (*leg.*) responsibility; liability.

вменяем|ый (∼, ∼а) *adj.* (*leg.*) of sound mind.

вменя|ть, ю *impf. of* ⇒**вменить**

вместе *adv.* together; at the same time; **в. с** (+*i.*) together with; **в. с тем** at the same time, also; **но/а в. с тем** but.

вместилищ|е, а *nt.* receptacle.

вместимост|ь, и *f.* capacity.

вместител|ьный (∼ен, ∼ьна) *adj.* capacious; roomy.

вме|стить(ся), щу(сь), стишь(ся) *pf. of* ⇒**∼щать(ся)**

вместо *prep.* +*g.* instead of; in place of.

вмешательств|о, а *nt.* interference; (*pol., mil., med.*) intervention; **политика ∼а** interventionism.

вмеша|ть, ю *pf.* (*of* ⇒**вмешивать**) (**в**+*a.*) **1** (*добавить*) to mix in. **2** (*coll.,* *fig.*) (*впутать*) to mix up (in), implicate (in).

вмеш|а́ться, а́юсь *pf.* (*of* ⇒**∼́иваться**) (**в** + *a.*) (*вторгнуться*) to interfere (in), meddle (with); (*для пресечения нежелательных последствий*) to intervene (in); **полице́йский ∼а́лся в дра́ку** a policeman intervened in the fight.

вме́шива|ть, ю *impf. of* ⇒**вмеша́ть**

вме́шива|ться, юсь *impf. of* ⇒**вмеша́ться**

вмеща́|ть, ю *impf.* (*of* ⇒**вмести́ть**) **1** (*контейнер*) to contain; to hold; (*дом, зал*) to accommodate; **э́та бо́чка ∼ет пятьдеся́т ли́тров** this barrel holds fifty litres. **2** (**в** + *a.*) to put, place (in, into).

вмеща́|ться, юсь *impf.* (*of* ⇒**вмести́ться**) **1** to fit, go in; **ва́ши ту́фли не ∼ются в мой чемода́н** your shoes will not go in my case. **2** *pass. of* ⇒**∼ть** 2

вмиг *adv.* in an instant; in a flash.

вмина́|ть, ю *impf. of* ⇒**вмять**

ВМК *m. indecl.* (*abbr. of* ***внутрима́точный контрацепти́в***) IUD (*intrauterine* (*contraceptive*) *device*).

ВМФ *m. indecl.* (*abbr. of* ***вое́нно-морско́й флот***) Navy.

вмя́тин|а, ы *f.* dent.

вмять, вомну́, вомнёшь *pf.* (*of* ⇒**вмина́ть**) to press in.

внаём, внаймы́ *adv.*: **отда́ть в.** to let, hire out, rent; **взять в.** to hire, rent; **сдаётся в.** 'to let'.

внаки́дку *adv.* (*coll.*): over one's shoulders.

внакла́де *adv.* (*coll.*): **оста́ться в.** to come off loser; **не оста́ться в.** (**от** + *g.*) to be none the worse off (for).

внакла́дку *adv.* (*coll.*): **пить чай в.** to drink tea with sugar in (*opp.* **вприку́ску**).

внача́ле *adv.* at first, in the beginning.

вне *prep.* + *g.* outside; out of; **объяви́ть в. зако́на** to outlaw; **в. о́череди** out of turn; **в. себя́** beside o.s.; **в. вся́ких сомне́ний** beyond any doubt.

вне... *comb. form* extra-.

внебра́чный *adj.* extra-marital; **в. ребёнок** illegitimate child.

вневре́менный *adj.* timeless.

внедре́ни|е, я *nt.* (*методов*) introduction; (*привычки*) inculcation.

внедр|и́ть, ю, и́шь *pf.* (*of* ⇒**∼я́ть**) **1** (*привычку*) to inculcate, instil. **2** (*методы*) to introduce.

внедр|и́ться, ю́сь, и́шься *pf.* (*of* ⇒**∼я́ться**) to take root.

внедря́|ть(ся), ю(сь) *impf. of* ⇒**внедри́ть(ся)**

внеза́пно *adv.* suddenly, all of a sudden.

внеза́пност|ь, и *f.* suddenness.

внеза́пный *adj.* sudden.

внеземно́й *adj.* alien, extra-terrestrial.

внекла́ссный *adj.* extra-curricular.

внема́точ|ный *adj.* (*med.*): **∼ная бере́менность** ectopic pregnancy.

вне́мл|ю, ешь *see* ⇒**внима́ть**

внеочередно́й *adj.* **1** out of turn; **зада́ть в. вопро́с** to ask a question out of order. **2** (*заседание*) extraordinary; (*рейс*) extra.

внепи́ковый *adj.* off-peak.

внепла́новый *adj.* (*econ.*) not provided for by the plan; extraordinary.

внесе́ни|е, я *nt.* **1** (*вещей*) bringing in, carrying in. **2** (*денег*) paying in, deposit. **3** (*включение*) entry, insertion. **4** (*предложения*) moving, submission.

внеслужéбный *adj.* leisure-time.

внес|ти́, у́, ёшь, *past* **∼́, ∼ла́** *pf.* (*of* ⇒**вноси́ть**) **1** (*принести внутрь*) to bring in, carry in; **в. ра́неных** to bring in the wounded. **2** (*fig.*) to introduce, put in; **в. я́сность в де́ло** to clarify a matter; **в. свой вклад в де́ло** to do one's bit; to make one's contribution. **3** (*деньги*) to pay in, deposit. **4** (*предложение*) to bring in, move, table. **5** (*вписать*) to insert, enter; **в. в спи́сок** to enter on a list. **6** (*причинить*) to bring about, cause; **в. раздо́ры** to cause bad feelings.

внестуди́йный *adj.* on-location, outside (*broadcast etc.*).

внеуро́чный *adj.* (*занятия*) extracurricular, leisure-time.

внешко́льн|ый *adj.* (*занятия*) extracurricular; **∼ое образова́ние** adult education.

вне́шне *adv.* outwardly.

вне́шн|ий *adj.* **1** outer, exterior; outward, external; outside; **в. вид** appearance. **2** (*иностранный*) foreign; **∼яя поли́тика** foreign policy.

вне́шност|ь, и *f.* appearance; exterior; **суди́ть по ∼и** to judge by appearances.

вншта́тник, а *m.* (*coll.*) freelancer; casual.

внешта́тный *adj.* freelance; casual.

вниз *adv.* down, downwards; **в. голово́й** head first; **идти́ в. по ле́стнице** to go downstairs; **в. по тече́нию** downstream; **в. по Во́лге** down the Volga.

внизу́ *adv.* below; downstairs; *prep.* + *g.*; **в. страни́цы** at the foot of the page.

вник|а́ть, а́ю *impf. of* ⇒**∼нуть**

вни́к|нуть, ну, нешь, *past* **∼, ∼ла** *pf.* (*of* ⇒**∼а́ть**) (**в** + *a.*) (*изучить*) to go carefully (into), investigate thoroughly; (*понять*) to understand, penetrate.

внима́ни|е, я *nt.* **1** (*сосредоточенность*) attention; heed; notice, note; **обраща́ть в.** (**на** + *a.*) (*i*) to pay attention (to); (*ii*) to draw attention (to); **удели́ть в. кому́-н.** to give s.o. attention; **оста́вить без ∼я** to ignore; **он весь в.** he is all ears; **принима́я во в.** taking into account; **благодарю́ за в.** thank you for listening. **2** (*забота*) kindness, consideration; **оказа́ть в. кому́-н.** to do a kindness to s.o. **3** (*int.*): **в.!** look out! mind out!; **в. на старт!** (*sport*) get set!

внима́тельност|ь, и *f.* **1** attentiveness. **2** (*заботливость*) thoughtfulness, consideration.

внима́тел|ьный (∼ен, ∼ьна) *adj.* **1** attentive. **2** (**к** + *d.*) (*заботливый*) thoughtful, considerate (towards).

внима́|ть, ю *and* **вне́млю** *impf.* (*of* ⇒**внять**) (+ *d.*) (*rhet.*) to heed; **он внял мо́ей про́сьбе** he heeded my request.

вничью́ *adv.* (*sport*) drawn; **па́ртия око́нчилась в.** the game ended in a draw; **на́ша кома́нда сыгра́ла сего́дня в.** our team drew today.

вно́ве *adv. as pred.* new, strange.

вновь *adv.* **1** (*опять*) afresh, anew; again. **2** (*недавно*) newly; **в. прибы́вший** newcomer.

вно|си́ть, шу́, ∼́сишь *impf. of* ⇒**внести́**

ВНП *m. indecl.* (*abbr. of* ***валово́й национа́льный проду́кт***) GNP (*Gross National Product*).

внук, а *m.* grandson; grandchild (*also fig.*).

вну́тренн|ий *adj.* **1** inner, interior; internal; intrinsic; **∼ие боле́зни** internal diseases; **в. мир** inner life, private world; **∼ие причи́ны** intrinsic causes; **∼ее сгора́ние** internal combustion; **в. смысл** inner meaning. **2** (*в государстве*) domestic, inland; **∼ие дохо́ды** inland revenue; **∼яя поли́тика** internal politics; **Министе́рство ∼их дел** Ministry of Internal Affairs.

вну́тренност|ь, и *f.* **1** interior. **2** (*pl. only*) entrails, intestines; internal organs.

внутри́ *adv. and prep.* + *g.* inside, within; **в. до́ма** inside the house.

внутри́... *comb. form* intra-.

внутриве́нный *adj.* (*med.*) intravenous.

внутрима́точный *adj.* intra-uterine.

внутрипарти́йный *adj.* within the Party, inner-Party.

внутрь *adv. and prep.* + *g.* within, inside; inwards; **открыва́ться в.** to open inwards; **войти́ в. до́ма** to go inside the house.

внуча́т|а, ∼ *no sg.* grandchildren.

внуча́тный *adj.*: **в. брат** second cousin; **в. племя́нник** great-nephew.

внуча́т|ый = ∼ный

вну́чк|а, и *f.* granddaughter.

внуша́емост|ь, и *f.* suggestibility.

внуш|а́ть, а́ю *impf. of* ⇒**∼и́ть**

внуше́ни|е, я *nt.* **1** (*psych.*) suggestion. **2** (*выговор*) reprimand.

внуши́тел|ьный (∼ен, ∼ьна) *adj.* imposing, impressive.

внуш|и́ть, у́, и́шь *pf.* (*of* ⇒**∼а́ть**) (+ *a.* and *d.*) to inspire (with); to instil (*Br.*), instill (*US*); to suggest; **его́ вид ∼и́л мне страх** the sight of him inspired me with fear; **в. уве́ренность в себе́** to instil self-confidence; **он уме́л в. слу́шателям, что он всегда́ прав** he had the power of suggesting to his audience that he was always right.

вню́ха|ться, юсь *pf.* (**в** + *a.*; *coll.*) to take a sniff (at) (*also fig.*).

внюхива|ться, юсь *impf. of* ⇒**внюхаться**

вня́т|ный (∼ен, ∼на) *adj.* distinct.

внят|ь *fut. not used, past* **∼л, ∼ла́, ∼́ло,** *imper.* **вонми́(те),** *pf. of* ⇒**внима́ть**

во[1] *prep.* = **в**

во[2] *particle* (*coll.*) **1** = **вот** 3; **в. каки́е де́ньги!** there's money for you! **2** (*очень* *хороший*): **книга в.!** it's a great book! **3** (*вот именно*): **в., я так и знал** I knew it all along. **4**: **в. как** greatly.

во́бл|а, ы *f.* vobla (*Caspian roach*).

вобр|а́ть, вберу́, вберёшь, *past* **~а́л, ~ала́, ~а́ло** *pf.* (*of* ⇒**вбира́ть**) (*воду*) to absorb, suck in; (*воздух*) to inhale.

вове́к(и) *adv.* for ever; **в. не** never.

вовлека́|ть, ю *impf. of* ⇒**вовле́чь**

вовлечённост|ь, и *f.* involvement.

вовл|е́чь, еку́, ечёшь, еку́т, *past* **~ёк, ~екла́** *pf.* to draw in, involve.

вовне́ *adv.* outside.

вовну́трь *adv. and prep.*+*g.* (*coll.*) inside.

во́время *adv.* in time, on time; **не в.** at the wrong time.

во́все *adv.* (*coll.*) completely; (+*neg.*) at all; **он в. не бога́тый челове́к** he is not at all a rich man.

вовсю́ *adv.* (*coll.*) like anything; to its (one's) utmost; **бежа́ть в.** to run like anything.

во-вторы́х *adv.* secondly, in the second place.

вогна́|ть, вгоню́, вго́нишь, *past* **~л, ~ла́, ~ло** *pf.* (*of* ⇒**вгоня́ть**) to drive in; **в. гвоздь в сте́ну** to drive a nail into the wall; **в. в гроб** to be the death of; **в. в депре́ссию** to make depressed; **в. в кра́ску** to make blush.

во́гнут|ый (~, ~а) *p.p.p. of* ⇒**вогну́ть** *and adj.* concave.

вогн|у́ть, у́, ёшь *pf.* (*of* ⇒**вгиба́ть**) to bend, curve inwards.

вод|а́, ы́, *a.* **~у,** *pl.* **~ы, ~ам** *f.* **1** water; **выводи́ть на чи́стую ~у** to show up, unmask; **как две ка́пли ~ы́ похо́жи** as like as two peas; **как с гу́ся в.** like water off a duck's back; **мно́го ~ы́ утекло́** much water has flowed under the bridge; it's been a long time; **как в ~у опу́щенный** downcast, dejected; **как в ~у гляде́л!** (*coll.*) I knew it! **2** (*pl.*) (*минеральные*) the waters; (*курорт*) watering-place, spa. **3** (*coll.*) (*болтовня*) waffle; **~у лить** to waffle (on).

водворе́ни|е, я *nt.* settlement; establishment.

водвор|и́ть, ю́, и́шь *pf.* **1** (*поселить*) to settle, install. **2** (*установить*) to establish.

водворя́|ть, ю *impf. of* ⇒**водвори́ть**

водеви́л|ь, я *m.* (*theatr.*) vaudeville; musical comedy.

води́тел|ь, я *m.* driver.

води́тельск|ий *adj.*: **~ие права́** driving licence (*Br.*), driver's license (*US*).

води́тельств|о, а (*obs.*) leadership.

во|ди́ть, жу́, ~дишь *impf.* (*indet. of* ⇒**вести́**) **1** (*see also* ⇒**вести́**) (*сопровождать*) to take; to lead; to conduct; (*машину*) to drive; (*самолёт*) to fly. **2** (*see also* ⇒**вести́**): **в. дру́жбу** (**с**+*i.*) to be friends with; **в. знако́мство** (**с**+*i.*) to keep up an acquaintance (with). **3** (+*i.*, **по**+*d.*; *see also* ⇒**вести́**) to pass (over, across); **в. глаза́ми** (**по**+*d.*) to cast one's eye (over) (*only* **в.** *used in this phr.*). **4** (*coll.*) (*животных*) to keep; **в. пчёл** to keep bees.

во|ди́ться, жу́сь, ~дишься *impf.* **1** (**с**+*i.*) to associate (with); (*о детях*) to play (with). **2** (*бывать*) to be, be found; **львы́ не ~дятся в Евро́пе** lions are not found in Europe; (*fig.*) **у него́ де́нег никогда́ не ~дится** he never has any money. **3** (*быть принятым*) to be the custom; to happen; **как ~дится** as usually happens.

води́ц|а, ы *f. dim. of* ⇒**вода́**

во́дк|а, и *f.* vodka.

воднолы́жник, а *m.* water-skier.

во́дн|ый *adj.* **1** water; **~ые лы́жи** (*i*) water-skiing, (*ii*) water-skis; **~ое по́ло** water polo; **в. пу́ть** waterways; **в. спорт** aquatic sports. **2** (*chem.*) aqueous.

водобоя́зн|ь, и *f.* (*med.*) hydrophobia, rabies.

водово́з, а *m.* water-carrier.

водоворо́т, а *m.* whirlpool; (*fig.*) maelstrom.

водоём, а *m.* reservoir.

водоизмеще́ни|е, я *nt.* (*naut.*) displacement.

водока́чк|а, и *f.* water-tower.

водола́з[1]**, а** *m.* diver; **в.-аквалангист** frogman.

водола́з[2]**, а** *m.* Newfoundland (dog).

водола́зк|а, и *f.* thin polo-necked sweater.

водола́з|ный *adj. of* ⇒**~**[1]; **в. костю́м** diving-suit.

Водоле́|й, я *m.* (*созвездие*) Aquarius.

водолече́бниц|а, ы *f.* hydropathic clinic.

водолече́бный *adj.* hydropathic.

водоме́р, а *m.* (*tech.*) water-gauge.

водоме́рк|а, и *f* pond skater (*Br.*), water strider (*US*).

водомёт, а *m.* water cannon.

водонапо́рн|ый *adj. only in phr.* **~ая ба́шня** water-tower.

водонепроница́ем|ый (~, ~а) *adj.* water-tight; waterproof.

водоно́с, а *m.* water-carrier.

водоотво́д, а *m.* drainage system.

водоотво́дн|ый *adj.* drainage; **~ая труба́** waste-pipe.

водоочисти́тельный *adj.* water-purifying.

водоочи́стн|ый *adj.*: **~ые сооруже́ния** water treatment plant.

водопа́д, а *m.* waterfall.

водопла́вающ|ий *adj.*: **~ие пти́цы** waterfowl; **~ая маши́на** amphibious vehicle.

водопо́|й, я *m.* **1** (*место*) watering-place. **2** (*поение скота*) watering.

водопрово́д, а *m.* water-supply system; plumbing; **дом с ~ом** house with running water.

водопрово́д|ный *adj. of* ⇒**~**; **~ная магистра́ль** water-main; **~ная сеть** water-supply; **~ная ста́нция** waterworks.

водопрово́дчик, а *m.* plumber.

водопроница́ем|ый (~, ~а) *adj.* permeable to water.

водоразде́л, а *m.* (*geog.*; *fig.*) watershed.

водоро́д, а *m.* (*chem.*) hydrogen.

водоро́дн|ый *adj.* hydrogen; **~ая бо́мба** hydrogen bomb.

во́доросл|ь, и *f.* (*bot.*) alga; **морска́я в.** seaweed.

водосли́в, а *m.* (*tech.*) spillway; sluice.

водоснабже́ни|е, я *nt.* water-supply.

водосто́к, а *m.* drain; (*на улице*) gutter.

водосто́|чный *adj. of* ⇒**~к**; **~чная труба́** drain-pipe.

водоупо́р|ный (~ен, ~на) *adj.* waterproof.

водоусто́йчивый *adj.* water-repellent.

водохо́дный *adj.* amphibious.

водохрани́лищ|е, а *nt.* reservoir.

во́дочк|а, и *f.* (*coll.*) *dim. of* ⇒**во́дка**

во́д|очный *adj. of* ⇒**~ка**

водружа́|ть, ю *impf. of* ⇒**водрузи́ть**

водру|зи́ть, жу́, зи́шь *pf.* (*of* ⇒**~жа́ть**) to hoist, erect.

водяни́ст|ый (~, ~а) *adj.* watery; (*fig.*, *coll.*) wishy-washy.

водя́нк|а, и *f.* (*med.*) dropsy.

водян|о́й[1] *adj.* **1** *adj. of* ⇒**вода́**. **2** (*живущий, растущий в воде*) water, aquatic; **~ы́е пти́цы** waterfowl; **~ы́е расте́ния** aquatic plants. **3** (*приводимый в движение водой*) water-driven, water-operated; **~а́я ме́льница** water-mill. **4**: **в. знак** watermark.

водян|о́й[2]**, о́го** *m.* water-sprite.

во|ева́ть, ю́ю, ю́ешь *impf.* (**с**+*i.*) **1** to wage war (with), make war (upon); to be at war. **2** (*coll.*) (*ссориться*) to quarrel (with).

воево́д|а, ы *m.* (*hist.*) voivode (*commander of an army in medieval Russia; also, in Muscovite period, governor of a town or province*).

воево́дств|о, а *nt.* **1** (*hist.*) office of voivode. **2** province (*in Poland*).

воедино *adv.* together; **собра́ть в.** to bring together.

воен... *comb. form, abbr. of* ***вое́нный***

военача́льник, а *m.* commander; leader in war.

воениза́ци|я, и *f.* militarization.

военизи́р|овать, ую *impf. and pf.* to militarize.

военкома́т, а *m.* (*abbr. of* ***вое́нный комиссариа́т***) military registration and enlistment office.

военко́р, а *m.* (*abbr. of* ***вое́нный корреспонде́нт***) war correspondent.

вое́нно-... *comb. form, abbr. of* ***вое́нный***

вое́нно-возду́шн|ый *adj.*: **~ые си́лы** Air Force(s).

вое́нно-морско́й *adj.* naval; **в. флот** the Navy.

военнообя́занн|ый, ого *m.* man liable for call-up (*including reservists*).

военнопле́нн|ый, ого *m.* prisoner of war.

вое́нно-полево́й *adj.* (*mil.*) field; **в. суд** court-martial.

военнослу́жащ|ий, его *m.* serviceman.

вое́нно-учёбный *adj.* military training.

вое́нн|ый *adj.* military; war; (*форма*) army; **в. врач** (army) medical officer; **~ое вре́мя** wartime; **в. городо́к** housing estate where servicemen and their families live; **в. заво́д** munitions factory; **на ~ую но́гу** on a war footing; **~ое положе́ние** martial law; **~ое учи́лище** military college; **в. челове́к** soldier, serviceman; *as n.* **в., ~ого** *m.* soldier, serviceman; **~ые** (*collect.*) the military.

вое́нщин|а, ы *f.* (*coll., pej.*) militarists, warmongers.

вожа́к, а́ *m.* **1** (*проводник*) guide. **2** (*руководитель*) leader.

вожа́т|ый, ого *m.* **1** (*проводник*) guide. **2** (*руководитель*) leader. **3** (*coll.*) (*водитель трамвая*) tram-driver.

вожделе́ни|е, я *nt.* desire, lust (*also fig.*).

вожделе́нный *adj.* (*poet.*) desired, longed-for.

вожделе́|ть, ю, ешь *impf.* (**к**+*d.*) **1** to long (for). **2** (*obs.*) to lust (after).

вожде́ни|е, я *nt.* (*сопровождение*) leading; (*машины*) driving; **в. корабля́** navigation; **в. самолёта** flying, piloting.

вожд|ь, я́ *m.* (*организации*) leader; (*племени*) chief.

вожжа́|ться, юсь *impf.* (**с**+*i.*; *coll.*) to bother o.s. (with), trouble o.s. (over).

во́жж|и, е́й *pl.* (*sg.* **~а́, ~и́** *f.*) reins.

во|жу́[1], ~́дишь *see* **⇒~ди́ть**

во|жу́[2], ~́зишь *see* **⇒~зи́ть**

ВОЗ *m.* (*indecl.*) (*abbr. of* ***Всеми́рная организа́ция здравоохране́ния***) WHO (*World Health Organization*).

воз, а, о ~́е, на ~у́, *pl.* **~ы́** *m.* **1** (*повозка*) cart, wagon; **что с ~́а упа́ло, то пропа́ло** (*prov.*) it is no use crying over spilt milk. **2** (*груз*) cartload. **3** (*fig., coll.*) (*множество*) load(s), heap(s); **в. вре́мени** loads of time.

возбран|и́ть, ю, и́шь *pf.* (*obs.*) to prohibit, forbid.

возбран|я́ть, я́ю *impf. of* **⇒~и́ть**

возбраня́|ться, ется *impf.* to be prohibited, be forbidden; **купа́ться тут не ~ется** swimming is permitted here.

возбуди́мост|ь, и *f.* excitability.

возбуди́м|ый (~, ~а) *adj.* excitable.

возбуди́тел|ь, я *m.* **1** agent; stimulus. **2** (*med.*) pathogen.

возбу|ди́ть, жу́, ди́шь *pf.* (*of* **⇒~жда́ть**) **1** to excite, rouse, arouse; **в. аппети́т** to whet the appetite. **2** (**про́тив**+*g.*) to stir up (against), incite (against). **3** (*leg.*) to institute; **в. де́ло** (**про́тив**+*g.*) to institute proceedings (against), bring an action (against); **в. иск** (**про́тив**+*g.*) to bring a suit (against); **в. хода́тайство** (**о**+*p.*) to submit a petition (for).

возбу|ди́ться, жу́сь, ди́шься *pf.* (*of* **⇒~жда́ться**) **1** (*о человеке*) to get excited. **2** (*об интересе*) to be aroused, stimulated.

возбужда́емост|ь, и *f.* excitability.

возбужда́|ть(ся), ю(сь) *impf. of* **⇒возбуди́ть(ся)**

возбужда́|ющий *pres. part. act. of* **⇒~ть; ~ющее сре́дство** (*med.*) stimulant.

возбужде́ни|е, я *nt.* excitement.

возбу|ждённый *p.p.p. of* **⇒~ди́ть** *and adj.* excited.

возбу|жу́(сь), ди́шь(ся) *see* **⇒~ди́ть(ся)**

возведе́ни|е, я *nt.* **1** (*в чин*) elevation. **2** (*здания*) raising; erection. **3** (*math.*) raising. **4**: **в. обвине́ния** (**на**+*a.*) bringing of an accusation (against).

возвед|у́, ёшь *see* **⇒возвести́**

возвели́чива|ть, ю *impf. of* **⇒возвели́чить**

возвели́ч|ить, у, ишь *pf.* (*of* **⇒~ивать**) to extol.

возве|сти́, ду́, дёшь, *past* **~́л, ~ла́** *pf.* (*of* **⇒возводи́ть**) **1** (*возвысить*) to elevate; **в. в сан патриа́рха** to elect to the patriarchate. **2** (*строить*) to raise, erect, put up; **в. высо́тный дом** to erect a skyscraper. **3** (*math.*) to raise; **в. во втору́ю сте́пень** to raise to the second power; **в. в куб** to cube. **4** (*обвинение*) to bring, level; **в. клевету́ на кого́-н.** to cast aspersions on s.o. **5** (**к**+*d.*) to trace (to), derive (from).

возве|сти́ть, щу́, сти́шь *pf.* (*of* **⇒~ща́ть**) to proclaim, announce; **в. побе́ду/о побе́де** to proclaim a victory.

возвеща́|ть, ю *impf. of* **⇒возвести́ть**

возве|щу́, сти́шь *see* **⇒~сти́ть**

возво|ди́ть, жу́, ~́дишь *impf. of* **⇒возвести́**

возво|жу́, ~́дишь *see* **⇒~ди́ть**

возвра́т, а *m.* return; repayment, reimbursement; **в. боле́зни** relapse; **в. со́лнца** (*astron.*) solstice; **без ~а** irrevocably.

возвра|ти́ть, щу́, ти́шь *pf.* (*of* **⇒~ща́ть**) **1** (*отдать обратно*) to return, give back; (*деньги*) to pay back. **2** (*получить обратно*) to recover, retrieve; **в. де́ньги, о́тданные взаймы́** to recover a loan.

возвра|ти́ться, щу́сь, ти́шься *pf.* (*of* **⇒~ща́ться**) to return; (*fig.*) to revert; **в. ко всем ста́рым привы́чкам** to revert to all one's old habits; **в. к разгово́ру** to resume a conversation.

возвра́т|ный *adj.* **1** *adj. of* **⇒~;** returnable. **2** (*med.*) recurring. **3** (*gram.*) reflexive.

возвраща́|ть(ся), ю(сь) *impf. of* **⇒возврати́ть(ся)** *and* **верну́ть(ся)**

возвраще́ни|е, я *nt.* return; **в. домо́й** home-coming.

возвра|щу́, ти́шь *see* **⇒~ти́ть**

возвы́|сить, шу, сишь *pf.* (*of* **⇒~ша́ть**) **1** (*работника*) to raise, elevate. **2**: **в. го́лос** to raise one's voice.

возвы́|ситься, шусь, сишься *pf.* (*of* **⇒~ша́ться**) to rise, go up; **они́ ~сились в на́шем мне́нии** they have risen in our estimation.

возвыша́|ть, ю *impf. of* **⇒возвы́сить**

возвыша́|ться, юсь *impf.* **1** *impf. of* **⇒возвы́ситься. 2** (*impf. only*) (**над**+*i.*) to tower (above) (*also fig.*).

возвыше́ни|е, я *nt.* **1** (*действие*) rise; raising; **в. Моско́вской Руси́** the rise of Muscovite Russia. **2** (*место*) elevation; raised place.

возвы́шенност|ь, и *f.* **1** (*geog.*) height; elevation. **2** (*чувств*) loftiness, sublimity.

возвы́шен|ный *p.p.p. of* **⇒возвы́сить** *and adj.* **1** (*высокий*) high; elevated. **2** (*благородный*) lofty, sublime, elevated; **~ные идеа́лы** lofty ideals; **в. стиль** elevated style.

возвы́|шу, сишь *see* **⇒~сить**

возгла́в|ить, лю, ишь *pf.* (*of* **⇒~ля́ть**) to head, be at the head of.

возглавля́|ть, ю *impf. of* **⇒возгла́вить**

во́зглас, а *m.* cry, exclamation.

возгла|си́ть, шу́, си́шь *pf.* (*of* **⇒~ша́ть**) to proclaim.

возглаша́|ть, ю *impf. of* **⇒возгласи́ть**

возглаше́ни|е, я *nt.* **1** (*объявление*) proclamation. **2** (*восклицание*) exclamation.

возгна́|ть, возгоню́, возго́нишь, *past* **~л, ~ла́, ~ло** *pf. of* **⇒возгоня́ть**

возго́нк|а, и *f.* (*chem.*) sublimation.

возгон|ю́, ~́ишь *see* **⇒возгна́ть**

возгоня́|ть, ю *impf.* (*chem.*) to sublimate.

возгора́емост|ь, и *f.* inflammability.

возгора́емый *adj.* inflammable.

возгора́ни|е, я *nt.* (*tech.*) inflammation, ignition; **то́чка ~я** flash-point.

возгора́|ться, юсь *impf. of* **⇒возгоре́ться**

возгор|ди́ться, жу́сь, ди́шься *pf.* to become proud; (+*i.*) to begin to pride o.s. (on).

возгор|е́ться, ю́сь и́шься *pf.* **1** to flare up (*also fig.*); **внеза́пно ме́жду ни́ми ~е́лась ссо́ра** suddenly there flared up a quarrel between them. **2** (+*i.*) (*каким-н. чувством*) to be inflamed (with); **она́ ~е́лась стра́стью к кино́** she was seized with a passion for the cinema.

возда|ва́ть, ю́, ёшь *impf. of* **⇒возда́ть**

возда́|м, шь, ст *see* **⇒~ть**

возда́|ть, м, шь, ст, ди́м, ди́те, ду́т, *past* **~л, ~ла́, ~ло** *pf.* (*of* **⇒~ва́ть**) (*дать*) to render; **в. кому́-н. до́лжное** to give s.o. his due; (*отплатить*) to repay.

воздая́ни|е, я *nt.* recompense; retribution.

воздвига́|ть, ю *impf.* to raise, erect.

воздвига́|ться, юсь *impf.* **1** *pass. of* ⇒**~ть. 2** to rear (up) (*intrans.*).

воздви́г|нуть, ну, нешь, *past* **~, ~ла** *pf. of* ⇒**~а́ть**

воздви́г|нуться, нусь, нешься, *past* **~ся, ~лась** *pf. of* ⇒**~а́ться**

Воздви́жени|е, я *nt.* (*eccl.*) Exaltation of the Cross (*Christian festival celebrated on 14 September*).

воздева́|ть, ю *impf. of* ⇒**возде́ть**

возде́йстви|е, я *nt.* influence; **оказа́ть мора́льное в.** (**на** + *a.*) to bring moral pressure to bear (upon); **он э́то сде́лал под физи́ческим ~ем** he did it under coercion.

возде́йств|овать, ую *impf. and pf.* (**на** + *a.*) to influence, affect; to exert influence, bring influence to bear (upon); to bring pressure to bear (upon).

возде́л|ать, аю *pf.* (*of* ⇒**~ывать**) to cultivate, till.

возде́лыва|ть, ю *impf. of* ⇒**возде́лать**

воздержа́вш|ийся *p.p. of* ⇒**воздержа́ться;** *as n.* **в., ~егося** *m.* abstainer; **предложе́ние бы́ло при́нято при трёх ~ихся** the motion was carried with three abstentions.

воздержа́ни|е, я *nt.* **1** abstinence. **2** (**от** + *g.*) abstention (from).

возде́ржанност|ь, и *f.* abstemiousness; temperance.

возде́ржан|ный (~, ~на) *adj.* (*в еде*) abstemious; (*в суждениях*) temperate.

воз|держа́ться, держу́сь, де́ржишься *pf.* (*of* ⇒**~де́рживаться**) (**от** + *g.*) **1** (*от замечания, курения*) to refrain (from); **в. от мя́са** to abstain from meat. **2** (*от голосования*) to abstain.

возде́ржива|ться, юсь *impf. of* ⇒**воздержа́ться**

возде́ржност|ь, и *f.* (*obs.*) = **возде́ржанность**

возде́рж|ный (~ен, ~на) *adj.* (*obs.*) = **~анный**

возде́|ть, ну, нешь *pf.* (*of* ⇒**~ва́ть**) *only in phr.* **в. ру́ки** (*obs.*) to raise one's hands.

во́здух, а *no pl., m.* **1** air; **на (откры́том) ~е** out of doors; **вы́йти на в.** to go out of doors; **в ~е** (*fig.*) in the air; **пови́снуть в ~е** to be unresolved; to be up in the air; **подня́ться в в.** to become airborne; **взлете́ть на в.** to explode. **2** (*атмосфера*) atmosphere.

воздухоохлажда́емый *adj.* air-cooled.

воздухоочисти́тел|ь, я *m.* extractor fan.

воздухопла́вани|е, я *nt.* aeronautics.

воздухопла́вател|ь, я *m.* aeronaut.

воздухопла́вательный *adj.* aeronautic.

воздухопроница́емый *adj.* gas-permeable.

возду́ш|ный *adj.* **1** air, aerial; **~ные за́мки** castles in the air; **в. змей** kite; **посла́ть ~ные поцелу́и** to blow kisses; **~ная прово́дка** overhead cable; **~ная трево́га** air-raid warning; **в. шар** balloon; **~ная я́ма** air-pocket. **2** (*приводимый в движение воздухом*) air-driven, air-operated; **в. насо́с** air-pump. **3 (~ен, ~на)** (*очень лёгкий*) airy, light; flimsy; **~ное пла́тье** flimsy dress.

воззва́ни|е, я *nt.* appeal.

возз|ва́ть, ову́, овёшь *pf.* (*of* ⇒**взыва́ть**) (**к** + *d.*, **о** + *p.*) to appeal (to), call (for); **он ~ва́л к избира́телям о подде́ржке** he appealed to the electors for their support.

возз|ову́, овёшь *see* ⇒**~ва́ть**

воззре́ни|е, я *nt.* (*мнение*) view, opinion; (*образ мыслей*) outlook.

воззр|и́ться, ю́сь, и́шься *pf.* (**на** + *a.*; *coll.*) to stare (at).

во|зи́ть, жу́, ~́зишь *impf.* (*indet. of* ⇒**везти́**) **1** to take, convey; to carry; (*тянуть*) to draw. **2** (+ *i.*, **по** + *d.*; *coll.*) to pass (over), run (over).

во|зи́ться, жу́сь, ~́зишься *impf.* **1** (*о детях*) to play noisily, romp. **2** (**с** + *i.*) (*с чем-н. трудным*) to take trouble (over); (*с детьми*) to spend time, busy o.s. (with); (*coll.*) (*копаться*) to potter; **он лю́бит в. в саду́** he likes pottering about in the garden.

возлага́|ть, ю *impf. of* ⇒**возложи́ть**

во́зле *prep.* + *g.* by, near; *adv.* nearby; **он стоя́л в.** he was standing nearby.

возлеж|а́ть, у́, и́шь *impf.* (*obs.*) to recline, lie.

возл|е́чь, я́гу, я́жешь, я́гут, *imper.* **~я́г,** *past* **~ёг, ~егла́** *pf.* (*obs.*) to lie down.

возлик|ова́ть, у́ю *pf.* to rejoice.

возлия́ни|е, я *nt.* **1** libation. **2** (*coll.*) (*выпивка*) drinking-bout.

возлож|и́ть, у́, ~́ишь *pf.* (*of* ⇒**возлага́ть**) **1** (*положить*) to lay; **в. вено́к на моги́лу** to lay a wreath on a grave. **2** (*поручить*) (+ *d.*) to entrust (to); **в. вину́/отве́тственность на** (+ *a.*) to lay the blame/responsibility on; **наро́д ~и́л все наде́жды на но́вого президе́нта** the people had pinned all their hopes on the new president.

возлю́бленн|ый *adj.* beloved; *as n.* (*i*) **в., ~ого** *m.* **1** boy-friend. **2** (*любовник*) lover. (*ii*) **~ая, ~ой** *f.* **3** girl-friend, sweetheart. **4** (*любовница*) mistress.

возме́зди|е, я *nt.* retribution.

возме|сти́ть, щу́, сти́шь *pf.* (*of* ⇒**~ща́ть**) to compensate (for), make up (for); **в. поте́рянное вре́мя** to make up for lost time; **в. расхо́ды** to refund expenses.

возмечта́|ть, ю *pf.* **1** (*obs.*) to dream, start dreaming. **2: в. о себе́** (*coll.*) to form a high opinion of o.s., become conceited.

возмеща́|ть, ю *impf. of* ⇒**возмести́ть**

возмеще́ни|е, я *nt.* **1** (*сумма*) compensation; (*leg.*) damages; **получи́ть в. убы́тков по суду́** to be awarded damages. **2** (*расходов*) refund, reimbursement.

возме|щу́, сти́шь *see* ⇒**~сти́ть**

возмо́жно *adv.* **1** possibly; (+ *comp.*) as … as possible; **в. лу́чше** as well as possible. **2** *as pred.* it is possible; **в., что мы за́втра уе́дем** we may possibly go away tomorrow.

возмо́жност|ь, и *f.* **1** possibility; **по (ме́ре) ~и** as far as possible. **2** (*удобный случай*) opportunity; **име́ть в. пое́хать в Росси́ю** to have the opportunity of going to Russia; **при пе́рвой ~и** at the first opportunity. **3** (*pl.*) (*средства*) means, resources; **у него́ бо́льшие ~и** he has great potentialities.

возмо́ж|ный (~ен, ~на) *adj.* **1** possible; **врач сде́лал для неё всё ~ное** the doctor did all in his power for her. **2** (*наибольший*) the greatest possible; **с ~ной то́чностью** with the greatest possible accuracy.

возмужа́лост|ь, и *f.* maturity; (*о мужчине*) manhood.

возмужа́лый *adj.* mature; grown up.

возмужа́|ть, ю *pf. of* ⇒**мужа́ть**

возмути́тел|ь, я *m.* destroyer; **в. споко́йствия** troublemaker.

возмути́тел|ьный (~ен, ~ьна) *adj.* disgraceful, outrageous, scandalous.

возму|ти́ть, щу́, ти́шь *pf.* (*of* ⇒**~ща́ть**) to anger, outrage.

возму|ти́ться, щу́сь, ти́шься *pf.* (*of* ⇒**~ща́ться**) (+ *i.*) to be indignant (at); to be outraged (at).

возмуща́|ть, ю *impf. of* ⇒**возмути́ть**

возмуща́|ться, юсь *impf. of* ⇒**возмути́ться**

возмуще́ни|е, я *nt.* indignation, outrage.

возмущён|ный (~, ~а́) *p.p.p. of* ⇒**возмути́ть** *and adj.* (+ *i.*) indignant (at).

возму|щу́, ти́шь *see* ⇒**~ти́ть**

вознагра|ди́ть, жу́, ди́шь *pf.* (*of* ⇒**~жда́ть**) (*за труд, за подвиг*) to reward; to recompense; (*возместить*) to compensate, make up (for).

вознагражда́|ть, ю *impf. of* ⇒**вознагради́ть**

вознагражде́ни|е, я *nt.* **1** (*за труд, за подвиг*) reward, recompense; (*компенсация*) compensation. **2** (*оплата*) fee, remuneration.

вознаме́рива|ться, юсь *impf. of* ⇒**вознаме́риться**

вознаме́р|иться, юсь, ишься *pf.* (*of* ⇒**~иваться**) (+*inf.*) to conceive the idea (of).

вознегод|ова́ть, у́ю *pf.* to become indignant.

возненави́|деть, жу, дишь *pf.* to come to hate.

вознесе́ни|е, я *nt.* ascent; **В.** (*eccl.*) Ascension (Day).

вознес|ти́, у́, ёшь, *past* **~́, ~ла́** *pf.* (*of* ⇒**возноси́ть**) (*poet.*) to raise, lift up; **в. моли́тву** to offer up a prayer.

вознес|ти́сь, у́сь, ёшься, *past* **~́ся, ~ла́сь** *pf.* (*of* ⇒**возноси́ться**) **1** (*poet.*)

(*подняться вверх*) to rise; to ascend. **2** (*возгордиться*) to become arrogant.
возник|а́ть, а́ю *impf.* (*of* ⇒**~́нуть**) **1** (*трудности, подозрение*) to arise, spring up; **у меня́ ~́ла мысль** the thought occurred to me. **2** (*coll.*) (*появляться*) to appear, pop up. **3** (*начинаться*) to begin.
возникнове́ни|е, я *m.* rise, beginning, origin.
возни́к|нуть, ну, нешь, *past* **~, ~ла** *pf. of* ⇒**~а́ть**
возни́ц|а, ы *m.* coachman, driver.
возно|си́ть, шу́, ~́сишь *impf. of* ⇒**вознести́**
возно|си́ться, шу́сь, ~́сишься *impf. of* ⇒**вознести́сь**
возно|шу́, ~́сишь *see* ⇒**~си́ть**
возн|я́, и́ *no pl., f.* (*coll.*) **1** (*шум*) row, noise; **мыши́ная в.** (*fig.*) petty intrigues. **2** (*хлопоты*) bother, trouble; **у него́ мно́го ~и́ с автомоби́лем** he has a lot of trouble with his car.
возоблада́|ть, ю *pf.* (**над** + *i.*) to prevail (over).
возобнов|и́ть, лю́, и́шь *pf.* (*of* ⇒**~ля́ть**) (*переговоры, отношения*) to resume; (*абонемент, контракт*) to renew.
возобновле́ни|е, я *nt.* resumption, renewal.
возобновля́|ть, ю *impf. of* ⇒**возобнови́ть**
возомн|и́ть, ю́, и́шь *pf.*: **в. о себе́** (*iron.*) to get a false idea of one's own importance; **в. себя́ авторите́том** to consider o.s. (*falsely*) an authority.
возра́д|оваться, уюсь *pf.* (+*d.*; *obs.*) to be delighted (at).
возража́|ть, ю *impf. of* ⇒**возрази́ть; не ~ю** I have no objection.
возраже́ни|е, я *nt.* objection; (*резкий ответ*) retort.
возра|зи́ть, жу́, зи́шь *pf.* (*of* ⇒**~жа́ть**) **1** (**про́тив** + *g. or* **на** + *a.*) to object (to); to take exception (to); **про́тив э́того не́чего в.** nothing can be said against it. **2** (*pf. only*) (*ответить резко*) to retort.
во́зраст, а *m.* age; **ребёнок в ~е двена́дцати лет** a twelve-year-old child; **моего́ ~а** of my age; **одного́ ~а** of the same age; **бра́чный в.** age of consent; **преде́льный в.** age-limit; **в. совершенноле́тия** age of majority; **быть на ~е** (*coll.*) to have come of age; **вы́йти из ~а** to pass the age, exceed the age-limit; **прекло́нный в.** declining years.
возраста́ни|е, я *nt.* growth, increase.
возраст|а́ть, а́ю *impf. of* ⇒**~и́**
возраст|и́, у́, ёшь, *past* **возро́с, возросла́** *pf.* (*of* ⇒**~а́ть**) to grow, increase.
возраст|но́й *adj. of* ⇒**во́зраст; ~на́я гру́ппа** age group.
возро|ди́ть, жу́, ди́шь *pf.* (*of* ⇒**~жда́ть**) (*хозяйство, город*) to regenerate; (*надежду, культуру*) to revive.
возро|ди́ться, жу́сь, ди́шься *pf.* (*of* ⇒**~жда́ться**) to revive (*intrans.*).
возрожда́|ть, ю *impf. of* ⇒**возроди́ть**
возрожда́|ться, юсь *impf. of* ⇒**возроди́ться**
возрожде́ни|е, я *nt.* regeneration; revival; **эпо́ха Возрожде́ния** Renaissance.
во́зчик, а *m.* carter, carrier.
возыме́|ть, ю, ешь *pf.* to conceive (*wish, intention, etc.*); **в. де́йствие** to take effect; **в. си́лу** to come into force.
возьм|у́(сь), ёшь(ся) *see* ⇒**взя́ть(ся)**
во́ин, а *m.* warrior; fighter.
во́инск|ий *adj.* **1** military; **~ая пови́нность** liability for military service; **в. по́езд** troop-train. **2** (*подобающий военному*) martial, warlike.
во́инствен|ный (~, ~на) *adj.* **1** (*no short forms*) (*народ*) warlike. **2** (*вид, тон*) bellicose.
во́инств|о, а *nt.* (*collect.*) host, army.
вои́нствующий *adj.* militant; (*pol., mil.*) hawkish.
вои́стину *adv.* really, indeed; **(Христо́с) в. воскре́с!** (*response at Orthodox Easter service*) He (Christ) is risen indeed!
во́ител|ь, я *m.* (*poet.*) warrior.
во́ительниц|а, ы *f.* (*poet.*) female warrior, Amazon.
во|й, я *no pl., m.* howl, howling; wail, wailing.
вой|ду́, дёшь *see* ⇒**~ти́**
во́йлок, а *m.* felt.
во́йлочный *adj.* felt.
войн|а́, ы́, *pl.* **~ы** *f.* war; (*ведение войны*) warfare; **вести́ ~у́** to wage war; **объяви́ть ~у́** to declare war.
во́йск|а́, ~ *pl.* (*sg.* **~́о, ~́а** *nt.*) troops; forces; **наёмные в.** mercenaries.
войсково́й *adj.* military.
во|йти́, йду́, йдёшь, *past* **~шёл, ~шла́** *pf.* (*of* ⇒**входи́ть**) (**в** + *a.*) (*вступить*) to enter; (*из данного места внутрь*) to go in(to); (*извне в данное место*) to come in(to); (*уместиться*) to go in, fit in; (*включиться*) to enter; **в. в исто́рию** to go down in history; **в. в лета́** to get on (in years); **в. в мо́ду** to become fashionable; **в. в систе́му** (*comput.*) to log on.
вока́л, а *m.* vocalism.
вокали́ст, а *m.* (*mus.*) vocalist.
вокали́ст|ка, ки *f. of* ⇒**~**
вока́льный *adj.* vocal; **в. ве́чер** an evening of song.
вокза́л, а *m.* (large) station; **железнодоро́жный в.** railway (*esp. main or terminus*) station; **морско́й в.** port arrival and departure building; **речно́й в.** river-boat station; river port.
вокза́л|ьный *adj. of* ⇒**~;** station.
во́кмен, а *m.* Walkman (*propr.*), personal stereo.
вокру́г *adv. and prep.* + *g.* round, around; (*по поводу*) about; **в. све́та** round the world; **верте́ться в. да о́коло** (*coll.*) to beat about the bush.
вол, а́ *m.* ox, bullock.
вола́н, а *m.* **1** (*оборка*) flounce (*on woman's skirt*). **2** (*для игры*) shuttlecock.
Во́лг|а, и *f.* the Volga (*river*).
волды́р|ь, я́ *m.* (*пузырь*) blister.
волево́й *adj.* (*человек, натура*) strong-willed; (*лицо, голос*) determined.
волеизъявле́ни|е, я *nt.* will; command; **по короле́вскому ~ю** by royal command.
волейбо́л, а *m.* volley-ball.
волейболи́ст, а *m.* volley-ball player.
волейболи́ст|ка, ки *f. of* ⇒**~**
во́лей-нево́лей *adv.* willy-nilly, whether one likes it or not.
во́лжский *adj.* Volga (*attr.*), of the Volga.
волк, а, *pl.* **~́и, ~о́в** *m.* wolf; **морско́й в.** (*coll.*) old salt; **смотре́ть ~́ом** (*fig.*) to scowl; **в. в ове́чьей шку́ре** wolf in sheep's clothing; **хоть ~́ом вы́ть** (*coll.*) it's enough to make you despair; **с ~а́ми жить, по-во́лчьи вы́ть** (*prov.*) when in Rome do as the Romans do.
волкода́в, а *m.* wolf-hound.
волн|а́, ы́, *pl.* **~́ы, ~́ам** *f.* wave; (*разбивающаяся у берега*) breaker.
волне́ни|е, я *nt.* **1** (*на воде*) choppiness. **2** (*fig.*) (*нервное*) agitation; (*радостное*) excitement; (*душевное*) emotion; **прийти́ в в.** to become agitated, excited. **3** (*usu. pl.*; *pol.*) disturbance(s); unrest.
волни́ст|ый (~, ~а) *adj.* wavy; **~ое желе́зо** corrugated iron; **~ая ме́стность** undulating ground.
волн|ова́ть, у́ю, *impf.* (*of* ⇒**вз~**) (*возбуждать*) to excite; (*беспокоить*) to worry; (*воду*) to disturb, agitate (*also fig.*); **его́ всё ~у́ет** he is easily excited; **не ну́жно в. больно́го** the patient must not be disturbed.
волн|ова́ться, у́юсь *impf.* **1** (*нервно*) to worry, be nervous; (*радостно*) to be excited; **она́ ~у́ется о де́тях** she worries about her children; **он всегда́ ~у́ется пе́ред экза́меном** he is always nervous before an examination. **2** (*вода*) to be agitated, choppy. **3** (*протестовать*) to protest; to be up in arms.
волнов|о́й *adj.* wave, undulatory; **~а́я тео́рия** (*phys.*) wave theory.
волноло́м, а *m.* breakwater.
волнообра́з|ный (~ен, ~на) *adj.* wavy, undulating.
волноре́з, а *m.* breakwater.
волну́шк|а, и *f.* coral milky cap (*mushroom*).
волн|у́ющий *pres. part. act. of* ⇒**~ова́ть** *and adj.* (*беспокоящий*) disturbing, worrying; (*захватывающий*) exciting, thrilling.
вол|о́вий *adj. of* ⇒**~; (*fig.*)** very strong; **~о́вья шку́ра** oxhide; **у него́ ~о́вья си́ла** he is as strong as an ox.
во́лок, а *m.* portage; **перепра́вить ~ом** to portage.
воло́к(ся), ла́(сь) *see* ⇒**воло́чь(ся)**
волоки́т|а, ы *f.* (*coll.*) red tape.

волокни́ст|ый (~, ~а) *adj.* (*растение*) fibrous; (*мясо*) stringy.

волок|но́, на́, *pl.* **~на, ~он, ~нам** *nt.* fibre (*Br.*), fiber (*US*).

во́локом *adv.* along the ground.

волок|о́нный *adj. of* ⇨**~но́; ~о́нная о́птика** fibre optics (*Br.*), fiber optics (*US*).

волонтёр, а *m.* volunteer.

волоо́кий *adj.* (*poet.*) ox-eyed, calf-eyed.

во́лос, а, *pl.* **~ы, воло́с, ~а́м** *m.* hair; (*pl.*) hair (*of the head*); **до седы́х воло́с** until old age; **рвать на себе́ ~ы** to tear one's hair; **при ви́де тру́па ~ы у меня́ ста́ли ды́бом** the sight of the corpse made my hair stand on end; **э́то притя́нуто за́ волосы** it is far fetched; **ни на́ волос** not a bit.

волоса́т|ый (~, ~а) *adj.* hairy.

волоси́нк|а, и *f.* (*coll.*) *dim. of* ⇨**во́лос; у него́ на голове́ три ~и** he's almost bald.

волос|о́к, ка́ *m.* **1** *dim. of* ⇨**во́лос; на в.** (**от**+*g.*) within a hairbreadth (of); **висе́ть, держа́ться на ~ке́** to hang by a thread. **2** (*в часах*) hair-spring. **3** (*в лампочке*) filament.

во́лост|ь, и, *pl.* **~и, ~е́й** *f.* (*hist.*) volost (*smallest administrative division of tsarist Russia*).

волосян|о́й *adj.* hair (*attr.*), of hair; **в. покро́в** (*anat.*) scalp.

волоч|и́ть, у́, ~ишь *impf.* to drag; **в. но́гу** to drag one's foot; **в. но́ги** to shuffle one's feet; **в. де́ло** to drag out an affair.

волоч|и́ться, у́сь, ~ишься, *impf.* **1** *pass. of* ⇨**~и́ть. 2** to drag (*intrans.*), to trail. **3** (**за**+*i.*; *coll.*) to run after; **три ме́сяца он уже́ ~ится за ней** he has been running after her for three months.

вол|о́чь, оку́, очёшь, оку́т, *past* **~о́к, ~окла́** *impf.* (*coll.*) to drag.

вол|о́чься, оку́сь, очёшься, оку́тся, *past* **~о́кся, ~окла́сь** *impf.* (*coll.*) = **волочи́ться** 2

волхв, а́ *m.* sorcerer; **три ~а́** the Magi.

волхв|ова́ть, у́ю *impf.* to practise (*Br.*), practice (*US*) sorcery.

волча́нк|а, и *f.* (*med.*) lupus.

волч|е́ц, ца́ *m.* (*bot.*) thistle.

во́лч|ий *adj. of* ⇨**волк;** wolf; **в. аппети́т** (*coll.*) voracious appetite; **в. зако́н** the law of the jungle; **~ья пасть** (*med.*) cleft palate.

волчи́х|а, и *f.* (*coll.*) she-wolf.

волчи́ц|а, ы *f.* she-wolf.

волч|о́к¹, ка́ *m.* top (*toy*); **верте́ться ~ко́м** to spin like a top.

волч|о́к², ка́ *m.* judas (*in door*).

волч|о́нок, о́нка, *pl.* **~а́та, ~а́т** *m.* wolf-cub.

волше́бник, а *m.* magician; wizard.

волше́бниц|а, ы *f.* enchantress.

волше́б|ный (~ен, ~на) *adj.* **1** magic (*attr.*); magical; **~ная па́лочка** magic wand; **~ное ца́рство** fairyland; **в. фона́рь** magic lantern. **2** (*fig.*) magical, bewitching; enchanting.

волшебств|о́, а́ *nt.* magic.

воль́ын|ить, ю, ишь *impf.* (*coll.*) to dawdle, delay.

волы́нк|а¹, и *f.* bagpipes.

волы́нк|а², и *f.* dawdling, delay; **тяну́ть ~у** to dawdle.

волы́нщик¹, а *m.* piper.

волы́нщик², а *m.* (*coll.*) dawdler, slacker.

волы́нщи|ца, цы *f. of* ⇨**~к¹,²**

вольго́т|ный (~ен, ~на) *adj.* (*coll.*) free-and-easy.

волье́р, а *m.* cage; enclosure.

волье́р|а, и *f.* = **волье́р**

во́льнича|ть, ю *impf.* (*pej.*) to take liberties.

во́льн|о *adv. of* **~ый;** (*as mil. command*) **в.!** stand at ease!

вольно́ *as pred.* (+*d. and inf.*) (*coll.*; *addressed to person complaining of misfortune*) **в. тебе́** it's of your own choosing; **ты простуди́лась? в. ж тебе́ бы́ло выходи́ть без пальто́** have you caught cold? well, you *would* go out without a coat.

вольноду́м|ец, ца *m.* free-thinker.

вольноду́м|ный (~ен, ~на) *adj.* free-thinking.

вольноду́мств|о, а *nt.* free-thinking.

вольнолюби́в|ый (~, ~а) *adj.* freedom-loving.

вольнонаёмный *adj.* **1** (*mil.*) civilian (*employed in or for mil. establishment*). **2** (*рабочий, труд*) hired; free-lance.

вольноотпу́щенник, а *m.* (*hist.*) freedman; emancipated serf.

вольноотпу́щенн|ый *adj.* (*hist.*) freed, emancipated; *as n.* **в., ~ого** *m.* = **~ик**

во́льност|ь, и *f.* **1** freedom; liberty; **поэти́ческая в.** poetic licence (*Br.*), poetic license (*US*); **позволя́ть себе́ ~и** to take liberties. **2** (*usu. pl.*; *hist.*) liberties, rights.

во́л|ьный *adj.* **1** (*свободный, независимый*) free; **~ьная пти́ца** one's own master, free agent. **2** (*не ограниченный*) free, unrestricted; **в. ры́нок** free market; **~ьная прода́жа** unrestricted sale. **3**: **в. перево́д** (*liter.*) free translation. **4** (*sport*) free, free-style; **~ьная борьба́** free-style wrestling; **в. стиль** (*in swimming*) free-style; **~ьные упражне́ния** floor routine (*in gymnastics*). **5** (**~ен, ~ьна́**) (*нескромный*) free, familiar (*in behaviour*). **6** (**~ен, ~ьна́,** *pl.* **~ьны́**) (*full form not used*) free, at liberty; **ты ~ен де́лать, что хо́чешь** you are at liberty to do as you wish.

вольт¹, а, *g. pl.* **в.** *m.* (*elec.*) volt.

вольт², а, о ~е, на ~у́ *m.* **1** (*в манежной езде, в фехтовании*) volte. **2** (*sl.*) (*подтасовка*) cheating (*at cards*); **вы́кинуть в.** (*fig., coll.*) to play a trick.

вольта́ж, а *m.* (*elec.*) voltage.

вольтме́тр, а *m.* (*elec.*) voltmeter.

вольфра́м, а *m.* (*chem.*) tungsten.

вольфра́м|овый *adj. of* ⇨**~**

вол|ью́, ёшь *see* ⇨**влить**

во́л|я, и *no pl., f.* **1** (*in var. senses*) will; **после́дняя в.** last will; **свобо́дная в.** free will; **в. к жи́зни** will to live; **си́ла ~и** will-power; **в. ва́ша** as you please, as you like; **по до́брой ~е** of one's own free will; **не по свое́й ~е** against one's will. **2** (*свобода*) freedom, liberty; **вы́пустить, отпусти́ть на ~ю** to set at liberty; **на ~е** at liberty; at large; **с ~и** (*prison sl.*) from outside; **дать ~ю** (+*d.*) to give free rein (to); give vent (to).

вон¹ *adv.* out; off, away; **вы́йти в.** to go away; **в. отсю́да!** get out!; **в. его́!** out with him!; **из рук в. пло́хо** abysmally.

вон² *particle* (*на отдалении*) there, over there; **в. он идёт** there he goes; (*подчёркивает меру, степень*) **в. как мно́го** what a lot; **в. ско́лько книг** what a lot of books; **во́н оно что** (*coll.*) really?; you don't say!

вон|жу́, зи́шь *see* ⇨**~зи́ть**

вонза́|ть, ю *impf. of* ⇨**вонзи́ть**

вонза́|ться, юсь 1 *impf. of* ⇨**вонзи́ться. 2** *pass. of* ⇨**~ть**

вон|зи́ть, жу́, зи́шь *pf.* (*of* ⇨**~за́ть**) (**в**+*a.*) to plunge, thrust (into).

вон|зи́ться, жу́сь, зи́шься *pf.* (*of* ⇨**~за́ться**) to pierce, penetrate; **стрела́ ~зи́лась ему́ в се́рдце** the arrow pierced his heart.

вонми́ *see* ⇨**внять**

вон|ь, и *no pl., f.* stink, stench.

воню́ч|ий (~, ~а) *adj.* stinking.

вонючк|а, и *f.* (*zool.*) skunk.

воня́|ть, ю *impf.* **1** (*coll.*) (+*i.*) to stink, reek (of); **весь дом ~ет чесноко́м** the whole house reeks of garlic. **2** (*pf.* **на~**) (*vulg.*) (*пердеть*) to fart.

вообража́|емый *pres. part. pass. of* ⇨**~ть** *and adj.* imaginary; fictitious.

вообража́л|а, ы *c.g.* (*coll.*) show-off.

вообража́|ть, ю *impf.* (*of* ⇨**вообрази́ть**) to imagine; **он ~ет, что все лю́бят его́** he imagines that everybody likes him; **он ~ет, что он вели́кий поэ́т** he fancies himself as a great poet; **она́ вообрази́ла себя́ хоро́шей певи́цей** she imagined herself to be a good singer.

воображе́ни|е, я *nt.* imagination; **у неё живо́е в.** she has a lively imagination.

вообрази́м|ый (~, ~а) *pres. part. pass. of* ⇨**вообрази́ть** *and adj.* imaginable.

вообра|зи́ть, жу́, зи́шь *pf. of* ⇨**~жа́ть; ~зи́(те)!** fancy!, (just) imagine!

вообще́ *adv.* **1** (*в общем*) in general; on the whole; **в. говоря́** generally speaking. **2** (*всегда*) always; **она́ вы́глядит бле́дной в., а не то́лько сего́дня** she always looks pale, not just today. **3** (*with neg.*) at all.

воодушев|и́ть, лю́, и́шь *pf.* (*of* ⇨**~ля́ть**) (**кого́-н. на**+*a.*) to inspire (to), rouse (to).

воодушев|и́ться, лю́сь, и́шься *pf.* (*of* ⇨**~ля́ться**) (+*i.*) to be inspired (by).

воодушевле́ни|е, я *nt.* **1** (*действие*) rousing; inspiriting.

2 (*увлечение*) enthusiasm, fervour (*Br.*), fervor (*US*); **говорить с большим ~ем** to speak with great fervour.

воодушевлён|ный (~, ~а́) *p.p.p. of* ⇒**воодушевить** *and adj.* enthusiastic, fervent.

воодушевля́|ть(ся), ю(сь) *impf. of* ⇒**воодушевить(ся)**

вооруж|а́ть(ся), а́ю(сь) *impf. of* ⇒**~и́ть(ся)**

вооруже́ни|е, я *nt.* **1** (*действие*) arming. **2** (*оружие*) arms, armament; **быть на ~и** to be deployed. **3** (*принадлежности*) equipment; **па́русное в.** (*naut.*) rig.

вооружён|ный (~, ~а́) *p.p.p. of* ⇒**вооружи́ть** *and adj.* armed; **в. до зубо́в** armed to the teeth; **~ные си́лы** armed forces.

вооруж|и́ть, у́, и́шь *pf.* (*of* ⇒**~а́ть**) **1** (+*i.*) to arm; to equip (with) (*also fig.*). **2** (**про́тив**+*g.*) to set (against).

вооруж|и́ться, у́сь, и́шься *pf.* (*of* ⇒**~а́ться**) to arm o.s.; (*fig.*) to equip o.s.; **в. терпе́нием** to resolve to be patient.

воо́чию *adv.* **1** with one's own eyes, for o.s.; **я в. убеди́лся в его́ гру́бости** I could see for myself how rude he was. **2** (*ясно*) clearly, plainly; **показа́ть в.** to show clearly.

во-пе́рвых *adv.* first, first of all, in the first place.

воп|и́ть, лю́, и́шь *impf.* (*coll.*) (*кричать*) to yell; (*плакать*) to howl; to wail.

вопи|ю́щий *adj.* appalling, scandalous; crying; **~ю́щее безобра́зие** crying shame; **~ю́щее противоре́чие** glaring contradiction.

вопло|ти́ть, щу́, ти́шь *pf.* (*of* ⇒**~ща́ть**) to embody, personify; **в. в себе́** to be the embodiment (of); **в. в жизнь** (*планы*) to realize.

вопло|ти́ться, щу́сь, ти́шься *pf.* (*of* ⇒**~ща́ться**) to be realized; to be fulfilled.

вопло|ща́|ть(ся), ю(сь) *impf. of* ⇒**воплоти́ть(ся)**

воплоще́ни|е, я *nt.* embodiment; **он — в. здоро́вья** he is the picture of health.

воплощён|ный *adj.* incarnate; personified; **он — ~ная добросо́вестность** he is conscientiousness personified.

вопл|ь, я *m.* cry, wail; wailing, howling.

вопреки́ *prep.*+*d.* (*несмотря на*) despite, in spite of; (*наперекор*) against, contrary to; **он вы́шел в. предписа́нию врача́** he went out against doctor's orders.

вопро́с, а *m.* **1** question; **зада́ть в.** to ask, put a question; **отве́тить на в.** to answer a question. **2** (*проблема*) question, problem; (*дело*) matter; **подня́ть, поста́вить в.** (**о**+*p.*) to raise the question (of); **поста́вить под в.** to call in question; **в. жи́зни и сме́рти** matter of life and death; **спо́рный в.** moot point; **что за в.!** what a question!, of course!; **э́то под ~ом** it's undecided, unresolved; **по ~у** +*g.* concerning.

вопроси́тельный *adj.* interrogative; **в. знак** question-mark; **в. взгляд** inquiring look.

вопро|си́ть, шу́, си́шь *pf.* (*of* ⇒**~ша́ть**) (*obs.*) to question, inquire (of).

вопро́сник, а *m.* questionnaire.

вопро́сный *adj.* containing questions; **в. лист** form.

вопроша́|ть, ю *impf. of* ⇒**вопроси́ть; ~ющий взгляд** inquiring look.

вопр|у́, ёшь *see* ⇒**впере́ть**

воп|ью́сь, ёшься *see* ⇒**впи́ться**

вор, а, *pl.* **~ы, ~о́в** *m.* thief; **карма́нный в.** pickpocket; **магази́нный в.** shoplifter; **ме́лкий в.** petty thief; **на ~е ша́пка гори́т** if the cap fits, wear it!

ворв|а́ться, у́сь, ёшься, *past* **~а́лся, ~ала́сь** *pf.* (*of* ⇒**врыва́ться**[2]) to burst (into); **он ~а́лся ко мне в ко́мнату** he burst into my room.

вори́шк|а, и *m.* (*pej.*) thief.

ворк|ова́ть, у́ю *impf.* (*о голубях*) to coo; (*fig.*) to bill and coo.

воркотн|я́, и́ *f.* (*coll.*) grumbling.

вороб|е́й, ья́ *m.* sparrow; **стре́ляный в.** (*fig.*) old hand.

вороб|ьи́ный *adj. of* ⇒**~е́й**

воро́ванный *adj.* stolen.

вороват|ый (~, ~а) *adj.* thievish; furtive; **в. взгляд** furtive glance.

вор|ова́ть, у́ю *impf.* **1** (*pf.* **с~**) to steal; **в. де́ньги у кого́-н.** to steal money from s.o. **2** *impf. only* to be a thief; **с ра́нних лет он ~у́ет** he has been a thief from his early years.

воро́вк|а, и *f. of* ⇒**вор**

воровски́ *adv.* (*coll.*) furtively.

воровск|о́й *adj.* of thieves; **в. язы́к, ~о́е арго́** thieves' cant.

воровств|о́, а́ *nt.* stealing; theft.

ворожб|а́, ы́ *no pl., f.* fortune-telling.

вороже|я́, и́ *f.* fortune-teller.

ворож|и́ть, у́, и́шь *impf.* (*of* ⇒**по~**) to tell fortunes.

во́рон, а *m.* raven.

воро́н|а, ы *f.* **1** crow. **2** (*fig.*) (*о человеке*) scatter-brain.

воро́н|ий (~ья, ~ье) *adj. of* ⇒**~а**

ворон|и́ть, ю́, и́шь *impf.* (*tech.*) to blue, burnish.

воро́нк|а, и *f.* **1** (*для переливания*) funnel (*for pouring liquids*). **2** (*mil.*) (*яма*) crater.

вороно́й *adj.* black (*of horses*).

во́рот[1]**, а,** *pl.* **~ы** *m.* (*одежды*) collar; **схвати́ть за́ в.** to seize by the collar; to collar.

во́рот[2]**, а** *m.* (*tech.*) winch; windlass.

воро́т|а (*coll.* **~а́), ~** *no sg.* **1** gate, gates; (*вход*) gateway; **въе́хать в в.** to enter the gates; **стоя́ть в ~ах** to stand in the gateway; **пришла́ беда́, отворя́й ~а́** (*prov.*) misfortunes never come singly; **показа́ть/дать от воро́т поворо́т** (*coll.*) to throw s.o. out; **оказа́ться за ~ами** to lose one's job. **2** (*sport*) goal, goal-posts.

вороти́л|а, ы *m.* (*coll.*) bigwig.

воро|ти́ть[1]**, чу́, ~тишь** *pf.* (*coll.*) to bring back; **сде́ланного не ~тишь** what's done can't be undone.

воро|ти́ть[2]**, чу́, ~тишь** *impf.* (*coll.*) (+*i.*) to be in charge (of), run; **он тут всем ~тит** he runs the whole show here; **нос, мо́рду в.** (**от**+*g.*) (*coll.*) to turn up one's nose (at); (*impers.*): **(с души́) меня́ ~тит от э́того де́ла** this business makes me sick.

воро|ти́ться, чу́сь, ~тишься *pf.* (*coll.*) to return.

воротни́к, а́ *m.* collar.

воротнич|о́к, ка́ *m.* collar; **бе́лые ~ки́** white-collar workers.

во́рох, а, *pl.* **~а́** *m.* heap, pile; (*fig., coll.*) heaps, masses.

воро́ча|ть, ю *impf.* (*coll.*) **1** to turn, move; **в. глаза́ми** to roll one's eyes. **2** (+*i.*; *fig.*) to be in charge (of); to have control (of); **в. миллио́нами** to deal in big money.

воро́ча|ться, юсь *impf.* (*coll.*) to turn, move (*intrans.*); **в. с бо́ку на́ бок** to toss and turn; **~йтесь!** (*coll.*) get a move on!

воро|чу́(сь), ~тишь(ся) *see* ⇒**~ти́ть(ся)**

ворош|и́ть, у́, и́шь *impf.* (*of* ⇒**раз~**) **1**: **в. се́но** to turn, ted hay. **2** (*fig., coll.*) (*прошлое*) to stir up.

ворс, а, *no pl., m.* pile; nap; **по ~у** with the pile, nap.

ворси́нк|а, и *f.* **1** (*text.*) hair. **2** (*physiol., bot.*) fibre (*Br.*), fiber (*US*).

ворси́ст|ый (~, ~а) *adj.* (*text.*) fleecy, with thick pile.

ворс|ова́ть, у́ю *impf.* (*of* ⇒**на~**) (*text.*) to comb (*cloth*) to raise a nap.

ворся́нк|а, и *f.* (*bot.*) teasel.

ворча́нь|е, я *nt.* grumbling; (*собаки*) growling.

ворч|а́ть, у́, и́шь *impf.* (**на**+*a.*) to grumble (at); (*о собаке*) to growl (at); **в. себе́ по́д нос** to mutter (into one's beard); **э́ти соба́ки ~а́т на всех чужи́х люде́й** these dogs always growl at strangers.

ворчли́в|ый (~, ~а) *adj.* querulous.

ворчу́н, а́ *m.* (*coll.*) grumbler.

восвоя́си *adj.* (*coll.*) (for) home; **убра́ться в.** to get out.

восемна́дцатый *adj.* eighteenth.

восемна́дцат|ь, и *num.* eighteen.

во́с|емь, ьми́, ьмью́ *and* **емью́** *num.* eight.

во́с|емьдесят, ьми́десяти *num.* eighty.

вос|емьсо́т, ьмисо́т, емьюста́ми (*coll.* **ьмиста́ми**) *num.* eight hundred.

во́семью *adv.* eight times (*in multiplication*).

воск, а *m.* wax.

воскли́кн|уть, у, ешь *pf. of* ⇒**восклица́ть**

восклица́ни|е, я *nt.* exclamation.

восклица́тельный *adj.* exclamatory; **в. знак** exclamation mark.

восклица́|ть, ю *impf.* (*of* ⇒**воскли́кнуть**) to exclaim.

В

восков|óй *adj.* wax; (*цвет*) waxen; **~áя свечá** wax candle; **~áя бумáга** greaseproof paper; **~óе лицó** waxen complexion.

воскрес|áть, áю *impf.* (*of* ⇒**~нуть**) to rise again, rise from the dead; (*fig.*) to revive.

воскресéни|е, я *nt.* resurrection.

воскресéнь|е, я *nt.* Sunday.

воскре|сúть, шý, сúшь *pf.* (*of* ⇒**~шáть**) to raise from the dead, resurrect; (*fig.*) to revive.

воскрéсник, а *m.* voluntary Sunday work.

воскрéс|нуть, ну, нешь, *past* **~, ~ла** *pf. of* ⇒**~áть**

воскрéсный *adj.* Sunday.

воскрешá|ть, ю *impf. of* ⇒**воскресúть**

воскрешéни|е, я *nt.* raising from the dead, resurrection; (*fig.*) revival.

вослéд = **вслед**

воспалéни|е, я *nt.* (*med.*) inflammation; **в. лёгких** pneumonia.

воспалён|ный (~, ~á) *p.p.p. of* ⇒**воспалúть** *and adj.* sore; inflamed (*also fig.*); **~ное воображéние** fevered imagination.

воспалúтельный *adj.* (*med.*) inflammatory; **в. процéсс** inflammation.

воспал|úть, ю, úшь *pf.* (*of* ⇒**~ять**) to inflame.

воспал|úться, ю́сь, úшься *pf.* (*of* ⇒**~яться**) to become inflamed.

воспал|ять(ся), яю(сь) *impf. of* ⇒**~úть(ся)**

воспар|úть, ю́, úшь *pf.* (*of* ⇒**~ять**) (*poet.*) to soar; **в. дýхом** (*iron.*) to be carried away.

воспаря|ть, ю *impf. of* ⇒**воспарúть**

воспевá|ть, ю *impf. of* ⇒**воспéть**

восп|éть, ою́, оёшь *pf.* (*of* ⇒**~евáть**) (*poet.*) to sing (of), extol (in song).

воспитáни|е, я *nt.* **1** upbringing; (*образование*) education. **2** (*воспитанность*) (good) breeding.

воспúтанник, а *m.* **1** pupil. **2** (*приёмыш*) ward.

воспúтанност|ь, и *f.* (good) breeding.

воспúтанный *p.p.p. of* ⇒**воспитáть** *and adj.* well brought up.

воспитáтел|ь, я *m.* teacher; (*приёмыша*) guardian.

воспитáтель|ница, ницы *f. of* ⇒**~**

воспитáтельный *adj.* educational; **в. дом** foundling hospital.

воспит|áть, áю *pf.* (*of* ⇒**~ывать**) **1** (*вырастить*) to bring up; **в. сы́на патриóтом** to bring one's son up to be a patriot; (*дать образование*) to educate. **2** (*привить*) to cultivate, foster.

воспúтыва|ть, ю *impf. of* ⇒**воспитáть**

воспламенéни|е, я *nt.* ignition.

воспламен|úть, ю́, úшь *pf.* (*of* ⇒**~ять**) to kindle, ignite; (*fig.*) to fire, inflame.

воспламен|úться, ю́сь, úшься *pf.* (*of* ⇒**~яться**) to catch fire, ignite; (*fig.*) to take fire, flare up.

воспламеняéмост|ь, и *f.* inflammability.

воспламеняéмый *adj.* inflammable.

воспламеня|ть(ся), ю(сь) *impf. of* ⇒**воспламенúть(ся)**

воспóлн|ить, ю, ишь *pf.* to fill in; **в. пробéлы в свои́х знáниях** to fill in the gaps in one's knowledge; (*недостатки*) to make up for.

восполня|ть, ю *impf. of* ⇒**воспóлнить**

воспóльз|оваться, уюсь *pf. of* ⇒**пóльзоваться**

воспоминáни|е, я *nt.* **1** recollection, memory; **жить ~ями** to live on memories. **2** *pl.* (*liter.*) memoirs; reminiscences.

воспослéд|овать, ую *pf.* (*obs.*) to follow, ensue.

восп|ою́, оёшь *see* ⇒**~éть**

воспрепя́тств|овать, ую *pf. of* ⇒**препя́тствовать**

воспре|тúть, щý, тúшь *pf.* (*of* ⇒**~щáть**) (+*a. or inf.*) to forbid, prohibit; **в. вход** prohibit entry.

воспрещá|ть, ю *impf. of* ⇒**воспретúть**

воспрещá|ться, юсь *impf.* to be prohibited; **«курúть ~ется»** 'No Smoking'; **«посторóнним вход ~ется»** No unauthorized entry.

воспрещéни|е, я *nt.* prohibition.

восприúмчив|ый (~, ~а) *adj.* **1** (*ум, натура*) receptive; impressionable. **2** (*подверженный*) susceptible.

восприм|ý, ~ешь *see* ⇒**воспринять**

воспринимá|ть, ю *impf. of* ⇒**воспринять**

воспри|нять, мý, ~мешь, *past* **~нял, ~нялá, ~няло** *pf.* (*of* ⇒**~нимáть**) **1** (*ощутить*) to perceive, apprehend; (*понять*) to grasp, take in. **2** (*понять как*) to take (for), interpret; **в. молчáние как знак соглáсия** to take silence as a mark of consent.

восприя́ти|е, я *nt.* (*phil., psych.*) perception.

воспроизведéни|е, я *nt.* **1** reproduction; **в. человéческого рóда** reproduction of the human species; **вéрное в. картúны Рýбенса** faithful reproduction of a painting by Rubens. **2** (*electronics*) playback, replay; **замéдленное/ускóренное в.** slow-motion/high-speed replay.

воспроизве|стú, дý, дёшь, *past* **~л, ~лá** *pf.* (*of* ⇒**воспроизводúть**) (*in var. senses*) to reproduce; **в. в пáмяти** to recall.

воспроизводúтельный *adj.* reproductive.

воспроизво|дúть, жý, ~дишь *impf. of* ⇒**воспроизвестú**

воспроизвóдств|о, а *nt.* (*econ.*) reproduction.

воспротúв|иться, люсь, ишься *pf. of* ⇒**протúвиться**

воспря́н|уть, у, ешь *pf.* **1**: **в. дýхом** to take heart. **2**: **в. ото снá** (*obs.*) to wake up.

воспылá|ть, ю *pf.* (+*i.*) to be inflamed (with); to blaze (with); **в. гнéвом** to blaze with anger; **в. любóвью** (**к**+*d.*) to be smitten with love (for).

воссéда|ть, ю *impf. of* ⇒**воссéсть**

восс|éсть, я́ду, я́дешь, *past* **~éл** *pf.* to sit (*in state, formally*); **в. на престóл** (*fig.*) to ascend the throne.

воссла́в|ить, лю, ишь *pf.* (*of* ⇒**~ля́ть**) to hymn, praise.

восславля́|ть, ю *impf. of* ⇒**воссла́вить**

воссоединéни|е, я *nt.* reunification.

воссоедин|úть, ю́, úшь *pf.* (*of* ⇒**~я́ть**) to reunite.

воссоединя́|ть, ю *impf. of* ⇒**воссоединúть**

воссозда|вáть, ю́, ёшь *impf. of* ⇒**~ть**

воссоздáни|е, я *nt.* reconstruction.

воссоз|дáть, дáм, дáшь, дáст, дадúм, дадúте, дадýт, *past* **~дáл, ~далá, ~дáло** *pf.* (*of* ⇒**~давáть**) to reconstruct, reconstitute.

восста|вáть, ю́, ёшь *impf. of* ⇒**~ть**

восстáв|ить, лю, ишь *pf.* (*obs.*) to set up, erect; **в. перпендикуля́р** (*math.*) to raise a perpendicular.

восставля́|ть, ю *impf. of* ⇒**восстáвить**

восстанáвлива|ть, ю *impf. of* ⇒**восстановúть**

восстáни|е, я *nt.* uprising, insurrection.

восстановúтел|ь, я *m.* renovator, restorer.

восстановúтельн|ый *adj.* restorative; **в. периóд** period of reconstruction; **~ые рабóты** restoration work.

восстанов|úть, лю́, ~ишь *pf.* (*of* ⇒**восстанáвливать**) **1** to restore; **в. мир** to restore peace; **в. в пáмяти** to recall, recollect; **в. когó-н. в правáх** to restore s.o.'s rights; **егó ~или в дóлжности завéдующего** he has been reinstated as manager. **2** (**прóтив**+*g.*) to set (against), antagonize. **3** (*chem.*) to reduce.

восстановлéни|е, я *nt.* **1** restoration, renewal; **в. в правáх** restoration of rights; **в. в дóлжности** reinstatement. **2** (*chem.*) reduction.

восстановля́|ть, ю *impf.* = **восстанáвливать**

восстá|ть, ну, нешь, *imper.* **~нь,** *pf.* (*of* ⇒**~вáть**) (**на**+*a.*, **прóтив**+*g.*) to rise (against); (*fig.*) to be up in arms (against), revolt against; **всё деревéнское населéние ~ло на врагá** the whole countryside rose against the enemy.

востóк, а *m.* **1** east; **на в., с ~а** to, from the east. **2** **В.** the East; the Orient; **Блúжний В.** the Middle East; **Дáльний В.** the Far East.

востокове́д, а *m.* orientalist.

востокове́дени|е, я *nt.* oriental studies.

восто́рг, а *m.* delight; rapture; **быть в ~е** (**от**+*g.*) to be delighted (with); **приходи́ть в в.** (**от**+*g.*) to go into raptures (over).

восторга́|ть, ю *impf.* to delight, enrapture.

восторга́|ться, юсь *impf.* (+*i.*) to be delighted (with); to go into, be in raptures (over); **она́ ~ется бале́том** she goes into raptures over the ballet.

восто́рженност|ь, и *f.* enthusiasm.

восто́ржен|ный (~, ~на) *adj.* (*поклонник*) enthusiastic; (*приём, отзыв*) rapturous.

восторжеств|ова́ть, у́ю *pf. of* ⇒**торжествова́ть**

восточногерма́нский *adj.* (*hist.*) East German.

восто́чн|ый *adj.* east, eastern; (*направление, ветер*) easterly; (*культура*) oriental; **В~ая Герма́ния** (*hist.*) East Germany; **~ая це́рковь** the Eastern Church.

востре́бовани|е, я *nt.* claiming, demand; **до ~я** poste restante; **посла́ть паке́т до ~я** to send a parcel poste restante.

востре́б|овать, ую *pf.* to claim (*from post office, etc.*).

вострепе|та́ть, щу́, ~щешь *pf.* (*obs.*) to begin to tremble.

востро́ *adv.* (*coll.*): **держа́ть у́хо в.** to keep a sharp look-out; to be on guard.

востроглазый *adj.* (*coll.*) sharp-eyed; bright-eyed.

востроно́сый *adj.* (*coll.*) sharp-nosed.

восхвале́ни|е, я *nt.* eulogy.

восхвал|и́ть, ю́, ~ишь *pf.* (*of* ⇒**~я́ть**) to laud, extol, eulogize.

восхваля́|ть, ю *impf. of* ⇒**восхвали́ть**

восхити́тел|ьный (~ен, ~ьна) *adj.* (*женщина, красота*) entrancing, ravishing; (*вечер, музыка*) delightful; (*вкус, запах*) delicious.

восхи|ти́ть, щу́, ти́шь *pf.* to delight, captivate.

восхи|ти́ться, щу́сь, ти́шься *pf.* (+*i.*) to be delighted (by); to be carried away (by); to admire.

восхища́|ть(ся), ю(сь) *impf. of* ⇒**восхити́ть(ся)**

восхище́ни|е, я *nt.* admiration; (*восторг*) delight, rapture; **прийти́ в в. от** (+*g.*) to be delighted with.

восхищён|ный (~, ~а́) *p.p.p. of* ⇒**восхити́ть** *and adj.* delighted, rapt; admiring.

восхи|щу́(сь), ти́шь(ся) *see* ⇒**~ти́ть(ся)**

восхо́д, а *m.* rising; **в. со́лнца** sunrise.

восходи́тел|ь, я *m.* mountain-climber.

восходи́тель|ница, ницы *f. of* ⇒**~**

восхо|ди́ть, жу́, ~дишь *impf.* **1** *impf. of* ⇒**взойти́**. **2** (*impf. only*) (**к**+*d.*) to go back (to), date (from); **в. к дре́вности** to go back to antiquity.

восход|я́щий *pres. part. of* ⇒**~и́ть** *and adj.* **~я́щая звезда́** (*fig.*) rising star.

восхожде́ни|е, я *nt.* ascent; **в. на Монбла́н** the ascent of Mont Blanc.

восше́стви|е, я *nt.* **(на престо́л)** accession (to the throne).

восьм|а́я *see* ⇒**~о́й**

восьмёрк|а, и *f.* **1** (*coll.*) (*цифра*) eight. **2** (*coll.*) (*автобус, трамвай*) number eight (*of buses, etc.*). **3** (*cards*) eight; **в. черве́й** eight of hearts.

во́сьмер|о, ы́х *num.* **1** eight; **нас бы́ло в.** there were eight of us; **в. сане́й** eight sledges. **2** (*пары*) eight pairs; **в. перча́ток** eight pairs of gloves.

восьми́... *comb. form* eight-, octo-.

восьмигра́нник, а *m.* (*math.*) octahedron.

восьмидесятиле́ти|е, я *nt.* **1** (*срок*) eighty years. **2** (*годовщина*) eightieth anniversary. **3** (*день рождения*) eightieth birthday.

восьмидесятиле́тний *adj.* **1** (*срок*) of eighty years; **в. юбиле́й** eightieth anniversary. **2** (*возраст*) eighty-year-old.

восьмидеся́тый *adj.* eightieth.

восьмикла́ссник, а *m.* eighth-form (*Br.*), eighth-grade (*US*) pupil.

восьмикла́ссни|ца, цы *f. of* ⇒**~к**

восьмикра́тный *adj.* eightfold; (*чемпион*) eight-times.

восьмиле́тний *adj.* **1** (*срок*) eight-year. **2** (*возраст*) eight-year-old.

восьмино́г = **осьмино́г**

восьмисо́тый *adj.* eight-hundredth.

восьмиуго́льник, а *m.* (*math.*) octagon.

восьмиуго́льный *adj.* octagonal.

восьмичасово́й *adj.* eight-hour; **в. рабо́чий день** eight-hour (working-)day.

восьм|о́й *adj.* eighth; **~а́я но́та** (*mus.*) quaver (*Br.*), eighth note (*US*); *as n.* **~а́я, ~о́й** *f.* an eighth.

восьму́шк|а, и *f.* (*coll.*) eighth part.

вот *particle* **1** (*здесь*) here (is), (*там*) there (is); (*это*) this is; **в. мой дом** here is my house, this is my house; **в. идёт авто́бус** here comes the bus; **в. мы пришли́** here we are; **в. где я живу́** this is where I live.
2 (*emph. prons.; unstressed*): **в. э́ти ту́фли ей нра́вились** *these* are the shoes she liked.
3 (*in excl.*) here's a ..., there's a ... (for you); **во́т тип!** there's a character (for you)!; **во́т так исто́рия!** here's a pretty kettle of fish!; **в. и всё** I've said it all, that's that; (*expr. surprise*) **во́т как!, во́т (оно) что!** really? you don't mean to say so!; **в. так та́к! в. тебе на́!** well!; well, I never!; (*surprise and disapproval*) **в. ещё!** no way!; what(ever) next!; (*approval and/or encouragement*) **в. та́к!, в.-в.!** that's right!; that's it!; **в. та́к** and that's that; (*accompanying blows*) **во́т тебе!** take that!; **вот тебе́ и...** so much for ...; **вот тебе́ и пое́здка в Пари́ж!** so much for the trip to Paris!; **в. тебе́ и на́!** well I never!; **в. и** (*указывает на завершение чего-н.*): **в. и пришли́** here we are.

вот-во́т *adv.* just, on the point of, any minute; **по́езд в.-в. придёт** the train is just coming.

воти́р|овать, ую *impf. and pf.* **1** (*принять голосованием*) to vote in favour (*Br.*), favor (*US*) of. **2** (**за** (+*a.*)/**про́тив** (+*g.*)) to vote (for/against).

votиро́вк|а, и *f.* voting.

votк|а́ть, у́, ёшь, *past* **~а́л, ~ала́, ~а́ло** *pf.* to interweave.

воткн|у́ть, у́, ёшь *pf.* (*of* ⇒**втыка́ть**) (**в**+*a.*) to stick (into); (*с большим усилием*) to drive (into); **в. кол в зе́млю** to drive a stake into the ground.

вотр|у́, ёшь *see* ⇒**вотре́ть**

во́тум, а *no pl., m.* vote; **в. (не)дове́рия** (+*d.*) vote of (no) confidence (in).

во́тчин|а, ы *f.* (*hist.*) inherited estate, ancestral lands (12th–18th c.).

вотще́ *adv.* (*obs.*) in vain.

воцаре́ни|е, я *nt.* accession (to the throne).

воцар|и́ться, ю́сь, и́шься *pf.* (*of* ⇒**~я́ться**) **1** to accede, come to the throne. **2** (*fig.*) to set in; **в лесу́ ~и́лась тишина́** in the forest silence fell.

воцаря́|ться, юсь *impf. of* ⇒**воцари́ться**

вош|ёл, ла́ *see* ⇒**войти́**

вошь, вши, *i.* **~ю,** *pl.* **вши, вше́й** *f.* louse.

воща́нк|а, и *f.* (*coll.*) (*бумага*) wax-paper; (*ткань*) waxed cloth.

вощёный *adj.* waxed.

вощи́н|а, ы *f.* **1** (*collect.*) empty honeycomb. **2** (*неочищенный воск*) unrefined beeswax.

вощ|и́ть, у́, и́шь *impf.* (*of* ⇒**на~**) to wax.

во́|ю, ешь *see* ⇒**выть**

вою́|ю, ешь *see* ⇒**воева́ть**

вояж, а *m.* (*obs. or iron.*) journey, travels.

вояжёр, а *m.* **1** (*obs. or iron.*) traveller. **2** (*obs.*) (*коммивояжёр*) commercial traveller, salesman.

воя́к|а, и *m.* (*coll., iron.*) (*воин*) warrior; (*задира*) fire-eater.

впада́|ть, ю *impf.* **1** *impf. of* ⇒**впасть**. **2** *impf. only* (*of rivers*) (**в**+*a.*) to fall (into), flow (into); **Ока́ ~ет в Во́лгу** the Oka flows into the Volga.

впаде́ни|е, я *nt.* (*место слияния рек*) confluence; (*устье*) mouth (*of rivers*).

впа́дин|а, ы *f.* cavity, hollow; **глазна́я в.** eye-socket.

впад|у́, ёшь *see* ⇒**впасть**

впа́ива|ть, ю *impf. of* ⇒**впая́ть**

впа́йк|а, и *f.* **1** (*действие*) soldering-in. **2** (*впаянная часть*) soldered-in piece.

впа́л|ый *adj.* hollow, sunken; **~ые щёки** hollow cheeks.

впа|сть, ду́, дёшь, *past* **~л, ~ла** *pf.* (*of* ⇒**~да́ть**) **1** (**в**+*a.*) to fall (into), lapse (into), sink (into); **в. в бе́дность** to fall into penury; **в. в грех** to lapse into sin; **в. в отча́яние** to fall into despair. **2** (*щёки, глаза*) to fall in, sink.

впа|я́ть, я́ю *pf.* (*of* **⇨~ивать**) to solder in.

вперв|о́й *adv.* (*coll.*) = **~ые**

впервы́е *adv.* for the first time, first; **когда́ я в. прие́хал в Ло́ндон** when I first came to London; **в. в жи́зни** for the first time in one's life; **в. слы́шу об э́том** it's the first I've heard of it.

вперева́лку *adv.* (*coll.*): **ходи́ть в.** to waddle.

вперего́нки *adv.* (*coll.*): **бе́гать в.** to run races.

вперёд *adv.* **1** forward(s), ahead; (*о часах*) (*coll.*) fast; **взад и в.** back and forth; **большо́й шаг в.** (*fig.*) a big step forward; **мои́ часы́ иду́т в.** my watch is fast. **2** (*coll.*) (*впредь*) in future, from now on; **в. будь осторо́жнее** be more careful in future. **3** (*авансом*) in advance; **заплати́ть в.** to pay in advance.

впереди́ 1 *adv.* in front, ahead. **2** *adv.* (*в будущем*) in (the) future; ahead; **у него́ всё в.** he has his whole life in front of him. **3** *prep.+g.* in front of, before.

впереме́жку *adv.* (*coll.*) alternately.

впереме́шку *adv.* (*coll.*) higgledy-piggledy.

впер|е́ть, вопру́, вопрёшь, *past* **~, ~ла** *pf.* (*of* **⇨впира́ть**) (*coll.*) **1** to barge in; **он про́сто ~ в дом, не дожда́вшись приглаше́ния** he simply barged into the house without waiting to be invited. **2** (*впихнуть*) to shove in, thrust in.

впер|е́ться, вопру́сь, вопрёшься, *past* **~ся, ~лась** *pf.* (*of* **⇨впира́ться**) (*coll.*) to barge in.

впер|и́ть, ю, и́шь *pf.* (*of* **⇨~я́ть**) (**в**+*a.*) to direct (upon); **в. взор/взгляд** to fasten one's gaze (upon).

впер|и́ться, ю́сь, и́шься *pf.* (*of* **⇨~я́ться**) (*obs.*) to stare (at), fasten one's eyes (upon).

впер|я́|ть(ся), ю(сь) *impf. of* **⇨вперить(ся)**

впечатле́ни|е, я *nt.* impression; **~я де́тства** childhood impressions; **произвести́ в.** (**на**+*a.*) to make an impression (upon); **его́ речь произвела́ в. на всех** his speech made an impression on everyone; **тако́е в., что/ бу́дто** it seems that.

впечатли́тельност|ь, и *f.* impressionability.

впечатли́тел|ьный (~ен, ~ьна) *adj.* impressionable.

впечатля́|ть, ю *impf.* to impress.

впечатля́ющий *adj.* impressive.

впива́|ть, ю *impf.* to drink in, enjoy (*esp. olfactory sensations*); (*fig.*) (*воспринимать*) to absorb.

впива́|ться, юсь *impf. of* **⇨впи́ться**

впира́|ть(ся), ю(сь) *impf. of* **⇨впере́ть(ся)**

впи́санный *p.p.p. of* **⇨вписа́ть** *and adj.* (*math.*) inscribed.

впи|са́ть, шу́, ~шешь *pf.* (*of* **⇨~сывать**) **1** to enter; to insert; **в. своё и́мя в спи́сок** to enter one's name on a list; **в. фра́зу в ру́копись статьи́** to insert a sentence into the manuscript of an article. **2** (*math.*) to inscribe.

впи|са́ться, шу́сь, ~шешься *pf.* (*of* **⇨~сываться**) (*гармонировать*) to fit in, blend in.

впи́ск|а, и *f.* (*coll.*) entry; insertion.

впи́сыва|ть(ся), ю(сь) *impf. of* **⇨вписа́ть(ся)**

впит|а́ть, а́ю *pf.* (*of* **⇨~ывать**) to absorb; (*fig.*) to absorb, take in.

впит|а́ться, а́ется *pf.* (*of* **⇨~ываться**) (**в**+*a.*) to soak (into).

впи́тыва|ть(ся), ю, ет(ся) *impf. of* **⇨впита́ть(ся)**

впи́|ться, вопью́сь, вопьёшься, *past* **~лся, ~ла́сь** *pf.* (*of* **⇨~ва́ться**) (**в**+*a.*) **1** (*вонзиться*) to stick (into); (*укусить*) to bite; (*ужалить*) to sting; **ко́шка ~ла́сь в неё когтя́ми** the cat stuck its claws into her; **гвоздь ~лся мне в но́гу** a nail stuck into my foot. **2**: **в. взо́ром, глаза́ми** to fix, fasten one's eyes (upon).

впих|а́ть, а́ю *pf.* (*coll.*) = **~ну́ть**

впи́хива|ть, ю *impf. of* **⇨впиха́ть** *and* **впихну́ть**

впих|ну́ть, ну́, нёшь *pf.* (*of* **⇨~ивать**) to stuff in, cram in; (*втолкнуть*) to shove; **в. кого́-н. в ко́мнату** to shove s.o. into a room.

ВПК *m. indecl.* (*abbr. of* ***вое́нно-промы́шленный ко́мплекс***) military-industrial complex.

вплавь *adv.* by swimming.

впле|сти́, ту́, тёшь, *past* **~л, ~ла́** *pf.* (*of* **⇨~та́ть**) (**в**+*a.*) to plait (into), intertwine.

вплета́|ть, ю *impf. of* **⇨вплести́**

впле|ту́, тёшь *see* **⇨~сти́**

вплотну́ю *adv.* close; (*fig.*) in earnest; **поста́вить стол в. к стене́** to put the table right against the wall; **приня́ться за де́ло в.** to tackle the matter in real earnest.

вплоть *adv.* **1**: **в. до** (+*g.*) (*до предела*) (right) up to; until; (*включая*) including. **2 в.** (**к**+*d.*) right against, right up to.

вплыва́|ть, ю *impf. of* **⇨вплыть**

вплы|ть, ву́, вёшь, *past* **~л, ~ла́, ~ло** *pf.* (*of* **⇨~ва́ть**) (*о человеке*) to swim in; (*о корабле*) to sail in.

впова́лку *adv.* (*coll.*) side by side.

вполглаза́ *adv.* (*coll.*): **спать в.** to sleep with one eye open; to doze.

вполго́лоса *adv.* in an undertone, under one's breath.

вполз|а́ть, а́ю *impf. of* **⇨~ти́**

вполз|ти́, у́, ёшь, *past* **~, ~ла́** *pf.* (*of* **⇨~а́ть**) to creep in, crawl in; (*подняться вверх*) to creep up, crawl up.

вполне́ *adv.* fully, entirely; quite; **э́того в. доста́точно** that is quite enough.

вполоборо́та *adv.* half-turned.

вполови́ну *adv.* (*coll.*) by half.

вполси́лы *adv.* (*coll.*) at half strength.

вполу́ха *adv.* (*coll.*) with half an ear.

впопа́д *adv.* (*coll.*) to the point; opportunely; **вы спроси́ли о́чень в.** your question was very much to the point.

впопыха́х *adv.* (*coll.*) **1** (*торопливо*) in a hurry, hastily. **2** (*в спешке*) in one's haste; **в. я оста́вил зо́нтик в по́езде** in my haste I left my umbrella on the train.

впо́ру *adv.* (*coll.*) *as pred.* **1** (*об одежде*) just right, exactly; **э́тот костю́м мне соверше́нно в.** this suit fits me perfectly. **2** (*остаётся лишь*) one can only; the only thing left; **в. всё бро́сить** one can only abandon everything; the only thing left is to abandon everything.

впорхн|у́ть, у́, ёшь *pf.* (*птица, бабочка*) to flit in(to), flutter in(to); (*fig.*) to fly (into).

впосле́дствии *adv.* subsequently; afterwards.

впотьма́х *adv.* (*coll.*) in the dark.

впра́вду *adv.* (*coll.*) really, in reality.

впра́ве *as pred.*: **быть в.** (+*inf.*) to have a right (to); **он был в. серди́ться на вас** he had a right to be angry with you.

впра́в|ить, лю, ишь *pf.* (*of* **⇨~ля́ть**) **1** (*med.*) (*кость*) to set. **2** (*рубашку*) to tuck in.

впра́вк|а, и *f.* (*med.*) setting.

вправля́|ть, ю *impf. of* **⇨впра́вить**

впра́во *adv.* (**от**+*g.*) to the right (of).

впредь *adv.* in future, henceforth; **в. до** until; **в. до распоряже́ния** until further notice.

впригля́дку *adv.* (*coll., joc.*) *only in phr.* **пить чай в.** to have tea without sugar.

вприку́ску *adv.* (*coll.*) *only in phr.* **пить чай в.** to drink unsweetened tea while holding a lump of sugar in the mouth (*opp.* **⇨внакла́дку**).

вприпры́жку *adv.* (*coll.*) skipping; hopping.

вприся́дку *adv.*: **пляса́ть в.** to dance squatting.

впри́тирку *adv.* (*coll.*) (**к**+*d.*) up close (to), touching.

впри́тык *adv.* (*coll.*) (**к**+*d.*) up close (to), abutting (on).

впро́голодь *adv.* half starving.

впрок *adv.* **1** (*про запас*) for future use; **загото́вить в.** to lay in, stock up on. **2** *as pred.* (*на пользу*) to advantage; **э́то не пойдёт ему́ в.** it will do him no good, he will do no good by it.

впроса́к *adv.* (*coll.*): **попа́сть в.** to put one's foot in it.

впросо́нках *adv.* (*coll.*) half asleep.

впро́чем *adv. and conj.* **1** (*однако, но*) however, but; **он у́мный челове́к, в. он иногда́ ошиба́ется** he is a clever man, but he sometimes makes mistakes. **2** (*выражает нерешимость*) or rather; but then again; **приезжа́йте за́втра, в., лу́чше бы́ло бы послеза́втра** come tomorrow, or, even better, the day after.

впры́гива|ть, ю *impf. of* **⇨впры́гнуть**

впры́г|нуть, ну, нешь *pf.* (*of* **⇨~ивать**) (**в, на**+*a.*) to jump (into, on).

впры́скивани|е, я *nt.* injection.

впры́скива|ть, ю *impf. of* **⇨впры́снуть**

впры́сн|уть, у, ешь *pf.* (*of* **⇨впры́скивать**) to inject.

впрягá|ть(ся), ю(сь) *impf. of* ⇨**впря́чь(ся)**

впрямь *adv.* (*coll.*) really, indeed.

впря|чь, гу́, жёшь, гу́т, *past* **впряг, ~глá, ~глó** *pf.* (*of* ⇨**~гáть**) (**в**+*a.*) to harness (to).

впря́|чься, гу́сь, жёшься, гу́тся, *past* **впря́гся, ~глáсь** *pf.* (*of* ⇨**~гáться**) (**в**+*a.*) to harness o.s. (to).

впу́ск, а *m.* admission, admittance.

впускá|ть, ю *impf. of* ⇨**впусти́ть**

впускн|óй *adj.* admittance; inlet; **~áя трубá** inlet pipe.

впу|сти́ть, щу́, ~́стишь *pf.* (*of* ⇨**~скáть**) to admit, let in.

впусту́ю *adv.* (*coll.*) for nothing, to no purpose.

впу́т|ать, аю 1 *pf.* (*of* ⇨**~ывать**) (*вплести*) to twist in. **2** *pf. of* ⇨**пу́тать** 4

впу́т|аться, аюсь 1 *pf.* (*of* ⇨**~ываться**) (*вцепиться*) to get twisted up (in). **2** *pf. of* ⇨**пу́таться** 4

впу́тыва|ть(ся), ю(сь) *impf. of* ⇨**впу́тать(ся)**

впу|щу́, ~́стишь *see* ⇨**~сти́ть**

впя́теро *adv.* five times; **в. бóльше** five times as much.

впятерóм *adv.* five (together).

враг, á *m.* enemy; (*collect*) the enemy.

вражд|á, ы *f.* enmity, hostility.

враждéб|ный (~ен, ~на) *adj.* hostile.

вражд|овáть, у́ю *impf.* (**с**+*i.*) to be at enmity (with), at odds (with).

врáжеский *adj.* (*mil.*) enemy; hostile.

врáжий *adj.* enemy; hostile.

враз *adv.* (*coll.*) **1** (*разом*) at once, at the same time, together. **2** (*сразу*) at once, immediately.

вразби́вку *adv.* (*coll.*) at random.

вразбрóд *adv.* (*coll.*) separately; in disunity.

вразбрóс *adv.* (*coll.*) separately.

вразвáлку *adv.* (*coll.*): **ходи́ть в.** to waddle.

вразнобóй *adv.* (*coll.*) haphazardly.

вразнóс *adv.*: **торговáть в.** to peddle.

вразрéз *adv.*: **идти́ в.** (**с**+*i.*) to go against.

вразуми́тел|ьный (~ен, ~ьна) *adj.* intelligible, clear, comprehensible.

вразум|и́ть, лю́, и́шь *pf.* (*of* ⇨**~ля́ть**) to make understand; (*убедить*) to reason with; **ничéм их не ~и́шь** they will never learn.

вразумля́|ть, ю *impf. of* ⇨**вразуми́ть**

врáк|и, ~ *no sg.* (*coll.*) nonsense, rubbish.

врал|ь, я́ *m.* (*coll.*) (*лгун*) liar; (*пустослов*) chatterbox.

вран|ьё, я́ *nt.* (*coll.*) (*ложь*) lies; (*вздор*) nonsense.

врасплóх *adv.*: **застáть, захвати́ть, засти́гнуть в.** to take unawares; to catch off guard.

врассыпну́ю *adv.* in all directions.

враст|áть, áю *impf.* (*of* ⇨**~и́**) to grow in(to); **~áющий нóготь** ingrowing nail; **в. в зéмлю** (*fig.*) to sink into the ground.

враст|и́, у́, ёшь, *past* **врос, вpx"рослá** *pf. of* ⇨**~áть**

врастя́жку *adv.* (*coll.*) **1** at full length; **упáсть в.** to fall flat. **2 говори́ть в.** to drawl.

врат|á, ~ *no sg.* (*poet., obs.*) = **ворóта**

вратáр|ь, я́ *m.* (*sport*) goalkeeper.

вр|ать, у, ёшь, *past* **~ал, ~алá, ~áло** *impf.* (*of* ⇨**на~** *and* **со~**) (*coll.*) **1** (*лгать*) to lie, tell lies. **2** (*говорить вздор*) to talk nonsense. **3** (*быть неточным*) to be wrong.

врач, á *m.* doctor, physician; **дéтский в.** paediatrician (*Br.*), pediatrician (*US*); **зубнóй в.** dentist; **в. óбщей прáктики** general practitioner.

врачéбный *adj.* medical.

врач|евáть, у́ю *impf.* (*of* ⇨**у~**) (*obs.*) to doctor, treat; (*fig.*) to heal.

вращáтельный *adj.* rotary.

вращá|ть, ю *impf.* to revolve, rotate; **в. глазáми** to roll one's eyes.

вращá|ться, юсь *impf.* to revolve, rotate (*intrans.*); **он ~ется в худóжественных кругáх** he moves in artistic circles.

вращéни|е, я *nt.* rotation; revolution.

вред, á *no pl., m.* (*человеку*) harm, injury; (*здоровью, зданию*) damage; **без ~á** (**для**+*g.*) without detriment (to); **во ~** (+*d.*) to the detriment of; **причини́ть в. комý-н.** to do harm to s.o.; to harm s.o.

вреди́тел|ь, я *m.* **1** (*agric.*) pest. **2** (*человек*) saboteur.

вреди́тель|ский *adj. of* ⇨**~** 2

вреди́тельств|о, а *nt.* **1** (*деятельность*) sabotage. **2** (*поступок*) act of sabotage.

вре|ди́ть, жу́, ди́шь *impf.* (*of* ⇨**по~**) (+*d.*) (*человеку*) to injure, harm, hurt; (*здоровью, зданию*) to damage.

врéднича|ть, ю *impf.* (*coll.*) to be nasty.

врéдно *adv. as pred.* it is harmful; **в. для здорóвья** it is bad for one's health.

врéдност|ь, и *f.* harm; (*человека*) (*coll.*) nastiness; (*условия производства*) hazards.

врéд|ный (~ен, ~нá, ~но) *adj.* harmful, unhealthy; (*производство*) hazardous; (*no short form*) (*человек*) (*coll.*) nasty.

врé|жу(сь), жешь(ся) *see* ⇨**~зать(ся)**

вре|жу́, ди́шь *see* ⇨**~ди́ть**

врé|зать, жу, жешь *pf.* (*of* ⇨**~зáть**) **1** to cut in; (*вставить*) to set in. **2** (*coll.*) (+*d.*) (*ударить*) to whack (s.o.). **3** (*sl.*) (*выпить*) to drink.

врез|áть, áю *impf. of* ⇨**~́ать**

врé|заться, жусь, жешься *pf.* (*of* ⇨**~зáться**) (**в**+*a.*) **1** (*воткнуться*) to cut (into); (*fig.*) (*ворваться*) to plunge, plough (*Br.*), plow (*US*) (into); **в. в толпу́** to run into a crowd; (*удариться*) to smash (into). **2** (*запечатлеться*) to be engraved (on); **черты́ её лицá ~зались в егó пáмять** her features were engraved on his memory. **3** (*pf. only*) (*coll.*) (*влюбиться*) to fall in love (with).

врез|áться, áюсь *impf. of* ⇨**~́аться**

врéзыва|ть(ся), ю(сь) *impf.* = **врезáть(ся)**

временáми *adv.* at times, now and then, now and again.

временни́к, á *m.* chronicle, annals.

временнóй *adj.* **1** (*phil.*) temporal. **2** (*gram.*) tense. **3** (*tech.*) time.

врéменн|ый *adj.* temporary; provisional; **В~ое прави́тельство** (*hist.*) the Provisional Government (*of Russia, March–November 1917*); **~ое прави́тельство** caretaker government; **~ое соглашéние** interim agreement.

временщи́к, á *m.* (*obs.*) favourite.

врéм|я, ени, енем, ени, *pl.* **~енá, ~ён, ~енáм** *nt.* **1** time; **~ от ~ени** from time to time; **в дáнное в.** at present, at the present moment; **в ми́рное в.** in peace-time; **(в) пéрвое в.** at first; **(в) послéднее в.** lately, of late; **в своё в.** (*i*) (*in ref. to past*) in one's time, once, at one time, (*ii*) (*in ref. to future*) in due course; in one's own time; **в скóром ~ени** in the near future, shortly, before long; **в то же (сáмое) в.** at the same time; **до поры́ до ~ени** for the time being; **за послéднее в.** lately; **на в.** for a while; **на пéрвое в.** for the time being; **однó в.** once (*in the past*); **с незапáмятных ~ён** from time immemorial; **с течéнием ~ени** in the course of time; **с ~енем** in time, with time; **всё в.** all the time, continually; **рáньше ~ени** prematurely; **сáмое в.** (+*inf. or* +*d.*; *coll.*) just the time (to, for); the (right) time (to, for); **скóлько ~ени?** what is the time?; **тем ~енем** meanwhile; **в. покáжет** time will tell. **2**: **в. гóда** season. **3** (*gram.*) tense. **4**: **в то в. как** while, whereas. **5**: **во в.** (+*g.*) during, in.

времяисчислéни|е, я *nt.* calendar (*system of reckoning time*).

время́нк|а, и *f.* **1** (*печка*) temporary stove. **2** (*сооружение*) (any) temporary structure or fitting.

времяпрепровождéни|е, я *nt.* pastime; way of spending one's time.

врéтищ|е, а *nt.* (*obs.*) sackcloth.

врóвень *adv.* (**с**+*i.*) level (with); **в. с краями** to the brim.

врóде 1 *prep.+g.* like; **у негó есть гáлстук в. моегó** he has a tie like mine; **нéчто в.** (*coll.*) a sort of, a kind of. **2** *particle* (*coll.*) (*кажется*) it looks as if.

врождён|ный (~, ~á) *adj.* (*способность*) innate; (*недостаток*) congenital.

врозь *adv.* (*obs.*) = **врозь**

врозь *adv.* separately, apart.

врó|ю(сь), ~ешь(ся) *see* ⇨**врыть(ся)**

вруб, а *m.* (*mining*) cut.

вруб|áть(ся), áю(сь) *impf. of* ⇨**~и́ть(ся)**

вруб|и́ть, лю́, ~́ишь *pf.* (*of*

⇒~ать) **1** to cut in(to). **2** (*coll.*) (*включить*) to turn on.

вруб|иться, люсь, ~ишься *pf.* (*of* ⇒**~аться**) (**в**+*a.*) **1** to cut one's way (into), hack one's way (through). **2** (*coll.*) (*понять*) to twig, cotton on.

врукопашную *adv.* (*о борьбе*) using bare hands or hand weapons; **схватиться в.** to engage in close combat.

врун, а́ *m.* (*coll.*) liar.

врун|ья, ьи *f. of* ⇒**~**

вруч|а́ть, а́ю *impf. of* ⇒**~и́ть**

вруче́ни|е, я *nt.* handing, delivery; (*медали*) presentation; (*leg.*) serving (*of summons, etc.*).

вручи́тел|ь, я *m.* bearer (*of message, writ, etc.*).

вруч|и́ть, у́, и́шь *pf.* (*of* ⇒**~а́ть**) (*письмо, посылку*) to hand, deliver; (*медаль*) to present; (*вверить*) to entrust; **в. суде́бную пове́стку** to serve a subpoena.

вручну́ю *adv.* by hand.

врыва́|ть, ю *impf. of* ⇒**врыть**

врыва́|ться[1], юсь *impf. of* ⇒**вры́ться**

врыва́|ться[2], юсь *impf. of* ⇒**ворва́ться**

вр|ыть, о́ю, о́ешь *pf.* (*of* ⇒**~ыва́ть**) (**в**+*a.*) (*дерево, куст*) to plant firmly; (*столб*) to sink in(to).

вр|ы́ться, о́юсь, о́ешься *pf.* (*of* ⇒**~ыва́ться[1]**) (**в**+*a.*) to dig o.s. (into), bury o.s. (in).

вряд (ли) *adv.* (*coll.*) hardly, it is unlikely; **в. ли сто́ит** it is hardly worth it; **они́ в. ли приду́т** they are unlikely to come.

вса|ди́ть, жу́, ~дишь, *pf.* (*of* ⇒**~живать**) **1** to thrust, plunge (into); **в. нож в спи́ну** (+*d.*) to stab in the back (*also fig.*); **в. пу́лю в лоб кому́-н.** to put a bullet in s.o.'s head. **2** (*coll.*) (*средства, деньги*) to put, sink (into); **он ~ди́л весь свой капита́л в одно́ риско́ванное предприя́тие** he has sunk all his capital in one doubtful venture.

вса́дник, а *m.* rider, horseman.

вса́дниц|а, ы *f.* rider, horsewoman.

вса́жива|ть, ю *impf. of* ⇒**всади́ть**

вса|жу́, ~дишь *see* ⇒**~ди́ть**

всамде́лишный *adj.* (*coll.*) real(-live), honest-to-goodness.

вса́сывани|е, я *nt.* suction; (*поглощение*) absorption.

вса́сыва|ть(ся), ю(сь), *impf. of* ⇒**всоса́ть(ся)**

все *see* ⇒**весь[1]**

все... *comb. form* all-, omni-, pan-; most (*gracious etc.*).

всё 1 *pron. see* ⇒**весь[1]**.
2 *adv.* always; all the time; **он в. отвеча́ет одно́ и то же** he always gives the same answer; **он в. руга́ется** he swears all the time.
3: **в. (ещё)** still; **дождь в. (ещё) идёт** it is still raining; **в. же** after all, nevertheless.
4 (*coll.*) only, all; **он провали́лся на экза́мене — в. из-за тебя́!** he has failed his examination — all because of you!
5 *as conj.* however, nevertheless; **как ни стара́юсь, в. не разбира́ю, что́ он говори́т** however hard I try, I cannot make out what he says.
6 *as particle* (*strengthening comp.*): **в. бо́лее и бо́лее** more and more; **он в. толсте́ет** he is getting fatter and fatter.
7 *predic.* (*coll.*) (*кончено*) that's it!

всеве́дени|е, я *nt.* omniscience.

всеве́дущ|ий (~, ~а) *adj.* omniscient.

всеви́дящий *adj.* all-seeing.

всевла́сти|е, я *nt.* absolute power.

всевла́стный *adj.* all-powerful.

всевозмо́жный *adj.* all kinds of; every possible; **в. това́р** goods of all kinds.

Всевы́шн|ий, ~его *n.* (*relig.*) the Almighty.

всегда́ *adv.* always.

всегда́шний *adj.* usual, customary.

всего́ 1 *pron. see* ⇒**весь[1]**; **бо́льше в.** (the) most; **лу́чше в.** (the) best; **ча́ще в.** most often. **2** *adv.* (*итого*) in all, all told; (*лишь*) only; **в. лишь, в. то́лько** (*coll.*) only; **в.-на́всего** only, all in all; **в. ничего́** (*coll.*) practically nothing; **то́лько и в.** (*coll.*) that's all.

Вседержи́тел|ь, я *m.* (*relig.*) the Almighty.

вседне́вный *adj.* (*obs.*) daily, everyday.

вседозво́ленност|ь, и *f.* permissiveness; **о́бщество ~и** the permissive society.

всезна́йк|а, и *c.g.* (*coll., iron.*) know-all.

вселе́ни|е, я *nt.* (*жильца*) installation; (*в дом*) moving in.

вселе́нн|ая, ой *no pl., f.* universe.

вселе́нский *adj.* universal; (*eccl.*) ecumenical; **в. собо́р** ecumenical council.

всел|и́ть, ю́, и́шь *pf.* (*of* ⇒**~я́ть**) **1** (*жильца*) to move (s.o.) in; to install. **2** (*fig., rhet.*) to instil (*Br.*), instill (*US*) (in); **в. страх** (**в**+*a.*) to strike fear (into).

всел|и́ться, ю́сь, и́шься *pf.* (*of* ⇒**~я́ться**) (**в**+*a.*) **1** (*в дом*) to move in(to). **2** (*fig.*) to be implanted (in).

вселя́|ть(ся), ю(сь) *impf. of* ⇒**всели́ть(ся)**

всем *see* ⇒**весь[1]**

всеме́рный *adj.* all possible.

все́меро *adv.* seven times.

всемеро́м *adv.* seven (together).

всеми́лостивейший *adj.* (*hist.*) most gracious.

всеми́рный *adj.* world (*attr.*); worldwide.

всемогу́ществ|о, а *nt.* omnipotence.

всемогу́щ|ий (~, ~а) *adj.* omnipotent, all-powerful; (*of God*) Almighty.

всенаро́дно *adv.* publicly.

всенаро́дный *adj.* national; nation-wide.

все́нощн|ая, ой *f.* (*eccl.*) vespers.

всео́буч, а *m.* (*abbr. of* ***всео́бщее обуче́ние***) universal education.

всео́бщ|ий *adj.* universal; general; **~ая во́инская пови́нность** universal military service; **~ая забасто́вка** general strike; **~ие вы́боры** general election.

всеобъе́млющ|ий (~, ~а) *adj.* all-embracing, comprehensive.

всеору́жи|е, я *nt. only in phr.* **во ~и** (+*g.*) fully armed (with); **во ~и зна́ний** armed with knowledge.

всеохва́тывающий = **всеобъе́млющий**

всеплане́тный *adj.* global, worldwide.

всепобежда́ющий *adj.* all-conquering.

всепоглоща́ющий *adj.* all-consuming (*also fig.*).

всепого́дный *adj.* all-weather.

всеросси́йский *adj.* all-Russian.

всерьёз *adv.* seriously, in earnest.

всесезо́нный *adj.* year-round.

всеси́л|ьный (~ен, ~ьна) *adj.* all-powerful.

всесою́зный *adj.* (*hist.*) All-Union (*with reference to former USSR*).

всесторо́нний *adj.* (*образование*) all-round; (*анализ*) thorough, detailed.

всё-таки *conj. and particle* still, all the same.

всеуслы́шани|е, я *nt. only in phr.* **во в.** publicly, for all to hear.

всех *see* ⇒**весь[1]**

всеце́ло *adv.* completely.

всеча́сный *adj.* (*obs.*) hourly.

всея́дный *adj.* omnivorous.

вска́кива|ть, ю *impf. of* ⇒**вскочи́ть**

вска́пыва|ть, ю *impf. of* ⇒**вскопа́ть**

вскара́бк|аться, аюсь *pf.* (*of* ⇒**кара́бкаться** *and* **~иваться**) (**на**+*a.*; *coll.*) to scramble (up, on to), clamber (up, on to).

вскара́бкива|ться, юсь *impf. of* ⇒**вскара́бкаться**

вска́рмлива|ть, ю *impf. of* ⇒**вскорми́ть**

вскачь *adv.* at a gallop.

вски́дыва|ть(ся), ю(сь) *impf. of* ⇒**вски́нуть(ся)**

вски́|нуть, ну, нешь *pf.* (*of* ⇒**~дывать**) (*кинуть*) to throw up; **в. на пле́чи** to shoulder; (*поднять*) to raise (*suddenly*); **в. глаза́** to look up suddenly.

вски́|нуться, нусь, нешься *pf.* (*of* ⇒**~дываться**) (**на**+*a.*; *coll.*) **1** (*подняться*) to leap up (on to). **2** (*fig.*) (*наброситься*) to turn (on), go (for).

вскипа́|ть, ю *impf. of* ⇒**вскипе́ть**

вскип|е́ть, лю́, и́шь *pf.* (*of* ⇒**~а́ть**) **1** (*вода*) to boil up. **2** (*fig.*) to flare up, fly into a rage; **в. негодова́нием** to flare with indignation.

вскипя|ти́ть, чу́, ти́шь *pf. of* ⇒**кипяти́ть**

вскипя|ти́ться, чу́сь, ти́шься *pf.* (*coll.*) to flare up, fly into a rage.

всклоко́чен|ный (~, ~а) *p.p.p. of* ⇒**всклоко́чить** *and adj.* (*coll.*) dishevelled, tousled.

всклоко́чива|ть, ю *impf. of* ⇒**всклоко́чить**

всклоко́ч|ить, у, ишь *pf.* (*of* ⇒**~ивать**) (*coll.*) to dishevel, tousle.

всклю́чива|ть, ю *impf. of* ⇒**всклю́чить**

всклю́ч|ить, у, ишь *pf.* (*of* ⇒**~ивать**) (*coll.*) to dishevel, tousle.

всколыхн|у́ть, у́, ёшь *pf.* to stir; (*fig.*) to stir up.

всколыхн|у́ться, у́сь, ёшься *pf.* to be stirred up; (*fig.*) to be roused.

вскользь *adv.* slightly; in passing; **упомяну́ть в.** to mention in passing.

вскопа́|ть, ю *pf.* (*of* ⇒**вска́пывать**) to dig over.

вско́ре *adv.* soon, shortly after.

вскорм|и́ть, лю́, ~́ишь *pf.* (*of* ⇒**вска́рмливать**) (*живо́тных*) to rear; (*дете́й*) to raise.

вскоч|и́ть, у́, ~́ишь *pf.* (*of* ⇒**вска́кивать**) **1** (**в, на**+*a.*, **с**+*g.*) to leap up (into, on to; from). **2** (*coll.*) (*ши́шка*) to come up (*of bumps, boils, etc.*).

вскри́кива|ть, ю *impf. of* ⇒**вскри́кнуть**

вскри́к|нуть, ну, нешь *pf.* (*of* ⇒**~ивать**) to cry out.

вскрич|а́ть, у́, и́шь *pf.* to exclaim.

вскро́|ю, ешь *see* ⇒**вскрыть**

вскруж|и́ть, у́, ~́ишь *pf. only in phr.* **в. го́лову кому́-н.** to turn s.o.'s head.

вскрыва́|ть(ся), ю, ет(ся) *impf. of* ⇒**вскры́ть(ся)**

вскры́ти|е, я *nt.* **1** (*паке́та*) opening, unsealing. **2** (*fig.*) (*фа́кта*) revelation, disclosure. **3** (*geog.*) (*рек*) opening (*of rivers after break-up of ice*). **4** (*med.*) (*нары́ва*) lancing. **5** (*med.*) (*тру́па*) autopsy, post-mortem.

вскр|ыть, о́ю, о́ешь *pf.* (*of* ⇒**~ыва́ть**) **1** (*паке́т*) to open, unseal. **2** (*fig.*) (*факт*) to reveal, disclose. **3** (*med.*) (*нары́в*) to lance. **4** (*med.*) (*труп*) to carry out a post-mortem on, dissect.

вскр|ы́ться, о́ется *pf.* (*of* ⇒**~ыва́ться**) **1** (*обнару́житься*) to come to light, be revealed. **2** (*geog.*) (*река́*) to become clear (of ice); become open. **3** (*med.*) to break, burst.

вскласть *adv.* (*coll.*) to one's heart's content.

вслед 1 *adv.* (**за**+*i.*) after; **посла́ть письмо́ в.** to forward a letter. **2** *prep.*+*d.* after; **смотре́ть в.** to follow with one's eyes.

вслéдствие *prep.*+*g.* in consequence of, owing to, due to.

вслепу́ю *adv.* blindly; **печа́тать в.** to touch-type.

вслух *adv.* aloud, out loud.

вслу́ш|аться, аюсь *pf.* (*of* ⇒**~иваться**) (**в**+*a.*) to listen attentively (to).

вслу́шива|ться, юсь *impf. of* ⇒**вслу́шаться**

всма́трива|ться, юсь *impf. of* ⇒**всмотре́ться**

всмотр|е́ться, ю́сь, ~́ишься *pf.* (*of* ⇒**всма́триваться**) (**в**+*a.*) to peer (at); to scrutinize.

всмя́тку *adv.*: **яйцо́ в.** soft-boiled, lightly-boiled egg.

всо́выва|ть, ю *impf. of* ⇒**всу́нуть**

всос|а́ть, у́, ёшь *pf.* (*of* ⇒**вса́сывать**) (*во́ду*) to soak up, absorb; (*fig.*) (*привы́чки*) to absorb, imbibe.

всос|а́ться, у́сь, ёшься *pf.* (*of* ⇒**вса́сываться**) (**в**+*a.*) **1** to fasten upon (*with mouth, lips, etc.*). **2** (*вода́*) to soak through (into), be absorbed.

вспа́ива|ть, ю *impf. of* ⇒**вспои́ть**

вспа́рхива|ть, ю *impf. of* ⇒**вспорхну́ть**

вспа́рыва|ть, ю *impf. of* ⇒**вспоро́ть**

вспа|ха́ть, шу́, ~́шешь *pf.* (*of* ⇒**~́хивать**) to plough up (*Br.*), plow up (*US*).

вспа́хива|ть, ю *impf. of* ⇒**вспаха́ть**

вспа́шк|а, и *f.* ploughing (*Br.*), plowing (*US*).

вспаш|у́, ~́ешь *see* ⇒**вспаха́ть**

вспе́нива|ть(ся), ю(сь) *impf. of* ⇒**вспе́нить(ся)**

вспе́н|ить, ю, ишь *pf.* (*of* ⇒**~ивать**) to make foam, make lather; **в. коня́** get one's horse into a lather.

вспе́н|иться, юсь, ишься *pf.* (*of* ⇒**~иваться**) to froth; to lather (*intrans.*).

вспетуш|и́ться, у́сь, и́шься *pf. of* ⇒**петуши́ться**

всплакн|у́ть, у́, ёшь *pf.* to shed a few tears, have a little cry.

всплеск, а *m.* splash.

всплёскива|ть, ю *impf. of* ⇒**всплесну́ть**

всплес|ну́ть, ну́, нёшь *pf.* (*of* ⇒**~́кивать**) to splash; **в. рука́ми** to throw up one's hands.

всплыва́|ть, ю *impf. of* ⇒**всплыть**

всплы|ть, ву́, вёшь, *past* **~л, ~ла́, ~́ло** *pf.* (*of* ⇒**~ва́ть**) to rise to the surface, surface; (*fig.*) (*факт*) to come to light; (*вопро́с*) to arise.

вспо|и́ть, ю́, и́шь *pf.* (*of* ⇒**вспа́ивать**) to nurse; to rear; **в. и вскорми́ть** (*fig., coll.*) to bring up.

вспола́скива|ть, ю *impf. of* ⇒**всполосну́ть**

всполосн|у́ть, у́, ёшь *pf.* (*of* ⇒**вспола́скивать**) to rinse.

всполо́х|и, ов *no sg.* (*зарни́ца*) (flashes of) summer lightning; (*collect.*) (*вспы́шки огня́*) flashes, glow (*from fire, explosion, etc.*).

всполош|и́ть, у́, и́шь *pf. of* ⇒**полоши́ть**

всполош|и́ться, у́сь, и́шься *pf. of* ⇒**полоши́ться**

вспомина́|ть(ся), ю, ет(ся) *impf. of* ⇒**вспо́мнить(ся)**

вспо́м|нить, ню, нишь *pf.* (*of* ⇒**~ина́ть**) (*де́тство*) to remember, recall, recollect; (**о**+*p.*, **что**) to remember.

вспо́м|ниться, нится *pf.* (*of* ⇒**~ина́ться**) to come back, be recalled; (*impers.*, +*d.*): **мне**, *etc.*, **~нилось** I, *etc.*, remembered.

вспомога́тельный *adj.* auxiliary; subsidiary; (*gram.*) auxiliary.

вспомоществова́ни|е, я *nt.* (*obs.*) relief, assistance.

вспомян|у́ть, у́, ~́ешь *pf.* (+*a. or* **о**+*p.*; *coll.*) to remember.

вспор|о́ть, ю́, ~́ешь *pf.* (*of* ⇒**вспа́рывать**) to rip open.

вспорхн|у́ть, у́, ёшь *pf.* to fly up.

вспоте́|ть, ю *pf.* (*of* ⇒**поте́ть**) to come out in a sweat; (*стекло́*) to mist over.

вспры́гива|ть, ю *impf. of* ⇒**вспры́гнуть**

вспры́г|нуть, ну, нешь *pf.* (*of* ⇒**~ивать**) (**на**+*a.*) to jump up (on to), spring up (on to).

вспры́скива|ть, ю *impf. of* ⇒**вспры́снуть**

вспры́с|нуть, ну, нешь *pf.* (*of* ⇒**~кивать**) **1** (+*i.*) to sprinkle (with). **2** (*fig., coll.*) (*отпра́здновать*) to celebrate.

вспу́гива|ть, ю *impf. of* ⇒**вспугну́ть**

вспуг|ну́ть, ну́, нёшь *pf.* (*of* ⇒**~́ивать**) to scare away; (*дичь*) to put up.

вспух|а́ть, а́ю *impf. of* ⇒**~́нуть**

вспу́х|нуть, ну, нешь *pf.* (*of* ⇒**~а́ть**) to swell up.

вспу́чива|ть, ю *impf. of* ⇒**вспу́чить**

вспу́ч|ить, у, ишь *pf.* (*of* ⇒**~ивать** *and* **пу́чить**) (*usu. impers.*) to distend; **у него́ живо́т ~ило** his abdomen is distended.

вспыл|и́ть, ю́, и́шь *pf.* to flare up; **в.** (**на**+*a.*) to fly into a rage (with).

вспы́льчив|ый (~, ~а) *adj.* hot-tempered; irascible.

вспы́хива|ть, ю *impf. of* ⇒**вспы́хнуть**

вспы́х|нуть, ну, нешь *pf.* (*of* ⇒**~ивать**) **1** (*ого́нь, свет*) to flash; (*бума́га*) to burst into flames, blaze up; (*fig.*) (*пожа́р*) to break out; (*ссо́ра, конфли́кт*) to flare up; (*па́ника, война́*) to break out. **2** (*покрасне́ть*) to blush.

вспы́шк|а, и *f.* flash; (*phot.*) flash (attachment); **электро́нная в.** flashgun; (*astron.*) flare; (*fig.*) (*гне́ва*) outburst, (*эне́ргии, отча́яния*) burst; (*боле́зни*) outbreak.

вспять *adv.* back(wards).

встава́ни|е, я *nt.* rising; **почти́ть ~ем** to stand in honour (*Br.*), honor (*US*) (of).

вста|ва́ть, ю́, ёшь *impf. of* ⇒**~ть**

вста́в|ить, лю, ишь *pf.* (*of* ⇒**~ля́ть**) to put in, insert; **в. в ра́му** to frame; **в. себе́ зу́бы** to have false teeth, dentures made.

вста́вк|а, и *f.* **1** (*де́йствие*) fixing, insertion; (*в ра́му*) framing; (*в опра́ву*) mounting. **2** (*в оде́жде*) inset. **3** (*в те́ксте*) insertion.

вставля́|ть, ю *impf. of* ⇒**вста́вить**

вставн|о́й *adj.* inserted; **~ы́е зу́бы**

false teeth, dentures; **~ые ра́мы** removable window-frames.

встарь *adv.* of old, in olden time(s).

вста|ть, ну, нешь *pf.* (*of* ⇒**~ва́ть**) **1** (*с постели*) to get up, rise; (*на ноги*) to stand up, rise, get up; (*солнце*) to rise; **он ра́но ~л сего́дня у́тром** he got up early this morning; **в. с ле́вой ноги́** to get out of bed on the wrong side; **в. из-за стола́** to rise, get up from the table; (*fig.*) **в. на свой но́ги** to stand on one's own feet; **в. гру́дью за** (+*a.*) to stand up for.
2 (*стать*) to stand; **в. на рабо́ту** to start work.
3 (**в** + *a.*) to go (into), fit (into); **большо́й шкаф не ~нет в э́ту ко́мнату** the large cupboard will not go into this room.
4 (*вопрос*) (*fig.*) to arise, come up.
5 (*возникнуть, появиться*) to appear, arise.
6 *impf. only* (*coll.*) (*часы*) to stop (working).

встрева́|ть, ю *impf. of* ⇒**встрять** *and* **встря́нуть**

встрево́жен|ный (~, ~на) *p.p.p. of* ⇒**встрево́жить** *and adj.* anxious.

встрево́ж|ить(ся), у(сь), ишь(ся) *pf. of* ⇒**трево́жить(ся)**

встрёпанный *p.p.p. and adj.* (*coll.*) dishevelled.

встреп|а́ть, лю́, ~лешь *pf.* (*coll.*) to dishevel.

встрепен|у́ться, у́сь, ёшься *pf.* **1** (*птицы*) to start (up), be roused. **2** (*сердце*) to give a start.

встрёпк|а, и *f.* (*coll.*) scolding.

встре́|тить, чу, тишь *pf.* (*of* ⇒**~ча́ть**) **1** (*человека*) to meet; (*сопротивление*) to meet with, encounter; (*обнаружить*) to come across.
2 (*предложение, речь*) to receive, greet; (*Пасху, 8 марта*) to celebrate; **в. Но́вый год** to see the New Year in.

встре́|титься, чусь, тишься *pf.* (*of* ⇒**~ча́ться**) (**с** + *i.*) **1** to meet (with), encounter, come across; **в. с затрудне́ниями** to encounter difficulties. **2** (*попасться*) to be found, occur. **3** (*собраться*) to gather, congregate.

встре́ч|а, и *f.* **1** meeting; (*приём*) reception; **в. в верха́х** (*pol.*) summit; **в. Но́вого го́да** New Year's Eve party.
2 (*sport*) match, meeting.

встреча́|ть, ю *impf. of* ⇒**встре́тить**

встреча́|ться, юсь *impf.* **1** *impf. of* ⇒**встре́титься. 2** *impf. only* (*бывать*) to be found; **в Шотла́ндии ещё ~ются ди́кие ко́шки** wild cats are still to be found in Scotland.

встре́чный *adj.* **1** (*поезд, машина*) proceeding from opposite direction; oncoming; **в. ве́тер** head wind; **в. по́езд** oncoming train; *as n.* **пе́рвый в.** the first person you meet, anyone; **(ка́ждый) в. и попере́чный** every Tom, Dick, and Harry. **2** (*предложение*) counter; **в. иск** (*leg.*) counter-claim; **в. план** counter-plan.

встро́енн|ый *adj.* built-in; **~ые програ́ммы** (*comput.*) firmware.

вструхн|у́ть, у́, ёшь *pf.* (*coll.*) to be alarmed.

встря́|нуть, ну, нешь *pf.* (*of* ⇒**встрева́ть**) (**в** + *a.*; *coll.*) to get mixed up (in); **в. в разгово́р** to butt in(to a conversation).

встря́ск|а, и *f.* shaking; (*fig.*) shock.

встря́|ть, ну, нешь = **встря́нуть**

встря́хива|ть(ся), ю(сь) *impf. of* ⇒**встряхну́ть(ся)**

встрях|ну́ть, ну́, нёшь *pf.* (*of* ⇒**~ивать**) to shake; (*fig.*) to shake up, rouse.

встрях|ну́ться, ну́сь, нёшься *pf.* (*of* ⇒**~иваться**) **1** to shake o.s. **2** (*fig.*) (*оживиться*) to rouse o.s.; to cheer up; **~ни́тесь!** pull yourself together. **3** (*coll.*) (*развлечься*) to have some fun.

вступа́|ть(ся), ю(сь) *impf. of* ⇒**вступи́ть(ся)**

вступи́тельн|ый *adj.* introductory; **в. взнос** entrance fee; **~ая ле́кция** inaugural lecture; **в. экза́мен** entrance exam.

вступ|и́ть, лю́, ~ишь *pf.* (*of* ⇒**~а́ть**) **1** (**в** + *a.*) (*войти, въехать*) to enter; (*стать членом*) to join; (*в спор, переговоры*) to enter into; **в. в бой** to join battle; **в. в де́йствие** (*договор, закон*) to come into force; **в. в брак** to marry; **в. в свои́ права́** to come into one's own; **в. в (зако́нную) си́лу** to become law; **в. в строй** (*завод*) to begin operating (*after being built*). **2** (**на** + *a.*) to mount, go up; **в. на престо́л** to ascend the throne.

вступ|и́ться, лю́сь, ~ишься *pf.* (*of* ⇒**~а́ться**) (**за** + *a.*) to stand up (for).

вступле́ни|е, я *nt.* **1** (*в город*) entry; (*в клуб*) joining. **2** (*в музыке*) prelude; (*в книге*) introduction.

всу́е *adv.* in vain.

всу́н|уть, у, ешь *pf.* (*of* ⇒**всо́вывать**) to stick in; (*незаметно*) to slip in.

всухомя́тку *adv.* (*coll.*): **есть в.** to live on, eat cold food without liquids.

всу́чива|ть, ю *impf. of* ⇒**всучи́ть**

всуч|и́ть, у́, ~ишь *pf.* (*of* ⇒**~ивать**) **1** (*вплести*) to entwine. **2** (+*d.*; *coll.*) (*заставить взять*) to foist (on), palm off (on).

всхли́п|нуть, ну, нешь *pf.* (*of* ⇒**~ывать**) to sob.

всхли́пывани|е, я *nt.* (*действие*) sobbing; (*звуки*) sobs.

всхли́пыва|ть, ю *impf. of* ⇒**всхли́пнуть**

всхо|ди́ть, жу́, ~дишь *impf. of* ⇒**взойти́**

всхо́д|ы, ов *no sg.* shoots.

всхо́жест|ь, и *f.* (*agric.*) germinating capacity.

всхо́жий *adj.* (*agric.*) capable of germinating.

всхрап|ну́ть, ну́, нёшь *pf.* **1** *pf. of* ⇒**~ывать. 2** (*coll.*) to have a nap.

всхра́пыва|ть, ю *impf.* (*of* ⇒**всхрапну́ть**) (*во сне*) to snore; (*о лошади*) to snort.

всы́п|ать, лю, лешь *pf.* (*of* ⇒**~а́ть**) **1** (**в** + *a.*) to pour (into). **2** (+*d.*; *coll.*) to give what for; (*бить*) to thrash; **в. по пе́рвое число́** to knock into the middle of next week.

всыпа́|ть, ю *impf. of* ⇒**всы́пать**

всы́пк|а, и *f.* (*выговор*) rating; (*порка*) thrashing.

всю́ду *adv.* everywhere.

вся *see* ⇒**весь**[1]

вськ *short form* (*obs.*) *of* ⇒**~и́й;** *as pron.* (*obs.*) everyone.

вся́к|ий *pron.* **1** any; **во ~ом слу́чае** in any case, at any rate; **без ~ого/~их** (*coll.*) without any argument; *as n.* anyone. **2** (*всевозможный*) all sorts of; every; **на в. слу́чай** just in case.

вся́ко *pron.* (*coll.*): **в. быва́ет** all sorts of things go on, happen.

вся́чески *adv.* (*coll.*) in every way possible.

вся́ческ|ий *adj.* (*coll.*) all kinds of.

вся́чин|а, ы *f.* (*coll.*): **вся́кая в.** all kinds of things.

вся́чинк|а, и *f.* (*coll.*): **жить со ~ой** to have one's up and downs.

Вт (*abbr. of* **ватт**) W, watt.

вта́йне *adv.* secretly, in secret.

вта́лкива|ть, ю *impf. of* ⇒**втолкну́ть**

вта́птыва|ть, ю *impf. of* ⇒**втопта́ть**

вта́скива|ть(ся), ю(сь) *impf. of* ⇒**втащи́ть(ся)**

втач|а́ть, а́ю *pf.* (*of* ⇒**~ивать**) (**в** + *a.*) to stitch in(to).

вта́чива|ть, ю *impf. of* ⇒**втача́ть**

вта́чк|а, и *f.* **1** (*действие*) stitching in. **2** (*вшитая часть*) patch.

втащ|и́ть, у́, ~ишь *pf.* (*of* ⇒**вта́скивать**) (**в** + *a.*, **на** + *a.*) to drag (into, on to).

втащ|и́ться, у́сь, ~ишься *pf.* (*of* ⇒**вта́скиваться**) (**в** + *a.*, **на** + *a.*) (*coll.*) to drag o.s. (into, on to).

втека́|ть, ет, ют *impf. of* ⇒**втечь**

втёмную *adv.* (*coll.*) without seeing one's cards; (*fig.*) blindly, in the dark; **де́йствовать в.** to take a leap in the dark.

втемя́ш|ить, у, ишь *pf.* (+*d.*; *coll.*) to impress (upon); **в. что-н. кому́-н. в башку́** to get sth. into s.o.'s skull.

втемя́ш|иться, ится *pf.* (+*d.*; *coll.*) (*о мысли*) to get into s.o.'s head.

втер|е́ть, вотру́, вотрёшь, *past* **~,** **~ла** *pf.* (*of* ⇒**втира́ть**) (**в** + *a.*) to rub in(to); **в. очки́ кому́-н.** (*fig., coll.*) to pull the wool over s.o.'s eyes.

втер|е́ться, вотру́сь, вотрёшься, *past* **~ся, ~лась** *pf.* (*of* ⇒**втира́ться**) **1** (**в** + *a.*; *coll.*) to insinuate *or* worm o.s. into; **ему́ удало́сь в. в дове́рие к премье́р-мини́стру** he succeeded in worming his way into the confidence of the Prime Minister.
2 (*впитаться*) to be absorbed.

вте|са́ться, шу́сь, ~шешься *pf.* (*of* ⇒**~сываться**) (**в** + *a.*; *coll.*) to insinuate o.s. in(to), brazen one's way in(to).

втёсыва|ться, юсь *impf. of* ⇒**втеса́ться**

вте|чь, чёт, ку́т, *past* **~к, ~кла́** *pf.* (*of* ⇒**~ка́ть**) to flow in(to).

втира́ни|е, я *nt.* **1** (*действие*) rubbing in. **2** (*лекарство*) embrocation, liniment.

втира́|ть(ся), ю(сь) *impf. of* ⇒**втере́ть(ся)**

вти́скива|ть(ся), ю(сь) *impf. of* ⇒**вти́снуть(ся)**

вти́с|нуть, ну, нешь *pf.* (*of* ⇒**~кивать**) (**в**+*a.*) to squeeze in(to).

вти́с|нуться, нусь, нешься *pf.* (*of* ⇒**~киваться**) (*coll.*) to squeeze (o.s.) in(to).

втих|аря́ *adv.* (*coll.*) = **~омо́лку**

втихомо́лку *adv.* (*coll.*) surreptitiously; on the quiet.

втих|у́ю *adv.* (*coll.*) = **~омо́лку**

втолкн|у́ть, у́, ёшь *pf.* (*of* ⇒**вта́лкивать**) (**в**+*a.*) to push in(to), shove in(to).

втолк|ова́ть, у́ю *pf.* (*of* ⇒**~о́вывать**) (+*d.*; *coll.*) to din (into), ram (into).

втолко́выва|ть, ю *impf. of* ⇒**втолкова́ть**

втоп|та́ть, чу́, ~чешь *pf.* (*of* ⇒**вта́птывать**) to trample in; **в. в грязь** (*fig.*) to drag in the mire, humiliate.

втора́чива|ть, ю *impf. of* ⇒**второчи́ть**

вторг|а́ться, а́юсь *impf. of* ⇒**~нуться**

вто́рг|нуться, нусь, нешься *past* **~ся, ~лась** *pf.* (*of* ⇒**~а́ться**) (**в**+*a.*) (*в страну*) to invade; (*в чужие владения*) to encroach (upon), trespass (on); (*в чужие дела*) to interfere (in); to intrude (into).

вторже́ни|е, я *nt.* invasion; encroachment; interference, intrusion.

вто́р|ить, ю, ишь *impf.* (+*d.*) **1** (*mus.*) to play, sing second part (to). **2** (*fig., pej.*) to echo, repeat.

втори́чн|ый *adj.* **1** (*второй*) second. **2** (*второстепенный*) secondary. **3**: **~ое сырьё** recyclable material.

вто́рник, а *m.* Tuesday; **во в.** on Tuesday; **на в.** for Tuesday; **в сле́дующий/про́шлый в.** next/last Tuesday.

вто́рни|чный *adj. of* ⇒**~к**

второго́дник, а *m.* pupil remaining in same form for second year.

второго́дни|ца, цы *f. of* ⇒**~к**

Второзако́ни|е, я *nt.* (*bibl.*) Deuteronomy.

втор|о́й *adj.* **1** second; **в. час** (it is) past one; **из ~ы́х рук** (at) second hand; (*не главный*) secondary; **на ~о́м пла́не** (*fig.*) in the background; **на ~ы́х ро́лях** playing supporting roles; **роль ~о́го пла́на** supporting role; **актёр ~о́го пла́на** supporting actor; **~а́я скри́пка** second fiddle. **2** *as n.* **~о́е, ~о́го** *nt.* main course (*of meal*). **3** *as particle* **~о́е** (*coll.*) in the second place.

второкла́ссник, а *m.* second-form (*Br.*), second-grade (*US*) pupil.

второкла́сsни|ца, цы *f. of* ⇒**~к**

второкла́ссный *adj.* second-class; (*pej.*) second-rate.

второку́рсник, а *m.* second-year student.

второку́рсни|ца, цы *f. of* ⇒**~к**

второочередно́й *adj.* secondary.

второпя́х *adv.* **1** hurriedly, in haste. **2** (*во время спешки*) in one's hurry.

второразря́дный *adj.* second-rate.

второсо́ртный *adj.* **1** (*товар*) of the second-best quality. **2** (*coll.*) (*актёр*) second-rate.

второстепе́н|ный (~ен, ~на) *adj.* secondary; minor.

второсырь|ё, я *nt.* recyclable material.

вторoч|и́ть, у́, и́шь *pf.* (*of* ⇒**втора́чивать**) to strap to one's saddle.

врав|и́ть, лю́, ~ишь *pf.* (*of* ⇒**~ливать**) (**в**+*a.*) to inveigle (into).

втра́влива|ть, ю *impf. of* ⇒**втрави́ть**

втре́ска|ться, юсь *pf.* (**в**+*a.*; *coll.*) to fall in love (with).

в-тре́тьих *adv.* thirdly, in the third place.

втри́дорога *adv.* (*coll.*) triple the price; **плати́ть в.** to pay through the nose.

втро́е *adv.* three times; **в. бо́льше** three times as big; **увели́чить в.** to triple.

втроём *adv.* three (together); **мы в.** the three of us.

втройне́ *adv.* three times as much, treble.

втуз, а *m.* (*abbr. of* ***вы́сшее техни́ческое уче́бное заведе́ние***) technical college.

вту́лк|а, и *f.* **1** (*tech.*) bush. **2** (*пробка*) plug, bung.

вту́не *adv.* (*obs.*) in vain; **оста́ться в.** to be in vain.

втык, а *m.* (*coll.*) dressing-down, rocket; **сде́лать в.** (+*d.*) to give s.o. a dressing-down; to tear s.o. off a strip.

втыка́|ть, ю *impf. of* ⇒**воткну́ть**

вты́чк|а, и *f.* (*coll.*) **1** sticking in. **2** (*пробка*) plug, bung.

втю́р|иться, юсь ишься *pf.* (**в**+*a.*; *coll.*) to fall in love (with); to fall for.

втя́гива|ть(ся), ю(сь) *impf. of* ⇒**втяну́ть(ся)**

втяжно́й *adj.* (*tech.*) suction.

втя|ну́ть, ну́, ~нешь *pf.* (*of* ⇒**~гивать**) **1** (*лодку*; *щёки, живот*) to draw (in, into, up), pull (in, into, up); (*воздух, жидкость*) to absorb, take in. **2** (*fig.*) (**в**+*a.*) to draw (into), involve (in); **в. в спор** to draw into an argument.

втя|ну́ться, ну́сь, ~нешься *pf.* (*of* ⇒**~гиваться**) (**в**+*a.*) **1** (*постепенно войти*) to draw (into), enter. **2** (*щёки*) to sag, fall in. **3** (*привыкнуть*) (*coll.*) to get accustomed (to), used (to). **4** (*увлечься*) to become keen (on).

вуайери́зм, а *m.* voyeurism.

вуайери́ст, а *m.* voyeur, peeping Tom.

вуайери́стский *adj.* voyeuristic.

вуале́тк|а, и *f.* veil.

вуали́р|овать, ую *impf.* (*of* ⇒**за~**) to veil, obscure, hide; **завуали́рованные угро́зы** veiled threats.

вуа́л|ь, и *f.* veil.

вуз, а *m.* (*abbr. of* ***вы́сшее уче́бное заведе́ние***) institution of higher education.

ву́зов|ец, ца̀ *m.* student (*at any institution of higher education*).

ву́зов|ка, ки *f. of* ⇒**~ец**

ву́з|овский *adj. of* ⇒**~**

вулка́н, а *m.* volcano; **де́йствующий, поту́хший в.** active, extinct volcano.

вулканиза́ци|я, и *f.* (*tech.*) vulcanization.

вулканизи́р|овать, ую *impf. and pf.* (*tech.*) to vulcanize.

вулкани́зм, а *m.* (*geol.*) volcanism.

вулканиз|ова́ть, у́ю = **~и́ровать**

вулкани́ческий *adj.* volcanic (*also fig.*).

вулкано́лог, а *m.* volcanologist.

вулканоло́ги|я, и *f.* volcanology.

вульгариза́ци|я, и *f.* vulgarization.

вульгаризи́р|овать, ую *impf. and pf.* to vulgarize.

вульгари́зм, а *m.* (*ling.*) vulgarism.

вульга́рност|ь, и *f.* vulgarity.

вульга́р|ный (~ен, ~на) *adj.* (*in var. senses*) vulgar.

вундерки́нд, а *m.* child prodigy.

вурдала́к, а *m.* vampire.

вход, а *m.* **1** (*действие*) entry. **2** (*место*) entrance. **3** (*допуск*) admission.

вхо|ди́ть, жу́, ~дишь *impf. of* ⇒**войти́**

вход|но́й *adj. of* ⇒**~**; **в. биле́т** entrance ticket; **~на́я пла́та** entrance fee.

вход|я́щий *pres. part. of* ⇒**~и́ть** *and adj.* (*почта*) incoming.

вхожде́ни|е, я *nt.* entry.

вхо́ж|ий (~, ~а) *adj.* (*coll.*): **быть ~им** (**в**+*a.*, **к**+*d.*) to be (well) received (at); to be well in (with).

вхолосту́ю *adv.* (*tech.*): **рабо́тать в.** to idle.

вцеп|и́ться, лю́сь, ~ишься *impf.* (*of* ⇒**~ля́ться**) (**в**+*a.*) to seize hold of (by).

вцепля́|ться, юсь *impf. of* ⇒**вцепи́ться**

вчера́ *adv.* yesterday.

вчера́шн|ий *adj.* (*дождь, суп*) yesterday's; **в. день** yesterday; (*fig.*) yesterday, the past; **жить ~им днём** to live in the past.

вчерне́ *adv.* in rough.

вче́тверо *adv.* four times; fourfold; **сложи́ть в.** to fold in four.

вчетверо́м *adv.* four (together).

в-четвёртых *adv.* fourthly, in the fourth place.

вчин|и́ть, ю, и́шь *pf.* (*of* ⇒**~я́ть**) (*leg.*; *obs.*): **в. иск** to bring an action.

вчиня́|ть, ю *impf. of* ⇒**вчини́ть**

вчисту́ю *adv.* (*coll.*) completely.

вчит|а́ться, а́юсь *pf.* (*of* ⇒**~ываться**) (**в**+*a.*) to get a grasp (of) (*a text*).

вчи́тыва|ться, юсь *impf.* **1** *impf. of*

⇒вчита́ться. 2 *impf. only* to try to grasp the meaning (of).

вчу́же *adv.* disinterestedly, vicariously.

вше́стеро *adv.* six times; six times as much.

вшестеро́м *adv.* six (together).

вшива́|ть, ю *impf. of* **⇒вшить**

вши́вк|а, и *f.* (*coll.*) **1** (*действие*) sewing in. **2** (*заплата*) patch.

вшивно́й *adj.* sewn-in.

вши́в|ый (~, ~а) *adj.* lousy, lice-ridden.

вширь *adv.* in breadth.

вшить, вошью́, вошьёшь *pf.* (*of* **⇒вшива́ть**) (**в**+*a.*) to sew in(to).

въеда́|ться, ю, ет(ся) *impf. of* **⇒въе́сться**

въе́длив|ый (~, ~а) *adj.* (*coll.*) corrosive; (*едкий*) caustic, acrid; (*человек*) pernickety.

въе́дчив|ый (~, ~а) *adj.* = **въе́дливый**

въезд, а *m.* **1** (*действие*) entry; **«В. запрещён»** 'No entry'. **2** (*место*) entrance.

въездн|о́й *adj. of* **⇒~; ~а́я ви́за** entry visa.

въезжа́|ть, ю *impf. of* **⇒въе́хать**

въе́|сться, стся, дя́тся, *past* **~лся** *pf.* (*of* **⇒~да́ться**) (**в**+*a.*) to eat (into).

въе́|хать, ду, дешь *pf.* (*of* **⇒~зжа́ть**) **1** (**в**+*a.*) to enter, ride in(to), drive in(to); (**на**+*a.*) (*наверх*) to ride up, drive up; **в. в мо́рду, в ры́ло** (+*d.*; *vulg.*) to slap in the face. **2** (*в дом*) to move in.

въя́в|е *adv.* = **~ь**

въявь *adv.* (*obs.*) really; **ви́деть в.** to see with one's own eyes.

вы, вас, вам, ва́ми, вас *pron.* (*pl. and formal mode of address to one person*) you; **быть на в.** (**с**+*i.*) to be on formal terms (with).

вы... *pref. indicating* **1** motion outwards. **2** action directed outwards. **3** acquisition (*as outcome of a series of actions*). **4** completion of a process.

выба́лтыва|ть, ю *impf. of* **⇒вы́болтать**

выбега́|ть, ю *impf. of* **⇒вы́бежать**

вы́бе|жать, гу, жишь, гут *pf.* (*of* **⇒~га́ть**) to run out.

вы́бел|ить, ю, ишь *pf. of* **⇒бели́ть** 3

вы́белк|а, и *f.* bleaching; whitening.

вы́бер|у, ешь *see* **⇒вы́брать**

выбива́|ть(ся), ю(сь) *impf. of* **⇒вы́бить(ся)**

выбира́|ть(ся), ю(сь) *impf. of* **⇒вы́брать(ся)**

вы́б|ить, ью, ьешь *pf.* (*of* **⇒~ива́ть**) **1** (*заставить выпасть*) to knock out; (*врага*) to drive out; to dislodge; **в. из колеи́** (*fig.*) to unsettle, upset. **2** (*очистить*) to beat (clean); **в. ковёр** to beat a carpet. **3** (*вычеканить*) to beat; to stamp; **в. меда́ль** to strike a medal. **4** (*уничтожить*) to beat down. **5** (*на барабане*) to beat out; to drum. **6** (*coll.*) (*добиться получения чего-либо*) to manage to get.

вы́б|иться, ьюсь, ьешься *pf.* (*of* **⇒~ива́ться**) **1** (**из**+*g.*) (*освободиться*) to get out (of); to break loose (from); **в. из коле́й** to go off the rails; **в. в лю́ди** to make one's way in the world; **в. из гра́фика** to get behind the schedule; **в. из сил** to wear o.s. out; to be exhausted. **2** (*показаться наружу*) to come out, show.

вы́боин|а, ы *f.* **1** (*на дороге*) rut, pot-hole. **2** (*на стене*) dent; groove.

вы́болта|ть, ю *pf.* (*of* **⇒выба́лтывать**) (*coll.*) to let out, blurt out.

вы́бор, а *m.* **1** choice; option. **2** (*ассортимент*) selection; assortment; **по своему́ ~у** of one's choice. **3** (*pl. only*) (*pol.*) election(s); **дополни́тельные ~ы** by-election.

вы́борк|а, и *f.* **1** (*статистическая*) selection; sample. **2** (*usu. in pl.*) (*цитата*) excerpt.

вы́борност|ь, и *f.* appointment by election.

вы́борн|ый *adj.* **1** (*кампания*) election (*attr.*); **в. бюллете́нь** ballot-paper. **2** (*орган, должность*) elective. **3** elected; *as n.* **в., ~ого** *m.* delegate.

вы́борочный *adj.* selective.

вы́борщик, а *m.* **1** (*pol.*) elector (*in indirect elections*); **колле́гия ~ов** electoral college. **2** (*работник*) selector.

вы́бор|ы, ов *see* **⇒~**

вы́бран|ить, ю, ишь *pf. of* **⇒брани́ть**

выбра́сыва|ть(ся), ю(сь) *impf. of* **⇒вы́бросить(ся)**

вы́б|рать, еру, ерешь *pf.* (*of* **⇒~ира́ть**) **1** to choose, select, pick out. **2** (*голосованием*) to elect. **3**: **в. пате́нт** (*leg.*) to take out a patent. **4** (*взять до последнего*) to take (everything) out. **5** (*время*) to find; **в. вре́мя для о́тдыха** to find time to rest. **6** (*naut.*) to haul in.

вы́б|раться, ерусь, ерешься *pf.* (*of* **⇒~ира́ться**) **1** (**из**+*g.*) to get out (of); **в. из затрудне́ний** to get out of a difficulty. **2** (*coll.*) (*найти возможность*) to (manage to) get to; to find time to; **в. в о́перу** to manage to get to the opera.

выбрива́|ть(ся), ю(сь) *impf. of* **⇒вы́брить(ся)**

вы́бр|ить, ею, еешь *pf.* (*of* **⇒~ива́ть**) to shave.

вы́бр|иться, еюсь, еешься *pf.* (*of* **⇒~ива́ться**) to shave, have a shave.

вы́брос, а *m.* **1** (*отходов*) discharge. **2** (*mil.*) landing. **3** (*in pl.*) emissions.

вы́бро|сить, шу, сишь *pf.* (*of* **⇒выбра́сывать**) **1** (*удалить из пределов*) to throw out. **2** (*старые вещи*) discard, throw away; (*отходы*) to discharge; **в. зря** to waste; **в. из головы́** to put out of one's head, dismiss. **3** (*с работы*) to kick out. **4** (*in var. senses*) to put out; **в. побе́ги** to throw out shoots; **в. флаг** to hoist a flag; **в. ло́зунг/това́р** to launch a slogan/product.

вы́бро|ситься, шусь, сишься *pf.* (*of* **⇒выбра́сываться**) to throw o.s. out, jump out; (*naut.*) **в. на мель, на́ берег** to run aground; **в. с парашю́том** to bale out.

вы́броск|а, и *f.* (*mil.*) (air)drop.

выбыва́ни|е, я *nt.* (*sport*) knock-out (*Br.*), elimination (*US*).

выбыва́|ть, ю *impf. of* **⇒вы́быть**

выбыти|е, я *nt.* departure.

вы́б|ыть, уду, удешь *pf.* (*of* **⇒~ыва́ть**) (**из**+*g.*) (*из города*) to leave; (*из соревнования*) to quit.

выва́лива|ть(ся), ю(сь) *impf. of* **⇒вы́валить(ся)**

вы́вал|ить, ю, ишь *pf.* (*of* **⇒~ивать**) (**из**+*g.*) **1** to empty out (of). **2** (*coll.*) (*толпа*) to pour out (of).

вы́вал|иться, юсь, ишься *pf.* (*of* **⇒~иваться**) (**из**+*g.*) to fall out, tumble out (of); (*coll.*) (*толпа*) to pour out (of).

вываля́|ть, ю *pf. of* **⇒валя́ть** 2

вываля́|ться, юсь *pf.* (**в**+*p.*) to get covered (*in mud, etc.*).

выва́рива|ть, ю *impf. of* **⇒вы́варить**

вы́вар|ить, ю, ишь *pf.* (*of* **⇒~ивать**) **1** (*кости*) to boil down; (*соль*) to extract by boiling. **2** (*мясо*) to boil thoroughly. **3** (*пятна*) to remove (*stains, etc.*) by boiling.

вы́варк|а, и *f.* decoction, extraction.

вы́вед|ать, аю *pf.* (*of* **⇒~ывать**) to find out; **в. секре́т у кого́-н.** to worm a secret out of s.o.

выведе́ни|е, я *nt.* **1** leading out, bringing out. **2** (*формулы*) deduction, conclusion. **3** (*цыплят*) hatching (out); (*растений*) growing; (*животных*) breeding, raising. **4** (*пятен*) removal (*of stains*); (*вредителей*) extermination (*of pests*).

выве́дыва|ть, ю *impf.* **1** *impf. of* **⇒вы́ведать. 2** *impf. only* to try to find out.

вы́вез|ти, у, ешь, *past* **~, ~ла** *pf.* (*of* **⇒вывози́ть**) **1** (*везя, удалить*) to take out, remove; (*везя, отправить*) to take; (*привезти с собой*) to bring. **2** (*econ.*) (*за границу*) to export. **3** (*coll.*) (*выручить*) to save, rescue.

вы́вер|ить, ю, ишь *pf.* (*of* **⇒~я́ть**) to adjust; to regulate.

вы́верк|а, и *f.* adjustment; regulation.

вы́вер|нуть, ну, нешь *pf.* (*of* **⇒~тывать** *and* **вывора́чивать**) **1** (*винт*) to unscrew; (*пробку*) to pull out. **2** (*coll.*) (*ногу*) to twist, wrench. **3** (*карман*) to turn (inside) out.

вы́вер|нуться, нусь, нешься *pf.* (*of* **⇒~тываться**) **1** (*винт*) to come unscrewed. **2** (*coll.*) (*выскользнуть*) to slip out. **3** (*coll.*) (*избежать*) to get out (of), extricate o.s. (from).

вы́верт, а *m.* (*coll.*) **1** (*движение*) caper; **танцева́ть с ~ами** to caper. **2** (*причуда*) mannerism; affectation; (*поведение*) antics.

вывёртыва|ть(ся), ю(сь) *impf. of* **⇒вы́вернуть(ся)**

выверя́|ть, ю *impf. of* **⇒вы́верить**

вы́ве|сить[1], шу, сишь *pf.* (*of*

⇨**~́шивать**) **1** (*объявление*) to put up; to post up. **2** (*бельё, флаг*) to hang out.

вы́ве|сить², шу, сишь *pf.* (*of* ⇨**~́шивать**) to weigh.

вы́веск|а, и *f.* **1** sign, signboard. **2** (*fig.*) screen, pretext; **под ~ой** (+*g.*) under the guise of.

вы́ве|сти, ду, дешь, *past* **~л, ~ла** *pf.* (*of* ⇨**выводи́ть**) **1** to lead out, bring out; **в. кого́-н. в лю́ди** to help s.o. on in life; **в. из заблужде́ния** to undeceive; **в. кого́-н. из себя́** to drive s.o. out of his wits; **в. из стро́я** to disable, put out of action (*also fig.*); **в. из терпе́ния** to exasperate; **в. на доро́гу** (*fig.*) to set on the right path; **в. на чи́стую во́ду** to bring out into the open. **2** (*исключить*) to turn out, force out; **в. из соста́ва прези́диума** to remove from the presidium. **3** (*пятна*) to remove; (*вредителей*) to exterminate (*pests*). **4** (*заключить*) to deduce, conclude. **5** (*птенцов*) to hatch (out); (*растения*) to grow (*plants*); (*животных*) to breed, raise. **6** (*в романе*) to depict, portray. **7** (*на картине*) to draw, trace out painstakingly. **8**: **в. балл, в. отме́тку** to give a mark.

вы́ве|стись, дется *pf.* (*of* ⇨**выводи́ться**) **1** (*выйти из употребления*) to go out of use; to lapse. **2** (*исчезнуть*) to disappear; to come out (*of stains*); to become extinct. **3** (*цыплята*) to hatch out (*intrans.*).

выве́триване|е, я *nt.* **1** airing. **2** (*geol.*) weathering.

выве́трива|ть(ся), ю, ет(ся) *impf. of* ⇨**вы́ветрить(ся)**

вы́ветр|ить, ю, ишь *pf.* (*of* ⇨**~́ивать**) **1** (*комнату*) to air; to ventilate; (*запах*) to remove (by ventilation). **2** (*geol.*) to weather.

вы́ветр|иться, ится *pf.* (*of* ⇨**~́иваться**) **1** (*geol.*) to weather. **2** (*запах, дым*) to disappear, disperse.

выве́шива|ть, ю *impf. of* ⇨**вы́весить**

вы́вин|тить, чу, тишь *pf.* (*of* ⇨**~́чивать**) to unscrew.

вы́вин|титься, тится *pf.* (*of* ⇨**~́чиваться**) to come unscrewed.

выви́нчива|ть(ся), ю, ет(ся) *impf. of* ⇨**вы́винтить(ся)**

вы́вих, а *m.* dislocation.

выви́хива|ть, ю *impf. of* ⇨**вы́вихнуть**

вы́вих|нуть, ну, нешь *pf.* (*of* ⇨**~́ивать**) to dislocate, put out (of joint); **он ~нул но́гу** he has dislocated his foot.

вы́вод, а *m.* **1** (*заключение*) deduction, conclusion. **2** (*elec.*) outlet. **3** (*выведение*) leading out, bringing out; **в. войск** withdrawal *or* pull-out of troops; **в. да́нных** (*comput.*) output.

выво|ди́ть(ся), жу́, ~́дит(ся) *impf. of* ⇨**вы́вести(сь)**

выводно́й *adj.* **1** (*tech.*) discharge. **2** (*anat.*) excretory.

вы́вод|ок, ка *m.* (*птиц*) brood (*also fig.*); (*из яиц*) hatch; (*кошки, суки*) litter.

выво|жу́¹, ~́дишь *see* ⇨**~ди́ть**

выво|жу́², ~́зишь *see* ⇨**~зи́ть**

вы́воз, а *m.* **1** (*отправление*) sending, dispatch. **2** (*экспорт*) export. **3** (*удаление*) removal.

вы́во|зить, жу, зишь *pf.* (**в**+*p.*; *coll.*) to cover (*in mud, snow, etc.*).

выво|зи́ть, жу́, ~́зишь *impf. of* ⇨**вы́везти**

вы́возк|а, и *f.* carting out; removal.

вывозно́й *adj.* (*тариф, пошлина*) export.

выволо́кива|ть, ю *impf. of* ⇨**вы́волочь**

вы́волочк|а, и *f.* (*coll.*) dressing-down.

вы́воло|чь, ку, чешь, кут, *past* **~к, ~кла** *pf.* (*of* ⇨**выволо́кивать**) (*coll.*) to drag out.

вывора́чива|ть, ю *impf. of* ⇨**вы́воротить** *and* **вы́вернуть**

вы́воро|тить, чу, тишь *pf.* (*of* ⇨**вывора́чивать**) (*coll.*) **1** (*вытащить*) to pull out, shake loose. **2** (*ногу*) to twist, wrench. **3** (*карман*) to turn (inside) out.

вы́гад|ать, аю *pf.* (*of* ⇨**~́ывать**) (*получить выгоду*) to gain; (*сберечь*) to save, economize; **что вы ~али на э́том?** what did you gain by it?

выга́дыва|ть, ю *impf. of* ⇨**вы́гадать**

вы́гарк|и, ов *no sg.* slag.

вы́гиб, а *m.* curve.

выгиба́|ть(ся), ю(сь) *impf. of* ⇨**вы́гнуть(ся)**

вы́гла|дить, жу, дишь *pf. of* ⇨**гла́дить 1**

вы́гля|деть¹, жу, дишь *pf.* (*coll.*) to discover; to spy out.

вы́гля|деть², жу, дишь *impf.* (*человек*) to look (like); **он ~дит о́чень мо́лодо** he looks very young; **она́ ~дит больно́й** she looks ill; **она́ пло́хо ~дит** she does not look well; (*показания*) to appear (to be).

выгля́дыва|ть, ю *impf. of* ⇨**вы́глянуть**

вы́гля|нуть, ну, нешь *pf.* (*of* ⇨**~́дывать**) **1** (*из окна*) to look out. **2** (*показаться*) to peep out, emerge; **из-за туч ~нуло со́лнце** the sun peeped out from behind the clouds.

вы́г|нать, оню, онишь *pf.* (*of* ⇨**~оня́ть**) **1** (*удалить*) to drive out; to expel; **в. с рабо́ты** (*coll.*) to sack (*Br.*), fire (*US*). **2** (*добыть перегонкой*) to distil (*Br.*), distill (*US*). **3** (*растения*) to force. **4** (*скот*) to send out to pasture.

выгнива́|ть, ю *impf. of* ⇨**вы́гнить**

вы́гни|ть, ю, ешь *pf.* (*of* ⇨**~ва́ть**) to rot away; to rot at the core.

вы́гнут|ый (~, ~а) *p.p.p. of* ⇨**~ь** *and adj.* curved; convex.

вы́гн|уть, у, ешь *pf.* (*of* ⇨**выгиба́ть**) to bend; **в. спи́ну** to arch the back.

вы́гн|уться, усь, ешься *pf.* (*of* ⇨**выгиба́ться**) to bend (*intrans.*).

вығова́рива|ть, ю *impf.* **1** *impf. of* ⇨**вы́говорить. 2** *impf. only* (+*d.*; *coll.*) to reprimand, tell off.

вы́говор, а *m.* **1** (*произношение*) accent; pronunciation. **2** (*порицание*) reprimand; rebuke.

вы́говор|ить, ю, ишь *pf.* (*of* ⇨**вы́гова́ривать**) **1** (*произнести*) to articulate, speak. **2** (*coll.*) (*условиться*) to manage to get (agreement to).

вы́говор|иться, юсь, ишься *pf.* (*coll.*) to speak out.

вы́год|а, ы *f.* (*польза*) advantage, benefit; (*прибыль*) profit, gain.

вы́годно *adv.* **1** advantageously. **2** *as pred.* it is profitable, it pays.

вы́год|ный (~ен, ~на) *adj.* (*дающий пользу*) advantageous, beneficial; (*прибыльный*) profitable.

вы́гон, а *m.* pasture.

вы́гонк|а, и *f.* distillation.

выгоня́|ть, ю *impf. of* ⇨**вы́гнать**

выгора́жива|ть, ю *impf. of* ⇨**вы́городить**

выгора́|ть, ет *impf. of* ⇨**вы́гореть**

вы́гор|еть¹, ит *pf.* (*of* ⇨**~а́ть**) **1** (*сгореть*) to burn down, burn out (*intrans.*). **2** (*выцвести*) to fade.

вы́гор|еть², ит *pf.* (*of* ⇨**~а́ть**) (*3rd person only or impers.*; *coll.*) (*удаться*) to succeed, come off.

вы́горо|дить, жу, дишь *pf.* (*of* ⇨**выгора́живать**) **1** (*участок*) to fence off. **2** (*fig., coll.*) (*приятеля*) to shield, screen.

вы́гравир|овать, ую *pf. of* ⇨**гравирова́ть**

вы́гре|б *see* ⇨**~сти**

выгреба́|ть, ю *impf. of* ⇨**вы́грести**

выгребн|о́й *adj.* refuse; **~а́я я́ма** cesspool.

вы́гре|сти¹, бу, бешь, *past* **~б, ~бла** *pf.* (*of* ⇨**~ба́ть**) (*удалить*) to rake out; to clear away.

вы́гре|сти², бу, бешь, *past* **~б, ~бла** *pf.* (*of* ⇨**~ба́ть**) (*выплыть*) to row (out), pull (out).

выгружа́|ть(ся), ю(сь) *impf. of* ⇨**вы́грузить(ся)**

вы́гру|зить, жу, зишь *pf.* (*of* ⇨**~жа́ть**) to unload.

вы́гру|зиться, жусь, зишься *pf.* (*of* ⇨**~жа́ться**) (*люди*) to disembark; (*корабль*) to unload.

вы́грузк|а, и *f.* unloading; (*людей*) disembarkation.

выгрыза́|ть, ю *impf. of* ⇨**вы́грызть**

вы́грыз|ть, у, ешь, *past* **~, ~ла** *pf.* (*of* ⇨**~а́ть**) to gnaw out.

вы́гул, а *m.* **1** range, pasture. **2**: **в. соба́к** dog walking; **«Вы́гул соба́к запрещён»** 'Dogs must be kept on a leash'.

выгу́лива|ть, ю *impf. of* ⇨**вы́гулять**

вы́гуля|ть, ю *pf.* (*of* ⇨**выгу́ливать**) to walk (*a dog, etc.*).

выда|ва́ть(ся), ю́(сь), ёшь(ся) *impf. of* ⇨**вы́дать(ся);** (*выделяться*)

(+*i.*) to stand out, be conspicuous (on account of).

выдав|ить, лю, ишь *pf.* (*of* ⇒**~ливать**) **1** (*выжать*) to press out, squeeze out (*also fig.*); **в. улыбку** to force a smile. **2** (*выломать*) to break, knock out.

выда́влива|ть, ю *impf. of* ⇒**вы́давить**

выда́ива|ть, ю *impf. of* ⇒**вы́доить**

выда́лблива|ть, ю *impf. of* ⇒**вы́долбить**

вы́дань|е, я *nt. only in phr.* (*coll., obs.*) **на в.** marriageable.

вы́да|ть, м, шь, ст, дим, дите, дут *pf.* (*of* ⇒**~ва́ть**) **1** (*дать*) to give (out), issue; (*изготовить*) to produce; **в. зарпла́ту** to pay out wages; **в. про́пуск** to issue a pass; **в. кого́-н. за́муж (за**+*a.*) to give s.o. in marriage (to); **в. у́голь на-гора́** to produce coal. **2** (*предать*) to give away, betray; (*в чужую страну*) to extradite. **3** (**за**+*a.*) to pass off (as), give out to be; **в. (себя́)** to pose (as); **в. себя́ за свяще́нника** to pose as a clergyman. **4** (*coll.*) (*сказать*) to say (*sth. unexpected or unpleasant*).

вы́да|ться, мся, шься, стся, димся, дитесь, дутся *pf.* (*of* ⇒**~ва́ться**) **1** to protrude, project, jut out; **скала́ ~ётся в мо́ре** the cliff juts out into the sea. **2** (*coll.*) (*случиться*) to happen; **как то́лько ~лся хоро́ший денёк, мы поéхали в дере́вню** on the first fine day that came along we went into the country. **3** (**в**+*a.*) (*быть похожим*) to take after; **он ~ётся в отца́** he takes after his father.

вы́дач|а, и *f.* **1** (*предоставление*) giving, issuing; (*изготовление*) production. **2** (*то, что выдано*) issue; (*товар*) production, output; (*выплата*) payment. **3** (*преступника*) extradition.

выдаю́щийся *pres. part. of* ⇒**выдава́ться** *and adj.* prominent, salient; (*fig.*) (*замечательный*) outstanding, eminent; prominent.

выдвига́|ть(ся), ю(сь) *impf. of* ⇒**вы́двинуть(ся)**

выдвиже́н|ец, ца *m.* worker promoted to an administrative post.

выдвиже́ни|е, я *nt.* **1** (*кандидата*) nomination. **2** (*по работе*) promotion.

выдвиже́н|ка, ки *f. of* ⇒**~ец**

выдвижно́й *adj.* sliding; (*tech.*) telescopic.

вы́двин|уть, ну, нешь *pf.* (*of* ⇒**~га́ть**) **1** (*стол, шкаф*) to move out, pull out; (*ящик*) to pull open. **2** (*fig.*) (*предложить*) to put forward, advance; **в. обвине́ние** to bring an accusation. **3** (*по работе*) to promote; **в. на до́лжность секретаря́** to promote to the post of secretary. **4** (*кандидата*) to nominate, propose; **в. чью-н. кандидату́ру, кого́-н. в кандида́ты** to propose s.o. as candidate.

вы́двин|уться, нусь, нешься *pf.* (*of* ⇒**~га́ться**) **1** (*вперёд*) to move forward; (*наружу*) to move, move out; (*ящик*) to slide in and out. **2** (*работник*) to rise, get on (in the world).

вы́двор|ить, ю, ишь *pf.* (*of* ⇒**~я́ть**) to throw out.

выдворя́|ть, ю *impf. of* ⇒**вы́дворить**

вы́дел, а *m.* apportionment.

вы́дел|ать, аю *pf.* (*of* ⇒**~ывать**) to treat, process.

выделе́ни|е, я *nt.* **1** (*physiol.*) secretion; (*обработанных веществ*) excretion. **2** (*chem.*) isolation. **3** (*средств*) allocation, assignment, apportionment.

выдели́тельный *adj.* (*physiol.*) secretory; excretory.

вы́дел|ить, ю, ишь *pf.* (*of* ⇒**~я́ть**) **1** (*отобрать*) to pick out, single out; (*mil.*) to detach, detail; (*comput.*) to highlight; (*typ.*) **в. курси́вом** to italicize. **2** (*средства*) to allocate, assign, earmark; (*время*) to allot. **3** (*physiol.*) to secrete; (*обработанные вещества*) to excrete. **4** (*chem.*) to isolate. **5** (*газ, вещества*) to emit.

вы́дел|иться, юсь, ишься *pf.* (*of* ⇒**~я́ться**) **1** (*отделиться от целого*) to split off, separate. **2** (+*i.*) to stand out (for); to make a mark (by); **он ~ился остроу́мием** he stood out by virtue of his wit. **3** (*пот*) to ooze out, exude; (*газ*) to be emitted.

вы́делк|а, и *f.* **1** (*производство*) manufacture. **2** (*качество*) workmanship. **3** (*кожи*) dressing, currying.

выде́лыва|ть, ю *impf. of* ⇒**вы́делать;** (*производить*) (*no pf.*) to make, produce; **что ты ~ешь?** (*coll.*) what are you up to?

выделя́|ть(ся), ю(сь) *impf. of* ⇒**вы́делить(ся)**

выдёргива|ть, ю *impf. of* ⇒**вы́дернуть**

вы́держанност|ь, и *f.* **1** (*последовательность*) consistency. **2** (*самообладание*) self-possession; (*стойкость*) firmness.

вы́держа|нный (~н, ~на) *p.p.p. of* ⇒**~ть** *and adj.* **1** (*последовательный*) consistent; **~нная поли́тика** consistent policy. **2** (*умеющий владеть собой*) self-possessed; (*стойкий*) firm. **3** (*сыр*) mature; (*дерево*) seasoned.

вы́держ|ать, у, ишь *pf.* (*of* ⇒**~ивать**) **1** (*под тяжестью, давлением*) to bear, hold; **лёд вас не ~ит** the ice will not hold you. **2** (*fig.*) (*вытерпеть*) to bear, stand (up to), endure; to contain o.s.; **не в.** to give in, break down; **я не мог э́того бо́льше в.** I could stand it no longer; **ва́ши мне́ния не ~ат кри́тики** your opinions will not stand up to criticism; **выраже́ние лица́ у него́ бы́ло тако́е коми́чное, что я не ~ал и рассмея́лся** his expression was so funny that I could not contain myself and burst out laughing. **3**: **в. экза́мен** to pass an examination. **4**: **в. не́сколько изда́ний** to run into several editions. **5** (*сыр, вино*) to keep, lay up; to mature; (*дерево*) to season. **6** (*соблюсти*) to maintain, sustain; **в. хара́ктер** to stand firm; **в. па́узу** to pause.

выде́ржива|ть, ю *impf. of* ⇒**вы́держать**

вы́держк|а¹, и *f.* **1** (*самообладание*) self-possession; (*терпение*) endurance. **2** (*phot.*) exposure.

вы́держк|а², и *f.* (*цитата*) excerpt, quotation.

вы́дер|нуть, ну, нешь *pf.* (*of* ⇒**~гивать**) to pull out.

выдира́|ть, ю *impf. of* ⇒**вы́драть¹**

выдира́|ться, юсь *impf. of* ⇒**вы́драться**

вы́до|ить, ю, ишь *pf.* (*of* ⇒**выда́ивать**) **1** (*корову*) to milk (dry). **2** (*молоко*) to obtain (by milking).

вы́долб|ить, лю, ишь *pf.* (*of* ⇒**выда́лбливать**) **1** to hollow out, gouge out. **2** (*coll.*) to learn by rote.

вы́дох, а *m.* exhalation.

вы́дохн|уть, у, ешь *pf.* (*of* ⇒**выдыха́ть**) to breathe out.

вы́дохн|уться, усь, ешься *pf.* (*of* ⇒**выдыха́ться**) (*духи*) to have lost fragrance, smell; (*вино*) to be flat; (*fig.*) (*актёр, талант*) to be past one's best, be played out.

вы́др|а, ы *f.* otter.

вы́д|рать¹, еру, ерешь *pf.* (*of* ⇒**~ира́ть**) (*вырвать*) to tear out.

вы́д|рать², еру, ерешь *pf.* (*of* ⇒**драть** 4) (*coll.*) (*выпороть*) to thrash.

вы́д|раться, ерусь, ерешься *pf.* (*of* ⇒**~ира́ться**) (*coll.*) to extricate o.s.

вы́дрессир|овать, ую *pf. of* ⇒**дрессирова́ть**

вы́дуб|ить, лю, ишь *pf. of* ⇒**дуби́ть**

выдува́льщик, а *m.* glass-blower.

выдува́|ть, ю *impf. of* ⇒**вы́дуть**

вы́дувк|а, и *f.* (*tech.*) (glass-)blowing.

выдувно́й *adj.* blown (*of glass*).

вы́думан|ный (~, ~а) *p.p.p. of* ⇒**вы́думать** *and adj.* made-up, fabricated; **~ная исто́рия** fabrication, fiction.

вы́дум|ать, аю *pf.* (*of* ⇒**~ывать**) to invent; to make up, fabricate; **он по́роха не ~ает** he will not set the Thames on fire.

вы́думк|а, и *f.* **1** invention; **голь на ~и хитра́** (*prov.*) necessity is the mother of invention. **2** (*изобретательность*) inventiveness. **3** (*вымысел*) invention, fabrication (*lie*).

вы́думщик, а *m.* (*coll.*) **1** inventor. **2** (*лгун*) lier, fibber.

выду́мыва|ть, ю *impf. of* ⇒**вы́думать**

вы́ду|ть, ю, ешь *pf.* (*of* ⇒**~ва́ть**) **1** to blow out. **2** (*impf.* **дуть**) (*tech.*) to blow.

выдыха́ни|е, я *nt.* exhalation.

выдыха́|ть(ся), ю(сь) *impf. of* ⇒**вы́дохнуть(ся)**

вы́еб|ать, у, ешь *pf. of* ⇒**еба́ть**

выеда́|ть, ю *impf. of* ⇒**вы́есть**

вы́еденн|ый *p.p.p. of* ⇒**вы́есть; не сто́ит ~ого яйца́** it is not worth a brass farthing.

вы́езд, а *m.* **1** (*отъезд*) departure.

2 (*место*) exit. **3**: **игра́ на ~е** (*sport*) away match.

вы́ез|дить, жу, дишь *pf.* (*of* ⇒**~жа́ть**) to break (in) (*horse*).

вы́ездк|а, и *f.* **1** (*лошади*) breaking-in. **2** (*в конном спорте*) dressage.

выезд|но́й *adj. of* ⇒**вы́езд; ~на́я се́ссия суда́** assizes; **в. матч** (*sport*) away match.

выезжа́|ть, ю *impf. of* ⇒**вы́ездить** *and* **вы́ехать**

вы́емк|а, и *f.* **1** (*действие*) taking out; (*писем*) collection; **в. докуме́нтов** seizure of documents. **2** (*грунта*) excavation. **3** (*углубление*) hollow; groove; (*archit.*) fluting. **4** (*rail.*) cutting.

вы́е|сть, м, шь, ст, дим, дите, дят *pf.* (*of* ⇒**~да́ть**) to eat away; (*coll.*) (*испортить*) to corrode.

вы́е|хать, ду, дешь *pf.* (*of* ⇒**~зжа́ть**) **1** (*уехать*) to depart, leave (*in or on a vehicle or on an animal*); (*из города, из ворот*) (*на машине*) to drive out; (*на лошади*) to ride out. **2** (*из квартиры*) to leave, move (out). **3** (**на**+*p.*) (*fig., coll., pej.*) to exploit, take advantage (of).

выжа́рива|ть, ю *impf. of* ⇒**вы́жарить**

вы́жар|ить, ю, ишь *pf.* (*of* ⇒**~́ивать**) (*coll.*) to bake (*pots, etc.*).

вы́ж|ать[1]**, му, мешь** *pf.* (*of* ⇒**~има́ть**) (*бельё*) to wring (out); (*лимон*) to squeeze; (*сок*) to squeeze out; **~атый лимо́н** (*fig.*) a has-been; (*fig.*) (*извлечь*) to wring (out), squeeze (out); (*штангу, гирю*) to lift.

вы́ж|ать[2]**, ну, нешь** *pf.* (*of* ⇒**~ина́ть**) to reap clean.

вы́жд|ать, у, ешь *pf.* (*of* ⇒**выжида́ть**) (+*g.*) to wait (for); to bide one's time.

вы́ж|ечь, гу, жешь *pf.* (*of* ⇒**~ига́ть**) **1** (*сжечь целиком*) to burn down; to burn out; (*солнце*) to scorch. **2** (*med.*) to cauterize. **3** (*сделать знак*) to make a mark, etc., by burning; **в. клеймо́** (**на**+*p.*) to brand.

вы́жжен|ный *p.p.p. of* ⇒**вы́жечь** *and adj.* **~ная земля́** scorched earth.

выжива́ни|е, я *nt.* survival.

выжива́|ть, ю *impf. of* ⇒**вы́жить**

вы́жиг|а, и *c.g.* (*coll.*) cunning rogue.

выжига́ни|е, я *nt.* **1** scorching; **в. по де́реву** poker-work. **2** (*med.*) cauterization.

выжига́|ть, ю *impf. of* ⇒**вы́жечь**

выжида́ни|е, я *nt.* waiting; temporizing.

выжида́тельн|ый *adj.* waiting; temporizing; **занима́ть ~ую пози́цию** to play a waiting game.

выжида́|ть, ю *impf. of* ⇒**вы́ждать**

вы́жим, а *m.* (*sport*) press-up.

выжима́ни|е, я *nt.* **1** (*ягод*) squeezing; (*белья*) wringing. **2** (*sport*) (weight-) lifting.

выжима́|ть, ю *impf. of* ⇒**вы́жать**[1]

вы́жимк|и, ов *no sg.* husks, marc; **льняны́е в.** linseed-cake.

выжина́|ть, ю *impf. of* ⇒**вы́жать**[2]

вы́жи|ть, ву, вешь *pf.* (*of* ⇒**~ва́ть**) **1** (*остаться в живых*) to survive. **2**: **в. из ума́** to lose possession of one's faculties. **3** (*coll.*) (*выгнать*) to drive out, hound out.

вы́з|вать, ову, овешь *pf.* (*of* ⇒**~ыва́ть**) **1** (*пригласить*) to call (out); to send for; (*потребовать явиться*) to summon; **в. врача́** to send for a doctor; **в. ученика́** to call out a pupil; **в. в суд** (*leg.*) to summon(s), subpoena. **2** (*на бой, на откровенность*) to challenge; **в. на ду́эль** to challenge to a duel. **3** (*гнев, любопытство*) to provoke, arouse; (*пожар, болезнь*) to cause; (*интерес*) to stimulate; (*спор*) to provoke; **в. к жи́зни** to cause.

вы́з|ваться, овусь, овешься *pf.* (*of* ⇒**~ыва́ться**) (+*inf.*) to volunteer; to offer; **в. помо́чь** to offer to help; **в. в экспеди́цию** to volunteer for an expedition.

вы́звезд|ить, ит *pf.* (*impers.*): **~ит, ~ило** the stars will be (were) out; it will be (was) a starlit night.

вы́звол|ить, ю, ишь *pf.* (*of* ⇒**~я́ть**) (*coll.*) to help out; **в. из беды́** to get s.o. out of trouble.

вызволя́|ть, ю *impf. of* ⇒**вы́зволить**

выздора́влива|ть, ю *impf. of* ⇒**вы́здороветь**

вы́здорове|ть, ю, ешь *pf.* (*of* ⇒**выздора́вливать**) to recover, get better.

выздоровле́ни|е, я *nt.* recovery; convalescence.

вы́зов, а *m.* **1** (*приглашение*) call. **2** (*требование явиться*) summons. **3** (*предложение вступить в борьбу*) challenge; **бро́сить в. кому́-н.** to throw down a challenge to s.o.

вы́золо|тить, чу, тишь *pf. of* ⇒**золоти́ть**

вы́золочен|ный (~, ~а) *p.p.p. of* ⇒**вы́золотить** *and adj.* gilt.

вызрева́|ть, ю *impf. of* ⇒**вы́зреть**

вы́зре|ть, ю, ешь *pf.* (*of* ⇒**~ва́ть**) to ripen.

вы́зубр|ить, ю, ишь *pf.* (*of* ⇒**зубри́ть**[2]) (*coll.*) to learn by heart.

вызыва́|ть(ся), ю(сь) *impf. of* ⇒**вы́звать(ся)**

вызыва́|ющий *pres. part. act. of* ⇒**~ть** *and adj.* defiant; provocative.

вы́игр|ать, аю *pf.* (*of* ⇒**~ывать**) (*войну, партию; много денег*) to win; **в. в лотере́ю** to win the lottery; (*получить пользу*) to gain; **в. вре́мя** to gain time; (*fig.*) (**в**+*p.*) to be positively assessed; **в. во мне́нии колле́г** to win the respect of one's colleagues.

вы́игрыва|ть, ю *impf. of* ⇒**вы́играть**

вы́игрыш, а *m.* **1** (*действие*) win; winning. **2** (*деньги*) winnings; (*премия*) prize; (*выгода*) gain; **быть в ~е** (*в игре*) to be winner; (*fig.*) to be the gainer, stand to gain.

вы́игрышный *adj.* **1** winning; **в. ход** winning move. **2** (*выгодный*) advantageous.

вы́и|скать, щу, щешь *pf.* (*coll.*) to track down, run to earth.

вы́и|скаться, щусь, щешься *pf.* (*coll., iron.*) to turn up, emerge.

вы́искива|ть, ю *impf.* to seek out, try to trace.

вы́|йти, йду, йдешь, *past* **~шел, ~шла** *pf.* (*of* ⇒**~ходи́ть**) **1** to go out; to come out; **она́ ~шла из ко́мнаты** she went out of/left the room; **он ~шел 5 мину́т наза́д** he went out/left 5 minutes ago; **в. в отста́вку** to retire; **в. в** (+*a.*) (*стать*) to become; **в. в фина́л** (*sport*) to reach the final; **в. из па́ртии/комите́та** to leave the party/committee; **в. из берего́в** to overflow its banks; **в. из бо́я** (*mil.*) to disengage; **в. из ваго́на** to alight from a carriage; **в. из во́зраста** to pass the age limit; **в. из грани́ц** (+*g.*), **из преде́лов** (+*g.*) (*fig.*) to exceed the bounds (of); **в. из себя́** to lose one's temper; **в. из систе́мы** (*comput.*) to log off; **в. из терпе́ния** to lose patience; **в. на прогу́лку** to go out for a walk; **в. на сце́ну** to come on to the stage.
2: **в. (в свет)** (*быть изданным*) to come out, appear.
3 (*о фотографии*) to come out; **вы хорошо́ ~шли на э́том сни́мке** you have come out well in this photo.
4: **в. (за́муж) (за**+*a.*) (*о женщине*) to marry.
5 (*получаться*) to come (out); to turn out (*also impers.*); to ensue; (*произойти*) to happen, occur; **не ~шел/~шла** (+*i. of n.; coll.*) he/she is lacking (in); **умо́м не ~шел** (*coll.*) he is not too bright; **в. победи́телем** to come out victor; **из него́ ~шел бы хоро́ший лётчик** he would have made a good pilot; **из э́того ничего́ не ~йдет** nothing will come of it; **~шло, что он винова́т** it turned out that he was to blame; **как бы чего́ не ~шло** (*coll.*) it will come to no good.
6 (*быть родом*) to be by origin; **она́ ~шла из крестья́н** she is of peasant origin, comes of peasant stock.
7 (*израсходоваться*) to be used up; (*of a period of time*) to have expired; **горчи́ца вся ~шла** the mustard is used up; **срок уже́ ~шел** time is up.

вы́ка|зать, жу, жешь *pf.* (*of* ⇒**~́зывать**) (*coll.*) to manifest, display (*abstract qualities*).

выка́зыва|ть, ю *impf. of* ⇒**вы́казать**

выка́лива|ть, ю *impf. of* ⇒**вы́калить**

вы́кал|ить, ю, ишь *pf.* (*of* ⇒**~́ивать**) (*tech.*) to fire.

выка́лыва|ть, ю *impf. of* ⇒**вы́колоть**

выка́пчива|ть, ю *impf. of* ⇒**вы́коптить**

выка́пыва|ть, ю *impf. of* ⇒**вы́копать**

вы́карабк|аться, аюсь *pf.* (*of* ⇒**~́иваться**) (*из ямы*) to scramble out; (*fig., coll.*) (*из бедности*) to get (o.s.) out; **в. из боле́зни** to get over an illness.

выкара́бкива|ться, юсь *impf. of* ⇒**вы́карабкаться**

выка́рмлива|ть, ю *impf. of* ⇒**вы́кормить**

вы́кат|ать, аю *pf. of* ⇒**ката́ть** 4

вы́кат|аться, аюсь *pf.* (*of* ⇒**~ываться**[1]) (*coll.*) (*выва́ляться*) to roll (*intrans.*).

вы́ка|тить, чу, тишь *pf.* (*of* ⇒**~тывать**[2]) **1** to roll out; (*что-либо на колёсах*) to wheel out. **2**: **в. глаза́** (*coll.*) to open one's eyes wide, stare. **3** (*coll.*) (*вы́ехать*) to come out.

вы́ка|титься, чусь, тишься *pf.* (*of* ⇒**~тываться**[2]) **1** to roll out (*intrans.*). **2** = **вы́катить** 3

выка́тыва|ться[1]**, юсь** *impf. of* ⇒**вы́кататься**

выка́тыва|ть(ся)[2]**, ю(сь)** *impf. of* ⇒**вы́катить(ся)**; **~йся** (*coll.*) be off!; get out!

вы́кач|ать, аю *pf.* (*of* ⇒**~ивать**) to pump out; (*fig., coll.*) (*де́ньги*) to extort.

выка́чива|ть, ю *impf. of* ⇒**вы́качать**

вы́качк|а, и *f.* pumping out; (*fig., coll.*) extortion.

выка́шива|ть, ю *impf. of* ⇒**вы́косить**

выка́шлива|ть(ся), ю(сь) *impf. of* ⇒**вы́кашлять(ся)**

вы́кашл|ять, яю *pf.* (*of* ⇒**~ивать**) to cough up.

вы́кашл|яться, яюсь *pf.* (*of* ⇒**~иваться**) (*coll.*) to clear one's throat.

выки́дыва|ть, ю *impf. of* ⇒**вы́кинуть**

вы́кидыш, а *m.* (*med.*) miscarriage.

вы́ки|нуть, ну, нешь *pf.* (*of* ⇒**~дывать**) **1** (*вы́бросить*) to throw out. **2** (*вы́весить*) to put out; **в. флаг** to hoist a flag. **3** (*coll., pej.*): **в. но́мер, штýку, фо́кус** to play a trick.

выкипа́|ть, ет *impf. of* ⇒**вы́кипеть**

вы́кип|еть, ит *pf.* (*of* ⇒**~а́ть**) to boil away.

вы́кипя|тить, чу, тишь *pf.* to boil out, boil through.

вы́кладк|а, и *f.* **1** (*веще́й, това́ра*) laying-out; lay-out. **2** (*облицо́вка*) facing. **3** (*mil.*) kit; **в по́лной ~е** in full marching order. **4** (*math.*) computation.

выкла́дыва|ть(ся), ю(сь) *impf. of* ⇒**вы́ложить(ся)**

вы́кл|евать, юю, юешь *pf.* (*of* ⇒**~ёвывать**) **1** (*глаза́*) to peck out. **2** (*корм*) to peck up.

выклёвыва|ть, ю *impf. of* ⇒**вы́клевать**

выклика́|ть, ю *impf. of* ⇒**вы́кликнуть**

вы́клик|нуть, ну, нешь *pf.* (*of* ⇒**~а́ть**) to call out.

выключа́тел|ь, я *m.* switch.

выключа́|ть(ся), ю(сь) *impf. of* ⇒**вы́ключить(ся)**

вы́ключ|ить, у, ишь *pf.* (*of* ⇒**~а́ть**) **1** (*свет, ра́дио*) to turn off, switch off. **2** (*исключи́ть*) to remove, exclude. **3** (*typ.*) to justify.

вы́ключ|иться, усь, ишься *pf.* (*of* ⇒**~а́ться**) **1** (*о све́те*) to go off. **2** (*о челове́ке*) to switch off.

вы́ключк|а, и *f.* (*typ.*): **~ строк** justification.

выкля́нчива|ть, ю *impf.* **1** *impf. of* ⇒**вы́клянчить. 2** *impf. only* **в. что-н. у кого́-н.** to try to get sth. out of s.o.

вы́клянч|ить, у, ишь *pf.* (*of* ⇒**~ивать**) (**у**+*g.*; *coll.*) to cadge (from, off), get (out of).

вы́к|овать, ую, уешь *pf.* (*of* ⇒**~о́вывать**) to forge (*also fig.*).

выко́выва|ть, ю *impf. of* ⇒**вы́ковать**

выковы́рива|ть, ю *impf. of* ⇒**вы́ковырять**

вы́ковыр|ять, яю *pf.* (*of* ⇒**~ивать**) (*вы́нуть*) to pluck out, pick out.

выкола́чива|ть, ю *impf. of* ⇒**вы́колотить**

вы́коло|тить, чу, тишь *pf* (*of* ⇒**выкола́чивать**) **1** (*пыль*) to knock out, beat out. **2** (*ковёр*) to beat. **3** (*coll.*) (*де́ньги*) to extort, wring out.

вы́кол|оть, ю, ешь *pf.* (*of* ⇒**выка́лывать**) to thrust out; **в. глаза́ кому́-н.** to poke out s.o.'s eyes.

вы́копа|ть, ю *pf.* (*of* ⇒**выка́пывать**) **1** (*impf. also* **копа́ть**) (*я́му*) to dig; (*извле́чь*) (*карто́фель*) to dig up, dig out; (*те́ло*) to exhume. **2** (*no impf.*) (*fig., coll.*) (*найти́*) to unearth.

вы́коп|тить, чу, тишь *pf.* (*of* ⇒**выка́пчивать**) to smoke (*trans.*).

вы́корм|ить, лю, ишь *pf.* (*of* ⇒**выка́рмливать**) to rear, bring up.

вы́кормыш, а *m.* **1** (*живо́тное*) orphaned animal, orphan. **2** (*pej.*) (*челове́к*) brat.

вы́корч|евать, ую *pf.* (*of* ⇒**~ёвывать**) (*де́рево*) to uproot; (*fig.*) (*престу́пность*) to root out.

выкорчёвыва|ть, ю *impf. of* ⇒**вы́корчевать**

вы́ко|сить, шу, сишь *pf.* (*of* ⇒**выка́шивать**) to mow clean.

выкра́дыва|ть(ся), ю(сь) *impf. of* ⇒**вы́красть(ся)**

выкра́ива|ть, ю *impf. of* ⇒**вы́кроить**

вы́кра|сить, шу, сишь *pf.* (*of* ⇒**~шивать**) (*сте́ну*) to paint; (*ткань, во́лосы*) to dye.

вы́кра|сть, ду, дешь, *past* **~л** *pf.* (*of* ⇒**~дывать**) to steal.

вы́кра|сться, дусь, дешься, *past* **~лся** *pf.* (*of* ⇒**~дываться**) (*coll.*) to steal away, steal out.

выкра́шива|ть, ю *impf. of* ⇒**вы́красить**

вы́крест, а *m.* (*obs.*) convert (*to Christianity, esp. of Jews*).

вы́кре|стить, щу, стишь *pf.* (*obs.*) to convert (*to Christianity*).

вы́кре|ститься, щусь, стишься *pf.* to be converted; to convert (*intrans.*) (*to Christianity*).

вы́крик, а *m.* cry, shout; yell.

выкри́кива|ть, ю *impf. of* ⇒**вы́крикнуть**

вы́крик|нуть, ну, нешь *pf.* (*of* ⇒**~ивать**) to cry out; (*сказа́ть крича́*) to yell.

вы́кристаллиз|оваться, уется *pf. of* ⇒**кристаллизова́ться**

вы́кро|ить, ю, ишь *pf.* (*of* ⇒**выкра́ивать**) **1** (*вы́резать*) to cut out. **2** (*fig.*) (*удели́ть*) to find; **в. вре́мя** to find time.

вы́кройк|а, и *f.* pattern.

выкрута́с|ы, ов *no sg.* (*coll.*) intricate movements; (*в по́черке*) flourishes; (*fig.*) (*чуда́чества*) peculiarities, idiosyncrasies; **говори́ть с ~ами** to speak affectedly; **челове́к с ~ами** eccentric.

вы́кру|тить, чу, тишь *pf.* (*of* ⇒**~чивать**) **1** (*ла́мпочку, винт*) to unscrew. **2** (*ру́ку*) to twist, wrench; (*coll., also fig.*) **ему́ ~тили ру́ку** they twisted his arm. **3** (*бельё*) to wring out.

вы́кру|титься, чусь, тишься *pf.* (*of* ⇒**~чиваться**) **1** (*винт*) to come unscrewed. **2** (*fig., coll.*) (*вы́путаться*) to extricate o.s., get o.s. out (of).

выкру́чива|ть(ся), ю(сь) *impf. of* ⇒**вы́крутить(ся)**

вы́куп, а *m.* **1** (*leg.*) redemption. **2** (*пла́та*) ransom.

выкуп|а́ть, а́ю *impf. of* ⇒**вы́купить**

вы́купа|ть(ся), ю(сь) *pf. of* ⇒**купа́ть(ся)**

вы́куп|ить, лю, ишь *pf.* (*of* ⇒**~а́ть**) **1** (*зало́жника*) to ransom. **2** (*ве́щи*) to redeem; **в. из-под зало́га** to get out of pawn.

выкупно́й *adj.* redemption, ransom.

выку́рива|ть, ю *impf. of* ⇒**вы́курить**

вы́кур|ить, ю, ишь *pf.* (*of* ⇒**~ивать**) **1** (*сигаре́ту*) to smoke. **2** (*зве́ря*) to smoke out; (*fig., coll.*) (*проти́вника*) to drive out.

вы́ку|сить, шу, сишь *pf.* (*of* ⇒**~сывать**) to bite through; **на-ка, ~си!** (*coll.*) you'll get nothing out of me!; you shan't have it!

выку́сыва|ть, ю *impf. of* ⇒**вы́кусить**

вы́куша|ть, ю *pf.* (*obs.*) to drink.

вы́ку|шу, сишь *see* ⇒**~сить**

вы́ку|ю, ешь *see* ⇒**вы́ковать**

выла́влива|ть, ю *impf. of* ⇒**вы́ловить**

вы́лазк|а, и *f.* **1** (*mil.*) sortie (*also fig.*). **2** (*прогу́лка*) outing, excursion.

вы́лака|ть, ю *pf.* (*of* ⇒**лака́ть**) to lap up.

выла́мыва|ть, ю *impf. of* ⇒**вы́ломать** *and* **вы́ломить**

выла́щива|ть, ю *impf. of* ⇒**вы́лощить**

вы́леж|ать, у, ишь *pf.* (*of* ⇒**~ивать**) (*coll.*) to stay in bed.

вы́леж|аться, усь, ишься *pf.* (*of* ⇒**~иваться**) (*coll.*) **1** (*отдохну́ть*) to have a thorough rest. **2** (*таба́к*) to ripen; to mature.

вылёжива|ть(ся), ю(сь) *impf. of* ⇒**вы́лежать(ся)**

вылеза́|ть, ю *impf. of* ⇒**вы́лезти**

вы́лез|ти, у, ешь, *past* **~, ~ла** *pf.* (*of* ⇒**~а́ть**) **1** (*ползя́*) to crawl out;

(*карабкаясь*) to climb out; (*coll.*) (*выйти*) to get out, alight. **2** (*выпасть*) to fall out, come out. **3** (**с**+*i.*; *coll., pej.*) to come out with; **он всегда́ ~ет с каки́м-н. глу́пым замеча́нием** he always comes out with some fatuous remark.

вы́лезт|ь = **~и**

вы́леп|ить, лю, ишь *pf. of* ⇒**лепи́ть**

вы́лет, а *m.* (*птицы*) flight; (*самолёта*) take-off; **зал ~а** departure lounge.

вылета́|ть, ю *impf. of* ⇒**вы́лететь**

вы́ле|теть, чу, тишь *pf.* (*of* ⇒**~та́ть**) **1** (*птица*) to fly out; (*самолёт*) to take off; (*fig., coll.*) to rush out, dash out; **в. из головы́** to slip one's mind; **в. в трубу́** (*coll.*) to go bankrupt. **2** (*fig., coll.*) (*с работы, из института*) to be kicked out.

выле́чива|ть(ся), ю(сь) *impf. of* ⇒**вы́лечить(ся)**

вы́леч|ить, у, ишь *pf.* (*of* ⇒**~́ивать**) (**от**+*g.*) to cure (of) (*also fig.*).

вы́леч|иться, усь, ишься *pf.* (*of* ⇒**~́иваться**) (**от**+*g.*) to be cured (of); to get over (*also fig.*); **он ~ился от наркома́нии** he has been cured of his drug-addiction.

вы́леч|у¹, ишь *see* ⇒**~ить**

вы́ле|чу², тишь *see* ⇒**~теть**

вылива́|ть(ся), ю, ет(ся) *impf. of* ⇒**вы́лить(ся)**

вы́ли|зать, жу, жешь *pf.* (*of* ⇒**~́зывать**) **1** (*о кошке*) to lick clean. **2** (*coll.*) (*квартиру*) to clean thoroughly.

выли́зыва|ть, ю *impf. of* ⇒**вы́лизать**

вы́линя|ть, ю *pf. of* ⇒**линя́ть**

вы́лит|ый (~, ~а) *p.p.p. of* ⇒**~ь**; (*fig., coll.; long form only*) **он — в. оте́ц** he is the spitting image of his father.

вы́л|ить, ью, ьешь *pf.* (*of* ⇒**~ива́ть**) **1** (*воду*) to pour out; (*ведро*) to empty (out). **2** (*tech.*) (*деталь*) to cast, found; to mould.

вы́л|иться, ьется *pf.* (*of* ⇒**~ива́ться**) **1** (*жидкость*) to run out, flow out; (*fig.*) to flow (from), spring (from). **2** (**в**+*a. or* **в фо́рму** +*g.*) (*принять образ*) to take the form (of); to be expressed, express itself (in).

вы́лов|ить, лю, ишь *pf.* (*of* ⇒**выла́вливать**) to fish out, catch.

вы́лож|ить, у, ишь *pf.* (*of* ⇒**выкла́дывать**) **1** (*товар, вещи*) to lay out, spread out; (*fig., coll.*) (*сказать*) to tell; to reveal. **2** (+*i.*) (*покрыть*) to cover, lay (with); **в. дёрном** to turf; **в. ка́мнем** to face with masonry.

вы́лож|иться, усь, ишься *pf.* (*of* ⇒**выкла́дываться**) (*coll.*) to give one's all.

вы́лом, а *m.* **1** (*действие*) breaking open; breaking off. **2** (*место*) breach.

вы́лома|ть, ю *pf.* (*of* ⇒**выла́мывать**) (*замок*) to break open; (*дверь*) to break down.

вы́лом|ить, лю, ишь *pf.* (*coll.*) = **вы́ломать**

вы́ломк|а, и *f.* breaking off.

вы́лощен|ный (~, ~а) *p.p.p. of* ⇒**вы́лощить** *and adj.* **1** (*паркет*) glossy. **2** (*coll., fig.*) (*человек, манеры*) polished, smooth.

вы́лощ|ить, у, ишь *pf.* (*of* ⇒**выла́щивать**) to polish.

вы́лу|дить, жу, дишь *pf.* (*of* ⇒**луди́ть**) to tin(-plate).

вы́лу|жу, дишь *see* ⇒**~дить**

вы́луп|ить, лю, ишь *pf.* (*of* ⇒**~ля́ть**) (*coll.*): **в. глаза́** to goggle.

вы́луп|иться, ится *pf.* (*of* ⇒**~ля́ться**) **1** (*птенцы*) to hatch (out). **2** (*coll.*) (*глаза*) to goggle; **в. на** (+*a.*) to stare at.

вылупля́|ть(ся), ю, ет(ся) *impf. of* ⇒**вы́лупить(ся)**

выл́ущива|ть, ю *impf. of* ⇒**вы́лущить**

вы́лущ|ить, у, ишь *pf.* (*of* ⇒**~́ивать**) **1** (*горошину*) to shell. **2** (*med.*) to remove (*by surgical operation*).

вы́л|ью, ьешь *see* ⇒**~ить**

вы́ма|зать, жу, жешь *pf.* (*of* ⇒**ма́зать** 2 *and* ⇒**~́зывать**) (+*i.*) (*покрыть*) to smear (with); (*coll.*) (*выпачкать*) to dirty.

вы́ма|заться, жусь, жешься *pf.* (*of* ⇒**ма́заться** 1 *and* **~́зываться**) (*coll.*) to get dirty, make o.s. dirty.

выма́зыва|ть(ся), ю(сь) *impf. of* ⇒**вы́мазать(ся)**

выма́лива|ть, ю *impf.* **1** *impf. of* ⇒**вы́молить. 2** *impf. only* to beg for.

выма́нива|ть, ю *impf. of* ⇒**вы́манить**

вы́ман|ить, ю, ишь *pf.* (*of* ⇒**~́ивать**) **1** (**у**+*g.*) (*получить обманом*) to cheat, swindle (out of); (*получить лестью*) to wheedle (out of). **2** (**из**+*g.*) to entice (from), lure (out of, from).

вы́мар|ать, аю *pf.* (*of* ⇒**~́ывать**) (*coll.*) **1** (*выпачкать*) to soil, dirty. **2** (*вычеркнуть*) to strike out, cross out.

выма́рива|ть, ю *impf. of* ⇒**вы́морить**

вы́марк|а, и *f.* deletion.

выма́рыва|ть, ю *impf. of* ⇒**вы́марать**

выма́тыва|ть(ся), ю(сь) *impf. of* ⇒**вы́мотать(ся)**

вы́ма|хать, шу, шешь *pf.* (*of* ⇒**выма́хивать**) (*coll.*) to grow (tall).

выма́хива|ть, ю *impf. of* ⇒**вы́махать**

вы́махн|уть, у, ешь *pf.* (*coll.*) to fly out; to leap out.

выма́чива|ть, ю *impf. of* ⇒**вы́мочить**

вы́м|ени, енем *see* ⇒**~я**

выме́нива|ть, ю *impf. of* ⇒**вы́менять**

вы́мен|ять, яю *pf.* (*of* ⇒**~́ивать**) (**на**+*a.*) to receive in exchange, barter (for).

вы́м|ереть, рет, рут *past* **~ер, ~ерла** *pf.* (*of* ⇒**~ира́ть**) **1** (*исчезнуть*) to die out, become extinct. **2** (*опустеть*) to become desolate, deserted.

вымерз|а́ть, а́ю *impf. of* ⇒**вы́мерзнуть**

вы́мерз|нуть, ну, нешь, *past* **~, ~ла** *pf.* (*of* ⇒**~а́ть**) **1** (*погибнуть от морозов*) to be killed by frost. **2** (*промёрзнуть насквозь*) to freeze (right through).

выме́рива|ть, ю *impf. of* ⇒**вы́мерить**

вы́мер|ить, ю, ишь *pf.* (*of* ⇒**~́ивать**) to measure.

вы́мер|ший *p.p. of* ⇒**~еть** *and adj.* extinct.

вымеря́|ть, ю = **выме́ривать**

вы́ме|сти, ту, тешь *past* **~л** *pf.* (*of* ⇒**~та́ть**) (*комнату*) to sweep out; (*мусор*) to sweep up, out.

вы́ме|стить, щу, стишь *pf.* (*of* ⇒**~ща́ть**) **1** (+*d.*) to retaliate, take revenge (against). **2** (**на**+*p.*) to vent; **в. зло́бу на ком-н.** to vent one's anger on s.o.

вы́мет|ать¹, аю *pf.* (*of* ⇒**~́ывать**) **1** to put out, cast out (*a net, etc.*). **2**: **в. икру́** to spawn.

вы́мет|ать², аю *pf.* (*of* ⇒**~́ывать**) **в. пе́тли** to make buttonholes.

вымета́|ть, ю *impf. of* ⇒**вы́мести**

вымета́|ться, юсь *impf.* (*coll.*) to clear out, clear off (*intrans.*).

вымётыва|ть, ю *impf. of* ⇒**вы́метать**

вымеща́|ть, ю *impf. of* ⇒**вы́местить**

вы́ме|щу, стишь *see* ⇒**~стить**

вымира́ни|е, я *nt.* dying out, extinction.

вымира́|ть, ю *impf. of* ⇒**вы́мереть**

вымога́тел|ь, я *m.* extortioner.

вымога́тельский *adj.* extortionate.

вымога́тельств|о, а *nt.* extortion.

вымога́|ть, ю *impf.* to extort; **в. де́ньги у кого́-н.** to extort money from s.o.

вы́моин|а, ы *f.* (*dial.*) gully.

вымока́|ть, ю *impf. of* ⇒**вы́мокнуть**

вы́мок|нуть, ну, нешь, *past* **~, ~ла** *pf.* (*of* ⇒**~а́ть**) to be drenched, be soaked; **мы ~ли до ни́тки** we are soaked to the skin.

вы́молв|ить, лю, ишь *pf.* to say, utter (*usu. with neg.*).

вы́мол|ить, ю, ишь *pf.* (*of* ⇒**выма́ливать**) to obtain (by asking, by entreaties).

вымора́жива|ть, ю *impf. of* ⇒**вы́морозить**

вы́мор|ить, ю, ишь *pf.* (*of* ⇒**мори́ть¹** *and* **выма́ривать**) to exterminate; **го́лодом в.** to starve out.

вы́моро|зить, жу, зишь *pf.* (*of* ⇒**вымора́живать**) **1** (*дом*) to cool; to air. **2** (*истребить*) to freeze to death (*trans.*).

вы́морочн|ый *adj.* (*leg.*) escheated; **~ое иму́щество** escheat.

вымо|стить, щу, стишь *pf.* (*of* ⇒**мостить**) to pave.

вымота|ть, ю *pf.* (*of* ⇒**выматывать**) (*coll.*) to use up; to exhaust; **в. душу** to wear out; **они ~ли ему нервы** they turned him into a nervous wreck.

вымота|ться, юсь *pf.* (*of* ⇒**выматываться**) (*coll.*) to be worn out.

вымоч|ить, у, ишь *pf.* (*of* ⇒**вымачивать**) to soak.

вымо|щу, стишь *see* ⇒**~стить**

вым|ою, оешь *see* ⇒**~ыть**

вымпел, а *m.* pennant.

вымр|ет, ут *see* ⇒**вымереть**

вымучен|ный (~, ~а) *p.p.p. of* ⇒**вымучить** *and adj.* (*улыбка, смех*) forced; (*liter.*) (*стиль*) laboured.

вымучива|ть, ю *impf. of* ⇒**вымучить**

вымуч|ить, у, ишь *pf.* (*of* ⇒**~ивать**) (**из** + *g.*) to wring (from), force (out of).

вымуштр|овать, ую *pf. of* ⇒**муштровать**

вымыва|ть, ю *impf. of* ⇒**вымыть**

вымыс|ел, ла *m.* **1** (*ложь*) invention, fabrication. **2** (*фантазия*) fantasy, flight of imagination.

вымы|слить, слю, слишь *pf.* (*of* ⇒**~шлять**) to think up, invent; to imagine.

вым|ыть, ою, оешь *pf.* (*of* ⇒**мыть** *and* **~ывать**) **1** (*сделать чистым*) to wash; **в. голову кому-н.** to wash s.o.'s hair; **в. посуду** to wash up. **2** (*размыть*) to wash away.

вым|ыться, оюсь, оешься *pf.* (*of* ⇒**мыться**) to wash o.s.

вымышлен|ный (~, ~а) *p.p.p. of* ⇒**вымыслить** *and adj.* fictitious, imaginary, invented; **под ~ным именем** under an assumed name.

вымышля|ть, ю *impf. of* ⇒**вымыслить**

вым|я, ени, ени, енем, ени, *pl.* **~ена, ~ён, ~енам** *nt.* udder.

вынашива|ть, ю *impf. of* ⇒**выносить**

вынесени|е, я *nt.* **1** (*вещей*) taking out. **2** (*решения*) taking. **3** (*благодарности*) giving, expressing. **4** (*на рассмотрение*) submitting. **5** (*приговора*) pronouncement.

вынес|ти, у, ешь, *past* **~, ~ла** *pf.* (*of* ⇒**выносить**) **1** (*удалить за пределы*) to carry out, take out; to take way; (*убрать*) to carry away; (*доставить*) to bring; **в. на берег** to wash ashore; **в. на поля** to enter in the margin (*of a book*); **в. под строку** to make a footnote; **в. сор из избы** to wash one's dirty linen in public. **2** (*fig.*) (*получить*) to take away, receive, derive; **в. приятное впечатление** to be favourably impressed. **3**: **в. вопрос (на собрание, на обсуждение)** to put, submit a question (to a meeting, for discussion). **4**: **в. на своих плечах** (*fig.*) to shoulder, take the full weight (of), bear the full brunt (of). **5** (*вытерпеть*) to bear, stand, endure. **6**: **в. благодарность** to express gratitude; **в. приговор** (+*d.*) to pass sentence (on), pronounce sentence (on); **в. решение** to decide; (*leg.*) to pronounce judgement.

вынес|тись, усь, ешься, *past* **~ся, ~лась** *pf.* (*of* ⇒**выноситься**) to fly out, rush out.

выни|зать, жу, жешь *pf.* (*of* ⇒**~зывать**) (*obs.*) to decorate, adorn (*with string of beads, pearls, etc.*).

вынизыва|ть, ю *impf. of* ⇒**вынизать**

вынима|ть, ю *impf. of* ⇒**вынуть**

вынима|ться, ется *impf.* (*coll.*) to come out; **этот ящик не ~ется** this drawer does not come out.

вынос, а *m.* **1** (*покойника*) bearing-out, carrying-out; **на в.** (*о еде*) to take away (*Br.*), to take out (*US*), to go (*US*). **2** (*способ запряжки лошадей*) trace; **лошадь под ~ом** trace-horse.

выно|сить, шу, сишь *pf.* (*of* ⇒**вынашивать**) (*ребёнка*) to bear, bring forth (*a child at full term*); (*план, мысль*) to nurture.

выно|сить, шу, ~сишь *impf.* **1** *impf. of* ⇒**вынести. 2** *impf. only* (+*neg.*) to be unable to bear, be unable to stand; **я его не ~шу** I can't stand him.

выно|ситься, шусь, ~сишься *impf. of* ⇒**вынестись**

выноск|а, и *f.* **1** (*действие*) taking out, carrying out. **2** (*примечание*) marginal note; (*под строкой*) footnote.

выносливост|ь, и *f.* (power of) endurance; staying-power.

вынослив|ый (~, ~а) *adj.* (*человек, растение*) hardy; (*оборудование*) robust, sturdy.

выносн|ой *adj.* **1** (*кабель*) detachable, removable; (*аппарат*) portable. **2** (*примечание*) inserted in footnote. **3**: **~ая лошадь** trace-horse.

выношен|ный (~, ~а) *p.p.p. of* ⇒**выносить** *and adj.* **в. ребёнок** child born at full term; **в. проект** (*fig.*) mature project.

выно|шу, сишь *see* ⇒**~сить**

выно|шу, ~сишь *see* ⇒**~сить**

выну|дить, жу, дишь *pf.* (*of* ⇒**~ждать**) **1** (+*inf.*) to force, compel; **его ~дили уехать из страны** he was forced to leave the country. **2** (**у** + *g.*) to extort, force (from, out of); **они ~дили у него признание** they have extorted a confession from him.

вынужда|ть, ю *impf. of* ⇒**вынудить**

вынужден|ный (~, ~а) *p.p.p. of* ⇒**вынудить** *and adj.* forced; **~ная посадка** (*aeron.*) forced landing.

вын|уть, у, ешь *pf.* (*of* ⇒**~имать**) **1** to take out; to pull out, extract. **2**: **~ь да положь** (*coll.*) (right) here and now, on the spot.

выныривa|ть, ю *impf. of* ⇒**вынырнуть**

выныр|нуть, ну, нешь *pf.* (*of* ⇒**~ивать**) to come to the surface; (*fig., coll.*) (*появиться*) to turn up.

вынюх|ать, аю *pf.* (*of* ⇒**~ивать**) to sniff out (*also fig.*).

вынюхива|ть, ю *impf. of* ⇒**вынюхать**

вынянч|ить, у, ишь *pf.* (*coll.*) to bring up, nurse.

выпад, а *m.* **1** (*враждебное выступление*) attack. **2** (*sport*) lunge, thrust.

выпада|ть, ю *impf. of* ⇒**выпасть**

выпадени|е, я *nt.* **1** (*зубов*) falling out; (*осадков*) falling. **2** (*med.*) prolapse.

выпалива|ть, ю *impf. of* ⇒**выпалить**

выпал|ить, ю, ишь *pf.* (*of* ⇒**~ивать**) (*coll.*) **1** (**в** + *a.*) to shoot, fire (at). **2** (*fig.*) (*сказать*) to blurt out.

выпалыва|ть, ю *impf. of* ⇒**выполоть**

выпарива|ть, ю *impf. of* ⇒**выпарить**

выпар|ить, ю, ишь *pf.* (*of* ⇒**~ивать**) to steam; to steam-clean.

выпархива|ть, ю *impf. of* ⇒**выпорхнуть**

выпарыва|ть, ю *impf. of* ⇒**выпороть**[1]

выпас, а *m.* pasture.

выпаса|ть, ю *impf.* to graze, pasture.

выпа|сть, ду, дешь, *past* **~л** *pf.* (*of* ⇒**~дать**) **1** (*упасть наружу*) to fall out. **2** (*дождь, снег*) to fall. **3** (+*d.*) (*задача*) to befall, fall (to); **ему ~л жребий спасти страну от кризиса** it fell to his lot to save the country from crisis; **мне ~ло счастье** (+*inf.*) I had the luck (to); **мне ~ло идти первому** it fell to me to go first. **4** (*случиться*) to occur, turn out; **ночь ~ла звёздная** it turned out a starry night. **5** (*sport*) to lunge, thrust.

выпа|хать, шу, шешь *pf.* (*of* ⇒**~хивать**) **1** (*истощить*) to exhaust (*soil*). **2** (*возделать*) to turn up with the plough.

выпахива|ть, ю *impf. of* ⇒**выпахать**

выпачка|ть, ю *pf.* to soil, dirty; to stain.

выпачка|ться, юсь *pf.* to make o.s. dirty.

выпа|шу, шешь *see* ⇒**~хать**

выпе|к *see* ⇒**~чь**

выпека|ть, ю *impf. of* ⇒**выпечь**

выпендрива|ться, юсь *impf.* (*coll.*) to show off.

вып|ереть, ру, решь, *past* **~ер, ~ерла** *pf.* (*of* ⇒**~ирать**) (*coll.*) **1** (*вытолкнуть*) to push out, shove out. **2** (*выдаться*) to stick out, bulge out, protrude. **3** (*выгнать*) to throw out, sling out.

выпест|овать, ую *pf. of* ⇒**пестовать**

выпечк|а, и *f.* baking.

выпечн|ой *adj.*: **~ые изделия** bakery products.

выпе|чь, ку, чешь, кут, *past* **~к, ~кла** *pf.* (*of* ⇒**~кать**) to bake.

выпива|ть, ю *impf.* **1** *impf. of* ⇒**выпить. 2** (*impf. only; coll.*) to be fond of the bottle.

выпивк|а, и *f.* (*coll.*) **1** (*попойка*)

drinking-bout. **2** (*collect.*) (*напитки*) drinks.

выпиво́н, а *m.* (*coll.*) booze-up, drinking session.

выпиво́х|а, и *c.g.* (*sl.*) tippler; boozer.

выпи́лива|ть, ю *impf. of* ⇒**вы́пилить**

вы́пил|ить, ю, ишь *pf.* (*of* ⇒**~́ивать**) to saw; to cut out, make (with a saw).

выпира́|ть, ю *impf. of* ⇒**вы́переть**

вы́пи|сать, шу, шешь *pf.* (*of* ⇒**~́сывать**) **1** (*списать*) to copy out; to excerpt. **2** (*написать, нарисовать тщательно*) to write out, draw carefully. **3** (*документ*) to write out; **в. квита́нцию** to write out a receipt. **4** (*вызвать письмом*) to send for (*in writing*). **5** (*из больницы*) to discharge. **6** (*газету, журнал*) to subscribe to.

вы́пи|саться, шусь, шешься *pf.* (*of* ⇒**~́сываться**) (*из больницы*) to be discharged; **он уже́ ~сался из больни́цы** he is already out of hospital; (*из квартиры*) to officially change one's place of residence.

вы́писк|а, и *f.* **1** (*списывание*) copying, excerpting. **2** (*цитата*) extract, excerpt. **3** (*книг, газет*) subscription. **4** (*из больницы*) discharge.

выпи́сыва|ть(ся), ю(сь) *impf. of* ⇒**вы́писать(ся)**

вы́пис|ь, и *f.* (*obs.*) extract, copy; **метри́ческая в.** birth certificate.

вы́п|ить, ью, ьешь *pf.* (*of* ⇒**выпива́ть** *and* ⇒**пить**) to drink.

выпи́хива|ть, ю *impf. of* ⇒**вы́пихнуть**

вы́пих|нуть, ну, нешь *pf.* (*of* ⇒**~́ивать**) (*coll.*) to shove out, bundle out.

вы́пи|шу, шешь *see* ⇒**~сать**

вы́плав|ить, лю, ишь *pf.* (*of* ⇒**~ля́ть**) to smelt.

вы́плавк|а, и *f.* **1** (*действие*) smelting. **2** (*металл*) smelted metal.

выплавля́|ть, ю *impf. of* ⇒**вы́плавить**

вы́пла|кать, чу, чешь *pf.* **1** (*излить в слезах*) to sob out. **2**: **в. (все) глаза́** to cry one's eyes out.

вы́пла|каться, чусь, чешься *pf.* (*coll.*) to have a good cry, have one's cry out.

вы́плат|а, ы *f.* payment.

вы́пла|тить, чу, тишь *pf.* (*of* ⇒**~́чивать**) **1** to pay (out). **2** (*долг*) to pay off.

выпла́чива|ть, ю *impf. of* ⇒**вы́платить**

вы́пла|чу[1], тишь *see* ⇒**~тить**

вы́пла|чу[2], чешь *see* ⇒**~кать**

выплёвыва|ть, ю *impf. of* ⇒**вы́плюнуть**

вы́пле|скать, щу, щешь *pf.* (*of* ⇒**~̈скивать**) to pour out.

выплёскива|ть, ю *impf. of* ⇒**вы́плескать** *and* **вы́плеснуть**

вы́плес|нуть, ну, нешь *pf.* (*of* ⇒**~̈кивать**) to pour out; **в. вместе с водо́й ребёнка** (*fig.*) to throw out the baby with the (bath-)water.

вы́пле|сти, ту, тешь *pf.* (*of* ⇒**~та́ть**) **1** (*ленту*) to undo, untie. **2** (*корзину*) to weave.

выплета́|ть, ю *impf. of* ⇒**вы́плести**

выплыва́|ть, ю *impf. of* ⇒**вы́плыть**

вы́плы|ть, ву, вешь *pf.* (*of* ⇒**~ва́ть**) **1** (*человек*) to swim out; (*корабль*) to sail out; (*fig.*): **она́ ~ла из ко́мнаты** she sailed out of the room. **2** (*всплыть*) to come to the surface; (*fig., coll.*) (*факты*) to emerge; to appear; to crop up.

вы́плюн|уть, у, ешь *pf.* (*of* ⇒**выплёвывать**) to spit out.

выпола́скива|ть, ю *impf. of* ⇒**вы́полоскать**

выполза́|ть, ю *impf. of* ⇒**вы́ползти**

вы́полз|ти, у, ешь, *past* **~, ~ла** *pf.* (*of* ⇒**~а́ть**) (**из** + *g.*) to crawl out, creep out (from); (*змея*) to slither out.

вы́полир|овать, ую *pf.* (*coll.*) to polish (up).

выполне́ни|е, я *nt.* (*работы, приказа*) execution, carrying-out; (*желания*) fulfilment.

выполни́м|ый (~, ~а) *adj.* practicable, feasible.

вы́полн|ить, ю, ишь *pf.* (*of* ⇒**~я́ть**) (*приказание, работу*) to carry out; (*обязанность, желание, план*) to fulfil (*Br.*), fulfill (*US*); (*рисунок*) to execute.

выполня́|ть, ю *impf. of* ⇒**вы́полнить**

вы́поло|скать, щу, щешь *pf.* (*of* ⇒**выпола́скивать**) to rinse out.

вы́пол|оть, ю, ешь *pf.* (*of* ⇒**выпа́лывать**) to weed out.

вы́пор|оть[1], ю, ешь *pf.* (*of* ⇒**выпа́рывать**) to rip out.

вы́пор|оть[2], ю, ешь *pf. of* ⇒**поро́ть[2]**

вы́порхн|уть, у, ешь *pf.* (*of* ⇒**выпа́рхивать**) (*птица*) to flit out; (*fig., coll.*) to dart out.

вы́потрош|ить, у, ишь *pf. of* ⇒**потроши́ть**

вы́прав|ить, лю, ишь *pf.* (*of* ⇒**~ля́ть**) **1** (*сделать прямым*) to straighten (out). **2** (*исправить*) to correct; (*улучшить*) to improve.

вы́прав|иться, люсь, ишься *pf.* (*of* ⇒**~ля́ться**) **1** (*выпрямиться*) to become straight. **2** (*стать лучше*) to improve (*intrans.*).

вы́правк|а, и *f.* bearing.

выправля́|ть(ся), ю(сь) *impf. of* ⇒**вы́править(ся)**

выпра́стыва|ть(ся), ю(сь) *impf. of* ⇒**вы́простать(ся)**

выпра́шива|ть, ю *impf.* **1** *impf. of* ⇒**вы́просить. 2** *impf. only* to try to get, beg for.

выпрова́жива|ть, ю *impf. of* ⇒**вы́проводить**

вы́прово|дить, жу, дишь *pf.* (*of* ⇒**выпрова́живать**) (*coll.*) to send packing; to show the door (to).

вы́про|сить, шу, сишь *pf.* (*of* ⇒**выпра́шивать**) (**у** + *g.*) to get (out of), obtain, elicit (by begging).

вы́проста|ть, ю *pf.* (*of* ⇒**выпра́стывать**) (*coll.*) (*освободить*) to free, work loose.

вы́проста|ться, юсь *pf.* (*of* ⇒**выпра́стываться**) (*coll.*) (*освободиться*) to free o.s., work (o.s.) free.

вы́про|шу, сишь *see* ⇒**~сить**

вы́п|ру, решь *see* ⇒**~ереть**

выпры́гива|ть, ю *impf. of* ⇒**вы́прыгнуть**

вы́прыг|нуть, ну, нешь *pf.* (*of* ⇒**~́ивать**) to jump out, spring out.

выпряга́|ть, ю *impf. of* ⇒**вы́прячь**

выпрями́тел|ь, я *m.* (*elec.*) rectifier.

вы́прям|ить, лю, ишь *pf.* (*of* ⇒**~ля́ть**) to straighten (out).

вы́прям|иться, люсь, ишься *pf.* (*of* ⇒**~ля́ться**) to become straight; **в. во весь рост** to draw o.s. up to one's full height.

выпрямля́|ть(ся), ю(сь) *impf. of* ⇒**вы́прямить(ся)**

вы́пря|чь, гу, жешь, гут, *past* **~г, ~гла** *pf.* (*of* ⇒**~га́ть**) to unharness.

выпукло-во́гнутый *adj.* (*phys.*) convexo-concave.

вы́пуклост|ь, и *f.* **1** (*неровность*) protuberance; bulge. **2** (*phys.*) convexity. **3** (*sg. only*; *fig.*) clarity, distinctness.

вы́пукл|ый (~, ~а) *adj.* **1** (*неровный*) protuberant; prominent, bulging. **2** (*phys.*) convex. **3** (*fig.*) clear, distinct.

вы́пуск, а *m.* **1** (*товаров*) output; (*денег, акций*) issue; (*газов*) discharge, emission; **в. из печа́ти** publication; **в. новосте́й** newscast; **сро́чный в. новосте́й** newsflash. **2** (*романа*) part, instalment (*Br.*), installment (*US*). **3** (*в школе, институте*) leavers; graduates. **4** (*сокращение*) cut, omission.

выпуска́|ть, ю *impf. of* ⇒**вы́пустить**

выпуска́|ющий *pres. part. act. of* ⇒**~ть;** *as n.* **в., ~ющего** *m.* person responsible for seeing newspaper *or* journal through press.

выпускни́к, а́ *m.* **1** (*окончивший учебное заведение*) graduate; **бы́вший в.** old boy. **2** (*на последнем курсе*) final-year student.

выпускни́|ца, цы *f. of* ⇒**~к**

выпуск|но́й *adj. of* ⇒**вы́пуск; в. кла́пан** (*tech.*) exhaust valve; **~на́я труба́** (*tech.*) exhaust pipe; **в. экза́мен** final examination, finals.

вы́пу|стить, щу, стишь *pf.* (*of* ⇒**~ска́ть**) **1** (*дать выйти*) to let out; (*заключённого, фильм*) to release; (*из учебного заведения*) to turn out; **в. во́ду из ва́нны** to let the water out of a bath; **в. из рук** to let go of; **в. из тюрьмы́** to release from prison; **в. раке́ту/снаря́д** to fire a rocket/shell; **в. (пулемётную) о́чередь** (*mil.*) to fire a burst. **2** (*деньги, акции*) to issue; (*продукцию*) to turn out, produce; **в. в прода́жу** to put on the market; **в. (в свет)** to publish.

3 (*исключить*) to cut (out), omit.
4 (*сделать шире, длиннее*) to let out, let down.
5 (*выставить*) to show; **в. свой ко́гти** to show one's claws.

вы́пут|ать, аю *pf.* (*of* ⇒**~ывать**) to disentangle.

вы́пут|аться, аюсь *pf.* (*of* ⇒**~ываться**) to disentangle o.s., extricate o.s. (*also fig.*).

выпу́тыва|ть(ся), ю(сь) *impf. of* ⇒**вы́путать(ся)**

вы́пуч|енный *p.p.p. of* ⇒**~ить** *and adj.* (*coll.*): **с ~енными глаза́ми** wide-eyed, goggle-eyed.

выпу́чива|ть, ю *impf. of* ⇒**вы́пучить**

вы́пуч|ить, у, ишь *pf.* (*of* ⇒**~ивать** *and* **пу́чить** 2); **в. глаза́** (*coll.*) to open one's eyes wide.

вы́пушк|а, и *f.* edging, braid, piping.

вы́пыт|ать, аю *pf.* (*of* ⇒**~ывать**) (**у**+*g.*) (*coll.*) (*информацию, секреты*) to elicit, extort (from).

выпы́тыва|ть, ю *impf.* (*coll.*) **1** *impf. of* ⇒**вы́пытать. 2** *impf. only* to try to discover (*by interrogation*); **в. секре́т у кого́-н.** to try to get a secret out of s.o.

вып|ь, и *f.* (*zool.*) bittern.

выпя́лива|ть(ся), ю(сь) *impf. of* ⇒**вы́пялить(ся)**

вы́пял|ить, ю, ишь *pf.* (*of* ⇒**~ивать**) (*coll.*) to stick out; **в. глаза́** to open one's eyes wide; (*уставиться*) to stare.

вы́пял|иться, юсь, ишься *pf.* (*of* ⇒**~иваться**) (*coll., pej.*) to stare.

вы́пя|тить, чу, тишь *pf.* (*of* ⇒**~чивать**) (*coll.*) **1** to stick out; **в. грудь** to stick out one's chest. **2** (*fig., pej.*) to over-emphasize.

вы́пя|титься, чусь, тишься *pf.* (*of* ⇒**~чиваться**) (*coll.*) to stick out (*intrans.*), protrude.

выпя́чива|ть(ся), ю(ся) *impf. of* ⇒**вы́пятить(ся)**

выраба́тыва|ть, ю *impf. of* ⇒**вы́работать**

вы́работа|ть, ю *pf.* (*of* ⇒**выраба́тывать**) **1** (*произвести*) to manufacture; to produce, make.
2 (*план*) to work out, draw up; (*привычку*) to develop. **3** (*coll.*) (*заработать*) to earn, make.

вы́работк|а, и *f.* **1** (*производство*) manufacture; production, making.
2 (*плана*) working-out, drawing-up.
3 (*продукция*) output, yield.
4 (*качество*) make; **хоро́шей ~и** well-made.

выра́внивани|е, я *nt.* smoothing-out, levelling; (*по прямой линии*) alignment.

выра́вниватель, я *m.* equalizer.

выра́внива|ть(ся), ю(сь) *impf. of* ⇒**вы́ровнять(ся)**

выража́|ть, ю *impf. of* ⇒**вы́разить**

выража́|ться, юсь *impf.* **1** *impf. of* ⇒**вы́разиться; мя́гко ~ясь** to put it mildly. **2** (*coll.*) (*ругаться*) to swear.

выраже́ни|е, я *nt.* expression; **усто́йчивое в.** set expression; **не стесня́ться в ~ях** to speak plainly; **говори́ть с ~м** to speak with feeling/expression.

выраже́н|ный (~, ~а) *p.p.p. of* ⇒**вы́разить** *and adj.* pronounced, marked.

вырази́тел|ь, я *m.* spokesperson; exponent.

вырази́тельност|ь, и *f.* expressiveness.

вырази́тел|ьный (~ен, ~ьна) *adj.* expressive.

вы́ра|зить, жу, зишь *pf.* (*of* ⇒**~жа́ть**) (*мысль, желание*) to express; (*передать*) to convey; (*общее мнение*) to voice.

вы́ра|зиться, жусь, зишься *pf.* (*of* ⇒**~жа́ться**) **1** (*сказать словами*) to express o.s.; **я непра́вильно ~зился** I did not put it the right way.
2 (*обнаружиться*) (**в**+*p.*) to manifest itself (in).

выраста́|ть, ю *impf. of* ⇒**вы́расти**

вы́р|асти, асту, астешь, *past* **~ос, ~осла** *pf.* (*of* ⇒**~аста́ть** *and* **расти́**) **1** to grow (up). **2** (**в**+*a.*) (*стать*) to grow (into), develop (into), become; **их дру́жба ~осла в любо́вь** their friendship grew into love. **3** (**из**+*g.*) to grow (out of) (*clothing*). **4** (*увеличиться*) to increase; **населе́ние за пять лет ~осло на два́дцать проце́нтов** in five years the population had increased by twenty per cent. **5** (*появиться*) to appear, rise up; **пе́ред на́шими глаза́ми ~ос Арара́т** Mount Ararat rose up before our eyes. **6**: **в. в чьих-н. глаза́х** to rise in s.o.'s estimation.

вы́ра|стить, щу, стишь *pf.* (*of* ⇒**~щивать**) (*детей*) to bring up; (*животных*) to rear, breed; (*растения*) to grow, cultivate.

выра́щива|ть, ю *impf. of* ⇒**вы́растить**

вы́рв|ать¹, у, ешь *pf.* (*of* ⇒**вырыва́ть¹**) **1** to pull out, tear out; **в. зуб** to pull out a tooth; (*отнять*) to snatch; **он ~ал кни́гу у меня́ из рук** he snatched the book out of my hands.
2 (*fig.*) (*добиться*) to extort, wring; **в. призна́ние у кого́-н.** to wring a confession out of s.o.

вы́рв|ать², у, ешь *pf. of* ⇒**рвать²**

вы́рв|аться, усь, ешься *pf.* (*of* ⇒**вырыва́ться**) **1** (**из**+*g.*) (*освободиться*) to tear o.s. away (from); to break out (from), break loose (from), break free (from); **в. из чьих-н. объя́тий** to tear o.s. away from s.o.'s embrace; (*уехать*) to get away (from); **едва́ ли мне уда́стся до ле́та в. из Москвы́** I shall hardly manage to get away from Moscow before the summer.
2 (*стон, замечание*) to break (from), burst (from), escape. **3** (*появиться*) to shoot up, shoot out. **4** (*быстро выйти*) to pull out in front of others.

вы́рез, а *m.* (*выемка*) cut; notch; (*в одежде*) neck; **пла́тье с больши́м ~ом** low-necked dress.

вы́ре|зать, жу, жешь *pf.* (*of* ⇒**~за́ть**) **1** (*опухоль; заметку из газеты*) to cut out; (*comput.*) to cut. **2** (*из дерева*) to cut, carve; (*на металле, на камне*) to engrave. **3** (*fig.*) (*убить*) to slaughter, butcher.

выреза́|ть, ю *impf. of* ⇒**вы́резать**

вы́резк|а, и *f.* **1** (*действие*) cutting-out, excision; carving; engraving.
2: **газе́тная в.** press-cutting. **3** (*мясо*) sirloin steak.

вырезно́й *adj.* carved.

вы́реш|ить, у, ишь *pf.* (*coll.*) to decide finally.

вы́рис|овать, ую *pf.* (*of* ⇒**~о́вывать**) to draw carefully, draw in detail.

вы́рис|оваться, уется *pf.* (*of* ⇒**~о́вываться**) to appear (in outline); to stand out; (*fig.*) (*ситуация*) to emerge.

вырисо́выва|ть(ся), ю, ет(ся) *impf. of* ⇒**вы́рисовать(ся)**

вы́ровня|ть, ю *pf.* (*of* ⇒**выра́внивать**) **1** (*шероховатое*) to smooth (out), level; (*шаг, дыхание*) to regulate.
2 (*по прямой линии*) to align. **3** (*mil.*) to draw up in line; **в. ряды́** to dress ranks.

вы́ровня|ться, юсь *pf.* (*of* ⇒**выра́вниваться**) **1** to become level; to become even; (*mil.*) to form up; to dress; (*sport*) to equalize. **2** (*fig.*) (*в занятиях*) to catch up, draw level. **3** (*fig.*) (*улучшиться*) to improve, get better.

вы́род|иться, ится *pf.* (*of* ⇒**вырожда́ться**) to degenerate.

вы́род|ок, ка *m.* (*coll.*) (*в какой-н. среде*) degenerate; (*в семье*) black sheep.

вырожда́|ться, ется *impf. of* ⇒**вы́родиться**

вырожде́н|ец, ца *m.* degenerate.

вырожде́ни|е, я *nt.* degeneration.

вы́рон|ить, ю, ишь *pf.* to drop

вы́р|ою, оешь *see* ⇒**~ыть**

выруба́|ть(ся), ю(сь) *impf. of* ⇒**вы́рубить(ся)**

вы́руб|ить, лю, ишь *pf.* (*of* ⇒**~а́ть**) **1** (*деревья*) to cut down, fell.
2 (*дыру, кусок льда*) to cut out.
3 (*фигуру*) to carve (out). **4** (*coll.*) (*выключить*) to switch off. **5** (*sl.*) to knock unconscious, knock out.

вы́руб|иться, люсь, ишься *pf.* (*of* ⇒**~а́ться**) (*sl.*) (*заснуть*) to fall asleep (from exhaustion), crash out; (*потерять сознание*) to lose consciousness.

вы́рубк|а, и *f.* **1** cutting down, felling; **в. ле́са** *or* **лесо́в** deforestation.
2 (*вырубленное место*) clearing.

вы́руга|ть(ся), ю(сь) *pf. of* ⇒**руга́ть(ся)**

выру́лива|ть, ю *impf. of* ⇒**вы́рулить**

вы́рул|ить, ю, ишь *pf.* (*of* ⇒**~ивать**) **1** (*из гаража, из узкого проезда*) to drive out. **2** (*aeron.*) to taxi.

выруча́|ть, ю *impf. of* ⇒**вы́ручить**

вы́руч|ить, у, ишь *pf.* (*of* ⇒**~а́ть**) **1** (*помочь*) to help out; to come to the help, aid (of). **2** (*coll.*) (*заработать*): **он ~ил мно́го де́нег** he has made a lot of money.

вы́ручк|а, и *f.* **1** help, assistance; **прийти́ на ~у** to come to the rescue.
2 (*деньги*) takings; earnings.

вырыва́|ть¹, ю *impf. of* ⇒**вы́рвать¹**

вырыва́|ть², ю *impf. of* ⇨**вы́рыть**

вырыва́|ться, юсь *impf. of* ⇨**вы́рваться**

вы́р|ыть, ою, оешь *pf.* (*of* ⇨**~ыва́ть²**) (*землю, яму*) to dig; (*предмет*) to dig up, dig out, unearth; **в. труп** to exhume a corpse.

вы́ря|дить, жу, дишь *pf.* (*coll.*) to dress up (*trans.*).

вы́ря|диться, жусь, дишься *pf.* (*of* ⇨**~жа́ться**) (*coll.*) to dress up (*intrans.*).

выряжа́|ть(ся), ю(сь) *impf. of* ⇨**вы́рядить(ся)**

вы́са|дить, жу, дишь *pf.* (*of* ⇨**~́живать**) **1** (*пассажира*) to drop off, set down; **в. на бе́рег** to put ashore; (*заставить выйти*) to throw off, out; **пья́ницу ~дили из авто́буса** the drunken man was made to get off the bus. **2** (*растение*) to transplant; (*рассаду*) to plant out.

вы́са|диться, жусь, дишься *pf.* (*of* ⇨**~́живаться**) (**из, с**+*g.*) to alight (from), get off; (*с судна, самолёта*) to disembark.

вы́садк|а, и *f.* **1** (*с судна*) debarkation, disembarkation; (*из автобуса*) alighting, getting off. **2** (*растения*) transplanting; planting out.

выса́жива|ть(ся), ю(сь) *impf. of* ⇨**вы́садить(ся)**

вы́са|жу, дишь *see* ⇨**~дить**

выса́сыва|ть, ю *impf. of* ⇨**вы́сосать**

высве́рлива|ть, ю *impf. of* ⇨**вы́сверлить**

вы́сверл|ить, ю, ишь *pf.* to drill, bore.

вы́све|тить, чу, тишь *pf.* (*of* ⇨**высве́чивать**) **1** (*осветить*) to light up, illuminate. **2** (*comput., also fig.*) to highlight.

высве́чива|ть, ю *impf. of* ⇨**вы́светить**

вы́свобо|дить, жу, дишь *pf.* **1** (*вынуть, освободить*) to free. **2** (*средства, рабочих*) to free up, release.

высвобожда́|ть, ю *impf. of* ⇨**вы́свободить**

высе́ива|ть, ю *impf. of* ⇨**вы́сеять**

высека́|ть, ю *impf. of* ⇨**вы́сечь²**

вы́се|ку, чешь *see* ⇨**~чь**

выселе́ни|е, я *nt.* eviction.

вы́сел|ить, ю, ишь *pf.* (*of* ⇨**~я́ть**) **1** (*из квартиры*) to evict. **2** (*переселить*) to evacuate, move.

вы́сел|иться, юсь, ишься *pf.* (*of* ⇨**~я́ться**) to move.

вы́сел|ок, ка *m.* settlement.

выселя́|ть(ся), ю(сь) *impf. of* ⇨**вы́селить(ся)**

вы́семен|иться, ится *pf.* (*agric.*) to go to seed.

вы́се|чь¹, ку, чешь, кут, *past* **~к, ~кла** *pf.* (*of* ⇨**се́чь¹**) (*бить*) to beat, flog.

вы́се|чь², ку, чешь, кут, *past* **~к, ~кла** *pf.* (*of* ⇨**~ка́ть**) (*фигуру*) to carve, carve out; **в. ого́нь** to strike fire (*from a flint*).

вы́се|ять, ю *pf.* (*of* ⇨**~́ивать**) (*agric.*) to sow.

вы́си|деть, жу, дишь *pf.* (*of* ⇨**~́живать**) **1** (*цыплят*) to hatch (out). **2** (*просидеть*) to stay; **мы ~дели до конца́ ле́кции** we sat the lecture out.

выси́жива|ть, ю *impf. of* ⇨**вы́сидеть**

вы́|ситься, сится *impf.* to tower (up), rise.

выска́блива|ть, ю *impf. of* ⇨**вы́скоблить**

вы́ска|зать, жу, жешь *pf.* (*of* ⇨**~́зывать**) to express; to state; **в. предположе́ние** to come out with a suggestion.

вы́ска|заться, жусь, жешься *pf.* (*of* ⇨**~́зываться**) **1** to speak out; to speak one's mind; to have one's say. **2** (**за**+*a.* or **про́тив**+*g.*) to speak (for *or* against); **никто́ не ~зался про́тив законопрое́кта** no one spoke against the bill.

выска́зывани|е, я *nt.* **1** (*действие*) speaking out; (*мнения*) expression. **2** (*суждение*) pronouncement; (*мнение*) opinion.

выска́зыва|ть(ся), ю(сь) *impf. of* ⇨**вы́сказать(ся)**

выска́кива|ть, ю *impf. of* ⇨**вы́скочить**

выска́льзыва|ть, ю *impf. of* ⇨**выскользнуть**

вы́скобл|ить, ю, ишь *pf.* (*of* ⇨**выска́бливать**) (*доску*) to scrape clean; (*краску*) to scrape off; (*надпись*) to erase, remove; (*med.*) to remove.

вы́скользн|уть, у, ешь *pf.* (*of* ⇨**выска́льзывать**) to slip out (*also fig.*).

вы́скоч|ить, у, ишь *pf.* (*of* ⇨**выска́кивать**) **1** (*выпрыгнуть*) to jump out; to leap out, spring out; (*выбежать*) to run out; (*fig., coll.*) (*с вопросом, замечанием*) to come out (with). **2** (*coll.*) (*чирей*) to come up. **3** (*coll.*) (*выпасть*) to drop out, fall out; **в. из головы́** to slip one's mind.

вы́скочк|а, и *c.g.* (*coll.*) upstart.

выскреба́|ть, ю *impf. of* ⇨**вы́скрести**

вы́скре|сти, бу, бешь, *past* **~б, ~бла** *pf.* **1** (*сковороду*) to scrape out, (*грязь*) scrape off. **2** (*золу*) to rake out.

вы́слан|ный (~, ~а) *p.p.p. of* ⇨**вы́слать;** *as n.* **в., ~ного** *m.*, **~ная, ~ной** *f.* exile, deportee.

вы́|слать, шлю, шлешь *pf.* (*of* ⇨**~сыла́ть**) **1** (*посылку, помощь*) to send, send out, dispatch. **2** (*pol.*) to exile; (*иностранца*) to deport.

вы́сле|дить, жу, дишь *pf.* (*of* ⇨**высле́живать**) to trace; to track down.

высле́жива|ть, ю *impf.* **1** *impf. of* ⇨**вы́следить. 2** *impf. only* to be on the track of; to shadow.

вы́сле|жу, дишь *see* ⇨**~дить**

вы́слуг|а, и *f.* period of service; **за ~у лет** for long service, for meritorious service.

выслу́жива|ть(ся), ю(сь) *impf. of* ⇨**вы́служить(ся)**

вы́служ|ить, у, ишь *pf.* **1** (*приобрести службой*) to qualify for, obtain; **он ~ил повыше́ние** he has qualified for promotion. **2** (*прослужить*) to serve (out).

вы́служ|иться, усь, ишься *pf.* **1** (*выдвинуться по службе*) to gain promotion, be promoted. **2** (*coll., pej.*) to gain favour (*Br.*), favor (*US*) (with), get in (with); **он ~ился пе́ред бригади́ром** he is well in with the foreman.

вы́слуша|ть, ю *pf.* (*of* ⇨**выслу́шивать**) **1** to hear out. **2** (*med.*) to listen to.

выслу́шивани|е, я *nt.* (*med.*) auscultation.

выслу́шива|ть, ю *impf. of* ⇨**вы́слушать**

высма́трива|ть, *impf. of* ⇨**вы́смотреть**

высме́ива|ть, ю *impf. of* ⇨**вы́смеять**

вы́сме|ять, ю, ешь *pf.* (*of* ⇨**~́ивать**) to deride, ridicule.

вы́смол|ить, ю, ишь *pf. of* ⇨**смоли́ть**

вы́сморка|ть(ся), ю(сь) *pf. of* ⇨**сморка́ть(ся)**

вы́смотр|еть, ю, ишь *pf.* (*of* ⇨**высма́тривать**) **1** (*осмотреть*) to scrutinize. **2** (*найти*) to spy out; to locate (*by eye*).

высо́выва|ть(ся), ю(сь) *impf. of* ⇨**вы́сунуть(ся)**

высо́к|ий (~, ~а́, ~́о) *adj.* (*дом, гора; цена, температура; качество, мнение*) high; (*человек*) tall; (*мысль, стиль*) lofty; (*гость*) distinguished; (*честь*) great; (*mus.*) high, high-pitched; **~ая вода́** high tide; **в ~ой сте́пени** highly.

высо́ко́ *adv.* **1** (*располагаться*) high (up); **лежа́ть в. над у́ровнем мо́ря** to be high above sea level. **2** *as pred.* it is high (up); it is a long way up; **окно́ бы́ло в. от земли́** the window was high up off the ground. **3**: **oцени́ть в.** to value highly.

высоко... *comb. form* high-, highly-.

высокоблагоро́ди|е, я *nt.* (**ва́ше**) **в.** (your) Honour, (your) Worship (*title, in tsarist Russia, of civil servants of the eighth to the sixth classes and of officers from the rank of major to that of colonel*).

высокого́рный *adj.* Alpine, mountain.

высокока́чественный *adj.* high-quality.

высококвалифици́рованный *adj.* highly qualified.

высокоме́ри|е, я *nt.* haughtiness, arrogance.

высокоме́р|ный (~ен, ~на) *adj.* haughty, arrogant.

высокоопла́чиваемый *adj.* highly-paid.

высокопа́р|ный (~ен, ~на) *adj.* (*liter.*) high-flown; bombastic.

высокопоста́вленный *adj.* high-ranking.

высокопревосходи́тельств|о, а *nt.*: **(ва́ше) в.** (your) Excellency (*title, in tsarist Russia, of officers and civil servants of the first and second class*).

высокопреосвяще́нств|о, а *nt.*: **(ва́ше) в.** (your) Eminence, (your) Grace (*title of archbishops and metropolitans of the Orthodox Church*).

высокопреподо́би|е, я *nt.*: **(ва́ше) в.** (your) Reverence (*title of archimandrites, abbots and archpriests of the Orthodox Church*).

высокопро́б|ный (~ен, ~на) *adj.* sterling; (*fig.*) sterling, of high quality.

высокопроизводи́тел|ьный (~ен, ~ьна) *adj.* highly productive.

высокора́звит|ый (~, ~а) *adj.* highly developed.

высокосо́ртный *adj.* high-grade.

высокотехнологи́чный *adj.* high-tech.

высокоуважа́емый *adj.* (*obs.*; *mode of address in letters*) honoured (*Br.*), honored (*US*) (Sir), respected (Sir).

высокочасто́тный *adj.* (*elec.*) high-frequency.

высокочти́мый *adj.* (*obs.*) highly esteemed.

высокоэффекти́в|ный (~ен, ~на) *adj.* high-efficiency.

вы́сос|ать, у, ешь *pf.* (*of* ⇒**выса́сывать**) **1** to suck out. **2** (*fig., coll.*) (*деньги, сведения*) to get out (of), extort (from); **в. все со́ки из** to exhaust, wear out; **в. из па́льца** to invent, fabricate; **всё э́то из па́льца ~ано** it is a complete fabrication.

высот|а́, ы́, *pl.* **~ы, ~** *f.* **1** (*здания, столба*) height; (*над земной поверхностью*) altitude; (*температуры, давления*) level; (*mus.*) pitch; **набра́ть ~у́** (*aeron.*) to gain altitude. **2** (*возвышенность*) height; **кома́ндные ~ы** commanding heights (*also fig.*). **3** (*искусства, мастерства*) high level; **дости́гнуть но́вых высо́т** to reach new heights. **4** (*fig.*): **на до́лжной ~е́** up to the mark; **быть на ~е́ положе́ния** to be equal to the occasion; **оказа́ться на ~е́ положе́ния** to rise to the occasion.

высо́тник, а *m.* (*строитель*) workman employed on the construction of high buildings; (*альпинист*) high-altitude mountaineer; (*лётчик*) high-altitude flier.

высо́тн|ый *adj.* **1** high-altitude. **2**: **~ое зда́ние** high-rise building, tower block.

высотоме́р, а *m.* altimeter.

вы́сох|нуть, ну, нешь, *past* **~, ~ла** *pf.* (*of* ⇒**высыха́ть**) **1** (*бельё*) to dry (out); (*река*) to dry up. **2** (*растение*) to wither, fade; (*fig.*) (*исхудать*) to waste away, fade away.

вы́сох|ший *p.p. act. of* ⇒**~нуть** *and adj.* dried-up; shrivelled; wizened.

высоча́йш|ий *adj.* **1** *superl. of* ⇒**высо́кий. 2** (*epithet of tsar or emperor*) imperial, royal; **проше́ние на ~ее и́мя** petition to His Imperial Majesty.

высоче́нный *adj.* (*coll.*) very high, (*человек*) very tall.

высо́честв|о, а *nt.*: **(ва́ше) в.** (your) Highness.

вы́сп|аться, люсь, ишься *pf.* (*of* ⇒**высыпа́ться²**) (*coll.*) to have a good sleep.

выспева́|ть, ю *impf. of* ⇒**вы́спеть**

вы́спе|ть, ю *pf.* (*coll.*) to ripen.

выспра́шива|ть, ю *impf. of* ⇒**вы́спросить**

выспрен|ний (~, ~ня) *adj.* high-flown; bombastic.

вы́спро|сить, шу, сишь *pf.* (*of* ⇒**выспра́шивать**) (*coll.*) **1** (*информацию*) to find out. **2** (*человека*) to interrogate; to pump.

вы́став|ить, лю, ишь *pf.* (*of* ⇒**~ля́ть**) **1** (*поставить наружу*) to put out, move out; (*картины, товары*) to exhibit, display; **в. на прода́жу** to put on sale; **в. на свет** to expose to the light; **в. напока́з** to show off, parade. **2** (*часовых*) to post. **3** (+*i.*) (*представить*) to represent (as), make out (as); **в. в плохо́м све́те** to represent in an unfavourable light; **его́ ~или тру́сом** he was made out to be a coward. **4** (*предложить*) to put forward; **в. свою́ кандидату́ру** to come forward as a candidate; **в. до́воды** to put forward arguments. **5** (*написать*) to put down, set down; **в. число́ на письме́** to date a letter. **6** (*coll.*) (*выгнать*) to send out, turn out, throw out; **в. со слу́жбы** to sack.

вы́став|иться, люсь, ишься *pf.* (*of* ⇒**~ля́ться**) **1** (*о художнике*) to exhibit. **2** (*coll.*) to stick out; to lean out; (*fig.*) to show off.

вы́ставк|а, и *f.* exhibition, show.

выставля́|ть, ю *impf. of* ⇒**вы́ставить**

выставля́|ться, юсь *impf. of* ⇒**вы́ставиться**

выставно́й *adj.* removable.

вы́став|очный *adj. of* ⇒**~ка**

выста́ива|ть(ся), ю, ет(ся) *impf. of* ⇒**вы́стоять(ся)**

вы́стега|ть¹, ю *pf. of* ⇒**стега́ть²**

вы́стега|ть², ю *pf.* (*coll.*) to thrash, flog.

вы́стел|ить, ю, ешь *pf.* = **вы́стлать**

вы́ст|елю, елешь *see* ⇒**~лать**

выстила́|ть, ю *impf. of* ⇒**вы́стлать**

вы́стира|ть, ю *pf. of* ⇒**стира́ть²**

вы́ст|лать, елю, елешь *pf.* (*покрыть*) to cover; (*вымостить*) to pave.

вы́сто|ять, ю, ишь *pf.* (*of* ⇒**выста́ивать**) **1** (*долго простоять*) to stand; **нам пришло́сь в. весь путь** we had to stand the whole way. **2** (*не сдаться*) to stand one's ground.

вы́сто|яться, ится *pf.* (*of* ⇒**выста́иваться**) to mature, ripen.

вы́страда|ть, ю *pf.* **1** (*пережить много страданий*) to suffer; to go through. **2** (*достигнуть страданиями*) to gain, achieve through suffering.

выстра́ива|ть(ся), ю(сь) *impf. of* ⇒**вы́строить(ся)**

выстра́чива|ть, ю *impf. of* ⇒**вы́строчить**

вы́стрел, а *m.* shot; **произвести́ в.** to fire a shot; **разда́лся в.** a shot rang out; **на в. (от**+*g.*) (*coll.*) within gunshot (of).

вы́стрел|ить, ю, ишь *pf.* to shoot, fire; **я ~ил в него́ три ра́за** I fired three shots at him.

вы́стри|г, гу, жешь *see* ⇒**~чь**

выстрига́|ть, ю *impf. of* ⇒**вы́стричь**

вы́стри|чь, гу, жешь, гут, *past* **~г, ~гла** *pf.* (*стрижкой удалить*) to cut, clip out; (*шерсть*) to shear.

вы́строга|ть, ю *pf.* (*of* ⇒**строга́ть**) **1** (*сделать гладким*) to plane, shave. **2** (*вырезать*) to carve

вы́стро|ить, ю, ишь *pf.* (*of* ⇒**выстра́ивать**) **1** to build. **2** (*mil.*) to draw up, form up.

вы́стро|иться, юсь, ишься *pf.* (*of* ⇒**выстра́иваться**) **1** (*mil.*) to form up (*intrans.*). **2** (*стоять рядами*) to stand in rows.

вы́строч|ить, у, ишь *pf.* (*of* ⇒**выстра́чивать**) to hemstitch.

вы́струга|ть, ю *pf.* = **вы́строгать**

вы́стука|ть, ю *pf.* (*of* ⇒**высту́кивать**) (*coll.*) to tap out; **в. мело́дию** to tap out a tune.

высту́кива|ть, ю *impf. of* ⇒**вы́стукать**

вы́ступ, а *m.* projection, ledge; **в. фро́нта** (*mil.*) salient.

выступа́|ть, ю *impf.* **1** *impf. of* ⇒**вы́ступить. 2** (*impf. only*) to project, jut out, stick out. **3** (*impf. only*) (*ходить с важным видом*) to strut.

вы́ступ|ить, лю, ишь *pf.* **1** (*выйти вперёд*) to come forward; to come out; **в. в похо́д** (*mil.*) to take the field. **2** (*выйти за пределы*) **(из**+*g.*) to go beyond; **в. из берего́в** to overflow its banks. **3** (*публично*) to appear (*publicly*); **(за**+*a.*, **про́тив**+*g.*) to come out (for, against); **в. в печа́ти** to appear in print; **в. с ре́чью** to make a speech; **в. по телеви́дению** to appear on television.

выступле́ни|е, я *nt.* **1** (*публичное*) appearance; (*речь*) speech; (*актёра*) performance. **2** (*отправление*) setting out.

вы́су|дить, жу, дишь *pf.* (*coll.*) to obtain by court decision.

высу́жива|ть, ю *impf. of* ⇒**вы́судить**

вы́су|жу, дишь *see* ⇒**~дить**

вы́сун|уть, у, ешь *pf.* (*of* ⇒**высо́вывать**) to put out, thrust out, stick out; **в. язы́к** to put/stick one's tongue out; **бежа́ть ~ув язы́к** (*coll.*) to run without pausing for breath.

вы́сун|уться, усь, ешься *pf.* (*of* ⇒**высо́вываться**) **1** (*о человеке*) to show o.s., thrust o.s. forward; **в. из окна́** to lean out of the window. **2** (*о ноге, руке*) to stick out.

высу́шива|ть, ю *impf. of* ⇒**вы́сушить**

вы́суш|ить(ся), у(сь), ишь(ся) *pf. of* ⇒**суши́ть(ся)**

вы́счита|ть, ю *pf.* (*of* ⇒**высчи́тывать**) to calculate.

высчи́тыва|ть, ю *impf. of* ⇒**вы́считать**

вы́с|ший *adj.* (*comp. and superl. of* ⇒**высо́кий**) (*самый высокий*) highest; (*самый главный*) supreme; (*более высокий*) higher; **~шего ка́чества** of the highest quality; **~шая матема́тика** higher mathematics; **~шая ме́ра наказа́ния** capital punishment; **суд ~шей инста́нции** higher court; **~шее образова́ние** higher education; **~шее о́бщество** (high) society; **~шее уче́бное заведе́ние** higher education establishment; **~шая шко́ла** higher education; **в ~шей сте́пени** in the highest degree.

высыла́|ть, ю *impf. of* ⇒**вы́слать**

вы́сылк|а, и *f.* **1** (*посылки, денег*) sending, dispatching. **2** (*диссидента*) exile; (*иностранца*) deportation.

вы́сып|ать, лю, лешь *pf.* (*of* ⇒**высыпа́ть**) **1** to pour out (*trans.*); (*нечаянно*) to spill. **2** (*coll.*) to pour out (*intrans.*). **3** (*сыпь*) to break out (*impers.*): **у него́ ~ало на всём те́ле** he has come out in a rash all over.

высыпа́|ть, ю *impf. of* ⇒**вы́сыпать**

вы́сып|аться, лется, лются *pf.* (*of* ⇒**высыпа́ться**[1]) to pour out; (*нечаянно*) to spill (*intrans.*).

высыпа́|ться[1], **ется** *impf. of* ⇒**вы́сыпаться**

высыпа́|ться[2], **юсь,** *impf. of* ⇒**вы́спаться**

высыха́|ть, ю *impf. of* ⇒**вы́сохнуть**

выс|ь, и *f.* (*в небе*) height; (*pl.*) (*вершины*) mountain tops.

выта́лкива|ть, ю *impf. of* ⇒**вы́толкать** *and* ⇒**вы́толкнуть**

выта́плива|ть, ю *impf. of* ⇒**вы́топить**

выта́птыва|ть, ю *impf. of* ⇒**вы́топтать**

вы́таращ|ить, у, ишь *pf. of* ⇒**тара́щить**

выта́скива|ть, ю *impf. of* ⇒**вы́тащить**

вы́тача|ть, ю *pf. of* ⇒**тача́ть**

выта́чива|ть, ю *impf. of* ⇒**вы́точить**

вы́тачк|а, и *f.* tuck, dart.

вы́тащ|ить, у, ишь *pf.* (*of* ⇒**выта́скивать**) **1** (*мебель из комнаты*) to drag out; (*из кармана, из сумки*) to pull out, extract; (*coll.*) (*убедить пойти*): **в. кого́-н.** to drag s.o. out, drag s.o. off; **они́ ~или его́ в кино́** they have dragged him off to the cinema; **в. кого́-н. из беды́** to help s.o. out of trouble. **2** (*coll.*) (*украсть*) to steal, pinch; **у меня́ ~или бума́жник** I have had my wallet stolen.

вы́твер|дить, жу, дишь *pf.* (*coll.*) to get/learn by heart.

вытве́ржива|ть, ю *impf. of* ⇒**вы́твердить**

вытворя́|ть, ю *impf.* (*coll.*) to get up to, be up to; **что ты ~ешь?** what are you up to?

вытека́|ть, ю *impf.* **1** *impf. of* ⇒**вы́течь. 2** (*impf. only*) (*река*) to flow (from, out of). **3** (*impf. only*) (*fig.*) (*вывод*) to result, follow (from).

вы́те|кут *see* ⇒**~чь**

вы́т|ереть, ру, решь, *past* **~ер, ~ерла** *pf.* (*of* ⇒**~ира́ть**) **1** (*руки, глаза, посуду, стол*) to wipe; (*грязь*) to wipe up; **в. пыль** to dust. **2** (*coll.*) (*износить*) to wear out, wear threadbare.

вы́терп|еть, лю, ишь *pf.* (*перенести*) to bear, endure; (*сдержаться*): **я е́ле ~ел, когда́ он сказа́л э́то** I could hardly stand it when he said that.

вы́терт|ый (~, ~а) *p.p.p. of* ⇒**вы́тереть** *and adj.* threadbare.

вы́те|сать, шу, шешь *pf.* to square off.

вытесне́ни|е, я *nt.* **1** ousting; (*замена собой*) supplanting. **2** (*phys.*) displacement.

вы́тесн|ить, ю, ишь *pf.* **1** (*врага*) to force out; to oust; (*заменить собой*) to supplant. **2** (*phys.*) to displace.

вытесня́|ть, ю *impf. of* ⇒**вы́теснить**

вытёсыва|ть, ю *impf. of* ⇒**вы́тесать**

вы́те|чь, чет, кут, *past* **~к, ~кла** *pf.* (*of* ⇒**~ка́ть**) to flow out, run out.

вы́те|шу, шешь *see* ⇒**~сать**

вытира́|ть, ю *impf. of* ⇒**вы́тереть**

вы́тисн|ить, ю, ишь *pf.* to stamp, imprint, impress.

вытисня́|ть, ю *impf. of* ⇒**вы́тиснить**

вытк|ать, у, ешь *pf.* to weave.

вы́толка|ть, ю *pf.* (*of* ⇒**выта́лкивать**) (*coll.*) to throw out; **его́ ~ли в ше́ю** (*sl.*) he was thrown out on his ear.

вы́толкн|уть, у, ешь *pf.* (*of* ⇒**выта́лкивать**) **1** to throw out. **2** (*пробку*) to push out, force out.

вы́топ|ить, лю, ишь *pf.* (*of* ⇒**выта́пливать**) **1** (*печь*) to heat. **2** (*сало*) to melt (down).

вы́топ|тать, чу, чешь *pf.* (*of* ⇒**выта́птывать**) to trample down.

вы́торг|овать, ую *pf.* **1** (*получить уступку*) to get a reduction (of); **он ~овал де́сять рубле́й из цены́ э́тих сапо́г** he got a reduction of ten roubles on the price of these boots; (*fig., coll.*) to manage to get; **он ~овал отсро́чку для оконча́ния диссерта́ции** he has managed to get an extension of time to finish his dissertation. **2** (*coll.*) (*заработать торговлей*) to make net, clear.

выторго́выва|ть, ю *impf.* **1** *impf. of* ⇒**вы́торговать. 2** to try to get (*by bargaining*); to haggle over.

вы́точен|ный (~, ~а) *p.p.p. of* ⇒**вы́точить** *and adj.* **сло́вно в.** (*черты лица*) chiselled; (*форма тела*) perfect, perfectly-formed.

вы́точ|ить, у, ишь *pf.* (*of* ⇒**выта́чивать**) **1** (*на токарном станке*) to turn. **2** (*coll.*) (*сделать острым*) to sharpen.

вы́трав|ить, лю, ишь *pf.* (*of* ⇒**трави́ть**[1] *and* ⇒**~ля́ть**) **1** (*тараканов*) to exterminate, destroy. **2** (*пятно*) to remove, get out. **3** (*надпись*) to etch. **4** (*посевы*) to trample down.

вытра́влива|ть, ю *impf.* (*coll.*) = **вытравля́ть**

вытравля́|ть, ю *impf. of* ⇒**вы́травить**

вы́треб|овать, ую *pf.* **1** (*получить*) to obtain. **2** (*заставить явиться*) to send for, summon(s); **в. кого́-н. в суд пове́сткой** to summons s.o.

вытрезви́тел|ь, я *m.* detoxification centre.

вы́трезв|ить, лю, ишь *pf.* (*of* ⇒**вытрезвля́ть**) to sober (up).

вы́трезв|иться, люсь, ишься *pf.* (*of* ⇒**вытрезвля́ться**) (*coll.*) to sober up (*intrans.*).

вытрезвля́|ть(ся), ю(сь) *impf. of* ⇒**вы́трезвить(ся)**

вы́т|ру, решь *see* ⇒**~ереть**

вытряса́|ть, ю *impf. of* ⇒**вы́трясти**

вы́тряс|ти, у, ешь, *past* **~, ~ла** *pf.* (*песок, мусор*) to shake out.

вытря́хива|ть, ю *impf. of* ⇒**вы́тряхнуть**

вы́тряхн|уть, у, ешь *pf.* (*of* ⇒**вытря́хивать**) **1** (*песок, мусор; скатерть*) to shake out. **2** (*coll.*) (*выгнать*) to throw out.

выту́рива|ть, ю *impf. of* ⇒**вы́турить**

вы́тур|ить, ю, ишь *pf.* (*of* ⇒**выту́ривать**) (*coll.*) to throw out, chuck out.

выть, во́ю, во́ешь *impf.* (*собака, волк, ветер*) to howl; (*сирена*) to wail; (*плакать*) to howl, wail.

вытьl|ё, я *no pl., nt.* howling; wailing.

вытя́гива|ть(ся), ю(сь) *impf. of* ⇒**вы́тянуть(ся)**

вы́тяжк|а, и *f.* **1** (*дыма, гноя*) drawing out, extraction. **2** (*chem.*) (*экстракт*) extract. **3** (*кожи, проволоки*) stretching, extension; **на ~у,** *see* ⇒**навы́тяжку**

вытяжн|о́й *adj.* for extracting, for drawing out; **в. трос** rip cord (*of parachute*); **~а́я труба́** ventilating pipe.

вы́тянут|ый (~, ~а) *p.p.p. of* ⇒**~ь** *and adj.* stretched; **~ое лицо́** (*fig.*) a long face.

вы́тян|уть, у, ешь *pf.* (*of* ⇒**вытя́гивать**) **1** (*вытащить*) to pull out. **2** (*ноги, руки*) to stretch (out); (*сделать длиннее*) to extend. **3** (*дым, гной*) to draw out, extract (*also fig.*); (*impers.*): **газ ~уло в окно́** the gas had escaped through the window; (*fig., coll.*) **в. всю ду́шу** (*+d. or* **у***+g.*) to wear (s.o.) out. **4** (*coll.*) (*выдержать*) to endure, stand, stick; **он до́лго не ~ет при тако́м кли́мате** he won't stick it for long in a climate like that. **5** (*coll.*) (*осуществить*) to fulfil (*Br.*), fulfill (*US*).

вы́тян|уться, усь, ешься *pf.* (*of* ⇒**вытя́гиваться**) **1** (*растянуться*) to stretch (*intrans.*); (*вдоль реки; на полу*) to stretch out; **лицо́ у неё**

~улось (*coll.*) her face fell. **2** (*coll.*) (*вырасти*) to grow, shoot up. **3** (*выпрямиться*) to stand erect; **в. во фронт** (*mil.*) to stand at attention.

выу́|дить, жу, дишь *pf.* (*of* ⇒**выу́живать**) **1** (*рыбу*) to catch. **2** (*деньги, секрет*) to extract, get out.

выу́жива|ть, ю *impf. of* ⇒**выудить**

вы́утюж|ить, у, ишь *pf. of* ⇒**утю́жить**

выученик, а *m.* (*coll.*) (*ученик*) pupil.

выу́чива|ть, ю *impf. of* ⇒**вы́учить**

вы́уч|ить, у, ишь *pf.* (*of* ⇒**учи́ть** *and* **~ивать**) **1** to learn. **2** (+*a. and d. or +inf.*) to teach; **он ~ил нас испа́нскому языку́** he taught us Spanish; **он ~ил её пра́вить маши́ной** he has taught her to drive (a car)

вы́уч|иться, усь, ишься *pf.* (*of* ⇒**учи́ться**) (+*d. or inf.*) to learn.

вы́учк|а, и *f.* (*о знаниях*) teaching; (*об умении*) training; **отда́ть на ~у** (+*d.*) to apprentice (to); **он прошёл хоро́шую ~у** he has had a sound training.

выха́жива|ть, ю *impf. of* ⇒**вы́ходить**

выхваля́|ться, юсь *impf.* (*coll., pej.*) to sing one's own praises, blow one's own trumpet.

вы́хва|тить, чу, тишь *pf.* **1** (*отнять*) to snatch out; to grab. **2** (*вытащить*) to pull out, draw; **в. нож** to draw a knife. **3** (*случайно взять*) to pull out.

выхва́тыва|ть, ю *impf. of* ⇒**вы́хватить**

вы́хвачен|ный (~, ~а) *p.p.p. of* ⇒**вы́хватить; ~ из жи́зни** true to life, taken from the life.

вы́хва|чу, тишь *see* ⇒**~тить**

вы́хлеста|ть, ю *pf.* (*coll.*) **1** (*высечь*) to flog, lash. **2** (*sl.*) (*выпить*) to drink off, drain.

вы́хлестн|уть, у, ешь *pf.* (*coll.*) **1** (*удалить*) to flick out. **2** (*выплеснуть*) to splash out.

вы́хлоп, а *m.* (*tech.*) exhaust (*apparatus*); (*действие*): **в. га́зов** emission of gases.

выхлопа́тыва|ть, ю *impf. of* ⇒**вы́хлопотать**

выхлопн|о́й *adj.* (*tech.*) exhaust; **~а́я труба́** exhaust pipe; **~ы́е га́зы** exhaust (fumes).

вы́хлопо|тать, чу, чешь *pf.* (*of* ⇒**выхлопа́тывать**) to obtain (*after much trouble*).

вы́ход, а *m.* **1** (*на улицу*) going out; (*чтобы покинуть*) leaving, departure; (*из партии*) leaving; (*поезда, корабля*) departure; **в. за́муж** marriage (*of woman*); **в. в отста́вку** retirement. **2** (*место выхода*) way out, exit; (*трубки*) outlet; (*способ*) way out; **из э́того положе́ния ~а не́ было** there was no way out of this situation; **знать все ходы́ и ~ы** to know all the ins and outs; **дать в.** (+*d.*) to give vent (to). **3** (*издания*) appearance; (*фильма*) release; (*theatr.*) entrance. **4** (*econ.*) output; yield. **5** (*comput.*) exit; logoff.

выхо́д|ец, ца *m.* **1** (*из другой страны*) immigrant; **сло́вно в. с того́ све́та** like an apparition, ghost. **2** (*из другой социальной среды*) person moving from one social group to another; **он — в. из крестья́н** he is of peasant origin.

вы́хо|дить¹, жу, дишь *pf.* (*of* ⇒**выха́живать**) **1** (*больного*) to tend, nurse. **2** (*ребёнка*) to rear, bring up; (*растения*) to grow.

вы́хо|дить², жу, дишь *pf.* (*of* ⇒**выха́живать**) (*coll.*) (*обойти всё*) to pass (through); to go all over.

выхо|ди́ть, жу́, ~дишь *impf.* **1** *impf. of* ⇒**вы́йти. 2** (*impf. only*) to look out (on), give (on), face; **его́ ко́мната ~дит о́кнами на у́лицу** his room looks onto the street. **3**: **не в. из головы́, из ума́** to be unforgettable, stick in one's mind. **4** *as pred.* **~дит** (*coll.*) it turns out.

вы́ходк|а, и *f.* (*pej.*) trick; escapade.

выходн|о́й *adj.* **1** exit; **~а́я дверь** street door. **2**: **в. день** day off; **~а́я оде́жда** 'best' clothes; **~о́е пла́тье** party dress, outfit; *as n.* (*i*) **в., ~о́го** *m.* (*день*) day off; (*ii*) **в., ~о́го** *m.*, **~а́я, ~о́й** *f.* (*coll.*) (*человек*) person having day off; **он сего́дня в.** it is his day off today. **3**: **~о́е посо́бие** (*also as n.* **~ы́е, ~ы́х**) severance pay. **4** (*theatr.*): **~а́я роль** bit part.

выход|я́щий *pres. part. of* ⇒**~и́ть; из ря́да вон ~я́щий** outstanding.

вы́хо|жу, дишь *see* ⇒**~дить**

выхо|жу́, ~дишь *see* ⇒**~ди́ть**

выхола́жива|ть, ю *impf. of* ⇒**вы́холодить**

выхола́щива|ть, ю *impf. of* ⇒**вы́холостить**

вы́хол|енный *p.p.p. of* ⇒**~ить** *and adj.* well-cared-for; well-groomed.

вы́хол|ить, ю, ишь *pf.* to care for, tend.

вы́холо|дить, жу, дишь *pf.* (*of* ⇒**выхола́живать**) to cool.

вы́холо|стить, щу, стишь *pf.* (*of* ⇒**выхола́щивать**) to castrate, geld; (*fig.*) (*идею, язык*) to emasculate.

вы́холо|щенный *p.p.p. of* ⇒**~стить** *and adj.* castrated, gelded; (*fig.*) emasculated; **~щенная ло́шадь** gelding.

вы́хухол|ь, я *m.* desman.

вы́царапа|ть, ю *pf.* (*coll.*) **1** (*написать*) to scratch; (+*a. and d.*) to scratch out; **в. глаза́ кому́-н.** to scratch s.o.'s eyes out. **2** (*fig.*) (*деньги*) to extract, get (out of).

выцара́пыва|ть, ю *impf. of* ⇒**вы́царапать**

вы́цве|сти, ту, тешь, *past* **~л** *pf.* to fade.

выцвета́|ть, ю *impf. of* ⇒**вы́цвести**

вы́цве|тший *p.p. of* ⇒**~сти** *and adj.* faded.

вы́це|дить, жу, дишь *pf.* **1** (*вылить*) to filter, rack (off); to decant. **2** (*fig., coll.*) (*выпить*) to drink off, drain.

выце́жива|ть, ю *impf. of* ⇒**вы́цедить**

вы́чекан|ить, ю, ишь *pf. of* ⇒**чека́нить**

вы́ч|ел, ла *see* ⇒**~есть**

вычёркива|ть, ю *impf. of* ⇒**вы́черкнуть**

вы́черкн|уть, у, ешь *pf.* (*слова*) to cross out; (*из списка*) to cross off; **в. из па́мяти** to erase from one's memory.

вы́черпа|ть, ю *pf.* (**из**+*g.*) **1** (*удалить*) to take out; (*из лодки*) to bail (out); **в. во́ду из ло́дки** to bail out a boat. **2** (*пруд*) to drain.

выче́рпыва|ть, ю *impf. of* ⇒**вы́черпать**

вы́чер|тить, чу, тишь *pf.* (*of* ⇒**выче́рчивать**) to draw; to trace.

вы́черчен|ный (~, ~а) *p.p.p. of* ⇒**вы́чертить** *and adj.* finely-shaped; **~ные бро́ви** finely-shaped eyebrows.

выче́рчива|ть, ю *impf. of* ⇒**вы́чертить**

вы́чер|чу, тишь *see* ⇒**~тить**

вы́че|сать, шу, шешь *pf.* (*of* ⇒**~сывать**) to comb out.

вы́ч|есть, ту, тешь, *past* **~ел, ~ла,** *pres. ger.* **~тя** *pf.* (*of* ⇒**~ита́ть**) **1** (*math.*) to subtract. **2** (*удержать*) to deduct, keep back.

вычёсыва|ть, ю *impf. of* ⇒**вы́чесать**

вы́чет, а *m.* deduction; **за ~ом** (+*g.*) except; minus.

вы́че|шу, шешь *see* ⇒**~сать**

вычисле́ни|е, я *nt.* calculation.

вычисли́тел|ь, я *m.* **1** (*прибор*) calculator. **2** (*человек*) computer specialist.

вычисли́тельн|ый *adj.* calculating, computing; **~ая маши́на** computer; **~ая те́хника** computers; **в. центр** computer centre (*Br.*), center (*US*).

вы́числ|ить, ю, ишь *pf.* to calculate, compute.

вычисля́|ть, ю *impf. of* ⇒**вы́числить**

вы́чи|стить, щу, стишь *pf.* (*of* ⇒**чи́стить** *and* **~ща́ть**) **1** to clean (up, out). **2** (*fig.*) to purge; to expel; **его́ ~стили из па́ртии** he has been expelled from the party.

вычита́ем|ое, ого *nt.* (*math.*) subtrahend.

вычита́ни|е, я *nt.* (*math.*) subtraction.

вы́чита|ть, ю *pf.* (*of* ⇒**вычи́тывать**) **1** (*coll.*) to find (*by reading, perusing*); **я ~л сообще́ние о его́ сме́рти в одно́й из вчера́шних газе́т** I found a report of his death in one of yesterday's newspapers. **2** (*typ.*) to read, proof-read.

вычита́|ть, ю *impf. of* ⇒**вы́честь**

вычи́тыва|ть, ю *impf. of* ⇒**вы́читать**

вычища́|ть, ю *impf. of* ⇒**вы́чистить**

вы́чи|щу, стишь *see* ⇒**~стить**

вы́ч|ту, тешь *see* ⇒**~есть**

вычу́р|ный (~ен, ~на) *adj.* fanciful; mannered; precious.

выша́гива|ть, ю *impf.* (*coll.*) to pace.

вышвы́рива|ть, ю *impf. of* ⇒**вы́швырнуть**

вы́швырн|уть, у, ешь *pf.* to throw

out, hurl out; (*fig., coll.*) (*выгнать*) to chuck out.

вы́ше 1 *comp. of* ⇒**высо́кий** *and* **высо́ко́**; higher, taller. **2** *prep.+g.* (*вверх от*) above, beyond; (*больше*) over; **в. восьми́десяти гра́дусов** over eighty degrees; **в. нуля́** above zero; **в. подозре́ния** above suspicion; (*за пределами*) beyond; **э́то в. моего́ понима́ния** it is beyond my comprehension; **зада́ча оказа́лась в. его́ сил** the task proved to be beyond him. **3** *adv.* (*liter.*) above; **смотри́ в.** see above.

выше... *comb. form* above-, afore-.

вышеизло́женный *adj.* foregoing.

вы́|шел, шла *see* ⇒**~йти**

вышелу́шива|ть, ю *impf. of* ⇒**вы́шелушить**

вы́шелуш|ить, у, ишь *pf.* to peel; to shell.

вышена́званный *adj.* aforenamed.

вышеозна́ченный *adj.* aforesaid, above-mentioned.

вышеприведённый *adj.* above-cited; **в. приме́р** the example above.

вышеска́занный *adj.* aforesaid.

вышестоя́щ|ий *adj.* higher; (*pol.*) **~ие о́рганы вла́сти** the higher organs of power.

вышеука́занный *adj.* foregoing.

вышеупомя́нутый *adj.* afore-mentioned.

вышиба́л|а, ы *m.* (*sl.*) bouncer, chucker-out.

вышиба́|ть, ю *impf. of* ⇒**вы́шибить**

вы́шиб|ить, у, ешь, *past* **~, ~ла** *pf.* (*coll.*) **1** (*выбить*) to knock out. **2** (*выгнать*) to chuck out.

вышива́льный *adj.* embroidery.

вышива́льщиц|а, ы *f.* needle-woman.

вышива́ни|е, я *nt.* embroidery, needle-work.

вышива́|ть, ю *impf. of* ⇒**вы́шить**

вы́шивк|а, и *f.* embroidery, needle-work.

вышивно́й *adj.* embroidered.

вышин|а́, ы́, *pl.* **~ы** *f.* height; **в ~е́** aloft, high up; **~о́й в ты́сячу ме́тров** a thousand metres high, up.

вы́ш|ить, ью, ьешь, *imper.* **~ей** *pf.* (*of* ⇒**~ива́ть**) to embroider.

вы́шк|а, и *f.* **1** (*часть здания*) turret. **2** (*башня*) (watch-)tower; **диспе́тчерская в.** (*aeron.*) control tower; **сторожева́я в.** watch-tower; **бурова́я в.** derrick. **3** (*sport*) high board. **4** (*coll.*) (*наказание*) the death penalty.

вы́школ|ить, ю, ишь *pf. of* ⇒**шко́лить**

вы́шлиф|овать, ую *pf.* **1** (*tech.*) to polish. **2** (*fig., coll.*) to polish, give a polish to; to smarten up.

вы́|шлю, шлешь *see* ⇒**~слать**

вышмы́гива|ть, ю *impf. of* ⇒**вы́шмыгнуть**

вы́шмыгн|уть, у, ешь *pf.* (*coll.*) to slip out.

вышны́рива|ть, ю *impf. of* ⇒**вы́шнырнуть**

вы́шнырн|уть, у, ешь *pf.* (*coll.*) to jump out.

вы́штукатур|ить, ю, ишь *pf.* to stucco.

вы́шу|тить, чу, тишь *pf.* to laugh at, make fun of.

вышу́чива|ть, ю *impf. of* ⇒**вы́шутить**

вы́щерб|ить, лю, ишь *pf.* (*of* ⇒**~ля́ть**) (*coll.*) to dent; to jag.

выщербля́|ть, ю *impf. of* ⇒**вы́щербить**

вы́щип|ать, лю, лешь *pf.* (*of* ⇒**выщи́пывать**) to pull out, pluck; **в. пе́рья у ку́рицы** to pluck a chicken.

вы́щипн|уть, у, ешь *pf.* to pull out; to pluck out.

выщи́пыва|ть, ю *impf. of* ⇒**вы́щипать**

вы́щупа|ть, ю *pf.* **1** (*med.*) to find (*by probing*). **2** (*coll.*) to run one's hands over; to ransack.

выщу́пыва|ть, ю *impf. of* ⇒**вы́щупать**

вы́|я, и *f.* (*obs. or rhet.*) neck.

вы́яв|ить, лю, ишь *pf.* (*of* ⇒**~ля́ть**) **1** (*талант, черты*) to display, reveal. **2** (*предать гласности*) to bring out; to make known. **3** (*недостатки*) to expose.

вы́яв|иться, люсь, ишься *pf.* (*of* ⇒**~ля́ться**) (*недостатки*) to come to light, be revealed, be exposed.

выявле́ни|е, я *nt.* revelation; (*недостатков*) exposure.

выявля́|ть(ся), ю(сь) *impf. of* ⇒**вы́явить(ся)**

выясне́ни|е, я *nt.* clarification; explanation.

вы́ясн|ить, ю, ишь *pf.* (*of* ⇒**выясня́ть**) (*сделать ясным*) to clarify, clear up, explain; **в. отноше́ния** to sort things out; (*установить*) to find out, ascertain.

вы́ясн|иться, ится *pf.* (*of* ⇒**выясня́ться**) (*объясниться*) to become clear; (*стать явным*) to turn out, prove (*intrans.*); **как ~илось, он лгал всё вре́мя** he was lying all the time as it turned out.

выясн|я́ть(ся), я́ю *impf. of* ⇒**вы́яснить(ся)**

Вьетна́м, а *m.* Vietnam.

вьетна́м|ец, ца *m.* Vietnamese.

вьетна́м|ка, ки *f. of* ⇒**~ец**

вьетна́м|ки, ок *no sg.* (*coll.*) flip-flops.

вьетна́мский *adj.* Vietnamese.

вью, вьёшь *see* ⇒**вить**

вью́г|а, и *f.* snow-storm, blizzard.

вью́|жный *adj. of* ⇒**~га**

вьюк, а *m.* pack; load.

вьюн, а́ *m.* climbing plant, climber.

вьюн|о́к, ка́ *m.* (*bot.*) bindweed, convolvulus.

вью́ч|ить, у, ишь *impf.* (*of* ⇒**на~**) to load (up).

вью́чн|ый *adj.* pack; **~ое живо́тное** beast of burden.

вью́шк|а, и *f.* damper.

вью́щ|ийся *pres. part. of* ⇒**ви́ться** *and adj.*: **~иеся во́лосы** curly hair; **~ееся расте́ние** (*bot.*) creeper, climber.

вя|жу́, ~жешь *see* ⇒**~за́ть**

вя́жущий *pres. part. act. of* ⇒**вяза́ть** *and adj.* **1** (*вкус*) astringent. **2** (*tech.*) binding, cementing.

вяз, а *m.* elm(-tree).

вяза́льн|ый *adj.* knitting; **в. крючо́к** crochet hook; **~ая спи́ца** knitting-needle.

вяза́льщик, а *m.* **1** (*трикотажа*) knitter, crocheter. **2** (*снопов*) binder.

вяза́ни|е, я *nt.* **1** (*трикотажа*) knitting, crocheting. **2** (*снопов*) binding, tying.

вя́занк|а, и *f.* (*coll.*) knitted garment (*jumper, etc.*).

вяза́нк|а, и *f.* bundle.

вя́заный *adj.* knitted.

вяза́нь|е, я *nt.* (*спицами*) knitting; (*крючком*) crocheting.

вя|за́ть, жу́, ~жешь *impf.* **1** (*pf.* **с~**) (*руки, ноги*) to tie, bind; (*снопы*) to bind; (*tech.*) to tie, clamp; **в. кому́-н. ру́ки** to tie s.o.'s hands. **2** (*pf.* **с~**) (*спицами*) to knit; (*крючком*) to crochet. **3** (*impf. only*) to be astringent; (*impers.*): **у меня́ ~жет во рту** my mouth feels constricted.

вя|за́ться, жу́сь, ~жешься *impf.* **1** (*coll.*) (**с** + *i.*) to agree, tally (with). **2**: **де́ло не вя́жется** things are not going well, not getting anywhere; **разгово́р не вя́жется** the conversation is not getting anywhere.

вя́зк|а, и *f.* **1** (*снопов*) tying, binding. **2** (*спицами*) knitting; (*крючком*) crocheting. **3** (*связка*) bunch, string; **в. ключе́й** bunch of keys.

вя́з|кий (~ок, ~ка́, ~ко) *adj.* **1** (*клейкий*) viscous, sticky. **2** (*топкий*) boggy.

вя́зкост|ь, и *f.* **1** viscosity, stickiness. **2** bogginess.

вя́з|нуть, ну, нешь, *past* **~, ~ла** *impf.* (**в** + *p.*) to get stuck (in).

вя́з|че *comp. of* ⇒**~кий, ~ко**

вязь, и *no pl., f.* **1** (*palaeog.*) (*письмо*) ornamental, ligatured script. **2** (*узор*) interwoven ornament (*in pattern*).

вя́ка|ть, ю *impf.* (*coll., pej.*) to talk nonsense, blather.

вя́леный *adj.* sun-dried.

вя́л|ить, ю, ишь *impf.* (*of* ⇒**про~**) to cure by drying in the sun.

вя́лост|ь, и *f.* (*кожи, тела*) flabbiness; limpness; (*fig.*) sluggishness; inertia; slackness.

вя́л|ый *adj.* **1** (*растение*) faded. **2 (~, ~а́, ~о)** (*кожа, тело*) flabby, flaccid; limp; (*fig.*) sluggish, inert; slack; **~ое настрое́ние** sluggish disposition; **в. ры́нок** (*econ.*) slack market.

вя́н|уть, у, ешь, *past* **~ул, ~ула** *and* **вял, вя́ла** *impf.* (*of* ⇒**за~**) (*растение*) to fade, wither; (*fig.*) (*красота, способности*) to fade; **у́ши ~ут от тако́го разгово́ра** it makes one sick to listen to such talk.

вя́щ|ий *adj.* (*obs. or joc.*) greater; **для ~ей предосторо́жности** to make assurance doubly sure; **для ~ей убеди́тельности** in order to be more convincing.

Г г

г (*abbr. of* **грамм**) g, gr, gram(me)(s).

г. *abbr. of* **1 год** year. **2 гора́** mountain; Mount, Mt. **3 го́род** city, town. **4 господи́н** Mr.

га (*abbr. of* **гекта́р**) ha, hectare(s).

Гаа́г|а, и *f.* The Hague.

габарди́н, а *m.* gaberdine.

габари́т, а *m.* (*tech.*) size, dimensions.

габари́т|ный *adj. of* ⇒**~; ~ные огни́** sidelights (*Br.*), sidemarker lights (*US*).

Габо́н, а *m.* Gabon.

гава́|ец, йца *m.* Hawaiian.

Гава́йи *m. indecl.* Hawaii.

гава́|йка, йки *f. of* ⇒**~ец**

гава́йский *adj.* Hawaiian.

Гава́н|а, ы *f.* Havana.

га́ван|ский *adj. of* ⇒**~ь**

га́ван|ь, и *f.* harbour (*Br.*), harbor (*US*).

га́вка|ть, ю *impf.* (*coll.*) to bark.

Гавр, а *m.* Le Havre.

га́врик, а *m.* (*sl.*) mate (*Br.*), buddy (*US*); **ма́ленький г.** little lad.

га́г|а, и *f.* eider-duck.

гага́ка|ть, ет *impf.* (*dial. or coll.; onomat., of geese*) to cackle.

гага́р|а, ы *f.* (*zool.*) diver (*Br.*), loon (*US*).

гага́рк|а, и *f.* (*zool.*) razorbill.

гага́т, а *m.* (*min.*) jet.

гага́чий *adj. of* ⇒**га́га; г. пух** eider-down.

гад, а *m.* **1** (*obs.*) amphibian, reptile. **2** (*fig., coll.*) louse, rat, skunk.

гада́лк|а, и *f.* fortune-teller.

гада́ни|е, я *nt.* **1** (*предсказывание*) fortune-telling; **г. по руке́** palmistry. **2** (*догадка*) guess-work.

гада́тел|ьный (~ен, ~ьна) *adj.* (*сомнительный*) doubtful; (*предположительный*) conjectural, hypothetical.

гада́|ть, ю *impf.* **1** (*pf.* **по~**) (**на** + *p. or* **по** + *d.*) (*предсказывать*) to tell fortunes (by); **г. на кофейной гу́ще** to make wild guesses. **2** *impf. only* (**о** + *p.*) (*предполагать*) to guess, conjecture, surmise.

Гаде́с, а *m.* Hades.

га́дин|а, ы *f.* = **гад** 2

га́|дить, жу, дишь *impf.* (*of* ⇒**на~**) **1** (*о животных*) to defecate. **2** (**на** + *a. or p.,* **в** + *p.*) (*пачкать*) to foul, defile. **3** (+ *d.; coll.*) (*вредить*) to play dirty tricks (on).

га́д|кий (~ок, ~ка́, ~ко) *adj.* nasty, vile, repulsive; **г. утёнок** ugly duckling.

га́дк|о[1] *adv. of* ⇒**~ий**

га́дко[2] *as pred.* **мне,** *etc.,* **г.** I, *etc.,* loathe (it); I, *etc.,* am repelled.

гадли́вост|ь, и *f.* aversion, disgust.

гадли́в|ый (~, ~а) *adj.*: **~ое чу́вство** (feeling of) disgust.

га́дост|ный (~ен, ~на) *adj.* disgusting; (*coll.*) poor, bad.

га́дост|ь, и *f.* **1** (*coll.*) (*дрянь*) filth, muck. **2** (*поступок*) dirty trick; **он спосо́бен на вся́кую г.** he is capable of the lowest trick; **говори́ть ~и** to say foul things.

гадю́к|а, и *f.* **1** (*змея*) adder, viper. **2** (*coll.*) (*человек*) repulsive person.

га́ечный *adj. of* ⇒**га́йка; г. ключ** spanner, wrench.

га́же *comp. of* ⇒**га́дкий**

газ[1]**, а** *m.* **1** gas; **г. (не́рвно)паралити́ческого де́йствия** nerve gas. **2** (*coll.*): **на по́лном ~е** (*or* **~у́**) at top speed; **дать г.** to step on the gas, step on it; **педа́ль ~а** accelerator, gas pedal; **сба́вить г.** to reduce speed; **быть под ~ом** to be tipsy. **3** (*pl.; med.*) wind; **скопле́ние ~ов** flatulence, wind.

газ[2]**, а** *no pl., m.* (*ткань*) gauze.

газго́льдер, а *m.* gasometer.

газе́л|ь, и *f.* (*zool.*) gazelle.

газе́т|а, ы *f.* newspaper; **г. табло́идного форма́та** tabloid.

газе́т|ный *adj. of* ⇒**~а; ~ная бума́га** news-print; **г. коро́ль** *or* **магна́т** press baron; **г. стиль** journalese.

газе́тчик, а *m.* **1** (*продавец*) newspaper-seller; newspaper-boy. **2** (*coll.*) (*журналист*) journalist.

га́зик, а *m.* jeep (*propr.*); 'Gazik' (*all-terrain vehicle produced by Gorky motor-vehicle works*).

газиро́ванный *adj.* carbonated.

гази́р|овать, ую (*and* **газир|ова́ть, у́ю)** *impf.* to carbonate.

газиро́вк|а, и *f.* (*coll.*) **1** (*газирование*) carbonation. **2** (*напиток*) carbonated water, soda (water).

газифика́ци|я, и *f.* **1** (*снабжение газовым топливом*) supplying with gas. **2** (*превращение в горючий газ*) gasification.

газифици́р|овать, ую *impf. and pf.* **1** (*снабдить газовым топливом*) to supply with gas; to install gas (in). **2** (*tech.*) (*превратить в горючий газ*) to gasify.

газобалло́н, а *m.* gas cylinder.

газ|ова́ть, у́ю *impf.* (*coll.*) to step on the gas; to put one's foot down (*Br.*).

газовщи́к, а́ *m.* gas-man.

га́зов|ый[1] *adj. of* ⇒**газ**[1]**; ~ая плита́** gas-cooker, gas-stove; **г. счётчик** gas-meter; **~ая ка́мера** gas chamber.

га́зовый[2] *adj. of* ⇒**газ**[2]

газогенера́тор, а *m.* (*tech.*) gas generator, gas producer.

газоли́н, а *m.* gasoline.

газоме́р, а *m.* gas-meter.

газомёт, а *m.* (*mil.*) gas projector.

газомото́р, а *m.* (*tech.*) gas-engine.

газо́н, а *m.* grassed area, lawn; **«по ~ам ходи́ть воспреща́ется»** 'Keep off the grass'.

газонепроница́емый *adj.* gas-proof, gas-tight.

газонокоси́лк|а, и *f.* lawn-mower.

газообра́з|ный (~ен, ~на) *adj.* (*phys.*) gaseous.

газопрово́д, а *m.* gas pipeline; gas-main.

газопрово́д|ный *adj. of* ⇒**~**

газохрани́лищ|е, а *nt.* gasometer.

ГАИ́ *f. indecl.* (*abbr. of* ***госуда́рственная автомоби́льная инспе́кция***) State Motor-Vehicle Inspectorate; traffic police.

Гаи́ти *m. indecl.* Haiti.

гаитя́н|ин, ина, *pl.* **~е, ~** *m.* Haitian.

гаитя́н|ка, ки *f. of* ⇒**~ин**

гаитя́нский *adj.* Haitian.

га́ишник, а *m.* (*coll.*) traffic-cop.

Гайа́н|а, ы *f.* Guyana.

гайа́н|ец, ца *m.* Guyanese.

гайа́н|ка, ки *f. of* ⇒**~ец**

гайа́нский *adj.* Guyanese.

гайдама́к, а *m.* (*hist.*) haydamak (*Ukrainian Cossack; also member of anti-Bolshevik Ukrainian cavalry detachment in 1918*).

гайдама́|цкий *adj. of* ⇒**~к**

гайду́к, а́ *m.* (*hist.*) heyduck (**1** *rebel against Turkish domination in the Balkans.* **2** *footman in house of wealthy landowner*).

га́йк|а, и *f.* nut; **бара́шковая г.** wing-nut; **закрути́ть ~и** (*fig.*) to put the screws on.

гаймори́т, а *m.* (*med.*) sinusitis.

гакабо́рт, а *m.* (*naut.*) taffrail.

гала́ *adj. indecl.* gala; **г.-представле́ние** gala performance.

гала́ктик|а, и *f.* (*astron.*) galaxy.

галантере́|йный *adj. of* ⇒**~я; г. магази́н** haberdashery, fancy-goods shop.

галантере́|я, и *f.* haberdashery, fancy goods.

гала́нтност|ь, и *f.* gallantry (= *courtliness*).

гала́нт|ный (~ен, ~на) *adj.* gallant (= *courtly*).

гала́т|ы, ов *pl.* (*bibl.*) Galatians.

гал|дёж, дежа́ *m.* (*coll.*) din, racket.

галд|е́ть, *1st pers. not used,* **и́шь** *impf.* (*coll.*) to make a din, racket.

гале́р|а, ы *f.* galley.

галере́|я, и *f.* (*in var. senses*) gallery.

галёрк|а, и *f.* (*theatr.; coll.*) gallery, 'the gods'.

гале́р|ный *adj. of* ⇒**~а**

гале́т|а, ы *f.* (*type of*) cracker.

га́лечник, а *m.* (*collect.*) pebbles, shingle.

га́лечный *adj.* pebble, shingle; pebbly, shingly.

Галиле́йск|ое мо́р|е, ~ого ~я *nt.* the Sea of Galilee.

Галиле́|я, и *f.* Galilee.

галиматья|я́, и́ *f.* (*coll.*) rubbish, nonsense.

Гали́си|я, и *f.* Galicia (*Spain*).

галифе́ *pl. indecl. or nt. indecl.* riding-breeches, jodhpurs; (*as adj.*): **брю́ки г.** riding-breeches, jodhpurs.

Гали́ци|я, и *f.* Galicia (*Eastern Europe*).

га́лк|а, и *f.* daw, jackdaw.

галл, а *m.* Gaul (*person*).

га́лли|й, я *m.* (*chem.*) gallium.

галлици́зм, а *m.* Gallicism.

Га́лли|я, и *f.* Gaul (*place*).

галлома́ни|я, и *f.* Gallomania.

галло́н, а *m.* gallon.

га́лльский *adj.* Gallic.

галлюцина́ци|я, и *f.* hallucination.

галлюцини́р|овать, ую *impf.* to have hallucinations.

галлюциноге́н, а *m.* hallucinogen.

галлюциноге́нный *adj.* hallucinogenic.

галоге́н, а *m.* (*chem.*) halogen.

гало́п, а *m.* gallop; **~ом** at a gallop; **лёгкий г.** canter; **скака́ть ~ом** to gallop.

галопи́р|овать, ую *impf.* to gallop.

га́лочк|а, и *f.* tick, check (*US*).

гало́ш|а, и *f.* **1** galosh; **сесть в ~у** (*coll.*) to get into a fix, into a spot. **2** (*sl.*) (*презерватив*) condom.

галс, а *m.* (*naut.*) tack; **пра́вым (ле́вым) ~ом** on the starboard (port) tack.

га́лстук, а *m.* tie; **г.-ба́бочка** bow-tie, dicky bow.

галу́н, а́ *m.* lace, galloon.

галу́шк|а, и *f.* (*cul.*) dumpling.

гальваниза́ци|я, и *f.* (*phys.*) galvanization.

гальванизи́р|овать, ую *impf. and pf.* (*phys.*) to galvanize.

гальвани́ческий *adj.* (*phys.*) galvanic.

гальвано́метр, а *m.* (*phys.*) galvanometer.

гальванопла́стик|а, и *f.* electroplating.

га́л|ька, ьки *f.* **1** (*g. pl.* **~ек**) pebble. **2** (*collect.*) pebbles, shingle.

гальюн, а *m.* (*naut.*) (the) heads (*toilet*).

гам, а *m.* (*coll.*) din, uproar.

гамадри́л, а *m.* (*zool.*) hamadryad (*baboon*).

гама́к, а́ *m.* hammock.

гама́ш|а, и *f.* gaiter, legging.

Га́мби|я, и *f.* Gambia.

га́мбургер, а *m.* (ham)burger.

га́мм|а¹, ы *f.* (*mus.*) scale; gamut (*also fig.*); **г. кра́сок** colour range (*Br.*), color range (*US*).

га́мм|а², ы *f.* gamma (*letter of Greek alphabet*); **г.-глобули́н** gamma globulin; **г.-лучи́** (*phys.*) gamma-rays.

Га́н|а, ы *f.* Ghana.

Ганг, а *m.* the Ganges (*river*).

га́нгли|й, я *m.* (*anat.*) ganglion.

гангре́н|а, ы *f.* gangrene.

гангрено́зный *adj.* gangrenous.

га́нгстер, а *m.* gangster.

гандбо́л, а *m.* handball.

гандболи́ст, а *m.* handball-player.

гандболи́ст|ка, ки *f. of* ⇒**~**

гандика́п, а *m.* (*sport*) handicap.

га́н|ец, ца *m.* Ghanaian.

ганзе́йский *adj.* (*hist.*) Hanseatic.

Ганно́вер, а *f.* Hanover.

га́нский *adj.* Ghanaian.

ганте́л|ь, и *f.* (*sport*) dumb-bell.

гара́ж, а́ *m.* garage.

гара́нт, а *m.* guarantor.

гаранти́йный *adj.* guarantee.

гаранти́р|овать, ую *impf. and pf.* **1** to guarantee, vouch for. **2** (**от**+*g.*) (*защитить*) to protect (against).

гара́нти|я, и *f.* guarantee; (*охрана*) safeguard.

Га́рвард, а *m.* Harvard.

гардеро́б, а *m.* **1** (*шкаф*) wardrobe. **2** (*помещение*) cloakroom. **3** (*collect.*) (*одежда*) wardrobe.

гардеро́бщик, а *m.* cloakroom attendant.

гардеро́бщи|ца, цы *f. of* ⇒**~к**

гарди́н|а, ы *f.* curtain.

гар|ево́й *adj. of* ⇒**~ь; ~ева́я доро́жка** cinder path.

гаре́м, а *m.* harem.

га́рк|ать, аю *impf. of* ⇒**~нуть**

га́рк|нуть, ну, нешь *pf.* (*of* ⇒**~ать**) (*coll.*) to bark (out), bawl (out); **г. на кого́-н.** to bark at s.o.

гармониза́ци|я, и *f.* (*mus.*) harmonization.

гармонизи́р|овать, ую *impf. and pf.* (*mus.*) to harmonize (*trans.*).

гармо́ник|а, и *f.* **1** accordion, concertina; **губна́я г.** mouth organ. **2**: **~ой, в ~у** *as adv.* pleated; concertina'ed. **3** (*phys.*) harmonic.

гармони́р|овать, ую *impf.* (**с**+*i.*) to be in harmony (with); (*о красках*) to tone (with), go (with).

гармони́ст, а *m.* accordion player, concertina player.

гармони́ческий *adj.* **1** (*mus.*) harmonic. **2** harmonious.

гармони́ч|ный (~ен, ~на) *adj.* harmonious.

гармо́ни|я, и *f.* **1** (*mus.*) harmony. **2** (*fig.*) harmony, concord.

гармо́н|ь, и *f.* (*coll.*) accordion, concertina.

гармо́шк|а, и *f.* = **гармо́нь**

гарнизо́н, а *m.* garrison.

гарнизо́н|ный *adj. of* ⇒**~; ~ная слу́жба** garrison duty.

гарни́р, а *m.* (*cul.*) garnish; (*из овощей*) vegetables; **на г.** as a side dish.

гарниту́р, а *m.* set; (*мебели*) suite.

гарниту́р|а, ы *f.* (*typ., comput.*): **шрифтова́я г.** fo(u)nt; **г. ру́сского/лати́нского шри́фта** Cyrillic/Latin fo(u)nt.

га́рпи|я, и *f.* harpy.

гарпу́н, а́ *m.* harpoon.

гарпу́н|ный *adj. of* ⇒**~; ~ная пу́шка** harpoon-gun.

га́рус, а *m.* worsted (yarn).

гарц|ева́ть, у́ю *impf.* to prance.

гар|ь, и *f.* **1** burning; **па́хнет ~ью** there's a smell of burning. **2** cinders, ashes.

га|си́ть, шу́, ~сишь *impf.* (*of* ⇒**по~**) **1** (*pf. also* **за~**) (*пожар, свет*) to put out, extinguish; **г. свет** to put out the light. **2**: **г. и́звесть** to slake lime. **3** (*чувства, звуки*) to suppress, stifle. **4** (*погашать*) to cancel; **г. долг** to liquidate a debt; **г. почто́вую ма́рку** to frank a postage stamp.

га́с|нуть, ну, нешь, *past* **~, ~ла** *impf.* (*of* ⇒**по~**) (*переставать гореть*) to be extinguished, go out; (*слабеть*) to grow feeble; (*о чувствах*) to fade, weaken.

гастри́т, а *m.* gastritis.

гастри́ческий *adj.* gastric.

гастролёр, а *m.* **1** artiste on tour. **2** (*coll.*) casual worker.
гастролир|овать, ую *impf.* to tour, be on tour (*of an artiste*).
гастрóл|ь, и *f.* (*usu. in pl.*) tour; engagement (*of touring artiste*).
гастрóльный *adj.* touring (*of artistes*).
гастронóм¹, а *m.* (*знаток вкусной еды*) gourmet.
гастронóм², а *m.* (*магазин*) grocer's (shop) (*Br.*), grocery store (*US*).
гастрономи́ческий *adj.* **1** gastronomical. **2**: **г. магази́н** grocer's (shop) (*Br.*), grocery store (*US*).
гастронóми|я, и *f.* **1** (*продукты*) high-quality cooked meats, fish, cheeses, etc. **2** (*гастрономический отдел*) delicatessen counter. **3** (*тонкий вкус в еде*) gastronomy.
ГАТТ *nt. indecl.* GATT (*abbr. of* General Agreement on Tariffs and Trade — *Генерáльное соглашéние о тари́фах и торгóвле*).
гат|ь, и *f.* road of brushwood; **бревéнчатая г.** corduroy road.
гáубиц|а, ы *f.* (*mil.*) howitzer.
гауптвáхт|а, ы *f.* (*mil.*) guardhouse, guardroom.
гáфел|ь, я *m.* (*naut.*) gaff.
гáч|и, ей *pl.* (*sg.* **~а, ~и** *f.*) (*dial.*) **1** (*брюки*) trousers. **2** (*ляжки*) haunches.
гашéни|е, я *nt.* (*огня*) extinguishing; (*извести*) slaking.
гашён|ый *p.p.p. of* ⇨**гаси́ть** *and adj.*: **~ая и́звесть** slaked lime.
гашéтк|а, и *f.* trigger.
гаши́ш, а *m.* hashish.
гвалт, а *m.* (*coll.*) row, uproar, rumpus.
гвардé|ец, йца *m.* (*mil.*) guardsman.
гвардéйский *adj.* (*mil.*) Guards'.
гвáрди|я, и *f.* (*mil.*) Guards; **~и** (*preceding* **капитáн** *etc., in titles of rank*) Guards.
Гватемáл|а, ы *f.* Guatemala.
гватемáл|ец, ьца *m.* Guatemalan.
гватемáл|ка, ки *f. of* ⇨**~ец**
гватемáльский *adj.* Guatemalan.
гвинé|ец, йца *m.* Guinean.
гвинé|йка, йки *f. of* ⇨**~ец**
гвинéйский *adj.* Guinean.
Гвинé|я, и *f.* Guinea.
гвоздевóй *adj.*: **г. материáл** feature item; **г. нóмер** main attraction, star turn.
гвóздик, а *m.* tack (*small nail*).
гвозди́к|а¹, и *f.* (*bot.*) pink(s); carnation(s); **турéцкая г., бородáтая г.** sweet william.
гвозди́к|а², и *f.* (*collect.*) (*пряность*) cloves.
гвóздик|и, ов *no sg.* (*каблуки*) stilettos.
гвоз|ди́ть, жý, ди́шь *impf.* (*coll.*) **1** (*бить*) to bang, bash; to bang away; **2** (*повторять*) to repeat, keep on.
гвозд|ь, я́, *pl.* **~и, ~éй** *m.* **1** nail; **~ём засéсть** (*fig.*) to become firmly fixed. **2** (+*g.*; *fig., coll.*) (*самое главное*) the crux (of); the highlight (of); **г. вопрóса** the crux of the matter; **г. прогрáммы** the highlight of the show; the main attraction. **3**: **(и) никаки́х ~éй!** (*coll.*) and that's that!
гг. *abbr. of* **1** ***гóды*** years. **2** ***городá*** cities, towns. **3** ***господá*** Messrs.; Mr and Mrs.
где *adv.* **1** (*interrog. and rel. adv.*) where; **г. бы ни** wherever; **г. бы то ни́ было** no matter where. **2** (*coll.*) (*где-н.*) somewhere; anywhere. **3**: **г...., г....** (*coll.*) in one place . . ., in another . . .; sometimes . . ., sometimes . . . . **4**: **г. (уж)** (+*d. and inf.*) (*coll.*) how should one, how is one to; **г. мне знать?** how should I know?
гдé-либо *adv.* anywhere.
гдé-нибудь *adv.* somewhere; anywhere.
гдé-то *adv.* somewhere.
ГДР *f. indecl.* (*abbr. of* ***Гермáнская Демократи́ческая Респýблика***) GDR (*German Democratic Republic*).
геби́ст, а *m.* (*coll.*) KGB man *or* agent.
Гебри́дск|ие óстров|á, ~их ~óв *no sg.* the Hebrides.
гегемóн, а *m.* leader.
гегемóни|я, и *f.* hegemony, supremacy.
гедони́зм, а *m.* hedonism.
гедони́ст, а *m.* hedonist.
гедонисти́ческий *adj.* hedonistic.
гей¹ *int.* hi!
ге|й², я *m.* (*sl.*) gay (*homosexual*); **г.-клуб** gay club.
гéйзер, а *m.* geyser.
гейм, а *m.* game.
гекзáметр, а *m.* hexameter.
геккóн, а *m.* (*zool.*) gecko.
гектáр, а *m.* hectare.
гекто... *comb. form* hecto-.
гéли|й, я *m.* (*chem.*) helium.
гелиóграф, а *m.* heliograph.
гелиотрóп, а *m.* (*bot. and min.*) heliotrope.
гелиоцентри́ческий *adj.* heliocentric.
гел|ь, я *m.* gel.
гематóлог, а *m.* haematologist (*Br.*), hematologist (*US*).
гематологи́ческий *adj.* haematological (*Br.*), hematological (*US*).
гематолóги|я, и *f.* haematology (*Br.*), hematology (*US*).
гемоглоби́н, а *m.* (*physiol.*) haemoglobin (*Br.*), hemoglobin (*US*).
геморрó|й, я *m.* (*med.*) haemorrhoids (*Br.*), hemorrhoids (*US*), piles.
гемофи́лик, а *m.* haemophiliac (*Br.*), hemophiliac (*US*).
гемофили́|я, и *f.* (*med.*) haemophilia (*Br.*), hemophilia (*US*).
ген, а *m.* (*physiol.*) gene.
ген... *comb. form, abbr. of* ***генерáльный***
генеалоги́ческий *adj.* genealogical.
генеалóги|я, и *f.* genealogy.
гéнезис, а *m.* origin, source, genesis.
генерáл, а *m.* general; **г.-майóр** major-general; **г.-лейтенáнт** lieutenant-general; **г.-полкóвник** colonel-general; **бригáдный г.** brigadier-general; **г.-губернáтор** governor-general.
генерали́ссимус, а *m.* generalissimo.
генералитéт, а *m.* (*collect.*) the generals; the top brass.
генерáльн|ый *adj.* (*in var. senses*) general; **г. конструктóр** chief designer; **~ая репети́ция** dress rehearsal; **~ое сражéние** decisive battle; **~ая убóрка** spring-clean; **г. штаб** general staff.
генерáльский *adj.* general's; **г. чин** rank of general.
генерáтор, а *m.* (*tech.*) generator.
генéтик, а *m.* geneticist.
генéтик|а, и *f.* genetics.
генети́ческий *adj.* genetic.
гениáльност|ь, и *f.* genius; greatness.
гениáл|ьный (~ен, ~ьна) *adj.* (*поэт, произведение*) brilliant; (*решение*) ingenious.
гéни|й, я *m.* (*талант, способность*) genius; (*человек*) a genius.
гениталi|и, й *no sg.* (*med.*) genitalia, genitals.
гéн|ный *adj. of* ⇨**~**; **~ная инженéрия** genetic engineering; **~ная дактилоскóпия** genetic fingerprinting.
генотерапи́|я, и *f.* gene therapy.
геноци́д, а *m.* genocide.
генсéк, а *m.* (*abbr. of* ***генерáльный секретáрь***) General-Secretary; Secretary-General.
Гéну|я, и *f.* Genoa.
гео... *comb. form, abbr. of* ***географи́ческий***
геóграф, а *m.* geographer.
географи́ческий *adj.* geographical.
геогрáфи|я, и *f.* geography.
геодези́ст, а *m.* land-surveyor.
геодези́ческий *adj.* geodesic, geodetic.
геодéзи|я, и *f.* geodesy, (land-) surveying.
геóлог, а *m.* geologist.
геологи́ческий *adj.* geological.
геолóги|я, и *f.* geology.
геометри́ческий *adj.* geometric(al).
геомéтри|я, и *f.* geometry.
геополи́тик|а, и *f.* geopolitics.
геополити́ческий *adj.* geopolitical.
георги́н, а *m.* (*bot.*) dahlia.
георги́н|а, ы *f.* = **~**
геофи́зик, а *m.* geophysicist.
геофи́зик|а, и *f.* geophysics.
геофизи́ческий *adj.* geophysical.
гепáрд, а *m.* cheetah.
гепати́т, а *m.* hepatitis.
герáльдик|а, и *f.* heraldry.
геральди́ческий *adj.* heraldic.
герáн|ь, и *f.* geranium.
герб, á *m.* arms, coat of arms.
гербáри|й, я *m.* herbarium.
гербици́д, а *m.* herbicide.
гéрбов|ый *adj.* **1** heraldic. **2** (*с гербом*) bearing a coat of arms; **~ая**

бума́га stamped paper; **~ая ма́рка** duty stamp. **3**: **г. сбор** stamp-duty.

гериатри́ческий *adj.* geriatric.

геркуле́с, а *m.* **1** (*человек*) (a) Hercules (*strong man*). **2** (*sg. only*) (*крупа*) rolled oats; porridge.

геркуле́совский *adj.* Herculean.

геркуле́сов|ый *adj.* oat; **~ая ка́ша** porridge; **~ое пече́нье** oat biscuits (*Br.*), oat cookies (*US*).

герма́н|ец, ца *m.* **1** Teuton; ancient German; **~цы** the Germanic, Nordic peoples. **2** (*coll.*) (*немец*) German.

германи́зм, а *m.* Germanism.

герма́ни|й, я *m.* (*chem.*) germanium.

германи́ст, а *m.* specialist in Germanic studies.

германи́стик|а, и *f.* Germanic studies.

Герма́ни|я, и *f.* Germany.

герма́нск|ий *adj.* **1** Germanic; Teutonic; **~ие языки́** Germanic languages. **2** (*coll.*) (*немецкий*) German.

гермафроди́т, а *m.* hermaphrodite.

гермети́чески *adv.*: **г. закры́тый** hermetically sealed.

гермети́ческ|ий *adj.* hermetic, sealed; air-tight; water-tight; **~ая каби́на** (*aeron.*) pressurized cabin.

Ге́рнси *m. indecl.* Guernsey.

герои́зм, а *m.* heroism.

геро́ик|а, и *f.* heroics; heroic spirit; (*стиль*) heroic style.

герои́н, а *m.* heroin.

герои́нщик, а *m.* (*coll.*) heroin addict.

герои́н|я, и *f.* heroine.

герои́ческий *adj.* heroic.

геро́|й, я *m.* hero; (*liter.*) (*действующее лицо*) character; **гла́вный г.** protagonist.

геро́йский *adj.* heroic.

геро́йств|о, а *nt.* heroism.

геро́льд, а *m.* (*hist.*) herald.

ге́рпес, а *m.* (*med.*) herpes.

геру́нди|й, я *m.* (*gram.*) gerund.

герц, а, *g. pl.* **г.** *m.* (*phys.*) hertz, cycle per second.

ге́рцог, а *m.* duke; **г. Эдинбу́ргский** the Duke of Edinburgh.

герцоги́н|я, и *f.* duchess.

ге́рцогский *adj.* ducal.

ге́рцогств|о, а *nt.* duchy.

геста́по *nt. indecl.* Gestapo.

геста́пов|ец, ца *m.* Gestapo agent.

гетероге́нный *adj.* heterogeneous.

гетеросексуали́ст, а *m.* heterosexual.

гетеросексуа́льный *adj.* heterosexual.

ге́тман, а *m.* (*hist.*) hetman.

ге́тр|ы, гетр *pl.* (*sg.* **~а, ~ы** *f.*) **1** gaiters. **2** (*sport, coll.*) football socks. **3** (*модные*) leg-warmers.

ге́тто *nt. indecl.* ghetto.

г-жа (*abbr. of* ***госпожа́***) (*замужняя*) Mrs; (*незамужняя*) Miss; (*замужняя или незамужняя*) Ms.

гиаци́нт, а *m.* (*bot.*) hyacinth.

ги́бел|ь, и *f.* **1** (*смерть*) death; (*уничтожение*) destruction, ruin; (*потеря*) loss; (*государства*) downfall. **2** (+*g.*; *coll.*) (*множество*) masses (of), swarms (of), hosts (of).

ги́бел|ьный (~ен, ~ьна) *adj.* disastrous, fatal.

ги́бк|ий (~ок, ~ка́, ~ко) *adj.* **1** flexible; (*тело*) supple, lithe; **г. диск** (*comput.*) floppy (disk); **г. стан** lithe body, figure. **2** (*ум*) adaptable, versatile. **3** (*политика*) flexible.

ги́бкост|ь, и *f.* **1** flexibility; (*тела*) suppleness. **2** (*ума*) versatility, resourcefulness. **3** (*политики*) flexibility.

ги́бл|ый *adj.* (*coll.*) (*место*) god-forsaken, wretched; (*безнадёжный*) hopeless; **~ое де́ло** a lost cause.

ги́б|нуть, ну, нешь, *past* **~, ~ла** *impf.* (*of* ⇒**по~**) to perish.

Гибралта́р, а *m.* Gibraltar.

Гибралта́рск|ий проли́в, ~ого ~а *m.* the Strait of Gibraltar.

гибри́д, а *m.* hybrid.

гибридиза́ци|я, и *f.* hybridization.

гига... *comb. form* giga-

гигаба́йт, а *m.* (*comput.*) gigabyte.

гига́нт, а *m.* giant; **(пласти́нка-)г.** LP, long-player.

гига́нтский *adj.* gigantic.

гигие́н|а, ы *f.* hygiene.

гигиени́ческ|ий *adj.* hygienic, sanitary; **~ая прокла́дка** sanitary towel (*Br.*), napkin (*US*).

гигро́метр, а *m.* hygrometer.

гид, а *m.* guide.

ги́др|а, ы *f.* (*myth., zool.*; *fig.*) hydra.

гидра́влик|а, и *f.* hydraulics.

гидравли́ческий *adj.* hydraulic.

гидра́нт, а *m.* hydrant.

гидра́т, а *m.* (*chem.*) hydrate.

гидро... *comb. form* hydro-.

гидро́граф, а *m.* hydrographer.

гидрографи́ческий *adj.* hydrographic.

гидрогра́фи|я, и *f.* hydrography.

гидродина́мик|а, и *f.* hydrodynamics.

гидрокостю́м, а *m.* wet suit.

гидро́лиз, а *m.* (*chem.*) hydrolysis.

гидроло́ги|я, и *f.* hydrology.

гидролока́тор, а *m.* sonar.

гидроо́кис|ь, и *f.* hydroxide.

гидросамолёт, а *m.* hydroplane.

гидроста́нци|я, и *f.* hydro-electric (power-)station.

гидроста́тик|а, и *f.* hydrostatics.

гидроте́хник, а *m.* hydraulic engineer.

гидроте́хник|а, и *f.* hydraulic engineering.

гидрофо́н, а *m.* (*naut.*) hydrophone.

гидроэлектри́ческий *adj.* hydro-electric.

гидроэлектроста́нци|я, и *f.* hydro-electric power-station.

гие́н|а, ы *f.* hyena.

гик, а *m.* (*coll.*) whoop.

ги́кань|е, я *nt.* whooping.

ги́к|ать, аю *impf.* (*of* ⇒**~нуть**) (*coll.*) to whoop.

ги́к|нуть, ну, нешь *pf.* (*of* ⇒**~ать**) to whoop.

гил|ь, и *f.* (*obs., coll.*) nonsense.

гильде́йский *adj. of* ⇒**ги́льдия**

ги́льди|я, и *f.* (*hist.*) guild.

ги́льз|а, ы *f.* cartridge-case; **папиро́сная г.** cigarette-paper.

гильоти́н|а, ы *f.* guillotine.

гильотини́р|овать, ую *impf. and pf.* to guillotine.

Гимала́|и, ев *no sg.* the Himalayas.

гимала́йский *adj.* Himalayan.

гимн, а *m.* hymn; **госуда́рственный г.** national anthem.

гимнази́ст, а *m.* grammar-school boy (*Br.*), high school boy.

гимнази́ст|ка, ки *f. of* ⇒**~**

гимна́зи|я, и *f.* grammar school (*Br.*), high school.

гимна́ст, а *m.* gymnast; **г. на трапе́ции** trapeze artist.

гимнастёрк|а, и *f.* soldier's blouse.

гимна́стик|а, и *f.* gymnastics; **худо́жественная г.** rhythmic gymnastics.

гимнасти́ческий *adj.* gymnastic; **г. зал** gymnasium.

гинеко́лог, а *m.* gynaecologist (*Br.*), gynecologist (*US*).

гинекологи́ческий *adj.* gynaecological (*Br.*), gynecological (*US*).

гинеколо́ги|я, и *f.* gynaecology (*Br.*), gynecology (*US*).

гине́|я, и *f.* guinea.

гипе́рбол|а, ы *f.* **1** hyperbole. **2** (*math.*) hyperbola.

гиперболи́ческий *adj.* **1** hyperbolical. **2** (*math.*) hyperbolic.

гиперинфля́ци|я, и *f.* hyperinflation.

гиперте́кст, а *m.* (*comput.*) hypertext.

гиперто́ник, а *m.* hypertensive, person with high blood pressure.

гипертони́|я, и *f.* (*med.*) hypertension, high blood pressure.

гипертрофи́рованный *adj.* (*biol.*) hypertrophied.

гипертрофи́|я, и *f.* (*biol.*) hypertrophy.

гипно́з, а *m.* hypnosis.

гипнотерапи́|я, и *f.* hypnotherapy.

гипнотизёр, а *m.* hypnotist.

гипнотизи́р|овать, ую *impf.* (*of* ⇒**за~**) to hypnotize.

гипноти́зм, а *m.* hypnotism.

гипно́тик, а *m.* hypnotic, (hypnotic) subject.

гипноти́ческий *adj.* hypnotic.

гипо́тез|а, ы *f.* hypothesis.

гипотену́з|а, ы *f.* (*math.*) hypotenuse.

гипотерми́|я, и *f.* hypothermia.

гипотети́ческий *adj.* hypothetical.

гиппопота́м, а *m.* hippopotamus.

гипс, а *m.* **1** (*min.*) gypsum. **2** (*art*) (*материал*) plaster of Paris; (*слепок*) plaster cast. **3** (*хирургическая повязка*) plaster cast, plaster.

ги́псовый *adj.* **1** (*завод*) gypsum. **2** (*статуя, повязка*) plaster.

гиреви́к, а́ *m.* (*sport*) weight-lifter.

гирля́нд|а, ы *f.* garland, wreath.

гироко́мпас, а *m.* gyrocompass.

гироско́п, а *m.* gyroscope.

гироскопи́ческий *adj.* gyroscopic.

ги́р|я, и *f.* (*для весов*) weight; (*sport*) weight, dumb-bell.

гистерэктоми́|я, и *f.* hysterectomy.

гистогра́мм|а, ы *f.* histogram.

гисто́лог, а *m.* histologist.

гистологи́ческий *adj.* histological.

гистоло́ги|я, и *f.* histology.

гита́р|а, ы *f.* guitar; **ритм-г.** rhythm guitar.

гитари́ст, а *m.* guitarist.

гитари́ст|ка, ки *f. of* ⇒**~**

ги́тлеров|ец, ца *m.* Hitlerite, Nazi; German soldier (*in Second World War*).

ги́тлеровский *adj.* Hitlerite, Nazi.

ги́чк|а, и *f.* (*naut.*) gig.

Глав... *and* **...глав...** *comb. forms, abbr. of* ***гла́вное управле́ние****, as* ***Главга́з*** **(*****Гла́вное управле́ние га́зового хозя́йства*****)**, ***Росглавко́ж*** **(*****Гла́вное управле́ние коже́венной промы́шленности Министе́рства лёгкой промы́шленности РФ*****)**.

глав... *comb. form, abbr. of* ***гла́вный***

глав|а́[1]**, ы́,** *pl.* **~ы** *f. and c.g.* **1** *f.* (*obs. or rhet.*) (*голова*) head. **2** *c.g.* (*начальник*) head, chief; **г. делега́ции** head of a delegation; **быть во ~е́** (+*g.*) to be at the head (of), lead; **во ~е́** (**с**+*i.*) under the leadership (of), led (by). **3**: **поста́вить во ~у́ угла́** to regard as of paramount importance. **4** *f.* (*archit.*) cupola.

глав|а́[2]**, ы́,** *pl.* **~ы** *f.* (*раздел книги*) chapter.

глава́р|ь, я́ *m.* leader; ringleader.

главе́нств|о, а *nt.* supremacy.

главе́нств|овать, ую *impf.* (**в**+*p.*, **над**+*i.*) to have command (over), hold sway (over).

главк, а *m.* (*abbr. of* ***гла́вный комите́т***) central directorate.

главнокома́ндующ|ий, его *m.* Commander-in-Chief (*abbr.* C.-in-C.); **верхо́вный г.** Supreme Commander.

гла́вн|ый *adj.* (*самый важный*) chief, main, principal; (*старший*) head, senior; **г. врач** head physician; **г. инжене́р** chief engineer; **~ая кни́га** ledger; **~ое предложе́ние** main clause; **~ое управле́ние** central directorate; **~ым о́бразом** chiefly, mainly, for the most part; *as n.* **~ое, ~ого** *nt.* the chief thing, the main thing; the essentials.

глаго́л, а *m.* verb.

глаго́лиц|а, ы *f.* (*ling.*) the Glagolitic alphabet.

глаголи́ческий *adj.* (*ling.*) Glagolitic.

глаго́льный *adj.* verbal.

гладиа́тор, а *m.* gladiator.

гладиа́торский *adj.* gladiatorial.

глади́льн|ый *adj.* ironing; **~ая доска́** ironing-board.

гладио́лус, а *m.* (*bot.*) gladiolus.

гла́|дить, жу, дишь *impf.* (*of* ⇒**по~**[1]) **1** (*pf. also* **вы́~**) (*выравнивать утюгом*) to iron, press. **2** (*ласково проводить рукой по чему-н.*) to stroke; **г. по голо́вке** (*coll.*) to pat on the back; **г. про́тив ше́рсти** to rub the wrong way.

гла́д|кий (~ок, ~ка́, ~ко) *adj.* **1** (*дорога*) smooth; (*волосы*) straight; (*ткань*) plain, unfigured; **с него́ взя́тки ~и** (*coll.*) you'll get nothing out of him. **2** (*речь*) fluent, facile.

гла́д|ко *adv. of* ⇒**~кий;** smoothly, swimmingly; **де́ло сошло́ г.** the affair went off smoothly; **г. вы́бритый** clean-shaven.

гладкоство́льный *adj.* (*of firearms*) smooth-bore.

глад|ь[1]**, и** *f.* (*поверхность*) smooth surface (*of water*); **тишь да г.** (*coll.*) peace and quiet.

глад|ь[2]**, и** *f.* (*вышивка*) satin-stitch; **вышива́ть ~ью** to satin-stitch.

гла́же, *comp. of* ⇒**гла́дкий, гла́дко**

гла́жень|е, я *nt.* ironing.

глаз, а, о ~е, в ~у́, *pl.* **~а́, ~, ~а́м** *m.* (*орган зрения*) eye; (*зрение*) eyesight; **дурно́й г.** evil eye; **невооружённый г.** naked eye; **не в бровь, а в г.** (*coll.*) to hit the mark, strike home; **в ~а́** to one's face; **я его́ в ~а́ не вида́л** I have never seen him; **в ~а́х** (+*g.*) in the eyes (of); **ни в одно́м ~у́** (*coll.*) not at all drunk; **за ~а́** (*i*) (*в отсутствие кого-либо*) in absence; **руга́ть кого́-н. за ~а́** to abuse s.o. behind his back, (*ii*) (*coll.*) (*с избытком*) enough, more than enough; **на ~а́, на ~а́х** before one's eyes; **не попада́йся мне на ~а́!** keep out of my sight!; **на г.** approximately, by eye; **с ~у на́ г.** tête-à-tête, cheek-by-jowl; **с г. доло́й** out of sight; **убира́йся с г. доло́й!** get out of my sight; **с г. доло́й — из се́рдца вон** out of sight, out of mind; **не спуска́ть г. с**+*g.* not to let out of one's sight; **смотре́ть во все ~а́** to be all eyes; **хоть г. вы́коли** it's pitch dark; **закрыва́ть ~а́** (**на**+*a.*) to close one's eyes (to), connive (at); **открыва́ть кому́-н. ~а́** (**на**+*a.*) to open s.o.'s eyes (to); **идти́ куда́ ~а́ глядя́т** to follow one's nose.

глаза́ст|ый (~, ~а) *adj.* (*coll.*) (*с большими глазами*) big-eyed; (*зоркий*) sharp-sighted.

глазе́|ть, ю *impf.* (*of* ⇒**по~**) (**на**+*a.*; *coll.*) to stare (at), gawk (at).

глазир|о́ванный *p.p.p. of* ⇒**~ова́ть** *and adj.* (*посуда*) glazed; (*бумага*) glossy; (*cul.*) (*торт*) iced, frosted (*US*); (*фрукты*) glacé, candied.

глазир|ова́ть, у́ю *impf. and pf.* to glaze; (*cul.*) to ice, frost (*US*); (*фрукты*) to candy.

глазиро́вк|а, и *f.* glazing; icing, frosting (*US*); **торт с ~ой** iced cake.

глазни́к, а́ *m.* (*coll.*) eye-doctor.

глазни́ц|а, ы *f.* eye-socket.

глазн|о́й *adj. of* ⇒**глаз; г. врач** oculist; **г. нерв** optic nerve; **~о́е я́блоко** eyeball.

глаз|о́к, ка́, *pl.* **~ки, ~ок** *and* **~ки́, ~ко́в** *m.* **1** (*pl.* **~ки**) *dim. of* ⇒**~;** **одни́м ~ко́м** with half an eye; **де́лать, стро́ить ~ки кому́-н.** to make eyes at s.o.; **аню́тины ~ки** (*bot.*) pansy. **2** (*pl.* **~ки́**) (*coll.*) peephole. **3** (*pl.* **~ки́**) (*растения*) bud; (*картофеля*) eye.

глазоме́р, а *m.* **1** (*определение размеров простым глазом*) measurement by eye. **2** (*способность к такому определению*) ability to judge by eye; **хоро́ший г.** good eye.

глазу́нь|я, ьи, *g. pl.* **~ий** *f.* fried eggs (*with yolk and white unmixed*).

глазу́р|ь, и *f.* **1** (*на посуде*) glaze. **2** (*cul.*) icing, frosting (*US*).

гла́нд|а, ы *f.* (*anat.*) tonsil; **удали́ть ~ы** to take out tonsils.

глас, а *m.* (*obs.*) voice; **г. вопию́щего в пусты́не** the voice of one crying in the wilderness.

гла|си́ть, шу́, си́шь *impf.* to say, run; **докуме́нт ~си́т сле́дующее** the paper runs as follows; **как ~си́т погово́рка** as the saying goes.

гла́сно *adv.* openly, publicly.

гла́сност|ь, и *f.* **1** (*известность*) publicity; **преда́ть ~и** to make public, make known, publish. **2** (*pol.*) *glasnost*, openness.

гла́сный[1] *adj.* (*открытый*) open, public; **г. суд** public trial.

гла́сн|ый[2] *adj.* (*ling.*) vowel, vocalic; *as n.* **г., ~ого** *m.* vowel.

глауко́м|а, ы *f.* glaucoma.

глаша́та|й, я *m.* **1** (*hist.*) town crier, public crier. **2** (*fig., rhet.*) herald.

гле́тчер, а *m.* glacier.

гли́н|а, ы *f.* clay; **фарфо́ровая г.** china clay.

гли́нист|ый *adj.* clayey; **~ая по́чва** loam.

глинобы́тный *adj.* adobe; mud.

глинозём, а *m.* (*chem.*) alumina.

глинтве́йн, а *m.* mulled wine.

гли́нян|ый *adj.* **1** (*сделанный из глины*) clay; earthenware; **~ая посу́да** earthenware crockery. **2** (*глинистый*) clayey.

гли́ссер, а *m.* (*naut.*) speed-boat.

глист, а́ *m.* (intestinal) worm.

глицери́н, а *m.* glycerine (*Br.*), glycerin (*US*).

глици́ни|я, и *f.* wisteria.

гл. об. (*abbr. of* ***гла́вным о́бразом***) mostly, chiefly.

глобализа́ци|я, и *f.* globalization.

глоба́льн|ый *adj.* global; (*fig.*) extensive, in-depth; **~ое потепле́ние** global warming.

гло́бус, а *m.* globe.

гло|да́ть, жу́, ~жешь *impf.* to gnaw (at) (*also fig.*).

гло́кеншпил|ь, я *m.* (*mus.*) glockenspiel.

глота́|ть, ю *impf.* to swallow.

гло́тк|а, и *f.* **1** (*anat.*) gullet. **2** (*coll.*) (*горло*) throat.

глот|о́к, ка́ *m.* gulp, mouthful; (*небольшое количество*) drop.

гло́х|нуть, ну, нешь, *past* **~, ~ла** *impf.* **1** (*pf.* **о~**) (*становиться глухим*) to become deaf. **2** (*pf.* **за~**) (*о звуках*) to die away, subside; (*о моторе*) to stall. **3** (*pf.* **за~**) (*о саде*) to become wild, go to seed.

глу́б|же *comp. of* ⇒**~о́кий** *and* **~око́**

глубин|а́, ы́, *pl.* **~ы** *f.* **1** depth; **на ~е́ 300 ме́тров** at a depth of 300 metres. **2** (*pl.*) (the) depths; **морски́е ~ы** the ocean depths. **3** (+*g.*) heart, interior (*also fig.*); **в ~е́ ле́са** in the heart of the forest; **в ~е́ души́** at heart, in one's heart of hearts; **от ~ы́ души́** with all one's heart.

глуби́нк|а, и *f.* (*coll.*) the sticks, the back of beyond; **жить в ~е** to live (way) out in the sticks.

глуби́нн|ый *adj.* **1** deep; deep-sea; **~ая бо́мба** depth charge; **г. лов ры́бы** deep-sea fishing. **2** (*отдалённый*) remote, out-of-the-way.

глубо́к|ий (~, ~а́, ~о́) *adj.* **1** (*in var. senses*) deep; **г. сон** deep sleep; **~ая таре́лка** soup-plate. **2** (*основательный*) profound; thorough; (*серьёзный*) serious; **~ие зна́ния** thorough knowledge; **~ая оши́бка** serious error. **3** (*время, возраст*) late; advanced; extreme; **до ~ой но́чи** (until) far into the night; **~ая ста́рость** extreme old age; **~ая стару́ха** a very old woman; **стоя́ла ~ая зима́** it was mid-winter; **~ой зимо́й** in the deep mid-winter. **4** (*очень сильный*) deep, profound, intense; **с ~им приско́рбием** (*in obituary formula*) with deep regret.

глубоко́[1] *adv.* deep; (*fig.*) deeply, profoundly.

глубо́ко́[2] *as pred.* it is deep.

глубоково́д|ный (~ен, ~на) *adj.* **1** (*глубокий*) deep-water. **2** (*производимый, живущий на большой глубине*) deep-water, deep-sea.

глубокомы́слен|ный (~, ~на) *adj.* thoughtful; serious.

глубокомы́сли|е, я *nt.* profundity.

глубокоуважа́емый *adj.* much-esteemed; (*в письмах*) dear.

глубоча́йший *superl. of* ⇒**глубо́кий**

глуб|ь, и *f.* depth; **г. реки́** the river-bottom.

глум|и́ться, лю́сь, и́шься *impf.* (**над**+*i.*) to mock (at).

глумле́ни|е, я *nt.* mockery.

глумли́в|ый (~, ~а) *adj.* (*coll.*) mocking.

глупе́|ть, ю *impf.* (*of* ⇒**по~**) to grow stupid.

глуп|е́ц, ца́ *m.* fool, blockhead.

глуп|и́ть, лю́, и́шь *impf.* (*of* ⇒**с~**) to make a fool of o.s.; to do sth. foolish.

глупова́т|ый (~, ~а) *adj.* silly; rather stupid.

глу́пост|ь, и *f.* **1** (*свойство*) foolishness, stupidity. **2** (*поступок*) foolish, stupid action; foolish, stupid thing. **3** (*usu. pl.*) (*вздор*) nonsense; **~и!** (stuff and) nonsense!

глу́п|ый (~, ~а́, ~о) *adj.* foolish, stupid; silly.

глупы́ш, а́ *m.* (*coll.*) silly; silly little thing.

глуха́р|ь, я́ *m.* **1** (*zool.*) capercailzie, woodgrouse. **2** (*coll.*) deaf person.

глу́хо[1] *adv. of* ⇒**глухо́й;** (*coll.*) = **на́глухо**

глу́хо[2] *as pred.* it is lonely, deserted.

глухова́т|ый (~, ~а) *adj.* **1** (*человек*) somewhat deaf, hard of hearing. **2** (*голос, звук*) somewhat indistinct, not very loud.

глух|о́й (~, ~а́, ~о) *adj.* **1** (*лишённый слуха*) deaf (*also fig.*); **он был ~ к на́шим мольба́м** he was deaf to our entreaties; *as n.* **г., ~о́го** *m.* deaf person. **2** (*звук*) muffled, indistinct. **3** (*ling.*) voiceless. **4** (*густо заросший*) thick, dense; wild; **г. лес** dense forest. **5** (*отдалённый*) remote, out-of-the-way; god-forsaken; **в ~о́й прови́нции** in the depths of the country; **~а́я у́лица** lonely street. **6** (*затаённый, скрытый*) concealed, hidden; **~о́е недово́льство** pent-up dissatisfaction; **~а́я не́нависть** secret hatred. **7** (*закрытый*) sealed; blank, blind; **~а́я стена́** blind wall. **8** (*застёгнутый*) buttoned-up, done up. **9** (*время, сезон*) quiet, dead; **~а́я пора́** slack period; **~а́я ночь** dead of night; **~а́я о́сень** late autumn.

глухома́н|ь, и *f.* (*coll.*) out-of-the-way place, backwoods.

глухонем|о́й *adj.* deaf and dumb; *as n.* **г., ~о́го** *m.* deaf mute; **язы́к (для) ~ы́х** sign language.

глухот|а́, ы *f.* deafness.

глу́|ше *comp. of* ⇒**~хо́й** *and* **~хо**

глуши́тел|ь, я *m.* **1** (*tech.*) silencer, muffler (*US*). **2** (*fig.*) suppressor.

глуш|и́ть, у́, и́шь *impf.* **1** (*pf.* **о~**) (*рыбу*) to stun, stupefy. **2** (*pf.* **за~**) (*звуки*) to muffle; **г. боль** to dull pain; **г. мото́р** to stop the engine. **3** (*pf.* **за~**) (*рост*) to choke, stifle. **4** (*pf.* **за~**) (*fig.*) to suppress, stifle; **г. кри́тику** to suppress criticism.

глуш|ь, и́ *f.* (*заросшая часть*) overgrown part; (*пустынное место*) backwoods (*also fig.*); **жить в ~и́** to live in the back of beyond.

глы́б|а, ы *f.* clod; lump, block.

глюк, а *m.* (*sl.*) hallucination.

глюко́з|а, ы *f.* glucose.

гля|де́ть, жу́, ди́шь *impf.* (*of* ⇒**по~**) **1** (**на**+*a.*) to look (at); to peer (at); to gaze (upon); **г. сквозь па́льцы** (**на**+*a.*) to shut one's eyes (to), turn a blind eye (to); **идти́ куда́ глаза́ ~дя́т** to follow one's nose. **2** (**на**+*a.*; *coll.*) (*брать пример с кого-н.*) to look to. **3** (*impf. only*) to show, appear. **4** (*impf. only*) (**на**+*a.*) (*быть обращённым в какую-н. сторону*) to look (on to), face, give (on to). **5** (*impf. only*) (+*i. or adv.*; *coll.*) (*иметь вид*) to look like, appear. **6** (**за**+*i.*; *coll.*) (*заботиться*) to look after, keep an eye on. **7**: **~ди́(те)** mind (out); **~ди́ не** (+*imper.*) mind you don't . . . **8**: **того́ и ~ди́** (*coll.*) it looks as if at any moment; **того́ и ~ди́ бу́дет бу́ря** it looks as if there's going to be a storm any moment now. **9**: **~дя** (**по**+*d.*, *coll.*) depending (on).

гля|де́ться, жу́сь, ди́шься *impf.* (*of* ⇒**по~**) (**в**+*a.*) to look at o.s. (in).

гля́дь *int.* lo and behold!; hey presto!

гля́н|ец, ца *m.* gloss, lustre (*Br.*), luster (*US*).

гля́|нуть, ну, нешь *pf.* (**на**+*a.*) glance (at).

глянцеви́т|ый (~, ~а) *adj.* glossy, lustrous.

гля́нцев|ый *adj.* glossy, lustrous; **~ая кра́ска** gloss paint.

гм *int.* hm!

г-н (*abbr. of* **господи́н**) Mr; Master; (*на конверте*) **~у** (+*d.*) Mr . . .; . . . Esq.; **~у В. Джо́нсу** W. Jones, Esq.

гна|ть, гоню́, го́нишь, *past* **~л, ~ла́, ~ло** *impf.* **1** (*det. of* ⇒**гоня́ть**) (*стадо*) to drive. **2** (*торопить*) to urge (on); (*coll.*) (*автомобиль*) to drive hard. **3** (*coll.*) (*быстро ехать*) to dash, tear. **4** (*преследовать*) to hunt, chase; (*fig.*) to persecute. **5** (*выгонять*) to turn out, turf out. **6** (*водку*) to distil (*Br.*), distill (*US*).

гна́|ться, гоню́сь, го́нишься, *past* **~лся, ~ла́сь, ~ло́сь** *impf.* (*det. of* ⇒**гоня́ться**) (**за**+*i.*) (*преследовать*) to pursue; (*стремиться*) to strive (for, after); (*fig.*) (*стараться быть не хуже*) to (try to) keep up with.

гнев, а *m.* anger, rage, wrath.

гне́ва|ться, юсь *impf.* (*of* ⇒**раз~**) (**на**+*a.*; *obs.*) to be angry (with).

гнев|и́ть, лю́, и́шь *impf.* (*of* ⇒**про~**) (*obs.*) to anger, enrage.

гне́в|ный (~ен, ~на́, ~но) *adj.* angry, irate.

гнедо́й *adj.* bay (*colour of horse*).

гнезд|и́ться, и́тся, я́тся *impf.* **1** to nest, build one's nest. **2** (*fig.*) (*о мыслях*) to take root; to be lodged.

гнезд|о́, а́, *pl.* **гнёзда** *nt.* **1** (*птицы*) nest. **2** (*животного*) den, lair (*also fig.*); **г. сопротивле́ния** (*mil.*) pocket of resistance. **3** (*tech.*) socket; seat; housing.

гнездова́ни|е, я *nt.* nesting; **пора́ ~я** nesting season.

гнездово́й *adj. of* ⇒**гнездо́**

гнездо́вь|е, я *nt.* nesting-site.

гнейс, а *m.* (*min.*) gneiss.

гне|сти́, ту́, тёшь *impf.* to oppress, weigh down; to press; **его́ ~ту́т забо́ты** he is weighed down by cares.

гнёт, а *m.* **1** (*obs.*) (*тяжесть*) press; weight. **2** (*fig.*) oppression, yoke; **г. ра́бства** the yoke of slavery.

гнету́щий *pres. part. act. of* ⇒**гнести́** *and adj.* oppressive.

гни́д|а, ы *f.* nit; (*fig.*) scumbag, worm.

гние́ни|е, я *nt.* decay, putrefaction, rot.

гнил|о́й (~, ~а́, ~о) *adj.* **1** rotten (*also fig.*); decayed; putrid. **2** (*погода*) damp, muggy; (*климат*) unhealthy.

гнилост|ный (~ен, ~на) *adj.* putrid.

гни́лост|ь, и *f.* rottenness (*also fig.*); putridity.

гнил|ь, и *f.* **1** (*что-н. гнилое*) rotten stuff. **2** (*плесень*) mould.

гниль|ё, я́ *nt.* (*collect.*) rotten stuff.

гни|ть, ю, ёшь *impf.* (*of* ⇒**с~**) to rot, decay.

гное́ни|е, я *nt.* suppuration.

гно|и́ть, ю́, и́шь *impf.* (*of* ⇒**с~**) to let rot, allow to decay; **г. наво́з** to ferment manure; **г. в тюрьме́** to leave to rot in prison.

гно|и́ться, ю́сь, и́шься *impf.* to suppurate, fester.

гно|й, я, в ~е *or* **в ~ю́** *m.* pus.

гнойни́к, а́ *m.* (*нарыв*) abscess; (*язва*) ulcer.

гно́йный *adj.* purulent.

гном, а *m.* gnome.

гносеоло́ги|я, и *f.* (*phil.*) gnosiology; theory of knowledge.

гно́стик, а *m.* Gnostic.

гностици́зм, а *m.* Gnosticism.

ГНС (*abbr. of* ***Госуда́рственная нало́говая слу́жба***) Inland Revenue (*Br.*); Internal Revenue Service, IRS (*US*).

гнус, а *m.* (*collect.*) midges.

гнуса́в|ить, лю, ишь *impf.* to speak through one's nose.

гнуса́вост|ь, и *f.* twang; nasal intonation.

гнуса́в|ый (~, ~а) *adj.* nasal.

гну́сност|ь, и *f.* **1** (*свойство*) vileness, foulness. **2** (*поступок*) vile, foul action.

гну́с|ный (~ен, ~на́, ~но) *adj.* vile, foul.

гну́т|ый *p.p.p. of* ⇒**гнуть** *and adj.* bent; **~ая ме́бель** bent-wood furniture.

гнуть, гну, гнёшь *impf.* (*of* ⇒**со~**) **1** (*проволоку*) to bend; (*деревья*) to bow; **г. спи́ну, ше́ю (пе́ред + *i.*)** (*coll.*) to cringe (before), kow-tow (to); **г. свою́ ли́нию** to stick to one's guns. **2** (*coll.*) (*направлять свои действия*) to drive at; **я не понима́ю, куда́ ты гнёшь** I don't know what you are driving at.

гнуть|ё, я́ *nt.* bending.

гну́ться, гнусь, гнёшься *impf.* (*of* ⇒**со~**) (*о материале, палке*) to bend; (*о деревьях*) to be bowed.

гнуш|а́ться, а́юсь *impf.* (*of* ⇒**по~**) **1** (+*g. or i.*) (*пренебрегать*) to abhor, have an aversion (to). **2** (+*inf.*) (*брезгать*) to disdain (to).

гобеле́н, а *m.* tapestry.

гобои́ст, а *m.* oboist.

гобои́ст|ка, ки *f. of* ⇒**~**

гобо́|й, я *m.* oboe.

говённый *adj.* (*vulg.*) shitty.

гове́нь|е, я *nt.* fasting (*as preparation for Communion*).

гов|е́ть, е́ю, е́ешь *impf.* (*eccl.*) to prepare for Communion (*by fasting*); (*coll.*) to fast, go without food.

говн|о́, а́ *nt.* (*vulg.*) shit.

говню́к, а́ *m.* (*vulg.*) shitbag, bastard.

го́вор, а *m.* **1** (*звуки разговора*) sound of voices; **г. волн** the murmur of the waves. **2** (*произношение*) mode of speech, accent. **3** (*диалект*) dialect.

говор|и́ть, ю́, и́шь *impf.* **1** (*impf. only*) (*владеть устной речью*) to speak, talk; **он ещё не ~и́т** he can't speak yet; **г. по-францу́зски** to speak French.
2 (*pf.* **сказа́ть**) (*выражать, сообщать*) to say; to tell; to speak, talk; **г. пра́вду** to tell the truth; **г. де́ло** to talk sense; **~я́т** they say, it is said; **что вы ~и́те?** (*expr. incredulity*) you don't mean to say so!; **~и́т Москва́!** (*introducing radio programme*) this is Radio Moscow!; **не́чего (и) г.** it goes without saying, needless to say; **что и г.** (*coll.*) it cannot be denied; **что ни ~и́** say what you like; **и не ~и́!** certainly!, of course!; **ина́че ~я́** in other words; **со́бственно ~я́** strictly speaking; **не ~я́ уже́ (о + *p.*)** not to mention.
3 (*pf.* **по~**) (**о + *p.***) (*беседовать*) to talk (about), discuss.
4 (*impf. only*) (*значить*) to mean, convey, signify; **э́то и́мя мне ничего́ не ~и́т** this name means nothing to me.
5 (*impf. only*) (**о + *p.***) (*свидетельствовать*) to point (to), indicate, testify (to); **всё ~и́т о том, что он поко́нчил с собо́й** everything points to his having committed suicide.
6 (*impf. only*): **г. в по́льзу** (+*g.*) to tell in favour (of); to support, back.

говор|и́ться, и́тся *impf. pass. of* ⇒**~и́ть; как ~и́тся** as they say, as the saying goes.

говорли́вост|ь, и *f.* garrulity, talkativeness.

говорли́в|ый (~, ~а) *adj.* garrulous, talkative.

говору́н, а́ *m.* (*coll.*) talker, chatterer.

говору́н|ья, ьи, *g. pl.* **~ий** *f. of* ⇒**~**

говя́дин|а, ы *f.* beef.

говя́жий *adj.* beef.

го́гол|ь, я *m.* (*zool.*) golden-eye (*Clangula bucephala*); **ходи́ть ~ем** to strut.

го́гот, а *m.* (*крик гусей*) cackle; (*coll.*) (*хохот*) loud laughter.

гогота́нь|е, я *nt.* cackling.

гого|та́ть, чу́, ~чешь *impf.* **1** (*о гусях*) to cackle. **2** (*coll.*) (*хохотать*) to cackle, roar with laughter.

год, а, в ~у́, о ~е, *pl.* **~ы** *and* **~а́,** *g.* **~о́в** *and* **лет** *m.* **1** (*g. pl.* **лет**) year; **високо́сный г.** leap year; **кру́глый г.** (*as adv.*) the whole year round; **в бу́дущем, про́шлом ~у́** next, last year; **в теку́щем ~у́** during the current year; **в г.** a year, per annum; **из ~а в г.** year in, year out; **г. о́т ~у** every year; **спустя́ три ~а** three years later; **че́рез три ~а** in three years' time; **бе́з ~у неде́ля** (*coll.*) only for a very short time; **мы ~ы не вида́лись** we have not met for years; **встреча́ть Но́вый г.** to see the New Year in; **ей пошёл пятна́дцатый г.** she is in her fifteenth year.
2 двадца́тые, тридца́тые, *etc.*, **~ы** (*g.* **~о́в**) the twenties, the thirties, etc.
3 ~а́ *and* **~ы, ~о́в** (*pl. only*) years, age, time; **шко́льные ~а́** schooldays; **в ~ы** (+*g.*) in the days (of); during; **в те ~ы** in those days; **в ~а́х** advanced in years; **не по ~а́м** beyond one's years, precocious(ly).

года́ми *adv.* for years (*on end*).

го|ди́ть, жу́, ди́шь *impf.* (*coll.*) to wait, loiter.

го|ди́ться, жу́сь, ди́шься *impf.*
1 (**на + *a.*, для + *g.*,** *or* **+ *d.***) (*быть полезным*) to be fit (for), be suited (for), do (for), serve (for); **э́та мате́рия ни на что, нигде́ не ~ди́тся** this material is no good (for anything); **не ~ди́тся** it's no good, it won't do. **2** (**в + *nom.-a.***) (*быть впору*) to serve (as), be suited to be; **он не ~ди́тся в офице́ры** he is not cut out to be an officer. **3** (**в + *nom.-a.***) (*подходить по возрасту*) to be old enough to be; **она́ ~ди́тся тебе́ в ма́тери** she is old enough to be your mother. **4**: **не ~ди́тся** (+*inf.*) it does not do (to), one should not.

годи́чн|ый *adj.* **1** (*относящийся к целому году*) lasting a year; **~ое путеше́ствие** a year's journey.
2 (*бывающий один раз в году*) annual, yearly; **~ые ко́льца** (*bot.*) annual rings.

го́дност|ь, и *f.* fitness, suitability; (*билета*) validity; **срок ~и** expiry date.

го́д|ный (~ен, ~на́, ~но) *adj.* fit, suitable, (*о билете*) valid; **г. к вое́нной слу́жбе** fit for military service; **г. к пла́ванию** seaworthy; **биле́т го́ден три ме́сяца** the ticket is valid for three months.

годова́лый *adj.* one year old, yearling.

годово́й *adj.* annual, yearly.

годовщи́н|а, ы *f.* anniversary.

го|й, я *m.* goy, gentile.

гол, а *m.* (*sport*) goal; **заби́ть г.** to score a goal.

Голго́ф|а, ы *f.* Calvary (*also fig.*).

голена́ст|ый (~, ~а) *adj.* **1** (*coll.*) long-legged. **2** *as pl. n.* (*zool.*) waders, Grallatores.

голени́щ|е, а *nt.* top (*of a boot*).

голеносто́пный *adj.*: **г. суста́в** ankle joint.

го́лен|ь, и *f.* shin.

голки́пер, а *m.* (*sport*) goalkeeper.

голла́нд|ец, ца *m.* Dutchman.

Голла́нди|я, и *f.* Holland.

голла́ндк|а, и *f.* Dutchwoman; Dutch girl.

голла́ндск|ий *adj.* Dutch; **~ая печь** tiled stove; **~ое полотно́** holland (*cloth*).

Голливу́д, а *m.* Hollywood.

голливу́дский *adj.* Hollywood (*attr.*).

голов|а́, ы́, *a.* **го́лову,** *pl.* **го́ловы, голо́в, ~а́м** *f. and c.g.* **1** *f.* head (*also fig.*); **на све́жую го́лову** while one is fresh; **быть ~о́й, на́ голову вы́ше кого́-н.** (*fig.*) to be head and shoulders above s.o.; **с ~ы́ до ног** from head to foot; **с ~о́й погрузи́ться, окуну́ться, уйти́ (во что-н.)** (*fig.*) to throw o.s. (into sth.), plunge (into sth.), get up to one's neck (in sth.); **свали́ть с больно́й ~ы́ на здоро́вую** to lay the blame on s.o. else; **че́рез чью-н. го́лову** (*fig.*) behind s.o.'s back; **у неё г. шла кру́гом** her head was going round and round; **у меня́ г. кру́жится** I feel giddy; **вы́дать (себя́) с ~о́й** to unconsciously show one's worse side; **намы́лить кому́-н. го́лову** to give s.o. a dressing-down; **го́лову пове́сить** to hang one's head.
2 *f.* (*единица счёта скота*) head (*of cattle*).
3 *f.* (*fig.*): **с ~ы́** per head.

4 *f.* (*fig.*) (*ум*) head; brain, mind; wits; **он па́рень с ~о́й** he's a bright lad; **лома́ть го́лову** to rack one's brains; **не теря́ть ~ы́** to keep one's head; **ей пришла́ в го́лову мысль** it occurred to her, it struck her.
5 *f.* (*fig.*) (*человек, как носитель каких-либо свойств*) head (= *person*); **горя́чая г.** hothead; **сме́лая г.** bold spirit.
6 *f.* (*fig.*) (*жизнь*) head, life; **на свою́ го́лову** to one's cost; **заплати́ть, поплати́ться за что-н. ~о́й** to pay for sth. with one's life; **отвеча́ть, руча́ться ~о́й за что-н.** to stake one's life on sth.
7 *c.g.* (*fig.*) (*начальник*) head; person in charge; **сам себе́ г.** one's own master.
8 *f.*: **г. са́хару** sugar-loaf; **г. сы́ру** a cheese; **г. капу́сты** head of cabbage.
9 *idiomatic phrr.*: **в пе́рвую го́лову** in the first place; first and foremost; **в ~а́х** at the head of the bed.

голова́стик, а *m.* tadpole.

голове́шк|а, и *f.* brand; smouldering (*Br.*), smoldering (*US*) piece of wood.

голо́вк|а, и *f.* **1** *dim. of* ⇒**голова́.** **2** (*гвоздя, булавки, спички, цветка*) head; **г. лу́ка** an onion, onion bulb; **г. чеснока́** head of garlic. **3** (*collect.*; *coll.*) heads, big shots. **4** (*pl.*) (*сапог*) vamp (*of boot*).

головн|о́й *adj.* **1** *adj. of* ⇒**голова́; ~а́я боль** headache; **г. плато́к** head-scarf; **г. убо́р** headgear, head-dress. **2** (*anat.*): **г. мозг** brain, cerebrum. **3** (*fig.*) head, leading.

головн|я́¹, и́, *g. pl.* **~е́й** *f.* (*обгорелое бревно*) charred log.

головн|я́², и́, *g. pl.* **~е́й** *f.* (*болезнь растений*) blight, smut, rust.

головокруже́ни|е, я *nt.* giddiness, dizziness (*also fig.*); vertigo.

головокружи́тельн|ый *adj.* dizzy, giddy (*also fig.*); **~ая высота́** dizzy height; **~ые перспекти́вы** breath-taking prospects.

головоло́мк|а, и *f.* puzzle, conundrum.

головоло́мный *adj.* puzzling; baffling; **г. вопро́с** puzzler.

головомо́йк|а, и *f.* (*coll.*) reprimand, dressing-down.

головоре́з, а *m.* (*coll.*) **1** (*бандит*) cutthroat; bandit; desperado. **2** (*сорвиголова*) daredevil; rascal.

голо́вушк|а, и *f. affectionate dim. of* ⇒**голова́; пропа́ла моя́ г.** I'm done for; I've had it.

гологра́мм|а, ы *f.* hologram.

голографи́ческий *adj.* holographic.

гологра́фи|я, и *f.* holography.

го́лод, а (у) *m.* **1** hunger; (*длительное недоедание*) starvation; **во́лчий г.** ravenous appetite; **умира́ть с ~у** to die of starvation; **мори́ть ~ом** to starve (*trans.*). **2** (*народное бедствие*) famine. **3** (*недостаток*) dearth, acute shortage; **шерстяно́й г.** wool shortage.

голода́ни|е, я *nt.* **1** (*недоедание*) starvation. **2** (*воздержание*) fasting.

голод|а́ть, а́ю *impf.* **1** (*скудно питаться*) to starve. **2** (*воздерживаться от пищи*) to fast, go without food. **3** (*быть на диете*) to diet.

голода́|ющий *pres. part. act. of* ⇒**~ть** *and adj.* starving, hungry; *as n.* **г., ~ющего** *m.*, **~ющая, ~ющей** *f.* starving person.

голо́д|ный (го́лоден, ~на́, ~но) *adj.* **1** (*желающий есть*) hungry; **сексуа́льно г.** sex-starved. **2** (*вызванный голодом*) hunger, starvation; **~ные бо́ли** hunger-pangs; **г. похо́д** hunger-march. **3** (*скудный*) meagre, scanty, poor; **г. год** lean year; **г. край** barren country; **г. паёк** starvation rations.

голодо́вк|а, и *f.* **1** (*голодание*) starvation. **2** (*в знак протеста*) hunger-strike; **объяви́ть ~у** to go on hunger-strike.

голодра́|нец, нца *m.* (*coll.*) beggar.

гололёд, а *m.* = **гололе́дица**

гололе́диц|а, ы *f.* black ice.

голоно́г|ий (~, ~а) *adj.* bare-legged; bare-foot.

го́лос, а, *pl.* **~а́** *m.* **1** voice; **во весь г.** at the top of one's voice; **быть в ~е** to be in good voice; **с ~а** by ear; **г. за ка́дром** voice-over. **2** (*mus.*) voice, part; **фу́га на четы́ре ~а** four-part fugue. **3** (*fig.*) (*мнение*) voice, word, opinion; **в оди́н г.** with one accord, unanimously; **име́ть свой г.** to have one's say. **4** (*pol.*) vote; **пра́во ~а** the vote, suffrage, franchise; **пода́ть г. (за** + *a.*) to vote (for), cast one's vote (for).

голоси́ст|ый (~, ~а) *adj.* loud-voiced; (*громкий*) loud.

голо|си́ть, шу́, си́шь *impf.* **1** (*coll.*) (*петь*) to sing loudly; (*выкрикивать*) to cry. **2** (*obs.*) (*плакать*) to wail; to keen; **г. по поко́йнику** to keen a dead person.

голосло́вно *adv.* without adducing any proof.

голосло́в|ный (~ен, ~на) *adj.* unsubstantiated, unfounded.

голосова́ни|е, я *nt.* voting; poll; **всео́бщее г.** universal suffrage; **поста́вить на г.** to put to the vote.

голос|ова́ть, у́ю *impf.* (*of* ⇒**про~**) **1** (**за** + *a.*, **про́тив** + *g.*) to vote (for, against); **г. нога́ми** to vote with one's feet. **2** (*ставить на голосование*) to put to the vote, vote on. **3** (*sl.*) (*останавливать машину*) to thumb a lift.

голосов|о́й *adj.* vocal; (*anat.*) **~ы́е свя́зки** vocal chords; **~а́я щель** glottis.

голу́беньк|ий, ого *m.* = **голубо́й** *as n.*

голубе́|ть, ю *impf.* (*of* ⇒**по~**) (*видеться*) to show blue; (*становиться голубым*) to turn blue.

голуб|е́ц, ца́ *m.* (*usu. pl.*) golubets (*rissole wrapped in cabbage-leaves*).

голубизн|а́, ы́ *f.* blueness.

голуби́к|а, и *f.* great bilberry, bog whortleberry (*Vaccinium uliginosum*).

голуби́н|ый *adj.* **1** *adj. of* ⇒**го́лубь; ~ая по́чта** pigeon post. **2** (*fig.*) dove-like.

голу́|бить, блю, бишь *impf.* (*of* ⇒**при~**) (*folk poet.*) to caress, fondle.

голу́бк|а, и *f.* **1** female pigeon, dove. **2** (*fig.*) (*ласковое обращение*) (my) dear, (my) darling.

голубогла́з|ый (~, ~а) *adj.* blue-eyed.

голуб|о́й *adj.* pale blue, sky-blue; **~а́я кровь** (*fig.*) blue blood; **~о́е то́пливо** 'blue fuel' (= *natural gas*); **г. экра́н** the small screen (*i.e. TV*); *as n.* **голуб|о́й, о́го** *m.* gay (= *homosexual*).

голуб|о́к, ка́ *m.* **1** *dim. of* ⇒**го́лубь;** *fig.* = **голу́бчик. 2** (*bot.*) columbine, aquilegia.

голу́бушк|а, и *f.* **1** (*coll.*; *as mode of address*) (my) dear. **2** *affectionate dim. of* ⇒**голу́бка** 1

голу́бчик, а *m.* (*coll.*; *as mode of address*) my dear; my dear fellow; my friend.

го́луб|ь, я, *g. pl.* **~е́й** *m.* pigeon, dove; **г. свя́зи** (*mil.*) carrier-pigeon.

голубя́тник, а *m.* pigeon-fancier.

голубя́т|ня, ни, *g. pl.* **~ен** *f.* dovecot(e), pigeon loft.

го́л|ый (~, ~а́, ~о) *adj.* **1** naked, bare (*also fig.*); **~ая голова́** (*i*) (*непокрытая*) bare head, (*ii*) (*лысая*) bald head; **~ая и́стина** the naked truth; **г. про́вод** naked wire; **~ыми рука́ми** with one's bare hands. **2** (*coll.*) poor; **~ как соко́л** poor as a church mouse.

голы́ш, а́ *m.* **1** (*coll.*) (*ребёнок*) naked child; (*человек*) naked person. **2** (*камень*) round flat stone.

гол|ь, и *no pl.*, *f.* **1** (*collect.*) the poor; **г. на вы́думки хитра́** necessity is the mother of invention. **2** (*obs.*) (*местность*) bare place, barren place.

гольф, а *m.* **1** golf; **игро́к в г.** golfer. **2**: **~ы** (*coll.*) (*брюки*) plus-fours; (*чулки*) knee-length socks.

гомеопа́т, а *m.* homoeopath(ist).

гомеопати́ческий *adj.* homoeopathic (*Br.*), homeopathic (*US*).

гомеопа́ти|я, и *f.* homoeopathy (*Br.*), homeopathy (*US*).

гомери́ческий *adj.*: **г. смех** Homeric laughter; resounding laughter.

го́мик, а *m.* (*coll.*, *pej.*) fairy, queer, poof(ter).

гомоге́нный *adj.* homogeneous.

го́мон, а *m.* (*coll.*) hubbub.

гомон|и́ть, ю́, и́шь *impf.* (*coll.*) to talk noisily, shout (*of large number of people*).

гомосе́к = **го́мик**

гомосексуали́зм, а *m.* homosexuality.

гомосексуали́ст, а *m.* homosexual; gay.

гомосексуали́ст|ка, ки *f. of* ⇒**~**

гомосексуали́стский *adj.* homosexual; gay.

гомосексуа́льный *adj.* homosexual; gay.

гон, а *m.* **1** dash, rush. **2** (*травля зверя*) hunt, chase, pursuit.

гонг, а *m.* gong.

гондо́л|а, ы *f.* **1** gondola. **2** (*aeron.*) car (*of balloon*).

гондолье́р, а *m.* gondolier.

гондо́н, а *m.* (*vulg.*) condom; French letter (*Br.*), rubber (*US*).
Гондура́с, а *m.* Honduras.
гондура́с|ец, ца *m.* Honduran.
гондура́с|ка, ки *f. of* ⇨**~ец**
гондура́сский *adj.* Honduran.
гоне́ни|е, я *nt.* persecution.
гон|е́ц, ца́ *m.* courier; (*fig.*) herald, harbinger.
гони́тел|ь, я *m.* persecutor.
го́нк|а, и *f.* **1** (*coll.*) haste, hurry. **2** (*sport; usu. pl.*) race; **гребны́е ~и** boat race; **г. вооруже́ний** arms race.
Гонко́нг, а *m.* Hong Kong.
Гонолу́лу *m. indecl.* Honolulu.
го́нор, а *m.* (*coll.*) arrogance, conceit.
гонора́р, а *m.* fee, honorarium; **а́вторский г.** royalties.
гонорé|я, и *f.* gonorrhoea (*Br.*), gonorrhea (*US*).
го́ночный *adj. of* ⇨**го́нка; г. автомоби́ль** racing car.
гонт, а *m.* (*collect.; tech.*) shingles.
гонтов|о́й *adj. of* ⇨**гонт; ~а́я кры́ша** shingle roof.
гонча́р, а́ *m.* potter.
гонча́рн|ый *adj.* potter's; **~ые изде́лия** pottery.
го́нч|ая, ей *f.* hound.
го́нщик, а *m.* **1** racing driver; **велосипеди́ст-г.** racing cyclist. **2** (*sl.*) (*лгун*) liar, story-teller.
гоню́(сь), го́нишь(ся) *see* ⇨**гна́ть(ся)**
гоня́|ть, ю *impf.* **1** (*indet. of* ⇨**гнать**) (*стада*) to drive; (*птиц*) to chase off. **2** (*coll.*) (*курьера*) to send on errands. **3** (**по**+*d.*; *coll.*) (*ученика*) to make run over, grill (on) (*sth. learnt, read, etc.*). **4**: **г. голубе́й** to race pigeons. **5**: **г. ло́дыря** (*coll.*) to kick one's heels.
гоня́|ться, юсь *impf.* (*indet. of* ⇨**гна́ться**) (**за**+*i.*) to chase, pursue; (*на охоте*) to hunt.
гоп *int.* hup!; jump!
гопа́к, а́ *m.* gopak (*Ukrainian dance*).
гопкомпа́ни|я, и *f.* (*sl.*) bunch of yobs.
го́пник, а *m.* (*sl.*) yob(bo).
гор... *comb. form, abbr. of* **1** ***городско́й*. 2 *го́рный***
гор|а́, ы́, *a.* **~у́,** *pl.* **~ы,** *a.* **~а́м** *f.* **1** mountain; hill; **г. Эвере́ст** Mount Everest; **г. с плеч** a load off one's mind; **ката́ться с ~ы́** to toboggan; **в ~у** uphill; **идти́ в ~у** to go uphill; (*fig.*) to go up in the world; **не за ~а́ми** (*fig.*) not far off; **по́д ~у** downhill (*also fig.*); **пир ~о́й** lavish, riotous feast; **наде́яться на кого́-н. как на ка́менную ~у** to place implicit faith in s.o.; **стоя́ть за кого́-н. ~о́й** to be solidly behind s.o. **2** (*fig.*) (*множество*) heap, pile, mass.
гора́зд (~а, ~о) *pred. adj.* (+*inf. or* **на**+*a.*; *coll.*) good (at), clever (at); **он на всё г.** he's a Jack of all trades; **кто во что г.** each in his own way; **он г. вы́пить** he is no mean drinker.
гора́здо *adv.* (+*comp. adjs. and advs.*) much, far, by far; **г. лу́чше** far better.
горб, а́, о ~е́, на ~у́ *m.* hump; **свои́м ~о́м** by the sweat of one's brow; **испыта́ть на своём ~у́** to learn by bitter experience.
горба́т|ый (~, ~а) *adj.* humpbacked, hunchbacked; gibbous; **г. мост** humpback bridge; **г. нос** hooked nose; **~ого моги́ла испра́вит** (*prov.*) can the leopard change his spots?
горби́нк|а, и *f.*: **нос с ~ой** aquiline nose.
го́рб|ить, лю, ишь *impf.* (*of* ⇨**с~**) to arch, hunch; **г. спи́ну** to arch one's back.
го́рб|иться, люсь, ишься *impf.* (*of* ⇨**с~**) (*о человеке*) to stoop; (*о спине*) to become bent.
горбоно́с|ый (~, ~а) *adj.* hook-nosed.
горбу́н, а́ *m.* hunchback.
горбу́ш|а, и *f.* humpback salmon.
горбу́шк|а, и *f.* crust (*of loaf*).
горделивост|ь, и *f.* haughtiness, pride.
горде́ли́в|ый (~, ~а) *adj.* haughty, proud.
горде́ц, а́ *m.* arrogant man.
го́рдиев *adj.*: **г. у́зел** Gordian knot.
гор|ди́ться, жу́сь, ди́шься *impf.* **1** (+*i.*) to be proud (of), pride o.s. (on). **2** (*быть высокомерным*) to put on airs.
го́рдост|ь, и *f.* pride.
го́рд|ый (~, ~а́, ~о, ~ы́) *adj.* proud.
гордя́чк|а, и *f.* arrogant woman.
го́р|е, я *nt.* **1** (*печаль*) grief, sorrow, woe; **на своё г.** to one's sorrow. **2** (*беда*) misfortune, trouble; **г. в том, что...** the trouble is that .... **3** *as pred.* (+*d.*; *coll.*) woe (unto), woe betide.
го́ре-... *comb. form* sorry, woeful; apology for a ...; **г.-поэ́т** poetaster.
гор|сва́ть, ю́ю, ю́ешь *impf.* (**о**+*p.*) to grieve (for).
горе́лк|а, и *f.* burner; **г. Бу́нзена** Bunsen burner; **при́мусная г.** Primus (*propr.*) stove.
горе́л|ки, ок *no sg.* (*game of*) catch.
горе́л|ый *adj.* burnt; **па́хло ~ым** there was a smell of burning.
горелье́ф, а *m.* (*art*) high relief.
горемы́к|а, и *c.g.* (*coll.*) unlucky individual, poor devil.
горемы́ч|ный (~ен, ~на) *adj.* hapless, ill-starred.
горе́ни|е, я *nt.* burning, combustion; (*fig.*) enthusiasm.
го́рест|ный (~ен, ~на) *adj.* (*печальный*) sad; (*жалкий*) pitiful.
го́рест|ь, и *f.* **1** sorrow, grief. **2** (*pl.*) misfortunes, troubles.
гор|е́ть, ю́, и́шь *impf.* **1** (*о доме*) to burn, be on fire. **2** (*о дровах, свете*) to burn, be alight; **в ку́хне у них ~е́л свет** the lights were burning in their kitchen; **~и́т ли пе́чка?** is the stove alight?; **де́ло ~и́т** things are going like a house on fire. **3** (+*i.*; *fig.*) to burn (with); **г. жела́нием** (+*inf.*) to be itching (to), be impatient (to). **4** (*блестеть*) to glitter, shine. **5** (*гнить*) to rot.
го́р|ец, ца *m.* mountain-dweller, highlander.
го́реч|ь, и *f.* **1** (*вкус*) bitter taste. **2** (*что-то горькое*) something bitter. **3** (*горькое чувство*) bitterness.
горже́тк|а, и *f.* boa.
горизо́нт, а *m.* horizon (*also fig.*); skyline.
горизонта́л|ь, и *f.* **1** horizontal; **по ~и** across (*in crossword*). **2** (*geog.*) contour line.
горизонта́л|ьный (~ен, ~ьна) *adj.* horizontal.
гори́лл|а, ы *f.* gorilla.
гори́ст|ый (~, ~а) *adj.* mountainous, hilly.
горихво́стк|а, и *f.* redstart (*bird*).
горицве́т, а *m.* (*bot.*) lychnis; ragged robin.
го́рк|а, и *f.* **1** hill, hillock. **2** (*шкаф*) cabinet, stand. **3** (*aeron.*) steep climb. **4** (*для детей*) slide.
го́ркн|уть, ет *impf.* (*of* ⇨**про~**) to go rancid.
горла́н|ить, ю, ишь *impf.* (*coll.*) to bawl.
горла́ст|ый (~, ~а) *adj.* (*coll.*) noisy, loudmouthed.
го́рлиц|а, ы *f.* turtle-dove.
го́рл|о, а *nt.* **1** throat; **дыха́тельное г.** windpipe; **драть г.** to bawl; **во всё г.** at the top of one's voice; **по г.** up to one's eyes; **сыт по г.** full up; (*fig.*) fed up; **приста́вить нож к чьему́-н. ~у** to hold a knife to s.o.'s throat; **промочи́ть г.** (*coll.*) to wet one's whistle; **слова́ застря́ли у меня́ в ~е** the words stuck in my throat. **2** (*сосуда*) neck.
горлови́н|а, ы *f.* mouth, orifice; **г. вулка́на** crater.
горлово́й *adj. of* ⇨**го́рло;** throat; guttural.
го́рлыш|ко, ка, *g. pl.* **~ек** *nt. dim. of* ⇨**го́рло**
гормо́н, а *m.* hormone.
гормона́льный *adj.* hormone, hormonal.
горн[1], а *m.* (*печь*) furnace, forge.
горн[2], а *m.* (*mus.*) bugle.
горни́л|о, а *nt.* crucible.
горни́ст, а *m.* bugler.
го́рниц|а, ы *f.* (*obs.*) chamber.
го́рничн|ая, ой *f.* (*в гостинице*) chambermaid; (*в доме*) maid.
горнов|о́й *adj. of* ⇨**горн[1]**; *as n.* **г., ~о́го** *m.* furnace-worker.
горнозаво́дский *adj.* mining.
горнолы́жник, а *m.* alpine skier.
горнолы́жный *adj.*: **г. спорт** alpine skiing.
горнопромы́шленност|ь, и *f.* mining industry.
горнопромы́шленный *adj.* mining.
горнорабо́ч|ий, его *m.* miner.
горноста́евый *adj.* ermine.
горноста́|й, я *m.* **1** (*zool.*) ermine; stoat. **2** (*мех*) ermine.
го́рн|ый *adj.* **1** *adj. of* ⇨**гора́;**

mountain; (*гористый*) mountainous; **~ая боле́знь** altitude sickness; **~ые лы́жи** downhill skis; **~ая цепь** mountain range. **2** (*минеральный*) mineral; **~ая поро́да** rock; **г. хруста́ль** rock crystal. **3** (*относящийся к разработке недр*) mining; **~ое де́ло** mining. **4**: **~ое со́лнце** artificial sunlight.

горня́к, а́ *m.* (*coll.*) **1** (*рабочий*) miner. **2** (*инженер*) mining engineer. **3** (*студент*) mining student.

горня́|цкий *adj. of* ⇒**~к** 1

го́род, а, *pl.* **~а́** *m.* **1** town; city; **г.-побрати́м** twin city; **вы́ехать за́ г.** to go out of town; **жить за́ ~ом** to live out of town, in the suburbs; **ни к селу́, ни к ~у** (*coll.*) for no reason at all, inappropriate(ly). **2** (*в играх*) base; home.

гор|оди́ть, ожу́, о́ди́шь *impf.* to enclose, fence; **огоро́д г.** to make unnecessary fuss; **г. чепуху́, чушь** to talk nonsense.

городи́ш|ко, ка, *g. pl.* **~ек** *m.* small town.

городи́щ|е, а *nt.* **1** very large town. **2** (*archaeol.*) site of ancient settlement.

город|ки́, ко́в *pl.* (*sg.* **~о́к, ~ка́** *m.*) gorodki (*game similar to skittles*).

городов|о́й, о́го *m.* (*hist.*) policeman.

город|о́к, ка́ *m.* small town; **вое́нный г.** military post; **университе́тский г.** campus.

городск|о́й *adj.* urban; city; municipal; (*coll.*) *as n.* **г., ~о́го** *m.* city-dweller, town-dweller.

городьб|а́, ы *f.* fence, hedge.

горожа́н|ин, ина, *pl.* **~е, ~** *m.* city-dweller, town-dweller; townsman.

горожа́н|ка, ки *f. of* ⇒**~ин;** townswoman.

гороско́п, а *m.* horoscope.

горо́х, а (у) *no pl., m.* **1** pea. **2** (*collect.*) peas; **как о́б стену г.** (*coll.*) like being up against a brick wall.

горо́хов|ый *adj.* **1** pea. **2** (*цвет*) greenish-khaki; pea-green; **чу́чело ~ое** scarecrow; **шут г.** buffoon, laughing-stock.

горо́ш|ек, ка *m.* **1** *dim. of* ⇒**горо́х; души́стый г.** (*bot.*) sweet peas. **2** (*collect.*) polka dots; **пла́тье в г.** polka-dot dress.

горо́шин|а, ы *f.* a pea.

го́рский *adj. of* ⇒**го́рец;** mountain, highland.

горсове́т, а *m.* town, city soviet.

го́рсточк|а, и *f.* handful.

горст|ь, и, *g. pl.* **~е́й** *f.* **1** cupped hand; **держа́ть ру́ку ~ью** to cup one's hand. **2** (*горсточка*) handful (*also fig.*).

горта́нный *adj.* **1** (*anat.*) laryngeal. **2** (*ling.*) guttural.

горта́н|ь, и *f.* larynx.

горте́нзи|я, и *f.* hydrangea.

го́рче *comp. of* ⇒**го́рький**

горч|и́ть, и́т *impf.* (*impers.*) to have a bitter taste.

горчи́ц|а, ы *f.* mustard.

горчи́чник, а *m.* mustard-plaster.

горчи́чниц|а, ы *f.* mustard-pot.

горчи́чн|ый *adj. of* ⇒**горчи́ца; г. газ** mustard gas; **~ое зерно́** mustard seed.

го́рше *comp. of* ⇒**го́рький**

горше́чник, а *m.* potter.

горше́чный *adj.* pottery; **г. това́р** pottery, earthenware.

горш|о́к, ка́ *m.* pot; **ночно́й г.** chamber pot; (*ребёнка*) potty.

горшо́чн|ый *adj.*: **~ое расте́ние** pot plant.

го́рьк|ая, ой *f.* vodka; **пить ~ую** (*coll.*) to hit the bottle.

го́р|ький (~ек, ~ька́, ~ько) *adj.* **1** (*comp.* **~че**) bitter; **~ькое ма́сло** rancid butter. **2** (*comp.* **~ше, ~ший**) (*fig.*) bitter; hard; **~ькие слёзы** bitter tears; **~ьким о́пытом узна́ть** to learn by bitter experience. **3** (*coll.*) (*несчастный*) hapless, wretched. **4**: **г. пья́ница** (*coll.*) inveterate drunkard.

го́рько[1] *adv.* bitterly.

го́рько[2] *as pred.* **1**: **у меня́ г. во рту** I have a bitter taste in my mouth. **2** it is bitter; **мне г.** I am sorry, I am grieved.

горю́ч|ее, его *nt.* fuel.

горю́чест|ь, и *f.* combustibility; inflammability.

горю́ч|ий *adj.* **1** combustible, inflammable. **2** (*folk poet.*): **~ие слёзы** bitter tears.

горя́ч|ий (~, ~а́, ~о́) *adj.* **1** hot (*also fig.*); **по ~им следа́м** (*i*) (+*g.*) hot on the heels (of), (*ii*) (*fig.*) forthwith; **под ~ую ру́ку** in the heat of the moment. **2** (*любовь*) passionate; (*желание*) ardent, fervent. **3** (*человек*) hot-tempered; (*лошадь*) mettlesome; **~ая голова́** hothead. **4** (*спор*) heated; (*речь*) impassioned. **5** (*время*) busy, hectic. **6** (*tech.*) high-temperature; **~ая обрабо́тка** heat treatment.

горяч|и́ть, у́, и́шь *impf.* (*of* ⇒**раз~**) to excite, arouse.

горяч|и́ться, у́сь, и́шься *impf.* (*of* ⇒**раз~**) to get excited, become impassioned, get het up.

горя́чк|а, и *f. and c.g.* **1** *f.* (*лихорадка*) fever. **2** *f.* (*возбуждение*) feverish activity; (*спешка*) feverish haste; **поро́ть ~у** (*coll.*) to act impetuously, in the heat of the moment. **3** *c.g.* (*coll.*) hothead; firebrand.

горя́чност|ь, и *f.* (*увлечение*) zeal, fervour, enthusiasm; (*несдержанность*) impulsiveness.

горячо́[1] *adv.* hot.

горячо́[2] *as pred.* it is hot.

гос... *comb. form, abbr. of* ***госуда́рственный***

госде́п, а *m.* (*abbr.*) = ***госдепарта́мент***

госдепарта́мент, а *m.* (*US*) State Department.

Госду́м|а, ы *f.* State Duma (*lower house of the Russian parliament*).

Госналогслу́жб|а, ы *f.* Inland Revenue (*Br.*), Internal Revenue Service (*US*).

го́спелз *m. indecl.* gospel music.

госпитализа́ци|я, и *f.* hospitalization.

госпитализи́р|овать, ую *impf. and pf.* to hospitalize.

го́спитал|ь, я *m.* hospital (*esp. mil.*).

госпита́льный *adj. of* ⇒**го́спиталь**

Госпла́н, а *m.* (*abbr. of* ***Госуда́рственная пла́новая коми́ссия***) State Planning Commission (*in former USSR*).

госпо́д|ень, ня, не *adj.* (*eccl.*) the Lord's; **моли́тва ~ня** the Lord's Prayer.

Го́споди *int.* good heavens!; good Lord!; good gracious!

господ|и́н, и́на, *pl.* **~а́, ~, ~а́м** *m.* **1** (*хозяин*) master; **сам себе́ г.** one's own master. **2** (*мужчина*) gentleman. **3** (*при фамилии*) Mr; **~а́** (*при обращении*) (*i*) gentlemen, (*ii*) ladies and gentlemen; (*при фамилии*) (*i*) Messrs, (*ii*) Mr and Mrs.

госпо́дский *adj.* manorial; **г. дом** manor-house.

госпо́дств|о, а *nt.* **1** (*власть*) supremacy, dominion, mastery. **2** (*преобладание*) predominance.

госпо́дств|овать, ую *impf.* **1** (*обладать властью*) to hold sway, exercise dominion. **2** (*преобладать*) to predominate, prevail. **3** (**над**+*i.*) (*возвышаться*) to command, dominate; to tower (above).

госпо́дств|ующий *pres. part. act. of* ⇒**~овать** *and adj.* **1** (*властвующий*) ruling; **г. класс** ruling class. **2** (*преобладающий*) predominant, prevailing. **3** (*возвышающийся*) commanding.

Госпо́дь, Го́спода, *voc.* **Го́споди** *m.* God, the Lord; **Г. его́ зна́ет** (the) Lord knows!

госпож|а́, и́ *f.* **1** (*хозяйка*) mistress. **2** (*женщина*) lady. **3** (*при фамилии; замужняя*) Mrs, Ms; (*незамужняя*) Miss, Ms.

госсекрета́р|ь, я́ *m.* Secretary of State.

гостево́й *adj.* guest, guests'.

гостеприи́м|ный (~ен, ~на) *adj.* hospitable.

гостеприи́мств|о, а *nt.* hospitality.

гости́н|ая, ой *f.* **1** (*комната*) living-room, sitting-room. **2** (*комплект мебели*) living-room suite.

гости́н|ец, ца *m.* (*coll.*) present.

гости́ниц|а, ы *f.* hotel.

гости́н|ичный *adj. of* ⇒**~ица**

гости́ный *adj.*: **г. двор** arcade, bazaar.

гости́ть, гощу́, гости́шь *impf.* (**у**+*g.*) to stay (with), be on a visit (to).

гост|ь, я, *g. pl.* **~е́й** *m.* guest, visitor; **кома́нда ~е́й** (*sport*) visiting team; **пойти́ в ~и** (**к**+*d.*) to visit; **быть в гостя́х (у)** to be a guest (at, of), be visiting; **в гостя́х хорошо́, а до́ма лу́чше** there's no place like home.

го́ст|ья, ьи, *g. pl.* **~ий** *f. of* ⇒**~ь**

госуда́рственност|ь, и *f.* State system; statehood.

госуда́рственн|ый *adj.* State, public;

г. переворо́т coup d'état; **~ая изме́на** high treason; **~ая нало́говая слу́жба** Inland Revenue (*Br.*), Internal Revenue Service (*US*); **~ое пра́во** public law; **~ая слу́жба** public service; **г. слу́жащий** civil servant; **Г. сове́т** (*hist.*) State Council; **~ые экза́мены** final examinations (*in higher education institutions*).

госуда́рств|о, а *nt.* State.

госуда́рын|я, и *f.* sovereign; **Г.** (*as form of address*) Your Majesty.

госуда́р|ь, я *m.* sovereign; **Г.** (*as form of address*) Your Majesty, Sire.

гот, а *m.* (*hist.*) Goth.

го́тик|а, и *f.* (*archit.*) Gothic style.

готи́ческий *adj.* (*art*) Gothic; **г. шрифт** Gothic script.

гото́ва́л|ьня, ьни, *g. pl.* **~ен** *f.* set of drawing instruments.

гото́в|ить, лю, ишь *impf.* **1** to prepare, make ready; (*обучать*) to train. **2** (*стряпать*) to cook.

гото́в|иться, люсь, ишься *impf.* **1** (**к**+*d.* or +*inf.*) to get ready (for, to); to prepare o.s. (for), make preparations (for). **2** (*предстоять*) to be at hand, in the offing.

гото́вност|ь, и *f.* **1** readiness, preparedness; **в боево́й ~и** ready for action. **2** (*согласие*) readiness, willingness.

гото́во *as pred.*: **и г.** (*coll.*) and that's that.

гото́в|ый (~, ~а) *adj.* **1** (**к**+*d.*) ready (for), prepared (for); **г. к де́йствию** ready for action; **я не ~** I'm not ready. **2** (**на**+*a.* or +*inf.*) (*согласный*) ready (for, to), prepared (for, to); willing (to); **мы ~ы на всё** we are prepared for anything; **она́ не ~а идти́** she is not willing to go. **3** (+*inf.*) (*находящийся в состоянии близком к чему-н.*) on the point (of), on the verge (of), ready (to). **4** (*окончательно сделанный*) ready-made, finished; ready-to-wear; **~ое пла́тье** ready-made clothes; **~ые изде́лия** finished articles.

го́тский *adj.* Gothic.

гофриро́ванн|ый *p.p.p. of* ⇨**гофрирова́ть** *and adj.*: **~ое желе́зо** corrugated iron; **~ая ю́бка** pleated skirt.

гофрир|ова́ть, у́ю *impf. and pf.* **1** (*железо*) to corrugate. **2** (*ткань*) to goffer.

гр. (*abbr. of* ***граждани́н*** *or* ***гражда́нка***) citizen.

граб, а *m.* (*bot.*) hornbeam.

грабё́ж, а́ *m.* robbery (*also fig., coll.*); (*дома*) burglary.

граби́ловк|а, и *f.* (*coll.*) **1** (*место*) rip-off establishment, clip-joint. **2** (*грабёж*) extortion, rip-off.

граби́тел|ь, я *m.* robber; **у́личный г.** mugger.

граби́тельский *adj.* **1** (*война*) predatory. **2** (*цены*) extortionate, exorbitant.

граби́тельств|о, а *nt.* (*obs.*) robbery.

гра́б|ить, лю, ишь *impf.* (*of* ⇨**о~**) to rob, pillage; (*fig.*) to rob.

гра́бленый *adj.* stolen.

гра́б|ли, лей *or* **~ель** *no sg.* rake.

граве́р, а *m.* engraver.

граве́р|ный *adj. of* ⇨**~; ное иску́сство** engraving.

гра́ви|й, я *m.* gravel.

грави́йн|ый *adj. of* ⇨**гра́вий; ~ые карье́ры** gravel pits.

гравирова́льн|ый *adj.* engraving; **~ая игла́** etching needle.

гравир|ова́ть, у́ю, у́ешь *impf.* (*of* ⇨**вы́~**) to engrave.

гравиро́вк|а, и *f.* engraving.

гравиро́вщик, а *m.* engraver.

гравитацио́нный *adj.* gravitation(al).

гравита́ци|я, и *f.* (*phys.*) gravitation.

гравю́р|а, ы *f.* engraving, print; (*офорт*) etching; **г. на де́реве** woodcut; **г. на лино́леуме** linocut; **г. на ме́ди** copper-plate engraving.

град[1], **а** *m.* **1** hail. **2** (*fig.*) (*поток*) hail, shower, torrent.

град[2], **а** *m.* (*arch. or poet.*) (*город*) city, town.

града́ци|я, и *f.* gradation, scale.

градие́нт, а *m.* gradient.

гра́дин|а, ы *f.* (*coll.*) hailstone.

гради́р|ня, ни, *g. pl.* **~ен** *f.* (water-) cooling tower.

градово́й *adj. of* ⇨**град**[1]

гра́дом *adv.* thick and fast; **уда́ры посы́пались г.** blows rained down.

градострои́тел|ь, я *m.* town-planner.

градострои́тельный *adj.* town-planning.

градострои́тельств|о, а *nt.* town-planning.

градуи́р|овать, ую *impf. and pf.* to calibrate.

гра́дус, а *m.* **1** (*единица измерения*) degree; **у́гол в 40 ~ов** angle of 40 degrees; **сего́дня 20 ~ов тепла́, моро́за** it is twenty degrees above, below zero today. **2**: **под ~ом** (*coll.*) tipsy.

гра́дусник, а *m.* thermometer.

гра́дус|ный *adj. of* ⇨**~; ~ная се́тка** (*geog.*) grid.

граждани́н, а, *pl.* **гра́ждане, гра́ждан** *m.* citizen.

гражда́н|ка[1], **ки** *f. of* ⇨**~и́н**

гражда́нк|а[2], **и** *f.* (*coll.*) civilian life; civvy street; **на ~е** in civvy street.

гражда́нск|ий *adj.* **1** (*leg., etc.*) civil; citizen's; civic; **г. иск** civil suit; **г. ко́декс** civil code; **~ое пра́во** civil law. **2** (*нецерковный, светский*) civil, secular; **г. брак** civil marriage, **~ая панихи́да** civil funeral rite. **3** (*невоенный*) civilian; **~ое пла́тье** civilian clothes, civvies, mufti. **4** (*подобающий гражданину*) civic, befitting a citizen; **~ие доброде́тели** civic virtues. **5**: **~ая война́** civil war.

гражда́нственност|ь, и *f.* **1** (*гражданское устройство*) civilization; civil society. **2** (*сознание гражданских обязанностей*) civic spirit.

гражда́нств|о, а *nt.* **1** citizenship, nationality; **права́ ~а** civic rights; **получи́ть права́ ~а** to be granted civic rights; (*fig.*) to achieve general recognition. **2** (*collect.*; *obs.*) (*граждане*) citizenry.

грамза́пис|ь, и *f.* gramophone recording.

грамм, а *m.* gramme, gram.

грамма́тик|а, и *f.* **1** (*раздел языкознания*) grammar. **2** (*учебник*) grammar(-book).

граммати́ст, а *m.* grammarian.

граммати́ческий *adj.* grammatical.

граммофо́н, а *m.* gramophone.

граммофо́н|ный *adj. of* ⇨**~; ~ная пласти́нка** gramophone record.

гра́мот|а, ы *f.* **1** (*умение читать и писать*) reading and writing, ability to read and write. **2** (*документ*) official document; deed.

гра́мотност|ь, и *f.* **1** (*умение читать и писать*) literacy (*also fig.*). **2** (*отсутствие грамматических ошибок*) grammatical correctness. **3** (*умелость*) competence.

гра́мот|ный (~ен, ~на) *adj.* **1** (*умеющий читать и писать*) literate; able to read and write. **2** (*без ошибок*) grammatically correct. **3** (*умелый*) competent. **4**: **полити́чески г.** politically aware.

грампласти́нк|а, и *f.* gramophone record (*Br.*), phonograph record (*US*).

гран, а *m.* grain (*unit of weight*); **в э́том нет ни ~а и́стины** there is not a grain of truth in it.

грана́т[1], **а** *m.* **1** (*плод*) pomegranate. **2** (*дерево*) pomegranate tree.

грана́т[2], **а** *m.* (*min.*) garnet.

грана́т|а, ы *f.* (*mil.*) shell, grenade; **ручна́я г.** hand-grenade.

грана́т|ный *adj. of* ⇨**~а; г. ого́нь** shell-fire.

грана́товый[1] *adj.* pomegranate.

грана́т|овый[2] **1** *adj. of* ⇨**~**[2]. **2** rich red.

гранатомё́т, а *m.* (*mil.*) grenade launcher.

грандио́зност|ь, и *f.* grandeur; immensity.

грандио́з|ный (~ен, ~на) *adj.* grandiose; mighty; vast.

гране́ни|е, я *nt.* cutting (*of precious stones, glass*).

гранё́н|ый *adj.* **1** (*алмаз*) cut, faceted; **~ое стекло́** cut glass. **2** (*рюмка, графин*) cut-glass.

грани́льный *adj.* lapidary; diamond-cutting.

грани́л|ьня, ьни, *g. pl.* **~ен** *f.* lapidary workshop; **г. алма́зов** diamond-cutting shop.

грани́льщик, а *m.* lapidary; **г. алма́зов** diamond-cutter.

грани́т, а *m.* granite.

грани́тный *adj.* granite.

гран|и́ть, ю́, и́шь *impf.*, to cut, facet.

грани́ц|а, ы *f.* **1** frontier, border; **за ~ей** abroad; **е́хать за ~у** to go abroad. **2** (*fig.*) boundary, limit; **вы́йти из ~** to overstep the mark; **в ~ах прили́чия** within the bounds of decency.

грани́ч|ить, у, ишь *impf.* (c+*i.*) **1** to border (on). **2** (*fig.*) to border (on), verge (on); **э́то ~ит с изме́ной** it borders on treason.

гра́нк|а, и *f.* (*typ.*) galley-proof.

грант, а *m.* grant.

гранули́р|овать, ую *impf. and pf.* to granulate.

грануля́ци|я, и *f.* (*tech., astron., med.*) granulation.

гран|ь, и *f.* **1** border, verge, brink; **на ~и сумасше́ствия** on the verge of insanity; **«поли́тика на ~и войны́»** brinkmanship. **2** (*geom.*) face; (*алмаза*) facet; (*линейки*) edge.

граф, а *m.* count.

граф|а́, ы́ *f.* (*столбец*) column; (*раздел*) section.

гра́фик[1], а *m.* **1** (*диаграмма*) graph, chart. **2** (*расписание*) schedule; **пло́тный г.** packed *or* heavy schedule; **скользя́щий г. рабо́ты** flexible working hours; flexitime; **то́чно по ~у** according to schedule.

гра́фик[2], а *m.* (*художник*) graphic artist.

гра́фик|а, и *f.* **1** (*art*) graphic art; (*comput.*) graphics; **экра́нная г.** on-screen graphics. **2** (*начертание букв*) script.

графи́н, а *m.* carafe; (*с пробкой*) decanter.

графи́н|я, и *f.* countess.

графи́т, а *m.* **1** (*min.*) graphite, black-lead. **2** (*карандаша*) pencil-lead.

графи́т|ный *adj.* = **~овый**

графи́товый *adj.* graphite.

граф|и́ть, лю́, и́шь *impf.* (*of* ⇒**раз~**) to rule (*paper*).

графи́ческий *adj.* graphic; **г. паке́т** (*comput.*) graphics package.

графлёный *adj.* (vertically) ruled.

графо́лог, а *m.* graphologist.

графоло́ги|я, и *f.* graphology.

графома́н, а *m.* graphomaniac; (*fig.*) pulp-writer, hack.

графома́ни|я, и *f.* graphomania.

графопострои́тел|ь, я *m.* plotter (*instrument*).

графопрое́ктор, а *m.* overhead projector.

гра́фский *adj. of* ⇒**граф**

гра́фств|о, а *nt.* county.

грацио́з|ный (~ен, ~на) *adj.* graceful.

гра́ци|я, и *f.* **1** (*изящество*) gracefulness. **2**: **Г.** (*myth.*) Grace. **3** (*корсет*) corselette.

грач, а́ *m.* (*zool.*) rook.

гребёнк|а, и *f.* comb; **стричь под ~у** to crop close; **стричь всех под одну́ ~у** to treat all alike, reduce all to the same level.

гре́б|ень, ня *m.* **1** (*для расчёсывания волос*) comb. **2** (*tech.*) comb; (*text.*) hackle. **3** (*птицы*) comb, crest; **петуши́ный г.** cock's comb. **4** (*волны, горы*) crest. **5** (*archit.*) ridge-piece, roof-tree. **6** (*agric.*) ridge.

греб|е́ц, ца́ *m.* rower, oarsman.

гребеш|о́к[1], ка́ *m.* = **гре́бень**

гребеш|о́к[2], ка́ *m.* (*zool.*) scallop.

гре́бл|я, и *f.* rowing.

гребни́ст|ый (~, ~а) *adj.* (high-) crested.

гребн|о́й *adj.* **1** rowing; **г. спорт** rowing; **~а́я шлю́пка** rowing boat (*Br.*), rowboat (*US*). **2**: **г. вал** propeller shaft; **г. винт** propeller screw; **~о́е колесо́** paddle wheel.

греб|о́к, ка́ *m.* **1** (*при гребле, плавании*) stroke. **2** (*весло*) blade (*of a mill-wheel or paddle-wheel*).

грегориа́нский = **григориа́нский**

грёз|а, ы *f.* day-dream, reverie.

гре́|жу *see* ⇒**~зить**

гре́|зить, жу, зишь *impf.* to dream; **г. наяву́** to day-dream.

гре́|зиться, жусь, зишься *impf.* (*of* ⇒**при~**) (*also impers.*, +*d.*) to dream; **мне ~зилось, что. . .** I used to dream that . . ..

гре́йдер, а *m.* **1** (*машина*) grader. **2** (*coll.*) (*дорога*) earth road (*levelled but unmetalled*).

грейпфру́т, а *m.* grapefruit.

грек, а *m.* Greek.

гре́ко-ки́прский *adj.* Greek-Cypriot.

гре́лк|а, и *f.* hot-water bottle; **электри́ческая г.** electric blanket.

грем|е́ть, лю́, и́шь *impf.* (*pf.* **про~**) to thunder, roar; (*о колоколах*) to peal; (*посудой*) to clatter; (*ключами*) to jangle; (*fig.*) to resound, ring out; **и́мя его́ ~е́ло по всей Евро́пе** his name resounded throughout Europe.

грему́ч|ий *adj.* roaring; **~ая змея́** rattlesnake; **~ая ртуть** (*chem.*) fulminate of mercury.

грему́шк|а, и *f.* rattle.

гренаде́р, а *m.* grenadier.

гре́нк|а, и *f.* (*coll.*) = **грено́к**

Гренла́нди|я, и *f.* Greenland.

гренла́ндский *adj.* Greenland.

грен|о́к, ка́ *m.* (*cul.*) croûton.

гре|сти́, бу́, бёшь, *past* **~б, ~бла́** *impf.* **1** to row; (*веслом, руками*) to paddle. **2** (*граблями*) to rake; **г. лопа́той де́ньги** (*coll.*) to rake in the shekels.

греть, гре́ю, гре́ешь *impf.* **1** (*intrans.*) to give out warmth. **2** (*trans.*) to warm, heat (up); (*предохранять от холода*) to keep warm; **г. (себе́) ру́ки** to warm one's hands; (*fig., coll., pej.*) to be on to a good thing.

гре́|ться, юсь, ешься *impf.* **1** (*человек*) to warm o.s.; (*вода, обед*) to warm, heat (up). **2** *pass. of* ⇒**греть**

грех, а́ *m.* **1** (*relig. or fig.*) sin; **первоpо́дный г.** original sin; **приня́ть на себя́ г.** to take the blame upon o.s.; **пода́льше от ~а́** get out of harm's way; **как на г.** as ill-luck would have it. **2** *as pred.* (+*inf.*; *coll.*) it is a sin, it is sinful; **не г.** (+*inf.*) there is no harm (in); **не г. вы́пить рю́мочку-две** there is no harm in (drinking) a glass or two. **3**: **с ~о́м попола́м** (only) just; **мы с ~о́м попола́м расшифрова́ли твой по́черк** we just managed to decipher your handwriting.

грехо́в|ный (~ен, ~на) *adj.* sinful.

грехопаде́ни|е, я *nt.* (*bibl.*) the Fall.

Гре́ци|я, и *f.* Greece.

гре́цкий *adj.*: **г. оре́х** walnut.

гре́ч|а, и *f.* (*coll.*) buckwheat.

греча́нк|а, и *f. of* ⇒**грек**

гре́ческий *adj.* Greek.

гречи́х|а, и *f.* buckwheat.

гре́чк|а, и *f.* (*coll.*) buckwheat.

гре́чнев|ый *adj.* buckwheat; **~ая ка́ша** buckwheat porridge.

греш|и́ть, у́, и́шь *impf.* **1** (*pf.* **со~**) to sin. **2** (*pf.* **по~**) (**про́тив**+*g.*; *fig.*) to sin (against).

гре́шник, а *m.* sinner.

гре́шни|ца, цы *f. of* ⇒**~к**

гре́ш|ный (~ен, ~на́, ~но, ~ны́) *adj.* sinful; culpable; **~ным де́лом** (*parenth.*) much as I regret it, I am ashamed to say.

греш|о́к, ка́ *m.* peccadillo.

гриб, а́ *m.* fungus; mushroom; **съедо́бный г.** mushroom, edible fungus; **несъедо́бный г.** inedible fungus; toadstool.

грибко́вый *adj.* fungoid.

грибни́ц|а, ы *f.* **1** (*часть гриба*) mushroom spawn. **2** (*coll.*) (*похлёбка*) mushroom soup.

грибн|о́й *adj. of* ⇒**гриб;** mushroom; **г. дождь** sun shower; **~а́я похлёбка** mushroom soup.

гриб|о́к, ка́ *m.* **1** *dim. of* ⇒**гриб.** **2** (*biol.*) fungus, microorganism. **3** (*для штопки чулок*) mushroom. **4** (*постройка*) shelter.

гри́в|а, ы *f.* mane.

гри́венник, а *m.* (*coll.*) (*сумма*) ten kopecks; (*монета*) ten-kopeck piece.

гри́вн|а, ы *f.* **1** (*hist.*) (*денежная единица*) grivna. **2** (*obs.*) (*гривенник*) ten kopecks.

григориа́нск|ий *adj.* Gregorian; **г. календа́рь, ~ое летоисчисле́ние** Gregorian Calendar.

гри́зли *m. indecl.* grizzly (bear)

гри́л|ь, я *m.* grill (*Br.*), broiler (*US*).

гриль-ба́р, а *m.* grillroom.

грим, а *m.* (*theatr.*) make-up; grease-paint.

грима́с|а, ы *f.* grimace; **де́лать ~ы** to make *or* pull faces.

грима́снича|ть, ю *impf.* to grimace; to make *or* pull faces.

гримёр, а *m.* (*theatr.*) make-up artist.

гримёрн|ая, ой *f.* (*theatr.*) make-up (room).

гримир|ова́ть, у́ю *impf.* **1** (*theatr.*) (*pf.* **на~**) to make up. **2** (*pf.* **за~**) (+*i.*) to make up (to look like); (+*i. or* **под**+*a.*; *fig.*) to make to appear, make out (as); **г. Наполео́на геро́ем, под геро́я** to paint Napoleon as a hero.

гримир|ова́ться, у́юсь *impf.* (*of* ⇒**за~**) (*theatr.*) to make up (*intrans.*);

(+*i.* or **под**+*a.*; *fig.*) to make o.s. out; **г. патрио́том, под патрио́та** to make o.s. out a patriot.

гримиро́вк|а, и *f.* (*theatr.*) making-up.

грим-убо́рн|ая, ой *f.* (*theatr., etc.*) dressing-room.

Гри́нвич, а *m.* Greenwich; **вре́мя по ~у** Greenwich (Mean) Time (*abbr.* GMT).

грипп, а *m.* influenza.

гриппо́зный *adj.* influenzal; **г. больно́й** flu victim *or* sufferer.

гриф¹, а *m.* **1** (*myth.*) griffin. **2** (*zool.*) vulture.

гриф², а *m.* (*mus.*) finger-board.

гриф³, а *m.* (*штемпель*) seal, stamp.

гриф⁴, а *m.* (*sport*) grip (*in wrestling*).

гри́фел|ь, я *m.* slate-pencil; (*карандаша*) lead.

гри́фельн|ый *adj.* slate; **~ая доска́** slate.

грифо́н, а *m.* **1** (*myth., archit.*) griffin. **2** (*собака*) griffon.

гроб, а, о ~е, в ~у́ *pl.* **~ы́** *and* **~а́** *m.* **1** coffin. **2** (*fig.*) the grave; **вогна́ть в г.** to drive to the grave; **до ~а, по г. жи́зни** (*coll.*) until the end of one's days; **стоя́ть одно́й ного́й в ~у́** to have one foot in the grave.

гро́б|ить, лю, ишь *impf.* (*sl.*) to ruin, mess up.

гробни́ц|а, ы *f.* tomb.

гробов|о́й *adj.* **1** *adj. of* **⇒гроб; ~а́я доска́** (*fig.*) the grave; **ве́рный до ~о́й доски́** faithful unto death. **2** (*мрачный*) sepulchral, deathly; **г. го́лос** sepulchral voice; **~о́е молча́ние** deathly silence.

гробовщи́к, а́ *m.* coffin-maker; undertaker.

грог, а *m.* grog.

гроз|а́, ы́, *pl.* **~ы** *f.* **1** (thunder)storm. **2** (*fig.*) (+*g.*) threat (to).

грозд|ь, и, *pl.* **~и, ~е́й** *and* **~ья, ~ьев** *f.* cluster, bunch (*of fruit or flowers*)

гро|зи́ть, жу́, зи́шь *impf.* **1** (*pf.* **при~**) (+*d. and i. or* +*inf.*) (*предупреждать с угрозой*) to threaten; **он ~зи́л мне револьве́ром** he was threatening me with a revolver; **г. уби́ть кого́-н.** to threaten to kill s.o. **2** (*pf.* **по~**) (+*i.*) (*делать угрожающий жест*) to make threatening gestures; **г. кулако́м кому́-н.** to shake one's fist at s.o. **3** (*no pf.*) (*предстоять*) to threaten; **ему́ ~зи́т банкро́тство** he is threatened with bankruptcy.

гро|зи́ться, жу́сь, зи́шься *impf.* (*of* **⇒по~**) (*coll.*) to threaten.

гро́з|ный (~ен, ~на́, ~но) *adj.* **1** (*угрожающий*) menacing, threatening. **2** (*ужасный*) dread, terrible; formidable; **~ная опа́сность** terrible danger. **3** (*coll.*) (*суровый*) stern, severe.

гроз|ово́й *adj. of* **⇒~а́; ~ова́я ту́ча** storm-cloud, thundercloud.

гром, а, *pl.* **~ы, ~о́в** *m.* thunder (*also fig.*); **уда́р ~а** thunderclap; **г. среди́ я́сного не́ба** a bolt from the blue; **мета́ть ~ы и мо́лнии** (*fig.*) to rant and rave.

грома́д|а, ы *f.* mass, bulk, pile (+*g.*); (*множество*) a mass (of), heaps (of).

грома́дин|а, ы *f.* (*coll.*) huge thing.

грома́д|ный (~ен, ~на) *adj.* huge, vast, enormous, colossal.

громи́л|а, ы *m.* (*coll.*) **1** (*вор*) burglar. **2** (*погромщик*) thug.

гром|и́ть, лю́, и́шь *impf.* (*of* **⇒раз~**) **1** to destroy; (*mil.*) to smash, rout. **2** (*fig., coll.*) (*критиковать*) to criticize, denounce.

гро́м|кий (~ок, ~ка́, ~ко) *adj.* **1** loud. **2** (*известный*) famous; (*пресловутый*) notorious. **3** (*напыщенный*) fine-sounding; **~кие слова́** (*iron.*) big words.

гро́мко *adv.* loud(ly); (*вслух*) aloud.

громкоговори́тел|ь, я *m.* loud-speaker.

гро́мкост|ь, и *f.* (*звука*) loudness, volume.

громов|о́й *adj.* **1** *adj. of* **⇒гром; ~ы́е раска́ты** peals of thunder. **2** (*громкий*) thunderous, deafening; **~ы́е рукоплеска́ния** thunderous applause. **3** (*уничтожающий*) crushing, smashing.

громогла́с|ный (~ен, ~на) *adj.* **1** loud; loud-voiced. **2** (*открытый*) public, open.

громоз|ди́ть, жу́, ди́шь *impf.* (*of* **⇒на~**) to pile up, heap up.

громоз|ди́ться, жу́сь, ди́шься *impf.* **1** (*возвышаться*) to tower. **2** (*coll.*) (*влезать*) to clamber up.

громо́зд|кий (~ок, ~ка) *adj.* cumbersome, unwieldy.

громоотво́д, а *m.* lightning-conductor (*also fig.*).

громоподо́б|ный (~ен, ~на) *adj.* thunderous.

гро́м|че *comp. of* **⇒~кий** *and* **~ко**

громыха́|ть, ю *impf.* (*coll.*) to rumble.

гросс, а *m.* gross.

гро́ссбух, а *m.* ledger.

гроссме́йстер, а *m.* grand master (*at chess*).

грот¹, а *m.* (*пещера*) grotto.

грот², а *m.* (*naut.*) mainsail.

грот-... *comb. form* (*naut.*) main-.

гроте́ск, а *m.* (*art*) grotesque.

гроте́скный *adj.* grotesque.

гроте́сковый *adj.* grotesque; **г. шрифт** (*typ.*) sanserif.

гро́х|ать(ся), аю(сь) *impf. of* **⇒~нуть(ся)**

гро́хн|уть, у, ешь *pf.* (*coll.*) **1** (*произвести сильный шум*) to crash, bang. **2** (*trans.*) (*бросить, уронить с шумом*) to drop with a crash, bang down. **3** (*рассмеяться*) to roar with laughter.

гро́хн|уться, усь, ешься *pf.* (*coll.*) to fall with a crash.

гро́хот¹, а *m.* crash, din.

гро́хот², а *m.* (*tech., agric.*) riddle, screen, sifter.

грохота́нь|е, я *nt.* crashing; rumbling.

грох|ота́ть, очу́, о́чешь *impf.* **1** to crash; roll, rumble; roar. **2** (*coll.*) (*хохотать*) to roar with laughter.

грош, а́ *m.* **1** (*obs.*) half-kopeck piece. **2** *pl.* **~и́, ~е́й** (*fig., coll.*) penny, cent; **э́то ~а́ ме́дного, ло́маного не сто́ит** it's not worth a brass farthing (*Br.*), two cents (*US*); **купи́ть за ~и́** to buy for a song; **рабо́тать за ~и́** to work for peanuts.

грошо́вый *adj.* (*coll.*) **1** (*очень дешёвый*) dirt-cheap; (*fig.*) (*плохого качества*) cheap, shoddy. **2** (*мелочный*) insignificant, trifling.

грубе́|ть, ю, ешь *impf.* (*of* **⇒о~**) to grow coarse, rude.

груб|и́ть, лю́, и́шь *impf.* (*of* **⇒на~**) (+*d.*) to be rude (to).

грубия́н, а *m.* (*coll.*) boor.

грубия́н|ка, ки *f. of* **⇒~**

гру́бо *adv.* **1** (*неискусно*) crudely. **2** (*невежливо*) rudely. **3** (*приблизительно*) roughly; **г. говоря́** roughly speaking.

грубова́т|ый (~, ~а) *adj.* rather coarse, rude.

гру́бост|ь, и *f.* **1** (*невежливость*) rudeness. **2** (*замечание*) rude remark; **говори́ть ~и** to be rude.

грубошёрстный *adj.* (*of cloth, etc.*) coarse.

гру́б|ый (~, ~а́, ~о) *adj.* **1** (*без изящества*) coarse, rough; **~ое сукно́** coarse fabric; **г. го́лос** gruff voice. **2** (*работа*) crude, rude. **3** (*недопустимый*) gross, flagrant; **г. обма́н** gross deception. **4** (*человек*) rude; coarse, crude; **~ое сло́во** rude, coarse word. **5** (*приблизительный*) rough; **в ~ых черта́х** in rough outline.

гру́д|а, ы *f.* heap, pile.

груда́ст|ый (~, ~а) *adj* (*coll.*) broad-chested; (*женщина*) big-breasted, big-bosomed.

груди́н|а, ы *f.* (*anat.*) breastbone.

груди́нк|а, и *f.* (*говядина*) brisket; (*баранина*) breast (*of lamb, etc.*).

грудни́ц|а, ы *f.* (*med.*) mastitis

грудн|о́й *adj. of* **⇒грудь; ~а́я жа́ба** (*med.*) angina pectoris; **~а́я железа́** (*anat.*) mammary gland; **~а́я кле́тка** (*anat.*) thorax; **г. ребёнок** baby.

грудобрю́шн|ый *adj.*: **~ая прегра́да** (*anat.*) diaphragm.

груд|ь, и́, о ~и, в (на) ~и́, *pl.* **~и ~е́й** *f.* **1** (*anat.*) chest; **стоя́ть ~ью (за**+*a.*) to stand up (for), champion; **г. с ~ью, г. на́ г. би́ться** to fight hand to hand **2** (*женщины*) breast; bosom, bust; **корми́ть ~ью** to breast-feed; **отня́ть от ~и́** to wean. **3** (*у рубашки*) (shirt)-front.

гружёный *adj.* loaded, laden.

груз, а *m.* **1** (*тяжесть*) weight; (*кладь*) load, cargo, freight; **поле́зный г.** payload. **2** (*fig.*) weight, burden.

грузд|ь, я́, *pl.* **~и, ~е́й** *m.* milk-agaric (*mushroom*).

грузи́л|о, а *nt.* sinker.

грузи́н, а, *g. pl.* **г.** *m.* Georgian.

грузи́н|ка, ки *f. of* **⇒~**

грузи́нский *adj.* Georgian.

гру|зи́ть, жу́, ~зи́шь *impf.* **1** (*pf.* **за~** *and* **на~**) to load; to lade, freight; **г. су́дно** to lade a ship. **2** (*pf.* **по~**) (в, на + *a.*) to load; **г. това́р на су́дно** to put a cargo aboard a ship.

гру|зи́ться, жу́сь, ~́зишься *impf.* (*of* ⇨**по~**) (*о судне*) to load (*intrans.*), take on cargo; (*о людях*) to board.

Гру́зи|я, и *f.* Georgia (*Transcaucasia*).

грузн|уть, у, ешь *impf.* to go down, sink.

гру́з|ный (~ен, ~на́, ~но) *adj.* (*тяжёлый*) weighty; (*громоздкий*) bulky; unwieldy; (*толстый*) corpulent.

грузови́к, а́ *m.* lorry (*Br.*), truck.

грузов|о́й *adj.* goods, cargo, freight; **~о́е движе́ние** goods traffic; **~о́е су́дно** cargo boat, freighter.

грузооборо́т, а *m.* turnover of goods.

грузоотправи́тел|ь, я *m.* shipper; consignor of goods.

грузо(-)пассажи́рский *adj.*: **г. автомоби́ль** utility vehicle.

грузоподъёмност|ь, и *f.* payload capacity; freight-carrying capacity.

грузоподъёмный *adj.*: **г. кран** (*loading*) crane.

грузополуча́тел|ь, я *m.* consignee.

грузопото́к, а *m.* goods traffic.

грузотакси́ *nt. indecl.* 'taxi-lorry' (*truck operated for hire from taxi-station*).

гру́зчик, а *m.* loader; (*в порту*) docker (*Br.*), stevedore.

грум, а *m.* groom.

грунт, а *m.* **1** (*почва*) soil, earth; (*дно*) bottom; **пересади́ть в г.** to plant out. **2** (*слой краски*) priming, primer.

грунт|ова́ть, у́ю *impf.* (*of* ⇨**за~**) to prime.

грунто́вк|а, и *f.* undercoat (*of paint*).

грунтов|о́й *adj. of* ⇨**грунт; ~ы́е во́ды** subsoil waters; **~а́я доро́га** dirt road.

гру́пп|а, ы *f.* (*in var. senses*) group; **г. кро́ви** (*med.*) blood group; **дошко́льная г.** playgroup; **операти́вная г.** task force.

группе́тто *nt. indecl.* (*mus.*) turn.

группир|ова́ть, у́ю *impf.* (*of* ⇨**с~**) to group; (*классифицировать*) to classify.

группир|ова́ться, у́ется *impf.* (*of* ⇨**с~**) to group, form groups.

группиро́вк|а, и *f.* **1** grouping; (*классификация*) classification; **г. сил** (*mil.*) distribution of forces. **2** (*совокупность лиц*) group, grouping.

группово́д, а *m.* group leader.

группов|о́й *adj.* group; **~ы́е заня́тия** group study, group work; **~ы́е и́гры** team games; **г. полёт** formation flying.

грусти́нк|а, и *f.* (*coll.*) slight sadness.

гру|сти́ть, щу́, сти́шь *impf.* to grieve, mourn; (**по** + *d.*) to pine (for).

гру́стно¹ *adv.* sadly, sorrowfully.

гру́стно² *as pred.* it is sad; **ей г.** she feels sad; **нам г. узна́ть, что. . .** we are sorry to hear that . . . .

гру́ст|ный (~ен, ~на́, ~но) *adj.* sad, melancholy.

груст|ь, и *f.* sadness, melancholy.

гру́ш|а, и *f.* **1** (*плод*) pear. **2** (*дерево*) pear-tree. **3**: **земляна́я г.** Jerusalem artichoke. **4**: **боксёрская г.** punchball.

гру́шевый *adj.* pear; **г. компо́т** stewed pears.

гры́ж|а, и *f.* (*med.*) hernia, rupture.

грыжево́й *and* **гры́жевый** *adj.* hernial; **г. банда́ж** truss.

гры́зл|о, а *nt.* bit (*of bridle*).

грызн|я́, и́ *f.* (*coll.*) **1** (*между животными*) fight. **2** (*ссора*) squabble.

грыз|ть, у́, ёшь, *past* **~, ~́ла** *impf.* **1** to gnaw; to nibble; **г. но́гти** to bite one's nails. **2** (*coll.*) (*бранить*) to nag (at). **3** (*fig.*) (*мучить*) to devour, consume; **нас ~́ло любопы́тство** we were consumed with curiosity.

гры́з|ться, у́сь, ёшься, *past* **~ся, ~лась** *impf.* **1** (*о животных*) to fight. **2** (*coll.*) (*ссориться*) to squabble, bicker.

грызу́н, а́ *m.* rodent.

гряд|а́, ы́, *pl.* **~́ы, ~, ~а́м** *f.* **1** (*гор*) ridge. **2** (*в огороде*) bed. **3** (*ряд*) row, series.

гря́дк|а, и *f. dim. of* ⇨**гряда́**

гряду́щ|ий *pres. part. act. of* ⇨**гря́сти́** *and adj.* coming, future; **~ие дни** days to come; **на сон г.** (*coll.*) at bedtime; *as n.* **~ее, ~его** *nt.* the future.

грязев|о́й *adj.* mud; **~а́я ва́нна** mud-bath.

грязелече́бниц|а, ы *f.* therapeutic mud-baths.

грязелече́ни|е, я *nt.* mud-cure.

грязне́|ть, ю *impf.* to get covered in mud, become dirty.

грязн|и́ть, ю́, и́шь *impf.* (*of* ⇨**на~**) **1** (*делать грязным*) to make dirty, soil; (*fig.*) to sully, besmirch. **2** (*мусорить*) to litter.

грязн|и́ться, ю́сь, и́шься *impf.* to become dirty.

гря́зн|о¹ *adv. of* ⇨**~ый**

гря́зно² *as pred.* it is dirty.

грязну́л|я, и *c.g.* (*coll.*) (*о ребёнке*) guttersnipe; (*о женщине*) slut.

гря́з|ный (~ен, ~на́, ~но) *adj.* **1** (*покрытый грязью*) muddy. **2** (*нечистый*) dirty; **~ное бельё** dirty washing (*also fig.*). **3** (*неопрятный*) untidy; slovenly; **~ная тетра́дь** untidy copy-book. **4** (*fig.*) (*непристойный*) dirty, filthy; **~ное де́ло** dirty business. **5** (*серовато-мутный*) mud-grey. **6** (*для мусора*) refuse, garbage; **~ное ведро́** refuse-pail, garbage-pail.

гряз|ь, и, о ~́и, в ~́и́ *f.* **1** mud (*also fig.*); **меси́ть г.** (*coll.*) to wade through mud; **заброса́ть ~́ью, смеша́ть с ~́ью; втопта́ть, затопта́ть в г.** (*fig.*) to sling mud (at). **2** (*pl.*) (*лечебное средство*) mud; mud-baths; mud-cure. **3** (*нечистота*) dirt, filth (*also fig.*).

гря́н|уть, у, ешь *pf.* **1** (*раздаться; начаться*) to burst out, crash out; **~ул гром** there was a clap of thunder; **~ул вы́стрел** a shot rang out. **2** (*запеть, заиграть*) to strike up (*a song, etc.*).

гря́н|уться, усь, ешься *pf.* to crash.

гря|сти́, ду́, дёшь (*impf.*) to approach.

гуа́шь, и *f.* (*art*) gouache.

губ|а́¹, ы́, *pl.* **~́ы, ~а́м** *f.* **1** lip; **наду́ть ~́ы** to pout; **по ~а́м кому́-н. пома́зать** (*coll.*) to raise false hopes in s.o.; **у него́ гу́ба не ду́ра** (*coll.*) he knows which side his bread is buttered; **молоко́ на ~а́х не обсо́хло** he is still green. **2** (*pl.*) (*концы клещей*) pincers.

губ|а́², ы́, *pl.* **~ы, ~а́м** *f.* bay, inlet (*in northern Russia*).

губ|а́³, ы́, *pl.* **~́ы, ~а́м** *f.* (*mil. sl.*) guardhouse.

губа́ст|ый (~, ~а) *adj.* (*coll.*) thick-lipped.

губерна́тор, а *m.* governor.

губерна́торск|ий *adj.* of a governor; (*joc.*) **положе́ние ху́же ~ого** a critical situation, a tight spot.

губерна́торств|о, а *nt.* governorship.

губе́рни|я, и *f.* (*hist.*) guberniya, province.

губи́тел|ь, я *m.* destroyer.

губи́тел|ьный (~ен, ~ьна) *adj.* (*последствия*) disastrous; (*мысль, климат*) harmful, destructive; (*влияние*) pernicious.

губ|и́ть, лю́, ~́ишь *impf.* (*of* ⇨**по~**) (*разрушать*) to destroy; (*портить*) to ruin, spoil.

гу́б|ка¹, ки *f. dim. of* ⇨**губа́¹**

гу́бк|а², и *f.* sponge; **мыть ~ой** to sponge.

губн|о́й *adj.* **1** lip; **~а́я пома́да** lipstick. **2** (*ling.*) labial.

гу́бчатый *adj.* porous, spongy; **г. каучу́к** foam rubber.

гуверна́нтк|а, и *f.* governess.

гувернёр, а *m.* tutor.

гугено́т, а *m.* (*hist.*) Huguenot.

гугни́в|ый (~, ~а) *adj.* (*coll.*) speaking through the nose.

гугу́ *only in phr.* **ни г.!** not a word!; **об э́том ни г.!** mum's the word!

гуд, а *m.* (*coll.*) buzzing; drone; hum.

гуде́ни|е, я *nt.* drone; hum; (*об автомобильном гудке*) honk.

гу|де́ть, жу́, ди́шь *impf.* **1** to drone; to hum; (*impers.*): **у меня́ ~де́ло в уша́х** there was a buzzing in my ears. **2** (*о гудке*) to hoot; to honk. **3** (*coll.*) (*болеть*) to ache. **4** (*sl.*) (*пить*) to drink, booze (*sl.*).

гуд|о́к, ка́ *m.* **1** (*устройство*) (*автомобиля*) horn; (*фабрики*) siren. **2** (*звук*) hoot(ing); honk; toot; **по ~ку́** when the whistle blows. **3** (*teleph.*) tone.

гудро́н, а *m.* tar.

гудрони́р|овать, ую *impf. and pf.* to tar; to tarmac.

гудро́н|ный *adj. of* ⇨**~; ~ное шоссе́** tarred, tarmacked highroad.

гуж, а́ *m.* tug (*part of harness*); **взя́лся за г., не говори́, что не дюж** (*prov.*) in for a penny in for a pound.

гужев|о́й *adj.* **1** *adj. of* ⇨**гуж. 2** cart; **~а́я доро́га** cart-track; **г. тра́нспорт** cartage, animal-drawn transport.

гу́зн|о, а *nt.* (*vulg.*) arse (*Br.*), ass (*US*), bum (*Br.*).

гул, а *m.* (*машин, голосов*) drone, hum; (*выстрелов*) rumble.

ГУЛА́Г *m. indecl.* (*abbr. of* ***Гла́вное управле́ние исправи́тельно-трудовы́х лагере́й***) GULAG, Main

Administration for Corrective Labour Camps.

гу́л|кий (~ок, ~ка́, ~ко) *adj.* **1** (*с резонансом*) resonant; echoing. **2** (*громкий*) booming, rumbling.

гулли́в|ый (~, ~а) *adj.* (*coll.*) gadabout.

гульб|а́, ы́ *f.* (*coll.*) idling; revelry.

гу́льден, а *m.* guilder (*Dutch unit of currency*).

гуля́к|а, и *c.g.* (*coll.*) idler; playboy.

гуля́нк|а, и *f.* (*coll.*) **1** (*празднество*) outdoor party. **2** (*пирушка*) feast.

гуля́н|ье, ья, *g. pl.* **~ий** *nt.* **1** (*прогулка*) walking; (going for a) walk. **2** (*празднество*) outdoor party.

гуля́|ть, ю *impf.* (*of* ⇒**по~**) **1** to walk, stroll; to take a walk, go for a walk; **г. по рука́м** to pass from hand to hand. **2** (*impf. only*) (*coll.*) (*иметь выходной день*) not to be working; **мы сего́дня ~ем** we have got the day off today. **3** (*coll.*) (*веселиться*) to make merry, have a good time. **4** (**с** + *i.*; *coll.*) (*быть в любовных отношениях*) to go out (with).

гуля́ш, а *m.* (*cul.*) goulash.

гуля́щ|ий *adj.* (*coll.*) idle; *as n.* **~ая, ~ей** *f.* streetwalker.

ГУМ, а *or* **гум, а** *m.* (*abbr. of* ***госуда́рственный универса́льный магази́н***) GUM, State Department Store.

гумани́зм, а *m.* humanism.

гумани́ст, а *m.* humanist.

гуманисти́ческий *adj.* humanist.

гуманита́рн|ый *adj.* **1** pertaining to the humanities; **~ые нау́ки** the humanities, the liberal arts; **~ое образова́ние** liberal education. **2** (*гуманный*) humane; **~ая по́мощь** humanitarian aid.

гума́нност|ь, и *f.* humanity, humaneness.

гума́н|ный (~ен, ~на) *adj.* humane.

гум|но́, на́, *pl.* **~на, ~ен** *and* **~ён, ~нам** *nt.* **1** (*ток*) threshing-floor. **2** (*сарай*) barn.

гу́мус, а *m.* (*agric.*) humus.

гунн, а *m.* (*hist.*) Hun.

гу́рк(х)а *m. indecl.* Gurkha.

гу́рк(х)ский *adj.* Gurkha.

гурма́н, а *m.* gourmet.

гурма́нств|о, а *nt.* connoisseurship (*of food and drink*).

гурт, а́ *m.* herd, drove; flock.

гуртовщи́к, а́ *m.* herdsman; drover.

гурто́м *adv.* (*coll.*) **1** (*оптом*) wholesale; in bulk. **2** (*гурьбой*) together; in a body, en masse.

гу́ру *m. indecl.* guru.

гурьб|а́, ы́ *f.* crowd, gang.

гуса́к, а́ *m.* gander.

гуса́р, а *m.* hussar.

гуса́рский *adj.* hussar.

гу́сениц|а, ы *f.* **1** (*zool.*) caterpillar. **2** (*трактора*) (caterpillar) track.

гу́сеничн|ый *adj.* (*zool.*, *tech.*) caterpillar; **~ая ле́нта** (*tech.*) caterpillar track; **г. тра́ктор** caterpillar tractor; **г. ход** caterpillar drive.

гус|ёнок, ёнка, *pl.* **~я́та** *m.* gosling.

гуси́н|ый *adj.* goose; **~ая ко́жа** goose-flesh; **~ые ла́пки** crow's feet.

гу́сл|и, ей *no sg.* (*mus.*) psaltery, gusli.

густе́|ть, ет *impf.* (*of* ⇒**по~**) (*о тумане, лесе*) to thicken, get thicker, get denser; (*о жидком*) (*pf.* **за~**) to thicken.

гу|сти́ть, щу́, сти́шь *impf.* to thicken (*trans.*).

гу́сто[1] *adv.* thickly, densely.

гу́сто[2] *as pred.* (*coll.*) there is much, there is plenty; **у меня́ де́нег не г.** I'm a bit hard up, a bit pushed.

густоволо́с|ый (~, ~а) *adj.* thick-haired, shaggy.

густ|о́й (~, ~а́, ~о) *adj.* **1** thick, dense; **~а́я листва́** thick foliage; **г. тума́н** dense fog; **~о́е населе́ние** dense population; **~ы́е бро́ви** bushy eyebrows. **2** (*о голосе, цвете*) deep, rich.

густоли́ственный *adj.* with thick foliage, leafy.

густонаселённый *adj.* densely populated.

густот|а́, ы́ *f.* **1** thickness, density. **2** (*голоса, цвета*) deepness, richness.

гусы́н|я, и *f.* (*female*) goose.

гус|ь, я, *pl.* **~и, ~ей** *m.* goose; **как с ~я вода́** like water off a duck's back; **хоро́ш гусь!** (*iron.*) a fine fellow indeed!

гусько́м *adv.* in (single) file, in crocodile.

гуся́тин|а, ы *f.* goose(-meat).

гуся́тник, а *m.* goose-pen.

гуся́тниц|а, ы *f.* casserole dish.

гутали́н, а *m.* shoe-polish.

гуто́р|ить, ю, ишь *impf.* (*dial.*) to natter.

гуттапе́рч|а, и *f.* gutta percha.

гуттапе́рч|евый *adj. of* ⇒**~а**

гу́щ|а, и *f.* **1** (*осадок*) dregs, lees, grounds, sediment; **кофе́йная г.** coffee grounds. **2** (*чаща*) thicket; (*fig.*) thick, centre, heart; **в са́мой ~е собы́тий** in the thick of things.

гу́ще *comp. of* ⇒**густо́й, гу́сто**

гущин|а́, ы́ *f.* (*coll.*) **1** (*густота*) thickness. **2** (*чаща*) thicket.

Гц (*abbr. of* ***герц***) Hz (hertz).

гэ́льский *adj.* Gaelic.

ГЭС *f. indecl.* (*abbr. of* ***гидроэлектроста́нция***) hydro-electric power-station.

Г

Дд

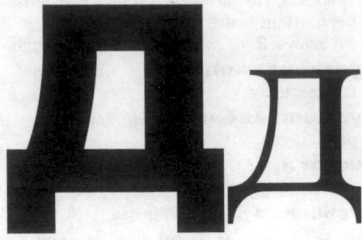

д. (*abbr. of* **дом**) house.

да[1] *particle* **1** yes. **2** (*interrog.*) yes?, is that so?, really?, indeed?; **он мно́го лет прожива́л в Пари́же. — Да? а я и не знал** he lived in Paris for many years. Really? I didn't know. **3** (*emph.*) why; well; **да не мо́жет быть!** why, that's impossible!; **д. нет!** of course not!; not likely!; **да в чём де́ло?** well, what's it all about? **4** *emph. pred.*: **когда́-н. да ко́нчится** it must end some time; **э́то что́-н. да зна́чит** there's sth. behind this. **5**: **(вот) э́то да!** (*coll.*) splendid!; super!

да[2] *particle* (+*3rd pers. pres. or fut. of v.*) (*пусть*) may, let; **да здра́вствует..!** long live . . .!

да[3] *conj.* **1** (*mainly in conventional phrr.*) (*и*) and; **день да ночь** day and night; **ко́жа да ко́сти** skin and bone.
2: **да (и** *or* **ещё)** and (besides); and what is more; **бы́ло за́ полночь, да и снег шёл** it was past midnight and (what is more) it was snowing; **принеси́те мне во́дки, да поскоре́е!** bring me some vodka, and (be) quick about it!; **он занима́лся, занима́лся, да и провали́лся на экза́мене** he studied and studied and then he (went and) failed his exam.
3: **да и то́лько** and that's all, and no more; **она́ ворчи́т, да и то́лько** she does nothing but grouse.
4 but; **я охо́тно проводи́л бы тебя́, да вре́мени не́ту** I would gladly come with you but I haven't the time.

дабы́ *conj.* in order (to, that).

дава́й(те) *as particle* **1** (+*inf. or 1st pers. pl. of fut.*) let's; **дава́йте приостано́вимся мину́точку-две** let's pause for a minute or two; **дава́йте заку́рим** let's light up. **2** (+*imper.*; *coll.*) come on; **дава́й, расскажи́ что-н.** come on, tell us a story.

да|ва́ть, ю, ёшь *impf. of* ⇒**дать**

да|ва́ться, ю́сь, ёшься *impf.* (*of* ⇒**~ться**) **1** *pass. of* ⇒**дава́ть.**
2 (*позволять поймать себя*) to let o.s. be caught; **не д.** (+*d.*) to dodge, evade.
3: **легко́ д.** to come easily, naturally; **ру́сский язы́к ему́ легко́ даётся** Russian comes easily to him.

да́веча *adv.* (*coll.*) lately, recently.

да́вешний *adj.* (*coll.*) recent; late.

дави́льный *adj.*: **д. пресс** winepress.

дави́л|ьня, ьни, *g. pl.* **~ен** *f.* winepress.

дав|и́ть, лю́, ~ишь *impf.* **1** (*also* **на**+*a.*) to press (upon); (*о сапоге*) to pinch; (*fig.*) (*угнетать*) to oppress, weigh (upon), lie heavy (on); (*impers.*): **се́рдце ~ит** (my) heart is heavy. **2** (*насекомых*) to crush; to trample; (*о машине*) to run over. **3** (*выжимать*) to squeeze (*juice out of fruit, etc.*).

дав|и́ться, лю́сь ~ишься *impf.* (*of* ⇒**по~**) **1** (+*i. or* **от**+*g.*) to choke (with); **д. от ка́шля** to choke with coughing. **2** (*coll.*) (*в автобусе*) to be squashed, crushed.

да́вка, и *f.* (*coll.*) throng, crush.

давле́ни|е, я *nt.* pressure (*also fig.*); **под ~ем** (+*g.*) under pressure (of); through stress (of).

да́вленый *adj.* pressed, crushed.

давне́нько *adv.* (*coll.*) quite a long time ago; for quite a long time.

да́вн|ий *adj.* **1** ancient; **в ~ие времена́** in ancient times.
2 (*существующий издавна*) of long standing; **с ~их пор, времён** of old, for a long time.

давни́шний *adj.* (*coll.*) = **да́вний**

давно́ *adv.* **1** (*много времени тому назад*) long ago; **он д. у́мер** he died long ago; **д. бы так** (*expr. approval of s.o.'s action*) not before (it was) time. **2** (*в течение долгого времени*) for a long time; long since; **мы д. живём в дере́вне** we have been living in the country for a long time.

давнопроше́дш|ий *adj.* remote (*in time*); **~ее вре́мя** (*gram.*) pluperfect tense.

да́вност|ь, и *f.* **1** (*древность*) antiquity; (*отдалённость*) remoteness. **2** (*длительное существование*) long standing. **3** (*leg.*) prescription.

давны́м-давно́ *adv.* (*coll.*) very long ago, ages (and ages) ago.

дагероти́п, а *m.* daguerreotype.

Дагеста́н, а *m.* Dagestan.

дагеста́н|ец, ца *m.* Dagestani.

дагеста́н|ка, ки *f. of* ⇒**~ец**

дагеста́нский *adj.* Dagestani.

да́же *particle* even; **е́сли д.** even if; **о́чень д. пло́хо** extremely bad.

да́йджест, а *m.* (*journ.*) digest.

дактили́ческий *adj.* (*liter.*) dactylic.

дактилоло́ги|я, и *f.* finger-speech.

дактилоскопи́|я, и *f.* dactyloscopy, identification by means of fingerprints; **ге́нная д.** genetic fingerprinting.

да́ктил|ь, я *m.* (*liter.*) dactyl.

дакти́льн|ый *adj.*: **~ая а́збука** sign language.

дала́й-ла́м|а, ы *m.* Dalai Lama.

да́лее *adv.* further; **не д., как вчера́, он был здесь** he was here only yesterday; **и так д.** (*abbr.* **и т. д.**) and so on, etcetera.

далёк|ий (~, ~а́, ~о́ *or* **~о)** *adj.* **1** (*in var. senses*) (*страна, выстрел*) distant; **д. путь** long journey; **~ое про́шлое** distant past; **д. от и́стины** wide of the mark; **я ~ от того́, что́бы жела́ть** I am far from wishing. **2** (*only with neg.*; *coll.*) (*умный*) clever, bright; **она́ не о́чень ~а́** she is not awfully bright.

далеко́ *and* **далёко**[1] *adv.* **1** (*о расстоянии*) far, far off; (**от**+*g.*) far (from); **д. зайти́** (*fig.*) to go too far, burn one's boats; **д. пойти́** (*fig.*) to go far (= *to be a success*). **2** (*fig.*) far, by a long way, by much; **д. за** (*of time*) long after; **д. не** far from; **она́ д. не краса́вица** she is far from beautiful.

далеко́ *and* **далёко**[2] *as pred.* it is far, it is a long way; (+*d.* **до**+*g. fig.*) to be far (from), be much inferior (to); **ему́ д. до соверше́нства** he is far from perfect.

далма́тский *adj.*: **д. дог** Dalmatian.

дал|ь, и, о ~и, в ~и́ *f.* **1** (*далёкое пространство*) distance; distant prospect. **2** (*coll.*) (*далёкое место*) distant spot. **3**: **така́я д.!** (*coll.*) it is so far, such a long way!

дальневосто́чный *adj.* Far Eastern.

дальне́йш|ий *adj.* further, furthest; **в ~ем** (*i*) (*в будущем*) in future, henceforth, (*ii*) (*ниже в тексте*) below, hereinafter.

да́льн|ий *adj.* **1** (*далёкий*) distant, remote; **Д. Восто́к** the Far East (*of former USSR*); **~ее пла́вание** long voyage; **~его де́йствия** long-range; **~его сле́дования** (*of a train*) long-distance. **2** (*о родстве*) distant. **3**: **без ~их слов** without more ado.

дальнобо́йност|ь, и *f.* (*mil.*) long range.

дальнобо́йный *adj.* (*mil.*) long-range.

дальнобо́йщик, а *m.* (*coll.*) long-distance lorry (*Br.*), truck driver.

дальнови́дност|ь, и *f.* foresight.

дальнови́д|ный (~ен, ~на) *adj.* far-sighted.

дальнозо́р|кий (~ок, ~ка) *adj.* long-sighted (*Br.*), far-sighted (*US*); (*fig.*) far-sighted.

дальнозо́ркост|ь, и *f.* long sight (*Br.*), far-sightedness (*US*); (*fig.*) far-sightedness.

дальноме́р, а *m.* range-finder.

да́льност|ь, и *f.* distance; range.

дальтони́зм, а *m.* colour-blindness (*Br.*), color-blindness (*US*), Daltonism.

дальто́ник, а *m.* colour-blind (*Br.*), color-blind (*US*) person.

да́льше *adj. and adv.* **1** *comp. of* **⇒далёкий. 2** (*adv.*) further; **ти́ше е́дешь, д. бу́дешь** (*prov.*) more haste, less speed; **д. не́куда** (*coll.*) that's the limit. **3** (*adv.*) (*продолжая начатое*) further; **расска́зывать д.** to go on (telling a story); **д.!** go on! **4** (*adv.*) (*затем*) then, next; **они́ не зна́ли, что д. де́лать** they did not know what to do next. **5** (*adv.*) (*долее*) longer; **ждать д. нельзя́ бы́ло** it was impossible to wait any longer.

да́м|а, ы *f.* **1** (*женщина*) lady. **2** (*в танцах*) partner. **3** (*игральная карта*) queen.

Дама́ск, а *m.* Damascus.

дама́ск, а *m.* damask.

да́мб|а, ы *f.* dike.

да́мк|а, и *f.* king (*at draughts* (*Br.*), *checkers* (*US*)).

дамо́клов *see* **⇒меч**

да́м|ский *adj. of* **⇒~а; ~ская су́мка** ladies' handbag; **д. кавале́р, д. уго́дник** ladies' man.

Дании́л, а *m.* (*bibl.*) Daniel.

Да́ни|я, и *f.* Denmark.

да́нн|ые, ых *no sg.* **1** (*also comput.*) data; (*факты*) facts, information; **необрабо́танные д.** raw data. **2** (*свойства*) qualities, gifts, potentialities. **3** (*основания*) grounds.

да́нн|ый *p.p.p. of* **⇒дать** *and adj.* given; present; in question; **в д. моме́нт** at the present moment, at present; **в ~ом слу́чае** in this case, in the case in question.

данти́ст, а *m.* dentist.

дан|ь, и *f.* **1** (*hist.*) tribute; **обложи́ть ~ью** to lay under tribute. **2** (*fig.*) (*моде, традиции*) tribute; debt; **отда́ть д.** (+*d.*) to pay tribute to, recognize.

дар, а, *pl.* **~ы́** *m.* **1** (*подарок*) gift, donation; **посме́ртный д.** bequest. **2** (+*g.*) (*способность*) gift (of); **д. ре́чи** (*i*) (*способность говорить свободно*) the gift of the gab, (*ii*) (*способность говорить*) speech, ability to speak.

дарвини́зм, а *m.* Darwinism.

дарвини́ст, а *m.* Darwinist.

Дардане́лл|ы, ~ *no sg.* the Dardanelles.

дарён|ый *adj.* received as a present; **~ому коню́ в зу́бы не смо́трят** (*prov.*) one should not look a gift horse in the mouth.

дари́тел|ь, я *m.* donor.

дар|и́ть, ю, ~ишь *impf.* (*of* **⇒по~**) **1** (+*d. and a.*) (*давать*) to give; **он ~и́л мне де́ньги** he gave me some money. **2** (+*a. and i.*) (*удостаивать*) to favour (with), bestow (upon); **д. кого́-н. улы́бкой** to bestow a smile upon s.o.

дармовщи́нк|а, и *f.*: **на ~у** (*coll.*) for nothing, for free.

дармое́д, а *m.* (*coll.*) parasite, sponger, scrounger.

дармое́днича|ть, ю *impf.* (*coll.*) to sponge, scrounge.

дармое́дств|о, а *nt.* (*coll.*) parasitism, sponging, scrounging.

дарова́ни|е, я *nt.* gift, talent.

дар|ова́ть, у́ю *impf. and pf.* to grant, confer.

дарови́т|ый (~, ~а) *adj.* gifted, talented.

дарово́й *adj.* free (of charge), gratuitous.

даровщи́нк|а, и *f.*: **на ~у** (*coll.*) for nothing, for free.

да́ром *adv.* **1** (*бесплатно*) free (of charge), gratis; **э́то вам д. не пройдёт** you'll pay for this. **2** (*напрасно*) in vain, to no purpose; **пропа́сть д.** to be wasted.

даронóсиц|а, ы *f.* (*eccl.*) pyx.

дарохрани́тельниц|а, ы *f.* (*eccl.*) tabernacle.

да́рственн|ый *adj.* **1** (*obs.*) (*подаренный*) received as a present. **2** (*удостоверяющий дар*) confirming a gift; **~ая на́дпись** dedicatory inscription; **~ая за́пись** (*leg.*) settlement, deed.

да́т|а, ы *f.* date.

да́тельный *adj.* (*gram.*) dative.

дати́р|овать, ую *impf. and pf.* to date (= (*i*) *affix a date to*, (*ii*) *establish the date of*).

датиро́вк|а, и *f.* dating.

да́тский *adj.* Danish.

датча́н|ин, ина, *pl.* **~е, ~** *m.* Dane.

датча́н|ка, ки *f. of* **⇒~ин**

да́тчик, а *m.* sensor.

дать, дам, дашь, даст, дади́м, дади́те, даду́т, *past* **дал, дала́, да́ло, да́ли** *pf.* (*of* **⇒дава́ть**) **1** to give; **д. взаймы́** to lend (*money*); **д. на во́дку, на чай** to tip; **д. конце́рт** to give a concert; **д. обе́д** to give a dinner; **д. уро́ки** to give lessons. **2** to give, administer; **д. лека́рство** to give medicine; **д. кому́-н. пощёчину** (*coll.*) to box s.o.'s ears. **3** (**по**+*d.*, **в**+*a.*; *coll.*) (*ударить*) to give (it); to hit; **д. кому́-н. по́ уху** to clip s.o. round the ear; **я те дам!** (*coll.*; *expr. vague threat*) I'll give you what-for!; I'll teach you! **4** (*fig.*) to give; **д. кля́тву** to take an oath; **д. нача́ло** (+*d.*) to give rise (to); **д. сло́во** to pledge one's word; **д. себе́ труд** (+*inf.*) to put o.s. to the trouble (of). **5** (*fig.*) to give, grant; **д. во́лю** (+*d.*) to give (free) rein (to), give vent (to); **д. газ** (*coll.*) to open the throttle; **д. доро́гу** (+*d.*) to make way (for); **не д. поко́я** (+*d.*) to give no peace; **д. кому́-н. сло́во** to give s.o. the floor (*at a meeting*); **д. ход** (+*d.*) to set in motion, get going; **д. ход кому́-н.** (*coll.*) to help s.o. on, give s.o. a leg-up. **6** *with certain nn. expr. action related to meaning of n.*; **д. залп** to fire a volley; **д. звоно́к** to ring (*a bell*); **д. отбо́й** to ring off (*on telephone*); **д. отпо́р** (+*d.*) to repulse; **д. течь** to spring a leak; **д. тре́щину** to crack. **7** (+*inf.*) (*позволить*) to let; **д. поня́ть** to give to understand; **д. себя́ знать, д. себя́ почу́вствовать** to make o.s. (itself) felt; **да́йте ему́ говори́ть** let him speak. **8**: **дай** + *1st pers. of fut. expr. decision to take some action*: **дай вы́купаюсь** I think I'll take a bath. **9**: **ни д. ни взять** (*i*) exactly the same, neither more nor less, (*ii*) as like as two peas.

да́ться, да́мся, да́шься *etc., past* **да́лся, дала́сь** *pf.* **1** *pf. of* **⇒дава́ться. 2** (+*d.*) (*стать предметом крайнего интереса*) to have become an obsession (with).

дацзыба́о *nt. indecl.* wall posters (*in China*).

да́ч|а[1]**, и** *f.* **1** (*действие*) giving. **2** (*порция*) helping, portion.

да́ч|а[2]**, и** *f.* **1** (*загородный дом*) dacha; **д.-(авто)прице́п** mobile home. **2**: **быть на ~е** to be in the country; **пое́хать на ~у** to go to the country.

да́ч|а[3]**, и** *f.* (*участок земли*) (piece of) woodland.

дачевладе́л|ец, ьца *m.* owner of a dacha.

дачевладе́л|ица, ицы *f. of* **⇒~ец**

да́чник, а *m.* (holiday) visitor (*in the country*).

да́ч|ный *adj. of* **⇒~а**[2]; **д. о́тдых** country holiday; **д. по́езд** suburban train.

дашна́к, а *m.* (*hist.*) Dashnak (*member of Armenian nationalist movement*).

ДВ *pl. indecl.* (*abbr. of* **дли́нные во́лны**) LW (*long wave*).

два (*f.* две), двух, двум, двумя́, о двух *num.* two; **два-три, две-три** two or three, a couple; **ни д. ни полтора́** (*coll.*) neither one thing nor another; **в двух слова́х** briefly, in short; **в д. счёта** in no time, in two ticks; **в двух шага́х** a short step away; **ка́ждые д. дня** every other day, on alternate days.

двадцати... *comb. form* twenty-.

двадцатиле́ти|е, я *nt.* **1** (*срок*) period of twenty years. **2** (*годовщина*) twentieth anniversary.

двадцатиле́тний *adj.* **1** (*срок*)

Д

twenty-year, of twenty years. **2** (*человек*) twenty-year-old.

двадцатипятиле́ти|е, я *nt.* **1** (*срок*) period of twenty-five years. **2** (*годовщина*) twenty-fifth anniversary.

двадца́т|ый *adj.* twentieth; **одна́ ~ая** a twentieth; **~ое января́** the twentieth of January; **~ые го́ды** the twenties.

два́дцат|ь, и́, *i.* **ью** *num.* twenty; **д. оди́н**, *etc.*, twenty-one, *etc.*; **д. одно́** (*card-game*) vingt-et-un.

два́дцатью *adv.* twenty times.

два́жды *adv.* twice; **д. два — четы́ре** twice two is four; **я́сно как д. два четы́ре** (*coll.*) as plain as a pikestaff.

двенадцатипе́рстн|ый *adj.*: **~ая кишка́** (*anat.*) duodenum.

двена́дцатый *adj.* twelfth.

двена́дцат|ь, и *num.* twelve.

двер|но́й *adj. of* ⇨**~ь; д. проём** doorway; **~на́я ру́чка** door-handle.

две́р|ца, ы, *g. pl.* **~ец** *f.* door (*of car, cupboard, etc.*).

двер|ь, и, о ~и, в ~и́, *pl.* **~и, ~е́й,** *i.* **~я́ми** *and* **~ьми́** *f.* door; **в ~я́х** in the doorway; **у ~е́й** close at hand; **при закры́тых ~я́х** behind closed doors, in camera.

две́сти, двухсо́т, двумста́м, двумяста́ми, о двухста́х *num.* two hundred.

дви́гател|ь, я *m.* motor, engine; (*fig.*) mover, motive force.

дви́гательн|ый *adj.* **1** motive; **~ая си́ла** moving force, impetus. **2** (*anat.*) motor; **боле́знь ~ых нейро́нов** motor neuron disease.

дви́га|ть, ю *and* **дви́жу** *impf.* (*of* ⇨**дви́нуть**) **1 (~ю)** to move. **2 (~ю)** (+*i.*) (*шевелить*) to move (*part of the body*); to make a movement (of). **3 (дви́жу)** (*приводить в движение*) to set in motion, get going (*also fig.*); **д. вперёд** (*fig.*) to advance, further.

дви́га|ться, юсь *and* **дви́жусь** *impf.* (*of* ⇨**дви́нуться**) **1** to move (*intrans.*); **д. вперёд** to advance (*also fig.*). **2** (*отправляться*) to start, get going. **3** *pass. of* ⇨**~ть**

движе́ни|е, я *nt.* **1** (*in var. senses*) movement; motion; **д. вперёд** forward movement, advance; **привести́ в д.** to set in motion; **д. сторо́нников ми́ра** peace movement; **д. «зелёных»** the green movement. **2** (*физическое*) movement, exercise. **3** (*дорожное*) traffic; **д. в одно́м направле́нии** one-way traffic; **пра́вила у́личного ~я** traffic regulations. **4**: **д. по слу́жбе** promotion, advancement. **5** (*внутреннее побуждение*) impulse.

дви́жимост|ь, и *f.* movables, chattels; personal property.

дви́жим|ый *adj.* movable; **~ое иму́щество** movable, personal property.

движко́в|ый *adj.* slide; **~ые регуля́торы** slide controls.

движ|о́к, ка́ *m.* **1** (*tech.*) slide, runner. **2** (*coll.*) (*двигатель*) (small) engine, motor.

дви́жущ|ий *pres. part. act. of* ⇨**дви́гать** *and adj.*: **~ие си́лы** driving force.

дви́|нуть, ну, нешь *pf.* **1** *pf. of* ⇨**~гать. 2** (*coll.*) (*ударить*) to hit, cosh.

дви́|нуться, нусь, нешься *pf. of* ⇨**~гаться**

дво́е, двои́х *num.* **1** (+*m. nn. denoting persons, pers. prons. in pl. or nn. used only in pl.*) two; **д. сынове́й** two sons; **нас бы́ло д.** there were two of us; **д. сане́й** two sledges; **д. су́ток** forty-eight hours. **2** (+*nn. denoting objects usu. found in pairs*) two pairs; **д. глаз** two pairs of eyes; **д. чуло́к** two pairs of stockings; **на свои́х (на) двои́х** on Shanks's pony.

двоебо́рь|е, я *nt.* (*sport*) biathlon.

двоебра́чи|е, я *nt.* bigamy.

двоевла́сти|е, я *nt.* diarchy.

двоеже́н|ец, ца *m.* bigamist (*of a man*).

двоежёнств|о, а *nt.* bigamy (*of man*).

двоему́жи|е, я *nt.* bigamy (*of woman*).

двоему́жниц|а, ы *f.* bigamist (*of a woman*).

двоето́чи|е, я *nt.* (*gram.*) colon.

дво́ечник, а *m.* (*coll.*) low-achiever (*pupil receiving an 'unsatisfactory' mark*).

дво́ечни|ца, цы *f. of* ⇨**~к**

дво|и́ться, ю́сь, и́шься *impf.* **1** (*разделяться надвое*) to divide in two (*intrans.*). **2** (*казаться двойным*) to appear double; **у него́ ~и́лось в глаза́х** he saw (objects) double.

двои́чн|ый *adj.* (*math.*) binary; **~ая ци́фра** binary digit, bit.

дво́йк|а, и *f.* **1** (*цифра*) two. **2** (*coll.*) (*автобус, трамвай*) No. 2 (*bus, tram, etc.*). **3** (*отметка*) 'two' (*out of five, acc. to marking system used in Russian educational establishments*). **4** (*игральная карта*) two; **д. треф** two of clubs.

двойни́к, а́ *m.* **1** (*кого-н.*) double. **2** (*coll.*) (*близнец*) twin. **3** (*elec.*) two-way adaptor.

двойн|о́й *adj.* double, twofold, binary; **д. подборо́док** double chin; **~а́я бухгалте́рия** double-entry book-keeping; **~а́я фами́лия** double-barrelled (*Br.*), double-barreled (*US*) surname.

дво́|йня, йни, *g. pl.* **~ен** *f.* twins.

двойня́шк|а, и *f.* (*coll.*) twin.

дво́йственност|ь, и *f.* **1** (*противоречивость*) ambivalence, duality. **2** (*двуличность*) duplicity.

дво́йствен|ный (~, ~на) *adj.* **1** (*чувство, мнение*) ambivalent; (*функция, роль*) dual; **~ное число́** (*gram.*) dual number. **2** (*двуличный*) two-faced. **3** (*касающийся двух, двоих*) bipartite.

двор, а́ *m.* **1** (*при одном доме*) yard; (*между домами*) courtyard. **2** (*крестьянское хозяйство*) homestead. **3**: **ско́тный д.** farmyard; **пти́чий д.** poultry-yard. **4**: **на ~е́** out of doors, outside; **по ~а́м, ко ~а́м** (*obs.*) to one's home, home(wards); **со ~а́** (*obs.*) from home. **5** (*королевский*) court; **при ~е́** at court. **6**: **быть ко ~у́** to be (found) suitable; **быть не ко ~у́** not to be wanted.

двор|е́ц, ца́ *m.* palace; **Д. бракосочета́ний** Wedding Palace.

дворе́цк|ий, ого *m.* butler, major-domo.

дво́рник, а *m.* **1** (*работник*) caretaker. **2** (*coll.*) (*в машине*) windscreen-wiper (*Br.*), windshield wiper (*US*).

дво́рницк|ий *adj. of* ⇨**дво́рник 1;** *as n.* **~ая, ~ой** *f.* caretaker's lodge.

дво́рничих|а, и *f.* (*coll.*) **1** (*жена дворника*) wife of caretaker. **2** (*женщина-дворник*) yardwoman.

дво́рн|я, и *f.* (*collect.*) servants, menials (*before 1861*).

дворня́г|а, и *f.* (*coll.*) mongrel (dog).

дворня́жк|а, и *f.* = **дворня́га**

дворо́в|ый *adj. of* ⇨**двор 1, 2; ~ые постро́йки** outbuildings, farm buildings; **~ая соба́ка** watch-dog.

дворцо́вый *adj. of* ⇨**дворе́ц; д. переворо́т** palace revolution.

дворян|и́н, и́на, *pl.* **~е, ~** *m.* nobleman.

дворя́н|ка, ки *f. of* ⇨**дворяни́н**

дворя́нск|ий *adj.* of the nobility; of the gentry; **~ое зва́ние** the rank of gentleman.

дворя́нств|о, а *nt.* (*collect.*) nobility, gentry.

двою́родный *adj.* related through grandparent; **д. брат** (first) cousin (*male*); **д. дя́дя** (first) cousin once removed.

двоя́кий *adj.* double, two-fold.

двоя́ко *adv.* in two ways.

двояково́гнутый *adj.* (*phys.*) concavo-concave.

двояковы́пуклый *adj.* (*phys.*) convexo-convex.

дву..., двух... *comb. form* bi-, di-, two-, double-.

двубо́ртный *adj.* double-breasted.

двувидово́й *adj.* (*gram.*) biaspectual.

двугла́в|ый *adj.* two-headed; **~ая мы́шца** (*anat.*) biceps; **д. орёл** double-headed eagle.

двугла́сн|ый, ого *m.* (*gram.*) diphthong.

двуго́рбый *adj.* two-humped; **д. верблю́д** Bactrian camel.

двугра́нный *adj.* two-sided; dihedral.

двугри́венн|ый, ого *m.* (*coll.*) twenty-kopeck piece.

двудо́льный *adj.* **1** two-part. **2** (*bot.*) dicotyledonous.

двужи́льный *adj.* **1** (*coll.*) (*сильный*) strong; hardy, tough. **2** (*tech.*) twin-core.

двузна́чный *adj.* **1** (*число*) two-digit. **2** (*слово, выражение*) ambiguous.

двуко́лк|а, и *f.* two-wheeled cart.

двукра́тный *adj.* twofold, double; (*повторный*) reiterated.

двули́к|ий (~, ~а) *adj.* two-faced (*also fig.*).

двули́чи|е, я *nt.* double-dealing, duplicity.

двули́чност|ь, и *f.* duplicity.

двули́ч|ный (~ен, ~на) *adj.* (*fig.*) two-faced; hypocritical.
двуно́гий *adj.* two-legged, biped.
двуо́кис|ь, и *f.* (*chem.*) dioxide; **д. углеро́да** carbon dioxide.
двупла́нный *adj.* two-dimensional.
двупо́лый *adj.* bisexual.
двуро́г|ий *adj.* two-horned; **~ая луна́** crescent moon.
двуру́чный *adj.* two-handed; two-handled.
двуру́шник, а *m.* double-dealer.
двуру́шнича|ть, ю *impf.* to play a double game.
двуру́шничеств|о, а *nt.* double dealing.
двусве́тный *adj.* with two tiers of windows.
двуска́тн|ый *adj.* with two sloping surfaces; **~ая кры́ша** gable roof.
двусло́жный *adj.* disyllabic.
двусме́нный *adj.* in two shifts, two-shift.
двусмы́сленност|ь, и *f.* **1** (*свойство*) ambiguity. **2** (*выражение*) double entendre.
двусмы́слен|ный (~, ~на) *adj.* ambiguous.
двуспа́льный *adj.* double (*of beds*).
двуство́лк|а, и *f.* double-barrelled gun (*Br.*), double-barreled gun (*US*).
двуство́льный *adj.* double-barrelled (*Br.*), double-barreled (*US*).
двуство́рчат|ый *adj.* bivalve; **~ые две́ри** folding doors.
двусти́ши|е, я *nt.* (*liter.*) distich, couplet.
двусто́пный *adj.* (*liter.*) of two feet (*verse*).
двусторо́н|ний (~ен, ~ня) *adj.* **1** double-sided; **~нее воспале́ние лёгких** double pneumonia; **ку́ртка ~ней но́ски** reversible jacket. **2** (*движение*) two-way. **3** (*соглашение*) bilateral.
двутавро́в|ый *adj.*: **~ая ба́лка** I-beam.
двууглеки́сл|ый *adj.* (*chem.*) bicarbonate; **д. на́трий, ~ая со́да** sodium bicarbonate.
двуутро́бк|а, и *f.* (*zool.*) marsupial.
двухгоди́чный *adj.* of two years' duration.
двухгодова́лый *adj.* two-year-old.
двухдне́вный *adj.* two-day.
двухколе́йный *adj.* (*rail.*) double-track.
двухколёсный *adj.* two-wheeled.
двухкра́сочный *adj.* two-tone.
двухле́тний *adj.* **1** (*срок*) of two years' duration. **2** (*ребёнок*) two-year-old. **3** (*bot.*) biennial.
двухле́тник, а *m.* (*bot.*) biennial.
двухма́чтовый *adj.* two-masted.
двухме́стн|ый *adj.* two-seater; **~ая каю́та** two-berth cabin; **д. но́мер** double room.
двухме́сячный *adj.* **1** (*срок*) of two months' duration. **2** (*ребёнок*) two-month-old. **3** (*издание*) bimonthly.
двухмото́рный *adj.* twin-engined.
двухнеде́льник, а *m.* (*coll.*) fortnightly (*magazine, etc.*).
двухнеде́льный *adj.* **1** (*срок*) of two weeks' duration. **2** (*ребёнок*) two-week-old. **3** (*издание*) fortnightly.
двухпала́тный *adj.* (*pol.*) bicameral, two-chamber.
двухпа́лубный *adj.* (*naut.*) having two decks.
двухпарти́йный *adj.* (*pol.*) two party; bipartisan.
двухпласти́ночный *adj.*: **д. альбо́м** double (*record*) album.
двухсотле́ти|е, я *nt.* bicentenary.
двухсотле́тний *adj.* **1** (*срок*) of two hundred years' duration. **2** (*годовщина*) bicentenary (*Br.*), bicentennial (*US*).
двухсо́тый *adj.* two-hundredth.
двухстепе́нн|ый *adj.*: **~ые вы́боры** indirect elections.
двухсу́точный *adj.* forty-eight-hour.
двухта́ктный *adj.* (*tech.*) two-stroke.
двухто́мник, а *m.* (*coll.*) two-volume book, work.
двухты́сячный *adj.* **1** two-thousandth. **2** (*ценою в две тысячи*) costing two thousand roubles.
двухцве́тный *adj.* two-coloured (*Br.*), two-colored (*US*).
двухчасово́й *adj.* **1** (*фильм*) two-hour. **2** (*coll.*) (*поезд*) two o'clock.
двухъя́русный *adj.* two-tier(ed).
двухэта́жный *adj.* two-storey (*Br.*), two-story (*US*); (*автобус*) double-decker.
двучле́н, а *m.* (*math.*) binomial.
двучле́нный *adj.* (*math.*) binomial.
двуязы́чи|е, я *nt.* bilingualism.
двуязы́ч|ный (~ен, ~на) *adj.* bilingual.
ДДТ *m. indecl.* (*abbr. of* ***дихлордифенилтрихлорэта́н***) DDT.
-де (*coll.*) *enclitic particle indicating attribution of utterance to another speaker*; **они́-де не мо́гут прийти́** (they say) they can't come.
дебарка́дер, а *m.* landing-stage.
дебати́р|овать, ую *impf.* to debate.
деба́т|ы, ов *no sg.* debate.
дебе́л|ый (~, ~а) *adj.* (*coll.*) plump, corpulent.
де́бет, а *m.* debit.
дебет|ова́ть, у́ю *impf. and pf.* to debit.
деби́л, а *m.* moron.
деби́т, а *m.* (*tech.*) yield, output (*of oil, etc.*).
дебито́р, а *m.* debtor.
деблоки́р|овать, ую *impf. and pf.* (*mil.*) to relieve, raise the blockade (of).
дебо́ш, а *m.* (*coll.*) uproar, shindy.
дебоши́р, а *m.* (*coll.*) rowdy, brawler, hell-raiser.
дебоши́р|ить, ю, ишь *impf.* (*coll.*) to kick up a row, create a shindy.
дебоши́рств|о, а *nt.* (*coll.*) rowdyism, hell-raising.
де́бр|и, ей *no sg.* **1** jungle; thickets. **2** (*глухое место*) the wilds. **3** (*fig.*) maze, labyrinth; **запу́таться в ~ях** (+*g.*) to get bogged down in.
дебю́т, а *m.* **1** début. **2** (*chess*) opening.
дебюта́нт, а *m.* débutant.
дебюта́нтк|а, и *f.* débutante.
дебюти́р|овать, ую *impf. and pf.* to make one's début.
дебю́т|ный *adj. of* ⇒**~**; **д. спекта́кль** (*theatr.*) début, first performance; **д. ход** (*chess*) opening move.
де́в|а, ы *f.* **1** (*obs.*) girl, maiden; unmarried girl; **ста́рая д.** (*coll.*) old maid. **2 Д.** (*relig.*) the Virgin. **3 Д.** (*созвездие*) Virgo.
девальва́ци|я, и *f.* devaluation.
девальви́р|овать, ую *impf. and pf.* to devalue.
дева́|ть, ю 1 *impf. of* ⇒**деть. 2** (*in past tense* = **деть**) to put, do (with); **куда́ ты ~л письмо́?** what have you done with the letter?
дева́|ться, юсь 1 *impf. of* ⇒**де́ться; она́ не зна́ла, куда́ д. от смуще́ния** she did not know where to put herself for embarrassment. **2** (*in past tense* = **де́ться**) (*исчезать*) to get to, disappear; **куда́ ~лись мои́ часы́?** where has my watch got to?
де́вер|ь, я, *pl.* **~ья́, ~е́й** *and* **~ьёв** (*coll.*) brother-in-law (*husband's brother*).
девиа́ци|я, и *f.* (*tech.*) deviation.
деви́з, а *m.* motto; (*в геральдике*) device.
деви́ц|а, ы *f.* (*obs.*) maiden; damsel.
деви́ческий = **де́ви́чий**
деви́честв|о, а *nt.* girlhood; maidenhood; **в ~е Ивано́ва** née Ivanova.
де́ви́ч|ий *adj.* girlish; maidenly; **~ья фами́лия** maiden name; **~ья па́мять** (*joc.*) a memory like a sieve.
де́вк|а, и *f.* **1** (*coll. and dial.*) (*девушка*) girl, wench, lass; **засиде́ться в ~ах** to remain on the shelf; **оста́ться в ~ах** to become an old maid. **2** (*coll.*) (*проститутка*) tart, whore.
Девома́тер|ь, и *f.* (*relig.*) the Virgin Mother.
дево́н, а *m.* (*geol.*) Devonian period.
дево́нский *adj.* (*geol.*) Devonian.
де́вочк|а, и *f.* (little) girl.
де́вственник, а *m.* virgin.
де́вственниц|а, ы *f.* virgin.
де́вственност|ь, и *f.* virginity; chastity; **обе́т ~и** vow of chastity.
де́вствен|ный (~, ~на) *adj.* **1** (*целомудренный*) virgin; **~ная плева́** (*anat.*) hymen. **2** (*невинный*) virginal; innocent. **3** (*fig.*) virgin; **д. лес** virgin forest.
де́вушк|а, и *f.* **1** (unmarried) girl. **2** (*coll.*) (*обращение*) miss.
девча́т|а, ~ *no sg.* (*coll.*) girls.
девчо́нк|а, и *f.* (*coll.*) girl.
девчу́рк|а, и *f.* (*coll.*) little girl.
девчу́шк|а, и *f.* (*coll.*) little girl.
девяно́ст|о *g., d., i. and p.* **а** *num.* ninety.
девяно́стый *adj.* ninetieth.
девятерно́й *adj.* ninefold.

Д

де́вятер|о, ы́х *num.* **1** nine; нас д. there are nine of us. **2** (*пары*) nine pairs.

девятикра́тный *adj.* ninefold.

девятиле́тний *adj.* **1** (*срок*) nine-year; of nine years' duration. **2** (*ребёнок*) nine-year-old.

девятиме́сячный *adj.* **1** (*срок*) nine-month. **2** (*ребёнок*) nine-month-old.

девятисо́тый *adj.* nine-hundredth.

девя́тк|а, и *f.* **1** (*цифра*) nine. **2** (*coll.*) (*автобус, трамвай*) No. 9 (*bus, tram, etc.*). **3** (*coll.*) (*группа из девяти единиц*) group of nine objects. **4** (*игральная карта*) nine.

девятна́дцатый *adj.* nineteenth.

девятна́дцат|ь, и *num.* nineteen.

девя́тый *adj.* ninth.

де́вят|ь, и́, *i.* **ью́** *num.* nine.

девятьсо́т, девятисо́т, девятиста́м, девятьюста́ми, о девятиста́х *num.* nine hundred.

де́вятью *adv.* nine times; **д. два — восемна́дцать** nine times two is eighteen.

дегаза́тор, а *m.* decontaminator.

дегазацио́нн|ый *adj. of* ⇨**дегаза́ция; ~ая часть** decontamination unit.

дегаза́ци|я, и *f.* decontamination.

дегази́р|овать, ую *impf. and pf.* to decontaminate.

дегенера́т, а *m.* degenerate.

дегенерати́вност|ь, и *f.* degeneracy.

дегенерати́в|ный (~ен, ~на) *adj.* degenerate.

дегенера́ци|я, и *f.* degeneration.

дегенери́р|овать, ую *impf. and pf.* to degenerate.

дёг|оть, тя *no pl., m.* tar; **ло́жка ~тя в бо́чке мёда** a fly in the ointment.

деграда́ци|я, и *f.* degradation.

деградиро|вать, ую *impf. and pf.* to become degraded.

дегтя́рн|ый *adj.* tar; **~ое мы́ло** coal-tar soap.

дегуманиза́ци|я, и *f.* dehumanization.

дегуманизи́р|овать, ую *impf. and pf.* to dehumanize.

дегуста́тор, а *m.* taster.

дегуста́ци|я, и *f.* tasting; **д. вин** wine-tasting.

дегусти́р|овать, ую *impf. and pf.* to carry out a tasting (of).

дед, а *m.* **1** grandfather; (*pl.*; *fig.*) grandfathers, forefathers. **2** (*coll.*) (*старик*) grand-dad, grandpa. **3**: **д.-моро́з** Father Christmas, Santa Claus.

де́довский *adj.* **1** grandfather's. **2** (*очень старый*) old-world; old-fashioned.

дедовщи́н|а, ы *f.* (*mil. sl.*) bullying, harassment (*of subordinates*).

дедукти́вный *adj.* deductive.

деду́кци|я, и *f.* deduction.

дедуци́р|овать, ую *impf. and pf.* to deduce.

де́душк|а, и *m.* grandfather, grandpa.

дееприча́сти|е, я *nt.* (*gram.*) gerund (*e.g.* **читáя, прочитáв**).

дееприча́ст|ный *adj. of* ⇨**~ие**

дееспосо́бност|ь, и *f.* **1** energy, activity. **2** (*leg.*) capability.

дееспосо́б|ный (~ен, ~на) *adj.* **1** able to function, active. **2** (*leg.*) capable.

дежу́р|ить, ю, ишь *impf.* **1** (*быть дежурным*) to be on duty. **2** (*неотлучно находиться*) to be in constant attendance, not to leave one's post.

дежу́рн|ый *adj.* **1** duty; on duty; **д. офице́р** (*mil.*) orderly officer; **д. пункт** (*mil.*) guard-room; **~ая апте́ка** chemist's shop open after normal closing hour *or* on holiday. **2**: **~ое блю́до** plat du jour. **3** (*избитый*) hackneyed. **4** *as n.* **д., ~ого** *m.*, **~ая, ~ой** *f.* man, woman on duty; **кто д.?** who is on duty? **5** *as n.* **~ая, ~ой** *f.* duty room.

дежу́рств|о, а *nt.* (being on) duty; **расписа́ние ~а** rota; (*mil.*) roster; **смени́ться с ~а** to come off duty, be relieved.

дезабилье́ *nt. indecl.* déshabillé.

дезавуи́р|овать, ую *impf. and pf.* to repudiate, disavow.

дезактива́ци|я, и *f.* decontamination.

дезактиви́р|овать, ую *impf. and pf.* to decontaminate.

дезерти́р, а *m.* deserter.

дезерти́р|овать, ую *impf. and pf.* to desert.

дезерти́рств|о, а *nt.* desertion.

дезинсекцио́нн|ый *adj. of* ⇨**дезинсе́кция; ~ые сре́дства** insecticides.

дезинсе́кци|я, и *f.* destruction of harmful insects.

дезинфекта́нт, а *m.* disinfectant.

дезинфекцио́нный *adj. of* ⇨**дезинфе́кция**

дезинфе́кци|я, и *f.* disinfection; (*coll.*) disinfectant.

дезинфици́р|овать, ую *impf. and pf.* to disinfect.

дезинформа́ци|я, и *f.* misinformation; (*намеренная*) disinformation.

дезинформи́р|овать, ую *impf. and pf.* to misinform.

дезодора́нт, а *m.* deodorant.

дезорганиза́ци|я, и *f.* disorganization; disruption.

дезорганиз|ова́ть, у́ю *impf. and pf.* to disrupt.

дезориента́ци|я, и *f.* disorientation.

дезориенти́р|овать, ую *impf. and pf.* to disorient; to cause to lose one's bearings, confuse.

дезориенти́р|оваться, уюсь *impf. and pf.* to lose one's bearings.

деи́зм, а *m.* deism.

деи́ст, а *m.* deist.

де́йственност|ь, и *f.* efficacy; effectiveness.

де́йствен|ный (~, ~на) *adj.* efficacious; effective.

де́йстви|е, я *nt.* **1** (*деятельность*) action, operation; activity; **ввести́ в д.** to bring into operation, bring into force. **2** (*функционирование*) functioning (*of a machine etc.*). **3** (*влияние*) effect; action; **под ~ем** (+*g.*) under the influence (of); **не ока́зывать никако́го ~я** to have no effect. **4** (*события, о которых идёт речь*) action (*of a story, etc.*); **д. происхо́дит во вре́мя Пе́рвой мирово́й войны́** the action takes place during the First World War. **5** (*часть пьесы*) act. **6** (*pl.*) (*поступки*) actions; (*mil.*) operations. **7** (*math.*) operation.

действи́тельно *adv.* really; indeed.

действи́тельност|ь, и *f.* **1** reality; **в ~и** in reality, in fact. **2** validity (*of a document*).

действи́тел|ьный (~ен, ~ьна) *adj.* **1** (*настоящий*) real, actual; true, authentic; **~ьное положе́ние веще́й** the true state of affairs; **э́то бы́ли его́ ~ьные слова́** these were his actual words; **~ьная слу́жба** (*mil.*) active service; **д. член Акаде́мии нау́к** (full) member of the Academy of Sciences. **2** (*имеющий силу*) valid; **удостовере́ние ~ьно на шесть ме́сяцев** the licence is valid for six months. **3**: **д. зало́г** (*gram.*) active voice.

де́йств|овать, ую *impf.* **1** (*impf. only*) (*совершать действия*) to act; (*функционировать*) to work, function; to operate; **телефо́н не ~ует** the telephone is not working, is out of order. **2** (*pf.* **по~**) (**на**+*a.*) (*влиять*) to affect, have an effect (upon), act (upon); **лека́рство ~ует** the medicine is taking effect; **д. кому́-н. на не́рвы** to get on s.o.'s nerves. **3** (*impf. only*) (+*i.*; *coll.*) (*использовать*) to work, operate; to use.

де́йствующ|ий *pres. part. act. of* ⇨**де́йствовать** *and adj.*: **~ая а́рмия** army in the field; **д. вулка́н** active volcano; **~ее лицо́** (*theatr., liter.*) character; **~ие ли́ца** (*theatr.*) dramatis personae.

дека... *comb. form* deca-.

де́к|а, и *f.* (*mus.*) **1** (*скрипки*) sounding-board. **2** (*магнитофона*) deck; **магнитофо́нная д.** tape deck.

декабри́ст, а *m.* (*hist.*) Decembrist.

декабри́ст|ский *adj. of* ⇨**~**

дека́бр|ь, я́ *m.* December.

дека́бр|ьский *adj. of* ⇨**~**

дека́д|а, ы *f.* **1** (*срок*) ten-day period. **2** (*фестиваль*) (ten-day) festival.

декада́нс, а *m.* decadence.

декаде́нт, а *m.* decadent.

декаде́нтский *adj.* decadent.

декаде́нтств|о, а *nt.* decadence.

дека́д|ный *adj. of* ⇨**~а**

дека́н, а *m.* dean (*of university*).

декана́т, а *m.* **1** (*должность*) office of dean (*of university*). **2** (*помещение*) dean's office.

дека́нств|о, а *nt.* (*of university*) duties of dean, deanship.

деклама́тор, а *m.* reciter, declaimer.

деклама́ци|я, и *f.* rccitation, declamation.

деклами́р|овать, ую *impf.* (*of* ⇨**про~**) to recite, declaim.

деклати́в|ный (~ен, ~на) *adj.* **1** (*торжественный*) declaratory; solemn. **2** (*pej.*) (*претенциозный*) made for effect, pretentious.

деклара́ци|я, и *f.* declaration; **нало́говая д.** tax return.

деклари́р|овать, ую *impf. and pf.* to declare, proclaim.

деклассированный *adj.* déclassé.

декоди́р|овать, ую *impf. and pf.* to decode.

декольте́ *nt. indecl.* décolleté (*also as adj.*); décolletage.

декольтиро́ванный *adj.* **1** (*о платье, женщине*) décolleté. **2** (*о плечах*) bare(d).

декомпре́сси|я, и *f.* decompression.

декомпре́ссор, а *m.* decompressor.

декорати́в|ный (~ен, ~на) *adj.* decorative, ornamental.

декора́тор, а *m.* (*помещения*) interior decorator; (*theatr.*) scene-painter.

декора́ци|я, и *f.* **1** (*theatr.*) set, scenery. **2** (*fig.*) window-dressing.

декори́р|овать, ую *impf. and pf.* to decorate.

деко́рум, а *m.* decorum.

декре́т, а *m.* **1** (*указ*) decree. **2** (*coll.*) (*декретный отпуск*) maternity leave; **уйти́ в д.** to take maternity leave.

декрети́р|овать, ую *impf. and pf.* to decree.

декре́тниц|а, ы *f.* (*coll.*) woman on maternity leave.

декре́т|ный *adj. of* ⇨~; **д. о́тпуск** maternity leave.

декстри́н, а *m.* (*chem.*) dextrine.

де́ланност|ь, и *f.* artificiality; affectation.

де́ланный *p.p.p. of* ⇨**де́лать** *and adj.* artificial, forced, affected.

де́ла|ть, ю *impf.* (*of* ⇨**с~**)
1 (*производить*) to make.
2 (*приводить в какое-н. состояние*) to make; **д. кого́-н. несча́стным** to make s.o. unhappy; **д. из кого́-н. посме́шище** to make a laughing-stock of s.o.
3 (*поступать*) to do; **д. не́чего** there is nothing for it; it can't be helped; **от не́чего д.** for want of anything better to do.
4 (+*var. nn.*) to make, do, give; **д. вид** to pretend, feign; **д. вы́воды** to draw conclusions; **д. вы́говор** (+*d.*) to reprimand; **д. гла́зки** (+*d.*; *coll.*) to make eyes (at); **д. комплиме́нт** (+*d.*) to pay a compliment; **д. предложе́ние** (+*d.*) to propose (*marriage*) (to); **д. уси́лия** to make an effort; **д. честь** (+*d.*) (*i*) to honour (*Br.*), honor (*US*), (*ii*) to do credit.
5 (*проходить расстояние*) to do, make.

де́ла|ться, юсь *impf.* (*of* ⇨**с~**)
1 (*становиться*) to become, get, grow.
2 (*происходить*) to happen; **что там ~ется?** what is going on?; **что с ней ~ется?** what is the matter with her?
3 (*coll.*) (*появляться*) to break out, appear.

делега́т, а *m.* delegate.

делега́т|ка, ки *f. of* ⇨~

делега́т|ский *adj. of* ⇨~

делега́ци|я, и *f.* delegation; group.

делеги́р|овать, ую *impf. and pf.* to delegate.

делёж, а́ *m.* sharing, division; partition.

делёж|ка, ки *f.* (*coll.*) = ~

деле́ни|е, я *nt.* **1** (*in var. senses*) division; **д. кле́ток** (*biol.*) cell-fission; **знак ~я** (*math.*) division sign. **2** (*на шкале*) point, degree, unit.

дел|е́ц, ьца́ *m.* (*pej.*) smart dealer.

Де́ли *m. indecl.* Delhi.

деликате́с, а *m.* delicacy; **магази́н ~ов** delicatessen.

делика́тност|ь, и *f.* (*in var. senses*) delicacy.

делика́т|ный (~ен, ~на) *adj.* (*in var. senses*) delicate.

дели́м|ое, ого *nt.* (*math.*) dividend.

дели́мост|ь, и *f.* divisibility.

дели́тел|ь, я *m.* divisor.

дел|и́ть, ю, ~ишь *impf.* **1** (*pf.* **раз~**) to divide; **д. по́ровну** to divide into equal parts; **д. шесть на́ три** to divide six by three. **2** (*pf.* **по~**) (**с**+*i.*) to share (with); **д. с кем-н. го́ре и ра́дость** to share s.o.'s sorrows and joys.

дел|и́ться, ю́сь ~ишься *impf.*
1 (*pf.* **раз~**) (**на**+*a.*) to divide (into).
2 (*impf. only*) (**на**+*a.*) to be divisible (by).
3 (*pf.* **по~**) (+*i.*, **с**+*i.*) to share (with); to communicate (to), impart (to); **д. куско́м хле́ба с кем-н.** to share a crust of bread with s.o.; **д. ве́стью с кем-н.** to impart news to s.o.; **д. впечатле́ниями с кем-н.** to compare notes with s.o.

де́л|о, а, *pl.* **~а́, ~, ~а́м** *nt.*
1 (*работа, занятие*) business, affair(s); **ме́жду ~ом** (*coll.*) at odd moments, between times; **по ~у, по ~а́м** on business; **э́то моё д.** that is my affair; **име́ть д.** (**с**+*i.*) to have to do (with), deal (with); **не вме́шивайтесь не в своё д.** mind your own business; **как (ва́ши) ~а́?** how are things going (with you)?, how are you getting on?; **за чем д. ста́ло?** what's holding things up?; **привести́ свои́ ~а́ в поря́док** to put one's affairs in order; **д. в шля́пе** (*coll.*) it's in the bag; **говори́ть д.** to talk sense; **вот э́то д.!** (*coll.*) now you're talking; **д. за ва́ми** it's up to you; **како́е мне до э́того д.?** what has this to do with me?; **что тебе́ за д.?** what does it matter to you?; **пе́рвым ~ом** in the first instance, first of all.
2 (*цель*) cause; **д. ми́ра** the cause of peace; **э́то д. его́ жи́зни** it's his life's work.
3 (+*adj.*) (*специальность*) occupation; (*obs.*) (*предприятие*) business, concern; **го́рное д.** mining.
4 matter, point; **д. вку́са** matter of taste; **д. че́сти** point of honour; **д. в том, что**... the point is that ...; **в то́м-то и д.** that's (just) the point; **не в э́том д.** that's not the point; **совсе́м друго́е д.** quite another matter; **д. идёт о**... (+*p.*) it is a matter of ....
5 (*факт*) fact, deed; thing; **на са́мом ~е** in actual fact, as a matter of fact; **и на слова́х и на ~е** in word and deed; **на слова́х**..., **на ~е же** in theory, nominally ... but actually; **в са́мом ~е** really, indeed.
6 (*поступок*) act, deed.
7 (*leg.*) (*судебное*) case; cause; **вести́ д.** to plead a cause; **возбуди́ть д.** (**про́тив**+*g.*) to bring an action (against), institute proceedings (against).
8 (*досье*) file, dossier; **ли́чное д.** personal file.
9 (*obs.*) (*сражение*) battle, fighting.
10 *idiomatic phr.*: **то и д.** continually, time and again.

делови́тост|ь, и *f.* business-like character, efficiency.

делови́т|ый (~, ~а) *adj.* business-like, efficient.

делов|о́й *adj.* **1** business; work; **~о́е письмо́** business letter; **~а́я пое́здка** business trip; **~о́е вре́мя** work time. **2** (*человек, тон*) business-like.

делопроизводи́тел|ь, я *m.* chief clerk.

делопроизво́дств|о, а *nt.* office work, clerical work.

де́льн|ый *adj.* **1** (*человек*) business-like, efficient. **2** (*проект, мысль*) sensible, practical; **~ое предложе́ние** sensible suggestion.

де́льт|а, ы *f.* delta.

дельтапла́н, а *m.* hang-glider (*craft*).

дельтапланери́зм, а *m.* hang-gliding.

дельтапланери́ст, а *m.* hang-glider (*person*).

дельтапланери́ст|ка, ки *f. of* ⇨~

дельтапла́нер|ный *adj. of* ⇨**~и́зм**; **д. спорт** hang-gliding.

дельтови́дный *adj.* delta-shaped; **д. самолёт** delta-wing aircraft.

дельфи́н, а *m.* dolphin.

дельфина́ри|й, я *m.* dolphinarium.

деля́г|а, и *m.* (*coll.*) person pursuing his own interests.

деля́нк|а, и *f.* (*участок земли*) plot (of land); (*участок леса*) piece (of woodland).

демаго́г, а *m.* demagogue.

демагоги́ческий *adj.* demagogic.

демаго́ги|я, и *f.* demagogy.

демаркацио́нн|ый *adj.*: **~ая ли́ния** line of demarcation.

демарка́ци|я, и *f.* demarcation.

дема́рш, а *m.* démarche, political initiative.

де́мбел|ь, я, *pl.* **~я́** *m.* (*mil. sl.*)
1 (*демобилизация*) demobilization, discharge. **2** (*солдат*) demobilized soldier.

демилитариза́ци|я, и *f.* demilitarization.

демилитаризи́р|овать ую *impf. and pf.* to demilitarize.

демисезо́нн|ый *adj.*: **~ое пальто́** light overcoat (*for spring and autumn wear*).

демиу́рг, а *m.* demiurge, creator.

демобилизацио́нный *adj.* demobilization.

демобилиза́ци|я, и *f.* demobilization.

демобилиз|ова́ть у́ю *impf. and pf.* to demobilize.

Д

демограф|и́ческий *adj. of* ⇒~́ия; **д. взрыв** population explosion.

демогра́фи|я, и *f.* demography.

демокра́т, а *m.* democrat.

демократиза́ци|я, и *f.* democratization.

демократизи́р|овать, ую *impf. and pf.* to democratize.

демократи́ческий *adj.* democratic.

демокра́ти|я, и *f.* democracy; **стра́ны наро́дной ~и** the People's Democracies.

де́мон, а *m.* demon.

демони́ческий *adj.* demonic, demoniacal.

демонстра́нт, а *m.* (*pol.*) demonstrator.

демонстра́нт|ка, ки *f. of* ⇒~

демонстрати́в|ный (~ен, ~на) *adj.* **1** (*вызывающий*) demonstrative, done for effect. **2** (*основанный на демонстрировании чего-либо*) demonstration; **~ная ле́кция** demonstration lecture. **3** (*mil.*) feint, decoy.

демонстра́тор, а *m.* demonstrator.

демонстра́ци|я, и *f.* **1** (*in var. senses*) demonstration; **д. му́скулов** (*pol.*) muscle-flexing. **2** (*публичный показ*) showing (*of a film, etc.*); **повто́рная д.** repeat, rerun. **3** (*mil.*) feint, manœuvre.

демонстри́р|овать, ую *impf. and pf.* **1** (*принять участие в демонстрации*) to demonstrate, make a demonstration. **2** (*pf. also* **про~**) (*показать*) to show, display; to give a demonstration (of); **д. но́вый кинофи́льм** to show a new film.

демонта́ж, а *m.* (*tech.*) dismantling.

демонти́р|овать, ую *impf. and pf.* (*tech.*) to dismantle.

деморализа́ци|я, и *f.* demoralization.

деморализ|ова́ть, у́ю *impf. and pf.* to demoralize.

де́мпинг, а *m.* (*econ.*) dumping.

де́мпфер, а *m.* (*tech.*) damper; shock absorber.

денатурализа́ци|я, и *f.* (*leg.*) denaturalization.

денатура́т, а *m.* methylated spirits.

денатури́р|овать, ую *impf. and pf.* (*chem.*) to denature.

денационализа́ци|я, и *f.* denationalization.

денационализи́р|овать, ую *impf. and pf.* to denationalize.

де́нди *m. indecl.* dandy.

дендра́ри|й, я *m.* arboretum.

дендроло́ги|я, и *f.* dendrology.

де́нежк|а, и *f.* **1** (*obs.*) (*старинная монета*) half-kopeck coin. **2** *usu. pl.* (*coll.*) (*деньги*) money; **пла́кали на́ши ~и** that's our money down the drain.

де́нежный *adj.* **1** monetary; money; **д. автома́т** cash dispenser; **д. знак** banknote; **д. перево́д** money order; **д. ры́нок** money-market; **д. штраф** fine; **д. я́щик** strong-box. **2** (*coll.*) (*богатый*) rich; **д. мешо́к** moneybags; **д. челове́к** a man of means.

ден|ёк, ька́ *m., dim. of* ⇒**день**

де́нно *adv.*: **д. и но́щно** day and night.

деномина́ци|я, и *f.* (*econ.*) denomination.

денонси́р|овать, ую *impf. and pf.* (*dipl.*) to renounce.

денщи́к, а́ *m.* (*mil., obs.*) batman.

де́нь, дня *m.* **1** day; afternoon; **в 4 ч. дня** at 4 p.m.; **днём** in the afternoon; **д.-деньско́й** all day long; **д. рожде́ния** birthday; **д. откры́тых двере́й** open day; **д. в д.** to the day; **д. ото дня** with every passing day, day by day; **в оди́н прекра́сный д.** one fine day; **во дни о́ны** in those days; **изо дня в д.** day after day; **на друго́й, сле́дующий д.** next day; **на днях** (*i*) the other day, (*ii*) one of these days, any day now; **не по дням, а по часа́м** hourly, fast, rapidly; **со дня на́ д.** daily, from day to day; **че́рез д.** every other day; **Д. сме́ха** April Fool's Day; **кану́н Дня всех святы́х** Halloween; **Д. поминове́ния** Remembrance Day; **второ́й д. Рождества́** Boxing Day. **2** (*pl.*) (*время; жизнь*) days; **его́ дни сочтены́** his days are numbered.

де́н|ьги, ег, ьгам *or* **ьга́м** *pl.* (*sg.* (*coll.*) **~ьга́, ~ьги́** *f.*) money; **кро́вные д.** hard-earned money; **ме́лкие д.** small change; **нали́чные д.** cash, ready money; **при ~ьга́х** in funds; **не при ~ьга́х** hard up; **ни за каки́е д.** not for all the tea in China.

деньжа́т|а, ~ *no sg.* (*coll.*) money, cash.

деньжо́н|ки, ок *no sg.* (*coll.*) money, cash.

департа́мент, а *m.* department.

депе́ш|а, и *f.* dispatch.

депо́ *nt. indecl.* (*rail.*) depot; shed, roundhouse; **пожа́рное д.** fire-station.

депози́т, а *m.* (*fin.*) deposit.

депози́т|ный *adj. of* ~

депози́тор, а *m.* (*fin.*) depositor.

депоне́нт, а *m* (*fin.*) depositor.

депони́р|овать, ую *impf. and pf.* (*fin., leg.*) to deposit.

депорта́ци|я, и *f.* deportation.

депорти́р|овать, ую *impf. and pf.* to deport.

депресня́к, а́ *m.* (*sl.*) depression, depressed mood.

депресси́вн|ый *adj. of* ⇒**депре́ссия; д. пери́од** (*econ.*) depression, slump; **~ое состоя́ние** (*econ. and psych.*) depression.

депре́сси|я, и *f.* **1** (*econ.*) depression, slump. **2** (*psych.*) depression.

депута́т, а *m.* deputy; delegate; **пала́та ~ов** Chamber of Deputies.

депута́ци|я, и *f.* deputation.

де́рвиш, а *m.* dervish.

дёрга|ть, ю *impf.* (*of* ⇒**дёрнуть**) **1** (*тянуть*) to pull, tug; **д. кого́-н. за рука́в** to tug at s.o.'s sleeve, pluck s.o. by the sleeve. **2** (*удалять*) to pull out; **д. зу́бы** (*i*) to pull out teeth, (*ii*) to have teeth out (*at the dentist's*). **3** (*impf. only*) (*беспокоить*) to harass, pester. **4** (*impf. only*) (*coll.*) (*вызывать резкое движение*) to cause to twitch; (*impers.*) to twitch; **его́ всего́ ~ло** he was twitching all over. **5** (*impf. only*) (+*i.*; *coll.*) (*резко двигать*) to jerk; **д. плеча́ми** to shrug one's shoulders.

дёрга|ться, юсь *impf.* (*of* ⇒**дёрнуться**) **1** *pass. of* ⇒**~ть. 2** to twitch; **рот у него́ непреста́нно ~ется** his mouth twitches incessantly.

дерга́ч, а́ *m.* (*zool.*) landrail, corncrake.

деревене́|ть, ю *impf.* (*of* ⇒**о~**) to grow stiff, numb.

дереве́нский *adj.* **1** (*магазин*) village. **2** (*тишина, пейзаж*) rural; (*житель, воздух*) country.

дереве́нщин|а, ы *c.g.* (*coll.*) (country) bumpkin.

дере́в|ня, ни, *g. pl.* **~е́нь** *f.* **1** (*селение*) village. **2** (*местность*) (the) country (*opp. the town*).

де́рев|о, а, *pl.* **~́ья, ~́ьев** *nt.* **1** (*растение*) tree; **за ~́ьями ле́са не ви́деть** not to see the wood for the trees. **2** (*sg. only*) (*древесина*) wood (*as material*).

деревообде́лочник, а *m.* woodworker.

деревообде́лочный *adj.* woodworking.

деревообрабо́тк|а, и *f.* woodworking.

деревýшк|а, и *f.* hamlet.

де́ревц|е, а, *pl.* **~а́** *and* **деревц|о́, а́** *nt.* sapling.

деревяни́ст|ый (~, ~а) *adj.* **1** (*bot.*) ligneous. **2** (*жёсткий*) hard (*of fruit, etc.*).

деревя́нн|ый *adj.* **1** wood; wooden. **2** (*fig.*) wooden; expressionless, dead; dull; **~ое выраже́ние лица́** wooden expression; **д. го́лос** expressionless voice.

деревя́шк|а, и *f.* **1** piece of wood. **2** (*coll.*) (*деревянная нога*) wooden leg.

держа́в|а, ы *f.* (*pol.*) power; **вели́кие ~ы** the Great Powers.

держа́вный *adj.* **1** (*царственный*) holding supreme power, sovereign. **2** (*сильный*) powerful.

держа́лк|а, и *f.* (*coll.*) handle.

держа́тел|ь, я *m.* **1** (*fin.*) holder. **2** (*приспособление*) holder.

держ|а́ть, у́, ~́ишь *impf.* **1** (*в руках*) to hold; (*не отпускать*) to hold on to; **~и́те во́ра!** stop thief! **2** (*поддерживать*) to hold up, support. **3** (*in var. senses*) (*заставлять находиться в каком-н. состоянии*) to keep, hold; **д. в посте́ли** to keep in bed; **д. банк** (*card-games*) to be banker; **д. курс (на** + *a.*) to hold course (for), head (for); (*fig.*) to be working (for); **д. путь (к** + *d.*, **на** + *a.*) to head (for), make (for); **д. пари́** to bet; **д. чью-н. сто́рону** to take s.o.'s side; **д. язы́к за зуба́ми** to hold one's tongue; **д. в ку́рсе** to keep posted; **д. в неве́дении** to keep in the dark. **4** (*животных*) to keep; **д. лошаде́й** to keep horses. **5**: **д. себя́** to behave. **6** + *certain nn.* = *to carry out*; **д. корректу́ру** to read proofs; **д. ре́чь** to make a speech; **д. экза́мен** to sit, take an examination.

держ|а́ться, у́сь, ~́ишься *impf.*

1 (**за**+*a.*) to hold (on to); **~итесь за перила** hold on to the banister.
2 (**на**+*p.*) to be held up (by), be supported (by); **д. на ниточке** to hang by a thread (*also fig.*).
3 (*находиться где-либо*) to keep, stay, be; **д. вместе** to stick together; **д. в стороне** to hold aloof.
4 (*стоять*) to hold o.s.; (*fig.*) (*вести себя*) to behave.
5 (*сохраняться*) to last; to hold together; **этот стол у вас еле ~ится** this table of yours is on its last legs.
6 (*не сдаваться*) to hold out, stand firm.
7 (+*g.*) (*придерживаться определённого направления*) to keep (to); **д. левой стороны** to keep to the left; **д. берега** to hug the shore.
8 (+*g.*) (*следовать чему-либо*) to adhere (to), stick (to); **д. темы** to stick to the subject; **д. убеждений** to have the courage of one's convictions.

дерзани|е, я *nt.* daring.

дерз|ать, аю *impf.* (*of* ⇒**~нуть**) to dare.

дерз|ить, *1st pers. not used,* **ишь** *impf.* (*of* ⇒**на~**) (+*d.*; *coll.*) to be impertinent (to), cheek.

дерз|кий (~ок, ~ка, ~ко) *adj.* **1** (*грубый*) impertinent, cheeky. **2** (*смелый*) daring, audacious.

дерзновени|е, я *nt.* (*obs.*) audacity.

дерзновен|ный (~ен, ~на) *adj.* daring, audacious.

дерзн|уть, у, ёшь *pf. of* ⇒**дерзать**

дерзост|ь, и *f.* **1** (*грубость*) impertinence; cheek; rudeness; **говорить ~и** to be impertinent, cheeky, rude. **2** (*смелость*) daring, audacity.

дериват, а *m.* (*tech.*) derivative.

деривaци|я, и *f.* **1** (*mil.*) drift. **2** (*ling.*) derivation.

дерматин, а *m.* leatherette.

дерматит, а *m.* dermatitis.

дерматолог, а *m.* dermatologist.

дерматологи|я, и *f.* dermatology.

дёрн, а *m.* turf.

дерн|овать, ую *impf.* to cover with turf; to make a turf edging round.

дерновый *adj. of* ⇒**дёрн**

дёрн|уть, у, ешь *pf.* **1** *pf. of* ⇒**дёргать; чёрт ~ет (~ул), нелёгкая ~ет (~ула)** *or* (*impers.*) **~ет (~уло) кого-н.** (+*inf.*; *coll.*) to be possessed (to do sth.); **чёрт меня ~ул дать слово** I don't know what possessed me to promise. **2** (*поехать*) to get going, get cracking. **3** (*coll.*) (*тронуться с места*) to go off. **4** (*coll.*) (*выпить*) to drink up; to take a swig. **5** (*coll.*) (*начать энергично делать что-н.*) to start vigorously to do sth.; **д. плясовую** to strike up a (dance) tune.

дёрн|уться, усь, ешься *pf.* (*of* ⇒**дёргаться**) to start up (with a jerk); to dart.

дер|у, ёшь *see* ⇒**драть**

дерьм|о, а *nt.* (*vulg.*) dung; (*fig.*) crap.

дерьмовый *adj.* (*coll.*) crappy (= *inferior*).

дерюг|а, и *f.* sackcloth, sacking.

дерюжный *adj.* sackcloth.

дерябн|уть, у, ешь *pf.* (*sl.*) (*выпить*) to drink up.

десант, а *m.* (*mil.*) **1** (*высадка войск*) landing. **2** (*войска*) landing force; **высадить, выбросить д.** to make a landing.

десантник, а *m.* paratrooper.

десантный *adj.* (*mil.*) landing.

десерт, а *m.* dessert.

десерт|ный *adj. of* ⇒**~; ~ная ложка** dessert spoon.

дескать *particle indicating reported speech* (*coll.*): **она, д., ничего подобного не хотела сказать** she said she had not meant anything of the kind.

десн|а, ы, *pl.* **~ы, дёсен** *f.* (*anat.*) gum.

десниц|а, ы *f* (*obs. or poet.*) right hand.

деспот, а *m.* despot.

деспотизм, а *m.* despotism.

деспотический *adj.* despotic.

деспотич|ный (~ен, ~на) *adj.* despotic.

деспоти|я, и *f.* despotism.

дестабилизaци|я, и *f.* destabilization.

дестабилизир|овать, ую *impf. and pf.* to destabilize.

деструктивный *adj.* destructive.

дест|ь, и, *g. pl.* **~ей** *f.* quire (*of paper*) (**русская д.** = 24 sheets; **метрическая д.** = 50 sheets).

десятер|о, ых *num.* **1** (+*m. nn. denoting persons, pers. prons. in pl. or nn. used only in pl.*) ten. **2** (*пары*) ten pairs.

десятибор|ец, ца *m.* decathlete.

десятиборь|е, я *nt.* (*sport*) decathlon.

десятизуб|ый *adj.*: **~ые кошки** (*mountaineering*) crampons.

десятикратный *adj.* tenfold.

десятилети|е, я *nt.* **1** (*срок*) decade. **2** (*годовщина*) tenth anniversary.

десятилетк|а, и *f.* ten-year secondary school (*Br.*), ten-year high school (*US*).

десятилетний *adj.* **1** (*срок*) ten-year, decennial. **2** (*ребёнок*) ten-year-old.

десятин|а, ы *f.* **1** (*мера*) dessiatine, desyatin (*old Russian land measure, equivalent to 2.7 acres or 1.09 hectares*). **2** (*налог*) tithe.

десятиугольник, а *m.* (*math.*) decagon.

десятичн|ый *adj.* decimal; **~ая дробь** decimal fraction.

десятка, и *f.* **1** (*цифра*) ten. **2** (*coll.*) (*автобус, трамвай*) No. 10 (*bus, tram, etc.*). **3** (*coll.*) (*группа из десяти единиц*) group of ten objects. **4** (*игральная карта*) ten.

десятник, а *m.* (*obs.*) foreman.

десят|ок, ка *m.* **1** (*десять*) ten. **2** (*десять лет*) ten years, decade (*of life*). **3** (*pl.*) (*math.*) tens. **4** (*pl.*) tens; **~ки людей** scores of people. **5**: **не робкого ~ка** plucky.

десят|ый *num.* tenth; **это дело ~ое** (*coll.*) it is of no consequence.

десят|ь, и, ью *num.* ten.

десятью *adv.* ten times; **д. два — двадцать** ten times two is twenty.

дет... *comb. form, abbr. of* ***детский***

детализaци|я, и *f.* working out in detail.

детализир|овать, ую *and* **детализ|овать, ую** *impf. and pf.* to work out in detail.

детал|ь, и *f.* **1** (*подробность*) detail. **2** (*часть машины*) part, component.

детал|ьный (~ен, ~ьна) *adj.* detailed; minute.

детвор|а, ы *no pl., f.* (*collect.*; *coll.*) children.

детдом, а *m.* children's home.

детдомов|ец, ца *m.* (*coll.*) resident of a children's home.

детдомов|ка, ки *f. of* ⇒**~ец**

детектив, а *m.* **1** (*человек*) detective. **2** (*роман*) detective story; whodunit. **3** (*фильм*) detective film.

детективный *adj.*: **д. роман** detective story.

детектор, а *m.* (*tech.*) detector.

детёныш, а *m.* young (*of animals*).

детергент, а *m.* detergent.

детерминизм, а *m.* determinism.

детерминист, а *m.* determinist.

дет|и, ~ей, ~ям, ~ьми, о ~ях *pl.* (*sg.* **дитя** *nt.*) children; **д. боярские,** *see* ⇒**боярский**

детин|а, ы *m.* (*coll.*) big fellow, hefty chap.

детищ|е, а, *g. pl.* **~** *nt.* child, offspring; (*fig.*) child, creation; brainchild.

деткомбинат, а *m.* (*coll.*) day nursery.

детный *adj.* (*coll.*) having children.

детонатор, а *m.* (*tech.*) detonator.

детонaци|я, и *f.* (*tech.*) detonation.

детонир|овать, ую *impf.* (*tech.*) to detonate.

детородный *adj.* genital.

деторождени|е, я *nt.* procreation.

детоубийств|о, а *nt.* infanticide (*action*).

детоубийц|а, ы *c.g.* infanticide (*agent*).

детплощадк|а, и *f.* playground.

детрит, а *m.* (*physiol.*) detritus.

детсад, а *m.* kindergarten, nursery school; **д.-ясли** day nursery.

детсадов|ец, ца *m.* (*coll.*) child attending kindergarten.

детск|ая, ой *f.* nursery.

детск|ий *adj.* **1** child's, children's; **д. дом** children's home; **д. сад** kindergarten, nursery school; **~ая смертность** infantile mortality; **д. труд** child labour (*Br.*), labor (*US*). **2** (*ребяческий*) childish; **д. лепет** baby-talk. **3**: **~ое место** (*anat.*) placenta.

детскост|ь, и *f.* childishness.

детств|о, а *nt.* childhood; **с ~а** from childhood, from a child; **впадать в д.** to lapse into dotage.

деть, дену, денешь *pf.* (*of* ⇒**девать**) to put, do (with); **куда ты дел моё перо?** what have you done with my pen?; **не знать, куда глаза д.** not to know where to look; **этого никуда не**

Д

де́нешь there's no getting away from it; there's no disputing it.

де́|ться, нусь, нешься *pf.* (*of* ⇒**дева́ться**) to get to, disappear.

де-фа́кто *adv.* de facto.

дефе́кт, а *m.* defect.

дефекти́в|ный (~ен, ~на) *adj.* handicapped; **д. ребёнок** handicapped child.

дефе́кт|ный (~ен, ~на) *adj.* imperfect, faulty.

дефекто́лог, а *m.* specialist in mental and physical handicaps (*in children*).

дефектол|оги́ческий *adj. of* ⇒**~о́гия**

дефектоло́ги|я, и *f.* study of mental defects and physical handicaps.

дефектоско́п, а *m.* (*tech.*) fault detector.

дефектоскопи́|я, и *f.* (*tech.*) fault detection.

дефили́р|овать, ую *impf.* (*of* ⇒**про~**) to march past, go in procession.

дефини́ци|я, и *f.* definition.

дефи́с, а *m.* hyphen.

дефици́т, а *m.* **1** (*econ.*) deficit; **д. торго́вого бала́нса** trade gap. **2** shortage, deficiency; **д. в то́пливе** fuel shortage.

дефици́т|ный (~ен, ~на) *adj.* **1** (*econ.*) (*предприятие*) showing a loss, unprofitable. **2** (*товар*) in short supply; scarce.

дефля́ци|я, и *f.* (*econ.*) deflation.

деформа́ци|я, и *f.* deformation.

деформи́р|овать, ую *impf. and pf.* (*исказить*) to deform; (*изменить форму чего-н.*) to change the form of.

деформи́р|оваться, уюсь *impf. and pf.* to change one's shape; to become deformed.

децентрализа́ци|я, и *f.* decentralization.

децентрализ|ова́ть, у́ю *impf. and pf.* to decentralize.

деци... *comb. form* deci-.

децибе́л, а *g. pl.* **д.** *m.* decibel.

децили́тр, а *m.* decilitre (*Br.*), deciliter (*US*).

децима́льный *adj.* decimal.

децимéтр, а *m.* decimetre (*Br.*), decimeter (*US*).

дешеве́|ть, ю *impf.* (*of* ⇒**по~**) to fall in price, become cheaper.

дешеви́зн|а, ы *f.* cheapness; low price.

дешёвк|а, и *f.* **1** low price; **купи́ть по ~е** to buy cheap. **2** (*fig.*) cheap stuff; worthless object.

деше́вле *comp. of* ⇒**дешёвый** *or* **дёшево; д. па́реной ре́пы** dirt-cheap.

дёшево *adv.* cheap, cheaply; (*fig.*) cheaply, lightly; **д. да гни́ло** cheap and nasty; **д. и серди́то** cheap but good; **д. отде́латься** to get off lightly; **э́то вам д. не пройдёт** this will cost you dear.

дешёв|ый (дёшев, дешева́, дёшево) *adj.* **1** cheap. **2** (*fig.*) cheap; empty, worthless; **~ая остро́та** cheap crack.

дешифри́р|овать, ую *impf. and pf.* to decipher, decode.

дешифро́вк|а, и *f.* decipherment, deciphering, decoding.

деэскала́ци|я, и *f.* (*mil., pol.*) de-escalation.

де-ю́ре *adv.* de jure.

дея́ни|е, я *nt.* (*obs. or rhet.*) act; action; **Дея́ния апо́столов** the Acts of the Apostles.

де́ятел|ь, я *m.* agent; **госуда́рственный д.** statesman; **обще́ственный д.** public figure.

де́ятельност|ь, и *f.* **1** activity, activities; work; **обще́ственная д.** public work; **педагоги́ческая д.** educational work, teaching. **2** (*physiol, psych., etc.*) activity, operation; **д. се́рдца** operation of the heart.

де́ятел|ьный (~ен, ~ьна) *adj.* active, energetic.

де́|яться, ется *impf.* (*coll.*) to happen; **что там ~ется?** what's going on?

джаз, а *m.* jazz.

джаз-анса́мбл|ь, я *m.* jazz-combo.

джаз-ба́нд, а *m.* jazz band.

джази́ст, а *m.* jazzman, jazz musician.

джазме́н, а *m.* = **джази́ст**

джаз-му́зык|а, и *f.* jazz.

джа́зовый *adj.* jazz.

джаку́зи *m. indecl.* jacuzzi (*propr.*).

джем, а *m.* jam (*Br.*), jelly (*US*).

дже́мпер, а *m.* jumper.

джентльме́н, а *m.* gentleman.

джентльме́нск|ий *adj.* gentlemanly; **~ое соглаше́ние** gentlemen's agreement.

джентльме́нств|о, а *nt.* gentlemanliness.

джерсе́йск|ий *adj.*: **~ая коро́ва** Jersey (cow).

Джéрси *m. indecl.* Jersey.

дже́рси́ *nt. indecl.* jersey (*material*).

джерсо́вый *adj. of* ⇒**дже́рси́**

джи́г|а, и *f.* jig.

джиги́т, а *m.* Dzhigit (*Caucasian horseman*).

джин, а *m.* gin (*liquor*); **д. с то́ником** gin and tonic.

джинн, а *m.* genie.

джи́нсо́вый *adj.* denim.

джи́нс|ы, ов *no sg.* jeans.

джип, а *m.* jeep (*propr.*).

джи́у-джи́тсу *nt. indecl.* ju-jitsu.

джо́ггинг, а *m.* jogging, fun-running; jog, fun-run.

джо́йстик, а *m.* (*comput.*) joystick.

джо́кер, а *m.* (*cards*) joker.

джо́нк|а, и *f.* junk (*Chinese sailing vessel*).

джо́ул|ь, я, *g. pl.* **~ей** *m.* (*phys.*) joule.

джу́нгл|и, ей *no sg.*, jungle; **ка́менные д.** concrete jungle.

джут, а *m.* jute.

джу́т|овый *adj. of* ⇒**~**

дзот, а *m.* (*abbr. of* ***де́рево-земляна́я огнева́я то́чка***) (*mil.*) earth-and-timber emplacement.

ДЗУ *nt. indecl.* (*abbr. of* ***долговре́менное запомина́ющее устро́йство***) (*comput.*) ROM (*read-only memory*).

дзэн-будди́зм, а *m.* Zen-Buddhism.

дзю(-)до́ *nt. indecl.* judo.

дзюдои́ст, а *m.* judoist, judoka.

диабе́т, а *m.* diabetes.

диабе́тик, а *nt.* diabetic.

диа́гноз, а *m.* diagnosis.

диагно́ст, а *m.* diagnostician.

диагно́стик|а, и *f.* diagnostics.

диагности́р|овать, ую *impf. and pf.* to diagnose; (*tech.*) to check.

диагона́л|ь, и *f.* diagonal; **по ~и** diagonally.

диагона́л|ьный (~ен, ~ьна) *adj.* diagonal.

диагра́мм|а, ы *f.* diagram; chart; **кругова́я д.** pie chart.

диаде́м|а, ы *f.* diadem.

диакрити́ческий *adj.*: **д. знак** (*ling.*) diacritical mark.

диале́кт, а *m.* dialect.

диалекта́льный *adj.* dialectal.

диалекти́зм, а *m.* (*ling.*) dialect word, expression.

диале́ктик, а *m.* (*phil.*) dialectician.

диале́ктик|а, и *f.* (*phil.*) dialectics.

диалекти́ческий *adj.* (*phil.*) dialectical.

диале́ктный *adj.* (*ling.*) dialectal.

диалектоло́ги|я, и *f.* (*ling.*) dialectology.

диало́г, а *m.* dialogue (*Br.*), dialog (*US*).

диалоги́ческий *adj.* having dialogue (*Br.*), dialog (*US*) form.

диало́гов|ый *adj.* (*comput.*) interactive; **~ое окно́** dialog box.

диама́т, а *m.* (*abbr. of* ***диалекти́ческий материали́зм***) dialectical materialism.

диа́метр, а *m.* diameter.

диаметра́льно *adv.*: **д. противополо́жный** diametrically opposite.

диаметра́льный *adj.* diametrical.

диапазо́н, а *m.* **1** (*mus.*) diapason, range. **2** (*fig.*) range, compass; **большо́й д. интере́сов** a wide range of interests. **3** (*tech.*; *fig.*) range; **д. волн** (*radio*) wave band.

диапозити́в, а *m.* (*phot.*) slide, transparency.

диа́спор|а, ы *f.* diaspora.

диатри́б|а, ы *f.* diatribe.

диафи́льм, а *m.* slide film.

диафра́гм|а, ы *f.* diaphragm.

ди́в|а, ы *f.* (*obs.*) diva, prima donna.

дива́н, а *m.* divan (*couch*); sofa; **д.-крова́ть** sofa bed.

дива́н|ный *adj. of* ⇒**~**

диверса́нт, а *m.* saboteur.

диверсифика́ци|я, и *f.* diversification.

диве́рси|я, и *f.* **1** (*mil.*) diversion. **2** sabotage.

дивертисме́нт, а *m.* (*theatr.*) variety show; divertissement (*ballet programme*).

дивиде́нд, а *m.* dividend.

дивизио́н, а *m.* (*mil.*) battalion.

дивизио́н|ный *adj.* **1** *adj. of* ⇨**диви́зия; д. кома́ндный пункт** division command post. **2** *adj. of* ⇨~

диви́зи|я, и *f.* (*mil.*) division.

див|и́ть, лю́, и́шь *impf.* (*coll.*) to amaze.

див|и́ться, лю́сь, и́шься *impf.* (*of* ⇨**по**~) (+*d.*) to be surprised, wonder, marvel (at); (**на**+*a.*) to look upon with wonder.

ди́в|ный (~ен, ~на) *adj.* **1** (*удивительный*) amazing; **что тут ~ного?** what's extraordinary about that? **2** (*прекрасный*) marvellous (*Br.*), marvelous (*US*), wonderful.

ди́в|о, а *nt.* wonder, marvel; **~у да́ться** to wonder, marvel; **что за д.!** how extraordinary!; **на д.** marvellously (*Br.*), marvelously (*US*); *as pred.* it is amazing; **не д.** it is no wonder.

дидакти́ческий *adj.* didactic.

дие́з, а *m.* (*and as indecl. adj.*) (*mus.*) sharp; **ре-д.** D sharp.

дие́т|а, ы *f.* diet; **посади́ть на ~у** to place on a diet; **сесть на ~у** to go on a diet; **сиде́ть на ~е** to be on a diet; **соблюда́ть ~у** to keep to a diet.

диете́тик|а, и *f.* dietetics.

диети́ческий *adj.* dietetic; **д. магази́н** health food shop.

дието́лог, а *m.* nutritionist.

диза́йн, а *m.* design.

диза́йнер, а *m.* designer.

диза́йнер|ский *adj. of* ⇨~

ди́зел|ь, я *m.* diesel engine.

ди́зельный *adj.* diesel.

дизентери́|я, и *f.* dysentery.

дика́р|ский *adj. of* ⇨**~ь**

дика́рств|о, а *nt.* shyness.

дика́р|ь, я́ *m.* **1** savage; (*некультурный человек*) barbarian. **2** (*coll.*) (*застенчивый человек*) shy, unsociable person.

ди́к|ий (~, ~а́, ~о) *adj.* **1** (*животное, растение*) wild; **~ая ко́шка** wild cat; **~ое я́блоко** crab-apple. **2** (*племя*) savage (*also as n.* **д., ~ого** *m.*). **3** (*необузданный*) wild; **~ие кри́ки** wild cries; **д. восто́рг** wild delight. **4** (*абсурдный*) absurd; preposterous, ridiculous. **5** (*застенчивый*) shy; unsociable. **6** (*страшный*) terrible, awful. **7** (*неофициальный*) unofficial.

ди́к|о[1] *adv.* **1** *adv. of* ⇨**~ий. 2** (*в испуге*) in fright; startled; **д. озира́ться** to look around wildly.

ди́ко[2] *as pred.* it is absurd, it is ridiculous; **д. задава́ть таки́е вопро́сы** it is ridiculous to ask such questions.

дикобра́з, а *m.* porcupine.

дико́вин|а, ы *and* **~ка, ~ки** *f.* (*coll.*) marvel, wonder; **э́то мне не в ~(к)у** I see nothing remarkable about it.

дико́винный *adj.* strange, unusual, remarkable.

дикорасту́щий *adj.* wild.

ди́кост|ь, и *f.* **1** (*леса*) wildness; (*человека*) savagery. **2** (*застенчивость*) shyness; unsociableness. **3** (*абсурдность*) absurdity; **э́то соверше́нная д.** it is quite absurd.

Ди́ксиленд, а *m.* Dixieland (jazz).

дикта́нт, а *m.* dictation.

дикта́т, а *m.* (*pol.*) diktat.

дикта́тор, а *m.* dictator.

дикта́торский *adj.* dictatorial.

дикта́торств|о, а *nt.* **1** dictatorship. **2** (*coll.*) dictatorial attitude.

диктату́р|а, ы *f.* dictatorship.

дикт|ова́ть, у́ю, у́ешь *impf.* (*of* ⇨**про**~) to dictate.

дикто́вк|а, и *f.* dictation; **под чью-н. ~у** to s.o.'s dictation; (*fig.*) at s.o.'s bidding.

ди́ктор, а *m.* announcer; (*последних известий*) newscaster.

диктофо́н, а *m.* Dictaphone (*propr.*).

ди́кци|я, и *f.* diction; enunciation.

диле́мм|а, ы *f.* dilemma.

ди́лер, а *m.* dealer.

дилета́нт, а *m.* dilettante, dabbler.

дилета́нтств|о, а *nt.* dilettantism.

дилижа́нс, а *m.* (*hist.*) stage-coach.

динами́зм, а *m.* dynamism.

дина́мик, а *m.* loudspeaker; **ба́совый д.** woofer; **высокочасто́тный д.** tweeter.

дина́мик|а, и *f.* dynamics.

динами́т, а *m.* dynamite.

динами́ческий *adj.* dynamic.

динами́чный *adj.* dynamic.

дина́мо *nt. indecl.* = **дина́мо-маши́на**

дина́мо-маши́н|а, ы *f.* dynamo.

дина́р, а *m.* dinar.

династи́ческий *adj.* dynastic.

дина́сти|я, и *f.* dynasty; **д. Тюдо́ров** the House of Tudor.

ди́нго *m. indecl.* (*zool.*) dingo.

диноза́вр, а *m.* dinosaur.

дио́д, а *m.*: **светоизлуча́ющий д.** light-emitting diode, LED.

дио́птри|я, и *f.* dioptre (*Br.*), diopter (*US*).

диора́м|а, ы *f.* diorama.

дип... *comb. form, abbr. of* ***дипломати́ческий***

дипкурье́р, а *m.* diplomatic courier.

дипло́м, а *m.* **1** (*документ*) diploma, certificate; degree. **2** (*coll.*) (*работа*) degree work, research.

диплома́нт, а *m.* prize-winner.

диплома́т, а *m.* **1** diplomat. **2** (*coll.*) attaché case, (rigid) briefcase.

дипломати́ческий *adj.* diplomatic; **д. ко́рпус** corps diplomatique.

дипломати́ч|ный (~ен, ~на) *adj.* (*fig.*) diplomatic.

диплома́ти|я, и *f.* diplomacy; **д. каноне́рок** gunboat diplomacy.

диплоМи́рованный *adj.* qualified, certificated.

дипло́мник, а *m.* student engaged on degree thesis.

дипло́м|ный *adj. of* ⇨**~; ~ная рабо́та** degree work, degree thesis.

директи́в|а, ы *f.* directive; instruction.

дире́ктор, а, *pl.* **~а́** *m.* director, manager; **д. шко́лы** head (master, mistress); principal.

директри́с|а, ы *f.* (*obs., coll.*) head mistress.

дире́кци|я, и *f.* management; board (of directors).

дирижа́бл|ь, я *m.* airship, dirigible.

дирижёр, а *m.* (*mus.*) conductor.

дирижёр|ский *adj. of* ⇨**~; ~ская па́лочка** (conductor's) baton.

дирижи́р|овать, ую *impf.* (+*i.*; *mus.*) to conduct.

дисгармони́р|овать, ую *impf.* **1** (*mus.*) to be out of tune. **2** (*fig.*) to clash, jar; to be out of keeping.

дисгармо́ни|я, и *g.* (*mus. and fig.*) disharmony; discord.

диск, а *m.* **1** (*also comput.*) disk; (*телефонный*) telephone dial. **2** (*sport*) discus. **3** (*mil.*) (cartridge-)drum (*of automatic weapon*). **4** (*грампластинка*) disc, record; **д.-гига́нт** long-playing record, LP.

ди́скант, а *m.* (*mus.*) treble.

дисквалифика́ци|я, и *f.* disqualification.

дисквалифици́р|овать, ую *impf. and pf.* to disqualify.

диске́т|а, ы *f.* (*comput.*) diskette; **пуста́я д.** blank diskette.

диск-жоке́|й, я *m.* disc-jockey.

ди́ско *nt. indecl.* disco music.

дискобо́л, а *m.* discus-thrower.

дисково́д, а *m.* (*comput.*) disk drive.

ди́сковый *adj.* disc-shaped.

дискомфо́рт, а *m.* discomfort.

дискомфо́ртный *adj.* uncomfortable.

диско́нт, а *m.* (*fin.*) discount.

дисконти́р|овать, ую *impf. and pf.* (*fin.*) to discount.

дискоте́к|а, и *f.* disco(theque) (*place*).

дискоте́|чный *adj. of* ⇨**~ка**

дискредити́р|овать, ую *impf. and pf.* to discredit.

дискриминацио́нный *adj.* discriminatory.

дискримина́ци|я, и *f.* discrimination; **д. же́нщин** sexism; **д. по во́зрасту** ageism.

дискримини́р|овать, ую *impf. and pf.* to discriminate against; **д. национа́льные меньшинства́** to discriminate against national minorities.

дискуссио́нн|ый *adj.* **1** *adj. of* ⇨**диску́ссия; д. клуб** debating club; **в ~ом поря́дке** as a basis for discussion. **2** (*спорный*) debatable, open to question.

диску́сси|я, и *f.* discussion.

дискути́р|овать, ую *impf.* (+*a. or* **о**+*p.*) to discuss.

Д

дисле́кси|я, и *f.* dyslexia.

дислока́ци|я, и *f.* **1** *(mil.)* deployment, distribution *(of troops)*. **2** *(geol.)* displacement. **3** *(med.)* dislocation.

дислоци́р|овать, ую *impf. and pf.* *(mil.)* to deploy *(troops)*.

диспансе́р, а *m.* *(med.)* clinic, (health) centre.

диспепси́|я, и *f.* dyspepsia.

диспе́тчер, а *m.* controller *(of movement of transport, etc.)*; *(comput.)* manager.

диспе́тчер|ский *adj. of* ⇨**~;** *(aeron.)*: **~ская вы́шка** control tower; **~ская слу́жба** flying control organization; *as n.* **~ская, ~ской** *f.* controller's office; *(aeron.)* control tower.

диспле́|й, я *m.* *(comput.)* display, VDU *(visual display unit)*.

диспропо́рци|я, и *f.* disproportion.

ди́спут, а *m.* (public) debate.

диссерта́нт, а *m.* defender of thesis.

диссерта́ци|я, и *f.* dissertation, thesis.

диссиде́нт, а *m.* *(pol.)* dissident; *(relig.)* nonconformist.

диссимиля́ци|я, и *f.* dissimilation.

диссона́нс, а *m.* *(mus. and fig.)* dissonance, discord.

диссони́р|овать, ую *impf.* to strike a discordant note, be discordant.

дистанцио́нн|ый *adj.*: **д. взрыва́тель, ~ая тру́бка** time fuse; **~ое управле́ние** remote control.

дистанци́р|оваться, уюсь *impf. and pf.* to distance o.s.

диста́нци|я, и *f.* **1** distance; **на большо́й, ма́лой ~и** at a great, short distance. **2** *(sport)* distance; **сойти́ с ~и** to withdraw, scratch. **3** *(mil.)* range. **4** *(rail.)* division, region.

дистилли́р|овать, ую *impf. and pf.* to distil *(Br.)*, distill *(US)*.

дистилля́ци|я, и *f.* distillation.

дистрибью́тор, а *m.* distributor, supplier.

дистрофи́|я, и *f.* *(med.)* dystrophy.

дисципли́н|а, ы *f.* *(in var. senses)* discipline.

дисциплина́рный *adj.* disciplinary; **д. батальо́н** penal battalion.

дисциплини́рова|нный *p.p.p. of* ⇨**~ть** *and adj.* disciplined.

дисциплини́р|овать, ую *impf. and pf.* to discipline.

дитя́, *g. and d.* **~ти,** *i.* **~тею,** *p.* **о ~ти,** *pl.* **де́ти** *nt.* child; baby.

дифира́мб, а *m.*: **петь ~ы** *(+d.)* to sing the praises (of), eulogize.

дифтери́т, и́та *m.* = **~и́я**

дифтери́|я, и *f.* diphtheria.

дифто́нг, а *m.* diphthong.

диффама́ци|я, и *f.* *(leg.)* defamation, libel.

дифференциа́л, а *m.* **1** *(math.)* differential. **2** *(tech.)* differential gear.

дифференциа́льн|ый *adj.* differential; **~ое исчисле́ние** *(math.)* differential calculus.

дифференци́р|овать, ую *impf. and pf.* to differentiate.

дича́|ть, ю *impf.* *(of* ⇨**о~)** to run wild, become wild; *(fig.)* to become unsociable.

дич|и́ться, у́сь, и́шься *impf.* *(+g.; coll.)* to be shy (of); to avoid.

дич|ь, и *f.* **1** *(collect.)* game; wildfowl. **2** *(глушь)* wilderness, wilds. **3** *(coll.)* *(вздор)* nonsense; **поро́ть д.** to talk nonsense.

диэле́ктрик, а *m.* *(phys.)* dielectric, non-conductor.

длин|а́, ы́ *f.* length; **в ~у́** longwise, lengthwise; **во всю ~у́** at full length; **ме́ры ~ы́** long measures; **~о́й в шесть ме́тров** six metres long *(Br.)*, six meters long *(US)*.

длинно... *comb. form* long-.

длинново́лновый *adj.* *(radio)* long-wave.

длиннот|а́, ы́, *pl.* **~ы** *f.* **1** *(obs. or coll.)* length. **2** *(pl.)* verbose, long-winded passages.

длиннофо́кусный *adj.*: **д. объекти́в** telephoto lens.

длинню́щий *adj.* *(coll.)* (terribly) long.

дли́н|ный (~ен, ~на́, ~но) *adj.* long; lengthy; **д. рубль** *(coll.)* easy money, quick money; **у него́ д. язы́к** he has a long tongue.

дли́тельност|ь, и *f.* duration.

дли́тел|ьный (~ен, ~ьна) *adj.* long, protracted, long-drawn-out.

дл|и́ться, и́тся *impf.* *(of* ⇨**про~)** to last.

для *prep.+g.* **1** *(в пользу кого, чего)* for (the sake of); **э́то д. тебя́** this is for you. **2** *(выражает цель)* for; **маши́на д. выка́чивания воды́** machine for pumping out water; **я э́то сде́лал то́лько д. ви́ду** I only did for appearances' sake; **д. того́, что́бы**. . . in order to . . . . **3** *(по отношению к)* for, to; **д. нас не сто́ит** for us it is not worth while; **вре́дно д. дете́й** bad for children; **непроница́емый д. воды́** waterproof. **4** *(по отношению к норме)* for, of; **он о́чень высо́к д. свои́х лет** he is very tall for his age; **э́то поведе́ние типи́чно д. них** such behaviour is typical of them.

днева́л|ить, ю, ишь *impf.* *(coll.)* to be on duty.

днева́льн|ый, ого *m.* *(mil.)* orderly, fatigue man.

днева́ть, дню́ю, дню́ешь *impf.* to spend the day; **д. и ночева́ть** to spend all one's time.

дневни́к, а́ *m.* diary, journal; **вести́ д.** to keep a diary.

дневн|о́й *adj.* **1** day; **в ~о́е вре́мя** during daylight hours; **д. свет** daylight; **~а́я сме́на** day shift; **д. спекта́кль** matinée. **2** *(одного дня)* day's, daily; **~а́я зарпла́та** day's pay.

днём *adv.* **1** in the day-time, by day. **2** *(после обеда)* in the afternoon; **сего́дня д.** this afternoon.

дни́щ|е, а *nt.* bottom *(of vessel or barrel)*.

ДНК *f. indecl.* *(abbr. of* ***дезоксирибонуклеи́новая кислота́****)* *(chem.)* DNA *(deoxyribonucleic acid)*.

дно, дна, *pl.* **до́нья, до́ньев** *nt.* bottom; **вверх дном** upside down; **пить до дна** to drink to the dregs; **(пей) до дна!** bottoms up!; **ни дна ему́ ни покры́шки!** *(coll.)* bad luck to him!

дноуглуби́тел|ь, я *m.* dredger.

до[1] *prep.+g.* **1** *(о пределе, границе)* to, up to; as far as; **от Ло́ндона до Москвы́** from London to Moscow; **дое́хать до Пари́жа** to go as far as Paris; **ю́бка до коле́н** knee-length skirt. **2** *(о временном пределе)* to, up to; until, till; **до шести́ часо́в** till six o'clock; **до сих пор** up to now, till now, hitherto; **до тех пор** till then, before; **до тех пор, пока́** until; **до свида́ния!** good-bye!; au revoir! **3** *(перед)* before; **до войны́** before the war; **до на́шей э́ры (до н. э.)** before Christ *(abbr.* BC); **до того́, как** before. **4** *(о пределе состояния)* to, up to, to the point of; **до бо́ли** until it hurt(s); **до того́. . ., что** to the point where; **мы до того́ уста́ли, что и засну́ть не удало́сь** we were too tired even to be able to sleep. **5** *(о количественном пределе)* under, up to (= *not over, not more than*); **де́ти до пяти́ лет** children under five; under-fives; **зараба́тывать до ты́сячи рубле́й** to earn up to a thousand roubles. **6** *(приблизительно)* about, approximately; **у нас в больни́це до двух ты́сяч ко́ек** in our hospital there are about two thousand beds. **7** *(относительно)* with regard to, concerning; **что до меня́** as far as I am concerned; **у меня́ есть до тебя́ де́ло** *(coll.)* I want (to see) you, I want a word with you; **не быть охо́тник до** not to be keen on, not to like; **мне,** *etc.*, **не до** *(coll.)* I, *etc.*, don't feel like, am not in the mood for; **мне не до разгово́ра** I am not in a mood for talk.

до[2] *nt. indecl.* *(mus.)* C.

до...[1] *vbl. pref.* **1** *expr. completion of action*: **дочита́ть кни́гу** to finish (reading) a book. **2** *indicates that action is carried to a certain point*: **дочита́ть до страни́цы 270** to read as far as page 270. **3** *expr. supplementary action*: **докупи́ть** to buy in addition. **4** *(+refl. vv.) expr. eventual attainment of object*: **дозвони́ться** to ring until one gets an answer.

до...[2] *pref. of nn. and adjs., used to indicate priority in chronological sequence* (pre-).

доба́в|ить, лю, ишь *pf.* *(of* ⇨**~ля́ть)** *(+a. or g.)* to add.

доба́вк|а, и *f.* **1** *(то, что добавлено)* addition. **2** *(в еде)* second helping.

добавле́ни|е, я *nt.* addition; *(к сочинению)* appendix, addendum.

добавля́|ть, ю *impf. of* ⇨**доба́вить**

доба́вочн|ый *adj.* additional, extra; *(teleph.)* extension; **~ое вре́мя** *(sport)* extra time; **д. нало́г** surtax; **д. три́дцать** extension 30.

добега́|ть, ю *impf. of* ⇨**добежа́ть**

добе́га|ться, юсь *pf.*: **~лся?** *(coll., iron.)* now you are in trouble!

добе|жа́ть, гу́, жи́шь, гу́т *pf.* *(of* ⇨**~га́ть)** *(до+g.)* to run (to, as far as); *(достигнуть)* to reach *(also fig.)*.

добела́ *adv.* **1** to white heat; **раскалённый д.** white-hot. **2** (*до белизны*) clean, white; **чёрного кобеля́ не отмо́ешь д.** (*prov.*) the leopard can't change his spots.

доберма́н(-пи́нчер), а *m.* Dobermann (pinscher).

добива́|ть, ю *impf. of* ⇒**доби́ть**

добива́|ться, юсь *impf.* **1** *impf. of* ⇒**доби́ться. 2** (+*g.*) to try to get, strive (for), aim (at).

добира́|ть, ю *impf. of* ⇒**добра́ть**

добира́|ться, юсь *impf. of* ⇒**добра́ться**

до|би́ть, бью, бьёшь *pf.* (*of* ⇒**~бива́ть**) to finish off, do for (*also in var. senses corresponding to meanings of pref. and simple v.*).

до|би́ться, бью́сь, бьёшься *pf.* (*of* ⇒**добива́ться**) (+*g.*) to get, obtain, secure; **д. своего́** to get one's way.

до́блест|ный (~ен, ~на) *adj.* valiant, valorous.

до́блест|ь, и *f.* valour (*Br.*), valor (*US*), gallantry.

до|бра́ть, беру́, берёшь, *past* **~бра́л, ~брала́, ~бра́ло** *pf.* (*of* ⇒**~бира́ть**) to finish collecting.

до|бра́ться, беру́сь, берёшься, *past* **~бра́лся, ~брала́сь, ~брало́сь** *pf.* (*of* ⇒**~бира́ться**) **1** (**до**+*g.*) to get (to), reach. **2** (*coll.*) to get (one's hands on); **я до тебя́ ~беру́сь!** I'll get you!

добра́чный *adj.* pre-marital.

добре|сти́, ду́, дёшь, *past* **~́л, ~ла́** *pf.* (**до**+*g.*) to get (to), reach (*slowly or with difficulty*).

добре́|ть[1], ю, ешь *impf.* (*of* ⇒**по~**) to become kinder.

добре́|ть[2], ю, ешь *impf.* (*of* ⇒**раз~**) (*coll.*) to put on weight.

добр|о́[1], а́ *nt.* **1** good; (*поступок*) good deed; **жела́ю вам ~а́** I wish you well; **от ~а́ ~а́ не и́щут** let well alone; **нет ху́да без ~а́** every cloud has a silver lining; **э́то не к ~у́** it is a bad omen, it bodes ill; **помина́ть ~о́м** to speak well (of), remember kindly. **2** (*collect.*, *coll.*) (*имущество*) goods, property. **3**: **дать/получи́ть добро́** to give/get the go-ahead.

добро́[2] *particle* (*coll.*) good; all right.

добро́[3]: **д. пожа́ловать!** welcome!

добро́[4] *as conj.* (+**бы**) it would be a different matter if; there would be some excuse if.

доброво́л|ец, ьца *m.* volunteer.

доброво́льно *adv.* voluntarily.

доброво́л|ьный (~ен, ~ьна) *adj.* voluntary.

доброво́льческий *adj.* volunteer.

доброде́тел|ь, и *f.* virtue.

доброде́тел|ьный (~ен, ~ьна) *adj.* virtuous.

доброду́ши|е, я *nt.* good-nature.

доброду́ш|ный (~ен, ~на) *adj.* good-natured; genial.

доброжела́тел|ь, я *m.* well-wisher.

доброжела́тел|ьный (~ен, ~ьна) *adj.* benevolent.

доброка́чествен|ный (~, ~на) *adj.* **1** of good quality. **2** (*med.*) benign.

добро́м *adv.* (*coll.*) voluntarily.

добропоря́доч|ный (~ен, ~на) *adj.* respectable.

добросерде́ч|ный (~ен, ~на) *adj.* good-hearted, kind.

добросо́вест|ный (~ен, ~на) *adj.* conscientious.

добрососе́дский *adj.* (good-) neighbourly (*Br.*), neighborly (*US*).

добрососе́дств|о, а *nt.* (good-) neighbourliness (*Br.*), neighborliness (*US*).

доброт|а́, ы́ *f.* goodness, kindness.

добро́тност|ь, и *f.* (good) quality; **д. сукна́** quality of cloth.

добро́т|ный (~ен, ~на) *adj.* of good, high quality; durable.

до́бр|ый (~, ~а́, ~о, ~́ы) *adj.* **1** (*хороший*) good; **~ое и́мя** good name; **д. знако́мый** good friend; **~ое у́тро!** good morning!; **всего́ ~ого!** good-bye!; all the best!; **в д. час!** good luck!; **по ~у́ по здоро́ву** while the going is (was) good. **2** (*отзывчивый*) kind, good; **бу́дьте ~ы́** (+*imper.*) please, would you be so kind as to. **3** (*coll.*) (*не меньший*) a good; **д. час** a good hour. **4**: **по ~ой во́ле** of one's own free will. **5**: **чего́ ~ого** (*introducing expr. of anticipation of unpleasant eventuality*) who knows; it may be.

добря́к, а́ *m.* (*coll.*) good-natured person.

добу|ди́ться, жу́сь, ~́дишься *pf.* (*coll.*) to wake, succeed in waking.

добыва́|ть, ю *impf. of* ⇒**добы́ть**

добы́тчик, а *m.* (*coll.*) **1** getter (*of minerals, etc.*). **2** (*кормилец*) bread-winner.

до|бы́ть, бу́ду, бу́дешь, *past* **~́был, ~была́, ~́было** *pf.* (*of* ⇒**~быва́ть**) **1** (*достать*) to get, obtain, procure. **2** (*из земли*) to extract, mine, quarry.

добы́ч|а, и *f.* **1** (*действие*) extraction (*of minerals*), mining, quarrying. **2** (*захваченное*) booty, spoils, loot. **3** (*охотника*) bag; (*рыболова*) catch. **4** (*добытое*) mineral products; output.

дова́рив|ать, аю *impf. of* ⇒**довари́ть**

довар|и́ть, ю́, ~́ишь *pf.* (*of* ⇒**~́ивать**) to finish cooking; to do to a turn.

довез|ти́, у́, ёшь, *past* **~́, ~ла́** *pf.* (*of* ⇒**довози́ть**) to take (to).

дове́ренност|ь, и *f.* warrant, power of attorney; **получи́ть де́ньги по ~и** to obtain money by proxy.

дове́р|енный *p.p.p. of* ⇒**~ить** *and adj.* trusted; **~енное лицо́** (*as n.* **д., ~енного** *m.*) agent, proxy; person empowered to act for s.o.

дове́ри|е, я *nt.* trust, confidence; **по́льзоваться чьим-н. ~ем** to enjoy s.o.'s confidence.

довери́тел|ь, я *m.* principal (*person empowering another to act for him*).

довери́тельный *adj.* confiding, trusting.

дове́р|ить, ю, ишь *pf.* (*of* ⇒**~я́ть**) (+*d.*) to entrust (to).

дове́р|иться, юсь, ишься *pf.* (*of* ⇒**~я́ться**) (+*d.*) to trust (in), confide (in).

до́верху *adv.* to the top; to the brim.

дове́рчивост|ь, и *f.* trusting nature, credulity.

дове́рчив|ый (~, ~а) *adj.* trustful, credulous.

доверш|а́ть, а́ю *impf. of* ⇒**~и́ть**

доверше́ни|е, я *nt.* completion; **в д. всего́** to crown all; on top of it all.

доверш|и́ть, у́, и́шь *pf.* (*of* ⇒**~а́ть**) to complete.

довер|я́ть, я́ю *impf.* **1** *impf. of* ⇒**~́ить. 2** (*impf. only*) (+*d.*) to trust, confide (in).

довер|я́ться, я́юсь *impf. of* ⇒**~́иться**

дове́с|ок, ка *m.* makeweight.

дове|сти́, ду́, дёшь, *past* **~́л, ~ла́** *pf.* (*of* ⇒**доводи́ть**) **1** (**до**+*g.*) to lead (to), take (to), accompany (to). **2** (**до**+*g.*) to bring (to); to drive (to), reduce (to); **д. до конца́** to see through (to the end); **д. до соверше́нства** to perfect; **д. до сумасше́ствия** to drive mad; **д. до слёз** to reduce to tears; **д. до све́дения** (+*g.*) to inform, let know, bring to the notice (of).

дове|сти́сь, дётся, *past* **~ло́сь** *pf.* (*of* ⇒**доводи́ться**) (*impers.*, +*d.*; *coll.*) to have occasion (to); to happen (to); **нам ~ло́сь заста́ть его́ до́ма** we happened to catch him in.

довин|ти́ть, чу́, ти́шь *pf.* (*of* ⇒**~́чивать**) to screw up.

дови́нчива|ть, ю *impf. of* ⇒**довинти́ть**

довле́|ть, ет *impf.* (**над**+*i.*; *vulg.*) to oppress, burden.

до́вод, а *m.* argument.

дово|ди́ть, жу́, ~́дишь *impf. of* ⇒**довести́**

дово|ди́ться, жу́сь, ~́дишься *impf.* **1** *impf. of* ⇒**довести́сь. 2** (+*d. and i.*) to be related (to as); **он ~́дится ей племя́нником** he is her nephew.

довое́нный *adj.* pre-war.

дово|зи́ть, жу́, ~́зишь *impf. of* ⇒**довезти́**

householdдово́льно[1] *adv.* **1** (*достаточно*) enough; *as pred.* it is enough; **с нас э́того д.** we've had enough of this; **д. спо́рить!** stop arguing! **2** (*порядочно*) quite, fairly; rather, pretty; **д. хоро́ший фильм** quite a good film.

дово́льно[2] *adv.* contentedly.

дово́л|ьный (~ен, ~ьна) *adj.* **1** contented, satisfied; **д. вид** contented expression. **2** (+*i.*) contented (with), satisfied (with), pleased (with); **д. собо́й** pleased with o.s., self-satisfied.

дово́льстви|е, я *nt.* (*mil.*) allowance.

дово́льств|о, а *nt.* **1** contentment. **2** (*coll.*) (*материальный достаток*) ease, prosperity.

дово́льств|оваться, уюсь *impf.* (*of*

⇨у~) (+*i.*) to be content (with), be satisfied (with).

довы́бор|ы, ов *no sg.* by-election.

дог, а *m.* mastiff; **да́тский д.** Great Dane; **далма́тский д.** Dalmatian.

догад|а́ться, а́юсь *pf.* (*of* **⇨~ываться**) to guess.

дога́дк|а, и *f.* surmise, conjecture; (*pl.*) guesswork; **теря́ться в ~ах** to be lost in conjecture.

дога́длив|ый (~, ~а) *adj.* quick-witted, bright.

дога́дыва|ться, юсь *impf.* **1** *impf. of* **⇨догада́ться. 2** (*impf. only*) to suspect.

догля|де́ть, жу́, ди́шь *pf.* (*coll.*) **1** (*досмотреть*) to watch to the end, see through. **2** (*присмотреть*) to keep an eye out; (**за**+*i.*) to keep an eye (on).

до́гм|а, ы *f.* dogma.

до́гмат, а *m.* **1** (*relig.*) doctrine, dogma; **д. непогреши́мости Па́пы** the doctrine of the infallibility of the Pope. **2** (*принцип*) tenet, foundation.

догмати́зм, а *m.* dogmatism.

догма́тик, а *m.* dogmatist.

догмати́ческий *adj.* dogmatic.

до|гна́ть, гоню́, го́нишь, *past* **~гна́л, ~гнала́, ~гна́ло** *pf.* (*of* **⇨~гоня́ть**) **1** to catch up (with) (*also fig.*). **2** (**до**+*g.*) to drive (to); (*fig., coll.*) to raise (to).

догова́рива|ть, ю *impf. of* **⇨договори́ть**

догова́рива|ться, юсь *impf.* **1** *impf. of* **⇨договори́ться. 2** (*impf. only*) (**о**+*p.*) to negotiate (about); **Высо́кие ~ющиеся сто́роны** (*dipl.*) the High Contracting Parties.

догово́р, а *and* (*coll.*) **до́говор**, *pl.* **~а́** *m.* agreement; (*pol.*) treaty, pact; **заключи́ть ми́рный д.** to conclude a peace treaty.

договорённост|ь, и *f.* agreement, understanding; (*pol.*) accord.

договор|и́ть, ю́, и́шь *pf.* (*of* **⇨догова́ривать**) to finish saying; to finish telling.

договор|и́ться, ю́сь, и́шься *pf.* (*of* **⇨догова́риваться**) **1** (**о**+*p.*) to come to an agreement, understanding (about); to arrange; **~и́лись!** agreed!; it's a deal! **2** (**до**+*g.*) to come (to); to talk (to the point of).

догово́рник, а *m.* (*coll.*) contract worker.

догово́рн|ый *adj.* agreed; contractual; **~ая цена́** agreed price; **на ~ых нача́лах** on a contractual basis.

догола́ *adv.* stark naked; **раздє́ться д.** to strip to the skin.

догоня́|ть, ю *impf. of* **⇨догна́ть**

догор|а́ть, а́ю *impf. of* **⇨~е́ть**

догор|е́ть, ю́, и́шь *pf.* (*of* **⇨~а́ть**) (*сгореть до какого-либо предела*) to burn down; (*сгореть до конца*) to burn out.

догружа́|ть, ю *impf. of* **⇨догрузи́ть**

догру|зи́ть, жу́, ~́зишь *pf.* (*of* **⇨~жа́ть**) **1** (*окончить погрузку*) to finish loading. **2** (*добавить к грузу*) to load in addition.

дода|ва́ть, ю́, ёшь *impf. of* **⇨~́ть**

дода́|ть, м, шь, ст, ди́м, ди́те, ду́т, *past* **до́да́л, ~ла́, до́дало** *pf.* (*of* **⇨~ва́ть**) to make up (the rest of); to pay up.

доде́л|ать, аю *pf.* (*of* **⇨~ывать**) to finish.

доде́лыва|ть, ю *impf. of* **⇨доде́лать**

доду́м|аться, аюсь *pf.* (*of* **⇨~ываться**) (**до**+*g.*) to hit (upon) (*afterthought*).

доду́мыва|ться, юсь *impf. of* **⇨доду́маться**

доеда́|ть, ю *impf. of* **⇨дое́сть**

доезжа́|ть, ю *impf. of* **⇨дое́хать**

дое́ни|е, я *nt.* milking.

до|е́сть, е́м, е́шь, е́ст, еди́м, еди́те, едя́т *pf.* (*of* **⇨~еда́ть**) to eat up, finish eating.

до|е́хать, е́ду, е́дешь *pf.* (*of* **⇨~езжа́ть**) (**до**+*g.*) to reach, arrive (at).

дож, а *m.* (*hist.*) doge.

дожа́рива|ть, ю *impf. of* **⇨дожа́рить**

дожа́р|ить, ю, ишь *pf.* (*of* **⇨~ивать**) to finish roasting, frying; to roast, fry to a turn.

дожд|а́ться, у́сь, ёшься, *past* **~а́лся, ~ала́сь, ~а́ло́сь** *pf.* **1** (+*g.*) to wait (for); **д. конца́ спекта́кля** to wait until the end of the show. **2**: **д. того́, что** to end up (by); **он ~а́лся того́, что ему́ указа́ли на дверь** he ended up by being shown the door.

дождева́льный *adj.*: **д. аппара́т** (*agric.*) water-sprinkler.

дождева́ни|е, я *nt.* (*agric.*) sprinkling.

дождеви́к, а́ *m.* (*coll.*) raincoat.

дождев|о́й *adj. of* **⇨дождь; ~а́я ка́пля** rain-drop; **~о́е о́блако** rain-cloud, nimbus.

до́ждик, а *m.* shower.

дожди́нк|а, и *f.* (*coll.*) rain-drop.

дождли́в|ый (~, ~а) *adj.* rainy.

дожд|ь, я́ *m.* **1** rain (*also fig.*); **под ~ём** in the rain; **ме́лкий д.** drizzle; **проливно́й д.** downpour; **кисло́тные ~и́** acid rain; **д. идёт** it is raining; **д. льёт как из ведра́** it's raining cats and dogs; it's bucketing down. **2** (*fig.*) rain, hail, cascade; **д. искр** cascade of sparks; **д. руга́тельств** torrent of abuse; **сы́паться ~ём** to rain down, cascade.

дожива́|ть, ю *impf.* **1** *impf. of* **⇨дожи́ть. 2** (*impf. only*) to live out; **д. свой век** to live out one's days.

дожида́|ться, юсь *impf.* (*of* **⇨дожда́ться**) (+*g.*) to wait (for).

до|жи́ть, живу́, живёшь, *past* **~́жил, ~жила́, ~́жило** *pf.* (*of* **⇨~жива́ть**) **1** (**до**+*g.*) (*прожить*) to live (till); to attain the age (of); **она́ ~жила́ до конца́ войны́** she lived to see the end of the war. **2** (**до**+*g.*) (*дойти до какого-либо состояния*) to come (to), be reduced (to); **до чего́ мы ~́жили!** what have we come to! **3** (*coll.*) (*пробыть*) to stay, spend (the rest of); **я доживу́ ле́то в Пари́же** I shall spend the rest of the summer in Paris.

до́з|а, ы *f.* dose.

дозапра́вк|а, и *f.* refuelling (*Br.*), refueling (*US*).

доза́тор, а *m.* dispenser.

до|зва́ться, зову́сь, зовёшься, *past* **~зва́лся, ~звала́сь, ~зва́ло́сь** *pf.* (*coll.*) to call until one gets an answer; **его́ не ~зовёшься** he never comes when he is called.

дозво́л|енный *p.p.p. of* **⇨~ить** *and adj.* permitted.

дозво́л|ить, ю, ишь *pf.* (*of* **⇨~я́ть**) (*obs. or coll.*) to permit, allow.

дозвол|я́ть, я́ю *impf. of* **⇨~ить**

дозвон|и́ться, ю́сь, и́шься *pf.* (*coll.*) (**до**+*g.*, **к**+*d.*) to ring until one gets an answer; to get through (*on telephone*); **я не мог к тебе́ д.** I rang you but could get no reply, could not get through.

дозвуково́й *adj.* subsonic.

дози́р|овать, ую *impf. and pf.* to measure out (in doses).

дозиро́вк|а, и *f.* dosage.

дозна|ва́ться, ю́сь, ёшься *impf.* **1** *impf. of* **⇨~́ться. 2** (*only impf.*) (**о**+*p.*) to inquire (about).

дозна́ни|е, я *nt.* (*leg.*) inquiry; inquest.

дозн|а́ться, а́юсь *pf.* (*of* **⇨~ава́ться**) to find out, ascertain.

дозо́р, а *m.* patrol.

дозо́р|ный *adj. of* **⇨~; ~ная шлю́пка** patrol boat; *as n.* **д., ~ного** *m.* (*mil.*) scout.

дозрева́|ть, ю *impf. of* **⇨дозре́ть**

дозре́лый *adj.* fully ripe.

дозр|е́ть, е́ю *pf.* (*of* **⇨~ева́ть**) to ripen.

доигр|а́ть, а́ю *pf.* (*of* **⇨~́ывать**) to finish (playing).

доигр|а́ться, а́юсь *pf.* (*of* **⇨~́ываться**) (**до**+*g.*) to play (until); (*fig.*) to get o.s. (into), land o.s. (in); **вот и ~а́лся!** now you've (he's, *etc.*) done it!

доі́грыва|ть(ся), ю(сь) *impf. of* **⇨доигра́ть(ся)**

до́йльный *adj.*: **д. аппара́т** milking machine.

до|иска́ться, ищу́сь, и́щешься *pf.* (*of* **⇨~и́скиваться**) (*coll.*) (+*g.*) **1** (*найти*) to find, discover. **2** (*узнать*) to find out, ascertain.

дои́скива|ться, юсь *impf.* **1** *impf. of* **⇨доиска́ться. 2** (*impf. only*) (+*g.*) to try to find out.

доистори́ческий *adj.* prehistoric.

до|и́ть, ю́, ~́ишь *impf.* (*of* **⇨по~**) to milk.

до|и́ться, ~́ится *impf.* **1** to give milk; **хорошо́ д.** to be a good milker. **2** *pass. of* **⇨~и́ть**

до́йк|а, и *f.* milking.

до́йн|ый *adj.* milch; **~ая коро́ва** milch cow (*also fig.*).

до|йти́, йду́, йдёшь, *past* **~шёл, ~шла́** *pf.* (*of* **⇨~ходи́ть**) **1** (**до**+*g.*) (*in var. senses*) to reach; **письмо́ ~шло́**

до меня́ то́лько сего́дня the letter only reached me today; **д. до све́дения** (+*g.*) to come to the attention (of); **д. до того́, что...** to reach a point where ...; **ру́ки не ~шли́ (до**+*g.*) I, *etc.*, had no time (for). **2** (*coll.*) (**до**+*g.*) (*произвести впечатление*) to make an impression (upon), get through (to), touch; **его́ про́поведь про́сто не ~шла́ до слу́шателей** his homily left his audience quite unmoved.
3 (*impers.*; *also* **де́ло ~йдёт, ~шло́ до**+*g.*) to come (to); **де́ло ~шло́ до проце́сса** it came to a court case.
4 (*coll.*) (*стать готовым*) to be done (= *to be cooked*); to be ripe.

док, а *m.* dock.

до́к|а, и *c.g.* (*coll.*) expert, authority.

доказа́тел|ьный (~ен, ~ьна) *adj.* demonstrative, conclusive.

доказа́тельств|о, а *nt.* **1** proof, evidence. **2** (*math.*) demonstration.

док|аза́ть, ажу́, а́жешь *pf.* (*of* ⇒**~а́зывать**) to demonstrate, prove; **счита́ть ~а́занным** to take for granted; **что и тре́бовалось д.** quod erat demonstrandum (*abbr.* Q.E.D.).

доказу́ем|ый (~, ~а) *adj.* demonstrable.

дока́зыва|ть, ю *impf.* **1** *impf. of* ⇒**доказа́ть. 2** (*impf. only*) to argue, try to prove.

дока́нчива|ть, ю *impf. of* ⇒**доко́нчить**

дока́пыва|ться, юсь *impf. of* ⇒**докопа́ться**

док|ати́ться, ачу́сь, а́тишься *pf.* (*of* ⇒**~а́тываться**) **1** (**до**+*g.*) to roll (to). **2** (*о звуках*) to roll, thunder, boom. **3** (*fig., coll.*) (**до**+*g.*) (*дойти до какого-либо состояния*) to sink (into), come (to); **д. до преступле́ния** to sink into crime.

дока́тыва|ться, юсь *impf. of* ⇒**докати́ться**

до́кер, а *m.* docker.

докла́д, а *m.* **1** report; lecture; paper; talk, address; **чита́ть д.** to give a report; to read a paper. **2** (*сообщение о приходе посетителя*) announcement; **войти́ без ~а** to enter unannounced.

докладн|о́й *adj.*: **~а́я запи́ска** report, memorandum; *as n.* **~а́я, ~о́й** *f.* = **~а́я запи́ска**

докла́дчик, а *m.* speaker, lecturer.

докла́дчи|ца, цы *f. of* ⇒**~к**

докла́дыва|ть(ся), ю(сь) *impf. of* ⇒**доложи́ть(ся)**

доко́ле (*and* **доко́ль**) *adv.* **1** (*interrog.*) how long. **2** (*rel.*) as long as; until.

докона́|ть, ю *pf.* (*coll.*) to finish off, be the end (of).

доко́нч|ить, у, ишь *pf.* (*of* ⇒**дока́нчивать**) to finish, complete.

докопа́|ться, юсь *pf.* (*of* ⇒**дока́пываться**) (**до**+*g.*) **1** to dig down (to). **2** (*fig.*) to get to the bottom (of); to find out, discover.

до́красна́ *adv.* to redness; to red heat; **раскалённый д.** red-hot.

докрич|а́ться, у́сь, и́шься *pf.* **1** to shout until one is heard. **2**: **д. до хрипоты́** to shout o.s. hoarse.

до́ктор, а, *pl.* **~а́** *m.* doctor.

доктора́нт, а *m.* person working for degree of doctor.

до́ктор|ский *adj. of* ⇒**~**; **~ская диссерта́ция** doctoral thesis.

до́кторш|а, и *f.* (*coll.*) **1** (*obs.*) (*жена врача*) doctor's wife. **2** (*женщина-врач*) woman-doctor.

доктри́н|а, ы *f.* doctrine.

доктринёр, а *m.* doctrinaire.

доктринёрский *adj.* doctrinaire.

доктринёрств|о, а *nt.* doctrinaire attitude.

доку́да *adv.* (*coll.*) **1** (*interrog.*) how far. **2** (*rel.*) as far as.

докуме́нт, а *m.* **1** document, paper; **предъяви́ть ~ы** to produce one's papers; (*comput.*) document. **2** (*leg.*) deed; instrument.

документали́ст, а *m.* documentary film-maker.

документа́льный *adj.* documentary; **д. фильм** documentary (film).

документа́ци|я, и *f.* **1** (*действие*) documentation. **2** (*collect.*) (*документы*) documents, papers, documentation.

документи́р|овать, ую *impf. and pf.* to document.

докуп|а́ть[1], а́ю *impf. of* ⇒**~и́ть**

докупа́|ть[2], ю *pf.* to finish bathing (*trans.*).

докуп|и́ть, лю́, ~ишь *pf.* (*of* ⇒**~а́ть[1]**) to buy in addition.

докуча́|ть, ю *impf.* (+*d. and i.*; *coll.*) to bother (with), pester (with), plague (with).

доку́члив|ый (~, ~а) *adj.* (*coll.*) tiresome, importunate.

доку́ч|ный (~ен, ~на) *adj.* (*coll.*) tiresome, boring.

дол, а *m.* (*poet.*) dale, vale; **за гора́ми, за ~а́ми** far and wide; **по гора́м, по ~а́м** up hill and down dale.

долбан|у́ть, у́, ёшь *pf.* (*coll.*) to hit hard.

долбёжк|а, и *f.* (*sl.*) swotting.

долб|и́ть, лю́, и́шь *impf.* **1** to hollow out; to gouge. **2** (*coll.*) (*повторять*) to repeat, say over and over. **3** (*sl.*) (*зубрить*) to swot (up); to learn by rote. **4** (**в**+*a.*) to bang (on).

долг, а, о ~е, в ~у́, *pl.* **~и́** *m.*
1 (*обязанность*) duty; **по ~у слу́жбы** in the performance of one's duty.
2 (*одолженное*) debt; **в д.** on credit; **войти́, влезть в ~и** to get into debt; **быть у кого́-н. в ~у́** to be indebted to s.o.; **отда́ть после́дний д.** to pay the last honours; **д. платежо́м кра́сен** one good turn deserves another.

до́л|гий (~ог, ~га́, ~го) *adj.* long, of long duration; **~гая пе́сня** (*fig.*) a long story; **отложи́ть в д. я́щик** to shelve, put off.

до́лго *adv.* long, (for) a long time.

долгове́ч|ный (~ен, ~на) *adj.* lasting; durable.

долгов|о́й *adj. of* ⇒**долг** 2; **~о́е обяза́тельство** promissory note.

долговре́мен|ный (~ен, ~на) *adj.* of long duration, prolonged.

долговя́з|ый (~, ~а) *adj.* (*coll.*) lanky.

долгогри́в|ый (~, ~а) *adj.* shaggy-maned.

долгожда́нный *adj.* long-awaited.

долгожи́тел|ь, я *m.* long-lived person.

долгожи́тель|ница, ницы *f. of* ⇒**~**

долгоигра́ющ|ий *adj.*: **~ая пласти́нка** long-playing (gramophone) record.

долголе́ти|е, я *nt.* longevity.

долголе́тний *adj.* of many years; long-standing.

долгоно́сик, а *m.* weevil.

долгосро́ч|ный (~ен, ~на) *adj.* (*кредит*) long-term; (*отпуск*) of long duration.

долгот|а́, ы́, *pl.* **~ы** *f.* **1** (*sg. only*) duration. **2** (*geog.*) longitude.

долготерпели́в|ый (~, ~а) *adj.* (*obs.*) long-suffering.

долготерпе́ни|е, я *nt.* long suffering.

долево́й[1] *adj.* lengthwise.

долев|о́й[2] *adj. of* ⇒**до́ля**

до́лее *comp. of* ⇒**до́лго**

долет|а́ть, а́ю *impf. of* ⇒**~е́ть**

доле|те́ть, чу́, ти́шь, *pf.* (*of* ⇒**~та́ть**) (**до**+*g.*) **1** (*летя, достигнуть какого-либо места*) to fly (to, as far as); to reach. **2** (*о брошенном предмете, звуках, запахе*) to reach.

должа́|ть, ю *impf.* (*of* ⇒**за~**) (*obs.*) **1** (**у**+*g.*) to borrow (from). **2** (+*d.*) to owe.

до́лж|ен (~на́, ~но́) *pred. adj.*
1 owing; **он д. мне три рубля́** he owes me three roubles. **2** (+*inf.*) (*обязан*): **я д. идти́** I must go, I have to go; **он д. был отказа́ться** he had to refuse. **3** (+*inf.*) (*предназначен*): **она́ ~на́ ско́ро прийти́** she should be here soon; **~но́ быть** probably; **вы с ним, ~но́ быть, уже́ знако́мы** you must have met him; you have probably met him.

должни́к, а́ *m.* debtor.

должни́|ца, цы *f. of* ⇒**~к**

до́лжно *as pred.* (+*inf.*) (*obs.*) one should, ought (to).

должностн|о́й *adj.* official; **~о́е лицо́** official, functionary, public servant; **~о́е преступле́ние** malfeasance in office.

до́лжност|ь, и, *g. pl.* **~е́й** *f.* post, office.

до́лжн|ый *adj.* due, fitting, proper; **~ым о́бразом** properly; *as n.* **~ое, ~ого** due; **воздава́ть д.** (+*d.*) to do justice.

долива́|ть, ю *impf. of* ⇒**доли́ть**

доли́н|а, ы *f.* valley.

доли́н|ный *adj. of* ⇒**~а**

дол|и́ть, ью́, ьёшь, *past* **~и́л, ~ила́, ~и́ло** *pf.* (*of* ⇒**~ива́ть**) **1** (*жидкость*) to add; to pour in addition. **2** (*сосуд*) to fill (up); to refill.

до́ллар, а *m.* dollar.

долож|и́ть[1], у́, ~ишь *pf.* (*of* ⇒**докла́дывать**) **1** (+*a. or* **о**+*p.*)

Д

(*сделать доклад*) to report; to give a report (on). **2** (**о**+*p.*) (*сообщить о приходе посетителя*) to announce (*a guest, etc.*).

долож|и́ть², у́, ~́ишь *pf.* (*of* ⇨**докла́дывать**) (*добавить*) to add.

долож|и́ться, у́сь, ~́ишься *pf.* (*of* ⇨**докла́дываться**) to announce one's arrival.

доло́й *adv.* (+*a.*; *coll.*) **1** down (with), away (with); **д. изме́нников!** down with the traitors!; **уйди́ с глаз д.!** out of my sight! **2** off (with); **ша́пки д.!** hats off!

долот|о́, а́, *pl.* **~́а, ~́** *nt.* chisel.

до́льк|а, и *f.* segment.

до́льше *adv.* longer.

до́л|я, и, *g. pl.* **~е́й** *f.* **1** (*часть*) part, portion; share; quota, allotment; **войти́ в ~ю** (**с**+*i.*) to go shares (with); **в его́ слова́х не́ было и ~и и́стины** there was not a grain of truth in his words. **2** (*anat., bot.*) lobe. **3** (*судьба*) lot, fate; **вы́пасть на чью-н. ~ю** to fall to s.o.'s lot.

дом, а (у), *pl.* **~а́** *m.* **1** (*жилое здание*) house; (*многоквартирный*) block (of flats) (*Br.*), apartment block (*US*); (*здание учреждения*) building; **д. культу́ры** palace of culture; ≈ arts (and leisure) centre; **д. о́тдыха** rest home, holiday home; **Д. учёных** Scientists' Club; **д. терпи́мости** brothel; **д.-музе́й**... ... House; **д.-музе́й Пу́шкина** Pushkin House. **2** (*своё жильё*) home; (*семья*) household; **вести́ д.** to keep house, run the house; **на ~у́** at home; **брать рабо́ту на́ д.** to take work home; **тоска́ по ~́у** homesickness. **3** (*династия*) house, lineage; **д. Рома́новых** the House of Romanov.

дом... *comb. form, abbr. of* **1** ***домо́вый.*** **2** ***дома́шний***

до́ма *adv.* at home, in; **быть как д.** to feel at home; **бу́дьте как д.** make yourself at home; **у него́ не все д.** he's not all there.

домаркси́стский *adj.* pre-Marxist.

дома́шн|ий *adj.* **1** house; home; domestic; **д. а́дрес** home address; **~ие забо́ты** household chores; **д. компью́тер** home computer; **~ее пла́тье** housecoat; **~яя рабо́тница** domestic (servant), maid; **~яя страни́ца** (*comput.*) home page; **~яя хозя́йка** housewife; **под ~им аре́стом** under house arrest. **2** (*самодельный*) home-made. **3** (*не дикий*) tame; domestic; **~ие живо́тные** domestic animals; **~ие пти́цы** poultry. **4** *as n.* **~ие, ~их** one's people, one's family.

до́менн|ый *adj. of* ⇨**до́мна; ~ая печь** blast furnace.

до́менщик, а *m.* blast-furnace operator.

до́мик, а *m. dim. of* ⇨**дом**

домина́нт|а, ы *f.* **1** (*mus.*) dominant. **2** (*fig.*) leitmotif.

доминика́н|ец, ца *m.* Dominican (monk).

Доминика́нск|ая Респу́блик|а, ~ой ~и *f.* the Dominican Republic.

доминио́н, а *m.* dominion.

домини́р|овать, ую *impf.* **1** to dominate, prevail (*fig.*). **2** (*geog.*) (**над**+*i.*) to dominate, command.

домино́ *nt. indecl.* **1** (*игра*) dominoes. **2** (*костюм*) domino.

доми́ш|ко, ~ка, *pl.* **~ки, ~ек, ~кам** *m.* (*coll.*) small, wretched house; hovel.

домко́м, а *m.* (*abbr. of* ***домо́вый комите́т***) house management committee.

домкра́т, а *m.* (*tech.*) jack.

до́мн|а, ы *f.* blast furnace.

домо... *comb. form* **1** home-. **2** *abbr. of* (*i*) ***домо́вый*** and (*ii*) ***дома́шний***

домови́т|ый (~, ~а) *adj.* thrifty, economical; **~ая хозя́йка** good housewife.

домовладе́л|ец, ьца *m.* house-owner; (*по отношению к нанимателю*) land-lord.

домово́дств|о, а *nt.* housekeeping; household management; home economics.

домов|о́й, о́го *m.* (*folklore*) brownie, house-sprite.

домо́в|ый *adj.* **1** house; household; **~ая кни́га** register of tenants; **~ая конто́ра** house-manager's office. **2** housing; **д. трест** housing trust.

домога́тельств|о, а *nt.* solicitation, demand, bid; **д. госпо́дства** bid for power; **сексуа́льное д.** sexual harassment.

домога́|ться, юсь *impf.* (+*g.*) to strive (for), solicit, covet.

домо́й *adv.* home, homewards; **нам пора́ д.** it's time for us to go home.

доморо́щенный *adj.* **1** (*виноград*) home-grown; (*лошадь*) home-bred. **2** (*fig.*) (*музыка, артист*) primitive; homespun.

домосе́д, а *m.* stay-at-home.

домострое́ни|е, я *nt.* house-building.

домострои́тельный *adj.* house-building.

домотка́ный *adj.* home-spun.

домоуправле́ни|е, я *nt.* house management (committee).

домофо́н, а *m.* electronic security system (*at entrance to building*); entryphone (*Br., propr.*).

домохозя́|ин, ина, *pl.* **~ева, ~ев** *m.* **1** (*домовладелец*) householder. **2** (*муж, ведущий домашнее хозяйство*) househusband.

домохозя́йк|а, и *f.* housewife.

домоча́д|ец, ца *m.* member of household.

до́мр|а, ы *f.* (*mus.*) domra (*Russian stringed instrument similar to mandolin*).

домрабо́тниц|а, ы *f.* domestic (servant), maid; **приходя́щая д.** home help; daily.

домри́ст, а *m.* domra-player.

дому́шник, а *m.* (*sl.*) burglar, housebreaker.

домч|а́ть, у́, и́шь *pf.* (*coll.*) to bring quickly (*in a vehicle, etc.*).

домч|а́ться, у́сь, и́шься *pf.* (*coll.*) to race (to), rush (to).

до́мыс|ел, ла *m.* conjecture.

донага́ *adv.* stark naked.

дона́шива|ть, ю *impf. of* ⇨**доноси́ть¹**

доне́льзя *adv.* to the utmost; in the extreme; **он д. упря́м** he is obstinate in the extreme.

донесе́ни|е, я *nt.* dispatch, report, message; **д. о боевы́х поте́рях** casualty report.

донес|ти́¹, у́, ёшь, *past* **~́, ~ла́** *pf.* (*of* ⇨**доноси́ть²**) (**до**+*g.*) to carry (to, as far as); (*звук, запах*) to carry, bear.

донес|ти́², у́, ёшь, *past* **~́, ~ла́** *pf.* (*of* ⇨**доноси́ть³**) **1** to report, announce; (+*d.*) to inform. **2** (**на**+*a.*) (*сделать донос*) to inform (on, against), denounce.

донес|ти́сь, у́сь, ёшься, *past* **~́ся, ~ла́сь** *pf.* (*of* ⇨**доноси́ться²**) **1** (*о звуках, запахах, новостях*) to reach; **до нас уже́ ~́ся слух** a rumour had already reached us. **2** (*coll.*) (*быстро доехать, добежать*) to reach quickly.

дон|е́ц, ца́ *m.* Don Cossack.

донжуа́н, а *m.* Don Juan, philanderer.

донжуа́нств|о, а *nt.* philandering.

до́низу *adv.* to the bottom.

донима́|ть, ю *impf. of* ⇨**доня́ть**

донкихо́тский *adj.* quixotic.

донкихо́тств|о, а *n.* quixotry.

до́нный *adj. of* ⇨**дно; д. лёд** ground ice.

до́нор, а *m.* (blood-)donor.

до́нор|ский *adj. of* ⇨**~; д. пункт** blood donation centre (*Br.*), center (*US*).

доно́с, а *m.* denunciation.

дон|оси́ть¹, ошу́, ~о́сишь *pf.* (*of* ⇨**дона́шивать**) **1** to wear out. **2**: **д. ребёнка** to bear at full term.

дон|оси́ть²,³, ошу́, ~о́сишь *impf. of* ⇨**донести́¹,²**

дон|оси́ться¹, ~о́сится *pf.* to wear out, be worn out.

дон|оси́ться², ~о́сится *impf. of* ⇨**донести́сь**

доно́счик, а *m.* informer.

доно́счи|ца, цы *f. of* ⇨**~к**

донско́й *adj.* (of the river) Don; **д. каза́к** Don Cossack.

до́нц|е, а *nt. dim. of* ⇨**дно**

доны́не *adv.* (*rhet.*) hitherto.

до|ня́ть, йму́, йме́шь, *past* **~́нял, ~няла́, ~́няло** *pf.* (*of* ⇨**~нима́ть**) (*coll.*) to weary, tire out, exasperate.

дообе́денный *adj.* pre-prandial.

дооктя́брьский *adj.* pre-October (*before the Russian Revolution of October 1917*).

допека́|ть, ю *impf. of* ⇨**допе́чь**

допетро́вский *adj.* pre-Petrine.

допе́|чь, ку́, чёшь, ку́т, *past* **~́к, ~кла́** *pf.* (*of* ⇨**~ка́ть**) **1** to bake until done; to finish baking. **2** (*fig., coll.*) (*донять*) to wear out, plague, pester.

допива́|ть, ю *impf. of* ⇨**допи́ть**

до́пинг, а *m.* **1** stimulant. **2** (*fig.*) (**психологи́ческий**) **д.** boost, shot in the arm.

до́пинговый *adj.*: **д. контро́ль** dope test; dope testing.

допи|са́ть, шу́, ~́шешь *pf.* (*of* ⇒**~́сывать**) **1** (*письмо*) to finish writing; (*картину*) to finish painting. **2** (*приписать*) to add.

допи́сыва|ть, ю *impf. of* ⇒**дописа́ть**

доп|и́ть, ью́, ьёшь, *past* **~́ил, ~ила́, ~́ило** *pf.* (*of* ⇒**~ива́ть**) to drink (up).

допла́т|а, ы *f.* additional payment; surcharge.

допл|ати́ть, ачу́, ~а́тишь *pf.* (*of* ⇒**~а́чивать**) to pay in addition, pay the remainder.

допла́чива|ть, ю *impf. of* ⇒**доплати́ть**

доплыва́|ть, ю *impf. of* ⇒**доплы́ть**

доплы́|ть, ву́, вёшь, *past* **~л, ~ла́, ~ло** *pf.* (*of* ⇒**~ва́ть**) (**до**+*g.*) (*вплавь*) to swim (to, as far as); (*на корабле*) to sail (to, as far as); (*fig.*) to reach.

допо́длинно *adv.* (*coll.*) for certain.

допо́длинный *adj.* (*coll.*) authentic, genuine.

допоздна́ *adv.* (*coll.*) till late.

дополне́ни|е, я *nt.* **1** supplement, addition; addendum. **2** (*gram.*) object; **прямо́е д.** direct object; **ко́свенное д.** indirect object.

дополни́тельно *adv.* in addition.

дополни́тельн|ый *adj.* supplementary, additional, extra; **~ое вре́мя** (*sport*) extra time; **д. окла́д** extra pay; **~ые цвета́** complementary colours (*Br.*), colors (*US*).

допо́лн|ить, ю, ишь *pf.* (*of* ⇒**~я́ть**) to supplement, add to; (*fig.*) to embellish (*a story, etc.*); **д. друг дру́га** to complement one another.

дополн|я́ть, я́ю, *impf. of* ⇒**~́ить**

допото́пный *adj.* antediluvian.

допра́шива|ть, ю *impf. of* ⇒**допроси́ть**

допризы́вник, а *m.* youth undergoing pre-conscription military training.

допризы́вный *adj.* pre-conscription.

допро́с, а *m.* (*leg.*) interrogation, examination; **перекрёстный д.** cross-examination.

допр|оси́ть, ошу́, о́сишь *pf.* (*of* ⇒**~а́шивать**) (*leg.*) to interrogate, question.

допр|оси́ться, ошу́сь, ~о́сишься *pf.* (*coll.*) (+*g.*) to get, obtain by asking.

до́пуск, а *m.* **1** right of entry, admittance. **2** (*tech.*) tolerance.

допуска́|ть, ю *impf. of* ⇒**допусти́ть**

допусти́м|ый (~, ~а) *adj.* permissible, admissible; **~ая нагру́зка** permissible load.

допу|сти́ть, щу́, ~́стишь *pf.* (*of* ⇒**~ска́ть**) **1** (**до**+*g.*, **к**+*d.*) to admit (to); **д. к ко́нкурсу** to allow to compete. **2** (*позволить*) to allow, permit; to tolerate. **3** (*предположить*) to grant, assume; **~́стим** let us suppose, let us assume. **4** (*сделать*): **д. оши́бку** to make a mistake; **д. беста́ктность** to make/commit a faux pas.

допуще́ни|е, я *nt.* (*доступ*) admission; (*предположение*) assumption; (*ошибки*) making.

допыт|а́ться, а́юсь *pf.* (*of* ⇒**~́ываться**) to find out.

допы́тыва|ться, юсь *impf. of* ⇒**допыта́ться**; (*impf. only*) to try to find out, try to elicit.

до́пьяна́ *adv.* (*coll.*) dead drunk; **напои́ть д.** to make dead drunk.

дораба́тыва|ть, ю *impf. of* ⇒**дорабо́тать**

дорабо́та|ть, ю *pf.* (*of* ⇒**дораба́тывать**) **1** (*завершить*) to finish, complete. **2** (**до**+*g.*) to work (until).

дораст|а́ть, а́ю *impf. of* ⇒**~и́**

дораст|и́, у́, ёшь, *past* **доро́с, доросла́** *pf.* (*of* ⇒**дораста́ть**) **1** (**до**+*g.*) to grow (to); (*fig.*) to attain (to), come up (to). **2 не д. что́бы** (+*inf.*) not to be old enough (to); **она́ ещё не доросла́, что́бы е́здить на велосипе́де** she is not old enough yet to ride a bicycle.

дорв|а́ться, у́сь, ёшься, *past* **~а́лся, ~ала́сь, ~а́ло́сь** *pf.* (**до**+*g.*; *coll.*) to fall upon, seize upon.

дореволюцио́нный *adj.* pre-revolutionary.

дорефо́рменный *adj.* pre-reform (*esp. with reference to the emancipation of serfs and other reforms in Russia in the 1860s*).

дори́ческий *adj.* (*archit.*) Doric.

доро́г|а, и *f.* **1** (*путь сообщения*) road; (*путь следования*) way (*also fig.*); **желе́зная д.** railway (*Br.*), railroad (*US*); **д. госуда́рственного значе́ния** national highway; **дать, уступи́ть кому́-н. ~у** to let s.o. pass, make way for s.o. (*also fig.*); **идти́ свое́й ~ой** to go one's own way; **пойти́ по плохо́й ~е** to be on the downward path; **стать кому́-н. поперёк ~и** to stand in s.o.'s way; **туда́ ему́ и д.** (*coll.*) it serves him right; **ска́тертью д.!** good riddance! **2** (*путешествие*) journey; **отпра́виться в ~у** to set out; **в ~е** on the journey, en route; **с ~и** after the journey, from the road. **3** (*путь развития*) (the) way, route; **показа́ть ~у** to show the way, direct; **сби́ться с ~и** to lose one's way; **нам с ни́ми бы́ло по ~е** we went the same way.

до́рого *adv.* dear, dearly; **д. обойти́сь** (+*d.*) to cost one dear; **д. бы я дал, что́бы…** (*coll.*) I would give anything to ….

дорогови́зн|а, ы *f.* high prices.

доро́гой *adv.* on the way, en route.

дорог|о́й (до́рог, дорога́, до́рого) *adj.* **1** dear, expensive; costly; **по ~о́й цене́** at a high price. **2** (*близкий сердцу*) dear; precious; *as n.* **д., ~о́го** *m.*, **~а́я, ~о́й** *f.* (my) dear.

дорогосто́ящий *adj.* costly.

доро́д|ный (~ен, ~на) *adj.* portly, burly.

дородово́й *adj.* antenatal.

дорожа́|ть, ет *impf.* (*of* ⇒**вз~** *and* **по~**) to rise (in price), go up.

доро́же *comp. of* ⇒**дорого́й** *and* **до́рого**

дорож|и́ть, у́, и́шь *impf.* (+*i.*) to value; to prize, set store (by).

дорож|и́ться, у́сь, и́шься *impf.* (*coll.*) to ask too high a price, overcharge.

доро́жк|а, и *f.* **1** path, walk; **велосипе́дная д.** cycle-path *or* way. **2** (*sport*) track; lane. **3** (*aeron.*) runway. **4** (*коврик*) strip (*of carpet, linoleum or fabric*); (*скатерть*) runner. **5** (*магнитофона*) track.

доро́жник, а *m.* road-worker.

доро́жно-тра́нспортн|ый *adj.*: **~ое происше́ствие** road *or* traffic accident.

доро́жн|ый *adj.* **1** *adj. of* ⇒**доро́га; д. знак** road sign; **д. отде́л** highways department; **~ая поли́ция** traffic police; **~ое строи́тельство** road-building. **2** (*для путешествия*) travel, travelling (*Br.*), traveling (*US*); **д. буди́льник** travel alarm; **~ые расхо́ды** travelling (*Br.*), traveling (*US*) expenses; **д. чек** traveller's cheque (*Br.*), traveler's check (*US*).

дорса́льный *adj.* dorsal.

ДОС *f. indecl.* (*abbr. of* ***ди́сковая операцио́нная систе́ма***) DOS (*disk operating system*).

доса́д|а, ы *f.* vexation, annoyance; **кака́я д.!** what a nuisance!

доса|ди́ть[1], жу́, ди́шь *pf.* (*of* ⇒**~жда́ть**) (+*d.*) (*раздражить*) to annoy, vex.

доса|ди́ть[2], жу́, ~́дишь *pf.* (*окончить посадку чего-н.*) to finish planting.

доса́длив|ый (~, ~а) *adj.* expressing vexation, irritation, disappointment; **д. жест** gesture of vexation.

доса́дно *as pred.* it is vexing, annoying.

доса́д|ный (~ен, ~на) *adj.* vexing, annoying.

доса́д|овать, ую *impf.* (**на**+*a.*) to be annoyed (with), be vexed (with).

досажда́|ть, ю *impf. of* ⇒**досади́ть[1]**

досе́ле *adv.* (*obs.*) up to now.

доси|де́ть, жу́, ди́шь *pf.* (*of* ⇒**~́живать**) (**до**+*g.*) to sit (until), stay (until).

доси́жива|ть, ю *impf. of* ⇒**досиде́ть**

доск|а́, и́, *a.* **~́у,** *pl.* **~́и,** *g.* **досо́к,** *d.* **~а́м** *f.* **1** board, plank; **д. для объявле́ний** notice-board; **д. почёта** board of honour; **ро́ликовая** *or* **ро́ллинговая д.** skateboard; **как д. (худо́й)** thin as a rake; **проче́сть от ~и́ до ~и́** to read from cover to cover; **ста́вить на одну́ ~́у** (**с**+*i.*) to put on a level (with); **пьян в ~́у** (*sl.*) dead drunk. **2** (*мраморная*) slab; (*металлическая*) plaque, plate.

доска|за́ть, жу́, ~́жешь *pf.* (*of* ⇒**~́зывать**) to finish telling.

доска́зыва|ть, ю *impf. of* ⇒**досказа́ть**

доскона́л|ьный (~ен, ~ьна) *adj.* thorough.

до|сла́ть, шлю́, шлёшь *pf.* (*of* ⇒**~сыла́ть**) to send in addition; to send the remainder.

дослéдовани|е, я *nt.* (*leg.*) further inquiry.

дослéд|овать, ую *impf. and pf.* (*leg.*) to submit to supplementary examination, further inquiry.

досло́вно *adv.* verbatim, word for word.

досло́вный *adj.* literal, verbatim; **д. перево́д** literal translation.

дослу́жива|ть(ся), ю(сь) *impf. of* ⇒**дослужи́ть(ся)**

дослуж|и́ть, у́, ~́ишь *pf.* (*of* ⇒**~́ивать**) (**до**+*g.*) to serve (until); to finish a period of service.

дослуж|и́ться, у́сь, ~́ишься *pf.* (*of* ⇒**~́иваться**) to obtain as a result of service; **д. до чи́на майо́ра** to rise to the rank of major; **д. до пéнсии** to qualify for a pension.

дослу́ша|ть, ю *pf.* (*of* ⇒**дослу́шивать**) to listen to (sth.) till the end.

дослу́шива|ть, ю *impf. of* ⇒**дослу́шать**

досма́трива|ть, ю, *impf. of* ⇒**досмотрéть**

досмо́тр, а *m.* examination; inspection.

досмотр|éть, ю́, ~́ишь *pf.* (*of* ⇒**досма́тривать**) **1** (**до**+*g.*) to watch, look at (to, as far as); **мы ~éли пьéсу до трéтьего а́кта** we saw the play as far as the third act. **2**: **не д.** to overlook; to allow to escape one's notice.

досмо́трщик, а *m.* inspector, examiner.

досовéтский *adj.* pre-Soviet.

доспева́|ть, ю *impf. of* ⇒**доспéть**

доспé|ть, ю, ешь *pf.* (*of* ⇒**~ва́ть**) to ripen, mature.

доспéх|и, ов *pl.* (*sg.* **~, ~а** *m.*) armour (*Br.*), armor (*US*).

досро́чный *adj.* ahead of schedule, early.

доста|ва́ть(ся), ю́(сь), ёшь(ся) *impf. of* ⇒**~́ть(ся)**

доста́в|ить, лю, ишь *pf.* (*of* ⇒**~ля́ть**) **1** (*груз, посылку*) to deliver; (*пассажиров*) to transport, convey. **2** (*возможность, случай*) to give, provide; (*удовольствие*) to give; (*трудности*) to cause.

доста́вк|а, и *f.* delivery.

доставля́|ть, ю *impf. of* ⇒**доста́вить**

доста́вщик, а *m.* delivery man.

доста́ива|ть, ю *impf. of* ⇒**достоя́ть**

доста́т|ок, ка *m.* **1** (*coll.*) (*достаточное количество*) sufficiency. **2** (*зажиточность*) prosperity; **жить в ~ке** to be comfortably off; **срéднего ~ка** middle-income. **3** (*pl. only*) (*доходы*) income.

доста́точно[1] *adv.* sufficiently, enough; (*значительно*) considerably.

доста́точно[2] *as pred.* it is enough; **д. сказа́ть** suffice it to say; **д. бы́ло одного́ взгля́да** one glance was enough.

доста́точност|ь, и *f.* sufficiency.

доста́точ|ный (~ен, ~на) *adj.* sufficient.

доста́|ть, ну, нешь *pf.* (*of* ⇒**~ва́ть**) (+*d.*) **1** (*взять*) to fetch; to take out; **д. плато́к из карма́на** to take a handkerchief out of one's pocket. **2** (+*g. or* **до**+*g.*) (*коснуться*) to touch; to reach; **д. руко́й до потолка́** to touch the ceiling. **3** (*получить*) to get, obtain. **4** (*impers.*, +*g.*; *coll.*) to suffice.

доста́|ться, нусь, нешься *pf.* (*of* ⇒**~ва́ться**) (+*d.*) **1** (*перейти в собственность*) to pass (to) (by inheritance); **ему́ ~лось большо́е имéние** he came into a large estate. **2** (*выпасть на долю*) to fall to one's lot. **3** (*impers.*; *coll.*): **ему́**, *etc.*, **~нется** he, *etc.*, will catch it.

достига́|ть, ю *impf. of* ⇒**дости́гнуть** *and* **дости́чь**

дости́г|нуть, ну, нешь, *past* **~, ~ла** *pf.* (*of* ⇒**~а́ть**) **1** (+*g.*) (*дойти, доехать*) to reach; **д. ста́рости** to reach old age. **2** (+*g.*) (*добиться*) to attain, achieve.

достижéни|е, я *nt.* achievement, attainment.

достижи́м|ый (~, ~а) *adj.* achievable, attainable.

дости́чь = **дости́гнуть**

достовéрност|ь, и *f.* authenticity; trustworthiness.

достовéр|ный (~ен, ~на) *adj.* reliable.

досто́инств|о, а *nt.* **1** (*хорошее качество*) merit, virtue. **2** (*sg. only*) (*уважение*) dignity; **чу́вство со́бственного ~а** self-respect. **3** (*econ.*) value; **монéты ма́лого ~а** coins of small denomination. **4** (*obs.*) (*титул, чин*) title, rank.

досто́йно *adv.* suitably, fittingly.

досто́|йный (~ин, ~йна) *adj.* **1** (+*g.*) (*стоящий*) worthy (of), deserving; **д. внима́ния** worthy of note; **д. похвалы́** praiseworthy. **2** (*заслуженный*) deserved; fitting, adequate; **~йная награ́да** deserved reward. **3** (*соответствующий*) suitable, fit. **4** (*почтенный*) worthy.

достопа́мят|ный (~ен, ~на) *adj.* memorable.

достопочтéнный *adj.* (*obs.*) venerable; (*iron.*) worthy.

достопримеча́тельност|ь, и *f.* sight; place, object of note; **осма́тривать ~и** to see the sights.

достопримеча́тел|ьный (~ен, ~ьна) *adj.* remarkable, notable.

достоя́ни|е, я *nt.* property.

досто|я́ть, ю́, и́шь *pf.* (*of* ⇒**доста́ивать**) to wait standing (until).

досту́ка|ться, юсь *pf.* (*coll.*) to get one's come-uppance.

до́ступ, а *m.* access, admission, admittance.

досту́п|ный (~ен, ~на) *adj.* **1** (*место*) accessible; easy of access. **2** (**для**+*g.*) open (to); available (to). **3** (*книга*) easily understood; intelligible. **4** (*цены*) moderate, reasonable; **~ные цéны** affordable prices. **5** (*человек*) affable, approachable.

достуч|а́ться, у́сь, и́шься *pf.* (*coll.*) to knock until one is heard.

досу́г, а *m.* **1** leisure, leisure-time; **на ~е** at leisure, in one's spare time. **2** *as pred.* (+*d. and inf.*; *coll.*) to have time (to, for); **где мне д. чита́ть?** what time have I for reading?

досу́ж|ий *adj.* (*coll.*) **1** leisure; **~ее врéмя** leisure-time, spare time. **2** (*пустой*) idle; **~ие разгово́ры** idle talk.

до́суха *adv.* (until) dry; **вы́тереть д.** to rub dry.

досчита́|ть, ю *pf.* (*of* ⇒**досчи́тывать**) **1** to finish counting. **2** (**до**+*g.*) to count (up to); **д. до ста** to count up to a hundred.

досчи́тыва|ть, ю *impf. of* ⇒**досчита́ть**

досыла́|ть, ю *impf. of* ⇒**досла́ть**

досып|а́ть, лю, лешь *pf.* (*of* ⇒**~а́ть**) to pour in, fill up.

досып|а́ть, а́ю *impf. of* ⇒**~ать**

до́сыта *adv.* (*coll.*) to satiety.

досьé *nt. indecl.* dossier, file.

досю́да *adv.* (*coll.*) as far as here, up to here.

досяга́емост|ь, и *f.* reach; (*mil.*) range; **вне предéлов ~и** beyond reach.

досяга́ем|ый (~, ~а) *adj.* attainable, accessible.

дот, а *m.* (*abbr. of* ***долговрéменная огнева́я то́чка***) (*mil.*) (*reinforced concrete*) pill-box.

дота́скива|ть(ся), ю(сь) *impf. of* ⇒**дотащи́ть(ся)**

дота́ци|я, и *f.* grant, subsidy.

дотащ|и́ть, у́, ~́ишь *pf.* (*of* ⇒**дота́скивать**) (*coll.*) (**до**+*g.*) to carry, drag (to).

дотащ|и́ться, у́сь, ~́ишься *pf.* (*of* ⇒**дота́скиваться**) (*coll.*) to drag o.s.

дотемна́ *adv.* until dark.

доти́р|овать, ую *impf. and pf.* to subsidize.

дотла́ *adv.* utterly, completely; **сгорéть д.** to burn to the ground.

дото́ле *adv.* (*obs.*) until then, hitherto.

дото́ш|ный (~ен, ~на) *adj.* (*coll.*) meticulous.

дотра́гива|ться, юсь *impf. of* ⇒**дотро́нуться**

дотро́н|уться, усь, ешься *pf.* (*of* ⇒**дотра́гиваться**) (**до**+*g.*) to touch.

дотя́гива|ть(ся), ю(сь), ешь(ся) *impf. of* ⇒**дотяну́ть(ся)**

дотян|у́ть, у́, ~́ешь *pf.* (*of* ⇒**дотя́гивать**) (**до**+*g.*) **1** to draw, drag, haul (to, as far as). **2** (*coll.*) (*дойти, доехать*) to reach, make. **3** (*протянуть*) to stretch out (to, as far as). **4** (*coll.*) (*выдержать*) to hold out (till); (*дожить*) to live (till); **он до утра́ не ~́ет** he won't last till morning. **5** (*coll.*) (*оттянуть*) to put off (till).

дотян|у́ться, у́сь, ~́ешься *pf.* (*of*

⇨**дотя́гиваться**) (**до**+*g.*) **1** to reach; to touch. **2** (*coll.*) to stretch (to), reach; **о́чередь ~у́лась до конца́ у́лицы** the queue stretched to the end of the street.

доу́чива|ть(ся), ю(сь) *impf. of* ⇨**доучи́ть(ся)**

доуч|и́ть, у́, ~́ишь *pf.* (*of* ⇨**~́ивать**) **1** (*кого-н.*) to finish teaching; (**до**+*g.*) to teach (up to). **2** (*что-н.*) to finish learning; (**до**+*g.*) to learn (up to, as far as).

доуч|и́ться, у́сь, ~́ишься *pf.* (*of* ⇨**~́иваться**) **1** (*завершить образование*) to complete one's studies, finish one's education. **2** (**до**+*g.*) (*проучиться*) to study (up to, till).

дох|а́, и́, *pl.* **~́и** *f.* fur-coat (*with fur on both sides*).

до́хл|ый (~, ~а́, ~о) *adj.* **1** (*мёртвый*) dead (*of animals*). **2** (*coll.*) (*хилый*) sickly (*of human beings*).

дохля́тин|а, ы *f.* (*coll.*) (*collect.*) carrion.

до́х|нуть, ну, нешь, *past* **~, ~ла** *impf.* (*of* ⇨**по~**) (*о животных*) to die; (*coll.*) (*о человеке*) to kick the bucket.

дохн|у́ть, у́, ёшь *pf.* to breathe, take a breath; **тут д. не́где** there is no room to breathe here.

дохо́д, а *m.* income; receipts; revenue.

дохо|ди́ть, жу́, ~́дишь *impf. of* ⇨**дойти́**

дохо́дност|ь, и *f.* profitability.

дохо́д|ный (~ен, ~на) *adj.* **1** profitable, lucrative, paying. **2** *adj. of* ⇨**~**

дохо́дчив|ый (~, ~a) *adj.* intelligible, easy to understand.

доходя́г|а, и *c.g.* (*sl.*) goner.

дохристиа́нский *adj.* pre-Christian.

доце́нт, а *m.* reader (*Br.*), associate professor (*US*).

до́чери, до́черью *see* ⇨**дочь**

доче́рн|ий *adj.* **1** daughter's. **2** (*о компании, предприятии*) daughter; branch.

до́чиста *adv.* **1** clean; **вы́мыть д.** to wash clean. **2** (*fig., coll.*) clean, completely; **его́ обыгра́ли д.** they cleaned him out (*at cards*).

дочит|а́ть, а́ю *pf.* (*of* ⇨**~́ывать**) **1** (*окончить чтение чего-н.*) to finish reading. **2** (**до**+*g.*) to read (to, as far as).

дочи́тыва|ть, ю *impf. of* ⇨**дочита́ть**

до́чк|а, и *f.* (*coll.*) = **дочь**

дочу́рк|а, и *f.* (*coll.*) *dim. of* ⇨**дочь**

доч|ь, ~́ери, *i.* **~́ерью,** *pl.* **~́ери, ~ере́й, ~еря́м, ~ерьми́, о ~еря́х** *f.* daughter.

дошко́льник, а *m.* pre-schooler.

дошко́льни|ца, цы *f. of* ⇨**~к**

дошко́льный *adj.* pre-school.

до́шлый *adj.* (*coll.*) cunning, shrewd.

доща́тый *adj.* made of planks, boards; **д. насти́л** duckboards.

доще́чк|а, и *f.* **1** *dim. of* ⇨**доска́. 2** door-plate, name-plate.

доя́рк|а, и *f.* milkmaid.

д-р *abbr. of* **1 до́ктор** Dr, Doctor. **2 дире́ктор** Director.

др.: и ~ (*abbr. of* **и други́е**) & co.; *et al.*

дра́г|а, и *f.* (*tech.*) dredge.

драги́р|овать, ую *impf. and pf.* (*tech.*) to dredge.

драго́й *adj.* (*obs. or poet.*) dear, precious.

драгоце́нност|ь, и *f.* **1** jewel; gem; (*pl.*) jewellery. **2** (*fig.*) treasure, object of great value; (*pl.*) valuables.

драгоце́н|ный (~ен, ~на) *adj.* precious (*also fig.*); **~ные ка́мни** precious stones.

драгу́н, а, *g. pl.* **~** *m.* dragoon.

дража́йш|ий (*obs.*) *superl. of* ⇨**дорого́й; ~ая полови́на** 'better half'.

драже́ *nt. indecl.* dragée; **шокола́дное д.** chocolate drop.

дразн|и́ть, ю́, ~́ишь *impf.* **1** (*собаку*) to tease; **его́ ~или тру́сом** they used to mock him by calling him a coward. **2** (*аппетит, любопытство*) to stimulate, arouse.

дра́|ить, ю, ишь *impf.* (*of* ⇨**на~**) (*naut.*) to scrub; to swab.

дра́йвер, а *m.* (*comput.*) driver.

дра́к|а, и *f.* fight; **у них дошло́ до ~и** they came to blows.

драко́н, а *m.* **1** dragon. **2** (*heraldry*) wyvern.

драко́новский *adj.* Draconian.

дра́м|а, ы *f.* **1** drama. **2** (*fig.*) crisis, calamity.

драматиза́ци|я, и *f.* dramatization.

драматизи́р|овать, ую *impf. and pf.* to dramatize.

драмати́зм, а *m.* **1** (*theatr.*) dramatic effect. **2** (*fig.*) dramatic character, quality; tension.

драмати́ческ|ий *adj.* **1** dramatic; drama, theatre (*Br.*), theater (*US*); **~ое иску́сство** dramatic art, art of the theatre (*Br.*), theater (*US*); **д. теа́тр** theatre (*Br.*), theater (*US*). **2** (*напыщенный*) dramatic, theatrical; **~им то́ном** in a dramatic tone. **3** (*fig.*) dramatic; tense.

драмати́ч|ный (~ен, ~на) *adj.* (*fig.*) dramatic.

драмату́рг, а *m.* playwright, dramatist.

драматурги́|я, и *f.* **1** dramatic art. **2** (*collect.*) plays, drama; **д. Че́хова** the plays of Chekhov.

драмкруж|о́к, ка́ *m.* dramatic circle.

драндуле́т, а *m.* (*coll., joc.*) jalopy, old banger.

дра́нк|а, и *f.* (*tech.*) **1** (*кровельная*) shingle. **2** (*штукатурная*) lath.

дра́ный *adj.* (*coll.*) tattered, ragged.

драп, а *m.* thick woollen cloth.

драпир|ова́ть, у́ю *impf.* (*of* ⇨**за~**) (+*i.*) to drape (with).

драпир|ова́ться, у́юсь *impf.* (*of* ⇨**за~**) **1** (**в**+*a., or i.*) to drape o.s. (in); (*fig.*) to affect, make a parade (of). **2** *pass. of* ⇨**~ова́ть**

драпиро́вк|а, и *f.* **1** (*действие*) draping. **2** (*занавеска*) curtain; hangings.

драпиро́вщик, а *m.* upholsterer.

дра́п|овый *adj. of* ⇨**~**

драпри́ *nt. indecl.* draperies; curtains.

дра́тв|а, ы *f.* waxed thread.

дра|ть, деру́, дерёшь, *past* **~л, ~ла́, ~́ло** *impf.* **1** (*impf. only*) (*рвать*) to tear (up, to pieces); **д. го́рло** (*coll.*) to bawl; **д. нос** (*coll.*) to turn up one's nose, put on airs. **2** (*pf.* **со~**) (*снимать*) to tear off; **д. шку́ру** to flay. **3** (*pf.* **за~**) (*убивать*) to kill (*of wild animals*). **4** (*pf.* **вы́~**) (*coll.*) (*сечь*) to flog, thrash; (*дёргать*) to tear out; **д. зу́бы** to pull out teeth. **5** (*pf.* **со~**) (**с**+*g.*; *fig., coll.*) (*брать высокую плату*) to fleece; to sting. **6** (*pf.* **по~**): **чёрт его́ (по)дери́!** damn him! **7** (*impf. only*) (*coll.*) (*раздражать*) to sting, irritate; **д. у́ши** (+*d.*) to jar (on); (*impers.*): **у меня́ в го́рле дерёт** I have a sore throat. **8** (*impf. only*) (*coll.*) (*убегать*) to run away, make off.

дра́|ться, деру́сь, дерёшься, *past* **~лся, ~ла́сь, ~́ло́сь** *impf.* **1** (**с**+*i.*) to fight (with); **д. на дуэ́ли** to fight a duel. **2** (*fig.*) (**за**+*a.*) to fight, struggle (for).

дра́хм|а, ы *f.* drachma (*Greek unit of currency*).

драчли́вост|ь, и *f.* pugnacity.

драчли́в|ый (~, ~a) *adj.* pugnacious.

драчу́н, а́ *m.* (*coll.*) pugnacious, quarrelsome fellow.

драчу́н|ья, ьи, *g. pl.* **~ий** (*coll.*) *f. of* ⇨**~**

дребеде́н|ь, и *f.* (*coll.*) nonsense; **сплошна́я д.** absolute rubbish.

дре́безг, а *m.* (*coll.*) **1** (*звук*) tinkling sound (*as of breaking glass, etc.*). **2** (*pl. only*): **разби́ть(ся) в (мо́лкие) ~и** to smash to smithereens.

дребезж|а́ть, и́т *impf.* to jingle, tinkle.

древеси́н|а, ы *f.* **1** (*плотная часть дерева*) wood. **2** (*лесоматериалы*) timber.

древесноволокни́ст|ый *adj.*: **~ая плита́** fibreboard (*Br.*), fiberboard (*US*).

древесностру́жечн|ый *adj.*: **~ая плита́** chipboard.

древе́сн|ый *adj. of* ⇨**де́рево; ~ая ма́сса** wood-pulp; **д. спирт** wood alcohol; **д. у́голь** charcoal.

дре́вк|о, а, *pl.* **~и, ~ов** *nt.* (*флага*) pole, staff; (*копья*) shaft.

древнегре́ческий *adj.* ancient, classical Greek.

древнееврейский *adj.* ancient, classical Hebrew.

древнеру́сский *adj.* Old Russian.

древнецерко́внославя́нский *adj.* (*ling.*) Old Church Slavonic.

дре́в|ний (~ен, ~ня) *adj.* ancient; **~няя исто́рия** ancient history; **~ние языки́** classical languages; *as n.* **~ние, ~них** the ancients.

дре́вност|ь, и *f.* **1** (*sg. only*) (*далёкое прошлое*) antiquity. **2** (*pl.*; *archaeol.*) antiquities.

дре́в|о, а, *pl.* **~еса́, ~е́с, ~еса́м** *nt.* (*obs. or poet.*) tree; **д. позна́ния** the tree of knowledge.

древови́д|ный (~ен, ~на) tree-like; **д. па́поротник** tree-fern.

дрези́н|а, ы *f.* (*rail.*) trolley (*Br.*), handcar (*US*).

дрейф, а *m.* (*naut.*) drift, leeway; **лечь в д.** to heave to; **лежа́ть в ~е** to lie to.

дре́йф|ить, лю, ишь *impf.* (*of* ⇒**с~**) (*coll.*) to be a coward.

дрейф|ова́ть, у́ю *impf.* (*naut.*) to drift; **~у́ющий лёд** drift ice.

дрел|ь, и *f.* (*tech.*) drill.

дрём|а, ы (*and* (*obs.*) **дрем|а́, ы́**) *f.* (*poet.*) drowsiness, sleepiness.

дрем|а́ть, лю́, ~лешь *impf.* to doze; to slumber; **не д.** (*also fig.*) to be watchful; to be wide awake.

дрем|а́ться, ~лется *impf.* (*impers.*, +*d.*) to feel sleepy, drowsy.

дремо́т|а, ы *f.* drowsiness.

дремо́тный *adj.* drowsy.

дрему́ч|ий (~, ~а) *adj.* (*poet.*) thick, dense; (*fig.*) utter, complete.

дрена́ж, а́ *m.* drainage.

дренажи́р|овать, ую *impf. and pf.* (*med.*) to drain.

дрена́ж|ный *adj. of* ⇒**~**; **~ная труба́** drain-pipe.

дрени́р|овать, ую *impf. and pf.* (*tech.*) to drain.

дресв|а́, ы *f.* gravel.

дрессиро́ванн|ый *p.p.p. of* ⇒**дрессирова́ть** *and adj.*: **~ые живо́тные** performing animals.

дрессир|ова́ть, у́ю *impf.* (*of* ⇒**вы́~**) to train (*animals*); (*fig.*) to school.

дрессиро́вк|а, и *f.* training.

дрессиро́вщик, а *m.* trainer.

дриа́д|а, ы *f.* (*myth.*) dryad.

дри́блинг, а *m.* (*sport*) dribbling.

дроби́лк|а, и *f.* (*tech.*) crusher.

дроби́льн|ый *adj.* (*tech.*) crushing; **~ая маши́на** crusher.

дроби́н|а, ы *f.* pellet.

дроб|и́ть, лю́, и́шь *impf.* (*of* ⇒**раз~**) **1** (*камень*) to break up, crush, smash (to pieces). **2** (*fig.*) (*силы*) to subdivide, split up.

дроб|и́ться, и́тся *impf.* (*of* ⇒**раз~**) **1** (*камень*) to break to pieces, smash, smash to pieces. **2** (*fig.*) (*силы*) to divide, split up.

дробле́ни|е, я *nt.* **1** crushing, breaking up. **2** (*fig.*) subdivision, splitting up.

дроблёный *adj.* splintered, crushed, ground.

дро́б|ный (~ен, ~на) *adj.* **1** separate; subdivided, split up. **2** (*частый и мелкий*) staccato, abrupt; **д. стук** staccato knocking; **д. дождь** fine rain. **3** (*math.*) fractional.

дробови́к, а́ *m.* shotgun.

дроб|ь, и, *pl.* **~и, ~е́й** *f.* **1** (*collect.*) (*для стрельбы*) small shot. **2** (*звуки*) drumming; tapping; patter; **бараба́нная ~** drum roll. **3** (*math.*) fraction. **4** (*черта*) slash.

дров|а́, ~, ~а́м *no sg.* firewood.

дро́вн|и, ~е́й *no sg.* (*peasant*) wood-sledge.

дровосе́к, а *m.* **1** woodcutter. **2** (*zool.*) longhorn beetle.

дров|яно́й *adj. of* ⇒**~а́**; **д. сара́й** woodshed; **д. склад** woodyard.

дро́г|и, ~ *no sg.* wagon, cart; **похоро́нные ~и** hearse.

дро́г|нуть[1], ну, нешь, *past* **~, ~ла** *impf.* to be chilled, freeze.

дро́гн|уть[2], у, ешь, *past* **~ул, ~ула** *pf.* **1** to shake, move; to quaver; (*о свете*) to flicker. **2** (*о человеке*) to waver, falter; **у меня́ рука́ не ~ет** (+*inf.*) I shall not hesitate to ....

дрожа́ни|е, я *nt.* trembling, vibration.

дрожа́тельный *adj.* tremulous, shivery; **д. парали́ч** (*med.*) Parkinson's disease.

дрож|а́ть, у́, и́шь *impf.* **1** to tremble; to shiver, shake; to quiver; to vibrate; (*о свете*) to flicker; **д. от хо́лода, испу́га** to shiver with cold, with fright. **2** (**за**+*a. or* **пе́ред**+*i.*; *fig.*) to tremble (for; before). **3** (**над**+*i.*) to grudge; **д. над ка́ждой копе́йкой** to count every penny.

дрожж|ево́й *adj. of* ⇒**~и**

дро́жж|и, е́й *no sg.* yeast, leaven; **ста́вить на ~а́х** to leaven; **пивны́е д.** barm, brewer's yeast.

дро́ж|ки, ~ек, ~кам *no sg.* droshky.

дрож|ь, и *f.* shivering, trembling; (*в голосе*) tremor, quaver.

дрозд, а́ *m.* thrush; **пе́вчий д.** song-thrush; **чёрный д.** blackbird; **дать ~а́** (+*d.*) to tear s.o. off a strip.

дрок, а *m.* (*bot.*) gorse.

дромаде́р, а *m.* (*zool.*) dromedary.

дро́ссел|ь, я *m.* (*tech.*) throttle, choke.

дро́тик, а *m.* **1** (*оружие*) spear, javelin. **2** (*в игре*) dart.

дрочи́л|а, ы *c.g.* (*vulg.*) wanker (= *masturbator*).

дрочи́ть, дро́чу́, дро́чи́шь *impf.* (*vulg.*) to wank, toss off.

дрочи́ться = **дрочи́ть**

друг[1], а, *pl.* **друзья́, друзе́й** *m.* friend; **д. до́ма** friend of the family; **д. по перепи́ске** pen friend *or* pal.

друг[2] (*short form of* ⇒**~о́й**) **д. ~а** each other, one another; **д. за ~ом** one after another; **д. с ~ом** with each other.

друг|о́й *adj.* **1** other, another; different; **и тот и д.** both; **ни тот ни д.** neither; **никто́ д.** none other; **э́то ~о́е де́ло** that is another matter; **~и́ми слова́ми** in other words; **с ~о́й стороны́** on the other hand; **на д. день** the next day; *as n.* **~и́е, ~и́х** others. **2** (*второй*) second.

дру́жб|а, ы *f.* friendship; **не в слу́жбу, а в ~у** out of friendship.

дружелю́би|е, я *nt.* friendliness.

дружелю́б|ный (~ен, ~на) *adj.* friendly, amicable.

дру́жеск|ий *adj.* friendly; **быть на ~ой ноге́** (**с**+*i.*) to be on friendly terms (with).

дру́жественн|ый *adj.* friendly, amicable; **~ая держа́ва** friendly power; (*comput.*) user-friendly.

дру́жеств|о, а *nt.* (*obs.*) friendship.

дружи́н|а, ы *f.* (*hist.*) **1** (*в древней Руси*) (prince's) armed force. **2** (*в царской армии*) militia unit, detachment. **3** (*отряд*) squad, team; **доброво́льная наро́дная д.** voluntary people's patrol (*in former USSR, assisting police in maintaining public order*).

дружи́нник, а *m.* (*hist.*) **1** (*в древней Руси*) member of (prince's) armed force. **2** (*в царской армии*) member of militia unit. **3** member of people's patrol, vigilante.

друж|и́ть, у́, ~ишь *impf.* (**с**+*i.*) to be friends (with), on friendly terms (with).

друж|и́ться, у́сь, ~и́шься *impf.* (*of* ⇒**по~**) (**с**+*i.*) to make friends (with).

дружи́щ|е, а *m.* (*coll.*) mate.

дру́жно *adv.* **1** harmoniously, in concord. **2** (*вместе*) (all) together, in concert; **раз, два, ~!** heave-ho!; all together!

дру́ж|ный (~ен, ~на́, ~но) *adj.* **1** (*единодушный*) amicable; harmonious. **2** (*одновременный*) simultaneous, concerted; **~ные уси́лия** concerted efforts.

друж|о́к, ка́ *m.* (*coll.*) pal; (*как обращение*) my dear.

друзья́ *see* ⇒**друг**

дры́г|ать, аю *impf.* (*of* ⇒**~нуть**) (+*i.*; *coll.*) to jerk, twitch.

дры́г|нуть, ну, нешь *pf. of* ⇒**~ать**

дры́х|нуть, ну, нешь, *past* **~** *and* **~нул, ~ла** *impf.* (*coll.*) to sleep.

дря́бл|ый (~, ~а́, ~о) *adj.* flabby.

дря́бн|уть, у, ешь *impf.* (*coll.*) to become flabby.

дрязг, а (у) *m.* (*collect.*; *obs. or dial.*) refuse, rubbish.

дря́зг|и, ~ *no sg.* (*coll.*) squabbles.

дрян|но́й (~ен, ~на́, ~но) *adj.* (*coll.*) worthless, rotten; good-for-nothing.

дрян|ь, и *f.* (*coll.*) **1** (*хлам*) trash, rubbish. **2** *as pred.* it is rotten, it is no good; **пого́да — д.** the weather is awful. **3** (*о человеке*) a bad lot, a good-for-nothing.

дряхле́|ть, ю *impf.* (*of* ⇒**о~**) to grow decrepit.

дря́хлост|ь, и *f.* decrepitude.

дря́хл|ый (~, ~а́, ~о) *adj.* decrepit, senile.

дуайе́н, а *m.* doyen.

дуали́зм, а *m.* (*phil.*) dualism.

дуб, а, *pl.* **~ы** *m.* **1** oak; **дать ~а** to snuff it; to kick the bucket. **2** (*coll.*) (*человек*) blockhead, numskull.

дуба́|сить, шу, сишь *impf.* (*of* ⇒**от~**) (*coll.*) **1** (*избивать*) to cudgel. **2** (**по**+*d. or* **в**+*a.*) (*ударять*) to bang (on).

дуби́льн|ый *adj.* tanning, tannic; **~ая кислота́** tannic acid.

дуби́л|ьня, ьни, *g. pl.* **~ен** *f.* tannery.

дуби́льщик, а *m.* tanner.

дуби́н|а, ы *f.* **1** club, cudgel. **2** (*coll.*) (*человек*) blockhead, numskull.

дуби́нк|а, и *f.* truncheon, baton.

дуб|и́ть, лю́, и́шь *impf.* (*of* ⇒**вы**~) to tan.

дублёнк|а, и *f.* (*coll.*) sheepskin coat.

дублёный *adj.* tanned; (*fig.*) leathery, weather-beaten.

дублёр, а *m.* (*theatr.*) understudy; (*cin.*) stand-in.

дубле́т, а *m.* duplicate.

дублика́т, а *m.* duplicate.

Ду́блин, а *m.* Dublin.

дубли́р|овать, ую *impf.* **1** (*pf.* **про**~) to duplicate; **д. роль** (*theatr.*) to understudy a part. **2** (*pf.* **с**~) (*cin.*) to dub.

дубл|ь, я *m.* (*cin.*) take.

дубня́к, а́ *m.* oak forest.

дубова́т|ый (~, ~а) *adj.* (*coll.*) (*грубый*) coarse; (*глупый*) stupid, thick.

дубо́в|ый *adj.* **1** oak; **д. лист** oak-leaf; **д. гроб** oak coffin. **2** (*fig., coll.*) (*грубый*) coarse; (*глупый*) thick; **~ая голова́** blockhead, numskull. **3** (*fig., coll.*) rock hard (= *inedible*).

дубра́в|а, ы *f.* **1** oak forest. **2** (*poet.*) leafy grove.

Дувр, а *m.* Dover.

дуг|а́, и́, *pl.* **~и** *f.* **1** (*часть упряжки*) shaft-bow. **2** (*часть кривой линии*) arc, arch; **бро́ви ~о́й** arched brows.

дуг|ово́й *adj. of* ⇒**~а́; ~ова́я ла́мпа** arc-lamp; **~ова́я сва́рка** arc welding.

дугообра́з|ный (~ен, ~на) *adj.* arched.

дуд|е́ть, *1st pers. not used,* **и́шь** *impf.* (*coll.*) to play the pipe, fife.

ду́дк|а, и *f.* pipe, fife; **пляса́ть под чью-н. ~у** (*fig.*) to dance to s.o.'s tune.

ду́дки *int.* (*coll.*) not if I know it!; not on your life!

ду́жк|а, и *f.* **1** *dim. of* ⇒**дуга́. 2** (*в крокете*) hoop. **3** (*ручка*) handle.

дука́т, а *m.* ducat.

ду́л|о, а *nt.* (*отверстие ствола*) muzzle; (*ствол*) barrel; **под ~ом пистоле́та** at gunpoint.

ду́л|ьце, ьца, *g. pl.* **~ец** *nt.* **1** *dim. of* ⇒**~о. 2** (*mus.*) mouthpiece (*of wind instruments*).

ду́м|а, ы *f.* **1** (*rhet. or poet.*) thought. **2** (**Д.**) Duma (*lower house of Russian parliament*).

ду́ма|ть, ю *impf.* (*of* ⇒**по**~) **1** (**о** + *p. or* **над** + *i.*) to think (about); to be concerned (about); **мно́го о себе́ д.** to have a high opinion of o.s. **2** (*impf. only*) **д., что...** to think, suppose that ...; **я ~ю!** of course!; I should think so! **3** (+ *inf.*) to think of, plan to; **он ~ет пое́хать в Ло́ндон** he is thinking of going to London; **и не ~ю** (+ *inf.*) I would not dream (of); **и д. не сме́й** (+ *inf.*) don't dare (to).

ду́ма|ться, ется *impf.* (*impers.*, + *d.*) to seem; **мне ~ется** I think, I fancy; **~ется** it seems.

ду́м|ец, ца *m.* member of Duma.

ду́мк|а, и *f.* **1** *dim. of* ⇒**ду́ма 1. 2** (*coll.*) small pillow.

Дуна́|й, я *m.* the Danube (*river*).

дунове́ни|е, я *nt.* puff, breath (*of wind*).

ду́н|уть, у, ешь *pf.* to blow.

ду́пел|ь, я *pl.* **~я́** *m.* (*zool.*) great snipe.

дупли́ст|ый (~, ~а) *adj.* hollow.

дупл|о́, а́, *pl.* **~а, ду́пел** *nt.* **1** (*в стволе дерева*) hollow. **2** (*в зубе*) cavity.

ду́р|а, ы *f. of* ⇒**дура́к**

дура́к, а́ *m.* **1** (*hist.*) (*шут*) jester, fool. **2** (*глупый человек*) fool, ass; **д. ~о́м** an utter fool; **не д.** (+ *inf.*) to love (*doing sth.*); **оста́вить в ~а́х** to make a fool of; **оста́ться в ~а́х** to be fooled, make a fool of o.s.; **валя́ть, лома́ть ~а́** to play the fool; to make a fool of o.s.; **на ~а́** for fun, for a joke; **~а́м зако́н не пи́сан** (*prov.*) fools rush in where angels fear to tread; **нашёл ~а́!** not likely!; no thanks!

дурале́|й, я *m.* = **дура́к** 2

дура́цкий *adj.* (*coll.*) stupid, foolish, idiotic; **д. колпа́к** dunce's cap.

дура́честв|о, а *nt.* folly, absurdity; prank.

дура́ч|ить, у, ишь *impf.* (*of* ⇒**о**~) to fool, dupe.

дура́ч|иться, усь, ишься *impf.* to play the fool.

дурач|о́к, ка́ *m.* **1** *affectionate dim. of* ⇒**дура́к. 2** (*coll.*) idiot, imbecile.

дура́шлив|ый (~, ~а) *adj.* (*coll.*) stupid.

дурдо́м, а *m.* (*coll.*) madhouse.

ду́р|ень, ня *m.* (*coll.*) fool, simpleton.

дуре́|ть, ю *impf.* (*of* ⇒**о**~) to become stupid.

дур|и́ть, ю́, и́шь *impf.* (*coll.*) **1** (*дурачиться*) to fool around; to play tricks. **2** (*упрямиться*) to be obstinate. **3** (*pf.* **за**~): **д. го́лову кому́-н.** to muddle, confuse s.o.

дурма́н, а *m.* **1** (*bot.*) thorn-apple (*Datura stramonium*). **2** (*coll.*) drug, narcotic; intoxicant.

дурма́н|ить, ю, ишь *impf.* (*of* ⇒**о**~) to stupefy.

дурне́|ть, ю *impf.* (*of* ⇒**по**~) to grow ugly.

ду́рно *adv. of* ⇒**дурно́й**

ду́рно *as pred.* (*impers.*, + *d.*): **мне,** *etc.*, **д.** I, *etc.*, feel faint, bad.

дур|но́й (~ен, ~на́, ~но) *adj.* **1** (*in var. senses*) (*плохой*) bad, evil; nasty; **д. вкус** nasty taste; **д. глаз** the evil eye; **~ны́е мы́сли** evil thoughts; **~ны́е привы́чки** bad habits; **д. сон** bad dream. **2**: **д. (собо́ю)** (*некрасивый*) ugly.

дурнот|а́, ы́ *f.* (*coll.*) faintness; nausea; **у́тренняя д.** morning sickness; **чу́вствовать ~у́** to feel faint, sick.

дурну́шк|а, и *f.* (*coll.*) plain girl, plain Jane.

ду́рост|ь, и *f.* (*coll.*) folly, stupidity.

дуршла́г, а *m.* (*cul.*) colander.

дур|ь, и *f.* (*coll.*) foolishness, stupidity.

ду́т|ый *p.p.p. of* ⇒**~ь** *and adj.* **1** (*полый*) hollow. **2** (*fig.*) (*преувеличенный*) inflated, exaggerated.

дуть, ду́ю, ду́ешь *impf.* **1** (*pf.* **по**~) to blow; **сего́дня ду́ет ве́тер с за́пада** there is a west wind today; **от окна́ ду́ет** there is a draught (*Br.*), draft (*US*) from the window; **в ус не ду́ет** (*coll.*) he does not give a damn. **2** (*pf.* **вы**~) (*изготовлять из стекла*) to blow.

дуть|ё, я́ *nt.* **1** (*tech.*) blowing, blast. **2** (*изготовление предметов из жидкого стекла*) (glass-)blowing.

ду́|ться, юсь, ешься *impf.* (*coll.*) (**на** + *a.*) to grumble (at), pout (at).

дух, а *m.* **1** (*relig., phil., and fig.*) spirit; **свято́й д.** the Holy Spirit, the Holy Ghost; **д. ве́ка** Zeitgeist (*spirit of the age*). **2** (*моральное состояние*) spirit(s); heart; mind; **настрое́ние ~а, расположе́ние ~а** mood, frame of mind; **быть в ~е** to be in good (high) spirits; **не в ~е** in low spirits; **па́дать ~ом** to lose heart; **собра́ться с ~ом** to take heart, pluck up one's courage; **прису́тствие ~а** presence of mind; **у меня́ ~у не хвата́ет** (+ *inf.*) I have not the heart (to); **э́то не в моём ~е** it is not to my taste; **что́-то в э́том ~е** sth. of the sort. **3** (*дыхание*) breath; (*coll.*) air; **перевести́ д.** to take breath; **испусти́ть д.** (*fig.*) to give up the ghost; **во весь д.** (*coll.*) at full speed, flat out; **одни́м ~ом** in one breath; (*fig.*) at one go, at a stretch; **о нём ни слу́ху ни ~у** nothing is heard of him. **4** (*призрак*) spectre (*Br.*), specter (*US*), ghost.

духа́н, а *m.* dukhan (*inn in Caucasus*).

дух|и́, о́в *no sg.* perfume, scent.

ду́хов *adj.*: **Д. день** (*eccl.*) Whit Monday.

духове́нств|о, а *nt.* (*collect.*) clergy, priesthood.

духови́д|ец, ца *m.* clairvoyant; medium.

духо́вк|а, и *f.* oven.

духовни́к, а́ *m.* (*eccl.*) confessor.

духо́вност|ь, и *f.* spirituality.

духо́вн|ый *adj.* **1** spiritual; inner; **~ые запро́сы** spiritual demands; **д. мир** inner world. **2** (*церковный*) ecclesiastical, church; religious; **~ое лицо́** ecclesiastic; **~ая му́зыка** sacred music; **д. оте́ц** confessor, spiritual director; **д. сан** holy orders. **3**: **~ое завеща́ние** (last) will, testament. **4**: **~ое о́ко** (the) mind's eye.

духов|о́й *adj.* **1** (*mus.*) wind; **д. инструме́нт** wind instrument; **д. орке́стр** brass band. **2** (*действующий посредством нагретого воздуха*) (hot-) air; **~о́е отопле́ние** hot-air heating; **~о́е ружьё** air-gun. **3** (*cul.*) steamed.

духот|а́, ы́ *f.* stuffiness, closeness.

душ, а *m.* shower; **приня́ть д.** to take a shower.

душ|а́, и́, *a.* **~у,** *pl.* **~и** *f.* **1** soul; (*fig.*) heart; **д. в ~у** at one, in harmony; **в ~е́** (*i*) inwardly, secretly, (*ii*) at heart; **для ~и** for one's private satisfaction; **за ~о́й** to one's name; **у него́ за ~о́й ни гроша́** he hasn't a penny to his name; **от ~и** from the heart; **от всей ~и** with all one's heart; **по ~е́** (+ *d.*) to one's liking; **по ~а́м говори́ть** (**с** + *i.*) to have a heart-to-heart talk (with); **вложи́ть ~у** (**в** + *a.*) to put one's heart (into); **изли́ть, отвести́ ~у** to pour out one's heart; **~и не ча́ять**

(**в**+*p.*) to think the world of; to dote on; **скóлько ~é угóдно** to one's heart's content; **~óй и тéлом** heart and soul; **ни ~óй, ни тéлом** in no wise, in no respect.
2 (*чувство*) feeling, spirit; **говори́ть с ~óй** to speak with feeling.
3 (*fig.*) (the) soul; moving spirit; inspiration; **д. óбщества** the life and soul of the party.
4 (*fig.*) (*человек*) spirit; **смéлая д.** a bold spirit.
5 (*fig.*) (*человек, при указании количества*) soul; **на ~у** per head; **потреблéние на ~у населéния** per-capita consumption; **ни (живóй) ~и́** not a (living) soul.
6: **душá моя́!** (*coll.*; *affectionate mode of address*) my dear, darling.

душев|áя, óй *f.* shower-room.

душевнобольн|óй *adj.* insane; mentally ill; *as n.* **д., ~óго** *m.*, **~áя, ~óй** *f.* insane person; mental patient.

душéвност|ь, и *f.* cordiality, friendliness.

душéвн|ый *adj.* **1** mental; **~ая болéзнь** mental illness; **~ое потрясéние** nervous shock.
2 (*сердечный*) sincere, heartfelt; **~ая бесéда** friendly chat; **д. человéк** understanding person.

душев|óй¹ *adj.* per head; **~óе потреблéние** per-capita consumption.

душевóй² *adj. of* ⇒**душ**

душегрéйк|а, и *f.* (*woman's*) sleeveless jacket (*usu. wadded or fur-lined*).

душегýб, а *m.* (*coll.*) murderer.

душегýб|ка, ки *f.* **1** *f. of* ⇒**~.**
2 (*лодка*) dugout (canoe). **3** (*hist.*) mobile gas-chamber.

душегýбств|о, а *nt.* (*coll.*) murder.

дýшеньк|а, и *c.g.* (*obs., coll.*) darling (*affectionate mode of address*).

душераздирáющий *adj.* heart-rending.

душеспаси́тел|ьный (~ен, ~ьна) *adj.* (*eccl. or iron.*) salutary, edifying.

дýшечк|а, и *c.g.* = **дýшенька**

душещипáтельный *adj.*: **д. фильм** tear-jerker, weepie.

души́ст|ый (~, ~а) *adj.* fragrant, sweet-scented.

душ|и́ть¹, ý, ~ишь *impf.* (*of* ⇒**за~**)
1 (*убивать*) to strangle; to stifle, smother, suffocate; (*fig.*) (*угнетать*) to stifle, suppress; **д. поцелýями** to smother with kisses. **2** (*impf. only*) (*лишать возможности дышать*) to choke; **егó ~ил гнéв** he choked with rage.

душ|и́ть², ý, ~ишь *impf.* (*of* ⇒**на~**) to scent, perfume.

душ|и́ться¹, ýсь, ~ишься *impf.*, *pass. of* ⇒**~и́ть¹**

душ|и́ться², ýсь, ~ишься *impf.* (*of* ⇒**на~**) (+*i.*) to perfume o.s. (with); **онá всегдá ~ится францýзскими духáми** she always uses French perfume.

души́ц|а, ы *f.* marjoram.

дýшк|а, и *c.g.* (*coll.*) dear (person); **он такóй д., онá такáя д.** he, she is such a dear.

душни́к, á *m.* vent (*in stove*).

дýшно *as pred.* it is stuffy; it is stifling, suffocating; **мне стáло д.** I felt suffocated.

дýш|ный (~ен, ~нá, ~но) *adj.* stuffy, close, sultry; stifling.

душ|óк, кá *m.* (*coll.*) **1** smell (*esp. of decaying matter*); **с ~кóм** high, tainted.
2 (*fig.*) smack, taint; tinge; **газéта с либерáльным ~кóм** (*pej.*) newspaper with a liberal tinge.

дуэ́л|ь, и *f.* duel; **вы́звать на д.** to challenge; **дрáться на ~и** to fight a duel.

дуэля́нт, а *m.* duellist (*Br.*), duelist (*US*).

дуэ́т, а *m.* duet.

ды́б|а, ы *f.* (*hist.*) rack (*instrument of torture*).

ды́б|иться, ится *impf.* **1** to stand on end. **2** (*о лошади*) to rear, prance.

ды́бом *adv.* on end; **вóлосы у негó встáли д.** his hair stood on end.

ды́бы́: на д. on to the hind legs; **станови́ться на д.** to rear, prance; (*fig.*) to kick, resist.

ды́лд|а, ы *c.g.* (*coll.*) lanky person, beanpole.

дым, а (у), о ~е, в ~ý, *pl.* **~ы́** *m.* smoke; **в д.** (*coll.*) completely.

дым|и́ть, лю́, и́шь *impf.* (*of* ⇒**на~**) to smoke (*intrans.*), emit smoke.

дым|и́ться, и́тся *impf.* to smoke (*intrans.*); (*of fog*) to billow.

ды́мк|а, и *f.* haze (*also fig.*).

ды́мный *adj.* (*наполненный дымом*) smoky; (*дымящийся*) smouldering (*Br.*), smoldering (*US*).

дымов|óй *adj. of* ⇒**дым; ~áя завéса** (*mil.*) smoke-screen; **~áя трубá** flue, chimney; (*парохода*) funnel, smoke-stack.

дым|óк, кá *m.* puff of smoke.

дымохóд, а *m.* flue.

ды́мчат|ый (~, ~а) *adj.* smoke-coloured (*Br.*), smoke-colored (*US*); (*очки*) tinted.

ды́нный *adj. of* ⇒**ды́ня**

ды́н|я, и *f.* melon.

дыр|á, ы́, *pl.* **~ы** *f.* **1** hole; **заткнýть ~ý** (*fig.*) to stop a gap. **2** (*fig., coll.*) (*глухое место*) hole.

ды́рк|а, и *f.* hole.

дырокóл, а *m.* hole-puncher, punch.

дыря́в|ить, лю, ишь *impf.* (*coll.*) to make a hole (in).

дыря́в|ый (~, ~а) *adj.* full of holes, holey; **~ая головá** a head like a sieve.

дыхáни|е, я *nt.* breathing; breath; **вторóе д.** (*fig.*) second wind; **искýсственное д.** artificial respiration.

дыхáтельн|ый *adj.* respiratory; **~ое гóрло** (*anat.*) windpipe; **~ые пути́** respiratory tract; **~ая трýбка** snorkel.

дыш|áть, ý, ~ишь *impf.* (+*i.*) to breathe; (*быть проникнутым чем-либо*) to exude; **éле д.** to be at one's last gasp; (*fig.*) to be on one's last legs.

ды́шл|о, а *nt.* shaft, pole, beam.

дья́вол, а *m.* devil; **какóго ~а?; за каки́м ~ом?; на кой ~?** (*coll.*) why the devil?; why the deuce?

дьявол|ёнок, ёнка, *pl.* **~я́та, ~я́т** *m.* (*coll.*) imp.

дья́вольский *adj.* devilish, diabolical; (*coll.*) damnable.

дья́вольщин|а, ы *f.* (*coll.*) devilment; **что за д.!** what the hell's going on?

дья́кон, а, *pl.* **~á, ~óв** *m.* (*eccl.*) deacon.

дья́конств|о, а *nt.* (*eccl.*) diaconate.

дьяч|óк, кá *m.* (*eccl.*) sacristan, sexton; reader.

дю́же *adv.* (*coll. or dial.*) terribly, awfully.

дю́ж|ий (~, ~á, ~е) *adj.* (*coll.*) hefty, strapping.

дю́жин|а, ы *f.* dozen; **чёртова д.** baker's dozen.

дю́жинный *adj.* ordinary, commonplace.

дюйм, а *m.* inch.

дюймóвый *adj.* one-inch.

дю́н|а, ы *f.* dune.

дюрáл|ь, я *m.* = **~юми́ний**

дюралюми́ни|й, я *m.* (*tech.*) Duralumin (*propr.*).

дя́гил|ь, я *m.* (*bot.*) angelica.

дя́деньк|а, и *m.* *affectionate form of* ⇒**дя́дя**

дя́дин *adj.* uncle's.

дя́дьк|а, и *m.* **1** *pej. form of* ⇒**дя́дя.**
2 (*coll.*) = **дя́дя** 2, 3

дя́дюшк|а, и *m.* (*coll.*) *affectionate form of* ⇒**дя́дя**; (*fig.*): **д. Сэм** Uncle Sam.

дя́д|я, и *m.* **1** (*родственник*) uncle.
2 (*coll.*) (*обращение*) mister (*as term of address*). **3** (*coll.*) (*мужчина*) guy.

дя́т|ел, ла *m.* woodpecker.

Ee

ЕАСТ *f. indecl.* (*abbr. of* ***Европе́йская ассоциа́ция свобо́дной торго́вли***) EFTA (*European Free Trade Association*).

ёбаный *adj.* (*vulg.*) fucking.

еб|а́ть, у́, ёшь *impf.* (*of* ⇒**вы́~**) (*vulg.*) to fuck; **ёб твою мать!** fuck you!; *int.* (*чёрт возьми*) fuck!; fucking hell!

Ева́нгели|е, я *nt.* (*collect.*) the Gospels; **е.** gospel (*also fig.*).

евангели́ст, а *m.* **1** (*составитель Евангелия*) Evangelist. **2** (*протестант*) (an) evangelical.

евангели́ческ|ий *adj.* evangelical; **~ая це́рковь** Evangelical Church.

ева́нгельский *adj.* gospel.

евге́ник|а, и *f.* eugenics.

е́внух, а *m.* eunuch.

евразийский *adj.* Eurasian.

Евра́зи|я, и *f.* Eurasia.

евре́|й, я *m.* Jew; (*древний*) Hebrew.

евре́йк|а, и *f.* Jewish woman, girl.

евре́йский *adj.* Jewish; **~ язы́к** Hebrew.

евре́йств|о, а *nt.* (*collect.*) Jewry, the Jews.

е́вро *nt. indecl.* euro (*currency unit*).

евро... *comb. form* Euro-.

Евро́п|а, ы *f.* Europe.

Европарла́мент, а *m.* Europarliament.

европе́|ец, йца *m.* European.

европеиза́ци|я, и *f.* Europeanization.

европеизи́р|овать, ую *impf. and pf.* to Europeanize.

европе́|йка, йки *f. of* ⇒**~ец**

европе́йский *adj.* European.

евроске́птик, а *m.* Euro-sceptic.

ЕВС *f. indecl.* (*abbr. of* ***Европе́йская валю́тная систе́ма***) EMS (*European Monetary System*).

ЕВФ *m. indecl.* (*abbr. of* ***Европе́йский валю́тный фонд***) EMF (*European Monetary Fund*).

Евфра́т, а *m.* the Euphrates (*river*).

евхари́сти|я, и *f.* (*eccl.*) Eucharist.

е́гер|ь, я, *pl.* **~и, ~ей** *and* **~я́, ~е́й** *m.* huntsman.

Еги́п|ет, та *m.* Egypt.

еги́петский *adj.* Egyptian.

египто́лог, а *m.* Egyptologist.

египтоло́ги|я, и *f.* Egyptology.

египтя́н|ин, ина, *pl.* **~е, ~** *m.* Egyptian.

египтя́н|ка, ки *f. of* ⇒**~ин**

его́ 1 *g. and a. sg. of* ⇒**он;** *g. sg. of* ⇒**оно́. 2** (*possessive pron.*) (*относящийся к человеку*) his; (*относящийся к предмету*) its.

егоз|а́, ы *c.g.* (*coll.*) fidget.

его|зи́ть, жу́, зи́шь *impf.* (*coll.*) **1** to fidget. **2** (**пе́ред** + *i.*) to fawn (upon).

егозли́в|ый (~, ~а) *adj.* (*coll.*) fidgety.

ед|а́, ы́ *f.* **1** (*пища*) food. **2** (*трапеза*) meal; **во вре́мя ~ы́** at meal-times, while eating.

еда́|ть *no pres., past* **~л, ~ла** (*coll.*) *freq. of* ⇒**есть¹**

едва́ *adv. and conj.* **1** (*adv.*) (*с трудом*) hardly, barely, only just; **мы е. попа́ли на по́езд** we only just caught the train. **2** (*adv.*) (*чуть*) hardly, scarcely, barely, only just; **печь е. гори́т** the fire is barely alight. **3 едва́-едва́** *emph. variant of* ⇒**е.** 1, 2. **4**: **е. ли** (*adv.*) hardly, scarcely (*in judgements of probability*); **е. ли он отка́жется от тако́го соблазни́тельного предложе́ния** he will hardly refuse such a tempting offer. **5**: **е. (ли) не** (*adv.*) nearly, almost, all but; **я е. не по́мер со́ смеху** I nearly died laughing. **6** (*conj.*) hardly, scarcely, barely; **е. ..., как** scarcely ... when; no sooner ... than; **е. самолёт взлете́л, как оди́н из мото́ров заéло** no sooner had the plane taken off than one of the engines seized up.

еди́м *see* ⇒**есть¹**

едине́ни|е, я *nt.* unity.

едини́ц|а, ы *f.* **1** (*цифра*) one; figure 1; (*math.*) unity. **2** (*in var. senses*) unit; **е. мо́щности** unit of power; **~ы вое́нно-морско́го фло́та** naval units. **3** (*отметка*) 'one' (*lowest mark in Russian university and school marking system*). **4** (*отдельное лицо*) individual; **(то́лько) ~ы** only a few, only a handful.

едини́чн|ый *adj.* **1** (*единственный*) single; **е. слу́чай** solitary instance; **~ые слу́чаи** isolated cases. **2** (*индивидуальный*) individual; **~ое се́льское хозя́йство** farming on an individual basis.

единобо́жи|е, я *nt.* monotheism.

единобо́рств|о, а *nt.* single combat.

единобра́чи|е, я *nt.* monogamy.

единобра́чный *adj.* monogamous.

единове́р|ец, ца *m.* co-religionist.

единове́р|ный (~ен, ~на) *adj.* (**с** + *i.*) of the same faith (as).

единовла́сти|е, я *nt.* autocracy, absolute rule.

единовла́ст|ный (~ен, ~на) *adj.* autocractic; dictatorial; **е. прави́тель** absolute ruler.

единовре́менно *adv.* **1** (*только один раз*) but once, once only. **2** (*одновременно*) simultaneously.

единовре́мен|ный (~ен, ~на) *adj.* **1** (*происходящий только один раз*) extraordinary, unique; **~ное посо́бие** extraordinary grant. **2** (**с** + *i.*) (*одновременный*) simultaneous (with).

единогла́си|е, я *nt.* unanimity.

единогла́сно *adv.* unanimously.

единогла́с|ный (~ен, ~на) *adj.* unanimous.

единоду́ши|е, я *nt.* unanimity.

единоду́ш|ный (~ен, ~на) *adj.* unanimous.

единокро́в|ный (~ен, ~на) *adj.* **1** (*от того же отца*) consanguineous; **е. брат** half-brother. **2** (*общего происхождения*) of the same stock.

единоли́чник, а *m.* individual peasant-farmer (*working his own holding*).

единоли́чн|ый *adj.* individual; personal; **~ое реше́ние** individual decision; **~ое хозя́йство** individual peasant holding.

единомы́сли|е, я *nt.* like-mindedness.

единомы́шленник, а *m.* **1** person who holds the same views; like-minded person; **мы с ним ~и по вопро́сам вне́шней поли́тики** we think the same way on matters of foreign policy. **2** (*сообщник*) confederate, accomplice.

единонасле́ди|е, я *nt.* (*leg.*) primogeniture.

единообра́зи|е, я *nt.* uniformity.

единообра́з|ный (~ен, ~на) *adj.* uniform.

единоро́г, а *m.* **1** (*myth.*) unicorn. **2** (*zool.*) narwhal.

единоро́дный *adj.* (*obs.*) only-begotten; **е. сын** only son.

единоутро́б|ный (~ен, ~на) *adj.* uterine; **е. брат** half-brother.

еди́нственно *adv.* only, solely; **е. возмо́жный ход** the only possible move; **она́ прису́тствовала е. из любопы́тства** she came solely out of curiosity.

еди́нствен|ный (~(ен), ~на) *adj.* only, sole; one and only; **е. сын** only son; **он е. оста́лся в живы́х** he was the sole survivor; **е. в своём ро́де** the only one of its kind, unique specimen; **~ное число́** (*gram.*) singular (number).

еди́нств|о, а *nt.* (*in var. senses*) unity.

еди́н|ый (~, ~а) *adj.* **1** (*единственный*) one; single, sole; **ни ~ой души́ там не́ было** there was not a soul there; **всё ~о** (*coll.*) it's all one; **все до ~ого** to a man. **2** (*один*) united, unified; **е. и недели́мый** one and indivisible. **3** (*общий*) common, single; **~ая во́ля** single will/purpose.

еди́те *see* ⇨**есть**[1]

е́д|кий (~ок, ~ка́, ~ко) *adj.* **1** caustic; acrid, pungent; **е. натр** (*chem.*) caustic soda; **е. за́пах** pungent smell. **2** (*fig.*) caustic, sarcastic.

е́дкост|ь, и *f.* **1** causticity; pungency; (*fig.*) sarcasm. **2** (*замечание*) sarcastic remark.

едо́к, а́ *m.* **1** (*лицо*) mouth; head; **у него́ в семье́ де́сять ~о́в** he has ten mouths to feed; **на ~а́** per head. **2** (*coll.*) (*том, кто ест*) (big) eater; **плохо́й е.** a poor eater.

е́д|у, ешь *see* ⇨**е́хать**

е́дучи *pres. ger.* (*coll.*) *of* ⇨**е́хать**

е́д|че *comp. of* ⇨**~кий**

едя́т *see* ⇨**есть**[1]

её 1 *g. and a. of* ⇨**она́. 2** (*possessive pron.*) (*относящийся к человеку*) (*при существительном*) her; (*без существительного*) hers; (*относящийся к предмету*) its.

ёж, ежа́ *m.* hedgehog; **~у́ поня́тно** (*coll.*) it's as plain as can be.

ежеви́к|а, и *f.* **1** (*collect.*) blackberries. **2** (*кустарник*) bramble, blackberry bush.

ежеви́|чный *adj. of* ⇨**~ка; ~чное варе́нье** blackberry preserve.

ежего́дник, а *m.* (*издание*) annual (publication), year-book; (*дневник*) diary; (*календарь*) calendar.

ежего́дный *adj.* annual, yearly.

ежедне́в|ный (~ен, ~на) *adj.* daily; everyday.

ежекварта́льник, а *m.* quarterly (publication).

ежекварта́льный *adj.* quarterly.

е́жели *conj.* (*obs. or coll.*) if.

ежеме́сячник, а *m.* monthly (publication).

ежеме́сячный *adj.* monthly.

ежеми́ну́т|ный (~ен, ~на) *adj.* **1** occurring every minute, at intervals of a minute. **2** (*непрерывный*) incessant, continual.

еженеде́льник, а *m.* weekly (publication).

еженеде́льный *adj.* weekly.

ежено́щный *adj.* nightly.

ежесеку́нд|ный (~ен, ~на) *adj.* **1** occurring every second. **2** (*coll.*) (*чрезвычайно частый*) incessant, continual.

ежесу́точный *adj.* daily.

ежеча́сный *adj.* hourly.

ёжик, а *m.* **1** *dim. of* ⇨**ёж. 2**: **стри́чься ~ом** to have a crew cut.

ёж|иться, усь, ишься *impf.* (*of* ⇨**съ~**) **1** (*от холода*) to shiver, huddle o.s. up. **2** (*fig., coll.*) (*от страха, стыда*) to shrink, cringe.

ежи́х|а, и *f.* female hedgehog.

ежо́в|ый *adj. of* ⇨**ёж; держа́ть в ~ых рукави́цах** (*coll.*) to rule with a rod of iron.

езд|а́, ы́ *f.* **1** ride, riding; (*на машине*) drive, driving; going; **е. на велосипе́де** bicycling. **2** *in phrr. indicating distance from one point to another*; journey, drive; **отсю́да до о́зера — до́брых три часа́ ~ы́** from here to the lake is a good three hours' journey.

е́з|дить, жу, дишь *impf.* **1** (*indet. of* ⇨**е́хать**) to go (*in or on a vehicle or on an animal*); to ride, drive; **е. верхо́м** to ride (on horseback). **2** (*уметь ездить*) to (be able to) ride, drive. **3** (**к**+*d.*) (*посещать*) to visit.

езд|ово́й *adj. of* ⇨**~а́; ~овы́е соба́ки** draught-dogs; *as n.* **е., ~ово́го** *m.* (*mil.*) driver.

ездо́к, а́ *m.* **1** rider; horseman. **2**: **туда́ я бо́льше не е.** I am not going there again.

езжа́|ть *no pres., past* **~л, ~ла** (*coll.*), *freq. of* ⇨**е́здить; ~й(те)** (*as imper. of* ⇨**е́хать**) go!; get going!

е́зжен|ый *adj.*: **~ая доро́га** beaten track.

Е́зр|а, ы *m.* (*bibl.*) Ezra.

ей *d. and i. of* ⇨**она́**

ей-Бо́гу *int.* (*coll.*) truly!; really and truly!

ёк|ать, аю *impf.* (*of* ⇨**~нуть**) (*coll.*) (*о сердце*) to miss a beat; to go pit-a-pat.

Екклезиа́ст, а *m.*: **кни́га ~а** Ecclesiastes.

ёкн|уть, у, ешь *pf. of* ⇨**ёкать**

ектен|ья́, ьи́, *g. pl.* **~и́й** *f.* (*eccl.*) ektenia (*part of Orthodox liturgy consisting of versicles and responses*).

ел, е́ла *see* ⇨**есть**[1]

е́ле *adv.* **1** (*с трудом*) hardly, barely, only just; **его́ речь была́ е. слышна́** his speech was hardly audible. **2** (*лишь только*) hardly, scarcely, barely, only just; **по́езд е. дви́гался** the train was scarcely moving. **3**: **е́ле-е́ле** *emph. variant of* ⇨**е.; он е.-е. спа́сся** he had a very narrow escape.

е́левый *adj.* (*bot.*) fir, spruce.

еле́|й, я *m.* (*eccl.*) anointing oil; unction; (*fig.*) unction; balm.

еле́й|ный *adj.* **1** (*eccl.*) *adj. of* ⇨**~. 2** (*fig.*) unctuous.

елизаве́ти́нский *adj.* Elizabethan.

ели́ко *adv.* (*obs.*) as far as, as much as; **е. возмо́жно** as far as possible.

елисе́йский *adj.* Elysian.

ёлк|а, и *f.* **1** fir(-tree), spruce; **рожде́ственская е.** Christmas-tree. **2** (*coll.*) (*праздник*) Christmas, New Year's party; (*int.*) **~и-па́лки!** (*coll.*) sugar!; flip(ping hell)!; hell's bells!

ел|о́вый *adj. of* ⇨**~ь; ~о́вые ши́шки** fir-cones.

ело́|зить, жу, зишь *impf.* (*coll.*) to crawl.

ёлочк|а, и *f.* **1** *dim. of* ⇨**ёлка. 2** herring-bone (pattern); **он но́сит зелёный пиджа́к ~ой, в ~у** he wears a green herring-bone jacket. **3** *pl.* (*typ.*) guillemets.

ёлочн|ый *adj. of* ⇨**ёлка; ~ые украше́ния** Christmas-tree decorations.

ел|ь, и *f.* spruce (*Picea*); fir(-tree).

е́льник, а *m.* **1** fir-grove, fir-plantation. **2** (*collect.*) fir-branches; fir-twigs.

ем *see* ⇨**есть**[1]

ём|кий (~ок, ~ка) *adj.* capacious.

ёмкост|ь, и *f.* (*вместимость*) capacity, cubic content; (*вместилище*) container.

ему́ *d. of* ⇨**он, оно́**

ено́т, а *m.* **1** (*zool.*) raccoon. **2** (*мех*) raccoon (fur).

ено́т|овый *adj. of* ⇨**~**

епанч|а́, и́, *g. pl.* **~е́й** *f.* (*hist.*) cloak, mantle.

епархиа́льный *adj.* (*eccl.*) diocesan.

епа́рхи|я, и *f.* (*eccl.*) diocese.

епи́скоп, а *m.* bishop.

епископа́льный *adj.* (*eccl.*) episcopalian.

епи́скопский *adj.* episcopal.

епи́скопств|о, а *nt.* episcopate.

ер, а *m.* (*obs.*) (hard) yer (*name of Russian letter* '**ъ**').

ерала́ш, а *m.* (*coll.*) jumble, muddle.

ерепе́н|иться, юсь, ишься *impf.* (*of* ⇨**взъ~**) (*coll.*) to bristle; to dig one's heels in (*fig.*).

е́рес|ь, и, *pl.* **~и, ~ей** *f.* **1** heresy. **2** (*coll.*) (*вздор*) nonsense.

ерети́к, а́ *m.* heretic.

ерети́ческий *adj.* heretical.

ёрза|ть, ю *impf.* (*coll.*) to fidget.

ермо́лк|а, и *f.* skull-cap.

еро́ш|ить, у, ишь *impf.* (*coll.*) to rumple, ruffle; to dishevel.

еро́ш|иться, ится *impf.* (*coll.*) to bristle, stick up.

ерунд|а́, ы́ *f.* (*coll.*) **1** (*чепуха*)

nonsense, rubbish; **говори́ть ~у́** to talk nonsense; **е. на по́стном ма́сле** twaddle, poppycock. **2** (*пустяк*) trifle, trifling matter; child's play.

ерунди́стик|а, и *f.* (*coll.*) nonsense.

ерунд|и́ть, *1st pers. sg. not used,* **~и́шь** *impf.* (*coll.*) to talk nonsense; to play the fool.

ерундо́в|ский *adj.* = **~ый**

ерундо́вый *adj.* (*coll.*) **1** (*глупый*) foolish. **2** (*незначительный*) trifling.

ёрш[1], ерша́ *m.* **1** (*рыба*) ruff. **2** (*щётка*) brush. **3** (*волосы*) hair sticking up; **~о́м** (*as adv.*) sticking up, on end.

ёрш[2], ерша́ *m.* (*coll.*) mixture of beer and vodka.

ерши́ст|ый (~, ~а) *adj.* (*coll.*) **1** bristling; sticking up. **2** (*fig.*) obstinate; unyielding.

ерш|и́ться, у́сь, и́шься *impf.* (*coll.*) **1** (*о волосах*) to stick up. **2** (*горячиться*) to grow heated, fly into a rage.

ершо́вый *adj. of* ⇒**ёрш[1]1**

еры́ *nt. indecl.* (*obs.*) yery (*name of Russian letter* **'ы'**).

ер|ь, я *m.* (*ling.*) (soft) yer (*name of Russian letter* **'ь'**).

ЕС *nt. indecl.* (*abbr. of* ***Европе́йское соо́бщество, сою́з*** EC, EU (*European Community, Union*).

есау́л, а *m.* (*hist.*) esaul (*Cossack captain*).

е́сли *conj.* if; **е. не** unless; **е. то́лько** provided; **е. бы не** but for, if it were not for; **е. бы не ты, он мог бы ко́нчить самоуби́йством** but for you he might have committed suicide; **е. бы** (*in exclamations*) if only; **что е...?** what if ...?; **что, е. бы** (*introducing suggestion of course of action*) what about, how about; **е. бы да кабы́** if ifs and ans were pots and pans.

ест *see* ⇒**есть[1]**

есте́ственник, а *m.* (natural) scientist.

есте́ственно[1] *adv.* **1** naturally. **2** *as particle* naturally, of course.

есте́ственно[2] *as pred.* it is natural.

есте́ствен|ный (~, ~на) *adj.* (*in var. senses*) natural; **~ные бога́тства** natural resources; **~ные нау́ки** natural sciences; **е. отбо́р** (*biol.*) natural selection.

естеств|о́, а́ *nt.* essence.

естествове́дени|е, я *nt.* (*obs.*) natural history; (natural) science.

естествозна́ни|е, я *nt.* (natural) science.

естествоиспыта́тел|ь, я *m.* (natural) scientist, naturalist.

есть[1], ем, ешь, ест, еди́м, еди́те, едя́т, *past* **ел, е́ла,** *imper.* **ешь,** *impf.* (*of* ⇒**съ~**) **1** (*принимать пищу*) to eat. **2** (*impf. only*) (*металл*) to corrode, eat away. **3** (*impf. only*) (*о дыме*) to sting, cause to smart. **4** (*impf. only*) (*coll.*) (*мучить*) to torment; to nag.

есть[2] 1 *3rd pers. sg.* (*also, rarely, substituted for all persons*) *pres. of* ⇒**быть; так и е.** (*coll.*) sure enough; yes, indeed; **как е.** (*coll.*) entirely, completely. **2** there is; there are; **у меня́, него́** *etc.*, **е.** I have, he has, *etc.*; **е. тако́е де́ло** (*coll.*) all right; O.K.

есть[3] *int.* (*mil.*) (*ответ подчинённого*) yes, sir; (*naut.*) aye-aye.

ефре́йтор, а *m.* (*mil.*) lance-corporal.

е́хать, е́ду, е́дешь *impf.* (*of* ⇒**по~**) (*det. of* ⇒**е́здить**) to go (*in or on a vehicle or on an animal*); to ride, drive; **е. верхо́м** to ride (*on horseback*); **е. по́ездом, на по́езде** to go by train; **да́льше е. не́куда** (*coll.*) that's the end, last straw.

ехи́дн|а, ы *f.* **1** (*zool.*) (*млекопитающее*) echidna. **2** (*змея*) Australian viper. **3** (*fig., coll.*) (*человек*) viper, snake.

ехи́днича|ть, ю *impf.* (*of* ⇒**съ~**) (*coll.*) to be malicious.

ехи́д|ный (~ен, ~на) *adj.* (*coll.*) malicious, spiteful.

ехи́дств|о, а *nt.* (*coll.*) malice, spite.

ехи́дств|овать, ую *impf.* (*coll.*) = **ехи́дничать**

ешь *see* ⇒**есть[1]**

ещё *adv.* **1** (*по-прежнему*) still; yet; **он е. мо́лод** he's still young; **е. не, нет е.** not yet; **всё е.** still; **пока́ е.** for the present, for the time being; **э́то е. ничего́!** that's nothing!
2 (*больше*) some more; any more; yet, further; again; **вам нали́ть е. (вина́** *etc.*)? may I pour you some more (wine, *etc.*)?; **есть е. хлеб?** is there any more bread?; **е. оди́н** one more, yet another; **е. раз** once more, again; **наде́юсь, е. приду́** I hope I shall come again.
3 (*уже*) already; as long ago as, as far back as; **е. в 1900-ом году́** in 1900 already; as long ago as 1900.
4 (*дополнительно*) else; **кто е. хо́чет ко́фе?** who else wants coffee?; **вы хоти́те е. что-нибу́дь?** do you want anything else?; **где вы е. бы́ли** where else have you been?
5 (+*comp.*) still, yet, even; **е. гро́мче** even louder; **е. и е.** more and more.
6 (+*prons. and advs.*) *as emph. particle*; **ты ви́дел кота́? — како́го е. кота́?** have you seen the cat? — What cat, for heaven's sake?
7: **е. бы** (*coll.*) (*i*) (*конечно, безусловно*) yes, rather!; you bet!, of course!; I'll say!, (*ii*) (*было бы удивительно, если бы*) it would be surprising if ...; **е. бы вы с ни́ми не сошли́сь** it would be surprising if you and they didn't get on; **е. чего́!** no way!, not likely!
8: **а е.** *expr. reproach or sarcastic criticism*: **сплётничать за мое́й спино́й, а е. друг** gossiping behind my back when you are supposed to be my friend.

ЕЭС *nt. indecl.* (*abbr. of* ***Европе́йское экономи́ческое соо́бщество***) EEC (*European Economic Community*).

е́ю *i. of* ⇒**она́**

ея́ *g. of* ⇒**она́** *in pre-1918 orthography.*

E

Жж

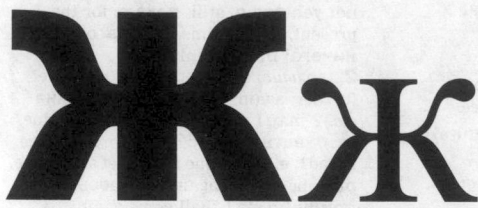

Ж (*abbr. of* ***Же́нская (убо́рная)***) Ladies (*lavatory*).

ж = **же**

жа́б|а¹, ы *f.* (*zool.*) toad.

жа́б|а², ы *f.* (*med.*) quinsy; **грудна́я ж.** angina pectoris.

жа́берный *adj.* (*zool.*) branchiate.

жа́б|ий *adj. of* **⇒~а¹**

жабо́ *nt. indecl.* jabot.

жа́бр|ы, ~ *pl.* (*sg.* **~а, ~ы** *f.*) (*zool.*) gills; **взять за ж.** (*fig., coll.*) to bring pressure to bear upon.

жа́ворон|ок, ка *m.* (*zool.*) lark; **полево́й ж.** skylark.

жа́дин|а, ы *c.g.* (*coll.*) greedy person.

жа́днича|ть, ю *impf.* (*coll.*) to be mean.

жа́дност|ь, и *f.* **1** (*к деньгам, еде, действию*) greed (for); greediness. **2** (*скупость*) avarice, meanness.

жа́д|ный (~ен, ~на́, ~но) *adj.* **1** (**к**+*d.*) greedy (for); avid (for); **он всегда́ был ~ным к но́вым зна́ниям** he was always greedy for knowledge. **2** (*скупой*) avaricious, mean.

жа́жд|а, ы *no pl., f.* thirst; (+*g.*; *fig.*) thirst, craving (for); **ж. зна́ний** thirst for knowledge.

жа́жд|ать, у, ешь *impf.* (+*g. or inf.*; *fig.*) to thirst (for, after), crave.

жаке́т, а *m.* (*ladies'*) jacket.

жаке́тк|а, и *f.* (*coll.*) = **жаке́т**

жале́|ть, ю *impf.* (*of* **⇒по~**) **1** (*чувствовать жалость*) to pity, feel sorry (for). **2** (**о**+*p. or* +*g.*; **что**) (*сожалеть*) to regret, be sorry (for, about); **~ю об утра́ченном вре́мени** I regret the waste of time; **~ю, что не оста́лся до конца́ ма́тча** I am sorry I did not stay till the end of the match. **3** (+*a. or g.*) (*скупиться*) to spare; to grudge; **не ~я сил** not sparing o.s., unsparingly.

жа́л|ить, ю, ишь *impf.* (*of* **⇒у~**) to sting; to bite.

жа́л|иться, юсь, ишься *impf.* (*coll.*) to sting; to bite.

жа́л|кий (~ок, ~ка́, ~ко) *adj.* pitiful, pathetic, wretched; **име́ть ж. вид** to be a sorry sight.

жа́лк|о¹ *adv. of* **⇒~ий**

жа́лко² *as pred.* (*impers.*) **1** (+*d. and a.*) (*о чувстве сострадания*) to pity, feel sorry (for); **мне ж. бра́та/А́нну** I feel sorry for my brother/Anna; **ей ж. бы́ло себя́** she felt sorry for herself. **2** (*о чувстве грусти*) (it is) a pity, a shame; **ж., что она́ не придёт** it's a pity she's not coming; (+*d. and g. or a.*) it grieves (me, *etc.*); to regret, feel sorry; **мне ста́ло ж. потра́ченного вре́мени** I began to regret the time wasted. **3** (+*g. or* +*inf.*) (*скупиться*) to grudge.

жа́л|о, а *nt.* **1** (*пчелы*) sting (*also fig.*). **2** (*булавки*) point.

жа́лоб|а, ы *f.* complaint; **пода́ть ~у** (**на**+*a.*) to make, lodge a complaint (about).

жа́лоб|ный (~ен, ~на) *adj.* **1** plaintive; mournful. **2** *adj. of* **⇒~а; ~ная кни́га** complaints book.

жа́лобщик, а *m.* person lodging a complaint.

жа́лова|нный *p.p.p. of* **⇒~ть** *and adj.* (*hist.*) granted, received as grant; **~нная гра́мота** letters patent, charter.

жа́ловань|е, я *nt.* salary.

жа́л|овать, ую *impf.* (*of* **⇒по~**) **1** (+*a. and i. or* +*d. and a.*) (*награждать*) to grant (to); to bestow, confer (on); to reward (with); **ж. сторо́нников землёй, ж. сторо́нникам зе́млю** to grant land to one's supporters, reward one's supporters with (grants of) land. **2** (*coll.*) (*любить*) to like, regard with favour (*Br.*), favor (*US*).

жа́л|оваться, уюсь *impf.* (*of* **⇒по~**) (**на**+*a.*) to complain (of, about); **ж. в суд** to go to law.

жа́лостлив|ый (~, ~а) *adj.* (*coll.*) **1** (*сострадательный*) compassionate, sympathetic. **2** (*печальный*) sad, mournful.

жа́лост|ный (~ен, ~на) *adj.* (*coll.*) **1** (*печальный*) plaintive, mournful. **2** (*сострадательный*) compassionate, sympathetic.

жа́лост|ь, и *f.* pity, compassion; **из ~и** (**к**+*d.*) out of pity (for); **кака́я ж.!** what a pity!; **ж. к себе́** self-pity.

жаль *as pred.* (*impers.*) **1** (+*d. and a.*) (*о чувстве сострадания*) to pity, feel sorry (for); **мне ж. тебя́** I pity you. **2** (*о чувстве грусти*) (it is) a pity, a shame; **ж., что вас там не бу́дет** it is a pity you will not be there; (+*d.*) it grieves (me, *etc.*); to regret, feel sorry; **нам ж. бы́ло расстава́ться** it grieved us to part. **3** (+*g. or* +*inf.*) (*скупиться*) to grudge; **(мне) ж. де́нег** I begrudge the money.

жалюзи́ *nt. indecl.* Venetian blind, jalousie.

жанда́рм, а *m.* gendarme.

жандарме́ри|я, и *f.* (*collect.*) gendarmerie.

жанр, а *m.* **1** (*вид произведений*) genre. **2** (*живопись на бытовые сюжеты*) genre-painting.

жанри́ст, а *m.* genre-painter.

жа́нр|овый *adj. of* **⇒~**

жар, а (у), о ~е, в ~у́ *no pl., m.* **1** heat; heat of the day; hot place; **в ~у́** (+*g.*) in the heat (of). **2** (*coll.*) (*горячие угли*) embers; **как ж. горе́ть** to gleam, glitter; **чужи́ми рука́ми ж. загреба́ть** to use others to pull one's chestnuts out of the fire. **3** (*лихорадка*) fever; (high) temperature. **4** (*fig.*) heat, ardour (*Br.*), ardor (*US*); **с ~ом приня́ться за что-н.** to set about sth. with a will.

жар|а́, ы *f.* heat; hot weather.

жарго́н, а *m.* jargon; slang.

жарго́н|ный *adj. of* **⇒~**

жа́рен|ое, ого *nt.* (*coll.*) fried food; (*мясо*) roast meat.

жа́реный *adj.* (*на сковороде*) fried; (*в духовке*) roast; (*на решётке*) grilled (*Br.*), broiled (*US*).

жа́р|ить, ю, ишь *impf.* **1** (*pf.* **за~** *or* **из~**) (*на сковороде*) to fry; (*в духовке*) to roast; (*на решётке*) to grill (*Br.*), broil (*US*). **2** (*о солнце*) to burn, scorch.

жа́р|иться, юсь, ишься *impf.* **1** (*pf.* **за~** *or* **из~**) to roast, fry (*intrans.*). **2**: **ж. на солнце** (*coll.*) to bask in the sun, sun o.s. **3** *pass. of* **⇒~ить**

жа́р|кий (~ок, ~ка́, ~ко) *adj.* **1** hot; (*знойный*) torrid; (*тропический*) tropical; **ж. пóяс** (*geog.*) torrid zone. **2** (*fig.*) hot, heated; ardent; passionate; **ж. спор** heated argument.

жáр|ко[1] *adv. of* ⇨**~кий**

жáрко[2] *as pred.* it is hot; **мне,** *etc.*, **ж.** I am, *etc.*, hot.

жарк|óе, óго *nt.* fried meat.

жарóв|ня, ни, *g. pl.* **~ен** *f.* brazier.

жар|овóй *adj. of* ⇨**~** 1

жаропонижáющ|ий *adj.* (*med.*) febrifugal; *as n.* **~ее, ~его** *nt.* febrifuge.

жаропрóчн|ый *adj.* ovenproof; **~ая кастрюля** casserole (dish).

жаростóйкий *adj.* (*tech.*) heat-resistant, heatproof.

жар-птúц|а, ы *f.* (*folklore*) the Fire-bird.

жáр|че *comp. of* ⇨**~кий** *and* **~ко**

жасмúн, а *m.* jasmine.

жáтв|а, ы *no pl., f.* reaping, harvesting; harvest (*also fig.*).

жáтв|енный *adj. of* ⇨**~а; ~енная машúна** harvester, reaping-machine.

жáтк|а, и *f.* harvester, reaping-machine.

жать[1], **жму, жмёшь** *impf.* (*no pf.*) **1** (*руку; лимон*) to press, squeeze; **ж. рýку** to shake (s.o.) by the hand. **2** (*сок*) to press out, squeeze out. **3** (*о платье, обуви*) to pinch, be tight; (*impers.*): **в плечáх жмёт** it is tight on the shoulders.

жать[2], **жну, жнёшь** *impf.* (*of* ⇨**с~**) to reap, cut, mow.

жáться, жмýсь, жмёшься *impf.* **1** (*сжиматься*) to huddle up; **ж. в ýгол** to skulk in a corner. **2** (**к**+*d.*) (*прижиматься*) to press close (to), draw closer (to). **3** (*coll.*) (*колебаться*) to hesitate, vacillate. **4** (*coll.*) (*скупиться*) to stint o.s.; to be stingy.

жбан, а *m.* (wooden) jug.

жвáчк|а, и *f.* **1** (*действие*) chewing, rumination. **2** (*пережёвываемая пища*) cud; **жевáть ~у** to chew the cud, ruminate; (*fig., coll.*) to bore everybody by repeating the same thing again and again. **3** (*coll.*) chewing-gum

жвáчн|ый *adj.* (*zool.*) ruminant; *as n.* **~ое, ~ого** *nt.* ruminant.

жгу, жжёшь, жгут *see* ⇨**жечь**

жгут, á *m.* **1** plait (*Br.*); braid. **2** (*med.*) tourniquet.

жгýчест|ь, и *f.* burning heat.

жгýч|ий (~, ~а, ~е) *adj.* burning hot (*also fig.*); **~ая боль** smart, smarting pain; **ж. брюнéт** person with jet-black hair and eyes; **ж. вопрóс** burning question.

ж. д. (*abbr. of* ***желéзная дорóга***) railway (*Br.*), railroad (*US*).

ждать, жду, ждёшь, *past* **ждал, ждалá, ждáло** *impf.* **1** (+*g.*) to wait (for); to await; **застáвить ж.** to keep waiting; **не застáвить себя ж.** to come quickly; **ж. не дождáться** (*coll.*) to wait impatiently, be on tenterhooks; **что нас ждёт?** what is in store for us?; **тогó и жди** (*coll.*) any time now, any minute. **2** (+*g.*) (*надеяться на, предполагать*) to expect. **3** (+**что**) to expect; **мы ждáли, что вы появúтесь на мúтинге** we expected you to come to the meeting.

же[1] *conj.* **1** (*при противопоставлении*) but; **идú, éсли тебé охóта, я же остáнусь здесь** you go, if you feel like it, but I shall stay here. **2** (*для присоединения*) and; **Окá впадáет в Вóлгу, Вóлга же в Каспúйское мóре** the Oka flows into the Volga, and the Volga flows into the Caspian Sea. **3** (*ведь*) after all; **расскажú ей — онá же твоя мать** tell her — she's your mother, after all.

же[2] *emph. particle*: **когдá же онú приéдут?** whenever will they come?; **что же ты дéлаешь?** whatever are you doing, what *are* you doing?

же[3] *particle expr. identity*: **тот же, такóй же** the same, idem; **тогдá же** at the same time; **там же** in the same place, ibidem; **Петросян, он же Петрóв** Petrosyan, alias Petrov.

жевáни|е, я *nt.* mastication; rumination.

жёваный *adj.* (*coll.*) chewed up; crumpled.

жевáтельн|ый *adj.* masticatory; **~ая резúнка** chewing gum.

жевáть, жую, жуёшь *impf.* to chew, masticate; (*о жвачных*) to ruminate; (*fig.*) **ж. жвáчку** *see* ⇨**жвáчка; ж. вопрóс** to chew over a question.

жёг, жгла *see* ⇨**жечь**

жезл, á *m.* (*символ власти*) rod, staff (of office); (*милиционера*) baton.

желáни|е, я *nt.* **1** (+*g.*) wish (for), desire (for); **бýдет по вáшему ~ю** it shall be as you wish; **при всём ~и** with the best will in the world. **2** (*просьба*) request. **3** (*вожделение*) desire, lust.

желá|нный *p.p.p. of* ⇨**~ть** *and adj.* wished for, longed for, desired, beloved; **ж. гость** welcome visitor.

желáтельно[1] *adv.* preferably.

желáтельно[2] *as pred.* it is desirable; it is advisable, preferable; **ж., чтóбы вы присýтствовали** it is desirable that you should be present, your presence is desirable.

желáтел|ьный (~ен, ~ьна) *adj.* desirable; advisable.

желатúн, а *no pl., m.* gelatin.

желатúновый *adj.* gelatinous.

желá|ть, ю *impf.* (*of* ⇨**по~**) **1** (+*g.*) to wish (for), desire. **2** (**чтóбы** *or* +*inf.*) to wish, want; **я ~ю, чтóбы вы прúняли учáстие в игрé** I want you to join in the game; **(не) ~ете ли вы познакóмиться с ним?** do you wish to meet him? **3** (+*d. and g. or inf.*) to wish (*s.o. sth.*); **~ю вам всяких благ** (*coll.*) I wish you every happiness; **~ю вам успéха** good luck!; **э́то оставляет ж. лýчшего, мнóгого** it leaves much to be desired.

желá|ющий *pres. part. act. of* ⇨**~ть; ~ющие** persons interested, those who so desire.

желвáк, á *m.* lump, tumour (*Br.*), tumor (*US*).

желé *nt. indecl.* jelly.

желез|á, ы, *pl.* **жéлезы, ~̀, ~áм** *f.* (*anat.*) gland; (*pl.*) (*coll.*) tonsils.

желéзистый[1] *adj.* (*anat.*) glandular.

желéзист|ый[2] **(~, ~а)** *adj.* ferrous, ferriferous; **ж. препарáт** iron preparation.

желéзк|а, и *f.* (*coll.*) piece of iron.

желёзк|а, и *f.* (*anat.*) glandule.

железнодорóжник, а *m.* railway worker.

железнодорóжн|ый *adj.* rail, railway, railroad (*US*); **~ая вéтка** branch line; **~ая перевóзка** rail transport; **~ое полотнó** permanent way; **ж. путь** (railway) track; **ж. ýзел** (railway) junction.

желéзн|ый *adj.* **1** iron (*also fig.*); (*chem.*) ferric, ferrous; **ж. блеск** (*min.*) haematite; **ж. век** the Iron Age; **~ое дéрево** (*bot.*) lignum vitae (*Guaiacum officinale*); **ж. зáнавес** the 'Iron Curtain'; **~ая кóмната** strong-room; **ж. лом** scrap iron; **за ~ой решёткой** (*coll.*) behind bars; **~ая рудá** iron-stone, iron-ore; **~ые товáры** ironmongery, hardware; **~ая травá** (*bot.*) vervain. **2**: **~ая дорóга** railway (*Br.*), railroad (*US*); **по ~ой дорóге** by rail; **~ая дорóга мéстного значéния** local line. **3** (*sl.*) (*надёжный*) reliable, dependable.

железнЯк, á *m.* (*min.*) iron-stone, iron clay.

желéз|о, а, *nt.* **1** iron; **ж. в болвáнках** pig-iron; **óкись ~а** (*chem.*) ferric oxide. **2** (*collect.*) iron; hardware.

желéзо... *comb. form* iron-, ferro-.

железобетóн, а *m.* (*tech.*) reinforced concrete, ferro-concrete.

железобетóн|ный *adj. of* ⇨**~**

железоплавúльный *adj.*: **ж. завóд** (*tech.*) iron foundry.

железопрокáтный *adj.*: **ж. завóд** (*tech.*) rolling mill.

жёлоб, а, *pl.* **~á, ~óв** *m.* (*водосточный*) gutter; (*для ссыпки чего-либо*) chute.

желоб|óк, кá *m.* (*tech.*) groove, channel, flute.

желтé|ть, ю *impf.* **1** (*pf.* **по~**) (*становиться жёлтым*) to turn yellow. **2** (*impf. only*) (*виднеться*) to be yellow, show up yellow.

желтé|ться, ется *impf.* to be yellow, show up yellow.

желтизн|á, ы́ *f.* yellowness; yellow.

жел|тúть, чý, тúшь *impf.* to colour (*Br.*), color (*US*) yellow.

желтовáт|ый (~, ~а) *adj.* yellowish.

желт|óк, кá *m.* yolk.

желтокóж|ий (~, ~а) *adj.* yellow-skinned.

желтолúц|ый (~, ~а) *adj.* sallow.

желторóт|ый (~, ~а) *adj.* **1** yellow-beaked. **2** (*fig.*) (*наивный*) inexperienced, green.

желтофиóл|ь, и *f.* (*bot.*) wallflower.

желт|óчный *adj. of* ⇨**~óк**

желтýх|а, и *f.* (*med.*) jaundice.

желтý|шный *adj. of* ⇨**~ха;** jaundiced.

жёлт|ый (~, ~а́, ~о and ~о́) *adj.* yellow; **~ая лихора́дка** yellow fever; **~ая пре́сса** the yellow press, the tabloids; **Жёлтые страни́цы** Yellow Pages (*propr.*).

желудёвый *adj. of* ⇨**жёлудь; ж. ко́фе** acorn coffee.

желу́д|ок, ка *m.* stomach; **несваре́ние ~ка** indigestion.

желу́доч|ек, ка *m.* (*anat.*) ventricle.

желу́дочно-кише́чный *adj.* gastro-intestinal.

желу́дочный *adj.* stomach; gastric; **ж. зонд** stomach pump; **ж. сок** gastric juice.

жёлуд|ь, я, *g. pl.* **~е́й** *m.* acorn.

жёлч|ный (~ен, ~на) *adj.* **1** bilious; **ж. ка́мень** gall-stone; **ж. пузы́рь** gall-bladder. **2** (*fig.*) peevish, irritable.

жёлч|ь (*coll.* **желчь**), **и** *no pl., f.* bile, gall (*also fig.*).

жема́н|иться, юсь, ишься *impf.* (*coll.*) to put on airs, behave affectedly.

жема́н|ный (~ен, ~на) *adj.* affected.

жема́нств|о, а *nt.* affectedness.

же́мчуг, а, *pl.* **~а́** *m.* (*collect.*) pearl(s).

жемчу́жин|а, ы *f.* pearl (*also fig.*).

жемчу́жниц|а, ы *f.* pearl-oyster.

жемчу́жн|ый *adj. of* ⇨**же́мчуг;** (*fig.*) pearly(-white); **~ое ожере́лье** pearl necklace.

жен... *comb. form, abbr. of* ***же́нский***

жен|а́, ы́, *pl.* **~ы, ~, ~ам** *f.* wife; **быть у ~ы́ под башмако́м** to be henpecked.

жена́т|ый (~) *adj.* married; **ж. (на**+*p.*) (*о мужчине*) married (to).

Жене́в|а, ы *f.* Geneva.

жен|и́ть, ю, ~ишь *impf. and pf.* (*pf. also* **по~**) to marry (off); **без меня́ меня́ ~или** (*fig., coll.*) I was roped in without being consulted.

жени́тьб|а, ы *no pl., f.* marriage.

жен|и́ться, ю́сь, ~ишься *impf. and pf.* (**на**+*p.*) (*о мужчине*) to marry, get married (to).

жени́х, а́ *m.* **1** fiancé; **смотре́ть ~о́м** (*coll.*) to look happy. **2** (*на свадьбе*) bridegroom. **3** (*поклонник*) suitor. **4** (*неженатый мужчина*) eligible bachelor.

женолю́б, а *nt.* ladies' man.

женолюби́в|ый (~) *adj.*: **ж. челове́к** ladies' man.

женолю́би|е, я *nt.* fondness for women.

женоненави́стник, а *m.* misogynist.

женоненави́стнический *adj.* misogynous.

женоненави́стничеств|о, а *nt.* misogyny.

женоподо́б|ный (~ен, ~на) *adj.* effeminate.

же́нск|ий *adj.* **1** woman's; female; feminine; **ж. вопро́с** the question of women's rights; **~ое ца́рство** petticoat government. **2** (*gram.*) feminine.

же́нственност|ь, и *f.* femininity.

же́нствен|ный (~, ~на) *adj.* feminine, womanly.

же́нщин|а, ы *f.* woman; **ж.-полице́йский** policewoman.

женьше́н|ь, я *m.* (*bot., med.*) ginseng.

жёрдочк|а, и *f.* (*coll.*) pole; (*в клетке*) perch.

жерд|ь, и, *pl.* **~и, ~е́й** *f.* pole; stake; **худо́й, как ж.** (*coll.*) thin as a lath.

жереб|ёнок, ёнка, *pl.* **~я́та, ~я́т** *m.* foal, colt.

жереб|е́ц, ца́ *m.* stallion.

жереб|и́ться, и́тся *impf.* (*of* ⇨**о~**) to foal.

жеребьёвк|а, и *f.* casting of lots; (*sport*) draw (*for play-off*).

жереб|я́чий *adj. of* ⇨**~ёнок; ж. смех** (*coll.*) horse-laugh.

жерл|о́, а́, *pl.* **~а, ~** *nt.* (*вулкана, печи*) mouth, orifice; (*пушки*) muzzle; **ж. вулка́на** crater.

жёрнов, а, *pl.* **~а́, ~о́в** *m.* millstone.

же́ртв|а, ы *f.* **1** sacrifice (*also fig.*); **принести́ ~у** (+*d.*) to make a sacrifice (to); **принести́ в ~у** to sacrifice. **2** (*пострадавший*) victim; **пасть ~ой** (+*g.*) to fall victim (to).

же́ртвенник, а *m.* sacrificial altar.

же́ртвенный *adj.* sacrificial.

же́ртвовател|ь, я *m.* donor.

же́ртв|овать, ую, *impf.* (*of* ⇨**по~**) **1** (*дарить*) to make a donation (of), present. **2** (+*i.*) (*подвергать опасности*) to sacrifice, give up.

жертвоприноше́ни|е, я *nt.* sacrifice.

жест, а *m.* gesture (*also fig.*).

жестикули́р|овать, ую *impf.* to gesticulate.

жестикуля́ци|я, и *f.* gesticulation.

жёст|кий (~ок, ~ка́, ~ко) *adj.* hard; tough; (*fig.*) rigid, strict; **ж. ваго́н** hard-seated carriage, 'hard' carriage; **~кая вода́** hard water; **~кие во́лосы** wiry hair; **ж. диск** (*comput.*) hard disk.

жёст|ко[1] *adv. of* ⇨**~кий**

жёстко[2] *as pred.* it is hard.

жесто́к|ий (~, ~а) *adj.* cruel; brutal; (*fig.*) severe, sharp.

жестокосе́рд|ный (~ен, ~на) *adj.* hard-hearted.

жестокосе́рд|ый (~, ~а) *adj.* = **~ный**

жесто́кост|ь, и *f.* cruelty, brutality.

жесто|ча́йший *superl. of* ⇨**~кий**

жёст|че *comp. of* ⇨**~кий** *and* **~ко**

жест|ь, и *f.* tin-plate.

жестя́нк|а, и *f.* **1** tin, can; **ж. из-под сарди́н** sardine tin. **2** (*coll.*) (*кусочек жести*) piece of tin-plate.

жест|яно́й *adj. of* ⇨**~ь; ~яна́я посу́да** tinware.

жестя́нщик, а *m.* tinman, tin-smith.

жето́н, а *m.* **1** (*медаль*) medal. **2** (*в транспорте*) token; **проездно́й ж.** travel token.

жечь, жгу, жжёшь, жгут, *past* **жёг, жгла** *impf.* **1** (*pf.* **с~**) to burn; **ж. му́сор** to burn refuse; (*дотла*) to burn down. **2** (*impf. only*) to burn, sting; (*impers.*): **от э́того ликёра жжёт го́рло** this liqueur burns one's throat.

же́чься, жгусь, жжёшься, жгу́тся, *past* **жёгся, жглась** *impf.* **1** to burn, sting (*intrans.*). **2** (*coll.*) to burn o.s.

жже́ни|е, я *nt.* burning sensation.

жжёнк|а, и *f.* hot punch.

жжёный *adj.* burnt, scorched; **ж. ко́фе** roasted coffee.

жжёшь *see* ⇨**жечь**

жива́ть *no pres.* (*coll.*) *freq. of* ⇨**жить**

жив|е́й, *see* ⇨**~о** 5

жив|е́ц, ца́ *m.* live bait, sprat.

живи́тел|ьный (~ен, ~ьна) *adj.* life-giving; (*воздух*) bracing.

жив|и́ть, лю́, и́шь *impf.* to give life to, animate; (*о воздухе*) to brace.

живи́ц|а, ы *f.* soft resin.

жи́вност|ь, и *no pl., f.* (*collect.; coll.*) small creatures.

жи́в|о *adv.* **1** (*ярко*) vividly. **2** (*оживлённо*) with animation. **3** (*остро*) keenly; extremely, exceedingly; **он ж. чу́вствовал оскорбле́ние** he felt deeply insulted. **4** (*coll.*) (*быстро*) quickly, promptly. **5 ж.!; ~е́й!** (*coll.*) get a move on!; look lively!

живодёр, а *m.* (*coll.*) knacker; (*fig.*) fleecer; profiteer.

живодёр|ня, ни, *g. pl.* **~ен** *f.* (*coll.*) knacker's yard.

живодёрств|о, а *nt.* (*coll.*) cruelty.

жив|о́й (~, ~а́, ~о) *adj.* **1** living, live, alive; **он ещё в ~ы́х** he is still alive; **оста́ться в ~ы́х** to survive; **~ (и) здоро́в** (*coll.*) safe and sound; **ни ~ ни мёртв** (*coll.*) petrified (*with fright, astonishment*); **ж. вес** live weight; **~а́я и́згородь** (quickset) hedge; **ж. инвента́рь** livestock; **шить на ~у́ю ни́тку** to tack; **на ~у́ю ни́тку** (*coll.*) hastily, anyhow; **ж. портре́т** (+*g.*) the living image (of); **~а́я ра́на** open wound; **ж. уголо́к** nature corner (*in a school*); **не́ было ви́дно ни (одно́й) ~о́й души́** there was not a living soul to be seen; **на нём не́ было ~о́го ме́ста** he was all battered and bruised; **забра́ть, заде́ть за ~о́е** to cut to the quick. **2** (*энергичный*) lively; keen; active; **ж. ум** lively mind; **проявля́ть ж. интере́с** (**к**+*d.*) to take a keen interest (in); **принима́ть ~о́е уча́стие** (**в**+*p.*) to take an active part (in); to feel keen sympathy with. **3** (*выразительный*) lively, vivacious; bright; **~ы́е глаза́** bright eyes. **4** (*остро переживаемый*) keen, poignant. **5** (*short form only;* +*i.*) *expr. raison d'être*: **он ~ одни́ми ша́хматами** he lives for chess alone; **чем она́ ~а́?** what makes her tick?

живокост|ь, и *f.* (*bot.*) larkspur.

живопи́с|ец, ца *m.* painter.

живопи́с|ный (~ен, ~на) *adj.* **1** (*относящийся к живописи*) pictorial. **2** (*красивый*) picturesque (*also fig.*); **~ное ме́сто** beauty spot.

живопис|ь, и *f.* **1** painting. **2** (*collect.*) paintings; **стенная ж.** murals.

живородящий *adj.* (*zool.*) viviparous.

живорождени|е, я *nt.* (*zool.*) viviparity.

живорыбный *adj.*: **ж. садок** fishpond.

живост|ь, и *f.* liveliness, vivacity; animation.

живот, а *m.* abdomen, belly; stomach; (*coll.*) tummy.

животвор|ить, ю, ишь *impf.* (*of* ⇒**о~**) (*obs.*) to revive.

животвор|ный (~ен, ~на) *adj.* life-giving.

животворящий *adj.* (*poet.*) life-giving.

животик, а *m.* (*coll.*) tummy.

животновод, а *m.* stockbreeder.

животноводств|о, а *nt.* stockbreeding, animal husbandry.

животноводческий *adj.* cattle-breeding, stock-raising.

животно|е, го *nt.* animal; **комнатное ж.** pet.

животный *adj.* **1** animal; **ж. жир** animal fat. **2** (*грубый*) bestial, brute.

животрепещущий *adj.* (*злободневный*) topical; stirring, exciting.

живучест|ь, и *f.* **1** vitality, tenacity of life. **2** (*fig.*) deep-rootedness.

живуч|ий (~, ~а) *adj.* **1** tenacious of life; (*bot.*) hardy; **он ~ как кошка** he has nine lives like a cat. **2** (*fig.*) (*обычай*) deep-rooted, enduring.

живчик, а *m.* **1** (*coll.*) (*человек*) lively person. **2** (*biol.*) spermatozoon. **3** (*coll.*) (*биение артерии*) perceptible pulsing of artery on temple; (*подёргивание века*) twitching of eyelid.

живьём *adv.* (*coll.*) alive; **петь ж.** to sing live; **постарайтесь схватить его ж.** try to catch him alive.

жиголо *m. indecl.* gigolo.

жид, а *m.* (*offens.*) Yid.

жид|кий (~ок, ~ка, ~ко) *adj.* **1** (*имеющий свойство течь*) liquid; fluid. **2** (*водянистый*) watery; weak, thin; **ж. чай** weak tea. **3** (*о волосах*) sparse, scanty; **~кая борода** straggly beard. **4** (*coll.*) (*о голосе, звуке*) weak, thin. **5** (*fig.*) (*о мускулах, об аргументах*) weak, feeble.

жидкокристаллический *adj.*: **ж. индикатор** liquid-crystal display, LCD.

жидкостный *adj.* (*tech.*) liquid; fluid.

жидкост|ь, и *f.* **1** liquid; fluid; **моющая ж.** washing-up liquid; **корректирующая ж.** correction fluid. **2** (*супа*) wateriness; (*голоса*) weakness, thinness (*also fig.*).

жиж|а, и *no pl.*, *f.* liquid; swill; slush.

жи|же *comp. of* ⇒**~дкий**

жижиц|а, ы *f.* (*coll.*) *dim. of* ⇒**жижа**

жизнедеятельност|ь, и *f.* (*biol.*) vital activity.

жизнедеятел|ьный (~ен, ~ьна) *adj.* **1** (*biol.*) active. **2** lively; energetic.

жизненност|ь, и *f.* **1** vitality. **2** (*реальность*) closeness to life; (*art*) lifelikeness.

жизнен|ный (~, ~на) *adj.* **1** (of) life; (*biol.*) vital; **~ные отправления** vital functions; **ж. путь** life; **ж. уровень** standard of living. **2** (*близкий к жизни, реальный*) close to life; lifelike. **3** (*fig.*) vital, vitally important; **ж. вопрос** question of vital importance; **~ные центры страны** nerve-centres of a country.

жизнеобеспечени|е, я *nt.*: **система ~я** life-support system.

жизнеописани|е, я *nt.* biography.

жизнерадостност|ь, и *f.* cheerfulness; joie de vivre.

жизнерадост|ный (~ен, ~на) *adj.* cheerful; vivacious.

жизнеспособност|ь, и *f.* (*biol.*) viability; (*fig.*) vitality.

жизнеспособ|ный (~ен, ~на) *adj.* capable of living; (*biol.*) viable; (*fig.*) vigorous, flourishing.

жизнесто|йкий (~ек, ~йка) *adj.* tenacious of life; tough, durable.

жизнеутверждающий *adj.* life-affirming.

жизн|ь, и *f.* life; (*существование*) existence; **ж. моя!** my love!; **зарабатывать на ж.** to earn one's living; **как ж.?** (*coll.*) how is life?; **лишить себя ~и** to take one's life; **не на ж., а на смерть** to the death; **ни в ж.** never, not for anything; **образ ~и** way of life; **вести широкий образ ~и** to live in style; **на всю ж.** for life; **провести что-н. в ж.** to put sth. into practice.

жиклёр, а *m.* (*tech.*) (carburettor) jet.

жил... *comb. form, abbr. of* **1** ***жилищный.*** **2** ***жилой*** 1

жил|а[1]**, ы** *f.* **1** (*кровеносный сосуд*) vein; (*сухожилие*) tendon, sinew; **тянуть ~ы** (**из** + *g.*; *coll.*) to torment, rack. **2** (*min.*) vein.

жил|а[2]**, ы** *c.g.* (*coll.*, *pej.*) skinflint.

жилет, а *m.* waistcoat (*Br.*), vest (*US*); **пуленепробиваемый ж.** bulletproof vest; **спасательный ж.** life-jacket.

жилетк|а, и *f.* (*coll.*) waistcoat (*Br.*), vest (*US*); **плакать в ~у** (+ *d.*) to cry on s.o.'s shoulders.

жилет|ный *adj. of* ⇒**~**

жил|ец, ьца *m.* tenant; **он не ж. (на белом свете)** (*coll.*) he is not long for this world.

жилист|ый (~, ~а) *adj.* **1** (*руки*) having prominent veins. **2** (*тело*) sinewy; (*старик*) wiry; **~ое мясо** stringy meat.

жил|ить, ю, ишь *impf.* (*coll.*) to swindle.

жил|ица, ицы *f. of* ⇒**~ец**

жиличк|а, и *f.* (*coll.*) = **жилица**

жилищ|е, а *nt.* dwelling, abode, (living) quarters.

жилищно-строительн|ый *adj.*: **~ое общество** building society.

жилищ|ный *adj. of* ⇒**~е**; **~ные условия** housing conditions; **~но-бытовые условия** living conditions.

жилк|а, и *f.* **1** (*anat.*, *geol.*) vein; (*zool.*, *bot.*) rib (*of insect's wing or of leaf*). **2** (*fig.*) streak; bent; **артистическая ж.** artistic streak.

жилмассив, а *m.* housing estate.

жиловат|ый (~, ~а) *adj.* (*coll.*) veiny.

жил|ой *adj.* **1** dwelling; residential; **ж. дом** dwelling house, block of flats; **ж. квартал** residential area; **~ая площадь** = **жилплощадь.** **2** (*обитаемый*) inhabited.

жилплощад|ь, и *f.* housing, accommodation.

жилстроительств|о, а *nt.* house-building.

жилфонд, а *m.* housing, accommodation.

жиль|ё, я *nt.* **1** (*селение*) habitation; dwelling; **мы не нашли никакого признака ~я** we could find no sign of life. **2** (*жилище*) lodging; (living) accommodation.

жим, а *m.* (*sport*) press (*in weight-lifting*).

жимолост|ь, и *f.* (*bot.*) honeysuckle.

жир, а (у), о ~е, в ~у, *pl.* **~ы** *m.* fat; grease; **с ~у беситься** (*coll.*) to become spoilt.

жираф, а *m.* giraffe.

жираф|а, ы *f.* = **~**

жире|ть, ю *impf.* (*of* ⇒**о~** *and* **раз~**) to grow fat, stout, plump.

жир|ный (~ен, ~на, ~но) *adj.* **1** (*пища, мясо*) fatty; (*chem.*) aliphatic; (*руки, волосы*) greasy; **~ная кислота** fatty acid, aliphatic acid; **~ное пятно** grease stain. **2** (*человек*) fat, plump. **3** (*земля*) rich; (*растительность*) lush. **4** (*typ.*) bold, heavy; **ж. шрифт** bold (-face) type.

жиро *nt. indecl.* (*fin.*) endorsement.

жир|овать[1]**, ую** *impf.* (*пропитывать жиром*) to lubricate, oil, grease.

жир|овать[2]**, ует** *impf.* (*о животных*) to fatten (*intrans.*).

жировик, а *m.* (*med.*) fatty tumour (*Br.*), tumor (*US*), lipoma.

жиров|ой *adj.* fatty, aliphatic; (*anat.*) adipose; **~ая ткань** adipose tissue.

житейск|ий *adj.* **1** worldly; of life, of the world; **~ая мудрость** worldly wisdom; **~ое море** the ups and downs of life. **2** (*обыденный*) everyday; **дело ~ое** (*coll.*) there's nothing extraordinary in that.

жител|ь, я *m.* inhabitant; dweller; **городской ж.** city dweller; **мирные ~и** civilians; civilian population.

житель|ница, ницы *f. of* ⇒**~**

жительств|о, а *nt.* residence; **вид на ж.** residence permit; **место ~а** residence, domicile; **место постоянного ~а** permanent address.

жити|е, я *nt.* (*жанр*) life, biography; **~я святых** Lives of the Saints.

житниц|а, ы *f.* granary (*also fig.*).

жит|о, а *no pl.*, *nt.* (*unground*) corn (*denotes rye in Ukraine, barley in northern Russia, spring-sown cereals in general in eastern Russia.*).

жить, живу, живёшь, *past* **жил, жила, жило (не жил, не жила, не жило)** *impf.* **1** to live; **ж. в Москве** to live in Moscow; **ж. весело** to have a

Ж

good time; **ж. припева́ючи** to be in clover; **ж. на широ́кую но́гу** to live in style; **ж. со дня на́ день** to live from hand to mouth; **жил-был** once upon a time there lived ....
2 (+*i. or* **на**+*a.*) to live (on); (+*i.*; *fig.*) to live (in, for); **нам не́ на что ж.** we have nothing to live on; **ж. на свой сре́дства** to support o.s., live on one's own means; **ж. наде́ждами** to live in hopes; **ж. иску́сством** to live for art.

жить|ё, я́ *nt.* (*coll.*) **1** (*жизнь*) life; existence; **~я́ тут нет от мух** the flies make life here impossible.
2 (*пребывание*) habitation, residence; **кварти́ра гото́ва для ~я́** the flat is ready for habitation.

житьё-бытьё, житья́-бытья́ *nt.* (*coll.*) life; existence.

жи́ться, живётся, *past* **жило́сь** *impf.* (*impers.*, +*d.*; *coll.*) to live, get on; **ей ве́село живётся** she enjoys her life; **как вам жило́сь в Аме́рике?** how did you get on in America?

ЖКИ *m. indecl.* (*abbr. of* ***жидкокристалли́ческий индика́тор***) LCD (*liquid-crystal display*).

жлоб, а *m.* (*coll.*) **1** (*скряга*) skinflint. **2** (*дуралей*) prat (*Br.*), jerk (*US*).

жмот, а *m.* (*coll.*) miser.

жму, жмёшь *see* **⇨жать¹**

жму́рик, а *m.* (*sl.*) goner, stiff.

жму́р|ить, ю, ишь *impf.* (*of* **⇨за~**): **ж. глаза́** to screw up one's eyes, narrow one's eyes.

жму́р|иться, юсь, ишься *impf.* (*of* **⇨за~**) to screw up one's eyes, narrow one's eyes.

жму́р|ки, ок *no sg.* blind man's buff.

жмых|и́, о́в *pl.* (*sg.* **~, ~а́** *m.*) (*agric.*) oil-cake.

жне́йк|а, и *f.* (*agric.*) harvester, reaping-machine.

жнец, а́ *m.* reaper.

жнив|ё, я́, *pl.* **~я** *nt.* **1** (*поле, где сжаты злаки*) stubble-field. **2** (*sg. only*) (*срезанные стебли злаков*) stubble.

жни́ц|а, ы *f. of* **⇨жнец**

жну, жнёшь *see* **⇨жать²**

жоке́|й, я *m.* jockey.

жоке́й|ский *adj. of* **⇨~**

жонглёр, а *m.* juggler.

жонглёрств|о, а *nt.* juggling (*also fig.*).

жонгли́р|овать, ую *impf.* (+*i.*) to juggle (with) (*also fig.*); **он лю́бит ж. ци́фрами** he likes juggling with figures.

жо́п|а, ы *f.* (*vulg.*) arse (*Br.*), ass (*US*); **ну ты и ж.!** you arsehole (*Br.*), asshole (*US*)!; **иди́** *or* **пошёл в ~у!** piss off!; **лени́вая ж.** lazy bugger (*Br.*), bum (*US*); **пья́н(ый) в ~у** pissed as a newt (*Br.*), drunk as a coot (*US*).

жратв|а́, ы́ *f.* (*sl.*) grub.

жр|ать, у́, ёшь, *past* **~ал, ~ала́, ~а́ло** *impf.* (*of* **⇨со~**) **1** (*о животных*) to eat. **2** (*sl.*) (*о человеке*) to guzzle, gobble.

жре́би|й, я *m.* **1** lot; **броса́ть, мета́ть ж.** to cast lots; **вы́нуть, тяну́ть ж.** to draw lots. **2** (*fig.*) lot, fate, destiny; **ж. бро́шен** the die is cast.

жрец, а́ *m.* (*pagan*) priest; (*fig.*) devotee.

жре́ческий *adj.* priestly.

жре́честв|о, а *nt.* priesthood.

жри́ц|а, ы *f.* priestess.

жу́желиц|а, ы *f.* (*zool.*) ground beetle.

жужжа́ни|е, я *nt.* hum, buzz, drone; humming, buzzing, droning.

жужж|а́ть, у́, и́шь *impf.* to hum, buzz, drone; (*о снарядах*) to whiz.

жуи́р, а *m.* playboy.

жук, а́ *m.* **1** beetle; **ма́йский ж.** may-bug, cockchafer. **2** (*coll.*) (*плут*) rogue, swindler.

жу́лик, а *m.* petty thief; cheat, swindler.

жуликова́т|ый (~, ~а) *adj.* (*coll.*) crooked.

жуль|ё, я́ *nt.* (*collect.*; *coll.*) rogues.

жу́льнича|ть, ю *impf.* (*of* **⇨с~**) (*coll.*) to cheat; to swindle.

жу́льнический *adj.* (*coll.*) crooked; underhand, dishonest.

жу́льничеств|о, а *nt.* (*coll.*) **1** (*в игре*) cheating. **2** (*плутовство*) underhand, dishonest action; sharp practice.

жу́пел, а *m.* bugbear, bogy.

журавл|и́ный *adj. of* **⇨~ь**; **~и́ные но́ги** spindle shanks.

жура́вл|ь, я *m.* **1** (*zool.*) crane; **не сули́ ~я́ в не́бе, а дай сини́цу в ру́ки** (*prov.*) a bird in the hand is worth two in the bush. **2** (*у колодца*) sweep, shadoof.

жур|и́ть, ю́, и́шь *impf.* (*coll.*) to reprove, take to task.

журна́л, а *m.* **1** (*периодическое издание*) magazine; periodical; journal. **2** (*книга для записи*) journal, diary; (*классный*) register; **ж. заседа́ний** minutes, minute-book.

журнали́ст, а *m.* journalist.

журнали́стик|а, и *f.* **1** (*деятельность*) journalism; **ж. с че́ковой кни́жкой** chequebook (*Br.*), checkbook (*US*) journalism. **2** (*collect.*) (*периодические издания*) periodical press.

журнали́стский *adj.* journalistic.

журна́л|ьный *adj. of* **⇨~**; **~ьная статья́** magazine article.

журча́ни|е, я *nt.* purling, babbling, murmur.

журч|а́ть, у́, и́шь *impf.* to babble, murmur (*of water*; *also fig.*, *poet.*).

жу́т|кий (~ок, ~ка́, ~ко) *adj.* terrible, terrifying; awe-inspiring, eerie.

жу́тко¹ *adv.* terrifyingly; (*coll.*) terribly, awfully.

жу́тко² *as pred.* **ж. поду́мать об э́том** it's terrible to think about it; **в лесу́ ж.** it's terrifying in the forest; (*impers.*, +*d.*): **мне,** *etc.*, **ж.** I, *etc.*, am terrified, feel awestruck.

жут|ь, и *f.* (*coll.*) **1** (*страх*) terror; awe. **2** *as pred.*: **~!** it is terrible!; **жара́ — про́сто ж.!** the heat is unbearable.

жу́хл|ый (~, ~а) *adj.* (*трава*) withered, dried-up; (*краски*) faded.

жу́х|нуть, нет, *past* **~, ~ла** *impf.* (*становиться сухим*) to wither, dry up; (*тускнеть*) to become tarnished.

жу́ч|ить, у, ишь *impf.* (*coll.*) to scold.

жу́чк|а, и *f.* (*coll.*) house-dog.

жуч|о́к, ка́ *m.* **1** *dim. of* **⇨жук.** **2** (*coll.*) (*пробка*) makeshift fuse.

жу|ю́, ёшь *see* **⇨жева́ть**

ЖЭК, а *or* **жэк, а** *m.* (*abbr. of* ***жили́щно-эксплуатацио́нная конто́ра***) housing office.

жюри́ *indecl. nt.* (*collect.*) judges (*of competition, etc.*).

Зз

З (*abbr. of* **за́пад**) W, West.

за *prep.* **I.** + *a. and i.* (+ *a.*: *indicates motion or action*; + *i.*: *indicates rest or state*).
1 (*позади*) behind; **за крова́ть, за крова́тью** behind the bed.
2 (*вне*) beyond; across, the other side of; **за боло́то, за боло́том** beyond the marsh; **за́ борт, за бо́ртом** overboard; **за́ угол, за угло́м** round the corner; **за́ городом** out of town; **за рубежо́м** abroad.
3 (*у*) at; **сесть за роя́ль** to sit down at the piano; **сиде́ть за роя́лем** to be at the piano.
4 (*занимаясь данным предметом*) at, to (*or translated by part.*); **приня́ться за рабо́ту** to set to work, get down to work; **заста́ть кого́-н. за рабо́той** to find s.o. at work, working; **сесть за кни́гу** to sit down with a book, get down to reading; **проводи́ть всё своё вре́мя за чте́нием** to spend all one's time reading.
5: **вы́йти за́муж за** (+ *a.*) (*of a woman*) to marry; **(быть) за́мужем за** (+ *i.*) (to be) married (to).
● **II.** + *a.* **1** (*свыше*) after (*of time*); over (*of age*); **далеко́ за́ полночь** long after midnight; **ему́ уже́ за со́рок** he is already over forty.
2 (*на расстоянии*): **самолёт разби́лся за ми́лю от дере́вни** the aeroplane crashed a mile from the village; **за два дня до его́ сме́рти** two days before his death; **за час** an hour before, an hour early.
3 (*в течение*) during, in the space of; **за́ ночь** during the night, overnight; **за су́тки** in the space of twenty-four hours; **за после́днее вре́мя** recently, lately, of late.
4 (*указывает на предмет, который охватывается*) by; **вести́ за́ руку** to lead by the hand.
5 (*in var. senses*) for; **плати́ть за биле́т** to pay for a ticket; **подписа́ть за дире́ктора** to sign for the director; **боя́ться, ра́доваться за кого́-н.** to fear, be glad for s.o.; **есть за трои́х** to eat (enough) for three; **за ва́ше здоро́вье!** your health!; cheers!
● **III.** + *i.* **1** (*после*) after; **друг за дру́гом** one after another; **год за го́дом** year after year; **сле́довать за кем-н.** to follow s.o.
2 (*fig.*) after; **следи́ть за детьми́** to look after children; **уха́живать за больны́м** to look after a sick person.
3 (*чтобы достать*) for; **идти́ за молоко́м** to go for milk; **посла́ть за до́ктором** to send for a doctor; **зайти́ за кем-н.** to call for s.o.
4 (*во время*) at, during; **за за́втраком** at breakfast.
5 (*по причине*) for, on account of, because of; **за неиме́нием, недоста́тком** (+ *g.*) for want of; **за темното́й** for the darkness, on account of the darkness; **за чем де́ло ста́ло?** what's up?
6 (+ *prons.*) (*выражает ответственность*): **за тобо́й пять рубле́й** you are owing five roubles; **о́чередь за ва́ми** it is your turn.
● **IV.** *as pred.* (*согласен*) for, in favour (*Br.*), favor (*US*).

за... *pref.* **I.** (*of vv.*) **1** *indicates commencement of action*: **зала́ять** to start barking. **2** *indicates direction of action beyond given point*: **заверну́ть за́ угол** to turn a corner. **3** *indicates continuation of action to excess*: **закорми́ть** to overfeed. **4** *forms pf. aspect of some vv.*
● **II.** (*of nn. and adjs.*) trans-; **Закавка́зье** Transcaucasia; **заатланти́ческий** transatlantic.

заале́|ть, ет *pf.* to begin to show red.

заале́|ться, ется = **~ть**

зааплоди́р|овать, ую *pf.* to break out into applause, start clapping.

зааренд|ова́ть, у́ю *pf.* (*of* ⇒**~о́вывать**) to rent, lease.

зааренд|о́выва|ть, ю *impf. of* ⇒**заарендова́ть**

заарка́н|ить, ю, ишь *pf. of* ⇒**арка́нить**

заарта́ч|иться, усь, ишься *pf.* (*coll.*) to become restive, stubborn.

заасфальти́р|овать, ую *pf. of* ⇒**асфальти́ровать**

заатланти́ческий *adj.* transatlantic.

заа́ха|ть, ю *pf.* (*coll.*) to begin to sigh, begin to groan.

заба́в|а, ы *f.* **1** (*игра*) game; (*развлечение*) pastime. **2** (*потеха*) amusement, fun; **он э́то сде́лал для ~ы** he did it for fun.

забавля́|ть, ю *impf.* to amuse, entertain, divert.

забавля́|ться, юсь *impf.* to amuse o.s.

заба́вник, а *m.* (*coll.*) amusing *or* entertaining person; humorist.

заба́вн|о[1] *adv. of* ⇒**~ый**

заба́вно[2] *as pred.* it is amusing, funny; **мне з.** I find it amusing, funny; **з.!** how funny!

заба́в|ный (~ен, ~на) *adj.* amusing; funny.

забаланси́р|овать, ую *pf. of* ⇒**баланси́ровать**

забаллоти́р|овать, ую *pf.* to blackball, reject, fail to elect.

заба́лтыва|ть, ю *impf. of* ⇒**заболта́ть**[1] 2

забальзами́р|овать, ую *pf. of* ⇒**бальзами́ровать**

забараба́н|ить, ю, ишь *pf.* to begin to drum.

забаррикади́р|овать, ую *pf. of* ⇒**баррикади́ровать**

забаст|ова́ть, у́ю *pf.* to go, come out on strike.

забасто́вк|а, и *f.* strike; **всео́бщая з.** general strike; **голо́дная з.** hunger strike.

забасто́в|очный *adj. of* ⇒**~ка**

забасто́вщик, а *m.* striker.

забасто́вщи|ца, цы *f. of* ⇒**~к**

забве́ни|е, я *nt.* oblivion; **преда́ть ~ю** to consign to oblivion.

забе́г, а *m.* (*sport*) race.

забега́ловк|а, и *f.* (*coll.*) snack bar.

забе́га|ть, ю *pf.* **1** (*начать бегать*) to start running. **2** (*о глазах*) to become shifty.

забега́|ть, ю *impf. of* ⇒**забежа́ть**

забе́га|ться, юсь *pf.* (*coll.*) to run o.s. to a standstill.

забе|жа́ть, гу́, жи́шь, гу́т *pf.* (*of* ⇒**~га́ть**) **1** (**в** + *a.*) to run in(to).

2 (**к**+*d.*; *coll.*) to drop in (to see). **3** (*убежать*) to run off; to stray. **4**: **з. сбо́ку** to come running from the side; **з. вперёд** to run ahead; (*fig., coll.*) to rush ahead.

забеле́|ть, ет *pf.* **1** (*начать белеть*) to begin to turn white. **2** (*показаться*) to appear white (in the distance).

забел|и́ть, ю́, ~и́шь *pf.* **1** to whiten, paint white. **2** (*coll.*) to add milk, cream (to); **з. чай молоко́м** to put milk in tea.

забере́мене|ть, ю *pf.* (*of* ⇒**бере́менеть**) to become pregnant.

забеспоко́|иться, юсь, ишься *pf.* to begin to worry.

забива́|ть(ся), ю(сь) *impf. of* ⇒**заби́ть(ся)**[1]

забинт|ова́ть, у́ю *pf.* (*of* ⇒**~о́вывать**) to bandage.

забинт|ова́ться, у́юсь *pf.* (*of* ⇒**~о́вываться**) to bandage o.s.

забинто́выва|ть(ся), ю(сь) *impf. of* ⇒**забинтова́ть(ся)**

забира́|ть(ся), ю(сь) *impf. of* ⇒**забра́ть(ся)**

заби́т|ый (~, ~а) *p.p.p. of* ⇒**~ь** *and adj.* cowed, downtrodden.

заб|и́ть[1]**, ью́, ьёшь** *pf.* (*of* ⇒**~ива́ть**) **1** (*вбить*) to drive in, hammer in, ram in; **з. себе́ в го́лову** to get (it) firmly fixed in one's head. **2** (*sport*) to score; **з. мяч** to kick the ball into the goal; **з. гол** to score a goal. **3** (*заделать*) to seal, stop up, block up; **з. ще́ли па́клей** to caulk up cracks with oakum. **4** (*закрыть проход*) to obstruct; (*заглушить*) to choke. **5** (+*i.*; *coll.*) (*наполнить*) to cram, stuff (with). **6** (*избить*) to beat up, knock senseless; (*fig.*) to render defenceless (*Br.*), defenseless (*US*). **7** (*coll.*) (*превзойти*) to beat (*at sth.*); to outdo, surpass. **8** (*убить*) to slaughter (*cattle*).

заб|и́ть[2]**, ью́, ьёшь** *pf.* (*in var. senses; trans. and intrans.*) to begin to beat (*in some cases forms pf. aspect of* ⇒**бить**); **з. трево́гу** to sound the alarm; **у нас из сква́жины ~и́ла нефть** we have struck oil.

заб|и́ться[1]**, ью́сь, ьёшься** *pf.* (*of* ⇒**~ива́ться**) **1** (**в**+*a.*) (*спрятаться*) to hide (in), take refuge (in). **2** (**в**+*a.*) (*проникнуть*) to get (into), penetrate. **3** (+*i.*) (*засориться*) to become cluttered (with), clogged (with).

заб|и́ться[2]**, ью́сь, ьёшься** *pf.* (*начать биться*) to begin to beat (*intrans.*).

забия́к|а, и *c.g.* (*coll.*) trouble-maker; bully.

заблаговре́менно *adv.* in good time; well in advance; **з. предупреди́ть** to warn in advance.

заблаговре́менный *adj.* timely, done in good time.

заблагорассу́д|иться, ится *pf.* (*impers.*) to like, think fit; to come into one's head; **он придёт, когда́ ему́ ~ится** he will come when he thinks fit, when he feels so disposed.

забле|сте́ть, щу́, сти́шь *and* **~щешь** *pf.* to begin to shine, glitter, glow.

забле́|ять, ю, ешь *pf.* to begin to bleat.

заблу|ди́ться, жу́сь, ~дишься *pf.* to lose one's way, get lost.

заблу́дш|ий *adj.* lost, stray; **~ая овца́** a lost sheep.

заблужда́|ться, юсь *impf.* to be mistaken.

заблужде́ни|е, я *nt.* error; delusion; **ввести́ в з.** to delude, mislead; **впасть в з.** to be deluded.

забода́|ть, ю *pf. of* ⇒**бода́ть**

забо́|й[1]**, я** *m.* (*mining*) (pit-)face.

забо́|й[2]**, я** *m.* (*убой*) slaughtering.

забо́йщик, а *m.* face-worker, getter (*in mine*).

забола́чива|ться, ется *impf. of* ⇒**заболо́титься**

заболева́емост|ь, и *f.* sickness rate; number of cases; **з. полиомиели́том утро́илась за про́шлую неде́лю** the number of polio cases has tripled during the last week.

заболева́ни|е, я *nt.* sickness, illness.

заболева́|ть[1]**, ю** *impf. of* ⇒**заболе́ть**[1]

заболева́|ть[2]**, ет** *impf. of* ⇒**заболе́ть**[2]

заболе́|ть[1]**, ю, ешь** *pf.* (*of* ⇒**~ва́ть**[1]) **1** to fall ill, fall sick; (+*i.*) to be taken ill (with), go down (with). **2** (+*i.*) (*увлечься*) to get mad keen (on).

забол|е́ть[2]**, ит** *pf.* (*of* ⇒**~ева́ть**[2]) (*начать болеть*) to (begin to) ache, hurt; **у меня́ ~е́л зуб** my tooth has started to ache.

заболо́|титься, тится *pf.* (*of* ⇒**забола́чиваться**) to turn into swamp (*intrans.*).

заболта́|ть[1]**, ю** *pf.* **1** (+*i.*) to begin to swing. **2** (*impf.* **заба́лтывать**) (*примешать*) to mix (in).

заболта́|ть[2]**, ю** *pf.* (*coll.*) to start chattering, nattering.

заболта́|ться[1]**, юсь** *pf.* (*coll.*) to begin to swing.

заболта́|ться[2]**, юсь** *pf.* (*coll.*) to become engrossed in conversation.

забо́р[1]**, а** *m.* (*ограда*) fence.

забо́р[2]**, а** *m.* (*воды*) taking.

забо́рист|ый (~, ~а) *adj.* (*coll.*) **1** (*пиво, табак*) strong. **2** (*fig.*) racy; **з. анекдо́т** risqué story.

забо́р|ный *adj.* **1** *adj. of* ⇒**~**[1]. **2** coarse, indecent; risqué.

забо́ртный *adj.* (*naut.*) outboard; **з. дви́гатель** outboard motor.

забо́т|а, ы *f.* **1** (*беспокойство*) care(s), trouble(s); **без ~** carefree; **ему́ ма́ло ~ы** what does he care? **2** (*уход*) care, attention(s); concern; **з. о челове́ке** concern for people's welfare.

забо́|тить, чу, тишь *impf.* to trouble, worry, cause anxiety.

забо́|титься, чусь, тишься *impf.* (*of* ⇒**по~**) (**о**+*p.*) **1** (*беспокоиться*) to worry, be troubled (about). **2** (*ухаживать*) to take care (of); to take trouble (about); to care (about); **он ни о чём не ~тится** he does not care about anything.

забо́тливост|ь, и *f.* solicitude, care, thoughtfulness.

забо́тлив|ый (~, ~а) *adj.* solicitous, thoughtful; caring.

забрако́в|анный *p.p.p. of* ⇒**~а́ть**; **з. това́р** rejects.

забрак|ова́ть, у́ю *pf. of* ⇒**браковáть**

забра́л|о, а *nt.* visor; **с откры́тым ~ом** openly, frankly.

забра́сыва|ть, ю *impf. of* ⇒**заброса́ть** *and* **забро́сить**

забра́|ть[1]**, заберу́, заберёшь,** *past* **~л, ~ла́, ~ло** *pf.* (*of* ⇒**забира́ть**) **1** (*взять*) to take (*in one's hands*); (*человека*) to take (with one); **з. во́жжи** to take the reins; **з. с собо́й ве́щи** to take one's things with one; **з. себе́ в го́лову** to take it onto one's head; **з. за живо́е** to touch to the quick. **2** (*арестовать*) to arrest; (*отнять*) to take away; to seize, appropriate. **3** (*coll.*) (*о чувствах*) to come over, seize; **его́ ~ла́ охо́та пое́хать в Аме́рику** he was seized with a desire to go to America. **4** (*сузить*) to take in (*part of a garment, etc.*). **5** (*уклониться в сторону*) to turn off, aside.

забра́|ть[2]**, заберу́, заберёшь,** *past* **~л, ~ла́, ~ло** *pf.* (*of* ⇒**забира́ть**) to stop up, block up.

забра́|ться, заберу́сь, заберёшься, *past* **~лся, ~ла́сь, ~ло́сь** *pf.* (*of* ⇒**забира́ться**) **1** (**в**+*a.*) to get (into); (**в, на**+*a.*) to climb (into, on to); **з. в чужо́й дом** to get into s.o. else's house. **2** (*уйти, уехать*) to get to; (*спрятаться*) to hide out, go into hiding; **куда́ они́ ~ли́сь?** where have they got to?

забре́|дить, жу, дишь *pf.* to become delirious.

забре́зж|ить, ит *pf.* to begin to dawn; to begin to appear; **чуть ~ил свет** it was barely light; (*impers.*): **~ило** it is just beginning to get light.

забре|сти́, ду́, дёшь, *past* **~л, ~ла́** *pf.* (*coll.*) **1** (*зайти*) to drop in. **2** (*бредя, уйти далеко*) to go astray, wander off.

забр|и́ть, е́ю, е́ешь *pf.* (*coll.*) to call up (into the army); **з. лоб** (+*d.*) = **з.**

заброни́р|овать, ую *pf.* (*of* ⇒**брони́ровать**) to reserve.

забронир|ова́ть, у́ю *pf.* (*of* ⇒**бронирова́ть**) to armour (*Br.*), armor (*US*).

забро́с, а *m.*: **в ~е** (*coll.*) in a state of neglect.

заброса́|ть, ю *pf.* (*of* ⇒**забра́сывать**) (+*a. and i.*) **1** (*заполнить*) to fill (up) (with); **з. я́му золо́й** to fill up a hole with ashes. **2** (*осыпать*) to shower (with), bespatter (with); **з. кого́-н. гря́зью** to sling mud at s.o. (*also fig.*); **з. кого́-н. бла́нками** to deluge s.o. with forms.

забро́|сить, шу, сишь *pf.* (*of* ⇒**забра́сывать**) **1** (*метнуть*) to throw (*with force or to a distance*); to cast (*also fig.*); **кто ~сил мя́чик в окно́?** who threw a ball through the window?; **вое́нная слу́жба ~сила его́ на**

Да́льний Восто́к military service took him to the Far East. **2** (*часть тела*) to throw; **з. го́лову наза́д** to throw one's head back. **3** (*pf. only*) (*затерять*) to mislay. **4** (*оставить*) to throw up, give up, abandon; to neglect, let go; **з. иссле́дования** to throw up one's research; **з. дете́й** to neglect children. **5** (*доставить в определённое место*) to take, bring.

забро́шенност|ь, и *f.* **1** (*сада*) neglect. **2** (*места*) desolation.

забро́|шенный *p.p.p. of* **⇒~сить** *and adj.* **1** (*сад, человек*) neglected. **2** (*место*) deserted, desolate.

забры́зг|ать¹, аю *pf.* (*of* **⇒~ивать**) (+*i.*) to splash; to bespatter (with).

забры́з|гать², жет *pf.* to begin to play (*of a fountain*).

забры́згива|ть, ю *impf. of* **⇒забры́згать¹**

заб|у́ду, у́дешь *see* **⇒~ы́ть**

забукси́р|овать, ую *pf.* to take in tow.

забулды́г|а, и *c.g.* (*coll.*) drunkard.

забуха́|ть, ет *impf. of* **⇒забу́хнуть**

забу́х|нуть, нет, *past* **~, ~ла** *pf.* (*of* **⇒~а́ть**) to swell (up) (*from damp*).

забыва́|ть(ся), ю(сь) *impf. of* **⇒забы́ть(ся)**

забы́вчив|ый (~, ~а) *adj.* forgetful; absent-minded.

заб|ы́ть, у́ду, у́дешь *pf.* (*of* **⇒~ыва́ть**) **1** (+*a. or* **о**+*p. or inf.*) to forget; **себя́ не з.** to take care of o.s. **2** (*случайно оставить*) to leave behind, forget (to bring); **вы опя́ть ~ы́ли биле́ты** you have forgotten the tickets again.

забыть|ё, я́, в ~и́ *nt.* **1** (*дремота*) drowsy state. **2** (*беспамятство*) half-conscious state, oblivion. **3** (*задумчивость*) (state of) distraction.

заб|ы́ться, у́дусь, у́дешься *pf.* (*of* **⇒~ыва́ться**) **1** (*задремать*) to doze off, drop off. **2** (*потерять сознание*) to become unconscious, lose consciousness. **3** (*замечтаться*) to sink into a reverie. **4** (*coll.*) (*выйти из границ приличия*) to forget o.s.

зав, а *m.* (*abbr. of* **~е́дующий**); (*coll.*) boss.

зав. (*abbr. of* ***заве́дующий***) manager.

зав... *comb. form, abbr. of* **1 *заве́дующий.* 2 *заводско́й, заво́дский***

зава́л, а *m.* obstruction, blockage.

зава́лива|ть(ся), ю(сь) *impf. of* **⇒завали́ть(ся)**

зава́линк|а, и *f.* zavalinka (*mound of earth round a Russian peasant hut serving as protection from the weather and oft. used for sitting out*).

завал|и́ть, ю́, ~́ишь *pf.* (*of* **⇒~́ивать**) **1** (*загромоздить*) to block up, obstruct; to fill (*so as to block up*); **з. вход мешка́ми с песко́м** to block up the entrance with sandbags. **2** (+*i.*; *coll.*) (*заполнить*) to pile (with); to fill cram-full (with); (*fig.*) (*переобременить*) to overload with; **прила́вок ~́ен коро́бками** the stall is piled high with boxes; **реда́кция ~́ена рабо́той** the editors are snowed under with work. **3** (*coll.*) (*запрокинуть*) to throw back; to tip up, cant. **4** (*coll.*) (*обрушить*) to knock down, demolish. **5** (*fig., coll.*) (*провалить*) to make a mess (of), muck up.

завал|и́ться, ю́сь, ~́ишься *pf.* (*of* **⇒~́иваться**) **1** (*упасть*) to fall; to collapse; **нож ~и́лся за шкаф** the knife has fallen behind the cupboard. **2** (*coll.*) (*лечь*) to lie down; **з. спать** to fall into bed. **3** (*coll.*) (*опрокинуться*) to overturn, tip up. **4** (*fig., coll.*) (*провалиться*) to come to grief.

заваля́|ться, ется *pf.* (*coll.*) to lie around.

заваля́щий *adj.* (*coll.*) long unsold, shop-soiled; worthless, useless.

зава́рива|ть(ся), ю, ет(ся) *impf. of* **⇒завари́ть(ся)**

завар|и́ть, ю́, ~́ишь *pf.* (*of* **⇒~́ивать**) **1** to make (*drinks, etc., by pouring on boiling water*); **з. чай** to brew tea; **з. ка́шу** (*fig.*) to start trouble; **ну и ~́ил ка́шу!** now the fat's in the fire. **2** (*coll.*) (*начать*) to start, initiate.

завар|и́ться, ~́ится *pf.* (*of* **⇒~́иваться**) **1** (*о напитках*) to brew. **2** (*coll.*) (*начаться*) to start; **~и́лось бо́льшое де́ло** there's big trouble brewing.

зава́рк|а, и *f.* **1** (*действие*) brewing (*of tea, etc.*). **2** (*coll.*) (*сухой чай*) enough tea for one brew; (*заваренный чай*) brew.

заварно́й *adj.* (*cul.*) boiled; **~ крем** custard.

заварух|а, и *f.* (*coll.*) commotion, stir.

заведе́ни|е, я *nt.* establishment, institution.

заве́д|овать, ую *impf.* (+*i.*) to manage, superintend; to be in charge (of).

заве́домо *adv.* wittingly; (+*adj.*) known to be; **з. зна́я** being fully aware; **переда́ть з. необосно́ванный слух** to pass on a rumour (*Br.*), rumor (*US*) known to be unfounded.

заве́домый *adj.* (*хорошо известный*) notorious; (*несомненный*) undoubted.

заве|ду́, дёшь *see* **⇒~сти́**

заве́дующ|ий, его *m.* (+*i.*) manager (of); head (of); person in charge (of); **з. уче́бной ча́стью** director of studies; **з. отде́лом** head of a department.

завез|ти́, у́, ёшь, *past* **~́, ~ла́** *pf.* (*of* **⇒завози́ть¹**) **1** (*привезти*) to deliver, drop off; **з. запи́ску по доро́ге домо́й** to deliver a note on the way home. **2** (*увезти*) to take (to a distance *or* out of one's way).

заверб|ова́ть, у́ю *pf. of* **⇒вербова́ть**

завере́ни|е, я *nt.* (*уверение*) assurance; (*заявление*) protestation.

завери́тел|ь, я *m.* witness (*to a signature, etc.*).

заве́р|ить, ю, ишь *pf.* (*of* **⇒~я́ть**) **1** (**в**+*p.*) (*уверить*) to assure (of). **2** (*удостоверить*) to certify; **з. по́дпись** to witness a signature.

заве́рк|а, и *f.* certification.

заверн|у́ть, у́, ёшь *pf.* (*of* **⇒завёртывать**) **1** (**в**+*a.*) (*обернуть*) to wrap (in); **~и́те его́ в одея́ло** wrap him in a blanket. **2** (*загнуть*) to tuck up, roll up (*sleeve, etc.*). **3** (*свернуть в сторону*) to turn (*intrans.*); **з. напра́во** to turn to the right. **4** (*coll.*) (*зайти*) to drop in, call in. **5** (*завинтить*) to screw tight; (*закрыть*) to turn off (*by screwing*); **з. га́йку** to screw a nut tight; **з. кран** to turn off a tap; **з. во́ду** to turn the water off.

заверн|у́ться, у́сь, ёшься *pf.* (*of* **⇒завёртываться**) **1** (**в**+*a.*) to wrap o.s. up (in), muffle o.s. (in). **2** *pass. of* **⇒~у́ть**

завер|те́ть, чу́, ~́тишь *pf.* **1** to begin to twirl. **2**: **з. кого́-н.** (*fig., coll.*) to turn s.o.'s head.

завер|те́ться, чу́сь, ~́тишься *pf.* **1** to begin to turn, begin to spin. **2** (*coll.*) to be in a whirl.

завёртыва|ть(ся), ю(сь) *impf. of* **⇒заверну́ть(ся)**

заверш|а́ть, а́ю *impf. of* **⇒~и́ть**

заверше́ни|е, я *nt.* completion; end; **в з.** in conclusion.

заверш|и́ть, у́, и́шь *pf.* (*of* **⇒~а́ть**) to complete, conclude, crown.

завер|я́ть, я́ю *impf. of* **⇒~ить**

заве́с|а, ы *f.* (*obs.*) curtain; **дымова́я з.** (*mil.*) smoke-screen; (*fig.*) veil, screen; **приподня́ть ~у** to lift the veil.

заве́|сить, шу, сишь *pf.* (*of* **⇒~шивать**) to curtain (off.).

заве|сти́, ду́, дёшь, *past* **~́л, ~ла́** *pf.* (*of* **⇒заводи́ть**) **1** (*привести*) to take, bring (*to a place*); to leave, drop off (*at a place*). **2** (*увести*) to take (to a distance *or* out of one's way). **3** (*основать*) to set up; to start; **з. де́ло** (*coll.*) to set up in business; **з. семью́** to start a family; **з. перепи́ску с кем-н.** to start up a correspondence with s.o. **4** (*приобрести*) to acquire. **5** (*ввести*) to institute, introduce (*as a custom*); **з. привы́чку** (+*inf.*) to get into the habit (of); **у нас так ~дено́** this is our custom. **6** (*часы*) to wind (up); (*машину*) to start; **з. мото́р** to start an engine.

заве|сти́сь, ду́сь, дёшься, *past* **~́лся, ~ла́сь** *pf.* (*of* **⇒заводи́ться**) **1** (*появиться*) to be; to appear; **в по́гребе ~ли́сь кры́сы** there are rats in the cellar. **2** (*установиться*) to be established, be set up; **~ло́сь обыкнове́ние** it has become a habit. **3** (*coll.*) to get wound up, get worked up. **4** (*о механизме*) to start (*intrans.*).

заве́т, а *m.* **1** (*rhet.*) behest, bidding, ordinance. **2**: **Ве́тхий, Но́вый з.** the Old, the New Testament.

заве́тн|ый *adj.* (*мечты*) cherished; (*разговор*) intimate; (*талисман*) secret; (*склад*) hidden; **стать кинозвездо́й — её ~ая мечта́** her secret ambition is to become a film-star.

заве́ш|ать, аю *pf.* (*of* **⇒~ивать**) (+*a. and i.*) to hang (all over); **он ~ал сте́ны своего́ кабине́та фотогра́фиями** he has hung the walls of his study with photographs.

заве́шива|ть, ю *impf. of* ⇒**заве́сить** *and* ⇒**заве́шать**
завеща́ни|е, я *nt.* will, testament.
завеща́тел|ь, я *m.* (*leg.*) testator.
завеща́тельниц|а, ы *f.* (*leg.*) testatrix.
завеща́|ть, ю *impf. and pf.* (+*a. and d.*) to leave (to), bequeath (to); (+*d.*+*inf.*) (*поручить*) to instruct.
завзя́тый *adj.* (*coll.*) inveterate, out-and-out.
завива́|ть(ся), ю(сь) *impf. of* ⇒**зави́ть(ся)**
зави́вк|а, и *f.* **1** (*действие*) waving; curling; **сде́лать себе́ ~у** to have one's hair waved. **2** (*причёска*) (hair-)wave.
зави́|деть, жу, дишь *pf.* (*coll.*) to catch sight of.
зави́дно *as pred.* (*impers.*, +*d.*) to feel envious.
зави́д|ный (~ен, ~на) *adj.* enviable.
зави́д|овать, ую *impf.* (*of* ⇒**по~**) (+*d.*) to envy; to be jealous of.
зави́дущий *adj.* (*coll.*) envious, covetous.
завизж|а́ть, у́, и́шь *pf.* to begin to scream, squeal.
завизи́р|овать, ую *pf. of* ⇒**визи́ровать**[1]
завин|ти́ть, чу́, ти́шь *pf.* (*of* ⇒**~́чивать**) to screw up.
завин|ти́ться, чу́сь, ти́шься *pf.* (*of* ⇒**~́чиваться**) to screw up (*intrans.*).
зави́нчива|ть(ся), ю(сь) *impf. of* ⇒**завинти́ть(ся)**
завира́|ться, юсь *impf. of* ⇒**завра́ться**
висá|ть, ю *impf.* (*aeron.*) to hover.
зави́|сеть, шу, сишь *impf.* (**от**+*g.*) to depend (on); **я помогу́ тебе́, наско́лько от меня́ ~сит** I will do everything in my power to help you.
зави́симост|ь, и *f.* dependence; **в ~и** (**от**+*g.*) depending (on), subject (to).
зави́сим|ый (~, ~а) *adj.* (**от**+*g.*) dependent (on).
зави́стлив|ый (~, ~а) *adj.* envious.
зави́стник, а *m.* envious person.
за́вист|ь, и *f.* envy; jealousy.
завит|о́й *and* **~́ый (за́вит, ~а́, за́вито)** *adj.* curled; waved.
завит|о́к, ка́ *m.* **1** (*локон*) curl, lock. **2** (*почерка*) flourish. **3** (*archit.*) volute, scroll.
зав|и́ть, ью́, ьёшь, *past* **~и́л, ~ила́, ~и́ло** *pf.* (*of* ⇒**~ива́ть**) to curl; to wave; to twist, wind.
зав|и́ться, ью́сь, ьёшься, *past* **~и́лся, ~ила́сь** *pf.* (*of* ⇒**~ива́ться**) **1** (*виться*) to curl, wave, twine (*intrans.*). **2** (*завить себе волосы*) to curl, wave one's hair; (*у парикмахера*) to have one's hair curled, waved.
завко́м, а *m.* (*abbr. of* ***заводско́й комите́т***) factory committee.
завладева́|ть, ю *impf. of* ⇒**завладе́ть**
завладе́|ть, ю *pf.* (*of* ⇒**~ва́ть**) (+*i.*) to take possession (of); to seize, capture (*also fig.*); **он ~л внима́нием слу́шателей** he captured the audience's attention.
завлека́тел|ьный (~ен, ~ьна) *adj.* (*coll.*) alluring; fascinating, captivating.
завлека́|ть, ю *impf. of* ⇒**завле́чь**
завле́|чь, ку́, чёшь, ку́т, *past* **~̈к, ~кла́** *pf.* (*of* ⇒**~ка́ть**) **1** (*заманить*) to lure, entice. **2** (*соблазнить*) to fascinate, captivate.
заво́д[1], а *m.* **1** factory, mill; works; **нефтеочисти́тельный з.** oil refinery. **2** (**ко́нский**) **з.** stud(-farm).
заво́д[2], а *m.* (*у часов*) winding mechanism; **игру́шка с ~ом** clockwork toy.
заводи́л|а, ы *c.g.* (*coll.*) instigator; live-wire.
заво|ди́ть, жу́, ~́дишь *impf. of* ⇒**завести́**
заво|ди́ться, жу́сь, ~́дишься *impf. of* ⇒**завести́сь**
заводн|о́й *adj.* **1** (*игрушка*) clockwork. **2** (*tech.*) winding, starting; **~а́я рукоя́тка, ру́чка** starting crank.
заводоуправле́ни|е, я *nt.* works management.
заво́д|ский *adj. of* ⇒**~**[1]; **~ская ло́шадь** stud-horse; *as n.* **з., ~ского** *m.* factory worker.
завод|ско́й = **~́ский**
заво́дчик, а *m.* factory-owner, mill-owner.
за́вод|ь, и *f.* creek, backwater.
завоева́ни|е, я *nt.* **1** (*действие*) winning. **2** (*захваченная территория*) conquest; (*fig.*) (*достижение*) achievement, attainment; **нове́йшие ~я те́хники** the latest achievements of technology.
завоева́тел|ь, я *m.* conqueror.
завоева́тельн|ый *adj.* aggressive; **~ая война́** war of conquest.
заво|ева́ть, ю́ю, ю́ешь *pf.* (*of* ⇒**~ёвывать**) to conquer; (*fig.*) to win, gain; **з. симпа́тии** to gain sympathy.
завоёвыва|ть, ю *impf. of* ⇒**завоева́ть;** to try to get.
заво́з, а *m.* delivery.
заво|зи́ть[1], жу́, ~́зишь *impf. of* ⇒**завезти́**
заво|зи́ть[2], жу́, ~́зишь *pf.* (*coll.*) to dirty, soil.
заво|зи́ться[1], жу́сь, ~́зишься *impf.*, *pass. of* ⇒**~зи́ть**[1]
заво|зи́ться[2], жу́сь, ~́зишься *pf.* (*coll.*) to begin to play about.
заво́зный *adj.* imported.
завола́кива|ть(ся), ю, ет(ся) *impf. of* ⇒**заволо́чь(ся)**
заволн|ова́ться, у́юсь *pf.* to become agitated.
заволо́|чь, ку́, чёшь, ку́т, *past* **~к, ~кла́** *pf.* (*of* ⇒**завола́кивать**) to cloud; to obscure; **тума́н ~к со́лнце** the sun was obscured by fog; **её глаза́ ~кло слеза́ми** her eyes were clouded with tears.
заволо́|чься, чётся, ку́тся, *past* **~кся, ~кла́сь** *pf.* (*of* ⇒**завола́киваться**) to cloud over, become clouded.
завоп|и́ть, лю́, и́шь *pf.* (*coll.*) to cry out, yell; to give a cry.
завора́жива|ть, ю *impf. of* ⇒**заворожи́ть**
завора́чива|ть[1], ю *impf.* = **завёртывать**
завора́чива|ть[2], ю *impf.* **1** *impf. of* ⇒**заворoти́ть. 2** (*impf. only*) (+*i.*; *coll.*) to be boss (of).
заворож|и́ть, у́, и́шь *pf.* (*of* ⇒**завора́живать**) to cast a spell (over), bewitch; (*fig.*) to fascinate.
заворо́т, а *m.* (*coll.*) **1** (*действие*) turn, turning. **2** (*дороги, реки*) bend.
завор|оти́ть, очу́, о́тишь *pf.* (*of* ⇒**завора́чивать**[2]) **1** (*свернуть в сторону*) to turn. **2** (*зайти*) to turn in; to drop in. **3** (*загнуть*) to roll up; to tuck up.
завр|а́ться, у́сь, ёшься, *past* **~а́лся, ~ала́сь** *pf.* (*of* ⇒**завира́ться**) (*coll.*) to become entangled in lies.
завсегда́ *adv.* (*coll.*) always.
завсегда́та|й, я *m.* habitué, frequenter, regular; **театра́льный з.** regular theatre-goer; **з. ба́ров** barfly.
за́втра *adv.* tomorrow; **до з.!** see you tomorrow!
за́втрак, а *m.* breakfast; **второ́й з.** elevenses, mid-morning snack.
за́втрака|ть, ю *impf.* (*of* ⇒**по~**) to (have) breakfast; (*среди дня*) to (have) lunch.
за́втрашний *adj.* tomorrow's; **з. день** tomorrow; (*poet.*) the morrow.
завуали́р|овать, ую *pf. of* ⇒**вуали́ровать**
за́вуч, а *m.* (*abbr. of* ***заве́дующий уче́бной ча́стью***) director of studies.
завхо́з, а *m.* (*abbr. of* ***заве́дующий хозя́йством***) bursar, steward.
завыва́|ть, ю *impf.* to howl.
завы́|сить, шу, сишь *pf.* (*of* ⇒**~ша́ть**) to raise too high; **з. отме́тку на экза́мене** to give too high a mark in an examination.
зав|ы́ть, о́ю, о́ешь *pf.* to begin to howl.
завыша́|ть, ю *impf. of* ⇒**завы́сить**
завя|за́ть[1], жу́, ~́жешь *pf.* (*of* ⇒**~́зывать**) **1** (*узел, шнурки*) to tie; (*пакет*) to tie up; (*галстук*) to knot; **з. шнурки́ боти́нок** to tie up one's shoe-laces. **2** (*палец*) to bind (up). **3** (*fig.*) (*начать*) to start; **з. бой** to join battle; **з. перепи́ску** to start a correspondence; **з. разгово́р** to strike up a conversation.
завяза́|ть[2], ю *impf. of* ⇒**завя́знуть**
завя|за́ться, ~́жется *pf.* (*of* ⇒**~́зываться**) **1** *pass. of* ⇒**~за́ть. 2** (*начаться*) to start; to arise.
завя́зк|а, и *f.* **1** (*то, чем завязывают*) string, lace, band. **2** (*начало*) beginning, start; (*романа*) opening.
завя́з|нуть, ну, нешь, *past* **~, ~ла**

pf. (*of* ⇒~а́ть[2]) to stick, get stuck; **з. в долга́х** to be up to one's ears in debt.

завя́зыва|ть(ся), ю, ет(ся) *impf. of* ⇒**завяза́ть(ся)**

за́вязь|ь, и *f.* (*bot.*) ovary.

завя́|нуть, ну, нешь, *past* ~**л** *pf. of* ⇒**вя́нуть**

загад|а́ть, а́ю *pf.* (*of* ⇒~ывать) **1**: **з. зага́дки** to ask riddles. **2** (*задумать*) to think of; ~**а́йте число́** think of a number. **3** (*замыслить*) to plan ahead, look ahead.

зага́|дить, жу, дишь *pf.* (*of* ⇒~**живать**) (*coll.*) to soil, dirty, befoul.

зага́дк|а, и *f.* riddle; (*fig.*) enigma; mystery.

зага́доч|ный (~ен, ~на) *adj.* enigmatic; mysterious.

зага́дыва|ть, ю *impf. of* ⇒**загада́ть**

зага́жива|ть, ю *impf. of* ⇒**зага́дить**

зага́р, а *m.* sunburn, (sun-)tan.

загаса́|ть, ет *impf. of* ⇒**зага́снуть**

зага|си́ть, шу́, ~сишь *pf. of* ⇒**гаси́ть** 1

зага́с|нуть, нет, *past* ~, ~**ла** *pf.* (*of* ⇒~**а́ть**) (*coll.*) to go out.

загво́здк|а, и *f.* (*coll.*) snag, obstacle; **вот в чём з.!** there's the rub!

заги́б, а *m.* **1** (*складка*) fold, crease; (*поворот*) bend. **2** (*в поведении*) deviation, quirk.

загиба́|ть(ся), ю(сь) *impf. of* ⇒**загну́ть(ся)**

заги́бщик, а *m.* (*pol.*; *coll.*) deviationist.

загипнотизи́р|овать, ую *pf. of* ⇒**гипнотизи́ровать**

загла́ви|е, я *nt.* title; heading; **под ~ем** entitled, headed.

загла́в|ный *adj. of* ⇒~**ие**; **з. лист** title-page; ~**ная бу́ква** capital letter; ~**ные бу́квы** initials; ~**ная роль** (*theatr.*) title-role; ~**ное сло́во** headword.

загла́|дить, жу, дишь *pf.* (*of* ⇒~**живать**) **1** (*сделать гладким*) to iron (out), press. **2** (*fig.*) (*смягчить*) to make up (for), make amends (for); **з. грехи́** to expiate one's sins.

загла́жива|ть, ю *impf. of* ⇒**загла́дить**

загла́зно *adv.* (*coll.*) behind s.o.'s back.

загла́зн|ый *adj.* (*coll.*) done, said in s.o.'s absence, behind s.o.'s back; ~**ая клевета́** scandal uttered about s.o. behind his back; backbiting.

загла́тыва|ть, ю *impf. of* ⇒**заглота́ть**

заглота́|ть, ю *pf.* (*of* ⇒**загла́тывать**) to swallow.

загло́хн|уть, у, ешь *pf. of* ⇒**гло́хнуть** 2, 3

заглуш|а́ть, а́ю *impf. of* ⇒~**и́ть**

заглуш|и́ть, у́, и́шь *pf.* (*of* ⇒**глуши́ть** *and* ~**а́ть**) **1** (*звуки*) to drown, deaden, muffle. **2** (*передачи*) to jam. **3** (*растения*) to choke. **4** (*fig.*) (*подавить*) to suppress, stifle.

загляде́нь|е, я *nt.* (*coll.*) lovely sight; sight for sore eyes.

загля|де́ться, жу́сь, ди́шься *pf.* (*of* ⇒~**дываться**) (**на** + *a.*; *coll.*) to stare (at); to be lost in admiration (of).

загля́дыва|ть, ю *impf. of* ⇒**загляну́ть**

загля́дыва|ться, юсь *impf. of* ⇒**загляде́ться**

загляну|у́ть, у́, ~ешь *pf.* (*of* ⇒**загля́дывать**) **1** (*взглянуть*) to peep; to glance; **она́ ~у́ла в окно́ и уви́дела, что де́ти засну́ли** she peeped in at the window and saw that the children had gone to sleep; **з. в газе́ты** to glance at the newspapers. **2** (*coll.*) (*зайти*) to look in, drop in; ~**и́те к нам, пожа́луйста!** please look in (on us)!

загна́ива|ть(ся), ю, ет(ся) *impf. of* ⇒**загнои́ть(ся)**

за́гнанный *p.p.p. of* ⇒**загна́ть** *and adj.* **1** (*замученный*) tired out, exhausted; **как з. зверь** at the end of one's tether. **2** (*запуганный*) down-trodden, cowed.

загна́|ть, загоню́, заго́нишь, *past* ~**л, ~ла́, ~ло** *pf.* (*of* ⇒**загоня́ть**[1]) **1** to drive in; **з. коро́в в хлев** to drive the cows into the shed, get the cows in; **з. мяч в воро́та** (*sport*) to score, shoot a goal. **2** (*заставить уйти, уехать*) to drive (off). **3** (*замучить*) to tire out, exhaust; to drive to exhaustion. **4** (*coll.*) (*вбить*) to drive home; **з. сва́и в зе́млю** to drive piles into the ground. **5** (*sl.*) (*продать*) to sell, flog (*Br.*).

загнива́ни|е, я *nt.* rotting, putrescence; (*fig.*) decay; (*med.*) suppuration.

загнива́|ть, ю *impf. of* ⇒**загни́ть**

загни́|ть, ю́, ёшь, *past* ~**л, ~ла́, ~ло** *pf.* (*of* ⇒~**ва́ть**) to begin to rot; to rot, decay (*also fig.*); (*med.*) to fester.

загно|и́ть, ю́, и́шь *pf.* (*of* ⇒**загна́ивать**) (*coll.*) **1** (*рану*) to allow to fester. **2** (*овощи*) to allow to rot, allow to decay.

загно|и́ться, и́тся *pf.* (*of* ⇒**загна́иваться**) to fester.

загн|у́ть, у́, ёшь *pf.* (*of* ⇒**загиба́ть**) **1** (*вверх*) to turn up; (*вниз*) to turn down; (*сгибать*) to bend, fold; to crease; **з. страни́цу** to dog-ear a page. **2** (*свернуть в сторону*) to turn (*intrans.*); **з. за́ угол** to turn a corner. **3** (*coll.*) (*сказать*) to utter; **ну и слове́чко ~у́л!** (*iron.*) what language!

загн|у́ться, у́сь, ёшься *pf.* (*of* ⇒**загиба́ться**) **1** (*вверх*) to turn up, stick up; (*вниз*) to turn down. **2** (*sl.*) (*умереть*) to turn up one's toes.

загова́рива|ть, ю *impf. of* ⇒**заговори́ть**[1]

загова́рива|ться, юсь *impf.* (*of* ⇒**заговори́ться**) **1** (*увлечься разговором*) to be carried away by a conversation. **2** (*impf. only*) (*говорить бессмыслицу*) to rave; to ramble (*in speech*).

за́говор, а *m.* **1** plot, conspiracy. **2** (*заклинание*) charm, spell.

заговор|и́ть[1]**, ю́, и́шь** *pf.* (*of* ⇒**загова́ривать**) **1** (*coll.*) (*утомить разговором*) to talk s.o.'s head off. **2** (*заколдовать*) to cast a spell (over); (**от** + *g.*) to put on a spell (against); **з. зу́бы кому́-н.** (*coll.*) to distract s.o. with smooth talk.

заговор|и́ть[2]**, ю́, и́шь** *pf.* (*начать говорить*) to begin to speak.

заговор|и́ться, ю́сь, и́шься *pf. of* ⇒**загова́риваться**

загово́рщик, а *m.* conspirator, plotter.

загово́рщи|ца, цы *f. of* ⇒~**к**

загово́рщицкий *adj.* (*coll.*) conspiratorial.

загово́рщический *adj.* = **загово́рщицкий**

за́годя *adv.* (*coll.*) in good time.

загол|и́ть, ю́, и́шь *pf.* (*of* ⇒~**я́ть**) to bare.

заголо́в|ок, ка *m.* **1** (*заглавие*) title; heading. **2** (*газетный*) headline.

заголя́|ть, ю *impf. of* ⇒**заголи́ть**

заго́н, а *m.* **1** (*действие*) driving in; rounding-up. **2** (*для скота*) enclosure; (*для овец*) pen. **3** (*полоса*) strip (of ploughed land). **4**: **быть в ~е** (*fig.*) to be kept down; **у кого́-н. в ~е** under s.o.'s thumb. **5**: **в ~е** (*sl.*) to one's credit, 'chalked up'; **у него́ в ~е три дня** he had three days' (work) to his credit.

заго́нщик, а *m.* (*hunting*) beater.

за|гоню́, го́нишь *see* ⇒~**гна́ть**

загоня́|ть[1]**, ю** *impf. of* ⇒**загна́ть**

загоня́|ть[2]**, ю** *pf.* (*coll.*) (*утомить*) to tire out; to work to death.

загора́жива|ть(ся), ю(сь) *impf. of* ⇒**загороди́ть(ся)**

загора́|ть(ся), ю(сь) *impf. of* ⇒**загоре́ть(ся)**

загор|ди́ться, жу́сь, ди́шься *pf.* (*coll.*) to become proud, become stuck-up.

загоре́лый *adj.* sunburnt; brown, bronzed.

загор|е́ть, ю́, и́шь *pf.* (*of* ⇒~**а́ть**) to become sunburnt, become brown; to acquire a tan.

загор|е́ться, ю́сь, и́шься *pf.* (*of* ⇒~**а́ться**) **1** (*начать гореть*) to catch fire; to begin to burn; (*impers.*): **в библиоте́ке ~е́лось** a fire broke out in the library. **2** (+*i.*; **от**+*g.*) to blaze (with), burn (with) (*fig.*); **его́ глаза́ ~е́лись от гне́ва** his eyes blazed with anger. **3** (*impers.*, +*d.*; *coll.*) to want very much; to have a burning desire; **ей ~е́лось уви́деть Рим** she had a burning desire to see Rome. **4** (*fig.*) (*возникнуть*) to break out, start; ~**е́лась дра́ка** a fight broke out.

загоро|ди́ть, жу́, ~ди́шь *pf.* (*of* ⇒**загора́живать**) **1** (*огородить*) to enclose, fence in. **2** (*преградить*) to barricade; to obstruct; **з. кому́-н. свет** to stand in s.o.'s light.

загоро|ди́ться, жу́сь, ~ди́шься *pf.* (*of* ⇒**загора́живаться**) to barricade o.s.; **з. ши́рмой** to screen o.s. off.

загоро́дк|а, и *f.* (*coll.*) **1** (*забор*) fence. **2** (*отгороженное место*) enclosure.

за́городн|ый *adj.* out-of-town; country; ~**ая экску́рсия** excursion into the country.

заго|сти́ться, щу́сь, сти́шься *pf.* (*coll.*) to outstay one's welcome.

заготови́тел|ь, я *m.* official in charge of (State) procurements.

загото|ви́тельный *adj. of* ⇒**~ка; з. аппара́т** official organization in charge of (State) procurements; **з. пункт** storage place; collection point.

загото́в|ить, лю, ишь *pf.* (*of* ⇒**~ля́ть**) **1** (*создать запас чего-либо*) to lay in; to make a stock (of), stockpile, store. **2** (*приготовить*) to prepare.

загото́вк|а, и *f.* **1** (*закупка государством*) (State) procurement (*of agricultural products, timber, etc.*). **2** (*запасание*) laying in; stocking up, stockpiling.

заготовля́|ть, ю *impf. of* ⇒**загото́вить**

загото́вщик, а *m.* = **заготови́тель**

заграба́ст|ать, аю *pf.* (*of* ⇒**~ывать**) (*coll., pej.*) to seize; to make off with.

заграба́стыва|ть, ю *impf. of* ⇒**заграба́стать**

заградител|ь, я *m.* (*naut.*) minelayer.

загради́тельный *adj.* (*mil.*) barrage; (*naut.*) mine-laying; **з. аэроста́т** barrage balloon; **з. ого́нь** defensive fire.

загра|ди́ть, жу́, ди́шь *pf.* (*of* ⇒**~жда́ть**) to block, obstruct; **з. путь** to bar the way.

загражда́|ть, ю *impf. of* ⇒**загради́ть**

загражде́ни|е, я *nt.* **1** (*действие*) blocking, obstruction. **2** (*преграда*) obstacle, barrier, obstruction.

заграни́ц|а, ы *f.* (*coll.*) foreign countries (*see also* ⇒**грани́ца**).

заграни́чный *adj.* foreign.

загреба́|ть, ю *impf. of* ⇒**загрести́**[1]; **чужи́ми рука́ми жар з.**, *see* ⇒**жар**

загребу́щий *adj.* (*coll.*) greedy.

загрем|е́ть[1], **лю́, и́шь** *pf.* (*coll.*) to crash down.

загрем|е́ть[2], **лю́, и́шь** *pf.* to begin to thunder.

загре|сти́[1], **бу́, бёшь,** *past* **~̈б, ~бла́** *pf.* (*of* ⇒**~ба́ть**) (*coll.*) to rake up; (*fig.*) to rake in; **з. жар** to bank up the fire; **з. де́ньги** to rake in the shekels.

загре|сти́[2], **бу́, бёшь,** *past* **~̈б, ~бла́** *pf.* to begin to row.

загри́в|ок, ка *m.* **1** (*у лошади*) withers. **2** (*coll.*) (*у человека*) nape (of the neck).

загримир|ова́ть(ся), у́ю(сь) *pf. of* ⇒**гримирова́ть(ся)**

загрипп|ова́ть, у́ю *pf.* (*coll.*) to catch flu, go down with the flu.

загро́бн|ый *adj.* **1** beyond the grave; **~ая жизнь** life after death. **2** (*о голосе*) sepulchral.

загроможда́|ть, ю *impf. of* ⇒**загромозди́ть**

загромоз|ди́ть, жу́, ди́шь *pf.* (*of* ⇒**загроможда́ть**) to block up, encumber; (*fig.*) to pack, cram; **з. расска́з подро́бностями** to cram a story with detail.

загрох|ота́ть, очу́, о́чешь *pf.* to begin to rumble, begin to rattle.

загрубе́лый *adj.* coarsened, calloused; (*fig.*) callous.

загрубе́|ть, ю *pf.* to become coarsened, calloused; (*fig.*) to become callous.

загружа́|ть, ю *impf. of* ⇒**загрузи́ть** 2, 3

загружа́|ться, юсь *impf. of* ⇒**загрузи́ться**

загру́женност|ь (*and* **загружённост|ь**), **и** *f.* **1** (*о транспорте*) utilized capacity (*of transport services, etc.*). **2** (*занятость*) workload, pressure of work.

загр|узи́ть, ужу́, у́зишь *pf.* **1** (*impf.* **грузи́ть**) to load. **2** (*impf.* **~ужа́ть**) (*tech.*) to feed, charge, prime; (*comput.*) (*компьютер*) to boot; (*программу, данные*) to load; (*скопировать*) to download; **з. то́пливо в печь** to stoke a furnace. **3** (*impf.* **~ужа́ть**) (*coll.*) (*занять работой*) to keep fully occupied, provide with a full-time job; (*заполнить работой*) to fill out (*a period of time*) with occupations.

загр|узи́ться, ужу́сь, у́зишься *pf.* (*of* ⇒**~ужа́ться**) **1** (+*i.*) to load up (with), take on. **2** (*coll.*) to take on a job, a commitment.

загру́зк|а, и *f.* **1** (*действие*) loading. **2** (*работа*) capacity, workload; **заво́д рабо́тает при по́лной ~е** the factory is working at full capacity.

загру́з|очный *adj. of* ⇒**~ка; з. ковш, я́щик** hopper.

загрунт|ова́ть, у́ю *pf. of* ⇒**грунтова́ть**

загру|сти́ть, щу́, сти́шь *pf.* to grow sad.

загрыза́|ть, ю *impf. of* ⇒**загры́зть**

загры́з|ть, у́, ёшь *past* **~, ~ла** *pf.* (*of* ⇒**~а́ть**) (*убить*) to kill; (*fig., coll.*) (*о человеке*) to nag, badger; (*о тоске*) to torment.

загрязне́ни|е, я *nt.* soiling; (*природы*) pollution.

загрязни́тел|ь, я *m.* polluter; pollutant.

загрязн|и́ть, ю́, и́шь *pf.* (*of* ⇒**~я́ть**) to soil, make dirty; (*природу*) to pollute.

загрязн|и́ться, ю́сь, и́шься *pf.* (*of* ⇒**~я́ться**) to make o.s. dirty, become dirty; (*о природе*) to become polluted.

загрязня́|ть(ся), ю(сь) *impf. of* ⇒**загрязни́ть(ся)**

ЗАГС, а *or* **загс, а** *m.* (*abbr. of* ***(отде́л) за́писи а́ктов гражда́нского состоя́ния***) registry office.

загуб|и́ть, лю́, ~̈ишь *pf.* **1** (*погубить*) to ruin; **з. чей-н. век, з. чью-н. жизнь** to make s.o.'s life a misery. **2** (*coll.*) (*истратить*) to squander.

загу́л, а *m.* (*coll.*) drinking-bout.

загуля́|ть, ю *pf.* (*coll.*) to take to drink, start drinking.

зад, а, о ~̈е, на ~у́, *pl.* **~ы́** *m.* **1** (*машины, дома*) back; **~̈ом напере́д** back to front. **2** (*животного*) hind quarters; rump; (*человека*) behind, buttocks; **бить ~̈ом** to buck (*of animal*).

зада́брива|ть, ю *impf. of* ⇒**задо́брить**

задава́к|а, и *c.g.* (*coll.*) snob, big-head.

задава́ла = **задава́ка**

зада|ва́ть, ю́, ёшь *impf. of* ⇒**~̈ть**

зада|ва́ться[1], **ю́сь, ёшься** *impf. of* ⇒**~̈ться**

зада|ва́ться[2], **ю́сь, ёшься** *impf.* (*coll.*) to give o.s. airs, put on airs.

задав|и́ть, лю́, ~̈ишь *pf.* to crush; (*о машине*) to run over, knock down.

зада́ни|е, я *nt.* task, job.

зада́рива|ть, ю *impf. of* ⇒**задари́ть**

задар|и́ть, ю́, ~̈ишь *pf.* (*of* ⇒**~̈ивать**) **1** (*осыпать подарками*) to load with presents. **2** (*подкупить*) to bribe.

зада́ром *adv.* (*coll.*) **1** (*бесплатно*) for nothing; very cheaply; **купи́ть з.** to buy for a song. **2** (*напрасно*) in vain, to no purpose.

зада́тк|и, ов *no sg.* instincts, inclinations.

зада́т|ок, ка *m.* deposit.

за|да́ть, да́м, да́шь, да́ст, дади́м, дади́те, даду́т, *past* **~̈дал, ~дала́, ~̈дало** *pf.* (*of* ⇒**~дава́ть**) to set; to give; **з. уро́к** to set a lesson; **з. вопро́с** to put a question; **з. корм коро́вам** to feed the cows; **з. тон** to set the tone; **з. стра́ху** (+*d.*) to strike terror (into); **я ему́ ~да́м!** (*coll.*) I'll give him what-for!

за|да́ться, да́мся, да́шься, да́стся, дади́мся, дади́тесь, даду́тся, *past* **~да́лся, ~дала́сь** *pf.* (*of* ⇒**~дава́ться**[1]) **1**: **з. це́лью, мы́слью** (+*inf.*) to set o.s. (to), make up one's mind (to); **з. вопро́сом** to ask o.s. the question. **2** (*coll.*) to turn out (well); to work out, succeed; **пое́здка не ~дала́сь** the trip was not a success.

зада́ч|а, и *f.* **1** (*math., etc.*) problem. **2** (*цель*) task; mission.

зада́чник, а *m.* book of (mathematical) problems.

задвига|ть, ю *pf.* to begin to move.

задвига́|ть, ю *impf. of* ⇒**задви́нуть**

задвига́|ться, юсь *impf.* **1** *impf. of* ⇒**задви́нуться. 2** (*impf. only*) to move, slide.

задви́жк|а, и *f.* bolt; catch, fastening.

задвижно́й *adj.* sliding.

задви́н|уть, у, ешь *pf.* (*of* ⇒**задвига́ть**) **1** (*переместить*) to push; **з. задви́жку** to shoot a bolt. **2** (*закрыть*) to bolt; to bar; to close; **з. за́навес** to draw a curtain (across).

задви́н|уться, усь, ешься *pf.* (*of* ⇒**задвига́ться**) to shut; to slide (*intrans.*)

задво́р|ки, ок *no sg.* **1** backyard; (*fig.*) out-of-the-way place, backwoods. **2**: **быть на ~ках** (*fig.*) to take a back seat; **на ~ках исто́рии** in the footnotes of history.

задева́|ть[1], ю *impf. of* ⇒**заде́ть**

задева́|ть[2], ю *pf. (coll.)* to mislay; **куда́ я ~л мои очки́?** where did I put my spectacles?

задева́|ться[1], юсь *impf., pass. of* ⇒**~ть[1]**

задева́|ться[2], юсь *pf. (coll.)* to disappear; **куда́ ты ~лся?** where did you disappear to?

заде́йств|овать, ую *pf.* **1** (*начать действовать*) to begin to function. **2** (*оборудование*) to make operational; (*людей*) to mobilize.

заде́л, а *m.* work already done; reserve, stock.

заде́л|ать, аю *pf.* (*of* ⇒**~ывать**) (*дыру, щель*) to block up, close up; **з. течь** to stop up a leak.

заде́л|аться, аюсь *pf.* (*of* ⇒**~ываться**) *(coll.)* to become; to turn; **он ~ался писа́телем** he has turned writer.

заде́лыва|ть(ся), ю(сь) *impf. of* ⇒**заде́лать(ся)**

задёрга|ть[1], ю *pf.* (+*a. or i.*) to begin to tug.

задёрга|ть[2], ю *pf.* (*лошадь*) to wear out (*by tugging on the reins*); (*fig., coll.*) to wear down (*by nagging, etc.*).

задёргива|ть, ю *impf. of* ⇒**задёрнуть**

задеревене́л|ый (~, ~а) *adj.* numb(ed), stiff.

задеревене́|ть, ю *pf. (coll.)* to become numb, become stiff.

задержа́ни|е, я *nt.* **1** (*автобуса*) stopping, holding back, detention, delay. **2** (*преступника*) detention, arrest. **3** (*отсрочка*) delay. **4** (*med.*): **з. мочи́** retention of urine.

задéржанн|ый, ого *m.* detainee.

задерж|а́ть, у́, ~́ишь *pf.* (*of* ⇒**~́ивать**) **1** (*остановить*) to stop, hold back, delay, detain; (*отсрочить*) to delay; **дождь ~а́л нача́ло ма́тча** the start of the match was delayed by rain. **2** (*удержать*) to withhold, keep back; **з. зарпла́ту** to stop wages; **з. дыха́ние** to hold one's breath; **з. шаги́** to slow down. **3** (*арестовать*) to detain, arrest.

задерж|а́ться, у́сь, ~́ишься *pf.* (*of* ⇒**~́иваться**) **1** (*на работе, в гостях*) to be held up, delayed; to stay too long. **2** (*у входа, перед магазином*) to linger. **3** (*не сделать вовремя*) to be late; **она́ ~а́лась с рабо́той** she was late finishing the work; she was late with the work.

заде́ржива|ть(ся), ю(сь) *impf. of* ⇒**задержа́ть(ся)**

заде́ржк|а, и *f.* delay; hold-up.

задёрн|уть, у, ешь *pf.* (*of* ⇒**задёргивать**) **1** (*дёрнуть*) to pull; to draw; **з. занаве́ски** to draw the curtains. **2** (*закрыть*) (+*i.*) to cover (with); to curtain off (with).

заде́|ть, ну, нешь *pf.* (*of* ⇒**~ва́ть[1]**) **1** (*коснуться*) to touch, brush (against); (*при ранении*) to graze; (*fig.*) (*обидеть*) to offend, wound; **его́ ~ло за живо́е** he was stung to the quick. **2** (*зацепиться*) to catch (on, against).

за́дешево *adv. (coll.)* very cheaply.

зади́р|а, ы *c.g. (coll.)* bully; trouble-maker.

задира́|ть(ся)[1], ю, ет(ся) *impf. of* ⇒**задра́ть(ся)**

задира́|ться[2], юсь *impf. (coll.)* to pick a quarrel.

зади́рист|ый (~, ~а) *adj. (coll.)* quarrelsome.

задненёбный *adj. (ling.)* velar.

заднепрохо́дный *adj. (anat.)* anal.

заднеязы́чный *adj. (ling.)* velar, back.

за́дн|ий *adj.* (*сиденье*) back, rear; (*ноги*) hind; **~яя мысль** ulterior motive; **з. план** background; **з. прохо́д** *(anat.)* anus; **~им умо́м кре́пок** *(coll.)* wise after the event; **з. фона́рь** tail-light; **з. ход** (*tech.*) backward movement; **дать з. ход** to go into reverse; to back up; **~им число́м** later, with hindsight; **поме́тить ~им число́м** to antedate; **быть без ~их ног** *(coll.)* to be falling off one's feet; **ходи́ть на ~их ла́пках (пе́ред**+*i.*) *(coll.)* to dance attendance (on).

за́дник, а *m.* **1** back, counter (*of shoe*). **2** (*theatr.*) backdrop.

за́дниц|а, ы *f. (vulg.)* arse (*Br.*), ass (*US*); backside.

задо́бр|ить, ю, ишь *pf.* (*of* ⇒**зада́бривать**) to cajole; to coax; to win over.

зад|о́к, ка́ *m.* back.

задолб|и́ть, лю́, и́шь *pf.* **1** (*начать долбить*) to begin to peck. **2** *(coll.)* (*выучить наизусть*) to learn off by rote.

задо́лго *adv.* long before; **он ко́нчил рабо́ту з. до ве́чера** he finished the work long before evening.

задолжа́|ть, ю *pf. of* ⇒**должа́ть**

задо́лженност|ь, и *f.* debts; **погаси́ть з.** to pay off one's debts.

задо́лжник, а *m. (coll.)* **1** (*по уплате*) debtor. **2** (*о студенте*) student who has fallen behind with taking exams.

задо́лжни|ца, цы *f. of* ⇒**~к**

за́дом *adv.* backwards; **е́хать з.** to reverse, back up.

задо́р, а *m.* fervour, ardour; passion.

задо́ринк|а, и *f. (coll.)*: **без сучка́, без ~и** *or* **ни сучка́, ни ~и** without a hitch.

задо́р|ный (~ен, ~на) *adj.* **1** (*пылкий*) fervent, ardent; impassioned. **2** (*запальчивый*) quick-tempered.

задох|ну́ться, ну́сь, нёшься, *past* **~́ся, ~́лась** *and* **~ну́лся, ~ну́лась** *pf.* (*of* ⇒**задыха́ться**) **1** (*умереть*) to suffocate; to choke; (*fig.*): **з. от гне́ва** to choke with anger. **2** (*тяжело дышать*) to pant; to gasp for breath.

задра́знива|ть, ю *impf. of* ⇒**задразни́ть**

задразн|и́ть, ю́, ~́ишь *pf. (coll.)* to tease unmercifully.

задра́ива|ть, ю *impf. of* ⇒**задра́ить**

задра́|ить, ю, ишь *pf.* (*of* ⇒**~ивать**) (*naut.*) to batten down.

задрапир|ова́ть(ся), у́ю(сь) *pf. of* ⇒**драпирова́ть(ся)**

зад|ра́ть, еру́, ерёшь, *past* **~ра́л, ~рала́, ~ра́ло** *pf.* (*of* ⇒**~ира́ть**) **1** (*растерзать*) to tear to pieces. **2** *(coll.)* (*поднять кверху*) to lift up; to pull up; **з. го́лову** to crane one's neck; **з. нос** (*fig.*) to cock one's nose. **3** (*ноготь*) to break; **з. ко́жу на па́льце** to split a finger.

зад|ра́ться, ерётся, *past* **~ра́лся, ~рала́сь, ~ра́ло́сь** *pf.* (*of* ⇒**~ира́ться**) **1** *(coll.)* (*о платье*) to ride up. **2** (*о ногте*) to break; to split (*intrans.*).

задрем|а́ть, лю́, ~́лешь *pf.* to doze off, begin to nod.

задри́пан|ный (~, ~а) *adj. (coll.)* bedraggled.

задрож|а́ть, у́, и́шь *pf.* to begin to tremble; (*от холода*) to begin to shiver.

задры́га|ть, ю *pf. (coll.)* to begin to jerk, begin to twitch.

задубе́|ть, ю *pf. (coll.)* to become stiff.

задува́|ть, ю *impf. of* ⇒**заду́ть**

заду́ма|ть, ю *pf.* (*of* ⇒**заду́мывать**) **1** (+*a. or inf.*) (*решить*) to plan; to intend; to conceive the idea (of). **2** (*число, желание*) to think of.

заду́ма|ться, юсь *pf.* to become thoughtful, pensive; to fall to thinking; **о чём вы ~лись?** what are you thinking about?

заду́мчивост|ь, и *f.* thoughtfulness, pensiveness; reverie.

заду́мчив|ый (~, ~а) *adj.* thoughtful, pensive.

заду́мыва|ть, ю *impf. of* ⇒**заду́мать**

заду́мыва|ться, юсь *impf.* (*погружаться в свои мысли*) to be thoughtful, be pensive; (*размышлять*) to meditate; to ponder; **не ~ясь, он согласи́лся** he agreed without a moment's thought.

задур|и́ть, ю́, и́шь *pf. of* ⇒**дури́ть** 3

заду́|ть, ю, ешь *pf.* (*of* ⇒**~ва́ть**) **1** (*погасить*) to blow out. **2** (*tech.*): **з. до́мну** to blow in a blast-furnace. **3** (*начать дуть*) to begin to blow.

задуше́в|ный (~ен, ~на) *adj.* (*искренний*) sincere; (*интимный*) intimate.

задуш|и́ть, у́, ~́ишь *pf. of* ⇒**души́ть[1]**

зад|ы́[1] *see* ⇒**~**

зад|ы́[2] = **~во́рки**

задым|и́ть, лю́, и́шь *pf.* **1** (*начать дымить*) to begin to (emit) smoke. **2** (*закоптить дымом*) to blacken with smoke.

задым|и́ться, и́тся *pf.* **1** (*начать дымиться*) to begin to (emit) smoke. **2** (*закоптеть*) to be blackened with smoke.

задымля́|ть(ся), ю, ет(ся) *impf. of* ⇒**задыми́ть(ся)** 2

задыха́|ться, юсь *impf. of* ⇒**задохну́ться**

задыш|а́ть, у́, ~́ишь *pf.* to begin to breathe.

З

заеб|а́ть, у́, ёшь *pf.* (*vulg.*) to wear out by pestering.

заеб|а́ться, у́сь, ёшься *pf.* (*vulg.*) to become completely exhausted; **я ~а́лся** I'm dead beat.

заеда́ни|е, я *nt.* (*tech.*) jamming.

заеда́|ть(ся), ю(сь) *impf. of* **⇒зае́сть(ся)**

зае́зд, а *m.* **1** calling in (*en route*). **2** (*sport*) race; (*отборочный*) heat.

зае́з|дить, жу, дишь *pf.* (*лошадь*) to override; (*fig.*) to wear out; to work too hard.

заезжа́|ть, ю *impf. of* **⇒зае́хать**

зае́зженный *adj.* (*coll.*) **1** (*фраза, анекдот*) hackneyed, trite. **2** (*вид, человек*) worn out.

зае́зж|ий *adj.* visiting; **~ая тру́ппа** touring company; **он здесь з. челове́к** he is just passing through.

заём, за́йма *m.* loan.

заёмн|ый *adj.* loan; **~ое письмо́** (*leg.*) acknowledgement of debt.

заёмщик, а *m.* borrower, debtor.

заёрза|ть, ю *pf.* (*coll.*) to begin to fidget.

зае́|сть[1], м, шь, ст, ди́м, ди́те, дя́т, *past* **~л** *pf.* (*of* **⇒~да́ть**) **1** (*укусами*) to bite to death; (*загрызть*) to kill; (*fig., coll.*) (*измучить*) to torment, oppress; **его́ ~ла тоска́** he fell a prey to melancholy. **2** (*impers.; tech.*) to jam; (*naut.*) to foul; **кана́т ~ло** the cable has fouled.

зае́|сть[2], м, шь, ст, ди́м, ди́те, дя́т, *past* **~л** *pf.* (*of* **⇒~да́ть**) (+*a.* and *i.*) to take (with); **он ~л лека́рство са́харом** he took the medicine with sugar.

зае́|сться, мся, шься, стся, ди́мся, ди́тесь, дя́тся, *past* **~лся** *pf.* (*of* **⇒~да́ться**) (*coll.*) to become fastidious, become fussy.

зае́|хать, ду, дешь *pf.* (*of* **⇒~зжа́ть**) **1** (**к**+*d.*) to call in (at); to drop in (on); (**в**+*a.*) to enter, ride into, drive into; (**за**+*a.*) to go beyond, past; (**за**+*i.*) to call for; to fetch, pick up. **2** (*уехать или попасть куда-нибудь далеко или куда не следует*) to get (to), go; **он ~хал в кана́ву** he landed in the ditch. **3** (+*d.* **в**+*a.*; *coll.*) to strike; **я ~хал ему́ в физионо́мию** I gave him a sock on the jaw.

зажа́р|ить(ся), ю(сь), ишь(ся) *pf. of* **⇒жа́рить(ся)**

зажа́т|ый *p.p.p. of* **⇒~ь** *and adj.* **(~, ~а)** (*coll.*) (*о человеке*) tense, up-tight.

заж|а́ть, му́, мёшь *pf.* (*of* **⇒~има́ть**) (*стиснуть*) to squeeze; to press; to clutch; (*заткнуть*) to stop up; **з. в руке́** to grip; **з. рот кому́-н.** (*fig.*) to stop s.o.'s mouth; **з. кри́тику** to suppress criticism.

заж|гу́, жёшь, гу́т *see* **⇒~е́чь**

зажд|а́ться, у́сь, ёшься, *past* **~а́лся, ~ала́сь, ~а́ло́сь** *pf.* (*coll.*) to be tired of waiting (for).

зажелте́|ть, ю, ешь *pf.* **1** (*начать желтеть*) to begin to turn yellow. **2** (*показаться*) to appear yellow (in the distance).

заж|е́чь, гу́, жёшь, гу́т, *past* **~ёг, ~гла́** *pf.* (*of* **⇒~ига́ть**) (*огонь, лампу*) to light; (*свет*) to turn on; **з. спи́чку** to strike a match; (*fig.*) (*страсть, интерес*) to kindle; (*публику*) to inflame.

заж|е́чься, гу́сь, жёшься, гу́тся, *past* **зажёгся, зажгла́сь** *pf.* (*of* **⇒~ига́ться**) (*об огне*) to begin to burn; (*о фонарях*) to go on, light up; (*fig.*) (*о чувствах*) to be aroused; (*о глазах*) to light up.

зажива́|ть(ся), ю(сь) *impf. of* **⇒зажи́ть(ся)**

зажив|и́ть, лю́, и́шь *pf.* (*of* **⇒~ля́ть**) to heal.

заживля́|ть, ю *impf. of* **⇒заживи́ть**

за́живо *adv.* alive; **з. погребённый** buried alive.

зажига́лк|а, и *f.* **1** (cigarette) lighter. **2** (*coll.*) (*бомба*) incendiary (bomb).

зажига́ни|е, я *nt.* **1** (*в машине*) ignition; **ключ (от) зажига́ния** ignition key. **2** (*действие*) lighting.

зажига́тел|ьный (~ен, ~ьна) *adj.* **1** incendiary; **~ьная бо́мба** fire bomb, incendiary (device); **буты́лка с ~ьной сме́сью** petrol bomb. **2** (*fig.*) stirring, rousing; **~ьная речь** rousing speech.

зажига́|ть(ся), ю(сь) *impf. of* **⇒заже́чь(ся)**

зажи́лива|ть, ю *impf. of* **⇒зажи́лить**

зажи́л|ить, ю, ишь *pf.* (*coll.*) to fail to return (*sth. borrowed*).

зажи́м, а *m.* **1** (*tech.*) clamp; clip. **2** (*elec.*) terminal. **3** (*fig.*) suppression; clamping down.

зажима́|ть, ю *impf. of* **⇒зажа́ть**

зажи́мист|ый (~, ~а) *adj.* (*coll.*) tight-fisted, stingy.

зажи́точност|ь, и *f.* prosperity; affluence.

зажи́точ|ный (~ен, ~на) *adj.* well-to-do; prosperous; affluent.

зажи́|ть, ву́, вёшь, *past* **за́жил, ~ла́, за́жило** *pf.* (*of* **⇒~ва́ть**) **1** (*о ране*) to heal (*intrans.*); to close up. **2** (*начать жить*) to begin to live; **з. по-но́вому** to begin a new life; **з. семе́йной жи́знью** to settle down; **з. трудово́й жи́знью** to begin to earn one's own living.

зажи́|ться, ву́сь, вёшься, *past* **~лся, ~ла́сь** *pf.* (*of* **⇒~ва́ться**) (*coll.*) to live to a great age; to exceed one's allotted span.

зажму́р|ить(ся), ю(сь), ишь(ся) *pf. of* **⇒жму́рить(ся)**

зажужж|а́ть, у́, и́шь *pf.* to begin to buzz; to begin to drone.

зажу́лива|ть, ю *impf. of* **⇒зажу́лить**

зажу́л|ить, ю, ишь *pf.* (*of* **⇒~ивать**) (*coll.*) to obtain by fraud.

заз|ва́ть, ову́, овёшь, *past* **~ва́л, ~вала́, ~ва́ло** *pf.* (*of* **⇒~ыва́ть**) (*coll.*) to press (to come); to press an invitation on.

зазвен|е́ть, и́т *pf.* to begin to ring.

зазвон|и́ть, ю́, и́шь *pf.* to begin to ring.

зазвуч|а́ть, у́, и́шь *pf.* to begin to sound; to begin to resound.

заздра́вный *adj.* to the health (of), in honour (of); **они́ вы́пили з. тост за посла́** they drank the ambassador's health.

зазева́|ться, юсь *pf.* (**на**+*a.*; *coll.*) to stand gaping (at); to gape (at).

зазелене́|ть, ю *pf.* **1** (*начать зеленеть*) to begin to turn green. **2** (*показаться*) to appear green (in the distance).

заземле́ни|е, я *nt.* (*elec.*) **1** (*действие*) earthing (*Br.*), grounding (*US*). **2** (*устройство*) earth (*Br.*), ground (*US*).

заземл|и́ть, ю, и́шь *pf.* (*elec.*) to earth.

заземл|я́ть, я́ю *impf. of* **⇒~и́ть**

зазерка́ль|е, я *nt.* illusion, fantasy.

зазим|ова́ть, у́ю *pf.* to winter; to pass the winter.

зазна|ва́ться, ю́сь, ёшься *impf. of* **⇒~́ться**

зазна́вшийся *adj.* (*coll.*) stuck-up, hoity-toity.

зазна́йка = **задава́ка**

зазна́йств|о, а *nt.* (*coll.*) conceit.

зазна́|ться, юсь *pf.* (*of* **⇒~ва́ться**) (*coll.*) to give o.s. airs, become conceited.

зазно́б|а, ы *f.* (*coll.*) sweetheart.

зазноб|и́ть, и́т *pf.* (*coll.*) (*impers.*): **его́ ~и́ло** he is beginning to be feverish.

заз|ову́, овёшь *see* **⇒~ва́ть**

зазо́р, а *m.* gap; (*tech.*) clearance.

зазо́р|ный (~ен, ~на) *adj.* (*coll.*) shameful, disgraceful.

зазре́ни|е, я *nt.*: **без ~я (со́вести)** (*coll.*) without a twinge of conscience.

зазу́брен|ный (~, ~а) *adj.* notched, jagged, serrated.

зазу́брива|ть, ю *impf. of* **⇒зазубри́ть**

зазу́брин|а, ы *f.* notch, jag.

зазубр|и́ть[1], ю́, и́шь *pf.* (*of* **⇒зубри́ть[1]** *and* **~ивать**) to notch, serrate.

зазубр|и́ть[2], ю́, ~ишь *pf.* (*of* **⇒зубри́ть[2]** *and* **~ивать**) (*sl.*) to learn by rote.

зазыва́л|а, ы *c.g.* (*fairground*) barker.

зазыва́|ть, ю *impf. of* **⇒зазва́ть**

зазывно́й *adj.* (*coll.*) inviting.

заигра́|ть, ю *pf.* **1** (*начать играть*) to begin to play; **з. весёлый моти́в** to strike up a lively tune. **2** (*заискриться*) to begin to sparkle. **3** (*impf.* **заи́грывать**) (*истрепать*) to wear out (*cards, etc.*); **з. пье́су** to do a play to death.

заигра́|ться, юсь *pf.* (*of* **⇒заи́грываться**) to become absorbed in playing.

заи́грыва|ть[1], ю *impf. of* **⇒заигра́ть** 3

заи́грыва|ть[2], ю *impf.* (**с**+*i.*; *coll.*) to flirt (with); to make advances (to) (*also fig.*).

заи́грыва|ться, юсь *impf. of* **⇒заигра́ться**

зайк|а, и *c.g.* stammerer, stutterer.

заика́ни|е, я *nt.* stammer(ing), stutter(ing).

заика́|ться, юсь *impf.* **1** to stammer, stutter; (*нерешительно говорить*) to falter (*in speech*). **2** (*pf.* **заикну́ться**) (**о** + *p.*; *coll.*) to hint (at), to mention in passing; **он никогда́ не ~ется о своей про́шлой жи́зни** he never breathes a word about his past life.

заикн|у́ться, у́сь, ёшься *pf. of* ⇒**заика́ться** 2

заимообра́зно *adv.* on credit, on loan.

заимообра́з|ный (~ен, ~на) *adj.* **1** (*взятый*) borrowed, taken on credit. **2** (*данный*) lent, loaned.

заи́мствовани|е, я *nt.* borrowing.

заи́мствован|ный (~, ~а) *p.p.p. of* ⇒**заи́мствовать; ~ное сло́во** (*ling.*) loan-word.

заи́мств|овать, ую *impf.* (*of* ⇒**по~**) to borrow.

заи́ндеве|ть, ет *pf.* (*of* ⇒**и́ндеветь**) (*coll.*) to be covered with hoar-frost.

заинтересо́ван|ный (~, ~а) *p.p.p. of* ⇒**заинтересова́ть** *and adj.* (**в** + *p.*) interested (in); **он ~ в возмо́жности торго́вых отноше́ний с Да́льним Восто́ком** he is interested in the possibility of trade relations with the Far East; **~ная сторона́** interested party; **он слу́шал с ~ным ви́дом** he listened with an interested expression on his face.

заинтерес|ова́ть, у́ю *pf.* to interest; to excite the curiosity (of).

заинтерес|ова́ться, у́юсь *pf.* (+ *i.*) to become interested; to take an interest (in).

заинтриг|ова́ть, у́ю *pf. of* ⇒**интригова́ть** 2

Заи́р, а *m.* Zaire.

заи́р|ец, ца *m.* Zairean.

заи́р|ка, ки *f. of* ⇒**~ец**

заи́рский *adj.* Zairean.

заи́скива|ть, ю *impf.* (**пе́ред** + *i.*) to try to ingratiate o.s. (with).

заи́скива|ющий *pres. part. act. of* ⇒**~ть** *and adj.* ingratiating.

заискр|и́ться, ю́сь, и́шься *pf.* to begin to sparkle.

зай|ду́, дёшь *see* ⇒**~ти́**

за́йк|а, и, *pl.* **~и, за́ек, ~ам** *m.* (*coll.*) little hare.

за́йма *see* ⇒**заём**

за́ймов|ый *adj. of* ⇒**заём; ~ая опера́ция** loan transaction.

займодержа́тел|ь, я *m.* bond holder.

займ|у́, ёшь *see* ⇒**заня́ть**

за|йти́, йду́, йдёшь, *past* **~шёл, ~шла́** *pf.* (*of* ⇒**~ходи́ть**[1]) **1** (**к** + *d.*, **в** + *a.*) (*посетить*) to call (on); to look in (at); to drop in (at); **по пути́ домо́й я ~шёл к Ивано́вым** I dropped in at the Ivanovs on the way home; **не забу́дьте з. в апте́ку** don't forget to look in at the chemist's.
2 (**за** + *i.*) (*чтобы взять*) to call for, fetch.
3 (**в** + *a.*) (*войти*) to go into, get into; (*попасть*) to get (*to a place*); to find o.s. (*in a place*); **мы ~шли́ в лес** we found ourselves in the forest.
4 (*о разговоре*) to turn to; **разгово́р ~шёл о выступле́нии президе́нта по ра́дио** the conversation turned to the President's radio broadcast.
5 (**за** + *a.*) (*скрыться за чем-н.*) to go behind; (*продолжаться*) to go on, continue (after); (*закатиться*) to set (*of sun, etc.*); **з. за́ угол** to turn a corner; **з. сли́шком далеко́** (*fig.*) to go too far.

за|йти́сь, йду́сь, йдёшься, *past* **~шёлся, ~шла́сь** *pf.* (*of* ⇒**заходи́ться**[2]) (*coll.*) to have an uncontrollable fit (*of crying, coughing, laughing, etc.*).

зайча́тин|а, ы *f.* hare (*as food*).

за́йчик, а *m.* (*coll.*) **1** *affectionate dim. of* ⇒**за́яц. 2** (*световой*) reflection of a sunray.

зайчи́х|а, и *f.* doe-hare.

зайч|о́нок, о́нка, *pl.* **~а́та, ~а́т** *m.* leveret.

закабал|и́ть, ю́, и́шь *pf.* (*of* ⇒**~я́ть**) to enslave.

закабал|и́ться, ю́сь, и́шься *pf.* (*of* ⇒**~я́ться**) (+ *d.*) to tie o.s. in slavery (to).

закабал|я́ть(ся), я́ю(сь) *impf. of* ⇒**~и́ть(ся)**

закавка́зский *adj.* Transcaucasian.

Закавка́зь|е, я *nt.* Transcaucasia.

закавы́к|а, и *f.* (*coll.*) = **закавы́чка**

закавы́чк|а, и *f.* (*coll.*)
1 (*препятствие*) obstacle, hitch.
2 (*намёк*) hint.

зака́дровый *adj.*: **з. го́лос** (*TV, cin.*) voice-over.

закады́чный *adj.*: **з. друг** (*coll.*) bosom friend.

зака́з[1]**, а** *m.* order; (*билетов, стола*) reservation; (*портрета*) commission; **на з.** to order; **мне де́лают костю́м на з.** I am having a suit made to measure; **по ~у** (+ *g.*) on s.o.'s order; **как по ~у** as if to order.

зака́з[2]**, а** *m.* (*obs.*) prohibition.

зака|за́ть[1]**, жу́, ~жешь** *pf.* (*of* ⇒**~зывать**) to order; (*билеты, стол*) to reserve; (*портрет*) to commission.

зака|за́ть[2]**, жу́, ~жешь** *pf.* (+ *inf. or a.*; *obs.*) to forbid.

зака́зник, а *m.* (*game*) reserve.

заказн|о́й *adj.* **1** made to order; made to measure. **2**: **~о́е письмо́** registered letter; **посла́ть письмо́ ~ы́м** to send a letter registered.

зака́зчик, а *m.* customer, client.

зака́зыва|ть, ю *impf. of* ⇒**заказа́ть**[1]

зака́ива|ться, юсь *impf. of* ⇒**зака́яться**

зака́л, а *m.* **1** (*tech.*) temper; (*fig.*) stamp, cast; **он челове́к ста́рого ~а** he is one of the old school. **2** (*fig.*) strength of character; guts, backbone.

закалён|ный (~, ~а́) *p.p.p. of* ⇒**закали́ть** *and adj.* hardened, hard; **з. в боя́х** battle-hardened.

зака́ллива|ть, ю *impf. of* ⇒**закали́ть**

закал|и́ть, ю́, и́шь *pf.* (*of* ⇒**~ивать** *and* **~я́ть**) (*tech.*) to temper; to case-harden; (*fig.*) to temper, harden; to make hard, hardy.

зака́лк|а, и *f.* tempering; hardening; (*sport*) conditioning.

зака́лыва|ть, ю *impf. of* ⇒**заколо́ть**

закаля́|ть, ю *impf. of* ⇒**закали́ть**

закамуфли́р|овать, ую *pf. of* ⇒**камуфли́ровать**

зака́нчива|ть(ся), ю, ет(ся) *impf. of* ⇒**зако́нчить(ся)**

зака́п|ать, аю *pf.* **1** to begin to drip; **дождь ~ал** it began to spot with rain. **2** (*impf.* **~ывать**) to spot, stain; **ты ~ала себе́ пла́тье черни́лами** you have spotted your dress with ink.

зака́пыва|ть(ся), ю(сь) *impf. of* ⇒**закопа́ть(ся)** *and* **зака́пать** 2

зака́рмлива|ть, ю *impf. of* ⇒**закорми́ть**

зака́т, а *m.* setting; **з. (со́лнца)** sunset; **он пришёл на ~е** he came at sunset; (*fig.*) decline; **на ~е дней** in one's declining years.

аката́|ть, ю *pf.* (*of* ⇒**зака́тывать**)
1 (*начать катать*) to begin to roll.
2 (**в** + *a.*) (*обмотать*) to roll up (in).
3 (*заровнять катком*) to roll. **4** (*coll.*) (*рукава*) to roll up. **5** (*банку, крышку*) to close, hermetically seal.

зака|ти́ть, чу́, ~тишь *pf.* (*of* ⇒**~тывать**) (*мяч*) to roll; (*коляску*) to wheel, push; **она́ ~ти́ла ему́ пощёчину** (*coll.*) she slapped his face; **з. исте́рику** (*coll.*) to go off into hysterics; **з. сце́ну** (*coll.*) to make a scene; **з. глаза́** to roll one's eyes.

зака|ти́ться, чу́сь, ~тишься *pf.* (*of* ⇒**~тываться**) **1** (*мяч*) to roll (*intrans.*). **2** (*солнце*) to set (*of heavenly bodies*); (*fig.*) (*слава*) to wane; to vanish, disappear; **его́ сла́ва давно́ ~ти́лась** his fame had long since waned; **моя́ звезда́ ~ти́лась** my luck has changed. **3** (*coll.*) (*отправиться*) to go off; **он ~ти́лся на неде́лю в Ло́ндон** he went off to London for a week. **4** (*coll.*) (*разразиться*) to burst out; **з. сме́хом** to go off into peals of laughter; **з. слеза́ми** to burst into tears.

зака́тный *adj.* sunset.

зака́тыва|ть, ю *impf. of* ⇒**заката́ть** *and* **закати́ть**

зака́тыва|ться, юсь *impf. of* ⇒**закати́ться**

закача́|ть, ю *pf.* **1** (*начать качать*) to begin to shake, begin to swing; **он ~л голово́й** he began shaking his head.
2 (*impers.*) to make feel sick by rocking; **меня́ ~ло** I feel sick.

закача́|ться, юсь *pf.* to begin to sway; **~ешься!** (*coll.*) (it's) great!

зака́шля|ться, юсь *pf.* to have a fit of coughing.

зака́|яться, юсь, ешься *pf.* (*of* ⇒**~иваться**) (+ *inf.*) to forswear; to swear to give up; **он ~ялся кури́ть** he has sworn that he will give up smoking.

заквá|сить, шу, сишь *pf.* (*of* ⇨**~шивать**) (*капусту*) to pickle; (*молоко*) to ferment, sour.

заквáск|а, и *f.* (*для теста*) leaven; (*для кефира*) culture; (*fig., coll.*): **у негó хорóшая з.** he's made of good stuff.

заквáшива|ть, ю *impf. of* ⇨**заквáсить**

закидá|ть, ю *pf.* (*of* ⇨**закúдывать**) (+*a. and i.*) **1** (*осыпать*) to bespatter (with); to shower (with); **з. камнями** to stone; **кандидáтов ~ли вопрóсами** the candidates were plied with questions; **з. грязью** (*fig.*) to sling mud (at). **2** (*заполнить*) to fill up (with); (*сверху*) to cover (with).

закидóн, а *m.* (*sl.*) (*каприз*) whim; (*странность*) quirk, oddity.

закúдыва|ть, ю *impf. of* ⇨**закидáть** *and* **закúнуть**

закúдыва|ться, ется *impf. of* ⇨**закúнуться**

закúн|уть, у, ешь *pf.* (*мяч в сетку, майку под кровать*) to throw; (*невод, удочку*) to cast; **з. нóгу нá ногу** to cross one's legs; **з. винтóвку зá спину** to sling a rifle on one's back; **з. удочку** (*fig., coll.*) to put out a feeler; **з. словéчко (о**+*p.*) (*coll.*) to throw out a hint (about); **~ьте словéчко за меня** put in a word for me; **судьбá ~ула меня в Россию** fate brought me to Russia.

закúн|уться, ется *pf.* **1** (*о голове*) to fall back. **2** (*о лошади*) to jib, shy.

закипá|ть, ет *impf. of* ⇨**закипéть**

закип|éть, ит *pf.* (*начать кипеть*) to begin to boil; (*кипеть*) to be on the boil; (*fig.*) (*о работе*) to be in full swing.

закисá|ть, ю *impf. of* ⇨**закúснуть**

закúс|нуть, ну, нешь, *past* **~, ~ла** *pf.* **1** to turn sour. **2** (*fig.*) to become apathetic.

зáкис|ь, и *f.* (*chem.*) protoxide; **з. азóта** nitrous oxide; **з. желéза** ferrous oxide.

заклáд, а *m.* **1** (*залог*) pawning; (*недвижимости*) mortgaging; **мой часы в ~е** my watch is in pawn. **2** (*пари*) bet, wager; **биться об з.** to bet, wager.

заклáдк|а[1], и *f.* (*фундамента*) laying; (*памятника*) laying the foundation.

заклáдк|а[2], и *f.* (*в книге*) bookmark (*also comput.*).

закладн|áя, óй *f.* (*leg.*) mortgage (-deed).

заклад|нóй *adj. of* ⇨**~**; **~áя квитáнция** pawn-ticket.

заклáдыва|ть, ю *impf. of* ⇨**заложúть**

заклáни|е, я *nt.* sacrifice; **идти (как) на з.** to go to the slaughter.

закл|евáть, юю, юёшь *pf.* **1** (*начать клевать*) to begin to peck; (*о рыбе*) to begin to bite. **2** (*клюя, убить*) to peck to death; (*fig., coll.*) to torment.

заклёвыва|ть, ю *impf. of* ⇨**заклевáть**

заклéива|ть(ся), ю, ет(ся) *impf. of* ⇨**заклéить(ся)**

заклé|ить, ю, ишь *pf.* to glue up; to stick up; **з. конвéрт** to seal an envelope.

заклé|иться, ится *pf.* to stick (*intrans.*).

заклейм|úть, лю, úшь *pf. of* ⇨**клеймúть**

заклепá|ть, ю *pf.* (*of* ⇨**заклёпывать**) (*tech.*) to rivet.

заклёпк|а, и *f.* (*tech.*) rivet.

заклёпыва|ть, ю *impf. of* ⇨**заклепáть**

заклинáни|е, я *nt.* **1** (*магические слова*) incantation; spell. **2** (*мольба*) entreaty.

заклинáтел|ь, я *m.* exorcist; **з. змей** snake-charmer.

заклинá|ть, ю *impf.* (*of* ⇨**заклясть**) **1** (*вызывать*) to invoke. **2** (*духов*) to exorcize. **3** (*заколдовывать*) to enchant, endow with magical powers. **4** (*impf. only*) (*умолять*) to entreat.

заклúнива|ть, ю *impf. of* ⇨**заклúнúть**

заклин|úть, ю, úшь (*also* **заклúн|ить, ю, ишь**) *pf.* **1** (*закрепить*) to wedge, fasten with a wedge. **2** (*лишить возможности вращаться*) to jam; (*also. impers.*): **дверь ~úло** the door jammed.

заключá|ть, ю *impf. of* ⇨**заключúть**

заключ|áться, áется *impf.* (*of* ⇨**~úться**) **1** *pass. of* ⇨**~áть. 2** (*impf. only*) (**в**+*p.*) to consist (of); to lie (in); **глáвное затруднéние ~áется в недостáтке дéнежных средств** the principal difficulty consists in the lack of funds. **3** (*заканчиваться*) to conclude, finish.

заключéни|е, я *nt.* **1** (*конец*) conclusion, end; (*завершение*) conclusion, ending; **в з.** in conclusion. **2** (*вывод*) conclusion, inference. **3** (*договора, сделки*) conclusion, signing. **4** (*лишение свободы*) confinement, detention; **тюрéмное з.** imprisonment.

заключён|ный (~, ~á) *p.p.p. of* ⇨**заключúть;** *as n.* **з., ~ного** *m., and* **~ная, ~ной** *f.* (*leg.*) prisoner, convict.

заключúтельн|ый *adj.* final, concluding; **з. аккóрд** (*mus.*) finale; **~ое слóво** concluding remarks.

заключ|úть, ý, úшь *pf.* (*of* ⇨**~áть**) **1** (+*i.*) (*закончить*) to conclude, end (with). **2** (*сделать вывод*) to conclude, infer. **3** (*принять*) to conclude, enter into; **з. брак** to contract marriage; **з. договóр** to conclude a treaty; **з. сдéлку** to strike a bargain. **4**: **з. в себé** to contain, enclose; to comprise; **з. в скóбки** to enclose in brackets. **5** (*лишить свободы*) to confine; **з. в тюрьмý** to imprison; **з. под стрáжу** to take into custody.

заключ|úться, úтся, áтся *pf. of* ⇨**~áться**

заклá|сть, нý, нёшь, *past* **~л, ~лá, ~ло** *pf. of* ⇨**заклинáть**

заклá|сться, нýсь, нёшься, *past* **~лся, ~лáсь, ~лось** *pf.* (*coll.*) to swear to give up.

заклáти|е, я *nt.* (*obs.*) **1** (*заклинание*) incantation. **2** (*клятва*) oath, pledge.

заклáтый *adj.*: **з. враг** sworn enemy.

зак|овáть, ую, уёшь *pf.* (*of* ⇨**~óвывать**) to chain; **з. в кандалы** to shackle, put in irons.

закóвыва|ть, ю *impf. of* ⇨**заковáть**

заковылá|ть, ю *pf.* (*coll.*) to begin to hobble.

заковырист|ый (~, ~а) *adj.* (*coll.*) tricky.

заковычк|а, и *f.* = **закавычка**

закодúровать *pf. of* ⇨**кодúровать**

заколáчива|ть, ю *impf. of* ⇨**заколотúть**

заколдóван|ный (~, ~а) *p.p.p. of* ⇨**заколдовáть** *and adj.* bewitched, enchanted; spellbound; (*fig.*) **з. круг** vicious circle.

заколд|овáть, ýю *pf.* to bewitch, enchant; to lay a spell (on).

заколдóвыва|ть, ю *impf. of* ⇨**заколдовáть**

заколеб|áться, ~люсь, ~лешься *pf.* to begin to shake; (*fig.*) to begin to waver, begin to vacillate.

закóлк|а, и *f.* hairgrip (*Br.*), bobby pin (*US*).

заколо|тúть, чý, ~тишь *pf.* (*of* ⇨**заколáчивать**) **1** (*досками*) to board up; (*гвоздями*) to nail up. **2** (*гвоздь*) to knock in, drive in. **3** (*забить до смерти*) to beat the life out of; to knock insensible. **4** (*начать колотить*) to begin to knock; **в дверь ~тúли** there was a knocking on the door.

заколо|тúться, чýсь, ~тишься *pf.* (*coll.*) to begin to beat; **сéрдце у неё ~тúлось** her heart began to thump.

закол|óть, ю, ~ешь *pf.* (*of* ⇨**закáлывать** *and* **колóть[2]**) **1** (*убить*) to stab (to death); (*животного*) to slaughter. **2** (*прикрепить*) to pin (up). **3** (*начать колоть*) to begin to chop. **4** (*impers.*): **у меня, etc., ~óло в бокý** I, *etc.*, have a stitch in my side.

закол|óться, юсь, ~ешься *pf.* to stab o.s.

заколы|хáться, ~шется *pf.* to begin to sway; to begin to wave, begin to flutter.

закольц|евáть, ýю, ýешь *pf. of* ⇨**кольцевáть**

закóн, а *m.* law; **свод ~ов** code, statute book; **объявúть вне ~а** to outlaw; **з. Бóжий** (*as school subject, etc.*) scripture, divinity; **з. пóдлости** Sod's Law, Murphy's Law; **неписаный з.** unwritten law.

закóнник, а *m.* (*coll.*) **1** (*юрист*) one versed in law, law expert, lawyer. **2** (*соблюдающий законы*) one who keeps to the letter of the law.

законнорождённый *adj.* legitimate (*child*).

закóнност|ь, и *f.* **1** (*документа, постановления*) lawfulness, legality. **2** (*соблюдение законов*) law and order.

закóн|ный (~ен, ~на) *adj.*

1 (*действия*) lawful, legal; (*документ, договор*) legal; **з. брак** lawful wedlock; **з. владе́лец** rightful owner. **2** (*fig.*) (*возмущение*) legitimate, understandable, natural.

законове́д, а *m.* jurist.

законове́дени|е, я *nt.* jurisprudence, law.

законода́тел|ь, я *m.* legislator; lawgiver; **з. мо́ды** trendsetter.

законода́тель|ница, ницы *f. of* ⇨~

законода́тельный *adj.* legislative.

законода́тельств|о, а *nt.* legislation.

закономе́рност|ь, и *f.* regularity; conformity with a law; normality.

закономе́р|ный (~ен, ~на) *adj.* **1** (*развитие, успех*) natural, logical. **2** (*fig.*) (*понятный*) legitimate, understandable, natural.

законопа́|тить, чу, тишь *pf. of* ⇨**конопа́тить**

законоположе́ни|е, я *nt.* (*leg.*) statute.

законопослуша́ни|е, я *nt.* law-abidingness.

законопослу́шный *adj.* law-abiding.

законопрое́кт, а *m.* (*pol., leg.*) bill.

законсерви́р|овать, ую *pf. of* ⇨**консерви́ровать**

законспекти́р|овать, ую *pf. of* ⇨**конспекти́ровать**

законспири́р|овать, ую *pf.* (*of* ⇨**конспири́ровать**) to keep secret, keep dark.

законтракт|ова́ть, у́ю *pf.* (*of* ⇨**контрактова́ть**) to contract (for), enter into a contract (for).

законтракт|ова́ться, у́юсь *pf.* (*of* ⇨**контрактова́ться**) to contract to work (for); to hire o.s. out (to).

законфу́|зиться, жусь, зишься *pf.* to show embarrassment.

зако́нченност|ь, и *f.* completeness.

зако́нчен|ный *p.p.p. of* ⇨**зако́нчить** *and adj.* (*дело*) finished; (*мысль, фраза*) complete; (*негодяй*) consummate; (*мастер*) accomplished; **он явля́ется ~ным прозаиком** he is an accomplished prose-writer; **з. лгун** consummate liar.

зако́нч|ить, у, ишь *pf.* (*of* ⇨**зака́нчивать**) to end, finish.

зако́нч|иться, ится *pf.* (*of* ⇨**зака́нчиваться**) to end, finish (*intrans.*).

закопа́|ть, ю *pf.* (*of* ⇨**зака́пывать**) **1** (*no impf.*) (*начать копать*) to begin to dig. **2** (*спрятать в земле*) to bury. **3** (*заполнить землёй*) to fill in.

закопа́|ться, юсь *pf.* (*of* ⇨**зака́пываться**) to bury o.s.

закопте́л|ый (~, ~а) *adj.* sooty; smutty.

закопт|е́ть, и́т *pf.* to become covered with soot.

закоп|ти́ть, чу́, ти́шь *pf.* (*of* ⇨**копти́ть**) **1** (*рыбу, окорок*) to smoke. **2** (*покрыть копотью*) to blacken with smoke.

закоп|ти́ться, чу́сь, ти́шься *pf.* **1** (*о рыбе, окороке*) to be smoked. **2** (*покрыться копотью*) to become covered with soot.

закорене́лый *adj.* (*предрассудок*) deep-rooted, ingrained; (*преступник*) inveterate.

закорене́|ть, ю, ешь *pf.* **1** (*fig.*) (*укорениться*) to take root. **2** (**в**+*p.*) to become steeped (in); **он ~л в греха́х** he became an inveterate sinner.

зако́р|ки, ок *no sg.* (*coll.*) back, shoulders; **он перенёс де́вочку че́рез ре́ку́ на ~ках** he carried the little girl across the river on his shoulders.

закорм|и́ть, лю́, ~́ишь *pf.* (*of* ⇨**зака́рмливать**) to overfeed; to stuff.

закорю́чк|а, и *f.* (*coll.*) **1** hook; (*в почерке*) flourish. **2** (*fig., coll.*) hitch, snag.

закосне́л|ый (~, ~а) *adj.* incorrigible, inveterate.

закосне́|ть, ю *pf. of* ⇨**косне́ть**

закостене́л|ый (~, ~а) *adj.* ossified; stiff.

закостене́|ть, ю *pf.* to ossify; (*fig.*): **он ~л от хо́лода** he became stiff with cold.

закостыля́|ть, ю *pf.* (*coll.*) to hobble, limp.

закоу́л|ок, ка *m.* **1** (*переулок*) back street, (dark) alley. **2** (*coll.*) (*уголок*) secluded corner; **обыска́ть все углы́ и ~ки** to search in every nook and cranny; **знать все ~ки** (*fig.*) to know all the ins and outs.

закочене́л|ый (~, ~а) *adj.* numb with cold.

закочене́|ть, ю, ешь *pf. of* ⇨**кочене́ть**

закра́дыва|ться, юсь *impf. of* ⇨**закра́сться**

закра́ива|ть, ю *impf. of* ⇨**закро́ить**

закра́па|ть, ю *pf.* **1** (*о каплях дождя*) to begin to fall. **2** (*покрыть крапинами*) to spot.

закра́пыва|ть, ю *impf. of* ⇨**закра́пать** 2

закра́|сить, шу, сишь *pf.* (*of* ⇨**~шивать**) to paint over, paint out.

закрасне́|ть, ю, ешь *pf.* **1** (*начать краснеть*) to begin to turn red. **2** (*показаться*) to appear red (in the distance).

закра́|сться, ду́сь, дёшься, *past* **~лся** *pf.* (*of* ⇨**~дываться**) to steal in, creep in; (*fig.*): **у меня́ ~лось подозре́ние** a suspicion crept into my mind.

закра́шива|ть, ю *impf. of* ⇨**закра́сить**

закрепи́тел|ь, я *m.* (*chem., phot.*) fixing agent, fixer.

закреп|и́ть, лю́, и́шь *pf.* (*of* ⇨**~ля́ть**) **1** to fasten, secure; (*naut.*) to make fast; (*phot.*) to fix. **2** (*fig.*) to consolidate; **мы ~и́ли прошлого́дние успе́хи** we have consolidated last year's successes. **3** (+*a.* **за**+*i.*) (*помещение*) to allot, assign (to); (*человека*) to appoint, attach (to); **з. за собо́й** to secure; **за на́ми ~и́ли одну́ из но́вых кварти́р** we have been assigned one of the new flats; **он ~и́л за собо́й места́ на за́втрашнее представле́ние** he has secured seats for tomorrow's performance.

закреп|и́ться, лю́сь, и́шься *pf.* (*of* ⇨**~ля́ться**) **1** (*о войсках*) (**на**+*a.*) to consolidate one's hold (on). **2** (*о слове, привычке*) to establish itself.

закре́пк|а, и *f.* fastener.

закрепля́|ть(ся), ю(сь) *impf. of* ⇨**закрепи́ть(ся)**

закрепо|сти́ть, щу́, сти́шь *pf.* to enslave.

закрепоща́|ть, ю *impf. of* ⇨**закрепости́ть**

закрепоще́ни|е, я *nt.* enslavement.

закристаллиз|ова́ться, у́ется *pf. of* ⇨**кристаллизова́ться**

закрич|а́ть, у́, и́шь *pf.* **1** (*начать кричать*) to begin to shout. **2** (*однократно*) to give a shout, cry out.

закро|и́ть, ю́, и́шь *pf.* (*of* ⇨**закра́ивать**) to cut out.

закро́|й, я *m.* cut; style (*of dress*).

закро́йны|й *adj.* for cutting clothes; **~е но́жницы** cutting-out scissors.

закро́йщик, а *m.* cutter.

закро́йщи|ца, цы *f. of* ⇨**~к**

за́кром, а, *pl.* **~а́** *m.* corn-bin; (*fig., rhet.*) granary.

закругле́ни|е, я *nt.* **1** (*действие*) rounding, curving. **2** (*изгиб*) curve.

закруглён|ный (~, ~а́) *p.p.p. of* ⇨**закругли́ть** *and adj.* rounded; (*liter.*) well-rounded.

закругл|и́ть, ю́, и́шь *pf.* (*of* ⇨**~я́ть**) to make round; to round off; **з. фра́зу** to round off a sentence.

закругл|и́ться, ю́сь, и́шься *pf.* (*of* ⇨**~я́ться**) **1** (*стать круглым*) to become round. **2** (*coll.*) (*закончить*) to round off, conclude.

закругля́|ть(ся), ю(сь) *impf. of* ⇨**закругли́ть(ся)**

закруж|и́ть, у́, ~́ишь *pf.* **1** to begin to whirl (*trans. and intrans.*); **з. кому́-н. го́лову** (*fig., coll.*) to turn s.o.'s head. **2** (*довести до головокружения*) to make giddy, make dizzy; (*о событиях, делах*) to confuse, throw off balance.

закруж|и́ться, у́сь, ~́ишься *pf.* **1** to begin to whirl, begin to go round; **у меня́ ~и́лась голова́** my head began to swim; **з. с дела́ми** to be run off one's feet. **2** *pf. of* ⇨**кружи́ться**

закру|ти́ть, чу́, ~́тишь *pf.* (*of* ⇨**закру́чивать**) **1** (*верёвку*) to twist; (*усы*) to twirl; (*вокруг*) to wind round; **они́ ~ти́ли ему́ ру́ки за́ спину** they twisted his arms behind his back. **2** (*кран*) to turn; (*гайку*) to screw in. **3** (*fig., coll.*) to turn s.o.'s head.

закру|ти́ться, чу́сь, ~́тишься *pf.* (*of* ⇨**закру́чиваться**) **1** to twist; to twirl; to wind round (*intrans.*). **2** (*coll.*) to be run off one's feet.

закру́тка = **самокру́тка**

закру́чива|ть(ся), ю(сь) *impf. of* ⇨**закрути́ть(ся)**

закрыва́|ть(ся), ю(сь) *impf. of* ⇨**закры́ть(ся)**

закры́ти|е, я *nt.* **1** closing; shutting; (*конец*) close. **2** (*mil.*) cover.

закры́т|ый (~, ~а) *p.p.p. of* ⇨**~ь** *and adj.* closed, shut; (*не для всех*) private; **с ~ыми глаза́ми** (*fig.*) blindly; **з. бассе́йн** indoor pool; **~ое голосова́ние** secret ballot; **при ~ых дверя́х** behind closed doors, in private; **~ое заседа́ние** private meeting; **~ое мо́ре** inland sea; **~ое пла́тье** high-necked dress; **в ~ом помеще́нии** indoors; **з. просмо́тр** private view.

закр|ы́ть, о́ю, о́ешь *pf.* (*of* ⇨**~ыва́ть**) **1** (*сделать недоступным*) to close, shut; **я ~ыл ему́ глаза́** I attended him on his deathbed; **з. глаза́** (**на**+*a.*) to shut one's eyes (to); **з. ско́бки** to close brackets; **з. счёт** to close an account. **2** (*выключить*) to shut off, turn off. **3** (*ликвидировать*) to close down, shut down. **4** (*покрыть*) to cover.

закр|ы́ться, о́юсь, о́ешься *pf.* (*of* ⇨**~ыва́ться**) **1** (*стать недоступным*) to close, shut; (*окончиться*) to end; (*перестать существовать*) to close down. **2** (*покрыть себя*) to cover o.s.; to take cover. **3** (*о ране*) to close up.

закули́сный *adj.* (occurring) behind the scenes; (*fig.*) secret; underhand, undercover.

закупа́|ть, ю *impf. of* ⇨**закупи́ть**

закуп|и́ть, лю́, ~́ишь *pf.* (*of* ⇨**~а́ть**) **1** (*скупить*) to buy up (wholesale). **2** (*запастись*) to lay in; to stock up with.

заку́пк|а, и *f.* purchase.

закупно́й *adj.* bought, purchased.

заку́порива|ть, ю *impf. of* ⇨**заку́порить**

заку́пор|ить, ю, ишь *pf.* **1** to cork; to stop up. **2** (*fig.*) to shut up; to coop up.

заку́порк|а, и *f.* **1** corking. **2** (*med.*) embolism, thrombosis.

заку́п|очный *adj. of* ⇨**~ка; ~очная цена́** purchase price.

заку́пщик, а *m.* purchaser; buyer.

заку́рива|ть(ся), ю, ет(ся) *impf. of* ⇨**закури́ть(ся)**

закур|и́ть, ю́, ~́ишь *pf.* (*of* ⇨**заку́ривать**) **1** (*сигарету*) to light up. **2** (*стать курильщиком*) to begin to smoke; **ещё не ко́нчив шко́лу он ~и́л** he began to smoke before he had left school.

закур|и́ться, ~́ится *pf.* (*of* ⇨**заку́риваться**) **1** (*о сигарете*) to begin to burn. **2** (*о вулкане*) to begin to smoke.

закуса́|ть, ю *pf.* (*coll.*) to bite.

заку|си́ть¹, шу́, ~́сишь *pf.* (*of* ⇨**~́сывать**) (*зажать зубами*) to bite; (*fig.*): **з. удила́** to break loose, lose control of o.s.; **з. язы́к** to hold one's tongue, to shut up.

заку|си́ть², шу́, ~́сишь *pf.* (*of* ⇨**~́сывать**) **1** (*поесть*) to have a snack, have a bite; **з. на́скоро** to snatch a hasty bite. **2** (+*a. and i.*) to take (with); **з. во́дку ры́бой** to drink vodka with fish hors d'oeuvres.

заку́ск|а, и *f.* (*usu. pl.*) hors d'oeuvre; snack; **на ~у** for a titbit; (*fig., coll.*) as a special treat.

заку́с|очный *adj. of* ⇨**~ка;** *as n.* **~очная, ~очной** *f.* snack bar.

заку́сыва|ть, ю *impf. of* ⇨**закуси́ть**

заку́т, а *m.* (*dial.*) **1** (*кладовая*) storeroom; (*fig.*) (*тесное помещение*) cramped space, room. **2** (*хлев*) shed (*for livestock*).

заку́та|ть, ю *pf.* (*of* ⇨**заку́тывать**) to wrap up, muffle; **з. в одея́ло** to tuck up (in bed).

заку́та|ться, юсь *pf.* (*of* ⇨**заку́тываться**) to wrap o.s. up, muffle o.s.

заку|ти́ть, чу́, ~́тишь *pf.* to begin to drink; to go drinking.

заку́тк|а, и *f.* (*dial.*) = **заку́т**

заку́т|ок, ка *m.* (*dial.*) = **заку́т**

закут|о́к, ка́ *m.* (*coll.*) nook, corner.

заку́тыва|ть(ся), ю(сь) *impf. of* ⇨**заку́тать(ся)**

зал, а *m.* hall; **з. ожида́ния** waiting room; **демонстрацио́нный з.** showroom; **з. вы́лета** (*airport*) departure lounge; **з. игровы́х автома́тов** amusement *or* video game arcade.

зала́|дить, жу, дишь *pf.* (*coll.*) **1** (+*inf.*) to take to; **он ~дил заходи́ть к нам по вечера́м** he has taken to calling in on us in the evening. **2**: **з. одно́ и то́ же** to harp on the same string.

зала́д|иться, ится *pf.* (*coll.*) to work out.

зала́мыва|ть, ю *impf. of* ⇨**заломи́ть**

залата́|ть, ю *pf. of* ⇨**лата́ть**

зал|га́ться, гу́сь, жёшься, гу́тся, *past* **~га́лся, ~гала́сь, ~гало́сь** *pf.* (*coll.*) to become entangled in lies.

залега́ни|е, я *nt.* **1** lying down. **2** (*geol.*) stratification, bedding.

залега́|ть, ю *impf. of* ⇨**зале́чь**

заледене́л|ый (~, ~а) *adj.* **1** (*покрывшийся льдом*) covered with ice; ice-bound. **2** (*холодный*) ice-cold, icy.

заледене́|ть, ю *pf.* (*of* ⇨**леденеть**) **1** (*покрыться льдом*) to be covered with ice; to freeze up, ice up. **2** (*стать холодным как лёд*) to become icy cold; (*закоченеть*) to become numb.

залежа́л|ый (~, ~а) *adj.* (*coll.*) **1** (*несвежий*) stale. **2** (*лежавший долго без употребления*) long unused.

залеж|а́ться, у́сь, и́шься *pf.* **1** (*пролежать слишком долго*) to lie too long; to lie idle a long time. **2** (*потерять свежесть*) to become stale.

залёжива|ться, юсь *impf. of* ⇨**залежа́ться**

за́леж|ь, и *f.* **1** (*geol.*) deposit, bed, seam. **2** (*agric.*) fallow land. **3** (*sg. only; collect.; coll.*) stale goods.

залеза́|ть, ю *impf. of* ⇨**зале́зть**

зале́з|ть, у, ешь, *past* **~, ~ла** *pf.* **1** (**на**+*a.*) (*на дерево, крышу*) to climb (up, on to). **2** (**в**+*a.*; *coll.*) (*в комнату*) to get (into); to break into; **з. кому́-н. в карма́н** to pick s.o.'s pocket; **з. в во́ду по го́рло** to get up to one's neck in water; **з. в долги́** to run into debt.

зален|и́ться, ю́сь, ~́ишься *pf.* (*coll.*) to grow lazy.

залепе|та́ть, чу́, ~́чешь *pf.* (*coll.*) to begin to babble.

залеп|и́ть, лю́, ~́ишь *pf.* (+*a. and i.*) to paste up, paste over; to glue up; **всю сте́ну ~и́ли афи́шами** the whole wall had been pasted over with bills; **глаза́ у него́ ~и́ло сне́гом** his eyes were stuck up with snow; **з. кому́-н. пощёчину** (*coll.*) to slap s.o.'s face.

залепля́|ть, ю *impf. of* ⇨**залепи́ть**

залета́|ть¹, ю *pf.* (*coll.*) to begin to fly.

залета́|ть², ю *impf. of* ⇨**залете́ть**

зале|те́ть, чу́, ти́шь *pf.* **1** (**в**+*a.*) to fly (into); (**за**+*a.*) to fly (over, beyond); **пти́ца ~те́ла в ко́мнату** a bird flew into the room; **мы ~те́ли за Се́верный по́люс** we flew over the North Pole. **2** (**в**+*a.*) to make a stopover (at), call in (at); **нам пришло́сь з. в Стокго́льм** we had to make a stopover at Stockholm. **3** (*fig., coll.*): **з. высоко́, з. далеко́** to go up in the world.

залётн|ый *adj.* (*coll.*): **~ая пти́ца** bird of passage (*also fig.*); **з. гость** unexpected visitor.

зале́чива|ть, ю *impf. of* ⇨**залечи́ть**

залеч|и́ть, у́, ~́ишь *pf.* **1** (*рану*) to heal. **2** (*coll.*): **з. (до́ смерти)** to doctor to death; to kill (*by unskilful treatment*).

залеч|и́ться, ~́ится *pf.* (*coll.*) to heal (up).

зал|е́чь, я́гу, я́жешь, я́гут, *past* **~ёг, ~егла́** *pf.* (*of* ⇨**~ега́ть**) **1** (*лечь*) to lie down; (*притаиться*) to lie low. **2** (*geol.*) to lie, be deposited; **здесь руда́ ~егла́ на глубине́ ста ме́тров** there is a deposit of ore here at a depth of a hundred metres (*Br.*), meters (*US*). **3** (*fig.*) (*морщина*) to form, develop.

зали́в, а *m.* bay; (*длинный*) gulf; (*маленький*) cove.

залива́|ть¹, ю *impf.* (*coll.*) to lie, tell lies.

залива́|ть²(ся), ю(сь) *impf. of* ⇨**зали́ть(ся)**

зали́вист|ый (~, ~а) *adj.* (*о звуке*) liquid, harmonious.

зали́вк|а, и *f.*: **з. бензи́на** filling up with petrol; **з. бето́на** stopping up, filling in with cement.

заливн|о́е, о́го *nt.* fish or meat in aspic.

заливн|о́й *adj.* **1**: **з. луг** water-meadow. **2** for pouring; **~а́я труба́** funnel. **3** (*cul.*) jellied; **~а́я ры́ба** fish in aspic.

зали|за́ть, жу́, ~́жешь *pf.* **1** to lick clean. **2**: **з. себе́ во́лосы** to slick down one's hair.

зали́зыва|ть, ю *impf. of* ⇨**зализа́ть**

зал|и́ть, ью́, ьёшь, *past* **~́ил, ~ила́, ~́ило** *pf.* (*of* ⇨**~ива́ть**)

1 (*покрыть жидкостью*) to flood, inundate; (*fig.*): **комнату ~ило светом** the room was flooded with light; **толпа ~ила улицы** the crowd filled the streets. **2** (*испачкать жидким*) (+*a.* and *i.*) to pour (over); to spill (on); **з. скатерть чернилами** to spill ink on the table-cloth; **з. тушью** to ink in. **3** (*потушить водой*) to quench, extinguish (*with water*); **з. пожар** to put out a fire; **з. горе (вином)** to drown one's sorrows. **4** (*наполнить, покрыть жидким*) to fill, cover with. **5** (*налить, наполнив что-н.*): **з. бензин в бак** to fill up with petrol (*Br.*), gas (*US*).

зал|иться, ьюсь, ьёшься, *past* **~ился, ~илась, ~илось** *pf.* (*of* ⇒**~иваться**) **1** (*покрыться водой*) to be flooded, inundated. **2** (*попасть*) to pour; to spill (*intrans.*); **вода ~илась мне за воротник** water has gone down my neck. **3** (*испачкаться*) to spill on o.s.; **ты весь ~ился супом** you have spilled soup all over yourself. **4** (+*i.*) (*зазвучать*) to break into, burst out (into); **собака ~илась лаем** the dog began to bark furiously; **з. песней** to break into a song; **з. слезами** to burst into tears, dissolve in tears. **5** to set (*of jellies*).

залихватск|ий *adj.* (*coll.*) devil-may-care; **~ая песня** rollicking song.

залог[1], а *m.* **1** deposit; pledge; security; (*leg.*) bail; **под з.** (+*g.*) on the security of; **отдать в з.** (*в ломбарде*) to pawn; (*дом*) to mortgage; **выкупить из ~а** to redeem; to pay off mortgage (on); **з. успеха** guarantee of success. **2** (*fig.*) (*доказательство*) pledge, token.

залог[2], а *m.* (*gram.*) voice.

залог|овый *adj. of* ⇒**~**; **~овое свидетельство** mortgage-deed.

залогодател|ь, я *m.* depositor; mortgagor.

залогодержател|ь, я *m.* pawnee.

залож|ить, у, ~ишь *pf.* (*of* ⇒**закладывать**) **1** (*положить за*) to put (behind); **он ~ил руки за спину** he put his hands behind his back. **2** (*положить основание чему-либо*) to lay (the foundation of). **3** (*coll.*) (*потерять*) to mislay. **4** (+*i.*) (*загромоздить*) to pile up, heap up (with); to block up (with); (*impers.*, +*d.*): **мне нос ~ило** my nose is blocked, is stuffed up. **5** (*место в книге*) to mark, put a marker in; **я ~ил страницу девяносто** I have put a marker in at page ninety. **6** (*запрячь*) to harness. **7** (*для хранения*) to lay in, store, put by. **8** (*часы*) to pawn; (*дом*) to mortgage. **9** (*sl.*) (*предать*) to betray.

заложник, а *m.* hostage.

заложни|ца, цы *f. of* ⇒**~к**

залом|ить, лю, ~ишь *pf.* (*of* ⇒**заламывать**) **1** to break off. **2** (*coll.*): **з. цену** to ask an exorbitant price; **з. шапку** to cock one's hat.

залосн|иться, ится *pf.* (*coll.*) to become shiny (from wear).

залп, а *m.* volley; salvo; **выстрелить ~ом** to fire a volley, salvo; **~ом** (*fig.*, *coll.*) without pausing for breath; **выпить ~ом** to drain at one draught.

залуча|ть, ю *impf. of* ⇒**залучить**

залуч|ить, у, ишь *pf.* (*coll.*) to entice, lure.

залысин|а, ы *f.* bald patch.

залюб|оваться, уюсь *pf.* (+*i.*) to be lost in contemplation (of).

заляпа|ть, ю *pf.* (*coll.*) to make dirty.

зам, а *m.* (*coll.*) *abbr. of* **~еститель**

зам. (*abbr. of* **заместитель**) deputy.

зам... *comb. form, abbr. of* **заместитель**

зама|зать, жу, жешь *pf.* (*of* ⇒**мазать** *and* **~зывать**) **1** (*покрыть краской*) to paint over; (*зачеркнуть*) to efface; (*fig.*) to slur over. **2** (*залепить*) to putty. **3** (*запачкать*) to daub, smear; to soil.

зама|заться, жусь, жешься *pf.* (*of* ⇒**мазаться** *and* **~зываться**) to smear o.s., to get dirty.

замазк|а, и *f.* **1** (*вещество*) putty. **2** (*действие*) puttying.

замазыва|ть(ся), ю(сь) *impf. of* ⇒**замазать(ся)**

заманива|ть, ю *impf. of* ⇒**заманить**

замалива|ть, ю *impf. of* ⇒**замолить**

замалчива|ть, ю *impf. of* ⇒**замолчать[2]**

заманива|ть, ю *impf. of* ⇒**заманить**

заман|ить, ю, ~ишь *pf.* to entice, lure; (*обманом*) to decoy.

заманчив|ый (~, ~а) *adj.* tempting, alluring.

замара|ть, ю *pf.* (*of* ⇒**марать** 1) **1** (*запачкать*) to soil, dirty; (*fig.*) to disgrace; **з. свою репутацию** to sully one's reputation. **2** (*зачеркнуть*) to blot out, efface.

замара|ться, юсь *pf. of* ⇒**мараться**

замарашк|а, и *c.g.* (*coll.*) grubby child.

замарива|ть, ю *impf. of* ⇒**заморить**

замарин|овать, ую *pf. of* ⇒**мариновать**

замаскир|овать, ую *pf. of* ⇒**маскировать**

замаскир|оваться, уюсь *pf. of* ⇒**маскироваться**

замаслива|ть(ся), ю(сь) *impf. of* ⇒**замаслить(ся)**

замасл|ить, ю, ишь *pf.* **1** (*смазать*) to oil, grease. **2** (*засалить*) to make oily, make greasy.

замасл|иться, юсь, ишься *pf.* to become oily, become greasy.

заматерел|ый (~, ~а) *adj.* hardened, inveterate.

заматере|ть, ю *pf.* to become hardened.

заматыва|ть(ся), ю(сь) *impf. of* ⇒**замотать(ся)**

замах, а *m.* backward swing (*of arm etc.*).

зама|хать, шу, ~шешь *pf.* to begin to wave.

замахива|ться, юсь *impf. of* ⇒**замахнуться**

замахн|уться, усь, ёшься *pf.* **1** (+*i.* and **на**+*a.*) (*палкой, рукой*) to raise threateningly; **он даже ~улся рукой на беззащитную старуху** he even lifted up his hand against a defenceless old woman. **2** (**на**+*a.*) (*fig.*, *coll.*) to set one's sights on.

замачива|ть, ю *impf. of* ⇒**замочить**

замашк|а, и *f.* (*coll.*, *pej.*) way, manner.

замащива|ть, ю *impf. of* ⇒**замостить**

зама|ять, ю, ешь *pf.* (*coll.*) to tire out, wear out.

зама|яться, юсь, ешься *pf.* (*coll.*) to be tired out, exhausted.

замаяч|ить, у, ишь *pf.* to loom; **вдали ~или огни гавани** the lights of the harbour loomed up in the distance.

замби|ец, йца *m.* Zambian.

замбийк|а, и *f.* Zambian.

замбийский *adj.* Zambian.

Замби|я, и *f.* Zambia.

замедлени|е, я *nt.* **1** (*действие*) slowing down, deceleration; (*mus.*) ritardando. **2** (*задержка*) delay; **без ~я** without delay, at once.

замедленн|ый *p.p.p. of* ⇒**замедлить** *and adj.* retarded; delayed; **бомба ~ого действия** delayed-action bomb, time bomb; (*fig.*) time bomb; **~ое воспроизведение** slow-motion replay.

замедл|ить, ю, ишь *pf.* **1** to slow down, retard; **з. шаг** to slacken one's pace; **з. ход** to reduce speed. **2** (**с**+*i.*) to delay (in); to be long (in); **з. с ответом** to delay in answering; **не з.** (+*inf.*) to be quick (to); **ответ не ~ил прийти** the answer was not long in coming.

замедл|иться, ится *pf.* to slow down; to slacken, become slower.

замедля|ть(ся), ю, ет(ся) *impf. of* ⇒**замедлить(ся)**

замен|а, ы *f.* **1** (*действие*) substitution; replacement; **з. смертной казни тюремным заключением** commutation of death sentence to imprisonment. **2** (*том, кто (или то, что) заменяет*) substitute.

замени|мый *pres. part. pass. of* ⇒**~ть** *and adj.* replaceable.

заменител|ь, я *m.* (+*g.*) substitute; **з. кожи** leather substitute; **з. сахара** sweetener.

замен|ить, ю, ~ишь *pf.* (*of* ⇒**~ять**) **1** (+*a.* and *i.*) to replace (by), substitute (for); **мы ~или керосин электричеством** we have replaced oil with electricity; **з. масло маргарином** to use margarine instead of butter. **2** (*занять место кого-то, чего-то*) to take the place of; **она ~ила ребёнку мать** she was (like) a mother to the child; **трудно будет з. его** it will be hard to replace him.

замен|ять, яю *impf. of* ⇒**~ить**

зам|ереть, ру, рёшь, *past* **~ер, ~ерла, ~ерло** *pf.* (*of* ⇒**~ирать**) **1** (*стать неподвижным*) to stand still; to freeze, be rooted to the spot; to die (*fig.*); **сердце моё ~ерло, когда дверь**

откры́лась my heart stopped beating when the door opened. **2** (*о звуке*) to die down, die away; **к полу́ночи стрельба́ ~ерла́** towards midnight firing died down.

замерза́ни|е, я *nt.* freezing; **то́чка ~я** freezing point; **на то́чке ~я** (*fig.*) at a standstill.

замерза́|ть, ю *impf. of* ⇨**замёрзнуть**

замёрз|нуть, ну, нешь, *past* **~, ~ла** *pf.* (*of* ⇨**~а́ть**) (*о реке, окне*) to freeze (up); (*умереть от мороза*) to freeze to death; (*о растениях*) to be killed by frost; **я ~** I'm frozen.

за́мертво *adv.* like one dead; **она́ упа́ла з.** she collapsed in a dead faint.

заме|си́ть, шу́, ~сишь *pf.* (*of* ⇨**~шивать**) to mix; **з. те́сто** to knead dough.

заме|сти́, ту́, тёшь, *past* **~л, ~ла́** *pf.* (*of* ⇨**~та́ть**[1]) **1** (*подмести*) to sweep up. **2** (*покрыть*) to cover (up); (*impers.*): **доро́гу ~ло́ сне́гом** the road is covered with snow; (*fig.*): **з. следы́** to cover up one's traces.

замести́тел|ь, я *m.* substitute; deputy; **з. дире́ктора** deputy director; **з. председа́теля** (*comm.*) vice-chairman; **быть ~ем** (+*g.*) to stand proxy (for), substitute (for).

замести́тельств|о, а *nt.* position of deputy; acting tenure of office; **по ~у** by proxy.

заме|сти́ть, щу́, сти́шь *pf.* (*of* ⇨**~ща́ть**) **1** (+*a. and i.*) (*заменить*) to replace (by); to substitute (for). **2** (*должность*) to fill. **3** (*заменить собой*) to deputize for, act for; to serve in place of.

замета́|ть[1]**, ю** *impf. of* ⇨**замести́**

замета́|ть[2]**, ю** *pf.* (*of* ⇨**замётывать**) to tack, baste.

заме|та́ться, чу́сь, ~чешься *pf.* to begin to rush about; (*в постели*) to begin to toss.

заме́|тить, чу, тишь *pf.* (*of* ⇨**~ча́ть**) **1** (*увидеть*) to notice; **~тили ли вы, что он ча́сто повторя́ется?** have you noticed that he often repeats himself? **2** (*обратить внимание (на)*) to take notice (of); (*пометить*) to make a note (of). **3** (*сказать*) to remark, observe; **«соверше́нно ве́рно» — ~тил он** 'perfectly true', he remarked.

заме́тк|а, и *f.* **1** (*знак*) mark. **2** (*запись*) note; **~и на поля́х** marginal notes; **взять на ~у** (*coll.*) to make a note (of). **3** (*краткое сообщение*) notice; paragraph; **ни одна́ газе́та не удосто́ила вы́ставку ~ой** not a single newspaper gave the exhibition a notice. **4**: **он у меня́ на ~е** (*coll.*) I'm keeping an eye on him.

заме́т|ный (~ен, ~на) *adj.* **1** (*видимый*) noticeable; (*ощутимый*) appreciable; **ме́жду ни́ми есть ~ная ра́зница в во́зрасте** there is an appreciable difference in age between them; **~но** (*as pred.*) it is noticeable; **~но, как он не лю́бит говори́ть о де́тстве** it is noticeable that he does not like talking about his childhood. **2** (*no short forms*) (*выдающийся*) prominent.

замётыва|ть, ю *impf. of* ⇨**замета́ть**[2]

замеча́ни|е, я *nt.* **1** remark, observation. **2** (*упрёк*) reprimand; reproof.

замеча́тельно *adv.* **1** (*with verbs*) splendidly, brilliantly, wonderfully. **2** (*with adjectives, adverbs*) remarkably. **3** *pred.*: **з.!** (it's) splendid!, wonderful!

замеча́тел|ьный (~ен, ~ьна) *adj.* remarkable; splendid, wonderful.

замеча́|ть, ю *impf. of* ⇨**заме́тить**

заме́чен|ный (~, ~а) *p.p.p. of* ⇨**заме́тить; з. (в** + *p.*) discovered, noticed, detected (in); **он был неоднокра́тно ~ во взя́точничестве** he was several times discovered taking bribes.

замечта́|ться, юсь *pf.* to give o.s. up to day-dreaming; to fall into a reverie; **он опя́ть ~лся** he is day-dreaming again.

замеша́тельств|о, а *nt.* confusion; embarrassment; **привести́ в з.** to throw into confusion; **прийти́ в з.** to be confused, be embarrassed.

замеша́|ть, ю *pf.* (**в** + *a.*) to mix up, entangle (in).

замеша́|ться, юсь *pf.* (**в** + *a.*) (*coll.*) **1** (*запутаться*) to become mixed up, entangled (in). **2** (*скрыться*) to mix (with), mingle (in, with); **з. в толпу́** to mingle with the crowd.

заме́шива|ть(ся), ю(сь) *impf. of* ⇨**замеси́ть** *and* **замеша́ть(ся)**

заме́шка|ться, юсь *pf.* (*coll.*) to linger, dawdle.

замеща́|ть, ю *impf. of* ⇨**замести́ть**

замеще́ни|е, я *nt.* **1** (*замена*) substitution; replacement. **2** (*должности*) filling; **бу́дет ко́нкурс на з. вака́нтной до́лжности** there will be a competition to fill the vacancy.

замза́в, а *m.* (*abbr. of* ***замести́тель заве́дующего***) assistant manager.

замина́|ть, ю *impf. of* ⇨**замя́ть**

зами́нк|а, и *f.* (*coll.*) **1** (*задержка*) hitch. **2** (*в речи*) hesitation.

замира́ни|е, я *nt.* dying out, dying down; **он ждал с ~ем се́рдца** he waited with a sinking heart.

замира́|ть, ю *impf. of* ⇨**замере́ть**

замире́ни|е, я *nt.* peace-making.

замир|и́ть, ю́, и́шь *pf.* (*of* ⇨**~я́ть**) (*врагов*) to pacify.

замиря́|ть, ю *impf. of* ⇨**замири́ть**

за́мкнут|ый (~, ~а) *adj.* **1** (*no short forms*) (*среда, жизнь*) isolated, secluded. **2** (*человек*) reserved, withdrawn; **он — о́чень з. челове́к** he is a very reserved person. **3**: **~ая цепь** (*elec.*) closed circuit.

замкн|у́ть, у́, ёшь *pf.* (*of* ⇨**замыка́ть**) to lock; to close; **з. ше́ствие, з. коло́нну** to bring up the rear.

замкн|у́ться, у́сь, ёшься *pf.* (*of* ⇨**замыка́ться**) **1** (*дверь*) to lock. **2** (*цепь*) to be joined at the ends; **круг ~у́лся** (*fig.*) everything fell into place. **3** to shut o.s. up; **з. в круг** to form a circle; (*fig.*) **з. в себе́** to become reserved, retire into o.s.

зам|ну́, нёшь *see* ⇨**~я́ть**

замоги́льный *adj.* sepulchral (*of voice*).

за́м|ок, ка *m.* castle; **возду́шные ~ки** castles in the air.

зам|о́к, ка́ *m.* **1** lock; **америка́нский з.** Yale lock; **вися́чий з.** padlock; **секре́тный з.** combination lock; **под ~ко́м** under lock and key; **за семью́ ~ка́ми** well and truly hidden. **2** (*archit.*) keystone. **3** (*винтовки*) bolt. **4** (*браслета*) clasp; (*серьги*) clip.

замока́|ть, ет *impf. of* ⇨**замо́кнуть**

замо́кн|уть, ет *pf.* to become drenched, become soaked.

замо́лв|ить, лю, ишь *pf.* (*coll.*): **з. слове́чко за** (+*a.*) to put in a word (for); **прошу́ вас з. слове́чко за меня́ у нача́льства** will you, please, put in a word for me with the authorities?

замол|и́ть, ю́, ~ишь *pf.* (*of* ⇨**зама́ливать**); **з. грехи́** to atone for one's sins by prayer.

замолка́|ть, ю *impf. of* ⇨**замо́лкнуть**

замо́лк|нуть, ну, нешь, *past* **~, ~ла** *pf.* to fall silent; to stop, cease (*speaking, etc.*); **внеза́пно пе́ние ~ло** suddenly the singing ceased.

замолч|а́ть[1]**, у́, и́шь** *pf.* to fall silent; (*fig.*) to cease corresponding.

замолч|а́ть[2]**, у́, и́шь** *pf.* (*of* ⇨**зама́лчивать**) (*coll.*) to keep silent about; to hush up.

замора́живани|е, я *nt.* freezing; **з. зарпла́ты/цен** wage-/price-freezing.

замора́жива|ть, ю *impf. of* ⇨**заморо́зить**

заморд|ова́ть, у́ю *pf.* (*coll.*) to torment.

замор|и́ть, ю́, и́шь *pf.* (*of* ⇨**зама́ривать**) (*coll.*) **1** (*работой*) to overwork. **2** (*не кормить досыта*) to underfeed; **з. червячка́** to have a bite, have a snack.

заморо́|женный *p.p.p. of* ⇨**~зить** *and adj.* frozen; iced; **~женное мя́со** frozen meat; **~женное шампа́нское** iced champagne.

заморо́|зить, жу, зишь *pf.* (*of* ⇨**замора́живать**) to freeze.

за́морозк|и, ов *no sg.* (light) frosts.

замо́рский *adj.* (*obs.*) oversea(s).

замо́рыш, а *m.* (*coll.*) weakling; runt.

замо|сти́ть, щу́, сти́шь *pf.* (*of* ⇨**мости́ть** *and* **зама́щивать**) to pave.

замо́тан|ный (~, ~а) *adj.* (*coll.*) fagged- *or* worn-out, shattered.

замота́|ть, ю *pf.* (*of* ⇨**зама́тывать**) **1** to wind, twist; (+*i.*) (*обмотать*) to wrap (in, with). **2** (*fig., coll.*) (*утомить*) to tire out.

замота́|ться, юсь *pf.* (*of* ⇨**зама́тываться**) **1** to wind round; (+*i.*) (*обмотать себя*) to wrap oneself (in). **2** (*fig., coll.*) (*устать*) to be tired out, be fagged out.

замоч|и́ть, у́, ~ишь *pf.* (*of* ⇒**зама́чивать** *and* **мочи́ть**) **1** (*слегка*) to wet; (*погрузить в воду*) to soak. **2** *see* ⇒**мочи́ть** 3

замо́чн|ый *adj. of* ⇒**замо́к; ~ая сква́жина** keyhole.

зампре́д, а *m.* (*abbr. of* ***замести́тель председа́теля***) vice-chairman; deputy chairman.

за́муж *adv.*: **вы́йти з. за кого́-н.** to marry s.o. (*of woman*); **вы́дать кого́-н. з.** (**за**+*a.*) to give s.o. in marriage (to); to marry off (to).

за́мужем *adv.*: **быть з.** (**за**+*i.*) to be married (to) (*of woman*).

заму́жеств|о, а *nt.* marriage (*of woman*); **у неё о́чень счастли́вое з.** she is very happily married.

заму́жняя *adj.* married (*of woman*).

замур|ова́ть, у́ю *pf.* to brick up; (*человека*) to immure.

замуро́выва|ть, ю *impf. of* ⇒**замурова́ть**

заму́сл|ить, ю, ишь = **замусо́лить**

замусо́лива|ть, ю *impf. of* ⇒**замусо́лить**

замусо́л|ить, ю, ишь *pf.* to beslobber.

заму|ти́ть, чу́, ти́шь *pf. of* ⇒**мути́ть; он воды́ не ~ти́т** he won't cause any trouble.

замухры́шк|а, и *c.g.* (*coll., pej.*) poor specimen.

заму́чива|ть, ю *impf. of* ⇒**заму́чить**

заму́ч|ить, у, ишь *pf.* (*of* ⇒**му́чить** *and* **~ивать**) to torment; (*утомить*) to wear out; (*разговорами*) to bore to tears; (*убить*) to torture to death.

заму́ч|иться, усь, ишься *pf.* (*of* ⇒**му́читься**) to be worn out.

за́мш|а, и *f.* chamois (leather); suede.

замшеви́дный *adj.* suedette.

за́мш|евый *adj. of* ⇒**~а**

замше́л|ый (~, ~а) *adj.* mossy, moss-covered.

замше́|ть, ет *pf.* to be overgrown with moss.

замыва́|ть, ю *impf. of* ⇒**замы́ть**

замыка́ни|е, я *nt.* locking; **коро́ткое з.** (*elec.*) short circuit.

замы́ка|ться, юсь *pf.* (*coll.*) to be tired out.

замыка́|ть(ся), ю(сь) *impf. of* ⇒**замкну́ть(ся)**

за́мыс|ел, ла *m.* (*план*) project, plan; design, scheme; (*смысл*) idea; **злы́е ~лы** evil designs.

замы́сл|ить, ю, ишь *pf.* (*of* ⇒**замышля́ть**) (+*a. or inf.*) to plan; to contemplate; **он ~ил самоубийство** he contemplated suicide; **они́ ~или убежа́ть под покро́вом темноты́** they had planned to escape under cover of darkness.

замыслова́т|ый (~, ~а) *adj.* intricate, complicated.

замыта́р|ить(ся), ю(сь), ишь(ся) *pf. of* ⇒**мыта́рить(ся)**

зам|ы́ть, о́ю, о́ешь *pf.* (*of* ⇒**~ыва́ть**) to wash off, wash out.

замышля́|ть, ю *impf. of* ⇒**замы́слить**

зам|я́ть, ну́, нёшь *pf.* (*of* ⇒**~ина́ть**) (*coll.*) to put a stop to; **з. разгово́р** to change the subject.

зам|я́ться, ну́сь, нёшься *pf.* (*coll.*) to stumble; to stop short (*in speech*).

за́навес, а *m.* curtain; **под з.** (*theatr.*) near the end of an act; (*fig.*) near the end, at the end.

занаве́|сить, шу, сишь *pf.* (*of* ⇒**~шивать**) to curtain; to cover.

занаве́ск|а, и *f.* curtain (*of light material*).

занаве́шива|ть, ю *impf. of* ⇒**занаве́сить**

зана́шива|ть, ю *impf. of* ⇒**заноси́ть**[2]

занеме́|ть, ю *pf.* to grow numb.

занемога́|ть, ю *impf. of* ⇒**занемо́чь**

занемо́|чь, гу́, жешь, гут, *past* **~г, ~гла́** *pf.* to fall ill, be taken ill.

занес|ти́, у́, ёшь, *past* **~, ~ла́** *pf.* (*of* ⇒**заноси́ть**[1]) **1** (*принести*) to bring; (*доставить мимоходом*) to drop off. **2** (*поднять*) to raise, lift; **з. но́гу в стре́мя** to raise one's foot into the stirrup. **3** (*записать*) to note down; **з. в протоко́л/спи́сок** to enter in the minutes/list. **4** (*coll.*) to carry (away); **куда́ его́ нелёгкая ~ла́?** where the devil has he got to?; (*impers.*): **каки́м ве́тром вас сюда́ ~ло́?** what wind blows you here? **5** (*impers.*): **з. сне́гом** to cover with snow; **доро́гу ~ло́ сне́гом** the road is snowed up.

занес|ти́сь, у́сь, ёшься, *past* **~ся, ~ла́сь** *pf.* (*of* ⇒**заноси́ться**[1]) (*coll., pej.*) to be carried away (*fig.*).

Занзиба́р, а *m.* Zanzibar.

занима́тел|ьный (~ен, ~ьна) *adj.* entertaining, diverting; absorbing.

занима́|ть[1]**, ю** *impf.* (*of* ⇒**заня́ть**) **1** (*город, квартиру*) to occupy; **крова́ть ~ет мно́го ме́ста** the bed takes up a lot of room; **он ~ет высо́кое положе́ние** (*fig.*) he occupies a high post. **2** (*увлекать*) to occupy; to interest; **она́ весь день ~ла дете́й** she kept the children occupied all day; **его́ ~ют бо́льше всего́ вопро́сы филосо́фии** his chief interest is in philosophy. **3** (*время*) to take; **э́то ~ет мно́го вре́мени** this takes a lot of time. **4** (*пост, должность*) to take up. **5**: **з. ме́сто кому́-н./для кого́-н.** to reserve a seat for s.o.; **з. пе́рвое ме́сто** to take first place.

занима́|ть[2]**, ю** *impf.* (*of* ⇒**заня́ть**) (*деньги*) to borrow.

занима́|ться[1]**, юсь** *impf.* (*of* ⇒**заня́ться**) (+*i.*) **1** to be occupied (with), be engaged (in); (*работать*) to work (at, on); (*учиться*) to study; **чем вы ~лись вчера́?** what were you doing yesterday?; **чем он ~ется?** what does he do? (*for a living*); **он ~ется подгото́вкой но́вой экспеди́ции** he is engaged in preparations for a new expedition; **до заму́жества она́ ~лась му́зыкой** before her marriage she was studying music; **она́ ~лась на трубе́** she was practising the trumpet. **2** (*посвящать себя*) to devote o.s. (to); **з. есте́ственными нау́ками** to devote o.s. to the natural sciences; **з. собо́й** to devote time to o.s. **3** (**с**+*i.*) (*помогать в учении*) to assist with (*study*).

занима́|ться[2]**, ется** *impf.* (*of* ⇒**заня́ться**) to catch fire.

за́ново *adv.* anew.

зано́з|а, ы *f.* splinter.

зано́зист|ый (~, ~а) *adj.* (*coll.*) (*поверхность*) splintery; (*fig.*) (*человек*) abrasive.

зано|зи́ть, жу́, зи́шь *pf.* to get a splinter into.

зано́с[1]**, а** *m.* drift; **сне́жный з.** snow-drift; **песча́ный з.** sand-drift.

зано́с[2]**, а** *m.* **1** (*доставка*) bringing, importing, import. **2** (*поднятие*) raising, lifting.

зано|си́ть[1]**, шу́, ~сишь** *impf. of* ⇒**занести́**

зано|си́ть[2]**, шу́, ~сишь** *pf.* (*of* ⇒**зана́шивать**) to wear out.

зано|си́ться[1]**, шу́сь, ~сишься** *impf. of* ⇒**занести́сь**

зано|си́ться[2]**, ~сится** *pf.* to be worn out; to wear out (*intrans.*).

зано́сный *adj.* alien, imported.

зано́счив|ый (~, ~а) *adj.* arrogant, haughty.

заноч|ева́ть, у́ю *pf.* (*coll.*) to stay for the night.

зану́д|а, ы *c.g.* (*coll.*) tiresome person, pain in the neck.

зану́дливый = **зану́дный**

зану́д|ный (~ен, ~на) *adj.* (*coll.*) tiresome.

занумер|ова́ть, у́ю *pf.* (*of* ⇒**нумерова́ть**) to number.

заня́ти|е, я *nt.* **1** (*дело*) occupation; pursuit. **2** (*pl.*) studies; (*usu. pl.*) (*урок*) lesson, class. **3** (*действие*) (*квартиры*) occupation; (*должности*) taking up.

заня́т|ный (~ен, ~на) *adj.* (*coll.*) entertaining, amusing.

занято́й *adj.* busy.

за́нятост|ь, и *f.* (*econ.*) employment; **по́лная з.** full employment.

за́нят|ый (~, ~а́, ~о) *p.p.p. of* ⇒**~ь** *and adj.* **1** occupied; **здесь ~о** this place is taken; **~о** (*телефон, туалет*) engaged; **на э́том заво́де ~о свы́ше ты́сячи рабо́чих** over a thousand people are employed in this factory; **быть ~ым собо́й** to be self-centred (*Br.*), -centered (*US*). **2** (*only short forms*) (*человек*) busy; **он сейча́с ~** he is busy at the moment.

зан|я́ть(ся), займу́(сь), займёшь(ся), *past* **~ял, ~я́лся, ~яла́(сь), ~яло, ~яло́сь** *pf. of* ⇒**занима́ть(ся);** (*impers.; coll.*): **у кого́-н. дух ~яло** to be out of breath; (*fig.*) to be (left) breathless; **от э́того у меня́ дух ~яло** it took my breath away.

З

заóблачный *adj.* beyond the clouds.

заоднó *adv.* **1** in concert, at one; **дéйствовать з.** to act in concert; **в э́том вопрóсе мужчи́ны — з. с жéнщинами** on this the men are in agreement with the women. **2** (*coll.*) (*одновременно*) at the same time; **купи́те з. и апельси́ны** buy oranges at the same time.

заозёрный *adj.* situated on the other side of the lake.

заокеáнский *adj.* transoceanic.

заор|áть, ý, ёшь *pf.* (*coll.*) to begin to bawl, begin to yell.

заострённый *p.p.p. of* ⇒**заостри́ть** *and adj.* pointed, sharp.

заостр|и́ть, ю́, и́шь *pf.* to sharpen; (*fig.*) to stress, emphasize; **з. внимáние** (**на** + *a.*) to focus attention (on).

заостр|и́ться, и́тся *pf.* to become sharp; to become pointed.

заостр|я́ть(ся), я́ю, я́ет(ся) *impf. of* ⇒**~и́ть(ся)**

заóчник, а *m.* student taking correspondence course; external student.

заóчно *adv.* **1** (*в отсутствие кого-н.*) in one's absence. **2** (*об обучении*) by correspondence course, externally.

заóчн|ый *adj.* **1** (*leg.*): **з. пригово́р** judgment by default. **2**: **з. курс** correspondence course; **~ое обучéние** distance learning.

зáпад, а *m.* **1** west. **2** (**З.**) (*pol.*) the West.

западá|ть, ю *impf. of* ⇒**запáсть**

зáпадник, а *m.* Westernizer, Westernist.

зáпадничеств|о, а *nt.* Westernism.

западногермáнский *adj.* (*hist.*) West German.

зáпадн|ый *adj.* west, western; (*направление, ветер*) westerly; **З~ая Гермáния** (*hist.*) West Germany.

западн|я́, и́, *g. pl.* **~éй** *f.* trap, snare; **попáсть в ~ю́** to fall into a trap (*also fig.*).

запáздывани|е, я *nt.* **1** lateness, being late. **2** (*tech.*) lag.

запáздыва|ть, ю *impf. of* ⇒**запоздáть** (*impf. only*; *tech.*) to be late, lag.

запáива|ть, ю *impf. of* ⇒**запая́ть**

запáйк|а, и *f.* soldering.

запак|овáть, ýю *pf.* to pack (up); to wrap up, do up.

запакóвыва|ть, ю *impf. of* ⇒**запаковáть**

запáко|стить, щу, стишь *pf. of* ⇒**пáкостить** 1

запáл, а *m.* **1** (*заряда*) fuse. **2** (*coll.*) (*пыл*) enthusiasm.

запáлива|ть, ю *impf. of* ⇒**запали́ть**[1]

запал|и́ть[1]**, ю́, и́шь** *pf.* (*of* ⇒**~́ивать**) (*coll.*) (*зажечь*) to set fire to, kindle; to light.

запал|и́ть[2]**, ю́, и́шь** *pf.* (*dial.*) **1** (*опоить*) to water (*a horse*) when overheated. **2** (*измучить*) to override (*a horse*).

запал|и́ть[3]**, ю́, и́шь** *pf.* (*coll.*) **1** (*начать палить*) to open fire. **2** (+*i.*) to hurl.

запáл|ьный *adj. of* ⇒**~ 1**; **~ьная свечá** sparking plug.

запáльчивост|ь, и *f.* (quick) temper.

запáльчив|ый (~, ~а) *adj.* quick-tempered.

запáмят|овать, ую *pf.* (*obs., coll.*) to forget.

запанибрáта *adv.* (*coll.*): **быть з. с кем-н.** to be hail-fellow-well-met with s.o.

запанибрáтский *adj.* (*coll.*) hail-fellow-well-met.

запáрива|ть(ся), ю(сь) *impf. of* ⇒**запáрить(ся)**

запáр|ить, ю, ишь *pf.* (*of* ⇒**~ивать**) **1** (*coll.*) (*лошадь*) to put into a sweat. **2** (*заварить*) to stew; to steam. **3** (*coll.*) (*утомить*) to exhaust.

запáр|иться, юсь, ишься *pf.* (*of* ⇒**~иваться**) **1** (*coll.*) (*покрыться потом*) to get into a sweat. **2** (*сильно устать*) to be worn out.

запарк|овáть, ýю *pf. of* ⇒**паркoвáть**

запарк|овáться, ýюсь *pf. of* ⇒**паркoвáться**

запарши́ве|ть, ю *pf. of* ⇒**парши́веть**

запáрыва|ть, ю *impf. of* ⇒**запорóть**

запáс, а *m.* **1** supply, stock; reserve; **про з.** for an emergency; **отложи́ть про з.** to put by; **истощи́ть з. терпéния** (*fig.*) to exhaust one's reserves of patience; **з. слов** vocabulary; **у меня́ день в ~е** I have one day in reserve, to spare. **2** (*mil.*) reserve; **егó уво́лили в з.** he has been transferred to the reserve. **3** (*в одежде*) hem; **вы́пустить з.** to let out.

запасá|ть(ся), ю(сь) *impf. of* ⇒**запасти́(сь)**

запáслив|ый (~, ~а) *adj.* thrifty; provident.

запасни́к[1]**, запасникá** *m.* (*mil.*; *coll.*) reservist.

запáсник[2]**, а** *m.* (*хранилище*) repository, depository; storeroom.

запасн|óй *adj.* **1** spare; (*игрок*) reserve; **з. вы́ход** emergency exit; **з. путь** siding; **з. стéржень** re-fill (*for pen*); **~áя часть** spare part; **з. я́корь** (*naut.*) sheet anchor, spare bower anchor. **2** *as n.* **з., ~óго** *m.* (*mil.*) reservist; (*sport*) reserve.

запáсн|ый *adj.* = **~óй**

запас|ти́, ý, ёшь, *past* **~́, ~лá** *pf.* (*of* ⇒**~áть**) (+*a. or g.*) to stock, store; to lay in a stock of.

запас|ти́сь, ýсь, ёшься, *past* **~́ся, ~лáсь** *pf.* (*of* ⇒**~áться**) (+*i.*) to provide o.s. (with); to stock up (on, with); **з. терпéнием** (*fig.*) to arm o.s. with patience.

запá|сть, дý, дёшь, *past* **~л** *pf.* (*of* ⇒**~дáть**) to fall (behind); (*о глазах*) to become sunken; **егó словá ~ли мне в дýшу** (*fig.*) his words are imprinted on my mind.

запатентовáть *pf. of* ⇒**патентовáть**

запат|овáть, ýю *pf. of* ⇒**патовáть**

зáпах, а *m.* smell.

запа|хáть, шý, ~́шешь *pf.* (*agric.*) **1** (*удобрения*) to plough in. **2** (*начать пахать*) to begin to plough.

запáхива|ть[1]**(ся), ю(сь)** *impf. of* ⇒**запахнýть(ся)**

запáхива|ть[2]**, ю** *impf. of* ⇒**запахáть**

запáхн|уть, у, ешь *pf.* to begin to (emit a) smell.

запахн|ýть, ý, ёшь *pf.* (*of* ⇒**запáхивать**[1]) **1** to wrap over (*folds of a garment*). **2** (*coll.*): **з. занавéску** to draw the curtain.

запахн|ýться, ýсь, ёшься *pf.* (**в** + *a.*) to wrap o.s. tighter (into).

запáчка|ть(ся), ю(сь) *pf. of* ⇒**пáчкать(ся)**

запаш|óк, кá *m.* (*coll.*) faint smell.

запая́|ть, ю *pf.* (*of* ⇒**запáивать**) to solder.

запéв, а *m.* introductory verse (*to song*).

запевáл|а, ы *c.g.* leader (of choir); (*fig., coll.*) leader, instigator.

запевá|ть, ю *impf.* **1** to lead the singing, set the tune. **2** *impf. of* ⇒**запéть**

запекáнк|а, и *f.* **1** bake; (*сладкая*) baked pudding; **ри́совая з.** rice pudding; **картóфельная з.** shepherd's pie. **2** (*наливка*) spiced brandy.

запекá|ть(ся), ю, ет(ся) *impf. of* ⇒**запéчь(ся)**

запеленá|ть, ю *pf. of* ⇒**пеленáть**

запéн|иться, ится *pf.* to begin to froth up, begin to foam (*intrans.*).

зап|ерéть, рý, рёшь, *past* **~́ер, ерлá, ~́ерло** *pf.* (*of* ⇒**~ирáть**) **1** (*дверь*) to lock; **з. на засóв** to bolt. **2** (*человека*) to lock in; to shut up. **3** (*преградить доступ*) to bar; to block up.

зап|ерéться, рýсь, рёшься, *past* **~́ерся́, ~ерлáсь, ~́ерлось** *pf.* (*of* ⇒**~ирáться**) **1** to lock o.s. in. **2** (*coll.*) (*не сознаться*) (**в** + *p.*) to refuse to admit; (*отказаться говорить*) to refuse to speak; to clam up. **3** (*дверь*) to lock.

зап|éть, ою́, оёшь *pf.* (*of* ⇒**~евáть**) **1** (*начать петь*) to begin to sing; **з. пéсню** to break into a song; **з. другóе** (*fig.*) to change one's tune. **2** (*coll.*) (*опошлить*) to do to death. **3** *pf. only* (*сказать при неблагоприятных обстоятельствах*) to say; **я посмотрю́, что ты тогдá ~оёшь** we'll see what you say then.

запечáт|ать, аю *pf.* (*of* ⇒**~ывать**) to seal.

запечатлевá|ть(ся), ю(сь) *impf. of* ⇒**запечатлéть(ся)**

запечатлé|ть, ю *pf.* **1** (*изобразить*) to portray, depict. **2** (*сохранить надолго в памяти*) to imprint, impress, engrave; **з. что-н. в пáмяти** (*fig.*) to imprint sth. on one's memory.

запечатлé|ться, юсь *pf.* (*fig.*) to imprint itself, stamp itself, etch itself; **черты́ егó лицá ~лись у неё в**

па́мяти his features etched themselves in her memory.

запеча́тыва|ть, ю *impf. of* ⇒**запеча́тать**

запе́|чь, кý, чёшь, кýт, *past* **~к, ~кла́** *pf.* (*of* ⇒**~ка́ть**) to bake.

запе́|чься, чётся, кýтся, *past* **~кся, ~кла́сь** *pf.* (*of* ⇒**~ка́ться**) **1** to bake (*intrans.*). **2** (*о крови*) to clot, coagulate. **3** (*о губах*) to become parched.

запива́|ть, ю *impf. of* ⇒**запи́ть**

запина́|ться, юсь *impf.* (*of* ⇒**запнýться**) (*споткнуться*) (**о**+*a.*) to stumble (on); (*в речи*) to stumble.

запи́нк|а, и *f.* hesitation (*in speech*).

запира́тельств|о, а *nt.* (*pej.*) denial, disavowal.

запира́|ть(ся), ю(сь) *impf. of* ⇒**запере́ть(ся)**

запи|са́ть, шý, ~шешь *pf.* (*of* ⇒**~сывать**) **1** (*занести на бумагу*) to note, make a note (of); to take down (in writing); (*концерт, фильм*) to record (*with apparatus*); **з. (на плёнку)** to tape; **з. (на ви́део)** to video; **з. ле́кцию** to take notes of a lecture. **2** (*включить в состав чего-либо*) to enter, register, enrol; **~ши́те меня́, пожа́луйста, на приём к врачý** please make an appointment with the doctor for me. **3** (+*a. and* **на**+*a.*; *leg.*) to make over (to); **он ~са́л всю со́бственность на свою́ племя́нницу** he made over all his property to his niece.

запи|са́ться, шýсь, ~шешься *pf.* (*of* ⇒**~сываться**) to register, enter one's name, enrol; **з. в клуб** to join a club; **з. к врачý** to make an appointment with the doctor.

запи́ск|а, и *f.* **1** note; **делова́я з.** memorandum, minute. **2**: **~и** (*pl.*) notes; memoirs; (*как название научных журналов*) transactions.

записн|о́й[1] *adj.*: **~а́я кни́жка** notebook.

записно́й[2] *adj.* (*coll.*) (*рьяный*) zealous; (*отъявленный*) inveterate.

запи́сыва|ть(ся), ю(сь) *impf. of* ⇒**записа́ть(ся)**

за́пис|ь, и *f.* **1** (*действие*) writing down; recording; registration. **2** (*в дневнике*) entry; (*comput.*) record; (*заметка*) note; (*на плёнку*) recording; (*leg.*) deed.

зап|и́ть, ью́, ьёшь, *past* **~и́л, ~ила́, ~и́ло** *pf.* (*of* ⇒**~ива́ть**) **1** (*coll.*; *past* **~и́л**) (*начать пить*) to take to drink; (*кутить*) to go on a drinking spree. **2** (*past* **~и́л;** +*a. and i.*) to wash down (with); to take (with, after); **з. табле́тку водо́й** to take a tablet with water.

запиха́|ть, ю *pf.* (*coll.*) to cram into.

запи́хива|ть, ю *impf. of* ⇒**запиха́ть**

запих|нýть, нý, нёшь *pf.* (*coll.*) = **~а́ть**

запи́чка|ть, ю *pf.* (*coll.*) to stuff, cram.

запи|шý, ~шешь *see* ⇒**~са́ть**

запла́кан|ный (~, ~а) *adj.* tear-stained; in tears.

запла́|кать, чу, чешь *pf.* to begin to cry.

запланир|овать, ую *pf. of* ⇒**плани́ровать**[1]

запла́т|а, ы *f.* patch (*in garments*); **наложи́ть ~у (на**+*a.*) to patch.

заплата́|ть, ю *pf.* (*of* ⇒**плата́ть**) (*coll.*) to patch.

запла|ти́ть, чý, ~тишь *pf. of* ⇒**плати́ть**

запла́|чу, чешь *see* ⇒**~кать**

запла|чý, ~тишь *see* ⇒**~ти́ть**

заплёван|ный (~, ~а) *p.p.p. of* ⇒**заплева́ть** *and adj.* bespattered (with spittle); dirty.

запл|ева́ть, юю́, юёшь *pf.* (*coll.*) to spit on; (*человека*) to spit at; (*fig.*) to rain curses on.

заплёвыва|ть, ю *impf. of* ⇒**заплева́ть**

запле|ска́ть, ска́ю, *and* **~щý, ~щешь** *pf.* **1** (*забрызгать*) to splash. **2** (*начать плескать*) to begin to splash.

заплёскива|ть, ю *impf. of* ⇒**заплеска́ть** *and* **заплеснýть**

запле́сневелый *adj.* mouldy (*Br.*), moldy (*US*), mildewed.

запле́сневе|ть, ет *pf. of* ⇒**пле́сневеть**

заплесн|ýть, ý, ёшь *pf.* (*of* ⇒**заплёскивать**) (*coll.*) to splash into; to swamp.

запле|сти́, тý, тёшь, *past* **~л, ~ла́** *pf.* (*of* ⇒**заплета́ть**) (*волосы*) to braid, plait.

заплета́|ть, ю *impf. of* ⇒**заплести́**

заплета́|ться, ется *impf.* (*о ногах*) to be unsteady, wobbly; **у него́ язы́к ~ется** his speech is indistinct.

запле́чный *adj.* over the shoulder; **з. мешо́к** rucksack.

запле́ч|ье, ья, *g. pl.* **~ий** *nt.* shoulder-blade.

запломбир|ова́ть, ýю *pf.* (*of* ⇒**пломбирова́ть**) **1**: **з. зуб** to stop, fill a tooth. **2** (*запечатать*) to seal.

заплута́|ться, юсь *pf.* (*coll.*) to lose one's way, stray.

заплы́в, а *m.* round, heat (*of water sports*).

заплыва́|ть, ю *impf. of* ⇒**заплы́ть**

заплы́|ть[1]**, вý, вёшь,** *past* **~л, ~ла́, ~ло** *pf.* (*о пловце*) to swim far out; (*о судне*) to sail away.

заплы́|ть[2]**, вý, вёшь,** *past* **~л, ~ла́, ~ло** *pf.* to be swollen; to be bloated; **~вшие жи́ром глаза́** bloated eyes.

запн|ýться, ýсь, ёшься *pf. of* ⇒**запина́ться**

заповеда|ть, ю *pf.* (*of* ⇒**запове́дывать**) (*rhet.*) to command.

запове́дник, а *m.* reserve; preserve; sanctuary; **госуда́рственный з.** national park.

запове́дный *adj.* **1** closed, protected; **з. лес** forest reserve. **2** (*fig.*) (*заветный*) secret, precious.

запове́дыва|ть, ю *impf. of* ⇒**запове́дать**

за́поведь, и *f.* precept; (*relig. and fig.*) commandment; **де́сять ~ей** the Ten Commandments.

запода́зрива|ть, ю *impf. of* ⇒**заподо́зрить**

заподо́зр|ить, ю, ишь *pf.* (+*a. and* **в**+*p.*) to suspect (of); **его́ ~или в прича́стности к за́говору** he was suspected of complicity in the plot.

запо́ем *adv.*: **пить з.** to drink like a fish; (*fig., coll.*) heavily, unrestrainedly; **чита́ть з.** to read avidly; **кури́ть з.** to smoke like a chimney.

запозда́лый *adj.* belated.

запозда́|ть, ю *pf.* (*of* ⇒**запа́здывать**) (**с**+*i.*) to be late (with); **он ~л с упла́той аре́нды** he is late in paying his rent.

запо́|й, я *m.* (addiction to periodic) hard drinking; **пить ~ем,** *see* ⇒**~ем**

запо́й|ный *adj. of* ⇒**~; з. пери́од** drunken bout; **з. пья́ница** chronic drunkard.

запола́скива|ть, ю *impf. of* ⇒**заполоска́ть** *and* **заполоснýть**

запо́лза|ть, ю *pf.* to begin to crawl.

заполза́|ть, ю *impf. of* ⇒**заползти́**

заполз|ти́, ý, ёшь, *past* **~, ~ла́** *pf.* (**в, под**+*a.*) to creep, crawl (into, under).

запо́лн|ить, ю, ишь *pf.* (*of* ⇒**~я́ть**) to fill in, fill up; **чем вы ~или вре́мя?** how did you fill in the time? **з. бланк** to fill in (*Br.*), out (*US*) a form; **з. пробе́л** to fill a gap.

запо́лн|иться, ится *pf.* (*of* ⇒**~я́ться**) to fill up (*intrans.*); **зал ~ился студе́нтами** the hall filled up with students.

заполня́|ть(ся), ю, ет(ся) *impf. of* ⇒**запо́лнить(ся)**

заполон|и́ть, ю́, и́шь *pf.* (*of* ⇒**~я́ть**) (*obs.*) to take captive; (*coll.*) (*дом, улицу*) to take over.

заполон|я́ть, я́ю *impf. of* ⇒**~и́ть**

заполо|ска́ть, щý, ~щешь *pf.* (*of* ⇒**запола́скивать**) (*coll.*) **1** (*начать полоскать*) to begin to rinse. **2** (*замыть*) to rinse out.

заполосн|ýть, ý, ёшь *pf.* (*of* ⇒**запола́скивать**) (*coll.*) to rinse out.

заполуч|а́ть, а́ю *impf. of* ⇒**~и́ть**

заполуч|и́ть, ý, ~ишь *pf.* (*of* ⇒**~а́ть**) (*coll.*) to get hold of; to pick up; **з. на́сморк** to pick up a cold.

заполя́рный *adj.* (*geog.*) **1** (*город*) polar. **2** (*путь*) trans-polar.

заполя́рь|е, я *nt.* (*geog.*) polar regions.

запомина́|ть(ся), ю(сь) *impf. of* ⇒**запо́мнить(ся); ~ющее устро́йство** computer memory.

запо́мн|ить, ю, ишь *pf.* (*of* ⇒**запомина́ть**) **1** (*текст, номер*) to memorize. **2** (*человека, картину, событие*) to remember.

запо́мн|иться, юсь, ишься *pf.* (*of* ⇒**запомина́ться**) to stick, remain in one's memory; **емý ~ился день**

землетрясе́ния the day of the earthquake remained in his memory.

за́понк|а, и *f.* cuff-link; stud.

запо́р[1], **а** *m.* **1** (*замок*) bolt; lock; **на ~(е)** locked; bolted (and barred). **2** (*coll.*) (*действие*) closing; locking; bolting.

запо́р[2], **а** *m.* (*med.*) constipation.

запора́шива|ть, ет *impf. of* ⇒**запороши́ть**

запоро́ж|ец, ца *m.* (*hist.*) Zaporozhian Cossack.

запор|о́ть, ю́, ~ешь *pf.* (*of* ⇒**запа́рывать**) (*coll.*) **1** (*засечь*) to flog to death. **2** (*испортить*) to spoil, ruin.

запорош|и́ть, и́т *pf.* (*of* ⇒**запора́шивать**) (+*i.*) to powder (with); (*impers.*): **доро́гу ~и́ло сне́гом** the road was powdered with snow; **глаза́ мои́ ~и́ло пы́лью** my eyes are full of dust.

запотева́|ть, ет *impf. of* ⇒**запоте́ть**

запоте́лый *adj.* (*coll.*) misted; steamed-up.

запоте́|ть, ет *pf.* (*of* ⇒**поте́ть** *and* **~ва́ть**) to mist over.

зап|ою́, оёшь *see* ⇒**~е́ть**

запра́вил|а, ы *m.* (*coll.*) boss.

запра́в|ить, лю, ишь *pf.* (*of* ⇒**~ля́ть**) **1** (*вставить*) to insert; **з. брю́ки в сапоги́** to tuck one's trousers into one's boots. **2** (*приготовить*) to prepare; **з. автомоби́ль бензи́ном** to fill a car up with petrol. **3** (+*i.*) (*добавить*) to mix in; (*сдобрить*) to season (with).

запра́в|иться, люсь, ишься *pf.* (*of* ⇒**~ля́ться**) **1 з. (горю́чим)** to refuel (*intrans.*). **2** (*coll.*) (*хорошо поесть*) to satisfy hunger; to eat one's fill.

запра́вк|а, и *f.* **1** (*приправа*) seasoning; **з. для сала́та** salad dressing. **2** (*машины*) refuelling (*Br.*), refueling (*US*). **3** (*coll.*) (*заправочная станция*) filling station.

заправля́|ть, ю *impf. of* ⇒**запра́вить;** (+*i.*) (*coll.*) to be in charge (of).

заправля́|ться, юсь *impf. of* ⇒**запра́виться**

запра́вочн|ый *adj.*: **з. пункт, ~ая ста́нция** filling station.

запра́вский *adj.* (*coll.*) real, true.

запра́вщик, а *m.* petrol station attendant.

запра́шива|ть, ю *impf. of* ⇒**запроси́ть**

запреде́льный *adj.* **1** lying beyond the bounds (of). **2** (*слава, цифра*) fantastic.

запресто́льный *adj.* (*eccl.*) situated behind the altar; **з. о́браз** altar-piece.

запре́т, а *m.* prohibition, ban; **быть под ~ом** to be banned; **наложи́ть з. (на**+*a.*) to place a ban (on).

запрети́тельный *adj.* prohibitive; prohibitory.

запре|ти́ть, щу́, ти́шь *pf.* (*of* ⇒**~ща́ть**) (*не позволять*) to prohibit, forbid; **врач ~ти́л мне кури́ть, врач ~ти́л мне куре́ние** the doctor has forbidden me to smoke; **«вход ~щён»** 'No Entry'; (*книгу, наркотики, оружие*) to ban.

запре́тн|ый *adj.* forbidden; **~ая зо́на** (*mil.*) restricted area; **~ая те́ма** taboo subject.

запреща́|ть, ю *impf. of* ⇒**запрети́ть**

запреща́|ться, ется *impf.* to be forbidden, to be prohibited; **«кури́ть ~ется»** 'No Smoking'.

запреще́ни|е, я *nt.* prohibition; ban; (*leg.*): **з. на иму́щество** distraint, arrest on property; **суде́бное з.** injunction.

заприме́|тить, чу, тишь *pf.* (*coll.*) **1** (*заметить*) to notice, perceive. **2** (*узнать*) to recognize, spot; **я ~тил его́ в толпе́ по кра́сной руба́шке** I spotted him in the crowd by his red shirt.

заприхо́д|овать, ую *pf. of* ⇒**прихо́довать**

запрограмми́р|овать, ую *pf. of* ⇒**программи́ровать**

запрода́ж|а, и *f.* sale.

запрода́жный *adj.* sale, selling.

запроекти́р|овать, ую *pf. of* ⇒**проекти́ровать**[1] 2

запроки́дыва|ть, ю *impf. of* ⇒**запроки́нуть**

запроки́н|уть, у, ешь *pf.* to throw back; **он захохота́л, ~ув го́лову** he threw back his head and guffawed.

запроки́н|уться, усь, ешься *pf.* to lean back, slump back.

запропа|сти́ть, щу́, сти́шь *pf.* (*coll.*) to mislay.

запропа|сти́ться, щу́сь, сти́шься *pf.* (*coll.*) to disappear; **куда́ ты ~сти́лся?** where on earth did you get to?

запропа́|сть, ду́, дёшь, *past* **~л** *pf.* (*coll.*) to get lost, disappear.

запро́с, а *m.* **1** inquiry; (*pol.*) question. **2** (*coll.*) (*о цене*) overcharging; **це́ны без ~а** fixed prices. **3** (*pl. only*) (*потребности*) needs, requirements.

запро|си́ть, шу́, ~сишь *pf.* (*of* ⇒**запра́шивать**) **1** (**о**+*p.*) to inquire (about); (+*a.*) (*попросить*) to request. **2**: **з. сли́шком высо́кую це́ну** (*coll.*) to ask an exorbitant price.

за́просто *adv.* (*coll.*) (*без формальностей*) without ceremony, without formality; (*coll.*) (*легко*) without any problem, easily.

запротоколи́р|овать, ую *pf.* to enter in the minutes.

запро|шу́, ~сишь *see* ⇒**~си́ть**

зап|ру́, рёшь *see* ⇒**~ере́ть**

запру́д|а, ы *f.* **1** (*плотина*) dam, weir. **2** (*водоём*) mill-pond.

запру|ди́ть[1], **жу́, ~ди́шь** *pf. of* ⇒**пруди́ть**

запру|ди́ть[2], **ди́т** *pf.* (*of* ⇒**запру́живать** (*fig., coll.*) (*заполнить*) to block (up); (*переполнить*) to fill to overflowing.

запру́жива|ть, ет *impf. of* ⇒**запруди́ть**[2]

запры́га|ть, ю *pf.* to begin to jump; (*coll.*): **се́рдце у неё ~ло** her heart began to thump.

запры́гива|ть, ю *impf. of* ⇒**запры́гнуть**

запры́гн|уть, у, ешь *pf.* (**за**+*a.*) to leap (over); (**на**+*a.*) to jump (onto).

запряга́|ть, ю *impf. of* ⇒**запря́чь**

запря́жк|а, и *f.* **1** (*действие*) harnessing. **2** (*упряжь*) harness.

запря́|тать, чу, чешь *pf.* (*coll.*) to hide.

запря́|таться, чусь, чешься *pf.* (*coll.*) to hide o.s.

запря́тыва|ть(ся), ю(сь) *impf. of* ⇒**запря́тать(ся)**

запря́|чь, гу́, жёшь, гу́т, *past* **~г, ~гла́** *pf.* (*of* ⇒**~га́ть**) to harness (*also fig.*); **з. воло́в** to yoke oxen.

запря́|чься, гу́сь, жёшься, гу́ться, *past* **~гся, ~гла́сь** *pf.* (*fig., coll.*) to harness o.s.; to buckle to, get down to.

запу́ганный *p.p.p. of* ⇒**запуга́ть** *and adj.* broken-spirited; frightened.

запуга́|ть, ю *pf.* to intimidate, cow; to frighten.

запу́гива|ть, ю *impf. of* ⇒**запуга́ть**

запу́дрива|ть, ю *impf. of* ⇒**запу́дрить**

запу́др|ить, ю, ишь *pf.* to powder.

за́пуск, а *m.* (*мотора*) starting; (*ракеты*) launch, launching; (*comput.*) running.

запус|ка́ть, ка́ю *impf. of* ⇒**~ти́ть**

запусте́лый *adj.* neglected; desolate.

запусте́ни|е, я *nt.* neglect; desolation.

запусте́|ть, ет *pf.* to fall into neglect; to become desolate.

запу|сти́ть[1], **щу́, ~стишь** *pf.* (*of* ⇒**~ска́ть**) **1** (+*i. and* **в**+*a.*; *coll.*) (*бросить*) to throw (at), fling (at); **он ~сти́л кирпичо́м в окно́** he flung a brick at the window. **2** (**в**+*a.*) (*засунуть*) to thrust (*hands, etc.*, into); **ко́шка ~сти́ла ко́гти в мышь** the cat dug its claws into the mouse; **з. ко́гти, ла́пы, ру́ки** (**в**+*a.*; *fig.*) to get one's hands on. **3** (*привести в действие*) to start (up); (*comput.*) to run; **з. мото́р** to start up the engine; **з. раке́ту** to launch a rocket. **4** (**в**+*a.*) (*coll.*) (*впустить*) to put (into), let loose (in); **з. коро́в на луг** to let cows loose in a meadow.

запу|сти́ть[2], **щу́, ~стишь** *pf.* (*of* ⇒**~ска́ть**) **1** (*оставить без ухода*) to neglect, allow to fall into neglect; **з. дела́** to neglect one's affairs; **з. сад** to neglect a garden. **2** (*дать развиться*) to allow to develop unchecked; **он ~сти́л на́сморк и тепе́рь заболе́л бронхи́том** he neglected his cold and now he is ill with bronchitis.

запу́тан|ный (~, ~на) *p.p.p. of* ⇒**запу́тать** *and adj.* tangled; (*fig.*) intricate, involved; **з. вопро́с** knotty question.

запу́та|ть, ю *pf.* (*of* ⇒**запу́тывать** *and* **пу́тать**) **1** (*нитки, волосы*) to tangle (up). **2** (*fig.*) (*человека*) to confuse; (*дело*) to complicate; to muddle; **его́ сообще́ние ~ло де́ло** his statement has complicated matters; **тако́го ро́да вопро́сы то́лько ~ют кандида́тов** questions of this kind will only confuse the candidates. **3** (**в** + *a.*; *fig.*) (*вовлечь*) to involve (in).

запу́та|ться, юсь *pf.* (*of* ⇒**запу́тываться** *and* **пу́таться**) **1** (*нитки, волосы*) to become entangled; to foul (*intrans.*); (**в** + *p.*) (*в сетях*) to entangle o.s. (in), be caught (in). **2** (**в** + *p.*; *fig.*) (*в деле*) to become entangled (in), become involved (in); (*дело, речь*) to become confused, complicated; (*сбиться с толку*) to get in a muddle; **з. в долга́х** to become involved in debts; **докла́дчик ~лся в слова́х** the lecturer became tied up in knots.

запу́тыва|ть(ся), ю(сь) *impf. of* ⇒**запу́тать(ся)**

запуш|и́ть, и́т *pf.* to cover lightly (*of snow or frost*).

запу́щен|ный (**~, ~на**) *p.p.p. of* ⇒**запусти́ть**[2] *and adj.* neglected.

запча́ст|и, е́й *pl.* (*sg.* **~ь, ~и** *f.*; *abbr. of* ***запасны́е ча́сти***) spare parts; spares.

запыла́|ть, ю *pf.* to blaze up, flare up.

запыл|и́ть, ю́, и́шь *pf.* (*of* ⇒**пыли́ть**) to cover with dust, make dusty.

запыл|и́ться, ю́сь, и́шься *pf.* (*of* ⇒**пыли́ться**) to become dusty.

запыха́|ться, юсь *impf.* (*coll.*) to puff, pant.

запыха́|ться, юсь *pf.* (*coll.*) to be out of breath.

запьяне́|ть, ю *pf.* (*coll.*) to get drunk.

запя́сть|е, я *nt.* wrist.

запят|а́я, о́й *f.* comma.

запятна́|ть, ю *pf. of* ⇒**пятна́ть**

зараба́тыва|ть(ся), ю(сь) *impf. of* ⇒**зарабо́тать(ся)**

зарабо́та|ть, ю *pf.* (*of* ⇒**зараба́тывать**) **1** (*приобрести работой*) to earn. **2** (*no impf.*) (*начать работать*) to begin to work; to start (up).

зарабо́та|ться, юсь *pf.* (*of* ⇒**зараба́тываться**) (*coll.*) **1** (*устать от работы*) to overwork, tire o.s. out with work. **2** (*проработать слишком долго*) to work late.

за́работн|ый *adj.*: **~ая пла́та** wages, pay, salary.

за́работ|ок, ка *m.* earnings; **лёгкий з.** easy money.

зара́внива|ть, ю *impf. of* ⇒**заровня́ть**

заража́емост|ь, и *f.* susceptibility to infection.

заража́|ть(ся), ю(сь) *impf. of* ⇒**зарази́ть(ся)**

зараже́ни|е, я *nt.* infection; (*местности*) contamination.

зара|жу́, зи́шь *see* ⇒**~зи́ть**

зара́з *adv.* (*coll.*) at once; at a sitting; at one fell swoop.

зара́з|а, ы *f.* **1** infection, contagion. **2** (*fig., coll.*) (*негодяй*) pest.

зарази́тел|ьный (~ен, ~ьна) *adj.* infectious; catching; **з. смех** infectious laughter.

зара|зи́ть, жу́, зи́шь *pf.* (*of* ⇒**~жа́ть**) (+ *i.*) to infect (with) (*also fig.*); (*местность*) to contaminate; **з. свои́м приме́ром** to infect with one's example.

зара|зи́ться, жу́сь, зи́шься *pf.* (*of* ⇒**~жа́ться**) (+ *i.*) to be infected (with); catch (*also fig.*).

зара́з|ный (~ен, ~на) *adj.* infectious; contagious; **з. больно́й** infectious case; *as n.* **з., ~ного** *m.*, **~ная, ~ной** *f.* infectious case.

зара́нее *adv.* beforehand; in good time; **заплати́ть з.** to pay in advance; **преступле́ние с з. обду́манным наме́рением** premeditated crime; **ра́доваться з.** (+ *d.*) to relish the prospect (of); to look forward (to).

зарапорт|ова́ться, у́юсь *pf.* (*coll.*) to let one's tongue run away with one.

зараста́|ть, ю *impf. of* ⇒**зарасти́**

зараст|и́, у́, ёшь, *past* **зарос́, заросла́** *pf.* **1** (+ *i.*) to be overgrown (with); **тропа́ заросла́ мхом** the path was overgrown with moss. **2** (*о ране*) to heal.

зарв|а́ться, у́сь, ёшься, *past* **~а́лся, ~ала́сь, ~а́ло́сь** *pf.* (*of* ⇒**зарыва́ться**[2]) (*coll.*) to go too far; to overstep the mark.

зарде́|ть, ю *pf.* (*poet.*) = **~ться** 1

зарде́|ться, юсь *pf.* **1** to redden, grow red. **2** (*от смущения*) to blush.

зарёван|ный (~, ~а) *adj.* (*coll.*) tearful.

за́рев|о, а *nt.* glow; **з. (от) пожа́ра** the glow of a fire.

зарегистри́р|овать, ую *pf.* (*of* ⇒**регистри́ровать**) to register.

зарегистри́р|оваться, уюсь *pf.* (*of* ⇒**регистри́роваться**) **1** to register o.s. **2** (*coll.*) (*в загсе*) to register one's marriage.

зарегистр|ова́ть(ся), у́ю(сь) *pf.* = **~и́ровать(ся)**

заре́з, а *m.* (*coll.*) (*as pred.*) disaster; **до ~у** extremely, badly, urgently; **мне до ~у ну́жно пять рубле́й** I badly need five roubles.

заре́|зать, жу, жешь *pf.* (*of* ⇒**зареза́ть** *and* **ре́зать**) **1** (*человека*) to murder; to knife; (*животное*) to slaughter; (*coll.*) (*о волке*) to devour, kill; **хоть заре́жь** (*coll.*) extremely, urgently; come what may. **2** (*fig.*) (*погубить*) to undo, be the undoing of; to do for; **без ножа́ з.** to do for; to make mincemeat of.

зареза́|ть(ся), ю(сь) *impf. of* ⇒**заре́зать(ся)**

заре́|заться, жусь, жешься *pf.* (*coll.*) to cut one's throat.

зарезерви́р|овать, ую *pf. of* ⇒**резерви́ровать**

зарека́|ться, юсь *impf. of* ⇒**заре́чься**

зарекоменд|ова́ть, у́ю *pf. only in phr.* **з. себя́** (+ *i.*) to prove o.s., show o.s. (to be); **хорошо́ з. себя́** to show to advantage.

заре|ку́сь, чёшься, ку́тся *see* ⇒**~́чься**

заре́чный *adj.* situated on the other side of the river.

заре́чь|е, я *nt.* part of town, etc., on the other side of a river.

заре́|чься, ку́сь, чёшься, ку́тся, *past* **~́кся, ~кла́сь** *pf.* (*of* ⇒**~ка́ться**) (+ *inf.*; *coll.*) to renounce; to promise to give up, vow to give up; **он ~́кся кури́ть** he has promised to give up smoking.

заржаве́|ть, ет *pf.* (*of* ⇒**ржа́веть**) to rust; to have got rusty.

заржа́влен|ный (~, ~а) *adj.* rusty.

зарис|ова́ть, у́ю *pf.* (*of* ⇒**~о́вывать**) to sketch.

зарисо́вк|а, и *f.* **1** (*действие*) sketching. **2** (*рисунок*) sketch.

зарисо́выва|ть, ю *impf. of* ⇒**зарисова́ть**

за́р|иться, юсь, ишься *impf.* (*of* ⇒**по~**) (**на** + *a.*; *coll.*) to hanker (after).

зарни́ц|а, ы *f.* summer lightning.

заровня́|ть, ю *pf.* (*of* ⇒**зара́внивать**) to level, even up; **з. я́му** to fill up a hole.

заро|ди́ть, жу́, ди́шь *pf.* (*of* ⇒**~жда́ть**) to generate, engender (*also fig.*).

заро|ди́ться, жу́сь, ди́шься *pf.* (*of* ⇒**~жда́ться**) (*возникнуть*) to arise, come into being; **у него́ ~ди́лось сомне́ние** a doubt arose in his mind.

заро́дыш, а *m.* (*biol.*) embryo; (*bot.*) bud; (*fig.*) embryo, germ; **подави́ть в ~е** to nip in the bud.

заро́дышевый *adj.* embryonic.

зарожда́|ть(ся), ю(сь) *impf. of* ⇒**зароди́ть(ся)**

зарожде́ни|е, я *nt.* conception; (*fig.*) origin.

заро|жу́, ди́шь *see* ⇒**~ди́ть**

заро́к, а *m.* (solemn) promise, vow, pledge, undertaking; **дать з.** to pledge o.s., give an undertaking.

зарон|и́ть, ю́, ~́ишь *pf.* **1** (*дать попасть*) to drop (behind); to let fall. **2** (*fig.*) (*вызвать*) to excite, arouse; **з. в ду́шу сомне́ния** to sow doubts in s.o.'s heart.

зарон|и́ться, ю́сь, ~́ишься *pf.* (**в** + *a.*; *obs.*) to sink in, make an impression (on).

за́росл|ь, и *f.* thicket.

зар|о́ю, о́ешь *see* ⇒**~ы́ть**

зарпла́т|а, ы *f.* (*abbr. of* ***за́работная пла́та***) wages, pay, salary; **сего́дня з.** today is pay day.

заруба́|ть, ю *impf. of* ⇒**заруби́ть**

зарубе́жный *adj.* foreign.

зарубе́жь|е, я *nt.* foreign countries; **бли́жнее ~** former Soviet republics.

заруб|и́ть, лю́, ~́ишь *pf.* (*of* ⇒**~а́ть**) **1** (*убить*) to hack to death. **2** (*сделать зарубку*) to notch, make an incision (on); **~и́ э́то себе́ на носу́, на лбу** (*coll.*) put that in your pipe and smoke it.

зару́бк|а, и *f.* notch; incision.

зарубц|ева́ться, у́ется *pf.* (*of* ⇒**рубцева́ться** *and* **~о́вываться**) to form a scar.

зарубцо́выва|ться, ется *impf. of* ⇒**зарубцева́ться**

заруми́нива|ть(ся), ю(сь) *impf. of* ⇒**заруми́нить(ся)**

заруми́н|ить, ю, ишь *pf.* to redden.

заруми́н|иться, юсь, ишься *pf.* **1** to redden (*intrans.*); (*о лице*) to colour (*Br.*), color (*US*). **2** (*coll.*) (*поджариться*) to brown, bake brown.

заруч|а́ться, а́юсь *impf. of* ⇒**~и́ться**

заруч|и́ться, у́сь, и́шься *pf.* (+*i.*) to secure; **з. подде́ржкой** to enlist support; **з. согла́сием** to obtain consent.

зару́чк|а, и *f.* (*coll.*) pull, protection.

зарыва́|ть, ю *impf. of* ⇒**зары́ть**

зарыва́|ться[1], юсь *impf. of* ⇒**зары́ться**

зарыва́|ться[2], юсь *impf. of* ⇒**зарва́ться**

зарыда́|ть, ю *pf.* to begin to sob.

зар|ы́ть, о́ю, о́ешь *pf.* (*of* ⇒**~ыва́ть**) to bury; **з. тала́нт в зе́млю** (*fig.*) to hide one's light under a bushel.

зар|ы́ться, о́юсь, о́ешься *pf.* (*of* ⇒**~ыва́ться[1]**) **1** to bury o.s.; **з. лицо́м в поду́шку** to bury one's head in the pillow; **з. в дере́вне** (*fig., coll.*) to bury o.s. in the country; **з. в кни́ги** to bury o.s. in one's books. **2** (*mil.*) to dig in.

зар|я́, и́, *a.* **~ю́** *and* (*rare*) **зо́рю,** *pl.* **зо́ри, зорь, ~я́м** *and* **зо́рям** *f.* **1** (*a.* **~ю́**) dawn, daybreak; **на ~е́** at dawn, at daybreak; **встать с ~ёй** to rise at crack of dawn; **что ты встал ни свет ни з.?** what made you get up at this unearthly hour? **2** (*a.* **~ю́**) **(вече́рняя) з.** sunset, evening glow; **от ~и́ до ~и́** from night to morning, all night long. **3** (*a.* **~ю́**) (*fig.*) (*начало*) start, outset; dawn, threshold. **4** (*a.* **зо́рю,** *d. pl.* **зо́рям**) (*mil.*) reveille; retreat; **бить зо́рю** to beat retreat.

заря́д, а *m.* **1** charge (*also elec.*); (*патрон*) cartridge; **холосто́й з.** blank cartridge. **2** (*fig.*) (*запас*) store, supply.

заря|ди́ть[1], жу́, ~ди́шь *pf.* (*of* ⇒**~жа́ть**) **1** (*орудие, фотоаппарат*) to load. **2** (*elec.*) (*батарею*) to charge; **~женные части́цы** charged particles.

заря|ди́ть[2], жу́, ди́шь *pf.* (*coll.*) to keep on, persist in; **с утра́ ~ди́л дождь** it has kept on raining since the morning; **он ~ди́л одно́ и то же** he keeps saying the same thing over and over again.

заря|ди́ться, жу́сь, ~ди́шься *pf.* (*of* ⇒**~жа́ться**) **1** (*о ружье*) to be loaded; (*elec.*) to be charged. **2** (*fig., coll.*) (*подбодрить себя*) to cheer o.s. up, revive o.s.

заря́дк|а, и *f.* **1** (*ружья*) loading; (*elec.*) charging. **2** (*упражнения*) exercises; drill.

заря́д|ный *adj. of* ⇒**~; з. я́щик** ammunition wagon.

заряжа́|ть(ся), ю(сь) *impf. of* ⇒**заряди́ть(ся)**

заря|жу́, ~ди́шь *see* ⇒**~ди́ть**

заса́д|а, ы *f.* ambush.

заса|ди́ть, жу́, ~дишь *pf.* (*of* ⇒**~живать**) **1** (+*a. and i.*) to plant (with); **з. сад плодо́выми дере́вьями** to plant a garden with fruit-trees. **2** (+*a.* and **в**+*a.*; *coll.*) (*воткнуть*) to plunge (into), drive (into). **3** (*coll.*) (*заключить*) to shut in, confine; to keep in; **з. (в тюрьму́)** to put in prison, lock up; **боле́знь на це́лый ме́сяц ~ди́ла меня́ в го́спиталь** illness kept me in hospital for a whole month. **4** (+*a. and* **за**+*a.*; *coll.*) to set (to); **его́ ~ди́ли за изуче́ние ру́сского языка́** he was set to learn Russian.

заса́дк|а, и *f.* planting.

заса́жива|ть, ю *impf. of* ⇒**засади́ть**

заса́жива|ться, юсь *impf.* **1** *impf. of* ⇒**засе́сть. 2** *pass. of* ⇒**~ть**

заса|жу́, ~дишь *see* ⇒**~ди́ть**

заса́лива|ть[1], ю *impf. of* ⇒**заса́лить**

заса́лива|ть[2], ю *impf. of* ⇒**засоли́ть**

заса́л|ить, ю, ишь *pf.* (*of* ⇒**~ивать[1]**) to soil, make greasy.

заса́сыва|ть, ю *impf. of* ⇒**засоса́ть**

заса́харен|ный *p.p.p. of* ⇒**заса́харить** *and adj.* candied; **~ные фру́кты** crystallized fruits, candied fruits.

заса́харива|ть, ю *impf. of* ⇒**заса́харить**

заса́хар|ить, ю, ишь *pf.* (*of* ⇒**~ивать**) to candy.

засверка́|ть, ю *pf.* to begin to sparkle, begin to twinkle.

засве|ти́ть, чу́, ~тишь *pf.* **1** (*лампаду*) to light. **2** (+*d.*; *coll.*) (*ударить*) to strike, hit. **3** (*плёнку*) to expose.

засве|ти́ться, ~тится *pf.* to light up (*also fig.*).

засветле́|ть, ю *pf.* to show up.

за́светло *adv.* (*coll.*) before nightfall, before dark.

засве|чу́, ~тишь *see* ⇒**~ти́ть**

засвиде́тельств|овать, ую *pf. of* ⇒**свиде́тельствовать** 3

засви|ста́ть, щу́, ~щешь *pf.* = **~сте́ть**

засви|сте́ть, щу́, сти́шь *pf.* to begin to whistle.

засе́в, а *m.* **1** (*действие*) sowing. **2** (*засеянная площадь*) sown area.

засева́|ть, ю *impf. of* ⇒**засе́ять**

заседа́ни|е, я *nt.* (*собрание*) meeting; (*совещание*) conference; (*суда*) session, sitting.

заседа́тел|ь, я *m.* assessor; **прися́жный з.** juror.

заседа́|ть, ю *impf.* to sit; to meet.

засе́ива|ть, ю *impf. of* ⇒**засе́ять**

засе́|к, кла *see* ⇒**~чь**

за́се́к|а, и *f.* abat(t)is.

засека́|ть, ю *impf. of* ⇒**засе́чь**

засекре́|тить, чу, тишь *pf.* **1** (*документы*) to place on secret list; to classify as secret, restrict. **2** (*человека*) to give access to secret documents; to admit to secret work.

засекре́ченный *p.p.p. of* ⇒**засекре́тить** *and adj.* secret; (*документы, сведения*) classified.

засекре́чива|ть, ю *impf. of* ⇒**засекре́тить**

засе|ку́, чёшь, ку́т *see* ⇒**~чь**

засе́|л, ла *see* ⇒**~сть**

заселе́ни|е, я *nt.* (*земли*) settlement; (*дома*) occupation.

заселённый *p.p.p. of* ⇒**засели́ть** *and adj.* populated; inhabited; **ре́дко з.** sparsely populated.

засел|и́ть, ю́, и́шь *pf.* (*of* ⇒**~я́ть**) (*землю*) to settle; to colonize; **з. но́вый дом** to occupy a new house.

засел|я́ть, я́ю *impf. of* ⇒**~и́ть**

засемен|и́ть, ю́, и́шь *pf.* to (begin to) mince (*of gait*).

зас|е́сть, я́ду, я́дешь, *past* **~е́л** *pf.* (*of* ⇒**~а́живаться**) (*coll.*) **1** (**за**+*a. or* +*inf.*) (*сесть надолго*) to sit down (to). **2** (*расположиться*) to sit firm, sit tight; to ensconce o.s.; **з. в тюрьму́** to go to prison. **3** (**в**+*p.*) (*застрять*) to lodge (in), stick (in); **пу́ля ~е́ла у него́ в боку́** a bullet had lodged in his side; **моти́в ~е́л у меня́ в голове́** (*fig.*) the tune has stuck in my head.

засе́чк|а, и *f.* **1** notch, mark. **2** (*typ.*) serif.

засе́|чь, ку́, чёшь, ку́т, *past* **~к, ~кла** *pf.* (*of* ⇒**~ка́ть**) **1** (*до смерти*) to flog to death. **2** (*сделать засечку на чём-либо*) to notch. **3** (*место*) to locate; (*время*) to note. **4** (*coll.*) (*увидеть*) to see; (*понять*) to grasp.

засе́|ять, ю, ешь *pf.* (*of* ⇒**~ва́ть** *and* ⇒**~ивать**) to sow.

заси|де́ть, ди́т *pf.* (*of* ⇒**~живать**) (*coll.*) to fly-spot.

заси|де́ться, жу́сь, ди́шься *pf.* (*of* ⇒**~живаться**) (*coll.*) to sit too long, stay too long; to sit up late; to stay late; **з. за рабо́той** to sit up late working; **з. в де́вках,** *see* ⇒**де́вка**

заси́женный *p.p.p. of* ⇒**засиде́ть** *and adj.* (*coll.*): **з. (му́хами)** fly-spotted, fly-blown.

заси́жива|ть(ся), юсь, ет(ся) *impf. of* ⇒**засиде́ть(ся)**

заси́ль|е, я *no pl.,* (*pej.*) domination, sway.

засине́|ть(ся), ю(сь) *pf.* **1** (*начать синеть*) to begin to turn blue. **2** (*показаться*) to appear blue (in the distance).

засия́|ть, ю *pf.* **1** (*начать сиять*) to begin to shine, begin to beam. **2** (*появиться*) to appear, come out; **ме́сяц ~л из-за туч** the moon appeared from behind the clouds.

заска|ка́ть, чу́, ~чешь *pf.* **1** to begin to jump, to break into a gallop. **2** (*impf.* **~кивать**) (**в**+*a.*) to gallop (away to, up to).

заска|ка́ться, чу́сь, ~чешься *pf.* (*coll.*) to gallop until exhausted.

заска́кива|ть, ю *impf. of* ⇒**заскака́ть** 2 *and* **заскочи́ть**

засквo|зи́ть, зи́т *pf.* to begin to show light through.

заскирд|ова́ть, у́ю *pf. of* **⇨скирдова́ть**

заско́к, а *m.* (*coll.*) crazy idea; **э́то у тебя́ з.?** have you gone crazy?; are you out of your mind?

заскору́злый *adj.* **1** (*кожа*) hardened, calloused. **2** (*fig.*) (*ум*) backward; (*привычки*) incorrigible.

заскору́з|нуть, ну, нешь, *past* **~, ~ла** *pf.* **1** (*руки*) to harden, coarsen, become calloused. **2** (*fig.*) to stagnate

заскоч|и́ть, у́, ~́ишь *pf.* (*of* **⇨заска́кивать**) **1** (**за**+*a.*, **на**+*a.*) to jump, spring (behind, onto). **2** (**в**+*a.*; *fig.*) to drop in (to, at).

заскуча́|ть, ю *pf.* **1** to get bored. **2** (**по**+*d.*) to begin to miss.

засла|сти́ть, щу́, сти́шь *pf.* (*of* **⇨~́щивать**) to sweeten.

за|сла́ть, шлю́, шлёшь *pf.* (*of* **⇨~сыла́ть**) to send, dispatch; **з. не по а́дресу** to send to the wrong address; **з. шпио́на** to send out a spy; **з. в глуби́нку** to exile.

засла́щива|ть, ю *impf. of* **⇨засласти́ть**

засле|зи́ться, зи́тся *pf.* to begin to water.

заслеп|и́ть, лю́, и́шь *pf.* (*of* **⇨~ля́ть**) (*coll.*) to blind.

заслепля́|ть, ю *impf. of* **⇨заслепи́ть**

засло́н, а *m.* **1** screen, barrier. **2** (*mil.*) covering force.

заслон|и́ть, ю́, и́шь *and* (*coll.*) **~́ишь** *pf.* (*of* **⇨~я́ть**) **1** (*закрыть*) to hide, cover; (*защитить*) to shield, screen. **2** (*fig.*) to push into the background.

заслон|и́ться, ю́сь, и́шся *and* (*coll.*) **~́ишься** *pf.* (*of* **⇨~я́ться**) (**от**+*g.*) to shield o.s., screen o.s. (from).

засло́нк|а, и *f.* oven-door; (*регулятор тяги*) damper.

заслон|я́ть(ся)[1], я́ю(сь) *impf. of* **⇨~и́ть(ся)**

заслоня́|ться[2], юсь *pf.* (*coll.*) to begin to pace up and down.

заслу́г|а, и *f.* service; contribution; **по ~ам** according to one's deserts; **их наказа́ли по ~ам** they got what they deserved; **у него́ больши́е ~и пе́ред родны́м го́родом** he has rendered great services to his home town.

заслу́женно *adv.* deservedly.

заслу́жен|ный (*and* ~́ный) *p.p.p. of* **⇨заслужи́ть** *and adj.* **1** (*награда*) deserved, merited. **2** (*артист*) meritorious, of merit; (*as honorific in former USSR*) Honoured. **3**: **~́ный профе́ссор** professor emeritus.

заслу́жива|ть, ю *impf.* (*of* **⇨заслужи́ть**) (+*g.*) to deserve, merit.

заслу́жива|ться, юсь *impf.* **1** *impf. of* **⇨заслужи́ться. 2** *pass. of* **⇨~ть**

заслуж|и́ть, у́, ~́ишь *pf.* (*of* **⇨~́ивать**) (+*a.*) to deserve, merit; (*выслужить*) to win, earn.

заслуж|и́ться, у́сь, ~́ишься *pf.* (*of* **⇨~́иваться**) (*coll.*) to serve for too long.

заслу́ш|ать, аю *pf.* (*of* **⇨~ивать**) **1** (*сообщение*) to hear, listen to (*a public or official pronouncement*). **2** (*coll.*) (*пластинку*) to wear out by excessive playing.

заслу́ш|аться, аюсь *pf.* (*of* **⇨~иваться**) (+*g.*) to listen spellbound (to).

заслу́шива|ть(ся), ю(сь) *impf. of* **⇨заслу́шать(ся)**

заслы́ш|ать, у, ишь *pf.* **1** to hear, catch. **2** (*coll.*) (*уловить обонянием*) to smell; **з. за́пах** to detect a smell.

заслы́ш|аться, ится *pf.* (*coll.*) to begin to be audible; to be able to be heard.

заслю́нива|ть, ю *impf. of* **⇨заслюни́ть**

заслюн|и́ть, ю́, и́шь *pf.* (*of* **⇨слюни́ть** *and* **~́ивать**) (*coll.*) to slobber over.

засма́лива|ть, ю *impf. of* **⇨засмоли́ть**

засма́трива|ть, ю *impf.* (**в**+*a.*; *coll.*) to look (into); to peep (into); **з. в окно́ к кому́-н.** to look in at s.o.'s window.

засма́трива|ться, юсь *impf. of* **⇨засмотре́ться**

засме́ива|ть, ю *impf. of* **⇨засмея́ть**

засме|я́ть, ю́, ёшь *pf.* (*coll.*) to ridicule.

засме|я́ться, ю́сь, ёшься *pf.* to begin to laugh.

засмол|и́ть, ю́, и́шь *pf.* (*of* **засма́ливать**) to tar; to caulk.

засмо́рканный *adj.* (*coll.*) snotty.

засмотр|е́ться, ю́сь, ~́ишься *pf.* (*of* **⇨засма́триваться**) (**на**+*a.*) to be lost in contemplation (of), be carried away (by the sight of).

засне́жен|ный (~, ~а) *adj.* snow-covered.

засн|иму́, и́мешь *see* **⇨~я́ть**

засн|у́ть, у́, ёшь *pf.* (*of* **⇨засыпа́ть[1]**) to go to sleep, fall asleep.

засн|я́ть, иму́, и́мешь, *past* **~я́л, ~яла́, ~я́ло** *pf.* to photograph, snap (*coll.*); (*cin. sl.*) to shoot.

засо́в, а *m.* bolt, bar.

засо́выва|ть, ю *impf. of* **⇨засу́нуть**

засо́л, а *m.* salting; pickling.

засол|и́ть, ю́, ~́ишь *pf.* (*of* **⇨заса́ливать[2]**) to salt; to pickle.

засо́льщик, а *m.* salter, pickler.

засоре́ни|е, я *nt.* (*пола*) littering; (*трубы*) obstruction, clogging up.

засор|и́ть, ю́, и́шь *pf.* (*of* **⇨~я́ть**) **1** (*трубу*) to clog, block up, stop. **2** (*пол*) to litter; (*глаза*) to get dirt into; (*fig.*): **з. чью-н. ду́шу** to poison s.o.'s mind.

засор|и́ться, и́тся *pf.* (*of* **⇨~я́ться**) to become obstructed, blocked up.

засоря́|ть(ся), ю, ет(ся) *impf. of* **⇨засори́ть(ся)**

засо́с, а *m.* sucking in.

засос|а́ть, у́, ёшь *pf.* (*of* **⇨заса́сывать**) **1** (*втянуть*) to suck in, engulf, swallow up (*also fig.*). **2** (*начать сосать*) to begin to suck.

засо́х|нуть, ну, нешь, *past* **~, ~ла** *pf.* (*of* **⇨засыха́ть**) **1** (*о булке, красках*) to dry (up). **2** (*о траве*) to wither.

за́спан|ный (~, ~а) *adj.* (*coll.*) sleepy.

засп|а́ть, лю́, и́шь, *past* **~а́л, ~ала́, ~а́ло** *pf.* (*coll.*) to forget about after sleeping; to sleep off.

засп|а́ться, лю́сь, и́шься, *past* **~а́лся, ~ала́сь, ~а́лось** *pf.* (*of* **⇨засыпа́ться[1]**) (*coll.*) to oversleep.

заспирт|ова́ть, у́ю *pf.* (*of* **⇨~о́вывать**) to preserve in alcohol.

заспирто́выва|ть, ю *impf. of* **⇨заспиртова́ть**

засп|лю́, и́шь *see* **⇨~а́ть**

заспо́р|ить, ю, ишь *pf.* to begin to argue.

заспо́р|иться, юсь, ишься *pf.* (*coll.*) to get carried away by argument.

заспор|и́ться, и́тся *pf.* (*coll.*) to go well; to be a success; to take off.

засрам|и́ть, лю́, и́шь *pf.* (*coll.*) to put to shame.

засра́н|ец, ца *m.* (*vulg.*) shit, turd (*person*).

засра́н|ка, ки *f. of* **⇨~ец**

заста́в|а, ы *f.* **1** (*пограничная застава*) border post. **2** (*hist., mil.*) (*шлагбаум*) barrier. **3** (*mil.*) picket; outpost.

заста|ва́ть, ю́, ёшь *impf. of* **⇨~́ть**

заста́в|ить[1], лю, ишь *pf.* (*of* **⇨~ля́ть[1]**) **1** (*загромоздить*) to cram, fill; **з. ко́мнату ме́белью** to cram a room with furniture. **2** (*загородить*) to block up, obstruct.

заста́в|ить[2], лю, ишь *pf.* (*of* **⇨~ля́ть[2]**) (+*a. and inf.*) (*принудить*) to compel, force, make; **он ~ил нас ждать себя́ два часа́** he kept us waiting for two hours.

заста́вк|а, и *f.* **1** (*typ.*) headpiece. **2** (*TV*) repeated image at the start of TV programme; logo; **музыка́льная з.** signature tune.

заставля́|ть[1,2], ю *impf. of* **⇨заста́вить[1,2]**

заста́ива|ться, юсь *impf. of* **⇨застоя́ться**

заста́|ну, нешь *see* **⇨~ть**

застаре́лый *adj.* inveterate; (*болезнь*) chronic.

заста́|ть, ну, нешь *pf.* (*of* **⇨~ва́ть**) to find; **вы его́ ~ли до́ма?** did you find him in?; **я ~л его́ ещё спя́щим** I found him still asleep; **з. врасплóх** to catch napping; **з. на ме́сте преступле́ния** to catch red-handed.

заста|ю́, ёшь *see* **⇨~ва́ть**

застега́|ть, ю *pf.* (*coll.*) **1** to begin to flog. **2**: **з. до́ смерти** to flog to death.

застёгива|ть, ю *impf. of* **⇨застегну́ть**

застёгива|ться, юсь *impf.* **1** *impf. of* **⇨застегну́ться. 2** *pass. of* **⇨~ть. 3** to fasten, do up (*intrans.*);

З

во́рот ~ется на пу́говицу the collar does up with a button.

застег|ну́ть, ну́, нёшь *pf.* (*of* ⇒**~́ивать**) to fasten, do up; **з. (на пу́говицы)** to button up.

застег|ну́ться, ну́сь, нёшься *pf.* (*of* ⇒**~́иваться**) to button o.s. up; **з. на все пу́говицы** to do up all one's buttons.

застёжк|а, и *f.* fastening; clasp; **з. «ве́лкро»** Velcro (*propr.*) fastener; **з.-мо́лния** zip fastener.

застекл|и́ть, ю́, и́шь *pf.* (*of* ⇒**~я́ть**) to glaze, fit with glass; **з. портре́т** to frame a portrait.

застекл|я́ть, я́ю *impf. of* ⇒**~и́ть**

застел|и́ть, ю́, ~́ешь *pf.* = **застла́ть 1**

застенографи́ровать *pf. of* ⇒**стенографи́ровать**

засте́н|ок, ка *m.* torture-chamber.

засте́нчив|ый (~, ~а) *adj.* shy; bashful.

застесня́|ться, юсь *pf.* (*coll.*) to come over all shy.

засти́|г, гла *see* ⇒**~чь**

засти|га́ть, га́ю *impf. of* ⇒**~́гнуть** *and* **~́чь**

засти́|гнуть = **~чь**

застила́|ть, ю *impf. of* ⇒**застла́ть**

застир|а́ть, а́ю *pf.* (*of* ⇒**~ывать**) (*coll.*) **1** (*отмыть*) to wash off. **2** (*испортить стиркой*) to ruin by washing.

засти́рыва|ть, ю *impf. of* ⇒**застира́ть**

за́|стить, щу, стишь *impf.* (*coll.*): **з. свет** to stand in the light.

засти́|чь, гну, гнешь, *past* **~г, ~гла** *pf.* (*of* ⇒**~га́ть**) to catch; to take unawares; **нас ~гла гроза́** we were caught by the storm.

заст|ла́ть, елю́, е́лешь *pf.* (*of* ⇒**~ила́ть**) **1** (+*i.*) to cover (with); **з. ковро́м** to carpet, lay a carpet (over). **2** (*fig.*) to hide from view; to cloud; **облака́ ~ла́ли со́лнце** clouds obscured the sun; **слёзы ~ла́ли её глаза́** tears dimmed her eyes. **3** (*кровать*) to make.

засто́|й, я *m.* stagnation (*fig.*); **в ~е** at a standstill; (*econ.*) depression.

засто́йный *adj.* stagnant (*fig.*).

засто́ль|е, я *nt.* (*coll.*) celebratory meal.

засто́льн|ый *adj.* table-, occurring at table; **~ая бесе́да** table-talk; **~ая пе́сня** drinking-song.

засто́порива|ть(ся), ю(сь) *impf. of* ⇒**засто́порить(ся)**

засто́пор|ить, ю, ишь, *pf.* (*of* ⇒**~ивать**) (*tech.*) to stop; (*fig., coll.*) to bring to a standstill.

засто́пор|иться, юсь, ишься *pf.* (*of* ⇒**~иваться**) (*tech.*) to stop (*of a machine*); (*fig., coll.*) to come to a standstill.

засто|я́ться, ю́сь, и́шься *pf.* (*of* ⇒**заста́иваться**) **1** (*простоять слишком долго*) to stand too long. **2** (*испортиться*) to stagnate.

застра́гива|ть, ю *impf. of* ⇒**застрога́ть**

застра́ива|ть, ю *impf. of* ⇒**застро́ить**

застрахо́ван|ный *p.p.p. of* ⇒**застрахова́ть** *and adj.* insured; *as n.* **з., ~ного** *m.* insured person.

застрах|ова́ть, у́ю *pf.* (*of* ⇒**страхова́ть** *and* **~о́вывать**) (**от**+*g.*) to insure (against).

застрах|ова́ться, у́юсь *pf.* (*of* ⇒**страхова́ться** *and* **~о́вываться**) to insure o.s.

застрахо́выва|ть(ся), ю(сь) *impf. of* ⇒**застрахова́ть(ся)**

застра́чива|ть, ю *impf. of* ⇒**застрочи́ть**

застраща́|ть, ю *pf.* (*coll.*) to frighten, intimidate.

застра́щива|ть, ю *impf. of* ⇒**застраща́ть**

застрева́|ть, ю *impf. of* ⇒**застря́ть**

застре́лива|ть(ся), ю(сь) *impf. of* ⇒**застрели́ть(ся)**

застрел|и́ть, ю́, ~́ишь *pf.* (*of* ⇒**~́ивать**) to shoot (dead).

застрел|и́ться, ю́сь, ~́ишься *pf.* (*of* ⇒**~́иваться**) to shoot o.s.; to blow one's brains out.

застре́льщик, а *m.* pioneer, leader; **з. но́вых мод** trendsetter.

застрога́|ть, ю *pf.* (*of* ⇒**застра́гивать**) to plane (down).

застро́енный *p.p.p. of* ⇒**застро́ить** *and adj.* built-up.

застро́|ить, ю, ишь *pf.* (*of* ⇒**застра́ивать**) to build on, develop.

застро́йк|а, и *f.* building; development; **пра́во ~и** building permit.

застроч|и́ть, у́, ~́ишь *pf.* **1** (*impf.* **застра́чивать**) (*зашить*) to sew up, stitch up. **2** (*coll.*) (*письмо*) to dash off. **3** (*coll.*) (*о пулемёте*) to blaze, rattle away (*of or with automatic weapons*).

застру́га́|ть, ю *pf.* = **застрога́ть**

застру́гива|ть, ю *impf. of* ⇒**застру́га́ть**

застря́|ну, нешь *see* ⇒**~ть**

застря́|ть, ну, нешь *pf.* (*of* ⇒**застрева́ть**) **1** to stick; **з. в грязи́** to get stuck in the mud; **слова́ ~ли у него́ в го́рле** the words stuck in his throat. **2** (*fig., coll.*) (*задержаться*) to be held up; to become bogged down.

засту|ди́ть, жу́, ~́дишь *pf.* (*of* ⇒**~́живать**) (*coll.*) to expose to cold; **~ го́рло** to get a sore throat.

засту|ди́ться, жу́сь, ~́дишься *pf.* (*of* ⇒**~́живаться**) (*coll.*) to catch cold, catch a chill.

засту́жива|ть(ся), ю(сь) *impf. of* ⇒**застуди́ть(ся)**

засту|жу́, ~́дишь *see* ⇒**~ди́ть**

за́ступ, а *m.* spade.

заступа́|ть(ся), ю(сь) *impf. of* ⇒**заступи́ть(ся)**

заступ|и́ть, лю́, ~́ишь *pf.* (*of* ⇒**~а́ть**): **з. (на пост)** (*coll.*) to take up (one's post); to start duty (*at the beginning of a shift*).

заступ|и́ться, лю́сь, ~́ишься *pf.* (**за**+*a.*) to stand up for; to plead (for).

засту́пник, а *m.* defender, intercessor.

засту́пни|ца, цы *f. of* ⇒**~к**

засту́пничеств|о, а *nt.* intercession.

застыва́|ть, ю *impf. of* ⇒**засты́ть**

засты|ди́ть, жу́, ди́шь *pf.* (*coll.*) to shame.

засты|ди́ться, жу́сь, ди́шься *pf.* (*coll.*) to become embarrassed.

засты|жу́, ди́шь *see* ⇒**~ди́ть**

засты́лый *adj.* (*coll.*) congealed; stiff.

засты́|ну, нешь *see* ⇒**~ть**

засты́|нуть = **~ть**

засты́|ть *and* **~нуть, ну, нешь** *pf.* (*of* ⇒**~ва́ть**) **1** (*о желе, цементе*) to set; (*о лаве*) to harden. **2** (*coll.*) (*о руках, трупе*) to become stiff; (*fig.*): **з. от у́жаса** to be paralysed with fright. **3** (*coll.*) (*о воде*) to freeze (*also fig.*).

засу|ди́ть, жу́, ~дишь *pf.* (*of* ⇒**~́живать**) (*coll.*) to condemn.

засуе|ти́ться, чу́сь, ти́шься *pf.* to begin bustling about, begin to fuss.

засу́жива|ть, ю *impf. of* ⇒**засуди́ть**

засу|жу́, ~́дишь *see* ⇒**~ди́ть**

засу́н|уть, у, ешь *pf.* (*of* ⇒**засо́вывать**) to stick in, thrust in; **з. ру́ки в карма́н** to thrust one's hands into one's pockets.

за́сух|а, и *f.* drought.

засухоусто́йчив|ый (~, ~а) *adj.* (*agric.*) drought-resistant.

засу́чива|ть, ю *impf. of* ⇒**засучи́ть**

засуч|и́ть, у́, ~́ишь *pf.* (*of* ⇒**~́ивать**) (**рукава́**, *etc.*) to roll up (*sleeves, etc.*).

засу́шива|ть(ся), ю(сь) *impf. of* ⇒**засуши́ть(ся)**

засуш|и́ть, у́, ~ишь *pf.* (*of* ⇒**~́ивать**) to dry up (*plants; also fig.*).

засуш|и́ться, у́сь, ~и́шься *pf.* (*of* ⇒**~́иваться**) to dry up (*intrans.*), shrivel.

засу́шлив|ый (~, ~а) *adj.* dry, droughty.

засчит|а́ть, а́ю *pf.* (*of* ⇒**~ывать**) to take into consideration; **з. в упла́ту до́лга** to reckon towards payment of a debt.

засчи́тыва|ть, ю *impf. of* ⇒**засчита́ть**

засыла́|ть, ю *impf. of* ⇒**засла́ть**

засы́лк|а, и *f.* sending, dispatching.

засы́п|ать[1], лю, лешь *pf.* (*of* ⇒**~а́ть[2]**) **1** (*яму*) to fill up. **2** (+*i.*) (*покрыть*) to cover (with), strew (with); **доро́жка была́ ~ана опа́вшими ли́стьями** the path was strewn with fallen leaves. **3** (+*i.*; *fig., coll.*): **з. вопро́сами** to bombard with questions; **з. поздравле́ниями** to shower congratulations (on). **4** (+*a. or g.* **в**+*a.*; *coll.*) to put (into); **з. овса́ в я́сли** to pour oats into the manger. **5** (*coll.*) (*студента*) to fail.

засы́п|ать[2], лю, лешь *pf.* (*of* ⇒**~а́ть[3]**) (*sl.*) to give away, betray.

засыпа́|ть[1], ю *impf. of* ⇒**засну́ть**

засыпа́|ть[2,3], **ю** *impf. of* ⇒**засы́пать**[1,2]

засы́п|аться, люсь, лешься *pf.* (*of* ⇒**～а́ться**[2]) **1** (*попасть куда-н. внутрь*) to get into; **песо́к ～ался мне в башмаки́** I have got sand into my shoes. **2** (+*i.*) (*наполниться чем-н. сыпучим*) to be filled (with); (*покрыться чем-н. сыпучим*) to be covered (with). **3** (*coll.*) (*попасться*) to be caught; (*sl.*) to be nabbed. **4** (*coll.*) (*провалиться*) to fail, come to grief, slip up.

засыпа́|ться[1], **юсь** *impf. of* ⇒**заспа́ться**

засыпа́|ться[2], **юсь** *impf. of* ⇒**засы́паться**

засы́пк|а, и *f.* **1** (*ямы*) filling up; (*семян*) strewing. **2** (*зерна*) pouring in, putting in.

засыха́|ть, ю *impf. of* ⇒**засо́хнуть**

зас|я́ду, я́дешь *see* ⇒**～е́сть**

затавр|и́ть, ю́, и́шь *pf.* (*of* ⇒**таври́ть**) to brand (*cattle, etc.*).

затаён|ный *p.p.p. of* ⇒**затаи́ть** *and adj.* secret; suppressed; **～ная мечта́** secret dream.

зата́ива|ть(ся), ю(сь) *impf. of* ⇒**затаи́ть(ся)**

зата|и́ть, ю́, и́шь *pf.* (*of* ⇒**～́ивать**) (*мечту, злобу*) to harbour (*Br.*), harbor (*US*), cherish; **з. оби́ду (на** + *a.*) to nurse a grievance (against); **з. дыха́ние** to hold one's breath.

зата|и́ться, ю́сь, и́шься *pf.* (*of* ⇒**～́иваться**) (*coll.*) to hide (*intrans.*); **з. в себе́** (*fig.*) to become reserved, withdraw into o.s.

зата́лкива|ть, ю *impf. of* ⇒**затолка́ть** *and* **затолкну́ть**

зата́плива|ть, ю *impf. of* ⇒**затопи́ть**[1]

зата́птыва|ть, ю *impf. of* ⇒**затопта́ть**

зата́сканный *p.p.p. of* ⇒**затаска́ть** *and adj.* worn-out; threadbare; (*fig.*) hackneyed, trite.

затаск|а́ть, а́ю *pf.* (*of* ⇒**～́ивать**[1]) (*coll.*) **1** (*одежду*) to wear out; (*fig.*) to make hackneyed, make trite. **2** (*по гостям, магазинам*) to drag about; **з. по суда́м** to drag through the courts.

затаск|а́ться, а́юсь *pf.* (*of* ⇒**～́иваться**) (*coll.*) to wear out, become worn out; to become dirty (with wear).

зата́скива|ть[1], **ю** *impf. of* ⇒**затаска́ть**

зата́скива|ть[2], **ю** *impf. of* ⇒**затащи́ть**

зата́скива|ться, юсь *impf. of* ⇒**затаска́ться**

зата́чива|ть, ю *impf. of* ⇒**заточи́ть**[1]

затащ|и́ть, у́, ～́ишь *pf.* (*of* ⇒**зата́скивать**[2]) (*coll.*) to drag off, drag away; (*fig.*): **они́ ～и́ли его́ в теа́тр** they have dragged him off to the theatre (*Br.*), theater (*US*).

затвердева́|ть, ю *impf. of* ⇒**затверде́ть**

затверде́лост|ь, и *f.* = **затверде́ние**

затверде́лый *adj.* hardened.

затверде́ни|е, я *nt.* **1** hardening. **2** (*med.*) callus.

затверде́|ть, ю *pf.* (*of* ⇒**～ва́ть**) (*о земле, цементе*) to harden, become hard; (*о жидкости*) to set.

затвер|ди́ть, жу́, ди́шь *pf.* (*of* ⇒**～́живать**) (*coll.*) to learn by rote.

затве́ржива|ть, ю *impf. of* ⇒**затверди́ть**

затво́р, а *m.* **1** (*винтовки*) bolt; breech-block; (*плотины*) flood-gate. **2** (*phot.*) shutter.

затвор|и́ть, ю́, ～́ишь *pf.* (*of* ⇒**～я́ть**) to shut, close.

затвор|и́ться, ю́сь, ～́ишься *pf.* (*of* ⇒**～я́ться**) **1** (*о двери*) to shut, close (*intrans.*). **2** (*о человеке*) to shut o.s. in, lock o.s. in. **3** (*eccl.*): **з. в монасты́рь, в монастыре́** to go into a monastery.

затво́рник, а *m.* hermit, recluse; **он живёт соверше́нным ～ом** (*fig.*) he is a complete recluse.

затво́рни|ца, цы *f. of* ⇒**～к**

затво́рни|ческий *adj. of* ⇒**～к;** solitary; **～ческая жизнь** the life of a recluse.

затво́рничеств|о, а *nt.* (*eccl.*) seclusion, solitary life.

затвор|я́ть(ся), я́ю(сь) *impf. of* ⇒**～и́ть(ся)**

затева́|ть, ю *impf. of* ⇒**зате́ять**

зате́йлив|ый (～, ～а) *adj.* **1** (*сложный*) intricate, involved; **～ая речь** involved discourse; **～ое украше́ние** intricate ornament. **2** (*замысловатый*) ingenious; inventive; **～ая игру́шка** ingenious toy.

зате́йник, а *m.* **1** (*шутник*) practical joker; humorist. **2** (*организатор массовых развлечений*) organizer of entertainments.

зате́|йный (～ен, ～йна) *adj.* (*coll.*) = **～йливый;** (*забавный*) amusing.

зате́йщик, а *m.* (*coll.*) instigator.

затёк, ла́ *see* ⇒**зате́чь**

затека́|ть, ю *impf. of* ⇒**зате́чь**

зате|ку́, чёшь, ку́т *see* ⇒**～чь**

зате́м *adv.* **1** (*после этого*) after that, then, next. **2** (*для этого*) for that reason; **з. что** because, since, as; **заче́м ты прие́хала? з., что слыха́ла, что ты заболе́л** why have you come? because I heard that you had been taken ill; **з. что́бы** in order that; **она́ прие́хала з., что́бы уха́живать за тобо́й** she has come (in order) to look after you.

затемне́ни|е, я *nt.* **1** (*действие*) darkening; obscuring (*also fig.*). **2** (*med.*) dark patch. **3** (*mil.*) black-out. **4** (*psych.*) black-out.

затемн|и́ть, ю́, и́шь *pf.* (*of* ⇒**～я́ть**) **1** to darken; to obscure (*also fig.*). **2** (*mil.*) to black-out.

затемн|и́ться, ю́сь, и́шься *pf.* (*of* ⇒**～я́ться**) to become dark; to become obscure; (*fig.*) to become obscured, become clouded.

за́темно *adv.* (*coll.*) before daybreak.

затемн|я́ть(ся), я́ю(сь) *impf. of* ⇒**～и́ть(ся)**

затен|и́ть, ю́, и́шь *pf.* (*of* ⇒**～я́ть**) to shade.

затен|я́ть, я́ю *impf. of* ⇒**～и́ть**

зат|ере́ть, ру́, рёшь, *past* **～ёр, ～ёрла** *pf.* (*of* ⇒**～ира́ть**) **1** (*стереть*) to rub out. **2** (*стеснить*) to block, jam; (*impers.*): **су́дно ～ёрло льда́ми** the ship was ice-bound; (*fig., coll.*): **з. кого́-н.** to keep s.o. down, impede s.o.'s career.

зат|ере́ться, ру́сь, рёшься, *past* **～ёрся, ～ёрлась** *pf.* (*of* ⇒**～ира́ться**) (*coll.*) (**в** + *a.*) to get (into), worm one's way (into).

зате́рива|ть(ся), ю(сь) *impf. of* ⇒**затеря́ть(ся)**

зате́рянный *p.p.p. of* ⇒**затеря́ть** *and adj.* forgotten, forsaken.

затер|я́ть, я́ю *pf.* (*of* ⇒**～́ивать**) (*coll.*) to lose, mislay.

затер|я́ться, я́юсь *pf.* (*of* ⇒**～́иваться**) to be lost, be mislaid; (*fig.*) to become forgotten; **моё перо́ ～я́лось** (*coll.*) my pen has vanished; **з. в толпе́** to be lost in a crowd.

зате|са́ть, шу́, ～́шешь *pf.* (*of* ⇒**～́сывать**) to rough hew; to sharpen (*stake, etc.*).

зате|са́ться, шу́сь, ～́шешься *pf.* (*of* ⇒**～́сываться**) (*coll.*) to worm one's way in, intrude.

затесн|и́ть, ю́, и́шь *pf.* (*of* ⇒**～я́ть**) (*coll.*) **1** to jostle, press. **2** (*fig.*) to oppress, persecute.

затесн|и́ться, ю́сь, и́шься *pf.* (*of* ⇒**～я́ться**) (*coll.*) to begin to crowd.

затесн|я́ть(ся), я́ю(сь) *impf. of* ⇒**～и́ть(ся)**

затёсыва|ть(ся), ю(сь) *impf. of* ⇒**затеса́ть(ся)**

зате́|чь, ку́, чёшь, ку́т, *past* **～̈к, ～кла́** *pf.* (*of* ⇒**～ка́ть**) **1** (**в** + *a.*; **за** + *a.*) to pour, flow, leak (into; behind). **2** (*распухнуть*) to swell up. **3** (*онеметь*) to become numb; **у меня́ нога́ ～кла́** my foot's gone numb.

зате́|я, и *f.* **1** (*замысел*) undertaking, enterprise, venture. **2** (*usu. pl.*) (*забавная*) piece of fun; escapade; practical joke; **без ～й** simply, unpretentiously.

зате́|ять, ю *pf.* (*of* ⇒**～ва́ть**) (*coll.*) (*путешествие*) to undertake; (*игру*) to organize; (*разговор, драку, спор*) to start.

затира́|ть(ся), ю(сь) *impf. of* ⇒**затере́ть(ся)**

зати́ск|ать, аю *pf.* (*of* ⇒**～ивать**) (*coll.*) to smother with caresses.

зати́скива|ть(ся), ю(сь) *impf. of* ⇒**зати́скать** *and* **зати́снуть(ся)**

зати́с|нуть, ну, нешь *pf.* (*of* ⇒**～кивать**) (*coll.*) to squeeze in.

зати́с|нуться, нусь, нешься *pf.* (*of* ⇒**～киваться**) (*coll.*) to squeeze (o.s.) in.

затих|а́ть, а́ю *impf. of* ⇒**～нуть**

зати́х|нуть, ну, нешь, *past* **～, ～ла** *pf.* (*of* ⇒**～а́ть**) (*о звуке, ветре, буре*) to

3

die down, abate; (*о человеке*) to quieten down (*Br.*), quiet down (*US*).

зати́шь|е, я *nt.* calm; lull.

затк|а́ть, у́, ёшь, *past* **~а́л, ~ала́, ~а́ло** *pf.* (+*a. and i.*) to cover all over with a woven pattern.

заткн|у́ть, у́, ёшь *pf.* (*of* ⇒**затыка́ть**) **1** (+*a. and i.*) to stop up; to plug; **з. буты́лку про́бкой** to cork a bottle; **з. рот, гло́тку кому́-н.** (*coll.*) to shut s.o. up; **~и́ гло́тку!** shut your mouth! **2** (*засунуть*) to stick, thrust; **з. кого́-н. за по́яс** (*fig., coll.*) to outdo s.o.

заткн|у́ться, у́сь, ёшься *pf.* (*coll.*) to shut up; **~и́сь!** shut up!

затмева́|ть, ю *impf. of* ⇒**затми́ть**

затме́ни|е, я *nt.* **1** (*astron.*) eclipse. **2** (*fig., coll.*) black-out.

затм|и́ть, и́шь *pf.* (*of* ⇒**~ева́ть**) **1** to obscure. **2** (*fig.*) to eclipse; to overshadow.

зато́ *conj.* (*coll.*) but then, but on the other hand; but to make up for it; **до́рого, з. хоро́шая вещь** it is expensive, but then it is good stuff.

затова́ренност|ь, и *f.* (*econ.*) glut.

затова́ренный *p.p.p. of* ⇒**затова́рить** *and adj.* (*econ.*) surplus.

затова́ривани|е, я *nt.* (*товаров*) stockpiling; (*магазина*) overstocking.

затова́рива|ть(ся), ю(сь) *impf. of* ⇒**затова́рить(ся)**

затова́р|ить, ю, ишь *pf.* (*of* ⇒**~ивать**) (*econ.*) to stockpile; to overstock.

затова́р|иться, юсь, ишься *pf.* (*of* ⇒**~иваться**) (*econ.*) **1** to be overstocked. **2** (*coll.*) to have a surplus.

затолка́|ть, ю *pf.* (*of* ⇒**зата́лкивать**) to jostle.

затолкн|у́ть, у́, ёшь *pf.* (*of* ⇒**зата́лкивать**) (*coll.*) to shove in.

зато́н, а *m.* **1** (*залив*) backwater. **2** (*место стоянки и ремонта судов*) boat yard.

затон|у́ть, у́, ~ешь *pf.* to sink (*intrans.*).

затоп|и́ть¹, лю́, ~ишь *pf.* (*of* ⇒**зата́пливать**) (*печь*) to light; (*включить отопление*) to turn on the heating.

затоп|и́ть², лю́, ~ишь *pf.* (*of* ⇒**~ля́ть**) **1** (*остров, окрестности*) to flood; to submerge. **2** (*судно*) to sink; **з. кора́бль** to scuttle a ship.

затопля́|ть, ю *impf. of* ⇒**затопи́ть²**

затоп|та́ть, чу́, ~чешь *pf.* (*of* ⇒**зата́птывать**) (*траву, цветы*) to trample down; (*костёр, папиросу*) to stamp out; (*убить*) to trample to death.

затоп|чу́, ~чешь *see* ⇒**~та́ть**

зато́р, а *m.* blocking, obstruction; **з. у́личного движе́ния** traffic-jam, congestion.

затормо|зи́ть, жу́, зи́шь *pf. of* ⇒**тормози́ть**

затормош|и́ть, у́, и́шь *pf.* (*coll.*) to pester.

заточ|а́ть, а́ю *impf. of* ⇒**~и́ть²**

заточе́ни|е, я *nt.* confinement; incarceration, captivity.

заточ|и́ть¹, у́, ~ишь *pf.* (*of* ⇒**зата́чивать**) to sharpen.

заточ|и́ть², у́, ~и́шь *pf.* (*of* ⇒**~а́ть**) to confine, shut up; to incarcerate.

затрав|и́ть, лю́, ~ишь *pf.* (*of* ⇒**трави́ть¹** *and* **~ливать**) to hunt down; (*fig., coll.*) to persecute.

затра́влива|ть, ю *impf. of* ⇒**затрави́ть**

затра́гива|ть, ю *impf. of* ⇒**затро́нуть**

затрапе́зный *adj.* (*coll.*) **1** (*будничный*) working-, every-day. **2** (*заношенный*) shabby.

затра́т|а, ы *f.* **1** (*действие*) expenditure. **2** (*usu. pl.*) (*расходы*) expenses, outlay.

затра́|тить, чу, тишь *pf.* (*of* ⇒**~чивать**) to expend, spend.

затра́чива|ть, ю *impf. of* ⇒**затра́тить**

затре́б|овать, ую *pf.* to request, require; to ask for.

затреп|а́ть, лю́, ~лешь *pf.* (*of* ⇒**~ывать**) to wear out; to make dirty (with wear); **з. чьё-н. и́мя** to give s.o. a bad name.

затреп|а́ться, лю́сь, ~лешься *pf.* (*of* **~ываться**) **1** to wear out (*intrans.*), be worn out. **2** (*fig.*): **я совсе́м ~а́лся** (*coll.*) I have stayed gossiping too long.

затрёпыва|ть(ся), ю(сь) *impf. of* ⇒**затрепа́ть(ся)**

затре́щин|а, ы *f.* (*coll.*) box on the ears.

затро́н|уть, у, ешь *pf.* (*of* ⇒**затра́гивать**) **1** (*нанести ущерб*) to affect; (*о пуле*) to touch, graze. **2** (*fig.*) to touch (on); **з. вопро́с** to broach a question; **з. чьё-н. самолю́бие** to wound s.o.'s self-esteem.

затрудне́ни|е, я *nt.* difficulty.

затруднённый *p.p.p. of* ⇒**затрудни́ть** *and adj.* laboured (*Br.*), labored (*US*).

затрудни́тельност|ь, и *f.* difficulty; straits.

затрудни́тел|ьный (~ен, ~ьна) *adj.* difficult; embarrassing.

затрудн|и́ть, ю́, и́шь *pf.* (*of* ⇒**~я́ть**) **1** (*кого-н.*) to trouble; to cause trouble (to); to embarrass. **2** (*что-н.*) to make difficult; to hamper.

затрудн|и́ться, ю́сь, и́шся *pf.* (*of* ⇒**~я́ться**) (+*inf. or i.*) to find difficulty (in); **з. отве́том** to find difficulty in replying; **он ~и́лся испо́лнить мою́ про́сьбу** he found difficulty in complying with my request.

затрудн|я́ть(ся), я́ю(сь) *impf. of* ⇒**~и́ть(ся)**

затума́н|ивать(ся), иваю(сь), иваешь(ся) *impf. of* ⇒**~ить(ся)**

затума́н|ить, ю, ишь *pf.* (*of* ⇒**~ивать**) **1** to befog; to cloud, dim; (*impers.*): **~ило горизо́нт** the horizon was obscured by fog; **слёзы ~или её глаза́** tears dimmed her eyes. **2** (*fig.*) to obscure.

затума́н|иться, юсь, ишься *pf.* (*of* ⇒**~иваться**) **1** to grow foggy, become clouded (with). **2** (*fig.*) to become obscure.

затуп|и́ть, лю́, ~ишь *pf.* (*of* ⇒**~ля́ть**) to blunt; to dull.

затуп|и́ться, лю́сь, ~ишься *pf.* (*of* ⇒**~ля́ться**) to become blunt(ed).

затупля́|ть(ся), ю(сь) *impf. of* ⇒**затупи́ть(ся)**

затуха́ни|е, я *nt.* extinction; (*tech.*) damping; fading.

затух|а́ть, а́ет *impf. of* ⇒**~нуть**

зату́х|нуть, нет, *past* **~, ~ла** *pf.* (*of* ⇒**~а́ть**) **1** (*перестать гореть*) to go out, be extinguished. **2** (*fig., coll.*) (*о звуке*) to die away.

затуш|ева́ть, у́ю *pf.* (*of* ⇒**~ёвывать**) **1** (*рисунок*) to shade. **2** (*fig., coll.*) to conceal; to gloss over.

затушёвыва|ть, ю *impf. of* ⇒**затушева́ть**

затуш|и́ть, у́, ~ишь *pf.* to put out, extinguish; (*fig.*) to suppress.

за́тхл|ый (~, ~а) *adj.* (*запах*) musty; (*воздух*) stale, stuffy; (*fig.*) stagnant.

затыка́|ть, ю *impf. of* ⇒**заткну́ть**

заты́л|ок, ка *m.* **1** back of the head. **2**: **станови́ться в з.** to form up in file.

заты́лочный *adj.* (*anat.*) occipital.

заты́чк|а, и *f.* (*coll.*) stopper; plug.

затя́гива|ть(ся), ю(сь) *impf. of* ⇒**затяну́ть(ся)**

затя́жк|а, и *f.* **1** (*при курении*) inhaling. **2** (*продление*) prolongation; (*coll.*) dragging out. **3** (*задержка*) delaying, putting off.

затяжн|о́й *adj.* long drawn-out, protracted; **~а́я боле́знь** protracted, lingering illness; **~ы́е дожди́** long periods of rain.

затя|ну́ть, ну́, ~нешь *pf.* (*of* ⇒**~гивать**) **1** (*узел, пояс*) to tighten; (*naut.*) to haul taut. **2** (*покрыть*) to cover; to close; (*impers.*): **не́бо ~ну́ло ту́чами** it has clouded over; **ра́ну ~ну́ло** the wound has closed. **3** (*coll.*) (*засосать*) to drag down, drag in; (*fig.*) (*вовлечь*) to inveigle. **4** (*coll.*) (*продлить*) to drag out, spin out. **5**: **з. пе́сню** (*coll.*) to strike up a song.

затя|ну́ться, ну́сь, ~нешься *pf.* (*of* ⇒**~гиваться**) **1** (*затянуть на себе*) to lace o.s. up; **з. по́ясом** to tighten one's belt; (*туго завязаться*) to tighten; **у́зел ~ну́лся** the knot tightened. **2** (*покрыться*) to be covered; to close (*intrans.*), heal over (of a wound). **3** (*coll.*) (*продлиться*) to drag on (*intrans.*); **вечери́нка ~ну́лась до полу́ночи** the party dragged on till midnight. **4** (*при курении*) to inhale.

зау́м|ный (~ен, ~на) *adj.* abstruse, esoteric, unintelligible.

зауны́в|ный (~ен, ~на) *adj.* doleful, plaintive.

заупоко́йн|ый *adj.* for the repose of the soul; **~ая слу́жба** requiem.

заупря́м|иться, люсь, ишься *pf.* to turn obstinate.

зауря́д|ный (~ен, ~на) *adj.*

(*обыкновенный*) ordinary, commonplace; (*посредственный*) mediocre.

заусе́ниц|а, ы *f.* **1** (*у ногтя*) agnail, hangnail. **2** (*tech.*) burr.

зау́трен|я, и *f.* (*eccl.*) prime.

заутю́жива|ть, ю *impf. of* **⇨заутю́жить**

заутю́ж|ить, у, ишь *pf.* to iron; **з. скла́дку** to iron a crease.

зау́ченный *p.p.p. of* **⇨заучи́ть** *and adj.* studied.

зау́чива|ть(ся), ю(сь) *impf. of* **⇨заучи́ть(ся)**

зау|чи́ть, чу́, ~́чишь *pf.* (*of* **⇨~́чивать**) **1** (*твёрдо выучить*) to learn by heart. **2** (*coll.*) (*человека*) to din learning into.

зауч|и́ться, у́сь, ~́ишься *pf.* (*of* **⇨~́иваться**) (*coll.*) to study too hard.

заушáтельский *adj.* disparaging, abusive.

заушáтельств|о, а *nt.* disparagement, abuse.

зау́шниц|а, ы *f.* (*med.*) mumps.

зафарши́р|ова́ть, у́ю *pf. of* **⇨фарширова́ть**

зафикси́р|овать, ую *pf. of* **⇨фикси́ровать**

зафрахт|ова́ть, у́ю *pf.* (*of* **⇨фрахтова́ть** *and* **~о́вывать**) to charter.

зафрахто́выва|ть, ю *impf. of* **⇨зафрахтова́ть**

заха́жива|ть, ю *freq. of* **⇨заходи́ть**[1]; **он частéнько к нам ~л** he often used to drop in (to see us).

заха́п|ать, аю *pf.* (*of* **⇨~ывать**) (*coll.*) to grab, lay hold of.

заха́пыва|ть, ю *impf. of* **⇨заха́пать**

Заха́ри|я, и *m.* (*bibl.*) Zechariah.

захва́лива|ть, ю *impf. of* **⇨захвали́ть**

захвал|и́ть, ю́, ~́ишь *pf.* (*coll.*) to praise to excess; to spoil by flattery.

захва́т, а *m.* **1** (*действие*) seizure, capture. **2** (*tech.*) claw.

захва́танный *p.p.p. of* **⇨захвата́ть** *and adj.* soiled by handling, thumbed; (*fig., coll.*) trite, hackneyed.

захват|а́ть, а́ю *pf.* (*of* **⇨~ывать**[2]) (*coll.*) to soil by handling; to thumb.

захва|ти́ть, чу́, ~тишь *pf.* (*of* **⇨~тывать**[1]) **1** (*взять*) to take; **з. горсть ви́шен** to take a handful of cherries; **они́ ~ти́ли с собо́й дете́й** they have taken the children with them. **2** (*завладеть*) to seize; to capture; **з. власть** to seize power; **мы ~ти́ли три́ста пле́нных** we took three hundred prisoners. **3** (*fig.*) (*увлечь*) to carry away; to thrill, excite; **кни́га меня́ ~ти́ла** I was thrilled by the book. **4** (*coll.*) (*застать, застигнуть*) to catch; **з. после́дний по́езд** to catch the last train; **я успе́л з. его́ в кабине́те** I managed to catch him in his office; **~ти́ла ли тебя́ гроза́?** were you caught by the storm? **5** (*болезнь, пожар*) to stop (*an illness, etc.*) in time. **6** (*impers.*): **от э́того у меня́ дух ~ти́ло** it took my breath away.

захва́тнический *adj.* (*pej.*) aggressive, expansionist.

захва́тчик, а *m.* invader; aggressor.

захва́тыва|ть[1]**, ю** *impf. of* **⇨захвати́ть**

захва́тыва|ть[2]**, ю** *impf. of* **⇨захвата́ть**

захва́тыва|ющий *pres. part. act. of* **⇨~ть**[1] *and adj.* (*fig.*) gripping; **слу́шать но́вости с ~ющим интере́сом** to listen to news with keen interest.

захвора́|ть, ю *pf.* (*coll.*) to be taken ill.

захиле́|ть, ю *pf. of* **⇨хиле́ть**

захире́лый *adj.* (*мальчик*) sickly, ailing; (*хозяйство*) ailing, run-down; (*талант*) faded.

захире́|ть, ю *pf. of* **⇨хире́ть**

захлеб|ну́ть, ну, нёшь *pf.* (*of* **⇨~́ывать**) (*coll.*) to swallow, take a mouthful of.

захлеб|ну́ться, ну́сь, нёшься *pf.* (*of* **⇨~́ываться**) **1** to choke (*intrans.*); to swallow the wrong way. **2** (*fig., coll.*): **з. от восто́рга** to be breathless with delight; **ата́ка ~ну́лась** (*mil.*) the attack misfired.

захлёбыва|ть, ю *impf. of* **⇨захлебну́ть**

захлёбыва|ться, юсь *impf.* (*of* **⇨захлебну́ться**) to choke (*intrans.*); (*fig.*): **з. от сме́ха** to choke with laughter; **говори́ть ~ющимся го́лосом** to speak in a voice choked with emotion.

захлест|ну́ть, ну́, нёшь *pf.* (*of* **⇨~́ывать**) **1** (*верёвку*) to fasten, secure. **2** (*о волнах*) to flow over, swamp, overwhelm; (*fig.*): **её ~ну́ла волна́ сча́стья** a wave of happiness flowed over her.

захлёстыва|ть, ю *impf. of* **⇨захлестну́ть**

захло́п|нуть, ну, нешь *pf.* (*of* **⇨~ывать**) **1** (*дверь*) to slam. **2** (*человека*) to shut in.

захло́п|нуться, нусь, нешься *pf.* (*of* **⇨~ываться**) to slam to; to close with a bang.

захло́пыва|ть(ся), ю(сь) *impf. of* **⇨захло́пнуть(ся)**

захмеле́|ть, ю *pf. of* **⇨хмеле́ть**

захо́д, а *m.* **1** (**со́лнца**) sunset. **2** (*куда-н.*) stopping (at), putting in (at); **э́тот парохо́д пришёл из Аме́рики без ~а в Шербу́р** this ship has arrived from America without calling at Cherbourg. **3** (*coll.*) attempt, go.

захо|ди́ть[1]**, жу́, ~́дишь** *impf. of* **⇨зайти́**

захо|ди́ть[2]**, жу́, ~́дишь** *pf.* to begin to walk; **он ~ди́л по ко́мнате** he began to pace up and down the room.

захо|ди́ться[1]**, жу́сь, ~́дишься** *pf.* (*coll.*) to tire o.s. out with walking, walk o.s. off one's feet.

захо|ди́ться[2]**, жу́сь, ~́дишься** *impf. of* **⇨зайти́сь**

захо́жий *adj.* (*coll.*) newly-arrived; **он — з. челове́к** he is a stranger.

захо|жу́, ~́дишь *see* **⇨~ди́ть**

захолоде́|ть, ю *pf.* (*coll.*) to become cold; (*impers.*) to turn cold.

захолу́ст|ный (~ен, ~на) *adj.* remote; (*жизнь, нравы*) provincial.

захолу́ст|ье, ья, *g. pl.* **~ий** (*coll.* **~ьев**) *nt.* out-of-the-way place; the sticks; (*провинция*) the provinces.

захороне́ни|е, я *nt.* burial.

захорон|и́ть, ю́, ~́ишь *pf.* (*of* **⇨хорони́ть**) to bury.

захо|те́ть(ся), чу́, ~́чешь, ~́чет(ся), ти́м, ти́те, тя́т(ся) *pf. of* **⇨хоте́ть(ся)**

захуда́л|ый (~, ~а) *adj.* impoverished; run-down.

заца́п|ать, аю *pf.* (*of* **⇨~ывать**) (*coll.*) to grab; to lay hold of.

заца́пыва|ть, ю *impf. of* **⇨заца́пать**

зацве|сти́, ту́, тёшь, *past* **~́л, ~ла́** *pf.* (*of* **⇨~та́ть**) to break into blossom.

зацвета́|ть, ю *impf. of* **⇨зацвести́**

зацве|ту́, тёшь *see* **⇨~сти́**

зацел|ова́ть, у́ю *pf.* (*coll.*) to smother with kisses, rain kisses on.

зацеп|и́ть, лю́, ~́ишь *pf.* (*of* **⇨~ля́ть**) **1** (*задеть*) to hook; **з. плот баgро́м** to hook a raft with a boat-hook. **2** (*coll.*) (**за**+*a.*) (*случайно задеть*) to catch (on); **з. ного́й за ка́мень** to catch one's foot on a stone.

зацеп|и́ться, лю́сь, ~́ишься *pf.* (*of* **⇨~ля́ться**) (**за**+*a.*) **1** to catch (on); **чуло́к у неё ~и́лся за гвоздь** her stocking caught on a nail. **2** (*coll.*) (*ухватиться*) to catch hold (of).

заце́пк|а, и *f.* (*coll.*) **1** (*крючок*) peg, hook. **2** (*предлог*) pretext. **3** (*протекция*) pull, protection. **4** (*помеха*) hitch, catch (*fig.*).

зацепля́|ть(ся), ю(сь) *impf. of* **⇨зацепи́ть(ся)**

заци́клива|ться, юсь *impf. of* **⇨заци́клиться**

заци́кл|иться, юсь, ишься *pf.* (*of* **⇨заци́кливаться**) (**на**+*p.*) (*coll.*) to get stuck (on).

зачаро́ванный *p.p.p. of* **⇨зачарова́ть** *and adj.* spell-bound.

зачар|ова́ть, у́ю *pf.* (*of* **⇨~о́вывать**) to bewitch, enchant, captivate.

зачаро́выва|ть, ю *impf. of* **⇨зачарова́ть**

зача|сти́ть, щу́, сти́шь *pf.* (*coll.*) **1** (+*inf.*) (*начать часто делать что-н.*) to take (to); **он ~сти́л игра́ть в те́ннис по вечера́м** he has taken to playing tennis in the evening; **они́ ~сти́ли к нам в го́сти** they have become regular visitors at our house. **2** (*начать быстро говорить, действовать*) to begin to go fast; **докла́дчик ~сти́л так, что переводи́ть его́ слова́ ста́ло невозмо́жно** the lecturer began to go so fast that it was impossible to translate; **дождь ~сти́л** it began to pour with rain.

зачастýю *adv.* (*coll.*) often, frequently.

зачáти|е, я *nt.* (*physiol.*) conception.

зачáт|ок, ка *m.* **1** embryo. **2** (*usu. pl.*; *fig.*) beginning, germ.

зачáточн|ый *adj.* rudimentary; **в ~ом состоя́нии** in embryo.

зач|áть, нý, нёшь, *past.* **~áл, ~алá, ~áло** *pf.* (*of* ⇒**~инáть**) to conceive (*trans. and intrans.*).

зачáх|нуть, ну, нешь, *past* **~нул** *and* **~, ~ла** *pf. of* ⇒**чáхнуть**

зача|щý, сти́шь *see* ⇒**~сти́ть**

зач|ёл, лá *see* ⇒**~éсть**

зачéм *interrog. and rel. adv.* why; what for; **з. ты пришлá?** why did you come? **вот з. пришлá** that's why I came.

зачéм-то *adv.* for some reason or other.

зачёркива|ть, ю *impf. of* ⇒**зачеркнýть**

зачерк|нýть, нý, нёшь *pf.* (*of* ⇒**~ивать**) to cross out, strike out.

зачерне́|ть, ю *pf.* **1** (*начать чернеть*) to begin to turn black. **2** (*показаться*) to appear black (in the distance).

зачерн|и́ть, ю́, и́шь *pf.* (*of* ⇒**черни́ть**1 *and* **~я́ть**) to blacken, paint black.

зачерн|я́ть, я́ю *impf. of* ⇒**~и́ть**

зачéрпа|ть, ю *pf.* to begin to ladle.

зачерп|нýть, нý, нёшь *pf.* (*of* ⇒**~ывать**) to scoop up; (*ложкой*) to ladle out.

зачéрпыва|ть, ю *impf. of* ⇒**зачерпнýть**

зачерстве́лый *adj.* stale, hard; (*fig.*) (*человек*) callous, hardened.

зачерстве́|ть, ю *pf. of* ⇒**черстве́ть** 1

зачер|ти́ть, чý, ~тишь *pf.* (*of* ⇒**~чивать**) **1** (*покрыть штрихами*) to cover with pencil-strokes. **2** (*составить чертёж*) to sketch.

зачéрчива|ть, ю *impf. of* ⇒**зачерти́ть**

зачер|чý, ~тишь *see* ⇒**~ти́ть**

заче|сáть, шý, ~шешь *pf.* **1** (*начать чесать*) to begin to scratch. **2** (*impf.* **~сывать**) (*волосы*) to comb back.

заче|сáться, шýсь, ~шешься *pf.* (*coll.*) **1** (*о человеке*) to begin to scratch o.s. **2** (*о части тела*) to begin to itch.

зач|éсть, тý, тёшь, *past* **~ёл, ~лá** *pf.* (*of* ⇒**~и́тывать**[1]) **1** to take into account, reckon as, credit; **з. дéсять рублéй в уплáту дóлга** to account ten roubles towards payment of a debt; **з. проведённый на воéнной слýжбе год за два гóда** to reckon a year spent on war service as two years. **2** (*+d. and a.*) (*одобрить*) to pass (*trans.*); **мы ~ли емý перевóд с францýзского** we passed him in French translation.

зачёсыва|ть, ю *impf. of* ⇒**зачесáть** 2

зачёт, а *m.* **1** reckoning; **в з. плáты** in payment. **2** (*экзамен*) test; **получи́ть з., сдать з.** (**по** *+d.*) to pass a test (in); **постáвить** (*+d.*) **з.** (**по** *+d.*) to pass (in); **постáвили мне з. по истóрии** they have passed me in history.

зачёт|ный *adj. of* ⇒**~** **1**: **~ная квитáнция** receipt. **2**: **~ная кни́жка** (student's) record book; **~ная сéссия** test period; **~ная стрельбá** classification shoot.

зачехл|и́ть, ю́, и́шь *pf. of* ⇒**зачехля́ть, чехли́ть**

зачехля́|ть, ю *impf.* (*of* ⇒**зачехли́ть**) = **чехли́ть**

зач|ешý, ~éшешь *see* ⇒**~есáть**

зачинáтел|ь, я *m.* (*rhet.*) pioneer, founder.

зачинá|ть, ю *impf. of* ⇒**зачáть**

зачи́нива|ть, ю *impf. of* ⇒**зачини́ть**

зачин|и́ть, ю́, ~ишь *pf.* (*of* ⇒**~ивать**) (*coll.*) (*брюки, крышу*) to mend; (*карандаш*) to sharpen.

зачи́нщик, а *m.* (*pej.*) instigator, ringleader.

зачислéни|е, я *nt.* enrolment.

зачи́сл|ить, ю, ишь *pf.* (*of* ⇒**~я́ть**) **1** (*записать*) to include; **з. в счёт** to enter in an account. **2** (*включить в состав*) to enrol, enlist; **з. в штат** to take on the staff.

зачи́сл|иться, юсь, ишься *pf.* (*of* ⇒**~я́ться**) (**в** *+a.*) to join, enter.

зачисл|я́ть(ся), я́ю(сь) *impf. of* ⇒**~ить(ся)**

зачи́|стить, щу, стишь *pf.* (*of* ⇒**~щáть**) **1** (*загладить*) to smooth out. **2** (*сделать чистым*) to clean up, clean out.

зачит|áть, áю *pf.* (*of* ⇒**~ывать**[2]) (*coll.*) **1** (*прочесть вслух*) to read out. **2** (*книгу*) to fail to return.

зачит|áться, áюсь *pf.* (*of* ⇒**~ываться**) to become engrossed in reading; to go on reading; **вчерá я ~áлся далекó зá пóлночь** last night I went on reading until long after midnight.

зачи́тыва|ть[1]**, ю** *impf. of* ⇒**зачéсть**

зачи́тыва|ть[2]**, ю** *impf. of* ⇒**зачитáть**

зачи́тыва|ться, юсь *impf. of* ⇒**зачитáться**

зачищá|ть, ю *impf. of* ⇒**зачи́стить**

зачи́|щу, стишь *see* ⇒**~стить**

зач|нý, нёшь *see* ⇒**~áть**

зачтён|ный (**~, ~á**) *p.p.p. of* ⇒**зачéсть**

зач|тý, тёшь *see* ⇒**~éсть**

зачумл|ённый (**~ён, ~енá**) *adj.* infected with plague.

зашáрка|ть, ю *pf.* (*coll.*) **1** (*impf.* **зашáркивать**) (*запачкать*) to scratch (*with one's feet*). **2** (*начать шаркать*) to begin to scrape (one's feet).

зашáркива|ть, ю *impf. of* ⇒**зашáркать** 1

зашварт|овáть, ýю *pf.* (*of* ⇒**~óвывать**) (*naut.*) to moor, tie up.

зашварт|овáться, ýюсь *pf.* (*of* ⇒**~óвываться**) (*naut.*) to moor, tie up (*intrans.*).

зашвартóвыва|ть(ся), ю(сь) *impf. of* ⇒**зашвартовáть(ся)**

зашвы́рива|ть, ю *impf. of* ⇒**зашвырнýть** *and* **зашвыря́ть**

зашвыр|нýть, нý, нёшь *pf.* (*of* ⇒**~ивать**) (*coll.*) to throw, fling.

зашвыр|я́ть, я́ю *pf.* (*of* ⇒**~ивать**) (*+a. and i.*; *coll.*) to shower (with); **з. когó-н. камня́ми** to stone s.o., throw stones at s.o.

зашиб|áть, áю *impf.* (*coll.*) **1** *impf. of* ⇒**~и́ть. 2** to drink (*intrans.*).

зашиб|áться, áюсь *impf. of* ⇒**~и́ться**

зашиб|и́ть, ý, ёшь, *past* **~, ~ла** *pf.* (*of* ⇒**~áть**) (*coll.*) **1** to bruise, knock, hurt; **он ~ себé колéно** he has bruised his knee. **2**: **з. деньгý** (*sl.*) to coin money.

зашиб|и́ться, ýсь, ёшься, *past* **~ся, ~лась** *pf.* (*of* ⇒**~áться**) (*coll.*) to bruise o.s., knock o.s.

зашивá|ть(ся), ю(сь) *impf. of* ⇒**заши́ть(ся)**

заш|и́ть, ью́, ьёшь *pf.* (*of* ⇒**~ивáть**) **1** (*дыру, пальто*) to mend. **2** (*упаковать*) to sew up; **з. посы́лку в холст** to sew up a parcel in sacking. **3** (*med.*) to stitch (up).

заш|и́ться, ью́сь, ьёшься *pf.* (*of* ⇒**зашивáться**) (*coll.*) to have too little time to do everything; **~ с делáми** to be snowed under with things to do.

зашифр|овáть, ýю *pf.* (*of* ⇒**шифровáть** *and* **~óвывать**) to encipher, put into code.

зашифрóвыва|ть, ю *impf. of* ⇒**зашифровáть**

за|шлю́, шлёшь *see* ⇒**~слáть**

зашнур|овáть, ýю *pf.* (*of* ⇒**шнуровáть** *and* ⇒**~óвывать**) to lace up.

зашнур|овáться, ýюсь *pf. of* ⇒**шнуровáться**

зашнурóвыва|ть, ю *impf. of* ⇒**зашнуровáть**

зашпакл|евáть, ю́ю *pf.* (*of* ⇒**шпаклевáть** *and* **~ёвывать**) to putty.

зашпаклёвыва|ть, ю *impf. of* ⇒**зашпаклевáть**

зашпи́л|ить, ю, ишь *pf.* (*of* ⇒**~ивать**) to pin up, fasten with a pin.

зашпи́лива|ть, ю *impf. of* ⇒**зашпи́лить**

заштемпел|евáть, ю́ю *pf.* (*of* ⇒**штемпелевáть**) to stamp, postmark.

заштóпа|ть, ю *pf.* (*of* ⇒**штóпать**) to darn.

заштрих|овáть, ýю *pf. of* ⇒**штриховáть**

заштукатýрива|ть, ю *impf. of* ⇒**заштукатýрить**

заштукатýр|ить, ю, ишь *pf.* (*of* ⇒**~ивать**) to plaster.

защеко|тáть, чý, ~чешь *pf.* (*coll.*) **1** (*измучить щекоткой*) to torment by tickling. **2** (*начать щекотать*) to begin to tickle.

защёлк|а, и *f.* (*в двери*) latch; (*в механизме*) catch.

защёлкива|ть, ю *impf. of* ⇒**защёлкнуть**

защёлк|нуть, ну, нешь *pf.* (*of* ⇒**~ивать**) (*coll.*) to latch.

защем|и́ть, лю́, и́шь *pf.* (*of* ⇒**~ля́ть**) **1** to pinch, jam, nip; **з. па́лец** to pinch one's finger. **2** (*impers.*; *coll.*): **у неё ~и́ло се́рдце** her heart aches.

защемля́|ть, ю *impf. of* ⇒**защеми́ть**

защип|ну́ть, ну́, нёшь *pf.* (*of* ⇒**~ывать**) to take (*with pincers, tongs, etc.*); to nip, tweak; (*волосы*) to curl; (*билеты*) to punch.

защи́пыва|ть, ю *impf. of* ⇒**защипну́ть**

защи́т|а, ы *no pl., f.* defence (*Br.*), defense (*US*); (**от, про́тив** + *g.*) protection (from, against); (*collect.*) the defence (*Br.*), defense (*US*) (*leg. and sport*); **в ~у** (+*g.*) in defence (*Br.*), defense (*US*) (of); **под ~ой** (+*g.*) under the protection (of); **з. окружа́ющей среды́** *or* **приро́ды** environmentalism, conservation.

защи|ти́ть(ся), щу́(сь), ти́шь(ся) *pf. of* ⇒**~ща́ть(ся)**

защи́тник, а *m.* **1** defender, protector; (*leg.*) counsel for the defence (*Br.*), defense attorney (*US*); **колле́гия ~ов** the Bar; **з. окружа́ющей среды́** *or* **приро́ды** environmentalist, conservationist. **2** (*sport*) (full-)back; **ле́вый, пра́вый з.** left, right back.

защи́тн|ый *adj.* protective; **~ые очки́** goggles; **з. цвет** khaki.

защища́|ть, ю *impf.* **1** (*impf. of* ⇒**защити́ть**) to defend, protect. **2** (*no pf.*) (*leg.*) to defend; **з. диссерта́цию** to defend a thesis (*before examiners*).

защища́|ться, юсь *impf.* (*of* ⇒**защити́ться**) **1** to defend o.s., protect o.s. **2** *pass. of* ⇒**~ть**

за́|щу, сти́шь *see* ⇒**~сти́ть**

заяви́тел|ь, я *m.* (*leg.*) declarant, deponent.

заяв|и́ть, лю́, ~ишь *pf.* (*of* ⇒**~ля́ть**) (+*a. or* **о**+*p. or* **что**) to announce, declare; **з. свои́ права́** (**на**+*a.*) to claim one's rights (to); **з. об ухо́де со слу́жбы** to announce one's resignation.

заяв|и́ться, лю́сь, ~ишься *pf.* (*coll.*) to appear, turn up.

зая́вк|а, и *f.* (**на**+*a.*) (*просьба*) application (for); (*о своих правах*) claim (for); demand (for); (*заказ*) order (for); **з. на изобрете́ние** patent application; **бланк ~и** application form.

заявле́ни|е, я *nt.* **1** (*сообщение*) statement, declaration. **2** (*просьба*) application; **пода́ть з.** to put in an application.

заявля́|ть, ю *impf. of* ⇒**заяви́ть**

зая́длый *adj.* (*coll.*) inveterate.

за́|яц, йца *m.* **1** hare; (*prov.*) **одни́м уда́ром уби́ть двух ~йцев** to kill two birds with one stone. **2** (*coll.*) (*пассажир*) stowaway; fare-dodger; **е́хать ~йцем** to travel without paying for a ticket.

за́я|чий *adj. of* ⇒**~ц**; **~чья губа́** (*med.*) harelip.

зва́ни|е, я *nt.* rank; title; **ры́царское з.** knighthood.

зва́ный *adj.* **1** (*гость*) invited. **2** (*с приглашением гостей*) with invited guests; **з. ве́чер** guest-night; **з. обе́д** dinner-party.

зва́тельный *adj.* (*gram.*): **з. паде́ж** vocative case.

зва|ть, зову́, зовёшь, *past* **~л, ~ла́, ~ло** *impf.* (*of* ⇒**по~**) **1** to call; **з. на по́мощь** to call for help. **2** (*приглашать*) to ask, invite. **3** (*impf. only*) (*называть*) to call; **как вас зову́т?** what is your name? **меня́ зову́т Влади́мир** my name is Vladimir; I am called Vladimir.

зва́|ться, зову́сь, зовёшься, *past* **~лся́, ~ла́сь, ~ло́сь** *impf.* (+*i.*; *obs.*) to be called; **её сестра́ ~ла́сь Татья́ной** her sister was called Tatyana.

звезд|а́, ы́, *pl.* **~ы, ~, ~ам** *f.* **1** star; **но́вая з.** (*astron.*) nova; (*fig.*): **з. экра́на** film star; **ве́рить в свою́ ~у́** to believe in one's lucky star; **роди́ться под счастли́вой ~о́й** to be born under a lucky star; **он ~ с не́ба не хвата́ет** (*coll., iron.*) he won't set the Thames on fire. **2** (*zool.*): **морска́я з.** starfish.

звёздно-полоса́тый *adj.*: **з. флаг** the Stars and Stripes, the Star-Spangled Banner (= *national flag of USA*).

звёзд|ный *adj. of* ⇒**~а́**; **з. дождь** meteor shower; shooting stars; **~ная ка́рта** celestial map; **~ная ночь** starlit night; **з. час** finest hour.

звездообра́з|ный (~ен, ~на) *adj.* star-shaped.

звездопа́д, а *m.* meteor shower; shooting stars.

звёздочк|а, и *f.* **1** *dim. of* ⇒**звезда́**. **2** asterisk.

-звёздочный *in comb.* -star; **пятизвёздочная гости́ница** five-star hotel.

звен|е́ть, ю́, и́шь *impf.* **1** to ring; **у неё ~е́ло в уша́х** there was a ringing in her ears. **2** (+*i.*): **з. моне́тами** to jingle coins; **з. стака́нами** to clink glasses.

звен|о́, а́, *pl.* **~ья, ~ьев** *nt.* **1** (*цепи*) link (*also fig.*). **2** (*fig.*) (*на работе*) team, section; (*aeron.*) flight.

звен|ьево́й *adj. of* ⇒**~о́**

звер|ёк[1], ька́ *m. dim. of* ⇒**~ь**

звер|ёк[2], ька́ *m.* (*sl.*) pusher, (drug-) dealer.

зверёныш, а *m.* (*coll.*) young of wild animal; cub; (*fig.*) little brute.

звере́|ть, ю, ешь *impf.* (*of* ⇒**о~**) to become brutalized.

звери́н|ец, ца *m.* menagerie.

звер|и́ный *adj. of* ⇒**~ь**; animal; savage.

зверобо́|й[1], я *m.* hunter, trapper.

зверобо́|й[2], я *m.* (*bot.*) St John's wort.

зверово́д, а *m.* fur farmer.

зверово́дств|о, а *nt.* fur farming.

зверово́д|ческий *adj. of* ⇒**~ство**

зверол́ов, а *m.* hunter, trapper.

зверол́ов|ный *adj. of* ⇒**~**; **з. про́мысел** hunting, trapping.

звероподо́б|ный (~ен, ~на) *adj.* bestial.

зверофе́рм|а, ы *f.* fur farm.

зве́рски *adv.* **1** brutally, bestially. **2** (*coll.*) terribly, awfully; **я з. уста́л** I am terribly tired.

зве́рский *adj.* **1** brutal, bestial. **2** (*coll.*) (*чрезвычайный*) terrific, tremendous; **у него́ з. аппети́т** he has a tremendous appetite.

зве́рств|о, а *nt.* brutality; atrocity; **~а** atrocities (*in war, etc.*).

зве́рств|овать, ую *impf.* to behave with brutality; to commit atrocities.

звер|ь, я, *pl.* **~и, ~е́й** *m.* **1** wild animal, wild beast; **пушно́й з.** fur-bearing animal. **2** (*fig.*) (*человек*) brute, beast; **смотре́ть ~ем** to look (very) savage, look (very) fierce.

зверь|ё, я́ *no pl., nt.* (*collect.*) wild animals, wild beasts; (*fig.*) brutes, beasts.

звон, а *m.* (ringing) sound, peal; **з. моне́т** chinking of coins; **з. стака́нов** clinking of glasses.

звона́р|ь, я́ *m.* bell-ringer.

звон|и́ть, ю́, и́шь *impf.* (*pf. of* ⇒**по~**) (**в**+*a.*) to ring; **з. кому́-н. (по телефо́ну)** to phone s.o., call s.o.; **вы не туда́ ~и́те** you've got the wrong number; **~я́т** s.o. is ringing.

звон|и́ться, ю́сь, и́шься *impf.* (*of* ⇒**по~**) to ring (*a doorbell*).

зво́н|кий (~ок, ~ка́, ~ко) *adj.* **1** ringing, clear; **~кая моне́та** hard cash, coin. **2** (*ling.*) voiced.

звон|ко́вый *adj. of* ⇒**~о́к**

зво́нниц|а, ы *f.* belfry (*of old Russian churches*).

звон|о́к, ка́ *m.* bell; **дать з.** to ring; **з. (по телефо́ну)** (phone) call; **встава́ть по ~ку́** to get up when the bell goes.

зво́н|че *and* (*coll.*) **~че́е** *comp. of* ⇒**~кий, ~ко**

звук, а *m.* sound; **пусто́й з.** (*fig.*) (mere) name, empty phrase; **я звал её, а она́ ни ~а** I kept calling her but she never uttered a sound; (*ling.*) **гла́сный з.** vowel; **согла́сный з.** consonant.

звук|ово́й *adj. of* ⇒**~**; **з. барье́р** sound barrier; **~ова́я волна́** sound wave; **~ова́я ка́рта** (*comput.*) sound card; **~ова́я сту́дия** sound studio; **з. фильм** sound-film, talkie.

звукоза́пис|ь, и *f.* sound recording.

звукоизоля́ци|я, и *f.* soundproofing.

звуконепроница́ем|ый (~, ~а) *adj.* soundproof.

звукоопера́тор, а *m.* (*cin.*) sound recordist, sound man.

звукоподража́ни|е, я *nt.* onomatopoeia.

звукоподража́тельный *adj.* onomatopoeic.

звукорежиссёр, а *m.* sound engineer.

звукоря́д, а *m.* (*mus.*) scale.

звукоснима́тел|ь, я *m.* pickup.

звукоула́вливател|ь, я *m.* (*mil.*) sound-locator.

звуча́ни|е, я *nt.* **1** sound(s). **2** (*значение*) significance.

звуч|а́ть, у́, и́шь *impf.* (*of* ⇒**про~**) **1** (*раздаваться*) to be heard; to sound; **вдали́ ~а́ли голоса́** voices could be heard in the distance; **э́тот пасса́ж ~и́т прекра́сно** (*mus.*) this passage sounds splendid. **2** (+*adv. or i.*; *fig.*) (*выражаться*) to sound; to express, convey; **з. трево́гой** to sound a note of alarm; **з. и́скренно** to ring true.

зву́ч|ный (~ен, ~на́, ~но) *adj.* sonorous.

звя́кань|е, я *nt.* jingling; tinkling.

звя́к|ать, аю *impf. of* ⇒**~нуть**

звя́к|нуть, ну, нешь *pf.* (*of* ⇒**~ать**) **1** (+*i.*) to jingle; to tinkle. **2** (+*d.*): **з. (по телефо́ну)** (*coll.*) to ring up; to give s.o. a buzz.

зга *only in phr.* **ни зги не ви́дно** it is pitch dark.

зда́ни|е, я *nt.* building.

здесь *adv.* **1** here. **2** (*coll.*) here, at this point (*of time*); in this; **з. мы засмея́лись** here we burst out laughing; **з. нет ничего́ смешно́го** there is nothing funny in this.

зде́шний *adj.* local; of this place; **вы з. жи́тель? нет, я не з.** are you a local? no, I am a stranger here.

здоро́ва|ться, юсь *impf.* (*of* ⇒**по~**) (**с**+*i.*) to greet; to say hello (to); **з. за́ руку** to shake hands (*in greeting*).

здорове́нн|ый *adj.* (*coll.*) burly, strapping; **~ая ба́ба** strapping woman; **з. го́лос** powerful voice.

здорове́|ть, ю, ешь *impf.* (*of* ⇒**по~**) (*coll.*) to become stronger.

здо́рово (*coll.*) **1** (*adv.*) (*отлично*) splendidly, magnificently; **ты з. порабо́тал** you have worked splendidly. **2** (*adv.*) (*очень сильно*) very, very much; **вчера́ они́ з. вы́пили** they had a great deal to drink yesterday. **3** (*int.*) great!; well done!

здоро́во[1] *int.* (*coll.*) hullo.

здоро́в|о[2] *adv. of* ⇒**~ый**[1]; healthily, soundly; **(за) з. живёшь** for no reason (at all).

здоро́в|ый[1] **(~, ~а)** *adj.* **1** healthy; **бу́дь(те) ~(ы)!** (*on parting*) take care!; (*to s.o. sneezing*) bless you! **2** (*полезный*) health-giving, wholesome; (*fig.*) sound, healthy; **з. кли́мат** healthy climate; **~ая иде́я** sound idea.

здоро́в|ый[2] **(~, ~а́, ~о́)** *adj.* (*coll.*) **1** (*сильный: о человеке*) robust, sturdy. **2** (*большой, сильный: о предметах*) strong, powerful; sound; **з. моро́з** sharp frost; **~ая трёпка** sound thrashing. **3** (*short form* +*inf.*) clever (at), good (at), expert (at); **он ~ льсти́ть же́нщинам** he is expert at flattering women.

здоро́вь|е, я *no pl., nt.* health; **пить за чьё-н. з.** to drink s.o.'s health; **за ва́ше з.!** your health!; **как ва́ше з.?** how are you?; **на з.** to your heart's content, as you please; **гру́ппа ~я** keep-fit group.

здоровя́к, а́ *m.* (*coll.*) person in the pink of health.

здрав... *comb. form, abbr. of* **здравоохрани́тельный**

здра́ви|е, я *nt.* (*obs.*) health; **~я жела́ю!** *soldiers' reply to senior officer's greeting.*

здра́виц|а, ы *f.* toast; **провозгласи́ть ~у за** (+*a.*) to propose a toast to.

здра́вниц|а, ы *f.* sanatorium.

здравомы́слящий *adj.* sensible.

здравоохране́ни|е, я *nt.* health care; public health; **Министе́рство ~я** Ministry of Health; **о́рганы ~я** (public) health services.

здравоохрани́тельный *adj.* health care; public health.

здравотде́л, а *m.* health department (*of local authority*).

здравпу́нкт, а *m.* first-aid station.

здра́вств|овать, ую *impf.* to be healthy; (*процветать*) to thrive, prosper; **~уй(те)!** how do you do; how are you; **да ~ует!** long live!

здра́в|ый (~, ~а) *adj.* sensible; **з. смысл** common sense; **~ и невреди́м** safe and sound; **быть в ~ом уме́** to be in one's right mind.

зе́бр|а, ы *f.* **1** (*zool.*) zebra. **2** (*место перехода*) zebra crossing (*Br.*).

зе́бр|овый *adj. of* ⇒**~а**

зев, а *m.* (*anat.*) pharynx.

зева́к|а, и *c.g.* idler, gaper.

зев|а́ть, а́ю *impf.* **1** (*pf.* **~ну́ть**) to yawn. **2** (*no pf.*) (*coll.*) to gape, stand gaping; **не ~а́й!** keep your wits about you! **3** (*pf.* **про~**) (*coll.*) to miss opportunities.

зева́|ться, ется *impf.* (*impers.*, +*d.*) (*coll.*) to have an urge to yawn; **мне сего́дня ~ется** I can't stop yawning today.

зев|ну́ть, ну́, нёшь *pf. of* ⇒**~а́ть** 1

зев|о́к, ка́ *m.* yawn.

зево́т|а, ы *f.* (fit of) yawning.

зелене́|ть, ю *impf.* **1** (*pf.* **по~**) (*становиться зелёным*) to turn green, come out green. **2** (*виднеться*) to show green.

зелен|и́ть, ю́, и́шь *impf.* (*of* ⇒**по~**) to make green, paint green.

зелёнк|а, и *f.* (*coll.*) 'brilliant green' (*an antiseptic embrocation*).

зеленова́т|ый (~, ~а) *adj.* greenish.

зеленогла́з|ый (~, ~а) *adj.* green-eyed.

зеленщи́к, а́ *m.* greengrocer.

зелён|ый (зе́лен, ~а́, зе́лено) *adj.* green (*also fig.*); **з. горо́шек** green peas; **з. лук** spring onions; **тоска́ ~ая** utter boredom; **~ое я́блоко** green apple; **з. юне́ц** greenhorn; **~ая у́лица** 'go' (*of traffic signals*); **дать ~ую у́лицу** (*fig.*) to give the go-ahead, green-light (to).

зе́лен|ь, и *no pl., f.* **1** (*зелёный цвет*) green colour (*Br.*), color (*US*). **2** (*collect.*) (*растительность*) greenery. **3** (*collect.*) (*овощи*) greens.

зе́л|ье, ья *g. pl.* **~ий** *nt.* **1** (*настой*) potion. **2** (*fig.*) (*яд*) poison. **3** (*fig., coll.*) (*человек*) pest (*sl.*).

зельц, а *m.* (*cul.*) brawn.

земе́льн|ый *adj.* land; **з. наде́л** allotment; **~ая ре́нта** ground-rent.

землеве́дени|е, я *nt.* physical geography.

землевладе́л|ец, ьца *m.* landowner.

землевладе́л|ьческий *adj. of* ⇒**~ец**

землевладе́ни|е, я *nt.* land-ownership.

земледе́л|ец, ьца *m.* arable farmer.

земледе́ли|е, я *nt.* arable farming.

земледе́льческий *adj.* agricultural.

землеко́п, а *m.* navvy.

землеме́р, а *m.* land-surveyor.

землеме́рный *adj.* geodetic; **з. шест** Jacob's staff.

землепа́шеств|о, а *nt.* (*obs.*) tillage.

землепа́ш|ец, ца *m.* (*obs.*) tiller.

землепо́льзовани|е, я *nt.* land-tenure.

землеро́йк|а, и *f.* (*zool.*) shrew.

землеро́йн|ый *adj.* excavating; **~ая маши́на** excavator.

землетрясе́ни|е, я *nt.* earthquake.

землечерпа́лк|а, и *f.* (*tech.*) dredger, excavator.

землечерпа́ни|е, я *nt.* (*tech.*) dredging.

земли́ст|ый (~, ~а) *adj.* earthy; (*о цвете лица*) sallow.

зем|ля́, ли́, *a.* **~лю,** *pl.* **~ли, ~е́ль, ~лям** *f.* **1** (*планета*) Earth; (*суша*) (dry) land; **уви́деть ~лю** to sight land; **упа́сть на ~лю** to fall to the ground. **2** (*владение*) land; soil (*fig.*); **поме́щичья з.** (*collect.*) landed estates; **на чужо́й ~ле́** on foreign soil. **3** (*почва*) earth, soil. **4** (*в Германии*) Land, state; (*в Австрии*) province.

земля́к, а́ *m.* fellow-countryman, compatriot.

земляни́к|а, и *no pl., f.* (*collect.*) wild strawberries.

земля́н|ин, ина, *pl.* **~е, ~** *m.* earth-dweller, earthling.

земляни́|чный *adj. of* ⇒**~ка**

земля́нк|а, и *f.* dug-out.

землян|о́й *adj.* **1** earthen, of earth; **~ые рабо́ты** excavations. **2** earth-; **~а́я гру́ша** Jerusalem artichoke; **з. оре́х** peanut; **з. червь** earth-worm.

земля́честв|о, а *nt.* **1** (*принадлежность к одной местности*) community. **2** (*объединение уроженцев одной местности*) association of fellow-countrymen.

земля́чк|а, и *f. of* ⇒**земля́к**

земново́дн|ый *adj.* amphibious; *as n.* (*zool.*) **~ые, ~ых** amphibia; *sg.* **~ое, ~ого** *nt.* amphibian.

земн|о́й *adj.* **1** earthly; terrestrial; **~а́я кора́** (earth-)crust; **з. шар** the globe. **2** (*fig.*) mundane.

зе́м|ский *adj.* **1** *of* ⇒**~ля́** 2; (*hist.*): **з. нача́льник** land captain (*holder of office established in 1889*); **~ское ополче́ние** militia; **З. собо́р** Assembly of the Land (*in Muscovite Russia*). **2** *of* ⇒**~ство**

зе́мств|о, а *nt.* zemstvo (*elective district council in Russia, 1864–1917*).

зени́т, а *m.* zenith (*also fig.*).

зени́тк|а, и *f.* (*mil.*; *coll.*) anti-aircraft gun.

зени́тн|ый *adj.* **1** (*astron.*) zenithal; **~ое расстоя́ние** zenith-distance. **2** (*mil.*) anti-aircraft.

зени́ц|а, ы *f.* (*arch.*) pupil (*of the eye*); **бере́чь как ~у о́ка** to guard most carefully; to treasure more than anything else in the world.

зе́ркал|о, а, *pl.* **~а́, зерка́л, ~а́м** *nt.* mirror (*also fig.*); **криво́е з.** distorting mirror.

зерка́льн|ый *adj. of* ⇒**зе́ркало;** (*fig.*) smooth; **~ое стекло́** plate glass; **~ое окно́** plate-glass window; **з. фотоаппара́т** reflex camera; **~ая пове́рхность** smooth surface; **з. карп** (*zool.*) mirror carp.

зерни́ст|ый (~, ~а) *adj.* granular; **~ая икра́** unpressed caviar(e).

зер|но́, на́, *pl.* **~̈на, ~̈ен, ~̈нам** *nt.* **1** (*пшеницы*) grain; (*мака*) seed; (*fig.*) grain; (*ядро*) kernel, core; **горчи́чное з.** mustard seed; **жемчу́жное з.** pearl; **ко́фе в ~̈нах** coffee beans; **з. и́стины** grain of truth. **2** (*collect.*, *sg. only*) grain, cereal.

зернобобо́в|ые, ых *no sg.* (*agric.*) grain legumes.

зернови́д|ный (~ен, ~на) *adj.* granular.

зерново́з, а *m.* grain carrier (*ship*).

зернов|о́й *adj.* grain, cereal; **~ы́е зла́ки** cereals; **~а́я торго́вля** grain trade.

зерносуши́лк|а, и *f.* (*agric.*) grain dryer.

зернохрани́лищ|е, а *nt.* granary.

зефи́р, а *m.* **1 (З.)** (*poet.*) (*ветер*) Zephyr. **2** (*ткань*) zephyr. **3** (*кондитерское изделие*) marshmallow.

зигза́г, а *m.* zigzag.

зигзагообра́зный *adj.* zig-zag.

зижди́тел|ь, я *m.* (*relig.*) the Creator.

зи́жд|иться, ется *impf.* (**на** + *p.*; *obs. or rhet.*) to be founded (on), based (on).

зим|а́, ы́, *a.* **~̆у,** *pl.* **~̆ы,** *d.* **~̆ам** *f.* winter; **на́ ~у** for the winter; **всю ~̆у** all winter; **ско́лько лет, ско́лько ~,** *see* ⇒**ле́то**

Зимба́бве *nt. indecl.* Zimbabwe.

зимбабви́|ец, йца *m.* Zimbabwean.

зимбабви́|йка, йки *f. of* ⇒**~ец**

зимбабви́йский *adj.* Zimbabwean.

зи́м|ний *adj. of* ⇒**~а́;** winter; (*погода*) wintry.

зим|ова́ть, у́ю *impf.* (*of* ⇒**пере~** *and* **про~**) to winter, pass the winter; **знать, где ра́ки ~у́ют,** *see* ⇒**рак**

зимо́вк|а, и *f.* **1** wintering; **оста́ться на ~у** to stay for the winter. **2** (*жильё*) winter camp.

зимо́вщик, а *m.* person who spends the winter in an uninhabited area; winterer.

зимо́вщи|ца, цы *f. of* ⇒**~к**

зимо́вь|е, я *nt.* winter quarters, winter hut.

зимо́й *adv.* in winter.

зиморо́д|ок, ка *m.* (*zool.*) kingfisher.

зипу́н, а́ *m.* homespun coat.

зия́ни|е, я *nt.* **1** gaping, yawning. **2** (*ling.*) hiatus.

зия́|ть, ю *impf.* to gape, yawn; **~ющая бе́здна** yawning abyss.

злак, а *m.* (*bot.*) grass; **хле́бные ~̆и** cereals.

зла́т|о, а *nt.* (*arch.*; *poet.*) gold.

Златовла́ск|а, и *f.* Goldilocks.

златогла́вый *adj.* gold-domed; with gold cupolas.

златоку́др|ый (~, ~а) *adj.* (*poet.*) golden-haired.

зла́чн|ый *adj.* (*coll.*): **~ое ме́сто** den of vice.

зле́йший *superl. of* ⇒**злой**

зл|ить, ю, ишь *impf.* (*of* ⇒**обо~** *and* **разо~**) to anger; to vex; to irritate.

зл|и́ться, юсь, и́шься *impf.* (*of* ⇒**обо~** *and* **разо~**) **1** (**на** + *a.*) to be in a bad temper; to be angry (with). **2** (*fig.*, *poet.*) to rage (*of a storm*).

зло¹, зла, *no pl. except g.* **зол** *nt.* **1** (*нечто дурное*) evil; harm; **отплати́ть ~м за добро́** to repay good with evil. **2** (*беда*) evil, misfortune, disaster; **из двух зол вы́брать ме́ньшее** to choose the lesser of two evils; **жела́ть кому́-н. зла** to bear s.o. malice. **3** (*sg. only*) (*досада*) malice, spite; vexation; **он э́то сде́лал то́лько со зла** he did it purely out of spite; **меня́ з. берёт** it annoys me, I feel annoyed.

зло² *adv. of* ⇒**~й**

зло́б|а, ы *f.* malice; spite; anger; **по ~е** out of spite; **со ~ой** maliciously; **з. дня** topic of the day, latest news.

зло́б|иться, люсь, ишься *impf.* (**на** + *a.*; *coll.*) to feel malice (towards); to be in a bad temper (with).

зло́б|ный (~ен, ~на) *adj* malicious, spiteful; bad-tempered.

злободне́вност|ь, и *f.* topical interest, topical character.

злободне́в|ный (~ен, ~на) *adj.* topical; **~ные вопро́сы** burning topics of the day.

зло́бств|овать, ую *impf.* to bear malice; (**на** + *a.*) to have it in (for).

злове́щ|ий (~, ~а) *adj.* ominous, ill-omened; sinister.

злово́ни|е, я *nt.* stink, stench.

злово́н|ный (~ен, ~на) *adj.* fetid, stinking.

зловре́д|ный (~ен, ~на) *adj.* harmful, pernicious.

злоде́|й, я *m.* villain, scoundrel (*also joc.*).

злоде́й|ка, ки *f. of* ⇒**~**

злоде́йский *adj.* villainous.

злоде́йств|о, а *nt.* **1** villainy. **2** (*поступок*) crime, evil deed.

злоде́йств|овать, ую *impf.* to act villainously.

злодея́ни|е, я *nt.* crime, evil deed.

злой (зол, зла, зло) *adj.* **1** (*о человеке*) evil; bad; **з. ге́ний** evil genius. **2** (*выражающий злобу*) wicked; malicious; malevolent; vicious; **зла́я улы́бка** malevolent smile; **со злым у́мыслом** with malicious intent; (*leg.*) of malice prepense. **3** (*short form only*) (**на** + *a.*) (*сердит*) angry (with) ; **она́ зла на всех** she is angry with everybody. **4** (*о животных*) fierce, savage; **«осторо́жно, зла́я соба́ка»** 'beware of the dog!' **5** (*coll.*) (*сильный*) bad, nasty; **з. ка́шель** bad cough; **з. моро́з** severe frost.

злока́чествен|ный (~, ~на) *adj.* (*med.*) malignant; **~ная о́пухоль** malignant tumour; **~ное малокро́вие** pernicious anaemia.

злоключе́ни|е, я *nt.* mishap, misadventure.

злоко́знен|ный (~, ~на) *adj.* (*obs.*) crafty, wily; malicious.

злонаме́рен|ный (~, ~на) *adj.* ill-intentioned.

злонра́ви|е, я *nt.* (*obs.*) bad character; depravity.

злонра́в|ный (~ен, ~на) *adj.* (*obs.*) having a bad character; depraved.

злопа́мятност|ь, и *f.* = **злопа́мятство**

злопа́мят|ный (~ен, ~на) *adj.* rancorous, unforgiving.

злопа́мятств|о, а *nt.* rancour (*Br.*), rancor (*US*).

злополу́ч|ный (~ен, ~на) *adj.* unlucky, ill-starred.

злопыха́тел|ь, я *m.* (*coll.*) spiteful critic.

злопыха́тельский *adj.* (*coll.*) spiteful, malevolent.

злопыха́тельств|о, а *nt.* (*coll.*) malevolence.

злора́д|ный (~ен, ~на) *adj.* gloating.

злора́дств|о, а *nt.* malicious pleasure, Schadenfreude.

злора́дств|овать, ую *impf.* to gloat.

злосло́ви|е, я *nt.* scandal, backbiting.

злосло́в|ить, лю, ишь *impf.* to say spiteful things.

зло́ст|ный (~ен, ~на) *adj.* **1** (*исполненный зла*) malicious. **2** (*сознательно недобросовестный*) conscious, intentional; **~ное банкро́тство** fraudulent bankruptcy; **з. неплате́льщик** persistent defaulter (*in payment of debt*). **3** (*закоренелый*) inveterate, hardened.

злост|ь, и *f.* malice, fury; **их з. берёт на него́** they are furious with him.

злосча́ст|ный (~ен, ~на) *adj.* ill-fated, ill-starred.

зло́т|ый, ого *m.* zloty (*Polish currency*).

злоумы́шленник, а *m.* plotter; criminal.

злоумы́шленный *adj.* (*obs.*) with criminal intent.

злоупотреб|и́ть, лю́, и́шь *pf.* (*of* ⇒**~ля́ть**) (+ *i.*) to abuse; (*сладким*) to indulge in to excess; **з. вла́стью** to abuse power; **з. чьим-н. внима́нием** to take up too much of s.o.'s time.

злоупотребле́ни|е, я *nt.* (+ *i.*) abuse (of); **з. дове́рием** breach of confidence.

З

злоупотреб|ля́ть, ля́ю *impf. of* **⇒~и́ть**

злоязы́чи|е, я *nt.* (*obs.*) slander, back-biting.

злоязы́ч|ный (~ен, ~на) *adj.* (*obs.*) slanderous.

злы́д|ень, ня *m.* (*dial.*) **1** (*obs.*) (*плут*) rogue, rascal. **2** (*злой человек*) wicked person; wicked creature.

злю́к|а, и *c.g.* (*coll.*) curmudgeon, crosspatch.

злю́чк|а, и *c.g.* = **злю́ка**

злю́щий *adj.* (*coll.*) furious.

змееви́д|ный (~ен, ~на) *adj.* serpentine; sinuous.

змееви́к, а́ *m.* **1** (*tech.*) coil(-pipe). **2** (*min.*) serpentine, ophite.

змеёныш, а *m.* young snake.

зме|и́ный *adj.* **1** *adj. of* **⇒~я́; ~и́ная ко́жа** snake-skin. **2** (*коварный*) cunning, crafty; wicked.

змеи́ст|ый (~, ~а) *adj.* serpentine, sinuous.

зме|и́ться, и́тся *impf.* to wind, coil; (*fig., poet. pej.*) to glide; **по её лицу́ ~и́лась улы́бка** a smile stole across her face.

змей, змея́ *m.* **1** (*obs. or coll.*) = **змея́. 2** (*myth.*) dragon, serpent. **3**: **(бума́жный) з.** kite; **запусти́ть змея́** to fly a kite.

зме́йк|а, и *f.* **1** *dim. of* **⇒змея́; бежа́ть ~ой** to glide. **2** (*typ.*) swung dash. **3** (*coll.*) (*молния*) zip(per).

зме|я́, и́, *pl.* **~и, ~й** *f.* snake (*also fig.*); **отогре́ть, пригре́ть ~ю на свое́й груди́** to cherish a snake in one's bosom.

зми́|й, я *m.* (*arch.*) serpent, dragon; the Serpent; **напи́ться до зелёного ~я** (*coll.*) to get blind drunk.

знава́ть *pres. not used, impf.* (*coll.*) *freq. of* **⇒знать**

знак, а *m.* **1** (*in var. senses*) sign; (*след*) mark; (*символ*) token, symbol; (*comput.*) character; **з. вста́вки** caret; **номерно́й з.** licence plate; **па́мятный з.** plaque; **~и препина́ния** punctuation marks; **~и отли́чия** decorations (and medals); **~и разли́чия** (*mil.*) badges of rank, insignia; **в з.** (+*g.*) as a mark (of), as a token (of), to show. **2** (*предзнаменование*) omen. **3** (*сигнал*) signal; **пода́ть з.** to give a signal.

знако́м|ить, лю, ишь *impf.* (*of* **⇒по~**) (+*a. and* **с**+*i.*) to acquaint s.o. (with); to introduce s.o. (to).

знако́м|иться, люсь, ишься *impf.* (*of* **⇒по~**) (**с**+*i.*) **1** (*с человеком*) to meet, make the acquaintance (*of a person*). **2** (*представляться*) to introduce o.s.; **~ьтесь!** (*informal mode of introduction*) may I introduce you? **3** (*с вещью*) to become acquainted (with), familiarize o.s. (with); to study, investigate; **з. с ме́стностью** to get to know a locality.

знако́мств|о, а *nt.* **1** (**с**+*i.*) (*между людьми*) acquaintance (with); **слу́жба ~** dating service. **2** (*collect.*) (circle of) acquaintances; **по ~у** by exploiting one's personal connections, by pulling strings. **3** (**с**+*i.*) (*знание*) familiarity (with), knowledge (of).

знако́м|ый (~, ~а) *adj.* **1** familiar; **его́ лицо́ мне ~о** his face is familiar. **2** (**с**+*i.*) familiar (with); **быть ~ым** (**с**+*i.*) to be acquainted (with), know; **я с ней ~ с де́тства** I have known her since childhood. **3** *as n.* **з., ~ого** *m.*, **~ая, ~ой** *f.* acquaintance, friend.

знамена́тел|ь, я *m.* (*math.*) denominator; **о́бщий з.** common denominator; **привести́ к одному́ ~ю** (*fig.*) to reduce to the common denominator.

знамена́тел|ьный (~ен, ~ьна) *adj.* **1** significant, momentous. **2** (*gram.*) principal.

зна́м|ени, енем, *etc., see* **⇒~я**

зна́мени|е, я *nt.* sign; **з. вре́мени** sign of the times.

знамени́тост|ь, и *f.* celebrity.

знамени́т|ый (~, ~а) *adj.* celebrated, famous, renowned; **печа́льно з.** infamous, notorious.

знамен|ова́ть, у́ю *impf.* to signify, mark.

знамено́с|ец, ца *m.* standard-bearer (*also fig.*).

знамёнщик, а *m.* (*mil.*) colour bearer.

зна́мо *as pred.* (*coll. or dial.*) it is well known.

зна́м|я, *g., d., and p.* ~ени, *i.* ~енем, *pl.* **~ёна, ~ён** *nt.* banner; standard; **под ~енем** (+*g.*; *fig., rhet.*) in the name of; **высо́ко держа́ть з. свобо́ды** to keep the flag of freedom flying.

зна́ни|е, я *nt.* **1** knowledge; **со ~ем де́ла** capably, competently. **2** (*pl. only*) learning; accomplishments.

зна́т|ный (~ен, ~на́, ~но) *adj.* **1** (*аристократический*) noble. **2** (*выдающийся*) outstanding, distinguished; **~ные лю́ди** celebrities, leading figures. **3** (*coll.*) (*отличный*) splendid; **~ные бли́нчики** splendid pancakes.

знато́к, а́ *m.* expert; connoisseur.

зна|ть¹, ~ю *impf.* to know, have a knowledge of; **~ете ли вы Алекса́ндрова?** do you know Alexandrov?; **з. в лицо́** to know by sight; **з. своё де́ло** to know one's job; **з. своё ме́сто** to know one's place; **з. ме́ру** to know when to stop; **не з. поко́я** to know no peace; **з. толк** (**в**+*p.*) to be knowledgeable (about); **з. себе́ це́ну** to know one's own value; **они́ не ~ли о на́ших наме́рениях** they were unaware of our intentions; **дать кому́-н. з.** to let s.o. know; **да́йте мне з. о вас** let me hear from you; **дать себя́ з.** to make itself felt; **он з. не хо́чет** he won't listen; **~й (себе́)** quite unconcerned; **она́ ~й себе́ пе́ла** she was singing away quite unconcerned; **то и ~й** (*coll.*) continually; **как з., почём з.?** who can tell?, how should I know?; **кто его́ ~ет, Бог его́ ~ет, чёрт его́ ~ет** (*coll.*) goodness knows!; God knows!; the devil (only) knows!; **вам лу́чше з.** you know best; **~ешь (ли), ~ете (ли)** (*coll.*) you know, do you know what?

знат|ь², и *no pl., f.* (*collect.*) the nobility, the aristocracy.

знать³ *as pred.* (*coll.*) evidently, it seems.

зна́|ться, юсь *impf.* (**с**+*i.*; *coll.*) to associate (with).

зна́хар|ка, ки *f. of* **⇒~ь**

зна́хар|ь, я *m.* sorcerer, witch-doctor; quack(-doctor).

зна́ч|ащий *pres. part. act. of* **⇒~ить** *and adj.* significant, meaningful.

значе́ни|е, я *nt.* **1** (*смысл*) meaning, significance. **2** (*важность*) importance, significance; **придава́ть большо́е з.** (+*d.*) to attach great importance (to); **э́то не име́ет ~я** it is of no importance. **3** (*math.*) value.

зна́чимост|ь, и *f.* significance.

зна́чим|ый (~, ~а) *adj.* significant.

зна́чит (*coll.*) so, then; well then; **он у́мер до войны́? з., вы не́ были с ним знако́мы** he died before the war? then you didn't know him.

значи́тел|ьный (~ен, ~ьна) *adj.* **1** (*большой*) considerable, sizeable; **в ~ьной сте́пени** to a considerable extent. **2** (*важный*) important; **игра́ть ~ьную роль** to play an important part. **3** (*выразительный*) significant, meaningful.

зна́ч|ить, у, ишь *impf.* **1** (*иметь смысл*) to mean, signify. **2** (*иметь значение*) to mean, have significance, be of importance; **ничего́ не ~ит** it is of no importance; **э́то о́чень мно́го ~ит для неё** it means a great deal to her.

зна́ч|иться, усь, ишься *impf.* to be; to be mentioned, appear; **з. в о́тпуску** to be on leave; **з. в спи́ске** to appear on a list.

знач|о́к, ка́ *m.* **1** badge. **2** (*пометка*) mark.

зна́|ющий *pres. part. act. of* **⇒~ть** *and adj.* expert; learned, erudite.

зноб|и́ть, и́т *impf.* (*impers.*): **меня́,** *etc.*, **~и́т** I, *etc.*, feel shivery, feverish.

зно|й, я *m.* intense heat; sultriness.

зно́|йный (~ен, ~йна) *adj.* hot, sultry; torrid; burning (*also fig.*).

зоб, а, *pl.* **~ы́, ~о́в** *m.* **1** (*птицы*) crop, craw. **2** (*med.*) goitre (*Br.*), goiter (*US*).

зов, а *m.* **1** call, summons. **2** (*coll.*) (*приглашение*) invitation.

зов|у́, ёшь *see* **⇒звать**

зодиа́к, а *m.* (*astron.*) zodiac; **зна́ки ~а** signs of the zodiac.

зодиака́льный *adj.* (*astron.*) zodiacal, of the zodiac.

зо́дчес|кий *adj. of* **⇒~тво**

зо́дчеств|о, а *nt.* architecture.

зо́дч|ий, его *m.* architect.

зол¹ *see* **⇒злой**

зол² *g. pl. of* **⇒зло¹**

зол|а́, ы́ *no pl., f.* ashes, cinders.

золо́вк|а, и *f.* sister-in-law (*husband's sister*).

золота́рник, а *m.* (*bot.*) golden rod.

золоти́льщик, а *m.* gilder.

золоти́ст|ый (~, ~а) *adj.* golden (*of colour*).

золо|ти́ть, чу́, ти́шь *impf.* (*of* ⇒**вы́~** *and* **по~**) to gild.

золо|ти́ться, ти́тся *impf.* **1** (*становиться золотистым*) to become golden. **2** (*виднеться*) to shine (*of sth. golden*).

зо́лотк|о, а *nt.* (*coll.*) sweetheart, sweetie(-pie).

золотни́к[1], а́ *m.* zolotnik (*old Russian measure of weight, equivalent to 4.26 grams*); **мал з., да до́рог** (*coll.*) small but precious.

золотни́к[2], а́ *m.* (*tech.*) slide valve.

зо́лот|о, а *no pl., nt.* gold; (*collect.*) gold (*coins, ware*); **«бе́лое з.»** 'white gold' (= *cotton*); **«голубо́е з.»** 'blue gold' (= *natural gas*); **«чёрное з.»** 'black gold' (= *oil*); (*fig.*): **она́ настоя́щее з.** she is pure gold, a treasure; **не всё то з., что блести́т** (*prov.*) all that glitters is not gold; **на вес ~а** worth its weight in gold.

золотоволо́с|ый (~, ~а) *adj.* golden-haired.

золотоиска́тел|ь, я *m.* gold-prospector; gold-digger.

золот|о́й *adj.* **1** gold; golden (*also fig.*); **~ы́х дел ма́стер** goldsmith; **з. песо́к** gold-dust; **з. запа́с** (*econ.*) gold reserves; **~а́я ры́бка** goldfish; **~о́е руно́** (*myth.*) golden fleece; **з. век** the Golden Age; **~о́е дно** (*fig.*) gold-mine; **~а́я молодёжь** gilded youth; **~ы́е ру́ки** skilful fingers; **~а́я середи́на** golden mean. **2** (*coll.*) (*дорогой*) invaluable, precious; **мой з.!** my precious! **3** *as n.* **з., ~о́го** *m.* gold coin.

золотоно́с|ный (~ен, ~на) *adj.* gold-bearing; **з. райо́н** gold-field.

золотопромы́шленност|ь, и *f.* gold-mining.

золоту́х|а, и *f.* (*med.*) scrofula.

золоту́шный *adj.* (*med.*) scrofulous.

золоче́ни|е, я *nt.* gilding.

золочёный *adj.* gilded, gilt.

Зо́лушк|а, и *f.* Cinderella.

зо́льник, а *m.* (*tech.*) ashpit; ashpan.

зо́н|а, ы *f.* **1** zone; area; **з. де́йствий** (*mil.*) zone of operations; **з. пораже́ния** (*mil.*) area under fire. **2** (*geol.*) stratum, layer. **3** (*sl.*) (*лагерь*) prison camp.

зона́льный *adj.* zone (*attr.*); (*характерный для определённой зоны*) regional.

зонд, а *m.* **1** (*med.*) probe. **2** (*meteor.*) weather-balloon.

зонда́ж, а *m.* sounding, probing; (*fig.*) sounding out.

зонди́р|овать, ую *impf.* (*of* ⇒**про~**) (*med. and fig.*) to sound, probe; **з. по́чву** (*fig.*) to explore the ground.

зо́н|ный *adj. of* ⇒**~а;** (*rail.*) regional.

зонт, а́ *m.* **1** umbrella. **2** (*навес*) awning.

зо́нтик, а *m.* umbrella; (*от солнца*) sunshade, parasol.

зо́нти|чный *adj. of* ⇒**~к;** (*bot.*) umbellate, umbelliferous.

зоо... *comb. form, abbr. of* ***зоологи́ческий***

зоо́лог, а *m.* zoologist.

зоологи́ческий *adj.* **1** zoological; **з. парк, з. сад** zoological garden(s). **2** (*fig.*) (*жестокий, грубый*) brutish, bestial.

зооло́ги|я, и *f.* zoology.

зоомагази́н, а *m.* pet-shop.

зоопа́рк, а *m.* zoo; **«сафа́ри» з.** safari park.

зооте́хник, а *m.* livestock specialist.

зооте́хник|а, и *f.* animal science.

зоотехни́ческий *adj.* (farm) animal-research; **з. институ́т** animal-research institute.

зооферм|а, ы *f.* fur farm.

зо́ри *see* ⇒**заря́**

зо́р|кий (~ок, ~ка́, ~ко) *adj.* **1** sharp-sighted. **2** (*fig.*) (*проницательный*) perspicacious, penetrating; (*бдительный*) vigilant.

зо́рю *see* ⇒**заря́**

зра́з|ы, ~ *pl.* (*sg.* (*rare*) **~а, ~ы** *f.*) (*cul.*) zrazy (*meat cutlets stuffed with rice, buckwheat kasha, etc.*).

зрач|о́к, ка́ *m.* pupil (*of the eye*).

зре́лищ|е, а *nt.* **1** (*предмет наблюдения*) sight. **2** (*представление*) spectacle; show; pageant.

зре́лищ|ный *adj. of* ⇒**~е; ~ные предприя́тия** places of entertainment.

зре́лост|ь, и *f.* (*винограда*) ripeness; (*человека*) maturity (*also fig.*); **полова́я з.** puberty; **аттеста́т ~и** school-leaving certificate.

зре́л|ый (~, ~а́, ~о) *adj.* (*виноград*) ripe; (*человек*) mature (*also fig.*); **дости́гнуть ~ого во́зраста** to reach maturity; **з. ум** mature mind; **по ~ом размышле́нии** on reflection, on second thoughts.

зре́ни|е, я *nt.* (eye)sight; **по́ле ~я** (*phys.*) field of vision; **обма́н ~я** optical illusion; **то́чка ~я** point of view; **под э́тим угло́м ~я** from this standpoint.

зре|ть[1], ю, ешь *impf.* (*of* ⇒**со~**) (*о плоде*) to ripen; (*о человеке*) to mature (*also fig.*); **у нас ~ет план** our plans are maturing.

зреть[2], зрю, зришь *impf.* (*of* ⇒**у~**) (*obs.*) **1** (*видеть*) to behold. **2** (**на** + *a.*) (*смотреть*) to gaze (upon).

зри́м|ый (~, ~а) *p.p.p. of* ⇒**зреть[2]** *and adj.* visible.

зри́тел|ь, я *m.* spectator, observer; **быть ~ем** to look on.

зри́тельн|ый *adj.* **1** visual; optic; **з. нерв** optic nerve; **~ая труба́** telescope. **2**: **з. зал** hall, auditorium.

зря *adv.* (*coll.*) to no purpose, for nothing; **болта́ть з.** to chatter idly; **рабо́тать з.** to work in vain.

зря́чий *adj.* sighted (*opp. blind*).

зуб, а *m.* **1** (*pl.* **~ы, ~о́в**) (*во рту*) tooth; **з. му́дрости** wisdom tooth; **вооружённый до ~о́в** armed to the teeth; **име́ть з. (про́тив), точи́ть ~ы** (**на** + *a.*; *coll.*) to have it in for s.o.; **положи́ть ~ы на по́лку** (*coll.*) to tighten one's belt; **не по ~а́м** beyond one's capacity; **э́то пробле́ма мне не по ~а́м** (*coll.*) I cannot get my teeth into this problem; **э́то у меня́ в ~а́х навя́зло** (*coll.*) it sticks in my gullet, I am sick and tired of it; **у тебя́ з. на́ з. не попада́ет** your teeth are chattering; **~ы заговори́ть** *see* ⇒**заговори́ть[1]**; **держа́ть язы́к за ~а́ми** to hold one's tongue. **2** (*pl.* **~ья, ~ьев**) (*зубец*) tooth, cog.

зуба́ст|ый (~, ~а) *adj.* (*coll.*) sharp-toothed; (*fig.*) sharp-tongued.

зуб|е́ц, ца́ *m.* tooth, cog; **з. ви́лки** prong.

зуби́л|о, а *nt.* (*tech.*) point-tool, chisel.

зу́бно-губно́й *adj.* (*ling.*) labio-dental.

зубн|о́й *adj.* **1** dental; **~а́я боль** tooth-ache; **з. врач** dentist; **~а́я па́ста** tooth-paste; **з. порошо́к** tooth-powder; **~а́я щётка** tooth-brush. **2** (*ling.*) dental.

зубовраче́бн|ый *adj. of* ⇒**зубно́й врач; з. кабине́т** dental surgery (*Br.*), dentist's office (*US*); **~ая шко́ла** dental school.

зубоврачева́ни|е, я *nt.* dentistry.

зуб|о́к, ка́, *pl.* **~ки́, ~о́к** *m. dim. of* ⇒**~; подари́ть на з.** (*coll.*) to bring a present for a (new-born) baby; **попа́сть на з. кому́-н.** (*coll., fig.*) to be torn to pieces by s.o.

зубоска́л|ить, ю, ишь *impf.* (*coll.*) to scoff, mock.

зубоска́льств|о, а *nt.* (*coll.*) scoffing, mocking.

зуботы́чин|а, ы *f.* (*vulg.*) sock on the jaw.

зубочи́стк|а, и *f.* toothpick.

зубр, а *m.* **1** (*zool.*) (European) bison. **2** (*fig.*) die-hard.

зубрёжк|а, и *f.* (*coll.*) cramming.

зубри́л|а, ы *c.g.* (*coll.*) crammer.

зубр|и́ть[1], ю́, ~и́шь *impf.* (*of* ⇒**за~**) to notch, serrate.

зубр|и́ть[2], ю́, ~и́шь *impf.* (*of* ⇒**вы́~** *and* **за~**) (*coll.*) to cram.

зубро́вк|а, и *f.* **1** (*злак*) sweet grass, holy grass. **2** (*водка*) zubrovka (*sweet-grass vodka*).

зубча́т|ый *adj.* **1** (*tech.*) toothed, cogged; **~ая желе́зная доро́га** rack-railway; **~ое колесо́** cogwheel; **~ая ре́йка** rack. **2** (*зазубренный*) jagged, indented.

зуд, а *m.* itch; (*fig.*) itch, urge.

зуд|е́ть, и́т *impf.* **1** (*coll.*) to itch (*intrans.*). **2** (*fig.*) to itch, feel an itch (*to do sth.*).

зу|ди́ть, жу́, ди́шь *impf.* (*coll.*) **1** (*надоедать*) to nag at. **2** (*зубрить*) to cram.

зу|ёк, йка́ *m.* (*zool.*) plover.

зулу́с, а *m.* Zulu.

зулу́с|ка, ки *f. of* ⇒**~**

зулу́сский *adj.* Zulu.

зу́ммер, а *m.* (*tech.*) buzzer; tone; **з. за́нятости** engaged tone.

ЗУПВ *nt. indecl.* (*abbr. of* ***запомина́ющее устро́йство с произво́льной вы́боркой***) (*comput.*) RAM (*random-access memory*).

зы́б|кий (~ок, ~ка́, ~ко) *adj.* (*поверхность*) rippling; (*почва*) unsteady, shaky; (*fig.*) unstable, vacillating.

зыбу́ч|ий *adj.* unsteady, unstable; **~ие пески́** quicksands.

З

зыб|ь, и, *pl.* **~и, ~е́й** *f.* (*on water*) ripple; **мёртвая з.** swell.

зы́ч|ный (~ен, ~на) *adj.* (*coll.*) loud, booming.

зэк, а *m.* (*sl.*) prisoner, convict.

зюйд, а *m.* (*naut.*) **1** (*юг*) south. **2** (*южный ветер*) southerly wind.

зюйдве́стк|а, и *f.* sou'wester (hat).

зя́б|кий (~ок, ~ка́, ~ко) *adj.* sensitive to cold.

зя́б|левый *adj. of* ⇨ **~ь; ~левая вспа́шка** autumn ploughing (*Br.*), plowing (*US*).

зя́блик, а *m.* chaffinch.

зя́б|нуть, ну, нешь, *past* **~, ~ла** *impf.* to suffer from cold, feel the cold.

зяб|ь, и *f.* (*agric.*) land ploughed (*Br.*), plowed (*US*) in autumn for spring sowing.

зят|ь, я, *pl.* **~ья́, ~ьёв** *m.* **1** (*муж дочери*) son-in-law. **2** (*муж сестры; муж золовки*) brother-in-law.

И и

и[1] *conj.* **1** and; **добро́ и зло** good and evil; *indicating temporal sequence*: **я встал и вы́мылся и побри́лся** I got up and washed and shaved; *introducing narrative*: **и наста́ло у́тро** and then came the morning; *emph. questions*: **и ра́зве э́то не пра́вда?** and is it not the truth?; *adversative*: **мужчи́на, и пла́чет!** a man, and crying!; **и так да́лее, и про́чее** (*abbr.* **и т. д., и пр.**) etcetera, and so on, and so forth.
2: **и**... **и** both ... and; **и тот и друго́й** both.
3 (*тоже*) too; (*with negation*) either; **она́ сказа́ла, что и муж придёт** she said that her husband would come too; **и он не знал** he did not know either.
4 (*даже*) even; **и знато́к ошиба́ется** even an expert may be mistaken; **я не мог бы и поду́мать об э́том** I would not (even) think of it.
5 (*emph.*) (*именно*): **в то́м-то и де́ло** that is the whole point.

и[2] *int.* (*expr. disagreement*; *coll.*) oh!; **и, по́лно!** that's quite enough!; (*iron.*) you don't say (so)!

иберийский *adj.* Iberian.

Ибе́ри|я, и *f.* Iberia.

и́бис, а *m.* (*zool.*) ibis.

и́бо *conj.* for.

и́в|а, ы *f.* willow; **корзи́ночная и.** osier; **плаку́чая и.** weeping willow.

ива́новск|ий *adj. only in phr.* **во всю ~ую** (*coll.*) with all one's might; extremely loudly; **крича́ть во всю ~ую** to shout at the top of one's voice; **скака́ть во всю ~ую** to go hell-for-leather.

ива́н-чай, ива́н-ча́я *no pl., m.* (*bot.*) rose-bay, willow-herb.

ивня́к, а́ *no pl., m.* **1** osier-bed. **2** (*collect.*) osier(s).

и́в|овый *adj. of* ⇒**~а**

и́волг|а, и *f.* (*zool.*) oriole.

иври́т, а *m.* (modern) Hebrew.

игл|а́, ы́, *pl.* **~́ы, ~** *f.* **1** (*для шитья*) needle. **2** (*bot.*) (*у хвойных деревьев*) needle; (*у растения*) thorn, prickle; **ело́вая и.** fir-needle. **3** (*ежа*) quill, spin. **4** (*проигрывателя*) needle, stylus.

игли́ст|ый (~, ~а) *adj.* prickly; covered with quills.

иглова́т|ый (~, ~а) *adj.* (*coll.*) prickly.

иглови́д|ный (~ен, ~на) *adj.* needle-shaped.

иглодержа́тел|ь, я *m.* needle-holder; (*проигрывателя*) cartridge.

иглообра́з|ный (~ен, ~на) *adj.* needle-shaped.

иглотерапе́вт, а *m.* acupuncturist.

иглотерапи́|я, и *f.* acupuncture.

иглоука́лывани|е, я *nt.* = **иглотерапи́я**

игнори́р|овать, ую *impf. and pf.* to ignore; to disregard.

и́г|о, а *nt.* yoke (*fig.*); **тата́рское и.** (*hist.*) the Tatar yoke.

иго́лк|а, и *f.* needle; **сиде́ть как на ~ах** to be on thorns, on tenterhooks; **каблуки́ на ~ах** stiletto heels.

иго́лочк|а, и *f. dim. of* ⇒**иго́лка;** (*coll.*) **оде́тый с ~и** spick and span; **костю́м с ~и** brand-new suit.

иго́льник, а *m.* (*футлярчик*) needle-case; (*подушечка*) pin-cushion.

иго́льн|ый *adj. of* ⇒**игла́; ~ое ушко́** eye of a needle.

иго́льчат|ый *adj.* **1** needle-shaped; **~ые каблуки́** stiletto heels. **2**: **и. при́нтер** (*comput.*) dot-matrix printer.

иго́рный *adj.* playing, gaming; **и. дом** gaming-house; **и. прито́н** gambling-den; **и. стол** gaming table.

игр|а́, ы́, *pl.* **~́ы** *f.* **1** (*действие*) play, playing; **гря́зная и.** foul play; **у скрипа́чки была́ блестя́щая и.** the violinist's performance was brilliant; **и. све́та на стене́** the play of light on the wall; **и. слов** play upon words; **биржева́я и.** stock exchange speculation; **и. приро́ды** freak, sport of nature.
2 (*занятие*) game; **аза́ртная и.** game of chance; **ко́мнатные ~́ы** indoor games, party games; **одино́чные ~́ы** (*tennis*) singles; **па́рные ~́ы** (*tennis*) doubles; **олимпи́йские ~́ы** Olympic games; (*fig.*) **опа́сная и.** dangerous game; **и. не сто́ит свеч** the game is not worth the candle; **игра́ть, вести́ большу́ю, кру́пную ~у́** to play for high stakes; **раскры́ть чью-н. ~у́** to uncover s.o.'s game.
3 (*sport, cards*) (*партия*) game (*part of set, match*, etc.); **взять ~у́ при свое́й пода́че** to win one's service.
4 (*cards*) hand; **сдать хоро́шую ~у́** to deal a good hand.
5 (*очередь*) turn (*to play*); **сейча́с твоя́ и.** it is your turn now.

игра́льн|ый *adj.* playing; **~ые ка́рты** playing cards; **~ые ко́сти** dice.

и́граный *adj.* (*coll.*) (already) used.

игра́|ть, ю *impf.* (*of* ⇒**сыгра́ть**) **1** to play; **и. пье́су** to put on a play; **и. роль** to play a part; **и. Ле́ди Макбе́т** to play, take the part of, Lady Macbeth; **э́то не ~ет ро́ли** it is of no importance, it does not signify; **и. симфо́нию** to play a symphony; **и. пе́рвую, втору́ю скри́пку** (*fig.*) to play first, second fiddle; **и. кому́-н. на́ руку** (*fig.*) to play into s.o.'s hands; **и. глаза́ми** to flash one's eyes; **и. слова́ми** to play upon words; **и. ферзём** to move the queen (*at chess*); **и. в ка́рты, те́ннис, футбо́л, ша́хматы** *etc.*, to play cards, tennis, football, chess, *etc.*; **и. в зага́дки** to talk in riddles; **и. в пря́тки** to play hide-and-seek; (*fig.*) to be secretive; **и. в скро́мность** to feign modesty; **и. на роя́ле, скри́пке** *etc.*, to play the piano, the violin, etc.; **и. на билья́рде** to play billiards; **и. на би́рже** to speculate on the Stock Exchange; **и. на** (+*p.*) to play on (*fig.*); **и. на чу́вствах толпы́** to play on the emotions of a crowd.
2 (*impf. only*) (+*i. or* **с**+*i.*) (*относиться несерьёзно*) to play with, toy with, trifle with (*also fig.*); **и. чьи́ми-н. чу́вствами** to trifle with s.o.; **и. с огнём** (*fig.*) to play with fire.
3 (*impf. only*) (*сверкать*) to play; to sparkle (*of wine, jewellery, etc.*); **улы́бка ~ла на её лице́** a smile played on her face.

игра́ючи *adv.* (*coll.*) effortlessly; with one's eyes closed.

игра́|ющий *pres. part. act. of* ⇒**~ть;** *as n.* **и., ~ющего** *m.* player.

и́грек, а *m.* (*the letter*) y; (*math.*) y (*second unknown quantity*).

игре́невый *adj.* skewbald.

игри́в|ый (~, ~а) *adj.* playful; (*coll.*) naughty, ribald.

игри́ст|ый (~, ~а) *adj.* sparkling (*of wine*).

игр|ово́й *adj. of* ⇒**~á; и. автома́т** one-armed bandit, fruit machine (*Br.*).

игро́к, á *m.* **1** (**в**+*a.*, **на**+*p.*) player (of); **и. в футбо́л** football-player; **хоро́ший и. на балала́йке** a good balalaika player. **2** (*в азартные игры*) gambler.

игроте́к|а, и *f.* (*собрание игр*) compendium (*Br.*), collection of children's games; (*комната*) games room.

игру́шечный *adj.* **1** toy; **и. парово́з** toy-engine. **2** (*coll.*) (*очень маленький*) tiny.

игру́шк|а, и *f.* toy; (*fig.*) plaything; **ёлочные ~и** Christmas tree decorations.

игуа́н|а, ы *f.* (*zool.*) iguana.

игу́мен, а *m.* (*eccl.*) Father Superior (*of monastery*).

игу́мен|ья, ьи, *g. pl.* **~ий** *f.* (*eccl.*) Mother Superior (*of a convent*).

идеа́л, а *m.* ideal.

идеализи́р|овать, ую *impf. and pf.* to idealize.

идеали́зм, а *m.* idealism.

идеали́ст, а *m.* idealist.

идеалисти́ческий *adj.* (*phil.*) idealist(ic).

идеалисти́ч|ный (~ен, ~на) *adj.* idealistic.

идеа́л|ьный (~ен, ~ьна) *adj.* **1** (*phil.*) ideal. **2** (*coll.*) ideal, perfect; **~ьное состоя́ние** perfect *or* mint condition.

иде́йк|а, и *f.* (*pej.*) *dim. of* ⇒**иде́я**

иде́йност|ь, и *f.* **1** ideological content. **2** (*прогрессивность*) 'progressive' character. **3** (*принципиальность*) principle, integrity.

иде́|йный (~ен, ~йна) *adj.* **1** (*идеологический*) ideological. **2** (*преданный какой-н. идее*) expressing an idea *or* ideas; committed, engagé; **~йная пье́са** play of ideas. **3** (*прогрессивный*) 'progressive'; **~йное иску́сство** 'progressive' art. **4** (*принципиальный*) high-principled, acting on principle.

идентифика́ци|я, и *f.* identification.

идентифици́р|овать, ую *impf. and pf.* to identify.

иденти́чност|ь, и *f.* identity.

иденти́ч|ный (~ен, ~на) *adj.* identical.

идеогра́мм|а, ы *f.* (*ling.*) ideogram.

идеогра́фи|я, и *f.* (*ling.*) ideography.

идео́лог, а *m.* ideologist.

идеологи́ческий *adj.* ideological.

идеоло́ги|я, и *f.* ideology.

идёт (*3rd pers. sg. pres. of* ⇒**идти́**) *as int.* (*coll.*) (all) right!

иде́|я, и *f.* **1** idea (*also coll.*); notion, concept; (*phil.*) Idea; **боро́ться за ~ю** to fight for an idea; **~я-фикс, навя́зчивая и.** obsession, idée fixe; **счастли́вая и.** happy thought. **2** (*главная мысль*) point, purport (*of a work of art*); **по ~е** (*coll.*) in principle.

идилли́ческий *adj.* idyllic.

иди́лли|я, и *f.* idyll (*liter. and fig.*).

идио́м|а, ы *f.* (*and* **~, ~а** *m.*) idiom.

идиома́тик|а, и *f.* (*ling.*) **1** (*учение об идиомах*) study of idiom(s). **2** (*collect.*) idiom, idiomatic expressions.

идиомати́ческий *adj.* idiomatic.

идиосинкрази́|я, и *f.* (*med.*) allergy.

идио́т, а *m.* idiot, imbecile (*med. and coll.*).

идиоти́зм, а *m.* idiocy, imbecility (*med. and coll.*).

идиоти́ческий *adj.* idiotic, imbecile.

идио́тский *adj.* idiotic, imbecile.

и́диш *m. indecl.* Yiddish (*language*).

и́дол, а *m.* idol (*also fig.*); **стоя́ть, сиде́ть ~ом** to stand, sit like a stuffed dummy.

идолопокло́нник, а *m.* idolater.

идолопокло́ннический *adj.* idolatrous.

идолопокло́нств|о, а *nt.* idolatry.

ид|ти́ (итти́), у́, ёшь, *past* **шёл, шла** *impf.* (*of* ⇒**пойти́**; *det. of* ⇒**ходи́ть**) **1** to go; (*impf. only*) (*приближаться*) to come; **и. в го́ру** to go uphill; **авто́бус ~ёт** the bus is coming; **кто ~ёт?** who goes there?; **и. гуля́ть** to go for a walk; **и. в прода́жу** to go for sale, be up for sale; **и. в но́гу** to keep in step (*also fig.*); **и. на охо́ту** to go hunting; **и. на сме́ну** (+*d.*) to take the place (of), succeed. **2** (**на**+*a.*) (*поступать*) to enter; (**в**+*nom.-a.*) to become; **и. на госуда́рственную слу́жбу** to enter Government service; **и. в лётчики** to become an airman. **3** (**в**+*a.*) (*употребляться*) to be used (for); (**на**+*a.*) to go to make; **и. в корм** to be used for fodder; **и. в лом** to go for scrap; **и. на ю́бку** to go to make a skirt. **4** (**из, от**+*g.*) (*о дыме, воде*) to come (from), proceed (from); **из трубы́ шёл чёрный дым** black smoke was coming from the chimney. **5** (*о новостях*) to go round; **шла молва́, что...** word went round that ..., rumour (*Br.*), rumor (*US*) had it that .... **6** (*coll.*) (*находить сбыт*) to sell, be sold; **хорошо́ и.** to be selling well; **и. за бесце́нок** to go for a song. **7** (*о механизме*) to go, run, work. **8** (*о дожде, снеге*) to fall; **дождь, снег ~ёт** it is raining, snowing. **9** (*о времени*) to pass; **шли го́ды** years passed; **ей ~ёт трídца́тый год** she is in her thirtieth year. **10** (*происходить*) to go on, be in progress; (*о спектакле*) to be on, be showing; **перегово́ры ~у́т** talks are in progress; **сего́дня ~ёт «Ревизо́р»** 'The Government Inspector' is on today. **11** (+*d. or* **к**+*d.*) (*быть к лицу*) to suit, become; **э́та шля́па ей не ~ёт** this hat does not become her. **12** (**в, на**+*a.*; *coll.*) (*о гвозде; о сапоге*) to go (in, on). **13** (+*i.* or **с**+*g.*) (*делать ход в игре*) to play, lead, move (*at chess, cards, etc.*); **и. ферзём** to move one's queen; **и. с черве́й** to lead a heart. **14** (**о**+*p.*) (*о разговоре*) to be (about); **де́ло ~ёт, речь ~ёт о том, что...** the point is that ..., it is a matter of ....

и́д|ы, ~ *no sg.* (*hist.*) Ides.

иегови́ст, а *m.* (*relig.*) Jehovah's witness.

Иезеки́л|ь, я *m.* (*bibl.*) Ezekiel.

иезуи́т, а *m.* (*eccl.*) Jesuit.

иезуи́тский *adj.* (*eccl.*) Jesuit; (*fig.*) Jesuitical.

ие́н|а, ы *f.* yen (*Japanese currency*).

иера́рх, а *m.* hierarch.

иерархи́ческий *adj.* hierarchic(al).

иера́рхи|я, и *f.* hierarchy.

иере́|й, я *m.* priest.

Иереми́|я, и *m.* (*bibl.*) Jeremiah.

иеро́глиф, а *m.* (*египетский*) hieroglyph; (*китайский, японский*) character.

иероглифи́ческий *adj.* hieroglyphic.

иеромона́х *m.* (*eccl.*) father (*priest in monastic order, as opposed to lay brother*).

Иерусали́м, а *m.* Jerusalem.

иждиве́н|ец, ца *m.* dependant; (*нахлебник*) sponger.

иждиве́ни|е, я *nt.* maintenance; **на чьём-н. ~и** at s.o.'s expense.

иждиве́н|ка, ки *f. of* ⇒**~ец**

иждиве́нчеств|о, а *nt.* dependence.

и́же *rel. pron.*: **и и́же с ним(и)** (*liter.*) (and others) of that ilk, and company.

и́жиц|а, ы *f.* 'izhitsa' (*last letter of Church Slavonic and pre-1918 Russian alphabet*); **прописа́ть ~у** (+*d.*) (*obs. or joc.*) to lecture, bring to book.

из (изо) *prep.*+*g.* from, out of; of. **1** (*обозначает источник действия*): **прие́хать из Ло́ндона** to come from London; **пить из ча́шки** to drink out of a cup; **узна́ть из газе́т** to learn from the newspapers; **из достове́рных исто́чников** from reliable sources, on good authority; **вы́йти из себя́** to be beside o.s.; **вы́йти из употребле́ния** to pass out of use, become obsolete; **он из крестья́н** he is of peasant origin. **2** (*обозначает часть целого*): **оди́н из её покло́нников** one of her admirers; **ни оди́н из ста** not one in a hundred; **мла́дший из всех** the youngest of all; **главне́йшие собы́тия из исто́рии Росси́и** the principal events in the history of Russia. **3** (*обозначает материал*): **из чего́ э́то сде́лано?** what is it made of?; **варе́нье из абрико́сов** apricot jam; **обе́д из трёх блюд** a three-course dinner; **ло́жки из серебра́** silver spoons; **буке́т из кра́сных гвозди́к** bouquet of red carnations; (*fig.*; *of human potential*) **из него́ вы́йдет хоро́ший труба́ч** he will make a good trumpet-player. **4** (*обозначает средство*): **изо всех сил** with all one's might; **из после́дних средств** with one's last penny. **5** (*обозначает причину*): **из благода́рности** in gratitude; **из ли́чных вы́год** for private gain; **из ре́вности** from jealousy; **мно́го шу́му из ничего́** a lot of fuss about nothing.

из... (*also* **изо..., изъ...** *and* **ис...**) *vbl. pref. indicating*: **1** motion outwards. **2** action over entire surface of object, in all directions. **3** expenditure of instrument *or* object in course of action; continuation *or* repetition of action to extreme point; exhaustiveness of action.

изб|а́, ы́, *a.* **~́у,** *pl.* **~ы** *f.* izba (*peasant's hut or cottage*).

избави́тел|ь, я *m.* deliverer.

избави́тель|ница, ~ницы *f. of* **⇒~**

изба́в|ить, лю, ишь *pf.* (*of* **⇒~ля́ть**) (**от**+*g.*) to save, deliver (from); **~ьте меня́ от ва́ших замеча́ний** spare me your remarks; **~ьте меня́!** leave me alone!; **~и Бог!** God forbid!

изба́в|иться, люсь, ишься *pf.* (*of* **⇒~ля́ться**) (**от**+*g.*) to be saved (from), escape; to get out (of); to get rid (of); **и. от привы́чки** to get out of a habit.

избавле́ни|е, я *nt.* deliverance.

избавля́|ть(ся), ю(сь) *impf. of* **⇒изба́вить(ся)**

избало́ванный *p.p.p. of* **⇒избалова́ть** *and adj.* spoilt.

избал|ова́ть, у́ю *pf.* (*of* **⇒балова́ть** *and* **~о́вывать**) to spoil (*a child, etc.*).

избал|ова́ться, у́юсь *pf.* (*of* **⇒~о́вываться**) to become spoilt.

избало́выва|ть(ся), ю(сь) *impf. of* **⇒избалова́ть(ся)**

избе́га|ть, ю *pf.* (*coll.*) to run about, run all over.

избег|а́ть, а́ю *impf.* (*of* **⇒~́нуть** *and* **избежа́ть**) (+*g. or inf.*) (*сторониться*) to avoid; (*избавляться*) to escape, evade; **и. встреча́ться с кем-н.** to avoid meeting s.o.; **и. штра́фа** to evade a penalty.

избе́га|ться, юсь *pf.* (*coll.*) to exhaust o.s. by running (about).

избе́г|нуть, ну, нешь, *past* **~нул** *and* **~, ~ла** *pf. of* **⇒~а́ть**

избежа́ни|е, я *nt.*: **во и.** (+*g.*) in order to avoid.

избе|жа́ть, гу́, жи́шь, гу́т *pf. of* **⇒~га́ть**

избива́|ть, ю *impf. of* **⇒изби́ть**

избие́ни|е, я *nt.* **1** (*убийство*) slaughter, massacre; **и. младе́нцев** (*bibl.*; *also fig. of persecutions*) Massacre of the Innocents. **2** (*leg.*) assault and battery; **и. гомосексуали́стов** gay-bashing.

избира́тел|ь, я *m.* elector, voter; **колеблю́щийся и.** floating voter.

избира́тельност|ь, и *f.* (*radio*) selectivity.

избира́тельн|ый *adj.* **1** electoral; **и. бюллете́нь** voting-paper; **~ая кампа́ния** election campaign; **и. о́круг** electoral district; **~ое пра́во** suffrage; franchise; **и. спи́сок** electoral roll, register of voters; **~ая у́рна** ballot-box; **и. уча́сток** polling station; **и. ценз** voting qualification. **2** (*tech.*) selective.

избира́|ть, ю *impf. of* **⇒избра́ть**

изби́т|ый *p.p.p. of* **⇒~ь** *and adj.*; (*fig.*) hackneyed, trite.

из|би́ть, обью́, обьёшь *pf.* (*of* **⇒~бива́ть**) **1** (*человека*) to beat unmercifully, beat up. **2** (*coll.*) (*дорогу, обувь*) to wear out, ruin.

изболе́|ть(ся), ю(сь) *pf.* (*coll.*) to be in torment.

избо́рник, а *m.* (*hist., liter.*) miscellany, anthology.

избороз|ди́ть, жу́, ди́шь *pf. of* **⇒борозди́ть**

избоче́н|иваться, иваюсь *impf. of* **⇒~иться**

избоче́н|иться, юсь, ишься *pf.* (*of* **⇒~иваться**) (*coll.*) to stand in a challenging pose (with one hip forward and one hand on it).

избра́ни|е, я *nt.* election.

избра́нник, а *m.* (*rhet.*) chosen one.

избра́нн|ица, ицы *f. of* **⇒~ик**

и́збран|ный *p.p.p. of* **⇒избра́ть** *and adj.* **1** (*отобранный*) selected; **~ные сочине́ния Пу́шкина** selected works of Pushkin; **вновь и.** ... elect; **вновь и. президе́нт** president elect. **2** (*лучший*) select; *as n.* **~ные, ~ных** *no sg.*, élite.

из|бра́ть, беру́, берёшь, *past* **~бра́л, ~брала́, ~бра́ло** *pf.* (*of* **⇒~бира́ть**) (+*a. and i.*) to elect (as, for); to choose; **его́ ~бра́ли чле́ном парла́мента** he has been elected a Member of Parliament.

избу́шк|а, и *f. dim. of* **⇒изба́**

избы́т|ок, ка *m.* (*излишек*) surplus, excess; (*обилие*) abundance, plenty; **в ~ке** in plenty; **от ~ка се́рдца, от ~ка чувств** from a fullness of heart.

избы́точ|ный (~ен, ~на) *adj.* **1** (*излишний*) surplus. **2** (*обильный*) abundant, plentiful.

изваа́ни|е, я *nt.* statue, sculpture; graven image.

изваа́|ть, ю *pf. of* **⇒вая́ть**

изве́д|ать, аю *pf.* (*of* **⇒~ывать**) to come to know, learn the meaning of; **и. го́ре** to taste grief.

изве́дыва|ть, ю *impf. of* **⇒изве́дать**

изве́ка *adv.* (*obs.*) of old.

и́зверг, а *m.* monster, fiend.

изверг|а́ть, а́ю *impf.* (*of* **⇒~́нуть**) to spew out, disgorge; (*fig.*) to eject, expel.

изверг|а́ться, а́юсь *impf.* (*of* **⇒~́нуться**) **1** to erupt (*of volcanoes*). **2** *pass. of* **⇒~а́ть**

изве́рг|нуть(ся), ну(сь), нешь(ся), *past* **~(ся)** *and* **~нул(ся), ~ла(сь)** *pf. of* **⇒~а́ть(ся)**

изверже́ни|е, я *nt.* **1** (*вулкана*) eruption. **2** (*fig.*) ejection, expulsion.

изве́рженный *p.p.p. of* **⇒изве́ргнуть** *and adj.* (*geol.*) igneous, volcanic.

изве́рива|ться, юсь *impf. of* **⇒изве́риться**

изве́р|иться, юсь, ишься *pf.* (*of* **⇒~иваться**) (**в**+*a. or p.*) to lose faith (in), lose confidence (in); **и. в люде́й, и. в лю́дях** to lose faith in people.

извер|ну́ться, ну́сь, нёшься *pf.* (*of* **⇒~́тываться** *and* **извора́чиваться**) (*coll.*) to dodge, take evasive action (*also fig.*); **и. при отве́те** to give an evasive answer.

извер|те́ться, чу́сь, ~́тишься *pf.* (*coll.*) (*стать ветреным*) to become flighty; (*стать непоседливым*) to become restless; (*стать непослушным*) to go to the bad.

извёртыва|ться, юсь *impf. of* **⇒изверну́ться**

изве|сти́, ду́, дёшь, *past* **~́л, ~ла́** *pf.* (*of* **⇒изводи́ть**) (*coll.*) **1** (*истратить*) to spend, use up; to waste. **2** (*погубить*) to destroy, exterminate. **3** (*измучить*) to vex, exasperate; to torment.

изве́сти|е, я *nt.* **1** (**о**+*p.*) news (of); **после́дние ~я** the latest news. **2** (*pl. only*) (*название издания*) proceedings, transactions; **~я Акаде́мии нау́к** Proceedings of the Academy of Sciences.

изве|сти́сь, ду́сь, дёшься, *past* **~́лся, ~ла́сь** *pf.* (*of* **⇒изводи́ться**) (*coll.*) **1** (*измучиться*) to consume o.s., eat one's heart out; to exhaust o.s., wear o.s. out; **и. от за́висти** to consume o.s. with envy. **2** (*исчезнуть*) to perish, disappear.

изве|сти́ть, щу́, сти́шь *pf.* (*of* **⇒~ща́ть**) to inform, notify; **она́ никого́ не извести́ла о своём прие́зде** she told nobody about her arrival.

извёстк|а, и *f.* (slaked) lime.

известк|ова́ть, у́ю *impf. and pf.* (*agric.*) to lime.

известко́вый *adj. of* **⇒и́звесть**

изве́стно 1 *as pred.* it is (well) known; **как и.** as is well known; **наско́лько мне и.** as far as I know. **2** (*as particle*; *coll.*) (*конечно*) of course, certainly.

изве́стност|ь, и *f.* **1** (*слава*) fame, reputation; (*лгуна, преступника*) notoriety; **приноси́ть и.** (+*d.*) to bring fame (to); **по́льзоваться гро́мкой ~ью** to be far-famed; **привести́ в и.** to make known, make public; **поста́вить кого́-н. в и.** to inform, notify. **2** (*coll.*) (*человек*) celebrity, prominent figure.

изве́ст|ный (~ен, ~на) *adj.* **1** (+*d.*) well-known (to); (+*i.*) (well-)known (for); (**за**+*a.*) (well-)known (as); **он ~ен свое́й бо́дростью** he is well known for his cheerfulness; **челове́к, и. как пья́ница** a well-known drunkard. **2** (*лгун, преступник*) infamous, notorious. **3** (*некоторый*) (a) certain; **~ным о́бразом** in a certain way; **в ~ных слу́чаях** in certain cases; **до ~ной сте́пени, в ~ной ме́ре** to a certain extent.

известня́к, а́ *m.* limestone.

известняко́вый *adj.* limestone.

и́звест|ь, и *f.* lime; **гашёная и.** slaked lime; **негашёная и.** quicklime; **хло́рная и.** chloride of lime; **раство́р ~и** mortar, grout; (*для побелки*) whitewash.

изветша́лый *adj.* (*obs.*) dilapidated.

изветша́|ть, ет *pf.* (*obs.*) to become completely dilapidated.

изве́ч|ный (~ен, ~на) *adj.* age-old, ancient.

извещá|ть, ю *impf. of* ⇒**известúть**

извещéни|е, я *nt.* notification, notice; (*comm.*) advice.

извúв, а *m.* bend.

извивá|ть, ю *impf. of* ⇒**извúть**

извивá|ться, юсь *impf.* (*of* ⇒**извúться**) **1** (*о змее, канате*) to coil (*intrans.*); (*о черве*) to wriggle. **2** (*impf. only*) (*о дороге, реке*) to twist, wind (*intrans.*); to meander.

извúлин|а, ы *f.* bend, twist; **~ы мóзга** (*anat.*) convolutions of the brain.

извúлист|ый (~, ~а) *adj.* winding, twisting, tortuous.

извинéни|е, я *nt.* **1** (*оправдание*) excuse. **2** (*просьба о прощении*) apology; **принять ~я** to accept an apology. **3** (*прощение*) pardon; **прошý ~я** I beg your pardon, I apologize.

извинúтел|ьный (~ен, ~ьна) *adj.* **1** (*простительный*) excusable, pardonable. **2** (*выражающий извинение*) apologetic.

извин|úть, ю, úшь *pf.* (*of* ⇒**~ять**) **1** (*простить*) to excuse; **~úте (меня)!** I beg your pardon; excuse me!; (I'm) sorry!; **~úте, что я опоздáл** sorry I'm late; **прошý и. меня за бестáктное замечáние** I apologize for my tactless remark; **~úте за выражéние** (*coll.*) if you will excuse the expression; **уж ~ú(те)!** (*coll.; expr. disagreement*) excuse me! **2** (*оправдать*) to excuse; **э́то ничéм нельзя́ и.** this is inexcusable.

извин|úться, ю́сь, úшься *pf.* (*of* ⇒**~яться**) **1** (**пéред** + *i.*) (*попросить прощения*) to apologize (to); **~úтесь за меня́** present my apologies, make my excuses. **2** (+*i.*) (*оправдаться*) to excuse o.s. (on account of, on the ground of); to make excuses.

извин|ять, я́ю *impf. of* ⇒**~úть**

извин|я́ться, я́юсь *impf. of* ⇒**~úться; ~я́юсь** (*coll.*) I apologize; (I'm) sorry!

извиня́|ющийся *pres. part. of* ⇒**~ться** *and adj.* apologetic.

из|вúть, овью́, овьёшь, *past* **~вúл, ~вилá, ~вúло** *pf.* (*of* ⇒**~вивáть**) to coil, twist, wind (*trans.*).

из|вúться, овью́сь, овьёшься, *past* **~вúлся, ~вилáсь** *pf. of* ⇒**~вивáться**

извлекá|ть(ся), ю *impf. of* ⇒**извлéчь(ся)**

извлечéни|е, я *nt.* **1** (*действие*) extraction. **2** (*выдержка*) extract, excerpt.

извлé|чь, кý, чёшь, кýт, *past* **~̈к, ~клá** *pf.* (*of* ⇒**~кáть**) to extract; (*fig.*) to derive, elicit; **и. урóк** (**из** + *g.*) to learn a lesson (from); **и. пóльзу, удовóльствие** (**из** + *g.*) to derive benefit, pleasure (from); **и. кóрень** (*math.*) to find the root.

извлé|чься, чётся, кýтся, *past* **~̈кся, ~клáсь** *pf.* (*of* ⇒**~кáться**) to be extracted; to come out.

извнé *adv.* from without.

изво|дúть(ся), жý(сь), ~́дишь(ся) *impf. of* ⇒**известú(сь)**

изво|зúть, жý, ~́зишь *pf.*: **и. в грязú** (*coll.*) to drag through the mud.

извóзчик, а *m.* **1** (*кучер*) carrier; **(легковóй) и.** cabman, cabby; **(ломовóй) и.** carter, drayman. **2** (*coll.*) (*экипаж*) cab; **éхать на ~е** to go in a cab.

извóл|ить, ю, ишь *impf.* (+*inf.*; *expr. ironical disapproval*) to deign, be pleased; **бáрин ~ит спать** the master is asleep; **а как вы ~ите поживáть?** and, pray, how are you?; **~ь(те)** kindly, please be good enough; **~ьте молчáть!** kindly be quiet!

изворáчива|ться, юсь *impf. of* ⇒**извернýться**

изворóт, а *m.* **1** (*поворот*) bend, twist. **2** (*pl.*; *fig.*) (*уловки*) tricks, wiles.

изворóтист|ый (~, ~а) *adj.* (*coll.*) = **изворóтливый**

изворóтлив|ый (~, ~а) *adj.* (*спорщик, ум*) versatile, resourceful; (*человек*) wily, shrewd.

извра|тúть, щý, тúшь *pf.* (*of* ⇒**~щáть**) **1** (*испортить*) to pervert. **2** (*ложно истолковать*) to misinterpret, misconstrue; **и. úстину** to distort the truth; **и. чью-н. мысль** to misinterpret s.o.

извращá|ть, ю *impf. of* ⇒**извратúть**

извращéн|ец, ца *m.* pervert.

извращéни|е, я *nt.* **1** (*ненормальность*) perversion. **2** (*искажение*) misinterpretation, distortion (*fig.*).

извращённый *p.p.p. of* ⇒**извратúть** *and adj.* perverted; unnatural.

изгá|дить, жу, дишь *pf.* (*of* ⇒**~живать**) (*coll.*) **1** (*испачкать*) to make dirty, soil. **2** (*fig.*) (*испортить*) to make a mess of.

изгá|диться, жусь, дишься *pf.* (*of* ⇒**~живаться**) (*coll.*) (*о погоде*) to turn nasty; (*о ребёнке, о деле*) to go to the bad; to be ruined.

изгáжива|ть(ся), ю(сь) *impf. of* ⇒**изгáдить(ся)**

изгúб, а *m.* bend, twist.

изгибá|ть(ся), ю(сь) *impf. of* ⇒**изогнýть(ся)**

изглá|дить, жу, дишь *pf.* (*of* ⇒**~живать**) to efface, wipe out (*also fig.*); **и. из пáмяти** to blot out of one's memory.

изглáжива|ть, ю *impf. of* ⇒**изглáдить**

изгнáни|е, я *nt.* **1** (*действие*) banishment; expulsion. **2** (*ссылка*) exile.

изгнáнник, а *m.* exile (*person*).

из|гнáть, гоню́, гóнишь, *past* **~гнáл, ~гналá, ~гнáло** *pf.* (*of* ⇒**~гоня́ть**) to banish, expel; (*сослать*) to exile; **и. из употреблéния** to prohibit the use of, ban.

изгó|й, я *m.* outcast.

изголóвь|е, я *nt.* head of the bed; **сидéть у ~я** to sit at the bedside; **служúть ~ем** to serve as a pillow.

изголодá|ться, юсь *pf.* **1** to be famished, starve. **2** (**по** + *d.*) (*fig.*) to yearn for.

из|гоню́, гóнишь *see* ⇒**~гнáть**

изгоня́|ть, ю *impf. of* ⇒**изгнáть**

изгóрб|иться, люсь, ишься *pf.* (*coll.*) to arch one's back.

úзгород|ь, и *f.* fence; **живáя и.** hedge.

изготáвлива|ть, ю *impf.* = **изготовля́ть**

изготовúтел|ь, я *m.* manufacturer, producer.

изготóв|ить, лю, ишь *pf.* (*of* ⇒**~ля́ть**) **1** to manufacture. **2** (*obs.*) (*приготовить*) to prepare.

изготóв|иться, люсь, ишься *pf.* (*of* ⇒**~ля́ться**) to get ready, prepare o.s.

изготóв|ка, ки *f.* = **~лéние; взять ружьё на ~ку** (*mil.*) to come to the ready.

изготовлéни|е, я *nt.* manufacture.

изготовля́|ть(ся), ю(сь) *impf. of* ⇒**изготóвить(ся)**

изгрыз|áть, áю *impf. of* ⇒**~ть**

изгры́з|ть, ý, ёшь *past* **~, ~ла** *pf.* (*of* ⇒**~áть**) to gnaw to shreds.

изда|вáть, ю́, ёшь, *impf. of* ⇒**~́ть**

изда|вáться, ётся *impf. of* ⇒**~́ться**

úздавна *adv.* for a long time; from time immemorial.

издал|екá (*more rarely* **~ёка**) *adv.* from afar; from a distance; **гóрод вúден и.** the town is visible from afar; **приéхать и.** to come from a distance; **говорúть и.** (*coll.*) to speak in a roundabout way.

úздал|и *adv.* = **~екá**

издáни|е, я *nt.* **1** (*книг*) publication; (*закона*) promulgation. **2** (*то, что издано*) edition; **пéрвое и.** first edition; **исправленное и.** revised edition; **репрúнтное и.** reprint.

издáтел|ь, я *m.* publisher.

издáтель|ский *adj. of* ⇒**~** *and* **~ство; ~ское дéло** publishing; **~ская фúрма** publishing house.

издáтельств|о, а *nt.* publishing house, publisher.

издá|ть, м, шь, ст, дúм, дúте, дýт, *past* **~л, ~лá, ~ло** *pf.* (*of* ⇒**~вáть**) **1** (*отпубликовать*) to publish; **и. закóн** to promulgate a law; **и. укáз** to issue an edict. **2** (*запах*) to produce, emit; (*звук*) to let out; **и. крик** to let out a cry.

издá|ться, стся, *past* **~лся, ~лáсь, ~лось** *pf.* to be published.

изд-во (*abbr. of* ***издáтельство***) publishing house.

издевáтельский *adj.* mocking.

издевáтельств|о, а *nt.* (*действие*) mockery; (*насмешка*) taunt, insult.

издевá|ться, юсь *impf.* (**над** + *i.*) to mock (at), scoff (at).

издёвк|а, и *f.* (*coll.*) taunt, insult.

издéли|е, я *nt.* **1** (*sg. only*) (*производство*) make; **кустáрного ~я** hand-made; **фáбричного ~я** factory-made. **2** (*предмет*) (manufactured) article; (*pl.*) wares.

издёрган|ный *p.p.p. of* ⇨**издёргать** *and adj.* harassed; **~ные нéрвы** shattered nerves.

издёрг|ать, аю *pf.* (*of* ⇨**~ивать**) (*coll.*) to harass; to overstrain.

издёрг|аться, аюсь *pf.* (*of* ⇨**~иваться**) (*coll.*) to become overwrought, become unhinged.

издёргива|ть(ся), ю(сь) *impf. of* ⇨**издёргать(ся)**

издерж|áть, ý, ~ишь *pf.* (*of* ⇨**~ивать**) (*деньги*) to spend; (*энергию*) to expend.

издерж|áться, ýсь, ~ишься *pf.* (*of* ⇨**~иваться**) (*coll.*) to have spent all one's money.

издéржива|ть(ся), ю(сь) *impf. of* ⇨**издержáть(ся)**

издéрж|ки, ек *pl.* (*sg.* **~ка, ~ки** *f.*) expenses; costs; **судéбные и.** (*leg.*) costs; **и. произвóдства** production costs.

издирá|ть, ю *impf. of* ⇨**изодрáть**

издóльщин|а, ы *f.* (*hist., econ.*) share-cropping.

издóх|нуть, ну, нешь *past* **~, ~ла** *pf.* (*of* ⇨**издыхáть**) (*о животных*) to die; (*sl.*) (*о людях*) to peg out, kick the bucket.

издрéвле *adv.* from the earliest times.

издроб|ить, лю, ишь *pf.* to pulverize, granulate.

издыхáни|е, я *nt.* (one's) last breath; **до послéднего ~я** to one's last breath; **при послéднем ~и** at one's last gasp.

издыхá|ть, ю *impf. of* ⇨**издóхнуть**

изжáр|ить(ся), ю(сь), ишь(ся) *pf. of* ⇨**жáрить(ся)**

изжёванный *p.p.p. of* ⇨**изжевáть** *and adj.* (*coll.*) **1** (*пальто*) crumpled. **2** (*fig.*) (*тема*) hackneyed.

изж|евáть, ýю, уёшь *pf.* (*of* ⇨**~ёвывать**) (*coll.*) to chew up.

изжёвыва|ть, ю *impf. of* ⇨**изжевáть**

ѝзжелта- *comb. form* yellowish-.

из|жéчь, ожгý, ожжёшь, ожгýт, *past* **~жёг, ~ожглá** *pf.* (*of* ⇨**~жигáть**) (*coll.*) **1** (*руки*) to burn all over; (*фартук*) to burn holes in. **2** (*топливо*) to use up.

из|жéчься, ожгýсь, ожжёшься, ожгýтся, *past* **~жёгся, ~ожглáсь** *pf.* (*of* ⇨**~жигáться**) (*coll.*) **1** to burn o.s. all over; to be covered with burns; **нóги у неё ~ожглѝсь от кислотѣ́** her legs were all covered with burns from the acid. **2** (*о топливе*) to be burned up, be used up.

изживá|ть, ю *impf. of* ⇨**изжить**

изжигá|ть(ся), ю(сь) *impf. of* ⇨**изжéчь(ся)**

изжити|е, я *nt.* elimination.

изжи|ть, вý, вёшь, *past* **~л, ~лá, ~ло** *pf.* (*of* ⇨**~вáть**) **1** (*искоренить*) to eliminate. **2**: **и. себя** to become obsolete.

изжóг|а, и *f.* heartburn.

из-за *prep.+g.* **1** from behind; **из-за двéри** from behind the door; **встать из-за столá** to rise from the table; **приéхать из-за мóря** to come from oversea(s); (*fig.*): **сплéтничать о ком-н. из-за углá** to gossip about s.o. behind his back. **2** (*по причине*) because of, through; **не засыпáть из-за шýма** to be unable to get to sleep because of the noise; **ссóриться из-за пустякóв** to fall out over trifles; **тóлько из-за тебя мы опоздáли** it was all because of you that we were late. **3** (*ради*) for; **жениться из-за дéнег** to marry for money.

иззя́б|нуть, ну, нешь, *past* **~, ~ла** *pf.* (*coll.*) to feel frozen, feel chilled to the marrow.

излагá|ть, ю *impf. of* ⇨**изложить**

изля́мыва|ть(ся), ю(сь) *impf. of* ⇨**изломáть(ся)**

излéнива|ться, юсь *impf. of* ⇨**излениться**

излен|иться, юсь, ~ишься *pf.* (*of* ⇨**~иваться**) (*coll.*) to grow incorrigibly lazy.

излёт, а *m.* (*tech.*): **пýля на ~е** spent bullet.

излечéни|е, я *nt.* **1** (*лечение*) medical treatment; **он был на ~и в Москвé** he was undergoing medical treatment in Moscow; **отпрáвить в гóспиталь на и.** to send to hospital for treatment. **2** (*выздоровление*) recovery.

излéчива|ть(ся), ю(сь) *impf. of* ⇨**излечить(ся)**

излечим|ый (~, ~а) *adj.* curable.

излеч|ить, ý, ~ишь *pf.* (*of* ⇨**~ивать**) to cure.

излеч|иться, ýсь, ~ишься *pf.* (*of* ⇨**~иваться**) (**от**+*g.*) to make a complete recovery (from); to be cured (of); (*fig.*) to rid o.s. (of), shake off.

изливá|ть(ся), ю(сь) *impf. of* ⇨**излить(ся)**

из|лить, олью, ольёшь, *past* **~лил, ~лилá, ~лило** *pf.* (*of* ⇨**~ливáть**) to pour out, give vent to; **и. свой гнев на** (+*a.*) to vent one's anger (on); **и. дýшу** to unbosom o.s.

из|литься, ольюсь, ольёшься, *past* **~лился, ~лилáсь, ~лилóсь** *pf.* (*of* ⇨**~ливáться**) **1** (*о чувствах*) (**в**+*p.*) to find expression (in). **2** (**в**+*p.*) (*выразить чувства*) to give vent to one's feelings (in); (**на**+*a.*) to vent itself (on); **егó гнев ~лился на всех окружáющих** his anger vented itself on all about him.

излиш|ек, ка *m.* **1** (*избыток*) surplus; remainder. **2** (*лишнее*) excess; **нам э́того хвáтит с ~ком** we have more than enough, enough and to spare; **и. осторóжности** excessive caution.

излишеств|о, а *nt.* excess; over-indulgence.

излишеств|овать, ую *impf.* to go to excess, over-indulge o.s.

излишне *adv.* (*слишком*) excessively; (*когда не нужно*) unnecessarily, superfluously.

излиш|ний (~ен, ~ня, ~не) *adj.* (*чрезмерный*) excessive; (*ненужный*) unnecessary, superfluous.

излия́ни|е, я *nt.* outpouring, effusion (*fig.*).

излов|ить, лю, ~ишь *pf.* (*coll.*) to catch.

изловч|иться, ýсь, ишься *pf.* (*coll.*) to contrive, manage; **он ~ился попáсть в цель** he managed to hit the target.

изложéни|е, я *nt.* exposition, account; **крáткое и.** synopsis, outline.

излож|ить, ý, ~ишь *pf.* (*of* ⇨**излагáть**) to expound, state; to set forth; **и. на бумáге** to commit to paper.

излóм, а *m.* **1** (*место перелома*) break, fracture. **2** (*изгиб*) sharp bend.

излóман|ный *p.p.p. of* ⇨**изломáть** *and adj.* **1** (*сломанный*) broken. **2** (*с изгибами*) winding, tortuous. **3** (*fig.*) unbalanced, unhinged; warped.

изломá|ть, ю *pf.* (*of* ⇨**изля́мывать**) **1** (*сломать*) to break, smash. **2** (*coll.*) (*измучить*) to break (*in health*); (*impers.*) to have (crippling) rheumatism; **всю спину у неё ~ло** she is crippled with rheumatism in her back. **3** (*fig., coll.*) (*испортить*) to warp, corrupt.

изломá|ться, юсь *pf.* (*of* ⇨**изля́мываться**) **1** to be broken, be smashed. **2** (*fig., coll.*) to be affected; to resort to hypocrisy.

излуч|áть, áю *impf.* to radiate (*also fig.*); **её глазá ~áли нéжность** her eyes radiated tenderness.

излуч|áться, áется *impf.* **1** (**из**+*g.*) to emanate (from). **2** *pass. of* ⇨**~áть**

излучéни|е, я *nt.* radiation; emanation.

излýчин|а, ы *f.* bend, wind.

излю́бленный *adj.* favourite (*Br.*), favorite (*US*).

измá|зать, жу, жешь, *pf.* (*of* ⇨**мáзать** 1 *and* **~зывать**) (*coll.*) to make dirty, smear; **и. пальтó крáской** to get paint all over one's coat.

измá|заться, жусь, жешься *pf.* (*of* ⇨**мáзаться** 1 *and* **~зываться**) (*coll.*) to get dirty; **он ~зался в крáске** he has got paint all over himself.

измáзыва|ть(ся), ю(сь) *impf. of* ⇨**измáзать(ся)**

измар|áть, áю *pf.* (*of* ⇨**~ывать**) to make dirty, soil.

измáрыва|ть, ю *impf. of* ⇨**измарáть**

измáтыва|ть(ся), ю(сь) *impf. of* ⇨**измотáть(ся)**

измáчива|ть(ся), ю(сь) *impf. of* ⇨**измочить(ся)**

измá|ять, ю *pf.* (*coll.*) to exhaust, tire out.

измá|яться, юсь *pf.* (*coll.*) to be exhausted, tired out.

измельчáни|е, я *nt.* growing small; growing shallow; (*fig.*) becoming shallow, becoming superficial.

измельчá|ть, ю *pf. of* ⇨**мельчáть**

измельч|ить, ý, ишь *pf. of* ⇨**мельчить**

измéн|а, ы *f.* betrayal; treachery; **госудáрственная и.** high treason;

супрýжеская и. unfaithfulness, (conjugal) infidelity.

изменéни|е, я *nt.* change, alteration; (*gram.*) inflexion.

измен|úть[1], ю, ˜ишь *pf.* (*of* ⇨**˜я́ть**) to change, alter; (*pol.*) **и. законопроéкт** to amend a bill.

измен|úть[2], ю, ˜ишь *pf.* (*of* ⇨**˜я́ть**) (+*d.*) (*родине, другу*) to betray; (*мужу*) to be unfaithful (to); (*fig.*) **зрéние ˜úло емý** his eyesight had failed him; **счáстье нам ˜úло** our luck is out.

измен|úться, ю́сь, ˜ишься *pf.* (*of* ⇨**˜я́ться**) to change, alter (*intrans.*); **и. к лýчшему, к хýдшему** to change for the better, for the worse.

измéнник, а *m.* traitor.

измéнни|ца, цы *f. of* ⇨**˜к**

измéннический *adj.* treacherous, traitorous.

измéнчивост|ь, и *f.* **1** changeableness; (*непостоянство*) inconstancy, fickleness. **2** (*biol.*) variability.

измéнчив|ый (˜, ˜а) *adj.* changeable; (*непостоянный*) inconstant, fickle; **˜ая погóда** changeable weather.

изменя́ем|ый *pres. part. pass. of* ⇨**изменя́ть** *and adj.* variable; **˜ые величúны** (*math.*) variables.

измен|я́ть(ся), я́ю(сь) *impf. of* ⇨**˜úть(ся)**

измерéни|е, я *nt.* **1** measurement, measuring; (*глубины моря*) sounding, fathoming; (*температуры*) taking. **2** (*math.*) dimension; **двух, трёх ˜й** two-, three-dimensional.

измерúм|ый (˜, ˜а) *adj.* measurable.

измерúтел|ь, я *m.* **1** measuring instrument, gauge. **2** (*econ.*) index.

измерúтельный *adj.* (for) measuring.

измéр|ить, ю, ишь *pf.* (*of* ⇨**˜я́ть**) to measure; **и. комý-н. температýру** to take s.o.'s temperature.

измер|я́ть, я́ю *impf. of* ⇨**˜ить**

изможде́ни|е, я *nt.* exhaustion.

измождён|ный (˜, ˜á) *adj.* (*лицо, вид*) emaciated; (*человек*) worn out.

измок|áть, áю *impf. of* ⇨**˜нуть**

измóк|нуть, ну, нешь *past* **˜, ˜ла** *pf.* (*of* ⇨**˜áть**) (*coll.*) to get soaked, get drenched.

измóр, а *no pl., m.*: **взять ˜ом** to reduce by starvation, starve out; (*fig., coll.*): **взять когó-н. ˜ом** to wear s.o. down.

измор|úть, ю́, úшь *pf.* (*coll.*) to wear out, exhaust.

и́зморoз|ь, и *f.* hoar-frost.

и́зморос|ь, и *f.* drizzle.

измотá|ть, ю *pf.* (*of* ⇨**измáтывать**) (*coll.*) to exhaust, wear out.

измотá|ться, юсь *pf.* (*of* ⇨**измáтываться**) (*coll.*) to be exhausted, worn out.

измочáлива|ть(ся), ю(сь) *impf. of* ⇨**измочáлить(ся)**

измочáл|ить, ю, ишь *pf.* (*of* ⇨**˜ивать**) (*coll.*) **1** (*истрепать*) to shred; to reduce to shreds. **2** (*измучить*) to exhaust, wear out.

измочáл|иться, юсь, ишься *pf.* (*of* ⇨**˜иваться**) (*coll.*) **1** (*истрепаться*) to become frayed, be in shreds. **2** (*измучиться*) to be worn to a shred, go to pieces.

измоч|úть, ý, ˜ишь *pf.* (*of* ⇨**измáчивать**) (*coll.*) to soak through.

измоч|úться, ýсь, ˜ишься *pf.* (*of* ⇨**измáчиваться**) (*coll.*) to be soaked through.

измýч|ать, аю *pf.* = **˜ить**

измýч|аться, аюсь *pf.* = **˜иться**

измýченный *p.p.p. of* ⇨**измýчить** *and adj.* worn out, tired out; **у вас и. вид** you look worn out.

измýчива|ть(ся), ю(сь) *impf. of* ⇨**измýчить(ся)**

измýч|ить, у, ишь *pf.* **1** (*pf. of* ⇨**˜ивать**) to torment; to tire out, exhaust. **2** *pf. of* ⇨**мýчить**

измýч|иться, усь, ишься *pf.* **1** *pf.* (*of* ⇨**˜иваться**) to be tired out, be exhausted. **2** *pf. of* ⇨**мýчиться**

измывáтельств|о, а *nt.* (*coll.*) mocking, scoffing.

измывá|ться, юсь *impf.* (**над**+*i. coll.*) to mock (at), scoff (at).

измы́зг|ать, аю *pf.* (*of* ⇨**˜ивать**) (*coll.*) **1** (*загрязнить*) to make dirty all over. **2** (*заносить*) to wear threadbare.

измы́зг|аться, аюсь *pf.* (*of* ⇨**˜иваться**) (*coll.*) **1** (*загрязниться*) to get dirty all over. **2** (*заноситься*) to become threadbare.

измы́згива|ть(ся), ю(сь) *impf. of* ⇨**измы́згать(ся)**

измы́лива|ть, ю *impf. of* ⇨**измы́лить**

измы́л|ить, ю, ишь *pf.* (*of* ⇨**˜ивать**) to use up (*soap*).

измы́сл|ить, ю, ишь *pf.* (*of* ⇨**измышля́ть**) **1** (*выдумать*) to fabricate, invent. **2** (*придумать*) to contrive.

измышлéни|е, я *nt.* fabrication, invention.

измышля́|ть, ю *impf. of* ⇨**измы́слить**

измя́т|ый *p.p.p. of* ⇨**˜ь** *and adj.* **1** (*бумага*) crumpled, creased. **2** (*fig.*) (*лицо*) haggard, jaded.

из|мя́ть(ся), омнý, омнёт(ся) *pf. of* ⇨**мя́ть(ся)[1]**

изнáнк|а, и *f.* the wrong side (*of material, clothing*); **с ˜и** on the inner side; **вы́вернуть на ˜у** to turn inside out; **и. жúзни** the seamy side of life.

изнасúловани|е, я *nt.* rape.

изнасúл|овать, ую *pf.* (*of* ⇨**насúловать** 2) to rape.

изначáльный *adj.* (*первобытный*) primordial; (*начальный*) initial.

изнáшивани|е, я *nt.* wear; wear and tear.

изнáшива|ть(ся), ю(сь) *impf. of* ⇨**износúть(ся)**

изнéженност|ь, и *f.* softness; effeteness.

изнéженный *p.p.p. of* ⇨**изнéжить** *and adj.* pampered; soft, effete.

изнéжива|ть(ся), ю(сь) *impf. of* ⇨**изнéжить(ся)**

изнéж|ить, у, ишь *pf.* (*of* ⇨**˜ивать**) to pamper, coddle.

изнéж|иться, усь, ишься *pf.* (*of* ⇨**˜иваться**) to go soft, become effete.

изнемогá|ть, ю *impf. of* ⇨**изнемóчь**

изнеможéни|е, я *nt.* exhaustion; **быть в ˜и** to be utterly exhausted; **рабóтать до ˜я** to work to the point of exhaustion.

изнеможён|ный (˜, ˜á) *adj.* exhausted.

изнемó|чь, гý, ˜жешь, ˜гут, *past* **˜г, ˜глá** *pf.* (*of* ⇨**˜гáть**) (**от**+*g.*) to be exhausted (from), worn out (from).

изнéрвнича|ться, юсь *pf.* (*coll.*) to get into a state of nerves.

изничтож|áть, áю *impf. of* ⇨**˜ить**

изничтóж|ить, у, ишь *pf.* (*of* ⇨**˜áть**) (*coll.*) to destroy, wipe out.

изнóс, а (у) *m.* (*coll.*) wear; wear and tear; **не знать ˜у (а)** to wear well; (+*d.*) **э́тим ботúнкам нет ˜у (а)** these boots will stand any amount of hard wear.

изно|сúть, шý, ˜сишь *pf.* (*of* ⇨**изнáшивать**) to wear out.

изно|сúться, шýсь, ˜сишься *pf.* (*of* ⇨**изнáшиваться**) to wear out (*intrans.*); (*fig., coll.*) to be used up, be played out.

износостóйкий *adj.* hard-wearing, wear-resistant.

изнóшенный *p.p.p. of* ⇨**износúть** *and adj.* worn out; **и. костю́м** threadbare suit.

изнурéни|е, я *nt.* (*physical*) exhaustion.

изнурённый *p.p.p. of* ⇨**изнурúть** *and adj.* (*physically*) exhausted, worn out; **у негó был и. вид** he looked worn out; **и. гóлодом** faint with hunger.

изнурúтел|ьный (˜ен, ˜ьна) *adj.* exhausting; gruelling; **˜ьная болéзнь** wasting disease.

изнур|úть, ю́, úшь *pf.* (*of* ⇨**˜я́ть**) to exhaust, wear out.

изнур|я́ть, я́ю *impf. of* ⇨**˜úть**

изнутрú *adv.* from within; **дверь запирáется и.** the door fastens on the inside.

изнывá|ть, ю *impf. of* ⇨**изны́ть**

изн|ы́ть, óю, óешь *pf.* (*of* ⇨**˜ывáть**) to languish, be exhausted; **и. от жáжды** to be tormented by thirst; **и. от тоскú** (**по**+*d.*; *poet.*) to pine (for).

изо *prep.* = **из**

изо...[1] *pref.* = **из...**

изо...[2] *comb. form* **1** iso-. **2** = *abbr. of* ***изобразúтельный***

изобáр|а, ы *f.* (*meteor.*) isobar.

изобú|деть, жу, дишь *pf.* (*coll.*) to hurt, insult.

изоби́ли|е, я *nt.* abundance, plenty, profusion; **рог ~я** cornucopia.

изоби́л|овать, ую *impf.* (+*i.*) to abound (in), be rich (in).

изоби́л|ьный (~ен, ~ьна) *adj.* **1** abundant. **2** (+*i.*) abounding in.

изоблич|а́ть, а́ю *impf.* **1** *impf. of* ⇒**~и́ть. 2** (*no pf.*) (**в**+*p. and a.*) to show (to be), point to (as being); **все его́ посту́пки ~а́ли в нём моше́нника** his every action pointed to his being a swindler; **его́ похо́дка ~а́ет в нём моряка́** one can tell by his gait that he is a sailor.

изобличе́ни|е, я *nt.* exposure.

изобличи́тельный *adj.* damning.

изоблич|и́ть, у́, и́шь *pf.* (*of* ⇒**~а́ть**) (+*a. and* **в**+*p*) to expose (as); to unmask; **его́ ~и́ли во лжи** he stands exposed as a liar.

изобража́|ть(ся), ю *impf. of* ⇒**изобрази́ть(ся)**

изображе́ни|е, я *nt.* **1** (*действие*) representation, portrayal. **2** (*предмет*) representation, portrayal; image; **и. в зе́ркале** reflection.

изобрази́тельн|ый *adj.* graphic; decorative; **~ые иску́сства** fine arts.

изобра|зи́ть, жу́, зи́шь *pf.* (*of* ⇒**~жа́ть**) **1** (+*i.*) to depict, portray, represent (as); **и. из себя́** (+*a.*; *coll.*) to make o.s. out (to be), represent o.s. (as); **и. Га́млета сла́бым челове́ком** to portray Hamlet as a weak character (*of actor or producer*); **и. из себя́ хоро́шего певца́** to make o.s. out a good singer. **2** (*копировать*) to imitate, take off. **3** (*выразить*) to express, show.

изобра|зи́ться, зи́тся *pf.* (*of* ⇒**~жа́ться**) (*на лице*) to be expressed; **на её лице́ ~зи́лось удивле́ние** a look of surprise came over her face.

изобре|сти́, ту́, тёшь *past* **~̆л, ~ла́** *pf.* (*of* ⇒**~та́ть**) (*создать что-либо новое*) to invent; (*придумать*) to devise, contrive.

изобрета́тел|ь, я *m.* inventor.

изобрета́тель|ница, ницы *f. of* ⇒**~**

изобрета́тельност|ь, и *f.* inventiveness.

изобрета́тел|ьный (~ен, ~ьна) *adj.* inventive; resourceful.

изобрета́тель|ский *adj. of* ⇒**~**

изобрета́тель|ство, ства *nt.* = **~ность**

изобрета́|ть, ю *impf. of* ⇒**изобрести́**

изобрете́ни|е, я *nt.* invention.

изо́гнут|ый *p.p.p. of* ⇒**~̆ь** *and adj.* bent, curved, winding.

изогн|у́ть, у́, ёшь *pf.* (*of* ⇒**изгиба́ть**) to bend, curve.

изогн|у́ться, у́сь, ёшься *pf.* (*of* ⇒**изгиба́ться**) to bend, curve (*intrans.*).

изо́дранный *p.p.p. of* ⇒**изодра́ть** *and adj.* tattered.

из|одра́ть, деру́, дерёшь, *past* **~одра́л, ~одрала́, ~одра́ло** *pf.* (*of* ⇒**~дира́ть**) (*coll.*) to tear to shreds.

изо|йти́, йду́, йдёшь, *past* **~шёл, ~шла́** *pf. of* ⇒**исходи́ть**[2]

изол|га́ться, гу́сь, жёшься, гу́тся, *past* **~га́лся, ~гала́сь, ~га́лось** *pf.* to become an inveterate, hardened liar.

изоли́рованный *p.p.p. of* ⇒**изоли́ровать** *and adj.* **1** isolated; separate. **2** (*tech.*) insulated.

изоли́р|овать, ую *impf. and pf.* **1** to isolate. **2** (*tech.*) to insulate.

изолиро́вк|а, и *f.* (*tech.*) **1** insulation. **2** (*coll.*) (*лента*) insulating tape.

изолиро́вочный *adj.* (*tech.*) insulating.

изоля́тор[1]**, а** *m.* (*tech.*) insulator.

изоля́тор[2]**, а** *m.* **1** (*med.*) isolation ward **2** (*в тюрьме*) solitary confinement cell.

изоляциони́зм, а *m.* (*pol.*) isolationism.

изоляциони́ст, а *m.* (*pol.*) isolationist.

изоля|цио́нный *adj. of* ⇒**~̆ция; ~цио́нная ле́нта** (*tech.*) insulating tape.

изоля́ци|я, и *f.* **1** isolation. **2** (*tech.*) insulation.

изоме́рный *adj.* (*chem.*) isomeric.

изомо́рфный *adj.* (*min.*) isomorphous.

изо́рванный *p.p.p. of* ⇒**изорва́ть** *and adj.* tattered, torn.

изорв|а́ть, у́, ёшь, *past* **~а́л, ~ала́, ~а́ло** *pf.* (*of* ⇒**изрыва́ть**[1]) to tear (to shreds).

изорв|а́ться, ётся, *past* **~а́лся, ~ала́сь, ~а́лось** *pf.* (*coll.*) to be in tatters.

изоте́рм|а, ы *f.* (*geog.*) isotherm.

изото́п, а *m.* (*chem.*) isotope.

изошу́тк|а, и *f.* (*coll.*) cartoon, humorous drawing.

изощре́ни|е, я *nt.* sharpening (*fig.*); refinement.

изощрённый *p.p.p. of* ⇒**изощри́ть** *and adj.* (*ум, вкус*) refined; (*слух*) keen, acute.

изощр|и́ть, ю́, и́шь *pf.* (*of* ⇒**~я́ть**) to cultivate, refine; **и. слух** to train one's ear; **и. ум** to cultivate one's mind.

изощр|и́ться, ю́сь, и́шься *pf.* (*of* ⇒**~я́ться**) **1** to acquire refinement. **2** (**в**+*p.*) to excel (in); **и. в приду́мывании каламбу́ров** to excel in punning.

изощр|я́ть(ся), я́ю(сь) *impf. of* ⇒**~и́ть(ся)**

из-под *prep.+g.* **1** from under; **у него́ укра́ли бума́жник из-под но́су** he had his wallet stolen from under his nose; **из-под полы́** on the sly; under the counter. **2** (*города*) from near; **мы прие́хали из-под Москвы́** we have come from near Moscow. **3** (*о вместилище*) for (*or not translated*); **ба́нка из-под варе́нья** jam-jar.

изра|зе́ц, ца́ *m.* tile.

изра|цо́вый *adj. of* ⇒**~е́ц**

Изра́ил|ь, я *m.* Israel.

изра́ильский *adj.* **1** Israeli. **2** (*hist.*) Israelitish.

израильтя́н|ин, ина, *pl.* **~е, ~** *m.* **1** Israeli. **2** (*hist.*) Israelite.

израильтя́н|ка, ки *f. of* ⇒**~ин**

изра́н|ить, ю, ишь *pf.* to cover with wounds.

израсхо́д|овать(ся), ую(сь) *pf. of* ⇒**расхо́довать(ся)**

и́зредка *adv.* now and then; from time to time.

изре́занный *p.p.p. of* ⇒**изре́зать** *and adj.*: **и. бе́рег** indented coastline.

изре́|зать, жу, жешь *pf.* (*of* ⇒**~зывать** *and* **~за́ть**) **1** (*на много частей*) to cut into pieces; to cut up; (*сделать на чём-н. много порезов*) to make cuts in. **2** (*geog.*) to cut across.

изрез|а́ть, а́ю *impf.* (*coll.*) *of* ⇒**~̆ать**

изре́зыва|ть, ю *impf. of* ⇒**изре́зать**

изрека́|ть, ю *impf. of* ⇒**изре́чь**

изрече́ни|е, я *nt.* dictum, saying.

изре́|чь, ку́, чёшь, ку́т, *past* **~̆к, ~кла́** *pf.* (*of* ⇒**~ка́ть**) (*obs. or iron.*) to speak (solemnly); to utter; **так ~̆к** thus he spake; **и. му́дрое сло́во** to utter a word of wisdom.

изреше|ти́ть, чу́, ти́шь *pf.* (*of* ⇒**~̆чивать**) to pierce with holes; **и. пу́лями** to riddle with bullets.

изреше́чива|ть, ю *impf. of* ⇒**изрешети́ть**

изрис|ова́ть, у́ю *pf.* (*of* ⇒**~о́вывать**) to cover with drawings.

изрисо́выва|ть, ю *impf. of* ⇒**изрисова́ть**

изруб|а́ть, а́ю *impf. of* ⇒**~и́ть**

изруб|и́ть, лю́, ~̆ишь *pf.* (*of* ⇒**~а́ть**) (*мясо*) to chop up; (*человека*) to hack to pieces.

изруга́|ть, ю *pf. of* ⇒**руга́ть**

изрыва́|ть[1]**, ю** *impf. of* ⇒**изорва́ть**

изрыва́|ть[2]**, ю** *impf. of* ⇒**изры́ть**

изрыг|а́ть, а́ю *impf.* (*of* ⇒**~ну́ть**) (*о человеке*) to vomit, throw up; (*о вулкане*) to spew forth; **пу́шки ~а́ли дым и пла́мень** the cannon were belching forth smoke and flames; (*fig.*): **и. руга́тельства** to let forth a stream of oaths.

изрыг|ну́ть, ну́, нёшь *pf. of* ⇒**~а́ть**

изры́т|ый *p.p.p. of* ⇒**~ь** (*поверхность*) pitted; **и. о́спой** pock-marked.

изр|ы́ть, о́ю, о́ешь *pf.* (*of* ⇒**~ыва́ть**[2]) to dig up; to dig through.

изря́дно *adv.* (*coll.*) fairly, pretty; tolerably; **я и. уста́л** I am pretty tired; **они́ вчера́ ве́чером и. вы́пили** they had a fair amount to drink last night.

изря́д|ный (~ен, ~на) *adj.* (*coll.*) fair, handsome; fairly large, tolerable; **~ое коли́чество** a fair amount; **и. пья́ница** a pretty heavy drinker.

изуве́р, а *m.* **1** (*фанатик*) bigot, fanatic. **2** (*изверг*) monster.

изуве́рский *adj.* **1** (*фанатичный*) bigoted, fanatical. **2** (*жестокий*) monstrous.

изуве́рств|о, а *nt.* **1** (*фанатизм*) fanaticism. **2** (*жестокость*) barbarity.

И

изуве́чива|ть, ю *impf. of* ⇒**изуве́чить**

изуве́ч|ить, у, ишь *pf.* (*of* ⇒**~ивать**) to maim, mutilate.

изуве́ч|иться, усь, ишься *pf.* (*coll.*) **1** (*изувечить себя*) to maim o.s., mutilate o.s. **2** (*получить увечья*) to be maimed.

изукра́|сить, шу, сишь *pf.* (*of* ⇒**~шивать**) to decorate (lavishly); **и. дом фла́гами** to bedeck a house with flags.

изукра́шива|ть, ю *impf. of* ⇒**изукра́сить**

изуми́тел|ьный (~ен, ~ьна) *adj.* amazing, astounding.

изум|и́ть, лю́, и́шь *pf.* (*of* ⇒**~ля́ть**) to amaze, astound.

изум|и́ться, лю́сь, и́шься *pf.* (*of* ⇒**~ля́ться**) to be amazed, astounded.

изумле́ни|е, я *nt.* amazement.

изумлённый *p.p.p. of* ⇒**изуми́ть** *and adj.* amazed, astounded; dumbfounded.

изумля́|ть(ся), ю(сь) *impf. of* ⇒**изуми́ть(ся)**

изумру́д, а *m.* emerald.

изумру́дный *adj.* **1** emerald. **2** (*цвет*) emerald(-green).

изуро́д|овать, ую *pf. of* ⇒**уро́довать**

изу́стно *adv.* (*obs.*) orally, by word of mouth.

изуч|а́ть, а́ю *impf.* (*of* ⇒**~и́ть**) to learn; (*impf. only*) to study; **он два го́да ~а́ет гре́ческий язы́к** he has been studying Greek for two years.

изуче́ни|е, я *nt.* study, studying.

изуч|и́ть, у́, ~ишь *pf.* (*of* ⇒**~а́ть**) **1** to learn; **за шесть ме́сяцев она ~и́ла и испа́нский и италья́нский языки́** in six months she had learned both Spanish and Italian. **2** (*понять*) to come to know (very well), come to understand; **он кра́йне за́мкнут, но я всё-таки ~и́л его́** he is extremely reserved, but I came to understand him in the end.

изъ... *pref.* = **из...**

изъеда́|ть, ю *impf. of* ⇒**изъе́сть**

изъе́денный *p.p.p. of* ⇒**изъе́сть** *and adj.*: **и. мо́лью** moth-eaten.

изъе́з|дить, жу, дишь *pf.* (*of* ⇒**~живать**) to travel all over, round; **мы ~дили весь свет** we have been all round the world.

изъе́зженный *p.p.p. of* ⇒**изъе́здить** *and adj.*, well-worn, rutted.

изъе́жива|ть, ю *impf. of* ⇒**изъе́здить**

изъе́|сть, м, шь, ст, ди́м, ди́те, дя́т, *past* **~л, ~ла** *pf.* (*of* ⇒**~да́ть**) **1** (*мех, шерсть*) to eat away. **2** (*металл*) to corrode.

изъяви́тельн|ый *adj., only in phr.* **~ое наклоне́ние** (*gram.*) indicative mood.

изъяв|и́ть, лю́, ~ишь *pf.* (*of* ⇒**~ля́ть**) to indicate, express; **и. своё согла́сие** to give one's consent.

изъявле́ни|е, я *nt.* expression.

изъявля́|ть, ю *impf. of* ⇒**изъяви́ть**

изъязв|и́ть, лю́, и́шь *pf.* (*of* ⇒**~ля́ть**) (*med.*) to ulcerate.

изъязвле́ни|е, я *nt.* (*med.*) ulceration.

изъязвлённый *p.p.p. of* ⇒**изъязви́ть** *and adj.* ulcered, ulcerous.

изъязвля́|ть, ю *impf. of* ⇒**изъязви́ть**

изъя́н, а *m.* defect, flaw; **това́р с ~ом** defective goods.

изъясн|и́ть, ю, и́шь *pf.* (*of* ⇒**~я́ть**) (*obs.*) to explain, expound.

изъясн|и́ться, ю́сь, и́шься *pf.* (*of* ⇒**~я́ться**) (*obs.*) to express o.s.; **и. в любви́** to declare one's love.

изъясн|я́ть(ся), я́ю(сь) *impf. of* ⇒**~и́ть(ся)**

изъя́ти|е, я *nt.* **1** (*действие*) withdrawal; removal. **2** (*исключение*) exception; **без вся́кого ~я** without exception; **в и. из пра́вил** as an exception to the rule.

из|ъя́ть, ыму́, ы́мешь *pf.* (*of* ⇒**~ыма́ть**) to withdraw; to remove; **и. из обраще́ния** to withdraw from circulation; **и. в по́льзу госуда́рства** to confiscate.

изыма́|ть, ю *impf. of* ⇒**изъя́ть**

из|ыму́, ы́мешь *see* ⇒**~ъя́ть**

изы́ск, а *m.* (*liter.*) pretentious novelty.

изыска́ни|е, я *nt.* **1** finding, procuring. **2** (*usu. pl.*) (*научные исследования*) investigation, research; (*предварительные исследования*) prospecting; survey.

изы́сканност|ь, и *f.* refinement.

изы́скан|ный 1 (~, ~а) *p.p.p. of* ⇒**изыска́ть. 2 (~, ~на)** *adj.* refined.

изыска́тел|ь, я *m.* prospector.

изыска́тельский *adj.* prospecting.

изы|ска́ть, щу́, ~щешь *pf.* (*of* ⇒**~скивать**) to find; to search out; **и. сре́дства на постро́йку домо́в** to find funds for house-building.

изы́скива|ть, ю *impf.* (*of* ⇒**изыска́ть**) to search out; to try to find.

изю́бр, а *m.* (*zool.*) Manchurian deer.

изю́м, а (у) *no pl., m.* raisins; sultanas; **э́то не фунт ~у!** (*joc.*) it is no joke.

изю́мин|а, ы *f.* raisin, sultana.

изю́мин|ка, ки *f., dim. of* ⇒**~а**; (*fig.*) pep, go, spirit; **с ~кой** spirited; **в ней нет ~ки** she has no go in her.

изя́ществ|о, а *nt.* elegance, grace.

изя́щ|ный (~ен, ~на) *adj.* elegant, graceful; (*obs.*) **~ные иску́сства** fine arts.

Иису́с, а *m.* (*bibl.*) Joshua; **И. (Христо́с)** Jesus Christ.

ика́ни|е, я *nt.* hiccupping.

ик|а́ть, а́ю *impf.* (*of* ⇒**~ну́ть**) to hiccup.

ик|ну́ть, ну́, нёшь *pf. of* ⇒**~а́ть**

ико́н|а, ы *f.* icon.

ико́н|ный *adj. of* ⇒**~а**

иконобо́р|ец, ца *m.* (*hist.*) iconoclast.

иконобо́рческий *adj.* (*hist.*) iconoclastic.

иконобо́рчеств|о, а *nt.* (*hist.*) iconoclasm.

иконогра́фи|я, и *f.* **1** iconography. **2** (*collect.*) portraits.

иконопи́с|ец, ца *m.* icon-painter.

иконопи́сный *adj.* **1** *adj. of* ⇒**и́конопись. 2** (*fig.*) icon-like (*severe, severely beautiful*).

и́конопис|ь, и *f.* icon-painting.

иконоста́с, а *m.* (*eccl.*) iconostasis.

ико́рный *adj. of* ⇒**икра́**[1]

ико́т|а, ы *f.* hiccups.

икр|а́[1], ы́ *no pl. f.* **1** (hard) roe; spawn; **мета́ть ~у́** to spawn; (*fig., coll.*) to rage. **2** (*кушанье*) caviar(e); (*из овощей*) pâté; **баклажа́нная и.** aubergine pâté.

икр|а́[2], ы, *pl.* **~ы** *f.* (*anat.*) calf.

икри́нк|а, и *f.* (*coll.*) grain of caviar(e).

икри́ст|ый (~, ~а) *adj.* containing much roe.

икр|и́ться, ю́сь, и́шься *impf.* to spawn.

икромета́ни|е, я *nt.* spawning.

икс, а *m.* (*the letter*) x; (*math*) x (*unknown quantity*).

ил, а *m.* silt.

и́ли *conj.* or; **и.... и.** either ... or.

и́лист|ый (~, ~а) *adj.* silty.

иллю́зи|я, и *f.* illusion.

иллюзо́р|ный (~ен, ~на) *adj.* illusory.

иллюмина́тор, а *m.* (*naut., aeron.*) porthole.

иллюмина́ци|я, и *f.* illuminations.

иллюмини́р|овать, ую *impf. and pf.* to illuminate.

иллюстрати́в|ный (~ен, ~на) *adj.* illustrative; **и. материа́л** illustration(s).

иллюстра́тор, а *m.* illustrator.

иллюстра́ци|я, и *f.* illustration.

иллюстри́р|ованный *p.p.p. of* ⇒**~овать** *and adj.* illustrated.

иллюстри́р|овать, ую *impf. and pf.* (*pf. also* **про~**) to illustrate (*also fig.*).

иль (*coll.*) = **и́ли**

и́льк|а, и *f.* (*zool.*) **1** (*животное*) fisher. **2** (*мех*) fisher.

и́льк|овый *adj. of* ⇒**~а**

ильм, а *m.* (*bot.*) elm (*Ulmus scabra*).

и́льм|овый *adj. of* ⇒**~**

им 1 *i. of prons.* ⇒**он, оно́. 2** *d. of pron.* ⇒**они́**

им. (*abbr. of* **и́мени**) named after; **стадио́н им. Ле́нина** Lenin Stadium.

има́м, а *nt.* imam (*Muslim priest or leader*).

имби́р|ный *adj. of* ⇒**~ь**

имби́р|ь, я́ *m.* ginger.

и́м|ени, енем *see* ⇒**~я**

име́ни|е, я *nt.* estate.

имени́нник, а *m.* person whose name-day it is.

имени́нни|ца, цы *f. of* ⇒**~к**

имени́н|ный *adj. of* ⇒**~ы; и. пиро́г** name-day cake.

имени́н|ы, ~ *no sg.* name-day (*day of saint after whom person is named*); **спра́вить и.** to celebrate one's name-day; **пойти́ на и. к кому́-н.** to go to s.o.'s name-day party.

имени́тельный *adj.* (*gram.*) nominative.

имени́т|ый (~, ~а) *adj.* distinguished.

и́менно *adv.* **1** (а) **и.** (*перед перечислением*) namely; to wit, videlicet (viz.); **нас там бы́ло тро́е, а и.: Петро́в, Ивано́в и я** there were three of us there, namely Petrov, Ivanov, and myself. **2** (*как раз, точно*) just, exactly; to be exact; **где и. она́ живёт?** where exactly does she live?; **в то вре́мя я был на Украи́не, а и. в Оде́ссе** I was in Ukraine then, in Odessa to be exact; **вот и. э́то я и говори́л** that's just what I was saying; **вот и.!** exactly!; precisely!

именн|о́й *adj.* **1** nominal; **~ые а́кции** (*fin.*) inscribed stock; **~о́е кольцо́** ring engraved with owner's name; **и. спи́сок** nominal roll; **и. чек** non-transferable cheque; **и. экземпля́р** autographed copy. **2** *adj. of* ⇒**и́мя** 3

имено́ван|ный *p.p.p. of* ⇒**именова́ть** *and adj.*; (*math.*): **~ное число́** concrete number.

имен|ова́ть, у́ю *impf.* (*of* ⇒**на~**) to name.

имен|ова́ться, у́юсь *impf.* (+*i.*) to be called; to be termed.

имену́емый *pres. part. pass. of* ⇒**именова́ть; царь Ива́н, и. Гро́зным** Tsar Ivan, called the Terrible.

име́|ть, ю, ешь *impf.* to have (*of abstract possession*); **и. возмо́жность** (+*inf.*) to have an opportunity (to), be in a position (to); **и. де́ло (с**+*i.*) to have dealings (with), have to do (with); **и. значе́ние (для**+*g.*) to matter (to), be important (to); **и. ме́сто** to take place; **и. на́глость, несча́стье** etc. (+*inf.*) to have the effrontery, the misfortune, *etc.* (to); **и. в виду́** (*не забывать*) to bear in mind, think of, (*подразумевать*) mean; **ничего́ не и. про́тив** (+*g.*) to have no objection(s) (to); **и. сто ме́тров в высоту́** to be 100 metres high.

име́|ться, ется *impf.* to be; to be present, be available (**~ется у, ~ются у** *are equivalent to* **есть у**); **в на́шем го́роде ~ется два кино́** there are two cinemas in our town; **бана́нов у нас не ~ется** we have no bananas; **и. нали́цо** to be available, be on hand.

име́|ющийся *pres. part. of* ⇒**~ться** *and adj.* available; present.

и́ми *i. of pron.* ⇒**они́**

и́мидж, а *m.* image.

имиджме́йкер, а *m.* image-maker.

имита́тор, а *m.* **1** (*человек*) mimic; impressionist. **2** (*устройство*) simulator; **и. полёта** flight simulator.

имита́ци|я, и *f.* **1** (*действие*) mimicry; mimicking. **2** (*предмет*) imitation; **и. же́мчуга** imitation pearl.

имити́р|овать, ую *impf.* to mimic, imitate.

иммане́нт|ный (~ен, ~на) *adj.* (*phil., theol.*) immanent.

иммигра́нт, а *m.* immigrant.

иммигра́нт|ка, ки *f. of* ⇒**~**

иммигра|цио́нный *adj. of* ⇒**~ция; ~цио́нные зако́ны** immigration laws.

иммигра́ци|я, и *f.* **1** immigration. **2** (*collect.*) (*иммигранты*) immigrants.

иммигри́р|овать, ую *impf. and pf.* to immigrate.

иммуниза́ци|я, и *f.* (*med.*) immunization.

иммунизи́р|овать, ую *impf. and pf.* (*med.*) to immunize.

иммуните́т, а *m.* (*med., leg.*) immunity.

иммý́н|ный (~ен, ~на) *adj.* (**к**+*d.*) immune (to); **~ная систе́ма** immune system.

иммуноло́ги|я, и *f.* immunology.

иммунотерапи́|я, и *f.* immunotherapy.

императи́в, а *m.* (*phil., gram.*) imperative.

императи́в|ный (~ен, ~на) *adj.* imperative.

импера́тор, а *m.* emperor.

импера́торский *adj.* imperial.

императри́ц|а, ы *f.* empress.

империали́зм, а *m.* imperialism.

империали́ст, а *m.* imperialist.

империалисти́ческий *adj.* imperialist(ic).

импе́ри|я, и *f.* empire.

импе́рский *adj.* imperial.

импи́чмент, а *m.* impeachment.

импланта́т, а *m.* (*med.*) implant.

импланта́ци|я и *f.* (*med.*) implantation.

импланти́р|овать, ую *impf. and pf.* (*med.*) to implant.

импоза́нт|ный (~ен, ~на) *adj.* imposing, striking.

импони́р|овать, ую *impf.* (+*d.*) to impress, strike (*fig.*); **его́ зна́ния ~овали всем знако́мым** everyone he knew was impressed by his learning.

и́мпорт, а *m.* **1** (*ввоз товаров*) import. **2** (*collect., coll.*) (*товары*) foreign goods.

импортёр, а *m.* importer.

импорти́р|овать, ую *impf. and pf.* (*econ.*) to import.

и́мпорт|ный *adj. of* ⇒**~; ~ные по́шлины** import duties; **~ные това́ры** (imported) goods.

импоте́нт, а *m.* impotent man.

импоте́нт|ный (~ен, ~на) *adj.* (*med.*) impotent.

импоте́нци|я, и *f.* (*med.*) impotence.

импреса́рио *m. indecl.* impresario.

импрессиони́зм, а *m.* (*art*) impressionism.

импрессиони́ст, а *m.* (*art*) impressionist.

импрессионисти́ческий *adj.* (*art*) impressionistic.

импрессиони́ст|ский *adj.* = **~и́ческий**

импровиза́тор, а *m.* improviser.

импровиза́торский *adj.* improvisational.

импровиза́ци|я, и *f.* improvisation.

импровизи́рова|нный *p.p.p. of* ⇒**~ть** *and adj.* improvised; impromptu, extempore.

импровизи́р|овать, ую *impf.* (*of* ⇒**сымпровизи́ровать**) to improvise; to extemporize.

и́мпульс, а *m.* (**к**+*d.*) impulse, impetus (for).

импульси́в|ный (~ен, ~на) *adj.* impulsive.

иму́ществ|енный *adj. of* ⇒**~о; и. ценз** property qualification.

иму́ществ|о, а *nt.* property, belongings; **дви́жимое и.** (*leg.*) personalty, personal estate; **недви́жимое и.** (*leg.*) realty, real estate.

иму́щий *adj.* propertied; well-off; **власть иму́щие** the powers that be.

и́м|я, *g., d., and p.* **~ени,** *i.* **~енем,** *pl.* **~ена́, ~ён, ~ена́м** *nt.* **1** name; (*личное название*) first, Christian name; **вы́мышленное и.** alias, false name; **по ~ени О́льга** Olga by name; **во и.** (+*g.*) in the name of; **посла́ть на и.** (+*g.*) to address to; **запиши́те счёт на моё и.** put it down to my account; **от ~ени** (+*g.*) on behalf of; **то́лько по ~ени** only in name, only nominally; **он тепе́рь изве́стен под други́м ~енем** he now goes by, under another name; **~енем зако́на** in the name of the law; **~ени** (+*g.*) named in honour (*Br.*), honor (*US*) of (*usu. not translated*); **Вое́нная акаде́мия ~ени Фру́нзе** the Frunze Military Academy; **называ́ть ве́щи свои́ми ~ена́ми** to call a spade a spade. **2** (*fig.*) (*репутация*) name, reputation; **челове́к с больши́м ~енем** a man with a big name; **у него́ европе́йское и.** he has a European reputation; **приобрести́ и.** to acquire, make a name; **замара́ть своё и.** to ruin one's good name; **кру́пные ~ена́ в о́бласти фи́зики** great names in the field of physics. **3** (*gram.*) noun, nomen (*any part of speech declined, as opposed to conjugated*); **и. прилага́тельное** adjective; **и. существи́тельное** noun, substantive; **и. числи́тельное** numeral.

имяре́к, а *m.* (*joc.*) so-and-so.

ин... *comb. form, abbr. of* **иностра́нный**

инакомы́сли|е, я *nt.* dissidence; nonconformism; heterodoxy.

инакомы́слящ|ий *adj.* dissident; nonconformist; heterodox; *as n.* **и., ~его** *m.* dissident.

инаугурацио́нный *adj.* inauguration, inaugural.

инаугура́ци|я, и *f.* inauguration.

инаугури́р|овать, ую *impf. and pf.* to inaugurate.

и́на́че 1 (*adv.*) differently, otherwise; **так и́ли и.** in either event, at all events; **не ина́че (как)** (*coll.*) precisely, of course; **не ина́че как полко́вник** none other than the colonel. **2** (*conj.*) otherwise, or (else); **спеши́те, и. вы опозда́ете** hurry up, or you will be late.

И

инвали́д, а *m.* invalid; disabled person; **и. войны́** disabled serviceman; **и. труда́** industrial invalid.

инвали́дност|ь, и *f.* disablement; invalidity; **посо́бие по ~и** invalidity allowance; **уво́литься по ~и** (*mil.*) to be invalided out.

инвали́д|ный *adj. of* ⇒**~; и. дом** home for the disabled.

инвалю́т|а, ы *f.* foreign currency.

инвалю́тный *adj.* foreign-currency.

инвекти́в|а, ы *f.* invective.

инвентариза́ци|я, и *f.* inventory making, stock-taking.

инвентариз|ова́ть, у́ю *impf. and pf.* to inventory, make an inventory.

инвента́р|ный *adj. of* ⇒**~ь; ~ная о́пись** inventory.

инвента́р|ь, я́ *m.* **1** (*предметы*) stock; equipment, appliances; **живо́й и.** livestock; **сельскохозя́йственный и.** agricultural implements; **торго́вый и.** stock-in-trade. **2** (*список*) inventory.

инве́рси|я, и *f.* inversion.

инвести́ровани|е, я *nt.* investment.

инвести́р|овать, ую *impf. and pf.* to invest.

инвеститу́р|а, ы *f.* investiture.

инвестицио́нный *adj.* investment.

инвести́ци|я, и *f.* investment.

инве́стор, а *m.* (*fin.*) investor.

ингаля́тор, а *m.* (*med.*) inhaler.

ингаля́ци|я, и *f.* (*med.*) inhaling.

ингредие́нт, а *m.* ingredient.

ингу́ш, а́, *g. pl.* **~е́й** *m.* Ingush.

Ингуше́ти|я, и *f.* Ingushetia.

ингу́ш|ка, ки *f. of* ⇒**~**

ингу́шский *adj.* Ingush.

Инд, а *m.* the Indus (*river*).

и́ндеве|ть, ет *impf.* (*of* ⇒**за~**) to become covered with hoar-frost.

инде́|ец, йца, *pl.* **~йцы, ~йцев** *m.* American Indian, Native American.

инде́йк|а, и *f.* turkey(-hen).

инде́|йский *adj. of* ⇒**~ец; и. пету́х** turkey-cock.

и́ндекс, а *m.* index; **и. цен** (*econ.*) price index; **почто́вый и.** post-code (*Br.*), zip code (*US*).

индекса́ци|я, и *f.* indexing.

индекси́р|овать, ую *impf. and pf.* to index.

инд|иа́нка, иа́нки *f. of* ⇒**~е́ец** *and* **~и́ец**

индиви́д, а *m.* individual.

индивидуализа́ци|я, и *f.* individualization.

индивидуализи́р|овать, ую *impf. and pf.* to individualize.

индивидуали́зм, а *m.* individualism.

индивидуали́ст, а *m.* individualist.

индивидуалисти́ческий *adj.* individualistic.

индивидуалисти́ч|ный (~ен, ~на) *adj.* individualistic

индивидуа́льност|ь, и *f.* individuality.

индивидуа́л|ьный (~ен, ~ьна) *adj.* individual; **в ~ьном поря́дке** individually; **и. слу́чай** individual case, single case.

индиви́дуум, а *m.* individual.

инди́го *nt. indecl.* indigo.

инди́|ец, йца, *pl.* **~йцы, ~йцев** *m.* Indian.

инди́йский *adj.* Indian.

Инди́йск|ий океа́н, ~ого ~а *m.* the Indian Ocean.

индикати́в, а *m.* (*gram.*) indicative.

индика́тор, а *m.* (*tech.*) indicator; (*comput.*) display; **жидкокристалли́ческий и.** liquid-crystal display, LCD; **светово́й и.** indicator light.

индифферéнтност|ь, и *f.* indifference.

индифферéнт|ный (~ен, ~на) *adj.* (**к**+*d.*) indifferent (to).

И́нди|я, и *f.* India.

индоевропе́йский *adj.* Indo-European.

Индокита́|й, я *m.* Indo-China.

индонези́|ец, йца, *pl.* **~йцы, ~йцев** *m.* Indonesian.

индонези́|йка, йки *f. of* ⇒**~ец**

индонези́йский *adj.* Indonesian.

Индоне́зи|я, и *f.* Indonesia.

индоссаме́нт, а *m.* (*fin.*) endorsement.

индосса́нт, а *m.* (*fin.*) endorser.

индосса́т, а *m.* (*fin.*) endorsee.

индосси́р|овать, ую *impf. and pf.* (*fin.*) to endorse.

индуи́зм, а *m.* Hinduism.

индуи́стский *adj.* Hindu.

индукти́вный *adj.* (*phil., phys.*) inductive.

инду́ктор, а *m.* (*elec.*) inductor.

индукци|о́нный *adj. of* ⇒**~я; ~о́нная кату́шка** induction coil.

инду́кци|я, и *f.* (*phil., phys.*) induction.

индульге́нци|я, и *f.* (*eccl.*) indulgence.

инду́с, а *m.* Hindu.

инду́с|ка, ки *f. of* ⇒**~**

инду́сский *adj.* Hindu.

индустриализа́ци|я, и *f.* industrialization.

индустриализи́р|овать, ую *impf. and pf.* to industrialize.

индустриа́льный *adj.* industrial.

индустри́|я, и *f.* industry.

индю́к, а́ *m.* turkey(-cock); **наду́лся как и.** (*coll.*) he got on his high horse.

индю́шк|а, и *f.* turkey(-hen).

индюш|о́нок, о́нка, *pl.* **~а́та, ~а́т** *m.* turkey-poult.

и́не|й, я *no pl., m.* hoar-frost, rime.

ине́ртност|ь, и *f.* inertness, sluggishness, inaction.

ине́рт|ный (~ен, ~на) *adj.* inert (*phys. and fig.*); (*fig.*) sluggish, inactive.

ине́рци|я, и *f.* (*phys. and fig.*) inertia; momentum; **дви́гаться по ~и** to move under its own momentum; (*fig.*): **де́лать что-н. по ~и** to do sth. from force of inertia, mechanically.

инжене́р, а *m.* engineer; **и.-меха́ник** mechanical engineer; **и.-строи́тель** civil engineer.

инжене́ри|я, и *f.* engineering; **ге́нная и.** genetic engineering.

инжене́рн|ый *adj.* engineering; **~ые войска́** (*mil.*) Engineers; **~ое де́ло** engineering.

инжи́р, а *m.* fig.

инжи́рный *adj.* fig.

и́нист|ый (~, ~а) *adj.* rimy, covered with hoar-frost.

инициа́л|ы, ов *pl.* (*sg.* **~, ~а** *m.*) initials.

инициати́в|а, ы *f.* initiative; **по со́бственной ~е** on one's own initiative.

инициати́в|ный *adj.* **1** initiating, originating; **~ная гру́ппа** action committee. **2** (**~ен, ~на**) full of initiative, enterprising; dynamic, go-getting.

инициа́тор, а *m.* initiator.

инкасса́тор, а *m.* (*fin.*) security guard (*delivering money to a bank*).

инкасси́р|овать, ую *impf. and pf.* (*fin.*) to cash.

инквизи́тор, а *m.* inquisitor.

инквизи́торский *adj.* inquisitorial.

инквизи́ци|я, и *f.* inquisition.

и́нк|и, ов *no sg.* the Incas.

инко́гнито 1 *adv.* incognito. **2** *n.*; *c.g. indecl.* incognito (*person*).

инкорпора́ци|я, и *f.* incorporation.

инкорпори́р|овать, ую *impf. and pf.* to incorporate.

инкримини́р|овать, ую *impf. and pf.* (+*d. and a.*) to charge (with); **ему́ ~уют поджо́г** he is being charged with arson.

инкруста́ци|я, и *f.* inlaid work, inlay.

инкрусти́р|овать, ую *impf. and pf.* to inlay.

инкуба́тор, а *m.* incubator.

инкубацио́нный *adj.* incubative, incubatory; **и. пери́од** (*med.*) incubation.

инкуба́ци|я, и *f.* incubation (*of chickens and med.*).

инове́р|ец, ца *m.* (*relig.*) adherent of different faith, creed.

инове́ри|е, я *nt.* (*relig.*) adherence to different faith, creed.

инове́рный *adj.* (*relig.*) belonging to different faith, creed.

иногда́ *adv.* sometimes.

иногоро́дн|ий *adj.* of, from another town; **~яя по́чта** mail for, from other towns.

инозе́мный *adj.* foreign.

ин|о́й *adj.* **1** (*другой*) different; other; **~ы́ми слова́ми** in other words; **не кто и., как; не что ~о́е, как** none other than; **тот и́ли и.** one or other, this or that. **2** (*некоторый*) some; **и. раз** sometimes; **и. (челове́к) мог и согласи́ться** some might agree.

и́нок, а *m.* monk.

и́нокин|я, и *f.* nun.

инокули́р|овать, ую *impf. and pf.* to inoculate.

инокуля́ци|я, и *f.* inoculation.

инопланéтный *adj.* alien, extraterrestrial.

инопланетя́н|ин, а, *pl.* **~е, ~** *m.* alien, extraterrestrial.

иноплемéнник, а *m.* (*obs.*) member of different tribe, nationality.

инорóд|ец, ца *m.* (*hist.*) non-Russian (*member of national minority in tsarist Russia*).

инорóд|ный (~ен, ~на) *adj.* alien; **~ное тéло** (*med. or fig.*) foreign body.

иносказáни|е, я *nt.* allegory.

иносказáтел|ьный (~ен, ~ьна) *adj.* allegorical.

инострáн|ец, ца *m.* foreigner.

инострáн|ка, ки *f. of* ⇨**~ец**

инострáнный *adj.* foreign.

инотдéл, а *m.* foreign department (*of Russian institutions*).

инофи́рм|а, ы *f.* foreign company.

и́ноческий *adj.* monastic.

и́ночеств|о, а *nt.* monasticism; monastic life.

иноязы́чный *adj.* **1** (*население*) speaking another language. **2** (*слово*) belonging to another language.

инсектици́д, а *m.* insecticide.

инсинуáци|я, и *f.* insinuation.

инсинуи́р|овать, ую *impf. and pf.* to insinuate.

инспекти́р|овать, ую *impf.* to inspect.

инспéктор, а, *pl.* **~á, ~óв** *m.* inspector; (*mil.*) inspecting officer; **и. манéжа** ringmaster; **портóвый и.** harbourmaster.

инспéктор|ский *adj. of* ⇨**~**

инспéкци|я, и *f.* **1** (*действие*) inspection; **и. на мéсте** (*mil.*) on-site inspection. **2** (*организация*) inspectorate.

инспири́р|овать, ую *impf. and pf.* to incite; to inspire; **кто ~овал э́ту статью́?** who inspired this article?; **и. слу́хи** to start rumours (*Br.*), rumors (*US*).

инстáнци|я, и *f.* (*leg.*) instance; (*pol.*) level of authority; **суд пéрвой ~и** court of first instance; (*mil.*) **комáндная и.** chain of command.

инсти́нкт, а *m.* instinct.

инстинкти́в|ный (~ен, ~на) *adj.* instinctive.

институ́т, а *m.* **1** (*общественное установление*) institution; **и. брáка** the institution of marriage. **2** (*учебное или научное заведение*) institute; school; **медици́нский и.** medical school; **педагоги́ческий и.** college of education.

институ́т|ский *adj. of* ⇨**~** 2

инструктáж, а *m.* instructing; (*mil., aeron.*) briefing.

инструкти́в|ный (~ен, ~на) *adj.* instructional.

инструкти́р|овать, ую *impf. and pf.* (*pf. also* **про~**) to instruct, brief.

инстру́ктор, а *m.* instructor.

инстру́ктор|ский *adj. of* ⇨**~**

инстру́кци|я, и *f.* instructions, directions.

инструмéнт, а *m.* (*mus.*; *tech.*) instrument; (*tech.*) tool, implement; (*sg.*; *collect.*) tools.

инструментали́ст, а *m.* (*mus.*) instrumentalist.

инструментáльн|ая, ой *f.* tool-shop.

инструментáльн|ый *adj.* **1** (*mus.*) instrumental. **2** (*tech.*) tool-making; **~ая стáль** tool steel.

инструментáльщик, а *m.* tool-maker, instrument-maker.

инструментáри|й, я *m.* (*collect.*) instruments, tools.

инструмент|овáть, у́ю *impf. and pf.* (*mus.*) to arrange for instruments; to orchestrate.

инструментóвк|а, и *f.* (*mus.*) instrumentation.

инсули́н, а *m.* (*med.*) insulin.

инсу́льт, а *m.* (*med.*) stroke.

инсцени́р|овать, ую *impf. and pf.* **1** (*роман*) to dramatize, adapt (for stage or screen). **2** (*fig.*) to feign, stage; **и. óбморок** to stage a faint.

инсцениро́вк|а, и *f.* **1** dramatization, adaptation (for stage or screen). **2** (*fig.*) pretence; act.

интегрáл, а *m.* (*math.*) integral.

интегрáльн|ый *adj.* integral; **~ое исчислéние** (*math.*) integral calculus.

интегрáци|я, и *f.* integration.

интегри́р|овать, ую *impf. and pf.* to integrate.

интеллéкт, а *m.* intellect; **иску́сственный и.** (*comput.*) artificial intelligence.

интеллектуáл, а *m.* intellectual.

интеллектуáльност|ь, и *f.* intellectuality.

интеллектуáл|ьный (~ен, ~на) *adj.* intellectual.

интеллигéнт, а *m.* member of the intelligentsia, intellectual.

интеллигéнт|ный (~ен, ~на) *adj.* cultured, educated.

интеллигéнт|ский *adj.* (*pej.*) *of* ⇨**~**

интеллигéнци|я, и *f.* (*collect.*) intelligentsia.

интендáнт, а *m.* (*mil.*) quartermaster.

интендáнтств|о, а *nt.* (*mil.*) quartermaster service, commissariat.

интенси́в|ный (~ен, ~на) *adj.* intensive.

интенсифици́р|овать, ую *impf. and pf.* to intensify.

интеракти́вный *adj.* interactive.

интервáл, а *m.* (*in var. senses*) interval; **и. строк** (*typ.*) line spacing.

интервéнт, а *m.* (*pol.*) interventionist.

интервéнци|я, и *f.* (*pol.*) intervention.

интервью́ *nt. indecl.* (*press*) interview; **взять ~ у** + *g.* to interview (*a person*).

интервьюéр, а *m.* (*press*) interviewer.

интервьюи́р|овать, ую *impf. and pf.* to interview.

интерéс, а *m.* **1** interest; **представля́ть и.** to be of interest; **прояви́ть и.** (**к** + *d.*) to show interest (in). **2** (*выгода*) interest; (*pl.*) interests; **какóй мне и.?** how do I stand to gain?; **в вáших ~ах поéхать** it is in your interest to go.

интерéсно *as pred.* it is, would be interesting; **и. знать, кто э́тот высóкий инострáнец** it would be interesting to know who the tall foreigner is; **и., что из негó вы́йдет** I wonder how he will turn out.

интерéс|ный (~ен, ~на) *adj.* **1** interesting; **в ~ном положéнии** (*euph.*) in the family way. **2** (*привлекательный*) striking, attractive.

интерес|овáть, у́ю *impf.* to interest.

интерес|овáться, у́юсь *impf.* (+*i.*) to be interested (in); (*coll.*) (*осведомляться*) to enquire.

интерлю́ди|я, и *f.* (*mus.*) interlude.

интермéди|я, и *f.* (*theatr.*) interlude.

интермéццо *nt. indecl.* (*mus.*) intermezzo.

интéрн, а *m.* (*med.*) houseman (*Br.*), intern (*US*).

интернáт, а *m.* **1** (*школа*) boarding school. **2** (*общежитие*) boarding house (*at private school*).

интернационáл, а *m.* **1** international (*organization*); **Пéрвый И.** (*hist.*) the First International. **2**: **И.** the 'Internationale'.

интернационализáци|я, и *f.* internationalization.

интернационализи́р|овать, ую *impf. and pf.* to internationalize.

интернационали́зм, а *m.* internationalism.

интернационали́ст, а *m.* internationalist.

интернационáльный *adj.* international.

Интернéт, а *m.* the Internet; **путешéствовать по ~у** to surf the Internet.

интерни́рова|нный *p.p.p. of* ⇨**~ть**; *as n.* **и., ~нного** *m.* internee.

интерни́р|овать, ую *impf. and pf.* to intern.

интерполи́р|овать, ую *impf. and pf.* to interpolate.

интерполя́ци|я, и *f.* interpolation.

интерпретáтор, а *m.* interpreter (*expounder*).

интерпретáци|я, и *f.* interpretation; **нóвая и. рóли Гáмлета** a new interpretation of the part of Hamlet.

интерпрети́р|овать, ую *impf. and pf.* to interpret.

интерфéйс, а *m.* (*comput.*) interface.

интерферéнци|я, и *f.* (*phys.*) interference.

интерьéр, а *m.* (*art*) interior.

инти́мност|ь, и *f.* intimacy.

инти́м|ный (~ен, ~на) *adj.* intimate.

интоксикáци|я, и *f.* (*med.*) intoxication; **алкогóльная и.** alcoholic poisoning.

интонáци|я, и *f.* intonation.

интони́р|овать, ую *impf.* to intone.
интри́г|а, и *f.* **1** (*политическая*) intrigue. **2** (*obs.*) (*любовная*) (love-) affair. **3** (*романа*) plot.
интрига́н, а *m.* intriguer, schemer.
интрига́н|ка, ки *f. of* ⇨~
интриг|ова́ть, у́ю *impf.* **1** (*no pf.*) to intrigue, carry on an intrigue. **2** (*pf.* **за~**) (*возбуждать интерес*) to intrigue, fascinate.
интрове́рт, а *m.* introvert.
интроду́кци|я, и *f.* (*mus.*) introduction.
интроспе́кци|я, и *f.* introspection.
интуити́в|ный (~ен, ~на) *adj.* intuitive.
интуи́ци|я, и *f.* intuition.
интури́ст, а *m.* foreign tourist.
инфанти́л|ьный (~ен, ~ьна) *adj.* infantile.
инфа́ркт, а *m.* (*med.*) heart attack; infarction.
инфекцио́нн|ый *adj.* infectious; **~ая больни́ца** isolation hospital.
инфе́кци|я, и *f.* infection.
инфильтра́ци|я, и *f.* infiltration.
инфинити́в, а *m.* (*gram.*) infinitive.
инфици́р|овать, ую *impf. and pf.* to infect.
инфляцио́нный *adj.* inflationary.
инфля́ци|я, и *f.* (*econ.*) inflation.
информати́в|ный (~ен, ~на) *adj.* informative.
информа́тик, а *m.* information scientist.
информа́тик|а, и *f.* information science, information technology.
информа́тор, а *m.* informant.
информ|ацио́нный *adj. of* ⇨**~а́ция**
информа́ци|я, и *f.* information; news item.
информи́р|овать, ую *impf. and pf.* to inform.
инфракра́сный *adj.* infrared.
инфраструкту́р|а, ы *f.* infrastructure.
инциде́нт, а *m.* incident; **пограни́чный и.** frontier incident.
инъекти́р|овать, ую, уешь *impf. and pf.* to inject.
инъе́кци|я, и *f.* injection.
и. о. (*abbr. of* ***исполня́ющий обя́занности***) +*g.* acting ….
Ио́в, а *m.* (*bibl.*) Job.
Ио́ил|ь, я *m.* (*bibl.*) Joel.
ио́н, а *m.* (*phys.*) ion.
Ио́н|а, ы *m.* (*bibl.*) Jonah.
иониза́ци|я, и *f.* (*phys., med.*) ionization.
иони́ческ|ий *adj.* Ionian, Ionic; **~ая коло́нна** Ionic column.
Иорда́н, а *m.* the Jordan (*river*).
иорда́н|ец, ца *m.* Jordanian.
Иорда́ни|я, и *f.* Jordan.
иорда́н|ка, ки *f. of* ⇨**~ец**
иорда́нский *adj.* Jordanian.
иподья́кон, а *m.* (*eccl.*) subdeacon.
ипоме́|я, и *f.* (*bot.*) morning glory.
ипоста́с|ь, и *f.* (*theol.*) hypostasis; **в ~и** (+*g.*) in the role of.
ипоте́к|а, и *f.* mortgage.
ипоте́|чный *adj. of* ⇨**~ка**
ипохо́ндрик, а *m.* hypochondriac.
ипохо́ндри|я, и *f.* hypochondria.
ипподро́м, а *m.* racecourse.
ипри́т, а *m.* mustard gas.
ИРА *f. indecl.* (*abbr. of* ***Ирла́ндская республика́нская а́рмия***) IRA (*Irish Republican Army*).
Ира́к, а *m.* Iraq.
ира́к|ец, ца *m.* Iraqi.
ира́кский *adj.* Iraqi.
Ира́н, а *m.* Iran.
ира́н|ец, ца *m.* Iranian.
ира́н|ка, ки *f. of* ⇨**~ец**
ира́нский *adj.* Iranian.
ира́|чка, чки *f. of* ⇨**~кец**
и́рбис, а *m.* (*zool.*) ounce.
ири́ди|й, я *m.* (*chem.*) iridium.
иридодиагно́стик|а, и *f.* iridology.
иридо́лог, а *m.* iridologist.
и́рис, а *m.* (*bot.*) iris.
ири́с, а *m.* toffee.
ири́ск|а, и *f.* (*coll.*) (a) toffee.
ирла́нд|ец, ца *m.* Irishman.
Ирла́нди|я, и *f.* Ireland.
ирла́нд|ка, ки *f. of* ⇨**~ец**
ирла́ндский *adj.* Irish.
ироке́з, а *m.* **1** Iroquois. **2** (*coll.*) (*причёска*) Mohican (*hairstyle*).
иронизи́р|овать, ую *impf.* (**над** + *i.*) to speak ironically (about).
ирони́ческий *adj.* ironic(al).
ирони́ч|ный (~ен, ~на) *adj.* = **~еский**
иро́ни|я, и *f.* irony.
иррациона́л|ьный (~ен, ~ьна) *adj.* irrational; **~ьное число́** (*math.*) irrational number, surd.
иррегуля́рн|ый *adj.* irregular; **~ые войска́** (*mil.*) irregulars.
ирригаци|я, и *f.* (*agric. and med.*) irrigation.
ис... *pref.* = **из...**
Иса́й|я, и *m.* (*bibl.*) Isaiah.
иск, а *m.* (*leg.*) suit, action; **предъяви́ть и. (к) кому́-н.** to sue, prosecute s.o., bring an action against s.o.; **отказа́ть в ~е** to reject a suit; **и. за клевету́** libel action.
искажа́|ть, ю *impf. of* ⇨**искази́ть**
искаже́ни|е, я *nt.* distortion, perversion.
искажённый *p.p.p. of* ⇨**искази́ть** *and adj.* distorted, perverted.
иска|зи́ть, жу́, зи́шь *pf.* (*of* ⇨**~жа́ть**) to distort, pervert, twist; to misrepresent; **боль ~зи́ла черты́ её лица́** pain has distorted her features; **и. чьи-н. слова́** to twist s.o.'s words; **и. фа́кты** to misrepresent the facts.
искале́ч|енный *p.p.p. of* ⇨**~ить** *and adj.* crippled, maimed.
искале́чива|ть, ю *impf. of* ⇨**искале́чить**
искале́ч|ить, у, ишь *pf.* (*of* ⇨**~ивать** *and* **кале́чить**) to cripple, maim.
искале́ч|иться, усь, ишься *pf. of* ⇨**кале́читься**
иска́лыва|ть, ю *impf. of* ⇨**исколо́ть**
иска́ни|е, я *nt.* **1** (+*g.*) search (for), quest (of). **2** (*pl.*) strivings.
иска́пыва|ть, ю *impf. of* ⇨**ископа́ть**
иска́тел|ь, я *m.* seeker, searcher; **и. же́мчуга** pearl-diver.
иска́тел|ьный (~ен, ~ьна) *adj.* ingratiating.
иска́тельств|о, а *nt.* (*arch.*) obsequiousness.
иска́ть, ищу́, и́щешь *impf.* **1** (+*a.*) to look for, search for; to seek (*sth. concr.*); **и. иго́лку, кварти́ру** to be looking for a needle, for a flat. **2** (+*g.*) to seek, look for, try to obtain (*sth. abstr.*); **и. слу́чая, сове́та** to seek an opportunity, seek advice.
исключ|а́ть, а́ю *impf. of* ⇨**~и́ть**
исключа́|я *pres. ger. of* ⇨**~ть** *and prep.+g.* excepting, with the exception of; **и. прису́тствующих** the present company excepted.
исключе́ни|е, я *nt.* **1** (*отклонение от нормы*) exception; **за ~ем** (+*g.*) with the exception (of). **2** (*из списка*) exclusion; (*из организации*) expulsion; **по ме́тоду ~я** by process of elimination.
исключи́тельно *adv.* **1** (*необыкновенно*) exceptionally. **2** (*только*) exclusively, solely. **3** (*liter.*) (*кроме последнего упоминаемого предмета*) exclusive; **до страни́цы семь и.** up to but not including page seven.
исключи́тел|ьный (~ен, ~ьна) *adj.* **1** (*необыкновенный*) exceptional; **и. слу́чай** exceptional case; **~ьной ва́жности** of exceptional importance. **2** (*не для всех*) exclusive; **~ьное пра́во** exclusive right, sole right. **3** (*coll.*) (*отличный*) excellent.
исключ|и́ть, у́, и́шь *pf.* (*of* ⇨**~а́ть**) **1** (*удалить*) to exclude; to eliminate; **и. из спи́ска** to strike off a list. **2** (*из организации*) to expel; to dismiss. **3** (*не допустить*) to rule out; **не ~ено́, что на́ши проигра́ют** our side could conceivably lose.
искове́рка|нный *p.p.p. of* ⇨**~ть** *and adj.* (*coll.*) corrupt(ed); **~нное сло́во** corrupted word, corruption.
исковерка|ть, ю *pf. of* ⇨**кове́ркать**
иск|ово́й *adj. of* ⇨**~**; **~ово́е заявле́ние** (*leg.*) statement of claim.
исколачива|ть, ю *impf. of* ⇨**исколоти́ть**
исколе|си́ть, шу́, си́шь *pf.* (*coll.*) to travel all over.
исколо|ти́ть, чу́, ~тишь *pf.* (*of* ⇨**исколачивать**) (*coll.*) **1** (*избить*) to beat; **и. кого́-н. до полусме́рти** to beat s.o. within an inch of his life.

2 (*испортить*) to damage by knocking in nails, etc.

исколо́ть, ю́, ´~ешь *pf.* (*of* ⇒**иска́лывать**) to prick all over, cover with pricks.

иско́мка|ть, ю *pf. of* ⇒**ко́мкать**

иско́м|ый *adj.* sought for; *as n.* **~ое, ~ого** *nt.* (*math.*) unknown quantity.

искони́ *adv.* (*rhet.*) from time immemorial.

иско́нный *adj.* (*права*) immemorial, age-old; (*население*) native, indigenous.

ископа́ем|ое, ого *nt.* **1** fossil (*also fig., iron.*). **2** (*also* **поле́зное ~**) mineral.

ископа́емый *adj.* fossilized.

ископа́|ть, ю *pf.* (*of* ⇒**иска́пывать**) to dig up.

искорёж|ить(ся), у(сь), ишь(ся) *pf. of* ⇒**корёжить(ся)**

искорене́ни|е, я *nt.* eradication.

искорен|и́ть, ю́, и́шь *pf.* (*of* ⇒**~я́ть**) to eradicate.

искорен|я́ть, я́ю *impf. of* ⇒**~и́ть**

и́скорк|а, и *f. dim. of* ⇒**и́скра**

и́скоса *adv.* (*coll.*) askance, sideways; **взгляд и.** sidelong glance.

и́скр|а, ы *f.* spark; (*fig.*) flash; **промелькну́ть, как и.** to flash by; **и. наде́жды** glimmer of hope; **у меня́ ~ы из глаз посы́пались** (*coll.*) I saw stars.

и́скренне *adv.* sincerely, candidly; **и. ваш, и. пре́данный вам** (*epistolary formula*) Yours sincerely; Yours faithfully.

и́скрен|ний (~ен, ~на, ~не *or* **~но)** *adj.* sincere, candid.

и́скренност|ь, и *f.* sincerity, candour.

искрив|и́ть, лю́, и́шь *pf.* (*of* ⇒**~ля́ть**) to bend; (*fig.*) to distort.

искривле́ни|е, я *nt.* bend; (*fig.*) distortion; **и. позвоно́чника** curvature of the spine.

искривля́|ть, ю *impf. of* ⇒**искриви́ть**

искри́ст|ый (~, ~а) *adj.* sparkling.

искр|и́ть, и́т *impf.* (*tech.*) to spark.

и́скр|иться, ´~ится *impf.* to sparkle; to scintillate (*also fig.*).

искровен|ённый *p.p.p. of* ⇒**~и́ть** *and adj.* blood-stained.

искровен|и́ть, ю́, и́шь *pf.* (*coll.*) **1** (*изранить*) to wound so as to draw blood. **2** (*выпачкать*) to stain with blood.

искр|ово́й *adj. of* ⇒**´~а**; **и. зазо́р, и. промежу́ток** (*elec.*) spark-gap.

искрогаси́тел|ь, я *m.* (*tech.*) spark-extinguisher.

искромётный *adj.* sparkling; (*fig.*): **и. взгляд** flashing glance.

искромса́|ть, ю *pf. of* ⇒**кромса́ть**

искрош|и́ть, у́, ´~ишь *pf.* (*of* ⇒**кроши́ть**) (*хлеб*) to crumble; (*мясо*) to chop up; (*fig.*) (*человека*) to cut to pieces (*with sabres*).

искрош|и́ться, ´~ится *pf.* (*of* ⇒**кроши́ться**) to crumble (*intrans.*).

искупа́|ть[1], ю *pf.* (*coll.*) to bath.

искуп|а́ть[2], а́ю *impf. of* ⇒**~и́ть**

искупа́|ться[1], юсь *pf.* (*coll.*) to bathe; to take a bath.

искупа́|ться[2], юсь *impf., pass. of* ⇒**~ть[2]**

искупи́тел|ь, я *m.* (*theol.*) redeemer.

искупи́тел|ьный (~ен, ~ьна) *adj.* expiatory, redemptive.

искуп|и́ть, лю́, ´~ишь *pf.* (*of* ⇒**~а́ть[2]**) **1** (*theol. and fig.*) (*вину, грех*) to expiate, atone for. **2** (*недостаток*) to make up for, compensate for.

искупле́ни|е, я *nt.* redemption, expiation, atonement.

иску́с, а *m.* test, ordeal.

искус|а́ть, а́ю *pf.* (*of* ⇒**~ывать**) (*о комарах*) to bite badly, all over; (*о пчёлах*) to sting badly, all over.

искуси́тел|ь, я *m.* tempter.

иску|си́ть, шу́, си́шь *pf. of* ⇒**~ша́ть**

иску|си́ться, шу́сь, си́шься *pf.* (*obs.*) **1** (*приобрести опыт*) (**в**+*p.*) to become expert (at), become a past master (in, of). **2** (*соблазниться*) to give in to temptation.

иску́сник, а *m.* (*coll.*) expert, past master.

иску́сни|ца, цы *f. of* ⇒**~к**

иску́с|ный (~ен, ~на) *adj.* skilful (*Br.*), skillful (*US*); expert.

иску́сственник, а *m.* (*coll.*) bottle-fed baby.

иску́сственни|ца, цы *f. of* ⇒**~к**

иску́сственност|ь, и *f.* artificiality.

иску́сствен|ный *adj.* **1** artificial; (*ткань, волокно*) synthetic, man-made; **~ное дыха́ние** artificial respiration; **и. интелле́кт** artificial intelligence; **~ное оплодотворе́ние** artificial insemination; **~ное пита́ние (младе́нца)** bottle feeding. **2 (~, ~на)** (*fig.*) (*смех*) artificial, feigned.

иску́сств|о, а *nt.* **1** art; **изобрази́тельные, изя́щные ~а** fine arts. **2** (*умение*) craftsmanship, skill; **и. верхово́й езды́** horsemanship; **де́лать что-н. из любви́ к ~у** to do sth. for its own sake.

искусствове́д, а *m.* art historian.

искусствове́дени|е, я *nt.* history of art, art history.

иску́сыва|ть, ю *impf. of* ⇒**искуса́ть**

искуша́|ть, ю *impf.* (*of* ⇒**искуси́ть**) to tempt; to seduce; **и. судьбу́** to tempt fate, tempt Providence.

искуше́ни|е, я *nt.* temptation; seduction; **ввести́ в и.** to lead into temptation; **подда́ться ~ю, впасть в и.** to yield to temptation.

искушённый *p.p.p. of* ⇒**искуси́ть** *and adj.* (*политик*) experienced; (*публика*) sophisticated.

исла́м, а *m.* Islam.

исла́мский *adj.* Islamic.

исла́нд|ец, ца *m.* Icelander.

Исла́нди|я, и *f.* Iceland.

исла́нд|ка, ки *f. of* ⇒**~ец**

исла́ндский *adj.* Icelandic.

испа́ко|стить, щу, стишь *pf. of* ⇒**па́костить**

испа́н|ец, ца *m.* Spaniard.

Испа́ни|я, и *f.* Spain.

испа́нк|а, и *f.* Spanish woman.

испа́нский *adj.* Spanish.

испаре́ни|е, я *nt.* **1** (*действие*) evaporation. **2** (*usu. pl.*) (*пар*) fumes.

испа́рин|а, ы *f.* perspiration.

испар|и́ть, ю́, и́шь *pf.* (*of* ⇒**~я́ть**) to evaporate (*trans.*).

испар|и́ться, ю́сь, и́шься *pf.* (*of* ⇒**~я́ться**) to evaporate; (*fig., joc.*) (*исчезнуть*) to vanish into thin air.

испар|я́ть(ся), я́ю(сь) *impf. of* ⇒**~и́ть(ся)**

испа́чка|ть(ся), ю(сь) *pf. of* ⇒**па́чкать(ся)**

испепел|и́ть, ю́, и́шь *pf.* (*of* ⇒**~я́ть**) to reduce to ashes, incinerate.

испепел|я́ть, я́ю *impf. of* ⇒**~и́ть**

испестр|ённый *p.p.p. of* ⇒**~и́ть** *and adj.* speckled, mottled; variegated.

испестр|и́ть, ю́, и́шь *pf.* (*of* ⇒**~я́ть**) to speckle; to mottle; to make variegated.

испестр|я́ть, я́ю *impf. of* ⇒**~и́ть**

испечённый *p.p.p. of* ⇒**испе́чь**; **вновь и.** (*coll.*) newly-fledged.

испе́|чь, ку́, чёшь, ку́т, *past* **´~к, ~кла́** *pf. of* ⇒**печь**

испе́|чься, чётся, ку́тся, *past* **´~кся, ~кла́сь** *pf. of* ⇒**пе́чься[1]**

испещр|и́ть, ю́, и́шь *pf.* (*of* ⇒**~я́ть**) (+*a. and i.*) to spot (with); to mark all over (with); **и. сте́ну на́дписями** to cover a wall with inscriptions.

испещр|я́ть, я́ю *impf. of* ⇒**~и́ть**

испи|са́ть, шу́, ´~шешь *pf.* (*of* ⇒**´~сывать**) **1** (*тетрадь*) to cover with writing; **он уже́ ~са́л два́дцать тетра́дей** he has already filled up twenty exercise books. **2** (*карандаш, бумагу*) to use up (in writing).

испи|са́ться, шу́сь, ´~шешься *pf.* (*of* ⇒**´~сываться**) (*coll.*) **1** (*о карандаше*) to be worn out; (*о ручке*) to run out. **2** (*о писателе*) to write o.s. out.

испи́сыва|ть(ся), ю(сь) *impf. of* ⇒**исписа́ть(ся)**

испито́й *adj.* (*coll.*) haggard, gaunt; hollow-cheeked.

испи́|ть, изопью́, изопьёшь, *past* **~л, ~ла́ ~ло** *pf.* **1** (*dial.*) to have a drink of, sup. **2** (*fig., rhet.*) to drain.

исповеда́л|ьня, ьни, *g. pl.* **~ен** *f.* (*eccl.*) confessional.

испове́дани|е, я *nt.* creed, confession (*of faith*).

испове́д|ать, аю *pf.* (*coll.*) = **~овать[1]**

испове́д|аться, аюсь *pf.* (*coll.*) = **~оваться[1]**

испове́д|овать[1], ую *impf. and pf.* **1** (*eccl.*) to hear the confession (of). **2** (*coll.*) (*расспрашивать*) to draw out.

испове́д|овать[2], ую *impf.* (*веру*) to profess.

испове́д|оваться[1], уюсь *impf. and*

pf. **1** (+*d.* *or* **у**+*g.*; *eccl.*) to confess, make one's confession (to). **2** (+*d.* *or* **пе́ред**+*i.*; *fig., coll.*) to confess; to unburden o.s. of; **он мне ~овался в свои́х сомне́ниях** he confessed his doubts to me.

испове́д|оваться², **уется** *impf. and pf., pass. of* ⇒**~овать²**

и́споведь, и *f.* (*eccl.*) confession; **быть на ~и** to be at confession.

испога́нива|ть, ю *impf. of* ⇒**испога́нить**

испога́н|ить, ю, ишь *pf.* (*of* ⇒**~ивать**) (*coll.*) to foul, defile.

и́сподволь *adv.* (*coll.*) in leisurely fashion; by degrees.

исподло́бья *adv.* from under the brows (*distrustfully, sullenly*).

исподни́зу *adv.* (*coll.*) from underneath.

исподтишка́ *adv.* (*coll., pej.*) in an underhand way; on the quiet, on the sly; **смея́ться и.** to laugh in one's sleeve.

испоко́н *adv.*; *only in phrr.* **и. ве́ку, и. веко́в** from time immemorial.

испо́лза|ть, ю *pf.* (*coll.*) to crawl all over.

исполи́н, а *m.* giant.

исполи́нский *adj.* gigantic.

исполко́м, а *m.* (*abbr. of* ***исполни́тельный комите́т***) executive committee.

исполне́ни|е, я *nt.* **1** (*желания*) fulfilment (*Br.*), fulfillment (*US*); (*приказа*) execution; (*долгов*) discharge; **привести́ в и.** to carry out, execute. **2** (*роли, музыки*) performance; (*theatr., mus.*) **в ~и** (+*g.*) (as) played (by), (as) performed (by).

испо́лненный *p.p.p. of* ⇒**испо́лнить** *and adj.* (+*g.*) full (of).

исполни́м|ый (~, ~а) *adj.* feasible, practicable, realizable.

исполни́тел|ь, я *m.* **1** executor; **суде́бный и.** bailiff. **2** (*theatr., mus., etc.*) performer; **соста́в ~ей** cast.

исполни́тель|ница, ницы *f. of* ⇒**~**

исполни́тельност|ь, и *f.* assiduity; expedition.

исполни́тел|ьный *adj.* **1** (*власть, директор, комитет*) executive; **и. лист** (*leg.*) writ, court order. **2 (~ен, ~ьна)** (*человек*) efficient and dependable.

испо́лн|ить¹, ю, ишь *pf.* (*of* ⇒**~я́ть**) **1** (*заказ*) to carry out, execute; (*желание*) to fulfil (*Br.*), fulfill (*US*); **и. обеща́ние** to keep a promise; **и. обя́занности** (+*g.*) to stand in (for); **и. про́сьбу** to grant a request. **2** (*роль, танец*) to perform; **и. роль** (+*g.*) to take the part (of).

испо́лн|ить², ю, ишь *pf.* (*of* ⇒**~я́ть**) (+*a. and i. or g.*) to fill (with); **сообще́ние о побе́де ~ило всех ра́достью (ра́дости)** the news of the victory delighted everyone.

испо́лн|иться, юсь, ишься *pf.* (*of* ⇒**~я́ться**) **1** (*осуществиться*) to be fulfilled. **2** (*impers.*, +*d.*; *expr. passage of time*): **ему́ ~илось семь лет** he is seven, he was seven last birthday; **~илось пять лет с тех пор, как он уе́хал в Аме́рику** five years have passed (it is five years) since he went to America.

исполн|я́ть(ся), я́ю(сь) *impf. of* ⇒**~́ить(ся)**; **~я́ющий обя́занности** (+*g.*) acting.

исполос|ова́ть, у́ю *pf. of* ⇒**полосова́ть**

испо́льзовани|е, я *nt.* use; (*сырья*) utilization; **повто́рное и.** recycling.

испо́льз|овать, ую *impf. and pf.* to use, make use of, utilize; to turn to account.

испо́льщик, а *m.* sharecropper.

испо́льщин|а, ы *f.* sharecropping.

испо́р|тить(ся), чу(сь), тишь(ся) *pf. of* ⇒**по́ртить(ся)**

испо́рченност|ь, и *f.* depravity.

испо́рчен|ный *p.p.p. of* ⇒**испо́ртить** *and adj.* **1** (*человек*) depraved; corrupted. **2** (*настроение, день*) ruined; (*товары*) spoiled; bad, rotten; **~ные зу́бы** rotten teeth; **~ное мя́со** tainted meat. **3** (*coll.*) (*ребёнок*) spoiled. **4** (*comput.*) corrupt.

испо́шл|ить, ю, ишь *pf.* (*coll.*) to vulgarize.

исправи́м|ый (~, ~а) *adj.* corrigible.

исправи́тельно-трудово́й *adj.* corrective labour (*Br.*), labor (*US*).

исправи́тельный *adj.* correctional; corrective; **и. дом** reformatory.

испра́в|ить, лю, ишь *pf.* (*of* ⇒**~ля́ть**) **1** (*ошибку*) to rectify, correct, emend. **2** (*починить*) to repair, mend. **3** (*человека, характер*) to reform.

испра́в|иться, люсь, ишься *pf.* (*of* ⇒**~ля́ться**) to improve (*intrans.*); to reform (*intrans.*), turn over a new leaf.

исправле́ни|е, я *nt.* **1** (*действие*) correcting; repairing. **2** (*улучшение*) improvement; correction.

испра́влен|ный *p.p.p. of* ⇒**испра́вить** *and adj.* improved, corrected; **~ное изда́ние** revised edition; **и. хара́ктер** reformed character.

исправля́|ть, ю *impf. of* ⇒**испра́вить**

исправля́|ться, юсь *impf. of* ⇒**испра́виться**

испра́вност|ь, и *f.* **1** (*хорошее состояние*) good condition; **в (по́лной) ~и** in good working order, in good repair. **2** (*работы, работника*) meticulousness; (*почты*) punctuality.

испра́в|ный (~ен, ~на) *adj.* **1** (*механизм*) in good order. **2** (*человек, работа*) meticulous.

испражне́ни|е, я *nt.* **1** (*действие*) defecation. **2** (*pl.*) (*экскременты*) faeces.

испражн|и́ться, ю́сь, и́шься *pf. of* ⇒**~я́ться**

испражн|я́ться, я́юсь *impf.* (*of* ⇒**~и́ться**) to defecate.

испра́шива|ть, ю *impf.* (*of* ⇒**испроси́ть**) to beg, solicit; **и. ми́лость** to ask a favour.

испро́б|овать, ую *pf.* **1** (*проверить*) to test, try out; **и. все возмо́жности** to try everything, leave no stone unturned. **2** (*coll.*) (*поесть для пробы*) to try.

испро|си́ть, шу́, ~́сишь *pf.* (*of* ⇒**испра́шивать**) to obtain (by asking).

испрям|и́ть, лю́, и́шь *pf.* (*of* ⇒**~ля́ть**) (*coll.*) to straighten (out).

испрямля́|ть, ю *impf. of* ⇒**испрями́ть**

испу́г, а (у) *m.* fright; alarm; **с ~у/с ~а** from fright.

испу́ганный *p.p.p. of* ⇒**испуга́ть** *and adj.* frightened, scared, startled.

испуга́|ть(ся), ю(сь) *pf. of* ⇒**пуга́ть(ся)**

испуска́|ть, ю *impf. of* ⇒**испусти́ть**

испу|сти́ть, щу́, ~́стишь *pf.* (*of* ⇒**~ска́ть**) (*свет, лучи*) to emit; (*стон*) to let out; **и. вздох** to heave a sigh; **и. дух** to breathe one's last; **и. крик** to utter a cry.

испыта́ни|е, я *nt.* **1** test, trial; (*fig.*) ordeal; **быть на ~и** to be on trial, be on probation. **2** (*экзамен*) examination; **вступи́тельные ~я, приёмные ~я** entrance examination.

испы́т|анный *p.p.p. of* ⇒**~а́ть** *and adj.* tried, well-tried.

испыта́тел|ь, я *m.* tester; **лётчик-и.** test pilot.

испыта́тельн|ый *adj.* (*полёт, машина*) test, trial; (*срок*) probationary; **~ая коми́ссия** examining board; **и. полёт** test-flight; **и. пробе́г** trial run; **и. срок, и. стаж** period of probation.

испыт|а́ть, а́ю *pf.* (*of* ⇒**~́ывать**) **1** (*проверить*) to test, put to the test; **и. чьё-н. терпе́ние** to try s.o.'s patience. **2** (*ощутить*) to feel, experience.

испыту́ющий *adj.*: **и. взгляд** searching look.

испы́тыва|ть, ю *impf. of* ⇒**испыта́ть**

иссека́|ть, ю *impf. of* ⇒**иссе́чь**

и́ссера- *comb. form* grey-; **и.-голубо́й** grey-blue.

иссече́ни|е, я *nt.* (*med.*) excision, removal.

иссе́|чь¹, ку́, чёшь, ку́т, *past* **~к, ~кла́** *pf.* (*of* ⇒**~ка́ть**) **1** (*из камня, мрамора*) to carve. **2** (*med.*) to excise, remove.

иссе́|чь², ку́, чёшь, ку́т, *past* **~к, ~кла́** *pf.* (*of* ⇒**~ка́ть**) **1** (*изрубить*) to cut up, cleave. **2** (*избить*) to whip, lash.

иссле́довани|е, я *nt.* **1** (*темы*) research; (*местности*) exploration; (*больного, проблемы*) examination; (*крови, состава*) analysis; **он занима́ется ~ями по ру́сской исто́рии** he is engaged in research on Russian history. **2** (*научный труд*) paper; study.

иссле́довател|ь, я *m.* researcher; (*страны*) explorer.

иссле́дователь|ница, ницы *f. of* ⇒**~**

иссле́довательский *adj.* research.

иссле́д|овать, ую *impf. and pf.* (*ситуацию, проблему*) to investigate;

(*тему*) to research into; (*страну*) to explore; (*кровь*) to analyse; (*больного*) to examine.

иссо́х|нуть, ну, нешь, *past* ~, ~**ла** *pf.* (*of* ⇒**иссыха́ть**) **1** (*о реке*) to dry up. **2** (*о растении*) to wither; (*fig.*) to fade away.

и́сстари *adv.* from of old, of yore; **так и. ведётся** it is an old custom.

исстрада́|ться, юсь *pf.* to become worn out, wretched (with suffering).

исстре́лива|ть, ю *impf. of* ⇒**исстреля́ть**

исстрел|я́ть, я́ю *pf.* (*of* ⇒~́ивать) (*патроны*) to use up.

исступле́ни|е, я *nt.* (*возбуждение*) frenzy; (*страсть*) ecstasy; **гне́вное и.** rage; **прийти́ в и.** to go into a frenzy.

исступлённост|ь, и *f.* state of frenzy, ecstasy.

исступлённый *adj.* (*возбуждённый*) frenzied; (*страстный*) ecstatic.

иссуш|а́ть, а́ю *impf. of* ⇒~**и́ть**

иссуш|и́ть, у́, ~́ишь *pf.* (*of* ⇒~**а́ть**) to dry up; (*fig.*) to consume, waste.

иссыха́|ть, ю *impf. of* ⇒**иссо́хнуть**

иссяк|а́ть, а́ю *impf. of* ⇒~́**нуть**

исся́к|нуть, ну, нешь, *past* ~, ~**ла** *pf.* (*of* ⇒~**а́ть**) to run dry, dry up; (*fig.*) (*терпение, силы*) to run out.

иста́плива|ть, ю *impf. of* ⇒**истопи́ть**

иста́ск|анный *p.p.p. of* ⇒~**а́ть** *and adj.* **1** (*одежда*) worn out; threadbare. **2** (*fig.*) (*лицо*) dissipated.

истаск|а́ть, а́ю *pf.* (*of* ⇒~́**ивать**) to wear out.

истаск|а́ться, а́юсь *pf.* (*of* ⇒~́**иваться**) (*coll.*) to wear out (*intrans.*); (*fig.*) to be played out.

иста́скива|ть(ся), ю(сь) *impf. of* ⇒**истаска́ть(ся)**

иста́чива|ть, ю *impf. of* ⇒**источи́ть**[1]

иста́|ять, ю, ешь *pf.* to melt (completely); (*fig.*) to wither away.

исте́блишмент, а *m.* the Establishment.

истека́|ть, ю *impf. of* ⇒**исте́чь**

исте́|кший *p.p. of* ⇒~**чь** *and adj.* past, preceding; **в тече́ние** ~**кшего го́да** during the past year.

истер|е́ть, изотру́, изотрёшь, *past* ~́, ~́**ла** *pf.* (*of* ⇒**истира́ть**) **1** (*сыр*) to grate. **2** (*одежду*) to wear out (*by rubbing*); **и. в порошо́к** to reduce to powder.

истер|е́ться, изотрётся, *past* ~́**ся,** ~́**лась** *pf.* (*of* ⇒**истира́ться**) to wear out (*intrans.*).

исте́рз|анный *p.p.p. of* ⇒~**а́ть** *and adj.* (~**ан,** ~**ана**) (*одежда*) tattered; (*fig.*) (*душа*) tormented.

истерза́|ть, ю *pf.* **1** (*разорвать на части*) to tear in pieces; to mutilate. **2** (*измучить*) to torment.

истéрик, а *m.* hysterical man.

исте́рик|а, и *f.* hysterics.

истери́ческий *adj.* hysterical; **и. припа́док** fit of hysterics.

истери́чк|а, и *f.* hysterical woman.

истери́ч|ный (~ен, ~на) *adj.* hysterical.

истери́|я, и *f.* (*med.*) hysteria; (*fig.*): **вое́нная и.** war hysteria.

истёртый *p.p.p. of* ⇒**истере́ть** *and adj.* worn, old.

ист|е́ц, ца́ *m.* (*leg.*) plaintiff.

истече́ни|е, я *nt.* **1** outflow; **и. кро́ви** haemorrhage (*Br.*), hemorrhage (*US*). **2** (*окончание*) expiry, expiration; **по** ~**и сро́ка гара́нтии** on the expiry of the guarantee period.

исте́|чь, ку́, чёшь, ку́т, *past* ~́**к,** ~**кла́** *pf.* (*of* ⇒~**ка́ть**) **1**: **и. кро́вью** to bleed profusely; (*fig., rhet.*) to pour out one's life-blood. **2** (*окончиться*) to expire, elapse; **вре́мя** ~**кло́** time is up; **срок гара́нтии истёк** the guarantee has expired.

и́стин|а, ы *f.* truth; **изби́тая и.** truism; **свята́я и.** God's truth; gospel truth.

и́стин|ный (~ен, ~на) *adj.* true, veritable.

истира́ни|е, я *nt.* abrasion.

истира́|ть(ся), ю *impf. of* ⇒**истере́ть(ся)**

ист|и́ца, и́цы *f. of* ⇒~**е́ц**

истле|ва́ть, ва́ю *impf. of* ⇒~**ть**

истле́|ть, ю *pf.* (*of* ⇒~**ва́ть**) **1** (*сгнить*) to rot, decay. **2** (*сгорать*) to smoulder to ashes.

истма́т, а *m.* (*abbr. of* ***истори́ческий материали́зм***) historical materialism.

и́стов|ый (~, ~а) *adj.* (*obs.*) (*настоящий*) true; (*благочестивый*) devout; (*усердный*) assiduous, punctilious.

исто́к, а *m.* source (*also fig.*).

истолкова́ни|е, я *nt.* (*смысла, слова*) interpretation; (*письменного памятника*) commentary.

истолкова́тел|ь, я *m.* interpreter, commentator.

истолкова́тель|ница, ницы *f. of* ⇒~

истолк|ова́ть, у́ю *pf.* (*of* ⇒~**о́вывать**) (*смысл, слово*) to interpret; (*письменный памятник*) to comment upon; **и. замеча́ние в дурну́ю сто́рону** to put a nasty construction on a remark.

истолко́выва|ть, ю *impf. of* ⇒**истолкова́ть**

истол|о́чь, ку́, чёшь, ку́т, *past* ~**о́к,** ~**кла́** *pf.* to pound, crush.

исто́м|а, ы *f.* languor.

истом|и́ть, лю́, и́шь *pf.* (*of* ⇒**томи́ть**) to exhaust, weary.

истом|и́ться, лю́сь, и́шься *pf.* (*of* ⇒**томи́ться**) (**от**+*g.*) to be exhausted, worn out (with, from); to be weary (of); **и. от жа́жды** to be faint with thirst.

истом|лённый *p.p.p. of* ⇒~**и́ть** *and adj.* exhausted, worn out.

истоп|и́ть, лю́, ~ишь *pf.* (*of* ⇒**иста́пливать**) **1** (*вытопить*) to heat up. **2** (*coll.*) (*израсходовать*) to spend, use up (*fuel*). **3** (*расплавить*) to melt down.

истопни́к, а́ *m.* stoker; (*котлов*) boilerman.

истоп|та́ть, чу́, ~́чешь *pf.* **1** (*измять*) to trample (down, over). **2** (*coll.*) (*износить*) to wear out (*footwear*).

исторг|а́ть, а́ю *impf. of* ⇒~**нуть**

исто́рг|нуть, ну, нешь, *past* ~, ~**ла** *pf.* (*of* ⇒~**а́ть**) **1** (*rhet.*) (*выбросить*) to throw out, expel; **и. из свое́й среды́** to ostracize. **2** (**у** *or* **из**+*g.*; *obs.*) to wrest, wrench (from); (*fig.*) to force (from), extort; **и. обеща́ние** to extort a promise.

исто́рик, а *m.* historian.

историо́граф, а *m.* historiographer.

историогра́фи|я, и *f.* historiography.

истори́ческ|ий *adj.* **1** historical; ~**ое лицо́** historical figure. **2** (*важный*) historic; ~**ое реше́ние** historic decision.

истори́ч|ный (~ен, ~на) *adj.* historical.

исто́ри|я, и *f.* **1** history; **войти́ в** ~**ю** to go down in history; **и. боле́зни** case history. **2** (*coll.*) (*рассказ*) story. **3** (*coll.*) (*событие*) incident, event; scene; **вчера́ со мной случи́лась заба́вная и.** a funny thing happened to me yesterday; **вот так и.!** here's a pretty kettle of fish!; **ве́чная** (*or* **обы́чная**) **и.!** the (same) old story!

истоск|ова́ться, у́юсь *pf.* (**по**+*d.*) to yearn (for); to be wearied with longing (for).

источ|а́ть, а́ю *impf.* (*of* ⇒~**и́ть**[2]) to give off, impart.

источ|и́ть[1]**, у́, ~́ишь** *pf.* (*of* ⇒**иста́чивать**) **1** (*истереть*) to grind down. **2** (*изъесть*) to eat away, gnaw through.

источ|и́ть[2]**, у́, ~́ишь** *pf. of* ⇒~**а́ть**

исто́чник, а *m.* **1** spring. **2** (*fig.*) source; **и. информа́ции** source of information; **ве́рный и.** reliable source; **и. све́та** source of light; **служи́ть** ~**ом** (+*g.*) to be a source (of).

исто́шный *adj.* (*coll.*) heart-rending.

истощ|а́ть(ся), а́ю(сь) *impf. of* ⇒~**и́ть(ся)**

истоще́ни|е, я *nt.* exhaustion; **война́ на и.** war of attrition.

истощ|ённый *p.p.p. of* ⇒~**и́ть** *and adj.* exhausted; (*исхудалый*) emaciated.

истощ|и́ть, у́, и́шь *pf.* (*of* ⇒~**а́ть**) to exhaust.

истощ|и́ться, у́сь, и́шься *pf.* (*of* ⇒~**а́ться**) to become exhausted (*also fig.*); **все на́ши запа́сы** ~**и́лись** all our supplies had run out.

истра́|тить, чу, тишь *pf. of* ⇒**тра́тить**

истра́|титься, чусь, тишься *pf.* (*coll.*) to overspend.

истреби́тел|ь, я *m.* **1** (*человек*) destroyer. **2** (*самолёт*) fighter; **и.-бомбардиро́вщик** fighter bomber. **3** (*лётчик*) fighter pilot.

истреби́тель|ный *adj.*

1 destructive. **2** *adj. of* ⇒**~** **2**; **~ная авиация** fighters (*collect.*).

истреб|ить, лю, ишь *pf.* (*of* ⇒**~лять**) (*посевы*) to destroy; (*крыс*) to exterminate.

истреблени|е, я *nt.* (*посевов*) destruction; (*крыс*) extermination.

истребля|ть, ю *impf. of* ⇒**истребить**

истр|ёпанный *p.p.p. of* ⇒**~епать** *and adj.* torn, frayed; worn.

истреп|ать, лю, ~лешь *pf.* (*of* ⇒**~ывать** *and* **трепать**) to tear, fray; to wear to rags; **и. нервы** (*coll.*) to fray one's nerves.

истреп|аться, ~лется *pf.* (*of* ⇒**истрёпываться** *and* **трепаться**) to tear, fray; to wear to rags.

истрёпыва|ть(ся), ю *impf. of* ⇒**истрепать(ся)**

истреска|ться, ется *pf.* (*coll.*) to crack, become cracked.

истукан, а *m.* idol, statue.

иступ|ить(ся), лю, ~ишь *pf. of* ⇒**тупить(ся)**

истый *adj.* true, genuine; **и. учёный** a true scholar; **и. любитель животных** a genuine animal-lover.

истык|ать, аю *pf.* (*of* ⇒**~ивать**) (*coll.*) to riddle, pierce all over.

истыкива|ть, ю *impf. of* ⇒**истыкать**

истязани|е, я *nt.* torture.

истязател|ь, я *m.* torturer.

истязатель|ница, ницы *f. of* ⇒**~**

истяза|ть, ю *impf.* to torture.

исхле|стать, щу, ~щешь *pf.* (*of* ⇒**~стывать**) (*coll.*) **1** (*избить*) to lash, flog. **2** (*привести в негодность*) to wear out (*a whip*).

исхлёстыва|ть, ю *impf. of* ⇒**исхлестать**

исхлопатыва|ть, ю *impf. of* ⇒**исхлопотать**

исхлопо|тать, чу, ~чешь *pf.* (*of* ⇒**исхлопатывать**) (*coll.*) to obtain (*by dint of application in the right quarters*).

исход, а *m.* **1** (*итог*) outcome; (*конец*) end; **быть на ~е** to be nearing the end, be coming to an end; **на ~е дня** towards evening; **день был на ~е** the day was drawing to a close. **2** (*bibl.*) **И.** (*the Book of*) Exodus.

исхо|дить[1], жу, ~дишь *pf.* (*обойти*) to go, walk all over.

исхо|дить[2], жу, ~дишь *impf.* (*of* ⇒**изойти**) **1** (*impf. only*) (**из**+*g.*) (*происходить*) to come (from); to emanate (from); **откуда исходит этот слух?** where does this rumour (*Br.*), rumor (*US*) come from? **2** (*impf. only*) (**из**+*g.*) (*основываться*) to proceed (from), base o.s. (on); **и. из необоснованных предположений** to proceed from unfounded assumptions. **3**: **и. кровью** to become weak through loss of blood; **и. слезами** to cry one's heart out.

исходн|ый *adj.* initial; **~ая точка**, **~ое положение** point of departure; **~ая стадия** initial phase.

исходящий *adj.* outgoing.

исхудалый *adj.* emaciated, wasted.

исхудани|е, я *nt.* emaciation.

исхуда|ть, ю *pf.* to become emaciated, become wasted.

исцарап|ать, аю *pf.* (*of* ⇒**~ывать**) to scratch badly; to scratch all over.

исцарапыва|ть, ю *impf. of* ⇒**исцарапать**

исцелени|е, я *nt.* **1** (*действие*) healing, cure. **2** (*выздоровление*) recovery.

исцел|имый *pres. part. pass. of* ⇒**~ить** *and adj.* curable.

исцелител|ь, я *m.* healer.

исцелитель|ница, ницы *f. of* ⇒**~**

исцел|ить, ю, ишь *pf.* (*of* ⇒**~ять**) to heal, cure.

исцел|ять, яю *impf. of* ⇒**~ить**

исчади|е, я *nt. esp. in phr.* **и. ада** devil incarnate.

исчах|нуть, ну, нешь, *past* **~**, **~ла** *pf.* to waste away.

исчез|ать, аю *impf.* (*of* ⇒**~нуть**) to disappear, vanish.

исчезновени|е, я *nt.* disappearance.

исчез|нуть, ну, нешь, *past* **~**, **~ла** *pf. of* ⇒**~ать**

исчёрк|ать, аю (*and* **~ать, ~аю**) *pf.* **1** (*рукопись, текст*) to cover with crossings-out. **2** (*бумагу*) to scribble all over.

исчерна- *comb. form* blackish-.

исчерп|ать, аю *pf.* (*of* ⇒**~ывать**) **1** to exhaust, drain; **и. все свои средства** to exhaust all one's resources; (*fig.*): **и. терпение** to exhaust s.o.'s patience. **2** (*довести до конца*) to settle, conclude; **и. вопрос** to settle a question; **и. повестку дня** to conclude the agenda.

исчерпыва|ть, ю *impf. of* ⇒**исчерпать**

исчерпыва|ющий *pres. part. act. of* ⇒**~ть** *and adj.* exhaustive.

исчер|тить, чу, ~тишь *pf.* (*of* ⇒**~чивать**) to cover with lines.

исчерчив|ать, ю *impf. of* ⇒**исчертить**

исчислени|е, я *nt.* calculation; (*math.*) calculus.

исчисл|ить, ю, ишь *pf.* (*of* ⇒**~ять**) to calculate.

исчисл|ять, яю *impf. of* ⇒**~ить**

исчисля|ться, ется *impf.* (+*i.* or **в**+*a.*) to amount to, come to; to be estimated (at); **убытки ~лись в сто рублей** the damages came to one hundred roubles; **потери ~ются тысячами** the casualties are estimated at thousands.

итак *conj.* thus; so then.

Итали|я, и *f.* Italy.

итальян|ец, ца *nt.* Italian.

итальян|ка, ки *f. of* ⇒**~ец**

итальянск|ий *adj.* Italian; **~ая забастовка** sit-down strike; work-to-rule.

ИТАР-ТАСС (*abbr. of* ***Информационное телеграфное агентство России — Телеграфное агентство Советского Союза***) ITAR-TASS (*official news agency of Russia*).

и т. д. (*abbr. of* ***и так далее***) etc., etcetera, and so on.

итеративный *adj.* (*ling.*) iterative.

итог, а *m.* **1** (*общая сумма*) sum, total; **общий и.** grand total. **2** (*fig.*) (*результат*) result; **подвести и.** to sum up; **в ~е** (*в конце концов*) in the end; (*в результате*) as a result; **в конечном ~е** in the end.

итого *adv.* in all, altogether.

итоговый *adj.* (*сумма*) total; (*завершающий*) final, concluding.

итож|ить, у, ишь *impf.* (*pf.* **подытожить**) to sum up, add up.

и т. п. (*abbr. of* ***и тому подобное***) etc., etcetera, and so on.

иттерби|й, я *m.* (*chem.*) ytterbium.

итти (*obs.*) = **идти**

иттри|й, я *m.* (*chem.*) yttrium.

Иуда, ы *m.* (*предатель*) Judas, traitor.

иудаизм, а *m.* Judaism.

иуде|й, я *m.* (*liter.*) Jew.

иудей|ка, ки *f. of* ⇒**~**

иудейский *adj.* (*hist. and relig.*) Judaic.

их[1] *a. and g. of* ⇒**они**

их[2] *possessive pron.* (*при существительном*) their; (*без существительного*) theirs; **их машина меньше, чем наша** their car is smaller than ours.

ихневмон, а *m.* (*zool.*) ichneumon.

ихний *possessive adj.* (*coll.*) their(s).

ихтиозавр, а *m.* ichthyosaurus.

ихтиолог, а *m.* ichthyologist.

ихтиологический *adj.* ichthyological.

ихтиологи|я, и *f.* ichthyology.

ишак, а *m.* donkey, ass; (*fig., coll.*) dogsbody (*Br.*), gofer (*US*).

иша|чий *adj. of* ⇒**~к**

ишач|ить, у, ишь *impf.* (*coll. pej.*) to slog, slave.

ишеми|я, и *f.* (*med.*) ischaemia (*Br.*), ischemia (*US*).

ишиас, а *m.* (*med.*) sciatica.

ишь *int.* (*coll.*) *expr. surprise or disgust*: look!; just look!; well I never!; **и. ты!** = **и.!** *or expr. disagreement or objection.*

ищейк|а, и *f.* bloodhound, tracker dog (*also fig., pej.*).

ищущий *pres. part. act. of* ⇒**искать** *and adj.*: **и. взгляд** searching look.

июл|ь, я *m.* July.

июль|ский *adj. of* ⇒**~**

июн|ь, я *m.* June.

июнь|ский *adj. of* ⇒**~**

Йй

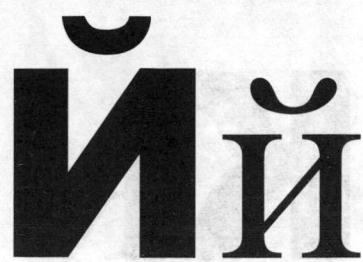

Йе́мен, а *m.* Yemen.
йе́мен|ец, ца *m.* Yemeni.
йе́мен|ка, ки *f. of* ⇨**~ец**
йе́менский *adj.* Yemeni.
йе́ти *m. indecl.* yeti, abominable snowman.
йог, а *m.* yogi.
йо́г|а, и *f.* yoga.
йо́гурт, а *m.* yog(h)urt.
йод, а *m.* iodine.
йо́дист|ый *adj.* (*chem.*) containing iodine; **й. ка́лий** potassium iodide; **~ая соль** iodized salt.
йо́д|ный *adj. of* ⇨**~**; **и. раство́р** tincture of iodine.
йот, а *m.* (*ling.*) *letter* J; yod (*name of sound* [j]).
йо́т|а, ы *f.* iota; **ни на ~у** not a jot, not an iota.
Йоха́ннесбург, а *m.* Johannesburg.

Кк

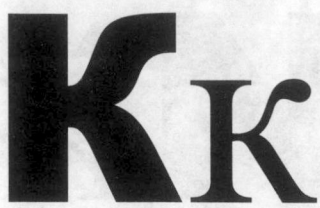

°К (*abbr. of* ***гра́дусов по Ке́львину***) K., degrees Kelvin; **273°К** 273K.

к, ко *prep.+d.* **1** (*при обозначении места*) to, towards; **мы подъезжа́ли к Москве́** we were nearing Moscow; **прислони́те ле́стницу к стене́** place the ladder against the wall; (*fig.*): **лицо́м к лицу́** face to face; **к лу́чшему** for the better; **моли́тва к Бо́гу** prayer to God; **любо́вь к де́тям** love of children; **письмо́ к дру́гу** letter to a friend; **к о́бщему удивле́нию** to everyone's surprise; **к (не)сча́стью** (un)fortunately; **к чёрту его́!** to hell with him!; **шля́па ей к лицу́** her hat becomes her; **к ва́шим услу́гам** at your service; (*при обозначении добавления*): **к трём приба́вить пять** to add three and five; **к тому́ же** besides, moreover.
2 (*при обозначении предельного срока*) to, towards; by; **зима́ подходи́ла к концу́** winter was drawing to a close; **к утру́** towards morning, by morning; **к пе́рвому января́** by the first of January; **я приду́ к восьми́ (часа́м)** I will be there by eight (o'clock); **к тому́ вре́мени** by then, by that time; **к сро́ку** on time.
3 (*при указании назначения*) for; **к чему́?** what for?; **э́то ни к чему́** it is no good, no use; **к обе́ду, к у́жину** *etc.*, for dinner, for supper, *etc.*
4 (*в названиях статей и т.д.*) on; on the occasion of; **к столе́тию со дня рожде́ния Льва Толсто́го** on (the occasion of) the centenary of the birth of Lev Tolstoy; **к вопро́су о**… *oft. requires no translation.*

к. (*abbr. of* ***копе́йка***) k, kopeck(s).

-ка *particle* (*coll.*) **1** *modifying force of imper.*: **скажи́-ка мне** come on now, tell me; **да́й-ка мне посмотре́ть** come on, let me take a look; **ну́-ка** well; **ну́-ка спо́йте что-н.!** come on, give us a song! **2** *with 1st pers. sg. of fut., expr. tentative decision*: **напишу́-ка ей письмо́** I think I'll write to her; **куплю́-ка тот га́лстук** maybe I'll buy that tie.

каба́к, а́ *m.* tavern; (*coll., fig.*) noisy place.

кабал|а́, ы́ *f.* servitude, bondage.

каба́л|ьный (~ен, ~ьна) *adj.* imposing bondage, enslaving; **~ьные усло́вия** crushing terms.

каба́н, а́ *m.* **1** (*дикая свинья*) wild boar. **2** (*самец свиньи*) boar.

каба́н|ий *adj. of* **⇨~**

кабар|га́, ги́, *g. pl.* **~о́г** *f.* (*zool.*) musk-deer.

кабаре́ *nt. indecl.* cabaret.

каба́|цкий *adj. of* **⇨~к**

кабач|о́к¹, ка́ *m.* **1** *dim. of* **⇨каба́к.** **2** (*coll.*) (*небольшой ресторан*) small restaurant.

кабач|о́к², ка́ *m.* (*растение*) (vegetable) marrow (*Br.*), squash (*US*).

каббалисти́ческий *adj.* (*relig. and fig.*) cab(b)alistic.

ка́бел|ь, я *m.* cable; **возду́шный к.** overhead cable.

ка́бель|ный *adj. of* **⇨~; ~ное телеви́дение** cable television.

ка́бельтов, а, *pl.* **~ы, ~ых, ~ым, ~ыми** *m.* (*naut.*) **1** (*мера*) cable('s length) (*measure = 185.2 metres*). **2** (*трос*) cable, hawser.

кабеста́н, а *m.* (*tech.*) capstan.

каби́н|а, ы *f.* (*в самолёте, для пассажиров*) cabin; (*в самолёте, для лётчика*) cockpit; (*грузовика*) cab; (*в туалете*) cubicle; (*телефонная; для голосования*) booth; (*для купальщиков*) bathing-hut; (*лифта*) cage.

кабине́т¹, а *m.* **1** (*в доме*) study; (*на работе*) office; (*врача*) surgery (*Br.*), office (*US*); **физи́ческий к.** physics laboratory (*in school*); **лингафо́нный к.** language laboratory. **2** (*комплект мебели*) suite.

кабине́т², а *m.* (*also* **к. мини́стров**) (*pol.*) cabinet.

кабине́т|ный *adj.* **1** *adj. of* **⇨~¹.** **2**: **к. роя́ль** baby grand (*piano*). **3** (*fig.*) theoretical; **к. учёный, страте́г** armchair scientist, strategist.

каби́н|ка, ки *f. dim. of* **⇨~а**

каблогра́мм|а, ы *f.* cable(gram).

каблу́к, а́ *m.* heel (*of footwear*); **ту́фли на высо́ком каблуке́** high-heeled shoes; **быть под ~о́м у кого́-н.** (*fig., coll.*) to be under s.o.'s thumb.

каблуч|о́к, ка́ *m. dim. of* **⇨каблу́к**

кабота́ж, а *m.* coastal shipping.

кабота́ж|ный *adj. of* **⇨~; ~ное пла́вание** coastwise navigation.

кабриоле́т, а *m.* cabriolet.

Кабу́л, а *m.* Kabul.

кабы́ *conj.* (*coll. and folk poet.*) if; **е́сли бы да к.,** *see* **⇨е́сли**

кавале́р¹, а *m.* **1** (*в танце*) partner; (*мужчина*) (gentle-)man. **2** (*coll.*) (*поклонник*) admirer, suitor.

кавале́р², а *m.*: **к. (о́рдена)** knight, holder (of an order); **Гео́ргиевский к.** holder of the St George Cross.

кавалер|и́йский *adj. of* **⇨~ия**

кавалери́ст, а *m.* cavalryman.

кавале́ри|я, и *f.* cavalry.

кавалька́д|а, ы *f.* cavalcade.

кавarда́к, а́ *m.* (*coll.*) mess, muddle.

ка́верз|а, ы *f.* (*coll.*) (*злая проделка*) mean trick, dirty trick; **устро́ить ~у кому́-н.** to play a mean trick on s.o.; (*трудность*) pitfall.

ка́вер|зить, жу, зишь *impf.* (*of* **⇨на~**) (*coll., pej.*) to play mean, dirty tricks.

ка́верзник, а *m.* (*coll.*) person who enjoys playing mean, dirty tricks.

ка́верзный *adj.* (*coll.*) **1** (*pej.*) (*человек*) given to playing mean, dirty tricks. **2** (*вопрос*) tricky, ticklish.

каве́рн|а, ы *f.* (*med. and geol.*) cavity.

Кавка́з, а *m.* Caucasus.

кавка́з|ец, ца *m.* Caucasian.

кавка́з|ка, ки *f. of* **⇨~ец**

кавка́зский *adj.* Caucasian.

кавы́ч|ки, ек, *sing.* **ка, ки** *f. pl.* inverted commas, quotation marks; **откры́ть к.** to quote; **закры́ть к.** to unquote; **в ~ках** in inverted commas, in quotes; (*fig., iron.*) so-called; **демокра́тия в ~ках** so-called 'democracy'.

кагебе́шник, а *m.* (*coll.*) KGB agent.

кагеби́ст, а *m.* = **кагебе́шник**

кагóр, а *m.* ≈ port (wine).

кагэбэ́шник, а *m.* = **кагебе́шник**

каде́нци|я, и *f.* (*mus.*)

1 (*гармонический оборот*) cadence. **2** (*виртуозная вставка*) cadenza.

кадéт¹, а *m.* cadet.

кадéт², а *m.* (*abbr. of* ***конституциóнный демокрáт***) (*pol., hist.*) Constitutional Democrat (*abbr.* Cadet).

кадéт|ский¹ *adj. of* ⇒~¹; **к. кóрпус** military school.

кадéт|ский² *adj. of* ⇒~²

кадúл|о, а *nt.* (*eccl.*) thurible, censer.

кадúл|ьный *adj.* **1** *adj. of* ⇒~**о. 2** of incense; **к. зáпах** smell of incense.

ка|дúть, жý, дúшь *impf.* (*eccl.*) to burn incense.

кáдк|а, и *f.* tub, vat.

кáдми|й, я *m.* (*chem.*) cadmium.

кáдочник, а *m.* cooper.

кáд|очный *adj. of* ⇒~**ка**

кадр, а *m.* (*cinema*) (*снимок*) frame; (*эпизод*) shot; **гóлос за** ~**ом** voice-over.

кадрúл|ь, и *f.* quadrille (dance).

кáдровый *adj.* **1** (*mil.*) (*офицер*) regular. **2** (*рабочий*) skilled; best.

кáдр|ы, ов *pl.* (*collect.*) **1** (*mil.*) (regular, peace-time) establishment; **он слýжит в** ~**ах** he is a regular (soldier). **2** (*работники*) personnel; **отдéл** ~**ов** personnel department (*of institution, factory, etc.*). **3** (*pol.*) cadres.

кадык, á *m.* (*coll.*) Adam's apple.

каёмк|а, и *f.* (*coll.*) *dim. of* ⇒**каймá**

каждéни|е, я *nt.* (*eccl.*) censing.

каждоднéвный *adj.* daily.

кáжд|ый *adj.* **1** every, each; **к. день** every day; ~**ые два дня** every two days; ~**ую веснý** every spring; **к. из них получúл по пять фýнтов** they received five pounds each; **на** ~**ом шагý** at every step. **2** *as n.* everyone; **всех и** ~**ого** (*coll.*) all and everyone, all and sundry.

кажúсь (*coll., dial.*) it seems, it would seem.

ка|жý¹, дúшь *see* ⇒~**дúть**

ка|жý², ~жешь *see* ⇒~**зáть**

кáжущийся *adj.* apparent.

казáк, á, *pl.* ~**ú** *m.* Cossack.

казáн, á *m.* (*dial.*) large cooking pot.

Казáн|ь, и *f.* Kazan.

казáрм|а, ы *f.* barracks.

казáрм|енный *adj. of* ⇒~**а;** (*fig., pej.*): **к. вид** barrack-like appearance; **к. режим,** ~**енное положéние** confinement to barracks.

ка|зáть, жý, ~жешь *impf.* (*coll.*) to show; **не к. глаз, нóсу** not to show up.

ка|зáться, жýсь, ~жешься *impf.* (*of* ⇒**показáться**) **1** to seem, appear; **он ~жется ýмным** he appears clever; **онá ~жется стáрше своúх лет** she looks older than she is. **2** (*impers.*): (**мне,** *etc.*) **~жется,** ~**зáлось** it seems, seemed (to me, *etc.*); apparently; **мне ~жется, что он был прав** I think he was right; **всё,** ~**зáлось, шло хорошó** everything seemed to be going well; **зáвтра, ~жется, начинáются егó канúкулы** apparently his holidays begin tomorrow; **вы, ~жется, из Москвы́?** you are from Moscow, I believe?; ~**зáлось бы** it would seem, one would think.

казáх, а *m.* Kazakh.

казáхский *adj.* Kazakh.

Казахстáн, а *m.* Kazakhstan.

казáцкий *adj.* Cossack.

казáчеств|о, а *nt.* (*collect.*) the Cossacks.

казáчий *adj.* Cossack.

казá|чка, чки *f. of* ⇒~**к**

казач|óк¹, кá *m.* **1** (*coll.*) *affectionate dim. of* ⇒**казáк. 2** (*hist.*) (*слуга*) page, boy-servant.

казач|óк², кá *m.* (*танец*) kazachok.

казá|шка, шки *f. of* ⇒~**х**

казеúн, а *m.* (*chem.*) casein.

казеúн|овый *adj. of* ⇒~

каземáт, а *m.* casemate; (*камера*) (prison) cell (*for one person*).

казённ|ый *adj.* **1** (*hist.*) fiscal; of State, of Treasury; ~**ое имýщество** State property; **на к. счёт** at public cost. **2** (*fig.*) (*бюрократический*) bureaucratic, formal; **к. язы́к** language of officialdom, official jargon. **3**: ~**ая часть** breech.

казинó *nt. indecl.* casino.

казн|á, ы́ *no pl., f.* **1** (*государственное имущество*) Exchequer, Treasury; public purse, public coffers. **2** (*obs.*) (*государство*) the State (*as a legal person*); **перейтú из чáстных рук в** ~**ý** to pass from private ownership to the State.

казначé|й, я *m.* **1** (*кассир*) treasurer, bursar (*Br.*). **2** (*mil.*) paymaster; (*naut.*) purser.

казначé|йский *adj.* **1** *of* ⇒~**. 2** *of* ⇒~**ство; к. билéт** treasury note.

казначéйств|о, а *nt.* Treasury, Exchequer.

казн|úть, ю, úшь *impf. and pf.* **1** to execute, put to death. **2** (*fig.*) (*наказывать*) to punish.

казн|úться, юсь, úшься *impf.* (*coll.*) to blame o.s.; to torment o.s. (*with remorse*).

казнокрáд, а *m.* embezzler of public funds.

казнокрáдств|о, а *nt.* embezzlement of public funds.

казн|ь, и *f.* execution, capital punishment; **смéртная к.** death penalty.

казуúст, а *m.* casuist (*also fig.*).

казуúстик|а, и *f.* casuistry (*also fig.*).

казуистúческий *adj.* casuistic(al).

кáзус, а *m.* **1** (*leg.*) exceptional case, special case. **2** (*coll.*) extraordinary occurrence; **вот так к.!** here's an amazing thing! **3**: **к. бéлли** casus belli.

кáзусный *adj.* involved, complex.

кáин|ов *adj.*: ~**ова печáть** the mark of Cain.

Каúр, а *m.* Cairo.

кайл|á, ы́ *f.* (miner's) hack.

кайл|ó, á *nt.* = ~**á**

ка|ймá, ймы́, *pl.* ~**ймы́,** ~**ём,** ~**ймáм** *f.* edging, border.

каймáн, а *m.* (*zool.*) cayman.

кайнозóйский *adj.* (*geol.*) Cenozoic.

кáйр|а, ы *f.* (*zool.*) guillemot.

кайф, а *m.* (*coll.*) kicks, 'high'; turn-on; buzz; **быть под** ~**ом** to be high *or* spaced out; **ловúть, поймáть к.** to get stoned; (*fig.*) bliss.

кайф|овáть, ýю *impf.* (*coll.*) **1** (*от наркотиков*) to be high; to get stoned *or* smashed (*on drugs* or *alcohol*). **2** (*получать удовольствие*) to enjoy o.s.

кайфóвый *adj.* (*coll.*) cool, far-out, mind-blowing.

кайфолóм, а *m.* (*sl.*) killjoy, party-pooper.

как¹ *adv. and particle* **1** how; **к. вам нрáвится Москвá?** how do you like Moscow?; **к. чýдно!** how wonderful!; **к. вы поживáете?** how do you do?; **к. (вáши) делá?** how are you getting on?; **забы́л, к. э́то дéлается** I have forgotten how to do this; **к. вам не сты́дно!** you ought to be ashamed!; **к. егó фамúлия, к. егó зовýт?** what is his name?, what is he called?; **к. называ́ется э́тот цветóк?** what is this flower called?; **к. вы дýмаете?** what do you think?; *expr. surprise and/or displeasure*: **к.! ты опя́ть здесь!** what! are you here again?; **к. же так?** how is that?; (*coll.*): **к. знать?** who knows?; (*coll.*): **к. сказáть** it all depends; (*coll.*): **к. есть** completely, utterly; **он к. есть дурáк** he is a complete fool; (*coll.*): **расскажú нам, к. и что** tell us all about it; (*coll.*): **к.-никáк** nevertheless, for all that; **к.-никáк, но мы попáли вóвремя** nevertheless, we managed to arrive in time; **к. же** (*coll. or iron.*) naturally, of course; **комý к.** it depends on the person. **2** (*о внезапном действии*) (*coll.*): **мы спокóйно слýшали рáдио, а — он к. вскóчит!** we were listening quietly to the wireless when all of a sudden he jumped up; **онá к. закричúт!** she suddenly cried out. **3**: **к. ни, к.… ни** however; **к. ни пóздно** however late it is; **к. он ни умён** clever as he is; **к. ни старáйтесь** however hard you may try, try as you may. **4** (*following* **бедá, прéлесть, страх, ужáсно,** *etc., in elliptical construction*; *coll.*) terribly, awfully, wonderfully, *etc.*; **онá прéлесть к. одéта** she is beautifully dressed.

как² *conj.* **1** (*выражает сравнение*) as; like; **бéлый, к. снег** white as snow; **он говорúт по-рýсски к. настоя́щий рýсский** he speaks Russian like a native; **бýдьте к. дóма** make yourself at home; **к. нарóчно** as luck would have it; **к. попáло** anyhow, at sixes and sevens; (*with comp.*): **к. мóжно, к. нельзя́** as … as possible; **к. мóжно скорéе** as soon as possible; **к. нельзя́ лýчше** as well as possible; (*в качестве*): **совéтую тебé э́то к. друг** I give this advice as a friend; **к. напримéр** as, for instance. **2**: **к.…, так и** both … and; **к. мáльчики, так и дéвочки** both the boys and the girls. **3** (*что*) *following vv. of perceiving not translated*: **я вúдел, к. онá ушлá** I saw her go out; **ты слы́шал, к. часы́ бúли пóлночь?** did you hear the clock strike midnight? **4** (*когда*) when; (*с тех пор, как*) since;

К

к. пойдёшь, зайди́ за мной when you go, call for me; **прошло́ два го́да, к. мы встре́тились** it is two years since we met; **к. то́лько** as soon as, when; **к. вдруг** when suddenly.
5 (+*neg.*) but, except, than; **что ему́ остава́лось де́лать, к. не созна́ться?** what could he do but confess?; **кому́, к. не мне знать э́то!** if anyone knows, I do!
6: **в то вре́мя к.**; **до того́ к.**; **ме́жду тем к.**; **тогда́ к.**, *see* ⇒**вре́мя, до, ме́жду, тогда́.**
7: **к. бу́дто, к. бы, к.-либо, к.-нибудь, к. ра́з, к.-то** *see separate entries.*

какаду́ *m. indecl.* (*zool.*) cockatoo.

кака́о *nt. indecl.* **1** (*порошок*) cocoa. **2** (*дерево*) cacao(-tree).

кака́о|вый *adj. of* ⇒~; **~вые бобы́** cocoa-beans.

ка́к|ать, аю *impf.* (*baby-talk*) to (do a) poo.

как бу́дто 1 *conj.* as if, as though; **она́ побледне́ла, к. б. уви́дела при́зрак** she turned pale as if she had seen a ghost; **к. б. вы не зна́ете!** as if you didn't know! **2** *particle* (*coll.*) (*вероятно*) apparently, it would seem; **они́ к. б. за́втра прие́дут** apparently they are coming tomorrow.

как бы 1 (+*inf.*) how; **к. б. э́то сде́лать?** how is it to be done, I wonder. **2**: **к. б. ни** however; **к. б. то ни́ было** however that may be, be that as it may. **3** as if, as though; **к. б. в шу́тку** as if in jest. **4**: **к. б. не** (*expr. anxious expectation*) what if, supposing; (*following v.*) (that, lest); **к. б. он не опозда́л** what if he is late!; **бою́сь, к. б. он не опозда́л** I am afraid (that) he may be late. **5** (*coll.*): **к. б. не так!** not likely, certainly not.

ка́к-либо *adv.* somehow.

ка́к-нибудь *adv.* **1** (*так или иначе*) somehow (or other). **2** (*coll.*) (*кое-как*) anyhow; **он всё де́лает к.-н.** he does things all anyhow. **3** (*coll.*) (*когда-нибудь*) some time; **загляни́те к.-н.** look in some time.

как-ника́к *adv.* (*coll.*) nevertheless, for all that.

како́в (~а́, ~о́, ~ы́) *pron.* (*interrog., and in exclamations expr. strong feeling*) what; of what sort; **к. результа́т?** what is the result?; **к. он?** what is he like?; **к. он собо́й?** what does he look like?; **а пого́да-то ~а́** what (*splendid, filthy*) weather!

каково́ *adv.* (*coll.*) how; **к. ему́ живётся?** how is he getting on?

каково́й *rel. pron.* (*obs.*) which.

как|о́й *pron.* **1** (*interrog. and rel.; and in exclamations*) what; **~и́е у вас впечатле́ния о Ло́ндоне?** what are your impressions of London?; **~о́е сего́дня число́?** what is today's date?; **~и́м о́бразом?** how?; **не зна́ю, ~у́ю кни́гу ему́ дать** I don't know what book to give him; **~а́я беда́!** what a misfortune, how unfortunate!; **~а́я на́глость!** what impudence!; **~а́я хоро́шенькая де́вушка!** what a pretty girl!
2: **(тако́й) к.** such as; **гнев, ~о́го он никогда́ не испы́тывал** anger such as he had never felt.
3: **к. ни** whatever, whichever; **к. есть, к. ни на есть** (*coll.*) whatever you please, any you please; **дай мне ~у́ю ни на есть кни́гу** give me any book you please.
4 (*expr. negation in rhetorical questions and retorts*): **к. он учёный?** what kind of scholar is that?; **~о́е там** nothing of the kind, quite the contrary; **ты хорошо́ спал? — ~о́е там!** did you sleep well? — I most certainly did not!
5: **к. тако́й?** which (exactly)?; **пришёл Ивано́в. — К. тако́й Ивано́в?** Ivanov is here. — Which Ivanov?
6 (*coll.*) any; **нет ли у вас ~о́го вопро́са?** have you any questions?

како́й-либо *pron.* = **како́й-нибудь** 1

как|о́й-нибудь *pron.* **1** some; any; **мы э́то сде́лаем ~и́м-н. спо́собом** we shall do it somehow; **да́йте мне хоть ~у́ю-н. кни́гу** give me a book, any one at all. **2** (*with numerals*) some (*and not more*), only; **за́мок нахо́дится в ~и́х-н. трёх киломе́трах отсю́да** the castle is some three kilometres (*Br.*), kilometers (*US*) from here; **~и́е-н. пять рубле́й** some five roubles.

как|о́й-то *pron.* **1** (*неизвестно какой*) some, a. **2** (*напоминающий*) a kind of; **э́то ~а́я-то боле́знь** it is a kind of disease.

какофони́ческий *adj.* cacophonous.

какофо́ни|я, и *f.* cacophony.

как ра́з *adv.* just, exactly; **к. р. то, что мне ну́жно** just what I need; **к. р. вас я иска́л** you are the very person I was looking for; *as pred.*: **э́ти ту́фли мне к. р.** these shoes are just right.

ка́к-то *adv.* **1** (*каким-то образом*) somehow; **он к.-то ухитри́лся сде́лать э́то** he managed to do it somehow; **в э́том до́ме к.-то всегда́ хо́лодно** somehow it is always cold in this house. **2** (*как*) how; **посмотрю́, к.-то он вы́вернется из э́того положе́ния** I wonder how he will get himself out of this situation. **3** (*coll.*): **к.-то (раз)** once. **4** (*а именно*) namely, as for example.

ка́ктус, а *m.* (*bot.*) cactus.

кал, а *m.* faeces (*Br.*), feces (*US*), excrement.

каламбу́р, а *m.* pun.

каламбури́ст, а *m.* punster.

каламбу́р|ить, ю, ишь *impf.* (*of* ⇒**с~**) to pun.

каламбу́рный *adj.* punning.

каланч|а́, и́, *g. pl.* **~е́й** *f.* watch-tower; **пожа́рная к.** fire observation tower; (*fig., coll.*) (*о человеке*) bean-pole.

кала́ч, а́ *m.* kalach (*kind of white, wheatmeal loaf*); **меня́ ~о́м туда́ не зама́нишь** (*coll.*) nothing will induce me to go there; (*fig., coll.*): **тёртый к.** person who has been around; old hand.

кала́чиком *adv.* (*coll.*) in the shape of a kalach; **лежа́ть к.** to lie curled up.

кала́ч|ный *adj. of* ⇒~

калейдоско́п, а *m.* kaleidoscope.

калейдоскопи́ческий *adj.* kaleidoscopic.

кале́к|а, и *c.g.* cripple.

календа́р|ный *adj. of* ⇒**~ь; к. ме́сяц** calendar month.

календа́р|ь, я́ *m.* calendar; (*sport*) fixture list.

кале́нд|ы, ~ *no sg.* (*hist.*) calends.

кале́ни|е, я *nt.* incandescence; **бе́лое к.** white heat; **довести́ до бе́лого ~я** (*fig., coll.*) to rouse to fury.

калён|ый *adj.* **1** red-hot. **2**: **~ые оре́хи** roasted nuts.

кале́ч|ить, у, ишь *impf.* (*of* ⇒**искале́чить**) to cripple, maim, mutilate; (*fig.*) to twist, pervert.

кале́ч|иться, усь, ишься *impf.* (*of* ⇒**искале́читься**) **1** to become a cripple. **2** *pass. of* ⇒**~ить**

кали́бр, а *m.* **1** calibre (*Br.*), caliber (*US*). **2** (*tech.*) gauge.

калибр|ова́ть, у́ю *impf.* (*tech.*) to calibrate.

калибро́вк|а, и *f.* (*tech.*) calibration.

ка́лиевый *adj.* (*chem.*) potassic, potassium.

ка́ли|й, я *m.* (*chem.*) potassium.

кали́йн|ый *adj.* (*chem.*) potassium; **~ое удобре́ние** potash fertilizer.

кали́льн|ый *adj.* (*tech.*): **к. жар** temperature of incandescence; **~ая се́тка** (incandescent) mantle.

кали́н|а, ы *no pl., f.* (*bot.*) guelder rose, viburnum.

кали́н|овый *adj. of* ⇒**~а**

кали́тк|а, и *f.* (wicket-)gate.

кал|и́ть, ю, и́шь *impf.* **1** (*tech.*) to heat. **2** (*орехи*) to roast.

кали́ф, а *m.* caliph; **к. на час** (*iron.*) king for a day.

калифорни́|ец, йца *m.* Californian.

калифорни́|йка, йки *f. of* ⇒**~ец**

калифорни́йский *adj.* Californian.

Калифо́рни|я, и *f.* California.

ка́лл|а, ы *f.* arum lily (*Br.*), calla lily (*US*).

каллиграфи́ческий *adj.* calligraphic.

каллигра́фи|я, и *f.* calligraphy.

калмы́к, а́ *m.* Kalmuck, Kalmyk.

калмы́цкий *adj.* Kalmuck, Kalmyk.

калмы́|чка, чки *f. of* ⇒**~к**

ка́л|овый *adj. of* ⇒~

ка́ломел|ь, и *f.* calomel.

калори́йност|ь, и *f.* **1** (*пищи*) calorie content. **2** (*phys.*) calorific value.

калори́йный *adj.* high-calorie; fattening.

калори́метр, а *m.* (*phys.*) calorimeter.

калориме́три|я, и *f.* (*phys.*) calorimetry.

калори́фер, а *m.* (*tech.*) heater, radiator.

кало́ри|я, и *f.* calorie.

кало́ш|а, и *f.* = **гало́ша**

калу́жниц|а, ы *f.* (*bot.*) king-cup, marsh marigold.

калы́м, а *no pl., m.* **1** (*ethnol.*) bride-money. **2** (*coll.*) earnings on the side.

калы́м|ить, лю, ишь *impf.* (*coll.*) to moonlight, do work on the side.

калы́мщик, а *m.* (*coll.*) moonlighter.

кальвини́зм, а *m.* Calvinism.

кальвини́ст, а *m.* Calvinist.
кальвини́стский *adj.* Calvinistic(al).
ка́л|ька, ьки, *g. pl.* **~ек** *f.* **1** (*бумага*) tracing-paper. **2** (*копия*) (tracing-paper) copy. **3** (*ling.*) loan translation, calque.
кальки́р|овать, ую *impf.* (*of* **⇒с~**) **1** to trace. **2** (*ling.*) to calque.
калькули́р|овать, ую *impf.* (*of* **⇒с~**) to calculate.
калькуля́тор, а *m.* calculator.
калькуля|цио́нный *adj. of* **⇒~ция; ~цио́нная ве́домость** cost sheet; cost record.
калькуля́ци|я, и *f.* calculation.
Кальку́тт|а, ы *f.* Calcutta.
кальма́р, а *m.* (*zool.*) squid.
кальсо́н|ы, ~ *no sg.* long johns.
ка́льциевый *adj.* (*chem.*) calcium, calcic.
ка́льци|й, я *m.* (*chem.*) calcium.
кальци́т, а *m.* (*min.*) calcite.
кальян, а *m.* hookah.
каля́ка|ть, ю *impf.* (*of* **⇒по~**) (*coll.*) to chat.
КамА́З, а *m.* lorry (*Br.*), truck (*US*) made at the *Ка́мский автомоби́льный заво́д*.
камари́ль|я, и *f.* (*liter.*) camarilla, clique.
кама́ринск|ая, ой *f.* kamarinskaya (*Russian folk-dance*).
ка́мбал|а, ы *f.* **1** flat-fish (*generic term*). **2** plaice; flounder.
Камбо́дж|а, и *f.* Cambodia.
камбоджи́|ец, йца *m.* Cambodian.
камбоджи́|йка, йки *f. of* **⇒~ец**
камбоджи́йский *adj.* Cambodian.
ка́мбуз, а *m.* (*naut.*) galley.
камво́льный *adj.* (*text.*) worsted.
каме́дистый *adj.* gummy.
каме́д|ь, и *f.* gum.
камел|ёк, ька́ *m.* fire-place.
каме́ли|я, и *f.* (*bot.*) camellia.
камене́|ть, ю *impf.* (*of* **⇒о~**) (*становиться твёрдым*) to become petrified, turn to stone; (*fig.*) (*о сердце*) to harden; (*от страха*) to be petrified.
камени́ст|ый (~, ~а) *adj.* stony.
каменноуго́льн|ый *adj.* coal; **к. бассе́йн** coal-field; **~ые рудники́** coal-mine.
ка́менн|ый *adj.* **1** stone-; stony; **к. век** the Stone Age; **~ая кла́дка** stone-work; **к. мешо́к** (*fig.*) prison; **~ая соль** rock-salt; **к. у́голь** coal. **2** (*fig.*) stony; **~ое се́рдце** stony heart.
каменоло́м|ня, ни, *g. pl.* **~ен** *f.* quarry.
каменотёс, а *m.* (stone)mason.
ка́менщик, а *m.* bricklayer; (*hist.*): **во́льный ~** Freemason.
ка́м|ень, ня, *pl.* **~ни, ~не́й** *and* (*obs.*) **~е́нья, ~е́ньев** *m.* stone; (*твёрдое образование*) tartar; **драгоце́нный к.** precious stone, gem; **зубно́й к.** dental tartar; **па́дать ~нем** to fall like a stone; **~ня на ~не не оста́вить** to raze to the ground; (*fig.*): **броса́ть ~нем (в** + *a.*) to cast stones (at); **у него́ к. на се́рдце лежи́т** a weight sits heavy on his heart; **держа́ть к. за па́зухой (на** + *a.*, **про́тив** + *g.*) to harbour (*Br.*), harbor (*US*) a grudge (against); **к. с души́ мое́й свали́лся** a load has been taken off my mind.
ка́мер|а, ы *f.* **1** chamber (*in var. senses*); (*в тюрьме*) cell; **морози́льная к.** freezer compartment (*of refrigerator*); **к. хране́ния (багажа́)** left-luggage office (*Br.*), baggage room (*US*). **2**: **(фотографи́ческая) к.** camera; **скры́той ~ой снима́ть** to film secretly. **3** (*шины*) inner tube; (*мяча*) bladder.
камерге́р, а *m.* chamberlain.
камерди́нер, а *m.* valet.
камери́стк|а, и *f.* lady's maid.
ка́мер|ный[1] *adj. of* **⇒~а**
ка́мерн|ый[2] *adj.* (*mus.*): **к. конце́рт** chamber concert; **~ая му́зыка** chamber music.
камерто́н, а *m.* tuning-fork.
ка́меш|ек, ка *m. dim. of* **⇒ка́мень;** pebble; (*fig., coll.*): **бро́сить/кида́ть к. в чей-н. огоро́д** to make digs at s.o.
каме́|я, и *f.* cameo.
камзо́л, а *m.* camisole (*men's short jacket*).
камика́дзе *m. indecl.* kamikaze pilot.
камила́вк|а, и *f.* (*eccl.*) kamelaukion (*Orthodox priest's headgear*).
ками́н, а *m.* fire-place; (open) fire; **электри́ческий к.** electric fire.
ками́н|ный *adj. of* **⇒~; ~ная по́лка** mantelpiece; **~ная решётка** fender, fireguard.
камк|а́, и́ *f.* (*text.*) damask.
камко́рдер, а *m.* camcorder.
камнедроби́лк|а, и *f.* stone-breaker, stone-crusher.
камнело́мк|а, и *f.* (*bot.*) saxifrage.
камнепа́д, а *m.* rockfall.
камо́рк|а, и *f.* (*coll.*) closet, tiny room; box room.
кампа́ни|я, и *f.* campaign.
кампучи́|ец, йца *m.* Kampuchean.
кампучи́|йка, йки *f. of* **⇒~ец**
кампучи́йский *adj.* Kampuchean.
Кампучи́|я, и *f.* Kampuchea.
камуфли́р|овать, ую *impf.* (*of* **⇒за~**) to camouflage.
камуфля́ж, а *no pl., m.* camouflage.
камфар|а́, ы *f.* camphor.
камфа́р|ный *adj. of* **⇒~а́**
ка́мф|ора = **~ара́**
Камча́тк|а, и *f.* Kamchatka.
камча́т(н)ый *adj.* (*о ткани*) damask, figured.
камы́ш, а́ *m.* reed, rush (*also collect.*).
камы́шниц|а, ы *f.* moorhen.
камыш|о́вый *adj. of* **⇒~**
кана́в|а, ы *f.* ditch; **сто́чная к.** gutter.
канавокопа́тел|ь, я *m.* (*tech.*) trench digger.
Кана́д|а, ы *f.* Canada.
кана́д|ец, ца, *g. pl.* **~цев** *m.* Canadian.
кана́д|ка, ки *f. of* **⇒~ец**
кана́дск|ий *adj.* Canadian; **~ая пи́хта** balsam fir.
кана́л, а *m.* **1** (*искусственное русло*) canal; (*морской*) channel. **2** (*fig.*) (*путь*) channel; **дипломати́ческие ~ы** diplomatic channels. **3** (*anat.*) duct, canal; **мочеиспуска́тельный к.** urethra. **4** (*телевизионный*) channel. **5** (*орудия*) bore.
канализа|цио́нный *adj. of* **⇒~ция; ~цио́нная труба́** sewer (-pipe).
канализа́ци|я, и *f.* sewerage system.
канализи́р|овать, ую *impf. and pf.* to provide with sewerage system.
кана́л|ья, ьи, *g. pl.* **~ий** *c.g.* (*coll.*) rascal, scoundrel.
канапе́ *nt. indecl.* canapé.
канаре́|ечный *adj.* **1** *adj. of* **⇒~йка. 2** (*цвет*) canary(-coloured).
канаре́йк|а, и *f.* canary.
Кана́рск|ие остров|а́, ~их ~о́в *no sg.* Canary Islands.
кана́т, а *m.* rope; cable.
кана́т|ный *adj. of* **⇒~; к. заво́д** rope-yard; **~ная доро́га** cable car.
канатохо́д|ец, ца *m.* tightrope-walker.
Ка́нберр|а, ы *f.* Canberra.
канв|а́, ы́ *no pl., f.* (*для вышивания*) canvas; (*fig.*) outline, design; **к. рома́на** the outline of a novel.
кандал|ы́, о́в *no sg.* shackles, fetters; **ручны́е к.** manacles; **закова́ть в к.** to put into irons.
канделя́бр, а *m.* candelabrum.
кандида́т, а *m.* candidate; **к. в чле́ны парла́мента** parliamentary candidate; **~ нау́к** (*educ.*) Doctor.
кандида́тск|ая, ой *f.* (*coll.*) (*диссертация*) doctoral thesis.
кандида́т|ский *adj. of* **⇒~; к. ми́нимум** qualifying examinations for admission to postgraduate study.
кандидату́р|а, ы *f.* candidature; **вы́ставить чью-н. ~у** to nominate s.o. for election; (*кандидат*) candidate.
кани́кул|ы, ~ *no sg.* (*школьные*) holidays (*Br.*), vacation (*US*); (*университетские*) vacation.
кани|куля́рный *adj. of* **⇒~кулы**
кани́стр|а, ы *f.* jerrycan.
каните́л|ить, ю, ишь *impf.* (*of* **⇒про~**) (*coll., pej.*) to drag out; **к. кого́-н.** to waste s.o.'s time.
каните́л|иться, юсь, ишься *impf.* (*of* **⇒про~**) (*coll., pej.*) to waste time; to mess about.
каните́л|ь, и *f.* **1** (*нить*) gold thread, silver thread. **2** (*fig., coll.*) (*дело*) long-drawn-out proceedings; **тяну́ть, разводи́ть к.** to drag out proceedings, procrastinate; **дово́льно ~и!** this has gone on, dragged on long enough!
каните́л|ьный (~ен, ~ьна) *adj.* (*coll.*) **1** long-drawn out; tedious. **2**: **к. челове́к** procrastinator. **3** *adj. of* **⇒~ь** 1
каните́льщик, а *m.* (*coll.*) time-waster.

канифо́л|ить, ю, ишь *impf.* (*of* ⇒**на~**) to rosin.

канифо́л|ь, и *f.* rosin.

канка́н, а *m.* cancan.

каннибáл, а *m.* cannibal.

каннибали́зм, а *m.* cannibalism.

канои́ст, а *m.* canoeist.

кано́н, а *m.* canon.

канона́д|а, ы *f.* cannonade.

каноне́рк|а, и *f.* gunboat.

каноне́рск|ий *adj.*: **~ая ло́дка** gunboat.

канониза́ци|я, и *f.* (*eccl.*) canonization.

канонизи́р|овать, ую *impf. and pf.* (*eccl. and fig.*) to canonize.

канониз|ова́ть, у́ю *impf. and pf.* = **~и́ровать**

кано́ник, а *m.* (*eccl.*) canon.

канони́ческ|ий *adj.* **1** (*eccl.*) canonical; (*liter.*) definitive. **2** (*eccl.*): **~ое пра́во** canon law.

канотье́ *nt. indecl.* boater (*hat*).

кано́э *nt. indecl.* canoe.

кант, а *m.* **1** (*оторочка*) edging, piping. **2** (*для рисунка*) mount.

канта́т|а, ы *f.* (*mus.*) cantata.

кант|ова́ть¹, у́ю *impf.* (*of* ⇒**о~**) (*рисунок*) to mount.

кант|ова́ть², у́ю *impf.* (*tech.*) (*груз*) to cant; **не к.!** keep upright!

канто́н, а *m.* canton.

кантона́льный *adj.* cantonal.

канто́нский *m.* Cantonese.

ка́нтор, а *m.* cantor.

кану́н, а *m.* eve; **к. Но́вого го́да** New Year's eve; **к. Рождества́** Christmas Eve.

ка́н|уть, у, ешь *pf.* (*obs.*) to drop, sink; **к. в ве́чность, к. в Ле́ту** (*fig.*) to sink into oblivion; **как в во́ду к.** to disappear without a trace, vanish into thin air.

канцеляри́ст, а *m.* clerk.

канцеля́ри|я, и *f.* clerical office.

канцеля́р|ский *adj. of* ⇒**~ия; ~ские принадле́жности/това́ры** stationery, office supplies; **~ская рабо́та** clerical work; **к. стол** office desk; **к. слог** officialese.

канцеля́рщин|а, ы *f.* (*coll.*) red tape.

канцероге́н, а *m.* carcinogen.

канцероге́нн|ый *adj.* carcinogenic; **~ое вещество́** carcinogen.

ка́нцлер, а *m.* chancellor.

канцтова́р|ы, ов *no sg.* (*abbr. of* ***канцеля́рские това́ры***) office supplies, stationery.

каньо́н, а *m.* (*geog.*) canyon.

каню́к, а́ *m.* (*zool.*) buzzard.

каню́ч|ить, у, ишь *impf.* (*coll., pej.*) to moan, whinge.

каоли́н, а *m.* china clay, kaolin.

кап... *comb. form, abbr. of* **1** ***капиталисти́ческий*. 2** ***капита́льный***

ка́п|ать, аю (*obs.* **~лю, ~лешь**) *impf.* (*of* ⇒**на~**) **1** (*no pf., 3rd pers. only*) (*падать каплями*) to drip, drop; to trickle; to dribble; to fall (in drops); **из глаз у неё ~али слёзы** tear-drops were falling from her eyes; **дождь ~ает** it is spotting with rain; **с потолка́ ~ало** there was a drip from the ceiling. **2** (*наливать каплями*) to pour out (*in drops*); **к. лека́рство в рю́мку** to pour medicine into a glass. **3** (+*i.*; *coll.*) (*проливать*) to spill; **ты ~аешь водо́й на ска́терть** you are spilling water on the cloth. **4** (*coll.*) (*доносить*) (**на**+*a.*) to tell on.

капе́лл|а, ы *f.* **1** (*хор*) choir. **2** (*часовня*) chapel; **к. Богома́тери** Lady chapel.

капелла́н, а *m.* chaplain.

капе́л|ь, и *f.* thaw.

ка́пельк|а, и *f.* **1** small drop; **к. росы́** dew-drop; **вы́пить всё до ~и** to drink to the last drop. **2** (*sg. only*; *fig.*) grain, minute quantity; **в нём нет ни ~и здра́вого смы́сла** he has not a grain of common sense; **она́ ни ~и не смути́лась** she was not the least bit put out; *as adv.*: **~у** (*coll.*) a little; **подожди́ ~у!** wait a moment.

капельме́йстер, а *m.* (*mus.*) conductor, bandmaster.

капельме́йстер|ский *adj. of* ⇒**~**; **~ская па́лочка** conductor's baton.

ка́пельниц|а, ы *f.* drip (feed).

ка́перс, а *m.* **1** (*bot.*) caper. **2** (*pl. only*; *cul.*) capers.

капилля́р, а *m.* (*phys., anat.*) capillary.

капилля́рный *adj.* (*phys., anat.*) capillary.

капита́л, а *m.* (*fin.*) capital; **стра́ны ~а** capitalist countries; (*fig.*): **полити́ческий к.** political capital.

капитализа́ци|я, и *f.* (*fin.*) capitalization.

капитализи́р|овать, ую *impf. and pf.* (*fin.*) to capitalize.

капитали́зм, а *m.* capitalism.

капитали́ст, а *m.* **1** capitalist. **2** (*coll.*) wealthy person.

капитали́ст|ка, ки *f. of* ⇒**~** 2

капиталисти́ческий *adj.* capitalist(ic).

капиталовложе́ни|е, я *nt.* capital investment.

капита́льн|ый *adj.* (*fin.*) capital; (*основной*) main, fundamental; (*самый важный*) most important; **к. вопро́с** fundamental question; **к. ремо́нт** major repairs, refurbishment; **~ая стена́** main wall.

капита́н, а *m.* captain.

капита́н|ский *adj. of* ⇒**~**; **к. мо́стик** (*naut.*) bridge.

капите́л|ь, и *f.* **1** (*archit.*) capital. **2** (*typ.*) small capitals.

капитули́р|овать, ую *impf. and pf.* (**пе́ред**+*i.*) to capitulate (to).

капитуля́ци|я, и *f.* capitulation.

ка́пищ|е, а *nt.* (*pagan*) temple; (*fig.*) den.

капка́н, а *m.* trap; **попа́сться в к.** to fall into a trap (*also fig.*).

капка́н|ный *adj. of* ⇒**~**; **к. про́мысел** trapping.

капли́ц|а, ы *f.* (*Roman Catholic*) chapel.

каплу́н, а́ *m.* capon.

ка́п|ля, ли, *g. pl.* **~ель** *f.* **1** drop; **по ~ле, к. за ~лей** drop by drop; **до ~ли** to the last drop; **похо́жи как две ~ли воды́** as like as two peas; (*fig.*): **к. в мо́ре** a drop in the ocean (*Br.*), bucket (*US*); **после́дняя к.** the last straw; **би́ться до после́дней ~ли кро́ви** to fight to the last. **2** (*pl.*; *med.*) drops. **3** (*fig., coll.*) drop, bit; **у него́ (нет) ни ~ли благоразу́мия** he hasn't a drop of sense.

ка́п|нуть, ну, нешь *pf.* to drop, let fall a drop.

ка́пор, а *m.* bonnet.

капо́т, а *m.* **1** (*машины*) bonnet (*Br.*), hood (*US*); **к. мото́ра** (*aeron.*) engine cowling. **2** (*obs.*) house-coat.

капра́л, а *m.* (*mil.*) corporal.

капра́л|ьский *adj. of* ⇒**~**

капра́льств|о, а *nt.* (*mil.*) rank of corporal.

капремо́нт, а *m.* major repairs, refurbishment.

капри́з, а *m.* caprice, whim; **к. судьбы́** twist of fate.

капри́зник, а *m.* capricious person, capricious child.

капри́знича|ть, ю *impf.* to behave capriciously; (*о ребёнке*) to play up.

капри́з|ный (~ен, ~на) *adj.* capricious.

капризу́л|я, и *c.g.* (*coll.*) capricious, self-willed child.

капри́ччио *nt.* (*mus.*) capriccio.

капро́н, а *m.* kapron (*synthetic fibre, similar to nylon*).

капро́н|овый *adj. of* ⇒**~**

ка́псул|а, ы *f.* capsule.

ка́псюл|ь, я *m.* (percussion) cap (*in explosives*).

каптёрк|а, и *f.* (*coll.*) store-room, depot.

капу́ст|а, ы *f.* cabbage; **брюссе́льская к.** Brussels sprouts; **спа́ржевая к.** broccoli; **кормова́я к.** kale; **цветна́я к.** cauliflower.

капу́стник, а *m.* **1** (*в огороде*) cabbage patch. **2** (*представление*) (satirical) revue.

капу́стниц|а, ы *f.* cabbage butterfly.

капу́ст|ный *adj. of* ⇒**~а**

капу́т *m. indecl.* (*coll.*) end, destruction; *used as adj. or adv.* done for, kaput; **тут ему́ и к.** he's done for; it's all up with him.

капуци́н, а *m.* **1** (*монах*) Capuchin (friar). **2** (*zool.*) capuchin monkey.

капюшо́н, а *m.* hood, cowl.

ка́р|а, ы *f.* (*rhet.*) punishment, retribution.

караби́н, а *m.* **1** (*винтовка*) carbine. **2** (*зацепка*) karabiner.

кара́бка|ться, юсь *impf.* (*of* ⇒**вс~**) to clamber.

карава́|й, я *m.* cottage loaf.

карава́н, а *m.* **1** (*верблюдов*) caravan. **2** (*судов*) convoy.

карава́н-сара́|й, я *m.* caravanserai.

кара́емый *adj.* (*leg.*) punishable.

Кар(а)и́бск|ое мо́р|е, ~ого ~я *m.* the Caribbean Sea; the Caribbean.

каракалпа́к, а *m.* (*ethnol.*) Karakalpak.

Кара́кас, а *m.* Caracas.
карака́тиц|а, ы *f.* **1** (*zool.*) cuttlefish. **2** (*fig., coll.*) (*человек*) short-legged, clumsy person.
кара́ковый *adj.* dark-bay.
кара́кул|евый *adj. of* ⇨**~ь**
кара́куль, я *no pl., m.* Persian lamb; astrakhan.
каракульч|а́, и́ *f.* astrakhan (fur); broadtail.
кара́кул|я, и *f.* scrawl, scribble.
карамбо́л|ь, я *m.* (*in billiards*) cannon.
караме́л|ь, и *no pl., f.* **1** (*collect.*) (*конфеты*) caramels. **2** (*жжёный сахар*) caramel.
караме́льк|а, и *f.* (*coll.*) caramel.
караме́ль|ный *adj. of* ⇨**~**
каранда́ш, а́ *m.* pencil.
каранда́ш|ный *adj. of* ⇨**~; к. рису́нок** pencil drawing.
каранти́н, а *m.* quarantine; **наложи́ть ~у на** (+*a.*) to place in quarantine.
каранти́н|ный *adj. of* ⇨**~; ~ное свиде́тельство** (*naut.*) bill of health.
карао́ке *nt. indecl.* karaoke.
карапу́з, а *m.* (*coll.*) chubby lad.
кара́с|ь, я́ *m.* (*fish*) crucian; **серебряный к.** Prussian carp.
кара́т, а *m.* carat.
кара́тел|ь, я *m.* member of punitive expedition.
кара́тельный *adj.* punitive.
карати́ст, а *m.* karate enthusiast, karateka.
карати́ст|ка, ки *f. of* ⇨**~**
кара́|ть, ю *impf.* (*of* ⇨**по~**) to punish.
карате́ *nt. indecl.* karate.
каратэи́ст, а *m.* = **карати́ст**
карау́л, а *m.* **1** guard; watch; **вступи́ть в к.** to mount guard; **нести́ к.** to be on guard duty; **почётный к.** guard of honour; **смени́ть к.** to relieve the guard. **2** *word of command*: **на к.!** present arms!; **взять на к.** to present arms. **3** *as int.* help!; **крича́ть к.** to shout for help.
карау́л|ить, ю, ишь *impf.* **1** (*охранять*) to guard. **2** (*coll.*) (*ожидать*) to lie in wait for, watch out for.
карау́л|ьный *adj. of* ⇨**~; ~ьная бу́дка** sentry-box; *as n.* **к., ~ьного** *m.* sentry, sentinel, guard.
карау́льщик, а *m.* (*coll.*) watchman, guard.
Кара́чи *m. indecl.* Karachi.
кара́ч|ки, ек *no sg.* (*coll.*): **на к., на ~ках** on all fours; **стать на к.** to get on all fours.
карби́д, а *m.* (*chem.*) carbide.
карбо́ван|ец, ца *m.* karbovanets (*Ukrainian unit of currency*).
карбо́лк|а, и *f.* (*coll.*) carbolic acid.
карбо́ловый *adj.* (*chem.*) carbolic.
карбона́т, а *m.* (*chem.*) carbonate.
карбору́нд, а *m.* carborundum.
карбу́нкул, а *m.* (*min., med.*) carbuncle.
карбюра́тор, а *m.* (*tech., chem*) carburettor (*Br.*), carburetor (*US*).
карг|а́, и́, *pl.* **~и́, ~, ~а́м** *f.* (*coll.*): **ста́рая к.** hag, crone.
кардамо́н, а *m.* (*bot.*) cardamom.
карда́нный *adj.*: **к. вал** (*tech.*) cardan shaft.
кардина́л, а *m.* (*eccl.*) cardinal.
кардина́л|ьный (~ен, ~ьна) *adj.* cardinal; fundamental.
кардина́л|ьский *adj. of* ⇨**~**
кардиогра́мм|а, ы *f.* cardiogram.
кардио́лог, а *m.* cardiologist.
кардиологи́ческий *adj.* cardiological.
кардиоло́ги|я, и *f.* cardiology.
кардиостимуля́тор, а *m.* (*med.*) pacemaker.
кардиохиру́рг, а *m.* heart surgeon.
кардиохирурги́|я, и *f.* heart surgery.
каре́ *nt. indecl.* (*mil.*) square.
каре́л, а *m.* Karelian.
Каре́ли|я, и *f.* Karelia.
каре́л|ка, ки *f. of* ⇨**~**
каре́льский *adj.* Karelian.
каре́т|а, ы *f.* carriage, coach; **почто́вая к.** stage-coach; **к. ско́рой по́мощи** ambulance.
каре́тк|а, и *f.* (*tech.*) carriage, frame.
кариати́д|а, ы *f.* (*archit.*) caryatid.
кари́бский *adj.* Caribbean.
ка́риес, а *m.* (*med.*) caries.
ка́рий *adj.* (*глаза*) brown, hazel; (*лошадь*) chestnut, dark-chestnut.
карикату́р|а, ы *f.* caricature, cartoon; (*fig.*) caricature.
карикатури́ст, а *m.* caricaturist, cartoonist.
карикату́р|ный *adj. of* ⇨**~а; ~ная фигу́ра** ludicrous figure.
карио́з, а *m.* = **ка́риес**
карио́зный *adj.* (*med.*) carious.
карка́с, а *m.* (*tech.*) frame; (*fig.*) framework.
карка́с|ный *adj. of* ⇨**~; к. дом** frame house.
ка́рк|ать, аю *impf.* **1** (*pf.* ⇨**ка́ркнуть**) to caw, croak. **2** (*pf.* ⇨**на~**) (*fig.*) to prophesy ill.
ка́рк|нуть, ну, нешь *pf. of* ⇨**~ать 1**
ка́рлик, а *m.* dwarf.
ка́рликов|ый *adj.* dwarf; **~ые племена́** the pygmies.
ка́рли|ца, цы *f. of* ⇨**~к**
ка́рм|а, ы *f.* (*relig.*) karma.
карма́н, а *m.* pocket; (*fig., coll.*): **э́то мне не по ~у** I can't afford it; **бить по ~у** to cost a pretty penny; **наби́ть себе́ к.** to line one's pockets; **то́щий к.** empty pocket; **держи́ к. ши́ре!** you've got a hope!; **не лезть за сло́вом в к.** to have a ready tongue.
карма́нник, а *m.* pickpocket.
карма́н|ный *adj. of* ⇨**~; к. вор** pickpocket; **~ные де́ньги** pocket money.
карма́нщик, а *m.* = **карма́нник**
карми́н, а *m.* carmine.
карми́нный *adj.* carmine.
карнава́л, а *m.* carnival.
карни́з, а *m.* (*archit.; mountaineering*) cornice.
карп, а *m.* (*рыба*) carp.
Карпа́т|ы, ~ *no sg.* the Carpathians.
карт, а *m.* (*sport*) go-cart.
ка́рт|а, ы *f.* **1** (*geog.*) map. **2** (*игральная*) (playing-)card; **игра́ть в ~ы** to play cards; **име́ть хоро́шие ~ы** to have a good hand; **его́ ка́рта би́та** (*fig.*) his game is up; **поста́вить на ~у** to stake, risk; **на ~е** at stake; **раскры́ть свои́ ~ы** to show one's hand (*also fig.*). **3** (*бланк*) form. **4** = **ка́рточка 1**; **магни́тная к.** swipe card.
карта́в|ить, лю, ишь *impf.* to be unable to pronounce 'r' and 'l' properly.
карта́вый *adj.* mispronouncing 'r' and 'l'.
карт-бла́нш *m. indecl.* carte blanche.
картёжник, а *m.* (*coll.*) card-player.
картёжный *adj.* (*coll.*) card-playing.
картезиа́нский *adj.* (*phil.*) Cartesian.
карте́л|ь, я *m.* (*fin.*) cartel.
ка́ртер, а *m.* (*tech.*) crankcase.
карте́ч|ный *adj. of* ⇨**~ь**
карте́ч|ь, и *f.* **1** (*mil.*) case-shot; grape-shot. **2** (*для охотничьего ружья*) buck-shot.
карти́н|а, ы *f.* **1** (*in var. senses*) picture. **2** (*theatr.*) scene; **жива́я к.** (*obs.*) tableau (vivant).
ка́ртинг, а *m.* go-carting.
карти́нк|а, и *f.* small picture; **как к.** very pretty.
карти́н|ный (~ен, ~на) *adj.* **1** *adj. of* ⇨**~а; ~ная галере́я** art gallery, picture-gallery. **2** (*красивый*) picturesque. **3** (*жест, поза*) theatrical, mannered.
карто́граф, а *m.* cartographer.
картографи́р|овать, ую *impf. and pf.* to map, draw a map of.
картографи́ческий *adj.* cartographic.
картогра́фи|я, и *f.* cartography.
карто́н, а *m.* card, cardboard.
карто́нк|а, и *f.* **1** (*ящик*) cardboard box; carton. **2** (*coll.*) (*кусок картона*) piece of card, cardboard.
карто́н|ный *adj. of* ⇨**~**; (*fig.*): **к. до́мик** house of cards.
картоте́к|а, и *f.* card-index.
картофелечи́стк|а, и *f.* potato peeler.
карто́фелин|а, ы *f.* (*coll.*) potato.
карто́фел|ь, я *no pl., m.* **1** (*collect.*) potatoes; **к. в мунди́ре** jacket potatoes; **жа́реный к.** fried potatoes; **молодо́й к.** new potatoes. **2** (*растение*) potato plant.
карто́фель|ный *adj. of* ⇨**~; ~ное пюре́** mashed potatoes.
ка́рточк|а, и *f.* **1** card; **визи́тная к.** visiting card, business card; **к. вин** wine-list; **продово́льственная к.** food-card, ration card. **2** (*проездной билет*) season ticket. **3** (*coll.*) photo.

ка́рточ|ный *adj.* **1** *adj. of* ⇒**ка́рта; к. долг** gambling-debt; **к. стол** card-table; (*coll.*): **к. до́мик** house of cards (*also fig.*); **к. фо́кус** card trick. **2** *adj. of* ⇒**~ка; к. катало́г** card index; **~ная систе́ма** rationing system.

карто́шк|а, и *f.* (*coll.*) **1** (*collect.*) (*картофель*) potatoes. **2** (*картофелина*) potato; **нос ~ой** bulbous nose.

ка́ртридж, а *m.* cartridge.

карту́з, а́ *m.* (peaked) cap.

карусе́л|ь, и *f.* merry-go-round, carousel.

Карфаге́н, а *m.* Carthage.

карфаге́нский *adj.* Carthaginian.

карфаге́нян|ин, ина, *pl.* **~е, ~** *m.* Carthaginian.

карфаге́нян|ка, ки *f. of* ⇒**~ин**

ка́рцер, а *m.* isolation cell.

карье́р[1]**, а** *m.* (*галоп*) career, full gallop; **во весь к.** at full speed; **пусти́ть ло́шадь в к., ~ом** to put a horse into full gallop; (*fig.*): **с ме́ста в к.** straight away, without more ado.

карье́р[2]**, а** *m.* (*каменоломня*) quarry; (*песочный*) sand-pit; **у́гольный к.** open-cast mine.

карье́р|а, ы *f.* career; **сде́лать ~у** to make good, get on.

карьери́зм, а *m.* careerism.

карьери́ст, а *m.* careerist.

карьери́стский *adj.* careerist.

карье́р|ный *adj. of* **1** ⇒**~**[1,2]**. 2** ⇒**~а**

каса́ни|е, я *nt.* contact; (*math.*): **то́чка ~я** point of contact.

каса́тельн|ая, ой *f.* (*math.*) tangent.

каса́тельно *prep.+g.* touching, concerning.

каса́тельств|о, а *nt.* (*liter.*) (**к**+*d.*) connection (with); **я не име́л никако́го ~а к э́тому заявле́нию** I had nothing to do with this statement.

каса́т|ка, ки *f.* **1** (*zool.*) swallow. **2** = **коса́тка**

каса́|ться, юсь *impf.* (*of* ⇒**косну́ться**) **1** (+*g.*) to touch. **2** (+*g.*; *fig.*) (*вопроса, темы*) to touch (on, upon); **к. больно́го вопро́са** to touch on a sore subject. **3** (+*g. or* **до**+*g.*; *fig.*) (*иметь отношение*) to concern, relate (to); **э́то тебя́ не ~ется** it is no concern of yours; **что ~ется** as to, as regards, with regard to.

ка́ск|а, и *f.* helmet.

каска́д, а *m.* **1** (*поток*) cascade; **к. красноре́чия** (*fig.*) flood of eloquence. **2** (*трюк*) stunt.

каскадёр, а *m.* stunt man.

Каспи́йск|ое мо́р|е, ~ого ~я *nt.* the Caspian Sea.

ка́сс|а, ы *f.* **1** (*ящик*) cash-box; (*аппарат в магазине*) till, cash register; (*место в магазине*) cash-desk; **уплати́ть в ~у** to pay at the cash-desk; **несгора́емая к.** safe. **2** (*деньги*) cash; **фильм де́лает ~у** the film is a box-office success. **3** (*железнодорожная*) booking-office; (*театральная*) box-office; **к. взаимопо́мощи** benefit fund, mutual aid fund; **сберега́тельная к.** savings bank.

касса|цио́нный *adj. of* ⇒**~́ция; ~цио́нная жа́лоба** appeal; **к. суд** Court of Appeal, Court of Cassation.

касса́ци|я, и *f.* (*leg.*) **1** cassation. **2**: **пода́ть на ~ю** to appeal.

кассе́т|а, ы *f.* cassette.

кассе́т|ный *adj. of* ⇒**~а; к. магнитофо́н** cassette recorder.

касси́р, а *m.* cashier.

касси́р|овать, ую *impf. and pf.* (*leg.*) to annul, quash.

касси́р|ша, ши *f.* (*coll.*) *of* ⇒**~**

ка́сс|овый *adj.* **1** *adj. of* ⇒**~а; ~овая кни́га** cash-book; **к. счёт** cash-account. **2**: **к. спекта́кль, фильм** a box-office success.

ка́ст|а, ы *f.* caste.

кастанье́т|ы, ~ *pl.* (*sg.* **~а, ~ы** *f.*) castanets.

кастеля́нш|а, и *f.* linen-keeper (*in institution*).

касте́т, а *m.* knuckleduster.

касто́рк|а, и *f.* (*coll.*) castor oil.

касто́ров|ый *adj.*: **~ое ма́сло** castor oil.

кастра́т, а *m.* eunuch; (*певец*) castrato.

кастра́ци|я, и *f.* castration.

кастри́р|овать, ую *impf. and pf.* to castrate.

кастрю́л|я, и *f.* saucepan.

катава́си|я, и *f.* (*coll.*) confusion, muddle.

катакли́зм, а *m.* cataclysm.

катако́мб|а, ы *f.* catacomb.

катала́жк|а, и *f.* (*coll.*) lock-up, nick (*Br.*).

катала́нский *adj.* Catalan (*of language*).

ката́лиз, а *m.* (*chem.*) catalysis.

катализа́тор, а *m.* catalyst (*also fig.*).

ката́лк|а, и *f.*: **де́тская к.** (*coll.*) baby buggy, pushchair.

катало́г, а *m.* catalogue (*Br.*), catalog (*US*).

каталогиза́тор, а *m.* cataloguer.

каталогизи́р|овать, ую *impf. and pf.* to catalogue (*Br.*), catalog (*US*).

катало́жн|ая, ой *f.* catalogue (*Br.*), catalog (*US*) room.

катало́|жный *adj. of* ⇒**~г**

катало́н|ец, ца *m.* Catalan, Catalonian.

Катало́ни|я, и *f.* Catalonia.

катало́н|ка, ки *f. of* ⇒**~ец**

катало́нский *adj.* Catalan; Catalonian.

катамара́н, а *m.* catamaran.

ката́ни|е, я *nt.* **1** (*мяча*) rolling. **2**: **к. в экипа́же** driving; **к. верхо́м** riding; **к. на ло́дке** boating; **к. на конька́х** skating; **к. на ро́ликах** roller skating; **фигу́рное к.** figure skating; **к. с гор** tobogganing.

ка́тань|е, я *nt., only in phr.* **не мытьём, так ~ем** (*coll.*) by hook or by crook.

катапу́льт|а, ы *f.* catapult.

катапульти́р|оваться, уюсь *impf. and pf.* (*о лётчике*) to eject.

Ката́р, а *m.* Qatar.

ката́р, а *m.* catarrh.

катара́кт, а *m.* (*geog.*) cataract.

катара́кт|а, ы *f.* (*med.*) cataract.

ка́тарсис, а *m.* catharsis.

катастро́ф|а, ы *f.* catastrophe, disaster; (*авария*) accident.

катастрофи́ческий *adj.* catastrophic.

катастрофи́ч|ный (~ен, ~на) *adj.* catastrophic.

кат|а́ть, а́ю *impf.* **1** (*indet. of* ⇒**~и́ть**) (*мяч*) to roll; (*велосипед, тачку*) to wheel, trundle. **2** (*человека*) to drive, take for a drive; (*на санках*) to take for a ride. **3** (*pf.* **с~**) (*из глины, теста*) to roll. **4** (*pf.* **вы́~**): **к. бельё** to mangle linen.

кат|а́ться, а́юсь *impf.* **1** (*indet. of* ⇒**~и́ться**) (*о мяче*) to roll (*intrans.*); (*coll.*): **к. от бо́ли** to roll in pain; **к. со́ смеху** to split one's sides with laughter; **к. с горы́** to slide down a hill. **2** (*на машине*) to go for a drive; **к. верхо́м** to ride, go riding; **к. на велосипе́де** to cycle, go cycling; **к. на конька́х** to skate, go skating; **к. на ло́дке** to go boating.

катафа́лк, а *m.* **1** (*подставка*) catafalque. **2** (*погребальная колесница*) hearse.

катафо́т, а *m.* Catseye (*Br. propr.*); reflector.

категори́чески *adv.* categorically; **к. отказа́ться** to refuse flatly.

категори́ческий *adj.* categorical.

категори́ч|ный (~ен, ~на) *adj.* categorical.

катего́ри|я, и *f.* category.

ка́тер, а, *pl.* **~а́** *m.* (*naut.*) boat; **мото́рный к.** motor-launch; **сторожево́й к.** patrol boat.

ка́тер|ный *adj. of* ⇒**~**

кате́тер, а *m.* (*med.*) catheter.

катехи́зис, а *m.* catechism.

ка|ти́ть, чу́, ~́тишь *impf.* (*of* ⇒**по~**) **1** *det. of* ⇒**~та́ть. 2** (*coll.*) (*быстро ехать*) to bowl along, tear.

ка|ти́ться, чу́сь, ~́тишься *impf.* (*of* ⇒**по~**) **1** *det. of* ⇒**~та́ться; к. по́д гору** (*fig.*) to go downhill. **2** (*течь*) to flow, stream; (*fig.*) to roll; **слёзы ~ти́лись по её щека́м** tears were rolling down her cheeks; **день ~́тится за днём** day after day rolls by. **3** (*coll.*): **~ти́сь; ~ти́тесь отсю́да!** get out!; clear off!

като́д, а *m.* (*phys.*) cathode.

като́дн|ый *adj.* (*phys.*) cathodic; **~ые лучи́** cathode rays; **~ая тру́бка** cathode-ray tube.

кат|о́к[1]**, ка́** *m.* (*ледяная площадка*) skating-rink.

кат|о́к[2]**, ка́** *m.* **1** (*машина*) roller. **2** (*для белья*) mangle.

като́лик, а *m.* (Roman) Catholic.

католици́зм, а *m.* (Roman) Catholicism.

католи́ческий *adj.* (Roman) Catholic.

католи́честв|о, а *nt.* (Roman) Catholicism.

католи́чк|а, и *f. of* ⇒**като́лик**

ка́торг|а, и *no pl., f.* penal servitude, hard labour (*Br.*), labor (*US*).
каторжа́н|ин, ина, *pl.* **~е, ~** *m.* convict; (*бывший на каторге*) ex-convict.
каторжа́н|ка, ки *f. of* ⇒**~ин**
ка́торжник, а *m.* convict.
ка́тор|жный *adj. of* ⇒**~га; ~жные работы** hard labour (*Br.*), labor (*US*); (*fig.*) drudgery; **~жная тюрьма́** convict prison.
кату́шк|а, и *f.* **1** reel, spool. **2** (*elec.*) coil.
катю́ш|а, и *f.* (*mil.*; *hist.*) Katyusha (*lorry-mounted multiple rocket launcher*).
кауза́льный *adj.* (*phil.*) causal.
кау́рый *adj.* (*лошадь*) light-chestnut.
каусти́ческий *adj.* (*chem.*) caustic.
каучу́к, а *m.* (india-)rubber, caoutchouc.
каучу́к|овый *adj of* ⇒**~;** rubber.
каучуконо́с, а *m.* (*bot.*) rubber plant.
кафе́ *nt. indecl.* café; **к.-моро́женое** ice-cream parlour (*Br.*), parlor (*US*).
ка́федр|а, ы *f.* **1** (*в церкви*) pulpit; (*для оратора*) rostrum, platform; **говори́ть с ~ы** to speak from the platform. **2** (*профессорство*) chair; **получи́ть ~у** to obtain a chair. **3** (*в университете*) department, sub-faculty; **заседа́ние ~ы** sub-faculty meeting.
кафедра́льный *adj.*: **к. собо́р** cathedral.
ка́фел|ь, я *m.* (*collect.*) Dutch tiles.
ка́фель|ный *adj. of* ⇒**~; ~ная печь** tiled stove; **~ная пли́тка** Dutch tile.
кафете́ри|й, я *m.* cafeteria.
кафта́н, а *m.* caftan.
кача́лк|а, и *f.* rocking-chair; **конь-к.** rocking-horse.
кача́ни|е, я *nt.* **1** rocking, swinging; **к. ма́ятника** swing of pendulum. **2** (*насосом*) pumping.
кач|а́ть, а́ю *impf.* (*of* ⇒**~ну́ть**) **1** (+*a.*) (*ребёнка, колыбель*) to rock; (+*i.*) (*головой, ногой*) to shake; (*impers.*): **его́ ~а́ло из стороны́ в сто́рону** he was reeling; **ло́дку ~а́ет** the boat is rolling. **2** (*coll.*) (*подбрасывать вверх*) to lift up, chair (*as mark of esteem or congratulation*); **к. права́** to demand one's rights. **3** (*насосом*) to pump. **4** (*pf.* ⇒**на~**) (*coll.*): **к. му́скулы** to do body-building exercises; to work out.
кач|а́ться, а́юсь *impf.* (*of* ⇒**~ну́ться**) **1** to rock, swing (*intrans.*); (*о лодке*) to roll, pitch. **2** (*при ходьбе*) to reel, stagger. **3** (*pf.* ⇒**на~**) (*coll.*) to practise body-building; to work out.
каче́л|и, ей *no sg.* (*child's*) swing; (*доска-качели*) see-saw.
ка́чественный *adj.* **1** (*различие, изменение*) qualitative. **2** (*товар*) quality.
ка́честв|о, а *nt.* **1** quality; **ни́зкого ~а** poor quality; low-grade; **в ~е** (+*g.*) in the capacity (of); **он рабо́тал в ~е сове́тника** he worked as/in the capacity of adviser; **в ~е исключе́ния** as a special concession. **2** (*chess*): **вы́играть, проигра́ть к.** to gain, lose an exchange.
ка́чк|а, и *f.* rocking; tossing; (*naut.*): **бортова́я к.** rolling; **килева́я к.** pitching.
ка́чкий *adj.* (*coll.*) unstable, wobbly.
кач|ну́ть(ся), ну́(сь), нёшь(ся) *pf. of* ⇒**~а́ть(ся)**
ка|чу́, ~тишь *see* ⇒**~ти́ть**
качу́рк|а, и *f.* (*zool.*) petrel.
ка́ш|а, и *f.* **1** kasha (*dish of cooked grain or groats*); porridge; **ма́нная к.** semolina; **ри́совая к.** boiled rice. **2** (*fig., coll.*) (*месиво*) jumble; (*путаница*) muddle; **с ним ~и не сва́ришь** you won't get anywhere with him; **у него́ к. во рту** he mumbles; **завари́ть ~у** to stir up trouble; **расхлёбывать ~у** to put things right.
кашало́т, а *m.* (*zool.*) sperm-whale.
кашева́р, а *m.* (*mil.*) cook.
ка́ш|ель, ля *m.* cough.
кашеми́р, а *m.* (*text.*) cashmere.
кашеми́р|овый *adj. of* ⇒**~**
каши́ц|а, ы *f.* (*coll.*) thin gruel.
ка́ш|ка¹, ки *f. dim. of* ⇒**~а;** pap.
ка́шк|а², и *f.* (*bot.*; *coll.*) clover.
ка́шлян|уть, у, ешь *pf.* to give a cough.
ка́шля|ть, ю *impf.* **1** to cough. **2** (*как болезнь*) to have a cough.
Кашми́р, а *m.* Kashmir.
кашми́р|ец, ца *m.* Kashmiri.
кашми́р|ка, ки *f. of* ⇒**~ец**
кашми́рский *adj.* Kashmiri.
кашне́ *nt. indecl.* scarf, muffler.
кашпо́ *nt. indecl.* decorative flower-pot holder.
кашта́н, а *m.* **1** (*орех*) chestnut; **таска́ть ~ы из огня́** (*fig.*) to pull the chestnuts out of the fire. **2** (*дерево*) chestnut-tree; **ко́нский к.** horse-chestnut.
кашта́н|овый *adj.* **1** *adj. of* ⇒**~.** **2** (*цвет*) chestnut(-coloured).
каю́к (*coll.*) *only in phr.* **к. (пришёл)** (+*d.*) it's the end (of); **ему́ к.** his number's up; he's done for.
каю́р, а *m.* dog-team (*or* reindeer-team) driver.
каю́т|а, ы *f.* cabin.
каю́т-компа́ни|я, и *f.* **1** (*на военном корабле*) wardroom. **2** (*на пассажирском судне*) officers' mess.
ка́|ющийся *pres. part. of* ⇒**~яться** *and adj.* repentant, contrite, penitent.
кая́к, а *m.* kayak.
ка́|яться, юсь, ешься *impf.* (*of* ⇒**по~**) **1** (**в**+*p.*) (*сожалеть*) to repent (of); **он сам тепе́рь ~ется** he is sorry himself now. **2** (**в**+*p.*) (*признаться*) to confess. **3** (*coll.*): **~юсь** I am sorry to say; I (must) confess; **я, ~юсь, совсе́м об э́том забы́л** I am sorry to say I had forgotten all about it.
КВ *pl. indecl.* (*abbr. of* ***коро́ткие во́лны***) SW (*short wave*).
кв. (*abbr. of* ***кварти́ра***) flat, apartment.
квадра́нт, а *m.* quadrant.
квадра́т, а *m.* (*math.*) square; **возвести́ в к.** to square; **в ~е** squared; (*fig., coll.*): **дура́к в ~е** doubly a fool.
квадра́тн|ый *adj.* square; **к. ко́рень** square root; **к. метр** square metre (*Br.*), meter (*US*); **~ые ско́бки** square brackets; **~ое уравне́ние** quadratic equation.
квадрату́р|а, ы *f.* (*math.*) quadrature; (*fig.*): **к. кру́га** squaring the circle.
квадриллио́н, а *m.* (*math.*) quadrillion.
кваза́р, а *m.* (*astron.*) quasar.
ква́зи... *comb. form* quasi-.
ква́кань|е, я *nt.* croaking.
ква́ка|ть, ю *impf.* to croak.
ква́кн|уть, у, ешь *pf.* to give a croak.
ква́кушк|а, и *f.* (*coll.*) frog.
квалификац|ио́нный *adj. of* ⇒**~́ия; ~ио́нная коми́ссия** board of experts.
квалифика́ци|я, и *f.* qualification; (*профессия*) profession.
квалифици́рова|нный (~н, ~на) *p.p.p. of* ⇒**~ть** *and adj.* **1** (*работник*) qualified, skilled. **2** (*труд*) skilled.
квалифици́р|овать, ую *impf. and pf.* **1** (*специалиста, спортсмена*) to rank, test. **2** (*оценить*) to categorize; **как к. тако́е поведе́ние?** how should one describe such conduct?
квант, а *m. and* **~́а, ~́ы** *f.* (*phys.*) quantum.
ква́нт|овый *adj. of* ⇒**~; ~овая тео́рия** quantum theory.
кварк, а *m.* (*phys.*) quark.
ква́рт|а, ы *f.* **1** (*liquid measure*) quart. **2** (*mus.*) fourth.
кварта́л, а *m.* **1** (*домов*) block. **2** (*часть города*) quarter; **к. кра́сных фонаре́й** red-light district; **кита́йский к.** Chinatown. **3** (*года*) quarter.
кварта́льный *adj.* quarterly; **к. отчёт** quarterly account.
кварте́т, а *m.* (*mus.*) quartet(te).
кварти́р|а, ы *f.* **1** flat (*Br.*), apartment (*US*). **2** (*снимаемое жильё*) lodgings; **жить на ~е** to live in lodgings. **3** *pl.* (*mil.*) quarters, billets; **зи́мние ~ы** winter quarters.
квартира́нт, а *m.* lodger, tenant.
квартира́нт|ка, ки *f. of* ⇒**~**
квартирме́йстер, а *m.* quartermaster.
кварти́р|ный *adj. of* ⇒**~а; ~ная пла́та** rent; **~ное расположе́ние** (*mil.*) billeting.
квартир|ова́ть, у́ю *impf.* **1** (*coll.*) to lodge, live. **2** (*mil.*) to be billeted, be quartered.
квартиронанима́тел|ь, я *m.* tenant.
квартпла́т|а, ы *f.* (*abbr. of* ***кварти́рная пла́та***) rent.
кварц, а *m.* (*min.*) quartz.
ква́рц|евый *adj. of* ⇒**~**
кварци́т, а *m.* (*min.*) quartzite.
квас, а, *pl.* **~ы́** *m.* kvass.
ква́|сить, шу, сишь *impf.* to pickle; to make sour.
квас|но́й *adj. of* ⇒**~; к. патриоти́зм** (*fig.*) jingoism.

К

квас|о́к, ка́ *m.* **1** *dim. of* ⇒**~**. **2** (*coll.*) sour tang.
квасцо́вый *adj.* (*chem.*) aluminous.
квасц|ы́, о́в *no sg.* (*chem.*) alum.
ква́шен|ый *adj.* sour, fermented; **~ая капу́ста** sauerkraut.
квашн|я́, и́, *g. pl.* **~е́й** *f.* **1** kneading trough. **2** (*coll.*) clumsy oaf.
Квебе́к, а *m.* Quebec.
кве́рху *adv.* up, upwards.
кви́нт|а, ы *f.* (*mus.*) fifth.
квинте́т, а *m.* (*mus.*) quintet(te).
квинтэссе́нци|я, и *f.* quintessence.
квит, ~ы *as pred.* (*coll.*) quits; **мы с тобо́й ~ы** we are quits.
квитанц|ио́нный *adj. of* ⇒**~ия**
квита́нци|я, и *f.* receipt; **бага́жная к.** luggage-ticket (*Br.*), baggage check (*US*).
кво́рум, а *m.* quorum.
кво́т|а, ы *f.* quota.
кВт (*abbr. of* ***килова́тт***) kW, kilowatt(s).
кг (*abbr. of* ***килогра́мм***) k, kg, kilo(s), kilogram(me)(s).
КГБ *m. indecl.* (*abbr. of* ***Комите́т госуда́рственной безопа́сности***) (*hist.*) KGB, State Security Committee.
кеба́б, а *m.* kebab.
кеба́бн|ая, ой *f.* kebab house.
кегельба́н, а *m.* bowling alley; skittle alley.
ке́гл|и, ей *pl.* (*sg.* **~я, ~и** *f.*) **1** skittles, ninepins; **спорти́вные к.** bowls. **2** (*sg.*) skittle; pin.
кегл|ь, я *m.* (*typ.*) point; **к. 8** 8 point.
кедр, а *m.* cedar; **гимала́йский к.** deodar; **лива́нский к.** cedar of Lebanon; **сиби́рский к.** Siberian pine.
кедро́вк|а, и *f.* (*zool.*) nutcracker.
кедр|о́вый *adj. of* ⇒**~**
ке́д|ы, ов *or* **~** *pl.* (*sg.* **кед, а** *m. or* **ке́д|а, ы** *f.*) trainers (*Br.*), sneakers (*US*).
кейф, а *m.* = **кайф**
кейф|ова́ть, у́ю *impf.* = **кайфова́ть**
кекс, а *m.* fruit-cake.
келе́йно *adv.* in secret, privately.
келе́йный *adj.* **1** *adj. of* ⇒**ке́лья.** **2** (*fig., pej.*) secret, private.
Кёльн, а *m.* Cologne.
кельт, а *m.* Celt.
ке́льтский *adj.* Celtic.
ке́л|ья, ьи, *g. pl.* **~ий** *f.* (*eccl.*) cell.
кем *i. of* ⇒**кто**
кема́р|ить, ю, ишь *impf.* (*sl.*) to kip (*Br.*); to grab some shut-eye.
Ке́мбридж, а *m.* Cambridge.
ке́мпинг, а *m.* camping-site, campsite.
кенгуру́ *m. indecl.* kangaroo.
кени́йский *adj.* Kenyan.
Ке́ни|я, и *f.* Kenya.
кенота́ф, а *m.* cenotaph.
кента́вр, а *m.* (*myth.*) centaur.
ке́пи *nt. indecl.* cap.
ке́пк|а, и *f.* cloth cap.
кера́мик, а *m.* = **керами́ст**
кера́мик|а, и *f.* ceramics.
керами́ст, а *m.* ceramicist.
керами́ческий *adj.* ceramic.
керати́н, а *m.* (*biol.*) keratin.
ке́рвел|ь, я *m.* (*bot.*) chervil; **ди́кий к.** cow-parsley.
керога́з, а *m.* paraffin stove.
кероси́н, а *m.* paraffin (*Br.*), kerosene (*US*).
кероси́нк|а, и *f.* (*coll.*) paraffin stove (*Br.*), kerosene stove (*US*).
кероси́н|овый *adj. of* ⇒**~**; **~овая ла́мпа** oil lamp.
ке́сарев *adj.* (*med.*): **~о сече́ние** Caesarean (*Br.*), Cesarean (*US*) section.
ке́сар|ь, я *m.* monarch, lord.
кессо́н, а *m.* (*tech.*) caisson.
кессо́н|ный *adj. of* ⇒**~**; **~ная боле́знь** caisson disease; the bends.
ке́т|а, ы́ *f.* Siberian salmon.
кетме́н|ь, я́ *m.* (*agric.*) ketmen (*kind of hoe used in Central Asia*).
ке́т|овый *adj. of* ⇒**~а**
ке́тч, а *m.* (*coll.*) all-in wrestling.
кетчи́ст, а *m.* (*coll.*) all-in wrestler.
ке́тчуп, а *m.* ketchup.
кефа́л|ь, и *f.* grey mullet.
кефи́р, а *m.* kefir.
киберне́тик, а *m.* cybernetician, cyberneticist.
киберне́тик|а, и *f.* cybernetics.
кибернети́ческий *adj.* cybernetic.
киберпростра́нств|о, а *nt.* cyberspace.
киби́тк|а, и *f.* **1** (*экипаж*) kibitka, covered wagon. **2** (*жилище*) nomad tent.
кибу́ц, а *m.* kibbutz.
кив|а́ть, а́ю *impf.* (*of* ⇒**~ну́ть**) **1**: **к. (голово́й)** to nod (one's head); (*как согласие*) to nod assent. **2** (**на** + *a.*) to nod at, motion (to); (*fig.*) to put the blame (on to).
ки́вер, а, *pl.* **~а́** *m.* shako.
ки́ви *f. & nt. indecl.* **1** (*f.*) (*zool.*) kiwi. **2** (*nt.*) kiwi fruit.
кив|ну́ть, ну́, нёшь *pf. of* ⇒**~а́ть**
кив|о́к, ка́ *m.* nod.
кида́л|а, ы *c.g.* (*sl.*) cheat, con man.
ки|да́ть, да́ю *impf.* (*of* ⇒**~нуть**) **1** to throw, fling, cast (*usage as for* **броса́ть**); **куда́ ни кинь** whichever way you turn. **2** (*sl.*) (*обманывать*) to cheat, con.
ки|да́ться, да́юсь *impf.* (*of* ⇒**~нуться**) **1** to throw o.s., fling o.s.; (*устремиться куда-н.*) to rush. **2** (+*i.*) to throw, fling. **3** *pass. of* ⇒**~да́ть**
Ки́ев, а *m.* Kiev.
киевля́н|ин, ина, *pl.* **~е, ~** *m.* Kievan.
киевля́н|ка, ки *f. of* ⇒**~ин**
ки́евский *adj.* Kiev; Kievan.
кизи́л, а *m.* (*bot.*) cornel.
ки|й, я́, *pl.* **~и́, ~ёв** *m.* (*sport*) cue.
кикбо́ксинг, а *m.* kick-boxing.
кики́мор|а, ы *f.* **1** (*folklore*) kikimora (*hobgoblin in female form*). **2** (*fig., coll.*): **вы́глядеть как к.** to look a fright.
кил|ево́й *adj. of* ⇒**~ь**; **~ева́я ка́чка** pitching.
ки́ллер, а *m.* contract killer, hit-man.
кило́ *nt. indecl.* (*coll.*) kilo, kilogram(me).
килоба́йт, а *m.* (*comput.*) kilobyte.
килова́тт, а *m.* (*elec.*) kilowatt.
килогра́мм, а *m.* kilogram(me).
килокало́ри|я, и *f.* large calorie.
киломе́тр, а *m.* kilometre (*Br.*), kilometer (*US*).
кил|ь, я *m.* (*naut.*) keel.
кильва́тер, а *m.* (*naut.*) wake; **идти́ в к.** (+*d.*) to follow in the wake (of).
ки́льк|а, и *f.* sprat.
кимоно́ *nt. indecl.* kimono.
кингсто́н, а *m.* (*naut.*) Kingston valve; **откры́ть ~ы** to scuttle (a ship).
кинемато́граф, а *m.* **1** (*как искусство*) cinematography. **2** (*кинотеатр*) cinema (*Br.*), movie theater (*US*).
кинематографи́ст, а *m.* cinematographer, film-maker.
кинематографи́ческий *adj.* cinematographic.
кинематогра́фи|я, и *f.* cinematography.
кинеско́п, а *m.* picture tube.
кине́тик|а, и *f.* (*phys.*) kinetics.
кинети́ческий *adj.* (*phys.*) kinetic.
кинжа́л, а *m.* dagger.
кинжа́л|ьный *adj.* **1** *adj. of* ⇒**~**. **2** (*mil.*) close-range, hand-to-hand.
кино́ *nt. indecl.* **1** (*как искусство*) the cinema. **2** (*здание*) cinema (*Br.*), movie theater (*US*). **3** (*coll.*) (*фильм*) film, movie.
кино... *comb. form, abbr. of* ***кино, кинематографи́ческий***
киноактёр, а *m.* film actor (*Br.*), movie actor (*US*).
киноактри́с|а, ы *f.* film actress (*Br.*), movie actress (*US*).
киноаппара́т, а *m.* movie camera.
киноаппарату́р|а, ы *f.* cinematographic equipment.
киноарти́ст, а *m.* = **киноактёр**
киноарти́стк|а, и *f.* = **киноактри́са**
кинобоеви́к, а́ *m.* hit film.
ки́новар|ь, и *f.* cinnabar, vermilion.
кинове́д, а *m.* film historian (*Br.*), movie historian (*US*).
кинове́дени|е, я *nt.* film studies (*Br.*), movie studies (*US*).
кинове́д|ческий *adj. of* ⇒**~ение**
кинодел|е́ц, ьца́ *m.* movie mogul.
кинодрамату́рг, а *m.* screenwriter.
киножурна́л, а *m.* newsreel.
кинозáл, а *m.* **1** (*здание*) cinema (*Br.*), movie theater (*US*). **2** (*зал*) auditorium.
кинозвезд|а́, ы́, *pl.* **~ы, ~, ~ам** *f.* film star (*Br.*), movie star (*US*).
кинозри́тел|ь, я *m.* cinema-goer.
кинока́мер|а, ы *f.* movie camera.
кинокарти́н|а, ы *f.* (*non-documentary*) film; motion picture; movie.

кинокоме́ди|я, и *f.* comedy film, movie.
кинокри́тик, а *m.* film critic.
киноле́нт|а, ы *f.* reel (of film).
кинолюби́тел|ь, я *m.* amateur film-maker, cineast(e).
киноман, а *m.* cinephile, film freak (*coll.*).
киномеха́ник, а *m.* projectionist.
кинообозрева́тел|ь, я *m.* film critic.
кинооперáтор, а *m.* camera-man.
киноплёнк|а, и *f.* cine film (*Br.*), movie film (*US*).
кинопро́б|а, ы *f.* screen test.
кинопрока́т, а *m.* film hire service.
кинопросмо́тр, а *m.* film screening.
кинорежиссёр, а *m.* film director.
кинорепортáж, а *m.* news film.
киносеа́нс, а *m.* (cinema) performance, showing.
киносту́ди|я, и *f.* film studio (*Br.*), movie studio (*US*).
киносцена́ри|й, я *m.* screenplay.
киносценари́ст, а *m.* scriptwriter; scripter.
киносъёмк|а, и *f.* filming, shooting.
киносъём|очный *adj. of* **⇨~ка; ~очная кома́нда** film crew; **к. аппара́т** film *or* movie camera.
кинотеа́тр, а *m.* cinema (*Br.*), movie theater (*US*).
киноустано́вк|а, и *f.* projecting machine.
кинофи́льм, а *m.* film, movie.
кинохро́ник|а, и *f.* newsreel.
ки́|нуть(ся), ну(сь), нешь(ся) *pf. of* **⇨~да́ть(ся)**
кио́ск, а *m.* kiosk, stall; **газе́тный к.** news-stand.
киоскёр, а *m.* stall-holder.
кио́т, а *m.* icon-case.
ки́п|а, ы *f.* **1** pile, stack. **2** (*мера*) pack, bale; **к. хло́пка** bale of cotton.
кипари́с, а *m.* (*bot.*) cypress.
кипе́ни|е, я *nt.* boiling; **то́чка ~я** boiling point.
кип|е́ть, лю́, и́шь *impf.* (*of* **⇨вс~**) to boil, seethe; **к. негодова́нием** (*fig.*) to seethe with indignation; **жизнь ~и́т** life is full; **рабо́та ~е́ла** work was in full swing.
Кипр, а *m.* Cyprus.
кипре́|й, я *m.* (*bot.*) willow-herb.
киприо́т, а *m.* Cypriot.
киприо́т|ка, ки *f. of* **⇨~**
ки́прский *adj.* Cypriot.
кипу́чест|ь, и *f.* ebullience, turbulence.
кипу́ч|ий (~, ~а) *adj.* **1** bubbling, seething. **2** (*fig.*) ebullient, turbulent; **~ая де́ятельность** feverish activity.
кипяти́льник, а *m.* kettle, boiler.
кипя|ти́ть, чу́, ти́шь *impf.* (*of* **⇨вс~**) to boil.
кипя|ти́ться, чу́сь, ти́шься *impf.* **1** to boil (*intrans.*). **2** (*fig., coll.*) to get excited. **3** *pass. of* **⇨~ти́ть**
кипят|о́к, ка́ *m.* boiling water.
кипячёный *adj.* boiled.
кир, а *m.* (*sl.*) booze, liquor.
кира́с|а, ы *f.* (*mil., hist.*) cuirass.
кираси́р, а *m.* (*mil., hist.*) cuirassier.
кирги́з, а *m.* Kyrgyz.
Кирги́зи|я, и *f.* Kyrgyzstan.
кирги́з|ка, ки *f. of* **⇨~**
кирги́зский *adj.* Kyrgyz.
ки́рз|а́, ы *and* **ы́** *f.* kersey.
ки́рз|о́вый *adj. of* **⇨~а́**
кири́ллиц|а, ы *f.* Cyrillic alphabet.
кирилли́ческий *adj.* Cyrillic.
ки́рк|а, и *f.* (Protestant) church.
кирк|а́, и́ *f.* pick(axe).
кирк|о́вый *adj. of* **⇨~а́**
кирпи́ч, а́ *m.* **1** brick. **2** (*collect.*) bricks. **3** (*coll.*) (*дорожный знак*) no-entry sign.
кирпи́ч|ик, ика *m.* **1** *dim. of* **⇨~.** **2** (*pl.*) (*игрушка*) bricks.
кирпи́ч|ный *adj. of* **⇨~; к. заво́д** brickworks; **к. цвет** terracotta.
ки́с|а, ы *f.* = **~ка**
кисе́|йный *adj. of* **⇨~я́**
кисе́л|ь, я́ *m.* kissel (*kind of blancmange*); (*fig., coll.*): **деся́тая** (*or* **седьма́я**) **вода́ на ~е́** distant relative; **за семь вёрст ~я́ хлеба́ть** to go on a fool's errand.
кисе́т, а *m.* tobacco pouch.
кисе|я́, и́ *f.* muslin.
ки́ск|а, и *f.* (*coll.*) puss, pussy-cat.
кис-ки́с *int.* puss-puss! (*when calling cat*).
ки́сленький *adj.* (*coll.*) slightly sour.
кисле́|ть, ю *impf.* (*coll.*) to become sour.
кисли́нк|а, и *f.* sour taste; **с ~ой** (*coll.*) slightly sour, sourish.
кислова́т|ый (~, ~а) *adj.* sourish; acidulous.
кислоро́д, а *m.* oxygen.
кислоро́дно-ацетиле́новый *adj.* oxy-acetylene.
кислоро́дный *adj.* (*chem.*) oxygen.
ки́сло-сла́д|кий (~ок, ~ка) *adj.* sweet-and-sour.
кислот|а́, ы́, *pl.* **~ы** *f.* **1** sourness; acidity. **2** (*chem.*) acid.
кисло́тност|ь, и *f.* (*chem.*) acidity.
кисло́тный *adj.* (*chem.*) acid; **к. дождь** acid rain.
ки́с|лый (~ел, ~ла́, ~ло) *adj.* **1** (*яблоко*) sour; (*fig.*): **~лое настрое́ние** sour mood. **2** (*закисший*) sour, fermented; **~лая капу́ста** sauerkraut. **3** (*chem.*) acid.
ки́с|нуть, ну, нешь, *past* **~, ~ла** *impf.* **1** (*молоко*) to turn sour. **2** (*fig., coll.*) (*человек*) to mope; to look sour.
кист|а́, ы́ *f.* (*med.*) cyst.
кисте́н|ь, я́ *m.* bludgeon, flail.
ки́сточк|а, и *f.* **1** (*для рисования*) brush; **к. для бритья́** shaving-brush. **2** (*на скатерти*) tassel. **3** (*винограда*) bunch.
кист|ь[1]**, и,** *pl.* **~и, ~е́й** *f.* **1** (*bot.*) cluster, bunch; **к. виногра́да** bunch of grapes. **2** (*для рисования*) brush; **маля́рная к.** paintbrush. **3** (*на скатерти*) tassel.
кист|ь[2]**, и,** *pl.* **~и, ~е́й** *f.* hand.
кит, а́ *m.* whale.
кита́|ец, йца, *pl.* **~йцы, ~йцев** *m.* Chinese.
Кита́|й, я *m.* China.
кита́йск|ий *adj.* Chinese; **~ая гра́мота** double Dutch.
кита́йско-... *comb. form* Sino-.
китая́нк|а, и *f. of* **⇨кита́ец**
ки́тел|ь, я, *pl.* **~я́, ~е́й** *m.* (*mil.*) tunic, jacket (*with high collar*).
китобо́|ец, йца *m.* (*судно*) whaler.
китобо́|й, я *m.* (*человек*; *судно*) whaler.
китобо́йн|ый *adj.* whaling; **к. про́мысел** whaling; **~ое су́дно** whaler.
кит|о́вый *adj. of* **⇨~; к. жир** blubber; **к. ус** whalebone, baleen
китоло́в, а *m.* (*человек*) whaler.
кито|ло́вный *adj.* = **~бо́йный**
китч, а *m.* kitsch.
кич|и́ться, у́сь, и́шься *impf.* (+*i.*) to boast (about); to strut.
кичли́вост|ь, и *f.* conceit; arrogance.
кичли́в|ый (~, ~а) *adj.* conceited, arrogant, strutting.
киш|е́ть, у́, и́шь *impf.* (+*i.*) to swarm (with), teem (with).
кише́чник, а *m.* (*anat.*) bowels, intestines; **очи́стить к.** to open the bowels.
киш|е́чный *adj. of* **⇨~е́чник** *and* **~ка́;** intestinal.
киш|ка́, ки́, *g. pl.* **~о́к** *f.* **1** (*anat.*) gut, intestine; **пряма́я к.** rectum; **слепа́я к.** caecum; **то́нкая, то́лстая к.** small, large intestine; (*fig., coll.*): **к. тонка́!** he, *etc.*, isn't up to that! **2** (*coll.*) (*для подачи воды*) hose; **поли́ть ~ко́й** to hose.
кишла́к, а́ *m.* kishlak (*village in Central Asia*).
кишми́ш, а́ *no pl., m.* (*виноград*) seedless grapes; (*изюм*) raisins, sultanas.
кишмя́ *adv., only in phr.* **к. кише́ть** to swarm.
клавеси́н, а *m.* (*mus.*) harpsichord.
клавиату́р|а, ы *f.* keyboard.
клавико́рд|ы, ов *no sg.* (*mus.*) clavichord.
кла́виш, а *m.* = **кла́виша**
кла́виш|а, и *f.* key (*of piano, computer, etc.*); **к. пробе́ла** space-bar.
кла́виш|ный *adj. of* **⇨~а; ~ные инструме́нты** keyboard instruments.
клад, а *m.* treasure; (*fig., coll.*) treasure(-house); **моя́ секрета́рша — настоя́щий к.** my secretary is a real treasure.
кла́дбищ|е, а *nt.* cemetery, graveyard; (*при церкви*) churchyard.
кладби́щенский *adj. of* **⇨кла́дбище; к. сто́рож** sexton.
кла́дез|ь, я *m., arch., now only in phr.* **к. прему́дрости** mine of information.
кла́дк|а, и *f.* laying; **ка́менная к.** masonry; **кирпи́чная к.** brickwork.
кладов|а́я, о́й *f.* (*для провизии*) pantry, larder; (*для товаров*) storeroom.

К

кладо́вк|а, и *f.* (*coll.*) small pantry, larder.

кладовщи́к, а́ *m.* storeman (*Br.*), warehouseman.

кладовщи́|ца, цы *f.* storewoman (*Br.*), warehousewoman.

кла|ду́, дёшь *see* ⇨**~сть**

кла́дчик, а *m.* bricklayer.

клад|ь, и *f.* (*sg. only*) load; **ручна́я к.** hand luggage (*Br.*), baggage (*US*).

кла́к|а, и *no pl., f.* (*collect.*) claque.

клакёр, а *m.* (*theatr.*) claqueur.

кла́ксо́н, а *m.* horn.

клан, а *m.* clan.

кла́ня|ться, юсь *impf.* (*of* ⇨**поклони́ться**) **1** (+*d. or* **с**+*i.*) to bow (to); (*приветствовать*) to greet; **к. в по́яс** to bow from the waist; (*fig.*): **мы с ним не ~емся** I am not on speaking terms with him. **2** (*передавать привет*) to send, convey greetings; **~йтесь ему́ от меня́** give him my regards. **3** (+*d. or* **пе́ред**+*i.*; *coll.*) (*униженно просить*) to cringe (before); to humiliate o.s. (before).

кла́пан, а *m.* **1** valve. **2** (*кармана*) flap.

кларне́т, а *m.* clarinet.

кларнети́ст, а *m.* clarinettist.

класс, а *m.* **1** class; **госпо́дствующий, пра́вящий к.** ruling class; **к. млекопита́ющих** (class of) mammalia; **игра́ высо́кого ~а** high-class play. **2** (*комната*) class-room.

кла́ссик, а *m.* **1** (*писатель*) writer of classics. **2** (*учёный*) classical scholar, classicist.

кла́ссик|а, и *f.* the classics.

кла́ссик|и, ов *dim. of* ⇨**кла́ссы**

классифика́ци|я, и *f.* classification.

классифици́р|овать, ую *impf. and pf.* to classify.

классици́зм, а *m.* classicism.

класси́ческий *adj.* (*музыка, образование, язык*) classical; (*работа, пример, одежда*) classic.

кла́сс|ный *adj.* (*of* ⇨**~**) **1**: **~ная доска́** blackboard; **~ная ко́мната** classroom; **~ная рабо́та** class work. **2**: **к. ваго́н** passenger coach. **3** (*sport*) first-class. **4** (*sl.*) (*отличный*) excellent, great.

кла́ссовост|ь, и *f.* class character.

кла́ссов|ый *adj.* (*pol.*) class; **~ая борьба́** class struggle; **~ое созна́ние** class-consciousness.

кла́сс|ы, ов *pl.* hopscotch.

кла|сть, ду́, дёшь, *past* **~л, ~ла** *impf.* (*of* ⇨**положи́ть**) **1** (*помещать*) to lay; to put; to place; **к. больно́го на носи́лки** to lay a patient on a stretcher; **к. са́хар в чай** to put sugar in one's tea; **к. на ме́сто** to replace; **к. не на ме́сто** to mislay; **к. на му́зыку** to set to music; **к. я́йца** to lay eggs; **к. нача́ло, к. коне́ц чему́-н.** to start sth., put an end to sth. **2** (*pf.* **сложи́ть**) (*строить*) to build. **3** (*назначать*) to assign, set aside; **мы ~дём пятьдеся́т рубле́й на э́ту пое́здку** we are setting aside fifty roubles for this trip.

клаустрофо́би|я, и *f.* claustrophobia.

кла́ца|ть, ю *impf.* (*coll.*) (*о зубах*) to chatter.

клёв, а *m.* biting, bite; **сего́дня хоро́ший к.** the fish are biting well today.

кл|ева́ть, юю́, юёшь *impf.* (*of* ⇨**~ю́нуть**) **1** (*о птице*) to peck. **2** (*о рыбе*) to bite; **вчера́ ры́ба не ~ева́ла** the fish were not biting yesterday. **3** (*coll.*): **к. но́сом** to nod (*from drowsiness*).

кл|ева́ться, ~юётся *impf.* to peck (one another).

кле́вер, а *m.* (*bot.*) clover.

кле́вер|ный *adj. of* ⇨**~**

клеве́т|а́, ы *f.* slander; (*в печати*) libel; **возвести́ на кого́-н. ~у́** to cast aspersions on s.o.

клеве|та́ть, щу́, ~щешь *impf.* (*of* ⇨**на~**) (**на**+*a.*) to slander; (*в печати*) to libel.

клеветни́к, а́ *m.* slanderer.

клеветн|и́ца, и́цы *f. of* ⇨**~и́к**

клеветни́ческ|ий *adj.* slanderous; libellous; **~ая кампа́ния** smear campaign.

клеве|щу́, ~щешь *see* ⇨**~та́ть**

клев|о́к, ка́ *m.* (*coll.*) peck.

клевре́т, а *m.* minion, creature.

клёвый *adj.* (*sl.*) brill, knockout, fantastic.

кле|ево́й *adj. of* ⇨**~й; ~ева́я кра́ска** size paint.

клеёнк|а, и *f.* oil-cloth.

клеёнчатый *adj.* oilskin.

кле́|ить, ю, ишь *impf.* (*pf.* **с~**) **1** to glue; to gum; to paste. **2**: **к. де́вушку** (*sl.*) to pick up a girl.

кле́|иться, ится *impf.* (*coll.*) **1** to become sticky. **2** (*fig.*; *usu. with neg.*) to get on, go well; **моя́ рабо́та не ~ится** my work is not going too well. **3** *pass. of* ⇨**~ить**

кле|й, я, о ~е, на ~ю́ *m.* glue; **мучно́й к.** paste; **пти́чий к.** bird-lime; **ры́бий к.** isinglass; fish-glue.

кле́йк|а, и *f.* glueing.

кле́йк|ий *adj.* sticky; **~ая ле́нта** adhesive tape.

клейкови́н|а, ы *f.* gluten.

кле́йкост|ь, и *f.* stickiness.

клеймёный *adj.* branded.

клейм|и́ть, лю́, и́шь *impf.* (*of* ⇨**за~**) to brand, stamp; (*fig.*) to brand, stigmatize; **к. позо́ром** to hold up to shame.

клеймле́ни|е, я *nt.* branding, stamping.

клейм|о́, а́, *pl.* **~а** *nt.* brand, stamp; **проби́рное к.** hall-mark; **фабри́чное к.** trade-mark; **к. позо́ра** (*fig.*) stigma.

кле́йстер, а *m.* paste.

клёкот, а *m.* screech.

клеко|та́ть, чу́, ~чешь *impf.* to screech.

клема́тис, а *m.* clematis.

кле́мм|а, ы *f.* (*elec.*) terminal.

клён, а *m.* maple.

кленóвый *adj. of* ⇨**клён**

клепа́льн|ый *adj.* riveting; **~ая маши́на** riveter, riveting machine.

клепа́льщик, а *m.* riveter (*operator*).

клёпаный *adj.* (*tech.*) riveted.

клепа́|ть[1], ю *impf.* (*tech.*) to rivet.

клеп|а́ть[2], лю́, ~лешь *impf.* (*of* ⇨**наклепа́ть**) (**на**+*a.*; *coll.*) to slander, cast aspersions (on).

клёпк|а[1], и *f.* (*действие*) riveting.

клёпк|а[2], и *f.* barrel stave; (*fig., coll.*): **у него́ одно́й ~и не хвата́ет** he has got a screw loose.

клептома́н, а *m.* kleptomaniac.

клептома́ни|я, и *f.* kleptomania.

клептома́н|ка, ки *f. of* ⇨**~**

клерикали́зм, а *m.* (*pol.*) clericalism.

клёст, а́ *m.* (*zool.*) crossbill.

клéтк|а, и *f.* **1** cage; (*для кур*) coop; (*для кроликов*) hutch. **2** (*на бумаге*) square; (*на ткани*) check. **3** (*anat.*): **грудна́я к.** thorax. **4** (*biol.*) cell.

клету́шк|а, и *f.* (*coll.*) closet, tiny room.

клетча́тк|а, и *f.* **1** (*bot., tech.*) cellulose. **2** (*anat.*) cellular tissue.

кле́тчатый *adj.* checked; **к. плато́к** checked head-scarf.

клет|ь, и, *pl.* **~и, ~е́й** *f.* **1** (*dial.*) (*кладовая*) store-room; shed. **2** (*в шахте*) cage.

клёцк|а, и *f.* (*cul.*) dumpling.

клёш, а *m.* (*and indecl. adj.*) flare; **брю́ки-к.** flared trousers, bell-bottomed trousers; **ю́бка-к.** flared skirt.

клешн|я́, и́, *g. pl.* **~е́й** *f.* claw, pincer.

клещ, а́ *m.* (*zool.*) tick.

клещ|и́, е́й *no sg.* **1** pincers, tongs; (*fig., coll.*): **э́того из меня́ ~а́ми не вы́тянешь** wild horses shall not drag it from me. **2** (*mil.*; *fig.*) pincers, pincer-movement.

кли́вер, а *m.* (*naut.*) jib.

клие́нт, а *m.* client.

клие́нт|ка, ки *f. of* ⇨**~**

клиенту́р|а, ы *f.* (*collect.*) clientèle.

кли́зм|а, ы *f.* (*med.*) enema; **ста́вить ~у** (+*d.*) to give (s.o.) an enema.

клик, а *m.* (*poet.*) cry, call.

кли́к|а, и *f.* clique.

кли́|кать, чу, чешь *impf.* (*of* ⇨**~кнуть**) **1** (*coll.*) (*призывать*) to call, hail. **2** (+*a. and i.*; *coll.*) (*называть*) to call (*name*); **его́ ~чут Ива́ном** he is called Ivan. **3** (*о птицах*) to honk.

кли́к|нуть, ну, нешь *pf. of* ⇨**~ать**

клику́ш|а, и *f.* hysterical woman.

клику́шеств|овать, ую *impf.* **1** to be hysterical. **2** (*fig.*) to stir up panic.

кли́макс, а *m.* = **климакте́рий**

климакте́ри|й, я *m.* menopause.

климактери́ческий *adj.* menopausal; **к. пери́од** menopause.

кли́мат, а *m.* climate.

климати́ческий *adj.* climatic.

клин, а, *pl.* **~ья, ~ьев** *m.* **1** wedge; **загна́ть к.** (**в**+*a.*) to drive a wedge (into); **борода́ ~ом** wedge-shaped beard; (*fig.*): **вбить к. (ме́жду)** to drive a wedge (between); **к. ~ом вышиба́ется** (*prov.*) like cures like; **свет не ~ом сошёлся**

there are plenty more fish in the sea. **2** (*archit.*) quoin. **3** (*кусок ткани*) gore; gusset.

кли́ник|а, и *f.* clinic.

клиници́ст, а *m.* clinician.

клини́ческий *adj.* clinical.

клинови́д|ный (~ен, ~на) *adj.* wedge-shaped; V-shaped.

клин|о́к, ка́ *m.* blade.

клинообра́з|ный (~ен, ~на) *adj.* wedge-shaped; **~ные письмена́** cuneiform characters.

клинопи́сный *adj.* cuneiform.

кли́нопис|ь, и *f.* cuneiform (characters, text).

кли́ныш|ек, ка *m.*: **боро́дка ~ком** goatee.

клип, а *m.* advertising video.

кли́пер, а *m.* (*naut.*) clipper.

кли́пс|ы, ~ *or* **ов** *pl.* (*sg.* **~, ~а** *m. or* **~а, ~ы** *f.*) clip-on earrings; clip-ons.

клир, а *m.* (*collect.*; *eccl.*) the clergy (*of a parish*).

кли́ринг, а *m.* (*fin.*) clearing, clearance.

кли́рос, а *m.* choir (*part of church*).

кли́тор, а *m.* (*anat.*) clitoris.

клич, а *m.* (*rhet.*) call; **боево́й к.** war-cry; **кли́кнуть к.** to issue a call.

кли́чк|а, и *f.* **1** (*домашнего животного*) name. **2** (*человека*) nickname.

клише́ *nt. indecl.* (*typ. and fig.*) cliché.

клиши́рованный *adj.* clichéd.

клоа́к|а, и *f.* cesspit, sewer (*also fig.*).

клобу́к, а́ *m.* (*eccl.*) klobuk (*headgear of Orthodox monk*).

клозе́т, а *m.* (*coll.*) water closet, W.C.

клок, а́, *pl.* **кло́чья, кло́чьев** *and* **~и́, ~о́в** *m.* **1** (*обрывок*) rag, shred; **разорва́ть в кло́чья** to tear to shreds, tatters. **2** (*пучок*) tuft, **к. се́на** wisp of hay.

кло́кот, а *no pl., m.* bubbling; gurgling.

клокота́ни|е, я *nt.* bubbling; gurgling.

клоко|та́ть, чу́, ~́чешь *impf.* to bubble; to gurgle; (*кипеть*) to boil up (*also fig.*); **в нём всё ~та́ло от гне́ва** he was seething with rage.

клон, а *m.* (*biol. etc.*) clone.

клони́р|овать, ую *impf. and pf.* to clone.

клон|и́ть, ю́, ~́ишь *impf.* **1** to bend; to incline; (*impers.*): **ло́дку ~и́ло на́ бок** the boat was heeling; **старика́ уже́ ~и́ло ко сну́** the old man was already nodding off. **2** (*fig., coll.*) to lead (*conversation*); **куда́ ты ~́ишь?** what are you driving at?

клон|и́ться, ю́сь, ~́ишься *impf.* **1** to bow, bend (*intrans.*). **2** (**к**+*d., fig.*) to be nearing; to be leading up (to), be heading (for); **день ~и́лся к ве́черу** the day was declining; **де́ло ~́ится к развя́зке** the affair is coming to a head; **к чему́ э́то ~́ится?** what is it leading up to?

клоп, а́ *m.* bedbug.

клопо́вник, а *m.* (*coll.*) bug-infested place.

клоп|о́вый *adj. of* ⇒**~**

кло́ун, а *m.* clown.

клоуна́д|а, ы *f.* clownery, clowning; clown acts.

кло́ун|ский *adj. of* ⇒**~; к. колпа́к** fool's cap.

клох|та́ть, чу́, ~́чешь *impf.* (*coll.*) to cluck.

клочкова́т|ый (~, ~а) *adj.* **1** (*шерсть*) tufted, shaggy. **2** (*стиль*) patchy, scrappy.

клоч|о́к, ка́ *m. dim. of* ⇒**клок; разорва́ть в ~ки́** to tear to shreds, tatters; **к. бума́ги** scrap of paper; **к. земли́** plot of land; **к. лазу́ри среди́ облако́в** a patch of blue sky between the clouds.

клуб¹, а *m.* **1** (*общество*) club; **к. люби́телей бе́га** jogging club; **к. здоро́вья** keep-fit club; **к. одино́ких серде́ц** Lonely Hearts Club. **2** (*здание*) club-house; **офице́рский к.** officers' mess.

клуб², а, *pl.* **~ы́, ~о́в** *m.* (*дыма*) puff; **~ы́ пы́ли** clouds of dust.

клу́б|ень, ня *m.* (*bot.*) tuber.

клуб|и́ть, и́т *impf.* to blow up, puff out; **к. пыль** to raise clouds of dust.

клуб|и́ться, и́тся *impf.* to swirl; to curl, wreathe.

клубнево́й *adj.* (*bot.*) tuberose.

клубни́к|а, и *f.* **1** (*растение*) (cultivated) strawberry. **2** (*collect.*) (cultivated) strawberries.

клубни́|чный *adj. of* ⇒**~ка; ~чное варе́нье** strawberry preserve.

клу́б|ный *adj. of* ⇒**~¹**

клуб|о́к, ка́ *m.* **1** ball; **сверну́ться ~ко́м, в к.** to roll o.s. up into a ball. **2** (*fig.*) (*запутанное сцепление чего-н.*) tangle, mass; **к. интри́г** network of intrigue; **к. противоре́чий** mass of contradictions. **3** (*fig.*) (*в горле*) lump; **у неё к. подступи́л к го́рлу** a lump rose in her throat.

клу́мб|а, ы *f.* (flower-)bed.

клу́ш|а, и *f.* **1** (*dial.*) broody hen. **2** (*человек*) clumsy person.

клык, а́ *m.* **1** (*у человека*) canine (tooth). **2** (*у животного*) fang; (*бивень*) tusk.

клюв, а *m.* beak; bill.

клюк|а́, и́ *f.* walking-stick.

клю́к|ать, аю *impf. of* ⇒**~нуть**

клю́кв|а, ы *f.* **1** (*растение*) cranberry. **2** (*collect.*) cranberries.

клю́кв|енный *adj. of* ⇒**~а; к. кисе́ль** cranberry jelly; **к. морс** cranberry drink.

клю́к|нуть, ну, нешь *pf.* (*of* ⇒**~ать**) (*coll.*) to take a drop.

клю́н|уть, у, ешь *pf. of* ⇒**клева́ть**

ключ¹, а́ *m.* **1** (*in var. senses*) key; **запере́ть на к.** to lock; **га́ечный к.** spanner, wrench; **францу́зский к.** monkey-wrench; **к.-шестигра́нник** Allen key; **к. к ши́фру** key to a cipher. **2** (*archit.*) keystone. **3** (*mus.*) key, clef; **басо́вый к.** bass clef; **скрипи́чный к.** treble clef.

ключ², а́ *m.* (*источник*) spring; source; **кипе́ть ~о́м** to bubble over; **бить ~о́м** to spout, jet; (*fig.*) to be in full swing.

ключ|ево́й¹ *adj. of* ⇒**~¹**; **~евы́е о́трасли промы́шленности** key industries; (*mil.*): **~евы́е пози́ции** key positions; **~ево́е сло́во** keyword; (*mus.*): **к. знак** clef.

ключ|ево́й² *adj. of* ⇒**~²**; **~ева́я вода́** spring water.

ключи́ц|а, ы *f.* (*anat.*) collar-bone.

клю́шк|а, и *f.* (*гольф*) (golf-)club; (*хоккей*) (hockey) stick; (*coll.*) walking-stick.

кл|юю́, юёшь *see* ⇒**~ева́ть**

кля́кс|а, ы *f.* blot, smudge.

кля|ну́, нёшь *see* ⇒**~сть**

кля́нч|ить, у, ишь *impf.* (*coll.*) (**у**+*g.*) to pester, nag (*s.o. for*); **к. де́ньги у кого́-н.** to pester s.o. for money.

кляп, а *m.* gag; **засу́нуть к. в рот** (+*d.*) to gag.

кля|сть, ну́, нёшь, *past* **~л, ~ла́, ~́ло** *impf.* to curse.

кля́|сться, ну́сь, нёшься, *past* **~лся, ~ла́сь** *impf.* (*of* ⇒**по~**) (**в**+*p.*, +*inf. or* +**что**) to swear, vow; **к. в ве́рности** to swear allegiance; **к. отомсти́ть** to vow vengeance; **к. че́стью** to swear on one's honour (*Br.*), honor (*US*).

кля́тв|а, ы *f.* oath, vow; **к. Гиппокра́та** Hippocratic oath; **ло́жная к.** perjury; **дать ~у** to take an oath.

кля́тв|енный *adj. of* ⇒**~а; дать ~енное обеща́ние** to promise on oath.

клятвопреступле́ни|е, я *nt.* perjury.

клятвопресту́пник, а *m.* perjurer.

кля́уз|а, ы *f.* (*coll.*) petty slander, malicious gossip.

кля́узник, а *m.* (*coll.*) scandalmonger; gossip.

кля́узнича|ть, ю *impf.* (*of* ⇒**на~**) (*coll.*) to spread slander; to gossip.

кля́узн|ый *adj.* (*coll.*) (*придирчивый*) captious, pettifogging; **~ое де́ло** malicious litigation.

кля́ч|а, и *f.* (*pej.*) (*лошадь*) (old) nag.

км (*abbr. of* **киломе́тр**) km, kilometre(s) (*Br.*), kilometer(s) (*US*).

КНДР *f. indecl.* (*abbr. of* ***Коре́йская Наро́дно-Демократи́ческая Респу́блика***) Korean People's Democratic Republic.

кне́л|и, ей *pl.* (*cul.*) quenelles.

кнел|ь, и *f.* (*collect.*; *cul.*) = **кне́ли**

кни́г|а, и *f.* book; **тебе́ и ~и в ру́ки** (*coll.*) you know best.

книгове́дени|е, я *nt.* bibliography.

книгоизда́тел|ь, я *m.* publisher.

книгоизда́тельский *adj.* publishing.

книгоизда́тельств|о, а *nt.* **1** (*заведение*) publishing-house. **2** (*действие*) publishing.

книголю́б, а *m.* bibliophile.

книгопеча́тани|е, я *nt.* (book-)printing.

книготорго́в|ец, ца *m.* bookseller.

книготорго́вл|я, и *f.* book trade.

К

книгохрани́лищ|е, а *nt.* **1** (*библиотека*) library. **2** (*в библиотеке*) book-stack.

кни́жечк|а, и *f.* booklet.

кни́жк|а, и *f.* **1** *dim. of* ⇨**книга; записна́я к.** notebook; **к.-календа́рь** pocket diary. **2** (*документ*) book, card; **забо́рная к.** ration book; **расчётная к.** pay-book; **че́ковая к.** cheque-book (*Br.*), check-book (*US*). **3**: **(сберега́тельная) к.** savings-bank book; **положи́ть де́ньги на ~у** to deposit money at a savings bank.

кни́жник, а *m.* **1** (*bibl.*) scribe. **2** (*любитель книг*) bibliophile. **3** (*торговец книгами*) bookseller.

кни́жн|ый *adj.* **1** *adj. of* ⇨**кни́га; к. знак** book-plate; **~ая по́лка** bookshelf; **к. шкаф** bookcase. **2** (*отвлечённый*) bookish; **~ая учёность** book-learning; **к. червь** bookworm.

кни́зу *adv.* downwards.

кни́ксен, а *m.* curts(e)y.

кно́пк|а, и *f.* **1** (*гвоздик*) drawing-pin (*Br.*), thumbtack (*US*); **прикрепи́ть ~ой** to pin. **2** (*застёжка*) press-stud, popper (*Br.*), snap (*US*). **3** (*elec.*) button; knob; **нажа́ть все ~и** (*fig., coll.*) to pull wires, do all in one's power.

кно́п|очный *adj. of* ⇨**~ка; к. телефо́н** push-button telephone.

КНР *f. indecl.* (*abbr. of* ***Кита́йская Наро́дная Респу́блика***) People's Republic of China.

кнут, а́ *m.* whip; **щёлкать ~о́м** to crack a whip; **поли́тика ~а́ и пря́ника** (*pol.*) carrot and stick policy.

кнутови́щ|е, а *nt.* whip-handle.

княги́н|я, и *f.* princess (*wife of prince*).

кня́жеств|о, а *nt.* principality.

кня́ж|ить, у, ишь *impf.* (*hist.*) to reign.

кня́жич, а *m.* prince (*prince's unmarried son*).

княж|на́, ны́, *g. pl.* **~о́н** *f.* princess (*prince's unmarried daughter*).

княз|ёк, ька́ *m.* **1** (*coll.*) princeling. **2** (*tech.*) roof-ridge.

княз|ь, я, *pl.* **~ья́, ~е́й** *m.* prince; **вели́кий к.** grand duke.

К° (*abbr. of* ***компа́ния***) Co., Company.

ко *see* ⇨**к**

коагуля́ци|я, и *f.* coagulation.

коалиц|ио́нный *adj. of* ⇨**~́ия**

коали́ци|я, и *f.* (*pol.*) coalition.

ко́бальт, а *m.* (*chem.*) cobalt.

ко́бальт|овый *adj. of* ⇨**~**

кобе́л|ь, я́ *m.* **1** (*male*) dog. **2** (*coll.*) lech(er).

кобе́н|иться, юсь, ишься *impf.* (*coll.*) to be capricious; to make faces.

ко́бз|а́, ~ы *f.* kobza (*Ukrainian musical instrument similar to guitar*).

кобза́р|ь, я́ *m.* kobza-player.

КОБО́Л, а *m.* (*comput.*) COBOL.

ко́бр|а, ы *f.* cobra.

кобур|а́, ы́ *f.* holster.

ко́бчик, а *m.* (*zool.*) merlin.

кобы́л|а, ы *f.* (*лошадь*) mare.

кобы́л|ий *adj. of* ⇨**~а**

кобы́лк|а¹, и *f.* (*лошадь*) filly.

кобы́лк|а², и *f.* (*mus.*) bridge (*of stringed instruments*).

ко́ваный *adj.* **1** forged; hammered. **2** (*fig.*) terse.

кова́р|ный (~ен, ~на) *adj.* crafty; treacherous.

кова́рств|о, а *nt.* craftiness; treachery.

кова́ть, кую́, куёшь *impf.* **1** (*pf.* **вы́~**) to forge (*also fig.*); (*железо*) to hammer; **к. побе́ду** to forge victory; **куй желе́зо, пока́ горячо́** (*prov.*) strike while the iron is hot. **2** (*pf.* **под~**) to shoe (*horses*).

ковбо́|й, я *m.* cowboy.

ковбо́йк|а, и *f.* (*coll.*) cowboy shirt.

ковбо́й|ский *adj. of* **~; к. фильм** western (*film*).

ков|ёр, ра́ *m.* carpet; (*маленький*) rug; mat; **к.-самолёт** magic carpet; **вы́звать на к.** (*coll.*) to call to account.

кове́рка|ть, ю *impf.* (*of* ⇨**ис~**) **1** (*портить*) to spoil, ruin. **2** (*fig.*) (*искажать*) to distort; to mangle, mispronounce; **к. чужу́ю мысль** to distort s.o. else's ideas; **к. слова́** to mangle words; **он ~ет францу́зский язы́к** he murders the French language.

ко́вк|а, и *f.* **1** forging. **2** (*лошадей*) shoeing.

ко́в|кий (~ок, ~ка́, ~ко) *adj.* malleable, ductile.

ко́вкост|ь, и *f.* malleability, ductility.

коври́г|а, и *f.* loaf.

коври́жк|а, и *f.* gingerbread; **ни за каки́е ~и** (*coll.*) not for love nor money.

ко́врик, а *m.* rug; **к. для ва́нной** bath mat.

ковро́вый *adj. of* ⇨**ковёр**

ковроочисти́тел|ь, я *m.* carpet cleaner.

коврочи́стк|а, и *f.* carpet sweeper.

ковче́г, а *m.* ark; **Но́ев к.** Noah's ark.

ковш, а́ *m.* **1** scoop, ladle. **2** (*tech.*) bucket.

ковы́л|ь, я́ *m.* (*bot.*) feather-grass.

ковыля́|ть, ю *impf.* (*coll.*) to hobble; (*о ребёнке*) to toddle.

ковыр|ну́ть, ну́, нёшь *pf. of* ⇨**~я́ть**

ковыр|я́ть, я́ю *impf.* (*of* ⇨**~ну́ть**) to dig into; (**в** + *p.*) to pick (at); **к. в зуба́х** to pick one's teeth.

ковыря́|ться, юсь *impf.* (*coll.*) **1** (**в** + *p.*) (*копаться*) to poke about (in). **2** (*медлить*) to tinker, potter about.

когда́¹ *adv.* **1** (*interrog. and rel.*) when; (*coll.*): **есть к.!** there's no time for it!; **есть к. мне болта́ть!** I've no time for talk! **2**: **к. (бы) ни** whenever; **к. бы вы ни пришли́, к. (вы) ни придёте** whenever you come. **3** (*coll.*): **к. . . ., к.** sometimes . . . sometimes; **я занима́юсь к. у́тром, к. ве́чером** sometimes I work in the morning, sometimes in the evening. **4** (*coll.*): **к. как** it depends. **5** (*coll.*) = **когда́-нибудь**

когда́² *conj.* **1** when; while, as; **я её встре́тил, к. шёл домо́й** I met her as I was going home. **2** (*coll.*) (*если*) if; **к. так, согла́сен с тобо́й** if that is the case, I agree.

когда́-либо *adv.* = **когда́-нибудь**

когда́-нибудь *adv.* **1** (*в будущем*) some time, some day. **2** (*в вопросах*) ever; **вы бы́ли к.-н. в Кита́е?** have you ever been to China?

когда́-то *adv.* **1** (*в прошлом*) once; some time; formerly. **2** (*в будущем*) some day (*indefinitely distant*); **к.-то ещё бу́дет тако́й прия́тный ве́чер** it will be a long time before we have such a pleasant evening again.

кого́ *a. and g. of* ⇨**кто**

кого́рт|а, ы *f.* cohort.

ко́г|оть, тя, *pl.* **~ти, ~те́й** *m.* claw; talon; **показа́ть свой ~ти** (*fig.*) to show one's teeth; **попа́сть в ~ти (к кому́-н.)** to fall into the clutches (of s.o.).

когти́ст|ый (~, ~а) *adj.* sharp-clawed.

ког|ти́ть, чу́, ти́шь *impf.* (*dial.*) to claw to pieces, tear with claws.

код, а *m.* code; **персона́льный к.** personal identification number, PIN; **по ~́у** in code.

ко́д|а, ы *f.* (*mus.*) coda.

кодеи́н, а *m.* (*pharm.*) codeine.

ко́декс, а *m.* (*leg. and fig.*) code; **мора́льный к.** moral code; **уголо́вный к.** criminal code.

коди́р|овать, ую *impf. and pf.* (*pf. also* **за~**) to encode.

кодифика́ци|я, и *f.* codification.

кодифици́р|овать, ую *impf. and pf.* (*leg.*) to codify.

ко́дл|а, ы *f.* (*sl.*) gang, band.

ко́дов|ый *adj. of* ⇨**код; ~ое назва́ние** code-name.

кодоско́п, а *m.* overhead projector.

ко́е-где́ (*and coll.* **кой-где́**) *adv.* here and there, in places.

ко́е-ка́к (*and coll.* **кой-ка́к**) *adv.* **1** (*плохо, небрежно*) anyhow. **2** (*с трудом*) somehow (or other), just; **к.-к. мы доплы́ли до того́ бе́рега** somehow we managed to swim to the other side.

ко́е-како́й (*and coll.* **кой-како́й**), **ко́е-како́го** *pron.* some.

ко́е-кто́ (*and coll.* **кой-кто́**), **ко́е-кого́** *pron.* somebody; some people.

ко́ечный *adj. of* ⇨**ко́йка; к. больно́й** in-patient.

ко́е-что́ (*and coll.* **кой-что́**), **ко́е-чего́** *pron.* something; (*немного*) a little.

ко́ж|а, и *f.* **1** (*у человека и животных*) skin; (*у крупных животных*) hide; (*anat.*) cutis; **гуси́ная к.** goose-flesh; (*fig., coll.*): **из ~и (вон) лезть** to go all out, do one's utmost; **к. да ко́сти** skin and bone. **2** (*материал*) leather; **свина́я к.** pig-skin; **теля́чья к.** calf. **3** (*плодов*) peel, rind; (*bot.*) epidermis.

ко́жанк|а, и *f.* (*coll.*) (*куртка*) leather jacket; (*пальто*) leather coat.

ко́жаный *adj.* leather.

кожгалантере́|я, и *f.* leather goods.

коже́венный *adj.* leather; tanning; **к. заво́д** tannery; **к. това́р** leather goods.

коже́вник, а *m.* currier, leather-dresser, tanner.

кожзамени́тел|ь, я *m.* imitation leather, leatherette.

кожими́т, а *m.* (*obs.*) imitation leather, leatherette.

ко́жиц|а, ы *f.* **1** (*тонкая кожа*) thin skin; **к. колбасы́** sausage-skin. **2** (*плодов*) peel, skin.

ко́жник, а *m.* (*coll.*) dermatologist.

ко́жный *adj.* skin; (*med.*) cutaneous.

кожур|а́, ы́ *f.* rind, peel, skin.

кожу́х, а́ *m.* **1** (*одежда*) sheepskin jacket. **2** (*tech.*) (*обшивка*) housing, casing, jacket.

коз|а́, ы́, *pl.* **~ы** *f.* **1** (*вид козлов*) goat. **2** (*самка козла*) nanny-goat. **3** (*coll.*) (*бойкая девочка*) tomboy.

коз|ёл, ла́ *m.* (*животное*) billy-goat; (*гимнастический снаряд*) horse; (*болван*) (*sl.*) prat (*Br.*), jerk (*US*); (*мерзавец*) (*sl.*) bastard; **к. отпуще́ния** scapegoat; **от него́ как от ~ла́ молока́** he is good for nothing.

козеро́г, а *m.* **1** (*zool.*) wild (mountain) goat, ibex. **2 К.** (*созвездие*) Capricorn; **тро́пик К~а** (*geog.*) Tropic of Capricorn.

ко́з|ий *adj. of* ⇒**~а́; ~ье молоко́** goat's milk.

козл|ёнок, ёнка, *pl.* **~я́та, ~я́т** *m.* kid.

коз|ли́ный *adj. of* ⇒**~ёл; ~ли́ная боро́дка** goatee; **к. го́лос** reedy voice.

козло́вый *adj.* goatskin.

ко́з|лы, ел, лам *no sg.* **1** (*сиденье*) (coach-)box. **2** (*подставка*) trestle(s); saw-horse.

козл|я́та, я́т *see* ⇒**~ёнок**

ко́зн|и, ей *pl.* (*sg.* (*rare*) **~ь, ~и** *f*) machinations, intrigues.

козово́д, а *m.* goat breeder.

козово́дств|о, а *nt.* goat-breeding.

козодо́|й, я *m.* (*zool.*) nightjar.

козу́л|я, и *f.* roe(buck).

козыр|ёк, ька́ *m.* (cap) peak; **взять под к.** (+*d.*) to salute.

козырно́й *adj. of* ⇒**ко́зырь**

козыр|ну́ть, ну́, нёшь *pf. of* ⇒**~я́ть**

ко́зыр|ь, я, *pl.* **~и, ~е́й** *m.* (*cards and fig.*) trump; **откры́ть свои́ ~и** (*fig.*) to lay one's cards on the table; **покры́ть ~ем** to trump; **ходи́ть с ~я** to lead trumps; (*fig.*) to play a trump card; **гла́вный к.** (one's) trump card.

козыр|я́ть[1], я́ю *impf.* (*of* ⇒**~ну́ть**) (*coll.*) **1** (*cards*) to lead trumps, play a trump; (*fig.*) to play one's trump card. **2** (+*i.*) (*хвастаться*) to show off.

козыр|я́ть[2], я́ю *impf.* (*of* ⇒**~ну́ть**) (+*d.*; *coll.*) to salute.

козя́вк|а, и *f.* (*coll.*) small insect, bug.

ко́итус, а *m.* coition, coitus; **к. прерыва́емый** coitus interruptus.

кой *interrog. and rel. pron.* (*obs.*) which; **до ко́их пор?** how long?; **ни в ко́ем слу́чае** on no account; (*coll.*): **на к. чёрт?** why in the world; what the devil for?

ко́йк|а, и *f.* **1** (*на судне*) berth, bunk. **2** (*в больнице*) bed.

койо́т, а *m.* coyote.

кок, а *m.* **1** (*повар*) (ship's) cook. **2** (*вихор*) quiff.

ко́к|а, и *f.* (*bot.*) coca.

кокаи́н, а *m.* cocaine.

кокаини́ст, а *m.* cocaine addict.

кокаини́ст|ка, ки *f. of* ⇒**~**

ко́ка-ко́л|а, ы *f.* Coca-Cola (*propr.*).

кока́рд|а, ы *f.* cockade.

ко́к|ать, аю *impf.* (*of* ⇒**~нуть**) (*coll.*) to crack, break.

ко́кер-спанье́л|ь, я *m.* cocker spaniel.

коке́тк|а, и *f.* coquette, flirt.

коке́тлив|ый (~, ~а) *adj.* coquettish, flirtatious.

коке́тнича|ть, ю *impf.* **1** (**с**+*i.*) to coquet(te), flirt (with). **2** (+*i.*) to show off, flaunt.

коке́тств|о, а *nt.* coquetry, flirting.

кокк, а *m.* (*med.*) coccus.

коклю́ш, а *m.* whooping-cough.

ко́к|нуть, ну, нешь *pf. of* ⇒**~ать**

ко́кон, а *m.* cocoon.

коко́с, а *m.* **1** (*дерево*) coconut palm. **2** (*плод*) coconut.

коко́с|овый *adj. of* ⇒**~; ~овое волокно́** coir; **~овое ма́сло** coconut oil; **к. оре́х** coconut; **~овая па́льма** coconut palm.

коко́тк|а, и *f.* courtesan.

кокс, а *m.* coke.

ко́кс|овый *adj. of* ⇒**~; ~овая печь** coke oven.

коксу́ющийся *adj.*: **к. у́голь** coking coal.

кокте́йл|ь, я *m.* cocktail; (*встреча*) cocktail party; **моло́чный к.** milk shake.

кол, а́ *m.* **1** (*pl.* **~ья, ~ьев**) stake, picket; **сажа́льный к.** dibber; **посади́ть на́ к.** to impale; (*coll.*): **стоя́ть ~о́м в го́рле** to stick in one's throat; **ему́ хоть к. на голове́ теши́** he is very pig-headed; **у него́ нет ни ~а́ ни двора́** he has neither house nor home. **2** (*pl.* **~ы́, ~о́в**) (*coll.*) (*низшая школьная отметка*) a 'very poor' (*mark*).

кол... *comb. form, abbr. of* ***коллекти́вный***

ко́лб|а, ы *f.* (*chem.*) retort.

колбас|а́, ы́, *pl.* **~ы** *f.* sausage; **кровяна́я к.** black pudding.

колба́сник, а *m.* sausage-maker.

колба́с|ный *adj. of* ⇒**~а́**

колго́т|ки, ок *no sg.* tights.

колдо́бин|а, ы *f.* (*coll.*) rut, pothole (*in road*).

колд|ова́ть, у́ю *impf.* to practise witchcraft.

колдовско́й *adj.* magical; (*fig.*) magical, bewitching.

колдовств|о́, а́ *nt.* witchcraft, sorcery, magic.

колду́н, а́ *m.* sorcerer, magician, wizard.

колду́н|ья, ьи, *g. pl.* **~ий** *f.* witch, sorceress.

колеба́ни|е, я *nt.* **1** (*phys.*) oscillation, vibration; **к. ма́ятника** swing of the pendulum. **2** (*изменение*) fluctuation, variation. **3** (*fig.*) (*сомнение*) hesitation, wavering, vacillation.

колеба́тельный *adj.* (*tech.*) oscillatory.

колеб|а́ть, ~лю, ~лешь *impf.* (*of* ⇒**по~**) to shake; (*fig.*): **к. обще́ственные усто́и** to shake the foundations of society.

колеб|а́ться, ~люсь, ~лешься *impf.* (*of* ⇒**по~**) **1** to shake to and fro, sway; (*phys.*) to oscillate. **2** (*изменяться*) to fluctuate, vary. **3** (*fig.*) (*не решаться*) to hesitate; to waver, vacillate.

коле́нк|а, и *f.* (*coll.*) knee.

коленко́р, а *m.* (*text.*) calico; (*coll.*): **э́то совсе́м друго́й к.** that's quite another matter.

коленко́р|овый *adj. of* ⇒**~**

коле́н|ный *adj. of* ⇒**~о;** (*anat.*): **к. суста́в** knee-joint; **~ная ча́шка** knee-cap.

коле́н|о, а *nt.* **1** (*pl.* **~и, ~ей, ~ям**) knee; **преклони́ть ~и** to genuflect; **стать на ~и (пе́ред)** to kneel (to); **стоя́ть на ~ях** to be kneeling, be on one's knees; **по к., по ~и** knee-deep, up to one's knees; (*coll.*): **ему́ мо́ре по к.** (*coll.*) he's not afraid of anything; **поста́вить кого́-н. на ~и** to bring s.o. to his knees. **2** (*pl. only*; **~и, ~ей, ~ям**) lap; **сиде́ть у кого́-н. на ~ях** to sit on s.o.'s lap. **3** (*pl.* **~ья, ~ьев**) (*tech.*) knee, joint; (*bot.*) joint, node; **к. трубы́** knee pipe, elbow pipe. **4** (*pl.* **~а, ~, ~ам**) (*изгиб*) bend (*of river, etc.*). **5** (*pl.* **~а, ~, ~ам**) (*поколение*) generation; **ро́дственники до пя́того ~а** cousins five times removed; **двена́дцать ~ изра́илевых** the twelve tribes of Israel. **6** (*pl.* **~а, ~, ~ам**) (*coll.*) (*в музыке*) part; (*в танце*) figure; (*pej.*): **вы́кинуть к.** to do sth. strange and unexpected.

коленопреклоне́ни|е, я *nt.* genuflection.

коле́нчатый *adj.* (*tech.*) elbow-shaped, cranked; **к. вал** crankshaft.

ко́лер, а *m.* (*art*) colour (*Br.*), color (*US*), shade.

колёсик|о, а *nt.* **1** *dim. of* ⇒**колесо́. 2** castor.

коле|си́ть, шу́, си́шь *impf.* (*coll.*) **1** (*много ездить*) to go all over, travel about. **2** (*двигаться не прямым путём*) to go in a haphazard way.

коле́сник, а *m.* wheelwright.

колесни́ц|а, ы *f.* chariot; **погреба́льная к.** hearse.

колёс|ный *adj.* **1** *adj. of* ⇒**~о́.** **2** (*экипаж*) wheeled, on wheels.

колес|о́, а́, *pl.* **~а** *nt.* **1** wheel; **запасно́е к.** spare wheel; **к. обозре́ния** Big Wheel (*fairground attraction*); **рулево́е к.** driving wheel; **цепно́е к.** sprocket; **вста́вить кому́-н. па́лки в ~а** to put a spoke in s.o.'s wheel; **кружи́ться, как бе́лка в ~е́** to run round in circles; **но́ги ~о́м** bandy legs; **кувырка́нье «~о́м»** cartwheel

К

(*acrobatics*); **ходи́ть ~о́м** to cartwheel. **2** *pl.* (*coll.*) (*автомобиль*) transport, a car; **быть на ~́ах** to have (one's own) transport.

коле́ч|ко, ка, *pl.* **~ки, ~ек, ~кам** *nt.* (*coll.*) ringlet.

коле|я́, и́ *f.* **1** rut; (*fig.*): **войти́ в ~ю́** to settle down (again); **вы́битый из ~и́** unsettled. **2** (*rail.*) track; gauge.

ко́ли (*and* **коль)** (*obs. or dial.*) if; (*coll.*): **к. на то пошло́** if it comes to that; if you put it like that; **коль ско́ро** if, as soon as.

коли́бри *c.g. indecl.* (*zool.*) humming-bird.

ко́лик|и, ~ *pl.* (*sg.* **~а, и** *f.*) (*med.*) colic.

коли́т, а *m.* (*med.*) colitis.

коли́чественн|ый *adj.* quantitative; **~ое числи́тельное** cardinal number.

коли́честв|о, а *nt.* quantity, amount; number.

ко́лк|а, и *f.* chopping.

ко́л|кий[1] (~ок, ~ка́ ~ко) *adj.* (*дрова*) easily split.

ко́л|кий[2] (~ок, ~ка́ ~ко) *adj.* (*хвоя*) prickly; (*fig.*) sharp, biting, caustic.

ко́лкост|ь, и *f.* **1** (*fig.*) sharpness. **2** (*замечание*) sharp, caustic remark; **говори́ть ~и** to make sharp remarks.

коллабораციони́ст, а *m.* (*pol.*; *pej.*) collaborator.

коллабораციони́ст|ский *adj. of* ⇒**~**

колла́ж, а *m.* collage.

колла́пс, а *m.* collapse.

колле́г|а, и *c.g.* colleague.

коллегиа́л|ьный (~ен, ~ьна) *adj.* joint, collective; corporate; **~ьное реше́ние** collective decision.

колле́ги|я, и *f.* board; **к. адвока́тов, к. правозасту́пников** the Bar; **к. вы́борщиков** electoral college.

колле́дж, а *m.* college.

колле́жский *adj.* (*in titles of officials in tsarist Russia*) collegiate; **к. сове́тник** collegiate counsellor.

коллекти́в, а *m.* collective, team; (*in many phrr. does not require separate translation*): **нау́чный к.** (the) scientists; **парти́йный к.** Party members.

коллективиза́ци|я, и *f.* collectivization.

коллективизи́р|овать, ую *impf. and pf.* to collectivize.

коллективи́зм, а *m.* collectivism.

коллективи́ст, а *m.* collectivist.

коллективи́стский *adj.* collectivist.

коллекти́в|ный (~ен, ~на) *adj.* collective; joint; **~ное владе́ние** joint ownership; **~ное хозя́йство** collective farm.

колле́ктор, а *m.* **1** (*elec.*) commutator. **2** (*канализационный*) manifold. **3**: **библиоте́чный к.** central library.

коллекционе́р, а *m.* collector.

коллекциони́р|овать, ую *impf.* to collect.

колле́кци|я, и *f.* collection.

ко́лли *c.g. indecl.* collie (*dog*).

колли́зи|я, и *f.* clash, conflict.

колло́ди|й, я *m.* (*chem.*) collodion.

колло́ид, а *m.* (*chem.*) colloid.

колло́идный *adj.* (*chem.*) colloidal.

колло́квиум, а *m.* **1** (*беседа со студентами*) oral examination. **2** (*научное собрание*) colloquium.

колоб|о́к, ка́ *m.* small round loaf.

колобро́|дить, жу, дишь *impf.* (*coll.*) **1** (*блуждать*) to roam, wander; (*слоняться*) to loaf. **2** (*вести себя шумно; озорничать*) to make a noise; to get up to mischief.

коловоро́т, а *m.* (*tech.*) brace.

коловраще́ни|е, я *nt.* turmoil.

коло́д|а[1], ы *f.* **1** (*бревно*) block, log. **2** (*корыто*) (water-)trough.

коло́д|а[2], ы *f.* (*карт*) pack (*of cards*).

коло́де|зный *adj. of* ⇒**~ц**

коло́д|ец, ца *m.* **1** well. **2** (*tech.*) shaft.

коло́дк|а, и *f.* **1** (*для сохранения формы обуви*) boot-tree; (*используемая при шитье обуви*) last. **2** (*tech.*) shoe. **3** (*pl.*; *hist.*) stocks; **наби́ть ~и на́ ноги кому́-н.** to put s.o. in stocks.

кол|о́к, ка́ *m.* (*mus.*) peg.

ко́локол, а, *pl.* **~а́, ~о́в** *m.* bell.

колоко́льный *adj. of* ⇒**ко́локол; к. звон** peal, chime.

колоко́л|ьня, ьни, *g. pl.* **~ен** *f.* bell-tower; (*coll.*): **смотре́ть со свое́й ~ьни на что-н.** to take a narrow, parochial view of sth.

колоко́льчик, а *m.* **1** small bell. **2** (*bot.*) campanula.

Коло́мбо *m. indecl.* Colombo.

колониали́зм, а *m.* colonialism.

колониа́льный *adj.* colonial.

колониза́тор, а *m.* colonizer.

колониза́ци|я, и *f.* colonization.

колонизи́р|овать, ую *impf. and pf.* to colonize.

колониз|ова́ть, у́ю *impf. and pf.* to colonize.

колони́ст, а *m.* colonist.

колони́ст|ка, ки *f. of* ⇒**~**

коло́ни|я, и *f.* colony; settlement.

коло́нк|а, и *f.* **1** *dim. of* ⇒**коло́нна. 2** (*для нагрева воды*) geyser (*Br.*), water heater. **3** (*на улице*) standpipe; water-pump. **4**: **бензи́новая к.** petrol pump (*Br.*), gas pump (*US*). **5** (*столбец*) column; **газе́тная полоса́ в шесть коло́нок** newspaper page with six columns; **к. цифр** column of figures. **6** (*coll.*) (*громкоговоритель*) (loud)speaker.

коло́нн|а, ы *f.* column; (*mil.*) **та́нковая к.** tank column.

колонна́д|а, ы *f.* colonnade.

коло́нный *adj.* columned.

колон|о́к, ка́ *m.* (*zool.*) Siberian weasel, kolinsky; (*мех*) kolinsky.

колонти́тул, а *m.* (*typ.*) running head; header.

колонци́фр|а, ы *f.* (*typ.*) page number.

колора́дский *adj.*: **к. жук** Colorado beetle.

колорату́р|а, ы *f.* (*mus.*) coloratura.

колорату́р|ный *adj. of* ⇒**~а**

колори́ст, а *m.* (*art*) colourist (*Br.*), colorist (*US*).

колори́т, а *m.* colouring, colour (*Br.*); coloring, color (*US*); (*fig.*): **ме́стный к.** local colour (*Br.*), color (*US*); **он прида́л расска́зу о встре́че я́ркий к.** he painted a glowing picture of the encounter.

колори́т|ный (~ен, ~на) *adj.* colourful (*Br.*), colorful (*US*); graphic (*also fig.*).

ко́лос, а, *pl.* **~́ья, ~́ьев** *m.* (*agric.*) ear, spike.

колоси́ст|ый (~, ~а) *adj.* (*agric.*) full of ears.

колос|и́ться, и́тся *impf.* (*agric.*) to form ears.

коло́сс, а *m.* colossus.

колосса́л|ьный (~ен, ~ьна) *adj.* colossal; (*coll.*) terrific, great.

коло|ти́ть, чу́, ~́тишь *impf.* (*of* ⇒**поколоти́ть**) **1** (*impf. only*) (**по** + *d.*, **в** + *a.*) to strike (on); to batter (on), pound (on); **к. в дверь** to bang on the door. **2** (*coll.*) (*бить*) to thrash, beat. **3** (*coll.*) (*разбивать*) to break, smash. **4** (*impf. only*) (*coll.*) to shake; (*impers.*): **его́ ~ти́ла лихора́дка** he was shaking with fever.

коло|ти́ться, чу́сь, ~́тишься *impf.* (*of* ⇒**поколоти́ться**) **1** (*impf. only*) (**о** + *a.*) to beat (against); to strike (against); **к. голово́й об сте́ну** to beat one's head against a wall. **2** (*impf. only*) (*coll.*) to pound; to shake; **се́рдце у неё ~ти́лось** her heart was pounding. **3** (*разбиваться*) to break, smash.

колоту́шк|а, и *f.* **1** (*tech.*) beetle. **2** (*у ночных сторожей*) (*wooden*) rattle.

ко́лот|ый[1] (~, ~а) *p.p.p. of* ⇒**~́ь[1]** *and adj.*; **к. са́хар** chipped sugar.

ко́лот|ый[2] (~, ~а) *p.p.p. of* ⇒**~́ь[2]** *and adj.*; **~ая ра́на** stab.

кол|о́ть[1], ю́, ~́ешь *impf.* (*of* ⇒**расколо́ть**) to break, chop, split; **к. дрова́** to chop wood; **к. оре́хи** to crack nuts.

кол|о́ть[2], ю́, ~́ешь *impf.* **1** (*pf.* **у~**) (*булавкой*) to prick; (*impers.*): **у меня́ ~́ет в боку́** I have a stitch in my side. **2** (*pf.* **за~**) (*ранить, убивать чем-нибудь острым*) to stab. **3** (*pf.* **за~**) (*животных*) to slaughter. **4** (*pf.* **у~**) (*fig.*) to sting, taunt; **к. глаза́ кому́-н.** (+ *i.*) to reproach s.o. with sth.; **пра́вда глаза́ ~́ет** (*prov.*) home truths are unpalatable. **5** (*pf.* **у~**) (*coll.*) (*лекарство, наркотики*) to inject.

ко́лоть|е, я (*and* **колоть|ё, я́**) *nt.* (*coll.*) stitch.

кол|о́ться[1], ю́сь, ~́ешься *impf.*, *pass. of* ⇒**~о́ть[1]**

кол|о́ться[2], ю́сь, ~́ешься *impf.* **1** (*причинять укол*) to prick (*intrans.*). **2** (*coll.*) (*быть наркоманом*) to be a junkie.

колошма́|тить, чу, тишь *impf.* (*of* ⇒**отколошма́тить**) (*coll.*) to beat, thrash.

колпа́к, а́ *m.* **1** cap; **ночно́й к.** nightcap; **шутовско́й к.** fool's cap; **к. колеса́** hubcap. **2** (*лампы*) lamp-shade; (*tech.*) cowl; **стекля́нный к.** bell-glass.

колпач|о́к, ка́ *m.* **1** *dim. of* ⇒**колпа́к. 2** (*калильная сетка*) (gas) mantle. **3** (*контрацептив*) (Dutch) cap (*Br.*), diaphragm.

колумба́ри|й, я *m.* columbarium.

колумби́|ец, йца *m.* Colombian.

колумби́|йка, йки *f. of* ⇒**~ец**

колумби́йский *adj.* Colombian.

Колу́мби|я, и *f.* Colombia.

колу́н, а́ *m.* (wood-)chopper, hatchet.

колупа́|ть, ю *impf.* (*coll.*) to pick, scratch.

колхо́з, а *m.* (*abbr. of* ***коллекти́вное хозя́йство***) collective farm.

колхо́зник, а *m.* member of collective farm.

колхо́зн|ица, ицы *f. of* ⇒**~ик**

колхо́з|ный *adj. of* ⇒**~; к. строй** collective farm system.

колча́н, а *m.* quiver.

колчеда́н, а *m.* (*min.*) pyrites.

колчено́гий *adj.* (*coll.*) **1** (*пёс*) lame. **2** (*стул*) rickety, wobbly.

колыбе́л|ь, и *f.* cradle; (*fig.*): **к. нау́ки** the cradle of learning; **с ~и** from the cradle; **от ~и до моги́лы** from the cradle to the grave.

колыбе́ль|ный *adj. of* ⇒**~; ~ная (пе́сня)** lullaby.

колыма́г|а, и *f.* (*obs.*) (*экипаж*) heavy, unwieldy carriage; (*coll.*) (*повозка*) old banger.

колы|ха́ть, ~шу, ~шешь *impf.* (*of* ⇒**~хну́ть**) to sway, rock.

колы|ха́ться, ~шется *impf.* (*of* ⇒**~хну́ться**) (*о ветках*) to sway; (*о море*) to heave; (*о флагах*) to flutter.

колых|ну́ть(ся), ну́(сь), нёшь(ся) *pf. of* ⇒**~а́ть(ся)**

ко́лыш|ек, ка *m.* peg.

коль *see* ⇒**ко́ли**

колье́ *m. indecl.* necklace.

коль|ну́ть, ьну́, ьнёшь *inst. pf. of* ⇒**~о́ть**^{2}

кольра́би *f. indecl.* (*bot.*) kohlrabi.

кольт, а *m.* colt (*pistol*).

кольц|ева́ть, у́ю *impf.* **1** (*of* ⇒**закольцева́ть**) (*дерево*) to girdle, ring-bark. **2** (*of* ⇒**окольцева́ть**) (*птицу*) to ring.

кольцев|о́й *adj.* annular; circular; **~а́я доро́га** ring road; **~а́я развя́зка** roundabout.

кольцеобра́з|ный (~ен, ~на) *adj.* ring-shaped.

кол|ьцо́ ~ьца́, *pl.* **~ьца, ~е́ц, ~ьцам** *nt.* ring; **сверну́ться ~ьцо́м** to coil up; **годи́чное к.** (*bot.*) ring; **обруча́льное к.** wedding ring; **трамва́йное к.** terminus.

ко́льчат|ый *adj.* annulate; **~ые че́рви** (*zool.*) Annelida.

кольчу́г|а, и *f.* shirt of mail, hauberk.

колю́ч|ий (~, ~а) *adj.* prickly; thorny; (*fig.*) sharp, biting; **~ая и́згородь** prickly hedge; **~ая про́волока** barbed wire; **к. язы́к** sharp tongue.

колю́чк|а, и *f.* (*coll.*) prickle; thorn; (*у ежа*) quill.

ко́люшк|а, и *f.* (*fish*) stickleback.

ко́л|ющий *pres. part. act. of* ⇒**~о́ть**^{2} *and adj.*; **~ющая боль** shooting pain.

коляд|а́, ы́ *f.* kolyada (*custom of house-to-house Christmas carol-singing*).

коляд|ова́ть, у́ю *impf.* to go round carol-singing.

коля́ск|а, и *f.* **1** (*экипаж*) carriage. **2**: (**де́тская**) **к.** pram (*Br.*), baby carriage (*US*); (*раскладная*) pushchair (*Br.*), stroller (*US*); **инвали́дная к.** wheelchair. **3** (*у мотоцикла*) side-car.

ком^{1}**, а,** *pl.* **~ья, ~ьев** *m.* lump; ball; **сне́жный к.** snow-ball; (*fig.*): **к. в го́рле** lump in the throat; **пе́рвый блин ~ом** (*prov.*) practice makes perfect.

ком^{2} *p. of* ⇒**кто**

ком... *comb. form, abbr. of* **1** ***коммунисти́ческий.*** **2** ***кома́ндный.*** **3** ***команди́р***

...ком *comb. form, abbr. of* **1** ***комите́т.*** **2** ***комисса́р.*** **3** ***комиссариа́т***

ко́м|а, ы *f.* (*med.*) coma.

кома́нд|а, ы *f.* **1** (*приказ*) command, order; **пода́ть ~у** to give a command. **2** (*начальствование*) command; **приня́ть ~у** (**над**+*i.*) to take command (of). **3** (*mil.*) (*отряд*) party, detachment, crew; (*naut.*) crew; **пожа́рная к.** fire-brigade. **4** (*sport*) team.

команди́р, а *m.* (*mil.*) commander, commanding officer; (*naut.*) captain.

командир|ова́ть, у́ю *impf. and pf.* to post; to dispatch, send on a mission.

командиро́вк|а, и *f.* **1** (*действие*) posting, dispatching (*on official business*). **2** (*поручение*) assignment; (*поездка*) business trip; **е́хать в ~у** to go on a business trip; **он в ~е** he is away on business; **я получи́л ~у в Казахста́н** I have been posted to Kazakhstan; **нау́чная к.** scientific mission.

командиро́в|очный *adj. of* ⇒**~ка; ~очные де́ньги** travelling (*Br.*), traveling (*US*) allowance; **~очное удостовере́ние** warrant, authority (*for travelling on official business*); *as n.* **~очные, ~очных** travel allowance, travelling (*Br.*), traveling (*US*) expenses.

кома́нд|ный *adj.* **1** *adj. of* ⇒**~а; к. пункт** command post; **к. соста́в** the officers (*of a military unit*). **2** (*fig.*) commanding; **~ные высо́ты** commanding heights.

кома́ндовани|е, я *nt.* **1** commanding, command; **приня́ть к.** (**над**+*i.*) to take command (of, over). **2** (*collect.*) command.

кома́нд|овать, ую *impf.* (*of* ⇒**с~**) **1** to give orders. **2** (+*i.*) (*быть командиром*) to command, be in command (of). **3** (*fig., coll.*) (+*i. or* **над**+*i.*) (*распоряжаться*) to order about. **4** (*fig.*) (**над**+*i.*) (*местностью*) to command.

кома́ндующ|ий, его *m.* commander.

кома́р, а́ *m.* mosquito; (*coll.*): **к. но́са не подто́чит** not a thing can be said against it.

комар|и́ный *adj. of* ⇒**~; к. уку́с** mosquito bite.

комато́зный *adj.* (*med.*) comatose.

комба́йн, а *m.* (*tech.*) combine; **зерново́й к.** combine harvester; **ку́хонный к.** food processor.

комба́йнер, а *m.* (*agric.*) combine operator.

комба́т, а *m.* (*abbr. of* ***команди́р батальо́на***) battalion commander.

комбико́рм, а, *pl.* **~а́** *m.* (*agric.*) mixed fodder.

комбина́т, а *m.* industrial complex; plant; **де́тский к.** day nursery.

комбина́тор, а *m.* (*pej.*) schemer; wheeler-dealer.

комбинато́рик|а, и *f.* (*math.*) combinatorics.

комбинато́рный *adj.* (*math.*) combinative.

комбинац|ио́нный *adj. of* ⇒**~ия**

комбина́ци|я^{1}**, и** *f.* **1** combination; (*econ.*) merger. **2** (*fig.*) scheme, system; (*pol., sport*) manœuvre.

комбина́ци|я^{2}**, и** *f.* (*женское бельё*) slip.

комбинезо́н, а *m.* overalls; dungarees.

комбини́рованный *adj.* combined.

комбини́р|овать, ую *impf.* (*of* ⇒**с~**) **1** to combine, arrange. **2** (*coll., pej.*) to scheme.

комбри́г, а *m.* (*abbr. of* ***команди́р брига́ды***) brigade commander.

комди́в, а *m.* (*abbr. of* ***команди́р диви́зии***) division(al) commander.

комедиа́нт, а *m.* **1** (*obs.*) actor. **2** (*pej.*) play-actor; hypocrite.

комеди́йный *adj.* (*liter., theatr.*) comic; comedy; **к. актёр** comedy actor, comedian.

коме́ди|я, и *f.* **1** comedy. **2** (*fig.*) farce; **лома́ть ~ю, разы́грывать ~ю** to put on an act.

ко́м|ель, ля *m.* butt, butt-end (*of tree, etc.*).

коменда́нт, а *m.* **1** (*mil*) commandant. **2** (*общественного здания*) manager; warden; **к. общежи́тия** warden of a hostel.

коменда́нт|ский *adj. of* ⇒**~; к. час** (*mil.*) curfew.

комендату́р|а, ы *f.* commandant's office.

коме́т|а, ы *f.* comet.

коми́зм, а *m.* comedy; **к. положе́ния** the funny side of a situation.

ко́мик, а *m.* **1** comic actor. **2** (*fig.*) comedian.

ко́микс, а *m.* (*книжка*) comic(-book); (*серия рисунков*) comic strip.

Коминте́рн, а *m.* (*hist.*) (*abbr. of* ***Коммунисти́ческий Интернациона́л***) Comintern.

комисса́р, а *m.* commissar, commissioner; **верхо́вный к.** high commissioner.

комиссариа́т, а *m.* commissariat.

комисса́р|ский *adj. of* ⇒**~**

комиссионе́р, а *m.* agent, broker.

К

комиссио́нк|а, и *f.* (*coll.*) second-hand shop.

комисс|ио́нный *adj. of* ⇒**~ия** 2; **к. магази́н** second-hand shop (*where goods are sold on commission*); *as n.* **~ио́нные, ~ио́нных** (*comm.*) commission.

коми́сси|я, и *f.* **1** commission, committee; **к. по разоруже́нию** disarmament commission; **сле́дственная к.** committee of investigation. **2** (*comm.*) commission; **брать на ~ю** to take on commission.

комите́т, а *m.* committee; **специа́льный к.** select committee; ad hoc committee.

коми́ческ|ий *adj.* **1** comic; **~ая о́пера** comic opera. **2** (*смешной*) comical, funny.

коми́ч|ный (~ен, ~на) *adj.* comical, funny.

ко́мка|ть, ю *impf.* (*of* ⇒**с~**) **1** (*pf. also* **иско́мкать**) to crumple. **2** (*fig., coll.*) to make a hash of, muff.

коммента́ри|й, я *m.* **1** (*разъяснительные замечания*) commentary. **2** (*pl.*) (*рассуждения*) comment; **~и изли́шни** comment is superfluous.

коммента́тор, а *m.* commentator.

комменти́р|овать, ую *impf. and pf.* to comment (upon).

коммерса́нт, а *m.* businessman.

комме́рци|я, и *f.* commerce, trade.

комме́рческий *adj.* commercial; **к. флот** mercantile marine.

коммивояжёр, а *m.* commercial traveller, travelling salesman (*Br.*), traveling salesman (*US*).

комму́н|а, ы *f.* commune.

коммуна́лк|а, и *f.* (*coll.*) communal flat (*Br.*), apartment (*US*).

коммуна́льн|ый *adj.* **1** communal; municipal; **~ая кварти́ра** 'communal' flat (*in which kitchen, bathroom, and toilet facilities are shared by a number of tenants*); **~ые услу́ги** public utilities; **~ое хозя́йство** municipal economy. **2** *adj. of* ⇒**комму́на**

коммуни́зм, а *m.* communism.

коммуника́бельност|ь, и *f.* sociableness, communicativeness.

коммуника́бел|ьный (~ен, ~ьна) *adj.* sociable, communicative.

коммуникати́вный *adj.* communicative.

коммуникацио́нн|ый *adj.*: **~ая ли́ния** line of communication.

коммуника́ци|я, и *f.* communication; (*mil.*) line of communication.

коммуни́ст, а *m.* communist.

коммунисти́ческий *adj.* communist.

коммуни́ст|ка, ки *f. of* ⇒**~**

коммута́тор, а *m.* **1** (*elec.*) commutator. **2** (*teleph.*) switchboard.

коммюнике́ *nt. indecl.* communiqué.

ко́мнат|а, ы *f.* room; **тёмная к.** (*phot.*) darkroom.

ко́мнатн|ый *adj.* **1** *adj. of* ⇒**ко́мната. 2** (*домашний*) indoor; **~ые и́гры** indoor games; **~ые расте́ния** house plants; **~ая соба́чка** lap-dog; **~ая температу́ра** room temperature.

комо́д, а *m.* chest of drawers.

ком|о́к, ка́ *m. dim. of* ⇒**~**; **сверну́ться в к.** to roll o.s. up into a ball; (*fig.*) **к. в го́рле** lump in the throat; **к. не́рвов** bundle of nerves.

комо́л|ый (~, ~а) *adj.* polled, hornless.

компа́кт-ди́ск, а *m.* compact disk, CD; **пройгрыватель** (*m.*) **для ~ов** compact disk *or* CD player.

компа́кт|ный (~ен, ~на) *adj.* compact; **к. диск** compact disk; (*fig.*) concise.

компане́йск|ий *adj.* (*coll.*) **1** (*общительный*) sociable, companionable. **2** (*одинаковый для всех*) equally shared; **расхо́ды на ~их нача́лах** expenses equally shared.

компа́ни|я, и *f.* (*in var. senses*) company; **доче́рняя к.** subsidiary; **води́ть ~ю с кем-н.** (*coll.*) to associate with s.o.; **расстро́ить ~ю** to break up a party; **соста́вить кому́-н. ~ю** to keep s.o. company; **я провёл ве́чер в ~и с Воло́дей** I spent the evening in Volodya's company; **он тебе́ не к.** he is not suitable company for you; **пойти́ це́лой ~ей** to go all together; **гуля́ть ~ей** to go about in a group; (*coll.*): **за ~ю** for company; **ну, ещё стака́нчик с тобо́й за ~ю!** well, just one more to keep you company!

компаньо́н, а *m.* **1** (*comm.*) partner. **2** (*товарищ*) companion.

компаньо́н|ка, ки *f.* **1** *f. of* ⇒**~. 2** (lady's) companion; chaperon(e).

компа́рти|я, и *f.* Communist Party.

ко́мпас, а *m.* compass.

ко́мпас|ный *adj. of* ⇒**~**; **~ная стре́лка** compass needle.

компатрио́т, а *m.* compatriot.

компатрио́т|ка, ки *f. of* ⇒**~**

компа́унд, а *m.* (*tech.*) compound.

компе́ндиум, а *m.* compendium, digest.

компенсацио́нный *adj.* compensatory.

компенса́ци|я, и *f.* compensation.

компенси́р|овать, ую *impf. and pf.* to compensate.

компете́нтност|ь, и *f.* competence.

компете́нт|ный (~ен, ~на) *adj.* competent; **к. исто́чник** reliable source.

компете́нци|я, и *f.* **1** (*область знания*) competence; **э́то не в мое́й ~и** it is beyond my scope. **2** (*круг полномочий*) jurisdiction.

компили́р|овать, ую *impf.* (*of* ⇒**с~**) (*pej.*) to rehash, cobble together.

компиляти́в|ный (~ен, ~на) *adj. of* ⇒**компиля́ция**; **к. труд** compilation.

компиля́тор, а *m.* (*pej.*) writer who rehashes the work of others; hack.

компиля́ци|я, и *f.* (*pej.*) rehash.

ко́мплекс, а *m.* (*in var. senses*) complex; (*набор*) set; **к. неполноце́нности** inferiority complex; **к. мероприя́тий** package of measures.

ко́мплексн|ый *adj.* **1** (*math.*) complex; **~ое число́** complex number. **2** all-embracing, all-in; **к. обе́д** table d'hôte dinner.

компле́кт, а *m.* **1** (*набор*) set; kit; **к. белья́** bedding, bed-clothes; **шрифтово́й к.** (*typ.*) fo(u)nt. **2** (*норма*) complement; specified number; **сверх ~а** above the specified number; **у нас ещё не хвата́ет двух челове́к до по́лного ~а** we are still two short of the full complement.

компле́ктный *adj.* complete.

комплект|ова́ть, у́ю *impf.* (*of* ⇒**у~**) **1** to complete; **к. журна́л** to acquire a complete set of a periodical. **2** (*штат*) to bring up to strength.

компле́кци|я, и *f.* build.

комплиме́нт, а *m.* compliment; **сде́лать к.** (+*d.*) to pay a compliment (to).

комплимента́рный *adj.* complimentary.

компози́тор, а *m.* (*mus.*) composer.

компози́ци|я, и *f.* composition; **класс ~и** (*mus.*) composition class.

компоне́нт, а *m.* component.

компон|ова́ть, у́ю *impf.* (*of* ⇒**скомпонова́ть**) to put together, arrange; **к. статью́** to put together an article.

компоно́вк|а, и *f.* putting together, arrangement.

компо́ст, а *m.* (*hort.*) compost.

компо́стер, а *m.* punch (*for bus tickets etc.*).

компости́р|овать, ую *impf.* (*of* ⇒**про~**) to punch (*bus tickets, etc.*).

компо́ст|ный *adj. of* ⇒**~**

компо́т, а *m.* compote, stewed fruit.

компре́сс, а *m.* (*med.*) compress; **согрева́ющий к.** hot compress; **поста́вить к.** to apply a compress.

компре́сси|я, и *f.* compression.

компре́ссор, а *m.* (*tech., med.*) compressor.

компрома́т, а *m.* (*abbr. of* ***компромети́рующий материа́л***) compromising material.

компромета́ци|я, и *f.* compromising.

компромети́р|овать, ую *impf.* (*of* ⇒**с~**) to compromise.

компроми́сс, а *m.* compromise; **идти́ на к.** to make a compromise, meet half-way.

компроми́сс|ный *adj. of* ⇒**~**; **~ное реше́ние** compromise settlement.

компью́тер, а *m.* computer; **ИБМ-совмести́мый к.** IBM-compatible computer; **к.-калькуля́тор** scientific calculator; **портати́вный к.** laptop (computer).

компьютериза́ци|я, и *f.* computerization.

компью́тер|ный *adj. of* ⇒**~**; **~ная гра́мотность** computer literacy.

компью́терщик, а *m.* (*coll.*) computer specialist; computer buff.

комсомо́л, а *m.* (*abbr. of* ***коммунисти́ческий сою́з молодёжи***) Komsomol (*Young Communist League*).

комсомо́л|ец, ьца *m.* Komsomol (member).

комсомо́л|ка, ки *f. of* ⇒**~ец**

комсомо́л|ьский *adj. of* ⇒**~**

кому́ *d. of* ⇒**кто**

комфо́рт, а *m.* comfort.

комфорта́бел|ьный (~ен, ~ьна) *adj.* comfortable.

комфо́ртный *adj.* comfortable.

кон, а, о ~е, на ~у́ *m.* **1** (*в азартных играх*) kitty; **поста́вить де́ньги на́ к.** to place one's stake, put one's money in (the kitty); **быть, стоя́ть на ~у́** (*fig.*) to be at stake. **2** (*партия*) game; round.

конве́йер, а *m.* (*tech.*) conveyor (*belt*); **сбо́рочный к.** assembly line.

конве́йер|ный *adj. of* ⇒**~**; **~ная систе́ма** conveyor (belt) system.

конве́кци|я, и *f.* (*phys.*) convection.

конве́нт, а *m.* (*pol.*) convention.

конвенц|ио́нный *adj. of* ⇒**~ия; к. тари́ф** agreed tariff.

конве́нци|я, и *f.* (*leg.*) convention, agreement.

конверге́нци|я, и *f.* convergence.

конве́рси|я, и *f.* conversion.

конве́рт, а *m.* **1** (*для писем*) envelope. **2** (*для пластинки*) sleeve. **3** (*для младенца*) sleeping bag, baby nest.

конверти́р|овать, ую *impf. and pf.* to convert.

конве́ртор, а *m.* (*tech.*) converter.

конво́ир, а *m.* escort.

конвои́р|овать, ую *impf.* to escort, convoy.

конво́|й, я *m.* escort, convoy; **вести́ под ~ем** to convoy, conduct under escort.

конво́й|ный *adj. of* ⇒**~**; **~ное су́дно** escort vessel; *as n.* **к., ~ного** *m.* escort.

конвульси́в|ный (~ен, ~на) *adj.* (*med.*) convulsive.

конву́льси|я, и *f.* (*med.*) convulsion.

конгениа́л|ьный (~ен, ~ьна) *adj.* congenial; (+*d.*) well suited (to), in harmony (with).

конгломера́т, а *m.* **1** conglomeration. **2** (*geol.*) conglomerate.

Ко́нго *nt. indecl.* the Congo.

конголе́з|ец, ца *m.* Congolese.

конголе́з|ка, ки *f. of* ⇒**~ец**

конголе́зский *adj.* Congolese.

конгре́сс, а *m.* congress; (*в США*) Congress.

конгрессме́н, а *m.* congressman.

конденса́тор, а *m.* condenser.

конденсацио́нн|ый *adj.* condensing, obtained by condensation; **~ая вода́** condensation water; **к. горшо́к** condensing vessel.

конденса́ци|я, и *f.* condensation.

конденси́р|овать, ую *impf. and pf.* to condense.

конденси́р|оваться, уется *impf. and pf.* to condense (*intrans.*).

конди́тер, а *m.* confectioner, pastry-cook.

конди́терск|ая, ой *f.* (*продающая конфеты*) confectioner's, sweet shop (*Br.*), candy store (*US*); (*продающая торты*) cake shop, pastry shop.

конди́терск|ий *adj.*: **~ие изде́лия** (*сахаристые*) confectionery; (*мучные*) cakes, pastries; **к. магази́н** = **~ая**

кондиционе́р, а *m.* air-conditioner.

кондициони́ровани|е, я *nt.* conditioning; **к. во́здуха** air conditioning.

кондициони́р|овать, ую *impf.* to condition.

конди́ци|я, и *f.* standard.

кондо́вый *adj.* of the good old-fashioned sort.

кондоми́ниум, а *m.* condominium.

ко́ндор, а *m.* (*zool.*) condor.

кондотье́р, а *m.* (*hist.*) soldier of fortune.

конду́ктор[1]**, а,** *pl.* **~а́, ~о́в** *m.* (*bus, tram*) conductor; (*rail.*) guard.

конду́ктор[2]**, а,** *pl.* **~ы, ~ов** *m.* (*elec.*) conductor.

конду́кторш|а, и *f.* (*coll.*) conductress.

конево́д, а *m.* horse-breeder.

конево́дств|о, а *nt.* horse-breeding.

конево́д|ческий *adj. of* ⇒**~ство**

кон|ёк, ька́ *m.* **1** *dim. of* ⇒**~ь**; **морско́й к.** (*zool.*) sea-horse. **2** (*fig., coll.*) hobby-horse; hobby; **сесть на своего́ ~ька́** to mount one's hobby-horse. **3** *see* ⇒**~ьки́**

кон|е́ц, ца́ *m.* **1** end; **о́стрый к.** point; **то́лстый к.** butt(-end); **то́нкий к.** tip; **в к.** (*coll.*) completely; **в ~це́ ~цо́в** in the end, after all; **и де́ло с ~цо́м** (*coll.*) and there's an end to it; **из ~ца́ в к.** from end to end, all over; **~цы́ с ~ца́ми своди́ть** (*coll.*) to make both ends meet; **на э́тот (тот) к.** (*coll.*) to this (that) end; **на худо́й к.** (*coll.*) at the worst, if the worst comes to the worst; **оди́н к.** (*coll.*) it comes to the same thing in the end; **со всех ~цо́в** from all quarters; **хорони́ть ~цы́** (*coll.*) to bury, remove traces; **и ~цы́ в во́ду** (*coll.*) and none will be the wiser; **пришёл ему́ к.** (*coll.*) that's the end of him; **отда́ть ~цы́** (*coll.*) to kick the bucket; **положи́ть к.** (+*d.*) to put an end to. **2** (*coll.*) (*расстояние, путь*) distance, way; **в оди́н к.** one way; **в о́ба ~ца́** there and back.

коне́чно *adv.* of course, certainly.

коне́чност|ь, и *f.* (*anat.*) extremity.

коне́ч|ный (~ен, ~на) *adj.* **1** final, last; ultimate; **~ная ста́нция** terminus; **~ная цель** ultimate aim; **в ~ном ито́ге, счёте** ultimately, in the last analysis. **2** (*имеющий конец*) finite.

кони́н|а, ы *no pl., f.* horse-flesh.

кони́ческий *adj.* conic(al).

конкистадо́р, а *m.* (*hist.*) conquistador.

конкла́в, а *m.* conclave.

конкорда́т, а *m.* concordat.

конкретизи́р|овать, ую *impf. and pf.* to give concrete expression to.

конкре́т|ный (~ен, ~на) *adj.* concrete; specific.

конку́р, а *m.* (*в конном спорте*) showjumping.

конкуре́нт, а *m.* competitor; rival.

конкуре́нт|ка, ки *f. of* ⇒**~**

конкурентоспосо́бност|ь, и *f.* competitiveness.

конкурентоспосо́б|ный (~ен, ~на) *adj.* competitive.

конкуре́нци|я, и *f.* competition; **вне ~и** unrivalled (*Br.*), unrivaled (*US*).

конкури́р|овать, ую *impf.* (**с**+*i.*) to compete (with).

конку́рн|ый *adj.*: **к. вса́дник** showjumper (*person*); **~ая ло́шадь** showjumper (*horse*).

ко́нкурс, а *m.* competition; contest; **к. красоты́** beauty contest; **уча́стник ~а** contestant; **объяви́ть к.** (**на**+*a.*) to announce a vacancy (for); **вне ~а** unrivalled; (*fig.*) in a class by itself.

конкурса́нт, а *m.* competitor; contestant.

конкурса́нт|ка, ки *f. of* ⇒**~**

ко́нкурс|ный *adj. of* ⇒**~**; **к. экза́мен** competitive examination.

ко́нник, а *m.* cavalryman.

ко́нниц|а, ы *f.* cavalry.

конногварде́|ец, йца *m.* (*mil.*) horse-guardsman.

коннозаво́дств|о, а *nt.* horse-breeding.

коннозаво́дчик, а *m.* owner of stud (-farm).

коннокаскадёр, а *m.* trick (*horseback*) rider.

конноспорти́вн|ый *adj.* equestrian; **~ая шко́ла** riding school.

ко́н|ный *adj. of* ⇒**~ь**; horse; mounted; equestrian; **~ная а́рмия** cavalry army; **к. двор** stables; **к. спорт** equestrianism; **~ная ста́туя** equestrian statue; **на ~ной тя́ге** horse-drawn.

конова́л, а *m.* **1** horse-doctor. **2** (*coll.*) (*плохой врач*) quack(-doctor).

ко́новязь|ь, и *f.* (*столб*) tethering-post.

конокра́д, а *m.* horse-thief.

конокра́дств|о, а *nt.* horse-stealing.

конопа́|тить, чу, тишь *impf.* (*of* ⇒**законопа́тить**) to caulk, stop up.

конопа́тк|а, и *f.* caulking.

конопа́тчик, а *m.* caulker.

конопа́т|ый (~, ~а) *adj.* (*coll.*) (*веснушчатый*) freckled; (*рябой*) pock-marked.

конопа́|чу, тишь *see* ⇒**~тить**

конопл|я́, и́ *f.* (*bot.*) hemp; (*наркотик*) cannabis.

конопля́нк|а, и *f.* (*zool.*) linnet.

конопля́|ный *adj. of* ⇒**~**; **~ное ма́сло** hempseed oil.

коносаме́нт, а *m.* (*comm.*) bill of lading.

консе́нсус, а *m.* consensus.

консерва́нт, а *m.* preservative.

консервати́в|ный (~ен, ~на) *adj.* conservative.
консервати́зм, а *m.* conservatism.
консерва́тор, а *m.* (*esp. pol.*) conservative.
консервато́ри|я, и *f.* conservatoire, academy of music.
консерва́торский *adj.* conservative.
консервато́р|ский *adj. of* ⇒**~ия**
консерва́ци|я, и *f.* **1** (*защита*) conservation. **2** (*предприятия*) temporary shut-down.
консерви́рован|ный (~, ~а) *p.p.p. of* ⇒**консерви́ровать** *and adj.*; **~ные фру́кты** bottled fruit, canned fruit.
консерви́р|овать, ую *impf. and pf.* (*pf. also* **за~**) **1** to preserve; to can; to bottle. **2**: **к. предприя́тие** to shut down an enterprise temporarily.
консе́рв|ный *adj. of* ⇒**~ы**; **~ная ба́нка** tin can; **к. нож** can-opener; **~ная фа́брика** cannery.
консе́рв|ы, ов *no sg.* canned food.
конси́лиум, а *m.* (*med.*) meeting between doctors.
консисте́нци|я, и *f.* (*phys., med.*) consistence.
ко́н|ский *adj. of* ⇒**~ь**; **~ские бобы́** horsebeans; **к. во́лос** horse-hair; **к. заво́д** stud(-farm); **~ские состяза́ния** horse-races; **к. хвост** 'pony-tail' (*hairstyle*).
консолида́ци|я, и *f.* consolidation.
консолиди́р|овать, ую *impf. and pf.* to consolidate.
консо́л|ь, и *f.* (*archit.*) **1** (*выступ*) cantilever. **2** (*подставка*) console table.
консоме́ *nt. indecl.* (*cul.*) consommé.
консона́нс, а *m.* (*mus.*) consonance.
консо́рциум, а *m.* (*fin.*) consortium.
конспе́кт, а *m.* outline, summary.
конспекти́в|ный (~ен, ~на) *adj.* concise, brief.
конспекти́р|овать, ую *impf.* (*of* ⇒**за~** *and* **про~**) to make a summary of.
конспирати́в|ный (~ен, ~на) *adj.* secret, clandestine.
конспира́тор, а *m.* conspirator.
конспира́ци|я, и *f.* secrecy.
конспири́р|овать, ую *impf.* (*of* ⇒**за~**) to observe the rules of security (*in an illegal organization*).
конста́нт|а, ы *f.* (*math., phys.*) constant.
Константино́пол|ь, я *m.* (*hist.*) Constantinople.
констата́ци|я, и *f.* ascertaining; establishment.
констати́р|овать, ую *impf. and pf.* to ascertain; to establish; **к. смерть** to certify death; **к. факт** to establish a fact.
конституционали́зм, а *m.* (*pol.*) constitutionalism.
конституциона́льный *adj.* (*med., physiol.*) constitutional.
конституцио́нный *adj.* (*pol.*) constitutional.
конститу́ци|я, и *f.* (*pol., med.*) constitution.
конструи́р|овать, ую *impf. and pf.* (*pf. also* **с~**) **1** (*строить*) to construct; (*проектировать*) to design. **2** (*создавать*) to form (*a government, etc.*).
конструктиви́зм, а *m.* (*art*) constructivism.
конструкти́в|ный (~ен, ~на) *adj.* **1** structural; construction. **2** (*критика*) constructive.
констру́ктор, а *m.* designer.
констру́ктор|ский *adj. of* ⇒**~**; **~ское бюро́** design office.
констру́кци|я, и *f.* **1** (*состав*) construction; design. **2** (*сооружение*) structure. **3** (*gram.*) construction.
ко́нсул, а *m.* consul.
ко́нсульский *adj.* consular.
ко́нсульств|о, а *nt.* consulate.
консульта́нт, а *m.* consultant, adviser; (*в вузе*) tutor.
консультати́вный *adj.* consultative, advisory.
консультац|и́онный *adj. of* ⇒**~и́я**; **~и́онное бюро́** advice bureau; **~и́онная пла́та** consultation fee.
консульта́ци|я, и *f.* **1** consultation; specialist advice. **2** (*учреждение*) advice bureau; **де́тская к.** children's clinic; **же́нская к.** ante-natal (*Br.*), prenatal (*US*) clinic; gynaecological (*Br.*), gynecological (*US*) clinic; **юриди́ческая к.** legal advice office. **3** (*в вузе*) tutorial.
консульти́р|овать, ую *impf.* **1** (*pf.* **про~**) to advise; (*в вузе*) to act as tutor (to). **2** (**с**+*i.*) (*obs.*) to consult.
консульти́р|оваться, уюсь *impf.* (*of* ⇒**про~**) (**с**+*i.*) to consult.
конта́кт, а *m.* **1** contact; **вступи́ть в к. с кем-н.** to come into contact, get in touch with s.o.; **быть в ~е** (**с**+*i.*) to be in touch (with). **2** (*elec.*) **к. приёмный** socket; **к. штыково́й** plug.
конта́кт|ный (~ен, ~на) *adj.* **1** (*tech.*) contact; **к. рельс** contact rail, live rail; **~ная сва́рка** point welding; **~ные ли́нзы** (*med.*) contact lenses. **2** (*coll.*) outgoing.
конте́йнер, а *m.* container.
контейнерово́з, а *m.* container ship *or* truck.
конте́кст, а *m.* context.
континге́нт, а *m.* **1** (*econ.*) quota. **2** contingent; batch; **к. войск** a military force; **к. новобра́нцев** batch, squad of recruits.
контине́нт, а *m.* continent.
континента́льный *adj.* continental.
конто́р|а, ы *f.* office, bureau.
конто́рк|а, и *f.* (writing-)desk, bureau.
конто́р|ский *adj. of* ⇒**~а**; **~ская кни́га** (account-)book.
конто́рщик, а *m.* (*obs.*) clerk.
ко́нтр|а[1]**, ы** *f.* (*coll.*): **быть в ~ах** (**с**+*i.*) to be at odds (with).
ко́нтр|а[2]**, ы** *c.g.* (*sl., hist.*) counter-revolutionary.
контраба́нд|а, ы *f.* **1** (*действие*) contraband, smuggling; **занима́ться ~ой** to smuggle. **2** (*товары*) contraband.
контрабанди́ст, а *m.* smuggler.
контрабанди́ст|ка, ки *f. of* ⇒**~**
контраба́ндный *adj.* contraband.
контраба́с, а *m.* (*mus.*) double-bass.
контрабаси́ст, а *m.* double-bass player.
контраге́нт, а *m.* contractor.
контр-адмира́л, а *m.* rear-admiral.
контра́кт, а *m.* contract.
контракта́ци|я, и *f.* contracting (for).
контракт|ова́ть, у́ю *impf.* (*of* ⇒**за~**) to contract for; **к. рабо́тников** to engage workmen.
контракт|ова́ться, у́юсь *impf.* (*of* ⇒**за~**) **1** to contract, undertake. **2** *pass. of* ⇒**~ова́ть**
контра́кт|овый *adj. of* ⇒**~**
контра́льто *nt. indecl.* (*mus.*) contralto.
контра́льто|вый *adj. of* ⇒**~**
контрама́рк|а, и *f.* complimentary ticket; free pass.
контрапу́нкт, а *m.* (*mus.*) counterpoint.
контрапункти́ческий *adj.* (*mus.*) contrapuntal.
контрапу́нкт|ный *adj.* = **~и́ческий**
контра́ст, а *m.* contrast; **по ~у** (**с**+*i.*) by contrast (with).
контрасти́р|овать, ую *impf.* (**с**+*i.*) to contrast (with).
контра́стност|ь, и *f.* (*TV etc.*) contrast.
контра́стный *adj.* contrasting.
контрата́к|а, и *f.* (*mil.*) counter-attack.
контратак|ова́ть, у́ю *impf. and pf.* to counter-attack.
контрацепти́в, а *m.* contraceptive; **внутрима́точный к.** intrauterine (contraceptive) device, IUD.
контрацепти́вный *adj.* contraceptive (*attr.*).
контрга́йк|а, и *f.* (*tech.*) lock-nut, check-nut.
контржу́рный *adj.*: **к. свет** backlighting.
контрибу́ци|я, и *f.* reparations; **наложи́ть ~ю** (**на**+*a.*) to impose reparations (on).
контрманёвр, а *m.* (*mil.*) counter-manœuvre.
контрме́р|а, ы *f.* countermeasure.
контрнаступле́ни|е, я *nt.* counter-offensive.
контрове́рз|а, ы *f.* controversy.
контролёр, а *m.* inspector; (*билетов*) ticket-collector.
контроли́р|овать, ую *impf.* (*of* ⇒**про~**) (*проверять*) to check; **к. биле́ты** to inspect tickets; (*держать под своим контролем*) to control.
контро́ллер, а *m.* (*elec., comput.*) controller.
контро́л|ь, я *m.* **1** control. **2** (*проверка*) check(ing); inspection;

(*tech., mil.*) monitoring; (*mil.*) verification; **ме́ры по ~ю** verification measures.

контро́льно-пропускно́й *adj.*: **к. пункт** checkpoint.

контро́ль|ный *adj. of* ⇒**~**; **~ная вы́шка** (*naut.*) conning tower; **~ная коми́ссия** control commission; **~ная рабо́та** test; **к. паке́т а́кций** (*fin.*) controlling interest.

контрразве́дк|а, и *f.* counter-espionage; counter-intelligence.

контрразве́дчик, а *m.* counter-intelligence agent.

контрреволюционе́р, а *m.* counter-revolutionary.

контрреволюцио́нный *adj.* counter-revolutionary.

контрреволю́ци|я, и *f.* counter-revolution.

контруда́р, а *m.* (*mil.*) counter-blow.

контрфо́рс, а *m.* (*archit.*) buttress.

конту́жен|ный (~, ~а) *p.p.p. of* ⇒**конту́зить** *and adj.*; **~ные** (*mil.*) shell-shock cases.

конту́|зить, жу, зишь *pf.* to contuse; (*при разрыве снаряда*) to shell-shock.

конту́зи|я, и *f.* contusion, bruising; (*при разрыве снаряда*) shell-shock.

ко́нтур, а *m.* **1** contour. **2** (*elec.*) circuit.

ко́нтур|ный *adj. of* ⇒**~**; **~ная ка́рта** contour map.

конур|а́, ы́ *f.* kennel; (*fig.*) hovel, dump.

ко́нус, а *m.* cone.

конусообра́з|ный (~ен, ~на) *adj.* conical.

конфедерати́вный *adj.* confederative.

конфедера́ци|я, и *f.* confederation.

конферансье́ *m. indecl.* (*theatr.*) compère, master of ceremonies (*abbr.* MC).

конфере́нц-за́л, а *m.* conference hall.

конфере́нци|я, и *f.* conference.

конфе́сси|я, и *f.* confession, faith.

конфе́т|а, ы *f.* sweet; **шокола́дная к.** chocolate; **коро́бка шокола́дных ~** box of chocolates.

конфе́т|ка, ки *f.* = **~а**

конфе́тниц|а, ы *f.* sweet dish *or* bowl.

конфе́т|ный *adj.* **1** *adj. of* ⇒**~а**; **~ная бума́жка** sweet wrapper. **2** (*coll., pej.*) sugary, treacly.

конфетти́ *nt. indecl.* confetti.

конфигура́ци|я, и *f.* configuration, conformation.

конфиденциа́льност|ь, и *f.* confidentiality.

конфиденциа́л|ьный (~ен, ~ьна) *adj.* confidential.

конфирма́ци|я, и *f.* (*eccl.*) confirmation.

конфирм|ова́ть, у́ю *impf. and pf.* (*eccl.*) to confirm.

конфиска́ци|я, и *f.* confiscation, seizure.

конфиск|ова́ть, у́ю *impf. and pf.* to confiscate.

конфли́кт, а *m.* conflict.

конфли́кт|ный *adj. of* ⇒**~**; **~ная коми́ссия** arbitration tribunal.

конфликт|ова́ть, у́ю *impf.* (**с**+*i.*) (*coll.*) to clash (with), come up (against).

конфо́рк|а, и *f.* ring (*on cooker*).

конфронта́ци|я, и *f.* confrontation, showdown.

конфу́з, а *m.* (*coll.*) discomfiture, embarrassment.

конфу́|зить, жу, зишь *impf.* (*of* ⇒**с~**) (*coll.*) to embarrass.

конфу́|зиться, жусь, зишься *impf.* (*of* ⇒**с~**) (*coll.*) to feel embarrassed.

конфу́злив|ый (~, ~а) *adj.* (*coll.*) bashful; shy.

конфу́з|ный (~ен, ~на) *adj.* (*coll.*) awkward, embarrassing.

концево́й *adj.* final, end.

концентра́т, а *m.* concentrate.

концентрацио́нный *adj.*: **к. ла́герь** concentration camp.

концентра́ци|я, и *f.* (*in var. senses*) concentration.

концентри́рова|нный *p.p.p. of* ⇒**~ть** *and adj.* concentrated.

концентри́р|овать, ую *impf.* (*of* ⇒**с~**) (*in var. senses*) to concentrate; (*mil.*) to mass; (*fig.*): **к. внима́ние на вопро́се** to concentrate one's attention on a question.

концентри́р|оваться, уюсь *impf.* (*of* ⇒**с~**) **1** to mass, collect (*intrans.*). **2** (*fig.*; **на**+*p.*) to concentrate.

концентри́ческий *adj.* concentric.

концептуа́л|ьный (~ен, ~ьна) *adj.* conceptual.

конце́пци|я, и *f.* conception, idea.

конце́рн, а *m.* (*econ.*) concern.

конце́рт, а *m.* (*mus.*) **1** concert; recital; **симфони́ческий к.** symphony concert; **быть на ~е** to be at a concert. **2** (*произведение*) concerto.

концерта́нт, а *m.* (concert) performer.

концерти́н|а, ы *f.* (*гармоника*) concertina.

концерти́но *nt. indecl.* **1** (*произведение*) concertino. **2** = **концерти́на**

концерти́р|овать, ую *impf.* to give concerts.

концертме́йстер, а *m.* (*mus.*) **1** (*первый скрипач*) leader (*of orchestra*) (*Br.*), concertmaster (*US*). **2** (*аккомпаниатор*) accompanist.

конце́рт|ный *adj. of* ⇒**~**; **к. роя́ль** concert grand (*piano*).

концессионе́р, а *m.* concessionaire.

конце́сси|я, и *f.* (*econ.*) concession.

концла́гер|ь, я *m.* (*abbr. of* ***концентрацио́нный ла́герь***) concentration camp.

концо́вк|а, и *f.* ending.

конч|а́ть(ся), а́ю(сь) *impf. of* ⇒**~́ить(ся)**

ко́нч|енный *p.p.p. of* ⇒**~ить;** *as int.* **~ено!** enough!; **всё ~ено!** it's all over!; **с ним всё ~ено** he's finished.

ко́нчен|ый *adj.* (*coll.*) decided, settled; **э́то де́ло ~ое** the matter is settled; **к. челове́к** (*coll.*) goner.

ко́нчик, а *m.* tip; point; **на ~е языка́** on the tip of one's tongue.

кончи́н|а, ы *f.* (*rhet.*) decease, demise.

ко́нч|ить, у, ишь *pf.* (*of* ⇒**~а́ть**) **1** to finish, end; **на э́том он ~ил** here he stopped; **я ~ил** that is all (I have to say); **к. шко́лу** to finish school course; **к. университе́т** to graduate; **к. самоуби́йством** to commit suicide; **к. пло́хо, ду́рно, скве́рно** to come to a bad end. **2** (**с**+*i.*) to be finished (with), give up. **3** (+*inf.*) to stop. **4** (*coll.*) to come (= *have an orgasm*).

ко́нч|иться, усь, ишься *pf.* (*of* ⇒**~а́ться**) (+*i.*) to end (in), finish (by); to come to an end; **де́ло ~илось ниче́м** it came to nothing.

конъюнктиви́т, а *m.* (*med.*) conjunctivitis.

конъюнкту́р|а, ы *f.* **1** state of affairs, juncture; **междунаро́дная к.** international situation. **2** (*econ.*) state of the market.

конъюнкту́р|ный *adj. of* ⇒**~а** 2; **~ные це́ны** (free) market prices.

конъюнкту́рщик, а *m.* (*coll., pej.*) opportunist.

кон|ь, я́, *pl.* **~́и, ~е́й** *m.* **1** horse; **боево́й к.** war-horse, charger; (*prov.*): **дарёному ~ю́ в зу́бы не смо́трят** never look a gift horse in the mouth. **2** (*гимнастический снаряд*) (vaulting-) horse; **к. с ру́чками** pommel-horse. **3** (*шахматы*) knight.

кон|ьки́, ько́в *pl.* (*sg.* **~ёк, ~ька́** *m.*) skates; **к. на ро́ликах, ро́ликовые к.** roller skates; **ката́ться на ~ька́х** to skate.

конькобе́ж|ец, ца *m.* skater.

конькобе́жный *adj.* skating; **к. спорт** skating.

конья́к, а́ (у́) *m.* brandy.

конья́|чный *adj. of* ⇒**~к**

ко́нюх, а *m.* groom, stable-man.

коню́ш|ня, ни, *g. pl.* **~ен** *f.* stable.

кооперати́в, а *m.* **1** (*организация*) cooperative society. **2** (*coll.*) (*магазин*) cooperative store; (*квартира*) flat in housing cooperative.

кооперати́вн|ый *adj.* cooperative; **~ое движе́ние** (*econ., pol.*) the cooperative movement; **~ое това́рищество** cooperative society.

коопера́тор, а *m.* member of the cooperative society.

коопера́ци|я, и *f.* **1** (*сотрудничество*) cooperation. **2** (*организация*) cooperative; **жили́щная к.** housing cooperative.

коопери́р|овать, ую *impf. and pf.* (*pf. also* **с~**) (*econ.*) to organize on cooperative lines.

коопери́р|оваться, уюсь *impf. and pf.* (*pf. also* ⇒**с~**) (*econ.*) **1** to cooperate. **2** *pass. of* ⇒**~овать**

коопта́ци|я, и *f.* co-option.

коопти́р|овать, ую *impf. and pf.* to co-opt.

координа́т|а, ы *f.* (*math.*) coordinate;

pl. (*coll.*) contact details (*address, telephone number, etc.*).

координа́тный *adj.* (*math.*) coordinate.

координа́тор, а *m.* coordinator.

координа́ци|я, и *f.* coordination.

координи́р|овать, ую *impf. and pf.* to coordinate.

копа́л, а *m.* copal.

копа́ни|е, я *nt.* digging.

коп|а́ть, а́ю *impf.* **1** (*pf.* **~ну́ть**) to dig. **2** (*pf.* **вы́~**) to dig up, dig out.

копа́|ться, юсь *impf.* **1** (**в**+*p.*) (*в сундуке*) to rummage (in); (*в песке*) to root around (in); (*fig.*): **к. в душе́** to be given to soul-searching. **2** (*coll.*; **с**+*i.*) (*канителиться*) to dawdle (over). **3** *pass. of* ⇒**~ть**

копе́ечк|а, и *f. dim. of* ⇒**копе́йка;** (*coll.*): **э́то влети́т тебе́ в ~у** it will cost you a pretty penny.

копе́ечн|ый *adj.* **1** one-kopeck; worth one kopeck. **2** (*о цене*) minor, trifling; **~ые расхо́ды** trifling expenses. **3** (*fig., coll.*) (*мелочный*) petty; twopenny-halfpenny.

копе́йк|а, и, *g. pl.* **копе́ек** *f.* kopeck; **к. в ~у** exactly; **до после́дней ~и** to the last farthing; **зашиби́ть, сколоти́ть ~у** to turn an honest penny; **к. рубль бережёт** (*prov.*) take care of the pence, the pounds will take care of themselves.

Копенга́ген, а *m.* Copenhagen.

коп|ёр, ра́ *m.* (*tech.*) pile-driver.

ко́п|и, ей *pl.* (*sg.* **~ь, ~и** *f.*) mines.

копи́лк|а, и *f.* money-box.

копи́рк|а, и *f.* (*coll.*) carbon paper; **писа́ть под ~у** to make a carbon copy.

копирова́льн|ый *adj.* copying; **~ая бума́га** carbon paper.

копи́р|овать, ую *impf.* (*of* ⇒**с~**) to copy; to imitate, mimic.

копиро́вк|а, и *f.* copying.

копиро́вщик, а *m.* copyist.

коп|и́ть, лю́, ~ишь *impf.* (*of* ⇒**на~**) to accumulate, amass; to store up; **к. де́ньги** to save up; (*fig.*): **к. си́лы** to save one's strength.

коп|и́ться, лю́сь, ~ишься *impf.* (*of* ⇒**на~**) to accumulate (*intrans.*).

ко́пи|я, и *f.* copy; **печа́тная к.** (*comput.*) hard copy; **резе́рвная к.** (*comput.*) backup; **заве́ренная к.** (*leg.*) attested copy; **снять ~ю** (**с**+*g.*) to copy, make a copy (of); (*fig.*): **он то́чная к. своего́ отца́** he is the very image of his father.

коп|на́, ны́, *pl.* **~ны, ~ён, ~на́м** *f.* shock, stook (*of corn*); **к. се́на** haycock; **к. воло́с** shock of hair.

копн|и́ть, ю́, и́шь *impf.* (*of* ⇒**с~**) (*agric.*) to shock, stook (*hay*).

коп|ну́ть, ну́, нёшь *pf. of* ⇒**~а́ть**

ко́пот|ь, и *f.* soot; lamp-black.

копош|и́ться, у́сь, и́шься *impf.* **1** (*о насекомых*) to swarm. **2** (*fig., coll.*) (*о мыслях*) to stir, creep in; **у меня́ в голове́ ~и́лось сомне́ние** a doubt was stirring in my head. **3** (*coll.*) (*возиться*) to potter about.

копт|е́ть¹, и́т *impf.* **1** (*о лампе*) to give off smoke; to smoke (*intrans.*). **2** (*obs.*) (*покрываться копотью*) to be blackened (*from smoke, with soot*).

коп|те́ть², чу́, ти́шь *impf.* (**над**+*i.*) (*coll.*) **1** (*корпеть*) to swot (at), plug away (at). **2** (*прозябать*) to vegetate, rot away (*fig.*).

копти́лк|а, и *f.* (*coll.*) oil-lamp (*of primitive design*).

копти́льный *adj.* for smoking.

копти́л|ьня, ьни, *g. pl.* **~ен** *f.* smoking-shed.

коп|ти́ть, чу́, ти́шь *impf.* **1** (*pf.* **за~**) (*мясо*) to smoke, cure in smoke. **2** (*pf.* **за~**) (*покрывать копотью*) to blacken (*with smoke*); **к. стекло́** to smoke glass; **к. не́бо** (*coll.*) to idle one's life away. **3** (*pf.* **на~**) (*о лампе*) to give off smoke; to smoke (*intrans.*).

копу́н, а́ *m.* (*coll.*) dawdler.

копу́ш|а, и *c.g.* (*coll.*) dawdler.

копче́ни|е, я *nt.* smoking, curing in smoke.

копчён|ый *adj.* smoked; **~ая селёдка** bloater.

ко́пчик, а *m.* (*anat.*) coccyx.

коп|чу́¹, ти́шь *see* ⇒**~те́ть²**

коп|чу́², ти́шь *see* ⇒**~ти́ть**

копы́тн|ый *adj.* **1** hoof (*attr.*). **2** (*zool.*) hoofed, ungulate; *as n.* **~ые, ~ых** ungulates.

копы́т|о, а *nt.* hoof.

коп|ь *see* ⇒**~́и**

коп|ьё¹, ья́, *pl.* **~́ья, ~́ий, ~́ьям** *nt.* spear, lance; (*sport*) javelin; **мета́ние ~ья́** (*sport*) javelin throwing; (*fig., iron.*): **~́ья лома́ть (из-за)** to do battle (over).

коп|ьё², я́ *nt.*: **у меня́ ни ~я́** (*coll.*) I haven't a penny.

копьемета́тел|ь, я *m.* javelin-thrower.

...кор *comb. form, abbr. of* ***корреспонде́нт***

кор|а́, ы́ *f.* **1** (*bot.*) bark. **2** (*anat.*): **к. головно́го мо́зга** cerebral cortex. **3** (*Земли*) crust; **земна́я к.** the earth's crust.

кораб|е́льный *adj. of* ⇒**~́ль; ~е́льная авиа́ция** shipborne aircraft; **к. лес** ship timber; **к. инжене́р** naval architect; **к. ма́стер** shipwright.

кораблевожде́ни|е, я *nt.* navigation.

кораблекруше́ни|е, я *nt.* shipwreck; **потерпе́ть к.** to be ship-wrecked.

кораблестрое́ни|е, я *nt.* shipbuilding.

кораблестрои́тел|ь, я *m.* shipbuilder.

кора́бл|ик, ика *m.* **1** *dim. of* ⇒**~ь. 2** (*игрушка*) toy boat. **3** (*zool.*) nautilus.

кора́бл|ь, я́ *m.* **1** ship, vessel; **лине́йный к.** battleship; **фла́гманский к.** flagship; **косми́ческий к.** spaceship; **челно́чный (косми́ческий) к.** space shuttle; **сади́ться на к.** to go on board (ship); **сжечь свой ~и́** (*fig.*) to burn one's boats; **большо́му ~ю́ большо́е пла́ванье** (*prov.*) a great ship asks deep waters. **2** (*archit.*) nave.

кора́лл, а *m.* coral.

кора́ллов|ый *adj.* **1** coral. **2** (*светло-красный*) coralline; coral-red; **~ые уста́** coral lips.

Кора́н, а *m.* the Koran.

корве́т, а *m.* (*naut.*) corvette.

ко́рд|а, ы *f.* lunge; **гоня́ть на ~е** to lunge (*a horse*).

кордебале́т, а *m.* corps de ballet.

корди́т, а *m.* cordite.

кордо́н, а *m.* cordon; **за к., за ~ом** (*coll.*) abroad.

кор|ево́й *adj. of* ⇒**~ь**

коре́|ец, йца *m.* Korean.

корёж|ить, у, ишь *impf.* (*of* ⇒**ис~**) (*coll.*) to bend, warp; (*impers.*): **его́ ~ило от бо́ли** he was writhing with pain.

корёж|иться, усь, ишься *impf.* (*coll.*) **1** (*pf.* ⇒**ис~**) to bend, warp (*intrans.*). **2** (*pf.* ⇒**с~**): **к. от бо́ли** to writhe with pain.

коре́йк|а, и *f.* smoked back bacon.

коре́йский *adj.* Korean.

корена́ст|ый (~, ~а) *adj.* thickset, stocky.

корени́т|ься, ся *impf.* (**в**+*p.*) to be rooted (in).

коренни́к, а́ *m.* shaft-horse.

коренн|о́й *adj.* radical, fundamental; **к. зуб** molar (tooth); **к. жи́тель** native; **~о́е населе́ние** indigenous population; **~а́я ло́шадь** = **~и́к**

ко́р|ень, ня, *pl.* **~ни, ~не́й** *m.* **1** (*in var. senses*) root; **в ~не** radically; **вы́рвать с ~нем** to uproot (*also fig.*); **красне́ть до ~не́й воло́с** to blush to the roots of one's hair; **пусти́ть ~ни** to take root (*also fig.*); **смотре́ть в к. чего́-н.** to get at the root of sth.; **хлеб на ~ню́** standing crop. **2** (*math.*) root; radical; **знак ~ня** radical sign; **куби́ческий к.** cube root.

коре́нь|я, ев *no sg.* roots (*of vegetables, herbs, etc., for culinary and medicinal purposes*).

ко́реш, а *m.* (*sl.*) pal, mate.

кореш|о́к, ка́ *m.* **1** (*книги*) spine. **2** (*чековой книжки*) counterfoil. **3** *dim. of* ⇒**ко́рень. 4** (*sl.*) (*приятель*) pal, mate.

Коре́|я, и *f.* Korea.

коре|я́нка, я́нки *f. of* ⇒**~́ец**

корзи́н|а, ы *f.* basket.

корзи́нк|а, и *f.* small basket, punnet.

корзи́н|ный *adj. of* ⇒**~а**

корзи́нщик, а *m.* basket-maker.

кориа́ндр, а *m.* coriander.

коридо́р, а *m.* corridor, passage.

кори́нк|а, и *no pl., f.* currants.

кори́нфский *adj.* (*archit.*) Corinthian.

кор|и́ть, ю́, и́шь *impf.* (+*a.* **за**+*a.*) to upbraid (for); (+*a. and i.*) to reproach (with).

кори́фе|й, я *m.* leading light.

кори́ц|а, ы *f.* cinnamon.

кори́чневый *adj.* brown.

ко́рк|а, и *f.* **1** (*хлеба*) crust. **2** (*апельсина*) peel, rind. **3** (*на коже*) scab. **4** (*fig.*): **прочита́ть от ~и до ~и** to read from cover to cover; **руга́ть,**

брани́ть кого́-н. на все ~и (*coll.*) to tear s.o. off a strip.

корм, а, о ~е, на ~е *and* **на ~у́,** *pl.* **~а́, ~о́в** *m.* **1** (*пища*) food, fodder; **пти́чий к.** birdseed. **2** (*действие*) feeding.

корм|а́, ы́ *f.* **1** (*naut.*) stern. **2** (*coll.*) bottom (*Br.*), arse (*Br.*), ass (*US*).

кормёжк|а, и *f.* (*coll.*) feeding.

корми́л|ец, ьца *m.* bread-winner.

корми́лиц|а, ы *f.* **1** *f. of* ⇒**корми́лец. 2** wet-nurse.

корми́л|о, а *nt.* (*naut. and fig.*) helm; (*fig., rhet.*): **быть у ~а правле́ния** to be at the helm.

корм|и́ть, лю́, ~ишь *impf.* **1** (*pf.* **на~** *and* **по~**) (*давать корм*) to feed; **к. с ло́жки** to spoon-feed, **к. гру́дью** to nurse, (breast-)feed; (*coll.*): **его́ хле́бом не ~и́, то́лько дай смотре́ть футбо́л** he is mad about watching football. **2** (*pf.* **про~**) (*содержать*) to keep, maintain.

корм|и́ться, лю́сь, ~ишься *impf.* **1** (*pf.* **по~**) (*есть*) to eat, feed (*intrans.*). **2** (*pf.* **про~**) (+*i.*) (*содержать себя*) to live (on); **к. уро́ками** to make a living by giving tuition.

кормле́ни|е, я *nt.* feeding.

корм|ово́й¹ *adj. of* ⇒**~а́; ~ово́е весло́** scull; **к. флаг** ensign; **~ова́я часть** after-part, stern-part; **~ова́я ру́бка** roundhouse.

корм|ово́й² *adj. of* ⇒**~;** fodder, forage; **~овы́е культу́ры, расте́ния** fodder crops; **~ова́я свёкла** mangel-wurzel.

корму́шк|а, и *f.* (*agric.*) (feeding-) trough; (*для птиц*) bird-table, bird-feeder.

ко́рмч|ий, его *m.* (*rhet.*) helmsman.

корна́|ть, ю *impf.* (*of* ⇒**о~** *and* **об~**) (*coll.*) to crop, cut too short.

корневи́щ|е, а *nt.* (*bot.*) rhizome.

кор|нево́й *adj. of* ⇒**~ень**

корнепло́д, а *m.* root vegetable.

ко́рнер, а, *pl.* **~ы** *or* **~а́** *m.* (*sport*) corner.

корне́т, а *m.* (*mil. and mus.*) cornet.

корнети́ст, а *m.* (*mus.*) cornet-player, cornetist.

корни́йский *adj.* = **корнуэ́льский**

корнишо́н, а *m.* (*cul.*) gherkin.

корнуэ́льский *adj.* Cornish (*of language*).

ко́роб, а, *pl.* **~а́** *m.* **1** basket (*of bast*). **2** (*fig., coll.*): **це́лый к. новосте́й** heaps of news; **наговори́ть с три ~а** to spin a long yarn.

коробе́йник, а *m.* pedlar.

коро́б|ить, лю, ишь *impf.* (*of* ⇒**по~**) **1** to warp. **2** (*fig.*) to jar upon, grate upon; (*impers.*): **меня́ ~ит от его́ акце́нта** his accent jars upon me.

коро́б|иться, ится *impf.* (*of* ⇒**по~** *and* **с~**) to warp, buckle.

коро́бк|а, и *f.* box, case; **дверна́я к.** door-frame; **к. скоросте́й** (*tech.*) gear-box; **черепна́я к.** (*anat.*) cranium.

короб|о́к, ка́ *m.* (small) box.

коро́бочк|а, и *f.* **1** *dim. of* ⇒**коро́бка. 2** (*bot.*) boll.

коро́бчатый *adj.* box-shaped.

коро́в|а, ы *f.* cow; **морска́я к.** sea-cow, manatee.

коро́в|ий *adj. of* ⇒**~а; ~ье ма́сло** butter.

коро́в|ка, ки *f. affectionate dim. of* ⇒**~а; бо́жья к.** lady-bird.

коро́вник, а *m.* cow-shed.

коро́вниц|а, ы *f.* (*obs.*) milk-maid.

короле́в|а, ы *f.* queen.

короле́вич, а *m.* (*obs. and folklore*) king's son.

короле́в|на, ны, *g. pl.* **~ен** *f.* (*obs. and folklore*) king's daughter.

короле́вск|ий *adj.* royal; **~ая ко́бра** king cobra; (*chess*): **к. слон** king's bishop.

короле́вств|о, а *nt.* kingdom.

корол|ёк, ька́ *m.* **1** (*zool.*): **желтоголо́вый к.** goldcrest, **красноголо́вый к.** firecrest. **2** (*апельсин*) blood-orange.

коро́л|ь, я́ *m.* king; (*fig.*) baron; **газе́тный к.** press baron.

коромы́с|ло, ла *g. pl.* **~ел** *nt.* **1** (*для вёдер*) yoke; (*у весов*) beam. **2** (*tech.*) rocking shaft, rocker arm. **3** (*coll.*): **дым стоя́л ~ом** all hell was let loose.

коро́н|а, ы *f.* **1** crown (*also fig.*). **2** (*astron.*) corona.

корона́рный *adj.* coronary.

коронаротромбо́з, а *m.* coronary (thrombosis).

корона|цио́нный *adj. of* ⇒**~ция**

корона́ци|я, и *f.* coronation.

коро́нк|а, и *f.* crown (*of tooth*).

коро́нный *adj.* crown, of state; (*theatr.*): **к. но́мер** best number.

корон|ова́ть, у́ю *impf. and pf.* to crown.

коро́ст|а, ы *f.* scab.

коросте́л|ь, я *m.* (*zool.*) corncrake.

корота́|ть, ю *impf.* (*of* ⇒**с~**) (*coll.*) to pass, while away (time).

коро́т|кий (ко́роток, коротка́, ко́ротко́, *pl.* **ко́ротки́)** *adj.* **1** short; **э́то пальто́ тебе́ ~ко́** this coat is too short for you; **~кая распра́ва** short shrift; **к. спи́сок** shortlist; **к. уда́р** short and sharp blow; (*coll.*): **ру́ки ко́ротки́!** just try!; you couldn't if you tried!; **ум ~ок** limited intelligence. **2** (*fig.*) (*дружественный*) close, friendly; (*coll.*): **быть на ~кой ноге́ с кем-н.** to be on friendly terms with s.o.

ко́ротк|о́¹ *see* ⇒**~ий**

ко́ротко² *adv.* **1** (*вкратце*) briefly; **к. говоря́** in short. **2** (*близко*): **к. узна́ть кого́-н.** to get to know s.o. well.

коротковолнови́к, а́ *m.* radio ham.

коротково́лновый *adj.* (*radio*) short-wave.

короткометра́жк|а, и *f.* (*coll.*) short (film); **рекла́мная к.** commercial, ad(vert).

короткометра́жный *adj.*: **к. фильм** short (film).

коροты́шк|а, и *c.g.* (*coll.*) shorty.

кор|о́че *comp. of* ⇒**~о́ткий** *and* **~о́тко** shorter; **к. говоря́** in short, to cut a long story short.

ко́рочк|а, и *f.* **1** *dim. of* ⇒**ко́рка. 2** (*coll.*) diploma.

корп|е́ть, лю́, и́шь *impf.* (**над, за** + *i.*) (*coll.*) to pore (over), sweat (over).

ко́рпи|я, и *f.* (*obs.*) lint.

корпорати́в|ный (~ен, ~на) *adj.* corporate.

корпора́ци|я, и *f.* corporation.

корпу́нкт, а *m.* press centre (*Br.*), center (*US*).

ко́рпус¹, а, *pl.* **~ы** *m.* **1** (*туловище*) body. **2** (*мера*) length (*of animal, as unit of measurement*); **на́ша ло́шадь опереди́ла други́х на три ~а** our horse won by three lengths.

ко́рпус², а, *pl.* **~а́, ~о́в** *m.* **1** (*mil.*) corps; **каде́тский, морско́й к.** military school, naval college; **дипломати́ческий к.** diplomatic corps. **2** (*здание*) building; block. **3** (*корабля*) hull; (*tech.*) frame, body, case.

корректи́в, а *m.* amendment, correction.

корректи́р|овать, ую *impf.* (*of* ⇒**про~**) to correct; **~ующая жи́дкость** correction fluid.

корректиро́вщик, а *m.* (*mil.*) **1** (*человек*) spotter. **2** (*самолёт*) spotter (aircraft).

корре́кт|ный (~ен, ~на) *adj.* correct, proper.

корре́ктор, а *m.* proof-reader; **орфографи́ческий к.** (*comput.*) spell-checker.

корректу́р|а, ы *f.* **1** (*исправление*) proof-reading, correction. **2** (*оттиск*) proof(-sheet); **держа́ть ~у** to read, correct proofs; **к. в гра́нках** galley proof(s); **к. в листа́х** page proof(s).

корректу́р|ный *adj. of* ⇒**~а; ~ные зна́ки** proof symbols; **к. о́ттиск** proof (-sheet).

корре́кци|я, и *f.* correction.

коррел́ят, а *m.* correlate.

коррелят́ивный *adj.* correlative.

корреля́ци|я, и *f.* correlation.

корреспонде́нт, а *m.* correspondent.

корреспонде́нт|ка, ки *f. of* ⇒**~**

корреспонде́нтский *adj.* correspondent's; press (*attr.*); **к. пункт** = **корпу́нкт**

корреспонде́нци|я, и *f.* **1** (*переписка; письма*) correspondence. **2** (*сообщение*) dispatch, report.

корри́д|а, ы *f.* bullfight.

корро́зи|я, и *f.* (*chem.*) corrosion.

коррумпи́рованност|ь, и *f.* corruptness, corruption.

коррумпи́ров|анный (~ан, ~ана) *adj.* corrupt.

корру́пци|я, и *f.* (*pol.*) corruption.

корса́ж, а *m.* bodice.

корса́р, а *m.* corsair.

корсе́т, а *m.* corset.

Ко́рсик|а, и *f.* Corsica.

корт, а *m.* (tennis-)court.

корте́ж, а *m.* procession, cortège; (*автомобилей*) motorcade.

кортизо́н, а *m.* (*med.*) cortisone.

К

ко́ртик, а *m.* dagger.

ко́рточ|ки, ек *no sg.*: **сиде́ть на ~ках, сесть на к.** to squat.

кору́нд, а *m.* (*min.*) corundum.

Ко́рфу *m. indecl.* Corfu.

корч|ева́ть, у́ю *impf.* to uproot, root out.

корчёвк|а, и *f.* uprooting, rooting out.

ко́рч|и, ей *pl.* (*sg.* **~а, ~и** *f.*) (*coll.*) convulsions, spasm; **му́читься в ~ах** to writhe with pain.

ко́рч|ить, у, ишь *impf.* (*of* ⇨**с~**) **1** to contort; (*coll.*): **к. грима́сы, ро́жи** to make, pull faces. **2** (*impf. only*) (*coll.*): **к. из себя́** to pose (as); **к. дурака́** to play the fool.

ко́рч|иться, усь, ишься *impf.* (*coll.*) to writhe.

корч|ма́, мы, *g. pl.* **~ём** *f.* (*obs.*) inn, tavern (*in Ukraine and Byelorussia*).

ко́ршун, а *m.* (*zool.*) kite; (*fig.*): **налете́ть, набро́ситься ~ом (на** + *a.*) to pounce (on), swoop (onto).

коры́ст|ный (~ен, ~на) *adj.* mercenary, selfish.

корыстолю́б|ец, ца *m.* mercenary-minded person.

корыстолюби́в|ый (~, ~а) *adj.* mercenary, selfish.

корыстолю́би|е, я *nt.* self-interest.

коры́ст|ь, и *f.* (*coll.*) **1** (*выгода*) profit, gain; **кака́я тебе́ в э́том к.?** what are you getting out of it? **2** (*корыстолюбие*) self-interest.

коры́т|о, а *nt.* tub; trough; **оста́ться у разби́того ~а** to be no better off than before, be back where one started.

кор|ь, и *f.* measles.

ко́рюшк|а, и *f.* smelt (*fish*).

коря́в|ый (~, ~а) *adj.* (*coll.*) **1** (*дуб, пальцы*) gnarled. **2** (*почерк, речь, стиль*) clumsy. **3** (*obs.*) (*лицо*) pock-marked.

коря́г|а, и *f.* (*ветвь*) dead branch, (*пень*) dead tree stump (*often submerged under water*).

кос|а́[1], **ы́,** *a.* **~у́,** *pl.* **~ы** *f.* (*волосы*) plait, pigtail, braid.

кос|а́[2], **ы́,** *a.* **~у́,** *pl.* **~ы** *f.* (*орудие*) scythe; **нашла́ к. на ка́мень** he (has) met his match; he ran (has run) into a brick wall.

кос|а́[3], **ы́,** *a.* **~у́,** *pl.* **~ы** *f.* (*geog.*) spit.

коса́р|ь[1], **я́** *m.* (*человек*) mower.

коса́р|ь[2], **я́** *m.* (*орудие*) chopper.

коса́тк|а, и *f.* killer whale.

ко́свенн|ый *adj.* indirect, oblique; **~ые ули́ки** circumstantial evidence; (*gram.*): **к. паде́ж** oblique case; **~ая речь** indirect speech.

косе́канс, а *m.* (*math.*) cosecant.

коси́лк|а, и *f.* mowing-machine, mower; **газо́нная к.** lawn mower.

ко́синус, а *m.* (*math.*) cosine.

ко|си́ть[1], **шу́, ~сишь** *impf.* (*of* ⇨**с~**) (*траву*) to mow; to cut; (*fig.*) (*людей*) to cut down; to wipe out; **~си́ ~са́ пока́ роса́** (*prov.*) make hay while the sun shines.

ко|си́ть[2], **шу́, си́шь** *impf.* (*of* ⇨**с~**) **1** (*о глазах*) to squint; **к. на о́ба гла́за** to have a squint in both eyes. **2** (+*a. or i.*) (*рот, глаза*) to twist, slant. **3** (*иметь косой вид*) to be crooked.

ко|си́ться, шу́сь, си́шься *impf.* (*of* ⇨**по~**) **1** (*о доме*) to slant. **2** (*coll.*) (**на** + *a.*) to cast a sidelong look (at); (*fig.*) to look askance (at).

коси́чк|а, и *f. dim. of* ⇨**коса́**[1]

косма́|тить, чу, тишь *impf.* (*coll.*) to tousle.

косма́т|ый (~, ~а) *adj.* shaggy.

косме́тик|а, и *f.* cosmetics, make-up.

космети́ческ|ий *adj.* cosmetic; **к. кабине́т** beauty parlour (*Br.*), parlor (*US*); **~ая ма́ска** face-pack; **к. ремо́нт** redecoration.

космети́чк|а, и *f.* (*coll.*) **1** (*человек*) beautician. **2** (*сумочка*) make-up bag.

космето́лог, а *m.* cosmetic surgeon.

косметоло́ги|я, и *f.* cosmetic surgery.

косми́ческ|ий *adj.* **1** space (*attr.*). **2** (*пыль, радиация*) cosmic; **к. кора́бль** spaceship; **~ое телеви́дение** satellite television broadcasting.

космого́ни|я, и *f.* cosmogony.

космодро́м, а *m.* cosmodrome, space centre (*Br.*), center (*US*).

космолёт, а *m.* (space) shuttle.

космона́вт, а *m.* astronaut, cosmonaut, spaceman.

космона́втик|а, и *f.* astronautics, space exploration.

космополи́т, а *m.* cosmopolite; cosmopolitan.

космополити́зм, а *m.* cosmopolitanism.

космополити́ческий *adj.* cosmopolitan.

ко́смос, а *m.* cosmos; outer space.

космоте́хник|а, и *f.* space technology.

ко́см|ы, ~ *no sg.* (*coll.*) locks, mane.

косне́|ть, ю *impf.* (*of* ⇨**за~**) (**в** + *p.*) to stagnate (in).

косноязы́чи|е, я *nt.* confused articulation.

косноязы́ч|ный (~ен, ~на) *adj.* speaking thickly.

косн|у́ться, у́сь, ёшься *pf. of* ⇨**каса́ться**

ко́с|ный (~ен, ~на) *adj.* (*ум*) inert, sluggish; (*образ жизни, общество*) stagnant.

ко́со *adv.* slantwise, askew; obliquely; **смотре́ть к.** to look askance, scowl.

кособо́к|ий (~, ~а) *adj.* (*coll.*) crooked, lop-sided.

Ко́сово *nt. indecl.* Kosovo.

косоворо́тк|а, и *f.* shirt (*with collar fastening at side*).

ко́совский *adj.* Kosovan, Kosovar.

косогла́зи|е, я *nt.* squint, cast in the eye.

косогла́з|ый (~, ~а) *adj.* cross-eyed, squint-eyed.

косого́р, а *m.* slope, hill-side.

кос|о́й (~, ~а́, ~о) *adj.* **1** slanting; oblique; **к. по́черк** sloping handwriting; **к. у́гол** (*math.*) oblique angle; **~а́я черта́** oblique stroke; **~а́я са́жень в плеча́х** (*coll.*) broad shoulders. **2** (*косоглазый*) squinting; cross-eyed. **3**: **к. взгляд** (*fig.*) sidelong glance.

косола́п|ый (~, ~а) *adj.* pigeon-toed; (*fig.*) clumsy.

Ко́ста-Ри́к|а, и *f.* Costa Rica.

косте́л, а *m.* (Roman Catholic) church.

костене́|ть, ю *impf.* (*of* ⇨**о~**) to grow stiff; to grow numb.

кост|ёр, ра́ *m.* bonfire; (*походный*) camp-fire; **заже́чь/разложи́ть к.** to make a fire; **сжечь на ~ре́** (*человека*) to burn at the stake.

костер|и́ть, ю́, и́шь *impf.* (*coll.*) = **кости́ть**

кости́ст|ый (~, ~а) *adj.* bony.

ко|сти́ть, щу́, сти́шь *impf.* (*coll.*) to scold.

костля́в|ый (~, ~а) *adj.* bony.

ко́стный *adj.* osseous; (*anat.*): **к. мозг** marrow.

ко́сточк|а, и *f.* **1** *dim. of* ⇨**кость; перемыва́ть ~и** (+*d.*) to gossip about, pull to pieces; **разбира́ть по ~ам что́-н.** to go through (a thing, matter) with a fine comb. **2** (*сливы, абрикоса*) stone (*Br.*), pit (*US*); (*лимона, винограда*) pip (*Br.*), seed (*US*). **3** (*на счётах*) ball (*of abacus*). **4** (*корсета*) bone.

косты́л|ь, я́ *m.* **1** crutch; **ходи́ть на ~я́х** to walk on crutches. **2** (*гвоздь*) spike.

костыля́|ть, ю *impf.* (*coll.*) **1** (*бить*) to cudgel. **2** (*хромать*) to hobble.

кост|ь, и, *pl.* **~и, ~е́й** *f.* **1** bone; **слоно́вая к.** ivory; (*fig., coll.*) **язы́к без ~е́й** loose tongue; **лечь ~ьми́** (*rhet.*) to fall in battle; **пересчита́ть кому́-н. ~и** to give s.o. a drubbing. **2** (*pl.*) (*в игре*) dice.

костю́м, а *m.* **1** (*одежда*) dress, clothes; **в ~е Ада́ма, Е́вы** (*joc.*) in one's birthday suit; **маскара́дный к.** fancy-dress. **2** (*пиджак и брюки; жакет и юбка*) suit; **вече́рний к.** dress suit; **купа́льный к.** swimsuit. **3** (*theatr.*) costume.

костюме́р, а *m.* (*theatr.*) wardrobe assistant.

костюме́р|ный *adj. of* ⇨**~**; *as n.* **~ная, ~ной** *f.* (*theatr.*) wardrobe (room).

костюме́рш|а, и *f.* (*coll., theatr.*) wardrobe mistress.

костюмиро́ва|нный *p.p.p. of* ⇨**~ть** *and adj.* **1** in costume; in fancy-dress. **2**: **к. бал, ве́чер** fancy-dress ball.

костюмир|ова́ть, у́ю *impf. and pf.* to dress (*in theatre or fancy-dress costume*).

костюмир|ова́ться, у́юсь *impf. and pf.* to put on costume; to put on fancy-dress.

костю́м|ный *adj. of* ⇨**~**; **~ная пье́са, дра́ма** period play, drama.

костя́к, а́ *m.* skeleton; (*fig.*) (+*g.*) backbone (of).

костян|о́й *adj.* (*made of*) bone; **~а́я мука́** bone-meal.

костя́шк|а, и *f.* **1** (*пальцев*) knuckle. **2** (*на счётах*) ball.

косу́л|я, и *f.* roe deer.

косы́нк|а, и *f.* (triangular) kerchief, scarf.

косьб|а́, ы́ *f.* mowing.

кося́к¹, а́ *m.* (*дверной*) (door-)post; jamb.

кося́к², а́ *m.* **1** (*лошадей*) herd. **2** (*рыб*) shoal, school; (*птиц*) flock.

кося́к³, а́ *m.* (*sl.*) (*с марихуаной*) joint.

кот, а́ *m.* **1** tom-cat; (*coll.*): **к. напла́кал** nothing to speak of; practically nothing; **купи́ть ~а́ в мешке́** to buy a pig in a poke. **2** (*sl.*) (*мужчина*) pimp.

кота́нгенс, а *m.* (*math.*) cotangent.

кот|ёл, ла́ *m.* **1** pot, cauldron; **о́бщий к.** communal pot. **2** (*tech.*) boiler.

котел|о́к, ка́ *m.* **1** pot. **2** (*mil.*) mess-tin. **3** (*шляпа*) bowler (hat).

коте́льн|ая, ой *f.* boiler-house.

коте́л|ьный *adj. of* ⇨**~** 2; **~ьное желе́зо** boiler plate.

коте́льщик, а *m.* boiler-maker.

кот|ёнок, ёнка, *pl.* **~я́та, ~я́т** *m.* kitten.

ко́тик, а *m.* **1** (*тюлень*) fur-seal. **2** (*мех*) sealskin. **3** *dim. of* ⇨**кот**

ко́тик|овый *adj. of* ⇨**~** 1, 2; **к. про́мысел** sealing; sealskin trade; **~овая ша́пка** sealskin cap.

котильо́н, а *m.* cotillion.

коти́р|овать, ую *impf. and pf.* (*fin.*) to quote.

коти́р|оваться, уюсь *impf. and pf.* **1** (*fin.*) (**в** + *a.*) to be quoted (at). **2** (*fig.*) to be rated.

котиро́вк|а, и *f.* (*fin.*) quotation.

кот|и́ться, и́тся *impf.* (*of* ⇨**о~**) (*о кошке*) to have kittens; (*о зайце, кролике*) to have young.

котле́т|а, ы *f.* burger; rissole; **(отбивна́я) к.** chop.

котле́тн|ая, ой *f.* burger bar.

котлова́н, а *m.* (*tech.*) foundation pit.

котлови́н|а, ы *f.* (*geog.*) hollow, basin.

кото́мк|а, и *f.* knapsack.

кото́р|ый *pron.* **1** *interrog. and rel.* (*о предметах*) which; **к. час?** what time is it?; **в ~ом часу́ он приходи́л?** what time did he call? **2** (*coll.*) (*не один*) some, quite a few; **к. раз я тебе́ э́то говорю́?** how many times have I told you!; **к. год он не пи́шет** he hasn't been writing for some years. **3** *rel.* (*о людях*) who. **4** (*coll.*): **к.... к.** some ... some (others); **~ые посети́тели сиде́ли, ~ые стоя́ли** some visitors were sitting, some standing.

кото́рый-либо *pron.* = **кото́рый-нибудь**

кото́рый-нибудь *pron.* some; one or other.

котте́дж, а *m.* cottage.

кот|я́та, я́т *see* ⇨**~ёнок**

ко́фе *m. indecl.* coffee; **раствори́мый к.** instant coffee; **к. в зёрнах** coffee beans.

кофева́рк|а, и *f.* coffee-maker.

кофеи́н, а *m.* caffeine.

кофе́йник, а *m.* coffee-pot.

кофе́йниц|а, ы *f.* coffee-grinder.

коф|е́йный *adj. of* ⇨**~е**

кофе́|йня, йни, *g. pl.* **~ен** *f.* coffee-house.

кофемо́лк|а, и *f.* coffee grinder.

ко́фт|а, ы *f.* (*woman's*) jacket, cardigan.

ко́фточк|а, и *f.* blouse.

коча́н, а́ (*and coll.* **кочна́)** *m.*: **к. капу́сты** head of cabbage.

коч|ева́ть, у́ю *impf.* **1** (*о племенах*) to be a nomad, to roam from place to place; (*fig.*) (*передвигаться*) to wander. **2** (*о животных*) to migrate.

кочёвк|а, и *f.* (*coll.*) **1** (*лагерь*) nomad camp. **2** (*действие*) wandering; nomadic existence; (*животных*) migrating.

коче́вник, а *m.* nomad.

кочево́й *adj.* **1** (*люди*) nomadic. **2** (*животные*) migratory.

коче́в|ье, ья, *g. pl.* **~ий** *nt.* **1** (*лагерь*) nomad encampment. **2** (*местность*) nomad territory.

кочега́р, а *m.* stoker, fireman.

кочега́рк|а, и *f.* stoke-hole, stoke-hold.

кочене́|ть, ю *impf.* (*of* ⇨**за~** *and* **о~**) to become numb; to stiffen.

кочер|га́, ги́, *g. pl.* **~ёг** *f.* poker.

кочеры́жк|а, и *f.* cabbage-stump.

ко́чет, а *m.* (*dial.*) cock.

ко́чк|а, и *f.* hummock; tussock.

кочкова́т|ый (~, ~а) *adj.* hummocky, tussocky.

коша́тник, а *m.* (*coll.*) cat-lover.

коша́тни|ца, цы *f. of* ⇨**~к**

кош|а́чий *adj. of* ⇨**~ка;** feline; **к. конце́рт** caterwauling; (*fig.*) hooting, barracking.

кошел|ёк, ька́ *m.* purse.

кошёлк|а, и *f.* (*coll.*) small basket.

коше́л|ь, я́ *m.* **1** (*obs.*) (*кошелёк*) purse. **2** (*coll.*) (*сумка*) bag.

кошени́л|ь, и *f.* (*краска*) cochineal.

коше́рный *adj.* kosher.

ко́шк|а, и *f.* **1** cat; **(к.-)манкс, бесхво́стая к.** Manx cat; (*fig., coll.*): **игра́ть в ~и-мы́шки** to play cat-and-mouse; **жить как к. с соба́кой** to lead a cat-and-dog life; **чёрная к. пробежа́ла ме́жду ни́ми** they have fallen out; **у него́ ~и скребу́т на се́рдце** he is heavy-hearted. **2** (*tech., naut.*) grapnel, drag. **3** (*pl.*) (*для лазания*) crampons; climbing-irons. **4** (*pl.*) (*плеть*) cat-o'-nine tails.

кошма́р, а *m.* **1** nightmare (*also fig.*). **2** *as pred.* (*coll.*) it is a nightmare.

кошма́р|ный (~ен, ~на) *adj.* nightmarish; (*fig.*) horrible, awful.

ко|шу́, си́шь *see* ⇨**~си́ть**

кощ́е|й, я *m.* **1** Koshchey (*an evil being in Russian folklore*). **2** (*fig., coll.*) (*скряга*) miser.

кощу́нствен|ный (~, ~на) *adj.* blasphemous.

кощу́нств|о, а *nt.* blasphemy.

кощу́нств|овать, ую *impf.* to blaspheme.

коэффицие́нт, а *m.* (*math.*) coefficient; (*tech.*): **к. поле́зного де́йствия** efficiency (*also fig.*); **к. у́мственных спосо́бностей** intelligence quotient, IQ.

КП *f. indecl.* (*abbr. of* ***Коммунисти́ческая па́ртия***) Communist Party.

КПД *m. indecl.* (*abbr. of* ***коэффицие́нт поле́зного де́йствия***) (*tech.*) efficiency (*also fig.*).

КПЗ *f. indecl.* (*abbr. of* ***ка́мера предвари́тельного заключе́ния***) remand prison.

КПП *m. indecl.* (*abbr. of* ***контро́льно-пропускно́й пункт***) checkpoint.

КПСС *f. indecl.* (*abbr. of* ***Коммунисти́ческая па́ртия Сове́тского Сою́за***) (*hist.*) CPSU (*Communist Party of the Soviet Union*).

кр. (*abbr. of* ***край***) kray, krai.

краб, а *m.* (*zool.*) crab.

кра́вч|ий, его *m.* (*hist.*) royal carver (*in Muscovite Russia*).

кра́г|и, ~ *pl.* (*sg.* **~а, ~и** *f.*) **1** leggings. **2** (*у перчаток*) cuffs.

кра́ден|ый *adj.* stolen; **~ое** (*collect.*) stolen goods.

кра|ду́, дёшь *see* ⇨**~сть**

краду́чись *adv.* stealthily; **идти́ к.** to creep, slink.

краеве́д, а *m.* local historian.

краеве́дени|е, я *nt.* local history.

краеве́д|ческий *adj. of* ⇨**~ение;** **к. музе́й** local-history/folk museum.

краево́й *adj. of* ⇨**край** 4

краеуго́льный *adj.* (*rhet.*) basic; **к. ка́мень** corner-stone.

кра́ж|а, и *f.* theft; **к. со взло́мом** burglary; **магази́нная к.** shoplifting; **квалифици́рованная к.** (*leg.*) aggravated theft.

кра|й, я, о ~е, в ~ю́, *pl.* **~я́, ~ёв** *m.* **1** (*поля, одежды*) edge; (*сосуда*) brim; (*пропасти*) brink (*also fig.*); **быть на ~ю́ моги́лы** to have one foot in the grave; **конца́-~ю нет** there is no end to it; **~ем у́ха слу́шать** to listen with half an ear; **на ~ю́ све́та** at the world's end; **че́рез к.** beyond measure; **хвати́ть че́рез к.** (*coll.*) to overstep the mark. **2** (*мяса*) side; **то́лстый к.** rib-steak; **то́нкий к.** chine (of beef), upper cut. **3** (*страна, область*) land, country; **в на́ших ~я́х** in our part of the world; **в чужи́х ~я́х** in foreign parts. **4** (*административная единица*) kray, krai.

край... *comb. form, abbr. of* ***краево́й***

крайко́м, а *m.* (*abbr. of* ***краево́й комите́т***) kray *or* krai committee.

кра́йне *adv.* extremely.

кра́йн|ий *adj.* **1** (*in var. senses*) extreme; (*последний*) last; **К. Се́вер** the Far North; **в ~ем слу́чае** in the last resort; **к. срок** deadline; **по ~ей ме́ре** at least; **~яя плоть** (*anat.*) foreskin. **2** (*sport*) outside, wing; **к. напада́ющий** outside forward, wing forward.

кра́йност|ь, и *f.* **1** (*крайняя степень*) extreme; **в ~и** in the last resort; **до ~и** in the extreme, extremely. **2** (*тяжёлое положение*) extremity; **быть в ~и** to be reduced to extremity.

крайце́нтр, а *m.* (*abbr. of* ***краево́й центр***) main city, capital of kray *or* krai.

Кра́ков, а *f.* Cracow.

краковя́к, а *m.* (*танец*) Cracovienne.

крал, а *see* ⇒**красть**

кра́л|я, и *f.* (*coll.*) (*красотка*) beauty; (*любовница*) lover.

крамо́л|а, ы *f.* sedition, subversion.

крамо́льник, а *m.* conspirator, plotter; rebel.

крамо́льный *adj.* seditious, subversive.

кран[1], **а** *m.* (*водопроводный*) tap, faucet (*US*); (*на трубопроводах*) valve; **шарово́й к.** ball valve; **запо́рный к.** stopcock; **к.-смеси́тель** mixer tap.

кран[2], **а** *m.* (*машина*) crane.

крановщи́к, а́ *m.* crane operator.

крановщи́|ца, цы *f. of* ⇒**~к**

кра́н|овый *adj. of* ⇒**~**[1,2]

крап, а *no pl., m.* (*пятна*) spots; specks.

кра́п|ать, ает *and* **лет** *impf.* to spatter; **дождь ~ает** it is spitting with rain (*Br.*).

крапи́в|а, ы *f.* (stinging-)nettle; (*collect.*) nettles.

крапи́вник, а *m.* (*zool.*) wren.

крапи́вниц|а, ы *f.* nettle-rash.

крапи́в|ный *adj. of* ⇒**~а**; **~ная лихора́дка** nettle-rash.

кра́пин|а, ы *f.* speck; spot.

кра́пин|ка, ки *f.* = **~а**

краплёный *adj.* (*of cards*) marked.

кра́пчат|ый (~, ~а) *adj.* speckled.

крас|а́, ы́ *f.* **1** beauty; (*iron.*): **во всей свое́й ~е́** in all one's glory. **2** (*rhet.*) glory.

краса́в|ец, ца *m.* handsome man; good-looker (*male*).

краса́виц|а, ы *f.* beauty; good-looker (*female*).

краса́вк|а, и *f.* deadly nightshade, belladonna.

краса́вчик, а *m.* (*coll.*) **1** = **краса́вец. 2** (*iron.*) dandy.

краси́вост|ь, и *f.* (mere) prettiness.

краси́в|ый (~, ~а) *adj.* beautiful; (*мужчина*) handsome; (*поступок, слова*) fine.

краси́льный *adj.* appertaining to dyes.

краси́л|ьня, ьни, *g. pl.* **~ен** *f.* dye-house, dye-works.

краси́льщик, а *m.* dyer.

краси́тел|ь, я *m.* dye(-stuff); **пищево́й к.** food colouring (*Br.*), coloring (*US*).

кра́|сить, шу, сишь *impf.* (*of* ⇒**по~**) **1** (*стену, губы*) to paint. **2** (*ткань, волосы*) to dye; (*дерево, стекло*) to stain. **3** (*impf. only*) (*украшать*) to adorn.

кра́|ситься, шусь, сишься *impf.* **1** (*pf.* **на~**) to make up one's face. **2** (*pf.* **по~**) to dye one's hair. **3** (*no pf.*) (*пачкать собой*) to run. **4** *pass. of* ⇒**~сить**

кра́ск|а, и *f.* **1** (*действие*) painting; dyeing. **2** (*материал*) paint; (*для ткани*) dye; **акваре́льная к.** water-colour (*Br.*), -color (*US*); **(водо-)эмульсио́нная к.** emulsion (*paint*); **ма́сляная к.** oil-paint; **типогра́фская к.** printer's ink; **писа́ть ~ами** to paint; **к. для ресни́ц** mascara. **3** (*pl., fig.*) (*колорит*) colours (*Br.*), colors (*US*); **ви́деть жизнь в ро́зовых ~ах** to be naive; **сгуща́ть ~и** (*coll.*) to lay it on thick. **4** (*румянец*) blush; **вогна́ть кого́-н. в ~у** (*coll.*) to make s.o. blush.

краскопу́льт, а *m.* = **краскораспыли́тель**

краскораспыли́тел|ь, я *m.* spray-gun.

красне́|ть, ю *impf.* (*of* ⇒**по~**) **1** (*становиться красным*) to redden, become red. **2** (*от стыда*) to blush; (*fig.*): **к. за** + *a.* to blush for. **3** (*impf. only*) (*виднеться*) to show red.

красне́|ться, юсь *impf.* to show red.

красноарме́|ец, йца *m.* (*hist.*) Red Army man.

красноарме́|йский *adj. of* ⇒**~ец, Кра́сная А́рмия**

краснобá|й, я *m.* (*coll.*) gasbag.

краснобáйств|о, а *nt.* (*coll.*) empty rhetoric.

краснова́т|ый (~, ~а) *adj.* reddish.

красногварде́|ец, йца *m.* (*hist.*) Red Guard.

красногварде́|йский *adj. of* ⇒**~ец**

краснодерéв|ец, ца *m.* cabinet-maker.

краснодерéв|щик, щика *m.* = **~ец**

краснокóж|ий (~, ~а) *adj.* red-skinned; *as n.* **к., ~его** *m.* (*offens.*) American Indian.

краснокрéстный *adj.* Red Cross.

краснолéсь|е, я *nt.* pine forest.

краснолúцый *adj.* red-faced.

красноречи́в|ый (~, ~а) *adj.* eloquent.

красноре́чи|е, я *nt.* eloquence.

краснот|а́, ы́ *f.* redness.

краснощёк|ий (~, ~а) *adj.* rosy-cheeked.

красну́х|а, и *f.* (*med.*) German measles.

кра́с|ный (~ен, ~на́, ~но) *adj.* **1** red (*also fig., pol.*); **Кра́сная А́рмия** Red Army; **~ное де́рево** mahogany; **Кра́сная Ша́почка** Little Red Riding Hood; **К. Крест** Red Cross; (*fig.*): **~ная строка́** (first line of) new paragraph; **проходи́ть ~ной ни́тью** to stand out, run through (*of theme*). **2** (*obs., folk poet. or coll.*) (*краси́вый*) beautiful; (*fig.*) fine; **~ная де́вица** bonny lass; (*prov.*): **долг платежо́м ~ен** one good turn deserves another.

крас|ова́ться, у́юсь *impf.* **1** to stand out (vividly). **2** (*coll.*) to flaunt oneself, show off.

красот|а́, ы́, *pl.* **~́ы** *f.* beauty; *as pred.* (*coll.*): **к.!** splendid!

красо́тк|а, и *f.* (*coll.*) good-looking girl; beauty.

кра́с|очный *adj.* **1** *adj. of* ⇒**~ка. 2 (~очен, ~очна)** colourful (*Br.*), colorful (*US*).

кра|сть, ду́, дёшь, *past* **~л, ~́ла** *impf.* (*of* ⇒**у~́**) to steal.

кра́|сться, ду́сь, дёшься, *past* **~лся, ~лась** *impf.* to steal, creep, sneak.

крат *only in phrr.* **во́ сто к.** hundredfold; **во мно́го к.** many times more.

кра́тер, а *m.* crater.

кра́т|кий (~ок, ~ка́, ~ко) *adj.* short; brief; **я бу́ду ~ок** I'll be brief; (*сжатый*) concise; **в ~ких слова́х** in short, briefly; **и ~кое** *Russian letter* **й.**

кра́тко *adv.* briefly.

кратковре́мен|ный (~ен, ~на) *adj.* of short duration, brief; **к. дождь** shower.

краткосро́ч|ный (~ен, ~на) *adj.* (*ссуда*) short-term; (*отпуск*) short.

кра́тн|ое, ого *nt.* (*math.*) multiple; **наиме́ньшее о́бщее к.** least common multiple.

кра́т|ный (~ен, ~на) *adj.* (+*d.*) divisible without remainder (by); **де́вять — число́, ~ное трём** nine is a multiple of three.

крат|ча́йший *superl. of* ⇒**~́кий**

кра́т|че *comp. of* ⇒**~кий** *and* **~ко**

крах, а *m.* (*fin. and fig.*) crash, collapse; (*fig.*) (*провал*) failure; **потерпе́ть к.** to fail.

крахма́л, а *m.* starch.

крахма́лист|ый (~, ~а) *adj.* containing starch.

крахма́л|ить, ю, ишь *impf.* (*of* ⇒**на~**) to starch.

крахма́л|ьный *adj. of* ⇒**~**; starched.

кра́чк|а, и *f.* (*zool.*) tern.

кра́ше (*liter.*) *comp. of* ⇒**краси́вый, краси́во**

кра́шени|е, я *nt.* dyeing.

кра́шен|ый *adj.* **1** (*стена*) painted; **~ое яйцо́** (decorated) Easter egg. **2** (*ткань*) dyed. **3** (*женщина*) made-up, wearing make-up; (*pej.*) painted; **~ая блонди́нка** peroxide blond.

краю́х|а, и *f.* (*coll.*) hunk of bread.

креве́тк|а, и *f.* (*zool.*) shrimp; prawn.

кре́дит, а *m.* (*book-keeping*) credit.

креди́т, а *m.* **1** credit; **в к.** on credit. **2** (*fig.*) (*доверие*) credibility. **3** (*pl.*) (*ассигнования*) finance.

креди́тк|а, и *f.* (*coll.*) credit card.

креди́т|ный *adj. of* ⇒**~**; **к. биле́т** banknote; **~ная ка́рточка/ка́рта** credit card.

кредит|ова́ть, у́ю *impf. and pf.* (*fin.*) to give credit (to).

кредито́р, а *m.* creditor.

кредитоспосо́бност|ь, и *f.* creditworthiness, credit rating.

кредитоспосо́б|ный (~ен, ~на) *adj.* creditworthy.

кре́до *nt. indecl.* credo, creed.

кре́йсер, а, *pl.* **~ы** *and* **~а́** (*mil.*) cruiser; **лине́йный к.** battle cruiser.

кре́йсер|ский *adj. of* ⇒**~**; **~ская ско́рость** cruising speed.

крейси́р|овать, ую *impf.* (*naut.*) **1** (*совершать рейсы*) to make regular scheduled trips from A to B; **теплохо́ды ~уют регуля́рно** motor vessels sail regularly. **2** (*mil.*) to patrol.

кре́кер, а *m.* cracker.

кре́кинг, а *m.* (*tech.*) cracking (*oil refining*).

крем, а *m.* (*in var. senses*) cream; **к.-брюле́** crème brûlée; **(сапо́жный) к.** shoe-polish; **увлажня́ющий к.** moisturizer; **защи́тный к.** sunblock.

крема́то́ри|й, я *m.* crematorium.

кремац|ио́нный *adj. of* ⇒**~ия**; **~ио́нная печь** incinerator.

крема́ци|я, и *f.* cremation.

крем|е́нь, ня́ *m.* flint.

кремлеве́д, а *m.* Kremlinologist; Kremlin-watcher.

кремлеве́дени|е, я *nt.* Kremlinology; Kremlin-watching.

кремл|ёвский *adj. of* ⇒**~ь**

кремлено́лог, а *m.* = **кремлеве́д**

кремленоло́ги|я, и *f.* Kremlinology, Kremlin-watching.

кремл|ь, я́ *m.* citadel; **(моско́вский) К.** the Kremlin.

кремнёв|ый *adj.* flint; **~ое ружьё** flint-lock.

кремнезём, а *m.* (*min., chem.*) silica.

кре́мниевый *adj.* (*chem.*) silicic.

кре́мни|й, я *m.* (*chem.*) silicon.

кремни́стый *adj.* **1** (*min.*) siliceous. **2** (*obs.*) stony.

кре́м|овый *adj.* **1** *adj. of* ⇒**~**. **2** (*цвет*) cream(-coloured).

крен, а *m.* (*naut.*) list, heel; (*aeron.*) bank; **дать к.** (*naut.*) to list, heel (over); (*aeron.*) to bank.

кре́ндел|ь, я, *pl.* **~и** *and* **~я́, ~е́й** *m.* (*cul.*) pretzel; **выпи́сывать ~я́** (*coll.*) to stagger, lurch.

крен|и́ть, ю́, и́шь *impf.* (*of* ⇒**на~**) to cause to heel, list.

крен|и́ться, ю́сь, и́шься *impf.* (*of* ⇒**на~**) (*naut.*) to list, heel (over); (*aeron.*) to bank.

креозо́т, а *m.* creosote.

крео́л, а *m.* Creole.

крео́л|ьский *adj. of* ⇒**~**

креп, а *m.* crêpe.

крепдеши́н, а *m.* crêpe de chine.

крепёжный *adj.* reinforcing; **к. лес** pit-props.

крепи́тельный *adj.* **1** (*воздух, сон*) refreshing. **2** (*tech.*) strengthening. **3** (*med.*) binding.

креп|и́ть, лю́, и́шь *impf.* **1** (*прочно прикреплять*) to fasten. **2** (*усиливать*) to strengthen. **3** (*med.*) to constipate.

креп|и́ться, лю́сь, и́шся *impf.* **1** to hold out. **2** *pass. of* ⇒**~и́ть**

кре́п|кий (~ок, ~ка́, ~ко) *adj.* (*чай, кофе; запах; ветер; организм; ткань*) strong; (*сон*) sound; (*забор*) sturdy, robust; (*мороз, удар*) hard; (*fig.*) (*стойкий*) firm; **~кие напи́тки** spirits; **~кое словцо́** (*coll.*) swear-word, strong language; **~ок на́ ухо** hard of hearing.

кре́пко *adv.* (*держать; завязать*) tight; (*построенный*) strongly; (*спать*) soundly; (*coll.*): **к.-на́крепко** very firmly; **к.-на́крепко завяза́ть** to tie really tight.

крепкоголо́в|ый (~, ~а) *adj.* (*coll.*) thick-headed.

крепколо́б|ый (~, ~а) *adj.* (*coll.*) thick-headed.

крепле́ни|е, я *nt.* **1** strengthening; fastening. **2** (*naut.*) lashing; furling. **3** (*лыжное*) binding.

креплёный *adj.* (*о вине*) fortified.

кре́пн|уть, у, ешь *impf.* (*of* ⇒**о~**) to get stronger.

крепостни́к, а́ *m.* advocate of serfdom; serf owner.

крепостни́|ческий *adj. of* ⇒**~к** *and* ⇒**~чество**

крепостни́честв|о, а *nt.* serfdom.

крепостн|о́й[1] *adj.* serf; **к. крестья́нин** (*peasant*) serf; **~о́е пра́во** serfdom; *as n.* **к., ~о́го** *m.* serf.

крепостно́й[2] *adj. of* ⇒**кре́пость**[2]

кре́пост|ь[1], **и** *f.* (*свойство*) strength.

кре́пост|ь[2], **и** *f.* (*mil.*) fortress.

крепча́|ть, ет *impf.* (*coll.*) (*о ветре*) to grow stronger, get up; (*о морозе*) to get harder.

кре́п|че *comp. of* ⇒**~кий** *and* **~ко**

крепы́ш, а́ *m.* (*coll.*) brawny fellow; (*о ребёнке*) sturdy child.

креп|ь, и *f.* (*mining*) timbering.

кре́с|ло, ла, *g. pl.* **~ел** *nt.* arm-chair, easy-chair; (*fig.*) (*должность*) post, office; **высо́кое к.** (*child's*) high chair; **инвали́дное к.** wheelchair; **к.-кача́лка** rocking chair; **к.-крова́ть** sofa bed; (*theatr.*) seat.

кресс-сала́т, а *m.* cress.

крест, а́ *m.* **1** cross; **поста́вить к.** (**на** + *p.*) to give up for lost. **2** (*жест*) the sign of the cross; **осени́ть себя́ ~о́м** to cross o.s.

крест|е́ц, ца́ *m.* (*anat.*) sacrum.

крести́льный *adj.* baptismal.

крести́н|ы, ~ *no sg.* christening.

крести́тел|ь, я *m.*: **Иоа́нн К.** (*relig.*) John the Baptist.

кре|сти́ть, щу́, ~стишь *impf.* **1** (*pf.* **к.** *or* **о~**) to baptize, christen; **~сти́ли его́ Гео́ргием** they baptized him George. **2** (*no pf.*) (+*a. and* **у**+*g.*) to be godfather, godmother (*to the child of*); **я у них ~сти́ла дочь** I was godmother to their daughter. **3** (*pf.* **пере~**) to make the sign of the cross over.

кре|сти́ться, щу́сь, ~стишься *impf.* **1** (*pf.* **к.** *or* **о~**) to be baptized, be christened. **2** (*pf.* **пере~**) to cross o.s.

крест-на́крест *adv.* crosswise.

кре́стник, а *m.* god-son, god-child.

кре́стниц|а, ы *f.* god-daughter, god-child.

кре́ст|ный *adj. of* ⇒**~**; **~ное зна́мение** sign of the cross; **к. ход** (religious) procession.

крёстн|ый *adj.*: **к. оте́ц** (*also as n.* **к., ~ого** *m.*) god-father; **~ая мать** (*also as n.* **~ая, ~ой** *f.*) god-mother; **~ые де́ти** god-children.

крестови́н|а, ы *f.* cross-shaped component; crosspiece; (*rail.*) frog.

кресто́вник, а *m.* (*bot.*) ragwort, groundsel.

крест|о́вый *adj. of* ⇒**~**; **к. похо́д** (*also fig.*) crusade.

крестоно́с|ец, ца *m.* crusader.

крестообра́з|ный (~ен, ~на) *adj.* cruciform.

крестоцве́т|ные, ых *nt. pl.* (*bot.*) cruciferae.

крестцо́вый *adj.* (*anat.*) sacral.

кресть́ян|ин, ина, *pl.* **~е, ~** *m.* peasant.

крестья́нк|а, и *f.* peasant (woman).

крестья́нский *adj.* peasant.

крестья́нств|о, а *nt.* (*collect.*) the peasants, peasantry.

крети́н, а *m.* cretin; (*fig., coll.*) idiot, imbecile.

кретини́зм, а *m.* cretinism; (*fig., coll.*) idiocy.

крето́н, а *m.* (*text.*) cretonne.

кре́чет, а *m.* (*zool.*) gyrfalcon.

креще́ндо *nt. indecl.* & *adv.* (*mus.*) crescendo.

креще́ни|е, я *nt.* **1** baptism, christening; **боево́е к.** (*fig.*) baptism of fire. **2** (*праздник*) Epiphany.

креще́н|ский *adj. of* ⇒**~ие** 2; **~ские моро́зы** hard frosts in the second half of January.

крещёный *adj.* baptized.

кре|щу́, ~стишь *see* ⇒**~сти́ть**

крив|а́я, о́й *f.* (*math., econ., etc.*) curve; **к. вы́везет** (*coll.*) I'll be fine.

криве́|ть, ю *impf.* (*of* ⇒**о~**) to lose an eye.

кривизн|а́, ы́ *f.* (*потолка*) crookedness; (*поверхности, линии*) curvature.

крив|и́ть, лю́, и́шь *impf.* (*of* ⇒**с~**) to bend, distort; (*coll.*): **к. гу́бы, рот** to twist one's mouth, curl one's lip; **к.** (*pf.* **по~**) **душо́й** to act against one's conscience.

крив|и́ться, лю́сь, и́шься *impf.* **1** (*pf.* **по~**) to become crooked, bent. **2** (*pf.* **с~**) (*coll.*) to make a wry face.

кривля́к|а, и *c.g.* (*coll.*) poseur, pseud.

кривля́нь|е, я *nt.* affectation.

кривля́|ться, юсь *impf.* to behave affectedly; to show off.

кривобо́к|ий (~, ~а) *adj.* lop-sided.

крив|о́й (~, ~а́, ~о) *adj.* **1** crooked; **~о́е зе́ркало** (*also fig.*) distorting mirror; **~а́я улы́бка** wry smile. **2** (*coll.*) (*слепой на один глаз*) one-eyed.

криволине́йный *adj.* (*math.*) curvilinear.

кривоно́г|ий (~, ~а) *adj.* bandy-legged, bow-legged.

кривото́лк|и, ов *no sg.* false rumours (*Br.*), rumors (*US*).

кривоши́п, а *m.* (*tech.*) crank; crankshaft.

кри́зис, а *m.* crisis.

кри́зис|ный *adj. of* ⇒**~**; **~ная ситуа́ция** crisis situation, crisis.

крик, а *m.* cry, shout; *pl.* clamour (*Br.*), clamor (*US*), outcry; **к. души́** emotional outpouring; **после́дний к. мо́ды** (*coll.*) the last word in fashion.

кри́кет, а *m.* cricket; **игро́к в к.** cricketer.

К

крикли́в|ый (~, ~a) *adj.* **1** (*ребёнок*) clamorous, bawling. **2** (*голос*) loud, penetrating. **3** (*fig., coll.*) (*наряд*) loud.

кри́кн|уть, у, ешь *inst. pf. of* ⇒**крича́ть**

крику́н, а́ *m.* (*coll.*) **1** shouter, bawler. **2** (*многоречивый человек*) babbler.

крику́н|ья, ьи *g. pl.* **~ий** *f. of* ⇒**~**

крил|ь, я *m.* krill.

кримина́л, а *m.* (*coll.*) **1** (*плохое поведение*) foul play. **2** (*преступление*) crime.

криминали́ст, а *m.* (*leg.*) specialist in crime detection.

криминали́стик|а, и *f.* (*science of*) crime detection.

кримина́л|ьный (~ен, ~ьна) *adj.* criminal.

криминоге́нный *adj.* criminogenic.

кримино́лог, а *m.* criminologist.

криминоло́ги|я, и *f.* criminology.

кримпле́н, а *m.* crimplene (*propr.*).

кримпле́н|овый *adj. of* ⇒**~**

кри́нка = **кры́нка**

криноли́н, а *m.* crinoline.

криптогра́мм|а, ы *f.* cryptogram.

криптографи́ческий *adj.* cryptographic.

криптогра́фи|я, и *f.* cryptography.

криста́лл, а *m.* **1** crystal; **маги́ческий к.** crystal ball. **2** (*comput.*) (silicon) chip.

кристаллиза́ци|я, и *f.* crystallization.

кристаллиз|ова́ть, у́ю *impf. and pf.* (*pf. also* **за~**) to crystallize (*trans.*).

кристаллиз|ова́ться, у́ется *impf.* (*of* ⇒**вы́~** *and* ⇒**за~**) to crystallize (*intrans.; also fig.*).

кристаллогра́фи|я, и *f.* crystallography.

криста́л|ьный *adj.* **1** crystalline. **2 (~ен, ~ьна)** (*fig.*) crystal-clear. **3** (*безупречный*) pure.

Крит, а *m.* Crete.

крите́ри|й, я *m.* criterion.

кри́тский *adj.* Cretan.

кри́тик, а *m.* critic.

кри́тик|а, и *f.* **1** criticism. **2** (*отрицательное суждение*) critique.

критика́н, а *m.* (*coll., pej.*) fault-finder, carper.

критика́нств|овать, ую *impf.* (*coll., pej.*) to engage in fault-finding; to carp.

критик|ова́ть, у́ю *impf.* to criticize.

критици́зм, а *m.* critical attitude.

крити́ческий *adj.* critical; **к. моме́нт** (*fig.*) crucial moment.

кри|ча́ть, чу́, чи́шь *impf.* (*of* ⇒**~кнуть**) **1** to cry, shout; to yell, scream; **к. (на** + *a.*) to shout (at); **к. о по́мощи** to call for help. **2 (о** + *p.*) (*coll.*) to make a song and dance (about), talk a lot (about).

крича́|щий *pres. part. act. of* ⇒**~ть** *and adj.* (*fig.*) loud; blatant.

кришна́ит, а *m.* Hare Krishna (follower).

кришна́ит|ский *adj. of* ⇒**~**

кров, а *m.* **1** (*obs.*) roof. **2** (*fig.*) roof, shelter; **оста́ться без ~а** to be left without a roof over one's head.

крова́в|ый *adj.* **1** (*режим, события*) bloody; (*fig.*): **~ая ба́ня** blood-bath. **2** (*одежда*) blood-stained.

крова́тк|а, и *f.*: **де́тская к.** cot (*Br.*), crib (*US*).

крова́т|ь, и *f.* bed; **двухъя́русная к.** bunk bed.

кро́в|ельный *adj. of* ⇒**~ля**

кро́вельщик, а *m.* roofer.

кровено́сн|ый *adj.* appertaining to the circulation of the blood; **~ая систе́ма** circulatory system; **к. сосу́д** blood-vessel.

крови́нк|а, и *f.* (*coll.*) drop of blood; **у него́ ни ~и в лице́** he is deathly pale.

кро́в|ля, ли, *g. pl.* **~ель** *f.* roof.

кро́вн|ый *adj.* **1** blood; **~ая месть** blood feud. **2** (*животное*) thoroughbred. **3** (*fig.*) vital, deep, intimate; **моё ~ое де́ло** an affair which concerns me closely; **~ые интере́сы** vital interests; **~ые де́ньги** money earned by the sweat of one's brow. **4** (*fig.*) grievous, deadly; **~ая оби́да** deadly insult.

кровожа́д|ный (~ен, ~на) *adj.* blood-thirsty.

кровоизлия́ни|е, я *nt.* (*med.*) haemorrhage (*Br.*), hemorrhage (*US*).

кровообраще́ни|е, я *nt.* circulation of the blood.

кровоостана́вливающ|ий *adj.*: **~ее сре́дство** styptic.

кровопи́йц|а, ы, *g. pl.* **~** *c.g.* (*fig., rhet.*) cruel oppressor.

кровоподтёк, а *m.* bruise.

кровопроли́ти|е, я *nt.* bloodshed.

кровопроли́т|ный (~ен, ~на) *adj.* bloody.

кровопуска́ни|е, я *nt.* (*med.*) blood-letting, phlebotomy.

кровосмеси́тельный *adj.* incestuous.

кровосмеше́ни|е, я *nt.* incest.

кровосо́с, а *m.* (*животное*) vampire bat; (*fig., coll.*) cruel oppressor.

кровотече́ни|е, я *nt.* bleeding; (*сильное*) haemorrhage (*Br.*), hemorrhage (*US*).

кровоточи́вост|ь, и *f.* (*med.*) haemophilia (*Br.*), hemophilia (*US*).

кровоточ|и́ть, и́т *impf.* to bleed.

кровоха́ркань|е, я *nt.* blood-spitting; (*med.*) haemoptysis (*Br.*), hemoptysis (*US*).

кров|ь, и, о ~и, в ~и́, *g. pl.* **~е́й** *f.* blood (*also fig.*); **в к., до ~и** till it bleeds; **изби́ть, разби́ть в к.** to draw blood; **пусти́ть к.** (+*d.*) to bleed (*trans.*); (*fig.*): **по ~и** by birth; **к. с молоко́м** (*coll.*) the very picture of health, blooming; **у него́ к. кипи́т** his blood is up; **страсть к игре́ у него́ в ~и́** gambling is in his blood; **по́ртить кому́-н. к.** to put s.o. out, annoy s.o.; **у меня́ се́рдце облива́ется ~ью** my heart bleeds.

кровяни́ст|ый (~, ~a) *adj.* containing some blood.

кров|яно́й *adj. of* ⇒**~ь**

кро|и́ть, ю́, и́шь *impf.* (*of* ⇒**с~**) to cut (out).

кро|й, я *m.* **1** cutting (out). **2** (*фасон*) cut (*of dress etc.*).

кро́йк|а, и *f.* cutting (out).

кроке́т, а *m.* **1** (*игра*) croquet. **2** (*cul.*) croquette.

кроке́т|ный *adj. of* ⇒**~**

кроки́ *nt. indecl.* (*план*) sketch-map; (*эскиз*) rough sketch.

крокоди́л, а *m.* crocodile.

крокоди́л|ов *and* **~овый** *adj. of* ⇒**~; ~овые слёзы** crocodile tears.

кро́кус, а *m.* (*bot.*) crocus.

кро́лик, а *m.* **1** (*животное*) rabbit. **2** (*мех*) rabbit fur.

кро́ли|ковый *and* **~чий** *adj. of* ⇒**~к; ~чий мех** rabbit fur.

крол|ь, я *m.* (*sport*) crawl (stroke).

крольча́тник, а *m.* rabbit-hutch.

крольчи́х|а, и *f.* doe-rabbit.

кро́ме *prep.* + *g.* **1** (*за исключением*) except. **2** (*в добавление*) besides, in addition to; **к. того́** besides, moreover, furthermore; (*coll.*): **к. шу́ток** joking apart.

кроме́шн|ый *adj.*: **ад к.** inferno; **тьма ~ая** (*fig.*) pitch darkness.

кро́мк|а, и *f.* edge; (*ткани*) selvage; **к. тротуа́ра** kerb.

кромса́|ть, ю *impf.* (*of* ⇒**ис~**) (*coll.*) to cut up carelessly.

кро́н|а[1], ы *f.* (*дерева*) crown.

кро́н|а[2], ы *f.* (*денежная единица*) crown.

кронпри́нц, а *m.* crown prince.

кронци́ркул|ь, я *m.* (*tech.*) calipers.

кро́ншнеп, а *m.* (*zool.*) curlew.

кронште́йн, а *m.* (*tech.*) (*полки*) bracket; (*балкона*) corbel.

кропа́|ть, ю *impf.* (*of* ⇒**на~**) (*coll.*) (*стихи*) to scribble.

кропи́л|о, а *nt.* (*eccl.*) aspergillum.

кроп|и́ть, лю́, и́шь *impf.* (*of* ⇒**о~**) **1** (*обрызгивать*) to besprinkle. **2** (*падать мелкими каплями*) to trickle, spot.

кропотли́в|ый (~, ~a) *adj.* **1** (*работа*) laborious. **2** (*человек*) painstaking, precise.

кросс, а *m.* (*sport*) cross-country (race).

кроссво́рд, а *m.* crossword.

кроссме́н, а *m.* cross-country runner.

кроссови́к, а́ *m.* = **кроссме́н**

кроссо́в|ки, ок *pl.* (*sg.* **~ка, ~ки** *f.*) trainers (*Br.*), sneakers (*US*).

крот, а́ *m.* **1** mole. **2** (*мех*) moleskin.

кро́т|кий (~ок, ~ка́, ~ко) *adj.* meek, mild.

кроты́вин|а, ы *f.* mole-hill.

крот|о́вый *adj.* **1** *of* ⇒**~; ~овая нора́** mole-hill. **2** (*из меха*) moleskin.

кро́тост|ь, и *f.* meekness, mildness.

кро́х|а[1], и *c.g.* (*coll.*) little tot (*child*).

кро́х|а́[2], кро́хи́, *a.* **~у,** *pl.* **~и, ~ам** *f.* (*obs.*) (*хлеба*) crumb; (*pl., fig.*) crumbs, scraps.

крохобо́р, а *m.* **1** (*скряга*) penny-pincher, skinflint. **2** (*obs.*) (*человек, занимающийся мелочами*) hair-splitter.

крохобо́рств|о, а *nt.* **1** (*скупость*) penny-pinching. **2** (*obs.*) (*внимание к мелочам*) hair-splitting.

крохобо́рств|овать, ую *impf.* **1** (*скупиться*) to penny-pinch. **2** (*obs.*) (*заниматься мелочами*) to split hairs.

кро́хотный *adj.* (*coll.*) tiny, minute.

кро́шечк|а, и *f. dim. of* ⇨**кро́шка**

кро́шеч|ный (~ен, ~на) *adj.* (*coll.*) tiny, minute.

крош|и́ть, у́, ~ишь *impf.* **1** (*pf.* **ис~, на~** *or* **рас~**) (*хлеб*) to crumb, crumble; (*нарезать*) to dice; (*fig.*) to hack to pieces. **2** (*pf.* **на~**) (+*i.*) (*сорить*) to drop, spill crumbs (of); **к. хле́бом на́ пол** to drop crumbs on to the floor.

крош|и́ться, ~ится *impf.* (*of* ⇨**ис~** *and* **рас~**) to crumble.

кро́шк|а, и *f.* **1** (*хлеба*) crumb. **2** (*fig.*) (*мелкая частица*) a tiny bit; **ни ~и** not a bit. **3** (*coll.*) (*о ребёнке*) little one.

круасса́н, а *m.* (*cul.*) croissant.

круг, а, *pl.* **~и́** *m.* **1** (*p. sg.* **в, на ~у́** = *circular area*; **в, на ~е** = *circumference*) circle; **движе́ние по ~у** movement in a circle; **~и́ (на воде́)** ripples (on water); **стать в к.** to form a circle; **у меня́ голова́ идёт ~ом** my head is spinning. **2** (*круглый предмет*) ring; **рези́новый к.** rubber ring; **спаса́тельный к.** life ring, life belt; **~и́ под глаза́ми** rings round the eyes. **3** (*sport*; *p. sg.* **на ~у́**) **бегово́й к.** race-course, ring; **к. почёта** lap of honour (*Br.*), honor (*US*). **4** (*fig.*; *p. sg.* **в ~у́**) (*сфера, область*) sphere, range; compass; **к. вопро́сов** range of questions; **вне ~а свои́х обя́занностей** outside one's province. **5** (*fig.*; *p. sg.* **в ~у́**) (*группа людей*) circle (*of persons*); **официа́льные ~и́** official quarters; **в семе́йном ~у́** in the family circle; **широ́кие ~и́ обще́ственности** the general public.

кру́гленьк|ий *adj.* (*coll.*) **1** *dim. of* ⇨**кру́глый; ~ая су́мма** a round sum. **2** (*толстый*) rotund, portly.

кругле́|ть, ю *impf.* (*of* ⇨**по~**) to become round.

круглова́т|ый (~, ~а) *adj.* roundish.

круглогоди́чный *adj.* = **круглогодово́й**

круглогодово́й *adj.* year-round.

круглоли́ц|ый (~, ~а) *adj.* round-faced.

круглосу́точный *adj.* round-the-clock, twenty-four-hour.

кру́гл|ый (~, ~а́, ~о) *adj.* **1** round; **к. год** all the year round; **~ая да́та** 10th, 20th, 30th, etc. anniversary; **к. отли́чник** student who gets only 'excellent' marks; **~ые ско́бки** round brackets; **~ые су́тки** day and night; **~ая су́мма** round sum; **в ~ых ци́фрах, для ~ого счёта** in round figures. **2** (*no short forms*) (*coll.*) complete, utter, perfect; **к. дура́к** utter fool; **~ое неве́жество** crass ignorance; **к., ~ая сирота́** orphan (*having neither father nor mother*).

кругов|о́й *adj.* circular; **~а́я пору́ка** mutual responsibility, guarantee; **~а́я ча́ша** loving-cup; **~а́я доро́га** roundabout route.

круговоро́т, а *m.* (*цикличность*) cycle; (*событий*) flow.

кругозо́р, а *m.* **1** prospect. **2** (*fig.*) horizon, range of interests.

круго́м¹ *adv.* **1** round, around; **он обошёл дом к.** he walked around the house; *int.* about turn! (*Br.*), about face! (*US*). **2** (*вокруг*) (all) round, round about; **к. всё бы́ло ти́хо** all around was still. **3** (*coll.*) (*совершенно*) completely, entirely; **он был к. в долга́х** he was head over heels in debt; **вы к. винова́ты** you are entirely to blame.

круго́м² *prep.* +*g.* round, around.

кругооборо́т, а *m.* circuit, circulation.

кругообра́з|ный (~ен, ~на) *adj.* circular.

кругосве́тный *adj.* round-the-world.

круж|ева́, ~ев, ~ева́м = **~ево**

кружевни́ц|а, ы *f.* lace-maker.

кружев|но́й *adj. of* ⇨**~а́** *and* **кру́жево**

кру́жев|о, а *nt.* lace.

круж|и́ть, у́, ~и́шь *impf.* **1** (*заставлять двигаться по кругу*) to whirl, spin round; (*fig.*): **к. кому́-н. го́лову** to turn s.o.'s head. **2** (*кружиться*) to circle. **3** (*coll.*) (*блуждать*) to wander.

круж|и́ться, у́сь, ~и́шься *impf.* (*of* ⇨**за~**) to whirl, spin round; (*о птицах*) to circle; **у меня́ ~ится голова́** my head is going round, I feel giddy.

кру́жк|а, и *f.* **1** (*сосуд*) mug; tankard. **2** (*коробка*) collecting-box.

кружковщи́н|а, ы *f.* clannishness, cliquishness.

круж|ко́вый *adj. of* ⇨**~о́к** 2

кру́жный *adj.* roundabout, circuitous.

круж|о́к, ка́ *m.* **1** *dim. of* ⇨**круг. 2** (*группа*) circle, club; (*учебный*) study group.

крýи́з, а *m.* cruise.

круи́з|ный *adj. of* ⇨**~**

круп¹, а *m.* (*med.*) croup.

круп², а *m.* (*лошади*) croup, crupper.

круп|а́, ы́, *pl.* **~ы** *f.* **1** (*collect.*) groats; **гре́чневая к.** buckwheat; **ма́нная к.** semolina; **овся́ная к.** oatmeal; **перло́вая к.** pearl-barley. **2** (*fig.*) (*снег*) sleet.

крупи́нк|а, и *f.* grain.

крупи́ц|а, ы *f.* grain, ounce; **у него́ нет ни ~ы́ здра́вого смы́сла** he hasn't a grain of common sense; **по ~ам** painstakingly.

крупне́|ть, ю *impf.* (*of* ⇨**по~**) to grow larger.

кру́пн|о *adv. of* ⇨**~ый; к. наре́зать** to cut into large pieces; **к. писа́ть** to write large; **к. поспо́рить (с**+*i.*) to have a slanging-match (with).

крупногабари́т|ный (~ен, ~на) *adj.* large.

крупнозерни́стый *adj.* coarse-grained, large-grained.

крупнокали́берный *adj.* large-calibre (*Br.*), -caliber (*US*).

крупномасшта́б|ный (~ен, ~на) *adj.* large-scale; (*fig.*) ambitious.

кру́п|ный (~ен, ~на́, ~но) *adj.* **1** (*большой*) large, big; (*крупномасштабный*) large-scale; (*fig.*) (*значительный*) prominent, outstanding; **~ные поме́щики** big landowners; **~ная промы́шленность** large-scale industry; **к. рога́тый скот** cattle; **~ный план** (*cinema*) close-up. **2** (*песок*) coarse. **3** (*важный*) important; (*серьёзный*) serious; **~ная неприя́тность** serious trouble; **к. разгово́р** (*fig.*) high words.

круп|о́зный *adj. of* ⇨**~¹**; **~о́зное воспале́ние лёгких** lobar pneumonia.

крупча́тк|а, и *f.* finest wheaten flour.

крупча́тый *adj.* granular.

крупье́ *m. indecl.* croupier.

крутизн|а́, ы́ *f.* **1** (*свойство*) steepness. **2** (*крутой спуск*) steep slope. **3** (*sl.*) (*замечательность*) coolness; (*крепкость*) toughness.

кру|ти́ть, чу́, ~тишь *impf.* (*of* ⇨**за~** *and* **с~**) **1** to twist; to twirl; **к. верёвку** to twist a rope; **к. папиро́су** to roll a cigarette; **к. усы́** to twirl one's moustache (*Br.*), mustache (*US*); **к. ру́ки кому́-н.** to twist s.o.'s arms; (*coll.*; +*i.*): **она́ ~тит им, как хо́чет** she twists him round her little finger. **2** (*кран, ручку*) to turn, wind. **3** (*кружить*) to whirl (*trans.*). **4** (*coll.*; **с**+*i.*) to go out (with), have an affair (with). **5**: **как ни ~ти́** (*coll.*) however hard you try.

кру|ти́ться, чу́сь, ~тишься *impf.* **1** (*вращаться*) to turn, spin, revolve. **2** (*кружиться*) to whirl. **3** (*fig., coll.*) (*быть в хлопотах*) to be in a whirl.

кру́то *adv.* **1** steeply. **2** (*внезапно*) suddenly; abruptly, sharply; **к. поверну́ть** to turn round sharply. **3** (*coll.*) harshly; **к. распра́виться с кем-н.** to give s.o. short shrift. **4** (*вполне*) thoroughly; **к. замеси́ть те́сто** to make a thick dough; **к. посоли́ть** to put (too) much salt (into). **5** (*туго*) tightly.

крут|о́й (~, ~а́, ~о) *adj.* **1** (*подъём*) steep; **к. вира́ж** (*aeron.*) steep turn **2** (*внезапный*) sudden, abrupt, sharp. **3** (*coll.*) (*характер*) severe; (*меры*) drastic. **4** (*cul.*) (*каша*) thick; **к. кипято́к** fiercely boiling water; **~о́е яйцо́** hard-boiled egg. **5** (*sl.*) (*замечательный*) cool; (*крепкий*) tough.

кру́ч|а, и *f.* steep slope.

кру́|че *comp. of* ⇨**~то́й** *and* **~то**

круче́ни|е, я *nt.* **1** (*text.*) twisting. **2** (*tech.*) torsion.

кручёный *adj.* **1** twisted. **2** (*sport*) spinning; with spin on.

кручи́н|а, ы *f.* (*folk poet.*) sorrow, woe.

кручи́н|иться, юсь, ишься *impf.* (*folk poet.*) to sorrow.

кру|чу́, ~тишь *see* ⇨**~ти́ть**

круше́ни|е, я *nt.* **1** (*авария*) crash; (*судна*) wreck; **потерпе́ть к.** (*поезд, самолёт*) to crash; (*корабль*) to be wrecked. **2** (*fig.*) (*надежд*; *коммунизма*) collapse.

круши́н|а, ы *f.* (*bot.*) buckthorn.

круш|ить, у́, и́шь *impf.* to destroy (*also fig.*).

крыжо́венный *adj.* gooseberry.

крыжо́вник, а *m.* **1** (*кустарник*) gooseberry bush(es). **2** (*collect.*) (*ягоды*) gooseberries.

крыла́т|ый *adj.* winged (*also fig.*): **∼ые слова́** pithy saying(s); (*tech.*): **∼ая га́йка** wing nut; **∼ая раке́та** cruise missile.

крыл|е́чко, е́чка *nt. dim. of* ⇒**∼ьцо́**

крыл|о́, а́, *pl.* **∼́ья, ∼́ьев** *nt.* (*птицы, самолёта, дома*) wing; (*мельницы*) sail, vane; (*автомобиля*) wing, mudguard (*Br.*), fender (*US*).

кры́лыш|ко, ка, *pl.* **∼ки, ∼ек, ∼кам** *nt. dim. of* ⇒**крыло́;** (*fig.*): **под ∼ком** under the wing (*of*).

крыл|ьцо́, ьца́, *pl.* **∼́ьца, ∼ец, ∼ьца́м** *nt.* porch.

Крым, а, о ∼е, в ∼у́ *m.* the Crimea.

кры́мский *adj.* Crimean.

кры́нк|а, и *f.* earthenware pot, pitcher.

кры́с|а, ы *f.* rat.

крыс|и́ный *adj. of* ⇒**∼́а; к. яд** rat poison.

крысоло́в, а *m.* rat-catcher.

крысоло́вк|а, и *f.* **1** (*капкан*) rat-trap. **2** (*собака*) ratter.

кры́т|ый *p.p.p. of* ⇒**∼ь** *and adj.* covered; sheltered; **к. ры́нок** covered market.

крыть, кро́ю, кро́ешь *impf.* (*of* ⇒**по∼**) **1** to cover; (*крышей*) to roof; (*краской*) to coat; (*cards*) to cover, trump. **2** (*coll.*) (*бранить*) to swear (at); **ему́ не́чем к.** he hasn't a leg to stand on.

кры́ться, кро́юсь, кро́ешься *impf.* **1** (**в**+*p.*) to be, lie (in). **2** (*таиться*) to be concealed.

кры́ш|а, и *f.* roof; (*в преступном мире*) protection; (*coll.*): **к. е́дет/пое́хала у**+*gen.*: **у него́ к. пое́хала** he's lost his marbles, gone mad.

кры́шк|а, и *f.* **1** (*кастрюли, банки, чемодана*) lid; (*люка*) cover. **2** (*sl.*) death, end; **ему́ к.** he's done for; he's finished.

крэк, а *m.* crack (*drug*).

крю|к, ка́ *m.* **1** (*pl.* **∼ки́, ∼ко́в**) hook; **(альпини́стский) к.** piton; (*pl.* **∼́чья, ∼́чьев**) (*для ношения клади*) hook. **2** detour; (*coll.*): **дать ∼́ку, сде́лать к.** to make a detour.

крю́ч|ить, ит *impf.* (*of* ⇒**с∼**) (*impers., coll.*): **его́ ∼ит (от бо́ли)** he is writhing (in pain).

крючкова́т|ый (∼, ∼а) *adj.* hooked.

крючкотво́р, а *m.* (*coll.*) pettifogger.

крючкотво́рств|о, а *nt.* (*coll.*) chicanery.

крюч|о́к, ка́ *m.* hook; **спусково́й к.** trigger.

крюшо́н, а *m.* cup, punch (*beverage*).

кря́ду *adv.* (*coll.*) running; in a row.

кряж, а *m.* **1** (*горный*) (mountain-)ridge. **2** (*дубовый*) block, log.

кря́жист|ый (∼, ∼а) *adj.* (*дуб*) thick; (*fig.*) (*о человеке*) thick-set.

кря́к|ать, аю *impf.* (*of* ⇒**∼нуть**) **1** to quack. **2** (*coll.*) to grunt.

кря́кв|а, ы *f.* wild duck, mallard.

кря́к|нуть, ну, нешь *inst. pf. of* ⇒**∼ать**

кряхт|е́ть, чу́, ти́шь *impf.* to groan.

ксёндз, а́ *m.* Roman Catholic (*esp. Polish*) priest.

ксенофо́б, а *m.* xenophobe.

ксенофо́би|я, и *f.* xenophobia.

ксерогра́фи|я, и *f.* xerography.

ксерокопи́р|овать, ую *impf. and pf.* to xerox, photocopy.

ксероко́пи|я, и *f.* Xerox (*propr.*), photocopy.

ксе́рокс, а *m.* **1** (*ксерография*) xerography. **2** (*устройство*) Xerox (-machine) (*propr.*), photocopier. **3** (*coll.*) (*копия*) xerox, photocopy.

кси́в|а, ы *f.* (*sl.*) document, official paper, ID.

ксилогра́фи|я, и *f.* **1** (*процесс*) wood-engraving. **2** (*гравюра*) woodcut.

ксилофо́н, а *m.* (*mus.*) xylophone.

кста́ти *adv.* **1** (*уместно*) to the point, apropos. **2** (*своевременно*) opportunely; **как раз к.** just at the right moment; **э́тот пода́рок оказа́лся о́чень к.** the present has proved most welcome. **3** (*coll.*) (*заодно*) at the same time, incidentally; **к. зайди́те пожа́луйста в апте́ку** will you please call at the chemist's at the same time. **4**: **к. (сказа́ть)** by the way; **к., где вы купи́ли э́тот га́лстук?** by the way, where did you buy that tie?

кти́тор, а *m.* churchwarden.

кто, кого́, кому́, кем, ком *pron.* **1** (*interrog.*) (*какой человек?*) who; **к. э́то тако́й?** who is that?; **к. из вас э́то сде́лал?** which of you did it? **2** (*rel.*) (*в придаточных*) who (*normally after pron. antecedent*); **тот, к.** he who; **те, к.** those who; **блаже́н, к...** blessed is he who ...; **спаса́йся, к. мо́жет!** every man for himself! **3** (*indef.*): **к. (бы) ни** who(so)ever; **к. ни придёт** whoever comes; **к. бы то ни́ был** whoever it may be. **4** (*indef.*): **к. ... к.** some ... others; (+*adv.*): **разбежа́лись к. куда́** they scattered in all directions; **к. где** all over the place; some here, some there; **как они́ устро́ились? — кто как** how did they settle in? — in all sorts of ways. **5** (*coll., indef.*) (*кто-нибудь*) anyone; **е́сли к. позвони́т, дай мне знать** if anyone rings, let me know; **к.-к., а он зна́ет, как писа́ть** he knows how to write, if anyone does; **к. кого́** until one side wins completely.

кто́-либо, кого́-либо *pron.* = **кто́-нибудь**

кто́-нибудь, кого́-нибудь *pron.* (*в вопросах*) anyone, anybody; (*в утверждениях*) someone, somebody.

кто́-то, кого́-то *pron.* someone, somebody.

куб[1]**, а,** *pl.* **∼ы́** *m.* **1** (*math.*) cube; **два в ∼́е** two cubed. **2** (*coll.*) (*кубический метр*) cubic metre (*Br.*), meter (*US*).

куб[2]**, а,** *pl.* **∼ы́** *m.* (*котёл*) boiler; (*перегонный*) still.

Ку́б|а, ы *f.* Cuba.

куба́н|ец, ца *m.* Kuban Cossack.

куба́нский *adj.* (*geog.*) (of the) Kuban.

ку́барем *adv.* (*coll.*) head over heels; **скати́ться к.** to roll head over heels.

кубату́р|а, ы *f.* cubic capacity.

куби́зм, а *m.* (*art*) cubism.

ку́бик, а *m.* **1** *dim. of* ⇒**куб. 2** (*pl.*) (*игрушка*) blocks, bricks. **3** (*coll.*) (*кубический сантиметр*) cubic centimetre (*Br.*), centimeter (*US*).

куби́н|ец, ца *m.* Cuban.

куби́н|ка, ки *f. of* ⇒**∼ец**

куби́нский *adj.* Cuban.

куби́ст, а *m.* (*art*) cubist.

куби́ст|ка, ки *f. of* ⇒**∼**

куби́ческий *adj.* cubic; **к. ко́рень** (*math.*) cube root.

ку́бковый *adj. of* ⇒**ку́бок; к. матч** cup match.

кубови́д|ный (∼ен, ∼на) *adj.* cube-shaped, cuboid.

куб|ово́й *adj. of* ⇒**∼**[2]

ку́бовый *adj.* indigo.

ку́б|ок, ка *m.* **1** (*бокал*) goblet. **2** (*sport*) cup; **переходя́щий к.** (*sport etc.*) (challenge) cup; **встре́ча на к.** cup-tie.

кубоме́тр, а *m.* cubic metre (*Br.*), meter (*US*).

ку́брик, а *m.* (*naut.*) crew's quarters.

кубы́шк|а, и *f.* (*coll.*) **1** clay pot with bulging sides. **2** (*coll.*) dumpy woman.

кува́лд|а, ы *f.* sledge-hammer.

Куве́йт, а *m.* Kuwait.

куве́йт|ец, ца *m.* Kuwaiti.

куве́йт|ка, ки *f. of* ⇒**∼ец**

куве́йтский *adj.* Kuwaiti.

кувши́н, а *m.* jug; pitcher.

кувши́нк|а, и *f.* (*bot.*) water-lily.

кувырк|а́ться, а́юсь *impf.* (*of* ⇒**∼ну́ться**) to turn somersaults, go head over heels.

кувырк|ну́ться, ну́сь, нёшься *inst. pf. of* ⇒**∼а́ться**

кувырко́м *adv.* (*coll.*) head over heels; topsy-turvy; **полете́ть к.** to go head over heels; **всё пошло́ к.** everything went haywire.

кугуа́р, а *m.* (*zool.*) puma, cougar.

куда́ *adv.* **1** (*interrog. and rel.*) where, whither; **к. ты идёшь?** where are you going?; **к. он положи́л мою́ кни́гу?** where did he put my book? **2**: **к. (бы) ни** wherever; **к. бы то ни́ было** anywhere; (*coll.*): **к. ни кинь** wherever one looks; **к. ни шло** come what may. **3** (*coll.*) (*для чего*) what for; **к. вам сто́лько багажа́?** what do you want so much luggage for? **4** (+*comp.*; *coll.*) (*гораздо*) much, far; **сего́дня мне к. лу́чше** I am much better today. **5** (*coll.*) (*выражает сомнение*) how (could that be; could you, he, *etc.*); **к ча́су я наме́рен дочита́ть до страни́цы 200 — к. тебе́!** I intend to reach page 200 by one o'clock — you'll never do it!; **они́ тебя́ узна́ли? — к. им** did they recognize you? how could they? **6** (*coll.*): **хоть к.** fine, excellent. **7** (*coll.*): **к. (уж) там** no way!

куда́-либо *adv.* = **куда́-нибудь**

куда́-нибудь *adv.* anywhere; somewhere.

куда́-то *adv.* somewhere.

куда́хтань|е, я *nt.* cackling, clucking.

куда́х|тать, чу, чешь *impf.* to cackle, cluck.

куде́л|ь, и *f.* (*text.*) tow.

куде́сник, а *m.* magician, sorcerer, fortune-teller.

кудла́т|ый (~, ~а) *adj.* (*coll.*) shaggy.

кудрева́т|ый (~, ~а) *adj.* rather curly; (*fig.*) (*стиль*) florid, ornate.

ку́др|и, е́й *no sg.* curls.

кудря́в|иться, ится *impf.* to curl.

кудря́в|ый (~, ~а) *adj.* **1** (*волосы*) curly; (*человек*) curly-headed. **2** (*дерево*) leafy, bushy; **~ая капу́ста** curly kale. **3** (*fig.*) (*стиль*) florid, ornate.

кудря́ш|ки, ек *no sg.* (*coll.*) ringlets.

кузе́н, а *m.* cousin.

кузи́н|а, ы *f.* cousin.

кузне́ц, а́ *m.* (black)smith; farrier.

кузне́чик, а *m.* grasshopper.

кузне́чн|ый *adj.* blacksmith's; **~ые мехи́** bellows.

ку́зниц|а, ы *f.* forge, smithy.

ку́зов, а, *pl.* **~ы** *and* **~а́** *m.* **1** (*короб*) basket. **2** (*автомобиля, экипажа*) body.

кузовн|о́й *adj. of* ⇨**ку́зов; ~ы́е рабо́ты** body repairs.

ку́зькин: показа́ть кому́-н. ~у мать (*coll.*) to teach s.o. what's what.

кукаре́ка|ть, ю *impf.* to crow.

кукареку́ (*onomat.*) cock-a-doodle-doo.

ку́киш, а *m.* (*coll.*) fig (*gesture of derision or contempt, consisting of thumb placed between index and middle fingers*); **показа́ть кому́-н. к.** *to make this gesture* (*cf.* to cock a snook, give the V-sign); **к. с ма́слом получи́ть** to get nothing.

ку́к|ла, лы, *g. pl.* **~ол** *f.* doll; (*в театре*) puppet; **теа́тр ~ол** puppet-theatre (*Br.*), -theater (*US*).

ку-клукс-кла́н, а *m.* Ku Klux Klan.

куклуксклáнов|ец, ца *m.* Ku Klux Klaner.

куклуксклáнов|ка, ки *f. of* ⇨**~ец**

кук|ова́ть, у́ю *impf.* **1** to (cry) cuckoo. **2** (*coll.*) (*бедствовать*) to live a miserable existence.

ку́колк|а, и *f.* **1** (*affectionate dim. of* ⇨**ку́кла**) dolly. **2** (*zool.*) chrysalis, pupa.

ку́кол|ь, я *m.* (*bot.*) cockle.

ку́кольник, а *m.* **1** (*артист*) actor in puppet-theatre (*Br.*), -theater (*US*). **2** (*изготовитель*) puppet-maker.

ку́кольни|ца, цы *f. of* ⇨**~к**

ку́кольный *adj.* doll's; **к. теа́тр** puppet-theatre (*Br.*), -theater (*US*).

ку́к|ситься, шусь, сишься *impf.* (*coll.*) to sulk; to be in the dumps.

кукуру́з|а, ы *f.* maize, (sweet)corn; **возду́шная к.** popcorn.

кукуру́з|ный *adj. of* ⇨**~а**

куку́шк|а, и *f.* cuckoo; **часы́ с ~ой** cuckoo-clock.

кула́к[1], **а́** *m.* (*кисть руки*) fist; **дойти́ до ~о́в** to come to blows; **смея́ться в ~** to laugh in one's sleeve.

кула́к[2], **а́** *m.* (*hist.*) kulak.

кула́к[3], **а́** *m.* (*tech.*) cam.

кула́|цкий *adj. of* ⇨**~к**[2]

кула́честв|о, а *nt.* (*collect.*) (*hist.*) the kulaks.

кула́чк|а, и *f. of* ⇨**кула́к**[2]

кула́чк|и *only in phrr.* **идти́ на к.** to come to blows; **би́ться на ~ах** to engage in fisticuffs.

кулач|ко́вый *adj. of* ⇨**~о́к**[2]; **к. вал** camshaft.

кула́|чный *adj. of* ⇨**~к**[1,3]; **к. бой** fisticuffs.

кула|чо́к[1], **чка́** *m. dim. of* ⇨**~к**[1]

кулач|о́к[2], **ка́** *m.* (*tech.*) cam

кулебя́к|а, и *f.* kulebyaka (*savoury pie*).

кул|ёк, ька́ *m.* (*paper*) bag.

ку́ли *m. indecl.* coolie.

кули́к, а́ *m.* (*zool.*) stint; sandpiper (*Calidris*).

кулина́р, а *m.* cookery specialist; master chef.

кулина́ри|я, и *f.* **1** (*искусство*) cookery. **2** (*магазин*) delicatessen.

кулина́рн|ый *adj.* culinary; **~ая кни́га** cookery-book (*Br.*), cook-book (*US*); **к. отде́л** delicatessen counter.

кули́с|ы, ~ *pl.* (*sg.* **~а, ~ы** *f.*) (*theatr.*) wings; **за ~ами** behind the scenes (*also fig.*).

кули́ч, а́ *m.* Easter cake.

кули́чк|и *only in phrr.* (*coll.*): **у чёрта на ~ах, к чёрту на к.** at (to) the world's end.

куло́н[1], **а** *m.* (*украшение*) pendant.

куло́н[2], **а** *m.* (*elec.*) coulomb.

кулуа́р|ный *adj. of* ⇨**~ы; (*fig.*)** behind-the scenes, backstage.

кулуа́р|ы, ов *sg. not used* (*pol.*) lobby; (*fig.*): **в ~ах** behind the scenes.

кул|ь, я́ *m.* sack.

кульби́т, а *m.* somersault.

ку́льман, а *m.* drawing-board.

кульминацио́нный *adj.* climactic; **к. пункт** culmination, climax.

кульмина́ци|я, и *f.* culmination.

культ, а *m.* cult; **к. ли́чности** personality cult; cult of personality.

культ... *comb. form, abbr. of* ***культу́рный***

культива́тор, а *m.* (*agric.*) cultivator (*machine*).

культива́ци|я, и *f.* (*agric.*) treatment of the ground with a cultivator.

культиви́ровани|е, я *nt.* cultivation (*also fig.*).

культиви́р|овать, ую *impf.* to cultivate (*also fig.*).

культма́ссов|ый *adj.*: **~ая рабо́та** education of the masses.

ку́льт|овый *adj. of* ⇨**~; ~овая му́зыка** religious music.

культтова́р|ы, ов *no sg.* recreational supplies; educational supplies.

культу́р|а, ы *f.* **1** culture; **Министе́рство ~ы** Ministry of Culture. **2** (*уровень*) standard, level; **к. ре́чи** standard of speech; **повы́сить ~у земледе́лия** to raise the standard of farming. **3** (*usu. pl.*) (*agric.*) (*растение*) crop; **зерновы́е ~ы** cereals; **кормовы́е ~ы** forage crops. **4** (*agric.*) (*разведение*) cultivation, growing; **к. карто́феля** potato-growing. **5**: **физи́ческая к.** physical education.

культури́зм, а *m.* body-building.

культури́ст, а *m.* body-builder.

культу́рно *adv.* in a civilized manner.

культу́рно-бытов|о́й *adj.*: **~о́е обслу́живание** culture and welfare service.

культу́рно-просвети́тельный *adj.* cultural and educational.

культу́рност|ь, и *f.* (level of) culture; cultivation; (*fig.*): **он отлича́лся ~ью** he was exceptionally cultivated.

культу́р|ный (~ен, ~на) *adj.* **1** (*человек, общество*) cultured, cultivated. **2** (*уровень, связи, обмен*) cultural. **3** (*agric., hort.*) (*не дикий*) cultured; cultivated.

культ|я́, и́ *f.* stump (*of limb*).

кум, а, *pl.* **~овья́, ~овьёв** *m.* godfather of one's child; father of one's god-child.

кум|а́, ы́ *f.* god mother of one's child; mother of one's god-child.

кума́ч, а́ *m.* red calico.

куме́ка|ть, ю *impf.* (*coll.*) to understand; to be with it.

куми́р, а *m.* idol (*also fig.*).

кумовств|о́, а́ *nt.* nepotism.

кумуляти́вный *adj.* cumulative.

ку́мушк|а, и *f.* **1** *affectionate of* ⇨**кума́**. **2** (*coll.*) (*сплетница*) gossip, scandal-monger.

кумы́с, а *m.* koumiss (*fermented mare's milk*).

куна́к, а́ *m.* friend (*among the mountain-dwellers of the Caucasus*).

кунжу́т, а *m.* (*bot.*) sesame.

кунжу́т|ный *adj. of* ⇨**~**

куни́ц|а, ы *f.* (*zool.*) marten.

кунстка́мер|а, ы *f.* collection of curiosities.

кун-фу́ *nt. indecl.* kung fu.

ку́п|а, ы *f.* clump (*of trees*).

купа́льник, а *m.* bathing costume (*Br.*), bathing suit (*US*), swimsuit.

купа́льный *adj.* bathing, swimming; **к. костю́м** bathing costume (*Br.*), bathing suit (*US*), swimsuit.

купа́л|ьня, ьни, *g. pl.* **~ен** *f.* (*enclosed*) bathing-place.

купа́льщик, а *m.* bather.

купа́льщи|ца, цы *f. of* ⇨**~к**

купа́|ть, ю *impf.* (*of* ⇨**вы́~**) to bathe; to bath.

купа́|ться, юсь *impf.* (*of* ⇨**вы́~**) (*плавать*) to swim, bathe; (*в ванне*) to have, take a bath; **к. в зо́лоте** to be rolling in money; **к. в луча́х сла́вы** to bask in glory.

купе́ *nt. indecl.* compartment (*of railway carriage*).

купе́йный *adj.*: **к. ваго́н** Pullman car.

К

купе́л|ь, и *f. (eccl.)* font.
куп|е́ц, ца́ *m.* merchant.
купе́ческ|ий *adj.* **1** merchant, mercantile; **~ое сосло́вие** the merchant class. **2** *(fig.)* vulgar.
купе́честв|о, а *nt. (collect.)* the merchants, the merchant class.
купин|а́, ы́ *f. (arch.)* bush; **неопали́мая к.** *(bibl.)* the burning bush.
куп|и́ть, лю́, ~ишь *pf. (of* **⇒покупа́ть) 1** *(вещь)* to buy, purchase. **2** *(coll.) (человека)* to buy.
купи́|ться, лю́сь, ~ишься *pf. (coll.)* **(на** + *a.*) to be taken in (by); **я ~лся на его́ улы́бку** I was taken in by his smile.
купле́т, а *m.* **1** *(строфа)* stanza, strophe, verse. **2** *(pl.) (сатирические песенки)* satirical ballad(s), song(s).
куплети́ст, а *m.* singer of satirical songs, ballads.
куплети́ст|ка, ки *f. of* **⇒~**
ку́пл|я, и *f.* purchase; **к.-прода́жа** *(comm.)* buying and selling.
ку́пол, а, *pl.* **~а́** *m.* cupola, dome.
куполообра́з|ный (~ен, ~на) *adj.* dome-shaped.
купо́н, а *m.* coupon; **стричь ~ы** to live on income from investments.
купоро́с, а *m. (chem.)* vitriol.
ку́пч|ая, ей *f. (also* **к. кре́пость)** *(leg.)* deed of purchase.
купчи́х|а, и *f.* **1** *f. of* **⇒купе́ц. 2** *(жена купца)* merchant's wife.
купю́р|а, ы *f.* **1** *(сокращение)* cut. **2** *(fin.) (деньги)* banknote; *(облигация)* band.
кур, а *m. (arch.)* cock; *now only in phr. (coll.)*: **как к. во́ щи (попа́сть)** (to get o.s.) into the soup.
ку́р|а, ы *f. (coll.)* = **~ица**
кураг|а́, и́ *f. (collect.)* dried apricots.
кура́ж|иться, усь, ишься *impf. (coll.)* to swagger, boast; **(над** + *i.*) to bully.
кура́нт|ы, ов *no sg.* chiming clock; chimes.
кура́тор, а *m.* **1** *(obs.) (попечитель)* curator. **2** *(студента)* (academic) supervisor; **к. информацио́нных служб** chief press officer.
курбе́т, а *m. (sport and fig.)* curvet.
ку́рв|а, ы *f. (vulg.)* whore, tart.
курга́н, а *m.* burial mound.
кургу́з|ый (~, ~а) *adj. (coll.)* **1** *(слишком короткий/тесный)* too short and/or tight. **2** *(куцый)* bob-tailed.
курд, а *m.* Kurd.
Курдиста́н, а *m.* Kurdistan.
ку́рдский *adj.* Kurdish.
курдя́нк|а, и *f. of* **⇒курд**
ку́рев|о, а *nt. (coll.)* tobacco, baccy; sth. to smoke; **у меня́ нет ~а** I haven't got any fags.
куре́ни|е, я *nt.* **1** *(действие)* smoking. **2** *(ладан)* incense.
куре́н|ь, я́ *m.* house, hut *(in Cossack villages)*.
ку́р|ий (~ья, ~ье) *adj.* chicken.
кури́лк|а[1], и *f. (coll.)* smoking-room.
кури́лка[2] *only in phr.* **жив к.!** there's life in the old dog yet.
кури́льниц|а, ы *f.* censer; incense-burner.
кури́л|ьня, ьни, *g. pl.* **~ен** *f.*: **к. о́пиума** opium-den.
кури́льщик, а *m.* smoker.
кури́льщи|ца, цы *f. of* **⇒~к**
кури́н|ый *adj. (яйцо)* hen's; *(бульон)* chicken; **~ая слепота́** *(med.)* night-blindness.
кури́р|овать, ую *impf.* to supervise.
кури́тельн|ый *adj.* smoking; **~ая бума́га** cigarette paper; **~ая (ко́мната)** smoking-room.
кур|и́ть, ю́, ~ишь *impf. (of* **⇒по~) 1** to smoke; **к. тру́бку** to smoke a pipe. **2** (+ *a. or i.*) to burn; **к. ла́даном** to burn incense.
кур|и́ться, ~ится *impf.* **1 (ку́рится)** *(гореть)* to burn. **2 (кури́тся)** *(о вулкане)* to emit smoke, steam; to smoke. **3** *pass. of* **⇒~и́ть**
ку́р|ица, ицы, *pl.* **~ы, ~** *f.* hen; *(fig., coll.)*: **мо́края к.** milksop; **~ам на́ смех** it would make a cat laugh; **де́нег у него́ ~ы не клюю́т** he is rolling in money.
курку́м|а, ы *f.* turmeric.
курно́с|ый (~, ~а) *adj.* snub-nosed.
курово́дств|о, а *nt.* poultry-breeding.
кур|о́к, ка́ *m.* cocking-piece; **взвести́ к.** to cock; **спусти́ть к.** to pull the trigger.
куроле́|сить, шу, сишь *impf. (of* **⇒на~)** *(coll.)* to play tricks, get up to mischief.
куропа́тк|а, и *f. (zool.)*: **(се́рая) к.** partridge; **бе́лая к.** willow grouse; **тундряна́я к.** ptarmigan.
куро́рт, а *m.* holiday resort; **водолече́бный к.** spa.
куро́ртник, а *m.* resort visitor, holidaymaker *(Br.)*, vacationer *(US)*.
куро́рт|ный *adj. of* **⇒~**
куросле́п, а *m. (bot.)* buttercup.
ку́рочк|а, и *f.* **1** *(молодая курица)* pullet. **2**: **водяна́я к.** moor-hen.
курс, а *m.* **1** course; **взять к. на се́вер** to steer northwards; *(pol.)* policy; **взять к. на демократиза́цию** to adopt a policy of democratization; **к. ле́кций/обуче́ния** course of lectures/instruction; **ускоре́нный к.** crash *or* intensive course; **быть на тре́тьем ~е** to be in the third year *(of a course of studies)*; **держа́ть к. (на** + *a.*) to head (for); **быть в ~е (де́ла)** to be au courant, be in the know; **держа́ть кого́-н. в ~е (чего́-н.)** to keep s.o. informed (about sth.). **2** *(fin.)* exchange rate; **к. рубля́ упа́л** the exchange rate of the rouble has fallen.
курса́нт, а *m.* **1** *(учащийся курсов)* student. **2** *(mil.)* cadet.
курси́в, а *m.* italic type, italics; **~ом** in italics.
курси́вный *adj. (typ.)* italic.
курси́р|овать, ую *impf.* **(ме́жду** + *i.*) to ply, run (between).
курсо́вк|а, и *f.* authorization for treatment and meals *(at health resort)*.
курс|ово́й *adj. of* **⇒~; ~ова́я ра́зница** difference in exchange rates; **~ова́я рабо́та** project; short dissertation.
курсо́р, а *m. (comput.)* cursor.
куртиза́нк|а, и *f.* courtesan.
ку́ртк|а, и *f.* jacket; anorak.
курча́в|иться, ится *impf.* to curl.
курча́в|ый (~, ~а) *adj. (волосы)* curly; *(человек)* curly-haired.
ку́р|ы *see* **⇒~ица**
курьёз, а *m.* curious, amusing incident; **для, ра́ди ~а** for fun.
курьёз|ный (~ен, ~на) *adj.* curious; funny.
курье́р, а *m. (в учреждении)* messenger; *(дипломатический)* courier.
курье́р|ский *adj.* **1** *adj. of* **⇒~. 2** fast; **к. по́езд** express.
куря́тин|а, ы *f.* chicken *(as meat)*.
куря́тник, а *m.* hen-house, hen-coop.
кур|я́щий *pres. part. act. of* **⇒~и́ть;** *as n.* **к., ~я́щего** smoker.
кус, а, *pl.* **~ы́** *m. (coll.)* large piece.
куса́|ть, ю *impf. (о собаке, о человеке)* to bite; *(о пчеле)* to sting.
куса́|ться, юсь *impf.* **1** *(о собаке)* to bite; *(о крапиве, о пчеле)* to sting. **2** *(кусать друг друга)* to bite one another. **3** *(coll.)* to be exorbitant; **э́то — хоро́шая вещь, но ~ется** it's good, but they sting you for it.
куса́ч|ки, ек *no sg.* pliers; wire-cutters.
куско́вой *adj.* broken in lumps; **к. са́хар** lump sugar.
кус|о́к, ка́ *m.* piece, bit; *(хлеба)* slice; *(сахара)* lump; *(мыла)* cake; **зарабо́тать к. хле́ба** to earn one's bread and butter.
куст[1], а́ *m.* bush, shrub; **спря́таться в ~ы́** *(fig.)* to scarper, make o.s. scarce.
куст[2], а́ *m. (econ.)* group.
куста́рник, а *m. (collect.)* bushes, shrubs; shrubbery.
куста́рнича|ть, ю *impf.* **1** to be a handicraftsman; to exercise a craft at home. **2** *(coll., pej.)* to use primitive methods; to work in an amateurish manner.
куста́рничеств|о, а *nt. (pej.)* work done by primitive methods; amateurish, inefficient work.
куста́рн|ый *adj.* **1** handicraft; **~ые изде́лия** craftwork. **2** *(fig., pej.)* amateurish, primitive.
куста́рщин|а, ы *f.* = **куста́рничество**
куста́р|ь, я́ *m.* craftsman.
кусти́ст|ый (~, ~а) *adj.* bushy.
куст|и́ться, и́тся *impf. (agric.)* to tiller.
кусторе́з, а *m.* hedge trimmer.
ку́та|ть, ю *impf. (of* **⇒за~) (в** + *a.*) to muffle up (in).
ку́та|ться, юсь *impf. (of* **⇒за~) (в** + *a.*) to muffle o.s. up (in).
кутёж, а́ *m.* drinking-bout; binge.
кутерьм|а́, ы́ *f. (coll.)* commotion.
кути́л|а, ы *m.* fast liver; hard drinker.
ку|ти́ть, чу́, ~тишь *impf. (of* **⇒~тну́ть)** to carouse; to go on the booze.

кут|ну́ть, ну́, нёшь *inst. pf. of* ⇨**~и́ть**

кутýзк|а, и *f.* (*coll.*) jail, lock-up.

куха́рк|а, и *f.* cook.

кýх|ня, ни, *g. pl.* **~онь** *f.* **1** (*помещение*) kitchen. **2** (*кушанье*) cooking, cuisine.

кýхонн|ый *adj.* kitchen; **~ая плита́** kitchen-range.

кýц|ый (~, ~а) *adj.* **1** (*животное*) tailless; bob-tailed. **2** (*одежда*) skimpy; (*fig.*) limited, abbreviated.

кýч|а, и *f.* **1** heap, pile; (*людей*) group; (*coll.*): **вали́ть всё в одну́ ~у** to lump everything together. **2** (*coll.*; +*g.*) heaps (of), piles (of); **у него́ к. де́нег** he has heaps of money.

кучево́й *adj.* (*meteor.*) cumulous.

кýчер, а, *pl.* **~á, ~о́в** *m.* coachman.

кучеря́в|ый (~, ~а) *adj.* (*coll.*) curly; curly-haired.

кýч|ка, ки *f. dim. of* ⇨**~а; к. люде́й** handful of people.

кýчный *adj.* (*of shots*) closely-grouped.

ку|чý, ~тишь *see* ⇨**~ти́ть**

куш, а *m.* (*coll.*) large sum (*of money*).

куша́к, á *m.* sash.

кýшань|е, я *nt.* food; dish.

кýша|ть, ю *impf.* (*of* ⇨**по~** *and* **с~**) (*in polite invitation to eat*) to eat, have.

куше́тк|а, и *f.* couch.

ку|ю́, ёшь *see* ⇨**кова́ть**

кхме́р|ы, ов *pl.* (*sg.* **~, а** *m.*) the Khmers; **кра́сные к.** the Khmer Rouge.

кэ́рри *nt. indecl.* curry.

кюве́т, а *m.* ditch (*at side of road*).

кюве́тк|а, и *f.* (*phot.*) cuvette, bath.

кюри́ *nt. indecl.* curie.

Л л

л (*abbr. of* **литр**) l, litre(s) (*Br.*), liter(s) (*US*).

лабиа́льный *adj.* (*ling.*) labial.

лабио-дента́льный *adj.* (*ling.*) labio-dental.

лабири́нт, а *m.* (*in var. senses*) labyrinth, maze.

лабора́нт, а *m.* laboratory assistant.

лабора́нт|ка, ки *f. of* ⇒∼

лаборато́ри|я, и *f.* laboratory.

лаборато́р|ный *adj. of* ⇒∼**ия**

лабрадо́р, а *m.* labrador (*dog*).

ла́бух, а *m.* (*sl.*) musician, 'muso'.

ла́в|а[1], ы *f.* (*вулканическая*) lava.

ла́в|а[2], ы *f.* (*горная выработка*) drift.

лава́нд|а, ы *f.* (*bot.*) lavender.

лава́ш, а *m.* lavash (*flat white loaf*).

лави́н|а, ы *f.* avalanche (*also fig.*).

лави́р|овать, ую *impf.* **1** (*naut.*) to tack. **2** (*fig.*) to manœuvre (*Br.*), maneuver (*US*).

ла́вк|а[1], и *f.* (*скамья*) bench.

ла́вк|а[2], и *f.* (*магазин*) small shop.

ла́вочк|а[1], и *f. dim. of* ⇒**ла́вка[1]**

ла́вочк|а[2], и *f. dim. of* ⇒**ла́вка[2]**; (*fig., coll.*) (*жульнические махинации*) racket, shady concern.

ла́вочник, а *m.* shop-keeper.

ла́вочни|ца, цы *f. of* ⇒∼**к**

лавр, а *m.* **1** (*bot.*) laurel; bay(-tree). **2** (*pl., fig.*) laurels; **пожина́ть** ∼́**ы** to win laurels; **почи́ть на** ∼́**ах** to rest on one's laurels.

ла́вр|а, ы *f.* monastery (*of highest rank*).

ла́вр|о́вый *adj. of* ⇒∼; ∼**о́вый вено́к** laurel wreath; (*fig.*) laurels; ∼**о́вый лист** bay leaf.

ла́вр|ский *adj. of* ⇒∼**а**

лавса́н, а *m.* lavsan (*synthetic fibre*).

ла́герник, а *m.* (*coll.*) inmate of camp.

ла́гер|ный *adj. of* ⇒∼**ь**

ла́гер|ь, я *m.* **1** (*pl.* ∼**я́**, ∼**е́й**) camp; (*mil.*): **располага́ться, стоя́ть** ∼**ем** to camp, be encamped; **снять л.** to break up, strike camp. **2** (*pl.* ∼**и**, ∼**ей**) (*fig.*) camp; **де́йствовать на два** ∼**я** to have a foot in both camps.

лагу́н|а, ы *f.* lagoon.

лад, а, о ∼́**е, в** ∼**у́**, *pl.* ∼**ы́**, ∼**о́в** *m.* **1** (*mus. and fig.*) (*согласие*) harmony, concord; **петь в л., не в л.** to sing in, out of tune; **запе́ть на друго́й л.** (*fig.*) to change one's tune; **жить в** ∼**у́** (**с**+*i.*) to live in harmony (with); **быть не в** ∼**а́х** (**с**+*i.*) to be at odds (with); (*coll.*) **идти́, пойти́ на л.** to go well, be successful. **2** (*способ*) manner, way; **на ра́зные** ∼**ы́** in various ways; **на свой л.** in one's own way; **на ста́рый л.** in the old style. **3** (*mus.*) (*струнного инструмента*) fret; (*гармоники*) key. **4** (*mus.*) (*тональность*) mode.

ла́дан, а *m.* incense; **дыша́ть на л.** (*fig., coll.*) to have one foot in the grave.

ла́данк|а, и *f.* amulet.

ла́|дить, жу, дишь *impf.* (**с**+*i.*) to get on (with), be on good terms (with); **они́ не** ∼**дят** they don't get on.

ла́д|иться, ится *impf.* (*coll.*) to go well, succeed.

ла́дно *adv.* (*coll.*) **1** *particle* **л.!** all right! OK! **2** (*мирно*) harmoniously. **3** (*удачно*) well; all right; **всё ко́нчилось л.** everything ended happily. **4**: **л. тебе́ крича́ть** that's enough of your shouting.

ла́д|ный (∼**ен,** ∼**на́,** ∼**но)** *adj.* (*coll.*) **1** (*хороший*) fine, excellent. **2** (*дружный*) harmonious.

ладо́н|ь, и *f.* palm (*of hand*); **быть (ви́дным) как на** ∼**и** to be clearly visible.

ладо́ши *only in phrr.* **бить, ударя́ть, хло́пать в л.** to clap one's hands.

ла́ды́ *particle* (*coll.*) = **ла́дно**

лад|ья́, ьи́, *g. pl.* ∼**е́й** *f.* **1** (*chess*) castle, rook. **2** (*лодка*) boat.

ла́ж|а, и *f.* (*sl.*) crap, garbage; **поро́ть** ∼**у** to talk crap.

лажо́вый *adj.* (*sl.*) crap(py), lousy.

ла́|жу[1], дишь *see* ⇒∼**дить**

ла́|жу[2], зишь *see* ⇒∼**зить**

лаз, а *m.* **1** (*отверстие*) hole, gap. **2** (*tech.*) manhole.

лаза́нь|я, и *f.* (*cul.*) lasagne.

лазаре́т, а *m.* (*mil.*) field hospital; (*naut.*) sick-bay.

ла́з|ать, аю *impf.* (*coll.*) = ∼**ить**

лазе́йк|а, и *f.* hole, gap; (*fig., coll.*) loophole; **оста́вить себе́** ∼**у** to leave o.s. a loophole.

ла́зер, а *m.* (*phys., tech.*) laser.

ла́зер|ный *adj. of* ⇒∼; **л. при́нтер** laser printer.

ла́|зить, жу, зишь *impf.* (*indet. of* ⇒**лезть**) **1** (**на**+*a.*, **по**+*d.*) to climb, clamber (on to, up); **л. на сте́ну** to climb a wall; **л. по дере́вьям** to climb trees; **л. по кана́ту** to swarm up a rope. **2** (**в**+*a.*) to climb (into), get (into); **л. в окно́** to get in through the window.

лазо́ревк|а, и *f.* (*zool.*) blue tit.

лазо́ревый *adj.* (*poet.*) sky-blue, azure; **л. ка́мень** (*min.*) lapis lazuli.

лазу́ревый *adj.* = **лазо́ревый, лазу́рный**

лазу́р|ный (∼**ен,** ∼**на)** *adj.* sky-blue, azure.

лазу́р|ь, и *f.* azure; **берли́нская л.** Prussian blue.

лазу́тчик, а *m.* (*mil., obs.*) spy, scout.

ла|й, я *m.* bark(ing).

ла́йб|а, ы *f.* (*one- or two-masted*) sailing boat (*used formerly in Baltic Sea and on rivers Dnieper and Dniester*).

ла́йк|а[1], и *f.* (*собака*) husky.

ла́йк|а[2], и *f.* (*кожа*) kid-skin.

ла́йк|овый *adj. of* ⇒∼**а[2]**; ∼**овые перча́тки** kid gloves.

ла́йнер, а *m.* (*naut., aeron.*) liner.

лак, а *m.* varnish, lacquer; **л. для воло́с** hair spray.

лака́|ть, ю *impf.* (*of* ⇒**вы**∼) to lap (up).

лаке́|й, я *m.* footman; lackey, flunkey (*also fig., pej.*).

лаке́й|ский *adj. of* ⇒∼; (*fig.*) servile.

лаке́йств|о, а *nt.* servility.

лаке́йств|овать, ую *impf.* (**пе́ред**+*i.*) to dance attendance (on), kow-tow (to).

лакиро́в|анный *p.p.p. of* ⇒∼**а́ть** *and adj.* varnished, lacquered; ∼**анная ко́жа** patent leather; ∼**анные ту́фли** patent-leather shoes.

лакир|овáть, ýю *impf.* (*of* ⇒**от~**) to varnish, lacquer; (*fig., pej.*) to varnish.

лакирóвк|а, и *f.* **1** (*действие*) varnishing, lacquering (*also fig., pej.*). **2** (*слой лака*) varnish. **3** (*fig.*) gloss, polish.

лáкмус, а *m.* (*chem.*) litmus.

лáкмус|овый *adj. of* ⇒**~; ~овая бумáга** litmus paper.

лáк|овый *adj. of* ⇒**~;** varnished, lacquered; **~овые тýфли** patent-leather shoes.

лáком|ить, лю, ишь *impf.* (*of* ⇒**по~**) (*obs.*) (+*i.*) to regale (with), treat (to).

лáком|иться, люсь, ишься *impf.* (*of* ⇒**по~**) (+*i.*) to feast (on).

лáкомк|а, и *c.g.* gourmand; **быть ~ой** (*о сладкоежке*) to have a sweet tooth.

лáкомств|о, а *nt.* dainty, delicacy, delicious food; (*сласти*) sweets.

лáком|ый (~, ~а) *adj.* **1** tasty, delicious; **л. кусóк** tasty morsel (*also fig.*). **2** (*coll.*) (**до**+*g.*) fond (of), partial (to).

лаконúзм, а *m.* laconicism; brevity.

лаконúческий *adj.* laconic.

лаконúч|ный (~ен, ~на) *adj.* = **~еский**

лакрúц|а, ы *f.* (*bot.*) liquorice.

лакрóсс, а *m.* lacrosse.

лактáци|я, и *f.* lactation.

лактóз|а, ы *f.* (*chem.*) lactose.

лáм|а[1]**, ы** *f.* (*zool.*) llama.

лáм|а[2]**, ы** *m.* (*relig.*) lama.

ламаúзм, а *m.* (*relig.*) Lamaism.

Ла-Мáнш, а *m.* the (English) Channel.

ламбрекéн, а *m.* pelmet.

лáмп|а, ы *f.* **1** lamp; **рудничная л.** Davy lamp; **л. дневнóго свéта** fluorescent lamp. **2** (*radio*) valve; tube.

лампáд|а, ы *f.* icon-lamp.

лампáдн|ый *adj.*: **~ое мáсло** lamp-oil.

лампáс, а *m.* stripe (*down side of trousers*).

лáмп|овый *adj. of* ⇒**~а**

лáмпочк|а, и *f.* **1** *dim. of* ⇒**лáмпа.** **2** (electric light) bulb; **л. в 100 ватт** 100-watt bulb. **3**: **это мне до ~и** (*sl.*) I couldn't care less about it.

лангéт, а *m.* thin steak.

лангýст, а *m.* (*also* **лангýст|а, ~ы** *f.*) spiny lobster; rock lobster.

ландó *nt. indecl.* landau.

ландшáфт, а *m.* landscape.

лáндыш, а *m.* lily of the valley.

ланúт|а, ы *f.* (*arch.*) cheek.

ланолúн, а *m.* (*pharm.*) lanolin.

ланцéт, а *m.* (*med.*) lancet; **вскрыть ~ом** to lance.

ланцетовúд|ный (~ен, ~на) *adj.* (*bot.*) lanceolate.

ланч, а *m.* lunch.

лан|ь, и *f.* fallow deer; (*самка*) doe (*of fallow deer*).

Лаóс, а *m.* Laos.

лаóс|ец, ца *m.* Laotian.

лаóс|ка, ки *f. of* ⇒**~ец**

лаóсский *adj.* Laotian.

лáп|а, ы *f.* **1** (*животного*) paw; (*птицы*) foot; (*fig., coll.*): (*нога*) big foot; (*рука*) big hand; **попáсть в ~ы к комý-н.** to fall into s.o.'s clutches; **дать на ~у комý-н.** to give a backhander; to bribe. **2** (*tech.*) tenon, dovetail. **3** (*якоря*) fluke. **4** (*ветвь*) bough (*of coniferous tree*).

лапидáр|ный (~ен, ~на) *adj.* lapidary, terse.

лáп|ка, ки *f. dim. of* ⇒**~а;** (*fig., coll.*): **стоять/ходúть на зáдних ~ках (пéред**+*i.*) to dance attendance (upon).

лаплáнд|ец, ца *m.* Lapp, Laplander.

Лаплáнди|я, и *f.* Lapland.

лаплáнд|ка, ки *f. of* ⇒**~ец**

лаплáндский *adj.* Lappish, Lapp.

лáп|оть, тя, *pl.* **~ти, ~тéй** *m.* **1** bast shoe; **ходúть в ~тях** to wear bast shoes. **2** (*coll.*) oaf, bumpkin

лáпочк|а, и *c.g.* (*coll.*) **1** (*в обращении*) (my) pet, darling, sweetheart. **2** (*о человеке*) sweetie; **онá такáя л.!** she's such a sweetie!

лапт|á, ы́ *f.* **1** (*игра*) lapta (*Russian ball game*). **2** (*бита*) lapta bat.

лáпушк|а, и *f.* (*coll.*) = **лáпочка 1**

лáпчат|ый (~, ~а) *adj.* **1** (*bot.*) palmate. **2** (*птица*) web-footed; **гусь л.** (*fig., coll.*) cunning fellow, sly one.

лапш|á, ú *f.* **1** noodles. **2** (*суп*) noodle soup.

лар|ёк, ькá *m.* stall.

лар|éц, цá *m.* casket.

ларингúт, а *m.* laryngitis

ларингоскóп, а *m.* laryngoscope.

ларинготомú|я, и *f.* laryngotomy.

лáрчик, а *m.* small casket; (*coll.*): **а л. прóсто открывáлся** the explanation was quite simple.

лáр|ы, ов *pl.* (*sg.* **~, ~а** *m.*): **л. и пенáты** lares and penates.

лар|ь, я *m.* bin.

лáск|а[1]**, и** *f.* **1** caress, endearment; (*pl.*) petting; **предварúтельные ~и** foreplay. **2** (*доброе отношение*) kindness.

лáс|ка[2]**, и,** *g. pl.* **~ок** *f.* (*zool.*) weasel.

ласкáтел|ьный (~ен, ~ьна) *adj.* **1** (*obs.*) (*улыбка*) tender; (*тон*) flattering, ingratiating. **2** (*gram.*) affectionate, expressing endearment; **~ьное úмя** pet name.

ласкá|ть, ю *impf.* to caress, fondle, pet; (*о ветре, о воде*) to caress.

ласкá|ться, юсь *impf.* **1** (**к**+*d.*) to show affection (towards); to snuggle up to; (*о собаке*) to fawn (on). **2** (*coll.*) to exchange caresses.

лáсков|ый (~, ~а) *adj.* affectionate, tender; (*fig.*) gentle; **л. вéтер** gentle wind.

лассó *nt. indecl.* lasso.

ласт, а *m.* flipper.

лáстик[1]**, а** *m.* (*ткань*) lasting.

лáстик[2]**, а** *m.* (*coll.*) (*для стирания написанного*) rubber (*Br.*), eraser.

лá|ститься, щусь, стишься *impf.* (**к**+*d.*) (*coll.*) to show affection (towards), fawn (on).

ластонóг|ое, ого *nt.* (*zool.*) pinniped.

лáсточк|а, и *f.* **1** swallow; **береговáя л.** sand-martin; **городскáя л.** (house) martin; **пéрвая л.** (*fig.*) the first signs; **однá л. веснú не дéлает** (*prov.*) one swallow does not make a summer. **2** (*в обращении*) sweetheart.

лáтан|ый (~, ~а) *adj.* (*coll.*) patched.

латá|ть, ю *impf.* (*of* ⇒**за~**) (*coll.*) to patch.

латвú|ец, йца *m.* Latvian.

латвú|йка, йки *f. of* ⇒**~ец**

латвúйский *adj.* Latvian.

Лáтви|я, и *f.* Latvia.

лáтекс, а *m.* latex.

латинúзм, а *m.* Latinism.

латúниц|а, ы *f.* Roman alphabet, Roman letters.

латиноамерикáн|ец, ца *m.* Latin-American.

латиноамерикáн|ка, ки *f. of* ⇒**~ец**

латиноамерикáнский *adj.* Latin-American.

латúнский *adj.* Latin; **Латúнская Амéрика** Latin America.

лáтк|а, и *f.* (*coll.*) patch.

латýк, а *m.* (*bot.*) lettuce.

латýнный *adj.* brass.

латýн|ь, и *f.* brass.

лáт|ы, ~ *no sg.* (*hist.*) armour (*Br.*), armor (*US*).

латы́н|ь, и *f.* Latin (*language*).

латы́ш, á, *pl.* **~и́, ~éй** *m.* Latvian.

латы́ш|ка, ки *f. of* ⇒**~**

латы́шский *adj.* Latvian.

лауреáт, а *m.* prize-winner; laureate; **л. Нóбелевской прéмии** Nobel prize-winner.

лафá *as pred.*; (*impers; coll.*): **тебé, емý,** *etc.* **л.** you are, he is *etc.*, in clover, having a wonderful time.

лафéт, а *m.* (*mil.*) gun-carriage.

лáцкан, а, *pl.* **~ы, ~ов** *m.* lapel.

лачýг|а, и *f.* hovel, shack.

лá|ять, ю, ешь *impf.* to bark; (*о гончих*) to bay.

лба, лбу *etc., see* ⇒**лоб**

лгать, лгу, лжёшь, лгут, *past* **лгал, лгалá, лгáло** *impf.* **1** (*pf.* **со~**) (*говорить неправду*) to lie; to tell lies. **2** (*pf.* **на~**) (**на**+*a.*) (*клеветать*) to slander.

лгун, á *m.* liar.

лгунúшк|а, и *m.* (*coll.*) paltry liar.

лгýн|ья, ьи, *g. pl.* **ий** *f. of* ⇒**~**

лебед|á, ы́ *f.* (*bot.*) goose-foot, orache.

лебед|ёнок, ёнка, *pl.* **~ята, ~ят** *m.* cygnet.

лебедúн|ый *adj. of* ⇒**лéбедь; ~ая пóступь** graceful gait; (*fig.*) **~ая пéсня** swan-song; **~ая шéя** swan-neck; (*tech.*) S-bend pipe.

лебёдк|а[1]**, и** *f.* (female) swan, pen (-swan).

лебёдк|а[2]**, и** *f.* (*tech.*) winch, windlass.

лéбед|ь, я, *pl.* **~и, ~éй** *m.* swan, cob (-swan).

лебе|зи́ть, жу́, зи́шь *impf.* (*coll.*) (**пе́ред** + *i.*) to fawn (on).

леб|я́жий *adj.* of ⇨ ~**едь; л. пух** swansdown.

лев[1], **льва** *m.* **1** (*животное*) lion; **морско́й л.** sea-lion. **2 Л.** (*созвездие*) Leo.

лев[2], **а** *m.* (*денежная единица*) lev (*Bulgarian monetary unit*).

лева́к, а́ *m.* **1** (*pol.*) leftist. **2** (*coll.*) black marketeer.

лева́цкий *adj.* (*pol., pej.*) ultra-left.

леве́|ть, ю *impf.* (*of* ⇨ **по**~) (*pol.*) to move to the left.

левиафа́н, а *m.* leviathan.

Леви́т, а *m.* (*bibl.*) Leviticus.

левита́ци|я, и *f.* levitation.

левко́|й, я *m.* (*bot.*) stock, gilly-flower.

левобере́жный *adj.* left-bank.

левре́тк|а, и *f.* Italian greyhound.

левш|а́, и́, *i.* ~**о́й,** *g. pl.* ~**е́й** *c.g.* left-hander.

ле́в|ый *adj.* **1** left; (*со стороны левой руки*) left-hand; (*naut.*) port; **л. борт** port side; ~**ая сторона́** left-hand side, (*of horse, carriage, etc.*) near side; (*of material*) wrong side; (*fig.*): **встать с** ~**ой ноги́** to get out of bed on the wrong side. **2** (*coll.*) (*незаконный*) illegal, unofficial; ~**ая рабо́та** work on the side. **3** (*pol.*) left-wing; *as n.* **л.,** ~**ого** *m.* left-winger; (*pl.; collect.*) the left.

лега́в|ая, ой *f.*: **(длинношёрстая) л.** setter; **(короткошёрстая) л.** pointer.

легализа́ци|я, и *f.* legalization.

легализ|и́ровать(ся), и́рую(сь) = ~**ова́ть(ся)**

легализ|ова́ть, у́ю *impf. and pf.* to legalize.

легализ|ова́ться, у́юсь *impf. and pf.* to become legalized.

лега́л|ьный (~**ен,** ~**ьна)** *adj.* legal.

лега́т, а *m.* legate.

лега́то *mus.* **1** *adv.* legato. **2** *n.; nt. indecl.* slur.

леге́нд|а, ы *f.* legend; (*на карте*) key, legend.

легенда́р|ный (~**ен,** ~**на)** *adj.* legendary.

легио́н, а *m.* legion; (*fig.*) (*очень много*) plethora.

легионе́р, а *m.* legionary.

леги́рова|нный *p.p.p. of* ⇨ ~**ть** *and adj.* alloy(ed).

леги́р|овать, ую *impf.* to alloy.

легислату́р|а, ы *f.* term of office.

легити́м|ный, (~**ен,** ~**на)** *adj.* (*власть*) legitimate.

лёг|кий (~**ок,** ~**ка́,** ~**ко́,** *pl.* ~**ки́** *or* ~**ки)** *adj.* **1** (*на вес*) light; **л. за́втрак** light breakfast; ~**кая промы́шленность** light industry. **2** (*нетрудный*) easy; **л. слог** simple style; **у него́ л. хара́ктер** he is easy to get on with; ~**кая атле́тика** (*sport*) athletics (*Br.*), track and field (*US*). **3** (*незначительный*) light; slight; ~**кая просту́да** slight cold; ~**кое чте́ние** light reading(-matter); (*coll.*): ~**ок на поми́не!** talk of the devil!; (*coll.*): **у него́** ~**кая рука́** he brings luck; **с ва́шей** ~**кой руки́** once you start(ed) the ball rolling; **же́нщина** ~**кого поведе́ния** woman of easy virtue.

легко́ *adv.* (*несильно*) lightly; (*без труда*) easily; (*слегка*) slightly; **э́то ему́ л. даётся** it comes easily to him; **л. косну́ться** to touch lightly; *as pred.* it is easy; **л. сказа́ть** easier said than done!

легкоатле́т, а *m.* (track-and-field) athlete.

легкоатлети́ческ|ий *adj.*: ~**ие соревнова́ния** track-and-field events.

легкоатле́т|ка, ки *f. of* ⇨ ~

легкове́ри|е, я *nt.* credulity, gullibility.

легкове́р|ный (~**ен,** ~**на)** *adj.* credulous, gullible.

легкове́с, а *m.* (*sport*) light-weight.

легкове́с|ный (~**ен,** ~**на)** *adj.* **1** light-weight; light. **2** (*fig., pej.*) (*поверхностный*) superficial.

легково́й *adj.* passenger (*conveyance*); **л. автомоби́ль** (motor) car.

легкову́шк|а, и *f.* (*coll.*) car, motor (*Br.*), auto (*US*).

лёгк|ое, ого *nt.* (*anat.*) lung; **воспале́ние одного́** ~**ого, обо́их** ~**их** single, double pneumonia.

легкомы́слен|ный (~**,** ~**на)** *adj.* thoughtless; flippant, frivolous; **л. посту́пок** thoughtless action.

легкомы́сли|е, я *nt.* thoughtlessness; flippancy, frivolity.

легкопла́в|кий (~**ок,** ~**ка)** *adj.* fusible.

лёгкост|ь, и *f.* **1** (*веса*) lightness. **2** (*нетрудность*) easiness. **3** (*свобода*) ease; **с** ~**ью** with ease.

легоне́нько *adv.* (*coll.*) **1** (*слегка*) slightly. **2** (*мягко*) gently.

лёгочный *adj.* (*med.*) pulmonary.

легча́|ть, ет *impf.* (*of* ⇨ **по**~) **1** (*слабеть*) to lessen, abate. **2** (*impers.,* + *d.*) to get better; to feel better.

ле́г|че *comp. of* ⇨ ~**кий** *and* ~**ко́**; (*as pred.*): **больно́му л.** the patient is feeling better; **мне от э́того не л.** I am none the better for it; (*coll.*): **час о́т часу не л.** things are getting worse by the minute; **л. на поворо́тах!** mind what you say!

лёд, льда, о льде́, на льду́ *m.* ice; **л. разби́т, л. сло́ман** (*fig.*) the ice is broken.

ледене́|ть, ю *impf.* (*of* ⇨ **за**~ *and* **о**~) (*intrans.*) **1** (*превращаться в лёд*) to freeze. **2** (*замерзать*) to become numb with cold; (*fig.*): **кровь** ~**ет** (one's) blood runs cold.

леден|е́ц, ца́ *m.* fruit-drop; **ки́слый л.** acid-drop.

леден|и́ть, и́т *impf.* (*of* ⇨ **о**~) (*о морозе*) to freeze (*trans.*); (*fig.*) (*об ужасе*) to chill.

леден|я́щий *pres. part. of* ⇨ ~**и́ть** *and adj.* chilling, icy.

ледери́н, а *m.* leatherette.

ле́ди *f. indecl.* lady.

ле́дник, а *m.* **1** (*погреб*) ice-house. **2** (*шкаф*) ice-box; **ваго́н-л.** refrigerator van.

ледни́к, а́ *m.* glacier.

леднико́вый *adj.* glacial; **л. пери́од** ice age.

ледови́тый *adj.*: **Се́верный Л. океа́н** the Arctic Ocean.

ледо́в|ый *adj.* ice; ~**ое пла́вание** Arctic voyage; ~**ое побо́ище** the Battle on the Ice (*fought on 5 April 1242 between the army of Alexander Nevsky and the Teutonic Knights*).

ледоко́л, а *m.* ice-breaker.

ледоко́л|ьный *adj. of* ⇨ ~

ледору́б, а *m.* ice-axe.

ледоста́в, а *m.* freezing-over (*of river*).

ледохо́д, а *m.* drifting of ice.

леды́шк|а, и *f.* (*coll.*) piece of ice.

лед|яно́й *adj.* **1** *adj. of* ⇨ ~; ~**яна́я гора́** ice slope (*for tobogganing*). **2** (*ветер; взгляд*) icy; ice-cold.

лёжа *adv.* lying down, in lying position.

лежа́к, а́ *m.* chaise longue, lounger.

лежа́лый *adj.* stale, old.

лежа́нк|а, и *f.* stove-bench (*a shelf on which it is possible to sleep, running along the side of a Russian stove*).

леж|а́ть, у́, и́шь *impf.* (*in var. senses*) to lie; (*о предметах*) to be (situated); **л. в больни́це** to be in hospital; **л. больны́м** to be laid up; **врач веле́л мне л.** the doctor told me to stay in bed; **л. на боку́, на печи́** (*fig., coll.*) to idle away one's time; **л. у кого́-н. на душе́** to be on one's mind; **э́то** ~**и́т у меня́ на со́вести** it lies heavy on my conscience; **у меня́ душа́ не** ~**и́т (к** + *d.*) I have a distaste, no appetite (for); **на нём** ~**и́т отве́тственность за э́то** it is his responsibility.

леж|а́ться, и́тся *impf.* (+ *d.*; *usu. with neg.*): **ему́ не** ~**а́лось в посте́ли** he would, could not stay in bed.

лежа́ч|ий *adj.* **1** lying, recumbent; **л. больно́й** bed-case; ~**его не бьют** never hit a man when he is down. **2** (*для лежания*) for lying down.

ле́жбищ|е, а *nt.* breeding ground (*of certain aquatic mammals*); **л. тюле́ней** seal-rookery.

лежебо́к|а, и *c.g.* (*coll.*) lazy-bones, lie-abed.

лёжк|а, и *f.* **1** (*coll.*) (*долгое лежание*) lying. **2** (*coll.*) (*положение*) lying position; **лежа́ть в** ~**у** to be on one's back (*of sick person*). **3** (*зверя*) lair.

лежмя́ *adv.* (*coll.*): **лежа́ть л.** to lie without getting up; to lie helpless.

ле́зви|е, я *nt.* blade.

лезги́нк|а, и *f.* lezginka (*Caucasian dance*).

лез|ть, у, ешь, *past* ~**,** ~**ла** *impf.* (*of* ⇨ **по**~) **1** (**на** + *a.*, **по** + *d.*) (*взбираться вверх*) to climb (up, on to); **л. на де́рево** to climb a tree. **2** (**в** + *a.*, **под** + *a.*) (*проникать*) to climb, clamber, crawl (through, into, under); **л. в окно́** to climb in the window. **3** (*тайком*) to sneak; **куда́** ~**ешь?** (*coll.*) where do you think you're going? **4** (**в** + *a.*) (*проникать рукой*) to thrust the hand (into). **5** (**в/на** + *a.*; *usu. with neg.*) (*быть впору*) to fit (into/onto).

6 (*сползать*) to slip out of position.
7 (*выпадать*) to fall out.
8 (*о ткани*) to come to pieces.
9 (*coll.*) (*вмешиваться*) to interfere; **л. не в своё дéло** to poke one's nose into s.o. else's affairs.
10: **л. нá стену** (*fig.*, *coll.*) to climb up the wall; **не л. в кармáн за слóвом** not to be at a loss for a word; **л. в буты́лку** (*coll.*) to be confrontational; **л. в дрáку** to be ready to pick a fight; **л. на глазá комý-н.** (*coll.*) to try to make o.s. noticed by s.o.; **л. в пéтлю** (*coll.*) to stick one's neck out.

ле|й, я *m.* leu (*Romanian monetary unit*).

лейбл, а *m.* (*mus.*) label.

лейбори́ст, а *m.* (*pol.*) Labourite (*Br.*), Laborite (*US*); labour supporter (*Br.*), labor supporter (*US*).

лейбори́стск|ий *adj.* (*pol.*) Labour (*Br.*), Labor (*US*); **~ая пáртия** Labour Party (*Br.*), Labor Party (*US*).

лéйк|а, и *f.* **1** (*для поливки*) watering-can. **2** (*coll.*) funnel.

лейкеми́|я, и *f.* (*med.*) leukaemia (*Br.*), leukemia (*US*).

лейкóз, а *m.* = **лейкеми́я**

лейкоплáстыр|ь, я *m.* sticking plaster (*Br.*), adhesive tape (*US*), Band-Aid (*propr.*) (*US*).

лейкоци́т, а *m.* (*physiol.*) leucocyte.

Лéйпциг, а *m.* Leipzig.

лейтенáнт, а *m.* lieutenant.

лейтмоти́в, а *m.* leitmotif.

лекáл|о, а *nt.* (*чертёжный инструмент*) French curve.

лекáрственн|ый *adj.* (*растение, настой*) medicinal; **л. препарáт** medicine, drug; **~ая фóрма** preparation.

лекáрств|о, а *nt.* medicine; **л. от кáшля** cough medicine.

лéкар|ь, я, *pl.* **~и, ~éй** *m.* (*obs. or joc.*) physician.

лéксик|а, и *f.* vocabulary; (*всего языка*) lexis.

лексикóграф, а *m.* lexicographer.

лексикографи́ческий *adj.* lexicographical.

лексикогрáфи|я, и *f.* lexicography.

лексикóлог, а *m.* lexicologist.

лексиколóги|я, и *f.* lexicology.

лексикóн, а *m.* **1** (*obs.*) (*словарь*) dictionary. **2** (*запас слов*) vocabulary.

лекси́ческий *adj.* lexical.

лéктор, а *m.* (*в учебном заведении*) lecturer; (*выступающий*) speaker.

лектóри|й, я *m.* **1** (*учреждение*) centre organizing public lectures.
2 (*помещение*) lecture-hall.

лéктор|ский *adj.* of ⇒**~**; *as n.* **~ская, ~ской** *f.* lecturers' common room.

лекциóнный *adj.* of ⇒**лéкция; л. зал** lecture-room; **л. курс** course of lectures.

лéкци|я, и *f.* lecture; **читáть ~ю** to lecture, deliver a lecture.

лелé|ять, ю *impf.* **1** to coddle, pamper.
2 (*fig.*) to cherish, foster; **л. мечтý** to cherish a hope.

лéмех, а, *pl.* **~á** (*and* **лемéх, á,** *pl.* **~и́**) *m.* ploughshare (*Br.*), plowshare (*US*).

лéмминг, а *m.* (*zool.*) lemming.

лемýр, а *m.* (*zool.*) lemur.

лён, льна *m.* (*bot.*) flax.

лени́в|ец, ца *m.* **1** lazy-bones.
2 (*zool.*) sloth.

лени́в|ый (~, ~а) *adj.* lazy, idle; (*походка, вид*) sluggish; (*о блюдах*) quick-to-prepare.

Ленингрáд, а *m.* (*hist.*) Leningrad.

лéнин|ец, ца *m.* Leninist.

ленини́зм, а *m.* Leninism.

лéнинский *adj.* (*книги*) of Lenin; (*принципы, партия*) Leninist.

лен|и́ться, ю́сь, ~ишься *impf.* **1** to be lazy, idle. **2** (+*inf.*) to be too lazy (to); **он ~и́лся им писáть** he had been too lazy to write to them.

лéност|ь, и *f.* laziness; sloth.

лéнт|а, ы *f.* (*украшение; орденская*) ribbon; (*магнитная*) tape; (*фильм*) film; **изоляциóнная л.** insulating tape; **патрóнная л.** cartridge belt; **ви́ться ~ой** to twist, meander.

лéнт|очный *adj. of* ⇒**~а; л. глист, л. червь** tape-worm; **~очная пилá** band-saw; **л. транспортёр** conveyor belt.

лентя́|й, я *m.* lazy-bones.

лентя́йнича|ть, ю *impf.* (*coll.*) to be lazy; to loaf.

ленц|á, ы́ *f.* (*coll.*) disposition to laziness; **он с ~óй** he is inclined to be lazy.

лéнчик, а *m.* saddle-tree.

лен|ь, и *f.* **1** laziness. **2** *as pred.* (+*d. and inf.*; *coll.*) to feel too lazy (to), not to feel like; **емý бы́ло л. вы́ключить рáдио** he was too lazy to turn the wireless off; **нáдо бы пойти́, да л.** I ought to go, but I don't feel like it; **все, комý не л.** anybody who wants.

леопáрд, а *m.* leopard.

леотáрд, а *m.* leotard.

лепест|óк, кá *m.* petal.

лéпет, а *m.* babble (*also fig.*).

лепе|тáть, чý, ~чешь *impf.* to babble.

лепёшк|а, и *f.* **1** flat cake; (*fig.*, *coll.*): **разби́ться, расшиби́ться в ~у** to strain every nerve, go through fire and water. **2** (*лекарственная*) tablet, lozenge.

леп|и́ть, лю́, ~ишь *impf.* **1** (*pf.* **вы́~** *and* **с~**) to model, fashion; to mould; **л. гнездó** to build a nest. **2** (*pf.* **на~**) (*coll.*) (*наклеить*) to stick (on).

леп|и́ться, лю́сь, ~ишься *impf.* (**по**+*d.*) to cling (to).

лéпк|а, и *f.* modelling (*Br.*), modeling (*US*).

лепни́н|а, ы *f.* (*collect.*) moulding(s) (*Br.*), molding(s) (*US*).

лепн|óй *adj.* modelled (*Br.*), modeled (*US*); moulded (*Br.*), molded (*US*); **~óе украшéние** stucco moulding (*Br.*), molding (*US*).

лéпт|а, ы *f.* mite; **внести́ свою́ ~у** to do one's bit.

лес, а (у), *pl.* **~á** *m.* **1** (**в ~ý**) (*большой*) forest, (*небольшой*) wood(s); **вы́йти из ~а (и́з ~у)** to come out of the wood; **крáсный, чёрный л.** coniferous, deciduous forest; **тропи́ческий л.** rainforest; **быть как в ~ý** (*fig.*, *coll.*) to be all at sea; **л. рýбят — щéпки летя́т** (*prov.*) you can't make omelettes without breaking eggs; **кто в л., к. по дровá** (to be, *etc.*) at sixes and sevens. **2** (**в ~е**) (*sg. only*; *collect.*) timber (*Br.*), lumber (*US*).

лес|á[1] *pl. of* ⇒**~**

лес|á[2], **óв** (*строительные*) scaffolding.

лéсá[3], **лéсы́,** *pl.* **лéсы** *or* **лёсы,** **лес** *or* **лёс** *f.* fishing-line.

лесби́йск|ий *adj.* lesbian; **~ая любóвь** lesbianism.

лесбия́нк|а, и *f.* lesbian.

лесбия́нский *adj.* lesbian.

лéсенк|а, и *f.* (*coll.*) *dim. of* ⇒**лéстница;** short flight of stairs; (*приставная*) short ladder.

леси́ст|ый (~, ~а) *adj.* wooded.

лéск|а, и *f.* fishing-line.

лесни́к, á *m.* forester.

лесни́честв|о, а *nt.* forest area.

лесни́ч|ий, его *m.* forestry officer; forest warden.

лес|нóй *adj. of* ⇒**~; л. двор, склад** timber-yard; **л. институ́т** forestry institute; **л. масси́в** forest tract; **~ны́е насаждéния** afforestation; **~нóе хозя́йство** forestry.

лесовóд, а *m.* forestry specialist.

лесовóдств|о, а *nt.* forestry.

лесовóз, а *m.* timber ship; timber lorry.

лесозавóд, а *m.* timber mill (*Br.*), lumber mill (*US*).

лесозаготóвк|а, и *f.* (*usu. pl.*) logging.

лесозащи́тный *adj.* appertaining to the protection of the forests.

лес|óк, кá *m.* small wood, copse, grove.

лесоматериáл, а *m.* timber (*Br.*), lumber (*US*).

лесонасаждéни|е, я *nt.* **1** (*разведение леса*) afforestation.
2 (*участок леса*) (forest) plantation.

лесопáрк, а *m.* wooded park.

лесопи́лк|а, и *f.* saw-mill.

лесопи́льный *adj.* sawing; **л. завóд** saw-mill.

лесопи́л|ьня, ьни, *g. pl.* **~ен** *f.* = **~ка**

лесоповáл, а *m.* tree felling.

лесополос|á, ы́ *f.* woodland belt, forest belt.

лесопосáд|ки, ок *pl.* forest plantations.

лесопромы́шленник, а *m.* timber merchant (*Br.*), lumber merchant (*US*).

лесопромы́шленност|ь, и *f.* timber industry (*Br.*), lumber industry (*US*).

лесорýб, а *m.* lumberjack.

лесосéк|а, и *f.* (wood-)cutting area.

лесосплáв, а *m.* timber rafting.

Л

лесосте́п|ь, и *f.* (*geog.*) forest-steppe.

лесоту́ндр|а, ы *f.* (*geog.*) forest-tundra.

леспромхо́з, а *m.* (*abbr. of* ***лесно́е промы́шленное хозя́йство***) (State) timber industry enterprise.

лёсс, а *m.* (*geol.*) loess.

ле́стниц|а, ы *f.* stairs, staircase; (*приставная*) ladder; **пара́дная л.** front staircase; **пожа́рная л.** fire-escape; **складна́я л.** steps, step-ladder; **служе́бная л.** career ladder.

ле́стни|чный *adj. of* ⇒**~ца; ~чная кле́тка** stairwell; **~чная площа́дка** landing.

ле́ст|ный (~ен, ~на) *adj.* flattering.

лест|ь, и *f.* flattery.

лёт, а, на ~у́, о ~е *m.* flight, flying; **на ~у́** in the air, on the wing; (*fig., coll.*) hurriedly, in passing; **хвата́ть на ~у́** to be quick to grasp.

Ле́т|а, ы *f.* (*myth.*) Lethe; **ка́нуть в ~у** to sink into oblivion.

лет|а́, ~ *pl.* **1** years; age; **с де́тских лет** from childhood; **мы одни́х лет** we are (of) the same age; **сре́дних лет** middle-aged; **быть в ~а́х** to be elderly, getting on (in years); **на ста́рости ~** in one's old age. **2** *g. pl.* (*as g. pl. of* ⇒**год**) years; **ско́лько вам ~?** how old are you?; **ему́ бо́льше, ме́ньше сорока́ ~** he is over, under forty; **прошло́ мно́го ~** many years (have) passed. **3** *pl. of* ⇒**ле́то**

лета́л|ьный (~ен, ~ьна) *adj.* lethal, fatal.

летарги́ческий *adj.* lethargic.

летарги́|я, и *f.* lethargy.

лета́тельный *adj.* flying; **л. аппара́т** aircraft.

лет|а́ть, а́ю *indet. of* ⇒**~е́ть**

лета́|ющий *pres. part. of* ⇒**~ть** *and adj.*; **~ющая таре́лка** flying saucer.

ле|те́ть, чу́, ти́шь *impf.* (*of* ⇒**по~**) **1** to fly. **2** (*fig.*) (*мчаться*) to fly; to rush, tear. **3** (*fig., coll.*) (*падать*) to fall, drop (*intrans.*); **ли́стья ~тя́т** the leaves are falling; **а́кции ~тя́т вниз** shares are plummeting. **4** (*coll.*) (*нарушаться*) to be ruined.

ле́тний *adj.* summer; **л. сад** pleasure garden(s).

ле́тник, а *m.* (*bot.*) annual.

лётн|ый *adj.* flying; **~ое де́ло** flying; **~ое по́ле** airfield; **л. соста́в** aircrew.

ле́т|о, а *nt.* summer; **ба́бье л.** Indian summer; (*coll.*): **ско́лько ~, ско́лько зим** it's been ages!

ле́том *adv.* in summer.

летопи́с|ец, ца *m.* chronicler, annalist.

летопи́сный *adj.* annalistic.

ле́топис|ь, и *f.* chronicle, annals.

летосчисле́ни|е, я *nt.* chronology.

лету́н, а́ *m.* **1** flyer, flier. **2** (*fig., coll.*) (*о человеке*) rolling-stone, drifter.

лету́чест|ь, и *f.* (*chem.*) volatility.

лету́ч|ий *adj.* **1** flying; **~ая мышь** bat; **л. отря́д** flying squad (*Br.*), SWAT team (*US*). **2** (*fig.*) (*разговор, встреча*) fleeting; brief. **3** (*chem.*) volatile.

лету́чк|а, и *f.* (*coll.*) **1** (*листок*) leaflet. **2** (*собрание*) emergency meeting. **3** (*отряд*) mobile unit.

лётчик, а *m.* pilot; **л.-испыта́тель** test-pilot; **л.-истреби́тель** fighter pilot.

лётчи|ца, цы *f. of* ⇒**~к**

лече́бниц|а, ы *f.* clinic.

лече́бный *adj.* **1** (*учреждение; средства*) medical. **2** (*свойства; мазь*) medicinal; **л. препара́т** medicine, drug.

лече́ни|е, я *nt.* (medical) treatment; **амбулато́рное л.** out-patient treatment.

леч|и́ть, у́, ~ишь *impf.* to treat (*medically*); **его́ ~ат от шо́ка** he is being treated for shock.

леч|и́ться, у́сь, ~ишься *impf.* **1** (**от**+*g.*) to receive, undergo (medical) treatment (for). **2** (**у**+*g.*) to be s.o.'s patient.

ле|чу́[1]**, ти́шь** *see* ⇒**~те́ть**

леч|у́[2]**, ~ишь** *see* ⇒**~и́ть**

лечь, ля́гу, ля́жешь, ля́гут, *past* **лёг, легла́,** *imper.* **ляг, ля́гте** *pf.* (*of* ⇒**ложи́ться**) **1** to lie (down); **л. в посте́ль, л. спать** to go to bed; **неуже́ли де́ти ещё не легли́?** aren't the children in bed yet?; **л. в больни́цу** to go (in)to hospital; **л. в осно́ву** (+*g.*) to underlie; to be the basis of; (*naut.*): **л. в дрейф** to lie to, heave to. **2** (**на**+*a.*) (*обременить*) to fall (on); (*fig.*): **отве́тственность ля́жет на вас** it will be your responsibility; **подозре́ние легло́ на него́** suspicion fell upon him; **л. на со́весть** to weigh on one's conscience.

ле́ш|ий, его *m.* wood-goblin.

лещ, а́ *m.* (*fish*) bream.

лещи́н|а, ы *f.* (*bot.*) hazel.

лже... *comb. form* pseudo-, false-, mock-.

лжесвиде́тел|ь, я *m.* false witness.

лжесвиде́тель|ница, ницы *f. of* ⇒**~**

лжесвиде́тельств|о, а *nt.* perjury.

лжесвиде́тельств|овать, ую *impf.* to commit perjury.

лжеуче́ни|е, я *nt.* false doctrine.

лжец, а́ *m.* liar.

лжёшь *see* ⇒**лгать**

лжи́вост|ь, и *f.* falsity, mendacity; untruthfulness.

лжи́в|ый (~, ~а) *adj.* **1** (*человек*) lying; mendacious. **2** (*улыбка*) false, deceitful.

ли (ль) 1 *interrog. particle* **возмо́жно ли?** is it possible?; **придёт ли он?** is he coming? **2** *conj.* whether, if; **не зна́ю, придёт ли он** I don't know whether he is coming; **посмотри́, идёт ли по́езд** go and see if the train is coming. **3**: **ли... ли** whether ... or; **сего́дня ли, за́втра ли** whether today or tomorrow.

лиа́н|а, ы *f.* (*bot.*) liana.

либера́л, а *m.* liberal; **л.-демокра́т** Liberal Democrat.

либерали́зм, а *m.* **1** liberalism. **2** (*pej.*) (*излишняя терпимость*) tolerance.

либера́льнича|ть, ю *impf.* (*of* ⇒**с~**) (**с**+*i.*; *coll., pej.*) to be too easy-going (with).

либера́л|ьный (~ен, ~ьна) *adj.* **1** liberal. **2** (*излишне терпимый*) (excessively) tolerant.

либери́|ец, йца *m.* Liberian.

либери́|йка, йки *f. of* ⇒**~ец**

либери́йский *adj.* Liberian.

Либе́ри|я, и *f.* Liberia.

ли́бо *conj.* or; **л.... л.** (either) ... or.

либретти́ст, а *m.* librettist.

либре́тто *nt. indecl.* libretto.

Лива́н, а *m.* (the) Lebanon.

лива́н|ец, ца *m.* Lebanese.

лива́н|ка, ки *f. of* ⇒**~ец**

лива́нский *adj.* Lebanese.

ли́в|ень, ня *m.* heavy shower, downpour; (*fig.*) **л. свинца́** hail of bullets.

ли́вер, а *m.* (*cul.*) offal.

ли́вер|ный *adj. of* ⇒**~; ~ная колбаса́** offal sausage.

ливи́|ец, йца *m.* Libyan.

ливи́|йка, йки *f. of* ⇒**~ец**

ливи́йский *adj.* Libyan.

Ли́ви|я, и *f.* Libya.

ливмя́ *adv.* (*coll.*): **л. лить** (*of rain*) to pour, come down in torrents.

ли́в|невый *adj. of* ⇒**~ень; ~невые во́ды** rainwater; **л. дождь** downpour.

ливре́|я, и *f.* livery.

ли́г|а, и *f.* league.

лигату́р|а[1]**, ы** *f.* (*chem.*) base metal (*added to precious metals to harden them*).

лигату́р|а[2]**, ы** *f.* (*ling. and med.*) ligature.

лигни́т, а *m.* (*min.*) lignite.

ли́дер, а *m.* leader.

ли́дерств|о, а *nt.* **1** (*партии, организации*) leadership. **2** (*в состязании*) first place, lead; **занима́ть л.** to be in the lead.

лиди́р|овать, ую *impf.* to lead, be in the lead.

ли|за́ть, жу́, ~жешь *impf.* (*of* ⇒**~зну́ть**) to lick; (*fig., coll.*): **л. пя́тки (но́ги, ру́ки) кому́-н.** to lick s.o.'s boots.

ли|за́ться, жу́сь, ~жешься *impf.* **1** (*о собаке*) to lick itself. **2** (*coll.*) (*целоваться*) to neck, snog, smooch.

лиз|ну́ть, ну́, нёшь *inst. pf. of* ⇒**~а́ть**

лизоблю́д, а *m.* (*coll., pej.*) lickspittle, bootlicker.

лик[1]**, а** *m.* **1** (*arch.*) face, countenance. **2** (*на иконах*) representation of face. **3**: **л. луны́** face of the moon.

лик[2]**, а** *m.* (*eccl., arch.*) assembly; **причи́слить к ~у святы́х** to canonize.

ликбе́з, а *m.* (*abbr. of* ***ликвида́ция безгра́мотности***) (*hist.*) campaign against illiteracy.

ликвида́тор, а *m.* (*comm., etc.*) liquidator.

ликвида́ци|я, и *f.* **1** (*comm.*) liquidation; **л. долго́в** settlement of debts. **2** (*pol., etc.*) (*отмена*) liquidation; elimination, abolition.

ликвиди́р|овать, ую *impf. and pf.* **1** (*comm.*) to liquidate, wind up. **2** (*отменять*) to liquidate; to eliminate, abolish.

ликвиди́р|оваться, уюсь *impf. and pf.* **1** to wind up (one's activities). **2** *pass. of* ⇒**~овать**

ликви́дност|ь, и *f.* (*fin.*) liquidity.

ликви́дн|ый *adj.* (*fin.*) liquid; **~ые акти́вы, сре́дства** liquid assets.

ликёр, а *m.* liqueur.

ликёрово́дочный *adj.*: **~ заво́д** distillery.

ликова́ни|е, я *nt.* rejoicing, jubilation, exultation.

лик|ова́ть, у́ю *impf.* to rejoice, exult.

лик|у́ющий *pres. part. of* ⇒**~ова́ть** *and adj.* jubilant, exultant, triumphant.

лилипу́т, а *m.* Lilliputian, midget.

ли́ли|я, и *f.* lily.

лилове́|ть, ю *impf.* (*of* ⇒**по~**) to turn violet.

лило́вый *adj.* violet.

лима́н, а *m.* estuary; (*солёное озеро*) salt marshes.

лими́т, а *m.* (*норма*) quota; (**на**+*a.*) (*ограничение*) limit (on); **л. на це́ны** limit on prices.

лимити́р|овать, ую *impf. and pf.* (*нормировать*) to establish a quota (*or* maximum) in respect of; (*ограничивать*) to limit.

лимо́н, а *m.* **1** (*плод*) lemon; **он был как вы́жатый л.** he was absolutely exhausted. **2** (*дерево*) lemon tree.

лимона́д, а *m.* **1** lemonade; lemon squash. **2** (*любой газированный напиток*) fizzy drink.

лимо́нн|ый *adj.* lemon; **~ая кислота́** (*chem.*) citric acid.

лимузи́н, а *m.* limousine.

ли́мф|а, ы *f.* (*physiol.*) lymph.

лимфати́ческий *adj.* (*physiol.*) lymphatic (*also fig., obs.*).

лингафо́нный *adj.*: **л. кабине́т** language laboratory.

лингви́ст, а *m.* linguist.

лингви́стик|а, и *f.* linguistics.

лингвисти́ческий *adj.* linguistic.

лине́йк|а, и *f.* **1** (*на бумаге*) (ruled) line; **писа́ть по ~ам** to write on the lines; **но́тные ~и** (*mus.*) staves. **2** (*инструмент*) ruler; **логарифми́ческая л.** slide-rule. **3** (*строй в шеренгу*) line; parade. **4** (*comput.*): **л. прокру́тки** scroll bar.

лине́йн|ый *adj.* **1** (*math.*) linear; **~ые ме́ры** long measures. **2** (*mil., naut.*) of the line; **л. кора́бль** battleship.

ли́нз|а, ы *f.* lens.

ли́ни|я, и *f.* line; (*fig.*): policy; **по ~и** (+*g.*) in connection with, in the sphere of; **вести́** (*coll. also* **гнуть**) **свою́ ~ю** to have one's own way; **вести́ ~ю на что-н.** to direct one's efforts towards sth.; **по ~и наиме́ньшего сопротивле́ния** on the line of least resistance.

линко́р, а *m.* (*abbr. of* ***лине́йный кора́бль***) battleship.

лино́ванный *adj.* lined, ruled.

лин|ова́ть, у́ю *impf.* (*of* ⇒**на~**) to rule.

линогравю́р|а, ы *f.* linocut.

лино́леум, а *m.* linoleum.

Линч, а *m.*: **зако́н ~а, суд ~а** lynch law.

линч|ева́ть, у́ю *impf. and pf.* to lynch.

лин|ь, я́ *m.* (*zool.*) tench.

ли́ньк|а, и *f.* moult(ing) (*Br.*), molt(ing) (*US*).

линю́ч|ий (~, ~а) *adj.* (*coll.*) liable to fade.

линя́лый *adj.* (*coll.*) faded, discoloured (*Br.*), discolored (*US*).

линя́|ть, ет *impf.* **1** (*pf.* **по~**) (*о материи*) to fade; (*о краске*) to run. **2** (*pf.* **вы́~**) (*о животных*) to moult (*Br.*), molt (*US*).

ли́п|а[1]**, ы** *f.* (*дерево*) lime(-tree).

ли́п|а[2]**, ы** *f.* (*sl.*) (*подделка*) forgery, fake, sham.

ли́п|ка, ки *f. dim. of* ⇒**~а**[1]; (*coll.*): **ободра́ть как ~ку** to fleece.

ли́п|кий (~ок, ~ка́, ~ко) *adj.* sticky, adhesive; **л. пла́стырь** sticking plaster.

ли́п|нуть, ну, нешь, *past* **~, ~ла** *impf.* (**к**+*d.*) to stick (to), adhere (to).

ли́п|овый[1] *adj. of* ⇒**~а**[1]

ли́повый[2] *adj.* (*sl.*) sham, fake, forged.

липу́чк|а, и *f.* (*coll.*) **1** (*липкая лента*) adhesive tape, Sellotape (*propr.*). **2** (*застёжка*) Velcro (*propr.*) (fastener).

ли́р|а[1]**, ы** *f.* (*музыкальный инструмент*) lyre.

ли́р|а[2]**, ы** *f.* (*денежная единица*) lira.

лири́зм, а *m.* lyricism.

ли́рик, а *m.* lyric poet.

ли́рик|а, и *f.* lyric poetry.

лири́ческ|ий *adj.* **1** (*поэзия, сопрано*) lyric. **2** (*настроение*) lyrical.

лири́ч|ный (~ен, ~на) *adj.* lyrical.

лис|а́, ы́, *pl.* **~ы** *f.* fox; **черно-бу́рая л.** silver fox.

лис|ёнок, ёнка, *pl.* **~я́та, ~я́т** *m.* fox-cub.

ли́с|ий *adj. of* ⇒**~а́**

лиси́ц|а, ы *f.* fox; vixen.

лиси́чк|а, и *f.* **1** *dim. of* ⇒**лиси́ца. 2** (*гриб*) chanterelle.

Лиссабо́н, а *m.* Lisbon.

лист[1]**, а́,** *pl.* **~ья, ~ьев** *m.* (*растения*) leaf.

лист[2]**, а́,** *pl.* **~ы́, ~о́в** *m.* **1** (*бумаги*) sheet; **в л.** in folio; **корректу́ра в ~а́х** page-proofs; **игра́ть с ~а́** (*mus.*) to sight-read. **2**: **исполни́тельный л.** (*leg.*) writ of execution; **опро́сный л.** questionnaire; **охра́нный л.** safe-conduct.

листа́|ть, ю *impf.* (*coll.*) to leaf through.

листв|а́, ы́ *f.* (*collect.*) leaves, foliage.

ли́ственниц|а, ы *f.* (*bot.*) larch.

ли́ственный *adj.* (*bot.*) deciduous.

листо́вк|а, и *f.* leaflet.

лист|ово́й *adj. of* ⇒**~; ~ово́е желе́зо** sheet iron.

лист|о́к, ка́ *m.* **1** *dim. of* ⇒**~**[1,2]. **2** (*листовка*) leaflet. **3** (*бланк*) form.

листопа́д, а *m.* fall of the leaves.

лит... *comb. form, abbr. of* ***литерату́рный***

литаври́ст, а *m.* = **лита́врщик**

лита́врщик, а *m.* kettledrummer.

лита́вр|ы, ~ *pl.* (*sg.* **~а, ~ы** *f.*) kettledrum; **бить в л.** (*fig.*) (*торжествовать*) to sound the trumpets.

Литв|а́, ы́ *f.* Lithuania.

лите́йный *adj.* founding, casting.

лите́йщик, а *m.* founder, caster.

ли́тер|а, ы *f.* (*typ.*) type.

литера́тор, а *m.* man of letters.

литерату́р|а, ы *f.* literature; **худо́жественная л.** fiction.

литерату́р|ный (~ен, ~на) *adj.* literary.

литературове́д, а *m.* literary critic.

литературове́дени|е, я *nt.* literary criticism.

литературове́дческий *adj.* literary.

ли́терный *adj.* marked with a letter.

ли́ти|й, я *m.* (*chem.*) lithium.

лито́в|ец, ца *m.* Lithuanian.

лито́в|ка, ки *f. of* ⇒**~ец**

лито́вский *adj.* Lithuanian.

лито́граф, а *m.* lithographer.

литографи́р|овать, ую *impf. and pf.* to lithograph.

литогра́фи|я, и *f.* **1** (*оттиск*) lithograph. **2** (*искусство*) lithography.

литогра́фский *adj.* lithographic.

лит|о́й *adj.* cast; **~а́я сталь** cast steel.

литр, а *m.* litre.

литра́ж, а́ *m.* capacity (*in litres*).

литро́вый *adj.* litre (*Br.*), liter (*US*) (*of one litre capacity*).

литурги́ческий *adj.* liturgical.

литурги́|я, и *f.* liturgy.

литфа́к, а *m.* (*abbr. of* ***литерату́рный факульте́т***) literature department.

Литфо́нд, а *m.* Writers' Foundation.

лить, лью, льёшь, *past* **лил, лила́, ли́ло,** *imper.* **лей** *impf.* **1** to pour (*trans. and intrans.*); **л. слёзы** to shed tears; **дождь льёт как из ведра́** it is raining cats and dogs; **л. во́ду на чью-н. ме́льницу** to play into s.o.'s hands. **2** (*tech.*) to found, cast, mould (*Br.*), mold (*US*).

лить|ё, я́ *no pl., nt.* (*tech.*) **1** (*действие*) casting. **2** (*collect.*) castings.

ли́|ться, льётся, *past* **~лся, ~ла́сь, ~ло́сь** *impf.* **1** to flow; to stream, pour. **2** *pass. of* ⇒**~ть**

лиф, а *m.* bodice.

лифт, а *m.* lift, elevator.

лифтёр, а *m.* lift operator.

лифтёр|ша, ши *f. of* ⇒**~**

ли́фчик, а *m.* **1** bra. **2** (*детский*) bodice.

лиха́ч, а́ *m.* **1** (*шофёр*) reckless driver; road-hog. **2** (*удалец*) daredevil.

лиха́честв|о, а *nt.* **1** (*шофёра*) reckless driving. **2** (*удальство*) recklessness.

лихв|а́, ы́ *f.* (*coll.*) interest; **отплати́ть с ~о́й** to repay with interest.

Л

ли́х|о[1], **а** *nt.* (*poet.*) evil, ill; **не помина́йте ~ом** (*coll.*) remember me (us) kindly; **узна́ть, почём фунт ~а** (*coll.*) to fall on hard times.

ли́х|о[2] *adv. of* ⇒**~о́й**[2]; **л. заломи́ть ша́пку** to cock one's hat at a jaunty angle.

лих|о́й[1] (**~, ~а́, ~о**) *adj.* (*dial. and folk poet.*) evil; **~а́ беда́ нача́ло** (*or* **нача́ть**) (*coll.*) the first step is the hardest.

лих|о́й[2] (**~, ~а́, ~о**) *adj.* (*coll.*) dashing, spirited; jaunty.

лихора́|дить, жу, дишь *impf.* **1** to be in a fever. **2** (*impers.*): **меня́ ~дит** I feel feverish.

лихора́дк|а, и *f.* **1** fever (*also fig.*); **сенна́я л.** hay fever. **2** (*на губах*) coldsore.

лихора́доч|ный (**~ен, ~на**) *adj.* feverish (*also fig.*).

ли́хост|ь, и *f.* (*coll.*) spirit, mettle; swagger.

ли́хтер, а *m.* (*naut.*) lighter.

лицев|о́й *adj.* **1** (*anat.*) facial. **2** exterior; **~а́я сторона́** (*здания*) façade, front; (*материи*) right side; (*монеты*) obverse. **3**: **~а́я ру́копись** illuminated manuscript. **4** (*book-keeping*): **л. счёт** personal account.

лицезр|е́ть, ю́, и́шь *impf.* (*obs. and iron.*) to behold.

лице́|й, я *m.* lycée.

лице́й|ский *adj. of* ⇒**~**

лицеме́р, а *m.* hypocrite.

лицеме́ри|е, я *nt.* hypocrisy.

лицеме́р|ить, ю, ишь *impf.* to play the hypocrite.

лицеме́р|ный (**~ен, ~на**) *adj.* hypocritical.

лице́нзи|я, и *f.* (*econ.*) licence (*Br.*), license (*US*).

лиц|о́, а́, *pl.* **~а** *nt.* **1** face; **черты́ ~а́** features; **сказа́ть в л. кому́-н.** to say to s.o.'s face; **знать кого́-н. в л.** to know s.o. by sight; **на нём ~а́ нет** he looks awful; **быть к ~у́** (+*d.*) to suit, become; (*fig.*) to become, befit; **нам не к ~у́ таки́е посту́пки** such actions do not become us; **~о́м к ~у́** face to face; **поста́вить ~о́м к ~у́** to confront; **они́ на одно́ л.** (*coll.*) they are as like as two peas; **ра́дость была́ напи́сана у неё на ~е́** joy was written all over her face; **показа́ть своё (настоя́щее) л.** to show one's true colours (*Br.*), colors (*US*); **пе́ред ~о́м** (+*g.*) in the face (of); **(исче́знуть) с ~а́ земли́** (to vanish) from the face of the earth. **2** (*наружная сторона*) exterior; (*материи*) right side; (*fig.*): **показа́ть това́р ~о́м** to show sth. to advantage; to make the best of sth. **3** (*человек*) person; **гражда́нское л.** civilian; **де́йствующее л.** (*theatr., liter.*) character; **де́йствующие ~а** dramatis personae; **должностно́е л.** official; **духо́вное л.** clergyman; **в ~е́** (+*g.*) in the person (of); **невзира́я на ~а** without respect of persons; **от ~а́** (+*g.*) in the name (of), on behalf (of). **4** (*индивидуальный облик*) identity.

личжи́ *m. indecl.* lychee.

личи́н|а, ы *f.* mask; (*fig.*) guise; **под ~ой** (+*g.*) in the guise (of).

личи́нк|а, и *f.* larva, grub; maggot.

ли́чно *adv.* personally, in person.

личн|о́й *adj.* face; **~ы́е му́скулы** facial muscles; **~о́е полоте́нце** face towel.

ли́чност|ь, и *f.* **1** (*индивидуальность*) personality. **2** (*человек*) person, individual; **тёмная л.** shady character; **удостовере́ние ~и** identity card; **установи́ть чью-н. л.** to establish s.o.'s identity. **3** (*pl.*) (*обидные замечания*) personal remarks, personalities; **переходи́ть на ~и** to get personal.

ли́чн|ый *adj.* personal; (*частный*) private; **~ое местоиме́ние** (*gram.*) personal pronoun; **~ая охра́на** body-guard; **л. секрета́рь** private secretary; **~ая со́бственность** personal property; **л. соста́в** staff.

лиша́|й, я́ *m.* **1** (*bot.*) lichen. **2** (*med.*) herpes; **опоя́сывающий л.** shingles; **стригу́щий л.** ringworm; **чешу́йчатый л.** psoriasis.

лиша́йник, а *m.* (*bot.*) lichen.

лиш|а́ть(ся), а́ю(сь) *impf. of* ⇒**~и́ть(ся)**

ли́ш|ек, ка *m.* (*coll.*) surplus; **с ~ком** odd, and more, just over; **де́сять миль с ~ком** ten odd miles, ten miles and a bit; **хвати́ть ~ку** (*coll.*) to have one too many.

лише́ни|е, я *nt.* **1** (*действие*) deprivation; **л. гражда́нских прав** (*leg.*) disenfranchisement. **2** (*usu. pl.*) (*недостаток*) privation, hardship.

лишён|ный (**~, ~а́, ~о́**) *p.p.p. of* ⇒**лиши́ть** *and adj.* (+*g.*) lacking (in), devoid (of); **он не лишён остроу́мия** he is not without wit.

лиш|и́ть, у́, и́шь *pf.* (*of* ⇒**~а́ть**) (+*g.*) to deprive (of); **л. кого́-н. насле́дства** to disinherit s.o.; **л. себя́ жи́зни** to take one's life.

лиш|и́ться, у́сь, и́шься *pf.* (*of* ⇒**~а́ться**) (+*g.*) to lose, be deprived (of); **л. зре́ния** to lose one's sight.

ли́шн|ий *adj.* **1** (*избыточный*) superfluous; unnecessary; unwanted; **бы́ло бы не ~е** (+*inf.*) it would not be out of place. **2** (*запасной*) spare, odd; **л. раз** once more; **с ~им** (*coll.*) and more, odd; **со́рок фу́нтов с ~им** forty pounds odd.

лишь *adv. and conj.* only; **не хвата́ет л. одного́** one thing only is lacking; **л. то́лько** as soon as; **л. бы** if only, provided that; **л. бы он мог прие́хать** provided that he can come.

лоб, лба, о лбе́, во (на) лбу́, *pl.* **лбы, лбов** *m.* forehead, brow; **стреля́ть в л.** to fire point-blank; **ата́ка в л.** frontal attack; **пусти́ть себе́ пу́лю в л.** to blow one's brains out; (*coll.*): **в л.** (*fig.*) straight; **сказа́ть/спроси́ть в л.** to tell/ask (s.o.) straight; **на лбу́ напи́сано** writ large on one's face; **что в л., что по́ лбу** it comes to the same thing.

ло́бби *nt. indecl.* (*pol.*) lobby.

лобби́ровани|е, я *nt.* (*pol.*) lobbying.

лобби́ст, а *m.* (*pol.*) lobbyist.

лобза́ни|е, я *nt.* (*obs.*) kiss.

лобза́|ть, ю *impf.* (*obs.*) to kiss.

ло́бзик, а *m.* fret-saw.

лобко́в|ый *adj.*: **~ая кость** (*anat.*) pubis.

ло́бн|ый *adj.* (*anat.*) frontal; **~ое ме́сто** (*hist.*) place of execution.

лобов|о́й *adj.* frontal; **~а́я ата́ка** (*mil.*) frontal attack; **~о́е стекло́** windscreen (*Br.*), windshield (*US*); **л. фона́рь** headlight.

лоб|о́к, ка́ *m.* (*anat.*) pubis.

лоботря́с, а *m.* (*coll.*) lazy-bones, idler.

лобыза́|ть, ю *impf.* (*obs.*) to kiss.

лов, а *m.* **1** = **~ля. 2** = **уло́в**

ловела́с, а *m.* (*coll.*) Lovelace, lady-killer.

лов|е́ц, ца́ *m.* (*рыболов*) fisherman; (*охотник*) hunter; **л. же́мчуга** pearl-diver.

лов|и́ть, лю́, ~ишь *impf.* (*of* ⇒**пойма́ть**) to (try to) catch; (*fig.*) **л. ры́бу в му́тной воде́** to fish in troubled waters; **л. чей-н. взгляд** to try to catch s.o.'s eye; **л. (удо́бный) моме́нт, слу́чай** to (try to) seize an opportunity; to look for an opportunity; **л. ка́ждое сло́во** to devour every word; **л. себя́ на чём-н.** to catch o.s. at sth.; **л. кого́-н. на сло́ве** to take s.o. at his word; **л. ста́нцию** (*radio*) to try to pick up a station.

ловка́ч, а́ *m.* (*coll.*) dodger.

ло́в|кий (**~ок, ~ка́, ~ко**) *adj.* **1** (*искусный*) adroit, dexterous, deft; **л. ход** master stroke. **2** (*хитрый*) cunning, smart.

ло́вко *adv.* (*искусно*) adroitly; **он л. устро́ился** he fixed himself up with a good job; **л. сде́лано!** well done!

ло́вкост|ь, и *f.* **1** (*искусность*) adroitness, dexterity, deftness; **л. рук** sleight of hand. **2** (*хитрость*) cunning, smartness.

ло́в|ля, ли, *g. pl.* **~ель** *f.* catching, hunting; **ры́бная л.** fishing; **л. си́лка́ми** snaring.

ловушк|а, и *f.* snare, trap (*also fig.*).

ло́в|че (*and* **~чее**) *comp. of* ⇒**~кий** *and* **~ко**

лог, а, в ~е *or* **в ~у́,** *pl.* **~а́, ~о́в** *m.* ravine.

логари́фм, а *m.* (*math.*) logarithm.

логарифми́ческ|ий *adj.* (*math.*) logarithmic; **~ая лине́йка** slide-rule.

ло́гик|а, и *f.* logic.

логи́ческий *adj.* logical.

логи́чност|ь, и *f.* logicality.

логи́ч|ный (**~ен, ~на**) *adj.* = **~еский**

ло́говищ|е, а *nt.* den, lair.

ло́гов|о, а *nt.* = **~ище**

логопе́д, а *m.* speech therapist.

логопед|и́ческий *adj. of* ⇒**~ия**

логопе́ди|я, и *f.* speech therapy.

логоти́п, а *m.* (*эмблема*) logo.

ло́дк|а, и *f.* boat; **подво́дная л.** submarine; **спаса́тельная л.** life-boat; **ката́ться на ~е** to go boating.

ло́дочк|а, и *f. dim. of* ⇒**ло́дка**

ло́дочник, а *m.* boatman.

ло́д|очный *adj. of* ⇒**~ка**

лоды́жк|а, и *f.* (*anat.*) ankle-bone.

ло́дырнича|ть, ю *impf.* (*coll.*) to loaf, idle.

ло́дыр|ь, я *m.* (*coll.*) loafer, idler.

ло́ж|а¹, и *f.* **1** (*theatr.*) box. **2** (*масонская*) lodge.

ло́ж|а², и *f.* (*ружья*) (gun-)stock.

ложби́н|а, ы *f.* (*geog.*) hollow, dip.

ло́ж|е, а *nt.* **1** (*obs.*) (*постель*) bed. **2** (*реки*) bed. **3** (*ружья*) gun-stock.

ло́жечк|а¹, и *f. dim. of* ⇒**ло́жка**

ло́жечк|а², и *f.*: **под ~ой** in the pit of the stomach.

лож|и́ться, у́сь, и́шься *impf. of* ⇒**лечь**

ло́жк|а, и *f.* **1** spoon; **десе́ртная л.** dessert-spoon; **столо́вая л.** table-spoon; **ча́йная л.** tea-spoon; **в час по ча́йной ~е** (*fig., coll.*) in dribs and drabs. **2** (*количество*) spoonful; **л. дёгтя в бо́чке мёда** a fly in the ointment.

ложно... *comb. form* pseudo-.

ло́жност|ь, и *f.* falsity, error.

ло́ж|ный (~ен, ~на) *adj.* false; **~ная скро́мность** false modesty; **~ная трево́га** false alarm.

ложь, лжи *f.* lie.

лоз|а́, ы́, *pl.* **~ы** *f.* **1** (*для наказания*) rod; **«волше́бная л.»** dowsing rod. **2** (*ивовая*) withe. **3** (*виноградная*) vine.

лозня́к, а́ *m.* willow-bush.

лозоиска́тел|ь, я *m.* dowser, water diviner.

лозоиска́тельств|о, а *nt.* dowsing, water divining.

ло́зунг, а *m.* **1** (*призыв*) slogan. **2** (*плакат*) banner.

локализа́ци|я, и *f.* localization.

локализ|ова́ть, у́ю *impf. and pf.* to localize.

лока́л|ьный (~ен, ~ьна) *adj.* local.

лока́тор, а *m.* locator.

лока́ут, а *m.* (*pol.*) lock-out.

локомоти́в, а *m.* locomotive.

ло́кон, а *m.* lock, curl, ringlet.

локотни́к, а́ *m.* arm (*of a chair*).

ло́к|оть, тя, *pl.* **~ти, ~те́й** *m.* elbow; **с про́дранными ~тя́ми** out at elbow(s); **рабо́тать ~тя́ми** (*coll.*) to elbow one's way; **чу́вство ~тя** (*fig.*) feeling of comradeship; **бли́зок л., да не уку́сишь** (*prov.*) so near and yet so far.

локтев|о́й *adj.* (*anat.*): **~а́я кость** ulna; funny-bone.

лом, а, *pl.* **~ы, ~о́в** *m.* **1** (*инструмент*) crow-bar. **2** (*sg. only; collect.*) (*ломаные предметы*) scrap, waste; **желе́зный л.** scrap-iron.

лома́к|а, и *c.g.* (*coll.*) poseur.

ло́маный *adj.* broken; **л. англи́йский язы́к** broken English.

лома́|ть, ю *impf.* (*of* ⇒**с~**) **1** to break. **2** (*no pf.*) (*fig.*): **л. себе́ го́лову (над** + *i.*) to rack one's brains (over); **л. ру́ки** to wring one's hands; **л. ша́пку (пе́ред** + *i.*) to bow obsequiously (to). **3** (*no pf.*): **л. ка́мень** to quarry stone. **4** (*no pf.*) (*о боли*) (*coll.*) to rack; to cause to ache; (*impers.*): **меня́ всего́ ~ло** I was aching all over.

лома́|ться, юсь *impf.* **1** (*pf.* **с~**) to break (*intrans*). **2** (*no pf.*) (*о голосе*) to crack, break. **3** (*pf.* **по~**) (*coll.*) (*кривляться*) to pose, put on airs.

ломба́рд, а *m.* pawn-shop; **заложи́ть в л.** to pawn.

ломба́рд|ный *adj. of* ⇒**~**; **~ная квита́нция** pawn ticket.

ло́мберный *adj.*: **л. стол** card-table.

лом|и́ть, лю́, ~ишь *impf.* (*coll.*) **1** (*ломать*) to break. **2** (*пробиваться*) to break through, rush. **3** (*impers.*) to cause to ache; **у меня́ ~ит спи́ну** my back aches.

лом|и́ться, лю́сь, ~ишься *impf.* **1** to be (near to) breaking; (**от** + *g.*) to burst (with), be crammed (with); **ве́тви ~ятся от плодо́в** the boughs are groaning with fruit. **2** (*coll.*) (*стремиться проникнуть*) to force one's way; **л. в откры́тую дверь** (*fig.*) to force an open door.

ло́мк|а, и *f.* breaking (*also fig.*).

ло́м|кий (~ок, ~ка́, ~ко) *adj.* fragile, brittle.

ломови́к, а́ *m.* drayman, carter.

ломов|о́й *adj.* dray, draught; **л. изво́зчик** = **ломови́к**; **~а́я ло́шадь** cart-horse, draught-horse; **~а́я подво́да** dray; *as n.* **л., ~о́го** *m.* = **ломови́к**

ломоно́с, а *m.* (*bot.*) clematis.

ломо́т|а, ы *f.* (*coll.*) ache.

лом|о́ть, тя́, *pl.* **~ти́, ~те́й** *m.* hunk, chunk.

ло́мтик, а *m.* slice; **ре́зать ~ами** to slice.

Ло́ндон, а *m.* London.

ло́ндон|ец, ца *m.* Londoner.

ло́ндон|ка, ки *f. of* ⇒**~ец**

ло́ндонский *adj.* London.

лонжеро́н, а *m.* (*aeron.*) (wing) spar.

ло́н|о, а *no pl., nt.* (*obs.*) bosom, lap; **л. семьи́** the bosom of the family; **на ~е приро́ды** in the open air.

ло́паст|ь, и, *pl.* **~и, ~е́й** *f.* blade (*of propeller, oar, etc.*).

лопа́т|а, ы *f.* spade, shovel.

лопа́тк|а, и *f.* **1** (*лопата*) shovel; (*садовника*) trowel; (*cul.*) spatula; blade (*of turbine*). **2** (*anat.*) shoulder-blade; (*часть туши*) shoulder; **положи́ть на о́бе лопа́тки** (*в борьбе*) to throw; (*fig.*) to beat; **бежа́ть во все ~и** (*coll.*) to run as fast as one's legs can carry one.

ло́па|ть, ю *impf.* (*of* ⇒**с~**) (*coll.*) to eat, gobble up.

ло́п|аться, аюсь *impf. of* ⇒**~нуть**

ло́п|нуть, ну, нешь *pf.* (*of* ⇒**~аться**) **1** (*о пузыре, шине, почке*) burst; (*о стекле*) to break, crack; (*о верёвке, струне*) to snap, break; **чуть не л. от сме́ха** to split one's sides with laughter, burst with laughter; (*fig.*): **у меня́ терпе́ние ~нуло** my patience is exhausted. **2** (*fig., coll.*) (*потерпеть неудачу*) to fail, be a failure; (*fin.*) to go bankrupt, crash.

лопо|та́ть, чу́, ~чешь *impf.* (*coll.*) to mutter, mumble.

лопоу́х|ий (~, ~а) *adj.* lop-eared.

лопу́х, а́ *m.* **1** (*bot.*) burdock. **2** (*sl.*) fool.

лорд, а *m.* lord; **пала́та ~ов** House of Lords.

лорд-ка́нцлер, а *m.* Lord Chancellor.

лорд-мэ́р, а *m.* Lord Mayor.

лорне́т, а *m.* lorgnette.

лорни́р|овать, ую *impf. and pf.* to quiz(z).

Лос-А́нджелес, а *m.* Los Angeles.

лоси́н|а, ы *f.* **1** (*кожа*) elk-skin. **2** (*pl.; hist.*) (*штаны*) buckskin breeches. **3** (*мясо*) elk.

лос|и́ный *adj. of* ⇒**~ь**

лоск, а *m.* lustre (*Br.*), luster (*US*), gloss, shine (*also fig.*).

ло́скут, а *no pl., m.* (*collect.*) rags, pieces.

лоску́т, а́, *pl.* **~ы, ~о́в** *and* **~ья, ~ьев** *m.* rag, shred, scrap.

лоску́тн|ый *adj.* patchwork; **~ое одея́ло** patchwork quilt.

лосн|и́ться, ю́сь, и́шься *impf.* to be glossy, shine.

лососёвый *adj.* salmon (*attr.*).

лососи́н|а, ы *f.* salmon (flesh).

ло́со́с|ь, я, *pl.* **ло́со́си, ло́сосе́й** *m.* salmon.

лос|ь, я, *pl.* **~и, ~е́й** *m.* elk.

лосьо́н, а *m.* lotion; (*после бритья*) aftershave.

лот¹, а *m.* (*naut.*) (sounding-)lead, plummet.

лот², а *m.* (*на аукционе*) lot.

лотере́|йный *adj. of* ⇒**~я**; **л. биле́т** lottery-ticket.

лотере́|я, и *f.* lottery, raffle; **разы́грывать в ~ю** to raffle, dispose of by lottery.

лото́ *nt. indecl.* lotto; bingo.

лот|о́к, ка́ *m.* **1** (*прилавок*) hawker's stand; (*ящик для торговли*) hawker's tray. **2** (*для ссыпания*) chute; (*для стока*) gutter; **ме́льничный л.** mill-race.

ло́тос, а *m.* (*bot.*) lotus.

лото́чник, а *m.* hawker.

лох, а *m.* (*sl.*) **1** (*мужлан*) country bumpkin. **2** (*дурак*) simpleton, half-wit.

лоха́нк|а, и *f* (wash-)tub.

лоха́н|ь, и *f.* (wash-)tub.

лохма́|тить, чу, тишь *impf.* (*of* ⇒**вз~**) (*coll.*) to tousle.

лохма́|титься, чусь, тишься *impf.* (*coll.*) to become dishevelled (*Br.*), disheveled (*US*).

лохма́т|ый (~, ~а) *adj.* **1** (*животное*) shaggy(-haired). **2** (*человек, волосы*) dishevelled (*Br.*), disheveled (*US*), tousled.

лохмо́ть|я, ев *no sg.* rags; **в ~ях** in rags, ragged.

ло́ци|я, и *f.* (*naut.*) sailing directions.

ло́цман, а *m.* **1** (*naut.*) pilot. **2** (*рыба*) pilot-fish.

лошадёнк|а, и *f.* (*pej.*) jade.

лошади́н|ый *adj.* of horses; equine; **~ая си́ла** horse-power.

лоша́дк|а, и *f. dim. of* ⇒**ло́шадь**

лоша́дник, а *m.* (*coll.*) horse-lover.

ло́шад|ь, и, *pl.* **~и, ~е́й, ~я́м,**

Л

~ьми́, ~я́х *f.* horse; **бегова́я, скакова́я л.** race-horse; **верхова́я л.** saddle-horse; **вью́чная л.** pack-horse; **заво́дская л.** stud-horse; **упряжна́я л.** draught horse; **чистокро́вная л.** thoroughbred; **сади́ться на л.** to mount; **ходи́ть за ~ью** to groom a horse.

лоша́к, а́ *m.* hinny.

лощён|ый *adj.* (*бумага*) glossy; **~ая пря́жа** glazed yarn; (*fig.*): **~ые мане́ры** polished manners.

лощи́н|а, ы *f.* (*geog.*) hollow, depression.

лощ|и́ть, у́, и́шь *impf.* (*of* ⇒**на~**) **1** (*натирать до блеска*) to polish. **2** (*наводить глянец*) to glaze.

лоя́льност|ь, и *f.* fairness; honesty; loyalty.

лоя́л|ьный (~ен, ~ьна) *adj.* (*справедливый*) fair; (*честный*) honest; (*верный*) loyal (*to the State authorities*).

ЛСД *m. indecl.* (*abbr. of* ***диэтилами́д лизерги́новой кислоты́***) LSD.

луб, а, *pl.* **~ья, ~ьев** *m.* (*bot.*) (lime) bast.

луб|о́к¹, ка́ *m.* **1** (*med.*) splint. **2** (*кусок луба*) strip of bast.

луб|о́к², ка́ *m.* **1** (*картинка*) cheap popular print. **2** (*литература*) popular literature.

луб|о́чный¹ *adj. of* ⇒**~о́к¹**

луб|о́чный² *adj. of* ⇒**~о́к²**; **~о́чная карти́нка** cheap popular print.

луб|яно́й *adj. of* ⇒**~**

луг, а, о ~е, на ~у́, *pl.* **~а́, ~о́в** *m.* meadow; **заливно́й л.** water-meadow.

луди́льщик, а *m.* tinsmith, tinman.

лу|ди́ть, жу́, ~ди́шь *impf.* (*of* ⇒**вы́~** *and* ⇒**по~**) (*tech.*) to tin.

лу́ж|а, и *f.* puddle, pool; **сесть в ~у** (*fig., coll.*) to get into a mess; to slip up.

лужа́йк|а, и *f.* (*полянка*) (forest) glade; (*газон*) lawn; **л. для игры́ в шары́** bowling green.

луже́ни|е, я *nt.* (*tech.*) tinning.

лужёный *adj.* tinned, tin-plate.

луж|о́к, ка́ *m. dim. of* ⇒**луг**

лу́з|а, ы *f.* (billiard-)pocket.

лук¹, а *m.* (*collect.*) (*растение*) onions; **голо́вка ~а** (*a single*) onion; **зелёный л.** spring onion(s) (*Br.*), scallion(s); **л.-поре́й** leek; **л.-шало́т** shallot; **л.-шнитт** chives.

лук², а *m.* (*оружие*) bow; **натяну́ть л.** to bend, draw a bow.

лук|а́, и́, *pl.* **~и** *f.* **1** (*реки, дороги*) bend. **2** (*седла*) pommel.

лука́в|ец, ца *m.* (*coll.*) crafty person; (*joc.*) slyboots.

лука́в|ить, лю, ишь *impf.* (*of* ⇒**с~**) to be cunning.

лука́вств|о, а *nt.* craftiness, slyness.

лука́в|ый (~, ~а) *adj.* **1** (*хитрый*) crafty, sly, cunning. **2** (*игривый*) arch.

лу́ковиц|а, ы *f.* **1** (*головка лука*) onion. **2** (*bot., anat.*) bulb. **3** (*купол*) 'onion' dome.

лу́кови|чный *adj. of* ⇒**~ца**; bulbous.

лукомо́рь|е, я *nt.* (*poet.*) cove, creek.

луко́ш|ко, ка, *pl.* **~ки, ~ек** *nt.* basket; punnet.

лун|а́, ы́, *pl.* **~ы** *f.* moon; (**Л.**) the Moon.

лу́на-па́рк, а *m.* funfair (*Br.*), amusement park.

лунати́зм, а *m.* sleep-walking, somnambulism.

луна́тик, а *m.* sleep-walker, somnambulist.

лунати́ческий *adj.* somnambulistic.

лу́нк|а, и *f.* hole; (*anat.*) alveolus, socket.

лу́нник¹, а *m.* (*bot.*) honesty.

лу́нник², а *m.* (*ракета*) lunar probe.

лу́н|ный *adj. of* ⇒**~а́**; (*astron.*) lunar; **~ное затме́ние** lunar eclipse; **~ная ночь** moonlit night; **л. свет** moonlight; **л. ка́мень** (*min.*) moonstone.

лунохо́д, а *m.* lunar rover, Moon buggy.

лун|ь, я́ *m.* (*zool.*) harrier; **седо́й, бе́лый, как л.** white as snow (*of hair*).

лу́п|а, ы *f.* magnifying glass.

луп|и́ть¹, лю́, ~ишь *impf.* **1** (*pf.* **об~**) to peel. **2** (*pf.* **с~**) (*fig., coll.*) to fleece; to take to the cleaners.

луп|и́ть², лю́, ~ишь *impf.* (*of* ⇒**от~**) (*coll.*) (*бить*) to thrash, flog.

луп|и́ться, ~ится *impf.* (*of* ⇒**об~**) to peel (off), scale; (*coll.*) (*отпадать*) to come off, chip (*of paint, plaster, etc.*).

лупогла́з|ый (~, ~а) *adj.* (*coll.*) pop-eyed, goggle-eyed.

лупц|ева́ть, у́ю *impf.* (*of* ⇒**от~**) (*coll.*) to beat, flog.

луч, а́ *m.* ray; beam; **рентге́новские, рентге́новы ~и́** X-rays; **л. наде́жды** (*fig.*) ray of hope.

луч|ево́й *adj.* **1** *adj. of* ⇒**~**. **2** radial. **3** (*anat.*): **~ева́я кость** radius. **4** (*med.*): **~ева́я боле́знь** radiation sickness.

лучеза́р|ный (~ен, ~на) *adj.* (*poet.*) radiant, resplendent.

лучи́н|а, ы *f.* splinter, chip (*of kindling wood; also collect.*).

лучи́ст|ый (~, ~а) *adj.* radiant.

луч|и́ться, и́тся *impf.* (*poet.*) to shine brightly, sparkle.

лучко́в|ый *adj.* bow-shaped; **~ая пила́** frame-saw.

лу́чник, а *m.* archer.

лу́чни|ца, цы *f. of* ⇒**~к**

лу́чше *adj. and adv.* **1** (*comp. of* ⇒**хоро́ший** *and* **хорошо́**) better; **тем л.** so much the better; **л. всего́, л. всех** best of all; **как мо́жно л.** as well as possible; *as pred.* it is better; **л. ли вам сего́дня?** are you better today?; **л. не спра́шивай** better not ask; **нам л. верну́ться** we had better go back. **2** *as particle* (*предпочтительнее*) rather, instead; **ты им скажи́ или, л., я позвоню́** you tell them, or, rather, I'll give them a ring; **дава́йте л. поговори́м об э́том** let's talk it over instead.

лу́чш|ий *adj.* (*comp. and superl. of* ⇒**хоро́ший**) better; best; **к ~ему** for the better; **в ~ем слу́чае** at best; **всего́ ~его!** all the best!

лущ|и́ть, у́, и́шь *impf.* (*pf.* **об~**) (*горох*) to shell, hull, pod; (*орехи*) to crack.

Лха́с|а, ы *f.* Lhasa.

лы́ж|а, и *f.* ski; **го́рные ~и** alpine skis; **бе́гать, ходи́ть на ~ах** to ski; **навостри́ть ~и** (*fig.*) to take to one's heels; **напра́вить ~и** (**к** + *d.*) (*fig.*) to head (for).

лы́жник, а *m.* skier.

лы́жни|ца, цы *f. of* ⇒**~к**

лы́ж|ный *adj. of* ⇒**~а**; **л. спуск** ski-run.

лыжн|я́, и́ *f.* ski-track.

лы́к|о, а, *pl.* **~и** *nt.* bast; **я не ~ом шит** I was not born yesterday; **он ~а не вя́жет** he's drunk to incoherence.

лысе́|ть, ю *impf.* (*of* ⇒**об~** *and* **по~**) to go bald.

лы́син|а, ы *f.* bald patch.

лысу́х|а, и *f.* (*zool.*) coot.

лы́с|ый (~, ~а́, ~о) *adj.* bald; (*гора*) bare.

ль = **ли**

льв|ёнок, ёнка, *pl.* **~я́та, ~я́т** *m.* lion cub.

льви́н|ый *adj. of* ⇒**лев¹**; **~ая до́ля** (*fig.*) the lion's share; (*bot.*): **л. зев, ~ая пасть** snap-dragon.

льви́ц|а, ы *f.* lioness.

льв|я́та *see* ⇒**~ёнок**

льго́т|а, ы *f.* privilege; advantage.

льго́тн|ый *adj.* privileged; favourable; **л. биле́т** concessionary ticket, free ticket; **~ые дни** (*comm.*) days of grace; **на ~ых усло́виях** on preferential terms.

льда *g. sg. of* ⇒**лёд**

льди́н|а, ы *f.* block of ice, ice-floe.

льди́нк|а, и *f.* piece of ice.

льди́ст|ый (~, ~а) *adj.* icy; ice-covered.

льна, льну *see* ⇒**лён**

льново́д, а *m.* flax grower.

льново́дств|о, а *nt.* flax growing.

льнопряде́ни|е, я *nt.* flax spinning.

льнопряди́льн|ый *adj.* flax-spinning; **~ая фа́брика** flax-mill.

льнуть, льну, льнёшь *impf.* (*of* ⇒**при~**) (**к** + *d.*) **1** to cling (to), stick (to). **2** (*fig., coll.*) (*из чувства любви*) to make up (to); (*sl.*) (*ради выгоды*) to try to get in (with).

льнян|о́й *adj.* **1** of flax; **~о́е ма́сло** linseed-oil; **~о́го цве́та** flaxen. **2** (*платье*) linen; **~а́я промы́шленность** linen industry.

льстец, а́ *m.* flatterer.

льсти́в|ый (~, ~а) *adj.* (*слова*) flattering; (*человек*) smooth-tongued.

льстить, льщу, льсти́шь *impf.* (*of* ⇒**по~**) **1** (+ *d.*) to flatter; to gratify; **э́то льсти́т его́ самолю́бию** it flatters his self-esteem. **2** (+ *a., with refl. pron. only*) to delude; **л. себя́ наде́ждой** to flatter o.s. with the hope.

лью, льёшь *see* ⇒**лить**

лэ́йбл, а *m.* = **лейбл**

ЛЭП *f. indecl.* (*abbr. of* ***ли́ния электропереда́чи***) power line.

любвеоби́л|ьный (~ен, ~ьна) *adj.* loving; full of love.

любе́знича|ть, ю *impf.* (**с** + *i.*) (*coll.*) to pay compliments (to).

любе́зност|ь, и *f.* **1** (*свойство*) courtesy; politeness, civility. **2** (*услуга*) kindness; **оказа́ть, сде́лать кому́-н. л.** to do s.o. a kindness. **3** (*комплимент*) compliment; **говори́ть ~и кому́-н.** to pay s.o. compliments.

любе́з|ный (~ен, ~на) *adj.* **1** (*вежливый*) courteous; polite; obliging. **2** (*милый*) kind, amiable; **л. чита́тель** gentle reader; **бу́дьте ~ны...** (*polite form of request*) be so kind as ....

лю́бер, а, *pl.* **~ы** *or* **а́** *m.* (*sl.*) hard guy (*esp. from Moscow suburb of Lyubertsy*).

люби́м|ец, ца *m.* favourite (*Br.*), favorite (*US*), darling.

люби́м|ица, ицы *f. of* ⇒**~ец**

люби́мчик, а *m.* (*pej.*) pet, blue-eyed boy.

люби́м|ый (~, ~а) *adj.* **1** (*дорогой*) beloved, loved. **2** (*предпочитаемый*) favourite (*Br.*), favorite (*US*).

люби́тел|ь, я *m.* **1** (+*g. or* +*inf.*) lover; **л. му́зыки** music-lover; **л. соба́к** dog-lover; **он л. спле́тничать** he loves gossiping. **2** (*непрофессионал*) amateur.

люби́тель|ница, ницы *f. of* ⇒**~**

люби́тельский *adj.* **1** amateur; **л. спекта́кль** amateur performance; **л. теа́тр** amateur dramatics. **2** (*pej.*) amateurish.

люби́тельств|о, а *nt.* amateurishness.

люб|и́ть, лю́, ~ишь *impf.* **1** (*мать, родину*) to love. **2** (*читать, музыку*) to like, be fond of. **3** (*о растениях*) (*coll.*) to like; **фиа́лки ~ят тень** violets like shade.

люб|ова́ться, у́юсь *impf.* (*of* ⇒**по~**) (+*i.*, **на**+*a.*) to admire; **л. на себя́ в зе́ркало** to admire o.s. in the looking glass.

любо́вник, а *m.* lover.

любо́вниц|а, ы *f.* lover, mistress.

любо́вн|ый *adj.* **1** love-; **~ая исто́рия** love-affair; **~ое письмо́** love letter. **2** (*отношение*) loving.

люб|о́вь, ви́, *i.* **~о́вью** *f.* (**к**+*d.*) love (for, of).

любозна́тел|ьный (~ен, ~ьна) *adj.* inquisitive.

любо́й 1 *adj.* any; (*из двоих*) either; **л. цено́й** at any price. **2** *as n.* anyone; (*из двоих*) either.

любопы́т|ный (~ен, ~на) *adj.* curious; interesting; (*impers.*; +*d. and inf.*): **~но знать, что с ним ста́ло** it would be interesting to know what happened to him; **~но, придёт ли она́** I wonder if she will come.

любопы́тств|о, а *nt.* curiosity; **пра́здное л.** idle curiosity.

любопы́тств|овать, ую *impf.* (*of* ⇒**по~**) to be curious.

лю́б|ящий *pres. part. act. of* ⇒**~и́ть** *and adj.* loving, affectionate; **л. Вас** (*в письмах*) yours affectionately.

люд, а *m.* (*collect.*; *coll.*) people.

лю́д|и, е́й, ~ям, ~ьми́, о ~ях *no sg.* **1** (*pl. of* ⇒**челове́к**) people; **вы́биться, вы́йти в л.** to rise in the world, get on in life; **вы́вести кого́-н. в л.** to put s.o. on his feet, set s.o. up; **уйти́ в л.** to go out into the world; **на ~ях** in the presence of others, in company. **2** (*mil.*) men. **3** (*кадры*) staff, people.

лю́д|ный (~ен, ~на) *adj.* **1** (*район*) populous, thickly-populated. **2** (*улица*) crowded.

людое́д, а *m.* **1** (*человек*) cannibal; (*животное*) man-eater; **тигр-л.** man-eating tiger. **2** (*в сказках*) ogre.

людое́дств|о, а *nt.* cannibalism.

людск|а́я, о́й *f.* (*obs.*) servants' hall.

людск|о́й *adj.* **1** human; **род л.** human race. **2** (*mil.*): **л. соста́в** personnel.

люк, а *m.* **1** (*naut.*) hatch, hatchway. **2** (*theatr.*) trap. **3**: **светово́й л.** sky-light.

люкс[1]**, а** *m.* (*phys.*) lux (*unit of light*).

люкс[2] *adj. indecl.* de luxe, luxury.

Люксембу́рг, а *m.* Luxembourg.

люксембу́ргский *m.* Luxembourg.

люксембу́рж|ец, ца *m.* Luxembourger.

лю́ксовый *adj.* (*coll.*) plush, luxury.

лю́льк|а, и *f.* cradle.

люмба́го *nt. indecl.* lumbago.

люминесце́нтн|ый *adj.* luminescent; **~ая ла́мпа** fluorescent lamp.

люминесце́нци|я, и *f.* (*phys.*) luminescence.

лю́мпен, а *m.* person living on the fringes of society.

люпи́н, а *m.* lupin.

лю́рекс, а *m.* lurex (*propr.*).

лю́стр|а, ы *f.* chandelier.

лютера́н|ин, ина, *pl.* **~е, ~** *m.* (*relig.*) Lutheran.

лютера́нский *adj.* (*relig.*) Lutheran.

лютера́нств|о, а *nt.* (*relig.*) Lutheranism.

лю́тик, а *m.* (*bot.*) buttercup.

лю́тн|евый *adj. of* ⇒**~я**

лю́т|ня, ни, *g. pl.* **~ен** *f.* (*mus.*) lute.

лю́т|ый (~, ~а́, ~о) *adj.* ferocious, fierce, cruel; (*мороз*) sharp; (*ненависть*) intense.

люф|а́, ы́ *f.* (*bot.*) loofah.

люце́рн|а, ы *f.* (*bot.*) lucerne.

ля *nt. indecl.* (*mus.*) A; **ля дие́з** A sharp; **ля бемо́ль** A flat.

ляг(те) *imper. of* ⇒**лечь**

ляг|а́ть, а́ю *impf.* (*of* ⇒**~ну́ть**) to kick.

ляга́|ться, юсь *impf.* to kick (*intrans.*); (*друг друга*) to kick one another.

ляг|ну́ть, ну́, нёшь *inst. pf. of* ⇒**~а́ть**

ля́|гу, жешь, гут *see* ⇒**лечь**

лягуша́тник, а *m.* **1** (*детский бассейн*) paddling pool. **2** (*sl.*) (*француз*) Frenchman; Frog (*offens.*).

лягуш|а́чий (*and* **~ечий**) *adj. of* ⇒**~ка**

лягу́шк|а, и *f.* frog.

лягуш|о́нок, о́нка, *pl.* **~а́та, ~а́т** *m.* young frog.

ля́жк|а, и *f.* thigh, haunch.

лязг, а *no pl.*, *m.* clank, clang.

ля́зга|ть, ю *impf.* (+*i.*) to clank, clang; **он ~л зуба́ми** his teeth were chattering; **л. це́пью** to rattle a chain.

ля́мк|а, и *f.* strap; **тяну́ть ~ами, на ~ах** to tow, take in tow; **тяну́ть ~у** (*fig.*, *coll.*) to toil, sweat.

ляп, а *m.* (*coll.*) blunder, gaffe.

ля́п|ать, аю *impf.* (*coll.*) **1** (*pf.* **на~**) to make hastily *or* any old how. **2** *impf. of* ⇒**~нуть**

ля́пис-лазу́р|ь, и *f.* lapis lazuli.

ля́п|нуть, ну, нешь *pf.* (*of* ⇒**~ать**) (*coll.*) to blurt out.

ля́псус, а *m.* blunder; slip (*of tongue, pen*).

ля́сы *only in phr.* (*coll.*): **точи́ть л.** to chatter, talk idly.

Мм

М *abbr. of* **1** ***метро́*** Metro, Underground (*Br.*), Subway (*US*). **2** ***Мужска́я (убо́рная)*** Gents, Gentlemen (*lavatory*).

М. (*abbr. of* ***Москва́***) Moscow.

м (*abbr. of* ***метр***) m, metre(s) (*Br.*), meter(s) (*US*).

м. (*abbr. of* ***мину́та***) min., minute(s).

мавзоле́|й, я *m.* mausoleum.

мавр, а *m.* Moor.

Маври́ки|й, я *m.* Mauritius.

маврита́н|ец, ца *m.* Mauritanian.

Маврита́ни|я, и *f.* Mauritania.

маврита́н|ка, ки *f. of* ⇒**~ец**

маврита́нский *adj.* Moorish.

маг[1], **а** *m.* (*чародей*) magician, wizard.

маг[2], **а** *m.* (*abbr. of* ***магнитофо́н***) (*coll.*) tape recorder.

магази́н, а *m.* **1** shop; **гастрономи́ческий м.** grocer's (shop) (*Br.*), grocery store (*US*); **универса́льный м.** department store. **2** (*в оружии*) magazine.

магази́н|ный *adj. of* ⇒**~**; **м. вор** shoplifter; **~ная коро́бка** magazine (*of fire-arm*).

магара́дж|а, и *m.* Maharaja(h).

магист|е́рский *adj. of* ⇒**~р** 1, 2

маги́стр, а *m.* **1** (*лицо*) holder of a master's degree. **2** (*учёная степень*) master's degree.

магистра́л|ь, и *f.* **1** (*водная, газовая*) main; (*железнодорожная*) main line. **2** (*улица*) arterial road, main road.

магистра́ль|ный *adj. of* ⇒**~**

магистра́т, а *m.* city, town council.

магистрату́р|а, ы *f.* magistracy.

маги́ческий *adj.* magic(al).

ма́ги|я, и *f.* magic.

магна́т, а *m.* magnate, tycoon.

магне́зи|я, и *f.* (*chem.*) magnesia.

магнети́зм, а *m.* magnetism.

магнети́ческий *adj.* magnetic.

магне́то *nt. indecl.* (*tech.*) magneto.

магнетро́н, а *m.* (*phys.*) magnetron.

ма́гниевый *adj.* magnesium.

ма́гни|й, я *m.* (*chem.*) magnesium.

магни́т, а *m.* magnet.

магни́тн|ый *adj.* magnetic; **~ая ка́рточка** smart card, swipe card; **м. железня́к** magnetite.

магнито́л|а, ы *f.* radio cassette player.

магнитоле́нт|а, ы *f.* magnetic tape.

магнитоте́к|а, и *f.* tape library.

магнитофо́н, а *m.* tape recorder; **видеокассе́тный м.** video (cassette) recorder, VCR; **кату́шечный м.** reel-to-reel tape recorder; **м.-пле́йер** personal stereo, Walkman (*propr.*).

магнитофо́н|ный *adj. of* ⇒**~**; **~ная за́пись** tape-recording; **~ная ле́нта, плёнка** magnetic, audio tape.

магнито-электри́ческий *adj.* electromagnetic.

магно́ли|я, и *f.* (*bot.*) magnolia.

магомета́н|ин, ина, *pl.* **~е, ~** *m.* Mohammedan.

магомета́нств|о, а *nt.* Mohammedanism.

мада́м *f. indecl.* madam(e).

Маде́йр|а, ы *f.* Madeira.

мадемуазе́л|ь, и *f.* mademoiselle.

маде́р|а, ы *f.* Madeira (wine).

маджо́нг, а *m.* mah-jong.

мадо́нн|а, ы *f.* madonna.

мадрига́л, а *m.* madrigal.

Мадри́д, а *m.* Madrid.

мадья́р, а, *pl.* **~ы, ~** *m.* Magyar.

мадья́р|ка, ки *f. of* ⇒**~**

мадья́рский *adj.* Magyar.

мает|а́, ы́ *f.* (*coll.*) trouble, bother.

мажо́р, а *m.* **1** (*mus.*) major key. **2** (*fig.*) (*бодрое настроение*) a cheerful mood; **быть в ~е** to be in high spirits.

мажордо́м, а *m.* major-domo.

мажо́рный *adj.* **1** (*mus.*) major. **2** (*fig.*) (*бодрый*) cheerful.

ма́занк|а, и *f.* (*dial.*) cottage of daubed brick or wood (*esp. in southern Russia*).

ма́заный *adj.* **1** (*coll.*) (*грязный*) dirty, stained, soiled. **2** (*из глины*) adobe.

ма́|зать, жу, жешь *impf.* **1** (*pf.* **на~, по~**) (*смазывать*) to oil, grease, lubricate. **2** (*pf.* **вы~, на~, по~**) (*намазывать*) to smear (with); **м. хлеб ма́слом** to spread butter on bread, butter bread. **3** (*pf.* **за~, из~;** *coll.*) (*пачкать*) to soil, stain. **4** (*pf.* **на~;** *coll.*) (*плохо рисовать*) to daub. **5** (*pf.* **про~**[2]; *coll.*) (*не попадать*) to miss.

ма́|заться, жусь, жешься *impf.* **1** (*pf.* **вы́~, за~, из~**) (*пачкаться*) to soil o.s., stain o.s. **2** (*coll.*) (*о предметах*) to soil, stain (*intrans.*). **3** (*pf.* **на~**) to make up; **она́ си́льно ~жется** (*coll.*) she makes up heavily. **4** (*pf.* **на~, по~**) (+*i.*) to apply (*ointment, cream, etc.*).

мазн|у́ть, у́, ёшь *pf.* **1** to dab. **2** (*coll.*) (*ударить по лицу*) to hit.

мазн|я́, и́ *f.* (*coll.*) poor painting, daub.

маз|о́к, ка́ *m.* **1** dab; (*кисти*) stroke; **класть после́дние ~ки́** (*fig.*) to put the finishing touches. **2** (*med.*) smear (*for microscopic examination*). **3** (*coll.*) (*промах*) miss (*in shooting, football, etc.*).

мазохи́зм, а *m.* (*med.*) masochism.

мазохи́ст, а *m.* masochist.

мазу́рк|а, и *f.* mazurka.

мазу́т, а *m.* (*tech.*) fuel oil.

маз|ь, и *f.* **1** (*лекарство*) ointment. **2** (*для смазки*) grease; **де́ло на ~и́** (*fig., coll.*) things are going swimmingly.

маис, а *m.* maize.

маи́с|овый *adj. of* ⇒**~**

ма|й, я *m.* May.

ма́йк|а, и *f.* sleeveless top; (*нижняя*) vest (*Br.*), undershirt (*US*).

ма́йн|а, ы *f.* myna(h) bird.

майо́лик|а, и *f.* majolica.

майоне́з, а *m.* (*cul.*) mayonnaise.

майо́р, а *m.* major (*mil. rank*).

майора́н, а *m.* (*bot.*) marjoram.

Майо́рк|а, и *f.* = **Мальо́рка**

майо́р|ский *adj. of* ⇒**~**

ма́й|ский *adj. of* ⇒**~**; **м. жук** may-bug, cockchafer.

ма́йя *c.g. indecl. and adj. indecl.* Maya.

мак, а *m.* **1** (*растение*) poppy. **2** (*collect.*) (*семена*) poppy-seed.

мака́к|а, и *f.* (*zool.*) macaque.

мака́о *m. indecl.* (*zool.*) macaw.

макаро́нник, а *m.* **1** (*запеканка*) pasta bake. **2** (*sl.*) (*итальянец*) Italian; wop (*offens.*).

макаро́н|ный *adj. of* ⇨**~ы; ~ные изде́лия** pasta.

макаро́н|ы, ~ *pl.* (*sg.* **~а, ~ы** *f.*) pasta.

мак|а́ть, а́ю *impf.* (*of* ⇨**~ну́ть**) to dip.

македо́н|ец, ца *m.* Macedonian.

Македо́ни|я, и *f.* Macedonia.

македо́н|ка, ки *f. of* ⇨**~ец**

македо́нский *adj.* Macedonian; **Алекса́ндр М.** Alexander the Great.

маке́т, а *m.* model; (*книги*) dummy.

макиавелли́зм, а *m.* Machiavellianism.

макиавеллисти́ческий *adj.* Machiavellian.

макинто́ш, а *m.* mackintosh.

макия́ж, а *m.* make-up.

ма́клер, а *m.* (*comm.*) broker.

ма́клерств|о, а *nt.* (*comm.*) brokerage.

мак|ну́ть, ну́, нёшь *pf. of* ⇨**~а́ть**

ма́ковк|а, и *f.* **1** (*плод мака*) poppy-head. **2** (*coll.*) (*головы*) crown. **3** (*coll.*) (*купол*) cupola.

ма́к|овый *adj. of* ⇨**~**

макраме́ *nt. indecl.* macramé.

макре́л|ь, и *f.* mackerel.

макрокома́нд|а, ы *f.* (*comput.*) macro.

макроко́см, а *m.* macrocosm.

макроскопи́ческий *adj.* macroscopic.

макроэконо́мик|а, и *f.* macroeconomics.

макроэкономи́ческий *adj.* macroeconomic.

ма́кси *nt. indecl.* maxi (*garment*); **ма́кси-ю́бка** maxi-skirt.

ма́ксим|а, ы *f.* maxim.

максимали́зм, а *m.* uncompromisingness.

максимали́ст, а *m.* uncompromising person.

максима́л|ьный (~ен, ~ьна) *adj.* maximum.

ма́ксимум, а *m.* **1** maximum. **2** *as adv.* at most; **м. сто рубле́й** a hundred roubles at most.

макулату́р|а, ы *f.* **1** (*на переработку*) paper for recycling. **2** (*coll., pej.*) (*о литературном произведении*) pulp literature.

маку́шк|а, и *f.* **1** (*дерева*) top. **2** (*головы*) crown; **у нас у́шки на ~е** (*fig.*) we are on our guard.

Мала́ви *nt. indecl.* Malawi.

малагаси́|ец, йца *m.* Malagasy.

малагаси́|йка, йки *f. of* ⇨**~ец**

малагаси́йский *adj.* Malagasy.

мала́|ец, йца *m.* Malay.

Мала́йзи|я, и *f.* Malaysia.

мала́|йка, йки *f. of* ⇨**~ец**

мала́йский *adj.* Malay, Malayan.

Мала́й|я, и *f.* Malaya.

малахи́т, а *m.* (*min.*) malachite.

мал|ева́ть, ю́ю, ю́ешь *impf.* (*of* ⇨**на~**) (*coll.*) to paint.

мале́йший *adj.* (*superl. of* ⇨**ма́лый**) least, slightest.

мал|ёк, ька́ *m.* young fish; (*collect.*) fry.

ма́леньк|ий *adj.* **1** little, small; **~ие лю́ди** humble folk; **идти́ по ~ому** (*baby talk*) to do a wee-wee. **2** (*незначительный*) slight. **3** (*малолетний*) young; *as n.* **м., ~ого** *m.*, **~ая, ~ой** *f.* the baby, the child; **~ие** the young.

мале́нько *adv.* (*coll.*) a little, a bit.

мале́ц, мальца́ *m.* (*coll.*) lad, boy.

Мали́ *nt. indecl.* Mali.

мали́н|а, ы *no pl., f.* **1** (*collect.*) (*ягоды*) raspberries. **2** (*кустарник*) raspberry-bush; raspberry-cane. **3** (*напиток*) raspberry juice. **4** (*sl.*) (*воровской притон*) (thieves') den. **5** (*fig., coll.*): **у нас житьё — м.** we are in clover.

мали́нник, а *no pl. m.* (*collect.*) raspberry-canes.

мали́н|ный *adj. of* ⇨**~а**

мали́новк|а, и *f.* (*zool.*) robin (redbreast).

мали́новый *adj.* **1** (*варенье*) raspberry. **2** (*цвет*) crimson.

ма́лк|а, и *f.* (*tech.*) bevel (square).

ма́ло *adv.* (*времени, денег*) little, not much; (*книг, людей*) few; (*недостаточно*) not enough; (*читать*) not much; **э́того ма́ло** this is not enough; **об э́том м. кто зна́ет** few (people) know about it; **я м. где быва́л** I have hardly been anywhere; **м. ли что!** what does it matter!; **м. ли что мо́жет случи́ться** anything may happen; **м. того́** moreover; **м. того́, что**… not only …, it is not enough that …; **м. того́, что он сам прие́хал, он привёз всех това́рищей** it was not enough that he came himself, but he had to bring all his friends.

малоблагоприя́т|ный (~ен, ~на) *adj.* unfavourable (*Br.*), unfavorable (*US*).

малова́ж|ный (~ен, ~на) *adj.* of little importance, insignificant.

малова́т (~а, ~о) *adj.* (*coll.*) on the small side; **м. ро́стом** undersized.

малова́то *adv.* (*coll.*) not quite enough; not very much.

малове́р, а *m.* sceptic (*Br.*), skeptic (*US*).

малове́ри|е, я *nt.* lack of faith, scepticism (*Br.*), skepticism (*US*).

малове́р|ный (~ен, ~на) *adj.* sceptical (*Br.*), skeptical (*US*).

маловероя́т|ный (~ен, ~на) *adj.* unlikely, improbable.

малове́с|ный (~ен, ~на) *adj.* light-weight.

маловод|ный (~ен, ~на) *adj.* (*река, озеро*) shallow; (*земля*) dry.

малово́дь|е, я *nt.* **1** (*недостаток воды*) shortage of water. **2** (*низкий уровень воды*) low water-level, shallowness.

маловы́год|ный (~ен, ~на) *adj.* unprofitable, unrewarding.

малогабари́т|ный (~ен, ~на) *adj.* small.

малоговоря́щий *adj.* not enlightening, not illuminating.

малогра́мот|ный (~ен, ~на) *adj.* **1** (*человек*) semiliterate. **2** (*чертёж*) crude. **3** (*техник*) incompetent.

малодостове́р|ный (~ен, ~на) *adj.* improbable; not well-founded.

малодохо́д|ный (~ен, ~на) *adj.* unprofitable.

малоду́шеств|овать, ую *impf.* (*падать духом*) to lose heart; (*проявлять малодушие*) to be faint-hearted.

малоду́ши|е, я *nt.* faint-heartedness.

малоду́ш|ный (~ен, ~на) *adj.* faint-hearted.

маложи́р|ный (~ен, ~на) *adj.* low-fat.

малозаме́т|ный (~ен, ~на) *adj.* **1** barely visible, barely noticeable. **2** (*обыденный*) ordinary, undistinguished.

малоземе́ль|е, я *nt.* shortage of (arable) land.

малознако́м|ый (~, ~а) *adj.* little-known, unfamiliar.

малозначи́тел|ьный (~ен, ~ьна) *adj.* of little significance, of little importance.

малоиму́щ|ий (~, ~а) *adj.* needy, indigent.

малокали́берный *adj.* (*о ружье*) small-calibre (*Br.*), -caliber (*US*); small-bore.

малокалори́йный *adj.* low-calorie.

малокро́ви|е, я *nt.* anaemia (*Br.*), anemia (*US*).

малокро́в|ный (~ен, ~на) *adj.* anaemic (*Br.*), anemic (*US*).

малоле́тн|ий *adj.* **1** young; juvenile. **2** *as n.* **м., ~его** *m.* (*ребёнок*) infant; (*подросток*) juvenile, minor.

малоле́тств|о, а *nt.* infancy; nonage, minority.

малолитра́жк|а, и *f.* (*coll.*) compact (car); mini.

малолитра́жный *adj.* of small (*cylinder*) capacity; **м. автомоби́ль** compact (car); mini.

малолю́дност|ь, и *f.* scarcity of people; (*на собрании*) poor attendance.

малолю́д|ный (~ен, ~на) *adj.* **1** (*улица*) not crowded, unfrequented; **~ное собра́ние** poorly attended meeting. **2** (*район*) thinly populated.

малолю́д|ье, ья *nt.* = **~ность**

мало-ма́льски *adv.* (*coll.*) in the slightest degree, at all.

малома́льский *adj.* (*coll.*) slightest, most insignificant.

малометра́жн|ый *adj.*: **~ая кварти́ра** small flat.

маломо́ч|ный (~ен, ~на) *adj.* (*econ.*) having small resources; **~ные крестья́не** poor peasants.

маломо́щ|ный (~ен, ~на) *adj.* **1** = **маломо́чный. 2** (*двигатель*) low-powered; weak.

М

малонадё́ж|ный (~ен, ~на) *adj.* unreliable.

малонаселё́нный *adj.* thinly, sparsely populated.

малообеспе́ченный *adj.* needy, poverty-stricken.

малоопла́чиваемый *adj.* (*работа*) low-paid, badly-paid.

малоснова́тел|ьный (~ен, ~ьна) *adj.* **1** (*слухи*) unfounded. **2** (*человек*) undependable.

малоподви́ж|ный (~ен, ~на) *adj.* not mobile, slow-moving.

мало-пома́лу *adv.* (*coll.*) little by little, bit by bit.

малопоня́т|ный (~ен, ~на) *adj.* hard to understand; obscure.

малопри́был|ьный (~ен, ~ьна) *adj.* barely profitable.

малоприго́д|ный (~ен, ~на) *adj.* of little use.

малора́звит|ый (~, ~а) *adj.* **1** (*страна, промышленность*) undeveloped; underdeveloped. **2** (*человек*) uneducated.

малоразгово́рчив|ый (~, ~а) *adj.* taciturn.

малоро́сл|ый (~, ~а) *adj.* undersized, stunted.

малоро́сс, а *m.* (*obs.*) Little Russian (*Ukrainian*).

малоросси́йский *adj.* (*obs.*) Little Russian (*Ukrainian*).

Малоро́сси|я, и *f.* (*obs.*) Little Russia, Ruthenia.

малосве́дущ|ий (~, ~а) *adj.* ill-informed.

малосеме́|йный (~ен, ~йна) *adj.* having a small family.

малоси́л|ьный (~ен, ~ьна) *adj.* **1** (*слабый*) weak, feeble. **2** (*tech.*) low-powered.

малосодержа́тел|ьный (~ен, ~ьна) *adj.* uninteresting; (*fig.*) empty, shallow.

малосо́л|ьный (~ен, ~ьна) *adj.* slightly salted.

малосостоя́тел|ьный (~ен, ~ьна) *adj.* unconvincing.

ма́лост|ь, и *f.* (*coll.*) **1** a bit; trifle. **2** *as adv.* a little, a bit; **м. поспа́ть** to take a nap.

малосуще́ствен|ный (~, ~на) *adj.* of small importance, immaterial.

малотира́жн|ый *adj.* small-circulation; **~ое изда́ние** limited edition.

малоубеди́тел|ьный (~ен, ~ьна) *adj.* unconvincing.

малоупотреби́тел|ьный (~ен, ~ьна) *adj.* infrequent, rarely used.

малоуспе́ш|ный (~ен, ~на) *adj.* unsuccessful.

малоформа́тный *adj.* miniature.

малоце́н|ный (~ен, ~на) *adj.* of little value.

малочи́сленност|ь, и *f.* small number; paucity.

малочи́слен|ный (~, ~на) *adj.* small (in numbers); scanty.

ма́л|ый[1] (~, ~а́, ~о́) *adj.* little, (too) small; **м. ро́стом** short, of small stature; **м. ход!** (*naut.*) slow speed (ahead)!; **э́ти сапоги́ мне ~ы́** these boots are too small for me; **от ~а до вели́ка** young and old alike; **с ~ых лет** from childhood; *as n.* **~ое, ~ого** *nt.* little; **са́мое ~ое** (*coll.*) at the least; **без ~ого** almost, all but; **за ~ым де́ло ста́ло** (*frequently iron.*) one small thing is lacking.

ма́л|ый[2], ого *m.* (*coll.*) (*мужчина*) fellow, chap; (*парень*) lad.

малы́ш, а́ *m.* (*coll.*) child, kid; little boy.

ма́льв|а, ы *f.* (*bot.*) mallow.

Мальо́рк|а, и *f.* Majorca.

Ма́льт|а, ы *f.* Malta.

мальти́йский *adj.* Maltese.

ма́льчик, а *m.* boy.

мальчи́шеский *adj.* **1** boyish. **2** (*pej.*) (*детский*) childish, puerile.

мальчи́шеств|о, а *nt.* boyishness; (*pej.*) childishness.

мальчи́шк|а, и *m.* (*coll.*) (little) boy.

мальчи́шник, а *m.* (*перед свадьбой*) stag-party (*Br.*), bachelor party (*US*).

мальчуга́н, а *m.* (*coll., affectionate*) little fellow.

малю́сенький *adj.* (*coll.*) tiny, wee.

малю́тк|а, и *c.g.* baby, tot.

маля́р, а́ *m.* (house-)painter, decorator.

маляри́йный *adj.* malarial.

маляри́|я, и *f.* (*med.*) malaria.

маля́р|ный *adj. of* ⇒**~**; **~ная кисть** paintbrush.

ма́м|а, ы *f.* mum, mummy (*Br.*), mommy (*US*).

мамалы́г|а, и *f.* polenta.

мама́ш|а, и *f.* (*coll.*) mummy (*Br.*), mommy (*US*).

ма́менькин *adj.* mother's; **м. сыно́к** (*coll., iron.*) mother's darling.

ма́мин *adj.* mother's.

ма́монт, а *m.* mammoth.

ма́монт|овый *adj. of* ⇒**~**; **~овое де́рево** (*bot.*) sequoia, Wellingtonia.

ма́мочк|а, и *f.* (*coll.*) mummy (*Br.*) mommy (*US*).

мана́т|ки, ок *no sg.* (*sl.*) possessions, one's bits and pieces.

манга́ни́т, а *m.* (*min.*) manganite.

ма́нго *nt. indecl.* (*bot.*) mango.

ма́нго|вый *adj. of* ⇒**~**

ма́нгровый *adj.* (*bot.*) mangrove.

мангу́ст|а, ы *f.* (*zool.*) mongoose.

мандари́н[1], а *m.* (*в Китае*) mandarin (*Chinese official*).

мандари́н[2], а *m.* (*дерево, плод*) mandarin(e), tangerine.

мандари́н|ный *adj. of* ⇒**~**[2]

мандари́н|овый *adj.* = **~ный**

мандари́н|ский *adj. of* ⇒**~**[1]

манда́т, а *m.* **1** (*документ*) warrant. **2** (*pol.*) mandate; credentials.

манда́т|ный *adj. of* ⇒**~**; **~ная коми́ссия** credentials committee; **~ная террито́рия** mandated territory.

мандоли́н|а, ы *f.* (*mus.*) mandolin.

мандолини́ст, а *m.* mandolin-player.

мандраго́р|а, ы *f.* (*bot.*) mandrake.

мандра́ж, а́ *m.* (*coll.*) butterflies, the jitters.

мандри́л, а *m.* (*zool.*) mandrill.

манё́вр, а *m.* **1** manœuvre (*Br.*), maneuver (*US*); manœuvres (*Br.*), maneuvers (*US*). **2** (*pl.*) (*rail.*) shunting.

манё́вренност|ь, и *f.* manœuvrability (*Br.*), maneuverability (*US*).

манё́вр|енный *adj. of* ⇒**~**; **~енная война́** mobile warfare; **~енный самолё́т** manœuvrable (*Br.*), maneuverable (*US*) aircraft.

маневри́р|овать, ую *impf.* (*of* ⇒**с~**) **1** to manœuvre (*Br.*), maneuver (*US*). **2** (+*i.*) (*распоряжаться*) to make good use (of), use to advantage.

мане́ж, а *m.* **1** riding-school, manège. **2** (*цирка*) ring; **инспе́ктор ~а** ringmaster. **3**: **спорти́вный м.** sports hall. **4**: **(де́тский) м.** play-pen.

манеке́н, а *m.* mannequin; dummy.

манеке́нщик, а *m.* male model.

манеке́нщиц|а, ы *f.* model.

мане́р, а *m.* (*coll.*) manner; **таки́м ~ом** in this manner, in this way; **на англи́йский м.** in the English manner.

мане́р|а, ы *f.* **1** manner, style; **м. вести́ себя́** way of behaving; **м. держа́ть себя́** bearing, carriage; **петь в ~е Кару́зо** to sing in the style of Caruso. **2** (*pl.*) manners; **у него́ плохи́е ~ы** he has no manners.

мане́рнича|ть, ю *impf.* (*coll.*) to behave affectedly.

мане́рност|ь, и *f.* affectation; preciosity.

мане́р|ный (~ен, ~на) *adj.* affected.

манже́т|а, ы *f.* cuff.

маниака́льный *adj.* maniacal; manic.

маникю́р, а *m.* manicure.

маникю́рш|а, и *f.* manicurist.

Мани́л|а, ы *f.* Manila.

мани́льск|ий *adj.*: **~ая бума́га** Manil(l)a paper.

манипули́р|овать, ую *impf.* (+*i.*) to manipulate.

манипуля́ци|я, и *f.* **1** manipulation. **2** (*fig.*) machination, intrigue.

ман|и́ть, ю́, ~́ишь *impf.* **1** (*pf.* **по~**) to beckon. **2** (*pf.* **вз~**) (*fig.*) (*привлекать*) to attract; (*соблазнять*) to lure, allure.

манифе́ст, а *m.* manifesto; proclamation.

манифеста́нт, а *m.* (*pol., etc.*) demonstrator.

манифеста́ци|я, и *f.* (street) demonstration.

манифести́р|овать, ую *impf. and pf.* to demonstrate, take part in a demonstration.

мани́шк|а, и *f.* (false) shirt-front, dicky.

ма́ни|я, и *f.* **1** mania; **м. вели́чия** megalomania. **2** (*fig.*) passion, craze; **у неё́ м. противоре́чить** she has a passion for contradicting.

ма́нк|а, и *f.* (*coll.*) semolina.

манки́р|овать, ую *impf. and pf.* (+*i.*) to neglect.

ма́нн|а, ы *f.* manna; **ждать** (+*g.*) **как ~ы небе́сной** to await with impatience.

ма́нн|ый *adj.*: **~ая ка́ша, крупа́** semolina.

манове́ни|е, я *nt.* (*obs.*) beck, nod; **~ем руки́** with a wave of one's hand.

мано́метр, а *m.* (*tech.*) pressure-gauge, manometer.

манометри́ческий *adj.* (*tech.*) manometric.

манса́рд|а, ы *f.* attic, garret.

манти́ль|я, и *f.* mantilla.

манти́сс|а, ы *f.* (*math.*) mantissa.

ма́нти|я, и *f.* cloak, mantle; robe, gown.

манто́ *nt. indecl.* (*lady's*) fur coat.

манускри́пт, а *m.* manuscript.

мануфакту́р|а, ы *f.* (*obs.*) **1** (*фабрика*) textile mill. **2** (*sg. only; collect.*) (*ткани*) textiles.

мануфакту́р|ный *adj. of* **⇨~а**

Маньчжу́ри|я, и *f.* Manchuria.

манья́к, а *m.* maniac.

маои́зм, а *m.* Maoism.

маои́стский *adj.* Maoist.

ма́ори *c.g. indecl.* Maori.

маори́йский *adj.* Maori.

марабу́ *nt. indecl.* (*zool.*) marabou.

мара́зм, а *m.* (*med.*) marasmus; **ста́рческий м.** senility; (*fig.*) decay.

мара́л, а *m.* (*zool.*) Siberian deer.

мараски́н, а *m.* maraschino (*liqueur*).

мара́|ть, ю *impf.* (*coll.*) **1** (*pf.* **за~**) (*пачкать*) to soil, dirty; (*fig.*) to sully, stain; **м. ру́ки** (**о**+*a.*) to soil one's hands (on). **2** (*pf.* **на~**) (*плохо писать, рисовать*) to scribble. **3** (*pf.* **вы́~**) (*вычёркивать*) to cross out, strike out.

мара́|ться, юсь *impf.* (*coll.*) (*pf.* **за~**) **1** (*пачкаться*) to get dirty. **2** (*fig.*) (*портить свою репутацию*) to soil one's hands. **3** *pass. of* **⇨~ть**

марафе́т, а *m.* **1** (*sl.*) coke (= *cocaine*). **2**: **навести́ м.** to spruce *or* tidy up.

марафо́н, а *m.* marathon.

марафо́н|ец, ца *m.* marathon runner.

марафо́нский *adj.*: **м. бег** (*sport*) marathon race.

ма́рган|ец, ца *m.* (*chem.*) manganese.

ма́рган|цевый *adj. of* **⇨~ец**

маргари́н, а *m.* margarine.

маргари́тк|а, и *f.* (*bot.*) daisy.

маргина́л, а *m.* person living on the fringes of society.

маргина́ли|и, ев *and* **ий** *no sg.* marginalia.

маргина́льный *adj.* marginal.

ма́рев|о, а *nt.* **1** (*мираж*) mirage. **2** (*туманная дымка*) heat haze.

маре́н|а, ы *f.* (*bot.*) madder.

ма́ри *indecl.* (*collect.*) the Mari (*inhabitants of Mari Autonomous Republic in former USSR, formerly the Cheremis*).

мари́|ец, йца *m.* Mari.

мари́йк|а, и *f. of* **⇨мари́ец**

мари́йский *adj.* Mari.

мари́н|а, ы *f.* (*art*) seascape.

марина́д, а *m.* (*соус*) marinade; (*маринованный продукт*) pickles.

марини́ст, а *m.* painter of seascapes.

марино́в|анный *p.p.p. of* **⇨~а́ть** *and adj.* (*cul.*) pickled.

марин|ова́ть, у́ю *impf.* **1** (*pf.* **за~**) to pickle. **2** (*pf.* **про~**) (*fig., coll.*) to put off, shelve.

марионе́т|ка, ки *f.* marionette; puppet (*also fig.*); **теа́тр ~ок** puppet-theatre (*Br.*), -theater (*US*).

марионе́т|очный *adj. of* **⇨~ка; ~очное госуда́рство** puppet state.

марихуа́н|а, ы *f.* marijuana.

ма́рк|а, и *f.* **1** (*почтовая*) (postage-) stamp. **2** (*денежная единица*) mark. **3** (*сорт*) brand, make; **фабри́чная м.** trade-mark; **како́й ~и?** what make? **4** (*качество*) grade, sort, brand; **това́р вы́сшей ~и** goods of the highest grade. **5** (*fig.*) (*репутация*) name, reputation; **держа́ть ~у** to maintain one's reputation.

маркёр, а *m.* (*in var. senses*) marker.

ма́ркетинг, а *m.* marketing.

маркетри́ *indecl. adj. and nt. n.* (*инкрустация по дереву*) marquetry.

марки́з, а *m.* marquis, marquess.

марки́з|а¹, ы *f.* (*человек*) marchioness.

марки́з|а², ы *f.* (*навес*) sun-blind; awning.

ма́р|кий (~ок, ~ка) *adj.* easily soiled.

маркир|ова́ть, у́ю *impf. and pf.* to mark.

маркси́зм, а *m.* Marxism.

маркси́зм-ленини́зм, а-а *m.* Marxism-Leninism.

маркси́ст, а *m.* Marxist.

маркси́стский *adj.* Marxist, Marxian.

маркси́стско-ле́нинский *adj* Marxist-Leninist.

маркше́йдер, а *m.* mine-surveyor.

ма́рл|евый *adj. of* **⇨~я; м. бинт** gauze bandage.

ма́рл|я, и *f.* gauze.

мармела́д, а *m.* (*конфеты*) fruit jellies.

маро́дёр, а *m.* **1** marauder, pillager. **2** (*coll.*) (*спекулянт*) profiteer.

маро́дёрск|ий *adj.* marauding; **~ие це́ны** (*fig., coll.*) exorbitant prices.

маро́дёрств|о, а *nt.* pillage, looting.

маро́дёрств|овать, ую *impf.* to maraud, pillage, loot.

марокка́н|ец, ца *m.* Moroccan.

марокка́н|ка, ки *f. of* **⇨~ец**

марокка́нский *adj.* Moroccan.

Маро́кко *nt. indecl.* Morocco.

ма́р|очный *adj. of* **⇨~ка; ~очное вино́** fine wine.

Марс, а *m.* (*astron., myth.*) Mars.

Марсе́л|ь, я *m.* Marseilles.

ма́рсел|ь, я *m.* (*naut.*) topsail.

Марселье́з|а, ы *f.* Marseillaise.

марсиа́н|ин, ина, *pl.* **~е, ~** *m.* Martian.

марсиа́нский *adj. of* **⇨Марс**

март, а *m.* March.

марте́н, а *m.* (*tech.*) open-hearth furnace.

марте́новский *adj.* (*tech.*) open-hearth.

мартинга́л, а *m.* (*в конской упряжи*) martingale.

мартироло́г, а *m.* martyrology.

ма́рт|овский *adj. of* **⇨~**

марты́шк|а, и *f.* marmoset; (*fig., coll.*) monkey.

марципа́н, а *m.* marzipan.

марш¹, а *m.* march; **м. проте́ста** protest march; **м. голо́дных** hunger march.

марш² *int.* (*команда*) forward!; **ша́гом м.!** quick march!; (*coll.*) off you go!

марш³, а *m.* (*лестница*) flight of stairs.

ма́ршал, а *m.* marshal.

ма́ршал|ьский *adj. of* **⇨~**

марши́р|ова́ть, у́ю *impf.* to march.

марширо́вк|а, и *f.* marching.

маршру́т, а *m.* route.

маршру́т|ный *adj. of* **⇨~; м. лист** itinerary; **м. по́езд** through goods-train; **~ное такси́** fixed-route taxi.

ма́ск|а, и *f.* mask; **противога́зовая м.** gas-mask; (*fig.*): **сбро́сить с себя́ ~у** to throw off the mask.

маскара́д, а *m.* masked ball; (*fig.*) masquerade.

маскара́д|ный *adj. of* **⇨~; м. костю́м** fancy dress.

маскир|ова́ть, у́ю *impf.* (*of* **⇨за~**) to mask, disguise; (*mil.*) to camouflage.

маскир|ова́ться, у́юсь *impf.* (*of* **⇨за~**) to disguise o.s.; (*mil.*) to camouflage o.s.

маскиро́вк|а, и *f.* masking, disguise; (*mil.*) camouflage.

ма́слениц|а, ы *f.* Shrovetide; carnival.

ма́слени|чный *adj. of* **⇨~ца**

маслёнк|а, и *f.* **1** (*посуда для сливочного масла*) butter-dish. **2** (*tech.*) oil-can.

масл|ёнок, ёнка, *pl.* **~я́та, ~я́т** *m.* *Boletus luteus* (*edible mushroom*).

ма́слен|ый *adj.* **1** buttered; oiled, oily, **~ая неде́ля** = **~ица; ~ые кра́ски** = **ма́сло** 3. **2** (*fig., coll.*) (*льстивый*) oily, unctuous. **3** (*fig., coll.*) (*сластолюбивый*) voluptuous, sensual.

масли́н|а, ы *f.* **1** (*дерево*) olive-tree. **2** (*плод*) olive.

ма́сл|ить, ю, ишь *impf.* (*of* **⇨на~** *and* **по~**) **1** (*мазать сливочным маслом*) to butter. **2** (*мазать растительным маслом*) to oil; (*смазывать*) to grease. **3** (*пищу*) to add butter to.

ма́сл|иться, ится *impf.* **1** to leave greasy marks. **2** (*coll.*) (*блестеть*) to shine; to glisten. **3** *pass. of* **⇨~ить**

ма́сличный *adj.* (*растение*) oil-yielding.

масли́|чный *adj. of* **⇨~на; М~чная гора́** Mount of Olives.

ма́с|ло, ла, *pl.* **~ла́, ~ел, ~ла́м** *nt.* **1**: **(сли́вочное) м.** butter. **2** (*растительное*) oil; **как по ~лу** (*fig., coll.*) swimmingly. **3** (*краски*) oil (paints); **писа́ть ~лом** to paint in oils.

маслобо́йк|а, и *f.* churn.

маслобо́йн|ый *adj.*: **м. заво́д** = **~я**

маслобо́|йня, йни, *g. pl.* **~ен** *f.* creamery.

маслоде́ли|е, я *nt.* butter manufacturing.

маслозаво́д, а *m.* creamery.

масломе́р, а *m.* oil gauge; dipstick.

маслопрово́д, а *m.* oil pipe, oil pipeline.

масляни́ст|ый (~, ~а) *adj.* oily.

ма́сл|яный *adj. of* ⇨**~о; ~яная кислота́** (*chem.*) butyric acid; **~яные кра́ски** oil paints.

масо́н, а *m.* Freemason, Mason.

масо́нский *adj.* Masonic.

масо́нств|о, а *nt.* Freemasonry.

ма́сс|а, ы *f.* **1** mass; *pl.* (*pol.*) the masses; **в ~е** on the whole. **2**: **древе́сная м.** wood-pulp. **3** (*coll.*) (*множество*) a lot, lots.

масса́ж, а *m.* massage; **то́чечный м.** shiatsu, acupressure.

массажи́ст, а *m.* masseur.

массажи́стк|а, и *f.* masseuse.

масси́в, а *m.* (*geog.*) massif, mountain-mass; (*fig.*) expanse; **жило́й м.** housing development; **лесно́й м.** forest tract.

масси́в|ный (~ен, ~на) *adj.* massive.

масси́ровани|е, я *nt.* massing, concentration.

масси́р|овать[1], ую *impf. and pf.* (*mil.*) to mass, concentrate.

масси́р|овать[2], ую *impf. and pf.* to massage.

масс-ме́дия *pl. indecl.* mass media.

массови́к, а́ *m.* organizer of popular cultural and recreational activities.

массо́вк|а, и *f.* (*coll.*) **1** (*собрание*) mass meeting. **2** (*экскурсия*) group outing. **3** (*theatr.*, *cin.*) crowd scene.

ма́ссов|ый *adj.* mass; **~ые аре́сты** mass arrests; **~ое произво́дство** mass production; **м. чита́тель** general reader.

маста́к, а́ *m.* (*coll.*) expert, past master.

ма́стер, а, *pl.* **~а́** *m.* **1** (*цеха*) foreman. **2** (*ремесленник*) craftsman, skilled workman; **золоты́х дел м.** goldsmith. **3** (**на**+*a.*, *or* +*inf.*) (*знаток*) expert, master (at, of); (*sport*) vet(eran); **м. (по ремо́нту)** repairman; **телевизио́нный м.** TV repairman; **м. спо́рта** 'master of sports' (*holder of sports qualification*); **м. на все ру́ки** person able to turn his hand to anything.

мастер|и́ть, ю, и́шь *impf.* (*of* ⇨**с~**) (*coll.*) to make, build; **мы ~и́м са́ни** we are making a sledge.

мастеров|о́й, о́го *m.* (*obs.*) workman, (factory-)hand.

мастерск|а́я, о́й *f.* (*столяра*) workshop; (*художника*) studio; (*на заводе*) shop; **авторемо́нтная м.** car repair garage.

мастерски́ *adv.* skilfully; in masterly fashion.

мастерско́й *adj.* masterly.

мастерств|о́, а́ *nt.* **1** (*ремесло*) trade, craft. **2** (*умение*) skill, craftsmanship.

мasти́к|а, и *f.* **1** (*смола*) mastic. **2** (*замазка*) putty. **3** (*для натирания полов*) floor-polish.

масти́к|овый *adj. of* ⇨**~а**

масти́т, а *m.* (*med.*) mastitis.

масти́т|ый (~, ~а) *adj.* venerable.

мастодо́нт, а *m.* mastodon.

мастурба́ци|я, и *f.* masturbation.

мастурби́р|овать, ую *impf.* to masturbate.

масты́рк|а, и *f.* (*sl.*) joint (= *marijuana cigarette*).

маст|ь, и, *pl.* **~и, ~е́й** *f.* **1** (*цвет шерсти*) colour (*Br.*), color (*US*). **2** (*cards*) suit; **ходи́ть в м.** to follow suit.

масшта́б, а *m.* scale; **м. — де́сять киломе́тров в сантиме́тре** the scale is ten kilometres (*Br.*), kilometers (*US*) to the centimetre (*Br.*), centimeter (*US*); (*fig.*): **в большо́м, ма́леньком ~е** on a large, small scale; **конфли́кт большо́го ~а** large-scale conflict.

масшта́бност|ь, и *f.* (*fig.*) (large) scale, range, dimensions.

масшта́б|ный (~ен, ~на) *adj.* **1** scale; **~ная моде́ль** scale model. **2** (*большой*) large-scale.

мат[1], а *m.* (*chess*) checkmate, mate; **объяви́ть м.** (+*d.*) to mate.

мат[2], а *m.* (*половик*) (floor-, door-)mat; (*sport*) mat.

мат[3], а *m.* (*coll.*) *only in phr.* **благи́м ~ом** at the top of one's voice.

мат[4], а *m.* (*брань*) foul language, abuse; **руга́ться ~ом** to use foul language.

матадо́р, а *m.* matador.

матема́тик, а *m.* mathematician.

матема́тик|а, и *f.* mathematics.

математи́ческий *adj.* mathematical.

матереуби́йств|о, а *nt.* matricide (*act*).

матереуби́йц|а, ы *c.g.* matricide (*agent*).

материа́л, а *m.* material; **м. (для печа́тания)** copy; **гвоздево́й м.** feature (item).

материали́зм, а *m.* materialism.

материализ|ова́ть(ся), у́ю(сь) *impf. and pf.* to materialize (*trans. and intrans.*).

материали́ст, а *m.* materialist.

материалисти́ческий *adj.* (*phil.*) materialist.

материалисти́ч|ный (~ен, ~на) *adj.* (*pej.*) materialistic.

материа́льност|ь, и *f.* materiality.

материа́льно-техни́ческий *adj.* (*mil.*) logistical.

материа́л|ьный (~ен, ~ьна) *adj.* material; **~ьные затрудне́ния** financial difficulties; **~ьное положе́ние** economic conditions; **~ьная часть** (*tech.*, *mil.*) equipment, matériel.

матери́к, а́ *m.* **1** (*континент*) continent. **2** (*суша*) mainland.

материко́вый *adj.* continental.

матери́нск|ий *adj.* maternal, motherly; **~ая пла́та** (*comput.*) motherboard.

матери́нств|о, а *nt.* (*состояние*) maternity, motherhood; (*чувство*) motherliness.

матер|и́ться, ю́сь и́шься *impf.* (*coll.*) to swear.

мате́ри|я[1], и *f.* **1** (*phil.*) matter. **2** (*med.*) matter, pus. **3** (*fig.*, *coll.*) subject, topic.

мате́ри|я[2], и *f.* (*text.*) material, cloth.

ма́терный *adj.* (*coll.*) obscene, abusive.

мате́рчатый *adj.* (*coll.*) made of cloth.

матерщи́н|а, ы *f.* (*coll.*) foul language.

матёр|ый (~, ~а) *adj.* **1** (*достигший полной зрелости*) full-grown, mature. **2** (*опытный*) experienced, practised. **3** (*неисправимый*) inveterate, out-and-out.

ма́тк|а, и *f.* **1** (*anat.*) uterus, womb. **2** (*самка*) female; (*пчелиная*) queen (bee).

ма́тов|ый *adj.* mat(t); **~ое стекло́** frosted glass.

ма́точный *adj.* (*anat.*) uterine.

матра́с, а *m.* mattress; **надувно́й м.** air bed, inflatable mattress.

матра́|ц = **~с**

матрёшк|а, и *f.* matrioshka, (set of) nested Russian dolls.

матриарха́льный *adj.* matriarchal.

матриарха́т, а *m.* matriarchy.

ма́триц|а, ы *f.* **1** (*typ.*) matrix. **2** (*tech.*) die, mould (*Br.*), mold (*US*).

ма́три|чный *adj. of* ⇨**~ца; м. при́нтер** dot-matrix printer.

матро́с, а *m.* sailor, seaman.

матро́ск|а[1], и *f.* (*блуза*) sailor top.

матро́ск|а[2], и *f.* (*coll.*) (*жена матроса*) sailor's wife.

ма́тушк|а, и *f.* (*coll.*) **1** (*мать*) mother; **~и (мои́)!** *excl. of surprise or fright.* **2** (*жена священника*) priest's wife. **3** (*обращение*) gran(ny), ma.

матч, а *m.* (*sport*) match; **междунаро́дный м.** (*cricket*, *rugby*) test (match); **повто́рный м.** return match.

мат|ь, *g.*, *d.*, *p.* **~ери,** *i.* **~ерью,** *pl.* **~ери, ~ере́й** *f.* **1** mother; **бу́дущая м.** expectant mother; **м.-одино́чка** single mother. **2** (*coll.*) *familiar term of address to a woman.*

ма́ть-и-ма́чех|а, и *f.* (*bot.*) coltsfoot.

ма́узер, а *m.* Mauser (*automatic pistol or rifle*).

мафио́зи *m. indecl.* Mafioso.

мафио́зник, а *m.* (*coll.*) = **мафио́зи**

мафио́зный *adj. of* ⇨**ма́фия**

мафио́зо *m. indecl.* = **мафио́зи**

ма́фи|я, и *f.* Mafia.

мах, а (у) *m.* (*рукой*) swing, stroke; (*колеса*) turn; (*крыла*) flap; (*coll.*): **дать ~у** to make a blunder; **одни́м ~ом, с одного́ ~у** at one stroke, in a trice; **с ~у** rashly, without thinking.

ма|ха́ть, шу́, ~шешь *impf.* (*of* ⇨**~хну́ть**) (+*i.*) (*рукой*) to wave; (*веткой*) to brandish; (*хвостом*) to wag; (*крыльями*) to flap.

махи́н|а, ы *f.* (*coll.*) bulky and cumbersome object.

махина́тор, а *m.* (*coll.*) schemer, wangler.

махина́ци|я, и *f.* machination, intrigue.

мах|ну́ть, ну́, нёшь *pf.* **1** *pf. of* ⇒**~а́ть; м. руко́й** (**на** + *a.*) (*fig., coll.*) to give up as a bad job. **2** (*coll.*) (*поехать*) to go, travel. **3** (*coll.*) (*броситься*) to rush; (*прыгнуть*) to leap.

махови́к, а́ *m.* fly-wheel.

махов|о́й *adj.* (*tech.*): **~о́е колесо́** fly-wheel.

ма́хонький *adj.* (*coll.*) titchy.

махо́рк|а, и *f.* makhorka (*inferior kind of tobacco*).

махро́в|ый *adj.* **1** (*bot.*) double. **2** (*неисправимый*) dyed-in-the-wool, out-and-out; **~ая порногра́фия** hard-core pornography. **3** (*ткань*) terry.

мац|а́, ы *no pl., f.* matzos (*Jewish biscuits for Passover*).

маче́те *nt. indecl.* machete.

ма́чех|а, и *f.* stepmother.

ма́чт|а, ы *f.* mast.

ма́чт|овый *adj. of* ⇒**~а**

маши́н|а, ы *f.* **1** (*механическое устройство*) machine (*also fig.*); **ку́хонная м.** food processor; **(посудо)мо́ечная м.** dishwasher. **2** (*автомобиль*) car; vehicle; **м. «ско́рой по́мощи»** ambulance; **пятидве́рная м.** hatchback; **служе́бная м.** company car.

машина́л|ьный (~ен, ~ьна) *adj.* mechanical (*fig.*); **м. отве́т** an automatic response.

машиниза́ци|я, и *f.* mechanization.

машинизи́р|овать, ую *impf. and pf.* to mechanize.

машини́ст, а *m.* **1** (*комбайна*) driver, operator (*workman in charge of machinery*). **2** (*локомотива*) engine-driver (*Br.*), engineer (*US*). **3** (*theatr.*) scene-shifter.

машини́стк|а, и *f.* typist; **м.-стенографи́стка** shorthand-typist.

маши́н|ка, ки *f. dim. of* ⇒**~а; (пи́шущая) м.** typewriter.

маши́нно-тра́кторн|ый *adj.*: **~ая ста́нция** (*hist.*) machine and tractor station.

маши́н|ный *adj. of* ⇒**~а; ~ная гра́фика** computer graphics; **~ное обуче́ние** computer-aided learning; **~ный перево́д** machine translation; **~ный язы́к** machine language.

машинопи́сный *adj.* typewritten; **м. текст** typescript.

маши́нопис|ь, и *f.* **1** (*печатание*) typing. **2** (*текст*) typescript.

машинострое́ни|е, я *nt.* mechanical engineering, machinery construction.

машинострo|и́тельный *adj. of* ⇒**~е́ние**

машиночита́емый *adj.* (*comput.*) machine-readable.

маэ́стро *m. indecl.* maestro; master.

мая́к, а́ *m.* **1** lighthouse; beacon (*also fig.*). **2** (*fig.*) (*человек*) leading light.

ма́ятник, а *m.* pendulum.

ма́|яться, юсь, ешься *impf.* (*coll.*) **1** (**с** + *i.*) (*трудиться*) to toil (with, over). **2** (*томиться*) to pine, suffer.

мая́ч|ить, у, ишь *impf.* (*coll.*) to loom (up), appear indistinctly.

мая́чник, а *m.* lighthouse-keeper.

м. б. (*abbr. of* ***мо́жет быть***) maybe, perhaps.

МБР *f. indecl.* (*abbr. of* ***межконтинента́льная баллисти́ческая раке́та***) ICBM (*intercontinental ballistic missile*).

МВД *nt. indecl.* (*abbr. of* ***Министе́рство вну́тренних дел***) Ministry of Internal Affairs; ≈ Home Office.

МВК *m. indecl.* (*abbr. of* ***механи́зм валю́тных ку́рсов***) ERM (*exchange rate mechanism*).

МВТ *nt. indecl.* (*abbr. of* ***Министе́рство вне́шней торго́вли***) Ministry of Foreign Trade.

МВФ *m. indecl.* (*abbr. of* ***Междунаро́дный валю́тный фонд***) IMF (*International Monetary Fund*).

мг (*abbr. of* ***миллигра́мм***) mg, milligram(s).

м. г. (*abbr. of* ***мину́вшего го́да***) last year.

мгл|а, ы *f.* **1** (*туман*) haze; mist. **2** (*темнота*) gloom, darkness.

мгли́ст|ый (~, ~а) *adj.* hazy.

мгнове́ни|е, я *nt.* instant, moment; **в м. о́ка** in the twinkling of an eye.

мгнове́н|ный (~ен, ~на) *adj.* **1** (*сразу возникающий*) instantaneous. **2** (*быстро проходящий*) momentary.

МГУ *m. indecl.* (*abbr. of* ***Моско́вский госуда́рственный университе́т***) Moscow State University.

ме́бел|ь, и *f.* furniture; (*fig.*): **для ~и** figurehead, fifth wheel (*said of a useless person*).

ме́бельщик, а *m.* furniture-maker.

меблиро́|ванный *p.p.p. of* ⇒**~ва́ть** *and adj.* furnished.

меблир|ова́ть, у́ю *impf. and pf.* to furnish.

меблиро́вк|а, и *f.* **1** (*действие*) furnishing. **2** (*мебель*) furniture, furnishings.

мегаба́йт, а *m.* (*comput.*) megabyte.

мегава́тт, а *m.* megawatt.

мегаге́рц, а *g. pl.* **м.** *m.* (*radio*) megahertz.

мегалома́ни|я, и *f.* megalomania.

мегато́нн|а, ы *f.* megaton.

мегафо́н, а *m.* megaphone.

меге́р|а, ы *f.* (*coll.*) shrew, termagant.

мёд, а, о ~е, в ~у́, *pl.* **~ы, ~о́в** *m.* **1** honey. **2** (*старинный напиток*) mead.

мед... *comb. form, abbr. of* ***медици́нский***

медали́ст, а *m.* medallist (*Br.*), medalist (*US*); medal winner.

медали́ст|ка, и *f. of* ⇒**~**

меда́л|ь, и *f.* medal.

медальо́н, а *m.* medallion, locket.

медбра́т, а *m.* male nurse.

медве́диц|а, ы *f.* she-bear; (*astron.*): **Больша́я М.** the Great Bear (Ursa Major); **Ма́лая М.** the Little Bear (Ursa Minor).

медве́дк|а, и *f.* (*zool.*) mole-cricket.

медве́д|ь, я *m.* bear (*also fig.*); **бамбу́ковый м.** (giant) panda; **бе́лый м.** polar bear.

медвеж|а́та *pl. of* ⇒**~о́нок**

медве́|жий *adj. of* ⇒**~дь; м. у́гол** (*coll.*) god-forsaken place; **~жья услу́га** well-meant action having opposite effect.

медвеж|о́нок, о́нка, *pl.* **~а́та, ~а́т** *m.* bear-cub; **плю́шевый м.** teddy (bear).

медвя́н|ый *adj.* **1** (*poet.*) honeyed. **2** (*имеющий запах мёда*) smelling of honey. **3**: **~ая роса́** honey-dew.

медиа́н|а, ы *f.* (*math.*) median.

ме́дик, а *m.* **1** (*врач*) physician, doctor. **2** (*студент*) medical student.

медикаме́нт, а *m.* medicine.

мединститу́т, а *m.* medical school.

медита́ци|я, и *f.* meditation.

медити́р|овать, ую *impf.* to meditate.

ме́диум, а *m.* medium, spiritualist.

медици́н|а, ы *f.* medicine.

медици́нский *adj.* medical.

мед|и́чка, и́чки *f.* (*coll.*) *of* ⇒**~и́к** 2

ме́дленно *adv.* slowly.

ме́длен|ный (~, ~на) *adj.* slow.

медли́тел|ьный (~ен, ~ьна) *adj.* sluggish; slow.

ме́дл|ить, ю, ишь *impf.* to linger; to tarry; (**с** + *i.*) to be slow (in); **он ~ит с отве́том** he is a long time replying.

ме́дник, а *m.* copper-smith.

ме́дно-кра́сный *adj.* copper-coloured (*Br.*), -colored (*US*).

меднолите́йный *adj.* copper-smelting.

ме́дный *adj.* **1** copper; **м. лоб** (*fig., coll.*) blockhead. **2** (*chem.*) cupric, cuprous; **м. купоро́с** copper sulphate, bluestone. **3** (*mus.*) brass.

медо́вый *adj. of* ⇒**мёд; м. ме́сяц** honeymoon.

медоно́сн|ый *adj.*: **пчела́ ~ая** honey-bee.

медосмо́тр, а *m.* medical (examination), checkup; **пройти́ м.** to have a checkup.

медпу́нкт, а *m.* first-aid station.

медсестр|а́, ы́ *f.* (*medical*) nurse.

меду́з|а, ы *f.* (*zool.*) jellyfish.

медуни́ц|а, ы *f.* (*bot.*) lungwort.

мед|ь, и *f.* **1** copper; **жёлтая м.** brass. **2** (*collect.*) (*монеты*) coppers.

медя́к, а́ *m.* (*coll.*) copper (coin).

медя́нк|а¹, и *f.* (*змея*) grass-snake.

медя́нк|а², и *f.* (*chem.*) verdigris.

меж = **ме́жду**

меж... *comb. form* inter-.

меж|а́, и́, *pl.* **~и, ~, ~а́м** *f.* boundary.

межве́домственный = **междуве́домственный**

М

межгородско́й *adj.* inter-city.

межгосуда́рственный *adj.* interstate.

междоме́ти|е, я *nt.* (*gram.*) interjection.

междоусо́би|е, я *nt.* civil strife; internecine strife (*esp. in medieval Russia*).

междоусо́б|ица, ицы *f.* (*obs.*) = **~ие**

междоусо́бный *adj.* internecine.

ме́жду *prep.* + *i.* (+*g. pl., obs.*) **1** between; **м. де́лом** at odd moments; **м. на́ми (говоря́)** between ourselves; between you and me; **м. про́чим** incidentally; **м. тем** meanwhile; **м. тем, как** while, whereas. **2** (*среди*) among, amongst.

междуве́домственный *adj.* interdepartmental.

междугоро́дный *adj.* inter-city; long-distance; **м. телефо́нный разгово́р** long-distance *or* trunk call.

междунаро́дный *adj.* international; **М. валю́тный фонд** International Monetary Fund.

междуря́дь|е, я *nt.* (*agric.*) space between rows.

междуца́рстви|е, я *nt.* interregnum.

межева́ни|е, я *nt.* surveying, survey (*of agricultural land*).

меж|ева́ть, у́ю *impf.* to survey (*agricultural land*); to establish the boundaries (of).

меж|ево́й *adj. of* ⇨**~а́; м. знак** landmark, boundary-mark.

меже́н|ь, и *f.* lowest water-level (*in river or lake*).

межеу́м|ок, ка *m.* (*coll.*) **1** (*недалёкий человек*) person of limited intelligence. **2** (*неопределимый человек, предмет*) neither one thing nor the other.

межеу́мочный *adj.* (*coll.*) ill-defined; neither one thing nor another.

межконтинента́льный *adj.* inter-continental; **м. баллисти́ческий снаря́д** intercontinental ballistic missile.

межли́чностный *adj.* interpersonal.

межнациона́льный *adj.* interethnic.

межплане́тный *adj.* interplanetary.

межправи́тельственный *adj.* intergovernmental.

межра́совый *adj.* interracial.

межсезо́нь|е, я *nt.* (*sport*) off-season.

мезозо́йский *adj.* (*geol.*) Mesozoic.

мезолити́ческий *adj.* (*archaeol.*) mesolithic.

мезо́н, а *m.* meson.

мезони́н, а *m.* attic.

мейнстри́м, а *m.* (*sl.*) the mainstream (*of culture, music*).

Ме́кк|а, и *f.* Mecca.

Ме́ксик|а, и *f.* Mexico.

мексика́н|ец, ца *m.* Mexican.

мексика́н|ка, ки *f. of* ⇨**~ец**

мексика́нский *adj.* Mexican.

мел, а, о ~е, в ~у́ *m.* chalk.

меланези́|ец, йца *m.* Melanesian.

меланези́|йка, йки *f. of* ⇨**~ец**

меланези́йский *adj.* Melanesian.

Мелане́зи|я, и *f.* Melanesia.

меланхо́лик, а *m.* melancholic.

меланхоли́ческий *adj.* melancholy.

меланхоли́ч|ный (~ен, ~на) *adj.* = **~еский**

меланхо́ли|я, и *f.* melancholy; (*med.*) melancholia.

мела́сс|а, ы *f.* (*чёрная патока*) molasses.

меле́|ть, ет *impf.* (*of* ⇨**об~**) to grow shallow.

мели́зм, а *m.* (*mus.*) grace note.

мелиор|ати́вный *adj. of* ⇨**~а́ция**

мелиора́тор, а *m.* (*agric.*) specialist in land improvement.

мелиора́ци|я, и *f.* (*agric.*) land improvement, reclamation.

мелиори́р|овать, ую *impf. and pf.* (*agric.*) to reclaim.

мел|и́ть, ю́, и́шь *impf.* (*of* ⇨**на~**) to chalk.

ме́л|кий (~ок, ~ка́, ~ко) *adj.* **1** (*небольшой*) small. **2** (*неглубокий*) shallow. **3** (*дождь; песок*) fine. **4** (*fig.*) (*человек*) petty, small-minded; **~кая душо́нка** petty person; **~кая со́шка** small fry.

ме́лко *adv.* **1** (*некрупно*) fine, into small particles. **2** (*неглубоко*) not deep.

мелкобуржуа́з|ный (~ен, ~на) *adj.* petty-bourgeois.

мелково́д|ный (~ен, ~на) *adj.* shallow.

мелково́дь|е, я *nt.* shallow water.

мелкозерни́ст|ый (~, ~а) *adj.* fine-grained.

мелкосо́бственнический *adj.* relating to small property holders.

мелкот|а́, ы́ *f.* (*collect.*; *coll.*) small fry.

мелкотра́вчат|ый (~, ~а) *adj.* (*coll., pej.*) petty, small-minded.

мелово́й *adj.* **1** (*состоящий из мела*) chalk, chalky. **2** (*белый как мел*) chalky, white as chalk. **3** (*geol.*) cretaceous.

мелоди́ческий *adj.* melodious, tuneful.

мелоди́ч|ный (~ен, ~на) *adj.* = **~еский**

мело́ди|я, и *f.* melody, tune.

мелодра́м|а, ы *f.* melodrama.

мелодрамати́ческий *adj.* melodramatic.

мел|о́к, ка́ *m.* piece of chalk; **восковы́е ~ки́** wax crayons.

мелома́н, а *m.* music-lover.

ме́лочност|ь, и *f.* pettiness, small-mindedness.

ме́лоч|ный (~ен, ~на) *adj.* **1** petty, trifling. **2** (*pej.*) (*человек*) petty, small-minded.

ме́лоч|ь, и, *pl.* **~и, ~е́й** *f.* **1** (*collect.*) (*мелкие предметы*) small items; small fry; **кру́пные я́блоки мы съе́ли, оста́лась м.** we had eaten the big apples, only the small ones were left. **2** (*collect.*) (*монеты*) (small) change. **3** (*pl.*) (*пустяки*) trifles, trivialities; **разме́ниваться на ~и, по ~а́м** to fritter away one's energies.

мел|ь, и, о ~и, на ~и́ *f.* shoal; bank; **песча́ная м.** sandbank; **на ~и́** aground; (*fig.*) on the rocks, high and dry; **сесть на м.** to run aground; **сиде́ть (как рак) на ~и́** (*fig., coll.*) to be on the rocks.

мельк|а́ть, а́ю *impf.* (*of* ⇨**~ну́ть**) **1** (*являться и исчезать*) to flash (past). **2** (*мерцать*) to twinkle. **3** (*о мыслях*) to flash.

мельк|ну́ть, ну́, нёшь, *inst. pf. of* ⇨**~а́ть; у меня́ ~ну́ла мысль** I had a sudden idea.

ме́льком *adv.* in passing, cursorily.

ме́льник, а *m.* miller.

ме́льниц|а, ы *f.* mill; **э́то вода́ на на́шу ~у** (*fig., coll.*) it's grist to our mill.

ме́льни|чный *adj. of* ⇨**~ца**

мельхио́р, а *m.* cupro-nickel, German silver.

мельхио́р|овый *adj. of* ⇨**~**

мельча́йший *superl. of* ⇨**ме́лкий**

мельча́|ть, ю *impf.* (*of* ⇨**из~**) **1** (*о реке*) to grow shallow. **2** (*становиться меньше*) to become small; to grow smaller. **3** (*fig.*) to become petty.

ме́л|ьче *comp. of* ⇨**~кий** *and* **~ко**

мельч|и́ть, у́, и́шь *impf.* (*of* ⇨**из~** *and* **раз~**) to crush, crumble.

мелю́, ме́лешь *see* ⇨**моло́ть**

мелюзг|а́, и́ *f.* (*collect.*; *coll.*) small fry.

мембра́н|а, ы *f.* (*tech.*) diaphragm.

мемора́ндум, а *m.* (*dipl.*) memorandum.

мемориа́л, а *m.* memorial.

мемориа́льный *adj.* memorial.

мемуа́р|ы, ов *no sg.* memoirs.

ме́н|а, ы *f.* exchange, barter.

ме́неджер, а *m.* manager; **м. по сбы́ту** sales manager.

ме́неджмент, а *m.* management.

ме́нее *adv.* (*comp. of* ⇨**ма́ло**) less; **тем не м.** none the less.

менестре́л|ь, я *m.* (*hist.*) minstrel.

мензу́рк|а, и *f.* (*pharm.*) measuring-glass.

менинги́т, а *m.* (*med.*) meningitis.

мени́ск, а *m.* (*math., phys.*) meniscus.

менов|о́й *adj.* (*econ.*) exchange; **~а́я торго́вля** barter.

менструа́льный *adj.* menstrual.

менструа́ци|я, и *f.* menstruation.

менструи́р|овать, ую *impf.* to menstruate.

мент, а *m.* (*sl.*) police officer, cop.

менталите́т, а *m.* mentality.

мента́льност|ь, и *f.* = **менталите́т**

менто́вк|а, и *f.* (*sl.*) police van.

менто́вск|ая, ой *f.* (*sl.*) cop-shop.

менто́л, а *m.* (*chem.*) menthol.

ме́нтор, а *m.* (*obs.*) mentor.

менту́р|а, ы *f.* (*sl.*) the fuzz.

менуэ́т, а *m.* minuet.

ме́ньше *comp. of* ⇨**ма́ленький** *and* **ма́ло** smaller, less.

меньшеви́зм, а *m.* (*pol.*) Menshevism.

меньшеви́к, а́ *m.* (*pol.*) Menshevik.

меньшеви́стский *adj.* (*pol.*) Menshevist.

ме́ньш|ий *adj.* (*comp. of* ⇨**ма́ленький, ма́лый**) lesser, smaller; younger; **по ~ей ме́ре** at least; **са́мое ~ее** at the least.

меньшинств|о́, а́ *nt.* minority.

меньшо́й *adj.* (*coll.*) youngest.

меню́ *nt. indecl.* menu; **всплыва́ющее/выпада́ющее ~** (*comput.*) pop-up/pull-down menu.

меня́ *a. and g. of* ⇨**я**

меня́л|а, ы *m.* (*coll.*) money-changer.

меня́льный *adj.* (*comm.*) money-changing.

меня́|ть, ю *impf.* **1** (*no pf.*) to change. **2** (+*a. and* **на**+*a.*; *pf.* **об~, по~**) to exchange (for).

меня́|ться, юсь *impf.* **1** (*no pf.*) to change; **м. в лице́** to change countenance. **2** (+*i.*; *pf.* **об~, по~**) to exchange; **м. с кем-н. ко́мнатами** to exchange rooms with s.o.

ме́р|а, ы *f.* measure; **вы́сшая м. наказа́ния** capital punishment; **~ы по укрепле́нию дове́рия** (*pol.*) confidence-building measures; **в ~у** (+*g.*) to the extent (of); **по ~е возмо́жности, по ~е сил** as far as possible; **по ~е того́, как** as, (in proportion) as; **по кра́йней, ма́лой, ме́ньшей ~е** at least; **в ~у** fairly; **ни в ко́ей ~е** under no circumstances; **сверх ~ы, чрез ~у, не в ~у** excessively, immoderately; **знать ~у** *see* ⇨**знать**[1]

ме́ргел|ь, я *m.* (*geol.*) marl.

мере́жк|а, и *f.* hem-stitch, open work.

мере́нг|а, и *f.* meringue.

мере́ть, мрёт, мрут, *past* **мёр, мёрла** *impf.* (*coll.*) **1** (*умирать*) to die (*in large numbers*); **мрут, как му́хи** they are dying/dropping like flies. **2** (*о сердце*) to stop beating.

мере́щ|иться, усь, ишься *impf.* (*of* ⇨**по~**) (*coll.*) **1** (+*d.*) (*казаться*) to seem (to), appear (to); **она́ мне ~ится** her image haunts me; **э́то тебе́ ~ится** you only imagine you see it. **2** (*obs.*) (*смутно видеться*) to appear dimly.

мерза́в|ец, ца *m.* (*coll.*) swine, bastard.

ме́рз|кий (~ок, ~ка́, ~ко) *adj.* disgusting, loathsome; abominable, foul.

мерзлот|а́, ы́ *f.* frozen condition of ground; **ве́чная м.** permafrost.

мёрзлый *adj.* frozen.

мёрз|нуть, ну, нешь, *past* **~, ~ла** *impf.* (*of* ⇨**за~**) to freeze.

ме́рзост|ь, и *f.* **1** (*свойство*) vileness, loathsomeness. **2** (*мерзкая вещь*) abomination.

меридиа́н, а *m.* meridian; **гри́нвичский м.** Greenwich meridian.

мери́л|о, а *nt.* standard, criterion.

ме́рин, а *m.* gelding; **врёт как си́вый м.** (*coll.*) he's a barefaced liar.

мерино́с, а *m.* **1** (*овца*) merino (sheep). **2** (*шерсть*) merino (wool).

мерино́совый *adj.* merino.

ме́р|ить, ю, ишь *impf.* **1** (*pf.* **с~**) to measure; **м. взгля́дом** to look up and down. **2** (*pf.* **по~, при~**) (*примерять*) to try on (*clothing, footwear*).

ме́р|иться, юсь, ишься *impf.* (*of* ⇨**по~**) (+*i.*) to measure (against); **м. ро́стом с кем-н.** to compare heights with s.o.

ме́рк|а, и *f.* **1** (*определённый размер*) measurements. **2** (*предмет для измерения*) measure; (*fig.*) yardstick; **подходи́ть ко всему́ с одно́й ~ой** (*fig.*) to apply the same standard to all alike.

меркантили́зм, а *m.* **1** (*econ.*) mercantilism. **2** (*fig.*) mercenary spirit.

меркант́ил|ьный *adj.* **1** mercantile. **2 (~ен, ~ьна)** (*fig., pej.*) mercenary.

ме́рк|нуть, нет, *past* **~нул** *and* **~, ~ла** *impf.* (*of* ⇨**по~**) to grow dark, grow dim; (*fig.*) to fade.

Мерку́ри|й, я *m.* (*myth., astron.*) Mercury.

мерла́н, а *m.* (*рыба*) whiting.

мерлу́шк|а, и *f.* lambskin.

ме́р|ный (~ен, ~на) *adj.* **1** measured; rhythmical. **2** (*tech.*) measuring.

мероприя́ти|е, я *nt.* **1** (*мера*) measure. **2** (*событие*) event, function.

мерси́ *particle* (*joc.*) ta.

ме́ртвен|ный (~, ~на) *adj.* deathly, ghastly.

мертве́|ть, ю *impf.* **1** (*pf.* **о~**) (*от холода*) to grow numb. **2** (*pf.* **по~**) (*от страха, горя*) to be benumbed.

мертве́ц, а́ *m.* corpse, dead person.

мертве́цк|ая, ой *f.* (*coll.*) mortuary, morgue.

мертве́цки *adv.* (*coll.*) *only in phrr.* **м. пьян** dead drunk; **напи́ться м.** to become dead drunk.

мертвечи́н|а, ы *f.* **1** (*collect.*) (*падаль*) carrion. **2** (*fig., coll.*) (a) dead thing.

мертв|и́ть, лю́, и́шь *impf.* to deaden.

мертворождённый *adj.* still-born.

мёртв|ый (~, ~а́, ~о, *pl.* **~ы;** *in fig. senses* **~о́, ~ы́)** *adj.* dead; **ни жив ни ~** more dead than alive; **~ая зыбь** (*naut.*) swell; **м. капита́л** (*fin.*) dead stock, unemployed capital; **~ая пе́тля** (*aeron.*) loop; **пить ~ую** (*coll.*) to drink hard; **спать ~ым сном** (*coll.*) to sleep like the dead; **быть на ~ой то́чке** to be at a standstill; **~ая хва́тка** mortal grip; **м. час** quiet time (*in sanatoria, etc.*).

мертвя́к, а́ *m.* (*sl.*) stiff (= *corpse*).

мерца́|ть, ю *impf.* to twinkle, glimmer, flicker.

ме́сив|о, а *nt.* **1** (*корм*) mash. **2** (*на дороге*) slush; (*полужидкая смесь*) mush.

ме|си́ть, шу́, ~́сишь *impf.* (*of* ⇨**с~**) to knead; **м. грязь** (*coll., joc.*) to wade through mud.

ме́сс|а, ы *f.* (*relig., mus.*) Mass.

мессиа́нский *adj.* Messianic.

мессиа́нств|о, а *nt.* Messianism.

месси́|я, и *m.* Messiah.

места́ми *adv.* (*coll.*) here and there, in places.

месте́ч|ко[1]**, ка,** *pl.* **~ки, ~ек, ~кам** *nt.* (*hist.*) small town (*in Ukraine and Byelorussia*).

месте́ч|ко[2]**, ка,** *pl.* **~ки, ~ек, ~кам** *nt. dim. of* ⇨**ме́сто; тёплое м.** (*coll.*) cushy job.

ме|сти́, ту́, тёшь, *past* **мёл, ~ла́** *impf.* **1** (*пол, двор*) to sweep; (*cop*) to sweep up. **2** (*развевать*) to whirl; (*impers.*): **~тёт** there is a snow-storm.

местко́м, а *m.* (*abbr. of* **ме́стный комите́т**) local (trade union) committee.

ме́стност|ь, и *f.* **1** (*дачная, сельская*) locality, district; area. **2** (*mil.*) (*гористая, открытая*) ground, country, terrain.

ме́стный *adj.* **1** local; **м. колори́т** local colour (*Br.*), color (*US*). **2** (*gram.*) locative.

-ме́стный *comb. form* -seated, -seater.

ме́ст|о, а, *pl.* **~а́, ~, ~а́м** *nt.* **1** place; site; **больно́е м.** (*fig.*) tender spot, sensitive point; **де́тское м.** (*anat.*) after-birth, placenta; **о́бщее м.** platitude; **пусто́е м.** blank (space); (*fig.*) a nobody, a nonentity; **сла́бое м.** (*fig.*) weakness, weak spot; **у́зкое м.** bottleneck; **м. де́йствия, м. происше́ствия** scene (of action); **на ~е преступле́ния** in the act, red-handed; **знать своё м.** (*fig.*) to know one's place; **име́ть м.** to take place; **поста́вить на своё м., указа́ть кому́-н. его́ м.** (*fig.*) to put s.o. in his place; **не находи́ть себе́ ~а** (*fig.*) to fret, worry; **не к ~у** (*fig.*) out of place; **по ~а́м!** to your places!; **ни с ~а!** don't move!; stay put!
2 (*в театре*) seat; (*на пароходе, поезде*) berth, seat.
3 (*свободное пространство*) space; room; **нет ~а** there is no room.
4 (*должность*) post, situation; job; **быть без ~а** to be out of work.
5 (*часть текста*) passage.
6 (*о багаже*) piece (*of luggage*).
7 (*pl.*) (*провинция*) the provinces, the country; **на ~а́х** in the provinces.

местожи́тельств|о, а *nt.* (place of) residence; **без определённого ~а** of no fixed abode.

местоиме́ни|е, я *nt.* (*gram.*) pronoun

местоиме́нный *adj.* (*gram.*) pronominal.

местонахожде́ни|е, я *nt.* location, the whereabouts.

местоположе́ни|е, я *nt.* site, situation, position.

местопребыва́ни|е, я *nt.* abode, residence.

месторожде́ни|е, я *nt.* (*geol.*) deposit.

мест|ь, и *f.* vengeance, revenge.

ме́сяц, а *m.* **1** month; **медо́вый м.** honeymoon. **2** (*луна*) moon; **молодо́й м.** new moon.

ме́сячн|ый *adj.* monthly; *as n.* **~ые, ~ых** *no sg.* (*coll.*) (menstrual) period.

метаболи́зм, а *m.* metabolism.

мета́лл, а *m.* metal; **презре́нный м.** filthy lucre.

металли́ст, а *m.* **1** metal-worker. **2** (*coll., mus.*) heavy metallist.

М

металли́ческий *adj.* metal; (*звук, привкус*) metallic.
металлоиска́тел|ь, я *m.* metal-detector.
металлоно́с|ный (~ен, ~на) *adj.* metalliferous.
металлообраба́тывающий *adj.* metal-working.
металлоплави́льный *adj.* smelting.
металлопрока́тный *adj.* (*tech.*) rolling.
металлопромы́шленност|ь, и *f.* metal industry.
металлоре́жущий *adj.* metal-cutting.
металлу́рг, а *m.* metallurgist.
металлурги́ческий *adj.* metallurgical; **м. заво́д** metal works, iron and steel works.
металлу́рги|я, и *f.* metallurgy.
метаморфо́з, а *m.* = **~а**
метаморфо́з|а, ы *f.* metamorphosis.
мета́н, а *m.* (*chem.*) methane.
мета́ни|е, я *nt.* **1** throwing, casting, flinging. **2**: **м. икры́** spawning.
метано́л, а *m.* (*chem.*) methanol.
мета́тел|ь, я *m.* (*sport*) thrower; **м. ди́ска** discus thrower.
мета́тельный *adj.* missile; **м. снаря́д** projectile.
ме|та́ть[1], чу́, ~чешь *impf.* (*of* **⇒~тну́ть**) **1** (*бросать*) to throw, cast, fling; **м. гро́мы и мо́лнии** (*fig., coll.*) to rage, fulminate; **рвать и м.** (*coll.*) to be in a rage; **м. жре́бий** to cast lots; **м. се́но** to stack hay. **2**: **м. икру́** to spawn. **3**: **м. банк** (*о банкомёте*) to keep the bank.
мета́|ть[2], ю *impf.* (*of* **⇒на~, с~**) (*шить*) to baste, tack; **м. пе́тли** to edge buttonholes.
ме|та́ться, чу́сь, ~чешься *impf.* (*по комнате*) to rush about; (*в постели*) to toss.
метафи́зик, а *m.* metaphysician.
метафи́зик|а, и *f.* metaphysics.
метафизи́ческий *adj.* metaphysical.
мета́фор|а, ы *f.* metaphor.
метафори́ческий *adj.* metaphorical.
мете́л|ить, ю, ишь *impf.* (*of* **⇒от~**) (*sl.*) to beat up, hit.
мете́л|ица, ицы *f.* (*poet.*) = **~ь**
метёлк|а, и *f.* **1** *dim. of* **⇒метла́; под ~у** (*fig., coll.*) entirely, to the last particle. **2** (*bot.*) panicle.
мете́л|ь, и *f.* snow-storm; blizzard.
метео... *comb. form, abbr. of* ***метеорологи́ческий***
метеопрогнози́ровани|е, я *nt.* weather forecasting.
метео́р, а *m.* **1** meteor. **2** (*судно*) hydrofoil.
метеори́т, а *m.* (*astron.*) meteorite.
метеори́ческий *adj.* meteoric.
метео́р|ный *adj. of* **⇒~**
метеоро́лог, а *m.* meteorologist; weather forecaster; (*coll.*) weatherman.
метеорологи́ческ|ий *adj.* meteorological; **~ая ста́нция** weather station.
метеороло́ги|я, и *f.* meteorology.
метеосво́дк|а, и *f.* weather report.
метеоста́нци|я, и *f.* meteorological station.
метиза́ци|я, и *f.* (*biol.*) cross-breeding.
мети́з|ы, ов *no sg.* (*abbr. of* ***металли́ческие изде́лия***) metal wares, hardware.
мети́л, а *m.* (*chem.*) methyl.
мети́с, а *m.* **1** (*biol.*) mongrel, half-breed. **2** (*anthrop.*) metis, mestizo.
ме́|тить[1], чу, тишь *impf.* (*of* **⇒по~**) (*ставить знак на чём-н.*) to mark.
ме́|тить[2], чу, тишь *impf.* (*of* **⇒на~[2]**) **1** (**в**+*a.*) (*стараться попасть*) to aim at; (*fig., coll.*; **в**+*nom.-a. pl.*) to aim (at), aspire (to); **он всегда́ ~тил в профессора́** it had always been his aim to become a professor. **2** (*fig.*; **в**+*a.*, **на**+*a.*) (*иметь в виду*) to drive (at), mean.
ме́|титься, чусь, тишься *impf. of* **⇒наме́титься** 2
ме́тк|а, и *f.* **1** (*действие*) marking. **2** (*знак*) mark.
ме́т|кий (~ок, ~ка́, ~ко) *adj.* well-aimed, accurate; **м. стрело́к** a good shot; (*fig.*): **~кое замеча́ние** apt remark.
ме́ткост|ь, и *f.* marksmanship; accuracy; (*fig.*) aptness.
мет|ла́, лы́, *pl.* **~лы, ~ел, ~лам** *f.* broom.
мет|ну́ть, ну́, нёшь *inst. pf. of* **⇒~а́ть[1]**
ме́тод, а *m.* method; **печа́тать слепы́м ~ом** to touch-type.
методи́зм, а *m.* (*relig.*) Methodism.
мето́дик|а, и *f.* method(s), system; principles; **м. преподава́ния ру́сского языка́** methods of teaching Russian; **м. пожа́рного де́ла** principles of fire-fighting.
методи́ст[1], а *m.* methodologist.
методи́ст[2], а *m.* (*relig.*) Methodist.
методи́ст|ка, ки *f. of* **⇒~[2]**
методи́ст|ский *adj. of* **⇒~[2]**
метод|и́ческий *adj.* **1** methodical, systematic. **2** *adj. of* **⇒~ика; м. приём** procedure.
методи́ч|ный (~ен, ~на) *adj.* methodical, orderly.
методологи́ческий *adj.* methodological.
методоло́ги|я, и *f.* methodology.
метр, а *m.* **1** (*единица длины; в стихе*) metre (*Br.*), meter (*US*). **2** (*линейка такой длины*) metre (*Br.*), meter (*US*) rule.
метра́ж, а *m.* **1** (*квартиры*) metric area. **2** (*ткани*) length in metres (*Br.*), meters (*US*).
метрдоте́л|ь, я *m.* head waiter.
ме́трик|а, и *f.* birth-certificate.
метри́ческий[1] *adj.* metric.
метри́ческий[2] *adj.* (*liter.*) metrical.
метри́ческ|ий[3] *adj.*: **~ая кни́га** register of births; **~ое свиде́тельство** birth-certificate.
метро́ *nt. indecl.* (*abbr. of* ***~полите́н***) **1** (*железная дорога*) underground (railway system) (*Br.*); the tube (*Br.*), subway (*US*). **2** (*coll.*) (*станция*) metro station; tube station (*Br.*), subway station (*US*).
метро... *comb. form, abbr. of* ***метрополите́нный***
метроно́м, а *m.* (*mus.*) metronome.
метрополите́н, а *m.* underground (railway) (*Br.*), subway (*US*).
метрополите́н|ный *adj. of* **⇒~**
метропо́ли|я, и *f.* mother country, centre (*of empire*).
ме|ту́, тёшь *see* **⇒~сти́**
ме́т|че *comp. of* **⇒~кий, ~ко**
ме́тчик, а *m.* (*tech.*) (*инструмент*) punch, stamp.
мех[1], а о ~е, в ~у́ (~е), на ~у́, *pl.* **~а́, ~о́в** *m.* fur; **на ~у́** fur-lined.
мех[2], а, *pl.* **~и́, ~о́в** *m.* **1** (*pl.*) (*кузнечные*) bellows. **2** (*мешок из шкуры животного*) wine-skin, water-skin.
механиза́тор, а *m.* **1** (*специалист по механизации*) specialist in mechanization. **2** (*agric.*) machine operator.
механиза́ци|я, и *f.* mechanization.
механизи́рова|нный *p.p.p. of* **⇒~ть** *and adj.* mechanized.
механизи́р|овать, ую *impf. and pf.* to mechanize.
механи́зм, а *m.* mechanism, gear(ing); (*pl.; collect.*) machinery (*also fig.*).
меха́ник, а *m.* mechanic.
меха́ник|а, и *f.* **1** (*наука, отрасль техники*) mechanics. **2** (*fig., coll.*) trick; knack; **подвести́ (***or* **подстро́ить) ~у кому́-н.** to play a trick on s.o.
механисти́ческий *adj.* (*phil.*) mechanistic.
механи́ческий *adj.* **1** mechanical; **м. моме́нт** momentum; **м. тка́цкий стано́к** power loom; **м. цех** machine shop. **2** (*phil.*) mechanistic.
механи́ч|ный (~ен, ~на) *adj.* (*fig.*) mechanical, automatic.
Ме́хико *m. indecl.* Mexico City.
мехово́й *adj. of* **⇒мех[1]; м. магази́н** furrier's.
меховщи́к, а́ *m.* furrier.
мецена́т, а *m.* patron.
мецена́тств|о, а *nt.* patronage of literature, of arts.
ме́ццо-сопра́но *indecl.* (*mus.*) **1** *nt.* (*голос*) mezzo-soprano. **2** *f.* (*певица*) mezzo-soprano.
ме́ццо-ти́нто *nt. indecl.* (*art*) mezzotint.
меч, а́ *m.* sword; **дамо́клов м.** sword of Damocles; **скрести́ть ~и́** (*fig., rhet.*) to cross swords.
ме́ченый *adj.* marked.
мече́т|ь, и *f.* mosque.
меч-ры́б|а, ы *f.* sword-fish.
мечт|а́, ы́ (*g. pl. not used*) *f.* **1** dream, day-dream. **2** (*предмет желаний*) dream, ambition.
мечта́ни|е, я *nt.* day-dreaming, reverie.

мечта́тел|ь, я *m.* dreamer; day-dreamer.

мечта́тель|ница, ницы *f. of* ⇒~

мечта́тел|ьный (~ен, ~ьна) *adj.* dreamy.

мечта́|ть, ю *impf.* (**о**+*p.*) to dream (of, about); **м. мно́го, высоко́** *etc.*, **о себе́** (*coll.*) to think much of o.s.

ме́|чу, тишь *see* ⇒**~тить**

ме|чу́, ~́чешь *see* ⇒**~та́ть**[1]

меша́лк|а, и *f.* (*coll.*) mixer, stirrer.

мешани́н|а, ы *f.* (*coll.*) jumble.

меша́|ть[1], **ю** *impf.* (*of* ⇒**по~**) **1** (+*d.* +*inf.*) (*препятствовать*) to prevent (from); to hinder, impede, hamper; **что ~ет вам прие́хать в Москву́?** what prevents you from coming to Moscow? **2** (+*d.*) (*беспокоить*) to disturb; **вам не ~ет, что я игра́ю на пиани́но?** does it disturb you when I play the piano?; **не ~ло бы** (+*inf.*) (*coll.*) it would not hurt (to).

меша́|ть[2], **ю** *impf.* **1** (*pf.* **по~**) (*чай, кашу*) to stir; **м. у́голь в пе́чке** to poke the fire; **м. в котле́** to stir the pot. **2** (*pf.* **с~**) (**с**+*i.*) (*вино с водой*) to mix (with), blend (with). **3** (*pf.* **с~**) (*путать*) to confuse, mix up.

меша́|ться, юсь *impf.* **1** (*coll.*; **в**+*a.*) to interfere (in), meddle (with); **не ~йтесь не в своё де́ло!** mind your own business! **2** (*pf.* **с~**) *pass. of* ⇒**~ть**[2]

ме́шка|ть, ю *impf.* (*coll.*; **с**+*i.*) to linger, dawdle, be slow.

мешкова́т|ый (~, ~а) *adj.* **1** (*одежда*) baggy. **2** (*человек*) awkward, clumsy.

мешкови́н|а, ы *f.* sacking, hessian.

ме́шкот|ный (~ен, ~на) *adj.* (*coll.*) **1** (*человек*) sluggish, slow. **2** (*дело*) long.

меш|о́к, ка́ *m.* bag; sack; **вещево́й м.** haversack, knapsack; kit-bag; **~ки́ под глаза́ми** bags under the eyes.

мешо́ч|ек, ка *m. dim. of* ⇒**мешо́к;** sac; **м. с ча́ем** tea bag.

мещан|и́н, и́на, *pl.* **~́е, ~́** *m.* **1** (*hist.*) petty bourgeois. **2** (*fig.*) philistine.

меща́нк|а, и *f. of* ⇒ **мещани́н**

меща́н|ский *adj. of* ⇒**~и́н;** (*fig.*) philistine; bourgeois, narrow-minded.

меща́нств|о, а *nt.* **1** (*collect.*) petty bourgeoisie, lower middle class. **2** (*fig.*) philistinism, narrow-mindedness.

мзд|а, ы *no pl., f.* (*arch., now joc.*) recompense, payment (*iron.* = *bribe*).

мздоим|ец, ца *m.* (*obs.*) bribe-taker.

мздоимств|о, а *nt.* (*obs.*) bribery.

ми *nt. indecl.* (*mus.*) E.

МИГ, а *or* **«миг», а** *m.* (*abbr. of* ***Микоя́н и Гуре́вич***) 'Mig' (*aircraft*).

миг, а *m.* moment, instant.

мига́лк|а, и *f.* (*coll.*) **1** (*коптилка*) flashing light. **2** (*на машине*) blinker.

мига́ни|е, я *nt.* **1** (*мерцание*) winking; twinkling. **2** (*непроизвольно*) blinking. **3** (*как знак*) winking.

миг|а́ть, а́ю *impf.* (*of* ⇒**~ну́ть**) **1** (*непроизвольно*) to blink. **2** (+*d.*) (*подавать знак*) to wink (at); (*fig.*) (*мерцать*) to wink, twinkle.

миг|ну́ть, ну́, нёшь *inst. pf. of* ⇒**~а́ть**

ми́гом *adv.* (*coll.*) in a flash; in a jiffy.

миграцио́нный *adj. of* ⇒**мигра́ция**

мигра́ци|я, и *f.* migration.

мигре́н|ь, и *f.* migraine.

мигри́р|овать, ую *impf.* to migrate.

МИД, а *m.* (*abbr. of* ***Министе́рство иностра́нных дел***) Ministry of Foreign Affairs; Foreign Office (*Br.*), State Department (*US*).

ми́ди *nt. indecl.* midi (*garment*); **ми́ди-ю́бка** midi-skirt.

ми́ди|я, и *f.* mussel.

мизансце́н|а, ы *f.* (*theatr.*) mise en scène, staging.

мизантро́п, а *m.* misanthrope.

мизантропи́ческий *adj.* misanthropic.

мизантро́пи|я, и *f.* misanthropy.

мизе́р|ный (~ен, ~на) *adj.* meagre (*Br.*), meager (*US*).

мизи́н|ец, ца *m.* (*на руке*) little finger; (*на ноге*) little toe.

мике́нский *adj.* Mycenean.

Мике́н|ы, ~ *no sg.* (*hist.*) Mycenae.

миколо́ги|я, и *f.* mycology.

микро... *comb. form* micro-

микроавто́бус, а *m.* minibus.

микроампе́р, а *m.* (*elec.*) microampere.

микро́б, а *m.* microbe.

микробио́лог, а *m.* microbiologist.

микробиоло́ги|я, и *f.* microbiology.

микроволно́в|ый *adj.*: **~ая пе́чка** microwave (oven).

микрокли́мат, а *m.* microclimate.

микрокомпью́тер, а *m.* microcomputer.

микроко́см, а *m.* microcosm.

микро́метр, а *m.* (*tech.*) micrometer.

микроме́три|я, и *f.* (*tech.*) micrometry.

микро́н, а *m.* (*phys.*) micron.

микроорганизм, а *m.* (*biol.*) micro-organism; **разлага́емый ~ами** biodegradable.

микроплёнк|а, и *f.* microfilm.

микропроце́ссор, а *m.* microprocessor.

микрорайо́н, а *m.* microrayon *or* microraion (*administrative subdivision of urban area*).

микроско́п, а *m.* microscope.

микроскопи́ческий *adj.* microscopic.

микроскопи́ч|ный (~ен, ~на) *adj.* = **~еский**

микроскопи́|я, и *f.* microscopy.

микрострукту́р|а, ы *f.* microstructure.

микросхе́м|а, ы *f.* microcircuit, microchip.

микрофи́льм, а *m.* microfilm.

микрофи́ш|а, и *f.* (micro)fiche.

микрофо́н, а *m.* microphone.

микрохирурги́|я, и *f.* microsurgery.

микроэконо́мик|а, и *f.* microeconomics.

микроэкономи́ческий *adj.* microeconomic.

микроэлектро́ник|а, и *f.* microelectronics.

микроэлеме́нт, а *m.* trace element.

ми́ксер, а *m.* (*cul.*) mixer, blender, liquidizer.

миксомато́з, а *m.* myxomatosis.

миксту́р|а, ы *f.* (liquid) medicine, mixture.

ми́кшер, а *m.* (*electronics*) mixer.

ми́кшерский *adj.*: **м. пульт** mixing desk.

микши́р|овать, ую *impf. and pf.* (*electronics*) to mix.

ми́ленький *adj.* **1** (*хорошенький*) pretty; (*дорогой*) dear. **2** (*в обращении*) darling.

милитариза́ци|я, и *f.* militarization.

милитари́зм, а *m.* militarism.

милитариз|ова́ть, у́ю *impf. and pf.* to militarize.

милитари́ст, а *m.* militarist.

милитаристи́ческий *adj.* militaristic.

милиц|е́йский *adj. of* ⇒**~́ия**

милиционе́р, а *m.* policeman (*in Russia*).

мили́ци|я, и *f.* police (*in Russia*).

миллиа́рд, а *m.* billion (= *thousand million*).

миллиарде́р, а *m.* billionaire.

миллиа́рдный *adj.* billionth.

миллиба́р, а *m.* (*meteor.*) millibar.

милливо́льт, а *m.* (*elec.*) millivolt.

миллигра́мм, а *m.* milligram(me).

миллили́тр, а *m.* millilitre (*Br.*), milliliter (*US*).

миллиме́тр, а *m.* millimetre (*Br.*), millimeter (*US*).

миллиметро́вк|а, и *f.* (*coll.*) graph paper.

миллио́н, а *m.* million.

миллионе́р, а *m.* millionaire.

миллио́нный *adj.* **1** millionth. **2** (*оцениваемый в миллионы*) worth millions. **3** (*исчисляемый миллионом*) million-strong.

ми́л|овать, ую *impf.* (*of* ⇒**по~**) to pardon, spare.

мил|ова́ться, у́юсь *impf.* (*coll.*) to exchange caresses.

милови́д|ный (~ен, ~на) *adj.* pretty, nice-looking.

мило́рд, а *m.* (mi)lord.

милосе́рди|е, я *nt.* mercy, charity.

милосе́рд|ный (~ен, ~на) *adj.* merciful, charitable.

ми́лостив|ый (~, ~а) *adj.* (*obs.*) gracious, kind; **м. госуда́рь** (*в обращении*) sir; (*в письме*) (Dear) Sir; **~ая госуда́рыня** madam; (*в письме*) (Dear) Madam.

ми́лостын|я, и *f.* alms.

М

ми́лост|ь, и *f.* **1** (*благодеяние*) favour (*Br.*), favor (*US*); **~и про́сим!** (*coll.*) welcome!; **скажи́(те) на м.!** (*coll., iron.*) you don't say (so)! **2** (*доброта*) kindness; charity; **сда́ться на м. победи́теля** to surrender unconditionally; **из ~и** out of charity. **3** (*obs.*) (*в обращении*): **ва́ша м.** your worship.

ми́лочк|а, и *f.* (*coll.*) dear, darling.

ми́л|ый (~, ~á, ~л) *adj.* **1** nice, sweet; lovable; **э́то о́чень ~о с ва́шей стороны́** it is very nice of you. **2** dear; *as n.* **м., ~ого** *m.*, **~ая, ~ой** *f.* dear, darling.

ми́л|я, и *f.* mile.

мим, а *m.* (*theatr.*) mime (artist).

ми́мик|а, и *f.* facial expressions.

мимикри́|я, и *f.* (*biol.*) mimicry.

мими́ст, а *m.* mimic.

мими́ст|ка, ки *f. of* ⇒~

мими́ческий *adj.* mimic.

ми́мо *adv. and prep. + g.* by, past; **пройти́, прое́хать м.** to pass by, to pass; **м.!** miss(ed)!

мимое́здом *adv.* (*coll.*) in passing.

мимо́з|а, ы *f.* (*bot.*) mimosa.

мимолёт|ный (~ен, ~на) *adj.* fleeting, transient.

мимохо́дом *adv.* in passing; **м. упомяну́ть** (*fig., coll.*) to mention in passing.

мин. (*abbr. of* **мину́та**) min., minute(s).

ми́н|а¹, ы *f.* **1** (*mil., naut.*) mine. **2** (*mil.*) (*снаряд миномёта*) mortar shell, bomb.

ми́н|а², ы *f.* (*выражение лица*) mien, expression; **сде́лать весёлую (хоро́шую) ~у при плохо́й игре́** to put a brave face on a sorry business.

минаре́т, а *m.* minaret.

миндалеви́дн|ый *adj.* almond-shaped; **~ая железа́** (*anat.*) tonsil.

минда́лин|а, ы *f.* **1** (*орех*) almond. **2** (*anat.*) tonsil.

минда́л|ь, я *m.* **1** (*дерево*) almond-tree. **2** (*collect.*) (*орехи*) almonds.

минда́ль|ный *adj. of* ⇒~

минёр, а *m.* (*mil.*) mine-layer.

минера́л, а *m.* mineral.

минера́лк|а, и *f.* (*coll.*) mineral water.

минералоги́ческий *adj.* mineralogical.

минерало́ги|я, и *f.* mineralogy.

минера́льный *adj.* mineral.

мине́т, а *m.* (*vulg.*) (*оральный секс*) blow-job.

Минздра́в, а *m.* (*abbr. of* ***Министе́рство здравоохране́ния***) Ministry of Health.

ми́ни *nt. indecl.* mini (*garment*).

миниатю́р|а, ы *f.* (*art, mus.*) miniature; (*theatr.*) short piece, play.

миниатюриза́ци|я, и *f.* miniaturization.

миниатюри́ст, а *m.* miniature-painter, miniaturist.

миниатю́р|ный (~ен, ~на) *adj.* **1** *adj. of* ⇒**~а. 2** (*fig.*) diminutive, tiny, dainty.

миниди́ск, а *m.* minidisc.

мини(-)компью́тер, а *m.* minicomputer.

минима́л|ьный (~ен, ~ьна) *adj.* minimum.

ми́нимум, а *m.* **1** minimum; **м. за́работной пла́ты** minimum wage; **прожи́точный м.** living wage. **2** (*as adv.*) at the least, at the minimum.

мини́р|овать, ую *impf. and pf.* (*mil., naut.*) to mine.

министе́рский *adj.* ministerial.

министе́рств|о, а *nt.* (*pol.*) ministry.

мини́стр, а *m.* (*pol.*) minister; **м.-президе́нт, премье́р-м.** Prime Minister, premier.

мини-футбо́л, а *m.* ≈ five-a-side.

мини-ЭВМ *f. indecl.* = **мини(-)компью́тер**

ми́ни-ю́бк|а (*and* минию́бк|а), и *f.* miniskirt.

ми́нн|ый *adj.* (*mil.*) mine; **~ое по́ле** minefield.

мин|ова́ть, у́ю *impf. and pf.* **1** (*пройти/проехать мимо*) to pass (by); **~у́я подро́бности** omitting details. **2** (*pf. only*) (*окончиться*) to be over, be past; **опа́сность ~ова́ла** the danger is past. **3** (*only with* **не** *+ g.*) (*избежать*) to escape, avoid; **не м. тебе́ тюрьмы́** you cannot escape being sent to prison.

мино́г|а, и *f.* (*zool.*) lamprey.

миноиска́тел|ь, я *m.* (*mil.*) mine-detector.

миномёт, а *m.* (*mil.*) mortar.

миномёт|ный *adj. of* ⇒~

миномётчик, а *m.* (*mil.*) mortar man.

минонос|ец, ца *m.* (*naut.*) torpedo-boat; **эска́дренный м.** destroyer.

мино́р, а *m.* **1** (*mus.*) minor key. **2** (*fig.*) (*грустное настроение*) the blues; **быть в ~е** to have the blues, be in the dumps.

мино́рн|ый *adj.* **1** (*mus.*) minor. **2** (*fig.*) (*грустный*) gloomy, depressed; **быть в ~ом настрое́нии** to have the blues, be in the dumps.

Минск, а *m.* Minsk.

мину́вш|ий *adj.* past; *as n.* **~ее, ~его** *nt.* the past.

ми́нус, а *m.* **1** (*math.*) minus. **2** (*fig., coll.*) (*недостаток*) shortcoming, drawback.

ми́нусовый *adj.* sub-zero; (*elec.*) negative.

мину́т|а, ы *f.* minute.

мину́т|ный *adj.* **1** *adj. of* ⇒**~а**; **~ная стре́лка** minute-hand. **2** momentary; **~ная встре́ча** brief encounter.

мин|у́ть, ~ешь *pf.* **1** (*past* **~у́л, ~у́ла**) = **минова́ть. 2** (*past* **~ул, ~у́ла**) (*+d.*) to pass (*only in expressions of age*); **ему́ ~уло два́дцать лет** he has turned twenty.

миока́рд, а *m.* myocardium; **инфа́ркт ~а** myocardial infarction.

миопи́|я, и *f.* (*med.*) myopia.

миоце́н, а *m.* the Miocene.

мир¹, а *m.* (*согласие*) peace; **про́чный м.** lasting peace; **заключи́ть м.** to make peace; **м. вам!** peace be with you!; **иди́те с ~ом** go in peace.

мир², а, *pl.* **~ы́** *m.* (*вселенная*) world (*also fig.*); universe; **академи́ческий м.** academia; **живо́тный м.** fauna; **расти́тельный м.** flora; **престу́пный м.** the underworld; **не от ~а сего́** (*coll.*) other-worldly, not of this world; **си́льные ~а сего́** (*obs., iron.*) people occupying a high position in society; **в ~у́** in the world (*opp. in a monastery*); **ходи́ть по́ ~у** to beg, live by begging; **пусти́ть по́ ~у** to ruin utterly.

мир³, а *m.* (*hist.*) mir (*Russian village community*).

мира́ж, а *m.* mirage (*also fig.*); optical illusion.

мира́кл|ь, я *m.* (*liter., theatr.*) miracle-play.

мир|и́ть, ю́, и́шь *impf.* **1** (*pf.* **по~**) (*враждующих*) to reconcile. **2** (*pf.* **при~**) (**с** *+ i.*) (*заставлять терпимо относиться*) to reconcile (to); **больша́я зарпла́та ~и́ла его́ с неприя́тными усло́виями рабо́ты** high wages reconciled him to unpleasant working conditions.

мир|и́ться, ю́сь, и́шься *impf.* (**с** *+ i.*) **1** (*pf.* **по~**) (*прекращать вражду*) to be reconciled (with), make it up (with). **2** (*pf.* **при~**) (*терпимо относиться*) to reconcile o.s. (to); **м. со свои́м положе́нием** to accept the situation.

ми́р|ный (~ен, ~на) *adj.* **1** *adj. of* ⇒**~¹**. **2** peaceful; peaceable; **~ное сосуществова́ние** (*pol.*) peaceful co-existence.

миров|а́я, о́й *f.* peaceful settlement; amicable agreement.

мировоззре́ни|е, я *nt.* (world-) outlook, Weltanschauung; (one's) philosophy (of life).

мир|ово́й¹ *adj. of* ⇒**~²**; **~ова́я война́** world war; (*coll., joc.*) (*отличный*) first-rate, first-class.

мирово́й² *adj.* (*obs.*) conciliatory; (*hist.*): **м. посре́дник** arbitrator; **м. судья́** Justice of the Peace.

мировосприя́ти|е, я *nt.* perception of the world.

мирозда́ни|е, я *nt.* the universe.

миролюби́вост|ь, и *f.* peaceable disposition.

миролюби́в|ый (~, ~а) *adj.* peaceable.

миролю́би|е, я *nt.* peaceableness.

мироощуще́ни|е, я *nt.* attitude, disposition.

миропома́зани|е, я *nt.* (*eccl.*) anointing.

миропонима́ни|е, я *nt.* = **мировоззре́ние**

миросозерца́ни|е, я *nt.* = **мировоззре́ние**

миротво́р|ец, ца *m.* peace-maker.

ми́рр|а, ы *f.* (*bot.*) myrrh.

мирско́й¹ *adj.* secular, lay; mundane, worldly.

мир|ско́й² *adj. of* ⇒**~³**; **~ска́я схо́дка** peasants' meeting.

мирт, а *m.* (*bot.*) myrtle.
ми́рт|овый *adj. of* ⇒**~**
ми́ск|а, и *f.* basin, bowl.
мисс *f. indecl.* Miss.
миссионе́р, а *m.* missionary.
миссионе́р|ка, ки *f. of* ⇒**~**
миссионе́р|ский *adj. of* ⇒**~**
миссионе́рств|о, а *nt.* missionary work.
ми́ссис *f. indecl.* missis, Mrs.
ми́сси|я, и *f.* mission.
ми́стер, а *m.* mister, Mr.
мисте́ри|я, и *f.* (*hist., theatr.*) mystery, miracle-play.
ми́стик, а *m.* mystic.
ми́стик|а, и *f.* mysticism; (*coll.*) mystery.
мистифика́тор, а *m.* hoaxer.
мистифика́ци|я, и *f.* hoax, leg-pull.
мистифици́р|овать, ую *impf. and pf.* to hoax, mystify.
мистици́зм, а *m.* mysticism.
мисти́ческий *adj.* mystic(al).
мистра́л|ь, я *m.* mistral (wind).
мит|ёк, ька́ *m.* (*sl.*) mityok, hippy artist.
мите́н|ки, ок *pl.* (*sg.* **~ка, ~ки** *f.*) mittens.
ми́тинг, а *m.* (political) mass-meeting; rally.
митинг|ова́ть, у́ю *impf.* (*coll.*) **1** to hold a mass-meeting (about). **2** (*pej.*) to discuss endlessly.
митинго́вый *adj. of* ⇒**ми́тинг**
митка́л|евый *adj. of* ⇒**~ь**
митка́л|ь, я́ *m.* (*text.*) calico.
ми́тр|а, ы *f.* (*eccl.*) mitre.
митрополи́т, а *m.* (*eccl.*) metropolitan.
митрополи́|чий *adj. of* ⇒**~т**
мит|ько́вый *adj. of* ⇒**~ёк**
миф, а *m.* myth (*also fig.*).
мифи́ческий *adj.* mythic(al).
мифологи́ческий *adj.* mythological.
мифоло́ги|я, и *f.* mythology.
ми́чман, а, *pl.* (*in naval usage*) **~а́, ~о́в** *m.* (*naut.*) **1** warrant officer. **2** (*в царской России*) midshipman.
мише́н|ь, и *f.* target (*also fig.*).
ми́шк|а, и *m.* (*dim. of* **Михаи́л**) **1** (*медведь*) (*pet-name for*) bear. **2** (*игрушка*) teddy bear.
мишур|а́, ы́ *f.* **1** tinsel. **2** (*fig.*) trumpery.
мишу́рный *adj.* tinsel (*attr.*); (*fig.*) tawdry, ostentatious.
младе́н|ец, ца *m.* baby, infant.
младе́нческий *adj.* infantile.
младе́нчеств|о, а *nt.* infancy, babyhood.
млад|о́й (~, ~а́, ~́о) *adj.* (*arch. or poet.*) young; **стар и ~** one and all (*without respect of age*).
младопи́сьменный *adj.*: **м. язы́к** language having newly acquired a written form.
мла́дост|ь, и *f.* (*arch. or poet.*) youth.
мла́дший *adj.* (*comp. and superl. of* ⇒**молодо́й**) **1** (*более молодой*) younger. **2** (*самый молодой*) the youngest. **3** (*по служебному положению*) junior; **м. лейтена́нт** second lieutenant.
млекопита́ющ|ее, его *nt.* (*zool.*) mammal.
мле|ть, ю *impf.* (**от**+*g.*) to be overcome (*with delight, fright, etc.*).
мле́чный *adj.* (*arch. or poet.*) milky; **м. сок** (*bot.*) latex; **М. Путь** (*astron.*) the Milky Way, the Galaxy.
млн. (*abbr. of* **миллио́н**) m, million(s).
млрд. (*abbr. of* **миллиа́рд**) b., billion(s) (= *thousand million*).
мм (*abbr. of* **миллиме́тр**) mm, millimetre(s) (*Br.*), millimeter(s) (*US*).
мне *d. and p. of* ⇒**я**
мнемо́ник|а, и *f.* mnemonics; system of mnemonics.
мнемони́ческий *adj.* mnemonic.
мне́ни|е, я *nt.* opinion.
мни́м|ый *adj.* **1** (*воображаемый*) imaginary (*also math.*); **~ая величина́** imaginary quantity. **2** (*притворный*) sham, pretended; **м. больно́й** hypochondriac.
мни́тельност|ь, и *f.* **1** (*ипохондрия*) hypochondria. **2** (*подозрительность*) mistrustfulness, suspiciousness.
мни́тел|ьный (~ен, ~ьна) *adj.* **1** (*ипохондрический*) hypochondriac. **2** (*подозрительный*) mistrustful, suspicious.
мн|ить, ю, ишь *impf.* **1** (*obs.*) to think, imagine. **2**: **м. мно́го о себе́** to think a lot of o.s.
мни́т|ься, ~ся *impf.* (*impers.; obs. or poet.*): **~ся** it seems, methinks.
мно́г|ие, их *adj. and n.* many; **во ~их отноше́ниях** in many respects.
мно́го *adv.* (+*g.*) much; many; a lot (of); **м. вре́мени** much time; **м. лет** many years; **о́чень м. знать** to know a great deal; **м. лу́чше** much better; **ни м., ни ма́ло** (*coll.*) neither more nor less.
много... *comb. form* many-, poly-, multi-.
многобо́жи|е, я *nt.* polytheism.
многобо́р|ец, ца *m.* all-round athlete, multi-eventer.
многобо́рь|е, я *nt.* multi-discipline event *or* competition.
многобра́чи|е, я *nt.* polygamy.
многобра́ч|ный (~ен, ~на) *adj.* polygamous.
многова́то *adv.* (*coll.*) a bit too much.
многовеково́й *adj.* centuries-old.
многовла́сти|е, я *nt.* = **многонача́лие**
многово́д|ный (~ен, ~на) *adj.* (*река*) full, having high water-level.
многоговоря́щий *adj.* revealing, suggestive.
многогра́нник, а *m.* (*math.*) polyhedron.
многогра́нный *adj.* (*math.*) polyhedral; (*fig.*) many-sided; multi-faceted.
многоде́т|ный (~ен, ~на) *adj.* having many children.
многодне́вный *adj.*: **м. путь** a journey lasting several days.
мно́г|ое, ого *nt.* much, a great deal; **во ~ом** in many respects.
многоже́н|ец, ца *m.* polygamist.
многожёнств|о, а *nt.* polygamy.
многозада́чный *adj.*: **м. режи́м (рабо́ты)** (*comput.*) multitasking.
многозначи́тельност|ь, и *f.* significance.
многозначи́тел|ьный (~ен, ~ьна) *adj.* significant.
многозна́ч|ный (~ен, ~на) *adj.* **1** (*math.*) multi-digit. **2** (*ling.*) polysemantic; **~ное сло́во** polyseme.
многокле́точный *adj.* (*biol.*) multi-cellular.
многокра́сочный *adj.* polychromatic, many-coloured (*Br.*), -colored (*US*).
многокра́т|ный (~ен, ~на) *adj.* **1** repeated; frequent. **2** (*gram.*) frequentative, iterative.
многоле́тний *adj.* **1** lasting *or* living many years; of many years' standing. **2** (*bot.*) perennial.
многоле́тник, а *m.* (*bot.*) perennial.
многоли́к|ий (~, ~а) *adj.* many-sided.
многолю́д|ный (~ен, ~на) *adj.* (*район*) populous; (*улица*) crowded.
многомиллиа́рдный *adj.* multibillion.
многомиллио́нный *adj.* multimillion; of many millions.
многому́жи|е, я *nt.* polyandry.
многонациона́л|ьный (~ен, ~ьна) *adj.* multi-national.
многонача́ли|е, я *nt.* multiple authority (*absence of clearly-defined spheres of authority*).
многоно́жк|а, и *f.* (*zool.*) centipede, millipede.
многообеща́ющий *adj.* **1** (*ученик*) promising, hopeful. **2** (*взгляд*) significant.
многообра́зи|е, я *nt.* variety, diversity.
многообра́з|ный (~ен, ~на) *adj.* varied, diverse.
многопарти́йный *adj.* multiparty.
многопо́ль|е, я *nt.* (*agric.*) crop-rotation system involving seven or eight fields.
многопо́ль|ный *adj. of* ⇒**~е**
многора́совый *adj.* multiracial.
многоречи́в|ый (~, ~а) *adj.* loquacious, verbose.
многосеме́|йный (~ен, ~йна) *adj.* having a large family.
многосери́йный *adj.* serial.
многосло́в|ный (~ен, ~на) *adj.* verbose.
многосло́жный *adj.* polysyllabic.
многосло́йн|ый *adj.* multi-layer; **~ая фане́ра** plywood.
многосторо́н|ний (~ен, ~ня) *adj.* **1** (*math.*) polygonal. **2** (*договор*) multilateral. **3** (*человек*) many-sided, versatile.

М

многострада́л|ьный (~ен, ~ьна) *adj.* long-suffering.

многоступе́нчатый *adj.* (*tech.*) multi-stage.

многотира́жк|а, и *f.* (*coll.*) factory newspaper; house organ.

многотира́жный *adj.* published in large editions; large-circulation.

многото́мный *adj.* multivolume.

многото́чи|е, я *nt.* (*typ.*) ellipsis.

многотру́д|ный (~ен, ~на) *adj.* arduous.

многоуважа́емый *adj.* respected; (*в письме*) dear.

многоуго́льник, а *m.* (*math.*) polygon.

многоуго́льный *adj.* (*math.*) polygonal.

многоцве́т|ный (~ен, ~на) *adj.* **1** multi-coloured (*Br.*), -colored (*US*). **2** (*typ.*) polychromatic.

многоцелево́й *adj.* multipurpose.

многочи́слен|ный (~, ~на) *adj.* numerous.

многочле́н, а *m.* (*math.*) multinomial.

многоэта́жный *adj.* multi-storey (*Br.*), multistory (*US*), high-rise.

мно́жественност|ь, и *f.* plurality.

мно́жественн|ый *adj.* plural; **~ое число́** (*gram.*) plural (number).

мно́жеств|о, а *nt.* a great number, a quantity; multitude; (*math.*) set.

мно́жим|ое, ого *nt.* (*math.*) multiplicand.

мно́жител|ь, я *m.* multiplier, factor.

мно́ж|ить, у, ишь *impf.* **1** (*pf.* **по~, у~**) (*math.*) to multiply. **2** (*pf.* **у~**) (*увеличивать*) to increase, augment.

мно́ж|иться, ится *impf.* (*of* ⇨**у~**) **1** to multiply, increase (*intrans.*). **2** *pass. of* ⇨**~ить**

мной, мно́ю *i. of* ⇨**я**

мобилиза|цио́нный *adj. of* ⇨**~ция**

мобилиза́ци|я, и *f.* mobilization.

мобилизо́ванност|ь, и *f.* complete readiness for action.

мобилизо́в|анный *p.p.p. of* ⇨**~а́ть**; *as n.* **м., ~анного** *m.* mobilized soldier.

мобилиз|ова́ть, у́ю *impf. and pf.* (*pf. also* **отмобилизова́ть**) (**на** + *a.*) to mobilize (for).

моби́л|ьный (~ен, ~ьна) *adj.* mobile.

моги́л|а, ы *f.* grave; **свести́ в ~у** to be the death of.

моги́льник, а *m.* (*archaeol.*) burial ground.

моги́льный *adj.* **1** *adj. of* ⇨**моги́ла. 2** sepulchral.

моги́льщик, а *m.* grave-digger.

мо|гу́, ~гут *see* ⇨**мочь**

могу́ч|ий (~, ~а) *adj.* mighty, powerful.

могу́ществен|ный (~, ~на) *adj.* powerful; potent.

могу́ществ|о, а *nt.* power, might.

мо́д|а, ы *f.* fashion, vogue; **выходи́ть из ~ы** to go out of fashion; **по после́дней ~е** in the latest fashion.

мода́льный *adj.* modal.

модели́зм, а *m.* modelling (*Br.*), modeling (*US*).

модели́р|овать, ую *impf. and pf.* (*pf. also* **с~**) (*одежду*) to design.

моде́л|ь, и *f.* model; (*платья*) design; (*для отливки*) pattern.

моделье́р, а *m.* fashion designer, couturier.

моде́ль|ный *adj.* **1** *adj. of* ⇨**~. 2** fashionable.

моде́льщик, а *m.* (*tech.*) modeller (*Br.*), modeler (*US*), pattern maker.

мо́де́м, а *m.* (*comput.*) modem.

моде́рн, а *m.* modernist style; *as indecl. adj.* modern; **м.-бале́т** modern dance.

модерниза́ци|я, и *f.* modernization; updating.

модернизи́р|овать, ую *impf. and pf.* to modernize; to update.

модерни́зм, а *m.* (*art*) modernism.

moderниз|ова́ть, у́ю *impf. and pf.* = **~и́ровать**

модерни́ст, а *m.* (*art*) modernist.

моде́рновый *adj.* (*coll.*) modern; trendy, with-it.

моде́рный = ⇨**моде́рновый**

моди́стк|а, и *f.* milliner.

модифика́ци|я, и *f.* modification.

модифици́р|овать, ую *impf. and pf.* to modify.

мо́дник, а *m.* (*coll.*) trendy dresser.

мо́дни|ца, цы *f. of* ⇨**~к**

мо́днича|ть, ю *impf.* (*coll.*) to dress in the latest fashion.

мо́д|ный (~ен, ~на́, ~но) *adj.* **1** fashionable, stylish. **2** *adj. of* ⇨**~а; м. журна́л** fashion magazine.

модули́р|овать, ую *impf.* (*mus. and tech.*) to modulate.

мо́дул|ь, я *m.* (*math.*) modulus; (*tech.*) module.

модуля́ци|я, и *f.* (*mus. and tech.*) modulation.

моёвк|а, и *f.* (*zool.*) kittiwake.

мо́жет *see* ⇨**мочь**

можжевёловый *adj.* juniper.

можжеве́льник, а *m.* (*bot.*) juniper.

мо́жно *pred.* (*impers.* + *inf.*) **1** (*возможно*) it is possible; **м. бы́ло э́то предви́деть** it could have been foreseen; **как м.** + *comp.* as ... as possible; **как м. скоре́е** as soon as possible. **2** (*разрешается*) it is permissible, one may; **м. идти́?** may I (we) go?

моза́ик|а, и *f.* mosaic; (*искусство*) mosaic work.

моза́ич|ный (~ен, ~на) *adj.* (*плитка*) mosaic; (*мебель*) inlaid.

Мозамби́к, а *m.* Mozambique.

мозамби́кский *adj.* Mozambican.

мозг, а, в ~у́, *pl.* **~и́, ~о́в** *m.* **1** brain (*also fig.*); (*fig.*) nerve centre (*Br.*), center (*US*); **головно́й м.** brain, cerebrum; **спинно́й м.** spinal cord. **2** (*anat.*) marrow; **до ~а косте́й** (*fig., coll.*) to the core.

мо́згл|ый (~, ~а) *adj.* (*coll.*) dank.

мозгля́в|ый (~, ~а) *adj.* (*coll.*) weakly, puny.

мозгови́т|ый (~, ~а) *adj.* (*coll.*) brainy.

мозгов|о́й *adj.* (*anat.*) cerebral; (*fig.*) brain; **~ая ата́ка** brainstorming session, brainstorm.

Мо́зел|ь, я *m.* the Moselle (*river*).

мозжеч|о́к, ка́ *m.* (*anat.*) cerebellum.

мозо́лист|ый (~, ~а) *adj.* calloused.

мозо́л|ить, ю, ишь *impf.* (*of* ⇨**на~**) to make calloused; **м. глаза́** (+ *d.*; *fig., coll.*) to plague (with one's presence).

мозо́л|ь, и *f.* corn; callus, callosity; **ру́ки в ~ях** calloused hands.

мозо́ль|ный *adj. of* ⇨**~; м. пла́стырь** corn-plaster.

мой *possessive pron.* (*при существительном*) my; (*без существительного*) mine; *as n.* **мой, мои́х** my people; **по-мо́ему** (*по моему мнению*) in my opinion; (*так, как я считаю правильным*) as I think right.

мо́йк|а, и *f.* **1** (*действие*) washing. **2** (*машина*) washer. **3** (*раковина*) sink.

мо́йщик, а *m.* washer; cleaner; **м. о́кон** window-cleaner; **м. посу́ды** dishwasher (*person*), washer-up.

мо́к|нуть, ну, нешь, *past* **~, ~ла** *impf.* **1** (*pf.* **вы́~**) (*становиться мокрым*) to become wet, become soaked. **2** (*лежать в воде*) to soak (*intrans.*). **3** (*о ране*) to weep.

мокри́ц|а, ы *f.* wood-louse.

мокрова́т|ый (~, ~а) *adj.* moist, damp.

мокро́т|а, ы *f.* (*med.*) phlegm.

мокрот|а́, ы́ *f.* humidity, moistness.

мо́кр|ый (~, ~а́, ~о) *adj.* wet; **м. снег** sleet; (*impers., pred.*): **~о** it is wet; **у неё глаза́ на ~ом ме́сте** (*coll.*) she is easily moved to tears.

мол[1]**, а** *m.* mole, pier.

мол[2] (*contraction of* ***мо́лвил***) (*coll.*) he says (said), they say (said), *etc.* (*indicating reported speech*); **он, м., никогда́ там не́ был** he said he had never been there.

молв|а́, ы́ *f.* (*obs.*) rumour (*Br.*), rumor (*US*), talk; **идёт м.** rumour (*Br.*), rumor (*US*) has it.

мо́лв|ить, лю, ишь *pf.* (*obs.*) to say.

молдава́н|ин, ина, *pl.* **~е, ~** *m.* Moldovan.

молдава́н|ка, ки *f. of* ⇨**~ин**

Молда́ви|я, и *f.* Moldavia.

молда́вский *adj.* Moldovan; Moldavian.

Молдо́в|а, ы *f.* Moldova.

моле́б|ен, на *m.* (*eccl.*) service; public prayer.

моле́кул|а, ы *f.* (*phys.*) molecule.

молекуля́рный *adj.* molecular.

моле́л|ьня, ьни, *g. pl.* **~ен** *f.* chapel, meeting-house.

моле́ни|е, я *nt.* **1** (*действие*) praying. **2** (*мольба*) entreaty, supplication.

молески́н, а *m.* (*text.*) moleskin.

молибде́н, а *m.* (*chem.*) molybdenum.

молибде́н|овый *adj. of* ⇒∼
моли́тв|а, ы *f.* prayer.
моли́твенник, а *m.* prayer-book.
моли́тв|енный *adj. of* ⇒∼а
мол|и́ть, ю́, ∼́ишь *impf.* (*a. and* **о**+*p.*) to pray (for), entreat (for), supplicate (for), beseech; **∼ю́ вас о по́мощи** I beg you to help me.
мол|и́ться, ю́сь, ∼́ишься *impf.* **1** (*pf.* **по∼**; +*d.*) to pray (to). **2** (*fig.*; **на**+*a.*) to idolize.
моллю́ск, а *m.* mollusc; shell-fish.
молниено́сно *adv.* with lightning speed, like lightning.
молниено́с|ный (∼ен, ∼на) *adj.* (quick as) lightning; **∼ная война́** blitzkrieg.
молниеотво́д, а *m.* lightning-conductor.
мо́лни|я, и *f.* **1** lightning. **2**: **(телегра́мма-)м.** express telegram. **3**: **(застёжка-)м.** zip-fastener (*Br.*), zipper (*US*).
молодёж|ный *adj. of* ⇒∼ь
молодёж|ь, и *f.* (*collect.*) youth; young people.
молоде́|ть, ю, ешь *impf.* (*of* ⇒**по∼**) to grow young again.
молод|е́ц, ца́ *m.* fine fellow; (*о женщине*) fine girl; *as int.*: **м.!** well done!
молоде́цкий *adj.* (*coll.*) dashing, spirited.
молоде́честв|о, а *nt.* spirit, mettle.
моло|ди́ть, жу́, ди́шь *impf.* to make look younger.
моло|ди́ться, жу́сь, ди́шься *impf.* to try to look younger than one's age.
молодня́к, а́ *m.* (*collect.*) **1** (*bot.*) saplings. **2** (*zool.*) young animals; cubs. **3** (*coll.*) the younger generation.
молодожён|ы, ов *pl.* (*sg.* **∼, ∼а** *m.*) **1** newly-married couple, newly-weds. **2** (*sg.*) newly-married man.
молод|о́й (мо́лод, ∼а́, мо́лодо) *adj.* **1** young; (*свойственный молодости*) youthful; **м. задо́р** youthful hotheadedness; **м. карто́фель** new potatoes; **м. ме́сяц** new moon. **2** *as n.* (*coll.*) **м., ∼о́го** *m.* bridegroom; **∼а́я, ∼о́й** *f.* bride; **∼ы́е, ∼ы́х** newly-married couple, newly-weds.
мо́лодост|ь, и *f.* youth; youthfulness.
молодцева́т|ый (∼, ∼а) *adj.* dashing.
моло́дчик, а *m.* (*coll.*) thug.
молодчи́н|а, ы *c.g.* (*coll.*) = **молоде́ц**
мо́лод|ь, и *f.* young; fry.
моложа́вост|ь, и *f.* youthful appearance (*for one's years*).
моложа́в|ый (∼, ∼а) *adj.* (*человек*) young-looking; (*вид*) youthful.
моло́|же *comp. of* ⇒**∼до́й**
моло́к|и, ∼ *pl.* soft roe, milt.
молок|о́, а́ *no pl.*, *nt.* milk.
молокво́з, а *m.* milk tanker.
молокосо́с, а *m.* (*coll.*) greenhorn, raw youth.
мо́лот, а *m.* hammer; **кузне́чный м.** sledge-hammer.
молоти́лк|а, и *f.* threshing-machine.
молоти́льщик, а *m.* thresher.
моло|ти́ть, чу́, ∼́тишь *impf.* (*of* ⇒**с∼**) to thresh.
молот|о́к, ка́ *m.* hammer; **отбо́йный м.** pneumatic drill; **прода́ть с ∼ка́** to sell by auction, auction.
молото́ч|ек, ка *m.* **1** *dim. of* ⇒**молото́к. 2** (*anat.*) malleus.
мо́лот|ый (∼, ∼а) *p.p.p. of* ⇒**моло́ть** *and adj.* ground.
моло́ть, мелю́, ме́лешь *impf.* (*of* ⇒**с∼**) to grind; **м. вздор** (*fig., coll.*) to talk nonsense *or* rot.
молотьб|а́, ы́ *f.* threshing.
молоча́|й, я *m.* (*bot.*) euphorbia.
моло́чн|ая, ой *f.* dairy; creamery.
моло́чник¹, а *m.* (*посуда*) milk-jug.
моло́чник², а *m.* (*разносчик молока*) milkman.
моло́чниц|а¹, ы *f.* milk-seller.
моло́чниц|а², ы *f.* (*med.*) thrush.
моло́чност|ь, и *f.* (*agric.*) yield (*of cow*).
моло́чн|ый *adj.* **1** *adj. of* ⇒**молоко́; м. брат** foster-brother; **∼ые изде́лия** dairy products; **∼ое стекло́** frosted glass; **∼ое хозя́йство** dairy-farm(ing). **2** milky; lactic; **∼ая кислота́** (*chem.*) lactic acid.
мо́лча *adv.* silently, in silence.
молчали́в|ый (∼, ∼а) *adj.* **1** (*человек*) taciturn, silent. **2** (*одобрение*) tacit, unspoken.
молча́ни|е, я *nt.* silence.
молч|а́ть, у́, и́шь *impf.* to be silent; (**о**+*p.*) to keep silent (about).
молч|ко́м *adv.* (*coll.*) = **∼а**
молчо́к *m. indecl.* (*coll.*) silence; **об э́том — м.!** not a word of (about) this!
мол|ь, и *f.* (clothes-)moth.
мольб|а́, ы́ *f.* entreaty, supplication.
мольбе́рт, а *m.* easel.
моля́щ|ийся, егося *m.* worshipper.
моме́нт, а *m.* **1** (*миг*) moment; instant; **в да́нный м.** at the present time; **на м. прове́рки** at the time of inspection; **лови́ м.!** now's your chance!; go for it! **2** (*черта*) feature, element, factor. **3** (*phys.*) moment.
момента́льно *adv.* in a moment, instantly.
момента́л|ьный (∼ен, ∼ьна) *adj.* instantaneous; **м. сни́мок** snapshot.
моме́нтами *adv.* (*coll.*) now and then.
Мона́ко *nt. indecl.* Monaco.
мона́рх, а *m.* monarch.
монархи́зм, а *m.* monarchism.
монархи́ст, а *m.* monarchist.
монархи́ст|ка, ки *f. of* ⇒∼
монархи́ческий *adj.* monarchic(al).
мона́рхи|я, и *f.* monarchy.
мона́рший *adj. of* ⇒**мона́рх**
монасты́рский *adj.* monastic.
монасты́р|ь, я́ *m.* monastery; **(же́нский) м.** convent, nunnery.
мона́х, а *m.* monk; friar; **постри́чься в ∼и** to take the monastic vows.
мона́хин|я, и *f.* nun; **постри́чься в ∼и** to take the veil.
мона́шенк|а, и *f.* (*coll.*) nun.
мона́шеский *adj.* monastic; (*fig., joc.*) monkish.
мона́шеств|о, а *nt.* **1** (*монашеская жизнь*) monasticism. **2** (*collect.*) (*монахи*) monks.
Монбла́н, а *m.* Mont Blanc.
монго́л, а *m.* Mongol, Mongolian.
Монго́ли|я, и *f.* Mongolia.
монго́л|ка, ки *f. of* ⇒∼
монго́льский *adj.* Mongolian.
моне́т|а, ы *f.* coin; **разме́нная м.** change; **плати́ть кому́-н. той же ∼ой** (*fig.*) to give s.o. a dose of his own medicine; **приня́ть за чи́стую ∼у** (*fig., coll.*) to take at face value, take in good faith.
монетари́ст, а *m.* (*econ.*) monetarist.
монетари́ст|ский *adj. of* ⇒∼
моне́тный *adj.* monetary; **м. двор** mint.
мони́ст|о, а *nt.* necklace.
монито́р, а *m.* (*TV, comput.*) monitor.
мо́но *nt. indecl.* mono.
монога́ми|я, и *f.* monogamy.
монога́м|ный (∼ен, ∼на) *adj.* monogamous.
моногра́мм|а, ы *f.* monogram.
моногра́фи|я, и *f.* monograph.
моно́кл|ь, я *m.* monocle.
моноли́т, а *m.* monolith.
моноли́тност|ь, и *f.* monolithic character, solidity.
моноли́т|ный (∼ен, ∼на) *adj.* monolithic (*also fig.*; *pol.*); (*fig.*) solid.
моноло́г, а *m.* monologue, soliloquy.
монома́н, а *m.* (*med.*) monomaniac.
монома́ни|я, и *f.* (*med.*) monomania.
моноплан, а *m.* monoplane.
монополиза́ци|я, и *f.* monopolization.
монополизи́р|овать, ую *impf. and pf.* to monopolize.
монополи́ст, а *m.* monopolist.
монополисти́ческий *adj.* monopolistic.
монопо́ли|я, и *f.* (*econ. and fig.*) monopoly.
монопо́л|ьный *adj. of* ⇒**∼ия; ∼ьное пра́во** exclusive rights.
моноре́льсовый *adj.* monorail.
моноспекта́кл|ь, я *m.* one-man/-woman show.
монотеи́зм, а *m.* monotheism.
монотеисти́ческий *adj.* monotheistic.
моноти́п, а *m.* (*typ.*) Monotype (*propr.*) machine (*machine that casts type letter by letter*).
моното́н|ный (∼ен, ∼на) *adj.* monotonous.
монофони́ческий *adj.* mono(phonic).
монохро́мный *adj.* monochrome.
моноци́кл, а *m.* unicycle.
монпансье́ *nt. indecl.* fruit drops.

М

Монреа́л|ь, я *m.* Montreal.
мо́нстр, а *m.* monster.
монта́ж, а́ *m.* **1** (*tech.*) (*действие*) assembling, mounting, installation. **2** (*cin.*) editing, montage; (*art, mus., liter.*) arrangement.
монта́жник, а *m.* (*на стройке*) rigger; (*на заводе*) fitter.
монта́жни|ца, цы *f. of* ⇨**~к**
Мо́нте-Ка́рло *m. indecl.* Monte-Carlo.
монтёр, а *m.* **1** fitter. **2** (*электромонтёр*) electrician.
монти́р|овать, ую *impf.* (*of* ⇨**с~**) **1** (*tech.*) to assemble, mount, fit. **2** (*cin.*) to edit; (*art, mus., liter.*) to arrange.
монуме́нт, а *m.* monument.
монумента́л|ьный (~ен, ~ьна) *adj.* monumental (*also fig.*).
мопе́д, а *m.* moped.
мопс, а *m.* pug(-dog).
мор, а *m.* (*obs. and coll.*) plague, wholesale deaths, high mortality.
морализи́р|овать, ую *impf.* to moralize.
морали́ст, а *m.* moralist.
морали́ст|ка, ки *f. of* ⇨**~**
мора́л|ь, и *f.* **1** (*нормы поведения*) (code of) morals, ethics. **2** (*coll.*) (*нравоучение*) moralizing; **чита́ть м.** to moralize, preach. **3** (*басни*) moral.
мора́л|ьный (~ен, ~ьна) *adj.* moral; ethical.
морато́ри|й, я *m.* (*leg., comm.*) moratorium.
морг, а *m.* morgue, mortuary.
морганати́ческий *adj.* morganatic.
морг|а́ть, а́ю *impf.* (*of* ⇨**~ну́ть**) to blink; to wink.
морг|ну́ть, ну́, нёшь *pf. of* ⇨**~а́ть; гла́зом не ~ну́в** (*coll.*) without batting an eyelid.
мо́рд|а, ы *f.* **1** snout, muzzle. **2** (*coll.*) (*лицо*) mug.
мордв|а́, ы́ *f.* (*collect.*) the Mordva, the Mordvins.
мордви́н, а *m.* Mordvin.
мордви́н|ка, ки *f. of* ⇨**~**
Мо́рдви|я, и *f.* = **Мордо́вия**
морде́нт, а *m.* (*mus.*) mordent.
мордобо́|й, я *m.* (*sl.*) fight.
Мордо́ви|я, и *f.* Mordvinia.
мордо́вский *adj.* Mordvinian.
мо́р|е, я, *pl.* **~я́, ~е́й** *nt.*: **за́ ~ем** overseas; **из-за ~я** from overseas; **на́ м.** at sea; **у ~я** by the sea; **ему́ м. по коле́но** (*coll.*) he's not afraid of anything.
море́н|а, ы *f.* (*geol.*) moraine.
море́н|ный *adj. of* ⇨**~а**
морёный *adj.* (*of wood*) stained.
морепла́вани|е, я *nt.* navigation, seafaring.
морепла́вател|ь, я *m.* navigator, seafarer.
морепла́вательный *adj.* nautical, navigational.
морехо́д, а *m.* seafarer.
морехо́дност|ь, и *f.* seaworthiness.
морехо́дный *adj.* nautical.
морехо́дств|о, а *nt.* (*obs.*) navigation.
морж, а́ *m.* walrus; (*coll.*) (*open-air*) winter bather.
моржева́ни|е, я *nt.* (*open-air*) winter bathing.
морж|ева́ть, у́ю *impf.* (*coll.*) to bathe in the open air in winter.
моржи́х|а, и *f. of* ⇨**морж**
морж|о́вый *adj. of* ⇨**~**
Мо́рзе *indecl.* Morse; **а́збука М.** Morse code.
морзя́нк|а, и *f.* (*coll.*) Morse code.
мори́лк|а, и *f.* (*tech.*) stain.
мор|и́ть[1], ю́, и́шь *impf.* **1** (*pf.* **вы́-** *and* **по~**) (*уничтожать*) to exterminate. **2** (*pf.* **у~**) (*изнурять*) to exhaust, wear out; **м. го́лодом** to starve.
мор|и́ть[2], ю́, и́шь *impf.* (*дерево*) to stain; **м. дуб** to fume oak.
морко́вк|а, и *f.* (*coll.*) a carrot.
морко́в|ный *adj. of* ⇨**~ь**
морко́в|ь, и *f.* carrots.
мормо́н, а *m.* (*relig.*) Mormon.
моров|о́й *adj.*: **~о́е пове́трие, ~а́я я́зва** plague, pestilence.
моро́жениц|а, ы *f.* **1** (*прибор*) ice-cream maker. **2** (*кафе*) ice-cream parlour (*Br.*), parlor (*US*).
моро́жен|ое, ого *nt.* ice(-cream); **м. в шокола́де** choc-ice.
моро́женщик, а *m.* ice-cream vendor.
моро́женщи|ца, цы *f. of* ⇨**~к**
моро́женый *adj.* frozen; (*картофель*) frost-damaged.
моро́з, а *m.* **1** frost; **у меня́ м. по ко́же подира́ет** (*or* **пошёл**) it makes (made) my flesh creep. **2** (*usu. in pl.*) intensely cold weather.
морози́лк|а, и *f.* (*coll.*) freezer compartment; freezer.
морози́льник, а *m.* freezer.
морози́льн|ый *adj.* freezing; **~ая ка́мера** deep-freeze.
морози́льщик, а *m.* (*coll.*) refrigerator ship.
моро́|зить, жу, зишь *impf.* (*of* ⇨**по~**) **1** to freeze, congeal. **2** (*impers.*): **~зит** it is freezing.
моро́зник, а *m.* hellebore.
моро́зн|ый *adj.* frosty; (*impers., pred.*): **~о** it is freezing.
морозосто́|йкий (~ек, ~йка) *adj.* (*bot.*) frost-resistant.
морозоусто́йчив|ый (~, ~а) *adj.* = **морозосто́йкий**
моро́к|а, и *f.* (*coll., fig.*) darkness, confusion; **с ним одна́ м.** you can get no sense out of him.
морос|и́ть, и́т *impf.* to drizzle.
моро́ч|ить, у, ишь *impf.* (*of* ⇨**об~**) (*coll.*) to fool, pull the wool over the eyes of; **м. го́лову кому́-н.** to take s.o. in.
моро́шк|а, и *f.* cloudberry (*Rubus chamaimorus*).
морс, а *m.* fruit drink.
морск|о́й *adj.* **1** sea; maritime; marine, nautical; **м. волк** (*coll.*) old salt; **~а́я звезда́** starfish; **м. ёж** (*zool.*) sea-urchin; **м. конёк** (*zool.*) sea-horse; **м. пейза́ж** seascape; **м. разбо́йник** pirate; **~а́я сви́нка** guinea-pig; **~а́я свинья́** porpoise. **2** naval; **~а́я пехо́та** marines; **м. флот** navy, fleet.
морти́р|а, ы *f.* (*mil.*) mortar.
морти́р|ный *adj. of* ⇨**~а**
морфе́м|а, ы *f.* (*ling.*) morpheme.
мо́рфи|й, я *m.* (*pharm.*) morphine.
морфологи́ческий *adj.* morphological.
морфоло́ги|я, и *f.* morphology.
морщи́н|а, ы *f.* (*на лице*) wrinkle; (*на ткани*) crease.
морщи́нист|ый (~, ~а) *adj.* wrinkled.
мо́рщ|ить, у, ишь *impf.* **1** (*pf.* **на~**) **м. лоб** to knit one's brow. **2** (*pf.* **с~**) to wrinkle, pucker; **м. гу́бы** to purse one's lips.
морщ|и́ть, и́т *impf.* to crease, ruck up (*intrans.*).
мо́рщ|иться, усь, ишься *impf.* **1** (*pf.* **на~**) to knit one's brow. **2** (*pf.* **по~** *and* **с~**) (*делать гримасы*) to make a wry face, wince. **3** (*pf.* **с~**) (*об одежде*) to crease, wrinkle.
моря́к, а́ *m.* sailor.
Москв|а́, ы́ *f.* **1** (*город*) Moscow; **М. не сра́зу стро́илась** (*prov.*) Rome wasn't built in a day. **2** (*река*) the Moskva.
москви́ч, а́ *m.* Muscovite.
москви́ч|ка, ки *f. of* ⇨**~**
моски́т, а *m.* mosquito.
моски́т|ный *adj. of* ⇨**~; ~ная се́тка** mosquito net.
Моско́ви|я, и *f.* (*hist.*) Muscovy.
моско́вк|а, и *f.* (*zool.*) coal tit.
моско́вск|ий *adj.* (of) Moscow; **~ая Русь** (*hist.*) Muscovy.
мост, ~а́, о ~е, на ~у́, *pl.* **~ы́** *m.* **1** (*через реку*) bridge. **2** (*автомобиля*) axle. **3** (*линия связи*) link.
мо́стик, а *m.* **1** *dim. of* ⇨**мост.** **2**: **капита́нский м.** (*naut.*) (*captain's*) bridge.
мости́льщик, а *m.* paver.
мо|сти́ть, щу́, сти́шь *impf.* **1** (*pf.* **вы́~, за~**) (*дорогу*) to pave. **2** (*pf.* **на~**) (*пол*) to lay.
мостк|и́, о́в *no sg.* **1** (*для перехода*) planked walkway. **2** (*площадка*) wooden platform.
мостов|а́я, о́й *f.* road(way), carriageway.
мост|ово́й *adj. of* ⇨**~**
мо́ськ|а, и *f.* (*coll.*) pug-dog.
мот, а *m.* prodigal, spendthrift.
мота́льный *adj.* (*tech.*) winding.
мот|а́ть[1], а́ю *impf.* **1** (*pf.* **за~, на~**) (*нитки, шерсть*) to wind, reel; **м. себе́ что-н. на ус** (*fig., coll.*) to make a mental note of sth. **2** (*pf.* **~ну́ть**) (+ *i.*; *coll.*) (*головой*) to shake (*head, etc.*). **3** (*coll.*) (*уходить*) to make off.
мота́|ть[2], ю *impf.* (*of* ⇨**про~**) (*coll.*) (*тратить*) to squander.
мота́|ться[1], ется *impf.* (*coll.*) (*болтаться*) to dangle.
мота́|ться[2], юсь *impf.* (*coll.*) (*хлопотать*) to rush about.

мотéл|ь, я *m.* motel.

моти́в¹, а *m.* **1** (*повод*) motive. **2** (*довод*) reason; **привести́ ~ы в пóльзу предложéния** to adduce reasons in support of an assertion.

моти́в², а *m.* **1** (*mus.*) tune, motif. **2** (*fig.*) motif.

мотиви́р|овать, ую *impf. and pf.* to give reasons (for), justify.

мотивирóвк|а, и *f.* reason(s), justification.

мот|нýть, нý, нёшь *pf. of* ⇒**~áть¹**

мото... *comb. form, abbr. of* **1** ***мотóрный¹***. **2** ***моторизóванный***. **3** ***мотоциклéтный***

мотобóт, а *m.* motor-boat.

мотóвк|а, и *f.* (*coll.*) *of* ⇒**мот**

мотовскóй *adj.* wasteful, extravagant.

мотовств|ó, á *nt.* wastefulness, extravagance.

мотогóн|ки, ок *no sg.* motor-cycle races.

мотогóнщик, а *m.* motor cycle racer.

мотогóнщи|ца, цы *f. of* ⇒**~к**

мотодрóм, а *m.* motor-cycle racing track.

мот|óк, кá *m.* skein, hank.

мотоклýб, а *m.* motorcycle club.

мотоколя́ск|а, и *f.* motorized wheel-chair.

мотокрóсс, а *m.* moto-cross, scramble.

мотокроссмéн, а *m.* moto-cross competitor.

мотопéд, а *m.* moped.

мотопехóт|а, ы *f.* motorized infantry.

мотопил|á, ы́ *f.* power saw.

мотопланёр, а *m.* powered glider.

мотóр, а *m.* motor; (*автомобиля, самолёта*) engine.

моторизáци|я, и *f.* motorization.

моторизóв|анный *p.p.p. of* ⇒**~áть** *and adj.* (*mil.*) motorized.

моториз|овáть, ýю *impf. and pf.* to motorize.

моторúст, а *m.* motor-mechanic.

моторúст|ка, ки *f. of* ⇒**~**

мотóрк|а, и *f.* (*coll.*) motor-boat.

мотóр|ный¹ *adj. of* ⇒**~**; **~ная установка** power plant, power unit.

мотóрный² *adj.* (*physiol., psych.*) motor.

моторóллер, а *m.* (motor-)scooter.

мотоспóрт, а *m.* motorcycle racing.

мототрюкáч, á *m.* motorcycle stunt rider.

мотоци́кл, а *m.* motor-cycle.

мотоциклéтный *adj. of* ⇒**мотоци́кл**

мотоциклúст, а *m.* motor-cyclist; biker.

мотоциклúст|ка, ки *f. of* ⇒**~**

мотошлéм, а *m.* crash helmet.

моты́г|а, и *f.* hoe, mattock.

моты́ж|ить, у, ишь *impf.* to hoe.

мотыл|ёк, ькá *m.* moth.

моты́л|ь¹, я́ *m.* (*личинка комара*) mosquito grub (*used to feed fish in aquaria*).

моты́л|ь², я́ *m.* (*tech.*) crank.

мох, мха *and* **мóха, о мхе** *and* **о мóхе, во (на) мхý,** *pl.* **мхи, мхов** *m.* moss.

мохéр, а *m.* mohair.

мохéр|овый *adj. of* ⇒**~**

мохнáт|ый (~, ~а) *adj.* hairy, shaggy; **~ое полотéнце** Turkish towel.

моциóн, а *m.* exercise; constitutional; **дéлать, совершáть м.** to take exercise.

моч|á, ú *f.* urine.

мочáлк|а, и *f.* loofah.

мочáл|о, а *nt.* bast.

мочеви́н|а, ы *f.* (*chem.*) urea.

мочевóй *adj.* urinary, uric; **м. пузы́рь** (*anat.*) bladder.

мочегóнный *adj.* (*med.*) diuretic.

мочеиспускáни|е, я *nt.* urination.

мочеиспускáтельный *adj.*: **м. канáл** (*anat.*) urethra.

мочёный *adj.* (*яблоки*) preserved.

мочеотделéни|е, я *nt.* urination.

мочеполовóй *adj.* (*anat.*) urino-genital.

мочетóчник, а *m.* (*anat.*) ureter.

моч|úть, ý, ~́ишь *impf.* **1** (*pf.* **на~, за~**) (*делать мокрым*) to wet, moisten. **2** (*pf.* **на~, за~**) (*бельё*) to soak; (*лён*) to ret; **м. селёдку** to souse herring. **3** (*pf.* **за~**) (*sl.*) (*убивать*) to kill.

моч|úться, ýсь, ~́ишься *impf.* (*of* ⇒**по~**) (*coll.*) to urinate.

мóчк|а¹, и *f.* (*белья, яблок*) soaking; (*льна*) retting.

мóчк|а², и *f.* (*anat.*) ear lobe.

мочь¹, могý, мóжешь, мóгут, *past* **мог, моглá** *impf.* (*of* ⇒**с~**) to be able; **мóжет быть, быть мóжет** perhaps, maybe; **мóжет** (*coll.*) = **мóжет быть; не мóжет быть!** impossible!; **как живёте-мóжете?** (*coll.*) how are you?; **мне не мóжется** I'm not very well.

моч|ь², и *f.* (*coll.*) power, might; **во всю м., изо всей ~́и, что есть ~́и** with all one's might, with might and main; **~́и нет (как)** it is unendurable, unbearable; **~́и нет, как хóлодно** it's so cold, I can stand it no longer.

мошéнник, а *m.* swindler, crook.

мошéннича|ть, ю *impf.* (*of* ⇒**с~**) to swindle.

мошéннический *adj.* fraudulent, crooked.

мошéнничеств|о, а *nt.* swindling; fraud; cheating.

мóшк|а, и *f.* midge.

мошк|á, ú *f.* (*collect.*) = **мошкарá**

мошкар|á, ы́ *f.* (*collect.*) (swarm of) midges.

мош|нá, ны́, *pl.* **~ны, ~óн** *f.* purse, pouch.

мошóнк|а, и *f.* (*anat.*) scrotum.

мощéни|е, я *nt.* paving.

мощённый *p.p.p. of* ⇒**мости́ть**

мощёный *adj.* paved.

мóщ|и, éй *no sg.* (*relig.*) relics.

мóщност|ь, и *f.* power; (*tech.*) capacity, rating; output; **двигатель ~ью в сто лошади́ных сил** hundred horsepower engine.

мóщ|ный (~ен, ~нá, ~но) *adj.* powerful, mighty; (*рост*) vigorous.

мо|щý, сти́шь *see* ⇒**~сти́ть**

мощ|ь, и *f.* power, might.

мó|ю, ешь *see* ⇒**мыть**

мóющ|ий *pres. part. act. of* ⇒**мыть** *and adj.* detergent; **~ие срéдства** detergents.

мóющ|ийся *adj.* washable; **~иеся обóи** washable wallpaper.

мраз|ь, и *no pl., f.* (*coll.*) dregs, scum.

мрак, а *m.* darkness, gloom (*also fig., rhet.*); **покры́то ~́ом неизвéстности** shrouded in mystery.

мракобéс, а *m.* obscurantist.

мракобéси|е, я *nt.* obscurantism.

мрáмор, а *m.* marble.

мрáморный *adj.* marble; (*fig.*) (white as) marble; (*бумага*) marbled.

мрачнé|ть, ю *impf.* (*of* ⇒**по~**) to grow dark; to grow gloomy.

мрáч|ный (~ен, ~нá, ~но) *adj.* **1** dark, sombre (*Br.*), somber (*US*). **2** (*fig.*) gloomy, dismal.

мрé|ть, ешь *impf.* (*coll.*) to be dimly visible.

мсти́тел|ь, я *m.* avenger.

мсти́тел|ьный (~ен, ~ьна) *adj.* vindictive.

мсти́ть, мщу, мстишь *impf.* (*of* ⇒**ото~**) **1** (+*d.*) to take revenge/ vengeance (on s.o.); **м. врагý** to take (revenge) on one's enemy. **2** (**за**+*a.*) to avenge; **м. за дрýга** to avenge one's friend. **3** (+*d. and* **за**+*a.*) to take revenge on s.o. for sth.; to avenge o.s. on s.o. for sth.

МТС *f. indecl.* (*abbr. of* ***маши́нно-трáкторная стáнция***) machinery and tractor station.

муáр, а *m.* moire, watered silk.

муáровый *adj.* moiré.

мудáк, á *m.* (*vulg.*) prick, arsehole (*Br.*), asshole (*US*) (*person*).

му|дéть, жý, ди́шь *impf.* (*of* ⇒**промудéть**) (*vulg.*) to talk balls or bollocks.

муджахи́д|ы, ов *no sg.* mujahidin, mujahedin, mujahedeen.

мýди, мудéй *pl.* (*sg.* **мудé** *nt. indecl.*) (*vulg.*) bollocks, balls (= *testicles*).

муди́ла *c.g.* (*vulg.*) = **мудáк**

муди́стик|а, и *f.* (*vulg.*) bollocks (= *nonsense*).

мудн|я́, ú *f.* (*vulg.*) (a load of) bollocks (= *nonsense*); **порóть ~ю́** to talk a load of bollocks.

мудрен|ée *comp. of* ⇒**~́ый** *only in phr.* (*coll.*): **ýтро вéчера м.** sleep on it.

мудрён|ый (~, ~á) *adj.* (*coll.*) **1** (*загадочный*) strange, queer, odd; **не ~ó, что...** it is no wonder that .... **2** (*трудный*) difficult, abstruse, complicated.

мудрéц, á *m.* (*rhet.*) sage, wise man.

мудр|úть, ю, и́шь *impf.* (*of* ⇒**на~**) (*coll.*) to complicate matters unnecessarily; **не ~йте!** don't try to be clever!

му́дрост|ь, и *f.* wisdom.

му́дрств|овать, ую *impf.* (*coll.*) to philosophize.

му́др|ый (~, ~а́, ~о) *adj.* wise.

муж, а *m.* **1** (*pl.* **~ья́, ~е́й, ~ья́м**) husband. **2** (*pl.* **~и́, ~е́й, ~а́м**) (*rhet.*) (*мужчина*) man; **госуда́рственный м.** statesman; **м. нау́ки** man of science; **учёный м.** scholar.

мужа́|ть, ю *impf.* (*of* ⇒**воз~**) **1** (*становиться взрослым*) to grow up, mature. **2** (*становиться сильнее*) to gain in strength; to become stronger.

мужа́|ться, юсь *impf.* to take heart, take courage; **~йтесь!** courage!

мужело́ж|ец, ца *m.* sodomite.

мужело́жств|о, а *nt.* sodomy.

мужен|ёк, ька́ *m.* (*coll.*) hubby.

мужененави́стниц|а, ы *f.* misandrist.

мужененави́стнический *adj.* misandrist, misandrous.

мужененави́стничеств|о, а *nt.* misandry.

мужеподо́б|ный (~ен, ~на) *adj.* mannish.

му́жествен|ный (~, ~на) *adj.* manly, steadfast.

му́жеств|о, а *nt.* courage, fortitude.

мужи́к, а́ *m.* **1** (*крестьянин*) muzhik, moujik (*Russian peasant*). **2** (*coll.*) (*мужчина*) bloke, guy.

мужикова́т|ый (~, ~а) *adj.* (*coll.*) loutish, boorish.

мужи́цкий *adj. of* ⇒**мужи́к 1**

мужск|о́й *adj.* (*голос, рукопожатие*) masculine; (*пол, клетка*) male; (*туалет, платье*) men's; **м. род** (*gram.*) masculine gender; **~а́я шко́ла** boys' school.

мужчи́н|а, ы *m.* man.

му́з|а, ы *f.* muse.

музееве́дени|е, я *nt.* museum management studies.

музе́|й, я *m.* museum; **м. восковы́х фигу́р** waxworks.

музе́й|ный *adj. of* ⇒**~**

му́зык|а, и *f.* music; **блатна́я м.** thieves' cant; **он испо́ртил всю ~у** he upset the apple-cart.

музыка́льност|ь, и *f.* musicality.

музыка́л|ьный (~ен, ~ьна) *adj.* music (*attr.*); musical.

музыка́нт, а *m.* musician; **у́личный м.** busker.

музыкове́д, а *m.* musicologist.

музыкове́дени|е, я *nt.* musicology.

му́к|а, и *f.* torment; torture; (*pl.*) pangs, throes; **родовы́е ~и** birth-pangs.

мук|а́, и́ *f.* (*пшеничная, кукурузная*) flour; (*костяная, рыбная*) meal.

мукомо́льный *adj.* flour-milling.

мул, а *m.* mule.

мула́т, а *m.* mulatto.

мула́т|ка, ки *f. of* ⇒**~**

мулине́ *nt. indecl.* stranded thread (*for embroidery*).

мулл|а́, ы́ *m.* mullah.

му́льтик, а *m.* (*coll.*) = **мультфи́льм**

мультимеди́йный *adj.* multimedia.

мультиме́диа *f. indecl.* multimedia.

мультиплика́тор, а *m.* animator, cartoonist.

мультиплика́ци|я, и *f.* (film) animation.

мультфи́льм, а *m.* cartoon, animation.

мультя́шк|а, и *f.* (*coll.*) = **мультфи́льм**

мумифици́р|овать, ую *impf. and pf.* to mummify.

му́ми|я, и *f.* mummy (*embalmed corpse*).

мунди́р, а *m.* full-dress uniform; **карто́фель в ~е** potatoes cooked in their jackets.

мундшту́к, а́ *m.* **1** (*сигареты, трубки*) mouth-piece; (*трубочка в которую вставляют сигарету*) cigarette-holder. **2** (*mus.*) mouth-piece.

муниципалите́т, а *m.* municipality; town council; **зда́ние ~а** town hall.

муниципа́льн|ый *adj.* municipal; **~ая кварти́ра** council flat.

мур|а́, ы *f.* (*coll.*) mess; nonsense.

мурав|е́й, ья́ *m.* ant.

мураве́йник, а *m.* ant-hill.

мура́в|ить, лю, ишь *impf.* to glaze (*pottery*).

муравье́д, а *m.* (*zool.*) ant-eater.

мурав|ьи́ный *adj.* **1** *adj. of* ⇒**~е́й. 2** (*chem.*) formic.

мура́шк|а, и *f.* (*coll.*) small insect; **~и по спине́ бе́гают** it gives one the creeps.

мурлы́|кать, чу, чешь *impf.* **1** (*о кошке*) to purr. **2** (*coll.*) (*о человеке*) to hum.

муска́т, а *m.* **1** (*орех*) nutmeg. **2** (*виноград*) muscadine, muscat. **3** (*вино*) muscatel, muscat.

муска́т|ный *adj. of* ⇒**~**; **м. оре́х** nutmeg.

му́скул, а *m.* muscle; **у него́ ни оди́н м. не дро́гнул** (*fig.*) he didn't move a muscle.

мускулату́р|а, ы *f.* (*collect.*) muscular system, musculature.

му́скули́ст|ый (~, ~а) *adj.* muscular, brawny.

му́скульный *adj.* muscular.

му́скус, а *m.* musk.

му́скусн|ый *adj.* musky; **~ая кры́са** musk-rat.

музли́н, а *m.* muslin.

мусли́н|овый *adj. of* ⇒**~**

му́сл|ить, ю, ишь *impf.* (*of* ⇒**на~**) (*coll.*) **1** (*смачивать слюной*) to wet, moisten; **м. ни́тку** to moisten a thread (*when threading a needle*). **2** (*пачкать слюной*) to beslobber; (*пачкать руками*) to soil (*with wet or sticky hands*); **м. кни́гу** to dog-ear, soil a book.

мусо́л|ить, ю, ишь *impf.* (*of* ⇒**за~, на~**) **1** = **му́слить. 2** (*fig.*) to spend much time (over); **м. вопро́с** to drag out a question.

му́сор, а *m.* rubbish (*Br.*), garbage (*US*).

му́сор|ить, ю, ишь *impf.* (*of* ⇒**на~**) (*coll.*) to make a mess.

му́сор|ный *adj. of* ⇒**~**; **м. я́щик** dustbin (*Br.*), garbage can (*US*).

мусорово́з, а *m.* dust-cart (*Br.*), garbage truck (*US*).

мусородроби́лк|а, и *f.* waste-disposal unit.

мусоропрово́д, а *m.* refuse chute.

мусоросжига́тельн|ый *adj.*: **~ая печь** incinerator.

мусороубо́рочн|ый *adj.* pertaining to refuse collection; **~ая маши́на** = **мусорово́з**

му́сорщик, а *m.* dustman (*Br.*), garbage collector (*US*).

мусс, а *m.* (*cul.*) mousse.

мусси́р|овать, ую *impf.* to exaggerate, inflate (*significance of sth.*).

муссо́н, а *m.* (*geog.*) monsoon.

муста́нг, а *m.* (*zool.*) mustang.

мусульма́н|ин, ина, *pl.* **~е, ~** *m.* Muslim.

мусульма́н|ка, ки *f. of* ⇒**~ин**

мусульма́нский *adj.* Muslim.

мусульма́нств|о, а *nt.* Islam.

мута́нт, а *m.* (*biol.*) mutant.

мута́нтный *adj.* (*biol.*) mutant.

мута́ци|я, и *f.* (*biol.*) mutation.

му|ти́ть, чу́, ти́шь *impf.* **1** (*pf.* **вз~, за~**) (*pres. also* **~тишь** *etc.*) (*жидкость*) to cloud. **2** (*pf.* **по~**) (*fig.*) (*возбуждать*) to stir up, upset. **3** (*pf.* **по~**) (*fig.*) (*чувства*) to dull, make dull. **4** (*impers.*): **меня́,** *etc.*, **~ти́т** I *etc.* feel sick.

му|ти́ться, чу́сь, ти́шься *impf.* **1** (*pf.* **за~**) (*pres. also* **~тишься** *etc.*) (*о жидкости*) to grow turbid. **2** (*pf.* **по~**) (*fig.*) to grow dull, dim. **3** (*impers.*; *coll.*): **у меня́ ~ти́тся в голове́** my head is going round.

мутне́|ть, ет *impf.* (*of* ⇒**по~**) to grow cloudy, grow muddy; (*fig.*) to grow dull.

му́тност|ь, и *f.* **1** cloudiness, muddiness. **2** (*fig.*) dullness.

му́т|ный (~ен, ~на́, ~но) *adj.* **1** cloudy, turbid; **в ~ной воде́ ры́бу лови́ть** (*fig.*) to fish in troubled waters. **2** (*fig.*) dull(ed); confused; **~ные глаза́** lacklustre (*Br.*), lackluster (*US*) eyes; **~ное созна́ние** dulled consciousness.

муто́вк|а[1], и *f.* whisk.

муто́вк|а[2], и *f.* (*bot.*) whorl.

му́тор|ный (~ен, ~на) *adj.* (*coll.*) dreary, sombre (*Br.*), somber (*US*); **у него́ бы́ло ~но на душе́** he was in a sombre (*Br.*), somber (*US*) mood.

му́т|ь, и *f.* **1** (*в бутылке*) sediment. **2** (*fig.*) (*в голове*) murk. **3** (*coll.*) (*ерунда*) nonsense, rubbish.

му́фт|а, ы *f.* **1** (*для рук*) muff. **2** (*tech.*) coupling; (*elec.*) connecting box; **м. сцепле́ния** clutch.

му́фти|й, я *m.* (*relig.*) mufti.

му́х|а, и *f.* fly; **кака́я м. его́ укуси́ла** (*fig., coll.*) what's bitten him?; **де́лать из ~и слона́** (*fig.*) to make a mountain out of a mole-hill; **быть под ~ой, с ~ой** (*coll.*) to be three sheets in the wind.

мухл|ева́ть, ю́ю *impf.* (*of* ⇒**с~**) (*coll.*) to cheat, swindle.

мухоло́вк|а, и *f.* **1** fly-paper. **2** (*bot.*) Venus's fly-trap, sundew. **3** (*zool.*) fly-catcher.

мухомо́р, а *m.* (*гриб*) fly agaric (*mushroom*).

муче́ни|е, я *nt.* torment, torture.

му́ченик, а *m.* martyr.

му́чени|ца, цы *f. of* ⇒**~к**

му́чени|ческий *adj. of* ⇒**~к; му́ка ~ческая** excruciating torment.

му́ченичеств|о, а *nt.* martyrdom.

му́ченск|ий *adj. only in phr.* **му́ка ~ая** (*coll.*) excruciating torment.

мучи́тел|ь, я *m.* torturer; tormentor.

мучи́тель|ница, ницы *f. of* ⇒**~**

мучи́тел|ьный (~ен, ~ьна) *adj.* excruciating; agonizing.

му́ч|ить, у, ишь *impf.* (*of* ⇒**за~, из~**) to torment; to worry, harass.

му́ч|иться, усь, ишься *impf.* (*of* ⇒**за~, из~**) **1** (+*i.*, **от**+*g.*) *pass. of* ⇒**~ить; м. от бо́ли** to be racked with pain. **2** (**из-за**+*g.*) to worry (about), feel unhappy. **3** (**над**+*i.*) to torment o.s. (over, about).

мучни́ст|ый (~, ~а) *adj.* farinaceous.

мучн|о́е, о́го *nt.* farinaceous foods.

мучно́й *adj. of* ⇒**мука́**

му́шк|а¹, и *f.* **1** *dim. of* ⇒**му́ха. 2** (*на лице*) beauty-spot.

му́шк|а², и *f.* (*оружия*) foresight; **взять на ~у** to take aim (at).

мушке́т, а *m.* musket.

мушкетёр, а *m.* musketeer.

муштр|а́, ы́ *f.* **1** (*mil.*) drill. **2** (*метод воспитания*) regimentation.

муштр|ова́ть, у́ю *impf.* (*of* ⇒**вы́~**) to drill.

муэдзи́н, а *m.* muezzin.

МФА *m. indecl.* (*abbr. of* ***междунаро́дный фонети́ческий алфави́т***) IPA (*International Phonetic Alphabet*).

мха, мху *see* ⇒**мох**

МХАТ, а *m.* (*abbr. of* ***Моско́вский худо́жественный академи́ческий теа́тр***) Moscow Arts Theatre (*Br.*), Theater (*US*).

мчать, мчу, мчишь *impf.* to rush, whirl along (*trans.*; *coll. also intrans.*).

мч|а́ться, усь, и́шься *impf.* to rush, race, tear along; **м. во весь опо́р** to go at full speed; **вре́мя ~и́тся** time flies.

мши́ст|ый (~, ~а) *adj.* mossy.

мще́ни|е, я *nt.* vengeance, revenge.

мы, *a., g., p.* **нас,** *d.* **нам,** *i.* **на́ми** *pron.* we; **мы с ва́ми** you and I.

мы́ка|ться, юсь *impf.* (*coll.*) to roam, wander.

мы́л|ить, ю, ишь *impf.* (*of* ⇒**на~**) to soap; to lather; **м. кому́-н. го́лову** (*fig., coll.*) to give s.o. a dressing-down.

мы́л|иться, юсь, ишься *impf.* (*of* ⇒**на~**) **1** (*о человеке*) to soap o.s. **2** (*о мыле*) to lather, form a lather.

мы́л|кий (~ок, ~ка́, ~ко) *adj.* freely lathering.

мы́л|о, а, *pl.* **~а́, ~, ~а́м** *nt.* **1** soap. **2** (*у лошади*) foam, lather.

мыловаре́ни|е, я *nt.* soap-making.

мылова́р|енный *adj. of* ⇒**~е́ние; м. заво́д** soap works.

мы́льниц|а, ы *f.* (*блюдечко*) soap-dish; (*коробочка*) soap-box.

мы́л|ьный *adj. of* ⇒**~о; м. ка́мень** soapstone; **~ьная о́пера** soap opera; **~ьные хло́пья** soap-flakes.

мыс, а *m.* (*geog.*) cape, promontory.

мы́сик, а *m.* **1** (*coll.*) protuberance; jutting out part. **2** (*о волосах*) widow's peak.

мы́сленн|ый *adj.* mental; **м. о́браз** mental image; **~ое пожела́ние** unspoken wish.

мы́слим|ый (~, ~а) *adj.* conceivable, thinkable.

мысли́тел|ь, я *m.* thinker.

мысли́тельный *adj.* intellectual, of thought; **м. проце́сс** thought process.

мы́сл|ить, ю, ишь *impf.* **1** (*думать*) to think; to reason. **2** (*представлять себе*) to conceive, imagine.

мысл|ь, и *f.* (**о**+*p.*) thought (of, about); (*идея*) idea; **за́дняя м.** ulterior motive; **о́браз ~ей** way of thinking, views; **у него́ э́того и в ~ях не́ было** it never even crossed his mind; **быть с кем-н. одни́х ~ей** to be of the same opinion as s.o.; **пода́ть м.** to suggest an idea; **собира́ться с ~ями** to collect one's thoughts.

мыта́р|ить, ю, ишь *impf.* (*of* ⇒**за~**) (*coll.*) to harass, torment, try.

мыта́р|иться, юсь, ишься *impf.* (*of* ⇒**за~**) (*coll.*) to be harassed; to have a hard time.

мыта́рств|о, а *nt.* ordeal, hardship.

мыть, мо́ю, мо́ешь *impf.* (*of* ⇒**вы́~, по~**) to wash.

мыть|ё, я́ *nt.* washing; **не ~ём, так ка́таньем** by hook or by crook.

мы́ться, мо́юсь, мо́ешься *impf.* (*of* ⇒**вы́~, по~**) **1** to wash (o.s.). **2** *pass. of* ⇒**мыть**

мыч|а́ть, у́, и́шь *impf.* **1** (*о корове*) to moo; (*о быке*) to bellow. **2** (*fig., coll.*) (*о человеке*) to mumble.

мыша́ст|ый (~, ~а) *adj.* mouse-coloured (*Br.*), -colored (*US*), mousey.

мышело́вк|а, и *f.* mouse-trap.

мы́шечный *adj.* muscular.

мыш|и́ный *adj. of* ⇒**~ь; ~и́ная возня́ (сует́а)** pointless fussing over trifles.

мы́шк|а¹, и *f. dim. of* ⇒**мышь**

мы́шк|а², и *f.* armpit; **под ~у, под ~ой** under one's arm; **взять под ~у** to put under one's arm; **нести́ под ~ой** to carry under one's arm.

мышле́ни|е, я *nt.* thinking, thought.

мыш|о́нок, о́нка, *pl.* **~а́та, ~а́т** young mouse.

мы́шц|а, ы *f.* muscle.

мыш|ь, и, *pl.* **~и, ~е́й** *f.* **1** (*also comput.*) mouse. **2**: **летýчая м.** bat.

мышья́к, а́ *m.* (*chem., pharm.*) arsenic.

мышьяко́вистый *adj.* (*chem.*) arsenious.

мышьяко́вый *adj.* (*chem.*) arsenic.

Мья́нм|а, ы *f.* Myanmar (*formerly Burma*).

Мэн: о́-в М., ~а М. *m.* the Isle of Man.

мэ́нский *adj.*: **м. язы́к** Manx (*language*).

мэр, а *m.* mayor.

мэ́ри|я, и *f.* **1** (*управление*) town council. **2** (*здание*) town hall.

мю́зикл, а *m.* musical.

мю́зик-хо́лл, а *m.* music-hall.

мя́г|кий (~ок, ~ка́, ~ко) *adj.* soft; (*fig.*) mild, gentle; (*о приговоре*) lenient; **м. ваго́н** (*rail.*) soft(-seated) carriage (*Br.*), sleeping car; **м. знак** (*ling.*) soft sign (*name of Russian letter* '**ь**'); **~кое кре́сло** easy chair.

мя́гко *adv.* softly; (*fig.*) mildly, gently; **м. выража́ясь** (*iron.*) to put it mildly, to say the least.

мягкосерде́чи|е, я *nt.* soft-heartedness.

мягкосерде́ч|ный (~ен, ~на) *adj.* soft-hearted.

мягкоте́л|ый (~, ~а) *adj.* soft; (*fig.*) spineless.

мя́г|че *comp. of* ⇒**~кий** *and* **~ко**

мягчи́тельный *adj.* (*med.*) emollient.

мягч|и́ть, у́, и́шь *impf.* (*of* ⇒**с~**) to soften.

мяки́н|а, ы *f.* chaff.

мя́киш, а *m.* inside, soft part (*of loaf*).

мя́к|нуть, ну, нешь, *past* **~, ~ла** *impf.* (*of* ⇒**раз~**) to soften; to become soft (*also fig.*).

мя́кот|ь, и *f.* **1** (*тела*) flesh. **2** (*плода*) pulp (*of fruit*).

мя́мл|ить, ю, ишь *impf.* (*coll.*) **1** (*pf.* **про~**) (*говорить невнятно*) to mumble. **2** (*no pf.*) (*действовать нерешительно*) to vacillate; to procrastinate.

мя́мл|я, и, *g. pl.* **~ей** *c.g.* (*coll.*) **1** (*тот, кто бормочет*) mumbler. **2** (*нерешительный человек*) ditherer, spineless person.

мяси́ст|ый (~, ~а) *adj.* fleshy; meaty.

мясн|а́я, о́й *f.* butcher's (shop).

мясни́к, а́ *m.* butcher.

мяс|но́й *adj. of* ⇒**~о; ~ны́е консе́рвы** tinned meat.

мя́с|о, а *nt.* meat; **пу́шечное м.** (*fig.*) cannon fodder; **сла́дкое м.** (*cul.*) sweetbread.

мясое́д, а *m.* (*eccl.*) season during which the eating of meat is permitted (*esp. from Christmas to Shrovetide*)

мясокомбина́т, а *m.* meat processing and packing factory.

мясору́бк|а, и *f.* mincing-machine.

мя|сти́сь, тýсь, тёшься *impf.* (*obs.*) to be disturbed.

мя́т|а, ы *f.* (*bot.*) mint; **пе́речная м.** peppermint.

мяте́ж, а́ *m.* mutiny, revolt.

мяте́жник, а *m.* mutineer, rebel.

М

мятéж|ный (~ен, ~на) *adj.* **1** rebellious, mutinous. **2** (*fig.*) restless; stormy.

мя́тн|ый *adj.* mint; **~ые леденцы́** peppermints.

мя́т|ый *p.p.p. of* ⇒**~ь**

мять, мну, мнёшь *impf.* **1** (*pf.* **раз~**) (*глину*) to work up, knead. **2** (*pf.* **из~, с~**) (*бумагу, платье*) to crumple; **м. траву́** to trample grass.

мя́ться[1], **мнётся** *impf.* (*of* ⇒**из~, по~** *and* **с~**) to become crumpled; to crease easily.

мя́ться[2], **мнусь, мнёшься** *impf.* (*coll.*) to vacillate, hesitate.

мяу́ка|ть, ю, *impf.* to mew, miaow.

мяч, á *m.* ball.

мя́чик, а *m. dim. of* ⇒**мяч**

Н н

на́[1] *int.* (*coll.*) here; here you are; here, take it; **на́ кни́гу!** here, take the book!; **вот тебе́ на́!** well, I never!; well, how d'you like that?

на[2] *prep.* **I.** + *a.* **1** on (to); to; into; over, through; **положи́те кни́гу на стол** put the book on the table; **сесть на авто́бус, по́езд** to board a bus, a train; **сесть на парохо́д** to go on board; **на Украи́ну** to (the) Ukraine; **на се́вер** to the North; **на се́вер от** (to the) north of; **на заво́д** to the factory; **на конце́рт** to a concert; **слепо́й на оди́н глаз** blind in one eye; **перевести́ на англи́йский** to translate into English; **положи́ть на му́зыку** to set to music; **сла́ва его́ греме́ла на весь мир** his fame resounded throughout the world.
2 (*о времени деятельности*) at; on; until, to (*or untranslated*); **на друго́й день, на сле́дующий день** (the) next day; **на Но́вый год** on New Year's day; **на Рождество́** at Christmas; **на Па́сху** at Easter; **отложи́ть на бу́дущую неде́лю** to put off until the following week; **на э́тот раз** this time, for this once.
3 (*при обозначении срока*) for; **на два дня** for two days; **собра́ние назна́чено на понеде́льник** the meeting is fixed for Monday; **уро́к на за́втра** the lesson for tomorrow; (*при обозначении цели, назначения*) for; **на́ зиму** for the winter; **на чёрный день** (*fig.*) for a rainy day; **на что э́то тебе́ ну́жно?** what do you want it for?; **ко́мната на двои́х** a room for two; **лес на постро́йку** building timber; **де́ньги на еду́** money for food; **учи́ться на инжене́ра** (*coll.*) to study engineering; **на беду́** unfortunately.
4 (*при обозначении меры*) by (*or untranslated*); **коро́че на дюйм** shorter by an inch; **купи́ть на вес** to buy by weight; **опозда́ть на час** to be an hour late; **ста́рше на три го́да** three years older; **четы́ре ме́тра (в длину́) на два (в ширину́)** four metres (long) by two (broad); (*при умножении, делении*) **помно́жить пять на три** to multiply five by three; **дели́ть на два** to divide into two.
5 (*при обозначении стоимости*) worth (*of sth.*); **ма́рок на рубль** a rouble's worth of stamps.
● **II.** + *p.* **1** on, upon; in; at; **на столе́** on the table; **на бума́ге** on paper (*also fig.*); **на Украи́не** in (the) Ukraine; **на се́вере** in the North; **на заво́де** at the factory; **на конце́рте** at a concert; **на со́лнце** in the sun; **на чи́стом, во́льном во́здухе** in the open air; **на дворе́, на у́лице** out of doors; **на рабо́те** at work; **на излече́нии** undergoing medical treatment; **на вёслах** under oars; **на мо́ре** at sea; **идти́ на паруса́х** to go sailing; **игра́ть на роя́ле** to play the piano; **висе́ть на потолке́** to hang from the ceiling; **жа́рить на ма́сле** to fry; **на свои́х глаза́х** before one's eyes; **на его́ па́мяти** within his recollection; **писа́ть на неме́цком языке́** to write in German; **оши́бка на оши́бке** blunder upon blunder.
2 (*во время чего-нибудь*) in (*or untranslated*); during; **на э́той неде́ле** this week; **на лету́** in flight, during (the) flight; **на кани́кулах** during the holidays.
3 (*при помощи чего-нибудь*) on (*or untranslated*); **на ва́те** padded; **матра́ц на рессо́рах** sprung mattress; **э́тот дви́гатель рабо́тает на не́фти** this engine runs on oil.
4 (*о транспорте*) by; **е́хать на по́езде/авто́бусе** to go by train/bus.

на... *as vbl. pref.* **I.** *forms pf. aspect.*
● **II.** *indicates* **1** action continued to sufficiency, to point of satisfaction or exhaustion. **2** action relating to determinate quantity or number of objects.

наб. (*abbr. of* ***на́бережная***) Embankment.

наба́в|ить, лю, ишь *pf.* (*of* ⇒**~ля́ть**) to add (to), increase; **н. ша́гу** to quicken one's pace.

наба́вк|а, и *f.* = **надба́вка**

набавля́|ть, ю, *impf. of* ⇒**наба́вить**

набалда́шник, а *m.* knob; walking-stick handle.

набальзами́р|овать, ую *pf. of* ⇒**бальзами́ровать**

наба́т, а *m.* alarm bell, tocsin; **бить (ударя́ть) (в) н.** to sound the alarm (*also fig.*).

наба́т|ный *adj. of* ⇒**~**

набе́г, а *m.* raid; foray.

набе́га|ть, ю, *pf.* (*coll.*) to cause o.s. (*heart trouble, etc.*) by running.

набега́|ть, ю, *impf. of* ⇒**набежа́ть**

набе́га|ться, юсь *pf.* to tire o.s. out with running about; (*вдоволь побегать*) to have one's fill of running.

набе|гу́, жи́шь, гу́т *see* ⇒**~жа́ть**

набедоку́р|ить, ю, ишь *pf. of* ⇒**бедоку́рить**

набе|жа́ть, гу́, жи́шь, гу́т *pf.* (*of* ⇒**~га́ть**) **1** (**на** + *a.*) to run into, smash into; (*о волнах*) to lap against.
2 (*сбежаться*) to come running (*together*). **3** (*о жидкостях*) to run into; to fill up; (*fig., coll.*) (*накопиться*) to accumulate. **4** (*о ветре*) to spring up.

набекре́нь *adv.* (*of hats*) aslant, tilted; **со шля́пой н.** with one's hat on one side; **у него́ мозги́ н.** (*coll., joc.*) he is crack-brained, crazy.

набел|и́ть(ся), ю́(сь), ~и́шь(ся) *pf. of* ⇒**бели́ть(ся)** 2

на́бело *adv.* clean, without corrections and erasures; **переписа́ть н.** to make a fair copy of.

на́бережн|ая, ой *f.* embankment.

набзд|е́ть, жу́, ди́шь *pf. of* ⇒**бздеть**

набива́|ть(ся), ю(сь) *impf. of* ⇒**наби́ть(ся)**

наби́вк|а, и *f.* stuffing, padding, packing.

набивно́й *adj.* **1** (*матрац*) stuffed.
2 (*о ткани*) printed.

набира́|ть(ся), ю(сь) *impf. of* ⇒**набра́ть(ся)**

наби́т|ый (~, ~а) *p.p.p. of* ⇒**~ь** *and adj.* packed, crowded; **зал ~ битко́м** the hall is crowded out; **н. дура́к** (*coll.*) complete fool.

наб|и́ть[1]**, ью́, ьёшь** *pf.* (*of* ⇒**~ива́ть**) **1** (+*a. and i.*) to stuff (with), pack (with), fill (with); **н. тру́бку** to fill one's pipe; **н. це́ну** to knock up the price; to bid up; **н. оско́мину** to set one's teeth on edge (*also fig.*); **н. ру́ку на чём-н.** (*fig.*) to become an expert, a dab hand (*Br.*). **2** (*text.*) to print.

наб|и́ть², ью́, ьёшь *pf.* (*of* ⇒**~ива́ть**): **н. гвозде́й в сте́ну** to drive (*a number of*) nails into a wall; **н. у́ток** to bag (*a number of*) duck; **н. посу́ды** to smash (*a lot of*) crockery; **н. мо́рду кому́-н.** (*coll.*) to smash s.o.'s face in.

наб|и́ться, ью́сь, ьёшься *pf.* (*of* ⇒**~ива́ться**) **1** (*скопиться*) to crowd (*into a place*); **битко́м н.** to be crowded out. **2** (*coll.*; +*d.*) (*навязаться*) to impose o.s. (upon), inflict o.s. (upon); **н. к кому́-н. в го́сти** to invite o.s. to s.o.'s house (*etc.*).

наблюда́тел|ь, я *m.* observer.

наблюда́тельност|ь, и *f.* powers of observation.

наблюда́тел|ьный *adj.* **1** (**~ен, ~ьна**) (*внимательный*) observant. **2** (*для наблюдения*) observation (*attr.*); **н. пункт** (*mil.*) observation post.

наблюда́|ть, ю *impf.* **1** (*следить глазами; изучать*) to observe; to watch. **2** (**за**+*i.*) (*детьми*) to take care (of), look after. **3** (**за** *and, obs.,* **над**+*i.*) to supervise, superintend; **н. за у́личным движе́нием** to control traffic; **н. за поря́дком** to be responsible for keeping order.

наблюда́|ться, юсь *impf.* **1** (*бывать*) to exist, be found. **2** (**у**+*g.*) to be under the observation of (*a doctor, etc.*).

наблюде́ни|е, я *nt.* **1** observation. **2** (*надзор*) supervision, superintendence.

на́божност|ь, и *f.* piety.

на́бож|ный (~ен, ~на) *adj.* devout, pious.

набо́йк|а, и *f.* **1** (*text.*) (*ткань*) printed cloth. **2** (*узор*) printed pattern on cloth. **3** (*обуви*) heel.

на́бок *adv.* on one side, awry.

наболе́|вший *p.p. of* ⇒**~ть** *and adj.* sore, painful (*also fig.*); **н. вопро́с** urgent question.

набол|е́ть, е́ет *pf.* to become painful; (*о вопросе*) to become urgent; **на душе́ наболе́ло** (*fig.*) my heart aches.

наболта́|ть, ю *pf.* (*coll.*) **1** (+*a. or g.*) (*глупостей*) to talk a lot (*of nonsense, etc.*). **2** (**на**+*a.*) (*наклеветать*) to gossip (about), talk (about); **на неё ~ли** they told a lot of lies about her.

набо́р, а *m.* **1** (*рабочих*) recruitment; (*скорости, высоты*) gaining, gathering. **2** (*typ.*) composition, type-setting. **3** (*комплект*) set, collection; **н. слов** mere verbiage. **4** (*украшение*) decorative plate (*on harness, belt, etc.*).

набо́рн|ая, ой *f.* type-setting office.

набо́рн|ый *adj.* type-setting; **~ая маши́на** typesetter (*machine*).

набо́рщик, а *m.* compositor, type-setter.

набра́сыва|ть, ю *impf. of* ⇒**наброса́ть** *and* **набро́сить**

набра́сыва|ться, юсь *impf. of* ⇒**набро́ситься**

набра́|ть, наберу́, наберёшь, *past* **~л, ~ла́, ~ло** *pf.* (*of* ⇒**набира́ть**) **1** (+*g. or a.*) (*собрать*) to gather; to collect, assemble; **н. у́гля** to take on coal; **н. но́мер** to dial a (*telephone*) number; **н. ско́рость** to pick up, gather speed; **н. высоту́** (*aeron.*) to gain height; to climb; **н. воды́ в рот** (*fig.*) to keep mum. **2** (*рабочих*) to recruit, enrol, engage. **3** (*typ.*) to compose, set up.

набра́|ться, наберу́сь, наберёшься, *past* **~лся, ~ла́сь, ~ло́сь** *pf.* (*of* ⇒**набира́ться**) **1** (*usu. impers.*) (*скопиться*) (*о людях*) to assemble, gather, collect; (*о пыли, деньгах, работе*) to accumulate; **~ло́сь мно́го наро́ду** a large crowd gathered. **2** (+*g.*) (*храбрости, сил*) to find, muster; (*знаний*) to acquire; (*coll., pej.*) (*привычек*) to pick up. **3** (*coll.*) (*напиться*) to get drunk.

набре|сти́, ду, дёшь, *past* **~́л, ~ла́** *pf.* **1** (**на**+*a.*) (*натолкнуться*) to come across; to happen upon; **я ~́л на интере́сную мысль** I have hit on an interesting idea. **2** (*собраться*) to collect, gather; **~ло́ мно́го наро́ду** a large crowd gathered.

наброса́|ть¹, ю *pf.* (*of* ⇒**набра́сывать**) **1** (*наметить*) to sketch, outline; **н. план** to outline a plan. **2** (*записать*) to jot down.

наброса́|ть², ю *pf.* (*бросить*) to throw about; to throw (*in successive instalments*).

набро́|сить, шу, сишь *pf.* (*of* ⇒**набра́сывать**) to throw (on, over); **н. шаль на пле́чи** to throw a shawl over one's shoulders.

набро́|ситься, шусь, сишься *pf.* (*of* ⇒**набра́сываться**) (**на**+*a.*) to fall upon; to go for; **соба́ка ~силась на меня́** the dog went for me; **н. на кого́-н. с вопро́сами** to deluge s.o. with questions; (*на работу, на еду*) to attack, get stuck into.

набро́с|ок, ка *m.* (*рисунок*) sketch; (*статьи*) draft.

набры́зга|ть, ю *pf.* (+*i. or g.*) to splash.

набрю́шник, а *m.* abdominal band.

набрю́шный *adj.* abdominal.

набух|а́ть, а́ю *impf. of* ⇒**~нуть**

набу́х|нуть, ну, нешь, *past* **~, ~ла** *pf.* (*of* ⇒**~а́ть**) to swell.

наб|ью́, ьёшь *see* ⇒**~и́ть**

нава́г|а, и *f.* (*zool.*) navaga (*a small fish of the cod family*).

наважде́ни|е, я *nt.* delusion; (*призрак*) hallucination.

нава́к|сить, шу, сишь *pf. of* ⇒**ва́ксить**

нава́лива|ть(ся), ю(сь) *impf. of* ⇒**навали́ть(ся)**

навал|и́ть, ю́, ~́ишь *pf.* (*of* ⇒**~́ивать**) (*наложить наверх*) to heap, pile; (*возложить*) to load (*also fig.*); *impers.*: **снегу́ ~и́ло по коле́но** the snow had piled up knee deep.

навал|и́ться, ю́сь, ~́ишься *pf.* (*of* ⇒**~́иваться**) (**на**+*a.*) **1** (*coll.*) (*на еду, на работу*) to attack, get stuck into. **2** (*на дверь, на человека*) to lean (on, upon); to bring all one's weight to bear (on). **3** (*насытаться*) to pile up (on); **на него́ ~и́лись забо́ты** he is inundated with worries.

нава́лом *adv.* piled up; **фру́ктов н.** loads of fruit.

наваля́|ть, ю *pf. of* ⇒**валя́ть** 5

нава́р, а *m.* **1** (*жир*) grease (*on the surface of soup*); (*жидкость*) stock. **2** (*coll.*) (*прибыль*) profit.

нава́рива|ть, ю *impf. of* ⇒**навари́ть¹**

нава́рист|ый (~, ~а) *adj.* (*жирный*) with large fat content (*of soup*); (*насыщенный*) saturated.

навар|и́ть¹, ю́, ~́ишь *pf.* (*of* ⇒**~́ивать**) (*металл*) to weld on.

навар|и́ть², ю́, ~́ишь *pf.* (+*g. or a.*) (*супа*) to cook, make (*a quantity of*); (*стали*) to found.

навева́|ть, ю *impf. of* ⇒**наве́ять**

наве́д|аться, аюсь *pf.* (*of* ⇒**~ываться**) (**к**+*d.*; *coll.*) to call (on).

наведе́ни|е, я *nt.* **1** (*орудия*) aiming; (*бинокля*) pointing. **2** (*лака, краски*) application. **3** (*порядка*) establishment; (*справок*) making; (*моста*) laying; (*fig.*): **«н. мосто́в»** bridge-building.

наве|ду́, дёшь *see* ⇒**~сти́**

наве́дыва|ться, юсь, *impf. of* ⇒**наве́даться**

навез|ти́¹, у́, ёшь, *past* **~́, ~ла́** *pf.* (*of* ⇒**навози́ть¹**) (**на**+*a.*) (*везя, натолкнуть*) to drive (on, against).

навез|ти́², у́, ёшь, *past* **~́, ла́** *pf.* (*of* ⇒**навози́ть²**) (*привезти*) to bring (*a quantity of*).

наве́к, *adv.* for ever.

наве́к|и = **~**

наверб|ова́ть, у́ю *pf. of* ⇒**вербова́ть**

наве́рно *adv.* **1** (*вводное слово*) probably, most likely; **он, н., не позвони́т** he probably won't phone. **2** (*несомненно*) for sure; certainly; **я э́то зна́ю н.** I know that for sure.

наве́рно|е *adv.* = **~**

наверн|у́ть, у́, ёшь *pf.* (*of* ⇒**навёртывать**) **1** (*навинтить*) to screw (on). **2** (*намотать*) to wind (round).

наверн|у́ться, у́сь, ёшься *pf.* (*of* ⇒**навёртываться**) **1** (*coll.*) (*подвернуться*) to turn up; (*о слезах*) to well up. **2** (*coll.*) (*о человеке*) to fall (over); (*о машине*) to turn over.

наверняка́ *adv.* (*coll.*) **1** (*несомненно*) for sure, certainly. **2** (*безошибочно*) safely, without taking risks; **бить н.** to take no chances; **держа́ть пари́ н.** to bet on a certainty.

наверста́|ть, ю *pf.* (*of* ⇒**навёрстывать**) to make up (for); **н. поте́рянное вре́мя** to make up for lost time; **н. упу́щенное** to repair an omission.

навёрстыва|ть, ю *impf. of* ⇒**наверста́ть**

навер|те́ть¹, чу́, ~́тишь *pf.* (*of* ⇒**~́тывать**) (*намотать*) to wind (round), twist (round).

навер|те́ть², чу́, ~́тишь *pf.* (*of*

⇨~чивать) (*вертя, наделать*) to drill (*a number of*) (*holes, etc.*).

навёртыва|ть, ю *impf. of* ⇨**наверну́ть** *and* **наверте́ть**[1]

навёртыва|ться, юсь *impf. of* ⇨**наверну́ться**

наве́рх *adv.* (*вверх*) up, upward; (*по лестнице*) upstairs; (*на поверхность*) to the top.

наверху́ *adv.* above; (*в верхнем этаже*) upstairs; (*fig.*) (*в руководстве*) at the top.

наве́рчива|ть, ю *impf. of* ⇨**наверте́ть**[2]

наве́с, а *m.* **1** (*крыша*) roof; (*из холста*) awning. **2** (*скалы*) overhang. **3** (*sport*) lob.

навеселе́ *adv.* (*coll.*) tipsy.

наве́|сить, шу, сишь *pf.* (*of* ⇨~**шивать**[1]) **1** (+*a. or g.*) (*дверь, замок*) to hang; (*повесить много*) to hang (*a number of*) pictures. **2** (*sport*) to lob.

навесн|о́й *adj.*: **~а́я дверь** door on hinges; **~а́я пе́тля** hinge.

наве|сти́[1], **ду́, дёшь,** *past* **~л, ~ла́** *pf.* (*of* ⇨**наводи́ть**) (**на**+*a.*) **1** (*указать направление*) to direct (at); (*орудие, прожектор*) to aim (at); **н. кого́-н. на мысль** to suggest an idea to s.o.; **н. на след** to put on the track. **2** (*лак, краску*) to apply; **н. лоск, гля́нец** to polish, gloss, glaze. **3** (*устроить, сделать*) to lay, put, make; **н. поря́док** to introduce order, establish order; **н. спра́вку** to make an inquiry; **н. ску́ку** to bore; **н. страх** to inspire fear.

наве|сти́[2], **ду́, дёшь,** *past* **~л, ~ла́** *pf.* (*of* ⇨**наводи́ть**) (*привести*) to bring (*a quantity of*).

наве|сти́ть, щу́, сти́шь *pf.* (*of* ⇨~**ща́ть**) to visit, call on.

наве́т, а *m.* slander, calumny.

наве́тренный *adj.* windward.

наве́чно *adv.* for ever.

наве́ш|ать[1], **аю** *pf.* (*of* ⇨~**ивать**[1]) (+*a. or g.*) (*повесить*) to hang (up), suspend.

наве́ш|ать[2], **аю** *pf.* (*of* ⇨~**ивать**[2]) (*конфет*) to weigh out (*a quantity of*).

наве́шива|ть[1], **и** *impf. of* ⇨**наве́сить** *and* **наве́шать**[1]

наве́шива|ть[2], **ю** *impf. of* ⇨**наве́шать**[2]

навеща́|ть, ю *impf. of* **навести́ть**

наве́|ять[1], **ю, ешь** *pf.* (*of* ⇨~**ва́ть**) (*вея, принести*) to blow; (*fig.*; +*a. and* **на**+*a.*) to cast (on, over), plunge (into); **его́ расска́з ~ял грусть на слу́шателей** his story plunged the audience into sadness.

наве́|ять[2], **ю, ешь** *pf.* (*of* ⇨~**ва́ть**) (*зерна*) to winnow (*a quantity of*).

на́взничь *adv.* backwards, on one's back.

навзры́д *adv.*: **пла́кать н.** to sob.

навива́|ть, ю *impf. of* ⇨**нави́ть**

навига́тор, а *m.* navigator.

навигац|ио́нный *adj. of* ⇨~**ия**

навига́ци|я, и *f.* navigation.

навин|ти́ть, чу́, ти́шь *pf.* (*of* ⇨~**чивать**) (**на**+*a.*) to screw (on).

нави́нчива|ть, ю *impf. of* ⇨**навинти́ть**

навис|а́ть, а́ю *impf.* (*of* ⇨~**нуть**) (**на**+*a.*, **над**+*i.*) to hang (over), overhang; (*fig.*) to impend, threaten; **над на́ми ~ла опа́сность** danger threatened us.

нави́с|нуть, ну, нешь, *past* **~, ~ла** *pf. of* ⇨~**а́ть**

нави́с|ший *p.p. act. of* ⇨~**нуть** *and adj.*: **~шие бро́ви** beetling brows.

нав|и́ть, ью, ьёшь, *past* **~и́л, ~ила́, ~и́ло** *pf.* (*of* ⇨~**ива́ть**) (+*a. or g.*) **1** (*намотать*) to wind (on). **2** (*наложить*) to load, stack (*straw, hay*).

навлека́|ть, ю *impf. of* ⇨**навле́чь**

навле|ку́, чёшь, ку́т *see* ⇨~**чь**

навле́|чь, ку́, чёшь, ку́т, *past* **~к, ~кла́** *pf.* (*of* ⇨~**ка́ть**) (**на**+*a.*) to bring (on); **н. на себя́ гнев** to incur anger.

наво|ди́ть, жу́, ~дишь *impf. of* ⇨**навести́**

наво́дк|а, и *f.* (*орудия*) aiming; (*света*) directing; **прямо́й ~ой** at point-blank.

наводне́ни|е, я *nt.* flood, flooding; (*товарами*) flooding, inundation.

наводн|и́ть, ю́, и́шь *pf.* (*of* ⇨~**я́ть**) (+*a. and i.*) to flood (with), inundate (with); (*fig.*): **н. ры́нок дешёвыми това́рами** to flood the market with cheap goods.

наводн|я́ть, я́ю *impf. of* ⇨~**и́ть**

наво́дчик, а *m.* **1** (*mil.*) gun-layer. **2** (*coll.*) tipper-off (*thieves' informant*).

наводя́щий *adj.*: **н. вопро́с** leading question.

наво́|жу, зишь *see* ⇨~**зить**

наво|жу́[1], **~дишь** *see* ⇨~**ди́ть**

наво|жу́[2], **~зишь** *see* ⇨~**зи́ть**

наво́з, а *m.* manure.

наво́|зить, жу, зишь *impf.* (*of* ⇨**у**~) to manure.

наво|зи́ть[1,2], **жу́, ~зишь** *impf. of* ⇨**навезти́**[1,2]

наво|зи́ть[3], **жу́, ~зишь** *pf.* (*coll.*) to get in (*a supply of*).

наво́зник, а *m.* dung-beetle.

наво́з|ный *adj. of* ⇨~; **н. жук** dung-beetle.

на́волочк|а, и *f.* pillow-case, pillow-slip.

навоня́|ть, ю, *pf.* (*coll.*; +*i.*) to stink (of).

навора́чива|ть, ю *impf. of* ⇨**наворoти́ть**

навор|ова́ть, у́ю *pf.* (*coll.*) to steal (*a quantity of*).

наворо|ти́ть, чу́, ~тишь *pf.* (*of* ⇨**навора́чивать**) (*coll.*; +*a. or g.*) to heap up, pile up.

наворо|чу́, ~тишь *see* ⇨~**ти́ть**

наворс|ова́ть, у́ю *pf. of* ⇨**ворсова́ть**

навостр|и́ть, ю́, и́шь *pf.* (*coll.*) to sharpen; **н. у́ши** to prick up one's ears; **н. лы́жи** to take to one's heels.

навостр|и́ться, ю́сь, и́шься *pf.* (**в**+*p. or* +*inf.*; *coll.*) to become good (at), become adept (at); **он ~и́лся пляса́ть** he has become a good dancer.

навощ|и́ть, у́, и́шь *pf. of* ⇨**вощи́ть**

навр|а́ть[1], **у́, ёшь,** *past* **~а́л, ~ала́, ~а́ло** *pf.* (*coll.*) **1** (*pf. of* ⇨**врать**) to tell lies. **2** (**в**+*p.*) to make mistakes (in); **н. в расска́зе** to get the story wrong. **3** (**на**+*a.*) to slander.

навр|а́ть[2], **у́, ёшь** *pf.* (*coll.*; +*a. or g.*) to tell (*a lot of*) (*sc. lies*); **н. вся́ких небыли́ц** to tell all manner of tales.

навре|ди́ть, жу́, ди́шь *pf.* (+*d.*) to do a great deal of harm (to).

навря́д (ли) *adv.* scarcely, hardly.

навсегда́ *adv.* for ever, for good; **раз и н.** once (and) for all.

навстре́чу *adv. and prep.* (+*d.*) to meet; towards; **он вы́шел н. гостя́м** he went out to meet the guests; **идти́ н. кому́-н.** to go to meet s.o.; (*fig.*) to help, show sympathy towards; **идти́ н. чьим-н. пожела́ниям** to meet s.o.'s wishes.

навы́ворот *adv.* (*coll.*) **1** inside out, wrong side out. **2** (*fig.*) the wrong way round.

на́вык, а *m.* skill.

навы́кат(е) *adv.*: **глаза́ н.** bulging eyes.

навы́лет *adv.* (right) through; **пу́ля проби́ла ему́ ру́ку н.** a bullet passed right through his arm.

навы́нос *adv.* to take-away (*Br.*), to go (*US*); for consumption off the premises.

навы́пуск *adv.* worn outside; **руба́ха н.** shirt worn outside of trousers.

навытя́жку *adv.*: **стоя́ть н.** to stand at attention.

навью́чива|ть, ю *impf. of* ⇨**навью́чить**

навью́ч|ить, у, ишь *pf.* (*of* ⇨**вью́чить** *and* ~**ивать**) to load (up).

навя|за́ть[1], **жу́, ~жешь** *pf.* (*of* ⇨~**зывать**) **1** (**на**+*a.*) (*привязать*) to tie on (to), fasten (to). **2** (*fig.*; +*d. and a.*) (*заставить принять*) to thrust (on); to foist (on); **н. кому́-н. сове́т** to thrust advice on s.o.

навя|за́ть[2], **жу́, ~жешь** *pf.* (*of* ⇨~**зывать**) (+*a. or g.*) (*чулки*) to knit (*a number of*).

навяз|а́ть[3], **а́ет** *impf. of* ⇨~**нуть**

навя|за́ться, жу́сь, ~жешься *pf.* (*of* ⇨~**зываться**) (*coll.*; +*d.*) to thrust o.s. (upon), intrude (upon).

навя́з|нуть, нет, *past* **~, ~ла** *pf.* (*of* ⇨~**а́ть**) to stick; **э́то ~ло у нас в зуба́х** (*fig.*) we are sick and tired of it.

навя́зчив|ый (~, ~а) *adj.* **1** (*человек*) importunate; annoying. **2** (*мысль*) persistent; **~ая иде́я** idée fixe, obsession.

навя́зыва|ть(ся), ю(сь) *impf. of* ⇨**навяза́ть(ся)**

нагада́|ть, ю *pf.* (*coll.*; +*a. or g.*) to foretell, predict.

нага́|дить, жу, дишь *pf. of* ⇨**га́дить**

нага́йк|а, и *f.* whip.

нага́н, а *m.* (Nagant) revolver.

нага́р, а *m.* (candle-)snuff.

нагиба́|ть(ся), ю(сь) *impf. of* ⇨**нагну́ть(ся)**

нагишо́м *adv.* (*coll.*) stark naked.

Н

нагла́|дить, жу, дишь *pf.* (*of* ⇒**~живать**) **1** (*платье, много белья*) to iron. **2** (*сделать гладким*) to smooth (out).

нагла́жива|ть, ю *impf. of* ⇒**нагла́дить**

нагла́зник, а *m.* **1** eye-shade. **2** (*в упряжи*) blinker.

нагле́|ть, ю *impf.* (*of* ⇒**об~**) to become impudent, become insolent.

нагле́ц, а́ *m.* impudent fellow, insolent fellow.

на́глост|ь, и *f.* impudence, insolence, impertinence.

наглота́|ться, юсь *pf.* (+*g.*) to swallow (*a large quantity of*).

на́глухо *adv.* tightly, securely; **застегну́ться н.** to do up all one's buttons.

на́гл|ый (~, ~а́, ~о) *adj.* impudent, insolent, impertinent.

нагля|де́ться, жу́сь, ди́шься *pf.* (**на**+*a.*) to see enough (of); **на э́тот вид гляжу́ — не ~жу́сь** I never tire of looking at this view.

нагля́дно *adv.* clearly, graphically.

нагля́дност|ь, и *f.* **1** clearness. **2** (*в обучении*) use of visual aids.

нагля́д|ный (~ен, ~на) *adj.* **1** (*очевидный*) clear; graphic, obvious. **2** (*no short forms*) (*в обучении*) visual; **~ные посо́бия** visual aids; **н. уро́к** object-lesson.

наг|на́ть¹, оню́, о́нишь, *past* **~на́л, ~нала́, ~на́ло** *pf.* (*of* ⇒**~оня́ть**) **1** (*догнать*) to overtake, catch up (with). **2** (*наверстать*) to make up (for). **3** (*fig., coll.*) (*внушить*) to inspire, arouse, occasion.

наг|на́ть², оню́, о́нишь *pf.* (+*a. or g.*) **1** (*овец*) to herd together (*a number of*). **2** (*спирта*) to distil (*Br.*) distill (*US*) (*a quantity of*).

нагне|сти́, ту́, тёшь *pf.* (*of* ⇒**~та́ть**) to compress, force; (*fig.*) (*ситуацию*) to inflame; (*напряжение*) to heighten.

нагнета́тельн|ый *adj.* (*tech.*): **н. кла́пан** pressure valve; **~ая труба́** force pipe.

нагнета́|ть, ю *impf. of* ⇒**нагнести́**

нагне|ту́, тёшь *see* ⇒**~сти́**

нагное́ни|е, я *nt.* (*med.*) festering, suppuration.

нагнои́т|ься, и́тся *pf.* (*med.*) to fester, suppurate.

нагн|у́ть, у́, ёшь *pf.* (*of* ⇒**нагиба́ть**) to bend.

нагн|у́ться, у́сь, ёшься *pf.* (*of* ⇒**нагиба́ться**) to bend (down), stoop.

нагова́рива|ть, ю *impf. of* ⇒**наговори́ть¹**

наговóр, а *m.* **1** (*клевета*) slander, calumny. **2** (*заклинание*) incantation.

наговор|и́ть¹, ю́, и́шь *pf.* (*of* ⇒**нагова́ривать**) **1** (*coll.*; **на**+*a.*) to slander, calumniate. **2**: **н. пласти́нку** to record (one's voice).

наговор|и́ть², ю́, и́шь *pf.* (+*a. or g.*) to talk, say a lot (of); **н. чепуху́** to talk a lot of nonsense.

наговор|и́ться, ю́сь, и́шься *pf.* to talk o.s. out; **они́ не мо́гут н.** they cannot talk enough.

наг|о́й (~, ~а́, ~о) *adj.* (*о человеке*) naked, nude; (*о части тела*) bare.

на́голо́ *adv.* bare; **остри́чь на́голо** to cut close to the skin, crop close; **с ша́шками наголо́** with drawn swords.

на́голову *adv.*: **разби́ть/разгроми́ть н.** to rout, smash.

наголода́|ться, юсь *pf.* to be half-starved.

нагоня́|й, я *m.* (*coll.*) scolding, rating.

нагоня́|ть, ю, *impf. of* ⇒**нагна́ть**

на-гора́ *adv.* (*mining*) to the surface, to the top.

нагора́жива|ть, ю *impf. of* ⇒**нагороди́ть**

нагор|а́ть, а́ет *impf. of* ⇒**~е́ть**

нагор|е́ть¹, и́т *pf.* (*of* ⇒**~а́ть**) **1** (*о свече*) to need snuffing. **2** (+*g.*) (*израсходоваться*) to be used up.

нагор|е́ть², и́т *pf.* (*of* ⇒**~а́ть**) (*impers.,* +*d.*; *coll.*): **тебе́ за э́то ~и́т** you'll get it hot for this.

наго́рн|ый *adj.* **1** mountainous, hilly. **2** (*берег реки*) high. **3**: **Н~ая про́поведь** (*bibl.*) Sermon on the Mount.

нагоро|ди́ть, жу́, ~дишь *pf.* (*of* ⇒**нагора́живать**) **1** (*настроить*) to build, erect (*in large quantity*). **2** (*coll.*) (*навалить*) to pile up, heap up. **3** (*fig.*) (*наговорить*) to talk, (*написать*) write (*a lot of nonsense*); **н. вздо́ра, чепухи́** to talk a lot of nonsense.

наго́рь|е, я *nt.* table-land, plateau.

нагот|а́, ы́ *f.* nakedness, nudity.

нагота́влива|ть, ю *impf. of* ⇒**нагото́вить**

нагото́ве *adv.* in readiness; ready to hand; **быть н.** to hold o.s. in readiness, be on call.

нагото́в|ить, лю, ишь *pf.* (*of* ⇒**нагота́вливать**) (+*a. or g.*) **1** (*запасти*) to lay in (*a supply of*). **2** (*приготовить*) to cook (*a large quantity of*).

награ́б|ить, лю, ишь *pf.* (+*a. or g.*) to amass by robbery.

награ́д|а, ы *f.* **1** reward, recompense; **в ~у** as a reward. **2** (*почётный знак, орден*) award; decoration; (*в школе*) prize.

награ|ди́ть, жу́, ди́шь *pf.* (*of* ⇒**~жда́ть**) (+*a. and i.*) **1** to reward (with). **2** (*орденом, медалью*) to decorate (with); to award, confer; (*fig.*) to endow (with); **н. кого́-н. о́рденом** to confer a decoration upon s.o., award s.o. a decoration; **приро́да ~ди́ла его́ вели́ким тала́нтом** nature has endowed him with great talent.

наград|но́й *adj. of* ⇒**~а**

наградн|ы́е, ы́х *pl. only* bonus.

награжда́|ть, ю *impf. of* ⇒**награди́ть**

награждённ|ый *p.p.p. of* ⇒**награди́ть;** *as n.* **н., ~ого** *m.* recipient (*of an award*).

нагре́в, а *m.* (*воды*) heating.

нагрева́ни|е, я *nt.* heating.

нагрева́тел|ь, я *m.* (*tech.*) heater.

нагрева́тельный *adj.* (*tech.*) heating.

нагрева́|ть(ся), ю(сь) *impf. of* ⇒**нагре́ть(ся)**

нагре́|ть, ю *pf.* (*of* ⇒**~ва́ть**) **1** to warm, heat; **н. ру́ки** (*fig.*) to feather one's nest. **2** (*coll.*) to swindle; **они́ ~ли меня́ на пять рубле́й** they swindled me out of five roubles.

нагре́|ться, юсь *pf.* (*of* ⇒**нагрева́ться**) (*стать тёплым*) to become warm; (*стать горячим*) to become hot; to warm up, heat up.

нагримир|ова́ть, у́ю *pf. of* ⇒**гримирова́ть**

нагроможда́|ть, ю *impf. of* ⇒**нагромозди́ть**

нагроможде́ни|е, я *nt.* pile, heap.

нагромоз|ди́ть, жу́, ди́шь *pf.* (*of* ⇒**громозди́ть** *and* **нагроможда́ть**) to pile up, heap up.

нагруб|и́ть, лю́, и́шь *pf. of* ⇒**груби́ть**

нагру́дник, а *m.* **1** (*детский*) bib. **2** (*рыцарский*) breastplate.

нагру́дн|ый *adj.* chest, breast; **н. знак** badge; **н. карма́н** breast pocket; **~ые мы́шцы** chest muscles.

нагружа́|ть(ся), ю(сь) *impf. of* ⇒**нагрузи́ть(ся)**

нагру|зи́ть, жу́, ~зишь *pf.* (*of* ⇒**грузи́ть** *and* **~жа́ть**) (+*a. and i.*) **1** to load (with). **2** (*fig.*) to burden (with).

нагру|зи́ться, жу́сь, ~зишься *pf.* (*of* ⇒**~жа́ться**) (+*i.*) to load o.s. (with), burden o.s. (with).

нагру́зк|а, и *f.* **1** (*действие*) loading. **2** (*груз*) load. **3** (*fig.*) work; commitments; **преподава́тельская н.** teaching load.

нагрязн|и́ть, ю́, и́шь *pf. of* ⇒**грязни́ть**

нагря́н|уть, у, ешь *pf.* (*вдруг появиться*) to appear unexpectedly; (**на**+*a.*) to descend (on).

нагу́л, а *m.* (*agric.*) fattening.

нагу́лива|ть, ю *impf. of* ⇒**нагуля́ть**

нагул|я́ть, я́ю *pf.* (*of* ⇒**~ивать**) to acquire, develop (*as result of feeding, exercise, etc.*); **н. жи́ру** (*agric.*) to fatten, put on weight; **н. брюшко́** (*fig., joc.*) to develop a paunch; **н. аппети́т** to work up an appetite.

нагуля́|ться, юсь *pf.* to have had a long walk.

над *prep.* +*i.* **1** (*выше*) over, above. **2** (*при обозначении предмета труда*) on; at; **рабо́тать над диссерта́цией** to be working on a dissertation; **смея́ться над** to laugh at.

над... *comb. form* super-, over-.

нада|ва́ть, ю́, ёшь *pf.* (*coll.*) **1** (+*d. and a. or g.*) to give (*a large quantity of*). **2** (*побить*) (+*d.*) to thrash.

надав|и́ть¹, лю́, ~ишь *pf.* (*of* ⇒**~ливать**) (**на**+*a.*) (*кнопку*) to press (on).

надав|и́ть², лю́, ~ишь *pf.* (*of* ⇒**~ливать**) (+*a. or g.*)

1 (*жидкость*) to squeeze out. **2** (*coll.*) (*мух*) to swat (*a quantity of*).

нада́влива|ть, ю *impf. of* ⇨**надави́ть**

нада́ива|ть, ю *impf. of* ⇨**надои́ть**

нада́рива|ть, ю *impf. of* ⇨**надари́ть**

надар|и́ть, ю́, ∼́ишь *pf.* (*of* ⇨**∼́ивать**) (*coll.*; +*d. and a. or g.*) to give (*a large quantity of*); **н. кому́-н. пода́рков** to shower s.o. with presents.

надба́в|ить, лю, ишь *pf.* = **наба́вить**

надба́вк|а, и *f.* (*повышение*) addition, increase; (*о цене*) extra charge; **н. к зарпла́те** rise (*Br.*), raise (*US*) (*in wages*).

надбавля́|ть, ю *impf. of* ⇨**надба́вить**

надбив|а́ть, ю *impf. of* ⇨**надби́ть**

надби́т|ый *p.p.p. of* ⇨**∼ь** *and adj.* cracked; chipped.

над|би́ть, обью́, обьёшь *pf.* (*of* ⇨**∼бива́ть**) to crack; to chip.

надвига́|ть(ся), ю(сь) *impf. of* ⇨**надви́нуть(ся)**

надви́н|уть, у, ешь *pf.* (*of* ⇨**надвига́ть**) to move, pull (up to, over).

надви́н|уться, усь, ешься *pf.* (*of* ⇨**надвига́ться**) **1** (*приблизиться*) to approach, draw near. **2** (*о шапке*) to slip, slide down (over).

надво́дный *adj.* above-water; **н. кора́бль** surface ship.

на́двое *adv.* **1** in two. **2**: **ба́бушка н. сказа́ла** (*coll.*) I wouldn't be too sure about that.

надво́рн|ый *adj.* situated outside; **∼ая постро́йка** outbuilding.

надгорта́нник, а *m.* (*anat.*) epiglottis.

надгро́би|е, я *nt.* gravestone.

надгро́бн|ый *adj.* grave; funeral, graveside; **∼ый ка́мень** gravestone; **∼ая на́дпись** epitaph; **∼ое сло́во** graveside oration.

надгрыз|а́ть, а́ю *impf. of* ⇨**∼́ть**

надгры́з|ть, у́, ёшь, *past* **∼, ∼ла** *pf.* (*of* ⇨**∼а́ть**) to nibble (at).

надда|ва́ть, ю́, ёшь *impf. of* ⇨**∼́ть**

надда́|ть, м, шь, ст, ди́м, ди́те, ду́т, *past* **∼л, ∼ла́, ∼ло** *pf.* (*of* ⇨**∼ва́ть**) (*coll.*; +*a. or g.*) to add, increase, enhance; **н. хо́ду** to increase the pace; **∼й!** get a move on!

надева́|ть, ю *impf. of* ⇨**наде́ть**

наде́жд|а, ы *f.* hope; **в ∼е на** (+*a.*) in the hope of; **пита́ть ∼у** (**на**+*a.*) to cherish hope (of); **подава́ть ∼ы** to promise well; **вся н. на** (+*a.*) (*coll.*) all my/our hope is on.

надёж|ный (∼ен, ∼на) *adj.* (*человек*) reliable, trustworthy; (*замок, фундамент*) solid, secure; (*средство*) safe.

наде́л, а *m.* allotment; land holding.

наде́ла|ть, ю *pf.* (+*a. or g.*) **1** (*пельменей*) to make (*a quantity of*). **2** (*coll.*; +*g.*) (*неприятностей*) to cause (*a lot of*); (*ошибок*) to make (*a lot of*). **3** (*coll.*) (*сделать что-то плохое*) to do (*sth. wrong*); **что ты ∼л?** what have you done?

надел|ённый *p.p.p of* ⇨**∼и́ть; он ∼ён больши́ми спосо́бностями** he is richly talented.

надел|и́ть, ю́, и́шь *pf.* (*of* ⇨**∼я́ть**) (+*a. and i.*) to provide (with); (*fig.*) to endow (with).

наделя́|ть, ю *impf. of* ⇨**надели́ть**

наде́|ну, нешь *see* ⇨**∼ть**

надёрг|ать, аю *pf.* (*of* ⇨**∼ивать**) (+*a. or g.*) to pull, pluck (*a quantity of*).

надёргива|ть, ю *impf. of* ⇨**надёргать** *and* **надёрнуть**

надерз|и́ть, *1st pers. not used,* **и́шь** *pf. of* ⇨**дерзи́ть**

надёр|нуть, ну, нешь *pf.* (*of* ⇨**∼гивать**) (**на**+*a.*) to pull (on, over).

над|еру́, ерёшь *see* ⇨**∼ра́ть**

наде́|ть, ну, нешь *pf.* (*of* ⇨**∼ва́ть**) to put on (*clothes, etc.*).

наде́|яться, юсь, ешься *impf.* (*of* ⇨**по∼**) **1** (**на**+*a.*) (*успех*) to hope (for); **н. на лу́чшее** to hope for the best. **2** (**на**+*a.*) (*друга, помощь*) to rely (on), count on. **3** (+*inf.*) to hope to.

надзе́мный *adj.* (*над поверхностью*) overground; (*на поверхности*) surface.

надзира́тел|ь, я *m.* overseer, supervisor; **тюре́мный н.** prison guard.

надзира́|ть, ю *impf.* (**за**+*i.*) to oversee, supervise.

надзо́р, а *m.* **1** supervision; (*за подозреваемым*) surveillance. **2** (*collect.*) (*орган*) inspectorate.

надив|и́ться, лю́сь, и́шься *pf.* (*coll.*; +*d. or* **на**+*a.*) to admire sufficiently.

надира́|ть, ю *impf. of* ⇨**надра́ть**

надира́|ться, юсь *impf. of* ⇨**надра́ться**

надка́лыва|ть, ю *impf. of* ⇨**надколо́ть**

надколе́нн|ый *adj.*: **∼ая ча́шка** knee-cap; (*anat.*) patella.

надкол|о́ть, ю́, ∼́ешь *pf.* (*of* ⇨**надка́лывать**) (*полено*) to crack.

надкры́ль|е, я *nt.* (*zool.*) wing-case.

надку|си́ть, шу́, ∼́сишь *pf.* (*of* ⇨**∼́сывать**) to take a bite of.

надку́сыва|ть, ю *impf. of* ⇨**надкуси́ть**

надла́мыва|ть(ся), ю(сь) *impf. of* ⇨**надломи́ть(ся)**

надлежа́щий *adj.* appropriate; fitting, proper.

надлеж|и́т, *past* **∼а́ло** (*impers.*, +*d. and inf.*) it is necessary, it is required; **вам н. яви́ться в де́сять часо́в** you are required to present yourself at ten o'clock.

надло́м, а *m.* **1** crack. **2** (*fig.*) breakdown; crack-up.

надлом|и́ть, лю́, ∼́ишь *pf.* (*of* ⇨**надла́мывать**) to break partly; to crack; (*fig.*) (*ослабить*) to overtax, damage.

надлом|и́ться, лю́сь, ∼́ишься *pf.* (*of* ⇨**надла́мываться**) to crack (*also fig.*); **здоро́вье у него́ ∼и́лось** his health has failed, broken down.

надло́м|ленный *p.p.p. of* ⇨**∼и́ть** *and adj.* broken (*also fig.*).

надме́нност|ь, и *f.* haughtiness, arrogance.

надме́н|ный (∼ен, ∼на) *adj.* haughty, arrogant.

надо[1] = **над**

на́до[2] +*d. and inf.* it is necessary; one must, one ought; (+*a. or g.*) there is need of; **не н.** (*i*) (*не нужно*) one need not, (*ii*) (*нельзя*) one must not; **мне н. идти́** I must go, I ought to go; **мне н. вина́** I need some wine; **так ему́ и н.** serves him right!; **н. быть** (*coll.*) probably; **н. же!** well, I never!; **что н.** (*as pred.*; *coll.*) excellent, great; **о́чень н.!** (*coll.*) (*выражение нежелания*) no thanks!

на́до|бно (*coll.*) = **∼**[2]

на́добност|ь, и *f.* necessity, need; **име́ть н. в чём-н.** to require sth.

на́доб|ный (∼ен, ∼на) *adj.* (*coll.*) necessary, needful.

надое́д|а, ы *c.g.* (*coll.*) pain (in the neck), nuisance.

надоеда́ла = **надое́да**

надоеда́|ть, ю *impf. of* ⇨**надое́сть**

надое́длив|ый (∼, ∼а) *adj.* annoying, boring, tiresome.

надое́|сть, м, шь, ст, ди́м, ди́те, дя́т *pf.* (*of* ⇨**∼да́ть**) **1** (+*d. and i.*) to get on the nerves (of), (*просьбами*) to pester (with), plague (with); to bore (with); **он мне до чёртиков ∼л** I'm sick to death of him. **2** (*impers.*, +*d. and inf.*): **мне,** *etc.*, **∼ло** I, *etc.*, am tired (of), sick (of); **нам ∼ло гуля́ть** we are tired of walking.

надо|и́ть, ю́, и́шь *pf.* (*of* ⇨**нада́ивать**) (+*a. or g.*) to obtain (*a quantity of milk*).

надо́|й, я *m.* (*agric.*) yield (*of milk*).

на́долб|а, ы *f.* stake; **противота́нковые ∼ы** anti-tank obstacles.

надо́лго *adv.* for a long time.

надо́мник, а *m.* homeworker.

надо́мни|ца, цы *f. of* ⇨**∼к**

надорв|а́ть, у́, ёшь, *past* **∼а́л, ∼ала́, ∼а́ло** *pf.* (*of* ⇨**надрыва́ть**) to tear slightly; (*fig.*) to (over)strain, overtax.

надорв|а́ться, у́сь, ёшься, *past* **∼а́лся, ∼ала́сь, ∼а́лось** *pf.* (*of* ⇨**надрыва́ться**) **1** (*о бумаге*) to tear slightly (*intrans.*). **2** (*о человеке*) to (over)strain o.s.; (*переутомиться*) to tire o.s. out.

надоу́м|ить, лю, ишь *pf.* (*of* ⇨**∼ливать**) (*coll.*) to advise.

надоу́млива|ть, ю *impf. of* ⇨**надоу́мить**

надпа́рыва|ть, ю *impf. of* ⇨**надпоро́ть**

надпи́лива|ть, ю *impf. of* ⇨**надпили́ть**

надпил|и́ть, ю́, ∼́ишь *pf.* (*of* ⇨**∼́ивать**) to make an incision in (*by sawing*).

надпи|са́ть, шу́, ∼́шешь *pf.* (*of* ⇨**∼́сывать**) (*книгу*) to inscribe.

надпи́сыва|ть, ю *impf. of* ⇒**надписа́ть**

на́дпис|ь, и *f.* inscription.

надпор|о́ть, ю́, ~́ешь *pf.* (*of* ⇒**надпа́рывать**) to unstitch, unpick (*a few stitches*).

надра́|ить, ю *pf. of* ⇒**дра́ить**

над|ра́ть, еру́, ерёшь, *past* **~ра́л, ~рала́, ~ра́ло** *pf.* (*of* ⇒**~ира́ть**) (+*a. or g.*) to tear off, strip (*a quantity of*); **н. у́ши кому́-н.** to pull s.o.'s ears.

над|ра́ться, еру́сь, ерёшься, *past* **~ра́лся, ~рала́сь, ~ра́лось** *pf.* (*of* ⇒**~ира́ться**) (*coll.*) to become sozzled.

надре́з, а *m.* cut, incision; (*зарубка*) notch.

надре́|зать, жу, жешь *pf.* (*of* ⇒**~за́ть** *and* **~зывать**) to make an incision (in).

надрез|а́ть, а́ю *impf. of* ⇒**~́ать**

надре́зыва|ть, ю *impf.* = **надреза́ть**

надруга́тельств|о, а *nt.* (**над**+*i.*) outrage (upon).

надруга́|ться, юсь *pf.* (**над**+*i.*) to commit an outrage (against).

надры́в, а *m.* **1** (*надорванное место*) slight tear, rent. **2** (*физический*) strain. **3** (*fig.*) (*нервный*) breakdown; crack-up. **4** (*возбуждённость*) hysteria.

надрыва́|ть(ся), ю(сь) *impf.* **1** *impf. of* ⇒**надорва́ть(ся). 2** (*no pf.*) (*стараться*) to exert o.s.; to break one's neck. **3** (*no pf.*) (*кричать*) to yell, bellow. **4**: **у меня́ се́рдце ~ется** my heart bleeds.

надры́вист|ый (~, ~а) *adj.* convulsive.

надры́в|ный (~ен, ~на) *adj.* (*истеричный*) hysterical.

надса́д|а, ы *f.* (*coll.*) strain; effort.

надса|ди́ть, жу́, ~́дишь *pf.* (*of* ⇒**~́живать**) (*coll.*) to (over)strain.

надса|ди́ться, жу́сь, ~́дишься *pf.* (*of* ⇒**~́живаться**) (*coll.*) to (over)strain o.s.

надса́д|ный (~ен, ~на) *adj.* (*coll.*) back-breaking; heavy; **н. ка́шель** hacking cough.

надса́жива|ть(ся), ю(сь) *impf. of* ⇒**надсади́ть(ся)**

надсма́трива|ть, ю *impf.* (**за**+*i. or* **над**+*i.*) to oversee, supervise.

надсмо́тр, а *m.* supervision; (*за подозреваемым*) surveillance.

надсмо́трщик, а *m.* overseer, supervisor; (*тюремный*) jailer.

надсмо́трщи|ца, цы *f. of* ⇒**~к**

надста́в|ить, лю, ишь *pf.* (*of* ⇒**~ля́ть**) to lengthen (*garment or part of garment*).

надста́вк|а, и *f.* added piece, extension.

надставля́|ть, ю *impf. of* ⇒**надста́вить**

надставно́й *adj.* put on.

надстра́ива|ть, ю *impf. of* ⇒**надстро́ить**

надстро́|ить, ю, ишь *pf.* (*of* ⇒**надстра́ивать**) **1** (*этаж*) to build on. **2** (*здание*) to raise the height (of).

надстро́йк|а, и *f.* **1** (*действие*) building on; raising. **2** (*надстроенная часть*) superstructure (*also phil.*).

надстро́чный *adj.* superscript.

надтре́снут|ый (~, ~а) *adj.* cracked (*also fig.*).

надува́л|а, ы *c.g.* (*coll.*) swindler, cheat.

надува́тельский *adj.* (*coll.*) swindling, underhand.

надува́тельств|о, а *nt.* (*coll.*) swindling, cheating.

надува́|ть(ся), ю(сь) *impf. of* ⇒**наду́ть(ся)**

надувн|о́й *adj.* pneumatic; **н. матра́ц** air bed; **~а́я рези́новая ло́дка** inflatable rubber dinghy.

надума́н|ный (~, ~на) *adj.* far-fetched, forced.

наду́м|ать, аю *pf.* (*coll.*) **1** (+*inf.*) (*решить*) to decide (to). **2** (*impf.* **~ывать**) (*придумать*) to think up, make up.

наду́мыва|ть, ю *impf. of* ⇒**наду́мать**

наду́т|ый (~, ~а) *p.p.p. of* ⇒**~ь** *and adj.* (*coll.*) **1** (*вены*) swollen. **2** (*высокомерный*) haughty; puffed up. **3** (*мрачный*) sulky. **4** (*стиль*) inflated, turgid.

наду́|ть, ю, ешь *pf.* (*of* ⇒**~ва́ть**) **1** (*шар, мяч, колесо*) to inflate, blow up; (*паруса*) to puff out; **н. велосипе́дную ка́меру** to inflate, blow up a bicycle tyre; (*impers.*; *pf. only*): **в ко́мнату ве́тром ~ло пы́ли** the wind filled the room with dust; **мне ~ло в у́хо** I have ear-ache from the draught; **н. гу́бы** (*coll.*) to pout one's lips. **2** (*coll.*) (*обмануть*) to dupe; to swindle.

наду́|ться, юсь, ешься *pf.* (*of* ⇒**~ва́ться**) **1** (*шар, мяч, колесо*) to inflate; (*паруса*) to fill out, swell out; (*вена, почка*) to swell. **2** (*fig., coll.*) (*принять важный вид*) to puff o.s. up. **3** (*fig., coll.*) (*обидеться*) to pout; to sulk. **4** (*coll.*; +*g.*) (*напиться*) to swig (*a quantity of*).

наду́ш|енный *p.p.p. of* ⇒**~и́ть** *and adj.* scented, perfumed.

надуш|и́ть(ся), у́(сь), ~́ишь(ся) *pf. of* ⇒**души́ть(ся)²**

надшива́|ть, ю *impf. of* ⇒**надши́ть**

над|ши́ть, ошью́, ошьёшь *pf.* (*of* ⇒**~шива́ть**) **1** (*удлинить*) to lengthen (*a garment*). **2** (*пришить*) to stitch on (to).

надым|и́ть, лю́, и́шь *pf. of* ⇒**дыми́ть**

надыш|а́ться, у́сь, ~́ишься *pf.* **1** (+*i.*) to breathe in, inhale. **2**: **не н.** (**на**+*a.*) to dote (on, upon).

наеда́|ться, юсь *impf. of* ⇒**нае́сться**

наедине́ *adv.* privately, in private; **н. с** (+*i.*) alone (with); **н. с собо́й** alone, by oneself.

нае́|ду, дешь *see* ⇒**~хать**

нае́зд, а *m.* **1** (*столкновение*) collision; **маши́на соверши́ла н. на пешехо́да** the car hit a pedestrian. **2** (*визит*) flying visit; **быва́ть ~ом/~ами** to pay short, infrequent visits.

нае́з|дить, жу, дишь *pf.* (*of* ⇒**~живать**) **1** (*проехать*) to cover, do (*driving or riding*); **мы ~дили сто миль** we covered a hundred miles. **2** (*coll.*) (*приобрести*) to make (= *gain, acquire by conveying*); **н. де́сять рубле́й** to make ten roubles. **3** (*дорогу*) to use (a road) a good deal. **4** (*лошадь*) to break in.

нае́здник, а *m.* horseman, rider.

нае́здни|ца, цы *f. of* ⇒**~к**

нае́здничеств|о, а *nt.* horsemanship.

наезжа́|ть, ю *impf.* **1** (*coll.*) to pay occasional visits. **2** *impf. of* ⇒**нае́хать**

нае́з|женный *p.p.p. of* ⇒**~дить** *and adj.* well-trodden, beaten; worn.

нае́зжива|ть, ю *impf. of* ⇒**нае́здить**

нае́з|жу, дишь *see* ⇒**~дить**

на|ём, ~́йма *m.* (*на короткий период, рабочих*) hire; (*в длительное пользование, квартиры*) renting; **взять в н.** to rent; **сдать в н.** to let.

наёмник, а *m.* **1** (*mil.*) mercenary. **2** (*наёмный работник*) hireling; (*fig.*) mercenary.

наёмный *adj.* hired; rented; **н. уби́йца** hit man.

наёмщик, а *m.* (*obs.*) tenant, lessee.

нае́|сться, мся, шься, стся, ди́мся, ди́тесь, дя́тся, *past* **~лся, ~лась** *pf.* (*of* ⇒**~да́ться**) **1** to eat one's fill. **2** (+*g. or i.*) to eat (a large quantity of), stuff o.s. (with).

нае́|хать, ду, дешь *pf.* (*of* ⇒**~зжа́ть**) **1** (**на**+*a.*) to run (into, over), collide (with); **на нас ~хал авто́бус** a bus ran into us, hit us. **2** (*coll.*) (*приехать*) to come, arrive (*unexpectedly or in numbers*). **3** (*sl.*) (**на**+*a.*) to go on (at), nag (at), give (s.o.) a hard time.

нажа́л|оваться, уюсь *pf.* (*coll.*; **на**+*a.*) to complain (of).

нажа́рива|ть, ю *impf. of* ⇒**нажа́рить**

нажа́р|ить¹, ю, ишь *pf.* (*of* ⇒**~ивать**) (*coll.*) (*сильно нагреть*) to overheat.

нажа́р|ить², ю, ишь *pf.* (*жаря, наготовить*) to fry, roast (*a quantity of*).

нажа́ти|е, я *nt.* (*на кнопку, на рычаг*) pressure.

наж|а́ть¹, му́, мёшь *pf.* (*of* ⇒**~има́ть**) **1** (+*a. or* **на**+*a.*) to press (on); **н. (на) кно́пку** to press the button. **2** (*fig., coll.*; **на**+*a.*) (*понудить*) to put pressure (upon). **3** (*fig., coll.*) (*энергично приняться за что-н.*) to press on, press ahead; **~мём и вы́полним э́ту рабо́ту!** let us press on and finish this job!

наж|а́ть², ну́, нёшь *pf.* (*of* ⇒**~ина́ть**) (+*a. or g.*) (*хлеба*) to reap, harvest (*a quantity of*).

нажда́к, а́ *m.* emery.

нажда́|чный *adj. of* ⇒**~к**; **~чная бума́га** emery paper.

наж|е́чь, гу́, жёшь, гу́т, *past* **~ёг, ~гла́** *pf.* (*of* ⇒**~ига́ть**) (+*a. or g.*) to burn (*a quantity of*).

нажи́в|а[1], **ы** *f.* gain, profit.

нажи́в|а[2], **ы** *f.* = **~ка**

нажива́|ть(ся), ю(сь) *impf. of* ⇒**нажи́ть(ся)**

нажив|и́ть, лю́, и́шь *pf.* (*of* ⇒**~ля́ть**) to bait.

нажи́вк|а, и *f.* bait.

наживля́|ть, ю *impf. of* ⇒**наживи́ть**

наживн|о́й *adj. only in phr.* **э́то де́ло ~о́е** (*coll.*) it'll come (with time).

нажи|ву́, вёшь *see* ⇒**~́ть**

нажига́|ть, ю *impf. of* ⇒**наже́чь**

нажи́м, а *m.* **1** pressure (*also fig.*); **сде́лать что-н. под ~ом** to do sth. under pressure. **2** (*tech.*) clamp.

нажима́|ть, ю *impf. of* ⇒**нажа́ть**[1]

нажина́|ть, ю *impf. of* ⇒**нажа́ть**[2]

нажира́|ться, юсь *impf. of* ⇒**нажра́ться**

наж|и́ть, иву́, ивёшь, *past* **~́ил, ~ила́, ~́ило** *pf.* (*of* ⇒**~ива́ть**) (*богатство*) to acquire, gain; (*fig., coll.*) (*болезнь*) to contract, get.

наж|и́ться, иву́сь, ивёшься, *past* **~и́лся, ~ила́сь** *pf.* (*of* ⇒**~ива́ться**) (**на**+*p.*) to become rich (from), make a fortune (from).

наж|му́, мёшь *see* ⇒**~а́ть**[1]

наж|ну́, нёшь *see* ⇒**~а́ть**[2]

нажр|а́ться, у́сь, ёшься *pf.* (*of* ⇒**нажира́ться**) **1** (*coll.*; +*g. or i.*) (*наесться*) to gorge o.s. (with). **2** (*sl.*) (*опьянеть*) to get very drunk, get sloshed.

наза́втра *adv.* (*coll.*) (the) next day.

наза́д *adv.* **1** (*оглянуться*) back; (*катиться*) backwards; (*на прежнее место*) back; **н.!** back!; stand back! **2**: **(тому́) н.** ago.

назади́ *adv.* (*coll.*) behind.

наза́льный *adj.* (*ling.*) nasal.

Назаре́т, а *m.* Nazareth.

назва́нива|ть, ю *impf.* (*coll.*) to keep ringing.

назва́ни|е, я *nt.* name; **под ~ем** named; **одно́ н.** (*coll.*) in name only; **ра́зве э́то о́тдых? одно́ н.** you can hardly call this rest; (*отдельное издание*) title.

назва́ный *adj.* (*брат, сестра*) sworn; (*сын, дочь*) adopted; (*fig.*): **он мой н. брат** he is my sworn brother.

наз|ва́ть[1], **ову́, овёшь,** *past* **~ва́л, ~вала́, ~ва́ло** *pf.* (*of* ⇒**~ыва́ть**) (+*a. and i.*) to call; to name; **они́ ~ва́ли дочь Татья́ной** they have called/named their daughter Tatyana; **он ~ва́л себя́ Никола́ем** he gave his name as Nicholas.

наз|ва́ть[2], **ову́, овёшь,** *past* **~ва́л, ~вала́, ~ва́ло** *pf.* (*coll.*; +*g.*) (*пригласить*) to invite (*a number of*).

наз|ва́ться[1], **ову́сь, овёшься,** *past* **~ва́лся, ~вала́сь** *pf.* (*of* ⇒**~ыва́ться**) (+*i.*) **1** (*получить какое-н. имя*) to call o.s.; to be named. **2** (*представиться*) to give one's name. **3** (*журналистом*) to claim to be.

наз|ва́ться[2], **ову́сь, овёшься,** *past* **~ва́лся, ~вала́сь** *pf.* (*coll.*) (*в гости*) to invite o.s.; (*помогать*) to volunteer.

назе́мн|ый *adj.* ground, surface; **~ые войска́** (*mil.*) ground troops; **~ая по́чта** surface mail.

на́земь *adv.* (down) to the ground.

назида́ни|е, я *nt.* (*liter.*) edification; **сказа́ть что-н. в н. кому́-н.** to say sth. for s.o.'s edification.

назида́тел|ьный (~ен, ~ьна) *adj.* edifying.

на́зло́ 1 *adv.* (*сделать*) out of spite. **2** *prep.* (+*d.*) (*родителям*) to spite.

назнач|а́ть, а́ю *impf. of* ⇒**~́ить**

назначе́ни|е, я *nt.* **1** (*даты, места*) fixing, setting; (*фондов*) allocation. **2** (*на работу*) appointment. **3** (*med.*) prescription. **4** (*цель*) purpose; **испо́льзовать что́-н. по ~ю** to use sth. properly, appropriately; **отвеча́ть своему́ ~ю** to serve its purpose; **отря́д осо́бого ~я** special task force. **5**: **ме́сто ~я** destination.

назна́ч|ить, у, ишь *pf.* (*of* ⇒**~а́ть**) **1** (*дату, место, размер*) to fix, set, appoint; **н. день встре́чи** to fix, appoint a day for a meeting; **н. кому́-н. свида́ние** to make a date with s.o.; **н. опла́ту** to fix a rate of pay; (*фонды*) to allocate. **2** (+*a. and i.*) to appoint, nominate; **его́ ~или дире́ктором** he has been appointed director. **3** (*med.*) to prescribe.

назо́йливост|ь, и *f.* importunity.

назо́йлив|ый (~, ~а) *adj.* importunate, troublesome.

назрева́|ть, ю *impf.* (*of* ⇒**назре́ть**) **1** (*о почке*) to ripen, mature; (*о нарыве*) to gather head. **2** (*fig.*) to become imminent; **кри́зис ~л** a crisis was brewing; **вопро́с назре́л** the question needs urgent discussion; **назре́ла необходи́мость чего́-н.** the need for sth. had become urgent.

назре́|ть, ю, ешь, *pf. of* ⇒**~ва́ть**

назубо́к *adv.* (*coll.*): **знать/вы́учить н.** to know/learn by heart.

называ́|емый *pres. part. pass. of* ⇒**~ть; так н.** so-called.

называ́|ть, ю *impf. of* ⇒**назва́ть**[1]; **н. ве́щи свои́ми имена́ми** to call a spade a spade.

называ́|ться, юсь *impf.* (*of* ⇒**назва́ться**[1]) (*носить какое-н. наименование, имя*) to be called; **как ~ется э́то село́?** what is this village called? what is the name of this village?; **что ~ется** (*coll.*) as they say, as it were.

наибо́лее *adv.* (the) most.

наибо́льший *adj.* the greatest; (*по величине*) the largest.

наи́вност|ь, и *f.* naivety.

наи́в|ный (~ен, ~на) *adj.* naive; (*простой*) artless.

наивы́сш|ий *adj.* the highest; **в ~ей сте́пени** to the utmost.

наи́гранн|ый 1 *p.p.p. of* ⇒**наигра́ть. 2** *adj.* (*fig.*) put on, assumed; forced; **~ая весёлость** assumed gaiety.

наигра́|ть, ю *pf.* (*of* ⇒**наи́грывать**) **1** (*coll.*) (*много денег*) to win, make (*by playing*). **2** (*coll.*) (*мелодию*) to play casually, sketchily. **3**: **н. пласти́нку** to make a record.

наигра́|ться, юсь *pf.* to play for a long time, for long enough.

наи́грыва|ть, ю *impf. of* ⇒**наигра́ть**

на́игрыш, а *m.* **1** (*мелодия*) tune. **2** (*coll.*) (*искусственность*) artificiality.

наизна́нку *adv.* inside out; **вы́вернуть н.** to turn inside out; **вывора́чиваться н.** (*fig., coll.*) (*стараться*) to put o.s. out; (*откровенничать*) to lay o.s. bare; to bare one's soul.

наизу́сть *adv.* by heart; from memory.

наилу́чший *adj.* (the) best.

наиме́нее *adv.* (the) least.

наименова́ни|е, я *nt.* name, appellation, designation; (*разновидность*) variety; **торго́вое н.** trade name.

наимен|ова́ть, у́ю *pf. of* ⇒**именова́ть**

наиме́ньший *adj.* (the) least; (*по величине*) the smallest.

наискосо́к *adv.* = **на́искось**

на́искось *adv.* obliquely, slantwise.

наи́ти|е, я *nt.* inspiration; **по ~ю** instinctively, intuitively.

наиху́дший *adj.* (the) worst.

найдёныш, а *m.* foundling.

найми́т, а *m.* hireling.

Найро́би *m. indecl.* Nairobi.

на|йти́[1], **~йду́, ~йдёшь,** *past* **~шёл, ~шла́** *pf.* (*of* ⇒**~ходи́ть**) to find; **н., что иде́я интере́сная/н. иде́ю интере́сной** to find the idea interesting; **как ты нашёл его́ по́сле о́тпуска?** how did you find him after his holiday?; (*открыть*) to discover; **н. себя́** to find o.s.; **н. себе́ моги́лу, смерть** (*rhet.*) to meet one's death.

на|йти́[2], **йду́, йдёшь,** *past* **~шёл, ~шла́** *pf.* (*of* ⇒**~ходи́ть**) **1** (**на**+*a.*) (*натолкнуться*) to come (across, upon); (*о чувствах*) to come over; **что э́то на неё ~шло́?** what has come over her?; (*закрыть собой*) to cover. **2** (*impers., coll.*) (*скопиться*) to gather, collect; **~шло́ мно́го наро́ду** a large crowd collected.

на|йти́сь, йду́сь, йдёшься, *past* **~шёлся, ~шла́сь** *pf.* (*of* ⇒**~ходи́ться**[1]) **1** (*обнаружиться*) (*после поисков*) to be found; to turn up; (*вызваться*) to volunteer. **2** (*не растеряться*) not to be at a loss; **я не ~шёлся, что сказа́ть** I was at a loss for what to say.

нака́вер|зить, жу, зишь *pf. of* ⇒**ка́верзить**

нака́з, а *m.* **1** (*obs.*) order; instructions. **2** (*pol.*) mandate.

наказа́ни|е, я *nt.* **1** punishment. **2** (*fig., coll.*) nuisance; **мне с ним (су́щее, пря́мо, про́сто) н.** he is a (perfect) nuisance to me.

нака|за́ть[1], **жу́, ~́жешь** *pf.* (*of* ⇒**~́зывать**) to punish.

нака|за́ть[2], **жу́, ~́жешь** *pf.* (*of*

Н

⇒~зывать) (*coll.* +*d.*) (*дать заказ*) to instruct, order.

наказу́емый *adj.* (*leg.*) punishable.

нака́зыва|ть, ю *impf. of* ⇒**наказа́ть**[1,2]

нака́л, а *m.* **1** incandescence. **2** (*fig.*) tension.

накал|ённый *p.p.p. of* ⇒~**и́ть** *and adj.* **1** incandescent; white-hot. **2** (*fig.*) strained, tense; **~ённая междунаро́дная обстано́вка** tense international situation.

нака́лива|ть(ся), ю(сь) *impf. of* ⇒**накали́ть(ся)**

накал|и́ть, ю́, и́шь *pf.* (*of* ⇒~**ивать**) to heat, incandesce; (*fig.*) (*ситуацию*) to inflame.

накал|и́ться, ю́сь, и́шься *pf.* (*of* ⇒~**иваться**) to glow, incandesce; (*fig.*) (*обстановка*) to become inflamed; **стра́сти ~и́лись** passions were running high.

нака́лыва|ть(ся), ю(сь) *impf. of* ⇒**наколо́ть(ся)**

наканифо́л|ить, ю, ишь *pf. of* ⇒**канифо́лить**

накану́не **1** (*adv.*) the day before. **2** (*prep.* +*g.*) on the eve (of); **н. Рождества́** on Christmas Eve.

нака́п|ать, аю *pf. of* ⇒**ка́пать**

нака́пливать(ся) *impf.* = **накопля́ть(ся)**

нака́пыва|ть, ю *impf. of* ⇒**накопа́ть**

нака́рка|ть, ю *pf.* (*coll.*) to bring down (evil) by one's own prophecies.

нака́т, а *m.* layer (*of beams or planks*).

накат|а́ть[1]**, а́ю** *pf.* (*of* ⇒~**ывать**) **1** (*катая, приготовить*) to roll out; (*дорогу*) to roll smooth. **2** (*no impf.*) (*coll.*) (*быстро написать*) to write hurriedly; **н. письмо́** to dash off a letter.

накат|а́ть[2]**, а́ю** *pf.* (*of* ⇒~**ывать**) (+*a. or g.*) (*бочек, брёвен*) to roll (*a quantity of*).

наката́|ться, юсь *pf.* (*coll.*) to have had enough (*of driving, riding*).

ната|ти́ть, чу́, ~тишь *pf.* (*of* ⇒~**тывать**) (**на**+*a.*) (*бочку*) to roll up (onto); (*coll.*) (*о чувстве*) to come over, overwhelm; (*coll.*) (*о гостях*) to descend, roll up.

нака|ти́ться, чу́сь, ~тишься *pf.* (*of* ⇒**нака́тываться**) to roll up.

нака́тыва|ть(ся), ю(сь) *impf. of* ⇒**наката́ть** *and* **накати́ть(ся)**

накач|а́ть[1]**, а́ю** *pf.* (*of* ⇒~**ивать**) (*шину, камеру*) to pump up, pump full.

накача́|ть[2]**, ю** *pf.* (*воды*) to pump (*a quantity of*).

накача́|ть[3]**, ю** *pf. of* ⇒**кача́ть**

накач|а́ться[1]**, а́юсь** *pf.* (*of* ⇒~**иваться**) (*coll.*) to become sozzled.

накача́|ться[2]**, юсь** *pf. of* ⇒**кача́ться**

нака́чива|ть(ся), ю(сь) *impf. of* ⇒**накача́ть(ся)**

накид|а́ть, а́ю *pf.* (*of* ⇒~**ывать**) = **наброса́ть**[2]

наки́дк|а, и *f.* **1** (*одежда*) cloak, mantle; wrap. **2** (*для подушки*) pillow-case. **3** (*прибавка*) increase; extra charge.

наки́дыва|ть(ся), ю(сь) *impf. of* ⇒**накида́ть** *and* **наки́нуть(ся)**

наки́|нуть, ну, нешь *pf.* (*of* ⇒~**дывать**) **1** (*шаль*) to throw on, throw over. **2** (*coll.*) (*прибавить*) to add.

наки́|нуться, нусь, нешься *pf.* (*of* ⇒~**дываться**) (**на**+*a.*) to fall (on, upon); (*на еду, на работу*) to attack, get stuck into.

накип|а́ть, а́ет *impf. of* ⇒~**е́ть**

накип|е́ть, и́т *pf.* (*of* ⇒~**а́ть**) to form a scum; to form a scale; (*fig., impers.*) to swell, boil; **в нём ~е́ла зло́ба** he is boiling with resentment.

на́кип|ь, и *f.* **1** (*пена*) scum. **2** (*осадок*) scale, deposit.

накла́дк|а, и *f.* **1** (*род парика*) hair-piece. **2** (*sl.*) (*ошибка*) blunder; **н. вы́шла** we made a blunder.

накладн|а́я, о́й *f.* invoice, way-bill.

накла́дно *adv.* (*coll.*) to one's disadvantage, to one's cost.

накладн|о́й *adj.* **1** super-imposed; **~о́е зо́лото** rolled gold; **н. карма́н** patch pocket; **~ы́е расхо́ды** overheads. **2** (*искусственный*) false; **~а́я борода́** false beard.

накла́дыва|ть, ю *impf. of* ⇒**наложи́ть**

наклеве|та́ть, щу́, ~щешь *pf. of* ⇒**клевета́ть**

наклёвыва|ться, ется *impf. of* ⇒**наклю́нуться**

накле́ива|ть, ю *impf. of* ⇒**накле́ить**

накле́|ить, ю, ешь *pf.* (*of* ⇒~**ивать**) to stick on, paste on.

накле́йк|а, и *f.* **1** (*действие*) sticking on, pasting on. **2** (*этикетка*) sticker.

наклепа́|ть[1]**, ю** *pf.* (*of* ⇒**наклёпывать**) to rivet.

наклеп|а́ть[2]**, лю́, ~лешь** *pf. of* ⇒**клепа́ть**[2]

наклёпк|а, и *f.* (*металлическая*) stud.

наклёпыва|ть, ю *impf. of* ⇒**наклепа́ть**[1]

накли|к|а́ть, а́ю *impf. of* ⇒~**ать**

накли́|кать, чу, чешь *pf.* (*of* ⇒~**ка́ть**); **н. на себя́** to bring upon o.s.; **н. беду́** (**на**+*a.*) to bring disaster (upon).

накло́н, а *m.* (*головы*) inclination; (*почерка*) slope, slant; (*покатая поверхность*) slope, incline.

наклоне́ни|е, я *nt.* (*gram.*) mood.

наклон|и́ть, ю́, ~ишь *pf.* (*of* ⇒~**я́ть**) to incline, bend.

наклон|и́ться, ю́сь, ~ишься *pf.* (*of* ⇒~**я́ться**) to stoop, bend.

накло́нност|ь, и *f.* (**к**+*d.*) inclination (towards), tendency (towards), propensity (for).

накло́нн|ый *adj.* inclined, sloping; **~ая пло́скость** inclined plane; **кати́ться по ~ой пло́скости** (*fig.*) to go downhill, go to the dogs (*morally*).

наклон|я́ть(ся), я́ю(сь) *impf. of* ⇒~**и́ть(ся)**

наклю́н|уться, ется *pf.* (*of* ⇒**наклёвываться**) **1** (*о птице*) to peck its way out of the shell. **2** (*coll.*) (*появиться*) to turn up; **слу́чай ~улся** an occasion came up.

накля́узнича|ть, ю *pf. of* ⇒**кля́узничать**

накова́л|ьня, ьни, *g. pl.* **~ен** *f.* anvil.

нако́жный *adj.* (*med.*) skin (*attr.*).

наколд|ова́ть, у́ю *pf.* (*беду*) to bring about (*by sorcery*).

наколе́нник, а *m.* knee-pad.

нако́лк|а, и *f.* **1** (*украшение*) head-dress (*fastened with pins*). **2** (*coll.*) (*татуировка*) tattoo.

накол|о́ть[1]**, ю́, ~ешь** *pf.* (*of* ⇒**нака́лывать**) (+*a. or g.*) to split (*a quantity of*); **н. дров** to chop (*a quantity of*) wood.

накол|о́ть[2]**, ю́, ~ешь** *pf.* (*of* ⇒**нака́лывать**) **1** to prick; **н. узо́р** to prick out a pattern. **2** (*насадить*) to pin down; **н. ба́бочку на була́вку** to pin down a butterfly. **3** (*убить*) to slaughter, kill (*a number of*).

накол|о́ться, ю́сь, ~ешься *pf.* (*of* ⇒**нака́лываться**) to prick o.s.

наконе́ц *adv.* at last, finally, in the end; **н.-то!** at last!, about time too!; (*ещё, кроме всего*) after all; (*выражает недовольство*) ever; **переста́ньте, н., спо́рить!** will you ever stop arguing!

наконе́чник, а *m.* tip, point; **н. стрелы́** arrow-head.

наконе́чный *adj.* final.

накопа́|ть, ю *pf.* (*of* ⇒**нака́пывать**) (+*a. or g.*) to dig up (*a number of*).

накопи́тел|ь, я *m.* (*comput.*) storage; **н. на ди́сках** disk drive.

накопи́тельств|о, а *nt.* acquisitiveness.

накоп|и́ть, лю́, ~ишь *pf.* (*of* ⇒**копи́ть, ~ля́ть** *and* ⇒**нака́пливать**) (+*a. or g.*) to accumulate, amass.

накоп|и́ться, лю́сь, ~ишься *pf.* (*of* ⇒~**ля́ться** *and* **нака́пливаться**) to accumulate.

накопле́ни|е, я *nt.* **1** accumulation. **2** (*pl.*) (*сбережения*) savings.

накопля́|ть(ся), ю(сь) *impf. of* ⇒**накопи́ть(ся)**

накоп|ти́ть[1]**, чу́, ти́шь** *pf. of* ⇒**копти́ть** 3

накоп|ти́ть[2]**, чу́, ти́шь** *pf.* (+*a. or g.*) (*рыбы*) to smoke (= *cure*) (*a quantity of*).

накорм|и́ть, лю́, ~ишь *pf. of* ⇒**корми́ть**

накоротке́ *adv.* (*coll.*) **1** (*недолго*) briefly. **2** (**от**+*g.*) close (to). **3** (*as predicate*): **быть н. с кем-н.** to be close to s.o., on good terms with s.o.

нако|си́ть, шу́, ~сишь *pf.* (+*a. or g.*) to mow (down) (*a quantity of*).

на́кось *see* ⇒**вы́кусить**

накра́дыва|ть, ю *impf. of* ⇒**накра́сть**

накра́пыва|ть, ет *impf.* (*impers. or* +**дождь**) to spit (*Br.*); (*всё утро*) to rain on and off; **ста́ло н.** it began to spit (*with rain*).

накра́|сить, шу, сишь *pf.* (*of* ⇒**~шивать**) **1** (*ногти, губы*) to paint. **2** (*лицо*) to make up.

накра́|ситься, шусь, сишься *pf. of* ⇒**кра́ситься**

накра́|сть, ду́, дёшь, *past* **~л** *pf.* (*of* ⇒**~дывать**) (+*a. or g.*) to steal (*a number of*).

накрахма́л|ить, ю, ишь *pf. of* ⇒**крахма́лить**

накра́шива|ть, ю *impf. of* ⇒**накра́сить**

накрен|и́ть, ю́, и́шь *pf.* **1** *pf. of* ⇒**крени́ть. 2** (*impf.* **~я́ть**) to tilt to one side, tilt.

накрен|и́ться, ю́сь, и́шься *pf.* **1** *pf. of* ⇒**крени́ться. 2** (*impf.* **~я́ться**) to tilt, list.

накрен|я́ть(ся), я́ю(сь) *impf. of* ⇒**~и́ть(ся)**

на́крепко *adv.* **1** fast, tight; **закры́ть н.** to shut fast. **2** (*coll.*) categorically; strictly; **приказа́ть н.** to give a strict order.

на́крест *adv.* crosswise; **сложи́ть ру́ки крест-н.** to cross one's arms.

накрич|а́ть, у́, и́шь *pf.* (**на**+*a.*) to shout (at).

накропа́|ть, ю *pf. of* ⇒**кропа́ть**

накрош|и́ть, у́, ~ишь *pf.* (*of* ⇒**кроши́ть**) **1** to crumble, shred (*a quantity of*). **2** (*насорить крошками*) to spill crumbs.

накр|о́ю, о́ешь *see* ⇒**~ы́ть**

накру|ти́ть, чу́, ~тишь *pf.* (*of* ⇒**~чивать**) **1** (*намотать*) (**на**+*a.*) to wind (around, onto). **2** (*верёвок*) to twist (*a quantity of*). **3** (*coll.*) to do, say (*sth. complicated or unusual*).

накру|ти́ться, чу́сь, ~тишься *pf.* (*of* ⇒**~чиваться**) **1** (*намотаться*) (**на**+*a.*) to wind around, twist around. **2** (*coll.*) (*завиться*) to curl one's hair. **3** (*no impf.*) (*измучиться*) to be exhausted.

накру́чива|ть(ся), ю(сь) *impf. of* ⇒**накрути́ть(ся)**

накрыва́|ть(ся), ю(сь) *impf. of* ⇒**накры́ть(ся)**

накр|ы́ть, о́ю, о́ешь *pf.* (*of* ⇒**~ыва́ть**) **1** (*закрыть*) to cover; **н. (на) стол** to lay the table; **н. к у́жину** to lay supper. **2** (*fig., coll.*) (*поймать*) to catch; **н. на ме́сте преступле́ния** to catch red-handed.

накр|ы́ться, о́юсь, о́ешься *pf.* (*of* ⇒**~ыва́ться**) **1** (+*i.*) to cover o.s. (with). **2** (*о планах*) to fall through.

накуп|а́ть, а́ю *impf. of* ⇒**~и́ть**

накуп|и́ть, лю́, ~ишь *pf.* (*of* ⇒**~а́ть**) (+*a. or g.*) to buy up (*a number or quantity of*).

наку́р|енный *p.p.p. of* ⇒**~и́ть** *and adj.* smoky, smoke-filled; **в. ко́мнате ~ено** the room is full of (tobacco) smoke.

накур|и́ть, ю́, ~ишь *pf.* (+*i.*) to fill with smoke, with fumes.

накур|и́ться, ю́сь, ~ишься *pf.* (*coll.*) to smoke a lot, too much; **н. до головно́й бо́ли** to smoke so much that one gets a headache.

накуроле́|сить, шу, сишь *pf. of* ⇒**куроле́сить**

наку́т|ать, аю *pf.* (*of* ⇒**~ывать**) (+*a. or g. and* **на**+*a.*) to put on (*clothing, etc.*); **мно́го ~али на ребёнка** the child was well wrapped up.

наку́тыва|ть, ю *impf. of* ⇒**наку́тать**

нала́влива|ть, ю *impf. of* ⇒**налови́ть**

налага́|ть, ю *impf. of* ⇒**наложи́ть**

нала́|дить, жу, дишь *pf.* (*of* ⇒**~живать**) **1** (*отрегулировать*) to regulate, adjust; (*исправить*) to repair, put right. **2** (*организовать*) to set going, arrange; **н. дела́** to get things going. **3** (*mus.*) (*coll.*) to tune.

нала́|диться, жусь, дишься *pf.* (*of* ⇒**~живаться**) to go right; **рабо́та ~дилась** the work is well in hand.

нала́дчик, а *m.* (*tech.*) adjuster.

нала́жива|ть(ся), ю(сь) *impf. of* ⇒**нала́дить(ся)**

налака́|ться, юсь *pf.* **1**: **н. молока́** to lap up one's fill of milk. **2** (*coll.*) (*опьянеть*) to get drunk.

на|лга́ть, лгу́, лжёшь, лгу́т, *past* **~лга́л, ~лгала́, ~лга́ло** *pf.* **1** to lie, tell lies. **2** (*impf.* ⇒**лгать** 2) (**на**+*a.*) to slander.

нале́во *adv.* **1** (**от**+*g.*) to the left (of); **н.!** (*mil.*) left turn! **2** (*coll.*) (*продавать*) on the side (= *illicitly*); **рабо́тать н.** to moonlight.

налега́|ть, ю *impf. of* ⇒**нале́чь**

налегке́ *adv.* **1** without luggage; **путеше́ствовать н.** to travel light. **2** (*в лёгкой одежде*) lightly clad.

належ|а́ться, у́сь, и́шься *pf.* (*coll.*) to have a good lie-down.

налез|а́ть, а́ю *impf. of* ⇒**~ть**[1,2]

нале́з|ть[1]**, у, ешь,** *past* **~, ~ла** *pf.* (*of* ⇒**~а́ть**) (*забраться*) to get in (*in large numbers, in quantities*).

нале́з|ть[2]**, ет** *pf.* (*of* ⇒**~а́ть**) **1** (*об одежде*) (**на**+*a.*) to fit, go on. **2** (*о шапке*) (**на**+*a.*) to slip, slide down (over).

нален|и́ть[1]**, лю́, ~ишь** *pf.* (*of* ⇒**лепи́ть** 2 *and* **~ля́ть**) to stick on.

нален|и́ть[2]**, лю́, ~ишь** *pf.* (+*a. or g.*) to model (*a number of*).

нален|ля́ть, ля́ю, *impf. of* ⇒**~и́ть**[1]

налёт[1]**, а** *m.* (*нападение*) raid; (*на квартиру, на магазин*) robbery, burglary; **возду́шный н.** air-raid; **с ~а** (*fig.*) (*не размышляя*) suddenly, without preparation; (*на ходу*) at full speed; **бить с ~а** to swoop down on.

налёт[2]**, а** *m.* (*тонкий слой*) deposit; thin coating; (*на бронзе*) patina; **зубно́й н.** dental plaque; (*fig.*) touch, soupçon; **с ~ом иро́нии** with a touch of irony.

налет|а́ть[1]**, а́ю** *impf. of* ⇒**~е́ть**[1,2]

налет|а́ть[2]**, а́ю** *pf.* to have flown (*so many hours, miles, etc.*).

нале|те́ть[1]**, чу́, ти́шь** *pf.* (*of* ⇒**~та́ть**[1]) **1** (**на**+*a.*) (*наброситься*) to fall (upon); (*о птице*) to swoop down (on); to fly (upon, against); (*натолкнуться*) to run (into). **2** (*о ветре, буре*) to spring up.

нале|те́ть[2]**, чу́, ти́шь** *pf.* (*of* ⇒**~та́ть**[1]) (*прилететь*) to fly in, drift in (*in quantities, in large numbers*).

налётчик, а *m.* burglar, robber; (*на банк*) raider.

на|ле́чь, ля́гу, ля́жешь, ля́гут, *imper.* **~ля́г,** *past* **~лёг, ~легла́** *pf.* (*of* ⇒**~лега́ть**) (**на**+*a.*) **1** (*прислониться*) to lean (on); **н. плечо́м на дверь** to try to force the door with one's shoulder. **2** (*направить усилия*) to apply o.s. (to), throw o.s. (into); **н. на вёсла** to ply one's oars; **н. на подчинённых** (*fig.*) to come down upon one's subordinates.

налива́|ть(ся), ю(сь) *impf. of* ⇒**нали́ть(ся)**

нали́вк|а, и *f.* fruit liqueur; **вишнёвая н.** cherry brandy.

наливн|о́й *adj.* **1**: **~о́е колесо́** overshot wheel; **~о́е су́дно** (*naut.*) tanker. **2** (*созревший*) ripe; (*сочный*) juicy.

нали|за́ться, жу́сь, ~жешься *pf.* (*coll.*) (*напиться*) to get sozzled.

нали́м, а *m.* (*zool.*) burbot.

налин|ова́ть, у́ю *pf. of* ⇒**линова́ть**

налип|а́ть, а́ет *impf. of* ⇒**~нуть**

нали́п|нуть, нет, *past* **~, ~ла** *pf.* (*of* ⇒**~а́ть**) (**на**+*a.*) to stick (to).

налито́й *adj.* **1** (*плод*) juicy, ripe. **2** (*щёки*) fleshy.

нал|и́ть, ью́, ьёшь, *past* **~ил, ~ила́, ~ило** *pf.* (*of* ⇒**~ива́ть**) **1** (*влить*) to pour out; (*наполнить*) (+*i.*) to fill (with); **н. бо́чку водо́й** to fill a barrel with water. **2** (*пролить*) to spill.

нал|и́ться, ью́сь, ьёшься, *past* **~и́лся, ~ила́сь, ~и́ло́сь** *pf.* (*of* ⇒**~ива́ться**) **1** (+*i.*) to fill (with); **н. кро́вью** to become bloodshot. **2** (*о плодах*) to ripen, become juicy.

налицо́ *adv.* present, available, on hand.

нали́честв|овать, ую *impf.* to be present, be on hand.

нали́чи|е, я *nt.* presence; **быть, оказа́ться в ~и** to be present, be available; **при ~и** (+*g.*) in the presence (of); given.

нали́чник, а *m.* **1** (*двери, окна*) casing, jambs and lintel. **2** (*для ключа*) lock-plate.

нали́чност|ь, и *f.* **1** (*деньги*) cash; **н. това́ров в магази́не** stock-in-trade. **2** (*присутствие*) presence; **быть в ~и** to be present.

нали́чн|ый *adj.* on hand, available; **~ые (де́ньги)** ready money, cash; **плати́ть ~ыми** to pay in cash, pay down; **за н. расчёт** for cash.

налов|и́ть, лю́, ~ишь *pf.* (+*a or g.*) to catch (*a number of*).

наловч|и́ться, у́сь, и́шься *pf.* (+*inf.*) to become proficient (in), become good (at).

нало́г, а *m.* tax; **доба́вочный н.** surtax; **подохо́дный н.** income tax; **н. на доба́вленную сто́имость** value added

Н

tax, VAT; **н. на при́быль** profits tax; **не облага́емый ~ом** tax-deductible.

нало́г|овый *adj. of* ⇒**~**; **~овая га́вань** tax haven; **~овая деклара́ция** tax return; **н. инспе́ктор** tax inspector; **~овое обложе́ние** taxation; **~овое убе́жище** tax haven.

налогообложе́ни|е, я *nt.* taxation.

налогоплате́льщик, а *m.* taxpayer.

налогоплате́льщи|ца, цы *f. of* ⇒**~к**

наложе́ни|е, я *nt.* imposition; **н. аре́ста** (*leg.*) seizure; **н. швов** (*med.*) suture, stitching.

нало́ж|енный *p.p.p. of* ⇒**~и́ть; ~енным платежо́м** cash on delivery (*abbr.* C.O.D.).

налож|и́ть[1], **у́, ~́ишь** *pf.* **1** (*impf.* **накла́дывать**) (*повязку; лак*) to apply; (*печать, визу*) affix; (*положить сверху*) to put on, over; **н. отпеча́ток на** + *a.* (*fig.*) to have a great influence (on). **2** (*impf.* **накла́дывать**) (*навалить*) to load, pack; **н. белья́ в корзи́ну** to load a basket with linen. **3** (*impf.* **налага́ть**) (**на** + *a.*) (*подвергнуть*) to lay (on), impose; **н. штраф** to impose a fine; **н. аре́ст на чьё-н. иму́щество** (*leg.*) to seize s.o.'s property.

налож|и́ть[2], **у́, ~́ишь** *pf.* (*of* ⇒**накла́дывать**) (+*a. or g.*) to put, lay (*a quantity of*).

нало́жниц|а, ы *f.* (*obs.*) concubine.

нало́|й, я *m.* = **анало́й**

налома́|ть, ю *pf.* (+*a. or g.*) to break (*a quantity of*); **н. бока́ кому́-н.** (*coll.*) to give s.o. a sound thrashing; **н. дров** (*coll., joc.*) to commit follies.

налощ|и́ть, у́, и́шь *pf. of* ⇒**лощи́ть**

нал|ью́, ьёшь *see* ⇒**~и́ть**

налюб|ова́ться, у́юсь *pf.* (+*i. or* **на** + *a.*) to gaze to one's heart's content (at) (*usu. with neg.*).

нал|я́гу, я́жешь, я́гут *see* ⇒**~е́чь**

наля́па|ть, ю *pf. of* ⇒**ля́пать**

нам *d. of* ⇒**мы**

намагни́|тить, чу, тишь *pf.* (*of* ⇒**~чивать**) to magnetize.

намагни́чива|ть, ю *impf. of* ⇒**намагни́тить**

нама́з, а *m.* Muslim prayer.

нама́|зать, жу, жешь *pf. of* ⇒**ма́зать** *and* **~зывать**

нама́|заться, жусь, жешься *pf.* **1** (*impf.* **~зываться**) (+*i.*) to rub o.s. (with). **2** *pf. of* ⇒**ма́заться**

нама́зыва|ть(ся), ю(сь) *impf. of* ⇒**нама́зать(ся)**

намал|ева́ть, ю́ю, ю́ешь *pf. of* ⇒**малева́ть**

намара́|ть, ю *pf. of* ⇒**мара́ть** 2

намарин|ова́ть, у́ю *pf.* (+*a. or g.*) to pickle (*a quantity of*).

нама́слива|ть, ю *impf.* = **ма́слить**

нама́сл|ить, ю, ишь *pf. of* ⇒**~ивать** *and* **ма́слить**

наматра́цник, а *m.* mattress cover.

нама́тывани|е, я *nt.* winding, reeling.

нама́тыва|ть(ся), ю(сь) *impf. of* ⇒**намота́ть(ся)**

нама́чива|ть, ю *impf. of* ⇒**намочи́ть**

наме́дни *adv.* (*coll.*) the other day, lately.

намёк, а *m.* hint; **то́нкий н.** gentle hint; **ко́свенный н.** innuendo; **сде́лать н.** to drop a hint; **с ~ом** (**на** + *a.*) with a suggestion (of).

намек|а́ть, а́ю *impf.* (*of* ⇒**~ну́ть**) (**на** + *a.*, **о** + *p.*) to hint (at), allude (to).

намек|ну́ть, ну́, нёшь *pf. of* ⇒**~а́ть**

намел|и́ть, ю́, и́шь *pf. of* ⇒**мели́ть**

наменя́|ть, ю *pf.* (+*a. or g.*) to obtain (*a quantity of*) by exchange.

намерева́|ться, юсь *impf.* (+*inf.*) to intend (to), mean (to).

наме́рен (~а, ~о) *adj. as pred.* **быть н.** (+*inf.*) to intend; **я н. за́втра е́хать** I intend to go tomorrow; **что вы ~ы де́лать?** what do you intend to do?

наме́рени|е, я *nt.* intention; purpose; **без вся́кого ~я** unintentionally.

наме́ренно *adv.* intentionally, deliberately.

наме́рен|ный (~, ~на) *adj.* intentional, deliberate.

намерз|а́ть, а́ет *impf. of* ⇒**~́нуть**

намёрз|нуть, нет, нут *past* **~, ~ла** *pf.* (*of* ⇒**~а́ть**) to freeze (on); **на ступе́ньках ~ло мно́го льда** a lot of ice had formed on the steps.

намёрз|нуться, нусь, нешься, *past* **~ся, ~лась** *pf.* (*coll.*) to get frozen.

на́мертво *adv.* tightly, fast.

наме|си́ть, шу́, ~́сишь *pf.* (+*a or g.*) to knead (*a quantity of*).

наме|сти́, ту́, тёшь, *past* **~́л, ~ла́** *pf.* (*of* ⇒**~та́ть**[1]) (+*a. or g.*) **1** (*подмести*) to sweep together (*a quantity of*). **2** (*о ветре*) to cause to drift; (*impers.*): **~ло́ мно́го сне́гу** big snowdrifts have formed.

наме́стник, а *m.* **1** (*заместитель*) deputy. **2** (*hist.*) (*правитель*) governor-general.

наме́стни|ческий *adj. of* ⇒**~к**

намётанный *adj.*: **н. глаз** an experienced, trained eye.

намета́|ть[1], **ю** *impf. of* ⇒**намести́**

намета́|ть[2], **ю** *pf. of* ⇒**мета́ть**[2]

наме|та́ть[3], **чу́, ~́чешь** *pf.* (+*a. or g.*) (*набросать*) to throw together (*a quantity of*).

наме|та́ть[4], **чу́, ~́чешь** *pf.* (*of* ⇒**~́тывать**) (*coll.*) (*сделать искусным*) to train; **н. глаз** to acquire a (good) eye; **н. ру́ку** (**на** + *a.*) to become proficient (in).

наме́|тить[1], **чу, тишь** *pf.* (*of* ⇒**~ча́ть**[1]) (*изобразить*) to sketch, outline.

наме́|тить[2], **чу, тишь** *pf.* **1** (*impf.* **~ча́ть**[2]) (*планировать*) to plan, project; to have in view; **н. пое́здку в Росси́ю** to plan a visit to Russia. **2** (*impf.* **~ча́ть**[2]) (*предположить*) to nominate; (*назначить*) to select; **его́ ~тили председа́телем** he has been nominated for chairman; **н. зда́ние к разруше́нию** to designate a building for demolition. **3** *pf. of* ⇒**ме́тить**[2]

наме́|титься, чусь, тишься *pf.* **1** (*impf.* ⇒**~ча́ться**) to begin to appear; to take shape. **2** (*impf.* ⇒**ме́титься**) (**в** + *a.*) to aim at.

намётк|а[1], **и** *f.* **1** (*действие*) basting, tacking. **2** (*нитка*) basting thread, tacking thread.

намётк|а[2], **и** *f.* (*план*) rough draft, preliminary outline.

намётыва|ть, ю *impf. of* ⇒**намета́ть**[4]

намеча́|ть[1], **ю** *impf. of* ⇒**наме́тить**[1]

намеча́|ть[2], **ю** *impf. of* ⇒**наме́тить**[2]

намеча́|ться, юсь *impf. of* ⇒**наме́титься**

наме́|чу, тишь *see* ⇒**~тить**

наме|чу́, чешь *see* ⇒**~та́ть**

намеш|а́ть, а́ю *pf.* (*of* ⇒**~́ивать**) (+*a. or g. and* **в** + *a.*) to add (to), mix in(to).

наме́шива|ть, ю *impf. of* ⇒**намеша́ть**

на́ми *i. of* ⇒**мы**

намиби́йский *adj.* Namibian.

Нами́би|я, и *f.* Namibia.

намина́|ть, ю *impf. of* ⇒**намя́ть**

намно́го *adv.* much, far (*with comparatives*); **н. лу́чше** much, far better; greatly, considerably (*with verbs*); **они́ н. улу́чшили свою́ рабо́ту** they improved their work greatly, considerably.

нам|ну́, нёшь *see* ⇒**~я́ть**

намозо́л|ить, ю, ишь *pf. of* ⇒**мозо́лить**

намок|а́ть, а́ю *impf.* (*of* ⇒**~́нуть**) to become wet, get wet.

намо́к|нуть, ну, нешь, *past* **~, ~ла** *pf. of* ⇒**~а́ть**

намоло|ти́ть, чу́, ~́тишь *pf.* (+*a. or g.*) to thresh (*a quantity of*).

нам|оло́ть, елю́, е́лешь *pf.* (+*a. or g.*) to grind, mill (*a quantity of*); **н. вздо́ру, чепухи́** (*coll.*) to talk a lot of nonsense.

намо́рдник, а *m.* muzzle.

намо́рщ|ить(ся), у(сь) ишь(ся) *pf. of* ⇒**мо́рщить(ся)**

намо|сти́ть, щу́, сти́шь *pf. of* ⇒**мости́ть** 2

намота́|ть[1], **ю** *pf. of* ⇒**мота́ть**[1]

намота́|ть[2], **ю** *pf.* (*of* ⇒**нама́тывать**) (+*a. or g.*) to wind (*a quantity of*).

намота́|ться, юсь *pf.* (*of* ⇒**нама́тываться**) **1** to be wound. **2** (*coll.*) (*устать*) to get tired.

намоч|и́ть, у́, ~́ишь *pf.* (*of* ⇒**нама́чивать**) **1** (*сделать мокрым*) to wet, moisten. **2** (+*a. or g.*) (*приготовить мочением*) to soak, steep. **3** (*intrans.; coll.*) (*налить на пол*) to spill water (on the floor, *etc.*).

намудр|и́ть, ю́, и́шь *pf. of* ⇒**мудри́ть**

наму́сл|ить, ю, ишь *pf. of* ⇒**му́слить**

намус|о́лить *pf.* = ~**лить**

наму́сор|ить, ю, ишь *pf. of* ⇒**му́сорить**

наму́ч|иться, усь, ишься *pf.* (*coll.*) to wear o.s. out; to have a hard time.

намы́в, а *m.* (*geol.*) alluvium.

намывно́й *adj.* (*geol.*) alluvial.

намы́ливать(ся) *impf.* = **мы́лить(ся)**

намы́л|ить(ся), ю(сь), ишь(сь) *pf. of* ⇒~**ивать(ся)** *and* **мы́лить(ся)**

нам|ы́ть, о́ю, о́ешь *pf.* (+*a. or g.*) **1** (*посуды*) to wash (*a quantity of*). **2** (*о реке*) to deposit.

нам|я́ть[1], ну́, нёшь *pf.* (*of* ⇒~**ина́ть**) (*давлением причинить боль*) to hurt (*by pressure or friction*), to crush; **н. кому́-н. бока́, ше́ю** to give s.o. a sound thrashing.

нам|я́ть[2], ну́, нёшь *pf.* (+*a. or g.*) **1** (*глины*) to mash (*a quantity of*). **2** (*траву*) to trample down (*a certain area of*).

нанесе́ни|е, я *nt.* **1** (*на карту*) drawing, plotting. **2** (*причинение*) infliction. **3** (*лака, краски*) application.

нанес|ти́[1], у́, ёшь, *past* ~, ~**ла́** *pf.* (*of* ⇒**наноси́ть**) **1** (*начертить*) (**на**+*a.*) to draw, plot (*on a map etc.*). **2** (*причинить*) to cause; to inflict; **н. оскорбле́ние** to insult; **н. уще́рб** to inflict damage; **н. визи́т** to pay a visit. **3** (*лак, краску*) to apply. **4** (+*a. and* **на**+*a.*) (*натолкнуть*) to dash (against); (*impers.*): **ло́дку ~ло́ на мель** the boat struck a shoal.

нанес|ти́[2], у́, ёшь, *past* ~, ~**ла́** *pf.* (+*a. or g.*) **1** (*принести*) to bring (*a quantity of*). **2** (*навалить*) to pile up (*a quantity of*); (*о снеге, песке*) (*usu. impers.*) to drift.

нанес|ти́[3], ёт, *past* ~**ла́** *pf.*: **н. яи́ц** to lay (*a number of*) eggs.

нани|за́ть, жу́, ~**жешь** *pf. of* ⇒**низа́ть** *and* ~**зывать**

нани́зыва|ть, ю *impf.* = **низа́ть**

нанима́тел|ь, я *m.* **1** (*квартиры*) tenant. **2** (*рабочей силы*) employer.

нанима́тель|ница, ницы *f. of* ⇒~

нанима́|ть(ся), ю(сь) *impf. of* ⇒**наня́ть(ся)**

на́нк|а, и *f.* (*text.*) nankeen.

на́нк|овый *adj. of* ⇒~**а**

на́ново *adv.* (*coll.*) anew, afresh.

нано́с, а *m.* (*geol.*) alluvium; (*песка, снега*) drift.

наносеку́нд|а, ы *f.* nanosecond.

нано|си́ть[1], шу́, ~**сишь** *impf. of* ⇒**нанести́**

нано|си́ть[2], шу́, ~**сишь** *pf.* (+*a. or g.*) to bring (*a quantity of*).

нано́с|ный (~ен, ~на) *adj.* **1** (*geol.*) alluvial. **2** (*fig.*) alien; borrowed.

нанотехноло́ги|я, и *f.* nanotechnology.

наню́х|аться, аюсь *pf.* (*of* ⇒~**иваться**) (+*g.*) **1** to smell to one's heart's content; to take snuff to one's heart's content. **2** (*до болезненного состояния*) to be intoxicated (with).

наню́хива|ться, юсь *impf. of* ⇒**наню́хаться**

на́н|ятый *p.p.p. of* ⇒~**я́ть**

на|ня́ть, найму́, наймёшь, *past* ~**нял,** ~**няла́,** ~**няло** *pf.* (*of* ⇒~**нима́ть**) (*квартиру*) to rent; (*машину, рабочих*) to hire; **н. на рабо́ту** to engage, take on.

на|ня́ться, найму́сь, наймёшься, *past* ~**ня́лся,** ~**няла́сь** *pf.* (*of* ⇒~**нима́ться**) to get a job.

наобеща́|ть, ю *pf.* (+*a. or g.*) to promise (much); **н. с три ко́роба** to promise the world.

наоборо́т *adv.* **1** (*обратной стороной*) back to front; **проче́сть сло́во н.** to read a word backwards. **2** (*не так*) the other way round; the wrong way (round); **он всё понима́ет н.** he take everything the wrong way. **3** (*при противопоставлении*) on the contrary; **как раз н.** quite the contrary; **и н.** and vice versa; **я не сержу́сь, а, н., рад, что вы пришли́** I am not angry; on the contrary, I am glad that you came.

наобу́м *adv.* (*не подумав*) without thinking; (*наудачу*) at random.

наор|а́ть, у́, ёшь *pf.* (**на**+*a.*; *coll.*) to shout (at).

нао́тмашь *adv.* (*размахнувшись*) with the back of the hand; **уда́рить н.** to strike a swinging blow.

наотре́з *adv.* flatly, point-blank.

напа́да|ть, ет *pf.* to fall (*in a certain quantity*); **в тече́ние но́чи ~ло мно́го сне́га** there was a heavy fall of snow during the night.

напада́|ть, ю *impf. of* ⇒**напа́сть**

напада́ющ|ий, его *m.* (*sport*) forward.

нападе́ни|е, я *nt.* **1** attack, assault. **2** (*sport, collect.*) forwards, forward-line.

напа́д|ки, ок, кам *no sg.* (*verbal*) attacks; **подверга́ться ~кам** to be under attack.

напа|ду́, дёшь *see* ⇒~**сть**

напа́ива|ть[1], ю *impf. of* ⇒**напои́ть**

напа́ива|ть[2], ю *impf. of* ⇒**напая́ть**

напа́ко|стить, щу, стишь *pf. of* ⇒**па́костить**

напа́лм, а *m.* (*chem.*; *mil.*) napalm.

напа́лм|овый *adj. of* ⇒~

напа́рник, а *m.* fellow worker, mate.

напа́рыва|ть(ся), ю(сь) *impf. of* ⇒**напоро́ть(ся)**

напас|ти́сь, у́сь, ёшься, *past* ~**ся,** ~**ла́сь** *pf.* (*coll.*; *usu.* +*neg.*) to lay in, save up enough; **на тебя́ еды́ не ~ёшься** you are eating us out of house and home.

напа́|сть[1], ду́, дёшь, *past* ~**л** *pf.* (*of* ⇒~**да́ть**) (**на**+*a.*) **1** to attack; to descend (on). **2** (*о чувстве*) to come (over); to grip, seize; **на нас ~л страх** fear seized us. **3** (*обнаружить*) to come (upon, across); **я ~л на интере́сную мысль в статье́** I came across an interesting thought in the article; **я ~л на иде́ю** an idea occurred to me.

напа́ст|ь[2], и *f.* (*coll.*) misfortune, disaster; **что за н.!** bother!

напа́чка|ть, ю *pf. of* ⇒**па́чкать**

напая́|ть, ю, ешь *pf.* (*of* ⇒**напа́ивать[2]**) to solder (onto).

напе́в, а *m.* tune, melody.

напева́|ть, ю *impf.* **1** *impf. of* ⇒**напе́ть. 2** to hum; to croon.

напе́в|ный (~ен, ~на) *adj.* melodious.

напека́|ть, ю *impf. of* ⇒**напе́чь[1]**

напербо́й *adv.* vying with one another.

напереве́с *adv.* in a horizontal position.

наперего́нки *adv.* racing one another; **бе́гать н.** to race (with) one another.

наперёд *adv.* (*coll.*) (*знать*) in advance; **за́дом н.** back to front.

напереко́р *adv. and prep.* (+*d.*) in defiance (of), counter (to).

напере́рез *adv.* (*and prep.*+*d.*) so as to cross one's path; **бежа́ть кому́-н. н.** to run to head s.o. off.

напереры́в *adv.* = **напербо́й**

на|пере́ть, пру́, прёшь, *past* ~**пёр,** ~**пёрла** *pf.* (*of* ⇒~**пира́ть**) (*coll.*; **на**+*a.*) to press (against).

напере|хва́т *adv.* **1** = ~**ре́з. 2** = ~**бо́й**

наперечёт *adv.* **1** (*помнить, знать*) through and through; every single one. **2** *as pred.* (*очень немного*) very few, not many.

напе́рсник, а *m.* (*obs.*) confidant.

напе́рсниц|а, ы *f.* (*obs.*) **1** confidante. **2** (*любовница*) mistress.

напёрст|ок, ка *m.* thimble.

наперстя́нк|а, и *f.* (*bot.*) foxglove.

напе́рч|ить, ~у, ~ишь *pf. of* ⇒**пе́рчить**

нап|е́ть, ою́, оёшь *pf.* (*of* ⇒~**ева́ть**) **1** (*песню, мелодию*) to hum, sing sketchily. **2**: **н. пласти́нку** to make a recording of one's voice. **3** (*coll.*; +*d. or* **в у́ши** +*d.*) to give s.o. a piece of one's mind.

напеча́та|ть(ся), ю(сь) *pf. of* ⇒**печа́тать(ся)**

напе́|чь[1], чёт, *past* ~**кло́** *pf.* (*of* ⇒~**ка́ть**) (*impers.*; *coll.*) (*опалить*) to burn, scorch (*with the sun*); **мне го́лову ~кло́** my head got scorched.

напе́|чь[2], ку́, чёшь, ку́т, *past* ~**к,** ~**кла́** *pf.* (+*a. or g.*) (*испечь*) to bake (*a number of*).

напива́|ться, юсь *impf. of* ⇒**напи́ться**

напи́лива|ть, ю *impf. of* ⇒**напили́ть**

напил|и́ть, ю́, ~ишь *pf.* (*of* ⇒~**ивать**) (+*a. or g.*) to saw (*a quantity of*).

напи́л|ок, ка *m.* (*coll.*) = ~**ьник**

напи́льник, а *m.* (*tech.*) file.

напира́|ть, ю *impf.* (*coll.*; **на**+*a.*) **1** *impf. of* ⇒**напере́ть.**

2 (*подчёркивать*) (**на**+*a.*) to emphasize, stress. **3** (*теснить*) to push.

написа́ни|е, я *nt.* **1** (*форма буквы*) way of writing (*a letter of the alphabet*). **2** (*правописание*) spelling. **3** (*статьи, книги*) writing.

напи|са́ть, шу́, ~́шешь *pf. of* **⇒писа́ть**

напит|а́ть, а́ю *pf.* **1** *pf. of* **⇒пита́ть.** **2** (*impf.* **~́ывать**) (+*i.*) (*пропитать*) to impregnate (with).

напит|а́ться, а́юсь *pf.* (*of* **~́ываться**) (+*i.*) to be impregnated (with).

напи́т|ок, ка *m.* drink, beverage; **тонизи́рующий н.** tonic, pick-me-up.

напи́тыва|ть(ся), ю(сь) *impf. of* **⇒напита́ть(ся)**

нап|и́ться, ью́сь, ьёшься, *past* **~и́лся, ~ила́сь, ~и́ло́сь** *pf.* (*of* **⇒~ива́ться**) **1** (+*g.*) (*утолить жажду*) to slake one's thirst (with, on); (*выпить*) to have a drink (of). **2** (*стать пьяным*) to get drunk.

напих|а́ть, а́ю *pf.* (*of* **⇒~́ивать**) (**в**+*a.*) to cram (into), stuff (into).

напи́хива|ть, ю *impf. of* **⇒напиха́ть**

напи́чка|ть, ю *pf. of* **⇒пи́чкать**

напи|шу́, ~́шешь *see* **⇒~са́ть**

напла́|кать, чу, чешь *pf.* (*coll.*) to make red, swollen from crying; **кот ~кал** very little; **у нас де́нег — кот ~кал** we have very little money.

напла́|каться, чусь, чешься *pf.* **1** (*поплакать много*) to cry a lot; to have a good cry. **2** (*coll.*) to have trouble; **он ещё ~чется** there is trouble in store for him yet; **она́ с ним ~чется** he will give her lots of trouble.

напластова́ни|е, я *nt.* (*geol.*) bedding, stratification.

наплева́тельский *adj.* (*coll.*) devil-may-care.

напл|ева́ть, юю́, юёшь *pf.* **1** (+*g.*) to spit (out). **2** (*fig., coll.*; **на**+*a.*) to wash one's hands (of); **н.!** to hell with it! who cares!; **н. на него́!** to hell with him!; **мне н.!** I couldn't care less!

напле|сти́, ту́, тёшь, *past* **~́л, ~ла́** *pf.* **1** (*impf.* **⇒наплета́ть**) (+*a. or g.*) to make by weaving (*a number of*). **2** (*pf. only*) (*coll.*) (*солгать*) to lie; **н. вздо́ру** (*fig., coll.*) to talk a lot of nonsense; (**на**+*a., coll.*) to slander.

наплета́|ть, ю *impf. of* **⇒наплести́**

напле́чник, а *m.* shoulder strap; (*sport*) shoulder pad.

напле́чный *adj.* (worn on the) shoulder.

напло|ди́ть, жу́, ди́шь *pf.* (*coll.*) to produce (*in great numbers*); to breed.

напло|ди́ться, ди́тся *pf.* (*coll.*) to multiply; to breed.

наплы́в, а *m.* **1** (*людей*) influx; (*чувств*) flood. **2** (*bot.*) canker; excrescence.

наплыва́|ть, ю *impf. of* **⇒наплы́ть**

наплы́|ть, ву́, вёшь, *past* **~л, ~ла́, ~ло** *pf.* (*of* **⇒~ва́ть**) **1** (**на**+*a.*) (*на мель*) to run (against), dash (against). **2** (*приплыв, скопиться*) to be washed up, form; **на него́ ~ли воспомина́ния** memories overwhelmed him. **3** (*о тучах*) (**на**+*a.*) to drift (in front of).

напова́л *adv.* outright, on the spot.

наподо́бие *prep.* (+*g.*) like, resembling, in the likeness of.

напо́|енный *p.p.p. of* **⇒~и́ть 1,** 2

напо|ённый *p.p.p. of* **⇒~и́ть** 3

напо|и́ть, ю, и́шь *pf.* (*of* **⇒пои́ть** *and* **⇒напа́ивать**[1]) **1** (*дать попить*) to give to drink; to water (*an animal*). **2** (*довести до опьянения*) to make drunk. **3** (*no impf.*) (*poet.*) (*наполнить*) to impregnate; to fill.

напока́з *adv.* for show; **вы́ставить н.** to show off (*also fig.*).

наполз|а́ть, а́ю *impf. of* **⇒~ти́**

наполз|ти́[1]**, у́, ёшь,** *past* **~́, ~ла́** *pf.* (*of* **⇒~а́ть**) (**на**+*a.*) to crawl (over, against).

наполз|ти́[2]**, у́, ёшь,** *past* **~́, ~ла́** *pf.* to crawl in (*in great numbers*).

наполне́ни|е, я *nt.* filling.

наполни́тел|ь, я *m.* (*tech.*) filler.

напо́лн|ить, ю, ишь *pf.* (*of* **⇒~я́ть**) (+*i.*) to fill (with).

напо́лн|иться, юсь, ишься *pf.* (*of* **⇒~я́ться**) (+*i.*) to fill (with) (*intrans.*)

наполн|я́ть(ся), я́ю(сь) *impf. of* **⇒~́ить(ся)**

наполови́ну *adv.* half; **зал ещё н. пуст** the hall is still half empty; **де́лать де́ло н.** to do a thing by halves.

напо́льн|ый *adj.* floor (*attr.*); **~ая ла́мпа** standard lamp; **~ые часы́** grandfather clock.

напома́|дить, жу, дишь *pf. of* **⇒пома́дить**

напомина́ни|е, я *nt.* **1** (*действие*) reminding. **2** (*что-н. напоминающее*) reminder.

напомина́|ть, ю *impf. of* **⇒напо́мнить**

напо́мн|ить, ю, ишь *pf.* (*of* **⇒напомина́ть**) **1** (+*d. and* **о**+*p. or* +*d. and a.*) (*заставить вспомнить*) to remind (of); **портре́т ~ил мне о про́шлом** *or* **~ил мне про́шлое** the portrait reminded me of the past. **2** (*иметь сходство*) to remind (of), recall (= *to resemble*); **он ~ил мне моего́ де́да** he reminded me of my grandfather.

напо́р, а *m.* (*воздуха, воды*) pressure (*also fig.*); **под ~ом** under pressure; **с ~ом** (*coll.*) vigorously.

напо́ристост|ь, и *f.* energy; push, go.

напо́рист|ый (~, ~а) *adj.* energetic; pushy.

напо́р|ный *adj. of* **⇒~** (*tech.*); **н. бак** pressure tank; **н. кла́пан** pressure valve; **н. насо́с** force pump; **~ная труба́** rising pipe, rising main.

напор|о́ть[1]**, ю ~́ешь** *pf.* (*of* **⇒напа́рывать**) (*coll.*) to tear, cut; **н. ру́ку на гвоздь** to cut one's hand on a nail.

напор|о́ть[2]**, ю, ~́ешь** *pf.* to rip (*a quantity of*); (*coll.*): **н. вздо́ру, чепухи́** to talk a lot of nonsense.

напор|о́ться, ю́сь, ~́ешься *pf.* (*of* **⇒напа́рываться**) (**на**+*a.*) **1** (*поранить себя*) to cut o.s. (on). **2** (*столкнуться*) to run (upon, against); (*fig.*) (*на неприятности*) to run (into, up against).

напо́р|тить[1]**, чу, тишь** *pf.* (+*a. or g.*) (*испортить*) to spoil (*a quantity of*).

напо́р|тить[2]**, чу, тишь** *pf.* (*coll.*) (+*d.*) (*навредить*) to injure, harm.

напосле́док *adv.* (*coll.*) in the end, finally, after all.

нап|ою́[1]**, оёшь** *see* **⇒~е́ть**

напо|ю́[2]**, и́шь** *see* **⇒~и́ть**

напр. (*abbr. of* ***наприме́р***) e.g., for example.

напра́в|ить, лю, ишь *pf.* (*of* **⇒~ля́ть**) **1** (**на**+*a.*) (*устремить*) to direct (to, at); **н. внима́ние (на**+*a.*) to direct one's attention (to); **н. свой путь** to head (for); **н. уда́р** to aim a blow (at). **2** (*отправить*) to send; **н. заявле́ние** to send in an application; (*к врачу, к юристу*) to refer. **3** (*отточить*) to sharpen; **н. бри́тву** to set a razor. **4** (*coll.*) (*организовать*) to organize.

напра́в|иться, люсь, ишься *pf.* (*of* **⇒~ля́ться**) **1** (**к**+*d.*, **в**+*a.*, **на**+*a.*) (*двинуться куда-н.*) to make (for). **2** (*coll.*) (*наладиться*) to get going, get under way (*fig.*).

напра́вк|а, и *f.* setting (*of razor, etc.*)

направле́ни|е, я *nt.* **1** (*линия, путь*) direction; **по ~ю (к**+*d.*) in the direction (of), towards; **взять н. на се́вер** to make for, head for the north. **2** (*mil.*) sector. **3** (*fig.*) (*в экономике, в политике*) trend, tendency; **н. ума́** turn of mind; **либера́льное н.** liberal tendency; (*группировка*) movement. **4** (*документ*) order, warrant; directive; **н. в санато́рий** warrant for stay at a sanatorium.

напра́вленност|ь, и *f.* direction, focus, purposefulness.

напра́в|ленный *p.p.p. of* **⇒~ить** *and adj.* **1** purposeful; unswerving. **2** (*radio*) directional.

направля́|ть, ю *impf. of* **⇒напра́вить**

направля́|ться, юсь *impf. of* **⇒напра́виться; ~емся в Му́рманск** we are bound for Murmansk.

направля́ющ|ая, ей *f.* (*tech.*) guide.

направля́|ющий *pres. part. act. of* **⇒~ть** *and adj.* (*tech.*) guiding, guide; leading; **н. ва́лик, н. ро́лик** guide roller.

напра́во *adv.* (**от**+*g.*) to the right (of); **н. и нале́во** freely, indiscriminately.

напрактик|ова́ться, у́юсь *pf.* (**в**+*p.*; *coll.*) to acquire skill (in).

напра́слин|а, ы *f.* (*coll.*) wrongful accusation, slander.

напра́сно *adv.* **1** (*бесполезно*) vainly, in vain; to no purpose. **2** (*несправедливо*) wrong, unjustly, mistakenly; **н. вы пришли́ без де́нег** it was a mistake for you to come without money.

напра́с|ный (~ен, ~на) *adj.* **1** (*бесполезный*) vain, idle; **~ная наде́жда** vain hope.

2 (*неосновательный*) unfounded.
3 (*ненужный*) needless.

напра́шива|ться, юсь *impf. of* ⇒**напроси́ться;** (*impf. only*) to arise, suggest itself; **~ется вопро́с** the question arises.

наприме́р for example, for instance.

напрока́|зить, жу, зишь *pf. of* ⇒**прока́зить**

напрока́знича|ть, ю *pf. of* ⇒**прока́зничать**

напрока́т *adv.* for hire, on hire; **взять н.** to hire, rent; **дать, отда́ть н.** to hire out, let.

напролёт *adv.* through, without a break; **рабо́тать всю ночь н.** to work the whole night through.

напроло́м *adv.* straight, regardless of obstacles (*also fig.*).

напропалу́ю *adv.* (*coll.*) regardless of the consequences; all out.

напроро́ч|ить, у, ишь *pf. of* ⇒**проро́чить**

напро|си́ться, шу́сь, ~сишься *pf.* (*of* ⇒**напра́шиваться**) (*coll.*) to thrust o.s. upon; (**на**+*a.*) to provoke; **н. на комплиме́нты** to fish for compliments.

напро́тив *adv. and prep.*+*g.* **1** opposite; **он живёт н. (на́шего до́ма)** he lives opposite (our house). **2** (+*d.*) (*наперекор*) in defiance (of); to contradict; **она́ всё де́лает мне н.** she does everything to spite me. **3** (*при противопоставлении*) on the contrary.

на́прочь *adv.* (*coll.*) completely.

нап|ру́, рёшь *see* ⇒**~ере́ть**

напру́жива|ть(ся), ю(сь) *impf. of* ⇒**напру́жить(ся)**

напру́ж|ить, у, ишь *pf.* (*of* ⇒**~ивать**) (*coll.*) to strain; to tense, tauten.

напру́ж|иться, усь, ишься *pf.* (*of* ⇒**~иваться**) (*coll.*) to become tense, become taut.

напряга́|ть(ся), ю(сь) *impf. of* ⇒**напря́чь(ся)**

напря|гу́, жёшь *see* ⇒**~чь**

напряже́ни|е, я *nt.* **1** (*затрата усилий*) effort, exertion; **рабо́тать с ~ем** to exert o.s.; (*трудное положение*) strain, tension. **2** (*phys., tech.*) strain; stress; (*elec.*) tension; voltage.

напряжённост|ь, и *f.* tension, strain.

напряжён|ный (~, ~на) *adj.* tense, strained; **~ные отноше́ния** strained relations; **~ная рабо́та** intensive work.

напрями́к *adv.* **1** (*пойти*) straight. **2** (*fig.*) (*сказать*) straight out, bluntly.

напряму́ю *adv.* = **напрями́к**

напря́|чь, гу́, жёшь, гу́т, *past* **~г, ~гла́** *pf.* (*of* ⇒**~га́ть**) (*мускулы*) to tense; (*голос, слух, внимание*) to strain (*also fig.*); **н. все си́лы** to strain every nerve.

напря́|чься, гу́сь, жёшься, гу́ться, *past* **~гся, ~гла́сь** *pf.* **1** (*о мускулах*) to become tense. **2** (*о человеке*) to exert o.s., strain o.s. **3** (*о взгляде, силах*) to be concentrated.

напуга́|ть(ся), ю(сь) *pf. of* ⇒**пуга́ть(ся)**

напу́др|ить(ся), ю(сь), ишь(ся) *pf. of* ⇒**пу́дрить(ся)**

напу́льсник, а *m.* wrist-band.

напуска́|ть(ся), ю(сь) *impf. of* ⇒**напусти́ть(ся)**

напускно́й *adj.* assumed, put on.

напу|сти́ть, щу́, ~стишь *pf.* (*of* ⇒**~ска́ть**) **1** (+*g.*) (*дыма, мух*) to let in; **н. воды́ в ва́нну** to fill a bath. **2** (*направить для нападения*) (**на**+*a.*) to let loose on, set on; **н. стра́ху на кого́-н.** (*coll.*) to strike fear into s.o. **3** (**на себя́**+*a.*) to affect, put on; **н. на себя́ ва́жность** to assume an air of importance.

напу|сти́ться, щу́сь, ~стишься *pf.* (*of* ⇒**~ска́ться**) (*coll.*; **на**+*a.*) to fly at, go for.

напу́та|ть, ю *pf.* (*coll.*, **в**+*p.*) to make a mess (of), make a hash (of); (*ошибиться*) to confuse, get wrong; **вы ~ли в а́дресе** you got the address wrong.

напу́тственн|ый *adj.* parting, farewell; **~ое сло́во** parting words.

напу́тстви|е, я *nt.* parting words, farewell speech.

напу́тств|овать, ую *impf. and pf.* to address (at parting); **н. до́брыми пожела́ниями** to bid farewell.

напух|а́ть, а́ет *impf. of* ⇒**~нуть**

напу́х|нуть, нет, *past* **~, ~ла** *pf.* (*of* ⇒**~а́ть**) to swell.

напу|щу́, ~стишь *see* ⇒**~сти́ть**

напы́ж|иться, усь, ишься *pf. of* ⇒**пы́житься**

напыл|и́ть, ю́, и́шь *pf. of* ⇒**пыли́ть**

напы́щенност|ь, и *f.* **1** (*надменность*) pomposity. **2** (*торжественность*) bombast.

напы́щен|ный (~, ~на) *adj.* **1** (*человек*) pompous. **2** (*стиль, речь*) bombastic, high-flown.

напя́лива|ть, ю *impf. of* ⇒**напя́лить**

напя́л|ить, ю, ишь *pf.* (*of* ⇒**~ивать**) **1** (*ткань*) to stretch on. **2** (*coll.*) (*одеть тесное*) to pull on, struggle into; (*одеть безвкусное*) to put on.

нар... *comb. form, abbr. of* ***наро́дный*** 4

нараба́тыва|ть, ю *impf. of* ⇒**нарабо́тать**

нарабо́та|ть, ю *pf.* (*of* ⇒**нараба́тывать**) (+*a. or g.*) (*coll.*) **1** (*сделать*) to make, turn out (*a quantity of*). **2** (*заработать*) to make, earn.

нарабо́та|ться, юсь *pf.* (*coll.*) to have worked enough; to have tired o.s. with work.

наравне́ *adv.* (**с**+*i.*) **1** (*на одной линии*) on a level (with); **ма́льчик шёл н. с солда́тами** the little boy kept pace with the soldiers. **2** (*одинаково*) equally (with); on an equal footing (with); together (with).

нара́д|оваться, уюсь *pf.* (+*d. or* **на**+*a.*; *usu.* +*neg.*) to rejoice, delight enough (in); **она́ не ~уется на сы́на** she dotes on her son.

нараспа́шку *adv.* (*coll.*) unbuttoned; **у него́ душа́ н.** (*fig.*) he wears his heart upon his sleeve.

нараспе́в *adv.* in a sing-song voice; drawlingly.

нараста́ни|е, я *nt.* (*процентов*) growth, accumulation; (*активности, шума*) increase.

нараст|а́ть, а́ю *impf. of* ⇒**~и́**

нарас|ти́, ту́, тёшь, *past* **наро́с, наросла́** *pf.* (*of* ⇒**~та́ть**) **1** (**на**+*p.*) to grow (on), form (on); **мох наро́с на камня́х** moss has grown on the stones. **2** (*увеличиться*) to increase; (*о звуке*) to swell. **3** (*накопиться*) to accumulate.

нара|сти́ть, щу́, сти́шь *pf.* (*of* ⇒**~щивать**) **1** (*мускулы*) to develop. **2** (*удлинить*) to lengthen; (*fig.*) (*увеличить*) to increase, augment.

нарасхва́т *adv.*: **продава́ться н.** to sell like hot cakes; **э́ту кни́гу покупа́ют н.** there is a great demand for this book.

нара́щивани|е, я *nt.* increase; build-up; **н. вооруже́ний** arms build-up.

нара́щива|ть, ю *impf. of* ⇒**нарасти́ть**

нарва́л, а *m.* (*zool.*) narwhal.

нарв|а́ть[1]**, у́, ёшь,** *past* **~а́л, ~ала́, ~а́ло** *pf.* (+*a. or g.*) **1** (*цветов*) to pick (*a quantity of*). **2** (*бумаги*) to tear (*a quantity of*).

нарв|а́ть[2]**, ёт,** *past* **~а́л, ~ала́, ~а́ло** *pf.* (*of* ⇒**нарыва́ть**) (*о нарыве*) to gather, come to a head.

нарв|а́ться, у́сь, ёшься, *past* **~а́лся, ~ала́сь, ~а́ло́сь** *pf.* (*of* ⇒**нарыва́ться**) (*coll.*; **на**+*a.*) to run into, run up (against).

на́рд|ы, ов *pl.* backgammon.

наре́|жу, жешь *see* ⇒**~зать**

наре́з, а *m.* **1** (*tech.*) thread; groove (*in rifling*). **2** (*hist., econ.*) lot, plot (*of land*).

наре́|зать, жу, жешь *pf.* (*of* ⇒**~за́ть**) **1** (+*a. or g.*) (*хлеба, сыр*) to cut; to slice. **2** (*tech.*) to thread; to rifle. **3** (*участки*) to allot, parcel out.

нарез|а́ть, а́ю *impf. of* ⇒**~ать**

наре́|заться, жусь, жешься *pf.* (*of* ⇒**~за́ться**) (*coll.*) to get drunk.

нарез|а́ться, а́юсь *impf. of* ⇒**~аться**

наре́зк|а, и *f.* **1** (*действие*) cutting (into pieces), slicing. **2** (*tech.*) thread; rifling.

нарезно́й *adj.* (*tech.*) threaded; rifled.

нарека́ни|е, я *nt.* censure; reprimand.

нарека́|ть, ю *impf. of* ⇒**наре́чь**

наре́чи|е[1]**, я** *nt.* (*диалект*) dialect.

наре́чи|е[2]**, я** *nt.* (*часть речи*) adverb.

наре́чный *adj.* adverbial.

наре́|чь, ку́, чёшь, ку́т, *past* **~к, ~кла́** *pf.* (*of* ⇒**~ка́ть**) (+*a. and i. or d. and a.*) to name; **ма́льчика ~кли́ Серге́ем, ма́льчику ~кли́ и́мя Серге́й** they named the boy Sergei.

нарза́н, а *m.* Narzan (*kind of mineral water*).

нарис|ова́ть, у́ю *pf. of* ⇒**рисова́ть**

нарица́тельн|ый *adj.* **1** (*econ.*)

nominal; **~ая сто́имость** nominal cost. **2** (*gram.*): **и́мя ~ое** common noun.

наркоби́знес, а *m.* drug trafficking.

наркодел|е́ц, ьца́ *m.* drug trafficker *or* pusher.

нарко́з, а *m.* **1** (*потеря чувствительности*) narcosis, anaesthesia (*Br.*), anesthesia (*US*). **2** (*средство*) anaesthetic (*Br.*), anesthetic (*US*); **ме́стный н.** local anaesthetic; **о́бщий н.** general anaesthetic.

нарко́лог, а *m.* expert in drug and alcohol abuse.

наркологи́ческий *adj.*: **н. диспансе́р** drug and alcohol abuse clinic.

нарколо́ги|я, и *f.* (study of) drug and alcohol abuse.

нарко́м, а *m.* (*abbr. of* ***наро́дный комисса́р***) (*hist.*) people's commissar.

наркома́н, а *m.* drug addict.

наркома́ни|я, и *f.* drug addiction.

наркома́н|ка, ки *f. of* ⇒**~**

наркома́т, а *m.* (*abbr. of* ***наро́дный комиссариа́т***) (*hist.*) people's commissariat.

наркома́фи|я, и *f.* drugs mafia.

наркосиндика́т, а *m.* drugs ring.

наркотизи́р|овать, ую *impf. and pf.* (*med.*) to anaesthetize (*Br.*), anesthetize (*US*).

нарко́тик, а *m.* narcotic; drug; **торго́вля ~ами** drug trafficking.

наркоти́ческ|ий *adj.* narcotic; **~ие сре́дства** narcotics, drugs.

наро́д, а (у) *m.* (*все жители*) people; (*нация*) nation; **~ы ми́ра** nations of the world; **англи́йский н.** the English people, the people of England; **челове́к из ~а** a man of the people; **на ми́тинге бы́ло ма́ло ~у** there were not many people at the meeting; **как говоря́т в ~е** as the expression goes; as they say.

наро|ди́ть, жу́, ди́шь *pf.* (*+a. or g.*) (*coll.*) to give birth to (*a number of*).

наро|ди́ться, жу́сь, ди́шься *pf.* (*of* ⇒**~жда́ться**) **1** (*coll.*) to be born. **2** (*fig.*) to come into being, arise.

наро́дник, а *m.* (*hist.*) narodnik, populist.

наро́дничес|кий *adj. of* ⇒**~тво**

наро́дничеств|о, а *nt.* (*hist.*) narodnik movement, populism.

наро́дно-освободи́тельный *adj.* popular liberation.

наро́дност|ь, и *f.* **1** (*народ*) nationality. **2** (*sg. only*) (*искусства*) national character; national traits.

народнохозя́йственный *adj.* pertaining to the national economy.

наро́дн|ый *adj.* **1** (*национальный*) national; **~ое хозя́йство** national economy; **н. поэ́т** national poet. **2** (*песня, искусство*) folk. **3** (*восстание, движение*) of the (*sc. common, working*) people, popular; **Н~ая во́ля** (*hist.*) Narodnaya volya ('The People's Will'); **Н. фронт** Popular Front. **4** *forms part of the official designation of certain Communist and former Communist states, also of certain organs of power and offices in the former USSR*; **стра́ны ~ой демокра́тии** 'the People's Democracies'; **Кита́йская Н~ая Респу́блика** the People's Republic of China; **н. заседа́тель** assessor (*in courts*); **н. суд** 'People's Court' (*court of first instance*). **5** (*в почётных званиях*) people's, officially recognized **н. арти́ст/худо́жник** people's actor/artist.

народовла́сти|е, я *nt.* 'people's power', government by the people.

народонаселе́ни|е, я *nt.* population.

нарожда́|ться, юсь *impf. of* ⇒**народи́ться**

нарожде́ни|е, я *nt.* birth, springing up; **н. ме́сяца** appearance of new moon.

наро́ст, а *m.* **1** (*грязи*) layer. **2** (*на растении*) excrescence, growth. **3** (*на котле*) scale.

нарочи́то *adv.* deliberately, intentionally.

нарочи́т|ый (~, ~а) *adj.* deliberate, intentional.

наро́чно *adv.* **1** (*намеренно*) on purpose, purposely; **как н.** (*coll.*) to make things worse; **н. не приду́маешь** it is quite something. **2** (*coll.*) (*в шутку*) for fun, pretending.

на́рочн|ый, ого *m.* courier; special messenger.

нарсу́д, а *m.* people's court.

на́рт|ы, ~ *pl.* (*sg.* **~а, ~ы** *f.*) sledge (*Br.*), sled (*US*) (*drawn by reindeer or dogs*).

наруб|и́ть, лю́, ~ишь *pf.* (*+a. or g.*) to chop (*a quantity of*).

нару́бк|а, и *f.* notch.

нару́жно *adv.* outwardly.

нару́жност|ь, и *f.* exterior; (outward) appearance; **н. обма́нчива** appearances are deceptive.

нару́жн|ый *adj.* (*стена, дверь*) external, exterior; (*изменение*) external; (*спокойствие*) outward; (*tech.*) male (*of screw thread*); **~ое (лека́рство)** medicine for external application.

нару́жу *adv.* outside, on the outside; **вы́йти н.** to come out; (*fig.*) to come to light, transpire.

нарука́вник, а *m.* oversleeve; armlet.

нарука́вн|ый *adj.* (worn on the) sleeve; **~ая повя́зка** arm-band.

нарумя́н|ить(ся), ю(сь), ишь(ся) *pf. of* ⇒**румя́нить(ся)**

нару́чник, а *m.* (*usu. pl.*) handcuff, manacle.

нару́чн|ый *adj.* worn on the arm; **~ые часы́** wrist-watch.

наруш|а́ть(ся), а́ю *impf. of* ⇒**~ить(ся)**

наруше́ни|е, я *nt.* **1** (*закона, дисциплины*) breach; violation; (*обещания*) breaking; **н. прав челове́ка** violation of human rights. **2** (*покоя*) disturbance; **н. су́точного ри́тма** jet lag.

наруши́тел|ь, я *m.* (*правила, закона*) transgressor, infringer.

наруши́тель|ница, ницы *f. of* ⇒**~**

нару́ш|ить, у, ишь *pf.* (*of* ⇒**~а́ть**) **1** (*сон, покой*) to break, disturb. **2** (*закон, обещание*) to break; **н. грани́цу** to cross a border illegally.

нару́ш|иться, ится *pf.* (*of* ⇒**~а́ться**) (*сон, покой, связь*) to be broken.

нарци́сс, а *m.* narcissus, daffodil.

на́р|ы, ~ *no sg.* plank-bed; bunk.

нары́в, а *m.* abscess; boil.

нарыва́|ть, ю *impf. of* ⇒**нарва́ть**[2]

нарыва́|ться, юсь *impf. of* ⇒**нарва́ться**

нар|ы́ть, о́ю, о́ешь *pf.* (*+a. or g.*) to dig (*a quantity of*).

наря́д[1]**, а** *m.* (*одежда*) attire, apparel, costume.

наря́д[2]**, а** *m.* **1** (*документ*) order, warrant. **2** (*mil.*) detail (*group of soldiers*). **3** (*mil.*) duty; **расписа́ние ~ов** roster; duty detail, orders.

наря|ди́ть[1]**, жу́, ~дишь** *pf.* (*of* ⇒**~жа́ть**) **1** (**в** *+a.*) to dress (in), array (in); **н. ёлку** to decorate a Christmas tree. **2** (*+i.*) to dress up (as).

наря|ди́ть[2]**, жу́, ~дишь** *pf.* (*of* ⇒**~жа́ть**) (*mil.*) to detail, appoint; **н. в карау́л** to put on guard.

наря|ди́ться, жу́сь, ~ди́шься *pf.* (*of* ⇒**~жа́ться**) **1** (**в** *+a.*) to array o.s. (in). **2** (*+i.*) to dress up (as).

наря́дност|ь, и *f.* elegance, smartness.

наря́д|ный (~ен, ~на) *adj.* (*человек*) well-dressed; elegant; (*одежда*) smart; (*комната*) well decorated.

наряду́ *adv.* (**с** *+i.*) side by side (with), equally (with); together (with); **де́ти н. со взро́слыми** grown-ups and children alike; **н. с э́тим** at the same time.

наряжа́|ть(ся), ю(сь) *impf. of* ⇒**наряди́ть(ся)**

нас *a., g., and p. of* ⇒**мы**

НА́СА *nt. indecl.* NASA (*abbr. of* National Aeronautics and Space Administration).

наса|ди́ть[1]**, жу́, ~дишь** *pf.* (*of* ⇒**~живать**) (*+a. or g.*) **1** (*растения*) to plant (*a quantity of*). **2** (*пассажиров*) to sit (*a number of*).

наса|ди́ть[2]**, жу́, ~дишь** *pf.* (*of* ⇒**~живать**) (*надеть*) to put; to stick, pin; **н. червяка́ на крючо́к** to fix a worm on to a hook.

наса|ди́ть[3]**, жу́, ~дишь** *pf.* (*of* ⇒**~жда́ть**) (*fig.*) to inculcate; to propagate.

наса́дк|а, и *f.* **1** (*действие*) setting, fixing, putting on. **2** (*часть прибора*) attachment; **набо́р наса́док** set of attachments. **3** (*для рыбы*) bait.

насажа́|ть, ю *pf.* = **насади́ть**[1]

насажда́|ть, ю *impf. of* ⇒**насади́ть**[3]

насажде́ни|е, я *nt.* **1** (*действие*) planting; (*fig.*) propagation, dissemination. **2** (*деревья*) plantation.

наса|ждённый *p.p.p. of* ⇒**~ди́ть**[3]

наса́|женный *p.p.p. of* ⇒**~ди́ть**[1,2]

наса́жива|ть, ю *impf. of* ⇒**насади́ть**[1,2]

наса́жива|ться, юсь *impf. of* ⇒**насе́сть**[1]

наса́лива|ть, ю *impf. of* **⇒насоли́ть**

наса́сыва|ть, ю *impf. of* **⇒насоса́ть**

наса́харива|ть, ю *impf. of* **⇒наса́харить**

наса́хар|ить, ю, ишь *pf.* (*of* **⇒~ивать**) to sugar, sweeten (*with sugar*).

насви́стыва|ть, ю *impf.* to whistle (*a tune*); (*о птицах*) to twitter.

наседа́|ть, ю *impf.* (*of* **⇒насе́сть²**) (**на**+*a.*) **1** (*о толпе*) to press. **2** (*о пыли*) to settle, collect.

насе́дк|а, и *f.* brood-hen, sitting hen.

насека́|ть, ю *impf. of* **⇒насе́чь**

насеко́м|ое, ого *nt.* insect.

насекомоя́дный *adj.* insectivorous.

населе́ни|е, я *nt.* **1** (*люди*) population; (*города, деревни*) inhabitants. **2** (*действие*) peopling, settling.

населённост|ь, и *f.* population density.

насел|ённый *p.p.p. of* **⇒~и́ть** *and adj.* **1** (*район*) densely populated; **н. пункт** (*official designation*) locality, place. **2** (*квартира*) inhabited.

насел|и́ть, ю́, и́шь *pf.* (*of* **⇒~я́ть**) to people, settle.

насел|я́ть, я́ю *impf.* **1** to inhabit. **2** *impf. of* **⇒~и́ть**

насе́ст, а *m.* roost, perch.

нас|е́сть¹, я́дет, *past* **~е́л** *pf.* (*of* **⇒~а́живаться**) to sit down (*in numbers*).

нас|е́сть², я́ду, я́дешь, *past* **~е́л** *pf. of* **⇒~еда́ть**

насе́чк|а, и *f.* **1** (*зарубка*) cut, incision; notch. **2** (*узор*) inlay.

насе́|чь, ку́, чёшь, ку́т, *past* **~к, ~кла́** *pf.* (*of* **⇒~ка́ть**) **1** to make incisions (in, on); to notch. **2** (*сталь, клинок*) to emboss; to damascene.

насе́|ять, ю, ешь *pf.* (+*a. or g.*) to sow (*a quantity of*).

наси|де́ть, жу́, ди́шь *pf.* (*of* **⇒~живать**) **1** (*о птице*) to hatch. **2** (*coll.*) (*о человеке*) to warm (*by sitting*).

наси|де́ться, жу́сь, ди́шься *pf.* (*coll.*) to sit long enough.

наси́|женный *p.p.p. of* **⇒~де́ть; ~женное яйцо́** fertilized egg; **~женное ме́сто** (*fig.*) familiar spot, old haunt.

наси́жива|ть, ю *impf. of* **⇒насиде́ть**

наси|жу́, ди́шь *see* **⇒~де́ть**

наси́ли|е, я *nt.* (*физическое*) violence; (*принуждение*) force.

наси́л|овать, ую *impf.* **1** (*принуждать*) to coerce, constrain. **2** (*pf.* **из~**) (*женщину*) to rape.

наси́лу *adv.* (*coll.*) with difficulty; (*едва*) hardly.

наси́льник, а *m.* **1** tyrant; aggressor. **2** (*над женщиной*) rapist.

наси́льно *adv.* by force, forcibly.

наси́льственн|ый *adj.* (*меры*) violent; (*выселение*) forcible; **~ая смерть** murder.

наска|за́ть, жу́, ~́жешь *pf.* (*coll.*; +*a. or g.*) to say, talk a lot (of); **н. новосте́й** to have a lot of news to tell.

наска|ка́ть, чу́, ~́чешь *pf.* (*of* **⇒~́кивать**) **1** (**на**+*a.*) to ride up (to). **2** (*прискакать*) to ride up, gallop up.

наска́кива|ть, ю *impf. of* **⇒наскака́ть** *and* **наскочи́ть**

наскanда́л|ить, ю, ишь *pf. of* **⇒сканда́лить**

наскво́зь *adv.* (*полностью*) through (and through); throughout; **промо́кнуть н.** to get wet through; (*пробить, прострелить*) through; **проби́ть сте́ну н.** to make a hole through the wall; **ви́деть (знать) кого́-н. н.** (*fig.*) to see through s.o.

наско́к, а *m.* **1** swoop; lunge; **де́йствовать ~ом** to act on impulse; **с ~а** (*fig., coll.*) hurriedly, on the spur of the moment. **2** (*fig., coll.*) attack.

наско́лько *adv.* **1** (*interrog.*) how?; **н. э́то серьёзно?** how serious is it?; (*in clauses*) **я не зна́ю, н. э́то сро́чно** I don't know how urgent it is. **2** (*rel.*) (*помню, знаю*) as far as; **н. мне изве́стно** as far as I know, to the best of my knowledge. **3** (*в такой степени*) so; **н. э́то трудне́е** it is so much more difficult; **н. он преуспе́л** he has been so successful.

на́скоро *adv.* (*coll.*) hastily, hurriedly.

наскоч|и́ть, у́, ~́ишь *pf.* (*of* **⇒наска́кивать**) (**на**+*a.*) **1** (*столкнуться*) to run (against), collide (with); **н. на неприя́тность** (*fig.*) to get into trouble. **2** (*fig., coll.*) (*с упрёками*) to fly (at).

наскреба́|ть, ю *impf. of* **⇒наскрести́**

наскре|сти́, бу́, бёшь, *past* **~́б, ~бла́** *pf.* (*of* **⇒~ба́ть**) to scrape up, scrape together; (*fig.*): **н. де́нег на пое́здку** to scrape up some money for a trip.

наску́ч|ить, у, ишь *pf.* (+*d.*) to bore; **мне э́то ~ило** I am sick of it.

насла|ди́ть, жу́, ди́шь *pf.* (*of* **⇒~жда́ть**) to delight, please.

насла|ди́ться, жу́сь, ди́шься *pf.* (*of* **⇒~жда́ться**) (+*i.*) to enjoy; to take pleasure (in), delight (in).

наслажда́|ть(ся), ю(сь) *impf. of* **⇒наслади́ть(ся)**

наслажде́ни|е, я *nt.* enjoyment, delight.

насла́ива|ться, юсь *impf. of* **⇒наслои́ться**

на|сла́ть¹, шлю́, шлёшь *pf.* (*of* **⇒~сыла́ть**) (*беду, болезни*) to send down.

на|сла́ть², шлю́, шлёшь *pf.* (+*a. or g.*) (*подарков*) to send (*a quantity of*).

насле́ди|е, я *nt.* legacy; (*культурное*) heritage.

насле|ди́ть, жу́, ди́шь *pf.* (*of* **⇒следи́ть²**) to leave (dirty) marks, traces.

насле́дник, а *m.* heir; (*fig.*) successor, inheritor.

насле́дниц|а, ы *f.* heiress.

насле́дный *adj.* first in the line of succession; **н. принц** Crown prince.

насле́довани|е, я *nt.* inheritance.

насле́д|овать, ую *impf. and pf.* **1** (*pf. also* **у~**) to inherit. **2** (+*d.*) to succeed (to).

насле́дственност|ь, и *f.* heredity.

насле́дственный *adj.* hereditary, inherited.

насле́дств|о, а *nt.* **1** inheritance, legacy; **получи́ть в н., по ~у** to inherit. **2** (*fig.*) heritage.

наслое́ни|е, я *nt.* **1** (*geol.*) stratification. **2** (*слой*) layer, deposit.

наслo|и́ться, ю́сь, и́шься *pf.* (*of* **⇒насла́иваться**) (**на**+*a.*) to be deposited (on), accumulate (on).

наслуж|и́ться, у́сь ~́ишься *pf.* (*coll.*) to have served for long enough.

наслу́ша|ться, юсь *pf.* (+*g.*) **1** (*услышать много*) to hear (a lot of). **2** (*вдоволь послушать*) to hear enough, listen to long enough; **я не ~юсь э́тих пе́сен** I cannot hear enough of these songs.

наслы́шан *adj. as pred.* (**о**+*p.*) familiar (with) by hearsay; **мы о вас мно́го ~ы** we have heard a lot about you.

наслы́ш|аться, усь, ишься *pf.* (**о**+*p.*) to have heard a lot (about).

наслы́шк|а, и *f.*: **по ~е** (*coll.*) by hearsay.

насма́рку *adv.* (*coll.*): **пойти́ н.** to come to nothing.

на́смерть *adv.* to death; **сража́ться н.** to fight to the death; **испуга́ть н.** (*fig.*) to frighten to death.

насмеха́|ться, юсь *impf.* (**над**+*i.*) to mock, ridicule.

насмеш|и́ть, у́, и́шь, *pf. of* **⇒смеши́ть**

насме́шк|а, и *f.* gibe, taunt; (*pl.*) mockery; **сказа́ть что-н. в ~у** to say sth. to hurt s.o.

насме́шлив|ый (~, ~а) *adj.* **1** (*тон, улыбка*) mocking, derisive. **2** (*человек*) sarcastic.

насме́шник, а *m.* (*coll.*) scoffer.

насме́шни|ца, цы *f. of* **⇒~к**

насме|я́ться, ю́сь, ёшься *pf.* **1** (*coll.*) to have a good laugh. **2** (**над**+*i.*) to laugh (at); **н. над чьи́ми-н. чу́вствами** to insult s.o.'s feelings.

на́сморк, а *m.* cold (*in the head*); **схвати́ть, получи́ть н.** to catch a cold.

насмотр|е́ться, ю́сь, ~́ишься *pf.* **1** (+*g.*) (*увидеть много*) to see a lot (of). **2** (**на**+*a.*) to have looked enough (at), to see enough (of); **не н.** not to tire of looking (at).

насоба́ч|иться, усь, ишься *pf.* (*coll.*; +*inf.*) to become adept (at), become good (at).

нас|ова́ть, ую́, уёшь *pf.* (*of* **⇒~о́вывать**) (*coll.*; +*g. or a.*) to shove in, stuff in (*a quantity of*); **н. конфе́т в карма́ны** to stuff sweets into one's pockets.

насовсе́м *adv.* (*coll.*) for good.

насо́выва|ть, ю *impf. of* **⇒насова́ть**

Н

насол|и́ть, ю́, ~и́шь *pf.* (*of* ⇨**наса́ливать**) **1** (+*a. or g.*) (*огурцов, грибов*) to salt, pickle (*a quantity of*). **2** (*coll.*) (*сильно посолить*) to put much salt (into). **3** (*fig.*; +*d.*) (*сделать неприятность*) to spite; to do a bad turn (to).

насор|и́ть, ю, и́шь *pf. of* ⇨**сори́ть**

насо́с, а *m.* pump.

насос|а́ть, у́, ёшь, *pf.* (*of* ⇨**наса́сывать**) (+*a. or g.*) **1** (*молока*) to suck (*a quantity of*). **2** (*бензина*) to pump.

насос|а́ться, у́сь, ёшься *pf.* (+*g.*) to have sucked one's fill.

насо́с|ный *adj. of* ⇨**~; н. агрега́т** pumping unit; **~ная ста́нция** pumping station.

насочин|и́ть, ю́, и́шь *pf.* (*coll.*) (+*a. or g.*) to talk a lot of nonsense; to make up (a lot of falsehoods).

на́спех *adv.* hastily; carelessly.

наспле́тнича|ть, ю *pf.* (*coll.*) (+*d.*) to gossip (to).

наср|а́ть, у, ёшь *pf. of* ⇨**сра́ть**

наст, а *m.* thin crust of ice over snow.

наста|ва́ть, ёт, ю́т *impf. of* ⇨**~́ть**

наставител|ьный (~ен, ~ьна) *adj.* edifying, instructive; **н. тон** didactic tone.

наста́в|ить[1], лю, ишь *pf.* (*of* ⇨**~ля́ть**) **1** (*платье*) to lengthen; (*кусок ткани*) to put on, add on; **н. нос кому́-н.** to fool, dupe s.o. **2** (**на**+*a.*) (*нацелить*) to aim (at), point (at); **н. револьве́р на кого́-н.** to point a revolver at s.o.

наста́в|ить[2], лю, ишь *pf.* (*of* ⇨**~ля́ть**) (*научить*) to edify; to exhort, admonish; **н. на путь и́стинный** to set on the right path; **н. кого́-н. на ум** to bring s.o. to his senses.

наста́в|ить[3], лю, ишь *pf.* (+*a. or g.*) (*стульев*) to set up, place (*a quantity of*); (*синяков*) to cause.

наста́вк|а, и *f.* addition.

наставле́ни|е, я *nt.* **1** (*действие, совет*) exhortation, admonition. **2** (*инструкция*) directions, instructions; (*mil.*) manual.

наставля́|ть, ю *impf. of* ⇨**наста́вить**

наста́вник, а *m.* (*воспитатель*) mentor; (*преподаватель*) teacher, instructor.

наста́вни|ческий *adj. of* ⇨**~к; н. тон** edifying tone.

наставно́й *adj.* (*рукава*) lengthened; (*труба*) added.

наста|ёт *see* ⇨**~ва́ть**

наста́ива|ть, ю *impf. of* ⇨**настоя́ть[1,2]**

наста́ива|ться, ется *impf. of* ⇨**настоя́ться[2]**

наста́|ть, нет, нут *pf.* (*of* ⇨**~ва́ть**) (*of times or seasons*) to come, begin.

на́стежь *adv.* wide open; **откры́ть н.** to open wide.

настели́ть = **настла́ть**

наст|елю́, е́лешь *see* ⇨**~ла́ть**

насте́нный *adj.* wall (*attr.*).

настиг|а́ть, а́ю *impf. of* ⇨**~нуть** *and* ⇨**насти́чь**

насти́гн|уть, у, ешь *pf.* = **насти́чь**

насти́л, а *m.* flooring; planking.

настила́|ть, ю *impf. of* ⇨**настла́ть**

насти́лк|а, и *f.* **1** (*действие*) laying, spreading. **2** = **насти́л**

насти́льн|ый *adj.* (*mil.*) grazing; **н. ого́нь** grazing fire; **~ая бо́мба** anti-personnel bomb.

настира́|ть, ю *pf.* (+*a. or g.*) (*coll.*) to wash, launder (*a quantity of*).

насти́|чь, гну, гнешь, *past.* **~г, ~гла** *pf.* (*of* ⇨**~га́ть**) to overtake (*also fig.*).

наст|ла́ть, елю́, ~е́лешь *pf.* (*of* ⇨**~ила́ть**) to lay, spread; **н. пол** to lay a floor; **н. соло́му** to spread straw.

насто́|й, я *m.* infusion.

насто́йк|а, и *f.* **1** (*спиртной напиток*) liqueur. **2** (*pharm.*) tincture.

насто́йчив|ый (~, ~а) *adj.* **1** (*человек*) persistent. **2** (*просьба, тон*) urgent, insistent.

насто́лько *adv.* so; so much; **н., наско́лько** as much as.

насто́льно-изда́тельский *adj.* desktop publishing; DTP.

насто́льн|ый *adj.* **1** table, desk; desktop; **~ая полигра́фия** desktop publishing; **~ая игра́** board game; **н. те́ннис** table tennis. **2** (*fig.*) for constant reference, in constant use; **~ая кни́га** bible.

настора́жива|ть(ся), ю(сь) *impf. of* ⇨**насторожи́ть(ся)**

настороже́ *adv.*: **быть н.** to be on one's guard; to be on the lookout.

насторожённост|ь, и *f.* (*and* **насторо́женность**) wariness.

насторо|жённый (*and* **~́женный**) *p.p.p. of* ⇨**~жи́ть** *and adj.* guarded, suspicious, wary.

насторож|и́ть, у́, и́шь *pf.* (*of* ⇨**настора́живать**) to put on one's guard; **н. слух, у́ши (н. внима́ние** *fig. only*) to prick up one's ears (*also fig.*).

насторож|и́ться, у́сь, и́шься *pf.* (*of* ⇨**настора́живаться**) to prick up one's ears.

настоя́ни|е, я *nt.* insistence; **по ~ю кого́-н.** at s.o.'s insistence.

настоя́тел|ь, я *m.* (*eccl.*) **1** (*монастыря*) prior, superior. **2** (*церкви*) senior priest.

настоя́тельниц|а, ы *f.* (*eccl.*) prioress, mother superior.

настоя́тел|ьный (~ен, ~ьна) *adj.* **1** (*требование*) persistent; insistent; **~ьная про́сьба** urgent request. **2** (*необходимость*) urgent, pressing.

насто|я́ть[1], ю́, и́шь *pf.* (*of* ⇨**наста́ивать**) (**на**+*p.*) to insist (on); **н. на своём** to insist on having it one's own way; **он ~я́л на том, что́бы пойти́ самому́** he insisted on going himself.

насто|я́ть[2], ю́, и́шь *pf.* (*of* ⇨**наста́ивать**) (*чай, травы*) to infuse.

насто|я́ться[1], ю́сь, и́шься *pf.* (*coll.*) to stand a long time.

насто|я́ться[2], и́тся, я́тся *pf.* (*of* ⇨**наста́иваться**) (*о чае, о травах*) to infuse, draw, brew.

настоя́щ|ий *adj.* **1** (*теперешний*) present; this; **в ~ее вре́мя** at present, now; **~ее вре́мя** (*gram.*) the present tense; *as n.* **~ее, ~его** *nt.* the present (time); **жить ~им** to live in the present. **2** (*подлинный*) real, genuine; **н. друг** real friend. **3** (*coll., pej.*) (*совершенный*) complete, utter, absolute; **он н. дура́к** he is an absolute fool.

настрада́|ться, юсь *pf.* to suffer much.

настра́ива|ть(ся), ю(сь) *impf. of* ⇨**настро́ить(ся)**

настра́чива|ть, ю *impf. of* ⇨**настрочи́ть[1]**

настреля́|ть, ю *pf.* (+*a. or g.*) to shoot (*a quantity of*).

настри́г, а *m.* (*agric.*) **1** (*действие*) shearing, clipping. **2** (*настриженная шерсть*) clip.

настри́|чь, гу́, жёшь, гу́т, *past* **~г, ~гла** *pf.* (+*a. or g.*) (*agric.*) to shear, clip (*a number of*).

на́строго *adv.* (*coll.*) strictly.

настрое́ни|е, я *nt.* **1** (*душевное состояние*) mood, temper, humour (*Br.*), humor (*US*); **припо́днятое/пода́вленное н.** high/low spirits; **челове́к ~я** a man of moods; **быть в плохо́м** *etc.*, **~и** to be in a bad, *etc.*, mood; **не в ~и** in a bad mood; **н. умо́в** state of opinion, public mood. **2** (+*inf.*) mood (for); **у меня́ нет ~я танцева́ть, я не в ~и танцева́ть** I am not in a mood for dancing; I don't feel like dancing.

настро́енност|ь, и *f.* mood.

настро́ен|ный (~, ~на) *adj.* **1** (*о настроении*): **он ~ оптимисти́чески** he is in optimistic mood. **2** (*о намерении*): **он ~ уе́хать** he intends to go away.

настро́|ить[1], ю, ишь *pf.* (*of* ⇨**настра́ивать**) **1** (*mus.*) (*пианино, рояль*) to tune; (*скрипку, флейту*) to tune up, tune. **2** (*приёмник*) to tune; **н. приёмник на сре́днюю волну́** to tune in to medium wave. **3** (*механизм*) to tune, adjust. **4** (*fig.*; **на**+*a.*) to dispose (to), incline (to); to incite; **н. кого́-н. на весёлый лад** to make s.o. happy, cheer s.o. up; **н. кого́-н. (про́тив**+*g.*) to incite s.o. (against).

настро́|ить[2], ю, ишь *pf.* (+*a. or g.*) (*построить*) to build (*a quantity of*).

настро́|иться, юсь, ишься *pf.* (*of* ⇨**настра́иваться**) (**на**+*a.*) to dispose o.s. (to); (+*inf.*) to make up one's mind (to); **я ~ился е́хать в Москву́** I made up my mind to go to Moscow.

настро́|й, я *m.* (*coll.*) mood.

настро́йк|а, и *f.* (*mus., radio*) tuning.

настро́йщик, а *m.* tuner.

настропал|и́ть, ю́, и́шь *pf.* (*of* ⇨**~я́ть**) (*coll.*) to incite, set on.

настропал|я́ть, я́ю *impf. of* ⇨**~и́ть**

настроч|и́ть[1], у́, и́шь *pf.* (*of*

⇒**настра́чивать**) (+*a. or g.*) to sew (*a quantity of*).

настроч|и́ть², у́, и́шь *pf. of* ⇒**строчи́ть** 2

настря́па|ть, ю *pf.* **1** (+*a. or g.*) (*еды*) to cook (*a quantity of*). **2** (*fig., coll.*) (*сочинить*) to cook up.

насту́к|ать, аю *pf.* (*of* ⇒**~ивать**) (*coll.*) to knock out, bash out (*on typewriter*).

насту́кива|ть, ю *impf. of* ⇒**насту́кать**

наступа́тельный *adj.* (*mil.*) offensive.

наступ|а́ть¹, а́ю *impf. of* ⇒**~и́ть¹,²**

наступа́|ть², ю *impf.* (*mil.*) to advance, be on the offensive; (*fig.*) (*на кого-н. с просьбами, требованиями*) to harass.

наступа́|ющий¹ *pres. part. act. of* ⇒**~ть¹** *and adj.* coming.

наступа́|ющий² *pres. part. act. of* ⇒**~ть²**; *as n.* **н., ~ющего** *m.* attacker.

наступ|и́ть¹, лю́, ~́ишь *pf.* (*of* ⇒**~а́ть¹**) (**на**+*a.*) to tread (on); **медве́дь** (*or* **слон**) **наступи́л ему́ на у́хо** he has absolutely no ear for music.

наступ|и́ть², ~́ит *pf.* (*of* ⇒**~а́ть¹**) (*о времени, состоянии*) to come, begin; (*о молчании, тишине*) to ensue; to set in; **~́ит вре́мя, когда́...** there will come a time, when....

наступле́ни|е¹, я *nt.* (*mil.*) offensive; attack; **перейти́ в н.** to assume the offensive.

наступле́ни|е², я *nt.* (*зимы*) coming, approach; onset; (*тишины*) ensuing.

насту́рци|я, и *f.* (*bot.*) nasturtium.

настуч|а́ть, у́, и́шь *pf. of* ⇒**стуча́ть** 3

насты́р|ный (~ен, ~на) *adj.* (*coll.*) persistent.

насул|и́ть, ю́, и́шь *pf.* (+*a. or g.*) (*coll.*) to promise (*much*).

насу́п|ить(ся), лю(сь), ишь(ся) *pf. of* ⇒**су́пить(ся)** *and* **~ливать(ся)**

насу́пливать(ся) = **су́пить(ся)**

насурьм|и́ть(ся), лю́(сь), и́шь(ся) *pf. of* ⇒**сурьми́ть(ся)**

на́сухо *adv.* dry; **вы́тереть н.** to wipe dry.

насуш|и́ть, у́, ~́ишь *pf.* (+*a. or g.*) to dry (*a quantity of*).

насу́щност|ь, и *f.* urgency.

насу́щ|ный (~ен, ~на) *adj.* vital, urgent; **хлеб н.** daily bread (*also fig.*).

нас|у́ю, уёшь *see* ⇒**~ова́ть**

насчёт *prep.*+*g.* about; as regards, concerning.

насчит|а́ть, а́ю *pf.* (*of* ⇒**~́ывать**) to count, number.

насчи́тыва|ть, ю *impf.* **1** *impf. of* ⇒**насчита́ть. 2** (*no pf.*) to number (= *to contain*); **э́тот го́род ~ет свы́ше ста ты́сяч жи́телей** this city has over one hundred thousand inhabitants.

насчи́тыва|ться, ется *impf.* (*impers.*) to number (= *to be, be contained*); **в на́шем селе́ ~ется не бо́лее двухсо́т жи́телей** the population of our village numbers no more than two hundred; **в го́роде ~ется де́сять больни́ц** the city has ten hospitals.

насыла́|ть, ю *impf. of* ⇒**насла́ть¹**

насы́п|ать, лю, лешь *pf.* (*of* ⇒**~а́ть**) **1** (+*a. or g.*) to pour (in, into); to fill (with); **н. муки́ в мешо́к** to pour flour into a bag; **н. мешо́к муко́й** to fill up a bag with flour. **2** (+*a. or g.* **на**+*a.*) (*посыпать*) to spread (on); **н. песку́ на доро́жку** to spread sand on the path. **3** (*холм*) to raise (*a heap or pile of sand, etc.*)

насып|а́ть, а́ю *impf. of* ⇒**~́ать**

насы́пк|а, и *f.* pouring (in), filling.

насыпно́й *adj.* poured; piled (up); **н. холм** artificial mound.

на́сып|ь, и *f.* embankment.

насы́|тить, щу, тишь *pf.* (*of* ⇒**~ща́ть**) **1** (*накормить*) to sate, satiate. **2** (*chem.*) to saturate, impregnate.

насы́|титься, щусь, тишься *pf.* (*of* ⇒**~ща́ться**) **1** (*наесться*) to be full; to be sated. **2** (*chem.*) to become saturated.

насыща́|ть(ся), ю(сь) *impf. of* ⇒**насы́тить(ся)**

насыще́ни|е, я *nt.* **1** satiety, satiation. **2** (*chem.*) saturation.

насы́щенност|ь, и *f.* **1** saturation. **2** (*fig.*) (*жизни*) richness.

насы́|щенный *p.p.p. of* ⇒**~тить** *and adj.* **1** saturated. **2** (*fig.*) (*содержательный*) rich.

ната́лкива|ть(ся), ю(сь) *impf. of* ⇒**натолкну́ть(ся)**

ната́плива|ть, ю *impf. of* ⇒**натопи́ть¹**

ната́птыва|ть, ю *impf. of* ⇒**натопта́ть**

ната́ск|анный *p.p.p. of* ⇒**~а́ть** *and adj.* (*ученик*) well-coached.

натаск|а́ть¹, а́ю *pf.* (*of* ⇒**~́ивать**) (*собак*) to train; (*fig., coll.*) (*учеников*) to coach, cram.

натаск|а́ть², а́ю *pf.* (*of* ⇒**~́ивать**) (+*a. or g.*) **1** (*принести*) to bring, lay in (*a quantity of*). **2** (*coll.*) (*извлечь*) to fish out, hook (*a quantity of*).

ната́скива|ть, ю *impf. of* ⇒**натаска́ть** *and* **натащи́ть¹**

натащ|и́ть¹, у́, ~́ишь *pf.* (*of* ⇒**ната́скивать**) (*натянуть*) to pull (on, over).

натащ|и́ть², у́, ~́ишь *pf.* (+*a. or g.*) (*притащить*) to bring (*a quantity of*).

натвор|и́ть, ю́, и́шь *pf.* (+*g.*; *coll., pej.*) to do, get up to; **н. вся́ких глу́постей** to get up to every sort of stupid trick; **что ты ~и́л!** what ever have you done?

на́те *int.* (*coll., addressed to more than one person or, politely, to one*) here (you are)!; there (you are)! (= *take it!*); **тепе́рь н. вам** and now see what's happened.

натёк, а *m.* **1** (*geol.*) deposit. **2** (*coll.*) pool (*of some liquid*).

натека́|ть, ет *impf. of* ⇒**натёчь**

нате́льн|ый *adj.* worn next to the skin; **~ое бельё** (*collect.*) underwear.

на|тере́ть¹, тру́, трёшь, *past* **~тёр, ~тёрла** *pf.* (*of* ⇒**~тира́ть**) **1** (*намазать*) to rub (in, on); **н. ру́ки вазели́ном** to rub vaseline into one's hands. **2** (*пол*) to polish. **3** (*повредить*) to rub sore; to chafe; **н. себе́ мозо́ль** to get a corn.

на|тере́ть², тру́, трёшь, *past* **~тёр, ~тёрла** *pf.* (+*a. or g.*) (*сыру*) to grate (*a quantity of*).

на|тере́ться, тру́сь, трёшься, *past* **~тёрся, ~тёрлась** *pf.* (*of* ⇒**~тира́ться**) (+*i.*) to rub o.s. (with).

натерп|е́ться, лю́сь, ~́ишься *pf.* (+*g.*; *coll.*) to have endured much; to have gone through much.

натёр|тый *p.p.p. of* ⇒**~е́ть¹,²**

нате́|чь, чёт, ку́т, *past* **~́к, ~кла́** *pf.* (*of* ⇒**~ка́ть**) (*о жидкости*) to accumulate.

натёш|иться, усь, ишься *pf.* (*coll.*) **1** to enjoy o.s., have a good time. **2** (**над**+*i.*) to have a good laugh (at).

натира́ни|е, я *nt.* **1** (*полов*) polishing. **2** (*coll.*) (*вещество*) embrocation, ointment.

натира́|ть(ся), ю(сь) *impf. of* ⇒**натере́ть(ся)**

на́тиск, а *m.* **1** (*войск*) onslaught, charge. **2** (*fig.*) pressure.

нати́ска|ть, ю *pf.* (+*a. or g.*) (*coll.*) to cram in, stuff in (*a quantity of*).

натк|а́ть, у́, ёшь, *past* **~а́л, ~ала́, ~а́ло** *pf.* (+*a. or g.*) to weave (*a quantity of*).

наткн|у́ть, у́, ёшь *pf.* (*of* ⇒**натыка́ть**) to stick, pin.

наткн|у́ться, у́сь, ёшься *pf.* (*of* ⇒**натыка́ться**) (**на**+*a.*) **1** to run (against), strike; to stumble (upon); **н. на гвоздь** to run against a nail; **н. на неожи́данное сопротивле́ние** (*fig.*) to meet with unexpected resistance. **2** (*fig.*) to stumble (upon, across), come (across); **н. на интере́сную мысль** to stumble across an interesting idea.

НА́ТО *nt. indecl.* NATO (*abbr. of* North Atlantic Treaty Organization — *Организа́ция Североатланти́ческого догово́ра*).

на́тов|ец, ца *m.* NATO member.

на́товский *adj. of* ⇒**НАТО**

натолкн|у́ть, у́, ёшь *pf.* (*of* ⇒**ната́лкивать**) (+*a.* **на**+*a.*) **1** to push (against), shove (against). **2** (*fig.*) to direct, lead (into, onto); **он ~у́л меня́ на мысль** he suggested the idea to me.

натолкн|у́ться, у́сь ёшься *pf.* (*of* ⇒**ната́лкиваться**) (**на**+*a.*) to run (against); (*fig.*) to run across.

натол|о́чь, ку́, чёшь, ку́т, *past* **~о́к, ~кла́** *pf.* (+*a. or g.*) to pound, crush (*a quantity of*).

натоп|и́ть¹, лю́, ~́ишь *pf.* (*of* ⇒**ната́пливать**) (*избу, печь*) to heat well, heat up.

натоп|и́ть², лю́, ~́ишь *pf.* (+*a. or g.*) **1** (*воску*) to melt (*a quantity of*). **2** (*молока*) to heat (*a quantity of*).

натоп|та́ть, чу́, ~́чешь *pf.* (*of* ⇒**ната́птывать**) (*coll.*; **в, на**+*p.*) to make dirty footmarks (in, on).

наторг|ова́ть, у́ю *pf.* (*coll.*) **1** (+*a. or g.*) (*приобрести*) to make, gain (*by* *commerce*). **2** (**на**+*a.*) (*о выручке*) to make; **он ~ова́л на 20 рубле́й** he made 20 roubles.

нато́ре|ть, ю *pf.* (**в**+*p.*; *coll.*) to become skilled (at, in), become expert (at, in).

наточ|и́ть, у́, ~́ишь *pf. of* ⇒**точи́ть**[1]

натоща́к *adv.* on an empty stomach.

натр, а *m.* (*chem.*) natron; **е́дкий н.** caustic soda.

натрав|и́ть[1], **лю́, ~́ишь** *pf.* (*of* ⇒**~́ливать**) (**на**+*a.*) (*собаку*) to set (on); (*fig.*) to set (against).

натрав|и́ть[2], **лю́, ~́ишь** *pf.* (*of* ⇒**~ля́ть**) (*сделать изображение*) to etch.

натрав|и́ть[3], **лю́, ~́ишь** *pf.* (+*a. or g.*) (*уничтожить*) to exterminate (*a quantity of*).

натра́влива|ть, ю *impf. of* ⇒**натрави́ть**[1]

натравля́|ть, ю, ешь *impf. of* ⇒**натрави́ть**[2]

натрениро́ван|ный (~, ~а) *adj.* trained.

натренир|ова́ть(ся), у́ю(сь) *pf. of* ⇒**тренирова́ть(ся)**

на́три|евый *adj. of* ⇒**~й**

на́три|й, я *m.* (*chem.*) sodium.

на́трое *adv.* in three.

нат|ру́, рёшь *see* ⇒**~ере́ть**

натру|ди́ть, жу́, ~ди́шь *pf.* (*of* ⇒**~́живать**) to tire out, overwork.

натру|ди́ться, жу́сь, ~ди́шься *pf.* (*coll.*) **1** (*утомиться*) to become tired out. **2** (*вдоволь потрудиться*) to have worked long enough; to have overworked.

натру́жива|ть, ю *impf. of* ⇒**натруди́ть**

натряс|ти́, у́, ёшь, *past* **~́, ~ла́** *pf.* (+*a. or g.*) to scatter, let fall (*a quantity of*).

нату́г|а, и *f.* effort, strain.

на́туго *adv.* (*coll.*) tightly; **ту́го-на́туго** very tightly.

нату́жива|ть(ся), ю(сь) *impf. of* ⇒**нату́жить(ся)**

нату́ж|ить, у, ишь *pf.* (*of* ⇒**~ивать**) (*coll.*) to tense, tighten.

нату́ж|иться, усь, ишься *pf.* (*of* ⇒**~иваться**) (*coll.*) to exert all one's strength; to strain.

нату́ж|ный (~ен, ~на) *adj.* (*coll.*) strained, forced.

нату́р|а, ы *f.* **1** (*характер*) nature. **2** (*натурщик*) (artist's) model, sitter. **3** (*econ.*) kind; **плати́ть ~ой** to pay in kind. **4** (*естественная обстановка*) natural setting; **рисова́ть с ~ы** to paint from life.

натурализа́ци|я, и *f.* naturalization.

натурали́зм, а *m.* naturalism.

натурализ|ова́ть, у́ю *impf. and pf.* to naturalize.

натурализ|ова́ться, у́юсь *impf. and pf.* to become naturalized.

натурали́ст, а *m.* naturalist.

натуралисти́ческий *adj.* naturalistic.

натура́льност|ь, и *f.* genuineness; naturalness.

натура́л|ьный (~ен, ~ьна) *adj.* **1** natural; **в ~ьную величину́** life-size. **2** (*настоящий*) (*мех, кожа, кофе*) real; (*смех*) genuine. **3** (*econ.*) in kind; **н. обме́н** barter.

нату́рщик, а *m.* (artist's) model, sitter.

нату́рщи|ца, цы *f. of* ⇒**~к**

нат́ыка|ть, ю *pf.* = **наткну́ть**

натыка́|ть(ся), ю(сь) *impf. of* ⇒**наткну́ть(ся)**

натюрмо́рт, а *m.* (*art*) still life.

натюрмо́рт|ный *adj. of* ⇒**~**

натя́гива|ть(ся), ю, ет(ся) *impf. of* ⇒**натяну́ть(ся)**

натяже́ни|е, я *nt.* pull, tension.

натя́жк|а, и *f.* **1** strained interpretation; **с ~ой** (*fig.*) at a stretch. **2** = **натяже́ние**

натяжн|о́й *adj.* (*tech.*) tension; **~о́е приспособле́ние** tension device, stretcher; **н. ро́лик** tension pulley; **н. рыча́г** tension lever.

натя́нутост|ь, и *f.* tension (*also fig.*)

натя́н|утый *p.p.p. of* ⇒**~у́ть** *and adj.* **1** tight. **2** (*fig.*) strained; forced; **~утые отноше́ния** strained relations; **~утое сравне́ние** far-fetched comparison.

натя|ну́ть, ну́, ~́нешь *pf.* (*of* ⇒**~́гивать**) **1** (*сделать тугим*) to stretch; to draw (tight); **н. лук** to draw a bow; **н. верёвку** (*naut.*) to haul a rope taut. **2** (*надеть*) to pull on; **н. ша́пку на́ уши** to pull a cap over one's ears.

натя|ну́ться, ~́нется, ~́нутся *pf.* (*of* ⇒**~́гиваться**) to stretch (*intrans.*).

науга́д *adv.* at random, by guess-work.

науго́льник, а *m.* (*tech.*) bevel, bevel square.

науда́чу *adv.* at random, by guess-work.

нау|ди́ть, жу́, ~́дишь *pf.* (+*a. or g.*) to hook, catch (*a number of*).

нау́к|а, и *f.* **1** (*система знаний*) science; (*учение*) learning; scholarship; **есте́ственные ~и** science; **гуманита́рные ~и** arts; **обще́ственные ~и** social sciences, social studies; **прикладны́е ~и** applied science. **2** (*coll.*) (*урок*) lesson; **э́то тебе́ н.!** let this be a lesson to you!

наукоёмкий *adj.* high-technology, high-tech.

нау|сти́ть, щу́, сти́шь *pf.* (*of* ⇒**~ща́ть**) (*obs.*) to incite, egg on.

нау́ськ|ать, аю *pf.* (*of* ⇒**~ивать**) (**на**+*a.*) to set (*dogs on*).

нау́ськива|ть, ю *impf. of* ⇒**нау́ськать**

наутёк *adv.*: **бро́ситься н., пусти́ться н.** (*coll.*) to take to one's heels.

нау́тро *adv.* next morning.

науч|и́ть, у́, ~́ишь *pf.* (*of* ⇒**учи́ть**) (+*a. and d. or* +*inf.*) to teach; **н. кого́-н. ру́сскому языку́** to teach s.o. Russian; **н. кого́-н. води́ть маши́ну** to teach s.o. to drive (a car).

науч|и́ться, у́сь, ~́ишься *pf.* (*of* ⇒**учи́ться**) (+*d. or inf.*) to learn.

нау́чно-иссле́довательск|ий *adj.* scientific research; **~ая рабо́та** (scientific) research work.

нау́чно-фантасти́ческий *adj.* science fiction.

нау́ч|ный (~ен, ~на) *adj.* scientific; **н. рабо́тник** researcher; **~ная фанта́стика** science fiction.

нау́шник[1], **а** *m.* **1** (*на шапке*) ear-flap; (*предмет одежды*) ear-muff. **2** (*для слушания*) ear-phone; (*in pl.*) head-phones.

нау́шник[2], **а** *m.* (*pej.*) (*доносчик*) informer, slanderer.

нау́шнича|ть, ю *impf.* (+*d. and* **на**+*a.*) to tell tales (to s.o. about), inform (s.o. on, about).

нау́шничеств|о, а *nt.* tale-bearing, informing.

науща́|ть, ю *impf. of* ⇒**науст́ить**

нау|щу́, сти́шь *see* ⇒**~сти́ть**

нафтали́н, а *m.* (*chem.*) naphthalene.

нафтали́н|ный *adj. of* ⇒**~**

нафтали́н|овый = **~ный; н. ша́рик** camphor ball, moth-ball.

наха́л, а *m.* impudent fellow, cheeky fellow.

наха́лк|а, и *f.* impudent woman, cheeky woman.

наха́льнича|ть, ю *impf.* to be impudent.

наха́л|ьный (~ен, ~ьна) *adj.* impudent, cheeky.

наха́льств|о, а *nt.* impudence, impertinence, effrontery; **име́ть н.** (+*inf.*) to have the cheek (to), have the face (to).

нахам|и́ть, лю́, и́шь *pf. of* ⇒**хами́ть**

нахва́лива|ть, ю *impf. of* ⇒**нахвали́ть**

нахвал|и́ть, ю́, ~́ишь *pf.* (*of* ⇒**~́ивать**) (*coll.*) to praise (highly).

нахвал|и́ться, ю́сь, ~́ишься *pf.* (*coll.*) **1** to boast a lot. **2** (+*i.*; *usu.* +*neg.*) to praise sufficiently; **я не могу́ им н.** I cannot speak too highly of him; I cannot praise him enough.

нахват|а́ть, а́ю *pf.* (*of* ⇒**~́ывать**) (*coll.*; +*a. or g.*) to pick up, get hold (of); (*fig.*) (*знаний*) to pick up, come by.

нахват|а́ться, а́юсь *pf.* (*of* ⇒**~́ываться**) (*coll., fig.*; +*g.*) (*слов, привычек, знаний*) to pick up.

нахва́тыва|ть(ся), ю(сь) *impf. of* ⇒**нахвата́ться**

нахлеба́|ться, юсь *pf.* (*coll.*; +*g.*) (*молока*) to drink (*a lot of*); (*горя*) to suffer (*a lot of*)

нахле́бник, а *m.* parasite, hanger-on.

нахле|ста́ть, щу́, ~́щешь *pf.* (*of* ⇒**~́стывать**) (*coll.*) to whip.

нахле|ста́ться, ~щу́сь, ~́щешься *pf.* (*of* ⇒**~́стываться**) (*sl.*) to get sloshed (*drunk*).

нахлёстыва|ть(ся), ю(сь) *impf. of* ⇒**нахлеста́ть(ся)**

нахлобу́чива|ть, ю *impf. of* ⇒**нахлобу́чить**

нахлобу́ч|ить, у, ишь *pf.* (*of* ⇒**~ивать**) (*coll.*) to pull down (over one's head *or* eyes).

нахлобу́ч|а, и *f.* (*coll.*) rating, dressing-down.

нахлы́н|уть, ет *pf.* (**на**+*a.*) to flow, gush (over, into); (*fig.*) to surge, crowd; **~ули слёзы** tears welled (in my, her, *etc.*, eyes); **на меня́ ~ули мы́сли** thoughts crowded into my mind.

нахму́р|енный *p.p.p. of* ⇒**~ить** *and adj.* frowning, scowling.

нахму́р|ить(ся), ю(сь), ишь(ся) *pf. of* ⇒**хму́рить(ся)**

нахо|ди́ть, жу́, ~дишь *impf. of* ⇒**найти́**

нахо|ди́ться[1]**, жу́сь, ~дишься** *impf. of* ⇒**найти́сь**

нахо|ди́ться[2]**, жу́сь, ~дишься** *impf.* to be (situated); **где ~дится ста́нция?** where is the station?; (*под наблюдением, стрессом*) to be.

нахо|ди́ться[3]**, жу́сь, ~дишься** *pf.* (*coll.*) (*устать от ходьбы*) to tire o.s. by walking; to have walked long enough.

нахо́дк|а, и *f.* **1** find; **Бюро́ нахо́док** lost property office (*Br.*), lost and found (*US*). **2** (*fig.*) (*подходящее*) godsend; (*приём*) device.

нахо́дчивост|ь, и *f.* **1** (*человека*) resourcefulness. **2** (*ответа*) quick-wittedness.

нахо́дчив|ый (~, ~а) *adj.* **1** (*человек*) resourceful. **2** (*ответ*) quick-witted.

нахожде́ни|е, я *nt.* **1** (*действие*) finding. **2**: **ме́сто ~я** the whereabouts.

нахоло|ди́ть, жу́, ди́шь *pf. of* ⇒**холоди́ть** 1

нахо́хл|иться, юсь, ишься *pf.* (*of* ⇒**хо́хлиться**) (*fig.*, *coll.*) to bristle (up).

нахохо|та́ться, чу́сь, ~чешься *pf.* (*coll.*) to have had a good laugh.

нахра́пист|ый (~, ~а) *adj.* (*coll.*, *pej.*) high-handed, pushy.

нахра́пом *adv.* (*coll.*) high-handedly, pushily.

нацара́п|ать, аю *pf.* (*of* ⇒**~ывать**) **1** to scratch. **2** (*fig.*, *coll.*) to scrawl, scribble.

нацара́пыва|ть, ю *impf. of* ⇒**нацара́пать**

наце|ди́ть, жу́, ~дишь *pf.* (+*a. or g.*) to strain.

наце́лен|ный (~, ~а) *adj.* (**на**+*a.*) striving for, aiming for.

наце́лива|ть(ся), ю(сь) *impf. of* ⇒**наце́лить(ся)**

наце́л|ить, ю, ишь *pf.* **1** (*impf.* **це́лить** *and* **~ивать**) (*оружие*) to aim, level. **2** (*impf.* **~ивать**) (*fig.*) (**на**+*a.*) (*на выполнение*) to aim, direct.

наце́л|иться, юсь, ишься *pf.* (*of* ⇒**~иваться**) **1** (**в**+*a.*) to aim (at), take aim (at). **2** (*fig.*; **на**+*a.*) to aim (at, for), strive (for). **3** (*fig.*, +*inf.*) to aim, strive (to do).

на́цело *adv.* (*coll.*) entirely, without remainder.

наце́нк|а, и *f.* mark-up; surcharge.

нацеп|и́ть, лю́, ~ишь *pf.* (*of* ⇒**~ля́ть**) **1** to fasten on; to attach (*by means of hook or pin*). **2** (*coll.*) (*надеть*) to put on.

нацеп|ля́ть, ля́ю *impf. of* ⇒**~и́ть**

наци́зм, а *m.* Nazism.

национализа́ци|я, и *f.* nationalization.

национализи́р|овать, ую *impf. and pf.* to nationalize.

национали́зм, а *m.* nationalism.

национали́ст, а *m.* nationalist.

националисти́ческий *adj.* nationalist(ic).

национали́ст|ка, ки *f. of* ⇒**~**

национа́льност|ь, и *f.* **1** (*принадлежность к нации*) nationality. **2** (*нация*) nation.

национа́льн|ый *adj.* national; **~ое меньшинство́** national minority; **~ые словари́** minority-language dictionaries.

наци́ст, а *m.* Nazi.

наци́ст|ка, ки *f. of* ⇒**~**

наци́стский *adj.* Nazi.

на́ци|я, и *f.* nation.

нацме́н, а *m.* (*coll.*) member of a national minority.

нацме́н|ка, ки *f. of* ⇒**~**

нач... *comb. form, abbr. of* **1** ***нача́льник.*** **2** ***нача́льствующий***

нача|ди́ть, жу́, ди́шь *pf. of* ⇒**чади́ть**

нача́л|о, а *nt.* **1** beginning; start; **в ~е четвёртого** soon after three (o'clock); **для ~а** to start with, for a start; **по ~у** at first; **положи́ть, дать н.** (+*d.*) to begin, commence; (*традиции, партии*) to establish.
2 (*источник*) origin, source; **вести́ н.** (**от**+*g.*), **взять н.** (**в**+*p.*) to originate (from, in).
3 (*pl.*) (*методы*) principle, basis; **рабо́тать на но́вых ~ах** to work on a new basis; (*принципы, основы*) basics, rudiments; **~а матема́тики** the rudiments of mathematics.
4: **быть под ~ом у кого́-н.** to be under s.o.; **отда́ть под н., под ~а** (+*d.*) to put under, place in the charge (of); **на ра́вных ~ах с кем-н.** on equal terms with s.o.
5 (*поэтическое, волевое*) nature.

нача́льник, а *m.* head, chief; superior; **н. свя́зи** chief signal officer; **н. отде́ла** head of a department, section.

нача́льнический *adj.* overbearing, imperious.

нача́льн|ый *adj.* **1** (*находящийся в начале*) initial, first; **~ая ско́рость** initial speed. **2** (*первоначальный*) primary, elementary; **~ая шко́ла** primary school (*Br.*), elementary school (*US*).

нача́льственный *adj.* overbearing, domineering.

нача́льств|о, а *nt.* **1** (*collect.*) (the) authorities, management. **2** (*власть начальника*) authority; **под ~ом кого́-н.** under s.o.'s authority. **3** (*coll.*) (*начальник*) head, boss.

нача́льствовани|е, я *nt.* command.

нача́льств|овать, ую *impf.* (**над**+*i.*) to command, be in command (of).

нача́льствующий *adj.*: **н. соста́в** (*в армии*) command personnel; (*в учреждении*) management.

нача́тк|и, ов *no sg.* rudiments, elements.

нач|а́ть, ну́, нёшь, *past* **~ал, ~ала́, ~ало** *pf.* (*of* ⇒**~ина́ть**) **1** to begin, start, commence; **н. с нача́ла** to begin at the beginning; **н. всё снача́ла** to start all over again, start afresh; **он на́чал моли́твой** (*or* **с моли́твы**) he began with a prayer. **2** (*новую пачку, тетрадь*) to start.

нач|а́ться, ну́сь, нёшься, *past* **~а́лся́, ~ала́сь** *pf.* (*of* ⇒**~ина́ться**) to begin, start.

начди́в, а *m.* (*abbr. of* ***нача́льник диви́зии***) division commander.

начека́н|ить, ю, ишь *pf.* (+*a. or g.*) to mint (*a quantity of*).

начеку́ *adv.* on the alert, on one's guard.

начерн|и́ть, ю́, и́шь *pf. of* ⇒**черни́ть** 1

на́черно *adv.* roughly; **написа́ть н.** to make a rough copy.

наче́рпа|ть, ю *pf.* (*of* ⇒**наче́рпывать**) (+*a. or g.*) to scoop up (*a quantity of*).

наче́рпыва|ть, ю *impf. of* ⇒**наче́рпать**

начерта́ни|е, я *nt.* (*действие*) drawing, tracing; (*букв*) outline.

начерта́тельн|ый *adj. only in phr.* **~ая геоме́трия** descriptive geometry.

начерта́|ть, ю *pf.* to draw, trace; (*fig.*) (*путь, будущее*) to outline; (*написать*) to inscribe.

начер|ти́ть, чу́, ~тишь *pf. of* ⇒**черти́ть**[1]

начёс, а *m.* **1** (*на ткани*) nap. **2** (*способ расчёсывания волос*) backcombing (*Br.*), teasing (*US*).

наче|са́ть, шу́, ~шешь *pf.* (+*a. or g.*) **1** to comb, card (*a quantity of*). **2** (*волосы*) to backcomb (*Br.*), tease (*US*).

начёсыва|ть, ю *impf. of* ⇒**начеса́ть**

начёт, а *m.* (*book-keeping*) recovery of unauthorized expenditure.

начётничеств|о, а *nt.* (*pej.*) dogmatism.

начётчик, а *m.* dogmatist.

начина́ни|е, я *nt.* undertaking, initiative.

начина́тел|ь, я *m.* originator, initiator.

начина́тельный *adj.* (*gram.*): **н. глаго́л** inceptive *or* inchoative verb.

начина́|ть(ся), ю(сь) *impf. of* ⇒**нача́ть(ся)**

начина́|ющий *pres. part. act. of* ⇒**~ть** *and adj.* (*писатель*) fledgling; *as n.* **н., ~ющего** *m.* beginner.

начина́я *as prep.* **1** (**с**+*g.*) (*о времени*) as from, starting from; (*в том числе*) starting with, including. **2** (**от**+*g.*) starting with, including.

начин|и́ть[1]**, ю́, и́шь** *pf.* (*of* ⇒**~я́ть**)

Н

(+*i.*) (*заполнить начинкой*) to fill (with), stuff (with).

начин|и́ть², ю́, ~и́шь *pf.* (+*a.* or *g.*) **1** (*починить*) to mend (*a quantity of*). **2**: **н. карандаше́й** to sharpen (*a number of*) pencils.

начи́нк|а, и *f.* (*cul.*) (*курицы, утки*) stuffing; (*пирожка*) filling.

начин|я́ть, я́ю *impf. of* ⇨**~и́ть¹**

начисле́ни|е, я *nt.* (*надбавка*) additional sum; extra; (*взимаемая сумма*) charge.

начи́сл|ить, ю, ишь *pf.* (*of* ⇨**~я́ть**) (*book-keeping*) (*надбавить*) to add (to s.o.'s account); (*взимать*) to charge; (*рабочие дни*) to calculate.

начисл|я́ть, я́ю *impf. of* ⇨**~ить**

начи́|стить¹, щу, стишь *pf.* (*of* ⇨**~ща́ть**) (*сапоги, кастрюлю*) to polish, shine (*trans.*).

начи́|стить², щу, стишь *pf.* (+*a.* or *g.*) (*овощи*) to peel (*a quantity of*).

на́чисто *adv.* **1** clean, fair; **переписа́ть н.** to make a fair copy (of). **2** (*coll.*) (*совсем*) completely, thoroughly; **н. отказа́ться** to refuse flatly. **3** (*coll.*) (*начистоту*) openly, without equivocation.

начистоту́ *adv.* (*coll.*) openly, without equivocation.

начи́танност|ь, и *f.* (*wide*) reading; erudition.

начи́тан|ный (~, ~на) *adj.* well-read, widely-read.

начита́|ть, ю *pf.* (*of* ⇨**начи́тывать**) (+*a.* or *g.*) to read (*a number of*).

начита́|ться, юсь *pf.* **1** (+*g.*) (*прочитать много*) to have read (*a lot of*). **2** (*почитать вдоволь*) to have read one's fill.

начи́тыва|ть, ю *impf. of* ⇨**начита́ть**

начища́|ть, ю *impf. of* ⇨**начи́стить**

нач|ну́, нёшь *see* ⇨**~а́ть**

наш, ~его, *f.* **~а, ~ей;** *nt.* **~е, ~его;** *pl.* **~и, ~их** *possessive pron.* (*при существительном*) our; (*без существительного*) ours; **~а взяла́!** (*coll.*) we've won!; **~е вам!** (*coll.*) hello there!; **знай ~их!** well done!; **(служи́ть) и ~им и ва́шим** (*coll.*) to run with the hare and hunt with the hounds; *as n.* **~и, ~их** (*родственники*) our folks, relatives; (*товарищи*) our people, people on our side; **его́ счита́ют одни́м из ~их** they regard him as one of us.

нашал|и́ть, ю́, и́шь *pf.* to be naughty.

нашаты́р|ный *adj. of* ⇨**~ь; н. спирт** liquid ammonia.

нашаты́р|ь, я́ *m.* (*chem.*) ammonium chloride.

нашёл *past of* ⇨**найти́;** (*coll.*): **н. когда́** (+*inf.*) this is a ridiculous time (to do sth.); **н. чего́ боя́ться** a ridiculous thing to be afraid of.

на́шенский *adj.* (*coll.*) = **наш**

нашеп|та́ть, чу́, ~чешь *pf.* (*of* ⇨**~тывать**) **1** (+*a.* or *g.*) to whisper (*a number of*) (*also fig.*). **2** (**на**+*a.*) (*наколдовать*) to put a spell (upon).

нашёптыва|ть, ю *impf. of* ⇨**нашепта́ть**

наше́стви|е, я *nt.* (*also fig.*) invasion, descent.

на́шивать *freq. of* ⇨**носи́ть**

нашива́|ть, ю *impf. of* ⇨**наши́ть**

наши́вк|а, и *f.* stripe, chevron.

нашивно́й *adj.* sewn on.

нашир|я́ться, юсь *pf. of* ⇨**шир|я́ться**

наш|и́ть, ью́, ьёшь *pf.* (*of* ⇨**~ива́ть**) **1** (*пришить*) to sew on. **2** (+*a.* or *g.*) (*сшить в каком-н. количестве*) to sew (*a quantity of*).

нашлёпа|ть, ю *pf.* (*coll.*) to slap; to spank.

на|шлю́, шлёшь *see* ⇨**~сла́ть**

нашпиг|ова́ть, у́ю *pf. of* ⇨**шпигова́ть**

нашпи́лива|ть, ю *impf. of* ⇨**нашпи́лить**

нашпи́л|ить, ю, ишь *pf.* (*of* ⇨**~ивать**) (*coll.*) to pin on.

нашум|е́ть, лю́, и́шь *pf.* to make much noise; (*fig.*) (*фильм, книга*) to cause a sensation.

нащип|а́ть, лю́, ~лешь *pf.* (+*a.* or *g.*) to pluck, pick (*a quantity of*).

нащу́п|ать, аю *pf.* (*of* ⇨**~ывать**) to find, discover (*by groping*).

нащу́пыва|ть, ю *impf.* (*of* ⇨**нащу́пать**) to grope (for, after); to fumble (for, after); to feel about (for) (*also fig.*); **н. по́чву** (*fig.*) to feel one's way, see how the land lies.

наэлектриз|ова́ть, у́ю *pf. of* ⇨**электризова́ть**

ная́беднича|ть, ю *pf. of* ⇨**я́бедничать**

наяву́ *adv.* waking; in reality; **гре́зить н.** to day-dream.

ная́д|а, ы *f.* (*myth.*) naiad.

ная́рива|ть, ю *impf.* (*coll.*) (*мелодию*) to bash out; (*с азартом делать*) to go hard at sth.

НДС *m. indecl.* (*abbr. of* ***нало́г на доба́вленную сто́имость***) VAT (*Value Added Tax*).

не¹ not; **я не зна́ю** I do not know; **я не знал** I did not know; **не враг** not an enemy; **не у́мный, а глу́пый** not clever, but stupid; **я не могу́ не сказа́ть** I can't but say; I must say; **не без волне́ния** with some excitement; **не до** (+*g.*) not time for; **мне не до шу́ток** I have no time for jokes; **не…, не** neither … nor; **не то** otherwise, or else.

не² *separable component of prons.* ⇨**не́кого** *and* **не́чего; мне не́ с кем разгова́ривать** I have no one to talk to; **не́ о чем бы́ло говори́ть** there was nothing to talk about.

не... *pref.* un-, in-, non-, mis-, dis-.

неавтоно́мный *adj.* (*comput.*) on-line.

неаккура́тност|ь, и *f.* **1** (*небрежность*) carelessness; inaccuracy. **2** (*неточность*) unpunctuality. **3** (*неопрятность*) untidiness.

неаккура́т|ный (~ен, ~на) *adj.* **1** (*небрежный*) careless; inaccurate. **2** (*неточный*) unpunctual. **3** (*неопрятный*) untidy.

неандерта́л|ец, ьца *m.* (*anthrop.*) Neanderthal man.

неандерта́льский *adj.* (*anthrop.*) Neanderthal.

неаполита́н|ец, ца *m.* Neapolitan.

неаполита́н|ка, ки *f. of* ⇨**~ец**

неаполита́нский *adj.* Neapolitan.

Неа́пол|ь, я *m.* Naples.

неаппети́т|ный (~ен, ~на) *adj.* unappetizing (*also fig.*).

небезопа́с|ный (~ен, ~на) *adj.* unsafe, insecure.

небезоснова́тел|ьный (~ен, ~ьна) *adj.* not unfounded.

небезразли́ч|ный (~ен, ~на) *adj.* not indifferent.

небезрезульта́т|ный (~ен, ~на) *adj.* not fruitless, not futile.

небезупре́ч|ный (~ен, ~на) *adj.* not irreproachable.

небезуспе́ш|ный (~ен, ~на) *adj.* not unsuccessful.

небезызве́ст|ный (~ен, ~на) *adj.* not unknown; (*iron.*) notorious; **~но, что…** it is no secret that ….

небезынтере́с|ный (~ен, ~на) *adj.* not without interest.

небелёный *adj.* unbleached.

небережли́в|ый (~, ~а) *adj.* thriftless, improvident.

неб|еса́ *pl. of* ⇨**~о**

небескоры́ст|ный (~ен, ~на) *adj.* not disinterested.

небе́сн|ый *adj.* heavenly, celestial; **~ые свети́ла** heavenly bodies; **н. свод** firmament; **Ца́рство ~ое** the Kingdom of Heaven; **~ого цве́та** sky-blue.

небесполе́з|ный (~ен, ~на) *adj.* of some use.

неблагови́д|ный (~ен, ~на) *adj.* unseemly, improper.

неблагода́рност|ь, и *f.* ingratitude.

неблагода́р|ный (~ен, ~на) *adj.* **1** (*человек*) ungrateful. **2** (*задача*) thankless.

неблагожела́тел|ьный (~ен, ~ьна) *adj.* malevolent, ill-disposed.

неблагозву́чи|е, я *nt.* disharmony, dissonance.

неблагозву́ч|ный (~ен, ~на) *adj.* inharmonious, disharmonious.

неблагонадёж|ный (~ен, ~на) *adj.* (*hist.*) unreliable (*esp. politically*).

неблагополу́чи|е, я *nt.* trouble.

неблагополу́чно *adv.* not successfully, not favourably (*Br.*), favorably (*US*); **дела́ у них обстоя́т н.** their affairs are in a bad way, things are not turning out happily for them.

неблагополу́ч|ный (~ен, ~на) *adj.* unfavourable (*Br.*), unfavorable (*US*), bad; **дело име́ло н. исхо́д** the affair had a bad ending; (*impers.*): **у нас ~но** things are going badly; we are in a bad way.

неблагопристо́йност|ь, и *f.* obscenity, indecency.

неблагопристо́|йный (~ен, ~йна) *adj.* obscene, indecent.

неблагоприя́т|ный (~ен, ~на) *adj.* unfavourable (*Br.*), unfavorable (*US*), inauspicious.

неблагоразу́м|ный (~ен, ~на) *adj.* imprudent, ill-advised, unwise.

неблагоро́д|ный (~ен, ~на) *adj.* ignoble, base; **н. мета́лл** base metal.

неблагоро́дств|о, а *nt.* baseness.

неблагоскло́н|ный (~ен, ~на) *adj.* unfavourable (*Br.*), unfavorable (*US*); (**к** + *d.*) ill-disposed (towards).

неблагоустро́ен|ный (~, ~на) *adj.* uncomfortable; badly planned.

нёбный *adj.* (*ling.*) palatal.

не́б|о, а, *pl.* **~еса́, ~е́с, ~еса́м** *nt.* sky; (*relig.*) heaven; **попа́сть па́льцем в н.** (*coll.*) to be wide of the mark; **жить ме́жду ~ом и землёй** not to have a roof above one's head; **под откры́тым ~ом** in the open (air); **с ~а свали́ться** (*fig., coll.*) to fall from the moon; **упа́сть с ~а на зе́млю** (*fig.*) to come down to earth.

нёб|о, а *nt.* (*anat.*) palate.

небога́т|ый (~, ~а) *adj.* **1** of modest means. **2** (*fig.*) modest.

небольш|о́й *adj.* small; not great; **о́чень ~ое расстоя́ние** a very short distance; **ты́сяча с ~и́м** a thousand odd; **де́ло ста́ло за ~и́м** one small thing is lacking.

небосво́д, а *m.* firmament; the vault of heaven.

небоскло́н, а *m.* horizon (*strictly*, sky immediately over the horizon).

небоскрёб, а *m.* skyscraper.

небо́сь *adv.* (*coll.*) **1** (*наверно*) probably, most likely, I dare say; **ты, н., мно́го книг чита́л** I suppose you've read lots of books. **2** (*obs.*) don't be afraid (= *не бойся*).

небре́жност|ь, и *f.* carelessness, negligence.

небре́ж|ный (~ен, ~на) *adj.* (*человек, работа*) careless; (*одежда, почерк*) untidy; (*тон, манера*) offhand.

небри́т|ый (~, ~а) *adj.* unshaven.

небыва́л|ый (~, ~а) *adj.* **1** (*не случавшийся прежде*) unprecedented. **2** (*вымышленный*) fantastic, imaginary. **3** (*coll.*) (*неопытный*) inexperienced.

небыва́льщин|а, ы *f.* (*obs. coll.*) = **небыли́ца**

небыли́ц|а, ы *f.* (*сказка*) fable; (*выдумка*) cock-and-bull story.

небыти|е́, я́ *nt.* non-existence.

небьющийся *adj.* unbreakable.

Нев|а́, ы́ *f.* the Neva (*river*).

неважне́цкий *adj.* (*coll.*) indifferent, so-so.

нева́жно *adv.* not too well, indifferently; **дела́ иду́т н.** things are not going too well.

нева́ж|ный (~ен, ~на́, ~но) *adj.* **1** (*незначительный*) unimportant. **2** (*посредственный*) poor, indifferent.

невдалеке́ *adv.* not far away, not far off.

невдомёк *adv.* (+*d.*) (*coll.*): **мне бы́ло н.** it never occurred to me, I never thought of it.

неве́дени|е, я *nt.* ignorance; **пребыва́ть в блаже́нном ~и** (*iron.*) to be in a state of blissful ignorance.

неве́домо *adv.* (*coll.*; + **что, как, когда́, куда́** *etc.*) God knows, no one knows; **он так и появи́лся, н. отку́да** he just turned up, God knows where from.

неве́дом|ый (~, ~а) *adj.* **1** unknown. **2** (*fig.*) (*таинственный*) mysterious.

неве́ж|а, и *c.g.* boor, lout.

неве́жд|а, ы *c.g.* ignoramus.

неве́жествен|ный (~, ~на) *adj.* ignorant.

неве́жеств|о, а *nt.* **1** ignorance. **2** (*coll.*) (*невежливость*) rudeness, bad manners.

неве́жливост|ь, и *f.* rudeness, impoliteness, bad manners.

неве́жлив|ый (~, ~а) *adj.* rude, impolite.

невезе́ни|е, я *nt.* (*coll.*) bad luck.

невезу́ч|ий (~, а) *adj.* (*coll.*) unlucky.

невели́к|ий (~, ~а́, ~о́) *adj.* **1** (*небольшой*) small, short. **2** (*незначительный*) slight, insignificant.

неве́ри|е, я *nt.* unbelief; lack of faith.

неве́рност|ь, и *f.* **1** (*неправильность*) incorrectness. **2** (*друга*) disloyalty; (*супруга*) infidelity, unfaithfulness.

неве́р|ный (~ен, ~на́, ~но) *adj.* **1** (*ошибочный*) incorrect; **~ная но́та** false note. **2** (*неуверенный*) unsteady, uncertain; **~ная похо́дка** unsteady gait; **н. слух** (*mus.*) unsure ear; **Фома́ н.** (*coll.*) a doubting Thomas. **3** (*друг*) faithless, disloyal; (*муж, жена*) unfaithful. **4** (*свет*) dim, flickering. **5** *as n.* **н., ~ного** *m.* (*relig.*) infidel.

невероя́ти|е, я *nt. now only in phr.* **до ~я** incredibly.

невероя́тно *adv.* incredibly, unbelievably.

невероя́тност|ь, и *f.* **1** improbability. **2** incredibility; **до ~и** incredibly, to an unbelievable extent.

невероя́т|ный (~ен, ~на) *adj.* **1** (*неправдоподобный*) improbable, unlikely. **2** (*чрезвычайный*) incredible, unbelievable (*also fig.*); (*impers., as pred.*): **~но** it is incredible, it is unbelievable; it is beyond belief.

неве́рующ|ий *adj.* (*relig.*) unbelieving; *as n.* **н., ~его** *m.*, **~ая, ~ей** *f.* unbeliever.

невес|ёлый (~́ел, ~ела́, ~́ело) *adj.* sad, gloomy, melancholy.

невесо́мост|ь, и *f.* weightlessness.

невесо́м|ый (~, ~а) *adj.* weightless (*also fig.*).

неве́ст|а, ы *f.* **1** fiancée; (*на свадьбе*) bride. **2** (*coll.*) (*неженатая девушка*) marriageable girl.

неве́стк|а, и *f.* **1** (*жена сына*) daughter-in-law. **2** (*жена брата*) sister-in-law.

неве́сть *adv.* (*coll.*; + **кто, что, ско́лько** *etc.*) God knows, goodness knows, heaven knows.

невеще́ственный *adj.* immaterial.

невзго́д|а, ы *f.* adversity, misfortune.

невзира́я *prep.* (**на** + *a.*) in spite of, regardless of.

невзлюб|и́ть, лю́, ~́ишь *pf.* to take a dislike to.

невзнача́й *adv.* (*coll.*) by chance; unexpectedly.

невзно́с, а *m.* non-payment (*of fees, etc.*).

невзра́ч|ный (~ен, ~на) *adj.* unprepossessing, unattractive; plain.

невзыска́тел|ьный (~ен, ~ьна) *adj.* modest, undemanding.

не́видал|ь, и *f.* (*coll.*) wonder; **вот н.!**; **э́ка(я) н.!** (*iron.*) that's nothing.

неви́дан|ный (~, ~а) *adj.* unprecedented.

невиди́мк|а, и *c.g and f.* **1** *c.g.* invisible being; **сде́латься ~ой** to become invisible; **челове́к-н.** invisible man; **ша́пка-н.** cap of darkness. **2** *f.* (*шпилька*) invisible hairpin.

невиди́м|ый (~, ~а) *adj.* invisible.

неви́д|ный (~ен, ~на) *adj.* **1** invisible. **2** (*coll.*) (*незначительный*) insignificant.

неви́дящ|ий *adj.* unseeing; **смотре́ть ~им взгля́дом** to look vacantly.

неви́нност|ь, и *f.* innocence; **де́вичья н.** virginity.

неви́н|ный (~ен, ~на) *adj.* innocent; (*девственный*) virgin(al); **~ная же́ртва** innocent victim; **~ные удово́льствия** innocent pleasures.

невино́в|ный (~ен, ~на) *adj.* (**в** + *p.*) innocent (of); (*leg.*) not guilty; **призна́ть ~ным** to acquit.

невку́с|ный (~ен, ~на́, ~но) *adj.* unpalatable.

невменя́емост|ь, и *f.* (*leg.*) irresponsibility.

невменя́ем|ый (~, ~а) *adj.* **1** (*leg.*) irresponsible. **2** (*coll.*) beside o.s.

невмеша́тельств|о, а *m.* (*pol.*) non-intervention, non-interference; **поли́тика ~а** (*pol.*) hands-off policy.

невмоготу́ *adv.* (*coll.*; +*d.*) unbearable (to, for), unendurable (to, for); **э́то мне н.** I can't stand it; this is more than I can stand; **ста́ло н.** it became unbearable; it became too much.

невмо́чь = **невмоготу́**

невнима́ни|е, я *nt.* **1** (*рассеянность*) inattention; carelessness. **2** (**к** + *d.*) (*пренебрежение*) lack of consideration (for).

невнима́тельност|ь, и *f.* inattention; (*небрежность*) thoughtlessness.

невнима́тел|ьный (~ен, ~ьна) *adj.* (*рассеянный*) inattentive; (*незаботливый*) thoughtless.

невня́т|ный (~ен, ~на) *adj.* indistinct, incomprehensible.

не́вод, а, *pl.* **~а́, ~о́в** *m.* seine, sweep-net.

невозбра́н|ный (~ен, ~на) *adj.* (*liter.*) free, unrestricted.

невозвра́т|ный (~ен, ~на) *adj.* irrevocable, irretrievable.

невозвращён|ец, ца *m.* (*pol.*) defector.

Н

невозвраще́ни|е, я *nt.* failure to return.

невозвраще́н|ка, ки *f. of* ⇨**~ец**

невозде́ланн|ый *adj.* uncultivated, untilled; **~ая земля́** waste land.

невозде́ржанност|ь, и *f.* (*в еде, потребностях*) intemperance; (*в поведении*) lack of self-restraint.

невозде́ржан|ный (~, ~на) *adj.* intemperate; unrestrained; **он ~ на язы́к** he has a loose tongue.

невозде́рж|ный (~ен, ~на) *adj.* = **невозде́ржанный**

невозмо́жност|ь, и *f.* impossibility; **до ~и** (*coll.*) to the last degree; **за ~ью** (+*g. or inf.*) owing to the impossibility (of).

невозмо́ж|ный (~ен, ~на) *adj.* **1** impossible; (*impers., pred.*): **~но** it is impossible; *as n.* **~ное, ~ного** *nt.* the impossible. **2** (*нестерпимый*) insufferable.

невозмути́м|ый (~, ~а) *adj.* **1** (*человек*) imperturbable. **2** (*тон*) calm, unruffled.

невознагради́м|ый (~, ~а) *adj.* **1** (*потеря*) irreparable. **2** (*услуга*) that can never be repaid.

невозобновля́емый *adj.* non-renewable.

нево́лей *adv.* (*obs.*) against one's will, forcibly.

нево́л|ить, ю, ишь *impf.* (*of* ⇨**при~**) (*coll.*) to force, compel.

нево́льник, а *m.* slave.

нево́льни|ца, цы *f. of* ⇨**~к**

нево́льничеств|о, а *nt.* slavery.

нево́льн|ичий *adj. of* ⇨**~ик; н. ры́нок** slave market; **н. труд** slave labour (*Br.*), labor (*US*).

нево́льно *adv.* involuntarily; unintentionally, unwittingly.

нево́льный *adj.* **1** (*вздох, трепет*) involuntary; (*ложь, обида*) unintentional. **2** (*вынужденный*) forced.

нево́л|я, и *f.* **1** (*плен*) bondage; captivity. **2** (*coll.*) (*необходимость*) necessity.

невообрази́м|ый (~, ~а) *adj.* unimaginable, inconceivable; **н. шум** (*fig.*) unimaginable din.

невооружённ|ый *adj.* unarmed; **~ым гла́зом** with the naked eye.

невоспи́танност|ь, и *f.* ill breeding; bad manners.

невоспи́тан|ный (~, ~на) *adj.* ill-bred; bad-mannered.

невоспламеня́ем|ый (~, ~а) *adj.* uninflammable, non-inflammable.

невосполни́м|ый (~, ~а) *adj.* irreplaceable.

невосприи́мчивост|ь, и *f.* **1** (*к знаниям*) lack of receptivity. **2** (*med.*) immunity.

невосприи́мчив|ый (~, ~а) *adj.* **1** (*к знаниям*) unreceptive. **2** (*med.*) (**к**+*d.*) immune (to).

невостре́бованный *adj.* unclaimed.

невпопа́д *adv.* (*coll.*) out of place, inopportunely; **отвеча́ть н.** to answer irrelevantly.

невпроворо́т *adv.* (*coll.*) **1** (*много*) a lot, a great deal. **2** (*слишком много*) too much; **э́то нам н.** it's too hard for us.

невразуми́тел|ьный (~ен, ~ьна) *adj.* unintelligible, incomprehensible.

невралги́ческий *adj.* neuralgic.

невралги́|я, и *f.* neuralgia; **н. седа́лищного не́рва** sciatica.

неврасте́ник, а *m.* neurasthenic.

неврастени́|ческий *adj. of* ⇨**~я**

неврастени́ч|ный (~ен, ~на) *adj.* neurasthenic (*person*).

неврастени́|я, и *f.* neurasthenia.

невреди́м|ый (~, ~а) *adj.* unharmed, intact; **цел и ~** safe and sound.

неври́т, а *m.* neuritis.

невро́з, а *m.* neurosis.

неврологи́ческий *adj.* neurological.

невроло́ги|я, и *f.* neurology.

невропато́лог, а *m.* neuropathologist.

невропатоло́ги|я, и *f.* neuropathology.

невро́тик, а *m.* neurotic.

невроти́ческий *adj.* neurotic.

невтерпёж *adv.* (+*d.*; *coll.*) unbearable; **мне,** *etc.*, **ста́ло н.** I, *etc.*, cannot stand it any longer; **мне,** *etc.*, **н. узна́ть** I, *etc.*, can't wait to find out.

невы́год|а, ы *f.* **1** (*недостаток*) disadvantage. **2** (*убыток*) loss.

невы́год|ный (~ен, ~на) *adj.* **1** (*положение*) disadvantageous, unfavourable (*Br.*), unfavorable (*US*); **показа́ть себя́ с ~ной стороны́** to show o.s. at a disadvantage; **ста́вить в ~ное положе́ние** to place at a disadvantage. **2** (*сделка*) unprofitable, unremunerative; (*impers., pred.*): **~но** it does not pay.

невы́держанност|ь, и *f.* **1** (*человека*) lack of self-control. **2** (*стиля*) unevenness.

невы́держан|ный (~, ~на) *adj.* **1** (*человек*) lacking self-control. **2** (*о стиле*) uneven. **3** (*о сыре, вине*) unmatured.

невы́езд, а *m.* constant (*usu. forced*) residence in one place; **дать подпи́ску о ~е** to give a written undertaking not to leave a place.

невыла́з|ный (~ен, ~на) *adj.* such that one cannot emerge from it; **~ная грязь** a veritable quagmire; **быть в ~ных долга́х** (*fig.*) to be up to the eyes in debt.

невыноси́м|ый (~, ~а) *adj.* unbearable, insufferable, intolerable.

невы́плат|а, ы *f.* non-payment.

невыполне́ни|е, я *nt.* non-fulfilment; (+*g.*) failure to carry out.

невыполни́м|ый (~, ~а) *adj.* impracticable; unrealizable.

невырази́м|ый (~, ~а) *adj.* inexpressible, beyond expression; *as n.* **~ые, ~ых** (*joc., euph.*) unmentionables (= *pants*).

невырази́тел|ьный (~ен, ~ьна) *adj.* inexpressive, expressionless.

невы́сказанный *adj.* unexpressed, unsaid.

невысо́к|ий (~, ~а́, ~о) *adj.* (*забор, потолок, голос*) rather low; (*человек*) rather short; **~ого ка́чества** of poor quality; **быть ~ого мне́ния** (**о**+*p.*) to have a low opinion (of).

невы́ход, а *m.* failure to appear; **н. на рабо́ту** absence (from work).

не́г|а, и *f.* **1** (*довольство*) comfort; abundance. **2** (*блаженство*) bliss, languor.

негаси́м|ый (~, ~а) *adj.* (*rhet.*) (*пламя, любовь*) eternal; (*лампада*) ever-burning.

негати́в, а *m.* (*phot.*) negative.

негати́в|ный (~ен, ~на) *adj.* negative.

негашён|ый *adj.*: **~ая и́звесть** quick-lime.

не́где *adv.* (+*inf.*) there is nowhere; **н. доста́ть э́ту кни́гу** this book is nowhere to be had; **я́блоку н. упа́сть** there's no room to move.

неги́б|кий (~ок, ~ка́, ~ко) *adj.* inflexible.

негла́с|ный (~ен, ~на) *adj.* secret.

неглиже́ *nt. indecl.* negligée.

неглубо́к|ий (~, ~а́) *adj.* rather shallow; (*fig.*) superficial.

неглу́п|ый (~, ~а́, ~о) *adj.* quite intelligent; **он о́чень ~** he is no fool.

него́ *a. and g. of* ⇨**он** *when governed by preps.*

него́дник, а *m.* (*coll.*) reprobate, scoundrel; ne'er-do-well.

него́дност|ь, и *f.* worthlessness; **привести́ в н.** to put out of commission.

него́д|ный (~ен, ~на) *adj.* **1** (*непригодный*) unfit, unsuitable. **2** (*недостойный*) worthless, good-for-nothing; **н. чек** dud cheque (*Br.*), check (*US*).

негодова́ни|е, я *nt.* indignation.

негод|ова́ть, у́ю *impf.* (**на**+*a.*, **про́тив**+*g.*) to be indignant (with).

негод|у́ющий *pres. part. act. of* ⇨**~ова́ть** *and adj.* indignant.

негодя́|й, я *m.* scoundrel, rascal.

негостеприи́м|ный (~ен, ~на) *adj.* inhospitable.

негоциа́нт, а *m.* (*obs.*) merchant.

негр, а *m.* black (man); **америка́нский н.** African American.

негра́мотност|ь, и *f.* illiteracy (*also fig.*).

негра́мот|ный (~ен, ~на) *adj.* **1** illiterate (*also fig.*); *as n.* **н., ~ного** *m.*, **~ная, ~ной** *f.* illiterate (*person*). **2** (*fig.*) crude, inexpert.

негрит|ёнок, ёнка, *pl.* **~ята, ~ят** *m.* black child.

негритя́нк|а, и *f.* black woman.

негритя́нский *adj.* black (*of person*).

негро́м|кий (~ок, ~ка́, ~ко) *adj.* quiet, low.

негума́нный *adj.* inhumane.

неда́вний *adj.* recent.

неда́вно *adv.* recently.

недалёк|ий (~, ~а́, ~о or ~о́) *adj.*

1 (*место*) nearby, not far off, near; (*путешествие, прогулка, расстояние*) short; **на ~ом расстоя́нии** at a short distance; (*недавний*) recent. **2** (*fig.*) (*глуповатый*) not bright, dull-witted.

недалеко́ (*and* **недалёко**) *adv.* not far, near; **за приме́ром идти́ н.** one does not have to search far for an example.

недальнови́дност|ь, и *f.* short-sightedness (*fig.*).

недальнови́д|ный (~ен, ~на) *adj.* short-sighted (*fig.*).

неда́ром *adv.* not for nothing; for good reason.

недви́жимост|ь, и *f.* (*leg.*) (immovable) property, real estate.

недви́жим|ый[1] *adj.* (*не способный двигаться*) immovable; **~ое иму́щество** = **~ость**

недви́жи́м|ый[2] **(~, ~а)** *adj.* (*неподвижный*) motionless.

недвусмы́слен|ный (~, ~на) *adj.* unequivocal, unambiguous.

недееспосо́бност|ь, и *f.* **1** (*leg.*) incapacity. **2** inability to function.

недееспосо́б|ный (~ен, ~на) *adj.* **1** (*leg.*) (*человек*) incapacitated. **2** (*организация*) unable to function.

недействи́тельност|ь, и *f.* **1** (*leg.*) invalidity. **2** (*obs.*) ineffectiveness.

недействи́тел|ьный (~ен, ~ьна) *adj.* **1** (*leg.*) invalid. **2** (*obs.*) ineffective, ineffectual.

неделика́т|ный (~ен, ~на) *adj.* indelicate, indiscreet.

недели́мост|ь, и *f.* indivisibility.

недели́м|ый (~, ~а) *adj.* indivisible; **~ое число́** prime number.

неде́льный *adj.* of a week's duration; **я вы́полню э́ту рабо́ту в н. срок** I will finish this work in a week's time; **н. о́тпуск** week's leave.

неде́л|я, и *f.* week; **~ями** for weeks (at a time); **на э́той ~е** this week.

недержа́ни|е, я *nt. only in phr.* **н. мочи́** (*med.*) irretention of urine.

недёшево *adv.* (*coll.*) at a considerable price, rather dear (*also fig.*).

недисциплини́рованност|ь, и *f.* indiscipline.

недисциплини́рован|ный (~, ~на) *adj.* undisciplined.

недобо́р, а *m.* shortage.

недоброжела́тел|ь, я *m.* ill-wisher.

недоброжела́тельност|ь, и *f.* malevolence, ill-will.

недоброжела́тел|ьный (~ен, ~ьна) *adj.* malevolent, ill-disposed.

недоброжела́тель|ство, ства *nt.* = **~ность**

недоброка́чественност|ь, и *f.* poor quality, bad quality.

недоброка́чествен|ный (~, ~на) *adj.* of poor quality, low-grade, bad.

недобросо́вестност|ь, и *f.* **1** (*нечестность*) bad faith; unscrupulousness. **2** (*небрежность*) carelessness.

недобросо́вест|ный (~ен, ~на) *adj.* **1** (*нечестный*) unscrupulous. **2** (*небрежный*) lacking in conscientiousness; careless.

недо́бр|ый *adj.* **1** (*человек, взгляд*) unkind; unfriendly. **2** (*сон*) bad; (*намерение, чувство*) evil; **~ая весть** bad news.

недове́ри|е, я *nt.* distrust; mistrust; **во́тум ~я** vote of no confidence.

недове́рчив|ый (~, ~а) *adj.* distrustful; mistrustful.

недове́с, а *m.* short weight.

недове́|сить, шу, сишь *pf.* (*of* ⇒**~шивать**) **1** (+*g.*) to give short weight (of). **2** to prove to be short-weight.

недове́шива|ть, ю *impf. of* ⇒**недове́сить**

недово́л|ьный (~ен, ~ьна) *adj.* (+*i.*) dissatisfied, discontented, displeased (with); *as n.* **н., ~ьного** *m.* malcontent.

недово́льств|о, а *nt.* dissatisfaction, discontent, displeasure.

недога́длив|ый (~, ~а) *adj.* slow (-witted).

недогля|де́ть, жу́, ди́шь *pf.* **1** (*опечатки*) to overlook, miss. **2** (**за**+*i.*) (*ребёнком*) to fail to keep an eye on; to not look after properly.

недоговорённост|ь, и *f.* **1** (*замалчивание*) reticence. **2** (*несогласованность*) lack of agreement.

недогру́зк|а, и *f.* underloading; (*fig.*) short time (*in factory or works*).

недода|ва́ть, ю́, ёшь *impf. of* ⇒**~́ть**

недо|да́ть, да́м, да́шь, да́ст, дади́м, дади́те, даду́т, *past* **~́дал, ~дала́, ~́дало** *pf.* (*of* ⇒**~дава́ть**) to give short; to deliver short; **он мне ~́дал три рубля́** he gave me three roubles short.

недода́ч|а, и *f.* (*денег*) deficiency in payment; (*товаров*) deficiency in supply.

недоде́лан|ный (~, ~на) *adj.* unfinished.

недоде́лк|а, и *f.* incompleteness.

недодерж|а́ть, у́, ~́ишь *pf.* (*phot.*) to under-expose.

недоде́ржк|а, и *f.* (*phot.*) under-exposure.

недоеда́ни|е, я *nt.* undernourishment, malnutrition.

недоеда́|ть, ю *impf.* to be undernourished, be underfed.

недозво́лен|ный (~, ~а) *adj.* illicit, unlawful.

недозре́лый *adj.* (*яблоко*) unripe; (*fig.*) (*человек*) immature.

недои́мк|а, и *f.* arrears.

недои́мщик, а *m.* person in arrears (*in paying taxes, etc.*).

недока́зан|ный (~, ~а) *adj.* not proved, unproven.

недоказа́тел|ьный (~ен, ~ьна) *adj.* unconvincing, inadequate.

недоказу́ем|ый (~, ~а) *adj.* indemonstrable.

недоко́нчен|ный (~, ~а) *adj.* unfinished, incomplete.

недолга́ *only in phr.* **(вот) и вся н.** (*coll.*) and that is all there is to it.

недо́л|гий (~ог, ~га́, ~го) *adj.* short, brief.

недо́лго *adv.* **1** not long; **н. ду́мая** without hesitation. **2** (*coll.*): **н. и** (+*inf.*) one can easily; it is easy (to), it is a simple matter (to); **тут и потону́ть н.** one could easily drown here.

недолгове́ч|ный (~ен, ~на) *adj.* short-lived, ephemeral.

недолёт, а *m.* (*mil.*) falling short (*of bullets, shells*).

недолю́блива|ть, ю *impf.* (+*a. or g.*; *coll.*) not to be overfond of; **они́ ~ли друг дру́га** there was no love lost between them.

недоме́р|ок, ка *m.* undersize object.

недомога́ни|е, я *nt.* indisposition.

недомога́|ть, ю *impf.* to be indisposed, be unwell.

недомо́лвк|а, и *f.* innuendo; allusion.

недомы́сли|е, я *nt.* thoughtlessness, failure to think things out.

недонесе́ни|е, я *nt.* failure to give information (*concerning crime committed or meditated*); **н. о преступле́нии** (*leg.*) misprision of felony.

недоно́с|ок, ка *m.* premature baby; (*fig., pej.*) blockhead.

недоно́шен|ный (~, ~а) *adj.* (*med.*) premature.

недооце́нива|ть, ю *impf. of* ⇒**недооцени́ть**

недооцен|и́ть, ю́, ~́ишь *pf.* (*of* ⇒**~́ивать**) to underestimate, underrate.

недооце́нк|а, и *f.* underestimation.

недопеч|ённый (~ён, ~ена́) *adj.* half-baked.

недополуч|а́ть, а́ю *impf. of* ⇒**~и́ть**

недополуч|и́ть, у́, ~́ишь *pf.* (*of* ⇒**~а́ть**) to receive less (than one's due)

недопусти́м|ый (~, ~а) *adj.* inadmissible, intolerable.

недорабо́тк|а, и *f.* incompleteness.

недора́звитост|ь, и *f.* under-development, backwardness.

недора́звитый *adj.* under-developed, backward.

недоразуме́ни|е, я *nt.* misunderstanding.

недо́рого *adv.* not dear, cheaply.

недор|ого́й (~́ог, ~ога́, ~́ого) *adj.* inexpensive; reasonable (*of price*).

недоро́д, а *m.* crop failure.

не́доросл|ь, я *m.* **1** (*hist.*) minor. **2** (*fig., coll.*) young ignoramus, young oaf.

недоса́лива|ть, ю *impf. of* ⇒**недосоли́ть**

недоска́занност|ь, и *f.* understatement.

недослы́ш|ать, у, ишь *pf.* **1** (+*a. or g.*) (*не услышать всего*) to fail to hear all of. **2** (*intrans.; coll.*) (*плохо слышать*) to be hard of hearing.

недосмо́тр, а *m.* oversight.

недосмотр|е́ть, ю́, ~́ишь *pf.*

1 (+*g.*) to overlook, miss. **2** (**за**+*i.*) not to look after properly.

недосол|и́ть, ю́, ~́ишь *pf.* (*of* ⇒**недоса́ливать**) to put too little salt in.

недос|па́ть, плю́, пи́шь *pf.* (*of* ⇒**~ыпа́ть**) not to get enough sleep.

недоста|ва́ть, ёт, *impf.* (*of* ⇒**~́ть**) (*impers.*, +*g.*) to be missing, be lacking, be wanting; **ему́ ~ёт о́пыта** he lacks experience; **мне о́чень ~ва́ло вас** I missed you very much; **э́того ещё ~ва́ло!** that would be (*or* is) the last straw!

недоста́т|ок, ка *m.* **1** (+*g. or* **в**+*p.*) shortage (of), lack (of); **за ~ком** (+*g.*) for want (of); **име́ть н. в рабо́чей си́ле** to be short-handed. **2** (*несовершенство*) shortcoming, imperfection; defect; **н. зре́ния** defective eyesight.

недоста́точно *adv.* **1** insufficiently. **2** (*pred.* +*g.*) (*не хватает*) not enough.

недоста́точност|ь, и *f.* insufficiency; inadequacy; **витами́нная н.** vitamin deficiency.

недоста́точ|ный (~ен, ~на) *adj.* insufficient; inadequate; **н. глаго́л** (*gram.*) defective verb.

недоста́|ть, нет *pf. of* ⇒**~ва́ть**

недоста́ч|а, и *f.* (*coll.*) lack, shortage.

недостаю́щий *adj.* missing.

недостижи́м|ый (~, ~а) *adj.* unattainable.

недостове́р|ный (~ен, ~на) *adj.* unreliable, apocryphal.

недосто́|йный (~ин, ~йна) *adj.* unworthy.

недосту́пност|ь, и *f.* inaccessibility.

недосту́п|ный (~ен, ~на) *adj.* inaccessible (*also fig.*); **э́то ~но моему́ понима́нию** it is beyond my comprehension.

недосу́г, а *m.* (*coll.*) lack of time; **придёт ли он на конце́рт? нет, ему́ н.** is he coming to the concert? No, he is busy.

недосчит|а́ться, а́юсь *pf.* (*of* ⇒**~́ываться**) (+*g.*) to find missing, miss; to be out (in one's accounts); **он ~а́лся десяти́ рубле́й** he found he was ten roubles short.

недосчи́тыва|ться, юсь *impf. of* ⇒**недосчита́ться**

недосыпа́|ть, ю *impf. of* ⇒**недоспа́ть**

недосяга́ем|ый (~, ~а) *adj.* unattainable.

недотёп|а, ы *c.g.* (*coll.*) duffer.

недотро́г|а, и *c.g.* (*coll.*) touchy person.

недоумева́|ть, ю *impf.* to be perplexed, be at a loss.

недоуме́ни|е, я *nt.* perplexity, bewilderment; **быть в ~и** to be in a quandary.

недоуме́нный *adj.* puzzled, perplexed.

недоу́м|ок, ка *m.* (*coll.*) half-wit, blockhead.

недоу́чк|а, и *c.g.* (*coll.*) half-educated person.

недохва́тк|а, и *f.* (*coll.*) shortage.

недочелове́к, а *m.* subhuman (*individual*).

недочёт, а *m.* **1** (*недостача*) deficit; shortage. **2** (*usu. pl.*) (*недостаток*) defect, shortcoming.

не́др|а, ~ *no sg.* **1** depths (*of the earth*); **н. земли́** bowels of the earth; **разве́дка ~** prospecting of mineral wealth. **2** (*fig.*) depths, heart.

недре́млющий *adj.* vigilant, watchful.

не́друг, а *m.* enemy, foe.

недружелю́б|ный (~ен, ~на) *adj.* unfriendly.

недру́ж|ный (~ен, ~на) *adj.* disunited; disjointed.

неду́г, а *m.* ailment, disease.

неду́рно *adv.* not badly, well enough; **н.!** not bad!

недур|но́й (~ён, ~на́, ~но) *adj.* **1** (*неплохой*) not bad. **2** (**собо́й**) (*довольно красивый*) not bad-looking.

недю́жинный *adj.* outstanding, exceptional.

неё *a. and g. of* ⇒**она́** *when governed by preps.*

нестесте́ствен|ный (~, ~на) *adj.* unnatural.

нежда́нно *adv.* unexpectedly; **н.-нега́данно** quite unexpectedly.

нежда́нный *adj.* unexpected.

нежела́ни|е, я *nt.* unwillingness.

нежела́тель|ный (~ен, ~ьна) *adj.* undesirable.

не́жели *conj.* (*obs.*) than.

нежена́тый *adj.* unmarried.

не́женк|а, и *c.g.* (*coll.*) mollycoddle.

нежив|о́й *adj.* **1** (*мёртвый*) lifeless, dead; **роди́ться ~ы́м** to be still-born. **2** (*неорганический*) inanimate, inorganic. **3** (*fig.*) (*вялый*) dull, lifeless.

нежи́знен|ный (~, ~на) *adj.* **1** (*нереальный*) impracticable. **2** (*неправдоподобный*) weird.

нежило́й *adj.* **1** (*необитаемый*) uninhabited. **2** (*негодный для жилья*) not fit for habitation; uninhabitable.

не́жит|ь[1]**, и** *f.* (*collect.*) (*in Russian folklore*) the spirits (*gnomes, goblins, etc.*).

не́ж|ить[2]**, у, ишь** *impf.* to pamper, coddle; to caress.

не́ж|иться, усь, ишься *impf.* to luxuriate; **н. на со́лнце** to bask in the sun.

не́жнича|ть, ю *impf.* (*coll.*) **1** to bill and coo, canoodle. **2** (*fig.*) to be over-indulgent.

не́жност|ь, и *f.* **1** (*ласковость*) tenderness. **2** (*тонкость*) delicacy. **3** (*pl. only*) (*нежные слова*) endearments; (*лесть*) compliments, flattery.

не́ж|ный (~ен, ~на́, ~но) *adj.* **1** tender; affectionate; **~ные взгля́ды** tender glances. **2** (*тонкий*) delicate (= *soft, fine; of colours, taste, skin, etc.*). **3** (*хрупкий*) delicate; **н. пол** the weaker sex.

незабве́н|ный (~ен, ~на) *adj.* unforgettable.

незабу́дк|а, и *f.* (*bot.*) forget-me-not.

незабыва́емост|ь, и *f.* unforgettableness.

незабыва́ем|ый (~, ~а) *adj.* unforgettable.

незаве́рен|ный (~, ~на) *adj.* uncertified.

незави́д|ный (~ен, ~на) *adj.* unenviable.

незави́симо *adv.* independently; **н. от** irrespective of.

незави́симост|ь, и *f.* independence.

незави́сим|ый (~, ~а) *adj.* independent.

незави́сящ|ий *only in phr.* **по ~им от нас** *etc.*, **обстоя́тельствам** (*or* **причи́нам**) owing to circumstances beyond our, *etc.*, control.

незада́ч|а, и *f.* (*coll.*) bad luck.

незада́члив|ый (~, ~а) *adj.* (*coll.*) unlucky.

незадо́лго *adv.* (**до**+*g.*, **пе́ред**+*i.*) shortly (before), not long (before).

незаконнорождённый *adj.* (*obs.*) illegitimate.

незако́нност|ь, и *f.* illegality, unlawfulness.

незако́н|ный (~ен, ~на) *adj.* illegal, unlawful; (*ребёнок*) illegitimate; **~ая жена́** common-law wife.

незакономе́р|ный (~ен, ~на) *adj.* exceptional.

незако́нченност|ь, и *f.* incompleteness, unfinished state.

незако́нчен|ный (~, ~на) *adj.* incomplete, unfinished.

незамедли́тельно *adv.* without delay.

незамедли́тель|ный (~ен, ~ьна) *adj.* immediate.

незамени́м|ый (~, ~а) *adj.* **1** irreplaceable. **2** (*очень нужный*) indispensable.

незамерза́ющий *adj.* non-freezing; ice-free; (*tech.*) anti-freeze.

незаме́тно *adv.* imperceptibly; **н., что́бы** ... you cannot tell that ...

незаме́т|ный (~ен, ~на) *adj.* **1** (*следы*) imperceptible. **2** (*человек*) unremarkable.

незаму́жняя *adj.* unmarried, single.

незамыслова́т|ый (~, ~а) *adj.* simple, uncomplicated.

незапа́мятн|ый *adj.* immemorial; **с ~ых времён** from time immemorial.

незапя́тнанный *adj.* unsullied, stainless.

незарабо́танный *adj.* unearned.

незара́з|ный (~ен, ~на) *adj.* non-contagious.

незаслу́жен|ный (~, ~на) *adj.* undeserved, unmerited.

незастро́енный *adj.* undeveloped, not built over.

незате́йлив|ый (~, ~а) *adj.* simple, unpretentious.

незауря́д|ный (~ен, ~на) *adj.* outstanding, exceptional.

не́зачем *adv.* (+*inf.*) there is no point (in), it is pointless; there is no need (to); **н.**

бо́льше ждать there is no point in waiting any longer.

незва́ный *adj.* uninvited.

незде́шний *adj.* **1** (*coll.*) not of these parts; **я н.** I am a stranger here. **2** (*неземной*) unearthly, supernatural, mysterious; **н. мир** the other world.

нездоро́вит|ься, ~ся *impf.* (*impers.*, +*d.*) to feel unwell.

нездоро́в|ый (~, ~а) *adj.* **1** unhealthy (*also fig.*). **2** *as pred.* unwell, poorly.

нездоро́вь|е, я *nt.* indisposition; ill-health.

неземно́й *adj.* unearthly.

незло́бив|ый (~, ~а) *adj.* mild, forgiving.

незлопа́мят|ный (~ен, ~на) *adj.* forgiving.

незнако́м|ец, ца *m.* stranger.

незнако́м|ка, ки *f. of* ⇒**~ец**

незнако́м|ый (~, ~а) *adj.* **1** unknown, unfamiliar. **2** (**с**+*i.*) unacquainted (with).

незна́ни|е, я *nt.* ignorance.

незна́чащий *adj.* insignificant.

незначи́тел|ьный (~ен, ~ьна) *adj.* insignificant, negligible, trivial.

незна́ющ|ий *adj.* (+*g.*) ignorant (of); **н. у́стали** indefatigable; **~ая грани́ц любо́вь** love that knows no bounds.

незре́лост|ь, и *f.* unripeness; (*fig.*) immaturity.

незре́л|ый (~, ~а) *adj.* unripe (*also fig.*); (*fig.*) immature.

незри́м|ый (~, ~а) *adj.* invisible.

незы́блем|ый (~, ~а) *adj.* unshakeable, stable.

неизбе́жност|ь, и *f.* inevitability.

неизбе́ж|ный (~ен, ~на) *adj.* inevitable, unavoidable; inescapable.

неизбы́в|ный (~ен, ~на) *adj.* unescapable, permanent.

неизве́дан|ный (~, ~на) *adj.* (*место*) unexplored; (*чувство*) new, not experienced before.

неизве́стност|ь, и *f.* **1** (*отсутствие сведений*) uncertainty; **быть в ~и** (**о**+*p.*) to be uncertain (about), be in the dark (about). **2** (*незаметное существование*) obscurity; **жить в ~и** to live in obscurity.

неизве́ст|ный (~ен, ~на) *adj.* unknown; **~но где, когда́,** *etc.*, no one knows where, when, *etc.* (= *somewhere, at some time, etc.*); *as n.* **н., ~ного** *m.*, **~ная, ~ной** *f.* unknown person; **~ное, ~ного** *nt.* (*math.*) unknown (quantity).

неизглади́м|ый (~, ~а) *adj.* indelible.

неи́зданный *adj.* unpublished.

неизлечи́м|ый (~, ~а) *adj.* incurable.

неизме́н|ный (~ен, ~на) *adj.* **1** (*постоянный*) invariable, immutable. **2** (*rhet.*) (*верный*) devoted, true.

неизменя́ем|ый (~, ~а) *adj.* unalterable.

неизмери́мо *adv.* immeasurably.

неизмери́мост|ь, и *f.* immeasurability; immensity.

неизмери́м|ый (~, ~а) *adj.* immeasurable; immense.

неизрече́нный *adj.* (*obs.*) ineffable.

неизъясни́м|ый (~, ~а) *adj.* (*трудно постигаемый*) inexplicable; (*невыразимый*) indescribable.

неиме́ни|е, я *nt.* lack, want; **за ~ем лу́чшего** for want of sth. better.

неимове́р|ный (~ен, ~на) *adj.* incredible, unbelievable.

неиму́щий *adj.* indigent, poor.

неинтере́с|ный (~ен, ~на) *adj.* uninteresting.

неискорени́м|ый (~, ~а) *adj.* ineradicable.

нeíскрен|ний (~ен, ~на) *adj.* insincere.

нeíскренност|ь, и *f.* insincerity.

неиску́с|ный (~ен, ~на) *adj.* unskilful, inexpert.

неискушённост|ь, и *f.* inexperience.

неискушён|ный (~, ~а) *adj.* inexperienced, unsophisticated.

неисповеди́м|ый (~, ~а) *adj.* (*liter.*) inscrutable, incomprehensible; **~ы пути́ Госпо́дни** the Lord/God works in mysterious ways.

неисполне́ни|е, я *nt.* failure to carry out, non-performance; **н. зако́на** failure to observe a law.

неисполни́м|ый (~, ~а) *adj.* impracticable; unrealizable.

неиспо́рченност|ь, и *f.* (*fig.*) innocence.

неиспо́рчен|ный (~, ~а) *adj.* (*fig.*) unspoiled, innocent.

неисправи́м|ый (~, ~а) *adj.* **1** (*человек*) incorrigible. **2** (*недостаток, ошибка*) irremediable, irreparable.

неиспра́вност|ь, и *f.* **1** (*машины*) disrepair. **2** (*неисполнительность*) carelessness; unreliability.

неиспра́в|ный (~ен, ~на) *adj.* **1** (*машина*) out of order; faulty, defective. **2** (*человек*) unreliable.

неиспы́танный *adj.* untried, untested.

неиссяка́ем|ый (~, ~а) *adj.* inexhaustible.

нeíстовств|о, а *nt.* **1** (*буйство*) fury, frenzy. **2** (*жестокость*) brutality, savagery.

нeíстовств|овать, ую *impf.* **1** (*о человеке; о буре*) to rage. **2** (*совершать зверства*) to commit brutalities.

нeíстов|ый (~, ~а) *adj.* furious, frenzied; **~ые аплодисме́нты** tempestuous applause.

неистощи́м|ый (~, ~а) *adj.* inexhaustible.

неистреби́м|ый (~, ~а) *adj.* ineradicable; undying.

неисчерпа́ем|ый (~, ~а) *adj.* inexhaustible.

неисчисли́м|ый (~, ~а) *adj.* innumerable; incalculable.

ней *d., i., and p. of* ⇒**она́** *when governed by preps.*

нейло́н, а *m.* nylon.

нейло́новый *adj.* nylon, made of nylon.

неймёт (*no other form in use*), *impf.*, *only in prov.* **(хоть) ви́дит о́ко, да зуб н.** there's many a slip 'twixt cup and lip.

неймётся *impf.* (*impers.*, +*d.*; *coll.*): **ему́ н.** he is set on it, there is no holding him; he will not sit still.

нейро́н, а *m.* (*physiol.*) neuron.

нейрохиру́рг, а *m.* neurosurgeon.

нейрохирурги́|я, и *f.* neurosurgery.

нейтрализа́тор, а *m.*: **каталити́ческий н.** catalytic converter.

нейтрализа́ци|я, и *f.* neutralization.

нейтрализ|ова́ть, у́ю *impf. and pf.* to neutralize.

нейтралите́т, а *m.* (*pol.*) neutrality.

нейтра́льност|ь, и *f.* neutrality.

нейтра́л|ьный (~ен, ~ьна) *adj.* neutral.

нейтро́н, а *m.* (*phys.*) neutron.

нейтро́н|ный *adj. of* ⇒**~**

неказíст|ый (~, ~а) *adj.* (*coll.*) unprepossessing.

нека́чественный *adj.* poor-quality.

неквалифици́рованный *adj.* unqualified; **н. рабо́чий** unskilled labourer (*Br.*), laborer (*US*).

не́кий *pron.* a certain; a kind of; **вас спра́шивал н. господи́н Па́влов** a (certain) Mr Pavlov was asking for you.

не́когда[1] *adv.* once, formerly; in the old days.

не́когда[2] *adv.* there is no time; **мне сего́дня н. разгова́ривать** I have no time to chat today.

не́кого, не́кому, не́кем, не́ о ком *pron.* (+*inf.*) there is nobody (to); **н. вини́ть** nobody is to blame; **ей не́ с кем пойти́** she has nobody to go with (her).

неколеби́мый = **непоколеби́мый**

некоммуника́бельност|ь, и *f.* uncommunicativeness; unsociableness.

некоммуника́бел|ьный (~ен, ~ьна) *adj.* uncommunicative; unsociable.

некомпете́нт|ный (~ен, ~на) *adj.* incompetent, unqualified.

некомпле́кт|ный (~ен, ~на) *adj.* incomplete; not up to strength.

неконтроли́руемый *adj.* uncontrollable.

некороно́ванный *adj.* uncrowned.

некорре́ктност|ь, и *f.* discourtesy, impoliteness.

некорре́кт|ный (~ен, ~на) *adj.* discourteous, impolite.

не́котор|ый *pron.* some; **он ~ое вре́мя не дви́гался с ме́ста** for a time he did not budge; **мы с ~ых пор живём здесь** we have been living here for some time; **~ым о́бразом** somehow, in some way; **в, до ~ой сте́пени** to some extent, to a certain extent; *as n.* **~ые, ~ых** some; some people.

некраси́в|ый (~, ~а) *adj.* **1** ugly,

Н

unattractive. **2** (*coll.*) (*поведение*) unseemly, not nice.

некредитоспосо́бност|ь, и *f.* insolvency.

некредитоспосо́б|ный (~ен, ~на) *adj.* insolvent.

некре́п|кий (~ок, ~ка́) *adj.* rather weak.

некрещёный *adj.* unbaptized, not baptized, non-Christian.

некро́з, а *m.* (*med.*) necrosis.

некроло́г, а *m.* obituary (notice).

некрома́нти|я, и *f.* necromancy.

некро́пол|ь, я *m.* necropolis.

некру́п|ный (~ен, ~на́, ~но) *adj.* medium-sized, not large.

некста́ти *adv.* (*прийти, сказать*) at the wrong moment, inopportunely; (*о замечании*) inopportune, inappropriate.

некта́р, а *m.* nectar.

не́кто *pron.* someone; **н. Петро́в** one Petrov, a certain Petrov.

не́куда *adv.* (+*inf.*) there is nowhere (to); **мне н. пойти́** I have nowhere to go.

некульту́рност|ь, и *f.* **1** (*низкий уровень культуры*) low level of civilization; uncivilized ways. **2** (*грубость*) bad manners, boorishness.

некульту́р|ный (~ен, ~на) *adj.* **1** (*нецивилизованный*) uncivilized; backward. **2** (*грубый*) rough (-mannered), boorish. **3** (*bot.*) uncultivated.

некуря́щ|ий *adj.* non-smoking; *as n.* **н., ~его** *m.* non-smoker; **ваго́н для ~их** non-smoking carriage.

нела́д|ный (~ен, ~на) *adj.* (*coll.*) wrong, bad; **у него́ ~но с го́рлом** there is sth. the matter with his throat; **будь он ~ен!** blast him!

нелад|ы́, о́в *no sg.* (*coll.*) **1** (*ссоры*) discord, disagreement; **у них н.** they are having problems. **2** (*проблема*) trouble, sth. wrong.

нела́сков|ый (~, ~а) *adj.* reserved, unfriendly.

нелега́л, а *m.* (*coll.*) illegal person (*person living somewhere illegally or doing sth. illegally*).

нелега́льност|ь, и *f.* illegality.

нелега́л|ьный (~ен, ~ьна) *adj.* illegal.

нелега́льщин|а, ы *f.* (*coll.*) (*деятельность*) illegal activities; (*литература*) illegal literature.

нелегити́м|ный (~ен, ~на) *adj.* illegitimate.

нелёгкая (*coll.*): **что за н. его́ сюда́ несёт?** what the deuce brings him here?

нелёг|кий (~ок, ~ка́) *adj.* **1** (*трудный*) difficult, not easy. **2** (*тяжёлый*) heavy, not light (*also fig.*).

неле́пост|ь, и *f.* absurdity, nonsense.

неле́п|ый (~, ~а) *adj.* absurd, ridiculous.

неле́ст|ный (~ен, ~на) *adj.* unflattering, uncomplimentary.

нелицеприя́т|ный (~ен, ~на) *adj.* (*liter.*) impartial.

нели́шний *adj.* not superfluous; not out of place; **нели́шне** (*coll.*) it's a good idea, it doesn't hurt, one ought; **нели́шне бы отдохну́ть** it wouldn't hurt to have a rest.-

нело́в|кий (~ок, ~ка́, ~ко) *adj.* **1** (*неуклюжий*) awkward; clumsy. **2** (*физически неудобный*) uncomfortable. **3** (*fig.*) awkward; embarrassing; **~кое молча́ние** awkward silence; **ему́ ~ко пригласи́ть её** he feels awkward about inviting her.

нело́вко *adv.* awkwardly; uncomfortably; **чу́вствовать себя́ н.** to feel ill at ease, feel awkward, feel uncomfortable.

нело́вкост|ь, и *f.* **1** (*свойство*) awkwardness, clumsiness (*also fig.*); **чу́вствовать н.** to feel awkward, feel uncomfortable. **2** (*поступок*) blunder, gaffe.

нелоги́чност|ь, и *f.* illogicality.

нелоги́ч|ный (~ен, ~на) *adj.* illogical.

нельзя́ *adv.* (+*inf.*) **1** (*нет возможности*) it is impossible; **н. не призна́ть** it is impossible not to admit, one cannot but admit. **2** (*запрещается*) it is not allowed; **здесь н. кури́ть** smoking is not allowed here. **3** (*нехорошо*) one ought not, one should not; **н. ложи́ться (спать) так по́здно** you ought not to go to bed so late. **4**: **как н.** (+*comp. adv.*) as … as possible; **как н. лу́чше** in the best possible way.

нелюбе́зност|ь, и *f.* ungraciousness; (*невежливость*) discourtesy.

нелюбе́з|ный (~ен, ~на) *adj.* ungracious, unobliging; (*невежливый*) discourteous.

нелюби́м|ый (~, ~а) *adj.* unloved.

нелюб|о́вь, ви́ *f.* (**к**+*d.*) dislike (for).

нелюбопы́т|ный (~ен, ~на) *adj.* **1** (*человек*) incurious, lacking curiosity. **2** (*беседа*) uninteresting.

нелюди́м, а *m.* unsociable person.

нелюди́м|ый (~, ~а) *adj.* unsociable.

нём *p. of* **⇨он, оно́**

нема́ло *adv.* **1** (+*g.*) (*времени, денег*) not a little; a good deal of; (*людей*) quite a few. **2** (*читать, гордиться*) a good deal, quite a lot.

немалова́ж|ный (~ен, ~на) *adj.* of no small importance.

нема́л|ый (~, ~а́) *adj.* considerable.

неме́дленно *adv.* immediately.

неме́длен|ный (~, ~на) *adj.* immediate.

неме́ркнущий *adj.* (*fig., rhet.*) unfading.

неме́|ть, ю *impf.* (*of* **⇨о~**) **1** (*становиться немым*) to become dumb, grow dumb. **2** (*pf. also* **за~**) (*цепенеть*) to become numb, grow numb.

не́м|ец, ца *m.* German.

неме́цк|ий *adj.* German; **~ая овча́рка** Alsatian (dog) (*Br.*), German shepherd.

немига́ющий *adj.* unwinking.

немилосе́рд|ный (~ен, ~на) *adj.* merciless, unmerciful (*also fig.*).

неми́лостив|ый (~, ~а) *adj.* ungracious; harsh.

неми́лост|ь, и *f.* disgrace, disfavour (*Br.*), disfavor (*US*); **впасть в н.** to fall into disgrace.

неми́л|ый (~, ~а́, ~о) *adj.* (*folk poet.*) unloved; hated.

немину́ем|ый (~, ~а) *adj.* inevitable, unavoidable.

не́м|ка, ки *f. of* **⇨~ец**

немно́г|ие *adj.* few, a few; *as n.* **н., ~их** few.

немно́го *adv.* **1** (+*g.*) (*времени, денег*) a little, some, not much; (*людей*) a few, not many. **2** (*слегка*) a little, somewhat, slightly; **я н. уста́л** I am a little tired; **н. спустя́** not long after.

немно́г|ое, ого *nt.* few things, little.

немногосло́в|ный (~ен, ~на) *adj.* laconic, brief, terse.

немно́жко *adv.* (*coll.*) a little; a trifle, a bit.

немну́щийся *adj.* (*text.*) crease-resistant; 'non-iron'.

нем|о́й (~, ~а́, ~о) *adj.* **1** dumb; **~а́я а́збука** deaf-and-dumb alphabet; *as n.* **н., ~о́го** *m.* mute; **~ы́е** (*collect.*) the dumb. **2** (*fig.*) silent; **н. фильм** silent film. **3** (*ling.*) mute.

не|молодо́й (~мо́лод, ~молода́, ~мо́лодо) *adj.* not young, elderly.

немо́лчный *adj.* (*poet.*) incessant, unceasing.

немот|а́, ы́ *f.* dumbness; muteness.

не́моч|ь, и *f.* (*coll.*) illness, sickness.

не́мощ|ный (~ен, ~на) *adj.* sick; feeble.

не́мощ|ь, и *f.* (*coll.*) sickness; feebleness.

нему́ *d. of* **он, оно́** *after preps.*

немудрён|ый (~, ~а́) *adj.* (*coll.*) simple, easy; **э́то де́ло ~ое** it is a simple matter; (*impers., as pred.*): **~о́** it is no wonder.

немы́слим|ый (~, ~а) *adj.* (*coll.*) unthinkable, inconceivable.

ненави́|деть, жу, дишь *impf.* to hate, detest, loathe.

ненави́стник, а *m.* hater.

ненави́стни|ца, цы *f. of* **⇨~к**

ненави́ст|ный (~ен, ~на) *adj.* hated; hateful.

не́навист|ь, и *f.* hatred, detestation.

ненавя́зчив|ый (~, ~а) *adj.* unobtrusive.

ненагля́дный *adj.* (*coll.*) beloved.

ненадёж|ный (~ен, ~на) *adj.* (*человек; сведение*) unreliable, untrustworthy; (*защита; лёд*) insecure.

нена́добност|ь, и *f.* uselessness; **за ~ью** as not wanted.

ненадо́лго *adv.* for a short while, not for long.

ненаме́ренно *adv.* unintentionally, unwittingly, accidentally.

ненаме́рен|ный (~, ~на) *adj.* unintentional, accidental.

ненападе́ни|е, я *nt.* non-aggression; **пакт о ~и** non-aggression pact.

ненаро́ком *adv.* (*coll.*) unintentionally, accidentally.

ненаруши́м|ый (~, ~а) *adj.* inviolable.

ненаси́льственный *adj.* non-violent.

нена́ст|ный (~ен, ~на) *adj.* (*погода*) bad, foul.

ненастоя́щий *adj.* (*мех*) artificial; (*деньги*) counterfeit.

нена́сть|е, я *nt.* bad, foul weather.

ненасы́т|ный (~ен, ~на) *adj.* insatiable (*also fig.*).

ненатура́л|ьный (~ен, ~ьна) *adj.* **1** (*человек, смех*) affected; not natural. **2** (*мех, шёлк*) artificial, imitation; (*свет*) artificial.

ненау́ч|ный (~ен, ~на) *adj.* unscientific.

ненорма́льност|ь, и *f.* abnormality.

ненорма́л|ьный (~ен, ~ьна) *adj.* **1** abnormal. **2** (*сумасшедший*) mad.

нену́ж|ный (~ен, ~на́, ~но) *adj.* (*мягкость*) unnecessary; (*книга, человек*) superfluous.

необду́ман|ный (~, ~на) *adj.* thoughtless, precipitate.

необеспе́ченн|ый *adj.* **1** without means, poor; unprovided for; **~ая жизнь** precarious existence. **2** (+*i.*) not provided (with).

необита́ем|ый (~, ~а) *adj.* uninhabited; **н. о́стров** desert island.

необозри́м|ый (~, ~а) *adj.* boundless, immense.

необосно́ванност|ь, и *f.* groundlessness.

необосно́ван|ный (~, ~на) *adj.* unfounded, groundless.

необрабо́тан|ный (~, ~а) *adj.* **1** (*земля*) uncultivated, untilled. **2** (*минерал*) raw, crude. **3** (*fig.*) (*статья*) unpolished; (*голос*) untrained.

необразо́ванност|ь, и *f.* lack of education.

необразо́ван|ный (~, ~на) *adj.* uneducated.

необрати́м|ый (~, ~а) *adj.* irreversible.

необу́здан|ный (~, ~на) *adj.* (*фантазия*) unbridled; (*нрав*) ungovernable.

необходи́мост|ь, и *f.* necessity; **по ~и** out of necessity; **това́ры пе́рвой ~и** essential goods.

необходи́м|ый (~, ~а) *adj.* necessary, essential; (*impers., as pred.*): **~о** it is necessary *or* imperative.

необщи́тел|ьный (~ен, ~ьна) *adj.* unsociable.

необъекти́в|ный (~ен, ~на) *adj.* not objective, biased.

необъясни́м|ый (~, ~а) *adj.* inexplicable, unaccountable.

необъя́т|ный (~ен, ~на) *adj.* immense, unbounded.

необыкнове́н|ный (~ен, ~на) *adj.* unusual, uncommon.

необыча́|йный (~ен, ~йна) *adj.* extraordinary, exceptional.

необы́ч|ный (~ен, ~на) *adj.* unusual; **~ные ви́ды вооруже́ний** unconventional weapons.

необяза́тел|ьный (~ен, ~ьна) *adj.* **1** (*предмет, курс*) not obligatory, optional. **2** (*человек*) unreliable.

неограни́чен|ный (~, ~на) *adj.* unlimited, unbounded; **~ная мона́рхия** absolute monarchy.

неоднозна́ч|ный (~ен, ~на) *adj.* **1** ambiguous, equivocal. **2** (*сложный*) complex, complicated.

неоднокра́тно *adv.* repeatedly.

неоднокра́т|ный (~ен, ~на) *adj.* repeated.

неоднoро́дност|ь, и *f.* heterogeneity.

неоднoро́д|ный (~ен, ~на) *adj.* heterogeneous; dissimilar.

неодобре́ни|е, я *nt.* disapproval.

неодобри́тел|ьный (~ен, ~ьна) *adj.* disapproving.

неодоли́м|ый (~, ~а) *adj.* (*враг, сила*) invincible; (*страсть, страх*) insuperable.

неодушевлённый *adj.* inanimate.

неожи́данност|ь, и *f.* **1** unexpectedness, suddenness. **2** (*событие*) surprise.

неожи́дан|ный (~, ~на) *adj.* unexpected, sudden.

неозо́йский *adj.* (*geol.*) Neozoic.

неоклассици́зм, а *m.* neoclassicism.

неокласси́ческий *adj.* neoclassical.

неоконча́тел|ьный (~ен, ~ьна) *adj.* inconclusive.

неоко́нченный *adj.* unfinished.

неоли́т, а *m.* (*archaeol.*) the neolithic period.

неолити́ческий *adj.* (*archaeol.*) neolithic.

неологи́зм, а *m.* neologism.

нео́н, а *m.* (*chem.*) neon.

нео́н|овый *adj. of* ⇒~; **~овая ла́мпа** neon lamp.

неопа́с|ный (~ен, ~на) *adj.* (*место, путешествие*) safe; (*болезнь, собака*) harmless.

неопера́бел|ьный (~ен, ~ьна) *adj.* (*med.*) inoperable.

неопери́вшийся *adj.* unfledged; (*fig.*) callow.

неопису́ем|ый (~, ~а) *adj.* indescribable.

неопла́т|ный (~ен, ~на) *adj.* that cannot be repaid; **я ваш н. должни́к** (*fig.*) I am eternally indebted to you.

неопо́знан|ный (~, ~а) *adj.* unidentified.

неопра́вданный *adj.* unjustified, unwarranted.

неопределённост|ь, и *f.* vagueness, uncertainty.

неопределён|ный (~ен, ~на) *adj.* **1** indefinite; **~ное наклоне́ние, ~ная фо́рма глаго́ла** (*gram.*) infinitive; **н. арти́кль** (*gram.*) indefinite article. **2** indeterminate; vague, uncertain.

неопредели́м|ый (~, ~а) *adj.* indefinable.

неопроверж́им|ый (~, ~а) *adj.* irrefutable.

неопря́тност|ь, и *f.* slovenliness; untidiness, sloppiness.

неопря́т|ный (~ен, ~на) *adj.* slovenly; untidy, sloppy.

нео́пытност|ь, и *f.* inexperience.

нео́пыт|ный (~ен, ~на) *adj.* inexperienced.

неорганизо́ванност|ь, и *f.* lack of organization; disorganization.

неорганизо́ван|ный (~, ~на) *adj.* unorganized; disorganized.

неоргани́ческий *adj.* inorganic.

неордина́р|ный (~ен, ~на) *adj.* unusual.

неосведомлённый *adj.* ill-informed.

неосла́б|ный (~ен, ~на) *adj.* unremitting, unabated.

неосмотри́тельност|ь, и *f.* imprudence.

неосмотри́тел|ьный (~ен, ~ьна) *adj.* imprudent, incautious.

неоснова́тел|ьный (~ен, ~ьна) *adj.* **1** unfounded, lacking foundation. **2** (*coll.*) (*легкомысленный*) frivolous.

неоспори́мост|ь, и *f.* incontestability, indisputability.

неоспори́м|ый (~, ~а) *adj.* unquestionable, incontestable, indisputable.

неосторо́жност|ь, и *f.* carelessness; imprudence.

неосторо́ж|ный (~ен, ~на) *adj.* careless; imprudent, incautious.

неосуществи́м|ый (~, ~а) *adj.* impracticable, unrealizable.

неосяза́ем|ый (~, ~а) *adj.* intangible.

неотврати́мост|ь, и *f.* inevitability.

неотврати́м|ый (~, ~а) *adj.* inevitable.

неотвя́з|ный (~ен, ~на) *adj.* importunate; obsessive.

неотвя́зчив|ый (~, ~а) *adj.* importunate; obsessive.

неотдели́м|ый (~, ~а) *adj.* inseparable.

неотёсан|ный (~, ~на) *adj.* **1** unpolished. **2** (*fig.*) (*грубый*) uncouth.

не́откуда *adv.* there is nowhere; **мне н. э́то получи́ть** there is nowhere I can get it from.

неотло́жк|а, и *f.* (*coll.*) ambulance service; (*машина*) ambulance.

неотло́жност|ь, и *f.* urgency.

неотло́ж|ный (~ен, ~на) *adj.* urgent, pressing; **~ная медици́нская по́мощь** emergency medical service.

неотлу́чно *adv.* constantly, permanently.

неотлу́ч|ный (~ен, ~на) *adj.* ever-present; permanent.

неотрази́м|ый (~, ~а) *adj.*

Н

irresistible (*also fig.*); **~ые до́воды** incontrovertible arguments.

неотсту́пност|ь, и *f.* persistence; importunity.

неотсту́п|ный (~ен, ~на) *adj.* persistent; importunate.

неотчётлив|ый (~, ~а) *adj.* vague, indistinct.

неотъе́млем|ый (~, ~а) *adj.* inalienable; **~ое пра́во** inalienable right; **~ая часть** integral part.

неофаши́зм, а *m.* neo-fascism.

неофаши́ст, а *m.* neo-fascist.

неофаши́стский *adj.* neo-fascist.

неофициа́л|ьный (~ен, ~ьна) *adj.* unofficial.

неохо́т|а, ы *f.* **1** reluctance. **2** (*+d.*, *as pred.*; *coll.*): **мне**, *etc.*, **н. идти́** I, *etc.*, have no wish to go, don't feel like going.

неохо́тно *adv.* reluctantly; unwillingly.

неоцени́м|ый (~, ~а) *adj.* inestimable, priceless, invaluable.

неощути́м|ый (~, ~а) *adj.* imperceptible.

Непа́л, а *m.* Nepal.

непа́л|ец, ьца *m.* Nepalese.

непа́л|ка, ки *fem. of* ⇒**~ец**

непа́льский *adj.* Nepalese.

непа́рный *adj.* odd (*not forming a pair*).

неларти́|йный (~ен, ~йна) *adj.* **1** (*человек*) non-Party. **2** (*поведение*) unbefitting a member of the Party.

непереводи́м|ый (~, ~а) *adj.* untranslatable.

непередава́ем|ый (~, ~а) *adj.* inexpressible, indescribable.

неперехо́дный *adj.* (*gram.*) intransitive.

непеча́тный *adj.* (*coll.*) unprintable.

непи́сан|ый *adj.* unwritten; **~ые пра́вила** unwritten rules.

неплатёж, а́ *m.* non-payment.

неплатёжеспосо́бност|ь, и *f.* (*fin.*) insolvency.

неплатёжеспосо́б|ный (~ен, ~на) *adj.* (*fin.*) insolvent.

неплате́льщик, а *m.* defaulter; person in arrears with payment (*of taxes, etc.*).

неплодоро́д|ный (~ен, ~на) *adj.* barren; infertile.

непло́хо *adv.* not badly, quite well.

неплох|о́й (~́, ~а́, ~́о) *adj.* not bad, quite good.

непобеди́м|ый (~, ~а) *adj.* invincible.

непова́дно *as pred.* (*impers.*, *+d. and inf.*; *coll.*): **чтобы н. бы́ло** to teach (s.o.) not (to do sth. again); **мальчи́шку вы́пороли, что́бы ему́ н. бы́ло кра́сть я́блоки** they gave the boy a thrashing to teach him not to steal apples again.

непови́н|ный (~ен, ~на) *adj.* innocent.

неповинове́ни|е, я *nt.* insubordination, disobedience.

неповоро́тлив|ый (~, ~а) *adj.* (*неуклюжий*) clumsy, awkward; (*медлительный*) sluggish, slow.

неповтори́м|ый (~, ~а) *adj.* unique.

непого́д|а, ы *f.* bad weather.

непогреши́мост|ь, и *f.* infallibility.

непогреши́м|ый (~, ~а) *adj.* infallible.

неподалёку *adv.* not far off.

непода́тлив|ый (~, ~а) *adj.* stubborn, intractable; unyielding, tenacious.

неподве́домствен|ный (~, ~на) *adj.* (*+d.*) not subject to the authority (of), beyond the jurisdiction (of).

неподви́жност|ь, и *f.* immobility.

неподви́ж|ный (~ен, ~на) *adj.* motionless, immobile, immovable (*also fig.*); fixed, stationary.

неподде́льност|ь, и *f.* genuineness; sincerity.

неподде́л|ьный (~ен, ~ьна) *adj.* genuine; unfeigned, sincere.

неподку́пност|ь, и *f.* incorruptibility, integrity.

неподку́п|ный (~ен, ~на) *adj.* incorruptible.

неподоба́ющий *adj.* unseemly, improper.

неподража́ем|ый (~, ~а) *adj.* inimitable.

неподсу́д|ный (~ен, ~на) *adj.* (*+d.*) not under the jurisdiction (of).

неподходя́щий *adj.* unsuitable, inappropriate.

неподчине́ни|е, я *nt.* insubordination; **н. суде́бному постановле́нию** (*leg.*) contempt of court.

непозволи́тел|ьный (~ен, ~ьна) *adj.* inadmissible, impermissible.

непознава́ем|ый (~, ~а) *adj.* (*phil.*) unknowable.

непокла́дист|ый (~, ~а) *adj.* obstinate, uncompromising.

непоко́|йный (~ен, ~йна) *adj.* (*obs.*, *coll.*) troubled; restless, disturbed.

непоколеби́м|ый (~, ~а) *adj.* steadfast, unshakeable.

непоко́рност|ь, и *f.* recalcitrance; unruliness.

непоко́р|ный (~ен, ~на) *adj.* recalcitrant; unruly.

непокры́т|ый (~, ~а) *adj.* uncovered, bare.

непола́дк|а, и *f.* **1** defect, fault. **2** (*in pl.*) (*нелады*) disagreement, quarrel.

неполнопра́в|ный (~ен, ~на) *adj.* not possessing full rights.

неполнот|а́, ы́ *f.* incompleteness.

неполноце́нност|ь, и *f.* inferiority; **ко́мплекс ~и** inferiority complex; **психи́ческая н.** mental deficiency.

неполноце́н|ный (~ен, ~на) *adj.* inferior; substandard; **у́мственно н.** mentally deficient; **физи́чески н.** physically handicapped.

непо́л|ный (~он, ~на́, ~но) *adj.* (*ведро, корзина*) not full; (*знания, перечень*) incomplete; **с тех пор прошло́ непо́лных два́дцать лет** since then not quite twenty years had passed; **~ная семья́** single-parent family; **рабо́тать ~ную неде́лю** to work part-time.

непоме́р|ный (~ен, ~на) *adj.* excessive, inordinate.

непонима́ни|е, я *nt.* incomprehension.

непоня́тливост|ь, и *f.* slowness, dimness.

непоня́тлив|ый (~, ~а) *adj.* slow (to grasp things), dim.

непоня́т|ный (~ен, ~на) *adj.* unintelligible, incomprehensible; (*impers.*, *as pred*): **~но** it is incomprehensible; **мне ~но, как он мог э́то сде́лать** I cannot understand how he could do it.

непопада́ни|е, я *nt.* miss (*in shooting*).

непоправи́м|ый (~, ~а) *adj.* irreparable, irremediable; irretrievable.

непоро́ч|ный (~ен, ~на) *adj.* pure, chaste; **~ное зача́тие** (*relig.*) the Immaculate Conception.

непоря́д|ок, ка *m.* disorder; violation of order.

непоря́доч|ный (~ен, ~на) *adj.* dishonourable (*Br.*), dishonorable (*US*).

непосвящённый *adj.* uninitiated.

непосе́д|а, ы *c.g.* (*coll.*) fidget; rolling stone.

непосе́дливост|ь, и *f.* restlessness.

непосе́длив|ый (~, ~а) *adj.* fidgety, restless.

непосеще́ни|е, я *nt.* (*+g.*) non-attendance (at).

непоси́л|ьный (~ен, ~ьна) *adj.* beyond one's strength, excessive.

непосле́довательност|ь, и *f.* inconsistency; inconsequence.

непосле́довател|ьный (~ен, ~ьна) *adj.* inconsistent; inconsequent.

непослуша́ни|е, я *nt.* disobedience.

непослу́ш|ный (~ен, ~на) *adj.* disobedient, naughty.

непосре́дственност|ь, и *f.* spontaneity, ingenuousness.

непосре́дствен|ный (~, ~на) *adj.* **1** (*результат*) immediate, direct; **в ~ной бли́зости (от** *+g.*) in the immediate vicinity (of). **2** (*fig.*) (*натура*) direct; spontaneous, ingenuous.

непостижи́м|ый (~, ~а) *adj.* incomprehensible, inscrutable; **уму́ ~о** it passes understanding.

непостоя́н|ный (~ен, ~на) *adj.* inconstant, changeable.

непостоя́нств|о, а *nt.* inconstancy.

непоти́зм, а *m.* nepotism.

непотопля́ем|ый (~, ~а) *adj.* unsinkable.

непотре́б|ный (~ен, ~на) *adj.* (*obs.*) obscene, indecent; **~ные слова́** obscenities.

непотре́бств|о, а *nt.* (*obs.*) obscenity; indecent conduct.

непоча́т|ый (~, ~а) *adj.* (*coll.*) untouched, not begun, entire; **н. край** (+*g.*) a wealth (of), a whole host (of).

непочте́ни|е, я *nt.* disrespect.

непочти́тел|ьный (~ен, ~ьна) *adj.* disrespectful.

непра́вд|а, ы *f.* untruth, lie; **все́ми пра́вдами и ~ами** by fair means or foul; by hook or by crook.

неправдоподо́би|е, я *nt.* improbability, unlikelihood.

неправдоподо́б|ный (~ен, ~на) *adj.* improbable, unlikely; implausible.

непра́вед|ный (~ен, ~на) *adj.* (*rhet.*) iniquitous, unjust.

непра́вильно *adv.* incorrectly, erroneously; *in conjunction with vv. frequently* = mis-; *e.g.*, **н. истолкова́ть** to misinterpret.

непра́вильност|ь, и *f.* **1** (*уклонение от нормы*) irregularity; anomaly. **2** (*ошибочность*) incorrectness.

непра́вил|ьный (~ен, ~ьна) *adj.* **1** (*развитие, черты, форма*) irregular; **н. глаго́л** irregular verb; **~ьная дробь** (*math.*) improper fraction. **2** (*расчёт, суждение*) incorrect, erroneous, wrong, mistaken; **н. подхо́д (к де́лу)** wrong approach, wrong attitude.

неправоме́рност|ь, и *f.* illegality.

неправоме́р|ный (~ен, ~на) *adj.* illegal.

неправомо́чност|ь, и *f.* (*leg.*) incompetence.

неправомо́ч|ный (~ен, ~на) *adj.* (*leg.*) not competent; lacking the necessary authority.

неправот|а́, ы́ *f.* **1** (*заблуждение*) error. **2** (*несправедливость*) wrongness; injustice.

непра́в|ый (~, ~а́, ~о) *adj.* **1** (*заблуждающийся*) wrong, mistaken. **2** (*несправедливый*) unjust.

непревзойдённый *adj.* unsurpassed; matchless.

непредвзя́т|ый (~, ~а) *adj.* unbiased.

непредви́денный *adj.* unforeseen.

непреднаме́рен|ный (~, ~на) *adj.* unpremeditated.

непредсказу́емост|ь, и *f.* unpredictability.

непредсказу́ем|ый (~, ~а) *adj.* unpredictable.

непредубеждённый *adj.* unprejudiced, unbiased.

непредуму́шленн|ый *adj.* unpremeditated; **~ое уби́йство** manslaughter.

непредусмотри́тельност|ь, и *f.* improvidence, short-sightedness.

непредусмотри́тел|ьный (~ен, ~ьна) *adj.* improvident, short-sighted.

непрезента́бел|ьный (~ен, ~ьна) *adj.* unpresentable.

непреклóнност|ь, и *f.* inflexibility; inexorability.

непреклóн|ный (~ен, ~на) *adj.* inflexible, unbending; inexorable, adamant.

непрело́ж|ный (~ен, ~на) *adj.* **1** (*нерушимый*) immutable, unalterable. **2** (*неоспоримый*) indisputable.

непреме́нно *adv.* **1** (*обязательно*) without fail; certainly; **они́ н. приду́т за́втра** they are sure to come tomorrow. **2** (*очень*) absolutely; **мне н. ну́жно поговори́ть с ним** it is absolutely essential that I speak to him.

непреме́н|ный (~ен, ~на) *adj.* (*условие*) necessary; (*следствие*) unavoidable; (*черта*) indispensable; **н. секрета́рь** (*hist.*) permanent secretary.

непреобори́м|ый (~, ~а) *adj.* (*liter.*) insuperable; irresistible.

непреодоли́м|ый (~, ~а) *adj.* insuperable, insurmountable; (*желание*) irresistible; **~ая си́ла** (*leg.*) force majeure.

непререка́ем|ый (~, ~а) *adj.* unquestionable, indisputable; **н. тон** peremptory tone.

непреры́вно *adv.* uninterruptedly, continuously.

непреры́вност|ь, и *f.* continuity.

непреры́в|ный (~ен, ~на) *adj.* uninterrupted, unbroken; continuous.

непреста́нно *adv.* incessantly, continually.

непреста́н|ный (~ен, ~на) *adj.* incessant, continual.

непреходя́щий *adj.* eternal.

неприве́тлив|ый (~, ~а) *adj.* (*человек, взгляд*) unfriendly, ungracious; (*местность*) bleak, forbidding.

непривлека́тел|ьный (~ен, ~ьна) *adj.* unattractive.

неприв́ычк|а, и *f.* (*coll.*) want of habit; **с ~и он бы́стро захмеле́л** being unaccustomed to strong drink, he quickly became drunk.

неприв́ыч|ный (~ен, ~на) *adj.* unaccustomed, unwonted; unusual.

неприглядн|ный (~ен, ~на) *adj.* unattractive, unsightly.

неприго́д|ный (~ен, ~на) *adj.* unfit, useless; unserviceable; (*для военной службы*) ineligible.

непригора́ющий *adj.* non-stick.

неприе́млем|ый (~, ~а) *adj.* unacceptable.

непри́знанный *adj.* unrecognized, unacknowledged.

неприкаса́ем|ый, ого *m.* untouchable, Harijan.

неприка́янный *adj.* (*coll.*) restless, unable to find anything to do; **ходи́ть, броди́ть,** *etc.*, **как н.** to go about, wander about, *etc.*, like a lost soul.

неприкоснове́нност|ь, и *f.* inviolability; **дипломати́ческая н.** diplomatic immunity.

неприкоснове́н|ный (~ен, ~на) *adj.* inviolable; **н. запа́с** (*mil.*) emergency ration, iron ration; **н. капита́л** reserve capital.

неприкра́шенный *adj.* plain, unvarnished.

неприкры́т|ый *adj.* undisguised; **~ая ложь** barefaced lie.

неприли́чи|е, я *nt.* indecency, impropriety, unseemliness.

неприли́ч|ный (~ен, ~на) *adj.* indecent, improper; unseemly, unbecoming.

непримени́м|ый (~, ~а) *adj.* inapplicable.

неприме́т|ный (~ен, ~на) *adj.* **1** (*разница*) imperceptible. **2** (*fig.*) (*человек*) unremarkable, undistinguished.

непримири́мост|ь, и *f.* irreconcilability; intransigence.

непримири́м|ый (~, ~а) *adj.* (*противоречия*) irreconcilable; (*характер*) intransigent, uncompromising.

непринуждённост|ь, и *f.* unconstraint; naturalness, ease.

непринуждён|ный (~, ~на) *adj.* natural, relaxed; laid-back.

неприсоедине́ни|е, я *nt.*: **поли́тика ~я** (*pol.*) policy of non-alignment.

неприсоедини́вш|ийся *adj.*: **~иеся стра́ны** non-aligned countries.

неприспосо́блен|ный (~, ~на) *adj.* (**к**+*d.*) unadapted (to); maladjusted.

непристо́йност|ь, и *f.* obscenity; indecency.

непристо́|йный (~ен, ~йна) *adj.* obscene; indecent.

неприступ|ный (~ен, ~на) *adj.* **1** (*скала*) inaccessible; (*крепость*) unassailable, impregnable. **2** (*fig.*) (*начальник*) inaccessible, unapproachable.

непритво́р|ный (~ен, ~на) *adj.* unfeigned, genuine.

непритяза́тел|ьный (~ен, ~ьна) *adj.* **1** (*простой*) unpretentious. **2** (*довольствующийся малым*) undemanding.

неприхотли́вост|ь, и *f.* **1** (*человека, вкуса*) unpretentiousness; modesty. **2** (*узора*) simplicity, plainness.

неприхотли́в|ый (~, ~а) *adj.* **1** (*человек*) unpretentious; modest, undemanding **2** (*рисунок*) simple, plain; **~ая пи́ща** frugal meal.

неприча́ст|ный (~ен, ~на) *adj.* (**к**+*d.*) not implicated (in), not involved (in).

неприя́знен|ный (~, ~на) *adj.* hostile, inimical.

неприя́зн|ь, и *f.* hostility, enmity.

неприя́тел|ь, я *m.* enemy; (*mil.*) the enemy.

неприя́тельский *adj.* hostile; (*mil.*) enemy.

неприя́тност|ь, и *f.* unpleasantness; trouble.

неприя́т|ный (~ен, ~на) *adj.* unpleasant, disagreeable.

непробу́д|ный (~ен, ~на) *adj.* from which there is no waking; **н. сон** deep sleep; **н. пья́ница** inveterate drunkard.

непроводни́к, а́ *m.* (*phys.*) non-conductor.

непрогля́д|ный (~ен, ~на) *adj.*

(*of darkness, fog, etc.*) impenetrable; pitch-dark.

непродолжи́тел|ьный (~ен, ~ьна) *adj.* of short duration, short-lived; **в ~ьном вре́мени** shortly, in a short time.

непродукти́в|ный (~ен, ~на) *adj.* unproductive.

непроду́ман|ный (~, ~на) *adj.* ill-considered.

непрое́зжий *adj.* impassable.

непрозра́чност|ь, и *f.* opacity.

непрозра́ч|ный (~ен, ~на) *adj.* opaque.

непроизводи́тел|ьный (~ен, ~ьна) *adj.* (*работа*) unproductive; (*расходы*) wasteful.

непроизво́л|ьный (~ен, ~ьна) *adj.* involuntary.

непрола́з|ный (~ен, ~на) *adj.* (*coll.*) impassable.

непромока́ем|ый (~, ~а) *adj.* waterproof; **н. плащ** waterproof (coat), raincoat.

непроница́емост|ь, и *f.* impenetrability; impermeability.

непроница́ем|ый (~, ~а) *adj.* **1** (*мрак, ночь; тайна*) impenetrable; (*для жидкостей, газов*) impermeable; **н. для зву́ка** sound-proof. **2** (*лицо*) inscrutable, impassive.

непропорциона́льност|ь, и *f.* disproportion.

непропорциона́л|ьный (~ен, ~ьна) *adj.* disproportionate.

непрости́тел|ьный (~ен, ~ьна) *adj.* unforgivable, unpardonable, inexcusable.

непротивле́ни|е, я *nt.* non-resistance.

непроходи́мо *adv.* (*coll.*) utterly, hopelessly.

непроходи́м|ый (~, ~а) *adj.* **1** (*лес, болото*) impassable. **2** (*fig., coll.*) (*совершенный*) complete, utter; **н. дура́к** utter fool.

непро́ч|ный (~ен, ~на) *adj.* fragile, flimsy; (*fig.*) precarious, unstable.

непро́шеный *adj.* (*coll.*) uninvited; unsolicited.

непрям|о́й (~, ~а́, ~о) *adj.* **1** (*путь*) indirect; circuitous. **2** (*fig., coll.*) (*человек, ответ*) evasive.

непутёвый *adj.* (*coll.*) good-for-nothing, useless.

непутём *adv.* (*coll.*) badly; **де́лать всё н.** to make a mess of everything.

непью́щий *adj.* teetotal.

нетрудоспосо́б|ный (~ен, ~на) *adj.* unable to work, disabled.

нерабо́ч|ий *adj.* non-working; **~ее вре́мя** time off, free time.

нера́венств|о, а *nt.* inequality, disparity.

неравно́ *particle expr. anticipation of disagreeable eventuality* (*coll.*); **н. опозда́ем** suppose we are late; **н. он зайдёт, а нас до́ма не бу́дет** what if he comes while we are out.

неравноду́ш|ный (~ен, ~на) *adj.* (**к**+*d.*) not indifferent (to).

неравноме́р|ный (~ен, ~на) *adj.* uneven, irregular.

неравнопра́в|ный (~ен, ~на) *adj.* not enjoying equal rights.

нера́в|ный (~ен, ~на́, ~но) *adj.* unequal.

нераде́ни|е, я *nt.* (*obs.*) = **neради́вость**

неради́вост|ь, и *f.* negligence, carelessness.

неради́в|ый (~, ~а) *adj.* negligent, careless.

неразбери́х|а, и *f.* (*coll.*) muddle, confusion.

неразбо́рчив|ый (~, ~а) *adj.* **1** (*почерк*) illegible, indecipherable. **2** (*fig.*) (*читатель, вкус*) undiscriminating; not fastidious; **н. в сре́дствах** unscrupulous; **сексуа́льно н.** promiscuous.

неразвит|о́й (нера́звит, ~а́, ~о) *adj.* undeveloped; (*умственно*) (intellectually) backward.

нера́звитост|ь, и *f.* lack of development; **у́мственная н.** backwardness.

неразга́данный *adj.* unsolved.

неразгово́рчив|ый (~, ~а) *adj.* taciturn, not talkative.

неразделённ|ый *adj.*: **~ая любо́вь** unrequited love.

неразделим|ый (~, ~а) *adj.* indivisible, inseparable.

неразде́л|ьный (~ен, ~ьна) *adj.* indivisible, inseparable; **~ьное иму́щество** (*leg.*) common estate.

неразличи́м|ый (~, ~а) *adj.* indistinguishable; indiscernible.

неразлу́ч|ный (~ен, ~на) *adj.* inseparable.

неразрешённый *adj.* **1** (*вопрос*) unsolved. **2** (*книга*) prohibited, banned.

неразреши́м|ый (~, ~а) *adj.* insoluble.

неразры́в|ный (~ен, ~на) *adj.* indissoluble.

неразу́ми|е, я *nt.* (*obs.*) folly, foolishness.

неразу́м|ный (~ен, ~на) *adj.* unreasonable; unwise; foolish.

нераска́янный *adj.* unrepentant.

нерасположе́ни|е, я *nt.* (**к**+*d.*) dislike (for), disinclination (for, to).

нерасполо́женный *adj.* (**к**+*d.*) ill-disposed (towards); unwilling (to), disinclined (to).

нераспоряди́тел|ьный (~ен, ~ьна) *adj.* inefficient, incompetent.

нераспростране́ни|е, я *nt.* non-proliferation (*esp. of nuclear weapons*).

нерассуди́тельност|ь, и *f.* irrationality; lack of common sense.

нерассуди́тел|ьный (~ен, ~ьна) *adj.* irrational, unreasoning; lacking common sense.

нерастворим|ый (~, ~а) *adj.* insoluble.

нерасторжи́м|ый (~, ~а) *adj.* indissoluble.

нерасторо́п|ный (~ен, ~на) *adj.* sluggish, slow.

нерасчётливост|ь, и *f.* **1** (*расточительность*) extravagance, wastefulness. **2** (*непредусмотрительность*) improvidence.

нерасчётлив|ый (~, ~а) *adj.* **1** (*расточительный*) extravagant, wasteful. **2** (*непредусмотрительный*) improvident.

нерациона́л|ьный (~ен, ~ьна) *adj.* irrational.

нерв, а *m.* (*anat. and fig.*) nerve; **гла́вный н.** (+*g.*) (*fig.*) nerve-centre (*Br.*), -center (*US*); **де́йствовать кому́-н. на ~ы** to get on s.o.'s nerves.

нерви́р|овать, ую *impf.* to get on s.o.'s nerves, irritate.

нерви́ческий *adj.* (*obs.*) nervous.

не́рвнича|ть, ю *impf.* to be *or* become fidgety, fret, be *or* become irritable.

нервнобольн|о́й, о́го *m.* person suffering from a nervous disorder.

не́рвно-паралити́ческ|ий *adj.* (*mil.*): **ОВ ~ого ти́па** nerve gas.

не́рвност|ь, и *f.* irritability, edginess.

не́рв|ный (~ен, ~на́, ~но) *adj.* **1** (*болезнь, тик; походка, жест; состояние*) nervous; **~ное волокно́** nerve-fibre (*Br.*), -fiber (*US*); **н. припа́док** fit of nerves; **~ная систе́ма** the nervous system; **н. у́зел** (*anat.*) ganglion; **н. центр** nerve-centre (*Br.*), -center (*US*). **2** (*человек*) nervous, highly strung. **3** (*работа*) nerve-racking.

нерво́з|ный (~ен, ~на) *adj.* nervy, irritable.

нервотрёпк|а, и *f.* (*coll.*) rigmarole, hassle.

нереа́л|ьный (~ен, ~ьна) *adj.* **1** (*местность*) unreal. **2** (*предложение*) impracticable.

нерегуля́р|ный (~ен, ~на) *adj.* irregular (*also mil.*).

нере́д|кий (~ок, ~ка́, ~ко) *adj.* not infrequent; not uncommon.

нере́дко *adv.* not infrequently, quite often.

нерента́бел|ьный (~ен, ~ьна) *adj.* unprofitable.

не́рест, а *m.* (*zool.*) spawning.

нерести́лищ|е, а *nt.* spawning-ground.

нереши́мост|ь, и *f.* indecision.

нереши́тельност|ь, и *f.* indecision; indecisiveness; **быть в ~и** to be undecided.

нереши́тел|ьный (~ен, ~ьна) *adj.* indecisive, irresolute.

нержаве́йк|а, и *f.* (*coll.*) stainless steel.

нержаве́ющ|ий *adj.* non-rusting; **~ая сталь** stainless steel.

неро́б|кий (~ок, ~ка́, ~ко) *adj.* not timid; **он челове́к ~кого деся́тка** he is no coward.

неро́вност|ь, и *f.* **1** (*поверхности*) unevenness, roughness. **2** (*дыхания*) irregularity. **3** (*линии*) crookedness. **4** (*характера*) instability, erraticness.

неро́в|ный (~ен, ~на́, ~но) *adj.*

1 (*поверхность*) uneven, rough; **н. грунт** rough country. **2** (*пульс, дыхание*) irregular. **3** (*линия*) crooked. **4** (*характер*) unstable, erratic.

неро́вн|я, и (*and* **неровн|я́, и́**) *c.g.* (*coll.*): **он ей н.** he is not her equal.

не́рп|а, ы *f.* (*zool.*) ringed seal.

нерукотво́р|ный (~ен, ~на) *adj.* (*relig. and poet.*) not made by hands.

неруши́м|ый (~, ~а) *adj.* indestructible.

неря́х|а, и *c.g.* sloven; (*coll.*) scruff.

неря́шеств|о, а *nt.* = **неря́шливость**

неря́шливост|ь, и *f.* **1** (*человека*) untidiness; scruffiness. **2** (*работы*) carelessness.

неря́шлив|ый (~, ~а) *adj.* **1** (*человек*) untidy; scruffy **2** (*работа*) careless, slipshod.

несваре́ни|е, я *nt. only in phr.* **н. желу́дка** indigestion.

несве́дущ|ий (~, ~а) *adj.* (**в** + *p.*) ignorant (about), not well-informed (about).

несве́ж|ий (~, ~а́, ~е) *adj.* **1** (*еда*) not fresh, stale. **2** (*fig.*) (*человек*) weary, wan. **3** (*бельё; воздух*) dirty.

несвобо́дн|ый *adj.*: **~ое сочета́ние** (*ling.*) set phrase.

несвоевре́мен|ный (~ен, ~на) *adj.* inopportune, untimely, unseasonable.

несво́йствен|ный (~ен, ~на) *adj.* not characteristic; **э́то ему́ ~но** it is not like him.

несвя́з|ный (~ен, ~на) *adj.* disconnected, incoherent.

несгиба́ем|ый (~, ~а) *adj.* unbending, inflexible.

несгово́рчив|ый (~, ~а) *adj.* intractable.

несгора́емый *adj.* fire proof; **н. шкаф** safe.

несде́ржан|ный (~, ~на) *adj.* unrestrained.

несе́ни|е, я *nt.* **1** (*обязанностей, службы*) performance, execution. **2** (*поклажи*) carrying, bearing. **3** (*потерь*) suffering. **4** (*наказания*) taking.

несерьёз|ный (~ен, ~на, ~но) *adj.* **1** (*человек*) frivolous. **2** (*замечание*) flippant. **3** (*дело, рана*) trivial. **4** (*болезнь*) mild.

несессе́р, а *m.* toilet-case.

несказа́н|ный (~ен, ~на) *adj.* indescribable, inexpressible.

нескла́диц|а, ы *f.* (*coll.*) nonsense.

нескла́д|ный (~ен, ~на) *adj.* **1** (*несвязный*) incoherent. **2** (*неуклюжий*) ungainly, awkward. **3** (*нелепый*) absurd.

несклоня́ем|ый (~, ~а) *adj.* (*gram.*) indeclinable.

не́скольк|о[1]**, их** *num.* some, several; a few; **в ~их слова́х** in a few words; **н. челове́к** several people.

не́сколько[2] *adv.* somewhat, rather, slightly; **они́ н. разочаро́ваны** they are rather disillusioned.

нескончáем|ый (~, ~а) *adj.* interminable, never-ending.

нескро́мност|ь, и *f.* **1** immodesty, lack of modesty. **2** indelicacy; indiscretion. **3** indiscreetness.

нескро́м|ный (~ен, ~на́, ~но) *adj.* **1** (*человек*) immodest; vain. **2** (*вопрос*) indiscreet. **3** (*анекдот, жест*) indecent.

нескрывáем|ый (~, ~а) *adj.* undisguised.

несло́ж|ный (~ен, ~на́, ~но) *adj.* simple, uncomplicated.

несльíхан|ный (~, ~на) *adj.* unheard-of, unprecedented.

несльíш|ный (~ен, ~на) *adj.* inaudible.

несменя́емост|ь, и *f.* irremovability (from office).

несменя́ем|ый (~, ~а) *adj.* irremovable.

несме́т|ный (~ен, ~на) *adj.* countless, incalculable, infinite.

несмолкáем|ый (~, ~а) *adj.* ceaseless, unremitting.

несмотря́ *prep.* (**на** + *a.*) in spite of, despite; notwithstanding; **н. ни на что** in spite of everything.

несмывáем|ый (~, ~а) *adj.* indelible, ineffaceable.

несно́с|ный (~ен, ~на) *adj.* intolerable, unbearable.

несоблюде́ни|е, я *nt.* non-observance.

несовершеннолéти|е, я *nt.* minority.

несовершеннолéтн|ий *adj.* under-age; *as n.* **н., ~его** *m.* minor.

несоверше́н|ный (~ен, ~на) *adj.* **1** imperfect, incomplete. **2** (*gram.*) imperfective.

несовмести́м|ый (~, ~а) *adj.* incompatible.

несоглáси|е, я *nt.* **1** disagreement; **н. во мне́ниях** difference of opinion; **н. ме́жду двумя́ ве́рсиями** discrepancy between two versions. **2** (*разлад*) discord. **3** (*sg. only*) (*отказ*) refusal.

несоглáс|ный (~ен, ~на) *adj.* **1** (**с** + *i.*) (*не разделяющий мнения*) in disagreement (with), not agreeing (with). **2** (**с** + *i.*) (*несоответствующий*) inconsistent (with), incompatible (with). **3** (*о звуках*) discordant.

несогласовáни|е, я *nt.* (*gram.*) non-agreement.

несогласо́ванност|ь, и *f.* lack of co-ordination.

несогласо́ван|ный (~, ~на) *adj.* uncoordinated.

несозву́ч|ный (~ен, ~на) *adj.* (+ *d.*) dissonant; out of tune (with).

несознáтельност|ь, и *f.* thoughtlessness; irresponsibility.

несознáтел|ьный (~ен, ~ьна) *adj.* irresponsible.

несоизмери́мост|ь, и *f.* incommensurability.

несоизмери́м|ый (~, ~а) *adj.* incommensurable, incommensurate.

несокруши́м|ый (~, ~а) *adj.* indestructible; (*вера, воля*) unshakeable.

несоли́д|ный (~ен, ~на) *adj.* unimpressive, light-weight.

несо́лоно *adv. only in phr.* (*coll.*): **уйти́ н. хлеба́вши** to get nothing for one's pains, go away empty-handed.

несомне́нно *adv.* undoubtedly, doubtless.

несомне́н|ный (~ен, ~на) *adj.* undoubted, indubitable, unquestionable.

несообрази́тел|ьный (~ен, ~ьна) *adj.* slow(-witted).

несообрáзност|ь, и *f.* **1** (*противоречие*) incongruity, incompatibility. **2** (*глупость*) stupidity, absurdity.

несообрáз|ный (~ен, ~на) *adj.* **1** (**с** + *i.*) (*несоответствующий*) incongruous (with), incompatible (with). **2** (*глупый*) stupid, absurd.

несоотве́тствен|ный (~, ~на) *adj.* (+ *d.*) incongruous (with), not corresponding (to).

несоотве́тстви|е, я *nt.* lack of correspondence, disparity.

несоразме́рност|ь, и *f.* disproportion.

несоразме́р|ный (~ен, ~на) *adj.* disproportionate.

несосвети́мый = **несусве́тный**

несостоя́тельност|ь, и *f.* **1** (*банкротство*) insolvency, bankruptcy; (*бедность*) poverty. **2** (*необоснованность*) groundlessness.

несостоя́тел|ьный (~ен, ~ьна) *adj.* **1** (*обанкротившийся*) insolvent, bankrupt; (*бедный*) poor. **2** (*необоснованный*) groundless, unsupported.

неспе́л|ый (~, ~á, ~о) *adj.* unripe.

неспе́ш|ный (~ен, ~на) *adj.* unhurried.

неподру́ч|ный (~ен, ~на) *adj.* (*coll.*) inconvenient, awkward.

неспоко́|йный (~ен, ~йна) *adj.* (*сон, характер*) restless; (*жизнь*) troubled; (*море, погода*) rough.

неспосо́бност|ь, и *f.* incapacity, inability.

неспосо́б|ный (~ен, ~на) *adj.* dull, not able; (**к** + *d.*, **на** + *a.*) incapable (of); **она́ ~на к языкáм** she has no aptitude for languages; **н. на ложь** incapable of a lie.

несправедли́вост|ь, и *f.* injustice, unfairness.

несправедли́в|ый (~, ~а) *adj.* **1** (*человек, суд*) unjust, unfair. **2** (*мнение*) incorrect, unfounded.

неспровоци́рованный *adj.* unprovoked.

неспростá *adv.* (*coll.*) not without purpose; with an ulterior motive.

несравне́нно *adv.* **1** incomparably. **2** (+*comp.*) far, by far; **н. лу́чше** far better.

несравне́н|ный (~ен, ~на) *adj.* incomparable.

несравни́м|ый (~, ~а) *adj.* incomparable.

Н

нестаби́льност|ь, и *f.* instability.

нестаби́л|ьный (~ен, ~ьна) *adj.* unstable.

нестерпи́м|ый (~, ~а) *adj.* unbearable, intolerable.

нес|ти́¹, у́, ёшь, *past* **~̈, ~ла́** *impf.* (*of* ⇒**по~**), *det.* **1** (*перемещать на себе*) to carry. **2** (*поддерживать*) to bear; to support. **3** (*fig.*) (*терпеть*) to bear; to suffer; to incur; **н. убы́тки** (*fin.*) to incur losses. **4** (*выполнять*) to perform; **н. дежу́рство** to be on duty. **5** (*fig.*) (*причинять*) to bear, bring; **н. ги́бель** to bring destruction. **6** (*impers., coll.*): **куда́ вас ~ёт?** wherever are you going? **7** (*impers., coll.*; +*i.*) (*пахнуть*) to stink (of), reek (of); **от него́ ~ёт чесноко́м** he reeks of garlic. **8** (*impers., coll.*): **его́,** *etc.*, **~ёт** he has, *etc.*, diarrhoea (*Br.*), diarrhea (*US*). **9** (*coll.*) (**вздор, чепуху́,** *etc.*) to talk (nonsense).

нес|ти́², ёт, *past* **~̈, ~ла́** *impf.* (*of* ⇒**с~**) (*яйцо*) to lay.

нес|ти́сь¹, у́сь, ёшься, *past* **~̈ся, ~ла́сь** *impf.* (*of* ⇒**по~**), *det.* **1** (*о человеке, машине*) to rush, tear, fly; (*по воздуху, воде*) to float, drift; (**по**+*d.*, **вдоль; над**) to skim (along; over). **2** (*о звуке, запахе*) to spread, be diffused.

нес|ти́сь², ётся, *past* **~̈ся, ~ла́сь** *impf.* (*of* ⇒**с~**) (*класть яйца*) to lay (eggs) (*intrans.*).

несто́|йкий (~ек, ~ка) *adj.* (*chem.*) unstable, non-persistent.

несто́ящий *adj.* (*coll.*) worthless, good-for-nothing.

нестроеви́к, а́ *m.* (*mil.*) non-combatant.

нестроево́й¹ *adj.* (*материал, лес*) unfit for building purposes.

нестроево́й² *adj.* (*mil.*) (*служба, команда*) non-combatant, administrative.

нестро́|йный (~ен, ~йна́, ~йно) *adj.* **1** (*человек*) clumsily built. **2** (*пение*) discordant, dissonant. **3** (*толпа*) disorderly.

несть (*obs.*) there is not.

несу́н, а *m.* (*coll.*) pilferer.

несура́зност|ь, и *f.* **1** (*глупость*) absurdity, senselessness. **2** (*неуклюжесть*) awkwardness.

несура́з|ный (~ен, ~на) *adj.* **1** (*глупый*) absurd, senseless. **2** (*неуклюжий*) awkward.

несусве́т|ный (~ен, ~на) *adj.* (*coll.*) extreme, utter; unimaginable; **~ная чепуха́** utter nonsense.

несу́шк|а, и *f.* (*coll.*) laying hen, hen in lay.

несуще́ствен|ный (~, ~на) *adj.* inessential, immaterial.

несу́щ|ий *pres. part. act. of* ⇒**нести́** *and adj.* (*tech.*) carrying; supporting; **н. винт** rotor (*of helicopter*); **~ая пове́рхность** lifting surface; (*aeron.*) airfoil.

несхо́д|ный (~ен, ~на) *adj.* **1** (*непохожий*) unlike, dissimilar. **2** (*coll.*) (*о цене*) unreasonable.

несчастли́в|ец, ца *m.* unlucky person, an unfortunate.

несчастли́в|ый (~, ~а) *adj.* **1** (*неудачный*) unfortunate, luckless. **2** (*печальный*) unhappy.

несча́ст|ный (~ен, ~на) *adj.* **1** unhappy; unfortunate, unlucky; **н. слу́чай** accident. **2** *as n.* **н., ~ного** *m.* wretch; an unfortunate.

несча́сть|е, я *nt.* **1** (*беда*) misfortune; **к ~ю** unfortunately. **2** (*несчастный случай*) accident.

несчёт|ный (~ен, ~на) *adj.* innumerable, countless.

несъедо́б|ный (~ен, ~на) *adj.* inedible; **н. гриб** toadstool.

нет¹ 1 (*при отрицании*) no; not; **вы его́ ви́дели? н.** you saw him? — No; **вы не ви́дели его́. н., ви́дел** you didn't see him? Yes, I did; **н. как н.** (*coll.; emph*) absolutely not, absolutely nothing; **н.-н. да и взгля́нет на меня́** he glanced at me from time to time. **2** nothing, naught; **свести на н.** to bring to naught; **свести́сь (сойти́) на н.** to come to naught.

нет² (+*g.*) (*не имеется*) (there) is no, (there) are no; **здесь н. собо́ра** there is no cathedral here; **у меня́ н. вре́мени** I have no time.

нетакти́ч|ный (~ен, ~на) *adj.* tactless.

нетбо́л, а *m.* netball.

нетвёрдо *adv.* **1** (*ходить*) unsteadily, not firmly. **2** (*fig.*) not definitely; **знать н.** to have a shaky knowledge of; **я н. уве́рен** I am not quite sure.

нетвёрд|ый (~, ~а́, ~о) *adj.* unsteady; shaky (*also fig.*).

нетерпёж, а́ *m.* (*coll.*) impatience.

нетерпели́в|ый (~, ~а) *adj.* impatient.

нетерпе́ни|е, я *nt.* impatience.

нетерпи́мост|ь, и *f.* intolerance.

нетерпи́м|ый (~, ~а) *adj.* **1** (*поступок*) intolerable. **2** (*человек*) intolerant.

нетле́н|ный (~ен, ~на) *adj.* imperishable.

нетороплив|ый (~, ~а) *adj.* leisurely, unhurried.

нето́чност|ь, и *f.* **1** (*свойство*) inaccuracy, inexactitude. **2** (*ошибка*) error, slip.

нето́ч|ный (~ен, ~на́, ~но) *adj.* inaccurate, inexact.

нетрадицио́н|ный (~ен, ~на) *adj.* unconventional.

нетре́бовател|ьный (~ен, ~ьна) *adj.* not exacting, undemanding; (*скромный*) unpretentious.

нетре́зв|ый (~, ~а́, ~о) *adj.* not sober, drunk; **в ~ом ви́де** in a state of intoxication.

нетривиа́л|ьный (~ен, ~ьна) *adj.* not trivial; outstanding, exceptional.

нетро́нут|ый (~, ~а) *adj.* (*почва, снег*) virgin; (*обед*) untouched; (*fig.*) (*натура*) unsullied, virginal.

нетрудово́й *adj.* **1** not derived from labour (*Br.*), labor (*US*); **н. дохо́д** unearned income. **2** (*человек*) not engaged in labour (*Br.*), labor (*US*).

нетрудоспосо́бност|ь, и *f.* disablement, disability.

нетрудоспосо́б|ный (~ен, ~на) *adj.* disabled; invalid.

не́тто *adj. indecl.* (*comm.*) net.

не́ту (*coll.*) = **нет²**

неубеди́тел|ьный (~ен, ~ьна) *adj.* unconvincing.

неу́бранный *adj.* **1** (*комната*) untidy. **2** (*пшеница*) unharvested.

неуваже́ни|е, я *nt.* disrespect, lack of respect; (*leg.*): **н. к суду́** contempt of court.

неуважи́тел|ьный (~ен, ~ьна) *adj.* **1** (*причина*) inadequate; not acceptable. **2** (*coll.*) (*непочтительный*) disrespectful.

неуве́ренност|ь, и *f.* uncertainty; **н. в себе́** lack of self-confidence.

неуве́рен|ный *adj.* **1 (~, ~а)** (*человек*) lacking confidence, unsure; **н. в себе́** lacking self-confidence, unsure of o.s. **2 (~, ~на)** (*походка, движение*) uncertain.

неувяда́|емый (~ем, ~ема) *adj.* = **~ющий**

неувяда́ющий *adj.* (*rhet.*) unfading, everlasting.

неувя́зк|а, и *f.* (*coll.*) (*в расчётах*) discrepancy; (*недоразумение*) misunderstanding.

неугаси́м|ый (~, ~а) *adj.* inextinguishable, unquenchable (*also fig.*).

неугомо́н|ный (~ен, ~на) *adj.* (*coll.*) indefatigable, irrepressible.

неуда́вшийся *adj.* unsuccessful.

неуда́ч|а, и *f.* failure.

неуда́члив|ый (~, ~а) *adj.* unlucky.

неуда́чник, а *m.* unlucky person, failure, loser.

неуда́чни|ца, цы *f. of* ⇒**~к**

неуда́ч|ный (~ен, ~на) *adj.* unsuccessful; (*несчастливый*) unfortunate; (*плохой*) bad; **~ное выраже́ние** unfortunate expression; **~ное нача́ло** bad start.

неудержи́м|ый (~, ~а) *adj.* irrepressible.

неудо́б|ный (~ен, ~на) *adj.* **1** (*одежда, постель*) uncomfortable. **2** (*fig.*) (*время*) inconvenient; (*положение*) awkward; embarrassing.

неудобовари́м|ый (~, ~а) *adj.* indigestible (*also fig.*).

неудобопроизноси́м|ый (~, ~а) *adj.* unpronounceable.

неудобочита́ем|ый (~, ~а) *adj.* difficult to read, obscure.

неудо́бств|о, а *nt.* **1** (*постели*) discomfort. **2** (*положения*) awkwardness; embarrassment.

неудовлетворе́ни|е, я *nt.* **1** non-compliance; **н. жа́лобы** failure to act on a complaint. **2** (*неудовлетворённость*) dissatisfaction.

неудовлетворённост|ь, и *f.* dissatisfaction, discontent.

неудовлетворён|ный *adj.* **1 (~, ~на)** (*человек*) dissatisfied, discontented. **2 (~, ~а́)** (*потребность*) unsatisfied.

неудовлетвори́тел|ьный (~ен, ~ьна) *adj.* unsatisfactory.

неудово́льстви|е, я *nt.* dissatisfaction, displeasure.

неуё́м|ный (~ен, ~на) *adj.* (*coll.*) irrepressible; **~ная печа́ль** uncontrollable grief.

неуже́ли *interrog. particle* really? is it possible?; **н. он так ду́мает?** does he really think that?; **н. ты не знал, что мы здесь?** did you really not know that we were here?; surely you knew that we were here?

неужи́вчивост|ь, и *f.* quarrelsome disposition.

неужи́вчив|ый (~, ~а) *adj.* difficult (to get on with); quarrelsome.

неу́жто *interrog. particle* (*coll.*) = **неуже́ли**

неузнава́емост|ь, и *f.* unrecognizability; **он похуде́л до ~и** he has lost so much weight that you would not recognize him.

неузнава́ем|ый (~, ~а) *adj.* unrecognizable.

неукло́н|ный (~ен, ~на) *adj.* steady, steadfast; undeviating.

неуклю́жест|ь, и *f.* clumsiness, awkwardness.

неуклю́ж|ий (~, ~а, ~е) *adj.* clumsy, awkward.

неукосни́тел|ьный (~ен, ~ьна) *adj.* strict, rigorous.

неукроти́м|ый (~, ~а) *adj.* indomitable.

неулови́м|ый (~, ~а) *adj.* **1** (*человек*) elusive, difficult to catch. **2** (*fig.*) (*звук*) imperceptible.

неулы́бчив|ый (~, ~а) *adj.* (*coll.*) unsmiling.

неуме́л|ый (~, ~а) *adj.* clumsy; unskilful (*Br.*), unskillful (*US*).

неуме́ни|е, я *nt.* inability; lack of skill.

неуме́ренност|ь, и *f.* **1** (*аппетита*) immoderation. **2** (*человека*) intemperance.

неуме́рен|ный (~, ~на) *adj.* **1** (*аппетит, восторг*) immoderate; excessive. **2** (*человек*) intemperate.

неуме́ст|ный (~ен, ~на) *adj.* **1** (*шутка*) inappropriate. **2** (*факт, информация*) irrelevant.

неумё́х|а, и *c.g.* (*coll.*) wally.

неу́м|ный (~ён, ~на́, ~но́) *adj.* foolish; (*решение*) unwise.

неумоли́м|ый (~, ~а) *adj.* implacable; inexorable.

неумолка́ем|ый (~, ~а) *adj.* incessant, unceasing.

неумо́л|чный (~чен, ~чна) *adj.* = **~ка́емый**

неумы́шлен|ный (~, ~на) *adj.* (*убийство*) unpremeditated; (*пренебрежение*) unintentional, inadvertent.

неупла́т|а, ы *f.* non-payment.

неупотреби́тел|ьный (~ен, ~ьна) *adj.* not in use.

неуравнове́шен|ный (~, ~на) *adj.* (*psych.*) unbalanced.

неурожа́|й, я *m.* bad harvest, crop failure.

неурожа́й|ный *adj. of* ⇒**~; н. год** lean year, bad harvest year.

неуро́чный *adj.* unearthly; **прийти́ в н. час** to come at an unearthly hour.

неуря́диц|а, ы *f.* (*coll.*) **1** (*беспорядок*) disorder, mess. **2** (*pl.*) (*ссора*) squabbling.

неуси́дчив|ый (~, ~а) *adj.* restless, not persevering.

неуспева́емост|ь, и *f.* poor progress (*in studies*).

неуспева́ющий *adj.* backward, not making satisfactory progress.

неуста́н|ный (~ен, ~на) *adj.* tireless, unwearying.

неусто́йк|а, и *f.* **1** (*leg.*) penalty (*for breach of contract*). **2** (*coll.*) failure.

неусто́йчивост|ь, и *f.* instability, unsteadiness.

неусто́йчив|ый (~, ~а) *adj.* unstable, unsteady.

неустрани́м|ый (~, ~а) *adj.* unremovable; **~ое препя́тствие** insurmountable obstacle.

неустраши́м|ый (~, ~а) *adj.* fearless, intrepid.

неустро́ен|ный (~, ~на) *adj.* unsettled; badly organized.

неустро́йств|о, а *nt.* disorder.

неусту́пчив|ый (~, ~а) *adj.* unyielding, uncompromising.

неусы́п|ный (~ен, ~на) *adj.* tireless, indefatigable.

неутеши́тел|ьный (~ен, ~ьна) *adj.* not comforting, depressing; **~ьные ве́сти** distressing news.

неуте́ш|ный (~ен, ~на) *adj.* inconsolable; disconsolate.

неутоли́м|ый (~, ~а) *adj.* (*жажда*) unquenchable; (*голод*) unappeasable; (*fig.*) insatiable.

неутоми́м|ый (~, ~а) *adj.* tireless, indefatigable.

не́уч, а *m.* (*coll.*) ignoramus.

неучти́вост|ь, и *f.* discourtesy, impoliteness, incivility.

неучти́в|ый (~, ~а) *adj.* discourteous, impolite, uncivil.

неую́т|ный (~ен, ~на) *adj.* bleak, comfortless.

неуязви́м|ый (~, ~а) *adj.* **1** (*позиция*) invulnerable. **2** (*доказательство*) unassailable.

неф, а *m.* (*archit.*) nave.

неформа́л, а *m.* (*coll.*) member of an unofficial organization.

неформа́л|ьный (~ен, ~ьна) *adj.* unofficial; informal.

нефри́т[1], а *m.* (*med.*) nephritis.

нефри́т[2], а *m.* (*min.*) nephrite, jade.

нефте... *comb. form* oil-, petro-.

нефтево́з, а *m.* oil-tanker (*truck*).

нефтедо́ллар, а *m.* petrodollar.

нефтеналивн|о́й *adj.* equipped for carrying oil in bulk; **~о́е су́дно** oil-tanker.

нефтено́с|ный (~ен, ~на) *adj.* oil-bearing.

нефтеперего́нный *adj.* oil-refining; **н. заво́д** oil refinery.

нефтеперераба́тывающий *adj.* oil-refining.

нефтепрово́д, а *m.* oil pipe-line.

нефтета́нкер, а *m.* oil-tanker (*ship*).

нефтехрани́лищ|е, а *nt.* oil-tank, oil reservoir.

нефт|ь, и *f.* oil, petroleum; **н.-сыре́ц** crude oil.

нефтя́ник, а *m.* oil(-industry) worker.

нефтя́нк|а, и *f.* (*coll.*) **1** (*двигатель*) oil-engine. **2** (*баржа*) oil-barge.

нефтян|о́й *adj.* oil; **~а́я вы́шка** derrick; **н. фонта́н** oil-gusher.

нехва́тк|а, и *f.* (*coll.*) shortage.

нехи́т|рый (~ёр, ~ра́, ~ро́) *adj.* **1** (*простодушный*) artless, guileless. **2** (*coll.*) (*простой*) simple; uncomplicated.

нехоро́ш|ий (~, ~а́, ~о́) *adj.* bad.

нехорошо́ *adv.* badly; **чу́вствовать себя́ н.** to feel unwell.

не́хотя *adv.* **1** (*неохотно*) reluctantly, unwillingly. **2** (*нечаянно*) inadvertently, unintentionally.

нецелесообра́з|ный (~ен, ~на) *adj.* inexpedient; pointless.

нецензу́р|ный (~ен, ~на) *adj.* unprintable; **~ные слова́** swear words, obscenities.

нечя́нност|ь, и *f.* **1** (*свойство*) unexpectedness. **2** (*неожиданное событие*) unexpected event, surprise.

нечя́нный *adj.* **1** (*неожиданный*) unexpected. **2** (*случайный*) accidental; unintentional.

не́чего, не́чему, не́чем, не́ о чем 1 *pron.* (+*inf.*) there is nothing (to); **мне н. чита́ть** I have nothing to read; **не́ о чем бы́ло говори́ть** there was nothing to talk about; **от н. де́лать** for want of sth. better to do, to while away the time; **н. сказа́ть!** (*coll., iron.*) indeed!; well, I declare! **2** *as pred.* (*impers.*; +*inf.*) (*незачем*) it's no good, it's no use; there is no need; **н. жа́ловаться** it's no use complaining; **н. и говори́ть, что…** it goes without saying that ….

нечелове́ческий *adj.* **1** (*усилия*) superhuman. **2** (*отношения*) inhuman.

нечести́в|ый (~, ~а) *adj.* impious, profane.

нече́стност|ь, и *f.* dishonesty.

нече́ст|ный (~ен, ~на́) *adj.* **1** (*человек*) dishonest. **2** (*поступок*) dishonourable (*Br.*), dishonorable (*US*); **~ная игра́** (*sport*) foul play.

не́чет, а *m.* (*coll.*) odd number.

нечё́т|кий (~ок, ~ка́) *adj.* (*почерк*) illegible; (*рисунок*) indistinct; (*изложение*) unclear; (*работа*) inaccurate, slipshod.

нечё́тный *adj.* odd.

нечистопло́т|ный (~ен, ~на) *adj.* **1** (*грязный*) dirty; (*неопрятный*) untidy, slovenly. **2** (*fig.*) (*нечестный*) unscrupulous.

нечистот|а́, ы́, *pl.* **~ы, ~** *f.*

Н

1 dirtiness. 2 *pl. only* (*отбросы*) sewage, garbage.

нечи́ст|ый (~, ~á, ~о) *adj.* 1 (*грязный*) unclean, dirty (*also fig.*); **~ое де́ло** suspicious affair; **~ая пи́ща** (*relig.*) unclean food. 2 (*с примесью чего-либо*) impure, adulterated; **~ая поро́да** impure breed; **~ое произноше́ние** defective pronunciation. 3 (*неаккуратный*) careless, inaccurate. 4 (*нечестный*) dishonourable (*Br.*), dishonorable (*US*); dishonest; **быть ~ым на́ руку** to be light-fingered. 5: **~ая си́ла** evil spirits.

не́чист|ь, и *f.* (*collect.*; *coll.*) 1 (*нечистая сила*) evil spirits. 2 (*fig., pej.*) (*презренные люди*) scum, vermin.

нечленоразде́л|ьный (~ен, ~ьна) *adj.* inarticulate.

не́что *pron.* (*nom. and a. cases only*) something.

нечувстви́тел|ьный (~ен, ~ьна) *adj.* (**к**+*d.*) insensitive (to).

нешу́точ|ный (~ен, ~на) *adj.* grave, serious; **де́ло ~ное** it is no joke; it is no laughing matter.

неща́д|ный (~ен, ~на) *adj.* merciless.

неэвкли́дов *adj.*: **~а геоме́трия** non-Euclidean geometry.

неэконо́м|ный (~ен, ~на) *adj.* uneconomical.

неэти́ч|ный (~ен, ~на) *adj.* unethical.

неэффекти́в|ный (~ен, ~на) *adj.* ineffective; inefficient.

нея́вк|а, и *f.* non-appearance, failure to appear.

неядови́тый *adj.* non-poisonous; (*chem.*) non-toxic.

нея́сност|ь, и *f.* vagueness, obscurity.

нея́с|ный (~ен, ~на́, ~но) *adj.* vague, obscure.

нея́сыт|ь, и *f.* tawny owl.

ни 1 *correlative conj.* **ни**… **ни** neither … nor; **ни тот ни друго́й** neither (the one nor the other); **ни то ни сё** neither one thing nor the other; **ни с того́, ни с сего́** all of a sudden; **ни за что, ни про что** for no reason at all. 2 *particle* not a; **ни оди́н, ни одна́, ни одно́** not a, not one, not a single; **на у́лице не́ было ни (одно́й) души́** there was not a soul about. 3 *separable component of prons.* **никако́й, никто́, ничто́** *following preps.*; **ни в како́м (ни в ко́ем) слу́чае** on no account; **ни за что (на све́те!)** in no circumstances; not for the world! 4 (*particle, in comb. with* **как, кто, куда́** *etc.*) = -ever; **как бы мы ни стара́лись** however hard we tried; **что бы он ни говори́л** whatever he might say.

ни́в|а, ы *f.* (corn-)field; **на ~е просвеще́ния** (*fig.*) in the field of education.

нивели́р, а *m.* (*tech.*) level.

нивели́р|овать, ую *impf. and pf.* (*tech. and fig.*) to level.

нивелиро́вк|а, и *f.* levelling.

нигде́ *adv.* nowhere.

Ни́гер, а *m.* 1 (*страна*) Niger. 2 (*река*) the Niger.

нигери́|ец, йца *m.* Nigerian.

нигери́|йка, йки *f. of* ⇒**~ец**

нигери́йский *adj.* Nigerian.

Ниге́ри|я, и *f.* Nigeria.

нигили́зм, а *m.* nihilism.

нигили́ст, а *m.* nihilist.

нигилисти́ческий *adj.* nihilistic.

нидерла́ндский *adj.* Dutch, Netherlands.

Нидерла́нд|ы, ов *no sg.* the Netherlands.

нижа́йший *superl. of* ⇒**ни́зкий; ваш н. слуга́** your very humble servant.

ни́же 1 *comp. of* ⇒**ни́зкий, ни́зко.** 2 *prep.* (+*g.*) *and adv.* below, beneath.

нижеподписа́вшийся *adj.* (the) undersigned.

нижеcле́дующий *adj.* following.

нижеупомя́нутый *adj.* undermentioned.

ни́жн|ий *adj.* lower; **~ее бельё** underclothes, underwear; **~яя пала́та** Lower Chamber, Lower House; **~яя ю́бка** slip; **н. эта́ж** ground floor (*Br.*), first floor (*US*).

ни|жу́, ~жешь *see* ⇒**~за́ть**

низ, а, *pl.* **~ы́** *m.* 1 bottom. 2 (*pl.*) (*общества*) lower classes. 3 (*pl.*; *mus.*) low notes.

ни|за́ть, жу́, ~жешь *impf.* (*of* ⇒**на~**) to string, thread; **н. слова́** to speak very smoothly.

низведе́ни|е, я *nt.* bringing down.

низверг|а́ть, а́ю *impf.* (*of* ⇒**~нуть**) to precipitate; (*fig.*) to overthrow.

низверг|а́ться, а́юсь *impf.* (*of* ⇒**~нуться**) 1 to crash down. 2 *pass. of* ⇒**~а́ть**

низве́рг|нуть(ся), ну(сь), нешь(ся), *past* **~(ся)** *and* **~нул(ся), ~ла(сь),** *pf. of* ⇒**~а́ть(ся)**

низверже́ни|е, я *nt.* overthrow.

низве|сти́, ду́, дёшь, *past* **~л, ~ла́** *pf.* (*of* ⇒**низводи́ть**) to bring down; (*fig.*) to bring low; to reduce.

низво|ди́ть, жу́, ~дишь *impf. of* ⇒**низвести́**

низи́н|а, ы *f.* low-lying area.

ни́з|кий (~ок, ~ка́, ~ко) *adj.* 1 low; **~кого происхожде́ния** of humble origin; **быть ~кого мне́ния о**+*p.* to have a low opinion of. 2 (*подлый*) base, mean; **н. посту́пок** shabby act.

низкока́чественный *adj.* low-quality.

низкоопла́чиваемый *adj.* poorly-paid.

низкопокло́нник, а *m.* toady, crawler.

низкопокло́ннича|ть, ю *impf.* (**пе́ред**+*i.*) to grovel (before).

низкопокло́нств|о, а *nt.* servility.

низкопро́б|ный (~ен, ~на) *adj.* 1 (*серебро*) base, low-grade. 2 (*товар, пьеса*) inferior; trashy. 3 (*делец*) unprincipled, immoral.

низкоро́сл|ый (~, ~а) *adj.* (*человек*) short; (*дерево*) undersized, stunted.

низкосо́рт|ный (~ен, ~на) *adj.* low-grade; poor-quality.

низлага́|ть, ю *impf. of* ⇒**низложи́ть**

низложе́ни|е, я *nt.* deposition, dethronement.

низлож|и́ть, у́, ~ишь *pf.* (*of* ⇒**низлага́ть**) to depose, dethrone.

ни́зменност|ь, и *f.* 1 (*geog.*) lowland (*not exceeding 200m above sea-level*). 2 (*подлость*) baseness.

ни́змен|ный (~, ~на) *adj.* 1 low-lying. 2 (*подлый*) low; base, vile; **~ные инсти́нкты** basic instincts.

низово́й[1] *adj.* (*geog.*) lower; situated down stream.

низово́й[2] *adj.* (*pol.*) grass-roots.

низо́в|ье, ья, *g. pl.* **~ьев** *nt.* the lower reaches (*of a river*).

низо|йти́, йду́, йдёшь, *past* **нисшёл, ~шла́** *pf.* (*of* ⇒**нисходи́ть**) (*obs.*) to descend.

ни́зом *adv.* (*coll.*) along the bottom; **е́хать н.** to take the lower road.

ни́зост|ь, и *f.* lowness; (*подлость*) baseness, meanness.

низри́н|уть, у, ешь *pf.* (*rhet.*) to throw down, overthrow.

низри́н|уться, усь, ешься *pf.* (*rhet.*) to crash down.

ни́зш|ий *superl. of* ⇒**ни́зкий;** lowest; **~ее образова́ние** primary education.

НИИ *m. indecl.* (*abbr. of* ***нау́чно-иссле́довательский институ́т***) research institute.

ника́к[1] *adv.* (*никаким образом*) by no means, in no way; **он н. не мог узна́ть её а́дрес** in no way could he discover her address; **н. нельзя́** it is quite impossible; **н. нет** (*mil.*) *respectful reply in negative to question.*

ника́к[2] *adv.* (*coll.*) (*кажется*) it seems, it would appear; **они́, н., уже́ пришли́** they are here already, it seems.

никак|о́й *pron.* no; **не**… **~о́го, ~о́й, ~и́х** no … whatever; **я не име́ю ~о́го представле́ния (поня́тия)** I have no idea, no conception; **~и́х возраже́ний!** no objections!; **учёный он н.** (*coll.*) he is no scholar; **и ~и́х (гвозде́й)!** (*coll.*) and that's that.

Никара́гуа *f. indecl.* Nicaragua.

никарагуа́н|ец, ца *m.* Nicaraguan.

никарагуа́н|ка, ки *f. of* ⇒**~ец**

никарагуа́нский *adj.* Nicaraguan.

ни́келевый *adj.* nickel.

никелиро́в|анный *p.p.p of* ⇒**~а́ть** *and adj.* nickel-plated.

никелир|ова́ть, у́ю *impf. and pf.* to plate with nickel, nickel.

никелиро́вк|а, и *f.* nickel-plating.

ни́кел|ь, я *m.* nickel.

ни́к|нуть, ну, нешь, *past* **~, ~ла** *impf.* (*of* ⇒**по~** *and* ⇒**с~**) to droop, flag (*also fig.*).

никогда́ *adv.* never; **как н.** as never before.

нико́|й *pron.* (*obs.*) no; *now only in phrr.*

~им о́бразом by no means, in no way; **ни в ко́ем слу́чае** on no account, in no circumstances.
никоти́н, а *m.* nicotine.
никоти́н|ный *adj. of* ⇒**~**
никоти́н|овый *adj.* = **~ный**
никто́, никого́, никому́, нике́м, ни о ком *pron.* nobody, no one; **там никого́ не́ было** there was nobody there; **н. друго́й** nobody else; **ни у кого́ нет э́того** no one has it.
никуда́ *adv.* nowhere; **э́то н. не годи́тся** (*fig.*) this won't do; it is no good at all; **н. не го́дный** good-for-nothing, worthless, useless.
никуды́ш|ный (~ен, ~на) *adj.* (*coll.*) = **никуда́ не го́дный.**
никчём|ный (~ен, ~на) *adj.* (*coll.*) useless, good-for-nothing.
Нил, а *m.* the Nile (*river*).
ним *i. of* ⇒**он, оно́;** *d. of* ⇒**они́** *after preps.*
нима́ло *adv.* not in the least, not at all.
нимб, а *m.* halo, nimbus.
ни́ми *i. of* ⇒**они́** *after preps.*
ни́мф|а, ы *f.* nymph.
нимфома́ни|я, и *f.* nymphomania.
нимфома́нк|а, и *f.* nymphomaniac.
нио́би|й, я *m.* (*chem.*) niobium.
ниотку́да *adv.* from nowhere; **н. не сле́дует, что**... it in no way follows that ....
нипочём *adv.* (*coll.*) **1** (+*d.*) it is nothing (to); **э́то ему́ н.** it is child's play to him; **ему́ н. провести́ це́лую ночь за рабо́той** he thinks nothing of spending a whole night working. **2** (*очень дёшево*) for nothing, dirt-cheap; **прода́ть н.** to sell for a song. **3** (*ни за что*) never, in no circumstances.
ни́ппел|ь, я, *pl.* **~я́, ~е́й** *m.* (*tech.*) nipple.
нирва́н|а, ы *f.* nirvana.
ниско́лько *adv.* not at all, not in the least; **ей от э́того бы́ло н. не лу́чше** she was none the better for it.
ниспада́|ть, ет *impf. of* ⇒**ниспа́сть**
ниспа́|сть, ду́, дёшь, *past* **~л, ~ла** *pf.* (*of* ⇒**~да́ть**) (*obs.*) to fall, drop.
ниспроверг|а́ть, а́ю *impf.* (*of* ⇒**~́нуть**) to overthrow.
ниспрове́рг|нуть, ну, нешь, *past* **~** *and* **~нул, ~ла** *pf. of* ⇒**~а́ть**
ниспроверже́ни|е, я *nt.* overthrow.
нисхо|ди́ть, жу́, ~́дишь *impf. of* ⇒**низойти́**
нисход|я́щий *pres. part. act. of* ⇒**~и́ть** *and adj.* **1** descending; **по ~я́щей ли́нии** in the line of descent, in a descending line. **2** (*ling.*) falling.
нитеви́д|ный (~ен, ~на) *adj.* thread-like, filiform.
ни́тк|а, и *f.* thread; **н. же́мчуга** string of pearls; **на живу́ю ~у** (*fig., coll.*) hastily, anyhow; **ши́то бе́лыми ~ами** (*fig., coll.*) transparent, obvious; **до (после́дней) ~и обобра́ть** (*fig., coll.*) to fleece, leave without a shirt to one's back; **промо́кнуть до ~и** (*fig.*) to get soaked to the skin.
ни́точк|а, и *f. dim. of* ⇒**ни́тка; по ~е разобра́ть** (*fig.*) to analyse minutely; **ходи́ть по ~е** (*fig.*) to toe the line.
нитра́т, а *m.* (*chem.*) nitrate.
нитри́т, а *m.* (*chem.*) nitrite.
нитробензо́л, а *m.* (*chem.*) nitrobenzene.
нитроглицери́н, а *m.* (*chem.*) nitroglycerine.
нитча́тк|а, и *f.* **1** (*червь*) roundworm. **2** (*bot.*) hair-weed, crow-silk.
ни́тчатый *adj.* filiform.
нит|ь, и *f.* **1** thread; **путево́дная н.** clue; **~́и дру́жбы** bonds of friendship; **проходи́ть кра́сной ~́ью** (*fig.*) to run through (*of theme, motif*). **2** (*bot., elec.*) filament. **3** (*med.*) suture.
ни́тяный *adj.* cotton.
них *a. and g. of* ⇒**они́** *when governed by preps.*
ниц *adv.* (*obs.*) face downwards; **пасть н.** to prostrate o.s., kiss the ground.
ничего́[1] *g. of* ⇒**ничто́**
ничего́[2] *adv.* **1** (*also* **н. себе́**) so-so; passably, not (too) badly; all right; **ко́рмят здесь н.** the food here is not too bad; **как вы чу́вствуете себя́? — н.** how do you feel? all right. **2** *as indecl. adj.* not (too) bad, passable, tolerable; **на́ша кварти́ра н.** our flat is not too bad; **па́рень он н.** he is not a bad chap.
нич|е́й (~ья́, ~ье́) *pron.* nobody's, no one's; **~ья́ земля́** no man's land; *as n.* **~ья́, ~ье́й** *f.* (*sport*) draw, drawn game; **сыгра́ть в ~ью** to play a drawn game, draw.
ниче́йный *adj.* (*coll.*) **1** no man's. **2** (*sport*) drawn.
ничко́м *adv.* prone, face downwards.
ничто́, ничего́, ничему́, ниче́м, ни о чём *pron.* **1** nothing; **э́то ничего́ не зна́чит** it means nothing; **ниче́м не ко́нчилось** it came to nothing; **ничего́ подо́бного!** nothing of the kind!; **э́то ничего́!** it's nothing!; it doesn't matter!; **ничего́!** (*coll.*) that's all right!; never mind! **2** (*ничтожество*) a nonentity, a nobody, nothing.
ничто́же *pron.* **н. сумня́ся, н. сумня́шеся** (*iron.*) without a second's hesitation.
ничто́жеств|о, а *nt.* **1** (*убожество*) poverty. **2** (*человек*) a nonentity, a nobody.
ничто́жност|ь, и *f.* **1** (*незначительность*) insignificance. **2** (*человек*) a nonentity, a nobody.
ничто́ж|ный (~ен, ~на) *adj.* (*незначительный*) insignificant; (*человек*) paltry, worthless.
ничу́ть *adv.* (*coll.*) not at all, not in the least, not a bit; **н. не быва́ло** not at all.
нич|ья́, е́й *f. see* ⇒**ниче́й**
ни́ш|а, и *f.* niche, recess; (*archit.*) alcove, bay.
нища́|ть, ю *impf.* (*of* ⇒**об~**) to be reduced to beggary.
ни́щенк|а, и *f.* beggar-woman.
ни́щенский *adj.* beggarly.
ни́щенств|о, а *nt.* **1** (*действие*) begging. **2** (*нищета*) beggary.
ни́щенств|овать, ую *impf.* **1** (*заниматься нищенством*) to beg, go begging. **2** (*жить в нищете*) to be destitute.
нищет|а́, ы́ *f.* **1** (*крайняя бедность*) poverty (*also fig.*). **2** (*collect.*) (*нищие люди*) beggars; the poor.
ни́щ|ий *adj.* **1** destitute; poverty-stricken; **н. ду́хом** poor in spirit. **2** *as n.* **н., ~его** *m.* beggar; pauper.
НКВД *m. indecl.* (*abbr. of* ***Наро́дный комиссариа́т вну́тренних дел***) (*hist.*) NKVD, People's Commissariat for Internal Affairs.
НЛО *m. indecl.* (*abbr. of* ***неопо́знанный лета́ющий объе́кт***) UFO (*unidentified flying object*).
но[1] *conj.* **1** but; *after concessive clause not translated or* still, nevertheless; **хотя́ он и бо́лен, но наме́рен прийти́** although he is ill, he (still) intends to come. **2** (*coll.*) *as nt. n.* a 'but'; snag, difficulty; **тут есть одно́ «но»** there is just one snag in it.
но[2] *int.* gee up!
Но́белевск|ий *adj.*: **~ая пре́мия** Nobel prize.
нова́тор, а *m.* innovator.
нова́тор|ский *adj. of* ⇒**~** *and* **~ство**
нова́торств|о, а *nt.* innovation.
Но́в|ая Гвине́|я, ~ой ~и *f.* New Guinea.
Но́в|ая Зела́нди|я, ~ой ~и *f.* New Zealand.
Но́в|ая Земл|я́, ~ой, ~и *f.* Novaya Zemlya.
Но́в|ая Шотла́нди|я, ~ой ~и *f.* Nova Scotia.
нове́йший *superl. of* ⇒**но́вый;** newest; (*последний*) latest.
нове́лл|а, ы *f.* novella.
новелли́ст, а *m.* novella-writer.
но́веньк|ий *adj.* **1** new. **2** *as n.* **н., ~ого** *m.* new boy; **~ая, ~ой** *f.* new girl.
новизн|а́, ы́ *f.* novelty; newness.
нови́к, а́ *m.* **1** (*hist.*) (*дворянин*) young courtier. **2** (*obs.*) (*новичок*) novice.
нови́нк|а, и *f.* new thing, novelty; **кни́жные ~и** new books; **э́то мне в ~у** it is a new experience for me.
нович|о́к, ка́ *m.* **1** (**в**+*p.*) novice (at), beginner (at). **2** (*в школе*) new boy; new girl.
новобра́н|ец, ца *m.* recruit.
новобра́чн|ая, ой *f.* bride.
новобра́чн|ые, ых *pl.* newly-weds.
новобра́чн|ый, ого *m.* bridegroom.
нововведе́ни|е, я *nt.* innovation.
нового́дн|ий *adj.* New Year's; **~яя ночь** New Year's Eve.
новогре́ческий *adj.*: **н. язы́к** Modern Greek.
новозаве́тный *adj.* of the New Testament.
новозела́нд|ец, ца *m.* New Zealander.
новозела́нд|ка, ки *f. of* ⇒**~ец**

Н

новозела́ндский *adj.* New Zealand.

новоиспечённый *adj.* (*coll., joc.*) new.

новокаи́н, а *m.* (*pharm.*) Novocaine (*propr.*).

новолу́ни|е, я *nt.* new moon.

новомо́д|ный (~ен, ~на) *adj.* in the latest fashion, up-to-date; (*fig., pej.*) newfangled.

новообразова́ни|е, я *nt.* new growth; new formation; (*med.*) neoplasm.

новообращённый *adj.* (*relig. and fig.*) newly converted.

новопреста́вленный *adj.* (*relig.*) the late, the late-lamented.

новоприбы́вш|ий *adj.* newly-arrived; *as n.* **н., ~его** *m.* new-comer.

новорождённ|ый *adj.* new-born; *as n.* **н., ~ого** *m.* the baby; (*med.*) neonate.

новосёл, а *m.* (*земли*) new settler; (*дома*) new occupant.

новосе́ль|е, я *nt.* **1** (*жилище*) new home. **2** (*празднование*) house-warming; **справля́ть н.** to give a house-warming party.

новостро́йк|а, и *f.* **1** (*действие*) erection of new buildings. **2** (*здание*) newly-erected building; **шко́ла-н.** new school.

но́вост|ь, и, *g. pl.* **~е́й** *f.* **1** (*известие*) news; **э́то что ещё за ~и!; вот ещё ~и!** (*coll.*) well, I like that!; did you ever! **2** = **нови́нка**

новоя́вленный *adj.* (*relig. or iron.*) newly brought to light.

но́вшеств|о, а *nt.* innovation, novelty.

но́в|ый (~, ~а́, ~о) *adj.* **1** new; **совершéнно н.** brand-new; **Н. год** New Year's Day; **Н. заве́т** the New Testament; **Н. свет** the New World; **что ~ого?** what's the news?; what's new? **2** (*современный*) modern; recent; **~ая исто́рия** modern history; **~ые языки́** modern languages.

нов|ь, и *f.* virgin soil.

ног|а́, и́, *a.* **~у,** *pl.* **~и, ног, ~а́м** *f.* (*ступня*) foot; (*до ступни*) leg; **вверх ~а́ми** head over heels; **без (за́дних) ног** (*coll.*) dead-beat; **в ~а́х посте́ли** at the foot of the bed; **идти́ в ~у (с+*i.*)** to keep step (with), keep pace (with) (*also fig.*); **идти́ н. за́ ~у** (*coll.*) to amble along; **к ~е́!** (*mil.*) order arms!; **положи́ть ~у на́ ~у** to cross one's legs; **сиде́ть н. на́ ~у** to sit with legs crossed; **поста́вить кого́-н. на́ ~и** (*fig.*) to set s.o. on his feet; **стать на́ ~и** (*fig.*) to stand on one's own feet; **жить на широ́кую (бо́льшую, ба́рскую) ~у** to live in (grand) style, live like a lord; **быть на коро́ткой ~е́ (с+*i.*)** to be on good terms (with); **хрома́ть на о́бе ~и́** to be lame in both legs; (*fig., coll.*) to go badly, creak; **верте́ться у кого́-н. под ~а́ми** to get under s.o.'s feet; **сбить с ног** to knock down; **встать с ле́вой ~и́** to get out of bed on the wrong side; **со всех ног** (*coll.*) as fast as one's legs will carry one; **е́ле ~и унести́** to escape by the skin of one's teeth; **он дава́й Бог ~и** (*coll.*) he took to his heels; **ног под собо́й не слы́шать (от ра́дости)** (*coll.*) to be beside o.s. (*with joy*); **ног под собо́й не чу́вствовать (от уста́лости,** *etc.*) to be barely able to stand (from tiredness, *etc*); **моéй ~и́ у вас не бу́дет** (*coll.*) I shall not set foot in your house again; **мы — ни ~о́й туда́** (*coll.*) we never go near the place; **стоя́ть одно́й ~о́й в моги́ле** to have one foot in the grave; **протяну́ть ~и** (*coll.*) to turn up one's toes.

ноготк|и́, о́в (*bot.*) marigold.

но́г|оть, тя, *pl.* **~ти, ~те́й** *m.* (finger-, toe-) nail.

ног|тево́й *adj. of* ⇒**~оть**

нож, а́ *m.* knife; **перочи́нный н.** penknife; **разрезно́й н.** paper-knife; **н.-пила́** bread-knife; **садо́вый н.** pruning-knife; **н. в спи́ну** (*fig.*) stab in the back; **э́то мне н. о́стрый** (*fig.*) for me this is sheer hell; **без ~а́ заре́зать** to do for; **быть на ~а́х (с+*i.*)** to be at daggers drawn (with); **под ~о́м** under the knife (= *during a surgical operation*); **пристава́ть к кому́-н. с ~о́м к го́рлу** to pester s.o.

нож|ево́й *adj. of* ⇒**~; н. ма́стер** cutler; **~евы́е изде́лия** cutlery.

но́жик, а *m.* (small) knife.

но́жк|а, и *f.* **1** *dim. of* ⇒**нога́; подста́вить ~у (+*d.*)** to trip up. **2** (*мебели, утвари*) leg; (*рюмки*) stem. **3** (*bot.*) stalk; (*гриба*) stem.

но́жниц|ы, ~ *pl.* **1** scissors, pair of scissors; (*большие*) shears. **2** (*econ.*) (*расхождение*) discrepancy.

ножно́й *adj. of* ⇒**нога́; н. то́рмоз** foot brake.

но́ж|ны ~ен, ~нам (*and* **нож|ны́, ~о́н, ~на́м)** *pl.* sheath; scabbard.

ножо́вк|а, и *f.* hacksaw.

ножо́вый = **ножево́й**

ноздрева́тост|ь, и *f.* porosity.

ноздрева́т|ый (~, ~а) *adj.* porous.

ноздр|я́, и́, *pl.* **~и, ~е́й** *f.* nostril

нока́ут, а *m.* (*sport*) knock-out.

нокаути́р|овать, ую *impf. and pf.* (*sport*) to knock out.

нокда́ун, а *m.* (*sport*) knock-down.

ноктю́рн, а *m.* (*mus.*) nocturne.

нолево́й = **нулево́й**

нол|ь, я́ *m.* = **нуль; ноль-ноль** *indicates timing of event at the hour exactly*; **экспре́сс в Берли́н отхо́дит в семна́дцать н.-н.** the express for Berlin departs at 17.00 hours.

нома́д, а *m.* (*hist.*) nomad.

номенклату́р|а, ы *f.* **1** (*совокупность названий терминов*) nomenclature. **2** (*hist.*) (*работники*) nomenklatura (*in the former USSR*).

номенклату́р|ный *adj. of* ⇒**~а**

но́мер, а *pl.* **~а́** *m.* **1** (*телефона, машины, дома*) number; (*газеты, журнала*) number, issue. **2** (*размер*) size; **како́й н. боти́нок вы но́сите?** what size do you take in shoes? **3** (*в гостинице*) room. **4** (*концерта*) item on the programme (*Br.*), program (*US*); number, turn; **со́льный н.** solo (number). **5** (*coll.*) trick; **вы́кинуть н.** to play a trick.

номерно́й *adj. of* ⇒**но́мер;** (*завод*) numbered (*as opp. to having a name*); **н. знак** number plate (*Br.*), license plate (*US*).

номер|о́к, ка́ *m.* **1** (*в гардеробе*) ticket. **2** (*в гостинице*) small room.

номина́л, а *m.* (*econ.*) face-value; **по ~у** at face-value.

номина́льн|ый *adj.* nominal; **~ая цена́** face value.

номина́ци|я, и *f.* nomination.

но́н|а, ы *f.* (*mus.*) ninth.

нор|а́, ы́, *pl.* **~ы, ~, ~ам** *f.* (*зайца*) burrow, hole; (*лисы*) lair.

Норве́ги|я, и *f.* Norway.

норвéж|ец, ца *m.* Norwegian.

норвéж|ка, ки *f. of* ⇒**~ец**

норвéжский *adj.* Norwegian.

норд, а *m.* (*naut.*) **1** (*направление*) north. **2** (*ветер*) north wind.

норд-ве́ст, а *m.* (*naut.*) **1** (*направление*) north-west. **2** (*ветер*) north-wester(-ly wind).

норд-о́ст, а *m.* (*naut.*) **1** (*направление*) north-east. **2** (*ветер*) north-easter(-ly wind).

но́рк|а[1]**, и** *f. dim. of* ⇒**нора́**

но́рк|а[2]**, и** *f.* (*зверь*) mink.

но́рк|овый *adj. of* ⇒**~а**[2]

но́рм|а, ы *f.* **1** (*поведения*) standard, norm; **в ~е** (*coll.*) fine. **2** (*величина*) rate; **н. вы́работки** rate of output; **сверх ~ы** in excess of planned rate.

нормализа́ци|я, и *f.* standardization; normalization.

нормализ|ова́ть, у́ю *impf. and pf.* (*орфографию*) to standardize; (*отношения*) to normalize.

норма́л|ь, и *f.* (*math., phys.*) normal.

норма́льно *as pred.* (*coll.*) it is all right, fine, OK.

норма́льност|ь, и *f.* normality.

норма́л|ьный (~ен, ~ьна) *adj.* normal.

норма́нд|ец, ца *m.* Norman (*inhabitant of Normandy*).

Норма́нди|я, и *f.* Normandy.

норма́нд|ка, ки *f. of* ⇒**~ец**

Норма́ндск|ие остров|а́, ~их ~о́в *no sg.* the Channel Islands.

норма́ндский *adj.* Norman.

норма́нн, а *m.* (*hist.*) Norseman; Norman.

норма́ннский *adj.* (*hist.*) Norse.

нормати́в, а *m.* (*econ.*) norm.

нормати́в|ный (~ен, ~на) *adj.* **1** *adj. of* ⇒**~;** corresponding to norm. **2** (*определяющий норму*) normative.

нормирова́ни|е, я *nt.* **1** regulation, normalization; **н. труда́** norm-fixing, norm-setting (*in production*). **2** (*продуктов*) rationing.

нормиро́в|анный *p.p.p. of* ⇒**~а́ть; н. рабо́чий день** fixed working hours; **~анное снабже́ние** rationing.

нормир|ова́ть, у́ю *impf. and pf.* **1** to regulate, normalize; **н. за́работную пла́ту** to fix wages. **2** (*продукты*) to ration, place on the ration.

но́ров, а *m.* **1** (*coll.*) (*упрямство*) obstinacy, capriciousness; **челове́к с**

~ом difficult person. **2** (*лошадей*) restiveness.

норови́ст|ый (~, ~а) *adj.* (*coll.*) restive; jibbing.

норов|и́ть, лю́, и́шь *impf.* (*coll.*) **1** (+*inf.*) to strive (to), aim (at). **2** (**в**+*nom.-a*) to strive to become; **он ~и́т в писа́тели** he has literary aspirations.

нос, а, о ~е, на ~у́, *pl.* **~ы́** *m.* **1** nose; **у меня́ идёт кровь ~ом (и́з ~у)** my nose is bleeding; **говори́ть в н.** to speak through one's nose; **~ом к ~у** (*coll.*) face to face; **на ~у́** (*coll.*) near at hand, imminent; **заруби́ э́то себе́ на ~у́!** put that in your pipe and smoke it!; **оста́вить с ~ом** (*coll.*) to dupe, make a fool of; **оста́ться с ~ом** (*coll.*) to be duped, be left looking a fool; **задра́ть н., подня́ть н.** (*coll.*) to put on airs; **клева́ть ~ом** (*coll.*) to nod; **натяну́ть н. кому́-н.** (*coll.*) to make a fool of s.o.; **н. вороти́ть** (**от**+*g.*) (*coll.*) to turn up one's nose (at); **пове́сить н. (на кви́нту)** (*coll.*) to be crestfallen, be discouraged; **показа́ть н.** (*coll.*) to cock a snook; **сова́ть н. не в своё де́ло** (*coll.*) to poke one's nose into other people's affairs; **ткнуть кого́-н. ~ом во что-н.** (*coll.*) to thrust sth. under s.o.'s nose; **уткну́ться ~ом во что-н.** (*coll.*) to bury o.s. in sth. **2** (*птицы*) beak. **3** (*naut.*) bow, head; prow.

noса́ст|ый (~, ~а) *adj.* big-nosed.

носа́т|ый (~, ~а) *adj.* = **носа́стый**

но́сик, а *m.* **1** *dim. of* ⇨**нос. 2** (*боти́нка*) toe. **3** (*ча́йника*) spout.

носи́л|ки, ок *no sg.* **1** (*для ра́неных*) stretcher. **2** (*для пассажи́ров*) sedan (-chair).

носи́льщик, а *m.* porter.

носи́тел|ь, я *m.* **1** (*fig.*) (*идей*) bearer; repository. **2** (*инфекции, гриппа*) carrier. **3** (*chem.*) vehicle. **4** (*тока*) transmitter. **5** (*языка*) speaker.

носи́тель|ница, ницы *f. of* ⇨~ 1

но|си́ть, шу́, ~сишь *impf.* **1** *indet. of* ⇨**нести́. 2** (*indet. only*) (*вещи; ребёнка*) to carry; (*большую тяжесть*) to bear (*also fig.*); **н. свою́ де́вичью фами́лию** to use one's maiden name; **н. кого́-н. на рука́х** (*indet. only*) to make a fuss of s.o., dote on s.o. **3** (*indet. only*) (*одежду, украшения*) to wear. **4** (*indet. only*) (*характер*) to have (*a certain character*), to be of (*a certain nature*).

но|си́ться, шу́сь, ~сишься *impf.* **1** *indet. of* ⇨**нести́сь; э́то ~сится в во́здухе** (*fig.*) it is in the air, it is rumoured (*Br.*), rumored (*US*). **2** (**с**+*i.*) (*с человеком*) to make a fuss (of); **н. с мы́слью** to be obsessed with an idea. **3** (*intr.*) (*одежда*) to wear; **э́та мате́рия хорошо́ ~сится** this material wears well.

но́ск|а¹, и *f.* **1** (*вещей*) carrying; bearing. **2** (*одежды*) wearing.

но́ск|а², и *f.* (*яиц*) laying.

но́с|кий¹ (~ок, ~ка) *adj.* (*одежда*) hard-wearing, durable.

но́ск|ий² ** *adj.*: **~ая ку́рица a good layer.

носов|о́й *adj.* **1** *adj. of* ⇨**нос; н. плато́к** (pocket) handkerchief. **2** (*ling.*) nasal. **3** (*naut.*) bow, fore; **~а́я часть (су́дна)** ship's bows.

носоглóтк|а, и *f.* (*anat.*) nasopharynx.

нос|о́к¹, ка́ *m.* **1** (*боти́нка, чулка*) toe. **2** *dim.of* ⇨~

нос|о́к², ка́, *pl.* **~ки́, ~ко́в** *or* **~о́к** *m.* (*чулок*) sock.

носоро́г, а *m.* rhinoceros.

носо́|чный *adj. of* ⇨**~к²**

ностальги́ческий *adj.* nostalgic.

ностальги́|я, и *f.* homesickness; (*о прошлом*) nostalgia.

но́т|а¹, ы *f.* (*mus.*) **1** note. **2** (*pl.*) (*текст*) (sheet) music; **игра́ть по ~ам (без нот)** to play from music (without music); **как по ~ам** (*fig.*) without a hitch, according to plan. **3** (*fig.*) (*оттенок*) note.

но́т|а², ы *f.* (*dipl.*) (diplomatic) note.

нотабе́н|а, ы *f. and* **нотабе́не** *nt. indecl.* nota bene (*abbr.* NB); **поста́вить ~у** to mark.

нотариа́льный *adj.* notarial.

нота́риус, а *m.* notary.

нота́ци|я¹, и *f.* (*coll.*) (*выговор*) lecture, reprimand; **прочита́ть кому́-н. ~ю** to read s.o. a lecture.

нота́ци|я², и *f.* (*система обозначений*) notation.

но́т|ка, ки *f. dim. of* ⇨**~а¹**

но́тн|ый *adj. of* ⇨**но́та¹; ~ая бума́га** manuscript paper.

но́утбук, а *m.* notebook (computer).

но́у-ха́у *nt. indecl.* know-how.

ноч|ева́ть, у́ю *impf.* (*of* ⇨**пере~**) to spend, pass the night.

ночёвк|а, и *f.* spending the night, passing the night.

ночле́г, а *m.* **1** (*место для ночёвки*) lodging for the night. **2** = **ночёвка**

ночле́жк|а, и *f.* (*coll.*) = **ночле́жный дом**

ночле́жник, а *m.* **1** (*coll.*) (*гость*) (overnight) visitor, guest. **2** (*бездомный человек*) vagrant.

ночле́|жный *adj. of* ⇨**~г; н. дом** night shelter; doss house (*Br.*), flophouse (*US*).

ночни́к, а́ *m.* night-light.

ночн|о́й *adj.* night; **~а́я ба́бочка** moth; (*euph.*) prostitute; **н. горшо́к** chamber-pot; **н. по́езд** overnight train; **~а́я руба́шка** (*мужская*) nightshirt; (*женская*) nightdress; **н. сто́лик** bedside table (*Br.*), night table (*US*); **~ы́е ту́фли** bedroom slippers; **~а́я фиа́лка** wild orchid.

ноч|ь, и, о ~и, в ~и́, *pl.* **~и, ~е́й** *f.* night; **глуха́я н.** the dead of night; **споко́йной ~и!** good-night!; **по ~а́м** by night, at night.

но́чью *adv.* by night.

но́ш|а, и, *f.* burden.

ноше́ни|е, я *nt.* **1** (*вещей*) carrying. **2** (*одежды*) wearing.

но́шеный *adj.* second-hand.

но́щно *adv. only in phr.* **де́нно и н.** (*coll.*) day and night.

но́|ю, ешь *see* ⇨**ныть**

но́ющ|ий *pres. part. act. of* ⇨**ныть; ~ая боль** ache.

ноя́бр|ь, я́ *m.* November.

ноя́бр|ьский *adj. of* ⇨~

нрав, а *m.* **1** (*характер*) disposition, temper; **быть** (+*d.*) **по ~у** to please. **2** (*pl.*) (*обычаи*) manners, customs, ways.

нра́в|иться, люсь, ишься *impf.* (*of* ⇨**по~**) (+*d.*) to please; **мне, ему́,** *etc.*, **~ится** I like, he likes, *etc.*; **мне о́чень ~ится э́та пье́са** I like this play very much; **вообще́-то она́ мне ~ится** I rather like her; (*impers.*): **ей не ~ится ката́ться на ло́дке** she does not like going in boats.

нра́в|ный (~ен, ~на) *adj.* (*coll.*) irritable, bad-tempered.

нравоучени́|е, я *nt.* **1** lecture; moral admonition. **2** (*liter.*) (*в басне*) moral.

нравоучи́тел|ьный (~ен, ~ьна) *adj.* (*басня*) with a moral; (*тон*) moralizing.

нра́вственност|ь, и *f.* morality; morals.

нра́вствен|ный (~, ~на) *adj.* moral.

н. ст. (*abbr. of* ***но́вый стиль***) NS, New Style (*of calendar*).

НТР *f. indecl.* (*abbr. of* ***нау́чно-техни́ческая револю́ция***) scientific and technological revolution.

ну *int. and particle* **1** well!; well ... then!; come on!; **ну, ну!** come, come!; come now! **2**: **(да) ну!** not really?; you don't mean to say so! **3** *выражает удивление, восхищение, негодование, иронию* well; what; why; **ну и...** what (a) ...!; here's ... (for you)!; there's ... (for you)!; **ну вот и..!** there you are, you see ...!; **ну, неуже́ли?!** what! really?; no? really?; **ну, пра́во!, ну, одна́ко же!** well, to be sure!; **ну и денёк!** what a day!; **ну и молоде́ц!** (*also iron.*) there's a good boy!; there's a clever chap!; **ну и ну!** (*coll.*) well, well! **4** *выражает согласие, уступку, примирение, облегчение* well; **ну вот** (*в повествовании*) well, well then; **ну что ж, ну́ так** well then; **ну хорошо́** all right then, very well then. **5**: **ну́ как** (+*fut.*) suppose, what if; **ну́ как они́ не приду́т во́-время?** suppose they don't come in time? **6** *as pred.* (+*inf.*) to start; **он ну крича́ть** he started yelling. **7**: **а ну́** (+*g.*) to hell (with)!; to the deuce (with)!; **а ну́ тебя́!** to hell with you!

нувори́ш, а *m.* nouveau riche.

нуг|а́, и *f.* nougat.

нуди́зм, а *m.* nudism, naturism.

нуди́ст, а *m.* nudist, naturist.

нуди́ст|ка, ки *f. of* ⇨~

ну́|дить, жу, дишь *impf.* (*obs., coll.*) **1** (*заставлять*) to force, compel. **2** (*утомлять*) to wear out.

ну|ди́ть, жу́, ди́шь *impf.* (*coll.*) to wear out (*with complaints, questions, etc.*).

ну́дност|ь, и *f.* tediousness.

ну́д|ный (~ен, ~на) *adj.* (*coll.*) tedious, boring.

нужд|а́, ы́, *pl.* **~ы** *f.* **1** (*бедность*) want, poverty. **2** (*необходимость*) need;

Н

necessity; **в слу́чае ~ы́** if necessary, if need be; **н. всему́ нау́чит** necessity is the mother of invention; **~ы́ нет, нет ~ы́** (*coll.*) no matter!; never mind.

нужда́емост|ь, и *no pl., f.* (**в**+*p.*) needs (in), requirements (in).

нужда́|ться, юсь *impf.* **1** (*жить в бедности*) to be in want; to be needy, hard-up. **2** (**в**+*p.*) to need, require; to be in need (of).

ну́жно (+*d.*) **1** (*impers.*; +*inf.* or +**что́бы**) it is necessary; (one) ought, (one) should, (one) must, (one) need(s); **н. бы́ло (бы) взять такси́** you should have taken a taxi; **н., что́бы она́ реши́лась** she ought to make up her mind. **2** (*impers.*, +*a.* or *g.*; *coll.*) I, *etc.*, need; **мне н. пять рубле́й** I need five roubles. **3** *see* ⇨**ну́жный**

ну́ж|ный (~ен, ~на́, ~но, ~ны́) *adj.* necessary; requisite; (*pred. forms* +*d.*) I, *etc.*, need; **что вам ~но?** what do you need?, what do you want?; **о́чень (мне) ~но!** (*coll.*, *iron.*) won't that be nice!; a fat lot of good that is!

ну́-ка *int.* (*coll.*) now then!; come on!

ну́ка|ть, ю *impf.* (*coll.*) to urge; to say 'come on'.

нул|ево́й *adj. of* ⇨**~ь;** (*math.*) zero; **н. вариа́нт** (*pol.*) zero option.

нул|ь, я́ *m.* **1** nought; (*о температуре*) zero; (*в играх*) nil; **своди́ться к ~ю́** (*fig.*) to come to nothing, come to nought. **2** (*человек*) nonentity.

нумера́ци|я, и *f.* numbering.

нумер|ова́ть, у́ю *impf.* (*of* ⇨**за~**) to number.

нумизма́т, а *m.* numismatist.

нумизма́тик|а, и *f.* numismatics.

нумизмати́ческий *adj.* numismatic.

ну́нци|й, я *m.* nuncio.

ну́те(-ка) *int.* well then!; come on!

ну́три|я, и *f.* (*zool.*) coypu; (*мех*) nutria.

нутр|о́, а́ *nt.* (*coll.*) **1** (*внутренняя часть*) inside, interior; (*внутренности*) insides. **2** (*fig.*) (*сущность*) core, kernel. **3** (*fig.*) (*инстинкт*) instinct(s), intuition; **~о́м понима́ть** to understand intuitively; **всем ~о́м** with one's whole being; **э́то мне не по ~у́** it goes against the grain with me.

нутряно́й *adj.* internal.

ны́не *adv.* **1** (*теперь*) now. **2** (*сегодня*) today.

ны́нешн|ий *adj.* (*coll.*) present; present-day; **н. президе́нт** the incumbent president; **~ее ле́то** this summer; **н. урожа́й** this year's harvest; **в ~ие времена́** nowadays.

ны́нче *adv.* (*coll.*) **1** (*сегодня*) today; **не н. за́втра** any day now. **2** (*теперь*) now.

ныр|ну́ть, ну́, нёшь *pf. of* ⇨**~я́ть**

ныр|о́к[1], ка́ *m.* (*coll.*) dive.

ныр|о́к[2], ка́ *m.* (*zool.*) pochard.

ныря́льщик, а *m.* diver.

ныря́льщи|ца, цы *f. of* ⇨**~к**

ныр|я́ть, я́ю *impf.* (*of* ⇨**~ну́ть**) to dive.

ны́тик, а *m.* (*coll.*) moaner, whinger.

ныть, но́ю, но́ешь *impf.* **1** (*болеть*) to ache. **2** (*coll.*) (*жаловаться*) to moan, whinge.

ныть|ё, я́ *nt.* (*coll.*) moaning, whining.

Нью-Йо́рк, а *m.* New York.

Ньюфа́ундле́нд, а *m.* Newfoundland.

н. э. (*abbr. of* **на́шей э́ры**) AD; **до н. э.** (*abbr. of* **до на́шей э́ры**) BC.

НЭП, а *or* **нэп, а** *m.* (*abbr. of* **но́вая экономи́ческая поли́тика**) (*hist.*) NEP (*New Economic Policy*).

нэ́п|овский *adj. of* ⇨**~**

нюа́нс, а *m.* nuance, shade.

ню́ни *only in phr.* **распусти́ть н.** (*coll.*) to snivel, whimper.

ню́н|я, и *c.g.* (*coll.*) sniveller, cry-baby.

Ню́рнберг, а *m.* Nuremberg.

нюх, а *m.* scent; (*fig.*) (**на**+*a.*) a nose (for).

ню́хательный *adj.*: **н. таба́к** snuff.

ню́ха|ть, ю *impf.* (*of* ⇨**по~**) (*цветок*) to smell; (*воздух*; *наркотик*) to sniff; **н. таба́к** to take snuff; **не ~л** (+*g.*) to have no experience (of); **по́роха не ~л** (*fig.*) he's still wet behind the ears.

нюхн|у́ть, у́, ёшь *inst. pf.* (*coll.*) to take a sniff of.

ня́нч|ить, у, ишь *impf.* to look after, mind.

ня́нч|иться, усь, ишься *impf.* (**с**+*i.*) **1** (*с внуками*) to look after, mind. **2** (*fig.*) (*с лодырем*) to fuss (over).

ня́ньк|а, и *f.* (*coll.*) = **ня́ня; у семи́ ня́нек дитя́ без гла́зу** (*prov.*) too many cooks spoil the broth.

ня́н|я, и *f.* **1** nanny; child-minder; **приходя́щая н.** babysitter. **2** (*coll.*) (*в больнице*) auxiliary nurse.

Oo

о¹ (об, обо) *prep.* **1** (+*p.*) (*указывает на предмет речи, мысли*) of, about, concerning; on; **о чём вы ду́маете?** what are you thinking about?; **ле́кция бу́дет о Пу́шкине** the lecture will be on Pushkin.
2 (+*p.*, *obs. or dial.*) (*указывает на наличие чего-н.*) with, having; **стол о трёх но́жках** a table with three legs, three-legged table; **па́лка о двух конца́х** a two-edged weapon.
3 (+*a.*) (*указывает на соприкосновение, столкновение*) against; on, upon; over; **опере́ться о сте́ну** to lean against the wall; **споткну́ться о ка́мень** to stumble on, over a stone; **бок о́ бок** side by side; **рука́ об руку** hand in hand.
4 (+*a. or p.*; *obs.*) (*о времени*) on, at, about; **об э́ту по́ру** about his time; **о Рождестве́** about Christmas-time.

о² *int.* oh!

о. (*abbr. of* ***о́стров***) I., Island, Isle

о... (*also* **об...**, **обо...** *and* **объ...**) *vbl. pref. indicating*: **1** transformation; process of becoming sth. **2** action applied to entire surface of object *or* to series of objects.

ОАЕ *f. indecl.* (*abbr. of* ***Организа́ция африка́нского еди́нства***) OAU (*Organization of African Unity*).

оа́зис, а *m.* oasis (*also fig.*).

об *prep. see* ⇒**о¹**

об... (*also* **обо...** *and* **объ...**) *vbl. pref.* **1** = **о... 2** indicating action *or* motion about an object.

о́ба, обо́их *m. and nt.*; **о́бе, обе́их** *f. num.* both; **гляде́ть в о., смотре́ть в о.** (*coll.*) to keep one's eyes open, be on one's guard; **обе́ими рука́ми** with both hands (*fig., coll.*); very willingly, readily.

оба́б|иться, люсь, ишься *pf.* (*coll.*) **1** (*о мужчине*) to become effeminate. **2** (*о женщине*) to let o.s. go.

обагр|и́ть, ю́, и́шь *pf.* (*of* ⇒**~я́ть**) to turn crimson (*trans.*); **о. кро́вью** to stain with blood.

обагр|и́ться, ю́сь, и́шься *pf.* (*of* ⇒**~я́ться**) to turn crimson; **о. (кро́вью)** to be stained with blood.

обагр|я́ть(ся), я́ю(сь) *impf. of* ⇒**~и́ть(ся)**

обалдева́|ть, ю *impf. of* ⇒**обалде́ть**

обалде́л|ый (~, ~а) *adj.* (*coll.*) crazed; stunned.

обалде́нный *adj.* (*sl.*) great, ace, brill.

обалде́|ть, ю *pf.* (*of* ⇒**~ва́ть**) (*coll.*) to go crazy; (*от удивления*) to be stunned.

обанкро́|титься, чусь, тишься *pf. of* ⇒**банкро́титься**

оба́яни|е, я *nt.* fascination, charm.

обая́тел|ьный (~ен, ~ьна) *adj.* fascinating, charming.

обва́л, а *m.* (*стены*) collapse; caving-in; (*камней*) rockfall; (*снежный*) avalanche.

обва́лива|ть¹, ю *impf. of* ⇒**обвали́ть**

обва́лива|ть², ю *impf. of* ⇒**обваля́ть**

обва́лива|ться, ется *impf. of* ⇒**обвали́ться**

обвал|и́ть, ю́, ~ишь *pf.* (*of* ⇒**~ивать¹**) **1** (*обрушить*) to cause to fall, cause to collapse. **2** (*завалить кругом*) to heap round; **о. избу́ камня́ми** to heap stones round a hut.

обвал|и́ться, ~ится *pf.* (*of* ⇒**~иваться**) to fall, collapse, cave in.

обвал|я́ть, я́ю *pf.* (*of* ⇒**~ивать²**) (+*a.*, **в**+*p.*) to roll (in); **о. котле́ту в сухаря́х** to roll a burger in bread-crumbs.

обва́рива|ть(ся), ю(сь) *impf. of* ⇒**обвари́ть(ся)**

обвар|и́ть, ю́, ~ишь *pf.* (*of* ⇒**~ивать**) **1** (*овощи*) to pour boiling water over. **2** (*руку*) to scald.

обвар|и́ться, ю́сь, ~ишься *pf.* (*of* ⇒**~иваться**) to scald o.s.

обвева́|ть, ю *impf. of* ⇒**обве́ять**

обве|ду́, дёшь *see* ⇒**~сти́**

обвенча́|ть(ся), ю(сь) *pf. of* ⇒**венча́ть(ся)¹**

обверн|у́ть, у́, ёшь *pf.* (*of* ⇒**обвёртывать**) (+*i.*) to wrap up (in).

обвер|те́ть, чу́, ~тишь *pf.* (*of* ⇒**~тывать**) (+*i.*) to wrap up (in); **о. ше́ю ша́рфом** to wrap a scarf about one's neck.

обвёртыва|ть, ю *impf. of* ⇒**обверну́ть** *and* **обверте́ть**

обве́|сить, шу, сишь *pf.* (*of* ⇒**~шивать¹**) to give short weight to; to cheat (*in weighing goods*).

обве|сти́, ду́, дёшь, *past* **~л, ~ла́** *pf.* (*of* ⇒**обводи́ть**) **1** (*провести вокруг*) to lead round, take round; **о. вокру́г па́льца** (*fig., coll.*) to twist round one's little finger. **2** (+*i.*) (*оградить*) to encircle (with); to surround (with); **о. рвом** to surround with a ditch; **о. взо́ром, глаза́ми** to look round (at), take in (*with one's eyes*). **3** (*очертить*) to outline; **о. чертёж ту́шью** to outline a sketch in ink. **4** (*sport*) to dodge; to get past.

обве́тр|енный *p.p.p. of* ⇒**~ить** *and adj.* (*скалы, лицо*) weather-beaten; (*губы*) chapped.

обве́тре|ть, ет *pf.* to become weather-beaten.

обве́трива|ть(ся), ю(сь) *impf. of* ⇒**обве́трить(ся)**

обве́тр|ить, ю, ишь *pf.* (*of* ⇒**~ивать**) to expose to the wind; (*impers.*): **мне ~ило гу́бы** my lips are chapped.

обве́тр|иться, юсь, ишься *pf.* (*of* ⇒**~иваться**) to become weather-beaten.

обветша́л|ый (~, ~а) *adj.* dilapidated.

обветша́|ть, ю *pf. of* ⇒**ветша́ть**

обве́ш|ать, аю *pf.* (*of* ⇒**~ивать²**) (*coll.*; +*i.*) to hang round (with), cover (with).

обве́шива|ть¹, ю *impf. of* ⇒**обве́сить**

обве́шива|ть², ю *impf. of* ⇒**обве́шать**

обве́|ять, ю, ешь *pf.* (*of* ⇒**~ва́ть**) **1** (+*i.*) to fan (with). **2** (*agric.*) to winnow.

обвива́|ть(ся), ю(сь) *impf. of* ⇒**обви́ть(ся)**

обвине́ни|е, я *nt.* **1** charge, accusation; **по ~ю (в**+*p.*) on a charge (of); **возвести́ на кого́-н. о.** (**в** + *p.*) to charge s.o. (with); **вы́нести о.** to find guilty. **2** (*leg.*) (*collect.*) the prosecution.

обвини́тел|ь, я *m.* accuser; (*leg.*) prosecutor; **госуда́рственный о.** public prosecutor.

обвини́тельный *adj.* accusatory; **о. акт** (bill of) indictment; **о. пригово́р** verdict of 'guilty'.

обвин|и́ть, ю́, и́шь *pf.* (*of* ⇒**~я́ть**) **1** (**в** + *p.*) to accuse (of), charge (with). **2** (*leg.*) to prosecute, indict.

обвиня́ем|ый, ого *m.* (*leg.*) the accused; defendant.

обвин|я́ть, я́ю *impf. of* ⇒**~и́ть**

обвис|а́ть, а́ет *impf.* (*of* ⇒**~́нуть**) to hang, droop; (*о человеческом теле*) to sag.

обви́сл|ый (~, ~а) *adj.* (*coll.*) (*усы, плечи*) drooping; (*щёки*) sagging, flabby.

обви́с|нуть, нет, *past* **~, ~ла** *pf. of* ⇒**~а́ть**

обви́|ть, обовью́, обовьёшь, *past* **~л, ~ла́ ~ло** *pf.* (*of* ⇒**~ва́ть**) to wind (round), entwine; **о. ше́ю рука́ми** to throw one's arms round s.o.'s neck.

обви́|ться, обовью́сь, обовьёшься, *past* **~лся, ~ла́сь** *pf.* (*of* ⇒**~ва́ться**) to wind round, twine round.

об-во (*abbr. of* ***о́бщество***) Soc., Society.

обво́д, а *m.* **1** (*ограждение*) enclosing, surrounding. **2** (*очертанием*) outlining.

обво|ди́ть, жу́, ~́дишь *impf. of* ⇒**обвести́**

обводне́ни|е, я *nt.* irrigation.

обводни́тельный *adj.* irrigation.

обводн|и́ть, ю́, и́шь *pf.* (*of* ⇒**~я́ть**) to irrigate.

обво́дный *adj.*: **о. кана́л** (*tech.*) by-pass.

обводн|я́ть, я́ю *impf. of* ⇒**~и́ть**

обвола́кива|ть(ся), ю(сь) *impf. of* ⇒**обволо́чь(ся)**

обволо́|чь, ку́, чёшь, ку́т, *past* **~к, ~кла́** *pf.* (*of* ⇒**обвола́кивать**) to cover; to envelop (*also fig.*).

обволо́|чься, ку́сь, чёшься, ку́тся, *past* **~кся, ~кла́сь** *pf.* (*of* ⇒**обвола́киваться**) (+*i.*; *coll.*) to become covered (with), enveloped (by, in).

обворо́жива|ть, ю *impf. of* ⇒**обворожи́ть**

обвор|ова́ть, у́ю *pf.* (*of* ⇒**~о́вывать**) (*coll.*) to rob.

обворо́выва|ть, ю *impf. of* ⇒**обворова́ть**

обворожи́тел|ьный (~ен, ~ьна) *adj.* fascinating, charming, enchanting.

обворож|и́ть, у́, и́шь *pf.* (*of* ⇒**обворо́живать**) to fascinate, charm, enchant.

обвя|за́ть¹, жу́, ~́жешь *pf.* (*of* ⇒**~́зывать**) to tie round; **о. верёвкой** to cord, rope; **о. го́лову платко́м** to tie a head-scarf round one's head.

обвя|за́ть², жу́, ~́жешь *pf.* (*of* ⇒**~́зывать**) (*обметать*) to edge in chain-stitch.

обвя|за́ться, жу́сь, ~́жешься *pf.* (*of* ⇒**~́зываться**) (+*i.*) to tie round o.s.; **о. верёвкой** to tie a rope round o.s.

обвя́зыва|ть(ся), ю(сь) *impf. of* ⇒**обвяза́ть(ся)**

обга́|дить, жу, дишь *pf.* (*of* ⇒**~живать**) (*vulg.*) to shit on, shit up.

обга́жива|ть, ю *impf. of* ⇒**обга́дить**

обгла́дыва|ть, ю *impf. of* ⇒**обглода́ть**

обгло́д|анный *p.p.p. of* ⇒**~а́ть; ~анная кость** picked bone, bare bone.

обгло|да́ть, жу́, ~́жешь *pf.* (*of* ⇒**обгла́дывать**) to pick, gnaw round.

обгова́рива|ть, ю *impf. of* ⇒**обговори́ть**

обговор|и́ть, ю́, и́шь *pf.* (*of* ⇒**обгова́ривать**) (*coll.*) to discuss.

обго́н, а *m.* passing, overtaking.

обгон|ю́, ~́ишь *see* ⇒**обогна́ть**

обгоня́|ть, ю *impf. of* ⇒**обогна́ть**

обгор|а́ть, а́ю *impf. of* ⇒**~е́ть**

обгоре́л|ый (~, ~а) *adj.* burnt; scorched.

обгор|е́ть, ю́, и́шь *pf.* to be burnt; (*на солнце*) to get burnt.

обгрыз|а́ть, а́ю *impf. of* ⇒**~́ть**

обгры́з|ть, у́, ёшь, *past* **~, ~ла** *pf.* (*of* ⇒**~а́ть**) to gnaw, nibble at.

обда|ва́ть(ся), ю́(сь), ёшь(ся) *impf. of* ⇒**обда́ть(ся)**

обд|а́ть, а́м, а́шь, а́ст, ади́м, ади́те, аду́т, *past* **~́ал, ~ала́, ~́ало** *pf.* (*of* ⇒**~ава́ть**) (+*i.*) **1** to pour over; **о. кого́-н. кипятко́м** to pour boiling water over s.o. **2** (*fig.*) to seize, cover; **о. взгля́дом презре́ния** to fix with a look of scorn; **меня́ ~́ало хо́лодом** (*impers.*) I came over cold.

обд|а́ться, а́мся, а́шься, а́стся, ади́мся, ади́тесь, аду́тся, *past* **~а́лся, ~ала́сь** *pf.* (*of* ⇒**~ава́ться**) (+*i.*) to pour over o.s.; **о. кипятко́м** to scald o.s.

обде́л|ать, аю *pf.* (*of* ⇒**~ывать**) **1** to finish; to dress (*leather, stone, etc.*); **о. драгоце́нные ка́мни** to set precious stones. **2** (*fig.*) to manage, arrange; **о. те́му** (*coll.*) to treat, handle a subject; **о. свои́ дели́шки** (*coll.*) to manage one's affairs with profit.

обдел|и́ть, ю́, ~ишь *pf.* (*of* ⇒**~я́ть**) (+*a. and i.*) to do out of one's (fair) share (of); **он ~и́л сестёр насле́дством** he did his sisters out of their share of the legacy.

обде́лыва|ть, ю *impf. of* ⇒**обде́лать**

обдел|я́ть, я́ю *impf. of* ⇒**~и́ть**

обдёргива|ть, ю *impf. of* ⇒**обдёрнуть**

обдёр|нуть, ну, нешь *pf.* (*of* ⇒**~гивать**) to adjust, pull down (*dress, skirt, etc.*).

обдер|у́, ёшь *see* ⇒**ободра́ть**

обдира́л|а, ы *m.* (*coll.*) swindler.

обдира́|ть, ю *impf. of* ⇒**ободра́ть**

обди́рный *adj.* peeled; hulled.

обдува́л|а, ы *m.* (*coll.*) cheat, trickster.

обдува́|ть, ю *impf. of* ⇒**обду́ть**

обду́манно *adv.* after careful consideration; deliberately (= *after deliberation*).

обду́манност|ь, и *f.* deliberation; careful consideration.

обду́ман|ный 1 (~, ~а) *p.p.p. of* ⇒**обду́мать. 2 (~, ~на)** *adj.* well-considered, carefully thought out; **с зара́нее ~ным наме́рением** deliberately; (*leg.*) of malice prepense.

обду́м|ать, аю *pf.* (*of* ⇒**~ывать**) to consider, think over.

обду́мыва|ть, ю *impf. of* ⇒**обду́мать**

обду́|ть¹, ю, ешь *pf.* (*of* ⇒**~ва́ть**) (*овеять*) to blow (on, round).

обду́|ть², ю, ешь *pf.* (*of* ⇒**~ва́ть**) (*coll.*) (*обмануть*) to cheat; to fool, dupe.

о́бе *see* ⇒**о́ба**

обе́га|ть, ю *pf.* (*of* ⇒**обега́ть**) **1** (*двор, город*) to run (all over, all round). **2** (*друзей*) to run round (to see); **за неде́лю до отъе́зда нам удало́сь о. всех знако́мых** in the week before our departure we managed to look in on all our acquaintances.

обега́|ть, ю *impf. of* ⇒**обе́гать** *and* **обежа́ть**

обе́д, а *m.* **1** lunch, dinner. **2** (*время*) lunch-time, dinner-time (= *midday*); **пе́ред ~ом** before lunch, dinner; in the morning; **по́сле ~а** after lunch, dinner; in the afternoon.

обе́да|ть, ю *impf.* (*of* ⇒**по~**) to have lunch, dinner.

обе́д|енный¹ *adj. of* ⇒**~; ~енное вре́мя** lunch, dinner time; **о. переры́в** lunch hour, lunch break; **о. стол** dinner table.

обе́д|енный² *adj. of* ⇒**~ня**

обедне́|вший *p.p. act. of* ⇒**~ть** *and adj.* impoverished.

обедне́|лый (~л, ~ла) *adj.* (*coll.*) = **~вший**

обедне́ни|е, я *nt.* impoverishment.

обедне́|ть, ю *pf. of* ⇒**бедне́ть**

обедн|и́ть, ю́, и́шь *pf.* (*of* ⇒**~я́ть**) to impoverish.

обе́д|ня, ни, *g. pl.* **~ен** *f.* (*eccl.*) Mass.

обедн|я́ть, я́ю *impf. of* ⇒**~и́ть**

обе|жа́ть, гу́, жи́шь, гу́т *pf.* (*of* ⇒**~га́ть**) **1** (*дом; магазины*) to run round. **2** (*мимо*) to run (past). **3** (*sport*) to outrun, pass.

обезбо́ливани|е, я *nt.* anaesthetization (*Br.*), anesthetization (*US*).

обезбо́лива|ть, ю *impf. of* ⇒**обезбо́лить**

обезбо́лива|ющий *pres. part. act. of* ⇒**~ть; ~ющее сре́дство** anaesthetic (*Br.*), anesthetic (*US*).

обезбо́л|ить, ю, ишь *pf.* (*of* ⇒**~ивать**) to anaesthetize (*Br.*), anesthetize (*US*).

обезво́|дить, жу, дишь *pf.* (*of* ⇒**~живать**) to dehydrate.

обезво́|женный *p.p.p. of* ⇒**~дить** *and adj.* dehydrated.

обезво́жива|ть, ю *impf. of* **⇒обезво́дить**

обезвре́|дить, жу, дишь *pf.* (*of* **⇒~живать**) (*человека*) to render harmless; (*бомбу*) to defuse; (*мину*) to deactivate.

обезвре́жива|ть, ю *impf. of* **⇒обезвре́дить**

обезгла́в|ить, лю, ишь *pf.* (*of* **⇒~ливать**) **1** to behead, decapitate. **2** (*fig.*) (*лишить главы*) to deprive of a head, of a leader.

обезгла́влива|ть, ю *impf. of* **⇒обезгла́вить**

обезде́неже|ть, ю *pf.* (*coll.*) to run short of money.

обездо́л|енный *p.p.p. of* **⇒~ить** *and adj.* unfortunate, hapless.

обездо́лива|ть, ю *impf. of* **⇒обездо́лить**

обездо́л|ить, ю, ишь *pf.* (*of* **⇒~ивать**) to deprive of one's share.

обезжи́р|енный *p.p.p. of* **⇒~ить** *and adj.* fat-free; skimmed.

обезжи́рива|ть, ю *impf. of* **⇒обезжи́рить**

обезжи́р|ить, ю, ишь *pf.* (*of* **⇒~ивать**) to remove fat (from); to skim.

обеззара́жива|ть, ю *impf. of* **⇒обеззара́зить**

обеззара́жива|ющий *p.p.p of* **⇒~ть** *and adj.* disinfectant.

обеззара́|зить, жу, зишь *pf.* (*of* **⇒~живать**) to disinfect.

обезземе́л|енный *p.p.p. of* **⇒~ить** *and adj.* landless, dispossessed.

обезземе́лива|ть, ю *impf. of* **⇒обезземе́лить**

обезземе́л|ить, ю, ишь *pf.* (*of* **⇒~ивать**) to dispossess (of land).

обезле́сени|е, я *nt.* deforestation.

обезле́си|ть, шь *pf.* to deforest.

обезли́чени|е, я *nt.* **1** depersonalization. **2** depriving of personal responsibility; removal of personal responsibility (from).

обезли́чива|ть, ю *impf. of* **⇒обезли́чить**

обезли́ч|ить, у, ишь *pf.* (*of* **⇒~ивать**) **1** (*лишить своих отличительных черт*) to deprive of individuality, depersonalize. **2** (*работу*) to do away with personal responsibility (for).

обезли́чк|а, и *f.* lack of personal responsibility.

обезлю́де|ть, ет *pf.* to become depopulated.

обезобра́жива|ть, ю *impf. of* **⇒обезобра́зить**

обезобра́|зить, жу, зишь *pf.* (*of* **⇒~живать** *and* **безобра́зить**) to disfigure.

обезопа́|сить, шу, сишь *pf.* (**от**+*g.*) to protect (against).

обезопа́|ситься, шусь, сишься *pf.* (**от**+*g.*) to secure o.s., protect o.s. (against).

обезору́жива|ть, ю *impf. of* **⇒обезору́жить**

обезору́ж|ить, у, ишь *pf.* (*of* **⇒~́ивать**) to disarm (*also fig.*).

обезу́ме|ть, ю *pf.* to lose one's senses, lose one's head; **о. от испу́га** to become panic-stricken.

обезья́н|а, ы *f.* monkey; (*бесхвостая*) ape.

обезья́н|ий *adj. of* **⇒~а;** (*zool.*) simian; (*fig.*) ape-like.

обезья́нник, а *m.* monkey-house.

обезья́нничань|е, я *nt.* (*coll.*) aping.

обезья́ннича|ть, ю *impf.* (*of* **⇒с~**) (*coll.*) to ape.

обели́ск, а *m.* obelisk.

обел|и́ть, ю́, и́шь *pf.* (*of* **⇒~я́ть**) to vindicate; to prove the innocence (of).

обел|и́ться, ю́сь, и́шься *pf.* (*of* **⇒~я́ться**) to vindicate o.s., prove one's innocence.

обел|я́ть(ся), я́ю(сь) *impf. of* **⇒~и́ть(ся)**

оберега́|ть(ся), ю(сь) *impf. of* **⇒оберéчь(ся)**

обере́|чь, гу́, жёшь, гу́т, *past* **~̆г, ~гла́** *pf.* (*of* **⇒~га́ть**) (**от**+*g.*) to guard (against), protect (from).

обере́|чься, гу́сь, жёшься, гу́тся, *past* **~̆гся, ~гла́сь** *pf.* (*of* **⇒~га́ться**) (**от**+*g.*) to guard o.s. (from, against), protect o.s. (from)

оберн|у́ть, у́, ёшь *pf.* (*of* **⇒обора́чивать**) **1** (*impf. also* **обёртывать**) (*шарф вокруг шеи*) to wind (round), twist (round); **о. вокру́г па́льца** (*coll.*) to twist round one's little finger. **2** (*impf. also* **обёртывать**) (*посылку*) to wrap up. **3** (*impf. also* **обёртывать**) (*повернуть*) to turn; **о. лицо́** (**к**+*d.*) to turn one's face (towards); **о. в свою́ по́льзу** (*fig.*) to turn to account, turn to advantage. **4** (*coll.*) (*опрокинуть*) to overturn, upturn. **5** (*comm.*) to turn over. **6** (*coll.*) (*проделать*) to work through, go through.

оберн|у́ться, у́сь, ёшься *pf.* (*of* **⇒обора́чиваться**) **1** (*impf. also* **обёртываться**) (*повернуться*) to turn; **о. лицо́м** to turn one's head. **2** (*impf. also* **обёртываться**) (*о делах*) to turn out; **собы́тия ~у́лись и́наче, чем мы ожида́ли** events turned out otherwise than we expected. **3** (*coll.*) (*сходить, съездить туда и обратно*) to (go and) come back; **я ~у́сь за два часа́** I shall be back in two hours. **4** (*coll.*) (*справиться с делами*) to manage, get by. **5** (*impf. also* **обёртываться**) (*coll.*) (+*i. or* **в**+*a.*) (*превратиться*) to turn into, become (*also fig.*); **о. вампи́ром** to turn into a vampire.

обёртк|а, и *f.* wrapper; (*книги*) dust-jacket, cover.

оберто́н, а *m.* (*mus.*) overtone.

обёрт|очный *adj. of* **⇒~ка; ~очная бума́га** wrapping paper.

обёртыва|ть(ся), ю(сь) *impf. of* **⇒оберну́ть(ся)**

обескро́в|ить, лю, ишь *pf.* (*of* **⇒~ливать**) to drain of blood; to bleed white; (*fig.*) to render lifeless.

обескро́в|ленный *p.p.p. of* **⇒~ить** *and adj.* bloodless; (*fig.*) anaemic (*Br.*), anemic (*US*), lifeless.

обескро́влива|ть, ю *impf. of* **⇒обескро́вить**

обескура́жива|ть, ю *impf. of* **⇒обескура́жить**

обескура́ж|ить, у, ишь *pf.* (*coll.*) to dishearten; to dismay.

обеспа́мяте|ть, ю *pf.* **1** (*лишиться памяти*) to lose one's memory. **2** (*впасть в обморок*) to lose consciousness.

обеспе́чени|е, я *nt.* **1** (*мира, успеха*) securing, guaranteeing; ensuring. **2** (+*i.*) (*углём*) providing (with), provision (of, with), supplying (of, with). **3** (*гарантия*) guarantee; security (= *pledge*). **4** (*материальные средства к жизни*) security; safeguard(s); **социа́льное о.** social security. **5** (*mil.*) security; protection. **6**: **програ́ммное о.** (*comput.*) software.

обеспе́ченност|ь, и *f.* **1** (+*i.*) being provided (with), provision (of, with); **о. школ учебниками** the provision of schools with text-books. **2** (*материальная*) (material) security.

обеспе́ч|енный *p.p.p. of* **⇒~ить** *and adj.* (**~ен, ~енна**) well-to-do; well provided for.

обеспе́чива|ть, ю *impf. of* **⇒обеспе́чить**

обеспе́ч|ить, у, ишь *pf.* (*of* **⇒~ивать**) **1** (*семью; старость*) to provide for. **2** (+*i.*) (*снабдить чем-н.*) to provide (with), guarantee supply (of); **о. экспеди́цию обору́дованием** to provide an expedition with equipment. **3** (*успех*) to secure, guarantee; to ensure. **4** (**от**+*g.*) (*obs.*) to protect (from).

обеспло́|дить, жу, дишь *pf.* (*of* **⇒~живать**) to sterilize; to render barren.

обеспло́жива|ть, ю *impf. of* **⇒обеспло́дить**

обеспоко́енност|ь, и *f.* worry, concern.

обеспоко́енный *adj.* worried, concerned.

обеспоко́|ить, ю, ишь *pf.* (*obs.*) to bother, touble.

обеспоко́|иться, юсь, ишься *pf.* (*obs.*) to be worried.

обесси́ле|ть, ю *pf.* to grow weak, lose one's strength.

обесси́лива|ть, ю *impf. of* **⇒обесси́лить**

обесси́л|ить, ю, ишь *pf.* (*of* **⇒~ивать**) to weaken.

обесcла́в|ить, лю, ишь *pf.* (*of* **⇒бессла́вить**) to defame.

обессме́р|тить, чу, тишь *pf.* to immortalize.

обессу́д|ить, *pf. now only used in imper.* **не ~ь(те)** (please) don't take it amiss; (please) don't be angry.

обесцве́|тить, чу, тишь *pf.* (*of* **⇒~чивать**) to decolorize, fade; (*fig.*) to tone down.

обесцве́|титься, чусь, тишься *pf.* (*of* **⇒~чиваться**) to fade; to

О

become colourless (*Br.*), colorless (*US*) (*also fig.*).

обесцвéчива|ть(ся), ю(сь) *impf. of* ⇒**обесцвéтить(ся)**

обесцéнени|е, я *nt.* depreciation.

обесцéн|енный *p.p.p. of* ⇒**~ить** *and adj.* depreciated.

обесцéнива|ть(ся), ю, ет(ся) *impf. of* ⇒**обесцéнить(ся)**

обесцéн|ить, ю, ишь *pf.* (*of* ⇒**~ивать**) to depreciate, cheapen.

обесцéн|иться, ится *pf.* (*of* ⇒**~иваться**) (*intrans.*) to depreciate.

обесчé|стить, щу, стишь *pf. of* ⇒**бесчéстить**

обéт, а *m.* (*rhet.*) vow, promise.

обетовáнн|ый *adj.*: **~ая земля́, о. край** the Promised Land.

обещáни|е, я *nt.* promise; **дать, сдержáть о.** to give, keep a promise (*or* one's word).

обещá|ть, ю *impf. and pf.* to promise.

обещá|ться, юсь *impf. and pf.* (*coll.*) to promise.

обжáловани|е, я *nt.* appeal; **о. приговóра** (*leg.*) appealing against a sentence.

обжáл|овать, ую *pf.* (*leg.*) to appeal (against).

обжáрива|ть, ю *impf. of* ⇒**обжáрить**

обжáр|ить, ю, ишь *pf.* (*of* ⇒**~ивать**) (*cul.*) to fry on both sides, to brown all over.

обжéчь, обожгу́, обожжёшь, обожгу́т, *past* **обжёг, обожглá** *pf.* (*of* ⇒**обжигáть**) **1** to burn, scorch; **о. себé пáльцы** to burn one's fingers (*also fig.*). **2** (*кирпич*) to fire, bake. **3** (*о крапиве*) to sting.

обжéчься, обожгу́сь, обожжёшься, обожгу́тся, *past.* **обжёгся, обожглáсь** *pf.* **1** (+*i. or* **на**+*p.*) to burn o.s. (on, with); **о. горя́чим чáем** to scald o.s. with hot tea; **о. крапи́вой** to be stung by a nettle. **2** (*fig., coll.*) (*потерпеть неудачу*) to burn one's fingers.

обживá|ть(ся), ю(сь) *impf. of* ⇒**обжи́ть(ся)**

óбжиг, а *m.* (*tech.*) firing, baking.

обжигá|ть(ся), ю(сь) *impf. of* ⇒**обжéчь(ся)**

обжирá|ться, юсь *impf. of* ⇒**обожрáться**

обжит|óй (*and* **~́ый**) *p.p.p. of* ⇒**~́ь**

обж|и́ть, иву́, ивёшь, *past* **~́ил, ~илá, ~́ило** *pf.* (*of* ⇒**~ивáть**) (*coll.*) to render habitable.

обж|и́ться, иву́сь, ивёшься, *past* **~и́лся, ~илáсь** *pf.* (*of* ⇒**~ивáться**) (*coll.*) to make o.s. at home, feel at home.

обжóр|а, ы *c.g.* (*coll.*) glutton.

обжóрлив|ый (~, ~а) *adj.* gluttonous.

обжóрств|о, а *nt.* gluttony.

обжу́лива|ть, ю *impf. of* ⇒**обжу́лить**

обжу́л|ить, ю, ишь *pf.* (*coll.*) to cheat, swindle.

обзаведéни|е, я *nt.* **1** (+*i.*) (*действие*) providing o.s. (with), fitting o.s. out. **2** (*coll.*) (*collect.*) (*вещи*) fittings, paraphernalia.

обзаве|сти́сь, ду́сь, дёшься, *past* **~́лся, ~лáсь** *pf.* (*of* ⇒**обзаводи́ться**) (+*i.*; *coll.*) to get o.s.; to set up; **о. семьёй** to start a family; **о. хозя́йством** to set up home.

обзаво|ди́ться, жу́сь, ~́дишься *impf. of* ⇒**обзавести́сь**

обзóр, а *m.* **1** (*сжатое сообщение*) survey, review, overview. **2** (*mil.*) field of view.

обзóр|ный *adj.* giving an overall view; **~ная лéкция, ~ная статья́** survey.

обзывá|ть, ю *impf. of* ⇒**обозвáть**

обивá|ть, ю *impf. of* **оби́ть**; **о. (все) порóги** (*fig.*) to leave no stone unturned.

оби́вк|а, и *f.* **1** (*действие*) upholstering. **2** (*материал*) upholstery.

обивнóй *adj.* for upholstery.

оби́д|а, ы *f.* **1** insult; (*чувство*) offence, (sense of) grievance, resentment; **быть на когó-н. в оби́де** to feel wronged by s.o., to be offended with s.o.; **затаи́ть ~у** to nurse a grievance; **проглоти́ть ~у** to swallow an insult; **не давáть себя́ в ~у** to (be able to) stick up for o.s.; **не в ~у будь скáзано** no offence meant. **2** (*coll.*) (*досада*) annoying thing, nuisance; **какáя о.!** what a nuisance!

оби́|деть, жу, дишь *pf.* (*of* ⇒**~жáть**) **1** to offend; to hurt (the feelings of), wound. **2** (*причинить ущерб*) to hurt; to do damage (to); **му́хи не ~дит** (*fig.*) he would not harm a fly. **3** (+*i.*; *following* **Бог, прирóда** *etc.*) to stint, begrudge; **прирóда не ~дела егó талáнтом** he has plenty of natural ability.

оби́|деться, жусь, дишься *pf.* (*of* ⇒**~жáться**) (**на**+*a.*) to take offence (at); to feel hurt (by), resent.

оби́д|ный (~ен, ~на) *adj.* **1** offensive; **мне ~но** I feel hurt, it pains me. **2** (*coll.*) (*досадный*) annoying; **~но** (*impers.*) it is a pity, it is a nuisance; **~но, что мы опоздáли** it is a pity that we are late.

оби́дчивост|ь, и *f.* touchiness, sensitivity.

оби́дчив|ый (~, ~а) *adj.* touchy, sensitive.

оби́дчик, а *m.* (*coll.*) offender.

обижá|ть, ю *impf. of* ⇒**оби́деть**

обижá|ться, юсь *impf. of* ⇒**оби́деться; не ~йтесь** don't be offended.

оби́|женный *p.p.p of* ⇒**~деть** *and adj.* offended, aggrieved; **быть ~женным** (**на**+*a.*) to have a grudge (against); **у негó был о. вид** he had an aggrieved air; **о. Бóгом, о. прирóдой** (*joc.*) not over-blessed (with talents); ill-starred.

оби́ли|е, я *nt.* abundance, plenty.

оби́л|овать, ую *impf.* (+*i.*; *obs.*) to abound (in).

оби́л|ьный (~ен, ~ьна) *adj.* abundant, plentiful; (+*i.*) rich (in); **~ьное угощéние** lavish entertainment; **о. урожáй** bumper crop; **день, о. происшéствиями** an eventful day.

обину́ясь *only in phr.* **не о.** (*obs.*) without a moment's hesitation.

обиня́к, á *m. only in phrr.* **говори́ть ~óм, ~áми** to beat about the bush; **говори́ть без ~óв** to speak plainly.

обирáл|а, ы *c.g.* (*coll.*) extortionist.

обирáловк|а, и *f.* (*coll.*) clip-joint.

обирá|ть, ю *impf. of* ⇒**обобрáть**

обитáем|ый (~, ~а) *adj.* inhabited; **~ая косми́ческая стáнция** manned space station.

обитáтел|ь, я *m.* inhabitant.

обитá|ть, ю *impf.* (**в**+*p.*) to live (in).

оби́тел|ь, и *f.* **1** (*obs.*) (*монастырь*) cloister. **2** (*joc.*) (*жилище*) abode, dwelling-place.

оби́|ть, обобью́, обобьёшь *pf.* (*of* ⇒**~вáть**) **1** (**с**+*g.*) (*ударами отделить*) to knock (off, down from); **о. плоды́ с я́блони** to knock down fruit from an apple-tree. **2** (+*i.*) (*покрыть*) to cover (with); **о. гвоздя́ми** to stud; **о. желéзом** to bind with iron. **3** (*coll.*) (*повредить*) to wear out; **о. подóл ю́бки** to wear the hem of a skirt; **о. штукату́рку** to chip off plaster.

обихóд, а *m.* **1** (*текущая жизнь*) everyday life. **2** (*употребление*) use; **пусти́ть в о.** to bring into (general) use; **вы́йти из ~а** to be no longer in use, fall into disuse.

обихóд|ный (~ен, ~на) *adj.* everyday; **~ное выражéние** colloquial expression.

обкáлыва|ть, ю *impf. of* ⇒**обколóть**

обкáп|ать, аю *pf.* (*of* ⇒**~ывать**[1]) (+*i.*) to let drops (of) fall on; to cover with drops (of).

обкáпыва|ть[1]**, ю** *impf. of* ⇒**обкáпать**

обкáпыва|ть[2]**, ю** *impf. of* ⇒**обкопáть**

обкáрмлива|ть, ю *impf. of* ⇒**обкорми́ть**

обкат|áть, áю *pf.* (*of* ⇒**~ывать**) **1** (*coll.*) (**в**+*p.*) (*катая, покрыть чем-н.*) to roll. **2** (*дорогу*) to roll smooth. **3** (*новую машину*) to run in (*Br.*), break in (*US*).

обкáтк|а, и *f.* (*дороги*) smoothing; (*машины*) running in (*Br.*), breaking in (*US*).

обкáтыва|ть, ю *impf. of* ⇒**обкатáть**

обклáдк|а, и *f.* facing; **о. дёрном** turfing.

обклáдыва|ть, ю *impf. of* ⇒**обложи́ть**

обкол|óть, ю́, ~́ешь *pf.* (*of* ⇒**обкáлывать**) **1** (*лёд*) to cut away. **2** (*руки*) to prick all over.

обкóм, а *m.* (*abbr. of* ***областнóй комитéт***) regional committee.

обкопá|ть, ю *pf.* (*of* ⇒**обкáпывать**[2]) (*coll.*) to dig round.

обкорм|и́ть, лю́, ~́ишь *pf.* (*of* ⇒**обка́рмливать**) to overfeed.

обкорна́|ть, ю *pf. of* ⇒**корна́ть**

обкра́дыва|ть, ю *impf. of* ⇒**обокра́сть**

обку́р|енный *p.p.p. of* ⇒**~и́ть(ся)** *and adj.*; **1**: **~енные па́льцы** tobacco-stained fingers. **2** (*sl.*) stoned (*from smoking marijuana etc.*).

обку́рива|ть(ся), ю(сь) *impf. of* ⇒**обкури́ть(ся)**

обкур|и́ть, ю́, ~́ишь *pf.* (*of* ⇒**~́ивать**) **1**: **о. тру́бку** to season a pipe. **2** (*coll.*) (*комнату*) to fill, envelop with (tobacco) smoke; (*пальцы*) to stain with tobacco.

обкур|и́ться, ю́сь, ~́ишься *pf.* (*of* ⇒**~́иваться**) **1** (*coll.*) (*курить слишком много*) to smoke too much. **2** (*sl.*) (*наркотиком*) to get stoned (*from smoking marijuana etc.*).

обкус|а́ть, а́ю *pf.* (*of* ⇒**~́ывать**) to bite round; to nibble.

обку́сыва|ть, ю *impf. of* ⇒**обкуса́ть**

обл. *abbr. of* **1** ***о́бласть*** oblast. **2** ***областно́й*** dial., dialectal.

обл... *comb. form, abbr. of* ***областно́й*** 1

обла́в|а, ы *f.* **1** (*охота*) battue; beating up. **2** (*fig.*) (*на преступников*) raid; round-up.

облага́емый *adj.* taxable.

облага́|ть, ю *impf. of* ⇒**обложи́ть**

облага́|ться, юсь *impf.* (*of* ⇒**обложи́ться**): **о. нало́гом** to be liable to tax, be taxable.

облагоде́тельств|овать, ую *pf.* (*iron.*) to do a great favour (*Br.*), favor (*US*).

облагора́жива|ть, ю *impf. of* ⇒**облагоро́дить**

облагоро́|дить, жу, дишь *pf.* (*of* ⇒**облагора́живать**) to ennoble.

облада́ни|е, я *nt.* possession.

облада́тел|ь, я *m.* possessor.

облада́|ть, ю *impf.* (+*i.*) to possess, have; **о. хоро́шим здоро́вьем** to enjoy good health; **о. пра́вом** to have the right.

обла́|зить, жу, зишь *pf.* (*coll.*) to climb all over.

о́блак|о, а, *pl.* **~а́, ~о́в** *nt.* cloud; **быть, носи́ться в ~а́х** (*fig.*) to live in the clouds; **свали́ться с ~о́в** (*fig.*) to appear from nowhere.

обла́мыва|ть(ся), ю(сь) *impf. of* ⇒**облома́ть(ся)**

обла́п|ить, лю, ишь *pf.* (*of* ⇒**~ливать**) (*coll.*) to hug.

обла́плива|ть, ю *impf. of* ⇒**обла́пить**

облапо́шива|ть, ю *impf. of* ⇒**облапо́шить**

облапо́ш|ить, у, ишь *pf.* (*of* ⇒**~ивать**) (*coll.*) to cheat, swindle.

обласка́|ть, ю *pf.* to be kind to.

областно́й *adj.* **1** oblast; provincial; regional. **2** (*ling.*) dialectal; regional.

о́бласт|ь, и, *g. pl.* **~е́й** *f.* **1** (*административная единица*) oblast; province. **2** (*часть страны*) region, district; belt; **о. вечнозелёных расте́ний** evergreen belt; **озёрная о.** lake district; (*в Германии*) -land; **Ре́йнская о.** the Rhineland; **Ру́рская о.** the Ruhr (*region*). **3** (*fig.*) (*отрасль*) field, sphere, realm, domain; **о. микробиоло́гии** the field of microbiology; **о. мифоло́гии** the realm of mythology.

обла́тк|а, и *f.* **1** (*eccl.*) wafer, host. **2** (*pharm.*) capsule.

облач|а́ть(ся), а́ю(сь) *impf. of* ⇒**~и́ть(ся)**

облаче́ни|е, я *nt.* **1** (**в**+*a.*) robing (in). **2** (*eccl.*) vestments, robes.

облач|и́ть, у́, и́шь *pf.* (*of* ⇒**~а́ть**) (**в**+*a.*) **1** (*eccl.*) to robe (in). **2** (*rhet. or coll., joc.*) to deck out (in).

облач|и́ться, у́сь, и́шься *pf.* (*of* ⇒**~а́ться**) **1** (*eccl.*) to robe, put on robes. **2** (*rhet. or coll., joc.*) to deck o.s. out.

облачк|о́, а, *pl.* **~а́, ~о́в** *nt. dim. of* ⇒**о́блако**

о́блачност|ь, и *f.* cloudiness.

о́блач|ный (~ен, ~на) *adj.* cloudy.

облега́|ть, ю *impf.* **1** *impf. of* ⇒**обле́чь**[1]. **2** (*об одежде*) to fit tightly; to cling to.

облега́|ющий *pres. part. act. of* ⇒**~ть** *and adj.* tight-fitting.

облегч|а́ть(ся), а́ю(сь) *impf. of* ⇒**~и́ть(ся)**

облегче́ни|е, я *nt.* **1** (*действие*) facilitation, lightening, easing. **2** (*чувство успокоения*) relief; **вздохну́ть с ~ем** to heave a sigh of relief.

облегч|и́ть, у́, и́шь *pf.* (*of* ⇒**~а́ть**) **1** (*груз, вес*) to lighten. **2** (*сделать менее трудным*) to make easier. **3** (*упростить*) to simplify. **4** (*успокоить*) to relieve; to alleviate; (*leg.*) to commute; **о. ду́шу** to relieve one's mind.

облегч|и́ться, у́сь, и́шься *pf.* (*of* **~а́ться**) **1** (*испытать успокоение*) to be relieved, find relief. **2** (*стать более лёгким*) to become easier; to become lighter. **3** (*coll., euph.*) (*освободить себе желудок*) to relieve o.s.

обледенéл|ый (~, ~а) *adj.* ice-covered.

обледене́ни|е, я *nt.* icing(-over); **пери́од ~я** Ice Age.

обледене́|ть, ю *pf.* to ice over, become covered with ice.

облез|а́ть, а́ет *impf. of* ⇒**~ть**

обле́зл|ый (~, ~а) *adj.* (*coll.*) shabby, bare; **~ая ко́шка** mangy cat.

обле́з|ть, ет, *past* **~, ~ла** *pf.* (*of* ⇒**~а́ть**) (*coll.*) **1** (*о мехе*) to fall out. **2** (*о кошке*) to grow mangy. **3** (*о краске, коже*) to peel off.

облека́|ть, ю *impf. of* ⇒**обле́чь**[2]

облека́|ться, юсь *impf. of* ⇒**обле́чься**

обле́нива|ться, юсь *impf. of* ⇒**облени́ться**

облен|и́ться, ю́сь, ~́ишься *pf.* (*of* ⇒**~́иваться**) to grow lazy.

облеп|и́ть, лю́, ~́ишь *pf.* (*of* ⇒**~ля́ть**) **1** (*прилипнуть*) to stick (to); (*fig.*) to cling (to); (*окружить*) to surround, throng; **нас ~и́ла ку́ча мальчи́шек** we were surrounded by a swarm of small boys. **2** (+*a. and i.*) (*заклеить*) to paste all over (with), plaster (with); **о. сте́ну объявле́ниями** to plaster a wall with notices.

облепи́х|а, и *f.* (*bot.*) sea buckthorn (*Hippophae rhamnoides*).

облепля́|ть, ю *impf. of* ⇒**облепи́ть**

облесе́ни|е, я *nt.* afforestation.

обле|си́ть, шу́, си́шь *pf.* to afforest.

облет|а́ть[1]**, а́ю** *impf. of* ⇒**~е́ть**

облет|а́ть[2]**, а́ю** *pf.* (*of* ⇒**~́ывать**) **1** to fly (all round, all over); **мы ~а́ли всю Евро́пу** we have flown all over Europe; **она́ ~а́ла всех подру́г** (*fig., coll.*) she flew round to all her girl-friends. **2** (*испытать*) to test (*an aircraft*).

обле|те́ть, чу́, ти́шь *pf.* (*of* ⇒**~та́ть**[1]) **1** (+*a. or* **вокру́г**+*g.*) to fly (round). **2** (*о новостях*) to spread (round, all over); **за полчаса́ весть о побе́де ~те́ла го́род** in half an hour the news of the victory had spread round the town. **3** (*о листьях*) to fall.

облётыва|ть, ю *impf. of* ⇒**облета́ть**[2]

облеч|ённый *p.p.p. of* ⇒**~ь**[2] *and adj.*: **о. вла́стью** invested with power.

обл|е́чь[1]**, ягу́, я́жешь, я́гут,** *past* **~ёг, ~егла́** *pf.* (*of* ⇒**~ега́ть**) (*окутать*) to cover, surround, envelop (*also fig.*); **ту́чи ~егли́ го́ру** rain-clouds enveloped the mountain.

обле́|чь[2]**, ку́, чёшь, ку́т,** *past* **~́к, ~кла́** *pf.* (*of* ⇒**~ка́ть**) (+*a.* **в**+*a. or* +*a. and i.*) (*одеть*) to clothe (in); (*доверием, властью*) to invest (with), vest (in); (*fig.*) shroud (in); **о. полномо́чиями** to invest with authority, commission; **о. та́йной** to shroud in mystery; **о. свою́ мысль непоня́тными слова́ми** to wrap one's idea in unintelligible words.

обле́|чься, ку́сь, чёшься, ку́тся, *past* **~́кся, ~кла́сь** *pf.* (*of* ⇒**~ка́ться**) (**в**+*a.*) to clothe o.s. (in), dress o.s. (in); (*fig.*) to take the form (of), assume the shape (of).

облива́ни|е, я *nt.* **1** (*действие*) spilling (over), pouring (over). **2** (*водная процедура*) shower-bath; sponge-down.

облива́|ть, ю *impf. of* ⇒**обли́ть**

облива́|ться, юсь *impf. of* ⇒**обли́ться; се́рдце у меня́ кро́вью ~ется** my heart bleeds.

обли́вк|а, и *f.* **1** (*действие*) glazing. **2** (*глазурь*) glaze.

обливно́й *adj.* glazed.

облигац|ио́нный *adj. of* ⇒**~́ия**

облига́ци|я, и *f.* (*fin.*) bond, debenture.

обли|за́ть, жу́, ~́жешь *pf.* (*of* ⇒**~́зывать**) to lick (all over); to lick clean; **па́льчики ~́жешь** (*fig., coll.*) (*sc.* it is, it will be) a real treat.

обли|за́ться, жу́сь, ~́жешься *pf.* (*of* ⇒**~́зываться**) **1** (*о человеке*) to smack one's lips (*also fig.*). **2** (*о животном*) to lick itself.

обли́зыва|ть, ю *impf. of* ⇒**облиза́ть; о. гу́бы** (*fig., coll.*) to smack one's lips.

обли́зыва|ться, юсь *impf. of* ⇒**облиза́ться**

о́блик, а *m.* **1** (*наружность*) look, appearance. **2** (*fig.*) (*характер*) cast of mind, character.

облиня́|ть, ю *pf.* (*coll.*) **1** (*утратить цвет*) to fade, lose colour (*also fig.*). **2** (*потерять шерсть, перья*) to moult (*Br.*), molt (*US*), lose hair *or* feathers.

облип|а́ть, а́ю *impf. of* ⇒**~нуть**

обли́п|нуть, ну, нешь, *past* **~, ~ла** *pf.* (*of* ⇒**~а́ть**) (+*i.*) to become stuck (in, with).

о́блит|ый (~, ~а́, ~о) *and* **обли́т|ый (~, ~а́, ~о)** *p.p.p. of* ⇒**обли́ть;** (*fig.*; +*i.*) covered (by), enveloped (in); **о. све́том луны́** bathed in moonlight.

обл|и́ть, оболью́, обольёшь, *past* **~ил, ~ила́, ~ило** *and* **~и́л, ~ила́, ~и́ло** *pf.* (*of* ⇒**~ива́ть**) **1** (*p.p.p.* **~итый**) (*намеренно*) to pour (over); (*случайно*) to spill (over); **о. ска́терть вино́м** to spill wine over the table-cloth; **о. презре́нием** (*fig.*) to pour contempt (on); **о. гря́зью, о. помо́ями** (*fig., coll.*) to vilify. **2** (*p.p.p.* **~и́тый**) (*глазурью*) to glaze.

обли́|ться, оболью́сь, обольёшься, *past* **~лся, ~ла́сь, ~ло́сь** *and* **~лось** *pf.* (*of* ⇒**~ва́ться**) (+*i.*) **1** to have a shower-bath; to sponge down; **о. холо́дной водо́й** to have a cold shower. **2** (*случайно*) to spill over o.s.; **о. по́том** to be bathed in sweat; **о. слеза́ми** to melt into tears.

облиц|ева́ть, у́ю, у́ешь *pf.* (*of* ⇒**~о́вывать**) (+*a. and i.*) to face, clad (with).

облицо́вк|а, и *f.* facing, cladding.

облицо́в|очный *adj. of* ⇒**~ка; о. кирпи́ч** facing brick, decorative tile.

облицо́выва|ть, ю *impf. of* ⇒**облицева́ть**

облич|а́ть, а́ю *impf.* (*of* ⇒**~и́ть**) **1** (*разоблачать*) to expose, unmask, denounce. **2** (*impf. only*) (*показывать*) to reveal, display, manifest; to point (to).

обличе́ни|е, я *nt.* exposure, unmasking, denunciation.

обличи́тел|ь, я *m.* exposer, unmasker, denouncer.

обличи́тельн|ый *adj.* denunciatory; **~ая речь, ~ая статья́** diatribe, tirade.

облич|и́ть, у́, и́шь *pf. of* ⇒**~а́ть**

обли́чь|е, я *nt.* **1** (*coll.*) (*лицо*) face. **2** (*облик*) aspect, appearance (*also fig.*).

облобыза́|ть, ю *pf.* (*obs., joc.*) to kiss.

обложе́ни|е, я *nt.* **1** (*налогом*) levying. **2** (*сбор*) levy.

облож|и́ть, у́, ~ишь *pf.* **1** (*impf.* **обкла́дывать**) (*положить вокруг*) to put (round); to edge; **о. больно́го поду́шками** to surround a patient with pillows. **2** (*impf.* **обкла́дывать**) (*покрыть*) to cover; **о. сте́ну пли́ткой** to tile a wall; (*impers.*): **круго́м ~и́ло (не́бо)** the sky is completely overcast. **3** (*impf.* **обкла́дывать**) (*окружить*) to surround. **4** (*impf.* **облага́ть**) to assess; **о. нало́гом** to tax. **5** (*impf.* **обкла́дывать**) (*coll.*) (*обругать*) to swear (at).

облож|и́ться, у́сь, ~ишься *pf.* **1** (*impf.* **обкла́дываться**) (*обложить себя*) (+*i.*) to put round o.s., surround o.s. (with). **2** (*покрыться*) (+*i.*) to be covered (with).

обло́жк|а, и *f.* (dust-)cover; (*для бумаг*) folder.

обложно́й *adj.*: **о. дождь** (*coll.*) incessant rain.

облока́чива|ться, юсь *impf. of* ⇒**облокоти́ться**

облоко|ти́ться, чу́сь, ~ти́шься *pf.* (*of* ⇒**облока́чиваться**) (на+*a.*) to lean one's elbow(s) (on, against).

обло́м, а *m.* **1** (*действие*) breaking off. **2** (*место*) break. **3** (*sl.*) (*неудача*) failure, misfortune; **в ~е** in a bad mood.

облома́|ть, ю *pf.* (*of* ⇒**обла́мывать**) **1** (*ветку*) to break off, snap. **2** (*fig., coll.*) (*уговорить*) to talk into, cajole.

облома́|ться, юсь *pf.* (*of* ⇒**обла́мываться**) **1** (*ветка*) to break off, snap. **2** (*sl.*) to fail.

облом|и́ть, лю́, ~ишь *pf.* to break off.

облом|и́ться, лю́сь, ~ишься *pf.* = **~а́ться**

обло́мовщин|а, ы *f.* Oblomovism, lethargy, apathy.

обло́м|ок, ка *m.* **1** fragment. **2** (*pl.*) débris, wreckage.

облуп|и́ть, лю́, ~ишь *pf. of* ⇒**лупи́ть**[1] *and* **~ливать**

облуп|и́ться, лю́сь, ~ишься *pf. of* ⇒**лупи́ться** *and* **~ливаться**

облу́п|ленный *p.p.p. of* ⇒**~и́ть** *and adj.* peeling; **знать как ~ленного** (*coll.*) to know inside out.

облу́плива|ть, ю *impf.* (*of* ⇒**облупи́ть**) **1** to peel; (*яйца*) to shell. **2** (*fig., coll.*) (*обобрать*) to fleece.

облу́плива|ться, юсь *impf.* (*of* ⇒**облупи́ться**) to peel (off); to come off.

облупл|я́ть(ся), я́ю(сь) *impf.* = **~ивать(ся)**

облуч|а́ть, а́ю *impf. of* ⇒**~и́ть**

облуче́ни|е, я *nt.* (*med.*) irradiation.

облуч|и́ть, у́, и́шь *pf.* (*of* ⇒**~а́ть**) to irradiate.

облуч|о́к, ка́ *m.* coachman's seat.

облущ|и́ть, у́, и́шь *pf. of* ⇒**лущи́ть**

облы́ж|ный (~ен, ~на) *adj.* (*coll.*) false.

облысе́|ть, ю, ешь *pf. of* ⇒**лысе́ть**

облюб|ова́ть, у́ю *pf.* (*of* ⇒**~о́вывать**) to pick, choose.

облюбо́выва|ть, ю *impf. of* ⇒**облюбова́ть**

обл|я́гу, я́жешь, я́гут *see* ⇒**~е́чь**[1]

обма́|зать, жу, жешь *pf.* (*of* ⇒**~зывать**) **1** (*покрыть*) to coat (with). **2** (*запачкать*) to smear (with); **о. себе́ ру́ки ма́слом** to cover one's hands with oil.

обма́|заться, жусь, жешься *pf.* (*of* ⇒**~зываться**) **1** (+*i.*) (*мазать себя*) to smear o.s.; (*пачкаться*) to get o.s. covered (with). **2** *pass. of* ⇒**~зать**

обма́зк|а, и *f.* coating.

обма́зыва|ть(ся), ю(сь) *impf. of* ⇒**обма́зать(ся)**

обма́кива|ть, ю *impf. of* ⇒**обмакну́ть**

обмак|ну́ть, ну́, нёшь, *past* **~ну́л** *pf.* (*of* ⇒**~ивать**) to dip.

обма́н, а *m.* fraud, deception; **о. зре́ния** optical illusion; **ввести́ в о.** to deceive.

обма́нк|а, и *f.* (*min.*) blende; **смоляна́я о.** pitchblende.

обма́н|ный (~ен, ~на) *adj.* fraudulent; **~ным путём** fraudulently.

обман|у́ть, у́, ~ешь *pf.* (*of* ⇒**~ывать**) to deceive; (*мошеннически*) to cheat, swindle; (*нарушить обещание*) to fail; to let s.o. down; **о. чьё-н. дове́рие** to betray s.o.'s trust; **о. чьи-н. наде́жды** to disappoint s.o.'s hopes.

обман|у́ться, у́сь, ~ешься *pf.* (*of* ⇒**~ываться**) to be deceived; **о. в свои́х ожида́ниях** to be disappointed in one's expectations.

обма́нчив|ый (~, ~а) *adj.* deceptive, delusive; **нару́жность ~а** appearances are deceptive.

обма́нщик, а *m.* deceiver; cheat, fraud.

обма́нщи|ца, цы *f. of* ⇒**~к**

обма́нывa|ть(ся), ю(сь) *impf. of* ⇒**обману́ть(ся)**

обмар|а́ть, а́ю *pf.* (*of* ⇒**~ывать**) (*coll.*) to soil, dirty.

обма́рыва|ть, ю *impf. of* ⇒**обмара́ть**

обма́тыва|ть(ся), ю(сь) *impf. of* ⇒**обмота́ть(ся)**

обма́хива|ть(ся), ю(сь) *impf. of* ⇒**обмахну́ть(ся)**

обмах|ну́ть, ну́, нёшь *pf.* (*of* ⇒**~ивать**) **1** (*лицо*) to fan. **2** (*удалить; очистить*) to dust (off); to brush (off); **о. сор со ска́терти** to brush crumbs off the cloth; **о. стол** to dust off the table.

обмах|ну́ться, ну́сь, нёшься *pf.* (*of* ⇒**~иваться**) to fan o.s.

обма́чива|ть(ся), ю(сь) *impf. of* ⇒**обмочи́ть(ся)**

обмеле́ни|е, я *nt.* shallowing, shoaling.

обмеле́|ть, ет *pf.* (*of* ⇒**меле́ть**) **1** (*стать мелководным*) to become shallow. **2** (*naut.*) (*сесть на мель*) to run aground.

обме́н, а *m.* (+*i.*) exchange (of); **о. мне́ниями** exchange of opinions; **о. веще́ств** (*biol.*) metabolism; **в о.** (на+*a.*) in exchange (for).

обме́нива|ть(ся), ю(сь) *impf. of* ⇒**обмени́ть(ся)** *and* **обменя́ть(ся)**

обмен|и́ть, ю́, ~ишь *pf.* (*of* ⇒**~ивать**) (*coll.*) to exchange (*accidentally or secretly*).

обмен|и́ться, ю́сь, ~ишься *pf.* (*of* ⇨**~иваться**) (+*i.*) (*coll.*) to exchange (*accidentally*).

обме́н|ный *adj. of* ⇨**~**

обмен|я́ть, я́ю *pf.* (*of* ⇨**меня́ть** 2 *and* **~ивать**) (+*a.* **на**+*a.*) to exchange (sth. for sth.).

обмен|я́ться, я́юсь *pf.* (*of* ⇨**меня́ться** 2 *and* **~иваться**) (+*i.*) to exchange; to swap; **о. взгля́дами** to exchange looks; **о. впечатле́ниями** to compare notes.

обме́р¹, а *m.* measurement.

обме́р², а *m.* false measure.

об|мере́ть, омру́, омрёшь, *past* **~мер, ~мерла́, ~мерло** *pf.* (*of* ⇨**~мира́ть**) (*coll.*) to faint; **о. от у́жаса** to be horror-struck; **я ~мер** my heart stood still.

обме́рива|ть, ю *impf. of* ⇨**обме́рить**

обме́р|ить¹, ю, ишь *pf.* (*of* ⇨**~ивать**) (*измерить*) to measure.

обме́р|ить², ю, ишь *pf.* (*of* ⇨**~ивать**) (*обмануть*) to cheat in measuring; to give short measure (to).

обме|сти́, ту́, тёшь, *past* **~л, ~ла́** *pf.* (*of* ⇨**~та́ть¹**) to sweep (off); to brush (off); to dust (off).

обмета́|ть¹, ю *impf. of* ⇨**обмести́**

обме|та́ть², чу́, ~чешь *pf.* (*of* ⇨**~тывать**) **1** to oversew. **2** (*impers.*; *coll.*): **у меня́ ~та́ло гу́бы** my lips are cracked (with cold sores).

обмётыва|ть, ю *impf. of* ⇨**обмета́ть²**

обмина́|ть, ю *impf. of* ⇨**обмя́ть**

обмира́|ть, ю *impf. of* ⇨**обмере́ть**

обмозг|ова́ть, у́ю *pf.* (*of* ⇨**~о́вывать**) (*coll.*) to think over, turn over (in one's mind).

обмозго́выва|ть, ю *impf. of* ⇨**обмозгова́ть**

обмок|а́ть, а́ю *impf. of* ⇨**~нуть**

обмо́к|нуть, ну, нешь, *past* **~, ~ла** *pf.* (*of* ⇨**~а́ть**) (*coll.*) to get soaking wet; to get wet all over.

обмола́чива|ть, ю *impf. of* ⇨**обмолоти́ть**

обмо́лв|иться, люсь, ишься *pf.* (*coll.*) **1** (*оговориться*) to make a slip in speaking. **2** (+*i.*) (*сказать*) to say; to utter; **не о. ни сло́вом** (**о**+*p.*) to say not a word (about).

обмо́лвк|а, и *f.* slip of the tongue.

обмоло́т, а *m.* (*agric.*) threshing.

обмоло|ти́ть, чу́, ~тишь *pf.* (*of* ⇨**обмола́чивать**) (*agric.*) to thresh.

обмора́жива|ть(ся), ю(сь) *impf. of* ⇨**обморо́зить(ся)**

обморо́же́ни|е, я *nt.* frost-bite.

обморо́|женный *p.p.p. of* ⇨**~зить** *and adj.* frost-bitten.

обморо́|зить, жу, зишь *pf.* (*of* ⇨**обмора́живать**); **я ~зил себе́ нос, ру́ки** *etc.* my nose is, hands, *etc.*, are frost-bitten.

обморо́|зиться, жусь, зишься *pf.* (*of* ⇨**обмора́живаться**) to suffer frost-bite, be frost-bitten.

о́бморок, а *m.* fainting-fit; **в глубо́ком ~е** in a dead faint; **упа́сть в о.** to faint.

обморо́ч|ить, у, ишь *pf. of* ⇨**моро́чить**

о́бморо|чный *adj. of* ⇨**~к**; **~чное состоя́ние** (*med.*) syncope.

обмота́|ть, ю *pf.* (*of* ⇨**обма́тывать**) (+*a. and i. or a.* **вокру́г**+*g.*) to wind (round); **о. ше́ю ша́рфом, о. шарф вокру́г ше́и** to wind a scarf round one's neck.

обмота́|ться, юсь *pf.* (*of* ⇨**обма́тываться**) **1** (+*i.*) to wrap o.s. (in). **2** *pass. of* ⇨**~ть**

обмо́тк|а, и *f.* (*elec.*) winding.

обмо́т|ки, ок *no sg.* puttees, leg-wrappings.

обмо́т|очный *adj. of* **1** ⇨**~ка. 2** ⇨**~ки**

обмоч|и́ть, у́, ~ишь *pf.* (*of* ⇨**обма́чивать**) to wet; **о. посте́ль** (*coll.*) to wet the bed.

обмоч|и́ться, у́сь, ~ишься *pf.* (*of* ⇨**обма́чиваться**) to wet o.s. (*also coll.*).

обм|о́ю, о́ешь *see* ⇨**~ы́ть**

обмундирова́ни|е, я *nt.* **1** (*действие*) fitting out (with uniform). **2** (*комплект форменной одежды*) uniform.

обмундир|ова́ть, у́ю *pf.* (*of* ⇨**~о́вывать**) to fit out (with uniform).

обмундиро́в|ка, ки *f.* = **~а́ние**

обмундиро́в|очный *adj. of* ⇨**~ка**; **~очные де́ньги** uniform allowance.

обмундиро́выва|ть, ю *impf. of* ⇨**обмундирова́ть**

обмыва́ни|е, я *nt.* **1** bathing, washing. **2** (*coll.*) celebration, drinking party.

обмыва́|ть(ся), ю(сь) *impf. of* ⇨**обмы́ть(ся)**

обмы́л|ок, ка *m.* (*coll.*) remnant of a bar of soap.

обм|ы́ть, о́ю, о́ешь *pf.* (*of* ⇨**~ыва́ть**) **1** to bathe, wash; **о. ра́ну** to bathe a wound. **2** (*coll.*) (*отметить выпивкой*) to celebrate, drink to.

обм|ы́ться, о́юсь, о́ешься *pf.* (*of* ⇨**~ыва́ться**) to bathe, wash.

обмяк|а́ть, а́ю *impf.* (*of* ⇨**~нуть**) (*coll.*) to become soft; (*fig.*) to become flabby.

обмя́к|нуть, ну, нешь, *past* **~, ~ла** *pf. of* ⇨**~а́ть**

об|мя́ть, омну́, омнёшь *pf.* (*of* ⇨**~мина́ть**) to press down; (*ногами*) to trample down.

обнагле́|ть, ю, ешь *pf. of* ⇨**нагле́ть**

обнадёжива|ть, ю *impf. of* ⇨**обнадёжить**

обнадёж|ить, у, ишь *pf.* (*of* ⇨**~ивать**) to reassure.

обнаж|а́ть(ся), а́ю(сь) *impf. of* ⇨**~и́ть(ся)**

обнаже́ни|е, я *nt.* **1** baring, uncovering. **2** (*fig.*) revealing. **3** (*geol.*): **о. го́рной поро́ды** outcrop.

обнаж|ённый *p.p.p. of* ⇨**~и́ть** *and adj.* naked, bare; nude.

обнаж|и́ть, у́, и́шь *pf.* (*of* ⇨**~а́ть**) **1** to bare, uncover; **о. го́лову** to bare one's head; **о. шпа́гу** to draw the sword. **2** (*fig.*) (*раскрыть*) to lay bare, reveal.

обнаж|и́ться, у́сь, и́шься *pf.* (*of* ⇨**~а́ться**) **1** to bare o.s., uncover o.s. **2** (*fig.*) (*стать явным*) to be revealed.

обнаро́довани|е, я *nt.* publication, promulgation.

обнаро́д|овать, ую *pf. and impf.* (*liter.*) to publish, promulgate.

обнаруже́ни|е, я *nt.* **1** displaying, revealing. **2** discovery; detection.

обнару́жива|ть(ся), ю(сь) *impf. of* ⇨**обнару́жить(ся)**

обнару́ж|ить, у, ишь *pf.* (*of* ⇨**~ивать**) **1** (*показать*) to display, reveal; **о. свою́ ра́дость** to betray one's joy. **2** (*найти*) to discover; to detect.

обнару́ж|иться, усь, ишься *pf.* (*of* ⇨**~иваться**) **1** (*оказаться*) to be revealed; to come to light. **2** (*найтись*) to turn up, be found.

обна́шива|ть, ю *impf. of* ⇨**обноси́ть¹**

обнес|ти́¹, у́, ёшь, *past* **~, ~ла́** *pf.* (*of* ⇨**обноси́ть²**) (+*i.*) to enclose (with); **о. и́згородью** to fence (in); **о. пери́лами** to rail in, off.

обнес|ти́², у́, ёшь, *past* **~, ~ла́** *pf.* (*of* ⇨**обноси́ть³**) (+*i.*) to serve round; **~ли́ ли вы всех госте́й шампа́нским?** have you served all the guests with champagne?

обнес|ти́³, у́, ёшь, *past* **~, ~ла́** *pf.* (*of* ⇨**обноси́ть⁴**) (+*a. and i.*) to pass over, leave out (*in serving sth.*); **меня́ ~ли́ вино́м** I have not had (= *been offered*) wine.

обнима́|ть(ся), ю(сь) *impf. of* ⇨**обня́ть(ся)**

обни́мк|а, и *f. only in phr.* **в ~у** (*coll.*) in an embrace, embracing one another, with arms around each other.

обнища́л|ый (~, ~а) *adj.* impoverished; beggarly.

обнища́ни|е, я *nt.* impoverishment.

обнища́|ть, ю *pf. of* ⇨**нища́ть**

обнов|и́ть, лю́, и́шь *pf.* (*of* ⇨**~ля́ть**) **1** (*памятник*) to renovate; (*жизнь, душу*) to revitalize; (*горечь*) to renew; (*гардероб, репертуар*) to update; to replenish; **2**: **о. свои́ зна́ния** (*fig.*) to refresh one's knowledge; **о. свои́ си́лы** (*fig.*) to regather one's strength. **3** (*coll., fig.*) (*впервые употребить*) to christen; to use *or* wear for the first time.

обнов|и́ться, лю́сь, и́шься *pf.* (*of* ⇨**~ля́ться**) to revive, be restored.

обно́вк|а, и *f.* (*coll.*) new acquisition (*usu. item of clothing*).

обновле́ни|е, я *nt.* renovation; revitalization; renewal; replenishment; **вне́шнее о.** face-lift.

обновля́|ть(ся), ю(сь) *impf. of* ⇨**обнови́ть(ся)**

обно|си́ть¹, шу́, ~сишь *pf.* (*of* ⇨**обна́шивать**) (*coll.*) (*новые ботинки*) to wear in.

обно|си́ть²,³,⁴, шу́, ~сишь *impf. of* ⇨**обнести́¹,²,³**

обно|си́ться, шу́сь, ~сишься *pf.*

O

(*coll.*) **1** (*износить свою одежду*) to have worn out all one's clothes; to be out at elbow. **2** (*стать удобным*) to become worn in, become comfortable (*of new clothes*).

обно́с|ки, ков *pl.* (*sg.* **~ок, ~ка** *m.*) (*coll.*) old clothes.

обню́х|ать, аю *pf.* (*of* ⇒**~ивать**) to sniff (around).

обню́хива|ть, ю *impf. of* ⇒**обню́хать**

обн|я́ть, иму́, и́мешь, *past* **~я́л, ~яла́, ~я́ло** *pf.* (*of* ⇒**~има́ть**) to embrace; to clasp in one's arms; (*fig.*) to envelop; **он шёл, ~я́в её за та́лию** he was walking with his arm round her waist; **о. взгля́дом** to survey; **о. умо́м** (*fig.*) to comprehend, take in.

обн|я́ться, иму́сь, и́мешься, *past* **~я́лся́, ~яла́сь, ~яло́сь** *pf.* (*of* ⇒**~има́ться**) to embrace; to hug (one another).

обо *prep.* = **о**[1]

обо... *vbl. pref.* = **о...** *and* **об...**

обобра́|ть, оберу́, оберёшь, *past* **~л, ~ла́ ~ло** *pf.* (*of* ⇒**обира́ть**) (*coll.*) **1** (*собрать*) to pick, gather. **2** (*ограбить*) to rob; (*sl.*) to clean out.

обобра́ться, оберу́сь, оберёшься *pf.* (*coll.*; +*g.*): **не оберёшься** beyond count, innumerable.

обобщ|а́ть, а́ю *impf. of* ⇒**~и́ть**

обобще́ни|е, я *nt.* generalization.

обобществ|и́ть, лю́, и́шь *pf.* (*of* ⇒**~ля́ть**) to collectivize.

обобществле́ни|е, я *nt.* collectivization.

обобществля́|ть, ю *impf. of* ⇒**обобществи́ть**

обобщ|и́ть, у́, и́шь *pf.* (*of* ⇒**~а́ть**) to generalize (from).

обобь|ю́, ёшь *see* ⇒**оби́ть**

обовь|ю́(сь), ёшь(ся) *see* ⇒**обви́ть(ся)**

обогати́тельный *adj.* (*mining tech.*) concentrating; **о. аппара́т** ore separator.

обога|ти́ть, щу́, ти́шь *pf.* (*of* ⇒**~ща́ть**) **1** to enrich. **2** (*mining tech.*) to concentrate; **о. руду́** to concentrate ore, dress ore.

обога|ти́ться, щу́сь, ти́шься *pf.* (*of* ⇒**~ща́ться**) to become rich; (+*i.*) to enrich o.s. (with).

обогаща́|ть(ся), ю(сь) *impf. of* ⇒**обогати́ть(ся)**

обогаще́ни|е, я *nt.* enrichment.

обогна́|ть, обгоню́, обго́нишь, *past* **~л, ~ла́, ~ло** *pf.* (*of* ⇒**обгоня́ть**) to pass, overtake; (*fig.*) to outstrip, outdistance.

обогн|у́ть, у́, ёшь *pf.* (*of* ⇒**огиба́ть**) **1** (*обойти, объехать*) to round; to skirt. **2** (*сгибая, надеть*) to bend round; **о. о́бруч вокру́г бо́чки** to hoop a barrel.

обоготворе́ни|е, я *nt.* deification, idolization.

обоготвор|и́ть, ю́, и́шь *pf.* (*of* ⇒**~я́ть**) to deify, idolize.

обоготвор|я́ть, я́ю *impf. of* ⇒**~и́ть**

обогре́в, а *m.* (*tech.*) heating.

обогрева́ни|е, я *nt.* heating, warming.

обогрева́тел|ь, я *m.* (*tech.*) heater.

обогрева́|ть(ся), ю(сь) *impf. of* ⇒**обогре́ть(ся)**

обогре́|ть, ю, ешь *pf.* (*of* ⇒**~ва́ть**) (*помещение*) to heat; (*человека*) to warm.

обогре́|ться, юсь, ешься *pf.* (*of* ⇒**~ва́ться**) to warm o.s.; (*о помещении*) to warm up.

о́бод, а, *pl.* **~ья, ~ьев** *m.* (*колеса, решета*) rim; (*бочки*) hoop.

обод|о́к, ка́ *m.* thin rim, thin border.

ободо́|чный *adj. of* ⇒**~к; ~чная кишка́** (*anat.*) colon.

ободра́н|ец, ца *m.* (*coll.*) ragamuffin, ragged fellow.

обо́др|анный *p.p.p. of* ⇒**~а́ть** *and adj.* ragged.

ободра́ть, обдеру́, обдерёшь, *past* **ободра́л, ободрала́, ободра́ло** *pf.* (*of* ⇒**обдира́ть**) **1** (*стену, прутик*) to strip; (*убитого зверя*) to skin; (*coll.*) (*лицо, руку*) to scratch; **о. кору́ с де́рева** to bark a tree. **2** (*fig., coll.*) to fleece.

ободре́ни|е, я *nt.* encouragement, reassurance.

ободри́тел|ьный (~ен, ~ьна) *adj.* encouraging, reassuring.

ободр|и́ть, ю́, и́шь *pf.* (*of* ⇒**~я́ть**) to cheer up; to encourage, reassure.

ободр|и́ться, ю́сь, и́шься *pf.* (*of* ⇒**~я́ться**) to cheer up, take heart.

ободр|я́ть(ся), я́ю(сь) *impf. of* ⇒**~и́ть(ся)**

обо́его, обо́ему (*no nom. or a.*), *m. and nt. num.* both; **обо́его по́ла** of both sexes.

обожа́ни|е, я *nt.* adoration.

обожа́тел|ь, я *m.* (*coll.*) admirer.

обожа́тель|ница, ницы *f. of* ⇒**~**

обожа́|ть, ю *impf.* to adore, worship.

обож|гу́, жёшь, гу́т *see* ⇒**обже́чь**

обожд|а́ть, у́, ёшь, *past* **~а́л, ~ала́, ~а́ло** *pf.* (*coll.*) to wait (for a while).

обожеств|и́ть, лю́, и́шь *pf.* (*of* ⇒**~ля́ть**) to deify, worship.

обожествле́ни|е, я *nt.* deification, worshipping.

обожествля́|ть, ю *impf. of* ⇒**обожестви́ть**

обожжённый *p.p.p. of* ⇒**обже́чь**

обожр|а́ться, у́сь, ёшься, *past* **~а́лся, ~ала́сь** *pf.* (*of* ⇒**обжира́ться**) (*coll.*) to guzzle, stuff o.s.

обо́з, а *m.* **1** (*повозок*) convoy. **2** (*mil.*) (*unit*) transport; **быть в ~е** (*fig.*) to bring up the rear.

обозва́|ть, обзову́, обзовёшь, *past* **~л, ~ла́, ~ло** *pf.* (*of* ⇒**обзыва́ть**) (+*a. and i.*) to call; **о. кого́-н. дурако́м** to call s.o. a fool.

обозл|ённый *p.p.p. of* ⇒**~и́ть** *and adj.* embittered.

обозл|и́ть, ю́, и́шь *pf.* **1** *pf. of* ⇒**злить. 2** to embitter.

обозл|и́ться, ю́сь, и́шься *pf. of* ⇒**зли́ться**

обозна|ва́ться, ю́сь, ёшься *impf. of* ⇒**~́ться**

обозна́|ться, юсь, ешься *pf.* (*of* ⇒**~ва́ться**) (*coll.*) to take s.o. for s.o. else; to be mistaken.

обознач|а́ть, а́ю *impf.* **1** (*no pf.*) (*значить*) to mean. **2** (*pf.* **~́ить**) (*отмечать*) to mark; **о. на ка́рте грани́цу** to mark a frontier on a map. **3** (*pf.* **~́ить**) (*делать заметным*) to reveal; to emphasize.

обознач|а́ться, а́ется *impf.* (*of* ⇒**~́иться**) **1** to appear; to reveal itself. **2** *pass. of* ⇒**~а́ть** 2, 3

обозначе́ни|е, я *nt.* **1** (*действие*) marking. **2** (*знак*) sign, symbol; **усло́вные ~я** conventional signs (*on maps, etc.*).

обозна́ч|ить, у, ишь *pf. of* ⇒**~а́ть** 2, 3

обозна́ч|иться, ится *pf. of* ⇒**~а́ться**

обозрева́тел|ь, я *m.* commentator; columnist (*see* ⇒**обозре́ние**); **полити́ческий о.** political correspondent (*of newspaper*).

обозрева́|ть, ю *impf. of* ⇒**обозре́ть**

обозре́ни|е, я *nt.* **1** (*действие*) surveying, viewing; looking round. **2** (*обзор*) survey; overview. **3** (*theatr.*) revue.

обозр|е́ть, ю, и́шь *pf.* (*of* ⇒**~ева́ть**) **1** to survey, view; to look round. **2** (*fig.*) to survey, review.

обозри́м|ый (~, ~а) *adj.* visible; **в ~ом бу́дущем** in the foreseeable future.

обо́|и, ев *no sg.* wall-paper; **окле́ить ~ями** to paper.

обой|дённый *p.p.p. of* ⇒**~ти́**

обо́йм|а, ы, *g. pl.* **~** *f.* (*mil.*) cartridge clip.

обо́|йный *adj. of* ⇒**~и**

обо|йти́, йду́, йдёшь, *past* **~шёл, ~шла́** *pf.* (*of* ⇒**обходи́ть**[1]) **1** (*пройти, окружая, минуя*) to go round. **2** (*пройти по всему пространству чего-либо*) to make the round (of), go (all) round; (*о враче*) to make (go) one's round(s); **слух ~шёл весь го́род** the rumour (*Br.*), rumor (*US*) spread all over the town. **3** (*избежать*) to avoid; to leave out; to pass over; **о. молча́нием** to pass over in silence; **о. зако́н** to get round (evade) a law; **о. затрудне́ние** to get round a difficulty. **4** (*coll., pej.*) (*обмануть*) to con.

обо|йти́сь, йду́сь, йдёшься, *past* **~шёлся, ~шла́сь** *pf.* (*of* ⇒**обходи́ться**) **1** (**с**+*i.*) to treat; **пло́хо о. с кем-н.** to treat s.o. badly. **2** (*coll.*) to cost, come to; **во ско́лько ~шёлся ваш костю́м?** how much did your suit come to? **3** (+*i.*) to manage (with, on), make do (with, on); **о. миллио́ном рубле́й** to make do with one million roubles; **без ва́шей по́мощи мы бы не ~шли́сь** without your aid we could not have managed. **4** (*закончиться*) to turn out, end; **всё ~шло́сь** everything worked out; **всё ~шло́сь благополу́чно** everything turned out all right; **как-н. ~йдётся!**

things will turn out all right somehow!; things will sort themselves out!

обо́йщик, а *m.* upholsterer.

о́бок *adv. and prep.* +*g. or d.* (*coll.*) close by; near.

обокра́|сть, обкраду́, обкрадёшь, *past* **~л, ~ла** *pf.* (*of* ⇒**обкра́дывать**) to rob.

оболва́нива|ть, ю *impf. of* ⇒**оболва́нить**

оболва́н|ить, ю, ишь *pf.* (*of* ⇒**~ивать**) (*coll.*) to make a fool of.

обо|лга́ть, лгу́, лжёшь, *past* **~лга́л, ~лгала́, ~лга́ло** *pf.* to slander.

оболо́чк|а, и *f.* **1** (*скорлупа*) shell; (*tech.*) casing. **2** (*anat.*) membrane; **ра́дужная о.** iris; **рогова́я о.** cornea; **сли́зистая о.** mucous membrane.

обо́лтус, а *m.* (*coll.*) blockhead, dunce

обольсти́тел|ь, я *m.* (*obs.*) seducer.

обольсти́тельниц|а, ы *f.* (*obs.*) seductress.

обольсти́тел|ьный (~ен, ~ьна) *adj.* seductive, captivating.

оболь|сти́ть, щу́, сти́шь *pf.* (*of* ⇒**~ща́ть**) **1** (*увлечь*) to captivate. **2** (*соблазнить*) to seduce.

оболь|сти́ться, щу́сь, сти́шься *pf.* (*of* ⇒**~ща́ться**) to be *or* labour (*Br.*), labor (*US*) under a delusion; (+*i.*) to flatter o.s. (with).

обольща́|ть(ся), ю(сь) *impf. of* ⇒**обольсти́ть(ся)**

обольще́ни|е, я *nt.* **1** (*действие*) seduction. **2** (*соблазн*) delusion.

оболь|ю́, ёшь *see* ⇒**обли́ть**

обомле́|ть, ю, ешь *pf.* (*coll.*) to be stupefied.

обомн|у́, ёшь *see* ⇒**обмя́ть**

обомр|у́, ёшь *see* ⇒**обмере́ть**

обомше́л|ый (~, ~а) *adj.* moss-grown.

обоня́ни|е, я *nt.* (sense of) smell; **име́ть то́нкое о.** to have a fine sense of smell.

обоня́тельный *adj.* (*anat.*) olfactory.

обоня́|ть, ю *impf.* to smell.

обора́чиваемост|ь, и *f.* (*fin., econ.*) turnover.

обора́чива|ть(ся), ю(сь) *impf. of* ⇒**оберну́ть(ся)** *and* **обороти́ть(ся)**

оборва́н|ец, ца *m.* ragamuffin.

обо́рв|анный *p.p.p. of* ⇒**~а́ть** *and adj.* torn, ragged.

оборв|а́ть, у́, ёшь, *past* **~а́л, ~ала́, ~а́ло** *pf.* (*of* ⇒**обрыва́ть**) **1** (*цветы, яблоки*) to tear off, pluck. **2** (*нитку*) to break; to snap. **3** (*fig.*) (*разговор; человека*) to cut short, interrupt; (*дружбу*) to break off.

оборв|а́ться, у́сь, ёшься, *past* **~а́лся, ~ала́сь, ~а́ло́сь** *pf.* (*of* ⇒**обрыва́ться**) **1** (*о верёвке*) to break; to snap. **2** (*о человеке*) to fall; (*о вещах*) to come away. **3** (*о жизни, песне*) to be cut short, come abruptly to an end.

обо́рвыш, а *m.* (*coll.*) ragamuffin.

обо́рк|а, и *f.* frill, flounce.

оборо́н|а, ы *no pl., f.* **1** defence (*Br.*), defense (*US*). **2** (*mil.*) defences (*Br.*), defenses (*US*).

оборони́тельный *adj.* defensive.

оборон|и́ть, ю, и́шь *pf.* (*of* ⇒**~я́ть**) to defend.

оборон|и́ться, ю́сь, и́шься *pf.* (*of* ⇒**~я́ться**) (**от**+*g.*) to defend o.s. (from).

оборо́н|ный *adj. of* ⇒**~а; ~ная промы́шленность** defence (*Br.*), defense (*US*) industry.

обороноспосо́бност|ь, и *f.* defensive capability.

обороноспосо́б|ный (~ен, ~на) *adj.* prepared for defence (*Br.*), defense (*US*).

оборон|я́ть(ся), я́ю(сь) *impf. of* ⇒**~и́ть(ся)**

оборо́т, а *m.* **1** turn; (*tech.*) revolution, rotation; **приня́ть дурно́й о.** (*fig.*) to take a turn for the worse. **2** (*употребление*) circulation; (*fin., comm.*) turnover; **ввести́, пусти́ть в о.** to put into circulation. **3** (*обратная сторона*) back; **смотри́ на ~е** please turn over. **4** (*выражение*) turn (of speech); **о. ре́чи** phrase, locution.

о́оборот|ень, ня *m.* werewolf.

оборо́тист|ый (~, ~а) *adj.* (*coll.*) resourceful.

оборо|ти́ть, чу́, ~тишь *pf.* (*of* ⇒**обора́чивать**) (*coll.*) to turn.

оборо|ти́ться, чу́сь, ~тишься *pf.* (*of* ⇒**обора́чиваться**) (*coll.*) **1** to turn (round). **2** (**в**+*a. or* +*i.*) to turn (into).

оборо́тлив|ый (~, ~а) *adj.* (*coll.*) resourceful.

оборо́т|ный *adj. of* ⇒**~; о. капита́л** (*fin., comm.*) working capital; **~ная сторона́** verso; reverse side (*also fig.*); **э ~ное** *name of letter* **'э'.**

обору́довани|е, я *nt.* **1** (*действие*) equipping. **2** (*приборы*) equipment; **вспомога́тельное о.** (*comput.*) peripherals, add-ons.

обору́д|овать, ую *impf. and pf.* to equip, fit out.

обоснова́ни|е, я *nt.* **1** (*действие*) substantiation. **2** (*довод*) basis, ground.

обосно́ванност|ь, и *f.* well-founded nature.

обосно́в|анный *p.p.p. of* ⇒**~а́ть** *and adj.* well-founded, well-grounded.

обосн|ова́ть, у́ю, уёшь *pf.* (*of* ⇒**~о́вывать**) to substantiate.

обосн|ова́ться, у́юсь, уёшься *pf.* (*of* ⇒**~о́вываться**) to settle.

обосно́выва|ть(ся), ю(сь) *impf. of* ⇒**обоснова́ть(ся)**

обосо́б|ить, лю, ишь *pf.* (*of* ⇒**~ля́ть**) to isolate.

обосо́б|иться, люсь, ишься *pf.* (*of* ⇒**~ля́ться**) to stand apart, keep aloof.

обособле́ни|е, я *nt.* isolation.

обосо́бленно *adv.* apart; aloof; **жить о.** to live by o.s.

обосо́б|ленный *p.p.p. of* ⇒**~ить** *and adj.* isolated, solitary.

обособля́|ть(ся), ю(сь) *impf. of* ⇒**обосо́бить(ся)**

обостре́ни|е, я *nt.* **1** (*чувств*) sharpening, intensification. **2** (*боли*) aggravation, exacerbation; (*отношений*) straining; (*кризиса, конфликта*) worsening, deepening.

обостр|ённый *p.p.p. of* ⇒**~и́ть** *and adj.* **1** (*о чертах лица*) sharp, pointed. **2** (*об ощущениях*) of heightened sensitivity; **о. слух** a keen ear. **3** (*об отношениях*) strained, tense.

обостр|и́ть, ю́, и́шь *pf.* (*of* ⇒**~я́ть**) **1** (*слух, аппетит, ощущение*) to sharpen, intensify. **2** (*боль*) to aggravate, exacerbate; (*отношения*) to strain.

обостр|и́ться, и́тся *pf.* (*of* ⇒**~я́ться**) **1** (*о чертах лица*) to become sharp, become pointed. **2** (*об ощущениях*) to become more sensitive, become keener. **3** (*о боли*) to become aggravated, become exacerbated; (*об отношениях*) to become strained; (*о кризисе, конфликте*) to worsen, deepen.

обостр|я́ть(ся), я́ет(ся) *impf. of* ⇒**~и́ть(ся)**

оботр|у́, ёшь *see* ⇒**обтере́ть**

обо́чин|а, ы *f.* (*дороги*) edge, side; (*тротуара*) kerb (*Br.*), curb (*US*).

обою́дност|ь, и *f.* mutuality, reciprocity.

обою́д|ный (~ен, ~на) *adj.* mutual, reciprocal; **по ~ному согла́сию** by mutual consent.

обоюдоо́стрый *adj.* double-edged, two-edged (*also fig.*).

обраба́тыва|ть, ю *impf. of* ⇒**обрабо́тать**

обраба́тыва|ющий *pres. part. act. of* ⇒**~ть** *and adj.*; **~ющая промы́шленность** manufacturing industry.

обрабо́та|ть, ю *pf.* (*of* ⇒**обраба́тывать**) **1** (*кожу*) to treat, process; **о. зе́млю** to work the land; **о. ра́ну** to dress a wound. **2** (*статью; голос*) to polish, perfect. **3** (*fig., coll.*) (*человека*) to work upon, win round; to brainwash.

обрабо́тк|а, и *f.* **1** (*кожи*) treatment, processing; **о. земли́** cultivation of land. **2** (*статьи*) polishing. **3** (*fig., coll.*) (*человека*) winning round; brainwashing.

обра́д|овать(ся), ую(сь) *pf. of* ⇒**ра́довать(ся)**

о́браз¹, а *m.* **1** (*вид*) shape, form; appearance; **по ~у своему́ и подо́бию** (*rhet. or joc.*) in one's own image. **2** (*liter.*) image; **мы́слить ~ами** to think in images. **3** (*liter.*) (*тип*) type; figure; **о. Га́млета** the Hamlet type. **4** (*порядок*) mode, manner; way; **о. жи́зни** way of life, mode of life; **о. правле́ния** form of government; **каки́м ~ом?** how?; **таки́м ~ом** thus; **гла́вным ~ом** mainly, chiefly, largely; **ра́вным ~ом** equally.

о́браз², а, *pl.* **~а́** *m.* (*икона*) icon.

образ|е́ц, ца́ *nt.* **1** model, pattern (*also fig.*); **ста́вить в о.** to set up as a model. **2** (*товарный*) specimen, sample; (*материи*) pattern.

образи́н|а, ы *f.* (*coll., pej.*) ugly mug; (*как бранное слово*) scum.

о́бразност|ь, и *f.* picturesqueness; (*liter.*) figurativeness; imagery.

о́браз|ный (~ен, ~на) *adj.* picturesque, vivid; (*liter.*) figurative; employing images.

образова́ни|е[1]**, я** *nt.* (*действие*) formation; **о. слов** word-formation; **о. па́ра** (*tech.*) production of steam.

образова́ни|е[2]**, я** *nt.* (*обучение*) education.

образо́ванност|ь, и *f.* education (= *educated state*).

образо́в|анный *p.p.p. of* ⇒**~а́ть** *and adj.*; **о. челове́к** an educated person.

образова́тел|ьный (~ен, ~ьна) *adj.* educational.

образ|ова́ть[1]**, у́ю** *impf.* (*in pres. tense*) *and pf.* (*of* ⇒**~о́вывать**) to form; to make up.

образ|ова́ть[2]**, у́ю** *pf.* (*of* ⇒**~о́вывать**) (*obs.*) to educate.

образ|ова́ться, у́ется *pf.* (*of* ⇒**~о́вываться**) **1** to form; to arise. **2** (*coll.*) to turn out well; **не беспоко́йтесь, всё ~у́ется!** don't worry, everything will be all right!

образо́выва|ть(ся), ю *impf. of* ⇒**образова́ть(ся)**

образу́м|ить, лю, ишь *pf.* (*coll.*) to bring to reason, make listen to reason.

образу́м|иться, люсь, ишься *pf.* (*coll.*) to come to one's senses, see reason.

образцо́в|ый (~, ~а) *adj.* model; exemplary; **~ое поведе́ние** exemplary conduct; **~ое хозя́йство** model farm.

обра́зчик, а *m.* specimen, sample; (*материи*) pattern.

обра́м|ить, лю, ишь *pf.* (*of* ⇒**~ля́ть**) to frame.

обрамле́ни|е, я *nt.* **1** (*действие*) framing. **2** (*рамка*) frame; (*fig.*) setting.

обрамля́|ть, ю *impf. of* ⇒**обра́мить**

обраста́ни|е, я *nt.* **1** overgrowing. **2** (*fig.*) accumulation, acquisition.

обраст|а́ть, а́ю *impf. of* ⇒**~и́**

обраст|и́, у́, ёшь, *past* **обро́с, обросла́** *pf.* (*of* ⇒**~а́ть**) (+*i.*) **1** (*покрыться растительностью*) to become (be) overgrown (with); **о. гря́зью** (*coll.*) to be coated with mud. **2** (*fig.*) (*создать вокруг себя*) to become (be) surrounded (by); to acquire, accumulate; **он обро́с нену́жной ме́белью** he has surrounded himself with superfluous items of furniture.

обрати́мост|ь, и *f.* reversibility.

обрати́м|ый (~, ~а) *adj.* reversible.

обра|ти́ть, щу́, ти́шь *pf.* (*of* ⇒**~ща́ть**) to turn; (**в**+*a.*) to turn (into); **о. внима́ние (на**+*a.*) to pay attention (to), take notice (of); **о. чьё-н. внима́ние (на**+*a.*) to call, draw s.o.'s attention (to); **о. на себя́ внима́ние** to attract attention (to o.s.); **о. в бе́гство** to put to flight; **о. в свою́ ве́ру** to convert (to one's faith); **о. в шу́тку** to turn into a joke.

обра|ти́ться, щу́сь, ти́шься *pf.* (*of* ⇒**~ща́ться**) **1** to turn; **о. лицо́м к стене́** to turn (one's face) towards the wall; **о. в бе́гство** to take to flight. **2** (**к**+*d.*) to turn (to), appeal (to); to apply (to); to accost; **она́ не зна́ла, к кому́ о. за по́мощью** she did not know to whom to turn for help; **о. с призы́вом к кому́-н.** to appeal to s.o.; **о. к юри́сту** to take legal advice; **о. к славянове́дению** to take up Slavonic studies. **3** (**в**+*a.*) (*превратиться*) to turn (into), become; **о. в ци́ника** to become a cynic; **о. в слух** (*fig.*) to be all ears; to prick up one's ears. **4** (**в**+*a.*) (*relig.*) to be converted (to).

обра́тно *adv.* **1** back; **туда́ и о.** there and back; **пое́здка туда́ и о.** round trip; **взять о.** to take back; **идти́ о., е́хать о.** to go back; to return, retrace one's steps. **2** (*наоборот*) conversely; inversely; **о. пропорциона́льный** inversely proportional.

обра́тн|ый *adj.* **1** reverse; **~ая сторона́** reverse (side); **о. а́дрес** sender's address; **о. биле́т** return (*Br.*), round-trip (*US*) ticket; **о. путь** return journey; **на о. путь** on the way back; **име́ющий ~ую си́лу** (*leg.*) retroactive, retrospective; **о. уда́р** backfire; **~ая связь** (*elec.*) feed-back. **2** (*противоположный*) opposite; **в ~ую сто́рону** in the opposite direction. **3** (*math.*) inverse; **~ое отноше́ние** inverse ratio.

обраща́|ть, ю *impf. of* ⇒**обрати́ть**

обраща́|ться, юсь *impf.* **1** *impf. of* ⇒**обрати́ться. 2** (*physiol., econ., etc.*) to circulate. **3** (**с**+*i.*) to treat; **пло́хо о. с кем-н.** to treat s.o. badly, maltreat s.o. **4** (**с**+*i.*) (*пользоваться*) to handle, manage (*an inanimate object*); **он, по-ви́димому, не уме́ет о. с автома́том** apparently he does not know how to handle a sub-machine-gun; **«о. осторо́жно!»** 'handle with care!'

обраще́ни|е, я *nt.* **1** (**к**+*d.*) appeal (to), address (to). **2** (**в**+*a.*) conversion (to, into); **о. в ве́ру** conversion to faith. **3** (*econ.*) circulation; **изъя́ть из ~я** to withdraw from circulation; **пусти́ть в о.** to put in circulation. **4** (**с**+*i.*) treatment (of); **плохо́е о.** ill-treatment. **5** (**с**+*i.*) (*пользование*) handling (of), use (of).

обревиз|ова́ть, у́ю *pf. of* ⇒**ревизова́ть**

обре́з[1]**, а** *m.* edge; **в о.** (*coll.*; +*g.*) only just enough; **де́нег у меня́ в о.** I have not a penny to spare.

обре́з[2]**, а** *m.* sawn-off (*Br.*), sawed-off (*US*) shotgun.

обре́за́ни|е, я *nt.* (*relig.*) circumcision.

обреза́ни|е, я *nt.* (*волос*) clipping, trimming.

обре́|зать, жу, жешь *pf.* (*of* ⇒**~зывать** *and* **~за́ть**) **1** (*ногти*) to clip, trim; **о. кому́-н. кры́лья** (*fig.*) to clip s.o.'s wings. **2** (*поранить*) to cut; **о. себе́ па́лец** to cut one's finger. **3** (*relig.*) to circumcise. **4** (*coll.*) (*прервать*) to cut short.

обрез|а́ть, а́ю *impf. of* ⇒**~́ать**

обре́|заться, жусь, жешься *pf.* (*of* ⇒**~за́ться** *and* **~зываться**) (*поранить себя*) to cut o.s.

обрез|а́ться, а́юсь *impf. of* ⇒**~́аться**

обрезно́й *adj.* (*tech.*) trimming.

обре́з|ок, ка *m.* scrap; (*pl.*) ends; clippings.

обре́зыва|ть(ся), ю(сь) *impf. of* ⇒**обре́зать(ся)**

обрека́|ть, ю *impf. of* ⇒**обре́чь**

обре|ку́, чёшь, ку́т *see* ⇒**~́чь**

обремени́тел|ьный (~ен, ~ьна) *adj.* burdensome, onerous.

обремен|и́ть, ю́, и́шь *pf.* (*of* ⇒**~я́ть**) to burden.

обремен|я́ть, я́ю *impf. of* ⇒**~и́ть**

обре|сти́, ту́, тёшь (*arch.* **обря́щу, обря́щешь**) *past* **~́л, ~ла́** *pf.* (*of* ⇒**~та́ть**) (*rhet.*) to find.

обрета́|ть, ю *impf. of* ⇒**обрести́**

обрета́|ться, юсь *impf.* (*obs., coll.*) to be; to pass one's time.

обрече́ни|е, я *nt.* doom.

обречённост|ь, и *f.* being doomed; **чу́вство ~и** feeling of doom.

обреч|ённый *p.p.p. of* ⇒**~́ь** *and adj.* doomed.

обре́|чь, ку́, чёшь, ку́т, *past* **~́к, ~кла́** *pf.* (*of* ⇒**~ка́ть**) (**на**+*a.*) to condemn, doom (to).

обрис|ова́ть, у́ю *pf.* (*of* ⇒**~о́вывать**) to outline, delineate, depict (*also fig.*).

обрис|ова́ться, у́ется *pf.* (*of* ⇒**~о́вываться**) to appear (in outline); to take shape.

обрисо́вк|а, и *f.* outlining, delineation, depicting.

обрисо́выва|ть(ся), ю, ет(ся) *impf. of* ⇒**обрисова́ть(ся)**

обри́т|ый *p.p.p. of* ⇒**~ь** *and adj.* shaven.

обр|и́ть, е́ю, е́ешь *pf.* (*голову*) to shave; (*усы*) to shave off.

обр|и́ться, е́юсь, е́ешься *pf.* to shave one's head.

обро́к, а *m.* (*hist.*) quit-rent.

оброн|и́ть, ю́, ~́ишь *pf.* **1** (*ключ*) to drop (*sc. and lose*). **2** (*замечание*) to let drop, let fall.

обруб|а́ть, а́ю *impf. of* ⇒**~и́ть**

обруб|и́ть[1]**, лю́, ~́ишь** *pf.* (*of* ⇒**~а́ть**) (*сук*) to chop off; (*хвост*) to dock.

обруб|и́ть[2]**, лю́, ~́ишь** *pf.* (*of* ⇒**~а́ть**) (*платок*) to hem.

обру́б|ок, ка *m.* stump.

обруга́|ть, ю *pf. of* ⇒**руга́ть**

обрусе́л|ый (~, ~а) *adj.* Russified, Russianized.

обрусе́ни|е, я *nt.* Russification, Russianization.

обрусе́|ть, ю *pf.* to become Russified, become Russianized.

обруси́|ть, шь *pf.* to Russify, Russianize.

о́бруч, а, *pl.* **~и, ~е́й** *m.* (*на бочке*; *гимнастический*) hoop; (*для волос*) hairband.

обруча́льн|ый *adj.*: **~ое кольцо́** wedding ring; **о. обря́д** betrothal.

обруч|áть(ся), áю(сь) *impf. of* **⇒~и́ть(ся)**

обручéни|е, я *nt.* betrothal.

обруч|и́ть, ý, и́шь *pf.* (*of* **⇒~áть**) to betroth.

обруч|и́ться, ýсь, и́шься *pf.* (*of* **⇒~áться**) (**с**+*i.*) to become engaged (to).

обрýшива|ть(ся), ю(сь) *impf. of* **⇒обрýшить(ся)**

обрýш|ить, у, ишь *pf.* (*of* **⇒~ивать**) to bring down, rain down.

обрýш|иться, усь, ишься *pf.* (*of* **⇒~иваться**) **1** (*о здании, крыше*) to come down, collapse, cave in. **2** (*fig.*) (**на**+*a.*) to come down (upon), fall (upon).

обры́в, а *m.* **1** precipice. **2** (*tech.*) break, rupture.

обрывá|ть(ся), ю(сь) *impf. of* **⇒оборвáть(ся)**

обры́вист|ый (~, ~а) *adj.* steep, precipitous.

обры́в|ок, ка *m.* (*бумаги*; *разговора*) scrap; (*верёвки*) piece; (*песни, мелодии*) snatch.

обры́воч|ный (~ен, ~на) *adj.* disjointed, fragmentary.

обры́зг|ать, аю *pf.* (*of* **⇒~ивать**) (+*i.*) (*водой*) to besprinkle (with); (*грязью*) to splash; to bespatter (with).

обры́згива|ть, ю *impf. of* **⇒обры́згать**

обры́ска|ть, ю *pf.* (*coll.*) to go through, hunt through.

обрю́згл|ый (~, ~а) *adj.* flabby, flaccid.

обрю́зг|нуть, ну, нешь, *past* **~, ~ла** *pf.* to become flabby, become flaccid.

обрю́зг|ший = **~лый**

обря́д, а *m.* rite, ceremony.

обря|ди́ть, жý, ~́дишь *pf.* (*of* **⇒~жáть**) (*coll., joc.*) (+*i.*) to get up (in).

обря|ди́ться, жýсь, ~́ди́шься *pf.* (*of* **⇒~жáться**) (*coll., joc.*) (+*i.*) to get o.s. up (in).

обря́дност|ь, и *f.* (*collect.*) rites, ritual, ceremonial.

обря́довый *adj.* ritual, ceremonial.

обряжá|ть(ся), ю(сь) *impf. of* **⇒обряди́ть(ся)**

обса|ди́ть, жý, ~́дишь *pf.* (*of* **⇒~́живать**) to plant round; **о. клáдбище ти́сами** to surround a cemetery with yew-trees.

обсáжива|ть, ю *impf. of* **⇒обсади́ть**

обсáсыва|ть, ю *impf. of* **⇒обсосáть**

обсемен|и́ть, ю́, и́шь *pf.* (*of* **⇒~я́ть**) (*agric.*) to sow (*a field*).

обсемен|и́ться, и́тся *pf.* (*of* **⇒~я́ться**) (*bot.*) to go to seed.

обсемен|я́ть(ся), я́ю, я́ет(ся) *impf. of* **⇒~и́ть(ся)**

обсерватóри|я, и *f.* observatory.

обска|кáть, чý, ~́чешь *pf.* (*of* **⇒~́кивать**) **1** (*проскакать вокруг*) to gallop round. **2** (*скача, обогнать*) to outgallop; (*fig., coll.*) to outdo, get the better of.

обскáкива|ть, ю *impf. of* **⇒обскакáть**

обскурáнт, а *m.* obscurant, obscurantist.

обскуранти́зм, а *m.* obscurantism.

обскуранти́стский *adj.* obscurantist.

обслéдовани|е, я *nt.* (+*g.*) (*осмотр*) inspection (of); (*исследование*) investigation (of); (*в больнице*) observation, tests.

обслéдовател|ь, я *m.* inspector, investigator.

обслéд|овать, ую *impf. and pf.* (*произвести осмотр*) to inspect; (*исследовать*) to investigate; **о. больнóго** to examine a patient.

обслýживани|е, я *nt.* service; (*tech.*) servicing, maintenance; **бытовóе о.** consumer service; **медици́нское о.** health service.

обслýжива|ть, ю *impf. of* **⇒обслужи́ть; о. станóк** to mind a machine; (*naut.*): **о. орýдия** to man the guns; **~ющий персонáл** ancillary staff.

обслуж|и́ть, ý, ~́ишь *pf.* (*of* **⇒~́ивать**) to serve; **о. потреби́теля** to serve a customer.

обслюн|и́ть, ю́, и́шь *pf.* (*coll.*) to slobber all over.

обсос|áть, ý, ёшь *pf.* (*of* **⇒обсáсывать**) **1** (*леденец*) to suck round. **2** (*fig., coll.*) to chew over.

обсóх|нуть, ну, нешь, *past* **~, ~ла** *pf.* (*of* **⇒обсыхáть**) to dry (off); **у негó молокó на губáх не ~ло** (*fig.*) he is still green.

обстáв|ить, лю, ишь *pf.* (*of* **⇒~ля́ть**) **1** (+*i.*) (*поставить что-либо вокруг*) to surround (with), encircle (with). **2** (+*i.*) (*меблировать*) to furnish (with). **3** (*fig.*) (*устроить*) to arrange; to organize. **4** (*coll.*) (*обогнать*) to get the better (of); (*обмануть*) to cheat.

обставля́|ть, ю *impf. of* **⇒обстáвить**

обстанóвк|а, и *f.* **1** (*квартиры*) furniture; décor. **2** (*theatr.*) set. **3** (*положение*) situation. **4** (*атмосфера*) atmosphere, environment.

обстир|áть, áю *pf.* (*of* **⇒~́ывать**) (*coll.*) to do all the washing for.

обсти́рыва|ть, ю *impf. of* **⇒обстирáть**

обстоя́тел|ьный (~ен, ~ьна) *adj.* **1** thorough, detailed. **2** (*coll.*) (*человек*) thorough, reliable.

обстоя́тельств|о¹, а *nt.* circumstance; **по незави́сящим от меня́ ~ам** for reasons beyond my control; **по семéйным ~ам** due to family circumstances; **ни при каки́х ~ах** in no circumstances; **смотря́ по ~ам** depending on the circumstances.

обстоя́тельств|о², а *nt.* (*gram.*) adverbial modifier.

обсто|я́ть, и́т *impf.* to be; to get on; **как ~и́т дéло?** how is it going?; **как ~я́т вáши делá?** how are you getting on?; **всё ~и́т благополýчно** all is well; everything is going all right; **вот как ~и́т дéло** that is the way it is; that's how matters stand.

обстрáгива|ть, ю *impf. of* **⇒обстрогáть**

обстрáива|ть(ся), ю(сь) *impf. of* **⇒обстрóить(ся)**

обстрéл, а *m.* firing, fire; **артиллери́йский о.** bombardment, shelling; **попáсть под о.** to come under fire.

обстрéлива|ть, ю *impf. of* **⇒обстреля́ть**

обстрéл|янный *p.p.p. of* **⇒~я́ть** *and adj.* seasoned, battle-hardened (*also fig.*); **~янная пти́ца** (*coll.*) old hand.

обстрел|я́ть, я́ю *pf.* (*of* **⇒~́ивать**) to fire (at, on); to bombard.

обстрогá|ть, ю *pf.* (*of* **⇒обстрáгивать**) to plane.

обстрó|ить, ю, ишь *pf.* (*of* **⇒обстрáивать**) to build (up)

обстрó|иться, юсь, ишься *pf.* (*of* **⇒обстрáиваться**) (*coll.*) **1** (*застроиться*) to be built (up). **2** (*выстроить для себя здания*) to build for o.s.

обстругá|ть, ю *pf.* = **обстрогáть**

обструкциони́зм, а *m.* (*pol.*) obstructionism.

обструкциони́ст, а *m.* (*pol.*) obstructionist.

обстрýкци|я, и *f.* (*pol.*) obstruction; filibustering.

обступ|áть, áю *impf. of* **⇒~и́ть**

обступ|и́ть, лю́, ~́ишь *pf.* (*of* **⇒~áть**) to surround; to cluster (round).

обсу|ди́ть, жý, ~́дишь *pf.* (*of* **⇒~ждáть**) to discuss; to consider.

обсуждá|ть, ю *impf. of* **⇒обсуди́ть**

обсуждéни|е, я *nt.* discussion.

обсýшива|ть(ся), ю(сь) *impf. of* **⇒обсуши́ть(ся)**

обсуш|и́ть, ý, ~ишь *pf.* (*of* **⇒~́ивать**) to dry (out).

обсуш|и́ться, ýсь, ~ишься *pf.* (*of* **⇒~́иваться**) to dry o.s., get dry.

обсчит|áть, áю *pf.* (*of* **⇒~́ывать**) to shortchange.

обсчит|áться, áюсь *pf.* (*of* **⇒~́ываться**) to make a mistake (*in counting*); **вы ~áлись на ты́сячу рублéй** you were a thousand roubles out (*Br.*), off (*US*).

обсчи́тыва|ть(ся), ю(сь) *impf. of* **⇒обсчитáть(ся)**

обсы́п|ать, лю, лешь *pf.* (*of* **⇒~áть**) (+*a. and i.*) to strew (with); to sprinkle (with).

обсып|áть, áю *impf. of* **⇒~́ать**

обсы́п|аться, люсь, лешься *pf.* = **осы́паться**

обсыхá|ть, ю *impf. of* **⇒обсóхнуть**

обтáива|ть, ет *impf. of* **⇒обтáять**

обтáчива|ть, ю *impf. of* **⇒обточи́ть**

обтá|ять, ет *pf.* (*of* **⇒~ивать**) **1** (*льдина*) to melt away. **2** (*дорога*) to become clear (*of ice*).

обтекáем|ый (~, ~а) *adj.* **1** (*tech.*) streamlined. **2** (*fig., coll.*) evasive.

обтека́|ть, ю *impf. of* ⇒**обте́чь**

обтер|е́ть, оботру́, оботрёшь, *past* ~̈, ~**ла** *pf.* (*of* ⇒**обтира́ть**) **1** (*высушить*) to wipe; to wipe dry. **2** (+*i.*) (*натереть*) to rub all over (with).

обтер|е́ться, оботру́сь, оботрёшься, *past* ~̈**ся,** ~**лась** *pf.* (*of* ⇒**обтира́ться**) **1** (*обтереть себя*) to wipe o.s. dry, dry o.s. **2** (*водой*) to sponge down. **3** (*coll.*) (*стать потёртым*) to wear thin.

обтерп|е́ться, лю́сь, ~́**ишься** *pf.* (*coll.*) to become acclimatized, become accustomed.

обтёс|анный *p.p.p. of* ⇒~**а́ть; гру́бо о.** rough-finished.

обте|са́ть, шу́, ~́**шешь** *pf.* (*of* ⇒~̈**сывать**) **1** (*бревно*) to trim. **2** (*fig., coll.*) (*человека*) to teach manners (to), lick into shape.

обте|са́ться, шу́сь, ~́**шешься** *pf.* (*of* ⇒~̈**сываться**) (*coll.*) to acquire (*polite*) manners, acquire polish.

обтёсыва|ть(ся), ю(сь) *impf. of* ⇒**обтеса́ть(ся)**

обте́|чь, ку́, чёшь, ку́т, *past* ~̈**к,** ~**кла́** *pf.* (*of* ⇒~**ка́ть**) **1** to flow round. **2** (*mil.*) to by-pass.

обтира́ни|е, я *nt.* **1** sponge-down. **2** (*coll.*) (*жидкость*) lotion.

обтира́|ть(ся), ю(сь) *impf. of* ⇒**обтере́ть(ся)**

обточ|и́ть, у́, ~́**ишь** *pf.* (*of* ⇒**обта́чивать**) to grind smooth; (*на станке*) to turn.

обто́чк|а, и *f.* smoothing; (*на станке*) turning.

обтрёп|анный *p.p.p. of* ⇒~**а́ть** *and adj.* **1** (*одежда*) frayed. **2** (*человек*) shabby.

обтреп|а́ть, лю́, ~́**лешь** *pf.* to fray.

обтреп|а́ться, лю́сь, ~́**лешься** *pf.* to become frayed, fray.

обтя́гива|ть, ю *impf. of* ⇒**обтяну́ть**

обтя́гивающий *adj.* skin-tight, figure-hugging.

обтя́жк|а, и *f.* **1** cover. **2**: **пла́тье в** ~**у** close-fitting dress.

обтя|ну́ть, ну́, ~́**нешь** *pf.* (*of* ⇒~́**гивать**) **1** (+*i.*) (*мебель*) to cover (with). **2** (*фигуру*) to fit close (to).

обува́|ть(ся), ю(сь) *impf. of* ⇒**обу́ть(ся)**

обу́вк|а, и *f.* (*coll.*) shoes.

обувн|о́й *adj. of* ⇒**о́бувь; о. магази́н** shoe shop; ~**а́я промы́шленность** boot and shoe industry.

о́був|ь, и *no pl., f.* footwear; shoes.

обу́гливани|е, я *nt.* carbonization.

обу́глива|ть(ся), ю, ет(ся) *impf. of* ⇒**обу́глить(ся)**

обу́гл|ить, ю, ишь *pf.* (*of* ⇒~**ивать**) to char; to carbonize.

обу́гл|иться, ится *pf.* (*of* ⇒~**иваться**) to become charred, char.

обу́жива|ть, ю *impf. of* ⇒**обу́зить**

обу́з|а, ы *f.* burden; **быть** ~**ой для кого́-н.** to be a burden to s.o.

обузд|а́ть, а́ю *pf.* (*of* ⇒~́**ывать**) (*лошадь*) to bridle; (*fig.*) to restrain, control; **о. свой хара́ктер** to restrain o.s.; **о. свои́ стра́сти** to curb one's passions.

обу́здыва|ть, ю *impf. of* ⇒**обузда́ть**

обу́|зить, жу, зишь *pf.* (*of* ⇒~**живать**) to make too tight.

обурева́|ть, ет *impf.* to grip; **его́** ~**ют сомне́ния** he is a prey to doubts.

обусло́в|ить, лю, ишь *pf.* (*of* ⇒~**ливать**) **1** (+*i.*) to make conditional (upon); **он** ~**ил своё согла́сие предоставле́нием маши́ны** he made his consent conditional upon the provision of a car. **2** (*явиться причиной*) to cause, bring about.

обусло́в|иться, люсь, ишься *pf.* (*of* ⇒~**ливаться**)

обусло́влива|ть, ю *impf. of* ⇒**обусло́вить**

обусло́влива|ться, юсь *impf.* (*of* ⇒**обусло́виться**) (+*i.*) to be conditional (upon); to depend (on); **разме́р** ~**ется тре́бованиями** the size is conditioned by the requirements.

обу́т|ый *p.p.p. of* ⇒~**ь; оде́тый и о.** clothed and shod.

обу́|ть, ю, ешь *pf.* (*of* ⇒~**ва́ть**) **1**: **о. кого́-н.** to put on s.o.'s boots (shoes) for him. **2** (*coll.*) (*снабдить обувью*) to provide with boots *or* shoes. **3** (*сапоги*) to put on.

обу́|ться, юсь, ешься *pf.* (*of* ⇒~**ва́ться**) **1** (*надеть обувь*) to put on one's boots, shoes. **2** (*снабдить себя обувью*) to provide o.s. with boots *or* shoes.

о́бух, а (*and* **обу́х, а́**) *m.* butt (*of an axe*); **меня́ то́чно** ~**ом по голове́** (*coll.*) you could have knocked me down with a feather.

обуч|а́ть(ся), а́ю(сь) *impf. of* ⇒~**и́ть(ся)**

обуче́ни|е, я *nt.* teaching; instruction, training; **совме́стное о.** (**лиц обо́его по́ла**) co-education; **о. по ме́сту рабо́ты** on-the-job *or* in-service training.

обуч|и́ть, у́, ~́**ишь** *pf.* (*of* ⇒**учи́ть** *and* ~**а́ть**) (**кого́-н. чему́-н.**) to teach (s.o. sth.); to instruct, train (s.o. in).

обуч|и́ться, у́сь, ~́**ишься** *pf.* (*of* ⇒**учи́ться** *and* ~**а́ться**) (+*d. or* +*inf.*) to learn.

обуя́|ть, ет *pf.* to seize; to grip; **его́** ~**л страх** fear had seized him.

обха́жива|ть, ю *impf.* (*coll.*) to cajole, try to get round.

обхва́т, а *m.* circumference, girth; **в** ~**е** in circumference.

обхва|ти́ть, чу́, ~́**тишь** *pf.* (*of* ⇒~́**тывать**) to encompass (with outstretched arms); to clasp.

обхва́тыва|ть, ю *impf. of* ⇒**обхвати́ть**

обхо́д, а *m.* **1** (*врача, почтальона*) round; (*милиционера*) beat; **пойти́ в о.** to make one's round(s). **2** (*кружный путь*) roundabout way; by-pass. **3** (*mil.*) turning movement. **4** (*уклонение*) evasion, circumvention (*of law, etc.*); **в о.** (+*g.*) round, bypassing; (*минуя*) evading.

обходи́тел|ьный (~**ен,** ~**ьна**) *adj.* courteous; well-mannered.

обхо|ди́ть[1], жу́, ~́**дишь** *impf. of* ⇒**обойти́**

обхо|ди́ть[2], жу́, ~́**дишь** *pf.* (*город, друзей*) to go all round.

обхо|ди́ться, жу́сь, ~́**дишься** *impf. of* ⇒**обойти́сь**

обхо́дн|ый *adj.* roundabout, circuitous; **о. путь** detour; ~**ым путём** in a roundabout way; ~**ое движе́ние** (*mil.*) turning movement.

обхо́дчик, а *m.* (*rail.*) trackman.

обхожде́ни|е, я *nt.* manners; (**с**+*i.*) treatment (of), behaviour (towards).

обче́сться, обочту́сь, обочтёшься, *past* **обчёлся, обочла́сь** *pf.* (*coll.*) = **обсчита́ться; (их) раз, два и обчёлся** (they) can be counted on the fingers of one hand.

обчи́|стить, щу, стишь *pf.* (*of* ⇒~**ща́ть**) **1** to clean; to brush. **2** (*fig., coll.*) (*обокрасть*) to clean out.

обчи́|ститься, щусь, стишься *pf.* (*of* ⇒~**ща́ться**) to clean o.s.; to brush o.s.

обчища́|ть(ся), ю(сь) *impf. of* ⇒**обчи́стить(ся)**

обша́рива|ть, ю *impf. of* ⇒**обша́рить**

обша́р|ить, ю, ишь *pf.* (*of* ⇒~**ивать**) to ransack.

обша́рпанный *adj.* dilapidated, run-down.

обшива́|ть, ю *impf. of* ⇒**обши́ть[1,2]**

обши́вк|а, и *f.* **1** (*воротника*) trim. **2** (*корабля*) plating. **3** (*дома*) cladding; (*стен*) panelling (*Br.*), paneling (*US*).

обши́в|очный *adj. of* ⇒~**ка**

обши́р|ный (~**ен,** ~**на**) *adj.* extensive (*also fig.*); (*комната*) spacious; (*пространство*) vast; **у него́** ~**ное знако́мство** he has a very wide circle of acquaintance.

об|ши́ть[1], ошью́, ошьёшь *pf.* (*of* ⇒~**шива́ть**) **1** (*одежду*) to edge, trim. **2** (*посылку*) to sew round. **3** (*корабль*) to plate; (*дом*) to clad; (*стены*) to panel.

об|ши́ть[2], ошью́, ошьёшь *pf.* (*of* ⇒~**шива́ть**) (*человека*) to make clothes for; **она́ сама́** ~**ши́ла всю семью́** she has made all the family's clothes herself.

обшла́г, а́, *pl.* ~**а́** *m.* cuff.

обща́г|а, и *f.* (*coll.*) = **общежи́тие 1**

обща́|ться, юсь *impf.* (**с**+*i.*) to associate (with), mix (with).

общевойсково́|й *adj.* (*mil.*) common to all arms; ~**е кома́ндование** combined command.

общедосту́п|ный (~**ен,** ~**на**) *adj.* **1** available to all. **2** (*цены*) moderate. **3** (*книга, лекция*) accessible, popular.

общежите́йский *adj.* everyday, ordinary.

общежи́ти|е, я *nt.* **1** (*рабочее*) hostel; (*студенческое*) hall of residence (*Br.*), dormitory (*US*). **2** (*общественный быт*) communal life; (*повседневная жизнь*) everyday life.

общеизвéст|ный (~ен, ~на) *adj.* well-known, generally known; (*преступник*) notorious.

общенарóд|ный (~ен, ~на) *adj.* national; public; **о. прáздник** public holiday.

общéни|е, я *nt.* relations, links; **ли́чное о.** personal contact.

общеобразовáтельны|й *adj.* of general education; **~е предмéты** general subjects.

общепоня́т|ный (~ен, ~на) *adj.* comprehensible to all.

общепри́знан|ный (~, ~а) *adj.* universally recognized.

общепри́нят|ый (~, ~а) *adj.* generally accepted.

общераспространённый *adj.* in general use, generally found.

общесою́зный *adj.* (*hist.*) All-Union (*in former USSR, common to or valid for the entire Union*).

общéственник, а *m.* social activist; person actively engaging in public life.

общéственни|ца, цы *f. of* ⇒**~к**

общéственност|ь, и *f.* (*collect.*) (the) public, the community; **англи́йская о.** the British public; **нау́чная о.** the scientific community.

общéственн|ый *adj.* **1** social, public; **~ая жизнь** public life; **~ое мнéние** public opinion; **~ые нау́ки** social sciences; **~ое питáние** public catering; **~ая сóбственность** public property, public ownership. **2** (*добровольный*) voluntary, unpaid; **на ~ых начáлах** on a voluntary basis; **~ые организáции** voluntary organizations.

óбществ|о, а *nt.* **1** society. **2** (*компания*) company; **в ~е когó-н.** in s.o.'s company; **попáсть в дурнóе о.** to fall into bad company.

обществовéдени|е, я *nt.* social science.

обществовéд|ческий *adj. of* ⇒**~ение**

общеупотреби́тел|ьный (~ен, ~ьна) *adj.* in general use.

общечеловéческий *adj.* common to all mankind.

óбщ|ий *adj.* general; common; **~ие вéщи** communal possessions; **о. враг** common enemy; **~ее дéло** common cause; **о. знакóмый** mutual acquaintance; **~ее мéсто** commonplace; **~ая рабóта** communal work; **~ее собрáние** general meeting; **~ее соглáсие** common consent; **~ая су́мма** sum total; **наибóльший о. дели́тель** (*math.*) the greatest common divisor; **наимéньшее ~ее крáтное** (*math.*) the least common multiple; **в ~ем** on the whole, in general; **не имéть ничегó ~его (с+*i.*)** to have nothing in common (with).

óбщи́н|а, ы *f.* (*общество*) community; (*коммуна*) commune.

общи́нн|ый *adj.* communal; **~ая землá** common (land).

общип|áть, лю́, ~лешь *pf.* (*of* ⇒**щипáть** 4 *and* **~ывать**) to pluck.

общи́пыва|ть, ю *impf. of* ⇒**общипáть**

общи́тельност|ь, и *f.* sociability.

общи́тел|ьный (~ен, ~ьна) *adj.* sociable.

óбщност|ь, и *f.* commonality; **о. интерéсов** commonality of interests.

объ... *vbl. pref.* = **о...** *and* **об...**

объегóрива|ть, ю *impf. of* ⇒**объегóрить**

объегóр|ить, ю, ишь, *pf.* (*of* ⇒**~ивать**) (*coll.*) to cheat, swindle.

объедá|ть(ся), ю(сь) *impf. of* ⇒**объéсть(ся)**

объедéни|е, я *nt.* **1** (*obs.*) (*обжорство*) overeating. **2** (*coll.*) sth. delicious; **тóрты э́ти — пря́мо о.** these cakes are simply delicious.

объединéни|е, я *nt.* **1** (*действие*) unification; amalgamation. **2** (*союз*) union, association.

объедин|ённый *p.p.p. of* ⇒**~и́ть** *and adj.* united; **Организáция Объединённых Нáций** United Nations (Organization).

объедини́тельный *adj.* unifying, uniting.

объедин|и́ть, ю́, и́шь *pf.* (*of* ⇒**~я́ть**) (*людей*) to unite; (*организации*) to amalgamate; **о. ресу́рсы** to pool resources; **о. уси́лия** to combine efforts.

объедин|и́ться, ю́сь, и́шься *pf.* (*of* ⇒**~я́ться**) **(с+*i.*)** to unite (with); amalgamate (with).

объедин|я́ть(ся), я́ю(сь) *impf. of* ⇒**~и́ть(ся)**

объéд|ки, ков *pl.* (*sg.* **~ок, ~ка** *m.*) (*coll.*) leftovers, scraps.

объéзд, а *m.* **1** (*действие*) travelling (*Br.*), traveling (*US*) round, riding round, going round. **2** (*место*) detour, diversion (*Br.*); **поéхать в о.** to make a detour.

объéз|дить[1], жу, дишь *pf.* (*of* ⇒**~жáть[1]**) (*страну*) to travel all over; (*друзей*) to go round visiting.

объéз|дить[2], жу, дишь *pf.* (*of* ⇒**~жáть[2]**) (*лошадей*) to break in.

объéздк|а, и *f.* (*лошадей*) breaking in.

объéздчик[1], а *m.* mounted patrol; **леснóй о.** forest warden.

объéздчик[2], а *m.* (*лошадей*) horse-breaker.

объезжá|ть[1], ю *impf. of* ⇒**объéздить[1]** *and* **объéхать**

объезжá|ть[2], ю *impf. of* ⇒**объéздить[2]**

объéзжий *adj.* roundabout, circuitous; **о. путь** detour.

объéкт, а *m.* **1** object. **2** (*mil.*) objective. **3** (*предприятие*) establishment; **строи́тельный о.** building site.

объекти́в, а *m.* (*opt.*) lens.

объекти́вност|ь, и *f.* objectivity.

объекти́в|ный (~ен, ~на) *adj.* objective.

объéкт|ный *adj. of* ⇒**~** 1

объéкт|овый *adj. of* ⇒**~** 3

объём, а *m.* volume (*also fig.*); (*величина*) size.

объёмист|ый (~, ~а) *adj.* (*coll.*) voluminous, bulky.

объём|ный (~ен, ~на) *adj.* **1** by volume, volumetric; (*изображение*) three-dimensional. **2** (*большой по объёму*) voluminous, bulky.

объé|сть, м, шь, ст, ди́м, ди́те, дя́т, *past* **~л** *pf.* (*of* ⇒**~дáть**) **1** to eat round; to nibble. **2** (*coll.*): **о. когó-н.** to eat s.o. out of house and home.

объé|сться, мся, шься, стся, ди́мся, ди́тесь, дя́тся, *past* **~лся** *pf.* (*of* ⇒**~дáться**) to overeat.

объé|хать, ду, дешь *pf.* (*of* ⇒**~зжáть[1]**) **1** (*болото*) to go round, skirt **2** (*грузовик*) to overtake, pass. **3** (*всю страну*) to travel over.

объяв|и́ть, лю́, ~ишь *pf.* (*of* ⇒**~ля́ть**) to declare, announce; **о. войну́** to declare war; **о. кóнкурс** to announce a competition; **о. собрáние откры́тым** to declare a meeting open; **о. вне закóна** to outlaw.

объяв|и́ться, лю́сь, ~ишься *pf.* (*of* ⇒**~ля́ться**) **1** (*coll.*) to turn up, appear. **2** (+*i.*) to announce o.s. (to be), declare o.s. (to be).

объявлéни|е, я *nt.* **1** declaration, announcement; (*вывеска*) notice; **о. войны́** declaration of war. **2** (*рекламное*) advertisement; **дать о. в газéту, помести́ть о. в газéте** to put an advertisement in a paper.

объявля́|ть(ся), ю(сь) *impf. of* ⇒**объяви́ть(ся)**

объяснéни|е, я *nt.* explanation; **о. в любви́** declaration of love.

объясни́м|ый (~, ~а) *adj.* explicable, explainable.

объясни́тельный *adj.* explanatory.

объясн|и́ть, ю, и́шь *pf.* (*of* ⇒**~я́ть**) to explain.

объясн|и́ться, ю́сь, и́шься *pf.* (*of* ⇒**~я́ться**) **1** to explain o.s.; **(с+*i.*)** to have a talk (with); to have it out (with); **о. в любви** (+*d.*) to make a declaration of love (to). **2** (*найти себе объяснение*) to become clear, be explained; **тепéрь всё ~и́лось** everything is now clear.

объясн|я́ть, я́ю *impf. of* ⇒**~и́ть**

объясн|я́ться, я́юсь *impf.* **1** *impf. of* ⇒**~и́ться. 2** to speak; to make o.s. understood; **умéете ли вы о. по-францу́зски?** can you make yourself understood in French?; **о. жéстами и знáками** to use sign language. **3** (+*i.*) to be explained (by), be accounted for (by); **э́тим ~я́ется егó стрáнное поведéние** that accounts for his strange behaviour.

объя́ти|е, я *nt.* embrace; **с распростёртыми ~ями** with open arms; **брóситься комý-н. в ~я** to fall into s.o.'s arms.

объя́т|ый *p.p.p. of* ⇒**~ь; о. плáменем** enveloped in flames; **о. стрáхом** terror-stricken; **о. ду́мой** wrapped in thought.

объя́|ть, обойму́, обоймёшь (*and coll.* **обыму́, обы́мешь**) *pf.* (*obs.*) to seize, grip, come over; **у́жас ~л его́** terror seized him.

обыва́тел|ь, я *m.* **1** (*hist.*) (*житель*) inhabitant, resident. **2** (*fig.*) (*мещанин*) philistine.

обыва́тельский *adj.* **1** (*obs.*) belonging to the local inhabitants. **2** (*fig.*) philistine; narrow-minded.

обыва́тельщин|а, ы *f.* philistinism; narrow-mindedness.

обыгр|а́ть, а́ю *pf.* (*of* ⇒**~ывать**) **1** (*соперника*) to beat (*at a game*); (*в шахматы*) to win; **о. кого́-н. на пять фу́нтов** to win five pounds from s.o. **2** (*theatr.*) to use with (good) effect, play up; (*fig.*) (*ошибку*) to turn to advantage, turn to account. **3** (*mus.*) to break in (*an instrument by playing*).

обы́грыва|ть, ю *impf. of* ⇒**обыгра́ть**

обы́денност|ь, и *f.* **1** (*свойство*) ordinariness. **2** (*событие*) everyday occurrence.

обы́денн|ый *adj.* ordinary; commonplace, everyday; **~ое происше́ствие** everyday occurrence.

обыкнове́ни|е, я *nt.* habit; **по ~ю** as usual; **по своему́ ~ю** as is his *etc.* wont; **име́ть о.** (+*inf.*) to be in the habit (of).

обыкнове́нно *adv.* usually, as a rule.

обыкнове́н|ный (~ен, ~на) *adj.* usual; ordinary; commonplace; **~ная исто́рия** everyday occurrence; **бо́льше ~ного** more than usual.

о́быск, а *m.* search; **о́рдер на о.** search warrant.

обы|ска́ть, щу́, ~щешь *pf.* (*of* ⇒**~скивать**) to search.

обы|ска́ться, щу́сь, ~щешься *pf.* (*coll.*) to carry out a search (in vain).

обы́скива|ть, ю *impf. of* ⇒**обыска́ть**

обы́ча|й, я *m.* custom; (*leg.*) usage; **по ~ю** in accordance with custom; **э́то у нас в ~е** it is our custom.

обы́чно *adv.* usually; as a rule; **как о.** as usual.

обы́ч|ный (~ен, ~на) *adj.* usual; ordinary.

обя́занност|ь, и *f.* duty; responsibility; **во́инская о.** military service; **исполня́ть ~и дире́ктора** to act as director; **исполня́ющий ~и дире́ктора** acting director.

обя́зан|ный (~, ~а) *adj.* **1** (+*inf.*) obliged, bound; **он ~ верну́ться** he is obliged to go back; it is his duty to go back. **2** (+*d.*) obliged, indebted (to); **я вам о́чень ~** I am very much obliged to you; **она́ вам ~а свое́й жи́знью** she owes her life to you.

обяза́тельно *adv.* without fail; definitely; **я о. приду́** I shall come without fail; **он о. там бу́дет** he is sure to be there, he is bound to be there; **не о.** not necessarily.

обяза́тельност|ь, и *f.* obligatoriness; binding force.

обяза́тел|ьный (~ен, ~ьна) *adj.* **1** obligatory; compulsory; binding; **~ьное обуче́ние** compulsory education; **~ьное постановле́ние** binding decree. **2** (*человек*) reliable.

обяза́тельств|о, а *nt.* **1** obligation; **долгово́е о.** promissory note; **взять на себя́ о.** (+*inf.*) to commit o.s. (to), undertake (to). **2** (*pl.*; *leg.*) liabilities.

обя|за́ть, жу́, ~жешь *pf.* (*of* ⇒**~зывать**) **1** to bind, oblige, commit; **о. кого́-н. яви́ться в определённое вре́мя** to bind s.o. to appear at a stated time. **2** to oblige; **вы меня́ о́чень ~жете** I shall be greatly indebted to you.

обя|за́ться, жу́сь, ~жешься *pf.* (*of* ⇒**~зываться**) to bind o.s., pledge o.s., undertake.

обя́зыва|ть, ю *impf. of* ⇒**обяза́ть**

обя́зыва|ться, юсь *impf. of* ⇒**обяза́ться; не хочу́ ни пе́ред ке́м о.** I wish to be beholden to no one.

ОВ *nt. indecl.* (*abbr. of* ***отравля́ющее вещество́***) (*mil.*) toxic chemical agent; **ОВ не́рвно-паралити́ческого ти́па** nerve gas.

о-в (*abbr. of* ***о́стров***) I., Island, Isle.

о-ва (*abbr. of* ***острова́***) Is, Islands, Isles.

ова́л, а *m.* **1** oval. **2** (*в комиксе*) balloon.

ова́л|ьный (~ен, ~ьна) *adj.* oval.

ова́ци|я, и *f.* ovation.

овдове́|вший *p.p. of* ⇒**~ть** *and adj.* widowed.

овдове́|ть, ю *pf.* to be widowed.

овева́|ть, ю *impf. of* ⇒**ове́ять**

ов|ён, на́ *m.* **1** (*obs.*) ram. **2** (*созвездие*) (**О.**) Aries.

ов|ёс, са́ *m.* oats.

ов|е́чий *adj. of* ⇒**~ца́; волк в ~е́чьей шку́ре** a wolf in sheep's clothing.

ове́чк|а, и *f. dim. of* ⇒**овца́**

овеществ|и́ть, лю́, и́шь *pf.* (*of* ⇒**~ля́ть**) to substantiate.

овеществля́|ть, ю *impf. of* ⇒**овеществи́ть**

ове́я|нный *p.p.p of* ⇒**~ть; о. сла́вой** covered in glory; **о. леге́ндами** surrounded by legends.

ове́|ять, ю, ешь *pf.* (*of* ⇒**~ва́ть**) (+*i.*) **1** to fan. **2** (*fig.*) (*окружить*) to surround (with), cover (with).

ОВИ́Р, а *m.* (*abbr. of* ***отде́л виз и регистра́ции***) visa and registration department.

овладева́|ть, ю *impf. of* ⇒**овладе́ть**

овладе́ни|е, я *nt.* (+*i.*) **1** seizure. **2** (*fig.*) (*усвоение*) mastery, mastering.

овладе́|ть, ю *pf.* (*of* ⇒**~ва́ть**) (+*i.*) **1** (*взять*) to seize; to take possession (of); **о. собо́й** to get control of o.s., regain self-control; **мно́ю ~ла ра́дость** I was overcome with joy. **2** (*fig.*) (*усвоить*) master.

о-во (*abbr. of* ***о́бщество***) Soc., Society.

о́вод, а, *pl.* **~ы, ~ов** (*and* **~а́, ~о́в**) gadfly.

овощево́дств|о, а *nt.* vegetable-growing.

овощехрани́лищ|е, а *nt.* vegetable store.

о́вощ|и, е́й *pl.* (*sg.* **~, ~а** *m.*) vegetables.

овощно́й *adj.* vegetable; **о. магази́н** greengrocer's (shop).

овра́г, а *m.* ravine, gully.

овра́жист|ый (~, ~а) *adj.* abounding in ravines.

овся́нк|а[1], и *f.* (*coll.*) **1** (*крупа*) oatmeal. **2** (*каша*) porridge (*Br.*), oatmeal (*US*).

овся́нк|а[2], и *f.* (*zool.*) yellow-hammer.

овсян|о́й *adj. of* ⇒**овёс; ~ое по́ле** field of oats.

овся́н|ый *adj.* made of oats; oatmeal; **~ая ка́ша** (oatmeal) porridge (*Br.*), oatmeal (*US*); **~ая крупа́** oatmeal.

овуля́ци|я, и *f.* (*biol.*) ovulation.

овц|а́, ы́, *pl.* **~ы, ове́ц, ~ам** *f.* sheep; (*самка*) ewe; **заблу́дшая о.** (*fig.*) lost sheep.

овцебы́к, а *m.* musk-ox.

овцево́д, а *m.* sheep-breeder.

овцево́дств|о, а *nt.* sheep-breeding.

ОВЧ *f. indecl.* (*abbr. of* ***о́чень высо́кая частота́***) VHF (*very high frequency*).

овча́р, а *m.* shepherd.

овча́рк|а, и *f.* sheep-dog; **неме́цкая о.** German shepherd (*dog*), Alsatian.

овча́р|ня, ни, *g. pl.* **~ен** *f.* sheep-fold.

овчи́н|а, ы *f.* sheepskin.

овчи́н|ка, ки *f. dim. of* ⇒**~а; ей не́бо с ~ку показа́лось** she was frightened out of her wits; **о. вы́делки не сто́ит** (*fig.*) the game is not worth the candle.

овчи́нный *adj.* sheepskin.

ога́р|ок, ка *m.* candle-end; (*pl.*) cinders.

огиба́|ть, ю *impf. of* ⇒**обогну́ть**

оглавле́ни|е, я *nt.* table of contents.

огла|си́ть, шу́, си́шь *pf.* (*of* ⇒**~ша́ть**) **1** (*объявить*) to proclaim, announce; **о. резолю́цию** to read out a resolution; **о. жениха́ и неве́сту** to publish banns of marriage. **2** (*obs.*) (*разгласить*) to divulge, make public. **3** (*наполнить громкими звуками*) to fill (*with loud cries, etc.*).

огла|си́ться, си́тся *pf.* (*of* ⇒**~ша́ться**) **1** (+*i.*) to resound (with). **2** (*obs.*) (*стать известным*) to become known; to be made public.

огла́ск|а, и *f.* publicity; **избега́ть ~и** to shun publicity; **преда́ть ~е** to make public, make known.

оглаша́|ть(ся), ю, ет(ся) *impf. of* ⇒**огласи́ть(ся)**

оглаше́ни|е, я *nt.* proclaiming, publication; **не подлежи́т ~ю** confidential (*classification of document*); (*eccl.*) (publication of) banns.

оглаше́нный *adj.*: **как о.** (*coll.*) like one possessed.

огло́б|ля, ли, *g. pl.* **~ель** *f.* shaft.

огло́х|нуть, ну, нешь, *past* **~, ~ла** *pf. of* ⇒**гло́хнуть** 1

оглуп|и́ть, лю́, ~и́шь *pf.* (*of* ⇒**~ля́ть**) **1** (*сделать глупым*) to fool, make a fool of; (*обмануть*) to deceive. **2** (*исказить*) to distort; to misrepresent.

оглупля́|ть, ю *impf.* **1** *impf. of*

⇒**оглупи́ть. 2** to try to fool, try to deceive.

оглуш|а́ть, а́ю *impf. of* ⇒**~и́ть**

оглуши́тел|ьный (~ен, ~ьна) *adj.* deafening.

оглуш|и́ть, у́, и́шь *pf.* **1** *pf. of* ⇒**глуши́ть** 1. **2** (*impf.* **~а́ть**) to deafen; (*ударом*) to stun (*also fig.*).

огля|де́ть, жу́, ди́шь *pf.* (*of* ⇒**~́дывать**) (*человека, горизонт*) to examine, inspect; (*оглядеться*) to look around.

огля|де́ться, жу́сь, ди́шься *pf.* (*of* ⇒**~́дываться**) **1** (*смотреть вокруг себя*) to look around. **2** (*в новом городе*) to get used to one's surroundings; (*fig.*) (*привыкнуть*) to adapt o.s., become acclimatized; **о. в темноте́** to become accustomed to the darkness.

огля́дк|а, и *f.* **1** looking back; **бежа́ть без ~и** to run without turning one's head; to run as fast as one can. **2** (*внимание*) care, caution; **без ~и** (*неосторожно*) carelessly; (*решительно*) decisively, resolutely; **де́йствовать с ~ой** to act cautiously, circumspectly.

огля́дыва|ть(ся), ю(сь) *impf. of* ⇒**огляде́ть(ся)** *and* **огляну́ть(ся)**

огля|ну́ть, ну́, ~́нешь *inst. pf.* (*of* ⇒**~́дывать**) to take a look over.

огля|ну́ться, ну́сь, ~́нешься *pf.* (*of* ⇒**~́дываться**) to turn (back) to look at sth.; to glance back.

огнев|о́й *adj. of* ⇒**ого́нь;** (*fig.*) fiery; **о. бой** (*mil.*) firing; **о. вал** (*mil.*) barrage; **~а́я заве́са** (*mil.*) curtain (of) fire; **~а́я коро́бка** fire-box; **~ы́е сре́дства** weapons; **~а́я то́чка** (*mil.*) emplacement.

огнеды́шащ|ий *adj.* fire-spitting; **~ая гора́** (*obs.*) volcano.

огнемёт, а *m.* (*mil.*) flame-thrower.

о́гненный *adj.* fiery (*also fig.*).

огнеопа́с|ный (~ен, ~на) *adj.* inflammable.

огнепокло́нник, а *m.* fire-worshipper.

огнепокло́нничеств|о, а *nt.* fire-worship.

огнеприпа́с|ы, ов *no sg.* ammunition.

огнесто́|йкий (~ек, ~йка) *adj.* fire-proof, fire-resistant.

огнестре́льн|ый *adj.*: **~ое ору́жие** fire-arm(s); **~ая ра́на** gunshot wound.

огнетуши́тел|ь, я *m.* fire-extinguisher.

огнеупо́р|ный (~ен, ~на) *adj.* fire-resistant, fire-proof; (*tech.*) refractory; **~ная гли́на** fire-clay; **о. кирпи́ч** fire-brick.

огнеупо́р|ы, ов *no sg.* (*tech.*) refractory materials.

огни́в|о, а *nt.* steel (*used formerly for striking fire from flint*).

ого́ *int.* oho!

огова́рива|ть(ся), ю(сь) *impf. of* ⇒**оговори́ть(ся)**

огово́р, а *m.* slander.

оговор|и́ть¹, ю́, и́шь *pf.* (*of* ⇒**огова́ривать**) (*оклеветать*) to slander.

оговор|и́ть², ю́, и́шь *pf.* (*of* ⇒**огова́ривать**) **1** (*заранее условиться о чём-либо*) to stipulate (for); to fix, agree (on); **мы ~и́ли усло́вия рабо́ты** we have fixed the conditions of work. **2** (*сделать оговорку*) to spell out; to specify.

оговор|и́ться, ю́сь, и́шься *pf.* (*of* ⇒**огова́риваться**) **1** (*сделать оговорку*) to make a reservation, make a proviso. **2** (*в речи*) to make a slip in speaking.

огово́р|ка, ки *f.* **1** reservation, proviso; **без ~ок** without reserve; **он согласи́лся, но с не́которыми ~ками** he agreed but made certain reservations. **2** (*в речи*) slip of the tongue.

оголе́ни|е, я *nt.* denudation.

огол|ённый *p.p.p. of* ⇒**~и́ть** *and adj.* bare, exposed.

огол|е́ц, ьца́ *m.* (*coll.*) lad, (young) fellow.

огол|и́ть, ю́, и́шь *pf.* (*of* ⇒**~я́ть**) to bare; (*провод*) to strip; (*шашку*) to draw; **о. фланг** (*mil.*) to expose one's flank.

огол|и́ться, ю́сь, и́шься *pf.* (*of* ⇒**~я́ться**) **1** to strip (o.s.). **2** (*о проводе*) to become exposed; (*о дереве*) to become bare.

оголте́л|ый (~, ~а) *adj.* (*coll.*) unbridled; mad, frenzied.

огол|я́ть(ся), я́ю(сь) *impf. of* ⇒**~и́ть(ся)**

огон|ёк, ька́ *m.* **1** (small) light; **блужда́ющий о.** will o' the wisp; **весёлый о.** merry twinkle; **зайти́ к кому́-н. на о.** (*coll.*) to drop in on s.o. (*seeing a light in the window*). **2** (*fig.*) (*увлечение*) zest, spirit.

ог|о́нь, ня́ *m.* **1** (*пламя*) fire (*also fig.*); **говори́ть с ~нём** to speak with fervour (*Br.*), fervor (*US*); **меж двух ~не́й** between two fires, between the devil and the deep blue sea; **пройти́ о. и во́ду** to go through fire and water; **из ~ня́ да в по́лымя** (*fig.*) out of the frying-pan into the fire. **2** (*mil.*) fire; firing; **отвеча́ть ~нём** to fire back. **3** (*свет*) light; **хвостово́й о.** (*aeron.*) tail light; **тако́го челове́ка днём с ~нём не найдёшь** (*coll.*) you will not find another like him in a month of Sundays.

огора́жива|ть(ся), ю(сь) *impf. of* ⇒**огороди́ть(ся)**

огоро́д, а *m.* kitchen-garden, vegetable garden; **бро́сить ка́мешек в чей-н. о.** (*fig., coll.*) to make disparaging remarks about s.o.

огоро|ди́ть, жу́, ~́дишь *pf.* (*of* ⇒**огора́живать**) to fence in, enclose.

огоро|ди́ться, жу́сь, ~́дишься *pf.* (*of* ⇒**огора́живаться**) to fence o.s. in.

огоро́дник, а *m.* market-gardener.

огоро́дни|ца, цы *f. of* ⇒**~к**

огоро́дничеств|о, а *nt.* market-gardening.

огоро́д|ный *adj. of* ⇒**~; ~ное хозя́йство** market-gardening, market-garden.

огоро́ш|ить, у, ишь *pf.* (*coll.*) to take aback, disconcert.

огорч|а́ть(ся), а́ю(сь) *impf. of* ⇒**~и́ть(ся)**

огорче́ни|е, я *nt.* distress; chagrin; **быть в ~и** to be in distress.

огорчи́тел|ьный (~ен, ~ьна) *adj.* distressing.

огорч|и́ть, у́, и́шь *pf.* (*of* ⇒**~а́ть**) to distress, upset.

огорч|и́ться, у́сь, и́шься *pf.* (*of* ⇒**~а́ться**) to be distressed; **не ~а́йтесь!** cheer up!

огра́б|ить, лю, ишь *pf. of* ⇒**гра́бить**

ограбле́ни|е, я *nt.* robbery; burglary; **у́личное о.** mugging.

огра́д|а, ы *f.* (*забор*) fence; (*решётка*) railings.

огра|ди́ть, жу́, ди́шь *pf.* (*of* ⇒**~жда́ть**) (**от**+*g.*) to guard (against, from), protect (against).

огра|ди́ться, жу́сь, ди́шься *pf.* (*of* ⇒**~жда́ться**) (**от**+*g.*) to defend o.s. (against); to protect o.s. (against).

огражда́|ть(ся), ю(сь) *impf. of* ⇒**огради́ть(ся)**

огражде́ни|е, я *nt.* barrier.

ограниче́ни|е, я *nt.* limitation, restriction.

ограни́ченност|ь, и *f.* limited nature; (*fig.*) narrowness, narrow-mindedness.

ограни́ч|енный *p.p.p. of* ⇒**~ить** *and adj.* limited; **о. челове́к** (*fig.*) narrow(-minded) person.

ограни́чива|ть(ся), ю(сь) *impf. of* ⇒**ограни́чить(ся)**

ограничи́тел|ь, я *m.* (*tech.*): **о. хо́да** catch, stop, stop piece, arresting device.

ограничи́тельный *adj.* restrictive, limiting.

ограни́ч|ить, у, ишь *pf.* (*of* ⇒**~ивать**) to limit, restrict, cut down; **о. себя́ в расхо́дах** to cut down one's expenditure.

ограни́ч|иться, усь, ишься *pf.* (*of* ⇒**~иваться**) (+*i.*) **1** (*удовлетвориться*) to limit o.s. (to), confine o.s. (to); **он ~ился кра́ткой ре́чью** he confined himself to a short speech. **2** (*остаться в каких-либо пределах*) to be limited (to), be confined (to).

огреба́|ть, ю *impf. of* ⇒**огрести́; о. де́ньги** (*coll.*) to rake in money.

огре|сти́, бу́, бёшь, *past* **~́б, ~бла́** *pf.* (*of* ⇒**~ба́ть**) to rake up.

огре́|ть, ю *pf.* (*coll.*) to whack.

огре́х, а *m.* (*coll.*) fault, imperfection (*in work*).

огро́м|ный (~ен, ~на) *adj.* huge; vast; enormous.

огрубе́л|ый (~, ~а) *adj.* coarse, hardened.

огрубе́|ть, ю *pf. of* ⇒**грубе́ть**

огру́з|нуть, ну, нешь, *past* **~, ~ла** *pf.* (*coll.*) to grow stout.

огрыз|а́ться, а́юсь *impf.* (*of* ⇒**~ну́ться**) (**на**+*a.*) to snap (at).

О

огрыз|ну́ться, ну́сь, нёшься *pf. of* ⇒**~а́ться**

огры́з|ок, ка *m.* (*яблока, сосиски*) leftover bit; (*карандаша*) stub.

огу́лом *adv.* (*coll.*) wholesale, indiscriminately.

огу́льно *adv.* without grounds; **о. обвиня́ть** to make a groundless accusation.

огу́л|ьный (~ен, ~ьна) *adj.* **1** (*без разбора*) wholesale, indiscriminate; **~ьное оха́ивание** wholesale disparagement. **2** (*необоснованный*) unfounded, groundless.

огур|е́ц, ца́ *m.* cucumber.

огуре́|чный *adj. of* ⇒**~ц**

огу́рчик, а *m. affectionate dim. of* ⇒**огуре́ц**

о́д|а, ы *f.* ode.

ода́лжива|ть, ю *impf. of* ⇒**одолжи́ть**

одарённост|ь, и *f.* endowments, (natural) gifts, talent.

одар|ённый *p.p.p. of* ⇒**~и́ть** *and adj.* gifted, talented.

ода́рива|ть, ю *impf. of* ⇒**одари́ть**

одар|и́ть, ю́, и́шь *pf.* **1** (*impf.* **~́ивать**) to give presents (to); **она́ ~и́ла всех дете́й игру́шками** she has given all the children toys. **2** (*impf.* **~я́ть**) (+*i.*) to endow (with); **приро́да ~и́ла его́ разнообра́зными спосо́бностями** nature has endowed him with a variety of talents.

одар|я́ть, я́ю *impf. of* ⇒**~и́ть**

одева́|ть(ся), ю(сь) *impf. of* ⇒**оде́ть(ся)**

одёж|а, и *f.* (*coll.*) clothes.

оде́жд|а, ы *f.* **1** clothes; clothing; **ве́рхняя о.** outer clothing, overcoat; **мужска́я о.** menswear; **фо́рменная о.** uniform. **2** (*tech.*) (*дороги*) surfacing.

одеколо́н, а *m.* eau-de-cologne.

одел|и́ть, ю́, и́шь *pf.* (*of* ⇒**~я́ть**) (+*i.*) to present (with).

одел|я́ть, я́ю *impf. of* ⇒**~и́ть**

од|ёр, ра́ *m.* (*coll.*) old hack (*horse*).

одёргива|ть, ю *impf. of* ⇒**одёрнуть**

одеревене́лый *adj.* numb; (*fig.*) lifeless.

одеревене́|ть, ю *pf. of* ⇒**деревене́ть**

одерж|а́ть, у́, ~́ишь *pf.* (*of* ⇒**~́ивать**) to gain; **о. верх** (**над**+*i.*) to gain the upper hand (over), prevail (over); **о. побе́ду** to gain a (the) victory, carry the day.

оде́ржива|ть, ю *impf. of* ⇒**одержа́ть**

одержи́м|ый (~, ~а) *adj.* (+*i.*) possessed (by); afflicted (by); **о. стра́хом** consumed with fear; **о. навя́зчивой иде́ей** obsessed by an idée fixe.

одёр|нуть, ну, нешь *pf.* (*of* ⇒**~гивать**) **1** (*рубашку, юбку*) to pull down, straighten. **2** (*fig., coll.*) (*человека*) to call to order; to silence; to snub.

одесси́т, а *m.* inhabitant of Odessa.

оде́т|ый *p.p.p. of* ⇒**~ь** *and adj.* (+*i.* or **в**+*a.*) dressed (in), clothed (in); with one's clothes on; **о. сне́гом** snow-clad; **хорошо́ о.** well-dressed.

оде́|ть, ну, нешь *pf.* (*of* ⇒**~ва́ть**) **1** (**в**+*a.*) to dress (in), clothe (in); **о. ребёнка в брю́ки** to dress a child in trousers; (+*i.*) (*покрыть*) to cover (with), wrap (in). **2** (*снабдить одеждой*) to clothe.

оде́|ться, нусь, нешься *pf.* (*of* ⇒**~ва́ться**) **1** to dress (o.s.); to clothe o.s.; **о. в вече́рнее пла́тье** to put on an evening dress. **2** (*покрыться*) (+*i.*) to be covered with.

одея́л|о, а *nt.* blanket; coverlet; **о-гре́лка** electric blanket; **стёганое о.** counterpane, quilt.

одея́ни|е, я *nt.* garb, attire.

оди́н, одного́ *m.*; **одна́, одно́й** *f.*; **одно́, одного́** *nt.*; *pl.* **одни́, одни́х** *num. and pron.* **1** (*число*) one; **о. стол** one table; **одни́ но́жницы** one pair of scissors; **одно́** one thing; **одно́ де́ло…, друго́е де́ло…** it is one thing …, another thing …; **о. за други́м** one after the other, one by one; **одни́… други́е** some …, (while) others; **с одно́й стороны́… с друго́й (стороны́)** on the one hand … on the other hand; **одно́ вре́мя** at one time; **о. раз** once; **одни́м сло́вом** in a word; **о.-два** one or two; **о. из ты́сячи** one in a thousand; **в о. го́лос** with one voice, with one accord; **в о. прекра́сный день** one fine day, once upon a time; **все до одного́** all to a man; **все, как о.** one and all; **о. на о.** in private; face to face; **по одному́** one by one, one at a time; in single file.
2 (*некий*) a, an; a certain; **я встре́тил одного́ моего́ бы́вшего колле́гу** I met an old colleague of mine.
3 (*без других*) alone; by o.s.; **да́йте ей сде́лать э́то одно́й** let her do it by herself; **я живу́ о.** I live alone.
4 (*без супруги*) single.
5 (*только*) only; **он о. зна́ет доро́гу** only he *or* he alone knows the way; **она́ чита́ет одни́ детекти́вные рома́ны** she reads nothing but detective stories.
6: **о., о. и тот же** the same, one and the same; **мы с ней одного́ во́зраста** she and I are the same age; **э́то одно́ и то же** it is the same thing.

одина́кий *adj.* (*obs., coll.*) identical.

одина́ково *adv.* equally, alike.

одина́ковост|ь, и *f.* identity (*of views, etc.*); sameness, uniformity.

одина́ков|ый (~, ~а) *adj.* (**с**+*i.*) identical (with), the same (as).

одина́рный *adj.* single.

одиннадцатиле́тний *adj.* eleven-year-old.

оди́ннадцатый *adj.* eleventh.

оди́ннадцат|ь, и *num.* eleven.

одино́к|ий (~, ~а) *adj.* **1** solitary; lonely; lone. **2** *as n.* **о., ~ого** *m.* single man, bachelor; **~ая, ~ой** *f.* single woman.

одино́ко *adv.* lonely; **чу́вствовать себя́ о.** to feel lonely.

одино́честв|о, а *nt.* solitude; loneliness.

одино́чк|а, и *c.g and f.* **1** *c.g.* lone person; **куста́рь-о.** craftsman working alone; **мать-о.** single mother; **оте́ц-о.** single father; **роди́тель-о.** single parent; **жить ~ой** to live alone; **в ~у** alone, on one's own; **по ~е** one by one. **2** *f.* (*coll.*) one-man cell, solitary confinement.

одино́чн|ый *adj.* **1** (*одного человека*) individual; one-man; **о. бой** single combat; **~ое заключе́ние** solitary confinement; **о. полёт** solo flight. **2** (*отдельный*) solitary; single; **о. вы́стрел** single shot.

одио́з|ный (~ен, ~на) *adj.* odious, offensive.

одиссе́|я, и *f.* (*fig.*) odyssey.

одича́л|ый (~, ~а) *adj.* (having gone) wild.

одича́ни|е, я *nt.* running wild.

одича́|ть, ю *pf. of* ⇒**дича́ть**

одна́жды *adv.* once; one day; **о. у́тром (ве́чером, но́чью)** one morning (evening, night).

одна́ко 1 *adv. and conj.* however; but; though. **2** *int.* you don't say so!; not really!

одноа́ктный *adj.* (*theatr.*) one-act.

однобо́к|ий (~, ~а) *adj.* one-sided (*also fig.*).

однобо́ртный *adj.* single-breasted.

одновале́нтный *adj.* (*chem.*) univalent, monovalent.

одновре́ме́нно *adv.* simultaneously, at the same time.

одновре́ме́нност|ь, и *f.* simultaneity.

одновр|е́ме́нный (~е́менен, ~е́ме́нна) *adj.* simultaneous.

одногла́зк|а, и *f.* (*zool.*) cyclops.

одногла́зый *adj.* one-eyed.

одногоди́чный *adj.* one-year, of one year's duration.

одного́д|ок, ка *m.* (**с**+*i.*; *coll.*) of the same age (as).

одного́рбый *adj.*: **о. верблю́д** dromedary, Arabian camel.

однодне́вк|а, и *f.* **1** (*насекомое*) insect living only one day. **2** (*coll., pej.*) a short-lived thing.

однодне́вный *adj.* one-day.

одноду́м, а *m.* person with idée fixe, obsessional.

однозву́ч|ный (~ен, ~на) *adj.* monotonous.

однозна́ч|ный (~ен, ~на) *adj.* **1** (*тождественный*) synonymous. **2** (*ling.*) monosemantic. **3** (*math.*) simple; **~ное число́** simple number, digit. **4** (*fig.*) (*недвусмысленный*) unambiguous; simple, straightforward.

одноимён|ный (~ен, ~на) *adj.* of the same name.

однока́шник, а *m.* (*coll.*) school-fellow.

однокла́ссник, а *m.* classmate.

однокла́ссни|ца, цы *f. of* ⇒**~к**

одноклёточный *adj.* (*biol.*) single-cell, unicellular.

одноклу́бник, а *m.* (*coll.*) fellow-member of club.

одноклу́бни|ца, цы *f. of* ⇒**~к**

одноколе́йный *adj.* single-track.
одноко́лк|а, и *f.* (*coll.*) gig.
одноко́нный *adj.* one-horse.
однокра́т|ный (~ен, ~на) *adj.* single; (*gram.*): **о. глаго́л** semelfactive verb.
одноку́рсник, а *m.* person in the same year of study.
одноку́рсни|ца, цы *f. of* ⇒**~к**
одноле́тний *adj.* **1** one-year. **2** (*bot.*) annual.
одноле́тник, а *m.* (*bot.*) annual.
одноле́т|ок, ка *m.* (**c**+*i.*) (*coll.*) of the same age (as).
одномáстный *adj.* of one colour.
одномáчтовый *adj.* single-masted.
одноме́стный *adj.* single-seated, single-seater.
одномото́рный *adj.* single-engine.
одноно́гий *adj.* one-legged.
однообрáзи|е, я *nt.* monotony.
однообрáзност|ь, и *f.* = **однообрáзие**
однообрáз|ный (~ен, ~на) *adj.* monotonous.
однопалáтный *adj.* (*pol.*) unicameral, single-chamber.
однопáлубный *adj.* single-deck.
одноплеме́нный *adj.* of the same tribe.
однополчáн|ин, ина, *pl.* **~е, ~** *m.* comrade-in-arms (*one serving in same regiment*).
однопо́лый *adj.* unisexual.
однопу́тный *adj.* one-track.
однорáзовый *adj.* (*шприц*) disposable; (*пропуск*) temporary, valid only once.
одноро́дност|ь, и *f.* homogeneity, uniformity.
одноро́д|ный (~ен, ~на) *adj.* **1** homogeneous. **2** (*похожий*) similar.
однору́кий *adj.* one-armed.
однорядк|а, и *f.* (*hist.*) single-breasted caftan.
односельчáн|ин, ина, *pl.* **~е, ~** *m.* fellow-villager.
односельчáн|ка, ки *f. of* ⇒**~ин**
односло́жно *adv.*: **говори́ть о.** to speak in monosyllables.
односло́ж|ный *adj.* **1** monosyllabic. **2 (~ен, ~на)** (*fig.*) terse, abrupt.
однoсло́йный *adj.* single-layer; one-ply, single-ply.
односпáльн|ый *adj.*: **~ая кровáть** single bed.
одноство́льн|ый *adj.*: **~ое ружьё** single-barrelled gun.
односторо́нн|ий *adj.* **1** (*ткань*) one-sided (*also fig.*); (*разоружение, договор*) unilateral. **2** (*ток*) one-way; **~ее движе́ние** one-way traffic; **о. ум** (*fig.*) one-track mind.
однoти́п|ный (~ен, ~на) *adj.* of the same type, of the same kind; **о. корáбль** sister-ship.
одното́мник, а *m.* single-volume edition.
одното́мный *adj.* one-volume.

однофáзный *adj.* (*elec.*) single-phase, monophase.
однофами́л|ец, ьца *m.* (**c**+*i.*) person having the same surname (as), namesake.
однофами́л|ица, ицы *f. of* ⇒**~ец**
одноцве́т|ный (~ен, ~на) *adj.* (*ткань*) plain; (*fig.*) monochrome.
одноцили́ндровый *adj.* one-cylinder.
одночáсь|е, я *nt.*: **в о.** (*coll.*) suddenly, in an instant.
одноэтáжный *adj.* single-storey (*Br.*), single-story (*US*).
одноязы́ч|ный (~ен, ~на) *adj.* monolingual.
одноя́русный *adj.* single-tier; (*geol.*) single-stage.
одобре́ни|е, я *nt.* approval.
одобри́тел|ьный (~ен, ~ьна) *adj.* approving; (*отзыв*) favourable (*Br.*), favorable (*US*).
одо́бр|ить, ю, ишь *pf.* (*of* ⇒**~я́ть**) to approve (of); **не о.** to disapprove (of).
одобр|я́ть, я́ю *impf. of* ⇒**~ить**
одолевá|ть, ю *impf. of* ⇒**одоле́ть**
одоле́|ть, ю *pf.* (*of* ⇒**~вáть**) **1** to overcome, conquer; **его́ ~л сон** he was overcome by sleepiness; **нас ~ло зловóние** the stench overpowered us. **2** (*fig.*) to master; to cope (with); to get through.
одолж|áть, áю *impf. of* ⇒**~и́ть**
одолжá|ться, юсь *impf.* (+*d. or* **у**+*g.*) to be obliged (to), be beholden (to).
одолже́ни|е, я *nt.* favour (*Br.*), favor (*US*), service; **сде́лайте мне о.** do me a favour (*Br.*), favor (*US*).
одолж|и́ть, у́, и́шь *pf.* (*of* ⇒**одáлживать** *and* **~áть**) **1** (+*d.*) to lend. **2** (*coll.*; **у**+*g.*) to borrow (from).
одомáшнени|е, я *nt.* domestication, taming.
одомáшн|енный *p.p.p. of* ⇒**~ить** *and adj.* domesticated.
одомáшнивa|ть, ю *impf. of* ⇒**одомáшнить**
одомáшн|ить, ю, ишь *pf.* (*of* ⇒**~ивать**) to domesticate, tame.
одр, á *m.* (*arch.*; *now only in certain phrr.*) bed, couch; **на сме́ртном ~е́** on one's death-bed.
одревесне́ни|е, я *nt.* lignification.
одряхле́|ть, ю *pf. of* ⇒**дряхле́ть**
одувáнчик, а *m.* (*bot.*) dandelion.
оду́м|аться, аюсь *pf.* (*of* ⇒**~ываться**) to change one's mind; to think better of it.
оду́мыва|ться, юсь *impf. of* ⇒**оду́маться**
одурáчива|ть, ю *impf. of* ⇒**одурáчить**
одурáч|ить, у, ишь *pf.* (*of* ⇒**дурáчить** *and* **~ивать**) (*coll.*) to make a fool (of), fool.
одуре́л|ый (~, ~а) *adj.* (*coll.*) dulled, besotted.
одуре́ни|е, я *nt.* stupefaction, torpor.
одуре́|ть, ю *pf. of* ⇒**дуре́ть**

одурмáнивa|ть, ю *impf. of* ⇒**одурмáнить**
одурмáн|ить, ю, ишь *pf.* (*of* ⇒**дурмáнить** *and* **~ивать**) to stupefy; (*наркотиком*) to drug.
óдур|ь, и *f.* (*coll.*) stupefaction, torpor; **со́нная о.** (*bot.*) deadly nightshade.
одуря́|ть, ю *impf.* (*coll.*) to stupefy; **~ющий зáпах** heavy scent.
одутловáт|ый (~, ~а) *adj.* puffy.
одухотворённост|ь, и *f.* spirituality.
одухотворённый *p.p.p. of* ⇒**одухотвори́ть** *and adj.* inspired; (*лицо*) spiritual.
одухотвор|и́ть, ю́, и́шь *pf.* (*of* ⇒**~я́ть**) **1** to inspire; to animate. **2** (*животных, природу*) to attribute soul (to).
одухотвор|я́ть, я́ю *impf. of* ⇒**~и́ть**
одушев|и́ть, лю́, и́шь *pf.* (*of* ⇒**~ля́ть**) to animate.
одушев|и́ться, лю́сь, и́шься *pf.* (*of* ⇒**~ля́ться**) to be animated.
одушевле́ни|е, я *nt.* animation.
одушевлённый *p.p.p. of* ⇒**одушеви́ть** *and adj.* **1** (*голос*) animated. **2** (*gram.*) animate.
одушевля́|ть(ся), ю(сь) *impf. of* ⇒**одушеви́ть(ся)**
оды́шк|а, и *f.* short breath; **страдáть ~ой** to be short-winded.
ожереб|и́ться, и́тся *pf. of* ⇒**жереби́ться**
ожере́ль|е, я *nt.* necklace.
ожесточ|áть(ся), áю(сь) *impf. of* ⇒**~и́ть(ся)**
ожесточе́ни|е, я *nt.* bitterness.
ожесточённост|ь, и *f.* = **ожесточе́ние**
ожесточённый *p.p.p. of* ⇒**ожесточи́ть** *and adj.* (*бой, спор*) bitter; (*человек*) embittered; hardened.
ожесточ|и́ть, у́, и́шь *pf.* (*of* ⇒**~áть**) to embitter; to harden.
ожесточ|и́ться, у́сь, и́шься *pf.* (*of* ⇒**~áться**) to become embittered; to become hardened.
оже́чь(ся) = **обже́чь(ся)**
оживáльный *adj.* (*archit.*) ogival.
оживá|ть, ю *impf. of* ⇒**ожи́ть**
ожив|и́ть, лю́, и́шь *pf.* (*of* ⇒**~ля́ть**) **1** (*человека; воспоминание*) to revive. **2** (*fig.*) (*общество, вечер*) to liven up, enliven; (*торговлю*) to revitalize; (*лицо, картину*) to brighten up.
ожив|и́ться, лю́сь, и́шься *pf.* (*of* ⇒**~ля́ться**) **1** (*человек, разговор*) to become animated, liven (up); (*взгляд*) to brighten up. **2** (*улица*) to come to life.
оживле́ни|е, я *nt.* **1** (*состояние*) animation, gusto. **2** (*действие*) reviving; enlivening.
оживлённый *p.p.p. of* ⇒**оживи́ть** *and adj.* animated; lively.
оживля́|ть(ся), ю(сь) *impf. of* ⇒**оживи́ть(ся)**
оживотвор|и́ть, ю́, и́шь *pf. of* ⇒**животвори́ть**

ожидáни|е, я *nt.* expectation; waiting; **обманýть ~я** to disappoint; **в ~и** (+*g.*) pending; **быть в ~и** (*о женщине*) (*euph.*) to be expecting; **сверх ~я** beyond expectation.

ожидá|ть, ю *impf.* (+*g.*) to wait (for); (*предвидеть*) to expect, anticipate; **о. ребёнка** to be expecting a baby; **мы э́того не ~ли** we were not expecting that; **как я и ~л** just as I expected.

ожирéни|е, я *nt.* obesity.

ожирé|ть, ю *pf. of* ⇒**жирéть**

ож|úть, иву́, ивёшь, *past* **~́ил, ~илá, ~́ило** *pf.* (*of* ⇒**~ивáть**) to come to life, revive (*also fig.*).

ожóг, а *m.* burn; (*жидкостью, паром*) scald.

оз. (*abbr. of* **óзеро**) L., Lake.

озабó|тить, чу, тишь *pf.* (*of* ⇒**~чивать**) to trouble, worry, cause anxiety.

озабó|титься, чусь, тишься *pf.* (*of* ⇒**~чиваться**) (+*i.*) to attend (to); to concern o.s. (with).

озабóченност|ь, и *f.* anxiety.

озабó|ченный *p.p.p. of* ⇒**~тить** *and adj.* anxious, worried.

озабóчива|ть(ся), ю(сь) *impf. of* ⇒**озабóтить(ся)**

озаглáв|ить, лю, ишь *pf.* (*of* ⇒**~ливать**) to entitle; (*главу, раздел*) to head.

озаглáвлива|ть, ю *impf. of* ⇒**озаглáвить**

озадáченност|ь, и *f.* perplexity, puzzlement.

озадáч|енный *p.p.p. of* ⇒**~ить** *and adj.* perplexed, puzzled.

озадáчива|ть, ю *impf. of* ⇒**озадáчить**

озадáч|ить, у, ишь *pf.* (*of* ⇒**~ивать**) to perplex, puzzle, take aback.

озар|úть, ю́, úшь *pf.* (*of* ⇒**~я́ть**) to light up, illuminate, illumine; **улы́бка ~úла её лицó** a smile lit up her face; **их ~úло** (*fig.*) it dawned upon them.

озар|úться, ю́сь, úшься *pf.* (*of* ⇒**~я́ться**) (+*i.*) to light up (with); **её лицó ~úлось рáдостью** her face lit up with joy.

озар|я́ть(ся), я́ю(сь) *impf. of* ⇒**~úть(ся)**

озверéл|ый (~, ~а) *adj.* brutal; brutalized.

озверé|ть, ю *pf. of* ⇒**зверéть**

озвýч|енный *p.p.p. of* ⇒**~ить; о. фильм** sound film.

озвýчива|ть, ю *impf. of* ⇒**озвýчить**

озвýч|ить, у, ишь *pf.* (*of* ⇒**~ивать**) (*cin.*) to add a sound-track to.

оздоровúтел|ьный (~ен, ~ьна) *adj.* health, sanitary; **~ьные мероприя́тия** health-improving measures; **о. лáгерь** health camp.

оздоров|úть, лю́, úшь *pf.* (*of* ⇒**~ля́ть**) **1** to make (more) healthy; **о. мéстность** to improve the sanitary conditions of a locality. **2** (*fig.*) (*улучшить*) to improve.

оздоровлéни|е, я *nt.* **1** making (more) healthy. **2** (*fig.*) (*улучшение*) improvement.

оздоровля́|ть, ю *impf. of* ⇒**оздоровúть**

озеленéни|е, я *nt.* planting with trees and gardens; greening.

озелен|úть, ю́, úшь *pf.* (*of* ⇒**~я́ть**) to plant with trees and gardens; to green.

озелен|я́ть, я́ю *impf. of* ⇒**~úть**

óземь *adv.* (*coll.*) to the ground, down.

озёрный *adj. of* ⇒**óзеро; о. райóн** lake district.

óзер|о, а, *pl.* **озёра, озёр** *nt.* lake; **о. Лох-Нéсс** Loch Ness.

озúм|ый *adj.* winter; **~ая культýра** winter crop; *as n.* **~ые, ~ых** winter crops.

óзим|ь, и *f.* winter crop.

озирá|ть, ю *impf.* (*obs.*) to view.

озирá|ться, юсь *impf.* to look round; to look back.

озлóб|ить, лю, ишь *pf.* (*of* ⇒**~ля́ть**) to embitter.

озлóб|иться, люсь, ишься *pf.* (*of* ⇒**~ля́ться**) to become embittered.

озлоблéни|е, я *nt.* bitterness, animosity.

озлóб|ленный *p.p.p. of* ⇒**~ить** *and adj.* embittered.

озлобля́|ть(ся), ю(сь) *impf. of* ⇒**озлóбить(ся)**

ознакóм|ить, лю, ишь *pf.* (*of* ⇒**~ля́ть**) (**с**+*i.*) to acquaint (with).

ознакóм|иться, люсь, ишься *pf.* (*of* ⇒**~ля́ться**) (**с**+*i.*) to familiarize o.s. with.

ознакомля́|ть(ся), ю(сь) *impf. of* ⇒**ознакóмить(ся)**

ознаменовáни|е, я *nt.* marking, commemoration; **в о.** (+*g.*) to mark, to commemorate, in commemoration (of).

ознамен|овáть, ýю *pf.* (*of* ⇒**~óвывать**) to mark, commemorate; to celebrate.

ознаменóвыва|ть, ю *impf. of* ⇒**ознаменовáть**

означá|ть, ю *impf.* to mean, signify, stand for; **что ~ют э́ти бýквы?** what do these letters stand for?

ознáченный *adj.* (*obs.*) the aforesaid.

ознóб, а *m.* shivering; chill; **почýвствовать о.** to feel shivery.

озноб|úть, лю́, úшь *pf.* (*of* ⇒**~ля́ть**) (*coll.*): **я ~úл себé ýши** *etc.*, my ears, *etc.*, are frozen.

ознобля́|ть, ю *impf. of* ⇒**ознобúть**

озоло|тúть, чý, тúшь *pf.* **1** to gild. **2** (*coll.*) (*обогатить*) to load with money, to pay s.o. handsomely.

озóн, а *m.* ozone.

озóнный *adj.* = **озóновый**

озонобезвред|ный (~ен, ~на) *adj.* ozone-friendly.

озóн|овый *adj. of* ⇒**~; ~овая ды́ра** hole in the ozone layer; **о. слой** ozone layer.

озорнúк, á *m.* (*coll.*) mischief-maker, rascal.

озорничá|ть, ю *impf.* (*of* ⇒**с~**) (*coll.*) to get up to mischief.

озорнóй *adj.* (*coll.*) mischievous.

озорств|ó, á *nt.* (*coll.*) mischief.

озя́б|нуть, ну, нешь, *past* **~, ~ла** *pf.* to be cold; **я ~!** I am frozen!

ой (*or* **ой-ой-ой**) *int. expr. surprise, fright or pain* o; oh; ow, ouch!; oops!

ок. (*abbr. of* **óколо**) approx., c., circa.

оказáни|е, я *nt.* rendering; showing.

ока|зáть, жý, ~́жешь *pf.* (*of* ⇒**~́зывать**) to render, show; **о. влия́ние** (**на**+*a.*) to influence, exert influence (upon); **о. внимáние** (+*d.*) to pay attention (to); **о. давлéние** (**на**+*a.*) to exert pressure (upon); **о. дéйствие** (**на**+*a.*) to have an effect (upon); to take effect; **о. пóмощь** (+*d.*) to help, give help; **о. предпочтéние** (+*d.*) to show preference (for), prefer; **о. содéйствие** (+*d.*) to render assistance; **о. сопротивлéние** (+*d.*) to offer, put up resistance (to); **о. услýгу** (+*d.*) to do, render a service; to do a good turn; **о. честь** (+*d.*) to do an honour (*Br.*), honor (*US*).

ока|зáться, жýсь, ~́жешься *pf.* (*of* ⇒**~́зываться**) **1** to turn out (to be), prove (to be); to be found (to be); **он ~зáлся отли́чным расскáзчиком** he proved to be a first-rate story-teller; **~зáлось, что онá всё врéмя лгалá** it turned out that she had been telling lies all the time. **2** (*очутиться*) to find o.s.; to be found; **я ~зáлся в больни́це** I found myself in hospital; **трёх экземпля́ров не ~зáлось** three copies were missing.

окáзи|я, и *f.* **1** (*возможность*) opportunity; **послáть письмó с ~ей** to send a letter with s.o. **2** (*coll.*) (*неожиданность*) unexpected happening; **что за о.!** what an odd thing!; how odd!

окáзыва|ть(ся), ю(сь) *impf. of* ⇒**оказáть(ся)**

окайм|úть, лю́, úшь *pf.* (*of* ⇒**~ля́ть**) (+*i.*) to border (with), edge (with).

окаймля́|ть, ю *impf. of* ⇒**окаймúть**

окáлин|а, ы *f.* (*tech.*) slag, dross.

окаменéлост|ь, и *f.* fossil.z

окаменéл|ый (~, ~а) *adj.* fossilized; petrified; (*fig.*) fixed, motionless.

окаменé|ть, ю *pf. of* ⇒**каменéть**

окант|овáть, ýю *pf. of* ⇒**кантовáть**[1]

окантóвк|а, и *f.* mount (*for pictures, etc.*).

окáнчива|ть(ся), ю(сь) *impf. of* ⇒**окóнчить(ся)**

óкань|е, я *nt.* okanie (*pronunciation of unstressed 'o' as 'o'*).

окáпыва|ть(ся), ю(сь) *impf. of* ⇒**окопáть(ся)**

окáрмлива|ть, ю *impf. of* ⇒**окормúть**

ока|тúть, чý, ~́тишь *pf.* (*of* ⇒**~́чивать**) to pour (over); **о. холóдной водóй** to pour cold water (over) (*also fig.*).

ока|тúться, чýсь, ~́тишься *pf.* (*of* ⇒**~́чиваться**) to pour over o.s.

о́ка|ть, ю *impf.* to pronounce unstressed 'o' as 'o' in Russian words.

ока́чива|ть(ся), ю(сь) *impf. of* ⇒**окати́ть(ся)**

окая́нный *adj.* damned, cursed.

окая́нств|о, а *nt.* (*eccl.*) sinfulness.

океа́н, а *m.* ocean.

Океа́ни|я, и *f.* Oceania; the South Sea Islands.

океано́граф, а *m.* oceanographer.

океанографи́ческий *adj.* oceanographic.

океаногра́фи|я, и *f.* oceanography.

океа́нский *adj.* ocean; oceanic; **о. парохо́д** ocean(-going) liner.

оки́дыва|ть, ю *impf. of* ⇒**оки́нуть**

оки́|нуть, ну, нешь *pf.* (*of* ⇒**~дывать**) to cast round; **о. взгля́дом, о. взо́ром** to take in at a glance; to glance over.

о́кис|ел, ла *m.* (*chem.*) oxide.

окисле́ни|е, я *nt.* (*chem.*) oxidation.

окисли́тел|ь, я *m.* (*chem.*) oxidizer, acidifier.

окисли́тельный *adj.* (*chem.*) oxidizing.

окисл|и́ть, ю́, и́шь *pf.* (*of* ⇒**~я́ть**) (*chem.*) to oxidize.

окисл|и́ться, и́тся *pf.* (*of* ⇒**~я́ться**) (*chem.*) to oxidize.

окисл|я́ть(ся), я́ю, я́ет(ся) *impf. of* ⇒**~и́ть(ся)**

о́кис|ь, и *f.* (*chem.*) oxide; **во́дная о.** hydroxide; **о. желе́за** ferric oxide; **о. углеро́да** carbon monoxide.

окказионали́зм, а *m.* (*ling.*) nonce-word.

оккульти́зм, а *m.* occultism.

окку́льтный *adj.* occult.

оккупа́нт, а *m.* invader, occupier.

оккупа|цио́нный *adj. of* ⇒**~ция; ~цио́нная а́рмия** army of occupation.

оккупа́ци|я, и *f.* (*mil.*) occupation.

оккупи́р|овать, ую *impf. and pf.* (*mil.*) to occupy.

окла́д[1]**, а** *m.* (*зарплата*) salary.

окла́д[2]**, а** *m.* (*иконы*) setting, framework.

окла́дист|ый (~, ~а) *adj.* (*борода*) broad and thick.

оклеве|та́ть, щу́, ~щешь *pf.* to slander, defame.

окле́ива|ть, ю *impf. of* ⇒**окле́ить**

окле́|ить, ю, ишь *pf.* (*of* ⇒**~ивать**) (+*i.*) to cover (with); to paste over (with); **о. ко́мнату обо́ями** to paper a room.

окле́йк|а, и *f.* glueing, pasting; **о. обо́ями** papering.

о́клик, а *m.* hail, call.

оклик|а́ть, а́ю *impf. of* ⇒**~нуть**

окли́к|нуть, ну, нешь *pf.* (*of* ⇒**~а́ть**) to hail, call (to).

окн|о́, а́, *pl.* **~а, о́кон, ~ам** *nt.* **1** (*also comput.*) window; **опускно́е о.** sash window; **слухово́е о.** dormer window; **ко́мната в три ~а́** a room with three windows; **о. вы́дачи** serving-hatch. **2** (*подоконник*) window-sill. **3** (*fig.*) (*отверстие*) gap, break.

о́к|о, а, *pl.* **о́чи, оче́й** *nt.* (*arch. or poet.*) eye; **в мгнове́ние ~а** in the twinkling of an eye; **о. за о.** an eye for an eye.

ок|ова́ть, ую́, уёшь *pf.* (*of* ⇒**~о́вывать**) to bind (*with metal*); (*fig.*) to fetter, shackle.

око́вк|а, и *f.* binding (*with metal*).

око́в|ы, ~ *no sg.* fetters (*also fig.*).

око́выва|ть, ю *impf. of* ⇒**окова́ть**

окола́чива|ться, юсь *impf.* (*coll.*) to lounge about, kick one's heels.

околд|ова́ть, у́ю *pf.* (*of* ⇒**~о́вывать**) to bewitch, entrance, enchant (*also fig.*).

околдо́выва|ть, ю *impf. of* ⇒**околдова́ть**

околева́|ть, ю *impf. of* ⇒**околе́ть**

околе́сиц|а, ы *and* **околё́сиц|а, ы** *f.* (*coll.*) nonsense, rubbish; **нести́ ~у** to talk nonsense.

околе́|ть, ю *pf.* (*of* ⇒**~ва́ть**) to die (*of animals and pej. of persons*).

око́лиц|а, ы *f.* outskirts (of a village); **вы́ехать за ~у** to leave the confines of a village; **на ~е** on the outskirts.

околи́чност|ь, и *f.* (*obs.*) circumlocution; innuendo; **говори́ть без ~ей** to speak plainly.

о́коло *prep.*+*g. and adv.* **1** (*рядом, возле*) by; (*вблизи*) close (to), near; (*вокруг*) around, about; **он сиде́л о. меня́** he was sitting by me; **никого́ нет о.** there is nobody about; **где́-н. о. (э́того ме́ста)** hereabouts, somewhere here; **(что́-н.) о. э́того, о. того́** thereabouts. **2** (*приблизительно*) about; **о. полу́ночи** about midnight; **о. шести́ ме́тров** about six metres (*Br.*), meters (*US*).

околопло́дник, а *m.* (*bot.*) pericarp, seed vessel.

околосерде́чн|ый *adj.* **~ая су́мка** (*anat.*) pericardium.

околпа́чива|ть, ю *impf. of* ⇒**околпа́чить**

околпа́ч|ить, у, ишь *pf.* (*of* ⇒**~ивать**) (*coll.*) to fool, dupe.

око́лыш, а *m.* cap-band.

око́льны|й *adj.* roundabout; **~е пути́** devious ways; **вы́ведать ~м путём** (*fig.*) to find out in a roundabout way.

окольц|ева́ть, у́ю *pf. of* ⇒**кольцева́ть** 2

оконе́чност|ь, и *f.* extremity.

око́нн|ый *adj. of* ⇒**окно́; ~ая ра́ма** window-frame; **~ое стекло́** window-pane.

оконфу́|зить, жу, зишь *pf.* (*coll.*) to embarrass, confuse.

оконча́ни|е, я *nt.* **1** (*завершение*) completion, conclusion; (*конец*) end; **о. сро́ка** expiration; **по ~и университе́та** on graduating; **о. сле́дует** (*note to serial article, story, etc.*) to be concluded. **2** (*gram.*) ending.

оконча́тельно *adv.* (*бесповоротно*) finally, definitively; (*совершенно*) completely.

оконча́тел|ьный (~ен, ~ьна) *adj.* (*бесповоротный*) final, definitive; (*совершенный*) complete.

око́нч|ить, у, ишь *pf.* (*of* ⇒**ока́нчивать**) to finish, end; **о. шко́лу** to leave school (*Br.*), to graduate from high school (*US*); **о. университе́т** to graduate.

око́нч|иться, ится *pf.* (*of* ⇒**ока́нчиваться**) to finish, end; to be over.

око́п, а *m.* (*mil.*) trench; entrenchment.

окопа́|ть, ю *pf.* (*of* ⇒**ока́пывать**) to dig round; (*картофель*) to earth up.

окопа́|ться, юсь *pf.* (*of* ⇒**ока́пываться**) **1** (*mil.*) to entrench (o.s.), dig in. **2** (*fig., iron.*) to find o.s. a comfortable hide-out.

око́п|ный *adj. of* ⇒**~; ~ная война́** trench warfare.

окорм|и́ть, лю́, ~ишь *pf.* (*of* ⇒**ока́рмливать**) **1** (*обкормить*) to overfeed. **2** (*отравить*) to poison with bad food.

окорна́|ть, ю *pf. of* ⇒**корна́ть**

о́коро|к, ка, *pl.* **~ка́** *m.* ham; (*баранины, телятины*) leg.

окосе́|ть, ю *pf.* (*coll.*) **1** to develop a squint. **2** (*ослепнуть*) to go blind in one eye. **3** (*опьянеть*) to get drunk.

окостенева́|ть, ю *impf. of* ⇒**окостене́ть**

окостене́л|ый (~, ~а) *adj.* ossified (*also fig.*).

окостене́|ть, ю *pf.* (*of* ⇒**костене́ть** *and* **~ва́ть**) to ossify (*also fig.*); (*окоченеть*) to stiffen.

око|ти́ться, ти́тся *pf. of* ⇒**коти́ться**

окочене́л|ый (~, ~а) *adj.* stiff with cold.

окочене́|ть, ю *pf. of* ⇒**кочене́ть**

око́ш|ко, ка, *pl.* **~ки, ~ек, ~кам** *nt. dim. of* ⇒**окно́**

окра́ин|а, ы *f.* **1** (*города*) outskirts; outlying districts; (*леса, деревни*) edge. **2** *pl.* (*страны*) border areas.

окра́|сить, шу, сишь *pf.* (*of* ⇒**~шивать**) (*стену, крышу*) to paint; (*ткань, волосы*) to dye; (*жизнь*) to colour (*Br.*), color (*US*); **слегка́ о.** to tinge, tint.

окра́ск|а, и *f.* **1** (*действие*) painting; dyeing. **2** (*цвет*) colouring (*Br.*), coloring (*US*), coloration; **защи́тная о.** (*zool.*) protective coloration. **3** (*fig.*) tinge, tint; (*pol.*) slant; **ирони́ческая о.** ironic tinge, touch of irony; **стилисти́ческая о.** stylistic nuance; **прида́ть чему́-н. другу́ю ~у** to put a different complexion on sth.

окра́шива|ть, ю *impf. of* ⇒**окра́сить**

окре́п|нуть, ну, нешь, *past* **~, ~ла** *pf. of* ⇒**кре́пнуть**

окре|сти́ть, щу́, ~стишь *pf.* **1** (*impf.* **крести́ть**) to baptize, christen. **2** (*coll.*; +*a. and i.*) to nickname; **его́ ~стили «медве́дем»** he was nicknamed 'the bear'.

окре|сти́ться, щу́сь, ~стишься *pf. of* ⇒**крести́ться** 1

окре́стност|ь, и *f.* **1** (*столицы, деревни*) environs. **2** (*окружающее пространство*) neighbourhood (*Br.*), neighborhood (*US*), vicinity.

окре́стный *adj.* **1** (*деревня, город*) neighbouring (*Br.*), neighboring (*US*). **2** (*люди, население*) local.

окриве́|ть, ю *pf. of* ⇒**криве́ть**

о́крик, а *m.* shout, cry.

окри́кива|ть, ю *impf. of* ⇒**окри́кнуть**

окри́к|нуть, ну, нешь *pf.* (*of* ⇒**~ивать**) to hail, shout (to).

окрова́в|ить, лю, ишь *pf.* (*of* ⇒**~ливать**) to stain with blood.

окрова́в|иться, люсь, ишься *pf.* (*of* ⇒**~ливаться**) to become bloodstained; to be soaked in blood; to spill blood on o.s.

окрова́в|ленный *p.p.p. of* ⇒**~ить** *and adj.* blood-stained; bloody.

окрова́влива|ть(ся), ю(сь) *impf. of* ⇒**окрова́вить(ся)**

окровен|и́ть, ю́, и́шь *pf.* (*coll.*) to stain with blood.

окроп|и́ть, лю́, и́шь *pf.* (*of* ⇒**кропи́ть** *and* **~ля́ть**) to sprinkle.

окропля́|ть, ю *impf. of* ⇒**окропи́ть**

окро́шк|а, и *f.* **1** okroshka (*cold kvass soup with chopped vegetables and meat or fish*). **2** (*fig., coll.*) (*смесь*) hodgepodge, jumble.

о́круг, а, *pl.* **~а́** *m.* (*in former USSR, territorial division for administrative, legal, military, etc., purposes*) okrug; region, district; circuit; **избира́тельный о.** electoral district.

окру́г|а, и *f.* (*coll.*) neighbourhood (*Br.*), neighborhood (*US*).

округле́|ть, ю *pf. of* ⇒**кругле́ть**

округл|и́ть, ю́, и́шь *pf.* (*of* ⇒**~я́ть**) **1** to make round; to round (off) (*also fig.*). **2** (*счёт, цифры*) to express in round numbers. **3** (*coll.*) (*имение, капитал*) to increase.

округл|и́ться, ю́сь, и́шься *pf.* (*of* ⇒**~я́ться**) **1** (*фигура, глаза*) to become round(ed). **2** (*счёт*) to be expressed in round numbers.

окру́глост|ь, и *f.* **1** (*свойство*) roundedness. **2** (*выпуклость*) protuberance, bulge.

окру́гл|ый (~, ~а) *adj.* rounded; (*лицо*) round.

округл|я́ть(ся), я́ю(сь) *impf. of* ⇒**~и́ть(ся)**

окруж|а́ть, а́ю *impf. of* ⇒**~и́ть**

окружа́|ющий *pres. part. act. of* ⇒**~ть** *and adj.* surrounding; **~ющая обстано́вка** surroundings; *as n.* **~ющее, ~ющего** *nt.* environment; **~ющие, ~ющих** the people around/surrounding one.

окруже́ни|е, я *nt.* **1** (*действие*) encirclement; **попа́сть в о.** (*mil.*) to be encircled, be surrounded. **2** (*среда*) surroundings; environment; milieu; **в ~и** (+*g.*) surrounded (by), in the midst (of); **он появи́лся в ~и боле́льщиков** he appeared surrounded by fans; (*люди*) the people around/surrounding one.

окруж|и́ть, у́, и́шь *pf.* (*of* ⇒**~а́ть**) to surround; to encircle; **о. кого́-н. забо́той** to lavish attentions on s.o.

окружн|о́й *adj.* **1** *adj. of* ⇒**о́круг; о. суд** circuit court. **2** operating (situated) about a circle; **~а́я желе́зная доро́га** circle line; **~а́я доро́га** circular road.

окру́жност|ь, и *f.* **1** circumference; (*замкнутая кривая*) circle; **име́ть де́сять ме́тров в ~и** to be ten metres (*Br.*), meters (*US*) in circumference; **на три ми́ли в ~и** within a radius of three miles, for three miles round. **2** (*obs.*) (*округа*) neighbourhood (*Br.*), neighborhood (*US*).

окру|ти́ть, чу́, ~тишь *pf.* (*of* ⇒**~чивать**) (+*i.*) to wind round.

окру́чива|ть, ю *impf. of* ⇒**окрути́ть**

окрыл|и́ть, ю́, и́шь *pf.* (*of* ⇒**~я́ть**) to inspire, encourage.

окрыл|я́ть, я́ю *impf. of* ⇒**~и́ть**

окры́с|иться, ишься *pf.* (**на**+*a.*; *coll.*) to snap (at).

О́ксфорд, а *m.* Oxford.

окта́в|а, ы *f.* octave.

окта́н, а *m.* (*chem.*) octane.

окта́нов|ый *adj.* (*chem.*) octane; **~ое число́** octane number, octane rating.

окта́эдр, а *m.* (*math.*) octahedron.

окте́т, а *m.* (*mus.*) octet.

октро́ир|овать, ую *impf. and pf.* to grant; to concede.

октябр|ёнок, ёнка, *pl.* **~я́та, ~я́т** *m.* (Little) Octobrist (*in former USSR, child aged 7–11 preparing for entry into Pioneers*).

октя́бр|ь, я́ *m.* October (*fig.* = *Russian revolution of October 1917*).

октя́брь|ский *adj. of* ⇒**~**

окули́ст, а *m.* optician, oculist.

окуля́р, а *m.* eye-piece.

окун|а́ть(ся), а́ю(сь) *impf. of* ⇒**~у́ть(ся)**

о́кун|евый *adj. of* ⇒**~ь**

окун|у́ть, у́, ёшь, *pf.* (*of* ⇒**~а́ть**) to dip; **о. ло́жку в па́току** to dip a spoon into the treacle.

окун|у́ться, у́сь, ёшься *pf.* (*of* ⇒**~а́ться**) **1** to dip (o.s.). **2** (*fig.*; **в**+*a.*) to plunge (into), become (utterly) absorbed (in), engrossed (in); **о. в спор** to plunge into an argument.

о́кун|ь, я, *pl.* **~и, ~е́й** *m.* (*zool.*) perch.

окупа́емост|ь, и *f.* viability.

окуп|а́ть(ся), а́ю(сь) *impf. of* ⇒**~и́ть(ся)**

окуп|и́ть, лю́, ~ишь *pf.* (*of* ⇒**~а́ть**) to compensate, repay, make up (for); **о. расхо́ды** to cover one's outlay.

окуп|и́ться, лю́сь, ~ишься *pf.* (*of* ⇒**~а́ться**) to be compensated, be repaid; (*fig.*) to pay; to be justified, be requited, be rewarded; **затра́ченные на́ми уси́лия ~и́лись** our efforts were rewarded.

окургу́|зить, жу, зишь *pf.* (*coll.*) to cut too short.

оку́ривани|е, я *nt.* fumigation.

оку́рива|ть, ю *impf. of* ⇒**окури́ть**

окур|и́ть, ю́, ~ишь *pf.* (*of* ⇒**~ивать**) to fumigate.

оку́р|ок, ка *m.* (*сигареты*) cigarette-end; (*сигары*) cigar-butt.

оку́т|ать, аю *pf.* (*of* ⇒**~ывать**) (+*i.*) **1** to wrap up (in). **2** (*fig.*) to shroud, cloak (in); **о. та́йной** to shroud in mystery.

оку́т|аться, аюсь, *pf.* (*of* ⇒**~ываться**) (+*i.*) **1** to wrap o.s. up (in). **2** (*fig.*) to shroud, cloak o.s. (in); **о. та́йной** to shroud o.s. in mystery.

оку́тыва|ть(ся), ю(сь) *impf. of* ⇒**оку́тать(ся)**

оку́чива|ть, ю *impf. of* ⇒**оку́чить**

оку́ч|ить, у, ишь *pf.* (*of* ⇒**~ивать**) (*agric.*) to earth up.

ола́д|ья, ьи, *pl.* **~ьи, ~ий** *f.* fritter; **карто́фельная о.** potato cake.

олеа́ндр, а *m.* oleander.

оледене́лый *adj.* frozen.

оледене́|ть, ю *pf. of* ⇒**ледене́ть**

оледен|и́ть, ю́, и́шь *pf. of* ⇒**ледени́ть**

оленево́д, а *m.* reindeer-breeder.

оленево́дств|о, а *nt.* reindeer-breeding.

оле́н|ий *adj. of* ⇒**~ь; ~ьи рога́** antlers; **о. лиша́й, о. мох** (*bot.*) reindeer moss.

оле́ни́н|а, ы *f.* venison.

оле́н|ь, я *m.* deer; **благоро́дный о.** stag, red deer; **се́верный о.** reindeer.

оли́в|а, ы *f.* (*obs.*) (*дерево*) olive-tree; (*плод*) olive.

оливи́н, а *m.* (*min.*) olivine, chrysolite.

оли́вк|а, и *f.* (*плод*) olive.

оли́вков|ый *adj.* **1** olive; **~ая ветвь** olive branch (*fig.*); **~ое ма́сло** olive oil. **2** (*цвет*) olive-green.

олига́рх, а *m.* oligarch.

олигархи́ческий *adj.* oligarchical.

олига́рхи|я, и *f.* oligarchy.

олигоце́н, а *m.* (*geol.*) Oligocene (epoch).

Оли́мп, а *m.* (Mt.) Olympus (*geog. and myth.*).

олимпиа́д|а, ы *f.* **1** (*олимпийские игры*) Olympics. **2** (*соревнования*) Olympiad.

олимпи́|ец, йца *m.* (*myth. and fig.*) Olympian.

олимпи́йски|й[1] *adj.* Olympic; **~е и́гры** Olympic Games, Olympics.

олимпи́йск|ий[2] *adj.* of Olympus; **~ое споко́йствие** (*fig.*) Olympian calm.

оли́ф|а, ы *f.* drying oil.

олицетворе́ни|е, я *nt.* personification; embodiment.

олицетвор|ённый *p.p.p. of* ⇒**~и́ть; он — ~ённая хи́трость** he is cunning personified.

олицетвор|и́ть, ю́, и́шь *pf.* (*of* ⇒**~я́ть**) to personify; to embody.

олицетвор|я́ть, я́ю *impf. of* ⇒**~и́ть**

о́лов|о, а *nt.* tin.

оловя́нн|ый *adj.* tin; **~ая посу́да** tinware; pewter; **~ая фо́льга** tin foil.

о́лух, а *m.* (*coll.*) blockhead, oaf; **о. царя́ небе́сного** complete idiot.

о́луш|а, и *f.* (*zool.*): **се́верная о.** gannet.

О́льстер, а *m.* Ulster.

ольх|а́, и́, *pl.* **~и** *f.* alder(-tree).
ольх|о́вый *adj. of* **⇒~а́**
оля́пк|а, и *f.* (*zool.*) dipper.
ом, а *m.* (*elec.*) ohm.
Ома́н, а *m.* Oman.
ома́р, а *m.* lobster.
оме́г|а, и *f.* omega; **от а́льфы до ~и** (*fig.*) from A to Z, from beginning to end.
оме́л|а, ы *f.* mistletoe.
омерзе́ни|е, я *nt.* loathing; **внуши́ть о.** (+*d.*) to inspire loathing (in).
омерзе́|ть, ю *pf.* to become loathsome; **мне э́тот пейза́ж ~л** I have come to loathe this view.
омерзи́тел|ьный (~ен, ~ьна) *adj.* loathsome, disgusting; (*coll.*) foul.
омертве́лост|ь, и *f.* stiffness, numbness; (*med.*) necrosis, mortification.
омертве́л|ый (~, ~а) *adj.* stiff, numb; (*med.*) necrotic; **~ая ткань** dead tissue.
омертве́ни|е, я *nt.* = **омертве́лость**
омертве́|ть, ю *pf. of* **⇒мертве́ть** 1
омертв|и́ть, лю́, и́шь *pf.* (*of* **⇒~ля́ть**) **1** to deaden. **2** (*econ.*) to withdraw from circulation.
омертвля́|ть, ю *impf. of* **⇒омертви́ть**
омёт, а *m.* stack (of straw).
омле́т, а *m.* omelette (*Br.*), omelet (*US*).
омме́тр, а *m.* (*elec.*) ohmmeter.
о́мнибус, а *m.* (*obs.*) (horse-drawn) omnibus.
омове́ни|е, я *nt.* ablution(s).
омола́жива|ть(ся), ю(сь) *impf. of* **⇒омолоди́ть(ся)**
омоло|ди́ть, жу́, ди́шь *pf.* (*of* **⇒омола́живать**) to rejuvenate.
омоло|ди́ться, жу́сь, ди́шься *pf.* (*of* **⇒омола́живаться**) to be rejuvenated.
омоложе́ни|е, я *nt.* rejuvenation.
ОМО́Н *m. indecl.* (*abbr. of* ***отря́д мили́ции осо́бого назначе́ния***) special forces unit; riot squad.
омо́ним, а *m.* (*ling.*) homonym.
омо́нов|ец, ца *m.* member of the special force.
омоч|и́ть, у́, ~ишь *pf.* (*obs.*) to wet; to moisten.
омоч|и́ться, у́сь, ~ишься *pf.* (*obs.*) to become wet; to become moist.
омрач|а́ть(ся), а́ю(сь) *impf. of* **⇒~и́ть(ся)**
омрач|и́ть, у́, и́шь *pf.* (*of* **⇒~а́ть**) to darken, cloud.
омрач|и́ться, у́сь, и́шься *pf.* (*of* **⇒~а́ться**) to darken, become clouded (*also fig.*).
о́мул|ь, я, *g. pl.* **~е́й** *m.* omul (*sea fish of salmon family, found also in Lake Baikal*).
о́мут, а *m.* **1** (*водоворот*) whirlpool; (*fig.*) whirl, maelstrom. **2** (*глубокое место*) deep place (*in river or lake*); **в ти́хом ~е че́рти во́дятся** (*prov.*) still waters run deep.
омыва́|ть, ю 1 *impf. of* **⇒омы́ть. 2** *impf.* (*geog.*) (*о морях*) to wash.
омыва́|ться, ется *impf.* (*geog.*) to be washed.
ом|ы́ть, о́ю, о́ешь *pf.* (*of* **⇒~ыва́ть**) (*rhet., obs.*) to wash; **о. кро́вью** to steep in blood.
он, его́, ему́, им, о нём *pron.* he.
она́, её, ей, ей (е́ю), о ней *pron.* she.
онани́зм, а *m.* masturbation.
онани́р|овать, ую *impf.* to masturbate.
онда́тр|а, ы *f.* (*животное*) musk-rat, musquash; (*мех*) musquash.
онда́тр|овый *adj. of* **⇒~а**
онеме́л|ый (~, ~а) *adj.* **1** (*немой*) dumb. **2** (*омертвелый*) numb.
онеме́|ть, ю *pf. of* **⇒неме́ть**
они́, их, им, и́ми, о них *pron.* they.
о́никс, а *m.* onyx.
онко́лог, а *m.* oncologist.
онкологи́ческий *adj.* oncological.
онколо́ги|я, и *f.* (*med.*) oncology.
онла́йновый *adj.* (*comput.*) online.
ОНО *nt. indecl.* (*abbr. of* ***отде́л наро́дного образова́ния***) education department (*of local authority*).
оно́, его́, ему́, им, о нём *pron.* **1** it. **2** (*это*) this, that; **о. и ви́дно** that is evident. **3** *as emph. particle* **о. коне́чно** well, of course; **вот о. что!** oh, I see!
onoма́стик|а, и *f.* (*ling.*) onomastics.
ономасти́ческий *adj.* onomastic.
онтогене́з, а *m.* (*biol.*) ontogenesis.
онтологи́ческий *adj.* (*phil.*) ontological.
онтоло́ги|я, и *f.* (*phil.*) ontology.
ону́ч|а, и *f.* onucha (*foot binding worn instead of sock*).
о́ный *pron.* (*obs.*) that; the above-mentioned; **во вре́мя о́но** in those days; (*joc.*) in days of old.
ОО́Н *f. indecl.* (*abbr. of* ***Организа́ция Объединённых На́ций***) UN (*United Nations Organization*).
оо́новский *adj.* (*coll.*) UN (*United Nations*).
ООП *f. indecl.* (*abbr. of* ***Организа́ция освобожде́ния Палести́ны***) PLO (*Palestine Liberation Organization*).
опада́|ть, ю *impf. of* **⇒опа́сть**
опада́|ющий *pres. part. act. of* **⇒~ть** *and adj.* (*bot.*) deciduous.
опа́здыва|ть, ю *impf.* **1** *impf. of* **⇒опозда́ть. 2** (*impf. only*) (*coll.*) (*о часах*) to be slow.
опа́ива|ть, ю *impf. of* **⇒опои́ть**
опа́л, а *m.* opal.
опа́л|а, ы *f.* disgrace, disfavour (*Br.*), disfavor (*US*); **быть в ~е** to be in disgrace, be out of favour (*Br.*), favor (*US*).
опа́лива|ть(ся), ю(сь) *impf. of* **⇒опали́ть(ся)**
опал|и́ть, ю́, и́шь *pf.* (*of* **⇒пали́ть**[1] *and* **~ивать**) to singe.
опал|и́ться, ю́сь, и́шься *pf.* (*of* **⇒~иваться**) to singe o.s.
опа́ловый *adj.* opal; (*цвет*) opaline.
опа́лубк|а, и *f.* (*tech.*) **1** (*обшивка*) casing, lining, sheathing, tubbing; **о. кры́ши** roof-boarding. **2** (*форма*) concrete mould, form.
опа́лый *adj.* (*coll.*) sunken; emaciated.
опа́льный *adj.* disgraced; in disgrace, out of favour (*Br.*), favor (*US*).
опа́мят|оваться, уюсь *pf.* (*coll.*) to come to one's senses; to collect o.s.
опа́р|а, ы *f.* **1** (*тесто*) leavened dough. **2** (*закваска*) leaven.
опарши́ве|ть, ю *pf. of* **⇒парши́веть**
опаса́|ться, юсь *impf.* **1** (+*g.*) (*бояться*) to fear, be afraid (of). **2** (+*g. or inf.*) (*избегать*) to beware (of); to avoid, keep off; **о. сли́шком мно́го пить** to beware of drinking to excess.
опасе́ни|е, я *nt.* fear; apprehension.
опа́ск|а, и *f.*: **с ~ой** (*coll.*) with caution, cautiously; warily.
опа́слив|ый (~, ~а) *adj.* (*coll.*) cautious; wary.
опа́сност|ь, и *f.* danger; peril; **вне ~и** out of danger.
опа́с|ный (~ен, ~на) *adj.* dangerous, perilous.
опа́|сть, ду́, дёшь *pf.* (*of* **⇒~да́ть**) **1** (*о листьях*) to fall (off). **2** (*о ветре, воде*) to subside; (*об опухоли*) to go down; (*о суфле*) to sink.
опаха́л|о, а *nt.* fan.
опа|ха́ть, шу́, ~шешь *pf.* (*of* **⇒~хивать**[1]) to plough round.
опа́хива|ть[1]**, ю** *impf. of* **⇒опаха́ть**
опа́хива|ть[2]**, ю** *impf. of* **⇒опахну́ть**
опах|ну́ть, ну́, нёшь *pf.* (*of* **⇒~ивать**[2]) to fan.
ОПЕ́К *f. indecl.* OPEC (*abbr. of* Organization of Petroleum-Exporting Countries — *Организа́ция стран-экспортёров не́фти*).
опе́к|а, и *f.* **1** guardianship (*also fig.*); (*над имуществом*) trusteeship; **быть под ~ой кого́-н.** to be under s.o.'s guardianship; **взять под ~у** to take into one's care; (*fig.*) to take charge (of), take under one's wing; **учреди́ть ~у над кем-н.** to place s.o. in care. **2** (*collect.*) (*лица*) guardians, board of guardians; **Междунаро́дная о.** International Trusteeship. **3** (*fig.*) (*забота*) care.
опека́|емый *pres. part. pass. of* **⇒~ть;** *as n.* **о., ~емого** *m.* ward.
опека́|ть, ю *impf.* **1** (*сирот*) to be guardian (to), have the wardship (of). **2** (*fig.*) (*младших*) to take care (of), watch (over).
опеку́н, а́ *m.* (*leg.*) guardian; (*над имуществом*) trustee.
опеку́н|ский *adj. of* **⇒~**
опеку́нств|о, а *nt.* guardianship.
опеку́н|ша, ши *f. of* **⇒~**
опён|ок, ка, *pl.* **~ки, ~ков** *m.* honey agaric (*mushroom*).
о́пер|а, ы *f.* opera; **«мы́льная о.»** soap (opera); **из друго́й ~ы, не из той ~ы** (*coll.*) quite a different matter.
опера́бел|ьный (~ен, ~ьна) *adj.* (*med.*) operable.
операти́вник, а *m.* detective.

операти́вност|ь, и *f.* energy, efficiency (*in getting things done*).

операти́в|ный *adj.* **1** (**~ен, ~на**) (*руководство*) energetic; efficient. **2** (*штаб, работа*) executive. **3** (*med.*) operative; surgical; **~ное вмеша́тельство** surgical intervention. **4** (*mil.*) operation(s), operational.

опера́тор, а *m.* **1** (*оборудования*) operator. **2** (*кинооператор*) cameraman. **3** (*врач-хирург*) surgeon.

опера|цио́нный *adj. of* ⇒**~ция; ~цио́нное отделе́ние** (*in hospital*) surgical wing; **~цио́нная систе́ма** (*comput.*) operating system; **о. стол** operating-table; *as n.* **~цио́нная, ~цио́нной** *f.* operating theatre (*Br.*), operating-room (*US*).

опера́ци|я, и *f.* (*med., mil., etc.*) operation; **перенести́ ~ю** to have, undergo an operation; to be operated (upon); **сде́лать ~ю** to perform an operation.

опере|ди́ть, жу́, ди́шь *pf.* (*of* ⇒**~жа́ть**) **1** (*в беге, в развитии*) to outstrip, leave behind. **2** (*успеть раньше*) to forestall.

опережа́|ть, ю *impf. of* ⇒**опереди́ть**

опере́ни|е, я *nt.* plumage; **хвостово́е о.** (*aeron.*) tail unit.

оперённый *adj.* feathered.

опере́т|очный *adj. of* ⇒**~та**

опере́тт|а, ы *f.* musical comedy, operetta.

опере́ть, обопру́, обопрёшь, *past* **опёр, оперла́** *pf.* (*of* ⇒**опира́ть**) (**o**+*a.*) to lean (against).

опере́ться, обопру́сь, обопрёшься, *past* **опёрся, оперла́сь** *pf.* (*of* ⇒**опира́ться**) (**на**+*a.*; **o**+*a.*) **1** to lean (on; against); **о. о подоко́нник** to lean against the window-sill. **2** (*fig.*) to rely on; to depend on.

опери́р|овать, ую *impf. and pf.* **1** (*med.*) to operate (upon). **2** (*mil.*) to operate, act. **3** (+*i.*) (*fin.*) to deal (in); (*fig.*) to use, handle; **о. недоста́точными да́нными** to operate with inadequate data.

опер|и́ть, ю́, и́шь *pf.* (*of* ⇒**~я́ть**) (*стрелу*) to feather; (*украсить*) to adorn with feathers.

опер|и́ться, ю́сь, и́шься *pf.* (*of* ⇒**~я́ться**) **1** (*о птицах*) to be fledged. **2** (*fig.*) to stand on one's own (two) feet.

о́перн|ый *adj.* opera (*attr.*); (*ария; жест*) operatic; **о. певе́ц, ~ая певи́ца** opera singer; **о. теа́тр** opera-house.

опёрт|ый (~, ~а́, ~о) *p.p.p. of* ⇒**опере́ть**

опер|ши́сь *past ger. of* ⇒**~е́ться; о.** (**на**+*a.*) leaning (on).

опер|я́ть(ся), я́ю(сь) *impf. of* ⇒**~и́ть(ся)**

опеча́л|ить(ся), ю(сь), ишь(ся) *pf. of* ⇒**печа́лить(ся)**

опеча́т|ать, аю *pf.* (*of* ⇒**~ывать**) to seal up.

опеча́т|ка, ки *f.* misprint; **спи́сок ~ок** (list of) errata.

опеча́тыва|ть, ю *impf. of* ⇒**опеча́тать**

опе́ш|ить, у, ишь *pf.* (*coll.*) to be taken aback.

опива́|ться, юсь *impf. of* ⇒**опи́ться**

о́пи|й, я *m.* opium.

о́пий|ный *adj. of* ⇒**~**

опи́лива|ть, ю *impf. of* ⇒**опили́ть**

опил|и́ть, ю́, ́~ишь *pf.* (*of* ⇒**́~ивать**) to saw; to file.

опи́л|ки, ок *no sg.* (*древесные*) sawdust; (*металлические*) (metal) filings.

опира́|ть(ся), ю(сь) *impf. of* ⇒**опере́ть(ся)**

описа́ни|е, я *nt.* description; account; **э́то не поддаётся ~ю** it is beyond description, it beggars description.

опи́с|анный *p.p.p. of* ⇒**~а́ть** *and adj.* (*math.*) circumscribed.

описа́тел|ьный (~ен, ~ьна) *adj.* descriptive.

описа́тельств|о, а *nt.* (*pej.*) (bare) description.

опи|са́ть, шу́, ́~шешь *pf.* (*of* ⇒**́~сывать**) **1** to describe. **2** (*сделать опись*) to list, inventory; **о. иму́щество** (*leg.*) to distrain property. **3** (*math.*) to describe, circumscribe.

опи|са́ться, шу́сь, ́~шешься *pf.* to make a slip of the pen.

опи́ск|а, и *f.* slip of the pen.

опи́сыва|ть, ю *impf. of* ⇒**описа́ть**

о́пис|ь, и *f.* list; inventory; **о. иму́щества** (*leg.*) distraint.

опи́|ться, обопью́сь, обопьёшься, *past* **́~лся, ~ла́сь, ́~ло́сь** *pf.* (*of* ⇒**~ва́ться**) (*coll.*) to drink to excess, drink o.s. stupid.

о́пиум, а *m.* opium.

о́пиум|ный *adj. of* ⇒**~**

опла́|кать, чу, чешь *pf.* (*of* ⇒**~кивать**) to mourn (over); to bewail, bemoan.

опла́кива|ть, ю *impf. of* ⇒**опла́кать**

опла́т|а, ы *f.* pay, payment; **почасова́я о.** payment by the hour; **сде́льная о.** piece work payment.

опла|ти́ть, чу́, ́~тишь *pf.* to pay (for); **о. расхо́ды** to foot the bill; **о. счёт** to settle the account, pay the bill; **о. убы́тки** to pay damages.

опла́|ченный *p.p.p. of* ⇒**~ти́ть; с ~ченным отве́том** reply-paid.

опла́чива|ть, ю *impf. of* ⇒**оплати́ть**

опла́|чу, чешь *see* ⇒**~кать**

опла|чу́, ́~тишь *see* ⇒**~ти́ть**

оплёв|анный *p.p.p. of* ⇒**~а́ть; как о.** as if in disgrace, feeling utterly humiliated.

опл|ева́ть, юю́, юёшь *pf.* (*of* ⇒**~ёвывать**) **1** (*coll.*) to cover with spittle. **2** (*fig.*) (*оскорбить*) to spit upon, humiliate.

оплёвыва|ть, ю *impf. of* ⇒**оплева́ть**

опле|сти́, ту́, тёшь, *past* **́~л, ~ла́** *pf.* (*of* ⇒**~та́ть**) to twine (round); to braid.

оплета́|ть, ю *impf. of* ⇒**оплести́**

оплеу́х|а, и *f.* (*coll.*) slap in the face.

опле́ч|ье, ья, *g. pl.* **~ий** *nt.* (*obs.*) shoulder(s) (*of garment*).

оплеши́ве|ть, ю *pf. of* ⇒**плеши́веть**

оплодотворе́ни|е, я *nt.* fertilization.

оплодотвори́тел|ь, я *m.* (*bot.*) fertilizer.

оплодотвор|и́ть, ю́, и́шь *pf.* (*of* ⇒**~я́ть**) to fertilize.

оплодотвор|я́ть, я́ю *impf. of* ⇒**~и́ть**

опломбир|ова́ть, у́ю *pf. of* ⇒**пломбирова́ть**

оплo´т, а *m.* (*rhet.*) stronghold, bulwark.

оплоша́|ть, ю *pf.* (*coll.*) to take a false step, blunder.

опло́шност|ь, и *f.* false step, blunder.

опло́ш|ный (~ен, ~на) *adj.* (*obs.*) **1** mistaken; **о. посту́пок** false step. **2** blundering.

оплыва́|ть, ю *impf. of* ⇒**оплы́ть**

оплы́|ть[1]**, ву́, вёшь,** *past* **~л, ~ла́, ~ло** *pf.* (*of* ⇒**~ва́ть**) **1** (*о лице*) to become swollen, swell up. **2** (*о свече*) to gutter. **3** (*о береге*) to collapse (*as a result of a landslide*).

оплы́|ть[2]**, ву́, вёшь,** *past* **~л, ~ла́, ~ло** *pf.* (*of* ⇒**~ва́ть**) (*на судне*) to sail round; (*без судна*) to swim round; **о. о́стров** to sail round an island; **о. о́зеро** to sail round (the edge of) a lake.

опове|сти́ть, щу́, сти́шь *pf.* (*of* ⇒**~ща́ть**) to notify, inform.

оповеща́|ть, ю *impf. of* ⇒**оповести́ть**

оповеще́ни|е, я *nt.* notification.

опога́н|ить, ю, ишь *pf. of* ⇒**пога́нить**

оподле́|ть, ю *pf. of* ⇒**подле́ть**

опо́|ек, йка *m.* calf(-leather).

опо́ечный *adj.* calf(-skin).

опозда́|вший *p.p. act. of* ⇒**~ть;** *as n.* **о., ~вшего** *m.* late-comer.

опозда́ни|е, я *nt.* lateness; delay; **без ~я** on time; **с ~ем на де́сять мину́т** ten minutes late.

опозда́|ть, ю *pf.* (*of* ⇒**опа́здывать**) to be late; **о. на ле́кцию** to be late for the lecture; **о. на полчаса́** to be half an hour late; **о. с упла́той нало́гов** to be late in paying taxes.

опознава́ни|е, я *nt.* identification; **о. самолётов** aircraft recognition.

опознава́тельный *adj.* distinguishing; **о. знак** landmark, (*naut.*) beacon; (*на крыльях самолёта*) marking.

опозна|ва́ть, ю́, ёшь *impf. of* ⇒**́~ть**

опозна́ни|е, я *nt.* (*leg.*) identification.

опозна́|ть, ю *pf.* (*of* ⇒**~ва́ть**) to identify.

опозо́рени|е, я *nt.* (*leg.*) defamation.

опозо́р|ить(ся), ю(сь), ишь(ся) *pf. of* ⇒**позо́рить(ся)**

опо|и́ть, ю́, и́шь *pf.* (*of* ⇨**опа́ивать**) to give (s.o.) too much to drink.

опо́йковый *adj.* calf(-skin).

опо́к|а, и *f.* (*tech.*) flask, mould box, casting box, box form; **литьё в ~ах** flask casting.

ополáскива|ть, ю *impf. of* ⇨**ополоска́ть** *and* **ополосну́ть**

ополз|а́ть, а́ю *impf. of* ⇨**~ти́**[1,2]

о́полз|ень, ня *m.* landslide, landslip.

о́полз|невый *adj. of* ⇨**~ень**

ополз|ти́[1]**, у́, ёшь,** *past* **~́, ~ла́** *pf.* (*of* ⇨**~а́ть**) (*проползти вокруг*) to crawl round.

ополз|ти́[2]**, ёт,** *past* **~́, ~ла́** *pf.* (*of* ⇨**~а́ть**) (*осесть*) to slip.

ополо|ска́ть, щу́, ~щешь *pf.* (*of* ⇨**опола́скивать**) = **~сну́ть**

ополосн|у́ть, у́, ёшь *pf.* (*of* ⇨**опола́скивать**) to rinse.

ополоу́ме|ть, ю *pf.* (*coll.*) to go crazy.

ополч|а́ть(ся), а́ю(сь) *impf. of* ⇨**~и́ть(ся)**

ополче́н|ец, ца *m.* militiaman; home guard.

ополче́ни|е, я *nt.* **1** militia; home guard. **2** (*collect.*; *hist.*) irregulars; levies.

ополч|и́ть, у́, и́шь *pf.* (*of* ⇨**~а́ть**) (**на**+*a.* *or* **про́тив**+*g.*; *coll.*) to arm (against); (*fig.*) to enlist the support of (against).

ополч|и́ться, у́сь, и́шься *pf.* (*of* ⇨**~а́ться**) (**на**+*a.* *or* **про́тив**+*g.*; *coll.*) to take up arms (against); (*fig.*) to be up in arms (against); to turn (against).

опо́мн|иться, юсь, ишься *pf.* (*прийти в сознание*) to come round; (*одуматься*) to come to one's senses.

опо́р, а *m. only in phr.* **во весь о.** at full speed, at top speed, full tilt.

опо́р|а, ы *f.* support (*also fig.*); (*моста*) pier; **то́чка ~ы** (*phys., tech.*) fulcrum.

опора́жнива|ть, ю *impf. of* ⇨**опоро́жни́ть**

опо́р|ки, ков *pl.* (*sg.* **~ок, ~ка** *m.*) down-at-heel shoes.

опо́р|ный *adj. of* ⇨**~а;** (*tech.*) bearing, supporting; **о. ка́мень** abutment stone; **о. пункт** (*mil.*) strong point; **~ная сва́я** bridge pile.

опор|о́жни́ть, о́жню, о́жни́шь *pf.* (*of* ⇨**опора́жнивать**) to empty; to drain (at a draught).

опорожня́|ть, ю *impf.* = **опора́жнивать**

опоро́с, а *m.* farrow (*of sow*).

опороси́|ться, тся *pf. of* ⇨**пороси́ться**

опоро́ч|ить, у, ишь *pf. of* ⇨**поро́чить**

опосре́дств|овать, ую *impf. and pf.* (*phil.*) to mediate.

опо́ссум, а *m.* (*zool.*) opossum.

опосты́ле|ть, ю *pf.* (*coll.*; +*d.*) to grow hateful (to), grow wearisome (to).

опохмел|и́ться, ю́сь, и́шься *pf.* (*of* ⇨**~я́ться**) (*coll.*) to take a hair of the dog that bit you.

опохмел|я́ться, я́юсь, *impf. of* ⇨**~и́ться**

опочива́л|ьня, ьни, *g. pl.* **~ен** *f.* (*obs.*) bedchamber.

опочива́|ть, ю *impf. of* ⇨**опочи́ть**

опочи́|ть, ю, ешь *pf.* (*of* ⇨**~ва́ть**) (*obs.*) **1** (*заснуть*) to go to sleep. **2** (*fig., poet.*) (*умереть*) to pass to one's rest.

опошле́|ть, ю *pf. of* ⇨**пошле́ть**

опо́шл|ить, ю, ишь *pf.* (*of* ⇨**~я́ть**) to vulgarize, debase.

опошля́|ть, ю *impf. of* ⇨**опо́шлить**

опоя́|сать, шу, шешь *pf.* (*of* ⇨**~сывать**) **1** to gird, engird(le). **2** (*fig.*) (*окружить собой*) to girdle.

опоя́|саться, шусь, шешься *pf.* (*of* ⇨**~сываться**) (+*i.*) to gird o.s. (with), gird on.

опоя́сыва|ть(ся), ю(сь) *impf. of* ⇨**опоя́сать(ся)**

оппозиционе́р, а *m.* member of the opposition.

оппози|цио́нный *adj. of* ⇨**~ция**

оппози́ци|я, и *f.* opposition.

оппоне́нт, а *m.* opponent.

оппони́р|овать, ую *impf.* (+*d.*) to oppose.

оппортуни́зм, а *m.* opportunism.

оппортуни́ст, а *m.* opportunist.

оппортунисти́ческий *adj.* opportunist.

оппортуни́ст|ка, ки *f. of* ⇨**~**

опра́в|а, ы *f.* frame; (*очков*) frames.

оправда́ни|е, я *nt.* **1** justification. **2** (*извинение*) excuse. **3** (*leg.*) acquittal, discharge.

оправда́тельный *adj.*: **о. пригово́р** verdict of 'not guilty'; **о. докуме́нт** voucher.

оправд|а́ть, а́ю *pf.* (*of* ⇨**~́ывать**) **1** (*показать себя достойным*) to justify, warrant; **о. ожида́ния** to come up to expectations; **о. себя́** to justify o.s.; **о. расхо́ды** to authorize expenses. **2** (*извинить*) to excuse; **о. посту́пок боле́знью** to excuse an action by reason of sickness. **3** (*leg.*) to acquit, discharge.

оправд|а́ться, а́юсь *pf.* (*of* ⇨**~́ываться**) **1** to justify o.s.; **о. незна́нием** (*leg.*) to plead ignorance. **2** to be justified; **моё предсказа́ние ~а́лось** my prediction has come true.

опра́вдыва|ть, ю *impf. of* ⇨**оправда́ть**

опра́вдыва|ться, юсь *impf.* **1** *impf. of* ⇨**оправда́ться. 2** to try to justify *or* vindicate o.s.

опра́в|ить, лю, ишь *pf.* (*of* ⇨**~ля́ть**) **1** (*платье, причёску, постель*) to put in order, straighten. **2** (*вставить в оправу*) to set, mount.

опра́в|иться, люсь, ишься *pf.* (*of* ⇨**~ля́ться**) **1** to put o.s. in order. **2** (**от**+*g.*) to recover (from).

оправля́|ть(ся), ю(сь) *impf. of* ⇨**опра́вить(ся)**

опра́стыва|ть(ся), ю *impf. of* ⇨**опроста́ть(ся)**

опра́шива|ть, ю *impf. of* ⇨**опроси́ть**

определе́ни|е, я *nt.* **1** definition; (*chem., phys., etc.*) determination. **2** (*leg.*) decision. **3** (*gram.*) attribute. **4** (*в кроссворде*) clue.

определён|ный (~ен, ~на) *adj.* **1** (*точно установленный*) definite; fixed; **о. за́работок** fixed wage; **о. член** (*gram.*) definite article. **2** (*некоторый*) certain; **в ~ных слу́чаях** in certain cases.

определи́м|ый (~, ~а) *adj.* definable.

определи́тел|ь, я *m.* **1** (*то, что определяет что-н.*) determining factor. **2** (*книга*) guide to identifying sth. **3** (*math.*) determinant.

определ|и́ть, ю́, и́шь *pf.* (*of* ⇨**~я́ть**) (*понятие*) to define; (*установить*) to determine; (*назначить*) to fix, appoint; **о. боле́знь** to diagnose a disease; **о. ме́ру наказа́ния** to fix a punishment; **о. расстоя́ние** to judge a distance.

определ|и́ться, ю́сь, и́шься *pf.* (*of* ⇨**~я́ться**) **1** to be formed; to take shape; to be determined. **2** (*aeron.*) to obtain a fix, find one's position.

определ|я́ть(ся), я́ю(сь) *impf. of* ⇨**~и́ть(ся)**

опресне́ни|е, я *nt.* desalination.

опресн|ённый *p.p.p. of* ⇨**~и́ть; ~ённая вода́** distilled water.

опресни́тел|ь, я *m.* (water-)distiller.

опресн|и́ть, ю́, и́шь *pf.* (*of* ⇨**~я́ть**) to desalinate.

опресн|я́ть, я́ю *impf. of* ⇨**~и́ть**

опри́чник, а *m.* (*hist.*) oprichnik (*member of oprichnina*).

опри́чнин|а, ы *f.* (*hist.*) oprichnina (*period of terror (1565–72) introduced in Russia by Ivan IV; also, the special administrative élite established by him, and the territory assigned to this élite*).

опри́чь *prep.* +*g.* (*obs.*) except, save.

опро́б|овать, ую *pf.* to test.

опроверг|а́ть, а́ю *impf. of* ⇨**~нуть**

опрове́рг|нуть, ну, нешь, *past* **~** *and* **~нул, ~ла** *pf.* (*of* ⇨**~а́ть**) to refute, disprove.

опроверже́ни|е, я *nt.* refutation; disproof; denial.

опрокидн|о́й *adj.*: **грузови́к с ~ы́м я́щиком** tip-up lorry (*Br.*), dump truck (*US*).

опроки́дыва|ть(ся), ю(сь) *impf. of* ⇨**опроки́нуть(ся)**

опроки́|нуть, ну, нешь *pf.* (*of* ⇨**~дывать**) **1** (*чашку*) to knock over; (*лодку*) to overturn. **2** (*mil.*) to overthrow. **3** (*fig.*) (*планы*) to upset; (*взгляды*) to refute.

опроки́|нуться, нусь, нешься *pf.* (*of* ⇨**~дываться**) (*о стакане*) to fall over, topple over; (*о лодке*) to capsize.

опроме́тчив|ый (~, ~а) *adj.* precipitate, rash, hasty.

о́прометью *adv.* headlong.

опро́с, а *m.* (*свидетелей*) questioning; **о. обще́ственного мне́ния** opinion poll.

опро|си́ть, шу́, ~́сишь *pf.* (*of*

⇨**опра́шивать**) (*свидетелей*) to question; (*общественное мнение*) to canvass, survey.

опро́с|ный *adj. of* ⇨**~**; **о. лист** questionnaire.

опроста́|ть, ю *pf.* (*of* ⇨**опра́стывать**) (*coll.*) to empty.

опроста́|ться, ется *pf.* (*of* ⇨**опра́стываться**) (*coll.*) to become empty.

опро|сти́ться, щу́сь, сти́шься *pf.* (*of* ⇨**~ща́ться**) to adopt the 'simple life'.

опростоволо́|ситься, шусь, сишься *pf.* (*coll.*) to make a gaffe, blunder.

опротест|ова́ть, у́ю *pf.* (*of* ⇨**~о́вывать**) **1**: **о. ве́ксель** (*fin.*) to protest a bill. **2** (*leg.*) to appeal (against).

опротесто́выва|ть, ю *impf. of* ⇨**опротестова́ть**

опроти́ве|ть, ю *pf.* to become loathsome, become repulsive.

опроща́|ться, юсь *impf. of* ⇨**опрости́ться**

опроще́ни|е, я *nt.* adoption of the 'simple life'.

опры́ск|ать, аю *pf.* (*of* ⇨**~ивать**) (+*i.*) to sprinkle (with); to spray (with).

опры́ск|аться, аюсь *pf.* (*of* ⇨**~иваться**) (+*i.*) to sprinkle o.s. (with); to spray o.s. (with).

опры́скивател|ь, я *m.* (*садовый*) sprinkler; (*для опрыскивания краской, химикатами*) sprayer.

опры́скива|ть(ся), ю(сь) *impf. of* ⇨**опры́скать(ся)**

опрыща́ве|ть, ю *pf. of* ⇨**прыща́веть**

опря́тност|ь, и *f.* neatness, tidiness.

опря́т|ный (~ен, ~на) *adj.* neat, tidy.

опт, а *m.* wholesale trade.

оптати́вный *adj.* (*gram.*) optative.

о́птик, а *m.* specialist in optics; maker of optical instruments.

о́птик|а, и *f.* **1** (*раздел физики*) optics. **2** (*collect.*) optical instruments.

оптима́л|ьный (~ен, ~ьна) *adj.* optimum, optimal.

оптими́зм, а *m.* optimism.

оптими́ст, а *m.* optimist.

оптимисти́ческий *adj.* optimistic.

о́птимум, а *m.* (*biol.*, *etc.*) optimum.

опти́ческ|ий *adj.* optic, optical; **~ое волокно́** optical fibre (*Br.*), fiber (*US*); **о. обма́н** optical illusion.

оптови́к, а́ *m.* wholesaler.

опто́вый *adj.* wholesale.

о́птом *adv.* wholesale; **о. и в ро́зницу** wholesale and retail.

опубликова́ни|е, я *nt.* publication; **о. зако́на** promulgation of a law.

опублик|ова́ть, у́ю *pf.* (*of* ⇨**публикова́ть** *and* **~о́вывать**) to publish; **о. зако́н** to promulgate a law.

опублико́выва|ть, ю *impf. of* ⇨**опубликова́ть**

о́пус, а *m.* (*mus.*) opus.

опуска́|ть(ся), ю(сь) *impf. of* ⇨**опусти́ть(ся)**

опускн|о́й *adj.* movable; **~а́я дверь** trapdoor.

опусте́лый *adj.* deserted.

опусте́|ть, ю *pf. of* ⇨**пусте́ть**

опу|сти́ть, щу́, ~́стишь *pf.* (*of* ⇨**~ска́ть**) **1** (*шторы*) to lower; to let down; **о. глаза́** to look down; **о. го́лову** (*fig.*) to hang one's head; **о. ру́ки** (*fig.*) to lose heart. **2** (*воротник*) to turn down. **3** (*пропустить*) to omit.

опу|сти́ться, щу́сь, ~́стишься *pf.* (*of* ⇨**~ска́ться**) **1** to lower o.s.; **о. в кре́сло** to sink into a chair; **о. на коле́ни** to go down on one's knees; **у него́ ру́ки ~сти́лись** (*fig.*) he has lost heart. **2** (*о солнце*) to sink, go down. **3** (*fig.*) (*разложиться*) to let o.s. go; to go to pieces.

опустош|а́ть, а́ю *impf. of* ⇨**~и́ть**

опустоше́ни|е, я *nt.* devastation, ruin.

опустоши́тел|ьный (~ен, ~ьна) *adj.* devastating.

опустош|и́ть, у́, и́шь *pf.* (*of* ⇨**~а́ть**) to devastate, lay waste, ravage.

опу́т|ать, аю *pf.* (*of* ⇨**~ывать**) to enmesh, entangle (*also fig.*); (*fig.*) to ensnare.

опу́тыва|ть, ю *impf. of* ⇨**опу́тать**

опух|а́ть, а́ю *impf. of* ⇨**~́нуть**

опу́хлый *adj.* (*coll.*) swollen.

опу́х|нуть, ну, нешь, *past* **~, ~ла** *pf.* (*of* ⇨**~а́ть**) to swell (up).

о́пухол|ь, и *f.* swelling; (*med.*) tumour (*Br.*), tumor (*US*); **~ мо́зга** brain tumour.

опуш|а́ть, а́ю *impf. of* ⇨**~и́ть**

опуш|и́ть, у́, и́шь *pf.* (*of* ⇨**~а́ть**) **1** (**ме́хом**) to edge, trim (with fur). **2** (*о снеге, инее*) to powder; to cover; **бо́роду у него́ ~и́ло сне́гом** his beard was powdered with snow.

опу́шк|а[1], и *f.* (*на одежде*) edging, trimming.

опу́шк|а[2], и *f.* (*леса*) edge.

опуще́ни|е, я *nt.* **1** lowering; letting down; **о. ма́тки** (*med.*) prolapse of the uterus. **2** (*пропуск*) omission.

опу́|щенный *p.p.p. of* ⇨**~сти́ть**; **как в во́ду о.** (*fig.*) crestfallen, downcast.

опыле́ни|е, я *nt.* (*bot.*) pollination; **перекрёстное о.** cross-pollination.

опы́ливател|ь, я *m.* (*agric.*) insecticide dust sprayer.

опы́лива|ть, ю *impf. of* ⇨**опыли́ть** 2

опыли́тел|ь, я *m.* **1** (*bot.*) pollinator. **2** (*agric.*) = **опы́ливатель**

опыл|и́ть, ю́, и́шь *pf.* **1** (*impf.* **~я́ть**) (*bot.*) to pollinate. **2** (*impf.* **~́ивать**) (*agric.*) to spray (with insecticide dust).

опыл|и́ться, и́тся *pf.* (*of* ⇨**~я́ться**) (*bot.*) to be pollinated.

опыл|я́ть, я́ю *impf. of* ⇨**~и́ть** 1

опыл|я́ться, я́ется *impf. of* ⇨**~и́ться**

о́пыт, а *m.* **1** experience; **на ~е, по ~у** by experience. **2** (*эксперимент*) experiment; test, trial; (*попытка*) attempt.

о́пытник, а *m.* experimenter.

о́пытност|ь, и *f.* experience.

о́пыт|ный *adj.* **1** (**~ен, ~на**) (*человек*) experienced. **2** (*экспериментальный*) experimental; **узна́ть ~ным путём** to learn by means of experiment; **~ная ста́нция** experimental station.

опьяне́лый *adj.* intoxicated.

опьяне́ни|е, я *nt.* intoxication.

опьяне́|ть, ю *pf. of* ⇨**пьяне́ть**

опьян|и́ть, ю́, и́шь *pf.* (*of* ⇨**пьяни́ть** *and* **~я́ть**) to intoxicate, make drunk; **успе́х ~и́л его́** success has gone to his head.

опьян|я́ть, я́ю *impf. of* ⇨**~и́ть**

опьяня́|ющий *pres. part. act. of* ⇨**~ть** *and adj.* intoxicating.

опя́ть *adv.* again.

опя́ть-таки *adv.* (*coll.*) **1** (*к тому же*) (and) what is more; **он холостя́к, о.-т. бога́тый челове́к** he is a bachelor, and what is more he is a rich man. **2** (*опять*) but again; however; **я постуча́л ещё раз, о.-т. ничего́ не послы́шалось** I knocked again, but again there was nothing to be heard.

ор, а *m.* (*coll.*) uproar.

ора́в|а, ы *f.* (*coll.*) crowd, horde.

ора́кул, а *m.* oracle.

ора́л|о, а *nt.* (*obs. and dial.*) plough (*Br.*), plow (*US*).

ора́льный *adj.* oral.

орангута́н(г), а *m.* orang-utan.

ора́нжевый *adj.* orange (*colour*).

оранжере́|йный *adj. of* ⇨**~я**; **~йное расте́ние** hothouse plant (*also fig.*).

оранжере́|я, и *f.* hothouse, greenhouse, conservatory.

ора́тор, а *m.* orator, (public) speaker.

орато́ри|я, и *f.* (*mus.*) oratorio.

ора́тор|ский *adj. of* ⇨**~**; oratorical; **~ское иску́сство** oratory.

ора́торств|овать, ую *impf.* to orate, speechify.

ор|а́ть, у́, ёшь *impf.* (*coll.*) to bawl, yell.

орби́т|а, ы *f.* **1** (*astron. and fig.*) orbit; **вы́вести на ~у** to put into orbit; **о. влия́ния** sphere of influence. **2** (*anat.*) eye-socket; **глаза́ у него́ вы́шли из ~** (*fig.*) his eyes leaped from their sockets.

орг... *comb. form, abbr. of* ***организацио́нный***

...орг *comb. form, abbr. of* ***организа́тор***

орга́зм, а *m.* (*physiol.*) orgasm.

о́рган, а *m.* (*biol.*, *pol.*, *etc.*) organ; **исполни́тельный о.** agency; **~ы вла́сти** organs of government; **половы́е ~ы** genitals.

орга́н, а *m.* (*mus.*) organ.

органа́йзер, а *m.* personal organizer.

организа́тор, а *m.* organizer.

организа́торский *adj.* organizational.

организа|цио́нный *adj. of* ⇨**~́ция**

организа́ци|я, и *f.* organization; **О.**

Объединённых На́ций United Nations Organization.

органи́зм, а *m.* organism.

организо́ванност|ь, и *f.* (good) organization; orderliness.

организо́ванн|ый *p.p.p. of* ⇒**организова́ть** *and adj.* organized; **~ая престу́пность** organized crime.

организ|ова́ть, у́ю *impf. and pf.* (*pf. also* **с~**) to organize.

организ|ова́ться, у́юсь *impf. and pf.* **1** to be organized. **2** (*в ансамбль, звено*) to organize o.s.

органи́ст, а *m.* organist.

органи́ческ|ий *adj.* organic; **~ая хи́мия** organic chemistry.

органи́ч|ный (~ен, ~на) *adj.* organic.

орга́н|ный *adj. of* ⇒**~**; **о. конце́рт** concerto for organ.

о́рги|я, и *f.* orgy.

оргте́хник|а, и *f.* (*abbr. of* ***организацио́нная те́хника***) office equipment.

орд|а́, ы́, *pl.* **~́ы, ~, ~́ам** *f.* (*hist. and fig.*) horde; **Золота́я о.** the Golden Horde.

о́рден[1]**, а,** *pl.* **~а́, ~о́в** *m.* (*знак отличия*) order; decoration; **о. Подвя́зки** Order of the Garter.

о́рден[2]**, а,** *pl.* **~ы, ~ов** *m.* **1** (*организация*) order; **иезуи́тский о.** Society of Jesus; **масо́нский о.** Masonic Order. **2** = **о́рдер**[2]

орденоно́с|ец, ца *m.* holder of an order *or* decoration.

орденоно́сный *adj.* decorated with an order.

о́рден|ский *adj. of* ⇒**~**; **~ская ле́нта** ribbon.

о́рдер[1]**, а,** *pl.* **~а́, ~о́в** *m.* order, warrant; (*leg.*) writ; **о. на о́быск** search warrant; **о. на поку́пку** coupon; **о. на кварти́ру** authorization to an apartment.

о́рдер[2]**, а,** *pl.* **~ы, ~ов** *m.* (*archit.*) order; **кори́нфский о.** Corinthian order.

ордина́р|ец, ца *m.* (*mil.*) orderly; batman.

ордина́р|ный (~ен, ~на) *adj.* ordinary.

ордина́т|а, ы *f.* (*math.*) ordinate.

ордина́тор, а *m.* (*med.*) registrar (*Br.*), resident (*US*).

ординату́р|а, ы *f.* (*med.*) registrarship (*Br.*), residency (*US*).

ор|ёл, ла́ *m.* eagle; **о. или ре́шка?** heads or tails?

орео́л, а *m.* halo, aureole.

оре́х, а *m.* **1** (*плод*) nut; **австрали́йский о.** macadamia; **америка́нский о.** Brazil nut; **гре́цкий о.** walnut; **кита́йский о.** peanut; **коко́совый о.** coconut; **лесно́й о., обыкнове́нный о.** hazel-nut; **муска́тный о.** nutmeg; **бу́дет тебе́ на ~и!; ему́ доста́лось (попа́ло) на ~и!** (*fig.*) you'll catch it!; he's caught it!; **разде́лать (отде́лать) кого́-н. под о.** (*coll.*) to give it s.o. hot. **2** (*дерево*) nut-tree. **3** (*древесина*) walnut; **шкаф из ~а** walnut cupboard.

оре́ховк|а, и *f.* (*zool.*) nutcracker.

оре́х|овый *adj. of* ⇒**~**; **~овое де́рево** nut-tree; (*древесина*) walnut; **о. шокола́д** nut chocolate.

оре́ш|ек, ка *m. dim. of* ⇒**оре́х**; **черни́льный о.** nut-gall.

оре́шник, а *m.* **1** (*кустарник*) (hazel) nut-tree. **2** (*заросль*) hazel-grove.

оригина́л, а *m.* **1** original. **2** (*coll.*) (*человек*) eccentric.

оригина́льнича|ть, ю *impf.* (*of* ⇒**с~**) (*coll.*) to put on an act, try to be clever.

оригина́льност|ь, и *f.* originality.

оригина́л|ьный (~ен, ~ьна) *adj.* original.

ориента́ци|я, и *f.* **1** (**на** + *a.*) orientation (toward). **2** (*fig.*) (**в** + *p.*) understanding (of), grasp (of); **у него́ хоро́шая о. в ю́жно-америка́нских дела́х** he has a firm grasp of South American affairs.

ориенти́р, а *m.* (*mil.*) reference point; guiding line; **(есте́ственный) о.** landmark.

ориенти́рова|нный *p.p.p. of* ⇒**~ть** *and adj.* knowledgeable.

ориенти́р|овать, ую *impf. and pf.* **1** to orient, orientate; (**в** + *p.*) to enlighten (concerning); **он не ~овал меня́ в экономи́ческом положе́нии** he did not put me in the picture about the economic position. **2** (**на** + *a.*) to direct (toward).

ориенти́р|оваться, уюсь *impf. and pf.* **1** to orient o.s.; to find one's bearings (*also fig.*); **я пло́хо ~уюсь** I have a poor sense of direction; **она́ ско́ро ~овалась в но́вой обстано́вке** (*fig.*) she soon found her feet in her new surroundings. **2** (**на** + *a.*) to head (for), make (for); (*fig.*) to direct one's attention (to, toward); **о. на рабо́чих слу́шателей** to cater for a working-class audience.

ориентиро́вк|а, и *f.* = **ориента́ция**

ориентиро́вочно *adv.* tentatively; approximately; **гру́бо о.** as a rough guide.

ориентиро́воч|ный *adj.* **1** position-finding. **2 (~ен, ~на)** (*приблизительный*) tentative; rough, approximate.

орке́стр, а *m.* **1** orchestra; (*духовой, джазовый*) band. **2** (*место перед сценой*) orchestra-pit.

оркестра́нт, а *m.* member of an orchestra *or* band.

оркестр|ова́ть, у́ю *impf. and pf.* to orchestrate.

оркестро́вк|а, и *f.* orchestration.

оркестро́вый *adj.* **1** *adj. of* ⇒**орке́стр. 2** orchestral.

Оркне́йск|ие остров|а́, ~их ~о́в *no sg.* the Orkney Islands; the Orkneys.

орла́н, а *m.* sea eagle.

орл|ёнок, ёнка, *pl.* **~я́та, ~я́т** *m.* eaglet.

орли́ный *adj. of* ⇒**орёл**; aquiline; **о. взгляд** eagle eye; **о. нос** aquiline nose.

орли́ц|а, ы *f.* female eagle.

орна́мент, а *m.* ornament.

орнамента́л|ьный (~ен, ~ьна) *adj.* ornamental.

орнамента́ци|я, и *f.* ornamentation.

орнаменти́р|овать, ую *impf. and pf.* to ornament.

орнито́лог, а *m.* ornithologist; **о.-люби́тель** bird-watcher.

орнитологи́ческий *adj.* ornithological.

орнитоло́ги|я, и *f.* ornithology.

оробе́лый *adj.* timid; frightened.

оробе́|ть, ю *pf. of* ⇒**робе́ть**

ороси́тельный *adj.* irrigation; irrigating; **о. кана́л** irrigation canal.

оро|си́ть, шу́, си́шь *pf.* (*of* ⇒**~ша́ть**) to irrigate; (*о дожде, росе*) to water; **о. слеза́ми** to wash with tears.

оро|ша́ть, ша́ю *impf. of* ⇒**~си́ть**

ороше́ни|е, я *nt.* irrigation; **поля́ ~я** sewage-farm.

ортодо́кс, а *m.* conformist.

ортодокса́льност|ь, и *f.* orthodoxy.

ортодокса́л|ьный (~ен, ~ьна) *adj.* orthodox.

ортодо́кси|я, и *f.* orthodoxy.

ортопе́д, а *m.* orthopaedist (*Br.*), orthopedist (*US*).

ортопеди́ческий *adj.* orthopaedic (*Br.*), orthopedic (*US*).

ортопе́ди|я, и *f.* orthopaedics (*Br.*), orthopedics (*US*).

ору́ди|е, я *nt.* **1** instrument; implement; tool (*also fig.*); **сельскохозя́йственные ~я** agricultural implements. **2** (*артиллерийское*) gun; **зени́тное о.** anti-aircraft gun.

оруд|и́йный *adj. of* ⇒**~ие 2**; **о. ого́нь** gun-fire; **о. око́п** gun-entrenchment; **о. расчёт** gun crew.

ору́д|овать, ую *impf.* (*coll.*; + *i.*) **1** to handle. **2** (*fig., pej.*) to be active; **он там всем ~ует** he bosses the whole show.

оруже́йник, а *m.* gunsmith, armourer (*Br.*), armorer (*US*).

оруж|е́йный *adj. of* ⇒**~ие**; **~е́йная пала́та** armoury (*Br.*), armory (*US*); **о. ма́стер** armourer (*Br.*), armorer (*US*).

оруженос|ец, ца *m.* armour-bearer, sword-bearer; (*fig.*) henchman.

ору́жи|е, я *nt.* weapon; (*collect.*) arms, weapons; **огнестре́льное о.** fire-arm(s); **стрелко́вое о.** small arms; **холо́дное о.** cold steel; **к ~ю!** to arms!; **бра́ться за о.** to take up arms; **подня́ть о.** (**на** + *a.*) to take up arms (against); **положи́ть о., сложи́ть о.** to lay down one's arms; **бить кого́-н. его́ же ~ем** (*fig.*) to beat s.o. at his own game.

орфографи́ческ|ий *adj.* orthographic(al); **о. корре́ктор** (*comput.*) spellchecker; **~ая оши́бка** spelling mistake.

орфогра́фи|я, и *f.* orthography, spelling.

орфоэпи́ческий *adj.*: **о. слова́рь** pronouncing dictionary.

орфоэ́пи|я, и *f.* orthoepy; (rules of) correct pronunciation.

орхиде́|я, и *f.* (*bot.*) orchid.

орясин|а, ы *f.* (*coll.*) rod, pole.

ос|á, ы́, *pl.* **~ы** *f.* wasp.

осáд|а, ы *f.* siege; **снять ~у** to raise a siege.

оса|ди́ть[1], жу́, ди́шь *pf.* (*of* ⇒**~ждáть**) to besiege, lay siege to; to beleaguer; **о. прóсьбами** to bombard with requests.

оса|ди́ть[2], жу́, ~дишь *pf.* (*of* ⇒**~ждáть**) (*chem.*) to precipitate.

оса|ди́ть[3], жу́, ~дишь *pf.* (*of* ⇒**~живать**) **1** to check, halt; to force back; **о. лóшадь** to rein in a horse. **2** (*fig.*): **о. когó-н.** to put s.o. in his place, take s.o. down a peg.

осáдк|а, и *f.* **1** (*о почве, стене*) set, settling. **2** (*naut.*) draught; **сýдно с небольшóй ~ой** vessel of shallow draught.

осáд|ный *adj. of* ⇒**~а; ~ная войнá** siege warfare; **~ное положéние** state of siege.

осáд|ок, ка *m.* **1** (*pl.*) (*атмосферные*) precipitation. **2** (*частицы*) sediment, deposition. **3** (*fig.*) after-taste; **у меня́ от э́того разговóра был неприя́тный о.** the conversation left an unpleasant taste in my mouth.

осáд|очный *adj. of* ⇒**~ок; ~очные порóды** (*geol.*) sedimentary rocks.

осаждá|ть, ю *impf. of* ⇒**осади́ть[1,2]**

осаждá|ться, ется *impf.* **1** (*об атмосферных осадках*) to fall. **2** (*chem.*) to be precipitated; to fall out.

осаждённый *p.p.p. of* ⇒**осади́ть[1,2]**

осáженный *p.p.p. of* ⇒**осади́ть[3]**

осáжива|ть, ю *impf. of* ⇒**осади́ть[3]**

осáнист|ый (~, ~а) *adj.* portly.

осáнк|а, и *f.* carriage, bearing.

осáнн|а, ы *f.* hosanna; **восклицáть, петь ~у комý-н.** (*fig.*) to sing s.o.'s praises.

осатаневá|ть, ю *impf. of* ⇒**осатанéть**

осатанéлый *adj.* (*coll.*) possessed; furious.

осатанé|ть, ю, ешь *pf.* (*of* ⇒**~вáть**) (*coll.*) **1** (*прийти в бешеное состояние*) to get mad, go into a frenzy. **2** (+*d.*) (*сильно надоесть*) to drive mad.

ОСВ *nt. indecl.* (*abbr. of* ***ограничéние стратеги́ческих вооружéний***): **переговóры по ОСВ** SALT (*Strategic Arms Limitation Treaty*) talks.

освáива|ть(ся), ю(сь) *impf. of* ⇒**освóить(ся)**

осведоми́тел|ь, я *m.* informant, informer.

осведоми́тель|ница, ницы *f. of* ⇒**~**

осведоми́тельн|ый *adj.* informative; (*conveying*) information; **~ая рабóта** information work, publicity work.

освéдом|ить, лю, ишь *pf.* (*of* ⇒**~ля́ть**) to inform.

освéдом|иться, люсь, ишься *pf.* (*of* ⇒**~ля́ться**) (**о**+*p.*) to inquire (about).

осведомлéни|е, я *nt.* informing, notification.

осведомлённост|ь, и *f.* knowledge, (possession of) information; **у негó хорóшая о. в исла́ндских сáгах** he is very knowledgeable about the Icelandic sagas.

осведомлён|ный (~, ~нá) *p.p.p. of* ⇒**освéдомить** *and adj.* (**в**+*p.*) well-informed (about), knowledgeable (about).

осведом|ля́ть(ся), ля́ю(сь) *impf. of* ⇒**освéдомить(ся)**

освеж|áть, áю *impf. of* ⇒**~и́ть**

освеж|евáть, ýю *pf. of* ⇒**свежевáть**

освежи́тел|ьный (~ен, ~ьна) *adj.* refreshing.

освеж|и́ть, ý, и́шь *pf.* (*of* ⇒**~áть**) **1** to refresh; to freshen; **о. кóмнату** to give a room an airing. **2** (*fig.*) to refresh, revive; **о. свои́ знáния** to refresh one's knowledge.

Освéнцим, а *m.* Auschwitz.

освети́тел|ь, я *m.* lighting technician.

освети́тельн|ый *adj.* lighting, illuminating; **о. прибóр** light; **~ая ракéта** (*aeron.*) flare.

осве|ти́ть, щý, ти́шь *pf.* (*of* ⇒**~щáть**) to light up; to illuminate; (*fig.*) to throw light on; (*в прессе*) to cover, report.

осве|ти́ться, щýсь, ти́шься *pf.* (*of* ⇒**~щáться**) to light up; to brighten; **её лицó ~ти́лось улы́бкой** (*fig.*) a smile lit up her face.

освещá|ть(ся), ю(сь) *impf. of* ⇒**освети́ть(ся)**

освещéни|е, я *nt.* light, lighting, illumination; (*в прессе*) coverage; **искýсственное о.** artificial light(ing); **электри́ческое о.** electric light.

освещённост|ь, и *f.* (*degree of, area of*) illumination.

осве|щённый *p.p.p. of* ⇒**~ти́ть; о. звёздами** star-lit; **о. лунóй** moonlit; **о. свечáми** candle-lit.

освидéтельств|овать, ую *pf. of* ⇒**свидéтельствовать** 4

осви|стáть, щý, ~щешь *pf.* (*of* ⇒**~стывать**) to hiss (off), catcall; **о. актёра** to hiss an actor off the stage.

осви́стыва|ть, ю *impf. of* ⇒**освистáть**

освободи́тел|ь, я *m.* liberator.

освободи́тель|ница, ницы *f. of* ⇒**~**

освободи́тельн|ый *adj.* liberation, emancipation; **~ая войнá** war of liberation.

освобо|ди́ть, жý, ди́шь *pf.* (*of* ⇒**~ждáть**) **1** (*город, страну, человека*) to free, liberate; (*заключённого*; *животное*) to release, set free; **о. арестóванного** to discharge a prisoner; **о. от воéнной слýжбы** to exempt from military service. **2** (*от должности*) to dismiss. **3** (*квартиру*) to vacate; (*место*; *полку от книг*) to clear, empty.

освобо|ди́ться, жýсь, ди́шься *pf.* (*of* ⇒**~ждáться**) **1** (**от**+*g.*) to free o.s. (of, from); to become free. **2** *pass. of* ⇒**~ди́ть**

освобождá|ть(ся), ю(сь) *impf. of* ⇒**освободи́ть(ся)**

освобождéни|е, я *nt.* **1** (*города*) liberation; (*заключённого*) release. **2** (*от должности*) dismissal. **3** (*квартиры*) vacation; (*полки*) clearing.

освобо|ждённый *p.p.p. of* ⇒**~ди́ть; о. от налóга** tax-free, exempt from tax.

освоéни|е, я *nt.* assimilation, mastery, familiarization; **о. нóвой тéхники** learning to handle new machinery; **о. крáйнего сéвера** the opening up of the Far North.

освó|ить, ю, ишь *pf.* (*of* ⇒**освáивать**) **1** to assimilate, master; to cope (with); to become familiar (with). **2** (*bot.*) to acclimatize.

освó|иться, юсь, ишься *pf.* (*of* ⇒**освáиваться**) **1** (**с**+*i.*) to familiarize o.s. (with). **2** to feel at home; **о. в нóвой средé** to get the feel of new surroundings.

освя|ти́ть, щý, ти́шь *pf.* **1** (*impf.* **святи́ть**) (*eccl.*) to consecrate; to bless, sanctify. **2** (*impf.* **~щáть**) (*fig.*) to sanctify, hallow.

освящá|ть, ю *impf. of* ⇒**освяти́ть**

освя|щённый *p.p.p. of* ⇒**~ти́ть; обы́чай, о. векáми** time-honoured (*Br.*), -honored (*US*) custom.

ос|евóй *adj. of* ⇒**~ь; axial.**

оседáни|е, я *nt.* **1** (*здания*) settling, subsidence; (*снега*) settling. **2** (*людей*) settlement.

оседá|ть, ю *impf. of* ⇒**осéсть**

осёдл|анный *p.p.p. of* ⇒**~áть**

оседлá|ть, ю *pf.* **1** (*impf.* **седлáть**) to saddle. **2** (*mil.*; *fig.*) gain control of.

осéдлост|ь, и *f.* settled (way of) life; **чертá ~и** (*hist.*) the Pale of Settlement (*area to which Jews were confined in tsarist Russia*).

осéдлый *adj.* settled (*opp. nomadic*).

осекá|ться, юсь *impf. of* ⇒**осéчься**

ос|ёл, лá *m.* donkey; ass (*also fig.*).

осел|óк, кá *m.* **1** (*для испытания*) touchstone (*also fig.*). **2** (*точильный*) whetstone.

осеменéни|е, я *nt.* insemination.

осемен|и́ть, ю́, и́шь *pf.* (*of* ⇒**~я́ть**) to inseminate.

осемен|я́ть, я́ю *impf. of* ⇒**~и́ть**

осен|и́ть, ю́, и́шь *pf.* (*of* ⇒**~я́ть**) **1** (*покрыть тенью*) to overshadow; (*fig.*) to shield; **о. крестóм** to make the sign of the cross (over). **2** (*fig.*) to dawn upon, strike; **егó ~и́ла мысль** it dawned upon him; (*impers.*): **меня́ внезáпно ~и́ло** it suddenly occurred to me.

осен|и́ться, ю́сь, и́шься *pf.* (*of* ⇒**~я́ться**) (*obs.*) *pass. of* ⇒**~и́ть; о. крестóм** to cross o.s.

осéнний *adj. of* ⇒**óсень;** autumnal.

óсен|ь, и *f.* autumn.

óсенью *adv.* in autumn.

осен|я́ть(ся), я́ю(сь) *impf. of* ⇒**~и́ть(ся)**

осер|ди́ться, жу́сь, ~ди́шься *pf.* (на + *a.*; *obs., coll.*) to become angry (with).

осерча́|ть, ю *pf. of* ⇒**серча́ть**

ос|е́сть, я́ду, я́дешь, *past* **~е́л, ~е́ла** *pf.* (*of* ⇒**~еда́ть**) **1** (*о здании*) to subside; (*о пыли, осадке*) to settle. **2** (*о людях*) to settle.

осети́н, а, *g. pl.* **о.** *m.* Ossetian, Ossete.

осети́н|ка, ки *f. of* ⇒**~**

осети́нский *adj.* Ossetian.

осётр, а́ *m.* sturgeon.

осетри́н|а, ы *f.* (flesh of) sturgeon.

осетро́вый *adj. of* ⇒**осётр**

осе́чк|а, и *f.* misfire; **дать ~у** to misfire (*also fig.*).

осе́|чься, ку́сь, чёшься, ку́тся, *past* **~кся, ~клась** *pf.* (*of* ⇒**~ка́ться**) (*coll.*) **1** to misfire (*also fig.*). **2** (*оборвать речь*) to stop short.

оси́лива|ть, ю *impf. of* ⇒**оси́лить**

оси́л|ить, ю, ишь *pf.* (*of* ⇒**~ивать**) **1** (*соперника*) to overpower. **2** (*coll.*) to master; to manage; **о. гре́ческий алфави́т** to master the Greek alphabet; **я е́ле ~ил ещё оди́н стака́н** I was hardly able to manage another glass.

оси́н|а, ы *f.* aspen.

оси́нник, а *m.* aspen wood.

оси́н|овый *adj. of* ⇒**~а; дрожа́ть как о. лист** to tremble like an aspen leaf.

ос|и́ный *adj. of* ⇒**~а́; ~и́ное гнездо́** (*fig.*) hornets' nest; **потрево́жить ~и́ное гнездо́** to stir up a hornets' nest; **~и́ная та́лия** wasp waist.

оси́плый *adj.* hoarse, husky.

оси́п|нуть, ну, нешь, *past* **~, ~ла** *pf.* to go hoarse.

осироте́лый *adj.* orphaned.

осироте́|ть, ю *pf.* to become an orphan, be orphaned.

оска́л, а *m.* bared teeth; grin.

оска́лива|ть(ся), ю(сь) *impf. of* ⇒**оска́лить(ся)**

оска́л|ить, ю, ишь *pf.* (*of* ⇒**скáлить** *and* **~ивать**): **о. зу́бы** to bare one's teeth.

оска́л|иться, юсь, ишься *pf.* (*of* ⇒**ска́литься** *and* **~иваться**) to bare one's teeth.

оскальпи́р|овать, ую *pf. of* ⇒**скальпи́ровать**

осканда́л|ить(ся), ю(сь), ишь(ся) *pf. of* ⇒**сканда́лить(ся)**

О́скар, а *m.* (*приз*) Oscar.

осквернéни|е, я *nt.* defilement; profanation.

оскверн|и́ть, ю́, и́шь *pf.* (*of* ⇒**~я́ть**) to defile; to profane.

оскверн|и́ться, ю́сь, и́шься *pf.* (*of* ⇒**~я́ться**) **1** to defile o.s. **2** *pass. of* ⇒**~и́ть**

оскверн|я́ть(ся), я́ю(сь) *impf. of* ⇒**~и́ть(ся)**

осклá|биться, блюсь, бишься *pf.* to grin.

оско́л|ок, ка *m.* splinter; fragment.

оско́ло|чный *adj. of* ⇒**~к; ~чная бо́мба** fragmentation bomb, anti-personnel bomb.

оско́мин|а, ы *f.* bitter taste (in the mouth); **наби́ть ~у** to set the teeth on edge (*also fig.*).

оскоп|и́ть, лю́, и́шь *pf.* (*of* ⇒**~ля́ть**) to castrate.

оскопля́|ть, ю *impf. of* ⇒**оскопи́ть**

оскорби́тельност|ь, и *f.* abusiveness.

оскорби́тел|ьный (~ен, ~ьна) *adj.* insulting, abusive.

оскорб|и́ть, лю́, и́шь *pf.* (*of* ⇒**~ля́ть**) to insult, offend.

оскорб|и́ться, лю́сь, и́шься *pf.* (*of* ⇒**~ля́ться**) to take offence; to be offended, be hurt.

оскорбле́ни|е, я *nt.* insult; **о. де́йствием** (*leg.*) assault and battery; **переноси́ть ~я** to bear insults.

оскорб|лённый *p.p.p. of* ⇒**~и́ть; ~лённая неви́нность** outraged innocence.

оскорбля́|ть(ся), ю(сь) *impf. of* ⇒**оскорби́ть(ся)**

оскудева́|ть, ю *impf. of* ⇒**оскуде́ть**

оскуде́лый *adj.* scarce, scanty.

оскуде́ни|е, я *nt.* scarcity; impoverishment.

оскуде́|ть, ю *pf.* (*of* ⇒**скуде́ть** *and* **~ва́ть**) (*о вещах*) to grow scarce; (*о стране*) to become impoverished.

ослабева́|ть, ю *impf. of* ⇒**ослабе́ть**

ослабе́лый *adj.* weakened, enfeebled.

ослабе́|ть, ю *pf.* (*of* ⇒**слабе́ть** *and* **~ва́ть**) (*о человеке, стране, решительности*) to weaken, become weak; (*о внимании, напряжении*) to slacken; (*о шуме, ветре*) to abate.

ослáб|ить, лю, ишь *pf.* (*of* ⇒**~ля́ть**) **1** to weaken. **2** (*сделать менее натянутым*) to slacken, relax; to loosen; **о. внима́ние** to relax one's attention; **о. нажи́м** to slacken pressure; **о. по́яс** to loosen a belt.

ослабле́ни|е, я *nt.* weakening; slackening, relaxation; **о. напряже́ния** slackening of tension.

ослабля́|ть, ю *impf. of* ⇒**ослáбить**

ослáб|нуть, ну, нешь, *past* **~, ~ла** *pf.* = **~е́ть**

ослáв|ить, лю, ишь *pf.* (*of* ⇒**~ля́ть**) (*coll.*) to defame, decry; to give a bad name.

ослáв|иться, люсь, ишься *pf.* (*of* ⇒**~ля́ться**) (*coll.*) to get a bad name.

ославля́|ть(ся), ю(сь) *impf. of* ⇒**ослáвить(ся)**

осл|ёнок, ёнка, *pl.* **~я́та, ~я́т** *m.* foal (*of ass*).

ослепи́тел|ьный (~ен, ~ьна) *adj.* blinding, dazzling.

ослеп|и́ть, лю́, и́шь *pf.* (*of* ⇒**~ля́ть**) to blind, dazzle (*also fig.*).

ослепле́ни|е, я *nt.* **1** blinding, dazzling. **2** (*fig.*) blindness; **де́йствовать в ~и** to act blindly.

ослепля́|ть, ю *impf. of* ⇒**ослепи́ть**

ослéп|нуть, ну, нешь, *past* **~, ~ла** *pf. of* ⇒**слéпнуть**

осли́злый *adj.* slimy.

осли́з|нуть, нет, *past* **~, ~ла** *pf.* to become slimy.

осли́ный *adj. of* ⇒**осёл;** ass's; (*fig.*) asinine.

осли́ц|а, ы *f.* she-ass.

О́сло *m. indecl.* Oslo.

осложне́ни|е, я *nt.* complication.

осложн|и́ть, ю́, и́шь *pf.* (*of* ⇒**~я́ть**) to complicate.

осложн|и́ться, и́тся *pf.* (*of* ⇒**~я́ться**) to become complicated; (*о болезни*) to develop complications.

осложн|я́ть(ся), я́ю, я́ет(ся) *impf. of* ⇒**~и́ть(ся)**

ослуша́ни|е, я *nt.* disobedience.

ослу́ш|аться, аюсь *pf.* (*of* ⇒**~иваться**) to disobey.

ослу́шива|ться, юсь *impf. of* ⇒**ослу́шаться**

ослу́шник, а *m.* (*obs.*) disobedient person.

ослы́ш|аться, усь, ишься *pf.* to mishear.

ослы́шк|а, и *f.* mishearing.

осма́н, а *m.* Ottoman.

осма́нский *adj.* Ottoman.

осма́трива|ть(ся), ю(сь) *impf. of* ⇒**осмотре́ть(ся)**

осме́ива|ть, ю *impf. of* ⇒**осмея́ть**

осмеле́|ть, ю *pf. of* ⇒**смеле́ть**

осме́лива|ться, юсь, *impf. of* ⇒**осме́литься**

осме́л|иться, юсь, ишься *pf.* (*of* ⇒**~иваться**) (+*inf.*) to dare; to take the liberty (of); **~юсь доложи́ть...** (*obs. polite formula*) I beg to report ....

осме|я́ть, ю́, ёшь *pf.* (*of* ⇒**~ивать**) to mock, ridicule.

о́сми|й, я *m.* (*chem.*) osmium.

осмол|и́ть, ю́, и́шь *pf. of* ⇒**смоли́ть**

о́смос, а *m.* (*phys.*) osmosis.

осмо́тр, а *m.* (*багажа*) examination, inspection; (*школы*) inspection; (*выставки*) looking round, visit; **медици́нский о.** medical (examination); checkup.

осмотр|е́ть, ю́, ~ишь *pf.* (*of* ⇒**осма́тривать**) (*багаж, больного*) to examine; (*школу*) to inspect; (*выставку*) to look round, look over.

осмотр|е́ться, ю́сь, ~ишься *pf.* (*of* ⇒**осма́триваться**) **1** to look round. **2** (*fig.*) to take one's bearings, see how the land lies.

осмотри́тельност|ь, и *f.* circumspection.

осмотри́тел|ьный (~ен, ~ьна) *adj.* circumspect.

осмо́трщик, а *m.* inspector.

осмы́сл|енный *p.p.p. of* ⇒**~ить** *and adj.* intelligent, sensible.

осмы́слива|ть, ю *impf. of* ⇒**осмы́слить**

осмы́сл|ить, ю, ишь *pf.* (*of* ⇒**~ивать** *and* **~я́ть**) (*истолковать*) to interpret; (*понять*) to comprehend.

О

осмысл|я́ть, я́ю *impf.* = **~́ивать**

осна|сти́ть, щу́, сти́шь *pf.* (*of* ⇒**~ща́ть**) (*naut.*) to rig; (*fig.*) to fit out, equip.

осна́стк|а, и *f.* (*naut.*) rigging.

оснаща́|ть, ю *impf. of* ⇒**оснасти́ть**

оснаще́ни|е, я *nt.* **1** (*действие*) rigging; fitting out. **2** (*оборудование*) equipment.

оснащённост|ь, и *f.* level of equipment.

осне́женный *adj.* snow-covered.

оснежённый *adj.* = **осне́женный**

оснеж|и́ть, у́, и́шь *pf.* (*poet.*) to cover with snow.

осно́в|а, ы *f.* **1** (*здания*) foundation; (*fig.*) basis, foundation; *pl.* fundamentals; **лежа́ть в ~е** (+*g.*) to be the basis (of). **2** (*gram.*) stem. **3** (*text.*) warp.

основа́ни|е, я *nt.* **1** (*действие*) founding, foundation. **2** (*chem., math., etc.*) base; (*здания*) foundation; **о. горы́** foot of a mountain; **разру́шить до ~я** to raze to the ground; **изучи́ть до ~я** (*fig.*) to study from A to Z. **3** (*fig.*) foundation, basis; ground, reason; **на како́м ~и вы э́то утвержда́ете?** on what grounds do you assert this?; **не без ~я** not without reason; **име́ть о. предполага́ть** to have reason to suppose; **с по́лным ~ем** with good reason.

основа́тел|ь, я *m.* founder.

основа́тель|ница, ницы *f. of* ⇒**~**

основа́тельност|ь, и *f.* soundness.

основа́тел|ьный (~ен, ~ьна) *adj.* **1** (*совет, причина*) well-founded; just; **~ьная жа́лоба** reasonable complaint. **2** (*постройка*) solid, sound; (*человек*) solid; (*осмотр*) thorough; **~ьные до́воды** sound arguments. **3** (*coll.*) (*вес, нагрузка*) considerable.

осн|ова́ть, ую́, уёшь *pf.* (*of* ⇒**~о́вывать**) **1** (*учредить*) to found. **2** (**на**+*p.*) to base (on).

осн|ова́ться, ую́сь, уёшься *pf.* (*of* ⇒**~о́вываться**) **1** (*поселиться*) to settle. **2** *pass. of* ⇒**~ова́ть**

основн|о́й *adj.* (*причина, цель*) main; (*принцип*) fundamental, basic; **о. капита́л** (*fin.*) fixed capital; **~а́я мысль** keynote; **~ы́е цвета́** primary colours; **в ~о́м** on the whole; basically.

основополо́жник, а *m.* founder, initiator.

осно́выва|ть, ю *impf. of* ⇒**основа́ть**

осно́выва|ться, юсь *impf.* **1** *impf. of* ⇒**основа́ться. 2** *impf. only* (**на**+*p.*) to base o.s. (on); to be based, founded (on); **о. на дога́дках** to base o.s. on conjecture.

осо́б|а, ы *f.* person, individual, personage; **ва́жная о.** (*iron.*) big-wig.

осо́бенно *adv.* especially; particularly; unusually; **не о.** not very, not particularly.

осо́бенност|ь, и *f.* peculiarity; **в ~и** especially, in particular, (more) particularly.

осо́бенн|ый *adj.* (e)special, particular, peculiar; **ничего ~ого** nothing in particular; nothing much.

особня́к, а́ *m.* private residence; mansion, detached house.

особняко́м *adv.* by o.s.; **держа́ться о.** to keep aloof.

осо́б|ый *adj.* special; particular; peculiar; **оста́ться при ~ом мне́нии** to reserve one's own opinion; **удели́ть ~ое внима́ние** (+*d.*) to give special attention (to).

о́соб|ь, и *f.* individual.

осо́бь *indecl. adj. only in phr.* **о. статья́** (*coll.*) quite another matter.

осове́лый *adj.* (*coll.*) dazed, dreamy.

осове́|ть, ю *pf.* (*coll.*) to fall into a dazed, dreamy state.

осовреме́нива|ть, ю *impf. of* ⇒**осовреме́нить**

осовреме́н|ить, ю, ишь *pf.* (*of* ⇒**~ивать**) to bring up to date; to modernize.

осозна|ва́ть, ю́, ёшь *impf. of* ⇒**~́ть**

осо́знанный *adj.* deliberate; conscious.

осозна́|ть, ю *pf.* (*of* ⇒**~ва́ть**) to realize.

осо́к|а, и *f.* (*bot.*) sedge.

осоко́р|ь, я *m.* (*bot.*) black poplar.

осолове́лый *adj.* (*coll.*) = **осове́лый**

осолове́|ть, ю, ешь *pf. of* ⇒**солове́ть**

о́сп|а, ы *f.* **1** smallpox; **ве́тряная о.** chicken-pox; **коро́вья о.** cow-pox; **чёрная о.** smallpox. **2** (*coll.*) pock-marks; **лицо́ в ~е** pock-marked face.

оспа́рива|ть, ю *impf.* **1** *impf. of* ⇒**оспо́рить. 2** *impf. only* to contend (for); **он ~ет зва́ние чемпио́на ми́ра** he is contending for the title of world champion.

о́сп|енный *adj. of* ⇒**~а; о. знак** pock-mark.

о́спин|а, ы *f.* pock-mark.

оспопривива́ни|е, я *nt.* vaccination.

оспо́р|ить, ю, ишь *pf.* (*of* ⇒**оспа́ривать**) to dispute, question; **о. завеща́ние** to dispute a will.

осрам|и́ть(ся), лю́(сь), и́шь(ся) *pf. of* ⇒**срами́ть(ся)**

ОССВ *no sg., indecl.* (*abbr. of* ***ограниче́ние и сокраще́ние стратеги́ческих вооруже́ний***): **перегово́ры по О.** START (*Strategic Arms Reduction Treaty*) talks.

ост, а *m.* (*naut.*) east.

оста|ва́ться, ю́сь, ёшься *impf. of* ⇒**оста́ться**

оста́в|ить, лю, ишь *pf.* (*of* ⇒**~ля́ть**) **1** to leave; (*покинуть*) to abandon; (*надежду*) to give up; (*перестать, бросить*) to stop, give up; **о. в поко́е** to leave alone, let alone; **о. на второ́й год** (*в школах*) to keep back; to make repeat a year; **о. госте́й ночева́ть/ обе́дать** to ask guests to stay the night/ stay to dinner; **~ь(те)!** stop that!; lay off! **2** (*охранить*) to reserve; to keep; **о. за собо́й пра́во** to reserve the right.

оставля́|ть, ю *impf. of* ⇒**оста́вить; ~ет жела́ть мно́гого** (*or* **лу́чшего**) it leaves much to be desired.

остальн|о́й *adj.* the rest of; **в ~о́м** in other respects; *as n.* **~ы́е** *pl.* the others; **~о́е** *nt.* the rest; **всё ~о́е** everything else.

остана́влива|ть(ся), ю(сь) *impf. of* ⇒**останови́ть(ся)**

оста́нк|и, ов *no sg.* remains.

останов|и́ть, лю́, ~́ишь *pf.* (*of* ⇒**остана́вливать**) **1** to stop. **2** (*сдержать*) to stop short, restrain. **3** (**на**+*p.*) (*направить*) to direct (to), concentrate (on); **о. взгляд** to rest one's gaze (on); **о. внима́ние** to concentrate one's attention (on).

останов|и́ться, лю́сь, ~ишься *pf.* (*of* ⇒**остана́вливаться**) **1** to stop; to come to a stop, come to a halt; **ни пе́ред чем не о.** (*fig.*) to stop at nothing. **2** (*переночевать*) to stay, put up, (*coll.*) stop; **о. у знако́мых** to stay with friends. **3** (**на**+*p.*) (*fig.*) (*в речи, докладе*) to dwell (on); (*о взгляде*) to settle (on), rest (on); **взор ма́льчика ~и́лся на но́вой игру́шке** the boy's gaze rested on the new toy.

остано́вк|а, и *f.* **1** (*в пути, работе*) stop; (*задержка*) stoppage; **о. за ва́ми** you are holding us up; **о. за ви́зами** there is a hold-up over the visas. **2** (*автобусная*) stop; **коне́чная о.** terminus; **мне на́до прое́хать ещё одну́ ~у** I have to go one stop further.

остано́в|очный *adj. of* ⇒**~ка; о. пункт** stop, stopping place.

оста́т|ок, ка *m.* **1** remainder; rest; (*ткани*) remnant; *pl.* remains; (*еды*) leftovers; **распрода́жа ~ков** clearance sale. **2** (*chem.*) residuum. **3** (*fin., comm.*) rest, balance. **4** (*math.*) remainder.

оста́то|чный *adj. of* ⇒**~к;** (*chem., tech.*) residual.

оста́|ться, нусь, нешься *pf.* (*of* ⇒**~ва́ться**) to remain; to stay; to be left (over); **о. в долгу́** to be in debt; **о. в живы́х** to survive, come through; **о. на́ ночь** to stay the night; **о. при своём мне́нии** to remain of the same opinion; **о. на второ́й год (в том же кла́ссе)** to repeat a year; **за ним ~лось пять фу́нтов** he owes five pounds; **по́сле него́ ~лись жена́ и тро́е дете́й** he left a wife and three children; **от обе́да ничего́ не ~лось** there is nothing left over from dinner; (*impers.*): **~ётся, ~лось** (+*d.*) it remains (remained), it is (was) necessary; **нам не ~лось ничего́ друго́го, как согласи́ться** we had no choice but to consent; **~лось то́лько заплати́ть** it remained only to pay.

остеклене́|ть, ет *pf. of* ⇒**стеклене́ть**

остекл|и́ть, ю, и́шь *pf.* (*of* ⇒**~я́ть**) to glaze.

остекл|я́ть, я́ю *impf. of* ⇒**~и́ть**

Осте́нде *m. indecl.* Ostend.

остеоартри́т, а *m.* osteoarthritis.

остеомиэли́т, а *m.* (*med.*) osteomyelitis.

остеопа́т, а *m.* osteopath.

остеопати́ческий *adj.* osteopathic.

остеопа́ти|я, и *f.* osteopathy.

остеопоро́з, а *m.* (*med.*) osteoporosis.

остепен|и́ть, ю, и́шь *pf.* (*of* ⇒**~я́ть**) to calm, mellow.

остепен|и́ться, ю́сь, и́шься *pf.* (*of* ⇒**~я́ться**) **1** (*стать степенным*) to settle down; to mellow. **2** (*coll., joc.*) (*получить учёную степень*) to get an academic degree.

остепеня́|ть(ся), ю(сь) *impf. of* ⇒**остепени́ть(ся)**

остервене́лый *adj.* frenzied.

остервене́ни|е, я *nt.* frenzy; **рабо́тать с ~ем** to work like a maniac.

остервен|е́ть, ю *pf. of* ⇒**стервене́ть**

остервен|и́ться, ю́сь, и́шься *pf.* to be frenzied.

остерега́|ть, ю *impf. of* ⇒**остере́чь**

остерега́|ться, юсь *impf.* (*of* ⇒**остере́чься**) (+*g. or inf.*) to beware (of); to be careful (of); **~йтесь соба́ки!** beware of the dog!; **~йся, что́бы не упа́сть!** mind you don't fall!

остере́|чь, гу́, жёшь, гу́т, *past* **~̈г, ~гла́** *pf.* (*of* ⇒**~га́ть**) to warn, caution.

остере́|чься, гу́сь, жёшься, гу́тся, *past* **~гся, ~гла́сь** *pf. of* ⇒**~га́ться**

Ост-И́нди|я, и *f.* the East Indies.

ости́ст|ый (~, ~а) *adj.* (*bot.*) bearded, awned.

о́стов, а *m.* **1** frame, framework (*also fig.*); (*корабля*) hull. **2** (*anat.*) skeleton.

усто́йчивост|ь, и *f.* (*naut.*) stability.

усто́йчив|ый (~, ~а) *adj.* (*naut.*) stable.

остолбене́лый *adj.* (*coll.*) dumbfounded.

остолбене́|ть, ю *pf. of* ⇒**столбене́ть**

остоло́п, а *m.* (*coll.*) blockhead.

осторо́жнича|ть, ю *impf.* (*of* ⇒**по~**) (*coll.*) to be overcareful.

осторо́жно *adv.* carefully; cautiously; **о.!** look out! mind out!; (*на посылке*) 'with care'.

осторо́жност|ь, и *f.* care; caution.

осторо́ж|ный (~ен, ~на) *adj.* careful; cautious; **бу́дьте ~ны!** take care!; be careful!

осточерте́|ть, ю *pf.* (+*d.*; *coll.*) to bore; **мне э́то ~ло** I am fed up with it.

остраки́зм, а *m.* ostracism; **подве́ргнуть ~у** to ostracize.

остра́стк|а, и *f.* (*coll.*) warning, caution; **для ~и** as a warning.

острига́|ть(ся), ю(сь) *impf. of* ⇒**остри́чь(ся)**

остри|ё, я́ *nt.* **1** (*иголки, штыка*) point; **о. клина** (*mil.*) spearhead of the attack. **2** (*ножа, бритвы*) (cutting) edge; **о. кри́тики** (*fig.*) the cutting edge of a criticism.

остр|и́ть¹, ю́, и́шь *impf.* (*делать острым*) to sharpen.

остр|и́ть², ю́, и́шь *impf.* (*of* ⇒**с~**) (*говорить остроты*) to be witty; to make witticisms, crack jokes; **о. на чужо́й счёт** to be witty at others' expense.

остри́|чь, гу́, жёшь, гу́т, *past* **~г, ~гла** *pf.* (*of* ⇒**стричь** *and* **~га́ть**) to cut; to clip.

остри́|чься, гу́сь, жёшься, гу́тся, *past* **~гся, ~глась** *pf.* (*of* ⇒**стри́чься** *and* **~га́ться**) to cut one's hair; to have one's hair cut.

о́стров, а, *pl.* **~а́** *m.* island; isle.

островитя́н|ин, ина, *pl.* **~е, ~** *m.* islander.

островитя́н|ка, ки *f. of* ⇒**~ин**

островно́й *adj.* island (*attr.*); insular.

остров|о́к, ка́ *m.* islet; **о. безопа́сности** traffic island.

остро́г, а *m.* **1** (*obs.*) (*тюрьма*) gaol. **2** (*hist.*) (*город*) stockaded town. **3** (*hist.*) (*ограда*) stockade, palisade.

острог|а́, и́ *f.* fish-spear, harpoon.

остроглаз|ый (~, ~а) *adj.* (*coll.*) sharp-sighted, keen-eyed.

острогу́бц|ы, ев (*tech.*) cutting nippers.

остроконе́ч|ный (~ен, ~на) *adj.* pointed.

остроли́ст, а *m.* (*bot.*) holly.

острonóс|ый (~, ~а) *adj.* sharp-nosed; (*fig.*) pointed, tapered.

острosло́в, а *m.* wit (*person*).

острosло́ви|е, я *nt.* wittiness.

острosло́в|ить, лю, ишь *impf.* to make witty remarks, crack jokes.

острosюже́т|ный (~ен, ~на) *adj.* gripping, tense.

остро́т|а, ы *f.* witticism, joke; **зла́я о.** sarcasm; **пло́ская о.** stupid joke; **то́нкая о.** subtle crack.

острот|а́, ы́ *f.* (*ножа, ума*) sharpness; (*зрения, слуха*) keenness; (*ситуации; боли*) acuteness; (*запаха*) pungency; (*чувства*) poignancy.

остроуго́л|ьный (~ен, ~ьна) *adj.* (*math.*) acute-angled.

остроу́ми|е, я *nt.* **1** wit; wittiness. **2** (*изобретательность*) ingenuity.

остроу́м|ный (~ен, ~на) *adj.* **1** witty. **2** (*изобретательный*) ingenious.

о́стр|ый (~ *and* **остёр, ~а́, ~о)** *adj.* (*нож, ум*) sharp; (*нос*) pointed (*also fig.*); (*ситуация; боль*) acute; (*зрение, слух*) keen; **~ое замеча́ние** pointed remark; **о. за́пах** acrid smell; **~ое зре́ние** keen eyesight; **о. интере́с (к**+*d.*) keen interest (in); **о. недоста́ток** acute shortage; **~ое положе́ние** critical situation; **о. со́ус** piquant sauce; **о. сыр** strong cheese; **о. у́гол** (*math.*) acute angle; **он остёр на язы́к** (*coll.*) he has a sharp tongue.

остря́к, а́ *m.* wit.

осту|ди́ть, жу́, ~̈дишь *pf.* (*of* ⇒**студи́ть** *and* **~жа́ть**) to cool.

остужа́|ть, ю *impf. of* ⇒**остуди́ть**

оступ|а́ться, а́юсь *impf. of* ⇒**~и́ться**

оступ|и́ться, лю́сь, ~̈ишься *pf.* (*of* ⇒**~а́ться**) to stumble.

остыва́|ть, ю *impf. of* ⇒**осты́ть**

осты́|ть, ну, нешь *pf.* (*of* ⇒**~ва́ть, сты́нуть 1, стыть**) to get cold; (*fig.*) to cool (down); **у вас чай ~л** your tea is cold.

ост|ь, и, *pl.* **~и, ~̈ей** *f.* (*bot.*) awn, beard.

осу|ди́ть, жу́, ~̈дишь *pf.* (*of* ⇒**~жда́ть**) **1** (*порицать*) to censure, condemn. **2** (*leg.*) (*на смерть, каторгу*) to condemn, sentence; (**за**+*a.*) to convict (of). **3** (**на**+*a.*) (*fig.*) (*обречь*) to condemn.

осужда́|ть, ю *impf. of* ⇒**осуди́ть**

осужде́ни|е, я *nt.* **1** censure, condemnation. **2** (*leg.*) conviction.

осуждённ|ый *p.p.p. of* ⇒**осуди́ть** *and adj.* condemned; convicted; *as n.* **о., ~ого** *m* convict.

осу́н|уться, усь, ешься *pf.* (*coll.*) (*о лице*) to grow thin, get pinched(-looking).

осуш|а́ть, а́ю *impf. of* ⇒**~и́ть**

осуше́ни|е, я *nt.* drainage.

осуш|и́тельный *adj. of* ⇒**~е́ние; о. кана́л** drainage canal.

осуш|и́ть, у́, ~̈ишь *pf.* (*of* ⇒**~а́ть**) (*болото; стакан*) to drain; (*следы дождя*) to dry; **о. глаза́** to dry one's eyes; **о. луга́** to drain meadows; **о. слёзы кому́-н.** to console s.o.; **о. стака́н пи́ва** to drain a glass of beer.

осуществи́м|ый (~, ~а) *adj.* practicable, feasible.

осуществ|и́ть, лю́, и́шь *pf.* (*of* ⇒**~ля́ть**) (*мечту*) to realize, bring about; (*намерение*) to carry out; (*решение*) to implement; (*контроль, руководство*) to exercise.

осуществ|и́ться, и́тся *pf.* (*of* ⇒**~ля́ться**) to be fulfilled, come true; **её де́тская мечта́ ~и́лась** her childhood dream has come true.

осуществле́ни|е, я *nt.* realization; accomplishment; implementation.

осуществля́|ть(ся), ю, ет(ся) *impf. of* ⇒**осуществи́ть(ся)**

осцилло́граф, а *m.* (*phys.*) oscillograph.

осцилля́тор, а *m.* (*phys.*) oscillator.

осчастли́в|ить, лю, ишь *pf.* (*of* ⇒**~ливать**) to make happy.

осчастли́влива|ть, ю *impf. of* ⇒**осчастли́вить**

осыпа|нный *p.p.p. of* ⇒**~ть; о. звёздами** star-studded, star-spangled.

осып|ать, лю, лешь *pf.* (*of* ⇒**~а́ть**) **1** (+*a. and i.*) (*покрыть*) to strew (with); to shower (on); (*fig.*) to heap (on); **о. кого́-н. бра́нью** to heap abuse on s.o.; **о. поцелу́ями** to smother with kisses; **о. кого́-н. уда́рами** to rain blows on s.o. **2** (*развалить*) to pull down, knock down. **3** (*листья*) to shed.

осып|аться, люсь, лешься *pf.* (*of* ⇒**~а́ться**) **1** (*о насыпи*) to crumble; (*о листьях*) to fall. **2** *pass. of* ⇒**осыпать**

осып|а́ть(ся), а́ю(сь) *impf. of* ⇒**~̈ать(ся)**

о́сып|ь, и *f.* scree.

ос|ь, и, *pl.* **~̈и, ~̈ей** *f.* **1** (*geom.*) axis; **земна́я о.** axis of the equator. **2** (*колеса*) axle.

осьмино́г, а *m.* (*zool.*) octopus.

О

осяза́ем|ый (~, ~а) *adj.* tangible; **~ые результа́ты** tangible results.

осяза́ние, я *nt.* touch; **чу́вство ~я** a sense of touch.

осяза́тел|ьный (~ен, ~ьна) *adj.* **1** tactile; **~ьные о́рганы** tactile organs. **2** (*fig.*) tangible, palpable; **~ьные результа́ты** tangible results.

осяза́|ть, ю *impf.* to feel.

от (ото) *prep.* + *g.* from; of; for. **1** (*указывает на исходную точку, источник чего-н.*): **от це́нтра го́рода** from the centre of the town; **от нача́ла до конца́** from beginning to end; **от Пу́шкина до Маяко́вского** from Pushkin to Mayakovsky; **от девяти́ (часо́в) до пяти́ (часо́в)** from nine (o'clock) to five (o'clock); **де́ти в во́зрасте от пяти́ до десяти́ лет** children from five to ten (years); **це́ны от рубля́ и вы́ше** prices from a rouble upward; **бли́зко от го́рода** near the town; **на се́вер от Москвы́** to the north of Moscow; **вре́мя от вре́мени** from time to time; **день ото дня** from day to day; **от всей души́** with all one's heart; **от и́мени** (+*g.*) on behalf (of); **узна́ть от дру́га** to learn from a friend; **я получи́л письмо́ от до́чери** I have received a letter from my daughter; **сын от пре́жнего бра́ка** a son by a previous marriage. **2** (*указывает на причину чего-н.*): **вскри́кнуть от ра́дости** to cry out for joy; **дрожа́ть от стра́ха** to tremble with fear; **умере́ть от го́лода** to die of hunger; **глаза́, кра́сные от слёз** eyes red with weeping. **3** (*указывает на дату документа*): **ва́ше письмо́ от пе́рвого а́вгуста** your letter of the first of August. **4** (*указывает на целое, которому принадлежит часть*): **ключ от две́ри** door key; **пу́говица от пиджака́** coat button; **цепо́чка от часо́в** watch-chain. **5** (*против*) for; against; **сре́дство от сенно́й лихора́дки** remedy for hay-fever; **миксту́ра от ка́шля** cough mixture; **защища́ть глаза́ от со́лнца** to shield one's eyes from the sun; **застрахова́ть от огня́** to insure against fire.

от... (*also* **ото...** *and* **отъ...**) *vbl. pref. indicating* **1** completion of action *or* task assigned. **2** action *or* motion away from given point. **3** (*vv. in form refl.*) action of negative character.

ота́плива|ть, ю *impf. of* ⇒**отопи́ть**

ота́р|а, ы *f.* large flock (*of sheep*).

отба́в|ить, лю, ишь *pf.* (*of* ⇒**~ля́ть**) to pour off.

отбавля́|ть, ю *impf. of* ⇒**отба́вить; хоть ~й** (*coll.*) more than enough.

отбараба́н|ить, ю, ишь *pf.* (*coll.*) to rattle off.

отбега́|ть, ю *impf. of* ⇒**отбежа́ть**

отбе|жа́ть, гу́, жи́шь, гу́т *pf.* (*of* ⇒**~га́ть**) to run off.

отбе́лива|ть, ю *impf. of* ⇒**отбели́ть**

отбел|и́ть, ю́, ~ишь *pf.* (*of* ⇒**~ивать**) to bleach.

отбе́лк|а, и *f.* bleaching.

отбива́|ть(ся), ю(сь) *impf. of* ⇒**отби́ть(ся)**

отбивн|о́й *adj.*: **~а́я котле́та** (*cul.*) chop.

отбира́|ть, ю *impf. of* ⇒**отобра́ть**

отби́ти|е, я *nt.* repulse; repelling.

отби́|ть, отобью́, отобьёшь *pf.* (*of* ⇒**~ва́ть**) **1** to beat off, repel; **о. ата́ку** to beat off an attack; **о. мяч** (*sport*) to return a ball; **о. уда́р** to parry a blow. **2** (*вернуть себе силой*) to retake, recapture; (*привлечь к себе*) to win over; (*coll.*): **о. у кого́-н.** to take off s.o., do s.o. out of; **о. пле́нных** to liberate prisoners; **о. покупа́телей** (*fig.*) to win customers; **он ~л у това́рища его́ де́вушку** he has taken his friend's girl. **3** (*удалить*) to remove, dispel; **о. у кого́-н. охо́ту к чему́-н.** to discourage s.o. from sth., take away s.o.'s inclination for sth. **4** (*отколоть*) to break off, knock off; **о. но́сик у ча́йника** to knock the spout off a tea-pot. **5** (*лезвие*) to whet, sharpen. **6**: **о. такт** to beat (out) time. **7** (*повредить ударами*) to damage by blows, by knocks; **о. ру́ку нело́вким уда́ром** to hurt one's hand with a clumsy blow. **8** (*обозначить ударами*) to mark out.

отби́|ться, отобью́сь, отобьёшься *pf.* (*of* ⇒**~ва́ться**) **1** (**от**+*g.*) to defend o.s. (against); to repel, beat off. **2** (*отстать*) to drop behind, straggle; **о. от ста́да** to stray from the herd; **о. от рук** (*coll.*) to get out of hand. **3** (*отломаться*) to break off.

отбла́гове|стить, щу, стишь *pf. of* ⇒**бла́говестить** 1

отблагодар|и́ть, ю́, и́шь *pf.* to show one's gratitude (to).

о́тблеск, а *m.* reflection.

отбо́|й, я *m.* **1** (*отталкивание*) repelling; **о. мяча́** (*sport*) return; **~ю нет** (**от**+*g.*; *coll.*) there is no end (of). **2** (*mil.*) (*сигнал*) retreat; **о. возду́шной трево́ги** all-clear signal; **бить о.** to beat a retreat (*also fig.*). **3** (*по телефону*) ringing off; **дать о.** to ring off.

отбо́й|ный *adj.*: **о. молото́к** miner's pick; **пневмати́ческий о. молото́к** pneumatic drill (*for coal-cutting*).

отбомб|и́ться, лю́сь, и́шься *pf.* (*coll.*) to have dropped one's load (of bombs).

отбо́р, а *m.* selection; **есте́ственный о.** (*biol.*) natural selection.

отбо́рн|ый *adj.* choice, select(ed); **~ые войска́** crack troops; **~ая ру́гань** choice swear-words.

отбо́рочн|ый *adj.*: **~ая коми́ссия** selection board; **~ое соревнова́ние** (*sport*) knock-out competition.

отбо́ярива|ться, юсь *impf.* (*of* ⇒**отбо́яриться**) (*coll.*) to try to escape, get out of.

отбо́яр|иться, юсь, ишься *pf.* (*of* ⇒**~иваться**) (*coll.*; **от**+*g.*) to escape (from), give the slip (to).

отбра́сыва|ть, ю *impf. of* ⇒**отбро́сить**

отбрива́|ть, ю *impf. of* ⇒**отбри́ть**

отбр|и́ть, е́ю, е́ешь *pf.* (*of* ⇒**~ива́ть**) (*coll.*) to rebuff, rebuke.

отбро́|сить, шу, сишь *pf.* (*of* ⇒**отбра́сывать**) **1** to throw off; to cast away; **о. тень** to cast a shadow. **2** (*mil.*) to repel. **3** (*отвергнуть*) to give up, reject, discard; **о. мысль** to give up an idea.

отбро́с|ы, ов *pl.* (*sg.* **~, ~а** *m.*) garbage, refuse; **о. произво́дства** industrial waste; **о. о́бщества** (*fig.*) dregs of society.

отбукси́р|овать, ую *pf.* to tow off.

отбыва́ни|е, я *nt.* serving; **о. сро́ка наказа́ния** serving of a sentence.

отбыва́|ть, ю *impf. of* ⇒**отбы́ть**

отбы́ти|е, я *nt.* departure.

от|бы́ть[1]**, бу́ду, бу́дешь**, *past* **~был, ~была́, ~было** *pf.* (*of* ⇒**~быва́ть**) to depart, leave.

от|бы́ть[2]**, бу́ду, бу́дешь**, *past* **~был, ~была́, ~было** *pf.* (*of* ⇒**~быва́ть**) to serve (a period of); **о. наказа́ние** to serve one's sentence; **о. во́инскую пови́нность** to do (one's) military service.

отва́г|а, и *f.* courage, bravery.

отва́|дить, жу, дишь *pf.* (*of* ⇒**~живать**) **1** (+*a.* **от**+*g.*) to break (of), make to stop; **о. кого́-н. от пья́нства** to break s.o. of drunkenness. **2** (*отпугнуть*) to scare away, drive off.

отва́жива|ть, ю *impf. of* ⇒**отва́дить**

отва́ж|иться, усь, ишься *pf.* (+*inf.*) to dare, venture; to have the courage (to).

отва́ж|ный (~ен, ~на) *adj.* courageous, brave.

отва́л[1]**, а** *m.*: **до ~а** (*coll.*) to satiety; **нае́сться до ~а** to stuff o.s.

отва́л[2]**, а** *m.* (*mining*) dump; (*шлака*) slag-heap.

отва́л[3]**, а** *m.* (*naut.*) putting off, casting off.

отва́лива|ть(ся), ю(сь) *impf. of* ⇒**отвали́ть(ся)**

отвал|и́ть, ю́, ~ишь *pf.* (*of* ⇒**~ивать**) **1** (*камень*) to heave off; to push aside. **2** (*naut.*) to put off, cast off. **3** (*coll.*) (*деньги*) to fork out, stump up.

отвал|и́ться, ю́сь, ~ишься *pf.* (*of* ⇒**~иваться**) **1** (*штукатурка*) to fall off. **2** (*coll.*) (*человек*) to lean back.

отва́льн|ая, ой *f.* (*coll.*) farewell party.

отва́р, а *m.* broth; decoction; **ячме́нный о.** barley-water.

отва́рива|ть, ю *impf. of* ⇒**отвари́ть**

отвар|и́ть, ю́, ~ишь *pf.* (*of* ⇒**~ивать**) to boil.

отварно́й *adj.* (*cul.*) boiled.

отве́д|ать, аю *pf.* (*of* ⇒**~ывать**) (+*a. or g.*) to taste; to try.

отве|дённый *p.p.p of* ⇒**~сти́**

отве́дыва|ть, ю *impf. of* ⇒**отве́дать**

отвез|ти́, у́, ёшь, *past* **~, ~ла́** *pf.* (*of* ⇒**отвози́ть**) (*везя, доставить*) to take; (*везя, убрать*) to take away.

отверг|а́ть, а́ю *impf. of* ⇒**~нуть**

отве́рг|нуть, ну, нешь, *past* ~ *and* **~нул, ~ла** *pf.* (*of* ⇒**~а́ть**) to reject, turn down.

отвердева́|ть, ет *impf. of* ⇒**отверде́ть**

отверде́лый *adj.* hardened.

отверде́|ть, ет *pf.* (*of* ⇒**~ва́ть**) to harden.

отве́р|женный *p.p.p.* (*obs.*) *of* ⇒**~гнуть** *and adj.* outcast; *as n.* **~женный, ~женного** *m.* outcast.

отвер|ну́ть, ну́, нёшь, *pf.* (*of* ⇒**~тывать**) **1** (*impf. also* **отвора́чивать**) to turn away, turn aside; **о. лицо́** to turn one's face away; **о. одея́ло** to turn down a blanket. **2** (*кран*) to turn on. **3** (*гайку*) to unscrew. **4** (*coll.*) (*отломать*) to twist off; **он едва́ не ~ну́л мне ру́ку** he almost twisted my arm off.

отвер|ну́ться, ну́сь, нёшься *pf.* (*of* ⇒**~тываться**) **1** (*impf. also* **отвора́чиваться**) to turn away, turn aside; **о. от кого́-н.** (*fig.*) to turn one's back upon s.o. **2** (*о кране*) to come on. **3** (*о гайке*) to come unscrewed.

отве́рсти|е, я *nt.* **1** opening; (*дыра*) hole; (*в автомате*) slot. **2**: **заднепрохо́дное о.** (*anat.*) anus.

отвер|те́ть, чу́, ~тишь *pf.* (*of* ⇒**~тывать**) (*coll.*) **1** (*гайку*) to unscrew. **2** (*отломать*) to twist off.

отверт|е́ться[1], **~ится** *pf.* (*of* ⇒**~ываться**) to come unscrewed.

отвер|те́ться[2], **чу́сь, ~тишься** *pf.* (*coll.*; **от**+*g.*) to get off; to get out (of), wriggle out (of); **нам удало́сь о.** we managed to get out of it.

отвёртк|а, и *f.* screwdriver; **кресто́вая о.** Phillips (*propr.*) *or* cross-head screwdriver.

отвёртыва|ть(ся), ю(сь) *impf. of* ⇒**отверну́ть(ся)** *and* **отверте́ть(ся)**

отве́с, а *m.* **1** (*tech.*) plumb. **2** (*склон*) (*vertical*) face, slope; **по ~у** plumb, perpendicularly.

отве́|сить, шу, сишь *pf.* (*of* ⇒**~шивать**) to weigh out; **о. фунт са́хару** to weigh out a pound of sugar; **о. покло́н** (+*d.*) to make a low bow (to); **о. пощёчину** (+*d.*) (*fig., coll.*) to deal s.o. a slap in the face.

отве́сно *adv.* plumb; sheer.

отве́с|ный (~ен, ~на) *adj.* (*линия*) perpendicular; (*скала*) steep.

отве|сти́, ду́, дёшь, *past* **~л, ~ла́** *pf.* (*of* ⇒**отводи́ть**) **1** (*ведя, доставить*) to lead, take, conduct; **о. ло́шадь в коню́шню** to lead a horse to the stable. **2** (*ведя, направить в сторону*) to draw aside, take aside; **о. от собла́зна** to lead out of temptation's way. **3** (*изменить направление движения чего-либо*) to deflect; **о. войска́** (*mil.*) to draw off one's troops; **о. во́ду** (**из**+*g.*) to drain; **о. ду́шу** to unburden one's heart; **о. обвине́ние** to justify o.s.; **о. уда́р** to parry a blow; **он не мог о. глаз от неё** he could not take his eyes off her; **о. глаза́ кому́-н.** (*fig.*) to distract s.o.'s attention, pull the wool over s.o.'s eyes. **4** (*отвергнуть*) to reject. **5** (*выделить*) to allot, assign.

отве́т, а *m.* **1** answer, reply, response; **держа́ть о.** to answer; **в о.** (**на**+*a.*) in reply (to), in response (to). **2** (*obs.*) (*ответственность*) responsibility; **быть в ~е** (**за**+*a.*) to be answerable (for); **призва́ть к ~у** to call to account.

ответв|и́ть, лю́, и́шь *pf.* (*of* ⇒**~ля́ть**) (*tech.*) to take off, tap, shunt.

ответв|и́ться, и́тся *pf.* (*of* ⇒**~ля́ться**) to branch off.

ответвле́ни|е, я *nt.* branch, offshoot (*also fig.*).

ответв|лённый *p.p.p. of* ⇒**~и́ть; ~лённая цепь** (*elec.*) branch circuit, derived circuit.

ответвля́|ть(ся), ю, ет(ся) *impf. of* ⇒**ответви́ть(ся)**

отве́|тить, чу, тишь *pf.* (*of* ⇒**~ча́ть**) **1** (**на**+*a.*) to answer, reply (to); **о. на письмо́** to answer a letter; **о. уро́к** to repeat one's lesson. **2** (**на**+*a.* +*i.*) to answer (with), return; **о. на чьё-н. чу́вство** to return s.o.'s feelings. **3** (**за**+*a.*) to answer (for), pay (for); **вы ~тите за э́ти слова́!** you will pay for these words!

отве́тный *adj.* given in reply; (*визит*) return; (*меры*) retaliatory.

отве́тственност|ь, и *f.* responsibility; **снять о. с кого́-н.** to relieve s.o. of responsibility; **привле́чь к ~и** (**за**+*a.*) to call to account, bring to book.

отве́тствен|ный (~, ~на) *adj.* **1** (*человек*; *работа*) responsible; **о. реда́ктор** editor-in-chief; **о. рабо́тник** executive. **2** (*решающий*) crucial; **о. моме́нт** crucial point.

отве́тств|овать, ую *impf. and pf.* (*obs.*) to answer, reply.

отве́тчик, а *m.* **1** (*leg.*) defendant. **2** (*coll.*) bearer of responsibility. **3**: **телефо́нный о.** answerphone, answering machine.

отве́тчи|ца, цы *f. of* ⇒**~к**

отвеча́|ть, ю *impf.* **1** *impf. of* ⇒**отве́тить. 2** (**за**+*a.*) to answer (for), be answerable (for). **3** (+*d.*) to answer (to), meet, be up (to); **о. тре́бованиям** to meet requirements.

отве́шива|ть, ю *impf. of* ⇒**отве́сить**

отви́лива|ть, ю *impf. of* ⇒**отвильну́ть**

отвильн|у́ть, у́, ёшь *pf.* (*of* ⇒**отви́ливать**) (*coll., pej.*; **от**+*g.*) to dodge.

отвин|ти́ть, чу́, ти́шь *pf.* (*of* ⇒**~чивать**) to unscrew.

отвин|ти́ться, чу́сь, ти́шься *pf.* (*of* ⇒**~чиваться**) to unscrew, come unscrewed.

отви́нчива|ть(ся), ю(сь) *impf. of* ⇒**отвинти́ть(ся)**

отвис|а́ть, а́ет *impf.* (*of* ⇒**~нуть**) to hang down, sag.

отви|се́ться, си́тся *pf.* (*coll.*): **дать пла́тью о.** to hang out a dress so as to remove the creases.

отви́слы|й *adj.* sagging, baggy; **с ~ми уша́ми** lop-eared.

отви́с|нуть, нет, нут, *past* **~, ~ла** *pf. of* ⇒**~а́ть**

отвлека́|ть(ся), ю(сь) *impf. of* ⇒**отвле́чь(ся)**

отвлече́ни|е, я *nt.* **1** (*абстракция*) abstraction. **2** (*от чего-н.*) distraction; **для ~я внима́ния** to distract attention.

отвлечён|ный (~, ~на) *adj.* abstract; **~ное и́мя существи́тельное** abstract noun.

отвле́|чь, ку́, чёшь, ку́т, *past* **~к, ~кла́** *pf.* (*of* ⇒**~ка́ть**) to distract, divert; **о. чьё-н. внима́ние** to divert s.o.'s attention.

отвле́|чься, ку́сь, чёшься, ку́тся, *past* **~кся, ~кла́сь** *pf.* (*of* ⇒**~ка́ться**) **1** to be distracted; **о. от те́мы** to digress; **его́ мы́сли ~кли́сь далеко́** his thoughts were far away. **2** (**от**+*g.*) (*абстрагироваться*) to abstract o.s. (from).

отво́д, а *m.* **1** (*человека, куда-н.*) leading, taking, conducting. **2** (*человека, в сторону*) taking aside; (*изменение направления*) deflection; diversion; **о. воды́** draining off of water; **о. войск** withdrawal of troops; **для ~а глаз** (*coll.*) as a blind. **3** (*отклонение*) rejection; (*leg.*) challenge; **дать о. кандида́ту** to reject a candidate. **4** (*выделение*) allotment, allocation.

отво|ди́ть, жу́, ~дишь *impf. of* ⇒**отвести́**

отво́дк|а, и *f.* **1** = **отво́д** 2. **2** (*tech.*) branch pipe.

отводно́й *adj.* drainage; **о. кана́л** drainage ditch; drain.

отво́д|ок, ка *m.* (*hort.*) cutting, layer.

отво|ева́ть[1], **ю́ю, ю́ешь** *pf.* (*of* ⇒**~ёвывать**) (**у**+*g.*) (*вернуть войной*) to win back (from), retake (from).

отво|ева́ть[2], **ю́ю, ю́ешь** *pf.* (*coll.*) **1** (*какое-н. время*) to fight, spend in fighting; **мы де́сять лет ~ева́ли** we have fought for ten years. **2** (*кончить воевать*) to finish fighting.

отвоёвыва|ть, ю *impf. of* ⇒**отвоева́ть**[1]

отво|зи́ть, жу́, ~зишь *impf. of* ⇒**отвезти́**

отвола́кива|ть, ю *impf. of* ⇒**отволо́чь**

отволо́|чь, ку́, чёшь, ку́т, *past* **~к, ~кла́** *pf.* (*of* ⇒**отвола́кивать**) (*coll.*) to drag away, drag aside.

отвора́чива|ть(ся), ю(сь) *impf. of* ⇒**отверну́ть(ся)** *and* **отвороти́ть(ся)**

отвор|и́ть, ю́, ~ишь *pf.* (*of* ⇒**~я́ть**) to open.

отвор|и́ться, ю́сь, ~ишься *pf.* (*of* ⇒**~я́ться**) to open.

отворо́т, а *m.* (*на пиджаке*) lapel; (*на брюках*) turn-up (*Br.*), cuff (*US*); (*сапога, рукава*) cuff.

отворо|ти́ть, чу́, ~тишь *pf.* (*of* ⇒**отвора́чивать**) to turn away, turn aside; **о. взгляд** to avert one's gaze.

отворо|ти́ться, чу́сь, ~тишься *pf.* (*of* ⇒**отвора́чиваться**) to turn

О

away, turn aside; **о. от кого́-н.** to look away from s.o.; (*fig.*) to turn one's back on s.o.

отвор|я́ть(ся), я́ю(сь) *impf. of* ⇒**~и́ть(ся)**

отврати́тел|ьный (~ен, ~ьна) *adj.* repulsive, disgusting.

отвра|ти́ть, щу́, ти́шь *pf.* (*of* ⇒**~ща́ть**) to avert, stave off.

отвра́т|ный (~ен, ~на) *adj.* (*coll.*) = **~и́тельный**

отвра|ща́ть, ща́ю *impf. of* ⇒**~ти́ть**

отвраще́ни|е, я *nt.* disgust, repugnance; **внуши́ть о.** (+*d.*) to disgust, repel; **пита́ть о.** (**к**+*d.*) to have an aversion (for), be repelled (by), loathe.

отвык|а́ть, а́ю *impf. of* ⇒**~нуть**

отвы́к|нуть, ну, нешь, *past* **~, ~ла** *pf.* (*of* ⇒**~а́ть**) (**от**+*g.*, *or* +*inf.*) (*от плохой привычки*) to break o.s. (of the habit of), give up; (*от работы, ходьбы*) to get out of the habit of, become unaccustomed to; (*от друзей, своей страны*) to become estranged from; **о. от куре́ния, о. кури́ть** to give up smoking.

отвя|за́ть, жу́, ~жешь *pf.* (*of* ⇒**~зывать**) to untie, unfasten.

отвя|за́ться, жу́сь, ~жешься *pf.* (*of* ⇒**~зываться**) **1** (*освободиться от привязи*) to come untied, come loose. **2** (*fig., coll.*; **от**+*g.*) (*отделаться*) to get rid (of), shake off, get shot (of). **3** (*fig., coll.*; **от**+*g.*) (*перестать надоедать*) to leave alone, leave in peace; stop nagging; **~жи́сь от меня́!** leave me alone!

отвя́зыва|ть(ся), ю(сь) *impf. of* ⇒**отвяза́ть(ся)**

отгад|а́ть, а́ю *pf.* (*of* ⇒**~ывать**) to guess.

отга́дк|а, и *f.* answer, solution (*to a riddle*).

отга́дчик, а *m.* (*coll.*) guesser, diviner.

отга́дчи|ца, цы *f. of* ⇒**~к**

отга́дыва|ть, ю *impf. of* ⇒**отгада́ть**

отгиба́|ть(ся), ю(сь) *impf. of* ⇒**отогну́ть(ся)**

отглаго́льный *adj.* (*gram.*) verbal.

отгла́|дить, жу, дишь *pf.* (*of* ⇒**~живать**) to iron.

отгла́жива|ть, ю *impf. of* ⇒**отгла́дить**

отглода́|ть, ю *pf.* (*coll.*) to bite off.

отгова́рива|ть(ся), ю(сь) *impf. of* ⇒**отговори́ть(ся)**

отговор|и́ть, ю́, и́шь *pf.* (*of* ⇒**отгова́ривать**) (**от**+*g.*, *or* +*inf.*) to dissuade (from); **я ~и́л его́ е́хать** I have talked him out of going.

отговор|и́ться, ю́сь, и́шься *pf.* (*of* ⇒**отгова́риваться**) (+*i.*) to excuse o.s. (on the ground of); to plead; **о. нездоро́вьем** (*coll.*) to plead ill-health.

отгово́рк|а, и *f.* excuse; (*предлог*) pretext.

отголо́с|ок, ка *m.* echo (*also fig.*).

отго́н¹, а *m.* (*скота*) driving (*to pasture*); **на ~е** at pasture.

отго́н², а *m.* **1** = **отго́нка²**. **2** (*продукт отгонки*) product of distillation.

отго́нк|а¹, и *f.* driving off.

отго́нк|а², и *f.* (*chem.*) distillation.

отгоня́|ть, ю *impf. of* ⇒**отогна́ть**

отгора́жива|ть(ся), ю(сь) *impf. of* ⇒**отгороди́ть(ся)**

отгоро|ди́ть, жу́, ~ди́шь *pf.* (*of* ⇒**отгора́живать**) to fence off, partition off; **о. ши́рмой** to screen off.

отгоро|ди́ться, жу́сь, ~ди́шься *pf.* (*of* ⇒**отгора́живаться**) to fence o.s. off; (*fig., coll.*; **от**+*g.*) to shut *or* cut o.s. off (from).

отго|сти́ть, щу́, сти́шь *pf.* (*coll.*; **у**+*g.*) to stay (with).

отграни́чива|ть, ю *impf. of* ⇒**отграни́чить**

отграни́ч|ить, у, ишь *pf.* (*of* ⇒**~ивать**) to delimit.

отгреба́|ть, ю *impf. of* ⇒**отгрести́**

отгрем|е́ть, и́т *pf.* to finish rumbling.

отгре|сти́¹, бу́, бёшь *past* **~б, ~бла́** *pf.* (*of* ⇒**~ба́ть**) (*мусор*) to rake away.

отгре|сти́², бу́, бёшь, *past* **~б, ~бла́** *pf.* (*of* ⇒**~ба́ть**) (*от берега*) to row off.

отгроха́|ть, ю *pf.* (*coll.*) **1** = **отгреме́ть. 2** to build, make, organize (*sth. impressive*).

отгружа́|ть, ю *impf. of* ⇒**отгрузи́ть**

отгру|зи́ть, жу́, ~зи́шь *pf.* (*of* ⇒**~жа́ть**) to ship, dispatch.

отгру́зк|а, и *f.* shipment, dispatching.

отгрыз|а́ть, а́ю *impf. of* ⇒**~ть**

отгры́з|ть, у́, ёшь, *past* **~, ~ла** *pf.* (*of* ⇒**~а́ть**) to bite off, gnaw off.

отгу́л, а *m.* day(s) off (*in compensation for overtime work*).

отгу́лива|ть, ю *impf. of* ⇒**отгуля́ть** 2

отгул|я́ть, я́ю *pf.* (*coll.*) **1** (*отпуск*) to have spent, to have finished; **мы ~я́ли о́тпуск** our holidays are over. **2** (*impf.* **~ивать**) to take (time) off; **о. день** to take a day off.

отда|ва́ть¹, ю́, ёшь *impf. of* ⇒**отда́ть**

отда|ва́ть², ёт *impf.* (*impers.* + *i.*; *coll.*) to taste (of); to smell (of); (*fig.*) to smack (of); **от него́ ~ёт во́дкой** he reeks of vodka; **э́то ~ёт суеве́рием** this smacks of superstition.

отда|ва́ться, ю́сь, ёшься *impf. of* ⇒**отда́ться**

отдав|и́ть, лю́, ~ишь *pf.* to crush; **о. кому́-н. но́гу** to tread on s.o.'s foot.

отдале́ни|е, я *nt.* **1** removal; (*fig.*) (*от товарищей*) estrangement. **2** (*расстояние*) distance; **держа́ть в ~и** to keep at a distance.

отдалённост|ь, и *f.* remoteness.

отдалён|ный (~, ~на) *adj.* distant, remote; **о. ро́дственник** distant relative; **~ное схо́дство** remote likeness.

отдал|и́ть, ю́, и́шь *pf.* (*of* ⇒**~я́ть**) **1** to remove; (*fig.*) (*от товарищей*) to estrange, alienate. **2** (*встречу*) to postpone, put off.

отдал|и́ться, ю́сь, и́шься *pf.* (*of* ⇒**~я́ться**) **1** (**от**+*g.*) (*от берега*) to move away (from); (*от друзей*) to become alienated (from); (*о шуме, воспоминаниях*) to become more distant. **2** (*fig.*) to digress; **о. от те́мы** to stray from the subject.

отдал|я́ть(ся), я́ю(сь) *impf. of* ⇒**~и́ть(ся)**

отда́ни|е, я *nt.*: **о. че́сти** (*mil.*) saluting.

отда́рива|ть(ся), ю(сь) *impf. of* ⇒**отдари́ть(ся)**

отдар|и́ть, ю́, и́шь *pf.* (*of* ⇒**~ивать**) (*coll.*) to give in return.

отдар|и́ться, ю́сь, и́шься *pf.* (*of* ⇒**~иваться**) (*coll.*) to make a present in return, repay a gift.

отд|а́ть, а́м, а́шь, а́ст, ади́м, ади́те, аду́т, *past* **~ал, ~ала́, ~ало** *pf.* (*of* ⇒**~ава́ть**) **1** (*дать обратно*) to give back, return; **о. до́лжное кому́-н.** to render s.o. his due; **о. после́дний долг** (+*d.*) to pay the last honours; **о. себе́ отчёт** (**в**+*p.*) to be aware (of), realize; **не о. себе́ отчёта** (**в**+*p.*) to fail to realize.
2 (*посвятить*) to devote; **о. жизнь нау́ке** to devote one's life to scholarship.
3 (+*a.* and *d.* or +*a.* **за**+*a.*) (*выдать замуж*) to give in marriage (to), give away.
4 (**в**+*a.*, **под**+*a.*) (*вручить*) to give, put, place (= *hand over for certain purpose*); **о. кни́гу в переплёт** to have a book bound, send a book to be bound; **о. ма́льчика в шко́лу** to send a boy to school; **о. под стра́жу** to give into custody; **о. под суд** to prosecute.
5 (*in comb. with certain nn.*) to give; to make (*or not requiring separate translation*); **о. покло́н** (*obs.*) to bow, make a bow; **о. прика́з** (+*d.*) to issue an order, give orders (to); **о. распоряже́ние** to give instructions; **о. честь** (*mil.*) (+*d.*) to salute.
6 (*coll.*) (*продать*) to sell, let have; **он мне э́то ~ал за бесце́нок** he let me have it for a song.
7 (*об оружии*) to kick, recoil.

отд|а́ться, а́мся, а́шься, а́стся, ади́мся, ади́тесь, аду́тся, *past* **~а́лся, ~ала́сь** *pf.* (*of* ⇒**~ава́ться**) **1** (+*d.*) (*победителю*) to give o.s. up (to); (*науке*) to devote o.s. (to); (*о женщине*) to give o.s. (to). **2** (*о голосе, об эхе*) to resound; to reverberate; to ring. **3** (*о боли*) to be felt.

отда́ч|а, и *f.* **1** (*книги*) return; (*долга*) payment, reimbursement. **2** (*эффективность*) efficiency, performance. **3** (*при выстреле*) recoil, kick. **4** (*приказа*) issuing, giving; (*чести*) (*mil.*) saluting.

отдежу́р|ить, ю, ишь *pf.* **1** (*кончить дежурить*) to come off duty. **2** (*известное время*) to spend on duty; **о. во́семь часо́в** to have had eight hours on (duty).

отде́л, а *m.* **1** department; **о. ка́дров** personnel department. **2** (*книги, журнала*) section, part.

отде́л|ать, аю *pf.* (*of* ⇒**~ывать**) **1** to finish, put the finishing touches (to); to decorate; **о. пла́тье кружева́ми** to trim a dress with lace. **2** (*coll.*) (*выругать*) to give a dressing down.

отде́л|аться, аюсь *pf.* (*of* ⇒**~ываться**) **1** (**от**+*g.*) to get rid (of), get shot (of). **2** (+*i.*) to escape (with), get off (with); **сча́стливо о.** to have a lucky escape; **о. цара́пиной** to get off with a scratch.

отделе́ни|е, я *nt.* **1** (*действие*) separation. **2** (*учреждение*) department, branch; **о. мили́ции** local police-station; **о. свя́зи** local post office. **3** (*вместилища*) compartment, section; (*представления*) part; **о. шка́фа** pigeon-hole; **маши́нное о.** (*naut.*) engine-room. **4** (*mil.*) section.

отдел|ённый[1] *p.p.p. of* ⇒**~и́ть**

отделённый[2] *adj. of* ⇒**отделе́ние** 4; **о. команди́р** section commander.

отдели́м|ый (~, ~а) *adj.* separable.

отдел|и́ть, ю́, ~ишь *pf.* (*of* ⇒**~я́ть**) **1** (*отнять*) to separate. **2** (*отграничить*) to separate off; **о. перегоро́дкой** to partition off.

отдел|и́ться, ю́сь, ~ишься *pf.* (*of* ⇒**~я́ться**) (*отодвинуться*) to move away, separate; (*оторваться*) to get detached; to come off; (*быть отграниченным от чего-либо*) to be separated.

отде́лк|а, и *f.* **1** (*действие*) finishing; trimming. **2** (*украшение*) finish, decoration; (*в комнате*) décor.

отде́лочник, а *m.* (interior) decorator.

отде́лочный *adj.* decorative.

отде́лыва|ть(ся), ю(сь) *impf. of* ⇒**отде́лать(ся)**

отде́льно *adv.* separately.

отде́льност|ь, и *f.*: **в ~и** taken separately, individually.

отде́льный *adj.* **1** separate, (*некоторый*) individual, (*единичный*) isolated. **2** (*mil.*) independent.

отдел|я́ть(ся), я́ю(сь) *impf. of* ⇒**~и́ть(ся)**

отдёргива|ть, ю *impf. of* ⇒**отдёрнуть**

отдёр|нуть, ну, нешь *pf.* (*of* ⇒**~гивать**) **1** (*в сторону*) to draw aside, pull aside; **о. занаве́ску** to draw back the curtain. **2** (*руку*) to pull back, withdraw.

отдира́|ть, ю *impf. of* ⇒**отодра́ть**

отдохн|у́ть, у́, ёшь *pf.* (*of* ⇒**отдыха́ть**) to rest; to have (take) a rest.

отдуба́|сить, шу, сишь *pf. of* ⇒**дуба́сить**

отдува́|ть, ю *impf. of* ⇒**отду́ть**

отдува́|ться, юсь *impf.* **1** to pant, puff. **2** (*fig.*, *coll.*; **за**+*a.*) to take the rap (for).

отду́м|ать, аю *pf.* (*of* ⇒**~ывать**) (*coll.*) to change one's mind; **мы ~али переезжа́ть** we have changed our mind about moving.

отду́мыва|ть, ю *impf. of* ⇒**отду́мать**

отду́|ть, ю, ешь *pf.* (*of* ⇒**~ва́ть**) **1** (*удалить дуновением*) to blow away. **2** (*coll.*) (*избить*) to thrash soundly.

отду́шин|а, ы *f.* air-hole, (air) vent; (*fig.*) outlet.

отду́шник, а *m.* air-hole, (air) vent.

о́тдых, а *m.* rest; relaxation; (*отпуск*) holiday (*Br.*), vacation (*US*); **день ~а** day of rest, rest day.

отдыха́|ть, ю *impf.* (*of* ⇒**отдохну́ть**) to be resting; (*быть в отпуске*) to be on holiday (*Br.*), vacation (*US*); (*проводить отпуск*) to holiday (*Br.*), vacation (*US*).

отдыха́|ющий *pres. part. of* ⇒**~ть;** *as n.* **о., ~ющего** *m.*; **~ющая, ~ющей** *f.* holiday-maker (*Br.*), vacationer (*US*).

отдыш|а́ться, у́сь, ~ишься *pf.* to recover one's breath.

отёк, а *m.* (*med.*) oedema (*Br.*), edema (*US*); **о. лёгких** emphysema.

отека́|ть, ю *impf. of* ⇒**оте́чь**

отёл, а *m.* calving.

отел|и́ться, ~ится *pf. of* ⇒**тели́ться**

оте́л|ь, я *m.* hotel.

оте́ль|ный *adj. of* ⇒**~**

отепл|и́ть, ю́, и́шь *pf.* (*of* ⇒**~я́ть**) to protect against the cold.

отепл|я́ть, я́ю *impf. of* ⇒**~и́ть**

от|е́ц, ца́ *m.* father (*also fig.*); **на́ши ~цы́** (*fig.*) our (fore)fathers; **О. небе́сный** (*relig.*) the heavenly Father; **о. семе́йства** (*coll.*) paterfamilias.

оте́ческий *adj.* fatherly, paternal.

оте́честв|енный *adj. of* ⇒**~о;** **~енная промы́шленность** home industry; **~енная война́** (*hist.*) the Patriotic War (*against Napoleon in 1812*); **Вели́кая ~енная война́** the Great Patriotic War (*World War II*).

оте́честв|о, а *nt.* native land, fatherland, homeland.

оте́|чь, ку́, чёшь, ку́т, *past* **~к, ~кла́** *pf.* (*of* ⇒**~ка́ть**) **1** (*опухнуть*) to swell, become swollen. **2** (*о свече*) to gutter.

от|жа́ть, отожму́, отожмёшь *pf.* (*of* ⇒**~жима́ть**) **1** (*бельё*) to wring out. **2** (*coll.*) (*толпу*) to push back.

от|же́чь, отожгу́, отожжёшь, *past* **~жёг, ~ожгла́** *pf.* (*of* ⇒**~жига́ть**) (*tech.*) to anneal.

отжива́|ть, ю *impf. of* ⇒**отжи́ть**

отжива́|ющий *pres. part. act. of* ⇒**~ть** *and adj.* moribund.

отжи́|вший *past part. act. of* ⇒**~ть** *and adj.* obsolete; outmoded.

о́тжиг, а *m.* (*tech.*) annealing.

отжига́|ть, ю *impf. of* ⇒**отже́чь**

отжима́|ть, ю *impf. of* ⇒**отжа́ть**

от|жи́ть, живу́, живёшь, *past* **~жил, ~жила́, ~жило** *pf.* (*of* ⇒**~жива́ть**) to become obsolete, die out; **о. свой век** to have had one's day; to go out of fashion.

отзвон|и́ть, ю́, и́шь *pf.* (*о звонаре*) to stop ringing; (*о часах*) to strike; **~и́л и с колоко́льни доло́й** (*coll.*) finished and done with.

о́тзвук, а *m.* echo (*also fig.*).

отзвуч|а́ть, и́т *pf.* (*о звуке*) to have faded away; to stop ringing.

о́тзыв, а *m.* **1** (*мнение*) opinion, judgement. **2** (*рекомендация*) reference; testimonial; **дать хоро́ший о. о ко́м-н.** to give s.o. a good reference. **3** (*рецензия*) review. **4** (*mil.*) reply (*to password*). **5** (*fig.*) = **о́тзвук**

отзы́в, а *m.* recall (*of diplomatic representative*).

отзыва́|ть, ю *impf.* **1** *impf. of* ⇒**отозва́ть. 2** (+*i.*) to taste (of); **о. го́речью** to have a bitter taste.

отзыва́|ться, юсь *impf.* **1** *impf. of* ⇒**отозва́ться. 2** (+*i.*) = **~ть**

отзы́вчив|ый (~, ~а) *adj.* responsive.

оти́т, а *m.* (*med.*) otitis.

ОТК *m. indecl.* (*abbr. of* ***отде́л техни́ческого контро́ля***) department of technical control.

отка́з, а *m.* **1** refusal; **получи́ть о.** to be refused, be turned down; **до ~а** to overflowing; **по́лный до ~а** jam-packed, full to capacity. **2** (**от**+*g.*) renunciation (of), giving up (of). **3** (*механизма*) failure; **де́йствовать без ~а** to run smoothly. **4** (*mus.*) natural.

отка|за́ть, жу́, ~жешь *pf.* (*of* ⇒**~зывать**) **1** (+*d. and* **в**+*p.*) to refuse, deny; **она́ ~за́ла ему́ в про́сьбе** she refused his request; **ему́ нельзя́ о. в тала́нте** there is no denying that he has talent; **не ~жи́те в любе́зности**... be so kind as .... **2** (*о механизме*) to fail, break down.

отка|за́ться, жу́сь, ~жешься *pf.* (*of* ⇒**~зываться**) **1** (**от**+*g. or* +*inf.*) to refuse, decline; to turn down; **о. от предложе́ния** to turn down a proposal; **о. от свои́х слов** to retract one's words; **о. от упла́ты до́лга** to repudiate a debt; **о. служи́ть** (*fig.*, *coll.*) to be out of order; **мои́ часы́ ~за́лись служи́ть** my watch would not go; **не ~жу́сь** (*coll.*) I don't mind if I do; **не ~за́лся бы** (*coll.*) I wouldn't say no. **2** (*отречься*) to renounce, give up; (*от права*) to relinquish; (*от власти*) to abdicate; **о. от борьбы́** to give up the struggle.

отка́зни|к, а *m.* refusenik.

отка́зни|ца, ~цы *f. of* ⇒**~к**

отка́зыва|ть(ся), ю(сь) *impf. of* ⇒**отказа́ть(ся)**

отка́лыва|ть(ся), ю(сь) *impf. of* ⇒**отколо́ть(ся)**

отка́пыва|ть, ю *impf. of* ⇒**откопа́ть**

отка́рмлива|ть, ю *impf. of* ⇒**откорми́ть**

отка́т, а *m.* (*mil.*) recoil.

отка|ти́ть, чу́, ~тишь *pf.* (*of* ⇒**~тывать**) (*бревно*) to roll away.

отка|ти́ться, чу́сь, ~тишься *pf.* (*of* ⇒**~тываться**) **1** (*мяч*) to roll away. **2** (*mil.*; *fig.*, *coll.*) to roll back, be forced back.

отка́тыва|ть(ся), ю(сь) *impf. of* ⇒**откати́ть(ся)**

откач|а́ть, а́ю *pf.* (*of* ⇒**~ивать**) **1** (*воздух, воду*) to pump out. **2** (*человека*) to resuscitate.

отка́чива|ть, ю *impf. of* ⇒**откача́ть**

откачн|у́ть, у́, ёшь *pf.* **1** to swing to one side. **2** (*fig.*, *coll.*; *impers.*) **его́ ~у́ло от бы́вших его́ собуты́льников** he has drifted away from his former drinking companions.

откачн|у́ться, у́сь, ёшься *pf.* (*coll.*) **1** (*о маятнике*) to swing to one side. **2** (*о человеке*) to reel back; to slump back. **3** (*fig.*; **от**+*g.*) (*прервать связь*) to turn away (from).

отка́шл|ивать, иваю *impf. of* ⇒**~януть**

отка́шл|иваться, иваюсь *impf. of* ⇒**~яться**

отка́шл|януть, яну, янешь *pf.* (*of* ⇒**~ивать**) to hawk up.

отка́шл|яться, яюсь *pf.* (*of* ⇒**~иваться**) to clear one's throat.

откидно́й *adj.* folding, collapsible.

отки́дыва|ть(ся), ю(сь) *impf. of* ⇒**отки́нуть(ся)**

отки́|нуть, ну, нешь *pf.* (*of* ⇒**~дывать**) **1** (*отбросить*) to throw away; to cast away (*also fig.*). **2** (*отогнуть*) to turn back, fold back.

отки́|нуться, нусь, нешься *pf.* (*of* ⇒**~дываться**) to lean back; to recline, settle back.

откла́дыва|ть, ю *impf. of* ⇒**отложи́ть**

откла́нива|ться, юсь *impf. of* ⇒**откла́няться**

откла́н|яться, яюсь *pf.* (*of* ⇒**~иваться**) (*obs.*) to take one's leave.

откле́ива|ть(ся), ю(сь) *impf. of* ⇒**откле́ить(ся)**

откле́|ить, ю, ишь *pf.* (*of* ⇒**~ивать**) to peel off.

откле́|иться, ится *pf.* (*of* ⇒**~иваться**) to come unstuck.

о́тклик, а *m.* **1** (*ответ на зов*) response; (*fig.*) (*в печати*) review, comment. **2** (*fig.*) (*эхо*) echo.

отклик|а́ться, а́юсь *impf.* (*of* ⇒**~́нуться**) (**на**+*a.*) to answer, respond (to) (*also fig.*).

откли́к|нуться, нусь, нешься *pf. of* ⇒**~а́ться**

отклоне́ни|е, я *nt.* **1** (*отход в сторону*) deviation; divergence; **о. от те́мы** digression. **2** (*отказ*) declining, refusal. **3** (*phys.*) deflection, declination; error; diffraction; **вероя́тное о.** probable error; **магни́тное о.** deflection of the needle; **у́гол ~я** angle of deviation.

отклон|и́ть, ю́, ~́ишь *pf.* (*of* ⇒**~я́ть**) **1** (*в сторону*) to deflect. **2** (*отказать*) to decline; **о. попра́вку** to vote down an amendment; **о. предложе́ние** to decline an offer. **3** (*побудить отказаться*) to discourage.

отклон|и́ться, ю́сь, ~́ишься *pf.* (*of* ⇒**~я́ться**) (*от курса*) to deviate; (*от удара*) to dodge; (*отодвинуться*) to move aside; **о. от те́мы** to digress.

отклоня́|ть(ся), ю(сь) *impf. of* ⇒**отклони́ть(ся)**

отключ|а́ть(ся), а́ю(сь) *impf. of* ⇒**~и́ть(ся)**

отключ|ённый *p.p.p. of* ⇒**~и́ть** *and adj.* (*elec.*) dead; **опера́ция проводи́мая на ~ённом се́рдце** open-heart operation.

отключ|и́ть, у́, и́шь *pf.* (*of* ⇒**~а́ть**) (*elec.*) to cut off, disconnect; **о. телефо́нный аппара́т** to cut off a telephone.

отключ|и́ться, у́сь, и́шься *pf.* (*of* ⇒**~а́ться**) **1** to become disconected. **2** (*coll.*) (*о человеке*) to switch off.

отковы́рива|ть, ю *impf. of* ⇒**отковыря́ть**

отковыр|я́ть, я́ю *pf.* (*of* ⇒**~́ивать**) to pick off.

откозыря́|ть, ю *pf.* (*coll.*; +*d.*) to salute.

отко́л|е *adv.* = **~ь**

отколо|ти́ть, чу́, ~́тишь *pf.* **1** (*отбить приколоченное*) to knock off. **2** (*избить*) to beat up.

откол|о́ть, ю́, ~́ешь *pf.* (*of* ⇒**отка́лывать**) **1** (*отломать*) to break off; (*отбить*) to chop off; (*от семьи*) to cut off. **2** (*булавку, чепец*) to unpin. **3** (*coll., pej.*): **о. глу́пость** to play a stupid trick; **о. словцо́** to make a wisecrack.

откол|о́ться, ю́сь, ~́ешься *pf.* (*of* ⇒**отка́лываться**) **1** (*отломаться*) to break off. **2** (*о булавке, чепце*) to come unpinned *or* undone. **3** (*fig.*) (*от семьи*) to break away; to cut o.s. off.

отколошма́|тить, чу, чишь *pf. of* ⇒**колошма́тить**

отколуп|а́ть, а́ю *pf.* (*of* ⇒**~́ывать**) (*coll.*) to pick off.

отколу́пыва|ть, ю *impf. of* ⇒**отколупа́ть**

отко́ль *adv.* (*obs.*) whence, where from.

откомандир|ова́ть, у́ю *pf.* (*of* ⇒**~о́вывать**) **1** to post (*to new duties or establishment*). **2** (**за**+*i.*) (*coll.*) to send (*to fetch*).

откомандиро́выва|ть, ю *impf. of* ⇒**откомандирова́ть**

откопа́|ть, ю *pf.* (*of* ⇒**отка́пывать**) **1** to dig out; (*труп*) to exhume, disinter. **2** (*fig., coll.*) (*найти*) to dig up, unearth.

отко́рм, а *m.* fattening (up).

откорм|и́ть, лю́, ~́ишь *pf.* (*of* ⇒**отка́рмливать**) to fatten (up).

отко́рм|ленный *p.p.p. of* ⇒**~и́ть** *and adj.* fat, fatted, fattened.

отко́с, а *m.* **1** (*покатый спуск*) slope, side (*of embankment etc.*); **о. холма́** hillside. **2** (*rail.*) embankment; **пусти́ть по́езд под о.** to derail a train.

открепи́ть, лю́, и́шь *pf.* (*of* ⇒**~ля́ть**) **1** (*цепь*) to unfasten, untie. **2** (*снять с учёта*) to strike off the register.

открепи́ться, лю́сь, и́шься *pf.* (*of* ⇒**~ля́ться**) **1** (*о замке*) to become unfastened. **2** (*сняться с учёта*) to remove one's name (*from a register etc.*).

открепля́|ть(ся), ю(сь) *impf. of* ⇒**открепи́ть(ся)**

откре|сти́ться, щу́сь, ~́стишься *pf.* (*of* ⇒**откре́щиваться**) (*coll.*; **от**+*g.*) to disown; to refuse to have anything to do (with).

откре́щива|ться, юсь *impf. of* ⇒**откре́сти́ться**

открове́ни|е, я *nt.* revelation.

открове́ннича|ть, ю *impf.* (*coll.*; **с**+*i.*) to be excessively candid/frank (with).

открове́нност|ь, и *f.* candour (*Br.*), candor (*US*), frankness; *pl.* (*coll.*) candid revelations.

открове́н|ный (~ен, ~на) *adj.* **1** (*искренний*) candid, frank. **2** (*нескрываемый*) open, unconcealed; **~ная неприя́знь** unconcealed hostility. **3** (*coll.*) (*о платье*) revealing.

откромса́|ть, ю *pf.* (*coll.*) to cut off (unevenly).

откру|ти́ть, чу́, ~́тишь *pf.* (*of* ⇒**~́чивать**) to untwist; **о. кран** to turn off a tap.

откру|ти́ться, чу́сь, ~́тишься *pf.* (*of* ⇒**~́чиваться**) **1** to come untwisted. **2** (*coll.*; **от**+*g.*) to get out (of).

откру́чива|ть(ся), ю(сь) *impf. of* ⇒**открути́ть(ся)**

открыва́лк|а, и *f.* (*coll.*) **1** (*для банок*) can-opener. **2** (*для бутылок*) bottle-opener.

открыва́|ть(ся), ю(сь) *impf. of* ⇒**откры́ть(ся)**

откры́л|ок, ка *m.* (*aeron.*) stub-wing.

откры́ти|е, я *nt.* **1** (*действие*) opening. **2** (*научное*) discovery.

откры́тк|а, и *f.* post-card; **о. с ви́дом** picture post-card.

откры́то *adv.* openly.

откры́т|ый *p.p.p. of* ⇒**~ь** *and adj.* open; **в ~ую** (*cards and fig.*) showing one's hand; **на ~ом во́здухе, под ~ым не́бом** out of doors, in the open air; **с ~ыми глаза́ми** (*fig.*) with open eyes; **о. дом** (*fig.*) open house; **~ое заседа́ние** public sitting; **~ое мо́ре** the open sea; **~ое письмо́** open letter; **~ое пла́тье** low-necked dress; **~ые го́рные рабо́ты** opencast mining; **~ая сце́на** open-air stage.

откр|ы́ть, о́ю, о́ешь *pf.* (*of* ⇒**~ыва́ть**) **1** to open; **о. кому́-н. глаза́ на что-н.** (*fig.*) to open s.o.'s eyes to sth.; **о. ми́тинг** to open a meeting; **о. ого́нь** (*mil.*) to open fire; **о. па́мятник** to unveil a monument; **о. счёт** to open an account. **2** (*обнажить*) to uncover, reveal (*also fig.*); **о. грудь** to bare one's breast; **о. ду́шу** to lay bare one's heart; **о. ка́рты** (*fig.*) to show one's hand; **о. секре́т** to reveal a secret. **3** (*обнаружить*) to discover; **о. Аме́рику** (*fig., iron.*) to retail stale news. **4** (*воду, газ*) to turn on.

откр|ы́ться, о́юсь, о́ешься *pf.* (*of* ⇒**~ыва́ться**) **1** (*дверь, глаза*) to open. **2** (*обнаружиться*) to come to light, be revealed; **пе́ред на́ми ~ы́лся великоле́пный вид** a magnificent view unfolded before us. **3** (+*d.*) (*кому-н.*) to confide (in, to).

отку́да *adv.* (*interrog.*) where from; (*rel.*) whence, from which; **о. вы?** where are you from?; **о. вы об э́том зна́ете?** how come you know about it?; **о. ни возьми́сь** (*coll.*) quite unexpectedly, out of the blue.

отку́да-либо *adv.* from somewhere or other.

откýда-нибудь *adv.* = **откýда-либо**

откýда-то *adv.* from somewhere.

óткуп, а, *pl.* **~á** *m.* (*hist.*) farming (*of revenues, etc.*); **взять на о.** to farm; **отдáть на о.** to farm out (*also fig.*).

откуп|áть(ся), áю(сь) *impf. of* ⇒**~и́ть(ся)**

откуп|и́ть, лю́, ~ишь *pf.* (*of* ⇒**~áть**) to pay up.

откуп|и́ться, лю́сь, ~ишься *pf.* (*of* ⇒**~áться**) (**от**+*g.*) to pay off.

откýпорива|ть, ю *impf. of* ⇒**откýпорить**

откýпор|ить, ю, ишь *pf.* (*of* ⇒**~ивать**) (*бутылку*) to uncork; (*банку*) to open.

откупщи́к, á *m.* tax-farmer

отку|си́ть, шý, ~сишь *pf.* (*of* ⇒**~сывать**) to bite off; (*щипцами*) to cut off.

откýсыва|ть, ю *impf. of* ⇒**откуси́ть**

откýша|ть, ю *pf.* (*obs.*) **1** (*окончить еду*) to have finished eating. **2** (*поесть*) to eat; (*попробовать*) to try (*food*); **позвáть о.** to invite to a meal.

отлагáтельств|о, а *nt.* delay; procrastination; **дéло не тéрпит ~а** the matter is urgent.

отлагá|ть(ся), ю(сь) *impf. of* ⇒**отложи́ть(ся)**

отлакир|овáть, ýю *pf. of* ⇒**лакировáть**

отлáмыва|ть(ся), ю(сь) *impf. of* ⇒**отломáть(ся)** *and* **отломи́ть(ся)**

отлегá|ть, ет *impf. of* ⇒**отлéчь**

отлеж|áть, ý, и́шь *pf.* (*of* ⇒**~ивать**): **я ~áл нóгу** my foot has gone to sleep.

отлеж|áться, ýсь, и́шься *pf.* (*of* ⇒**~иваться**) **1** (*отдохнуть*) to lie up; to rest (*in bed*). **2** (*об овощах, фруктах*) to lie, be stored (*in order to ripen*).

отлёжива|ть(ся), ю, ет(ся) *impf. of* ⇒**отлежáть(ся)**

отлеп|и́ть, лю́, ~ишь *pf.* (*of* ⇒**~ля́ть**) (*coll.*) to unstick, peel off.

отлеп|и́ться, ~ится *pf.* (*of* ⇒**~ля́ться**) (*coll.*) to come unstuck, peel off.

отлепля́|ть(ся), ю, ет(ся) *impf. of* ⇒**отлепи́ть(ся)**

отлёт, а *m.* flying away; (*самолёта*) departure; **быть на ~е** to be about to leave; **держáть на ~е** to hold in one's outstretched hand; **держáться на ~е** (*coll.*) to hold o.s. aloof; **дом на ~е** house standing by itself.

отлетá|ть[1], ю *pf.* **1** (*кончить летать*) to stop flying. **2** (*coll.*) to have been flying (*for a given period*); **он ~л двáдцать лет** he has twenty years' flying experience.

отлет|áть[2], áю *impf. of* ⇒**~éть**

отле|тéть, чý, ти́шь *pf.* (*of* ⇒**~тáть[2]**) **1** (*улететь*) to fly (away, off); (*fig.*) (*исчезнуть*) to fly, vanish. **2** (*о мяче*) to rebound, bounce back. **3** (*coll.*) (*о пуговице*) to come off.

отл|éчь, я́жет, я́гут *past* **~ёг, ~еглá** *pf.* (*of* ⇒**~егáть**) (*о боли, тревоге*) to pass; (*coll.; impers.*) **у неё ~еглó от сéрдца** she felt relieved.

отли́в[1], а *m.* (*моря*) ebb, ebb-tide.

отли́в[2], а *m.* (*оттенок*) tint; **с золоты́м ~ом** shot with gold.

отливá|ть[1], ю *impf. of* ⇒**отли́ть**

отливá|ть[2], ет *impf.* (+*i.*) to be shot (*with a colour*).

отли́вк|а, и *f.* (*tech.*) **1** (*действие*) casting, founding. **2** (*изделие*) cast, ingot, moulding (*Br.*), molding (*US*).

отливн|óй *adj.* (*tech.*) cast, founded, moulded (*Br.*), molded (*US*); **~áя печь** founding furnace.

отлип|áть, áет *impf. of* ⇒**~нуть**

отли́п|нуть, нет, *past* **~, ~ла** *pf.* (*of* ⇒**~áть**) (*coll.*) to come off, come unstuck.

отли́ть, отолью́, отольёшь, *past* **óтли́л, отлилá, óтли́ло** *pf.* (*of* ⇒**отливáть[1]**) **1** (+*a. or g.*) (*молока*) to pour off; (*выкачать*) to pump out; (*отхлынуть*) to flood back. **2** (*tech.*) to cast, found.

отлич|áть, áю *impf. of* ⇒**~и́ть**

отлич|áться, áюсь *impf.* **1** (*pf.* **~и́ться**) to distinguish o.s., excel (*also joc., iron.*). **2** (*impf. only*) (**от**+*g.*) to differ (from). **3** (*impf. only*) (+*i.*) to be notable (for).

отли́чи|е, я *nt.* **1** difference, distinction; **знак ~я** distinguishing feature; (*mil.*) order, decoration; **в о. от** (+*g.*) unlike, in contrast to. **2** (*оценка*) distinction; (*заслуга*) distinguished services; **получи́ть дипло́м с ~ем** to obtain a distinction.

отличи́тельный *adj.* distinctive; distinguishing; **о. при́знак** distinguishing feature.

отлич|и́ть, ý, и́шь *pf.* (*of* ⇒**~áть**) **1** to distinguish; **о. однó от другóго** to tell one thing from another. **2** (*выделить из числа других*) to single out.

отлич|и́ться, ýсь, и́шься *pf. of* ⇒**~áться**

отли́чник, а *m.* **1** student obtaining 'excellent' marks. **2**: **о. произвóдства** exemplary worker.

отли́чни|ца, цы *f. of* ⇒**~к**

отли́чно 1 *adv.* excellently; perfectly; extremely well; **о. знать** to know perfectly well; **он о. понимáет по-рýсски** he understands Russian perfectly. **2** *n.; nt. indecl.* 'excellent' mark (*in school, etc.*).

отли́ч|ный (~ен, ~на) *adj.* **1** (**от**+*g.*) (*иной*) different (from). **2** (*превосходный*) excellent; perfect; extremely good; **~но!** excellent!

отлóг|ий (~, ~а) *adj.* sloping.

отлóгост|ь, и *f.* slope.

отлó|же *comp. of* ⇒**~гий**

отложéни|е, я *nt.* (*geol., med.*) deposit.

отлож|и́ть, ý, ~ишь *pf.* **1** (*impf.* **отклáдывать**) (*положить в сторону*) to put aside, set aside; (*сохранить*) to put away, put by; **о. на чёрный день** to put by for a rainy day. **2** (*impf.* **отклáдывать** *and obs.* **отлагáть**) (*отсрочить*) to put off, postpone; **о. пáртию** to adjourn a game; **о. в дóлгий я́щик** to shelve. **3** (*impf.* **отклáдывать**) (*о птицах*) to lay. **4** (*impf.* **отклáдывать**) (*obs.*) (*лошадей*) to unharness. **5** (*impf.* **отлагáть**) (*chem., geol.*) to deposit.

отлож|и́ться, ýсь, ~ишься *pf.* (*of* ⇒**отлагáться**) **1** (*obs.;* **от**+*g.*) to detach o.s. (from); to separate (from); (*pol.*) to secede. **2** (*chem., geol.*) to deposit; to be deposited.

отложнóй *adj.*: **о. воротни́к** turn-down collar.

отломá|ть, ю *pf.* (*of* ⇒**отлáмывать**) to break off.

отломá|ться, юсь *pf.* (*of* ⇒**отлáмываться**) to break off.

отлом|и́ть(ся), лю́(сь), ~ишь(ся) *pf.* = **~áть(ся)**

отлуп|и́ть, лю́, ~ишь *pf. of* ⇒**лупи́ть[2]**

отлупц|евáть, ýю *pf. of* ⇒**лупцевáть**

отлуч|áть(ся), áю(сь) *impf. of* ⇒**отлучи́ть(ся)**

отлучéни|е, я *nt.* (*eccl. and fig.*) excommunication.

отлуч|и́ть, ý, и́шь *pf.* (*of* ⇒**~áть**) (*obs.;* **от**+*g.*) to separate *or* remove (from); **о. (от цéркви)** (*eccl.*) to excommunicate.

отлуч|и́ться, ýсь, и́шься *pf.* (*of* ⇒**~áться**) to absent o.s.

отлýчк|а, и *f.* absence; **самовóльная о.** (*mil.*) absence without leave (*abbr.* AWOL); **быть в ~е** to be absent, be away.

отлы́нива|ть, ю *impf.* (*coll.;* **от**+*g.*) to shirk.

отмáлчива|ться, юсь *impf. of* ⇒**отмолчáться**

отмáтыва|ть, ю *impf. of* ⇒**отмотáть**

отма|хáть[1], шý, ~шешь *pf.* (*of* ⇒**~хивать**): **о. рýки** to tire one's arms by waving.

отмахá|ть[2], ю *pf.* (*coll.*) to cover (*a distance*); **за день мы ~ли свы́ше тридцати́ миль** in the day we covered more than thirty miles.

отмáхива|ть(ся), ю(сь) *impf. of* ⇒**отмахáть[1]** *and* **отмахнýть(ся)**

отмах|нýть, нý, нёшь *pf.* (*of* ⇒**~ивать**) (*coll.*) to wave away, brush off (*with one's hand*).

отмах|нýться, нýсь, нёшься *pf.* (*of* ⇒**~иваться**) (**от**+*g.*) **1** = **~нýть; о. от комарóв** to brush mosquitoes off. **2** (*fig.*) to brush aside.

отмáчива|ть, ю *impf. of* ⇒**отмочи́ть**

отмеж|евáть, ýю *pf.* (*of* ⇒**~ёвывать**) to mark off, draw a boundary line (between).

отмеж|евáться, ýюсь *pf.* (*of* ⇒**~ёвываться**) (**от**+*g.*) to dissociate o.s. (from); to refuse to acknowledge.

отмежёвыва|ть(ся), ю(сь) *impf. of* ⇒**отмежевáть(ся)**

о́тмел|ь, и *f.* sandbank.

отме́н|а, ы *f.* abolition; repeal; cancellation; **о. крепостно́го пра́ва** abolition of serfdom; **о. зако́на** repeal of a law; **о. спекта́кля** cancellation of a show.

отмен|и́ть, ю́, ~́ишь *pf.* (*of* ⇒**~я́ть**) (*налог*) to abolish; (*закон*) to repeal; (*решение, приказание*) to revoke; (*заседание*) to cancel.

отме́н|ный (~ен, ~на) *adj.* excellent.

отмен|я́ть, я́ю *impf. of* ⇒**~и́ть**

отмер|е́ть, отомрёт, *past* **о́тмер, ~ла́, о́тмерло** *pf.* (*of* ⇒**отмира́ть**) to die off; (*fig.*) to die out, die away.

отмерз|а́ть, а́ет *impf. of* ⇒**~́нуть**

отмёрз|нуть, нет, *past* **~, ~ла** *pf.* (*of* ⇒**~а́ть**) to freeze; **ру́ки у меня́ ~ли** my hands are frozen.

отме́рива|ть, ю *impf. of* ⇒**отме́рить**

отме́р|ить, ю, ишь *pf.* (*of* ⇒**~ивать** *and* **~я́ть**) to measure off.

отмер|я́ть, я́ю *impf.* = **~́ивать**

отме|сти́, ту́, тёшь, *past* **~́л, ~ла́** *pf.* (*of* ⇒**~та́ть**) to sweep aside (*also fig.*).

отме́стк|а, и *f.* (*coll.*) revenge; **в ~у** in revenge.

отмета́|ть, ю *impf. of* ⇒**отмести́**

отмете́л|ить, ю, ишь *pf. of* ⇒**мете́лить**

отме́тин|а, ы *f.* mark; (*на лбу лошади*) star.

отме́|тить, чу, тишь *pf.* (*of* ⇒**~ча́ть**) **1** (*место в книге*) to mark, note; (*присутствующих; высоту*) to make a note (of); **о. пти́чкой** to tick off. **2** (*достоинства*) to point to, mention, record; **о. чьи-н. по́двиги** to point to s.o.'s feats. **3** (*регистрировать*) to record. **4** (*день рождения*) to celebrate.

отме́|титься, чусь, тишься *pf.* (*of* ⇒**~ча́ться**) to sign one's name; to register.

отме́тк|а, и *f.* **1** (*знак*) mark; (*запись*) note. **2** (*оценка*) mark.

отмеча́|ть(ся), ю(сь) *impf. of* ⇒**отме́тить(ся)**

отмира́ни|е, я *nt.* dying off; dying away.

отмира́|ть, ет *impf. of* ⇒**отмере́ть**

отмобилиз|ова́ть, у́ю *pf. of* ⇒**мобилизова́ть**

отмок|а́ть, а́ет *impf. of* ⇒**~́нуть**

отмо́к|нуть, нет, *past* **~, ~ла** *pf.* (*of* ⇒**~а́ть**) **1** (*стать мокрым*) to grow wet. **2** (*отделиться*) to soak off.

отмолч|а́ться, у́сь, и́шься *pf.* (*of* ⇒**отма́лчиваться**) (*coll.*) to keep silent, say nothing.

отмора́жива|ть, ю *impf. of* ⇒**отморо́зить**

отморо́жени|е, я *nt.* frost-bite.

отморо́|женный *p.p.p of* ⇒**~зить** *and adj.* frost-bitten.

отморо́|зить, жу, зишь *pf.* (*of* ⇒**отмора́живать**) to injure by frost-bite; **я ~зил себе́ у́ши** my ears are frost-bitten.

отмота́|ть, ю *pf.* (*of* ⇒**отма́тывать**) to unwind.

отмоч|и́ть, у́, ~́ишь *pf.* (*of* ⇒**отма́чивать**) **1** (*марку*) to soak off. **2** (*кожу*) to soak, steep. **3** (*coll.*) (*глупость*) to do, say (*sth. ludicrous or outrageous*).

отмсти́ть = **отомсти́ть**

отмще́ни|е, я *nt.* (*obs.*) vengeance.

отмыва́|ть(ся), ю(сь) *impf. of* ⇒**отмы́ть(ся)**

отмыка́|ть(ся), ю *impf. of* ⇒**отомкну́ть(ся)**

отм|ы́ть, о́ю, о́ешь *pf.* (*of* ⇒**~ыва́ть**) **1** (*руки*) to wash clean. **2** (*грязь*) to wash off, wash away. **3** (*fig.*): **о. де́ньги** to launder money.

отм|ы́ться, о́юсь, о́ешься *pf.* (*of* ⇒**~ыва́ться**) **1** (*о человеке*) to wash o.s. clean. **2** (*о руках*) to become/get clean. **3** (*о грязи*) to come out, come off.

отмы́чк|а, и *f.* master key; (*воровская*) jemmy (*Br.*), jimmy (*US*).

отмяк|а́ть, а́ет *impf. of* ⇒**~́нуть**

отмя́к|нуть, нет, *past* **~, ~ла** *pf.* (*of* ⇒**~а́ть**) to grow soft.

отне́кива|ться, юсь *impf.* (*coll.*) to refuse.

отнес|ти́, у́, ёшь, *past* **~́, ~ла́** *pf.* (*of* ⇒**относи́ть**) **1** (**в**+*a.*, **к**+*d.*) (*доставить*) to take (to). **2** to carry away, carry off; (*impers.*): **ло́дку ~ло́ тече́нием** the boat was carried away by the current; (*переместить*) to move. **3** (*coll.*) (*отсечь*) to cut off. **4** (**к**+*d.*) to ascribe (to), attribute (to), refer (to); **ру́копись ~ли́ к пя́тому ве́ку** the manuscript was believed to date from the fifth century; **мы ~ли́ его́ раздражи́тельность на счёт глухоты́** we put his irritability down to his deafness.

отнес|ти́сь, у́сь, ёшься, *past* **~́ся, ~ла́сь** *pf.* (*of* ⇒**относи́ться**) (**к**+*d.*) to treat; to regard; **хорошо́ о. к кому́-н.** to treat s.o. well, be nice to s.o.; **скепти́чески о. к предположе́нию** to be sceptical about a hypothesis; **как вы ~ли́сь к э́той ле́кции?** what did you think of the lecture?

отникелир|ова́ть, у́ю *pf. of* ⇒**никелирова́ть**

отнима́|ть(ся), ю *impf. of* ⇒**отня́ть(ся)**

относи́тельно 1 *adv.* relatively. **2** *prep.* (+*g.*) concerning, about, with regard to.

относи́тельност|ь, и *f.* relativity; **тео́рия ~и Эйнште́йна** Einstein's Theory of Relativity.

относи́тел|ьный (~ен, ~ьна) *adj.* relative; **~ьное местоиме́ние** (*gram.*) relative pronoun.

отно|си́ть, шу́, ~́сишь *impf. of* ⇒**отнести́**

отно|си́ться, шу́сь, ~́сишься *impf.* **1** *impf. of* ⇒**отнести́сь. 2** *impf. only* (**к**+*d.*) to concern, have to do (with), relate (to); **э́то к де́лу не ~́сится** that's beside the point, that is irrelevant. **3** *impf. only* (**к**+*d.*) to date (from); **храм э́тот ~́сится к двена́дцатому ве́ку** this church dates from the twelfth century.

отноше́ни|е, я *nt.* **1** (**к**+*d.*) attitude (to); treatment (of); **внима́тельное о. к ста́рым** consideration for the old; **у него́ стра́нное о. к же́нщинам** he has a strange attitude to women. **2** (*связь*) relation; respect; **име́ть о. к чему́-н.** to bear a relation to sth., have a bearing on sth.; **не име́ть ~я** (**к**+*d.*) to bear no relation (to), have nothing to do (with); **в ~и** (+*g.*), **по ~ю** (**к**+*d.*) with respect (to), with regard (to); **в не́которых ~ях** in some respects. **3** (*pl.*) (*связи между людьми*) relations; terms; **дипломати́ческие ~я** diplomatic relations; **быть в дру́жеских ~ях** (**с**+*i.*) to be on friendly terms (with); **вы́яснить ~я** (**с**+*i.*) to have it out (with). **4** (*math.*) ratio; **в прямо́м (обра́тном) ~и** in direct (inverse) ratio. **5** (*деловая бумага*) letter, memorandum.

отны́не *adv.* henceforth, henceforward.

отню́дь *adv.* by no means, not at all.

отня́ти|е, я *nt.* taking away; **о. руки́** amputation of an arm; **о. от груди́** weaning.

от|ня́ть, ниму́, ни́мешь *past* **~́нял, ~няла́, ~́няло** *pf.* (*of* ⇒**~нима́ть**) **1** to take (away); **о. от груди́** to wean; **о. жизнь у кого́-н.** to take s.o.'s life; **от шести́ о. три** to take away three from six; **э́то ~́няло у меня́ три часа́** it took me three hours. **2** (*ампутировать*) to amputate.

от|ня́ться, ни́мется, *past* **~ня́лся, ~няла́сь** *pf.* (*of* ⇒**~нима́ться**) to be paralysed; **у него́ ~няла́сь пра́вая рука́** he has lost the power of his right arm; **у неё ~ня́лся язы́к** she has lost the power of speech.

ото *prep.* = **от**

ото... *vbl. pref.* = **от...**

отобе́да|ть, ю *pf.* to have finished dinner.

отобража́|ть, ю *impf. of* ⇒**отобрази́ть**

отображе́ни|е, я *nt.* reflection; representation.

отобра|зи́ть, жу́, зи́шь *pf.* (*of* ⇒**~жа́ть**) to reflect; to represent.

от|обра́ть, беру́, берёшь, *past* **~обра́л, ~обрала́, ~обра́ло** *pf.* (*of* ⇒**отбира́ть**) **1** (*отнять*) to take (away). **2** (*выбрать*) to select, pick out.

отовсю́ду *adv.* from everywhere, from every quarter.

от|огна́ть[1], гоню́, го́нишь, *past* **~огна́л, ~огнала́, ~огна́ло** *pf.* (*of* ⇒**~гоня́ть**) to drive away, chase away.

от|огна́ть[2], гоню́, го́нишь, *past* **~огна́л, ~огнала́, ~огна́ло** *pf.* (*of* ⇒**~гоня́ть**) (*chem.*) to distil (*Br.*), distill (*US*) (off).

отогн|у́ть, у́, ёшь *pf.* (*of* ⇒**отгиба́ть**) to bend back.

отогн|у́ться, у́сь, ёшься *pf.* (*of* ⇒**отгиба́ться**) to bend back.

отогрева́|ть(ся), ю(сь) *impf. of* ⇒**отогре́ть(ся)**

отогре́|ть, ю *pf.* (*of* ⇨**~ва́ть**) to warm.

отогре́|ться, юсь *pf.* (*of* ⇨**~ва́ться**) to warm o.s.

отодвига́|ть(ся), ю(сь) *impf. of* ⇨**отодви́нуть(ся)**

отодви́|нуть, ну, нешь *pf.* (*of* ⇨**~га́ть**) **1** to move aside. **2** (*fig.*) (*отсрочить*) to put off, put back.

отодви́|нуться, нусь, нешься *pf.* (*of* ⇨**~га́ться**) **1** to move aside. **2** (*о сроке*) to be postponed.

от|одра́ть, деру́, дерёшь, *past* **~одра́л, ~одрала́, ~одра́ло** *pf.* (*of* ⇨**~дира́ть**) **1** (*оторвать*) to tear off, rip off. **2** (*coll.*) (*высечь*) to flog.

отож(д)еств|и́ть, лю́, и́шь *pf.* (*of* ⇨**~ля́ть**) to identify.

отож(д)ествля́|ть, ю *impf. of* ⇨**отож(д)естви́ть**

отожжённый *p.p.p. of* ⇨**отже́чь** *and adj.* (*tech.*) annealed.

от|озва́ть, зову́, зовёшь, *past* **~озва́л, ~озвала́, ~озва́ло** *pf.* (*of* ⇨**~зыва́ть**) **1** to take aside. **2** (*посла*) to recall.

от|озва́ться, зову́сь, зовёшься, *past* **~озва́лся, ~озвала́сь, ~озва́ло́сь** *pf.* (*of* ⇨**~зыва́ться**) **1** (**на**+*a.*) to answer; to respond (to). **2** (**о**+*p.*) to speak (of); **рецензе́нты хорошо́ ~озвали́сь о его́ второ́й кни́ге** his second book was well received by (received good notices from) the reviewers. **3** (**на**+*a.*) to tell (on, upon); **деторожде́ние ~озвало́сь на её здоро́вье** child-bearing has told on her health.

ото|йти́, йду́, йдёшь, *past* **~шёл, ~шла́** *pf.* (*of* ⇨**отходи́ть**[1]) **1** to move away; to move off; (*о поезде*) to leave, depart. **2** (*оставить свою прежнюю позицию*) to withdraw; to recede; (*mil.*) to withdraw, fall back; (*fig.*; **от**+*g.*) to move away (from); to digress (from), diverge (from); **он далеко́ ~шёл от пре́жних взгля́дов** he has moved a long way from his earlier views. **3** (*о пятнах*) to come out; (**от**+*g.*) to come away (from), come off; **обо́и ~шли́ от стены́** the paper has come off (the wall). **4** (*прийти в обычное состояние*) to recover (normal state); (*impers., coll.*): **у меня́ ~шло́ от се́рдца** I felt better; I felt relieved. **5** (**к**+*d.*) (*перейти в чью-либо собственность*) to pass (to), go (to). **6** (*выделиться*) to be lost (*in processing*). **7** (*obs.*) (*пройти*) to pass; **ле́то ~шло́** summer was over; **о. в ве́чность** (*rhet.*) to pass away.

отомкн|у́ть, у́, ёшь *pf.* (*of* ⇨**отмыка́ть**) to unlock, unbolt.

отомкн|у́ться, ётся *pf.* (*of* ⇨**отмыка́ться**) to open.

отом|сти́ть, щу́, сти́шь *pf. of* ⇨**мстить**

отопи́тельный *adj.* heating; **о. сезо́н** cold season.

отоп|и́ть, лю́, ~шь *pf.* (*of* ⇨**ота́пливать** *and* **отопля́ть**) to heat.

отопле́ни|е, я *nt.* heating.

отопля́|ть, ю *impf. of* ⇨**отопи́ть**

отора́чива|ть, ю *impf. of* ⇨**отороч́ить**

ото́рванност|ь, и *f.* isolation; loneliness; **чу́вствовать о. от цивилиза́ции** to feel cut off from civilization.

оторв|а́ть, у́, ёшь, *past* **~а́л, ~ала́, ~а́ло** *pf.* (*of* ⇨**отрыва́ть**[1]) (*пуговицу*) to tear off; (*отвлечь*) to tear away (*fig.*); **о. кого́-н. от рабо́ты** to tear s.o. away from his work; **с рука́ми о.** (*coll.*) to seize eagerly.

оторв|а́ться, у́сь, ёшься, *past* **~а́лся, ~ала́сь, ~а́ло́сь** *pf.* (*of* ⇨**отрыва́ться**) **1** (*о пуговице*) to come off, be torn off. **2** (*aeron.*): **о. от земли́** to take off. **3** (*fig.*; **от**+*g.*) (*от друзей*) to be cut off (from), lose touch (with); (*от соперников*; *от отряда*) to break away (from); **о. от проти́вника** to lose contact with the enemy. **4** (*fig.*; **от**+*g.*) to tear o.s. away (from); **от э́той кни́ги я не мог о.** I could not tear myself away from this book. **5** (*sl.*) (*развлечься*) to relax, have a good time.

оторопе́лый *adj.* (*coll.*) dumbfounded.

оторопе́|ть, ю *pf.* (*coll.*) to be struck dumb.

о́тороп|ь, и *f.* (*coll.*) confusion, fright; **меня́ о. взяла́** I was dumbfounded.

оторо́ч|и́ть, у́, и́шь *pf.* (*of* ⇨**отора́чивать**) to edge, trim.

оторо́чк|а, и *f.* edging, trimming.

ото|сла́ть, шлю́, шлёшь *pf.* (*of* ⇨**отсыла́ть**) **1** to send off, dispatch; **о. де́ньги** to send a remittance. **2** (**к**+*d.*) to refer (to); **о. чита́теля к предыду́щему то́му** to refer the reader to the preceding volume.

отосп|а́ться, лю́сь, и́шься, *past* **~а́лся, ~ала́сь** *pf.* (*of* ⇨**отсыпа́ться**[2]) to have a (good) long sleep; **о. по́сле доро́ги** to sleep off a journey.

отоше́дший *p.p. of* ⇨**отойти́**

ото|шёл, шла́ *see* ⇨**~йти́**

ото|шлю́, шлёшь *see* ⇨**~сла́ть**

отоща́лый *adj.* (*coll.*) emaciated.

отоща́|ть, ю *pf. of* ⇨**тоща́ть**

отпада́|ть, ю *impf. of* ⇨**отпа́сть**

отпа́ива|ть[1]**, ю** *impf. of* ⇨**отпая́ть**

отпа́ива|ть[2]**, ю** *impf. of* ⇨**отпои́ть**

отпа́рива|ть, ю *impf. of* ⇨**отпа́рить**

отпари́р|овать, ую *pf. of* ⇨**пари́ровать**

отпа́р|ить, ю, ишь *pf.* (*of* ⇨**~ивать**) **1** to steam; **о. брю́ки** to press trousers through a damp cloth. **2** (*обои*) to steam off.

отпа́рыва|ть, ю *impf. of* ⇨**отпоро́ть**

отпа́|сть, ду́, дёшь, *past* **~л** *pf.* (*of* ⇨**~да́ть**) **1** (*отделиться*) to fall off, drop off. **2** (*fig.*; **от**+*g.*) to drop out (of); **мно́гие чле́ны ~ли от па́ртии** many members have dropped out of the party. **3** (*fig.*) (*утратить силу*) to pass, fade; **у него́ ~ла охо́та к путеше́ствию по А́фрике** his desire to travel in Africa has passed; **вопро́с об э́том ~л** the question no longer arises.

отпа|я́ть, я́ю *pf.* (*of* ⇨**~ивать**[1]) to unsolder.

отпева́ни|е, я *nt.* funeral service.

отпева́|ть, ю *impf. of* ⇨**отпе́ть**

от|пере́ть, опру́, опрёшь, *past* **~пер, ~перла́, ~перло** *pf.* (*of* ⇨**~пира́ть**) to unlock; to open.

от|пере́ться[1]**, опрётся**, *past* **~пёрся, ~перла́сь** *pf.* (*of* ⇨**~пира́ться**) to open.

от|пере́ться[2]**, опру́сь, опрёшься**, *past* **~пёрся, ~перла́сь** *pf.* (*of* ⇨**~пира́ться**) (*coll.*; **от**+*g.*) to deny; to disown.

отпе́т|ый *p.p.p. of* ⇨**~ь** *and adj.* (*coll.*) arrant, inveterate.

отп|е́ть, ою́, оёшь *pf.* (*of* ⇨**~ева́ть**) to read the funeral service (for, over).

отпеча́т|ать, аю *pf.* **1** (*impf.* **печа́тать**) to print (off). **2** (*impf.* **~ывать**) to imprint; **о. па́льцы на стекле́** to leave finger-prints on glass; **о. следы́** to leave footprints. **3** (*impf.* **~ывать**) (*помещение*) to open (up).

отпеча́т|аться, ается *pf.* to leave an imprint; to be imprinted.

отпечатле́|ться, ется *pf.* (*obs.*) to leave its mark.

отпеча́т|ок, ка *m.* imprint (*also fig.*); **о. па́льца** finger-print.

отпеча́тыва|ть(ся), ю, ет(ся) *impf. of* ⇨**отпеча́тать(ся)**

отпива́|ть, ю *impf. of* ⇨**отпи́ть**

отпи́лива|ть, ю *impf. of* ⇨**отпили́ть**

отпил|и́ть, ю́, ~ишь *pf.* (*of* ⇨**~ивать**) to saw off.

отпира́тельств|о, а *nt.* denial, disavowal.

отпира́|ть(ся), ю(сь) *impf. of* ⇨**отпере́ть(ся)**

отпи|са́ть, шу́, ~шешь *pf.* (*of* ⇨**~сывать**) (*obs.*) **1** (*завещать*) to bequeath, leave. **2** (*конфисковать*) to confiscate.

отпи|са́ться, шу́сь, ~шешься *pf.* (*of* ⇨**~сываться**) to make a (purely) formal reply.

отпи́ск|а, и *f.* (*pej.*) formal reply.

отпи́сыва|ть(ся), ю(сь) *impf. of* ⇨**отписа́ть(ся)**

от|пи́ть, опью́, опьёшь, *past* **~пил, ~пила́, ~пи́ло** *pf.* (*of* ⇨**~пива́ть**) (+*a. or g.*) to take a sip (of).

отпи́хива|ть(ся), ю(сь) *impf. of* ⇨**отпихну́ть(ся)**

отпих|ну́ть, ну́, нёшь *pf.* (*of* ⇨**~ивать**) (*coll.*) to push off; to shove aside.

отпих|ну́ться, ну́сь, нёшься *pf.* (*of* ⇨**~иваться**) (*coll.*) to push off (*esp. in a boat*).

отпла́т|а, ы *f.* repayment.

отпла|ти́ть, чу́, ~тишь *pf.* (*of*

⇒∼́чивать) (+*d.*) to pay back (to); repay; **о. кому́-н. той же моне́той** to pay s.o. in his own coin.

отпла́чива|ть, ю *impf. of* **⇒отплати́ть**

отплёвыва|ть, ю *impf. of* **⇒отплю́нуть**

отплёвыва|ться, юсь *impf.* to spit (*also fig., to express disgust*).

отплёскива|ть, ю *impf. of* **⇒отплесну́ть**

отплес|ну́ть, ну́, нёшь *pf.* (*of* **⇒отплёскивать**) **1** (*о воде, о волне*) to splash back. **2** (*coll.*) (*жидкость*) to pour off.

отплыва́|ть, ю *impf. of* **⇒отплы́ть**

отплы́ти|е, я *nt.* sailing, departure.

отплы́|ть, ву́, вёшь, *past* **∼л, ∼ла́, ∼ло** *pf.* (*of* **⇒∼ва́ть**) (*о корабле*) to sail, set sail; (*о плывущих людях*) to swim off.

отплю́н|уть, у, ешь *pf.* (*of* **⇒отплёвывать**) to spit (out), expectorate.

отпля|са́ть, шу́, ∼́шешь *pf.* (*of* **⇒∼́сывать**) (*coll.*) **1** (*гопак*) to perform. **2** (*кончить плясать*) to finish dancing.

отпля́сыва|ть, ю *impf. of* **⇒отпляса́ть**

о́тповед|ь, и *f.* reproof, rebuke.

отпо|и́ть, ю́, и́шь *pf.* (*of* **⇒отпа́ивать²**) **1** (*кончить поить*) to finish watering. **2** (*вырастить*) to fatten (on liquids). **3** (*coll.*; +*i.*) (*вылечить*) to cure by giving to drink; **о. отра́вленного молоко́м** to give milk to s.o. suffering from poisoning.

отполз|а́ть, а́ю *impf. of* **⇒∼ти́**

отполз|ти́, у́, ёшь, *past* **∼́, ∼ла́** *pf.* (*of* **⇒∼а́ть**) to crawl away.

отполир|ова́ть, у́ю *pf. of* **⇒полирова́ть**

отпо́р, а *m.* repulse; rebuff; **дать о.** (+*d.*) to repulse; **встре́тить о.** to be repulsed; to meet with a rebuff.

отпор|о́ть, ю́, ∼́ешь *pf.* (*of* **⇒отпа́рывать**) to rip off.

отпотева́|ть, ю *impf. of* **⇒отпоте́ть**

отпоте́|ть, ю *pf.* (*of* **⇒поте́ть** *and* **∼ва́ть**) to mist over, be covered with moisture.

отпочк|ова́ться, у́ется *pf.* (*of* **⇒∼о́вываться**) (*biol.*) to gemmate, propagate by gemmation; (*fig.*) to detach o.s.

отпочко́выва|ться, ется *impf. of* **⇒отпочкова́ться**

отправи́тел|ь, я *m.* sender.

отправи́тель|ница, ницы *f. of* **⇒∼**

отпра́в|ить, лю, ишь *pf.* (*of* **⇒∼ля́ть**) to send; (*по почте*) to post (*Br.*), mail (*US*); to send off; **о. на тот свет** to send to kingdom come; **о. есте́ственные потре́бности** to relieve nature.

отпра́в|иться, люсь, ишься *pf.* (*of* **⇒∼ля́ться**) to set out, set off, start; (*о поезде*) to leave, depart; **о. на боковую́** (*coll.*) to turn in, go to bed.

отпра́вк|а, и *f.* sending off; (*по почте*) posting; (*товаров*) dispatch; (*поезда*) departure.

отправле́ни|е, я *nt.* **1** (*действие*) sending. **2** (*почтовое, заказное*) item. **3** (*поезда*) departure. **4** (*организма*) function (*of the body*). **5** (*исполнение*) exercise, performance; **о. обя́занностей** exercise of one's duties.

отправля́|ть, ю *impf.* **1** *impf. of* **⇒отпра́вить. 2** (*impf. only*) to exercise, perform (*duties, functions*).

отправля́|ться, юсь *impf.* **1** *impf. of* **⇒отпра́виться. 2** (*fig.*; **от**+*g.*) to proceed (from).

отправн|о́й *adj.*: **о. пункт, ∼а́я то́чка** starting-point.

отпра́здн|овать, ую *pf. of* **⇒пра́здновать**

отпра́шива|ться, юсь *impf.* (*of* **⇒отпроси́ться**) to ask (for) leave.

отпресс|ова́ть, у́ю *pf. of* **⇒прессова́ть**

отпро|си́ться, шу́сь, ∼́сишься *pf.* (*of* **⇒отпра́шиваться**) **1** (*попросить о разрешении*) to ask (for) leave. **2** (*получить разрешение*) to obtain leave.

отпры́гива|ть, ю *impf. of* **⇒отпры́гнуть**

отпры́г|нуть, ну, нешь *pf.* (*of* **⇒∼ивать**) (*назад*) to jump back; (*в сторону*) to jump aside.

о́тпрыск, а *m.* (*bot. and fig.*) offshoot, scion.

отпряга́|ть, ю *impf. of* **⇒отпря́чь**

отпря́дыва|ть, ю *impf. of* **⇒отпря́нуть**

отпря́|нуть, ну, нешь *pf.* (*of* **⇒∼дывать**) to recoil, start back.

отпря́|чь, гу́, жёшь, гу́т, *past* **∼г, ∼гла́** *pf.* (*of* **⇒∼га́ть**) to unharness.

отпу́гива|ть, ю *impf. of* **⇒отпугну́ть**

отпуг|ну́ть, ну́, нёшь *pf.* (*of* **⇒∼́ивать**) to frighten off, scare away.

о́тпуск, а, в ∼е *or* **в ∼у́,** *pl.* **∼а́, ∼о́в** *m.* **1** leave, holiday(s) (*Br.*), vacation (*US*); (*mil.*) leave, furlough; **в ∼е, в ∼у́** on leave; **о. без сохране́ния содержа́ния** unpaid leave; **о. по боле́зни** sick-leave. **2** (*товаров*) issue, delivery, distribution.

отпуска́|ть, ю *impf. of* **⇒отпусти́ть**

отпускни́к, а́ *m.* holiday-maker (*Br.*), person on vacation (*US*); (*mil.*) soldier on leave.

отпускн|о́й *adj.* **1** *adj. of* **⇒о́тпуск 1**; **∼ы́е де́ньги** holiday pay; **∼о́е свиде́тельство** authorization of leave (*of absence*); (*mil.*) leave pass. **2** (*econ.*): **∼а́я цена́** selling price.

отпу|сти́ть, щу́, ∼́стишь *pf.* (*of* **⇒∼ска́ть**) **1** (*позволить кому-н. уйти; перестать держать*) to let go; (*в сад*) to let out; (*освободить*) to set free; to release; (*дать отпуск*) to give leave (of absence); **∼сти́ мою́ ру́ку!** let go (of) my arm!; **о. на пра́здник** to release for the holiday; **о. комплиме́нт** (*coll.*) to make a compliment; **о. шу́тку** (*coll.*) to crack a joke.

2 (*ослабить*) to relax, slacken; **о. по́вод ло́шади** to give a horse its head; (*impers., coll.*): **боль ∼сти́ло** the pain has eased. **3** (*отрастить*) to (let) grow; **о. (себе́) бо́роду** to grow a beard. **4** (*выдать*) to issue, give out; (*продать*) to serve. **5** (*назначить*) to assign, allot. **6** (*простить*) to remit; to forgive; **о. кому́-н. грехи́** (*eccl.*) to give s.o. absolution.

отпуще́ни|е, я *nt.* remission; **о. грехо́в** (*eccl.*) absolution; **козёл ∼я** (*coll.*) scapegoat.

отраба́тыва|ть, ю *impf. of* **⇒отрабо́тать**

отрабо́та|нный *p.p.p. of* **⇒∼ть** *and adj.* (*tech.*) worked out; waste, spent, exhaust; **о. газ** waste gas, exhaust gas.

отрабо́та|ть¹, ю *pf.* (*of* **⇒отраба́тывать**) **1** (*долг*) to work off. **2** (*coll.*) (*какое-н. время*) to work. **3** to work through, give a work-out to.

отрабо́та|ть², ю *pf.* (*кончить работать*) to finish one's work.

отрабо́тк|а, и *f.* working off, paying by work.

отрабо́точн|ый *adj.*: **∼ая систе́ма** statute labour, corvée.

отра́в|а, ы *f.* poison.

отрави́тел|ь, я *m.* poisoner.

отрави́тель|ница, ницы *f. of* **⇒∼**

отрав|и́ть, лю́, ∼́ишь *pf.* (*of* **⇒∼ля́ть**) to poison (*also fig.*).

отрав|и́ться, лю́сь, ∼́ишься *pf.* (*of* **⇒∼ля́ться**) to poison o.s.

отравле́ни|е, я *nt.* poisoning.

отравля́|ть(ся), ю(сь) *impf. of* **⇒отрави́ться**

отравля́ющий *adj.* toxic.

отра́д|а, ы *f.* joy, delight; comfort.

отра́д|ный (∼ен, ∼на) *adj.* gratifying, pleasing; comforting.

отража́тел|ь, я *m.* reflector.

отража́тельн|ый *adj.* (*tech.*) reflecting, deflecting; **∼ая засло́нка, о. лист, ∼ая плита́** deflector (plate), baffle (plate).

отража́|ть(ся), ю(сь) *impf. of* **⇒отрази́ть(ся)**

отраже́ни|е, я *nt.* **1** reflection. **2** (*нападения*) repelling; warding off.

отра|зи́ть, жу́, зи́шь *pf.* (*of* **⇒∼жа́ть**) **1** to reflect (*also fig.*). **2** (*нападение*) to repel; to ward off.

отра|зи́ться, жу́сь, зи́шься *pf.* (*of* **⇒∼жа́ться**) **1** to be reflected. **2** (*fig.*; **на**+*p.*) to affect; to tell (on); **пое́здка в го́ры благоприя́тно ∼зи́лась на его́ рабо́те** the mountain trip had a beneficial effect on his work.

отрапорт|ова́ть, у́ю *pf. of* **⇒рапортова́ть**

отраслево́й *adj. of* **⇒о́трасль**

о́трасл|ь, и *f.* branch; **о. промы́шленности** branch of industry.

отраст|а́ть, а́ю *impf. of* **⇒∼и́**

отраст|и́, у́, ёшь, *past* **отро́с, отросла́** *pf.* (*of* **⇒∼а́ть**) to grow.

отра|сти́ть, щу́, сти́шь *pf.* (*of* **⇒∼́щивать**) to (let) grow; **о. во́лосы**

to grow one's hair long; **о. брю́хо** (*coll.*) to develop a paunch.

отра́щива|ть, ю *impf. of* ⇨**отрасти́ть**

отреаги́р|овать, ую *pf.* (*coll.*) *of* ⇨**реаги́ровать** 2

отре́бь|е, я *nt.* (*collect.*) rabble.

отрегули́р|овать, ую *pf. of* ⇨**регули́ровать**

отредакти́р|овать, ую *pf. of* ⇨**редакти́ровать**

отре́з, а *m.* **1** cut; **ли́ния ~а** line of the cut. **2** (*кусок ткани*) length (*of material*); **о. на пла́тье** dress length.

отрез|а́ть, а́ю *impf. of* ⇨**~́ать**

отре́|зать, жу, жешь *pf.* (*of* ⇨**~за́ть**) **1** to cut off (*also fig.*); **проти́вник ~зал нам отступле́ние** the enemy had cut off our retreat. **2** (*coll.*) (*резко ответить*) to snap back.

отрезве́|ть, ю *pf. of* ⇨**трезве́ть**

отрезви́тельный *adj.* sobering (*also fig.*).

отрезв|и́ть, лю́, и́шь *pf.* (*of* ⇨**~ля́ть**) to sober (*also fig.*).

отрезв|и́ться, лю́сь, и́шься *pf.* (*of* ⇨**~ля́ться**) to become sober, sober up.

отрезвле́ни|е, я *nt.* sobering (up).

отрезвля́|ть(ся), ю(сь) *impf. of* ⇨**отрезви́ть(ся)**

отрезно́й *adj.* detachable; **о. тало́н** tear-off coupon.

отре́з|ок, ка *m.* (*ткани*) piece, cut; (*пути*) section; (*hist.*) (*земли*) portion (*of land*); (*math.*) segment; **о. вре́мени** stretch of time.

отрека́|ться, юсь *impf. of* ⇨**отре́чься**

отрекоменд|ова́ть, у́ю *pf. of* ⇨**рекомендова́ть**

отрекоменд|ова́ться, у́юсь *pf. of* ⇨**рекомендова́ться**

отремонти́р|овать, ую *pf. of* ⇨**ремонти́ровать**

отрепети́р|овать, ую *pf. of* ⇨**репети́ровать**

отре́пь|е, я, *pl.* **~я, ~ев** *nt.* (*collect.*) rags; **ходи́ть в о., в ~ях** to be in rags.

отрече́ни|е, я *nt.* (**от** + *g.*) renunciation (of); **о. от престо́ла** abdication.

отре́|чься, ку́сь, чёшься, ку́тся, *past* **~́кся, ~кла́сь** *pf.* (*of* ⇨**~ка́ться**) (**от** + *g.*) to renounce, disavow, give up; **о. от престо́ла** to abdicate.

отреш|а́ть(ся), а́ю(сь) *impf. of* ⇨**~и́ть(ся)**

отрешённост|ь, и *f.* estrangement, aloofness.

отреш|и́ть, у́, и́шь *pf.* (*of* ⇨**~а́ть**) (*liter.*) (**от** + *g.*) to release (from); **о. от до́лжности** to dismiss, suspend.

отреш|и́ться, у́сь, и́шься *pf.* (*of* ⇨**~а́ться**) (*liter.*) (**от** + *g.*) to renounce, give up; **я не мог о. от мы́сли** I could not get rid of the idea.

отри́н|уть, у, ешь *pf.* (*obs.*) to reject.

отрица́ни|е, я *nt.* denial; negation; (*ling.*) negative.

отрица́тел|ьный (~ен, ~ьна) *adj.* negative.

отрица́|ть, ю *impf.* to deny; to disclaim; **о. вино́вность** (*leg.*) to plead not guilty.

отро́г, а *m.* (*geog.*) spur.

о́троду *adv.* (*coll.*): **не… о.** never in one's life; never in one's born days; **я о. не вида́л ничего́ подо́бного** I have never seen the like.

отро́дь|е, я *nt.* (*coll., pej.*) spawn, offspring.

отродя́сь *adv.* (*coll.*) = **о́троду**

о́трок, а *m.* (*obs. and iron.*) boy, lad; adolescent.

отрокови́ц|а, ы *f.* (*obs. and iron.*) girl; adolescent.

отро́ст|ок, ка *m.* **1** (*bot.*) shoot, sprout. **2** (*tech.*) branch, extension. **3** (*anat.*) appendix.

о́троческий *adj.* adolescent.

о́трочеств|о, а *nt.* adolescence.

отруб|а́ть, а́ю *impf. of* ⇨**~и́ть**

о́труб|и, е́й *no sg.* bran.

отруб|и́ть, лю́, ~́ишь *pf.* (*of* ⇨**~а́ть**) **1** (*сук*) to chop off. **2** = **отре́зать** 2

о́труб|ный *adj. of* ⇨**~и**

отруга́|ть, ю *pf. of* ⇨**руга́ть**

отру́гива|ться, юсь *impf.* (*coll.*) to return abuse.

отры́в, а *m.* **1** tearing off. **2** (*fig.*) alienation, isolation; loss of contact; **в ~е (от** + *g.*) out of touch (with); **учи́ться без ~а от произво́дства** to study while continuing (normal) work; **о. от земли́** (*aeron.*) take-off; **о. от проти́вника** (*mil.*) disengagement.

отрыва́|ть[1], ю *impf. of* ⇨**оторва́ть**

отрыва́|ть[2], ю *impf. of* ⇨**отры́ть**

отрыва́|ться, юсь *impf. of* ⇨**оторва́ться**

отры́вист|ый (~, ~а) *adj.* jerky, abrupt; (*речь*) curt.

отрывно́й *adj.* perforated; **о. календа́рь** tear-off calendar.

отры́в|ок, ка *m.* (*разговора*) fragment; (*книги*) excerpt; passage; **о. из фи́льма** film clip.

отры́вочн|ый (~ен, ~на) *adj.* fragmentary, scrappy.

отры́гива|ть, ю *impf. of* ⇨**отрыгну́ть**

отрыг|ну́ть, ну́, нёшь *pf.* (*of* ⇨**~́ивать**) (+*a. or g.*) to belch.

отры́жк|а, и *f.* **1** belch. **2** (*fig.*) survival, throw-back.

отр|ы́ть, о́ю, о́ешь *pf.* (*of* ⇨**~ыва́ть[2]**) to dig up; to unearth (*also fig.*).

отря́д, а *m.* **1** (*mil.*) detachment; (*группа*) group, party, brigade; **передово́й о.** (*fig.*) vanguard. **2** (*biol.*) order.

отря|ди́ть, жу́, ди́шь *pf.* (*of* ⇨**~жа́ть**) to dispatch, send; (*mil.*) to detail.

отряжа́|ть, ю *impf. of* ⇨**отряди́ть**

отряс|а́ть, а́ю *impf. of* ⇨**~ти́**

отряс|ти́, у́, ёшь, *past* **~, ~ла́** *pf.* (*of* ⇨**~а́ть**) (*obs.*) to shake off; **о. прах от ног свои́х** (*fig.*) to shake off the dust from one's feet.

отря́хива|ть(ся), ю(сь) *impf. of* ⇨**отряхну́ть(ся)**

отрях|ну́ть, ну́, нёшь *pf.* (*of* ⇨**~ивать**) to shake down, shake off; **о. снег с воротника́** to shake snow off one's collar.

отрях|ну́ться, ну́сь, нёшься *pf.* (*of* ⇨**~́иваться**) to shake o.s. down.

отса|ди́ть, жу́, ~́дишь *pf.* (*of* ⇨**~́живать**) **1** (*кусты*) to transplant, plant out. **2** (*человека*) to seat apart.

отса́дк|а, и *f.* (*hort.*) transplanting, planting out.

отса́жива|ть, ю *impf. of* ⇨**отсади́ть**

отса́жива|ться, юсь *impf. of* ⇨**отсе́сть**

отсалют|ова́ть, у́ю *pf. of* ⇨**салютова́ть**

отса́сывани|е, я *nt.* suction.

отса́сыва|ть, ю *impf. of* ⇨**отсоса́ть**

о́тсвет, а *m.* reflection; reflected light.

отсве́чива|ть, ю *impf.* **1** to be reflected; (+*i.*) to shine (with); **фона́рь с у́лицы ~л в окне́** the light of the street-lamp was reflected in the window. **2** (*coll.*) (*о человеке*) to stand in the light.

отсебя́тин|а, ы *f.* (*coll.*) words of one's own; sth. of one's own devising; (*theatr.*) ad-libbing.

отсе́в, а *m.* **1** (*действие*) sifting, selection. **2** (*высевки*) siftings, residue.

отсе́ива|ть(ся), ю(сь) *impf. of* ⇨**отсе́ять(ся)**

отсе́к, а *m.* **1** (*naut., etc.*) compartment; (*в библиотеке*) carrel. **2** (*astronautics*) module.

отсека́|ть, ю *impf. of* ⇨**отсе́чь**

отсе́ле *adv.* (*obs.*) hence, from here.

отсел|и́ть, ю́, и́шь *pf.* (*of* ⇨**~я́ть**) to move further out.

отсел|и́ться, ю́сь, и́шься *pf.* (*of* ⇨**~я́ться**) to move further out.

отсе́л|ь = **~е**

отсел|я́ть(ся), я́ю(сь) *impf. of* ⇨**~и́ть(ся)**

отс|е́сть, я́ду, я́дешь, *past* **~е́л** *pf.* (*of* ⇨**~а́живаться**) to seat o.s. apart; (**от** + *g.*) to move away (from).

отсече́ни|е, я *nt.* cutting off, severance; **дать го́лову на о.** (*coll.*) to stake one's life.

отсе́|чь, ку́, чёшь, ку́т, *past* **~к, ~кла́** *pf.* (*of* ⇨**~ка́ть**) to cut off, chop off.

отсе́|ять, ю, ешь *pf.* (*of* ⇨**~ивать**) **1** to sift, screen. **2** (*fig.*) to eliminate, screen out.

отсе́|яться, юсь, ешься *pf.* (*of* ⇨**~иваться**) **1** to be separated. **2** (*fig.*) to fall off, fall away; **бо́льшая часть слу́шателей ~ялась** the greater part of the audience had fallen away.

отси|де́ть, жу́, ди́шь *pf.* (*of* ⇨**~́живать**) **1** (*просидеть*) to stay (for); to sit out; **он ~де́л де́сять лет в тюрьме́** he has done ten years (in prison). **2** (*вызвать онемение части тела*) to make numb by sitting; **я ~дéл себé нóгу** I have pins and needles in my leg.

отси|дéться, жу́сь, ди́шься *pf.* (*of* ⇒**~живаться**) (*coll.*) to sit tight.

отси́жива|ть(ся), ю(сь) *impf. of* ⇒**отсидéть(ся)**

отскáблива|ть, ю *impf. of* ⇒**отскобли́ть**

отска|кáть, чу́, ~чешь *pf.* (*coll.*) to gallop, cover by galloping.

отскáкива|ть, ю *impf. of* ⇒**отскочи́ть**

отскобл|и́ть, ю́, ~и́шь *pf.* (*of* ⇒**отскáбливать**) to scratch off.

отскóк, а *m.* rebound.

отскоч|и́ть, у́, ~ишь *pf.* (*of* ⇒**отскáкивать**) **1** (*отпрыгнуть*) to jump aside, jump away; (*о мяче*) to rebound, bounce back. **2** (*coll.*) (*отделиться*) to come off, break off.

отскребá|ть, ю *impf. of* ⇒**отскрести́**

отскре|сти́, бу́, бёшь, *past* **~б, ~блá** *pf.* (*of* ⇒**~бáть**) to scrape off.

отслáива|ть, ю *impf. of* ⇒**отслои́ть**

отслáива|ться, ется *impf. of* ⇒**отслои́ться**

отслоéни|е, я *nt.* (*geol.*) exfoliation.

отсло|и́ть, ю́, и́шь *pf.* (*of* ⇒**отслáивать**) to peel away, strip away.

отсло|и́ться, и́тся *pf.* (*of* ⇒**отслáиваться**) (*geol.*) to exfoliate; to scale off.

отслу́жива|ть, ю *impf. of* ⇒**отслужи́ть**

отслуж|и́ть, у́, ~ишь *pf.* (*of* ⇒**~ивать**) **1** (*о человеке*) to serve; to serve one's time. **2** (*coll.*) (*о вещах*) to be worn out. **3** (*eccl.*) to conduct (*a service*).

отсовéт|овать, ую *pf.* (+*d. and inf.*) to dissuade (from).

отсоедин|и́ть, ю́, и́шь *pf.* (*of* ⇒**~я́ть**) to disconnect.

отсоединя́|ть, ю *impf. of* ⇒**отсоедини́ть**

отсортир|овáть, у́ю *pf.* (*of* ⇒**~óвывать**) to sort (out).

отсортирóвыва|ть, ю *impf. of* ⇒**отсортировáть**

отсос|áть, у́, ёшь *pf.* (*of* ⇒**отсáсывать**) (+*a. or g.*) to suck off; to draw off.

отсóх|нуть, нет, *past* **~, ~ла** *pf.* (*of* ⇒**отсыхáть**) to dry up, to wither.

отсрóчива|ть, ю *impf. of* ⇒**отсрóчить**

отсрóч|ить, у, ишь *pf.* (*of* ⇒**~ивать**) **1** to postpone, defer. **2** (*coll.*) (*документ*) to extend (*period of validity of a document*).

отсрóчк|а, и *f.* **1** postponement, deferment. **2** (*coll.*) (*документа*) extension (*of period of validity of document*).

отставáни|е, я *nt.* lag.

отста|вáть, ю́, ёшь *impf. of* ⇒**~ть**

отстáв|ить, лю, ишь *pf.* (*of* ⇒**~ля́ть**) **1** to set aside, put aside. **2**: **о.!** (*mil.*) as you were!

отстáвк|а, и *f.* (*mil.*) retirement; (*hist.*) (*с государственной службы*) resignation; **вы́йти в ~у** to retire; to resign; **подáть в ~у** to tender one's resignation; **в ~е** retired, in retirement.

отставля́|ть, ю *impf. of* ⇒**отстáвить**

отставнóй *adj.* (*mil.*) retired.

отстáива|ть, ю *impf. of* ⇒**отстоя́ть**[1]

отстáива|ться, ется *impf. of* ⇒**отстоя́ться**

отстáлост|ь, и *f.* (*fig.*) backwardness.

отстáлый *adj.* (*fig.*) backward; **у́мственно о.** mentally retarded; **физи́чески о.** physically handicapped.

отстá|ть, ну, нешь *pf.* (*of* ⇒**~вáть**) **1** (**от**+*g.*) (*оказаться позади*) to fall behind; to lag behind; (*умственно*) to be backward, be retarded; **о. в рабóте** to be behind in (with) one's work; **о. от клáсса** to be behind (the rest of) one's class; **о. от вéка, о. от совремéнности** to be behind the times.
2 (**от**+*g.*) (*отделиться*) to become detached (from); **о. от гру́ппы** to become detached from a group; **о. от пóезда** to be left behind by the train (*sc., at a station en route*); **обóи ~ли от стены́** the wallpaper came off.
3 (**от**+*g.*) (*потерять связь*) to lose touch (with); to break (with); **я ~л от всех свои́х знакóмых воéнного врéмени** I have lost touch with all my war-time acquaintances.
4 (*coll.*; **от**+*g.*) (*отвыкнуть*) to give up; **о. от привы́чки** to break o.s. of a habit.
5 (*о часах*) to be slow; **о. на полчасá** to be half an hour slow.
6 (*coll.*; **от**+*g.*) (*перестать надоедать*) to leave alone; **~нь от меня́!** leave me alone!

отста|ю́щий *pres. part. of* ⇒**~вáть;** *as n.* **о., ~ю́щего** *m.* backward pupil; **рабóта с ~ю́щими** remedial work.

отстегá|ть, ю *pf.* (*of* ⇒**стегáть**[1]) to beat, lash.

отстёгива|ть(ся), ю *impf. of* ⇒**отстегну́ть(ся)**

отстег|ну́ть, ну́, нёшь *pf.* (*of* ⇒**~ивать**) **1** (*крючок*) to unfasten, undo; (*пуговицы*) to unbutton. **2** (*sl.*) (*деньги*) to pay out.

отстег|ну́ться, нётся *pf.* (*of* ⇒**~иваться**) to come unfastened, come undone.

отстир|áть, áю *pf.* (*of* ⇒**~ывать**) to wash off.

отстир|áться, áется *pf.* (*of* ⇒**~ываться**) to wash off, come out in the wash.

отсти́рыва|ть(ся), ю *impf. of* ⇒**отстирáть(ся)**

отстó|й, я *m.* sediment, deposit.

отстóйник, а *m.* settling tank.

отсто|я́ть[1]**, ю́, и́шь** *pf.* (*of* ⇒**отстáивать**) (*город*) to defend; (*свои взгляды, права*) to stand up for.

отсто|я́ть[2]**, ю́, и́шь** *pf.* (*простоять*) to stand through; **мы ~я́ли весь спектáкль** we stood through the entire show.

отсто|я́ть[3]**, ю, и́шь** *impf.* (**от**+*g.*) to be ... distant (from); **стáнция ~и́т от цéнтра гóрода на два киломéтра** the station is two kilometres (away) from the centre of the town.

отсто|я́ться, и́тся *pf.* (*of* ⇒**отстáиваться**) **1** (*chem.*) to settle. **2** (*fig.*) to settle, become stabilized.

отстрадá|ть, ю *pf.* **1** (*кончить страдать*) to finish suffering. **2** (*какое-н. время*) to have suffered.

отстрáива|ть(ся), ю(сь) *impf. of* ⇒**отстрóить(ся)**

отстранéни|е, я *nt.* **1** pushing aside. **2** (*увольнение*) dismissal, discharge.

отстран|и́ть, ю́, и́шь *pf.* (*of* ⇒**~я́ть**) **1** (*отодвинуть*) to push aside; **о. от себя́ все забóты** to lay aside all one's cares. **2** (*уволить*) to dismiss, discharge.

отстран|и́ться, ю́сь, и́шься *pf.* (*of* ⇒**~я́ться**) (**от**+*g.*) to move away (from); (*fig.*) to keep out of the way (of), keep aloof (from); **о. от удáра** to dodge a blow; **о. от дóлжности** to relinquish a post.

отстран|я́ть(ся), я́ю(сь) *impf. of* ⇒**~и́ть(ся)**

отстрéлива|ть[1]**, ю** *impf. of* ⇒**отстрели́ть**

отстрéлива|ть[2]**, ю** *impf. of* ⇒**отстреля́ть**

отстрéлива|ться, юсь *impf. of* ⇒**отстреля́ться**[1]

отстрел|и́ть, ю́, ~ишь *pf.* (*of* ⇒**~ивать**[1]) (*палец*) to shoot off.

отстрел|я́ть, я́ю *pf.* (*of* ⇒**~ивать**[2]) (*зверя*) to shoot (*for commercial purposes, etc.*).

отстрел|я́ться[1]**, я́юсь** *pf.* (*of* ⇒**~иваться**) **1** (**от**+*g.*) to defend o.s. (against) (by shooting). **2** (*ответить стрельбой на стрельбу*) to return fire, fire back.

отстрел|я́ться[2]**, я́юсь** *pf.* (*coll.*) **1** (*закончить стрельбу*) to have finished firing; to have completed a practice (shoot). **2** (*окончить какие-н. дела*) to be finished with sth. (*e.g. exams*).

отстригá|ть, ю *impf. of* ⇒**отстри́чь**

отстри́|женный *p.p.p. of* ⇒**~чь**

отстри́|чь, гу́, жёшь, гу́т, *past* **~г, ~гла** *pf.* (*of* ⇒**~гáть**) to cut off, clip.

отстр|óить, óю, óишь *pf.* (*of* ⇒**~áивать**) to complete the construction of, finish building.

отстр|óиться, óюсь, óишься *pf.* (*of* ⇒**~áиваться**) (*coll.*) to finish building.

отсту́к|ать, аю *pf.* (*of* ⇒**~ивать**) (*coll.*) (*ритм*) to tap out; **о. мелóдию** to bash out a tune; **о. на маши́нке** to bash out on a typewriter.

отсту́кива|ть, ю *impf. of* ⇒**отсту́кать**

óтступ, а *m.* (*typ.*) indentation.

отступ|áть(ся), áю(сь) *impf. of* ⇒**~и́ть(ся)**

отступ|и́ть, лю́, ~ишь *pf.* (*of*

⇒**~а́ть**) **1** (*отойти назад*) to step back; to recede. **2** (*mil.*) to retreat, fall back. **3** (*fig.*) (*от своего*) to back down; (**от**+*g.*) to go back (on); to give up; **о. от реше́ния** to go back on a decision. **4** (*fig.*; **от**+*g.*) (*от чего-н. установленного*) to deviate (from); **о. от обы́чая** to depart from custom; **о. от те́мы** to digress. **5** (*typ.*) to indent.

отступ|и́ться, лю́сь, ~́ишся *pf.* (*of* ⇒**~а́ться**) (*coll.*; **от**+*g.*) to give up, renounce; **о. от своего́ сло́ва** to go back on one's word; **они́ все ~и́лись от него́** they have all given him up.

отступле́ни|е, я *nt.* **1** (*mil. and fig.*) retreat. **2** (*от темы*) deviation; digression.

отсту́пник, а *m.* apostate.

отсту́пни|ца, цы *f. of* ⇒**~к**

отсту́пничеств|о, а *nt.* apostasy.

отступн|о́й *adj.*: **~ы́е де́ньги** (*or as n.* **~о́е, ~о́го** *nt.*) indemnity, compensation.

отступ|я́ *ger. of* ⇒**~и́ть,** *as adv.* (**от**+*g.*) off, away (from); **о. два-три ме́тра** two or three metres off; **немно́го о. от до́ма** a little way away from the house.

отсу́тстви|е, я *nt.* absence; (+*g.*) lack (of); **в его́ о.** in his absence; **за ~ем** (+*g.*) (*кого-н.*) in the absence of; (*чего-н.*) for lack (of), for want (of); **находи́ться в ~и** to be absent; **блиста́ть свои́м ~ем** to be conspicuous by one's absence.

отсу́тств|овать, ую *impf.* (*о человеке*) to be absent; (*о доказательстве*) to be lacking.

отсу́тств|ующий *pres. part. of* ⇒**~овать** *and adj.* absent (*also fig.*); **о. вид** blank expression; *as n.* **о., ~ующего** *m.* absentee.

отсчёт, а *m.* reading (*on an instrument*).

отсчит|а́ть, а́ю *pf.* (*of* ⇒**~́ывать**) to count out, count off; **о. кому́-н. де́сять рубле́й** to count out ten roubles to s.o.

отсчи́тыва|ть, ю *impf. of* ⇒**отсчита́ть**

отсыла́|ть, ю *impf. of* ⇒**отосла́ть**

отсы́лк|а, и *f.* **1** dispatch; **о. де́нег** remittance. **2** (*в тексте*) reference.

отсы́п|ать, лю, лешь *pf.* (*of* ⇒**~а́ть**) (+*a. or g.*) to pour off; to measure off.

отсып|а́ть, а́ю *impf. of* ⇒**~́ать**

отсы́п|аться, лется *pf.* (*of* ⇒**~а́ться**[1]) to pour out.

отсып|а́ться[1]**, а́ется** *impf. of* ⇒**~́аться**

отсып|а́ться[2]**, а́юсь** *impf. of* ⇒**отоспа́ться**

отсыре́лый *adj.* damp.

отсыре́|ть, ю *pf. of* ⇒**сыре́ть**

отсыха́|ть, ет *impf. of* ⇒**отсо́хнуть**

отсю́да *adv.* from here; hence (*also fig.*); (*fig.*) from this; **о. сле́дует, что...** from this it follows that ....

Отта́в|а, ы *f.* Ottawa.

отта́ива|ть, ю *impf. of* ⇒**отта́ять**

отта́лкивани|е, я *nt.* (*phys.*) repulsion.

отта́лкива|ть(ся), ю(сь) *impf. of* ⇒**оттолкну́ть(ся)**

отта́лкива|ющий *pres. part. act. of* ⇒**~ть** *and adj.* repulsive, repellent.

отта́птыва|ть, ю *impf. of* ⇒**оттопта́ть**

оттаска́|ть, ю *pf.* (*of* ⇒**таска́ть** 2) to pull; **о. кого́-н. за́ во́лосы** to pull s.o.'s hair.

отта́скива|ть, ю *impf. of* ⇒**оттащи́ть**

отта́чива|ть, ю *impf. of* ⇒**отточи́ть**

оттащ|и́ть, у́, ~́ишь *pf.* (*of* ⇒**отта́скивать**) to drag aside (away), pull aside (away).

отта́|ять, ю, ешь *pf.* (*of* ⇒**~ивать**) (*trans. and intrans.*) to thaw out.

оттека́|ть, ет *impf. of* ⇒**оттечь**

оттен|и́ть, ю, и́шь *pf.* (*of* ⇒**~я́ть**) **1** to shade (in). **2** (*fig.*) to set off, make more prominent.

отте́н|ок, ка *m.* (*цвета*) shade, hue; (*fig.*) shade, nuance; **о. значе́ния** shade of meaning; **он говори́л с ~ком иро́нии** there was a note of irony in his voice.

оттен|я́ть, я́ю *impf. of* ⇒**~и́ть**

о́ттепел|ь, и *f.* thaw.

оттер|е́ть, ототру́, ототрёшь *past* **~̈, ~̈ла** *pf.* (*of* ⇒**оттира́ть**) **1** (*грязь*) to rub off, rub out. **2** (*руку*) to restore sensation to by rubbing. **3** (*coll.*) (*оттеснить*) to press back, push aside.

оттер|е́ться, ототрётся, *past* **~̈ся, ~̈лась** *pf.* (*of* ⇒**оттира́ться**) to rub out; to come out (*by rubbing*).

оттесн|и́ть, ю́, и́шь *pf.* (*of* ⇒**~я́ть**) to drive back; to press back; to push aside, shove aside (*also fig.*); **о. проти́вника** (*mil.*) to force the enemy back; **о. конкуре́нта** (*fig.*) to edge a competitor out.

оттесн|я́ть, я́ю *impf. of* ⇒**~и́ть**

отте́|чь, чёт, ку́т *past* **оттёк, ~кла́** to flow away.

оттира́|ть(ся), ю, ет(ся) *impf. of* ⇒**оттере́ть(ся)**

о́ттиск, а *m.* **1** (*подковы*) impression. **2** (*статьи*) off-print. **3** (*корректурный*) proof.

отти́скива|ть, ю *impf. of* ⇒**отти́снуть**

отти́с|нуть, ну, нешь *pf.* (*of* ⇒**~кивать**) **1** (*coll.*) (*оттеснить*) to push aside. **2** (*отпечатать*) to print.

оттого́ *adv.* that is why; **о. мы и не могли́ прие́хать** that's why we couldn't come; **о.... что** because; **я о. опозда́л, что мото́р не заводи́лся** I was late because the engine would not start.

отто́ле *adv.* (*obs.*) thence, from there.

оттолкн|у́ть, у́, ёшь *pf.* (*of* ⇒**отта́лкивать**) **1** (*стул*) to push away, push aside. **2** (*fig.*) (*друзей*) to antagonize, alienate.

оттолкн|у́ться, у́сь, ёшься *pf.* (*of* ⇒**отта́лкиваться**) **1** (**от**+*g.*) to push off (from). **2** (*fig.*; **от**+*g.*) to take as a starting-point.

отто́л|ь = **~е**

оттома́нк|а, и *f.* ottoman.

оттоп|та́ть, чу́, ~́чешь *pf.* (*of* ⇒**отта́птывать**) (*coll.*) **1** to hurt, damage (*by much walking*). **2**: **о. кому́-н. но́гу** to tread (heavily) on s.o.'s foot.

оттопы́р|енный *p.p.p. of* ⇒**~ить** *and adj.* (*coll.*) protruding, sticking out; (*карманы*) bulging.

оттопы́рива|ть(ся), ю, ет(ся) *impf. of* ⇒**оттопы́рить(ся)**

оттопы́р|ить, ю, ишь *pf.* (*of* ⇒**~ивать**) (*coll.*) to stick out; **о. ло́кти** to stick out one's elbows.

оттопы́р|иться, ится *pf.* (*of* ⇒**~иваться**) (*coll.*) to protrude, stick out; (*о карманах*) to bulge.

отторг|а́ть, а́ю *impf. of* ⇒**~́нуть**

отто́рг|нуть, ну, нешь, *past* **~, ~ла** *pf.* (*of* ⇒**~а́ть**) to tear away, seize; (*med.*) to reject.

отторже́ни|е, я *nt.* tearing away, seizure; (*med.*) rejection (*of a transplanted organ*).

отточ|и́ть, у́, ~́ишь *pf.* (*of* ⇒**отта́чивать**) to sharpen; (*fig.*) to hone.

оттреп|а́ть, лю́, ~́лешь *pf.* (*of* ⇒**оттрёпывать**) (*coll.*) to punish (*by pulling by the ears or hair*).

оттрёпыва|ть, ю *impf. of* ⇒**оттрепа́ть**

оттруб|и́ть, лю́, и́шь *pf.* (*coll.*) to slave away (*for a certain period*).

отту́да *adv.* from there.

отту|зи́ть, жу́, зи́шь *pf. of* ⇒**тузи́ть**

оттяга́|ть, ю *pf.* (*coll.*) to gain by a lawsuit.

оття́гива|ть(ся), ю(сь) *impf. of* ⇒**оттяну́ть(ся)**

оття́жк|а, и *f.* **1** (*coll.*) (*отсрочка*) delay, procrastination. **2** (*naut.*) rope, stay.

оття|ну́ть, ну́, ~́нешь *pf.* (*of* ⇒**~́гивать**) **1** to pull, drag (away). **2** (*mil.*) (*отряд*) to draw off. **3** (*coll.*) (*отсрочить*) to delay; **что́бы о. вре́мя** to gain time. **4** (*карман*) to stretch, weigh down. **5** (*coll.*) (*плечи*) to weigh down on, tire.

оття|ну́ться, ну́сь, ~́нешься *pf.* (*of* ⇒**~́гиваться**) **1** (*о кармане*) to sag. **2** (*mil.*) to draw off. **3** (*sl.*) (*развлечься*) to relax, have a good time.

оттяп|а́ть, аю *pf.* (*of* ⇒**~́ывать**) (*coll.*) to chop off.

оття́пыва|ть, ю *impf. of* ⇒**оттяпа́ть**

оту́жина|ть, ю *pf.* to have finished supper.

отума́нива|ть, ю *impf. of* ⇒**отума́нить**

отума́н|ить, ю, ишь *pf.* (*of* ⇒**~ивать**) **1** to blur; to dim; **её глаза́ ~ило слеза́ми** her eyes were dimmed with tears. **2** (*fig.*) to cloud, dull; **моё созна́ние ~ило вино́м** wine had clouded my reason.

отупе́лый *adj.* (*coll.*) stupefied, dulled.

отупе́ни|е, я *nt.* stupefaction, dullness, torpor.

отупе́|ть, ю *pf.* (*coll.*) to grow dull, sink into torpor.

О

отутю́жива|ть, ю *impf. of* ⇒**отутю́жить**

отутю́ж|ить, у, ишь *pf.* (*of* ⇒**~ивать**) to iron (out).

отуч|а́ть(ся), а́ю(сь) *impf. of* ⇒**~и́ть(ся¹)**

оту́чива|ться, юсь *impf. of* ⇒**отучи́ться²**

отуч|и́ть, у́, ~ишь *pf.* (*of* ⇒**~а́ть**) (**от**+*g. or* +*inf.*) to break (of); **о. от груди́** to wean.

отуч|и́ться¹, у́сь, ~ишься *pf.* (*of* ⇒**~а́ться**) (**от**+*g. or* +*inf.*) (*отвыкнуть*) to break o.s. (of).

отуч|и́ться², у́сь, ~ишься *pf.* (*of* ⇒**~иваться**) (*кончить учиться*) to have finished one's lessons; to finish learning.

отфутбо́лива|ть, ю *impf. of* ⇒**отфутбо́лить**

отфутбо́л|ить, ю, ишь *pf.* (*of* ⇒**~ивать**) (*coll.*) to refer (s.o.) to another person or body.

отха́жива|ть, ю *impf. of* ⇒**отходи́ть²,³**

отха́рк|ать, аю *pf.* (*of* ⇒**~ивать**) to expectorate.

отха́ркива|ть, ю *impf. of* ⇒**отха́ркать**

отха́ркива|ться, юсь *impf. of* ⇒**отха́ркнуться**

отха́ркива|ющий *pres. part. act. of* ⇒**~ть; ~ющее (сре́дство)** (*med.*) expectorant.

отха́ркн|уть, у, ешь *pf.* to hawk up.

отха́рк|нуться, нусь, нешься *pf.* (*of* ⇒**~иваться**) (*coll.*) to clear one's throat.

отхва|ти́ть, чу́, ~тишь *pf.* (*of* ⇒**~тывать**) (*coll.*) **1** (*отрезать*) to snip off; (*отрубить*) to chop off; **он ~ти́л себе́ па́лец топоро́м** he chopped his finger off with an axe. **2** (*достать*) to get hold of.

отхва́тыва|ть, ю *impf. of* ⇒**отхвати́ть**

отхлеб|ну́ть, ну́, нёшь *pf.* (*of* ⇒**~ывать**) (*coll.*; +*a. or g.*) to take a sip (of); to take a mouthful (of).

отхлёбыва|ть, ю *impf. of* ⇒**отхлебну́ть**

отхле|ста́ть, щу́, ~щешь *pf.* (*coll.*) to give a lashing.

отхлы́н|уть, у, ешь *pf.* to rush back, flood back (*also fig.*).

отхо́д, а *m.* **1** departure. **2** (*mil.*) withdrawal. **3** (**от**+*g.*) (*отклонение*) deviation (from); (*разрыв*) break (with). **4** *see* ⇒**~ы**

отхо|ди́ть¹, жу́, ~дишь *impf. of* ⇒**отойти́**

отхо|ди́ть², жу́, ~дишь *pf.* (*of* ⇒**отха́живать**) (*coll.*) (*вылечить*) to nurse back to health.

отхо|ди́ть³, жу́, ~дишь *pf.* (*of* ⇒**отха́живать**) (*coll.*) **1** (*ноги*) to tire, hurt (*by walking*). **2** (*весь день*) to spend (*time*) walking. **3** (*кончить ходить*) to finish walking

отхо́дн|ая, ой *f.* prayer for the dying; **справля́ть ~ую кому́-н.** (*fig.*) to write s.o. off.

отхо́дчив|ый (~, ~а) *adj.* not bearing grudges.

отхо́д|ы, ов (*tech.*) waste (products).

отхо́ж|ий *adj.*: **~ее ме́сто** (*coll.*) latrine, earth closet; **о. про́мысел** (*hist.*) seasonal work (*outside peasant's own village*).

отцве|сти́, ту́, тёшь, *past* **~л, ~ла́** *pf.* (*of* ⇒**~та́ть**) to finish blossoming, fade (*also fig.*); **она́ ~ла́** she has lost her bloom.

отцве|та́ть, та́ю *impf. of* ⇒**~сти́**

отце|ди́ть, жу́, ~дишь *pf.* (*of* ⇒**~живать**) to strain off.

отце́жива|ть, ю *impf. of* ⇒**отцеди́ть**

отцеп|и́ть, лю́, ~ишь *pf.* (*of* ⇒**~ля́ть**) to unhook; to uncouple.

отцеп|и́ться, лю́сь, ~ишься *pf.* (*of* ⇒**~ля́ться**) **1** to come unhooked; to come uncoupled. **2** (*fig., coll.*) to leave alone; **~и́сь ты от меня́!** leave me alone!

отцепля́|ть(ся), ю(сь) *impf. of* ⇒**отцепи́ть(ся)**

отцеуби́йств|о, а *nt.* patricide (*act*).

отцеуби́йц|а, ы *c.g.* patricide (*agent*).

отцикл|ева́ть, ю́ю *pf. of* ⇒**циклева́ть**

отцо́в *adj.* one's father's.

отцо́вск|ий *adj.* one's father's; paternal.

отцо́вств|о, а *nt.* paternity.

отча́ива|ться, юсь *impf. of* ⇒**отча́яться**

отча́лива|ть, ю *impf. of* **отча́лить**; **~й!** (*coll.*) clear off!; beat it!

отча́л|ить, ю, ишь *pf.* (*of* ⇒**~ивать**) (*naut.*) to cast off.

отча́сти *adv.* partly.

отча́яни|е, я *nt.* despair.

отча́ян|ный (~, ~на) *adj.* (*положение, взор, крик*) desperate; (*смелый до безрассудности*) daring, reckless; (*coll.*) (*ужасный*) terrible, awful.

отча́|яться, юсь, ешься *pf.* (*of* ⇒**~иваться**) (+*inf. or* **в**+*p.*) to despair (of).

о́тче (*obs.*) *voc. of* ⇒**оте́ц**; **О. наш** Our Father (*prayer*).

отчего́ *adv.* why; **вот о.** that's why.

отчего́-либо *adv.* for some reason or other.

отчего́-нибудь = **отчего́-либо**

отчего́-то *adv.* for some reason.

отчека́нива|ть, ю *impf. of* ⇒**отчека́нить**

отчека́н|ить, ю, ишь *pf.* (*of* ⇒**чека́нить** *and* **~ивать**) **1** to coin, mint. **2** (*fig.*) (*слова*) to articulate.

отчёркива|ть, ю *impf. of* ⇒**отчеркну́ть**

отчерк|ну́ть, ну́, нёшь *pf.* (*of* ⇒**~̈ивать**) to mark off.

отчерп|ну́ть, ну́, нёшь *pf.* (*of* ⇒**~ывать**) (+*a. or g.*) to ladle out.

отчёрпыва|ть, ю *impf. of* ⇒**отчерпну́ть**

о́тчеств|о, а *nt.* patronymic; **как его́ по ~у** what is his patronymic?

отчёт, а *m.* account; **дать о.** (**в**+*p.*) to give an account (of), report (on); **взять де́ньги под о.** to take money on account; **отдава́ть себе́ о.** (**в**+*p.*) to be aware (of), realize.

отчётливост|ь, и *f.* intelligibility, clarity, distinctness.

отчётлив|ый (~, ~а) *adj.* intelligible, clear, distinct.

отчётно-вы́борн|ый *adj.*: **~ое собра́ние** meeting held to hear reports and elect new officials.

отчётност|ь, и *f.* **1** (*счетоводство*) book-keeping. **2** (*документы*) accounts.

отчёт|ный *adj. of* ⇒**~**; **о. год** financial year, current year; **о. докла́д** report.

отчи́зн|а, ы *f.* (*poet.*) native land; fatherland.

о́тчий *adj.* (*obs., poet.*) paternal.

о́тчим, а *m.* step-father.

отчисле́ни|е, я *nt.* **1** (*вычет*) deduction. **2** (*увольнение*) dismissal.

отчи́сл|ить, ю, ишь *pf.* (*of* ⇒**~я́ть**) **1** (*вычесть*) to deduct; **о. часть зарпла́ты в упла́ту подохо́дного нало́га** to deduct part of wages for income-tax payment. **2** (*уволить*) to dismiss.

отчи́сл|иться, юсь, ишься *pf.* (*of* ⇒**~я́ться**) (**от**+*g.*) to leave; to resign from.

отчисл|я́ть(ся), я́ю(сь) *impf. of* ⇒**~ить(ся)**

отчи́|стить, щу, стишь *pf.* (*of* ⇒**~ща́ть**) **1** (*пятно*) to clean off; to brush off. **2** (*одежду*) to clean.

отчи́|ститься, щусь, стишься *pf.* (*of* ⇒**~ща́ться**) **1** (*о грязи*) to come off, come out. **2** (*об одежде*) to become clean.

отчит|а́ть, а́ю *pf.* (*of* ⇒**~ывать**) (*coll.*) to tell off.

отчит|а́ться, а́юсь *pf.* (*of* ⇒**~ываться**) (**в**+*p.*) to give an account (of), report (on); **о. пе́ред избира́телями** to report back to the electors.

отчи́тыва|ть(ся), ю(сь) *impf. of* ⇒**отчита́ть(ся)**

отчища́|ть(ся), ю(сь) *impf. of* ⇒**отчи́стить(ся)**

отчуди́ть, жу́, ди́шь *pf.* (*coll.*) to do sth. strange.

отчужда́|ть, ю *impf.* **1** (*leg.*) to alienate. **2** (*fig.*) to alienate, estrange.

отчужде́ни|е, я *nt.* **1** (*leg.*) alienation. **2** (*fig.*) estrangement.

отчуждённост|ь, и *f.* estrangement.

отшага́|ть, ю *pf.* (*coll.*) to walk; to tramp.

отшагн|у́ть, у́, ёшь *pf.* (*coll.*) (*в сторону*) to step aside; (*назад*) to step back.

отшатн|у́ться, у́сь, ёшься *pf.* (*of* ⇒**отша́тываться**) (**от**+*g.*) **1** (*от удара*) to start back (from); to recoil (from). **2** (*fig.*) (*прекратить общение*) to give up; to break (with); **о. от дру́га** to give up a friend.

отша́тыва|ться, юсь *impf. of* ⇒**отшатну́ться**

отшы́рива|ть, ю *impf. of* ⇒**отшвырну́ть**

отшвыр|ну́ть, ну́, нёшь *pf.* (*of* ⇒**~́ивать**) to fling away; to throw off.

отше́льник, а *m.* hermit; recluse.

отше́льни|ца, цы *f. of* ⇒**~к**

отше́льни|ческий *adj. of* ⇒**~к**

отше́льничеств|о, а *nt.* a hermit's life, a recluse's life (*also fig., iron.*).

отши́б, а *m. only in phr.* **на ~е** at a distance (*from a settlement*); **жить на ~е** (*fig.*) to live alone.

отшиб|а́ть, а́ю *impf. of* ⇒**~и́ть**

отшиб|и́ть, у́, ёшь, *past* **~́, ~́ла** *pf.* (*of* ⇒**~а́ть**) (*coll.*) **1** (*отбить*) to break off; to knock off; **о. ру́чку у ча́йника** to knock the handle off a teapot; **у меня́ ~́ло па́мять** my memory has failed me. **2** (*повредить*) to hurt; **о. себе́ ру́ку** to hurt one's arm.

отши́ть, отошью́, отошьёшь *pf.* (*coll.*) to snub, rebuff.

отшлёп|ать, аю *pf.* (*of* ⇒**~ывать**) (*coll.*) to spank

отшлёпыва|ть, ю *impf. of* ⇒**отшлёпать**

отшлифо|ва́ть, у́ю *pf.* (*of* ⇒**~о́вывать**) to grind; (*fig.*) to polish.

отшлифо́выва|ть, ю *impf. of* ⇒**отшлифова́ть**

отшпи́лива|ть(ся), ю(сь) *impf. of* ⇒**отшпи́лить(ся)**

отшпи́л|ить, ю, ишь *pf.* (*of* ⇒**~ивать**) to unpin, unfasten.

отшпи́л|иться, ится *pf.* (*of* ⇒**~иваться**) to come unpinned, come unfastened.

отштукату́р|ить, ю, ишь *pf. of* ⇒**штукату́рить**

отшум|е́ть, лю́, и́шь *pf.* to finish making a noise.

отшу|ти́ться, чу́сь, ~́тишься *pf.* (*of* ⇒**~́чиваться**) to make a joke in reply.

отшу́чива|ться, юсь *impf. of* ⇒**отшути́ться**

отщепе́н|ец, ца *m.* renegade.

отщепе́н|ка, ки *f. of* ⇒**~ец**

отщеп|и́ть, лю́, и́шь *pf.* (*of* ⇒**~ля́ть**) to chip off.

отщепля́|ть, ю *impf. of* ⇒**отщепи́ть**

отщип|а́ть, лю́, ~́лешь *pf.* (*of* ⇒**~́ывать**) to pinch off, nip off.

отщи́пыва|ть, ю *impf. of* ⇒**отщипа́ть**

отъ... *vbl. pref.* = **от...**

отъеда́|ть(ся), ю(сь) *impf. of* ⇒**отъе́сть(ся)**

отъе́зд, а *m.* departure; **быть в ~е** to be away.

отъе́з|дить, жу, дишь *pf.* (*coll.*) to have spent (*time*) in driving, riding.

отъезжа́|ть, ю *impf. of* ⇒**отъе́хать**

отъезжа́|ющий *pres. part. of* ⇒**~ть;** *as n.* **о., ~ющего** *m.* departing person.

отъе́зжий *adj.* (*obs.*) distant.

отъёмный *adj.* removable, detachable.

отъе́|сть, м, шь, ст, ди́м, ди́те, дя́т, *past* **~л, ~ла** *pf.* (*of* ⇒**~да́ть**) to bite off and eat.

отъе́|сться, мся, шься, стся, ди́мся, ди́тесь, дя́тся, *past* **~лся, ~лась** *pf.* (*of* ⇒**~да́ться**) to put on weight; to feed well.

отъе́|хать, ду, дешь *pf.* (*of* ⇒**~зжа́ть**) to depart.

отъя́вленный *adj.* (*coll., pej.*) thorough, inveterate, out-and-out.

от|ъя́ть, ыму́, ы́мешь *pf.* (*obs.*) = **~ня́ть**

отыгр|а́ть, а́ю *pf.* (*of* ⇒**~́ывать**) to win back.

отыгр|а́ться, а́юсь *pf.* (*of* ⇒**~́ываться**) **1** to win (having lost); to get back what one has lost. **2** (*fig., coll.*) (*выйти из затруднительного положения*) to get out of a situation.

оты́грыва|ть(ся), ю(сь) *impf. of* ⇒**отыгра́ть(ся)**

о́тыгрыш, а *m.* **1** (*действие*) winning back. **2** (*то, что отыграно*) sum won back.

оты|ска́ть, щу́, ~́щешь *pf.* (*of* ⇒**~́скивать**) to find; to track down, run to earth.

оты|ска́ться, щу́сь, ~́щешься *pf.* (*of* ⇒**~́скиваться**) to turn up, appear.

оты́скива|ть, ю *impf.* **1** *impf. of* ⇒**отыска́ть. 2** (*impf. only*) to look for, try to find.

оты́скива|ться, юсь *impf. of* ⇒**отыска́ться**

отяго|ти́ть, щу́, ти́шь *pf.* (*of* ⇒**~ща́ть**) to burden.

отягоща́|ть, ю *impf. of* ⇒**отяготи́ть**

отягч|а́ть, а́ю *impf. of* ⇒**~и́ть; ~а́ющие (вину́) обстоя́тельства** aggravating circumstances.

отягч|и́ть, у́, и́шь *pf.* (*of* ⇒**~а́ть**) to aggravate.

отяжеле́|ть, ю *pf.* to become heavy.

о́фис, а *m.* office.

о́фис|ный *adj. of* ⇒**~**

офице́р, а *m.* officer.

офице́р|ский *adj. of* ⇒**~; ~ское собра́ние** officers' mess.

офице́рств|о, а *nt.* **1** (*collect.*) the officers. **2** (*чин*) commissioned rank.

официа́льн|ый *adj.* official; **~ое лицо́** an official.

официа́нт, а *m.* waiter.

официа́нтк|а, и *f.* waitress.

официо́з, а *m.* semi-official organ (*of press*).

официо́з|ный (~ен, ~на) *adj.* semi-official.

оформи́тел|ь, я *m.* designer; **о. витри́ны** window-dresser; **о. спекта́кля** set designer.

оформи́тель|ница, ницы *f. of* ⇒**~**

офо́рм|ить, лю, ишь *pf.* (*of* ⇒**~ля́ть**) **1** to design; **о. витри́ну** to dress a window; **о. пье́су** to design the sets for a play. **2** (*узаконить*) to register officially, legalize; **о. вступле́ние в брак** to register a marriage; **о. догово́р** to draw up an agreement. **3** (*на работу*) to enrol (*Br.*), enroll (*US*), take on.

офо́рм|иться, люсь, ишься *pf.* (*of* ⇒**~ля́ться**) **1** (*об идеях*) to take shape. **2** (*узакониться*) to be registered; to legalize one's position. **3** (*на работу*) to be taken on, join the staff.

оформле́ни|е, я *nt.* **1** design; **сцени́ческое о.** staging. **2** (*узаконение*) registration, legalization.

оформля́|ть(ся), ю(сь) *impf. of* ⇒**офо́рмить(ся)**

офо́рт, а *m.* etching.

офса́йд, а *m.* (*sport*) offside.

офсе́т, а *m.* (*typ.*) offset process.

офтальмо́лог, а *m.* ophthalmologist.

офтальмологи́ческий *adj.* ophthalmological.

офтальмоло́ги|я, и *f.* ophthalmology.

оф(ф)шо́рный *adj.* (*fin.*) offshore.

ох *int.* oh!; ah!

оха́ива|ть, ю *impf. of* ⇒**оха́ять**

оха́льник, а *m.* (*coll.*) (*озорник*) mischief-maker; (*нахал*) impudent fellow.

оха́л|ьный (~ен, ~ьна) *adj.* mischievous.

о́хань|е, я *nt.* (*coll.*) moaning, groaning.

оха́пк|а, и *f.* armful; **взять в ~у** (*coll.*) to take in one's arms.

охарактериз|ова́ть, у́ю *pf. of* ⇒**характеризова́ть**

о́х|ать, аю *impf.* (*of* ⇒**~нуть**) (*от боли*) to moan, groan; (*от печали*) to sigh.

оха́|ять, ю *pf.* (*of* ⇒**ха́ять** *and* **~ивать**) (*coll.*) to criticize, pan.

охва́т, а *m.* **1** scope, range. **2** (*включение*) inclusion. **3** (*mil.*) outflanking, envelopment.

охва|ти́ть, чу́, ~́тишь *pf.* (*of* ⇒**~́тывать**) **1** (*обхватить*) to envelop; to enclose; **дом ~ти́ло пла́менем** the house was enveloped in flames. **2** (*о чувстве*) to grip, seize; **их ~ти́л у́жас** they were seized with panic. **3** (+*i.*) (*coll.*) (*включить*) to draw (in), involve (in); **о. молодёжь обще́ственной рабо́той** to draw young people into social work. **4** (*fig.*) (*понять*) to comprehend, take in. **5** (*mil.*) to outflank, envelop.

охва́тн|ый *adj.*: **~ое движе́ние** (*mil.*) flanking movement, enveloping movement.

охва́тыва|ть, ю *impf. of* ⇒**охвати́ть**

охва́|ченный *p.p.p. of* ⇒**~ти́ть; о. у́жасом** terror-stricken.

охво́стье, я *nt.* (*collect.*) **1** chaff, husks. **2** (*fig.*) rabble.

охладева́|ть, ю *impf. of* ⇒**охладе́ть**

охладе́лый *adj.* (*obs.*) cold; grown cold.

охладе́|ть, ю *pf.* (*of* ⇒**~ва́ть**) to grow cold; (*fig.*; **к** + *d.*) (*к человеку*) to grow cold (towards); (*к футболу*) to lose interest (in).

охлади́тел|ь, я *m.* (*tech.*) cooler, refrigerator; condenser.

О

охлади́тельный *adj.* cooling.

охла|ди́ть, жу́, ди́шь *pf.* (*of* ⇨**~жда́ть**) to cool, cool off (*also fig.*); **о. чей-н. пыл** to damp s.o.'s ardour.

охла|ди́ться, жу́сь, ди́шься *pf.* (*of* ⇨**~жда́ться**) to become cool, cool down (*also fig.*).

охлажда́|ть(ся), ю(сь) *impf. of* ⇨**охлади́ть(ся)**

охлажда́|ющий *pres. part. act. of* ⇨**~ть** *and adj.* cooling, refrigerating; **~ющая жи́дкость** coolant.

охлажде́ни|е, я *nt.* **1** cooling (off); **с возду́шным ~ем** air-cooled. **2** (*fig.*) coolness.

охмеле́|ть, ю *pf.* (*of* ⇨**хмеле́ть**) (*coll.*) to get drunk.

охмел|и́ть, ю́, и́шь *pf.* (*of* ⇨**~я́ть**) to make intoxicated (*also fig.*).

охмел|я́ть, я́ю *impf. of* ⇨**~и́ть**

охмур|и́ть, ю́, и́шь *pf.* (*of* ⇨**~я́ть**) (*coll.*) to cheat, trick, deceive.

охмуря́|ть, ю *impf. of* ⇨**охмури́ть**

о́х|нуть, ну, нешь *pf. of* ⇨**~ать**

охоло|сти́ть, щу́, сти́шь *pf.* to castrate, geld.

охора́шива|ться, юсь *impf.* (*coll.*) to smarten o.s. up.

охо́т|а[1]**, ы** *f.* hunt, hunting; chase; **о. с ружьём** shooting; **псо́вая о.** riding to hounds; **соколи́ная о.** falconry.

охо́т|а[2]**, ы** *f.* **1** (**к**+*d. or* +*inf.*) desire, wish, inclination; **у него́ бо́льше нет ~ы писа́ть** he no longer has any desire to write; **по свое́й ~е** of one's own accord; **что ему за о.!** what makes him do it!; **о. тебе́ спо́рить с ним!** (*coll.*) what makes you argue with him! **2** (*период течки*) heat (*in female animals*).

охо́|титься, чусь, тишься *impf.* (**на**+*a. or* **за**+*i.*) to hunt; (*fig.*; **за**+*i.*) to hunt for.

охо́тк|а, и *f.*: **в ~у** (*coll.*) with pleasure, eagerly.

охо́тник[1]**, а** *m.* hunter.

охо́тник[2]**, а** *m.* **1** (**до**+*g. or* +*inf.*) lover (of); enthusiast (for); **он большо́й о. до грибо́в** he is a great mushroom lover. **2** (*доброволец*) volunteer; **есть ли ~и пойти́?** are there any volunteers to go?

охо́тнич|ий *adj.* hunting; **о. биле́т** hunting permit; **~ья соба́ка** hound, gun-dog; **о. расска́з** (*joc.*) tall story.

охо́тно *adv.* willingly, gladly, readily.

охо́ч|ий (~, ~а) *adj.* (+*inf.*; *coll.*) inclined (to), keen (to), having an urge (to).

о́хр|а, ы *f.* ochre (*Br.*), ocher (*US*).

охра́н|а, ы *f.* **1** (*помещения*) guarding; (*природы*) protection; **о. труда́** health and safety measures. **2** (*группа людей*) guard; **ли́чная о.** body-guard; **пограни́чная о.** frontier guard.

охране́ни|е, я *nt.* safeguarding; protection.

охрани́тельный *adj.* protective.

охран|и́ть, ю́, и́шь *pf.* (*of* ⇨**~я́ть**) (*границу, помещение*) to guard; (*природу*; *интересы*) to protect.

охра́нк|а, и *f.* (*coll.*) Okhranka (*Secret Police Department in tsarist Russia*).

охра́нник, а *m.* guard.

охра́нни|ца, цы *f. of* ⇨**~к**

охра́н|ный *adj. of* ⇨**~а**; **~ная гра́мота, о. лист** safe-conduct, pass; **~ная зо́на** (*mil.*) restricted area.

охран|я́ть, я́ю *impf. of* ⇨**~и́ть**

охри́плый *adj.* (*coll.*) hoarse.

охри́п|нуть, ну, нешь, *past* **~, ~ла** *pf.* (*of* ⇨**хри́пнуть**) to become hoarse.

охроме́|ть, ю *pf.* (*of* ⇨**хроме́ть**) (*coll.*) to go lame.

оху́лк|а, и *only in phrr.* **~и на́ руку не класть (положи́ть)** to have one's wits about one; **он ~и на́ руку не поло́жит** (*coll.*) he is no fool.

оцара́па|ть, ю *pf.* (*of* ⇨**цара́пать**) to scratch.

оцара́па|ться, юсь *pf.* to scratch o.s.

оцело́т, а *m.* (*zool.*) ocelot.

оце́нива|ть, ю *impf. of* ⇨**оцени́ть**

оцен|и́ть, ю́, ~ишь *pf.* (*of* ⇨**~ивать**) **1** (*определить цену чего-н.*) to estimate the value of, value; (*назначить цену чему-н.*) to price; (*определить ценность, значительность чего-н.*) to evaluate, appraise. **2** (*признать достоинства чего-н.*) to appreciate; **о. что-н. по досто́инству** to appreciate sth. at its true value.

оце́нк|а, и *f.* **1** (*имущества*) valuation; (*работы*) evaluation, appraisal; **о. обстано́вки** (*mil.*) estimate of the situation. **2** (*мнение о ценности*) appreciation; **дать настоя́щую ~у чему́-н.** to give sth. a proper appreciation. **3** (*отметка*) mark, grade.

оце́н|очный *adj. of* ⇨**~ка**

оце́нщик, а *m.* valuer.

оце́нщи|ца, цы *f. of* ⇨**~к**

оцепене́лый *adj.* dazed, benumbed.

оцепене́ни|е, я *nt.* stupor.

оцепене́|ть, ю *pf. of* ⇨**цепене́ть**

оцеп|и́ть, лю́, ~ишь *pf.* (*of* ⇨**~ля́ть**) to surround; to cordon off.

оцепле́ни|е, я *nt.* **1** (*действие*) surrounding; cordoning off. **2** (*люди*) cordon.

оцепля́|ть, ю *impf. of* ⇨**оцепи́ть**

оцинко́в|анный *p.p.p. of* ⇨**~а́ть** *and adj.* zinc-coated, galvanized.

оцинк|ова́ть, у́ю *pf.* (*of* ⇨**~о́вывать**) to (coat with) zinc, galvanize.

оцинко́выва|ть, ю *impf. of* ⇨**оцинкова́ть**

оча́г, а́ *m.* **1** hearth (*also fig.*); **ку́хонный о.** kitchen range; **дома́шний о.** (*fig.*) hearth, home. **2** (*fig.*) centre, seat; **о. войны́** seat of war; **о. землетрясе́ния** earthquake centre.

очарова́ни|е, я *nt.* charm, fascination.

очарова́тел|ьный (~ен, ~ьна) *adj.* charming, fascinating.

очар|ова́ть, у́ю *pf.* (*of* ⇨**~о́вывать**) to charm, fascinate.

очаро́выва|ть, ю *impf. of* ⇨**очарова́ть**

очеви́д|ец, ца *m.* eye-witness.

очеви́дно *adv.* obviously, evidently; **вы, о., не согла́сны** you obviously do not agree.

очеви́д|ный (~ен, ~на) *adj.* obvious, evident.

очелове́чива|ть(ся), ю(сь) *impf. of* ⇨**очелове́чить(ся)**

очелове́ч|ить, у, ишь *pf.* (*of* ⇨**~ивать**) to humanize.

очелове́ч|иться, усь, ишься *pf.* (*of* ⇨**~иваться**) to become human.

о́чень *adv.* (*при прилагательных и наречиях*) very; (*при глаголах*) very much.

очерви́ве|ть, ет *pf. of* ⇨**черви́веть**

очередни́к, а́ *m.* person on the waiting list (*esp. for a flat*).

очередни́|ца, цы *f. of* ⇨**~к**

очередн|о́й *adj.* **1** next; next in turn; **о. вопро́с** the next question; **о. вы́пуск** latest issue (*of a journal, etc.*); **~а́я зада́ча** the immediate task. **2** usual; regular; **~ы́е неприя́тности** the usual trouble; **о. о́тпуск** regular holidays.

очерёдност|ь, и *f.* prescribed order.

о́черед|ь, и, *pl.* **~и, ~е́й** *f.* **1** turn; **пропусти́ть свою́ о.** to miss one's turn; **о. за ва́ми** it is your turn; **в свою́ о.** in one's turn; **на ~и** next (in turn); **по ~и** in turn, in order, in rotation; **в пе́рвую о.** in the first place, in the first instance; **в поря́дке ~и** when one's turn comes. **2** (*ряд*) queue (*Br.*), line (*US*); **стоя́ть в ~и** (**за**+*i.*) to queue (for) (*Br.*), stand in line (for) (*US*). **3** (*mil.*): (**пулемётная**) **о.** burst; **батаре́йная о.** (battery) salvo.

о́черк, а *m.* essay, sketch, study; (*контур*) outline; **~и ру́сской исто́рии** studies in Russian history.

очёркива|ть, ю *impf. of* ⇨**очеркну́ть**

очерки́ст, а *m.* essayist.

очерк|ну́ть, ну́, нёшь *pf.* (*of* ⇨**~ивать**) to place a circle round.

очерн|и́ть, ю́, и́шь *pf. of* ⇨**черни́ть** 2

очерстве́лый *adj.* hardened, callous.

очерстве́|ть, ю *pf. of* ⇨**черстве́ть** 2

очерта́ни|е, я *nt.* outline.

очер|ти́ть, чу́, ~тишь *pf.* (*of* ⇨**~чивать**) to outline; **~тя́ го́лову** (*coll.*) without thinking, headlong.

очёрчива|ть, ю *impf. of* ⇨**очерти́ть**

очёс, а *m.* (*collect.*) = **очёски**

оче|са́ть, шу́, ~шешь *pf.* (*of* ⇨**~сывать**) to comb out.

очёс|ки, ков *pl.* (*sg.* **~ок, ~ка** *m.*) combings; flocks; **льняны́е о.** flax tow.

очёсыва|ть, ю *impf. of* ⇨**очеса́ть**

очёчник, а *m.* spectacle case (*Br.*), eyeglass case (*US*).

о́чи *pl. of* ⇨**о́ко**

очи́нива|ть, ю *impf. of* ⇨**очини́ть**

очин|и́ть, ю́, ~ишь *pf.* (*of*

⇨∼ивать *and* **чини́ть²**) to sharpen, point.

очи́нк|а, и *f.* sharpening; **маши́нка для ∼и карандаше́й** pencil-sharpener.

очисти́тельн|ый *adj.* purifying, cleansing; **о. заво́д** refinery; **∼ое сре́дство** cleanser, detergent.

очи́|стить, щу, стишь *pf.* (*of* **⇨∼ща́ть**) **1** (*патрон, тарелку, обувь*) to clean; (*воду, спирт*) to purify; (*совесть*) to salve, clear; (*душу*) to cleanse, purify. **2** (**от**+*g.*) (*стол*) to clear (of); to free; **о. почто́вый я́щик** to clear a letter-box; **о. кише́чник** to open bowels. **3** (*картошку, яблоко*) to peel. **4** (*coll.*) (*обкрасть*) to clean out.

очи́|ститься, щусь, стишься *pf.* (*of* **⇨∼ща́ться**) (**от**+*g.*) to become clear (of).

очи́стк|а, и *f.* **1** (*обуви*) cleaning; (*души*) cleansing, purification; (*воды*) purification; (*овощей*) peeling; **для ∼и со́вести** (*coll.*) to salve one's conscience. **2** (**от**+*g.*) clearing, clearance (of); freeing (of); (*mil.*) mopping-up.

очи́стк|и, ов *no sg.* peelings.

очища́|ть(ся), ю(сь) *impf. of* **⇨очи́стить(ся)**

очище́ни|е, я *nt.* cleansing; purification.

очи́|щенный *p.p.p. of* **⇨∼стить;** *as n.* **∼щенная, ∼щенной** *f.* (*coll.*) vodka.

очка́рик, а *m.* (*coll.*) person who wears glasses.

очк|и́, о́в *no sg.* glasses, spectacles (*Br.*), eyeglasses (*US*); (*защитные*) goggles.

очк|о́¹, а́, *pl.* **∼и́, ∼о́в** *nt.* **1** (*на картах или кости*) pip. **2** (*sport*) point; **дать де́сять/сто ∼о́в вперёд (кому́-н.)** to be ten/a hundred times better (than s.o.); to surpass. **3** (*отверстие*) hole; **смотрово́е о.** peep-hole.

очк|о́², а́ *nt.*: **втере́ть кому́-н. ∼и́** (*coll.*) to pull the wool over s.o.'s eyes.

очковтира́тельств|о, а *nt.* (*coll.*) deception.

очко́|вый¹ *adj. of* **⇨∼¹**; **∼вая систе́ма** points system (of scoring).

очко́в|ый² *adj.*: **∼ая змея́** cobra.

очн|у́ться, у́сь, ёшься *pf.* **1** (*после сна*) to wake. **2** (*после обморока*) to come to (o.s.), regain consciousness.

о́чн|ый *adj.* **1** (*opp.* **зао́чный**) internal (*instruction, student, etc., as opposed to* external, extra-mural). **2**: **∼ая ста́вка** (*leg.*) confrontation.

очу́вств|оваться, уюсь *pf.* (*obs.*) to come to (o.s.), regain consciousness.

очуме́лый *adj.* (*coll.*) mad, off one's head; **бежа́ть, как о.** to run like mad.

очуме́|ть, ю *pf.* (*coll.*) to go mad, go off one's head.

очут|и́ться, ∼ишься *pf.* to find o.s.; to come to be; **о. в нело́вком положе́нии** to find o.s. in an awkward position; **как вы здесь ∼и́лись?** how did you come to be here?

очу́ха|ться, юсь *pf.* (*coll.*) to come to, regain consciousness.

ошале́лый *adj.* (*coll.*) crazy, crazed.

ошале́|ть, ю *pf. of* **⇨шале́ть**

ошара́шива|ть, ю *impf. of* **⇨ошара́шить**

ошара́ш|ить, у, ишь *pf.* (*of* **⇨∼ивать**) (*coll.*) to strike dumb, flabbergast.

ошварт|ова́ть, у́ю *pf. of* **⇨швартова́ть**

оше́йник, а *m.* (*animal's*) collar; **соба́чий о.** dog-collar.

ошеломи́тел|ьный (∼ен, ∼ьна) *adj.* stunning.

ошелом|и́ть, лю́, и́шь *pf.* (*of* **⇨∼ля́ть**) to stun.

ошеломле́ни|е, я *nt.* stupefaction.

ошеломля́|ть, ю *impf. of* **⇨ошеломи́ть; ∼ющий** stunning.

ошельм|ова́ть, у́ю *pf. of* **⇨шельмова́ть**

ошиб|а́ться, а́юсь *impf. of* **⇨∼и́ться**

ошиб|и́ться, у́сь, ёшься, *past* **∼ся, ∼лась** *pf.* (*of* **⇨∼а́ться**) to be mistaken, make a mistake, make mistakes.

оши́бк|а, и *f.* mistake; error; **по ∼е** by mistake.

оши́боч|ный (∼ен, ∼на) *adj.* erroneous, mistaken.

ошива́|ться, юсь *impf.* (*coll.*) to hang about.

оши́ка|ть, ю *pf.* (*of* **⇨ши́кать** 2) (*coll.*) to hiss off the stage.

ошмёт|ки, ков *pl.* (*sg.* **∼ок, ∼ка** *m.*) (*coll.*) worn-out shoes; rags.

ошпа́рива|ть, ю *impf. of* **⇨ошпа́рить**

ошпа́р|ить, ю, ишь *pf.* (*of* **⇨∼ивать, шпа́рить** 1) to scald.

оштраф|ова́ть, у́ю *pf. of* **⇨штрафова́ть**

оштукату́р|ить, ю, ишь *pf. of* **⇨штукату́рить**

ощен|и́ться, и́тся *pf. of* **⇨щени́ться**

ощe'рива|ть(ся), ю(сь) *impf. of* **⇨ощe'рить(ся)**

ощe'р|ить, ю, ишь *pf. of* **⇨щe'рить**

ощe'р|иться, юсь, ишься *pf. of* **⇨щe'риться**

ощети́нива|ться, юсь *impf. of* **⇨ощети́ниться**

ощети́н|иться, юсь, ишься *pf.* (*of* **⇨∼иваться** *and* **щети́ниться**) to bristle (*also fig.*).

ощип|а́ть, лю́, ∼лешь *pf.* (*of* **⇨щипа́ть** 4 *and* **∼ывать**) to pluck.

ощи́пыва|ть, ю *impf. of* **⇨ощипа́ть**

ощу́п|ать, аю *pf.* (*of* **⇨∼ывать**) to feel.

ощу́пыва|ть, ю *impf. of* **⇨ощу́пать**

о́щуп|ь, и *f.*: **на о.** to the touch; by touch; **идти́ на о.** to grope one's way.

о́щупью *adv.* **1** by groping one's way; by touch; **иска́ть о.** to grope for; **пробра́ться о.** to grope one's way. **2** (*fig.*) blindly.

ощут|и́мый (∼и́м, ∼и́ма) *adj.* = **∼и́тельный**

ощути́тел|ьный (∼ен, ∼ьна) *adj.* **1** (*запах, похолодание*) perceptible, noticeable. **2** (*fig.*) (*недостатки, расходы*) appreciable.

ощу|ти́ть, щу́, ти́шь *pf.* (*of* **⇨∼ща́ть**) to feel, sense; **о. го́лод** to feel hunger; **он ∼ти́л её отсу́тствие** he felt her absence.

ощуща́|ть, ю *impf. of* **⇨ощути́ть**

ощуще́ни|е, я *nt.* **1** (*physiol.*) sensation. **2** (*страха, радости*) feeling, sense.

оягн|и́ться, и́тся *pf. of* **⇨ягни́ться**

О

П п

па *nt. indecl.* (*dance*) step.

паб, а *m.* pub.

пабли́сити *nt. indecl.* publicity.

па́в|а, ы *f.* peahen.

павиа́н, а *m.* baboon.

павильо́н, а *m.* **1** pavilion. **2** (*cin.*) film studio.

павли́н, а *m.* peacock.

павли́н|ий *adj. of* ⇒~

па́вод|ок, ка *m.* flood (*esp. resulting from melting of snow*).

пагина́ци|я, и *f.* pagination.

па́год|а, ы *f.* pagoda.

па́губ|а, ы *f.* ruin, destruction.

па́губ|ный (~ен, ~на) *adj.* (*влияние*) pernicious; (*последствия*) fatal.

па́дал|ь, и *f.* (*usu. collect.*) carrion.

па́дан|ец, ца *m.* windfall, faller (*fallen fruit*).

па́да|ть, ю *impf.* **1** (*pf.* **пасть** *and* **упа́сть**) to fall; (*о настроении*) to sink; (*о нравах*) to decline; **баро́метр ~л** the barometer was falling; **~ет снег** it is snowing; **се́рдце у меня́ ~ло** my spirits were sinking; **п. ду́хом** to lose heart; **п. в о́бморок** to faint; **п. от уста́лости** to be ready to drop.
2 (*pf.* **пасть**) (*fig.*; **на**+*a.*) to fall (on, to); **отве́тственность ~ет на вас** the responsibility falls on you.
3 (*impf. only*) (*ling.*) (*об ударении*) to fall, be; **ударе́ние ~ет на пе́рвый слог** the stress is on the first syllable.
4 (*impf. only*) (*о волосах, зубах*) to fall out, drop out.
5 (*pf.* **пасть**) (*о животных*) to die.

па́да|ющий *pres. part. of* ⇒**~ть** *and adj.* (*phys.*) incident; **~ющие звёзды** shooting stars.

паде́ж, а́ *m.* (*gram.*) case.

падёж, а́ *m.* murrain, cattle plague.

паде́ж|ный *adj. of* ⇒~; **~ное оконча́ние** case ending.

паде́ни|е, я *nt.* **1** fall; (*настроения*) sinking; (*нравов*) decline; **мора́льное п.** degradation. **2** (*phys.*) incidence; **у́гол ~я** angle of incidence.

па́д|кий (~ок, ~ка) *adj.* (**на**+*a. or* **до**+*g.*) having a weakness (for); susceptible (to); **п. на де́ньги** mercenary; **он ~ок до сла́дкого** he has a sweet tooth.

па́дуб, а *m.* holly.

паду́ч|ий *adj.* (*obs.*) falling; **~ая звезда́** shooting star; **~ая (боле́знь)** epilepsy.

па́дчериц|а, ы *f.* step-daughter.

паево́й *adj. of* ⇒**пай**[1]; **п. взнос** share.

па|ёк, йка́ *m.* ration.

паж, а́ *m.* (*hist.*) page.

паз, а, о ~е, в ~у́, *pl.* **~ы, ~о́в** *m.* (*tech.*) groove.

па́зух|а, и *f.* **1** bosom; **за ~ой** in one's bosom; **держа́ть ка́мень за ~ой** (*fig.*) to bear a grudge; **жить как у Христа́ за ~ой** to live in clover. **2** (*anat.*) sinus. **3** (*bot.*) axil.

па́ин|ька, ьки, *g. pl.* **~ек** *c.g.* (*coll.*) good child; **будь п.!** be a good boy (girl)!; **п.-ма́льчик** good (little) boy.

па|й[1]**, я,** *pl.* **~и́, ~ёв** *m.* share; **това́рищество на ~я́х** joint-stock company; **на ~я́х** (*fig., coll.*) on an equal footing, going shares.

пай-...[2] *c.g. indecl.* (*coll.*) good child; **п.-ма́льчик** good (little) boy.

па́йк|а, и *f.* solder(ing).

пайко́вый *adj. of* ⇒**паёк;** rationed.

па́йщик, а *m.* shareholder.

пак, а *no pl., m.* pack-ice.

пакга́уз, а *m.* warehouse; **тамо́женный п.** bonded warehouse.

паке́т, а *m.* **1** (*свёрток*) parcel, package. **2** (*письмо*) (official) letter. **3** (*мешок*) (paper) bag. **4** (*comput.*) package.

Пакиста́н, а *m.* Pakistan.

пакиста́н|ец, ца *m.* Pakistani.

пакиста́н|ка, ки *f. of* ⇒**~ец**

пакиста́нский *adj.* Pakistani.

па́кл|я, и *f.* tow; oakum.

пак|ова́ть, у́ю *impf.* (*of* ⇒**у~**) to pack.

па́ко|стить, щу, стишь *impf.* (*coll.*) **1** (*pf.* **за~** *and* **на~**) (*пачкать*) to soil, dirty. **2** (*pf.* **ис~**) (*портить*) to spoil, mess up. **3** (*pf.* **на~**) (+*d.*) (*делать пакости*) to play dirty tricks (on).

па́кост|ный (~ен, ~на) *adj.* nasty.

па́кост|ь, и *f.* **1** (*о поступке*) dirty trick; **де́лать ~и** (+*d.*) to play dirty tricks (on). **2** (*дрянь*) filth. **3** (*о слове*) obscenity, filthy word.

пакт, а *m.* pact; **п. о ненападе́нии** non-aggression pact.

паланти́н, а *m.* fur tippet, stole.

пала́т|а, ы *f.* **1** (*pl. only; obs.*) (*дворец*) palace. **2** (*obs.*) (*комната*) chamber, hall; **Оруже́йная п.** Armoury Museum (*in Moscow*); **у него́ ума́ п.** (*coll.*) he is as wise as Solomon. **3** (*в больнице*) ward. **4** (*pol.*) chamber, house; **ве́рхняя, ни́жняя п.** Upper, Lower Chamber; **п. ло́рдов** House of Lords; **п. о́бщин** House of Commons. **5** (*название некоторых государственных учреждений*): **Кни́жная п.** Book Chamber (*bibliographical centre in Moscow*); **Торго́вая п.** Chamber of Commerce.

палатализа́ци|я, и *f.* (*ling.*) palatalization.

палатализ|ова́ть, у́ю *impf. and pf.* (*ling.*) to palatalize.

палата́льный *adj.* (*ling.*) palatal.

пала́тк|а, и *f.* **1** tent; (*большая*) marquee; **в ~ах** under canvas. **2** (*ларёк*) stall, booth.

пала́т|ный *adj. of* ⇒**~а; ~ная сестра́** ward sister.

пала́ч, а́ *m.* executioner; (*fig.*) butcher.

пала́ш, а́ *m.* broadsword.

па́левый *adj.* straw-coloured (*Br.*), -colored (*US*), pale yellow.

палёны|й *adj.* singed, scorched; **па́хнет ~м** there is a smell of burning.

палео́граф, а *m.* palaeographer (*Br.*), paleographer (*US*).

палеографи́ческий *adj.* palaeographic (*Br.*), paleographic (*US*).

палеогра́фи|я, и *f.* palaeography (*Br.*), paleography (*US*).

палеозо́йский *adj.* (*geol.*) Palaeozoic (*Br.*), Paleozoic (*US*).

палеоли́т, а *m.* (*archaeol.*) palaeolithic period (*Br.*), paleolithic period (*US*).

палеолити́ческий *adj.* (*archaeol.*) palaeolithic (*Br.*), paleolithic (*US*).

палеонтóлог, а *m.* palaeontologist (*Br.*), paleontologist (*US*).

палеонтологи́ческий *adj.* palaeontological (*Br.*), paleontological (*US*).

палеонтолóги|я, и *f.* palaeontology (*Br.*), paleontology (*US*).

Палести́н|а, ы *f.* Palestine.

палести́н|ец, ца *m.* Palestinian.

палести́н|ка, ки *f. of* ⇨**~ец**

палести́нский *adj.* Palestinian.

пáлех, а *m.* lacquerwork.

пáлехский *adj.* (made in) Palekh (*place famed for its lacquerwork*).

пáл|ец, ьца *m.* **1** finger; **п. ноги́** toe; **большóй п.** thumb; **указáтельный п.** forefinger, index (finger); **срéдний п.** middle finger, third finger, **безымя́нный п.** fourth finger, ring-finger; (*fig.*): **п. о п. не удáрить, ~ьцем не шевельнýть** (*coll.*) to not lift a finger; **емý ~ьца в рот не клади́** (*coll.*) he is not to be trusted, he needs to be watched; **~ьцы ломáть** to tear one's hair; **смотрéть сквозь ~ьцы на что-н.** (*coll.*) to shut one's eyes to sth.; **знать что-н. как свой пять ~ьцев** (*coll.*) to know sth. like the back of one's hand; **обвести́ когó-н. вокрýг ~ьца** (*coll.*) to twist s.o. round one's (little) finger; **вы́сосать из ~ьца** (*coll.*) to fabricate, concoct; **он ~ьцем никогó не трóнет** he wouldn't hurt a fly; **попáсть ~ьцем в нéбо** (*coll.*) to be wide of the mark.
2 (*tech.*) pin, peg; cam, cog, tooth.

палимпсéст, а *m.* palimpsest.

палиндрóм, а *m.* palindrome.

палисáд, а *m.* **1** paling. **2** (*mil.*) palisade. **3** = **палисáдник**

палисáдник, а *m.* small front garden.

палисáндр, а *m.* rosewood.

палисáндр|овый *adj. of* ⇨**~**

пали́тр|а, ы *f.* palette.

пал|и́ть¹**, ю́, и́шь** *impf.* **1** (*pf.* **с~**) to burn, scorch. **2** (*pf.* **о~**) to singe.

пал|и́ть²**, ю́, и́шь** *impf.* (*coll.*) (*стрелять*) to fire (*from gun*); **~и́!** (*word of command*) fire!

пáлиц|а, ы *f.* club, cudgel.

пáлк|а, и *f.* stick; **встáвить комý-н. ~и в колёса** to put a spoke in s.o.'s wheel; **из-под ~и** under the lash; **п. о двух концáх** two-edged weapon; **э́то п. о двух концáх** it cuts both ways.

паллиати́в, а *m.* palliative.

паллиати́вный *adj.* palliative.

палóмник, а *m.* pilgrim (*also fig.*).

палóмнича|ть, ю *impf.* to go on (a) pilgrimage.

палóмничеств|о, а *nt.* pilgrimage (*also fig.*).

пáлочк|а, и *f.* **1** *dim. of* ⇨**пáлка; барабáнная п.** drumstick; **волшéбная п.** magic wand; **дирижёрская п.** conductor's baton; **пахýчая п.** joss-stick; **ры́бная п.** fish finger. **2** (*med.*) bacillus.

пáл|очный *adj. of* ⇨**~ка; ~очная дисципли́на** discipline of the rod.

пáлтус, а *m.* halibut, turbot.

пáлуб|а, ы *f.* deck; **полётная п.** flight deck.

пáлуб|ный *adj. of* ⇨**~а; п. груз** deck cargo.

пáлый *adj.* **1** (*dial.*) (*скот*) dead. **2** (*coll.*) (*листья*) fallen.

пальб|á, ы́ *f.* firing; **пýшечная п.** cannonade.

пáльм|а, ы *f.* palm(-tree).

пáльм|овый *adj. of* ⇨**~а; ~овое дéрево** boxwood.

пал|ьнýть, ьнý, ьнёшь *inst. pf.* (*of* ⇨**~и́ть**²) to fire a shot; to discharge a volley.

пальти́ш|ко, ка, *pl.* **~ки, ~ек** *nt.* (*coll., pej.*) *dim. of* ⇨**пальтó**

пальтó *nt. indecl.* (over)coat.

пальцеви́д|ный (~ен, ~на) *adj.* finger-shaped.

пáльчик, а *m. dim. of* ⇨**пáлец**

пал|я́щий *pres. part. act. of* ⇨**~и́ть**¹ *and adj.* burning, scorching.

пампáс|овый *adj. of* ⇨**~ы; ~овая травá** pampas grass.

пампáс|ы, ов *no sg.* (*geog.*) pampas.

памфлéт, а *m.* lampoon.

памфлети́ст, а *m.* lampoonist.

пáмятк|а, и *f.* (list of) instructions, guidelines; **п. по ухóду** care-label.

пáмятлив|ый (~, ~а) *adj.* (*coll.*) having a good memory.

пáмятник, а *m.* monument; (*на могиле*) tombstone; (*статуя*) statue; (*археологический*) relic; **~и пи́сьменности** ancient manuscripts.

пáмят|ный (~ен, ~на) *adj.* **1** (*незабываемый*) memorable. **2** (*для напоминания*) serving to assist the memory; **~ная доскá** memorial plate, plaque; **~ная кни́жка** notebook, memorandum book.

пáмят|овать, ую *impf.* (*obs.*; **о** + *p.*) to remember.

пáмят|ь, и *f.* **1** (*also comput.*) memory; **у негó кýриная п.** he has a memory like a sieve; **на моéй ~и** within my memory; **говори́ть на п.** to speak from memory; **вдруг мне пришлó на п., что…** suddenly I remembered that …; **по ~и** from memory; **по стáрой ~и** from force of habit.
2 (*воспоминание*) memory, recollection, remembrance; **вéчная п. емý!** may his memory live for ever!; **остáвить по себé дóбрую п.** to leave fond memories of o.s.; **в п.** (+*g.*) in memory (of); **подари́ть на п.** to give as a keepsake.
3 (*сознание*) mind, consciousness; **быть без ~и** to be unconscious; **быть от когó-н. без ~и** (*coll.*) to be head over heels in love with s.o., be crazy about s.o.
4 (*eccl.*; +*g.*) commemoration of death (of), feast (of)

пан, а, *pl.* **~ы́** *m.* (*hist.*) Polish landowner; **ли́бо п., ли́бо пропáл** (*prov.*) all or nothing.

пан… *comb. form* pan-.

панаги́|я, и *f.* (*eccl.*) panagia (*image worn round neck by Orthodox bishops*).

Панáм|а, ы *f.* Panama.

панáм|а, ы *f.* panama (hat).

панамерикáнский *adj.* Pan-American.

панáмский *adj.* Panamanian.

панацé|я, и *f.* panacea; **п. от всех зол** (*fig.*) universal panacea.

панбáрхат, а *m.* panne (*dress material*).

пáнд|а, ы *f.* panda.

панеги́рик, а *m.* panegyric, eulogy.

панегири́ст, а *m.* panegyrist, eulogist.

панегири́ческий *adj.* panegyrical, eulogistic.

панéл|ь, и *f.* **1** (*тротуар*) pavement (*Br.*), sidewalk (*US*). **2** (*обшивка*) panel, panelling (*Br.*), paneling (*US*), wainscot(ing). **3**: **п. прибóров** instrument panel; dashboard.

панéль|ный *adj. of* ⇨**~; ~ная обши́вка** panelling (*Br.*), paneling (*US*), wainscoting.

панибрáтский *adj.* (*coll.*) (over-) familiar.

панибрáтств|о, а *nt.* (*coll.*) (undue) familiarity.

пáник|а, и *f.* panic; **впасть в ~у** to become panic-stricken, panic.

паникади́л|о, а *nt.* (*eccl.*) chandelier.

паникёр, а *m.* panic-monger, scaremonger, alarmist.

паникёр|ский *adj. of* ⇨**~**

паникёрств|о, а *nt.* alarmism.

паникёрств|овать, ую *impf.* (*no pf.*) (*coll.*) to panic.

паник|овáть, ýю *impf.* (*no pf.*) (*coll.*) to panic.

панирóвочн|ый *adj.*: **~ые сухари́** (*cul.*) breadcrumbs.

панихи́д|а, ы *f.* funeral service; requiem; **граждáнская п.** civil funeral.

панихи́д|ный *adj. of* ⇨**~а;** (*fig.*) funereal.

пани́ческий *adj.* **1** (*проникнутый паникой*) panic-stricken; **п. страх** utter terror. **2** (*выражающий панику*) alarming. **3** (*coll.*) (*легко поддающийся панике*) panicky.

панк, а *m.* (*also as indecl. adj.*) punk.

панк… *comb. form* punk-.

панк|овáть, ýю *impf.* (*sl.*) to be a punk, live like a punk.

пáнков|ский *adj.* = **~ый**

пáнк|овый *adj. of* ⇨**~**

панкреати́ческий *adj.* (*anat.*) pancreatic.

паннó *nt. indecl.* panel.

панóптикум, а *m.* waxworks.

панорáм|а, ы *f.* panorama.

панорáмный *adj.* panoramic.

пансиóн, а *m.* **1** (*hist.*) (*школа*) boarding school. **2** (*obs.*) (*гостиница*) boarding-house. **3** (*полное содержание*) (full) board and lodging; **кóмната с ~ом** room and board; **жить на ~е** to have full board and lodging, live en pension.

пансионáт, а *m.* boarding-house, guest-house.

пансионéр, а *m.* **1** (*hist.*) (*в школе*) boarder. **2** (*obs.*) (*в гостинице*) guest.

пансионéр|ка, ки *f. of* ⇨**~**

пáн|ский *adj. of* ⇨**~**

панслави́зм, а *m.* (*hist.*) Pan-Slavism.

П

пантало́н|ы, ~ *no sg.* (*obs.*) **1** (*брюки*) trousers (*Br.*), pants (*US*). **2** (*женские трусы*) drawers, knickers (*Br.*).

пантáлы́к, а (у) *m.* (*coll.*) *only in phrr.* **сбить с ~у** to confuse; **сби́ться с ~у** to become confused, be at one's wit's end.

пантеи́зм, а *m.* pantheism.

пантеи́ст, а *m.* pantheist.

пантеисти́ческий *adj.* pantheistic.

пантео́н, а *m.* pantheon.

панте́р|а, ы *f.* panther.

пантó граф, а *m.* (*tech.*) pantograph.

пантоми́м|а, ы *f.* mime.

пантомими́ческий *adj.* pantomimic.

пантоми́м|ный *adj.* = **~и́ческий**

па́нт|ы, ов *no sg.* antlers of young Siberian stag (*as used in preparation of medicament*).

па́нцирн|ый *adj.* **1** armour-clad (*Br.*), armor-clad (*US*). **2** (*zool.*) testaceous.

па́нцир|ь, я *m.* **1** (*hist.*) coat of mail, armour (*Br.*), armor (*US*). **2** (*zool.*) shell, test.

панъевропе́йский *adj.* Pan-European.

па́п|а[1], ы *m.* (*coll.*) dad, daddy, papa (*US*).

па́п|а[2], ы *m.*: **п. ри́мский** (the) Pope.

папа́й|я, и *f.* papaya, paw-paw.

папара́цци *pl. indecl.* paparazzi.

папа́х|а, и *f.* papakha (*Caucasian fur hat*).

папа́ш|а, и *m.* (*coll.*) = **па́па**

па́перт|ь, и *f.* church-porch, parvis.

папи́зм, а *m.* papism.

папилько́тк|а, и *f.* paper or rag for curling the hair.

папиро́с|а, ы *f.* cigarette (*of Russian type, with cardboard mouthpiece*).

папиро́с|ный *adj. of* **⇒~а; ~ная бума́га** (*для папирос*) cigarette paper; (*тонкая бумага*) tissue paper.

папи́рус, а *m.* papyrus.

папи́рус|ный *adj. of* **⇒~**

папи́ст, а *m.* papist.

па́пк|а, и *f.* folder, file.

па́поротник, а *m.* fern.

па́прик|а, и *f.* paprika.

па́пский *adj.* papal.

па́пств|о, а *nt.* papacy.

Па́пуа-Но́вая Гвине́я, -Но́вой Гвине́и *f.* Papua New Guinea.

папуа́с, а *m.* Papua New Guinean.

папуа́с|ка, ки *f. of* **⇒~**

папуа́сский *adj.* Papua New Guinean.

папье́-маше́ *nt. indecl.* papier-mâché.

пар[1], а, о ~е, в ~у́, *pl.* **~ы** *m.* **1** steam; **стоя́ть под ~а́ми** to be under steam, have steam up; **на всех ~а́х** (*fig.*) full steam ahead, at full speed; **с лёгким па́ром!** greeting to s.o. coming out of the shower/bath. **2** (*видимое испарение*) vapour (*Br.*), vapor (*US*). **3** (*pl.*) (*спирта, бензина*) fumes.

пар[2], а, *pl.* **~ы́** *m.* (*agric.*) fallow; **находи́ться под ~ом** to lie fallow.

па́р|а, ы *f.* **1** (*сапог, чулок, ножниц*) pair; (*два предмета, двое людей*) couple; **супру́жеская п.** married couple; **ходи́ть ~ами** to walk in couples; **е́хать на ~е** to drive a pair (*of horses*); **на ~у мину́т** for a couple of minutes; **п. пустяко́в!** it's child's play!; **на ~у слов** for a few words; **она́ ему́ не п.** she is no match for him; **два сапога́ п.** (*coll., pej.*) they make a pair. **2** (*костюм*) suit (*of clothes*). **3** (*coll.*) (*отметка*) a 'two' (*out of five*).

пара́бол|а[1], ы *f.* (*math.*) parabola.

пара́бол|а[2], ы *f.* (*притча*) parable.

параболи́ческий[1] *adj.* (*math.*) parabolic.

параболи́ческий[2] *adj.* parabolical.

парагва́|ец, йца *m.* Paraguayan.

Парагва́|й, я *m.* Paraguay.

парагва́|йка, йки *f. of* **⇒~ец**

парагва́йский *adj.* Paraguayan.

пара́граф, а *m.* paragraph.

пара́д, а *m.* **1** (*шествие*) parade; (*mil.*) review; **возду́шный п.** air display; fly-past. **2** (*coll., joc.*) (*нарядная одежда*) ceremonial get-up; **быть при по́лном ~е** to be in one's best bib and tucker.

паради́гм|а, ы *f.* paradigm.

пара́дно-выходн|о́й *adj.*: **~а́я фо́рма вне стро́я** (*mil.*) ceremonial walking-out dress.

пара́дност|ь, и *f.* magnificence; ostentation.

пара́д|ный (~ен, ~на) *adj.* **1** (*торжественный*) ceremonial; **п. костю́м** ceremonial dress; **~ная фо́рма** full dress (uniform). **2** (*пышный*) gala; **п. спекта́кль** gala night. **3** (*главный*) main, front; **~ная дверь** front door; **п. подъе́зд** main entrance; *as n.* **~ное, ~ного** *nt. and* **~ная, ~ной** *f.* front door.

парадо́кс, а *m.* paradox.

парадокса́л|ьный (~ен, ~ьна) *adj.* paradoxical.

парази́т, а *m.* (*biol. and fig.*) parasite.

паразити́зм, а *m.* (*biol. and fig.*) parasitism.

паразити́р|овать, ую *impf.* to live as a parasite.

паразити́ческий *adj.* (*biol. and fig.*) parasitic(al).

парази́тный *adj.* (*biol.*) parasitic.

парализо́ванност|ь, и *f.* paralysis.

парализо́в|анный *p.p.p. of* **⇒~а́ть** *and adj.* paralysed (*also fig.*).

парализ|ова́ть, у́ю *impf. and pf.* to paralyse (*also fig.*).

парали́тик, а *m.* paralytic.

паралити́ческий *adj.* paralytic.

парали́ч, а́ *m.* paralysis; **он разби́т ~о́м** he is completely paralysed.

парали́чный *adj.* paralytic; **п. больно́й** paralytic.

паралла́кс, а *m.* (*astron.*) parallax.

параллелепи́пед, а *m.* (*math.*) parallelepiped.

параллели́зм, а *m.* parallelism.

параллелогра́мм, а *m.* (*math.*) parallelogram.

паралле́л|ь, и *f.* parallel; **провести́ п.** (**ме́жду** + *i.*) to draw a parallel (between).

паралле́льно *adv.* (**c** + *i.*) **1** parallel (with). **2** (*одновременно*) simultaneously (with), at the same time (as).

паралле́л|ьный (~ен, ~ьна) *adj.* parallel; **~ьные бру́сья** (*sport*) parallel bars; **~ьная медици́на** alternative *or* complementary medicine; **п. телефо́н** shared line, party line.

пара́метр, а *m.* parameter.

парандж|а́, и́ *f.* yashmak.

парано́ик, а *m.* (*med.*) paranoiac.

параноти́ческий *adj.* (*med.*) paranoid; paranoiac.

парано́й|я, и *f.* (*med.*) paranoia.

паранорма́льный *adj.* paranormal.

парапе́т, а *m.* parapet.

парапсихоло́ги|я, и *f.* parapsychology.

парати́ф, а *m.* paratyphoid.

парафи́н, а *m.* paraffin (wax).

парафи́н|овый *adj. of* **⇒~**

парафи́р|овать, ую *impf. and pf.* (*dipl.*) to initial.

пара́ш|а, и *f.* (*prison sl.*) **1** (*горшок*) chamber pot. **2** (*ложь*) lie.

парашю́т, а *m.* parachute; **на ~е** by parachute; **прыжо́к с ~ом** parachute jump; **пры́гать с ~ом** to parachute.

парашюти́зм, а *m.* parachute jumping (*as sport*); sky-diving.

парашюти́р|овать, ую *impf.* (*of* **⇒с~**) (*aeron.*) to pancake.

парашюти́ст, а *m.* parachute jumper; sky-diver; **п.-деса́нтник** paratrooper.

парашю́т|ный *adj. of* **⇒~; ~но-деса́нтные войска́** paratroops; **п. спорт** parachute jumping; sky-diving.

пардо́н *int.* (I beg your) pardon.

парен|ёк, ька́ *m.* young boy, young chap.

па́рени|е, я *nt.* (*белья*) steaming; (*веником*) beating; (*cul.*) stewing.

паре́ни|е, я *nt.* (*в небе*) floating, hovering.

па́рен|ый *adj.* stewed; **деше́вле ~ой ре́пы** (*coll.*) dirt-cheap; **про́ще ~ой ре́пы** (*coll.*) very easy, a piece of cake.

па́р|ень, ня, *pl.* **~ни, ~не́й** *m.* **1** (*юноша*) boy, lad. **2** (*coll.*) (*мужчина*) chap (*Br.*), fellow, guy; **свой п.** a good guy.

пари́ *nt. indecl.* bet; **держа́ть п., идти́ на п.** to bet, lay a bet; **п. держу́, что...** I bet that ...

Пари́ж, а *m.* Paris.

парижа́н|ин, ина, *pl.* **~е, ~** *m.* Parisian.

парижа́н|ка, ки *f. of* **⇒~ин;** Parisienne.

пари́жский *adj.* Parisian.

пари́к, а́ *m.* wig.

парикма́хер, а *m.* hairdresser; (*мужской*) barber.

парикма́херск|ая, ой *f.* hairdresser's; hair-dressing salon; (*мужская*) barber's (shop).

пари́лк|а, и *f.* (*coll.*) = **пари́льня**

пари́л|ьня, ьни, *g. pl.* **~ен** *f.* steam-room (*in baths*).

пари́р|овать, ую *impf. and pf.* (*pf. also* **от~**) to parry, counter.

паритéт, а *m.* parity.

паритéт|ный *adj. of* ⇒~; **на ~ных началах (с**+*i.*) on a par (with), on an equal footing (with).

пáр|ить, ю, ишь *impf.* (*no pf.*) **1** (*бельё*) to steam. **2** (*в бане*) to beat about with a besom. **3** (*cul.*) to stew. **4** (*impers.*): **~ит** it is sultry.

пар|и́ть, ю́, и́шь *impf.* (*no pf.*) to soar, swoop, hover; **п. в облака́х** (*fig.*) to live in the clouds.

пáр|иться, юсь, ишься *impf.* **1** (*pf.* **по~**) (*в бане*) to steam, sweat. **2** (*cul.*) to stew.

пáри|я, и, *g. pl.* **~й** *c.g.* pariah, outcast.

парк, а *m.* **1** (*сад*) park; **разбить п.** to lay out a park. **2** (*место стоянки*) yard, depot; (*mil.*) park, depot; **артиллери́йский п.** ordnance depot; **трамва́йный п.** tram depot. **3** (*подвижной состав*) fleet; stock; pool; **автомоби́льный п.** fleet of motor vehicles; **вагóнный п.** rolling-stock.

пáрк|а[1], **и** *f.* (*одежда*) parka.

пáрк|а[2], **и** *f.* (*coll.*) (*белья*) steaming.

паркéт, а *m.* parquet; parquetry.

паркéт|ный *adj. of* ⇒~; **п. пол** parquet floor.

паркéтчик, а *m.* specialist in laying parquet floors.

пáркинг, а *m.* car park.

паркова́ни|е, я *nt.* parking.

парк|ова́ть, у́ю *v.t. impf.* (*of* ⇒**запаркова́ть**) to park.

парк|ова́ться, у́юсь *v.i. impf.* (*of* ⇒**запаркова́ться**) to park.

паркóвк|а, и *f.* (*coll.*) parking.

паркóвочный *adj.*: **п. автома́т** *or* **счётчик** parking meter.

пáрк|овый *adj. of* ⇒~; **~овые культу́ры** park plants.

парла́мент, а *m.* parliament.

парламентари́зм, а *m.* parliamentarism.

парламентáри|й, я *m.* parliamentarian.

парламентáрный *adj.* parliamentarian.

парламентёр, а *m.* (*mil.*) envoy; bearer of a flag of truce.

парламентёр|ский *adj. of* ⇒~; **п. флаг** flag of truce.

парла́ментский *adj.* parliamentary; **п. закóн** Act of Parliament; **п. запрóс** interpellation.

парн|áя, óй *f.* = **пари́льня**

парни́к, á *m.* hotbed, polytunnel; (*из стекла*) greenhouse; **в ~é** under glass.

парник|óвый *adj. of* ⇒~; **~óвые растéния** hothouse plants; **п. эффéкт** greenhouse effect.

парни́шк|а, и *m.* (*coll.*) boy, lad.

парн|óй *adj.* **1** (*свежий*) fresh; **~óе молокó** milk fresh from the cow; **~óе мя́со** fresh meat. **2** (*coll.*) (*воздух*) steamy.

парнокопы́тн|ые, ~ых *pl.* (*sg.* **~ое, ~ого** *nt.*) (*zool.*) Artiodactyla, artiodactyls.

пáрн|ый *adj.* pair; forming a pair; twin; **п. носóк, п. сапóг,** *etc.*, pair, fellow (*other one of pair of socks, boots, etc.*); **~ая грéбля** sculling; **~ая игрá** (*в теннис, бадминтон*) doubles game; **~ое катáние** (*на коньках*) pair skating.

паровóз, а *m.* (steam-)engine, locomotive.

паровóз|ный *adj. of* ⇒~; **~ная бригáда** engine crew; **~ное депó** engine-shed.

паровозоремóнтный *adj.* engine-repair, locomotive-repair.

паров|óй[1] *adj.* **1** *adj. of* ⇒**пар**[1]; **~áя маши́на** steam-engine; **~áя прáчечная** steam laundry. **2** (*cul.*) steamed.

паровóй[2] *adj.* (*поле*) lying fallow.

парод|и́йный *adj. of* ⇒**~́ия**

пароди́р|овать, ую *impf. and pf.* to parody.

пароди́ст, а *m.* mimic, impressionist.

парóди|я, и *f.* **1** (*произведение*) parody. **2** (*скетч*) skit. **3** (**на**+*a.*) (*на справедливость*) travesty, caricature.

пароксизм, а *m.* paroxysm.

парóл|ь, я *m.* password.

парóм, а *m.* ferry(-boat); **перепрáвить на ~е** to ferry.

парóм|ный *adj. of* ⇒~

парóмщик, а *m.* ferryman.

парообрáзный *adj.* vaporous.

парообразовáни|е, я *nt.* (*phys., tech.*) steam-generation, vaporization.

парораспредели́тельн|ый *adj.*: **~ая корóбка** (*tech.*) steam-box.

паросилов|óй *adj.*: **~áя установка** (*tech.*) steam power plant.

парострýйный *adj.* steamjet.

пароход, а *m.* steamer, steamship; **колёсный п.** paddle-boat *or* steamer; **океáнский п.** ocean liner.

парохóд|ный *adj. of* ⇒~; **~ное óбщество** steamship company.

парохóдств|о, а *nt.* **1** (*судоходство*) navigation, shipping. **2** (*предприятие*) steamship-line.

парт... *comb. form, abbr. of* ***парти́йный***

пáрт|а, ы *f.* (school) desk; **сесть за ~у** (*fig.*) to become a student, begin one's studies.

партакти́в, а *m.* (*pol.*) party activists.

партбилéт, а *m.* (*pol.*) party (-membership) card.

партеногенéз, а *m.* (*zool.*) parthenogenesis.

партéр, а *m.* (*theatr.*) the stalls.

парти́|ец, йца *m.* party member.

партизáн, а, *g. pl.* ~ *m.* (*на войне*) partisan; (*против режима*) guerrilla.

партизáн|ить, ю, ишь *impf.* (*coll.*) to be a partisan, fight with the partisans.

партизáн|ский *adj.* **1** *adj. of* ⇒~; **~ская войнá** guerrilla warfare; **~ское движéние** the Resistance (movement) (*e.g. against Germany during World War II*); **п. отря́д** partisan detachment. **2** (*fig., pej.*) unplanned, haphazard.

партизáнств|о, а *nt.* guerrilla warfare.

партизáнщин|а, ы *f.* **1** guerrilla warfare. **2** (*fig., pej.*) unplanned work, haphazard work.

парти́йност|ь, и *f.* **1** (*следование духу партии*) party spirit. **2** (*принадлежность к партии*) party membership.

парти́йн|ый *adj.* (*pol.*) **1** party; **п. билéт** party-membership card; **п. стаж** length of party membership; **~ая ячéйка** party cell. **2** *as n.* **п., ~ого** *m.* party member.

партитýр|а, ы *f.* (*mus.*) score.

пáрти|я[1], **и** *f.* (*pol.*) party.

пáрти|я[2], **и** *f.* **1** (*группа лиц*) party, group. **2** (*в производстве*) batch; lot; (*груза*) consignment; (*отправленных товаров*) shipment. **3** (*sport*) game; set. **4** (*mus.*) part. **5** (*obs.*) (*брак*) (good) match (*marriage*); **сдéлать хорóшую ~ю** to make a good match.

партком, а *m.* party committee.

партнёр, а *m.* partner.

партнёрств|о, а *nt.* partnership; **войти́ в п. (с**+*i.*) to go into partnership (with).

партнёр|ша, ши *f.* (*coll.*) *of* ⇒~

партóрг, а *m.* (*abbr. of* ***парти́йный организáтор***) party organizer.

парторганизáци|я, и *f.* party organization.

партстáж, а *m.* length of party membership.

партсъéзд, а *m.* party congress.

пáрус, а, *pl.* **~á** *m.* sail; **идти́ под ~áми** to sail, be under sail; **подня́ть ~á, постáвить ~á** to make sail, set sail; **на всех ~áх** in full sail (*also fig.*).

паруси́н|а, ы *f.* canvas, sail-cloth.

паруси́новый *adj.* canvas.

пáрусник, а *m.* **1** (*судно*) sailing vessel. **2** (*спортсмен*) sailor.

пáрус|ный *adj. of* ⇒~; **п. спорт** sailing.

парфóрсн|ый *adj.*: **~ая ездá** circus riding.

парфюмéр, а *m.* perfumer.

парфюмéри|я, и *f.* (*промышленность*) perfumery; (*духи*) perfumes; (*косметика*) cosmetics; (*отдел духов*) perfume department; (*отдел косметики*) cosmetics department.

парфюмéр|ный *adj. of* ⇒**~ия**; **п. магази́н** (*только духи*) perfumery, perfumer's shop; (*косметика*) cosmetics shop; **~ная фáбрика** perfume factory.

парч|á, и́, *g. pl.* **~éй** *f.* brocade.

парч|óвый *adj. of* ⇒**~á**

парш|á, и́ *f.* mange; (*струпья*) scab.

парши́ве|ть, ю *impf.* (*of* ⇒**за~** *and* **о~**) to become mangy; to be covered with scabs.

парши́в|ец, ца *m.* (*coll.*) lousy fellow.

парши́в|ый (~, ~а) *adj.* **1** mangy; **~ая овцá** (*fig.*) black sheep. **2** (*coll.*) (*дрянной*) rotten, lousy.

пас[1], **а** *m.* (*cards*) pass; **объяви́ть п.** to pass; *as int.* **я п.** (I) pass; **в э́том дéле я п.** (*fig., coll.*) I'm no good at this; this is not in my line.

П

пас², **а** *m.* (*sport*) pass.
па́сек|а, **и** *f.* apiary.
па́сечник, **а** *m.* bee-keeper.
па́сквил|ь, **я** *m.* libel, lampoon; squib.
па́сквильный *adj.* libellous (*Br.*), libelous (*US*).
пасквиля́нт, **а** *m.* lampoonist, slanderer.
паску́д|ный (**~ен**, **~на**) *adj.* (*coll.*) foul, filthy.
паслён, **а** *m.* (*bot.*) solanum; morel; **сла́дко-го́рький п.** bitter-sweet; **чёрный п.** deadly nightshade.
па́смур|ный (**~ен**, **~на**) *adj.* **1** (*день*) dull, cloudy; overcast. **2** (*fig.*) (*лицо*) gloomy, sullen.
пас|ова́ть¹, **у́ю** *impf.* (*of* ⇒**с~**) **1** (*also pf. in past tense*) (*cards*) to pass. **2** (*fig.*) (*сдаваться*) to give up, give in; **п. пе́ред тру́дностями** to give in to difficulties.
пас|ова́ть², **у́ю** *impf. and pf.* (*sport*) to pass.
паспарту́ *nt. indecl.* mount.
па́спорт, **а**, *pl.* **~а́** *m.* **1** passport. **2** (*машины, аппарата*) registration certificate.
па́спорт|ный *adj. of* ⇒**~**; **п. стол** passport office.
пасс, **а** *m.* pass (*in hypnotism*).
пасса́ж, **а** *m.* **1** (*галерея*) arcade. **2** (*mus.*) passage.
пассажи́р, **а** *m.* passenger.
пассажи́р|ка, **ки** *f. of* ⇒**~**
пассажи́р|ский *adj. of* ⇒**~**
пасса́т, **а** *m.* (*meteor.*) trade wind.
пассати́ж|и, **ей** *pl.* (combination) pliers.
пасса́т|ный *adj. of* ⇒**~**; **п. ве́тер** trade wind.
пасси́в, **а** *m.* **1** (*comm.*) liabilities. **2** (*gram.*) passive voice.
пасси́вност|ь, **и** *f.* passivity.
пасси́в|ный (**~ен**, **~на**) *adj.* **1** passive; **~ное избира́тельное пра́во** (*pol.*) eligibility. **2** (*econ.*): **п. бала́нс** unfavourable (*Br.*), unfavorable (*US*) balance.
па́сси|я, **и** *f.* (*obs., coll.*) passion; **бы́вшая п.** old flame.
па́ст|а, **ы** *f.* paste; **зубна́я п.** toothpaste; **тома́тная п.** tomato purée; (*в ручке*) ink (*in ballpoint pen*).
па́стбищ|е, **а** *nt.* pasture.
па́стбищный *adj.* pasture; grazing.
па́ств|а, **ы** *f.* (*eccl.*) flock, congregation.
пасте́л|ь, **и** *f.* **1** (*collect.*) (*карандаши*) pastel(s). **2** (*рисунок*) pastel (drawing).
пасте́льный *adj.* (*картина*) (drawn in) pastel; (*цвет*) pastel, soft.
пастериза́ци|я, **и** *f.* pasteurization.
пастеризо́в|анный *p.p.p. of* ⇒**~а́ть** *and adj.* pasteurized.
пастериз|ова́ть, **у́ю** *impf. and pf.* to pasteurize.
пастерна́к, **а** *m.* parsnip.
пас|ти́, **у́**, **ёшь**, *past* **~**, **~ла́** *impf.* (*no pf.*) (*скот*) to graze, pasture; (*гусей*) to tend.
пастил|а́, **ы́**, *pl.* **~́ы** *f.* pastila (*sort of fruit fudge*).
пас|ти́сь, **ётся**, *past* **~́ся**, **~ла́сь** *impf.* (*no pf.*) to graze; to browse; (*coll., fig.*) to hang about.
па́стор, **а** *m.* (*Protestant*) minister, pastor.
пастора́л|ь, **и** *f.* **1** (*liter.*) pastoral. **2** (*mus.*) pastorale.
пастора́льный *adj.* pastoral, bucolic.
па́сторский *adj.* pastoral.
пасту́х, **а́** *m.* (*коров*) herdsman; (*овец*) shepherd.
пасту́|шеский *adj. of* ⇒**~х**; **п. по́сох** shepherd's crook.
пасту́|ший *adj. of* ⇒**~х**; **~шья су́мка** (*bot.*) shepherd's purse.
пасту́шк|а, **и** *f.* shepherdess.
пастуш|о́к, **ка́** *m.* **1** *affectionate dim. of* ⇒**пасту́х**. **2** (*poet.*) swain. **3** (*zool.*): **водяно́й п.** water-rail.
па́стыр|ский *adj. of* ⇒**~ь**; (*eccl.*) pastoral.
па́стыр|ь, **я** *m.* **1** (*obs.*) (*пастух*) shepherd. **2** (*eccl.*) pastor.
па|сть¹, **ду́**, **дёшь**, *past* **~л**, **~́ла** *pf. of* ⇒**~́дать 1** (*pf. only*) (*погибнуть*) to die, fall; **п. же́ртвой чего́-н.** to fall victim to. **2** (*о крепости, о городе*) to fall, surrender. **3**: **п. ду́хом** to despair.
паст|ь², **и** *f.* (*зверя*) mouth; jaws.
пастьб|а́, **ы** *f.* pasturage.
Па́сх|а, **и** *f.* **1** (*в иудаизме*) Passover. **2** (*в христианстве*) Easter. **3 п.** (*cul.*) paskha (*sweet cream-cheese dish eaten at Easter*).
пасха́льн|ый *adj. of* ⇒**Па́сха**; **~ое яйцо́** Easter egg.
па́сын|ок, **ка** *m.* stepson, stepchild.
пасья́нс, **а** *m.* patience (*card-game*); **раскла́дывать п.** to play patience.
пат¹, **а** *m.* (*в шахматах*) stalemate.
пат², **а** *m.* (*cul.*) paste.
пате́нт, **а** *m.* (**на** + *a.*) (*на изобретение*) patent (for); (*торговый*) licence (*Br.*), license (*US*) (for); **владе́лец ~а** patentee.
патенто́в|анный *p.p.p. of* ⇒**~а́ть** *and adj.* patent; **~анное сре́дство** patent medicine.
патент|ова́ть, **у́ю** *impf.* (*of* ⇒**за~**) to patent; to take out a patent for.
пате́тик|а, **и** *f.* (the) passionate element; emotionalism.
патети́ческий *adj.* passionate; emotional.
патети́ч|ный (**~ен**, **~на**) *adj.* = **~еский**
патефо́н, **а** *m.* (*small, portable*) gramophone.
пати́н|а, **ы** *f.* (*archaeol., tech.*) patina.
патиссо́н, **а** *m.* custard marrow (*Br.*), squash (*US*).
па́тл|ы, **~** *pl.* (*sg.* **~а**, **~ы** *f.*) (*coll.*) locks (*of hair*).
пат|ова́ть, **у́ю** *impf.* (*of* ⇒**за~**) (*в шахматах*) to stalemate.
па́ток|а, **и** *f.* treacle; syrup; **све́тлая п.** golden syrup; **чёрная п.** molasses.
пато́лог, **а** *m.* pathologist.
патологи́ческ|ий *adj.* pathological; **~ая анато́мия** (anatomical) pathology.
патоло́ги|я, **и** *f.* pathology.
патологоана́том, **а** *m.* (anatomical) pathologist.
па́то|чный *adj. of* ⇒**~ка**; treacly.
патриа́рх, **а** *m.* (*ethnol. and eccl.*) patriarch.
патриарха́льност|ь, **и** *f.* patriarchal character.
патриарха́л|ьный (**~ен**, **~ьна**) *adj.* patriarchal.
патриарха́т, **а** *m.* (*ethnol.*) patriarchy.
патриа́рхи|я, **и** *f.* (*eccl.*) patriarchate.
патриа́р|ший *adj. of* ⇒**~х** (*eccl.*).
патрио́т, **а** *m.* patriot.
патриоти́зм, **а** *m.* patriotism.
патриоти́ческий *adj.* patriotic.
патриоти́ч|ный (**~ен**, **~на**) *adj.* = **~еский**
патрио́т|ка, **ки** *f. of* ⇒**~**
патрициа́нский *adj. of* ⇒**патри́ций**
патри́ци|й, **я** *m.* (*hist.*) patrician.
патро́н¹, **а** *m.* **1** (*покровитель*) patron. **2** (*хозяин*) boss. **3** (*святой*) patron saint.
патро́н², **а** *m.* **1** (*mil.*) cartridge. **2** (*tech.*) chuck (*of drill, lathe*), holder. **3** (*лампочки*) socket. **4** (*образец*) (*tailor's*) pattern.
патрона́ж, **а** *m.* **1** (*покровительство*) patronage. **2** (*med.*) home visiting (*by health service worker*).
патрона́ж|ный *adj. of* ⇒**~ 2**; **~ная сестра́** district nurse (*Br.*), visiting nurse (*US*).
патро́нник, **а** *m.* (*mil.*) (cartridge-) chamber.
патро́н|ный *adj. of* ⇒**~²**; **~ная ги́льза** cartridge case; **~ная су́мка** cartridge pouch.
патронта́ш, **а** *m.* bandolier, ammunition belt.
па́труб|ок, **ка** *m.* (*tech.*) branch pipe.
патрули́р|овать, **ую** *impf.* (*no pf.*) (*mil.*) to patrol.
патру́л|ь, **я́** *m.* patrol.
патру́ль|ный *adj. of* ⇒**~**; *as n.* **п.**, **~ного** *m.* patrol.
па́уз|а, **ы** *f.* pause; interval; (*mus.*) rest.
пау́к, **а́** *m.* spider.
паути́н|а, **ы** *f.* cobweb, spider's web; (*fig.*) web; **п. лжи** web/tissue of lies.
пау́|чий *adj. of* ⇒**~к**
па́фос, **а** *m.* **1** (+*g.*) enthusiasm (for), zeal (for). **2** (*сущность*) spirit; emotional content; **п. рома́на** the spirit of a novel.
пах, **а**, **о** **~́е**, **в ~у́** *m.* (*anat.*) groin.
паха́н, **а́** *m.* (*sl.*) **1** (*отец*) father, old man. **2** (*группы*) head, boss.
па́ханы|й *adj.* ploughed (*Br.*), plowed (*US*) (up); **~е зе́мли** ploughland (*Br.*), plowland (*US*).
па́хар|ь, **я** *m.* ploughman (*Br.*), plowman (*US*).
па|ха́ть, **шу́**, **~́шешь** *impf.* **1** (*pf.* **вс~**) to plough (*Br.*), plow (*US*), till. **2** (*coll.*) (*работать*) to slave (away).

пáх|нуть, ну, нешь, *past* ~ *or* ~**нул,** ~**ла** *impf.* (*no pf.*) (+*i.*) to smell (of); ~**нет лýком** there is a smell of onions; (*fig.*; *usu. impers.*) to savour (*Br.*), savor (*US*) (of), smack (of); ~**нет бедóй** this means trouble; ~**ло ссóрой** a quarrel was in the air.

пахн|ýть, ёт *pf.* (*no impf.*) (+*i.*; *coll.*) to puff, blow; ~**ýл зáпах** a smell wafted over; (*impers.*): ~**ýло хóлодом** there came a cold blast; ~**ýло веснóй** there was a smell of spring.

паховóй *adj.* (*anat.*) inguinal.

пáхот|а, ы *f.* **1** (*действие*) ploughing (*Br.*), plowing (*US*), tillage. **2** (*земля*) ploughland (*Br.*), plowland (*US*).

пáхотный *adj.* arable.

пáхт|а, ы *f.* buttermilk; **жир** ~**ы** butterfat.

пáхтань|е, я *nt.* **1** (*действие*) churning. **2** (*пахта*) buttermilk.

пáхта|ть, ю *impf.* to churn.

пахýч|ий (~, ~а) *adj.* strong-smelling.

пацáн, á *m.* (*coll.*) boy, lad.

пациéнт, а *m.* patient.

пациéнт|ка, ки *f. of* ⇒~

пацифи́зм, а *m.* pacifism.

пацифи́ст, а *m.* pacifist.

пацифи́ст|ка, ки *f. of* ⇒~

пáче *adv.* (*arch.*) more; *now only in phrr.* **тем п.** the more so, the more reason; **п. чáяния** contrary to expectation; beyond expectation.

пáчк|а, и *f.* **1** (*писем, газет*) bundle; (*папирос, чая, печенья*) packet (*Br.*), pack; ~**ами** (*coll.*) in great numbers. **2** (*балерины*) tutu.

пáчка|ть, ю *impf.* (*pf.* **за**~, **ис**~, *and* **на**~) to dirty, soil, stain, sully (*also fig.*); **п. рýки** (*fig.*) to soil one's hands; **п. чьё-н. дóброе и́мя** to sully s.o.'s good name.

пáчка|ться, юсь *impf.* (*of* ⇒**за**~, **ис**~, *and* **на**~) **1** (*человек*) to make o.s. dirty; to soil o.s. **2** (*вещь*) to become dirty.

пáш|ня, ни, *g. pl.* ~**ен** *f.* arable land; ploughland (*Br.*), plowland (*US*).

пашóт, а *m.*: **яйцó-п.** poached egg.

паштéт, а *m.* pâté.

паэ́ль|я, и *f.* (*cul.*) paella.

пáюсн|ый *adj.*: ~**ая икрá** pressed caviar(e).

паяльник, а *m.* soldering iron.

пая́льн|ый *adj.* soldering; ~**ая лáмпа** blow lamp; ~**ая трýбка** blowpipe.

пая́льщик, а *m.* solderer.

паясничa|ть, ю *impf.* (*no pf.*) (*coll.*) to clown, play the fool.

пая́|ть, ю *impf.* (*no pf.*) to solder.

пая́ц, а *m.* **1** (*клоун*) (*circus*) clown. **2** (*fig., pej.*) clown.

ПВО *f. indecl.* (*abbr. of* ***противовоздýшная оборóна***) (*mil.*) anti-aircraft defences (*Br.*), defenses (*US*).

пеáн, а *m.* paean.

пев|éц, цá *m.* singer; (*fig.*) celebrator.

певи́ц|а, ы *f. of* ⇒**певéц**

певýч|ий (~, ~а) *adj.* melodious.

пéвч|ий 1 *adj.* singing; ~**ая пти́ца** songbird. **2** *as n.* **п.,** ~**его** *m.* chorister.

пегáнк|а, и *f.* (*zool.*) shelduck.

пéг|ий (~, ~а) *adj.* skewbald.

пед... *comb. form, abbr. of* ***педагоги́ческий***

педагóг, а *m.* teacher.

педагóгик|а, и *f.* pedagogy, pedagogics.

педагоги́ческий *adj.* pedagogic(al); educational; **п. институ́т** college of education (*Br.*), teachers' college (*US*).

педагоги́ч|ный (~ен, ~на) *adj.* sensible, wise (*in sphere of education*).

педáл|ь, и *f.* pedal; **нажáть на п.** to pedal; **рабóтать** ~**ью** to treadle; **нажáть на все** ~**и** (*fig., coll.*) to go flat out.

педáль|ный *adj. of* ⇒~

педáнт, а *m.* pedant.

педанти́зм, а *m.* pedantry.

педанти́чност|ь, и *f.* pedantry.

педанти́ч|ный (~ен, ~на) *adj.* pedantic.

педáнт|ка, ки *f. of* ⇒~

педвýз, а *m.* = **пединститýт**

пéдел|ь, я *m.* (*hist.*) official in charge of student discipline.

педерáст, а *m.* p(a)ederast, sodomite.

педерáсти|я, и *f.* p(a)ederasty, sodomy.

педиáтр, а *m.* paediatrician (*Br.*), pediatrician (*US*).

педиатри́ческий *adj.* paediatric (*Br.*), pediatric (*US*).

педиатри́|я, и *f.* paediatrics (*Br.*), pediatrics (*US*).

пéдик, а *m.* (*coll., pej.*) queer, poof (*Br.*).

педикю́р, а *m.* pedicure.

педикю́рш|а, и *f.* pedicure.

пединститýт, а *m.* = **педагоги́ческий институ́т**

педóметр, а *m.* pedometer.

педофи́л, а *m.* paedophile (*Br.*), pedophile (*US*).

педофили́|я, и *f.* paedophilia (*Br.*), pedophilia (*US*).

педсовéт, а *m.* staff meeting (*at school*).

педучи́лищ|е, а *nt.* (primary and preschool) college of education (*Br.*), teachers' college (*US*).

пéйджер, а *m.* pager.

пейзáж, а *m.* **1** landscape; scenery. **2** (*картина*) landscape.

пейзажи́ст, а *m.* landscape painter.

пейзажи́ст|ка, ки *f. of* ⇒~

пейзáж|ный *adj. of* ⇒~; ~**ная жи́вопись** landscape painting.

пéйс|ы, ов *pl.* long sidelocks (*of orthodox Jews*), payess (*US*).

пёк, пеклá *see* ⇒**печь**[1]

пекáрн|ый *adj.* baking; ~**ое ремеслó** bakery trade.

пекáр|ня, ни, *g. pl.* ~**ен** *f.* bakery, bakehouse.

пéкар|ский *adj. of* ⇒~**ь**; ~**ские дрóжжи** baker's yeast.

пéкар|ь, я, *pl.* ~**я́**, ~**éй** *and* ~**и**, ~**ей** *m.* baker.

Пеки́н, а *m.* Peking; Beijing.

пеклевáнн|ый *adj.* finely ground; ~**ая мукá** rye flour (of the best quality); **п. хлеб** fine rye bread.

пéкл|о, а *nt.* **1** (*сильный жар*) scorching heat; **попáсть в сáмое п.** (*fig., coll.*) to get into the thick of it. **2** (*ад*) hell, hellfire.

пекти́н, а *m.* (*chem.*) pectin.

пекý, пекýт *see* ⇒**печь**[1]

пелен|á, ы́, *pl.* ~**ы́**, ~̈, ~**áм** *f.* shroud; **с** ~̈ (*obs., fig.*) from the cradle; **у негó (слóвно) п. (с глаз) упáла** the scales fell from his eyes.

пеленá|ть, ю *impf.* (*of* ⇒**за**~ *and* **с**~) to swaddle.

пéленг, а *m.* (*naut., aeron.*) bearing.

пеленгáтор, а *m.* (*naut., aeron.*) direction finder.

пеленг|овáть, ýю *impf. and pf.* (*naut., aeron.*) to take the bearings (of).

пелён|ка, ки *f.* (*usu. pl.*) swaddling clothes; **с пелёнок** (*fig.*) from the cradle.

пелери́н|а, ы *f.* cape, pelerine.

пеликáн, а *m.* pelican.

пельмéн|и, ей *pl.* (*sg.* ~**ь**, ~**я** *m.*) (*cul.*) pelmeni (*kind of ravioli*).

пéмз|а, ы *f.* pumice(-stone).

пéн|а, ы *f.* **1** (*на море*) foam; (*на бульоне*) scum; (*на пиве*) froth, head; **мы́льная п.** soapsuds; **говори́ть с** ~**ой у рта, с** ~**ой на губáх** (*fig.*) to foam at the mouth; **п. для вáнны** bubble bath. **2** (*на лошади*) lather.

пенáл, а *m.* pencil-box.

пенáльти *m. indecl.* (*в футболе*) penalty; **они́ вы́играли по п.** they won on penalties.

пенáт|ы, ов *no sg.* (*myth. and fig.*) penates; **вернýться к (свои́м), родны́м** ~**ам** to return to one's hearth and home.

пéни|е, я *nt.* singing; **п. (птиц)** (birds') song; **п. петухá** cock's crow.

пéнист|ый (~, ~а) *adj.* foamy; frothy.

пенитенциáрный *adj.* (*leg.*) penitentiary.

пéн|ить, ю, ишь *impf.* to froth (up).

пéн|иться, ится *impf.* to foam; to froth (up) (*intrans.*).

пеницилли́н, а *m.* penicillin.

пéнк|а, и *f.* (*на молоке*) skin; **снять** ~**и** (**с**+*g.*) to skim; (*fig.*) to take the pickings (of).

пéнни *nt. indecl.* penny.

пéн|ный *adj.* = ~**истый**

пенопла́ст, а *m.* foam plastic.

пенопла́ст|овый *adj. of* ⇒~

пеностекл|ó, á *nt.* glass fibre (*Br.*), fiber (*US*).

пеностек|óльный *adj. of* ⇒~**лó**

пéночк|а, и *f.* (*zool.*) warbler (*Phylloscopus*).

пенс, а *m.* penny.

пенсионéр, а *m.* pensioner.

пенсионéр|ка, ки *f. of* ⇒~

пенсиóнн|ый *adj. of* ⇒**пéнсия;**

~ая кни́жка pension book; **п. во́зраст** retirement age; **п. фонд** pension fund.

пе́нси|я, и *f.* pension; **он на ~и** he is retired; **вы́йти на ~ю** to retire; **его́ отпра́вили на ~ю** he was pensioned off; **п. по ста́рости** old-age pension; **п. по инвали́дности** invalidity pension.

пенсне́ *nt. indecl.* pince-nez.

пента́метр, а *m.* (*liter.*) pentameter.

пе́нтюх, а *m.* (*coll.*) lout, bumpkin.

пенчингбо́л, а *m.* punchball.

пень, пня *m.* **1** stump; **стоя́ть как п.** (*coll.*) to be rooted to the ground. **2** (*coll.*) (*человек*) blockhead.

пеньк|а́, и́ *f.* hemp.

пенько́вый *adj.* hempen.

пеньюа́р, а *m.* peignoir, negligee.

пе́н|я, и *f.* fine.

пеня́|ть, ю *impf.* (*of* ⇒**по~**) (+*d.* or **на**+*a.*; *coll.*) to blame, reproach; **~й на себя́!** you have only yourself to blame!

пе́п|ел, ла *m.* ash(es); **подня́ться из ~ла** to rise from the ashes.

пепели́щ|е, а *nt.* **1** site of fire. **2** (*fig.*) (hearth and) home; **верну́ться на ста́рое п.** to return to one's old home.

пе́пельниц|а, ы *f.* ash-tray.

пе́пельно-се́рый *adj.* ash-grey.

пе́пельн|ый *adj.* ashy; **~ого цве́та** ash-grey.

пе́пси-ко́л|а, ы *f.* Pepsi-Cola (*propr.*).

пепси́н, а *m.* (*physiol.*) pepsin.

пепси́новый *adj.* peptic.

пер. (*abbr. of* ***переу́лок***) Lane.

перва́ч, а́ *m.* (*coll.*) **1** (*товар*) top quality foodstuff. **2** (*самогон*) strong home-distilled vodka.

перве́йший *adj.* (*coll.*) primary; very best.

пе́рвен|ец, ца *m.* first-born.

пе́рвенств|о, а *nt.* first place; (*sport*) championship; **завоева́ть п. ми́ра по футбо́лу** to win the world championship at football.

пе́рвенств|овать, ую *impf.* (*no pf.*) to take first place; (**над**+*i.*) to take precedence (over).

пе́рвенст|вующий *pres. part. act. of* ⇒**~вовать** *and adj.* pre-eminent; primary.

перви́чн|ый *adj.* (*главный*) primary; (*первоначальный*) initial; (*организации*) grass-root; **п. пери́од боле́зни** initial period of illness; **~ые поро́ды** (*geol.*) primary rocks.

первобы́т|ный (~ен, ~на) *adj.* (*ethnol. and fig.*) primitive; primordial; primeval.

пе́рв|ое, ого *nt.* first course (*of a meal*).

первозда́нный *adj.* primordial; (*geol.*) primitive, primary; **п. хао́с** primordial chaos (*also fig., iron.*).

первоисто́чник, а *m.* (*сведений*) primary source; (*основа*) origin.

первокла́ссник, а *m.* first-former (*Br.*), first-grader (*US*).

первокла́ссни|ца, цы *f. of* ⇒**~к**

первокла́ссный *adj.* first-class, first-rate.

первоку́рсник, а *m.* first-year student, freshman.

первоку́рсни|ца, цы *f. of* ⇒**~к**

Первома́|й, я *m.* May Day.

первома́йский *adj. of* ⇒**Первома́й**

пе́рво-на́перво *adv.* (*coll.*) first of all.

первонача́льно *adv.* originally.

первонача́л|ьный (~ен, ~ьна) *adj.* **1** (*самый первый*) original. **2** (*являющийся началом*) initial; **~ьная причи́на** (*phil.*) first cause. **3** (*элементарный*) elementary. **4**: **~ьные чи́сла** (*math.*) prime numbers.

первоо́браз, а *m.* prototype.

первообра́зный *adj.* prototypal.

первоосно́в|а, ы *f.* (*phil.*) first principle.

первооткрыва́тел|ь, я *m.* discoverer.

первоочередн|о́й *adj.* immediate; **~а́я зада́ча** immediate task.

первоочерёдн|ый = **~о́й**

первопеча́тник, а *m.* printing pioneer.

первопеча́тн|ый *adj.* **1** printed early, belonging to the first years of printing; **~ые кни́ги** incunabula. **2** (*издание*) first printed.

первоприча́н|а, ы *f.* (*phil.*) first cause.

первопрохо́д|ец, ца *m.* (*also fig., rhet.*) pioneer; trailblazer.

первопрохо́дческий *adj.* trail-blazing, pioneering.

первопу́т|ок, ка *m.* (*coll.*) the first sledging (*of the winter*); **е́хать по ~ку** to traverse a road after the first snowfall.

перворазря́дник, а *m.* (*sport*) first-rank player.

перворазря́дный *adj.* first-class, first-rank.

перворо́дный *adj.* (*obs.*) **1** first-born. **2** (*первозданный*) primal; **п. грех** (*eccl.*) original sin.

перворо́дств|о, а *nt.* **1** (*leg.*) primogeniture. **2** (*fig.*) (*первенство*) primacy.

перворождённый *adj.* first-born.

первосвяще́нник, а *m.* high priest; pontiff.

первосо́рт|ный (~ен, ~на) *adj.* **1** top-quality. **2** (*coll.*) (*превосходный*) first-class, first-rate.

первостате́|йный (~ен, ~йна) *adj.* (*coll.*) first-rate, first-class.

первостепе́н|ный (~ен, ~на) *adj.* paramount.

пе́рвост|ь, и *f.*: **по ~и** (*coll.*) in the beginning, at first.

первоцве́т, а *m.* (*bot.*) primrose.

пе́рв|ый *adj.* **1** first; (*по времени*) earliest, first; **~ое (число́ ме́сяца)** the first (of the month); **~ого января́** on the first of January; **полови́на ~ого** half past twelve; **в ~ом часу́** between twelve and one; **он п. вошёл** he was the first to enter; **быть ~ым, идти́ ~ым** to come first, lead; **~ое вре́мя** at first; **~ое де́ло, ~ым де́лом** (*coll.*) first of all, first thing; **не ~ой мо́лодости** not in one's first youth; **п. план** foreground; **~ая по́мощь** first aid; **п. рейс** maiden voyage; **~ая скри́пка** first violin; **п. эта́ж** ground floor (*Br.*), first floor (*US*); **в ~ую о́чередь** in the first place; **из ~ых рук** first-hand; **на п. взгляд, с ~ого взгля́да** at first sight; **при ~ой возмо́жности** at the first opportunity, as soon as possible; **с ~ого ра́за** from the first; **п. блин ко́мом** (*prov.*) practice makes perfect. **2** (*лучший*) best.

перга́мент, а *m.* parchment.

пер|де́ть, жу́, ди́шь *impf.* (*vulg.*) to fart.

пере... *vbl. pref. indicating* **1** *action across or through sth.* (trans-). **2** *repetition of action* (re-). **3** *superiority, excess, etc.* (over-, out-). **4** *extension of action to encompass many or all objects or cases of a given kind.* **5** *division into two or more parts.* **6** (*reflexives*) reciprocity of action.

переадрес|ова́ть, у́ю *pf.* (*of* ⇒**~о́вывать**) to re-address; to forward.

переадресо́выва|ть, ю *impf. of* ⇒**переадресова́ть**

перебази́р|овать, ую *pf.* to shift; to relocate.

перебази́р|оваться, уюсь *pf.* to relocate.

перебаллотиро́вк|а, и *f.* second ballot.

переба́рщива|ть, ю *impf. of* ⇒**переборщи́ть**

перебега́|ть, ю *impf. of* ⇒**перебежа́ть**

перебе|жа́ть, гу́, жи́шь, гу́т *pf.* (*of* ⇒**~га́ть**) **1** (**че́рез**+*a.*) to cross (running); **п. (че́рез) у́лицу** to run across the street; **п. кому́-н. доро́гу** to cross s.o.'s path. **2** (*fig., coll.*; **к**+*d.*) (*к противнику*) to go over (to), desert (to).

перебе́жк|а, и *f.* (*mil.*) bound, rush.

перебе́жчик, а *m.* deserter; (*fig.*) turncoat.

перебе́жчи|ца, цы *f. of* ⇒**~к**

перебе́лива|ть, ю *impf. of* ⇒**перебели́ть**

перебел|и́ть, ю, и́шь *pf.* (*of* ⇒**~и́вать**) **1** to whitewash again. **2** (*obs.*) (*переписать начисто*) to make a fair copy (of).

перебе|си́ться, шу́сь, ~сишься *pf.* **1** (*взбеситься*) to go mad, run wild. **2** (*coll.*) (*успокоиться*) to settle down, having sown one's wild oats.

перебива́|ть(ся), ю(сь) *impf. of* ⇒**переби́ть(ся)**[1,2]

переби́вк|а, и *f.* re-upholstering.

перебинт|ова́ть[1]**, у́ю** *pf.* (*of* ⇒**~о́вывать**) (*поменять повязку*) to change the dressing (on), put a new dressing (on).

перебинт|ова́ть[2]**, у́ю** *pf.* (*of* ⇒**~о́вывать**) (*забинтовать многих*) to dress, bandage (*all, a quantity of*).

перебинто́выва|ть, ю *impf. of* ⇒**перебинтова́ть**

перебира́|ть[1](ся), ю(сь) *impf. of* ⇒**перебра́ть(ся)**

перебира́|ть[2], ю *impf.* **1** (*касаться пальцами*) to finger; **п. стру́ны** to run one's fingers over the strings. **2** (+*i.*) (*ногами, пальцами*) to move (*in turn or in a regular manner*).

переб|и́ть[1], ью́, ьёшь *pf.* (*of* ⇒**~ива́ть**) **1** (*мебель*) to re-upholster. **2** (*подушку*) to beat up again.

переб|и́ть[2], ью́, ьёшь *pf.* (*of* ⇒**~ива́ть**) **1** (*говорящего*) to interrupt. **2** (*перехватить*) to intercept; **п. кому́-н. доро́гу** to cross s.o.'s path; **п. поку́пку** (*coll.*) to outbid for sth. **3** (*заглушить*) to stifle, suppress; **п. аппети́т** to spoil one's appetite.

переб|и́ть[3], ью́, ьёшь *pf.* **1** (*убить*) to slaughter. **2** (*разбить, сломать*) to break.

переб|и́ться[1], ётся *pf.* (*of* ⇒**~ива́ться**) (*посуда*) to break.

переб|и́ться[2], ью́сь, ьёшься *pf.* (*of* ⇒**~ива́ться**) (*coll.*) **1** (*с трудом прожить*) to make ends meet; **п. с хле́ба на квас** to live from hand to mouth. **2** (*обойтись*) to survive, manage.

перебо́|й, я *m.* (*перерыв*) interruption; (*задержка*) hold up; (*двигателя*) misfire; (*сердца*) irregularity; **пульс с ~ями** irregular pulse.

перебо́йный *adj.* intermittent.

переболе́|ть[1], ю *pf.* (+*i.*) to have had, have been down (*with an illness*); **де́ти все ~ли коклю́шем** the children have all been down with whooping-cough.

перебол|е́ть[2], и́т *pf.* (*о сердце, душе*) to recover.

перебо́рк|а[1], и *f.* **1** sorting out. **2** (*tech.*) re-assembly.

перебо́рк|а[2], и *f.* (*перегородка*) partition; (*naut.*) bulk-head.

перебор|о́ть, ю́, ~ешь *pf.* (*no impf.*) to overcome.

переборщ|и́ть, у́, и́шь *pf.* (*of* ⇒**перeба́рщивать**) (**в**+*p.*; *coll.*) to go too far; to overdo it; to go over the top.

перебра́нива|ться, юсь *impf.* (**с**+*i.*; *coll.*) to have words (with).

перебран|и́ться, ю́сь, и́шься *pf.* (**с**+*i.*; *coll.*) to quarrel (with), fall out (with).

перебра́нк|а, и *f.* (*coll.*) wrangle, squabble; slanging match (*Br.*).

перебра́сыва|ть(ся), ю(сь) *impf. of* ⇒**перебро́сить(ся)**

пере|бра́ть, беру́, берёшь, *past* **~бра́л, ~брала́, ~бра́ло** *pf.* (*of* ⇒**~бира́ть**) **1** (*сортировать*) to sort; (*пересмотреть*) to look through. **2** (*fig.*) (*в уме*) to turn over (in one's mind). **3** (*взять слишком много*) to take too much. **4** (*tech.*) (*паркет, машину*) to (dismantle and) reassemble.

пере|бра́ться, беру́сь, берёшься, *past* **~бра́лся, ~брала́сь, ~бра́ло́сь** *pf.* (*coll.*) **1** (*перейти*) to get over, cross. **2** (*переселиться*) to move.

перебр|оди́ть, о́дит *pf.* to have fermented; to have risen.

перебро́са́|ть, ю *pf.* to throw one after another.

перебро́|сить, шу, сишь *pf.* (*of* ⇒**перебра́сывать**) **1** (*мяч*) to throw over; **п. мост че́рез ре́ку** to throw a bridge across a river. **2** (*переместить*) to transfer (*troops, etc.*).

перебро́|ситься, шусь, сишься *pf.* (*of* ⇒**перебра́сываться**) **1** (+*i.*) to throw one to another; **п. не́сколькими слова́ми** (*fig.*) to exchange a few words. **2** (*распространиться*) to spread. **3** (*переместиться*) to be transferred.

перебро́ск|а, и *f.* transfer.

перебыва́|ть, ю *pf.* to have called, have been; **он везде́ ~л** he has been all over the world.

перева́л, а *m.* **1** (*действие*) passing, crossing. **2** (*geog.*) (*место*) pass.

перева́л|ец, ьца *m.*: **ходи́ть с ~ьцем** (*coll.*) to waddle.

перева́лива|ть, ю *impf. of* ⇒**перевали́ть**

перева́лива|ться[1], юсь *impf. of* ⇒**перевали́ться**

перева́лива|ться[2], юсь *impf.* (*no pf.*) to waddle.

перевал|и́ть, ю́, ~ишь *pf.* (*of* ⇒**~ивать**) **1** (*переместить*) to transfer, shift. **2** (*перейти*) to cross; (*impers.*; *coll.*) (*о пределе*) to be past; **~и́ло за по́лночь** it is past midnight; **ей ~и́ло за со́рок (лет)** she has turned forty; she is past forty.

перевал|и́ться, ю́сь, ~ишься *pf.* (*of* ⇒**~иваться[1]**) to roll over; **п. на пра́вый бок** to roll over on to one's right side.

перева́лк|а, и *f.* **1** (*действие*) transshipment, conveyance. **2** (*место*) transshipping point.

перева́л|очный *adj. of* ⇒**~ка; пункт** staging post.

перева́рива|ть, ю *impf. of* ⇒**перевари́ть;** (*with neg., coll.*) to be unable to stand; **я его́ не ~ю** I can't stand him.

перевар|и́ть[1], ю́, ~ишь *pf.* (*of* ⇒**~ивать**) **1** (*заново*) to cook again; to boil again. **2** (*чрезмерно*) to overcook, overdo.

перевар|и́ть[2], ю́, ~ишь *pf.* (*of* ⇒**~ивать**) to digest; **п. прочи́танное** (*fig.*) to digest what one has read.

переве́д|аться, аюсь *pf.* (*of* ⇒**~ываться**) (*obs.*; **с**+*i.*) to get even (with).

переве́дыва|ться, юсь *impf. of* ⇒**переве́даться**

перевез|ти́, у́, ёшь, *past* **~, ~ла́** *pf.* (*of* ⇒**перевози́ть**) **1** (*переместить*) (*людей через реку*) to take across, transport across. **2** (*везя, доставить*) (*детей на дачу*) to transport, take (*from A to B*).

переверн|у́ть, у́, ёшь *pf.* (*of* ⇒**перевёртывать** *and* **перевора́чивать**) **1** (*с одной стороны на другую*) to turn over; (*вверх дном*) to turn upside down. **2** (*изменить*) to change radically, transform. **3** (*потрясти*) to shake, stun. **4** (*в уме*) to turn over. **5** (*привести в беспорядок*) to turn upside down.

переверн|у́ться, у́сь, ёшься *pf.* (*of* ⇒**перевёртываться** *and* **перевора́чиваться**) to turn over; **он ~ётся в гробу́** (*joc.*) he would turn in his grave.

перевер|те́ть, чу́, ~тишь *pf.* (*of* ⇒**~тывать** *and* **~чивать**) (*coll.*) to overwind.

перевёртыва|ть(ся), ю(сь) *impf. of* ⇒**переверну́ть(ся)** *and* **переверте́ть**

переве́рчива|ть, ю *impf. of* ⇒**переверте́ть**

переве́с, а *m.* preponderance; advantage; **чи́сленный п.** numerical superiority; **взять п. в чём-н.** to gain the upper hand in sth.

переве́|сить[1], шу, сишь *pf.* (*of* ⇒**~шивать**) (*пальто*) to hang somewhere else; **п. карти́ну с одно́й стены́ на другу́ю** to move a picture from one wall to another.

переве́|сить[2], шу, сишь *pf.* (*of* ⇒**~шивать**) **1** (*взвесить заново*) to weigh again. **2** (*превзойти весом*) to outweigh, outbalance (*also fig.*); (*fig.*) (*оказаться более весомым*) to tip the scales.

переве́|ситься, шусь, сишься *pf.* (*of* ⇒**~шиваться**) to lean over.

переве|сти́[1], ду́, дёшь, *past* **~л, ~ла́** *pf.* (*of* ⇒**переводи́ть**) **1** (*ведя, переместить*) to take across; **п. дете́й че́рез у́лицу** to take children across the road. **2** (*в другое место*) to transfer, move, switch, shift; **п. на другу́ю рабо́ту** to transfer to another post; **п. де́ньги** to transfer money; **п. стре́лку** to shunt, switch; **п. стре́лку часо́в вперёд (наза́д)** to put a clock on (back). **3** (**с**+*g.* **на**+*a.*) to translate (from into); (**в, на**+*a.*) (*в другие единицы*) to convert (to), express (as, in); **п. с ру́сского языка́ на англи́йский** to translate from Russian into English; **п. в метри́ческие ме́ры** to convert to metric units. **4** (*взгляд, разговор*) to shift; **п. разгово́р на другу́ю те́му** to change the subject. **5** (*art*) to transfer, copy. **6**: **п. дух/дыха́ние** to take breath.

переве|сти́[2], ду́, дёшь, *past* **~л, ~ла́** *pf.* (*of* ⇒**переводи́ть**) (*coll.*) **1** (*истребить*) to exterminate. **2** (*деньги*) to spend, use up.

переве|сти́сь[1], ду́сь, дёшься, *past* **~лся, ~ла́сь** *pf.* (*of* ⇒**переводи́ться**) to move, be transferred.

переве|сти́сь[2], дётся, *past* **~лся, ~ла́сь** *pf.* (*of* ⇒**переводи́ться**) (*coll.*) **1** (*израсходоваться*) to come to an end; **де́ньги у меня́ ~ли́сь** my money was all gone. **2** (*исчезнуть*) to disappear.

переве́ш|ать[1], аю *pf.* (*of* ⇒**~ивать**) (*взвесить*) to weigh (*all or a quantity of*).

переве́ш|ать[2], аю *pf.* (*убить*) to hang (*a number of*).

П

перевéшива|ть, ю *impf. of* ⇨**перевéсить** *and* **перевéшать**[1]

перевéшива|ться, юсь *impf. of* ⇨**перевéситься**

перевивá|ть(ся), ю, ет(ся) *impf. of* ⇨**перевúть(ся)**

перевидá|ть, ю *pf.* (*coll.*) to have seen (*also fig.*).

перевирá|ть, ю *impf. of* ⇨**переврáть**

перев|úть[1]**, ью́, ьёшь,** *past* **~úл, ~илá, ~úло** *pf.* (*of* ⇨**~ивáть**) (*свить заново*) to weave again.

перев|úть[2]**, ью́, ьёшь,** *past* **~úл, ~илá, ~úло** *pf.* (*of* ⇨**~ивáть**) (+*i.*) (*вплести*) to interweave (with), intertwine (with).

перев|úться, ьётся, *past* **~úлся, ~илáсь, ~лóсь** *pf.* (*of* ⇨**~ивáться**) to interweave, intertwine.

перевóд[1]**, а** *m.* **1** (*в другое место*) transfer, move, switch, shift; **п. дéнег** remittance; **почтóвый п.** postal order; **п. стрéлки** shunting, switching; **п. стрéлки часóв вперёд (назáд)** putting a clock on (back). **2** (*с одного языка на другой*) translation; (*в другие единицы*) conversion; **п. мер** conversion of measures; **синхрóнный п.** simultaneous interpreting.

перевóд[2]**, а** *m.* (*coll.*) spending, using up; **пустóй п. дéнег** squandering, wasting.

перево|дúть(ся), жу́(сь), ~дишь(ся) *impf. of* ⇨**перевестú(сь)**

переводн|óй *adj. of* ⇨**перевóд**[1]; **~áя бумáга** carbon paper; transfer paper; **~áя картúнка** transfer.

перевóд|ный *adj. of* ⇨**~**[1]; **п. ромáн** novel in translation; **п. бланк** postal order form.

перевóдчик, а *m.* translator; (*устный*) interpreter.

перевóдчи|ца, цы *f. of* ⇨**~к**

перевóз, а *m.* **1** (*действие*) transportation. **2** (*место*) ferry.

перево|зúть, жу́, ~зишь *impf. of* ⇨**перевезтú**

перевóзк|а, и *f.* transportation, conveyance.

перевóз|очный *adj. of* ⇨**~ка; ~очные срéдства** means of transportation, conveyance.

перевóзчик, а *m.* **1** (*через реку*) ferryman; boatman; (*человек, организация, занимающиеся перевозкой грузов*) carrier. **2** (*zool.*) common sandpiper.

переволн|овáться, у́юсь *pf.* (*coll.*) to be alarmed; to suffer prolonged anxiety.

перевооруж|áть(ся), áю(сь) *impf. of* ⇨**~úть(ся)**

перевооружéни|е, я *nt.* (*армии*) re-armament; (*производства*) re-equipment.

перевооруж|úть, у́, úшь *pf.* (*of* ⇨**~áть**) (*армию*) to re-arm; (*производство*) to re-equip.

перевооруж|úться, у́сь, úшься *pf.* (*of* ⇨**~áться**) to re-arm (*intrans.*).

перевопло|тúть, щу́, тúшь *pf.* (*of* ⇨**~щáть**) to reincarnate; (*fig.*) to transform.

перевопло|тúться, щу́сь, тúшься *pf.* (*of* ⇨**~щáться**) to be reincarnated; (*fig.*) to undergo a transformation.

перевоплощá|ть(ся), ю(сь) *impf. of* ⇨**перевоплотúть(ся)**

перевоплощéни|е, я *nt.* reincarnation; (*fig.*) transformation.

переворáчива|ть(ся), ю(сь) *impf. of* ⇨**перевернýть(ся)**

переворóт, а *m.* **1** revolution; **госудáрственный п.** coup d'état; **дворцóвый п.** palace coup. **2** (*geol.*) cataclysm.

перевορош|úть, у́, úшь *pf.* (*coll.*) **1** to turn (over) (*also fig.*); **п. сéно** to turn hay; **п. свою́ пáмять** to search through one's memories. **2** (*fig.*) (*перестроить*) to turn upside down.

перевоспитáни|е, я *nt.* re-education; rehabilitation.

перевоспит|áть, áю *pf.* (*of* ⇨**~ывать**) to re-educate; (*преступника*) to rehabilitate.

перевоспит|áться, áюсь *pf.* (*of* ⇨**~ываться**) to re-educate o.s.; (*преступник*) to be re-educated.

перевоспúтыва|ть(ся), ю(сь) *impf. of* ⇨**перевоспитáть(ся)**

перевр|áть, у́, ёшь, *past* **~áл, ~алá, ~áло** *pf.* (*of* ⇨**перевирáть**) (*coll.*) to garble, confuse; to misinterpret; **п. цитáту** to misquote.

перевыбирá|ть, ю *impf. of* ⇨**перевы́брать**

перевы́бор|ы, ов *no sg.* re-election.

перевы́б|рать, еру, ерешь *pf.* (*of* ⇨**~ирáть**) to re-elect.

перевыполнéни|е, я *nt.* over-fulfilment (*Br.*), -fulfillment (*US*).

перевы́полн|ить, ю, ишь *pf.* (*of* ⇨**~я́ть**) to over-fulfil (*Br.*), -fulfill (*US*).

перевыполн|я́ть, я́ю *impf. of* ⇨**~ить**

перевя|зáть[1]**, жу́, ~жешь** *pf.* (*of* ⇨**~зывать**) **1** (*рану*) to dress, bandage. **2** (*коробку*) to tie up, cord.

перевя|зáть[2]**, жу́, ~жешь** *pf.* (*of* ⇨**~зывать**) (*свитер*) to knit again.

перевя́зк|а, и *f.* dressing, bandage.

перевя́з|очный *adj. of* ⇨**~ка; п. материáл** dressing; **п. пункт** dressing station.

перевя́зыва|ть, ю *impf. of* ⇨**перевязáть**

пéревязь, и *f.* **1** (*mil., hist.*) shoulder-belt, baldric. **2** (*med.*) sling.

перегáр, а *m.* (*coll.*) (*вкус*) taste of alcohol; (*запах*) smell of alcohol; **от негó неслó ~ом** he reeked of alcohol.

перегúб, а *m.* **1** bend, twist; (*линия*) fold. **2** (*fig.*) (*преувеличение*) exaggeration; (*в политике, в руководстве*): **допустúть п. в чём-н.** to carry sth. too far.

перегибá|ть(ся), ю(сь) *impf. of* ⇨**перегнýть(ся)**

перегля́дыва|ться, юсь *impf. of* ⇨**переглянýться**

перегля|нýться, нýсь, ~нешься *pf.* (*of* ⇨**~дываться**) (**с**+*i.*) to exchange glances (with).

перегн|áть, перегоню́, перегóнишь, *past* **~áл, ~алá, ~áло** *pf.* (*of* ⇨**перегоня́ть**) **1** (*обогнать*) to outdistance, leave behind; (*fig.*) to overtake, surpass. **2** (*скот*) to drive (*somewhere else; from A to B*). **3** (*chem.*) to distil (*Br.*), distill (*US*).

перегнивá|ть, ет *impf. of* ⇨**перегнúть**

перегн|úть, иёт, *past* **~úл, ~илá, ~úло** *pf.* (*of* ⇨**~ивáть**) to rot through.

перегнó|й, я *m.* humus.

переґ|нýть, нý, нёшь *pf.* (*of* ⇨**~ибáть**) to bend; (*fig., coll.*) to go too far; **он ~нýл с крúтикой** he went too far with his criticism; **п. пáлку** (*fig.*) to go too far.

перег|нýться, нýсь, нёшься *pf.* (*of* ⇨**~ибáться**) **1** (*о человеке*) to lean over, bend over. **2** (*о ветви*) to bend.

перевáрива|ть, ю *impf. of* ⇨**переговорúть**[2]

перевáрива|ться, юсь *impf.* (**с**+*i.*) to exchange remarks (with).

переговор|úть[1]**, ю́, úшь** *pf.* (**о**+*p.*) to talk (about); to talk over, discuss; **п. по телефóну** to speak over the telephone.

переговор|úть[2]**, ю́, úшь** *pf.* (*of* ⇨**перевáривать**) (*coll.*) to out-talk.

переговóрн|ый *adj.*: **~ая бýдка** telephone booth; **п. (телефóнный) пункт** trunk-call office.

переговóр|ы, ов *no sg.* negotiations, talks; **вестú п.** (**с**+*i.*) to negotiate, hold talks (with); **идýт п.** negotiations are in progress.

перегóн[1]**, а** *m.* (*действие*) driving.

перегóн[2]**, а** *m.* (*участок пути*) stage (*between two railway stations*).

перегóнк|а, и *f.* (*chem.*) distillation.

перегóн|ный *adj. of* ⇨**~ка; п. завóд** distillery.

перегоня́|ть, ю *impf. of* ⇨**перегнáть**

перегорáжива|ть, ю *impf. of* ⇨**перегородúть**

перегор|áть, áет *impf. of* ⇨**~éть**

перегорéлый *adj.* (*coll.*) burnt out.

перегор|éть, úт *pf.* (*of* ⇨**~áть**) **1** (*о лампочке*) to burn out. **2** (*о балке*) to burn through. **3** (*о навозе*) to rot through.

перегоро|дúть, жу́, ~дúшь *pf.* (*of* ⇨**перегорáживать**) to partition off.

перегорóдк|а, и *f.* **1** partition. **2** (*fig.*) barrier.

перегрéв, а *m.* overheating.

перегревá|ть(ся), ю(сь) *impf. of* ⇨**перегрéть(ся)**

перегрé|ть, ю *pf.* (*of* ⇨**~вáть**) to overheat.

перегрé|ться, юсь *pf.* (*of* ⇨**~вáться**) to overheat; (*на солнце*) to spend too long in the sun.

перегружа́|ть, ю *impf. of* ⇒**перегрузи́ть**

перегру́женност|ь, и *f.* **1** (*на транспорте*) overcrowding. **2** (*ученика*) strain.

перегру|зи́ть¹, жу́, ~зи́шь *pf.* (*of* ⇒**~жа́ть**) to overload; **п. рабо́той** to overwork.

перегру|зи́ть², жу́, ~зи́шь *pf.* (*of* ⇒**~жа́ть**) to load (*somewhere else; from A to B*); to transship; **п. с по́езда на парохо́д** to load from a train on to a ship.

перегру́зк|а¹, и *f.* overloading; (*usu. pl.*) strain, stress.

перегру́зк|а², и *f.* transfer, transshipping.

перегруппир|ова́ть, у́ю *pf.* (*of* ⇒**~о́вывать**) to re-group.

перегруппиро́вк|а, и *f.* re-grouping.

перегруппир|о́вывать, о́вываю *impf. of* ⇒**~ова́ть**

перегрыза́|ть, ю *impf. of* ⇒**перегры́зть**

перегры́з|ть, у́, ёшь, *past* **~, ~ла** *pf.* (*of* ⇒**~а́ть**) to gnaw through, bite through.

перегры́з|ться, у́сь, ёшься, *past* **~ся, ~лась** *pf.* (*no impf.*) (**из-за** + *g.*; *coll.*; *of dogs*) to fight (over); (*fig.*) to quarrel (over), wrangle (about).

пе́ред *and* **пе́редо** *prep.* + *i.* **1** (*при обозначении места*) in front of; before; **п. до́мом** in front of the house; (*also fig.*): **п. опа́сностью/тру́дностями** in the face of danger/difficulties. **2** (*раньше*) before; **п. обе́дом** before dinner; **п. тем, как** (*conj.*) before. **3** (*в присутствии*) in the presence of, in front of; **п. учи́телем** in front of the teacher. **4** (*в отношении; по сравнению*) to; **извини́ться п. кем-н.** to apologize to s.o.; **что он пе́ред ва́ми?** what is he compared with you?

перёд, пе́реда, *pl.* **~а́, ~о́в** *m.* front, fore-part.

переда|ва́ть(ся), ю, ёт(ся) *impf. of* ⇒**переда́ть(ся)**

переда́|точный *adj. of* ⇒**~ча; п. вал** (*tech.*) countershaft; **п. механи́зм** driving gear, drive; **~точное число́** (*tech.*) gear ratio.

переда́тчик, а *m.* transmitter.

переда́|ть¹, м, шь, ст, ди́м, ди́те, ду́т, *past* **пе́редал, ~ла́, пе́редало** *pf.* (*of* ⇒**~ва́ть**) **1** (*отдать через кого-н.*) to pass; (*вручить*) to hand; (*свои права, коллекцию*) to hand over; to transfer; **п. по насле́дству** to hand down; **п. де́ло в суд** to take a matter to law, sue. **2** (*сообщить*) to tell; to communicate; **переда́йте ему́, что я приезжа́ю за́втра** tell him I shall be arriving tomorrow; (*распространить*) to transmit, convey; **п. по ра́дио/телеви́дению** to broadcast (on the radio/television); **п. благода́рность** to convey thanks; **п. инфе́кцию** to communicate infection; **п. поруче́ние** to deliver a message; **п. приве́т** to send one's regards; **~й(те) им (мой) приве́т** give them my regards; remember me to them. **3** (*воспроизвести*) to reproduce (*a sound, a thought, etc.*).

переда́|ть², м, шь, ст, ди́м, ди́те, ду́т, *past* **пе́редал, ~ла́, пе́редало** *pf.* (*of* ⇒**~ва́ть**) (*больше чем нужно*) to pay too much, give too much; **вы пе́редали три рубля́** you have paid three roubles too many.

переда́|ться, стся, ду́тся, *past* **~лся, ~ла́сь** *pf.* (*of* ⇒**~ва́ться**) **1** to pass; (*о тревоге, болезни*) to be transmitted, be communicated; (*по наследству*) to be inherited; **корь ~ла́сь ему́ от сосе́дских дете́й** he picked up measles from the children next door. **2** (+*d.*; *obs.*) (*противнику*) to go over (to).

переда́ч|а, и *f.* **1** (*действие*) passing; transmission; communication; transfer, transference; **без пра́ва ~и** not transferable; **Петро́ву для ~и Ивано́ву** (*form of address on letter*) (Mr) Ivanov, c/o (Mr) Petrov. **2** (*больному, заключённому*) parcel. **3** (*по телевидению, по радио*) broadcast; **пряма́я п.** live broadcast; (*программа*) programme (*Br.*), program (*US*); **сегодня́ ве́чером интере́сная п.** there's an interesting programme on tonight. **4** (*tech.*) drive; gear(ing); transmission; **ремённая п.** belt drive.

передвига́|ть(ся), ю(сь) *impf. of* ⇒**передви́нуть(ся)**

передвиже́ни|е, я *nt.* (*войск*) movement; (*срока*) alteration; **сре́дства ~я** means of conveyance.

передви́ж|ка, ки *f.* **1** = **~е́ние. 2** *as adj.* travelling (*Br.*), traveling (*US*), mobile; **библиоте́ка-п.** mobile library (*Br.*), bookmobile (*US*); **теа́тр-п.** strolling players.

передви́жник, а *m.* (*art*) Peredvizhnik, Wanderer (*member of Russian school of realist painters of second half of nineteenth century*).

передвижн|о́й *adj.* **1** (*перегородка*) movable. **2** (*библиотека*) mobile, travelling (*Br.*), traveling (*US*); **~а́я вы́ставка** travelling exhibition.

передви́|нуть, ну, нешь *pf.* (*of* ⇒**~га́ть**) to move, shift (*also fig.*); **п. сро́ки экза́менов** to alter the date of examinations.

передви́|нуться, нусь, нешься *pf.* (*of* ⇒**~га́ться**) to move, shift.

переде́л, а *m.* re-partition; re-distribution.

переде́л|ать¹, аю *pf.* (*of* ⇒**~ывать**) (*сделать заново*) to redo; (*сделать по-иному*) to alter; (*fig.*) to re-fashion, recast; **п. пла́тье** to alter a dress.

переде́л|ать², аю *pf.* (*coll.*) (*сделать*) to do; **я ~ал все дела́** I have done all I had to do.

передел|и́ть, ю́, ~ишь *pf.* (*of* ⇒**~я́ть**) to re-divide.

переде́лк|а, и *f.* **1** alteration; **отда́ть что-н. в ~у** to have sth. altered; **попа́сть в ~у** (*coll.*) to get into a pretty mess; **побыва́ть в ~ах** (*coll.*) to be in a mess. **2** (*произведения*) adaptation.

переде́лыва|ть, ю *impf. of* ⇒**переде́лать¹**

передел|я́ть, я́ю *impf. of* ⇒**~и́ть**

передёргива|ть(ся), ю(сь) *impf. of* ⇒**передёрнуть(ся)**

передерж|а́ть¹, у́, ~ишь *pf.* (*of* ⇒**~ивать**) **1** (*кушанье*) to overdo; to overcook. **2** (*phot.*) to over-expose.

передерж|а́ть², у́, ~ишь *pf.* (*of* ⇒**~ивать**) (*coll.*): **п. экза́мен** to take an examination again.

переде́ржива|ть, ю *impf. of* ⇒**передержа́ть**

переде́ржк|а¹, и *f.* (*phot.*) over-exposure.

переде́ржк|а², и *f.* (*coll.*) (*переэкзаменовка*) re-examination.

переде́ржк|а³, и *f.* (*coll.*) (*жульничество*) cheating (*at cards*); juggling (*with facts*).

передёр|нуть, ну, нешь *pf.* (*of* ⇒**~гивать**) **1** (*передвинуть*) to pull aside. **2** (*сжульничать*) to cheat (*at cards*). **3** (*fig.*): **п. фа́кты** to juggle with facts. **4** (*impers.*): **его́ ~нуло от бо́ли** he was convulsed with pain.

передёр|нуться, нусь, нешься *pf.* (*of* ⇒**~гиваться**) (*coll.*) to flinch, wince.

переднеприводно́й *adj.*: **п. автомоби́ль** front-wheel drive vehicle.

пере́дн|ий *adj.* front; **~ие коне́чности** fore-legs; **п. край** in the front line (*also fig.*); **п. план** foreground.

пере́дник, а *m.* apron.

пере́дн|яя, ей *f.* (entrance) hall, lobby.

пе́редо = **пе́ред**

передов|а́я, ~о́й *f.* **1** (*статья*) leading article, leader; editorial. **2** (*mil.*) forward position.

передове́р|ить, ю, ишь *pf.* (*of* ⇒**~я́ть**) (+*d.*) to transfer trust (to); (*leg.*) to transfer power of attorney (to); **п. догово́р** to sub-contract (to).

передовер|я́ть, я́ю *impf. of* ⇒**~ить**

передови́к, а́ *m.* leading worker.

передови́ц|а, ы *f.* (*coll.*) leading article, leader; editorial.

передов|о́й *adj.* (*отряд*) forward; (*технология*) advanced; (*взгляды*) progressive; **~а́я статья́** leading article, leader; editorial.

передозиро́вк|а, и *f.* (*med.*) overdose.

перед|о́к, ка́ *m.* front (*of carriage, etc.*).

передо́м *adv.* (*coll.*) in front.

передо́х|нуть, нет, *past* **~, ~ла** *pf.* (*no impf.*) (*издохнуть*) to die off (*usu. of animals*).

передохн|у́ть, у́, ёшь *pf.* (*of* ⇒**передыха́ть**) (*coll.*) to pause for breath, take a short rest.

передра́знива|ть, ю *impf. of* ⇒**передразни́ть**

передразн|и́ть, ю́, ~ишь *pf.* (*of* ⇒**~ивать**) to take off, mimic.

пере|дра́ться, деру́сь, дерёшься, *past* **~дра́лся, ~драла́сь, ~дра́ло́сь** *pf.* (*no impf.*) (*coll.*) to fight, brawl (*of many people, etc.*).

передро́г|нуть, ну, нешь, *past* **~,**

П

~ла *pf.* (*no impf.*) (*coll.*) to get chilled through.

передря́г|а, и *f.* (*coll.*) scrape.

переду́м|ать, аю *pf.* (*of* ⇒**~ывать**) **1** (*изменить решение*) to change one's mind. **2** (*обдумать многое*) to do a great deal of thinking.

переду́мыва|ть, ю *impf. of* ⇒**переду́мать**

передыха́|ть, ю *impf. of* ⇒**передохну́ть**

передышк|а, и *f.* breathing-space; (*в работе*) break, breather.

перееда́ни|е, я *nt.* overeating.

перееда́|ть, ю *impf. of* ⇒**перее́сть**

перее́зд[1], **а** *m.* (*место*) crossing.

перее́зд[2], **а** *m.* (*переселение*) move.

переезжа́|ть, ю *impf. of* ⇒**перее́хать**

перее́|сть[1], **м, шь, ст, ди́м, ди́те, дя́т,** *past* **~л** *pf.* (*of* ⇒**~да́ть**) (*объедаться*) to overeat.

перее́|сть[2], **ст, дя́т,** *past* **~л** *pf.* (*of* ⇒**~да́ть**) (*разрушить*) to corrode, eat away.

перее́|хать, ду, дешь *pf.* (*of* ⇒**~зжа́ть**) **1** (+*a. or* **че́рез**+*a.*) (*дорогу*) to cross. **2** (*задавить*) to run over, knock down. **3** (*переселиться*) to move.

пережа́рива|ть, ю *impf. of* ⇒**пережа́рить**[1]

пережа́р|ить[1], **ю, ишь** *pf.* (*of* ⇒**~ивать**) (*изжарить слишком долго*) to overdo, overroast.

пережа́р|ить[2], **ю, ишь** *pf.* (*изжарить многое*) to roast (*all or a number of*).

пережд|а́ть, у́, ёшь, *past* **~а́л, ~ала́, ~а́ло** *pf.* (*of* ⇒**пережида́ть**) to wait through; **мы ~а́ли грозу́** we waited till the storm was over.

переж|ева́ть, ую́, уёшь *pf.* (*of* ⇒**~ёвывать**) to masticate, chew.

пережёвыва|ть, ю *impf.* **1** *impf. of* ⇒**пережева́ть. 2** (*fig.*) to repeat over and over again.

пережен|и́ться, ~́ится *pf.* (*coll.*) to marry; **все её бра́тья ~и́лись** all her brothers have married.

переж|е́чь, гу́, жёшь, гу́т, *past* **~ёг, ~гла́** *pf.* (*of* ⇒**~ига́ть**) **1** (*израсходовать сверх меры*) to burn more than one's quota (*of fuel, etc.*). **2** (*шнур*) to burn through. **3** (*испортить излишним обжиганием*) to heat to excess. **4** (*сжечь многое*) to burn.

пережива́ни|е, я *nt.* (*события*) experience; (*душевное состояние*) feeling.

пережива́|ть, ю *impf.* **1** *impf. of* ⇒**пережи́ть. 2** (*impf. only*) (**за**+*a.*) (*coll.*) to be upset, worry (for, on behalf of).

пережига́|ть, ю *impf. of* ⇒**пережéчь**

пережида́|ть, ю *impf. of* ⇒**пережда́ть**

пережит|ое, о́го *nt.* one's past.

пережи́т|ок, ка *m.* relic, vestige, survival.

пережи́|ть, ву́, вёшь, *past* **пе́режил, ~ла́, пе́режило** *pf.* (*of* ⇒**~ва́ть**) **1** to live through; **п. жизнь** to live one's life through. **2** (*испытать*) to experience; to go through; (*выдержать*) to endure, suffer; **тяжело́ п. что-н.** to take sth. hard; **она́ ещё не совсе́м ~ла́ потрясе́ние** she has still not completely got over the shock; (*остаться в живых*) to survive; **мне оби́дно, но ничего́, переживу́** I'm upset, but I'll survive. **3** (*прожить дольше*) to outlive, survive.

перезаб|ы́ть, у́ду, у́дешь *pf.* (*no impf.*) (*coll.*) to forget.

перезагру|жа́ть, жа́ю *impf. of* ⇒**~зи́ть**

перезагр|узи́ть, ужу́, у́зишь *pf.* (*of* ⇒**~ужа́ть**) (*comput.*) to reboot.

перезакла́дыва|ть, ю *impf. of* ⇒**перезаложи́ть**

перезаключ|а́ть, а́ю *impf. of* ⇒**~и́ть**

перезаключ|и́ть, у́, и́шь *pf.* (*of* ⇒**~а́ть**) to renew; **п. догово́р** to renew a contract.

перезалож|и́ть, у́, ~́ишь *pf.* (*of* ⇒**перезакла́дывать**) (*кольцо*) to re-pawn; (*дом*) to remortgage.

перезап|иса́ть, ишу́, и́шешь *pf.* (*of* ⇒**~и́сывать**) (*comput.*) to overwrite.

перезапи́сыва|ть, ю *impf. of* ⇒**перезаписа́ть**

перезаря|ди́ть, жу́, ~ди́шь *pf.* (*of* ⇒**~жа́ть**) **1** (*аккумулятор*) to re-charge. **2** (*револьвер, фотоаппарат*) to re-load.

перезаря́дк|а, и *f.* re-charging; re-loading.

перезаряжа́|ть, ю *impf. of* ⇒**перезаряди́ть**

перезва́нива|ть, ю *impf. of* ⇒**перезвони́ть**

перезво́н, а *m.* ringing, chime.

перезвон|и́ть, ю, и́шь *pf.* (*of* ⇒**перезва́нивать**) to ring back (*Br.*), call back (*US*).

перезим|ова́ть, у́ю *pf.* (*of* ⇒**зимова́ть**) to winter, pass the winter.

перезнако́м|ить, лю, ишь *pf.* (*coll.*; **с**+*i.*) to acquaint (with), introduce (to).

перезнако́м|иться, люсь, ишься *pf.* (*no impf.*) (*coll.*) to become acquainted (with), be introduced (to).

перезрева́|ть, ю *impf. of* ⇒**перезре́ть**

перезре́лый *adj.* overripe; (*fig.*) passé, past one's prime.

перезре́|ть, ю *pf.* (*of* ⇒**~ва́ть**) **1** to become overripe. **2** (*fig.*) to be past one's prime.

переигр|а́ть[1], **а́ю** *pf.* (*of* ⇒**~́ывать**) **1** (*партию*) to play again. **2** (*coll.*) (*изменить*) to change; to reconsider.

переигр|а́ть[2], **а́ю** *pf.* (*of* ⇒**~́ывать**) (*theatr.*; *coll.*) to overact, overdo.

переигр|а́ть[3], **а́ю** *pf.* (*of* ⇒**~́ывать**) (*сыграть многое*) to play, act, perform (*all or a number of*).

переигр|а́ть[4], **а́ю** *pf.* (*of* ⇒**~́ывать**) (*coll., sport*) to outplay; to beat.

переи́грыва|ть, ю *impf. of* ⇒**переигра́ть**[1,2,3,4]

переизбира́|ть, ю *impf. of* ⇒**переизбра́ть**

переизбра́ни|е, я *nt.* re-election.

переиз|бра́ть, беру́, берёшь, *past* **~бра́л, ~брала́, ~бра́ло** *pf.* (*of* ⇒**~бира́ть**) to re-elect.

переизда|ва́ть, ю́, ёшь *impf. of* ⇒**~́ть**

переизда́ни|е, я *nt.* **1** (*действие*) re-publication. **2** (*книга*) new edition, reprint.

переизда́|ть, м, шь, ст, ди́м, ди́те, ду́т, *past* **~л, ~ла́, ~ло** *pf.* (*of* ⇒**~ва́ть**) to re-publish, reprint.

переимен|ова́ть, у́ю *pf.* (*of* ⇒**~о́вывать**) (**в**+*a.*) to rename.

переимено́выва|ть, ю *impf. of* ⇒**переименова́ть**

переи́мчив|ый (~, ~а) *adj.* (*coll.*) imitative.

переина́чива|ть, ю *impf. of* ⇒**переина́чить**

переина́ч|ить, у, ишь *pf.* (*of* ⇒**~ивать**) to alter; to modify.

пере|йти́, йду́, йдёшь, *past* **~шёл, ~шла́** *pf.* (*of* ⇒**~ходи́ть**) **1** (+*a. or* **че́рез**+*a.*) (*переправиться*) to cross; to get across, get over, go over; **п. грани́цу** to cross the frontier; **п. через мо́ст** to go across a bridge.
2 (**в, на**+*a. or* **к**+*d.*) (*в другое место*) to pass (to); **п. в сосе́днюю ко́мнату** to go into the next room; **п. в наступле́ние** to switch to the offensive, assume the offensive; **п. в ру́ки** (+*g.*) to pass into the hands (of); **п. из рук в ру́ки** to change hands; **п. на другу́ю рабо́ту** to change one's job; **п. на сто́рону проти́вника** to go over to the enemy.
3 (**в**+*a.*) (*превратиться*) to turn (into); **их ссо́ра ~шла́ в дра́ку** their quarrel turned into a fight.

перека́лива|ть, ю *impf. of* ⇒**перекали́ть**

перекал|и́ть, ю, и́шь *pf.* (*of* ⇒**~́ивать**) (*tech.*) to overtemper; (*coll.*) to overheat.

перека́лыва|ть, ю *impf. of* ⇒**переколо́ть**

перека́пыва|ть, ю *impf. of* ⇒**перекопа́ть**

перека́рмлива|ть, ю *impf. of* ⇒**перекорми́ть**

перека́т[1], **а** *m.* (*мелководный участок*) shoal.

перека́т[2], **а** *m.* (*грома*) roll, peal (*of thunder*).

перекати́-по́л|е, я *nt.* **1** (*bot.*) tumbleweed. **2** (*fig.*) (*о человеке*) rolling stone.

перека|ти́ть, чу́, ~́тишь *pf.* (*of* ⇒**~́тывать**) (*бочку*) to roll; (*велосипед*) to wheel.

перека|ти́ться, чу́сь, ~́тишься *pf.* (*of* ⇒**~́тываться**) to roll.

перека́тыва|ть(ся), ю(сь) *impf. of* ⇒**перекати́ть(ся)**

перекач|а́ть, а́ю *pf.* (*of* ⇒**~́ивать**) to pump over, pump across.

перека́чива|ть, ю *impf. of* ⇒**перекача́ть**

перека́шива|ть(ся), ю, ет(ся) *impf. of* ⇒**перекоси́ть(ся)**

переквалифика́ци|я, и *f.* retraining.

переквалифици́р|овать, ую *impf. and pf.* to retrain.

переквалифици́р|оваться, уюсь *impf. and pf.* to retrain.

перекид|а́ть, а́ю *pf.* (*of* ⇒**~́ывать**) to throw (one after another).

перекидно́й *adj.*: **п. мо́стик** footbridge; **п. календа́рь** desk calendar.

переки́дыва|ть(ся), ю(сь) *impf. of* ⇒**перекида́ть** *and* ⇒**переки́нуть(ся)**

переки́|нуть, ну, нешь *pf.* (*of* ⇒**~дывать**) to throw (over).

переки́|нуться, нусь, нешься *pf.* (*of* ⇒**~дываться**) **1** (*быстро переместиться*) to leap (over). **2** (*огонь*) to spread. **3** (+*i.*) (*мячом*) to throw (one to another); (*словами*) to bandy, exchange.

перекипя|ти́ть, чу́, ти́шь *pf.* to boil again.

пе́рекис|ь, и *f.* (*chem.*) peroxide.

перекла́дин|а, ы *f.* **1** (*брус*) cross-beam, cross-piece, transom. **2** (*sport*) horizontal bar.

перекладн|ы́е, ы́х *pl.* (*hist.*) post-chaise.

перекла́дыва|ть, ю *impf. of* ⇒**переложи́ть**

перекле́ива|ть, ю *impf. of* ⇒**перекле́ить**

перекле́|ить[1], ю, ишь *pf.* (*of* ⇒**~ивать**) (*наклеить заново*) to re-stick; to glue again.

перекле́|ить[2], ю, ишь *pf.* (*of* ⇒**~ивать**) (*склеить многое*) to stick (*a number of*).

переклик|а́ться, а́юсь *impf.* (**с**+*i.*) **1** (*pf.* **~́нуться**) to call to one another. **2** (*no pf.*) (*fig.*) (*быть подобным*) to have sth. in common (with).

перекли́к|нуться, нусь, нешься *pf. of* ⇒**~а́ться** 1

перекли́чк|а, и *f.* roll-call; **де́лать ~у** to call the roll.

переключа́тел|ь, я *m.* (*tech.*) switch.

переключ|а́ть(ся), а́ю(сь) *impf. of* ⇒**~и́ть(ся)**

переключе́ни|е, я *nt.* switching; (*скорости*) changing (*Br.*), shifting (*US*).

переключ|и́ть, у́, и́шь *pf.* (*of* ⇒**~а́ть**) (*tech. and fig.*; **на**+*a.*) to switch (over to); **п. ско́рость** to change gear (*Br.*), shift gears (*US*); **п. внима́ние на...** to switch one's attention to ...; **п. разгово́р на другу́ю те́му** to change the subject; **п. телеви́зор/ра́дио на другу́ю програ́мму** to switch over, change channels (*on the TV/radio*).

переключ|и́ться, у́сь и́шься *pf.* (*of* ⇒**~а́ться**) (*tech. and fig.*; **на**+*a.*) to switch (over to); **компа́ния ~и́лась на э́кспорт телеви́зоров** the company switched to the export of televisions; **внима́ние пу́блики ~и́лось на говоря́щего** attention switched to the speaker; **п. на бли́жний свет** to dip (*Br.*), dim (*US*) one's headlights.

перек|ова́ть, ую́, уёшь *pf.* (*of* ⇒**~о́вывать**) **1** (*коня*) to reshoe. **2** (*изделие*) to reforge; **п. мечи́ на ора́ла** to beat swords into ploughshares (*Br.*), plowshares (*US*) (*also fig.*).

переко́выва|ть, ю *impf. of* ⇒**перекова́ть**

переκол|о́ть[1], ю́, ~́ешь *pf.* (*of* ⇒**перека́лывать**) **1** (*приколоть иначе*) to pin (*somewhere else*). **2** (*покрыть уколами*) to prick all over.

перекол|о́ть[2], ю́, ~́ешь *pf.* (*of* ⇒**перека́лывать**) (*расколоть*) to chop, hew.

перекопа́|ть, ю *pf.* (*of* ⇒**перека́пывать**) **1** (*картофель; огород*) to dig up. **2** (*чемодан*) to rummage through. **3** (*дорогу*) to dig a ditch across.

перекорм|и́ть, лю́, ~́ишь *pf.* (*of* ⇒**перека́рмливать**) to overfeed.

перекóр|ы, ов *no sg.* (*coll.*) squabble.

перекоря́|ться, юсь *impf.* (*no pf.*) (*coll.*) to squabble.

переко́с, а *m.* **1** (*искривление*) warping. **2** (*fig.*) (*тенденциозность*) slant.

переко|си́ть[1], шу́, ~́сишь *pf.* (*of* ⇒**перека́шивать**) (*сделать косым*) to warp; (*fig.*) to distort, slant; (*impers.*): **око́нную ра́му ~́сило** the window-frame has warped; **от зло́бы его́ ~́сило** his face was distorted with malice.

переко|си́ть[2], шу́, ~́сишь *pf.* (*скосить многое*) to mow (*all of, a large area of*).

переко|си́ться, ~́сится, ~́сятся *pf.* (*of* ⇒**перека́шиваться**) to warp, be warped; (*fig.*) to become distorted.

перекоч|ева́ть, у́ю *pf.* (*of* ⇒**~ёвывать**) **1** (*о таборе*) to move on. **2** (*coll.*) (*перейти*) to move, migrate.

перекочёвыва|ть, ю *impf. of* ⇒**перекочева́ть**

перекó|шенный *p.p.p. of* ⇒**~си́ть** *and adj.* distorted, twisted.

перекра́ива|ть, ю *impf. of* ⇒**перекрои́ть**

перекра́|сить[1], шу, сишь *pf.* (*of* ⇒**~шивать**) (*стену*) to repaint; (*в другой цвет*) to paint another colour (*Br.*), color (*US*); (*волосы*) to re-dye.

перекра́|сить[2], шу, сишь *pf.* (*of* ⇒**~шивать**) (*покрасить многое*) (*рамы*) to paint; (*рубашки*) to dye.

перекра́|ситься, шусь, сишься *pf.* (*of* ⇒**~шиваться**) **1** to change colour (*Br.*), color (*US*). **2** (*fig.*) to become a turncoat.

перекра́шива|ть(ся), ю(сь) *impf. of* ⇒**перекра́сить(ся)**

перекре|сти́ть[1], щу́, ~́стишь *pf.* (*of* ⇒**крести́ть** 3) to make the sign of the cross over.

перекре|сти́ть[2], щу́, ~́стишь *pf.* (*of* ⇒**~́щивать**) (*расположить крест-накрест*) to criss-cross.

перекре|сти́ть[3], щу́, ~́стишь *pf.* (*of* ⇒**~́щивать**) (*coll.*) (*дать новое имя*) to rechristen, rename.

перекре|сти́ться[1], щу́сь, ~́стишься *pf.* (*of* ⇒**крести́ться** 2) (*о человеке*) to cross o.s.

перекре|сти́ться[2], ~́стится *pf.* (*of* ⇒**~́щиваться**) (*о линиях*) to cross, intersect.

перекрёстн|ый *adj.* cross; **п. допро́с** cross-examination; **п. ого́нь** (*mil.*) cross-fire; **~ая ссы́лка** cross-reference.

перекрёст|ок, ка *m.* cross-roads, crossing; **крича́ть на всех ~ках** (*coll.*) to shout from the house-tops.

перекре́щива|ть(ся), ю(сь) *impf. of* ⇒**перекрести́ть[2,3](ся)[2]**

перекри́кива|ть, ю *impf. of* ⇒**перекрича́ть**

перекри|ча́ть, чу́, чи́шь *pf.* (*of* ⇒**~́кивать**) (*шум*) to shout above; (*человека*) to shout down.

перекро|и́ть, ю́, и́шь *pf.* (*of* ⇒**перекра́ивать**) to cut out again; (*fig.*) (*статью, план*) to rehash; to re-shape; **п. ка́рту ми́ра** to re-draw the map of the world.

перекру|ти́ть, чу́, ~́тишь *pf.* (*of* ⇒**~́чивать**) **1** (*крутя, испортить*) to overwind. **2** (*перевязать*) to tie. **3** (*скрутить*) to fasten.

перекру́чива|ть, ю *impf. of* ⇒**перекрути́ть**

перекрыва́|ть, ю *impf. of* ⇒**перекры́ть**

перекры́ти|е, я *nt.* **1** (*archit.*) ceiling; (*между этажами*) floor. **2** (*tech.*) damming (of a river).

перекр|ы́ть[1], о́ю, о́ешь *pf.* (*of* ⇒**~ыва́ть**) (*покрыть заново*) to re-cover.

перекр|ы́ть[2], о́ю, о́ешь *pf.* (*of* ⇒**~ыва́ть**) **1** (*coll.*) (*превзойти*) to exceed; **п. реко́рд** to break a record. **2** (*дорогу*) to close; (*воду*) to cut off; (*реку*) to dam.

перекувы́ркива|ть(ся), ю(сь) *impf. of* ⇒**перекувырну́ть(ся)**

перекувыр|ну́ть, ну́, нёшь *pf.* (*of* ⇒**~́кивать**) (*coll.*) to upset, overturn.

перекувыр|ну́ться, ну́сь, нёшься *pf.* (*of* ⇒**~́киваться**) (*coll.*) **1** (*упасть*) to topple over. **2** (*перевернуться кувырком*) to turn a somersault.

перекуп|а́ть, а́ю *impf. of* ⇒**~и́ть**

перекупа́|ться, юсь *pf.* (*coll.*) to bathe too long, stay in (the water) too long.

перекуп|и́ть, лю́, ~́ишь *pf.* (*of* ⇒**~а́ть**) (*купить то, что хотел купить другой*) to buy (*sth. sought by others*); to outbid for; (*купить все или много*) to buy up (*all or a lot*).

переку́пщик, а *m.* second-hand dealer.

переку́р, а *m.* (*coll.*) smoking break; (*перерыв вообще*) break; **пойдём на п.** let's take five.

переку́рива|ть, ю *impf. of* ⇒**перекури́ть**

П

перекур|и́ть, ю́, ∽́ишь *pf.* (*of* **⇒∽́ивать**) (*coll.*) to break for a smoke; (*передохнуть*) to take a break.

переку|си́ть, шу́, ∽́сишь *pf.* (*of* **⇒∽́сывать**) **1** to bite through. **2** (*coll.*) (*закусить*) to have a bite, have a snack.

перекýсыва|ть, ю *impf. of* **⇒перекуси́ть**

перелага́|ть, ю *impf. of* **⇒переложи́ть**

перела́мыва|ть(ся), ю, ет(ся) *impf. of* **⇒переломи́ть(ся)**

перележ|а́ть, у́, и́шь *pf.* to lie too long.

перелез|а́ть, а́ю *impf. of* **⇒∽́ть**

переле́з|ть, у, ешь, *past* **∽, ∽ла** *pf.* (*of* **⇒∽а́ть**) to climb over, get over.

переле́с|ок, ка *m.* copse, coppice.

перелёт, а *m.* **1** (*самолёта*) flight. **2** (*птиц*) migration. **3** (*снаряда*) shot over the target.

перелет|а́ть, а́ю *impf. of* **⇒∽е́ть**

переле|те́ть, чу́, ти́шь *pf.* (*of* **⇒∽та́ть**) **1** (+*a. or* **че́рез**+*a.*) to fly over. **2** (*дальше нужного*) to fly too far; to overshoot (the mark).

перелётн|ый *adj.*: **∽ая пти́ца** bird of passage (*also fig.*); migratory bird.

пере|ле́чь, ля́гу, ля́жешь, ля́гут, *past* **∽лёг, ∽легла́** *pf.* (*no impf.*) to lie somewhere else; to move; **п. с дива́на на крова́ть** to move from the sofa to the bed.

перели́в, а *m.* (*цвета*) tint, tinge; (*цветов*) play (of colours (*Br.*), colors (*US*)); (*голоса*) modulation.

перелива́ни|е, я *nt.* **1** decantation. **2** (*med.*) transfusion.

перелива́|ть¹, ю *impf. of* **⇒перели́ть**

перелива́|ть², ет *impf.* (*о цветах*) to play.

перелива́|ться¹, ется *impf. of* **⇒перели́ться**

перелива́|ться², ется *impf.* (*о цветах*) to play; (*о голосах*) to modulate.

перели́вчат|ый (∽, ∽а) *adj.* iridescent; (*о голосе*) modulating; (*о шёлке*) shot.

перелист|а́ть, а́ю *pf.* (*of* **⇒∽́ывать**) **1** to leaf through. **2** (*бегло просмотреть*) to look through, flick through.

перели́стыва|ть, ю *impf. of* **⇒перелиста́ть**

перел|и́ть¹, ью́, ьёшь, *past* **∽и́л, ∽ила́, ∽и́ло** *pf.* (*of* **⇒∽ива́ть**) **1** to pour (*somewhere else*; *from A into B*); to decant; **п. молоко́ из кастрю́ли в кувши́н** to pour milk from a saucepan into a jug. **2** (*med.*) to transfuse; **п. кровь** (+*d.*) to administer a blood transfusion (to). **3** (*через край*) to let overflow.

перел|и́ть², ью́, ьёшь, *past* **∽и́л, ∽ила́, ∽и́ло** *pf.* (*of* **⇒∽ива́ть**) **1** (*деталь*) to re-cast. **2** (*литьём превратить во что-н. иное*) to melt down; **п. колокола́ на пу́шки** to melt down bells for guns.

перел|и́ться, ьётся, *past* **∽и́лся, ∽ила́сь, ∽и́ло́сь** *pf.* (*of* **⇒∽ива́ться**) **1** (*литься в другое место*) to flow. **2** (*вылиться*) to overflow, run over.

перелиц|ева́ть, у́ю *pf.* (*of* **⇒∽о́вывать**) **1** (*пальто*) to turn (*to disguise wear*); to have (*a garment etc.*) turned. **2** (*fig.*) (*придать новый вид*) to give a new face to.

перелицо́выва|ть, ю *impf. of* **⇒перелицева́ть**

перелов|и́ть, лю́, ∽́ишь *pf.* to catch (*all or a number of*).

переложе́ни|е, я *nt.* (*mus.*) arrangement; **п. в стихи́** versification.

перелож|и́ть, у́, ∽́ишь *pf.* **1** (*impf.* **перекла́дывать** *and* **перелага́ть**) to put somewhere else; to shift, move; (*fig.*) to shift, transfer; **п. отве́тственность на кого́-н.** to shift the responsibility on to s.o. **2** (*impf.* **перекла́дывать**) (+*a. and i.*) to interlay (with); **п. посу́ду соло́мой** to interlay crockery with straw. **3** (*impf.* **перекла́дывать**) (*печь*) to re-lay. **4** (*impf.* **перелага́ть**) (**в, на**+*a.*) to set (to), arrange (for); to put (into); **п. на му́зыку** to set to music; **п. в стихи́** to put into verse. **5** (*impf.* **перекла́дывать**) (+*g.*) (*положить слишком много*) to put in too much; **вы ∽и́ли со́ли в суп** you have put too much salt in the soup.

перело́м, а *m.* **1** break, breaking; (*кости*) fracture. **2** (*fig.*) (*поворотный пункт*) turning point; (*резкая перемена*) sudden change.

перелома́|ть, ю *pf.* to break (*all or a number of*); (*fig., coll.*) to prevail over (*s.o.*).

перелома́|ться, ется *pf.* (*coll.*) to break, be broken.

перелом|и́ть, лю́, ∽́ишь *pf.* (*of* **⇒перела́мывать**) **1** to break in two. **2** (*fig.*) to break, master; **п. себя́** to master o.s.; to restrain one's feelings; **п. кому́-н. во́лю** to break s.o.'s will; **п. ход собы́тий** to turn events around.

перелом|и́ться, ∽́ится *pf.* (*of* **⇒перела́мываться**) to break in two; to be fractured.

перело́м|ный *adj. of* **⇒∽; п. моме́нт** critical moment, crucial moment.

перема́|зать, жу, жешь *pf.* (*of* **⇒∽зывать**) (*coll.*; +*i.*) to smear (with), make dirty (with).

перема́|заться, жусь, жешься *pf.* (*of* **⇒∽зываться**) (*coll.*) to besmear o.s., get dirty.

перема́зыва|ть(ся), ю(сь) *impf. of* **⇒перема́зать(ся)**

перема́лыва|ть(ся), ю, ет(ся) *impf. of* **⇒перемоло́ть(ся)**

перема́нива|ть, ю *impf. of* **⇒перемани́ть**

переман|и́ть, ю́, ∽́ишь *pf.* (*of* **⇒∽́ивать**) (*coll.*) to entice; **п. на свою́ сто́рону** to win over.

перема́тыва|ть, ю *impf. of* **⇒перемота́ть**

перема́хива|ть, ю *impf. of* **⇒перемахну́ть**

перемах|ну́ть, ну́, нёшь *pf.* (*of* **⇒∽́ивать**) (*coll.*) to jump over, leap over.

перемежа́|ть, ю *impf.* (*no pf.*) (+*a. and i.* or **с**+*i.*) to alternate; **он ∽л угро́зы (с) обеща́ниями** he alternated threats and promises.

перемежа́|ться, ется *impf.* (*no pf.*) (+*i. or* **с**+*i.*) to alternate; **снег ∽лся (с) дождём** snow alternated with rain, it snowed and rained by turns.

перемеж|ева́ть, у́ю *pf.* (*of* **⇒∽ёвывать**) to re-survey.

перемежёвыва|ть, ю *impf. of* **⇒перемежева́ть**

переме́н|а, ы *f.* **1** change. **2** (*в школе*) break (*Br.*), recess (*US*); **больша́я п.** long (*sc.* midday) break.

перемен|и́ть, ю́, ∽́ишь *pf.* (*of* **⇒∽я́ть**) to change; **п. пози́цию** to shift one's ground (*also fig.*); **п. тон** (*fig.*) to change one's tune.

перемен|и́ться, ю́сь, ∽́ишься *pf.* (*of* **⇒∽я́ться**) to change; **п. в лице́** to change countenance.

переме́нн|ый *adj.* variable; **∽ая величина́** (*math.*) variable (quantity); **∽ая пого́да** changeable weather; **п. ток** (*elec.*) alternating current; **с ∽ым успе́хом** with varying success.

переме́нчив|ый (∽, ∽а) *adj.* (*coll.*) changeable.

перемен|я́ть(ся), я́ю(сь) *impf. of* **⇒∽и́ть(ся)**

пере|мере́ть, мрёт, *past* **пе́ремер, ∽мерла́, пе́ремерло** *pf.* (*coll.*) to perish.

перемерз|а́ть, а́ю *impf. of* **⇒∽́нуть**

перемёрз|нуть, ну, нешь *pf.* (*of* **⇒∽а́ть**) (*coll.*) **1** (*озябнуть*) to get chilled, freeze. **2** (*о растениях*) to be killed by the frost.

переме́рива|ть, ю *impf. of* **⇒переме́рить**

переме́р|ить¹, ю, ишь *pf.* (*of* **⇒∽ивать**) (*измерить заново*) to re-measure.

переме́р|ить², ю, ишь *pf.* (*примерить*) to try on.

переме|сти́ть, щу́, сти́шь *pf.* (*of* **⇒∽ща́ть**) to move (*somewhere else*); (*на другую работу*) to transfer.

переме|сти́ться, щу́сь, сти́шься *pf.* (*of* **⇒∽ща́ться**) to move.

переме́|тить, чу, тишь *pf.* (*of* **⇒∽ча́ть**) **1** (*пометить заново*) to mark again. **2** (*пометить многое*) to mark (*a quantity of*).

переметн|у́ться, у́сь, ёшься *pf.* (*no impf.*) **1** (*перебежать*) to dash across. **2** (*к противнику*) (*coll.*) to go over, desert.

перемётн|ый *adj.*: **∽ая сума́** (*coll.*) turncoat.

перемеч|а́ть, ю *impf. of* **⇒переме́тить**

перемеш|а́ть, а́ю *pf.* (*of* **⇒∽́ивать**) **1** to (inter)mix, intermingle; **п. ка́рты** to shuffle cards; **п. у́гли в пе́чке** to poke the fire. **2** (*coll.*)

(*нарушить порядок*) to mix up; (*obs.*) (*спутать*) to confuse; **он, по-видимому, ~а́л на́ши фами́лии** he evidently got our names mixed up.

перемеш|а́ться, а́ется *pf.* (*of* ⇒**~иваться**) to get mixed (up); **всё у него́ в голове́ ~а́лось** he has got everything mixed up.

переме́шивани|е, я *nt.* mixing.

переме́шива|ть(ся), ю, ет(ся) *impf. of* ⇒**перемеша́ть(ся)**

перемеща́|ть(ся), ю(сь) *impf. of* ⇒**перемести́ть(ся)**

перемеще́ни|е, я *nt.* (*изменение положения*) transference, shift; (*движение*) movement; (*по службе*) transfer.

переме|щённый *p.p.p. of* ⇒**~сти́ть; ~щённые ли́ца** (*pol.*) displaced persons.

перемя́гива|ться, юсь *impf. of* ⇒**перемигну́ться**

перемиг|ну́ться, ну́сь, нёшься *pf.* (*of* ⇒**~иваться**) (*coll.*; **с**+*i.*) to wink (at); **п. ме́жду собо́й** to wink at each other.

перемина́|ться, юсь *impf.* (*no pf.*): **п. с ноги́ на́ ногу** (*coll.*) to shift from one foot to the other.

переми́ри|е, я *nt.* armistice, truce.

перемнож|а́ть, а́ю *impf. of* ⇒**~ить**

перемно́ж|ить, у, ишь *pf.* (*of* ⇒**~а́ть**) to multiply.

перемога́|ть, ю *impf.* (*coll.*) **1** (*pf.* **перемо́чь**) (*преодолеть*) to overcome (*an illness, etc.*). **2** (*стараться преодолеть*) to try to overcome (*an illness, etc.*).

перемога́|ться, юсь *impf.* (*coll.*) to try to overcome an illness; **три дня он ~лся, но в конце́ концо́в ему́ пришло́сь вы́звать врача́** he held out for three days, but in the end he had to call in the doctor.

перемок|а́ть, а́ю *impf. of* ⇒**~нуть**

перемо́к|нуть, ну, нешь, *past* **~, ~ла** *pf.* (*of* ⇒**~а́ть**) (*coll.*) to get drenched.

перемо́лв|ить, лю, ишь *pf.* (*no impf.*): **п. сло́во** (**с**+*i.*; *coll.*) to exchange a word (with).

перемо́лв|иться, люсь, ишься *pf.* (*no impf.*) (+*i.*; **с**+*i.*; *coll.*) to exchange words (with); **п. не́сколькими слова́ми с сосе́дом** to exchange a few words with a neighbour.

перем|оло́ть, елю́, е́лешь *pf.* (*of* ⇒**~а́лывать**) (*кофе, зерно*) to grind, mill; (*fig.*) (*разрушить*) to pulverize.

перем|оло́ться, е́лется *pf.* (*of* ⇒**~а́лываться**): **~е́лется — мука́ бу́дет** (*prov.*) it will all come right in the end.

перемота́|ть, ю *pf.* (*of* ⇒**перема́тывать**) **1** (*на что-н. другое*) to wind; to reel. **2** (*намотать заново*) to re-wind.

перемо́|чь, гу́, ~жешь *pf. of* ⇒**~га́ть**

перему́ч|иться, усь, ишься *pf.* (*no impf.*) (*coll.*) to have suffered very much.

перемыва́|ть, ю *impf. of* ⇒**перемы́ть; п. ко́сточки кому́-н.** to gossip about s.o.

перем|ы́ть, о́ю, о́ешь *pf.* (*of* ⇒**~ыва́ть**) **1** (*вымыть заново*) to wash up again. **2** (*вымыть многое*) to wash (up) (*all or a quantity of*).

перемы́чк|а, и *f.* (*tech.*) **1** (*соединение*) crosspiece. **2** (*заграждение*) cofferdam.

перенапряга́|ть(ся), ю(сь) *impf. of* ⇒**перенапря́чь(ся)**

перенапряже́ни|е, я *nt.* **1** overstrain. **2** (*в сети*) increased voltage, surge.

перенапря́|чь, гу́, жёшь, *past* **~г, ~гла́** *pf.* (*of* ⇒**~га́ть**) to overstrain.

перенапря́|чься, гу́сь, жёшься, *past* **~гся, ~гла́сь** *pf.* (*of* ⇒**~га́ться**) to overstrain o.s.

перенаселе́ни|е, я *nt.* overpopulation.

перенаселённост|ь, и *f.* overpopulation; (*квартиры*) overcrowding.

перенасел|ённый *p.p.p. of* ⇒**~и́ть** *and adj.* overpopulated; (*квартира*) overcrowded.

перенасел|и́ть, ю́, и́шь *pf.* (*of* ⇒**~я́ть**) to overpopulate.

перенасел|я́ть, я́ю *impf. of* ⇒**~и́ть**

перенасы́щенный *adj.* (*chem.*) supersaturated.

перене́рвнича|ть, ю *pf.* (*coll.*) to worry a lot.

перенесе́ни|е, я *nt.* **1** (*в другое место*) transference. **2** (*собрания*) postponement.

перенес|ти́[1], у́, ёшь, *past* **~, ~ла́** *pf.* (*of* ⇒**переноси́ть**) **1** (*через пространство*) to carry (*somewhere else*); (*поместить в другое место*) to move, transfer; **п. столи́цу в Москву́** to move the capital to Moscow. **2**: **п. сло́во** (*typ.*) to carry over (*part of word*) to the next line. **3** (*отсрочить*) to put off, postpone; to carry over.

перенес|ти́[2], у́, ёшь, *past* **~, ~ла́** *pf.* (*of* ⇒**переноси́ть**) (*выдержать*) to endure, bear, stand; **п. боле́знь** to have an illness; **я э́того не мог п.** I couldn't stand that.

перенес|ти́сь, у́сь, ёшься, *past* **~ся, ~ла́сь** *pf.* (*of* ⇒**переноси́ться**) to be carried, be borne; (*fig.*) (*мысленно*) to be carried away.

перенима́|ть, ю *impf. of* ⇒**переня́ть**

перено́с, а *m.* **1** transfer; moving. **2** (*typ.*) hyphenation at the end of a line; word division; (*знак*) hyphen (*at the end of a line*); **знак ~а** hyphen. **3** (*заседания*) postponement.

переноси́м|ый (~, ~а) *pres. part. pass. of* ⇒**переноси́ть** *and adj.* bearable, endurable.

перено|си́ть(ся), шу́(сь), ~сишь(ся) *impf. of* ⇒**перенести́(сь)**

перено́сиц|а, ы *f.* bridge of the nose.

перено́ск|а, и *f.* carrying over; carriage.

переносно́й = **перено́сный** 1

перено́сный *adj.* **1** (*приёмник*) portable. **2** (*ling.*) figurative.

перено́счик, а *m.* carrier.

переноч|ева́ть, у́ю *pf.* (*of* ⇒**ночева́ть**) to spend the night.

перенумер|ова́ть, у́ю *pf.* (*of* ⇒**перенумеро́вывать**) **1** (*много*) to number (*many things*). **2** (*заново*) to renumber.

перенумеро́выва|ть, ю *impf. of* ⇒**перенумерова́ть**

пере|ня́ть, йму́, йме́шь, *past* **пе́ренял, ~няла́, пе́реняло** *pf.* (*of* ⇒**~нима́ть**) to imitate, copy; **п. о́пыт** to assimilate experience; **п. привы́чку** to adopt, pick up a habit (*from s.o. else*).

переоборуд|овать, ую *impf. and pf.* to re-equip, to refit.

переобремен|и́ть, ю́, и́шь *pf.* (*of* ⇒**~я́ть**) to overburden.

переобремен|я́ть, я́ю *impf. of* ⇒**~и́ть**

переобува́|ть(ся), ю(сь) *impf. of* ⇒**переобу́ть(ся)**

переобу́|ть, ю, ешь *pf.* (*of* ⇒**~ва́ть**) to change s.o.'s shoes; **п. ту́фли** to change one's shoes.

переобу́|ться, юсь, ешься *pf.* (*of* ⇒**~ва́ться**) to change one's shoes, boots, *etc.*

переобуча́|ть, ю *impf. of* ⇒**переобучи́ть**

переобуче́ни|е, я *nt.* retraining.

переобу|чи́ть, чу́, ~чишь *pf.* (*of* ⇒**~ча́ть**) to retrain.

переодева́|ть(ся), ю(сь) *impf. of* ⇒**переоде́ть(ся)**

переоде́тый *adj.* disguised.

переоде́|ть, ну, нешь *pf.* (*of* ⇒**~ва́ть**) **1** (*платье, свитер*) to change; (*ребёнка, больного*) to change s.o.'s clothes; **они́ ~ли де́вочку в наря́дное пла́тье** they changed the little girl into a party frock; **п. пла́тье** to change one's dress. **2** (+*i. or* **в**+*a.*) to dress up, disguise (as, in); **п. де́вочку ма́льчиком** to dress up a little girl as a boy.

переоде́|ться, нусь, нешься *pf.* (*of* ⇒**~ва́ться**) **1** to change (one's clothes). **2** (+*i. or* **в**+*a.*) to disguise o.s. *or* dress up (as, in); **она ~лась в ма́льчика** she disguised herself as a boy.

переориенти́р|овать, ую *impf. and pf.* to reorient.

переориенти́р|оваться, уюсь *impf. and pf.* to reorient (oneself).

переосвиде́тельств|овать, ую *impf. and pf.* (*med.*) to re-examine.

переосмысле́ни|е, я *nt.* re-examination.

переосмы́сл|ить, ю, ишь *pf.* (*of* ⇒**~я́ть**) to re-examine.

переосмысля́|ть, ю *impf. of* ⇒**переосмы́слить**

переосна|сти́ть, щу́, сти́шь *pf.* (*of* ⇒**переоснаща́ть**) to re-equip, refit.

переоснащá|ть, ю *impf. of* **⇒переоснастúть**

переоцéнива|ть, ю *impf. of* **⇒переоценúть**

переоцен|úть, ю́, ~ишь *pf.* (*of* **⇒~ивать**) **1** (*оценить слишком высоко*) to overestimate, overrate. **2** (*оценить заново*) to revalue, reappraise.

переоцéнк|а, и *f.* **1** overestimation. **2** revaluation, reappraisal; **п. цéнностей** reappraisal of values (*also fig.*).

перепáд, а *m.* (*температур, давления*) differential, difference.

перепáда|ть, ет *pf.* (*coll.*) to fall (*one after another*).

перепадá|ть, ет *impf. of* **⇒перепáсть**

перепáива|ть, ю *impf. of* **⇒перепоúть**

перепáлк|а, и *f.* (*coll.*) exchange of fire, skirmish (*also fig.*).

перепáрхива|ть, ю *impf. of* **⇒перепорхнýть**

перепá|сть, дёт, *past* **~л** *pf.* (*of* **⇒~дáть**) (*coll.*) **1** to fall intermittently; **дождь ~дёт** there will be rain at intervals, it will be showery. **2** (*impers.*; +*d.*) to fall to one's lot.

перепа|хáть, шý, ~шешь *pf.* (*of* **⇒~хивать**) (*вспахать заново*) to plough (*Br.*), plow (*US*) (up) again; (*вспахать целиком*) to plough (*Br.*), plow (*US*) over.

перепáхива|ть, ю *impf. of* **⇒перепахáть**

перепáчка|ть, ю *pf.* to make all dirty.

перепáчка|ться, юсь *pf.* to make o.s. dirty (all over).

перепéв, а *m.* (*повторение*) repetition, rehash.

пéрепел, а, *pl.* **~á** *m.* (*zool.*) quail.

перепелен|áть, áю *pf.* (*of* **⇒~ёывать**): **п. ребёнка** to change a baby.

перепелёныва|ть, ю *impf. of* **⇒перепеленáть**

перепёлк|а, и *f.* (*zool.*) female quail.

перепеля́тник, а *m.* sparrow-hawk.

перепечáт|ать, аю *pf.* (*of* **⇒~ывать**) **1** (*старое издание*) to reprint. **2** (*рукопись*) to type (out).

перепечáтк|а, и *f.* **1** (*действие*) reprinting; **п. воспрещáется** copyright reserved. **2** (*текст*) reprint.

перепечáтыва|ть, ю *impf. of* **⇒перепечáтать**

перепивá|ть(ся), ю(сь) *impf. of* **⇒перепúть(ся)**

перепúлива|ть, ю *impf. of* **⇒перепилúть**

перепил|úть¹, ю́, ~ишь *pf.* (*of* **⇒~ивать**) (*пополам*) to saw in two.

перепил|úть², ю́, ~ишь *pf.* (*всё, многое*) to saw (*all or a number of*).

перепи|сáть¹, шý, ~шешь *pf.* (*of* **⇒~сывать**) **1** (*заново*) to re-write; (*на машинке*) to re-type; **п. нáбело** to make a fair copy (of). **2** (*списать*) to copy.

перепи|сáть², шý, ~шешь *pf.* (*of* **⇒~сывать**) (*сделать список*) to make a list (of), list; **п. всех присýтствующих** to take the names of all those present.

перепúск|а, и *f.* **1** (*действие*) copying; (*на машинке*) typing. **2** (*корреспонденция*) correspondence; **быть в ~е** (**с**+*i.*) to be in correspondence (with). **3** (*collect.*) (*все письма*) correspondence, letters.

перепúсчик, а *m.* copyist.

перепúсыва|ть, ю *impf. of* **⇒переписáть**

перепúсыва|ться, юсь *impf.* (**с**+*i.*) to correspond (with).

пéрепис|ь, и *f.* **1** (*населения*) census. **2** (*имущества*) inventory.

переп|úть, ью́, ьёшь, *past* **~úл, ~илá, ~úло** *pf.* (*of* **⇒~ивáть**) (*coll.*) **1** (*выпить слишком много*) to drink excessively. **2** (*выпить больше другого*) to out-drink; to drink under the table.

переп|úться, ью́сь, ьёшься, *past* **~úлся, ~илáсь, ~úлóсь** *pf.* (*of* **⇒~ивáться**) (*coll.*) to get completely drunk.

переплáв|ить¹, лю, ишь *pf.* (*of* **⇒~ля́ть**) (*руду*) to smelt.

переплáв|ить², лю, ишь *pf.* (*of* **⇒~ля́ть**) (*по воде*) to float; (*на плоту*) to raft.

переплавля́|ть, ю *impf. of* **⇒переплáвить**

перепланúр|овáть, ую, ýю *pf.* (*of* **⇒~óвывать**) to re-plan.

перепланирóвк|а, и *f.* re-planning.

перепланирóвыва|ть, ю *impf. of* **⇒перепланúровáть**

переплáт|а, ы *f.* overpayment.

перепла|тúть, чý, ~тишь *pf.* (*of* **⇒~чивать**) to overpay; to pay too much.

переплáчива|ть, ю *impf. of* **⇒переплатúть**

переплёвыва|ть, ю *impf. of* **⇒переплю́нуть**

перепле|стú, тý, тёшь, *past* **~ёл, ~лá** *pf.* (*of* **⇒~тáть**) **1** (*книгу*) to bind. **2** (+*i.*) (*нити, верёвки*) to interlace (with), interknit (with). **3** (*косы*) to braid again, plait again (*Br.*).

перепле|стúсь, тётся, *past* **~ёлся, ~лáсь** *pf.* (*of* **⇒~тáться**) **1** (*стебли, верёвки*) to interlace, interweave. **2** (*fig.*) (*события*) to be interwoven.

переплёт, а *m.* **1** (*действие*) binding; **отдáть кнúгу в п.** to have a book bound. **2** (*обложка*) binding, book-cover. **3** (*двери, окна*) transom. **4** (*coll.*) (*затруднительное положение*) mess, scrape; **попáсть в п.** to get into a mess, get into trouble.

переплетá|ть(ся), ю *impf. of* **⇒переплестú(сь)**

переплетéни|е, я *nt.* **1** (*нитей*) weave. **2** (*событий*) interweaving.

переплётн|ая, ой *f.* (*also* **п. мастерскáя**) bindery.

переплётчик, а *m.* bookbinder.

переплывá|ть, ю *impf. of* **⇒переплы́ть**

переплы́|ть, вý, вёшь, *past* **~л, ~лá, ~ло** *pf.* (*of* **⇒~вáть**) (*вплавь*) to swim (across); (*на пароходе*) to sail (across).

переплю́н|уть, у, ешь *pf.* (*of* **⇒переплёвывать**) (*coll.*) to spit further than; (*fig.*) to do better than, surpass.

переподготáвлива|ть, ю *impf. of* **⇒переподготóвить**

переподготóв|ить, лю, ишь *pf.* (*of* **⇒переподготáвливать**) to retrain.

переподготóвк|а, и *f.* further training; retraining.

перепо|úть, ю́, ~úшь *pf.* (*of* **⇒перепáивать**) **1** (*животное*) to give too much to drink. **2** (*coll.*) (*человека*) to make drunk.

перепó|й, я *m.* (*coll.*) **1** excessive drinking, boozing. **2** (*после выпивки*) hangover.

переполз|áть, áю *impf. of* **⇒~тú**

переполз|тú, ý, ёшь, *past* **~, ~лá** *pf.* (*of* **⇒~áть**) to crawl across; to creep across.

переполнéни|е, я *nt.* (*сосуда*) overfilling; (*автобуса*) overcrowding; (*comput.*) overflow.

перепóлн|ить, ю, ишь *pf.* (*of* **⇒~я́ть**) (*сосуд*) to overfill; (*автобус*) to overcrowd.

перепóлн|иться, ится *pf.* (*of* **⇒~я́ться**) (*о сосуде*) to be overfilled; (*об автобусе*) to be overcrowded; **её сéрдце ~илось рáдостью** her heart overflowed with joy.

переполн|я́ть(ся), я́ю, я́ет(ся) *impf. of* **⇒~ить(ся)**

переполóх, а *m.* commotion, rumpus.

переполош|úть, ý, úшь *pf.* (*coll.*) to alarm.

переполош|úться, ýсь, úшься *pf.* (*coll.*) to be thrown into panic.

перепóнк|а, и *f.* membrane; **барабáнная п.** (*anat.*) ear-drum, tympanum.

перепончатокры́лы|й *adj.* (*zool.*) hymenopterous; *as n.* **~е, ~х** Hymenoptera.

перепóнчатый *adj.* membraneous, membranous; (*zool.*) webbed; web-footed.

перепоруч|áть, áю *impf. of* **⇒~úть**

перепоруч|úть, ý, ~ишь *pf.* (*of* **⇒~áть**) (+*d.*) to turn over (to), reassign (to); **п. ведéние дéла другóму защúтнику** to turn over one's case to another lawyer.

перепорхн|ýть, ý, ёшь *pf.* (*of* **⇒перепáрхивать**) to flutter, flit (*somewhere else*; *from A to B*).

перепоя́|сать, шу, шешь *pf.* (*of* **⇒~сывать**) (*одежду*) to gird, belt.

перепоя́сыва|ть, ю *impf. of* **⇒перепоя́сать**

перепрáв|а, ы *f.* (*действие*) crossing; (*место*) crossing(-place); (*брод*) ford.

перепрáв|ить¹, лю, ишь *pf.* (*of*

⇨**~ля́ть**) **1** (*перевезти*) to convey, transport; to take across. **2** (*письмо*) to forward (*mail*).

перепра́в|ить[2], лю, ишь *pf.* (*of* ⇨**~ля́ть**) (*исправить*) to correct.

перепра́в|иться, люсь, ишься *pf.* (*of* ⇨**~ля́ться**) to cross, get across; (*вплавь*) to swim across; (*на пароходе*) to sail across.

переправля́|ть(ся), ю(сь) *impf. of* ⇨**перепра́вить(ся)**

перепрева́|ть, ю *impf. of* ⇨**перепре́ть**

перепре́|ть, ю *pf.* (*of* ⇨**~ва́ть**) **1** (*гнить*) to rot. **2** (*coll.*) (*о еде*) to be overdone.

перепро́б|овать, ую *pf.* (*еду*) to taste (*all or a quantity of*); (*fig.*) (*средства*) to try.

перепрода|ва́ть, ю́, ёшь *impf. of* ⇨**~́ть**

перепродав|е́ц, ца́ *m.* re-seller.

перепрода́ж|а, и *f.* re-sale.

перепрода́|ть, м, шь, ст, ди́м, ди́те, ду́т, *past* **перепро́дал, ~ла́, перепро́дало** *pf.* (*of* ⇨**~ва́ть**) to re-sell.

перепроизво́дств|о, а *nt.* overproduction.

перепры́гива|ть, ю *impf. of* ⇨**перепры́гнуть**

перепры́г|нуть, ну, нешь *pf.* (*of* ⇨**~ивать**) (+*a. or* **че́рез**+*a.*) to jump (over).

перепря|га́ть, га́ю *impf. of* ⇨**~́чь**

перепря́жк|а, и *f.* changing of horses.

перепря́|чь, гу́, жёшь, гу́т, *past* **~г, ~гла́** *pf.* (*of* ⇨**~га́ть**) (*запрячь заново*) to re-harness.

перепу́г, а (у) *m.* (*coll.*): **с ~у, от ~у** in one's fright.

перепуга́|ть, ю *pf.* (*no impf.*) to frighten, give a fright.

перепуга́|ться, юсь *pf.* (*no impf.*) to get a fright.

перепу́т|ать, аю *pf.* (*of* ⇨**~ывать**) **1** (*нити*) to entangle. **2** (*fig.*) (*имена, факты*) to confuse, mix up, muddle up.

перепу́т|аться, ается *pf.* (*of* ⇨**~ываться**) **1** (*нити*) to get entangled. **2** (*fig.*) (*мысли*) to get confused, get mixed up.

перепу́тыва|ть(ся), ю, ет(ся) *impf. of* ⇨**перепу́тать(ся)**

перепу́ть|е, я *nt.* cross-roads; **быть на п.** (*fig.*) to be at the cross-roads.

перераба́тыва|ть(ся), ю(сь) *impf. of* ⇨**перерабо́тать(ся)**

перерабо́та|ть[1], ю *pf.* (*of* ⇨**перераба́тывать**) **1** (*сырьё*) to process; (*преобразовать*) to convert (to); to treat; **п. свёклу в са́хар** to convert beet to sugar; **п. пи́щу** to digest food. **2** (*переделать*) to re-make; (*fig.*) (*статью*) to revise, re-cast, re-shape.

перерабо́та|ть[2], ю *pf.* (*of* ⇨**перераба́тывать**) to exceed fixed hours of work, work overtime; (*coll.*) (*переутомиться*) to overwork.

перерабо́та|ться, юсь *pf.* (*of* ⇨**перераба́тываться**) (*coll.*) to overwork.

перерабо́тк|а[1], и *f.* **1** (*сырья*) processing, treatment. **2** (*переделка*) re-making; (*вторичное использование*) recycling; (*fig.*) revising, re-casting, re-shaping.

перерабо́тк|а[2], и *f.* (*время*) overtime work.

перераспределе́ни|е, я *nt.* re-distribution.

перераспредел|и́ть, ю́, и́шь *pf.* (*of* ⇨**~я́ть**) to re-distribute.

перераспредел|я́ть, я́ю *impf. of* ⇨**~и́ть**

перераста́ни|е, я *nt.* **1** outgrowing. **2** (**в**+*a.*) growing (into), development (into).

перераст|а́ть, а́ю *impf. of* ⇨**~и́**

перераст|и́, у́, ёшь, *past* **перерос́, переросла́** *pf.* (*of* ⇨**~а́ть**) **1** (*стать выше*) to outgrow, (over)top; (*превзойти*) to outstrip (*in height, also fig.*); **в трина́дцать лет она́ уже́ переросла́ отца́** at thirteen she had already outgrown her father; **п. своего́ учи́теля** to outstrip one's teacher. **2** (*fig.*; **в**+*a.*) (*превратиться*) to grow (into), develop (into), turn (into). **3** (*оказаться по возрасту старше, чем нужно*) to be too old (for); **для де́тского са́да он перерос́** he is too old for kindergarten.

перерасхо́д, а *m.* **1** (*денег, энергии*) overspending, over-expenditure. **2** (*fin.*) (*в банковском счёте*) overdraft.

перерасхо́д|овать, ую *pf.* (*no impf.*) **1** (*деньги, энергию*) to overspend, spend to excess. **2** (*fin.*) (*в банковском счёте*) to overdraw.

перерасчёт, а *m.* recalculation; (*в другие единицы*) conversion.

перерв|а́ть, у́, ёшь, *past* **~а́л, ~ала́, ~а́ло** *pf.* (*of* ⇨**перерыва́ть[1]**) to break (in two), tear asunder.

перерв|а́ться, у́сь, ёшься, *past* **~а́лся, ~ала́сь, ~а́ло́сь** *pf.* (*of* ⇨**перерыва́ться**) to break (in two).

перерегистра́ци|я, и *f.* re-registration.

перерегистри́р|овать, ую *impf. and pf.* to re-register.

перерегистри́р|оваться, уюсь *impf. and pf.* to re-register.

перере́|зать[1], жу, жешь *pf.* (*of* ⇨**~за́ть** *and* **~зывать**) **1** (*верёвку*) to cut (in two). **2** (*fig.*) (*путь, доступ*) to cut off; **п. путь неприя́телю** to bar the enemy's way.

перере́|зать[2], жу, жешь *pf.* (*убить*) to kill, slaughter (*all or a number of*).

перерез|а́ть, а́ю *impf. of* ⇨**~́ать[1]**

перере́зыва|ть, ю *impf.* = **перереза́ть**

перереш|а́ть[1], а́ю *impf. of* ⇨**~и́ть**

перереш|а́ть[2], а́ю *pf.* to solve (*all or a number of problems*).

перереш|и́ть, у́, и́шь *pf.* (*of* ⇨**~а́ть[1]**) **1** (*решить по-другому*) to decide, settle in a different way. **2** (*передумать*) to change one's mind, reconsider one's decision.

переро|ди́ть, жу́, ди́шь *pf.* (*of* ⇨**~жда́ть**) to regenerate.

переро|ди́ться, жу́сь, ди́шься *pf.* (*of* ⇨**~жда́ться**) **1** (*о человеке*) to be re-born. **2** (*о городе, месте*) to be regenerated. **3** (*biol. and fig.*) (*измениться к худшему*) to degenerate.

перерожда́|ть(ся), ю(сь) *impf. of* ⇨**переродиться**

перерожде́ни|е, я *nt.* **1** regeneration. **2** (*к худшему*) degeneration.

переро́ст|ок, ка *m.* (*coll.*) child who is older than the rest of the class.

переруб|а́ть, а́ю *impf. of* ⇨**~и́ть**

переруб|и́ть, лю́, ~́ишь *pf.* (*of* ⇨**~а́ть**) to chop in two.

переруга́|ться, юсь *pf.* (*coll.*; **с**+*i.*) to fall out (with).

переру́гива|ться, юсь *impf.* (*coll.*; **с**+*i.*) to quarrel (with), squabble (with).

переры́в, а *m.* break; **обе́денный п.** lunch break; **без ~а** without a break; **с ~ами** off and on.

перерыва́|ть[1], ю *impf. of* ⇨**перерва́ть**

перерыва́|ть[2], ю *impf. of* ⇨**перерыть**

перерыва́|ться, юсь *impf. of* ⇨**перерва́ться**

перер|ы́ть, о́ю, о́ешь *pf.* (*of* ⇨**~ыва́ть[2]**) **1** (*улицу*) to dig up. **2** (*fig., coll.*) (*комнату, литературу*) to rummage (*through*).

переря|ди́ть, жу́, ~́ди́шь *pf.* (*of* ⇨**~́живать**) (+*i.*; *coll.*) to disguise (as), dress up (as).

переря|ди́ться, жу́сь, ~́ди́шься *pf.* (*of* ⇨**~́живаться**) (+*i.*; *coll.*) to disguise o.s. *or* dress up (as).

переря́жива|ть(ся), ю(сь) *impf. of* ⇨**переряди́ть(ся)**

переса|ди́ть, жу́, ~́дишь *pf.* (*of* ⇨**~́живать**) **1** (*заставить пересесть*) to move, make s.o. change his seat; (*на другой поезд*) to transfer. **2**: **п. кого́-н. че́рез что-н.** to help s.o. across sth. **3** (*bot.*) to transplant. **4** (*med.*) (*сердце*) to transplant; (*кожу*) to graft.

переса́дк|а, и *f.* **1** (*bot.*) transplantation. **2** (*med.*) transplant; grafting; **опера́ция по ~е се́рдца** heart transplant operation. **3** (*переход на другой поезд, автобус*) change; **сде́лать ~у** to change (*trains, buses, etc.*).

переса́жива|ть, ю *impf. of* ⇨**пересади́ть**

переса́жива|ться, юсь *impf. of* ⇨**пересе́сть**

переса́лива|ть, ю *impf. of* ⇨**пересоли́ть**

переда|ва́ть, ю́, ёшь *impf. of* ⇨**~́ть**

переда́|ть, м, шь, ст, ди́м, ди́те, ду́т, *past* **~л, ~ла́, ~́ло** *pf.* (*of* ⇨**~ва́ть**) **1** (*помещение*) to re-let; to sub-let. **2** (*cards*) to re-deal. **3** (*экзамен*) to resit (*Br.*), retake.

пересека́|ть(ся), ю, ет(ся) *impf. of* ⇨**пересе́чь(ся)**

П

переселе́н|ец, ца *m.* settler.

переселе́ни|е, я *nt.* **1** (*на новую территорию*) migration; re-settlement. **2** (*в новую квартиру*) move (*to new place of residence*).

переселе́н|ка, ки *f. of* ⇨**~ец**

переселе́н|ческий *adj. of* ⇨**~ец; ~ческая организа́ция** emigration, re-settlement organization.

пересел|и́ть, ю́, и́шь *pf.* (*of* ⇨**~я́ть**) to move; (*на новую территорию*) to resettle.

пересел|и́ться, ю́сь, и́шься *pf.* (*of* ⇨**~я́ться**) to move; (*на новую территорию*) to migrate.

пересел|я́ть(ся), я́ю(сь) *impf. of* ⇨**~и́ть(ся)**

перес|е́сть, я́ду, я́дешь *pf.* (*of* ⇨**~а́живаться**) **1** (*на другое место*) to change one's seat. **2** (*сделать пересадку*) to change (*trains, etc.*).

пересече́ни|е, я *nt.* crossing, intersection; **то́чка ~я** point of intersection.

перес|ечённый *p.p.p. of* ⇨**~е́чь; ~ечённая ме́стность** (*geog.*) broken terrain; **бег по ~ечённой ме́стности** cross-country race *or* run.

пересе́|чь, ку́, чёшь, ку́т, *past* **~к, ~кла́** *pf.* (*of* ⇨**~ка́ть**) **1** (*перейти*) to cross; to traverse; **п. у́лицу** to cross the road; **п. путь неприя́телю** (*fig.*) to cut the enemy off, bar the enemy's way. **2** (*город, местность*) to cross, cut across.

пересе́|чься, чётся, ку́тся, *past* **~кся, ~кла́сь** *pf.* (*of* ⇨**~ка́ться**) to cross, intersect.

переси|де́ть, жу́, ди́шь *pf.* (*of* ⇨**~живать**) **1** (*coll.*) to out-sit; **он ~де́л всех други́х госте́й** he outstayed all the other guests. **2** (*просидеть слишком долго*) to sit too long.

переси́жива|ть, ю *impf. of* ⇨**пересиде́ть**

переси́лива|ть, ю *impf. of* ⇨**переси́лить**

переси́л|ить, ю, ишь *pf.* (*of* ⇨**~ивать**) (*человека*) to overpower; (*fig.*) (*усталость*) to overcome, master.

переска́з, а *m.* **1** (*содержания романа*) re-telling, narration. **2** (*изложение*) exposition.

переска|за́ть, жу́, ~жешь *pf.* (*of* ⇨**~зывать**) **1** to re-tell, narrate. **2** (*рассказать подробно*) to retail, relate; **п. слу́хи** to retail rumours (*Br.*), rumors (*US*).

переска́зыва|ть, ю *impf. of* ⇨**пересказа́ть**

переска́кива|ть, ю *impf. of* ⇨**перескочи́ть**

перескоч|и́ть, у́, ~ишь *pf.* (*of* ⇨**перска́кивать**) **1** (*+a. or* **че́рез** *+a.*) to jump (over); (*fig.*) (*пропустить*) to skip (over). **2** (*fig.*) to skip; **п. с одно́й те́мы на другу́ю** to skip from one topic to another.

пересла|сти́ть, щу́, сти́шь *pf.* (*of* ⇨**~щивать**) to make too sweet, put too much sugar (into).

пере|сла́ть, шлю́, шлёшь *pf.* (*of* ⇨**~сыла́ть**) (*отправить*) to send; (*деньги*) to remit; (*по другому адресу*) to forward.

пересла́щива|ть, ю *impf. of* ⇨**пересласти́ть**

пересма́трива|ть, ю *impf. of* ⇨**пересмотре́ть**

пересме́ива|ться, юсь *impf.* (*coll.*; **с** *+i.*) to exchange smiles (with).

пересме́н|а, ы *f.* period of time between shifts.

пересме́шк|а, и *f.* (*coll.*) mockery, banter.

пересме́шник, а *m.* **1** (*coll.*) mocker. **2** (*zool.*) mocking-bird.

пересмо́тр, а *m.* **1** (*программы*) revision. **2** (*предложения*) reconsideration; (*leg.*) review (*of a sentence*); re-trial.

пересмотр|е́ть[1], ю́, ~ишь *pf.* (*of* ⇨**пересма́тривать**) **1** (*книгу, документ*) to look through; to go over again. **2** (*решение*) to re-consider; (*leg.*) to review. **3** (*ища что-либо*) to go through (*in search of sth.*).

пересмотр|е́ть[2], ю́, ~ишь *pf.* to have seen (*all or a quantity of*); to have gone all through.

переснима́|ть, ю *impf. of* ⇨**пересня́ть**

пересн|я́ть, иму́, и́мешь, *past* **~я́л, ~яла́, ~я́ло** *pf.* (*of* ⇨**~има́ть**) **1** (*фотографировать заново*) to photograph again. **2** (*копировать*) to make a copy of. **3** (*фильм*) to reshoot.

пересо́л, а *m.* excess of salt.

пересол|и́ть, ю́, ~ишь *pf.* (*of* ⇨**переса́ливать**) **1** to put too much salt (into). **2** (*fig., coll.*) to go too far.

пересо́х|нуть, нет, *past* **~, ~ла** *pf.* (*of* ⇨**пересыха́ть**) (*о белье*) to dry out; (*о земле, речке*) to dry up, become parched.

пересп|а́ть, лю́, и́шь, *past* **~а́л, ~ала́, ~а́ло** *pf.* (*coll.*) **1** (*проспать слишком долго*) to oversleep. **2** (*переночевать*) to spend the night. **3** (**с** *+i.*; *euph.*) to sleep (with).

переспе́лый *adj.* overripe.

переспо́р|ить, ю, ишь *pf.* to defeat in argument.

переспра́шива|ть, ю *impf. of* ⇨**переспроси́ть[1]**

переспро|си́ть[1], шу́, ~сишь *pf.* (*of* ⇨**переспра́шивать**) (*повторить вопрос*) to ask again; (*попросить повторить*) to ask to repeat.

переспро|си́ть[2], шу́, ~сишь *pf.* (*всех, многих*) to question (*all or a number of*).

пересо́р|ить, ю, ишь *pf.* to set at odds.

пересо́р|иться, юсь, ишься *pf.* (**с** *+i.*) to quarrel (with), fall out (with).

переста|ва́ть, ю́, ёшь *impf. of* ⇨**~ть**

переста́в|ить, лю, ишь *pf.* (*of* ⇨**~ля́ть**) to move, shift; **п. ме́бель** to re-arrange the furniture; **п. слова́ во фра́зе** to transpose the words in a sentence.

переставля́|ть, ю *impf. of* ⇨**переста́вить**

переста́ива|ть, ю *impf. of* ⇨**перестоя́ть**

перестано́вк|а, и *f.* **1** re-arrangement, transposition. **2** (*math.*) permutation.

перестара́|ться, юсь *pf.* (*coll.*) to overdo it.

перестар́|ок, ка *m.* (*coll.*) person over age (*for given purpose*).

переста́|ть, ну, нешь *pf.* (*of* ⇨**~ва́ть**) (*+inf.*) to stop, cease; **они́ ~ли разгова́ривать** they stopped talking; **~ньте!** stop it!

перестел|и́ть, ю́, ~ешь *pf.* = **перестла́ть**

перестила́|ть, ю *impf. of* ⇨**перестели́ть** *and* **перестла́ть**

перестир|а́ть[1], а́ю *pf.* (*of* ⇨**~ывать**) (*заново*) to wash again.

перестир|а́ть[2], а́ю *pf.* (*no impf.*) (*всё, многое*) to wash (*all or a number of*).

перести́рыва|ть, ю *impf. of* ⇨**перестира́ть[1]**

перест|ла́ть, елю́, е́лешь *pf.* (*of* ⇨**~ила́ть**) to re-lay; **п. пол в ко́мнате** to re-floor a room; **п. посте́ль** to re-make a bed.

пересто|я́ть, ю́, и́шь *pf.* (*of* ⇨**переста́ивать**) to stand too long; (*испортиться*) to go off.

перестрада́|ть, ю *pf.* (*no impf.*) to have suffered.

перестра́ива|ть(ся), ю(сь) *impf. of* ⇨**перестро́ить(ся)**

перестрах|ова́ть, у́ю *pf.* (*of* ⇨**~о́вывать**) to re-insure.

перестрах|ова́ться, у́юсь *pf.* (*of* ⇨**~о́вываться**) **1** to re-insure o.s. **2** (*fig., pej.*) to play safe.

перестрахо́вк|а, и *f.* **1** re-insurance. **2** (*fig., pej.*) playing safe.

перестрахо́вщик, а *m.* (*pej.*) adherent of policy of 'playing safe'.

перестрахо́вщи|ца, цы *f. of* ⇨**~к**

перестрахо́выва|ть(ся), ю(сь) *impf. of* ⇨**перестрахова́ть(ся)**

перестре́лива|ть, ю *impf. of* ⇨**перестреля́ть**

перестре́лива|ться, юсь *impf.* to fire (at each other); to shoot it out.

перестре́лк|а, и *f.* exchange of fire, shoot-out.

перестрел|я́ть, я́ю *pf.* (*of* ⇨**~ивать**) **1** (*убить*) to shoot (down). **2** (*израсходовать стрельбой*) to use up, expend (*in shooting*).

перестро́|ечный *adj. of* ⇨**~йка**

перестро́|ить, ю, ишь *pf.* (*of* ⇨**перестра́ивать**) **1** (*дом*) to rebuild, reconstruct. **2** (*план, работу*) to re-design, re-fashion, re-shape; to reorganize; **п. фра́зу** to reshape a sentence. **3** (*mil.*) to re-form. **4** (*mus., radio*) to re-tune.

перестро́|иться, юсь, ишься *pf.* (*of* ⇨**перестра́иваться**) **1** to re-form; to reorganize o.s.; to restructure. **2** (*mil.*) to re-form. **3** (*radio*) (**на** *+a.*) to switch over (to), tune (on to); **п. на**

коро́ткую волну́ to switch over to short wave.

перестро́йк|а, и *f.* **1** (*здания*) rebuilding, reconstruction; (*pol., econ.*) perestroika. **2** (*реорганизация*) reorganization. **3** (*mil.*) re-formation. **4** (*mus., radio*) re-tuning.

перестука́вани|е, я *nt.* communication by tapping (*in prison, etc.*).

перестукива|ться, юсь *impf.* (**с**+*i.*) to communicate (with) by tapping (*in prison, etc.*).

переступ|а́ть, а́ю *impf.* **1** *impf. of* ⇒**~и́ть. 2** (*impf. only*) to move slowly; **он е́ле ~а́л (нога́ми)** his feet would hardly carry him; **п. с ноги́ на́ ногу** to shift from one foot to the other.

переступ|и́ть, лю́, ~ишь *pf.* (*of* ⇒**~а́ть**) (+*a. or* **че́рез**+*a.*) to step over; (*fig.*) to overstep; **п. поро́г** to cross the threshold; **п. зако́н** to break the law; **п. грани́цы прили́чия** to overstep the bounds of decency.

пересу́д, а *m.* (*coll.*) re-trial.

пересу́д|ы, ов *no sg.* (*coll.*) gossip.

пересу́шива|ть, ю *impf. of* ⇒**пересуши́ть**[1]

пересуш|и́ть[1]**, у́, ~ишь** *pf.* (*of* ⇒**~ивать**) (*больше, чем нужно*) to overdry.

пересуш|и́ть[2]**, у́, ~ишь** *pf.* (*no impf.*) (*всё, многое*) to dry (*all or a quantity of*).

пересчёт, а *m.* re-count.

пересчит|а́ть[1]**, а́ю** *pf.* (*of* ⇒**~ывать**) **1** to re-count; **п. ко́сти (рёбра) кому́-н.** (*fig., coll.*) to give s.o. a drubbing. **2** (**на**+*a.*) to convert (to), express (in terms of).

пересчит|а́ть[2]**, а́ю** *pf.* (*no impf.*) (*многое*) to count.

пересчи́тыва|ть, ю *impf. of* ⇒**пересчита́ть**[1]

пересыла́|ть, ю *impf. of* ⇒**пересла́ть**

пересы́лк|а, и *f.* sending; forwarding; **п. де́нег** remittance; **сто́имость ~и** postage; **п. беспла́тно** post free.

пересыл|очный *adj. of* ⇒**~ка; п. пункт** transit point.

пересы́льн|ый *adj.* transit; **~ая тюрьма́** transit prison.

пересы́п|ать[1]**, лю, лешь** *pf.* (*of* ⇒**~а́ть**) to pour (*dry substance*) into another container; **п. зерно́ в мешки́** to pour off grain into bags.

пересы́п|ать[2]**, лю, лешь** *pf.* (*of* ⇒**~а́ть**) (+*i.*) **1** to powder (with). **2** (*fig.*) to (inter)lard, intersperse (with); **п. речь руга́тельствами** to lard one's speech with profanities.

пересып|а́ть, а́ю *impf. of* ⇒**~ать**

пересыха́|ть, ет *impf. of* ⇒**пересо́хнуть**

перета́плива|ть, ю *impf. of* ⇒**перетопи́ть**[1]

перетаск|а́ть, а́ю *pf.* (*of* ⇒**~ивать**) **1** to carry away. **2** (*fig., coll.*) (*украсть*) to pinch (*Br.*); to lift.

перета́скива|ть, ю *impf. of* ⇒**перетаска́ть** *and* **перетащи́ть**

перетас|ова́ть, у́ю *pf.* (*of* ⇒**~о́вывать**) to re-shuffle (*cards, also fig.*).

перетасо́выва|ть, ю *impf. of* ⇒**перетасова́ть**

перетащ|и́ть, у́, ~ишь *pf.* (*of* ⇒**перета́скивать**) **1** (*волоча*) to drag over; (*неся*) to carry over; (*переместить*) to move, shift; **п. сунду́к на черда́к** to move a trunk into the attic. **2** (*fig., coll.*) (*помочь переменить место работы, жительства*) to get (s.o.) to move (*closer to o.s., with regard to their job or to where they live*).

перетека́|ть, ет *impf. of* ⇒**перете́чь**

пере|тере́ть, тру́, трёшь, *past* **~тёр, ~тёрла** *pf.* (*of* ⇒**~тира́ть**) **1** (*трением разделить надвое*) to wear through. **2** (*повредить трением*) to wear out, wear down. **3** (*растирая, привести в другой вид*) to grind; (*на тёрке*) to grate.

пере|тере́ться, трётся, *past* **~тёрся, ~тёрлась** *pf.* (*of* ⇒**~тира́ться**) to wear through.

перетерп|е́ть, лю́, ~ишь *pf.* (*coll.*) to suffer, endure.

перете́|чь, чёт, ку́т, *past* **~к, ~кла́** *pf.* (*of* ⇒**~ка́ть**) to overflow.

перетира́|ть(ся), ю, ет(ся) *impf. of* ⇒**перетере́ть(ся)**

перето́к, а *m.* flow.

перето́лк|и, ов *no sg.* (*coll.*) tittle-tattle.

перетолк|ова́ть[1]**, у́ю** *pf.* (*no impf.*) (*coll.*) to talk over, discuss; **на́до нам с тобо́й об э́том п.** we must talk it over.

перетолк|ова́ть[2]**, у́ю** *pf.* (*of* ⇒**~о́вывать**) (*coll.*) (*истолковать неверно*) to misinterpret.

перетолко́выва|ть, ю *impf. of* ⇒**перетолкова́ть**[2]

перетоп|и́ть[1]**, лю́, ~ишь** *pf.* (*of* ⇒**перета́пливать**) (*масло*) to melt.

перетоп|и́ть[2]**, лю́, ~ишь** *pf.* (*coll.*) (*печь*) to heat; to kindle.

перетрево́ж|ить, у, ишь *pf.* (*no impf.*) (*coll.*) to disturb, alarm.

перетрево́ж|иться, усь, ишься *pf.* (*no impf.*) (*coll.*) to be alarmed, become anxious.

пере|тру́, трёшь, тёр, тёрла *see* ⇒**~тере́ть**

перетру́|сить, шу, сишь *pf.* (*no impf.*) (*coll.*) to have a fright; to take fright.

перетряс|а́ть, а́ю *impf. of* ⇒**~ти́**

перетряс|ти́, у́, ёшь, *past* **~, ~ла́** *pf.* (*of* ⇒**~а́ть**) to shake up.

пере́ть, пру, прёшь, *past* **пёр, пёрла** *impf.* (*coll.*) **1** (*идти*) to go, make one's way. **2** (*напролом*) to push, press. **3** (*тащить*) to drag. **4** (*проявляться*) to come out; to show. **5** (*pf.* **с~**) (*красть*) to steal, pinch (*Br.*).

перетя́гивани|е, я *nt.*: **п. кана́та** (*sport*) tug-of-war.

перетя́гива|ть, ю *impf. of* ⇒**перетяну́ть**

перетя|ну́ть[1]**, ну́, ~нешь** *pf.* (*of* ⇒**~гивать**) **1** to pull, draw (*somewhere else; from A to B*); **п. ло́дку от одного́ бе́рега к друго́му** to pull the boat from one bank to the other. **2** (*fig., coll.*) to pull over, attract; **п. на свою́ сто́рону** to win over, gain support of. **3** (*крепко стянуть*) to tighten. **4** (*быть более тяжёлым*) to outbalance, outweigh.

перетя|ну́ть[2]**, ну́, ~нешь** *pf.* (*of* ⇒**~гивать**) (*натянуть заново*) to retighten.

переубе|ди́ть, ди́шь *pf.* (*of* ⇒**~жда́ть**) to make (*s.o.*) change his, her, *etc.* mind.

переубе|ди́ться, ди́шься *pf.* (*of* ⇒**~жда́ться**) to change one's mind.

переубежда́|ть(ся), ю(сь) *impf. of* ⇒**переубеди́ть(ся)**

переу́л|ок, ка *m.* lane, side-street.

переусе́рдств|овать, ую *pf.* (*no impf.*) (*coll.*) to be over-diligent, show excess of zeal.

переустро́йств|о, а *nt.* reconstruction.

переутом|и́ть, лю́, и́шь *pf.* (*of* ⇒**~ля́ть**) to tire out; to overwork.

переутом|и́ться, лю́сь, и́шься *pf.* (*of* ⇒**~ля́ться**) to tire o.s. out; to overwork; (*pf. only*) to be run down.

переутомле́ни|е, я *nt.* exhaustion; overwork.

переутомля́|ть(ся), ю(сь) *impf. of* ⇒**переутоми́ть(ся)**

переуч|е́сть, ту́, тёшь, *past* **~ёл, ~ла́** *pf.* (*of* ⇒**~и́тывать**) to take stock.

переучёт, а *m.* stock-taking.

переу́чива|ть(ся), ю(сь) *impf. of* ⇒**переучи́ть(ся)**

переучи́тыва|ть, ю *impf. of* ⇒**переуче́сть**

переуч|и́ть, у́, ~ишь *pf.* (*of* ⇒**~ивать**) to teach again.

переуч|и́ться, у́сь, ~ишься *pf.* (*of* ⇒**~иваться**) **1** to re-learn. **2** (*coll.*) (*больше, чем нужно*) to study too much.

переформати́р|овать, ую *impf. and pf.* (*comput.*) to reformat.

переформир|ова́ть, у́ю *pf.* (*of* ⇒**~о́вывать**) (*mil.*) to re-form.

переформиро́выва|ть, ю *impf. of* ⇒**переформирова́ть**

перефрази́р|овать, ую *impf. and pf.* to paraphrase.

перефразиро́вк|а, и *f.* paraphrase.

перехва́лива|ть, ю *impf. of* ⇒**перехвали́ть**

перехвал|и́ть, ю́, ~ишь *pf.* (*of* ⇒**~ивать**) to over-praise.

перехва́т, а *m.* interception.

перехва|ти́ть, чу́, ~тишь *pf.* (*of* ⇒**~тывать**) **1** (*задержать*) to intercept, catch; **я ~ти́л его́ по доро́ге на рабо́ту** I caught him on the way to work. **2** (*обвязать*) to tie. **3** (*coll.*) (*перекусить*) to grab (*sth. to eat*). **4** (*coll.*) (*взять взаймы*) to borrow (*for a short time*). **5** (*coll.*) (*проявить неумеренность*) to overshoot the mark.

П

перехва́тчик, а *m.* (*aeron.*) interceptor.

перехва́тыва|ть, ю *impf. of* ⇒**перехвати́ть**

перехворá|ть, ю *pf.* (*no impf.*) (+*i.*) to have had; to have been down (with) (*sc.* an illness).

перехитр|и́ть, ю́, и́шь *pf.* to outwit.

перехо́д, а *m.* **1** (*действие; место*) crossing; (*к другому состоянию, к другой системе*) transition, switch(over); **подзе́мный п.** underpass, subway. **2** (*mil.*) (day's) march. **3** (*relig.*) conversion.

перехо|ди́ть[1], жу́, ~дишь *impf. of* ⇒**перейти́**

перехо|ди́ть[2], жу́, ~дишь *pf.* (*no impf.*) (*coll.*) (*исходить*) to go all over.

перехо|ди́ть[3], жу́, ~дишь *pf.* (*no impf.*) (*coll.*) (*в играх*) to have one's turn again, make one's move again.

переходни́к, а́ *m.* (*coll.*) adaptor.

перехо́дный *adj.* **1** (*период*) transitional. **2** (*gram.*) transitive. **3** (*tech.*) transient.

переход|я́щий *pres. part. of* ⇒**~и́ть** *and adj.* **1** transient, transitory; **п. ку́бок** (*sport*) challenge cup. **2** (*дождь*) intermittent. **3** (*fin.*) brought forward, carried over.

пе́р|ец, ца *m.* pepper; **стручко́вый п.** capsicum; **зада́ть кому́-н. ~цу** (*coll.*) to give it s.o. hot.

перецара́па|ться, юсь *pf.* **1** to scratch o.s. **2** (*взаимно*) to scratch each other.

пе́реч|ень, ня *m.* (*список*) list; (*перечисление*) enumeration.

перечёркива|ть, ю *impf. of* ⇒**перечеркну́ть**

перечерк|ну́ть, ну́, нёшь *pf.* (*of* ⇒**~ивать**) to cross (out); (*fig.*) (*уничтожить*) to cancel.

перечер|ти́ть, чу́, ~тишь *pf.* (*of* ⇒**~чивать**) **1** (*заново*) to draw again. **2** (*скопировать*) to copy, trace.

перечёрчива|ть, ю *impf. of* ⇒**перечерти́ть**

перече|са́ться, ~шешься *pf.* (*no impf.*) (*coll.*) **1** (*заново*) to do one's hair again. **2** (*иначе*) to do one's hair differently.

пере|че́сть[1], чту́, чтёшь, *past* **~чёл, ~чла́** *pf.* = **~счита́ть[2]**; **их мо́жно по па́льцам п.** you could count them on the fingers of one hand.

пере|че́сть[2], чту́, чтёшь, *past* **~чёл, ~чла́** *pf.* = **~чита́ть**

перечи́нива|ть, ю *impf. of* ⇒**перечини́ть[1]**

перечин|и́ть[1], ю́, ~ишь *pf.* (*of* ⇒**~ивать**) (*заново*) to mend again, repair again.

перечин|и́ть[2], ю́, ~ишь *pf.* (*всё или многое*) to mend, repair (*all or a number of*).

перечисле́ни|е, я *nt.* **1** enumeration. **2** (*fin.*) transferring.

перечи́сл|ить, ю, ишь *pf.* (*of* ⇒**~я́ть**) **1** to enumerate. **2** (*перевести*) to transfer; **его́ ~или в запа́с** he has been transferred to the reserve; **п. на теку́щий счёт** (*fin.*) to transfer to one's current account.

перечисл|я́ть, я́ю *impf. of* ⇒**~ить**

перечит|а́ть[1], а́ю *pf.* (*of* ⇒**~ывать**) (*заново*) to re-read.

перечит|а́ть[2], а́ю *pf.* (*всё или многое*) to read (*all or a quantity of*); **он ~а́л все кни́ги в библиоте́ке** he has read all the books in the library.

перечи́тыва|ть, ю *impf. of* ⇒**перечита́ть[1]**

пере́ч|ить, у, ишь *impf.* (*no pf.*) (+*d.*; *coll.*) to contradict; to go against.

пе́речниц|а, ы *f.* pepper-pot.

пе́ре|чный *adj. of* ⇒**~ц**

перечу́вств|овать, ую *pf.* (*no impf.*) to feel, experience.

переша́гива|ть, ю *impf. of* ⇒**перешагну́ть**

перешаг|ну́ть, ну́, нёшь *pf.* (*of* ⇒**~ивать**) to step over; **п. (че́рез) поро́г** to cross the threshold.

переше́|ек, йка *m.* isthmus.

перешёптыва|ться, юсь *impf.* to whisper to one another.

перешиб|а́ть, а́ю *impf. of* ⇒**~и́ть**

перешиб|и́ть, у́, ёшь, *past* **~, ~ла** *pf.* (*of* ⇒**~а́ть**) (*coll.*) to break, fracture.

перешива́|ть, ю *impf. of* ⇒**переши́ть**

переши́вк|а, и *f.* alteration (*of clothes*).

переш|и́ть, ью́, ьёшь *pf.* (*of* ⇒**~ива́ть**) to alter; to have altered.

перещеголя́|ть, ю *pf.* (*no impf.*) (*coll.*) to outdo, surpass.

переэкзамен|ова́ть, у́ю *pf.* (*of* ⇒**~о́вывать**) to re-examine.

переэкзамен|ова́ться, у́юсь *pf.* (*of* ⇒**~о́вываться**) to resit (*Br.*), retake an examination.

переэкзамено́вк|а, и *f.* resit (*Br.*), repeat examination (*US*).

переэкзамено́выва|ть(ся), ю(сь) *impf. of* ⇒**переэкзаменова́ть(ся)**

периге́|й, я *m.* (*astron.*) perigee.

периге́ли|й, я *m.* (*astron.*) perihelion.

перика́рд, а *m.* (*anat.*) pericardium.

пери́л|а, ~ *no sg.* rail(ing); handrail; (*лестницы*) banisters.

пери́метр, а *m.* (*math.*) perimeter.

пери́н|а, ы *f.* feather-bed.

пери́од, а *m.* **1** period; **леднико́вый п.** (*geol.*) ice age. **2** (*игры*) half.

периодиза́ци|я, и *f.* division into periods.

перио́дик|а, и *f.* (*collect.*) periodicals.

периоди́ческ|ий *adj.* periodic(al); recurring; **~ая дробь** recurring decimal; **п. журна́л** periodical, magazine; **~ое явле́ние** recurrent phenomenon.

периоди́чност|ь, и *f.* periodicity.

периоди́ч|ный (~ен, ~на) *adj.* periodic(al).

перипети́|я, и *f.* upheaval.

периско́п, а *m.* periscope.

пе́ристо-кучево́й *adj.* (*meteor.*) cirro-cumulus.

пе́ристы|й *adj.* **1** (*zool., bot.*) pinnate. **2** (*похожий на перья*) feather-like; **~е облака́** fleecy clouds; cirri.

перитони́т, а *m.* (*med.*) peritonitis.

перифери́йный *adj.* provincial.

перифери́ческий *adj.* peripheral.

перифери́|я, и *f.* **1** periphery. **2** (*collect.*) (*местность, удалённая от центра*) the provinces; the outlying districts. **3** (*comput.*) peripherals, peripheral devices.

перифра́з|а, ы *f.* periphrasis.

перифрази́р|овать, ую *impf. and pf.* to use a periphrasis (for).

перифрасти́ческий *adj.* periphrastic.

пёрк|а, и *f.* (*tech.*) (drill) bit.

перка́л|ь, и *f.* (*and* **~я**, *m.*) (*text.*) percale.

перколя́тор, а *m.* (coffee) percolator.

перку́сси|я, и *f.* (*med.*) percussion.

перл, а *m.* pearl (*fig.*).

перламу́тр, а *m.* mother-of-pearl.

перламу́тр|овый *adj. of* ⇒**~**

пе́рлин|ь, я *m.* (*naut.*) hawser.

перло́в|ый *adj.*: **~ая крупа́** pearl barley.

перлюстра́ци|я, и *f.* censorship (*opening and inspection of correspondence*).

перлюстри́р|овать, ую *impf. and pf.* to censor (*correspondence*).

перманéнт, а *m.* perm, permanent wave.

перманéнт|ный (~ен, ~на) *adj.* permanent.

перна́т|ый (~, ~а) *adj.* feathered; *as n. pl.* **~ые, ~ых** birds.

пёр|нуть, ну, нешь (*inst. pf. of* ⇒**~де́ть**) (*vulg.*) to fart.

пер|о́, а́, *pl.* **~ья, ~ьев** *nt.* **1** (*птицы*) feather; **ни пу́ха, ни ~а́!** good luck! **2** (*hist.*) quill; (*стальное*) nib; **взя́ться за п.** (*fig.*) to take up the pen; **владе́ть ~о́м** to wield a skilful (*Br.*), skillful (*US*) pen; **про́ба ~а́** (*fig.*) first attempt at writing.

перочи́нный *adj.*: **п. нож** pen-knife.

перпендикуля́р, а *m.* (*math.*) perpendicular.

перпендикуля́р|ный (~ен, ~на) *adj.* perpendicular.

перро́н, а *m.* platform (*at railway station*).

перс, а *m.* Persian.

пе́рс|и, ей *no sg.* (*arch. or poet.*) breast, bosom.

перси́дский *adj.* Persian.

Перси́дск|ий зали́в, ~ого ~а *m.* the Persian Gulf.

пе́рсик, а *m.* **1** (*плод*) peach. **2** (*дерево*) peach-tree.

пе́рсик|овый *adj. of* ⇒**~**; peachy; **~овое де́рево** peach-tree.

Пе́рси|я, и *f.* Persia.

перс|ия́нка, ия́нки *f. of* ⇒**~**

персо́н|а, ы *f.* person; **ва́жная п.** (*coll.*) big wig; **яви́ться со́бственной ~ой** (*iron.*) to appear in person; **п. гра́та**

persona grata; **обе́д на́ шесть ~** dinner for six.

персона́ж, а *m.* (*liter.*) character; (*fig.*) personage.

персона́л, а *m.* personnel, staff.

персона́льный *adj.* personal; individual; **п. компью́тер** personal computer.

персонифика́ци|я, и *f.* personification.

персонифици́р|овать, ую *impf. and pf.* to personify.

перспекти́в|а, ы *f.* **1** (*art*) perspective. **2** (*вид*) vista, prospect. **3** (*fig.*) prospect, outlook; **что в ~е?** what is in prospect?, what are the prospects?; **име́ть ~у** to have prospects, have a future (before one).

перспекти́в|ный *adj.* **1** (*art*) perspective. **2** (*план*) long-term, long-range; **~ное плани́рование** (*econ.*) long-term planning. **3 (~ен, ~на)** (*многообещающий*) having prospects; promising; **~ная молода́я балери́на** a promising young ballerina.

перст, а́ *m.* (*obs.*) finger; **оди́н, как п.** all alone.

пе́рст|ень, ня *m.* ring.

Перу́ *f. indecl.* Peru.

перуа́н|ец, ца *m.* Peruvian.

перуа́н|ка, ки *f. of* **⇒~ец**

перуа́нский *adj.* Peruvian.

перу́н|ы, ов *no sg.* (*obs., poet.*) (*гром*) thunderbolts; (*fig.*) fulminations; **мета́ть п.** to fulminate.

перфе́кт, а *m.* (*gram.*) perfect (tense).

перфока́рт|а, ы *f.* punched card.

перфоле́нт|а, ы *f.* punched tape.

перфора́тор, а *m.* (*tech.*) **1** (*для пробивания отверстий*) perforator; punch. **2** (*для бурения горных пород*) drill, boring machine.

перфора́ци|я, и *f.* (*tech.*) **1** (*отверстий*) perforation, punching. **2** (*в горной породе*) drilling, boring.

перфори́р|овать, ую *impf. and pf.* (*tech.*) **1** (*сделать множество отверстий*) to perforate, punch. **2** (*сделать скважины в горной породе*) to drill, bore.

перха́|ть, ю *impf.* (*no pf.*) (*coll.*) to cough (*in order to clear the throat*).

перхо́т|а, ы *f.* (*coll.*) tickling in the throat.

пе́рхот|ь, и *f.* dandruff.

перцо́вк|а, и *f.* pepper vodka.

перцо́вый *adj. of* **⇒пе́рец**

перча́тк|а, и *f.* glove; **бро́сить ~у** (*fig.*) to throw down the gauntlet.

перчи́нк|а, и *f.* peppercorn.

пе́рч|ить, ~у́, ~и́шь *impf.* (*of* **⇒на~** *and* **по~**) to pepper.

перш|и́ть, и́т *impf.* (*coll.*; *impers.*): **у меня́ в го́рле ~и́т** I have a tickle in my throat.

пёрыш|ко, ка, *pl.* **~ки, ~ек, ~кам** *nt.* (*coll.*) *dim. of* **⇒перо́; лёгкий, как п.** light as a feather.

пёс, пса *m.* (*coll.*) dog; (*astron.*): **созве́здие Большо́го Пса** Canis Major; **созве́здие Ма́лого Пса** Canis Minor; (*coll.*): **п. зна́ет** the devil only knows.

пе́сенк|а, и *f.* song; **его́ п. спе́та** (*coll.*) he is done for; he has had it.

пе́сенник, а *m.* **1** (*сборник*) song-book. **2** (*певец*) singer. **3** (*композитор*) song-writer.

пе́с|енный *adj. of* **⇒~ня**

песе́т|а, ы *f.* peseta.

пес|е́ц, ца́ *m.* (*животное*) Arctic fox; (*мех*) Arctic fox fur.

пёс|ий *adj. of* **⇒~**

пёсик, а *m.* (*coll.*) *dim. of* **⇒пёс;** doggie.

песка́р|ь, я́ *m.* gudgeon (*fish*).

пескостру́йный *adj.* (*tech.*) sand-blast.

песнопе́в|ец, ца *m.* (*poet.*) poet, bard.

песнопе́ни|е, я *nt.* **1** (*eccl.*) psalm; canticle. **2** (*poet.*) poetry, poesy.

песн|ь, и, *g. pl.* **~ей** *f.* **1** (*obs.*) song; **П. ~е́й** the Song of Songs, Song of Solomon. **2** (*liter.*) canto, book.

пе́с|ня, ни, *g. pl.* **~ен** *f.* song; **до́лгая п.** (*fig., coll.*) a long story; **э́та п. стара́** (*coll.*) it's the same old story.

пес|о́к, ка́ *m.* **1** sand; **золото́й п.** gold dust; **са́харный п.** granulated sugar; **стро́ить на ~ке́** (*fig.*) to build on sand. **2** (*pl.*) sands; **зыбу́чие ~ки́** quicksands.

песо́чник, а *m.* (*zool.*) sand-piper.

песо́чниц|а, ы *f.* sand-pit (*Br.*), sand-box (*US*).

песо́чн|ый *adj.* **1** *adj. of* **⇒песо́к;** sandy; **~ые часы́** sand-glass, hour-glass. **2** (*cul.*) short; **~ое пече́нье** shortbread.

пессими́зм, а *m.* pessimism.

пессими́ст, а *m.* pessimist.

пессимисти́ческий *adj.* pessimistic.

пессимисти́ч|ный (~ен, ~на) *adj.* = **~еский**

пессими́ст|ка, ки *f. of* **⇒~**

пест, а́ *m.* pestle.

пе́стик[1]**, а** *m.* (*bot.*) pistil

пе́стик[2]**, а** *m. dim. of* **⇒пест**

пестици́д, а *m.* pesticide.

пе́ст|овать, ую *impf.* (*of* **⇒вы́~**) **1** (*obs.*) to nurse. **2** (*fig.*) to cherish, foster.

пестр|е́ть[1]**, е́ет** *impf.* (*no pf.*) **1** (*становиться пёстрым*) to become many-coloured (*Br.*), many-colored (*US*). **2** (+*i.*) to be bright (with); **корабли́ ~е́ли фла́гами** the ships were bright with bunting. **3** (*виднеться*) to show colourfully (*Br.*), colorfully (*US*) (*of objects of different colours*).

пестр|е́ть[2]**, и́т** *impf.* (*no pf.*) **1** (*попадаться на глаза*) to strike the eye; **~я́т афи́ши на стена́х** posters on the walls strike the eye. **2** (*coll.*) (*быть слишком пёстрым*) to be too gaudy, be flashy. **3** (+*i.*) (*изобиловать*) to abound (in).

пестр|и́ть, ю́, и́шь *impf.* (*no pf.*) **1** (*делать пёстрым*) to make gaudy; to make colourful (*Br.*), colorful (*US*). **2** (*impers.*): **у меня́ ~и́ло в глаза́х** I was dazzled (*sc.* by the colours).

пестрот|а́, ы́ *no pl., f.* diversity of colours (*Br.*), colors (*US*); (*fig.*) mixed character.

пёстр|ый (~, ~а́, ~о *and* **~о́)** *adj.* **1** variegated, multi-coloured (*Br.*), -colored (*US*). **2** (*fig., coll.*) mixed; **п. соста́в населе́ния** mixed population. **3** (*fig.*) florid; **п. слог** florid style.

пес|цо́вый *adj. of* **⇒~е́ц**

песча́ник, а *m.* (*geol.*) sandstone.

песча́нк|а, и *f.* **1** (*грызун*) gerbil. **2** (*птица*) sanderling.

песча́н|ый *adj.* sandy; **~ая коса́** sandbar; **п. холм** dune.

песчи́нк|а, и *f.* grain of sand.

пета́рд|а, ы *f.* **1** (*hist. mil.*) petard. **2** (*фейерверк*) banger (*Br.*), fire-cracker (*US*).

петербу́ргский *adj.* St Petersburg.

петербу́рж|ец, ца *m.* St Petersburger.

пети́ци|я, и *f.* petition.

петли́ц|а, ы *f.* **1** (*для пуговицы*) buttonhole. **2** (*нашивка*) tab (*on uniform collar*).

пе́т|ля, ли, *g. pl.* **~ель** *f.* **1** loop; **мёртвая п.** (*aeron.*) loop; **сде́лать мёртвую ~лю** to loop the loop. **2** (*fig.*) noose; **лезть в ~лю** to put one's head in the noose. **3** (*для пуговицы*) buttonhole. **4** (*в вязании*) stitch; **спусти́ть ~лю** to drop a stitch. **5** (*двери*) hinge; **дверь соскочи́ла с ~ель** the door has come off its hinges.

петля́|ть, ю *impf.* (*coll.*) to dodge.

петру́шк|а[1]**, и** *f.* (*растение*) parsley.

петру́шк|а[2]**, и** *m. and f.* **1** *m.* (*кукла*) Punch. **2** *m.* (*представление*) Punch-and-Judy show; **брось валя́ть ~у!** stop being a fool! **3** *f.* (*fig., coll.*) (*нечто нелепое, странное, смешное*) foolishness, absurdity, **кака́я-то п. получи́лась** an absurd thing happened.

пету́н|ия, ии *f.* (*bot.*) petunia.

пету́н|ья, ьи, *g. pl.* **~ий** *f.* = **~ия**

пету́х, а́ *m.* cock; **до ~о́в** before cock-crow; **встать с ~а́ми** to rise with the lark; **пусти́ть ~а́** (*mus. sl.*) to let out a squeak (*on a high note*); **пусти́ть кра́сного ~а́** to start a fire.

пету́|ший *adj. of* **⇒~х; п. гре́бень** cockscomb.

петуши́ный *adj. of* **⇒пету́х; п. бой** cockfight(ing); **п. го́лос** (*fig.*) squeaky voice.

петуш|и́ться, у́сь, и́шься *impf.* (*of* **⇒вс~**) (*coll.*) to get on one's high horse.

петуш|о́к, ка́ *m.* cockerel.

пе́т|ый *p.p.p. of* **⇒~ь;** (*coll.*): **п. дура́к** perfect fool.

петь, пою́, поёшь *impf.* (*of* **⇒про~** *and* **⇒с~**) to sing; **п. ба́сом** to have a bass voice; **п. вполго́лоса** to hum; **п. другу́ю пе́сню** to sing another tune; **п. Ла́заря** (*coll., pej.*) to bemoan one's fate, grumble, complain; **п. сла́ву** (+*d.*) to sing the praises (of).

пехо́т|а, ы *f.* infantry; **морска́я п.** (the) marines.

пехоти́н|ец, ца *m.* infantryman.

пехо́тный *adj.* infantry.

печа́л|ить, ю, ишь *impf.* (*of* ⇒**о~**) to grieve, sadden.

печа́л|иться, юсь, ишься *impf.* (*of* ⇒**о~**) to grieve, be sad.

печа́л|ь, и *f.* grief, sorrow; **(вот) не́ было ~и!** what a nuisance!; **кака́я п.!** how sad!; **не твоя́ п.** it's no concern of yours; **тебе́ что за п.?** what has that to do with you?

печа́л|ьный (~ен, ~ьна) *adj.* **1** sad, doleful. **2** (*прискорбный*) bad, regrettable; **п. коне́ц** bad end; **~ьные результа́ты** unfortunate results; **оста́вить по себе́ ~ьную па́мять** to leave a bad reputation.

печа́тани|е, я *nt.* printing.

печа́та|ть, ю *impf.* (*of* ⇒**на~**) to print; (*на машинке*) to type.

печа́та|ться, юсь *impf.* (*of* ⇒**на~**) **1** to have (*literary compositions, etc.*) published; **в три́дцать лет он ещё нигде́ не ~лся** at thirty he had not yet had anything published. **2** (*находиться в печати*) to be at the printer's.

печа́тк|а, и *f.* signet.

печа́тник, а *m.* printer.

печа́тн|ый *adj.* **1** printing; **~ое де́ло** printing; **п. лист** quire, printer's sheet; **п. стано́к** printing-press. **2** (*напечатанный*) printed; in the press; **~ая кни́га** printed book (*opp. manuscript*). **3**: **писа́ть по ~ому, ~ыми бу́квами** to (write in) print; to write in block capitals.

печа́т|ь¹, и *f.* (*для оттискивания*) seal, stamp (*also fig.*); **наложи́ть п. (на** + *a.*) to affix a seal (to); **носи́ть п.** (+ *g.*) to bear the stamp (of); **на мои́х уста́х п. молча́ния** my lips are sealed.

печа́т|ь², и *f.* **1** (*печатание*) print(ing); **вы́йти из ~и** to come out, be published. **2** (*вид напечатанного*) print, type; **ме́лкая п.** small print; **кру́пная п.** large print; **убо́ристая п.** close print. **3** (*пресса*) (the) press; **свобо́да ~и** freedom of the press; **име́ть благоприя́тные о́тзывы в ~и** to have a good press.

пече́ни|е, я *nt.* baking.

печёнк|а, и *f.* **1** liver (*of animal, as food*). **2** (*coll.*) liver; **сиде́ть (у кого́-н.) в ~ах** to plague (s.o.).

печёночник, а *m.* (*bot.*) liverwort.

печён|очный *adj. of* ⇒**~ка** *and* **пе́чень;** hepatic.

печёный *adj.* (*cul.*) baked.

пе́чен|ь, и *f.* liver.

пече́нь|е, я *nt.* (*collect.*) biscuits (*Br.*), cookies (*US*).

пе́чк|а, и *f.* stove; **танцева́ть от ~и** (*coll., iron.*) to begin again from the beginning.

печ|но́й *adj. of* ⇒**~ь²**; **~на́я труба́** chimney, flue.

печь¹, пеку́, печёшь, пеку́т, *past* **пёк, пекла́** *impf.* (*of* ⇒**ис~**) to bake; **со́лнце пекло́** there was a scorching sun.

печ|ь², и, о ~и, в ~и́, *pl.* **~и, ~е́й** *f.* **1** stove; (*духовка*) oven. **2** (*tech.*) furnace; (*обжиговая*) kiln; **до́менная п.** blast-furnace; **кремацио́нная п.** incinerator.

пе́чься¹, печётся, пеку́тся, *past* **пёкся, пекла́сь** *impf.* (*of* ⇒**ис~**) to bake.

пе́чься², пеку́сь, печёшься, пеку́тся, *past* **пёкся, пекла́сь** *impf.* (*no pf.*) (**о** + *p.*) to take care (of), look after.

пешедра́лом *adv.* (*coll.*) = **пешко́м**

пешехо́д, а *m.* pedestrian.

пешехо́дный *adj.* pedestrian; **п. мост** foot-bridge.

пе́ший *adj.* **1** pedestrian. **2** (*mil.*) unmounted, foot.

пе́шк|а, и *f.* (*in chess, also fig.*) pawn.

пешко́м *adv.* on foot.

пещёр|а, ы *f.* cave.

пещёр|ный *adj. of* ⇒**~а; п. челове́к** cave-dweller, cave-man.

ПЗУ *nt. indecl.* (*abbr. of* ***постоя́нное запомина́ющее устро́йство***) (*comput.*) ROM (*read-only memory*).

пи *nt. indecl.* (*math.*) pi (π).

пиани́но *nt. indecl.* (upright) piano.

пиани́ссимо *adv.* (*mus.*) pianissimo.

пиани́ст, а *m.* pianist.

пиани́ст|ка, ки *f. of* ⇒**~**

пиа́но *adv.* (*mus.*) piano.

пиано́л|а, ы *f.* (*mus.*) pianola.

пиа́стр, а *m.* piastre.

пива́|ть, ю *impf.* (*coll.*) *freq. of* ⇒**пить**

пивба́р, а *m.* (*coll.*) pub.

пивн|а́я, о́й *f.* pub.

пив|но́й *adj. of* ⇒**~о; ~ны́е дро́жжи** brewer's yeast; **~на́я кру́жка** beer mug.

пи́в|о, а *nt.* beer; **с ним ~а не сва́ришь** (*fig., coll.*) he's an awkward customer.

пивова́р, а *m.* brewer.

пивоваре́ни|е, я *nt.* brewing.

пивова́ренн|ый *adj.*: **п. заво́д** brewery; **~ая промы́шленность** brewing.

пи́галиц|а, ы *f.* (*zool.*) lapwing, peewit; (*fig., coll.*) pipsqueak.

пигме́|й, я *m.* pygmy (*also fig.*).

пигме́нт, а *m.* pigment.

пигмента́ци|я, и *f.* pigmentation.

пиджа́к, а́ *m.* jacket, coat.

пиджа́|чный *adj. of* ⇒**~к; п. костю́м, ~чная па́ра** (lounge-)suit.

пи́дор, а *m.* (*vulg., pej.*) queer, poof (*Br.*).

пиете́т, а *m.* reverence.

пижа́м|а, ы *f.* pyjamas.

пижо́н, а *m.* (*coll.*) fop; (*sl., pej.*) twit.

пизд|а́, ы́ *f.* (*vulg.*) cunt.

пии́т, а *m.* (*arch.*) poet.

пик¹, а *m.* (*geog.*) peak; (*fig.*) pinnacle.

пик², а 1 *m.* peak (*of work, traffic, etc.*); **п. нагру́зки** (*elec.*) peak load. **2** *adj. indecl.* **часы́ пик** rush-hour.

пи́к|а¹, и *f.* (*оружие*) pike, lance.

пи́к|а², и *f.* (*cards*) spade; **да́ма ~** the queen of spades; **пойти́ ~ой** to play a spade.

пи́к|а³, и *f. only in phr.* **сде́лать что-н. в ~у кому́-н.** to do a thing to spite s.o.

пика́нтност|ь, и *f.* piquancy, savour, zest.

пика́нт|ный (~ен, ~на) *adj.* (*соус*) piquant, spicy; (*fig.*) (*новость, анекдот*) juicy; spicy; (*женщина*) attractive, sexy.

пика́п, а *m.* pick-up (truck).

пике́¹ *nt. indecl.* (*text.*) piqué.

пике́² *nt. indecl.* (*aeron.*) dive; **перейти́ в п.** to go into a dive.

пике́|йный *adj. of* ⇒**~¹**

пике́т¹, а *m.* (*группа бастующих*) picket.

пике́т², а *m.* (*карточная игра*) piquet.

пикети́р|овать, ую *impf.* to picket.

пике́тчик, а *m.* picket.

пики́ровани|е, я *nt.* (*aeron.*) dive, diving.

пики́р|овать, ую *impf. and pf.* (*pf. also* **с~**) (*aeron.*) to dive, swoop.

пикир|ова́ть, у́ю *impf. and pf.* (*agric.*) to thin out.

пики́р|оваться, уюсь *impf.* (*no pf.*) (**с** + *i.*) to exchange insults; to squabble.

пикиро́вк|а¹, и *f.* (*agric.*) thinning.

пикиро́вк|а², и *f.* (*coll.*) squabbling.

пикиро́вщик, а *m.* dive-bomber.

пики́р|ующий *pres. part of* ⇒**~овать** *and adj.*; **п. бомбардиро́вщик** dive-bomber.

пи́кколо *nt. indecl.* piccolo.

пикни́к, а́ *m.* picnic.

пи́кн|уть, у, ешь *pf.* (*coll.*) to let out a squeak; (*fig.*) to make a sound (of protest); **попро́буй то́лько п.** (*with implied threat*) one sound out of you!; **п. не сметь** to not dare utter a word.

пи́к|овый *adj.* **1** *adj. of* ⇒**~а²**; **~овая да́ма** queen of spades; **~овая масть** spades. **2** (*fig., coll.*) awkward; **попа́сть в ~овое положе́ние** to get into a pretty mess; **оста́ться при ~овом интере́се** to get nothing for one's pains.

пи́ксел, а *m.* pixel.

пиктогра́мм|а, ы *f.* pictogram; (*comput.*) icon.

пи́кул|и, ей *no sg.* pickles.

пи́кш|а, и *f.* haddock.

пил|а́, ы́, *pl.* **~ы, ~** *f.* **1** saw; **ажу́рная п.** jig-saw; **ле́нточная п.** band-saw; **лучко́вая п.** bow saw. **2** (*fig.*) (*человек*) nagger.

пила́в, а *m.* (*cul.*) pilaff, pilau.

пила́-ры́ба, пилы́-ры́бы *f.* saw-fish.

пилёный *adj.* sawn; **п. лес** timber; **п. са́хар** lump sugar.

пилигри́м, а *m.* pilgrim.

пили́ка|ть, ю *impf.* (*coll.*) to scrape (*on a fiddle, etc.*).

пил|и́ть, ю́, ~ишь *impf.* **1** to saw. **2** (*fig., coll.*) (*упрекать*) to nag (at).

пи́лк|а, и *f.* **1** (*действие*) sawing. **2** (*ручная пила*) fret-saw. **3** (*для ногтей*) nail-file.

пиломатериа́л|ы, ов *no sg.* saw-timber.

пило́н, а *m.* (*archit.*) pylon.

пилообра́зный *adj.* serrated, notched.
пилора́м|а, ы *f.* power-saw bench.
пило́т, а *m.* pilot; **п.-сме́ртник** suicide pilot.
пилота́ж, а *m.* pilotage; **вы́сший п.** aerobatics.
пилоти́р|овать, ую *impf.* to pilot; to man.
пило́тк|а, и *f.* (*mil.*) forage cap.
пиль *int.* (*command to hounds*) take!
пи́льщик, а *m.* sawyer, wood-cutter.
пилю́л|я, и *f.* pill (*also fig.*); **проглоти́ть ~ю** (*fig.*) to swallow the pill.
пиля́стр|а, ы *f.* (*archit.*) pilaster.
пина́|ть, ю *impf. of* ⇨**пнуть**
пингви́н, а *m.* penguin.
пинг-по́нг, а *m.* ping-pong.
пине́тк|а, и *f.* (*baby's*) bootee.
пи́ни|я, и *f.* store pine.
пин|о́к, ка́ *m.* (*coll.*) kick.
пи́нт|а, ы *f.* pint.
пинце́т, а *m.* (*tech.*) pincers; (*med.*) tweezers.
пи́нчер, а *m.* (*собака*) pinscher.
пио́н, а *m.* (*bot.*) peony.
пионе́р, а *m.* pioneer; **(ю́ный) пионе́р** (Young) Pioneer (*in former USSR, member of Communist children's organization*).
пионе́р|ка, ки *f. of* ⇨**~**
пионе́р|ский *adj. of* ⇨**~**
пиоре́|я, и *f.* (*med.*) pyorrhoea (*Br.*), pyorrhea (*US*).
пипе́тк|а, и *f.* pipette; medicine dropper.
пи-пи́ (*baby talk*): **сде́лать п.** to do a wee(-wee).
пир, а, о ~е, в ~у́, *pl.* **~ы́** *m.* feast, banquet; **п. горо́й, п. на весь мир** sumptuous feast.
пирами́д|а, ы *f.* pyramid.
пирамида́л|ьный (~ен, ~ьна) *adj.* pyramidal; **п. то́поль** Lombardy poplar.
пирамидо́н, а *m.* (*pharm.*) pyramidon, amidopyrine; headache tablets.
пира́нь|я, и *f.* (*zool.*) piranha.
пира́т, а *m.* pirate; **возду́шный п.** air pirate, skyjacker.
пира́тский *adj.* (*судно*) pirate; (*обычаи*) piratical; (*издание*) pirated.
пира́тств|о, а *nt.* piracy.
Пирене́|и, -ев *no sg.* the Pyrenees.
пирене́йский *adj.* Pyrenean.
пири́т, а *m.* (*min.*) pyrites.
пир|ова́ть, у́ю *impf.* to feast, banquet.
пиро́г, а́ *m.* pie; **п. с мя́сом** meat pie; **возду́шный п.** soufflé.
пиро́г|а, и *f.* pirogue, canoe.
пирожко́в|ая, ой *f.* snack-bar.
пиро́жник, а *m.* pastry-cook.
пиро́жни|ца, цы *f. of* ⇨**~к**
пиро́жн|ое, ого *nt.* (fancy) cake, pastry.
пирож|о́к, ка́ *m.* pasty (*Br.*), patty, pie.
пироте́хник|а, и *f.* pyrotechnics.
пиротехни́ческий *adj.* pyrotechnic.
пи́рров *adj.*: **~а побе́да** Pyrrhic victory.
пиру́шк|а, и *f.* (*coll.*) carousal; binge.
пиру́эт, а *m.* pirouette.
пи́ршеств|о, а *nt.* feast, banquet.
пи́ршеств|овать, ую *impf.* to feast, banquet.
писа́к|а, и *m.* (*coll.*) scribbler, hack writer.
писа́ни|е, я *nt.* **1** (*действие*) writing. **2** (*текст*) writing, screed; **(свяще́нное) п.** Holy Scripture, Holy Writ.
пи́сан|ый *adj.* written; **~ая краса́вица** a picture (of beauty); **говори́ть как по-~ому** to speak fluently.
пи́сар|ь, я, *pl.* **~я́** *m.* (*obs.*) clerk.
писа́тел|ь, я *m.* writer, author.
писа́тель|ница, ницы *f. of* ⇨**~**
писа́тель|ский *adj. of* ⇨**~**
пи́са|ть, ю *impf.* (*vulg.*) to piss.
пи|са́ть, шу́, ~́шешь *impf.* (*of* ⇨**на~**) **1** to write; **п. на маши́нке** to type; **п. про́зой, стиха́ми** to write prose, verse; **п. дневни́к** to keep a diary; **п. под дикто́вку** to take dictation; **не про нас ~́сано** (*coll.*) (*i*) (*недоступно нашему пониманию*) it is Greek to us, (*ii*) (*предназначено не для нас*) it is not (intended, meant) for us; **~ши́ пропа́ло** it is as good as lost. **2** (+*i.*) (*красками*) to paint (in); **п. портре́ты ма́слом** to paint portraits in oils.
пи|са́ться, ~́шется *impf.* **1** to be spelled *or* spelt; **как ~́шется э́то сло́во?** how do you spell this word? **2** (*impers.*; +*d.*) to feel an inclination for writing; **мне сего́дня не ~́шется** I don't feel like writing today.
пис|е́ц, ца́ *m.* (*hist.*) scribe.
писк, а *m.* (*ребёнка, мыши*) squeak; (*цыплят*) cheep.
пискли́в|ый (~, ~а) *adj.* squeaky.
пискля́в|ый (~, ~а) *adj.* (*coll.*) = **пискли́вый**
пи́скн|уть, у, ешь *inst. pf.* (*of* ⇨**пища́ть**) (*coll.*) to give a squeak, cheep; **то́лько ~и у меня́!** (*with implied threat*) one squeak out of you!
писсуа́р, а *m.* urinal.
пистоле́т, а *m.* pistol; **п.-пулемёт** sub-machine-gun.
писто́н, а *m.* **1** (*в патроне*) (percussion) cap. **2** (*mus.*) valve.
писчебума́жны|й *adj.*: **п. магази́н** stationer's (shop); **~е принадле́жности** stationery.
пи́сч|ий *adj.*: **~ая бума́га** writing paper.
письмена́, письмён, ~м *no sg.* characters, letters; **дре́вние еги́петские п.** ancient Egyptian characters.
пи́сьменно *adv.* in writing; **изложи́ть п.** to set down in writing.
пи́сьменност|ь, и *f.* **1** (*литературные памятники*) literature; (*collect.*) literary texts. **2** (*средства письменного общения*) the written language.
пи́сьменн|ый *adj.* **1** (*употребляемый для писания*) writing; **п. стол** writing-table, bureau. **2** (*написанный*) written; **в ~ом ви́де, в ~ой фо́рме** in writing, in written form; **п. знак** letter; **п. экза́мен** written examination.
письм|о́, а́, *pl.* **~́а, пи́сем, ~́ам** *nt.* **1** letter; **заказно́е п.** registered letter. **2** (*умение писать*) writing; **иску́сство ~а́** art of writing. **3** (*система графических знаков*) script; (*почерк*) hand(-writing); **ара́бское п.** Arabic script; **ме́лкое п.** small hand. **4** (*стиль*) style (*of painting*).
письмоно́с|ец, ца *m.* postman.
пита́ни|е, я *nt.* **1** (*действие*) feeding, nutrition; (*характер пищи*) diet; **уси́ленное п.** high-calorie diet; **недоста́точное п.** malnutrition; (*пища*) food. **2** (*tech.*) feed, supply. **3** (*elec.*) power supply.
пита́тельност|ь, и *f.* nutritiousness.
пита́тел|ьный (~ен, ~ьна) *adj.* **1** nourishing, nutritious; **п. крем** skin cream; **~ьная среда́** (*biol.*) culture medium; (*fig.*) breeding-ground; **~ьное вещество́** nutrient. **2** (*tech.*) feed, supply; **~ьная труба́** feed pipe, supply pipe.
пита́|ть, ю *impf.* (*of* ⇨**на~**) **1** to feed; to nourish (*also fig.*); **п. больно́го** to feed a patient; **п. наде́жду** to nourish the hope; **п. отвраще́ние (к**+*d.*) to have an aversion (for); **п. привя́занность** to be attached (to), cultivate an attachment (to). **2** (*tech.*) to supply; **п. го́род электроэне́ргией** to supply a city with electricity.
пита́|ться, юсь *impf.* (+*i.*) to feed (on), live (on); **хорошо́ п.** to be well fed, eat well; **п. наде́ждами** to live on hope.
пит-бу́л|ь, я *m.* pit bull terrier.
питека́нтроп, а *m.* (*anthrop.*) pithe, canthropus, Java man.
Пи́тер, а *m.* (*coll.*) St. Petersburg.
пи́тер|ский *adj. of* ⇨**П~**
пито́м|ец, ца *m.* **1** (*воспитанник*) charge. **2** (*студент*) pupil; (*бывший студент*) alumnus.
пито́м|ица, ицы *f. of* ⇨**~ец**
пито́мник, а *m.* nursery (*for plants or animals*; *also fig.*); **древе́сный п.** arboretum.
пито́н, а *m.* python.
пить, пью, пьёшь, *past* **пил, пила́, пи́ло** *impf.* (*of* ⇨**вы́~**) to drink; **мне п. хо́чется** I am thirsty; **п. за** (+*a.*), **за здоро́вье** (+*g.*) to drink to, to the health (of); **п. го́рькую, п. мёртвую** (*coll.*) to drink hard; **как п. дать** (*coll.*) for sure.
пить|ё, я́ *nt.* **1** (*действие*) drinking. **2** (*напиток*) drink.
питьев|о́й *adj.* drinkable; **~а́я вода́** drinking water.
пифаго́ров *adj.*: **~а теоре́ма** Pythagoras' theorem.
пих|а́ть, а́ю *impf.* (*of* ⇨**~ну́ть**) (*coll.*) **1** (*толкать*) to push, shove, jostle. **2** (*запихивать*) to shove, cram; **п. ве́щи в чемода́н** to cram things into a suitcase.
пиха́|ться, юсь *impf.* (*coll.*) to push and shove; to jostle one another.

П

пих|ну́ть, ну́, нёшь *pf. of* ⇒**~а́ть**
пи́хт|а, ы *f.* fir(-tree).
пи́хт|овый *adj. of* ⇒**~а**
пи́цц|а, ы *f.* pizza.
пиццери́|я, и *f.* pizza parlour, pizzeria.
пиццика́то *nt. indecl.* (*mus.*) pizzicato; *adv., adj.* pizzicato.
пи́чка|ть, ю *impf.* (*of* ⇒**на~**) (*coll.*) to stuff, cram (*also fig.*).
пичу́г|а, и *f.* (*coll.*) bird.
пичу́жк|а, и *f.* (*coll.*) = **пичу́га**
пиччика́то = **пиццика́то**
пи́шущ|ий *pres. part. act. of* ⇒**писа́ть** *and adj.*; **п. э́ти стро́ки** the present writer; **~ая маши́нка** typewriter.
пи́щ|а, и *no pl., f.* food; **п. для ума́** food for thought.
пища́л|ь, и *f.* (*hist.*) (h)arquebus.
пищ|а́ть, у́, и́шь *impf.* (*of* ⇒**пи́скнуть**) **1** (*о мыши, о двери*) to squeak; (*о цыплятах*) to cheep. **2** (*coll.*) (*жаловаться*) to whine.
пище... *comb. form, abbr. of* ***пищево́й***
пищеваре́ни|е, я *nt.* digestion; **расстро́йство ~я** indigestion.
пищевари́тельный *adj.* digestive; **п. кана́л** alimentary canal.
пищево́д, а *m.* (*anat.*) oesophagus (*Br.*), esophagus (*US*), gullet.
пищ|ево́й *adj. of* ⇒**~а; ~евы́е проду́кты** foodstuffs.
пищекомбина́т, а *m.* catering combine.
пи́щик, а *m.* **1** (*дудочка*) pipe for luring birds. **2** (*mus.*) reed.
пия́вк|а, и *f.* leech.
ПК *m. indecl.* (*abbr. of* ***персона́льный компью́тер***) PC (*personal computer*).
пл. (*abbr. of* ***пло́щадь***) Sq., Square.
плав, а *m.*: **на ~у́** afloat.
пла́вани|е, я *nt.* **1** swimming; **синхро́нное п.** synchronized swimming. **2** (*на судне*) sailing; navigation; **су́дно да́льнего ~я** ocean-going ship; **отпра́виться в п., пусти́ться в п.** to put out to sea.
пла́вательный *adj.* swimming; natatorial, natatory; **п. бассе́йн** swimming pool.
пла́ва|ть, ю *impf.* **1** *indet. of* ⇒**плыть. 2** (*держаться на воде*) to float.
плавба́з|а, ы *f.* (*abbr. of* ***плаву́чая ба́за***) factory ship.
плавико́вый *adj.*: **п. шпат** (*min.*) fluorspar.
плави́льн|ый *adj.* (*tech.*) melting, smelting; **~ая печь** smelting furnace.
плави́л|ьня, ьни, *g. pl.* **~ен** *f.* foundry, smeltery.
плави́льщик, а *m.* smelter.
пла́в|ить, лю, ишь *impf.* to smelt.
пла́в|иться, ится *impf.* to melt; to fuse (*intrans.*).
пла́вк|а, и *f.* fusing; fusion.
пла́в|ки, ок *no sg.* swimming trunks.
пла́в|кий, ок, ка *adj.* fusible; **п. предохрани́тель, ~кая про́бка** (*elec.*) fuse; **~кая про́волока** fuse wire.
плавле́ни|е, я *nt.* melting, fusion; **то́чка ~я** melting point.
пла́вленый *adj.*: **п. сыр** processed cheese.
пла́вн|и, ей *no sg.* (*reed-covered*) flats (*on lower reaches of rivers Dnieper, Kuban, etc.*).
плавни́к, а́ *m.* fin; flipper; **спинно́й п.** dorsal fin.
пла́вност|ь, и *f.* smoothness; facility.
пла́в|ный (~ен, ~на) *adj.* **1** smooth; **~ная речь** flowing speech. **2** (*ling.*) liquid.
плаву́нчик, а *m.* (*zool.*) phalarope.
плаву́чест|ь, и *f.* buoyancy.
плаву́ч|ий *adj.* floating; **~ая льди́на** ice-floe; **п. мая́к** lightship.
плагиа́т, а *m.* plagiarism.
плагиа́тор, а *m.* plagiarist.
пла́зм|а, ы *f.* (*biol. and phys.*) plasma.
пла́кальщик, а *m.* (*hired*) mourner.
пла́кальщи|ца, цы *f. of* ⇒**~к**
плака́т, а *m.* poster.
плакати́ст, а *m.* poster artist.
плака́т|ный *adj. of* ⇒**~**
пла́|кать, чу, чешь *impf.* to cry, weep; **п. навзры́д** to sob; **хоть ~чь!** it is enough to make you weep!; (*о том, что пропало*): **~кал твой о́тпуск!** that's your holiday down the drain!
пла́|каться, чусь, чешься *impf.* (*coll.*) (**на** + *a.*) to complain (of), lament; **п. на свою́ судьбу́** to bemoan one's fate.
плакир|ова́ть, у́ю *impf. and pf.* (*tech.*) to plate.
пла́кс|а, ы *c.g.* (*coll.*) cry-baby.
плакси́в|ый (~, ~а) *adj.* (*coll.*) (*ребёнок*) given to crying; whining; (*голос, лицо, улыбка*) pathetic.
плаку́н-трав|а́, ы́ *f.* (*bot.*) purple loosestrife (*Lythrum salicaria*).
плаку́ч|ий *adj.* weeping; **~ая и́ва** weeping willow.
пламене́|ть, ю *impf.* (*poet.*) to flame, blaze; **п. стра́стью** to burn with passion.
пла́менност|ь, и *f.* ardour (*Br.*), ardor (*US*).
пла́менн|ый *adj.* **1** flaming, fiery. **2** (*fig.*) (*страстный*) ardent, burning.
пла́мен|ь, и *m.* (*obs., poet.*) = **пла́мя**
пла́м|я, ени *nt.* flame; (*яркое*) blaze; **вспы́хнуть ~енем** to burst into flame.
план, а *m.* **1** (*намерение; чертёж, карта*) plan; **уче́бный п.** curriculum; **по ~у** according to plan. **2** (*место*): **пере́дний п.** foreground; **за́дний п.** background; **кру́пный п.** close-up (*in filming*); (*fig.*): **вы́двинуть на пе́рвый п.** to bring to the forefront; **отодви́нуть на за́дний п.** to put on the back burner. **3** (*fig.*) (*область*) area.
планёр, а *m.* (*aeron.*) glider.
планери́зм, а *m.* gliding.
планери́ст, а *m.* glider-pilot.
планёр|ный *adj. of* ⇒**~; п. спорт** gliding.
плане́т|а, ы *f.* **1** planet. **2** (*Земля*) (the) planet (= *Earth*).
планета́ри|й, я *m.* planetarium.
плане́т|ный *adj. of* ⇒**~а;** planetary.
планиме́тр, а *m.* (*surveying*) planimeter.
планиметр|и́ческий *adj.* **1** *of* ⇒**~. 2** *of* ⇒**~ия**
планиме́три|я, и *f.* (*math.*) plane geometry.
плани́ровани|е¹, я *nt.* planning; **п. городо́в** town-planning.
плани́ровани|е², я *nt.* (*aeron.*) gliding; glide.
плани́р|овать¹, ую *impf.* (*of* ⇒**за~**) to plan.
плани́р|овать², ую *impf.* (*of* ⇒**с~**) (*aeron.*) to glide (down).
планир|ова́ть, у́ю *impf.* (*of* ⇒**рас~**) to lay out (*a park, etc.*).
планиро́вк|а, и *f.* laying out; lay-out.
планиро́вщик, а *m.* planner.
пла́нк|а, и *f.* lath, slat.
планкто́н, а *m.* (*biol.*) plankton.
планови́к, а́ *m.* planner.
пла́новост|ь, и *f.* planned character.
пла́нов|ый *adj.* **1** planned, systematic; **~ое хозя́йство** planned economy. **2** planning (*attr.*); **~ая коми́ссия** planning commission.
планоме́рност|ь, и *f.* systematic character.
планоме́р|ный (~ен, ~на) *adj.* systematic, planned.
планта́тор, а *m.* planter.
планта́ци|я, и *f.* plantation.
планше́т, а *m.* **1** (*surveying*) plane-table. **2** (*сумка для карт*) map-case.
планше́тный *adj.*: **п. графопострои́тель** flatbed plotter; **п. ска́нер** flatbed scanner.
планши́р, а *m.* (*naut.*) gunwale.
планши́р|ь, я *m.* = **~**
пласт, а́ *m.* layer; sheet; (*archit.*) course; (*geol.*) stratum, bed; **лежа́ть ~о́м** to lie flat on one's back.
пласта́|ть, ю *impf.* to cut in layers.
пла́стик, а *m.* plastic (*material*).
пла́стик|а, и *f.* **1** (*collect.*) the plastic arts. **2** (*движения тела*) eurhythmics. **3** (*пластичность*) gracefulness, grace.
пла́стиковый *adj.* plastic.
пластили́н, а *m.* plasticine (*propr.*).
пласти́н|а, ы *f.* plate.
пласти́нк|а, и *f.* **1** plate; (**граммофо́нная**) **п.** gramophone record; (*phot.*) (photographic) plate. **2** (*bot.*) blade. **3** (*coll.*) (*зубной протез*) plate.
пласти́нчатый *adj.* lamellar, lamellate.
пласти́ческ|ий *adj.* plastic; **~ая ма́сса** plastic; **~ая хирурги́я** plastic surgery.
пласти́чност|ь, и *f.* plasticity.
пласти́ч|ный (~ен, ~на) *adj.* **1** (*материал, вещество*) plastic; pliant. **2** (*плавный*) rhythmical; fluent, flowing; (*изящный*) graceful; (*гармоничный*) harmonious; **п. жест** flowing gesture.
пластма́сс|а, ы *f.* (*abbr. of* ***пласти́ческая ма́сса***) plastic.

пластма́сс|овый *adj. of* ⇒**~а**

пласт|ова́ть, у́ю *impf.* **1** (*накладывать пластами*) to lay in layers. **2** (*резать пластами*) to cut in layers.

пласту́н, а́ *m.* (*hist.*) dismounted Cossack.

пласту́н|ский *adj. of* ⇒**~; переполза́ние по-~ски** (*mil.*) the leopard crawl.

пла́стыр|ь, я *m.* (*med.*) plaster.

плат, а *m.* (*obs.*) = **~о́к**

пла́т|а[1]**, ы** *f.* **1** (*за труд*) pay; salary; **за́работная п.** wages. **2** (*за получение, использование чего-н.*) payment, charge; fee; **входна́я п.** entrance fee; **кварти́рная п.** rent; **п. за прое́зд** fare.

пла́т|а[2]**, ы** *f.* (*comput.*) card, board; **графи́ческая п.** graphics card; **звукова́я п.** sound card; **монта́жная п.** circuit board.

плата́н, а *m.* plane(-tree).

плата́|ть, ю *impf.* (*of* ⇒**за~**) (*coll.*) to patch.

платёж, а́ *m.* payment; **нало́женным ~о́м** cash on delivery.

платёжеспосо́бност|ь, и *f.* solvency.

платёжеспосо́б|ный (~ен, ~на) *adj.* solvent.

платёж|ный *adj. of* ⇒**~; п. бала́нс** balance of payments; **~ная ве́домость** pay-roll; **п. день** pay-day; **~ное поруче́ние** payment order.

плате́льщик, а *m.* payer.

пла́тин|а, ы *f.* (*min.*) platinum.

пла́тин|овый *adj. of* ⇒**~а**

пла|ти́ть, чу́, ~́тишь *impf.* (*of* ⇒**за~**) **1** to pay; **п. нали́чными** to pay in cash, pay in ready money; **п. нату́рой** to pay in kind. **2** (*fig.*; + *i.* **за** + *a.*) to pay back, return; **п. кому́-н. услу́гой за услу́гу** to make it up to s.o., return a favour (*Br.*), favor (*US*).

пла|ти́ться, чу́сь, ~́тишься *impf.* (*of* ⇒**по~**) (+ *i.* **за** + *a.*) to pay (with for); **п. жи́знью за свои́ оши́бки** to pay for one's mistakes with one's life.

пла́тн|ый *adj.* **1** paid; requiring payment, chargeable; **~ая доро́га** toll road. **2** paying; (*школа*) fee-paying; (*больница*) private; **п. посети́тель** paying guest.

плато́ *nt. indecl.* plateau.

плат|о́к, ка́ *m.* (*на плечи*) shawl; (*на голову*) headscarf, kerchief; **носово́й п.** (pocket) handkerchief.

платони́ческий *adj.* (*phil.*) Platonic; (*fig.*) platonic.

платфо́рм|а, ы *f.* **1** (*перрон*) platform. **2** (*вагон*) (open) goods truck (*Br.*), flatcar (*US*). **3** (*fig., pol.*) platform. **4** (*comput.*) platform.

пла́ть|е, я, *g. pl.* **~ев** *nt.* **1** (*женское*) dress; (*длинное*) gown; **вече́рнее п.** evening dress. **2** (*одежда*) clothes, clothing.

плат|яно́й *adj. of* ⇒**~́ье; п. шкаф** wardrobe; **~яна́я щётка** clothes-brush.

плафо́н, а *m.* **1** (*archit.*) (*потолок*) plafond. **2** (*абажур*) shade (*for lamp suspended from ceiling*).

пла́х|а, и *f.* block; (*hist.*) executioner's block; **взойти́ на ~у** to mount the scaffold.

плац, а, о ~́е, на ~у́ *m.* (*mil.*) parade ground; **уче́бный п.** drill square.

плацда́рм, а *m.* **1** (*mil.*) bridgehead; beachhead. **2** (*pol.*; *fig.*) base.

плаце́нт|а, ы *f.* (*anat.*) placenta.

плацка́рт|а, ы *f.* ticket for reserved seat *or* (*в спальном вагоне*) berth.

плацка́рт|ный *adj. of* ⇒**~а; п. ваго́н** carriage with numbered reserved seats; **~ное ме́сто** reserved seat.

плац-пара́д, а *m.* (*mil.*) parade ground.

плач, а *m.* weeping, crying; **П. Иереми́и** (*bibl.*) Lamentations.

плаче́в|ный (~ен, ~на) *adj.* **1** mournful, sad; **име́ть п. вид** to be a sorry sight. **2** (*fig.*) lamentable, deplorable, sorry; **в ~ном состоя́нии** in a sorry state.

плашко́ут, а *m.* (*naut.*) lighter.

плашко́утный *adj.*: **п. мост** pontoon bridge.

плашмя́ *adv.* flat; flatways; prone; **лежа́ть п.** to lie flat.

плащ, а́ *m.* **1** (*непромокаемое пальто*) raincoat. **2** (*накидка*) cloak.

плащ-пала́тк|а, и *f.* cape (*doubling as a tent*).

плебе́|й, я *m.* (*hist.*) plebeian.

плебе́йский *adj.* plebeian.

плебисци́т, а *m.* plebiscite.

плебс, а *m.* (*collect.*; *hist.*) plebs.

плев|а́, ы́ *f.* (*anat.*) membrane, film, coat; **де́вственная п.** hymen.

плева́тельниц|а, ы *f.* spittoon.

плева́ть, плюю́, плюёшь *impf.* (*of* ⇒**плю́нуть**) **1** to spit; **п. в потоло́к** (*fig., joc.*) to idle, fritter away the time. **2** (**на** + *a.*; *coll.*) to spit (upon); to not care a rap about; **им п. на всё** they don't give a damn about anything.

плева́ться, плюю́сь, плю, *g. pl.* **пёшься** *impf.* (*coll.*) to spit.

пле́вел, а, *g. pl.* **п.** *m.* (*bot.*) darnel; (*fig.*) weed.

плев|о́к, ка́ *m.* spit(tle).

пле́вр|а, ы *f.* (*anat.*) pleura.

плеври́т, а *m.* (*med.*) pleurisy.

плёв|ый *adj.* (*coll.*) **1** (*негодный*) worthless; rubbishy; **п. челове́к** good-for-nothing. **2** (*пустяковый*) trifling, trivial; **де́ло ~ое** trifling matter.

плед, а *m.* travelling rug (*Br.*), lap robe (*US*).

плее́р, а *m.* personal stereo, Walkman (*propr.*).

плейбо́|й, я *m.* playboy.

пле́йер = **плее́р**

плейстоце́н, а *m.* (*geol.*) Pleistocene.

плейстоце́н|овый *adj. of* ⇒**~**

племенно́й *adj.* **1** (*быт, языки*) tribal. **2** (*скот*) pedigree.

пле́м|я, ени, *pl.* **~ена́, ~ён, ~ена́м** *nt.* tribe; **молодо́е п.** the younger generation; **на племя́** for breeding.

племя́нник, а *m.* nephew.

племя́нниц|а, ы *f.* niece.

плен, а, о ~́е, в ~у́ *m.* captivity; **быть в ~у́** to be in captivity; **взять в п.** to take prisoner; **попа́сть в п.** (**к** + *d.*) to be taken prisoner (by).

плена́рный *adj.* plenary.

плене́ни|е, я *nt.* (*obs.*) capture; (*состояние*) captivity.

плени́тельност|ь, и *f.* fascination.

плени́тел|ьный (~ен, ~ьна) *adj.* captivating, charming.

плен|и́ть, ю́, и́шь *pf.* (*of* ⇒**~я́ть**) **1** (*obs.*) (*взять в плен*) to take prisoner. **2** (*fig.*) (*очаровать*) to captivate, charm.

плен|и́ться, ю́сь, и́шься *pf.* (*of* ⇒**~я́ться**) (+ *i.*) to be captivated (by), be fascinated (by).

плёнк|а, и *f.* (*тонкий слой*) film (*also phot.*); (*магнитофонная*) tape.

пле́нник, а *m.* prisoner, captive.

пле́нн|ый *adj.* captive; *as n.* **п., ~ого** *m.* captive, prisoner.

плён|очный *adj. of* ⇒**~ка;** filmy.

пле́нум, а *m.* plenum, plenary session.

плен|я́ть(ся), я́ю(сь) *impf. of* ⇒**~и́ть(ся)**

плёс, а *m.* (*участок реки*) reach (*of river*); (*водное пространство*) stretch (*of river or lake*).

пле́сенный *adj.* mouldy (*Br.*), moldy (*US*).

пле́сен|ь, и *f.* mould (*Br.*), mold (*US*).

плеск, а *m.* splash; **п. волн** lapping of waves.

пле|ска́ть, щу́, ~́щешь *impf.* (*of* ⇒**~сну́ть**) to splash; (*о волнах*) to lap; **п. о бе́рег** to lap against the shore; **п. на кого́-н. водо́й** to splash s.o. (with water).

пле|ска́ться, щу́сь, ~́щешься *impf.* to splash; (*о волнах*) to lap.

пле́снев|еть, еет *impf.* (*of* ⇒**за~**) to grow mouldy (*Br.*), moldy (*US*).

плес|ну́ть, ну́, нёшь *pf. of* ⇒**~ка́ть**

пле|сти́, ту́, тёшь, *past* **~́л, ~ла́** *impf.* (*of* ⇒**с~**) (*волосы*) to braid, plait; (*корзину, венок*) to weave; **п. небыли́цы** (*coll., pej.*) to spin yarns; **п. паути́ну** to spin a web; **п. вздор, п. чепуху́** (*coll., pej.*) to talk rubbish.

пле|сти́сь, ту́сь, тёшься, *past* **~́лся, ~ла́сь** *impf.* (*coll.*) to trudge, plod (along).

плете́ни|е, я *nt.* **1** braiding, plaiting; weaving; **п. слове́с** (*iron.*) verbiage. **2** (*плетёная вещь*) wicker-work.

плетёнк|а, и *f.* **1** (*корзина*) (wicker) basket. **2** (*хлеб*) twist (*of bread*).

плетён|ый *adj.* wicker; **~ая корзи́н(к)а** wicker basket.

плет|ень, ня́ *m.* wattle fencing.

плётк|а, и *f.* lash.

плет|ь, и, *pl.* **~́и, ~е́й** *f.* lash.

плечев|о́й *adj.* (*anat.*) humeral; **~а́я кость** humerus.

пле́чик|и, ов *no sg.* (*coll.*) (coat-)hanger.

плéчик|о, а, *pl.* **~и, ~ов** *nt.* **1** shoulder-strap. **2** *dim. of* ⇒**плечó**

плечи́ст|ый (~, ~а) *adj.* broad-shouldered.

плеч|ó, á, *pl.* **~и, ~, ~áм** *nt.* shoulder; **всё э́то у меня́ за ~áми** (*fig.*) all that is behind me; **~óм к ~ý** shoulder to shoulder; **взять нá ~и** to shoulder; **имéть гóлову на ~áх** to have a good head on one's shoulders; **вы́нести на свои́х ~áх** to bear (the full brunt of); **э́то емý не по ~ý** he is not up to it; **с ~á** straight from the shoulder; **у меня́ (слóвно) горá с ~ свали́лась** that's a weight off my mind; **с ~ долóй!** that's done, thank goodness; **с чужóго ~á** (*of clothing*) worn, second-hand; **пожáть ~áми** to shrug one's shoulders.

плеши́ве|ть, ю *impf.* (*of* ⇒**о~**) to grow bald.

плеши́в|ый (~, ~а) *adj.* bald.

плеши́н|а, ы *f.* bald patch.

плеш|ь, и *f.* bald patch.

плея́д|ы, ~ *pl.* (*sg.* **~а, ~ы** *f.*) **1 П.** (*astron.*) Pleiades. **2** (*sg.*; *fig.*) (*группа*) pleiad; galaxy.

пли *int.* (*see* ⇒**пали́ть**) (*mil.*; *obs.*) fire!

пли́нтус, а *m.* **1** (*archit.*) plinth. **2** (*между стеной и полом*) skirting board (*Br.*), baseboard (*US*).

плиоцéн, а *m.* (*geol.*) Pl(e)iocene.

плис, а *m.* velveteen.

пли́с|овый *adj. of* ⇒**~**

плиссé *indecl.* **1** *adj.* pleated; **ю́бка п.** pleated skirt. **2** *n.*; *nt.* pleat(s).

плиссир|овáть, ýю *impf.* (*no pf.*) to pleat.

плит|á, ы́, *pl.* **~ы** *f.* **1** (*металлическая*) plate; (*каменная*) slab; (*для настилки полов*) flag(-stone); **моги́льная п.** gravestone, tombstone; **мрáморная п.** marble slab. **2** (*печь*) stove; cooker.

пли́тк|а, и *f.* **1** *dim. of* ⇒**плитá;** (*облицовочная*) tile, (thin) slab; **п. шоколáда** bar of chocolate. **2** (*печь*) small stove.

плитня́к, á *m.* flagstone.

плитотектóник|а, и *f.* (*geol.*) plate tectonics.

пли́т|очный *adj. of* ⇒**~ка; п. пол** tiled floor.

плов, а *m.* (*cul.*) pilaff, pilau.

плов|éц, цá *m.* swimmer; **п. на доскé** surfer.

пловýчий *adj.* = **плавýчий**

плов|чи́ха, чи́хи *f. of* ⇒**~éц**

плод, á *m.* **1** fruit (*also fig.*); **приноси́ть п.** to bear fruit; **запрéтный п.** (*fig.*) forbidden fruit. **2** (*biol.*) foetus (*Br.*), fetus (*US*).

пло|ди́ть, жý, ди́шь *impf.* (*of* ⇒**рас~**) to produce, procreate; to engender (*also fig.*).

пло|ди́ться, ди́тся *impf.* (*of* ⇒**рас~**) to multiply; to propagate.

плóдный *adj.* **1** (*biol.*) fertile. **2** (*оплодотворённый*) fertilized.

плодови́тост|ь, и *f.* fertility, fecundity.

плодови́т|ый (~, ~а) *adj.* (*животное, дерево*) prolific (*also fig.*); (*почва*) fertile; (*собрание*) fruitful; **п. писáтель** prolific writer.

плодовóдств|о, а *nt.* fruit-growing.

плодовóд|ческий *adj. of* ⇒**~ство**

плодóв|ый *adj. of* ⇒**плод; ~ое дéрево** fruit-tree; **п. сад** orchard.

плодонóжк|а, и *f.* (*bot.*) fruit stem.

плодоно|си́ть, ~сит *impf.* (*no pf.*) to bear fruit.

плодонóс|ный (~ен, ~на) *adj.* fruit-bearing, fruitful.

плодоóвощ|и, éй *no sg.* fruit and vegetables.

плодоовощнóй *adj.* fruit and vegetable.

плодорóди|е, я *nt.* fertility.

плодорóд|ный (~ен, ~на) *adj.* fertile.

плодосмéнн|ый *adj.*: **~ая систéма** (*agric.*) rotation of crops.

плодотвóр|ный (~ен, ~на) *adj.* fruitful.

плóмб|а, ы *f.* **1** (*на товарах, на дверях*) seal. **2** (*в зубе*) filling; **стáвить ~у** to fill a tooth.

пломби́р, а *m.* 'plombières' (*ice cream with candied fruit*).

пломбир|овáть, ýю *impf.* **1** (*pf.* **о~**) (*товары*) to seal. **2** (*pf.* **за~**) (*зуб*) to fill.

плóс|кий (~ок, ~кá, ~ко) *adj.* **1** flat; plane; **~кая грудь** flat chest; **~кая повéрхность** plane surface. **2** (*fig.*) (*пошлый*) trivial, tame; **~кая шýтка** feeble joke.

плоскогóрь|е, я *nt.* plateau; tableland.

плоскогрýд|ый (~, ~а) *adj.* flat-chested.

плоскогýбц|ы, ев *no sg.* pliers.

плоскодóнк|а, и *f.* flat-bottomed boat; punt.

плоскодóнный *adj.* flat-bottomed.

плоскостнóй *adj.* plane.

плоскостóпи|е, я *nt.* (*med.*) flat-foot, flat feet.

плóскост|ь, и, *pl.* **~и, ~éй** *f.* **1** (*свойство*) flatness. **2** (*поверхность*) plane (*also fig.*); **наклóнная п.** inclined plane; **кати́ться по наклóнной ~и** (*fig.*) to go downhill. **3** (*банальность*) platitude.

плот, á, о ~é, на ~ý *m.* raft.

плотв|á, ы́ *f.* (*fish*) roach.

плоти́н|а, ы *f.* dam.

плотнé|ть, ю *impf.* (*of* ⇒**по~**) to thicken.

плóтник, а *m.* carpenter.

плóтнича|ть, ю *impf.* to work as a carpenter.

плóтничеств|о, а *nt.* carpentry.

плóтничный *adj.* carpentry.

плóтно *adv.* **1** close(ly), tightly; **п. заколоти́ть дверь** to board up a door. **2**: **п. поéсть** to eat heartily.

плóтност|ь, и *f.* **1** (*тумана, населения*) density (*also phys.*). **2** (*человека*) solidity.

плóт|ный (~ен, ~нá, ~но) *adj.* **1** (*туман, население*) dense (*also phys.*). **2** (*бумага*) thick, solid, strong; (*человек*) thick-set, solidly built. **3** (*папка*) tightly-filled. **4** (*coll.*) (*завтрак*) hearty.

плотоя́д|ный (~ен, ~на) *adj.* **1** carnivorous. **2** (*fig.*) (*сладострастный*) lustful; voluptuous.

плóтский *adj.* (*arch.*) carnal, fleshly.

плóттер, а *m.* (*comput.*) plotter.

плот|ь, и *f.* flesh; **во ~и́** in the flesh; **дья́вол во ~и́** the devil incarnate; **п. от ~и** flesh of one's flesh; **п. и кровь** (one's) flesh and blood; **крáйняя п.** (*anat.*) foreskin, prepuce.

плóхо 1 *adv.* bad(ly); ill; **п. вести́ себя́** to behave badly; **п. обращáться** (**с** + *i.*) to ill-treat; **чýвствовать себя́ п.** to feel unwell; **п. пáхнуть** to smell bad; **п. кóнчить** (*coll.*) to come to a bad end. **2** *n.*; *nt. indecl.* bad mark; **я опя́ть получи́л п. по áлгебре** I have got a bad mark in algebra again.

плоховáто *adv.* (*coll.*) rather badly, not too well.

плоховáт|ый (~, ~а) *adj.* (*coll.*) rather bad, not too good.

плох|óй (~, ~á, ~о) *adj.* bad; poor; **~áя погóда** bad weather; **~óе настроéние** bad mood; **п. рабóтник** a poor workman; **~óе пищеварéние** poor digestion; **с ним шýтки ~и** he is not one to be trifled with; *as pred.*: **емý óчень ~о** he is in a very bad way.

плошá|ть, ю *impf.* (*of* ⇒**с~**) (*coll.*) to make a mistake, slip up.

плóшк|а, и *f.* **1** (*coll.*) saucer. **2** (*obs.*) lampion.

площáдк|а, и *f.* **1** ground, area; **дéтская п.** children's playground; **спорти́вная п.** sports ground; **строи́тельная п.** building site; **тéннисная п.** tennis court; **киносъёмочная п.** (*film*) set; **п. для игры́ в гольф** golf course. **2** (*лестничная*) landing (*on staircase*). **3** (*в вагоне*) platform; **пусковáя п.** launch pad (*of rocket*).

площадн|óй *adj.* vulgar, coarse; **~áя брань** vulgar language.

плóщад|ь, и, *pl.* **~и, ~éй** *f.* **1** (*в городе*) square. **2** (*пространство*) area; space; **жилáя п.** living space; **посевнáя п.** area under crops. **3** (*math.*) area.

плó|ще *comp. of* ⇒**~ский, ~ско**

плуг, а, *pl.* **~и́** *m.* plough (*Br.*), plow (*US*).

плýнжер, а *m.* (*tech.*) plunger.

плут, á *m.* **1** (*мошенник*) cheat. **2** (*joc.*) rogue.

плутá|ть, ю *impf.* (*coll.*) to stray.

плути́шк|а, и *m.* (*coll.*) little rascal, imp.

плýтн|и, ей *pl.* (*sg.* **~я, ~и** *f.*) (*coll.*) tricks.

плутовáт|ый (~, ~а) *adj.* cunning.

плут|овáть, ýю *impf.* (*of* ⇒**с~**) (*coll.*) to cheat.

плутóвк|а, и *f. of* ⇒**плут, плути́шка**

плутовск|óй *adj.* **1** (*мошеннический*) knavish. **2** (*coll.*) (*улыбка, глаза*) roguish, mischievous. **3** (*liter.*) picaresque.

плутовств|о́, а́ *nt.* cheating.

плутокра́т, а *m.* plutocrat.

плутократи́ческий *adj.* plutocratic.

плутокра́ти|я, и *f.* plutocracy.

плуто́ни|й, я *m.* plutonium.

плы|ть, ву́, вёшь, *past* **~л, ~ла́, ~́ло** *impf.* (*det. of* ⇒**пла́вать**) **1** (*о человеке, о животном*) to swim; (*об облаках, о звуках*) to float; **п. сто́я** to tread water; **всё ~́ло пе́ред мои́ми глаза́ми** everything was swimming before my eyes. **2** (*ехать на судне*) to sail; **п. на вёслах** to row; **п. под паруса́ми** to sail; **п. по во́ле волн** to drift.

плюга́в|ый (~, ~а) *adj.* (*coll.*) unprepossessing; (*fig.*) trivial.

плюма́ж, а *m.* plume (*on hat*).

плю́н|уть, у, ешь *pf. of* ⇒**плева́ть; п. не́куда** no room to swing a cat.

плюрали́зм, а *m.* (*phil. & pol.*) pluralism.

плюралисти́ческий *adj.* (*phil. & pol.*) pluralistic.

плюс, а *m.* **1** plus; *as connective in math. expressions:* **два п. два равно́ четырём** two plus two equals four. **2** (*fig., coll.*) (*преимущество*) advantage; **э́тот прое́кт не без ~́ов** this scheme has some advantages.

плюс|на́, ны́, *pl.* **~́ны, ~́ен, ~́нам** *f.* (*anat.*) metatarsus.

плю́с|овый *adj. of* ⇒**~**

плю́х|ать(ся), аю(сь) *impf. of* ⇒**~нуть(ся)**

плю́х|нуть, ну, нешь *pf.* (*of* ⇒**~ать**) (*coll.*) to flop (down); **п. в кре́сло** to flop into an arm-chair.

плю́х|нуться, нусь, нешься *pf.* (*of* ⇒**~аться**) = **~нуть**

плюш, а *m.* plush.

плю́ш|евый *adj. of* ⇒**~**

плю́шк|а, и *f.* bun.

плющ, а́ *m.* ivy.

плющи́льный *adj.* (*tech.*) flattening, laminating; **п. стано́к** flatting mill, rolling mill.

плю́щ|ить, у, ишь *impf.* (*of* ⇒**с~**) (*tech.*) to flatten, laminate.

пляж, а *m.* beach.

пляс, а *no pl., m.* (*coll.*) dance.

пля|са́ть, шу́, ~́шешь *impf.* (*of* ⇒**с~**) to dance.

пля́ск|а, и *f.* (*действие*) dancing; (*танец*) dance (*esp. folk-dance*); **п. свято́го Ви́та** (*med.*) St. Vitus's dance, chorea.

плясов|о́й *adj.* dancing; *as n.* **~а́я, ~о́й** *f.* dance tune.

плясу́н, а́ *m.* (*coll.*) dancer; **кана́тный п.** rope-dancer.

плясу́н|ья, ьи, *g. pl.* **~ий** *f. of* ⇒**~**

пневмати́ческий *adj.* pneumatic.

пневмони́|я, и *f.* pneumonia.

пнуть, пну, пнёшь *pf.* (*of* ⇒**пина́ть**) (*coll.*) to kick.

ПО (*abbr. of* ***програ́ммное обеспе́чение***) (*comput.*) software.

по *prep.* **I.** *+d.* **1** (*на поверхности*) on; (*вдоль*) along; **идти́ по траве́** to walk on the grass; **е́хать по у́лице** to go along the street; **идти́ по следа́м** (*+g.*) to follow in the tracks (of); **хло́пнуть по спине́** to slap on the back; **по всему́, по всей** all over.
2 (*в разные места*) round, about; **ходи́ть по магази́нам** to go round the shops; **размести́ть войска́ по го́роду** to quarter troops about the town.
3 (*посредством*) by, on, over; **по во́здуху** by air; **по желе́зной доро́ге** by rail; **по по́чте** by post; **по ра́дио** over the radio; **по телефо́ну** on, over the telephone; **переда́ть по ра́дио** to broadcast.
4 (*в соответствии, согласно*) according to; by; in accordance with; **по пра́ву** by right(s); **по расписа́нию** according to schedule; **жени́ться по любви́** to marry for love; **звать по и́мени** to call by first name; **рабо́тать по пла́ну** to work according to plan; **су́дя по результа́там** judging by results; **по мне** as far as I am concerned; **жить по сре́дствам** to live within one's means; **по Плато́ну** according to Plato.
5 (*в отношении*) by, in (= *in respect of*); **по профе́ссии** by profession; **по происхожде́нию он армяни́н** he is of Armenian origin; **лу́чший по ка́честву** better in quality; **това́рищ по ору́жию** comrade-in-arms; **това́рищ по шко́ле** school-mate; **ро́дственник по ма́тери** a relative on one's mother's side.
6 (*в области*) at, on, in (= *in the field of*); **чемпио́н по ша́хматам** champion at chess, chess champion; **ле́кции по европе́йской исто́рии** lectures on European history; **специали́ст по я́дерной фи́зике** specialist in nuclear physics.
7 (*из-за*) by (reason of); on account of; from; **по боле́зни** on account of sickness; **по рассе́янности** from absent-mindedness; **его́ прости́ли по мо́лодости лет** he was pardoned by reason of his youth; **по незави́сящим от меня́ причи́нам** for reasons beyond my control.
8 (*указывает на предмет действия*) at, for (*or not translated*); **стреля́ть по проти́внику** to fire at the enemy; **охо́та по кру́пному зве́рю** big game hunting; **скуча́ть по де́тям** to miss one's children; **тоска́ по до́му, по ро́дине** homesickness; **по а́дресу** (*+g.*) to the address (of); **э́то по его́ а́дресу** (*fig.*) this is meant for him.
9 (*указывает время*) on; in; **по понеде́льникам** on Mondays; **по пра́здникам** on holidays; **она́ рабо́тает по утра́м** she works (in the) mornings.
● **II.** (*в разделительном значении*) (*+d., but also +a., esp. in coll. usage*) **по одному́ (одно́й); по пяти́, по шести́,** *etc.*; **по оди́ннадцати,** *etc.*; **по двадцати́,** *etc.*; **по ста; по пятисо́т,** *etc.*; **по полтора́ (полторы́);** (*+a.*) **по́ два (две), по́ три, по четы́ре, по две́сти, по три́ста, по четы́реста; да́йте им по** (*sc.* **одному́) я́блоку** give them an apple each; **мы получи́ли по три фу́нта** we received three pounds each; **по рублю́ шту́ка** one rouble each; **по де́сять (десяти́) рубле́й шту́ка** ten roubles each; **по́ два, по́ двое** in twos, two by two.
● **III.** *+a.* **1** (*до*) to, up to; **по по́яс в воде́** up to the waist in water; **за́нят по го́рло** up to one's eyes in work; **по́ уши в долга́х** up to one's ears in debt; **по́ уши влюблён** head over heels in love; **по сего́дня** up to today; **по пе́рвое ма́я** up to (and including) the first of May.
2 (*following vv. of motion; coll.*) (*за*) for (= *to fetch, to get*); **идти́ по́ воду** to go for water.
● **IV.** *+p.* **1** (*после*) on, after; **по оконча́нии рабо́ты** after work; **по прибы́тии** on arrival; **по рассмотре́нии** on examination.
2 (*after vv. of grieving, mourning, etc.*) for; **пла́кать по му́же** to mourn (for) one's husband; **носи́ть тра́ур по ком-н.** to be in mourning for s.o.
3: по нём, *etc.*, as he, *etc.*, likes, is used.

по- *+d. of adj. or ending* **...ски** *forms adv. indicating* **1** *manner of action, conduct, etc., as* **жить по-ста́рому** to live in the old style; **рабо́тать по-това́рищески** to work in a comradely fashion. **2** *use of given language, as* **говори́ть по-ру́сски** to speak Russian. **3** *accordance with opinion or wish, as* **по-мо́ему** in my opinion; **пусть бу́дет по-ва́шему** (let it be) as you wish.

по...[1] *as vbl. pref.* **1** *forms pf. aspect.* **2** *indicates action of short duration or of incomplete character, as* **порабо́тать** to do a little work; **поспа́ть** to have a sleep. **3** (*+suff.* **...ыва..., ...ива...**) *indicates action repeated at intervals or of indet. duration, as* **позва́нивать** to keep ringing.

по...[2] *pref. modifying comp. adj. or adv., as* **погро́мче** a little louder.

п. о. (*abbr. of* ***почто́вое отделе́ние***) PO, Post Office.

побагрове́|ть, ю *pf. of* ⇒**багрове́ть**

поба́ива|ться, юсь *impf.* (*+g. or inf.; coll.*) to be rather afraid.

поба́лива|ть, ю *impf.* (*coll.*) (*немного*) to ache a little; (*иногда*) to ache on and off.

по-ба́рски *adv.* like a lord.

побасёнк|а, и *f.* (*coll.*) tale, story.

побе́г[1]**, а** *m.* (*бегство*) flight; escape.

побе́г[2]**, а** *m.* (*bot.*) sprout, shoot.

побе́га|ть, ю *pf.* to have a run.

побегу́шк|и: быть у кого́-н. на ~ах (*coll.*) to run errands for s.o.; (*fig.*) to be at s.o.'s beck and call.

побе́д|а, ы *f.* victory; **одержа́ть ~у** to gain a victory.

победи́тел|ь, я *m.* victor; (*sport*) winner.

победи́тель|ница, ницы *f. of* ⇒**~**

побед|и́ть, и́шь *pf.* (*of* ⇒**побежда́ть**) (*врага*) to conquer; (*соперника*) to defeat, beat; **на́ша кома́нда победи́ла** our team won; (*fig.*) to master, overcome.

побе́дный *adj.* victorious, triumphant; **п. гол** winning goal.

победоно́с|ный (~ен, ~на) *adj.* victorious, triumphant.

побе|жа́ть, гу́, жи́шь, гу́т *pf.* **1** *pf. of* ⇒**бежа́ть. 2** to break into a run.

побежда́|ть, ю *impf. of* ⇒**победи́ть**

побе́жк|а, и *f.* pace, gait.

побеле́|ть, ю *pf. of* ⇒**беле́ть**

побел|и́ть, ю́, ~́ишь *pf. of* ⇒**бели́ть** 1

побе́лк|а, и *f.* whitewashing.

побере́жный *adj.* coastal.

побере́жь|е, я *nt.* coast, seaboard.

побере́|чь, гу́, жёшь, гу́т, *past* **~́г, ~гла́** *pf.* (*coll.*) to look after, take care (of); **п. здоро́вье** to take care of one's health; **~ги́ мой ве́щи до моего́ возвраще́ния** look after my things until I come back.

побере́|чься, гу́сь, жёшься, гу́ться, *past* **~́гся, ~гла́сь** *pf.* to take care of o.s.; **~ги́сь!** mind out!

побесе́д|овать, ую *pf.* to have a (little) talk, have a chat.

побеспоко́|ить, ю, ишь *pf. of* ⇒**беспоко́ить** 2; **позво́льте вас п.** may I trouble you?

побеспоко́|иться, юсь, ишься *pf.* **1** *pf. of* ⇒**беспоко́иться** 2. **2** to be rather worried.

побира́|ться, юсь *impf.* (*coll.*) to beg, live by begging.

поб|и́ть, ью́, ьёшь *pf.* **1** *pf. of* ⇒**бить** 1, 2; **п. реко́рд** to break a record. **2** (*повредить*) to beat down, damage; (*о морозе*) to nip. **3** (*разбить*) to break, smash (*a number of*). **4** (*убить*) to kill (*a number of*).

поб|и́ться, ьётся *pf.* **1** *pf. of* ⇒**би́ться. 2** to break.

поблагодар|и́ть, ю́, и́шь *pf. of* ⇒**благодари́ть**

побла́жк|а, и *f.* indulgence; allowance(s); **де́лать ~у** (+*d.*) to indulge, make allowance(s) (for).

побледне́|ть, ю *pf. of* ⇒**бледне́ть**

поблёклый *adj.* faded; withered.

поблёк|нуть, ну, нешь, *past* **~, ~ла** *pf. of* ⇒**блёкнуть**

поблёскива|ть, ю *impf.* to gleam.

побли́зости *adv.* nearby; **п.** (**от**+*g.*) near (to).

побож|и́ться, у́сь, и́шься *pf. of* ⇒**божи́ться**

побо́|и, ев *no sg.* beating; **терпе́ть п.** to take a beating.

побо́ищ|е, а *nt.* slaughter, carnage; bloody battle; **ледо́вое п.** *see* ⇒**ледо́вый**

поболта́|ть, ю *pf.* (*coll.*) to have a chat.

побо́рник, а *m.* champion, upholder.

побо́рни|ца, цы *f. of* ⇒**~к**

побор|о́ть, ю́, ~́ешь *pf.* to overcome.

побо́р|ы, ов *pl.* (*sg.* **~, ~а** *m.*) (*obs.*) (*налоги*) requisitions; (*вымогательство*) extortion.

побо́чн|ый *adj.* secondary; **п. эффе́кт** side effect; **п. насле́дник** collateral heir; **п. проду́кт** by-product; **~ая рабо́та** side-line; **п. сын** (*obs.*) illegitimate son.

побо|я́ться, ю́сь, и́шься *pf.* (+*g. or inf.*) to be afraid.

побран|и́ть, ю́, и́шь *pf.* to give a scolding, tick off.

побран|и́ться, ю́сь, и́шься *pf.* (**с**+*i.*; *coll.*) to have a quarrel, have words (with).

побрата́|ться, юсь *pf. of* ⇒**брата́ться**

побрати́м, а *m.* **1** (*obs.*) sworn brother. **2** (*город*) twin town.

по-бра́тски *adv.* like a brother; fraternally.

по|бра́ть, беру́, берёшь, *past* **~бра́л, ~брала́, ~бра́ло** *pf.* (*coll.*) to take (a quantity of); **чёрт ~бери́!** damn!

побре́зга|ть, ю *pf. of* ⇒**бре́згать**

побре́зг|овать, ую *pf. of* ⇒**бре́зговать**

побре|сти́, ду́, дёшь, *past* **~́л, ~ла́** *pf.* to plod.

побр|и́ть(ся), е́ю(сь) *pf. of* ⇒**бри́ть(ся)**

побро|ди́ть¹, жу́, ~́дишь *pf.* (*погулять*) to wander for some time.

побро|ди́ть², ~́дит *pf.* (*о пиве*) to ferment for some time.

поброса́|ть, ю *pf.* **1** (*бросить как попало*) to throw. **2** (*покинуть*) to desert, abandon.

побря́к|ать, аю *pf.* (*of* ⇒**~ивать**) (+*i.*; *coll.*) to rattle.

побря́кива|ть, ю *impf. of* ⇒**побря́кать**

побряку́шк|а, и *f.* (*coll.*) (*безделушка*) trinket; (*погремушка*) rattle.

побуди́тельн|ый *adj.* stimulating; **~ая причи́на** motive, incentive; **~ые сре́дства** stimulants.

побу|ди́ть¹, жу́, ~́дишь *pf.* **1** (*попытаться разбудить*) to try to wake. **2** (*разбудить*) to wake, rouse.

побу|ди́ть², жу́, ~ди́шь *pf.* (*of* ⇒**~жда́ть**) (**к**+*d. or* +*inf.*) (*склонить*) to induce (to), prompt (to); **что ~би́ло вас уйти́?** what made you go?

побу́дк|а, и *f.* (*mil.*) reveille.

побужда́|ть, ю *impf. of* ⇒**побуди́ть²**

побужде́ни|е, я *nt.* motive; inducement; incentive; **по со́бственному ~ю** of one's own accord.

побуре́|ть, ю *pf. of* ⇒**буре́ть**

побыва́льщин|а, ы *f.* (*obs.*) true story.

побыва́|ть, ю *pf.* **1** (*посетить*) to have been, have visited; **он ~л всю́ду** he has been everywhere; **в про́шлом году́ мы ~ли в Норве́гии и в Шве́ции** last year we were in Norway and Sweden. **2** (*coll.*) (*зайти*) to drop in, call in; **он ~л у друзе́й** he dropped in to see some friends.

побы́вк|а, и *f.* leave, furlough; **прие́хать домо́й на ~у** to come home on leave.

по|бы́ть, бу́ду, бу́дешь, *past* **~́был, ~была́, ~́было** *pf.* to stay (*for a short time*); **мы ~́были в Ло́ндоне два дня** we stayed in London for two days.

пова́|дить, жу, дишь *pf.* (*of* ⇒**~живать**) (*coll.*, *pej.*) to accustom; to train.

пова́|диться, жусь, дишься *pf.* (+*inf.*; *coll.*, *pej.*) to get into the habit (of); to take to going (*somewhere*); **он ~ди́лся к нам ходи́ть** he took to visiting us; **он ~ди́лся туда́ ходи́ть** he took to going there.

пова́дк|а, и *f.* (*coll.*) habit.

пова́дно *only in phr.* **что́бы не́ было п.** (+*d.*) (in order) to teach not to do so (again).

пова́жива|ть, ю *impf. of* ⇒**пова́дить**

повал|и́ть¹, ю́, ~́ишь *pf. of* ⇒**вали́ть¹**

повал|и́ть², ю́, ~́ишь *pf.* to begin to throng, begin to pour; **дым ~и́л из трубы́** smoke began to pour from the chimney; **снег ~и́л хло́пьями** snow began to fall in flakes.

повал|и́ться, ю́сь, ~ишься *pf. of* ⇒**вали́ться**

пова́льно *adv.* without exception.

пова́льн|ый *adj.* general, mass; **п. о́быск** general search; **~ая боле́знь** epidemic.

пова́нива|ть, ет *impf.* (*coll.*) to smell slightly.

по́вар, а, *pl.* **~а́** *m.* cook; **п.-ма́стер** master chef.

пова́ренн|ый *adj.* culinary; **~ая кни́га** cookery book (*Br.*), cook book (*US*); **~ая соль** table salt.

повар|ёнок, ёнка, *pl.* **~я́та, ~я́т** *m.* (*coll.*) kitchen-boy.

поварёшк|а, и *f.* (*coll.*) ladle, strainer.

повари́х|а, и *f. of* ⇒**по́вар**

пова́рнича|ть, ю *impf.* (*coll.*) to cook, be a cook.

пова́р|ня, ни, *g. pl.* **~ен** *f.* (*obs.*) kitchen.

поварско́й *adj. of* ⇒**по́вар**

по-ва́шему *adv.* **1** (*по вашему мнению*) in your opinion. **2** (*как вы хотите*) as you wish.

пове́д|ать, аю *pf.* (*of* ⇒**~ывать**) to tell, relate; **п. та́йну** to disclose a secret.

поведе́ни|е, я *nt.* behaviour (*Br.*), behavior (*US*).

пове́дыва|ть, ю *impf. of* ⇒**пове́дать**

повез|ти́, у́, ёшь, *past* **~́, ~ла́** *pf. of* ⇒**везти́**

повелева́|ть, ю *impf.* **1** (+*i.*, *obs.*) to command, rule. **2** (+*d. and inf.*) to enjoin; **так ~ет мне со́весть** thus my conscience enjoins.

повеле́ни|е, я *nt.* (*obs.*) command, injunction.

повел|е́ть, ю́, и́шь *pf.* to order, command.

повели́тел|ь, я *m.* (*rhet.*) sovereign, master.

повели́тельниц|а, ы *f.* (*rhet.*) sovereign, mistress, lady.

повели́тел|ьный (~ен, ~ьна)

adj. imperious, peremptory; **п. жест** imperious gesture; **п. тон** peremptory tone; **~ьное наклоне́ние** (*gram.*) imperative mood.

повенча́|ть(ся), ю(сь) *pf. of* ⇒**венча́ть(ся)**

поверг|а́ть, а́ю *impf. of* ⇒**~́нуть**

пове́рг|нуть, ну, нешь, *past* **~** *and* **~нул, ~ла** *pf.* (*of* ⇒**~а́ть**) **1** (*obs.*) (*опрокинуть*) to throw down, lay low; (*победить*) to conquer. **2** (**в**+*a.*) to plunge (into); **п. в отча́яние** to plunge into despair.

пове́р|енный *p.p.p. of* ⇒**~ить²**; *as n.* **п., ~енного** *m.* **1** (*also* **~енная, ~енной** *f.*) (*наперсник*) confidant(e). **2** (*уполномоченное лицо*) attorney; **п. в дела́х** chargé d'affaires.

пове́р|ить¹, ю, ишь *pf. of* ⇒**ве́рить**

пове́р|ить², ю, ишь *pf.* (*of* ⇒**~я́ть**) **1** (+*d.*) to confide (to), entrust (to); **п. кому́-н. та́йну** to confide a secret to s.o. **2** (*obs.*) (*проверить*) to check (up); to verify.

пове́рк|а, и *f.* **1** check, check-up; checking up, verification; (*math.*) proof. **2** (*mil.*) roll-call.

повер|ну́ть, ну́, нёшь *pf.* (*of* ⇒**~́тывать**) to turn; (*fig.*) to change; **п. разгово́р** to change the subject.

повер|ну́ться, ну́сь, нёшься *pf.* (*of* ⇒**~́тываться**) to turn; **п. круго́м** to turn round, turn about; **п. спино́й** (**к**+*d.*) to turn one's back (upon); **п. к лу́чшему** to take a turn for the better.

пове́р|очный *adj. of* ⇒**~ка; ~очные испыта́ния** tests.

повёртыва|ть(ся), ю(сь) *impf. of* ⇒**поверну́ть(ся)**

пове́рх *prep.*+*g.* over, above; on top of; **смотре́ть п. очко́в** to look over the top of one's spectacles.

пове́рхностност|ь, и *f.* superficiality.

пове́рхностн|ый *adj.* **1** surface, superficial; **~ая зака́лка** (*tech.*) case-hardening; **~ое натяже́ние** (*tech.*) surface tension; **~ая ра́на** superficial injury; **~ое унаво́живание** (*agric.*) top dressing. **2** (**~ен, ~на**) (*fig.*) superficial.

пове́рхност|ь, и *f.* surface.

по́верху *adv.* on the surface, on top.

пове́р|ье, ья, *g. pl.* **~ий** *nt.* popular belief, superstition.

повер|я́ть, я́ю *impf. of* ⇒**~́ить²**

пове́с|а, ы *m.* (*coll.*) rake, playboy.

повеселе́|ть, ю *pf.* to cheer up, become cheerful.

по-весе́ннему *adv.* as in spring.

пове́|сить(ся), шу(сь), сишь(ся) *pf. of* ⇒**ве́шать(ся)¹**

пове́снича|ть, ю *impf.* (*coll.*) to lead a wild life.

повествова́ни|е, я *nt.* narrative, narration.

повествова́тельный *adj.* narrative.

повеств|ова́ть, у́ю *impf.* (**о**+*p.*) to narrate, recount, relate.

пове|сти́¹, ду́, дёшь, *past* **~́л, ~ла́** *pf. of* ⇒**вести́ 1**

пове|сти́², ду́, дёшь, *past* **~́л, ~ла́** *pf.* (*of* ⇒**поводи́ть¹**) (+*i.*) to move; **п. бровя́ми** to raise one's eye-brows; **он и бро́вью не ~́л** he did not turn a hair.

пове|сти́сь, ду́сь, дёшься, *past* **~́лся, ~ла́сь** *pf. of* ⇒**вести́сь; уж так ~ло́сь** (*coll.*) such is the custom.

пове́стк|а, и *f.* notice, notification; **п. на заседа́ние** notice of meeting; **п. в суд** summons, writ, subpoena; **п. дня** agenda, order of the day; **на ~е дня** on the agenda (*also fig.*).

по́вест|ь, и, *pl.* **~и, ~е́й** *f.* story, tale.

пове́три|е, я *nt.* **1** (*obs.*) (*эпидемия*) epidemic. **2** (*fig.*) (*мода*) craze.

пове́шени|е, я *nt.* hanging.

пове́|шенный *p.p.p. of* ⇒**~сить;** *as n.* **п., ~шенного** *m.* hanged man.

пове́|ять, ет *pf.* **1** (*начать веять*) to begin to blow; (*подуть слегка*) to blow softly. **2** (*impers.,* +*i.*) to breathe (of); (*fig.*) to begin to be felt; **~яло весно́й** spring was in the air.

повздо́р|ить, ю, ишь *pf. of* ⇒**вздо́рить**

повзросле́|ть, ю *pf.* to grow up.

повива́льн|ый *adj.* (*obs.*) obstetric; **~ая ба́бка** midwife; **~ое иску́сство** midwifery.

повида́|ть, ю *pf.* (*coll.*) to see.

повида́|ться, юсь *pf. of* ⇒**вида́ться**

по-ви́димому *adv.* apparently, seemingly.

пови́дл|о, а *nt.* jam.

повили́к|а, и *f.* (*bot.*) dodder.

повин|и́ться, ю́сь, и́шься *pf. of* ⇒**вини́ться**

пови́нн|ая, ой *f.* confession, acknowledgement of guilt; **принести́ ~ую** to acknowledge one's guilt, own up; **яви́ться с ~ой** to give o.s. up.

пови́нност|ь, и *f.* duty, obligation; **во́инская п.** compulsory military service, conscription.

пови́н|ный (~ен, ~на) *adj.* guilty.

повин|ова́ться, у́юсь *impf.* (*in past tense also pf.*) (+*d.*) to obey.

повинове́ни|е, я *nt.* obedience.

повис|а́ть, а́ю *impf. of* ⇒**~́нуть**

пови|се́ть, шу́, си́шь *pf.* to hang for a time.

пови́с|нуть, ну, нешь, *past* **~, ~ла** *pf.* (*of* ⇒**~а́ть**) **1** (**на**+*p.*) to hang (by). **2** (*склониться*) to hang down, droop; **п. в во́здухе** (*fig.*) to hang in mid-air; (*о шутке*) to fall flat.

повиту́х|а, и *f.* (*obs.*) midwife.

повлажне́|ть, ю *pf. of* ⇒**влажне́ть**

повле́|чь, ку́, чёшь, ку́т, *past* **~́к, ~кла́** *pf.* (**за собо́й**) to entail, bring in one's train; **п. за собо́й неприя́тные после́дствия** to have unpleasant consequences.

повлия́|ть, ю *pf. of* ⇒**влия́ть**

по́вод¹, а, *pl.* **~ы** *m.* (**к**+*d.*) occasion, cause, ground (for, of); **п. к войне́** casus belli; **дать п.** (+*d.*) to give occasion (to), give cause (for); **без вся́кого ~а** without cause; **по ~у** (+*g.*) apropos (of), as regards, concerning; **по како́му ~у?** in what connection? why?

по́вод², а, о ~е, на ~у́, *pl.* **~ья, ~ьев** *m.* rein; **быть у кого́-н. на ~у́** (*fig.*) to be under s.o.'s thumb.

пово|ди́ть¹, жу́, ~́дишь *impf. of* ⇒**повести́²**

пово|ди́ть², жу́, ~́дишь *pf.* (*человека*) to lead; (*животное*) to walk.

повод|о́к, ка́ *m.* lead (*Br.*), leash (*US*).

поводы́р|ь, я́ *m.* leader, guide.

пово́зк|а, и *f.* cart.

пово́лжский *adj.* situated on the Volga.

поволо́к|а, и *f.* shroud.

повора́чива|ть(ся), ю(сь) *impf. of* ⇒**повороти́ть(ся); ~йся!, ~йтесь!** (*coll.*) get a move on!, look sharp!

поворож|и́ть, у́, и́шь *pf. of* ⇒**ворожи́ть**

поворо́т, а *m.* turn(ing); **огни́ ~а** direction indicator lamps (*of car*); (*fig.*) turning-point; **п. реки́** bend in a river; **пе́рвый п. напра́во** the first turning to the right; **на ~е доро́ги** at the turn of the road; **п. к лу́чшему** turn for the better.

поворо|ти́ть(ся), чу́(сь), ~́тишь(ся) *pf. of* ⇒**повора́чивать(ся)** to turn.

поворо́тливост|ь, и *f.* **1** nimbleness, agility. **2** (*tech., naut.*) manoeuvrability (*Br.*), maneuverability (*US*).

поворо́тлив|ый (~, ~а) *adj.* **1** nimble, agile. **2** (*tech., naut.*) manoeuvrable (*Br.*), maneuverable (*US*).

поворо́тн|ый *adj.* rotary, rotating, revolving; (*fig.*) crucial, decisive; **п. круг** turn-table; **п. мост** swing bridge; **~ое сиде́нье** swivel seat; **п. моме́нт, п. пункт** turning-point.

повре|ди́ть, жу́, ди́шь *pf.* **1** *pf. of* ⇒**вреди́ть. 2** (*pf. of* ⇒**~жда́ть**) (*испортить*) to damage; (*поранить*) to injure, hurt; **п. себе́ но́гу** to hurt one's leg.

повре|ди́ться, жу́сь, ди́шься *pf.* (*of* ⇒**~жда́ться**) (*испортиться*) to be damaged; (*пораниться*) to be injured; **п. в уме́** (*coll.*) to become mentally deranged.

поврежда́|ть(ся), ю(сь) *impf. of* ⇒**повреди́ть(ся)**

поврежде́ни|е, я *nt.* damage; injury.

повре|ждённый *p.p.p. of* ⇒**~ди́ть**

повремен|и́ть, ю́, и́шь *pf.* (*coll.*) to wait a little; (**с**+*i.*) to delay (over).

повреме́нн|ый *adj.* **1** (*издание*) periodical. **2** (*работа*) reckoned on time basis; **~ая опла́та** payment by time (*by the hour, etc.*).

повседне́вно *adv.* daily, every day.

повседне́вност|ь, и *f.* daily routine.

повседне́вн|ый *adj.* daily; everyday; **~ая рабо́та** daily task; **п. слу́чай** everyday occurrence.

повсеме́стно *adv.* everywhere.

повсеме́ст|ный (~ен, ~на) *adj.* universal, general.

повска|ка́ть, ~́чет *pf.* to jump up one after another.

повска́кива|ть, ет *pf.* = **повскака́ть**

П

повста́н|ец, ца *m.* insurgent, rebel.

повста́нческий *adj.* insurgent, rebel.

повстреча́|ть, ю *pf.* (*coll.*) to meet, run into.

повстреча́|ться, юсь *pf.* (*coll.*) (+*d.* or **с**+*i.*) to meet, run into; **мне ∼лся знако́мый, я ∼лся со знако́мым** I met an acquaintance.

повсю́ду *adv.* everywhere.

повто́р, а *m.* replay.

повторе́ни|е, я *nt.* **1** (*действия*) repetition. **2** (*события*) recurrence. **3** (*урока*) revision.

повтори́тельный *adj.* repeat; recapitulatory; **п. курс** refresher course.

повтор|и́ть, ю́, и́шь *pf.* (*of* ⇒**∼я́ть**) **1** to repeat. **2** (*уроки*) to revise.

повтор|и́ться, ю́сь, и́шься *pf.* (*of* ⇒**∼я́ться**) **1** (*повторить сказанное*) to repeat o.s. **2** (*о событиях*) to reoccur; (*о болезни*) to recur.

повто́р|ный (∼ен, ∼на) *adj.* (*визит*) second, repeated; (*заболевание*) recurring.

повтор|я́ть(ся), я́ю(сь) *impf. of* ⇒**∼и́ть(ся)**

повы́|сить, шу, сишь *pf.* (*of* ⇒**∼ша́ть**) **1** to raise, heighten; **п. вдвое́, втрое́** to double, treble; **п. в пять раз**, *etc.*, to raise five-fold, *etc.*; **п. давле́ние** to increase pressure; **п. го́лос** to raise one's voice (*also fig.*, *in anger*); (*улучшить*) to improve; **п. кого́-н. в чьём-н. мне́нии** to raise s.o. in s.o.'s estimation. **2** (*работника*) to promote, advance; **п. кого́-н. по слу́жбе** to give s.o. promotion.

повы́|ситься, шусь, сишься *pf.* (*of* ⇒**∼ша́ться**) **1** to rise; (*увеличиться*) to increase; (*улучшиться*) to improve; **п. в чьём-н. мне́нии** to rise in s.o.'s estimation; **на́ши а́кции ∼сились** our shares have gone up; (*fig.*) our stock has risen. **2** (*по службе*) to be promoted, receive advancement.

повыша́|ть(ся), ю(сь) *impf. of* ⇒**повы́сить(ся)**

повы́ше *comp. adj. and adv.* a little higher (up); (*о росте человека*) a little taller.

повыше́ни|е, я *nt.* rise, increase; **п. по слу́жбе** advancement, promotion.

повы́|шенный *p.p.p. of* ⇒**∼сить** *and adj.* heightened; increased; **∼шенное настро́ение** state of excitement; **∼шенная температу́ра** a (raised) temperature; **∼шенная чувстви́тельность** heightened sensibility.

повя|за́ть¹, жу́, ∽жешь *pf.* (*of* ⇒**∽зывать**) to tie; **п. га́лстук** to tie a tie.

повя|за́ть², жу́, ∽жешь *pf.* to do a little knitting, knit for a while.

повя|за́ться, жу́сь, ∽жешься *pf.* (*of* ⇒**∽зываться**) (+*i.*) to tie o.s. (with); **п. (платко́м)** to tie a scarf on one's head.

повя́зк|а, и *f.* **1** (*лента*) band. **2** (*бинт*) bandage.

повя́зыва|ть(ся), ю(сь) *impf. of* ⇒**повяза́ть(ся)**

погада́|ть, ю *pf. of* ⇒**гада́ть**

пога́н|ить, ю, ишь *impf.* (*of* ⇒**о∼**) (*coll.*) to pollute, defile.

пога́н|ка, ки *f.* **1** = **∼ый гриб. 2** (*zool.*) grebe.

пога́н|ый (∼, ∼а) *adj.* **1** foul, unclean; **п. гриб** toadstool; **∼ая пи́ща** (*relig.*) unclean food; **∼ое ведро́** refuse pail. **2** (*coll.*) (*отвратительный*) foul, vile; **∼ое настрое́ние** foul mood.

по́ган|ь, и *f.* (*collect.*; *pej.*) filth.

погаса́|ть, ю *impf.* to go out, be extinguished.

пога|си́ть, шу́, ∽сишь *pf.* (*of* ⇒**гаси́ть** *and* **∼ша́ть**) to liquidate, cancel; **п. долг** to clear a debt; **п. ма́рку** to cancel a stamp.

пога́с|нуть, ну, нешь, *past* **∼, ∼ла** *pf. of* ⇒**га́снуть**

погаша́|ть, ю *impf. of* ⇒**погаси́ть**

погаше́ни|е, я *nt.* (*долга*) paying off, clearing (*of a debt*).

пога́|шенный *p.p.p. of* ⇒**∼си́ть** *and adj.* used (*of postage stamps, etc.*); cashed.

погиба́|ть, а́ю *impf. of* ⇒**∽нуть**

поги́бел|ь¹, и *f.* (*obs.*) (*гибель*) ruin, perdition.

поги́бел|ь², и *f.* (*coll.*): **согну́ться в три ∼и** to be hunched up; (*fig.*) to be cowed.

поги́бельный *adj.* (*obs.*) ruinous, fatal.

поги́б|нуть, ну, нешь, *past* **∼, ∼ла** *pf.* (*of* ⇒**ги́бнуть** *and* **∼а́ть**) to perish; (*naut. and fig.*) to be lost; **кора́бль ∼ со всей кома́ндой** the ship was lost with all hands.

поги́б|ший *p.p. of* ⇒**∼нуть** *and adj.* lost, ruined.

погла́|дить¹, жу, дишь *pf. of* ⇒**гла́дить**

погла́|дить², жу, дишь *pf.* to do a little ironing.

погла́жива|ть, ю *impf.* to stroke (*every so often*).

поглазе́|ть, ю *pf. of* ⇒**глазе́ть**

погло|ти́ть, щу́, ∽тишь *pf.* (*of* ⇒**∼ща́ть**) to soak up, absorb (*also fig.*); **п. во́ду** to absorb water; **п. чьё-н. внима́ние** to engross s.o.; **п. рома́н** to devour a novel.

поглоща́|ть, ю *impf. of* ⇒**поглоти́ть**

поглупе́|ть, ю *pf. of* ⇒**глупе́ть**

погля|де́ть, жу́, ди́шь *pf.* **1** *pf. of* ⇒**гляде́ть. 2** (*взглянуть*) to have a look. **3** (*некоторое время*) to look for a while.

погля|де́ться, жу́сь, ди́шься *pf. of* ⇒**гляде́ться**

погля́дыва|ть, ю *impf.* **1** (**на**+*a.*) to glance from time to time (at). **2** (**за**+*i.*; *coll.*) to keep an eye (on).

по|гна́ть, гоню́, го́нишь, *past* **∼гна́л, ∼гнала́, ∼гна́ло** *pf.* to drive; (*начать гнать*) to begin to drive.

по|гна́ться, гоню́сь, го́нишься, *past* **∼гна́лся, ∼гнала́сь, ∼гнало́сь** *pf.* (**за**+*i.*) to run (after); to give chase; (*fig.*) to strive (after, for); **п. за эффе́ктами** to strive for effect.

погни́|ть, ю, ёшь, *past* **∼л, ∼ла́, ∼ло** *pf.* to rot, decay.

погн|у́ть, у́, ёшь *pf.* to bend.

погн|у́ться, ётся *pf.* to bend (*intrans.*).

погнуша́|ться, юсь *pf. of* ⇒**гнуша́ться**

погова́рива|ть, ю *impf.* (**о**+*p.*) to talk (of); **∼ют** there is talk (of); **∼ют о его́ жени́тьбе** there is talk of his marrying.

поговор|и́ть, ю́, и́шь *pf.* to have a talk.

погово́рк|а, и *f.* saying; **войти́ в ∼у** to become proverbial.

пого́д|а, ы *f.* weather; **кака́я бы ни была́ п.** rain or shine; **э́то не де́лает ∼ы** that is not what counts; **ждать у мо́ря (***or* **у́ моря) ∼ы** to wait for sth. to turn up.

пого|ди́ть, жу́, ди́шь *pf.* (*coll.*) to wait a little; **∼ди́те!** wait a moment!, one moment!; **немно́го ∼дя́** a little later.

пого́д|ки, ков *pl.* (*sg.* **∼ок, ∼ка** *m.*) brothers or sisters born at a year's interval; **мы с ней п.** there is a year's difference between us.

пого́дный¹ *adj.* annual, yearly.

пого́д|ный² *adj. of* ⇒**∼а**

пого́жий *adj.* fine, lovely (*of weather*).

поголо́вно *adv.* one and all; (all) to a man.

поголо́вн|ый *adj.* general, universal; **п. нало́г** poll-tax; **∼ая пе́репись** universal census.

поголо́вь|е, я *nt.* (*total*) number, head (*of live-stock*).

поголубе́|ть, ю *pf. of* ⇒**голубе́ть**

пого́н, а, *g. pl.* **∼** *m.* (*mil.*) shoulder-strap.

пого́нный *adj.* linear.

пого́нщик, а *m.* driver; **п. му́лов** muleteer.

пого́н|я, и *f.* pursuit, chase.

погоня́|ть¹, ю *impf.* (*торопить*) to urge on, drive (*also fig.*).

погоня́|ть², ю *pf.* (*заставить бежать*) to drive (*for a certain time*).

погор|а́ть, а́ю *impf. of* ⇒**∼е́ть¹**

погоре́л|ец, ьца *m.* person who has lost everything in a fire; fire victim.

погор|е́ть¹, ю́, и́шь *pf.* (*of* ⇒**∼а́ть**) (*coll.*) **1** (*о человеке*) to lose all one's possessions in a fire. **2** (*об имуществе*) to be burnt. **3** (*провалиться*) to fail; **п. на воровстве́** to be caught thieving.

погор|е́ть², и́т *pf.* (*некоторое время*) to burn for a while.

погоряч|и́ться, у́сь, и́шься *pf.* to get heated (*fig.*), get worked up.

пого́ст, а *m.* (*obs.*) country churchyard.

пого|сти́ть, щу́, сти́шь *pf.* (**у**+*g.*) to stay for a while (at, with).

погран... *comb. form* frontier(-), border(-).

пограни́чник, а *m.* border guard, frontier guard.

пограни́чно-пропускно́й *adj.*: **п. пункт** border control post.

пограни́чн|ый *adj.* (*страны*) border, frontier; (*участка*) boundary; **п. столб**

border post; boundary post; **~ая стра́жа** border guards.

по́греб, а, *pl.* **~а́** *m.* cellar (*also fig.*); **ви́нный п.** wine-cellar.

погреба́льн|ый *adj.* funeral; **п. звон** knell; **~ое пе́ние** dirge.

погреба́|ть, ю *impf. of* ⇒**погрести́**[1]

погребе́ни|е, я *nt.* burial, interment.

погребе́|ц, ца́ *m.* (*obs.*) provisions hamper.

погрему́шк|а, и *f.* rattle.

погре|сти́[1], **бу́, бёшь,** *past* **~б, ~бла́** *pf.* (*of* ⇒**~ба́ть**) (*похоронить*) to bury.

погре|сти́[2], **бу́, бёшь,** *past* **~б, ~бла́** *pf.* (*грести некоторое время*) to row a little.

погре́|ть, ю *pf.* to warm.

погре́|ться, юсь *pf.* to warm o.s.

погреш|а́ть, а́ю *impf. of* ⇒**~и́ть**

погреш|и́ть, у́, и́шь *pf.* (*of* ⇒**~а́ть**) (**про́тив** + *g.*) to sin (against); to err.

погре́шност|ь, и *f.* error, mistake.

погро|зи́ть, жу́, зи́шь *pf. of* ⇒**грози́ть** 2

погро|зи́ться, жу́сь, зи́шься *pf. of* ⇒**грози́ться**

погро́м, а *m.* pogrom; (*coll.*) chaos.

погро́мщик, а *m.* person organizing *or* taking part in a pogrom.

погромых|а́ть, а́ю *pf.* (*of* ⇒**~ивать**) to rumble intermittently.

погромы́хива|ть, ю *impf. of* ⇒**погромыха́ть**

погружа́|ть(ся), ю(сь) *impf. of* ⇒**погрузи́ть(ся); ~емый нагрева́тель** immersion heater.

погруже́ни|е, я *nt.* submergence; immersion; (*подводной лодки*) dive, diving.

погру́|женный *and* **~жённый** *p.p.p. of* ⇒**~зи́ть; п. в во́ду** immersed (in water); **п. в размышле́ния** deep in thought; **п. в себя́** wrapped up in o.s.

погру|зи́ть, жу́, ~зи́шь *pf.* (*of* ⇒**~жа́ть**) **1** (**в** + *a.*) to immerse; (*в темноту*) to plunge. **2** *pf. of* ⇒**грузи́ть** 2

погру|зи́ться, жу́сь, ~зи́шься *pf.* **1** (**в** + *a.*) to sink (into), plunge (into); (*о подводной лодке*) to submerge, dive; (*fig.*) to be plunged (in); to be absorbed (in), be buried (in), be lost (in); **п. в темноту́** to be plunged into darkness; **п. в чте́ние** to be absorbed in reading; **п. в размышле́ния** to be deep in thought. **2** *pf. of* ⇒**грузи́ться**

погру́зк|а, и *f.* loading.

погру́зочный *adj.* loading; **п. жёлоб** loading chute.

погряз|а́ть, а́ю *impf. of* ⇒**~нуть**

погря́з|нуть, ну, нешь, *past* **~, ~ла** *pf.* (*of* ⇒**~а́ть**) (**в** + *p.*) to be stuck (in); to be bogged down (in); (*в разврате*) to wallow (in); **п. в долга́х** to be up to one's eyes in debt.

погуб|и́ть, лю́, ~ишь *pf. of* ⇒**губи́ть**

погу́дк|а, и *f.* (*coll.*) tune, melody; **ста́рая п. на но́вый лад** (*fig.*) the (same) old story.

погу́лива|ть, ю *impf.* (*coll.*) **1** (*гулять*) to walk up and down. **2** (*веселиться*) to go on the spree from time to time.

погуля́|ть, ю *pf. of* ⇒**гуля́ть**

погусте́|ть, ет *pf. of* ⇒**густе́ть**

под[1], **а, о ~е, на ~у́** *m.* (*печи*) hearth, floor.

под[2] (*also* **подо**) *prep.* **1** (+ *a. and i.*) (*ниже*) under; **поста́вить п. стол** to put under the table; **находи́ться п. столо́м** to be under the table; **п. аре́стом** under arrest; **п. ви́дом** (+ *g.*) in the guise (of); **п. влия́нием** (+ *g.*) under the influence (of); **п. вопро́сом** open to question; **по́д гору** downhill; **п. замко́м** under lock and key; **п. землёй** underground; **быть п. ружьём** to be under arms; **взять кого́-н. по́д руку** to take s.o.'s arm; **п. руко́й** (close) at hand, to hand; **отда́ть п. суд** to prosecute; **п. усло́вием** on condition. **2** (+ *a. and i.*) (*около*) in the environs of, near; **жить п. Москво́й** to live near Moscow; **пое́хать на да́чу п. Москву́** to go to a dacha near Moscow. **3** (+ *a. and i.*) (*для*) for; (to serve) as; **помеще́ние под шко́лой** premises occupied by a school; **отвести́ помеще́ние п. шко́лу** to earmark premises for a school; **ба́нка п. варе́нье** jam-jar; **по́ле п. пшени́цей** wheat-field. **4** (+ *a.*) (*о времени*) towards; on the eve of; **п. ве́чер** towards evening; **п. Но́вый год** on New Year's Eve; **ему́ п. пятьдеся́т (лет)** he is getting on for fifty. **5** (+ *a.*) (*в сопровождении*) to (the accompaniment of); **танцева́ть п. му́зыку** to dance to music. **6** (+ *a.*) (*наподобие*) in imitation of; **э́то сде́лано п. оре́х** it is imitation walnut; **он пи́шет п. Турге́нева** he writes in imitation of (*the style of*) Turgenev. **7** (+ *a.*) (*в обмен*) on (= *in exchange for*); **п. зало́г** on security; **п. распи́ску** on receipt. **8** (+ *i.*) (*при обозначении понятия*) by; **что на́до понима́ть п. э́тим выраже́нием?** what is meant by this expression?; **что п. э́тим подразумева́ется?** what is implied by this? **9** (+ *i.*; *cul.*) in, with; **ры́ба п. бешаме́лью** fish cooked in white sauce; **говя́дина п. хре́ном** beef with horse-radish.

под...[1] (*also* **подо...** *and* **подъ...**) *as vbl. pref. indicates* **1** *action from beneath or affecting lower part of sth., as* **подчеркну́ть** to underline. **2** *motion upwards, as* **подня́ть** to raise. **3** *motion towards, as* **подъе́хать** to approach. **4** *action carried out or event occurring in slight degree, as* **подкра́сить** to touch up; **подожи́ть** to begin to heal up. **5** *supplementary action, as* **подрабо́тать** to earn additionally. **6** *underhand action, as* **подкупи́ть** to bribe.

под...[2] (*also* **подо...** *and* **подъ...**) *as pref. of nn. and adjs.* under-, sub-.

подава́льщик, а *m.* **1** (*официант*) waiter. **2** (*рабочий, занятый подачей чего-н.*) supplier.

подава́льщиц|а, ы *f.* waitress.

пода|ва́ть(ся), ю́(сь), ёшь(ся) *impf. of* ⇒**пода́ть(ся)**

подав|и́ть[1], **лю́, ~ишь** *pf.* (*of* ⇒**~ля́ть**) **1** (*восстание; стон*) to suppress; to repress. **2** (*fig.*) (*ослабить, угнетать*) to depress; to crush, overwhelm. **3** (*mil.*) to neutralize.

подав|и́ть[2], **лю́, ~ишь** *pf.* (*no impf.*) **1** (*coll.*) (*раздавить многое, многих*) to press, trample (*a quantity of*). **2** (*подвергнуть давлению в течение некоторого времени*) to press, squeeze for a time.

подав|и́ться, лю́сь, ~ишься *pf. of* ⇒**дави́ться**

подавле́ни|е, я *nt.* **1** suppression; repression. **2** (*mil.*) neutralization.

пода́вленност|ь, и *f.* depression.

пода́в|ленный *p.p.p. of* ⇒**~и́ть** *and adj.* **1** (*стон, смех*) suppressed, stifled. **2** (*человек, настроение*) depressed, dispirited.

пода́влива|ть, ю *impf.* to exert slight pressure from time to time.

подавля́|ть, ю *impf. of* ⇒**подави́ть**[1]

подавля́|ющий *pres. part. act. of* ⇒**~ть** *and adj.* overwhelming.

пода́вно *adv.* even more so, all the more.

пода́гр|а, ы *f.* gout.

пода́грик, а *m.* gout sufferer.

подагри́ческий *adj.* gouty.

пода́льше *adv.* (*coll.*) a little farther.

подар|и́ть, ю́, ~ишь *pf. of* ⇒**дари́ть**

пода́р|ок, ка *m.* present, gift; **получи́ть в п.** to receive as a present.

пода́рочный *adj.* gift (*attr.*).

пода́тел|ь, я *m.* bearer (*of a letter, etc.*).

пода́тливост|ь, и *f.* **1** pliancy, pliability. **2** (*fig.*) (*уступчивость*) complaisance.

пода́тлив|ый (~, ~а) *adj.* **1** pliant, pliable. **2** (*fig.*) (*уступчивый*) complaisant.

по́дат|ь, и, *pl.* **~и, ~ей** *f.* (*hist.*) tax, duty, assessment.

по|да́ть, да́м, да́шь, да́ст, дади́м, дади́те, даду́т *past* **~дал, ~дала́, ~дало** *pf.* (*of* ⇒**~дава́ть**) **1** to give; **п. го́лос** to call, make a sound; **п. го́лос за** (+ *a.*) to vote for; to vote; **п. знак** to give a sign; **п. по́мощь** to lend a hand; **п. приме́р** to set an example; **п. ру́ку** (+ *d.*) to offer one's hand; **п. сигна́л** to give the signal; **~да́йте ей пальто́** help her on with her coat. **2** (*еду*) to serve; **п. на стол** to serve up; **обе́д ~дан** dinner is served. **3** (*sport*): **п. мяч** to serve. **4** (*заявление, жалобу*) to serve, present, hand in; **п. апелля́цию** to appeal; **п. жа́лобу** to lodge a complaint; **п. заявле́ние** to hand in an application; **п. телегра́мму** to send a telegram; **п. в отста́вку** to tender one's resignation; **п. в суд** (**на** + *a.*) to bring an action (against). **5** (*liter., theatr.*) (*представить, изобразить*) to present, display.

по|да́ться, да́мся, да́шься,

П

да́стся, дади́мся, дади́тесь, даду́тся, *past* **~да́лся, ~дала́сь, ~дало́сь** *pf.* (*of* ⇒**~дава́ться**) **1** (*подвинуться*) to move; **п. наза́д** to draw back; **п. в сто́рону** to move aside. **2** (**на**+*a.*; *coll.*) (*отправиться*) to make (for), set out (for). **3** (*coll.*) (*уступить*) to give way, yield (*also fig.*).

пода́ч|а, и *f.* **1** giving, presenting; **п. го́лоса** voting; **п. заявле́ния** sending in of application. **2** (*sport*) service, serve. **3** (*tech.*) feed, feeding, supply.

пода́чк|а, и *f.* (*coll.*) **1** (*кусок еды*) scraps. **2** (*fig.*) (*человеку*) hand-out.

подая́ни|е, я *nt.* alms.

подба́в|ить, лю, ишь *pf.* (*of* ⇒**~ля́ть**) (+*a. or g.*) to add; **п. са́хару в ко́фе** to put (more) sugar in coffee; **п. ро́му в чай** to lace tea with rum.

подба́вк|а, и *f.* (*coll.*) addition.

подбавля́|ть, ю *impf. of* ⇒**подба́вить**

подба́лтыва|ть, ю *impf. of* ⇒**подболта́ть**

подбега́|ть, ю *impf. of* ⇒**подбежа́ть**

подбе|жа́ть, гу́, жи́шь, гу́т *pf.* (*of* ⇒**~га́ть**) (**к**+*d.*) to run up (to), come running up (to).

подберёзовик, а *m.* brown mushroom (*Boletus scaber*).

подбива́|ть, ю *impf. of* ⇒**подби́ть**

подби́вк|а, и *f.* **1** (*пальто*) lining. **2** (*обуви*) re-soling.

подбира́|ть(ся), ю(сь) *impf. of* ⇒**подобра́ть(ся)**

подби́т|ый *p.p.p. of* ⇒**~ь**; **п. ва́той** wadded; **п. ме́хом** fur-lined; **п. глаз** black eye.

под|би́ть, обью́, обьёшь *pf.* (*of* ⇒**~бива́ть**) **1** (+*i.*) (*пальто*) to line (with). **2** (*обувь*) to re-sole. **3** (*ушибить*) to injure; **п. кому́-н. глаз** to give s.o. a black eye. **4** (*самолёт, утку*) to shoot down. **5** (+*inf. or* **на**+*a.*; *coll.*) (*подстрекать*) to incite (to).

подбодр|и́ть, ю́, и́шь *pf.* (*of* ⇒**~я́ть**) to cheer up.

подбодр|и́ться, ю́сь, и́шься *pf.* (*of* ⇒**~я́ться**) to cheer up, take heart.

подбодр|я́ть(ся), я́ю(сь) *impf. of* ⇒**~и́ть(ся)**

подболта́|ть, ю *pf.* (*of* ⇒**подба́лтывать**) (+*a. or g.*) to mix in, stir in; **п. молока́ в суп** to stir milk into soup.

подбо́р, а *m.* **1** selection, assortment; **(как) на п.** choice, well-matched. **2**: **в п.** (*typ.*) run on.

подбо́рк|а, и *f.* set, selection.

подборо́д|ок, ка *m.* chin.

подбоче́нива|ться, юсь *impf. of* ⇒**подбоче́ниться**

подбоче́нившись *adv.* with one's arms akimbo, with one's hands on one's hips.

подбоче́н|иться, юсь, ишься *pf.* (*of* ⇒**~иваться**) to place one's arms akimbo.

подбра́сыва|ть, ю *impf. of* ⇒**подбро́сить**

подбро́|сить, шу, сишь *pf.* (*of* ⇒**подбра́сывать**) **1** to throw up, toss up; (**под**+*a.*) to throw (under); **п. моне́ту** to toss up. **2** (+*a. or g.*) to throw in, throw on; **п. резе́рвы** (*mil.*) to throw in one's reserves; **п. дров в печь** to throw more wood on the fire. **3** (*положить скрытно*) to place surreptitiously.

подва́л, а *m.* **1** (*в здании*) cellar; basement. **2** (*в газете*) feuilleton.

подва́лива|ть, ю *impf. of* ⇒**подвали́ть**

подвал|и́ть, ю́, ~́ишь *pf.* (*of* ⇒**~́ивать**) **1** (*coll.*) (+*a. or g.*) to heap up. **2** (+*a. or g.*) (*coll.*) to add; (*impers.*): **наро́ду ~и́ло** still more people came. **3** (*naut.*; **к**+*d.*) to come in (to), steam in (to).

подва́л|ьный *adj. of* ⇒**~**; **п. эта́ж** basement.

подве́домствен|ный (~, ~на) *adj.* (+*d.*) dependent (on), within the jurisdiction (of).

подвез|ти́, у́, ёшь, *past* **~́, ~ла́** *pf.* (*of* ⇒**подвози́ть**) **1** (*довезти*) to bring, take (with one); to give a lift (*on the road*). **2** (+*a. or g.*) (*доставить*) to bring up, transport.

подвене́чн|ый *adj.*: **~ое пла́тье** wedding dress.

подверг|а́ть(ся), а́ю(сь) *impf. of* ⇒**~́нуть(ся)**

подве́рг|нуть, ну, нешь, *past* **~** *and* **~нул, ~ла** *pf.* (*of* ⇒**~а́ть**) (+*d.*) to subject (to); to expose (to); **п. испыта́нию** to put to the test; **п. опа́сности** to expose to danger, endanger; **п. сомне́нию** to call in question; **п. штра́фу** to fine.

подве́рг|нуться, нусь, нешься, *past* **~ся** *and* **~нулся, ~лась** *pf.* (*of* ⇒**~а́ться**) (+*d.*) to undergo, be subjected to.

подве́рженност|ь, и *f.* (+*d.*) susceptibility (to).

подве́ржен|ный (~, ~а) *adj.* (+*d.*) (*влиянию ветров*) subject (to); (*простуде*) prone (to), susceptible (to).

подвер|ну́ть, ну́, нёшь *pf.* (*of* ⇒**~́тывать**) **1** (*подвинтить*) to screw up a little; **п. винт** to tighten a screw. **2** (*подоткнуть*) to tuck in, tuck up; **п. одея́ло** to tuck in a blanket; **п. брю́ки** to tuck up one's trousers. **3** (*повредить*) to twist, sprain; **п. но́гу** to sprain one's ankle.

подвер|ну́ться, ну́сь, нёшься *pf.* (*of* ⇒**~́тываться**) **1** to be twisted, sprained; **нога́ у меня́ ~ну́лась** I have sprained my ankle. **2** (*fig., coll.*) (*попасться*) to turn up, show up; **он кста́ти ~ну́лся** he turned up just at the right moment.

подвёртыва|ть(ся), ю(сь) *impf. of* ⇒**подверну́ть(ся)**

подве́|сить, шу, сишь *pf.* (*of* ⇒**~шивать**) to hang up, suspend.

подве́|ситься, шусь, сишься *pf.* (*of* ⇒**~шиваться**) (**на**+*p.*) to hang (on to, on by), be suspended (from).

подве́ск|а, и *f.* **1** (*действие*) hanging up, suspension. **2** (*украшение*) pendant.

подвесно́й *adj.* hanging, suspended; overhead; **п. конве́йер** overhead conveyor; **п. мост** suspension bridge; **п. мото́р** outboard motor.

подве́с|ок, ка *m.* pendant.

подве|сти́, ду́, дёшь, *past* **~́л, ~ла́** *pf.* (*of* ⇒**подводи́ть**) **1** (**к**+*d.*) (*человека*) to lead up (to); (*поезд*) to bring up (to); (*дорогу*) to extend (to). **2** (**под**+*a.*) to place (under); **п. ми́ну под мост** to mine a bridge; **п. про́чную ба́зу под свой до́воды** to place one's arguments on a sound footing. **3** (*покрасить*): **п. бро́ви** to pencil one's eyebrows; **п. глаза́** to put on eyeliner; **п. гу́бы** to put on lipstick. **4** (*сделать общий вывод*) to put together; **п. бала́нс** (+*g.*) to balance; **п. ито́ги** to reckon up; to sum up (*also fig.*). **5** (*coll.*) (*поставить в трудное положение*) to let down; to put in a spot. **6** (*impers.*; *coll.*): **у меня́ живо́т ~ло́** I'm absolutely famished.

подве́тренный *adj.* leeward.

подве́шива|ть(ся), ю(сь) *impf. of* ⇒**подве́сить(ся)**

подвива́|ть(ся), ю(сь) *impf. of* ⇒**подви́ть(ся)**

по́двиг, а *m.* exploit, feat; heroic deed.

подви́га|ть, ю *pf.* (+*i.*) to move a little.

подвига́|ть(ся), ю(сь) *impf. of* ⇒**подви́нуть(ся)**

подви́гн|уть, у, ешь *pf.* (**на**+*a.*) (*rhet., obs.*) to rouse (to).

подви́д, а *m.* (*biol.*) subspecies.

подви́жник, а *m.* **1** (*relig.*) ascetic; zealot. **2** (*fig.*) zealot, devotee.

подви́жничеств|о, а *nt.* **1** (*relig.*) asceticism. **2** (*fig.*) selfless devotion (*to a cause*).

подвижн|о́й *adj.* mobile; movable; (*tech.*) travelling (*Br.*), traveling (*US*); **п. го́спиталь** mobile hospital; **~ы́е и́гры** outdoor games; **п. масшта́б** sliding scale; **п. пра́здник** (*eccl.*) movable feast; **п. соста́в** (*rail.*) rolling stock.

подви́жност|ь, и *f.* **1** mobility. **2** (*человека*) liveliness.

подви́ж|ный (~ен, ~на) *adj.* **1** (*группа войск*) mobile. **2** (*ребёнок*) lively; **~ное лицо́** mobile features.

подвиза́|ться, юсь *impf.* (*rhet. or iron.*) to work; to pursue an occupation; **п. на юриди́ческом по́прище** to follow the law; **п. на сце́не** to tread the boards.

подвин|ти́ть, чу́, ти́шь *pf.* (*of* ⇒**~́чивать**) **1** to screw up, tighten. **2** (*fig., coll.*) to urge, goad.

подви́|нуть, ну, нешь *pf.* (*of* ⇒**~га́ть**) **1** to move; to push; **~ньте стул!** pull up a chair! **2** (*fig.*) (*продвинуть*) to advance, push forward.

подви́|нуться, нусь, нешься *pf.* (*of* ⇒**~га́ться**) **1** to move; **~ньтесь и да́йте мне сесть!** move up and let me sit down! **2** (*fig.*) (*продвинуться*) to advance, progress.

подви́нчива|ть, ю *impf. of* ⇒**подвинти́ть**

под|ви́ть, овью́, овьёшь, *past* **~ви́л, ~вила́, ~ви́ло** *pf.* (*of* ⇒**~вива́ть**) to curl slightly, frizz.

под|виться, овьюсь, овьёшься, *past* **~вился, ~вилась, ~вилось** *pf.* (*of* ⇒**~виваться**) to curl one's hair slightly, frizz one's hair.

подвласт|ный (~ен, ~на) *adj.* (+*d.*) subject to, under the control of.

подвод, а *m.* (*tech.*) supply, feed, admission; (*elec.*) lead, feeder.

подвод|а, ы *f.* cart.

подво|дить, жу, ~дишь *impf. of* ⇒**подвести**

подводник, а *m.* (*моряк*) submariner; (*водолаз*) diver.

подводн|ой *adj.*: **~ая труба** (*tech.*) feed pipe.

подводн|ый *adj.* submarine; underwater; **п. кабель** submarine cable; **п. камень** reef, rock; **~ая лодка** submarine; **~ое течение** undercurrent.

подвоз, а *m.* transport; supply.

подво|зить, жу, ~зишь *impf. of* ⇒**подвезти**

подворот|ня, ни, *g. pl.* **~ен** *f.* **1** (*щель*) space between gate and ground. **2** (*доска*) board attached to bottom of gate. **3** (*проём для проезда, прохода*) gateway, passageway.

подвох, а *m.* (*coll.*) dirty trick.

подвыпи|вший *p.p. of* ⇒**~ть** *and adj.* (*coll.*) tipsy.

подвып|ить, ью, ьешь *pf.* (*coll.*) to become tipsy.

подвя|зать, жу, ~жешь *pf.* (*of* ⇒**~зывать**) to tie up.

подвязк|а, и *f.* (*женская*) garter; (*мужская*) suspender (*Br.*), garter (*US*).

подвязыва|ть, ю *impf. of* ⇒**подвязать**

подга|дить, жу, дишь *pf.* (*coll.*) **1** to spoil the effect (of), make a mess (of). **2** (+*d.*) to play a dirty trick (on).

подгиба|ть(ся), ю, ет(ся) *impf. of* ⇒**подогнуть(ся)**

подгля|деть, жу, дишь *pf.* (*of* ⇒**~дывать**) (**в**+*a.*; *coll.*) to peep (at); to spy (on), watch furtively.

подглядыва|ть, ю *impf. of* ⇒**подглядеть**

подгнива|ть, ет *impf. of* ⇒**подгнить**

подгни|ть, ёт, *past* **~л, ~ла, ~ло** *pf.* (*of* ⇒**~вать**) to begin to rot, rot slightly.

подговарива|ть, ю *impf. of* ⇒**подговорить**

подговор|ить, ю, ишь *pf.* (*of* ⇒**подговаривать**) (**на**+*a. or* +*inf.*) to put up (to), incite (to).

подголовник, а *m.* head-rest.

подголос|ок, ка *m.* **1** (*mus.*) second part, supporting voice. **2** (*coll., pej.*) yes-man.

подгоня|ть, ю *impf. of* ⇒**подогнать**

подгор|ать, ает *impf. of* ⇒**~еть**

подгорелый *adj.* slightly burnt.

подгор|еть, ит *pf.* (*of* ⇒**~ать**) to burn slightly.

подгородный *adj.* situated on the outskirts of a town.

подготавлива|ть(ся), ю(сь) *impf. of* ⇒**подготовить(ся)**

подготовительный *adj.* preparatory.

подготов|ить, лю, ишь *pf.* (*of* ⇒**подготавливать** *and* **~лять**) (**для**+*g.*, **к**+*d.*) to prepare (for); **п. почву** (*fig.*) to pave the way.

подготов|иться, люсь, ишься *pf.* (*of* ⇒**подготавливаться** *and* **~ляться**) (**к**+*d.*) to prepare (for), get ready (for).

подготовк|а, и *f.* **1** (**к**+*d.*) preparation (for), training (for); **артиллерийская п.** artillery preparation, preparatory bombardment. **2** (**в**+*p. or* **по**+*d.*) grounding (in), schooling (in).

подготовленност|ь, и *f.* preparedness.

подготовля|ть(ся), ю(сь) *impf. of* ⇒**подготовить(ся)**

подгреба|ть, ю *impf. of* ⇒**подгрести**

подгре|сти[1], бу, бёшь, *past* **~б, ~бла** *pf.* (*of* ⇒**~бать**) (*листья*) to rake up.

подгре|сти[2], бу, бёшь, *past* **~б, ~бла** *pf.* (*of* ⇒**~бать**) (**к**+*d.*) (*приблизиться*) to row up (to).

подгруд|ок, ка *m.* dewlap.

подгрупп|а, ы *f.* sub-group.

подгузник, а *m.* nappy (*Br.*), diaper (*US*).

подгуля|ть, ю *pf.* (*coll.*) **1** to have had a little too much to drink. **2** (*joc.*) (*не удаться*) to be rather poor.

подда|вать(ся), ю(сь), ёшь(ся) *impf. of* ⇒**поддать(ся)**

поддакива|ть, ю *impf.* (*of* ⇒**поддакнуть**) (+*d.*; *coll.*) to say yes (to), assent (to) (*also pej.*).

поддак|нуть, ну, нешь *pf. of* ⇒**~ивать**

подданн|ый *p.p.p. of* ⇒**поддать;** *as n.* **п., ~ого** *m., and* **~ая, ~ой** *f.* subject, national.

подданств|о, а *nt.* citizenship, nationality.

под|дать, дам, дашь, даст, дадим, дадите, дадут, *past* **~дал, ~дала, ~дало** *pf.* (*of* ⇒**~давать**) **1** (*мяч*) to strike; (*ногой*) to kick. **2** (*в игре в шашки*) to give away. **3** (+*g.*; *coll.*) (*усилить*) to add, increase; **п. жару** to add fuel to the fire; **п. пару** to increase steam; **п. газу** to get a move on. **4** (*coll.*) (*выпить*) to booze, tipple.

под|даться, дамся, дашься, дастся, дадимся, дадитесь, дадутся, *past* **~дался, ~далась** *pf.* (*of* ⇒**~даваться**) **1** (+*d.*) to yield (to), give way (to), give in (to); **дверь не ~далась** the door would not give; **п. искушению** to yield to temptation; **не ~даваться описанию** to beggar description; **п. отчаянию** to give way to despair; **п. угрозам** to give in to threats. **2** (*coll.*) (*дать себя поймать*) to give o.s. up.

поддева|ть, ю *impf. of* ⇒**поддеть**

поддел|ать, аю *pf.* (*of* ⇒**~ывать**) to forge; to counterfeit; **п. подпись** to forge a signature.

поддел|аться, аюсь *pf.* (*of* ⇒**~ываться**) **1** (**под**+*a.*) to imitate, put on. **2** (**к**+*d.*; *coll.*) to ingratiate o.s. (with).

подделк|а, и *f.* forgery; counterfeit, fake; **п. под жемчуг** imitation pearls.

подделывател|ь, я *m.* forger; counterfeiter.

подделыва|ть(ся), ю(сь) *impf. of* ⇒**подделать(ся)**

поддельн|ый *adj.* forged, counterfeit; (*неискренний*) sham; **~ые драгоценности** imitation jewellery; **~ая монета** counterfeit coin; **п. паспорт** forged passport.

поддёргива|ть, ю *impf. of* ⇒**поддёрнуть**

поддержани|е, я *nt.* maintenance; **п. мира** peacekeeping; **войска по ~ю мира** peacekeeping force.

поддерж|ать, у, ~ишь *pf.* (*of* ⇒**~ивать**) **1** to support (*also fig.*); to back, second; **морально п.** to give moral support; **п. резолюцию** to second a resolution. **2** (*не дать прекратиться*) to keep up, maintain; **п. огонь** to keep up the fire; **п. разговор** to keep up a conversation; **поддерживать отношения** (**с**+*i.*) to keep in touch (with).

поддержива|ть, ю *impf.* **1** *impf. of* ⇒**поддержать. 2** (*impf. only*) to bear, support.

поддержк|а, и *f.* **1** (*действие*) support; backing; seconding. **2** (*опора*) support, prop.

поддёр|нуть, ну, нешь *pf.* (*of* ⇒**~гивать**) to pull up.

подде|ть, ну, нешь *pf.* (*of* ⇒**~вать**) **1** (**под**+*a.*; *coll.*) to put on under, wear under; **~нь(те) свитер под куртку** put a sweater on under your jacket. **2** (*зацепить*) to hook; to catch up. **3** (*fig., coll.*) (*человека*) to catch out; to have a dig at s.o.

поддон, а *m.* (*для кирпичей*) pallet; (*подставка*) stand, tray.

поддонник, а *m.* saucer (*placed under flowerpot*).

поддразнива|ть, ю *impf. of* ⇒**поддразнить**

поддразн|ить, ю, ~ишь *pf.* (*of* ⇒**~ивать**) (*coll.*) to tease.

поддувал|о, а *nt.* damper (*of stove, furnace*).

поддува|ть, ю *impf.* **1** (*снизу, сбоку*) to blow (*from underneath*). **2** (*слегка*) to blow slightly.

по-дедовски *adv.* (*coll.*) as of old.

подейств|овать, ую *pf. of* ⇒**действовать** 2

поделa|ть, ю *pf.* (*no impf.*) (*coll.*) to do; **ничего не ~ешь** it can't be helped; **ничего не могу с ними п.!** I can't do anything with them.

подел|ить(ся), ю(сь), ~ишь(ся) *pf. of* ⇒**делить(ся)**

поделк|а, и *f.* **1** (*случайная работа*) odd job. **2** (*изделие*) hand-made article;

П

~и из дéрева hand-made wooden articles.

поделóм *adv.* (*coll.*): **п. емý,** *etc.*, it serves him, *etc.*, right.

подéлыва|ть *impf.* (*coll.*) *only used in question* **что ~ешь? что ~ете?** how are you getting on?

подёнк|а, и *f.* (*zool.*) mayfly.

подённо *adv.* by the day.

подённ|ый *adj.* by the day; **~ая оплáта** pay by the day; **~ая рабóта** day-labour (*Br.*), -labor (*US*).

подёнщик, а *m.* day-labourer (*Br.*), -laborer (*US*).

подёнщин|а, ы *f.* day-labour (*Br.*), -labor (*US*).

подёнщи|ца, цы *f. of* ⇨**~к**

подёрг|ать, аю *pf. of* ⇨**~ивать**

подёргивани|е, я *nt.* twitch(ing).

подёргива|ть, ю *impf.* **1** (*impf. of* ⇨**подёргать**) (+*a. or* **за**+*a.*) to pull (at), tug (at). **2** (*impf. only*) (+*i.*) to twitch.

подёргива|ться, юсь *impf.* to twitch.

подéржанный *adj.* second-hand.

подерж|áть, ý, ~ишь *pf.* (*в руках*) to hold for some time; (*у себя*) to keep for some time.

подерж|áться, ýсь, ~ишься *pf.* **1** (**за**+*a.*) to hold (on to) for some time. **2** (*сохраниться*) to hold (out), last.

подёрн|уть, ет *pf.* to cover, coat; (*impers.*): **рекý ~уло льдом** the river was coated with ice.

подёрн|уться, ется *pf.* (+*i.*) to be covered (with).

подешевé|ть, ет *pf. of* ⇨**дешевéть**

поджáрива|ть(ся), ю, ет(ся) *impf. of* ⇨**поджáрить(ся)**

поджáрист|ый (~, ~а) *adj.* well-done; crisp.

поджáр|ить, ю, ишь *pf.* (*of* ⇨**~ивать**) (*на сковороде*) to fry; (*в духовке*) to roast; (*на рашпере*) to grill (slightly); **п. хлеб** to toast bread.

поджáр|иться, ится *pf.* (*of* ⇨**~иваться**) to fry, roast (slightly).

поджáр|ый (~, ~а) *adj.* (*coll.*) lean, wiry.

под|жáть, ожмý, ожмёшь *pf.* (*of* ⇨**~жимáть**) **1** to draw in; **п. гýбы** to purse one's lips; **п. хвост** to have one's tail between one's legs (*also fig.*); **сидéть ~жáв нóги** to sit cross-legged. **2** (*coll.*) (*вынудить торопиться*) to force to hurry.

поджелýдочн|ый *adj.*: **~ая железá** (*anat.*) pancreas.

под|жéчь, ожгý, ожжёшь, ожгýт, *past* **~жёг, ~ожглá** *pf.* (*of* ⇨**~жигáть**) **1** to set fire (to), set on fire. **2** (*coll.*) (*еду*) to burn slightly.

поджигáтел|ь, я *m.* **1** incendiary, arsonist. **2** (*fig.*) instigator; **п. войны́** warmonger.

поджигáтель|ница, ницы *f. of* ⇨**~**

поджигáтельский *adj.* inflammatory.

поджигá|ть, ю *impf. of* ⇨**поджéчь**

поджидá|ть, ю *impf.* to wait (for).

поджи́л|ки, ок *no sg.* knee tendons; **у меня́ от стрáха п. затрясли́сь** (*fig., coll.*) I was shaking in my shoes.

поджимá|ть, ю *impf. of* ⇨**поджáть**

поджóг, а *m.* arson; arson attack.

подзаб|ы́ть, ýду, ýдешь *pf.* (*coll.*) to forget partially; **я ~ы́л рýсский язы́к** my Russian is a little rusty.

подзаголóв|ок, ка *m.* sub-title, sub-heading.

подзадóрива|ть, ю *impf. of* ⇨**подзадóрить**

подзадóр|ить, ю, ишь *pf.* (*of* ⇨**~ивать**) (*coll.*) to egg on.

подзарабóта|ть, ю *pf.* (*coll.*) to earn in addition.

подзаты́льник, а *m.* (*coll.*) clip round the ear.

подзащи́тн|ый, ого *m.* (*leg.*) client.

подземéл|ье, ья, *g. pl.* **~ий** *nt.* cave; (*тюрьма*) dungeon.

подзéмк|а, и *f.* (*coll.*) underground (railway), tube.

подзéмный *adj.* underground, subterranean; **п. толчóк** earth tremor.

подзеркáльник, а *m.* pier table.

подзóл, а *m.* (*agric.*) podzol.

подзóр, а *m.* **1** carved cornice (*in Russian wooden architecture*). **2** (*покрывала*) edging, trimming.

подзóрн|ый *adj.*: **~ая трубá** spy-glass, telescope.

подзу|ди́ть, жý, ~дишь *pf.* (*of* ⇨**~живать**) (*coll.*) to egg on.

подзýжива|ть, ю *impf. of* ⇨**подзуди́ть**

подзывá|ть, ю *impf. of* ⇨**подозвáть**

поди́[1] (*coll.*) = ***пойди́*** **(***imper. of* ⇨**пойти́); п. сюдá!** come here!

поди́[2] (*coll.*) **1** (*наверное*) probably; I dare say; I shouldn't wonder; *or translated* must (be), is sure (to be); **ты, п., устáла** you must be tired; **он, п., забы́л** he has probably forgotten. **2** (*выражение удивления*) (*also* **нá п.**); **п. ты, рáзве он э́то сказáл?** go on, he never said that?; impossible! he couldn't have said that!; **вот п. ж ты** just imagine; well, who would have thought it possible. **3** *particle*+*imper.* just try; **п. удержи́ егó** just try to stop him.

подив|и́ться, лю́сь, и́шься *pf. of* ⇨**диви́ться**

подирá|ть, ет *impf.*: **морóз по кóже ~ет** (*coll.*) it makes one's flesh creep; it gives one the creeps.

подкáлыва|ть, ю *impf. of* ⇨**подколóть**

подкáпыва|ть(ся), ю(сь) *impf. of* ⇨**подкопáть(ся)**

подкараýлива|ть, ю *impf.* (*of* ⇨**подкараýлить**) (*coll.*) to be on the watch (for), lie in wait (for).

подкараýл|ить, ю, ишь *pf. of* ⇨**подкараýливать**

подкáрмлива|ть, ю *impf. of* ⇨**подкорми́ть**

подка|ти́ть, чý, ~тишь *pf.* (*of* ⇨**~тывать**) **1** (*мяч*) to roll; (*велосипед*) to wheel. **2** (*coll.*) (*об экипаже*) to roll up, drive up. **3** (*coll.*): **у меня́ ком ~ти́л к гóрлу** I felt a lump rise in my throat.

подка|ти́ться, чýсь, ~тишься *pf.* (*of* ⇨**~тываться**) (**под**+*a.*) to roll (under).

подкáтыва|ть(ся), ю(сь) *impf. of* ⇨**подкати́ть(ся)**

подкач|áть, áю *pf.* (*of* ⇨**~ивать**) (*coll.*) to make a mess (of things).

подкáчива|ть, ю *impf. of* ⇨**подкачáть**

подкáшива|ть(ся), ю, ет(ся) *impf. of* ⇨**подкоси́ть(ся)**

подки́дыва|ть, ю *impf. of* ⇨**подки́нуть**

подки́дыш, а *m.* foundling, abandoned baby.

подки́|нуть, ну, нешь *pf.* (*of* ⇨**~дывать**) = **подбрóсить**

подклáдк|а, и *f.* lining.

подкладнó|й *adj.* put under; **~е сýдно** bed-pan.

подклáд|очный *adj. of* ⇨**~ка; п. материáл** lining (material).

подклáдыва|ть, ю *impf. of* ⇨**подложи́ть**

подклáсс, а *m.* (*biol.*) sub-class.

подклéива|ть, ю *impf. of* ⇨**подклéить**

подклé|ить, ю, ишь *pf.* (*of* ⇨**~ивать**) **1** (**под**+*a.*) to glue (under), paste (under). **2** (*починить*) to glue up, paste up.

подключ|áть(ся), áю(сь) *impf. of* ⇨**~и́ть(ся)**

подключ|и́ть, ý, и́шь *pf.* (*of* ⇨**~áть**) (**к**+*d.*) **1** (*tech.*) to link up (to), connect up (to). **2** (*fig.*) to attach (to); to involve; **егó ~и́ли ко вторóму кýрсу** he has been attached to the second year; **к рабóте ~и́ли специали́стов** specialists were involved in the work.

подключ|и́ться, ýсь, и́шься *pf.* (*of* ⇨**~áться**) **1** (*tech.*) to be connected up. **2** (*fig.*) to get involved, become a participant.

подкóв|а, ы *f.* (horse-)shoe.

подк|овáть, ую́, уёшь *pf.* (*of* ⇨**ковáть** *and* **~óвывать**) **1** to shoe. **2** (**в**+*p.*; *fig., coll.*) (*подготовить*) to ground (in), give a grounding (in).

подкóвыва|ть, ю *impf. of* ⇨**подковáть**

подковы́рива|ть, ю *impf. of* ⇨**подковырнýть**

подковыр|нýть, нý, нёшь *pf.* (*of* ⇨**~ивать**) **1** to pick (*a sore, etc.*). **2** (*fig., coll.*) (*человека*) to catch out.

подкóжный *adj.* (*жир*) subcutaneous; (*укол*) hypodermic.

подколóдн|ый *adj.*: **змея́ ~ая** (*fig., coll.*) snake in the grass.

подкол|óть, ю́, ~ешь *pf.* (*of* ⇨**подкáлывать**) **1** (*волосы*) to pin up. **2** (*дрова*) to chop up. **3** (*документ к делу*) to attach, append.

подкоми́сси|я, и *f.* sub-committee.

подкомитéт, а *m.* sub-committee.

подконтрóл|ьный (~ен, ~ьна) *adj.* under control; (+*d.*) under the control of.

подкóп, а *m.* **1** (*действие*) undermining. **2** (*подземный ход*) underground passage. **3** (*fig., coll.*) (*происки*) intrigue(s).

подкопá|ть, ю *pf.* (*of* ⇒**подкáпывать**) **1** to dig under. **2** (*fig., coll.*) to undermine.

подкопá|ться, юсь *pf.* (*of* ⇒**подкáпываться**) (**под**+*a.*) **1** (*о животных*) to burrow (under). **2** (*fig., coll.*) to undermine.

подкорм|и́ть, лю́, ~ишь *pf.* (*of* ⇒**подкáрмливать**) to feed up; to fatten (up).

подкóрмк|а, и *f.* feeding; fattening.

подкóс, а *m.* (*tech.*) strut, brace, angle brace.

подко|си́ть, шу́, ~сишь *pf.* (*of* ⇒**подкáшивать**) **1** (*траву*) to cut. **2** (*о пуле, ударе*) to fell, lay low (*also fig.*); **э́то оконча́тельно ~си́ло (меня́, его́,** *etc.*) that was the last straw; that was the final blow.

подкос|и́ться, ~ится *pf.* (*of* ⇒**подкáшиваться**) to give way, buckle.

подкрáдыва|ться, юсь *impf. of* ⇒**подкрáсться**

подкрá|сить, шу, сишь *pf.* (*of* ⇒**~шивать**) (*стену*) to tint, colour (*Br.*), color (*US*); (*губы*) to touch up.

подкрá|ситься, шусь, сишься *pf.* (*of* ⇒**~шиваться**) to touch up one's make-up.

подкрá|сться, дýсь, дёшься *pf.* (*of* ⇒**~дываться**) (**к**+*d.*) to steal up (to), sneak up (to).

подкрáшива|ть(ся), ю(сь) *impf. of* ⇒**подкрáсить(ся)**

подкреп|и́ть, лю́, и́шь *pf.* (*of* ⇒**~ля́ть**) **1** (*забор; теорию*) to reinforce, support (*also fig.*). **2** (*накормить*) to fortify (*with food and/or drink*); **п. себя́ пéред дорóгой** to fortify o.s. for a journey. **3** (*mil.*) to reinforce.

подкреп|и́ться, лю́сь, и́шься *pf.* (*of* ⇒**~ля́ться**) to fortify o.s. (*with food and/or drink*).

подкреплéни|е, я *nt.* **1** (*забора; теории*) reinforcement, support. **2** (*едой, питьём*) sustenance. **3** (*mil.*) reinforcement.

подкрепля́|ть(ся), ю(сь) *impf. of* ⇒**подкрепи́ть(ся)**

подкузьм|и́ть, лю́, и́шь *pf.* (*coll.*) to do a bad turn; to do (down).

пóдкуп, а *m.* bribery; corruption.

подкуп|áть, áю *impf. of* ⇒**~и́ть**

подкуп|и́ть, лю́, ~ишь *pf.* (*of* ⇒**~áть**) **1** (*деньгами*) to bribe. **2** (*fig.*) (*добротой*) to win over.

подлá|диться, жусь, дишься *pf.* (*of* ⇒**~живаться**) (**к**+*d.*; *coll.*) **1** (*приспособиться*) to adapt o.s. (to), fit in (with). **2** (*постараться угодить*) to humour (*Br.*), humor (*US*); to make up (to).

подлáжива|ться, юсь *impf. of* ⇒**подлáдиться**

подлáмыва|ться, ется *impf. of* ⇒**подломи́ться**

пóдле *prep.*+*g.* by the side of, beside.

подлёдный *adj.* under the ice.

подлеж|áть, ý, и́шь *impf.* (+*d.*) to be liable (to), be subject (to); **э́тот дом ~и́т снóсу** this house is to be pulled down; **«не ~и́т оглашéнию»** (*classification of document*) 'Confidential'; **не ~и́т сомнéнию** it is beyond doubt.

подлежáщ|ее, его *nt.* (*gram.*) subject.

подлежá|щий *pres. part. act. of* ⇒**~ть** *and adj.* (+*d.*) liable (to), subject (to); **п. обложéнию сбóром** dutiable; **не п. обложéнию сбóром** duty-free; **не п. оглашéнию** confidential; off the record.

подлез|áть, áю *impf. of* ⇒**~ть**

подлéз|ть, у, ешь *pf.* (*of* ⇒**~áть**) (**под**+*a.*) to crawl (under), creep (under).

подлéс|ок, ка *m.* undergrowth.

подлет|áть, áю *impf. of* ⇒**~éть**

подле|тéть, чý, ти́шь *pf.* (*of* ⇒**~тáть**) (**к**+*d.*) to fly up (to); (*fig.*) to rush up (to).

подлé|ть, ю, ешь *impf.* (*of* ⇒**о~**) (*coll.*) to grow mean; to become a scoundrel.

подлéц, á *m.* scoundrel, villain, rascal.

подлéчива|ть(ся), ю(сь) *impf. of* ⇒**подлечи́ть(ся)**

подлеч|и́ть, ý, ~ишь *pf.* (*of* ⇒**~ивать**) (*coll.*) to treat.

подлеч|и́ться, ýсь, ~ишься *pf.* (*of* ⇒**~иваться**) (*coll.*) to take medical treatment.

подливá|ть, ю *impf. of* ⇒**подли́ть**

подли́вк|а, и *f.* sauce; (*салатная*) dressing; (*мясная*) gravy.

подливн|óй *adj.*: **~óе колесó** (*tech.*) undershot wheel.

подли́з|а, ы *c.g.* (*coll.*) toady.

подли|зáться, жýсь, ~жешься *pf.* (*of* ⇒**~зываться**) (**к**+*d.*; *coll.*) to lick s.o.'s boots; to suck up (to).

подли́зыва|ться, юсь *impf. of* ⇒**подлизáться**

пóдлинник, а *m.* original (*opp. copy*).

пóдлинно *adv.* really; genuinely; **п. хорóший фильм** a really good film.

пóдлинност|ь, и *f.* authenticity.

пóдлин|ный (~ен, ~на) *adj.* **1** (*не поддельный*) genuine; authentic; (*не копия*) original; **«с ~ным верно»** 'certified true copy'. **2** (*истинный*) true, real; **п. учёный** a true scholar.

подлипáла = **подли́за**

под|ли́ть, олью́, ольёшь, *past* **~ли́л, ~лилá, ~ли́ло** *pf.* (*of* ⇒**~ливáть**) (+*a. or g.* **в**+*a.*) to add (to); **п. мáсла в огóнь** (*fig.*) to add fuel to the fire.

пóдлича|ть, ю *impf.* to act meanly.

подлóг, а *m.* forgery.

подлóдк|а, и *f.* submarine; sub.

подлож|и́ть, ý, ~ишь *pf.* (*of* ⇒**подклáдывать**) **1** (**под**+*a.*) to lay under. **2** (+*a. or g.*) (*добавить*) to add; **~и́те дровá** *or* **дров** put some more wood on. **3** (*положить скрытно*) to put furtively; **п. свинью́ комý-н.** to play a dirty trick on s.o.

подлóж|ный (~ен, ~на) *adj.* counterfeit, forged.

подлокóтник, а *m.* elbow-rest; arm (*of chair*).

подлом|и́ться, ~ится *pf.* (*of* ⇒**подлáмываться**) (**под**+*i.*) to break (under).

пóдлост|ь, и *f.* **1** (*свойство*) meanness, baseness. **2** (*поступок*) mean trick, low-down trick.

подлýнный *adj.* sublunar.

пóдл|ый (~, ~á, ~о) *adj.* mean, base, despicable.

подмá|зать, жу, жешь *pf.* (*of* ⇒**~зывать**) to grease, oil; (*fig., coll.*) to grease s.o.'s palm.

подмá|заться, жусь, жешься *pf.* (*of* ⇒**~зываться**) (*coll.*) **1** (*подкраситься*) to touch up one's make-up. **2** (**к**+*d.*) (*подделаться*) to curry favour (*Br.*), favor (*US*) (with); to make up (to).

подмáзыва|ть(ся), ю(сь) *impf. of* ⇒**подмáзать(ся)**

подмал|евáть, ю́ю, ю́ешь *pf.* (*of* ⇒**~ёвывать**) (*coll.*) to tint, colour (*Br.*), color (*US*); to touch up.

подмалёвыва|ть, ю *impf. of* ⇒**подмалевáть**

подмандáтн|ый *adj.* (*pol.*) mandated; **~ая территóрия** mandated territory.

подмáнива|ть, ю *impf. of* ⇒**подмани́ть**

подман|и́ть, ю́, ~ишь *pf.* (*of* ⇒**~ивать**) to call (to); to beckon.

подмáслива|ть, ю *impf. of* ⇒**подмáслить**

подмáсл|ить, ю, ишь *pf.* (*of* ⇒**~ивать**) **1** to add butter to. **2** (*coll.*) (*подкупить*) to bribe; to grease s.o.'s palm.

подмастéрь|е, я, *g. pl.* **~ев** *m.* apprentice.

подмáхива|ть, ю *impf. of* ⇒**подмахнýть**

подмах|нýть, нý, нёшь *pf.* (*of* ⇒**~ивать**) (*coll.*) to scribble a signature on.

подмáчива|ть, ю *impf. of* ⇒**подмочи́ть**

подмéн, а *m.* substitution (*of sth. false for sth. real*).

подмéн|а, ы *f.* = **~**

подмéнива|ть, ю *impf. of* ⇒**подмени́ть**

подмен|и́ть, ю́, ~ишь *pf.* (*of* ⇒**~ивать** *and* **~я́ть**) (+*a. and i.*) to substitute (for) (*intentionally*); **ктó-то на вечери́нке ~и́л мне шля́пу** s.o. at the party took my hat (and left his instead).

подмен|я́ть, я́ю *impf. of* ⇒**~и́ть**

подмерз|áть, áет *impf. of* ⇒**~нуть**

подмёрз|нуть, нет, *past* **~, ~ла** *pf.* (*of* ⇒**~áть**) to freeze slightly.

П

подме|си́ть, шу́, ~́сишь *pf.* (*of* ⇒**~́шивать**[1]) to add, mix in.

подме|сти́, ту́, тёшь, *past* **~́л, ~ла́** *pf.* (*of* ⇒**~та́ть**[1]) **1** (*место*) to sweep. **2** (*мусор*) to sweep up.

подмета́|ть[1]**, ю** *impf. of* ⇒**подмести́**

подме|та́ть[2]**, чу́, ~́чешь** *pf.* (*of* ⇒**~́тывать**) (*подшить*) to baste, tack.

подме́|тить, чу, тишь *pf.* (*of* ⇒**~ча́ть**) to notice.

подмётк|а, и *f.* sole; **в ~и кому́-н. не годи́ться** (*coll.*) to not be fit to hold a candle to s.o.

подмётыва|ть, ю *impf. of* ⇒**подмета́ть**[2]

подмеча́|ть, ю *impf. of* ⇒**подме́тить**

подмеш|а́ть, а́ю *pf.* (*of* ⇒**~́ивать**[2]) to stir in, mix in.

подме́шива|ть[1]**, ю** *impf. of* ⇒**подмеси́ть**

подме́шива|ть[2]**, ю** *impf. of* ⇒**подмеша́ть**

подми́гива|ть, ю *impf. of* ⇒**подмигну́ть**

подмиг|ну́ть, ну́, нёшь *pf.* (*of* ⇒**~́ивать**) (+*d.*) to wink (at).

подмина́|ть, ю *impf. of* ⇒**подмя́ть**

подмо́г|а, и *f.* (*coll.*) help, assistance.

подмок|а́ть, а́ю *impf. of* ⇒**~нуть**

подмо́к|нуть, ну, нешь, *past* **~, ~ла** *pf.* (*of* ⇒**~а́ть**) to get slightly wet.

подмора́жива|ть, ет *impf. of* ⇒**подморо́зить**

подморо́женный *adj.* frost-bitten, frozen (slightly).

подморо́з|ить, ит *pf.* (*of* ⇒**подмора́живать**) to freeze; **к ве́черу ~ило** towards evening it began to freeze.

подмоско́вный *adj.* (situated) near Moscow.

подмо́стк|и, ов *no sg.* **1** (*леса*) scaffolding, staging. **2** (*theatr.*) (*сцена*) stage; boards.

подмо́ч|енный *p.p.p. of* ⇒**~и́ть** *and adj.* **1** (*влажный*) slightly wet, damp. **2** (*испорченный*) damaged (*also fig.*); **~енная репута́ция** tarnished reputation.

подмоч|и́ть, у́, ~́ишь *pf.* (*of* ⇒**подма́чивать**) **1** (*намочить*) to wet slightly, damp, dampen. **2** (*испортить*) to damage.

подмыва́|ть, ю *impf.* **1** *impf. of* ⇒**подмы́ть. 2** (*impers.*) to urge; **меня́ так и ~ет** (+*inf.*) I feel an urge (to); I can hardly keep (from).

подм|ы́ть, о́ю, о́ешь *pf.* (*of* ⇒**~ыва́ть**) **1** (*ребёнка*) to wash s.o.'s bottom. **2** (*берег*) to wash away, undermine.

подмы́шк|а, и *f.* arm-pit (*of article of clothing*).

подмы́ш|ки, ек *no sg.* arm-pits (*see also* ⇒**мы́шка**[2]).

под|мя́ть, омну́, омнёшь *pf.* (*of* ⇒**~мина́ть**) to crush.

поднадзо́р|ный (~ен, ~на) *adj.* under surveillance.

поднаж|а́ть, му́, мёшь *pf.* (**на**+*a.*; *coll.*) (*на дверь*) to press, put pressure (on); (*на отстающих*) to chivvy; **поднажми́!** hurry up!

поднату́ж|иться, усь, ишься *pf.* (*coll.*) to make a big effort.

подна́чива|ть, ю *impf. of* ⇒**подна́чить**

подна́ч|ить, у, ишь *pf.* (*of* ⇒**~ивать**) (*coll.*) to egg on.

поднебе́сн|ая, ой *f.* (*folk poet.*) the earth.

поднебе́сь|е, я *nt.* (*folk poet.*) the heavens.

поднево́л|ьный (~ен, ~ьна) *adj.* **1** (*человек*) dependent; subordinate; not free. **2** (*труд*) forced.

поднес|ти́, у́, ёшь, *past* **~́, ~ла́** *pf.* (*of* ⇒**подноси́ть**) **1** (*нести*) (**к**+*d.*) to take (to), bring (to). **2** (+*d. and a.*) (*подарить*) to present (with); to take (as a present); (*угостить*) to treat (to); **п. кому́-н. буке́т цвето́в** to present s.o. with a bouquet.

поднима́|ть(ся), ю(сь) *impf. of* ⇒**подня́ть(ся)**

поднов|и́ть, лю́, и́шь *pf.* (*of* ⇒**~ля́ть**) (*краску*) to freshen up, touch up; (*мебель*) to renovate.

подновля́|ть, ю *impf. of* ⇒**поднови́ть**

подного́тн|ая, ой *f.* (*coll.*) all there is to know; the ins and outs; **он зна́ет про них всю ~ую** he knows all (there is to know) about them.

подно́жи|е, я *nt.* **1** (*горы, башни*) foot. **2** (*пьедестал*) pedestal.

подно́жк|а[1]**, и** *f.* (*автобуса*) step, footboard.

подно́жк|а[2]**, и** *f.* (*в борьбе*) backheel; **дать кому́-н. ~у** to trip s.o. up.

подно́жн|ый *adj.*: **п. корм** pasture, pasturage; **быть на ~ом корму́** to be at grass.

подно́с, а *m.* tray; (*серебряный*) salver; **ча́йный п.** tea-tray.

подно|си́ть, шу́, ~́сишь *impf. of* ⇒**поднести́**

подно́ск|а, и *f.* transporting, bringing.

подно́счик, а *m.* **1** carrier; **п. патро́нов** ammunition carrier. **2** (*в трактире*) innkeeper's assistant, drinks server.

подноше́ни|е, я *nt.* **1** (*действие*) presenting, giving. **2** (*подарок*) present, gift; **цвето́чные ~я** floral tributes.

подня́ти|е, я *nt.* (*действие по глаголу поднять*) raising; (*действие по глаголу подняться*) rising; **п. за́навеса** curtain-rise; **голосова́ть ~ем рук** to vote by show of hands.

под|ня́ть, ниму́, ни́мешь, *past* **~́нял, ~няла́, ~́няло** *pf.* (*of* ⇒**~нима́ть**) **1** to raise; to lift; **п. настрое́ние** (+*g.*) to cheer up, raise the spirits (of); **п. ору́жие** to take up arms; **п. паруса́** to set sail; **п. флаг** to hoist a flag; **п. целину́** to open up virgin lands; **п. я́корь** to weigh anchor; **п. на во́здух** to blow up; **п. на́ смех** to make a laughing-stock (of). **2** (*подобрать*) to pick up; **п. пе́тли** to pick up stitches. **3** (*возбудить*) to rouse, stir up; **п. восста́ние** to stir up rebellion; **п. ссо́ру** to pick a quarrel; **п. на́ ноги** to rouse. **4** (*улучшить*) (*fig.*) to improve; to enhance.

под|ня́ться, ниму́сь, ни́мешься, *past* **~ня́лся, ~няла́сь** *pf.* (*of* ⇒**~нима́ться**) **1** (*о температуре, ценах, солнце*) to rise; (*по лестнице*) to go up; (*встать*) to get up; **п. на́ ноги** to rise to one's feet; **п. в ата́ку** to go in to the attack; **п. в гало́п** to break into a gallop. **2** (**на**+*a.*) (*гору*) to climb, ascend, go up. **3** (*возникнуть*) to arise; to break out, develop; **~няла́сь ссо́ра** a quarrel arose; **~няла́сь дра́ка** a fight started. **4** (*econ.*; *fig.*) (*улучшиться*) to improve; to recover.

подо *prep.* = **под**[2]

подо...[1] *as vbl. pref.* = **под...**[1]

подо...[2] *as pref. of nn. and adjs.* = **под...**[2]

подоба́|ть, ет *impf.* (*impers.*; +*d. and inf.*) to become, befit.

подоба́|ющий *pres. part. act. of* ⇒**~ть** *and adj.* proper, fitting.

подо́би|е, я *nt.* **1** likeness; **по своему́ о́бразу и ~ю** in one's own image. **2** (*math.*) similarity.

подо́блачный *adj.* under the clouds.

подо́бно *adv.* (+*d.*) like; **п. тому́, как** just as.

подо́б|ный (~ен, ~на) *adj.* like; similar; **~ное поведе́ние** such behaviour (*Br.*), behavior (*US*); **~ные треуго́льники** (*math.*) similar triangles; **я никогда́ не встреча́л ~ного дурака́** I have never met such a fool; **ничего́ ~ного!** (*coll.*) nothing of the kind!; **и тому́ ~ное** (*abbr.* **и т. п.**) and so on, and such like.

подобостра́сти|е, я *nt.* servility.

подобостра́ст|ный (~ен, ~на) *adj.* servile.

подо́бранност|ь, и *f.* neatness, tidiness.

подо́бр|анный *p.p.p. of* ⇒**~а́ть** *and adj.* neat, tidy.

под|обра́ть, беру́, берёшь, *past* **~обра́л, ~обрала́, ~обра́ло** *pf.* (*of* ⇒**~бира́ть**) **1** (*поднять*) to pick up. **2** (*ноги*) to tuck up; (*вожжи*) to take up; **п. во́лосы** to put up one's hair. **3** (*выбрать*) to select, pick; **п. дже́мпер под цвет костю́ма** to choose a jumper to match a suit.

под|обра́ться, беру́сь, берёшься, *past* **~обра́лся, ~обрала́сь, ~обра́ло́сь** *pf.* (*of* ⇒**~бира́ться**) **1** (*составиться, образоваться*) to get together, be formed. **2** (**к**+*d.*) (*незаметно подойти*) to steal up (to), approach stealthily. **3** (*coll.*) (*оправить себя*) to make o.s. tidy.

подобре́|ть, ю *pf. of* ⇒**добре́ть**[1]

по-добрососе́дски: жить п. (**с**+*i.*) to have good-neighbourly relations (with).

подобру́-поздоро́ву *adv.* (*coll.*) while the going is good.

под|огна́ть, гоню́, го́нишь, *past* **~огна́л, ~огнала́, ~огна́ло** *pf.* (*of* ⇒**~гоня́ть**) **1** (**к**+*d.*) (*заставить *приблизиться*) to drive (to). **2** (*coll.*) (*заставить идти быстрее*) to drive on, urge on, hurry. **3** (**к**+*d.*) (*приспособить*) to adjust (to), fit (to).

под|огну́ть, огну́, огнёшь *pf.* (*of* ⇒**~гиба́ть**) to tuck in; to bend under.

под|огну́ться, огнётся *pf.* (*of* ⇒**~гиба́ться**) to bend (under); **коле́ни у него́ ~огну́лись** his legs gave way (*from fatigue, etc.*).

подогре́в, а *m.* (*tech.*) heating.

подогрева́тел|ь, я *m.* (*tech.*) heater.

подогрева́тельный *adj.* (*tech.*) heating.

подогрева́|ть, ю *impf. of* ⇒**подогре́ть**

подогре́|ть, ю *pf.* (*of* ⇒**~ва́ть**) to warm up, heat up; (*fig.*) (*возбудить*) to rouse.

пододвига́|ть, ю *impf. of* ⇒**пододви́нуть**

пододви́|нуть, ну, нешь *pf.* (*of* ⇒**~га́ть**) (**к**+*d.*) to move up (to), push up (to).

пододея́льник, а *m.* blanket cover, duvet cover.

подожд|а́ть, у́, ёшь, *past* **~а́л, ~ала́, ~а́ло** *pf.* (+*a. or g.*) to wait (for).

под|озва́ть, зову́, зовёшь, *past* **~озва́л, ~озвала́, ~озва́ло** *pf.* (*of* ⇒**~зыва́ть**) to call over; (*жестом*) to beckon.

подозрева́|емый *pres. part. pass. of* ⇒**~ть** *and adj.* suspected; suspect.

подозрева́|ть, ю *impf.* (*no pf.*) to suspect (*s.o. or that sth. is the case*); **я ~ю его́ в преступле́нии** I suspect him of a crime; **я ~ю, что он соверши́л преступле́ние** I suspect that he has committed a crime.

подозре́ни|е, я *nt.* suspicion; **оста́ться вне ~й** to remain above suspicion; **по ~ю** (**в**+*p.*) on suspicion (of); **быть под ~ем, на ~и** to be under suspicion.

подозри́тельно *adv.* suspiciously; **вести́ себя́ п.** to behave suspiciously; **смотре́ть п.** (**на**+*a.*) to regard with suspicion.

подозри́тельност|ь, и *f.* suspiciousness.

подозри́тел|ьный (~ен, ~ьна) *adj.* suspicious.

подо|и́ть, ю́, ~и́шь *pf. of* ⇒**дои́ть**

подо́йник, а *m.* milk-pail.

подо|йти́, йду́, йдёшь, *past* **~шёл, ~шла́** *pf.* (*of* ⇒**подходи́ть**) **1** (**к**+*d.*) (*приблизиться*) to approach (*also fig.*); to come up (to), go up (to); **по́езд ~шёл к ста́нции** the train pulled in to the station; **джу́нгли ~шли́ к са́мому поселе́нию** the jungle came right up to the settlement; **крити́чески п. к вопро́су** to approach a question critically, adopt a critical approach to a question. **2** (*годиться*) (+*d.*) to do (for); to suit; (*по размеру*) to fit; **э́тот пиджа́к о́чень мне ~йдёт** this coat will suit me very well.

подоко́нник, а *m.* window-sill.

подо́л, а *m.* **1** (*платья*) hem; **держа́ться за чей-н. п.** to cling to s.o.'s skirts. **2** (*горы*) (*dial.*) lower part, lower slopes; foot.

подо́лгу *adv.* for a long time; for ages; for long periods of time; **они́ п. не разгова́ривали друг с дру́гом** they had long periods of not speaking to each other.

подоль|сти́ться, щу́сь, сти́шься *pf.* (**к**+*d.*; *coll.*) to ingratiate o.s. (with).

подольща́|ться, юсь *impf. of* ⇒**подольсти́ться**

по-дома́шнему *adv.* simply; without ceremony.

подо́н|ки, ков *pl.* (*sg.* **~ок, ~ка** *m.*) dregs (*also fig.*); (*fig.*) scum; riff-raff.

подопе́чн|ый *adj.* **1** under wardship; **~ая террито́рия** (*pol.*) trust territory. **2** *as n.* **п., ~ого** *m.*, **~ая, ~ой** *f* ward.

подоплёк|а, и *f.* (*coll.*) the real cause, the underlying cause.

подо́пытный *adj.* experimental; **п. кро́лик** (*fig.*) guinea-pig.

подорв|а́ть, у́, ёшь, *past* **~а́л, ~ала́, ~а́ло** *pf.* (*of* ⇒**подрыва́ть**[1]) **1** to blow up. **2** (*fig.*) to undermine; to damage severely; **п. чей-н. авторите́т** to undermine s.o.'s authority; **п. здоро́вье** to damage one's health.

подорожа́|ть, ет *pf. of* ⇒**дорожа́ть**

подоро́жник, а *m.* **1** (*bot.*) plantain. **2** (*coll.*) (*пища в дорогу*) provisions taken on a journey. **3** (*obs.*) (*разбойник*) highwayman. **4** (*zool.*): **лапла́ндский п.** Lapland bunting.

подоро́жный *adj.* roadside; **п. столб** milestone.

подоси́новик, а *m.* (*bot.*) orange-cap boletus (*mushroom*) (*Boletus versipellis*).

подо|сла́ть, шлю́, шлёшь *pf.* (*of* ⇒**подсыла́ть**) to send, dispatch (*secretly*).

подосно́в|а, ы *f.* real cause, underlying cause.

подоспева́|ть, ю *impf. of* ⇒**подоспе́ть**

подоспе́|ть, ю *pf.* (*of* ⇒**~ва́ть**) (*coll.*) to arrive, appear (in time).

под|остла́ть, стелю́, сте́лешь *pf.* (*of* ⇒**~стила́ть**) (**под**+*a.*) to lay (under), stretch (under).

подотде́л, а *m.* section, subdivision.

подоткн|у́ть, у́, ёшь *pf.* (*of* ⇒**подтыка́ть**) to tuck in, tuck up; **п. простыню́** to tuck in a sheet; **п. ю́бку** to tuck up one's skirt.

подотря́д, а *m.* (*biol.*) sub-order.

подотчёт|ный (~ен, ~на) *adj.* **1** (+*d.*) accountable (to). **2** (*fin.*) on account.

подо́хн|уть, у, ешь *pf.* (*of* ⇒**до́хнуть** *and* **подыха́ть**) **1** (*о животных*) to die. **2** (*coll.*) (*о людях*) to peg out, kick the bucket.

подохо́дный *adj.*: **п. нало́г** income tax.

подо́шв|а, ы *f.* **1** (*ноги, обуви*) sole. **2** (*холма*) foot. **3** (*tech.*) base.

подпада́|ть, ю *impf. of* ⇒**подпа́сть**

подпа́ива|ть, ю *impf. of* ⇒**подпои́ть**

подпа́лива|ть, ю *impf. of* ⇒**подпали́ть**

подпа́лин|а, ы *f.* scorch-mark; **ло́шадь с ~ой** dappled horse.

подпал|и́ть, ю́, и́шь *pf.* (*of* ⇒**~ивать**) (*coll.*) **1** (*немного опалить*) to singe, scorch. **2** (*поджечь*) to set on fire.

подпа́рыва|ть(ся), ю, ет(ся) *impf. of* ⇒**подпоро́ть(ся)**

подпа́с|ок, ка *m.* shepherd boy.

подпа́|сть, ду́, дёшь, *past* **~л** *pf.* (*of* ⇒**~да́ть**) (**под**+*a.*) to fall (under); **п. под чьё-н. влия́ние** to fall under s.o.'s influence.

подпева́л|а, ы *c.g.* (*coll.*) yes-man.

подпева́|ть, ю *impf.* (+*d.*) to join (in singing); (*fig.*) to echo.

под|пере́ть, опру́, опрёшь, *past* **~пёр, ~пёрла** *pf.* (*of* ⇒**~пира́ть**) to prop up.

подпи́лива|ть, ю *impf. of* ⇒**подпили́ть**

подпил|и́ть, ю́, ~ишь *pf.* (*of* ⇒**~ивать**) **1** (*подрезать пилой*) to saw; (*напильником*) to file. **2** (*укоротить пилой*) to saw a little off; (*напильником*) to file down.

подпи́л|ок, ка *m.* file.

подпира́|ть, ю *impf. of* ⇒**подпере́ть**

подписа́вш|ий, его *m.* signatory.

подписа́ни|е, я *nt.* signing.

подпи|са́ть, шу́, ~шешь *pf.* (*of* ⇒**~сывать**) **1** (*поставить подпись* (*на*)) to sign. **2** (*добавить*) to add (*to sth. written*); **п. ещё одно́ подстро́чное примеча́ние** to add another footnote. **3** (*включить в число подписчиков*) to subscribe; **п. кого́-н. на журна́л** to take out a magazine subscription for s.o.

подпи|са́ться, шу́сь, ~шешься *pf.* (*of* ⇒**~сываться**) **1** (**под**+*i.*) to sign; (*fig.*) (*согласиться*) to subscribe (to). **2** (**на**+*a.*) to subscribe (to, for); **п. на журна́л** to subscribe to a magazine.

подпи́ск|а, и *f.* **1** (*на журнал*) subscription. **2** (*письменное обязательство*) written undertaking; signed statement; **дать ~у о невы́езде** to give a written undertaking not to leave a place.

подписно́й *adj.* subscription (*attr.*).

подпи́счик, а *m.* (**на**+*a.*) subscriber (to).

подпи́счи|ца, цы *f. of* ⇒**~к**

подпи́сыва|ть(ся), ю(сь) *impf. of* ⇒**подписа́ть(ся)**

по́дпис|ь, и *f.* **1** signature; **поста́вить свою́ п.** (**под**+*i.*) to put one's signature (to); **за ~ью** (+*g.*) signed (by). **2** (*надпись*) caption; inscription.

подплыва́|ть, ю *impf. of* ⇒**подплы́ть**

подплы́|ть, ву́, вёшь, *past* **~л, ~ла́ ~ло** *pf.* (*of* ⇒**~ва́ть**) **1** (**к**+*d.*) (*вплавь*) to swim up (to); (*на лодке*) to sail up (to). **2** (**под**+*a.*) to swim under.

подпо|и́ть, ю́, ~́ишь *pf.* (*of* ⇒**подпа́ивать**) (*coll.*) to make tipsy.

подполз|а́ть, а́ю *impf. of* ⇒**~ти́**

подполз|ти́, у́, ёшь, *past* **~́, ~ла́** *pf.* (*of* ⇒**~а́ть**) (**к**+*d.*) to creep up (to); to crawl up (to); (**под**+*a.*) to creep (under); to crawl (under).

подполко́вник, а *m.* lieutenant-colonel.

подпо́ль|е, я *nt.* **1** cellar. **2** (*fig.*) underground (*organization, activities*); **уйти́ в п.** to go underground.

подпо́льный *adj.* underground (*also fig.*).

подпо́льщик, а *m.* member of an underground organization.

подпо́льщи|ца, цы *f. of* ⇒**~к**

подпо́р|а, ы *f.* prop, support.

подпо́рк|а, и *f.* = **подпо́ра**

подпо́р|ный *adj. of* ⇒**~а; ~ная сте́нка** retaining wall.

подпор|о́ть, ю́, ~́ешь *pf.* (*of* ⇒**подпа́рывать**) to rip; to unpick, unstitch.

подпор|о́ться, ~́ется *pf.* (*of* ⇒**подпа́рываться**) to rip; to come unpicked, come unstitched.

подпо́р|тить, чу, тишь *pf.* (*coll.*) to spoil slightly.

подпору́чик, а *m.* (*hist.*) second lieutenant.

подпо́чв|а, ы *f.* subsoil, substratum.

подпо́чвенн|ый *adj.* subsoil; subterranean; **~ая вода́** underground water.

подпоя́|сать, шу, шешь *pf.* (*of* ⇒**~сывать**) to belt.

подпоя́|саться, шусь, шешься *pf.* (*of* ⇒**~сываться**) to belt o.s.; to put on a belt.

подпоя́сыва|ть(ся), ю(сь) *impf. of* ⇒**подпоя́сать(ся)**

подпра́в|ить, лю, ишь *pf.* (*of* ⇒**~ля́ть**) to touch up.

подправля́|ть, ю *impf. of* ⇒**подпра́вить**

подпрогра́мм|а, ы *f.* (*comput.*) subroutine.

подпру́г|а, и *f.* girth.

подпры́гива|ть, ю *impf. of* ⇒**подпры́гнуть**

подпры́г|нуть, ну, нешь *pf.* (*of* ⇒**~ивать**) to leap up, jump up.

подпу́нкт, а *m.* sub-clause.

подпуска́|ть, ю *impf. of* ⇒**подпусти́ть**

подпу|сти́ть, щу́, ~́стишь *pf.* (*of* ⇒**~ска́ть**) **1** (*дать приблизиться*) to allow to approach; **п. на расстоя́ние вы́стрела** to allow to come within range. **2** (+*a. or g.*; *coll.*) (*добавить*) to add in. **3** (*coll.*) (*сказать*) to get in, put in.

подраба́тыва|ть, ю *impf. of* ⇒**подрабо́тать**

подрабо́та|ть, ю *pf.* (*of* ⇒**подраба́тывать**) (*coll.*) **1** (+*a. or g.*) (*денег*) to earn additionally. **2** (*вопрос*) to work out, develop.

подра́внива|ть, ю *impf. of* ⇒**подровня́ть**

подра́гива|ть, ю *impf.* (*coll.*) to shake, tremble intermittently.

подража́ни|е, я *nt.* imitation.

подража́тел|ь, я *m.* imitator.

подража́тель|ница, ницы *f. of* ⇒**~**

подража́тел|ьный (~ен, ~ьна) *adj.* imitative.

подража́тельств|о, а *nt.* (*pej.*) imitativeness.

подража́|ть, ю *impf.* (*no pf.*) (+*d.*) to imitate.

подразде́л, а *m.* subsection.

подразделе́ни|е, я *nt.* **1** subdivision. **2** (*mil.*) sub-unit.

подраздел|и́ть, ю́, и́шь *pf.* (*of* ⇒**~я́ть**) to subdivide.

подраздел|я́ть, я́ю *impf. of* ⇒**~и́ть**

подразумева́|ть, ю *impf.* to mean.

подразумева́|ться, ется *impf.* to be implied, be meant; **что ~ется под э́тим выраже́нием?** what is meant by this expression?; **(само́ собо́й) ~ется** it is understood, it goes without saying.

подра́мник, а *m.* stretcher (*frame for canvas*).

подра́м|ок, ка *m.* = **~ник**

подраст|а́ть, а́ю *impf. of* ⇒**~и́; ~а́ющее поколе́ние** the rising generation.

подраст|и́, у́, ёшь, *past* **подро́с, подросла́** *pf.* to grow (a little).

по|дра́ть(ся), деру́(сь), дерёшь(ся), *past* **~дра́л(ся), ~драла́(сь), ~дра́ло(сь)** *pf. of* ⇒**дра́ть(ся)**

подре́|зать, жу, жешь *pf.* (*of* ⇒**~за́ть**) **1** (*волосы*) to cut; (*ногти, куст*) to clip, trim; (*деревья*) to prune, lop; **п. кому́-н. кры́лья** (*fig.*) to clip s.o.'s wings. **2** (+*g.*) to cut off in addition; **п. хле́ба** to cut some more bread.

подреза́|ть, ю *impf. of* ⇒**подре́зать**

подрем|а́ть, лю́, ~́лешь *pf.* to have a nap; to doze.

подрис|ова́ть, у́ю *pf.* (*of* ⇒**~о́вывать**) **1** (*подправить*) to touch up. **2** (*добавить*) to add, put in (*on a painting, etc.*).

подрисо́выва|ть, ю *impf. of* ⇒**подрисова́ть**

подро́бно *adv.* minutely, in detail; at (great) length.

подро́бност|ь, и *f.* detail; **вдава́ться в ~и** to go into detail; **во всех ~ях** in every detail.

подро́б|ный (~ен, ~на) *adj.* detailed, minute.

подровня́|ть, ю *pf.* (*of* ⇒**подра́внивать**) (*сделать более ровным*) to level; (*бороду, волосы*) to trim.

подро́ст|ок, ка *m.* adolescent, teenager.

подруб|а́ть, а́ю *impf. of* ⇒**~и́ть**

подруб|и́ть[1], лю́, ~́ишь *pf.* (*of* ⇒**~а́ть**) to hew.

подруб|и́ть[2], лю́, ~́ишь *pf.* (*of* ⇒**~а́ть**) to hem.

подру́г|а, и *f.* (*female*) friend; **п. по шко́ле** school-friend.

по-дру́жески *adv.* in a friendly way; as a friend.

подруж|и́ться, у́сь, и́шься *pf. of* ⇒**дружи́ться**

подру́жк|а, и *f. affectionate dim. of* ⇒**подру́га; п. неве́сты** bridesmaid.

подру́лива|ть, ю *impf. of* ⇒**подрули́ть**

подрул|и́ть, ю́, и́шь *pf.* (*of* ⇒**~́ивать**) **1** (**к**+*d.*) (*о самолёте*) to taxi up (to). **2** (*о машине*) to drive up (to).

подрумя́нива|ть(ся), ю(сь) *impf. of* ⇒**подрумя́нить(ся)**

подрумя́н|ить, ю, ишь *pf.* (*of* ⇒**~ивать**) **1** (*румянами*) to rouge; to touch up with rouge. **2** (*сделать румяным*) to make ruddy, make rosy; **моро́з ~ил им щёки** the frost brought a flush to their cheeks. **3** (*cul.*) to brown.

подрумя́н|иться, юсь, ишься *pf.* (*of* ⇒**~иваться**) **1** (*румянами*) to apply rouge, use rouge. **2** (*на морозе*) to become ruddy, become rosy; to flush, become flushed. **3** (*cul.*) to brown.

подру́чн|ый *adj.* **1** (*инструмент*) at hand, to hand; (*средства*) improvised, makeshift. **2** *as n.* **п., ~ого** *m.* assistant, mate.

подры́в, а *m.* undermining; (*fig.*) injury, detriment; **п. самолю́бия** a blow to one's pride; **п. здоро́вья** sapping of health; **п. торго́вли** injury to trade.

подрыва́|ть[1], ю *impf. of* ⇒**подорва́ть**

подрыва́|ть[2], ю *impf. of* ⇒**подры́ть**

подрывни́к, а́ *m.* (*mil.*) member of demolition squad.

подрывн|о́й *adj.* blasting, demolition; (*fig.*) subversive; **~а́я рабо́та** demolition work; **~а́я де́ятельность** subversive activities.

подр|ы́ть, о́ю, о́ешь *pf.* (*of* ⇒**~ыва́ть[2]**) to undermine.

подря́д[1] *adv.* in succession; running; on end; **три го́да п.** three years running; **не́сколько дней п. шёл дождь** it rained for days on end.

подря́д[2], а *m.* contract; **по ~у** by contract; **взять п. на постро́йку плоти́ны** to contract to build a dam; **сдать п. (на**+*a.*), **сдать с ~а** to put out to contract.

подря|ди́ть, жу́, ди́шь *pf.* (*of* ⇒**~жа́ть**) (*coll.*) to hire.

подря|ди́ться, жу́сь, ди́шься *pf.* (*of* ⇒**~жа́ться**) (*coll.*) to contract, undertake.

подря́д|ный *adj. of* ⇒**~[2]**

подря́дчик, а *m.* contractor.

подряжа́|ть(ся), ю(сь) *impf. of* ⇒**подряди́ть(ся)**

подря́сник, а *m.* cassock.

подса|ди́ть[1], жу́, ~́дишь *pf.* (*of* ⇒**~́живать**) **1** (**в, на**+*a.*) to help (into, on to); **п. кого́-н. на ло́шадь** to help s.o. on to a horse. **2** (**к**+*d.*) to place next (to); меня́ ~ди́ли к глухо́й да́ме I was placed next to a deaf lady.

подса|ди́ть[2], жу́, ~́дишь *pf.* (*of* ⇒**~́живать**) (+*a. or g.*) (*растения*) to plant some more.

подсадн|о́й *adj.*: **~а́я у́тка** decoy duck.

подса́жива|ть, ю *impf. of* ⇒**подсади́ть**

подса́жива|ться, юсь *impf. of* ⇒**подсе́сть**

подса́лива|ть, ю *impf. of* ⇒**подсоли́ть**

подсве́чник, а *m.* candlestick.

подсви́стыва|ть, ю *impf.* (+*d.*) to whistle as accompaniment to.

подсева́|ть, ю *impf. of* ⇒**подсе́ять**

подсека́|ть, ю *impf. of* ⇒**подсе́чь**

подсе́кци|я, и *f.* sub-section.

под|се́сть, ся́ду, ся́дешь, *past* **~се́л** *pf.* (*of* ⇒**~са́живаться**) (**к**+*d.*) to sit down (near, next to), take a seat (near, next to).

подсе́|чь, ку́, чёшь, ку́т, *past* **~к, ~кла́** *pf.* (*of* ⇒**~ка́ть**) **1** to hew; to hack (down). **2** (*fig.*) (*о горе*) to lay low.

подсе́|ять, ю, ешь *pf.* (*of* ⇒**~ва́ть**) (+*a. or g.*) to sow (*in addition*); to undersow.

подси|де́ть, жу́, ди́шь *pf.* (*of* ⇒**~́живать**) **1** to lie in wait (for). **2** (*fig., coll.*) to scheme, intrigue (against).

подси́живани|е, я *nt.* (*coll.*) scheming, intriguing.

подси́жива|ть, ю *impf. of* ⇒**подсиде́ть**

подси́нива|ть, ю *impf. of* ⇒**подсини́ть**

подсин|и́ть, ю́, и́шь *pf.* (*of* ⇒**~ивать**) to blue, apply blueing to.

подска́блива|ть, ю *impf. of* ⇒**подскобли́ть**

подска|за́ть, жу́, ~́жешь *pf.* (*of* ⇒**~́зывать**) (+*d.*+*a.*) **1** (*негромко напомнить*) to prompt (s.o. with sth.) (*also fig.*). **2** (*решение*) to suggest. **3** (*coll.*) (*сказать*) to tell.

подска́зк|а, и *f.* prompting.

подска́зчик, а *m.* (*coll.*) prompter.

подска́зыва|ть, ю *impf. of* ⇒**подсказа́ть**

подска|ка́ть, чу́, ~́чешь *pf.* (*of* ⇒**~́кивать[1]**) (**к**+*d.*) to come galloping up (to).

подска́кива|ть[1], ю *impf. of* ⇒**подскака́ть**

подска́кива|ть[2], ю *impf. of* ⇒**подскочи́ть**

подскобл|и́ть, ю́, ~и́шь *pf.* (*of* ⇒**подска́бливать**) to scrape off.

подскоч|и́ть, у́, ~ишь *pf.* (*of* ⇒**подска́кивать[2]**) **1** (**к**+*d.*) to run up (to), come running (to). **2** to jump up, leap up; **п. от ра́дости** to jump with joy; **це́ны ~или** prices soared.

подскреба́|ть, ю *impf. of* ⇒**подскрести́**

подскре|сти́, бу́, бёшь, *past* **~́б, ~бла́** *pf.* (*of* ⇒**~ба́ть**) (*удалить*) to scrape; (*очистить*) to scrape clean.

подсла|сти́ть, щу́, сти́шь *pf.* (*of* ⇒**~́щивать**) to sweeten.

подсла́щива|ть, ю *impf. of* ⇒**подсласти́ть**

подсле́дственный *adj.* (*leg.*) under investigation.

подслепова́т|ый (~, ~а) *adj.* weak-sighted.

подслу́жива|ться, юсь *impf. of* ⇒**подслужи́ться**

подслуж|и́ться, у́сь, ~́ишься *pf.* (*of* ⇒**~́иваться**) (**к**+*d.*; *coll.*) to fawn (upon); to worm o.s. into the favour (*Br.*), favor (*US*) (of).

подслу́ш|ать, аю *pf.* (*of* ⇒**~ивать**) to overhear; to eavesdrop (on).

подслу́шива|ть, ю *impf. of* ⇒**подслу́шать**

подсма́трива|ть, ю *impf. of* ⇒**подсмотре́ть**

подсме́ива|ться, юсь *impf.* (**над**+*i.*) to laugh (at), make fun (of).

подсмотр|е́ть, ю́, ~́ишь *pf.* (*of* ⇒**подсма́тривать**) to spy.

подсне́жник, а *m.* (*bot.*) snowdrop.

подсо́бн|ый *adj.* subsidiary; secondary; auxiliary; ancillary; **~ое предприя́тие** subsidiary enterprise; **п. рабо́чий** ancillary worker.

подсо́выва|ть, ю *impf. of* ⇒**подсу́нуть**

подсоедин|и́ть, ю́, и́шь *pf.* (*of* ⇒**~я́ть**) (*телефон*) to connect up; (*стиральную машину*) to plumb in.

подсоедин|я́ть, я́ю *impf. of* ⇒**~и́ть**

подсозна́ни|е, я *nt.* the subconscious.

подсозна́тел|ьный (~ен, ~ьна) *adj.* subconscious.

подсол|и́ть, ю́, ~́ишь *pf.* (*of* ⇒**подса́ливать**) to add more salt (to).

подсо́лнечник, а *m.* sunflower.

подсо́лнечн|ый[1] *adj. of* ⇒**~ик; ~ое ма́сло** sunflower oil.

подсо́лнечн|ый[2] *adj.* in the sun; **~ая сторона́** the sunny side; *as n.* **~ая, ~ой** *f.* (*obs.*) the universe.

подсо́лнух, а *m.* (*coll.*) **1** (*цветок*) sunflower. **2** (*семена*) sunflower-seeds.

подсо́х|нуть, ну, нешь *pf.* (*of* ⇒**подсыха́ть**) to dry out (a little).

подспо́рь|е, я *nt.* (*coll.*) help, support.

подспу́дн|ый *adj.* latent; secret, hidden; **~ые си́лы** latent strength; **~ые мы́сли** secret thoughts.

подста́в|ить, лю, ишь *pf.* (*of* ⇒**~ля́ть**) **1** (**под**+*a.*) to put (under), place (under); **п. го́лову под струю́ воды́ из кра́на** to put one's head under a tap; **п. но́жку кому́-н.** to trip s.o. up (*also fig.*). **2** (+*d.*) to bring up (to), put up (to); to hold up (to); **п. кому́-н. стул** to offer s.o. a seat. **3** (*fig.*) to expose; **п. ферзя́ под уда́р** (*chess*) to expose one's queen; (*coll.*) to set s.o. up. **4** (*math.*) to substitute.

подста́вк|а, и *f.* stand; (*для бутылки, стакана*) coaster.

подставля́|ть, ю *impf. of* ⇒**подста́вить**

подставн|о́й *adj.* false; **~о́е лицо́** dummy, figure-head.

подстака́нник, а *m.* glass-holder.

подстано́вк|а, и *f.* (*math.*) substitution.

подста́нци|я, и *f.* sub-station.

подстёгива|ть, ю *impf. of* ⇒**подстегну́ть**

подстег|ну́ть[1], ну́, нёшь *pf.* (*of* ⇒**~́ивать**) (*пристегнуть снизу*) to fasten underneath.

подстег|ну́ть[2], ну́, нёшь *pf.* (*of* ⇒**~́ивать**) (*коня*) to whip up, urge forward, urge on (*also fig.*).

подстерега́|ть, ю *impf. of* ⇒**подстере́чь**

подстере́|чь, гу́, жёшь, гу́т, *past* **~́г, ~гла́** *pf.* (*of* ⇒**~га́ть**) to be on the watch (for), lie in wait (for).

подстила́|ть, ю *impf. of* ⇒**подостла́ть**

подсти́лк|а, и *f.* bedding.

подстора́жива|ть, ю *impf.* (*of* ⇒**подсторожи́ть**) (*coll.*) to be on the watch for.

подсторож|и́ть, у́, и́шь *pf. of* ⇒**подстора́живать**

подстра́ива|ть, ю *impf. of* ⇒**подстро́ить**

подстрах|ова́ть, у́ю *pf.* (*of* ⇒**подстрахо́вывать**) **1** (*гимнаста*) to stand by ready to help. **2** (*fig.*) to (take measures to) protect; to provide with additional insurance.

подстрахо́выва|ть, ю *impf. of* ⇒**подстрахова́ть**

подстрека́тел|ь, я *m.* instigator.

подстрека́тельский *adj.* inflammatory.

подстрека́тельств|о, а *nt.* instigation, incitement.

подстрек|а́ть, а́ю *impf. of* ⇒**~ну́ть**

подстрек|ну́ть, ну́, нёшь *pf.* (*of* ⇒**~а́ть**) **1** (**к**+*d.*) to incite (to). **2** (*возбудить*) to excite; **п. любопы́тство** to excite one's curiosity.

подстре́лива|ть, ю *impf. of* ⇒**подстрели́ть**

подстрел|и́ть, ю́, ~́ишь *pf.* (*of* ⇒**~́ивать**) to wound (*by a shot*); to wing.

подстрига́|ть(ся), ю(сь) *impf. of* ⇒**подстри́чь(ся)**

подстри́|женный *p.p.p. of* ⇒**~чь; ко́ротко ~женные во́лосы** (closely) cropped hair.

подстри́|чь, гу́, жёшь, гу́т, *past* **~г, ~гла** *pf.* (*of* ⇒**~га́ть**) (*волосы*) to cut; (*куст*) to clip, trim; (*дерево*) to prune; **п. бо́роду** to trim one's beard; **п. газо́н** to cut the grass; to mow the lawn; **п. но́гти** to cut one's nails.

подстри́|чься, гу́сь, жёшься, гу́ться, *past* **~гся, ~глась** *pf.* (*of* ⇒**~га́ться**) to trim one's hair; to have a hair-cut.

подстро́|ить, ю, ишь *pf.* (*of* ⇒**подстра́ивать**) **1** (**к**+*d.*) to build on (to); **п. фли́гель к до́му** to build a wing on to a house. **2** (*скрипку*) to tune (up). **3** (*fig., coll.*) to contrive; (*pej.*) to arrange; **п. шýтку** (+*d.*) to play a trick (on); **э́то дéло ~ено** it's a put-up job.

подстрóчник, а *m.* word-for-word translation.

подстрóчн|ый *adj.* subscript; **п. перевóд** word-for-word translation; **~ое примечáние** footnote.

пóдступ, а *m.* (*geog.*; *fig.*) approach; **к немý и ~а нет** he is quite inaccessible.

подступ|áть(ся), áю(сь) *impf. of* ⇨**~и́ть(ся)**

подступ|и́ть, лю́, ~ишь *pf.* (*of* ⇨**~áть**) (**к**+*d.*) to approach, come up (to), come near; **слёзы ~и́ли к её глазáм** tears came to her eyes.

подступ|и́ться, лю́сь, ~ишься *pf.* (*of* ⇨**~áться**) (**к**+*d.*) to approach; **к немý не ~ишься** he is quite inaccessible.

подсуди́м|ый, ого *m.* (*leg.*) defendant; the accused.

подсýдност|ь, и *f.* jurisdiction.

подсýд|ный (~ен, ~на) *adj.* (+*d.*) within the jurisdiction (of); **~ое дéло** case due to come before the court; (*преступление*) crime.

подсýм|ок, ка *m.* (*mil.*) cartridge pouch.

подсýн|уть, у, ешь *pf.* (*of* ⇨**подсóвывать**) **1** (**под**+*a.*) to shove (under). **2** (+*d. and a.*; *coll.*) to slip (into); to palm off (on, upon); **они́ мне ~ули не ту кни́гу** they palmed off the wrong book on me.

подсýшива|ть, ю *impf. of* ⇨**подсуши́ть**

подсуш|и́ть, ý, ~ишь *pf.* (*of* ⇨**~ивать**) to dry a little.

подсчёт, а *m.* calculation; count.

подсчит|áть, áю *pf.* (*of* ⇨**~ывать**) to count up, reckon up; to calculate.

подсчи́тыва|ть, ю *impf. of* ⇨**подсчитáть**

подсылá|ть, ю *impf. of* ⇨**подослáть**

подсып|áть, áю *impf. of* ⇨ **~ать**

подсы́п|ать, лю, лешь *pf.* (*of* ⇨**~áть**) (+*a. or g.*) to add, pour in.

подсыхá|ть, ю *impf. of* ⇨**подсóхнуть**

подтáива|ть, ет *impf. of* ⇨**подтáять**

подтáлкива|ть, ю *impf. of* ⇨**подтолкнýть**

подтáплива|ть, ю *impf. of* ⇨**подтопи́ть**

подтáскива|ть, ю *impf. of* ⇨**подтащи́ть**

подтас|овáть, ýю *pf.* (*of* ⇨**~óвывать**) to shuffle unfairly; (*fig.*) to juggle (with); **п. фáкты** to juggle with facts.

подтасóвк|а, и *f.* unfair shuffling; (*fig.*) juggling.

подтасóвыва|ть, ю *impf. of* ⇨**подтасовáть**

подтáчива|ть, ю *impf. of* ⇨**подточи́ть**

подтащ|и́ть, ý, ~ишь *pf.* (*of* ⇨**подтáскивать**) (**к**+*d.*) to drag up (to).

подтá|ять, ет *pf.* (*of* ⇨**~ивать**) to thaw a little, melt a little.

подтверди́тельн|ый *adj.* confirmatory; **послáть ~ое письмó** to send a letter to confirm.

подтвер|ди́ть, жý, ди́шь *pf.* (*of* ⇨**~ждáть**) to confirm; to corroborate, bear out; **п. получéние чегó-н.** to acknowledge receipt of sth.

подтвер|ди́ться, ди́тся *pf.* (*of* ⇨**~ждáться**) to be confirmed.

подтверждá|ть(ся), ю, ет(ся) *impf. of* ⇨**подтверди́ть(ся)**

подтверждéни|е, я *nt.* confirmation; corroboration.

подтёк, а *m.* bruise.

подтекá|ть, ет *impf.* **1** *impf. of* ⇨**подтéчь. 2** (*impf. only*) to leak; to be leaking.

подтéкст, а *m.* subtext, concealed meaning; **угадáть п.** to read between the lines.

под|терéть, отрý, отрёшь, *past* **~тёр, ~тёрла** *pf.* (*of* ⇨**~тирáть**) to wipe (up).

подтé|чь, чёт, кýт, *past* **~к, ~клá** *pf.* (*of* ⇨**~кáть**) (**под**+*a.*) to flow (under), run (under).

подтирá|ть, ю *impf. of* ⇨**подтерéть**

подтолкн|ýть, ý, ёшь *pf.* (*of* ⇨**подтáлкивать**) **1** to push slightly; **п. лóктем** to nudge. **2** (*fig.*) to urge on.

подтоп|и́ть, лю́, ~ишь *pf.* (*of* ⇨**подтáпливать**) (*coll.*) to heat a little.

подточ|и́ть, ý, ~ишь *pf.* (*of* ⇨**подтáчивать**) **1** (*сделать острее*) to sharpen slightly. **2** (*повредить, разъедая*) to eat away, gnaw; (*о воде*) to undermine (*also fig.*); **тюрéмное заключéние ~и́ло егó здорóвье** imprisonment has undermined his health.

подтрýнива|ть, ю *impf. of* ⇨**подтруни́ть**

подтрун|и́ть, ю́, и́шь *pf.* (*of* ⇨**~ивать**) (**над**+*i.*) to tease.

подтыкá|ть, ю *impf. of* ⇨**подоткнýть**

подтя́гива|ть(ся), ю(сь) *impf. of* ⇨**подтянýть(ся)**

подтя́ж|ки, ек *no sg.* braces (*Br.*), suspenders (*US*).

подтя́нутост|ь, и *f.* smartness.

подтя́н|утый *p.p.p. of* ⇨**~ýть** *and adj.* smart.

подтя|нýть, нý, ~нешь *pf.* (*of* ⇨**~гивать**) **1** (*пояс*) to tighten. **2** (**к**+*d.*) (*подтащить*) to pull up (to), haul up (to); **п. лóдку к бéрегу** to haul up a boat on shore. **3** (*mil.*) to bring up, move up. **4** (*fig.*, *coll.*) (*ученика*) to take in hand, pull up, chase up.

подтя|нýться, нýсь, ~нешься *pf.* (*of* ⇨**~гиваться**) **1** to gird o.s. more tightly; **п. пóясом** to tighten one's belt. **2** (*на перекладине*) to pull o.s. up (*on gymnastic apparatus, etc.*). **3** (*mil.*) to move up, move in. **4** (*fig.*, *coll.*) (*об ученике*) to pull o.s. together, take o.s. in hand.

подýма|ть, ю *pf.* **1** *pf. of* ⇨**дýмать; п. (тóлько), ~й(те) (тóлько)!** just think!; **~ешь** (*as iron. int.*; *coll.*) I say!; what do you know?; **~ешь, какáя блестя́щая мысль!** well, what a brainwave!; **и не ~ю!** I wouldn't dream of it; **мóжно п.** one might think. **2** (*немного*) to think a little, for a while.

подýмыва|ть, ю *impf.* (**о**+*p. or* +*inf.*; *coll.*) to think (of, about); **п. об отъéзде, п. уéхать** to think of leaving.

по-дурáцки *adv.* (*coll.*) foolishly, like a fool.

подурáч|иться, усь, ишься *pf.* (*coll.*) to fool about, play the fool.

подурнé|ть, ю *pf. of* ⇨**дурнéть**

подý|ть, ю, ешь *pf.* **1** *pf. of* ⇨**дуть 1. 2** (*начать дуть*) to begin to blow.

подýчива|ть(ся), ю(сь) *impf. of* ⇨**подучи́ть(ся)**

подуч|и́ть, ý, ~ишь *pf.* (*of* ⇨**~ивать**) **1** (+*a. and d.*) to teach, instruct (in); **п. когó-н. стрельбé** to give s.o. a few lessons in shooting. **2** (*урок*) to learn. **3** (*inf.*; *coll.*) (*подговорить*) to egg on (to), put up (to).

подуч|и́ться, ýсь, ~ишься *pf.* to learn (a little more, a little better).

подýшечк|а, и *f. dim. of* ⇨**подýшка; п. для булáвок** pincushion.

подуш|и́ть, ý, ~ишь *pf.* to spray with perfume.

подуш|и́ться, ýсь, ~ишься *pf.* to put some perfume on.

подýшк|а, и *f.* (*в постели*) pillow; (*диванная*) cushion; **воздушная п.** air-cushion.

подýшн|ый *adj.*: **~ая пóдать** (*hist.*) poll-tax.

подфáрник, а *m.* sidelight (*Br.*), sidemarker light (*US*).

подхали́м, а *m.* toady.

подхалимáж, а *m.* (*coll.*) toadying, grovelling (*Br.*), groveling (*US*).

подхали́мнича|ть, ю *impf.* (*coll.*) to toady.

подхали́мств|о, а *nt.* = **подхалимáж**

подхалтýрива|ть, ю *impf. of* ⇨**подхалтýрить**

подхалтýр|ить, ю, ишь *pf.* (*of* ⇨**~ивать**) (*coll.*) to earn on the side.

подхва|ти́ть, чý, ~тишь *pf.* (*of* ⇨**~тывать**) to catch (up); to pick up; to take up; **п. сýмку** to catch up one's bag; **п. мяч** to catch a ball; **п. нáсморк** to catch, pick up a cold; **п. пéсню** to catch up a melody, join in a song.

подхвáтыва|ть, ю *impf. of* ⇨**подхвати́ть**

подхлест|нýть, нý, нёшь *pf.* (*of* ⇨**~ывать**) to whip up (*also fig.*, *coll.*).

подхлёстыва|ть, ю *impf. of* ⇨**подхлестнýть**

подхóд, а *m.* approach.

подхо|ди́ть, жý, ~дишь *impf. of* ⇨**подойти́**

подходя́|щий *pres. part. of* ⇨**~и́ть** *and adj.* suitable, appropriate; **п. момéнт** the right moment.

подцеп|и́ть, лю́, ~ишь *pf.* (*of* ⇒**~ля́ть**) to hook on, couple on; (*fig., joc.*) to pick up; **п. на́сморк** to pick up a cold.

подцепля́|ть, ю *impf. of* ⇒**подцепи́ть**

подча́с *adv.* sometimes, at times.

подчёркива|ть, ю *impf. of* ⇒**подчеркну́ть**

подчерк|ну́ть, ну́, нёшь *pf.* (*of* ⇒**~ивать**) **1** to underline. **2** (*fig.*) to emphasize, stress.

подчине́ни|е, я *nt.* **1** subordination; submission, subjection; **быть в ~и (у)** to be subordinate (to). **2** (*gram.*) subordination.

подчинённост|ь, и *f.* subordination.

подчин|ённый 1 *p.p.p. of* ⇒**~и́ть;** (+*d.*) under, under the command (of). **2** *adj.* subordinate; **~ённое госуда́рство** tributary state; *as n.* **п., ~ённого** *m.* subordinate.

подчини́тельный *adj.* (*gram.*) subordinating.

подчин|и́ть, ю́, и́шь *pf.* (*of* ⇒**~я́ть**) (+*d.*) to subordinate (to), subject (to); to place under the command (of); **п. свое́й во́ле** to bend to one's will.

подчин|и́ться, ю́сь, и́шься *pf.* (*of* ⇒**~я́ться**) (+*d.*) to submit (to); **п. прика́зу** to obey an order.

подчин|я́ть(ся), я́ю(сь) *impf. of* ⇒**~и́ть(ся)**

подчи́|стить, щу, стишь *pf.* (*of* ⇒**~ща́ть**) **1** (*вычистить*) to clean (up). **2** (*стереть*) to rub out, erase.

подчи́стк|а, и *f.* **1** cleaning (up). **2** erasure.

подчисту́ю *adv.* (*coll.*) completely, without remainder; **мы съе́ли всё п.** we left our plates clean.

подчища́|ть, ю *impf. of* ⇒**подчи́стить**

подше́фный *adj.* aided, assisted; (+*d.*) under the patronage (of), sponsored (by), supported (by).

подшиб|а́ть, а́ю *impf. of* ⇒**~и́ть**

подшиб|и́ть, у́, ёшь, *past* **~, ~ла** *pf.* (*of* ⇒**~а́ть**) to knock down; **п. кому́-н. глаз** to give s.o. a black eye.

подши́б|ленный *p.p.p. of* ⇒**~и́ть; п. глаз** black eye.

подшива́|ть, ю *impf. of* ⇒**подши́ть**

подши́вк|а, и *f.* **1** (*действие*) hemming; lining; soling. **2** (*у платья*) hem. **3** (*бумаг*) filing; **п. газе́ты** newspaper file.

подши́пник, а *m.* (*tech.*) bearing; **ро́ликовый п.** roller bearing; **ша́риковый п.** ball bearing.

под|ши́ть, ошью́, ошьёшь *pf.* (*of* ⇒**~шива́ть**) **1** (*пришить*) to sew on, in; (*платье, платок*) to hem; (*с изнанки*) to line; (*обувь*) to sole. **2** (*бумаги*) to file.

подшта́нник|и, ов *no sg.* (*coll.*) (*men's*) drawers.

подшто́п|ать, аю *pf.* (*of* ⇒**~ывать**) to darn.

подшто́пыва|ть, ю *impf. of* ⇒**подшто́пать**

подшу|ти́ть, чу́, ~тишь *pf.* (*of* ⇒**~чивать**) (**над** + *i.*) to make fun of; to mock; to play a trick (on).

подшу́чива|ть, ю *impf. of* ⇒**подшути́ть**

подъ...[1] *as vbl. pref.* = **под...**[1]

подъ...[2] *as pref. of nn. and adjs.* = **под...**[2]

подъеда́|ть, ю *impf. of* ⇒**подъе́сть**

подъе́зд, а *m.* **1** (*вход*) entrance, doorway. **2** (*к реке*) approach(es).

подъезд|но́й *adj. of* ⇒**~ 2; ~на́я алле́я** drive; **~на́я доро́га** access road.

подъе́зд|ный *adj. of* ⇒**~ 1**

подъезжа́|ть, ю *impf. of* ⇒**подъе́хать**

подъём, а *m.* **1** (*груза*) lifting; (*флага*) raising. **2** (*в гору*) ascent. **3** (*aeron.*) climb. **4** (*fig.*) (*рост, развитие*) development, rise, **промы́шленный п.** boom, upsurge; **круто́й п. произво́дства** a sharp rise in production; **на ~е** on the up and up. **5** (*fig.*) élan; enthusiasm, animation; **говори́ть с больши́м ~ом** to speak with great animation; **лёгок на п.** quick off the mark; **тяжёл на п.** sluggish, slow to start. **6** (*ноги*) instep. **7** (*после сна*) rising time; (*mil.*) reveille.

подъёмник, а *m.* lift (*Br.*), elevator (*US*), hoist.

подъёмн|ый *adj.* **1** lifting; **п. кран** crane; **~ое окно́** sash window. **2: п. мост** drawbridge. **3: ~ые (де́ньги)** relocation expenses.

подъ|е́сть, ем, е́шь е́ст, еди́м, еди́те, едя́т, *past* **~е́л** *pf.* (*of* ⇒**~еда́ть**) (*coll.*) to eat up, finish off.

подъе́|хать, ду, дешь *pf.* (*of* ⇒**~зжа́ть**) (**к** + *d.*) **1** (*приблизиться*) to drive up (to), draw up (to). **2** (*coll.*) (*приехать ненадолго*) to call (on). **3** (*fig., coll.*) (*подольститься*) to get round.

подыгр|а́ть, а́ю *pf.* (*of* ⇒**~ывать**) (+*d.*; *coll.*) **1** (*mus.*) to accompany. **2** (*theatr.*) to play up (to).

подыгр|а́ться, а́юсь *pf.* (*of* ⇒**~ываться**) (**к** + *d.*; *coll.*) to get round.

поды́грыва|ть, ю *impf. of* ⇒**подыгра́ть**

поды́грыва|ться, юсь *impf.* **1** *impf. of* ⇒**подыгра́ться. 2** (*impf. only*) to try to get round.

подыма́|ть(ся), ю(сь) *impf.* (*coll.*) = **поднима́ть(ся)**

поды|ска́ть, щу́, ~щешь *pf.* (*of* ⇒**~скивать**) to seek out, find.

поды́скива|ть, ю *impf.* **1** *impf. of* ⇒**подыска́ть. 2** (*impf. only*) to seek, try to find.

подыто́жива|ть, ю *impf. of* ⇒**подыто́жить**

подыто́ж|ить, у, ишь *pf.* (*of* ⇒**~ивать** *and* **ито́жить**) to sum up.

подыха́|ть, ю *impf. of* ⇒**подо́хнуть**

подыш|а́ть, у́, ~ишь *pf.* to breathe; **вы́йти п. све́жим во́здухом** to go out for a breath of fresh air.

поеда́|ть, ю *impf. of* ⇒**пое́сть**

поеди́н|ок, ка *m.* duel.

поедо́м *adv.*: **п. есть кого́-н.** (*coll.*) to make s.o.'s life a misery (by nagging).

по́езд, а, *pl.* **~а́** *m.* train; **~ом** by train; **п. да́льнего сле́дования** long-distance train; **п. прямо́го сообще́ния** through train.

пое́з|дить, жу, дишь *pf.* to travel about.

пое́здк|а, и *f.* trip, excursion, outing, tour; **ознакоми́тельная п.** fact-finding tour.

поездно́й *adj. of* ⇒**по́езд**

поезжа́й(те): *used as imper. of* ⇒**е́хать** *and* **пое́хать**

поёмн|ый *adj.* under water at flood times; **~ые луга́** water-meadows.

по|е́сть, е́м, е́шь, е́ст, еди́м, еди́те, едя́т, *past* **~е́л** *pf.* (*of* ⇒**~еда́ть**) **1** to eat (up). **2** (*немного*) to eat a little; to take some food, have a bite. **3** (*о кроликах, насекомых*) to eat, devour.

пое́|хать, ду, дешь *pf.* (*of* ⇒**е́хать**) to go (*in or on a vehicle or on an animal*); (*отправиться*) to set off, depart; **~хали!** (*coll.*) let's go!; **ну, ~хал!** (*coll.*) now he's off!

пожале́|ть, ю *pf. of* ⇒**жале́ть**

пожа́л|овать, ую *pf. of* ⇒**жа́ловать; добро́ п.!** welcome!; **~уйте** *formula of polite request;* **~уйте сюда́!** this way, please!; **~уйте в столо́вую!** dinner (supper, *etc.*) is served!

пожа́л|оваться, уюсь *pf. of* ⇒**жа́ловаться**

пожа́луй *adv.* perhaps; very likely; it may be; **мы, п., пое́дем** we shall very likely go; **п., ты прав** you may be right; **по мне п.** (*coll.*) it's all right by me.

пожа́луйста *particle* **1** (*при просьбе*) please; **сади́тесь, п.** please sit down. **2** (*при согласии*) certainly!, by all means!, with pleasure! (*or not translated*); **мо́жно посмотре́ть э́ти сни́мки? — п.** may I look at these photos? Certainly; **переда́йте мне, п., кни́гу. — п.** would you mind passing me the book? — There you are. **3** (*в ответ на «спасибо»*) don't mention it; not at all.

пожа́р, а *m.* fire; **как на п. бежа́ть** (*coll.*) to run like hell; **не на п.!** (*coll.*) hold your horses!; there's no hurry!

пожа́рищ|е[1]**, а** *m.* (*coll.*) big fire.

пожа́рищ|е[2]**, а** *nt.* (*место*) site of a fire.

пожа́рник, а *m.* (*coll.*) fireman.

пожа́р|ный *adj. of* ⇒**~; ~ная кома́нда** fire-brigade; **~ная ле́стница** fire escape; **~ная маши́на** fire-engine; **в ~ном поря́дке** (*coll., joc.*) hastily, in slapdash fashion; **на вся́кий п. слу́чай** (*coll., joc.*) in case of dire need; just in case; *as n.* **п., ~ного** *m.* fireman.

пожа́ти|е, я *nt.*: **п. руки́** handshake.

по|жа́ть[1]**, жму́, жмёшь** *pf.* (*of* ⇒**~жима́ть**) to press, squeeze; **п. ру́ку** (+*d.*) to shake hands (with); **п. плеча́ми** to shrug one's shoulders.

по|жа́ть[2]**, жну́, жнёшь** *pf.* (*of* ⇒**~жина́ть**) to reap (*also fig.*); **п. сла́ву** to win renown; **п. плоды́ чужо́го**

П

труда́ (*fig.*) to reap where one has not sown; **что посе́ешь, то и ~жнёшь** (*prov.*) one must reap as one has sown.

по|жа́ться, жму́сь, жмёшься *pf.* (*of* ⇨**~жима́ться**) to shrink up, huddle up.

пож|ева́ть, ую́, уёшь *pf.* (*of* ⇨**~ёвывать**) to chew.

пожёвыва|ть, ю *impf. of* ⇨**пожева́ть**

пожела́ни|е, я *nt.* wish, desire.

пожела́|ть, ю *pf. of* ⇨**жела́ть**

пожелте́лый *adj.* yellowed.

пожелте́|ть, ю *pf. of* ⇨**желте́ть**

пожен|и́ть, ю́, ~ишь *pf. of* ⇨**жени́ть**

пожен|и́ться, ~имся *pf.* (*pl. used only; of two people*) to get married.

поже́ртвовани|е, я *nt.* donation.

поже́ртв|овать, ую *pf. of* ⇨**же́ртвовать**

по|же́чь, жгу́, жжёшь, жгу́т, *past* **~жёг, ~жгла́** *pf.* to burn up; to destroy by fire.

пожи́в|а, ы *f.* (*coll.*) gain, profit.

пожива́|ть, ю *impf.* to live; **как (вы) ~ете?** how are you (getting on)?

пожив|и́ться, лю́сь, и́шься *pf.* (+*i.*; *coll.*) to live (off), profit (by); **п. на счёт друго́го** to make good at another's expense.

пожи́|вший *p.p. act. of* ⇨**~ть** *and adj.* (*usu. pej.*) experienced.

пожи́зненн|ый *adj.* life(long); for life; **~ое заключе́ние** life imprisonment; **~ая ре́нта** life annuity.

пожило́й *adj.* elderly.

пожима́|ть(ся), ю(сь) *impf. of* ⇨**пожа́ть[1](ся)**

пожина́|ть, ю *impf. of* ⇨**пожа́ть[2]**

пожира́|ть, ю *impf. of* ⇨**пожра́ть; п. глаза́ми** to devour with one's eyes.

пожи́тк|и, ов *no sg.* (*coll.*) belongings; (one's) things; **со все́ми ~ами** bag and baggage.

по|жи́ть, живу́, живёшь, *past* **~жил, ~жила́, ~жило** *pf.* **1** to live (*for a time*); to stay; **мы ~жили три го́да в Ки́еве** we lived for three years in Kiev. **2** (*coll.*) to live it up; **~живём-уви́дим** we shall see what we shall see.

пожм|у́, ёшь *see* ⇨**пожа́ть[1]**

пожн|у́, ёшь *see* ⇨**пожа́ть[2]**

пожр|а́ть, у́, ёшь, *past* **~а́л, ~ала́, ~а́ло** *pf.* (*of* ⇨**пожира́ть**) to devour.

по́з|а, ы *f.* pose, attitude, posture; (*fig.*) pose; **приня́ть каку́ю-н. ~у** to strike an attitude, adopt a pose; **приня́ть ~у вели́кого учёного** to pose as a great scholar; **э́то то́лько п.** it is a mere pose.

позаба́в|ить, лю, ишь *pf.* to amuse a little.

позаба́в|иться, люсь, ишься *pf.* to amuse o.s. a little.

позабо́|титься, чусь, тишься *pf. of* ⇨**забо́титься**

позабыва́|ть, ю *impf. of* ⇨**позабы́ть**

позаб|ы́ть, у́ду, у́дешь *pf.* (*of* ⇨**~ыва́ть**) (+*a. or* **о**+*p.*; *coll.*) to forget (about).

позави́д|овать, ую *pf. of* ⇨**зави́довать**

поза́втрака|ть, ю *pf. of* ⇨**за́втракать**

позавчера́ *adv.* the day before yesterday.

позавчера́|шний *adj. of* ⇨**~**

позади́[1] *adv.* (*of place*; *fig. of time*) behind; **оста́вить п.** to leave behind; **наиху́дшие времена́ оста́лись п.** the worst times are past.

позади́[2] *prep.*+*g.* behind.

поза́имств|овать, ую *pf. of* ⇨**заи́мствовать**

позапро́шлый *adj.* before last; **п. год** the year before last.

поза́р|иться, юсь, ишься *pf. of* ⇨**за́риться**

по|зва́ть, зову́, зовёшь, *past* **~зва́л, ~звала́, ~зва́ло** *pf. of* ⇨**звать**

по-зве́рски *adv.* brutally, like a beast.

позволе́ни|е, я *nt.* permission; **с ва́шего ~я** with your permission; **с ~я сказа́ть** if one may say so; **э́тот, с ~я сказа́ть, вождь** (*iron.*) this apology for a leader; this, if one may so call him, leader.

позволи́тел|ьный (~ен, ~ьна) *adj.* permissible.

позво́л|ить, ю, ишь *pf.* (*of* ⇨**~я́ть**) (+*d. of person and inf.*, +*a. of inanimate object*) to allow, permit; **е́сли доктора́ ~ят мне пое́хать, я уви́жу вас в Москве́** if the doctors allow me to travel, I shall see you in Moscow; **п. себе́** (+*inf.*) to venture, take the liberty (of); (+*a.*) to be able to afford; **п. себе́ сде́лать замеча́ние** to venture a remark; **п. себе́ пое́здку в Пари́ж** to be able to afford a trip to Paris; **~ь(те)** (*i*) *polite form of request* **~ьте предста́вить до́ктора Х.** allow me to introduce Doctor X., (*ii*) *expr. of disagreement or objection* **~ьте, что э́то зна́чит?** excuse me, what does that mean?

позвол|я́ть, я́ю *impf. of* ⇨**~ить**

позвон|и́ть(ся), ю́(сь), и́шь(ся) *pf. of* ⇨**звони́ть(ся)**

позвон|о́к, ка́ *m.* (*anat.*) vertebra.

позвоно́чник, а *m.* (*anat.*) spine, backbone.

позвоно́чн|ый *adj.* (*anat.*) vertebral; **п. столб** spinal column; *as n.* **~ые, ~ых** (*zool.*) vertebrates.

поздн|ее *comp. of* ⇨**~ий** *and* **~о** later.

поздне́йший *adj.* (*более поздний*) later; (*самый поздний*) latest.

по́здн|ий *adj.* late; **до ~ей но́чи** until late at night, late into the night; **~о** it is late.

по́здно *adv.* late.

поздоро́ва|ться, юсь *pf. of* ⇨**здоро́ваться**

поздорове́|ть, ю *pf. of* ⇨**здорове́ть**

поздоро́в|иться, ится *pf. only in phr.* (*coll.*): **не ~ится ему́,** *etc.* (**от**+*g.*) much good will it do him, *etc.*; he, *etc.* will be in trouble.

поздрави́тел|ь, я *m.* bearer of congratulations, well-wisher.

поздрави́тельн|ый *adj.* congratulatory; **~ая ка́рточка** greetings card.

поздра́в|ить, лю, ишь *pf.* (*of* ⇨**~ля́ть**) (**с**+*i.*) to congratulate (on, upon); **п. кого́-н. с днём рожде́ния** to wish s.o. many happy returns of the day; **п. кого́-н. с Но́вым го́дом** to wish s.o. a happy New Year.

поздравле́ни|е, я *nt.* congratulation, greeting(s).

поздравля́|ть, ю *impf. of* ⇨**поздра́вить**

позёвыва|ть, ю *impf.* (*coll.*) to yawn (from time to time).

позелене́|ть, ю *pf. of* ⇨**зелене́ть 1**

позелен|и́ть, ю́, и́шь *pf. of* ⇨**зелени́ть**

поземе́льный *adj.* land; **п. нало́г** land-tax.

позёмк|а, и *f.* blizzard accompanied by ground wind.

позёр, а *m.* poseur; pseud.

по́з|же *comp. of* ⇨**~дний** *and* **~дно;** later (on).

по-зи́мнему *adv.* as in winter, as for winter; **оде́т п.** (dressed) in winter clothes.

пози́р|овать, ую *impf.* (+*d.*) to pose (for); (*fig.*) to pose.

позити́в, а *m.* (*phot.*) positive.

позитиви́зм, а *m.* (*phil.*) positivism.

позитиви́ст, а *m.* (*phil.*) positivist.

позити́в|ный (~ен, ~на) *adj.* positive.

позитро́н, а *m.* (*phys.*) positron, positive electron.

позицио́нн|ый *adj. of* ⇨**пози́ция; ~ая война́** trench warfare.

пози́ци|я, и *f.* position; **выжида́тельная п.** wait-and-see attitude; **заня́ть ~ю** (*mil.*) to take up a position; (*fig.*) to take one's stand; **с ~и си́лы** from (a position of) strength.

позла|ти́ть, щу́, ти́шь *pf.* (*of* ⇨**~ща́ть**) (*obs. or fig.*) to gild.

позлаща́|ть, ю *impf. of* ⇨**позлати́ть**

позл|и́ть, ю́, и́шь *pf.* to tease a little.

познава́ем|ый (~, ~а) *pres. part. pass. of* ⇨**познава́ть** *and adj.* knowable.

познава́тельный *adj.* cognitive; (*обучающий*) educational; **п. проце́сс** cognition.

позна|ва́ть, ю́, ёшь *impf. of* ⇨**~ть**

позна|ва́ться, ю́сь, ёшься *impf.* (*no pf.*) to become known; **друзья́ ~ю́тся в беде́** (*prov.*) a friend in need is a friend indeed.

познако́м|ить(ся), лю(сь), ишь(ся) *pf. of* ⇨**знако́мить(ся)**

познако́м|ленный *p.p.p. of* ⇨**~ить**

позна́ни|е, я *nt.* **1** (*phil.*) cognition;

теория ~я epistemology. **2** (*pl.*) knowledge.

позна́|ть, ю *pf.* (*of* ⇒**~ва́ть**) to get to know; to become acquainted with; (*phil.*) to cognize; **п. го́ре** to become acquainted with grief; to know grief; to experience grief.

позоло́т|а, ы *f.* gilding, gilt.

позоло|ти́ть, чу́, ти́шь *pf. of* ⇒**золоти́ть**

позо́р, а *m.* shame, disgrace; **быть ~ом (для)** to be a disgrace (to); **вы́ставить на п.** to put to shame; **покры́ть себя́ ~ом** to disgrace o.s.

позо́р|ить, ю, ишь *impf.* (*of* ⇒**о~**) to disgrace.

позо́р|иться, юсь, ишься *impf.* (*of* ⇒**о~**) to disgrace o.s.

позо́рищ|е, а *nt.* (*coll.*) shameful event, disgrace.

позо́р|ный (~ен, ~на) *adj.* shameful, disgraceful; ignominious; **п. столб** pillory; **поста́вить к ~ному столбу́** (*fig.*) to pillory.

позуме́нт, а *m.* galoon, braid; **золото́й п.** gold braid.

позы́в, а *m.* urge; **п. на рво́ту** urge to be sick, (feeling of) nausea.

позыва́|ть, ет *impf.* (*impers.*) to feel an urge, feel a need; **меня́ ~ет на рво́ту** I feel an urge to be sick.

позывн|о́й *adj.*: **п. сигна́л** (*radio*) call sign; *as n.* **~ы́е, ~ы́х** call sign.

поигра́|ть, ю *pf.* to have a game, play a little.

пои́грыва|ть, ю *impf.* (*coll.*) to play now and then.

по́илк|а, и *f.* **1** (*скота*) feeding-trough; feeding-bowl. **2** (*больного*) feeding-vessel.

поимённо *adv.* by name.

поимённый *adj.* nominal; **п. спи́сок** list of names.

поимен|ова́ть, у́ю *pf.* to name, call out by name.

по́имк|а, и *f.* capture.

поиму́щественный *adj.*: **п. нало́г** property tax.

по-ино́му *adv.* differently, in a different way.

поинтерес|ова́ться, у́юсь *pf.* (+*i.*) to be curious (about); to display interest (in); **он ~ова́лся узна́ть, кто вы** he was curious to find out who you are.

по́иск, а *m.* **1** (*pl.*) search (*also comput.*); **в ~ах** (+*g.*) in search (of), in quest (of). **2** (*mil.*) (reconnaissance) raid.

пои|ска́ть, щу́, ~щешь *pf.* to look for, search for; **~щи́те хороше́нько** have a good look.

по́исков|ый *adj.*: **~ая систе́ма** (*comput.*) search engine.

пои́стине *adv.* indeed, in truth.

по|и́ть, ю́, ~и́шь *impf.* (*of* ⇒**на~**) to give to drink; (*скота*) to water; **п. вино́м** to treat to wine; **п. и корми́ть семью́** to maintain the family.

по|ищу́, и́щешь *see* ⇒**~иска́ть**

пой|ду́, дёшь *see* ⇒**~ти́**

по́йл|о, а *nt.* swill, mash; **п. для свине́й** pig-swill.

по́йм|а, ы, *g. pl.* **~** *f.* flood-lands; water-meadow.

пойма́|ть, ю *pf. of* ⇒**лови́ть**

пойм|у́, ёшь *see* ⇒**поня́ть**

по́йнтер, а *m.* (*dog*) pointer.

пой|ти́, ду́, дёшь, *past* **пошёл, пошла́** *pf.* **1** *pf. of* ⇒**идти́** *and* **ходи́ть; пошёл!** off you go!; **пошёл вон!** be off!; off with you!; **уж е́сли на то пошло́** if it comes to that; for that matter; **(так) не ~дёт** (*coll.*) that won't work. **2** (*начать ходить*) to begin to (be able to) walk. **3** (*coll.*) (*начать*) to begin. **4** (**в**+*a.*) to take after; **он пошёл в отца́** he takes after his father.

пока́[1] *adv.* for the present, for the time being; **п. что** (*coll.*) in the meanwhile; **п. ещё, п.-то ещё** (*coll.*) not for a while yet; **э́то п. всё** that is all for now; **не беспоко́йтесь, п.-то ещё он появи́тся** don't worry, he won't turn up for a while yet; **ну, п.!** (*coll.*) cheerio!; bye!

пока́[2] *conj.* **1** while; **нам на́до попроси́ть его́, п. он тут** we must ask him while he is here. **2**: **п. не** until, till, before; **не на́до уходи́ть, п. она́ не придёт** we must not go until she comes; **п. ещё не по́здно** before it's too late.

пока́з, а *m.* (*фильма*) showing; (*эксперимента*) demonstration; (*fig.*) (*жизни*) portrayal.

показа́ни|е, я *nt.* (*usu. pl.*) **1** (*свидетельство*) testimony, evidence. **2** (*leg.*) deposition; affidavit; **дава́ть п.** to testify, give evidence. **3** (*прибора*) reading.

показа́тел|ь, я *m.* **1** indicator; index. **2** (*math.*) exponent, index.

показа́тел|ьный (~ен, ~ьна) *adj.* **1** (*характерный*) significant; instructive, revealing; **о́чень ~ьное заявле́ние** a very significant pronouncement. **2** (*образцовый*) model; demonstration; **п. проце́сс** show-trial; **п. уро́к** object-lesson; **~ьное хозя́йство** model farm. **3** (*math.*) exponential.

пока|за́ть, жу́, ~жешь *pf.* (*of* ⇒**~зывать**) **1** to show; to display, reveal; **п. себя́** to prove o.s. *or* one's worth; **он ~за́л себя́ хоро́шим ора́тором** he has shown himself to be a good speaker; **п. свои́ зна́ния** to display one's knowledge; **они́ ~за́ли де́вочку врачу́** they took the little girl to the doctor; **он ~за́л вид, что се́рдится** he feigned anger. **2** (*о приборе*) to show, register, read. **3** (**на**+*a.*) to point (at, to); **п. кому́-н. на дверь** (*fig., coll.*) to show s.o. the door. **4** (*leg.*) to testify, give evidence.

пока|за́ться, жу́сь, ~жешься *pf.* **1** *pf. of* ⇒**каза́ться. 2** (*pf. of* ⇒**~зываться**) to show o.s.; to appear; to come in sight; **из-за облако́в ~за́лась луна́** the moon appeared from behind the clouds; **п. врачу́** to see a doctor. **3** *pass. of* ⇒**~за́ть**

показно́й *adj.* (*сочувствие*) affected; (*роскошь*) ostentatious.

показу́х|а, и *f.* (*coll.*) show; **э́то сплошна́я п.** it's all put on, just for show.

пока́зыва|ть(ся), ю(сь) *impf. of* ⇒**показа́ть(ся)**

пока́лыва|ть, ю *impf.* to prick occasionally; (*impers.*): **у меня́ ~ет в боку́** I have occasional stabbing pains in my side.

покаля́ка|ть, ю *pf. of* ⇒**каля́кать**

пока́мест *adv. and conj.* (*coll.*) = **пока́**

покара́|ть, ю *pf. of* ⇒**кара́ть**

іпоката́|ть[1]**, ю** *pf.* to roll.

поката́|ть[2]**, ю** *pf.* to take for a drive; **п. дете́й** to take the children out.

поката́|ться, юсь *pf.* to go for a drive; **п. на ло́дке** to go out boating.

пока|ти́ть, чу́, ~тишь *pf.* **1** *pf. of* ⇒**кати́ть. 2** (*мяч*) to start (rolling), set rolling. **3** (*coll.*) (*отправиться*) to set off (*by car, bicycle*).

пока|ти́ться, чу́сь, ~тишься *pf.* **1** *pf. of* ⇒**кати́ться; п. со́ смеху** (*coll.*) to roar with laughter. **2** (*начать катиться*) to start rolling.

пока́тост|ь, и *f.* slope, incline; declivity.

пока́т|ый (~, ~а) *adj.* sloping; slanting; **п. лоб** receding forehead.

покача́|ть, ю *pf.* to rock, swing (for a time); **п. голово́й** to shake one's head.

покача́|ться, юсь *pf.* to rock, swing (for a time); to have a swing.

пока́чива|ться, юсь *impf.* to rock slightly; **идти́ ~ясь** to walk unsteadily.

покачн|у́ть, у́, ёшь *pf.* to shake.

покачн|у́ться, у́сь, ёшься *pf.* **1** to sway, totter, give a lurch. **2** (*fig., coll.*) (*ухудшиться*) to totter, go downhill.

пока́шлива|ть, ю *impf.* to have a slight cough; to cough intermittently.

пока́шля|ть, ю *pf.* to cough.

покая́ни|е, я *nt.* **1** (*eccl.*) (*исповедь*) confession. **2** (*раскаяние*) penitence, repentance; **принести́ п.** (**в**+*p.*) to repent (of).

покая́н|ный (~ен, ~на) *adj.* penitential.

пока́|яться, юсь, ешься *pf. of* ⇒**ка́яться**

поквarта́льно *adv.* quarterly.

поквита́|ться, юсь *pf.* (**с**+*i.*; *coll.*) to get even (with); **тепе́рь мы с ва́ми ~лись** now we're quits; **я ещё с ним ~юсь** I'll get even with him yet.

по́кер, а *m.* poker (*card-game*).

по́кер|ный *adj. of* ⇒**~**

покива́|ть, ю *pf.* to nod (*several times*).

покида́|ть, ю *impf. of* ⇒**поки́нуть**

поки́нут|ый *p.p.p. of* ⇒**~ь** *and adj.* deserted; abandoned.

поки́|нуть, ну, нешь *pf.* (*of* ⇒**~да́ть**) to leave; to desert, abandon, forsake.

поклада́я *only in phr.* **не п. рук** indefatigably.

покла́дист|ый (~, ~а) *adj.* complaisant, obliging.

покла́ж|а, и *f.* (*coll.*) load; luggage.

поклёп, а *m.* (*coll.*) slander, calumny; **взвести́/возвести́ п.** (**на**+*a.*) to slander, cast aspersions (on).

покли́|кать, чу, чешь *pf.* (*coll.*) to call (to).

П

поклóн, а *m.* **1** bow; **сдéлать п.** to bow (*in greeting*); **класть ~ы** to bow (*in prayer*); **идтú на п., идтú с ~ом к комý-н.** to go cap in hand to s.o. **2** (*fig.*) (*привет*) greeting; **послáть ~ы** to send one's compliments, send one's kind regards.

поклонéни|е, я *nt.* worship.

поклон|úться, ю́сь, ~ишься *pf. of* ⇒**клáняться**

поклóнник, а *m.* admirer; (*relig.*) worshipper.

поклóнни|ца, цы *f. of* ⇒**~к**

покланя́|ться, юсь *impf.* (+*d.*) to worship.

покля́|сться, нýсь, нёшься *pf. of* ⇒**кля́сться**

покóвк|а, и *f.* (*tech.*) forging; forged piece.

покóем *adv.* (*obs.*) in the shape of the letter **п.**

покó|ить, ю, ишь *impf.* (*obs.*) to tend, cherish.

покó|иться, юсь, ишься *impf.* **1** (**на**+*p.*) to rest (on, upon), repose (on, upon), be based (on, upon); **п. на догáдке** to be based on conjecture. **2** (*об умерших*) to lie; **здесь ~ится прах** (+*g.*) here lies (the body of).

покó|й¹, я *m.* rest, peace; **вéчный п.** (*fig., poet.*) eternal rest; **остáвить в ~е** to leave in peace; **уйтú на п., удалúться на п.** to retire.

покó|й², я *m.* (*obs.*) (*комната*) room, chamber; **приёмный п.** reception ward (*in hospital*).

покóйник, а *m.* the deceased.

покóйни|ца, цы *f. of* ⇒**~к**

покóйницк|ая, ой *f.* mortuary.

покó|йный¹ (~ен, ~йна) *adj.* **1** (*спокойный*) calm, quiet; **бýдьте ~йны** don't be alarmed; don't (you) worry. **2** (*удобный*) comfortable; restful; **~йной нóчи!** good night!

покóйн|ый² *adj.* (*умерший*) (the) late; **п. корóль** the late king; *as n.* **п., ~ого** *m.*, **~ая, ~ой** *f.* the deceased.

поколеб|áть, ~лю, ~лешь *pf. of* ⇒**колебáть**

поколеб|áться, ~люсь, ~лешься *pf.* **1** *pf. of* ⇒**колебáться. 2** to waver (for a time), hesitate (for a time).

поколéни|е, я *nt.* generation; **из ~я в п.** from generation to generation.

поколо|тúть(ся), чý(сь), ~тишь(ся) *pf. of* ⇒**колотúть(ся)**

покóнч|ить, у, ишь *pf.* (**с**+*i.*) **1** (*завершить*) to finish off; to finish (with), be through (with), have done (with); **с э́тим ~ено** that's done with. **2** (*уничтожить*) to put an end (to); to do away (with); **п. с собóй** to put an end to one's life; to do away with o.s.; **п. жизнь самоубúйством** to commit suicide.

покорéни|е, я *nt.* conquest.

покорúтел|ь, я *m.* conqueror; **п. сердéц** lady-killer.

покор|úть, ю́, úшь *pf.* (*of* ⇒**~я́ть**) to conquer, subdue; **п. чьё-н. сéрдце** to win s.o.'s heart.

покор|úться, ю́сь, úшься *pf.* (*of* ⇒**~я́ться**) (+*d.*) to submit (to); to resign o.s. (to); **п. своéй ýчасти** to resign o.s. to one's lot.

покорм|úть(ся), лю́(сь), ~ишь(ся) *pf. of* ⇒**кормúть(ся)**

покóрн|ейший *superl. of* ⇒**~ый**

покóрно *adv.* humbly; submissively, obediently; **п. благодарю́** (*coll.*) thank you; **благодарю́ п.** (*iron.*; *expr. refusal and/or astonishment*) thank you (very much)!

покóрност|ь, и *f.* submissiveness, obedience.

покóр|ный (~ен, ~на) *adj.* **1** (+*d.*) submissive (to), obedient; **п. судьбé** resigned to one's fate. **2** (*in conventional expressions of politeness*; *obs.*) humble, obedient; **ваш п. слугá** your obedient servant.

покорóб|ить(ся), лю, ит(ся) *pf. of* ⇒**корóбить(ся)**

покóрств|овать, ую *impf.* (*obs., poet.*) (+*d.*) to submit (to).

покор|я́ть(ся), я́ю(сь) *impf. of* ⇒**~úть(ся)**

покóс, а *m.* **1** (*действие*) mowing; (*время косьбы*) haymaking. **2** (*место косьбы*) meadow(-land).

покосú|вшийся *p.p. of* ⇒**~ться** *and adj.* rickety, ramshackle.

покоc|úться, шýсь, сúшься *pf. of* ⇒**косúться**

покрáж|а, и *f.* **1** (*кража*) theft. **2** (*obs.*) (*вещи*) stolen goods.

покрáп|ать, лет *pf.* (*o дожде*) to spit.

покрáпыва|ть, ет *impf.*; (*impers.*): **~л дождь, ~ло** it was spitting (with rain) off and on.

покрá|сить(ся), шу(сь), сишь(ся) *pf. of* ⇒**крáсить(ся)**

покрáск|а, и *f.* painting, colouring.

покраснé|ть, ю *pf. of* ⇒**краснéть** 1,2

покрив|úть(ся), лю́(сь), úшь(ся) *pf. of* ⇒**кривúть(ся)**

покрúкива|ть, ю *impf.* (**на**+*a.*; *coll.*) to shout (at) (*a little, for a time*).

покритик|овáть, ýю *pf.* (*coll.*) to criticize.

покрóв¹, а *m.* **1** cover; covering; (*fig.*) cloak, shroud, pall; **пóчвенный п.** top-soil; **снéжный п.** blanket of snow; **под ~ом нóчи** under cover of night. **2** (*fig., obs.*) protection; **взять под свой п.** to take under one's protection.

Покрóв², á *m.* (*eccl.*) (Feast of) the Protection, Protective Veil (of the Virgin).

покровúтел|ь, я *m.* patron, protector.

покровúтельниц|а, ы *f.* patroness, protectress.

покровúтельствен|ный (~, ~на) *adj.* **1** protective; **~ная систéма** (*econ.*) protectionism; **~ная окрáска** (*zool.*) protective colouring (*Br.*), coloring (*US*). **2** (*снисходительный*) condescending, patronizing.

покровúтельств|о, а *nt.* protection, patronage; **О́бщество ~а живóтным** Society for the Prevention of Cruelty to Animals; **под ~ом** (+*g.*) under the patronage (of), under the auspices (of).

покровúтельств|овать, ую *impf.* (+*d.*) to protect, patronize.

покрó|й, я *m.* cut (*of garment*); **все на одúн п.** (*fig.*) all in the same style.

покрош|úть, ý, ~ишь *pf.* (+*a. or g.*) (*хлеб*) to crumble; (*лук*) to chop.

покруглé|ть, ю *pf. of* ⇒**круглéть**

покруж|úть, ý, ~úшь *pf.* (*coll.*) **1** to circle several times. **2** (*плутать*) to roam, wander (*a while*).

покрупнé|ть, ю *pf. of* ⇒**крупнéть**

покрывáл|о, а *nt.* **1** (*кусок ткани*) cover; (*на кровать*) bedspread, counterpane. **2** shawl; (*вуаль*) veil. **3** (*туманное, дымное*) layer, covering, veil.

покрывá|ть(ся), ю(сь) *impf. of* ⇒**покры́ть(ся)**

покры́ти|е, я *nt.* **1** covering; **п. дорóги** road surfacing; **п. кры́ши** roofing. **2** (*возмещение*) covering, discharge, payment; **п. расхóдов** defrayment of expenses.

покр|ы́ть, óю, óешь *pf.* (*of* ⇒**крыть** *and* **~ывáть**) **1** to cover; **п. кры́шей** to roof; **п. крáской** to coat with paint; **п. лáком** to varnish, lacquer; **п. позóром** to cover with shame; **п. тáйной** to shroud in mystery. **2** (*возместить*) to meet, pay off; **п. расхóды** to cover expenses, defray expenses. **3** (*звуки*) to drown. **4** (*не выдать*) to shield, cover up (for); to hush up. **5** (*расстояние*) to cover.

покр|ы́ться, óюсь, óешься *pf.* (*of* ⇒**~ывáться**) (+*i.*) **1** (*накрыть себя*) to cover o.s. (with). **2** (*заполниться, усеяться*) to be, get covered (with).

покры́шк|а, и *f.* **1** (*coll.*) cover(ing). **2** (*автомобиля*) tyre (*Br.*), tire (*US*).

покýда *adv. and conj.* (*coll.*) = **покá**

покупáтел|ь, я *m.* (*дома, машины*) buyer, purchaser; (*в магазине*) customer.

покупáтель|ница, ницы *f. of* ⇒**~**

покупáтельн|ый *adj.* purchasing; **~ая спосóбность** (*econ.*) purchasing power.

покупáтель|ский *adj. of* ⇒**~**

покупá|ть¹, ю *impf. of* ⇒**купúть**

покупá|ть², ю *pf.* (*ребёнка*) to bath (*Br.*), bathe (*US*).

покупá|ться, юсь *pf.* (*в море*) to bathe (*Br.*), to go bathing; (*в ванне*) to take a bath.

покýпк|а, и *f.* **1** (*действие*) buying; purchasing, purchase. **2** (*вещь*) purchase; **вы́годная п.** bargain; **дéлать ~и** to go shopping.

покуп|нóй *adj.* **1** bought (*opp. home-made or received as a gift*). **2** = **~áтельный; ~нáя ценá** purchase price.

покýрива|ть, ю *impf.* (*coll.*) to smoke (a little, from time to time).

покур|úть, ю́, ~ишь *pf.* **1** *pf. of* ⇒**курúть. 2** to have a smoke; **давáй ~им** let's have a smoke.

покуса́|ть, ю *pf.* to bite; (*о пчёлах*) to sting.

поку|си́ться, шу́сь, си́шься *pf.* (*of* ⇒**~ша́ться**) (**на**+*a.*) **1** (*попытаться сделать что-н.*) to attempt, make an attempt (upon); **п. на чью-н. жизнь** make an attempt on s.o.'s life. **2** (*попытаться завладеть чем-н.*) to encroach (on, upon); **п. на чьи-н. права́** to encroach on s.o.'s rights.

поку́ша|ть, ю *pf. of* ⇒**ку́шать**

покуша́|ться, юсь *impf. of* ⇒**покуси́ться**

покуше́ни|е, я *nt.* attempt; **п. на жизнь** (+*g.*) (*or* **на**+*a.*) attempt upon the life (of).

пол[1]**, а, о ~́е, на ~у́,** *pl.* **~ы́** *m.* floor.

пол[2]**, а** *m.* sex; **обо́его ~́а** of both sexes.

пол... *comb. form, abbr. of* ***полови́на***; half (*as in* **полчаса́** half an hour; **полдеся́того** half past nine; **полдю́жины** half a dozen, *etc.*).

пол|а́, ы́, *pl.* **~́ы** *f.* skirt, flap, lap; **из-под ~ы́** on the sly, under cover; **торгова́ть из-под ~ы́** to sell under the counter.

полага́|ть, ю *impf.* to suppose, think; **~ют, что он умира́ет** he is believed to be dying; **на́до п.** it is to be supposed; one must suppose.

полага́|ться, юсь *impf.* **1** *impf. of* ⇒**положи́ться. 2** (*impers.*): **~ется** one is supposed (to); **так ~ется** it is the custom; **не ~ется** it is not done; **здесь ~ется снима́ть шля́пу** one is supposed to take off one's hat here. **3**: **~ется** (+*d.*) to be due (to); **нам э́то ~ется** it is our due; we have a right to it.

пола́|дить, жу, дишь *pf.* (**с**+*i.*) to come to an understanding (with); to get on (with).

пола́ком|ить(ся), лю(сь), ишь(ся) *pf. of* ⇒**ла́комить(ся)**

пола́т|и, ей *no sg.* sleeping-bench (*on high raised platform in peasant hut*).

по́лб|а, ы *f.* (*bot.*) spelt, German wheat.

полбеды́ *f. indecl., as pred.* (*coll.*) a minor misfortune; **э́то ещё п.** it is not so very serious.

полве́ка, полуве́ка *m.* half a century.

полго́да, полуго́да *m.* half a year, six months; **с п., о́коло полуго́да** for about six months.

полго́ря *nt. indecl.* = **полбеды́**

по́лдень, полу́дня *and* **по́лдня** *m.* noon, midday; **за п.** (*or* **за́ полдень**) past noon; **к полу́дню** towards noon.

полдне́вный *adj. of* ⇒**по́лдень**

по́лдник, а *m.* (afternoon) snack.

по́лдннича|ть *impf.* (*coll.*) to have an (afternoon) snack.

полдоро́г|и *f.* half-way; **встре́титься на ~е** to meet half-way; **останови́ться на ~е** to stop half-way (*also fig.*).

по́л|е, я, *pl.* **~я́, ~е́й** *nt.* **1** field; **спорти́вное п.** playing field; **п. би́твы, п. сраже́ния** battle-field; **п. зре́ния** field of vision. **2** (*art*) ground; (*heraldry*) field. **3** (*pl.*) (*чистая полоса*) margin; **заме́тки на ~я́х** notes in the margin. **4** (*pl.*) (*шляпы*) brim.

полеве́|ть, ю *pf. of* ⇒**леве́ть**

полёвк|а, и *f.* field-vole.

полево́дств|о, а *nt.* field-crop cultivation.

полев|о́й *adj.* field; **п. бино́кль** field glasses; **~а́я мышь** field-mouse; **~ы́е усло́вия** field conditions; **~ы́е цветы́** wild flowers.

полега́ни|е, я *nt.* (*agric.*) lodging (*of crops*).

полега́|ть, ю *impf. of* ⇒**поле́чь** 3

полего́ньку *adv.* (*coll.*) by easy stages.

полегча́|ть, ет *pf. of* ⇒**легча́ть; больно́му ~ло** the patient is feeling better; **у меня́ на душе́ ~ло** I feel a load off my mind.

поле́гче *comp. of* ⇒**лёгкий** *and* **легко́ 1** (*somewhat, a little*) lighter. **2** a little easier, a little less difficult; **п.!** take it easy!, ease up a bit!, not so fast!

полеж|а́ть, у́, и́шь *pf.* to lie down (*for a while*).

поле́з|ный (~ен, ~на) *adj.* useful; helpful; (*пища*) wholesome, health-giving; **~ное де́йствие** efficiency, duty (*of a machine*); **~ная жила́я пло́щадь** actual living space; **э́то лека́рство о́чень ~но от ка́шля** this medicine is very good for coughs; **чем могу́ быть ~ен?** can I help you?

поле́з|ть, у, ешь, *past* **~, ~ла** *pf.* **1** *pf. of* ⇒**лезть. 2** (*начать лезть*) to start to climb.

полемизи́р|овать, ую *impf.* (**с**+*i.*) to engage in polemics (with).

поле́мик|а, и *f.* polemic(s); dispute, controversy; **вступи́ть в ~у** (**с**+*i.*) to enter into polemics (with).

полеми́ст, а *m.* polemicist.

полеми́ческий *adj.* polemic(al).

полеми́ч|ный (~ен, ~на) *adj.* polemical.

поле́нива|ться, юсь *impf.* (*coll.*) to be rather lazy.

полен|и́ться, ю́сь, ~́ишься *pf.* (+*inf.*) to be too lazy to.

поле́ни́ц|а, ы *c.g.* (*folk poet.*) hero, heroine.

поле́нниц|а, ы *f.* (*поленьев*) pile; (*дров*) stack.

поле́н|о, а, *pl.* **~ья, ~ьев** log.

поле́сь|е, я *nt.* wooded locality; woodlands.

полёт, а *m.* flight; flying; **фигу́рный п.** aerobatics; **вид с пти́чьего ~а** bird's-eye view; **п. фанта́зии** flight of fancy.

полета́|ть, ю *pf.* to fly (*for a while*), do some flying.

поле|те́ть, чу́, ти́шь *pf.* **1** *pf. of* ⇒**лете́ть. 2** (*начать лететь*) to start to fly; to fly off. **3** (*fig., coll.*) (*упасть*) to fall, go headlong.

по-ле́тнему *adv.* as in summer, as for summer; **одет п.** (dressed) in summer clothes.

полеч|и́ть, у́, ~́ишь *pf.* to treat (*for a while*).

полеч|и́ться, у́сь, ~́ишься *pf.* to undergo treatment (*for a while*).

пол|е́чь, я́гу, я́жешь, я́гут, *past* **~ёг, ~егла́** *pf.* **1** to lie down (*in numbers*). **2** (*fig.*) (*погибнуть*) to fall, be killed (*in numbers*). **3** (*impf.* **~ега́ть**) (*agric.*) to be lodged (*of standing crops*).

по́лз|ать, аю *impf., indet. of* ⇒**~ти́**

ползко́м *adv.* crawling, on all fours.

полз|ти́, у́, ёшь, *past* **~, ~ла́** *impf.* **1** to crawl, creep (along); **по́езд ~** the train was crawling. **2** (*о жидкости*) to ooze (out). **3** (*fig., coll.*) (*о слухах*) to spread. **4** (*coll.*) (*о ткани*) to fray.

ползун|о́к, ка́ *m.* **1** (*coll.*) child who can only crawl, not walk. **2** *pl.* (*coll.*) (*одежда*) rompers.

ползу́ч|ий *adj.* creeping; **~ие расте́ния** (*bot.*) creepers.

поли... *comb. form* poly-.

полиа́ндри|я, и *f.* polyandry.

полиартри́т, а *m.* (*med.*) polyarthritis.

поли́в|а, ы *f.* glaze.

полива́|ть(ся), ю(сь) *impf. of* ⇒**поли́ть(ся)**

поливитами́н|ы, ов *no sg.* multivitamins.

поли́вк|а, и *f.* watering.

поливн|о́й *adj.* requiring irrigation; **~ы́е зе́мли** irrigation area.

полига́ми|я, и *f.* polygamy.

полигло́т, а *m.* polyglot.

полиго́н, а *m.* (*mil.*) (artillery *or* bombing) range; **испыта́тельный п.** proving ground, testing area; **уче́бный п.** training ground.

полиграфи́ст, а *m.* printer.

полиграфи́ческий *adj.* printing.

полиграфи́|я, и *f.* printing.

поликли́ник|а, и *f.* clinic; health centre (*Br.*), center (*US*).

полилове́|ть, ю *pf. of* ⇒**лилове́ть**

полиме́р, а *m.* (*chem.*) polymer.

полимериза́ци|я, и *f.* (*chem.*) polymerization.

полинези́|ец, йца *m.* Polynesian.

полинези́|йка, йки *f. of* ⇒**~ец**

полинези́йский *adj.* Polynesian.

Полине́зи|я, и *f.* Polynesia.

полиненасы́щенн|ый *adj.*: **~ые жиры́** polyunsaturated fats.

полино́м, а *m.* (*math.*) polynomial.

полиня́лый *adj.* faded, discoloured (*Br.*), discolored (*US*).

полиня́|ть, ет *pf. of* ⇒**линя́ть**

полиомиели́т, а *m.* (*med.*) polio(myelitis).

поли́п, а *m.* polyp.

полипропиле́н, а *m.* polypropylene.

полирова́льный *adj.* polishing; **п. стано́к** buffing machine.

полир|ова́ть, у́ю *impf.* (*of* ⇒**от~**) to polish.

полиро́вк|а, и *f.* polish(ing).

полиро́вочный *adj.* polishing.

по́лис, а *m.* policy; **страхово́й п.** insurance policy.

полисеми́|я, и *f.* (*ling.*) polysemy.

полисме́н, а *m.* policeman; constable.

полисодержа́тел|ь, я *m.* policyholder.

поли́стный *adj.* per sheet.

полит... *comb. form, abbr. of* ***полити́ческий***

политбюро́ *nt. indecl.* the Politburo.

политеи́зм, а *m.* polytheism.

политеи́ст, а *m.* polytheist.

политеисти́ческий *adj.* polytheistic.

полите́хник, а *m.* student of polytechnic.

полите́хникум, а *m.* polytechnic (school).

политехни́ческий *adj.* polytechnic.

политзаключённ|ый, ого *m.* political prisoner.

политиза́ци|я, и *f.* politicization.

политизи́р|овать, ую *impf. and pf.* to politicize.

поли́тик, а *m.* politician.

поли́тик|а, и *f.* **1** policy; **п. на гра́ни войны́** 'brinkmanship'; **проводи́ть ~у** to carry out a policy. **2** (*наука*) politics; **п. си́лы** power politics.

политика́н, а *m.* (*pej.*) politician, intriguer.

политика́нств|о, а *nt.* politicking, intrigue.

политика́нств|овать, ую *impf.* to intrigue.

полити́ческ|ий *adj.* political; **п. де́ятель** political figure, politician; **~ая корре́ктность** political correctness; **~ие нау́ки** political science; **~ое убе́жище** political asylum; **~ая эконо́мия** political economy; *as n.* **п., ~ого** (*coll.*) political prisoner.

полити́ч|ный (~ен, ~на) *adj.* (*coll.*) politic.

политкаторжа́н|ин, ина, *pl.* **~е, ~** *m.* political convict (*in pre-1917 Russia*).

политкаторжа́н|ка, ки *f. of* **⇒~ин**

полито́лог, а *m.* political scientist.

политоло́ги|я, и *f.* political science.

политрабо́тник, а *m.* political worker.

политру́к, а *m.* (*abbr. of* ***полити́ческий руководи́тель***) political instructor (*in former USSR, in units of armed forces*).

политуправле́ни|е, я *nt.* Political Administration.

политу́р|а, ы *f.* polish, varnish.

политучёб|а, ы *f.* political education.

пол|и́ть, ью́, ьёшь, *past* **~и́л, ~ила́, ~и́ло** *pf.* (*of* **⇒~ива́ть**) **1** (*+a. and i.*) (*смочить*) to pour (on, upon); **п. что-н. водо́й** to pour water on sth.; **п. цветы́** to water the flowers. **2** (*начать лить*) to begin to pour.

пол|и́ться, ью́сь, ьёшься, *past* **~и́лся, ~ила́сь, ~и́ло́сь** *pf.* (*of* **⇒~ива́ться**) **1** (*+i.*) (*полить себя*) to pour over o.s. **2** (*начать литься*) to begin to flow.

политэконо́ми|я, и *f.* political economy.

политэмигра́нт, а *m.* political refugee.

полиурета́н, а *m.* polyurethane.

полифони́ческий *adj.* polyphonic.

полифони́|я, и *f.* (*mus.*) polyphony.

полихлорвини́л, а *m.* PVC (*polyvinyl chloride*).

полицейме́йстер, а *m.* (*hist.*) chief of police.

полице́йск|ий *adj.* police; **п. уча́сток** police-station; *as n.* **п., ~ого** *m.* policeman, police-officer.

поли́ци|я, и *f.* police.

поли́чн|ое, ого *nt.*: **пойма́ть с ~ым** to catch red-handed.

полишине́л|ь, я *m.* Punch(inello); **секре́т ~я** open secret.

полиэтиле́н, а *m.* polythene.

полиэтиле́н|овый *adj. of* **⇒~**

полк, а́, о ~е́, в ~у́ *m.* regiment; **на́шего ~у́ при́было** (*coll.*) our ranks have swollen.

по́лк|а¹, и *f.* **1** shelf; **кни́жная п.** bookshelf. **2** (*в поезде*) berth.

по́лк|а², и *f.* (*огорода*) weeding.

полко́вник, а *m.* colonel.

полково́д|ец, ца *m.* commander; military leader.

полково́й *adj.* regimental.

пол-ли́тра, полули́тра *m.* half a litre (*Br.*), liter (*US*).

поллюта́нт, а *m.* pollutant.

поллю́ци|я, и *f.* (*physiol.*) nocturnal emission.

полмиллио́на, полумиллио́на *m.* half a million.

полмину́ты, полумину́ты *f.* half a minute.

полне́йший *adj.* sheer, utter(most).

полне́|ть, ю *impf.* (*of* **⇒по~**) to grow stout, put on weight.

полнёхон|ький (~ек, ~ька) *adj.* (*coll.*) brim-full, crammed, packed.

полн|и́ть, ю́, и́шь *impf.* (*coll.*) to make look fat; **э́то пла́тье её ~и́т** this dress makes her look fat.

по́лно¹ *adv.* brim-full, full to the brim.

по́лно² *adv.* (*coll.*) **1** (*перестань!*) enough (of that)!; that will do!; **п. ворча́ть!** stop grumbling! **2** (*что вы говорите?*) you don't mean that!; come come!

полно́ *adv.* (*+g.*) (*coll.*) lots; **в ко́мнате полно́ наро́ду** the room is packed with people.

полнове́сност|ь, и *f.* **1** full weight. **2** (*fig.*) soundness.

полнове́с|ный (~ен, ~на) *adj.* **1** full-weight. **2** (*fig.*) sound.

полновла́сти|е, я *nt.* sovereignty.

полновла́ст|ный (~ен, ~на) *adj.* sovereign; **п. хозя́ин** sole master.

полново́д|ный (~ен, ~на) *adj.* deep.

полново́дь|е, я *nt.* high water.

полнозву́ч|ный (~ен, ~на) *adj.* sonorous.

полнокро́ви|е, я *nt.* (*med.*) plethora.

полнокро́в|ный (~ен, ~на) *adj.* **1** (*med.*) plethoric. **2** (*fig.*) full-blooded.

полнолу́ни|е, я *nt.* full moon.

полнометра́жный *adj.*: **п. фильм** feature-length film.

полномо́чи|е, я *nt.* authority, power; (*leg.*) proxy; **чрезвыча́йные ~я** emergency powers; **срок ~й** term of office; **превыше́ние ~й** exceeding one's commission; **дать ~я** (*+d.*) to empower.

полномо́ч|ный (~ен, ~на) *adj.* plenipotentiary; **п. представи́тель** plenipotentiary.

полнопра́ви|е, я *nt.* full rights; competency.

полнопра́в|ный (~ен, ~на) *adj.* enjoying full rights; **п. член** full member.

полноро́дный *adj.* (*leg.*) full (*brother or sister*).

по́лностью *adv.* fully, in full; completely.

полнот|а́, ы́ *no pl., f.* **1** fullness, completeness; **п. вла́сти** absolute power. **2** (*тучность*) stoutness, corpulence.

по́лноте *int.* (*coll.*) = **по́лно²**

полноце́нност|ь, и *f.* full value.

полноце́н|ный (~ен, ~на) *adj.* **1** (*рубль*) of full value. **2** (*fig.*) (*лётчик*; *школа*) proper; fully-fledged; (*работа*) valuable.

полно́чи *f. indecl.* half the (a) night.

полно́чный *adj.* midnight.

по́лночь, по́лночи *and* **полу́ночи** *f.* midnight; **за́ п.** after midnight.

по́л|ный (~он, ~на́, ~но́) *adj.* **1** (*+g. or i.*) (*наполненный*) full (of); (*совершенный*) complete, entire, total; absolute; **~ным го́лосом** at the top of one's voice; **сказа́ть ~ным го́лосом** (*fig.*) to say outright; **~ное затме́ние** total eclipse; **п. карма́н** (*+g.*) a pocketful (of); **п. пансио́н** full board and lodging; **~ное собра́ние сочине́ний** complete works; **п. ход вперёд!** full speed ahead!; **идти́ ~ным хо́дом** to go at full speed; (*fig.*) to be in full swing; **~ная ча́ша** (*fig.*) plenty; **в ~ной ме́ре** fully, in full measure; **в ~ном расцве́те сил** in one's prime; **они́ пришли́ в ~ном соста́ве** they came in full force; **на ~ном ходу́** at full speed. **2** (*толстый*) stout, portly; plump.

полны́м-полно́ *adv.* chock-full, jam-packed; **в авто́бусе бы́ло п.-п наро́ду** the bus was jam-packed with people.

по́ло *nt. indecl.* (*sport*) polo; **во́дное п.** water polo.

поло́в|а, ы *f.* chaff.

полови́к, а́ *m.* mat; long narrow carpet, runner.

полови́н|а, ы *f.* half; **два с ~ой** two and a half; **п. шесто́го** half past five; **в пе́рвой ~е девятна́дцатого ве́ка** in the first half of the nineteenth century; **во второ́й ~е дня** in the afternoon; **на ~е доро́ги** halfway; **п. две́ри** leaf of a door.

полови́нк|а, и *f.* **1** half. **2** (*двери*) leaf.

полови́нн|ый *adj.* half; **~ая но́та** (*mus.*) minim (*Br.*), half note (*US*); **п. окла́д** half-pay; **заплати́ть за что-н. в ~ом разме́ре** to pay half-price for sth.

половинчат|ый (~, ~а) *adj.* **1** halved; half-and-half; **п. кирпич** half-brick. **2** (*fig.*) half-hearted; undecided; **~ое решение** half-baked decision.

половиц|а, ы *f.* floor board.

половник, а *m.* (*coll.*) ladle.

половодь|е, я *nt.* flood, high water (*at time of spring thaw*).

полов|ой[1] *adj.* floor; **~ая тряпка** floorcloth.

полов|ой[2] *adj.* sexual; **~ое бессилие** impotence; **~ое влечение** sexual attraction; **~ая зрелость** puberty; **~ые органы** genitals, sexual organs; **~ая связь** sexual intercourse.

полов|ой[3], **ого** *m.* (*obs.*) waiter.

полог, а *m.* bed-curtain; **под ~ом ночи** (*poet.*) under cover of night.

полог|ий (~, ~а) *adj.* gently sloping.

положени|е, я *nt.*
1 (*местонахождение*) position; whereabouts.
2 (*тела*) position; posture; attitude; **в сидячем ~и** in a sitting position.
3 (*состояние*) position; condition, state; situation; (*социальное*) status; (*обстоятельство*) circumstances; **семейное п.** marital status; **военное п.** martial law; **перевести на мирное п.** to transfer to a peace-time footing; **осадное п.** state of siege; **чрезвычайное п.** state of emergency; **п. вещей** state of affairs; **при таком ~и дел** as things stand; **быть на высоте ~я** to be on top of the situation; **выходить из ~я** to find a way out; **войти в чьё-н. п.** to understand s.o.'s position; **быть в стеснённом ~и** to be in straitened circumstances; **быть в (интересном) ~и** (*coll., euph.*) to be in the family way, be expecting.
4 (*устав*) regulations, statute; **по ~ю** according to the regulations.
5 (*тезис*) thesis; tenet; (*договора*) clause, provisions.

полож|енный *p.p.p. of* **⇒~ить** *and adj.* agreed, determined; **в п. час** at a time agreed.

положено *pred.* (*coll., impers.*) one is supposed to, it is customary; **как п.** as is customary; **этого делать не п.** one is not supposed to do that.

положим let us assume; **п., что вы правы** let us assume that you are right.

положительно *adv.* **1** positively; favourably; **п. ответить** (*i*) (*утвердительно*) to answer in the affirmative, (*ii*) (*согласиться*) to agree, consent; **отнестись п.** (**к**+*d.*) to take a favourable view (of). **2** (*coll.*) positively, absolutely; **она п. ничего не понимает** she understands absolutely nothing.

положител|ьный (~ен, ~ьна) *adj.* **1** positive; **~ьная степень сравнения** (*gram.*) positive degree; **п. электрический заряд** positive electric charge. **2** (*утвердительный*) affirmative; **п. ответ** affirmative reply. **3** (*благоприятный*) favourable (*Br.*), favorable (*US*); **п. герой** (*liter.*) positive hero; **~ьная оценка** favourable (*Br.*), favorable (*US*) reception. **4** (*coll.*) (*совершенный*) complete, absolute; **п. дурак** complete fool.

полож|ить, у, ~ишь *pf. of* **⇒класть; п. жизнь** to lay down one's life; **п. оружие** to lay down one's arms.

полож|иться, усь, ~ишься *pf.* (*of* **⇒полагаться**) (**на**+*a.*) to rely (upon), count (upon).

полоз[1], **а,** *pl.* **полозья, полозьев** *m.* (*саней*) (sledge) runner.

полоз[2], **а** *m.* (*змея*) grass-snake.

пол|ок[1], **ка** *m.* (*в русской бане*) sweating shelf.

пол|ок[2], **ка** *m.* (*obs.*) (*телега*) dray.

полома|ть, ю *pf.* (*coll.*) to break.

полома|ться, юсь *pf. of* **⇒ломаться**

поломк|а, и *f.* **1** (*действие*) breakage; (*машины*) breakdown. **2** (*место*) damaged part; damage.

поломойк|а, и *f.* (*coll.*) charwoman

полон, а *m.* (*arch.*) captivity.

полонез, а *m.* polonaise.

полони|й, я *m.* (*chem.*) polonium.

полон|ить, ю, ишь *pf.* (*arch.*) to take captive.

полос|а, ы, *a.* **полосу,** *pl.* **полосы, полос, ~ам** *f.* **1** (*какого-н. цвета*) stripe; streak; **материя (с) белыми и голубыми ~ами** material in blue and white stripes. **2** (*воды, бумаги*) strip. **3** (*от удара*) weal. **4** (*область*) region; zone, belt; strip; **ничейная п.** no man's land; **оборонительная п.** defence zone; **чернозёмная п.** black-earth belt. **5** (*agric.; obs.*) (*участок земли*) patch, strip. **6** (*период*) period; phase; **~ой, ~ами** (*as adv. of time*) in patches; **п. хорошей погоды** spell of fine weather; **п. неудач** run of bad luck. **7** (*typ.*) page.

полосатик, а *m.* (*zool.*) rorqual.

полосат|ый (~, ~а) *adj.* striped.

полоск|а, и *f. dim. of* **⇒полоса; в ~у** striped

полоскани|е, я *nt.* **1** (*действие*) rinse, rinsing; (*горла*) gargling. **2** (*жидкость*) gargle.

полоскательниц|а, ы *f.* slop-basin (*Br.*), slop-bowl (*US*).

полоскательн|ый *adj.*: **~ая чашка** slop-basin (*Br.*), slop-bowl (*US*).

поло|скать, щу, ~щешь *impf.* (*of* **⇒вы~**) to rinse; **п. горло** to gargle.

поло|скаться, щусь, ~щешься *impf.* **1** (*в воде*) to paddle. **2** (*на ветру*) to flutter, flap.

полосн|уть, у, ёшь *pf.* (*no impf.*) (*coll.*) to slash.

полос|овать, ую *impf.* (*of* **⇒ис~**) (*coll.*) to flog.

полост|ь[1], **и,** *g. pl.* **~ей** *f.* (*anat.*) cavity.

полост|ь[2], **и,** *g. pl.* **~ей** *f.* (*покрывало*) travelling (*Br.*), traveling (*US*) rug.

полотен|це, ца, *g. pl.* **~ец** *nt.* towel; **посудное п.** tea-towel; **п. на ролике** roller towel.

полотёр, а *m.* floor-polisher.

полотнищ|е, а *nt.* **1** (*ткани*) width; **парус в пять ~** sail of five panels. **2** (*пилы*) flat (part), blade.

полот|но, на, *pl.* **~на, ~ен, ~нам** *nt.* **1** (*ткань*) linen; **бледный как п.** white as a sheet. **2** (*картина*) canvas. **3** (*дороги*) roadbed. **4** (*tech.*) (*пилы*) blade.

полотняный *adj.* linen.

пол|оть, ю, ~ешь *impf.* (*of* **⇒вы~**) to weed.

полоуми|е, я *nt.* craziness.

полоум|ный (~ен, ~на) *adj.* (*coll.*) crazy.

полош|ить, у, ишь *impf.* (*of* **⇒вс~**) (*coll.*) to alarm.

полош|иться, усь, ишься *impf.* (*of* **⇒вс~**) (*coll.*) to be alarmed.

полпред, а *m.* (*abbr. of* ***полномочный представитель***) (ambassador) plenipotentiary.

полпути *m. indecl.*: **на п.** half-way; **вернуться с п.** to turn back half-way; **остановиться на п.** (*fig.*) to stop half-way.

полслов|а, на ~е *nt.*: **п. от него не услышишь** you cannot get a word out of him; **можно вас на п.?** may I have a word with you?

полставки *f. indecl.*: **на п.** part-time.

полтергейст, а *m.* poltergeist.

полтин|а, ы *f.* (*coll.*) = **~ник; два с ~ой** two roubles fifty kopecks.

полтинник, а *m.* **1** (*сумма*) fifty kopecks. **2** (*монета*) fifty-kopeck piece.

полтора, полутора *m. and nt.* one and a half; **в п. раза больше** half as much again.

полтораста, полутораста *num.* a hundred and fifty.

полтор|ы *f.* = **~а; п. тысячи** one and a half thousand.

полу... *comb. form* half-, semi-, demi-.

полубак, а *m.* (*naut.*) forecastle.

полубессознател|ьный (~ен, ~ьна) *adj.* semi-unconscious.

полубог, а *m.* demigod.

полуботин|ки, ок *pl.* (*sg.* **~ок, ~ка** *m.*) shoes.

полуваттный *adj.* (*elec.*) half-watt.

полувоенный *adj.* paramilitary.

полугласн|ый, ого *m.* (*ling.*) semivowel.

полугоди|е, я *nt.* half year, six months.

полугодичный *adj.* half-yearly; six-month.

полугодовалый *adj.* six-month(s)-old.

полугодовой *adj.* half-yearly, six-monthly; **п. отчёт** half-yearly report.

полуграмот|ный (~ен, ~на) *adj.* semi-literate.

полуграци|я, и *f.* pantie-girdle.

полуденный *adj.* midday.

полу|дить, жу, ~дишь *pf. of* **⇒лудить**

полужёсткий *adj.* (*tech.*) semi-rigid.

полужив|ой (~, ~а, ~о) *adj.* half dead; more dead than alive.

полузащит|а, ы *f.* (*collect.; sport*) half-backs, midfield players.

полузащитник, а *m.* (*sport*) half-back, midfield player; **центральный ~** centre half (*Br.*), center half (*US*).

полуим|я, ени, *pl.* **~ена, ~ён, ~енам** *nt.* (*obs., coll.*) pet name.

П

полуке́д|ы, ов *or* **~** *no sg.* plimsolls (*Br.*), sneakers (*US*).

полукро́вк|а, и *f.* half-breed (*animal*).

полукру́г, а *m.* semicircle.

полукру́глый *adj.* semicircular.

полулеж|а́ть, у́, и́шь *impf.* to recline.

полумгл|а́, ы́ *f.* (*туман*) mist; (*неполная мгла*) half-light.

полуме́р|а, ы *f.* half-measure.

полумёртв|ый (~, ~а́) *adj.* half-dead.

полуме́сяц, а *m.* half moon; crescent.

полуме́сячный *adj.* fortnight's (*Br.*), half a month's (*US*).

полумра́к, а *m.* semi-darkness.

полунаго́й *adj.* half-naked.

полуноск|и́, о́в *no sg.* ankle socks.

полуно́чни|к, а *m.* (*coll.*) nightbird.

полуно́чни|ца, цы *f. of* **⇒~к**

полуно́чнича|ть, ю *impf.* (*coll.*) to burn the midnight oil.

полу́но́чный *adj.* midnight.

полуоборо́т, а *m.* half-turn.

полуоде́т|ый (~, ~а) *adj.* half-dressed, half-clothed.

полуосвещ|ённый (~ён, ~ена́) *adj.* half-lit.

полуо́стров, а *m.* peninsula.

полуостровно́й *adj.* peninsular.

полуотво́рен|ный (~, ~а) *adj.* half-open; (*дверь, окно*) ajar (*pred.*).

полуоткры́т|ый (~, ~а) *adj.* half-open; (*дверь, окно*) ajar (*pred.*).

полупальто́ *nt. indecl.* short overcoat, car coat.

полуподва́льный *adj.*: **п. эта́ж** semi-basement.

полупокло́н, а *m.* slight bow.

полупроводни́к, а́ *m.* (*phys.*) semi-conductor.

полупроводнико́вый *adj.* transistor(ized).

полупрофессиона́л, а *m.* semi-professional.

полупрофессиона́льный *adj.* semi-professional.

полупья́н|ый (~, ~а́, ~о) *adj.* tipsy.

полуразру́шен|ный (~, ~а) *adj.* tumbledown, dilapidated.

полусапо́ж|ки, ек *pl.* (*sg.* **~ек, ~ка** *m.*) half-boots.

полусве́т¹, а *m.* (*сумерки*) twilight.

полусве́т², а *m.* (*общества*) demi-monde.

полусерьёз|ный (~ен, ~на) *adj.* half-serious; half in joke.

полусло́в|о, а *nt.*: **оборва́ть кого́-н. на ~е** to cut s.o. short; **останови́ться на ~е** to stop short, stop in the middle of a sentence; **поня́ть с ~а** to be quick on the uptake.

полусме́рт|ь, и *f.*: **до ~и** (*fig., coll.*) to death; **изби́ть кого́-н. до ~и** to beat s.o. within an inch of his life; **испуга́ться до ~и** to be frightened to death.

полус|о́н, на́ *m.* half sleep; drowsiness; **в ~не́** half-asleep.

полусо́нный *adj.* half-asleep; dozing.

полуспу́щенный *adj.*: **п. флаг** flag at half-mast.

полуста́н|ок, ка *m.* (*rail.*) halt.

полуте́н|ь, и, о ~и, в ~и́ *f.* penumbra.

полуто́н, а, *pl.* **~ы** *and* **~а́** *m.* **1** (*mus.*) semitone. **2** (*art*) half-tint.

полу́торк|а, и *f.* (*coll.*) thirty-hundredweight lorry.

полу́торн|ый *adj.* of one and a half; **в ~ом разме́ре** half as much again.

полутьм|а́, ы́ *f.* semi-darkness; twilight.

полутяжёлый *adj.* light heavyweight; cruiserweight (*Br.*).

полуста́в, а *m.* (*palaeog.*) semi-uncial.

полуфабрика́т, а *m.* (*изделие*) semi-finished product; (*пищевой*) semi-prepared foodstuff.

полуфина́л, а *m.* semi-final.

полуфинали́ст, а *m.* semi-finalist.

полуфинали́ст|ка, ки *f. of* **⇒~**

полуфина́л|ьный *adj. of* **⇒~; ~ьные встре́чи** semi-finals.

получасово́й *adj.* (*о продолжительности*) half-hour('s); (*о повторяемости*) half-hourly.

получа́тел|ь, я *m.* recipient.

получа́тель|ница, ницы *f. of* **⇒~**

получ|а́ть(ся), а́ю(сь) *impf. of* **⇒~и́ть(ся)**

получе́ни|е, я *nt.* receipt; obtaining; **распи́ска в ~и** receipt; **по ~и** on receipt, on receiving.

получ|и́ть, у́, ~ишь *pf.* (*of* **⇒~а́ть**) to get, receive, obtain; **п. на́сморк** to catch a cold; **п. обра́тно** to recover, get back; **п. призна́ние** to obtain recognition; **п. прика́з** to receive an order; **п. примене́ние** to come into use, effect; **п. удово́льствие** to derive pleasure.

получ|и́ться, у́сь, ~ишься *pf.* (*of* **⇒~а́ться**) **1** (*оказаться*) to turn out, prove, be; **результа́ты ~и́лись нева́жные** the results are poor; **~и́лось, что он был прав** it turned out that he was right, he proved right. **2** (*coll.*) (*оказаться удачным*) to work out; (*о снимке*) to come out. **3**: **из э́того ничего́ не ~ится** nothing will come of it.

полу́чк|а, и *f.* (*coll.*) **1** (*действие*) receipt. **2** (*за работу*) pay (packet), sum paid.

полу́чше *adv.* a little better.

полуша́ри|е, я *nt.* hemisphere.

полушёпот, а *m.* **говори́ть ~ом** to speak in undertones.

полуше́рст|ь, и *f.* wool mixture.

полу́шк|а, и *f.* (*obs.*) quarter-kopeck piece; **не име́ть ни ~и** to be penniless.

полушу́б|ок, ка *m.* (knee-length) sheepskin coat.

полушутя́ *adv.* half in joke.

полцены́ *f. indecl.*: **за п.** at half price; for half its value.

полчаса́, получа́са *m.* half an hour; **ка́ждые п.** every half-hour.

по́лчищ|е, а *nt.* (*войско*) horde; (*fig.*) (*насекомых*) swarm.

полшага́ *m. indecl.* half-pace.

по́л|ый *adj.* **1** hollow. **2**: **~ая вода́** flood-water.

по́лымя *nt.* (*dial.*) flame; **из огня́ да в п.** (*prov.*) out of the frying-pan into the fire.

полы́н|ный *adj. of* **⇒~ь; ~ная во́дка** absinthe.

полы́н|ь, и *f.* wormwood.

полын|ья́, ьи́, *g. pl.* **~е́й** *f.* polynya (*unfrozen patch of water in the midst of ice*).

полысе́|ть, ю *pf. of* **⇒лысе́ть**

полыха́|ть, ет *impf.* to blaze.

по́льз|а, ы *f.* use; advantage, benefit, profit; **кака́я от э́того п.?** what good will it do?; what use is it?; **что ~ы говори́ть об э́том?** what's the use of talking about it?; **извлека́ть из чего́-н. ~у** to benefit from sth.; to profit by sth.; **принести́ ~у** (+*d.*) to be of benefit (to); **для ~ы** (+*g.*) for the benefit (of); **в ~у** (+*g.*) in favour (*Br.*), favor (*US*) (of), on behalf (of); **э́то говори́т не в ва́шу ~у** it does not speak well for you; **два-ноль в ~у Дина́мо** (*sport*) 2–0 to Dynamo; **пойти́ на ~у кому́-н.** to be of benefit to s.o.

по́льзовани|е, я *nt.* use; **многокра́тного ~я** reusable; **о́бщего ~я** in general use.

по́льзовател|ь, я *m.* user; **коне́чный п.** end-user.

по́льз|оваться, уюсь *impf.* (+*i.*) **1** to make use (of), use, utilize. **2** (*pf.* **вос~**) (*извлекать выгоду*) to profit (by); **п. слу́чаем** to take an opportunity. **3** (*обладать*) to enjoy; **п. дове́рием** (+*g.*) to enjoy the confidence (of); **п. права́ми** to enjoy rights; **п. успе́хом** to enjoy success, be a success.

по́льк|а¹, и Pole, Polish woman.

по́льк|а², и *f.* (*танец*) polka.

по́льск|ий *adj.* Polish; *as n.* (*obs.*) **п., ~ого** *m.* polonaise.

поль|сти́ть, щу́, сти́шь *pf. of* **⇒льсти́ть**

По́льш|а, и *f.* Poland.

полюб|и́ть, лю́, ~ишь *pf.* to come to like, grow fond (of); (*влюбиться*) to fall in love (with).

полюб|и́ться, лю́сь, ~ишься *pf.* (*coll.*) (+*d.*) to catch the fancy (of); **она́ мне сра́зу же ~и́лась** I was immediately attracted by her, I took an immediate liking to her.

полюб|ова́ться, у́юсь *pf. of* **⇒любова́ться; ~у́йся, ~у́йтесь** (**на**+*a.*; *coll., iron.*) just look; **~у́йся на э́того дурака́!** just look at that fool!

полюбо́вно *adv.* amicably; **реши́ть, ко́нчить де́ло п.** to come to an amicable agreement.

полюбо́в|ный (~ен, ~на) *adj.* amicable.

полюбопы́тств|овать, ую *pf. of* **⇒любопы́тствовать**

по-людски́ *adv.* (*coll.*) as others do; **жить п.** to live as other people do; to live like a (normal) human being.

по́люс, а *m.* (*geog., phys., and fig.*) pole;

Се́верный п. North Pole; **они́ — два ~а** they are poles apart.

поля́к, а *m.* Pole.

поля́н|а, ы *f.* glade, clearing.

поляриза́ци|я, и *f.* (*phys.*) polarization.

поляриз|ова́ть, у́ю *impf. and pf.* (*phys.*) to polarize.

поля́рник, а *m.* polar explorer.

поля́рни|ца, цы *f. of* ⇒**~к**

поля́рност|ь, и *f.* (*phys.*) polarity.

поля́рн|ый *adj.* **1** polar, arctic; **П~ая звезда́** Pole-star, North star; **Се́верный п. круг** Arctic Circle. **2** (*fig.*) polar, diametrically opposed.

пом. (*abbr. of* ***помо́щник***) assistant.

пом... *comb. form, abbr. of* ***помо́щник***

пома́ва|ть, ю *impf.* (*obs.*) (+*i.*) to wave, brandish.

пома́д|а, ы *f.* pomade; **губна́я п.** lipstick.

пома́|дить, жу, дишь *impf.* (*of* ⇒**на~**) (*coll.*) to pomade; **п. во́лосы** to grease one's hair; **п. гу́бы** to put lipstick on.

пома́дк|а, и *f.* (*collect.*) fruit candy; **сли́вочная п.** fudge.

пома́зани|е, я *nt.* (*eccl.*) anointing.

пома́занник, а *m.* (*eccl.*) anointed sovereign.

пома́|зать, жу, жешь *pf.* **1** *pf. of* ⇒**ма́зать** 1,2. **2** (*eccl.*) to anoint.

пома́|заться, жусь, жешься *pf. of* ⇒**ма́заться**

помаз|о́к, ка́ *m.* (small) brush.

помале́ньку *adv.* (*coll.*) **1** little by little, gradually, gently; **рабо́тать п.** to take one's time over one's work. **2** (*терпимо*) tolerably, so-so, all right; **жить п.** to live tolerably.

пома́лкива|ть, ю *impf.* (*coll.*) to hold one's tongue, keep quiet.

по-мальчи́шески *adv.* in a boyish way, like a boy.

поман|и́ть, ю́, ~ишь *pf. of* ⇒**мани́ть**

пома́рк|а, и *f.* (*исправление*) correction (*by hand*); (*вычеркнутое место*) crossing-out.

пома́сл|ить, ю, ишь *pf. of* ⇒**ма́слить**

пома|ха́ть, шу́, ~шешь *pf.* (+*i.*) to wave (*for a while, a few times*).

пома́хива|ть *impf.* (+*i.*) to wave, brandish, swing (*from time to time*); **соба́ка ~ла хвосто́м** the dog would wag his tail.

поме́дл|ить, ю, ишь *pf.* (**с**+*i.*; *coll.*) to linger (over).

помел|о́, а́, *pl.* **~ья, ~ьев** *nt.* mop; (*ведьмы*) broomstick.

поме́ньше *comp. of* ⇒**ма́ленький** *and* **ма́ло** (*по размеру*) somewhat smaller, a little smaller; (*по количеству*) somewhat less, a little less.

поменя́|ть(ся), ю(сь) *pf. of* ⇒**меня́ть(ся)** 2

помера́н|ец, ца *m.* **1** (*плод*) Seville *or* sour orange. **2** (*дерево*) sour orange.

помера́н|цевый *adj. of* ⇒**~ец**; **~цевые цветы́** orange-blossom.

по|мере́ть, мру́, мрёшь, *past* **~мер, ~мерла́, ~мерло** *pf.* (*of* ⇒**~мира́ть**) (*coll.*) to die; **п. со́ смеху** to split one's sides (with laughing).

помере́щ|иться, усь, ишься *pf. of* ⇒**мере́щиться**

помёрз|нуть, ну, нешь, *past* **~, ~ла** *pf.* (*провести время в холоде*) to freeze; (*о растениях*) to be killed by frost.

поме́р|ить(ся), ю(сь), ишь(ся) *pf. of* ⇒**ме́рить(ся)**

поме́рк|нуть, ну, нешь, *past* **~, ~ла** *pf. of* ⇒**ме́ркнуть**

помертве́лый *adj.* deathly pale; (*fig.*) lifeless.

помертве́|ть, ю *pf. of* ⇒**мертве́ть**

помести́тельност|ь, и *f.* spaciousness; capaciousness.

помести́тел|ьный (~ен, ~ьна) *adj.* spacious, roomy; capacious.

поме|сти́ть, щу́, сти́шь *pf.* (*of* ⇒**~ща́ть**) **1** (*поселить*) to lodge, accommodate; to put up; **мы могли́ бы их п. в свобо́дную ко́мнату** we could put them into the spare room. **2** (*поставить*) to put, place; (*fin.*) to invest; **п. объявле́ние в газе́те** to put an advertisement in a paper; **п. сбереже́ния в сберка́ссу** to put one's savings in a savings bank.

поме|сти́ться, щу́сь, сти́шься *pf.* (*of* ⇒**~ща́ться**) **1** (*жить*) to find room; to put up; (*о вещах*) to go in; **в э́тот я́щик мои́ ве́щи не ~стя́тся** my things will not go into this drawer. **2** *pass. of* ⇒**~сти́ть**

поме́стн|ый *adj.*: **~ое дворя́нство** landed gentry.

поме́ст|ье, ья, *g. pl.* **~ий** *nt.* estate.

по́мес|ь, и *f.* **1** hybrid; cross; **п. терье́ра и овча́рки, п. терье́ра с овча́ркой** a cross between a terrier and a sheepdog. **2** (*fig.*) mixture, hotchpotch.

поме́сячно *adv.* by the month; monthly, each month.

поме́сячный *adj.* monthly.

помёт, а *m.* **1** (*кал*) dung; droppings. **2** (*выводок*) litter, brood; (*о поросятах*) farrow.

поме́т|а, ы *f.* mark, note; **сде́лать ~ы на поля́х** to make notes in the margin.

поме́|тить, чу, тишь *pf.* (*of* ⇒**~ча́ть**) to mark; to date; **п. га́лочкой** to tick; **я ~тил письмо́ 2-м января́** I dated my letter the 2nd of January.

поме́тк|а, и *f.* = **поме́та**

поме́х|а, и *f.* **1** hindrance; obstacle; **быть ~ой** (+*d.*) to hinder, impede. **2** (*pl. only*) (*radio, TV*) interference.

помеча́|ть, ю *impf. of* ⇒**поме́тить**

поме́шан|ный (~, ~а) *adj.* **1** mad, crazy; insane; *as n.* **п., ~ного** *m.* madman; **~ная, ~ной** *f.* madwoman. **2** (**на**+*p.*; *fig., coll.*) mad (on, about), crazy (about); **они́ ~ы на бри́дже** they are mad about bridge.

помеша́тельств|о, а *nt.* **1** madness, craziness; lunacy, insanity. **2** (**на**+*p.*; *fig., coll.*) craze (for).

помеша́|ть[1,2], ю *pf. of* ⇒**меша́ть[1,2]**

помеша́|ться, юсь *pf.* **1** to go mad, go crazy. **2** (**на**+*p.*; *fig., coll.*) to become mad (on, about), become crazy (about).

помеща́|ть, ю *impf. of* ⇒**помести́ть**

помеща́|ться, юсь *impf.* **1** (*impf. only*) (*находиться*) to be; to be located, be situated; (*храниться*) to be housed; **где ~ется ваш кабине́т?** where is your office? **2** (*impf. only*): **на э́том стадио́не ~ется се́мьдесят ты́сяч челове́к** this stadium holds seventy thousand people. **3** *impf. of* ⇒**помести́ться**

помеще́ни|е, я *nt.* **1** (*действие*) placing, location; (*капитала*) investment. **2** (*жильё*) room, lodging, apartment; (*для учреждения*) premises; **жило́е п.** housing.

поме́щик, а *m.* landowner.

поме́щи|ца, цы *f. of* ⇒**~к**

поме́щи|чий *adj. of* ⇒**~к**; **п. дом** manor-house.

помза́в, а *m.* (*abbr. of* ***помо́щник заве́дующего***) assistant manager.

помидо́р, а, *g. pl.* **~ов** *m.* tomato.

помидо́р|ный *adj. of* ⇒**~**

поми́ловани|е, я *nt.* (*leg.*) pardon, forgiveness; **про́сьба о ~и** appeal (for pardon).

поми́л|овать, ую *pf.* to pardon, forgive; **поми́луй(те)!** for pity's/goodness sake!; **Го́споди, ~уй!** Lord, have mercy (upon us)!

поми́мо *prep.*+*g.* **1** (*кроме*) apart from; besides; **п. всего́ про́чего** apart from anything else; **п. други́х соображе́ний** other considerations apart. **2** (*минуя*) without the knowledge (of), unbeknown (to); **всё э́то реши́лось п. меня́** all this was decided without my knowledge.

поми́н, а *m.* (*coll.*) mention; **лёгок на ~е** talk of the devil; **его́ и в ~е нет** there is no trace of him.

помина́льны|й *adj.*: **п. обе́д** funeral repast, wake; **~е обря́ды** funeral rites.

помина́ни|е, я *nt.* (*eccl.*) **1** (*молитва*) prayer (for the dead *or* for sick persons). **2** (*список*) list of names of dead and sick persons.

помина́|ть, ю *impf. of* ⇒**помяну́ть**; **не ~й(те) меня́ ли́хом!** remember me kindly!; **а его́ ~й, как зва́ли!** (*coll.*) he just vanished into thin air.

поми́н|ки, ок *no sg.* funeral repast, wake.

поминове́ни|е, я *nt.* (*eccl.*) prayer for the dead *and/or* for the sick; remembrance (of the dead *and/or* the sick) in prayer.

помину́тно *adv.* (*coll.*) continually, constantly.

помину́т|ный (~ен, ~на) *adj.* **1** occurring every minute; (*fig., coll.*) (*очень частый*) continual, constant. **2** (*оплата*) by the minute.

помира́|ть, ю *impf. of* ⇒**помере́ть**

помир|и́ть(ся), ю́(сь), и́шь(ся) *pf. of* ⇒**мири́ть(ся)**

помна́ч, а *m.* (*abbr. of* ***помо́щник нача́льника***) assistant chief.

по́мн|ить, ю, ишь *impf.* (+*a. or* **о**+*p.*)

П

to remember; **не п. себя́ (от**+*g.*) to be beside o.s. (with).

по́мн|иться, ится *impf.* (*impers.*+*d.*) I, *etc.*, remember; **мне ещё ~ится день пожа́ра** I still remember the day of the fire; **наско́лько мне ~ится** as far as I can remember; **~ится, э́то произошло́ в декабре́** as I remember, it happened in December.

помно́гу *adv.* (*coll.*) in plenty, in large quantities; in large numbers.

помнож|а́ть, а́ю *impf. of* ⇒**~́ить**

помно́ж|ить, у, ишь *pf.* (*of* ⇒**мно́жить** *and* ⇒**~а́ть**) to multiply; **п. два на́ три** to multiply two by three.

помога́|ть, ю *impf. of* ⇒**помо́чь**

пом|огу́, о́жешь, о́гут *see* ⇒**~о́чь**

по-мо́ему *adv.* **1** (*по моему мнению*) in my opinion. **2** (*как я хочу*) as I wish.

помо́|и, ев *no sg.* slops; **обли́ть кого́-н. ~ями** (*fig., coll.*) to fling mud at s.o.

помо́й|ка, ки, *g. pl.* **помо́ек** *f.* rubbish dump (*Br.*), garbage dump (*US*); (*яма*) cesspit.

помо́|йный *adj. of* ⇒**~и; ~йное ведро́** slop-pail; **~йная я́ма** cesspit.

помо́л, а *m.* grinding; **мука́ кру́пного, ме́лкого ~а** coarse-ground, fine-ground flour.

помо́лв|ить, лю, ишь *pf.* (+*a.* **с**+*i., or* +*a.* **за**+*a.*; *obs.*) to betrothe (to); **она́ ~лена с Ива́ном** *or* **за Ива́на** she is engaged to Ivan.

помо́лвк|а, и *f.* betrothal, engagement.

помол|и́ться, ю́сь, ~́ишься *pf. of* ⇒**моли́ться.**

помолоде́|ть, ю *pf. of* ⇒**молоде́ть**

помолч|а́ть, у́, и́шь *pf.* to be silent for a while.

помо́р, а *m.* coast-dweller (*esp. of Russian inhabitants of coasts of White Sea*).

помор|и́ть, ю, и́шь *pf. of* ⇒**мори́ть**[1]

помо́р|ка, ки *f. of* ⇒**~**

помо́рник, а *m.* (*zool.*) skua.

поморо́|зить, жу, зишь *pf. of* ⇒**моро́зить**

помо́р|ский *adj. of* ⇒**~** *and* **~ье**

помо́рщ|иться, усь, ишься *pf. of* ⇒**мо́рщиться**

помо́рь|е, я *nt.* seaboard, coastal region; **Балти́йское П.** Pomerania (*southern coast of Baltic Sea*); **Се́верное П.** White Sea Coast.

помо́ст, а *m.* platform, rostrum; (*эшафот*) scaffold.

по́моч|и, е́й *no sg.* **1** leading strings; **быть, ходи́ть на ~а́х** (*fig.*) to be in leading strings. **2** (*подтяжки*) braces (*Br.*), suspenders (*US*).

помоч|и́ться, у́сь, ~́ишься *pf. of* ⇒**мочи́ться**

по́моч|ь, и *f.* **1** (*obs.*) = **по́мощь. 2** (*obs.*) mutual aid (*afforded one another by villagers*).

помо́|чь, гу́, жешь, гут, *past* **~г, ~гла́** *pf.* (*of* ⇒**~га́ть**) **1** (+*d.*) to help, aid, assist; **~ги́(те) ей наде́ть пальто́** help her on with her coat. **2** (*о лекарстве*) to relieve, bring relief; **инъе́кции ~гли́ от бо́ли** the injections relieved the pain.

помо́щник, а *m.* **1** helper. **2** (*заместитель*) assistant; **п. дире́ктора** assistant director; **п. капита́на** (*naut.*) mate; **п. команди́ра** second in command; **п. судьи́** (*sport*) linesman.

помо́щни|ца, цы *f. of* ⇒**~к 1**

по́мощ|ь, и *f.* help, assistance; **оказа́ть п.** to help, assist; **пода́ть ру́ку ~и** (+*d.*) to lend a hand; **позва́ть на п.** to call for help; **прийти́ на п.** (+*d.*) to come to the aid (of); **на п.!** help!; **с ~ью** (+*g.*), **при ~и** (+*g.*) with the help (of), by means (of); **ско́рая п.** ambulance; **каре́та ско́рой ~и** (*obs.*) ambulance; **п. на дому́** home visiting (*by doctors to patients*); **пе́рвая п.** first aid; **п. иностра́нным госуда́рствам** foreign aid.

по́мп|а[1]**, ы** *f.* (*пышность*) pomp, state.

по́мп|а[2]**, ы** *f.* (*насос*) pump.

помпе́зност|ь, и *f.* pomposity.

помпе́з|ный (~ен, ~на) *adj.* pompous.

помпо́н, а *m.* pompon.

помрач|а́ть(ся), а́ет(ся) *impf. of* ⇒**~и́ть(ся)**

помраче́ни|е, я *nt.* darkening, obscuring.

помрач|и́ть, и́т *pf.* (*of* ⇒**~а́ть**) to darken, obscure, cloud.

помрач|и́ться, и́тся *pf.* (*of* ⇒**~а́ться**) to grow dark, become obscured, become clouded.

помрачне́|ть, ю *pf. of* ⇒**мрачне́ть**

помре́ж, а *m.* (*abbr. of* ***помо́щник режиссёра***) (*theatr.*) assistant producer; (*cin.*) assistant director.

пому|ти́ть(ся), чу́, ти́шь, ти́т(ся) *pf. of* ⇒**мути́ть(ся)**

помутне́|ть, ет *pf. of* ⇒**мутне́ть**

пому́ч|ить, у, ишь *pf.* to make suffer, torment (*for a time*).

пому́ч|иться, усь, ишься *pf.* to suffer (*for a while*).

помч|а́ть, у́, и́шь *pf.* **1** to begin to whirl, rush. **2** (*coll.*) = **~а́ться**

помч|а́ться, у́сь, и́шься *pf.* to begin to rush, begin to tear along.

помыка́|ть, ю *impf.* (+*i.*; *coll.*) to order about.

по́мыс|ел, ла *m.* (*мысль*) thought; (*намерение*) intention; **благи́е ~лы** good intentions.

помы́сл|ить, ю, ишь *pf.* (*of* ⇒**помышля́ть**) (**о**+*p.*) to think (of, about), contemplate; **об э́том и п. мы не сме́ли** we dared not even dream of it.

пом|ы́ть(ся), о́ю(сь), о́ешь(ся) *pf. of* ⇒**мыть(ся)**

помышле́ни|е, я *nt.* (*obs.*) (*мысль*) thought; (*намерение*) intention, design.

помышля́|ть, ю *impf. of* ⇒**помы́слить**

помян|у́ть, у́, ~́ешь *pf.* (*of* ⇒**помина́ть**) **1** (*упомянуть*) to mention, make mention (of); **п. добро́м кого́-н.** to speak well of s.o.; **~и́ моё сло́во** (*coll.*) mark my words. **2** (*помолиться*) to pray (for), remember in one's prayers. **3** (*устроить поминки*) to give a funeral repast (for, in memory of).

помя́т|ый *p.p.p. of* ⇒**~ь** *and adj.* (*coll.*) flabby, baggy.

пом|я́ть, ну́, нёшь *pf.* to rumple slightly; to crumple slightly.

пом|я́ться[1]**, ну́сь, нёшься** *pf. of* ⇒**мя́ться**[1]

пом|я́ться[2]**, ну́сь, нёшься** *pf.* (*coll.*) (*проявить нерешительность*) to vacillate, hum and ha (*for a while*).

пона... *vbl. pref. indicating action performed gradually or by instalments.*

по-над *prep.*+*i.* (*dial.*) along, by.

понаде́|яться, юсь, ешься *pf.* (**на**+*a.*; *coll.*) to count (upon), rely (on).

пона́добиться, люсь, ишься *pf.* to be, become necessary; **е́сли ~ится** if necessary.

понапра́сну *adv.* (*coll.*) in vain.

понаслы́шке *adv.* (*coll.*) by hearsay.

по-настоя́щему *adv.* properly.

поначалу *adv.* (*coll.*) at first, in the beginning.

по-на́шему *adv.* **1** (*по нашему мнению*) in our opinion. **2** (*как мы хотим*) as we wish.

понево́ле *adv.* against one's will.

понеде́льник, а *m.* Monday.

понеде́льно *adv.* by the week, each week; weekly.

понеде́льный *adj.* weekly.

поне́же *conj.* (*arch.*) because, since.

понемно́гу *adv.* **1** (*немного*) little, a little at a time. **2** (*постепенно*) little by little.

понемно́жку *adv.* = **понемно́гу;** (*in answer to question* **как пожива́ете?**) (doing) all right, not bad, so-so.

понес|ти́, у́, ёшь, *past* **~̈, ~ла́** *pf.* **1** *pf. of* ⇒**нести́. 2** (*о лошадях*) to bolt.

понес|ти́сь, у́сь, ёшься, *past* **~̈ся, ~ла́сь** *pf.* **1** *pf. of* ⇒**нести́сь. 2** to rush off, tear off, dash off.

по́ни *m. indecl.* pony.

понижа́|ть(ся), ю(сь) *impf. of* ⇒**пони́зить(ся)**

пони́же *adv.* rather lower; rather shorter.

пониже́ни|е, я *nt.* fall, drop; lowering; reduction; **п. давле́ния** drop in pressure; **п. зарпла́ты** wage-cut; **п. цен** reduction, fall in prices; **п. по слу́жбе** demotion.

пони́|зить, жу, зишь *pf.* (*of* ⇒**~жа́ть**) (*голос*) to lower; (*цены*) to reduce; **п. по слу́жбе** to demote.

пони́|зиться, жусь, зишься *pf.* (*of* ⇒**~жа́ться**) to fall, drop, go down, be reduced.

понизо́вь|е, я *nt.* lower reaches.

по́низу *adv.* low; along the ground.

поника́|ть, ю *impf. of* ⇒**пони́кнуть**

пони́к|нуть, ну, нешь, *past* **~, ~ла** *pf.* (*of* ⇒**ни́кнуть** *and* **~а́ть**) to droop; **п. голово́й** to hang one's head.

понима́ни|е, я *nt.* **1** understanding, comprehension; **э́то вы́ше моего́ ~я** it is beyond me. **2** (*толкование*) interpretation, conception; **но́вое п. исто́рии** a new interpretation of history; **в моём ~и** as I see it.

понима́|ть, ю *impf.* (*of* ⇒**поня́ть**) **1** to understand; to comprehend; to realize; **~ю!** I see! **2** (*толковать*) to interpret; **непра́вильно п.** to misunderstand; **как вы ~ете э́тот посту́пок?** what do you make of this action? **3** (*impf. only*) (+*a.* or **в**+*p.*) (*знать толк*) to be a (good) judge (of), know (about); **я ничего́ не ~ю в му́зыке** I know nothing about music.

по-но́вому *adv.* in a new fashion; **нача́ть жить п.** to start life afresh, turn over a new leaf.

поножо́вщин|а, ы *f.* (*coll.*) knife-fight; knifing.

понома́р|ь, я́ *m.* sexton, sacristan.

поно́с, а *m.* diarrhoea (*Br.*), diarrhea (*US*).

поно|си́ть[1]**, шу́, ~́сишь** *impf.* (*оскорблять*) to abuse, revile.

поно|си́ть[2]**, шу́, ~́сишь** *pf.* **1** (*ребёнка*) to carry (*for a while*). **2** (*свитер*) to wear (*for a while*).

поно́с|ный (~ен, ~на) *adj.* (*obs.*) abusive, defamatory.

поноше́ни|е, я *nt.* abuse, defamation.

поно́|шенный *p.p.p. of* ⇒**~си́ть**[2] *and adj.* worn, shabby, threadbare; **п. вид** (*fig.*) worn-out appearance.

понра́в|иться, люсь, ишься *pf. of* ⇒**нра́виться**

понтёр, а *m.* (*cards*) punter.

понто́н, а *m.* **1** (*судно*) pontoon. **2** (*мост*) pontoon bridge.

понто́н|ный *adj. of* ⇒**~; ~ный мост** pontoon bridge.

понуди́тельный *adj.* impelling, pressing; coercive.

пону́|дить, жу, дишь *pf.* (*of* ⇒**~жда́ть**) to force, compel, coerce; **его́ ~дили к реше́нию** he was forced into a decision.

понужда́|ть, ю *impf. of* ⇒**пону́дить**

понука́|ть, ю *impf.* (*coll.*) to urge on, goad.

пону́р|ить, ю, ишь *pf.*: **п. го́лову** to hang one's head.

пону́р|иться, юсь, ишься *pf.* to hang one's head.

пону́рый *adj.* downcast.

по́нчик, а *m.* doughnut (*Br.*), donut (*US*).

по́нчо *nt. indecl.* poncho.

поны́не *adv.* (*liter.*) to this day, until now.

понюха|ть, ю *pf. of* ⇒**ню́хать**

поню́шк|а, и *f.*: **п. табаку́** pinch of snuff; **ни за ~у табаку́** (*fig., coll.*) for nothing, to no purpose.

поня́ти|е, я *nt.* **1** (*общая мысль*) conception. **2** (*представление*) notion, idea; **име́ть п. (о**+*p.*) to have an idea (about, of); **~я не име́ю!** (*coll.*) I've no idea!; I haven't a clue!; **не име́ю ни мале́йшего ~я!** I haven't the faintest idea! **3** (*usu. pl.*) (*понимание*) notions; level (of understanding); **счита́ться с ~ями слу́шателей** to take into account one's audience level.

поняти́йный *adj.* conceptual.

поня́тливост|ь, и *f.* comprehension, understanding.

поня́тлив|ый (~, ~а) *adj.* sharp, quick (on the uptake).

поня́тност|ь, и *f.* clearness, intelligibility.

поня́т|ный (~ен, ~на) *adj.* **1** (*обоснованный*) understandable; **~но, что**… it is understandable that…; it is natural that…; **~но** (*coll.*) of course, naturally; **я, ~но, не мог согласи́ться** of course, I could not consent; **~ное де́ло** (*coll.*) of course, naturally. **2** (*ясный*) clear, intelligible; **~но?** (*coll.*) (do you) see?; is that clear?; **~но!** (*coll.*) I see!; I understand!

понят|о́й, о́го *m.* witness (*at an official search, etc.*).

пон|я́ть, пойму́, поймёшь, *past* **~́ял, ~яла́, ~́яло** *pf.* (*of* ⇒**~има́ть**) to understand; to comprehend; (*осознать*) to realize; **п. намёк** to take a hint; **дать п.** to give to understand.

пообе́да|ть, ю *pf. of* ⇒**обе́дать**

пообеща́|ть, ю *pf.* (*of* ⇒**обеща́ть**) to promise.

поо́даль *adv.* at some distance, a little way away.

поодино́чке *adv.* one at a time, one by one.

поосторо́жнича|ть, ю *pf. of* ⇒**осторо́жничать**

поочерёдно *adv.* in turn, by turns.

поочерёдный *adj.* alternating; taken in turn.

поощре́ни|е, я *nt.* (*действие*) encouragement; (*награда*) incentive, spur.

поощри́тел|ьный (~ен, ~ьна) *adj.* encouraging.

поощр|и́ть, ю́, и́шь *pf.* (*of* ⇒**~я́ть**) to encourage.

поощр|я́ть, я́ю *impf. of* ⇒**~и́ть**

поп[1]**, а́** *m.* (*coll.*) (*священник*) (*Russian*) priest.

поп[2]**, а́** *m.* (*в игре в городки*) pin; **поста́вить на ~а́** (*coll.*) to place upright.

поп-... *comb. form* pop-.

по́п|а, ы *f.* (*coll.*) (*baby's*) bottom.

попада́ни|е, я *nt.* hit (*on target*); **прямо́е п.** direct hit.

попа́да|ть, ет *pf.* to fall (*of a number of objects*).

попада́|ть(ся), ю(сь) *impf. of* ⇒**попа́сть(ся)**

попадь|я́, и́ *f.* (*coll.*) priest's wife.

попа́|ло: как п. *etc., see* ⇒**~сть** 3

поп-анса́мбл|ь, я *m.* pop group.

попа́рно *adv.* in pairs, two by two.

поп-а́рт, а *m.* pop art.

попа́|сть, ду́, дёшь, *past* **~л** *pf.* (*of* ⇒**~да́ть**) **1 (в**+*a.*) to hit; **п. в цель** to hit the target; **не п. в цель** to miss; **пу́ля ~ла ему́ в лоб** the bullet hit him in the forehead. **2 (в**+*a.*) (*оказаться*) to get (to), find o.s. (in); **(на**+*a.*) to hit (upon), come (upon); **п. в Ло́ндон** to get to London; **п. на по́езд** to catch a train; **п. домо́й** to get home; **п. в плен** to be taken prisoner; **п. кому́-н. в ру́ки** to fall into s.o.'s hands; **п. под суд** to be brought to trial; **не туда́ п.** to get the wrong number (*on telephone*); **п. на рабо́ту** to land a job; **п. впроса́к** to put one's foot into it; **п. в беду́** to get into trouble, come to grief; **п. в са́мую то́чку** to hit the nail on the head; (*impers.*; *coll.*): **ему́ ~ло** he caught it (hot); **ему́ ~дёт!** he'll catch it! **3** (*coll.*): **~ло** *gives indef. force to certain prons. and advs.*: **как ~ло** anyhow; helter-skelter; **что ~ло** any old thing; **где ~ло** anywhere; **он э́то сде́лал чем ~ло** he made it with whatever came to hand.

попа́|сться, ду́сь, дёшься, *past* **~лся** *pf.* (*of* ⇒**~да́ться**) **1** (+*d.*) to come across; **он мне ~лся навстре́чу на у́лице** I ran into him in the street; **п. кому́-н. на глаза́** to catch s.o.'s eye; **что ~дётся** anything; **пе́рвый ~вшийся** the first person one happens to meet. **2** (*быть пойманным*) to be caught; **(в**+*a.*) to get (into); **п. в кра́же** to be caught stealing; **п. с поли́чным** to be taken red-handed; **п. на у́дочку** to swallow the bait (*also fig.*); **п. в беду́** to get into trouble; **смотри́, бо́льше не ~ди́сь!** don't let me catch you again!

попа́хива|ть, ет *impf.* (*coll.*) (+*i.*) to smell slightly (of).

попеня́|ть, ю *pf. of* ⇒**пеня́ть**

попере́к *adv. and prep.*+*g.* across; **положи́те их п.** lay them crosswise; **де́рево упа́ло п. доро́ги** the tree fell across the road; **стоя́ть у кого́-н. п. доро́ги** to be in s.o.'s way; **стать кому́-н. п. го́рла** to stick in s.o.'s throat; **вдоль и п.** far and wide; **знать что-н. вдоль и п.** to know sth. inside out.

попереме́нно *adv.* in turn, by turns.

попере́чин|а, ы *f.* cross-beam, cross-piece, cross-bar.

попере́чник, а *m.* diameter; **шесть ме́тров в ~е** six metres in diameter, six metres across.

попере́чн|ый *adj.* transverse, cross-; **~ая ба́лка** cross-beam; **п. разре́з, ~ое сече́ние** cross-section; **(ка́ждый) встре́чный и п.** anybody and everybody; (every) Tom, Dick, and Harry.

поперхн|у́ться, у́сь, ёшься *pf.* (+*i.*) to choke (over).

попе́рч|ить, ~́у, ~́ишь *pf. of* ⇒**пе́рчить**

попече́ни|е, я *nt.* care; charge; **быть на ~и** (+*g.*) to be in the charge (of); **оста́вить дете́й на п. отца́** to leave children in care of their father; **отложи́ть п. о чём-н.** (*liter.*) to cease caring about sth.

попечи́тел|ь, я *m.* guardian; (*comm.*) trustee.

попечи́тель|ница, ницы *f. of* ⇒**~**

попечи́тельств|о, а *nt.* guardianship; (*comm.*) trusteeship.

поп-звезд|а́, ы, *pl.* **~́ы, ~́, ~́ам** *f.* pop star.

П

попива́|ть, ю *impf.* (*coll.*) to have a little drink (of); **стать п.** to take to drink.

попира́|ть, ю *impf. of* ⇒**попра́ть**

попи́скива|ть, ю *impf.* to cheep, give a cheep.

попи́сыва|ть, ю *impf.* (*coll.*) to write (*from time to time*); (*iron.*) to do a bit of writing.

по́пито *p.p.p. of* ⇒**попи́ть** (*coll.*); **нема́ло бы́ло п.** a fair quantity was drunk.

по|пи́ть, пью́, пьёшь, *past* **~пи́л, ~пила́, ~пи́ло** *pf.* to have a drink.

по́пк|а[1], и *m.* (*coll.*) (*попугай*) parrot; Polly.

по́пк|а[2], и *f.* (*coll.*) = **по́па**

попко́рн, а *m.* popcorn.

попла́ва|ть, ю *pf.* to have, take a swim.

поплав|ко́вый *adj. of* ⇒**~о́к; ~ко́вая ка́мера** float chamber (*of carburettor*); **п. кран** ballcock.

поплав|о́к, ка́ *m.* **1** float. **2** (*coll.*) (*ресторан*) floating restaurant.

попла́|кать, чу, чешь *pf.* to cry (*a little, for a while*); to shed a few tears.

попла|ти́ться, чу́сь, ~тишься *pf. of* ⇒**плати́ться**

попле|сти́сь, ту́сь, тёшься, *past* **~лся, ~ла́сь** *pf.* (*coll.*) to push off; to drag o.s. along; **я тепе́рь ~ту́сь домо́й** I shall push off home now.

попли́н, а *m.* (*text.*) poplin.

попли́н|овый *adj. of* ⇒**~**

поплотне́|ть, ю *pf. of* ⇒**плотне́ть**

поплы́|ть, ву́, вёшь, *past* **~л, ~ла́, ~ло** *pf.* (*о человеке*) to strike out, start swimming; (*о судне*) to set sail.

попля|са́ть, шу́, ~шешь *pf.* (*coll.*) to have a bit of dancing; **ты у меня́ ~шешь!** (*coll.*) you'll pay for this!

поп-му́зык|а, и *f.* pop music.

попо́вич, а *m.* (*coll.*) priest's son.

попо́в|на, ны, *g. pl.* **~ен** *f.* (*coll.*) priest's daughter.

попо́вник, а *m.* (*bot.*) marguerite, white ox-eye.

попо́вский *adj. of* ⇒**поп[1]**

попо́йк|а, и *f.* (*coll.*) drinking-bout.

попола́м *adv.* in two, in half; half-and-half; **раздели́ть п.** to divide in two, divide in half, halve; **дава́йте запла́тим п.** let's go halves; **ви́ски п. с водо́й** whisky and water half-and-half.

по́полз|ень, ня *m.* (*zool.*) nuthatch.

поползнове́ни|е, я *nt.* **1** feeble impulse; half-formed intention; **я име́л п. вы́сказать своё мне́ние, но в конце́ концо́в сдержа́лся** I had half a mind to say what I thought but in the end I restrained myself. **2** (**на** + *a.*) pretension(s) (to).

пополз|ти́, у́, ёшь, *past* **попо́лз, ~ла́** *pf.* to begin to crawl.

пополне́ни|е, я *nt.* **1** replenishment; re-stocking; (*коллекции*) enlargement; **п. горю́чим** re-fuelling. **2** (*mil.*) reinforcement.

пополне́|ть, ю *pf. of* ⇒**полне́ть**

попо́лн|ить, ю, ишь *pf.* (*of* ⇒**~я́ть**) to replenish, fill up; to re-stock; (*коллекцию*) to enlarge; (*mil.*) to reinforce; **п. горю́чим** to re-fuel; **п. свой зна́ния** to supplement one's knowledge.

попо́лн|иться, ится *pf.* (*of* ⇒**~я́ться**) **1** to increase. **2** *pass. of* ⇒**~ить**

пополн|я́ть(ся), я́ю, я́ет(ся) *impf. of* ⇒**~ить(ся)**

пополу́дни *adv.* in the afternoon, p.m.; **в два часа́ п.** at 2 p.m.

пополу́ночи *adv.* after midnight, a.m.; **в два часа́ п.** at 2 a.m.

попо́мн|ить, ю, ишь *pf.* (*coll.*) **1** to remember; **~и(те) моё сло́во** mark my words. **2** (+*d.*) to remind; **я тебе́ э́то ~ю!** I'll get even with you!

попо́н|а, ы *f.* horse-cloth.

попо́тч|евать, ую *pf. of* ⇒**по́тчевать**

поп-пев|е́ц, ца́ *m.* pop singer.

поп-пев|и́ца, и́цы *f. of* ⇒**~е́ц**

поправе́|ть, ю *pf. of* ⇒**праве́ть**

поправи́м|ый (~, ~а) *adj.* rectifiable, remediable.

попра́в|ить, лю, ишь *pf.* (*of* ⇒**~ля́ть**) **1** (*починить*) to mend, repair. **2** (*ошибку, ученика*) to correct, set right, put right. **3** (*шляпу*) to adjust, set straight; **п. причёску** to tidy one's hair. **4** (*улучшить*) to improve, better; **п. своё здоро́вье** to restore one's health.

попра́в|иться, люсь, ишься *pf.* (*of* ⇒**~ля́ться**) **1** (*исправить свою ошибку*) to correct o.s. **2** (*выздороветь*) to get better, recover; **я совсе́м ~ился** I am completely recovered. **3** (*пополнеть*) to put on weight; to look better; **он о́чень ~ился** he has put on a lot of weight; he looks much better. **4** (*о делах*) to improve.

попра́вк|а, и *f.* **1** (*починка*) mending, repairing. **2** (*ошибки*) correction; amendment; **п. к резолю́ции** amendment to a resolution; **внести́ ~и в законопрое́кт** to amend a bill. **3** (*шляпы*) adjustment. **4** (*выздоровление*) recovery; **де́ло идёт на ~у** things are improving; things are on the mend.

поправле́ни|е, я *nt.* **1** (*ошибки*) correction, correcting. **2** (*здоровья*) recovery; (*дел*) improvement; **он вы́ехал на Кавка́з для ~я здоро́вья** he has gone to the Caucasus for his health.

поправля́|ть(ся), ю(сь) *impf. of* ⇒**попра́вить(ся)**

попра́ни|е, я *nt.* trampling; (*fig.*) flouting, disregarding.

попра́ть (*fut. not used*) *pf.* (*of* ⇒**попира́ть**) (*rhet.*) (*топтать*) to trample (upon); (*fig.*) (*закон*) to flout; (*права*) to disregard.

по-пре́жнему *adv.* as before; as usual.

попрёк, а *m.* reproach.

попрек|а́ть, а́ю *impf.* (*of* ⇒**~ну́ть**) (+*a. and i. or* +*a.* **за** + *a.*) to reproach (with).

попрек|ну́ть, ну́, нёшь *pf. of* ⇒**~а́ть**

по́прищ|е, а *nt.* field; profession; **вое́нное п.** soldiering; **литерату́рное п.** the world of letters; **вступи́ть на но́вое п.** to embark on a new career.

по-приятельски *adv.* as a friend; in a friendly manner.

попро́б|овать, ую *pf. of* ⇒**про́бовать**

попро|си́ть(ся), шу́(сь), ~сишь(ся) *pf. of* ⇒**проси́ть(ся)**

по́просту *adv.* (*coll.*) simply; **п. говоря́** to put it bluntly.

попроша́йк|а, и *c.g.* **1** (*coll., pej.*) cadger. **2** (*obs.*) (*нищий*) beggar.

попроша́йнича|ть, ю *impf.* **1** (*coll., pej.*) to cadge. **2** (*obs.*) (*нищенствовать*) to beg.

попроша́йничеств|о, а *nt.* **1** (*coll., pej.*) cadging. **2** (*obs.*) (*выпрашивание милостыни*) begging.

попроща́|ться, юсь *pf.* (**с** + *i.*) to take leave (of), say good-bye (to).

попры́гива|ть, ю *impf.* (*coll.*) to hop about.

попрыгу́н (*oblique cases not used*) *m.* (*coll., joc.*) fidget.

попрыгу́н|ья, ьи *f. of* ⇒**~**

попры́ска|ть, ю *pf.* (+*i.*) to sprinkle (with).

попры́ска|ться, юсь *pf. of* ⇒**пры́скаться**

попря́|тать, чу, чешь *pf.* (*coll.*) to hide (*many objects*).

попря́|таться, чусь, чешься *pf.* (*coll.*) (*о многих*) to hide (o.s.).

попс|а́, ы *f.* (*coll.*) **1** popular culture; sth. trendy. **2** (*mus.*) pop music.

попсо́вый *adj.* (*mus., coll.*) pop.

попуга́|й, я *m.* parrot.

попуга́йнича|ть, ю *impf.* (*coll.*) to parrot.

попуга́йчик, а *m.* parakeet; **волни́стый п.** budgerigar; budgie.

попуга́|ть, ю *pf.* (*coll.*) to frighten a little.

попу́др|ить, ю, ишь *pf.* to powder.

попу́др|иться, юсь, ишься *pf.* to powder one's face.

попули́ст, а *m.* populist.

попули́стский *adj.* populist.

популяриза́тор, а *m.* popularizer.

популяриза́ци|я, и *f.* popularization.

популяризи́р|овать, ую *impf. and pf.* to popularize.

популяриз|ова́ть, у́ю *impf. and pf.* = **~и́ровать**

популя́рност|ь, я *f.* popularity.

популя́р|ный (~ен, ~на) *adj.* popular.

популя́ци|я, и *f.* population (*of plants, animals*).

попурри́ *nt. indecl.* (*mus.*) pot-pourri.

попусти́тельств|о, а *nt.* (*pej.*) tolerance; connivance; **при ~е** (+*g.*) with the connivance (of).

попусти́тельств|овать, ую *impf.* (+*d.*) (*pej.*) to tolerate, put up (with); to connive (at); **почему́ она́ ~ует его́ пья́нству?** why does she put up with his drunkenness?

по-пусто́му *adv.* (*coll.*) in vain, to no purpose.

по́пусту *adv.* (*coll.*) = **по-пусто́му**

попу́та|ть, ет *pf.* (*coll., joc.*) to beguile; **чёрт ~л** it's the devil's work.

попу́тно *adv.* on one's way; at the same time; (*fig.*) in passing; incidentally; **мо́жно п. заме́тить, что…** it may be observed in passing that ….

попу́тн|ый *adj.* **1** accompanying; (*машина*) passing; **п. ве́тер** fair wind, favourable (*Br.*), favorable (*US*) wind; **~ая струя́** backwash. **2** (*fig.*) passing, incidental; **~ое замеча́ние** passing remark.

попу́тчик, а *m.* fellow-traveller (*Br.*), traveler (*US*) (*also fig., pol.*).

попыта́|ть, ю *pf.* (+*a. or g.*; *coll.*) to try (out); **п. сча́стья** to try one's luck.

попыта́|ться, юсь *pf. of* ⇒**пыта́ться**

попы́тк|а, и *f.* attempt, try; **предприня́ть ~у** to make an attempt; **со второ́й ~и** at the second attempt.

попы́хива|ть, ю *impf.* (*coll.*) to let out puffs; **п. тру́бкой, п. из тру́бки** to puff away at a pipe.

попя́|тить(ся), чу(сь), тишь(ся) *pf. of* ⇒**пя́тить(ся)**

попя́тн|ый *adj.*: **идти́ на п.** *or* **на ~ую** (*coll.*) to go back on one's word; to back-pedal.

по́р|а, ы *f.* pore.

пор|а́, ы́, *a.* **~у** *f.* **1** time, season; **весе́нняя п.** springtime; **осе́нняя п.** autumn; **вече́рней ~о́й** of an evening; **в ~у** at just the right time; **не в ~у** at the wrong time; **в ту ~у** then, at that time; **до ~ы́, до вре́мени** for the time being; **до каки́х ~?** till when?, till what time?; **до каки́х ~ вы оста́нетесь здесь?** how long will you be here?; **до сих ~** till now, up to now; **на пе́рвых ~а́х** at first; **с да́вних ~** long, for a long time, for ages; **с каки́х ~?, с кото́рых ~?** since when?; **с тех ~, как…** (ever) since …; **с э́тих ~** since then, since that time. **2** *as pred.* it is time; **давно́ п.** it is high time; **п. спать!** (it is) bedtime!

порабо́та|ть, ю *pf.* to do some work.

поработи́тел|ь, я *m.* (*rhet.*) enslaver.

порабо|ти́ть, щу́, ти́шь *pf.* (*of* ⇒**~ща́ть**) (*rhet.*) to enslave.

порабоща́|ть, ю *impf. of* ⇒**поработи́ть**

порабоще́ни|е, я *nt.* enslavement.

поравня́|ться, юсь *pf.* (**с**+*i.*) to pull alongside (of).

поради́ть, ю *pf. of* ⇒**раде́ть**

пора́д|овать(ся), ую(сь) *pf. of* ⇒**ра́довать(ся)**

поража́|ть(ся), ю(сь) *impf. of* ⇒**порази́ть(ся)**

пораже́н|ец, ца *m.* defeatist.

пораже́ни|е, я *nt.* **1** (*неудача в борьбе*) defeat; **не име́ть ~й** (*sport*) to be unbeaten. **2** (*mil.*) hitting (*the target, the objective*). **3** (*med.*) lesion. **4**: **п. в права́х** (*leg.*) disfranchisement.

пораже́нческий *adj.* defeatist.

пораже́нчеств|о, а *nt.* defeatism.

порази́тел|ьный (~ен, ~ьна) *adj.* striking; staggering, startling.

пора|зи́ть, жу́, зи́шь *pf.* (*of* ⇒**~жа́ть**) **1** (*победить*) to defeat; to rout. **2** (*mil.*) (*ударить*) to hit, strike; **п. кинжа́лом** to stab with a dagger. **3** (*med.*) to affect, strike. **4** (*fig.*) (*удивить*) to strike; to stagger; **меня́ ~зи́л её мра́чный вид** I was struck by her gloomy appearance; **нас ~зи́ли све́дения об их помо́лвке** we were staggered by the news of their engagement.

пора|зи́ться, жу́сь, зи́шься *pf.* (*of* ⇒**~жа́ться**) to be staggered, be astounded.

по-ра́зному *adv.* differently, in different ways.

порайо́нный *adj.* (by) area.

пора́н|ить, ю, ишь *pf.* to wound, injure, hurt (*slightly*).

пора́н|иться, юсь, ишься *pf.* to injure, hurt o.s. (*slightly*).

пораст|а́ть, а́ет *impf. of* ⇒**~и́**

пораст|и́, ёт, *past* **поро́с, поросла́** *pf.* (+*i.*) to become overgrown (with).

порв|а́ть, у́, ёшь, *past* **~а́л, ~ала́, ~а́ло** *pf.* **1** to tear slightly. **2** (*impf.* **порыва́ть**) (**с**+*i.*; *fig.*) to break (with); to break off (with); **она́ давно́ ~ала́ с ним** she broke with him long ago; **п. дипломати́ческие отноше́ния** to break off diplomatic relations.

порв|а́ться, ётся, *past* **~а́лся, ~ала́сь, ~а́ло́сь** *pf.* **1** (*о верёвке*) to break (off), snap. **2** (*об одежде*) to tear. **3** (*impf.* **порыва́ться**[1]) (*fig.*) to be broken (off).

поре́де|ть, ет *pf. of* ⇒**реде́ть**

поре́з, а *m.* cut.

поре́|зать, жу, жешь *pf.* **1** (*поранить*) to cut; **п. себе́ па́лец** to cut one's finger. **2** (+*a. or g.*) (*нарезать*) to cut (*a quantity of*); **п. хле́ба** to cut some bread. **3** (+*a. or g.*) (*убить*) to kill, slaughter (a number of).

поре́|заться, жусь, жешься *pf.* to cut o.s.

поре́|й, я *m.* leek.

порекоменд|ова́ть, у́ю *pf. of* ⇒**рекомендова́ть**

пореш|и́ть, у́, и́шь *pf.* **1** (*coll.*) (*решить*) to make up one's mind. **2** (*obs.*) (*кончить*) to decide, finish, settle; **вот мы ~и́ли де́ло** now we have settled the matter. **3** (*fig., coll.*) (*убить*) to finish off, do away (with), do for.

поржа́ве|ть, ет *pf. of* ⇒**ржа́веть**

по́ристост|ь, и *f.* porosity.

по́рист|ый (~, ~а) *adj.* porous.

порица́ни|е, я *nt.* censure; reprimand; **досто́йный ~я** reprehensible; **вы́разить п.** (+*d.*) to censure; **вы́нести обще́ственное п.** (+*d.*) to reprimand publicly.

порица́тел|ьный (~ен, ~ьна) *adj.* disapproving; reproving.

порица́|ть, ю *impf.* to censure; to reprimand.

по́рк|а[1]**, и** *f.* unstitching, unpicking.

по́рк|а[2]**, и** *f.* (*coll.*) flogging, thrashing; (*хлыстом*) whipping, lashing.

порно́граф *m.* pornographer.

порнографи́ческий *adj.* pornographic.

порногра́фи|я, и *f.* pornography.

порножурна́л, а *m.* pornographic *or* girlie magazine.

порномагази́н, а *m.* sex shop.

порнофи́льм, а *m.* porno film, blue movie.

порну́х|а, и *f.* (*coll.*) porn, pornography.

по́ровну *adv.* equally, in equal parts; **раздели́ть п.** to divide equally, into equal parts.

поро́г, а *m.* **1** threshold (*also fig.*); **переступи́ть п.** to cross the threshold; **я их на п. не пущу́** they shall not darken my door; **п. бе́дности** poverty line; **стоя́ть на ~е сме́рти** to be at death's door. **2** (*geog.*) rapids.

поро́д|а, ы *f.* **1** (*животных*) breed; (*деревьев*) species; (*fig.*) (*людей*) kind, sort, type; **коро́ва джерсе́йской ~ы** Jersey cow; **они́ как раз одно́й и той же ~ы** they are of exactly the same type. **2** (*geol.*) rock; **го́рная п.** rock; (*пласт*) layer, stratum.

поро́дистост|ь, и *f.* (pure) breeding.

поро́дист|ый (~, ~а) *adj.* thoroughbred, pedigree.

поро|ди́ть, жу́, ди́шь *pf.* (*of* ⇒**~жда́ть**) to give rise (to), spawn, engender.

породн|ённый *p.p.p. of* ⇒**~и́ть**; **~ённые города́** twinned cities.

породн|и́ть(ся), ю(сь), и́шь(ся) *pf. of* ⇒**ródни́ть(ся)**

порожда́|ть, ю *impf. of* ⇒**породи́ть**

порожде́ни|е, я *nt.* result, outcome.

поро́жист|ый (~, ~а) *adj.* full of rapids.

поро́жний *adj.* (*coll.*) empty.

порожня́к, а́ *m.* empty vehicles.

порожняко́вый *adj.*: **п. соста́в** = **порожня́к**

порожняко́м *adv.* (*coll.*) empty, without a load.

по́рознь *adv.* separately, apart.

порозове́|ть, ю *pf. of* ⇒**розове́ть**

поро́й (*and* **поро́ю)** *adv.* at times, now and then.

поро́к, а *m.* **1** (*человека*) vice. **2** (*вещи*) defect; flaw, blemish; **~и ре́чи** speech defects; **п. се́рдца** heart disease.

пороло́н, а *m.* foam rubber.

порос|ёнок, ёнка, *pl.* **~я́та, ~я́т** *m.* piglet; **моло́чный п.** (*cul.*) sucking-pig.

поро|си́ться, си́тся *impf.* (*of* ⇒**о~**) to farrow.

по́росл|ь, и *f.* verdure, shoots.

поросяти́н|а, ы *f.* sucking-pig (*meat*).

порос|я́чий *adj. of* ⇒**~ёнок**

пор|о́ть[1]**, ю, ~ешь** *impf.* (*of* ⇒**рас~**) (*платье*) to unstitch, unpick; **п. вздор, ерунду́, чушь** (*coll.*) to talk nonsense; **п. горя́чку** (*coll.*) to be in a (tearing) hurry.

пор|о́ть², ю́, ~́ешь *impf.* (*of* ⇒**вы́~²**) (*coll.*) (*бить*) to flog, thrash; (*хлыстом*) to whip, lash.

пор|о́ться, ~́ется *impf.* (*of* ⇒**рас~**) to come unstitched, come undone; to rip.

по́рох, а (у), *pl.* **~а́, ~о́в** *m.* gunpowder; powder; **он как п.** he is hot-blooded; **ему́ ~а не хвата́ет** (*coll.*) he has not got it in him, he is not up to it; **п. да́ром тра́тить** to spend one's wits to no purpose; **держа́ть п. сухи́м** (*fig.*) to keep one's powder dry; **ни синь ~а** (*coll.*) not a trace; **~ом па́хнет** (*fig.*) there's a smell of gunpowder in the air; there is trouble brewing.

пороховни́ц|а, ы *f.* (*hist.*) powder-flask; **есть ещё по́рох в ~ах** he is/we are *etc.* still going strong.

порохов|о́й *adj. of* ⇒**по́рох; ~а́я бо́чка** powder-keg.

поро́ч|ить, у, ишь *impf.* (*of* ⇒**о~**) **1** (*признавать негодным*) to discredit; **п. чьи-н. вы́воды** to discredit s.o.'s conclusions. **2** (*бесчестить*) to bring into disrepute; to denigrate, blacken, smear; **п. чью-н. репута́цию** to blacken s.o.'s reputation.

поро́чност|ь, и *f.* **1** (*безнравственность*) depravity. **2** (*неправильность*) fallaciousness.

поро́ч|ный (~ен, ~на) *adj.* **1** (*безнравственный*) depraved; wanton. **2** (*неправильный*) faulty; fallacious; **п. круг** vicious circle.

поро́ш|а, и *f.* newly-fallen snow.

пороши́нк|а, и *f.* grain of powder

порош|и́ть, и́т *impf.* (*о снеге*) to fall in powdery form; (*impers.*): **~и́ло** it was snowing lightly.

порош|ко́вый *adj. of* ⇒**~о́к**

порошкообра́з|ный (~ен, ~на) *adj.* powdery.

порош|о́к, ка́ *m.* powder; **стира́льный п.** washing-powder; **стере́ть в п.** to grind into dust; (*fig., coll.*) to make mincemeat (of).

поро́ю = **поро́й**

порт, а, о ~́е, в ~у́, *pl.* **~́ы, ~о́в** *m.* port; (*гавань*) harbour; (*comput.*) port; **вое́нный п.** naval port, naval dockyard; **возду́шный п.** airport; **морско́й п.** seaport.

порта́л, а *m.* (*archit.*) portal.

порта́л|ьный *adj. of* ⇒**~; п. кран** gantry crane.

портати́вност|ь, и *f.* portability, portableness.

портати́в|ный (~ен, ~на) *adj.* portable; **п. компью́тер** laptop computer; **п. телефо́н** mobile phone.

портве́йн, а *m.* port (*wine*).

по́ртер, а *m.* porter, stout.

по́ртик, а *m.* portico.

по́р|тить, чу, тишь *impf.* (*of* ⇒**ис~**) **1** (*аппетит, вечер, настроение, ребёнка*) to spoil; (*машину, здоровье, зрение*) to damage; **не ~тите себе́ не́рвы** don't take it to heart. **2** (*развращать*) to corrupt.

по́р|титься, чусь, тишься *impf.* (*of* ⇒**ис~**) **1** (*о здоровье, погоде, отношениях*) to deteriorate; (*о продуктах*) to go off; (*о зубах*) to decay; to rot; **не п. от жары́** to be heatproof; **отноше́ния ста́ли п.** relations have begun to deteriorate. **2** (*о механизме*) to get out of order. **3** (*нравственно*) to become corrupt.

порт|ки́, ко́в *or* **~о́к** *no sg.* (*coll.*) = **~ы́**

портмоне́ *nt. indecl.* (*obs.*) purse.

портни́х|а, и *f.* dressmaker.

портно́вский *adj.* tailor's, tailoring.

портн|о́й, о́го *m.* tailor.

портня́жн|ый *adj.* tailor's; **~ое де́ло** tailoring.

портови́к, а́ *m.* docker.

порто́вый *adj. of* ⇒**порт; п. го́род** port; **п. рабо́чий** docker.

портпле́д, а *m.* hold-all (*Br.*), traveling bag (*US*).

портре́т, а *m.* portrait; **п. во весь рост** full-length portrait; **поясно́й п.** half-length portrait; **он — живо́й п. своего́ отца́** he is the image of his father.

портрети́ст, а *m.* portrait-painter, portraitist.

портрети́ст|ка, ки *f. of* ⇒**~**

портре́т|ный *adj. of* ⇒**~; ~ная галере́я** portrait gallery.

портсига́р, а *m.* cigarette-case.

португа́л|ец, ьца *m.* Portuguese.

Португа́ли|я, и *f.* Portugal.

португа́л|ка, ки *f. of* ⇒**~ец**

португа́льский *adj.* Portuguese.

портула́к, а *m.* (*bot.*) purslane.

портупе́|я, и *f.* (*mil.*) sword-belt.

портфе́л|ь, я *m.* **1** brief-case; **п.-диплома́т** attaché case. **2** (*pol., comm.*) portfolio; **мини́стр без ~я** Minister without Portfolio.

портше́з, а *m.* sedan(-chair).

порт|ы́, о́в *no sg.* (*coll.*) trousers.

портье́ *m. indecl.* (*hotel*) porter, doorman.

портье́р|а, ы *f.* portière; (*heavy*) curtain.

портя́нк|а, и *f.* foot binding; puttee.

поруб|и́ть, лю́, ~́ишь *pf.* **1** (*в большом количестве*) to chop down (*all or a large number of*). **2** (*некоторое время*) to do a bit of chopping.

пору́бк|а, и *f.* tree-felling, wood-chopping.

поруга́ни|е, я *nt.* desecration; **отда́ть на п.** to desecrate.

пору́ганн|ый *adj.* desecrated; **~ая честь** outraged honour (*Br.*), honor (*US*).

поруга́|ть, ю *pf.* (*coll.*) to scold, swear (at).

поруга́|ться, юсь *pf.* **1** to swear, curse. **2** (**с** + *i.*; *coll.*) to fall out (with).

пору́к|а, и *f.* bail; guarantee; surety; **кругова́я п.** collective guarantee; **взять на ~и** to stand bail (for); **отпусти́ть на ~и** to release on bail.

по-ру́сски *adv.* (in) Russian; **говори́ть п.** to speak Russian.

поруч|а́ть, а́ю *impf. of* ⇒**~и́ть**

поруче́йник, а *m.* **1** (*zool.*) marsh sandpiper. **2** (*bot.*) water parsnip.

поруче́н|ец, ца *m.* special messenger.

поруче́ни|е, я *nt.* (*задание*) errand; (*весомое*) mission, assignment; **по ~ю** (+*g.*) on the instructions (of); (*от имени*) per procurationem (p.p.).

по́руч|ень, ня *m.* (*usu. in pl.*) handrail.

пору́чик, а *m.* (*obs.*) lieutenant.

поручи́тел|ь, я *m.* guarantor.

поручи́тельств|о, а *nt.* guarantee; (*залог*) bail.

поруч|и́ть, у́, ~́ишь *pf.* (*of* ⇒**~а́ть**) **1** (*возложить на кого-н. исполнение чего-н.*) to charge, commission; to instruct; **он ~и́л мне переда́ть вам де́ньги** he charged me to hand you the money. **2** (*вверить кого-, что-н. заботе кого-н.*) to entrust; **ма́льчика ~и́ли тата́рской ня́не** the little boy has been entrusted to the care of a Tartar nanny.

поруч|и́ться, у́сь, ~́ишься *pf. of* ⇒**руча́ться**

порфи́р, а *m.* (*min.*) porphyry.

порфи́р|а, ы *f.* (the) purple (*as monarch's robe*).

порфи́р|ный *adj.* **1** *adj. of* ⇒**~. 2** (*obs.*) purple.

порх|а́ть, а́ю *impf.* (*of* ⇒**~ну́ть**) to flutter, fly about.

порх|ну́ть, ну́, нёшь *pf. of* ⇒**~а́ть**

порцио́нный *adj.* à la carte.

по́рци|я, и *f.* portion; (*кушанья*) helping; **две ~и ды́ни** two portions of melon, melon for two.

по́рч|а, и *f.* **1** (*продуктов*) spoiling; (*машины*) damage; **п. отноше́ний** deterioration of relations. **2** (*нравов*) corruption.

по́рш|ень, ня *m.* (*tech.*) (*двигателя*) piston; (*насоса*) plunger.

порш|нево́й *adj. of* ⇒**~́ень; ~нево́е кольцо́** piston ring; **п. сте́ржень** piston rod.

поры́в¹, а *m.* **1** (*ветра*) gust; rush. **2** (*fig.*) (*чувства*) fit; upsurge; **благоро́дный п.** noble impulse; **п. гне́ва** fit of temper; **под влия́нием ~а** on an impulse, on the spur of the moment.

поры́в², а *m.* (*действие*) breaking; (*место*) break.

порыва́|ть, ю *impf. of* ⇒**порва́ть**

порыва́|ться¹, юсь *impf. of* ⇒**порва́ться**

порыва́|ться², юсь *impf.* **1** (*делать порывистые движения*) to make jerky movements. **2** (+*inf.*) (*пытаться*) to try, endeavour.

поры́висто *adv.* fitfully, by fits and starts.

поры́вистост|ь, и *f.* impetuosity, violence.

поры́вист|ый (~, ~а) *adj.* **1** (*ветер*) gusty. **2** (*движение*) jerky. **3** (*fig.*) (*характер*) impetuous, violent; (*дыхание*) fitful.

порыже́лый *adj.* (*coll.*) reddish-brown (*as result of fading*).

порыже́|ть, ю *pf. of* ⇒**рыже́ть**

пор|ы́ться, о́юсь, о́ешься *pf.* (**в** + *p.*; *coll.*) to rummage (in, among); **п. в па́мяти** to give one's memory a jog.

порыхле́|ть, ю *pf. of* ⇒**рыхле́ть**

по-ры́царски *adv.* in a chivalrous manner.

порябе́|ть, ю *pf. of* ⇒**рябе́ть**

поря́дков|ый *adj.* ordinal; **~ое числи́тельное** ordinal numeral.

поря́дком *adv.* (*coll.*) **1** (*очень*) very, really; **мне п. надое́л э́тот фильм** I found it a really boring film. **2** (*как следует*) properly, thoroughly; **он не объясни́л п., как туда́ попа́сть** he did not explain properly how to get there.

поря́д|ок, ка *m.* order. **1** (*правильное состояние, расположение*) **привести́ в п.** to put in order; **привести́ себя́ в п.** to tidy o.s. up; **следи́ть за ~ком** to keep order; **всё в ~ке!** everything is all right!; **э́то в ~ке веще́й** it is in the order of things; **не в ~ке** out of order, not right; **к ~ку!** (*at a meeting*) order!
2 (*последовательность*): **алфави́тный п.** alphabetical order; **де́ло идёт свои́м ~ком** things are taking their (regular, normal) course; **по ~ку** in order, in succession; **п. дня** agenda; **стоя́ть в ~ке дня** to be on the agenda.
3 (*способ*) manner, way; procedure; **в ~ке** (+*g.*) by way (of), on the basis (of); **в администрати́вном ~ке** administratively; **в обяза́тельном ~ке** without fail; **в спе́шном ~ке** quickly; **в устано́вленном ~ке** in accordance with established procedure; **зако́нным ~ком** legally; **пресле́довать суде́бным ~ком** to prosecute; **п. вы́боров** election procedure; **п. голосова́ния** voting procedure.
4 (*mil.*) (*построение*): **боево́й п.** battle order.
5 (*pol.*) (*система, строй*): **ста́рый п.** the old order; **устано́вленный п.** the established order.
6 (*pl.*) (*обычаи*) customs, usages, observances.
7: **~ка**+*g.* (*coll.*) approximately, about, in the order of; **~ка десяти́ до́лларов** about ten dollars.
8 (*math.*) order.

поря́дочно *adv.* **1** decently; honestly; **они́ поступи́ли вполне́ п.** they acted perfectly decently. **2** (*coll.*) (*довольно*) fairly, pretty; (*довольно много*) a fair amount; **она́ п. уста́ла** she was pretty tired; **мы п. вы́пили** we had a fair amount to drink. **3** (*coll.*) (*довольно хорошо*) fairly well, quite decently; **он поёт п.** he sings quite decently.

поря́дочност|ь, и *f.* decency; honesty.

поря́доч|ный (~ен, ~на) *adj.* **1** (*честный*) decent; honest; **~ные лю́ди** decent folk. **2** (*coll.*) (*значительный*) fair, considerable; **они́ живу́т на ~ном расстоя́нии отсю́да** they live a fair distance from here; **он — п. плут** he is pretty much of a rogue.

пос. (*abbr. of* ***посёлок***) settlement.

поса́д, а *m.* **1** (*hist.*) (*торговая часть города*) trading quarter. **2** (*obs.*) (*пригород*) suburb.

поса|ди́ть, жу́, ~́дишь *pf. of* ⇒**сади́ть** *and* **сажа́ть**

поса́дк|а, и *f.* **1** (*семян*) planting. **2** (*на судно*) embarkation; (*на поезд, автобус*) boarding. **3** (*aeron.*) landing; **вы́нужденная п.** forced landing.

поса́дочн|ый *adj.* **1** planting. **2** (*aeron.*) landing; **~ая площа́дка** landing ground; **~ая фа́ра** landing light. **3** (*aeron.*): **п. биле́т** boarding pass.

поса́|женный *p.p.p. of* ⇒**~ди́ть**

посажёный *adj.* proxy (*for parent of bride or bridegroom at wedding ceremony*), sponsor.

поса́пыва|ть, ю *impf.* (*coll.*) to snuffle; (*во сне*) to breathe heavily.

поса́сыва|ть, ю *impf.* (*coll.*) to suck (at) (*from time to time*).

поса́хар|ить, ю, ишь *pf. of* ⇒**са́харить**

посва́та|ть(ся), ю(сь) *pf. of* ⇒**сва́тать(ся)**

посвеже́|ть, ю *pf. of* ⇒**свеже́ть**

посве|ти́ть, чу́, ~́тишь *pf.* **1** to shine for a while. **2** (+*d.*) to hold a light (for); **я тебе́ ~чу́ до угла́ переу́лка** I will light you to the corner of the lane.

посветле́|ть, ю *pf. of* ⇒**светле́ть**

по́свист, а *m.* whistle; whistling.

посви|ста́ть, щу́, ~́щешь *pf.* to whistle (to).

посви|сте́ть, щу́, сти́шь *pf.* to whistle, give a whistle.

посви́стыва|ть, ю *impf.* to whistle (*softly, from time to time*).

по-сво́ему *adv.* in one's own way; **де́лайте п., поступа́йте п.** have it your own way.

по-сво́йски *adv.* (*coll.*) **1** in one's own way; **он всегда́ поступа́ет п.** he always pleases himself. **2** (*по-родственному*) in a familiar way, as between friends.

посвя|ти́ть, щу́, ти́шь *pf.* (*of* ⇒**~ща́ть**) **1** (+*a.* **в**+*a.*) to let (into); **мы вас ~ти́м в на́шу та́йну** we will let you into our secret. **2** (+*a. and d.*) (*жизнь*) to devote (to), give up (to); (*книгу*) to dedicate (to); **п. себя́ нау́ке** to devote o.s. to (the cause of) learning; **он ~ти́л пе́рвую кни́гу свое́й ма́тери** he dedicated his first book to his mother. **3** (+*a.* **в**+*nom.-a.*) (*в сан*) to ordain, consecrate; **п. в ры́цари** to knight, confer a knighthood (upon).

посвяща́|ть, ю *impf. of* ⇒**посвяти́ть**

посвяще́ни|е, я *nt.* **1** (*в тайну*) initiation. **2** (*в книге*) dedication. **3** (*в сан*) ordination; consecration; **п. в ры́цари** knighting.

посе́в, а *m.* **1** (*действие*) sowing. **2** (*то, что посеяно*) crops; **пло́щадь ~ов** sown area, area under crops.

посевн|о́й *adj.* sowing; **~а́я пло́щадь** sown area, area under crops; *as n.* **~а́я, ~о́й** *f.* sowing campaign.

поседе́лый *adj.* grown grey, grizzled.

поседе́|ть, ю *pf. of* ⇒**седе́ть**

посейча́с *adv.* (*coll.*) up to now, up to the present.

поселе́н|ец, ца *m.* **1** settler. **2** (*сосланный*) deportee.

поселе́ни|е, я *nt.* **1** (*действие*) settling. **2** (*место*) settlement. **3** (*ссылка*) deportation; **отпра́вить на п.** to deport.

поселе́н|ка, ки *f. of* ⇒**~ец**

посел|и́ть, ю́, и́шь *pf.* (*of* ⇒**~я́ть**) **1** to settle; to lodge. **2** (*возбудить*) to arouse, engender; **п. вражду́ ме́жду друзья́ми** to engender enmity between friends.

посел|и́ться, ю́сь, и́шься *pf.* (*of* ⇒**~я́ться**) to settle, take up residence.

посел|ко́вый *adj. of* ⇒**~́ок**

посёл|ок, ка *m.* village; settlement.

посел|я́ть(ся), я́ю(сь) *impf. of* ⇒**~и́ть(ся)**

посему́ *adv.* (*obs.*) therefore.

посеребр|ённый *p.p.p. of* ⇒**~и́ть** *and adj.* silver-plated.

посеребр|и́ть, ю́, и́шь *pf. of* ⇒**серебри́ть**

посереди́не *adv. and prep.*+*g.* in the middle (of).

посере́|ть, ю *pf. of* ⇒**сере́ть**

посети́тел|ь, я *m.* visitor; **ежедне́вный п. пивно́й** habitué of a bar, regular.

посети́тель|ница, ницы *f. of* ⇒**~**

посети́тель|ский *adj. of* ⇒**~**

посе|ти́ть, щу́, ти́шь *pf.* (*of* ⇒**~ща́ть**) to visit; **п. ле́кции** to attend lectures.

посе́т|овать, ую *pf. of* ⇒**се́товать**

посе́|чься, чётся, ку́тся *pf. of* ⇒**се́чься**

посеща́емост|ь, и *f.* attendance; **плоха́я п.** poor attendance.

посеща́|ть, ю *impf. of* ⇒**посети́ть**

посеще́ни|е, я *nt.* visit; (*лекций*) attendance.

посе́|ять, ю *pf. of* ⇒**се́ять**

посиве́|ть, ю *pf. of* ⇒**сиве́ть**

посиде́л|ки, ок *no sg.* young people's gathering (*in the old Russian village, for recreation on winter evenings*).

поси|де́ть, жу́, ди́шь *pf.* to sit (*for a while*).

поси́л|ьный (~ен, ~ьна) *adj.* within one's powers, feasible; **~ьная зада́ча** feasible task; **оказа́ть ~ьную по́мощь** to do what one can to help.

посине́лый *adj.* gone blue.

посине́|ть, ю *pf. of* ⇒**сине́ть**

посин|и́ть, ю́, и́шь *pf. of* ⇒**сини́ть**

поска|ка́ть[1], чу́, ~́чешь *pf. of* ⇒**скака́ть**

поска|ка́ть[2], чу́, ~́чешь *pf.* to hop, jump.

поскользн|у́ться, у́сь, ёшься *pf.* to slip.

поско́льку *conj.* **1** as far as; **п. мне изве́стно** as far as I know; **мы путеше́ствуем посто́льку, п. позволя́ют сре́дства** we travel (just) as much as we can afford. **2** (*так как*) in so far as, since; so long as; **п. вы гото́вы подписа́ть, гото́в и я** so long as you are ready to sign, I am too.

поско́нный *adj.* hempen.

по́скон|ь, и *f.* **1** (*bot.*) male hemp-plant; (*волокно*) hemp fibre (*Br.*), fiber (*US*).

П

2 (*obs.*) (*холст*) home-spun hempen sacking.

поскорée *adv.* somewhat quicker; *int.* ~! quick!

поскрёбк|и, ов *no sg.* scrapings, leftovers (*of food*).

поскуп|и́ться, лю́сь, и́шься *pf. of* ⇨скупи́ться

послаблéни|е, я *nt.* indulgence; leniency.

послáн|ец, ца *m.* messenger, envoy.

послáни|е, я *nt.* 1 (*официальное*) dispatch; (*дружеское*) message. 2 (*liter.*) epistle; Послáния (*bibl.*) the Epistles.

послáнник, а *m.* envoy, minister.

пóсл|анный *p.p.p. of* ⇨~áть; *as n.* п., ~анного *m.* messenger, envoy.

посла|сти́ть, щу́, сти́шь *pf. of* ⇨сласти́ть

по|слáть, шлю́, шлёшь *pf.* (*of* ⇨~сылáть) 1 to send; п. за дóктором to send for the doctor; п. по пóчте to post; п. привéт to send one's regards; п. когó-н. к чёрту (*fig., coll.*) to tell s.o. to go to hell. 2 (*sport, etc.*) (*подвинуть*) to move (*part of the body*).

пóсле *adv. and prep.* + *g.* after; afterwards, later (on); (*after a neg.*) since; п. войны́ after the war; мы с ним не видáлись п. войны́ he and I have not seen one another since the war; он пришёл п. всех he came last; п. всегó after all, when all is said and done; п. чегó whereupon; п. тогó, как after; п. тогó, как мы посмотрéли фильм, мы поéхали домóй after seeing the film we went home.

после... *comb. form* post-.

послевоéнный *adj.* post-war.

послéд, а *m.* (*anat.*) placenta.

после|ди́ть, жу́, ди́шь *pf.* (за + *i.*) to look (after), see (to) (*for a while*).

послéдк|и, ов *no sg.* (*coll.*) remnants, leftovers.

послéдн|ий *adj.* 1 last; (*решение, слово*) final; (в) ~ее врéмя, за ~ее врéмя lately, of late, recently; (в) п. раз for the last time. 2 (*самый новый*) (the) latest; ~ие извéстия the latest news; ~яя мóда the latest fashion. 3 (*из упомянутых*) the latter. 4 (*coll.*) (*самый плохой*) worst, lowest; э́то ужé ~ее дéло! it's the end!; it's the very limit!; ~яя кáпля the last straw; ругáться ~ими словáми to use foul language. 5 *as n.* ~ее, ~его *nt.* the last; the uttermost.

послéдовател|ь, я *m.* follower.

послéдователь|ница, ницы *f. of* ⇨~

послéдовательност|ь, и *f.* 1 (*порядок*) succession, sequence; п. времён (*gram.*) sequence of tenses; в стрóгой ~и in strict sequence. 2 (*логичность*) consistency.

послéдовател|ьный (~ен, ~ьна) *adj.* 1 (*следующий один за другим*) successive, consecutive. 2 (*логичный*) consistent, logical.

послéд|овать, ую *pf. of* ⇨слéдовать

послéдстви|е, я *nt.* consequence; остáвить жáлобу без ~й to take no action on a complaint.

послéдующий *adj.* subsequent.

послéдыш, а *m.* 1 (*coll.*) (*последний ребёнок*) youngest child (*in a family*). 2 (*fig., pej.*) (*последний сторонник*) belated follower.

послезáвтра *adv.* the day after tomorrow.

послезáвтра|шний *adj. of* ⇨~

послеобéденный *adj.* after-dinner.

послереволюциóнный *adj.* post-revolutionary.

послеродовóй *adj.* post-natal.

послесловú|е, я *nt.* afterword, postface; concluding remarks.

послóвиц|а, ы *f.* proverb, saying; войти́ в ~у to become proverbial.

послóвичный *adj.* proverbial.

послуж|и́ть[1], у́, ~ишь *pf. of* ⇨служи́ть

послуж|и́ть[2], у́, ~ишь *pf.* to serve (*for a while*).

послужнóй *adj.*: п. спи́сок service record.

послушáни|е, я *nt.* 1 obedience. 2 (*eccl.*) work of penance; назнáчить комý-н. п. to impose a penance on s.o.

послýша|ть(ся), ю(сь) *pf. of* ⇨слýшать(ся)

пóслушник, а *m.* novice, lay brother.

пóслушниц|а, ы *f.* novice, lay sister.

послýш|ный (~ен, ~на) *adj.* obedient.

послы́ш|аться, усь, ишься *pf. of* ⇨слы́шаться

послюн|и́ть, ю́, и́шь *pf. of* ⇨слюни́ть

посмáтрива|ть, ю *impf.* (на + *a.*) to look (at) from time to time.

посмéива|ться, юсь *impf.* to chuckle, laugh softly; п. в кулáк to laugh up one's sleeve.

посмéнно *adv.* in turns, by turns; by shifts.

посмéнн|ый *adj.* by turns, in shifts; ~ая рабóта shift work.

посмéртный *adj.* posthumous.

посмé|ть, ю *pf. of* ⇨сметь

посмéшищ|е, а *nt.* laughing-stock.

посмеяни|е, я *nt.* (*rhet.*) mockery, ridicule; отдáть когó-н. на п. to make a laughing-stock of s.o.

посмотр|éть(ся), ю́(сь), ~ишь(ся) *pf. of* ⇨смотрéть(ся)

поснимá|ть, ю *pf.* (*coll.*) 1 to take off, take away (all *or* a number of); порá нам п. все рождéственские украшéния it is time we took down all the Christmas decorations. 2 (*phot.*) to take some pictures; (*cin.*) to do some shooting.

по-собáчьи *adv.* like a dog.

посóби|е, я *nt.* 1 (*денежная помощь*) allowance, benefit; п. по безрабóтице unemployment benefit, the dole; п. на детéй child benefit; п. по болéзни sick benefit, sick pay; п. по инвали́дности disability allowance. 2 (*учебник*) textbook; (*учебный предмет*) (educational) aid; наглядные ~я visual aids; учéбные ~я educational supplies; school text-books.

пособ|и́ть, лю́, и́шь *pf.* (*of* ⇨~ля́ть) (*coll.*) (+ *d.*) (*помочь*) to aid; (*облегчить*) to relieve; п. гóрю to assuage grief.

пособля́|ть, ю *impf. of* ⇨пособи́ть

посóбник, а *m.* accomplice; abettor.

посóбни|ца, цы *f. of* ⇨~к

посóбничеств|о, а *nt.* (+ *g.*) complicity (in); aiding and abetting.

посóве|ститься, щусь, стишься *pf. of* ⇨сóвеститься

посовéт|овать(ся), ую(сь) *pf. of* ⇨совéтовать(ся)

посодéйств|овать, ую *pf. of* ⇨содéйствовать

пос|óл[1], лá *m.* (*дипломатический представитель*) ambassador.

посóл[2], а *m.* (*действие*) salting.

посол|и́ть, ю́, ~и́шь *pf. of* ⇨соли́ть

посоловéлый *adj.* bleary, bleared.

посоловé|ть, ю *pf. of* ⇨соловéть

посóльс|кий *adj.* 1 ambassadorial, ambassador's. 2 *adj. of* ⇨~тво; п. автомоби́ль embassy car.

посóльств|о, а *nt.* embassy.

по-сосéдски *adv.* in a neighbourly way.

пóсох, а *m.* 1 (*чабана*) staff, crook. 2 (*епископа*) crosier.

посóх|нуть, нет, *past* ~, ~ла *pf.* (*о многом*) to wither.

посош|óк, кá *m.* 1 *dim. of* ⇨пóсох. 2 (*coll., joc.*) one for the road (*final drink before departure*).

посп|áть, лю́, и́шь, *past* ~áл, ~алá, ~áло *pf.* to have a sleep, have a nap.

поспевá|ть[1], ет *impf. of* ⇨поспéть[1]

поспевá|ть[2], ю *impf. of* ⇨поспéть[2]

поспé|ть[1], ет *pf.* (*of* ⇨~вáть[1]) (*coll.*) 1 (*созреть*) to ripen. 2 (*стать готовым*) to be done.

поспé|ть[2], ю *pf.* (*of* ⇨~вáть[2]) (*coll.*) (*успеть*) to have time; (к + *d.*, на + *a.*) to be in time (for); (за + *i.*) to keep up (with), keep pace (with); ~ли ли вы? were you in time?, did you make it?; онá éле-éле ~ла на пóезд she just caught the train; мы не могли́ п. за ни́ми we could not keep up with them.

поспешá|ть, ю *impf.* (*coll.*) to hurry.

поспéшеств|овать, ую *impf.* (+ *d.*; *arch.*) to help, assist.

поспеш|и́ть, у́, и́шь *pf. of* ⇨спеши́ть; ~и́шь, людéй насмеши́шь (*prov.*) more haste, less speed.

поспéшно *adv.* in a hurry, hurriedly, hastily; п. отступи́ть to beat a hasty retreat; п. уйти́ to hurry off, hurry away.

поспéшност|ь, и *f.* haste.

поспéш|ный (~ен, ~на) *adj.* hasty, hurried.

посплéтнича|ть, ю *pf.* to have a gossip.

поспóр|ить, ю, ишь *pf.* 1 *pf. of* ⇨спóрить. 2 (с + *i.*) (*побороться*) to contend (with). **3** (*заключить пари*) to bet, have a bet.

поспосо́бств|овать, ую *pf. of* ⇒**спосо́бствовать**

посрам|и́ть, лю́, и́шь *pf.* (*of* ⇒**~ля́ть**) to disgrace.

посрам|и́ться, лю́сь, и́шься *pf.* (*of* ⇒**~ля́ться**) to disgrace o.s.

посрамле́ни|е, я *nt.* disgrace.

посрамля́|ть(ся), ю(сь) *impf. of* ⇒**посрами́ть(ся)**

посреди́ *adv. and prep.* + *g.* in the middle (of), in the midst (of); **п. у́лицы** in the middle of the street; **п. толпы́** in the midst of the crowd.

посреди́не *adv.* = **посереди́не**

посре́дник, а *m.* **1** mediator, intermediary; go-between **2** (*comm.*) middle-man.

посре́днича|ть, ю *impf.* to act as a go-between, mediate.

посре́днический *adj.* intermediary; mediation (*attr.*).

посре́дничеств|о, а *nt.* mediation.

посре́дственно 1 *adv.* so-so, mediocrely, not particularly well; **он п. игра́ет в те́ннис** he is not particularly good at tennis. **2** *n.*; *nt. indecl.* fair, satisfactory (*as examination mark*); **я сдал экза́мен по фи́зике на п.** I got a 'fair' in physics.

посре́дственност|ь, и *f.* (*свойство, о человеке*) mediocrity.

посре́дствен|ный (~, ~на) *adj.* **1** mediocre, middling. **2** (*отметка*) fair, satisfactory.

посре́дств|о, а *nt.* (*obs.*) mediation; **при ~е, че́рез п.** (+*g.*) by means of; thanks to.

посре́дством *prep.* +*g.* by means of; with the aid of.

посре́дствующий *adj.* (*liter.*) intermediate; connecting.

посс|а́ть, у́, и́шь *3rd pers. pl.* **у́т** (*vulg.*) *pf. of* ⇒**ссать**

поссо́р|ить(ся), ю(сь), ишь(ся) *pf. of* ⇒**ссо́рить(ся)**

пост[1], а́, о ~е́, на ~у́, *pl.* **~ы́** *m.* post; **наблюда́тельный п.** observation post; **быть на своём ~у́, стоя́ть на ~у́** to be at one's post; **занима́ть высо́кий п.** to hold a high post.

пост[2], а́, о ~е́ *m.* **1** (**в ~е́**) (*воздержание от пищи*) fasting; (*fig., coll.*) abstinence. **2** (**в ~у́**) (*eccl.*) fast; **Вели́кий п.** Lent.

поста́в|ить[1], лю, ишь *pf. of* ⇒**ста́вить**

поста́в|ить[2], лю, ишь *pf.* (*of* ⇒**~ля́ть**) (*снабдить*) to supply.

поста́вк|а, и *f.* supply; delivery; **ма́ссовая п.** bulk delivery.

поставля́|ть, ю *impf. of* ⇒**поста́вить[2]**

поставщи́к, а́ *m.* supplier.

постаме́нт, а *m.* pedestal, base.

постана́влива|ть, ю *impf.* = **постановля́ть**

постанов|и́ть, лю́, ~ишь *pf.* (*of* ⇒**постана́вливать** *and* **~ля́ть**) to decide, resolve; to decree.

постано́вк|а, и *f.* **1** (*столба*) erection; (*паруса*) raising. **2** (*дела, работы*) arrangement, organization; **п. вопро́са** formulation of a question; **у неё хоро́шая п. головы́** she holds her head well; **п. го́лоса** (*mus.*) voice training. **3** (*theatr.*) staging, production; **вчера́ мы ви́дели «Ча́йку» Че́хова в но́вой ~е** yesterday we saw a new production of Chekhov's 'Seagull'.

постановле́ни|е, я *nt.* **1** (*решение*) decision, resolution; **вы́нести п.** to pass a resolution. **2** (*распоряжение*) decree; **изда́ть п.** to issue a decree.

постановля́|ть, ю *impf. of* ⇒**постанови́ть**

постано́в|очный *adj. of* ⇒**~ка** 3; **~очная пье́са** play suitable for staging.

постано́вщик, а *m.* (*пьесы*) producer; (*фильма*) director.

постара́|ться, юсь *pf. of* ⇒**стара́ться**

постаре́|ть, ю *pf. of* ⇒**старе́ть**

по-ста́рому *adv.* **1** (*как раньше*) as before. **2** (*как в старые времена*) as of old.

постате́йный *adj.* paragraph-by-paragraph.

постел|и́ть, ю́, ~ешь *pf.* (*coll.*) = **постла́ть**

посте́л|ь, и *f.* **1** bed; **лечь в п.** to get into bed; **лежа́ть в ~и** to be in bed; **встать с ~и** to get out of bed; **постла́ть п.** to make up a bed; **прико́ванный к ~и** bed-ridden. **2** (*geol., tech.*) bed; bottom.

посте́ль|ный *adj. of* ⇒**~**; **~ное бельё** bed-clothes; **~ные принадле́жности** bedding; **п. режи́м** confinement to bed.

постепе́нно *adv.* gradually, little by little.

постепе́нност|ь, и *f.* gradualness; **п. разви́тия** gradual development.

постепе́н|ный (~ен, ~на) *adj.* gradual.

постепе́нов|ец, ца *m.* gradualist.

постепе́новщин|а, ы *f.* (*pol., pej.*) gradualism.

постесня́|ться, юсь *pf. of* ⇒**стесня́ться**

постиг|а́ть, а́ю *impf. of* ⇒**~нуть** *and* **пости́чь**

пости́гнуть = **пости́чь**

постиже́ни|е, я *nt.* comprehension, grasp.

постижи́м|ый (~, ~а) *adj.* comprehensible.

постила́|ть, ю *impf. of* ⇒**постла́ть**

постимпрессиони́зм, а *m.* post-Impressionism.

постимпрессиони́ст, а *m.* post-Impressionist.

постиндустриа́льный *adj.* post-industrial.

постира́|ть, ю *pf.* **1** (*coll.*) to wash. **2** (*некоторое время*) to do some washing.

по|сти́ться, щу́сь, сти́шься *impf.* to fast.

пости́|чь, гну, гнешь, *past* **~г** *and* (*obs.*) **~гнул, ~гла** *pf.* (*of* ⇒**~га́ть**) **1** (*понять*) to comprehend, grasp. **2** (*о горе, о несчастье*) to befall, strike; **их ~гло ещё одно́ несча́стье** yet another misfortune has befallen them.

посткоммунисти́ческий *adj.* post-Communist.

пост|ла́ть, елю́, е́лешь, *past* **~ла́л, ~лала́, ~ла́ло** *pf.* (*of* ⇒**стлать** *and* **~ила́ть**) to spread, lay; **п. ковёр** to lay a carpet; **п. посте́ль** to make one's bed.

постмодерни́зм, а *m.* postmodernism.

постмоде́рновый *adj.* postmodern.

по́стник, а *m.* (*obs.*) faster, person observing fast.

по́стни|ца, цы *f. of* ⇒**~к**

по́стнича|ть, ю *impf.* to fast.

по́стничеств|о, а *nt.* fasting.

по́ст|ный (~ен, ~на́, ~но) *adj.* **1** Lenten; **п. день** (*eccl.*) fast-day; **п. обе́д** meatless dinner. **2** (*coll.*) (*о мясе*) lean. **3** (*fig., coll., joc.*) (*хмурый*) glum. **4** (*fig., coll., joc.*) (*ханжеский*) pious, sanctimonious.

постов|о́й *adj. of* ⇒**пост[1]**; **~а́я бу́дка** sentry-box; **п. милиционе́р** militia-man on point-duty; **~а́я слу́жба** sentry duty; *as n.* **п., ~о́го** *m.* = **п. милиционе́р**

посто́й[1], ~те (*coll.*) stop!; wait!

посто́|й[2], я *m.* billeting, quartering; **поста́вить на п.** to billet, quarter.

посто́льку *conj.* **п., поско́льку** in so far as …

посторон|и́ться, ю́сь, ~ишься *pf. of* ⇒**сторони́ться**

посторо́нн|ий *adj.* **1** (*побочный*) extraneous, outside; **~ие вопро́сы** side issues; **без ~ей по́мощи** unaided; **~ее те́ло** foreign body. **2** (*чужой*) strange; *as n.* **п., ~его** *m.* stranger; outsider; **«~им вход запрещён»** 'unauthorized persons not admitted'.

постоя́л|ец, ьца *m.* (*obs.*) (*квартирант*) lodger; (*в гостинице*) guest.

постоя́лый *adj.*: **п. двор** (*obs.*) coaching inn.

постоя́нн|ая, ой *f.* (*math.*) constant.

постоя́нно *adv.* constantly, continually.

постоя́н|ный *adj.* **1** constant, continual; **п. ка́шель** continual cough; **п. посети́тель** constant visitor. **2** (*не временный*) constant; permanent, invariable; **п. а́дрес** permanent address; **~ная а́рмия** regular army; **~ная величина́** (*math.*) constant; **п. жи́тель** permanent resident; **~ная рабо́та** a permanent job; **п. ток** (*elec.*) direct current. **3** (**~ен, ~на**) (*не изменчивый*) constant, unchanging; **она́ далеко́ не ~на во вку́сах** she is far from constant in her tastes.

постоя́нств|о, а *nt.* constancy; permanency.

посто|я́ть[1], ю́, и́шь *pf.* (*некоторое время*) to stand (*for a while*).

посто|я́ть[2], ю́, и́шь *pf.* (**за** + *a.*) (*защитить*) to stand up (for).

пострада́|вший *p.p. of* ⇒**~ть**; *as n.* **п., ~вшего** *m.* victim.

пострадá|ть, ю *pf. of* ⇒**страдáть**

постранúчный *adj.* by the page, per page.

пострáнств|овать, ую *pf.* to do some travelling.

постращá|ть, ю *pf. of* ⇒**стращáть**

пострéл, а *m.* (*coll.*) little imp, little rascal.

пострéлива|ть, ю *impf.* to fire intermittently.

постреля́|ть, ю *pf.* **1** (*некоторое время*) to do some shooting. **2** (+*a. or g.*; *coll.*) (*застрелить многих*) to shoot, bag (*a number of*).

постригá|ть(ся), ю(сь) *impf. of* ⇒**пострúчь(ся)**²

пострижéни|е, я *nt.* taking of monastic vows; (*о женщине*) taking of the veil.

пострú|чь, гý, жёшь, гýт, *past* ~**г,** ~**гла** *pf.* **1** (*волосы, ногти*) to cut, trim; (*человека*) to give (s.o.) a hair-cut. **2** (*eccl.*): **п. в монáхи/монáхини** to make, ordain a monk/nun.

пострú|чься¹**, гýсь, жёшься, гýтся,** *past* ~**гся,** ~**глась** *pf.* to have a hair-cut.

пострú|чься²**, гýсь, жёшься, гýтся,** *past* ~**гся,** ~**глась** *pf.* (*of* ⇒~**гáться**) to take monastic vows; (*о женщине*) to take the veil.

построéни|е, я *nt.* **1** construction. **2** (*mil.*) formation.

постро́|ечный *adj. of* ⇒~**йка**

постро́|ить(ся), ю(сь), ишь(ся) *pf. of* ⇒**стро́ить(ся)**

постро́йк|а, и *f.* **1** (*действие*) building, erection, construction. **2** (*здание*) building. **3** (*obs.*) (*место*) building-site.

постро́мк|а, и *f.* trace (*part of harness*).

постро́чный *adj.* by the line, per line.

постскрúптум, а *m.* postscript.

постýка|ть, ю *pf.* to knock (*for a while*).

постýкива|ть, ю *impf.* to knock (*from time to time*), tap; (*о дожде*) to patter.

постулáт, а *m.* (*math., phil.*) postulate.

постулúр|овать, ую *impf. and pf.* to postulate.

поступáтельн|ый *adj.* forward, advancing; ~**ое движéние** forward movement; **п. ход** onward march.

поступ|áть(ся), áю(сь) *impf. of* ⇒~**úть(ся)**

поступ|úть, лю́, ~́ишь *pf.* (*of* ⇒~**áть**) **1** to act; **в дáнных обстоя́тельствах он прáвильно** ~**úл** in the circumstances he acted rightly, did right; **онú с ним плóхо** ~**úли** they have treated him badly. **2** (**в, на**+*a.*) (*зачислиться*) to enter, join; **п. в шкóлу** to go to school; **п. в университéт** to enter the university; **п. на рабóту** to start work; **п. на воéнную слýжбу** to join up, enlist. **3** (*о посланном*) (*дойти*) to come through; to be received; ~**úла жáлоба** a complaint has been received, has come in; ~**úло ли егó заявлéние?** has his application come through, been received?; **п. в продáжу** to go on sale, come on the market; **п. в произво́дство** to go into production.

поступ|úться, лю́сь, ~́ишься *pf.* (*of* ⇒~**áться**) (+*i.*) to waive, forgo; to give up.

поступлéни|е, я *nt.* **1** (*в университет*) entering; (*в партию, клуб*) joining; **п. на воéнную слýжбу** enlisting, joining up. **2** (*денежное*) receipt; (*в библиотеке*) acquisition.

постýп|ок, ка *m.* action; deed; (*pl., collect.*) behaviour (*Br.*), behavior (*US*).

пóступ|ь, и *f.* gait; step, tread; **мéрная п.** measured tread.

постуч|áть(ся), ý(сь), úшь(ся) *pf. of* ⇒**стучáть(ся)**

постфáктум *adv.* post factum, after the event.

посты|дúть, жý, дúшь *pf.* (*coll.*) to reprimand slightly, pull up.

посты|дúться, жýсь, дúшься *pf. of* ⇒**стыдúться;** ~**дúтесь!** you ought to be ashamed (of yourself)!

постыд|ный (~**ен,** ~**на)** *adj.* shameful.

постыл|ый (~**,** ~**а)** *adj.* (*coll.*) hateful, repellent.

посýд|а, ы *f.* **1** (*collect.*) crockery; **глúняная п., фая́нсовая п.** earthenware; **кýхонная п.** kitchen utensils; **жаропрóчная п.** bakeware; **стекля́нная п.** glassware; **фарфóровая п.** china; **чáйная п.** tea-service. **2** (*coll.*) (*отдельный предмет*) vessel, crock.

посýдин|а, ы *f.* **1** vessel, crock. **2** (*coll.*) (*лодка*) old tub.

посу|дúть, жý, ~́дишь *pf.* to judge, consider; ~**дú сам** judge for yourself.

посýд|ный *adj. of* ⇒~**а; п. магазúн** china-shop; ~**ное полотéнце** dish-cloth, tea-towel; **п. шкаф** dresser, china cupboard.

посудомóечн|ый *adj.*: ~**ая машúна** dishwasher, dishwashing machine.

посудомóйк|а, и *f.* **1** (*машина*) dishwasher, dishwashing machine. **2** (*работница*) dishwasher.

посýл, а *m.* **1** (*coll.*) (*обещание*) promise. **2** (*obs.*) (*взятка*) bribe.

посул|úть, ю, úшь *pf. of* ⇒**сулúть**

посýточно *adv.* by the day, for every 24 hours.

посýточн|ый *adj.* 24-hour, round-the-clock; **у них** ~**ое дежýрство** they have a 24-hour spell of duty; ~**ая оплáта** pay by the day.

пóсуху *adv.* (*coll.*) on dry land.

посчастлúв|иться, ится *pf.* (*impers.*+*d.*) to have the luck (to); to be lucky enough (to).

посчитá|ть, ю *pf.* to count (up).

посчитá|ться, юсь *pf.* **1** (**с**+*i.*; *coll.*) to get even (with). **2** *pf. of* ⇒**считáться**

посылá|ть, ю *impf. of* ⇒**послáть**

посы́лк|а¹**, и** *f.* **1** (*действие*) sending. **2** (*вещь*) parcel. **3** (*pl.*) (*побегушки*) errands; **быть на** ~**ах (у**+*g.*) to run errands (for).

посы́лк|а²**, и** *f.* (*phil.*) premise.

посы́лочн|ый *adj.* parcel; ~**ая фúрма** mail-order firm.

посы́льн|ый *adj.* **1** dispatch; ~**ое сýдно** dispatch-boat. **2** *as n.* **п.,** ~**ого** *m.* messenger.

посып|áть, áю *impf. of* ⇒~**ать**

посы́п|ать, лю, лешь *pf.* (*of* ⇒~**áть**) (+*i.*) to strew (with); to sprinkle (with); **п. сóлью** to sprinkle with salt.

посы́п|аться, лется *pf.* to begin to fall; (*fig.*) to rain down.

посягáтельств|о, а *nt.* (**на**+*a.*) encroachment (on, upon), infringement (of); **п. на свобóду** infringement of liberty.

посяг|áть, áю *impf. of* ⇒~**нýть**

посяг|нýть, нý, нёшь *pf.* (*of* ⇒~**áть**) (**на**+*a.*) to encroach (on, upon), infringe (on, upon); **п. на чью-н. жизнь** to make an attempt on s.o.'s life.

пот, а, о ~́е, в ~**ý,** *pl.* ~**ы́,** ~**óв** *m.* sweat, perspiration; **весь в** ~**ý** all of a sweat, bathed in sweat; **в ~́е лицá** by the sweat of one's brow; **~́ом и крóвью** with blood and sweat; **трудúться до седьмóго (четвёртого) ~́а** (*coll.*) to sweat one's guts out.

потаённый *adj.* = **потайнóй**

потайнóй *adj.* secret; hidden.

потакá|ть, ю *impf.* (*no pf.*) (+*d.*; *coll.*) to indulge; **п. ребёнку в капрúзах, п. капрúзам ребёнка** to indulge a child's whims.

потанц|евáть, ýю *pf.* to have a dance.

потáскан|ный (~**,** ~**на)** *adj.* (*coll.*) **1** (*костюм*) shabby, threadbare. **2** (*fig.*) (*вид*) worn, seedy.

потаскýн, а *m.* (*coll.*) lecher, rake.

потаскýх|а, и *f.* (*coll.*) strumpet, trollop.

потасóвк|а, и *f.* (*coll.*) **1** (*драка*) brawl, fight. **2** (*побои*) beating, hiding; **задáть комý-н.** ~**у** to give s.o. a hiding.

потáчк|а, и *f.* indulgence.

потáш, á *m.* potash.

потащ|úть, ý, ~́ишь *pf.* to begin to drag.

потащ|úться, ýсь, ~́ишься *pf.* to begin slowly to make one's way.

по-твоéму *adv.* **1** (*по твоему мнению*) in your opinion. **2** (*как ты хочешь*) as you wish.

потвóрств|о, а *nt.* indulgence, pandering.

потвóрств|овать, ую *impf.* (+*d.*) to show indulgence (towards), pander (to).

потёк, а *m.* stain; damp patch.

потём|ки, ок *no sg.* darkness.

потемнéни|е, я *nt.* darkening; dimness.

потемнé|ть, ю *pf. of* ⇒**темнéть**

потéни|е, я *nt.* sweating, perspiration.

потенциáл, а *m.* potential.

потенциáл|ьный (~**ен,** ~**ьна)** *adj.* potential.

потенциóметр, а *m.* (*elec.*) potentiometer.

потéнци|я, и *f.* (*liter.*) potentiality.

потеплéни|е, я *nt.* warm(er) spell.

потеплé|ть, ет *pf. of* ⇒**теплéть**

по|терéть, трý, трёшь, *past* ~**тёр,** ~**тёрла** *pf.* to rub.

по|терéться, трýсь, трёшься, *past* ~**тёрся,** ~**тёрлась** *pf. of* ⇒**терéться**

потерпé|вший *p.p. act. of* ⇒~**ть;** *as n.* **п.,** ~**вшего** *m.* victim; survivor; **п. от пожáра** fire victim; **п. кораблекрушéние** shipwreck survivor.

потерп|éть, лю́, ~ишь *pf.* **1** (*проявить терпение*) to be patient (*for a while*). **2** (*терпеть*) to tolerate, stand (for); **я не ~лю́ никакóй нáглости** I won't stand for any cheek. **3** (*стерпеть*) to suffer, undergo; **п. кораблекрушéние** to be shipwrecked; **п. поражéние** to sustain a defeat, be defeated; **п. убы́тки** to suffer losses.

потёртост|ь, и *f.* **1** (*место на коже*) sore spot. **2** (*поношенность*) shabbiness.

потёр|тый *p.p.p. of* ⇒~**éть** *and adj.* **1** (*одежда*) shabby, threadbare. **2** (*coll.*) (*вид, лицо*) washed-out.

потéр|я, и *f.* loss; *pl.* (*mil.*) losses; **п. аппети́та** loss of appetite; **п. врéмени** waste of time; **спи́сок ~ь** (*mil.*) casualty list.

потéр|янный *p.p.p. of* ⇒~**я́ть** *and adj.* (*fig.*) lost; **у неё был п. вид** she had a lost expression.

потеря́|ть(ся), ю(сь) *pf. of* ⇒**теря́ть(ся)**

потесн|и́ть, ю́, и́шь *pf. of* ⇒**тесни́ть**

потесн|и́ться, ю́сь, и́шься *pf.* to squeeze up, move closer together (*so as to make room for others*).

потé|ть, ю *impf.* **1** (*pf.* **вс~**) to sweat, perspire. **2** (*pf.* **за~** *and* **от~**) to mist over, steam up. **3** (*impf. only*) (**над** + *i.*; *fig.*) to sweat (over), toil (over).

потéх|а, и *f.* (*coll.*) fun, amusement; **устрóить что-н. для ~и** to do sth. for fun.

потé|чь, кý, чёшь, кýт, *past* ~**к,** ~**клá** *pf.* to begin to flow.

потешá|ть, ю *impf.* to amuse.

потешá|ться, юсь *impf.* **1** to amuse o.s. **2** (**над** + *i.*) to make fun (of).

потéш|ить, у, ишь *pf.* **1** *pf. of* ⇒**тéшить. 2** to amuse (for a while).

потéш|иться, усь, ишься *pf.* **1** *pf. of* ⇒**тéшиться. 2** to have a bit of fun.

потéш|ный (~ен, ~на) *adj.* (*coll.*) funny, amusing.

потúр, а *m.* (*eccl.*) chalice.

потирá|ть, ю *impf.* to rub.

потихóньку *adv.* (*coll.*) **1** (*медленно*) slowly. **2** (*тихо*) softly, noiselessly. **3** (*тайно*) on the sly, secretly.

потли́вост|ь, и *f.* disposition to sweat, perspire.

потли́в|ый (~, ~а) *adj.* sweaty.

потни́к, á *m.* saddle-cloth.

пóт|ный (~ен, ~нá, ~но) *adj.* **1** sweaty, damp with perspiration. **2** (*о стакане*) misted, steamed-up.

потов|óй *adj. of* ⇒**пот; ~ы́е жéлезы** sweat glands.

потогóнн|ый *adj.*: **~ое (срéдство)** (*med.*) sudorific; **~ая систéма трудá** slave labour (*Br.*), labor (*US*).

потóк, а *m.* **1** stream; flow; **гóрный п.** mountain stream; **людскóй п.** stream of people; **п. слов** flow of words; **п. сознáния** stream of consciousness; **лить ~и слёз** to shed floods of tears. **2** (*система производства*) production line. **3** (*учащихся*) group.

потолкá|ться, юсь *pf.* (*coll.*) to knock about.

потолк|овáть, ýю *pf.* (**с** + *i.*; *coll.*) to have a talk (with).

потол|óк, кá *m.* ceiling; **взять что-н. с ~кá** (*joc.*) to make sth. up.

потолстé|ть, ю *pf. of* ⇒**толстéть**

потóм *adv.* (*после*) afterwards; (*позже*) later (on); (*затем*) then, after that; **мы п. придём** we shall come later; **ну, что вы сдéлали п.?** well, what did you do then?

потóм|ок, ка *m.* descendant; *pl.* offspring, progeny.

потóмственный *adj.* hereditary; **он п. серéбряных дел мáстер** he comes of a family of silversmiths.

потóмств|о, а *nt.* (*collect.*) posterity, descendants.

потомý 1 *adv.* that is why; **я был в отпускý, п. я и не знал об э́том** I was on leave, that is why I did not know about it. **2** *conj.*: **п. что; п.... что** because, as; **я не знал об э́том, п. что был в отпускý** I did not know about it because I was on leave; **я п. не знал об э́том, что был в отпускý** (*division of conj. alters emphasis*) the reason I did not know about it was that I was on leave.

потон|ýть, ý, ~ешь *pf. of* ⇒**тонýть**

потóп, а *m.* flood, deluge; **всеми́рный п.** (*bibl.*) the Flood.

потоп|и́ть[1], лю, ~ишь *pf.* to heat (*for a while*).

потоп|и́ть[2], лю́, ~ишь *pf.* (*of* ⇒~**ля́ть**) to sink.

потоплéни|е, я *nt.* sinking.

потопля́|ть, ю *impf. of* ⇒**потопи́ть[2]**

потоп|тáть, чý, ~чешь *pf. of* ⇒**топтáть**

поторáплива|ть, ю *impf.* (*coll.*) to hurry, urge on.

поторáплива|ться, юсь *impf.* (*coll.*) to hurry; **~йтесь!** get a move on!

поторг|овáться, ýюсь *pf.* (*coll.*) to bargain, haggle.

потороп|и́ть(ся), лю́(сь), ~ишь(ся) *pf. of* ⇒**торопи́ть(ся)**

потó|чный *adj. of* ⇒~**к; ~чная ли́ния** production line; **мáссовое ~чное производствó** mass production.

потрáв|а, ы *f.* damage (*caused to crops by cattle*).

потрав|и́ть[1], лю́, ~ишь *pf. of* ⇒**трави́ть[1]4**

потрав|и́ть[2], лю́, ~ишь *pf. of* ⇒**трави́ть[2]**

потрá|тить(ся), чу(сь), тишь(ся) *pf. of* ⇒**трáтить(ся)**

потрáф|ить, лю, ишь *pf.* (*of* ⇒~**ля́ть**) (+ *d. or* **на** + *a.*; *coll.*) to please, satisfy; **им не ~ишь** there's no pleasing them.

потрафля́|ть, ю *impf. of* ⇒**потрáфить**

потрéб|а, ы *f.* (*obs.*) need, want.

потреби́тел|ь, я *m.* **1** (*лицо, организация, потребляющие продукты*) consumer, user. **2** (*pej.*) user of other people.

потреби́тель|ница, ницы *f. of* ⇒~ 2

потреби́тель|ский *adj. of* ⇒~; **~ская кооперáция** (*collect.*) consumers' co-operatives; **~ские товáры** consumer goods.

потреб|и́ть, лю́, и́шь *pf.* (*of* ⇒~**ля́ть**) to consume, use.

потреблéни|е, я *nt.* consumption, use; **товáры ширóкого ~я** consumer goods; **чрезмéрное п.** overconsumption.

потребля́|ть, ю *impf. of* ⇒**потреби́ть**

потрéбност|ь, и *f.* need, requirement; **жи́зненные ~и** the necessities of life; **физи́ческая п.** physical need; **испы́тывать п. в чём-н.** to feel a need for sth.

потрéб|ный (~ен, ~на) *adj.* (*liter.*) necessary, required, requisite.

потрéб|овать(ся), ую, ует(ся) *pf. of* ⇒**трéбовать(ся)**

потревóж|ить(ся), у(сь), ишь(ся) *pf. of* ⇒**тревóжить(ся)**

потрёп|анный *p.p.p. of* ⇒~**áть** *and adj.* **1** (*рубаха, книга*) shabby; tattered. **2** (*fig.*) (*вид*) worn, seedy.

потреп|áть(ся), лю́, ~лет(ся) *pf. of* ⇒**трепáть(ся)**

потрéска|ться, ется *pf. of* ⇒**трéскаться**

потрéскива|ть, ю *impf.* to crackle.

потрóга|ть, ю *pf.* to touch, run one's hand over; **п. пáльцем** to finger.

потрох|á, óв *no sg.* giblets.

потрош|и́ть, ý, и́шь *impf.* (*pf.* **вы~**) to gut, clean.

потру|ди́ться, жýсь, ~дишься *pf.* **1** to take pains; to do some work. **2 ~ди́сь, ~ди́тесь** (+ *inf.*) (*official or joc. injunction*) be so kind as (to); **~ди́тесь зайти́ ко мне зáвтра** be so kind as to call on me tomorrow; **~ди́сь, ~ди́тесь вы́йти!** kindly leave the room!

потряс|áть, áю *impf. of* ⇒~**ти́**

потрясá|ющий *pres. part. act. of* ⇒~**ть** *and adj.* (*coll.*) staggering, stupendous, tremendous.

потрясéни|е, я *nt.* shock; (*социальное*) upheaval.

потряс|ти́[1], ý, ёшь, *past* ~, ~**лá** *pf.* (*of* ⇒~**áть**) **1** to shake; to rock; **п. до основáния** to rock to its foundations. **2** (+ *i.*) (*взмахнуть*) to brandish, shake; **п. кулакóм** to shake one's fist. **3** (*fig.*) (*удивить*) to shake; to stagger, stun.

потряс|ти́[2], ý, ёшь, *past* ~, ~**лá** *pf.* to shake (*a little, a few times*).

потря́хива|ть, ю *impf.* (+ *i.*) to shake (*a little, from time to time*); to jolt.

потýг|а, и *f.* **1** muscular contraction; **родовы́е ~и** birth-pangs. **2** (*fig.*)

(*неудачная попытка*) attempt; **~и на остроу́мие** attempts to be funny.

поту́п|ить, лю, ишь *pf.* (*of* ⇒**~ля́ть**) to lower, cast down; **~я взор** with downcast eyes.

потуп|и́ть, лю́, ~ишь *pf.* to blunt.

поту́п|иться, люсь, ишься *pf.* (*of* ⇒**~ля́ться**) to look down, cast down one's eyes.

потупля́|ть(ся), ю(сь) *impf. of* ⇒**поту́пить(ся)**

по-туре́цки *adv.* in Turkish; in the Turkish fashion; **сиде́ть п.** to sit cross-legged.

потускне́лый *adj.* tarnished; (*fig.*) lack-lustre (*Br.*), -luster (*US*).

потускне́|ть, ю *pf. of* ⇒**тускне́ть**

потусторо́нний *adj.*: **п. мир** the other world.

потуха́ни|е, я *nt.* extinction.

потух|а́ть, а́ю *impf. of* ⇒**~нуть**

поту́х|нуть, ну, нешь, *past* **~, ~ла** *pf.* (*of* ⇒**ту́хнуть**[1] *and* **~а́ть**) to go out; (*fig.*) to be extinguished, die out.

поту́х|ший *p.p. act. of* ⇒**~нуть** *and adj.* extinct; (*fig.*) lifeless, lack-lustre (*Br.*), -luster (*US*); **п. вулка́н** extinct volcano.

потучне́|ть, ю *pf. of* ⇒**тучне́ть**

потуш|и́ть[1]**, у́, ~ишь** *pf. of* ⇒**туши́ть**[1]

потуш|и́ть[2]**, у́, ~ишь** *pf.* (*мясо*) to stew (*for a while*).

по́тч|евать, ую *impf.* (*of* ⇒**по~**) (+*i.*; *coll.*) to regale (with), treat (to).

потяга́|ться, юсь *pf. of* ⇒**тяга́ться**

потя́гива|ть, ю *impf.* (*coll.*) **1** (*верёвку*) to pull (at); to tug (at); **п. папиро́су** to draw at a cigarette. **2** (*пиво*) to sip.

потя́гива|ться, юсь *impf. of* ⇒**потяну́ться**

потян|у́ть, у́, ~ешь *pf.* to begin to pull.

потян|у́ться, у́сь, ~ешься *pf.* (*of* ⇒**тяну́ться** *and* **потя́гиваться**) to stretch o.s.; (*растянуться*) to stretch out.

поу́жина|ть, ю *pf. of* ⇒**у́жинать**

поумне́|ть, ю *pf. of* ⇒**умне́ть**

поуро́чн|ый *adj.* **1**: **~ая опла́та** piece-work payment. **2** (*по урокам*) by the lesson.

поутру́ *adv.* (*coll.*) in the morning.

поуча́|ть, ю *impf.* **1** (*obs.*) (*учить*) to teach, instruct. **2** (*coll., iron.*) (*наставлять*) to preach (at), lecture.

поуче́ни|е, я *nt.* (*liter.*) exhortation, homily; (*coll., iron.*) preaching; sermon, sermonizing.

поучи́тел|ьный (~ен, ~ьна) *adj.* instructive.

поуч|и́ть, у́, ~ишь *pf.* **1** to do a bit of teaching. **2** (+*a. and d.*) to give a bit of instruction (in); to give a few tips (on).

поуч|и́ться, у́сь, ~ишься *pf.* to study (*for a while*); to do a bit of studying.

пофарт|и́ть, и́т *pf. of* ⇒**фарти́ть**

пофор|си́ть, шу́, си́шь *pf.* (+*i.*; *coll.*) to show off, parade.

поха́бник, а *m.* (*coll.*) foul-mouthed person.

поха́бнича|ть, ю *impf.* (*coll.*) to use foul language, use obscenities.

поха́б|ный (~ен, ~на) *adj.* (*coll.*) dirty, smutty.

поха́бщин|а, ы *f.* (*coll.*) smut(tiness), filth.

пожа́жива|ть, ю *impf.* (*coll.*) **1** (*ходить, не торопясь*) to pace; to stroll. **2** (*заходить*) to come, go (*from time to time*).

похвал|а́, ы́ *f.* praise; **отозва́ться с ~о́й** (**о**+*p.*) to praise, speak favourably (*Br.*), favorably (*US*) (of).

похва́лива|ть, ю *impf.* (*coll.*) to praise.

похвал|и́ть(ся), ю́(сь), ~ишь(ся) *pf. of* ⇒**хвали́ть(ся)**

похвальб|а́, ы́ *f.* (*coll.*) bragging, boasting.

похва́л|ьный (~ен, ~ьна) *adj.* **1** (*заслуживающий похвалы*) praiseworthy, commendable. **2** (*содержащий похвалу*) laudatory; **~ьная гра́мота** certificate of merit.

похваля́|ться, юсь *impf.* (+*i.*; *coll.*) to boast (of, about), brag (about).

похва́рыва|ть, ю *impf.* (*coll.*) to be frequently unwell.

похва́ста|ть(ся), ю(сь) *pf. of* ⇒**хва́стать(ся)**

похе́р|ить, ю, ишь *pf.* (*obs., coll.*) to cross out, cancel.

похити́тел|ь, я *m.* thief; kidnapper; abductor; hijacker.

похити́тель|ница, ницы *f. of* ⇒**~**

похи́|тить, щу, тишь *pf.* (*of* ⇒**~ща́ть**) (*вещь*) to steal; (*человека*) to kidnap; to abduct; (*самолёт*) to hijack.

похища́|ть, ю *impf. of* ⇒**похи́тить**

похище́ни|е, я *nt.* theft; kidnapping; abduction; hijacking.

похлёбк|а, и *f.* soup, broth.

похло́па|ть, ю *pf.* to slap, clap (a few times).

похлопо|та́ть, чу́, ~чешь *pf. of* ⇒**хлопота́ть**

похме́ль|е, я *nt.* hangover; **быть с ~я** to have a hangover; **в чужо́м пиру́ п.** unpleasantness suffered through no fault of one's own.

похо́д[1]**, а** *m.* **1** (*mil.*) march; (*naut.*) cruise; **на ~е** on the march. **2** (*mil.*; *fig.*) campaign; **кресто́вый п.** crusade. **3** (*прогулка*) walking tour, hike.

похо́д[2]**, а** *m.* (*coll.*) (*излишек*) overweight.

похода́тайств|овать, ую *pf. of* ⇒**хода́тайствовать**

похо|ди́ть[1]**, жу́, ~дишь** *impf.* (**на**+*a.*) to resemble, look like.

похо|ди́ть[2]**, жу́, ~дишь** *pf.* to walk (*for a while*).

похо́дк|а, и *f.* gait, walk, step.

похо́д|ный *adj. of* ⇒**~**[1]; **п. го́спиталь** field hospital; **~ная крова́ть** camp-bed; **~ная ку́хня** mobile kitchen, field kitchen; **~ная пе́сня** marching song; **п. поря́док** marching order; **~ная ра́ция** walkie-talkie set.

по́ходя *adv.* (*coll.*) **1** as one goes along; on the march; **мы е́ли п.** we ate as we went along. **2** (*fig.*) (*мимоходом*) in passing; in an offhand manner.

похожде́ни|е, я *nt.* adventure, escapade; **любо́вное п.** (love) affair.

похо́ж|ий (~, ~а) *adj.* **1** resembling, alike; (**на**+*a.*) like; **он ~ на де́да** he is like his grandfather; **они́ о́чень ~и друг на дру́га** they are very much alike; **э́то на неё не ~е** (*fig.*) that's not like her; **э́то ни на что́ не ~е** (*fig., pej.*) it's like nothing on earth; it is unheard of. **2** (*coll.*): **~е** it appears, it would appear; **~е на то, что...** it looks as if...; **он, ~е, бо́лен** it would appear he is ill.

по-хозя́йски *adv.* thriftily.

похолода́ни|е, я *nt.* fall of temperature, cold spell.

похолода́|ть, ю *pf. of* ⇒**холода́ть**

похолоде́|ть, ю *pf. of* ⇒**холоде́ть**

похорон|и́ть, ю́, ~ишь *pf. of* ⇒**хорони́ть**

похоро́нн|ый *adj.* **1** funeral; **~ое бюро́** undertaker's. **2** (*fig., coll.*) funereal.

по́хор|оны, о́н, она́м *no sg.* funeral; burial.

по-хоро́шему *adv.* in an amicable way.

похороше́|ть, ю *pf. of* ⇒**хороше́ть**

похотли́вост|ь, и *f.* lewdness, lasciviousness.

похотли́в|ый (~, ~а) *adj.* lustful, lewd, lascivious.

похотни́к, а́ *m.* (*obs., coll.*) clitoris.

по́хот|ь, и *f.* lust.

похохо|та́ть, чу́, ~чешь *pf.* to laugh (*a little, for a while*); to have a laugh.

похрабре́|ть, ю *pf. of* ⇒**храбре́ть**

похра́пыва|ть, ю *impf.* (*coll.*) (*о человеке*) to snore (softly, gently); (*о лошади*) to snort (softly, gently).

похристо́с|оваться, уюсь *pf. of* ⇒**христо́соваться**

похуде́|ть, ю *pf. of* ⇒**худе́ть**

похул|и́ть, ю́, и́шь *pf.* (*obs.*) to scold.

поцара́па|ть, ю *pf.* to scratch slightly.

поцара́па|ться, юсь *pf.* to get slightly scratched.

поца́рств|овать, ую *pf.* to reign (*for some time*).

поцел|ова́ть(ся), у́ю(сь) *pf. of* ⇒**целова́ть(ся)**

поцелу́|й, я *m.* kiss.

поцеремо́н|иться, юсь, ишься *pf. of* ⇒**церемо́ниться**

почасови́к, а́ *m.* employee who is paid by the hour.

почасово́й *adj.* by the hour.

поча́т|ок, ка *m.* (*bot.*) ear; spadix; **п. кукуру́зы** corn-cob.

по́чв|а, ы *f.* **1** soil, ground, earth. **2** (*fig.*) (*основа*) foundation, basis; **на ~е** (+*g.*) owing (to), because (of); **вы́бить ~у из-под чьих-н. ног** to cut the ground from under s.o.'s feet; **подгото́вить ~у** to prepare the ground, pave the way; **стоя́ть на твёрдой ~е, не теря́ть ~ы под нога́ми** to be on firm ground.

по́чв|енный *adj. of* ⇒**~а**

почвове́д, а *m.* soil scientist.

почвове́дени|е, я *nt.* soil science.

почём¹ *interrog. and rel. adv.* (*coll.*) how much; **п. сего́дня я́блоки?** how much are apples today?; **узна́ть, п. фунт ли́ха** (*coll.*) to fall upon hard times.

почём² *interrog. adv.* (*only used with parts of v.* **знать** *coll.*) how?; **п. знать?** who knows?; how is one to know?; **п. я зна́ю?** how should I know?

почему́ 1 *interrog. and rel. adv.* why; **п. вы так ду́маете?** why do you think that? **2** *as conj.* (and) so; which is why; **она́ простуди́лась, п. и оста́лась до́ма** she has caught a cold, which is why she has stayed at home.

почему́-либо = **почему́-нибудь**

почему́-нибудь *adv.* for some reason or other.

почему́-то *adv.* for some reason.

по́черк, а *m.* handwriting; (*fig.*) hallmark.

почерне́лый *adj.* darkened.

почерне́|ть, ю *pf. of* ⇒**черне́ть**

почерп|а́ть, а́ю *impf. of* ⇒**~ну́ть**

почерп|ну́ть, ну́, нёшь *pf.* (*of* ⇒**~а́ть**) **1** (+*a. or g.*) (*воды*) to draw. **2** (*fig.*) (*сведения*) to glean, pick up.

почерстве́|ть, ю *pf. of* ⇒**черстве́ть**

поче|са́ть(ся), шу́(сь), ~шешь(ся) *pf. of* ⇒**чеса́ть(ся)**

по́чест|ь, и *f.* honour (*Br.*), honor (*US*); **возда́ть ~и, оказа́ть ~и** (+*d.*) to pay homage (to).

по|че́сть, чту́, чтёшь, *past* **~чёл, ~чла́** *pf.* (*of* ⇒**~чита́ть¹**) (*obs.*) to consider, think; **он ~чёл свои́м до́лгом вы́ступить** he considered it his duty to speak.

почёсыва|ть, ю *impf.* (*coll.*) to scratch (*from time to time*).

почёт, а *m.* honour (*Br.*), honor (*US*); respect, esteem; **быть в ~е у кого́-н., по́льзоваться ~ом у кого́-н.** to stand high in s.o.'s esteem.

почёт|ный *adj.* **1** (*пользующийся почётом*) honoured (*Br.*), honored (*US*); **п. гость** guest of honour (*Br.*), honor (*US*). **2** (*избираемый в знак почёта*) honorary; **п. член** honorary member. **3** (**~ен, ~на**) (*являющийся проявлением почёта; доставляющий почёт*) honourable (*Br.*), honorable (*US*); **п. карау́л** guard of honour (*Br.*), honor (*US*); **п. мир** honourable (*Br.*), honorable (*US*) peace.

по́ч|ечный¹ *adj. of* ⇒**~ка¹**

по́чечн|ый² *adj.* (*anat., med.*) nephritic; renal; **~ые ка́мни** kidney-stones.

почива́|ть, ю *impf.* (*obs.*) **1** to sleep. **2** *impf. of* ⇒**почи́ть**

почи́|вший *p.p. of* ⇒**~ть;** *as n.* **п., ~вшего** *m.*, **~вшая, ~вшей** *f.* the deceased.

почи́н, а *m.* **1** (*инициатива*) initiative; **взять на себя́ п.** to take the initiative. **2** (*начало*) beginning, start.

почин|и́ть, ю́, ~ишь *pf.* (*of* ⇒**чини́ть¹** *and* (*coll.*) **~я́ть**) to repair, mend.

почи́нк|а, и *f.* repairing, mending; **отда́ть что́-н. в ~у** to have sth. repaired, mended.

почин|я́ть, я́ю *impf.* (*coll.*) *of* ⇒**~и́ть**

почи́|стить(ся), щу(сь), стишь(ся) *pf. of* ⇒**чи́стить(ся)**

почита́й *adv.* (*coll.*) **1** (*почти*) almost. **2** (*пожалуй*) it seems; very likely.

почита́ни|е, я *nt.* **1** (*уважение*) honouring (*Br.*), honoring (*US*); (+*g.*) respect (for). **2** (*культ*) reverence, worship.

почита́тел|ь, я *m.* admirer; worshipper.

почита́тель|ница, ницы *f. of* ⇒**~**

почита́|ть¹, ю *impf. of* ⇒**поче́сть**

почита́|ть², ю *impf.* **1** (*уважать*) to honour (*Br.*), honor (*US*), respect. **2** (*как святыню*) to revere.

почита́|ть³, ю *pf.* **1** (*немного*) to read (*a little, for a while*). **2** (*coll.*) (*прочитать*) to read.

почи́тыва|ть, ю *impf.* (*coll.*) to read (now and then).

почи́|ть, ю, ешь *pf.* (*of* ⇒**~ва́ть**) (*rhet.*) to rest; (*fig.*) to pass away; **п. на ла́врах** to rest on one's laurels.

почи́ще *adv.* **1** cleaner. **2** (*fig., coll.*) better; stronger, more vividly; **он вы́разился п. остальны́х** he expressed himself more vividly than the others.

по́чк|а¹, и *f.* (*bot.*) bud.

по́ч|ка², ки *f.* **1** (*anat.*) kidney; **иску́сственная п.** (*med.*) kidney machine. **2** (*pl.; cul.*) kidneys.

почкова́ни|е, я *nt.* (*biol.*) budding; gemmation.

по́чт|а, ы *f.* **1** (*система*) post; **возду́шная п.** air mail; **электро́нная п.** e-mail; **посла́ть по ~е, ~ой** to send by post, post; **с у́тренней (с вече́рней) ~ой** by the morning (evening) post; **с обра́тной ~ой** by return (of post). **2** (*письма*) (the) post, (the) mail; **пришла́ ли п.?** has the post come? **3** (*учреждение*) post office.

почтальо́н, а *m.* postman.

почта́мт, а *m.* main post office (*of city or town*).

почте́ни|е, я *nt.* respect, esteem; deference; **относи́ться с ~ем (к)** to treat with respect; **с соверше́нным ~ем** (*epistolary formula*) respectfully yours.

почте́н|ный (~ен, ~на) *adj.* **1** estimable; venerable; **~ная рабо́та** estimable work; **п. во́зраст** venerable age. **2** (*fig., coll.*) (*значительный*) considerable.

почти́ *adv.* almost, nearly; **п. ничего́** next to nothing; **п. что** = **п.**

почти́тельност|ь, и *f.* respect, deference.

почти́тел|ьный (~ен, ~ьна) *adj.* respectful, deferential.

по|чти́ть, чту́, чти́шь, чтят *or* **чту́т** pf. to honour (*Br.*), honor (*US*).

почтови́к, а́ *m.* (*coll.*) postal worker.

почт|о́вый *adj. of* ⇒**~а; ~о́вая бума́га** note-paper; **п. ваго́н** mail-van (*Br.*), mail car (*US*); **п. го́лубь** carrier-pigeon, homing pigeon; **п. и́ндекс** post-code (*Br.*), Zip code (*US*); **~о́вая ка́рточка** postcard; **~о́вая ма́рка** (postage) stamp; **~о́вое отделе́ние** post-office; **~о́вые отправле́ния** things sent by post; **п. перево́д** postal order; **п. по́езд** mail train; **~о́вые расхо́ды** postage; **п. я́щик** (*i*) letter-box, postbox (*Br.*), mailbox (*US*); (*comput.*) mailbox; (*ii*) = **я́щик** 3; **е́хать на ~о́вых** (*hist.*) to travel by post-chaise.

поч|ту́¹, тёшь *see* ⇒**~е́сть**

поч|ту́², ти́шь *see* ⇒**~ти́ть**

почу́вств|овать, ую *pf. of* ⇒**чу́вствовать**

почу́д|иться, ится *pf. of* ⇒**чу́диться**

почу́|ять, ю *pf. of* ⇒**чу́ять**

пошаба́ш|ить, у, ишь *pf. of* ⇒**шаба́шить**

поша́лива|ть, ю *impf.* (*coll.*) **1** to act up; to play up (*also fig.*); **се́рдце у меня́ ~ет** I have trouble with my heart; **моя́ маши́на ~ет** my car is acting up. **2** (*fig.*) (*заниматься разбоем*) to engage in robbery; **в э́том райо́не ~ют** your wallet isn't safe in these parts.

пошал|и́ть, ю́, и́шь *pf.* to get up to mischief (*for a while*).

поша́р|ить, ю, ишь *pf. of* ⇒**ша́рить**

пошатн|у́ть, у́, ёшь *pf.* to shake (*also fig.*); **п. чью-н. ве́ру** to shake s.o.'s faith; (*impers.*): **меня́ ~у́ло** I was shaken.

пошатн|у́ться, у́сь, ёшься *pf.* **1** to sway, totter, stagger. **2** (*fig.*) to be shaken; **её здоро́вье ~у́лось** her health has suffered.

поша́тыва|ться, юсь *impf.* to sway, totter, stagger.

пошеве́лива|ться, юсь *impf.* (*coll.*) to stir (*from time to time*); **ну, ~йся!** come on!, get a move on!

пошевел|и́ть(ся), ю́(сь), ~и́шь(ся) *pf. of* ⇒**шевели́ть(ся)**

пошевельн|у́ть(ся), у́(сь), ёшь(ся) *pf.* = **пошевели́ть(ся)**

по́шевн|и, ей *no sg.* (*dial.*) (wide) sledge.

пош|ёл, ла́ *see* ⇒**пойти́**

пошеп|та́ть, чу́, ~чешь *pf.* to say in a whisper; to whisper.

пошеп|та́ться, чу́сь, ~чешься *pf.* (*coll.*) to converse in whispers.

поши́б, а *m.* (*coll.*) manners; ways.

поши́в, а *m.* = **поши́вка**

поши́вк|а, и *f.* sewing.

поши́вочн|ый *adj.* sewing; **~ая мастерска́я** (sewing) workshop.

пошле́|ть, ю *impf.* (*of* ⇒**о~**) (*coll.*) to become vulgar.

по́шлин|а, ы *f.* duty; **и́мпортная п.** import duty; **э́кспортная п.** export duty; **ге́рбовая п.** stamp-duty; **суде́бная п.** costs, legal expenses; **тамо́женная п.** customs duties; **обложи́ть ~ой** to impose duty (on).

по́шлин|ный *adj. of* ⇒**~а**

по́шлост|ь, и *f.* **1** (*свойство*)

П

vulgarity, commonness. **2** (*замечание*) trite remark, banality; **говорить ~и** to utter banalities.

пóшл|ый (~, ~á, ~о) *adj.* **1** (*низкий*) vulgar; **у негó óчень ~ые вкýсы** he has very vulgar tastes. **2** (*банальный*) trite, banal; **~ая пóвесть** banal story.

пошля́к, á *m.* (*coll.*) vulgar person.

поштýчно *adv.* by the piece.

поштýчн|ый *adj.* by the piece; **~ая оплáта** piecework payment.

пошум|éть, лю́, и́шь *pf.* to make a bit of a noise.

пошу|ти́ть, чý, ~тишь *pf. of* ⇒**шути́ть**

пощáд|а, ы *f.* mercy; **без ~ы** without mercy.

пощa|ди́ть, жý, ди́шь *pf. of* ⇒**щади́ть**

пощеко|тáть, чý, ~чешь *pf. of* ⇒**щекотáть**

пощёлкивани|е, я *nt.* clicking.

пощёлкива|ть, ю *impf.* (+*i.*) to click; **п. пáльцами** to snap one's fingers.

пощёчин|а, ы *f.* slap in the face (*also fig.*); **дать ~у** (+*d.*) to slap in the face.

пощип|áть, лю́, ~лешь *pf.* **1** (+*a. or g.*) (*травы*) to nibble. **2** (*coll.*) (*выщипать*) to pull out, pull up. **3** (*fig., joc.*) (*пограбить*) to pinch (from), rob. **4** (*fig., joc.*) (*раскритиковать*) to pick holes in; to tear a strip off.

пощи́пыва|ть, ю *impf.* (*coll.*) (*траву*) to nibble (*from time to time*); (*о морозе*) to nip; (*impers.*): **пощи́пывает в гóрле** I have/he has *etc.* a tickle in the throat.

пощýпа|ть, ю *pf. of* ⇒**щýпать**

поэ́зи|я, и *f.* poetry.

поэ́м|а, ы *f.* (narrative) poem (*usu. of large proportions*).

поэ́т, а *m.* poet.

поэтáпный *adj.* phased.

поэтéсс|а, ы *f.* poetess.

поэтизи́р|овать, ую *impf. and pf.* to wax poetic (about).

поэ́тик|а, и *f.* **1** (*теория*) poetics; theory of poetry. **2** (*стиль*) poetic style.

поэти́ческий *adj.* (*in var. senses*) poetic(al).

поэти́ч|ный (~ен, ~на) *adj.* (*fig.*) poetic(al).

поэ́тому *adv.* therefore, and so.

по|ю́¹, ёшь *see* ⇒**петь**

по|ю́², ~и́шь *see* ⇒**пои́ть**

появ|и́ться, лю́сь, ~ишься *pf.* (*of* ⇒**~ля́ться**) to appear.

появлéни|е, я *nt.* appearance.

появля́|ться, юсь *impf. of* ⇒**появи́ться**

пóяс, а, *pl.* **~á, ~óв** *m.* **1** belt; **спасáтельный п.** lifebelt; **заткнýть зá п.** (*coll.*) to outdo. **2** (*талия*) waist; **кла́няться в п.** to bow from the waist; **по п.** up to the waist, waist-deep, waist-high. **3** (*pl.* **~ы**) (*geog., econ.*) zone, belt.

пояснéни|е, я *nt.* explanation.

поясни́тельный *adj.* explanatory.

поясн|и́ть, ю́, и́шь *pf.* (*of* ⇒**~я́ть**) to explain, elucidate.

поясни́ц|а, ы *f.* small of the back; **боль, прострéл в ~е** lumbago.

поясни́чный *adj.* (*anat.*) lumbar.

поясн|óй *adj.* **1** *adj. of* ⇒**пóяс 1; п. ремéнь** (waist-)belt. **2** to the waist, waist-high; **~áя вáнна** hip-bath; **п. поклóн** bow from the waist; **п. портрéт** half-length portrait. **3** (*geog., econ.*) zonal; **п. тари́ф** zonal tariff.

поясн|я́ть, я́ю *impf. of* ⇒**~и́ть**

пр. *abbr. of* **1** ***проéзд*** Passage. **2** ***проспéкт*** Avenue. **3** ***прóчее;*** **и ~** etc., etcetera, and so on.

прабáб|ка, ки *f.* = **~ушка**

прабáбушк|а, и *f.* great-grandmother.

прáвд|а, ы *f.* **1** truth; the truth; **п.-мáтка** (*coll.*) the simple truth; **сýщая п.** the honest truth; **э́то п.** it is true; it is the truth; **по ~е сказáть, ~у говоря́** to tell the truth; **вáша п.** you are right; **что п., то п.** there's no denying the truth; **всéми ~ами и непрáвдами** by fair means or foul. **2** (*справедливость*) justice; **искáть ~ы** to seek justice. **3**: **п.?** is that so?; really?; **п. (ли)?** is it true?; **п. ли, что он умирáет?** is it true that he is dying?; **не п. ли?** *in interrog. sentences indicates that affirmative answer is expected*; **вы погаси́ли свет, не п. ли?** you (did) put out the light, didn't you? **4** (*as concessive conj.*) true; **п., я емý не написáл, но я вот-вóт собирáлся позвони́ть** true, I had not written to him, but I was on the point of phoning.

правди́вост|ь, и *f.* **1** (*рассказа*) truth; veracity. **2** (*человека*) truthfulness; uprightness.

правди́в|ый (~, ~а) *adj.* **1** true; veracious; **п. расскáз** true story. **2** (*человек*) truthful; upright; **п. отвéт** honest answer.

правдоподóби|е, я *nt.* verisimilitude; probability, likelihood; plausibility.

правдоподóб|ный (~ен, ~на) *adj.* probable, likely; plausible.

прáведник, а *m.* righteous man; **спать сном ~а** to sleep the sleep of the just.

прáведн|ица, ицы *f. of* ⇒**~ик**

прáвед|ный (~ен, ~на) *adj.* **1** (*благочестивый*) righteous; upright. **2** (*справедливый*) just.

правёж, á *m.* (*hist.*) flogging (*of insolvent debtor*).

правé|ть, ю *impf.* (*of* ⇒**по~**) (*pol.*) to become more conservative, swing to the right.

прáвил|о, а *nt.* **1** rule; regulation; **граммати́ческие ~а** grammatical rules; **~а ýличного движéния** traffic regulations; **как п.** as a rule; **по всем ~ам** according to all the rules. **2** (*принцип*) rule, principle; **взять за п.** to make it a rule; **взять себé за п.** (+*inf.*) to make a point (of).

прáвильно *adv.* **1** (*верно*) rightly; correctly; **п. ли идýт вáши часы́?** is your watch right? **2** (*регулярно*) regularly.

прáвильност|ь, и *f.* **1** (*верность*) rightness; correctness. **2** (*регулярность*) regularity.

прáвил|ьный (~ен, ~ьна) *adj.* **1** (*верный*) right, correct; **п. отвéт** the right answer; **~ьная дробь** proper fraction; **~ьно** (*as pred.*) it is correct; **~ьно!** that's right! **2** (*регулярный*) regular; **~ьное движéние поездóв** regular train service(s); **~ьное спряжéние** (*gram.*) regular conjugation; **~ьные черты́ лицá** regular features.

прави́тел|ь, я *m.* ruler.

прави́тель|ница, ницы *f. of* ⇒**~**

прави́тельственн|ый *adj.* governmental; government; **~ое решéние** governmental decision; **~ое учреждéние** government establishment.

прави́тельств|о, а *nt.* government.

прáв|ить¹, лю, ишь *impf.* (*no pf.*) (+*i.*) **1** (*государством*) to rule (over), govern. **2** (*машиной*) to drive; **п. рулём** to steer.

прáв|ить², лю, ишь *impf.* (*no pf.*) **1** (*исправлять*) to correct; **п. корректýру** to read, correct proofs. **2** (*бритву*) to set.

прáвк|а, и *f.* **1** (*исправление*) correcting; **п. корректýры** proof-reading. **2** (*бритвы*) setting.

правлéни|е, я *nt.* **1** (*действие*) government; **óбраз ~я** form of government. **2** (*орган*) board, governing body; **быть члéном ~я** to be on the board.

прáвленый *adj.* corrected; **п. экземпля́р** fair copy.

прáвнук, а *m.* great-grandson.

прáвнучк|а, и *f.* great-granddaughter.

прáв|о¹, а, *pl.* **~á** *nt.* **1** (*наука*) law; **граждáнское п.** civil law; **оби́чное п.** common law; **уголóвное п.** criminal law; **изучи́ть п.** to study law. **2** (*свобода*) right; **(води́тельские) ~á** driving licence (*Br.*), driver's license (*US*); **п. вéто** (right of) veto; **п. гóлоса, избирáтельное п.** the vote, suffrage; **п. убéжища** asylum, right of sanctuary; **~á человéка** human rights; **п. на наслéдство** right of inheritance; **по ~у** by rights; **с пóлным ~ом** rightfully; **быть в ~е** (+*inf.*) to have the right (to), be entitled (to); **воспóльзоваться свои́м ~ом (на**+*a.*) to exercise one's right (to); **имéть п. (на**+*a.*) to have the right (to), be entitled (to).

прáво² *adv.* (*coll.*) really; **я, п., не знáю, кудá онá дéлась** I really do not know where she has got to.

правобережный *adj.* situated on the right bank, right-bank.

правовéд, а *m.* lawyer, jurist.

правовéдени|е, я *nt.* jurisprudence.

правовéрност|ь, и *f.* orthodoxy.

правовéр|ный (~ен, ~на) *adj.* (*relig.*) **1** orthodox. **2** *as n.*: **~ные** the faithful.

правов|óй *adj.* legal; lawful; **~óе госудáрство** (*pol.*) state based on the rule of law.

правозащи́тник, а *m.* human rights activist.

правозащи́тни|ца, цы *f. of* ⇒**~к**

правомéр|ный (~ен, ~на) *adj.* (*действие, поступок*) lawful, rightful; (*вопрос, сомнение*) legitimate.

правомо́чи|е, я *nt.* competence.

правомо́ч|ный (~ен, ~на) *adj.* competent, authorized.

правонаруше́ни|е, я *nt.* infringement of the law, offence, delinquency.

правонаруши́тел|ь, я *m.* law-breaker, offender; **ю́ный п.** juvenile delinquent.

правонаруши́тель|ница, ницы *f. of* ⇒~

правоохрани́тельн|ый *adj.* law-enforcement; **~ые о́рганы** law-enforcement agencies.

правописа́ни|е, я *nt.* spelling, orthography.

правопоря́д|ок, ка *m.* law and order.

правосла́ви|е, я *nt.* (*relig.*) Orthodoxy.

правосла́вн|ый *adj.* (*relig.*) orthodox; **~ая це́рковь** Orthodox Church; *as n.* **п., ~ого** *m.*, **~ая, ~ой** *f.* member of the Orthodox Church.

правоспосо́бност|ь, и *f.* (*leg.*) (legal) capacity.

правоспосо́б|ный (~ен, ~на) *adj.* (*leg.*) capable.

правосу́ди|е, я *nt.* justice.

правот|а́, ы́ *f.* rightness; (*leg.*) innocence.

пра́в|ый[1] *adj.* **1** (*по направлению*) right; right-hand; (*naut.*) starboard; **п. борт** starboard side; **~ая рука́** (*fig.*) right-hand man. **2** (*pol.*) right-wing, right; **~ая па́ртия** party of the right.

пра́в|ый[2] **(~, ~а́, ~о)** *adj.* **1** (*правильный*) right, correct; **вы не совсе́м ~ы** you are not quite right. **2** (*справедливый*) righteous, just; **~ое де́ло** a just cause. **3** (*leg.*) innocent, not guilty.

пра́в|ящий *pres. part. act. of* ⇒**~ить** *and adj.* ruling; **~ящие кла́ссы** the ruling classes.

Пра́г|а, и *f.* Prague.

прагмати́зм, а *m.* pragmatism.

прагма́тик, а *m.* pragmatist.

прагмати́ческий *adj.* pragmatic.

пра́дед, а *m.* **1** great-grandfather. **2** (*pl.*) ancestors, forefathers.

праде́довск|ий *adj. of* ⇒**пра́дед; ~ие времена́** ancestral times.

праде́душк|а, и *m. dim. of* ⇒**пра́дед**

пра́зднеств|о, а *nt.* festival; festivities.

пра́здник, а *m.* **1** (public) holiday; (*религиозный*) (religious) feast, festival; **по ~ам** on high days and holidays; **с ~ом!** happy holiday!; **бу́дет и на на́шей у́лице п.** (*fig.*) our day will come. **2** (*день радости, торжества*) festive occasion; **по слу́чаю ~а** to celebrate the occasion.

пра́здничн|ый *adj.* holiday; festive; **п. день** holiday; **п. наря́д** holiday attire; **~ое настрое́ние** festive mood.

пра́здновани|е, я *nt.* celebration.

пра́здн|овать, ую *impf.* (*of* ⇒**от~**) to celebrate.

празднросло́ви|е, я *nt.* idle talk, empty talk.

пра́здност|ь, и *f.* **1** idleness, inactivity. **2** (*разговора*) emptiness.

пра́зд|ный (~ен, ~на) *adj.* **1** (*бездельный*) idle, inactive; **~ная жизнь** a life of idleness. **2** (*пустой*) idle, empty; **~ное любопы́тство** idle curiosity; **п. разгово́р** empty talk. **3** (*бесполезный*) idle, vain, useless; **~ные попы́тки** idle attempts.

пра́ктик, а *m.* **1** (*работник*) practical worker; **он хоро́ший п., но слаб в теорети́ческих зна́ниях** he is a good practical worker but his theoretical knowledge is weak. **2** (*человек*) practical person.

пра́ктик|а, и *f.* **1** practice; **на ~е** in practice; **вам нужна́ ещё разгово́рная п.** you need more conversational practice. **2** (*форма обучения*) practical work. **3** (*obs.*) (*работа врача, юриста*) practice.

практика́нт, а *m.* trainee.

практик|ова́ть, у́ю *impf.* **1** to practise (*Br.*), practice (*US*). **2** (*obs.*) (*о враче, о юристе*) to practise (*Br.*), practice (*US*).

практик|ова́ться, у́юсь *impf.* **1** (*pf.* **на~**) (**в**+*p.*) to practise (*Br.*), practice (*US*); **п. в игре́ на скри́пке** to practise the violin; **п. в ру́сском языке́** to practise speaking Russian. **2** *pass. of* ⇒**~ова́ть; э́тот приём бо́льше не ~у́ется** this method is no longer used.

пра́ктикум, а *m.* practical work (*in universities, colleges*).

практи́ческ|ий *adj.* practical; **~ие заня́тия** practical training; **~ая медици́на** applied medicine.

практи́чност|ь, и *f.* practicality.

практи́ч|ный (~ен, ~на) *adj.* practical.

прама́тер|ь, и *f.* (*rhet.*) the first mother; mother of the human race.

пра́от|ец, ца *m.* forefather; **отпра́виться к ~цам** (*joc.*) to be gathered to one's forefathers.

пра́порщик, а *m.* **1** warrant officer. **2** (*в царской армии*) ensign.

праро́дител|ь, я *m.* primogenitor.

праславя́нский *adj.* (*ling.*) Common Slavonic.

прах, а *no pl., m.* **1** (*rhet.*) (*пыль*) dust, earth; **обрати́ть в п., пове́ргнуть в п.** to reduce to dust, to ashes; **отрясти́ п. с ног** (*fig.*) to shake the dust from one's feet; **пойти́ ~о́м, рассы́паться ~о́м** to go to rack and ruin; **п. и суета́** a hollow sham. **2** (*умершего*) ashes, remains; **здесь поко́ится п.** (+*g.*) here lies; **мир ~у его́** may he rest in peace.

пра́чечн|ая, ой *f.* laundry; **п.-автома́т, автомати́ческая п.** launderette.

пра́чк|а, и *f.* laundress.

пращ|а́, и́, *g. pl.* **~е́й** *f.* sling (*weapon*).

пра́щур, а *m.* ancestor, forefather.

пре...[1] *adj. pref. indicating superl. degree* very, most, exceedingly.

пре...[2] *vbl. pref. indicating action in extreme degree or superior measure* sur-, over-, out- (*cf.* ⇒**пере...**).

преа́мбул|а, ы *f.* preamble.

пребыва́ни|е, я *nt.* stay, sojourn; **ме́сто постоя́нного ~я** permanent residence, permanent address; **п. в до́лжности, п. на посту́** tenure of office, period of office.

пребыва́|ть, ю *impf.* **1** (*быть*) to be; (*жить*) to reside; **п. в отсу́тствии** to be absent. **2** (*быть в каком-н. состоянии*) to be; **п. в неве́дении** to be in the dark; **п. у вла́сти** to be in power.

превали́р|овать, ую *impf.* (**над**+*i.*) to prevail (over).

превенти́вный *adj.* preventive.

превзо|йти́, йду́, йдёшь, *past* **~шёл, ~шла́** *pf.* (*of* ⇒**превосходи́ть**) (**в**+*p. or* +*i.*) to surpass (in); to excel (in); **п. все ожида́ния** to exceed all expectations; **п. самого́ себя́** to surpass o.s.; **п. чи́сленностью** to outnumber.

превозмога́|ть, ю *impf. of* ⇒**превозмо́чь**

превозмо́|чь, гу́, ~жешь, ~гут, *past* **~г, ~гла́** *pf.* (*of* ⇒**~га́ть**) to overcome, surmount.

превознес|ти́, у́, ёшь, *past* **~, ~ла́** *pf.* (*of* ⇒**превозноси́ть**) to extol.

превозно|си́ть, шу́, ~сишь *impf. of* ⇒**превознести́**

превозно|си́ться, шу́сь, ~сишься *impf.* (*obs.*) to put on airs; to have a high opinion of o.s.

превосходи́тельств|о, а *nt.* (*as title*) Excellency.

превосхо|ди́ть, жу́, ~дишь *impf. of* ⇒**превзойти́**

превосхо́д|ный (~ен, ~на) *adj.* **1** superb, outstanding. **2**: **~ная сте́пень** (*gram.*) superlative degree.

превосхо́дств|о, а *nt.* superiority.

превосходя́|щий *pres. part. of* ⇒**~и́ть** *and adj.* superior.

превра|ти́ть, щу́, ти́шь *pf.* (*of* ⇒**~ща́ть**) (**в**+*a.*) (*перевести*) to turn (to, into), convert (into); **п. я́рды в ме́тры** to convert yards into metres (*Br.*), meters (*US*); **п. в ка́мень** to turn to stone; **п. в шу́тку** to turn into a joke.

превра|ти́ться, щу́сь, ти́шься *pf.* (*of* ⇒**~ща́ться**) (**в**+*a.*) to turn (into), change (into); **п. в слух** to be all ears.

превра́тно *adv.* wrongly; **п. истолкова́ть** to misinterpret; **вы меня́ п. по́няли** you misunderstood me.

превра́тност|ь, и *f.* **1** (*ложность*) wrongness, falsity. **2** (*невзгода*) vicissitude; **~и судьбы́** vicissitudes of fate.

превра́т|ный (~ен, ~на) *adj.* **1** (*ложный*) wrong, false; **у него́ бы́ло ~ное поня́тие о том, что произошло́** he had a false impression of what happened. **2** (*изменчивый*) fickle, perverse; **~ная судьба́** perverse fate.

превраща́|ть(ся), ю(сь) *impf. of* ⇒**преврати́ть(ся)**

превраще́ни|е, я *nt.* transformation, conversion.

превы́|сить, шу, сишь *pf.* (*of* ⇒**~ша́ть**) to exceed; **п. власть, п. полномо́чия** to exceed one's authority.

превыша́|ть, ю *impf. of* ⇒**превы́сить**

превы́ше *adv.* far above; **п. всего́** above all.

превыше́ни|е, я *nt.* exceeding; **п. вла́сти** exceeding one's authority; **п. своего́ креди́та в ба́нке** overdrawing.

прегра́д|а, ы *f.* barrier; obstacle.

прегра|ди́ть, жу́, ди́шь *pf.* (*of* ⇒**~жда́ть**) to bar, obstruct, block; **п. путь кому́-н.** to bar s.o.'s way.

прегражда́|ть, ю *impf. of* ⇒**прегради́ть**

прегреш|а́ть, а́ю *impf. of* ⇒**~и́ть**

прегреше́ни|е, я *nt.* sin, transgression.

прегреш|и́ть, у́, и́шь *pf.* (*of* ⇒**~а́ть**) to sin, transgress.

пред[1], а *n.* (*sl.*) = **председа́тель**

пред[2] *prep.* = **пе́ред**

пред...[1] *pref.* pre-, fore-, ante-.

пред...[2] *comb. form, abbr. of* ***председа́тель***

...пред *comb. form, abbr. of* ***представи́тель***

преда|ва́ть(ся), ю́(сь), ёшь(ся) *impf. of* ⇒**преда́ть(ся)**

преда́ни|е[1], я *nt.* (*легенда*) legend.

преда́ни|е[2], я *nt.* (*действие*) handing over, committing; **п. земле́** committing to the earth; **п. сме́рти** putting to death; **п. суду́** bringing to trial.

пре́данно *adv.* (*служить*) loyally; (*смотреть*) devotedly.

пре́данност|ь, и *f.* devotion.

пре́дан|ный (~, ~на) *p.p.p. of* ⇒**преда́ть** *and adj.* (+*d.*) devoted (to); (*делу*) dedicated (to); **п. друг** staunch friend; **п. Вам** (*epistolary formula*) yours faithfully, yours truly.

преда́тел|ь, я *m.* traitor.

преда́тельниц|а, ы *f. of* ⇒**преда́тель**

преда́тельский *adj.* treacherous (*also fig.*).

преда́тельств|о, а *nt.* treachery, betrayal.

пре|да́ть, да́м, да́шь, да́ст, дади́м, дади́те, даду́т, *past* **~дал, ~дала́, ~дало** *pf.* (*of* ⇒**~дава́ть**) **1** (+*d.*) (*отдать*) to hand over (to), commit (to); **п. гла́сности** to make known, make public; **п. забве́нию** to consign to oblivion; **п. земле́** to commit to the earth; **п. огню́** to commit to the flames; **п. суду́** to bring to trial. **2** (*изменить*) to betray.

пре|да́ться, да́мся, да́шься, да́стся, дади́мся, дади́тесь, даду́тся, *past* **~да́лся, ~дала́сь** *pf.* (*of* ⇒**~дава́ться**) (+*d.*) **1** (*отдаться*) to give o.s. up (to); **п. отча́янию** to give way to despair; **п. страстя́м** to abandon o.s. to one's passions. **2** (*подчиниться кому-н.*) to entrust o.s. (to); to put o.s. in the hands (of); **п. врагу́** to go over to the enemy.

предба́нник, а *m.* (*в бане*) dressing-room; (*fig., coll.*) hall, ante-chamber.

предвари́лк|а, и *f.* (*coll.*) lock-up (*place of detention before trial*).

предвари́тельно *adv.* in advance, beforehand; as a preliminary.

предвари́тел|ьный (~ен, ~ьна) *adj.* (*замечания, работа*) preliminary; (*продажа, заказ*) advance; **~ьное заключе́ние** (*leg.*) detention on remand; **~ьные перегово́ры** preliminary talks; **п. пока́з** preview; **~ьная прода́жа биле́тов** advance sale of tickets, advance booking; **~ьное сле́дствие** (*leg.*) preliminary investigation, inquest; **по ~ьному соглаше́нию** by prior arrangement; **~ьное усло́вие** precondition.

предвар|и́ть, ю́, и́шь *pf.* (*of* ⇒**~я́ть**) **1** (*опередить*) to forestall, anticipate. **2** (*obs.*) (*уведомить заранее*) to forewarn, tell beforehand.

предвар|я́ть, я́ю *impf. of* ⇒**~и́ть**

предве́сти|е, я *nt.* presage, portent.

предве́стник, а *m.* forerunner, precursor; herald, harbinger; presage, portent.

предве́ч|ный (~ен) *adj.* (*theol.*; *epithet of God*) everlasting; existing from before time.

предвеща́|ть, ю *impf.* (*no pf.*) herald, presage, portend; **ту́чи ~ли грозу́** the clouds heralded a storm; **э́то ~ет хоро́шее** this bodes well, this augurs well.

предвзя́тост|ь, и *f.* prejudice, bias.

предвзя́т|ый (~, ~а) *adj.* prejudiced, biased.

предви́дени|е, я *nt.* foresight; (*предсказание*) prediction.

предви́|деть, жу, дишь *impf.* (*no pf.*) to foresee; (*предсказать*) to predict.

предви́д|еться, ится *impf.* (*no pf.*) to be foreseen; to be expected.

предвку|си́ть, шу́, ~сишь *pf.* (*of* ⇒**~ша́ть**) to look forward (to), anticipate (with pleasure).

предвкуша́|ть, ю *impf. of* ⇒**предвкуси́ть**

предвкуше́ни|е, я *nt.* (*pleasurable*) anticipation; **в ~и** (+*g.*) in anticipation (of).

предводи́тел|ь, я *m.* leader.

предводи́тельств|о, а *nt.* leadership.

предводи́тельств|овать, ую *impf.* (+*i.*) to lead, be the leader (of).

предвое́нный *adj.* pre-war.

предвозве|сти́ть, щу́, сти́шь *pf.* (*of* ⇒**~ща́ть**) to foretell.

предвозве́стник, а *m.* herald; harbinger, precursor.

предвозвеща́|ть, ю *impf. of* ⇒**предвозвести́ть**

предвосхи́|тить, щу, тишь *pf.* (*of* ⇒**~ща́ть**) to anticipate.

предвосхища́|ть, ю *impf. of* ⇒**предвосхи́тить**

предвосхище́ни|е, я *nt.* anticipation.

предвы́борн|ый *adj.* (pre-)election; **~ая кампа́ния** election campaign; **~ое собра́ние** (pre-)election meeting.

предго́р|ье, ья, *g. pl.* **~ий** *nt.* foothills.

предгрозов|о́й *adj.*: **~а́я мо́лния** lightning before a storm.

предгро́зь|е, я *nt.* time before a storm (*also fig.*).

преддве́ри|е, я *nt.* threshold (*also fig.*); **в ~и** (+*g.*) on the threshold (of); in the period just before, in the run-up to.

преде́л, а *m.* limit; bound; **в ~ах** (+*g.*) within, within the limits (of), within the bounds (of); **за ~ами** (+*g.*) outside, beyond; **в ~ах го́рода** within the city; **в ~ах досяга́емости** within reach; **в ~ах го́да** within the year; **за ~ами страны́** outside the country; **вы́йти за ~ы го́рода** to go outside the city boundary; **вы́йти за ~ы** (+*g.*) to exceed the bounds (of); **э́то за ~ами мои́х сил** it is beyond my power; **на ~е сил** at the limit of one's strength; **не́рвы на ~е** my/his, *etc.* nerves are at breaking point; **п. жела́ний** pinnacle of (one's) desires; **п. насыще́ния** saturation point; **п. про́чности** (*tech.*) breaking point; **положи́ть п.** (+*d.*) to put an end (to), terminate.

преде́л|ьный *adj.* **1** *adj. of* ⇒**~**; **п. во́зраст** age-limit; **~ьная ли́ния** boundary line; **п. срок** time-limit, deadline; **п. у́гол** critical angle. **2** (*крайний*) maximum; utmost; **~ьная ско́рость** maximum speed; **с ~ьной я́сностью** with the utmost clarity.

предержа́щ|ий *only in phr.* **вла́сти ~ие** the powers that be.

предзнаменова́ни|е, я *nt.* omen, augury.

предика́т, а *m.* (*gram.*) predicate.

предикати́вный *adj.* (*gram.*) predicative; **п. член** predicate.

предисло́ви|е, я *nt.* preface, foreword; **без ~й** (*coll.*) straight away.

предлага́|ть, ю *impf. of* ⇒**предложи́ть**

предлежа́ни|е, я *nt.* (*med.*): **ягоди́чное п. плода́** breech delivery *or* presentation.

предло́г[1], а *m.* pretext; **под ~ом** (+*g.*) on the pretext (of); **он ушёл под ~ом того́, что его́ ждут** he left on the pretext that s.o. was waiting for him.

предло́г[2], а *m.* (*gram.*) preposition.

предложе́ни|е[1], я *nt.* **1** (*помощи*) offer; (*идея*) suggestion, proposition; (*брака*) proposal (of marriage); **сде́лать п. кому́-н.** to propose (marriage) to s.o. **2** (*на заседании*) proposal, motion; **внести́ п.** to introduce a motion; **отклони́ть п.** to turn down a proposal. **3** (*econ.*) supply; **зако́н спро́са и ~я** law of supply and demand.

предложе́ни|е[2], я *nt.* **1** (*gram.*) sentence; **гла́вное п.** main clause; **прида́точное п.** subordinate clause; **вво́дное п.** parenthesis. **2** (*phil.*) proposition.

предлож|и́ть, у́, ~ишь *pf.* (*of* ⇒**предлага́ть**) **1** (*помощь, услуги*) to offer. **2** (*решение, проект*) to propose; to suggest; **п. резолю́цию** to move a resolution; **п. тост** to propose a toast; **п. кого́-н. в председа́тели** to propose s.o. for chairman; **п. внима́нию** to call attention (to); **мы ~и́ли ей обрати́ться**

к врачу́ we suggested that she should see a doctor. **3** (*задать*) to put, set; **п. вопро́с** to put a question; **п. зада́чу** to set a problem. **4** (*потребовать*) to order, require; **им ~или освободи́ть кварти́ру** they have been ordered to vacate their apartment.

предло́жный *adj.* (*gram.*) prepositional; **п. паде́ж** prepositional case.

предме́ст|ье, ья, *g. pl.* **~ий** *nt.* suburb.

предме́т, а *m.* **1** object; (*вещь*) article, item; (*pl.*) goods; **~ы дома́шнего обихо́да** household goods; **~ы пе́рвой необходи́мости** necessities; **~ы широ́кого потребле́ния** consumer goods. **2** (*тема*) subject, topic, theme; (+*g.*) object (of); **п. насме́шек** object of ridicule; **п. спо́ра** point at issue. **3** (*в школе*) subject; **обяза́тельный п.** compulsory subject; **факультати́вный п.** optional subject. **4** (*цель*) object; **на п.** (+*g.*) with the object (of).

предме́т|ный *adj. of* **⇒~; п. уро́к** object-lesson; **п. катало́г** subject catalogue; **п. указа́тель** subject index.

предмо́стн|ый *adj.*: **п. плацда́рм, ~ое укрепле́ние** bridge-head.

предназнача́|ть, а́ю *impf. of* **⇒~́ить**

предназначе́ни|е, я *nt.* **1** (*ресурсов*) earmarking. **2** (*судьба*) destiny.

предназна́ч|ить, у, ишь *pf.* (*of* **⇒~а́ть**) (**для**+*g.*, *or* **на**+*a.*) to destine (for), intend (for), mean (for); (*специально выделить*) to earmark (for), set aside (for); **мы ~или э́ти де́ньги для поку́пки автомоби́ля** we set aside this money to buy a car.

преднаме́ренно *adv.* deliberately.

преднаме́ренност|ь, и *f.* premeditation.

преднаме́рен|ный (~, на) *adj.* premeditated; deliberate.

предначерта́ни|е, я *nt.* outline, plan; **п. судьбы́** predestination.

предначе́рт|анный *p.p.p. of* **⇒~а́ть; п. судьбо́й** predestined.

предначерта́|ть, ю *pf.* to outline; to plan beforehand; to foreordain.

предо = **пред**

пре́д|ок, ка *m.* forefather, ancestor; (*pl.*) forebears; (*pl., sl.*) parents.

предоперацио́нный *adj.* (*med.*) pre-operative.

предопределе́ни|е, я *nt.* **1** (*действие*) predetermining. **2** (*судьба*) predestination.

предопредел|и́ть, ю́, и́шь *pf.* (*of* **⇒~я́ть**) to predetermine; (*судьбу*) to predestine, foreordain.

предопредел|я́ть, я́ю *impf. of* **⇒~и́ть**

предоста́в|ить, лю, ишь *pf.* (*of* **⇒~ля́ть**) **1** (+*d. and inf.*) (*дать право*) to let; to leave; **нам ~или сами́м реши́ть де́ло** we were left to decide the matter for ourselves; **п. кого́-н. самому́ себе́** to leave s.o. to his own devices, to his own resources. **2** (*дать*) to give, grant; **п. креди́т** to give credit; **п. пра́во** to concede a right; **п. возмо́жность** to afford an opportunity, give a chance; **п. кому́-н. сло́во** to call upon s.o. to speak; **они́ ~или ко́мнату в на́ше распоряже́ние** they have put a room at our disposal.

предоставля́|ть, ю *impf. of* **⇒предоста́вить**

предостерега́|ть, ю *impf. of* **⇒предостере́чь**

предостереже́ни|е, я *nt.* warning, caution.

предостере́|чь, гу́, жёшь, гу́т, *past* **~́г, ~гла́** *pf.* (*of* **⇒~га́ть**) (**от**+*g.*) to warn (against), caution (against).

предосторо́жност|ь, и *f.* **1** (*осторожное поведение*) caution; **ме́ры ~и** precautionary measures, precautions. **2** (*мера*) precaution.

предосуди́тельност|ь, и *f.* reprehensibility.

предосуди́тел|ьный (~ен, ~ьна) *adj.* wrong, reprehensible.

предотвра|ти́ть, щу́, ти́шь *pf.* (*of* **⇒~ща́ть**) to prevent, avert; to stave off; **п. войну́** to avert a war; **п. опа́сность** to stave off, avert danger.

предотвраща́|ть, ю *impf. of* **⇒предотврати́ть**

предотвраще́ни|е, я *nt.* prevention, averting; staving off.

предохране́ни|е, я *nt.* (**от**+*g.*) protection (against), preservation (from).

предохрани́тел|ь, я *m.* guard, safety device; **(пла́вкий) п.** (*elec.*) fuse.

предохрани́тельн|ый *adj.* **1** preventive; **~ые ме́ры** precautionary measures, precautions; **~ая приви́вка** preventive inoculation. **2** (*tech.*) safety; protective; **п. кла́пан** safety-valve; **~ая коро́бка** fuse box; **~ые очки́** safety goggles.

предохран|и́ть, ю́, и́шь *pf.* (*of* **⇒~я́ть**) (**от**+*g.*) to protect (from, against).

предохран|и́ться, ю́сь, и́шься *pf.* (*of* **⇒~я́ться**) (**от**+*g.*) to protect o.s. (from, against).

предохран|я́ть(ся), я́ю(сь) *impf. of* **⇒~и́ть(ся)**

предписа́ни|е, я *nt.* order, injunction; (*pl.*) directions, instructions; (*med.*) prescription; **по ~ю врача́** on doctor's orders.

предпи|са́ть, шу́, ~́шешь *pf.* (*of* **⇒~́сывать**) **1** (+*d. and inf.*) to order, direct, instruct (to). **2** (*med.*) (+*d. and a.*) to prescribe (*s.o. sth.*).

предпи́сыва|ть, ю *impf. of* **⇒предписа́ть**

предпле́ч|ье, ья, *g. pl.* **~ий** *nt.* (*anat.*) forearm.

предплюс|на́, ны́, *pl.* **~́ны, ~́ен** *f.* (*anat.*) tarsus.

предполага́емый *pres. part. pass. of* **⇒предполага́ть** *and adj.* proposed.

предполага́|ть, ю *impf.* **1** *impf. of* **⇒предположи́ть. 2** (*impf. only*) to intend, propose; **мы ~ем оста́вить дете́й у ба́бушки** we propose to leave the children at their grandmother's. **3** (*impf. only*) (*иметь своим условием*) to presuppose; **успе́х в э́том де́ле ~ет хоро́шую пого́ду** the success of this business presupposes good weather.

предполага́|ться, ется *impf.* **1** to be planned; **сва́дьба ~лась ле́том** the wedding was planned for the summer. **2** (*impers.*): **~ется** it is proposed, it is intended; **~ется проложи́ть отсю́да автостра́ду** it is proposed to build a motorway from here.

предположе́ни|е, я *nt.* **1** (*допущение*) supposition, assumption. **2** (*намерение*) intention; **у меня́ есть п. жени́ться** I intend to marry.

предположи́тельно *adv.* **1** hypothetically; supposedly, presumably. **2** (*in parenthesis*) (*вероятно*) probably; **мы прие́дем в Ло́ндон, п., к десяти́ часа́м** we shall be in London probably by ten o'clock.

предположи́тельный *adj.* (*дата, результат*) hypothetical; (*доход*) estimated, anticipated.

предполож|и́ть, у́, ~́ишь *pf.* (*of* **⇒предполага́ть**) to suppose, assume; **~́им, что он опозда́л на по́езд** (let us) suppose he missed the train.

предпо|сла́ть, шлю́, шлёшь *pf.* (*of* **⇒~сыла́ть**) (+*d. and a.*) to preface (with); **а́втор ~сла́л кни́ге обраще́ние к чита́телю** the author prefaced the book with an address to the reader.

предпосле́дний *adj.* penultimate, last but one, next to last; one from the bottom (*on list*).

предпосыла́|ть, ю *impf. of* **⇒предпосла́ть**

предпосы́лк|а, и *f.* **1** prerequisite, precondition. **2** (*phil.*) premise.

предпоч|е́сть, ту́, тёшь, *past* **~ёл, ~ла́** *pf.* (*of* **⇒~ита́ть**) (+*a. and d.*) to prefer; **п. говя́дину бара́нине** to prefer beef to lamb; **я ~ёл бы идти́ пешко́м** I would rather walk; (+*inf.*) to choose to; **он ~ёл уйти́** he chose to leave.

предпочита́|ть, ю *impf. of* **⇒предпоче́сть**

предпочте́ни|е, я *nt.* preference; **оказа́ть п., отда́ть п.** (+*d.*) to show a preference (for), give preference.

предпочти́тельно *adv.* rather, preferably; (*в основном*) mainly.

предпочти́тел|ьный (~ен, ~ьна) *adj.* preferable.

предпра́здничн|ый *adj.* (pre-) holiday; **~ая суета́** holiday rush.

предприи́мчивост|ь, и *f.* enterprise.

предприи́мчив|ый (~, ~а) *adj.* enterprising.

предпринима́тел|ь, я *m.* entrepreneur; businessman.

предпринима́тель|ский *adj. of* **⇒~; п. капита́л** venture capital.

предпринима́тельств|о, а *no pl., nt.* enterprise; **свобо́дное п.** free enterprise; **ча́стное п.** private enterprise.

П

предпринимá|ть, ю *impf. of* ⇒**предпринять**

предпри|нять, мý, ~мешь, *past* **~нял, ~нялá, ~няло** *pf.* (*of* ⇒**~нимáть**) to undertake; (*mil., etc.*) to launch; **п. атáку** to launch an attack; **п. шаги́** to take steps.

предприя́ти|е, я *nt.*
1 (*предпринятое дело*) undertaking, enterprise; (*инициатива*) venture; **рискóванное п.** risky undertaking, venture. **2** (*econ.*) enterprise, concern, business; (*завод, фабрика*) works; **мéлкое п.** small business; **индустриáльное п.** (industrial) works; **совмéстное п.** joint venture.

предрасполагá|ть, ю *impf. of* ⇒**предрасположи́ть**

предрасположéни|е, я *nt.* (**к**+*d.*) predisposition (to).

предрасполó**женност|ь, и** *f.* = **предрасположéние**

предрасполó**ж|енный** *p.p.p. of* ⇒**~и́ть;** (**к**+*d.*) predisposed (to), prone (to); **ребёнок ~ен к простýде** the child is prone to colds.

предрасполож|и́ть, ý, ~ишь *pf.* (*of* ⇒**предрасполагáть**) (**к**+*d.*) to predispose (to).

предрассвéтн|ый *adj.* occurring before dawn; **~ая мгла** early morning mist.

предрассýд|ок, ка *m.* prejudice.

предрекá|ть, ю *impf. of* ⇒**предрéчь**

предрé|чь, кý, чёшь, кýт, *past* **~к, ~клá** *pf.* (*of* ⇒**~кáть**) to foretell.

предреш|áть, áю *impf. of* ⇒**~и́ть**

предреш|и́ть, ý, и́шь *pf.* (*of* ⇒**~áть**) **1** (*заранее решить*) to decide beforehand. **2** (*предопределить*) to predetermine.

предродовóй *adj.* antenatal (*Br.*), prenatal.

председáтел|ь, я *m.* (*собрания, правления*) chairman; (*общества*) president.

председáтель|ский *adj. of* ⇒**~; ~ское мéсто** the chair (*at a meeting*); **заня́ть ~ское мéсто** to take the chair.

председáтельств|о, а *nt.* chairmanship; presidency.

председáтельств|овать, ую *impf.* to be in the chair, preside.

предсéрди|е, я *nt.* (*anat.*) auricle.

предсказáни|е, я *nt.* prediction.

предсказáтел|ь, я *m.* forecaster; soothsayer.

предска|зáть, жý, ~жешь *pf.* (*of* ⇒**~зывать**) to foretell, predict.

предскáзыва|ть, ю *impf. of* ⇒**предсказáть**

предсмéртн|ый *adj.* occurring before death; **~ое желáние** dying wish.

предста|вáть, ю́, ёшь *impf. of* ⇒**~ть**

представи́тел|ь, я *m.*
1 representative; (*должностное лицо*) (+*g.*) spokesman (for); **полномóчный п.** plenipotentiary. **2** (*bot., etc.*) specimen.

представи́тель|ница, ницы *f. of* ⇒**~** 1

представи́тельност|ь, и *f.* imposingness; imposing appearance, presence.

представи́тельный[1] *adj.* (*pol., leg.*) representative.

представи́тел|ьный[2] **(~ен, ~ьна)** *adj.* (*внушительный*) imposing.

представи́тельств|о, а *nt.*
1 representation, representing.
2 (*collect.*) representation, representatives; **дипломати́ческое п.** diplomatic representatives; **торгóвое п.** trade mission.

предстáв|ить, лю, ишь *pf.* (*of* ⇒**~ля́ть**) **1** (*причинить*) to present; **п. трýдности** to offer difficulty; **п. интерéс** to be of interest. **2** (*предъявить*) to produce, submit; **п. доказáтельства** to produce evidence. **3** (+*a. and d.*) (*познакомить*) to introduce (to), present (to). **4** (**к**+*d.*) to recommend (for), put forward (for); **п. когó-н. к óрдену** to recommend s.o. for a decoration. **5: п. (себé)** to imagine; **~ь(те) себé, какáя э́то былá досáда!** (just) imagine what a nuisance that was!; **~ьте (себé)!** just imagine! **6** (*изобразить*) to represent, display; **п. чтó-то в смешнóм ви́де** to hold sth. up to ridicule. **7** (*theatr.*) to perform; to play.

предстáв|иться, люсь, ишься *pf.* (*of* ⇒**~ля́ться**) **1** (*возникнуть*) to present itself, arise; **~ился слýчай поéхать в Москвý** a chance arose to go to Moscow; **я им сообщý, как тóлько ~ится возмóжность** I will inform them as soon as an opportunity arises.
2 (*impers.*+*d.*) (*показаться*) to seem (to); **э́то тебé тóлько ~илось** it was just your imagination. **3** (+*d.*) (*познакомиться*) to introduce o.s. (to).
4 (+*i.*) (*притвориться*) to pretend (to be); **п. больны́м** to feign sickness.
5 (*произвести впечатление*) to appear.

представлéни|е, я *nt.* **1** (*действие*) presentation; **п. прóпуска** presentation of a permit; (*для знакомства*) introduction; **п. нóвого сотрýдника** introduction of a new colleague.
2 (*заявление*) (written) declaration, statement; representation; **~я бы́ли сдéланы всем прави́тельствам** representations have been made to all the governments. **3** (*theatr.*) performance.
4 (*psych.*) representation.
5 (*понимание*) idea, notion, conception; **дать п.** (**о**+*p.*) to give an idea (of); **я не имéю ни малéйшего ~я** I have not the faintest idea.

представля́|ть, ю *impf.* **1** *impf. of* ⇒**предстáвить. 2** (*impf. only*) (*страну, интересы*) to represent; **он ~ет США в ООН** he represents the USA at the UN. **3** (*являться*) to represent, be, constitute; **п. угрóзу** to represent a threat. **4: п. собóй** (*являться*) to represent, be; to constitute; **э́то ~ет собóй исключéние** this constitutes an exception.

представля́|ться, юсь *impf. of* ⇒**предстáвиться**

предстáтельн|ый *adj.*: **~ая железá** (*anat.*) prostate (gland).

предстá|ть, ну, нешь *pf.* (*of* ⇒**~вáть**) (**пéред**+*i.*) to appear (before); **п. пéред судóм** to appear in court.

предсто|я́ть, и́т *impf.* (+*d.*) to be in prospect (for), lie ahead (of), be at hand; to be in store (for); **~я́ла сурóвая зимá** a hard winter lay ahead; **нам ~и́т мнóго неприя́тностей** we are in for a lot of trouble; **емý ~и́т предстáвить диссертáцию к пéрвому ию́ня** he has to submit his dissertation by the first of June.

предстоя́|щий *pres. part. of* ⇒**~ть** *and adj.* forthcoming; impending; **~щие вы́боры** the forthcoming elections; **онá страши́лась ~щего медици́нского осмóтра** she was dreading the impending medical (examination).

предтéч|а, и *c.g.* forerunner, precursor; **Иоáнн П.** John the Baptist.

предубе|ди́ть, ди́шь *pf.* (*of* ⇒**~ждáть**) to prejudice, bias.

предубеждá|ть, ю *impf. of* ⇒**предубеди́ть**

предубеждéни|е, я *nt.* prejudice, bias.

предубе|ждённый *p.p.p. of* ⇒**~ди́ть** *and adj.* prejudiced, biased.

предувéдом|ить, лю, ишь *pf.* (*of* ⇒**~ля́ть**) to inform beforehand, give advance notice; to warn, forewarn; **вам слéдовало п. их о вáшем приéзде** you should have informed them that you were coming.

предуведомлéни|е, я *nt.* notice in advance; warning, forewarning.

предуведомля́|ть, ю *impf. of* ⇒**предувéдомить**

предугад|áть, áю *pf.* (*of* ⇒**~ывать**) to guess (in advance); (*предсказать*) to foretell.

предугáдыва|ть, ю *impf. of* ⇒**предугадáть**

предудáрный *adj.* (*ling.*) pre-tonic.

предумы́шленност|ь, и *f.* premeditation.

предумы́шлен|ный (~, ~на) *adj.* premeditated.

предупреди́тельност|ь, и *f.* courtesy; attentiveness.

предупреди́тел|ьный *adj.*
1 (*меры*) preventive, precautionary.
2 (~ен, ~ьна) (*человек*) courteous; attentive; obliging.

предупре|ди́ть, жý, ди́шь *pf.* (*of* ⇒**~ждáть**) **1** (**о**+*p.*) to let know beforehand (about), notify in advance (about), warn (about); to give notice (of, about); **п. об увольнéнии за недéлю** to give a week's notice (*of dismissal*).
2 (*предотвратить*) to prevent, avert; **п. авáрию** to prevent an accident.
3 (*опередить*) to anticipate; to forestall; **п. замечáние** to anticipate a remark; **я как раз э́то хотéл сказáть, но вы ~ди́ли меня́** that is just what I was about to say, but you took the words out of my mouth.

предупреждá|ть, ю *impf. of* ⇒**предупреди́ть**

предупреждéни|е, я *nt.*
1 (*извещение*) notice; notification.

2 (*предотвращение*) prevention. **3** (*просьбы*) anticipating; forestalling. **4** (*предостережение*) warning; (*взыскание*) caution; **получи́ть вы́говор с ~ем** (*leg.*) to be dismissed with a caution.

предусма́трива|ть, ю *impf. of* ⇒**предусмотре́ть**

предусмотр|е́ть, ю́, ~́ишь *pf.* (*of* ⇒**предусма́тривать**) (*предвидеть*) to envisage, foresee; (*обеспечить*) to provide (for), make provision (for); **п. все возмо́жности** to provide for every eventuality.

предусмотри́тельност|ь, и *f.* foresight, prudence.

предусмотри́тел|ьный (~ен, ~ьна) *adj.* prudent; far-sighted; **~ьная поли́тика** far-sighted policy

предустано́вленный *adj.* (*obs.*) pre-established, predetermined.

преду́тренний *adj.* occurring immediately before morning; **п. час** the hour before dawn.

предчу́встви|е, я *nt.* presentiment; (*дурного*) foreboding, premonition.

предчу́вств|овать, ую *impf.* to have a presentiment (of, about), have a premonition (of, about); **я ~овал, что вы сего́дня появи́тесь** I had a feeling that you would turn up today.

предше́ственник, а *m.* predecessor; forerunner, precursor.

предше́ств|овать, ую *impf.* (+*d.*) to go in front (of); to precede; **её сме́рти ~овала дли́тельная боле́знь** her death was preceded by a long illness.

предше́ствующий *adj.* previous; foregoing.

предъяви́тел|ь, я *m.* bearer; **п. и́ска** plaintiff.

предъяви́тель|ница, ницы *f. of* ⇒**~**

предъяв|и́ть, лю́, ~́ишь *pf.* (*of* ⇒**~ля́ть**) **1** to show, produce, present; **п. биле́т** to show one's ticket; **п. доказа́тельства** to produce evidence, present proofs. **2** (*leg., etc.*) to bring (forward); **п. иск** (**к**+*d.*) to bring a suit (against); **п. обвине́ние** (+*d.* **в**+*p.*) to charge (with), bring an accusation (against s.o. of); **ему́ ~́или обвине́ние в поджо́ге** he is charged with arson; **п. пра́во** (**на**+*a.*) to lay claim (to); **п. тре́бование** (**к**+*d.*) to lay claim (to); **п. высо́кие тре́бования** (**к**+*d.*) to make big demands (of, on).

предъявле́ни|е, я *nt.* **1** showing, producing, presentation; **вход разреша́ется по ~и удостовере́ния ли́чности** entry is permitted on presentation of identity card. **2** (*leg., etc.*) bringing; **п. и́ска** bringing of a suit.

предъявля́|ть, ю *impf. of* ⇒**предъяви́ть**

предыду́щ|ий *adj.* previous, preceding; *as n.* **~ее, ~его** *nt.* the foregoing.

предысто́ри|я, и *f.* prehistory.

пре́емник, а *m.* successor.

пре́емни|ца, цы *f. of* ⇒**~к**

пре́емственност|ь, и *f.* succession; (*традиций, культуры*) continuity.

пре́емствен|ный (~, ~на) *adj.* successive.

пре́емств|о, а *nt.* succession.

пре́жде 1 *adv.* (*opp.* **пото́м**) (*сначала*) before; first; **п. чем** *as conj.* before; **на́до бы́ло ду́мать об э́том п.** you should have thought about it before; **ты до́лжен дое́сть ка́шу, п. чем взять ды́ню** you must eat up your kasha before you have any melon. **2** *adv.* (*opp.* **тепе́рь**) (*раньше*) formerly, in former times; before; **п. он преподава́л в интерна́те** he taught in a boarding-school before. **3** *prep.* +*g.* before; **они́ пришли́ п. нас** they arrived before us; **п. всего́** first of all, to begin with; (*самое важное*) first and foremost.

преждевре́менно *adv.* prematurely; (*умереть*) before one's time.

преждевре́менност|ь, и *f.* prematurity, untimeliness.

преждевре́мен|ный (~ен, ~на) *adj.* premature, untimely; **~ные ро́ды** (*med.*) premature birth.

пре́жн|ий *adj.* previous, former; **в ~ее вре́мя** in the old days, in former times.

презе́нт, а *m.* (*obs. or joc.*) present.

презента́бел|ьный (~ен, ~ьна) *adj.* presentable.

презента́ци|я, и *f.* presentation; launch; **п. това́ра** sales presentation; **п. кни́ги** book launch.

презент|ова́ть, у́ю *impf. and pf.* (*obs. or joc.*) to present.

презервати́в, а *m.* condom.

президе́нт, а *m.* president.

президе́нт|ский *adj. of* ⇒**~**; **~ские вы́боры** presidential elections.

президе́нтств|о, а *nt.* presidency.

прези́диум, а *m.* presidium.

презира́|ть, ю *impf.* **1** (*impf. only*) to despise, hold in contempt. **2** (*pf.* **презре́ть**) to disdain; **п. опа́сность** to scorn danger.

презре́ни|е, я *nt.* disdain, contempt, scorn.

презре́н|ный (~, ~на) *adj.* contemptible, despicable; **п. мета́лл** (*coll.*) filthy lucre.

презр|е́ть, ю́, и́шь *pf. of* ⇒**презира́ть**

презри́тел|ьный (~ен, ~ьна) *adj.* contemptuous, scornful, disdainful.

презу́мпци|я, и *f.* (*phil., leg.*) presumption; **п. невино́вности** presumption of innocence.

преиму́щественно *adv.* mainly, chiefly, principally.

преиму́щественный *adj.* **1** (*главный*) primary, prime, principal. **2** (*предпочтительный*) preferential, priority.

преиму́ществ|о, а *nt.* **1** advantage; **име́ть п.** (**пе́ред**+*i.*) to have an advantage (over); **получи́ть п.** (**пе́ред**+*i.*) to gain an advantage (over); **они́ име́ют то п., что у них телефо́н** they have the advantage of being on the telephone. **2** (*предпочтение*) preference; **по ~у** for the most part, chiefly.

преиспо́дн|яя, ей *f.* the nether regions, the underworld.

преиспо́лн|енный *p.p.p. of* ⇒**~ить** *and adj.* (+*g. or i.*) filled (with), full (of); **п. опа́сности** fraught with danger; **п. реши́мости** firmly resolved.

преиспо́лн|ить, ю, ишь *pf.* (*of* ⇒**~я́ть**) (+*a. and g. or i.*) to fill (s.o./sth. with).

преиспо́лн|иться, юсь, ишься *pf.* (*of* ⇒**~я́ться**) (+*g. or i.*) to be filled (with), become full (of).

преиспо́лн|я́ть(ся), я́ю(сь) *impf. of* ⇒**~ить(ся)**

прейскура́нт, а *m.* price-list.

преклоне́ни|е, я *nt.* (**пе́ред**+*i.*) admiration (for), worship (of).

преклон|и́ть, ю́, и́шь *pf.* (*of* ⇒**~я́ть**) to incline, bend; (*знамя*) to lower; **п. го́лову** to bow (one's head); **п. коле́на** to genuflect.

преклон|и́ться, ю́сь, и́шься *pf.* (*of* ⇒**~я́ться**) (**пе́ред**+*i.*) **1** to bow down (before). **2** (*fig.*) to admire, worship.

преклóнный *adj.*: **п. во́зраст** old age, declining years.

преклон|я́ть(ся), я́ю(сь) *impf. of* ⇒**~и́ть(ся)**

прекосло́ви|е, я *nt.* (*obs.*) contradiction; **без вся́кого ~я** without contradiction.

прекосло́в|ить, лю, ишь *impf.* (+*d.*) to contradict.

прекра́сно *adv.* **1** excellently; (*знать, понимать*) perfectly well; **они́ п. зна́ют, что э́то запрещено́** they know perfectly well that it is forbidden. **2** *as int.* excellent!; splendid!

прекраснοду́ши|е, я *nt.* (*iron.*) starry-eyed idealism.

прекраснοду́ш|ный (~ен, ~на) *adj.* (*iron.*) starry-eyed.

прекра́с|ный (~ен, ~на) *adj.* **1** (*красивый*) beautiful, fine; **п. пол** the fair sex; **в оди́н п. день** one fine day, once upon a time; *as n.* **~ное, ~ного** *nt.* (*phil.*) the beautiful. **2** (*отличный*) excellent, capital, first-rate.

прекра|ти́ть, щу́, ти́шь *pf.* (*of* ⇒**~ща́ть**) to stop; (*положить конец*) to put a stop (to), put an end (to); (*отношения*) to break off, sever, cut off; **п. войну́** to end the war; **п. вое́нные де́йствия** to cease hostilities; **п. знако́мство** (**с**+*i.*) to break (it off) (with); **п. обсужде́ние вопро́са** to drop the subject; **п. ого́нь** (*mil.*) to cease fire; **п. платежи́** to suspend, stop payments; **п. подпи́ску** to discontinue a subscription, stop subscribing; **п. пода́чу га́за** to cut off the gas (supply); **п. рабо́ту** to down tools; **п. рабо́тать** to stop work(ing); **п. сноше́ния** (**с**+*i.*) to sever relations (with).

прекра|ти́ться, ти́тся *pf.* (*of* ⇒**~ща́ться**) to cease, end.

прекраща́|ть(ся), ю, ет(ся) *impf. of* ⇒**прекрати́ть(ся)**

прекраще́ни|е, я *nt.* stopping, cessation, discontinuance; **п. вое́нных**

П

де́йствий cessation of hostilities; **п. войны́** ending of war; **п. де́ла** dismissal of a case; **п. огня́** cease-fire; **п. платеже́й** suspension of payments.

прела́т, а *m.* prelate.

преле́стно *adv.* (*петь, танцевать*) charmingly; **она́ п. вы́глядит** she looks lovely.

преле́ст|ный (~ен, ~на) *adj.* charming, delightful, lovely.

пре́лест|ь, и *f.* charm, delight; **кака́я п.!** how lovely!; **~и жи́зни в дере́вне** the delights of living in the country; **моя́ п.!** my sweetheart!

прелом|и́ть, лю́, ~́ишь *pf.* (*of* ⇒**~ля́ть**) **1** (*phys.*) to refract. **2** (*fig.*) to interpret, put a construction (upon).

прелом|и́ться, ~́ится *pf.* (*of* ⇒**~ля́ться**) **1** (*phys.*) to be refracted. **2** (*fig.*) to be interpreted; to take on a different aspect.

преломле́ни|е, я *nt.* **1** (*phys.*) refraction. **2** (*fig.*) interpretation, construction.

преломля́|ть(ся), ю, ет(ся) *impf. of* ⇒**преломи́ть(ся)**

пре́лост|ь, и *f.* rottenness, mouldiness (*Br.*), moldiness (*US*).

пре́л|ый (~, ~а) *adj.* rotten, fusty.

прел|ь, и *f.* rot, mouldiness (*Br.*), moldiness (*US*), mould (*Br.*), mold (*US*).

прель|сти́ть, щу́, сти́шь *pf.* (*of* ⇒**~ща́ть**) **1** (*привлечь*) to attract; **он ~сти́л свои́х слу́шателей красноре́чием** he attracted his audience with his eloquence. **2** (*увлечь*) to lure, entice; **п. обеща́ниями** to lure with promises.

прель|сти́ться, щу́сь, сти́шься *pf.* (*of* ⇒**~ща́ться**) (+*i.*) to be attracted (by); to be tempted (by), fall (for); **мы ~сти́лись предложе́нием пое́хать на юг** we were tempted by the offer of going to the south.

прельща́|ть(ся), ю(сь) *impf. of* ⇒**прельсти́ть(ся)**

прелюбоде́|й, я *m.* adulterer.

прелюбоде́й|ка, ки *f. of* ⇒**~**

прелюбоде́йств|овать, ую *impf.* to commit adultery.

прелюбодея́ни|е, я *nt.* adultery.

прелю́ди|я, и *f.* (*mus. and fig.*) prelude.

премиа́льн|ый *adj. of* ⇒**пре́мия; ~ая систе́ма** bonus system; *as n.* (*pl.*) **~ые, ~ых** bonus.

преми́н|уть, у, ешь *pf. only with neg.* (+*inf.*) to not fail (to); **я не ~у зайти́ к вам** I shall not fail to call in to see you; (*не замедлить*) to be quick to.

премирова́ни|е, я *nt.* (*победителя*) awarding of a prize; (*работника*) awarding of a bonus.

премиро́в|анный *p.p.p. of* ⇒**~а́ть** *and adj.* prize-winning, prize; *as n.* **п., ~анного** *m.* prize-winner.

премир|ова́ть, у́ю *impf. and pf.* (*победителя*) to award a prize (to); (*работника*) to give a bonus (to).

пре́ми|я, и *f.* **1** (*победителю*) prize; (*работнику*) bonus; **Но́белевская п.** Nobel Prize; **п. О́скара** Oscar. **2** (*fin.*) (*в страховании*) premium; **страхова́я п.** insurance premium.

премно́го *adv.* (*obs.*) very; **п. благода́рен** I am very grateful.

прему́дрост|ь, и *f.* wisdom; **~и** (+*g.*) (*iron.*) subtleties (of), tricks (of).

прему́др|ый (~, ~а) *adj.* (very) wise, sage.

премье́р, а *m.* **1** prime minister, premier. **2** (*theatr.*) leading actor, lead.

премье́р|а, ы *f.* (*theatr.*) première, opening night.

премье́р-мини́стр, а *m.* prime minister, premier.

премье́рш|а, и *f.* (*theatr.*) leading lady, lead.

пренебрега́|ть, ю *impf. of* ⇒**пренебре́чь**

пренебреже́ни|е, я *nt.* **1** (*презрение*) scorn, contempt, disdain; **обнару́жить, вы́казать своё п.** (**к**+*d.*) to show one's contempt (for). **2** (*невнимание*) neglect, disregard; **п. свои́ми обя́занностями** neglect of one's duties, dereliction of duty.

пренебрежи́тельност|ь, и *f.* scorn.

пренебрежи́тел|ьный (~ен, ~ьна) *adj.* scornful, disdainful.

пренебре́|чь, гу́, жёшь, гу́т, *past* **~́г, ~гла́** *pf.* (*of* ⇒**~га́ть**) (+*i.*) **1** (*презреть*) to scorn, despise; **п. опа́сностью** to scorn danger; **п. сове́том** to scorn advice. **2** (*обязанностями*) to neglect, disregard.

пре́ни|е, я *nt.* rotting.

пре́ни|я, й *no sg.* debate; **откры́ть, прекрати́ть п.** to open, close a debate.

преоблада́ни|е, я *nt.* predominance.

преоблада́|ть, ет *impf.* to predominate; to prevail.

преоблада́|ющий *pres. part. act. of* ⇒**~ть** *and adj.* predominant; prevalent.

преобража́|ть(ся), ю(сь) *impf. of* ⇒**преобрази́ть(ся)**

преображе́ни|е, я *nt.* **1** transformation. **2** (*relig.*) the Transfiguration.

преобра|зи́ть, жу́, зи́шь *pf.* (*of* ⇒**~жа́ть**) to transform.

преобра|зи́ться, жу́сь, зи́шься *pf.* (*of* ⇒**~жа́ться**) to be transformed.

преобразова́ни|е, я *nt.* **1** (*во что-н. другое*) transformation. **2** (*реформа*) reform; reorganization.

преобразова́тел|ь, я *m.* **1** (*реорганизатор*) reformer. **2** (*elec.*) converter; transformer.

преобраз|ова́ть, у́ю *pf.* (*of* ⇒**~о́вывать**) **1** to transform (*also phys., tech.*). **2** (*реформировать*) to reform; (*реорганизовать*) to reorganize.

преобразо́выва|ть, ю *impf. of* ⇒**преобразова́ть**

преодолева́|ть, ю *impf. of* ⇒**преодоле́ть**

преодоле́|ть, ю *pf.* (*of* ⇒**~ва́ть**) to overcome, get over; **п. препя́тствия** to surmount obstacles; **п. тру́дности** to overcome difficulties.

преодоли́м|ый (~, ~а) *adj.* surmountable.

преосвяще́нств|о, а *nt.*: **его́ п.** (*title of bishop*) his Grace.

препара́т, а *m.* (*chem., pharm.*) preparation.

препари́р|овать, ую *impf. and pf.* (*biol., pharm.*) to prepare, make a preparation (of).

препина́ни|е, я *nt.*: **зна́ки ~я** (*gram.*) punctuation marks.

препира́тельств|о, а *nt.* altercation, wrangling, squabbling.

препира́|ться, юсь *impf.* (**с**+*i.*; *coll.*) to wrangle (with), squabble (with).

преподава́ни|е, я *nt.* teaching, tuition, instruction.

преподава́тел|ь, я *m.* teacher; (*вуза*) lecturer, instructor.

преподава́тель|ница, ницы *f. of* ⇒**~**

преподава́тель|ский *adj. of* ⇒**~; п. соста́в** teaching staff.

препода|ва́ть, ю́, ёшь *impf.* to teach.

препода́|ть, м, шь, ст, ди́м, ди́те, ду́т, *past* **препо́дал, ~ла́, препо́дало** *pf.* to give (*advice, a lesson, etc.*); **п. уро́к кому́-н.** to teach s.o. a lesson.

преподнесе́ни|е, я *nt.* presentation.

преподнес|ти́, у́, ёшь, *past* **~́, ~ла́** *pf.* (*of* ⇒**преподноси́ть**) (+*a. and d.*) to present (with); (*сведения*) to convey; (*сюрприз*) to give; **он ~́ нам неприя́тную но́вость** he brought us a piece of bad news; **п. что-н. кому́-н. в гото́вом ви́де** (*fig.*) to hand sth. to s.o. on a plate.

преподно|си́ть, шу́, ~́сишь *impf. of* ⇒**преподнести́**

преподо́би|е, я *nt.*: **его́ п.** (*title of priest*) his Reverence, the Reverend.

преподо́бный *adj.* (*title of canonized monks*) Saint; Venerable.

препо́н|а, ы *f.* obstacle, impediment.

препоруч|а́ть, а́ю *impf. of* ⇒**~и́ть**

препоруч|и́ть, у́, ~́ишь *pf.* (*of* ⇒**~а́ть**) (*obs.*) to entrust.

препоя́|сать, шу, шешь *pf.* (*of* ⇒**~сывать**) (*obs.*) to gird; **п. свои́ чре́сла** (*fig., rhet.*) to gird up one's loins.

препоя́сыва|ть, ю *impf. of* ⇒**препоя́сать**

препроводи́тельный *adj.* accompanying (*document, etc.*).

препрово|ди́ть, жу́, ди́шь *pf.* (*of* ⇒**~жда́ть**) to send, forward, dispatch.

препровожда́|ть, ю *impf. of* ⇒**препроводи́ть**

препровожде́ни|е¹, я *nt.* (*документов*) sending, dispatching.

препровожде́ни|е², я *nt.* (*времени*) passing; **для ~я вре́мени** to pass the time.

препя́тстви|е, я *nt.* **1** obstacle, impediment, hindrance; **чини́ть кому́-н. ~я** to put obstacles in s.o.'s way. **2** (*sport*) obstacle; **бег с ~ями, ска́чки с ~ями** steeple-chase; **взять п.** to clear an obstacle; (*fig.*) to clear a hurdle.

препя́тств|овать, ую *impf.* (*of* **⇒вос~**) (+*d.*) to hinder, impede; to stand in the way (of).

прерв|а́ть, у́, ёшь, *past* **~а́л, ~ала́, ~а́ло** *pf.* (*of* **⇒прерыва́ть**) (*прекратить*) to break off, sever; (*перебить*) to interrupt, to cut short; **п. молча́ние** to break a silence; **п. ора́тора** to interrupt a speaker; **п. на полусло́ве** to cut (s.o.) short; **п. дипломати́ческие отноше́ния** to break off diplomatic relations; **п. перегово́ры** to break off negotiations; **п. рабо́ту** to take a break; **нас ~а́ли** (*of telephone conversation*) we have been cut off.

прерв|а́ться, ётся, *past* **~а́лся, ~ала́сь, ~а́ло́сь** *pf.* (*of* **⇒прерыва́ться**) **1** (*о разговоре*) to be interrupted; (*о знакомстве*) to be broken off. **2** (*о голосе, от волнения*) to break.

пререка́ни|е, я *nt.* altercation, wrangle, argument; **вступи́ть в п. с кем-н.** to start an argument with s.o.

пререка́|ться, юсь *impf.* (**с**+*i.*) to argue (with).

пре́ри|я, и *f.* prairie.

прерогати́в|а, ы *f.* prerogative.

прерыва́тел|ь, я *m.* (*elec.*) (circuit) breaker, cut-out.

прерыва́|ть(ся), ю, ет(ся) *impf. of* **⇒прерва́ть(ся)**

прерыва́|ющийся *pres. part. of* **⇒~ться; ~ющимся го́лосом** with a catch in one's voice.

преры́висто *adv.* in a broken way; **говори́ть п.** to speak in a faltering way; **дыша́ть п.** to gasp.

преры́вист|ый (~, ~а) *adj.* (*дыхание, звук*) intermittent; (*линия*) broken, dotted.

пресви́тер, а *m.* (*eccl.*) presbyter.

пресвитериа́нский *adj.* (*relig.*) Presbyterian.

пресвитериа́нств|о, а *nt.* (*relig.*) Presbyterianism.

пресека́|ть(ся), ю, ет(ся) *impf. of* **⇒пресе́чь(ся)**

пресече́ни|е, я *nt.* stopping, suppression.

пресе́|чь, ку́, чёшь, ку́т, *past* **~к, ~кла** *pf.* (*of* **⇒~ка́ть**) to cut short, stop; **п. в ко́рне** to nip in the bud.

пресе́|чься, чётся, ку́тся, *past* **~кся, ~кла́сь** *pf.* (*of* **⇒~ка́ться**) **1** (*прекратиться*) to stop. **2** (*о голосе, от волнения*) to break.

пресле́довани|е, я *nt.* **1** (*погоня*) pursuit. **2** (*притеснение*) persecution, victimization; **ма́ния ~я** persecution complex. **3** (*leg.*): **суде́бное п.** prosecution.

пресле́довател|ь, я *m.* **1** (*тот, кто гонится за кем-н.*) pursuer. **2** (*тот, кто притесняет кого-н.*) persecutor.

пресле́дователь|ница, ницы *f. of* **⇒~**

пресле́д|овать, ую *impf.* **1** (*врага, зверя*) to pursue; (*fig.*) (*о мыслях, о чувствах*) to haunt; **подозре́ние ~ует меня́** a suspicion haunts me. **2** (*fig.*) (*интересы, замысел, женщину*) to pursue; **п. цель** to pursue an end. **3** (*притеснять*) to persecute. **4** (*leg.*) to prosecute.

преслову́тый *adj.* notorious; (*iron.*) celebrated.

пресмыка́тельств|о, а *nt.* grovelling (*Br.*), groveling (*US*), crawling.

пресмыка́|ться, юсь *impf.* (**пе́ред**+*i.*) to grovel (before), cringe (before).

пресмыка́ющ|ееся, егося *nt.* reptile.

пресново́дный *adj.* freshwater.

пре́с|ный (~ен, ~на́, ~но) *adj.* **1** (*вода*) fresh, sweet. **2** (*хлеб*) unleavened. **3** (*пища*) flavourless (*Br.*), flavorless (*US*), tasteless; (*fig.*) insipid, vapid; **~ные остро́ты** feeble jokes.

преспоко́йно *adv.* (*coll.*) **1** (*без шума*) very quietly. **2** (*без тревоги*) calmly, coolly.

пресс, а *m.* press.

пре́сс|а, ы *f.* (*collect.*) the press; **ло́жа ~ы** press gallery.

пресс-атташе́ *m. indecl.* press attaché.

пресс-бюро́ *nt. indecl.* press department.

пре́ссинг, а *m.* (psychological) pressure.

пресс-конфере́нци|я, и *f.* press conference.

пресс|ова́ть, у́ю *impf.* (*of* **⇒с~** *and* **от~**) to press, compress.

прессо́вк|а, и *f.* pressing, compressing.

прессовщи́к, а́ *m.* presser, press operator.

пресс-папье́ *nt. indecl.* **1** (*тяжёлый предмет*) paper-weight. **2** (*с промокательной бумагой*) blotter.

пресс-рели́з, а *m.* press release.

пресс-секрета́р|ь, я́ *m.* press secretary.

пресс-слу́жб|а, ы *f.* press service.

пресс-центр, а *m.* press office.

преста́в|иться, люсь, ишься *pf.* (*obs.*) to pass away.

престаре́л|ый *adj.* aged, old; **дом (для) ~ых** old people's home.

прести́ж, а *m.* prestige; **поте́ря ~а** loss of face; **охраня́ть свой п.** to save one's face.

прести́ж|ный (~ен, ~на) *adj.* prestigious.

престо́л, а *m.* **1** throne; **вступи́ть на п.** to come to the throne; **отре́чься от ~а** to abdicate. **2** (*eccl.*) altar; **Па́пский п.** Holy See, See of Rome.

престолонасле́ди|е, я *nt.* succession to the throne.

престолонасле́дник, а *m.* successor to the throne.

престо́л|ьный *adj. of* **⇒~; п. го́род** capital (city).

преступ|а́ть, а́ю *impf. of* **⇒~и́ть**

преступ|и́ть, лю́, ~́ишь *pf.* (*of* **⇒~а́ть**) to transgress, trespass (against); **п. зако́н** to break the law.

преступле́ни|е, я *nt.* crime, offence; **п. про́тив челове́чества** crime against humanity; (*leg.*) (*тяжкое*) felony; **должностно́е п.** malfeasance; **уголо́вное п.** criminal offence.

преступ́ник, а *m.* criminal; **вое́нный п.** war criminal.

престу́пни|ца, цы *f. of* **⇒~к**

престу́пност|ь, и *f.* **1** (*свойство*) criminality. **2** (*collect.*) crime; **организо́ванная п.** organized crime; **рост ~и** increase in crime.

престу́п|ный (~ен, ~на) *adj.* criminal.

пресы́|тить, щу, тишь *pf.* (*of* **⇒~ща́ть**) (*obs.*) (+*i.*) to satiate (with); to sate (with).

пресы́|титься, щусь, тишься *pf.* (*of* **⇒~ща́ться**) (+*i.*) to be satiated (with); to have had a surfeit (of).

пресыща́|ть(ся), ю(сь) *impf. of* **⇒пресы́тить(ся)**

пресыще́ни|е, я *nt.* satiety; surfeit; **до ~я** to satiety.

пресы́щенност|ь, и *f.* satiety; surfeit.

пресы́|щенный *p.p.p. of* **⇒~тить** *and adj.* satiated; surfeited, sated, replete.

претворе́ни|е, я *nt.* conversion; **п. в жизнь, в де́ло** realization, putting into practice.

претвор|и́ть, ю́, и́шь *pf.* (*of* **⇒~я́ть**) **1** (*obs.*) (**в**+*a.*) to turn (into), change (into), convert (into). **2**: **п. в жизнь, п. в де́ло** to realize, carry out, put into practice.

претвор|и́ться, и́тся *pf.* (*of* **⇒~я́ться**) **1** (**в**+*a.*) to turn (into), become. **2**: **п. в жизнь** to be realized, come true; **моя́ мечта́ ~и́лась в жизнь** my dream has come true.

претвор|я́ть(ся), я́ю, я́ет(ся) *impf. of* **⇒~и́ть(ся)**

претенде́нт, а *m.* (**на**+*a.*) (*на престол*) pretender, claimant (to); (*на наследство*) claimant (to); (*на должность*) candidate (for); (*sport*) contestant; **он п. на ру́ку принце́ссы** he aspires to the hand of the princess.

претенде́нт|ка, ки *f. of* **⇒~**

претенд|ова́ть, у́ю *impf.* (**на**+*a.*) (*на престол, на ум*) to have pretensions (to); (*на наследство*) to lay claim (to); (*на должность*) to aspire (to); **он ~у́ет на пост мини́стра иностра́нных дел** he aspires to the position of Minister of Foreign Affairs.

прете́нзи|я, и *f.* **1** (*заявление прав*) claim; **име́ть ~ю (на**+*a.*) to claim, lay claim (to), make claims (on); **заяви́ть ~ю** to lodge a claim. **2** (*на ум, на остроумие*) pretension; **челове́к с ~ями, без ~й** a pretentious, an unpretentious person; **быть в ~и на кого́-н.** to have a grievance against s.o. **3** (*жалоба*) complaint.

претенцио́зност|ь, и *f.* pretentiousness, affectation.

претенцио́з|ный (~ен, ~на) *adj.* pretentious, affected.

претерпева́|ть, ю *impf. of* **⇒претерпе́ть**

претерп|е́ть, лю́, ~́ишь *pf.* (*of* **⇒~ева́ть**) (*подвергнуться*) to

П

undergo; (*вытерпеть*) to suffer, endure; **план ~ёл измене́ния** the plan has undergone changes; **п. лише́ния** to endure privations.

прет|и́ть, и́т *impf.* (+*d.*) to sicken; **э́та пи́ща мне ~и́т** I am nauseated by this food; **мне ~и́т его́ высокоме́рие** his arrogance sickens me.

преткнове́ни|е, я *nt.*: **ка́мень ~я** stumbling-block.

преториа́нский *adj.* (*hist.*) praetorian.

пре|ть, ю *impf.* **1** (*pf.* **со~**) (*гнить*) to rot. **2** (*impf. only*) (*становиться влажным*) to become damp. **3** (*pf.* **у~**) (*пища*) to stew.

преувеличе́ни|е, я *nt.* exaggeration; overstatement.

преувели́чива|ть, ю *impf. of* ⇒**преувели́чить**

преувели́ч|ить, у, ишь *pf.* (*of* ⇒**~ивать**) to exaggerate; to overstate.

преуменьш|а́ть, а́ю *impf. of* ⇒**~́ить**

преуменьше́ни|е, я *nt.* underestimation; understatement.

преуме́ньш|ить, у, ишь *pf.* (*of* ⇒**~а́ть**) (*представить меньшим*) to underestimate, minimize; (*представить менее важным*) to belittle; to understate; **п. опа́сность** to underestimate the danger; **п. чью-н. по́мощь** to belittle s.o.'s assistance.

преуспева́|ть, ю *impf.* **1** *impf. of* ⇒**преуспе́ть. 2** (*impf. only*) to thrive, prosper, flourish.

преуспева́|ющий *pres. part. act. of* ⇒**~ть** *and adj.* successful, prosperous.

преуспе́|ть, ю *pf.* (*of* ⇒**~ва́ть**) (**в**+*p.*) to succeed (in), be successful (in); **п. в жи́зни** to get on in life.

преуспея́ни|е, я *nt.* (*obs.*) success.

префе́кт, а *m.* prefect.

префекту́р|а, ы *f.* prefecture.

префера́нс, а *m.* preference (*card-game*).

пре́фикс, а *m.* (*gram.*) prefix.

префикса́льный *adj.* (*gram.*) with a prefix.

префикса́ци|я, и *f.* (*gram.*) prefixation.

преходя́щий *adj.* transient.

прецеде́нт, а *m.* precedent; **установи́ть п.** to establish, set a precedent.

прецизио́нный *adj.* (*tech.*) precision; **п. прибо́р** precision instrument.

при *prep.*+*p.* **1** (*около*) by, at; (*в присутствии*) in the presence of; **при доро́ге** by the road(-side); **би́тва при Бородино́** the battle of Borodino; **письмо́ бы́ло подпи́сано при мне** the letter was signed in my presence; **не на́до так выража́ться при де́тях** you should not use such language in front of the children.
2 (*под эгидой*) attached to, affiliated to, under the auspices of (*usu. not translated*); **он рабо́тает при университе́те** he is attached to the university; **при магази́не есть кафе́** there is a café attached to the shop.
3 (*с собой*) by, with; about, on; **у него́ не́ было при себе́ де́нег** he had no money on him; **у вас есть при себе́ перочи́нный нож?** do you have a pen-knife about you?
4 (*при наличии*) with; (*несмотря на*) for, notwithstanding; **при таки́х тала́нтах он далеко́ пойдёт** with such talent he will go far; **при уча́стии** (+*g.*) with the participation (of); **при жела́нии всего́ мо́жно доби́ться** where there's a will there's a way; **при всех его́ досто́инствах, он мне не нра́вится** for all his virtues, I do not like him; **при всём том** (*i*) with it all, moreover, (*ii*) for all that; **при чём тут я?** what has it to do with me?; **я тут ни при чём** it has nothing to do with me.
5 (*во время, в эпоху*) in the time of, in the days of; under (*sc.* the rule of); during; **при Ива́не Гро́зном** during the reign of, in the time of Ivan the Terrible; **при Рома́новых** under the Romanovs; **при мне бы́ло не так** in my day it was not like this.
6 (*указывает на обстоятельства*) by; **при дневно́м све́те** by daylight; **при све́те ла́мпы** by lamplight.
7 (*когда*) when; on; in case of; **при перехо́де че́рез у́лицу** when crossing the street; **при слу́чае** when the occasion arises, at convenience; **при ана́лизе** on analysis; **при маляри́и** in case of malaria; **при усло́вии(, что)** under the condition (that).
8 (*благодаря*) with; **при по́мощи рыбако́в нам удало́сь оттолкну́ть ло́дку** with the aid of the fishermen we succeeded in pushing the boat off.

при...[1] *vbl. pref. indicating* **1** *completion of action or motion up to given terminal point, as* **прие́хать** to arrive. **2** *action of attaching, as* **пристро́ить** to build on. **3** *direction of action towards speaker, as* **пригласи́ть** to invite. **4** *direction of action from above downward, as* **придави́ть** to press down. **5** *incompleteness or tentativeness of action, as* **приоткры́ть** to open slightly. **6** *exhaustiveness of action, as* **приучи́ть** to train. **7** (+*suffixes* **...ыва...**, **...ива...**) *accompaniment, as* **припля́сывать** to dance (to a tune).

при...[2] *as pref. of nn. and adjs.* (*esp. geog.*) *indicates juxtaposition or proximity, as* **приозе́рье** lake-side; **прибре́жный, примо́рский** coastal.

приба́в|ить, лю, ишь *pf.* (*of* ⇒**~ля́ть**) **1** (+*a. or g.*) to add; **к пяти́ п. три** to add three to five; **п. (в ве́се)** to put on (weight); **за три ме́сяца она́ ~ила де́сять килогра́мов** she put on ten kilos in three months. **2** (+*g.*) (*увеличить*) to increase; **п. жа́лованья** to increase a salary; **п. ша́гу** to hasten one's steps. **3** (**в**+*p.*) (*одежду*) to lengthen, widen; **на́до п. в рукава́х** the sleeves need to be lengthened. **4** (*coll.*, *fig.*) (*сказать неправду*) to make sth. up, exaggerate.

приба́в|иться, ится *pf.* (*of* ⇒**~ля́ться**) to increase; (*о воде*) to rise; (*о луне*) to wax; **п. в ве́се** to put on weight; **день ~ился** the days are getting longer; (*impers.*): **воды́ ~илось** the water has risen; **наро́ду ~илось** the crowd has grown.

приба́вк|а, и *f.* **1** (*действие*) addition. **2** (*надбавка*) increase, supplement; **получи́ть ~у** to get a rise (*Br.*), raise (*US*).

прибавле́ни|е, я *nt.* addition; **п. семе́йства** addition to the family; **сказа́ть в п.** to say in addition, add.

прибавля́|ть(ся), ю, ет(ся) *impf. of* ⇒**приба́вить(ся)**

приба́вочн|ый *adj.* **1** additional. **2** (*econ.*) surplus; **~ая сто́имость** surplus value.

приба́лт, а *m.* (*coll.*) Balt.

прибалти́йский *adj.* Baltic (= *adjacent to the Baltic Sea*).

Приба́лтик|а, и *f.* the Baltic States.

приба́лт|ка, ки *f.* (*coll.*) *of* ⇒**~**

приба́утк|а, и *f.* humorous catchphrase.

прибега́|ть[1]**, ю** *impf. of* ⇒**прибе́гнуть**

прибега́|ть[2]**, ю** *impf. of* ⇒**прибежа́ть**

прибе́г|нуть, ну, нешь, *past* **~, ~ла** *pf.* (*of* ⇒**~а́ть**[1]) (**к**+*d.*) to resort (to), have resort (to); **п. к си́ле** to resort to force.

прибедн|и́ться, ю́сь, и́шься *pf.* (*of* ⇒**~я́ться**) (*coll.*) **1** (*притвориться бедным*) to feign poverty. **2** (*преуменьшить свои успехи*) to show false modesty.

прибедн|я́ться, я́юсь *impf. of* ⇒**~и́ться**

прибе|жа́ть, гу́, жи́шь, гу́т *pf.* (*of* ⇒**~га́ть**[2]) (*бегом или торопясь*) to come running; **пе́рвым к фи́нишу ~жа́л Борзо́в** Borzov was the first to finish the race.

прибе́жищ|е, а *nt.* refuge; **после́днее п.** (*fig.*) last resort; **найти́ п.** (**в**+*p.*) to take refuge (in).

приберега́|ть, ю *impf. of* ⇒**прибере́чь**

прибере́|чь, гу́, жёшь, гу́т, *past* **~́г, ~гла́** *pf.* (*of* ⇒**~га́ть**) to save up.

прибива́|ть, ю *impf. of* ⇒**приби́ть**[1]

прибира́|ть(ся), ю(сь) *impf. of* ⇒**прибра́ть(ся)**

приб|и́ть[1]**, ью́, ьёшь** *pf.* (*of* ⇒**~ива́ть**) **1** (*гвоздями*) to nail; **п. до́ску к стене́** to nail a board to a wall. **2** (*о дожде*) to beat down, flatten; **град ~и́л посе́вы** the hail has flattened the corn. **3** (*usu. impers.*) (*волной, течением*) to wash up; **труп ~и́ло к бе́регу** a body was washed ashore.

приб|и́ть[2]**, ью́, ьёшь** *pf.* (*sl.*) to beat up.

прибл. (*abbr. of* ***приблизи́тельно***) approx., approximately.

приближа́|ть, ю *impf. of* ⇒**прибли́зить**

приближа́|ться, юсь *impf.* **1** *impf. of* ⇒**прибли́зиться. 2** (*impf. only*) (**к**+*d.*) to approximate (to); **п. к и́стине** to approximate to the truth.

приближе́ни|е, я *nt.* **1** (*действие*)

approach; approaching, drawing near. **2** (*math.*) approximation.

приближённост|ь, и *f.* proximity.

приближённый[1] *adj.* approximate, rough.

приближённ|ый[2] *adj.* (**к**+*d.*) close (to); **~ые к королю́ ли́ца** people close to the king; *as n.* **п., ~ого** *m.* retainer; (*pl.*) retinue.

приблизи́тельно *adv.* approximately, roughly.

приблизи́тельност|ь, и *f.* approximateness.

приблизи́тел|ьный (~ен, ~ьна) *adj.* approximate, rough.

прибли́|зить, жу, зишь *pf.* (*of* **⇒~жа́ть**) **1** (*придвинуть ближе*) to bring nearer, move nearer; (*сделать близким*) to bring closer; **п. кни́гу к глаза́м** to bring a book nearer one's eyes. **2** (*ускорить*) to hasten, advance; **я наме́рен п. мой отъе́зд** I intend to hasten my departure.

прибли́|зиться, жусь, зишься *pf.* (*of* **⇒~жа́ться**) (**к**+*d.*) to approach, draw near; to draw nearer (to), come nearer (to).

приблу́дный *adj.* (*coll.*; *of animals*) stray.

прибо́|й, я *m.* surf, breakers.

приболе́|ть, ю, ешь *pf.* (*coll.*) to be unwell.

прибо́р, а *m.* **1** instrument, device, apparatus, appliance. **2** (*комплект*) set; **бри́твенный п.** shaving things; **ча́йный п.** tea-service. **3** (*для оборудования*) fittings; **печно́й п.** stove fittings.

прибо́р|ный *adj of* **⇒~**; **~ная доска́** dashboard; (*aeron.*) instrument panel.

приборострое́ни|е, я *nt.* instrument-making.

при|бра́ть, беру́, берёшь, *past* **~бра́л, ~брала́, ~бра́ло** *pf.* (*of* **⇒~бира́ть**) **1** (*привести в порядок*) to clear up, clean up, tidy (up); **п. ко́мнату, п. в ко́мнате** to do a room; **п. на столе́** to clear the table; **п. кого́-н. к рука́м** to take s.o. in hand; **п. что-н. к рука́м** to lay one's hands on sth. **2** (*убрать*) to put away; **~бери́ игру́шки — пора́ спать!** put your toys away, it's time for bed!

при|бра́ться, беру́сь, берёшься, *past* **~бра́лся, ~брала́сь, ~брало́сь** *pf.* (*of* **⇒~бира́ться**) to tidy o.s. up; to have a clear-up of one's things.

прибре́жн|ый *adj.* **1** (*у берега моря*) coastal; **~ая полоса́** coastal strip. **2** (*у берега реки*) riverside.

прибре́жь|е, я *nt.* littoral; coastal strip.

прибре|сти́, ду́, дёшь, *past* **~л, ~ла́** *pf.* (*coll.*) to come trudging (along).

прибыва́|ть, ю *impf. of* **⇒прибы́ть**

при́был|ь, и *f.* **1** profit; **валова́я п.** gross profit; **чи́стая п.** net profit; **п. до упла́ты нало́га** pre-tax profit. **2** (*fig.*) benefit, gain; **кака́я мне в э́том п.?** (*coll.*) what do I get out of it? **3** (*увеличение*) increase, rise; **п. населе́ния** increase of population; **вода́ идёт на п.** the water is rising.

при́быльност|ь, и *f.* profitability, lucrativeness.

при́был|ьный (~ен, ~ьна) *adj.* profitable, lucrative.

прибы́ти|е, я *nt.* arrival.

при|бы́ть[1]**, бу́ду, бу́дешь,** *past* **~был, ~была́, ~было** *pf.* (*of* **⇒~быва́ть**) (*прийти, приехать*) to arrive.

при|бы́ть[2]**, бу́дет,** *past* **~был, ~была́, ~было** *pf.* (*of* **⇒~быва́ть**) (*увеличиться*) to increase, grow; (*о воде*) to rise, swell; (*о луне*) to wax; **вода́ ~была́** the water has risen; **на́шего полку́ ~было** our numbers have grown.

прива́|дить, жу, дишь *pf.* (*of* **⇒~живать**) **1** to train (*a bird, etc., by putting out food*). **2** (**к**+*d.*) (*привыкнуть*) to train, accustom (to); (*привлечь к себе*) to win over, win the trust of.

прива́жива|ть, ю *impf. of* **⇒прива́дить**

прива́л, а *m.* **1** (*остановка*) halt, stop. **2** (*место остановки*) stopping-place.

прива́лива|ть, ю *impf. of* **⇒привали́ть**

привал|и́ть, ю́, ~ишь *pf.* (*of* **⇒~ивать**) **1** (*прислонить*) to lean, rest; **п. дрова́ к забо́ру** to pile logs against the fence. **2** (*о судне*) to come alongside. **3** (*coll.*) (*появиться, прийти*) to turn up; **на матч ~и́ло мно́го наро́ду** a lot of people turned up at the match; **сча́стье нам ~и́ло** fortune smiled on us.

прива́рива|ть, ю *impf. of* **⇒привари́ть**

привар|и́ть, ю́, ~ишь *pf.* (*of* **⇒~ивать**) (**к**+*d.*) to weld on (to).

прива́рк|а, и *f.* welding.

прива́т-доце́нт, а *m.* privat-docent (*freelance university lecturer*).

приватиза́тор, а *m.* privatizer.

приватиза́ци|я, и *f.* privatization.

приватизи́р|овать, ую *impf.* & *pf.* to privatize.

прива́т|ный (~ен, ~на) *adj.* (*obs.*) private.

приведе́ни|е, я *nt.* **1** bringing; **п. к прися́ге** administration of oath, swearing in. **2** putting; **п. в движе́ние** setting in motion; **п. в исполне́ние** carrying out, putting into effect; **п. в поря́док** putting in order. **3** (*math.*) reduction; **п. к о́бщему знамена́телю** reduction to a common denominator. **4** adducing; **п. приме́ров** adducing of instances.

привез|ти́, у́, ёшь, *past* **~, ~ла́** *pf.* (*of* **⇒привози́ть**) to bring (*not on foot*); (*товар, почту*) to deliver.

привере́длив|ый (~, ~а) *adj.* fussy, finicky.

привере́дник, а *m.* fussy person; finicky person.

привере́дни|ца, цы *f. of* **⇒~к**

привере́днича|ть, ю *impf.* (*coll.*) to be hard to please; to be fussy.

приве́ржен|ец, ца *m.* adherent; follower.

приве́рженност|ь, и *f.* (**к**+*d.*) adherence (to); devotion (to).

приве́ржен|ный (~, ~а) *adj.* (**к**+*d.*) attached (to), devoted (to).

приверн|у́ть, у́, ёшь *pf.* (*of* **⇒приверты́вать**) **1** (*вертя, прикрепить*) to screw tight, tighten, clamp. **2** (*вертя, убавить*) to turn down; **п. фити́ль** to turn a wick down.

привер|те́ть, чу́, ~тишь *pf.* (*of* **⇒~тывать**) to screw tight, tighten, clamp.

привёртыва|ть, ю *impf. of* **⇒приверну́ть** *and* **приверте́ть**

приве́|сить, шу, сишь *pf.* (*of* **⇒~шивать**) to hang up.

приве́с|ок, ка *m.* (*coll.*) **1** (*довесок*) makeweight. **2** (*fig.*) appendage.

приве|сти́, ду́, дёшь, *past* **~л, ~ла́** *pf.* (*of* **⇒приводи́ть**) **1** to bring; (*о дороге*) to lead, take; **он ~л с собо́й неве́сту** he has brought his fiancée (with him); **п. кого́-н. к прися́ге** to swear s.o. in; **не ~ди́ Бог!** God forbid! **2** (**к**+*d.*; *fig.*) to lead (to), bring (to), result (in); **э́то к добру́ не ~дёт** no good will come of it. **3** (**в**+*a.*) to put, set (*or translated by v. corresponding to n. governed by* **в**); **п. в бе́шенство** to throw into a rage, drive mad; **п. в движе́ние, в де́йствие** to set in motion, set going; **п. в затрудне́ние** to cause difficulties, put in a difficult position; **п. в изумле́ние** to astonish, astound; **п. в исполне́ние** to carry out, put into effect; **п. в хоро́шее настрое́ние** to put in a good mood; **п. в отчая́ние** to reduce to despair; **п. в поря́док** to put in order, tidy (up); to arrange, fix; **п. в соотве́тствие** (**с**+*i.*) to bring into line (with); **п. в у́жас** to horrify; **п. в чу́вство** to bring to, bring round. **4** (*слова, доказательства*) to adduce, cite; **п. приме́р** to give an example.

приве|сти́сь, дётся, *past* **~ло́сь** *pf.* (*of* **⇒приводи́ться**) (*impers.*+*d.*; *coll.*) (*случиться*) to happen, chance; **мне ~ло́сь посети́ть э́тот го́род до войны́** I happened to visit this town before the war; (*выпасть на долю*) to fall to s.o.'s lot.

приве́т, а *m.* greeting(s); regards; **п.!** (*coll.*) hi!; (*выражает недоумение*) you're joking!; **переда́ть п., слать п.** to send one's regards; **переда́йте п. ва́шим колле́гам** remember me to your colleagues, my regards to your colleagues; **п. из Москвы́!** greetings from Moscow!; **он с ~ом** (*coll.*) he is odd.

приве́тливост|ь, и *f.* affability; cordiality.

приве́тлив|ый (~, ~а) *adj.* friendly; affable; cordial.

приве́тственн|ый *adj.* welcoming; **~ая речь** speech of welcome.

приве́тстви|е, я *nt.* **1** greeting, salutation. **2** (*речь*) speech of welcome.

приве́тств|овать, ую *impf.* **1** (*in past tense also pf.*) to greet; to welcome. **2** (*fig.*) to welcome; **п. предложе́ние** to welcome a suggestion. **3** (*also pf.*) (*mil.*) to salute.

привé|шенный *p.p.p. of* ⇒**~сить; у негó язы́к хорошó ~шен** (*coll.*) he has a ready tongue.

привéшива|ть, ю *impf. of* ⇒**привéсить**

прививá|ть(ся), ю, ет(ся) *impf. of* ⇒**приви́ть(ся)**

приви́вк|а, и *f.* **1** (**от, прóтив**+*g.*; *med.*) inoculation (against); vaccination. **2** (*bot.*) grafting.

привидéни|е, я *nt.* ghost, spectre (*Br.*), specter (*US*); apparition.

приви́|деться, дится *pf. of* ⇒**ви́деться** 3

привилегирóванност|ь, и *f.* privilege(s).

привилегирóванный *adj.* privileged.

привилéги|я, и *f.* privilege; (*для ветеранов, инвалидов*) benefit.

привин|ти́ть, чý, ти́шь *pf.* (*of* ⇒**~́чивать**) to screw on.

приви́нчива|ть, ю *impf. of* ⇒**привинти́ть**

привирá|ть, ю *impf. of* ⇒**приврáть**

приви́ти|е, я *nt.* inculcation, fostering.

прив|и́ть, ью́, ьёшь, *past* **~и́л, ~илá, ~и́ло** *pf.* (*of* ⇒**~ивáть**) (+*a. and d.*) **1** (*med.*) to inoculate (with); **п. комý-н. óспу** to vaccinate s.o. against smallpox. **2** (*bot.*) to graft. **3** (*fig.*) (*заставить усвоить*) to inculcate (in); to cultivate (in), foster (in); **п. комý-н. вкус к стихáм** to inculcate in s.o. a taste for poetry.

прив|и́ться, ьётся, *past* **~и́лся, ~илáсь** *pf.* (*of* ⇒**~ивáться**) **1** (*о вакцине, черенке*) to take. **2** (*fig.*) (*идеи, теория*) to find acceptance; (*мода, интерес*) to catch on; **э́ти взгля́ды ~и́лись не всю́ду** these views did not find universal acceptance.

при́вкус, а *m.* (*посторонний вкус*) after-taste; (*характерный вкус*) flavour (*Br.*), flavor (*US*); (*fig.*) trace; flavour (*Br.*), flavor (*US*); **егó словá имéли п. нáглости** his words smacked of insolence.

привлекáтельност|ь, и *f.* attractiveness.

привлекáтел|ьный (~ен, ~ьна) *adj.* attractive.

привлекá|ть, ю *impf. of* ⇒**привлéчь**

привлечéни|е, я *nt.* **1** (*внимания, людей*) attraction. **2** (*методов*) application. **3**: **п. к судý** taking to court; **п. к ответственности** calling to account.

привлé|чь, кý, чёшь, кýт, *past* **~̈к, ~клá** *pf.* (*of* ⇒**~кáть**) **1** to attract; **п. внимáние** to attract attention. **2** (*сделать участником*) to draw in, involve; **п. на свою́ стóрону** to win over (*to one's side*); **п. к рабóте** to involve in work. **3** (*leg.*) to have up; **п. к судý** to take to court; to put on trial; **п. к отвéтственности/отвéту (за**+*a.*) to make answer (for), call to account (for).

привнес|ти́, ý, ёшь, *past* **~̈, ~лá** *pf.* (*of* ⇒**привноси́ть**) (**в**+*a.*) to introduce (into); **п. элемéнт коми́зма в описáние** to introduce an element of comedy into the description

привно|си́ть, шý, ~́сишь *impf. of* ⇒**привнести́**

привóд[1]**, а** *m.* (*leg.*) taking into custody; arrest.

при́вóд[2]**, а** *m.* (*tech.*) drive; **ремённый п.** belt drive.

приво|ди́ть(ся), жу, ~́дишь, ~́дит(ся) *impf. of* ⇒**привести́(сь)**

приводнéни|е, я *nt.* splash-down.

приводн|и́ться, ю́сь, и́шься *pf.* (*of* ⇒**~я́ться**) to land (on water), splash down.

приводн|óй *adj.* (*tech.*) driving, drive; **п. вал** driving shaft; **п. механи́зм** driving gear; **п. ремéнь** drive belt.

приводн|я́ться, я́юсь *impf. of* ⇒**~и́ться**

приво|жý[1]**, ~́дишь** *see* ⇒**~ди́ть**

приво|жý[2]**, ~́зишь** *see* ⇒**~зи́ть**

привóз, а *m.* **1** (*действие*) bringing; (*доставка*) delivery. **2** (*coll.*) (*то, что привезено*) delivery, load.

приво|зи́ть, жý, ~́зишь *impf. of* ⇒**привезти́**

привозн|óй *adj.* imported.

привóзн|ый = **~óй**

привó|й, я *m.* (*agric.*) graft.

привокзáльн|ый *adj.* (*около вокзала*) by, near the station; (*на вокзале*) at the station; **~ое кафé** station café.

приволáкива|ть, ю *impf. of* ⇒**приволочи́ть** *and* **приволóчь**

приволáкива|ться, юсь *impf. of* **1** ⇒**приволочи́ться** *and* **приволóчься. 2** ⇒**приволокнýться**

приволокн|ýться, ýсь, ёшься *pf.* (*of* ⇒**приволáкиваться**) (**за**+*i.*; *coll.*) to flirt (with).

приволоч|и́ть(ся), ý(сь), и́шь(ся) *pf.* = **~ь(ся)**

привол|óчь, кý, чёшь, кýт, *past* **~к, ~клá** *pf.* (*of* ⇒**приволáкивать**) (*coll.*) to drag (over).

приволó|чься, кýсь, чёшься, кýтся, *past* **~кся, ~клáсь** *pf.* (*of* ⇒**приволáкиваться**) (*coll.*) to drag o.s.

привóль|е, я *nt.* **1** (*просторное место*) wide open spaces; **степнóе п.** the wide open steppe. **2** (*свобода*) freedom.

привóльн|ый *adj.* free; **~ая жизнь** free and easy life.

приворáжива|ть, ю *impf. of* ⇒**приворожи́ть**

привораж|и́ть, ý, и́шь *pf.* (*of* ⇒**привора́живать**) to bewitch, cast a spell on; (*fig.*) to bewitch, charm.

привра́тник, а *m.* doorman, porter.

привр|áть, ý, ёшь, *past* **~áл, ~алá, ~áло** *pf.* (*of* ⇒**привирáть**) (*coll.*) to make up; to exaggerate.

привскáкива|ть, ю *impf. of* ⇒**привскочи́ть**

привскоч|и́ть, ý, ~́ишь *pf.* (*of* ⇒**привскáкивать**) to start, jump up.

привста|вáть, ю́, ёшь *impf. of* ⇒**~́ть**

привстá|ть, ну, нешь *pf.* (*of* ⇒**~вáть**) to half-rise.

привходя́щ|ий *adj.*: **~ие обстоя́тельства** attendant circumstances.

привыкáни|е, я *nt.* (**к**+*d.*) getting accustomed, used (to).

привык|áть, áю *impf. of* ⇒**~́нуть**

привы́к|нуть, ну, нешь, *past* **~, ~ла** *pf.* (*of* ⇒**~áть**) (**к**+*d. or* +*inf.*) **1** (*освоиться*) to get accustomed (to), get used (to); **онá скóро ~ла к нóвому дóму** she soon got used to the new house. **2** (*получить привычку*) to get into the habit (of); **он ~ ругáться** he has got into the habit of swearing.

привы́чк|а, и *f.* habit; **войти́ в ~у** to become a habit; **имéть ~у (к**+*d.*) to be accustomed (to); to be in the habit (of); **приобрести́ ~у** (+*inf.*) to get into the habit (of); **он человéк ~и** he is a man of habit; **сдéлать что-н. по ~е** to do sth. out of habit.

привы́чност|ь, и *f.* habitualness.

привы́ч|ный (~ен, ~на) *adj.* **1** (*обычный*) habitual, usual, customary. **2** (**к**+*d.*) (*привыкший*) accustomed (to), used (to); **ничегó, он человéк п.** it's all right, he's used to it.

привя́занност|ь, и *f.* **1** (**к**+*d.*) (*чувство*) attachment (to); affection (for, towards). **2** (*fig.*) object of affection; **стáрая п.** old flame.

привя́з|анный *p.p.p. of* ⇒**~áть** *and adj.* (**к**+*d.*) attached (to).

привя|зáть, жý, ~́жешь *pf.* (*of* ⇒**~́зывать**) (**к**+*d.*) **1** to tie (to), fasten (to), attach (to); **п. верёвку/ собáку к забóру** to tie a rope/the dog to the fence; **п. ремни́** to fasten belts. **2** (**к себé**; *fig.*) to win over, endear o.s. to.

привя|зáться, жýсь, ~́жешься *pf.* (*of* ⇒**~́зываться**) (**к**+*d.*) **1** to become attached (to); **онá óчень к вам ~зáлась** she has become very attached to you. **2** to attach o.s. (to); **на дорóге какóй-то ни́щий ~зáлся к нам** a beggar attached himself to us on the road. **3** (*coll.*) (*надоесть*) to pester, bother.

привязн|óй *adj.* fastened, secured; **п. ремéнь** seat-belt.

привя́зчив|ый (~, ~а) *adj.* **1** (*склонный к привязанности*) affectionate. **2** (*надоедливый*) annoying, bothersome.

при́вяз|ь, и *f.* tie; lead, leash; tether; **на ~и** on a leash.

привя́зыва|ть(ся), ю(сь) *impf. of* ⇒**привязáть(ся)**

пригáр, а *m.* (*coll.*) burnt place (*of cooked food*).

при́гар|ь, и *f.* taste of burning.

пригвождá|ть, ю *impf. of* ⇒**пригвозди́ть**

пригвоз|ди́ть, жý, ди́шь *pf.* (*of* ⇒**пригвождáть**) (**к**+*d.*) to nail (to); (*fig.*) to pin (down); **п. к мéсту** to root to the spot.

пригибá|ть(ся), ю(сь) *impf. of* ⇒**пригнýть(ся)**

пригла́|дить, жу, дишь *pf.* (*of* ⇨**~живать**) to smooth.

прига́жива|ть, ю *impf. of* ⇨**пригла́дить**

пригласи́тельный *adj.* invitation; **п. биле́т** invitation card.

пригла|си́ть, шу́, си́шь *pf.* (*of* ⇨**~ша́ть**) **1** to invite, ask; **п. на обе́д** to invite, ask to dinner; **п. кого́-н. на та́нец** to ask s.o. to dance, ask s.o. for a dance; **п. в го́сти** to invite, ask round; **его́ ~си́ли на рабо́ту в но́вой шко́ле** he has been offered a job in a new school. **2** (*врача*) to call.

приглаша́|ть, ю *impf. of* ⇨**пригласи́ть**

приглаше́ни|е, я *nt.* **1** invitation; **по ~ю** by invitation; **разосла́ть ~я** to send out invitations. **2** (*на работу*) offer (*of employment*).

приглуш|а́ть, а́ю *impf. of* ⇨**~и́ть**

приглуш|и́ть, у́, и́шь *pf.* (*of* ⇨**~а́ть**) (*звук*) to muffle, deaden; (*голос, речь*) to mute; (*свет, радио*) to turn down; (*огонь*) to choke, damp; (*тоску*) to relieve.

пригля|де́ть, жу́, ди́шь *pf.* (*of* ⇨**~дывать**) (*coll.*) **1** (*подыскать*) to find, look out (*Br.*). **2** (**за**+*i.*) to look after; **п. за детьми́** to look after children.

пригля|де́ться, жу́сь, ди́шься *pf.* (*of* ⇨**~дываться**) (*coll.*) **1** (**к**+*d.*) (*внимательно посмотреть*) to look closely (at), scrutinize. **2** (**к**+*d.*) (*привыкнуть*) to get accustomed (to), get used (to); **п. к темноте́** to get accustomed to darkness. **3** (+*d.*) (*надоесть*) to tire, bore; **мне ~де́лись фи́льмы о войне́** I am tired of war films.

пригля́дыва|ть(ся), ю(сь) *impf. of* ⇨**пригляде́ть(ся)**

приглян|у́ться, у́сь, ~ешься *pf.* (+*d.*; *coll.*) to take one's fancy, attract; **она́ сра́зу ~у́лась ему́** he was attracted by her instantly.

при|гна́ть¹, гоню́, го́нишь, *past* **~гна́л, ~гнала́, ~гна́ло** *pf.* (*of* ⇨**~гоня́ть**) (*гоня, доставить*) to drive.

при|гна́ть², гоню́, го́нишь, *past* **~гна́л, ~гнала́, ~гна́ло** *pf.* (*of* ⇨**~гоня́ть**) (*приладить*) to fit, adjust.

пригн|у́ть, у́, ёшь *pf.* (*of* ⇨**пригиба́ть**) to bend down, bow.

пригн|у́ться, у́сь, ёшься *pf.* (*of* ⇨**пригиба́ться**) (*о человеке*) to bend down; (*о ветке*) to bend.

пригова́рива|ть¹, ю *impf.* to keep saying, keep repeating (*as accompaniment to given action*).

пригова́рива|ть², ю *impf. of* ⇨**приговори́ть**

пригово́р, а *m.* (*судьи*) sentence; **вы́нести п.** to pass sentence; **отмени́ть п.** to quash a sentence; **обвини́тельный п.** guilty verdict; **оправда́тельный п.** verdict of 'not guilty'; (*присяжных*) verdict; (*fig.*) (*истории*) judgement, verdict.

приговор|и́ть, ю́, и́шь *pf.* (*of* ⇨**пригова́ривать²**) (**к**+*d.*) to sentence (to), condemn (to).

приго|ди́ться, жу́сь, ди́шься *pf.* (+*d.*) to prove useful (to), come in handy; to stand in good stead.

приго́дност|ь, и *f.* fitness, suitability.

приго́д|ный (~ен, ~на) *adj.* (**к**+*d.*) fit (for), suitable (for), good (for); **ни к чему́ не п.** good-for-nothing, worthless.

приго́ж|ий (~, ~а) *adj.* **1** (*folk poet.*) (*девушка*) comely. **2** (*coll.*) (*погода*) fine.

приголу́б|ить, лю, ишь *pf.* (*of* ⇨**голу́бить** *and* **~ливать**) to caress, fondle.

приголу́блива|ть, ю *impf. of* ⇨**приголу́бить**

приго́н, а *m.* driving home, bringing in.

приго́нк|а, и *f.* fitting, adjusting; **п. часте́й** (*tech.*) assembling.

пригоня́|ть, ю *impf. of* ⇨**пригна́ть**

пригор|а́ть, а́ет *impf. of* ⇨**~е́ть**

пригоре́лый *adj.* burnt.

пригор|е́ть, и́т *pf.* (*of* ⇨**~а́ть**) to be burnt; **молоко́ ~е́ло** the milk is burnt.

при́город, а *m.* suburb.

при́городный *adj.* suburban; **п. по́езд** local train.

приго́р|ок, ка *m.* hillock, knoll.

при́горш|ня, ни, *g. pl.* **~ен** *and* **~ней** *f.* handful; **пить во́ду ~нями** to drink water from cupped hands.

пригорю́нива|ться, юсь *impf. of* ⇨**пригорю́ниться**

пригорю́н|иться, юсь, ишься *pf.* (*of* ⇨**~иваться**) (*coll.*) to become sad.

приго́тавлива|ть(ся), ю(сь) *impf.* = **приготовля́ть(ся)**

приготови́тельный *adj.* preparatory.

пригото́в|ить, лю, ишь *pf.* (*of* ⇨**пригота́вливать** *and* **~ля́ть**) to prepare; **п. обе́д** to cook, prepare a dinner; **п. роль** to learn a part.

пригото́в|иться, люсь, ишься *pf.* (*of* ⇨**пригота́вливаться** *and* **~ля́ться**) (+*inf.*) to prepare (to); (**к**+*d.*) to prepare (o.s.) (for).

приготовле́ни|е, я *nt.* preparation; **без ~я** extempore.

приготовля́|ть(ся), ю(сь) *impf. of* ⇨**пригото́вить(ся)**

пригреба́|ть, ю *impf. of* ⇨**пригрести́**

пригрева́|ть(ся), ю(сь) *impf. of* ⇨**пригре́ть(ся)**

пригре́|зиться, жусь, зишься *pf. of* ⇨**гре́зиться**

пригре|сти́, бу́, бёшь, *past* **~б, ~бла́** *pf.* (*of* ⇨**~ба́ть**) (*coll.*) **1** (*листья*) to rake up. **2** (**к**+*d.*) (*приблизиться, гребя*) to row (towards).

пригре́|ть, ю, ешь *pf.* (*of* ⇨**~ва́ть**) **1** to warm. **2** (*fig.*) (*приютить*) to give shelter (to), take to one's care.

пригре́|ться, юсь, ешься *pf.* (*of* ⇨**~ва́ться**) (*coll.*) to warm o.s.; to warm up.

пригро|зи́ть, жу́, зи́шь *pf. of* ⇨**грози́ть 1**

пригу́б|ить, лю, ишь *pf.* to take a sip (of), taste.

прида|ва́ть, ю́, ёшь *impf. of* ⇨**прида́ть**

придав|и́ть, лю́, ~ишь *pf.* (*of* ⇨**~ливать**) to press; (*повредить*) to squash; (*fig.*) (*удручить*) to weigh down on.

прида́влива|ть, ю *impf. of* ⇨**придави́ть**

прида́ни|е, я *nt.* giving, imparting; **для ~я хра́брости** to give courage; **для ~я зако́нной си́лы** (+*d.*; *leg.*) to give legal status (to); to make legal.

прида́н|ое, ого *nt.* **1** (*имущество*) dowry; (*одежда*) trousseau. **2** (*для новорождённого*) layette.

прида́т|ок, ка *m.* appendage, adjunct.

прида́точн|ый *adj.* **1** additional, supplementary. **2** (*gram.*) subordinate; **~ое предложе́ние** subordinate clause.

прида́|ть, м, шь, ст, ди́м, ди́те, ду́т, *past* **при́дал, ~ла́, при́дало** *pf.* (*of* ⇨**~ва́ть**) **1** to add; (*mil.*) to attach. **2** (*усилить*) to increase, strengthen; **п. бо́дрости** (+*d.*) to hearten, put heart (into); **п. ду́ху** (+*d.*) to inspire, encourage. **3** (+*a.* *and* *d.*) (*свойство, состояние*) to give (to), impart (to); (*fig.*) to attach (to); **п. вкус** to give piquancy (to); **п. лоск** to impart lustre (*Br.*), luster (*US*) (to); **п. значе́ние** to attach importance (to); **п. фо́рму** to give shape (to).

прида́ч|а, и *f.* **1** (*действие*) adding; (*mil.*) attaching. **2** (*то, что придано*) addition, supplement; **в ~у** in addition.

придвига́|ть(ся), ю(сь) *impf. of* ⇨**придви́нуть(ся)**

придви́|нуть, ну, нешь *pf.* (*of* ⇨**~га́ть**) to move (up), draw (up); **~нь(те) кре́сло к пе́чке** draw your chair up to the stove.

придви́|нуться, нусь, нешься *pf.* (*of* ⇨**~га́ться**) (**к**+*d.*) to move.

придво́рн|ый *adj.* court; **п. врач** court physician; **п. шут** court jester; *as n.* **п., ~ого** *m.* courtier.

приде́л, а *m.* (*eccl.*) (*постройка*) side-chapel.

приде́л|ать, аю *pf.* (*of* ⇨**~ывать**) (**к**+*d.*) to fix (to), attach (to).

приде́лыва|ть, ю *impf. of* ⇨**приде́лать**

придерж|а́ть, у́, ~ишь *pf.* (*of* ⇨**~ивать**) to hold back (*also fig.*); **п. това́р** to hold back goods; **п. язы́к** to hold one's tongue.

приде́ржива|ть, ю *impf. of* ⇨**придержа́ть**

приде́ржива|ться, юсь *impf.* **1** (**за**+*a.*) to hold on (to); **п. за по́ручень** to hold on to the rail. **2** (+*g.*) to hold (to), keep (to) (*also fig.*); (*fig.*) to stick (to), adhere (to); (*моды, советов*) to follow; **п. пра́вой стороны́** to keep to the right; **п. догово́ра** to adhere to an agreement; **п. мне́ния** to hold the opinion, be of the opinion; **п. пра́вил** to stick to, follow the rules; **п. те́мы** to stick to the subject.

приди́р|а, ы *c.g.* (*coll.*) quibbler, fault-finder.

придира́|ться, юсь *impf. of* ⇨**придра́ться**

приди́рк|а, и *f.* (*coll.*) quibble; (*pl.*) fault-finding, nagging, carping.

придир́чивост|ь, и *f.* captiousness.

придир́чив|ый (~, ~а) *adj.* fault-finding, carping, nagging.

придорóжный *adj.* roadside, wayside.

при|драться, дерýсь, дерёшься, *past* **~дрáлся, ~дралáсь, ~дрáлóсь** *pf.* (*of* ⇒**~дирáться**) (к+*d.*) **1** (*упрекнуть*) to find fault (with), carp (at); to nag (at), pick (on); **п. к комý-н. из-за пустякóв/по пустякáм** to find fault with s.o. over trifles. **2** (*воспользоваться как предлогом*) (*coll.*) to seize (on, upon).

придýм|ать, аю *pf.* (*of* ⇒**~ывать**) **1** (*отговорку, выход*) to think of, think up; (*приспособление*) to devise, invent; (*сказку, песню*) to make up; (*музыку*) to compose, make up; **п. развлечéние** to devise an entertainment; **он ~ал, как вы́йти из кри́зиса** he thought of how to get out of the crisis; **наконéц я ~ал, что дéлать** at last I have thought of what to do. **2** (*вообразить*) to imagine.

придýмыва|ть, ю *impf. of* ⇒**придýмать**

придурковáт|ый (~, ~а) *adj.* (*coll.*) daft, dopey.

придýр|ок, ка *m.* (*sl.*) idiot, fool.

при́дур|ь, и *f.*: **с ~ью** (*coll.*) slightly mad, touched.

придуш|и́ть, ý, ~́ишь *pf.* (*coll.*) to strangle, smother.

придыхáни|е, я *nt.* (*ling.*) (*в речи*) aspiration.

придыхáтельн|ый *adj.* (*ling.*) aspirate; *as n.* **п., ~ого** *m.* aspirate.

при|дý *see* ⇒**~йти́**

приедá|ться, ется *impf. of* ⇒**приéсться**

приéзд, а *m.* arrival, coming; **с ~ом!** welcome!

приезжá|ть, ю *impf. of* ⇒**приéхать**

приезжáющ|ий *pres. part. of* ⇒**приезжáть;** *as n.* **п., ~его** *m.*, **~ая, ~ей** *f.* newcomer, (new) arrival.

приéзж|ий *adj.* newly arrived; visiting; *as n.* **п., ~его** *m.*, **~ая, ~ей** *f.* newcomer; (*гость*) visitor.

приём, а *m.* **1** (*действие*) receiving; reception; **часы́ ~а** (reception) hours, calling hours; (*врача*) surgery (hours) (*Br.*), office hours (*US*). **2** (*гостей*) reception, welcome; **оказáть комý-н. радýшный п.** to accord s.o. a hearty welcome. **3** (*в партию, клуб*) admittance. **4** (*собрание приглашённых*) reception. **5** (*лекарства*) dose. **6** (*отдельное действие*) go; motion, movement; **в оди́н п.** at one go; **вы́пить стакáн в два ~а** to drain a glass in two draughts (*Br.*), drafts (*US*); **испóлнить комáнду в три ~а** to execute a command in three movements. **7** (*способ*) method, way, mode; (*уловка*) device, trick (*also pej.*); (*sport*) hold, grip; **лечéбный п.** method of treatment. **8** (*radio, TV*) reception.

приёмк|а, и *f.* receipt.

приéмлемост|ь, и *f.* acceptability; admissibility.

приéмлем|ый (~, ~а) *adj.* acceptable; admissible.

приёмн|ая, ой *f.* **1** (*для ожидания*) waiting-room. **2** (*где принимают гостей*) reception room.

приёмник[1], а *m.* (*радиоприёмник*) radio (set); (*для приёма сигналов*) receiver.

приёмник[2], а *m.* (*учреждение*) reception centre (*Br.*), center (*US*).

приёмн|ый *adj.* **1** receiving; reception; **п. день** visiting day; **~ые часы́** (reception) hours; (*врача*) surgery (hours) (*Br.*), office hours (*US*); **п. покóй** casualty ward. **2** selection; entrance; **~ая коми́ссия** selection committee; **п. экзáмен** entrance examination. **3** foster, adoptive; **п. отéц** foster-father; **~ая мать** foster-mother; **п. сын** adopted son, foster-son.

приёмщик, а *m.* examiner, inspector (*of goods at a factory*).

приёмщи|ца, цы *f. of* ⇒**~к**

приёмыш, а *m.* adopted child, foster-child.

при|éсться, éстся, едя́тся, *past* **~éлся, ~éлась** *pf.* (*of* ⇒**~едáться**) (+*d.*; *coll.*) to pall (on), bore; **мне ~éлась э́та рабóта** I am fed up with this work.

приé|хать, ду, дешь *pf.* (*of* ⇒**~зжáть**) to arrive, come (*not on foot*).

прижáт|ый *p.p.p. of* ⇒**~ь; быть ~ым к стенé** (*fig.*) to have one's back to the wall.

приж|áть, мý, мёшь *pf.* (*of* ⇒**~имáть**) **1** (к+*d.*) to press (to), clasp (to); **п. к землé** to pin down; **п. к груди́** to clasp to one's bosom; **п. к стенé** (*fig.*) to drive into a corner. **2** (*fig.*) to press, bring pressure to bear (upon); **п. должникóв** to press one's debtors.

приж|áться, мýсь, мёшься *pf.* (*of* ⇒**~имáться**) (к+*d.*) (*прислониться*) to press o.s. (to, against); (*к матери*) to cuddle up (to), snuggle up (to), nestle up (to); **п. к стенé** to flatten o.s. against the wall.

при|жéчь, жгý, жжёшь, жгýт, *past* **~жёг, ~жглá** *pf.* (*of* ⇒**~жигáть**) to cauterize, sear.

приживáл|ка, ки *f. of* ⇒**~ьщик**

приживáльщик, а *m.* hanger-on, sponger.

приживáльщи|ца, цы *f. of* ⇒**~к**

приживá|ть(ся), ю(сь) *impf. of* ⇒**прижи́ть(ся)**

прижигáни|е, я *nt.* (*med.*) cauterization, searing.

прижигá|ть, ю *impf. of* ⇒**прижéчь**

прижи́зненный *adj.* occurring during one's lifetime.

прижимá|ть(ся), ю(сь) *impf. of* ⇒**прижáть(ся)**

прижи́мист|ый (~, ~а) *adj.* (*coll.*) tight-fisted, stingy.

прижи́мк|а, и *f.* (*fig., coll.*) pressure; clamping down.

приж|и́ть, ивý, ивёшь, *past* **~́ил, ~илá, ~́ило** *pf.* (*of* ⇒**~ивáть**) (*coll.*) to beget (*usu. of extra-marital unions*).

приж|и́ться, ивýсь, ивёшься, *past* **~и́лся, ~илáсь** *pf.* (*of* ⇒**~ивáться**) **1** (*прожив, привыкнуть*) to settle down, get acclimatized (*Br.*), acclimated (*US*). **2** (*о растениях*) to take root.

приз, а, *pl.* **~ы́** *m.* prize; **переходя́щий п.** challenge prize; **получи́ть п.** to win a prize; **присуди́ть п.** (+*d.*) to award a prize (to).

призадýм|аться, аюсь *pf.* (*of* ⇒**~ываться**) to become thoughtful, become pensive.

призадýмыва|ться, юсь *impf. of* ⇒**призадýматься**

приза|ня́ть, йму́, ймёшь, *past* **~́нял, ~нялá, ~́няло** *pf.* (*coll.*) to borrow (*a small sum*).

призвáни|е, я *nt.* (*назначение*) vocation, calling; **слéдовать своемý ~ю** to follow one's vocation; (*склонность*) aptitude; (*музыки, театра*) mission, purpose.

при|звáть, зовý, зовёшь, *past* **~звáл, ~звалá, ~звáло** *pf.* (*of* ⇒**~зывáть**) (*позвать явиться*) to call, summon; (*позвать делать что-н.*) to call upon, appeal; **п. на пóмощь** to call for help; **п. на воéнную слýжбу** to call up (*for mil. service*); **п. к поря́дку** to call to order.

при|звáться, зовýсь, зовёшься, *past* **~звáлся, ~звалáсь, ~звáлóсь** *pf.* (*of* ⇒**~зывáться**) (*coll.*) to be called up.

при́звук, а *m.* additional sound.

призéмист|ый (~, ~а) *adj.* stocky, squat; thickset.

приземлéни|е, я *nt.* (*aeron.*) landing, touch-down.

приземл|и́ть, ю, и́шь *pf.* (*of* ⇒**~я́ть**) (*aeron.*) to land.

приземл|и́ться, ю́сь, и́шься *pf.* (*of* ⇒**~я́ться**) (*aeron.*) to land, touch down.

приземля́|ть(ся), ю(сь) *impf. of* ⇒**приземли́ть(ся)**

призёр, а *m.* prize-winner.

при́зм|а, ы *f.* prism; **сквозь ~у** (+*g.*; *fig.*) in the light (of).

призмати́ческий *adj.* prismatic.

призна|вáть(ся), ю́(сь), ёшь(ся) *impf. of* ⇒**признáть(ся)**

при́знак, а *m.* sign; indication; **п. болéзни** symptom; **служи́ть ~ом** (+*g.*) to be a sign (of); **обнарýживать ~и** (+*g.*) to show signs (of); **имéются все ~и тогó, что** there is every indication that; **не подавáть ~ов жи́зни** to show no sign of life.

признáни|е, я *nt.* **1** (*заявление*) confession, declaration; admission, acknowledgement; **невóльное п.** involuntary admission; **п. вины́** avowal of guilt; **п. в любви́** declaration of love; **по óбщему ~ю** by general admission. **2** (*оценка по достоинству*) recognition; **получи́ть п.** to obtain, win recognition.

при́зн|анный *p.p.p. of* ⇒**~áть** *and adj.* acknowledged, recognized.

признáтельност|ь, и *f.* gratitude.

призна́тел|ьный (~ен, ~ьна) *adj.* grateful.
призна́|ть, ю *pf.* (*of* ⇒**~ва́ть**) **1** (*узнать*) to recognize; to spot, identify; **вы меня́ не ~ли?** did you not recognize me? **2** (*leg., pol.*) to recognize; **п. прави́тельство** to recognize a government. **3** (*сознать*) to admit, acknowledge; **п. себя́ вино́вным** (*leg.*) to plead guilty; **п. свою́ оши́бку** to admit one's mistake. **4** (*считать*) to deem; **п. ну́жным** to deem (it) necessary; **п. недействи́тельным** to declare invalid; **п. (не)вино́вным** to find (not) guilty.
призна́|ться, юсь *pf.* (*of* ⇒**~ва́ться**) (**в**+*p.*) to confess (to); **п. в любви́** to make a declaration of love; **п. в преступле́нии** to confess to a crime.
призов|о́й *adj. of* ⇒**приз; ~ы́е де́ньги** prize-money; **~о́е ме́сто** medal position.
призо́р, а *m.*: **без ~а** (*coll.*) untended, neglected.
при́зрак, а *m.* spectre (*Br.*), specter (*US*), ghost, apparition.
при́зрачност|ь, и *f.* illusoriness.
при́зрач|ный (~ен, ~на) *adj.* **1** spectral, ghostly. **2** (*fig.*) (*мнимый*) illusory, imagined; **~ная опа́сность** imagined danger.
призрева́|ть, ю *impf. of* ⇒**призре́ть**
призре́ни|е, я *nt.* care, charity; **дом ~я бе́дных** alms-house, poor people's home.
призр|е́ть, ю́, ~и́шь *pf.* (*of* ⇒**~ева́ть**) to support by charity.
призы́в, а *m.* **1** (*просьба*) call, appeal; **откли́кнуться на чей-н. п.** to respond to s.o.'s call. **2** (*лозунг*) slogan; **первома́йские ~ы** May Day slogans. **3** (*mil.*) call-up, conscription.
призыва́|ть(ся), ю(сь) *impf. of* ⇒**призва́ть(ся)**
призывни́к, а́ *m.* conscript.
призывно́й *adj.* call-up; **п. во́зраст** call-up age.
призы́вный *adj.* summoning; inviting; **п. клич** call.
при́иск, а *m.* mine; **золоты́е ~и** gold-field(s).
при|иска́ть, ищу́, и́щешь *pf.* (*of* ⇒**~и́скивать**) (*coll.*) to find.
прии́скива|ть, ю *impf.* (*coll.*) **1** *impf. of* ⇒**приискать. 2** (*impf. only*) to look for, search for.
приисково́й *adj. of* ⇒**прииск**
при|йти́, ду́, дёшь, *past* **~шёл, ~шла́** *pf.* (*of* ⇒**~ходи́ть**) to come; to arrive; **п. пе́рвым** to come first; **п. в восто́рг** (**от**+*g.*) to go into raptures (over); **п. в у́жас** to be horrified; **п. в я́рость** to fly into a rage; **п. в го́лову кому́-н., на ум кому́-н.** to occur to s.o., strike s.o., cross one's mind; **мысль ~шла́ мне в го́лову** the idea occurred to me; **п. в себя́, п. в чу́вство** to come round, regain consciousness; (*fig.*) to come to one's senses; **п. к концу́** to come to an end; **п. к соглаше́нию** to come to an agreement.
при|йти́сь, ду́сь, дёшься, *past* **~шёлся, ~шла́сь** *pf.* (*of* ⇒**~ходи́ться**) **1** (**по**+*d.*) to fit; **пальто́ ~шло́сь мне по разме́ру** the coat fitted me; **п. кому́-н. по вку́су, по нра́ву** to be to s.o.'s taste, liking. **2** (**на**+*a.*; *о датах, событиях*) to fall (on); **Па́сха ~шла́сь на 28-ое ма́рта** Easter fell on the 28th of March; (**по**+*d.*; *попасть*): **уда́р ~шёлся по лицу́** the blow landed on my, his, *etc.* face. **3** (*impers.*+*d.*) (*оказаться нужным*) to have (to); **нам ~шло́сь подожда́ть ещё два часа́** we had to wait another two hours; **ей ~дётся неме́дленно верну́ться в Москву́** she will have to return to Moscow immediately. **4** (*impers.*+*d.*) (*выпасть на долю*) to happen (to), fall to the lot (of); **мне ~шло́сь быть ря́дом в тот моме́нт, когда́ он упа́л в о́бморок** I happened to be standing by when he fainted; **им ту́го ~шло́сь** they had a rough time; **ему́ ~шло́сь тяжело́** he had a hard time; **как ~дётся** (*coll.*) anyhow; **где ~дётся** anywhere; in all sorts of places; **что ~дётся** anything; whatever comes along. **5** (*impers.*; **на**+*a. or* **с**+*g.*; *coll.*) (*причитаться*) to be owing (to, from); **на ка́ждого ~шло́сь по фу́нту** they got a pound each; **с вас ~дётся де́сять рубле́й** there is ten roubles to come from you.
прика́з, а *m.* **1** order, command; **вы́полнить п.** to carry out an order; **отда́ть п.** to give an order; **по ~у** by order. **2** (*hist.*) office, department.
приказа́ни|е, я *nt.* (*приказ*) order, command; (*указание*) instruction.
прика|за́ть, жу́, ~́жешь *pf.* (*of* ⇒**~́зывать**) (+*d.*) to order; to give orders; **он ~за́л подчинённым, что́бы зако́нчили рабо́ту к ве́черу** he ordered his subordinates to finish the work by evening; **дире́ктор ~за́л соста́вить но́вый гра́фик** the director ordered a new schedule to be worked out; **генера́л ~за́л атакова́ть** the general gave orders to attack; the general ordered an attack; **п. до́лго жить** (*coll.*) to pass on, depart this life; **что ~́жете?** what do you wish?, what can I do for you?; **как ~́жете** as you wish; **как ~́жете понима́ть э́то?** how am I supposed to take this?
приказ|но́й *adj.* commanding; **в ~но́м поря́дке** in the form of an order.
прика́зчик, а *m.* (*obs.*) **1** (*продавец*) salesman. **2** (*в имении*) steward.
прика́зыва|ть, ю *impf. of* ⇒**приказа́ть**
прика́лыва|ть, ю *impf. of* ⇒**приколо́ть**
прика́нчива|ть, ю *impf. of* ⇒**прико́нчить**
прикарма́нива|ть, ю *impf. of* ⇒**прикарма́нить**
прикарма́н|ить, ю, ишь *pf.* (*of* ⇒**~ивать**) (*coll.*) to pocket.
прика́рмлива|ть, ю *impf.* **1** *impf. of* ⇒**прикорми́ть. 2** (*impf. only*) (*дополнительно кормить*) to give additional food (*during the weaning period*).
прикаса́|ться, юсь *impf. of* ⇒**прикосну́ться**
прика|ти́ть, чу́, ~́тишь *pf.* (*of* ⇒**~́тывать**) **1** (**к**+*d.*) (*бочку*) to roll up (to); (*тачку*) to wheel up (to). **2** (*coll.*) (*приехать*) to roll up, turn up.
прика́тыва|ть, ю *impf. of* ⇒**прикати́ть**
прики́д, а *m.* (*sl.*) stylish clothing, gear.
прики́дыва|ть(ся), ю(сь) *impf. of* ⇒**прики́нуть(ся)**
прики́|нуть, ну, нешь *pf.* (*of* ⇒**~дывать**) **1** (*добавить*) to throw in, add. **2** (*приблизительно сосчитать*) to estimate (approximately); **п. в уме́** (*fig.*) to weigh (up), ponder.
прики́|нуться, нусь, нешься *pf.* (*of* ⇒**~дываться**) (+*i.*; *coll.*) to pretend (to be), feign; **п. больны́м** to pretend to be ill, feign illness; **он ~нулся, что не ви́дит меня́** he pretended that he could not see me.
прикла́д[1], а *m.* (*ружья*) butt.
прикла́д[2], а *m.* (*для шитья одежды, обуви*) trimmings.
прикладн|о́й *adj.* applied; **~о́е иску́сство** applied arts; **~а́я програ́мма** (*comput.*) application (program); **~а́я фи́зика** applied physics.
прикла́дыва|ть(ся), ю(сь) *impf. of* ⇒**приложи́ть(ся)**
прикле́ива|ть(ся), ю, ет(ся) *impf. of* ⇒**прикле́ить(ся)**
прикле́|ить, ю, ишь *pf.* (*of* ⇒**~ивать**) to stick; to glue; **п. ма́рку** to stick on a stamp; **п. афи́шу к стене́** to stick (up) a bill on a wall.
прикле́|иться, ится *pf.* (*of* ⇒**~иваться**) (**к**+*d.*) to stick (to), adhere (to).
приклеп|а́ть, а́ю *pf.* (*of* ⇒**~́ывать**) to rivet.
приклёпыва|ть, ю *impf. of* ⇒**приклепа́ть**
приклон|и́ть, ю́, ~и́шь *pf.*: **п. го́лову** to lay one's head; **ему́ не́где п. го́лову** he has nowhere to lay his head.
приключ|а́ться, а́ется *impf. of* ⇒**~и́ться**
приключе́ни|е, я *nt.* adventure.
приключе́нческий *adj.* adventure; **п. рома́н** adventure novel.
приключ|и́ться, и́тся *pf.* (*of* ⇒**~а́ться**) (*coll.*) to happen, occur.
прикноп|и́ть, лю́, ~и́шь *pf.* to pin up (*with a drawing pin*).
прико́в|анный *p.p.p. of* ⇒**~а́ть; п. к посте́ли** bed-ridden.
прик|ова́ть, ую́, уёшь *pf.* (*of* ⇒**~о́вывать**) (**к**+*d.*) **1** to chain (to). **2** (*fig.*) (*взгляд*) to fix; (*внимание*) to rivet; **карти́на ~ова́ла на́ше внима́ние** our attention was riveted on the picture; **п. к себе́ всео́бщее внима́ние** to attract everybody's attention; **страх ~ова́л нас к ме́сту** fear rooted us to the spot; **боле́знь ~ова́ла его́ к посте́ли** illness confined him to his bed.
прико́выва|ть, ю *impf. of* ⇒**прикова́ть**
прико́л, а *m.* **1** stake; **стоя́ть на ~е**

П

(*naut.*) to be tied up, moored; **на ~е** laid up (*also fig.*). **2** (*sl.*) (*анекдот*) funny story, anecdote; (*выходка*) trick, strange action; **для ~а** for a laugh.

прикола́чива|ть, ю *impf. of* **⇒приколоти́ть**

приколо|ти́ть, чу́, ~́тишь *pf.* (*of* **⇒прикола́чивать**) to nail, fasten with nails.

прикол|о́ть, ю́, ~́ешь *pf.* (*of* **⇒прика́лывать**) **1** to pin, fasten with a pin. **2** (*coll.*) (*человека*) to stab; **п. штыко́м** to bayonet.

прикомандир|ова́ть, у́ю *pf.* (*of* **⇒~о́вывать**) (**к**+*d.*) to attach (to), second (to).

прикомандиро́выва|ть, ю *impf. of* **⇒прикомандирова́ть**

прико́нч|ить, у, ишь *pf.* (*of* **⇒прика́нчивать**) (*coll.*) **1** (*израсходовать*) to use up. **2** (*fig.*) (*умертвить*) to finish off.

прикоп|и́ть, лю́, ~́ишь *pf.* (+*a. or g.*; *coll.*) to save (up), put by.

прико́рм, а *m.* **1** (*для рыб, птиц*) lure, bait. **2** (*для детей*) additional food.

прикорм|и́ть, лю́, ~́ишь *pf.* (*of* **⇒прика́рмливать**) to lure (*by putting out food*).

прико́рм|ка, ки *f.* = **~**

прикорн|у́ть, у́, ёшь *pf.* (*coll.*) to curl up.

прикоснове́ни|е, я *nt.* **1** touch; **то́чка ~я** point of contact. **2** (*obs.*) concern; **я не име́ю никако́го ~я к э́тому де́лу** this affair is no concern of mine, is nothing to do with me.

прикоснове́нност|ь, и *f.* (**к**+*d.*) (*liter.*) concern (in), involvement (in).

прикоснове́н|ный (~, ~на) *adj.* (**к**+*d.*) (*liter.*) concerned (in), involved (in), implicated (in); **он был ~ к убийству** he was implicated in a murder.

прикосн|у́ться, у́сь, ёшься *pf.* (*of* **⇒прикаса́ться**) (**к**+*d.*) to touch (lightly).

прикра́с|а, ы *f.* (*usu. pl.*) (*coll.*) embellishment; **без ~** unvarnished.

прикра́|сить, шу, сишь *pf.* (*of* **⇒~шивать**) to embellish, embroider (*in speech*).

прикра́шива|ть, ю *impf. of* **⇒прикра́сить**

прикреп|и́ть, лю, и́шь *pf.* (*of* **⇒~ля́ть**) (**к**+*d.*) **1** to fasten (to). **2** (*fig.*) to attach (to); **п. де́тский сад к поликли́нике** to attach a kindergarten to a health centre (*Br.*), center (*US*).

прикреп|и́ться, лю́сь, и́шься *pf.* (*of* **⇒~ля́ться**) (**к**+*d.*) to register (at, with).

прикрепле́ни|е, я *nt.* **1** fastening. **2** (*fig.*) attachment. **3** (*регистрация*) registration.

прикрепля́|ть(ся), ю(сь) *impf. of* **⇒прикрепи́ть(ся)**

прикри́кива|ть, ю *impf. of* **⇒прикри́кнуть**

прикри́к|нуть, ну, нешь *pf.* (*of* **⇒~ивать**) (**на**+*a.*) to shout (at), raise one's voice (at).

прикру|ти́ть, чу́, ~́тишь *pf.* (*of* **⇒~́чивать**) **1** (**к**+*d.*) (*привязать*) to tie (to), bind (to), fasten (to). **2** (*coll.*) (*фитиль*) to turn down.

прикру́чива|ть, ю *impf. of* **⇒прикрути́ть**

прикрыва́|ть(ся), ю(сь) *impf. of* **⇒прикры́ть(ся)**

прикры́ти|е, я *nt.* cover; (*конвой*) escort; (*fig.*) screen, cloak; **под ~ем** (+*g.*) under cover (of); **артиллери́йское п.** artillery cover.

прикр|ы́ть, о́ю, о́ешь *pf.* (*of* **⇒~ыва́ть**) **1** (+*i.*) (*покрыть*) to cover (with); to screen; **п. кастрю́лю кры́шкой** to put the lid on a saucepan. **2** (*защитить*) to protect, shield; **п. глаза́ руко́й** to shade, shield one's eyes (with one's hand); (*о войсках*) to cover; **п. наступле́ние артилле́рией** to cover an attack with an artillery barrage. **3** (*fig.*) (*скрыть*) to cover (up), conceal, screen; **п. своё неве́жество** to conceal one's ignorance. **4** (*coll.*) (*ликвидировать*) to close down, wind up. **5** (*coll.*) (*закрыть неплотно*) to close (*a door, etc.*) to.

прикр|ы́ться, о́юсь, о́ешься *pf.* (*of* **⇒~ыва́ться**) **1** (+*i.*) to cover o.s. (with); (*fig.*) to use as a cover, take refuge (in), shelter (behind); **он ~ы́лся боле́знью** he took refuge in being ill. **2** (*coll.*) (*ликвидироваться*) to close down, go out of business. **3** (*coll.*) (*закрыться неплотно*) to close to.

прикуп|а́ть, а́ю *impf. of* **⇒~и́ть**

прикуп|и́ть, лю́, ~́ишь *pf.* (*of* **⇒~а́ть**) (+*a. or g.*) to buy (*some more*).

прику́пк|а, и *f.* additional purchase.

прику́рива|ть, ю *impf. of* **⇒прикури́ть**

прикур|и́ть, ю́, ~́ишь *pf.* (*of* **⇒~́ивать**) (**у кого́-н.**) to get a light (*from s.o.'s cigarette*).

прику́с, а *m.* bite.

прику|си́ть, шу́, ~́сишь *pf.* (*of* **⇒~́сывать**) to bite; **п. (себе́) язы́к** to bite one's tongue; (*fig., coll.*) to hold one's tongue, keep one's mouth shut.

прику́сыва|ть, ю *impf. of* **⇒прикуси́ть**

прила́в|ок, ка *m.* counter; (*на рынке*) stall; **рабо́тник ~ка** counter hand, salesman; **из-под ~ка** (*fig.*) under the counter.

прилага́|емый *pres. part. pass. of* **⇒~ть** *and adj.* accompanying; enclosed; **п. почто́вый перево́д** the enclosed postal order.

прилага́тельн|ое *adj.*: **имя ~ое** (*or as n.* **~ое, ~ого** *nt.*) adjective.

прилага́|ть, ю *impf. of* **⇒приложи́ть**

прила́|дить, жу, дишь *pf.* (*of* **⇒~живать**) (**к**+*d.*) to fit (to), adjust (to).

прила́жива|ть, ю *impf. of* **⇒прила́дить**

приласка́|ть, ю *pf.* to caress, pet; (*отнестись хорошо*) to show kindness to.

приласка́|ться, юсь *pf.* (**к**+*d.*) to snuggle up (to).

прилгн|у́ть, у́, ёшь *pf.* (*coll.*) to add made-up bits (*when recounting sth.*).

прилега́|ть, ет *impf.* (**к**+*d.*) **1** (*pf.* **приле́чь**[1]) (*об одежде*) to fit closely. **2** (*no pf.*) (*примыкать*) to be adjacent (to), border (upon); **сад ~ет к те́ннисному ко́рту** the garden is adjacent to the tennis court.

прилега́|ющий *pres. part. of* **⇒~ть** *and adj.* **1** close-fitting, tight-fitting. **2** (**к**+*d.*) adjoining, adjacent (to).

прилежа́ни|е, я *nt.* diligence, assiduousness; application.

прилежа́щий *adj.* (*math.*) adjacent.

приле́ж|ный (~ен, ~на) *adj.* diligent, assiduous.

прилеп|и́ть, лю́, ~́ишь *pf.* (*of* **⇒~ля́ть**) (**к**+*d.*) to stick (to, on).

прилеп|и́ться, лю́сь, ~́ишься *pf.* (*of* **⇒~ля́ться**) (**к**+*d.*) to stick (to, on).

прилепля́|ть(ся), ю(сь) *impf. of* **⇒прилепи́ть(ся)**

прилёт, а *m.* arrival (*by air*).

прилет|а́ть, а́ю *impf. of* **⇒~е́ть**

приле|те́ть, чу́, ти́шь *pf.* (*of* **⇒~та́ть**) **1** to arrive (*by air*), fly in. **2** (*fig., coll.*) (*быстро прибыть*) to fly, come flying.

при|ле́чь[1]**, ля́жет, ля́гут**, *past* **~лёг, ~легла́** *pf. of* **⇒~лега́ть**

при|ле́чь[2]**, ля́гу, ля́жешь, ля́гут**, *past* **~лёг, ~легла́** *pf.* **1** (*лечь ненадолго*) to lie down, have a lie-down (*Br.*). **2** (*о злаках*) to be laid flat.

прили́в, а *m.* **1** rising tide; (*fig.*) (*людей, денег*) influx; **волна́ ~а** tidal wave; **п. и отли́в** ebb and flow. **2** (*med.*) congestion; **п. кро́ви** rush of blood; (*fig.*): **п. эне́ргии, негодова́ния** surge of energy, indignation.

прилива́|ть, ет *impf. of* **⇒прили́ть**

прили́вный *adj.* tidal.

прили́з|анный *p.p.p. of* **⇒~а́ть; ~анные во́лосы** slicked-down hair.

прили|за́ть, жу́, ~́жешь *pf.* (*of* **⇒~́зывать**) **1** (*шерсть*) to lick smooth. **2** (*волосы*) to slick down.

прили́зыва|ть, ю *impf. of* **⇒прилиза́ть**

прилип|а́ть, а́ю *impf. of* **⇒~́нуть**

прили́п|нуть, ну, нешь, *past* **~, ~ла** *pf.* (*of* **⇒~а́ть**) (**к**+*d.*) to stick (to), adhere (to); (*coll.*) (*надоедать*) to pester; **п. к телеви́зору** (*coll.*) to be glued to the television.

прили́пчив|ый (~, ~а) *adj.* (*coll.*) **1** sticking, adhesive. **2** (*fig.*) (*надоедливый*) boring, tiresome. **3** (*болезнь*) catching; (*мелодия*) catchy.

прили́стник, а *m.* (*bot.*) stipule.

при|ли́ть, льёт, *past* **~ли́л, ~лила́, ~ли́ло** *pf.* (*of* **⇒~лива́ть**) (**к**+*d.*) to flow (to); (*о крови*) to rush (to); **кровь ~лила́ к её щека́м** blood rushed to her cheeks.

прили́честв|овать, ует *impf.* (+*d.*) to befit, become.

прили́чи|е, я *nt.* decency, propriety; decorum; **соблюда́ть ~я** to observe the proprieties.

прили́ч|ный (~ен, ~на) *adj.* **1** decent, proper; decorous, seemly. **2** (+*d.*; *obs.*) (*подходящий*) fitting; appropriate (to). **3** (*coll.*) (*достаточно хороший*) decent, fair; **~ная зарпла́та** a decent wage; (*достаточно большой*) sizeable.

приложе́ни|е, я *nt.* **1** (*применение*) application; **п. нау́ки к промы́шленности** the application of science to industry. **2** (*печати*) affixing. **3** (*документов к письме*) enclosure; (*comput.*) attachment. **4** (*к журналу, к газете*) supplement. **5** (*к книге*) appendix; (*к документу*) addendum. **6** (*gram.*) apposition. **7** (*comput.*) (*прикладная программа*) application.

прилож|и́ть, у́, ~́ишь *pf.* **1** (*impf.* **прикла́дывать**) (**к**+*d.*) (*положить*) to put (to), hold (to); **п. ру́ку ко лбу** to put one's hand to one's head; **п. ру́ки чему́-н.** to put one's hand (to), take a hand (in); **ума́ не ~у́** (*coll.*) I can't work it out; (*не знаю*) I have no idea. **2** (*impf.* **прикла́дывать** *and* **прилага́ть**) (*прибавить*) to add; (*к письму*) to enclose; (*печать*) to affix. **3** (*impf.* **прилага́ть**) (*использовать*) to apply; **п. си́лу** to apply force; **п. все уси́лия** to make every effort; **п. всё стара́ние** to do one's best.

прилож|и́ться, у́сь, ~́ишься *pf.* (*of* ⇒**прикла́дываться**) **1** (+*i.*, **к**+*d.*) to put (to); **п. гла́зом к замо́чной сква́жине** to put one's eye to the keyhole; **п. (губа́ми)** to kiss. **2** (*прицелиться*) to take aim. **3** (*прибавиться*) to come; **остально́е ~́ится** the rest will come. **4** (*coll.*) to drink (*a small quantity of liquor*).

прилуне́ни|е, я *nt.* (*aeron.*) moon landing.

прилун|и́ться, ю́сь, и́шься *pf.* to land on the moon.

прильн|у́ть, у́, ёшь *pf. of* ⇒**льнуть**

при́м|а, ы *f.* (*mus.*) **1** (*ведущая партия*) lead. **2** (*тон*) tonic. **3** (*струна*) first string, top string.

при́ма-балери́на, при́мы-балери́ны *f.* prima ballerina.

примадо́нн|а, ы *f.* prima donna.

прима́|заться, жусь, жешься *pf.* (*of* ⇒**~зываться**) (**к**+*d.*; *coll.*, *pej.*) to attach o.s. (to), get in (with).

прима́зыва|ться, юсь *impf. of* ⇒**прима́заться**

прима́нива|ть, ю *impf. of* ⇒**примани́ть**

приман|и́ть, ю́, ~́ишь *pf.* (*of* ⇒**~́ивать**) (*coll.*) to lure; to entice.

прима́нк|а, и *f.* bait; (*fig.*) enticement, allurement.

прима́с, а *m.* (*eccl.*) primate.

прима́т[1], а *m.* (*phil.*) primacy; pre-eminence.

прима́т[2], а *m.* (*zool.*) primate.

прима́чива|ть, ю *impf. of* ⇒**примочи́ть**

примелька́|ться, юсь *pf.* to become familiar; **её лицо́ мне о́чень ~лось** her face is very familiar to me.

примене́ни|е, я *nt.* application; (*употребление*) use, employment; **на́ши ме́тоды получи́ли широ́кое п.** our methods have been widely adopted; **непра́вильное п.** misuse; **в ~и** (**к**+*d.*) in application (to).

примени́мост|ь, и *f.* applicability.

примени́м|ый (~, ~а) *adj.* applicable.

примени́тельно *adv.* (**к**+*d.*) (*соответственно с*) in conformity (with); (*по отношению к*) as applied (to).

примен|и́ть, ю́, ~́ишь *pf.* (*of* ⇒**~я́ть**) to apply; to employ, use; **п. свои́ зна́ния** to apply one's knowledge; **п. на пра́ктике** to put into practice.

примен|и́ться, ю́сь, ~́ишься *pf.* (*of* ⇒**~я́ться**) (**к**+*d.*) to adapt o.s. (to), conform (to).

применя́|ть(ся), ю(сь) *impf. of* ⇒**примени́ть(ся)**

приме́р, а *m.* **1** example, instance; **привести́ п.** to give an example; **привести́ в п.** to cite as an example; **к ~у** (*coll.*) for example. **2** (*образец*) example; model; **брать п. с кого́-н., сле́довать чьему́-н. ~у** to follow s.o.'s example; **подава́ть п.** to set an example; **показа́ть п.** to give an example, give the lead; **для ~а** as an example; **по ~у** (+*g.*) after the example (of), on the pattern (of); **не в п.** (+*d.*) unlike; (+*comp.*) far more, by far; **не в п. про́чим** unlike the others; **не в п. лу́чше** far better.

примерз|а́ть, а́ю *impf. of* ⇒**~́нуть**

примёрз|нуть, ну, нешь, *past* **~, ~ла** *pf.* (*of* ⇒**~а́ть**) (**к**+*d.*) to freeze (to).

приме́р|ить, ю, ишь *pf.* (*of* ⇒**ме́рить** 2 *and* **~я́ть**) to try on.

приме́р|иться, юсь, ишься *pf.* (*of* ⇒**~я́ться**) (*coll.*) to assess the situation before doing sth.; to get into position.

приме́рк|а, и *f.* trying on; fitting.

приме́рно *adv.* **1** (*отлично*) in exemplary fashion; **п. вести́ себя́** to be an example. **2** (*приблизительно*) approximately, roughly.

приме́р|ный (~ен, ~на) *adj.* **1** (*отличный*) exemplary, model. **2** (*приблизительный*) approximate, rough.

приме́рочн|ая, ой *f.* fitting-room.

пример|я́ть(ся), я́ю(сь) *impf. of* ⇒**~́ить(ся)**

при́мес|ь, и *f.* admixture; dash; (*fig.*) touch; **без ~ей** unadulterated.

приме́т|а, ы *f.* (*признак*) sign, token; mark; (*суеверная*) omen; **име́ть на ~е** to have one's eye (on); **осо́бые ~ы** distinguishing marks.

примет|а́ть, а́ю *pf.* (*of* ⇒**~́ывать**) to tack (on), stitch (on).

приме́|тить, чу, тишь *pf.* (*of* ⇒**~ча́ть**) to notice.

приме́тливост|ь, и *f.* power(s) of observation.

приме́тлив|ый (~, ~а) *adj.* (*coll.*) observant.

приме́тно *adv.* perceptibly, noticeably; **он п. похуде́л** he has grown perceptibly thinner.

приме́т|ный (~ен, ~на) *adj.* **1** (*след, волнение*) perceptible, noticeable. **2** (*человек, внешность*) conspicuous, prominent.

примётыва|ть, ю *impf. of* ⇒**примета́ть**

примеча́ни|е, я *nt.* note, comment; (*сноска*) footnote.

примеча́тельност|ь, и *f.* noteworthiness.

примеча́тел|ьный (~ен, ~ьна) *adj.* noteworthy, notable, remarkable.

примеча́|ть, ю *impf.* **1** *impf. of* ⇒**приме́тить. 2** (*impf. only*) (**за**+*i.*; *coll.*) to keep an eye (on).

примеш|а́ть, а́ю *pf.* (*of* ⇒**~́ивать**) (+*a. or g.*) to add, admix; (*fig.*) to bring.

приме́шива|ть, ю *impf. of* ⇒**примеша́ть**

примина́|ть, ю *impf. of* ⇒**примя́ть**

примире́ни|е, я *nt.* reconciliation.

примире́нческий *adj.* compromising.

примире́нчеств|о, а *nt.* conciliatoriness, appeasement.

примири́тел|ь, я *m.* conciliator, peace-maker.

примири́тел|ьный (~ен, ~ьна) *adj.* conciliatory.

примир|и́ть, ю́, и́шь *pf.* (*of* ⇒**~я́ть**) to reconcile; **п. супру́гов** to reconcile a husband and wife.

примир|и́ться, ю́сь, и́шься *pf.* (*of* ⇒**~я́ться**) (**с**+*i.*) **1** (*с кем-н.*) to be reconciled (to), make it up (with). **2** (*с чем-н.*) to reconcile o.s. (to); **п. с неудо́бствами** to reconcile o.s. to discomforts.

примир|я́ть(ся), я́ю(сь) *impf. of* ⇒**~и́ть(ся)**

примити́в, а *m.* **1** (*art*) primitive. **2** (*вещь*) primitive artefact. **3** (*coll.*) (*человек*) primitive person.

примитиви́зм, а *m.* (*art*) primitivism.

примитиви́ст, а *m.* (*art*) primitive.

примити́в|ный (~ен, ~на) *adj.* primitive.

примкн|у́ть, у́, ёшь *pf.* (*of* ⇒**примыка́ть**) (**к**+*d.*) **1** (*плотно придвинуть, присоединить*) to fix (to), attach (to); **п. штыки́!** fix bayonets! **2** (*fig.*) (*присоединиться*) to join, attach o.s. (to); to side (with).

примо́лк|нуть, ну, нешь, *past* **~, ~ла** *pf.* (*coll.*) to go quiet, fall silent.

примо́рский *adj.* seaside; (*растение, климат*) maritime; **п. куро́рт** seaside resort.

примо́рь|е, я *nt.* seaside.

примо|сти́ть, щу́, сти́шь *pf.* (*coll.*) to find room (for), stick (*in crowded or inconvenient surroundings*).

примо|сти́ться, щу́сь, сти́шься *pf.* (*coll.*) to find room for o.s.; to perch o.s..

примоч|и́ть, у́, ~́ишь *pf.* (*of* ⇒**прима́чивать**) (*больное место*) to bathe; (*смочить*) to moisten; **п. себе́ глаз** to bathe one's eye.

примо́чк|а, и *f.* wash, lotion.

при́мул|а, ы *f.* primula, primrose.

при́мус, а *m.* Primus(-stove) (*propr.*).

при́мус|ный *adj. of* ⇒**~**

примч|áть, ý, ѝшь *pf.* (*coll.*) **1** (*принести*) to bring in a hurry, hurry along with. **2** = **~áться**

примч|áться, ýсь, ѝшься *pf.* to come tearing along.

примыкá|ть, ю *impf.* **1** *impf. of* ⇨**примкнýть. 2** (*impf. only*) (**к**+*d.*) to adjoin, abut (upon).

при|мя́ть, мнý, мнёшь *pf.* (*of* ⇨**~минáть**) to crush, flatten; (*ногами*) to trample down, tread down.

принадлеж|áть, ý, ѝшь *impf.* **1** (+*d.*) to belong (to); **п. по прáву** to belong by right. **2** (**к**+*d.*) (*быть членом*) to belong (to), be a member (of); **п. к аэроклýбу** to belong to a flying club; (*входить в состав*) to be among; to be one/some of; **симфóнии Чайкóвского ~áт к лýчшим произведéниям мировóй мýзыки** the symphonies of Tchaikovsky are among the best of the world's musical compositions. **3**: **Гермáнии ~ѝт ведýщая роль** Germany has a leading role. **4**: **п. кѝсти/перý** (+*g.*) to be the work of.

принадлéжност|ь, и *f.* **1** (**к**+*d.*) belonging (to), membership (of); **п. к ассоциáции** membership of an association. **2** (*pl.*) accessories; equipment; gear; **туалéтные ~и** toiletries; **канцеля́рские ~и** stationery. **3** (*свойство*) characteristic.

прина|лéчь, ля́гу, ля́жешь, ля́гут, *past* **~лёг, ~леглá** *pf.* (**на**+*a.*; *coll.*) **1** (*навалиться*) to rest lightly (upon). **2** (*усердно приняться*) to apply o.s. (to), go (at) with a will.

принаря|дѝть, жý, ~дѝшь *pf.* (*of* ⇨**~жáть**) (*coll.*) to dress up, deck out, smarten up.

принаря|дѝться, жýсь, ~дѝшься *pf.* (*of* ⇨**~жáться**) (*coll.*) to get dressed up; to smarten up.

принаряжá|ть(ся), ю(сь) *impf. of* ⇨**принарядѝть(ся)**

принев óлива|ть, ю *impf. of* ⇨**принев óлить**

принев óл|ить, ю, ишь *pf.* (*of* ⇨**~ивать**) (+*inf.*; *coll.*) to force (to), make; **онѝ ~или егó женѝться** they made him marry.

принес|тѝ, ý, ёшь, *past* **~, ~лá** *pf.* (*of* ⇨**приносѝть**) **1** (*неся, доставить*) to bring (*also fig.*); to fetch; **п. обрáтно** to bring back; **п. благодáрность** to express gratitude; **п. в жéртву** to sacrifice; **п. извинéния** to apologize; **п. кля́тву** to take an oath. **2** (*приплод, урожай*) to bear, yield; (*причинить*) to bring in; **п. плоды́** to yield fruit; **п. большóй дохóд** to bring in big revenue, show a large return; **п. пóльзу** to be of use, be of benefit; **п. результáт** to yield/give results; (*о чём-н. нежелательном*): **откýда тебя́ ~лó в такóй час?** where have you come from at this hour?

принес|тѝсь, ýсь, ёшься, *past* **~ся, ~лáсь** *pf.* (*of* ⇨**приносѝться**) (*coll.*) **1** (*о звуке, о запахе*) to be borne, carried; (*об известии*) to arrive. **2** (*стремительно прибыть*) to come tearing along.

принижá|ть, ю *impf. of* ⇨**принѝзить**

принижéни|е, я *nt.* disparagement, belittling.

принѝ|женный *p.p.p. of* ⇨**~зить** *and adj.* humbled, submissive.

принѝ|зить, жу, зишь *pf.* (*of* ⇨**~жáть**) **1** (*унизить*) to humble, humiliate. **2** (*умалить значение*) to disparage, belittle.

приник|áть, áю *impf. of* ⇨**~нуть**

принѝк|нуть, ну, нешь, *past* **~, ~ла** *pf.* (*of* ⇨**~áть**) (**к**+*d.*) to press o.s. (against, to); (*прильнуть*) to nestle up (against, to); **мы ~ли к земле́** we pressed ourselves to the ground; **п. ýхом к замóчной сквáжине** to press one's ear to the keyhole; **ребёнок ~ к мáтери** the child nestled up to its mother.

принимá|ть, ю *impf. of* ⇨**приня́ть**

принимá|ться, юсь *impf. of* ⇨**приня́ться**

принорáвлива|ть(ся), ю(сь) *impf. of* ⇨**принорóвить(ся)**

принорóв|ѝть, лю́, ѝшь *pf.* (*of* ⇨**принорáвливать**) to adapt, adjust; **п. переéзд к лéтним канѝкулам** to time a move to coincide with the summer holidays.

принорóв|ѝться, лю́сь, ѝшься *pf.* (*of* ⇨**принорáвливаться**) (**к**+*d.*) to adapt o.s. (to), accommodate o.s. (to).

прино|сѝть(ся), шý(сь), ~сишь(ся) *impf. of* ⇨**принестѝ(сь)**

приношéни|е, я *nt.* gift, offering.

прѝнтер, а *m.* (*comput.*) printer.

принудѝтел|ьный (~ен, ~ьна) *adj.* compulsory, forced, coercive; **~ьные мéры** coercive measures; **~ьные рабóты** forced labour (*Br.*), labor (*US*); **п. сбор** levy; **в ~ьном поря́дке** by order.

принý|дить, жу, дишь *pf.* (*of* ⇨**~ждáть**) to force, compel, coerce.

принуждá|ть, ю *impf. of* ⇨**принýдить**

принуждéни|е, я *nt.* compulsion, coercion; **по ~ю** under duress.

принуждённост|ь, и *f.* constraint; stiffness.

принуждённый *p.p.p. of* ⇨**принýдить** *and adj.* constrained, forced; **п. смех** forced laughter.

принц, а *m.* prince.

принцéсс|а, ы *f.* princess.

прѝнцип, а *m.* principle; **в ~е** in principle; **из ~а** on principle.

принципиáльно *adv.* **1** (*из принципа*) on principle; on a question of principle; **п. отказáться** to refuse on principle. **2** (*в принципе*) in principle. **3**: **п. отличáться** to differ fundamentally.

принципиáльност|ь, и *f.* adherence to principle(s).

принципиáл|ьный (~ен, ~ьна) *adj.* **1** of principle; based on, guided by principle; **п. вопрóс** question of principle; **п. человéк** man of principle; **имéть ~ьное значéние** to be a matter of principle. **2** (*в основном*) in principle; general; **онѝ дáли ~ьное соглáсие** they consented in principle. **3** (*коренной*): **~ьное разлѝчие** fundamental difference.

принюх|аться, аюсь *pf.* (*of* ⇨**~иваться**) (*coll.*) **1** (**к**+*d.*) (*привыкнуть к запаху*) to get used to the smell (of). **2** (*о собаке*) to sniff.

принюхива|ться, юсь *impf. of* ⇨**принюхаться**

приня́ти|е, я *nt.* **1** (*пищи, лекарства, решения, присяги*) taking; (*поста, позы*) taking up. **2** (*предложения, сочувствия*) acceptance. **3** (*гостей, пациентов*) receiving. **4** (*в партию*) admission, admittance; **п. граждáнства** naturalization.

прѝнят|ый *p.p.p. of* ⇨**приня́ть; ~о** (+*inf.*) it is accepted, it is usual (*to do sth.*); **не ~о** it is not done, it is not accepted.

при|ня́ть, мý, ~мешь, *past* **~нял, ~нялá, ~няло** *pf.* (*of* ⇨**~нимáть**) **1** to take; (*взять как дар; согласиться*) to accept; **п. вáнну/душ** to take, have a bath/shower; **п. лекáрство** to take medicine; **п. мéры** to take measures; **п. мéры предосторóжности** to take precautions; **п. монáшество** to take monastic vows, become a monk; to take the veil; **п. намéрение** to form the intention; **п. подáрок** to accept a present; **п. прися́гу** to take the oath; **п. решéние** to take, reach a decision; **п. учáстие** (**в**+*p.*) to take part (in); participate (in); **п. христиáнство** to adopt Christianity; **п. во внимáние** to take into consideration; **не п. во внимáние** to disregard; **п. в шýтку** to take as a joke; **п. всерьёз** to take seriously; **п. за прáвило** to make it a rule; **п. (блѝзко) к сéрдцу** to take to heart; **п. что-н. на себя́** to take upon o.s. **2** (*пост*) to take up; **п. нóвое назначéние** to take up a new appointment; **п. комáндование** (+*i.*) to take command (of); **п. духóвный сан** to take holy orders; **п. делá** (**от**+*g.*) to take over duties (from). **3** (*через голосование*) to accept; **п. закóн** to pass a law; **п. резолю́цию** to pass, adopt, carry a resolution. **4** (**в, на**+*a.*) (*зачислить*) to admit (to); to accept (for); **п. в пáртию** to admit to a party; **п. на слýжбу** to accept for a job. **5** (*посетителей, пациентов, заказ*) to receive; **онѝ ~няли нас радýшно** they gave us a warm welcome, a cordial reception. **6** (*приобрести*) to assume, take (on); **болéзнь ~нялá серьёзный харáктер** the illness assumed a grave character; **переговóры ~няли благоприя́тный оборóт** the talks took a favourable turn. **7** (+*a.* **за**+*a.*) (*счесть по ошибке*) to take (for); **я ~нял вас за шотлáндца** I took you for a Scotsman. **8** (*при родах*) to deliver (*at birth of child*); **п. рóды** to deliver a baby.

при|ня́ться, мýсь, ~мешься, *past* **~нялся́, ~нялáсь** *pf.* (*of* ⇨**~нимáться**) **1** (+*inf.*) (*начать*) to begin; to start. **2** (**за**+*a.*) to set (to), get down (to); **п. за рабóту** to set to work; **п. за чтéние** to get down to reading; **гóсти ~нялѝсь за дессéрт** the guests began their dessert. **3** (**за**+*a.*; *coll.*) (*за лентяя*) to take in hand. **4** (*о растениях*) to take root; (*о прививках*) to take.

приободр|и́ть, ю́, и́шь *pf.* (*of* ⇒**~я́ть**) to cheer up, encourage, hearten.

приободр|и́ться, ю́сь, и́шься *pf.* (*of* ⇒**~я́ться**) to cheer up.

приободр|я́ть(ся), я́ю(сь) *impf. of* ⇒**~и́ть(ся)**

приобре|сти́, ту́, тёшь, *past* **~л, ~ла́** *pf.* (*of* ⇒**~та́ть**) **1** (*дом, друзей, машину*) to acquire; (*авторитет, репутацию*) to gain; **п. о́пыт** to gain experience. **2** (*свойство*) to take on, assume; **пробле́ма ~ла́ осо́бое значе́ние** the problem took on a special significance.

приобрета́|ть, ю *impf. of* ⇒**приобрести́**

приобрете́ни|е, я *nt.* **1** (*действие*) acquisition, acquiring. **2** (*то, что приобретено*) acquisition, gain; (*для науки*) find.

приобщ|а́ть(ся), а́ю(сь) *impf. of* ⇒**~и́ть(ся)**

приобщ|и́ть, у́, и́шь *pf.* (*of* ⇒**~а́ть**) **1** (**к**+*d.*) (*познакомить*) to introduce (to); **п. ребёнка к иску́сству** to introduce a child to art. **2** (*присоединить*) to join, attach; **п. к де́лу** to file. **3** (*eccl.*) to administer the sacrament (to).

приобщ|и́ться, у́сь, и́шься *pf.* (*of* ⇒**~а́ться**) (**к**+*d.*) **1** (*включиться*) to join (in), become involved (in); **п. к обще́ственной жи́зни** to join in social life. **2** (*познакомиться*) to become familiar with.

приоде́|ть, ну, нешь *pf.* (*coll.*) to dress up, smarten up.

приоде́|ться, нусь, нешься *pf.* (*coll.*) to dress up; to get dressed up; to smarten o.s. up.

прио́р, а *m.* (*eccl.*) prior.

приорите́т, а *m.* priority.

приорите́т|ный, (~ен, ~на) *adj.* most important, priority.

приоса́нива|ться, юсь *impf. of* ⇒**приоса́ниться**

приоса́н|иться, юсь, ишься *pf.* (*coll.*) to assume a dignified air.

приостана́влива|ть(ся), ю(сь) *impf. of* ⇒**приостанови́ть(ся)**

приостанов|и́ть, лю́, ~ишь *pf.* (*of* ⇒**приостана́вливать**) to halt, suspend.

приостанов|и́ться, лю́сь, ~ишься *pf.* (*of* ⇒**приостана́вливаться**) to halt, come to a halt; (*о человеке*) to pause.

приостано́вк|а, и *f.* halt, suspension.

приотвор|и́ть, ю́, ~ишь *pf.* (*of* ⇒**~я́ть**) to open slightly, half-open; **п. дверь** to half-open the door, set the door ajar.

приотвор|и́ться, ~ится *pf.* (*of* ⇒**~я́ться**) to open slightly, half-open.

приотвор|я́ть(ся), я́ю, я́ет(ся) *impf. of* ⇒**~и́ть(ся)**

приоткрыва́|ть(ся), ю, ет(ся) *impf. of* ⇒**приоткры́ть(ся)**

приоткр|ы́ть(ся), о́ю, о́ет(ся) *pf.* = **приотвори́ть(ся)**

приохо́|тить, чу, тишь *pf.* (**к**+*d.*; *coll.*) to give a taste (for).

приохо́|титься, чусь, тишься *pf.* (**к**+*d.*; *coll.*) to acquire a taste (for), take (to).

припада́|ть, ю *impf.* **1** *impf. of* ⇒**припа́сть**[1]. **2** (*impf. only*) to have a slight limp; **п. на ле́вую но́гу** to have a slight limp in the left leg.

припа́д|ок, ка *m.* fit; attack; **не́рвный п.** attack of nerves; **серде́чный п.** heart attack; **эпилепти́ческий п.** epileptic fit; **п. бе́шенства** fit of rage.

припа́дочн|ый *adj.* subject to fits; **~ые явле́ния** fits; *as n.* **п., ~ого** *m.* person subject to fits.

припа́ива|ть, ю *impf. of* ⇒**припая́ть**

припа́йк|а, и *f.* soldering.

припа́рк|а, и *f.* (*med.*) poultice.

припас|а́ть, а́ю *impf. of* ⇒**~ти́**

припас|ти́, у́, ёшь, *past* **~, ~ла́** *pf.* (*of* ⇒**~а́ть**) (+*a. or g.*; *coll.*) to store, lay in (*a supply of*); **п. консе́рвов** to lay in tinned food.

припа́|сть[1], **ду́, дёшь**, *past* **~л** *pf.* (*of* ⇒**~да́ть**) (**к**+*d.*) (*к земле, к груди*) to press o.s. (to); (*склониться*) to fall down (before); **п. к чьим-н. нога́м** to prostrate o.s. before s.o.; **п. у́хом** to press one's ear (to).

припа́|сть[2], **дёт**, *past* **~л** *pf.* (*coll., obs.*) (*появиться*) to appear, show itself.

припа́с|ы, ов *no sg.* stores, supplies; **боевы́е п.** ammunition; **вое́нные п.** munitions; **съестны́е п.** provisions, victuals.

припа́хива|ть, ет *impf.* (*coll.*) to smell.

припая́|ть, ю *pf.* (*of* ⇒**припа́ивать**) (**к**+*d.*) to solder (to).

припе́в, а *m.* refrain.

припева́|ть, ю *impf.* to hum; **жить ~ючи** (*coll.*) to be in clover; to live the life of Riley.

припёк, а *m.*: **на ~е** (*coll.*) right in the sun, exposed to the full heat of the sun.

припёк|а, и *f.*: **сбо́ку п.** (*coll.*) superfluous, unnecessary.

припека́|ть, ет *impf.* (*coll.*) (*о солнце*) to be very hot, beat down.

при|пере́ть, пру́, прёшь, *past* **~пёр, ~пёрла** *pf.* (*of* ⇒**~пира́ть**) **1** (**к**+*d.*) to press (against); **п. стул к две́ри, п. дверь сту́лом** to put a chair against the door; **п. кого́-н. к сте́нке** (*fig., coll.*) to drive s.o. into a corner. **2** (*coll.*) (*дверь, окно*) to close. **3** (*coll.*) (*принести*) to drag. **4** (*coll.*) (*прийти*) to turn up.

при|пере́ться, пру́сь, прёшься, *past* **~пёрся, ~пёрлась** *pf.* (*coll.*) to turn up.

припеча́т|ать, аю *pf.* (*of* ⇒**~ывать**) (*coll.*) to seal; **п. сургучо́м** to apply sealing-wax (to).

припеча́тыва|ть, ю *impf. of* ⇒**припеча́тать**

припира́|ть, ю *impf. of* ⇒**припере́ть**

припи|са́ть, шу́, ~шешь *pf.* (*of* ⇒**~сывать**) **1** (*написать в добавление*) to add. **2** (**к**+*d.*) (*причислить, записать*) to register (at). **3** (+*d.*) to attribute (to); to ascribe (to); to put down (to); **п. стихотворе́ние Пу́шкину** to attribute a poem to Pushkin; **п. неуда́чу ле́ни** to put a failure down to laziness.

припи́ск|а, и *f.* **1** (*добавление*) addition; postscript; **п. к завеща́нию** (*leg.*) codicil. **2** (*регистрация*) registration; **порт ~и** (*naut.*) port of registration.

припи́сыва|ть, ю *impf. of* ⇒**приписа́ть**

припла́т|а, ы *f.* additional payment; surcharge; **без вся́ких ~** no extras.

припла|ти́ть, чу́, ~тишь *pf.* (*of* ⇒**~чивать**) to pay in addition.

припла́чива|ть, ю *impf. of* ⇒**приплати́ть**

приплe|сти́, ту́, тёшь, *past* **~л, ~ла́** *pf.* (*of* ⇒**~та́ть**) **1** to plait in. **2** (*fig., coll.*) to drag in; **не сле́довало п. э́то сюда́** there was no need to drag that in.

приплe|сти́сь, ту́сь, тёшься, *past* **~лся, ~ла́сь** *pf.* (*coll.*) to drag o.s. along.

приплета́|ть, ю *impf. of* ⇒**приплести́**

припло́д, а *m.* issue, increase (*of animals*).

приплыва́|ть, ю *impf. of* ⇒**приплы́ть**

приплы́|ть, ву́, вёшь, *past* **~л, ~ла́, ~ло** *pf.* (*of* **~ва́ть**) (*вплавь*) to swim up; (*на лодке*) to sail up.

приплю́снут|ый *p.p.p. of* ⇒**~ь** *and adj.*: **п. нос** flat nose.

приплю́сн|уть, у, ешь *pf.* (*of* ⇒**приплю́щивать**) to flatten.

приплюс|ова́ть, у́ю *pf.* (*of* ⇒**~о́вывать**) (*coll.*) to add on.

приплюсо́выва|ть, ю *impf. of* ⇒**приплюсова́ть**

приплю́щива|ть, ю *impf. of* ⇒**приплю́снуть**

припля́сыва|ть, ю *impf.* to trip, skip; **идти́ ~я по тротуа́ру** to trip along the pavement.

приподнима́|ть(ся), ю(сь) *impf. of* ⇒**приподня́ть(ся)**

приподнятост|ь, и *f.* elation; animation.

припо́дн|ятый *p.p.p. of* ⇒**~я́ть** *and adj.* (*оживлённый*) elated; animated; (*торжественный*) elevated.

приподн|я́ть, иму́, и́мешь, *past* **~ял, ~яла́, ~яло** *pf.* (*of* ⇒**~има́ть**) to raise slightly; to lift slightly.

приподн|я́ться, иму́сь, и́мешься, *past* **~я́лся, ~яла́сь** *pf.* (*of* ⇒**~има́ться**) to raise o.s. (a little); **п. на цы́почках** to stand on tiptoe; **п. на носки́** to rise on one's toes.

припоздн|и́ться, ю́сь, и́шься *pf.* (*coll.*) to be late.

припо́|й, я *m.* solder.

П

приполз|áть, áю *impf. of* ⇒**~тú**

приполз|тú, ý, ёшь, *past* **~, ~лá** *pf.* (*of* ⇒**~áть**) to creep up, crawl up.

припоминá|ть(ся), ю(сь) *impf. of* ⇒**припóмнить(ся)**

припóм|нить, ню, нишь *pf.* (*of* ⇒**~инáть**) **1** to remember, recollect, recall; **я не ~ню, когдá мы встрéтились в пéрвый раз** I do not recall when we first met. **2** (+*d.*) to remind; **я э́то тебé ~ню!** (*coll.*) you won't forget this!; I'll get even with you for this!

припóмн|иться, юсь, ишься *pf.* (*of* ⇒**припоминáться**) **1** (*детство, прошлое*) to be remembered, recalled; to come into one's memory; **мне ~илось, что/как...** I recalled that/how .... **2** (+*d.*): **э́то тебé ~ится** you'll pay for this.

приправ|а, ы *f.* flavouring (*Br.*), flavoring (*US*), seasoning; (*соус*) dressing; **п. к салáту** salad dressing.

припрáв|ить, лю, ишь *pf.* (*of* ⇒**~ля́ть**) (+*i.*) to season (with), flavour (*Br.*), flavor (*US*) (with); (*соусом*) to dress (with).

приправля́|ть, ю *impf. of* ⇒**припрáвить**

припры́гива|ть, ю *impf.* (*coll.*) to hop, skip.

припря́|тать, чу, чешь *pf.* (*of* ⇒**~тывать**) (*coll.*) to put by, store up (*for future use*).

припря́тыва|ть, ю *impf. of* ⇒**припря́тать**

припýгива|ть, ю *impf. of* ⇒**припугнýть**

припуг|нýть, нý, нёшь *pf.* (*of* ⇒**~́ивать**) (*coll.*) to intimidate, scare.

припýдрива|ть(ся), ю(сь) *impf. of* ⇒**припýдрить(ся)**

припýдр|ить, ю, ишь *pf.* (*of* ⇒**~ивать**) **1** to powder. **2** (*tech.*) to dust.

припýдр|иться, юсь, ишься *pf.* (*of* ⇒**~иваться**) to powder o.s.

при́пуск, а *m.* (*tech.*) allowance, margin; **п. на усáдку** shrinkage allowance; **остáвить п. (на**+*a.*) to allow (for).

припускá|ть, ю *impf. of* ⇒**припусти́ть**

припу|сти́ть, щý, ~́стишь *pf.* (*of* ⇒**~скáть**) **1** (**к**+*d.*) to put (to) (*for coupling or feeding*); **п. телёнка к корóве** to put a calf to the cow. **2** (*платье*) to let out. **3** (*coll.*) (*погнать*) to urge on. **4** (*coll.*) (*побежать быстрее*) to quicken one's pace. **5** (*coll.*) (*о дожде*) to come down harder.

припýт|ать, аю *pf.* (*of* ⇒**~ывать**) **1** (*привязать*) to tie on, fasten. **2** (**к**+*d.*; *fig., coll.*) (*упомянуть некстати; вмешать*) to drag in (to), implicate (in).

припýтыва|ть, ю *impf. of* ⇒**припýтать**

припух|áть, áет *impf. of* ⇒**~́нуть**

припýхлост|ь, и *f.* (slight) swelling.

припýхлый *adj.* (slightly) swollen.

припýх|нуть, нет, *past* **~, ~ла** *pf.* (*of* ⇒**~áть**) to swell up a little.

прирабáтыва|ть, ю *impf. of* ⇒**прирабóтать**

прирабóта|ть, ю *pf.* (*of* ⇒**прирабáтывать**) to earn extra.

при́работ|ок, ка *m.* extra earnings.

прирáвнива|ть, ю *impf. of* ⇒**приравня́ть**

приравн|я́ть, я́ю *pf.* (*of* ⇒**~́ивать**) (**к**+*d.*) to equate (with).

прираст|áть, áю *impf. of* ⇒**~и́**

прираст|и́, ý, ёшь, *past* **прирóс, прирослá** *pf.* (*of* ⇒**~áть**) **1** (**к**+*d.*) to adhere (to); (*о пересаженной ткани, о черенке*) to take; **п. к мéсту, п. к землé** (*fig.*) to become rooted to the spot, to the ground. **2** (*увеличиться*) to increase; (*проценты*) to accrue.

приращéни|е, я *nt.* (*увеличение*) increase, increment; (*черенка*) taking.

приревн|овáть, ýю *pf.* to be jealous; **п. когó-нибудь (к**+*d.*) to be jealous because of s.o.'s attachment to; **онá ~овáла мýжа к своéй прия́тельнице** she was jealous of her husband's interest in her friend.

прирез|áть, áю *impf. of* ⇒**~́ать²**

прирé|зать¹, жу, жешь *pf.* (*of* ⇒**~зывать**) (*coll.*) (*убить*) to kill; to cut the throat (of).

прирé|зать², жу, жешь *pf.* (*of* ⇒**~зáть** *and* **~зывать**) (*добавить*) to add on; **п. учáсток к огорóду** to add on a piece to a garden.

прирéз|ок, ка *m.* additional piece (*of land*).

прирéзыва|ть, ю *impf. of* ⇒**прирéзать**

прирóд|а, ы *f.* **1** nature. **2** (*характер*) nature, character; **от ~ы** by nature, congenitally; **по ~е** by nature, naturally; **э́то в ~е вещéй** it is in the nature of things.

прирóдн|ый *adj.* **1** (*созданный природой*) natural; **~ые богáтства** natural resources; **п. газ** natural gas. **2** (*по рождению*) born; **п. англичáнин** an Englishman by birth. **3** (*врождённый*) inborn, innate; **п. ум** native wit.

природобезврéд|ный (~ен, ~на) *adj.* environment-friendly.

природовéдени|е, я *nt.* natural history.

природосберегáющий *adj.* environment-friendly.

прирождённый *adj.* **1** (*о способностях*) inborn, innate. **2** (*о человеке*) a born; **п. лгун** a born liar.

прирóст, а *m.* increase, growth.

прируч|áть, áю *impf. of* ⇒**~и́ть**

приручéни|е, я *nt.* taming; domestication.

прируч|и́ть, ý, и́шь *pf.* (*of* ⇒**~áть**) to tame (*also fig.*); to domesticate.

присáжива|ться, юсь *impf. of* ⇒**присéсть**

присáлива|ть, ю *impf. of* ⇒**присоли́ть**

присáсыва|ться, юсь *impf. of* ⇒**присосáться**

присвáива|ть, ю *impf. of* ⇒**присвóить**

при́свист, а *m.* **1** whistle. **2** (*свистящий призвук*) sibilance, hissing in one's speech.

присви́стыва|ть, ю *impf.* **1** to whistle. **2** (*говорить с присвистом*) to sibilate.

присвоéни|е, я *nt.* **1** (*власти*) appropriation; **незакóнное п.** misappropriation. **2** (*звания*) awarding, conferment.

присвó|ить, ю, ишь *pf.* (*of* ⇒**присвáивать**) **1** (*завладеть*) to appropriate; **незакóнно п. срéдства** to misappropriate funds. **2** (+*a. and d.*) (*дать*) to give, award, confer; **п. и́мя** (+*d. and g.*) to name (after); **емý ~или стéпень дóктора** he has been given the degree of Doctor.

приседáни|е, я *nt.* squatting.

приседá|ть, ю *impf. of* ⇒**присéсть**

присéст, а *m.*: **в оди́н п., за оди́н п.** (*coll.*) at one sitting, at a stretch.

при|сéсть, ся́ду, ся́дешь, *past* **~сéл** *pf.* **1** (*impf.* **~сáживаться**) (*сесть*) to sit down, take a seat. **2** (*impf.* **~седáть**) (*на корточки*) to squat; (*от страха*) to cower. **3** (*impf.* **~седáть**) (*сделать реверанс*) to curts(e)y, drop curts(e)ys.

при́сказк|а, и *f.* **1** (*к сказке*) introduction. **2** (*прибаутка*) saying.

приска|кáть, чý, ~́чешь *pf.* to come galloping, arrive at a gallop; (*fig., coll.*) to rush, tear.

прискóрби|е, я *nt.* sorrow, regret; **к моемý ~ю** to my regret.

прискóрб|ный (~ен, ~на) *adj.* regrettable, deplorable.

прискýч|ить, у, ишь *pf.* (+*d.*; *coll.*) to bore, tire.

при|слáть, шлю́, шлёшь *pf.* (*of* ⇒**~сылáть**) to send.

прислóвь|е, я *nt.* (*coll.*) saying (*introduced into a speech, etc.*).

прислон|и́ть, ю́, ~́ишь *pf.* (*of* ⇒**~я́ть**) (**к**+*d.*) to lean (against), rest (against).

прислон|и́ться, ю́сь, ~́ишься *pf.* (*of* ⇒**~я́ться**) (**к**+*d.*) to lean (against), rest (against).

прислон|я́ть(ся), я́ю(сь) *impf. of* ⇒**~и́ть(ся)**

прислýг|а, и *f.* **1** maid, servant. **2** (*collect.; obs.*) servants, domestics. **3** (*mil.*) crew; **орýди́йная п.** gun crew.

прислýжива|ть, ю *impf.* (+*d.*; *obs.*) to wait (upon), attend.

прислýжива|ться, юсь *impf. of* ⇒**прислужи́ться**

прислуж|и́ться, ýсь, ~́ишься *pf.* (*of* ⇒**~́иваться**) (**к**+*d.*; *obs.*) to worm o.s. into the favour (of), fawn (upon).

прислýжник, а *m.* **1** (*obs.*) (*слуга*) servant. **2** (*coll.*) lickspittle; fawner.

прислýжничеств|о, а *nt.* subservience, servility.

прислýш|аться, аюсь *pf.* (*of* ⇒**~иваться**) (**к**+*d.*) **1** to listen (to). **2** (*fig.*) (*принять во внимание*) to listen (to); to heed; **п. к чьему́-н. сове́ту** to listen to s.o.'s advice. **3** (*coll.*) (*привыкнуть к каким-н. звукам*) to get used to the sound (of).

прислу́шива|ться, юсь *impf. of* ⇒**прислу́шаться**

присма́трива|ть(ся), ю(сь) *impf. of* ⇒**присмотре́ть(ся)**

присмире́|ть, ю *pf.* to grow quiet, calm down.

присмир|и́ть, ю́, и́шь *pf.* (*of* ⇒**~я́ть**) to quieten (*Br.*), quiet (*US*).

присмир|я́ть, ю *impf. of* ⇒**~и́ть**

присмо́тр, а *m.* care; supervision; **п. за детьми́** child-minding.

присмотр|е́ть, ю́, ~ишь *pf.* (*of* ⇒**присма́тривать**) **1** (**за**+*i.*) to look after, keep an eye (on); **п. за ребёнком** to mind the baby. **2** (*coll.*) (*подыскать*) to look for; **п. себе́ рабо́ту** to look for a job. **3** *pf. only* (*найти*) to find.

присмотр|е́ться, ю́сь, ~ишься *pf.* (*of* ⇒**присма́триваться**) (**к**+*d.*) **1** (*внимательно посмотреть*) to look closely (at); **п. к кому́-н.** to size s.o. up. **2** (*привыкнуть*) to get accustomed (to), get used (to).

присн|и́ться, ю́сь, и́шься *pf. of* ⇒**сни́ться**

приснопа́мят|ный (~ен, ~на) *adj.* (*obs.*) memorable, unforgettable.

при́сн|ые, ~ых *n. pl.* associates.

присове́т|овать, ую *pf.* = **посове́товать**

присовокуп|и́ть, лю́, и́шь *pf.* (*of* ⇒**~ля́ть**) to add; **п. бума́гу к де́лу** to file a paper.

присовокупля́|ть, ю *impf. of* ⇒**присовокупи́ть**

присоедине́ни|е, я *nt.* **1** addition. **2** (*pol.*) annexation. **3** (**к**+*d.*) joining, associating o.s. (with); (*к мнению*) adherence (to). **4** (*elec.*) connection.

присоедин|и́ть, ю́, и́шь *pf.* (*of* ⇒**~я́ть**) **1** to add; to join. **2** (*pol.*) to annex. **3** (*elec.*) to connect.

присоедин|и́ться, ю́сь, и́шься *pf.* (*of* ⇒**~я́ться**) (**к**+*d.*) **1** to join; **пора́ нам п. к остальны́м** it is time we joined the others. **2** (*согласиться*) to endorse, associate o.s. (with); **п. к мне́нию** to subscribe to an opinion.

присоедин|я́ть(ся), я́ю(сь) *impf. of* ⇒**~и́ть(ся)**

присол|и́ть, ю́, ~и́шь *pf.* (*of* ⇒**приса́ливать**) (*coll.*) to salt, add salt (to).

присос|а́ться, у́сь, ёшься *pf.* (*of* ⇒**приса́сываться**) (**к**+*d.*) to stick (to), adhere to (*by suction*).

присосе́|диться, жусь, дишься *pf.* (**к**+*d.*; *coll.*) to sit down next (to).

присо́ск|а, и *f.* (*biol.*) sucker.

присо́х|нуть, нет, *past* **~, ~ла** *pf.* (*of* ⇒**присыха́ть**) (**к**+*d.*) to adhere (*in drying*) (to); to stick (to), dry (on).

приспева́|ть, ет *impf. of* ⇒**приспе́ть**

приспе́|ть, ет *pf.* (*of* ⇒**~ва́ть**) (*coll.*) (*о времени*) to come, draw nigh, be ripe.

приспе́шник, а *m.* stooge, henchman.

приспе́шни|ца, цы *f. of* ⇒**~к**

приспи́ч|ить, ит *pf.* (*impers.*+*d. and inf.*; *coll.*) to be impatient (to); **им ~ило уходи́ть** they were impatient to be off.

приспоса́блива|ть(ся), ю(сь) *impf.* = **приспособля́ть(ся)**

приспосо́б|ить, лю, ишь *pf.* (*of* ⇒**~ля́ть**) to adapt, convert; **п. шко́лу под больни́цу** to convert a school into a hospital.

приспосо́б|иться, люсь, ишься *pf.* (*of* ⇒**~ля́ться**) (**к**+*d.*) to adapt o.s. (to).

приспособле́н|ец, ца *m.* time-server.

приспособле́ни|е, я *nt.* **1** (*действие*) adaptation, accommodation; **п. к кли́мату** acclimatization. **2** (*устройство*) device; appliance.

приспособле́н|ка, ки *f. of* ⇒**~ец**

приспосо́бленност|ь, и *f.* fitness, suitability.

приспособле́нческий *adj.* time-serving.

приспособле́нчеств|о, а *nt.* time-serving.

приспособля́емост|ь, и *f.* adaptability.

приспособля́|ть(ся), ю(сь) *impf. of* ⇒**приспосо́бить(ся)**

приспуска́|ть, ю *impf. of* ⇒**приспусти́ть**

приспу|сти́ть, щу́, ~стишь *pf.* (*of* ⇒**~ска́ть**) to lower a little; **п. флаг** to lower a flag to half-mast.

приспу́|щенный *p.p.p. of* ⇒**~сти́ть; ~щенные фла́ги** flags at half-mast.

при́став, а, *pl.* **~а́** *m.* (*hist.*) police-officer; **суде́бный п.** bailiff.

пристава́ни|е, я *nt.* pestering; molestation.

приста|ва́ть, ю́, ёшь *impf. of* ⇒**приста́ть**

приста́в|ить, лю, ишь *pf.* (*of* ⇒**~ля́ть**) **1** (**к**+*d.*) to put (to, against), lean (against); **п. ле́стницу к стене́** to put a ladder against the wall. **2** (*пришить, приделать*) to add (*a piece of material, etc.*). **3** (**к**+*d.*) (*назначить для ухода*) to appoint to look after; **п. проводника́ к тури́стам** to appoint a guide to look after tourists.

приста́вк|а, и *f.* attachment; (*gram.*) prefix.

приставля́|ть, ю *impf. of* ⇒**приста́вить**

приставн|о́й *adj.* added, attached; attachable; **~а́я ле́стница** step ladder.

при́стально *adv.* intently; **п. смотре́ть** (**на**+*a.*) to look intently (at); to stare (at), gaze (at).

при́стал|ьный (~ен, ~ьна) *adj.* fixed, intent; **п. взгляд** intent look; stare, gaze; **с ~ьным внима́нием** intently.

приста́нищ|е, а *nt.* refuge, shelter.

при́стан|ь, и, *pl.* **~и, ~е́й** *f.* **1** landing-stage, jetty; pier; wharf. **2** (*fig., poet.*) haven.

приста́|ть, ну, нешь *pf.* (*of* ⇒**~ва́ть**) **1** (**к**+*d.*) (*прилипнуть*) to stick (to), adhere (to). **2** (**к**+*d.*) (*присоединиться*) to join; to attach o.s. (to); **п. к гру́ппе экскурса́нтов** to join a party of tourists. **3** (**к**+*d.*; *coll.*) (*о болезни*) to be passed on (to); **к де́тям ~ла ветря́нка** the children have picked up chickenpox. **4** (**к**+*d.*) (*надоесть*) to pester, bother; **п. с предложе́ниями** to pester with suggestions. **5** (**к**+*d.*; *naut.*) to put in (to), come alongside. **6** *pf. only* (*impers.*+*d.*; *coll.*) to befit; **не ~ло тебе́ так говори́ть** you ought not to speak like that. **7** *pf. only* (+*d.*; *obs., coll.*) (*прийтись к лицу*) to become, suit.

пристёгива|ть, ю *impf. of* ⇒**пристегну́ть**

пристег|ну́ть, ну́, нёшь *pf.* (*of* ⇒**~ивать**) **1** to fasten; to button up. **2** (*fig., coll.*) (*добавить*) to drag in.

пристежн|о́й *adj.* detachable; **руба́шка с ~ы́м воротничко́м** shirt with separate collar.

присто́йност|ь, и *f.* decency, propriety, decorum.

присто́|йный (~ен, ~йна) *adj.* decent, proper, decorous, seemly.

пристра́ива|ть(ся), ю(сь) *impf. of* ⇒**пристро́ить(ся)**

пристра́сти|е, я *nt.* (**к**+*d.*) **1** (*склонность*) passion (for); **у неё п. к верхово́й езде́** she has a passion for riding. **2** (*предвзятость*) partiality (for, towards), bias (towards)

пристра|сти́ть, щу́, сти́шь *pf.* (**к**+*d.*; *coll.*) to instil a passion (for); **его́ докла́д ~сти́л меня́ к исто́рии И́ндии** his talk instilled in me a passion for the history of India.

пристра|сти́ться, щу́сь, сти́шься *pf.* (**к**+*d.*) to develop a passion (for).

пристра́стност|ь, и *f.* partiality, bias.

пристра́ст|ный (~ен, ~на) *adj.* partial, biased.

пристра́чива|ть, ю *impf. of* ⇒**пристрочи́ть**

пристре́лива|ть, ю *impf. of* ⇒**пристрелить** *and* **пристреля́ть**

пристре́лива|ться, юсь *impf. of* ⇒**пристреля́ться**

пристрел|и́ть, ю́, ~ишь *pf.* (*of* ⇒**~ивать**) to shoot (down).

пристре́лк|а, и *f.* (*mil.*) adjustment (of fire), ranging; **вести́ ~у** to find the range.

пристре́льный *adj.* (*mil.*): **п. ого́нь** straddling fire.

пристрел|я́ть, я́ю *pf.* (*of* ⇒**~ивать**) (*mil.*) to adjust.

пристрел|я́ться, я́юсь *pf.* (*of* ⇒**~иваться**) (*mil.*) to adjust fire; to find the range.

пристро́|ить, ю, ишь *pf.* (*of* ⇒**пристра́ивать**) **1** (**к**+*d.*) to add (*to a building*), build on (to). **2** (*coll.*) (*поместить*) to place, settle; (*устроить*) to fix up; **п. кого́-н. на слу́жбу** to settle s.o. in a job.

пристро́|иться, юсь, ишься *pf.* (*of* ⇒**пристра́иваться**) **1** (*coll.*)

П

(*поместиться*) to settle o.s.; (*на работу*) to get a job, get fixed up; **он ~ился в контóру** he has got a job in an office. **2** (**к**+*d.*; *mil.*) to form up (with).

пристрóйк|а, и *f.* annex, extension.

пристроч|и́ть, у́, ~́ишь *pf.* (*of* ⇒**пристрáчивать**) (**к**+*d.*) to sew on (to).

пристру́нива|ть, ю *impf. of* ⇒**пристру́нить**

пристру́н|ить, ю, ишь *pf.* (*of* ⇒**~ивать**) (*coll.*) to take in hand.

присту́кива|ть, ю *impf. of* ⇒**присту́кнуть**

присту́к|нуть, ну, нешь *pf.* (*of* ⇒**~ивать**) **1** (+*i.*; *coll.*) to tap; **п. каблукáми** to tap one's heels. **2** (*coll.*) (*убить*) to club to death; to kill (*with a blow*).

при́ступ, а *m.* **1** (*mil.*) assault, storm; **пойти́ на п.** to go in to the assault; **взять ~ом** to take by storm. **2** (*припадок*) fit, attack; **п. гнéва** fit of temper; **п. гри́ппа** bout of influenza; **п. кáшля** fit, bout of coughing. **3** (*obs.*, *coll.*) access; **к нему́ ~у нет** he is inaccessible, unapproachable.

приступ|áть(ся), áю(сь) *impf. of* ⇒**~и́ть(ся)**

приступ|и́ть, лю́, ~́ишь *pf.* (*of* ⇒**~́ать**) (**к**+*d.*) to set about, get down (to), start; **п. к дéлу** to set to work, get down to business.

приступ|и́ться, лю́сь, ~́ишься *pf.* (*of* ⇒**~áться**) (**к**+*d.*; *coll.*) to approach, accost, go up (to).

присту́п|ок, ка *m.* (*coll.*) step.

присты|ди́ть, жу́, ди́шь *pf. of* ⇒**стыди́ть**

пристя́жк|а, и *f.* **1**: **в ~е** (*о лошади*) in traces. **2** (*лошадь*) trace-horse, outrunner.

пристяжн|áя, óй *f.* trace-horse, outrunner.

прису|ди́ть, жу́, ~́дишь *pf.* (*of* ⇒**~ждáть**) **1** (+*a.* *and* **к**+*d.* *or* +*a.* *and d.*) to sentence (to), condemn (to); **п. когó-н. к заключéнию** to sentence s.o. to imprisonment; **п. к штрáфу, п. штраф** (+*d.*) to fine, impose a fine (on). **2** (+*d.*) to award; to confer (on); **емý ~ди́ли стéпень дóктора** a doctorate has been conferred on him.

присуждá|ть, ю *impf. of* ⇒**присуди́ть**

присуждéни|е, я *nt.* awarding; conferment.

прису́тственн|ый *adj.* (*obs.*): **п. день** working-day; **~ое мéсто** (*obs.*) office, work-place.

прису́тстви|е, я *nt.* presence; **в ~и детéй** in the presence of the children, in front of the children; **п. дýха** presence of mind.

прису́тств|овать, ую *impf.* (**на**+*p.*) to be present (at), attend.

прису́тств|ующий *pres. part. act. of* ⇒**~овать** *and adj.* present; *as n.* **~ующие, ~ующих** those present.

прису́щ|ий (~, ~а) *adj.* (+*d.*) inherent (in); characteristic; **~ая ей щéдрость** her characteristic generosity.

присчит|áть, áю *pf.* (*of* ⇒**~́ывать**) to add on.

присчи́тыва|ть, ю *impf. of* ⇒**присчитáть**

присылá|ть, ю *impf. of* ⇒**прислáть**

присы́лк|а, и *f.* sending.

присы́п|ать, лю, лешь *pf.* (*of* ⇒**~áть**) **1** (+*a. or g.*) (*добавить*) to pour some more. **2** (+*a. and i.*) (*посыпать тонким слоем*) to sprinkle (with).

присып|áть, áю *impf. of* ⇒**~́ать**

присы́пк|а, и *f.* **1** (*действие*) sprinkling. **2** (*порошок*) powder.

присыхá|ть, ет *impf. of* ⇒**присóхнуть**

прися́г|а, и *f.* oath; **лóжная п.** perjury; **дать ~у** to swear; **приня́ть ~у** to take the oath; **привести́ к ~е** to swear in, administer the oath (to); **под ~ой** on oath, under oath.

присяг|áть, áю *impf.* (*of* ⇒**~нýть**) (**в**+*p.*) to swear (to); to swear an oath; **п. в вéрности** (+*d.*) to swear allegiance (to).

присяг|нýть, нý, нёшь *pf. of* ⇒**~áть**

прися́жн|ый *adj.* **1**: **п. повéренный** (*hist.*) barrister; **п. заседáтель** juror; *as n.* **п., ~ого** *m.* = **п. заседáтель; суд ~ых** jury. **2** (*coll.*) born, inveterate; **п. ворчýн** born grumbler.

притá|иться, ю́сь, и́шься *pf.* to hide; to conceal o.s.

притáптыва|ть, ю *impf.* **1** *impf. of* ⇒**притоптáть. 2** *impf. only* (*coll.*) to tap (with) one's heels.

притáскива|ть, ю *impf. of* ⇒**притащи́ть**

притащ|и́ть, у́, ~́ишь *pf.* (*of* ⇒**притáскивать**) to bring, drag, haul.

притащ|и́ться, у́сь, ~́ишься *pf.* (*coll.*) to drag o.s.

притвор|и́ть, ю́, ~́ишь *pf.* (*of* ⇒**~я́ть**) to set ajar; to leave not quite shut.

притвор|и́ться[1], **~́ится** *pf.* (*of* ⇒**~я́ться**) (*о двери*) to be ajar, to be not quite shut.

притвор|и́ться[2], **ю́сь, и́шься** *pf.* (*of* ⇒**~я́ться**) (+*i.*) to pretend (to be); to feign; **п. больны́м** to pretend to be ill, feign illness; **п. безрази́чным** to feign indifference.

притвóр|ный (~ен, ~на) *adj.* pretended, feigned; **~ное невéжество** feigned ignorance; **~ные слёзы** crocodile tears.

притвóрств|о, а *nt.* pretence; sham.

притвóрщик, а *m.* sham, faker.

притвóрщи|ца, цы *f. of* ⇒**~к**

притвор|я́ть(ся), я́ю(сь) *impf. of* ⇒**~и́ть(ся)**

притекá|ть, ет *impf. of* ⇒**притéчь**

притерп|éться, лю́сь, ~́ишься *pf.* (**к**+*d.*; *coll.*) to get accustomed (to), get used (to).

притёр|тый *adj.*: **~тая прóбка** ground-in stopper (*of bottle*); **~тое стеклó** ground glass.

притеснéни|е, я *nt.* oppression.

притесни́тел|ь, я *m.* oppressor.

притесни́тель|ница, ницы *f. of* ⇒**~**

притесни́тел|ьный (~ен, ~ьна) *adj.* oppressive.

притесн|и́ть, ю́, и́шь *pf.* (*of* ⇒**~я́ть**) to oppress, keep down.

притесн|я́ть, я́ю *impf. of* ⇒**~и́ть**

притé|чь, чёт, кýт, *past* **~́к, ~клá** *pf.* (*of* ⇒**~кáть**) to flow in, pour in.

прити́скива|ть, ю *impf. of* ⇒**прити́снуть**

прити́с|нуть, ну, нешь *pf.* (*of* ⇒**~кивать**) (*coll.*) to press, squeeze; **п. пáлец двéрью** to pinch one's finger in the door.

притих|áть, áю *impf. of* ⇒**~́нуть**

прити́х|нуть, ну, нешь, *past* **~, ~ла** *pf.* (*of* ⇒**~áть**) to quieten (*Br.*), quiet (*US*) down; to grow quiet.

приткн|ýть, ý, ёшь *pf.* (*of* ⇒**притыкáть**) (*coll.*) to stick; **~и свой вéщи кудá хóчешь** stick your things anywhere you like.

приткн|ýться, ýсь, ёшься *pf.* (*coll.*) to perch o.s.; to find room for o.s.

притóк, а *m.* **1** (*geog.*) tributary. **2** (*воздуха, воды, денег*) inflow; (*людей*) influx.

при́толок|а, и *f.* lintel.

притóм *conj.* (and) besides; and what's more.

притом|и́ть, лю́, и́шь *pf.* (*coll.*) to tire.

притом|и́ться, лю́сь, и́шься *pf.* (*coll.*) to get tired.

притóн, а *m.* den; **воровскóй п.** den of thieves; **игóрный п.** gambling-den.

притóп|нуть, ну, нешь *pf.* (*of* ⇒**~ывать**) to stamp one's foot; **п. каблукáми** to tap one's heels.

притоп|тáть, чý, ~́чешь *pf.* (*of* ⇒**притáптывать**) to tread down.

притóпыва|ть, ю *impf. of* ⇒**притóпнуть**

приторáчива|ть, ю *impf. of* ⇒**притoрочи́ть**

при́торност|ь, и *f.* sickly sweetness, excessive sweetness.

при́тор|ный (~ен, ~на) *adj.* sickly sweet, cloying (*also fig.*); **~ная улы́бка** unctuous smile.

притороч|и́ть, у́, и́шь *pf.* (*of* ⇒**приторáчивать**) to strap.

притрáгива|ться, юсь *impf. of* ⇒**притрóнуться**

притрóн|уться, усь, ешься *pf.* (*of* ⇒**притрáгиваться**) (**к**+*d.*) to touch; **они́ не ~улись к ýжину** they have not touched their supper.

притул|и́ться, ю́сь, и́шься *pf.* (*coll.*) to find room for o.s.; to find shelter.

притуп|и́ть, лю́, ~́ишь *pf.* (*of* ⇒**~ля́ть**) to blunt; (*fig.*) to dull, deaden.

притуп|и́ться, ~́ится *pf.* (*of* ⇒**~ля́ться**) to become blunt; (*fig.*) (*о памяти, зрении*) to fail.

притупля́|ть(ся), ю, ет(ся) *impf. of* ⇒**притупи́ть(ся)**

притуш|и́ть, у́, ~ишь *pf.* (*coll.*) (*огонь*) to damp; **п. фа́ры** to dip lights.

при́тч|а, и *f.* parable; **что за п.?** (*coll.*) what an extraordinary thing!; **п. во язы́цех** (*joc.*) the talk of the town.

притыка́|ть, ю *impf. of* ⇒**приткну́ть**

притяга́тельност|ь, и *f.* attractiveness.

притяга́тел|ьный (~ен, ~ьна) *adj.* attractive, magnetic.

притя́гива|ть, ю *impf. of* ⇒**притяну́ть**

притяжа́тельный *adj.* (*gram.*) possessive.

притяже́ни|е, я *nt.* (*phys.*) attraction; **зако́н земно́го ~я** law of gravity.

притяза́ни|е, я *nt.* claim, pretension; **име́ть ~я** (**на**+*a.*) to have claims (to, on).

притяза́тел|ьный (~ен, ~ьна) *adj.* demanding, exacting.

притяза́|ть, ю *impf.* (**на**+*a.*) to lay claim (to).

притя́н|утый *p.p.p. of* ⇒**~у́ть; п. за́ уши, п. за́ волосы** (*fig.*) far-fetched.

притя|ну́ть, ну́, ~нешь *pf.* (*of* ⇒**~гивать**) **1** to drag (up), pull (up); **п. за́ уши, за́ волосы доказа́тельства** to adduce far-fetched arguments. **2** (*fig.*) (*привлечь*) to draw, attract; **п. как магни́т** to attract like a magnet. **3** (*coll.*) (*вызвать*) to summon; **п. к отве́ту** to call to account; **п. к суду́** to have up, sue.

приугото́в|ить, лю, ишь *pf.* (*of* ⇒**~ля́ть**) (*obs.*) to prepare, have in store.

приуготовля́|ть, ю *impf. of* ⇒**приугото́вить**

приуда́р|ить, ю, ишь (*of* ⇒**~я́ть**) **1** (*ударить*) to deal a light blow. **2** (*coll.*) (*начать делать что-н. быстрее*) to get cracking. **3** (**за**+*i.*; *coll.*) to go (after), pursue (= *begin courting*).

приудар|я́ть, я́ю *impf. of* ⇒**~ить**

приукра́|сить, шу, сишь *pf.* (*of* ⇒**~шивать**) (*coll.*) (*наряд*) to adorn; (*успехи*) to exaggerate; (*рассказ*) to embellish, embroider.

приукра́шива|ть, ю *impf. of* ⇒**приукра́сить**

приуменьш|а́ть, а́ю *impf. of* ⇒**~ить**

приуме́ньш|ить, ~у́, ~и́шь *pf.* (*of* ⇒**~а́ть**) to diminish, lessen, reduce.

приумнож|а́ть(ся), а́ю, ~а́ет(ся) *impf. of* ⇒**~ить(ся)**

приумноже́ни|е, я *nt.* increase, augmentation.

приумно́ж|ить, у, ишь *pf.* (*of* ⇒**~а́ть**) to increase, augment, multiply.

приумно́ж|иться, ится *pf.* (*of* ⇒**~а́ться**) to increase, multiply.

приумо́лк|нуть, ну, нешь, *past* **~, ~ла** *pf.* (*coll.*) to fall silent (*for a while*).

приун|ы́ть, о́ю, о́ешь *pf.* (*coll.*) to become depressed, become gloomy.

приуро́чива|ть, ю *impf. of* ⇒**приуро́чить**

приуро́ч|ить, у, ишь *pf.* (*of* ⇒**~ивать**) (**к**+*d.*) to time (for, to coincide with); **~или изда́ние кни́ги к прибы́тию а́втора** publication of the book was timed to coincide with the author's arrival.

приуса́дебный *adj.* adjoining the farm(-house); **п. уча́сток (колхо́зника)** personal plot (of collective farmer).

приути́х|нуть, ну, нешь, *past* **~, ~ла** *pf.* to quieten (*Br.*), quiet (*US*) down; (*о буре*) to abate; (*о ветре*) to fall, drop.

приуч|а́ть(ся), а́ю(сь) *impf. of* ⇒**~и́ть(ся)**

приуч|и́ть, у́, ~ишь *pf.* (*of* ⇒**~а́ть**) (**к**+*d. or* +*inf.*) to train (to), school (to, in); **п. кого́-н. к дисципли́не** to inculcate discipline in s.o.

приуч|и́ться, у́сь, ~ишься *pf.* (*of* ⇒**~а́ться**) (+*inf.*) to train o.s. (to); to accustom o.s. (to).

прифран|ти́ться, чу́сь, ти́шься *pf.* (*coll.*) to dress up.

прифронтов|о́й *adj.* (*mil., pol.*) forward, front-line; **~а́я полоса́** forward area; **~ы́е госуда́рства** front-line states.

прихва́рыва|ть, ю *impf.* (*coll.*) to be unwell off and on.

прихвастн|у́ть, у́, ёшь *pf.* (*coll.*) to boast a little, brag a little.

прихва|ти́ть, чу́, ~тишь *pf.* (*of* ⇒**~тывать**) (*coll.*) **1** (*взять*) to catch up, seize up. **2** (*привязать*) to tie up, fasten. **3** (*о морозе*) to touch, nip.

прихва́тыва|ть, ю *impf. of* ⇒**прихвати́ть**

прихворн|у́ть, у́, ёшь *pf.* (*coll.*) to be indisposed, be unwell.

при́хвост|ень, ня *m.* (*coll.*) hanger-on, stooge.

прихлеба́тел|ь, я *m.* (*coll.*) sponger.

прихлеба́тель|ница, ницы *f. of* ⇒**~**

прихлеба́тельств|о, а *nt.* (*coll.*) sponging.

прихлебн|у́ть, у́, ёшь *pf.* to take a sip.

прихлёбыва|ть, ю *impf.* (*coll.*) to sip.

прихло́п|нуть, ну, нешь *pf.* (*of* ⇒**~ывать**) (*coll.*) **1** (*дверь*) to slam. **2** (*придавить*) to squash, pinch; **п. па́лец две́рью** to pinch one's finger in the door. **3** (*sl.*) (*убить*) to kill.

прихло́пыва|ть, ю *impf.* **1** *impf. of* ⇒**прихло́пнуть. 2** *impf. only* to clap.

прихлы́н|уть, у, ешь *pf.* (**к**+*d.*) to rush (towards), surge (towards); (*fig.*) (*о воспоминаниях*) to come flooding back.

прихо́д[1]**, а** *m.* (*прибытие*) coming, arrival.

прихо́д[2]**, а** *m.* (*доход*) receipts; **п. и расхо́д** credit and debit.

прихо́д[3]**, а** *m.* (*eccl.*) parish; **како́в поп, тако́в и п.** (*prov.*) like master, like man.

прихо|ди́ть, жу́, ~дишь *impf. of* ⇒**прийти́**

прихо|ди́ться, жу́сь, ~дишься *impf.* **1** *impf. of* ⇒**прийти́сь. 2** *impf. only* (+*d. and i.*) to be (*in a given degree of relationship to*); **я ей ~жу́сь дя́дей** I am her uncle. **3**: **раз на раз/день на́ день не ~дится** no two occasions/days are ever the same.

прихо́д|ный *adj. of* ⇒**~**[2]; **~ная кни́га** receipt-book.

прихо́д|овать, ую *impf.* (*of* ⇒**за~**) (*book-keeping*) to enter (*in a receipt-book*).

прихо́до-расхо́дн|ый *adj.* credit and debit; **~ая кни́га** account-book.

прихо́дский *adj.* parish; **п. свяще́нник** parish priest.

приход|я́щий *pres. part. act. of* ⇒**~и́ть** *and adj.* non-resident; **п. больно́й** outpatient; **~я́щая домрабо́тница** cleaning woman; **~я́щая ня́ня** babysitter.

прихожа́н|ин, ина, *pl.* **~е** *m.* parishioner.

прихожа́н|ка, ки *f. of* ⇒**~ин**

прихо́ж|ая, ей *f.* (entrance) hall, lobby.

прихора́шива|ться, юсь *impf.* (*coll.*) to spruce o.s. up.

прихотли́вост|ь, и *f.* capriciousness, whimsicality.

прихотли́в|ый (~, ~а) 1 (*человек*) capricious, whimsical. **2** (*узор*) intricate.

при́хот|ь, и *f.* whim, caprice, fancy.

прихра́мыва|ть, ю *impf.* to limp, hobble.

прице́л, а *m.* **1** (back-)sight; **п. для бомбомета́ния** bomb sight; **взять на п.** to take aim (at), aim (at); (*fig.*) to keep a watch on. **2** (*действие*) aiming.

прице́лива|ться, юсь *impf. of* ⇒**прице́литься**

прице́л|иться, юсь, ишься *pf.* (*of* ⇒**~иваться**) to take aim.

прице́л|ьный *adj. of* ⇒**~; ~ьная бомбардиро́вка** precision bombing; **~ьная ли́ния** line of sight; **п. ого́нь** aimed fire.

прице́нива|ться, юсь *impf. of* ⇒**прицени́ться**

прицен|и́ться, ю́сь, ~ишься *pf.* (*of* ⇒**~иваться**) (**к**+*d.*; *coll.*) to ask the price (of).

прице́п, а *m.* trailer.

прицеп|и́ть, лю́, ~ишь *pf.* (*of* ⇒**~ля́ть**) (**к**+*d.*) **1** to hitch (to), hook on (to); (*вагоны*) to couple (to). **2** (*coll.*) (*брошку, бант*) to pin on (to), fasten (to).

прицеп|и́ться, лю́сь, ~ишься *pf.* (*of* ⇒**~ля́ться**) (**к**+*d.*) **1** to stick (to), cling (to). **2** (*fig., coll.*) (*пристать*) to pester; to nag (at).

прице́пк|а, и *f.* **1** hitching, hooking on; coupling. **2** (*coll.*) pestering; nagging.

прицепля́|ть(ся), ю(сь) *impf. of* ⇒**прицепи́ть(ся)**

прицепно́й *adj.*: **п. ваго́н** trailer.

прича́л, а *m.* **1** (*действие*) mooring, making fast. **2** (*верёвка*) mooring line. **3** (*место*) berth, moorage; **у ~ов** at its, her moorings.

прича́лива|ть, ю *impf. of* ⇒**прича́лить**

прича́л|ить, ю, ишь *pf.* (*of* ⇒**~ивать**) **1** (**к**+*d.*) to moor (to). **2** (*intrans.*) to moor.

прича́л|ьный *adj. of* ⇒**~; п. кана́т** mooring line.

прича́сти|е¹, я *nt.* (*gram.*) participle.

прича́сти|е², я *nt.* (*eccl.*) **1** communion; the Eucharist. **2** (*причащение*) making one's communion, communicating.

прича|сти́ть, щу́, сти́шь *pf.* (*of* ⇒**~ща́ть**) (*eccl.*) to give communion.

прича|сти́ться, щу́сь, сти́шься *pf.* (*of* ⇒**~ща́ться**) (*eccl.*) to receive communion.

прича́стност|ь, и *f.* (**к**+*d.*) connection (with); involvement (with).

прича́ст|ный¹ (~ен, ~на) *adj.* (**к**+*d.*) connected (with), involved (in); **быть ~ным** (**к**+*d.*) to be connected (with), be involved (in).

прича́стный² *adj.* (*gram.*) participial.

причаща́|ть(ся), ю(сь) *impf. of* ⇒**причасти́ть(ся)**

причаще́ни|е, я *nt.* (*eccl.*) receiving communion.

причём *conj.* moreover, and (*or translated by means of participial clause*); **бы́ло о́чень темно́, п. я пло́хо ориенти́ровалась в ме́стности** it was very dark and I didn't know the area well.

приче|са́ть, шу́, ~́шешь *pf.* (*of* ⇒**~́сывать**) to comb; **п. го́лову** to brush, comb one's hair; **п. кого́-н.** to brush, comb s.o.'s hair.

приче|са́ться, шу́сь, ~́шешься *pf.* (*of* ⇒**~́сываться**) to brush, comb one's hair; (*у парикмахера*) to have one's hair done.

причёск|а, и *f.* hair style, hair-do.

при|че́сть, чту́, чтёшь, *past* **~чёл, ~чла́** *pf.* (*of* ⇒**~чи́тывать**) **1** (*coll.*) (*присчитать*) to add on. **2** (*obs.*) (*отнести к числу кого-чего-н.*) to number, reckon.

причёсыва|ть(ся), ю(сь) *impf. of* ⇒**причеса́ть(ся)**

приче́тник, а *m.* (*eccl.*) junior deacon.

причи́н|а, ы *f.* (*пожара, болезни*) cause; (*основание*) reason; **по той или ино́й ~е** for some reason or other; **по той просто́й ~е, что** for the simple reason that; **по ~е** (+*g.*) by reason (of), on account (of), owing (to), because (of).

причинда́л|ы, ов *no sg.* (*coll.*) things, gear.

причин|и́ть, ю́, и́шь *pf.* (*of* ⇒**~я́ть**) to cause.

причи́нност|ь, и *f.* causality.

причи́нн|ый *adj.* causal, causative; **~ая связь** causation; **~ое ме́сто** (*coll.*) private parts.

причин|я́ть, я́ю *impf. of* ⇒**~и́ть**

причи́сл|ить, ю, ишь *pf.* (*of* ⇒**~я́ть**) (**к**+*d.*) **1** (*присчитать*) to add on (to). **2** (*отнести к числу кого-чего-н.*) to number (among), rank (among); **его́ ~или к са́мым выдающимся матема́тикам** he was ranked among the foremost mathematicians.

причисл|я́ть, я́ю *impf. of* ⇒**~ить**

причита́ни|е, я *nt.* (ritual) lamentation.

причита́|ть, ю *impf.* (**по**+*p.*) to lament (for); to bewail.

причита́|ться, ется *impf.* (+*d.*; **с**+*g.*) to be due (to; from); **вам ~ется два рубля́** there is two roubles due to you, you have two roubles to come; **с вас ~ется два рубля́** you have two roubles to pay.

причи́тыва|ть, ю *impf. of* ⇒**приче́сть**

причмо́кива|ть, ю *impf. of* ⇒**причмо́кнуть**

причмо́к|нуть, ну, нешь *pf.* (*of* ⇒**~ивать**) to smack one's lips.

причт, а *m.* (*collect.*) the clergy of a parish.

причу́д|а, ы *f.* caprice, whim, fancy.

причу́д|иться, ится *pf. of* ⇒**чу́диться**

причу́дливост|ь, и *f.* **1** (*замысловатость*) fantasticality. **2** (*coll.*) (*капризность*) capriciousness, whimsicality.

причу́длив|ый (~, ~а) *adj.* **1** (*замысловатый*) intricate; fantastical. **2** (*coll.*) (*капризный*) capricious, whimsical.

причу́дник, а *m.* (*coll.*) odd person.

причу́дни|ца, цы *f. of* ⇒**~к**

пришварт|ова́ть, у́ю *pf.* (*of* ⇒**~о́вывать**) (**к**+*d.*) to moor (to), make fast (to).

пришварт|ова́ться, у́юсь *pf.* (*of* ⇒**~о́вываться**) (**к**+*d.*) to moor (to), tie up (at).

пришварто́выва|ть(ся), ю(сь) *impf. of* ⇒**пришвартова́ть(ся)**

прише́л|ец, ьца *m.* **1** (*пришлый человек*) newcomer, stranger. **2** (*инопланетянин*) alien.

пришепётыва|ть, ю *impf.* (*coll.*) to lisp slightly.

пришёптыва|ть, ю *impf.* (*coll.*) to whisper (*while doing sth.*).

прише́стви|е, я *nt.* advent, coming; **до второ́го ~я** (*joc.*) till doomsday.

пришиб|и́ть, у́ ёшь, *past* **~́, ~́ла** *pf.* (*coll.*) **1** to strike dead. **2** (*fig.*) (*удручить*) to crush; to dispirit.

пришиб|ленный *p.p.p. of* ⇒**~и́ть** *and adj.* (*coll.*) crushed; crest-fallen.

пришива́|ть, ю́ *impf. of* ⇒**приши́ть**

пришивно́й *adj.* sewn on.

приш|и́ть, ью́, ьёшь *pf.* (*of* ⇒**~ива́ть**) **1** (*пуговицу*) to sew on. **2** (*доску*) to nail on. **3** (+*a.* *and* **к**+*d.* *or* +*a.* *and d.*; *fig., coll.*) to pin (on).

пришко́льный *adj.* (adjoining a) school.

при́шлый *adj.* newly arrived; strange.

пришпи́лива|ть, ю *impf. of* ⇒**пришпи́лить**

пришпи́л|ить, ю, ишь *pf.* (*of* ⇒**~ивать**) to pin.

пришпо́рива|ть, ю *impf. of* ⇒**пришпо́рить**

пришпо́р|ить, ю, ишь *pf.* (*of* ⇒**~ивать**) to spur; to put, set spurs (to).

прищёлкива|ть, ю *impf. of* ⇒**прищёлкнуть**

прищёлк|нуть, ну, нешь *pf.* (*of* ⇒**~ивать**): **п. кнуто́м** to crack the whip; **п. па́льцами** to snap one's fingers.

прищем|и́ть, лю́, и́шь *pf.* (*of* ⇒**~ля́ть**) to pinch, catch; **п. себе́ па́лец две́рью** to pinch one's finger in the door.

прищемля́|ть, ю *impf. of* ⇒**прищеми́ть**

прищеп|и́ть, лю́, и́шь *pf.* (*of* ⇒**~ля́ть**) (*bot.*) to graft.

прище́пк|а, и *f.* (clothes-)peg (*Br.*), clothespin (*US*).

прищепля́|ть, ю *impf. of* ⇒**прищепи́ть**

прище́п|ок, ка *m.* = **~ка**

прищу́рива|ть(ся), ю(сь) *impf. of* ⇒**прищу́рить(ся)**

прищу́р|ить, ю, ишь *pf.* (*of* ⇒**~ивать**); **п. глаза́** = **~иться**

прищу́р|иться, юсь, ишься *pf.* (*of* ⇒**~иваться**) to screw up one's eyes.

прию́т, а *m.* **1** shelter, refuge. **2**: **де́тский п.** orphanage.

прию|ти́ть, чу́, ти́шь *pf.* to shelter, give refuge.

прию|ти́ться, чу́сь, ти́шься *pf.* to take shelter.

приязнен|ный (~, ~на) *adj.* (*obs.*) friendly, amicable.

прия́зн|ь, и *f.* (*obs.*) friendliness, goodwill.

прия́тел|ь, я *m.* friend.

прия́тельниц|а, ы *f.* (*female*) friend.

прия́тельский *adj.* friendly, amicable.

прия́т|ный (~ен, ~на) *adj.* nice, pleasant, pleasing; **п. на вид** nice-looking; (*impers., pred.*): **~но** it is pleasant; it is nice; **о́чень ~но** pleased to meet you; how do you do?

при|я́ть, му́, ~́мешь *pf.* (*obs.*) = **~ня́ть**

про *prep.* +*a.* **1** (*о*) about; **мы говори́ли про вас** we were talking about you. **2** (*coll.*) (*для*) for; **э́то не про нас** this is not for us. **3**: **про себя́** to o.s.; **чита́ть про себя́** to read to o.s.

про...¹ *vbl. pref. indicating* **1** *action through, across or past object, as* **прострели́ть** to shoot through; **прое́хать** to pass (by). **2** *overall or exhaustive action, as* **прогре́ть** to warm thoroughly. **3** *duration of action throughout given period of time, as* **просиде́ть всю ночь** to sit up all night. **4** *loss or failure, as* **проигра́ть** to lose (*a game*).

про...² *as pref. of nn. and adjs.* pro-.

проанализи́р|овать, ую *pf. of* ⇒**анализи́ровать**

про́б|а, ы *f.* **1** (*машины*) trial, test; try-out; (*металла*) assay; (*theatr.*) audition; **п. го́лоса** voice test; **п. сил** trial of strength; **взять на ~у** to take on trial; **путём ~ и оши́бок** by trial and error. **2** (*для анализа*) sample. **3** (*драгоценного металла*) standard (*measure of purity of gold*); **зо́лото 56-о́й ~ы** 14 carat gold; **зо́лото 96-о́й ~ы** pure gold, 24 carat gold. **4** (*клеймо*) hallmark.

пробавля́|ться, юсь *impf.* (*coll.*) to subsist (on), make do (on).

проба́лтыва|ть(ся), ю(сь) *impf. of* ⇒**проболта́ть(ся)**

проба|си́ть, шу́, си́шь *pf.* (*coll.*) to speak in a bass, deep voice.

пробе́г, а *m.* **1** (*действие*) run. **2** (*sport*) race; **лы́жный п.** ski-run. **3** (*пройденное расстояние*) mileage, distance covered.

пробе́га|ть, ю *pf.* (*coll.*) to run about (*for a certain time*).

пробега́|ть, ю *impf. of* ⇒**пробежа́ть**

пробе|жа́ть, гу́, жи́шь, гу́т *pf.* (*of* ⇒**∼га́ть**) **1** (*мимо*) to run past; (*через*) to run through; (*по*) to run along; **п. па́льцами по клавиату́ре** to run one's fingers over the keyboard. **2** (*преодолеть пространство*) to run; to cover; **по́езд ∼жа́л шестьдеся́т миль ро́вно за час** the train covered sixty miles in exactly one hour. **3** (*fig.*) (*пронестись*) to run, flit (over, down, across); **хо́лод ∼жа́л по её спине́** a chill ran down her spine. **4** (*fig., coll.*) (*бегло прочитать*) to look through, skim.

пробе|жа́ться, гу́сь, жи́шься, гу́тся *pf.* to run, take a run.

пробе́жк|а, и *f.* run, jog.

пробе́л, а *m.* **1** blank, gap; **запо́лнить ∼ы** to fill in the blanks. **2** (*недостаток*) deficiency, gap; **∼ы в зна́ниях** gaps in one's knowledge.

пробива́|ть(ся), ю(сь) *impf. of* ⇒**проби́ть(ся)**

проби́вк|а, и *f.* piercing; punching.

пробивн|о́й *adj.* **1** piercing, punching; **∼а́я си́ла** penetrating power (*of missile*). **2** (*coll.*) (*энергичный*) go-getting, pushy.

пробира́|ть(ся), ю(сь) *impf. of* ⇒**пробра́ть(ся)**

проби́рк|а, и *f.* test-tube.

проби́рн|ый *adj.* testing; assaying; **п. ка́мень** touchstone; **∼ое клеймо́** hallmark; **∼ая пала́та** assay office.

проби́р|овать, ую *impf.* to test, assay.

про|би́ть[1], бью́, бьёшь, *past* **∼би́л, ∼би́ла, ∼би́ло** *pf. of* ⇒**бить** 9

про|би́ть[2], бью́, бьёшь *pf.* (*of* ⇒**∼бива́ть**) to make a hole (in); to pierce; to punch; **п. сте́ну** to breach a wall; **п. ши́ну** to puncture a tyre; **п. путь, доро́гу** to open the way (*also fig.*); **п. себе́ доро́гу** (*fig.*) to carve one's way.

про|би́ться, бью́сь, бьёшься *pf.* (*of* ⇒**∼бива́ться**) **1** to fight one's way through; to break, strike through; **п. сквозь толпу́** to fight one's way through the crowd. **2** (*о растениях*) to appear, push up.

про́бк|а, и *f.* **1** (*материал*) cork (*substance*). **2** (*для бутылок*) cork; stopper; (*в раковину*) plug; **глуп как п.** daft as a brush. **3** (*elec.*) fuse. **4** (*fig.*) (*на улице*) traffic jam; congestion.

про́бковый *adj.* cork.

пробле́м|а, ы *f.* problem.

проблема́тик|а, и *f.* (*collect.*) problems.

проблемати́ческий *adj.* problematic(al).

проблемати́чност|ь, и *f.* problematical character.

проблемати́ч|ный (∼ен, ∼на) *adj.* = **∼еский**

про́блеск, а *m.* flash; ray, gleam (*also fig.*); **п. наде́жды** ray of hope.

пробле́скива|ть, ю *impf. of* ⇒**проблесну́ть**

пробле|сну́ть, ну́, нёшь *pf.* (*of* ⇒**∼кивать**) to flash, gleam.

проблужда́|ть, ю *pf.* to wander, rove, roam (*for a certain time*).

про́бный *adj.* **1** trial, test; **п. ка́мень** touchstone; **п. полёт** test flight; **п. экземпля́р** specimen copy. **2** (*с клеймом пробы*) hallmarked.

про́б|овать, ую *impf.* (*of* ⇒**по∼**) **1** (*проверять*) to test; **п. пи́щу** to taste, try food. **2** (+*inf.*) (*стараться*) to try (to), attempt (to).

прободе́ни|е, я *nt.* (*med.*) perforation.

пробо́ин|а, ы *f.* hole (*esp. caused by missile*).

пробо́|й, я *m.* clamp, hasp.

проболе́|ть[1], ю *pf.* to be ill (*for a certain time*).

пробол|е́ть[2], и́т *pf.* to hurt (*for a certain time*).

проболта́|ть, ю *pf.* (*of* ⇒**проба́лтывать**) (*coll.*) **1** (*с друзьями*) to chat away. **2** (*выболтать*) to blab (out).

проболта́|ться[1], юсь *pf.* (*of* ⇒**проба́лтываться**) (*coll.*) to shoot one's mouth off, let the cat out of the bag.

проболта́|ться[2], юсь *pf.* (*coll.*) (*бездельничать*) to idle, loaf.

пробо́р, а *m.* parting (*Br.*), part (*US*) (*of the hair*); **прямо́й п.** middle part(ing); **косо́й п.** side part(ing).

пробормо|та́ть, чу́, ∼чешь *pf. of* ⇒**бормота́ть**

про́бочник, а *m.* (*coll.*) corkscrew.

про|бра́ть, беру́, берёшь, *past* **∼бра́л, ∼брала́, ∼бра́ло** *pf.* (*of* ⇒**∼бира́ть**) **1** to penetrate; **моро́з ∼бра́л меня́ до косте́й** I was chilled to the marrow; **их ∼бра́л страх** fear had struck them. **2** (*coll.*) (*выбранить*) to scold.

про|бра́ться, беру́сь, берёшься, *past* **∼бра́лся, ∼брала́сь, ∼брало́сь** *pf.* (*of* ⇒**∼бира́ться**) **1** (*с трудом*) to fight, force one's way. **2** (*тихо*) to steal (through, past); **п. о́щупью** to feel one's way; **п. на цы́почках** to tiptoe (through).

пробро|ди́ть, жу́, ∼дишь *pf.* to wander (*for a certain time*).

пробубн|и́ть, ю́, и́шь *pf. of* ⇒**бубни́ть**

пробу|ди́ть, жу́, ∼дишь *pf.* (*of* ⇒**буди́ть** *and* **∼жда́ть**) to wake; to awaken, rouse, arouse (*also fig.*).

пробу|ди́ться, жу́сь, ∼дишься *pf.* (*of* ⇒**∼жда́ться**) to wake up, awake (*also fig.*).

пробужда́|ть(ся), ю(сь) *impf. of* ⇒**пробуди́ть(ся)**

пробужде́ни|е, я *nt.* waking up, awakening.

пробура́в|ить, лю, ишь *pf.* (*of* ⇒**∼ливать, бура́вить**) to bore, drill, perforate.

пробура́влива|ть, ю *impf. of* ⇒**пробура́вить**

пробур|и́ть, ю́, и́шь *pf. of* ⇒**бури́ть**

пробурч|а́ть, у́, и́шь *pf. of* ⇒**бурча́ть**

проб|ы́ть, у́ду, у́дешь, *past* **∼ыл, ∼ыла́** *pf.* to stay, remain; to be (*for a certain time*); **он ∼ыл у нас три неде́ли** he stayed with us for three weeks.

прова́йдер, а *m.* (*comm.*) provider.

прова́л, а *m.* **1** (*действие*) collapse. **2** (*geog.*) gap; hole. **3** (*неудача*) failure; **п. па́мяти** failure of memory; **по́лный п.** a complete flop.

прова́лива|ть, ю *impf.* **1** *impf. of* ⇒**провали́ть. 2**: **∼й!** (*coll.*) clear off!; beat it!; hop it!

прова́лива|ться, юсь *impf. of* ⇒**провали́ться**

провал|и́ть, ю́, ∼ишь *pf.* (*of* ⇒**∼ивать**) **1** (*крышу*) to cause to collapse, knock down. **2** (*fig., coll.*) (*дело*) to ruin, make a mess (of). **3** (*fig.*) (*предложение*) to reject; **п. кандида́та на экза́мене** to fail a candidate in an examination.

провал|и́ться, ю́сь, ∼ишься *pf.* (*of* ⇒**∼иваться**) **1** to collapse, fall through; **потоло́к ∼и́лся** the ceiling has come down. **2** (*fig., coll.*) (*потерпеть неудачу*) to fail, fall through; (*на экзамене*) to fail. **3** (*coll.*) (*исчезнуть*) to disappear, vanish; **он как сквозь зе́млю ∼и́лся** he vanished into thin air.

провانса́л|ь, я *m.* mayonnaise, salad dressing.

прова́нск|ий *adj.*: **∼ое ма́сло** olive oil.

прова́рива|ть, ю *impf. of* ⇒**провари́ть**

провар|и́ть, ю́, ∼ишь *pf.* (*of* ⇒**∼ивать**) to boil thoroughly.

прове́д|ать, аю *pf.* (*of* ⇒**∼ывать**) (*coll.*) **1** (*навестить*) to come to see, call on. **2** (**о** + *p.*) (*узнать*) to find out (about), learn (of, about).

проведе́ни|е, я *nt.* **1** (*человека*) leading, taking; (*судна*) piloting. **2** (*дороги*) building; (*электричества*) installation. **3** (*операции*) carrying out, through; (*заседания*) conducting; **п. кампа́нии** (*mil., pol.*) conduct of a campaign; **п. в жизнь** putting into effect, implementation. **4** (*черты*) drawing.

прове́дыва|ть, ю *impf. of* ⇒**прове́дать**

провез|ти́, у́, ёшь, *past* **∼, ∼ла́** *pf.* (*of* ⇒**провози́ть**) **1** (*везя, доставить*) to convey, transport; **п. контраба́ндой** to smuggle. **2** (*перевезти с собой*) to bring (with one).

провентили́р|овать, ую *pf. of* ⇒**вентили́ровать**

прове́р|енный *p.p.p. of* ⇒**∼ить** *and adj.* proved, of proved worth.

прове́р|ить, ю, ишь *pf.* (*of* ⇒**∼я́ть**) **1** to check; to verify; **п. биле́ты** to

examine tickets; **п. ка́ссу** to check the till; **п. тетра́ди** to correct exercise-books.
2 (*на практике*) to test; **п. свой си́лы** to try one's strength.

прове́рк|а, и *f.* **1** checking; examination; verification; check-up. **2** (*на практике*) testing.

провер|ну́ть, ну́, нёшь *pf.* (*of* ⇒**~тывать**) (*coll.*) **1** (*доску; дыру*) to bore, drill. **2** (*мотор*) to crank. **3** (*fig.*) (*сделать быстро*) to rush through (*discussion of a question, etc.*).

прове́рочн|ый *adj.* checking, verifying; **~ая рабо́та** test paper.

провер|те́ть, чу́, ~тишь *pf.* (*of* ⇒**~тывать**) (*coll.*) to bore, drill.

провёртыва|ть, ю *impf. of* ⇒**проверну́ть** *and* **проверте́ть**

провер|я́ть, я́ю *impf. of* ⇒**~ить**

прове́с, а *m.* sag; dip (*of wire*).

прове|сти́, ду́, дёшь, *past* **~л, ~ла́** *pf.* (*of* ⇒**проводи́ть**[1])
1 (*человека*) to lead, take; (*машину*) to take; (*судно*) to pilot.
2 (*дорогу*) to build; (*электричество*) to install.
3 (*реформы, опыты*) to carry out; (*кампанию*) to carry on; (*урок, заседание*) to conduct, hold; **п. бесе́ду** to give a talk.
4 (*резолюцию, законопроект*) to carry through; to carry, pass, get through; (*решение*) to implement.
5 (*идею*) to advance, put forward.
6 (*book-keeping*) to register; **п. по кни́гам** to book; **п. по ка́ссе** to register, ring up on the till.
7 (*черту*) to draw; **п. грани́цу** to draw a boundary-line.
8 (+*i.*) (*рукой*) to pass over, run over; **она́ ~ла́ руко́й по лбу** she passed her hand over her forehead.
9 (*время*) to spend, pass; **что́бы п. вре́мя** to pass the time.
10 (*coll.*) (*обмануть*) to take in, trick, fool.

прове́трива|ть(ся), ю(сь) *impf. of* ⇒**прове́трить(ся)**

прове́тр|ить, ю, ишь *pf.* (*of* ⇒**~ивать**) to air; to ventilate.

прове́тр|иться, юсь, ишься *pf.* (*of* ⇒**~иваться**) **1** (*о комнате, об одежде*) to have an airing; (*fig., coll.*) (*о человеке*) to have a change of scene.
2 *pass. of* ⇒**~ить**

провиа́нт, а *m.* provisions.

прови́дени|е, я *nt.* foresight.

провиде́ни|е, я *nt.* (*relig.*) Providence.

прови́|деть, жу, дишь *impf.* to foresee.

прови́д|ец, ца *m.* (*obs., rhet.*) seer, prophet.

прови́д|ица, ицы *f. of* ⇒**~ец**

прови́зи|я, и *no pl., f.* provisions.

прови́зор, а *m.* pharmacist.

провизо́р|ный (~ен, ~на) *adj.* provisional; temporary.

провин|и́ться, ю́сь, и́шься *pf.* (**в** + *p.*) to be guilty (of); to commit an offence; **п. пе́ред кем-н.** to wrong s.o.; **в чём мы ~и́лись?** what have we done wrong?

прови́нност|ь, и *f.* (*coll.*) fault; offence.

провинциа́л, а *m.* provincial (*person*).

провинциали́зм, а *m.* provincialism.

провинциа́л|ка, ки *f. of* ⇒**~**

провинциа́льност|ь, и *f.* provinciality.

провинциа́л|ьный (~ен, ~ьна) *adj.* provincial (*also fig.*).

прови́нци|я, и *f.* **1** (*область*) province. **2** (*удалённая местность*) the provinces; **жить в глухо́й ~и** to live in the depths of the country.

провира́|ться, юсь *impf. of* ⇒**провра́ться**

провис|а́ть, а́ет *impf. of* ⇒**~нуть**

прови́с|нуть, нет *pf.* (*of* ⇒**~а́ть**) to sag.

про́вод, а, *pl.* **~а́** *m.* wire, lead; **заземля́ющий п.** earth(-wire); **п. под напряже́нием** live wire.

проводи́мост|ь, и *f.* (*elec.*) conductivity.

прово|ди́ть[1]**, жу́, ~дишь** *impf.*
1 *impf. of* ⇒**провести́. 2** *impf. only* (*phys., elec.*) to conduct.

прово|ди́ть[2]**, жу́, ~дишь** *pf.* (*of* ⇒**~жа́ть**) to accompany; to see off; **п. кого́-н. домо́й** to take, see s.o. home; **п. кого́-н. до двере́й** to see s.o. to the door; **п. глаза́ми** to follow with one's eyes.

прово́дк|а, и *f.* **1** (*судна*) piloting; (*машины*) taking. **2** (*дороги*) building; (*электричества*) installation. **3** (*collect.; elec.*) wiring, wires.

проводни́к[1]**, а́** *m.* **1** (*провожатый*) guide. **2** (*в поезде*) conductor; guard (*Br.*).

проводни́к[2]**, а́** *m.* **1** (*phys., elec.*) conductor. **2** (*fig.*) (*культуры, идей*) transmitter.

проводни́|ца, цы *f. of* ⇒**~к**[1]

про́вод|ы, ов *no sg.* seeing-off; send-off.

провожа́т|ый, ого *m.* guide, escort.

провожа́|ть, ю *impf. of* ⇒**проводи́ть**[2]

прово́з, а *m.* carriage, conveyance, transport; **пла́та за п.** payment for carriage.

провозве|сти́ть, щу́, сти́шь *pf.* (*of* ⇒**~ща́ть**) (*rhet.*) to proclaim.

провозве́стник, а *m.* (*rhet.*) proclaimer.

провозве́стни|ца, цы *f. of* ⇒**~к**

провозвеща́|ть, ю *impf. of* ⇒**провозвести́ть**

провозгла|си́ть, шу́, си́шь *pf.* (*of* ⇒**~ша́ть**) to proclaim; **п. тост** to propose a toast; **его́ ~си́ли королём** he was proclaimed king.

провозглаша́|ть, ю *impf. of* ⇒**провозгласи́ть**

провозглаше́ни|е, я *nt.* proclamation; declaration.

прово|зи́ть, жу́, ~зишь *impf. of* ⇒**провезти́**

прово|зи́ться[1]**, жу́сь, ~зишься** *pf.* **1** (*coll.*) (*играя*) to play about.
2 (**с** + *i.*) (*в хлопотах*) to spend (*a certain time*) (over, in seeing to); **я ~зи́лся це́лый ме́сяц с получе́нием ви́зы** I spent a whole month over obtaining the visa.

прово|зи́ться[2]**, жу́сь, ~зишься** *impf. pass., of* ⇒**~зи́ть**

провока́тор, а *m.* **1** agent provocateur. **2** (*fig.*) instigator, provoker.

провокацио́нный *adj.* provocative.

провока́ци|я, и *f.* provocation.

про́волок|а, и *f.* wire; **колю́чая п.** barbed wire.

про́волочк|а, и *f. dim. of* ⇒**про́волока;** short wire, fine wire.

проволо́чк|а, и *f.* (*coll.*) delay.

про́воло|чный *adj. of* ⇒**~ка; ~чная сеть** wire netting.

провоня́|ть, ет *pf.* (+*i.*; *coll.*) to stink (of).

прово́рност|ь, и *f.* = **прово́рство**

прово́р|ный (~ен, ~на) *adj.*
1 (*быстрый*) quick, swift, expeditious.
2 (*ловкий*) agile, nimble, adroit, dexterous.

провор|ова́ться, у́юсь *pf.* (*coll.*) to be caught stealing, embezzling.

проворо́н|ить, ю, ишь *pf.* (*coll.*) to miss, let slip, lose; **п. свою́ о́чередь** to miss one's turn.

прово́рств|о, а *nt.* **1** (*быстрота*) quickness, swiftness. **2** (*ловкость*) agility, nimbleness, adroitness, dexterity.

проворч|а́ть, у́, и́шь *pf.* to mutter.

провоци́р|овать, ую *impf. and pf.* (*pf. also* **с~**) to provoke.

провр|а́ться, у́сь, ёшься, *past* **~а́лся, ~ала́сь, ~а́ло́сь** *pf.* (*of* ⇒**провира́ться**) (*coll.*) to give o.s. away; to slip up (*in lying*).

провя́л|ить, ю, ишь *pf. of* ⇒**вя́лить**

прогад|а́ть, а́ю *pf.* (*of* ⇒**~ывать**) (*coll.*) to miscalculate.

прога́дыва|ть, ю *impf. of* ⇒**прогада́ть**

прога́лин|а, ы *f.* glade.

проги́б, а *m.* (*tech.*) (*действие*) sagging; (*место*) sag.

прогиба́|ть(ся), ю(сь) *impf. of* ⇒**прогну́ть(ся)**

прогла́|дить[1]**, жу, дишь** *pf.* (*of* ⇒**~живать**) to iron (out).

прогла́|дить[2]**, жу, дишь** *pf.* (*некоторое время*) to iron.

прогла́жива|ть, ю *impf. of* ⇒**прогла́дить**[1]

прогла́тыва|ть, ю *impf. of* ⇒**проглоти́ть; говори́ть, ~я слова́** to swallow one's words.

прогло|ти́ть, чу́, ~тишь *pf.* (*of* ⇒**прогла́тывать**) to swallow (*also fig.*); **п. язы́к** to lose one's tongue; **п. кни́гу** to devour a book; **язы́к ~тишь** it makes your mouth water.

прогля|де́ть, жу́, ди́шь *pf.* (*of* ⇒**~дывать**) **1** (*просмотреть*) to look through, skim through; **п. глаза́** (*coll.*) to wear one's eyes out. **2** *pf. only* (*не заметить*) to overlook.

прогля́дыва|ть, ю *impf. of* ⇨**прогляде́ть** *and* **прогляну́ть**

прогля|ну́ть, ~́нет *pf.* (*of* ⇨**~́дывать**) to peep (out, through); to be perceptible; **со́лнце ~ну́ло из-за облако́в** the sun peeped out from behind the clouds; **в её взгля́де ~ну́ла тоска́** there was a touch of wistfulness in her look.

про|гна́ть, гоню́, го́нишь, *past* **~гна́л, ~гнала́, ~гна́ло** *pf.* (*of* ⇨**~гоня́ть**) **1** (*заставить уйти*) to drive away (*also fig.*); (*fig.*) to banish; **п. с глаз доло́й** to banish from one's sight; **п. забо́ты** to banish care. **2** (*заставить идти*) to drive (through); **п. коро́в в по́ле** to drive the cows into the field. **3** (*coll.*) (*с работы*) to sack, fire.

прогне́ва|ть, ю *pf.* (*obs.*) to anger.

прогне́ва|ться, юсь *pf.* (*obs.*) (**на** + *a.*) to become angry (with).

прогнев|и́ть, лю́, и́шь *pf. of* ⇨**гневи́ть**

прогнива́|ть, ю *impf. of* ⇨**прогни́ть**

прогн|и́ть, ию́, иёшь, *past* **~и́л, ~ила́, ~и́ло** *pf.* (*of* ⇨**~ива́ть**) to rot through.

прогно́з, а *m.* prognosis; forecast; **п. пого́ды** weather forecast.

прогн|у́ть, у́, ёшь *pf.* (*of* ⇨**прогиба́ть**) to weigh down, cause to sag.

прогн|у́ться, у́сь, ёшься *pf.* (*of* ⇨**прогиба́ться**) to cave in, sag.

прогова́рива|ть(ся), ю(сь) *impf. of* ⇨**проговори́ть(ся)**

проговор|и́ть, ю́, и́шь *pf.* (*of* ⇨**прогова́ривать**) **1** (*сказать*) to say, utter; **п. сквозь зу́бы** to mutter; **он ни сло́ва не ~и́л** he did not utter a word. **2** (*некоторое время*) to speak, talk.

проговор|и́ться, ю́сь, и́шься *pf.* (*of* ⇨**прогова́риваться**) to shoot one's mouth off, let the cat out of the bag.

проголода́|ть, ю *pf.* to starve, go hungry.

проголода́|ться, юсь *pf.* to get hungry, grow hungry.

проголос|ова́ть, у́ю *pf. of* ⇨**голосова́ть**

прого́н¹, а *m.* **1** (*archit.*) (*опорная балка*) purlin; (*моста*) bearer, baulk. **2** (*archit.*) (*лестничная клетка*) stairwell.

прого́н², а *m.* (*дорога*) cattle track.

прого́н³, а *m.* (*theatr. sl.*) run-through (= *first full rehearsal of play in order of scenes*).

прого́н|ный *adj. of* ⇨**~ы; ~ные (де́ньги)** (*obs.*) travel allowance.

прого́н|ы, ов *no sg.* (*obs.*) fare (*for journey by post-chaise*).

прогоня́|ть, ю *impf. of* ⇨**прогна́ть**

прогор|а́ть, а́ю *impf. of* ⇨**~е́ть¹**

прогор|е́ть¹, ю́, и́шь *pf.* (*of* ⇨**~а́ть**) **1** (*сгореть совсем*) to burn through; to burn to a cinder. **2** (*coll.*) (*разориться*) to go bankrupt, go bust.

прогор|е́ть², и́т *pf.* (*некоторое время*) to burn.

прого́рклый *adj.* rancid.

прого́рк|нуть, нет *past* **~, ~ла** *pf. of* ⇨**го́ркнуть**

прого|сти́ть, щу́, сти́шь *pf.* to stay.

програ́мм|а, ы *f.* programme (*Br.*), program (*US*); (*comput.*) program, application; **учёбная п.** syllabus; curriculum.

программи́р|овать, ую *impf.* (*of* ⇨**за~**) to programme (*Br.*), program (*US*); (*comput.*) to program.

программи́ст, а *m.* (computer) programmer.

программи́ст|ка, ки *f. of* ⇨**~**

програ́мм|ный *adj.* **1** *adj. of* ⇨**~а; ~ное обеспе́чение** (*comput.*) software. **2** (*tech.*) programmed (*Br.*), programed (*US*); automatically operated.

прогрева́|ть(ся), ю(сь) *impf. of* ⇨**прогре́ть(ся)**

прогрем|е́ть, лю́, и́шь *pf. of* ⇨**греме́ть**

прогре́сс, а *m.* progress.

прогресси́в|ный (~ен, ~на) *adj.* progressive.

прогресси́р|овать, ую *impf.* to progress, make progress; (*о болезни*) to grow progressively worse.

прогре́сси|я, и *f.* (*math.*) progression.

прогре́|ть, ю *pf.* (*of* ⇨**~ва́ть**) to heat, warm up.

прогре́|ться, юсь *pf.* (*of* ⇨**~ва́ться**) to warm up.

прогу́л, а *m.* (*на работе*) absence; (*в школе*) truancy.

прогу́лива|ть, ю *impf.* **1** *impf. of* ⇨**прогуля́ть. 2** *impf. only* to walk; **п. ло́шадь** to walk a horse.

прогу́лива|ться, юсь *impf.* **1** *impf. of* ⇨**прогуля́ться. 2** *impf. only* to stroll, saunter.

прогу́лк|а, и *f.* **1** (*хождение*) walk; stroll. **2** (*поездка*) outing; (*в автомобиле*) drive; (*верхом*) ride.

прогу́л|очный *adj. of* ⇨**~ка; ~очная зо́на** pedestrian precinct; **~очная ло́дка** pleasure-boat.

прогу́л|ьный *adj. of* ⇨**~; ~ьное вре́мя** time off work (*without good cause*).

прогу́льщик, а *m.* (*на работе*) absentee; (*в школе*) truant.

прогу́льщи|ца, цы *f. of* ⇨**~к**

прогуля́|ть, ю *pf.* (*of* ⇨**прогу́ливать**) **1** (*на работе*) to be absent from work; (*школу*) to play truant. **2** (*пропустить*) to miss; **п. обе́д** to miss one's dinner; **п. уро́ки** to bunk off school (*Br.*), play hookey (*US*). **3** *pf. only* (*некоторое время*) to walk; to stroll.

прогуля́|ться, юсь *pf.* (*of* ⇨**прогу́ливаться**) to take a walk, stroll.

прод... *comb. form, abbr. of* ***продово́льственный***

прода|ва́ть, ю́, ёшь *impf. of* ⇨**~́ть**

прода|ва́ться, ю́сь, ёшься *impf.* **1** (*impf. only*) to be on sale, be for sale; **дом ~ётся** the house is for sale; **~ётся мотоци́кл** (*formula of advertisement of sale*) 'motor-cycle for sale'. **2** (*impf. only*) to sell; **дёшево п.** to sell cheap, go cheap; **его́ но́вый рома́н хорошо́ ~ётся** his new novel is selling well. **3** *impf. of* ⇨**~́ться**

продав|е́ц, ца́ *m.* **1** seller; vendor. **2** (*в магазине*) salesman, shop-assistant.

продав|и́ть, лю́, ~́ишь *pf.* (*of* ⇨**~́ливать**) to break (through); to crush.

прода́влива|ть, ю *impf. of* ⇨**продави́ть**

продавщи́ц|а, ы *f.* **1** seller; vendor. **2** saleswoman, shop-assistant.

прода́ж|а, и *f.* sale; **опто́вая п.** wholesale; **п. в ро́зницу** retail; **пусти́ть в ~у** to put on sale; **поступи́ть в ~у** to go/be on sale; **нет в ~е** out of stock; sold out; **п. по телефо́ну** telesales.

прода́жност|ь, и *f.* corruptness, corruption.

прода́ж|ный *adj.* **1** sale; selling; **~ная цена́** selling price. **2** **(~ен, ~на)** (*fig.*) corrupt; **~ная же́нщина** prostitute.

прода́лблива|ть, ю *impf. of* ⇨**продолби́ть**

прода́|ть, м, шь, ст, ди́м, ди́те, ду́т, *past* **про́дал, ~ла́, про́дало** *pf.* (*of* ⇨**~ва́ть**) **1** to sell; **п. о́птом** to sell wholesale; **п. в ро́зницу** to sell retail; **п. с торго́в** to auction; **п. в креди́т** to sell on credit. **2** (*fig., pej.*) to sell, sell out.

прода́|ться, мся, шься, стся, ди́мся, ди́тесь, ду́тся, *past* **~лся, ~ла́сь** *pf.* (*of* ⇨**~ва́ться**) to sell o.s.

продвига́|ть(ся), ю(сь) *impf. of* ⇨**продви́нуть(ся)**

продвиже́ни|е, я *nt.* **1** advancement. **2** (*mil.*; *fig.*) progress, advance.

продви́нут|ый (~, ~а) *adj.* advanced.

продви́|нуть, ну, нешь *pf.* (*of* ⇨**~га́ть**) **1** to move forward, push forward. **2** (*fig.*) to promote, advance; **п. по слу́жбе** to promote; **п. де́ло** to expedite a matter.

продви́|нуться, нусь, нешься *pf.* (*of* ⇨**~га́ться**) **1** to advance (*also fig.*); to move on, move forward; to push on; **п. вперёд** (*mil. and fig.*) to gain ground, make headway, make an advance. **2** (*по службе*) to be promoted.

продева́|ть, ю *impf. of* ⇨**проде́ть**

продежу́р|ить, ю, ишь *pf.* to be on duty (*for a certain time*).

продеклами́р|овать, ую *pf. of* ⇨**деклами́ровать**

проде́л|ать, аю *pf.* (*of* ⇨**~ывать**) **1** (*отверстие, проход*) to make. **2** (*работу, упражнения*) to do, perform, accomplish.

проде́лк|а, и *f.* trick; prank.

проде́лыва|ть, ю *impf. of* ⇨**проде́лать**

продемонстри́р|овать, ую *pf. of* ⇨**демонстри́ровать**

продёргива|ть, ю *impf. of* ⇨**продёрнуть**

продерж|а́ть, у́, ~́ишь *pf.* (*чемодан*) to hold (*for a certain time*); (*человека*) to keep (*for a certain time*); **его́ ~а́ли два**

ме́сяца в больни́це he was kept in hospital for two months.

продерж|а́ться, у́сь, ~́ишься *pf.* to hold out.

продёр|нуть, ну, нешь *pf.* (*of* ⇒**~гивать**) (*coll.*) **1** to pass, run; **п. ни́тку в иго́лку** to thread a needle. **2** (*fig.*) (*покритиковать*) to tear to shreds.

проде́|ть, ну, нешь *pf.* (*of* ⇒**~ва́ть**) to pass, run; **п. ни́тку в иго́лку** to thread a needle.

продефили́р|овать, ую *pf. of* ⇒**дефили́ровать**

продешев|и́ть, лю́, и́шь *pf.* (*coll.*) to sell too cheap.

продикт|ова́ть, у́ю *pf. of* ⇒**диктова́ть**

продира́|ть(ся), ю(сь) *impf. of* ⇒**продра́ть(ся)**

продлева́|ть, ю *impf. of* ⇒**продли́ть**

продле́ни|е, я *nt.* extension, prolongation.

продл|ённый *p.p.p. of* ⇒**~и́ть; шко́ла с ~ённым днём** extended-day school.

продл|и́ть, ю́, и́шь *pf.* (*of* ⇒**~ева́ть**) to extend, prolong; **п. срок де́йствия ви́зы** to extend a visa.

продл|и́ться, и́тся *pf. of* ⇒**дли́ться**

продма́г, а *m.* (*abbr. of* ***продово́льственный магази́н***) grocery (store).

продово́льств|енный *adj. of* ⇒**~ие; п. магази́н** grocery (store); **~енные райо́ны** food-producing areas; **п. склад** food store; (*mil.*) ration store, ration dump; **~енная ка́рточка** ration book, ration card; **~енные това́ры** food-stuffs.

продово́льстви|е, я *nt.* food-stuffs, provisions; (*mil.*) rations; **но́рма ~я** ration scale.

продолб|и́ть, лю́, и́шь *pf.* (*of* ⇒**прода́лбливать**) to make a hole (in), chisel through.

продолгова́т|ый (~, ~а) *adj.* oblong; **п. мозг** (*anat.*) medulla oblongata.

продолжа́тел|ь, я *m.* continuer, successor.

продолжа́тель|ница, ницы *f. of* ⇒**~**

продолж|а́ть, а́ю *impf.* **1** to continue, go on; **п. свою́ рабо́ту** to continue, go on with one's work; **п. рабо́тать** to continue to work, go on working. **2** *impf. of* ⇒**~́ить**

продолж|а́ться, а́ется *impf.* (*of* ⇒**~́иться**) to continue, last, go on; **восста́ние ~а́ется уже́ второ́й год** the insurrection is now in its second year.

продолже́ни|е, я *nt.* **1** continuation; **забо́р слу́жит ~ем стены́** the fence serves as a continuation of the wall. **2** (*рассказа*) continuation; sequel; **п. сле́дует** to be continued. **3**: **в п.** (*+g.*) in the course (of), during, for, throughout; **в п. почти́ двух лет я ни ра́зу её не вида́л** for almost two years I did not see her once.

продолжи́тельност|ь, и *f.* duration, length.

продолжи́тел|ьный (~ен, ~ьна) *adj.* long; prolonged, protracted.

продо́лж|ить, у, ишь *pf.* (*of* ⇒**~а́ть**) to extend, prolong.

продо́лж|иться, ится *pf. of* ⇒**~а́ться**

продо́льн|ый *adj.* longitudinal; (*naut.*) fore-and-aft; **~ая ось** longitudinal axis; **~ая пила́** rip-saw.

продохн|у́ть, у́, ёшь *pf.* (*coll.*) to breathe freely.

продразвёрстк|а, и *f.* (*hist.*) requisitioning of farm produce.

про|дра́ть, деру́, дерёшь, *past* **~дра́л, ~драла́, ~дра́ло** *pf.* (*of* ⇒**~дира́ть**) (*coll.*) to tear; to wear holes (in); **п. глаза́** to open one's eyes.

про|дра́ться, деру́сь, дерёшься, *past* **~дра́лся, ~драла́сь, ~дра́ло́сь** *pf.* (*of* ⇒**~дира́ться**) (*coll.*) **1** (*разорваться*) to tear; to wear into holes; **у меня́ ло́кти ~дра́лись** my coat is out at the elbows. **2** (*протиснуться*) to squeeze through, force one's way through.

продрем|а́ть, лю́, ~́лешь *pf.* to doze (*for a certain time*).

продро́г|нуть, ну, нешь, *past* **~, ~ла** *pf.* to be chilled to the marrow.

продува́|ть, ю *impf.* **1** *impf. of* ⇒**проду́ть. 2** (*impf. only*) to blow (*from all sides*); **прия́тно ~л ветеро́к** there was a pleasant breeze.

продува́|ться, юсь *impf. of* ⇒**проду́ться**

продувн|о́й *adj.* (*coll.*) crafty, sly.

проду́кт, а *m.* **1** product; **побо́чный п.** by-product. **2** *pl.* produce; provisions, food-stuffs; **моло́чные ~ы** dairy produce; **натура́льные ~ы** wholefoods.

продукти́вно *adv.* productively; with a good result, to good effect.

продукти́вност|ь, и *f.* productivity.

продукти́в|ный (~ен, ~на) *adj.* productive; (*fig.*) fruitful.

продукто́вый *adj.* food; **п. магази́н** grocery (store).

проду́кци|я, и *f.* production, output.

продума́|нный *p.p.p. of* ⇒**~ть** *and adj.* well thought-out, considered.

проду́м|ать, аю *pf.* (*of* ⇒**~ывать**) (*вопрос*) to think over; (*план*) to think out.

проду́мыва|ть, ю *impf. of* ⇒**проду́мать**

проду́|ть, ю, ешь *pf.* (*of* ⇒**~ва́ть**) **1** to blow through; to clean by blowing. **2** (*impers.+a.*) to be in a draught (*Br.*), draft (*US*); **придви́ньте стул, а то вас ~ет** bring your chair up, or else you will be in a draught. **3** (*coll.*) (*проиграть*) to lose (*at games*).

проду́|ться, юсь, ешься *pf.* (*of* ⇒**~ва́ться**) (*coll.*) to lose (*at games*).

проду́шин|а, ы *f.* air-hole, vent.

продыря́в|ить, лю, ишь *pf.* (*of* ⇒**~ливать**) to make a hole (in), pierce.

продыря́в|иться, ится *pf.* (*of* ⇒**~ливаться**) to become full of holes.

продыря́влива|ть(ся), ю, ет(ся) *impf. of* ⇒**продыря́вить(ся)**

продю́сер, а *m.* producer.

проеда́|ть(ся), ю(сь) *impf. of* ⇒**прое́сть(ся)**

прое́зд, а *m.* **1** (*место*) passage, thoroughfare; **«~а нет!»** 'no thoroughfare!' **2** (*в транспорте*) trip, journey.

прое́з|дить, жу, дишь *pf.* (*of* ⇒**~жа́ть**) **1** (*лошадь*) to exercise. **2** (*coll.*) (*истратить*) to spend on a journey; **мы ~дили сто рубле́й** we got through a hundred roubles on the journey. **3** *pf. only* to spend (*a certain time*) driving, riding, travelling (*Br.*), traveling (*US*); **они́ ~дили тро́е су́ток** they had travelled for three days and nights.

прое́з|диться, жусь, дишься *pf.* (*coll.*) to have spent all one's money on a journey.

проездн|о́й *adj.* travelling (*Br.*), traveling (*US*); **п. биле́т** ticket; **~а́я пла́та** fare.

прое́здом *adv.* en route, while passing through.

проезжа́|ть, ю *impf. of* ⇒**прое́здить** *and* **прое́хать**

прое́зж|ий *adj.*: **~ая доро́га** thoroughfare, public road; **~ие лю́ди** passers-by; *as n.* **п., ~его** *m.* passer-by.

прое́кт, а *m.* **1** (*здания*) design. **2** (*предварительный текст*) draft; **п. догово́ра** draft treaty. **3** (*замысел*) plan, project.

проекти́ровани|е, я *nt.* designing; **автоматизи́рованное п.** CAD, computer-aided design.

проекти́р|овать[1], ую *impf.* **1** (*pf.* **с~**) to design; **п. теа́тр** to design a theatre (*Br.*), theater (*US*). **2** (*pf.* **за~**) (*fig.*) to plan; **мы ~уем уе́хать весно́й** we plan to go away in the spring.

проекти́р|овать[2], ую *impf.* (*math.*) to project.

проектиро́вк|а, и *f.* = **проекти́рование**

проектиро́вщик, а *m.* designer.

проектиро́вщи|ца, цы *f. of* ⇒**~к**

прое́ктн|ый *adj.* **1** planning, designing; **~ое бюро́** planning office. **2** (*предусмотренный*) planned; **~ая мо́щность** (*tech.*) rated capacity.

прое́ктор, а *m.* projector.

проекцио́нный *adj.*: **п. фона́рь** projector.

прое́кци|я, и *f.* **1** (*math.*) projection. **2** (*на экран*) projection.

проём, а *m.* (*archit.*) aperture; embrasure; **дверно́й п.** doorway.

прое́|сть, м, шь, ст, ди́м, ди́те, дя́т, *past* **~л** *pf.* (*of* ⇒**~да́ть**) **1** to eat through. **2** (*coll.*) (*деньги*) to spend on food.

прое́|сться, мся, шься, стся, ди́мся, ди́тесь, дя́тся *past* **~лся** *pf.* (*of* ⇒**~да́ться**) (*coll.*) to spend all one's money on food.

прое́|хать, ду, дешь *pf.* (*of* ⇒**~зжа́ть**) **1** (*на транспорте*) to pass (by, through); to drive (by, through), ride (by, through). **2** (*по ошибке*) to pass, go past. **3** (*расстояние*) to go, do, make, cover.

проé|хаться, дусь, дешься *pf.* (*coll.*) to go for a drive, ride.

проеци́р|овать, ую *impf. and pf.* (*изображение*) to project.

прожáр|енный *p.p.p. of* ⇒**~ить** *and adj.* (*cul.*) well-done.

прожáрива|ть(ся), ю(сь) *impf. of* ⇒**прожáрить(ся)**

прожáр|ить, ю, ишь *pf.* (*of* ⇒**~ивать**) to fry, roast thoroughly.

прожáр|иться, юсь, ишься *pf.* (*of* ⇒**~иваться**) **1** to fry, roast thoroughly. **2** (*coll.*) to roast (*in the sun*).

прожд|áть, ý, ёшь, *past* **~áл, ~алá, ~áло** *pf.* (+*a. or g*) to wait (for), spend (*a certain time*) waiting (for).

прож|евáть, ýю, уёшь *pf.* (*of* ⇒**~ёвывать**) to chew well.

прожёвыва|ть, ю *impf. of* ⇒**прожевáть**

прожéкт, а *m.* **1** (*obs.*) = **проéкт. 2** (*iron.*) (hare-brained) scheme.

прожектёр, а *m.* (*iron.*) schemer.

прожектёрств|о, а *nt.* (*iron.*) (hare-brained) scheming.

прожéктор, а, *pl.* **~ы** *and* **~á** *m.* searchlight, floodlight.

прожéктор|ный *adj. of* ⇒**~**

про|жéчь, жгý, жжёшь, жгýт, *past* **~жёг, ~жглá** *pf.* (*of* ⇒**~жигáть**) **1** (*огнём, кислотой*) to burn a hole in. **2** (*лампу*) to burn, leave alight (*for a certain time*).

про|жжённый *p.p.p. of* ⇒**~жéчь** *and adj.* (*coll.*) out-and-out.

проживáни|е, я *nt.* residence, stay.

проживá|ть, ю *impf.* **1** (*иметь жилище*) to live, reside. **2** *impf. of* ⇒**прожи́ть**

проживá|ться, юсь *impf. of* ⇒**прожи́ться**

прожигáтел|ь, я *m.*: **п. жи́зни** fast liver.

прожигáтель|ница, ницы *f. of* ⇒**~**

прожигá|ть¹, ю *impf. of* ⇒**прожéчь**

прожигá|ть², ю *impf.*: **п. жизнь** to lead a fast life.

прожи́лк|а, и *f.* vein.

прожи́ти|е, я *nt.*: **на п.** to live on; **хватáет ли у них дéнег на п.?** have they enough to live on?

прожи́точный *adj.* sufficient to live on; **п. ми́нимум** living wage, subsistence wage.

про|жи́ть, живý, живёшь, *past* **~́жил, ~жилá, ~́жило** *pf.* (*of* ⇒**~живáть**) **1** (*пробыть живым*) to live; **он ~́жил сто лет** he lived to be a hundred (*years of age*). **2** (*провести*) to spend; **мы ~́жили мéсяц áвгуст на берегý мóря** we spent the month of August at the seaside. **3** (*истратить*) to spend, run through (*money*).

про|жи́ться, живýсь, живёшься, *past* **~жи́лся, ~жилáсь** *pf.* (*of* ⇒**~живáться**) (*coll.*) to have spent all one's money.

прожóрливост|ь, и *f.* voracity, gluttony.

прожóрлив|ый (~, ~а) *adj.* voracious, gluttonous.

прожужж|áть, ý, и́шь *pf.* to buzz, drone, hum; **п. ýши комý-н.** (*coll.*) to drone on at s.o.

прóз|а, ы *f.* prose; **п. жи́зни** the prosaic side of life.

прозаи́зм, а *m.* prosaic expression (*in poetry*).

прозáик, а *m.* prose-writer, prosaist.

прозаи́ческий *adj.* **1** (*произведение*) prose. **2** (*вкус, жизнь*) prosaic; matter-of-fact.

прозаи́чност|ь, и *f.* prosaicness.

прозаи́ч|ный (~ен, ~на) *adj.* prosaic; humdrum.

прозаклáдыва|ть, ю *impf. and pf.* (*coll.*) to stake, wager.

прозвáни|е, я *nt.* nickname; **по ~ю** nicknamed.

про|звáть, зовý, зовёшь, *past* **~звáл, ~звалá, ~звáло** *pf.* (*of* ⇒**~зывáть**) to nickname.

прóзвищ|е, я *nt.* nickname.

прозвон|и́ть, ю́, и́шь *pf.* **1** (*издать звон*) to ring out, peal. **2** (*объявить звоном*) to announce by ringing; **~и́ли обéд** the bell (gong, *etc.*) went for dinner.

прозвуч|áть, и́т *pf. of* ⇒**звучáть**

прозевá|ть, ю *pf. of* ⇒**зевáть** 3; (*coll.*) to miss.

прозéктор, а *m.* prosector, dissector.

прозели́т, а *m.* proselyte.

прозели́т|ка, ки *f. of* ⇒**~**

прозим|овáть, ýю *pf. of* ⇒**зимовáть**

прознá|ть, ю *pf.* (+*a. or* **о**+*p.*; *coll.*) to find out (about).

прозодéжд|а, ы *f.* (*abbr. of* ***произвóдственная одéжда***) working clothes; overalls.

прозонди́р|овать, ую *pf. of* ⇒**зонди́ровать**

прозорли́вост|ь, и *f.* sagacity, perspicacity, intuition.

прозорли́в|ый (~, ~а) *adj.* sagacious, perspicacious.

прозрáчност|ь, и *f.* transparency.

прозрáч|ный (~ен, ~на) *adj.* transparent (*also fig.*); (*вода, воздух*) clear, pellucid; **п. намёк** transparent hint.

прозревá|ть, ю *impf. of* ⇒**прозрéть**

прозрéни|е, я *nt.* **1** recovery of sight. **2** (*fig.*) insight.

прозр|éть, ю́, и́шь *pf.* (*of* ⇒**~евáть**) **1** to recover one's sight. **2** (*fig.*) to see the light.

прозывá|ть, ю *impf. of* ⇒**прозвáть**

прозывá|ться, юсь *impf.* to be nicknamed.

прозябáни|е, я *nt.* vegetative, miserable existence.

прозябá|ть, ю *impf.* (*о человеке*) to vegetate; to drag out a miserable existence.

прозя́б|нуть, ну, нешь, *past* **~, ~ла** *pf.* (*coll.*) to be chilled.

проигнори́р|овать, ую *pf.* to ignore.

проигр|áть, áю *pf.* (*of* ⇒**~́ывать**) **1** (*потерпеть неудачу*) to lose; **п. судéбный процéсс** to lose a case; **мы ничегó не ~áли, приéхав автóбусом** we lost nothing in coming by bus. **2** (*сыграть*) to play (through, over); **п. концéрт** to play through a concerto. **3** *pf. only* (*некоторое время*) to play.

проигр|áться, áюсь *pf.* (*of* ⇒**~́ываться**) to lose all one's money (*at gambling*).

прои́грывател|ь, я *m.* record-player; **п. для компáкт-ди́сков** CD player.

прои́грыва|ть(ся), ю(сь) *impf. of* ⇒**проигрáть(ся)**

прóигрыш, а *m.* loss; **остáться в ~е** to be the loser, come off loser.

произведéни|е, я *nt.* **1** (*искусства, литературы*) work; **и́збранные ~я Л. Н. Толстóго** selected works of L. N. Tolstoy. **2** (*math.*) product.

произве|сти́, дý, дёшь, *past* **~́л, ~лá** *pf.* (*of* ⇒**производи́ть**) **1** (*сделать*) to make; (*ремонт, опыты*) to carry out; **п. вы́стрел** to fire a shot; **п. смотр** (+*d.*) to review. **2** (*родить*) to give birth (to); **п. на свет** to bring into the world. **3** (*вызвать*) to cause, produce; **п. впечатлéние** (**на**+*a.*) to create an impression (on, upon); **п. сенсáцию** to cause a sensation. **4** (**в**+*nom.-a.*) to promote (to, to the rank of); **егó ~ли́ в подполкóвники** he has been promoted (to the rank of) lieutenant-colonel.

производи́тел|ь, я *m.* **1** producer; **мéлкие ~и** small producers. **2** (*самец*) sire; **жеребéц-п.** stud-horse; **бы́к-п.** breeding bull. **3**: **п. рабóт** clerk of the works (*Br.*), construction superintendent (*US*).

производи́тельност|ь, и *f.* productivity.

производи́тел|ьный (~ен, ~ьна) *adj.* productive.

произво|ди́ть, жý, ~́дишь *impf.* **1** *impf. of* ⇒**произвести́. 2** *impf. only* (*изготовлять*) to produce.

произвóдн|ый *adj.* derivative, derived; **~ое слóво** derivative; *as n.* **~ая, ~ой** *f.* (*math.*) derivative.

произвóдственник, а *m.* production worker.

произвóдственни|ца, цы *f. of* ⇒**~к**

произвóдств|енный *adj. of* ⇒**~о**; production; industrial.

произвóдств|о, а *nt.* **1** (*товаров*) production, manufacture; **срéдства ~а** means of production; **япóнского ~а** Japanese-made. **2** (*завод*) factory, works. **3** (*ремонта, опыта*) carrying-out. **4** (**в**+*nom.-a.*) promotion (to, to the rank of).

производ|я́щий *pres. part. act. of* ⇒**~и́ть** *and adj.* (*econ.*) producing, producer.

произвóл, а *m.* **1** (*необоснованность*) arbitrariness. **2** (*своеволие*) arbitrary rule.

произво́льно *adv.* **1** (*необоснованно*) arbitrarily. **2** (*по желанию*) at will.

произво́льност|ь, и *f.* arbitrariness.

произво́л|ьный (~ен, ~ьна) *adj.* arbitrary.

произнесе́ни|е, я *nt.* pronouncing; utterance, delivery.

произнес|ти́, у́, ёшь, *past* **~̈, ~ла́** *pf.* (*of* ⇒**произноси́ть**) **1** (*выговорить*) to pronounce; to articulate. **2** (*сказать*) to pronounce, say, utter; **п. пригово́р** to pronounce sentence; **п. речь** to deliver a speech; **он не ~̈ ни сло́ва** he did not utter a word.

произноси́тельный *adj.* pronunciation.

произно|си́ть, шу́, ~́сишь *impf. of* ⇒**произнести́**

произноше́ни|е, я *nt.* pronunciation.

произо|йти́, йду́, йдёшь, *past* **~шёл, ~шла́** *pf.* (*of* ⇒**происходи́ть**) **1** (*случиться*) to happen, occur, take place. **2** (**от, из-за** + *g.*) (*по причине*) to arise (from), result (from); **ава́рия ~шла́ от небре́жности** the crash resulted from carelessness. **3** (**из, от** + *g.*) (*родиться*) to come (from, of), be descended (from).

произраста́ни|е, я *nt.* growth.

произраст|а́ть, а́ет *impf. of* ⇒**~и́**

произраст|и́, ёт, *past* **произро́с, произросла́** *pf.* (*of* ⇒**~а́ть**) to grow, spring up.

проиллюстри́р|овать, ую *pf.* (*of* ⇒**иллюстри́ровать**) to illustrate.

проинструкти́р|овать, ую *pf.* (*of* ⇒**инструкти́ровать**) to instruct, give instructions (to).

проинтервьюи́р|овать, ую *pf.* (*of* ⇒**интервьюи́ровать**) to interview.

проинформи́р|овать, ую *pf.* (*of* ⇒**информи́ровать**) to inform.

прои|ска́ть, щу́, ~́щешь *pf.* to look (for), spend (*a certain time*) in search (of).

про́иск|и, ов *no sg.* intrigues; machinations.

проистека́|ть, ю *impf. of* ⇒**происте́чь**

происте́|чь, ку́, чёшь, ку́т, *past* **~̈к, ~кла́** *pf.* (*of* ⇒**~ка́ть**) (**из, от** + *g.*) to spring (from), result (from).

происхо|ди́ть, жу́, ~́дишь *impf.* **1** *impf. of* ⇒**произойти́. 2** *impf. only* to go on, be going on; **что тут ~́дит?** what is going on here?

происхожде́ни|е, я *nt.* origin; (*по рождению*) birth; **п. ви́дов** (*biol.*) origin of species; **он по ~ю армяни́н** he is (an) Armenian by birth.

происше́стви|е, я *nt.* event, incident, happening, occurrence; (*авария*) accident.

пройдо́х|а, и *c.g.* (*coll.*) scoundrel, rascal.

про́йм|а, ы *f.* armhole.

про|йти́, йду́, йдёшь, *past* **~шёл, ~шла́** *pf.* (*of* ⇒**~ходи́ть**[1]) **1** (*передвинуться*) to pass (by, through); to go (by, through); **п. ми́мо** to pass by, go by, go past; (+*g.*; *fig.*) to overlook, disregard; **п. торже́ственным ма́ршем** to march past; **п. по мосту́** to cross a bridge; **п. в жизнь** to be put into effect. **2** (*по ошибке*) to pass, go past. **3** (*расстояние*) to go, do, cover; **п. две ты́сячи миль за неде́лю** to do two thousand miles in a week. **4** (*о новостях, слухах*) to travel, spread. **5** (*о дожде, снеге*) to fall. **6** (*о времени*) to pass, elapse, go, go by; **~шёл це́лый год** a whole year had passed. **7** (*миновать*) to be over; (*прекратиться*) to pass (off), stop, let up; **~шло́ ле́то** summer was over; **боль ~шла́** the pain passed (off); **дождь ~шёл** the rain stopped. **8** (+*a.* *or* **че́рез** + *a.*) to pass, go through, get through; **пье́са не ~шла́ че́рез цензу́ру** the play did not pass the censorship. **9** (*завершиться*) to go, go off; **как ~шёл ваш докла́д?** how did your lecture go?; **заседа́ние ~шло́ уда́чно** the meeting went off successfully. **10** (**в** + *nom.-a.*) (*оказаться в числе принятых*) to become, be made; to be taken (on); **она́ ~шла́ в штат** she has been taken on the staff. **11** (*coll.*) (*курсы*) to do, take; **п. хи́мию** to do chemistry; **мы уже́ ~шли́ вое́нную слу́жбу** we have already done military service; **п. ку́рс лече́ния** to take a course of treatment.

про|йти́сь, йду́сь, йдёшься, *past* **~шёлся, ~шла́сь** *pf.* (*of* ⇒**~ха́живаться**) **1** to walk, stroll; (*прогуляться*) to take a stroll; **п. по ко́мнате** to pace up and down the room. **2** (*coll.*) (*сплясать*) to dance. **3** (**по** + *d.*; *coll.*) to run (over), go (over); **п. по кла́вишам** to run one's fingers over the keys. **4**: **п. на чей-н. счёт, п. по чьему́-н. а́дресу** (*coll.*) to give s.o. a bad write-up.

прок, а (у) *m.* (*coll.*) use, benefit; **что в э́том ~́у?** what is the good of it?

прокажённ|ый *adj.* leprous; *as n.* **п., ~ого** *m.*, **~ая, ~ой** *f.* leper.

прока́з|а[1]**, ы** *f.* (*болезнь*) leprosy.

прока́з|а[2]**, ы** *f.* (*шалость*) mischief, prank, trick.

прока́|зить, жу, зишь *impf.* (*of* **на~**) (*coll.*) to be up to mischief, play pranks.

прока́злив|ый (~, ~а) *adj.* mischievous.

прока́зник, а *m.* mischief-maker; prankster.

прока́знича|ть, ю *impf.* (*of* ⇒**на~**) = **прока́зить**

прока́лива|ть, ю *impf. of* ⇒**прокали́ть**

прокал|и́ть, ю́, и́шь *pf.* (*of* ⇒**~́ивать**) (*tech.*) to temper, anneal; to calcine, fire.

прока́лк|а, и *f.* (*tech.*) tempering.

прока́лыва|ть, ю *impf. of* ⇒**проколо́ть**

проканите́л|ить(ся), ю(сь), ишь(ся) *pf. of* ⇒**канители́ть(ся)**

прока́пчива|ть, ю *impf. of* ⇒**прокопти́ть**

прока́пыва|ть, ю *impf. of* ⇒**прокопа́ть**

прокарау́л|ить, ю, ишь *pf.* **1** (*coll.*) (*упустить*) to let slip, let go while on guard; **он ~ил аресто́ванного** he let the prisoner escape. **2** (*некоторое время*) to be on guard.

прока́т[1]**, а** *m.* (*tech.*) **1** (*действие*) rolling. **2** (*изделия*) rolled iron.

прока́т[2]**, а** *m.* hire.

прокат|а́ть[1]**, а́ю** *pf.* (*of* ⇒**~ывать**) **1** (*бельё*) to spread flat with a roller. **2** (*tech.*) (*сталь*) to roll, laminate.

прокат|а́ть[2]**, а́ю** *pf.* (*детей*) to take out (*for a drive, etc.*) (*for a certain time*).

прокат|а́ться[1]**, а́ется** *pf.* (*of* ⇒**~ываться**) (*tech.*) to roll out.

прокат|а́ться[2]**, а́юсь** *pf.* to go out (*for a drive, etc.*) (*for a certain time*).

прока|ти́ть, чу́, ~́тишь *pf.* (*of* ⇒**~́тывать**) **1** (*для развлечения*) to take out; to take for a drive, ride. **2** (*мяч*) to roll. **3** (*проехать*) to roll by, past. **4** (*coll.*) (*критиковать*) to criticize.

прока|ти́ться, чу́сь, ~́тишься *pf.* (*of* ⇒**~́тываться**) **1** (*о мяче*) to roll (*also fig., of thunder, etc.*). **2** (*для развлечения*) to go for a drive, go for a spin.

прока́тк|а, и *f.* (*tech.*) rolling, lamination.

прока́тн|ый[1] *adj.* (*tech.*) rolling; **~ое желе́зо** rolled iron; **п. стан** rolling mill.

прока́тный[2] *adj.* (*автомобиль*) hired, let out on hire.

прока́тчик, а *m.* rolling mill operative.

прока́тыва|ть(ся), ю(сь) *impf. of* ⇒**проката́ть(ся)**[1] *and* **прокати́ть(ся)**

прока́шлива|ть(ся), ю(сь) *impf. of* ⇒**прока́шлять(ся)**

прока́шл|ять, яю *pf.* **1** (*кашлять*) to cough. **2** (*impf.* **~ивать**) (*откашлянуть*) to cough up.

прока́шл|яться, яюсь *pf.* (*of* ⇒**~иваться**) to clear one's throat.

прокип|е́ть, и́т *pf.* to boil thoroughly.

прокипя|ти́ть, чу́, ти́шь *pf.* to boil thoroughly.

прокис|а́ть, а́ет *impf. of* ⇒**~́нуть**

проки́с|нуть, нет *pf.* (*of* ⇒**~а́ть**) to turn (sour).

прокла́дк|а, и *f.* **1** (*действие*) laying; building, construction; **п. доро́ги** road building; **п. трубопрово́да** pipe laying. **2** (*tech.*) (*деталь*) washer, gasket; packing, padding. **3** (*coll.*) (*гигиеническая*) sanitary towel.

прокладн|о́й *adj.* packing; **кни́га с ~ы́ми листа́ми** book with blank sheets (*for notes*).

прокла́дыва|ть, ю *impf. of* ⇒**проложи́ть**

проклама́ци|я, и *f.* (political) leaflet.

прокламир|овать, ую *impf. and pf.* to proclaim.

прокле́ива|ть, ю *impf. of* ⇒**прокле́ить**

прокле́|ить, ю, ишь *pf.* (*of* ⇒**~ивать**) to paste, glue; (*бумагу, холст*) to size.

проклина́|ть, ю *impf.* **1** *impf. of* **⇒прокля́сть. 2** (*coll.*) to curse, swear at.

прокл|я́сть, яну́, янёшь, *past* **~́ял, ~яла́, ~́яло** *pf.* (*of* **⇒~ина́ть**) to curse, damn.

прокля́ти|е, я *nt.* **1** (*осуждение*) damnation; **преда́ть ~ю** to consign to perdition. **2** (*слово, выражение*) curse. **3** *as int.* **п.!** damn it!; damnation!

про́кл|ятый *p.p.p. of* **⇒~я́сть; будь я ~ят, е́сли...** I'll be damned if...; **будь он ~ят!** damn him!

прокля́тый *adj.* damned; cursed.

проковы́рива|ть, ю *impf. of* **⇒проковыря́ть**

проковыр|я́ть, я́ю *pf.* (*of* **⇒~́ивать**) to pick a hole (in).

проко́л, а *m.* **1** (*в шине*) puncture. **2** (*на билете; на ухе*) hole. **3** (*действие*) (*шины*) puncturing; (*ушей*) piercing. **4** (*coll.*) (*неудача*) failure; (*оплошность*) blunder.

проколо́ть, ю́, ~́ешь *pf.* (*of* **⇒прока́лывать**) **1** (*шину*) to puncture. **2** (*уши*) to pierce. **3** (*дыру*) to pierce, prick.

прокомменти́р|овать, ую *pf.* to comment (upon).

прокомпости́р|овать, ую *pf. of* **⇒компости́ровать**

проконспекти́р|овать, ую *pf. of* **⇒конспекти́ровать**

проконсульти́р|овать(ся), ую(сь) *pf. of* **⇒консульти́ровать(ся)**

проконтроли́р|овать, ую *pf. of* **⇒контроли́ровать**

прокопа́|ть, ю *pf.* (*of* **⇒прока́пывать**) **1** (*канаву*) to dig. **2** (*холм*) to dig through.

прокопа́|ться, юсь *pf.* (*coll., pej.*) to dawdle, mess about (*for a certain time*).

прокопте́лый *adj.* (*coll.*) sooty, soot-covered.

прокоп|ти́ть, чу́, ти́шь *pf.* (*of* **⇒прока́пчивать**) **1** (*пищу*) to smoke, cure in smoke. **2** (*coll.*) (*стены*) to foul with smoke, soot.

проко́рм, а *m.* nourishment, sustenance.

прокорм|и́ть(ся), лю́(сь), ~́ишь(ся) *pf. of* **⇒корми́ть(ся)**

прокорректи́р|овать, ую *pf. of* **⇒корректи́ровать**

проко́с, а *m.* swathe.

прокра́дыва|ться, юсь *impf. of* **⇒прокра́сться**

прокра́|сить, шу, сишь *pf.* (*of* **⇒~шивать**) to paint, cover with paint.

прокра́|сться, ду́сь, дёшься *pf.* (*of* **⇒~дываться**) to steal; **п. ми́мо** to steal by, past.

прокра́шива|ть, ю *impf. of* **⇒прокра́сить**

прокрич|а́ть, у́, и́шь *pf.* **1** to shout, cry; to give a shout, raise a cry. **2** (**о**+*p.*; *coll.*) to trumpet.

прокру|ти́ть, чу́, ~́тишь *pf.* (*of* **⇒прокру́чивать**) (*coll.*) **1** (*пластинку, запись*) to play. **2** (*мысленно*) to turn over.

прокру́чива|ть, ю *impf. of* **⇒прокрути́ть**

прокурату́р|а, ы *f.* office of public prosecutor.

проку́рива|ть, ю *impf. of* **⇒прокури́ть**

прокур|и́ть, ю́, ~́ишь *pf.* (*of* **⇒~́ивать**) (*coll.*) **1** (*деньги*) to spend on smoking. **2** (*комнату*) to fill with tobacco smoke.

прокуро́р, а *m.* public prosecutor; counsel for the prosecution (*in criminal cases*); **речь ~а** speech for the prosecution.

прокуро́р|ский *adj. of* **⇒~**

проку́с, а *m.* bite.

проку|си́ть, шу́, ~́сишь *pf.* (*of* **⇒~́сывать**) to bite through.

проку́сыва|ть, ю *impf. of* **⇒прокуси́ть**

проку|ти́ть, чу́, ~́тишь *pf.* (*of* **⇒~́чивать**) (*coll.*) **1** (*истратить*) to squander, dissipate. **2** (*провести в кутежах*) to revel.

проку|ти́ться, чу́сь, ~́тишься *pf.* (*of* **⇒~́чиваться**) (*coll.*) to dissipate one's money.

проку́чива|ть(ся), ю(сь) *impf. of* **⇒прокути́ть(ся)**

пролага́|ть, ю *impf. of* **⇒проложи́ть**

прола́з|а, ы *c.g.* (*coll.*) scoundrel, rascal.

прола́мыва|ть(ся), ю, ет(ся) *impf. of* **⇒пролома́ть(ся)** *and* **проломи́ть(ся)**

пролега́|ть, ет *impf.* to lie, run; **доро́га ~ла вдоль бе́рега кана́ла** the path lay by the canal.

пролеж|а́ть, у́, и́шь *pf.* (*of* **⇒~́ивать**) to lie; to spend (*a certain time*) lying; **она́ всю зи́му ~а́ла в посте́ли** she spent the whole winter in bed; **посы́лка неде́лю ~а́ла на по́чте** the parcel lay for a week in the post office.

про́леж|ень, ня *m.* (*med.*) bedsore.

пролёжива|ть, ю *impf. of* **⇒пролежа́ть**

пролез|а́ть, а́ю *impf. of* **⇒~ть**

проле́з|ть, у, ешь, *past* **~, ~ла** *pf.* (*of* **⇒~а́ть**) **1** (*проникнуть куда-н.*) to get through, climb through. **2** (**в**+*a.*; *fig., coll., pej.*) (*хитростью*) to worm o.s. (into, on to); **он ~ в чле́ны комите́та** he has wormed his way on to the committee.

пролёт[1], а *m.* (*птицы, самолёта*) flight.

пролёт[2], а *m.* **1** (*открытое пространство*) open space. **2** (*archit.*) (*между опорами*) bay; **п. мо́ста** span. **3** (*лестницы*) stair-well. **4** (*coll.*) (*между железнодорожными станциями*) stage.

пролетариа́т, а *m.* proletariat.

пролета́ри|й, я *m.* proletarian; **~и всех стран, соединя́йтесь!** workers of the world, unite!

пролета́рский *adj.* proletarian.

пролет|а́ть[1], а́ю *impf. of* **⇒~е́ть**

пролет|а́ть[2], а́ю *pf.* to fly (*for a certain time*).

проле|те́ть, чу́, ти́шь *pf.* (*of* **⇒~та́ть[1]**) **1** (*какое-н. расстояние*) to fly, cover. **2** (*мимо*) to fly (by, through, past) (*also fig.*); **кани́кулы ~те́ли** the holidays flew by. **3** (*fig.*) (*мелькнуть*) to flash, flit; **у неё в голове́ ~те́ла мысль** a thought flashed through her mind. **4**: **п. как фане́ра над Пари́жем** (*coll.*) to fail; to miss an opportunity.

пролётк|а, и *f.* droshky, (horse-)cab.

пролётн|ый *adj.*: **~ая пти́ца** bird of passage.

прол|е́чь, я́жет, я́гут; ёг, егла́ *pf.* (*of* **⇒пролега́ть**) to lie, run, stretch; **доро́га пролегла́ по реке́** the road lay by the river.

проли́в, а *m.* (*geog.*) strait, sound.

пролива́|ть, ю *impf. of* **⇒проли́ть**

проливно́й *adj.*: **п. дождь** pouring rain; **шёл п. дождь** it was pouring.

проли́ти|е, я *nt.* shedding; **п. кро́ви** bloodshed.

прол|и́ть, ью́, ьёшь, *past* **~́ил, ~ила́, ~́ило** *pf.* (*of* **⇒~ива́ть**) to spill, shed; **п. чью-н. кровь** to shed s.o.'s blood; **п. слёзы** (**по**+*d. or p.*, **о**+*p.*) to shed tears (over); **п. свет** (**на**+*a.*; *fig.*) to shed light (on).

проло́г, а *m.* prologue (*Br.*), prolog (*US*).

пролож|и́ть, у́, ~́ишь *pf.* (*of* **⇒прокла́дывать**) **1** (*impf. also* **пролага́ть**) to lay; to build, construct; **п. доро́гу** to build a road; (*fig.*) to pave the way; **п. себе́ доро́гу че́рез толпу́** to hack one's way through the crowd; **п. путь** (*fig.*) to pave the way; **п. но́вые пути́** (*fig.*) to blaze new trails. **2** (**ме́жду**+*i. or* +*a. and i.*) to interlay; to insert (between); **п. кни́гу бе́лыми листа́ми** to interleave a book.

проло́м, а *m.* **1** (*действие*) breaking; breach, break; (*отверстие*) break; gap. **2** (*med.*) fracture.

пролома́|ть, ю *pf.* (*of* **⇒прола́мывать**) to break (through); **п. лёд** to break the ice.

пролома́|ться, ется *pf.* (*of* **⇒прола́мываться**) to break.

пролом|и́ть, лю́, ~́ишь *pf.* (*of* **⇒прола́мывать**) to break (through); **п. дыру́** to make a hole; **п. че́реп** to fracture one's skull.

пролом|и́ться, ~́ится *pf.* (*of* **⇒прола́мываться**) to break, give way; **осторо́жно, лёд ~́ился** look out! the ice has given way.

пролонга́ци|я, и *f.* prolongation.

пролонги́р|овать, ую *impf. and pf.* to prolong.

пром... *comb. form, abbr. of* ***промы́шленный***

прома́|зать[1], жу, жешь *pf.* (*of* **⇒~зывать**) to smear thoroughly; to oil thoroughly.

прома́|зать[2], жу, жешь *pf. of* **⇒ма́зать** 5

прома́зыва|ть, ю *impf. of* **⇒прома́зать[1]**

прома́ргива|ть, ю *impf. of* **⇒проморга́ть**

П

промарин|овáть, у́ю *pf.* (*of* ⇨**мариновáть**) (*coll.*) to delay, hold up, shelve.

промáсл|енный *p.p.p. of* ⇨**~ить** *and adj.* oiled, greased; oily, greasy; **~енная бумáга** oil-paper.

промáслива|ть, ю *impf. of* ⇨**промáслить**

промáсл|ить, ю, ишь *pf.* (*of* ⇨**~ивать**) to oil, treat with oil, grease.

промáтыва|ть(ся), ю(сь) *impf. of* ⇨**промотáть(ся)**

прóмах, а *m.* miss; (*fig.*) slip, blunder; **дать п.** to be unlucky; **он мáлый не п.** (*coll.*) he's nobody's fool.

промáхива|ться, юсь *impf. of* ⇨**промахну́ться**

промах|ну́ться, ну́сь, нёшься *pf.* (*of* ⇨**~иваться**) to miss; (*fig., coll.*) to (make a) blunder.

промáчива|ть, ю *impf. of* ⇨**промочи́ть**

промедлéни|е, я *nt.* delay; procrastination.

промéдл|ить, ю, ишь *pf.* to delay; to procrastinate.

промéж *prep.* (+*g. or i.*) (*coll.*) between; among; **п. нас** between ourselves.

промéжност|ь, и *f.* (*anat.*) perineum.

промежу́т|ок, ка *m.* (*между событиями*) interval; (*между предметами*) space; **п. врéмени** period, stretch of time.

промежу́точный *adj.* (*положение*) intermediate; (*период*) intervening.

промелькн|у́ть, у́, ёшь *pf.* **1** to flash; (*о времени*) to fly by; **п. в головé** to flash through one's mind. **2** (*появиться*) to be faintly perceptible; **в егó словáх ~у́ло разочаровáние** there was a shade of disappointment in his words.

проме́нива|ть, ю *impf. of* ⇨**променя́ть**

промен|я́ть, я́ю *pf.* (*of* ⇨**~ивать**) (**на**+*a.*) to exchange, swap (for); to trade (for), barter (for).

промéр, а *m.* **1** measurement. **2** (*ошибка*) error in measurement.

промерз|áть, áю *impf. of* ⇨**~нуть**

промёрзлый *adj.* frozen.

промёрз|нуть, ну, нешь, *past* **~, ~ла** *pf.* (*of* ⇨**~áть**) to freeze through.

промéрива|ть, ю *impf. of* ⇨**промéрить**

промéр|ить, ю, ишь *pf.* (*of* ⇨**~ивать** *and* **~я́ть**) **1** to measure. **2** (*pf. only*) (*ошибиться*) to make an error in measurement.

промер|я́ть, я́ю *impf.* = **~ивать**

проме|си́ть, шу́, ~сишь *pf.* (*of* ⇨**~шивать**) to knead well, thoroughly.

промéшива|ть, ю *impf. of* ⇨**промеси́ть**

промéшка|ть, ю *pf.* (*coll.*) to linger, dawdle.

проминá|ть(ся), ю(сь) *impf. of* ⇨**промя́ть(ся)**

промкомбинáт, а *m.* industrial combine.

промóзглый *adj.* dank.

промóин|а, ы *f.* pool, gully (*formed by flood, rain, etc.*).

промокáтельн|ый *adj.*: **~ая бумáга** blotting-paper.

промок|áть[1], áю *impf.* **1** *impf. of* ⇨**~нуть. 2** *impf. only* to let water through, not be waterproof; **э́ти боти́нки ~áют** these boots are not waterproof.

промок|áть[2], áю *impf. of* ⇨**~ну́ть**

промокáшк|а, и *f.* (*coll.*) blotting-paper.

промóк|нуть, ну, нешь, *past* **~, ~ла** *pf.* (*of* ⇨**~áть[1]**) to get soaked, get drenched; **п. до костéй** to get soaked to the skin.

промок|ну́ть, ну, нёшь *pf.* (*of* ⇨**~áть[2]**) (*coll.*) to blot.

промóлв|ить, лю, ишь *pf.* to say, utter.

промолч|áть, у́, и́шь *pf.* to keep silent, say nothing.

проморгá|ть, ю *pf.* (*of* ⇨**промáргивать**) (*coll.*) to miss, overlook; **п. удóбный слу́чай** to miss an opportunity, let a chance slip.

проморо|и́ть, ю́, и́шь *pf.* (*coll.*) **1** (**гóлодом**) to starve (*for a certain time*). **2** (*подвергнуть лишениям*) to impose privations (upon) (*for a certain time*).

промотá|ть, ю *pf.* (*of* ⇨**мотáть[2]** *and* **промáтывать**) to squander.

промотá|ться, юсь *pf.* (*of* ⇨**промáтываться**) (*coll.*) to squander one's money.

промоч|и́ть, у́, ~ишь *pf.* (*of* ⇨**промáчивать**) to (make/get) wet (through); to soak, drench; **п. нóги** to get one's feet wet; **п. гóрло** (*coll.*) to wet one's whistle.

промтовáр|ный *adj. of* ⇨**~ы; п. магази́н** shop selling manufactured goods.

промтовáр|ы, ов *no sg.* manufactured goods.

прому|дéть, жу́, ди́шь *pf. of* ⇨**мудéть**

промч|áться, у́сь, и́шься *pf.* **1** to tear (by, past, through); **п. стрелóй** to dart (by, past), flash (by, past). **2** (*о времени*) to fly (by).

промывáни|е, я *nt.* washing (out); (*med.*) bathing, irrigation; **п. мозгóв** brain-washing.

промывá|ть, ю *impf. of* ⇨**промы́ть**

промы́вк|а, и *f.* washing.

прóмыс|ел, ла *m.* **1** (*охота*) hunting, catching; **охóтничий п.** hunting; game-shooting; **пушнóй п.** trapping; **ры́бный п.** fishing. **2** (*занятие*) trade, business; **гóрный п.** mining; **кустáрный п.** cottage industry; **пушнóй п.** fur trade. **3** *pl.* (*предприятие*) fields, mines; **нефтяны́е ~лы** oil-fields; **соляны́е ~лы** salt-mines.

прóмысл, а *m.* (*relig.*) Providence.

промы́сл|ить, ю, ишь *pf.* (*of* ⇨**промышля́ть**) (*coll.*) to get, come by.

промыслóв|ый *adj.* **1** *adj. of* ⇨**прóмысел** 1; **~ые пти́цы** game-birds. **2** *adj. of* ⇨**прóмысел** 2, 3; **~ая кооперáция** producers' co-operative; **п. налóг** business tax; **~ая ры́ба** marketable fish.

пром|ы́ть, óю, óешь *pf.* (*of* ⇨**~ывáть**) **1** to wash well, thoroughly; **п. мозги́** (+*d., fig.*) to brain-wash. **2** (*med.*) to bathe. **3** (*tech.*) to wash; **п. зóлото** to pan out gold.

промы́шленник, а *m.* manufacturer, industrialist.

промы́шленност|ь, и *f.* industry.

промы́шленный *adj.* industrial.

промышля́|ть, ю *impf.* **1** *impf. of* ⇨**промы́слить. 2** (+*i.*) to earn one's living (by).

промя́мл|ить, ю, ишь *pf. of* ⇨**мя́млить** 1

про|мя́ть, мну́, мнёшь *pf.* (*of* ⇨**~минáть**) **1** to crush. **2** (*coll.*) (*лошадь, собаку*) to limber up; **п. нóги** to stretch one's legs.

про|мя́ться, мну́сь, мнёшься *pf.* (*of* ⇨**~минáться**) (*coll.*) to stretch one's legs.

пронáшива|ть(ся), ю, ет(ся) *impf. of* ⇨**проноси́ть(ся)[1]**

пронес|ти́, у, ёшь, *past* **~, ~лá** *pf.* (*of* ⇨**проноси́ть[3]**) **1** to carry (by, past, through). **2**: **~лó!** the danger is over!

пронес|ти́сь, у́сь, ёшься, *past* **~ся, ~лáсь** *pf.* (*of* ⇨**проноси́ться[2]**) **1** to rush (by, past, through); (*об облаках*) to scud (past). **2** (*о времени*) to fly by. **3** (*о слухах*) to spread.

пронз|áть, áю *impf. of* ⇨**~и́ть**

пронзи́тел|ьный (~ен, ~ьна) *adj.* piercing.

прон|зи́ть, жу́, зи́шь *pf.* (*of* ⇨**~зáть**) to pierce.

прони|зáть, жу́, ~жешь *pf.* (*of* ⇨**~зывать**) to pierce; to permeate, penetrate; (*fig.*) to run through; **свет ~зáл темноту́** the light pierced the darkness; **однá идéя ~зáла все егó произведéния** one idea ran through all his works.

прони́зыва|ть, ю *impf. of* ⇨**пронизáть**

прони́зыва|ющий *pres. part. act. of* ⇨**~ть** *and adj.* piercing.

проник|áть, áю *impf. of* ⇨**~нуть**

проникновéни|е, я *nt.* **1** penetration. **2** = **проникновéнность**

проникновéнност|ь, и *f.* feeling; heartfelt conviction; **говори́ть с ~ью** to speak with feeling.

проникновéн|ный (~ен, ~на) *adj.* full of feeling; heartfelt.

прони́кнут|ый (~, ~а) *adj.* (+*i.*) imbued (with), full (of).

прони́к|нуть, ну, нешь, *past* **~, ~ла** *pf.* (*of* ⇨**~áть**) (**в**+*a.*) to penetrate (*also fig.*); (**чéрез**+*a.*) to percolate (through); **п. в чьи-н. намéрения** to fathom s.o.'s designs; **п. в суть дéла** to get to the bottom of the matter.

пронима|ть, ю *impf. of* ⇒**пронять**

проницаемост|ь, и *f.* permeability.

проницаем|ый (~, ~а) *adj.* permeable.

проницательност|ь, и *f.* penetration; perspicacity; insight, shrewdness.

проницател|ьный (~ен, ~ьна) *adj.* perspicacious; shrewd; penetrating, piercing; **п. взор** penetrating gaze.

проница|ть, ю *impf.* (*obs.*) to penetrate.

проно|сить[1]**, шу́, ~сишь** *pf.* (*of* ⇒**пронашивать**) (*износить до дыр*) to wear out, wear to shreds.

проно|сить[2]**, шу́, ~сишь** *pf.* (*некоторое время*) to wear (*for a certain time*).

проно|сить[3]**, шу́, ~сишь** *impf. of* ⇒**пронести**

проно|ситься[1]**, ~сится** *pf.* (*of* ⇒**пронашиваться**) to wear through, wear to shreds.

проно|ситься[2]**, шу́сь, ~сишься** *impf. of* ⇒**пронестись**

проныр|а, ы *c.g.* (*coll.*) string-puller.

пронырлив|ый (~, ~а) *adj.* wily, sharp.

пронюх|ать, аю *pf.* (*of* ⇒**~ивать**) (*coll.*) to smell out, nose out, get wind (of).

пронюхива|ть, ю *impf. of* ⇒**пронюхать**

про|нять, йму́, ймёшь, *past* **~нял, ~няла́, ~няло** *pf.* (*of* ⇒**~нимать**) (*coll.*) **1** to penetrate. **2** (*fig.*) to get at; **его ничем не ~ймёшь** you can't get through to him.

прообраз, а *m.* prototype.

пропаганд|а, ы *f.* propaganda; promotion, advocacy.

пропагандир|овать, ую *impf.* to propagandize; to advocate.

пропагандист, а *m.* propagandist.

пропагандист|ка, ки *f. of* ⇒**~**

пропагандист|ский *adj. of* ⇒**~**

пропада|ть, ю *impf. of* ⇒**пропасть**

пропаж|а, и *f.* **1** (*исчезновение*) loss. **2** (*предмет*) lost object, missing object.

пропалыва|ть, ю *impf. of* ⇒**прополоть**

пропан, а *m.* propane.

пропаст|ь, и *f.* **1** precipice (*also fig.*); abyss; **на краю ~и** (*fig.*) on the brink of disaster. **2** (*coll.*) (*множество*) a mass (of), masses (of); **у него п. денег** he has masses of money.

пропа|сть, ду́, дёшь, *past* **~л** *pf.* (*of* ⇒**~дать**) **1** (*потеряться*) to be missing; to be lost; **п. без вести** (*mil.*) to be missing; **пиши ~ло** (*coll.*) it is as good as lost. **2** (*исчезнуть*) to disappear, vanish; **куда вы ~ли?** where did you vanish to? **3** (*погибнуть*) to be lost, be done for; (*о цветах*) to die; **теперь мы ~ли!** now we're done for!; **~ди пропадом!** (*coll.*) to hell with it! **4** (*пройти бесполезно*) to be wasted; **п. даром** to go to waste.

пропа|хать[1]**, шу́, ~шешь** *pf.* (*of* ⇒**~хивать**) **1** to plough (*Br.*), plow (*US*). **2** (*fig., coll.*) to plough (*Br.*), plow (*US*) through.

пропа|хать[2]**, шу́, ~шешь** *pf.* (*некоторое время*) to plough (*Br.*), plow (*US*).

пропахива|ть, ю *impf. of* ⇒**пропахать**[1]

пропах|нуть, ну, нешь, *past* **~, ~ла** *pf.* to become permeated with the smell (of).

пропашк|а, и *f.* (*agric.*) tilling between rows.

пропашн|ой *adj.*: **~ые культуры** crops requiring tilling between rows.

пропащ|ий *adj.* (*coll.*) **1** (*безнадёжный*) hopeless; good-for-nothing; **он п. человек** he's a hopeless case; **это ~ее дело** it's a lost cause. **2** (*потерянный*) lost.

пропека|ть(ся), ю, ет(ся) *impf. of* ⇒**пропечь(ся)**

пропеллер, а *m.* propeller.

проп|еть[1]**, ою́, оёшь** *pf.* **1** *pf. of* ⇒**петь. 2**: **п. голос** (*coll.*) to lose one's voice (*from singing*); to sing o.s. hoarse.

проп|еть[2]**, ою́, оёшь** *pf.* (*некоторое время*) to sing; **п. несколько нот** to sing a few notes.

пропечат|ать, аю *pf.* (*of* ⇒**~ывать**) (*coll.*) (*огласить в печати*) to expose (*in the press*).

пропечатыва|ть, ю *impf. of* ⇒**пропечатать**

пропе|чь, ку́, чёшь, ку́т, *past* **~к, ~кла́** *pf.* (*of* ⇒**~кать**) to bake well, thoroughly.

пропе|чься, чётся, ку́тся, *past* **~кся, ~кла́сь** *pf.* (*of* ⇒**~каться**) to bake well, get baked through.

пропива|ть(ся), ю(сь) *impf. of* ⇒**пропить(ся)**

пропил, а *m.* (saw-)kerf, slit, notch.

пропилива|ть, ю *impf. of* ⇒**пропилить**

пропил|ить, ю́, ~ишь *pf.* (*of* ⇒**~ивать**) to saw through.

пропи|сать, шу́, ~шешь *pf.* (*of* ⇒**~сывать**) **1** (*лекарство*) to prescribe. **2** (*жильца*) to register; **п. паспорт** to stamp a passport. **3** (*+d.; coll.*) (*наказать*) to give it hot, tear off a strip. **4** (*некоторое время*) to write.

пропи|саться, шу́сь, ~шешься *pf.* (*of* ⇒**~сываться**) to register (*intrans.*).

прописк|а, и *f.* **1** (*регистрация*) registration; **п. паспорта** stamping of a passport. **2** (*помета в паспорте*) residence permit.

прописн|ой *adj.* **1** (*буква*) capital; **писаться с п. буквы** to be written with a capital letter. **2** (*тривиальный*) commonplace, trivial; **~ая истина** truism.

прописыва|ть(ся), ю(сь) *impf. of* ⇒**прописать(ся)**

пропис|ь, и *f.* **1** *usu. pl.* (*образцы письма*) sample(s) of writing. **2** (*fig., pej.*) (*банальность*) platitude.

прописью *adv.* in words, in full.

пропитани|е, я *nt.* subsistence, sustenance; **заработать себе на п.** to earn one's living.

пропит|ать, аю *pf.* (*of* ⇒**~ывать**) **1** (*прокормить*) to keep, provide (for). **2** (*+i.*) to impregnate (with), steep (in); **п. маслом** to oil.

пропит|аться, аюсь *pf.* (*of* ⇒**~ываться**) (*+i.*) to become saturated (with).

пропитк|а, и *f.* (*tech.*) impregnation.

пропитыва|ть(ся), ю(сь) *impf. of* ⇒**пропитать(ся)**

про|пить, пью, пьёшь, *past* **~пил, ~пила́, ~пило** *pf.* (*of* ⇒**~пивать**) **1** (*деньги*) to spend on drink, squander on drink. **2** (*coll.*) (*талант*) to ruin (*through excessive drinking*).

про|питься, пью́сь, пьёшься, *past* **~пился, ~пила́сь, ~пило́сь** *pf.* (*of* ⇒**~пиваться**) (*coll.*) to ruin o.s. (*through excessive drinking*).

пропих|аться, аюсь *pf.* = **~нуться**

пропихива|ть(ся), ю(сь) *impf. of* ⇒**пропихнуть(ся)**

пропих|нуть, ну́, нёшь *pf.* (*of* ⇒**~ивать**) (*coll.*) to shove through, force through.

пропих|нуться, ну́сь, нёшься *pf.* (*of* ⇒**~иваться**) (*coll.*) to shove, force one's way through.

проплава|ть, ю *pf.* (*вплавь*) to swim (*for a certain time*); (*на судне*) to sail (*for a certain time*).

пропла|кать, чу, чешь *pf.* to cry, weep (*for a certain time*); **п. глаза** (*coll.*) to cry one's eyes out.

проплыва|ть, ю *impf. of* ⇒**проплыть**

проплы|ть, ву́, вёшь, *past* **~л, ~ла́, ~ло** *pf.* (*of* ⇒**~вать**) **1** (*вплавь*) to swim (by, past, through); (*на судне*) to sail (by, past, through); (*о предмете*) to float, drift (by, past, through); (*fig., joc.*) (*пройти*) to sail (by, past). **2** (*расстояние*) to cover (*a certain distance*).

проповедник, а *m.* **1** preacher. **2** (*+g.; fig.*) advocate (of).

проповед|овать, ую *impf.* **1** to preach. **2** (*fig.*) to advocate, propagate.

проповед|ь, и *f.* **1** sermon; homily. **2** (*+g.; fig.*) advocacy (of), propagation (of).

пропойный *adj.* (*coll.*) drunken, besotted.

пропойц|а, ы *m.* (*coll.*) drunkard.

прополаскива|ть, ю *impf. of* ⇒**прополоскать**

прополз|ать, аю *impf. of* ⇒**~ти**

прополз|ти, у́, ёшь, *past* **~, ~ла́** *pf.* (*of* ⇒**~ать**) to creep, crawl (by, past, through).

прополис, а *m.* propolis.

прополк|а, и *f.* weeding.

прополо|скать, щу́, ~щешь *pf.* (*of* ⇒**прополаскивать**) to rinse, swill; **п. горло** to gargle.

пропол|оть, ю́, ~ешь *pf.* (*of* ⇒**пропалывать**) to weed.

пропорциональност|ь, и *f.* proportionality; (*соразмерность*) proportion; **обра́тная п.** inverse proportion.

пропорциона́л|ьный (~ен, ~ьна) *adj.* **1** proportional; proportionate; **~ьное представи́тельство** proportional representation. **2** (*обладающий правильными пропорциями*) well-proportioned.

пропо́рци|я, и *f.* proportion.

пропоте́лый *adj.* sweat-soaked.

пропоте́|ть, ю *pf.* **1** (*сильно вспотеть*) to sweat profusely. **2** (*пропитаться потом*) to be soaked in sweat.

про́пуск, а *m.* **1** *no pl.* (*действие*) admission. **2** (*pl.* **~и** *and* **~а́**) (*документ*) pass, permit. **3** (*pl.* **~а́**) (*mil.*) password. **4** (*pl.* **~и**) (+*g.*) (*непосещение*) non-attendance (at), absence (from). **5** (*pl.* **~и**) (*пустое место*) blank, gap.

пропуска́|ть, ю *impf.* **1** *impf. of* ⇒**пропусти́ть. 2** *impf. only* to let pass; **п. во́ду** to leak; **не п. воды́** to be waterproof; **э́та бума́га ~ет черни́ла** this paper absorbs ink.

пропускн|о́й *adj.*: **п. пункт** check-point; **~а́я спосо́бность** capacity.

пропу|сти́ть, щу́, ~́стишь *pf.* (*of* ⇒**~ска́ть**) **1** (*дать пройти*) to let pass, let through; to make way (for); (*впустить*) to let in, admit; (*обслужить*) to put through, deal with; **п. на перро́н** to let on to the platform; **вы́ставка ~сти́ла пять миллио́нов посети́телей** the exhibition had five million visitors. **2** (**че́рез** + *a.*) to run (through), pass (through); **п. че́рез фильтр** to filter. **3** (*при чтении, письме*) to omit, leave out; to skip. **4** (*не явиться*) to miss; **п. ле́кцию** to miss a lecture; (*упустить*) to miss, let slip; **п. удо́бный слу́чай** to miss an opportunity. **5** (*coll.*) (*выпить*) to drink.

пропылесо́с|ить, ишь *pf. of* ⇒**пылесо́сить**

пропых|те́ть, чу́, ти́шь *pf. of* ⇒**пыхте́ть**

прора́б, а *m.* (*abbr. of* ***производи́тель рабо́т***) clerk of the works (*Br.*), construction superintendent (*US*).

праба́тыва|ть, ю *impf. of* ⇒**прорабо́тать**[1]

прорабо́та|ть[1]**, ю** *pf.* (*of* ⇒**праба́тывать**) (*coll.*) **1** (*изучить*) to work (at), study. **2** (*критиковать*) to pick holes (in).

прорабо́та|ть[2]**, ю** *pf.* (*некоторое время*) to work.

прорабо́тк|а, и *f.* **1** (*изучение*) study, studying. **2** (*критика*) panning.

прораста́ни|е, я *nt.* germination; sprouting.

прораст|а́ть, а́ет *impf. of* ⇒**~и́**

прорас|ти́, ёт, *past* **проро́с, проросла́** *pf.* (*of* ⇒**~а́ть**) to germinate, sprout, shoot (*of plant*).

про́рв|а, ы *f.* (*coll.*) **1** (+*g.*) (*много*) masses (of), heaps (of). **2** (*обжора*) glutton.

прорв|а́ть, у́, ёшь, *past* **~а́л, ~ала́, ~а́ло** *pf.* (*of* ⇒**прорыва́ть**[1]) **1** to break through; to tear, make a hole (in); **п. блока́ду** to run the blockade; **п. ли́нию оборо́ны проти́вника** to break through the enemy's defence line; (*impers.*): **~а́ло плоти́ну** the dam has burst; **я ~а́л носо́к** I have a hole in my sock. **2** (*impers.*; *coll.*) to lose patience.

прорв|а́ться, у́сь, ёшься, *past* **~а́лся, ~ала́сь, ~а́ло́сь** *pf.* (*of* ⇒**прорыва́ться**[1]) **1** (*сломаться*) to break, burst (open). **2** (*разорваться*) to tear. **3** (*силой проложить себе путь*) to break (out, through); to force one's way (through).

прореаги́р|овать, ую *pf. of* ⇒**реаги́ровать**

проре|ди́ть, жу́, ди́шь *pf.* (*of* ⇒**~́живать**) (*agric.*) to thin out.

проре́жива|ть, ю *impf. of* ⇒**прореди́ть**

проре́з, а *m.* cut; slit, notch; **ме́лкий п.** nick.

проре́|зать, жу, жешь *pf.* (*of* ⇒**~зывать** *and* **~за́ть**) to cut through (*also fig.*).

проре́|заться, жется *pf.* (*of* ⇒**ре́заться, ~зываться** *and* **~за́ться**) (*о зубах*) to cut, come through; **у неё уже́ ~зались зу́бы** she has already cut her teeth.

прорез|а́ть(ся), а́ю, ет(ся) *impf. of* ⇒**~́ать(ся)**

прорези́нива|ть, ю *impf. of* ⇒**прорези́нить**

прорези́н|ить, ю, ишь *pf.* (*of* ⇒**~ивать**) to rubberize.

проре́зыва|ть(ся), ю, ет(ся) *impf. of* ⇒**проре́зать(ся)**

про́рез|ь, и *f.* opening, aperture.

проре́ктор, а *m.* pro-rector, vice-principal (*of university*).

прорепети́р|овать, ую *impf. of* ⇒**репети́ровать**

проре́х|а, и *f.* **1** (*дыра*) tear. **2** (*у брюк*) flies. **3** (*fig., coll.*) (*недостаток*) gap, deficiency.

прорецензи́р|овать, ую *pf. of* ⇒**рецензи́ровать**

проржа́ве|ть, ет *pf.* to rust through.

прорица́ни|е, я *nt.* soothsaying, prophecy.

прорица́тел|ь, я *m.* soothsayer, prophet.

прорица́|ть, ю *impf.* to prophesy.

проро́к, а *m.* prophet.

пророн|и́ть, ю́, ~́ишь *pf.* to utter; **он не ~и́л ни зву́ка** he did not utter a sound.

проро́ческий *adj.* prophetic, oracular.

проро́честв|о, а *nt.* prophecy.

проро́честв|овать, ую *impf.* (**о** + *p.*) to prophesy.

проро́ч|ить, у, ишь *impf.* (*of* **на~**) to prophesy, predict.

проруб|а́ть, а́ю *impf. of* ⇒**~и́ть**

проруб|и́ть, лю́, ~́ишь *pf.* (*of* ⇒**~а́ть**) to hack through, cut through.

про́руб|ь, и *f.* ice-hole.

проро́х|а, и *f.* (*coll.*) blunder, mistake.

проры́в, а *m.* **1** break; (*mil.*) break-through, breach. **2** (*fig.*) (*нарушение хода работы*) hitch, hold-up; **по́лный п.** breakdown.

прорыва́|ть[1]**, ю** *impf. of* ⇒**прорва́ть**

прорыва́|ть[2]**, ю** *impf. of* ⇒**проры́ть**

прорыва́|ться[1]**, юсь** *impf. of* ⇒**прорва́ться**

прорыва́|ться[2]**, юсь** *impf. of* ⇒**проры́ться**

прор|ы́ть, о́ю, о́ешь *pf.* (*of* ⇒**~ыва́ть**[2]) to dig through.

прор|ы́ться, о́юсь, о́ешься *pf.* (*of* ⇒**~ыва́ться**[2]) to dig one's way through, burrow through.

проса|ди́ть[1]**, жу́, ~́дишь** *pf.* (*of* ⇒**~́живать**) (+*i.*; *coll.*) (*проколоть*) to stick (into); **п. но́гу гвоздём** to get a nail stuck in one's foot.

проса|ди́ть[2]**, жу́, ~́дишь** *pf.* (*of* ⇒**~́живать**) (*coll.*) (*деньги*) to squander, lose.

проса́жива|ть, ю *impf. of* ⇒**просади́ть**

проса́лива|ть[1]**, ю** *impf. of* ⇒**проса́лить**

проса́лива|ть[2]**, ю** *impf. of* ⇒**просоли́ть**

проса́л|ить, ю, ишь *pf.* (*of* ⇒**~ивать**[1]) to grease.

проса́чивани|е, я *nt.* **1** percolation; oozing, exudation. **2** (*fig.*) (*наружу*) leakage; (*внутрь*) infiltration.

проса́чива|ться, ется *impf. of* ⇒**просочи́ться**

просва́та|ть, ю *pf.* (*о родителях невесты*) to promise in marriage.

просве́рлива|ть, ю *impf. of* ⇒**просверли́ть**

просверл|и́ть, ю́, и́шь *pf.* (*of* ⇒**~́ивать**) (*дыру*) to drill, bore; (*доску*) to drill through, bore through.

просве́т, а *m.* **1** shaft of light; (*fig.*) ray of hope. **2** (*archit.*) light; aperture, opening.

просвети́тел|ь, я *m.* **1** educator, teacher. **2** (*hist.*) representative of the Enlightenment.

просвети́тель|ница, ницы *f. of* ⇒**~**

просвети́тельн|ый *adj.* educational; **~ая филосо́фия** (*hist.*) philosophy of the Enlightenment.

просвети́тель|ский *adj. of* ⇒**~**

просвети́тельств|о, а *nt.* enlightenment.

просве|ти́ть[1]**, щу́, ти́шь** *pf.* (*of* ⇒**~ща́ть**) to educate; to enlighten.

просве|ти́ть[2]**, чу́, ~́тишь** *pf.* (*of* ⇒**~́чивать**[1]) (*med.*) to X-ray.

просветле́ни|е, я *nt.* **1** (*погоды*) clearing up, brightening up. **2** (*fig.*) lucid moment.

просветл|ённый *p.p.p. of* ⇒**~и́ть** *and adj.* (*fig.*) clear, lucid.

просветле́|ть, ю *pf.* **1** (*о погоде*) to clear up, brighten up. **2** (*fig.*) to brighten; **п. от ра́дости** to light up with joy. **3** (*fig.*) (*о сознании*) to become lucid.

просветл|и́ть, ю́, и́шь *pf.* (*of* ⇒**~я́ть**) to clarify.

просветл|я́ть, я́ю *impf. of* ⇒**~и́ть**

просве́чива|ть[1], ю *impf. of* ⇒**просвети́ть[2]**

просве́чива|ть[2], ет *impf.* **1** (*быть прозрачным*) to be translucent. **2** (**че́рез, сквозь**+*a.*) (*быть видным*) to be visible (through), show (through), appear (through); (*о солнце*) to shine (through); **шрам ~л че́рез её чуло́к** the scar showed through her stocking.

просвеща́|ть, ю *impf. of* ⇒**просвети́ть[1]**

просвеще́ни|е, я *nt.* **1** (*образование*) education; **наро́дное п.** public education. **2** enlightenment; **эпо́ха П~я** (*hist.*) the Age of the Enlightenment.

просвещённост|ь, и *f.* enlightenment, culture.

просве|щённый *p.p.p. of* ⇒**~ти́ть[1]** *and adj.* enlightened; educated, cultured; **~щённое мне́ние** expert opinion; **п. челове́к** educated person.

просвир|а́, ы́, *pl.* **про́свиры, про́свир, про́свирам** *f.* (*eccl.*) (communion) bread; host.

просви́р|ня, ни, *g. pl.* **~ен** *f.* woman baking communion bread.

просвирня́к, а́ *m.* (*bot.*) marsh mallow.

просви|сте́ть, щу́, сти́шь *pf.* **1** to whistle; **п. мело́дию** to whistle a tune. **2** (*о пуле*) to whistle (by, past).

про́сед|ь, и *f.* streak(s) of grey.

просе́ива|ть, ю *impf. of* ⇒**просе́ять**

про́сек|а, и *f.* cutting (*in a forest*).

просёл|ок, ка *m.* country road, cart-track.

просе́|ять, ю, ешь *pf.* (*of* ⇒**~ивать**) to sift; **~янный игро́к** (*sport*) seed.

просигнализи́р|овать, ую *pf. of* ⇒**сигнализи́ровать**

просигна́л|ить, ю, ишь *pf. of* ⇒**сигна́лить**

проси|де́ть[1], жу́, ди́шь *pf.* (*of* ⇒**~живать**) to sit (*for a certain time*); **п. ночь у посте́ли больно́го** to sit up all night with a patient.

проси|де́ть[2], жу́, ди́шь *pf.* (*of* ⇒**~живать**) (*брюки*) to wear out the seat (of); to wear into holes (*by sitting*).

проси́жива|ть, ю *impf. of* ⇒**просиде́ть**

про́син|ь, и *f.* (*coll.*) bluish tint.

проси́тел|ь, я *m.* applicant; petitioner.

проси́тель|ница, ницы *f. of* ⇒**~**

проси́тельный *adj.* pleading.

про|си́ть, шу́, ~сишь *impf.* (*of* ⇒**по~**) **1** (+*a. of person asked*; +*a. or g. of thing sought, or* **о**+*p.*) to ask (for), beg; **~шу́ (вас)** please; **п. кого́-н. о по́мощи** to ask s.o. for help, ask s.o.'s assistance; **п. вре́мени на размышле́ние** to ask for time to think (sth.) over; **п. разреше́ния** to ask permission; **п. сове́та** to ask (for) advice; **п. извине́ния у кого́-н.** to apologize to s.o. **2** (**за**+*a.*) (*вступаться*) to intercede (for). **3** (*приглашать*) to invite; **вас ~сят к столу́** please take your places at the table; **«~сят не кури́ть»** 'no smoking'.

про|си́ться, шу́сь, ~сишься *impf.* (*of* ⇒**по~**) **1** (+*inf. or* **в**+*a.*, **на**+*a.*) to ask (for); to apply (for); **п. в о́тпуск** to apply for leave. **2** (*fig., coll.*) to ask (for); **п. с языка́** to be on the tip of one's tongue; **зака́т так и ~си́лся на карти́ну** the sunset was just asking to be painted.

просия́|ть, ю *pf.* **1** (*о солнце*) to begin to shine. **2** (**от**+*g.*) to beam (with), light up (with); **она́ ~ла от сча́стья** she beamed with joy; **лицо́ у него́ ~ло** his face lit up.

проска|ка́ть, чу́, ~чешь *pf.* to gallop (by, past, through).

проска́кива|ть, ю *impf. of* ⇒**проскочи́ть**

проска́льзыва|ть, ю *impf. of* ⇒**проскользну́ть**

просквоз|и́ть, и́т *pf.* (*impers.*; *coll.*): **меня́**, *etc.*, **~и́ло** I, *etc.*, have caught cold from being in a draught (*Br.*), draft (*US*).

просклоня́|ть, ю *pf. of* ⇒**склоня́ть[2]**

проскользн|у́ть, у́, ёшь *pf.* (*of* ⇒**проска́льзывать**) (*coll.*) to slip in, creep in (*also fig.*); **~у́ло мно́го оши́бок** many errors have crept in.

проскоч|и́ть, у́, ~ишь *pf.* (*of* ⇒**проска́кивать**) **1** (*пробежать*) to rush by, tear by. **2** (**че́рез**+*a.*) to slip (through). **3** (**сквозь**+*a.*, **ме́жду**+*i.*) to fall (through, between); **п. ме́жду па́льцами** to fall through one's fingers. **4** (*fig., coll.*) to slip in, creep in; **~и́ло не́сколько оши́бок** a few errors crept in. **5** (*не остановиться где нужно*) to overshoot.

проскрип|е́ть, лю́, и́шь *pf.* **1** *pf. of* ⇒**скрипе́ть. 2** (*coll.*) to creak along.

проскурня́к, а́ *m.* (*bot.*) marsh mallow.

проскуча́|ть, ю *pf.* to have a dull, boring time; **мы ~ли всю неде́лю** we had a dull week.

прosла́б|ить, ит *pf. of* ⇒**сла́бить**

просла́в|ить, лю, ишь *pf.* (*of* ⇒**~ля́ть**) to glorify; to bring glory (to); to make famous.

просла́в|иться, люсь, ишься *pf.* (*of* ⇒**~ля́ться**) (+*i.*) to become famous (for); **он ~ился остро́тами** he became famous for his witticisms.

прославле́ни|е, я *nt.* glorification.

просла́в|ленный *p.p.p. of* ⇒**~ить** *and adj.* renowned, celebrated.

прославля́|ть(ся), ю(сь) *impf. of* ⇒**просла́вить(ся)**

просла́ива|ть, ю *impf. of* ⇒**прослои́ть**

просле|ди́ть, жу́, ди́шь *pf.* (*of* ⇒**~живать**) **1** (*выследить*) to track (down). **2** (*исследовать*) to trace (through); to trace back, retrace; **п. разви́тие па́пства** to trace the development of the papacy.

просле́д|овать, ую *pf.* to proceed, go in state.

просле́жива|ть, ю *impf. of* ⇒**проследи́ть**

просле|зи́ться, жу́сь, зи́шься *pf.* to shed a few tears.

просло|и́ть, ю́, и́шь *pf.* (*of* ⇒**просла́ивать**) (+*i.*) to interlay (with), sandwich (with).

просло́йк|а, и *f.* **1** layer, stratum (*also fig.*). **2** (*geol.*) seam, streak.

прослуж|и́ть, у́, ~ишь *pf.* **1** to work, serve (*for a certain time*); **он ~и́л три го́да на Да́льнем Восто́ке** he served for three years in the Far East. **2** (*пробыть в употреблении*) to last (*for a certain time*); **э́то пальто́ ~ит мне ещё оди́н год** this coat will last me another year.

прослу́ш|ать, аю *pf.* **1** (*impf.* **слу́шать**) to hear (through); **п. курс ле́кций** to attend a course of lectures. **2** (*impf.* **~ивать**) (*med.*) to listen to; **п. чьё-н. се́рдце** to listen to s.o.'s heart. **3** (*impf.* **~ивать**) (*coll.*) to miss, not to catch; **прости́те, я ~ал, что вы сказа́ли** I am sorry, I did not catch what you said.

прослу́шивани|е, я *nt.* audition.

прослу́шива|ть, ю *impf. of* ⇒**прослу́шать**

прослы́|ть, ву́, вёшь, *past* **~л, ~ла́, ~ло** *pf.* (+*i.*) to pass (for), be reputed.

прослы́ш|ать, у, ишь *pf.* (*coll.*) to find out, hear; **я то́лько что ~ал о ва́шем несча́стном слу́чае** I have only just heard about your accident.

просма́лива|ть, ю *impf. of* ⇒**просмоли́ть**

просма́трива|ть, ю *impf. of* ⇒**просмотре́ть**

просмол|и́ть, ю́, и́шь *pf.* (*of* ⇒**просма́ливать**) to tar; to coat with tar.

просмо́тр, а *m.* **1** survey; view, viewing; **п. докуме́нтов** examination of papers; **закры́тый п.** private view; **предвари́тельный п.** preview. **2** (*ошибка*) oversight.

просмотр|е́ть, ю́, ~ишь *pf.* (*of* ⇒**просма́тривать**) **1** to survey; to view. **2** (*читая*) to look over, look through; (*бегло*) to glance over, glance through; **п. ру́копись** to glance through a manuscript. **3** (*пропустить*) to overlook, miss.

прос|ну́ться, ну́сь, нёшься *pf.* (*of* ⇒**~ыпа́ться[1]**) to wake up, awake.

про́с|о, а *nt.* millet.

просо́выва|ть(ся), ю(сь) *impf. of* ⇒**просу́нуть(ся)**

просоди́ческий *adj.* (*liter.*) prosodic.

просо́ди|я, и *f.* (*liter.*) prosody.

просол|и́ть, ю́, ~ишь *pf.* (*of* ⇒**проса́ливать[2]**) to salt; **п. мя́со** to corn meat.

просо́х|нуть, ну, нешь, *past* **~, ~ла** *pf.* (*of* ⇒**просыха́ть**) to get dry, dry out.

просоч|и́ться, и́тся *pf.* (*of* ⇒**проса́чиваться**) **1** to percolate; to filter; to leak; to seep out. **2** (*fig.*) to filter through; to leak out; **~и́лись**

П

сведения о поражении news of the defeat filtered through.

просп|áть¹, лю, йшь, *past* **~áл, ~алá, ~áло** *pf.* (*of* ⇒**просыпáть²**) **1** (*не проснуться вовремя*) to oversleep. **2** (*пропустить*) to miss, pass (*due to being asleep*).

просп|áть², лю, йшь, *past* **~áл, ~алá, ~áло** *pf.* (*некоторое время*) to sleep (*for a certain time*).

просп|áться, люсь, йшся, *past* **~áлся, ~алáсь, ~áлось** *pf.* (*coll.*) to sleep it off (*sc. one's drunkenness*).

проспéкт¹, а *m.* (*улица*) avenue.

проспéкт², а *m.* **1** (*справочное издание*) brochure, prospectus. **2** (*план*) outline, résumé.

проспóрива|ть, ю *impf. of* ⇒**проспóрить¹**

проспóр|ить¹, ю, ишь *pf.* (*of* ⇒**~ивать**) (*деньги*) to lose (*in a bet*).

проспóр|ить², ю, ишь *pf.* (*некоторое время*) to argue.

проспрягá|ть, ю *pf. of* ⇒**спрягáть**

просрóч|енный *p.p.p. of* ⇒**~ить** *and adj.* overdue.

просрóчива|ть, ю *impf. of* ⇒**просрóчить**

просрóч|ить, у, ишь *pf.* (*of* ⇒**~ивать**) to exceed the time limit; **п. óтпуск** to overstay one's leave; **п. платёж** to fail to pay in time.

просрóчк|а, и *f.* delay; expiry of a time limit.

простáв|ить, лю, ишь *pf.* (*of* ⇒**~лять**) to put down (*in writing*); to state, fill in; **п. дáту (в, на**+*p.*) to date.

проставля|ть, ю *impf. of* ⇒**простáвить**

простагландин, а *m.* prostaglandin.

простáива|ть, ю *impf. of* ⇒**простоять**

простáк, á *m.* simpleton.

простáт|а, ы *f.* (*anat.*) prostate (gland).

простег|áть, áю *pf.* (*of* ⇒**~ивать**) to quilt.

простёгива|ть, ю *impf. of* ⇒**простегáть**

простéйш|ий *superl. of* ⇒**простóй;** *pl. as n.* **~ие, ~их** (*zool.*) protozoa.

простéн|ок, ка *m.* (*archit.*) pier.

прóстенький *adj.* (*coll.*) quite simple; plain, unpretentious.

прос|терéть, трý, трёшь, *past* **~тёр, ~тёрла** *pf.* (*of* ⇒**~тирáть¹**) **1** to extend, hold out, reach out; **п. рýку** to hold out one's hand. **2** (*fig.*) to raise, stretch; **они слишком далекó ~тёрли свои трéбования** they raised their demands too high.

прос|терéться, трётся, *past* **~тёрся, ~тёрлась** *pf.* (*of* ⇒**~тирáться**) to stretch, extend; **п. на сóтни миль** to stretch for hundreds of miles.

простирá|ть¹, ю *impf. of* ⇒**простерéть**

простирá|ть², ю *pf.* (*некоторое время*) to wash.

простир|áть³, áю *pf.* (*of* ⇒**~ывать**) (*coll.*) (*хорошо выстирать*) to wash well, thoroughly.

простирá|ться, ется *impf. of* ⇒**простерéться**

простирн|ýть, ý, ёшь *pf.* (*coll.*) to give a wash.

простирыва|ть, ю *impf. of* ⇒**простирáть³**

простител|ьный (~ен, ~ьна) *adj.* pardonable, excusable.

проституир|овать, ую *impf. and pf.* to prostitute.

проститýтк|а, и *f.* prostitute.

проститýци|я, и *f.* prostitution.

про|сти́ть, щý, сти́шь *pf.* (*of* ⇒**~щáть**) **1** to forgive, pardon; **п. грехи́** to forgive sins; **~сти́те (меня́)!** excuse me!; I beg your pardon! **2** (*долг*) to remit; **п. долг комý-н.** to remit s.o.'s debt. **3**: **~сти́(те)!** (*obs.*) good-bye!

про|сти́ться, щýсь, сти́шься *pf.* (*of* ⇒**~щáться**) (**с**+*i.*) to say good-bye (to), bid farewell (to).

прóсто *adv.* simply; **п. по привычке** purely out of habit; **п. так** for no particular reason; **это п. невероятно** it is simply incredible; **я п. не знáю** I really don't know.

простовáтост|ь, и *f.* simplicity, simple-mindedness.

простовáт|ый (~, ~а) *adj.* simple, simple-minded.

простоволóс|ый (~, ~а) *adj.* bare-headed.

простодýши|е, я *nt.* simple-heartedness; ingenuousness, artlessness.

простодýш|ный (~ен, ~на) *adj.* simple-hearted; ingenuous, artless.

прост|óй¹ (~, ~á, ~o) *adj.* **1** (*нетрудный*) simple; easy; **вам ~о критиковáть** it is easy for you, all very well for you to criticize. **2** (*однородный*) simple (= *unitary*); **~óе предложéние** (*gram.*) simple sentence; **~óе числó** (*math.*) prime number. **3** (*обыкновенный*) simple; ordinary; **~ым глáзом** with the naked eye; **п. нарóд** the common people. **4** (*без претензий*) simple, plain; unaffected, unpretentious; **~ые лю́ди** ordinary people; homely people; **~ые манéры** unaffected manners; **п. óбраз жи́зни** plain living. **5** (*не более как*) mere; **~óе любопы́тство** mere curiosity; **п. смéртный** a mere mortal; **по той ~óй причи́не, что** for the simple reason that.

простó|й², я *m.* downtime, idle time; stoppage; **плáта за п.** demurrage.

простоквáш|а, и *f.* thick soured milk.

простолюди́н, а *m.* man of the common people.

прóсто-нáпросто *adv.* (*coll.*) simply.

простонарóд|ный (~ен, ~на) *adj.* of the common people.

простонарóдь|е, я *nt.* the common people.

простон|áть, ý, ~ешь *pf.* **1** (*издать стон*) to groan. **2** (*некоторое время*) to groan (*for a certain time*).

простóр, а *m.* **1** (*пространство*) spaciousness; space, expanse; **степны́е ~ы** the expanses of the steppe(s). **2** (*свобода*) freedom, scope.

просторéчи|е, я *nt.* popular speech; **в ~и** in common parlance.

просторéч|ный (~ен, ~на) *adj. of* ⇒**~ие**

простóр|ный (~ен, ~на) *adj.* spacious, roomy; (*об одежде*) loose-fitting.

простосердéчи|е, я *nt.* simple-heartedness.

простосердéч|ный (~ен, ~на) *adj.* simple-hearted.

простот|á, ы́ *f.* simplicity.

простофи́л|я, и *c.g.* (*coll.*) duffer, ninny.

просто|я́ть, ю́, и́шь *pf.* (*of* ⇒**простáивать**) **1** (*некоторое время*) to stay, stand; **пóезд ~я́л на запаснóм пути́ всю ночь** the train stood in a siding all night. **2** (*бездействовать*) to stand idle, lie idle. **3** (*о здании*) to stand, last.

прострáн|ный (~ен, ~на) *adj.* **1** (*обширный*) extensive, vast. **2** (*многословный*) verbose.

прострáнственный *adj.* spatial.

прострáнств|о, а *nt.* space; (*неограниченная протяжённость*) expanse; **воздýшное п.** air space; **безвоздýшное п.** (*phys.*) vacuum; **пустóе п.** void; **боя́знь ~а** (*med.*) agoraphobia.

прострáци|я, и *f.* prostration.

прострáчива|ть, ю *impf. of* ⇒**простро́чить**

прострéл, а *m.* **1** (*coll.*) (*боль*) lower-back pain, lumbago. **2** (*sport*) low cross.

прострéлива|ть, ю *impf.* **1** *impf. of* ⇒**прострели́ть. 2** *impf. only* (*mil.*) to rake, sweep with fire.

прострéлива|ться, ется *impf.* (*mil.*) to be exposed to fire.

прострел|и́ть, ю́, ~ишь *pf.* (*of* ⇒**~ивать**) **1** (*выстрелом пробить насквозь*) to shoot through. **2** (*sport*) to cross low.

простроч|и́ть, ý, ~ишь *pf.* (*of* ⇒**прострáчивать, строчи́ть**) to stitch; to back-stitch.

простýд|а, ы *f.* (chest) cold; **схвати́ть ~у** (*coll.*) to catch (a) cold.

просту|ди́ть, жý, ~дишь *pf.* (*of* ⇒**~жáть**) to let catch cold; **п. себé гóрло** to get a sore throat.

просту|ди́ться, жýсь, ~дишься *pf.* (*of* ⇒**~жáться**) to catch (a) cold.

простýдный *adj.* catarrhal.

простужá|ть(ся), ю(сь) *impf. of* ⇒**простуди́ть(ся)**

простý|женный *p.p.p. of* ⇒**~ди́ть** *and adj.*: **я вновь ~жен** I have caught another cold.

простýк|ать, аю *pf.* (*of* ⇒**~ивать**) (*med.*) to tap.

простýкива|ть, ю *impf. of* ⇒**простýкать**

проступ|áть, áет *impf. of* ⇒**~и́ть**

проступ|и́ть, ~ит *pf.* (*of* ⇒**~áть**) to appear, show through, come through; **сыры́е пя́тна ~или на стенáх** damp patches have appeared on the walls; **пот ~и́л у него́ на лбу** perspiration stood out on his forehead.

просту́п|ок, ка *m.* misdeed; (*leg.*) misdemeanour (*Br.*), misdemeanor (*US*).

простыва́|ть, ю *impf. of* **⇒просты́ть**

просты́н|ный *adj. of* **⇒~я́; ~ное полотно́** sheeting.

простын|я́, и́, *pl.* **про́стыни, ~ь, ~я́м** *f.* sheet.

просты́|ть, ну, нешь *pf.* (*of* **⇒~ва́ть**) **1** to get cold; to cool; **и след ~л** (+*g.*; *coll.*) not a trace (of). **2** (*coll.*) (*простудиться*) to catch cold.

просу́н|уть, у, ешь *pf.* (*of* **⇒просо́вывать**) (**в**+*a.*) to push (through, in), shove (through, in), thrust (through, in).

просу́н|уться, усь, ешься *pf.* (*of* **⇒просо́вываться**) to push through, force one's way through.

просу́шива|ть(ся), ю(сь) *impf. of* **⇒просуши́ть(ся)**

просуш|и́ть, у́, ~ишь *pf.* (*of* **⇒~ивать**) to dry thoroughly, properly.

просуш|и́ться, у́сь, ~ишься *pf.* (*of* **⇒~иваться**) to (get) dry.

просу́шк|а, и *f.* drying

просуществ|ова́ть, у́ю *pf.* (*прожить*) to exist; (*продлиться*) to last, endure.

просфор|а́, ы́ *f.* (*eccl.*) (communion) bread; host.

просце́ниум, а *m.* (*theatr.*) proscenium.

просчёт, а *m.* **1** (*действие*) counting (up), reckoning (up). **2** (*ошибка*) error (*in counting, reckoning*).

просчит|а́ть, а́ю *pf.* (*of* **⇒~ывать**) **1** (*подсчитать*) to count (up), reckon (up). **2** (*ошибиться*) to miscount; **вы ~а́ли пятьдеся́т рубле́й** you have given fifty roubles too much.

просчит|а́ться, а́юсь *pf.* (*of* **⇒~ываться**) **1** (*при счёте*) to miscount; **мы ~а́лись на два́дцать рубле́й** we are out by twenty roubles. **2** (*fig.*) to miscalculate.

просчи́тыва|ть(ся), ю(сь) *impf. of* **⇒просчита́ть(ся)**

про́сып, а *m.*: **без ~у** (*coll.*) without waking, without stirring.

просы́п|ать, лю, лешь *pf.* (*of* **⇒~а́ть**[1]) to spill.

просып|а́ть[1]**, а́ю** *impf. of* **⇒~ать**

просып|а́ть[2]**, а́ю** *impf. of* **⇒проспа́ть**[1]

просы́п|аться, лется *pf.* (*of* **⇒~а́ться**[2]) to spill, get spilled.

просып|а́ться[1]**, а́юсь** *impf. of* **⇒просну́ться**

просып|а́ться[2]**, а́ется** *impf. of* **⇒~аться**

просыха́|ть, ю *impf. of* **⇒просо́хнуть**

про́сьб|а, ы *f.* request; **обраща́ться с ~ой** to make a request; **у меня́ к вам п.** I have a favour (*Br.*), favor (*US*) to ask you; **по моей ~е** at my request; **«п. не кури́ть!»** 'no smoking, please!'

просяно́й *adj.* millet.

прота́лин|а, ы *f.* thawed patch (*of earth*).

прота́лкива|ть, ю *impf. of* **⇒протолкну́ть**

прота́лкива|ться, юсь *impf. of* **⇒протолка́ться** *and* **протолкну́ться**

протанц|ева́ть, у́ю *pf.* **1** to dance; **п. вальс** to dance a waltz, do a waltz. **2** (*некоторое время*) to dance.

прота́плива|ть, ю *impf. of* **⇒протопи́ть**

прота́птыва|ть, ю *impf. of* **⇒протопта́ть**

протара́н|ить, ю, ишь *pf.* (*of* **⇒тара́нить**) **1** (*mil.*) to ram. **2** (*fig.*) to break through, smash.

прота́скива|ть, ю *impf. of* **⇒протащи́ть**

прота́чива|ть, ю *impf. of* **⇒проточи́ть**

протащ|и́ть, у́, ~ишь *pf.* (*of* **⇒прота́скивать**) **1** to pull (through, along), drag (through, along), trail. **2** (*coll., pej.*) (*обманным путём*) to push through. **3** (*coll.*) (*подвергнуть критике*) to criticize severely, tear to pieces.

прота́|ять, ет *pf.* to thaw through.

протеже́ *c.g. indecl.* protégé(e).

протежи́р|овать, ую *impf.* (+*d.*) to favour (*Br.*), favor (*US*); to pull strings (for).

проте́з, а *m.* prosthesis; artificial limb; **зубно́й п.** false tooth, denture.

протези́р|овать, ую *impf. and pf.* to equip with a prosthetic appliance; to make a prosthetic appliance.

проте́зн|ый *adj.* prosthetic; **~ая мастерска́я** orthopaedic (*Br.*), orthopedic (*US*) workshop.

протеи́н, а *m.* (*chem.*) protein.

протека́|ть, ет *impf.* **1** *impf. of* **⇒проте́чь. 2** *impf. only* (*о реке, струе*) to flow, run. **3** *impf. only* (*о крыше*) to leak, be leaky.

проте́ктор, а *m.* **1** (*obs.*) (*покровитель*) protector, patron. **2** (*tech.*) (*покрышки*) tread (*of pneumatic tyre*).

протектора́т, а *m.* protectorate.

протекциони́зм, а *m.* **1** (*pol., econ.*) protectionism. **2** (*coll.*) favouritism (*Br.*), favoritism (*US*).

протекциони́ст, а *m.* protectionist.

проте́кци|я, и *f.* patronage, influence; **оказа́ть кому́-н. ~ю** to use one's influence on s.o.'s behalf, pull strings for s.o.

проте́|кший *p.p. act. of* **⇒~чь** *and adj.* past, last.

про|тере́ть, тру́, трёшь, *past* **~тёр, ~тёрла** *pf.* (*of* **⇒~тира́ть**) **1** (*одежду*) to rub a hole (in); to wear into holes. **2** (*через сито*) to rub through, grate. **3** (*окна*) to rub over, wipe over. **4**: **п. глаза́** (*coll.*) to rub one's eyes.

про|тере́ться, трётся, *past* **~тёрся, ~тёрлась** *pf.* (*of* **⇒~тира́ться**) to wear through, wear into holes.

протерп|е́ть, лю́, ~ишь *pf.* to wait, last out; to endure.

протесн|и́ться, ю́сь, и́шься *pf.* to push one's way (through), elbow one's way (through), barge (through).

проте́ст, а *m* **1** protest; **заяви́ть п.** to make a protest. **2** (*leg.*) objection.

протеста́нт[1]**, а** *m.* protester, objector.

протеста́нт[2]**, а** *m.* (*relig.*) Protestant.

протестанти́зм, а *m.* = **протеста́нтство**

протеста́нт|ка, ки *f. of* **⇒~**

протеста́нтский *adj.* (*relig.*) Protestant.

протеста́нтств|о, а *nt.* (*relig.*) Protestantism.

протест|ова́ть, у́ю *impf.* (**про́тив**+*g.*) to protest (against).

проте́чк|а, и *f.* leak.

проте́|чь, чёт, ку́т, *past* **~к, ~кла́** *pf.* (*of* **⇒~ка́ть**) **1** to ooze, seep. **2** (*о времени*) to elapse, pass; **кани́кулы бы́стро ~кли́** the holidays flew by. **3** (*о болезни*) to take its course.

про́тив *prep.* +*g.* **1** against; **п. тече́ния** against the current; **за и п.** for and against, pro and con; **име́ть что-н. п.** to have sth. against; to mind, object; **вы ничего́ не име́ете п. того́, что я курю́?** do you mind my smoking?; **вы ничего́ не бу́дете име́ть п., е́сли я закурю́?** will you mind if I smoke? **2** (*прямо перед*) opposite; facing; **друг п. дру́га** facing one another; **останови́тесь, пожа́луйста, п. це́ркви** please stop opposite the church. **3** (*вопреки*) contrary to; **п. на́ших ожида́ний** contrary to our expectations. **4** (*coll.*) (*по сравнению*) as against; according to; **в э́том году́ п. про́шлого** this year as against last (year).

про́тив|ень, ня *m.* (*неглубокий*) baking sheet, baking tray; (*глубокий*) roasting pan.

проти́в|иться, люсь, ишься *impf.* (*of* **⇒вос~**) (+*d.*) to oppose; to resist, stand up (against).

проти́вник, а *m.* **1** opponent, adversary; **п. коммуни́зма** anticommunist. **2** (*collect.; mil.*) the enemy.

проти́вно[1] *adv.* in a disgusting way.

проти́вно[2] *prep.* +*d.* against; contrary to; **поступа́ть п. свое́й со́вести** to go against one's conscience.

проти́вн|ый[1] *adj.* **1** (*противоположный*) opposite; contrary; **~ое мне́ние** a contrary opinion; **в ~ом слу́чае** otherwise; **доказа́тельство от ~ого** the rule of contraries. **2** (*враждебный*) opposing, opposed; **~ые сто́роны** opposing sides.

проти́вн|ый[2] **(~ен, ~на)** *adj.* (*отвратительный*) nasty, disgusting; **п. за́пах** nasty smell; **он мне ~ен** I find him offensive.

противо... *comb. form* anti-, contra-, counter-.

противоалкого́льный *adj.* temperance; **п. зако́н** prohibition.

противобо́рств|о, а *nt.* struggle; (*pol.*) confrontation.

противобо́рств|овать, ую *impf.* (+*d.*) to oppose; to fight (against).

противове́с, а *m.* (*tech. and fig.*) counterbalance, counterpoise.

противовозду́шн|ый *adj.* anti-aircraft; **~ая оборо́на** air defence (*Br.*), defense (*US*).

противога́з, а *m.* gas-mask.

противоде́йстви|е, я *nt.* opposition, counteraction.

противоде́йств|овать, ую *impf.* (+*d.*) to oppose, counteract.

противоесте́ствен|ный (~, ~на) *adj.* unnatural.

противозако́нност|ь, и *f.* illegality.

противозако́н|ный (~ен, ~на) *adj.* unlawful; (*leg.*) illegal.

противозача́точн|ый *adj.* contraceptive; **~ое сре́дство** contraceptive.

противолежа́щий *adj.* (*math.*) opposite; **п. у́гол** alternate angle.

противоло́дочный *adj.* (*naut.*) anti-submarine.

противообще́ственный *adj.* antisocial.

противопехо́тн|ый *adj.* (*mil.*): **~ая ми́на** antipersonnel mine.

противоподло́дочный *adj.* (*naut.*) anti-submarine.

противопожа́рн|ый *adj.* anti-fire; **~ая дверь** fire door; **~ые ме́ры** fire-prevention measures; **~ая слу́жба** fire service.

противопоказа́ни|е, я *nt.* **1** (*leg.*) contradictory evidence. **2** (*med.*) contra-indication.

противопока́занный *adj.* (*med.*) contra-indicated.

противополага́|ть, ю *impf. of* **⇒противоположи́ть**

противоположе́ни|е, я *nt.* opposition.

противополож|и́ть, у́, ~́ишь *pf.* (*of* **⇒противополага́ть**) (+*d.*) to contrast (with).

противополо́жност|ь, и *f.* **1** (*несходство*) opposition; contrast; **в п.** (+*d.*) as opposed (to), by contrast (with). **2** (*что-н. противоположное*) opposite, antithesis; **по́лная п.** complete antithesis; **пряма́я п.** exact opposite.

противополо́ж|ный (~ен, ~на) *adj.* **1** (*берег*) opposite. **2** (*мнение*) opposed, contrary; **диаметра́льно п.** diametrically opposed.

противопоста́в|ить, лю, ишь *pf.* (*of* **⇒~ля́ть**) (+*d.*) **1** (*направить против*) to oppose (with), counter (with); **си́ле п. си́лу** to oppose force with force. **2** (*сравнить*) to contrast (with), set off (against).

противопоставле́ни|е, я *nt.* (+*d.*) **1** (*направление против*) opposition (to). **2** (*сравнение*) contrasting (with), setting off (against).

противопоставля́|ть, ю *impf. of* **⇒противопоста́вить**

противоправи́тельственный *adj.* anti-government(al).

противопра́в|ный (~ен, ~на) *adj.* illegal.

противораке́тн|ый *adj.* (*mil.*) anti-missile; **~ая раке́та** anti-missile missile.

противоречи́вост|ь, и *f.* contradictoriness; discrepancy.

противоречи́в|ый (~, ~а) *adj.* contradictory; discrepant, conflicting; **~ые сообще́ния** conflicting reports.

противоре́чи|е, я *nt.* **1** (*несоответствие*) contradiction; inconsistency; **~я в показа́ниях** contradictions in evidence. **2** (*возражение*) contrariness; defiance; **дух ~я** spirit of defiance, contrariness. **3** (*конфликт*) conflict, clash; **находи́ться в ~и (с**+*i.*) to be at variance (with), conflict (with).

противоре́ч|ить, у, ишь *impf.* (+*d.*) **1** (*возражать*) to contradict; **он всё ~ил ма́тери** he was always contradicting his mother. **2** (*несоответствовать*) to be at variance (with), conflict (with), be contrary (to); **э́то ~ит действи́тельности** it is contrary to the facts; **их показа́ния ~ат одно́ друго́му** their evidence is conflicting.

противосамолётный *adj.* (*mil.*) anti-aircraft.

противостолбня́чный *adj.* (*med.*) anti-tetanus.

противостоя́ни|е, я *nt.* **1** (*astron.*) opposition. **2** (*pol.*) confrontation.

противосто|я́ть, ю, и́шь *impf.* (+*d.*) **1** (*сопротивляться*) to resist, withstand. **2** (*различаться по сути*) to be at variance. **3** (*astron.*) to be in opposition.

противота́нковый *adj.* anti-tank.

противото́к, а *m.* (*tech.*) counter-current, counterflow.

противоуго́нный *adj.* anti-theft.

противохими́ческий *adj.* (*mil.*) anti-gas.

противоцинго́тный *adj.* (*med.*) anti-scorbutic.

противошу́м|ы, ов *no sg.* ear defenders.

противоя́ди|е, я *nt.* antidote.

протира́|ть(ся), ю, ет(ся) *impf. of* **⇒протере́ть(ся)**

проти́рк|а, и *f.* cleaning rag.

проти́ск|аться, аюсь *pf.* (*of* **⇒~иваться**) to push one's way through, elbow one's way through.

проти́скива|ть, ю *impf. of* **⇒проти́снуть**

проти́скива|ться, юсь *impf. of* **⇒проти́скаться**

проти́с|нуть, ну, нешь *pf.* (*of* **⇒~кивать**) to push through, shove through.

проти́с|нуться, нусь, нешься *pf.* = **~каться**

протк|ну́ть, у́, ёшь *pf.* (*of* **⇒протыка́ть**) to pierce.

протодья́кон, а *m.* (*eccl.*) archdeacon.

протозо́а *pl. indecl.* (*zool.*) Protozoa.

протоиере́|й, я *m.* (*eccl.*) archpriest.

протоисто́ри|я, и *f.* prehistory.

прото́к, а *m.* **1** channel. **2** (*anat.*) duct.

протоко́л, а *m.* **1** (*заседания*) minutes; report; **вести́ п.** to take the minutes; **занести́ в п.** to enter in the minutes. **2** (*leg.*) statement; charge-sheet; **п. дозна́ния, п. допро́са** examination record; **соста́вить п.** to draw up a report. **3** (*dipl.*) protocol.

протоколи́р|овать, ую *impf. and pf.* (*pf. also* **за~**) to minute; to record.

протоко́л|ьный *adj. of* **⇒~**

протолка́|ться, юсь *pf.* (*of* **⇒прота́лкиваться**) (*coll.*) to force, jostle one's way (through).

протолкн|у́ть, у́, ёшь *pf.* (*of* **⇒прота́лкивать**) to push through, press through; (*fig.*): **п. де́ло** to push a matter forward.

протолкн|у́ться, у́сь, ёшься *pf.* = **протолка́ться**

прото́н, а *m.* (*phys.*) proton.

прото́н|ный *adj. of* **⇒~**

протоп|и́ть, лю́, ~́ишь *pf.* (*of* **⇒прота́пливать**) to heat thoroughly.

протопла́зм|а, ы *f.* (*biol.*) protoplasm.

протопо́п, а *m.* (*obs.*) archpriest.

протоп|та́ть, чу́, ~́чешь *pf.* (*of* **⇒прота́птывать**) **1** to beat, make (*by walking*); **п. тропи́нку** to make a path. **2** (*обувь*) to wear out.

проторг|ова́ть, у́ю *pf.* (*coll.*) to lose (*in trading*).

проторг|ова́ться, у́юсь *pf.* (*coll.*) to suffer losses (*in trading*); (*разориться*) to be ruined.

протор|ённый *p.p.p. of* **⇒~и́ть** *and adj.* well-trodden; **~ённая доро́жка** beaten track.

про́тор|и, ей *no sg.* (*obs.*) expenses.

протор|и́ть, ю́, и́шь *pf.* (*of* **⇒~я́ть**) to beat; **п. путь** to blaze a trail.

протор|я́ть, я́ю *impf. of* **⇒~и́ть**

прототи́п, а *m.* prototype.

прото́ч|енный *p.p.p. of* **⇒~и́ть; п. червя́ми** worm-eaten.

проточ|и́ть, у́, ~ишь *pf.* (*of* **⇒прота́чивать**) **1** (*о насекомых*) to gnaw through, eat through. **2** (*о текучей воде*) to wash. **3** (*на токарном станке*) to turn.

прото́чн|ый *adj.* flowing, running; **~ая вода́** running water; **п. пруд** pond fed by springs.

протра́в|а, ы *f.* (*chem.*) mordant.

протра́л|ить, ю, ишь *pf. of* **⇒тра́лить**

протрезв|и́ть, лю́, и́шь *pf.* (*of* **⇒~ля́ть**) to sober (*s.o.*) up.

протрезв|и́ться, лю́сь, и́шься *pf.* (*of* **⇒~ля́ться**) to sober up.

протрезвля́|ть(ся), ю(сь) *impf. of* **⇒протрезви́ть(ся)**

протубера́н|ец, ца *m.* (*astron.*) solar flare.

протур|и́ть, ю́, и́шь *pf.* (*coll.*) to drive away, chuck out.

протух|а́ть, а́ет *impf. of* **⇒~́нуть**

протýх|нуть, нет, нут, *past* **~, ~ла** *pf.* (*of* ⇒**~áть**) (*мясо, рыба*) to go bad.

протýх|ший *p.p. act. of* ⇒**~нуть** *and adj.* rotten; bad.

протыкá|ть, ю *impf. of* ⇒**проткнýть**

протя́гива|ть(ся), ю(сь) *impf. of* ⇒**протянýть(ся)**

протяжéни|е, я *nt.* **1** extent; (*пространство*) expanse, area; **на большóм ~и** over a wide area; **на всём ~и** (+*g.*) along the whole length (of), all along. **2**: **на ~и** (+*g.*) during, for the duration (of).

протяжённост|ь, и *f.* extent, length.

протяжён|ный (~, ~на) *adj.* extensive.

протя́жност|ь, и *f.* slowness; **п. рéчи** drawl.

протя́ж|ный (~ен, ~на) *adj.* long drawn-out; **~ное произношéние** drawl.

протя|нýть, нý, ~нешь *pf.* (*of* ⇒**~гивать**) **1** (*верёвку*) to stretch; (*линию связи*) to extend. **2** (*руки, ноги*) to stretch out; (*газету, книгу*) to hold out; **п. рýку пóмощи** to extend a helping hand; **п. нóги** (*fig., coll.*) to turn up one's toes. **3** (*дело*) to protract. **4** (*звуки, слова*) to drawl out. **5** (*pf. only*) (*прожить*) to last; **больнóй недóлго ~нет** the patient won't last long.

протя|нýться, нýсь, ~нешься *pf.* (*of* ⇒**~гиваться**) **1** (*о руках*) to stretch out; to reach out; **п. на дивáне** to stretch out on the sofa. **2** (*о дороге, о пространстве*) to extend, stretch, reach. **3** *pf. only* (*продлиться*) to last, go on.

проýл|ок, ка *m.* (*coll.*) lane.

проýчива|ть, ю *impf. of* ⇒**проучи́ть**[1]

проуч|и́ть[1]**, ý, ~ишь** *pf.* (*of* ⇒**~ивать**) (*coll.*) (*наказать*) to teach (a lesson); **я егó ~ý!** I'll teach him!

проуч|и́ть[2]**, ý, ~ишь** *pf.* (*некоторое время*) (*уроки*) to study, learn up (*for a certain time*); (*детей*) to teach (*for a certain time*).

проуч|и́ться, ýсь, ~ишься *pf.* to spend (*a certain time*) in study.

проф... *comb. form, abbr. of* **1** ***профессионáльный***. **2** ***профсою́зный***

профáн, а *m.* ignoramus; (*неспециалист*) layman.

профанáци|я, и *f.* profanation.

профани́р|овать, ую *impf. and pf.* to profane.

профершпи́л|иться, юсь, ишься *pf.* (*coll.*) to lose all one's money, be ruined.

профессионáл, а *m.* professional.

профессионали́зм, а *m.* professionalism.

профессионáльн|ый *adj.* **1** professional, occupational; **п. дипломáт** career diplomat; **~ое заболевáние** occupational disease; **~ое образовáние** vocational training; **~ая ориентáция** career guidance; **п. риск** occupational hazard; **п. секрéт** trade secret; **п. сою́з** trade union. **2** (*компетентный*) professional (*opp. amateur*).

профéсси|я, и *f.* profession, occupation, trade; **по ~и** by profession, by trade.

профéссор, а, *pl.* **~á** *m.* professor.

профéссорск|ий *adj.* **1** professorial. **2** *as n.* **~ая, ~ой** *f.* staff common room.

профéссорств|о, а *nt.* professorship, chair.

профессýр|а, ы *f.* **1** professorship, chair. **2** (*collect.*) the professors.

профилáктик|а, и *f.* **1** (*med.*) prophylaxis. **2** (*collect.*) preventive measures, precautions.

профилакти́ческий *adj.* **1** (*med.*) prophylactic. **2** preventive, precautionary.

профилактóри|й, я *m.* sanatorium, health farm.

прóфил|ь, я *m.* **1** (*вид сбоку*) profile; side-view; **в п.** in profile. **2** (*сечение*) section; **поперéчный п.** cross-section. **3** (*специфический характер*) type; **шкóлы рáзного ~я** schools of various types.

прóфиль|ный *adj. of* ⇒**~**; **~ное желéзо** section iron; **п. резéц, п. фрéзер** (*tech.*) profile cutter, forming tool.

профильтр|овáть, ýю *pf. of* ⇒**фильтровáть**

профин|ти́ть, чý, ти́шь *pf.* (*coll.*) to squander.

профи́т, а *m.* (*coll.*) benefit.

профитрóл|ь, я *m.* (*cul.*) profiterole.

профкóм, а *m.* (*abbr. of* ***профсою́зный комитéт***) trade-union committee.

профконсультáнт, а *m.* careers adviser.

профóрг, а *m.* (*abbr. of* ***профсою́зный организáтор***) trade-union organizer.

профóрм|а, ы *f.* form, formality; **чи́стая п.** pure, mere formality; **для ~ы, рáди ~ы** for form's sake, as a matter of form.

профсою́з, а *m.* trade union.

профсою́зный *adj.* trade-union.

прохáжива|ться, юсь *impf. of* ⇒**пройти́сь**

прохва|ти́ть, чý, ~тишь *pf.* (*of* ⇒**~тывать**) (*coll.*) **1** (*о холоде, о ветре*) to penetrate; **меня́ ~ти́ло на сквозняке́** I caught a chill from being in a draught (*Br.*), draft (*US*). **2** (*прокусить*) to bite through. **3** (*fig.*) (*раскритиковать*) to tear to pieces.

прохвáтыва|ть, ю *impf. of* ⇒**прохвати́ть**

прохворá|ть, ю *pf.* (*coll.*) to be ill (*for a certain time*); to be laid up (*for a certain time*).

прохвóст, а *m.* (*coll.*) scoundrel.

прохлáд|а, ы *f.* coolness.

прохлáд|ец, ца *m.*: **с ~цем** (*coll.*) (*без усердия; вяло*) without making much effort; listlessly; (*равнодушно*) coolly.

прохлади́тельн|ый *adj.* refreshing, cooling; **~ые напи́тки** soft drinks.

прохла|ди́ться, жýсь, ди́шься *pf.* (*coll.*) to cool off.

прохлáд|ный (~ен, ~на) *adj.* **1** cool; (*impers., pred.*): **~но** it is cool. **2** (*fig.*) cool; **отношéния у них стáли ~ными** there has been a cooling-off between them.

прохлáд|ца, цы *f.* = **~ец**

прохлаждá|ться, юсь *impf.* (*coll.*) to take it easy.

прохóд, а *m.* **1** (*действие*) passage; **прáво ~а** right of way; **не давáть ~а** (+*d.*) to give no peace, pester; **мне от негó ~а нет** I cannot get rid of him, shake him off. **2** (*место*) passageway; (*между рядами*) gangway, aisle; **кры́тый п.** covered way. **3** (*anat.*) duct; **зáдний п.** anus.

проходи́м|ец, ца *m.* rogue, rascal.

проходи́м|ка, ки *f. of* ⇒**~ец**

проходи́мост|ь, и *f.* **1** (*о дорогах*) passability. **2** (*об автомобиле*) cross-country ability.

проходи́м|ый (~, ~а) *adj.* passable.

прохо|ди́ть[1]**, жý, ~дишь** *impf.* **1** *impf. of* ⇒**пройти́**. **2** *impf. only* (**чéрез** + *a.*) to lie (through), go (through), pass (through); **канáл ~дит чéрез джýнгли** the canal passes through jungle.

прохо|ди́ть[2]**, жý, ~дишь** *pf.* (*некоторое время*) to walk; **мы ~ди́ли весь день** we have spent the whole day walking.

прохóдк|а, и *f.* (*mining*) working; sinking (*of shaft*); drift.

проходн|óй *adj. of* ⇒**прохóд**; passage; **п. балл** pass mark; **~áя бýдка** entrance check-point, entrance lodge; **~áя кóмната** inter-communicating room.

прохóдчик, а *m.* (*mining*) shaft sinker; drifter.

прохождéни|е, я *nt.* passing, passage; **п. торжéственным мáршем** (*mil.*) march past.

прохóж|ий *adj.* passing, in transit; *as n.* **п., ~его** *m.*, **~ая, ~ей** *f.* passer-by.

процветáни|е, я *nt.* prosperity, well-being; flourishing.

процветá|ть, ю *impf.* to prosper, flourish, thrive.

процe|ди́ть, жý, ~дишь *pf.* (*of* ⇒**~живать**) **1** to filter, strain. **2**: **п. сквозь зýбы** to say through clenched teeth.

процедýр|а, ы *f.* **1** procedure. **2** (*usu. pl.*) (*med.*) treatment.

процедýрный *adj.* procedural.

процéжива|ть, ю *impf. of* ⇒**процеди́ть**

процéнт, а *m.* **1** percentage; per cent; **сто ~ов** one hundred per cent; **рабóтать на ~ах** to work on a percentage basis. **2** (*доход с капитала*) interest; **размéр ~а** rate of interest; **просты́е, слóжные ~ы** (*math.*) simple, compound interest.

процéнт|ный *adj. of* ⇒**~**; interest-bearing; **~ное отношéние** percentage;

П

∼ные облига́ции interest-bearing bonds.

проце́сс, а *m.* **1** process. **2** (*leg.*) trial; legal action, legal proceedings; lawsuit. **3** (*med.*) active condition; **п. в лёгких** active pulmonary tuberculosis.

проце́сси|я, и *f.* procession.

проце́ссор, а *m.* (*comput.*) processor; **центра́льный п.** central processing unit.

процессуа́льн|ый *adj. of* **⇒проце́сс** 2; **∼ые но́рмы** legal procedure.

процити́р|овать, ую *pf. of* **⇒цити́ровать**

про́черк, а *m.* dash, line.

прочёркива|ть, ю *impf. of* **⇒прочеркну́ть**

прочерк|ну́ть, ну́, нёшь *pf.* (*of* **⇒∼́ивать**) to strike through, draw a line through.

прочер|ти́ть, чу́, ∼́тишь *pf.* (*of* **⇒∼́чивать**) to draw.

проче́рчива|ть, ю *impf. of* **⇒прочерти́ть**

проче|са́ть, шу́, ∼́шешь *pf.* (*of* **⇒∼́сывать**) **1** to comb out thoroughly. **2** (*mil.*; *fig.*) to comb.

прочёск|а, и *f.* screening (*as a security measure*).

про|че́сть, чту́, чтёшь, *past* **∼чёл, ∼чла́** *pf.* = **∼чита́ть**

прочёсыва|ть, ю *impf. of* **⇒прочеса́ть**

прочёт, а *m.* (*coll.*) error (*in counting*).

про́ч|ий *adj.* other; **и ∼ее (***abbr.* **и пр., и проч.)** etcetera, and so on; **∼ие** (the) others; **ме́жду ∼им** by the way; **поми́мо всего́ ∼его** in addition.

прочи́|стить, щу, стишь *pf.* (*of* **⇒∼ща́ть**) to clean out.

прочита́|ть¹, ю *pf. of* **⇒чита́ть**

прочита́|ть², ю *pf.* (*некоторое время*) to read.

прочи́тыва|ть, ю *impf.* (*coll.*) to read through, peruse.

про́ч|ить, у, ишь *impf.* (**в**+*a.*) to intend (for), destine (for); **его́ ∼или в свяще́нники** he was intended for the church.

прочища́|ть, ю *impf. of* **⇒прочи́стить**

про́чно *adv.* firmly, soundly, solidly, well.

про́чност|ь, и *f.* firmness, soundness, stability, solidity; durability; strength; **п. на уда́р** (*tech.*) shock resistance; **запа́с ∼и, коэффицие́нт ∼и** safety factor, safety margin.

про́ч|ный (∼ен, ∼на́, ∼но) *adj.* firm, sound, stable, solid; durable, lasting; **∼ные зна́ния** sound knowledge; **∼ная кра́ска** fast dye; **∼ное сча́стье** lasting happiness; **∼ная ткань** durable fabric.

прочте́ни|е, я *nt.* **1** reading; perusal; **по ∼и** (+*g.*) on reading. **2** (*истолкование*) interpretation, reading.

прочу́вствова|нный *p.p.p. of* **⇒∼ть** *and adj.* full of emotion; heart-felt.

прочу́вств|овать, ую *pf.* to feel deeply, acutely, keenly; **п. свою́ роль** to get the feel of one's part.

прочь *adv.* **1** away, off; **(поди́) п.!** go away!; be off!; **(пошёл) п. отсю́да!** get out of here!; **п. с глаз мои́х!** get out of my sight!; **п. с доро́ги!** (get) out of the way!, make way!; **ру́ки п.!** hands off! **2** *as pred.* averse (to); **не п.** (+*inf.*; *coll.*) to have no objection (to); to be not averse (to); **я не п. пойти́ туда́** I have no objection to (*or* I wouldn't mind) going there; **он не п. вы́пить стака́нчик** he is not averse to taking a drop.

прошвыр|ну́ться, ну́сь, нёшься *pf.* (*coll.*) to go for a stroll.

проше́дш|ий *p.p. act. of* **⇒пройти́** *and adj.* past; last; **∼им ле́том** last summer; **∼ее вре́мя** (*gram.*) past tense; *as n.* **∼ее, ∼его** *nt.* the past.

проше́ни|е, я *nt.* application, petition; **пода́ть п.** to submit an application, forward a petition.

прошеп|та́ть, чу́, ∼́чешь *pf. of* **⇒шепта́ть**

проше́стви|е, я *nt.*: **по ∼и** (+*g.*) after the lapse (of), after the expiry (of).

прошиб|а́ть, а́ю *impf. of* **⇒∼и́ть**

прошиб|и́ть, у́, ёшь, *past* **∼́, ∼́ла** *pf.* (*of* **⇒∼́а́ть**) (*coll.*) **1** to break through. **2**: **его́ ∼ пот** he broke into a sweat; **её ∼́ла слеза́** she shed a tear.

прошива́|ть, ю *impf. of* **⇒проши́ть**

проши́вк|а, и *f.* lace trim.

прош|и́ть, ью́, ьёшь *pf.* (*of* **⇒∼ива́ть**) **1** (*пришить*) to sew, stitch (on); (*некоторое время*) to sew (*for a certain time*). **2** (*coll.*) (*прострелить*) to pelt, pepper.

прошлого́дний *adj.* last year's; of last year.

про́шл|ый *adj.* **1** (*происходивший раньше*) past; former; **э́то де́ло ∼ое** it's a thing of the past; *as n.* **∼ое, ∼ого** *nt.* the past; **далёкое ∼ое** the distant past; **отойти́ в ∼ое** to become a thing of the past. **2** (*предшествовавший настоящему*) last; **в ∼ом году́** last year; **на ∼ой неде́ле** last week.

прошмы́гива|ть, ю *impf. of* **⇒прошмыгну́ть**

прошмыг|ну́ть, ну́, нёшь *pf.* (*of* **⇒∼́ивать**) (*coll.*) (*человек*) to slip (by, past, through); (*животное*) to scurry past.

прошнур|ова́ть, у́ю *pf. of* **⇒шнурова́ть** 2

прошпакл|ева́ть, ю́ю, ю́ешь *pf.* (*of* **⇒∼ёвывать**) to putty; (*naut.*) to caulk.

прошпаклёвыва|ть, ю *impf. of* **⇒прошпаклева́ть**

прошта́ф|иться, люсь, ишься *pf.* (*coll.*) to be at fault.

проштуди́р|овать, ую *pf. of* **⇒штуди́ровать**

прошум|е́ть, лю́, и́шь *pf.* **1** to roar past. **2** (*fig.*) to become famous.

проща́й(те) good-bye!; farewell!

проща́льн|ый *adj.* farewell, parting; **∼ая пиру́шка** farewell party; **∼ые слова́** parting words.

проща́ни|е, я *nt.* farewell; parting, leave-taking; **на п.** at parting.

проща́|ть(ся), ю(сь) *impf. of* **⇒прости́ть(ся)**

про́ще *comp. of* **⇒просто́й** *and* **про́сто;** simpler; plainer; easier.

прощелы́г|а, и *c.g.* (*coll.*) rogue.

проще́ни|е, я *nt.* forgiveness; (*преступника*) pardon; (*грехов*) absolution; **проси́ть ∼я у кого́-н.** to ask s.o.'s pardon; **прошу́ ∼я!** I beg your pardon!; (I am) sorry!

прощён|ый *adj.*: **∼ое воскресе́нье** last Sunday before Lent.

прощу́п|ать, аю *pf.* (*of* **⇒∼ывать**) **1** to feel; to detect (*by feeling*). **2** (*fig., coll.*) to size up, suss out.

прощу́пыва|ть, ю *impf. of* **⇒прощу́пать**

проэкзамен|ова́ть(ся), у́ю(сь) *pf. of* **⇒экзаменова́ть(ся)**

прояви́тел|ь, я *m.* (*phot.*) developer.

прояв|и́ть, лю́, ∼́ишь *pf.* (*of* **⇒∼ля́ть**) **1** to show, display; **п. забо́ту (о**+*p.*) to show concern (for, about); **п. интере́с (к**+*d.*) to show interest (in); **п. себя́** to show one's worth; **п. себя́** (+*i.*) to show o.s., prove (to be); **он ∼ил себя́ пре́данным колле́гой** he proved to be a loyal colleague. **2** (*phot.*) to develop.

прояв|и́ться, ∼́ится *pf.* (*of* **⇒∼ля́ться**) **1** (*обнаружиться*) to show (itself), reveal itself, manifest itself. **2** (*phot.*) to be developed.

проявле́ни|е, я *nt.* display, manifestation; **при пе́рвом ∼и** (+*g.*) at the first sign(s) of.

проявля́|ть(ся), ю, ет(ся) *impf. of* **⇒прояви́ть(ся)**

проя́сне|ть, ет *pf.* (*о небе*) to clear; (*impers.*): **∼ло** it cleared up.

проясне́|ть, ет *pf.* **1** to brighten (up); **лицо́ ма́льчика вдруг ∼ло** the boy's face suddenly brightened up. **2** (*о мыслях, о положении*) to become clear.

проясн|и́ть, ю́, и́шь *pf.* (*of* **⇒∼я́ть**) **1** (*мысли, положение*) to clarify. **2** (*голову*) to clear. **3** (*душу, лицо*) to brighten up.

проясн|и́ться, и́тся *pf.* (*of* **⇒∼я́ться**) **1** (*о погоде*) to clear (up); **днём ∼и́лось** in the afternoon it cleared up. **2** (*о мыслях, о положении*) to become clear.

проясн|я́ть, я́ю *impf. of* **⇒∼и́ть**

проясн|я́ться, я́ется *impf. of* **⇒∼и́ться**

пруд, а́, в ∼у́, *pl.* **∼ы́** *m.* pond.

пру|ди́ть, жу́, ∼́ди́шь *impf.* (*of* **⇒за∼**) to dam (up); **хоть пруд ∼ди́** (*coll.*) in abundance; **де́нег у них — хоть пруд ∼ди́** they are rolling in money.

пружи́н|а, ы *f.* spring; **гла́вная п.** mainspring (*also fig.*); **п.-волосо́к** hairspring.

пружи́нистост|ь, и *f.* springiness, elasticity.

пружи́нист|ый (∼, ∼а) *adj.* springy, elastic.

пружи́н|ить, ю, ишь *impf.* **1** (*trans.*)

to tense. **2** (*intrans.*) to be elastic, possess spring; **хорошо́ п.** to be well sprung.

пружи́нк|а, и *f.* **1** (*часов*) mainspring; hairspring. **2** (*противозачаточное средство*) loop, coil.

пружи́н|ный *adj. of* ⇒**~а; ~ные весы́** spring balance; **п. матра́ц** spring mattress.

пруса́к, а́ *m.* (*coll.*) cockroach.

прусса́к, а́ *m.* Prussian.

прусса́|чка, чки *f. of* ⇒**~к**

Пру́сси|я, и *f.* Prussia.

пру́сский *adj.* Prussian.

прут, а́ *m.* **1** (*pl.* **~ья, ~ьев**) twig; switch; **и́вовый п.** withe, withy. **2** (*pl.* **~ы́, ~о́в**) (*tech.*) bar.

пру́тик, а *m. dim. of* ⇒**прут; волше́бный п.** dowsing rod.

пры́гал|ка, ки (*also pl.* **~ки, ~ок**) *f.* (*coll.*) skipping-rope (*Br.*), jump rope (*US*).

пры́гани|е, я *nt.* jumping, leaping; skipping.

пры́г|ать, аю *impf.* (*of* ⇒**~нуть**) **1** to jump, leap, spring; to bound; **п. на одно́й ноге́** to hop on one leg; **п. со скака́лкой** to skip; **п. от ра́дости** to jump with, for joy. **2** (*о мяче*) to bounce.

пры́г|нуть, ну, нешь *pf. of* ⇒**~ать**

прыгу́н, а́ *m.* (*sport*) jumper; **п. в во́ду** diver; **п. в длину́** long-jumper.

прыгу́н|ья, ьи, *g. pl.* **~ий** *f. of* ⇒**~**

прыжко́в|ый *adj.*: **~ая вы́шка** diving board.

прыж|о́к, ка́ *m.* **1** jump, leap, spring. **2** (*sport*) jump; **~ки́** jumping; **акробати́ческие ~ки́** tumbling; **~ки́ на бату́те** trampolining; **~ки́ в во́ду** diving; **~ки́ с парашю́том** parachute jumping, sky-diving; **п. в высоту́** high jump; **п. в длину́** long jump; **п. с упо́ром** vault(ing); **п. с шесто́м** pole-vault; **п. с ме́ста** standing jump; **п. с разбе́га** running jump.

пры́ска|ть, ю *impf. of* ⇒**пры́снуть**

пры́ска|ться, юсь *impf.* (*of* ⇒**по~**) (+*i.*; *coll.*) to (be)sprinkle *or* spray o.s. (with).

пры́с|нуть, ну, нешь *pf.* (*of* ⇒**~кать**) (*coll.*) **1** (+*i.*) to sprinkle (with); to spray (with). **2** (*политься струёй*) to spurt, gush; **п. (со́ смеху)** (*fig.*) to burst out laughing.

пры́т|кий (~ок, ~ка́, ~ко) *adj.* quick, lively, sharp.

пры́т|ь, и *f.* (*coll.*) **1** (*быстрота*) speed; **во всю п.** at full speed. **2** (*подвижность*) energy, liveliness; **отку́да у него́ така́я п.?** where does he get his energy from?

прыщ, а́ *m.* pimple, spot; **лицо́ в ~а́х** pimply, spotty face.

прыща́ве|ть, ю *impf.* (*of* ⇒**о~**) to become covered in pimples, spots.

прыща́в|ый (~, ~а) *adj.* pimply, spotty.

прыщева́т|ый (~, ~а) *adj.* a bit pimply, spotty.

прюне́л|евый *adj. of* ⇒**~ь**

прюне́л|ь, и *f.* (*text.*) prunella.

пря́да|ть, ю *impf.* (*obs. or dial.*): **п. уша́ми** (*of, or in the manner of, a horse*) to move its ears.

пряде́ни|е, я *nt.* spinning.

пря́деный *adj.* spun.

пряди́льный *adj.* spinning; **п. стано́к** spinning loom.

пряди́л|ьня, ьни, *g. pl.* **~ен** *f.* (*obs.*) spinning mill.

пряди́льщик, а *m.* spinner.

пряди́льщи|ца, цы *f. of* ⇒**~к**

пряд|ь, и *f.* **1** (*пучок волос*) lock (*of hair*). **2** (*нить*) strand.

пря́ж|а, и *no pl., f.* yarn; **шерстяна́я п.** woollen yarn.

пря́жк|а, и *f.* buckle.

пря́лк|а, и *f.* spinning-wheel.

прям|а́я, о́й *f.* **1** straight line; **провести́ ~у́ю** to draw a straight line; **расстоя́ние по ~о́й** distance as the crow flies. **2** (*sport*) straight; **фи́нишная п.** home straight.

прямизн|а́, ы́ *f.* straightness.

прямико́м *adv.* (*coll.*) straight.

пря́мо *adv.* **1** straight (on); **иди́те п.!** (go) straight on!; **держа́ться п.** to hold o.s. straight *or* erect. **2** (*непосредственно*) straight, directly; **п. к де́лу** to the point; **попа́сть п. в цель** to hit the bull's eye (*also fig.*); **смотре́ть п. в глаза́ кому́-н.** to look s.o. straight in the face. **3** (*fig.*) (*откровенно*) straight; frankly, openly; **сказа́ть что-н. кому́-н. п. в лицо́** to say sth. to s.o.'s face; **мы ему́ п. сказа́ли, что э́то ему́ не уда́стся** we told him straight that he would not succeed. **4** (*coll.*) (*совершенно*) real; really; **он п. идио́т** he is a real idiot; **я п. не зна́ю, что с ней ста́ло** I really don't know what has become of her.

прямоду́ши|е, я *nt.* directness, straightforwardness.

прямоду́ш|ный (~ен, ~на) *adj.* direct, straightforward.

прям|о́й (~, ~а́, ~о) *adj.* **1** (*без изгибов*) straight; (*вертикальный*) upright, erect; **~а́я кишка́** (*anat.*) rectum; **п. пробо́р** parting in the middle; **п. у́гол** (*math.*) right angle; **п. у́зел** reef knot. **2** (*без промежуточных пунктов*) through; direct; **по́езд ~о́го сообще́ния** through train; **п. про́вод** direct (*telephone*) line. **3** (*непосредственный*) direct; **~ы́е вы́боры** direct elections; **~о́е дополне́ние** (*gram.*) direct object; **п. нало́г** direct tax; **п. насле́дник** heir in a direct line; **п. нача́льник** immediate superior; **~о́е попада́ние** (*mil.*) direct hit; **~а́я противополо́жность** direct opposite; **~а́я речь** (*gram.*) direct speech; **п. смысл сло́ва** the literal sense of a word. **4** (*откровенный*) straightforward, frank. **5** (*coll.*) (*верный*) real; **п. убы́ток** sheer loss; **п. расчёт пойти́ самому́** it is really worth while going o.s.

прямолине́йност|ь, и *f.* straightforwardness.

прямолине́|йный (~ен, ~йна) *adj.* **1** rectilinear. **2** (*fig.*) straightforward; direct.

прямот|а́, ы́ *f.* straightforwardness; plain dealing.

прямоуго́льник, а *m.* (*math.*) rectangle.

прямоуго́льный *adj.* right-angled; rectangular; **п. треуго́льник** right-angled triangle.

пря́ник, а *m.* spice cake; gingerbread; **медо́вый п.** honey-cake.

пря́ни|чный *adj. of* ⇒**~к**

пря́ност|ь, и *f.* spice.

пря́|нуть, ну, нешь *pf.* (*obs.*) to jump aside.

пря́ный *adj.* spicy (*also fig.*); (*запах*) heady.

пря|сть[1], ду́, дёшь, *past* **~л, ~ла́, ~ло** *impf.* (*of* ⇒**с~**) to spin.

пря́|сть[2], ду́, дёшь, *past* **~л, ~ла́, ~ло** *impf.* = **~дать**

пря́|тать, чу, чешь *impf.* (*of* ⇒**с~**) to hide, conceal.

пря́|таться, чусь, чешься *impf.* (*of* ⇒**с~**) to hide; to conceal o.s.; to take refuge.

пря́т|ки, ок *no sg.* hide-and-seek; **игра́ть в п.** to play hide-and-seek.

пря́х|а, и *f.* spinner.

псалмопе́в|ец, ца *m.* psalmodist.

псал|о́м, ма́ *m.* psalm.

псало́мщик, а *m.* (*eccl.*) (psalm-)reader; sexton.

псалты́р|ь, и *f. and* (*coll.*) **п., ~я́** *m.* (*eccl.*) Psalter.

пса́р|ня, ни, *g. pl.* **~ен** *f.* kennel.

псар|ь, я́ *m.* huntsman (*person in charge of hounds*).

псевдо... *comb. form* pseudo-.

псевдогеро́йческий *adj.* (*liter.*) mock-heroic.

псевдони́м, а *m.* pseudonym; (*comput.*) alias.

пси́н|а, ы *f.* (*coll.*) **1** (*мясо*) dog's flesh. **2** (*запах*) doggy smell. **3** (*пёс*) dog.

пси́ный *adj.* dog's; doggy.

псих, а *m.* (*abbr. of* **психопа́т**) (*coll.*) loony, nutcase.

психбольни́ц|а, ы *f.* mental hospital.

психиа́тр, а *m.* psychiatrist.

психиатри́ческий *adj.* psychiatric.

психиатри́|я, и *f.* psychiatry.

пси́хик|а, и *f.* state of mind; psyche; **нездоро́вая п.** unhealthy state of mind; **вре́дно де́йствовать на ~у** to have a harmful effect on the psyche.

психи́чески *adv.* mentally, psychically, psychologically; **п. больно́й** mentally ill; *as n.* **п. больно́й, п. больно́го** *m.* mental patient.

психи́ческ|ий *adj.* mental; **~ая боле́знь** mental illness.

психоана́лиз, а *m.* psychoanalysis.

психоанали́тик, а *m.* psychoanalyst.

психоаналити́ческий *adj.* psychoanalytic(al).

псих|ова́ть, у́ю *impf.* (*coll.*) to be hysterical; to go mad.

П

психо́з, а *m.* (*med.*) psychosis; **вое́нный п.** war hysteria.

психолингви́стик|а, и *f.* psycholinguistics.

психо́лог, а *m.* psychologist.

психологи́ческий *adj.* psychological.

психоло́ги|я, и *f.* psychology.

психонevро́з, а *m.* (*med.*) psychoneurosis.

психопа́т, а *m.* psychopath; (*coll.*) lunatic.

психопатологи́ческий *adj.* psychopathological.

психопатоло́ги|я, и *f.* psychopathology.

психосомати́ческий *adj.* psychosomatic.

психотерапе́вт, а *m.* psychotherapist.

психотерапевти́ческий *adj.* psychotherapeutic.

психотерапи́|я, и *f.* psychotherapy.

психоти́ческий *adj.* psychotic.

психофизиоло́ги|я, и *f.* psychophysiology.

психофизи́ческий *adj.* psychophysical.

психу́шк|а, и *f.* (*coll.*) loony bin.

псо́в|ый *adj.*: **~ая охо́та** the chase, hunting (*with hounds*).

псориа́з, а *m.* psoriasis.

пта́шк|а, и *f.* little bird; birdie; **ра́нняя п.** (*fig.*) early bird.

птен|е́ц, ца́ *m.* chick; fledg(e)ling (*also fig.*).

птерода́ктил|ь, я *m.* pterodactyl.

пти́ц|а, ы *f.* bird; **боло́тная п.** wader; **дома́шняя п.** (*collect.*) poultry; **хи́щные ~ы** birds of prey; **ва́жная п.** (*fig.*, *coll.*) big noise.

птицево́д, а *m.* poultry farmer, poultry breeder.

птицево́дств|о, а *nt.* poultry farming, poultry-keeping.

птицево́дческий *adj.* poultry-farming, poultry-keeping.

птицело́в, а *m.* fowler.

птицело́вств|о, а *nt.* fowling.

птицефе́рм|а, ы *f.* poultry farm.

пти́ч|ий *adj. of* ⇒**пти́ца; п. двор** poultry-yard; **вид с ~ьего полёта** bird's-eye view; **жить на ~ьих права́х** to live precariously without any rights.

пти́чк|а[1]**, и** *f. dim. of* ⇒**пти́ца**

пти́чк|а[2]**, и** *f.* tick; **ста́вить ~у** to tick.

пти́чник[1]**, а** *m.* (*помещение*) poultry-yard, hen-run; hen-house.

пти́чник[2]**, а** *m.* (*работник*) poultryman.

пти́чниц|а, ы *f.* poultrywoman.

птомаи́н, а *m.* (*chem.*) ptomaine.

ПТУ *nt. indecl.* (*abbr. of* ***профессиона́льно-техни́ческое учи́лище***) vocational technical school.

пуа́нт, а *m.* ballet shoe; **на ~ах** on the tips of the toes (*also fig.*).

пу́блик|а, и *f.* (*collect.*) (the) public; (*зрители, слушатели*) (the) audience.

публика́ци|я, и *f.* **1** (*действие*) publication. **2** (*объявление*) advertisement, notice; **помести́ть ~ю в газе́те** to place an advertisement in a newspaper; **п. о сме́рти** obituary notice.

публик|ова́ть, у́ю *impf.* (*of* ⇒**о~**) to publish.

публици́ст, а *m.* publicist; commentator on current affairs.

публици́стик|а, и *f.* sociopolitical journalism.

публицисти́ческий *adj.* publicistic.

публи́чк|а, и *f.* (*coll.*) public library.

публи́чно *adv.* publicly; in public; openly.

публи́чност|ь, и *f.* publicity.

публи́чн|ый *adj.* public; **~ая библиоте́ка** public library; **п. дом** brothel.

пу́гал|о, а *nt.* scarecrow.

пу́ган|ый *adj.* (*coll.*) scared; **~ая воро́на (и) куста́ бои́тся** (*prov.*) once bitten twice shy.

пуга́|ть, ю *impf.* (*of* ⇒**ис~, на~**) **1** to frighten, scare. **2** (+*i.*) to threaten (with).

пуга́|ться, юсь *impf.* (*of* ⇒**ис~, на~**) (+*g.*) to be frightened (of), be scared (of); to take fright (at); (*о лошади*) to shy (at).

пуга́ч, а́ *m.* **1** toy-pistol. **2** (*zool.*) screech owl.

пугли́вост|ь, и *f.* fearfulness, timidity.

пугли́в|ый (~, ~а) *adj.* fearful, timid.

пугн|у́ть, у́, ёшь *pf.* to give a fright, give a scare.

пу́говиц|а, ы *f.* button.

пу́гови|чный *adj. of* ⇒**~ца**

пу́говк|а, и *f.* (*small*) button.

пуд, а, *pl.* **~ы́, ~о́в** *m.* pood (*old Russian measure of weight, equivalent to 16.38 kilogrammes*).

пу́дел|ь, я, *pl.* **~и, ~ей** *or* **~я́, ~е́й** *m.* poodle.

пу́динг, а *m.* pudding.

пудлинг|ова́ть, у́ю *impf. and pf.* (*tech.*) to puddle.

пудо́вый *adj.* one pood in weight.

пу́др|а, ы *f.* powder; **са́харная п.** icing sugar (*Br.*), powdered sugar (*US*).

пу́дрениц|а, ы *f.* powder-compact.

пу́дреный *adj.* powdered.

пу́др|ить, ю, ишь *impf.* (*of* ⇒**на~**) to powder.

пу́др|иться, юсь, ишься *impf.* (*of* ⇒**на~**) to use powder, powder one's face.

пуза́н, а́ *m.* (*coll.*) person with a paunch, pot-bellied person.

пуза́т|ый (~, ~а) *adj.* (*coll.*) pot-bellied.

пу́з|о, а *nt.* (*coll.*) belly, paunch.

пузыр|ёк, ька́ *m.* **1** (*бутылочка*) vial. **2** (*пузырь*) bubble.

пузы́р|иться, ится *impf.* (*coll.*) **1** to bubble; to effervesce. **2** (*об одежде*) to blow up.

пузы́рник, а *m.* (*bot.*) senna-pod.

пузы́рчат|ый (~, ~а) *adj.* (*coll.*) covered with bubbles.

пузы́р|ь, я́ *m.* **1** (*шарик*) bubble; **мы́льный п.** soap-bubble; **пуска́ть мы́льные ~и́** to blow bubbles. **2** (*волдырь*) blister. **3** (*anat.*) bladder; **жёлчный п.** gall-bladder; **мочево́й п.** (urinary) bladder. **4** (*мешок*) bag.

пук, а, *pl.* **~и́** *m.* (*цветов*) bunch; (*бумаги, соломы, прутьев*) bundle; (*волос*) tuft.

пу́к|ать, аю *impf.* (*of* ⇒**~нуть**) (*coll.*) to fart.

пу́к|нуть, ну, нешь *pf. of* ⇒**~ать**

пул|ево́й *adj. of* ⇒**~я**

пулемёт, а *m.* machine-gun.

пулемёт|ный *adj. of* ⇒**~**

пулемётчик, а *m.* machine-gunner.

пуленепробива́емый *adj.* bullet-proof.

пулесто́йкий *adj.* bullet-proof.

пуло́вер, а *m.* pullover.

пульвериза́тор, а *m.* atomizer, sprayer.

пульвериза́ци|я, и *f.* spraying.

пу́льк|а[1]**, и** *f. dim. of* ⇒**пу́ля**

пу́льк|а[2]**, и** *f.* (*cards*) pool.

пу́льп|а, ы *f.* (*anat.*) pulp.

пульс, а *m.* pulse; **счита́ть п.** to take the pulse.

пульса́р, а *m.* pulsar.

пульса́ци|я, и *f.* pulsation, pulse.

пульси́р|овать, ую *impf.* to pulsate; (*о боли*) to throb.

пульт, а *m.* **1** (*пюпитр*) desk, stand; **дирижёрский п.** conductor's stand. **2** (*диспетчерский*) control panel.

пу́л|я, и *f.* bullet; **лить, отлива́ть ~и** (*fig.*, *coll.*) to tell lies.

пуля́рк|а, и *f.* fatted fowl.

пу́м|а, ы *f.* puma.

пуни́ческий *adj.* (*hist.*) Punic.

пункт, а *m.* **1** point; spot; **населённый п.** inhabited area; **исхо́дный п., нача́льный п.** starting point; **коне́чный п.** terminus, terminal; **кульминацио́нный п.** culmination, climax. **2** (*организационный центр*) station, centre (*Br.*), center (*US*); post, point; **медици́нский п.** first-aid station; **наблюда́тельный п.** observation post, point; **перегово́рный п.** (*collect.*) public (telephone) call-boxes; **призывно́й п.** recruiting centre (*Br.*), center (*US*). **3** (*документа*) point; paragraph, item; **по ~ам** point by point; **соглаше́ние из трёх ~ов** a three-point agreement. **4** (*typ.*) full point.

пу́нктик, а *m.* (*coll.*) **1** *dim. of* ⇒**пункт. 2** (*fig.*) eccentricity, peculiarity; **он — челове́к с ~ом** he is a bit odd.

пункти́р, а *m.* dotted line.

пункти́рн|ый *adj.*: **~ая ли́ния** dotted line.

пунктуа́льност|ь, и *f.* punctuality.

пунктуа́л|ьный (~ен, ~ьна) *adj.* punctual.

пунктуа́ци|я, и *f.* punctuation.

пу́нкци|я, и *f.* (*med.*) puncture.
пу́ночк|а, и *f.* (*zool.*) snow-bunting.
пунсо́н, а *m.* (*tech.*) punch, die, stamp.
пунцо́вый *adj.* crimson.
пунш, а *m.* punch (*drink*).
пуп, а́ *m.* (*coll.*) belly button, navel; **п. земли́** the hub of the universe.
пупа́вк|а, и *f.* stinking mayweed.
пупови́н|а, ы *f.* (*anat.*) umbilical cord.
пуп|о́к, ка́ *m.* **1** navel. **2** (*у птиц*) gizzard.
пупо́чный *adj.* (*anat.*) umbilical.
пупс, а *m.* (*coll.*) baby doll.
пупы́рыш|ек, ка *m.* (*coll.*) pimple.
пург|а́, и́ *no pl., f.* snow-storm, blizzard.
пури́зм, а *m.* purism.
пури́ст, а *m.* purist.
пури́ст|ка, ки *f. of* ⇒**~**
пурита́н|ин, ина, *pl.* **~е, ~** *m.* puritan.
пурита́н|ка, ки *f. of* ⇒**~ин**
пурита́нский *adj.* puritan; (*fig.*) puritanical.
пурита́нств|о, а *nt.* puritanism.
пу́рпур, а *m.* purple.
пурпу́рный *adj.* purple.
пурпу́р|овый *adj.* = **~ный**
пуск, а *m.* starting (up); setting in motion.
пуска́й *particle and conj.* (*coll.*) = **пусть**
пуска́|ть(ся), ю(сь) *impf. of* ⇒**пусти́ть(ся)**
пусков|о́й *adj.* starting; **п. пери́од** initial phase (*of working of factory, etc.*); **~а́я рукоя́тка** starting crank; **~о́е устро́йство** starter; **~а́я площа́дка** (rocket) launching platform.
пустельг|а́, и́ *f. and c.g.* **1** *f.* (*zool.*) kestrel. **2** *c.g.* (*coll.*) good-for-nothing.
пусте́|ть, ет *impf.* (*of* ⇒**о~**) to (become) empty; to become deserted.
пу|сти́ть, щу́, ~́стишь *pf.* (*of* ⇒**~ска́ть**) **1** (*дать свободу*) to let go; **п. на во́лю** to set free; **п. кро́вь кому́-н.** to bleed s.o.
2 (*разрешить идти*) to let; to allow, permit; **п. кого́-н. в о́тпуск** to let s.o. go on leave; **нас не ~сти́ли в пала́ту** they would not let us into the ward; **~сти́те соба́ку на двор** let the dog out.
3 (*разрешить войти*) to let in, allow to enter; **не п.** to keep out.
4 (*привести в движение*) to start, set in motion, set going, set working; **п. во́ду** to turn on water; **п. заво́д** to start up a factory; **п. слух** to start a rumour (*Br.*), rumor (*US*); **п. фейерве́рк** to let off fireworks; **п. часы́** to start a clock.
5 (*заставить или дать возможность двигаться*) to set, put; to send; **п. себе́ пу́лю в лоб** to blow out one's brains, put a bullet through one's head; **п. в обраще́ние** to put in circulation; **п. ло́шадь во весь опо́р** to give a horse his head; **п. в прода́жу** to offer for sale; **п. в произво́дство** to put in production; **п. в ход** to start, launch, set going, set in train; **п. в ход все сре́дства** to move heaven and earth; **п. кора́бль ко дну** to send a ship to the bottom; **п. по́ миру** to ruin utterly.
6 (+*a. or i.*) (*бросить*) to throw; **п. ка́мнем в окно́** to throw a stone at a window; **п. пыль в глаза́** to cut a dash, show off.
7 (*bot.*) to put forth, put out; **п. ко́рни** to take root (*also fig.*); **п. ростки́** to shoot, sprout.
пу|сти́ться, щу́сь, ~́стишься *pf.* (*of* ⇒**~ска́ться**) (**в**+*a. or* +*inf.*; *coll.*) **1** (*отправиться*) to set out, start; **п. в путь** to set out, get on the way.
2 (*начать*) to begin, start; to set to; **п. в оправда́ния** to start making excuses; **п. в пляс** to break into a dance.
пустобрёх, а *m.* (*coll.*) chatterbox, windbag.
пустова́т|ый (~, ~а) *adj.* **1** (*помещение*) rather empty. **2** (*роман*) fatuous.
пуст|ова́ть, у́ет *impf.* to be empty, stand empty; (*о земле*) to lie fallow.
пустоголо́в|ый (~, ~а) *adj.* empty-headed.
пустозво́н, а *m.* (*coll.*) windbag.
пустозво́н|ить, ю, ишь *impf.* (*coll.*) to engage in idle talk.
пустозво́нств|о, а *nt.* (*coll.*) idle talk.
пуст|о́й (~, ~а́, ~́о) *adj.* **1** empty; **п. взгляд** vacant look; **~о́е ме́сто** blank space; **на п. желу́док** on an empty stomach; **с ~ы́ми рука́ми** empty-handed. **2** (*fig.*) (*несерьёзный*) idle; shallow; frivolous; **~а́я болтовня́** idle talk; **п. челове́к** shallow person. **3** (*fig.*) (*напрасный*) vain, ungrounded; **~а́я зате́я** vain enterprise; **~ы́е мечты́** castles in the air; **~а́я отгово́рка** lame excuse; **~ы́е слова́** mere words; **~ы́е угро́зы** empty threats, bluster.
пустоме́л|я, и *c.g.* (*coll.*) idle talker, windbag.
пустопоро́жний *adj.* (*coll.*) empty, vacant.
пустосло́в, а *m.* (*coll.*) windbag.
пустосло́ви|е, я *nt.* (*coll.*) idle talk, verbiage.
пустосло́в|ить, лю, ишь *impf.* (*coll.*) to engage in idle talk.
пустот|а́, ы́, *pl.* **~́ы** *f.* **1** emptiness; void; (*phys.*) vacuum. **2** (*fig.*) emptiness, shallowness. **3** (*полое место*) cavity.
пустоте́лый *adj.* hollow.
пустоцве́т, а *m.* barren flower (*also fig.*).
пу́стош|ь, и *f.* waste (plot of) land, waste ground.
пусты́нник, а *m.* hermit.
пусты́нни|ца, цы *f. of* ⇒**~к**
пусты́н|ный (~ен, ~на) *adj.* **1** (*необитаемый*) uninhabited; **п. о́стров** desert island. **2** (*безлюдный*) deserted.
пу́стын|ь, и *f.* hermitage, monastery.
пусты́н|я, и *f.* desert, wilderness.
пусты́р|ь, я́ *m.* wasteland, vacant plot (of land).
пусты́шк|а, и *f.* (*coll.*) **1** (*у младенца*) dummy (*Br.*), pacifier (*US*). **2** (*fig.*) shallow person.
пусть 1 *particle* let; **п. бу́дет так!** so be it!; **п. она́ сама́ реши́т** let her decide herself; **п.** *x* **ра́вен 3** (*math.*) let $x = 3$. **2** *as conj.* though, even if; **п. им бу́дет проти́вно, но я до́лжен вы́сказать своё мне́ние** even if they hate it, I must express my opinion. **3** *particle* (*coll.*) (*ладно*) all right, very well.
пустя́к, а́ *m.* trifle; **спо́рить из-за ~о́в** to split hairs; **па́ра ~о́в!** (*coll.*) child's play!; **~и́!** (*i*) (*ничего*) it's nothing!; never mind!; (*ii*) (*вздор*) nonsense!; rubbish!
пустяко́вый *adj.* trifling, trivial.
пустя́чный *adj.* = **пустяко́вый**
путა́н|а, ы *f.* (*coll.*) tart, whore.
пу́таник, а *m.* muddle-head (*person*).
пу́таниц|а, ы *f.* muddle, confusion; mess, tangle.
пу́таный *adj.* **1** (*объяснение*) muddled, confused; confusing. **2** (*coll.*) (*человек*) muddle-headed. **3** (*нитки*) tangled.
пу́та|ть, ю *impf.* (*of* ⇒**с~, за~**) **1** (*нитки*) to tangle. **2** (*сбивать с толку*) to confuse, muddle; **он всё ~л слу́шателей примене́нием анало́гий** he always muddled his audience by his use of analogy. **3** (*смешивать*) to confuse, mix up; **ты ещё ~ешь на́ши имена́** you are still mixing our names up. **4** (*pf.* **в~**) (**в**+*a.*; *coll.*) (*вовлекать*) to implicate (in), mix up (in).
пу́та|ться, юсь *impf.* (*of* ⇒**с~, за~**) **1** (*о нитках*) to get tangled. **2** (*о мыслях*) to get confused. **3** (*сбиваться с толку*) to get mixed up, get muddled; **п. в расска́зе** to give a muddled account. **4** (*pf.* **в~**) (**в**+*a.*; *coll.*) (*вовлекаться*) to get mixed up (in); **п. в тёмные дели́шки** to get mixed up in shady business. **5** *impf. only* (*coll.*) (*болтаться*) to mooch about. **6** (**с**+*i.*; *coll.*) (*общаться*) to get mixed up (with); (*находиться в любовных отношениях*) to carry on (with).
путёвк|а, и *f.* **1** (*удостоверение*) pass, authorization; **сде́лать зая́вку на ~у в санато́рий** to apply for a place in a sanatorium; **п. в жизнь** a start in life. **2** place on a package holiday; **я купи́л ~у в Ита́лию** I have booked a package holiday to Italy. **3** (*водителя транспорта*) schedule of duties.
путеводи́тел|ь, я *m.* guide, guide-book.
путево́дн|ый *adj.* guiding; **~ая звезда́** guiding star; (*fig.*) lodestar; **~ая нить** guiding light.
путев|о́й *adj.* travelling (*Br.*), traveling (*US*), itinerary; **~ы́е заме́тки** travel notes; **~а́я ка́рта** road-map; **п. обхо́дчик, п. сто́рож** (*rail.*) trackman; **~а́я ско́рость** (*aeron.*) ground speed.
путе́|ец, йца *m.* (*coll.*) railway engineer.
путём[1] *prep.* (+*g.*) by means of, by dint of.
путём[2] *adv.* (*coll.*) (*как следует*) properly; coherently; **он ничего́ п. не уме́ет объясни́ть** he cannot explain anything coherently.
путеобхо́дчик, а *m.* (*rail.*) trackman.
путепрово́д, а *m.* (*над дорогой*) overpass, flyover; (*под дорогой*) underpass.
путеше́ственник, а *m.* traveller (*Br.*), traveler (*US*).
путеше́ственни|ца, цы *f. of* ⇒**~к**

путеше́стви|е, я *nt.* **1** journey; trip; (*морской*) voyage; cruise. **2** *pl.* (*liter.*) travels.

путеше́ств|овать, ую *impf.* to travel, go on travels; (*по морю*) to voyage; **п. по Интерне́ту** to surf the Internet.

пути́н|а, ы *f.* fishing season.

пу́тлищ|е, а *nt.* stirrup strap.

пу́тник, а *m.* traveller (*Br.*), traveler (*US*).

пу́тни|ца, цы *f. of* ⇒**~к**

пу́тн|ый *adj.* (*coll.*) sensible; **из него́ ничего́ ~ого не вы́йдет** you'll never make a man of him.

путч, а *m.* (*pol.*) putsch.

пу́ты, пут *no sg.* **1** hobbles. **2** (*fig.*) fetters, chains.

пут|ь, и́, *i.* **ём, о ~и́,** *pl.* **~и́, ~е́й, ~я́м** *m.* **1** (*дорога*) way, track, path; (*aeron.*) track; (*astron.*) race; (*fig.*) road, course; **во́дный п.** water-way; **морски́е ~и́** shipping-routes, sea-lanes; **~и́ сообще́ния** communications; **жи́зненный п.** (*fig.*) life; **на пра́вильном ~и́** on the right track; **сби́ться с (ве́рного) ~и́** to lose one's way; (*fig.*) to go astray.
2 (*rail.*) track; **запа́сный п.** siding.
3 (*путешествие*) journey; voyage; **в ~и́** on one's way, en route; **в четырёх днях ~и́ (от** + *g.*) four days' journey (from); **на обра́тном ~и́** on the way back; **по ~и́** on the way; **нам с ва́ми по ~и́** we are going the same way; **держа́ть п. (на** + *a.*) to head (for), make (for); **счастли́вого ~и́!** bon voyage!
4 *pl.* (*anat.*) passage, duct; **дыха́тельные ~и́** respiratory tract.
5 (*fig.*) (*средство*) way, means; **каки́м ~ём?** how?, in what way?; **ми́рным ~ём** amicably, peaceably; **око́льным ~ём, око́льными ~я́ми** in, by a roundabout way; **найти́ ~и́ и сре́дства** to find ways and means; **пойти́ по ~и́** (+ *g.*) to take the path (of).
6 (*coll.*) (*польза*) use, benefit; **без ~и́** in vain, uselessly.

пуф, а *m.* pouf(fe).

пух, а, о ~е, в ~у́ *m.* down; fluff; **в п. и прах** (*coll.*) completely, utterly; **разряди́ться в п. и прах** to put on all one's finery; **разби́ть в п. и прах** to put to complete rout; **ни ~а, ни пера́!** (*coll.*) good luck!

пу́хл|ый (~, ~а́, ~о) *adj.* (*человек*) chubby, plump; (*книга, досье*) fat.

пухля́к, а́ *m.* (*zool.*) willow tit.

пу́х|нуть, ну, нешь, *past* **~, ~ла** *impf.* to swell.

пухови́к, а́ *m.* feather-bed.

пухо́вк|а, и *f.* powder-puff.

пухо́вый *adj.* downy; (*платок*) angora; (*подушка*) down.

пучегла́з|ый (~, ~а) *adj.* goggle-eyed.

пучи́н|а, ы *f.* gulf, abyss (*also fig.*); (*морская бездна*) the deep.

пу́ч|ить, у, ишь *impf.* (*coll.*) **1** (*pf.* **вс~**) to become swollen; (*impers.*): **у него́ живо́т ~ит** he is troubled with wind. **2** (*pf.* **вы́~**): **п. глаза́** to goggle.

пуч|о́к, ка́ *m.* **1** (*газет, верёвки*) bundle; (*цветов*) bunch. **2** (*coll.*) (*причёска*) bun.

пу́ш|ечный *adj. of* ⇒**~ка**[1]; **п. ого́нь** gunfire, cannon fire; **~ечное мя́со** cannon-fodder.

пуши́нк|а, и *f.* bit of fluff; **п. сне́га** snow-flake.

пуши́ст|ый (~, ~а) *adj.* fluffy, downy.

пуш|и́ть, у́, и́шь *impf.* (*of* ⇒**рас~**) **1** to fluff up. **2** (*coll.*) (*ругать*) to swear at.

пу́шк|а[1], **и** *f.* **1** gun, cannon; **стреля́ть из пу́шек по воробья́м** (*prov.*) to use a sledgehammer to crack a nut. **2** (*sl.*) (*пистолет*) gun, shooter.

пу́шк|а[2], **и** *f.* (*coll.*): **на ~у** (*i*) (*обманным путём*) by a trick; (*ii*) (*бесплатно*) for nothing.

пушка́р|ь, я́ *m.* (*obs., coll.*) gunner.

пушни́н|а, ы *f.* (*collect.*) furs.

пушно́й *adj.* **1** (*животное*) fur-bearing; **п. зверь** (*collect.*) fur-bearing animals. **2** fur (*attr.*); **п. про́мысел** fur trade; **п. това́р** furs.

пуш|о́к, ка́ *m.* fluff.

пу́щ|а, и *f.* dense forest, virgin forest.

пу́ще *adv.* (*coll.*) more; **п. всего́** most of all.

пу́щ|ий *adj. only in phr.* **для ~ей ва́жности** for greater show.

пуэрторика́н|ец, ца *m.* Puerto Rican.

пуэрторика́н|ка, ки *f. of* ⇒**~ец**

пуэрторика́нский *adj.* Puerto Rican.

Пуэ́рто-Ри́ко *nt. indecl.* Puerto Rico.

ПХВ *m. indecl.* (*abbr.*) = ***полихлорвини́л***

Пхенья́н, а *m.* Pyongyang.

пчел|а́, ы́, *pl.* **~ы** *f.* bee; **рабо́чая п.** worker bee.

пчел|и́ный *adj. of* ⇒**~а́; п. воск** beeswax; **~и́ная ма́тка** queen bee; **п. рой** swarm of bees; **п. у́лей** beehive.

пчелово́д, а *m.* bee-keeper, apiarist.

пчелово́дств|о, а *nt.* bee-keeping, apiculture.

пчелово́дческий *adj.* bee-keeping.

пче́льник, а *m.* bee-garden, apiary.

пшени́ц|а, ы *f.* wheat; **ярова́я п.** spring wheat; **ози́мая п.** winter wheat.

пшени́чный *adj.* wheat(en).

пшён|ный *adj. of* ⇒**~о́**

пшен|о́, а́ *nt.* millet.

пшик, а *m.* (*coll.*) nothing; **оста́лся оди́н п.** nothing was left.

пыж, а́ *m.* wad (*used in loading fire-arm from muzzle*).

пы́жик, а *m.* (*телёнок*) young deer; (*мех*) fur of young deer.

пы́жиковый *adj.* deerskin.

пы́ж|иться, усь, ишься *impf.* (*of* ⇒**на~**) (*coll.*) **1** (*важничать*) to be puffed up, strut. **2** (*стараться*) to go all out.

пыл, а, о ~е, в ~у́ *m.* **1** (*coll.*) heat; **пирожки́ с ~у** hot pasties. **2** (*fig.*) heat, ardour (*Br.*), ardor (*US*); **ю́ный п.** youthful ardour (*Br.*), ardor (*US*); **в ~у́ сраже́ния** in the heat of the battle.

пыла́|ть, ю *impf.* **1** to blaze, flame. **2** (*о лице*) to glow. **3** (+ *i.*; *fig.*) to burn (with); **п. стра́стью** to be afire with passion.

пылесо́с, а *m.* vacuum cleaner, Hoover (*propr.*).

пылесо́с|ить, ишь *impf.* (*of* ⇒**про~**) to vacuum(-clean), hoover.

пыли́нк|а, и *f.* speck of dust.

пыл|и́ть, ю́, и́шь *impf.* **1** (*pf.* **на~**) to raise dust. **2** (*pf.* **за~**) to cover with dust, make dusty.

пыл|и́ться, ю́сь, и́шься *impf.* (*of* ⇒**за~**) to get dusty, get covered with dust; to gather dust (*also fig.*).

пы́л|кий (~ок, ~ка́, ~ко) *adj.* (*желание, речь*) ardent, passionate; (*воображение*) fervid.

пы́лкост|ь, и *f.* ardour, (*Br.*), ardor (*US*), passion.

пыл|ь, и, о ~и, в ~и́ *f.* dust; **водяна́я п.** spray; **у́гольная п.** coal-dust; slack; **смести́ п. (с** + *g.*) to dust.

пы́льник[1], **а** *m.* (*bot.*) anther.

пы́льник[2], **а** *m.* (*пальто*) dust-coat.

пы́л|ьный (~ен, ~ьна́, ~ьно) *adj.* **1** dusty; **~ьная тря́пка** (*coll.*) duster. **2**: **п. котёл** (*agric.*) dust bowl.

пыльц|а́, ы́ *f.* (*bot.*) pollen.

пыре́|й, я *m.* (*bot.*) couch-grass.

пырн|у́ть, у́, ёшь *pf.* (*coll.*) to jab; **п. ножо́м** to thrust a knife (into); **п. рога́ми** to butt.

пыта́|ть, ю *impf.* **1** to torture (*also fig.*); (*fig.*) to torment. **2** (*coll.*) (*пробовать*) to try; **п. сча́стье** to try one's luck.

пыта́|ться, юсь *impf.* (*of* ⇒**по~**) to try, attempt.

пы́тк|а, и *f.* torture, torment (*also fig.*); **ору́дие ~и** instrument of torture.

пытли́вост|ь, и *f.* inquisitiveness.

пытли́в|ый (~, ~а) *adj.* inquisitive.

пы́|хать, шу, шешь *impf.* **1** (**жа́ром**) to blaze. **2** (*fig.*): **п. гне́вом** to blaze with anger; **п. здоро́вьем** to be a picture of health.

пых|те́ть, чу́, ти́шь *impf.* **1** to puff, pant. **2** (*coll.*) (**над** + *i.*) to sweat (over).

пы́шк|а, и *f.* **1** doughnut (*Br.*), donut (*US*). **2** (*fig., coll.*) (*ребёнок*) chubby child; (*женщина*) plump woman.

пы́шност|ь, и *f.* **1** splendour (*Br.*), splendor (*US*), magnificence. **2** (*волос*) luxuriance; (*теста*) lightness.

пы́ш|ный (~ен, ~на́, ~но) *adj.* **1** (*великолепный*) splendid, magnificent. **2** (*пушистый*) fluffy; light; luxuriant; **~ные во́лосы** fluffy hair; **п. пиро́г** light pie; **~ные рукава́** puffed sleeves.

пьедеста́л, а *m.* **1** pedestal (*also fig.*); **вознести́ на п.** (*fig.*) to place on a pedestal. **2** (*победителя*) rostrum.

пье́ксы, пьекс *no sg.* ski boots.

пье́с|а, ы *f.* **1** (*theatr.*) play. **2** (*mus.*) piece.

пьяне́|ть, ю, ешь *impf.* (*of* ⇒**о~**) to get drunk, get intoxicated.

пьян|и́ть, ю́, и́шь *impf.* (*of* ⇒**о~**) to make drunk, intoxicate; (*fig.*) to intoxicate.

пья́ниц|а, ы *c.g.* drunkard; **го́рький п.** hard drinker.

пья́нк|а, и *f.* (*coll.*) drinking-bout, binge, booze-up.

пья́нств|о, а *nt.* drunkenness.

пья́нств|овать, ую *impf.* to drink heavily.

пья́н|ый (~, ~а́, ~о) *adj.* drunk; drunken; intoxicated; **по ~ой ла́вочке, с ~ых глаз** (*coll.*) one over the eight; *as n.* **п., ~ого** *m.* (a) drunk.

пэр, а *m.* peer.

пюпи́тр, а *m.* lectern; **но́тный п.** music-stand.

пюре́ *nt. indecl.* (*cul.*) purée; **карто́фельное п.** mashed potatoes.

пяд|ь, и, *pl.* **~и, ~е́й** *f.* span; **ни ~и не уступи́ть** (*fig.*) not to yield an inch; **будь он семи́ ~е́й во лбу** (*fig.*) be he a Solomon.

пя́л|ить, ю, ишь *impf.*: **п. глаза́** (**на**+*a.*; *coll.*) to stare (at).

пя́л|ьцы, ец *no sg.* tambour; (*для кружева*) lace-frame.

пяст|ь, и *f.* (*anat.*) metacarpus.

пят|а́, ы́, *pl.* **~ы, ~, ~а́м** *f.* **1** (*obs.*) heel; **ахилле́сова п.** Achilles' heel; **ходи́ть за кем-н. по ~а́м** to follow on s.o.'s heels; **под ~о́й** (+*g.*; *fig.*) under the heel (of); **с, от головы́ до́ ~** from top to toe, all over, altogether. **2** (*tech.*) abutment.

пята́к, а́ *m.* (*coll.*) five-copeck piece.

пятач|о́к¹, ка́ *m.* (*coll.*) **1** = **пята́к. 2** small (round) area; **аэродро́м с п.** pocket handkerchief aerodrome.

пятач|о́к², ка́ *m.* (*coll.*) (*у свиньи*) snout.

пятёрк|а, и *f.* **1** (*цифра*) five. **2** (*отметка*) five, 'A' (*highest mark in Russian educational marking system*). **3** (*coll.*) (*пять рублей*) five-rouble note, fiver. **4** (*cards*) five. **5** (*coll.*) (*автобус, трамвай*) No 5 (*bus, tram, etc.*). **6** (*coll.*) group of five (*people, objects*).

пятерн|я́, и́, *g. pl.* **~е́й** *f.* (*coll.*) hand.

пя́тер|о, ы́х *num.* (*collect.*) five.

пятиалты́нн|ый, ого *m.* (*obs.*) fifteen-kopeck piece.

пятибо́р|ец, ца *m.* pentathlete.

пятибо́рь|е, я *nt.* (*sport*) pentathlon.

пятигра́нник, а *m.* (*math.*) pentahedron.

пятигра́нный *adj.* (*math.*) pentahedral.

пятидве́рн|ый *adj.*: **~ая маши́на** hatchback.

пятидесятиле́ти|е, я *nt.* **1** (*срок*) fifty years. **2** (*годовщина*) fiftieth anniversary; (*день рождения*) fiftieth birthday.

пятидесятиле́тний *adj.* **1** (*срок*) fifty-year, of fifty years. **2** (*человек*) fifty-year-old.

пятидеся́тник, а *m.* (*relig.*) Pentecostalist.

Пятидеся́тниц|а, ы *f.* (*eccl.*) Pentecost.

пятидеся́тни|ца, цы *f. of* **⇒~к**

пятидеся́т|ый *adj.* fiftieth; **~ые го́ды** the fifties.

пятидне́вк|а, и *f.* five-day period; five-day week.

пятикла́ссник, а *m.* fifth-former (*Br.*), fifth-grader (*US*).

пятикла́ссни|ца, цы *f. of* **⇒~к**

Пятикни́жи|е, я *nt.* (*eccl., liter.*) Pentateuch.

пятиконе́чн|ый *adj.*: **~ая звезда́** five-pointed star.

пятикра́тный *adj.* fivefold.

пятиле́ти|е, я *nt.* **1** (*срок*) five years. **2** (*годовщина*) fifth anniversary.

пятиле́тк|а, и *f.* (*econ.*) five-year plan.

пятиле́тний *adj.* **1** (*срок*) five-year; **п. план** (*econ.*) five-year plan. **2** (*ребёнок*) five-year-old.

пятисотле́ти|е, я *nt.* **1** (*срок*) five centuries. **2** (*годовщина*) quincentenary.

пятисо́тый *adj.* five-hundredth.

пя́|тить, чу, тишь *impf.* (*of* **⇒по~**) to back, move back.

пя́|титься, чусь, тишься *impf.* (*of* **⇒по~**) to back, move backward(s); (*о лошади*) to jib.

пятиуго́льник, а *m.* (*math.*) pentagon.

пятиуго́льный *adj.* pentagonal.

пятиэта́жный *adj.* five-storey (*Br.*), five-story (*US*).

пя́тк|а, и *f.* heel (*also of sock or stocking*); **лиза́ть кому́-н. ~и** to lick s.o.'s boots; **показа́ть ~и** to show a clean pair of heels; **у меня́ душа́ в ~и ушла́** my heart sank to my boots.

пятнадцатиле́тний *adj.* **1** (*срок*) fifteen-year. **2** (*мальчик*) fifteen-year-old.

пятна́дцатый *adj.* fifteenth.

пятна́дцат|ь, и *num.* fifteen.

пятна́|ть, ю *impf.* (*of* **⇒за~**) **1** to spot, stain; (*fig.*) to stain, blemish. **2** (*coll.*) (*играя в пятнашки*) to catch (*at tag*).

пятна́ш|ки, ек *no sg.* (*coll.*) (*children's game*) tag.

пятни́ст|ый (~, ~а) *adj.* spotted, dappled; **п. оле́нь** spotted deer.

пя́тниц|а, ы *f.* Friday; **по ~ам** on Fridays, every Friday; **у него́ семь ~ на неде́ле** he keeps changing his mind.

пят|но́, на́, *pl.* **~на, ~ен, ~нам** *nt.* **1** (*место иной окраски*) spot; patch; (*запачканное место*) stain; **роди́мое п.** birth-mark; **со́лнечные ~на** (*astron.*) sun-spots. **2** (*fig.*) blot, stain; blemish.

пя́тныш|ко, ка, *pl.* **~ки, ~ек, ~кам** *nt.* speck.

пят|о́к, ка́ *m.* (+*g.*; *coll.*) five (*similar objects*).

пя́т|ый *adj.* fifth; **глава́ ~ая** chapter five; **п. но́мер** number five, size five; **~ое число́ (ме́сяца)** the fifth (*day of the month*); **в ~ом часу́** after four (o'clock).

пят|ь, и́, ью *num.* five.

пятьдеся́т, пяти́десяти, пятью́десятью *num.* fifty.

пятьсо́т, пятисо́т, пятиста́м *num.* five hundred.

пя́тью *adv.* five times; **п. шесть** five times six.

Рр

р. *abbr. of* **1** ***река*** R., River. **2** ***рубль*** r., rouble(s).

раб, а́ *m.* slave (*also fig.*).

раб... *comb. form, abbr. of* ***рабо́чий*** *adj.* 1

раб|а́, ы́ *f.* (*female*) slave.

раблезиа́нский *adj.* (*liter.*) Rabelaisian.

рабовладе́л|ец, ьца *m.* slave-owner.

рабовладе́льческий *adj.* slave-owning.

раболе́пи|е, я *nt.* servility.

раболе́п|ный (~ен, ~на) *adj.* servile.

раболе́пств|о, а *nt.* servility.

раболе́пств|овать, ую *impf.* (**перед** + *i.*) to fawn (on), kowtow (to).

рабо́т|а, ы *f.* **1** (*действие*) work, working; (*функционирование*) functioning, running; **обеспе́чить норма́льную ~у** (+ *g.*) to ensure normal functioning (of). **2** (*занятие, труд*) work; labour (*Br.*), labor (*US*); **дома́шняя р.** homework; **принуди́тельные ~ы** forced labour (*Br.*), labor (*US*); **сельскохозя́йственные ~ы** agricultural work; **совме́стная р.** collaboration; **взять в ~у** (*coll.*) to take to task. **3** (*как источник заработка*) work, job; **постоя́нная р.** regular work; **случа́йная р.** casual work, odd job(s); **иска́ть ~у** to look for a job; **снять с ~ы** to lay off, dismiss; **быть без ~ы, не име́ть ~ы** to be out of work. **4** (*качество работы*) work, workmanship.

рабо́та|ть, ю *impf.* **1** (**на** + *a.*; **над** + *i.*) to work (for; on); **вре́мя ~ет на нас** time is on our side; **он ~ет над но́вым рома́ном** he is working on a new novel. **2** (*функционировать*) to work, run, function; **не р.** not to work, be out of order; **р. на не́фти** to run on oil. **3** (*быть открытым*) to be open; **галере́я не ~ет по воскресе́ньям** the gallery is not open on Sundays. **4** (+ *i.*) (*управлять*) to work, operate; **р. вёслами** to ply the oars; **р. рычаго́м** to operate a lever.

рабо́та|ться, ется *impf.* (*impers.*; *coll.*): **сего́дня хорошо́ ~ется** work is going well today; **вчера́ мне не ~лось** I didn't feel like working yesterday.

рабо́тник, а *m.* worker; (*учреждения*) employee; **нау́чный р.** researcher; **р. иску́сства** person working in the arts; **р. физи́ческого труда́** manual worker.

рабо́тниц|а, ы *f.* (*female*) worker; (*учреждения*) (*female*) employee; **дома́шняя р.** (house)maid; home help.

рабо́тный *adj.*: **р. дом** (*obs.*) workhouse.

работода́тел|ь, я *m.* employer.

работома́н, а *m.* workaholic.

работома́н|ка, ки *f. of* ⇒~

работорго́в|ец, ца *m.* slave-trader, slaver.

работорго́вл|я, и *f.* slave-trade.

работоспосо́бност|ь, и *f.* ability to work; capacity for work.

работоспосо́б|ный (~ен, ~на) *adj.* **1** (*могущий работать*) able to work, able-bodied. **2** (*способный много работать*) able to work hard, hardworking.

работя́г|а, и *c.g.* (*coll.*) hard worker; slogger.

работя́щий *adj.* (*coll.*) hard-working, industrious.

рабо́ч|ий¹, его *m.* worker; workman; **~ие** (*collect.*; *as social class*) the workers; **сезо́нный р.** seasonal worker; **р. от станка́** factory worker.

рабо́ч|ий² *adj.* **1** (*относящийся к рабочим*) workers', working-class; **~ее движе́ние** working-class movement; **р. класс** the working class; **р. по́езд** workmen's train. **2** (*выполняющий работу*) work, working; **~ая ло́шадь** draught-horse; **р. мураве́й** worker ant; **~ая пчела́** worker bee; **~ие ру́ки** hands; **~ая си́ла** manpower; **р. скот** draught animals. **3** (*предназначенный для работы*) working; **~ее вре́мя** working time, working hours; **р. день** working day (*Br.*), workday (*US*); **р. костю́м, ~ее пла́тье** working clothes; **~ее ме́сто** (*i*) (*помещение*) working place, workplace, (*ii*) (*пост*) job; **~ая ста́нция** (*comput.*) work station. **4**: **в ~ем поря́дке** while working, without breaking off from work.

ра́б|ский *adj.* **1** *adj. of* ⇒~; **р. труд** slave labour (*Br.*), labor (*US*). **2** (*fig.*) (*раболепный*) servile.

ра́бств|о, а *nt.* slavery, servitude.

рабфа́к, а *m.* (*hist.*) (*abbr. of* ***рабо́чий факульте́т***) 'rabfak'; workers' school (*educational establishment in existence during the first years after the Russian Revolution, set up to prepare workers and peasants for higher education*).

рабы́н|я, и, *g. pl.* **~ь** *f.* (*female*) slave.

равви́н, а *m.* rabbi.

равенду́к, а *m.* (*text.*) duck.

ра́венств|о, а *nt.* equality; parity; **знак ~а** (*math.*) equals sign.

равио́ли *nt. and pl. indecl.* ravioli.

равне́ни|е, я *nt.* **1** dressing, alignment; **р. нале́во!, р. напра́во!** (*mil. words of command*) eyes left!, eyes right! **2** (**на** + *a.*) emulation (of).

равни́н|а, ы *f.* plain.

равни́н|ный *adj. of* ⇒**~а**; **р. жи́тель** plainsman; **~ная ме́стность** flat country.

равно́¹ *adv.* **1** alike, in like manner. **2** *as conj.* **р. как (и), (а) р. и** as well as; and also; (*after neg.*) nor; **золото́й брасле́т, р. как и други́е её драгоце́нности, пропа́л** a gold bracelet, as well as other jewellery of hers, had disappeared.

равно́² *nt. pred. form of* ⇒**ра́вный.** **1** (*math.*) make(s), equals, is; **три плюс три р. шести́** three plus three equals six. **2**: **всё р.** it is all the same, it makes no difference; *as adv.* all the same; **всё р., что** it is just the same as, it is equivalent to; **мне всё р.** I don't mind; it's all the same, all one to me; **я всё р. вам позвоню́** I will ring you all the same; **не всё ли р.?** what difference does it make?

равно... *comb. form* equi-, iso-.

равнобе́дренный *adj.* (*math.*) isosceles.

равновели́к|ий (~, ~а) *adj.* (*math.*) equivalent; **~ие треуго́льники** equivalent triangles.

равнове́си|е, я *nt.* equilibrium (*also fig.*); balance; **душе́вное р.** mental equilibrium; **полити́ческое р.** balance of power; **вы́вести из ~я** to disturb the equilibrium (of), upset the balance (of); **привести́ в р.** to balance; **сохраня́ть р.** to keep one's balance.

равноде́йствующ|ая, ей *f.* (*math., phys.*) resultant (force).

равноде́нстви|е, я *nt.* equinox; **весе́ннее, осе́ннее р.** vernal, autumnal equinox.

равноду́ши|е, я *nt.* indifference.

равноду́ш|ный (~ен, ~на) *adj.* (**к**+*d.*) indifferent (to).

равнозна́ч|ный (~ен, ~на) *adj.* equivalent.

равноме́рност|ь, и *f.* evenness; uniformity.

равноме́р|ный (~ен, ~на) *adj.* even; uniform; **~ная ско́рость** uniform speed.

равнопра́ви|е, я *nt.* (possession of) equal rights; equality.

равнопра́в|ный (~ен, ~на) *adj.* possessing, enjoying equal rights; equal.

равноси́л|ьный (~ен, ~ьна) *adj.* **1** of equal strength; equally matched. **2** (+*d.*) equal (to), equivalent (to), tantamount (to); **э́то ~ьно изме́не** it is tantamount to treachery; it amounts to treachery.

равносторо́нний *adj.* (*math.*) equilateral.

равноце́н|ный (~ен, ~на) *adj.* of equal value, of equal worth; equivalent.

ра́в|ный (~ен, ~на́, ~но́) *adj.* equal; **~ным о́бразом** equally, likewise; **при про́чих ~ных усло́виях** other things being equal; **ему́ нет ~ного** he has no equal.

равня́|ть, ю *impf.* (*of* ⇒**с~**) **1** (*делать равным*) to make equal; **р. счёт** (*sport*) to equalize. **2** (**с**+*i.*; *coll.*) to compare (with), equate (with).

равня́|ться, юсь *impf.* **1** (**по**+*d.*) (*mil.*) to dress; **~йсь!** (*word of command*) eyes right!; **р. в заты́лок** to cover off. **2** (**с**+*i.*; *coll.*) to compete (with), compare (with), match. **3** *impf. only* (+*d.*) to equal, be equal (to); (*fig.*) to be equivalent (to), be tantamount (to), amount (to); **два́жды пять ~ется десяти́** twice five is ten.

рагу́ *nt. indecl.* (*cul.*) ragout; **кита́йское р.** chop suey.

рад (~а, ~о) *pred. adj.* (+*d.*; +*inf.*; **что**) glad (of; to; that); **я был о́чень р. слу́чаю поговори́ть с ни́ми** I was very glad of the opportunity to talk to them; **о́чень р. (познако́миться с ва́ми)!** pleased to meet you!; **и не р., сам не р.** (*coll.*) I, *etc.*, regret it; I, *etc.*, am sorry; **и не р., что пошёл** I'm sorry I went; **р. не р.** (*coll.*) willy-nilly; like it or not; **р.-радёшенек** (*coll.*) pleased as Punch, chuffed.

ра́д|а, ы *f.* rada (= *council; popular assembly in Ukraine, Byelorussia, Lithuania and Poland at var. times in history*).

рада́р, а *m.* radar.

рада́р|ный *adj. of* ⇒**~**

раде́ни|е, я *nt.* (*coll.*) zeal.

раде́|ть, ю, ешь *impf.* (*obs.*) **1** (*pf.* **по~**) (+*d.*) to oblige; (**о**+*p.*) to be concerned (about). **2** *impf. only* (*relig.*; *of some Russian sects*) to carry out rites.

ра́дж|а, и *m.* rajah.

ра́ди *prep.*+*g.* for the sake of; **чего́ р.?** what for?; **шу́тки р.** for fun; **р. Бо́га** (*coll.*) for God's sake, for goodness' sake.

радиа́льный *adj.* (*math., tech.*) radial.

радиа́тор, а *m.* radiator.

радиацио́нный *adj.* radiation.

радиа́ци|я, и *f.* radiation.

ра́диевый *adj.* radium.

ра́ди|й, я *m.* (*chem.*) radium.

радика́л[1], а *m.* (*math., chem.*) radical.

радика́л[2], а *m.* (*pol.*) radical.

радикали́зм, а *m.* (*pol.*) radicalism.

радика́льност|ь, и *f.* **1** (*pol.*) radicalism. **2** (*решительность*) radical nature, drastic nature, sweeping character.

радика́л|ьный (~ен, ~ьна) *adj.* **1** (*pol.*) radical. **2** (*решительный*) radical, drastic, sweeping; **~ьные измене́ния** sweeping changes; **~ьные ме́ры** drastic measures; **~ьное сре́дство** drastic remedy.

радикули́т, а *m.* radiculitis; back pain.

ра́дио *nt. indecl.* **1** (*средство связи*) radio; **по р.** by radio, over the air; **переда́ть по р.** to broadcast; **слу́шать р.** to listen in. **2** (*радиоприёмник*) radio.

радио... *comb. form* radio-.

радиоакти́вност|ь, и *f.* (*chem., phys.*) radio-activity.

радиоакти́в|ный (~ен, ~на) *adj.* (*chem., phys.*) radio-active.

радиобесе́д|а, ы *f.* phone-in.

радиобиоло́ги|я, и *f.* radio-biology.

радиовеща́ни|е, я *nt.* broadcasting.

радиовеща́тельн|ый *adj.* broadcasting; **~ая ста́нция** broadcasting station, transmitter.

радиоволн|а́, ы́, *pl.* **~́ы, ~а́м** *f.* radio-wave.

радиогра́мм|а, ы *f.* radio-telegram.

радио́граф, а *m.* radiographer.

радиографи́ческий *adj.* radiographic.

радиогра́фи|я, и *f.* radiography.

радиожурнали́ст, а *m.* (*radio*) broadcaster.

радиожурнали́ст|ка, ки *f. of* ⇒**~**

радиозо́нд, а *m.* radio-sounding apparatus.

радио́л|а, ы *f.* radiogram (*Br.*), radio phonograph (*US*).

радио́лог, а *m.* radiologist.

радиологи́ческ|ий *adj.* radiological; **~ая устано́вка** radiological unit.

радиоло́ги|я, и *f.* radiology.

радиолока́тор, а *m.* radar set.

радиолок|ацио́нный *adj. of* ⇒**~а́ция**

радиолока́ци|я, и *f.* radar.

радиолюби́тел|ь, я *m.* radio enthusiast, 'ham'.

радиома́чт|а, ы *f.* radio-mast.

радиомая́к, а́ *m.* radio-beacon.

радиомо́ст, а *m.* satellite (radio) link-up.

радиопеленга́тор, а *m.* radio direction finder.

радиопеленга́ци|я, и *f.* radio direction-finding.

радиопереда́тчик, а *m.* (radio) transmitter.

радиопереда́ч|а, и *f.* radio transmission, broadcast.

радиоперехва́т, а *m.* radio interception.

радиопостано́вк|а, и *f.* radio show.

радиоприёмник, а *m.* radio (set).

радиору́бк|а, и *f.* (*naut., aeron.*) radio room, radio cabin.

радиосвя́з|ь, и *f.* radio communication.

радиосе́т|ь, и *f.* radio network.

радиосигна́л, а *m.* radio signal.

радиослу́шател|ь, я *m.* (radio) listener.

радиоста́нци|я, и *f.* radio station.

радиотелегра́ф, а *m.* radio telegraph.

радиотелеграфи́|я, и *f.* radio-telegraphy.

радиотелефо́н, а *m.* radio-telephone.

радиотерапи́|я, и *f.* radio-therapy.

радиоте́хник, а *m.* radio mechanic.

радиоте́хник|а, и *f.* radio engineering.

радио|техни́ческий *adj. of* ⇒**~те́хника**

радиотрансляцио́нный *adj.* broadcasting.

радиоуглеро́дный *adj.*: **р. ана́лиз** carbon dating.

радиоу́з|ел, ла́ *m.* radio relay centre.

радиоуправля́емый *adj.* radio-controlled, remote-controlled.

радиофици́р|овать, ую *impf. and pf.* to install radio (in), equip with radio.

радиохими́ческий *adj.* radiochemical.

радиохи́ми|я, и *f.* radiochemistry.

ради́р|овать, ую *impf. and pf.* to radio.

ради́ст, а *m.* radio operator.

ради́ст|ка, ки *f. of* ⇒**~**

ра́диус, а *m.* radius; **р. де́йствия** range.

ра́д|овать, ую *impf.* (*of* ⇒**об~, по~**) to gladden, make happy.

ра́д|оваться, уюсь *impf.* (*of* ⇒**об~, по~**) (+*d.*) to be glad (at), be happy (at), rejoice (in).

ра́дост|ный (~ен, ~на) *adj.* glad, joyous, joyful; **~ное изве́стие** glad tidings, good news.

ра́дост|ь, и *f.* gladness, joy; **к всео́бщей ~и** to everybody's delight; **р. жи́зни** joie de vivre; **не чу́вствовать себя́ от ~и** to be beside o.s. with joy; **на ~ях** (+*g.*, *coll.*) in celebration (of), to celebrate; **с ~ью** with pleasure, gladly; **моя́ р., р. моя́** my darling.

Р

ра́дуг|а, и *f.* rainbow.

ра́дужно *adv.* cheerfully; **р. смотре́ть** (**на**+*a.*) to look on the bright side (of).

ра́дужн|ый *adj.* **1** (*переливчатый*) iridescent, opalescent; **~ая оболо́чка (глаза)** (*anat.*) iris. **2** (*светлый, радостный*) cheerful; optimistic; **~ые наде́жды** high hopes; **~ое настрое́ние** high spirits.

раду́ши|е, я *nt.* cordiality.

раду́ш|ный (~ен, ~на) *adj.* cordial.

ра|ёк, йка́ *m.* (*theatr.*; *obs.*) gallery; the gods.

раж, а *m.* (*coll.*) rage, passion; **войти́ в р., прийти́ в р.** to fly into a rage.

раз[1], **а,** *pl.* **~ы́, ~** *m.* **1** time; occasion; **оди́н р., ка́к-то р.** once; **два ~а** twice; **мно́го р.** many times; **ещё р.** once again, once more; **не р.** more than once; time and again; **ни ~у** not once, never; **р. (и) навсегда́** once (and) for all; **р. в день** once a day; **вся́кий р.** every time, each time; **вся́кий р., когда́** whenever; **ино́й р.** sometimes, now and again; **во второ́й р.** for the second time; **в друго́й р.** another time, some other time; **в са́мый р.** (*coll.*) at the right moment; just right; **р. за ~ом** time after time; **на э́тот р.** this time, on this occasion, for (this) once; **с пе́рвого ~а** from the very first; **во́т тебе (и) р.!** (*coll.*) well, I never!; **как р.** just, exactly; **как р. то** the very thing. **2** (*num.*) one.

раз[2] *adv.* once, one day.

раз[3] *conj.* if; since; **р. вы бу́дете во Фра́нции, не смо́жете ли вы прие́хать и сюда́?** if you are going to be in France, can't you come here too?

раз[1]**... (***also* **разо..., разъ...** *and* **рас...)** *vbl. pref. indicating* **1** *division into parts* (dis-, un-). **2** *distribution, direction of action in different directions* (dis-). **3** *action in reverse* (un-). **4** *termination of action or state.* **5** *intensification of action.*

раз[2]**... (***also* **разо..., разъ...** *and* **рас...)** (*coll.*) *adj. pref. indicating high degree of a quality.*

разбави́тел|ь, я *m.* thinner.

разба́в|ить, лю, ишь *pf.* (*of* ⇒**~ля́ть**) to dilute.

разбавля́|ть, ю *impf. of* ⇒**разба́вить**

разбаза́рива|ть, ю *impf. of* ⇒**разбаза́рить**

разбаза́р|ить, ю, ишь *pf.* (*of* ⇒**~ивать**) (*coll.*) to squander.

разба́лива|ться, юсь *impf. of* ⇒**разболе́ться**

разба́лтыва|ть(ся), ю(сь) *impf. of* ⇒**разболта́ть(ся)**

разбе́г, а *m.* run, running start; **пры́гнуть с ~у** to take a running jump; **прыжо́к с ~у** running jump; **р. при взлёте** (*aeron.*) take-off run.

разбега́|ться, юсь *impf. of* ⇒**разбежа́ться**

разбе|жа́ться, гу́сь, жи́шься, гу́тся *pf.* (*of* ⇒**~га́ться**) **1** (*взять разбег*) to take a run, run up. **2** (*в разные стороны*) to scatter, disperse. **3** (*о мыслях*) to be scattered; **глаза́ у меня́ ~жа́лись** I was dazzled.

разбере|ди́ть, жу́, ди́шь *pf. of* ⇒**береди́ть**

разбива́|ть(ся), ю(сь) *impf. of* ⇒**разби́ть(ся)**

разби́вк|а, и *f.* **1** (*парка*) laying out. **2** (*людей*) arranging.

разбинт|ова́ть, у́ю *pf.* (*of* ⇒**~о́вывать**) to remove a bandage (from).

разбинто́выва|ть, ю *impf. of* ⇒**разбинтова́ть**

разбира́тельств|о, а *nt.* (*leg.*) examination, investigation; **суде́бное р.** court examination.

разбира́|ть, ю *impf.* **1** *impf. of* ⇒**разобра́ть. 2** (*impf. only*) to be fastidious; **не ~я** indiscriminately.

разбира́|ться, юсь *impf. of* ⇒**разобра́ться**

разбитно́й *adj.* (*coll.*) bright, sprightly; sharp.

разби́т|ый *p.p.p. of* ⇒**~ь** *and adj.* (*coll.*) jaded, down.

раз|би́ть, обью́, обьёшь *pf.* (*of* ⇒**~бива́ть**) **1** (*impf. also* **бить**) (*окно, чашку*) to break, smash; **р. вдре́безги** to smash to smithereens. **2** (*разделить*) to divide (up); to break up; **р. на гру́ппы** to divide up into groups. **3** (*расположить*) to lay out, mark out; **р. ла́герь** to pitch a camp. **4** (*повредить*) to damage severely, hurt badly; to fracture; **р. кому́-н. нос в кровь** to make s.o.'s nose bleed. **5** (*победить*) to beat, defeat, smash (*also fig.*); **р. чьи-н. до́воды** to destroy s.o.'s arguments.

раз|би́ться, обью́сь, обьёшься *pf.* (*of* ⇒**~бива́ться**) **1** (*расколоться*) to break, get broken, get smashed. **2** (*разделиться*) to divide; to break up. **3** (*пораниться*) to hurt o.s. badly; to smash o.s. up.

разблоки́р|овать, ую *pf.* to unblock.

разбогате́|ть, ю, ешь *pf. of* ⇒**богате́ть**

разбо́|й, я *m.* robbery; **морско́й р.** piracy.

разбо́йник, а *m.* **1** robber; **морско́й р.** pirate; **р. с большо́й доро́ги** highwayman. **2** (*шалун*) scamp; scallywag.

разбо́йни|ца, цы *f. of* ⇒**~к**

разбо́йнича|ть, ю *impf.* to rob, plunder.

разбо́йни|чий *adj. of* ⇒**~к; р. прито́н** den of thieves.

разболе́|ться[1]**, юсь, ешься** *pf.* (*of* ⇒**разба́ливаться**) (*coll.*) to become ill; **он совсе́м ~лся** his health has completely cracked.

разбол|е́ться[2]**, и́тся** *pf.* (*of* ⇒**разба́ливаться**) to begin to ache badly.

разбо́лт|анный *p.p.p. of* ⇒**~а́ть**[1] *and adj.* (*fig.*) disorderly.

разболта́|ть[1]**, ю** *pf.* (*of* ⇒**разба́лтывать**) **1** (*размешать*) to mix in. **2** (*ослабить*) to loosen.

разболта́|ть[2]**, ю** *pf.* (*of* ⇒**разба́лтывать**) (*coll.*) (*секрет*) to blab out, give away.

разболта́|ться, юсь *pf.* (*of* ⇒**разба́лтываться**) **1** (*о муке*) to mix in (*as result of stirring*). **2** (*о гайке*) to come loose, work loose. **3** (*fig.*) (*об ученике*) to get out of hand; to come unstuck.

разбомб|и́ть, лю́, и́шь *pf.* (*no impf.*) to destroy by bombing.

разбо́р, а *m.* **1** (*механизма*) stripping, dismantling. **2** (*бумаг, вещей*) sorting out. **3**: **р. де́ла** (*leg.*) investigation (*of a case*). **4** (*gram.*) parsing; analysis. **5** (*статья*) critique. **6** (*выбор*) selectiveness; **без ~у** indiscriminately, promiscuously; **с ~ом** discriminatingly, fastidiously. **7** (*obs.*) (*сорт, качество*) sort, quality; **пе́рвого, второ́го ~а** first, second quality.

разбо́рк|а, и *f.* **1** (*бумаг*) sorting out. **2** (*механизма*) stripping, dismantling. **3** (*coll.*) (*ссора*) quarrel, fight, argument.

разбо́рный *adj.* collapsible.

разбо́рчивост|ь, и *f.* **1** (*требовательность*) fastidiousness; scrupulousness. **2** (*чёткость*) legibility.

разбо́рчив|ый (~, ~а) *adj.* **1** (*требовательный*) fastidious, exacting; discriminating; scrupulous. **2** (*чёткий*) legible.

разбран|и́ть, ю́, и́шь *pf.* (*coll.*) (*человека*) to reprimand; (*работу*) to slam.

разбран|и́ться, ю́сь, и́шься *pf.* (**с**+*i.*; *coll.*) to fall out (with); to quarrel (with), squabble (with).

разбра́сыва|ть, ю *impf. of* ⇒**разброса́ть**

разбра́сыва|ться, юсь *impf.* **1** *impf. of* ⇒**разброса́ться. 2** (*fig.*) to dissipate one's energies; to try to do too much at once.

разбреда́|ться, ется *impf. of* ⇒**разбрести́сь**

разбре|сти́сь, дётся, *past* **~лся, ~ла́сь** *pf.* (*of* ⇒**~да́ться**) to disperse; **р. по дома́м** to disperse and go home.

разбро́д, а *m.* disorder.

разброни́р|овать, ую *pf.* to cancel reservation (of).

разбро́санност|ь, и *f.* **1** sparseness; scattered nature. **2** (*fig.*) disconnectedness, incoherence.

разбро́с|анный *p.p.p. of* ⇒**~а́ть** *and adj.* **1** sparse, scattered; straggling. **2** (*fig.*) disconnected, incoherent.

разброса́|ть, ю *pf.* (*of* ⇒**разбра́сывать**) to throw about; to scatter, spread, strew; **р. наво́з** to spread manure; **р. де́ньги на ве́тер** to squander one's money.

разброса́|ться, юсь *pf.* (*of* ⇒**разбра́сываться**) (*о больном*) to throw o.s. about.

разбры́з|гать, жу, жешь *pf.* (*of* ⇒**~гивать**) to splash; to spray.

разбры́згивател|ь, я *m.* sprinkler.

разбры́згива|ть, ю *impf. of* ⇒**разбры́згать**

разбу|ди́ть, жу́, ~́дишь *pf. of* ⇒**буди́ть**

разбух|а́ть, а́ет *impf. of* ⇒**~нуть**

разбу́х|нуть, нет, *past* **~, ~ла** *pf.* (*of* ⇒**~а́ть**) to swell (*also fig.*).

разбуш|ева́ться, у́юсь *pf.* **1** (*о буре*) to rage; to blow up; (*о море*) to run high. **2** (*coll.*) (*о человеке*) to fly into a rage.

разбуя́н|иться, юсь, ишься *pf.* (*coll.*) to fly into a rage.

разва́жнича|ться, юсь *pf.* (*coll.*) to put on airs.

разва́л, а *m.* **1** (*распад*) breakdown, disintegration; (*беспорядок*) disorder. **2** (*рынок*) flea market, open-air bazaar.

разва́л|ец, ьца *m.* (*coll.*): **ходи́ть с ~ьцем** to shamble; **рабо́тать с ~ьцем** to go slow.

разва́лива|ть(ся), ю(сь) *impf. of* ⇒**развали́ть(ся)**

разва́лин|а, ы *f.* **1** *pl.* ruins; **лежа́ть в ~ах** to be in ruins; **преврати́ть в ~ы** to reduce to ruins. **2** (*fig., coll.*) (*о человеке*) wreck, ruin.

развал|и́ть, ю́, ~́ишь *pf.* (*of* ⇒**~́ивать**) **1** to pull down (*a building, etc.*). **2** (*fig.*) (*хозяйство*) to ruin.

развал|и́ться, ю́сь, ~́ишься *pf.* (*of* ⇒**~́иваться**) **1** (*распасться*) to fall down, collapse. **2** (*fig.*) (*прийти в упадок*) to go to pieces, fall to pieces, break down. **3** (*coll.*) (*сидеть, раскинувшись*) to lounge, sprawl.

развалю́х|а, и *f.* (*coll.*) ruin, wreck.

разва́рива|ть(ся), ю, ет(ся) *impf. of* ⇒**развари́ть(ся)**

развар|и́ть, ю́, ~́ишь *pf.* (*of* ⇒**~́ивать**) to boil soft.

развар|и́ться, ~́ится *pf.* (*of* ⇒**~́иваться**) to be boiled soft; **р. в ка́шу** to be boiled to a pulp.

разварно́й *adj.* boiled.

ра́зве 1 *interrog. particle, neutral or indicating that neg. answer is expected; + neg. indicates that affirmative answer is expected* **р. они́ все вместя́тся в э́ту маши́ну?** will they (really) all get in this car?; **р. ты не знал, что он ру́сский?** didn't you know that he is Russian?; surely you knew that he is Russian? **2** *interrog. particle, expr. hesitation about course of action to be followed* (*+inf.*; *coll.*) **р. отложи́ть нам пое́здку?** perhaps we had better postpone the trip? **3 р. (что), р. (то́лько)** *as adv.* only; perhaps; *as conj.* except that, only; **кро́ме р.** (*+g.*) except perhaps, with the possible exception (of); **он вы́глядит так же как всегда́, р. что похуде́л** he looks the same as ever, except that he has lost weight. **4** *conj.* (*coll.*) (*если не*) unless.

развева́|ть, ет *impf.* **1** (*дым, дождь*) to blow about. **2** (*флаги*) to make flutter.

развева́|ться, ется *impf.* (*флаг*) to flutter; (*волосы, плащ*) to blow about.

разве́д... *comb. form, abbr. of* ***разве́дывательный***

разве́д|ать, аю *pf.* (*of* ⇒**~ывать**) **1** (**о** *+p.*; *coll.*) to find out (about), ascertain. **2** (*mil.*) to reconnoitre (*Br.*), reconnoiter (*US*). **3** (*geol.*) to prospect (for); *pf. only* to locate; **р. нефть** to prospect for oil.

разведе́ни|е[1], я *nt.* (*скота*) breeding, rearing; (*сада*) cultivation; (*костра*) making.

разведе́ни|е[2], я *nt.* (*моста*) opening; (*сока*) dilution.

разведённ|ый *p.p.p. of* ⇒**развести́** *and adj.* divorced; *as n.* **р., ~ого** *m.*, **~ая, ~ой** *f.* divorcee.

разве́дк|а, и *f.* **1** (*geol., etc.*) prospecting. **2** (*mil.*) (*для получения сведений*) reconnaissance. **3** (*mil.*) (*войсковая группа*) reconnaissance party. **4** (*pol.*) secret service, intelligence service.

разве́дочн|ый *adj.* (*geol.*) prospecting, exploratory; **~ая сква́жина** test well.

разве́дчик[1], а *m.* **1** (*mil.*) scout. **2** (*pol.*) secret-service agent; intelligence officer. **3** (*geol.*) prospector.

разве́дчик[2], а *m.* (*самолёт*) reconnaissance aircraft.

разве́дчиц|а, ы *f.* **1** (*mil.*) (*female*) scout. **2** (*pol.*) (*female*) intelligence officer.

разве́дывательный *adj.* **1** (*mil.*) reconnaissance; **р. бой** probing attack; reconnaissance in force; **р. дозо́р** reconnaissance patrol; **р. отря́д** reconnaissance detachment. **2** (*pol.*) intelligence; **р. отде́л** intelligence section.

разве́дыва|ть, ю *impf. of* ⇒**разве́дать**

развез|ти́[1], у́, ёшь, *past* **~́, ~ла́** *pf.* (*of* ⇒**развози́ть**) (*доставить*) to convey, deliver.

развез|ти́[2], у́, ёшь, *past* **~́, ~ла́** *pf.* (*of* ⇒**развози́ть**) (*coll.*) **1** (*изнурить*) to exhaust, wear out; (*impers.*): **от жары́ нас ~ло́** we were exhausted from the heat. **2** (*сделать непригодным для езды*) to make impassable, make unfit for traffic; (*impers.*): **доро́гу ~ло́ от дожде́й** the road was made impassable by rain.

разве́ива|ть(ся), ю(сь) *impf. of* ⇒**разве́ять(ся)**

развенч|а́ть, а́ю *pf.* (*of* ⇒**~́ивать**) **1** (*царя*) to dethrone. **2** (*fig.*) (*кумир*) to debunk.

разве́нчива|ть, ю *impf. of* ⇒**развенча́ть**

развере|ди́ть, жу́, ди́шь *pf. of* ⇒**вереди́ть**

разверз|а́ть(ся), а́ю, а́ет(ся) *impf. of* ⇒**~́нуть(ся)**

разве́рз|нуть, ну, нешь, *past* **~, ~ла** *pf.* (*of* ⇒**~а́ть**) (*obs., poet.*) to open wide.

разве́рз|нуться, нется, *past* **~ся, ~лась** *pf.* (*of* ⇒**~а́ться**) (*obs., poet.*) to open wide, yawn, gape.

развёрн|утый *p.p.p. of* ⇒**~у́ть** *and adj.* **1** (*предпринятый в широких масштабах*) extensive, large-scale. **2** (*подробный*) detailed; **~утая програ́мма** detailed, comprehensive programme (*Br.*), program (*US*). **3** (*mil.*) deployed.

развер|ну́ть, ну́, нёшь *pf.* (*of* ⇒**~́тывать** *and* **развора́чивать**) **1** (*бумагу*) to unfold; (*ковёр*) to unroll; (*свёрток*) to unwrap; (*знамя*) to unfurl. **2** (*mil.*) to deploy. **3** (*fig.*) (*проявить*) to show, display. **4** (*fig.*) (*разбить*) to develop; to expand; **р. аргумента́цию** to develop a line of argument; **р. торго́влю** to expand trade. **5** (*машину*) to turn (around). **6** (*выставку*) to set up.

развер|ну́ться, ну́сь, нёшься *pf.* (*of* ⇒**~́тываться** *and* **развора́чиваться**) **1** (*о бумаге*) to come unfolded; (*о ковре*) to come unrolled; (*о свёртке*) to come undone. **2** (*mil.*) to deploy. **3** (*fig.*) (*проявиться*) to show *or* display o.s. **4** (*fig.*) (*развиться*) to develop; to spread; to expand. **5** (*о машине*) to turn (around). **6** (*о виде*) to open up.

разверст|а́ть, а́ю *pf.* (*of* ⇒**~́ывать**) to distribute, allot.

развёрстк|а, и *f.* allotment, apportionment.

развёрстыва|ть, ю *impf. of* ⇒**разверста́ть**

разве́р|стый *p.p.p. of* ⇒**~знуть** *and adj.* (*obs., poet.*) open, yawning, gaping; **~стая пасть** gaping maw.

развер|те́ть, чу́, ~́тишь *pf.* (*of* ⇒**~чивать**) **1** (*винт*) to unscrew. **2** (*tech.*) (*дыру*) to ream. **3** (*колесо*) to turn, set in motion.

развёртк|а[1], и *f.* **1** (*math.*) development. **2** (*tech.*) reaming. **3** (*electronics*) scanning.

развёртк|а[2], и *f.* (*tech.*) (*инструмент*) reamer.

развёртывани|е, я *nt.* **1** unfolding; unrolling; unwrapping. **2** (*mil.*) deployment. **3** (*fig.*) development, expansion.

развёртыва|ть(ся), ю(сь) *impf. of* ⇒**разверну́ть(ся)**

разве́рчива|ть, ю *impf. of* ⇒**разверте́ть**

разве́с, а *m.* weighing out.

развесел|и́ть, ю́, и́шь *pf. of* ⇒**весели́ть**

развесел|и́ться, ю́сь, и́шься *pf.* to cheer up.

развесёлый *adj.* (*coll.*) merry, gay.

разве́сист|ый (~, ~а) *adj.* branchy; **р. кашта́н** spreading chestnut.

разве́|сить[1], шу, сишь *pf.* (*of* ⇒**~шивать**) (*муку*) to weigh out.

разве́|сить[2], шу, сишь *pf.* (*of* ⇒**~шивать**) **1** (*картины*) to hang. **2** (*ветви*) to spread; **р. у́ши** (*fig., coll.*) to listen open-mouthed.

разве́|сить[3], шу, сишь *pf.* (*of* ⇒**~шивать**) (*бельё*) to hang out.

разве́ск|а, и *f.* **1** = **разве́с. 2** (*картин*) hanging.

развесно́й *adj.* sold by weight.

разве|сти́[1], ду́, дёшь, *past* **~́л, ~ла́** *pf.* (*of* ⇒**разводи́ть**) **1** (*ведя, доставить*) to take, conduct; **р. дете́й по дома́м** to take the children to their homes. **2** (*в разные стороны*) to part, separate; **р. мост** to raise a bridge, swing a bridge open; **р. рука́ми** to throw out one's hands, shrug one's shoulders. **3** (*супругов*) to divorce. **4** (*сок*) to dilute; (*порошок*) to dissolve.

разве|сти́², ду́, дёшь, *past* **~л, ~ла́** *pf.* (*of* **⇒разводи́ть**) **1** (*животных*) to breed, rear; (*сад*) to cultivate; **р. парк** to lay out a park. **2** (*разжечь*) to start; **р. костёр** to make a camp fire; **р. ого́нь** to light a fire; **р. пары́** to get up steam. **3** (*fig., coll.; pej.*) to start; **р. чепуху́** to start talking nonsense.

разве|сти́сь¹, ду́сь, дёшься, *past* **~лся, ~ла́сь** *pf.* (*of* **⇒разводи́ться**) (**с**+*i.*) to divorce, get divorced (from).

разве|сти́сь², дётся, *past* **~лся, ~ла́сь** *pf.* (*of* **⇒разводи́ться**) (*о животных*) to breed, multiply.

разветв|и́ться, и́тся *pf.* (*of* **⇒~ля́ться**) to branch; to fork.

разветвле́ни|е, я *nt.* **1** (*действие*) branching; forking. **2** (*место*) branch; fork (*of road, etc.*).

разветвля́|ться, ется *impf. of* **⇒разветви́ться**

разве́ш|ать, аю *pf.* (*of* **⇒~ивать**) to hang.

разве́шива|ть, ю *impf. of* **⇒разве́сить** *and* **разве́шать**

разве́|ять, ю, ешь *pf.* (*of* **⇒~ивать**) to scatter, disperse; (*fig.*) (*грусть, сомнения*) to dispel; **р. миф** to shatter a myth.

разве́|яться, юсь, ешься *pf.* (*of* **⇒~иваться**) **1** (*о тумане*) to disperse; (*fig.*) (*о тоске*) to be dispelled. **2** (*о человеке*) to relax.

развива́|ть(ся), ю(сь) *impf. of* **⇒разви́ть(ся)**

разви́лин|а, ы *f.* fork.

разви́лист|ый (~, ~а) *adj.* forked.

развин|ти́ть, чу́, ти́шь *pf.* (*of* **⇒~чивать**) to unscrew.

развин|ти́ться, чу́сь, ти́шься *pf.* (*of* **⇒~чиваться**) **1** to come unscrewed. **2** (*fig.*) to come unstuck.

разви́нченност|ь, и *f.* (*coll.*) unbalance.

разви́н|ченный *p.p.p. of* **⇒~ти́ть** *and adj.* (*coll.*) **1** (*человек*) unbalanced, unnerved. **2** (*походка*) unsteady, lurching.

разви́нчива|ть(ся), ю(сь) *impf. of* **⇒развинти́ть(ся)**

разви́ти|е, я *nt.* development; evolution.

развит|о́й (ра́звит, ~а́, ра́звито) *adj.* **1** developed. **2** (*духовно*) (intellectually) mature; adult.

разви́т|ый (~, ~а́, ~о) *p.p.p. of* **⇒~ь**

раз|ви́ть¹, овью́, овьёшь, *past* **~ви́л, ~вила́, ~ви́ло** *pf.* (*of* **⇒~вива́ть**) (*верёвку*) to unwind, untwist.

раз|ви́ть², овью́, овьёшь, *past* **~ви́л, ~вила́, ~ви́ло** *pf.* (*of* **⇒~вива́ть**) (*усилить*) to develop; **р. мускулату́ру** to develop one's muscles; **р. мысль** to develop an idea; **р. ско́рость** to gather speed.

раз|ви́ться¹, овьётся, *past* **~ви́лся, ~вила́сь** *pf.* (*of* **⇒~вива́ться**) (*о верёвке*) to untwist; (*о волосах*) to lose its curl.

раз|ви́ться², овью́сь, овьёшься, *past* **~ви́лся, ~вила́сь** *pf.* (*of* **⇒~вива́ться**) (*о мускулах, о таланте, об индустрии*) to develop.

развлека́тел|ьный (~ен, ~ьна) *adj.* entertaining; **~ьное чте́ние** light reading.

развлека́|ть(ся), ю(сь) *impf. of* **⇒развле́чь(ся)**

развлече́ни|е, я *nt.* entertainment; amusement.

развле́|чь, ку́, чёшь, ку́т, *past* **~к, ~кла́** *pf.* (*of* **⇒~ка́ть**) **1** (*повеселить*) to entertain, amuse. **2** (*отвлечь*) to divert.

развле́|чься, ку́сь, чёшься, ку́тся, *past* **~кся, ~кла́сь** *pf.* (*of* **⇒~ка́ться**) **1** (*повеселиться*) to have a good time; to amuse o.s. **2** (*отвлечься*) to be diverted, be distracted.

разво́д¹, а *m.* divorce; **дать р. кому́-н.** to give s.o. a divorce; **проце́сс о ~е** divorce proceedings; **они́ в ~е** they are divorced.

разво́д², а *m.* (*mil.*): **р. карау́лов** guard mounting; **р. часовы́х** posting of sentries.

разво́д³, а *m.* (*животных*) breeding.

разво|ди́ть(ся), жу́(сь), ~дишь(ся) *impf. of* **⇒развести́(сь)**

разво́дк|а, и *f.* separation; **р. мо́ста** raising of a bridge; **р. пилы́** saw setting.

разводно́й *adj.*: **р. ключ** adjustable spanner, monkey wrench; **р. мост** drawbridge.

разво́д|ы, ов *no sg.* **1** (*узор*) design, pattern. **2** (*пятна*) stains; **черни́льные р.** ink-stains.

разво́дь|е, я, *g. pl.* **~ев** *nt.* patch of ice-free water.

разво|ева́ться, ю́юсь, ю́ешься *pf.* (*coll.*) to bluster.

разво́з, а *m.* conveyance.

разво|зи́ть, жу́, ~зишь *impf. of* **⇒развезти́**

разво|зи́ться, жу́сь, ~зишься *pf.* (*coll.*) to kick up a din.

разво́зк|а, и *f.* conveying; delivery.

разволн|ова́ть, у́ю *pf.* to excite, agitate.

разволн|ова́ться, у́юсь *pf.* to get excited, get agitated.

развора́чива|ть, ю *impf. of* **⇒разверну́ть** *and* **развороти́ть**

развора́чива|ться, юсь *impf. of* **⇒разверну́ться**

развор|ова́ть, у́ю *pf.* (*of* **⇒~о́вывать**) to loot, clean out.

разворо́выва|ть, ю *impf. of* **⇒разворова́ть**

разворо́т, а *m.* **1** (*машины*) U-turn. **2** (*coll.*) (*развитие*) development; **р. торго́вли** growth of trade. **3** (*в книге*) double page, centrefold (*Br.*), centerfold (*US*).

разворо|ти́ть, чу́, ~тишь *pf.* (*of* **⇒развора́чивать**) **1** (*кучу*) to destroy; (*привести в беспорядок*) to turn upside down. **2** (*разломать*) to smash up, break up.

разворош|и́ть, у́, и́шь *pf.* to turn upside down, scatter.

развра́т, а *m.* (*половой*) debauchery, dissipation; (*духовный*) corruption, depravity.

разврати́тел|ь, я *m.* debaucher, seducer, corrupter.

развра|ти́ть, щу́, ти́шь *pf.* (*of* **⇒~ща́ть**) **1** to debauch, corrupt. **2** (*fig.*) (*духовно*) to corrupt.

развра|ти́ться, щу́сь, ти́шься *pf.* (*of* **⇒~ща́ться**) to give o.s. up to debauchery; (*духовно*) to become corrupted.

развра́тник, а *m.* debauchee, profligate, libertine.

развра́тни|ца, цы *f. of* **⇒~к**

развра́тнича|ть, ю *impf.* to lead a depraved life.

развра́тност|ь, и *f.* depravity, profligacy; corruptness.

развра́т|ный (~ен, ~на) *adj.* debauched, depraved; corrupt.

развраща́|ть(ся), ю(сь) *impf. of* **⇒разврати́ть(ся)**

развращённост|ь, и *f.* corruptness, depravity.

развра|щённый *p.p.p. of* **⇒~ти́ть** *and adj.* corrupt; depraved.

развью́чива|ть, ю *impf. of* **⇒развью́чить**

развью́ч|ить, у, ишь *pf.* (*of* **⇒~ивать**) to unload, unburden.

развя|за́ть, жу́, ~жешь *pf.* (*of* **⇒~зывать**) to untie, undo; to unleash; **р. кому́-н. ру́ки** to untie s.o.'s hands (*also fig.*); **р. войну́** to unleash war.

развя|за́ться, жу́сь, ~жешься *pf.* (*of* **⇒~зываться**) **1** to come untied, come undone; **у него́ ~за́лся язы́к** (*fig.*) his tongue has been loosened. **2** (**с**+*i.*; *fig.*) to have done (with), be through (with).

развя́зк|а, и *f.* **1** (*liter.*) denouement. **2** (*завершение*) outcome, upshot; **счастли́вая р.** happy ending; **де́ло идёт к ~е** things are coming to a head. **3**: **р. движе́ния, кольцева́я (тра́нспортная) р.** (traffic) roundabout.

развя́з|ный (~ен, ~на) *adj.* (unduly) familiar; free-and-easy.

развя́зыва|ть(ся), ю(сь) *impf. of* **⇒развяза́ть(ся)**

разгад|а́ть, а́ю *pf.* (*of* **⇒~ывать**) (*тайну, замысел*) to guess; (*загадку*) to solve; (*сны*) to interpret; (*шифр*) to break; (*человека*) to figure out.

разга́дк|а, и *f.* solution (*of a riddle, etc.*).

разга́дыва|ть, ю *impf. of* **⇒разгада́ть**

разга́р, а *m.*: **в ~е** (+*g.*) at the height (of); **в по́лном ~е** in full swing; **в ~е бо́я** in the heat of the battle.

разгиба́|ть(ся), ю(сь) *impf. of* ⇒**разогну́ть(ся); не ~я спины́** without a let-up.

разгильдя́|й, я *m.* (*coll.*) sloven; sloppy individual.

разгильдя́йнича|ть, ю *impf.* (*coll.*) to be slovenly, be sloppy; to be slipshod.

разглаго́льствовани|е, я *nt.* (*coll.*) big talk.

разглаго́льств|овать, ую *impf.* (*coll.*) to hold forth; to talk big.

разгла́|дить, жу, дишь *pf.* (*of* ⇒**~живать**) to smooth out; to iron out, press.

разгла́|диться, дится *pf.* (*of* ⇒**~живаться**) (*платье*) to become smoothed out; (*морщины*) to drop out.

разгла́жива|ть(ся), ю, ет(ся) *impf. of* ⇒**разгла́дить(ся)**

разгла|си́ть, шу́, си́шь *pf.* (*of* ⇒**~ша́ть**) **1** to divulge, give away, let out. **2** (**о**+*p.*; *coll.*) to trumpet, broadcast.

разглаша́|ть, ю *impf. of* ⇒**разгласи́ть**

разглаше́ни|е, я *nt.* divulging, (unauthorized) disclosure.

разгля|де́ть, жу́, ди́шь *pf.* to make out, discern.

разгля́дыва|ть, ю *impf.* to examine closely, scrutinize.

разгне́ва|ть, ю *pf.* (*obs.*) to anger, incense.

разгне́ва|ться, юсь *pf. of* ⇒**гне́ваться**

разгова́рива|ть, ю *impf.* (**с**+*i.*) to talk (to, with), speak (to, with), converse (with); **переста́ньте р.!** stop talking!; **они́ друг с дру́гом не ~ют** they are not on speaking terms.

разгов|е́ться, е́юсь, е́ешься *pf.* (*of* ⇒**~ля́ться**) to break a (period of) fast.

разговля́|ться, юсь *impf. of* ⇒**разгове́ться**

разгово́р, а (у) *m.* **1** talk, conversation; **перемени́ть р.** to change the subject; **об э́том и ~у быть не мо́жет** there can be no question about it, **без ~ов!** and no argument! **2** *pl.* (*coll.*) (*толки*) gossip.

разговор|и́ть, ю́, и́шь *pf.* (*coll.*) to dissuade.

разговор|и́ться, ю́сь, и́шься *pf.* **1** (**с**+*i.*) to get into conversation (with). **2** (*увлечься разговором*) to warm to one's theme.

разгово́рник, а *m.* phrase-book.

разгово́р|ный *adj.* **1** colloquial; **р. язы́к** spoken language. **2**: **~ная каби́на** telephone booth (*in post office*); **р. уро́к** conversation class.

разгово́рчивост|ь, и *f.* talkativeness.

разгово́рчив|ый (~, ~а) *adj.* talkative.

разго́н, а *m.* **1** (*толпы*) dispersal; dissolution; **р. собра́ния** breaking up of a meeting. **2**: **быть в ~е** (*coll.*) to be out. **3** (*sport*) run, running start; **прыжо́к с ~а** running jump. **4** (*расстояние*) distance. **5** (*машины*) acceleration. **6** (*coll.*) (*выговор*) scolding.

разго́нист|ый (~, ~а) *adj.* (*coll.*) spaced-out.

разгоня́|ть(ся), ю(сь) *impf. of* ⇒**разогна́ть(ся)**

разгора́жива|ть, ю *impf. of* ⇒**разгороди́ть**

разгор|а́ться, а́ется *impf. of* ⇒**~е́ться**

разгор|е́ться, и́тся *pf.* (*of* ⇒**~а́ться**) **1** (*об огне*) to flare up. **2** (*fig.*) (*о битве*) to flare up; **~е́лся спор** a heated argument developed; **стра́сти ~е́лись** feeling ran high, passions rose. **3** (*fig.*) (*о щеках*) to flush.

разгоро|ди́ть, жу́, ~ди́шь *pf.* (*of* ⇒**разгора́живать**) to partition off.

разгоряч|и́ть, у́, и́шь *pf. of* ⇒**горячи́ть**

разгоряч|и́ться, у́сь, и́шься *pf.* (*of* ⇒**горячи́ться**) (**от**+*g.*) to be flushed (with); **р. от вина́** to be flushed with wine.

разгра́б|ить, лю, ишь *pf.* to plunder, pillage, loot.

разграбле́ни|е, я *nt.* plunder, pillage.

разграниче́ни|е, я *nt.* **1** (*размежевание*) demarcation, delimitation. **2** (*определение*) differentiation.

разграни́чива|ть, ю *impf. of* ⇒**разграни́чить**

разграничи́тельн|ый *adj.*: **~ая ли́ния** line of demarcation, dividing line.

разграни́ч|ить, у, ишь *pf.* (*of* ⇒**~ивать**) **1** (*размежевать*) to delimit, demarcate. **2** (*точно определить*) to differentiate, distinguish.

разграф|и́ть, лю́, и́шь *pf.* (*of* ⇒**графи́ть** *and* **~ля́ть**) to rule (*in squares, columns, etc.*).

разграфля́|ть, ю *impf. of* ⇒**разграфи́ть**

разгреба́|ть, ю *impf. of* ⇒**разгрести́**

разгре|сти́, бу́, бёшь, *past* **~б, ~бла́** *pf.* (*of* ⇒**~ба́ть**) to rake (aside, away); to shovel (aside, away).

разгро́м, а *m.* **1** (*неприятеля*) crushing defeat, rout. **2** (*coll.*) (*беспорядок*) havoc, devastation; **карти́на ~а** scene of devastation; **в кварти́ре был по́лный р.** there was complete chaos in the flat.

разгром|и́ть, лю́, и́шь *pf. of* ⇒**громи́ть**

разгружа́|ть(ся), ю(сь) *impf. of* ⇒**разгрузи́ть(ся)**

разгру|зи́ть, жу́, ~зи́шь *pf.* (*of* ⇒**~жа́ть**) **1** to unload. **2** (**от**+*g.*; *fig., coll.*) to relieve (of); **р. от доба́вочных обя́занностей** to relieve of extra commitments.

разгру|зи́ться, жу́сь, ~зи́шься *pf.* (*of* ⇒**~жа́ться**) **1** to unload. **2** (**от**+*g.*; *fig., coll.*) to be relieved (of).

разгру́зк|а, и *f.* **1** unloading. **2** (*fig., coll.*) relieving.

разгру́зочн|ый *adj.* unloading; **р. день** dieting day, day of fasting; **~ые рабо́ты** unloading operations.

разгруппир|ова́ть, у́ю *pf.* (*of* ⇒**~о́вывать**) to divide into groups, group.

разгруппиро́выва|ть, ю *impf. of* ⇒**разгруппирова́ть**

разгрыза́|ть, ю *impf. of* ⇒**разгры́зть**

разгры́з|ть, у́, ёшь, *past* **~, ~ла** *pf.* (*of* ⇒**~а́ть**) to crack (*with one's teeth*); **р. оре́х** to crack a nut.

разгу́л, а *m.* **1** revelry. **2** (+*g.*; *fig.*) wave (of); outburst (of); **р. антисемити́зма** a wave of anti-semitism.

разгу́лива|ть, ю *impf.* **1** to stroll about, walk about. **2** *impf. of* ⇒**разгуля́ть**

разгу́лива|ться, юсь *impf. of* ⇒**разгуля́ться**

разгу́ль|е, я *nt.* (*coll.*) merry-making.

разгу́л|ьный (~ен, ~ьна) *adj.* (*coll.*) wild, fast; **вести́ ~ьную жизнь** to lead a wild life.

разгул|я́ть, я́ю *pf.* (*of* ⇒**~ивать**) (*coll.*) **1** (*развлечь*) to amuse so as to keep awake. **2** (*отогнать*) to dispel; **р. чью-н. хандру́** to dispel s.o.'s gloom.

разгул|я́ться, я́юсь *pf.* (*of* ⇒**~иваться**) (*coll.*) **1** to spread o.s.; to let o.s. go, live it up; (*fig.*) (*о ветре*) to get up. **2** (*о ребёнке*) to wake up, stop feeling sleepy. **3** (*о погоде*) to clear up, improve; **день ~я́лся** it has turned out a fine day.

разда|ва́ть(ся), ю́(сь), ёшь(ся) *impf. of* ⇒**разда́ть(ся)**

раздав|и́ть, лю́, ~ишь *pf.* (*of* ⇒**~ливать**) **1** (*насекомых*) to crush, squash; (*о машине*) to run over. **2** (*fig.*) to crush, overwhelm. **3** (*coll.*) (*выпить*) to down, sink (*alcoholic beverages*).

разда́влива|ть, ю *impf. of* ⇒**раздави́ть**

разда́рива|ть, ю *impf. of* ⇒**раздари́ть**

раздар|и́ть, ю́, ~ишь *pf.* (*of* ⇒**~ивать**) (+*d.*) to give away (to), make a present of (*many things*).

разда́точн|ый *adj.* distributing, distribution; **~ая ве́домость** list of those due to receive (*gifts, money, etc.*); **р. пункт** distribution centre (*Br.*), center (*US*).

разда́тчик, а *m.* distributor, dispenser.

разда́тчи|ца, цы *f. of* ⇒**~к**

разда́|ть[1]**, м, шь, ст, ди́м, ди́те, ду́т,** *past* **~л, ~ла́, ~ло** *or* **ро́здал, ~ла́, ро́здало** *pf.* (*of* ⇒**~ва́ть**) to distribute, give out, serve out, dispense; **р. ми́лостыню** to dispense charity; **р. кни́ги** to give out books.

разда́|ть[2]**, м, шь, ст, ди́м, ди́те, ду́т,** *past* **~л, ~ла́, ~ло** *or* **ро́здал, ~ла́, ро́здало** *pf.* (*of* ⇒**~ва́ть**) (*coll.*) (*обувь*) to stretch; (*одежду*) to enlarge, widen, let out.

разда́|ться[1]**, стся, ду́тся,** *past* **~лся, ~ла́сь, ~ло́сь** *pf.* (*of* ⇒**~ва́ться**) to be heard; to resound; to ring (out); **~лся вы́стрел** a shot rang out; **~лся стук (в дверь)** a knock at the door was heard.

разда́|ться², мся, шься, стся, ди́мся, ди́тесь, ду́тся, *past* **~лся, ~ла́сь, ~ло́сь** *pf.* (*of* ⇒**~ва́ться**) (*coll.*) **1** (*расступиться*) to make way. **2** (*растянуться*) to stretch, expand. **3** (*потолстеть*) to put on weight.

разда́ч|а, и *f.* distribution.

раздва́ива|ть(ся), ю(сь) *impf. of* ⇒**раздвои́ть(ся)**

раздвига́|ть(ся), ю, ет(ся) *impf. of* ⇒**раздви́нуть(ся)**

раздвижно́й *adj.* expanding; sliding; **р. за́навес** (*theatr.*) draw curtain; **р. стол** leaf table, expanding table.

раздви́|нуть, ну, нешь *pf.* (*of* ⇒**~га́ть**) to move apart, slide apart; **р. занаве́ски** to draw back the curtains; **р. стол** to extend a table.

раздви́|нуться, нется *pf.* (*of* ⇒**~га́ться**) to move apart, slide apart; **за́навес ~нулся** the curtain was drawn back; (*в театре*) the curtain rose; **толпа́ ~нулась** the crowd made way.

раздвое́ни|е, я *nt.* division into two; bifurcation; **р. ли́чности** (*med.*) split personality.

раздво́|енный (*and* **раздвоённый**) *p.p.p. of* ⇒**~и́ть** *and adj.* forked; bifurcated; **~енное копы́то** cloven hoof; **~енное созна́ние** split mind.

раздво|и́ть, ю́, и́шь *pf.* (*of* ⇒**раздва́ивать**) to divide into two; to bisect.

раздво|и́ться, ю́сь, и́шься *pf.* (*of* ⇒**раздва́иваться**) to bifurcate, fork, split, become double.

раздева́лк|а, и *f.* (*coll.*) **1** (*гардероб*) cloak-room. **2** (*в банях*) changing-room.

раздева́льный *adj.* (*for*) undressing.

раздева́л|ьня, ьни, *g. pl.* **~ен** *f.* = **~ка**

раздева́ни|е, я *nt.* undressing.

раздева́|ть(ся), ю(сь) *impf. of* ⇒**разде́ть(ся)**

разде́л, а *m.* **1** (*имущества*) division; (*земли*) allotment. **2** (*часть*) section, part (*of book, etc.*).

разде́л|ать, аю *pf.* (*of* ⇒**~ывать**) **1** (*тушу*) to dress, prepare; **р. гря́дки** to prepare (flower-)beds (*for sowing*); **р. под дуб** to grain in imitation of oak; **р. кого́-н. под оре́х** (*coll.*) to give it s.o. hot. **2** (*coll.*) (*избить*) to beat up.

разде́л|аться, аюсь *pf.* (*of* ⇒**~ываться**) (**с** + *i.*) **1** (*с поручениями*) to be through (with); (*с кредиторами*) to settle (accounts) (with); **р. с долга́ми** to pay off debts. **2** (*fig.*) to settle accounts (with), get even (with), make short work of.

разделе́ни|е, я *nt.* division; **р. труда́** division of labour (*Br.*), labor (*US*).

раздели́м|ый (~, ~а) *adj.* divisible.

раздели́тельн|ый *adj.* **1** dividing, separating; **~ая черта́** dividing line. **2** (*gram.*) disjunctive; distributive; partitive; **р. сою́з** disjunctive conjunction; **~ое местоиме́ние** distributive pronoun; **роди́тельный р. паде́ж** partitive genitive.

раздел|и́ть, ю́, ~ишь *pf.* (*of* ⇒**~я́ть**) **1** (*деньги*) to divide. **2** (*разъединить*) to separate, part. **3** (*мнение, убеждение*) to share.

раздел|и́ться, ~ится *pf.* (*of* ⇒**~я́ться**) **1** (**на** + *a.*) to divide (into); to be divided; **нам придётся р. на две гру́ппы** we shall have to divide into two groups; **мне́ния ~и́лись** opinions were divided. **2** (*прекратить совместную жизнь*) to separate, part company. **3** *pf. only* (**на** + *a.*) to be divisible (by); **число́ со́рок де́вять ~ится на семь** forty-nine is divisible by seven.

разде́лыва|ть(ся), ю(сь) *impf. of* ⇒**разде́лать(ся)**

разде́льн|ый *adj.* **1** (*отдельный*) separate; **~ое обуче́ние** separate education for boys and girls. **2** (*отчётливый*) clear, distinct.

раздел|я́ть, я́ю *impf. of* ⇒**~и́ть**

раздел|я́ться, я́ется *impf. of* ⇒**~и́ться**

раздёрг|ать, аю *pf.* (*of* ⇒**~ивать**) (*coll.*) to tear up.

раздёргива|ть, ю *impf. of* ⇒**раздёргать** *and* **раздёрнуть**

раздёр|нуть, ну, нешь *pf.* (*of* ⇒**~гивать**) to draw apart, pull apart; **р. занаве́ски** to draw back the curtains.

разде́т|ый *p.p.p. of* ⇒**~ь** *and adj.* **1** unclothed, undressed. **2** (*плохо одетый*) poorly clothed, ill-clad.

разде́|ть, ну, нешь *pf.* (*of* ⇒**~ва́ть**) to undress; **его́ ~ли на у́лице** he was robbed of his clothes in the street.

разде́|ться, нусь, нешься *pf.* (*of* ⇒**~ва́ться**) to undress, get undressed; (*снять пальто, шапку*) to take off one's things.

раздира́|ть, ю *impf.* **1** *impf. of* ⇒**разодра́ть. 2** *impf. only* (*fig.*) to rend, tear, lacerate, harrow.

раздира́|ться, ю, ет(ся) *impf. of* ⇒**разодра́ться**

раздира́|ющий *pres. part. act. of* ⇒**~ть** *and adj.*; **р. (ду́шу)** heart-rending, heart-breaking, harrowing.

раздобре́|ть, ю *pf. of* ⇒**добре́ть²**

раздо́бр|иться, юсь, ишься *pf.* (*coll.*) to become generous, become kind.

раздобыва́|ть, ю *impf. of* ⇒**раздобы́ть**

раздо|бы́ть, бу́ду, бу́дешь, *past* **~бы́л** *pf.* (*of* ⇒**~быва́ть**) (*coll.*) to get, procure, get hold of.

раздо́ль|е, я *nt.* **1** (*простор*) expanse. **2** (*fig.*) (*свобода*) freedom; **им р.** they are quite free to do as they please.

раздо́л|ьный (~ен, ~ьна) *adj.* free.

раздо́р, а *m.* discord, dissension; **я́блоко ~а** bone of contention; **се́ять р.** to breed strife.

раздоса́д|овать, ую *pf.* to vex.

раздраж|а́ть(ся), а́ю(сь) *impf. of* ⇒**~и́ть(ся)**

раздража́|ющий *pres. part. act. of* ⇒**~ть** *and adj.* irritating, annoying; *as n.* **~ющее, ~ющего** *nt.* irritant.

раздраже́ни|е, я *nt.* irritation.

раздражи́тел|ь, я *m.* (*med.*) irritant.

раздражи́тельност|ь, и *f.* irritability; shortness of temper.

раздражи́тел|ьный (~ен, ~ьна) *adj.* irritable; short-tempered.

раздраж|и́ть, у́, и́шь *pf.* (*of* ⇒**~а́ть**) **1** to irritate, annoy. **2** (*med.*) to irritate.

раздраж|и́ться, у́сь, и́шься *pf.* (*of* ⇒**~а́ться**) **1** to get irritated, get annoyed. **2** (*med.*) to become inflamed.

раздразн|и́ть, ю́, ~ишь *pf.* **1** (*рассердить*) to tease. **2** (*возбудить*) to stimulate; **р. чей-н. аппети́т** to whet s.o.'s appetite.

раздрако́нива|ть, ю *impf. of* ⇒**раздрако́нить**

раздрако́н|ить, ю, ишь *pf.* (*of* ⇒**~ивать**) (*coll.*) to scold, chastise severely.

раздроб|и́ть, лю́, и́шь *pf.* **1** *pf. of* ⇒**дроби́ть. 2** (*impf.* **~ля́ть**) (**в** + *a.*; *math.*) to turn (into), reduce (to); **р. гра́ммы в сантигра́ммы** to turn grams into centigrams.

раздроб|и́ться, и́тся *pf. of* ⇒**дроби́ться**

раздробле́ни|е, я *nt.* **1** breaking, smashing to pieces. **2** (*math.*) reduction.

раздро́б|ленный (*and* **раздроблённый**) *p.p.p. of* ⇒**~и́ть** *and adj.* (*fig.*) fragmented.

раздробля́|ть, ю *impf. of* ⇒**раздроби́ть**

раздруж|и́ться, у́сь, и́шься *pf.* (*coll.*) to break it off (with), to break off friendly relations (with).

раздува́льный *adj.*: **р. мех** (*tech.*) bellows.

раздува́|ть(ся), ю(сь) *impf. of* ⇒**разду́ть(ся)**

разду́м|ать, аю *pf.* (*of* ⇒**~ывать**) to change one's mind; (+ *inf.*) to decide not (to); **я ~ал подава́ть заявле́ние на э́то ме́сто** I decided not to apply for that job; I changed my mind about applying for that job.

разду́м|аться, аюсь *pf.* (**о** + *p.*; *coll.*) to be absorbed in thinking (about).

разду́мыва|ть, ю *impf.* **1** *impf. of* ⇒**разду́мать. 2** *impf. only* (**о** + *p.*) to ponder (on, over), consider; **я давно́ ~ю, купи́ть маши́ну и́ли нет** for a long time I have been considering whether or not to buy a car; **не ~я** without a moment's thought.

разду́мь|е, я *nt.* **1** meditation; thought, thoughtful mood; **в глубо́ком р.** deep in thought. **2** hesitation; **меня́ взяло́ р.** I can't make up my mind.

разду́т|ый *p.p.p. of* ⇒**~ь** *and adj.* (*fig., coll.*) exaggerated; inflated; excessive.

разду́|ть, ю, ешь *pf.* (*of* ⇒**~ва́ть**) **1** (*разжечь*) to blow; to fan; **р. пла́мя** (*fig.*) to fan the flames. **2** (*надуть*) to blow (out); **р. щёки** to blow out one's cheeks; (*impers.*): **у него́ ~ло щёку** his cheek is swollen. **3** (*fig., coll.*) (*преувеличить*) to exaggerate; to inflate, swell; **р. поте́ри** to exaggerate losses. **4** (*развеять*) to blow about; (*impers.*): **~ло бума́ги по́ полу** the papers had blown all over the floor.

разду́|ться, юсь, ешься *pf.* (*of* ⇒**~ва́ться**) to swell.

раздуш|и́ть, у́, ~́ишь *pf.* (*coll.*) to drench in perfume.

разева́|ть, ю *impf. of* ⇒**рази́нуть**

разжа́лоб|ить, лю, ишь *pf.* to move (to pity).

разжа́лоб|иться, люсь, ишься *pf.* to be moved to pity.

разжа́ловани|е, я *nt.* demotion.

разжа́л|овать, ую *pf.* (*mil.*) to demote; **р. в солда́ты** to reduce to the ranks.

раз|жа́ть, ожму́, ожмёшь *pf.* (*of* ⇒**~жима́ть**) (*руки*) to unclasp; (*пружину*) to release; (*кулак, зубы*) to unclench.

раз|жа́ться, ожмётся *pf.* (*of* ⇒**~жима́ться**) (*о пружине*) to come loose; (*о кулаке, губах*) to relax.

разж|ева́ть, ую́, уёшь *pf.* (*of* ⇒**~ёвывать**) **1** to chew; (*fig., coll.*) to chew over. **2** (*fig.*) (*разъяснить*) to spell out.

разжёвыва|ть, ю *impf. of* ⇒**разжева́ть**

раз|же́чь, ожгу́, ожжёшь, ожгу́т, *past* **~жёг, ~ожгла́** *pf.* (*of* ⇒**~жига́ть**) **1** (*заставить гореть*) to kindle. **2** (*fig.*) to kindle, rouse, stir up; **р. стра́сти** to arouse passion.

раз|же́чься, ожжётся, ожгу́тся, *past* **~жёгся, ~ожгла́сь** *pf.* (*of* ⇒**~жига́ться**) **1** (*начать гореть*) to begin to burn. **2** (*fig.*) to be kindled, aroused.

разжи́в|а, ы *f.* (*coll.*) gain, profit.

разжива́|ться, юсь *impf. of* ⇒**разжи́ться**

разжига́ни|е, я *nt.* kindling (*also fig.*).

разжига́|ть(ся), ю, ет(ся) *impf. of* ⇒**разже́чь(ся)**

разжи|ди́ть, жу́, ди́шь *pf.* (*of* ⇒**~жа́ть**) to dilute, thin

разжижа́|ть, ю *impf. of* ⇒**разжиди́ть**

разжиже́ни|е, я *nt.* dilution, thinning.

разжима́|ть(ся), ю, ет(ся) *impf. of* ⇒**разжа́ть(ся)**

разжире́|ть, ю *pf. of* ⇒**жире́ть**

разж|и́ться, иву́сь, ивёшься, *past* **~и́лся, ~ила́сь** *pf.* (*of* ⇒**~ива́ться**) (*coll.*) **1** (*разбогатеть*) to get rich. **2** (+*i.*) (*раздобыть*) to come by, get hold of.

раззаво́д, а *m.*: **на р.** (*sl.*) for breeding.

раззадо́рива|ть(ся), ю(сь) *impf. of* ⇒**раззадо́рить(ся)**

раззадо́р|ить, ю, ишь *pf.* (*of* ⇒**~ивать**) (*coll.*) to stir up, excite.

раззадо́р|иться, юсь, ишься *pf.* (*of* ⇒**~иваться**) (*coll.*) to get excited, get worked up.

раззва́нива|ть, ю *impf. of* ⇒**раззвони́ть**

раззвон|и́ть, ю́, и́шь *pf.* (*of* ⇒**раззва́нивать**) (**о**+*p.*; *coll.*) to trumpet, proclaim (from the housetops).

раззнако́м|ить, лю, ишь *pf.* to alienate.

раззнако́м|иться, люсь, ишься *pf.* (**с**+*i.*) to break off one's acquaintance (with), break (with).

раззуд|е́ться, и́тся *pf.* (*coll.*) to begin to itch (*also fig.*).

раззя́в|а, ы *c.g.* = **рази́ня**

рази́н|уть, у, ешь *pf.* (*of* ⇒**разева́ть**) (*coll.*) to open wide (*the mouth*); to gape; **слу́шать, ~ув рот** to listen open-mouthed.

рази́н|я, и *c.g.* (*coll., pej.*) scatter-brain.

рази́тел|ьный (~ен, ~ьна) *adj.* striking.

ра|зи́ть[1], жу́, зи́шь *impf.* (*liter.*) (*бить*) to strike, hit.

раз|и́ть[2], и́т *impf.* (*impers.*+*i.*; *coll.*) (*пахнуть*) to reek (of), stink (of); **из ко́мнаты ~и́ло чесноко́м** the room reeked of garlic.

разлага́|ть(ся), ю(сь) *impf. of* ⇒**разложи́ть(ся)**

разла́д, а *m.* **1** (*в работе*) disorder. **2** (*раздор*) discord, dissension.

разла́|дить, жу, дишь *pf.* (*of* ⇒**~живать**) (*механизм*) to put out of commission; (*coll.*) to mess up.

разла́|диться, дится *pf.* (*of* ⇒**~живаться**) (*о механизме*) to get out of order; (*coll.*) to go wrong.

разла́жива|ть(ся), ю, ет(ся) *impf. of* ⇒**разла́дить(ся)**

разла́ком|ить, лю, ишь *pf.* (+*i.*; *coll.*) to give s.o. a taste (for).

разла́ком|иться, люсь, ишься *pf.* (+*i.*; *coll.*) to get a taste (for).

разла́мыва|ть(ся), ю, ет(ся) *impf. of* ⇒**разлома́ть(ся)** *and* **разломи́ть(ся)**

разлёжива|ться, юсь *impf.* (*coll., pej.*) to lie about.

разлез|а́ться, а́ется *impf. of* ⇒**~́ться**

разле́з|ться, ется, *past* **~ся, ~лась** *pf.* (*of* ⇒**~а́ться**) (*coll.*) to come to pieces; to fall apart.

разле́нива|ться, юсь *impf. of* ⇒**разлени́ться**

разлен|и́ться, ю́сь, ~́ишься *pf.* (*of* ⇒**~́иваться**) (*coll.*) to become sunk in sloth.

разлеп|и́ть, лю́, ~́ишь *pf.* (*of* ⇒**~ля́ть**) to unstick.

разлеп|и́ться, ~́ится *pf.* (*of* ⇒**~ля́ться**) to come unstuck.

разлепля́|ть(ся), ю, ет(ся) *impf. of* ⇒**разлепи́ть(ся)**

разлёт, а *m.* flying away, departure.

разлет|а́ться, а́юсь *impf. of* ⇒**~е́ться**

разле|те́ться, чу́сь, ти́шься *pf.* (*of* ⇒**~та́ться**) **1** (*о птицах*) to fly away; to scatter (*in the air*). **2** (*coll.*) (*разбиться*) to smash, shatter. **3** (*fig., coll.*) (*исчезнуть*) to vanish, be shattered; **её мечты́ ~те́лись** her dreams were shattered. **4** (*coll.*) (*набрать скорость*) to speed up. **5** (*о новостях*) to spread. **6** (*coll., pej.*) (*прийти спешно*) to come rushing (*with a request or suggestion*).

разл|е́чься, я́гусь, я́жешься, *past* **~ёгся, ~егла́сь** *pf.* (*coll.*) to sprawl; to stretch o.s. out.

разли́в, а *m.* **1** (*вина*) bottling. **2** (*реки*) flood; overflow.

разлива́ни|е, я *nt.* pouring out.

разлива́нн|ый *adj. only in phr.* **~ое мо́ре** (*joc.*) oceans, lashings (*usu. of alcoholic beverages*).

разлива́тельн|ый *adj.*: **~ая ло́жка** ladle.

разлива́|ть(ся), ю, ет(ся) *impf. of* ⇒**разли́ть(ся)**

разли́вк|а, и *f.* **1** bottling. **2** (*tech.*) teeming, casting.

разливно́й *adj.* on tap, on draught (*Br.*), draft (*US*).

разлин|ова́ть, у́ю *pf.* (*of* ⇒**~о́вывать**) to rule (*paper, etc.*).

разлино́выва|ть, ю *impf. of* ⇒**разлинова́ть**

разли́ти|е, я *nt.* (*вина*) pouring out; (*по бутылкам*) bottling; (*реки*) overflowing; (*распространение*) broadcasting; **р. жёлчи** (*med.*) bilious attack.

раз|ли́ть, олью́, ольёшь, *past* **~ли́л, ~лила́, ~ли́ло** *pf.* (*of* ⇒**~лива́ть**) **1** (*налить*) to pour out; **р. по буты́лкам** to bottle; **р. чай** to pour out tea. **2** (*пролить*) to spill; **р. водо́й** to pour water (over), douse, drench; **их водо́й не ~ольёшь** (*coll.*) they are thick as thieves. **3** (*fig.*) (*распространить*) to spread, broadcast.

раз|ли́ться, ольётся, *past* **~ли́лся, ~лила́сь** *pf.* (*of* ⇒**~лива́ться**) **1** (*пролиться*) to spill; **суп ~ли́лся по ска́терти** the soup has spilled over the table-cloth. **2** (*о реке*) to overflow. **3** (*med.*): **у него́ ~лила́сь жёлчь** he had a bilious attack. **4** (*fig.*) (*распространиться*) to spread; **по её лицу́ ~лила́сь улы́бка** a smile spread across her face.

различ|а́ть, а́ю *impf. of* ⇒**~и́ть**

различа́|ться, юсь *impf.* to differ.

разли́чи|е, я *nt.* distinction; difference; **де́лать р.** (**ме́жду**+*i.*) to make distinctions (between); **без ~я** without distinction.

различи́тельный *adj.* distinctive; **р. при́знак** distinguishing feature.

различ|и́ть, у́, и́шь *pf.* (*of* ⇒**~а́ть**) **1** (*установить различие*) to distinguish; to tell the difference (between). **2** (*воспринять*) to discern, make out.

разли́ч|ный (~ен, ~на) *adj.* **1** (*несходный*) different; **у нас бы́ли ~ные мне́ния** our opinions differed **2** (*разнообразный*) various, diverse; **~ные лю́ди** all manner of people; **по ~ным соображе́ниям** for various reasons.

разложе́ни|е, я *nt.* **1** (*на составные части*) breaking down; (*math.*) expansion; (*phys.*) resolution. **2** (*гниение*) decomposition, decay; putrefaction. **3** (*fig.*) (*деморализация*) demoralization; disintegration.

Р

разложи́|вшийся *p.p. act. of* ⇒**~ться** *and adj.* **1** decomposed, decayed. **2** (*fig.*) (*морально*) demoralized.

разлож|и́ть¹, у́, ~ишь *pf.* (*of* ⇒**раскла́дывать**) **1** (*положить по разным местам*) to put; **р. свои́ ве́щи по я́щикам** to put one's things in their respective drawers. **2** (*в определённом порядке*) to lay out, to spread (out); **р. ого́нь** to make a fire; **р. ска́терть** to spread a table-cloth; **р. складну́ю крова́ть** to put up a camp bed. **3** (*распределить*) to distribute, apportion; **р. при́быль** to distribute, share out profits.

разлож|и́ть², у́, ~ишь *pf.* (*of* ⇒**разлага́ть**) **1** (*на составные части*) to break down; (*math.*) to expand; (*phys.*) to resolve; **р. вещество́ на составны́е ча́сти** to break a substance down into its component parts. **2** (*fig.*) (*деморализовать*) to break down, demoralize.

разлож|и́ться¹, у́сь, ~ишься *pf.* (*of* ⇒**раскла́дываться**) (*coll.*) (*разместить свои вещи*) to lay one's things out.

разлож|и́ться², у́сь, ~ишься *pf.* (*of* ⇒**разлага́ться**) **1** (*chem.*) to decompose; (*math.*) to expand. **2** (*сгнить*) to decompose, rot, decay; **труп уже́ ~и́лся** the body has already decomposed. **3** (*fig.*) (*деморализоваться*) to become demoralized; to crack up, go to pieces.

разло́м, а *m.* **1** (*действие*) breaking. **2** (*место*) break.

разлома́|ть, ю *pf.* (*of* ⇒**разла́мывать**) to break (in pieces); **р. дом** to pull down a house.

разлома́|ться, ется *pf.* (*of* ⇒**разла́мываться**) to break (in pieces); to break up.

разлом|и́ть, лю́, ~ишь *pf.* (*of* ⇒**разла́мывать**) **1** to break (in pieces). **2** (*impers.; coll.*): **меня́ всего́ ~и́ло** every bone in my body aches.

разлом|и́ться, ~иться *pf.* (*of* ⇒**разла́мываться**) to break in pieces.

разлу́к|а, и *f.* **1** separation; **жить в ~е** (**с**+*i.*) to live apart (from), be separated (from). **2** (*расставание*) parting; **час ~и** hour of parting.

разлуч|а́ть(ся), а́ю(сь) *impf. of* ⇒**~и́ть(ся)**

разлуч|и́ть, у́, и́шь *pf.* (*of* ⇒**~а́ть**) (+*a.* *and* **с**+*i.*) to separate (from), part (from).

разлуч|и́ться, у́сь, и́шься *pf.* (*of* ⇒**~а́ться**) (**с**+*i.*) to separate, part (from).

разлюб|и́ть, лю́, ~ишь *pf.* (*человека*) to cease to love, stop loving; (*гулять; Москву*) to cease to like.

размагни́|тить, чу, тишь *pf.* (*of* ⇒**~чивать**) (*tech.*) to demagnetize.

размагни́|титься, чусь, тишься *pf.* (*of* ⇒**~чиваться**) **1** (*tech.*) to become demagnetized. **2** (*fig., coll.*) to lose one's grip; to become unbalanced.

размагни́чива|ть(ся), ю(сь) *impf. of* ⇒**размагни́тить(ся)**

разма́|зать, жу, жешь *pf.* (*of* ⇒**~зывать**) **1** to spread, smear; **р. варе́нье по всему́ лицу́** to get jam all over one's face. **2** (*coll.*) (*доклад*) to pad out.

разма́|заться, жется *pf.* (*of* ⇒**~зываться**) to spread; to get smeared.

размазн|я́, и́, *g. pl.* **~е́й** *f. and c.g.* (*coll.*) **1** *f.* gruel; (*fig.*) slush. **2** *c.g.* (*fig.*) (*человек*) ninny, wishy-washy person.

разма́зыва|ть(ся), ю, ет(ся) *impf. of* ⇒**разма́зать(ся)**

размал|ева́ть, ю́ю, ю́ешь *pf.* (*of* ⇒**~ёвывать**) (*coll.*) to daub.

размалёвыва|ть, ю *impf. of* ⇒**размалева́ть**

разма́лыва|ть, ю *impf. of* ⇒**размоло́ть**

разма́рива|ть(ся), ю(сь) *impf. of* ⇒**размори́ть(ся)**

разма́тыва|ть(ся), ю, ет(ся) *impf. of* ⇒**размота́ть(ся)**

разма́х, а *m.* **1** (*сила взмаха*) sweep; **со всего́ ~у** with all one's might; **уда́рить с ~у** to strike with all one's might. **2** (*рук, крыльев*) span; **р. кры́льев** (*aeron.*) wing-span, wing-spread. **3** (*tech.*) (*величина колебания*) swing, amplitude (*of pendulum*). **4** (*fig*) scope, range; **широ́кий р.** grand scale; **они́ живу́т с ~ом** they live in style, they do things in a big way.

разма́хива|ть, ю *impf.* (+*i.*) to swing; to brandish; **р. рука́ми** to gesticulate.

разма́хива|ться, юсь *impf. of* ⇒**размахну́ться**

размах|ну́ться, ну́сь, нёшься *pf.* (*of* ⇒**~иваться**) **1** to swing one's arm (*to strike or as if to strike*). **2** (*fig., coll.*) to do things in a big way.

разма́чива|ть, ю *impf. of* ⇒**размочи́ть**

разма́шист|ый (~, ~а) *adj.* sweeping; **р. жест** sweeping gesture; **р. по́черк** bold hand.

размежева́ни|е, я *nt.* demarcation, delimitation.

размеж|ева́ть, у́ю, у́ешь *pf.* (*of* ⇒**~ёвывать**) to divide out, delimit (*also fig.*); **р. сфе́ры влия́ния** to delimit spheres of influence.

размеж|ева́ться, у́юсь, у́ешься *pf.* (*of* ⇒**~ёвываться**) **1** to fix the boundaries; (*fig.*) to delimit the functions, spheres of action. **2** (*fig.*) (*с идейными противниками*) to dissociate oneself (*from*).

размежёвыва|ть(ся), ю(сь) *impf. of* ⇒**размежева́ть(ся)**

размельч|а́ть, а́ю *impf. of* ⇒**~и́ть**

размельч|и́ть, у́, и́шь *pf.* (*of* ⇒**~а́ть**) to divide into particles; to pulverize.

разме́н, а *m.* exchange; **р. де́нег** changing of money.

разме́нива|ть(ся), ю(сь) *impf. of* ⇒**разменя́ть(ся)**

разме́нн|ый *adj.*: **~ая моне́та** small change.

размен|я́ть, я́ю *pf.* (*of* ⇒**~ивать**) to change; **р. сторублёвку** to change a hundred-rouble note.

размен|я́ться, я́юсь *pf.* (*of* ⇒**~иваться**) (*coll.*) **1** (+*i.*) to exchange; **р. пе́шками** (*in chess*) to exchange pawns. **2** (*fig.*) (**на ме́лочи, по мелоча́м**) to dissipate one's talents.

разме́р, а *m.* **1** (*масштаб*) dimensions; **воро́нка ~ом в де́сять квадра́тных ме́тров** a crater measuring ten square metres (*Br.*), meters (*US*). **2** (*одежды, обуви*) size; (*pl.*) measurements; **како́й ваш р.?** what size do you take? **3** (*зарплаты, процентов*) rate, amount; **получа́ть зарпла́ту в ~е десяти́ рубле́й в день** to be paid at the rate of ten roubles per day. **4** (*степень*) scale, extent; (*pl.*) proportions; **в широ́ких ~ах** on a large scale; **увели́читься до огро́мных ~ов** to assume enormous proportions. **5** (*ритм стиха, музыки*) rhythm.

разме́р|енный *p.p.p. of* ⇒**~ить** *and adj.* measured; **~енная похо́дка** measured tread.

разме́р|ить, ю, ишь *pf.* (*of* ⇒**~я́ть**) to measure off.

размер|я́ть, я́ю *impf. of* ⇒**~ить**

разме|си́ть, шу́, ~сишь *pf.* (*of* ⇒**~шивать**) to knead.

разме|сти́, ту́, тёшь, *past* **~л, ~ла́** *pf.* (*of* ⇒**~та́ть¹**) **1** (*дорожку*) to sweep clean. **2** (*снег*) to shovel, sweep away.

разме|сти́ть, щу́, сти́шь *pf.* (*of* ⇒**~ща́ть**) **1** (*поместить по местам*) to place, accommodate; **р. делега́тов по гости́ницам** to accommodate the delegates in hotels; **р. войска́ по кварти́рам** to quarter troops. **2** (*распределить между многими*) to distribute.

разме|сти́ться, щу́сь, сти́шься *pf.* (*of* ⇒**~ща́ться**) **1** (*занять места*) to take one's seat. **2** (*поместиться*) to be housed, located.

размета́|ть¹, ю *impf. of* ⇒**размести́**

разме|та́ть², чу́, ~чешь *pf.* (*of* ⇒**~тывать**) to scatter, disperse.

разме|та́ться, чу́сь, ~чешься *pf.* **1** (*coll.*) (*в бреду*) to toss. **2** (*на диване*) to sprawl.

разме́|тить, чу, тишь *pf.* (*of* ⇒**~ча́ть**) to mark.

размётыва|ть, ю *impf. of* ⇒**размета́ть²**

размеча́|ть, ю *impf. of* ⇒**разме́тить**

размеш|а́ть, а́ю *pf.* (*of* ⇒**~ивать**) to stir.

разме́шива|ть, ю *impf. of* ⇒**размеси́ть** *and* **размеша́ть**

размеща́|ть(ся), ю(сь) *impf. of* ⇒**размести́ть(ся)**

размеще́ни|е, я *nt.* **1** (*по местам*) placing, accommodation; (*между многими*) distribution, allocation; **р. войск по кварти́рам** quartering, billeting of troops; **р. вооружённых сил** stationing of armed forces; **р. промы́шленности** location of industry. **2** (*fin.*) (*капитала*) placing, investment.

размина́|ть(ся), ю(сь) *impf. of* ⇒**размя́ть(ся)**

размини́ровани|е, я *nt.* (*mil.*) mine clearing.

размини́р|овать, ую *pf.* to clear of mines.

разми́нк|а, и *f.* (*sport*) limbering-up; warm-up.

размин|у́ться, у́сь, ёшься *pf.* (*coll.*) **1** (**с**+*i.*) to pass (*without meeting*); to miss; **мы, должно́ быть, ~у́лись с ним на доро́ге** we must have passed one another on the road. **2** (*о письмах*) to cross. **3** (*обойти, объехать*) to (be able to) pass; **на э́том уча́стке доро́ги маши́нам нельзя́ р.** it is impossible for cars to pass on this part of the road.

размнож|а́ть(ся), а́ю, а́ет(ся) *impf. of* ⇒**~́ить(ся)**

размноже́ни|е, я *nt.* **1** duplicating; photocopying. **2** (*biol.*) reproduction, propagation.

размно́ж|ить, у, ишь *pf.* (*of* ⇒**~а́ть**) **1** (*распечатать в многих экземплярах*) to duplicate; to photocopy. **2** (*животных*) to breed, rear.

размно́ж|иться, ится *pf.* (*of* ⇒**~а́ться**) (*biol.*) to reproduce; to breed.

размозж|и́ть, у́, и́шь *pf.* to smash.

размок|а́ть, а́ет *impf. of* ⇒**~́нуть**

размо́к|нуть, нет, *past* **~, ~ла** *pf.* (*of* ⇒**~а́ть**) to get soaked; to get sodden.

размо́л, а *m.* **1** grinding. **2**: **мука́ кру́пного, ме́лкого ~а** coarse-ground flour; finely ground flour.

размо́лвк|а, и *f.* tiff, disagreement.

раз|моло́ть, мелю́, ме́лешь *pf.* (*of* ⇒**разма́лывать**) to grind.

разморáжива|ть(ся), ю(сь) *impf. of* ⇒**разморо́зить(ся)**

размор|и́ть, и́т *pf.* (*of* ⇒**разма́ривать**) (*coll.*) to exhaust; (*impers.*): **её ~и́ло на со́лнце** the sun wore her out.

размор|и́ться, ю́сь, и́шься *pf.* (*of* ⇒**разма́риваться**) (*coll.*) to be worn out.

разморо́|зить, жу, зишь *pf.* (*of* ⇒**размора́живать**) to defrost.

разморо́|зиться, жусь, зишься *pf.* (*of* ⇒**размора́живаться**) to defrost.

размота́|ть, ю *pf.* (*of* ⇒**разма́тывать**) to unwind, uncoil, unreel.

размота́|ться, ется *pf.* (*of* ⇒**разма́тываться**) to unwind, uncoil, unreel; to come unwound.

размоч|и́ть, у́, ~́ишь *pf.* (*of* ⇒**разма́чивать**) to soak, steep.

размы́в, а *m.* washing away, erosion.

размыва́|ть, ю *impf. of* ⇒**размы́ть**

размыка́ни|е, я *nt.* (*elec.*) breaking, break, disconnection.

размы́ка|ть, ю *pf.* (*of* ⇒**размы́кивать**) (*coll.*) to shake off; **р. го́ре** (*poet.*) to shake off one's grief.

размыка́|ть, ю *impf. of* ⇒**разомкну́ть**

размы́кива|ть, ю *impf. of* ⇒**размы́кать**

размы́сл|ить, ю, ишь *pf.* (*of* ⇒**размышля́ть**) (**о**+*p.*) to reflect (on, upon), meditate (on, upon), ponder (over).

разм|ы́ть, о́ю, о́ешь *pf.* (*of* ⇒**~ыва́ть**) to wash away; (*geol.*) to erode.

размышле́ни|е, я *nt.* reflection, meditation, thought; **по зре́лом ~и** on second thoughts, on reflection; **быть погружённым в ~я** to be lost in thought.

размышля́|ть, ю *impf. of* ⇒**размы́слить**

размягч|а́ть(ся), а́ю(сь) *impf. of* ⇒**~и́ть(ся)**

размягче́ни|е, я *nt.* softening.

размягч|и́ть, у́, и́шь *pf.* (*of* ⇒**~а́ть**) to soften.

размягч|и́ться, у́сь, и́шься *pf.* (*of* ⇒**~а́ться**) to soften, grow soft.

размя́к|нуть, ну, нешь, *past* **~, ~ла** *pf. of* ⇒**мя́кнуть**

раз|мя́ть, омну́, омнёшь *pf.* (*of* ⇒**мять** *and* **~мина́ть**) **1** (*глину*) to knead; (*картошку*) to mash. **2**: **р. но́ги** (*coll.*) to stretch one's legs.

раз|мя́ться, омну́сь, омнёшься *pf.* (*of* ⇒**~мина́ться**) **1** to grow soft (*as result of kneading*). **2** (*coll.*) to stretch one's legs; (*sport*) to limber up, loosen up.

разна́шива|ть(ся), ю, ет(ся) *impf. of* ⇒**разноси́ть(ся)**[1]

разне́жива|ть(ся), ю(сь) *impf. of* ⇒**разне́жить(ся)**

разне́ж|ить, у, ишь *pf.* (*of* ⇒**~ивать**) (*coll.*) **1** (*избаловать*) to spoil, pamper. **2** (*заставить расчувствоваться*) to appeal to the tender feelings (of).

разне́ж|иться, усь, ишься *pf.* (*of* ⇒**~иваться**) (*coll., pej.*) **1** (*избаловаться*) to become spoilt. **2** (*предаться неге*) to grow lazy, soft. **3** (*расчувствоваться*) to go soft.

разнемо́|чься, гу́сь, ~жешься, ~гутся, *past* **~гся, ~гла́сь** *pf.* (*coll.*) to become ill, be taken ill.

разне́рвнича|ться, юсь *pf.* (*coll.*) to become very nervous.

разнес|ти́, у́, ёшь, *past* **~́, ~ла́** *pf.* (*of* ⇒**разноси́ть**[2]) **1** to carry, convey; to take round; **р. газе́ты** to deliver newspapers; **р. слух** to spread a rumour. **2** (*записать*) to enter, note down; **р. цита́ты на ка́рточки** to note down quotations on cards. **3** (*coll.*) (*разбить*) to smash, break up. **4** (*рассеять*) to scatter, disperse. **5** (*coll.*) (*раздуть*) to cause to swell; (*impers.*): **его́ щёку ~ло́** his cheek is swollen. **6** (*fig., coll.*) (*разбранить*) to slam.

разнес|ти́сь, ётся, *past* **~́ся, ~ла́сь** *pf.* (*of* ⇒**разноси́ться**[2]) **1** (*о слухах*) to spread. **2** (*о звуках*) to resound.

разнима́|ть, ю *impf. of* ⇒**разня́ть**

ра́зн|иться, юсь, ишься *impf.* to differ.

ра́зниц|а, ы *f.* difference; disparity; **без ~ы** (*sl.*) it makes no difference; **кака́я р.?** (*coll.*) what difference does it make?

разнобо́|й, я *m.* lack of co-ordination; difference, disagreement.

разнове́с, а *m.* (*collect.*) set of weights.

разнови́дност|ь, и *f.* variety.

разновре́мен|ный (~ен, ~на) *adj.* taking place at different times.

разногла́си|е, я *nt.* **1** (*во мнениях*) difference, disagreement; **р. во взгля́дах** difference of opinion. **2** (*противоречие*) discrepancy; **р. в показа́ниях** conflicting evidence.

разноголо́сиц|а, ы *f.* discordance, dissonance (*also fig., coll.*); **р. во мне́ниях** dissent.

разноголо́с|ый (~, ~а) *adj.* discordant.

разнокали́бер|ный (~ен, ~на) *adj.* **1** (*mil.*) of different calibres. **2** (*fig., coll.*) mixed, heterogeneous.

разнома́ст|ный (~ен, ~на) *adj.* **1** (*разного цвета*) of different colours (*Br.*), colors (*US*). **2** (*cards*) of different suits.

разномы́сли|е, я *nt.* (*liter.*) difference of opinion(s).

разнообра́зи|е, я *nt.* variety, diversity; **для ~я** for a change.

разнообра́|зить, жу, зишь *impf.* to vary, diversify.

разнообра́зност|ь, и *f.* = **разнообра́зие**

разнообра́з|ный (~ен, ~на) *adj.* various, varied, diverse.

разноплеме́нный *adj.* (*obs.*) of different races, tribes.

разнорабо́ч|ий, его *m.* unskilled labourer (*Br.*), laborer (*US*).

разноречи́в|ый (~, ~а) *adj.* contradictory, conflicting.

разноре́чи|е, я *nt.* (*liter.*) contradiction.

разноро́дност|ь, и *f.* heterogeneity.

разноро́д|ный (~ен, ~на) *adj.* heterogeneous.

разно́с, а *m.* **1** carrying; delivery (*of mail, etc.*). **2** (*fig., coll.*) (*внушение*) dressing-down.

разно|си́ть[1]**, шу́, ~́сишь** *pf.* (*of* ⇒**разна́шивать**) to wear in (*footwear*).

разно|си́ть[2]**, шу́, ~́сишь** *impf. of* ⇒**разнести́**

разно|си́ться[1]**, ~́сится** *pf.* (*of* ⇒**разна́шиваться**) (*об обуви*) to become comfortable.

разно|си́ться[2]**, ~́сится** *impf. of* ⇒**разнести́сь**

разно́ск|а, и *f.* delivery.

разносклоня́емый *adj.* (*gram.*) irregularly declined.

разно́сн|ый[1] *adj.*: **~ая кни́га** delivery book; **~ая торго́вля** street-trading.

разно́сн|ый[2] *adj.* (*coll.*) (*ругательный*) abusive; **~ая реце́нзия** scathing review; **~ые слова́** swear-words.

разносо́л, а *m.* (*cul.*) **1** (*obs.*) (*маринад*) pickle(s). **2** (*pl. only*) (*coll.*) (*изысканная еда*) dainties, delicacies.

разноспряга́емый *adj.* (*gram.*) irregularly conjugated.

Р

разносторо́н|ний *adj.* **1** (*math.*) scalene. **2** **(~ен, ~ня)** (*fig.*) many-sided; versatile; **~нее образова́ние** all-round education.

разносторо́нност|ь, и *f.* versatility.

ра́зност|ь, и *f.* **1** (*math.*) difference. **2** difference, diversity; **ра́зные ~и** (*coll.*) this and that.

разно́счик, а *m.* (*газет, телеграмм*) delivery man; (*новостей*) bearer; (*инфекции*) carrier; (*торговец*) pedlar, hawker.

разноти́п|ный (~ен, ~на) *adj.* of different types, diverse.

разнохара́ктер|ный (~ен, ~на) *adj.* diverse, varied.

разноцве́т|ный (~ен, ~на) *adj.* of different colours (*Br.*), colors (*US*); multi-coloured (*Br.*), multi-colored (*US*).

разночи́н|ец, ца *m.* (*hist.*) raznochinets (*in 19th century, Russian intellectual not of gentle birth*).

разночи́н|ный *adj. of* ⇒**~ец**

разночте́ни|е, я *nt.* (*philol.*) variant reading.

разношёрст|ный (~ен, ~на) *adj.* **1** (*животные*) of different colours (*Br.*), colors (*US*). **2** (*fig., coll.*) mixed; ill-assorted.

разноязы́ч|ный (~ен, ~на) *adj.* polyglot.

разну́зд|анный *p.p.p. of* ⇒**~а́ть** *and adj.* unbridled, unruly.

разнузд|а́ть, а́ю *pf.* (*of* ⇒**~́ывать**) to unbridle.

разну́здыва|ть, ю *impf. of* ⇒**разнузда́ть**

ра́зн|ый *adj.* **1** (*взгляды*) different, differing. **2** (*разнообразный*) various, diverse; **~ого ро́да** of various kinds; *as n.* **~ое, ~ого** *nt.* (*на повестке дня*) any other business.

разню́х|ать, аю *pf.* (*of* ⇒**~ивать**) (*coll.*) to smell out (*also fig.*); (*fig.*) to nose out, ferret out.

разню́хива|ть, ю *impf. of* ⇒**разню́хать**

раз|ня́ть, ниму́, ни́мешь, *past* **~ня́л, ~няла́, ~ня́ло** *pf.* (*of* ⇒**~нима́ть**) **1** (*индейку; машину*) to take to pieces, dismantle. **2** (*драчунов*) to part, separate. **3** (*пальцы, руки*) to unclench.

разо... *vbl. pref.* = **раз...**

разоби́|деть, жу, дишь *pf.* (*coll.*) to offend greatly.

разоби́|деться, жусь, дишься *pf.* (*coll.*) to take offence.

разоблач|а́ть(ся), а́ю(сь) *impf. of* ⇒**~и́ть(ся)**

разоблаче́ни|е, я *nt.* exposure, unmasking.

разоблачи́тел|ь, я *m.* unmasker.

разоблач|и́ть, у́, и́шь *pf.* (*of* ⇒**~а́ть**) **1** (*eccl. or joc.*) to disrobe, divest. **2** (*fig.*) to expose, unmask.

разоблач|и́ться, у́сь, и́шься *pf.* (*of* ⇒**~а́ться**) **1** (*eccl. or joc.*) to disrobe. **2** (*fig.*) to be exposed, be unmasked.

раз|обра́ть, беру́, берёшь, *past* **~обра́л, ~обрала́, ~обра́ло** *pf.* (*of* ⇒**~бира́ть**) **1** (*механизм*) to take to pieces, dismantle; **р. дом** to pull down a house. **2** (*раскупить*) to buy up; (*взять*) to take. **3** (*привести в порядок*) to sort out. **4** (*ссору, дело*) to investigate, look into. **5** (*gram.*) to parse; to analyse (*Br.*), analyze (*US*). **6** (*понять*) to make out, understand; **я не могу́ р. его́ по́черк** I cannot make out his handwriting; **мы не мо́жем р., в чём де́ло** we cannot understand what it is all about. **7** (*fig., coll.*) (*охватить*) to fill (with), seize (with); **её ~обрала́ ре́вность** she was filled with jealousy; **его́ ~обра́ло** he was drunk.

раз|обра́ться, беру́сь, берёшься, *past* **~обра́лся, ~обрала́сь** *pf.* (*of* ⇒**~бира́ться**) **1** (*coll.*) (*после поездки*) to sort out one's things. **2** (**в**+*p. or coll.* **с**+*i.*) (*исследовать*) to investigate, look into; (*понимать*) to understand; **р. в пчелово́дстве** to know about bee-keeping; **я в нём не ~обра́лся** I could not make him out.

разобщ|а́ть(ся), а́ю(сь) *impf. of* ⇒**~и́ть(ся)**

разобще́ни|е, я *nt.* separation.

разобщённо *adv.* apart, separately; **де́йствовать р.** to act independently.

разобщ|и́ть, у́, и́шь *pf.* (*of* ⇒**~а́ть**) **1** to separate; (*fig.*) to estrange, alienate. **2** (*tech.*) to disconnect, uncouple, disengage.

разобщ|и́ться, у́сь, и́шься *pf.* (*of* ⇒**~а́ться**) (*tech.*) to become disconnected.

ра́зов|ый *adj.* valid for one occasion (only); **~ого по́льзования** disposable.

раз|огна́ть, гоню́, го́нишь, *past* **~огна́л, ~огнала́, ~огна́ло** *pf.* (*of* ⇒**~гоня́ть**) **1** to drive away; to disperse; (*fig.*) to dispel; **р. демонстра́цию** to break up a demonstration; **р. го́ре** to dispel grief. **2** (*coll.*) (*автомобиль*) to drive at high speed, race.

раз|огна́ться, гоню́сь, го́нишься, *past* **~огна́лся, ~огнала́сь, ~огна́ло́сь** *pf.* (*of* ⇒**~гоня́ться**) to gather speed; to gather momentum.

разогн|у́ть, у́, ёшь *pf.* (*of* ⇒**разгиба́ть**) to unbend, straighten; **р. спи́ну** to straighten one's back.

разогн|у́ться, у́сь, ёшься *pf.* (*of* ⇒**разгиба́ться**) to straighten o.s. up.

разогре́в, а *m.* (*tech.*) initial heating; firing (*of furnace*).

разогрева́ни|е, я *nt.* warming-up.

разогрева́|ть(ся), ю(сь) *impf. of* ⇒**разогре́ть(ся)**

разогре́|ть, ю *pf.* (*of* ⇒**~ва́ть**) to warm up.

разогре́|ться, юсь *pf.* (*of* ⇒**~ва́ться**) to warm up, grow warm.

разоде́т|ый *p.p.p. of* ⇒**~ь** *and adj.* dressed up; **весь р.** all dressed up, in one's best bib and tucker.

разоде́|ть, ну, нешь *pf.* (*coll.*) to dress up.

разоде́|ться, нусь, нешься *pf.* (*coll.*) to dress up; **р. в пух и прах** to be dressed to kill.

разодолж|а́ть, а́ю *impf. of* ⇒**~и́ть**

разодолж|и́ть, у́, и́шь *pf.* (*of* ⇒**~а́ть**) (*coll.*) to give a nasty surprise.

раз|одра́ть, деру́, дерёшь, *past* **~одра́л, ~одрала́, ~одра́ло** *pf.* (*of* ⇒**~дира́ть**) to tear up.

раз|одра́ться, дерётся, *past* **~одра́лся, ~одрала́сь, ~одра́ло́сь** *pf.* (*of* ⇒**~дира́ться**) (*coll.*) to tear.

разозл|и́ть, ю́, и́шь *pf.* (*of* ⇒**злить**) to make angry, enrage.

разозл|и́ться, ю́сь, и́шься *pf.* (*of* ⇒**зли́ться**) to get angry, get in a rage.

раз|ойти́сь, ойду́сь, ойдёшься, *past* **~ошёлся, ~ошла́сь** *pf.* (*of* ⇒**расходи́ться**) **1** (*уйти*) to go away; (*рассеяться*) to disperse; **толпа́ ~ошла́сь** the crowd broke up; **ту́чи ~ошли́сь** the clouds dispersed. **2** (**с**+*i.*) (*расстаться*) to part (from); (*о супругах*) to separate (from); **мы ~ошли́сь друзья́ми** we parted friends; **он ~ошёлся с жено́й** he has separated from his wife. **3** (*о линиях, о дорогах*) to branch off, diverge; (*о лучах*) to radiate. **4** (*разминуться*) to pass (*without meeting*). **5** (**с**+*i.*) (*обнаружить разногласие*) to be at variance (with), conflict (with); **р. во мне́нии с кем-н.** to disagree with s.o. **6** (*раствориться*) to dissolve; (*растаять*) to melt. **7** (*распродаться*) to be sold out; (*о деньгах*) to be spent; (*о запасах*) to be used up. **8** (*coll.*) (*приобрести скорость*) to gather speed. **9** (*coll.*) (*дать волю себе*) to get going, get worked up; **бу́ря ~ошла́сь** the storm raged. **10** (*разъединиться*) to come apart.

раз|о́к, ка́ *m.* (*coll.*) *dim. of* ⇒**~; ещё р.** once more; **р. друго́й** once or twice.

ра́зом *adv.* (*coll.*) at once, at one go.

разомкн|у́ть, у́, ёшь *pf.* (*of* ⇒**размыка́ть**) to open, unfasten; (*tech.*) to break, disconnect.

разомле́|ть, ю *pf.* (*coll.*) to languish, grow languid.

разонра́в|иться, люсь, ишься *pf.* (*coll.*; +*d.*) to cease to please, lose its attraction (for).

разопрева́|ть, ю *impf. of* ⇒**разопре́ть**

разопре́|ть, ю *pf.* (*of* ⇒**~ва́ть**) **1** (*о еде*) to become soft (*in cooking*). **2** (*coll.*) (*о человеке*) to be worn out, done in (*from heat*).

разо́р, а *m.* (*coll.*) ruin, destruction.

разор|а́ться, у́сь, ёшься *pf.* (*coll.*) to start shouting.

разорв|а́ть, у́, ёшь, *past* **~а́л, ~ала́, ~а́ло** *pf.* (*of* ⇒**разрыва́ть**[1]) **1** (*письмо*) to tear up; (*пакет, конверт*) to tear open; (*одежду*) to tear. **2** (*impers.*) (*взорвать*) to blow up, burst; **котёл ~а́ло** the boiler has burst. **3** (*fig.*) (*прекратить*) to break (off), sever; **р.**

дипломати́ческие отноше́ния to break off diplomatic relations.

разорв|а́ться, у́сь, ёшься, *past* **~а́лся, ~ала́сь, ~а́ло́сь** *pf.* (*of* ⇒**разрыва́ться**) **1** (*о верёвке*) to break, snap; (*об одежде*) to tear, become torn. **2** (*взорваться*) to blow up; to explode. **3** (*об отношениях*) to be broken off, severed. **4** (*coll.*; *usu.* + *neg.*) to be everywhere at once; **я не могу́ р.** I can't be everywhere at once; **хоть ~и́сь!** however hard I try, tried!

разоре́ни|е, я *nt.* (*города*) destruction, ravage; (*народа*) ruin.

разори́тел|ь, я *m.* destroyer.

разори́тель|ница, ницы *f. of* ⇒~

разори́тел|ьный (~ен, ~ьна) *adj.* ruinous; wasteful.

разор|и́ть, ю́, и́шь *pf.* (*of* ⇒**~я́ть**) **1** (*опустошить*) to destroy, ravage. **2** (*довести до нищеты*) to ruin, bring to ruin.

разор|и́ться, ю́сь, и́шься *pf.* (*of* ⇒**~я́ться**[1]) **1** (*прийти в упадок*) to be ruined. **2** (*впасть в нищету*) to go broke, ruin o.s. **3** (*coll.*) (**на** + *a.*) to spend all one's money (on).

разоруж|а́ть(ся), а́ю(сь) *impf. of* ⇒**~и́ть(ся)**

разоруже́ни|е, я *nt.* (*действие*) disarming; (*политика*) disarmament.

разоруж|и́ть, у́, и́шь *pf.* (*of* ⇒**~а́ть**) to disarm.

разоруж|и́ться, у́сь, и́шься *pf.* (*of* ⇒**~а́ться**) to disarm.

разор|я́ть(ся)[1], я́ю(сь) *impf. of* ⇒**~и́ть(ся)**

разоря́|ться[2], юсь *impf.* (*coll.*, *pej.*) (*много говорить*) to rant.

разо|сла́ть, шлю́, шлёшь *pf.* (*of* ⇒**рассыла́ть**) to send out.

разосп|а́ться, лю́сь, и́шься, *past* **~а́лся, ~ала́сь, ~а́ло́сь** *pf.* (*coll.*) to be fast asleep.

разостла́ть (*and* **расстели́ть**), **расстелю́, рассте́лешь** *pf.* (*of* ⇒**расстила́ть**) to spread (out), lay.

разостла́|ться (*and* **расстели́ться**), **рассте́лется** *pf.* (*of* ⇒**расстила́ться**) to spread.

разохо́|тить, чу, тишь *pf.* (**к** + *d.*, **на** + *a.*; *coll.*) to stimulate (to), arouse an inclination (to, for).

разохо́|титься, чусь, тишься *pf.* (+ *inf.*; *coll.*) to take a liking (to), feel an inclination (for); **спе́рва́ он не хоте́л танцева́ть, а тепе́рь ~тился** he did not want to dance at first, but now he is keen to.

разочарова́ни|е, я *nt.* disappointment.

разочаро́в|анный *p.p.p. of* ⇒**~а́ть** *and adj.* disappointed; (**в** + *prep.*) disillusioned (with).

разочар|ова́ть, у́ю *pf.* (*of* ⇒**~о́вывать**) to disappoint.

разочар|ова́ться, у́юсь *pf.* (*of* ⇒**~о́вываться**) (**в ком-н., в чём-н.**) to be disappointed (in s.o., with sth.).

разочаро́выва|ть(ся), ю(сь) *impf. of* ⇒**разочарова́ть(ся)**

разраба́тыва|ть, ю *impf. of* ⇒**разрабо́тать**

разрабо́та|ть, ю *pf.* (*of* ⇒**разраба́тывать**) **1** (*agric.*) to cultivate. **2** (*mining*) to work, exploit. **3** (*подготовить*) to work out, work up; to develop; to elaborate; **р. ме́тоды** to devise methods; **р. пла́ны** to work out plans.

разрабо́тк|а, и *f.* **1** (*agric.*) cultivation. **2** (*mining*) working, exploitation; **откры́тая р.** open-cast mining. **3**: **нефтяна́я р.** oilfield; **р. гра́вия** gravel pit; **р. сла́нца** slate quarry. **4** (*проекта*) working out, working up; elaboration.

разра́внива|ть, ю *impf. of* ⇒**разровня́ть**

разража́|ться, юсь *impf. of* ⇒**разрази́ться**

разра|зи́ться, жу́сь, зи́шься *pf.* (*of* ⇒**~жа́ться**) (*о грозе, о катастрофе*) to break out, burst out; **р. слеза́ми** to burst into tears; **р. сме́хом** to burst out laughing.

разраст|а́ться, а́ется *impf. of* ⇒**~и́сь**

разраст|и́сь, ётся, *past* **разро́сся, разросла́сь** *pf.* (*of* ⇒**~а́ться**) to grow; to spread; **де́ло разросло́сь** the business has grown; **сире́нь разросла́сь** the lilac has spread.

разрев|е́ться, у́сь, ёшься *pf.* (*coll.*) to start howling.

разре|ди́ть, жу́, ди́шь *pf.* (*of* ⇒**~жа́ть**) **1** (*рассаду*) to thin out, weed out. **2** (*воздух*) to rarefy.

разрежа́|ть, ю *impf. of* ⇒**разреди́ть**

разре|жённый *p.p.p. of* ⇒**~ди́ть** *and adj.* rarefied.

разре́з, а *m.* **1** (*отверстие*) cut; slit; **ю́бка с ~ом** slit skirt. **2** (*сечение*) section; **попере́чный р.** cross-section; **р. глаз** shape of one's eyes. **3** (*fig.*, *coll.*) (*точка зрения*) point of view; **в ~е** (+ *g.*) from the point of view (of), in the context (of).

разре́|зать, жу, жешь *pf.* (*of* ⇒**~за́ть**) to cut; to slit.

разрез|а́ть, а́ю *impf. of* ⇒**~ать**

разрезн|о́й *adj.* **1** cutting; **р. нож** paper-knife; **~а́я пила́** rip saw. **2** (*имеющий разрезы*) slit, with slits.

разреш|а́ть, а́ю *impf. of* ⇒**~и́ть**

разреш|а́ться, а́юсь *impf.* **1** *impf. of* ⇒**~и́ться. 2** *impf. only* to be allowed; **здесь кури́ть не ~а́ется** no smoking (is allowed here).

разреше́ни|е, я *nt.* **1** (*право*) permission; **с ва́шего ~я** with your permission, by your leave. **2** (*документ*) permit, authorization; **р. на въезд** entry permit. **3** (*проблемы*) solution. **4** (*спора*) settlement. **5** (*tech.*) (*степень детализации*) resolution.

разреши́м|ый (~, ~а) *adj.* solvable.

разреш|и́ть, у́, и́шь *pf.* (*of* ⇒**~а́ть**) **1** (+ *d.*) to allow, permit; **~и́те пройти́** allow me to pass; do you mind letting me pass? **2** (*книгу, фильм*) to authorize; **р. кни́гу к печа́ти** to authorize the printing of a book. **3** (*проблему*) to solve. **4** (*конфликт*) to settle; **р. сомне́ния** to resolve doubts.

разреш|и́ться, у́сь, и́шься *pf.* (*of* ⇒**~а́ться**) **1** (*о проблеме*) to be solved. **2** (*о конфликте*) to be settled. **3** (**от бре́мени**) (+ *i.*; *obs.*) to be delivered (of); **она́ ~и́лась де́вочкой** she was delivered of a girl.

разрис|ова́ть, у́ю *pf.* (*of* ⇒**~о́вывать**) to cover with drawings.

разрисо́выва|ть, ю *impf. of* ⇒**разрисова́ть**

разровня́|ть, ю *pf.* (*of* ⇒**разра́внивать**) to level.

разро́зн|енный *p.p.p. of* ⇒**~ить** *and adj.* **1** (*лишенный единства*) uncoordinated. **2**: **р. компле́кт** incomplete set; **~енные тома́** odd volumes.

разро́знива|ть, ю *impf. of* ⇒**разро́знить**

разро́зн|ить, ю, ишь *pf.* (*of* ⇒**~ивать**) to break a set (of).

разруб|а́ть, а́ю *impf. of* ⇒**~и́ть**

разруб|и́ть, лю́, ~ишь *pf.* (*of* ⇒**~а́ть**) to cut, cleave; **р. го́рдиев у́зел** to cut the Gordian knot.

разруга́|ть, ю *pf.* (*coll.*) (*человека*) to reprimand; (*работу*) to slam.

разруга́|ться, юсь *pf.* (**с** + *i.*; *coll.*) to quarrel (with).

разрумя́нива|ть(ся), ю(сь) *impf. of* ⇒**разрумя́нить(ся)**

разрумя́н|ить, ю, ишь *pf.* (*of* ⇒**~ивать**) **1** (*покрыть румянами*) to rouge. **2** (*покрыть румянцем*) to flush, redden; **моро́з ~ил её щёки** the frost brought a flush to her cheeks.

разрумя́н|иться, юсь, ишься *pf.* (*of* ⇒**~иваться**) **1** (*покрыться румянами*) to put rouge on. **2** (*покрыться румянцем*) to blush; to be flushed.

разру́х|а, и *f.* ruin, collapse.

разруш|а́ть(ся), а́ю, а́ет(ся) *impf. of* ⇒**~и́ть(ся)**

разруше́ни|е, я *nt.* destruction; (*pl.*) havoc.

разруши́тел|ьный (~ен, ~ьна) *adj.* destructive.

разру́ш|ить, у, ишь *pf.* (*of* ⇒**~а́ть**) **1** to destroy; to ruin. **2** (*fig.*) to ruin, frustrate; **р. чьи-н. наде́жды** to ruin s.o.'s hopes.

разру́ш|иться, ится *pf.* (*of* ⇒**~а́ться**) to go to ruin, be destroyed, collapse.

разры́в, а *m.* **1** (*пространство*) break; gap; (*прореха*) tear; (*отношений*) breaking, severance; (*с кем-н.*) break-up; (*несоответствие*) gap; **р. ме́жду поколе́ниями** generation gap. **2** (*снаряда*) burst, explosion.

разрыва́|ть[1], ю *impf. of* ⇒**разорва́ть**

разрыва́|ть[2], ю *impf. of* ⇒**разры́ть**

разрыва́|ться, юсь *impf. of* ⇒**разорва́ться**

разрывно́й *adj.* explosive.

разр|ы́ть, о́ю, о́ешь *pf.* (*of*

Р

⇒~ыва́ть²) **1** to dig up. **2** (*fig., coll.*) to turn upside-down, rummage through.

разрыхле́ни|е, я *nt.* loosening.

разрыхли́тел|ь, я *m.* baking powder, soda.

разрыхл|и́ть, ю́, и́шь *pf.* (*of* ⇒~я́ть) to loosen; to hoe.

разрыхл|я́ть, я́ю *impf. of* ⇒~и́ть

разря́д¹, а *m.* (*электричества*) discharge.

разря́д², а *m.* (*категория*) category, sort; (*в профессии, в спорте*) rank, class; **пе́рвого ~а** first-class.

разря|ди́ть¹, жу́, ~́дишь *pf.* (*of* ⇒~жа́ть) (*coll.*) to dress up.

разря|ди́ть², жу́, ди́шь *pf.* (*of* ⇒~жа́ть) **1** (*elec.*) to discharge; **р. атмосфе́ру** (*fig.*) to clear the air. **2** (*ружьё*) to unload; (*стреляя*) to discharge.

разря|ди́ться¹, жу́сь, ~́дишься *pf.* (*of* ⇒~жа́ться) to dress up.

разря|ди́ться², ди́тся *pf.* (*of* ⇒~жа́ться) **1** (*elec.*) to run down; (*fig.*) to clear, ease; **атмосфе́ра ~ди́лась** the atmosphere has become less tense. **2** (*об оружии*) to be unloaded; (*стреляя*) to be discharged.

разря́дк|а, и *f.* **1** (*электричества*) discharging; (*ружья*) unloading; **р. напряжённости** (*pol.*) lessening of tension, détente. **2** (*typ.*) letter-spacing.

разря́дник, а *m.* sportsman with an official ranking.

разря́дниц|а, ы *f.* sportswoman with an official ranking.

разряжа́|ть(ся), ю(сь) *impf. of* ⇒**разряди́ть(ся)**

разубе|ди́ть, жу́, ди́шь *pf.* (*of* ⇒~жда́ть) (**в**+*p.*) to dissuade (from).

разубе|ди́ться, жу́сь, ди́шься *pf.* (*of* ⇒~жда́ться) (**в**+*p.*) to change one's mind (about).

разубежда́|ть(ся), ю(сь) *impf. of* ⇒**разубеди́ть(ся)**

разува́|ть(ся), ю(сь) *impf. of* ⇒**разу́ть(ся)**

разувере́ни|е, я *nt.* dissuasion.

разуве́р|ить, ю, ишь *pf.* (*of* ⇒~я́ть) (**в**+*p.*) to cause s.o. to lose faith, stop believing (in); to persuade to the contrary; **он меня́ ~ил в том, что э́того мо́жно доби́ться** he persuaded me that it could not be achieved.

разуве́р|иться, юсь, ишься *pf.* (*of* ⇒~я́ться) (**в**+*p.*) to lose faith (in).

разуверя́|ть(ся), ю(сь) *impf. of* ⇒**разуве́рить(ся)**

разузна|ва́ть, ю́, ёшь *impf.* **1** *impf. of* ⇒**разузна́ть. 2** *impf. only* to make inquiries (about).

разузна́|ть, ю *pf.* (*of* ⇒~ва́ть) to find out.

разукра́|сить, шу, сишь *pf.* (*of* ⇒~шивать) to adorn; to decorate; to embellish.

разукра́|ситься, шусь, сишься *pf.* (*of* ⇒~шиваться) to adorn *or* decorate o.s.

разукра́шива|ть(ся), ю(сь) *impf. of* ⇒**разукра́сить(ся)**

разукрупн|и́ть, ю́, и́шь *pf.* (*of* ⇒~я́ть) to break up into smaller units.

разукрупн|я́ть, я́ю, я́ет *impf. of* ⇒~и́ть

ра́зум, а *m.* reason; (*интеллект*) intellect; **у него́ ум за р. зашёл** (*coll.*) he is, was at his wit's end.

разуме́ни|е, я *nt.* **1** (*obs.*) (*понимание*) understanding. **2** (*мнение*) opinion, viewpoint; **по моему́ ~ю** to my mind, as I see it.

разуме́|ть, ю *impf.* **1** (*obs.*) (*понимать*) to understand. **2** (**под**+*i.*) (*подразумевать*) to understand (by), mean (by).

разуме́|ться, ется *impf.* (**под**+*i.*) to be understood (by), be meant (by); **под э́тим ~ется**... by this is meant ...; **(са́мо собо́й) ~ется** it stands to reason; it goes without saying, of course; **он, ~ется, не знал, что вы уже́ пришли́** he, of course, did not know that you were already here.

разу́мник, а *m.* (*coll.*) clever chap, clever boy.

разу́мниц|а, ы *f.* (*coll.*) clever girl.

разу́м|ный (~ен, ~на) *adj.* **1** (*существо*) rational, intelligent. **2** (*парень*) intelligent, clever. **3** (*поступок*) reasonable; **э́то (вполне́) ~но** it is (perfectly) reasonable.

разу́|ть, ю, ешь *pf.* (*of* ⇒~ва́ть); **р. кого́-н.** to take s.o.'s shoes off.

разу́|ться, юсь, ешься *pf.* (*of* ⇒~ва́ться) to take one's shoes off.

разу́чива|ть(ся), ю(сь) *impf. of* ⇒**разучи́ть(ся)**

разуч|и́ть, у́, ~́ишь *pf.* (*of* ⇒~́ивать) to learn (up); **р. роль** to learn, study one's part.

разуч|и́ться, у́сь, ~́ишься *pf.* (*of* ⇒~́иваться) (+*inf.*) to forget (how to), lose the art (of); **я ~и́лся ходи́ть на лы́жах** I have forgotten how to ski.

разъ... *vbl. pref.* = **раз...**

разъеда́|ть(ся), ю(сь) *impf. of* ⇒**разъе́сть(ся)**

разъедине́ни|е, я *nt.* **1** separation. **2** (*elec.*) disconnection, breaking.

разъедин|и́ть, ю́, и́шь *pf.* (*of* ⇒~я́ть) **1** (*друзей*) to separate. **2** (*elec.*) to disconnect, break; **нас ~и́ли** we were cut off (*on telephone*).

разъедин|и́ться, ю́сь, и́шься *pf.* (*of* ⇒~я́ться) to separate, part; (*о проводах*) to come apart, be disconnected; (*о людях*) to become disunited, estranged.

разъедин|я́ть(ся), я́ю(сь) *impf. of* ⇒~и́ть(ся)

разъе́зд, а *m.* **1** (*людей*) departure. **2** (*pl.*) (*поездки*) travels. **3** (*mil.*) mounted patrol. **4** (*rail.*) siding.

разъездн|о́й *adj.*: **~ы́е де́ньги** travelling expenses; **р. путь** (*rail.*) siding.

разъезжа́|ть, ю *impf.* to drive (about, around), ride (about, around); to travel; **р. по дела́м слу́жбы** to travel about on business.

разъезжа́|ться, юсь *impf. of* ⇒**разъе́хаться**

разъе́|сть, ст, дя́т, *past* **~л** *pf.* (*of* ⇒~да́ть) to eat away; to corrode (*also fig.*); **его́ ~ли сомне́ния** he was consumed with doubts.

разъе́|сться, мся, шься, стся, ди́мся, ди́тесь, дя́тся, *past* **~лся** *pf.* (*of* ⇒~да́ться) (*coll.*) to get fat (*from good living*).

разъе́|хаться, дусь, дешься *pf.* (*of* ⇒~зжа́ться) **1** (*уехать*) to depart; to disperse. **2** (*о супругах*) to separate, cease living together. **3** (*о машинах*) to (be able to) pass. **4** (*разминуться*) to pass one another (*without meeting*); to miss one another. **5** (*coll.*) (*о лыжах*) to slide apart. **6** (*coll.*) (*об одежде*) to fall to pieces, fall apart.

разъяр|и́ть, ю́, и́шь *pf.* (*of* ⇒~я́ть) to infuriate.

разъяр|и́ться, ю́сь, и́шься *pf.* (*of* ⇒~я́ться) to fly into a rage.

разъяр|я́ть(ся), я́ю(сь) *impf. of* ⇒~и́ть(ся)

разъясне́ни|е, я *nt.* explanation.

разъясни́тельный *adj.* explanatory.

разъясн|и́ть, ю́, и́шь *pf.* (*of* ⇒~я́ть) to explain.

разъясн|и́ться, и́тся *pf.* (*of* ⇒~я́ться) to become clear, be cleared up; (*о погоде*) to become clear, clear up.

разъясн|я́ть(ся), я́ю, я́ет(ся) *impf. of* ⇒~и́ть(ся)

разыгр|а́ть, а́ю *pf.* (*of* ⇒~́ывать) **1** (*исполнить*) to play (through); to perform; **р. дурака́** to play the fool. **2** (*игру, карту*) to play. **3** (*в лотерее*) to raffle. **4** (*coll.*) (*одурачить*) to play a trick (on).

разыгр|а́ться, а́юсь *pf.* (*of* ⇒~́ываться) **1** (*увлечься игрой*) to be carried away by a game, by play. **2** (*о музыканте, об актёре*) to warm up. **3** (*о ветре, о буре*) to get up; (*о чувствах*) to run high.

разы́грыва|ть(ся), ю(сь) *impf. of* ⇒**разыгра́ть(ся)** 2, 3

разыска́ни|е, я *nt.* **1** finding, searching out. **2** (*исследование*) (piece of) research.

разы|ска́ть, щу́, ~́щешь *pf.* to find (after searching).

разы|ска́ться, щу́сь, ~́щешься *pf.* (*найтись*) to turn up, be found.

разы́скива|ть, ю *impf.* to hunt, search for.

разы́скива|ться, юсь *impf.* to be searched, hunted for; **р. поли́цией** to be wanted by the police.

ра|й, я, о ~́е, в ~ю́ *m.* paradise.

рай... *comb. form, abbr. of* **райо́нный**

райко́м, а *m.* (*abbr. of* ***райо́нный комите́т***) district committee.

райо́н, а *m.* **1** region. **2** (*административная единица*) district.

райо́н|ный *adj. of* ⇒~

ра́й|ский *adj. of* ⇒~; (*fig.*) heavenly; **~ская пти́ца** bird of paradise.

райсове́т, а *m.* district soviet (*council*).

рак, а *m.* **1** (*zool.*) (*речной*) crayfish (*Br.*), crawfish (*US*); (*морской*) spiny lobster; **кра́сный как р.** red as a lobster. **2** (*med.*)

cancer; (*bot.*) canker. **3 Р.** (*astrol., astron.*) Crab, Cancer; **тро́пик ∼а** (*geog.*) Tropic of Cancer.

ра́к|а, и *f.* (*eccl.*) shrine (*of a saint*).

раке́т|а[1], **ы** *f.* **1** (*для сигналов; фейерверк*) rocket; **пусти́ть ∼у** to let off a rocket. **2** (*mil.*) rocket, ballistic missile; **зени́тная р.** surface-to-air missile; **крыла́тая р.** cruise missile; **межконтинента́льная р.** intercontinental ballistic missile (ICBM). **3** (*космическая*) rocket; **р.-носи́тель** launch vehicle. **4** (*coll.*) (*судно*) hydrofoil.

раке́т|а[2], **ы** *f.* = **∼ка**

раке́т|ка, ки *f.* (*sport*) racket.

раке́тниц|а, ы *f.* rocket projector; Very pistol, signal pistol.

раке́тный *adj.* rocket(-powered); missile.

ракетодро́м, а *m.* rocket launch site.

раке́тчик, а *m.* missile specialist.

раки́т|а, ы *f.* (*bot.*) crack willow.

раки́тник, а *m.* (*куст*) broom; (*заросль*) broom plantation.

ра́ковин|а, ы *f.* **1** (*моллюска*) shell; **ушна́я р.** (*anat.*) aural cavity. **2** (*для умывания*) sink; wash-basin; **уса́дочная р.** air hole, blow hole.

ра́к|овый *adj. of* ⇒**∼;** (*med.*) cancerous.

ракообра́зн|ые, ых *pl.* (*sg.* **∼ое, ∼ого** *nt.*) (*zool.*) Crustacea.

раку́рс, а *m.* (*art*) foreshortening; **в ∼е** foreshortened.

раку́шечник, а *m.* (*geol.*) coquina, shell rock.

раку́шк|а, и *f.* shell; seashell.

ра́лли *nt. indecl.* rally.

ралли́ст, а *m.* rallyist, rally driver.

ра́м|а, ы *f.* **1** frame; **око́нная р.** window-frame, sash; **вста́вить в ∼у** to frame. **2** (*машины*) chassis.

рамада́н, а *m.* = **рамаза́н**

рамаза́н, а *m.* (*relig.*) Ramadan.

рам|ена́, е́н, ена́м *no sg.* (*arch. or poet.*) shoulders.

ра́мк|а, и *f.* frame; (*текста*) border; **объявле́ние о сме́рти в тра́урной ∼е** black-bordered obituary announcement.

ра́м|ки, ок (*pl. only*) framework; limits; **в ∼ках** (+*g.*) within the framework (of), within the limits (of); **вы́йти за р.** (+*g.*) to exceed the limits (of).

ра́мп|а, ы *f.* (*theatr.*) footlights.

ра́н|а, ы *f.* wound.

ранг, а *m.* class, rank.

рангоу́т, а *m.* (*naut.*) masts and spars.

рангоу́т|ный *adj. of* ⇒**∼; ∼ное де́рево** (*naut.*) spar.

ра́нее *adv.* = **ра́ньше**

ране́ни|е, я *nt.* **1** (*действие*) wounding; injuring. **2** (*рана*) wound; injury.

ра́нен|ый *adj.* wounded; injured; *as n.* **р., ∼ого** *m.* injured man; wounded man; casualty; *pl.* the injured; the wounded.

ра́н|ец, ца *m.* (*походный, солдатский*) knapsack, pack; (*ученический*) satchel.

ранжи́р, а *m.*: **по ∼у** in order of size.

рани́м|ый (∼, а) *adj.* vulnerable.

ра́н|ить, ю, ишь *impf. and pf.* to wound; to injure.

ра́нн|ий *adj.* early; **∼им у́тром** early in the morning; **∼яя пти́чка** (*fig.*) early bird; **с ∼его де́тства** from early childhood; **с ∼их лет** from (one's) earliest years.

ра́но[1] *pred.* it is early; **ещё р. ложи́ться спать** it is too early for bed.

ра́но[2] *adv.* early; **р. и́ли по́здно** sooner or later.

рант, а, о ∼е, на ∼у́ *m.* welt; **сапоги́ на ∼у́** welted boots.

рантье́ *m. indecl.* rentier.

ран|ь, и *f.* (*coll.*) early hour; **куда́ ты направля́ешься в таку́ю р.?** where are you bound for at this ungodly hour?

ра́ньше *adv.* **1** earlier; **как мо́жно р.** as early as possible; as soon as possible. **2** (+*g.*) (*прежде*) before; **до Ло́ндона он не доéдет р. ве́чера** he will not reach London before evening. **3** (*сперва, сначала*) first (of all). **4** (*прежде*) before, formerly; **р. мы жи́ли в дере́вне** we used to live in the country.

рапи́р|а, ы *f.* foil.

ра́порт, а *m.* report.

рапорт|ова́ть, у́ю *impf. and pf.* (*pf. also* ⇒**отрапортова́ть**) to report.

рапс, а *m.* (*bot.*) rape.

рапсо́ди|я, и *f.* (*mus.*) rhapsody.

рарите́т, а *m.* rarity, curiosity.

рас... *vbl. pref.* = **раз...**

ра́с|а, ы *f.* race.

раси́зм, а *m.* racism.

раси́ст, а *m.* racist.

раси́ст|ка, ки *f. of* ⇒**∼**

раси́стский *adj.* racist.

раска́ива|ться, юсь *impf. of* ⇒**раска́яться**

раскал|ённый *p.p.p. of* ⇒**∼и́ть** *and adj.* scorching, burning hot; **р. добела́** white-hot; **р. до́красна́** red-hot.

раскал|и́ть, ю́, и́шь *pf.* (*of* ⇒**∼я́ть**) to bring to a great heat; **р. добела́** to make white-hot; **р. до́красна́** to make red-hot.

раскал|и́ться, ится *pf.* (*of* ⇒**∼я́ться**) to glow, become hot; **р. добела́** to become white-hot; **р. до́красна́** to become red-hot.

раска́лыва|ть(ся), ю(сь) *impf. of* ⇒**расколо́ть(ся)**

раскал|я́ть(ся), я́ет(ся) *impf. of* ⇒**∼и́ть(ся)**

раска́пыва|ть, ю *impf. of* ⇒**раскопа́ть**

раска́рмлива|ть, ю *impf. of* ⇒**раскорми́ть**

раска́т, а *m.* roll, peal; **р. гро́ма** peal of thunder.

раскат|а́ть, а́ю *pf.* (*of* ⇒**∼́ывать**) **1** (*ковёр*) to unroll. **2** (*тесто*) to roll (out); (*дорогу*) to smooth out; to level.

раскат|а́ться, а́ется *pf.* (*of* ⇒**∼́ываться**) **1** (*о ковре*) to unroll. **2** (*о тесте*) to roll out.

раска́тист|ый (∼, ∼а) *adj.* (*гром*) rolling, booming; **р. смех** peal(s) of laughter.

раска|ти́ть, чу́, ∼́тишь *pf.* (*of* ⇒**∼́тывать**) **1** (*придать скорость*) to set rolling. **2** (*в разные стороны*) to roll away.

раска|ти́ться, чу́сь, ∼́тишься *pf.* (*of* ⇒**∼́тываться**) **1** (*приобрести скорость*) to gather momentum. **2** (*в разные стороны*) to roll away.

раска́тыва|ть, ю *impf.* **1** *impf. of* ⇒**раската́ть** *and* **раскати́ть.** **2** (*coll.*) (*ездить много*) to drive (about, around), ride (about, around).

раска́тыва|ться, юсь *impf. of* ⇒**раската́ться** *and* **раскати́ться**

раскач|а́ть, а́ю *pf.* (*of* ⇒**∼́ивать**) **1** (*качели*) to swing; to rock. **2** (*расшатать*) to loosen, shake loose. **3** (*fig., coll.*) (*заставить действовать*) to shake up, stir up.

раскач|а́ться, а́юсь *pf.* (*of* ⇒**∼́иваться**) **1** (*о качелях*) to swing; (*о лодке*) to rock. **2** (*расшататься*) to shake loose. **3** (*fig., coll.*) (*начать действовать*) to bestir o.s.

раска́чива|ть(ся), ю(сь) *impf. of* ⇒**раскача́ть(ся)**

раска́шля|ться, юсь *pf.* to have a fit of coughing.

раска́яни|е, я *nt.* repentance.

раска́|яться, юсь *pf.* (*of* ⇒**∼иваться**) (**в**+*p.*) to repent (of).

расквартирова́ни|е, я *nt.* quartering, billeting.

расквартир|ова́ть, у́ю *pf.* (*of* ⇒**∼о́вывать**) to quarter, billet.

расквартиро́выва|ть, ю *impf. of* ⇒**расквартирова́ть**

расква́|сить, шу, сишь *pf.* (*of* ⇒**∼шивать**) (*coll.*) to punch (*and draw blood from*); **р. кому́-н. нос** to give s.o. a bloody nose.

расква́шива|ть, ю *impf. of* ⇒**расква́сить**

расквита́|ться, юсь *pf.* (**с**+*i.*; *coll.*) to settle accounts (with) (*also fig.*); (*fig.*) to get even (with).

раскид|а́ть, а́ю *pf.* (*of* ⇒**∼́ывать**) to scatter.

раски́дист|ый (∼, ∼а) *adj.* branchy, spreading.

раскидно́й *adj.* folding.

раски́дыва|ть, ю *impf. of* ⇒**раскида́ть** *and* **раски́нуть**

раски́дыва|ться, юсь *impf. of* ⇒**раски́нуться**

раски́|нуть, ну, нешь *pf.* (*of* ⇒**∼дывать**) **1** (*руки*) to stretch (out). **2** (*ковёр*) to spread (out); (*лагерь*) to set up; (*палатку*) to pitch. **3**: **р. умо́м** to consider, think over.

раски́|нуться, нусь, нешься *pf.* (*of* ⇒**∼дываться**) **1** to spread out, stretch out. **2** (*coll.*) to sprawl.

раскис|а́ть, а́ю *impf. of* ⇒**∼́нуть**

раски́с|нуть, ну, нешь, *past* **∼, ∼ла** *pf.* (*of* ⇒**∼а́ть**) **1** (*о тесте*) to rise (*from fermentation*). **2** (*fig., coll.*) (*стать вялым*) to become limp.

Р

расклáд, а *m.* disposition, arrangement; (*сил, средств*) apportionment.

расклáдк|а, и *f.* **1** (*вещей*) laying out, arrangement. **2** (*огня*) making; (*кровати, матраса*) unfolding, laying out (*ready for use*). **3** (*распределение*) apportionment.

расскладн|óй *adj.* folding; **~áя кровáть** camp bed (*Br.*), cot (*US*).

раскладýшк|а, и *f.* (*coll.*) camp bed (*Br.*), cot (*US*).

расклáдыва|ть(ся), ю(сь) *impf. of* **⇒разложи́ть(ся)**[1]

расклáнива|ться, юсь *impf. of* **⇒расклáняться**

расклáн|яться, яюсь *pf.* (*of* **⇒~иваться**) **1** to exchange bows (*on meeting or leave-taking*). **2** (*об актёре*) to take a bow.

расклéива|ть(ся), ю(сь) *impf. of* **⇒расклéить(ся)**

расклé|ить, ю, ишь *pf.* (*of* **⇒~ивать**) **1** (*конверт*) to unstick. **2** (*афиши*) to stick, paste (*in various places*).

расклé|иться, юсь, ишься *pf.* (*of* **⇒~иваться**) **1** to come unstuck. **2** (*fig., coll.*) (*о деле*) to fall through, fail to come off. **3** (*fig., coll.*) (*о человеке*) to be off colour (*Br.*), color (*US*); **он совсéм ~ился** he has gone to pieces.

расклéйк|а, и *f.* (*афиш*) sticking, pasting.

расклéйщик, а *m.* bill-sticker.

расклеп|áть, áю *pf.* (*of* **⇒~ывать**) **1** (*конструкцию*) to unrivet, unclench. **2** (*заклёпку*) to hammer out, flatten.

расклёпыва|ть, ю *impf. of* **⇒расклепáть**

раскóванный *adj.* relaxed, uninhibited.

раск|овáть, ую, уёшь *pf.* (*of* **⇒~óвывать**) **1** (*человека*) to unchain, unfetter; (*лошадь*) to unshoe. **2** (*железо*) to hammer out, flatten.

раск|овáться, уюсь, уёшься *pf.* (*of* **⇒~óвываться**) **1** (*о лошади*) to cast a shoe. **2** (*о человеке*) to free o.s. (*from fetters*).

раскóвыва|ть(ся), ю(сь) *impf. of* **⇒расковáть(ся)**

расковы́рива|ть, ю *impf. of* **⇒расковыря́ть**

расковыр|я́ть, я́ю *pf.* (*of* **⇒~ивать**) to pick at.

раскóка|ть, ю *pf.* (*coll.*) to drop and break.

раскóл, а *m.* **1** (*relig., hist.*) schism, dissent. **2** (*pol., etc.*) split, division.

расколáчива|ть, ю *impf. of* **⇒расколоти́ть**

расколо|ти́ть, чý, ~тишь *pf.* (*of* **⇒расколáчивать**) (*coll.*) to smash; to break.

раскол|óть, ю́, ~ешь *pf.* **1** *pf. of* **⇒колóть**[1]. **2** (*impf.* **раскáлывать**) (*fig.*) to disrupt, break up.

раскол|óться, ю́сь, ~ешься *pf.* (*of* **⇒раскáлываться**) to split (*also fig.*).

раскóльник, а *m.* **1** (*relig., hist.*) schismatic, dissenter. **2** (*pol.; fig.*) splitter.

раскóльническ|ий *adj.* **1** (*relig., hist.*) schismatic, dissenting. **2**: **~ая тáктика** (*pol.*) splitting tactics.

раскопá|ть, ю *pf.* (*of* **⇒раскáпывать**) to dig up, unearth (*also fig.*); (*archaeol.*) to excavate.

раскóпк|а, и *f.* (*действие*) digging up; *pl.* (*archaeol.*) excavations.

раскорм|и́ть, лю́, ~ишь *pf.* (*of* **⇒раскáрмливать**) to fatten.

раскорч|евáть, ýю *pf.* (*of* **⇒~ёвывать**) to uproot.

раскорчёвыва|ть, ю *impf. of* **⇒раскорчевáть**

раскоря́к|а, и *c.g.* (*coll.*) bow-legged person.

раскóсый *adj.* (*глаза*) slanting.

раскошéлива|ться, юсь *impf. of* **⇒раскошéлиться**

раскошéл|иться, юсь, ишься *pf.* (*of* **⇒~иваться**) (*coll.*) to loosen one's purse-strings; to fork out.

раскрáдыва|ть, ю *impf. of* **⇒раскрáсть**

раскрáива|ть, ю *impf. of* **⇒раскрои́ть**

раскрá|сить, шу, сишь *pf.* (*of* **⇒~шивать**) to paint, colour (*Br.*), color (*US*).

раскрáск|а, и *f.* **1** (*действие*) painting, colouring (*Br.*), coloring (*US*). **2** (*расцветка*) colours (*Br.*), colors (*US*), colour scheme (*Br.*), color scheme (*US*).

раскраснé|ться, юсь *pf.* to flush, go red (in the face).

раскрá|сть, дý, дёшь, *past* **~л** *pf.* (*of* **⇒~дывать**) to loot, clean out.

раскрáшива|ть, ю *impf. of* **⇒раскрáсить**

раскрепо|сти́ть, щý, сти́шь *pf.* (*of* **⇒~щáть**) to set free, liberate, emancipate.

раскрепо|сти́ться, щýсь, сти́шься *pf.* (*of* **⇒~щáться**) to free *or* liberate o.s.

раскрепощá|ть(ся), ю(сь) *impf. of* **⇒раскрепости́ть(ся)**

раскрепощéни|е, я *nt.* liberation, emancipation; **р. жéнщины** emancipation of women.

раскритик|овáть, ýю *pf.* to criticize severely, slam.

раскрич|áться, ýсь, и́шься *pf.* **1** to start shouting, start crying. **2** (**на**+*a.*) to shout (at).

раскро|и́ть, ю́, и́шь *pf.* (*of* **⇒раскрáивать**) **1** (*ткань*) to cut out. **2** (*fig., coll.*) to cut open; **р. комý-н. чéреп** to split s.o.'s skull.

раскрош|и́ть(ся), ý, ~ит(ся) *pf. of* **⇒кроши́ть(ся)**

раскру|ти́ть, чý, ~тишь *pf.* (*of* **⇒~чивать**) **1** (*развить*) to untwist, untwine, undo. **2** (*колесо*) to spin, rotate.

раскру|ти́ться, чýсь, ~тишься *pf.* (*of* **⇒~чиваться**) **1** (*развиться*) to come untwisted, come undone. **2** (*начать крутиться*) to start spinning, rotating.

раскрýчива|ть(ся), ю, ет(ся) *impf. of* **⇒раскрути́ть(ся)**

раскрывá|ть(ся), ю(сь) *impf. of* **⇒раскры́ть(ся)**

раскры́ти|е, я *nt.* **1** opening. **2** (*обнаружение*) exposure, disclosing.

раскр|ы́ть, óю, óешь *pf.* (*of* **⇒~ывáть**) **1** (*открыть*) to open (wide); **р. зóнтик** to put up an umbrella; **р. кни́гу** to open a book; **р. скóбки** to open brackets. **2** (*сделать видным*) to expose, bare. **3** (*обнаружить*) to reveal, disclose, lay bare; (*найти*) to discover; **р. секрéт** to disclose a secret; **р. свои́ кáрты** (*fig.*) to show one's cards *or* one's hand.

раскр|ы́ться, óюсь, óешься *pf.* (*of* **⇒~ывáться**) **1** to open. **2** (*раскрыть себя*) to uncover o.s. **3** (*обнаружиться*) to come out; to come to light.

раскудáх|таться, чусь, чешься *pf.* (*coll.*) to set up a cackling.

раскулáчивани|е, я *nt.* dispossession of the kulaks, de-kulakization.

раскулáчива|ть, ю *impf. of* **⇒раскулáчить**

раскулáч|ить, у, ишь *pf.* (*of* **⇒~ивать**) to dispossess (*a kulak*).

раскумéка|ть, ю *pf.* (*coll.*) to learn, find out.

раскуп|áть, áю *impf. of* **⇒~и́ть**

раскуп|и́ть, лю́, ~ишь *pf.* (*of* **⇒~áть**) to buy up.

раскýпорива|ть, ю, ет *impf. of* **⇒раскýпорить**

раскýпор|ить, ю, ишь *pf.* (*of* **⇒~ивать**) to uncork, open.

раскýрива|ть(ся), ю, ет(ся) *impf. of* **⇒раскури́ть(ся)**

раскур|и́ть, ю́, ~ишь *pf.* (*of* **⇒~ивать**) **1** (*заставить куриться*) to puff at (*a pipe or cigarette*). **2** (*зажечь*) to light up.

раскур|и́ться, ю́сь, ~ишься *pf.* (*of* **⇒~иваться**) **1** (*о трубке, сигарете*) to draw. **2** *pf. only* (*coll.*) (*начать курить много*) to start smoking away.

раску|си́ть, шý, ~сишь *pf.* (*of* **⇒~сывать**) **1** (*конфету*) to bite into. **2** *pf. only* (*coll.*) (*узнать, понять*) to suss out.

раскýсыва|ть, ю *impf. of* **⇒раскуси́ть**

раскýт|ать, аю *pf.* (*of* **⇒~ывать**) to unwrap.

раскýт|аться, аюсь *pf.* (*of* **⇒~ываться**) to unwrap o.s.

раску|ти́ться, чýсь, ~тишься *pf.* (*coll.*) to take to going on drinking-bouts.

раскýтыва|ть(ся), ю(сь) *impf. of* **⇒раскýтать(ся)**

рáсовый *adj.* racial.

распáд, а *m.* **1** disintegration, break-up; (*fig.*) collapse. **2** (*chem.*) decomposition.

распада́|ться, ется *impf. of* **⇒распа́сться**

распа́ива|ть(ся), ю, ет(ся) *impf. of* **⇒распая́ть(ся)**

распак|ова́ть, у́ю *pf.* (*of* **⇒~о́вывать**) to unpack.

распак|ова́ться, у́юсь *pf.* (*of* **⇒~о́вываться**) **1** (*о посылке*) to come undone. **2** (*coll.*) to unpack (one's things).

распако́выва|ть(ся), ю(сь) *impf. of* **⇒распакова́ть(ся)**

распал|и́ть, ю́, и́шь *pf.* (*of* **⇒~я́ть**) **1** to make burning hot. **2** (*fig.*) to inflame; **р. гне́вом** to incense.

распал|и́ться, ю́сь, и́шься *pf.* (*of* **⇒~я́ться**) **1** to get burning hot. **2** (+*i.*; *fig.*) to burn (with); **р. гне́вом** to be incensed.

распал|я́ть(ся), я́ю(сь) *impf. of* **⇒~и́ть(ся)**

распа́рива|ть(ся), ю(сь) *impf. of* **⇒распа́рить(ся)**

распа́р|ить, ю, ишь *pf.* (*of* **⇒~ивать**) **1** (*кожу*) to steam out; (*овощи*) to stew well. **2** (*coll.*) (*разогреть до пота*) to cause to sweat.

распа́р|иться, юсь, ишься *pf.* (*of* **⇒~иваться**) **1** (*о коже*) to steam out; (*об овощах*) to be well stewed. **2** (*разогреться до пота*) to break into a sweat.

распа́рыва|ть(ся), ю, ет(ся) *impf. of* **⇒распоро́ть(ся)**

распа́|сться, дётся, *past* **~лся** *pf.* (*of* **⇒~да́ться**) **1** to disintegrate, fall to pieces; (*fig.*) to break up; to collapse; **коали́ция ~лась** the coalition broke up. **2** (*chem.*) to decompose.

распа|ха́ть, шу́, ~́шешь *pf.* (*of* **⇒~́хивать**) to plough up (*Br.*), plow up (*US*).

распа́хива|ть, ю *impf. of* **⇒распаха́ть** *and* **распахну́ть**

распа́хива|ться, юсь *impf. of* **⇒распахну́ться**

распах|ну́ть, ну́, нёшь *pf.* (*of* **⇒~́ивать**) to open wide; to fling open, throw open; **широко́ р. две́ри** (+*d.*) to open wide the doors (to) (*also fig.*).

распах|ну́ться, ну́сь, нёшься *pf.* (*of* **⇒~́иваться**) **1** (*о двери, од окне*) to fly open, swing open. **2** (*распахнуть полы своей одежды*) to throw open one's coat. **3** (*о полях*) to open up, out.

распа́шк|а, и *f.* ploughing up (*Br.*), plowing up (*US*).

распашн|о́й *adj.* (*dial.*) for ploughing up (*Br.*), plowing up (*US*); **~а́я земля́** ploughland (*Br.*), plowland (*US*).

распашо́нк|а, и *f.* (*baby's*) vest (*Br.*), undershirt (*US*).

распа|я́ть, я́ю *pf.* (*of* **⇒~́ивать**) to unsolder.

распа|я́ться, я́ется *pf.* (*of* **⇒~́иваться**) to come unsoldered.

распева́|ть, ю *impf.* **1** *impf. of* **⇒распе́ть. 2** to sing (*loudly, gaily*).

распека́|ть, ю *impf. of* **⇒распе́чь**

распелен|а́ть, а́ю *pf.* (*of* **⇒~́ывать**) to unswaddle.

распелёныва|ть, ю *impf. of* **⇒распелена́ть**

распере́ть, разопру́, разопрёшь, *past* **распёр, распёрла** *pf.* (*of* **⇒распира́ть**) (*coll.*) to burst open, cause to burst.

распетуш|и́ться, у́сь, и́шься *pf.* (*coll.*) to get into a temper; to have one's hackles up.

расп|е́ть, ою́, оёшь *pf.* (*of* **⇒~ева́ть**) (*mus.*) **1** (*пропеть*) to sing through. **2** (*голос*) to practise.

расп|е́ться, ою́сь, оёшься *pf.* (*coll.*) **1** (*начать петь свободно*) to warm up. **2** (*начав петь, увлечься*) to sing away.

распеча́т|ать, аю *pf.* (*of* **⇒~ывать**) **1** (*вскрыть*) to unseal; **р. письмо́** to open a letter. **2** (*напечатать во многих экземплярах*) to print off. **3** (*comput.*) to print (out).

распеча́т|аться, ается *pf.* (*of* **⇒~ываться**) to come unsealed, to come open.

распеча́тк|а, и *f.* printout; (*действие*) printing out.

распеча́тыва|ть(ся), ю, ет(ся) *impf. of* **⇒распеча́тать(ся)**

распе́|чь, ку́, чёшь, ку́т, *past* **~́к, ~кла́** *pf.* (*of* **⇒~ка́ть**) (*coll.*) to tell off.

распива́|ть, ю *impf. of* **⇒распи́ть**

распи́вочно *adv.*: **прода́жа питья́ р.** sale of liquor for consumption on the premises.

распи́л, а *m.* saw cut.

распи́лива|ть, ю *impf. of* **⇒распили́ть**

распил|и́ть, ю́, ~́ишь *pf.* (*of* **⇒~́ивать**) to saw up.

распи́лк|а, и *f.* sawing.

распило́вк|а, и *f.* = **распи́лка**

распина́|ть, ю *impf. of* **⇒распя́ть**

распина́|ться, юсь *impf.* (*coll.*) (**за кого́-н.** *or* **пе́ред кем-н.**) to put o.s. out (*sc. on s.o.'s behalf*).

распира́|ть, ю *impf. of* **⇒распере́ть**

расписа́ни|е, я *nt.* time table, schedule.

распи|са́ть, шу́, ~шешь *pf.* (*of* **⇒~́сывать**) **1** (*сведения*) to enter; to note down; **р. счета́ по кни́гам** to enter bills in the account-book. **2** (*распределить*) to assign, allot. **3** (*разрисовать*) to paint. **4** (*fig., coll.*) (*изобразить*) to paint a picture (of).

распи|са́ться, шу́сь, ~́шешься *pf.* (*of* **⇒~́сываться**) **1** to sign (one's name); (**в**+*p.*) to sign (for); **р. в получе́нии заказно́го письма́** to sign for a registered letter. **2** (*coll.*) (*регистировать брак*) to register one's marriage. **3** (**в**+*p.*; *fig.*) (*признаться*) to acknowledge, testify (to); **р. в со́бственном неве́жестве** to acknowledge one's own ignorance.

распи́ск|а, и *f.* receipt; **р. в получе́нии** (+*g.*) receipt (for); **сдать письмо́ под ~у** to make s.o. sign for a letter.

расписно́й *adj.* painted, decorated.

распи́сыва|ть(ся), ю(сь) *impf. of* **⇒расписа́ть(ся)**

рас|пи́ть, разопью́, разопьёшь, *past* **~пи́л, ~пила́, ~пи́ло** *pf.* (*of* **⇒~пива́ть**) (*coll.*) to drink (*together with s.o.*); **р. буты́лку (с кем-н.)** to split a bottle (with s.o.).

распих|а́ть, а́ю *pf.* (*of* **⇒~́ивать**) (*coll.*) **1** (*растолкать*) to push aside. **2** (*рассовать*) to shove; **р. я́блоки по карма́нам** to stuff apples into one's pockets.

распи́хива|ть, ю *impf. of* **⇒распиха́ть**

распла́в|ить, лю, ишь *pf.* (*of* **⇒~ля́ть**) to melt, fuse.

распла́в|иться, ится *pf.* (*of* **⇒~ля́ться**) to melt, fuse.

расплавле́ни|е, я *nt.* melting, fusion.

расплавля́|ть(ся), ю, ет(ся) *impf. of* **⇒распла́вить(ся)**

распла́|каться, чусь, чешься *pf.* to burst into tears.

распланир|ова́ть, у́ю *pf. of* **⇒планирова́ть**

распласт|а́ть, а́ю *pf.* (*of* **⇒~́ывать**) **1** (*разделить в пласты*) to split, divide into layers. **2** (*широко раскрыть*) to spread; **р. кры́лья** to spread one's wings.

распласт|а́ться, а́юсь *pf.* (*of* **⇒~́ываться**) to sprawl.

распла́стыва|ть(ся), ю(сь) *impf. of* **⇒распласта́ть(ся)**

распла́т|а, ы *f.* payment; (*fig.*) retribution; **час ~ы** day of reckoning.

распла|ти́ться, чу́сь, ~́тишься *pf.* (*of* **⇒~́чиваться**) **1** (**с**+*i.*) to pay off; to settle accounts (with), get even (with) (*also fig.*); **р. с долга́ми** to pay off one's debts; **р. по ста́рым счета́м** to pay off old scores. **2** (**за**+*a.*; *fig.*) to pay (for).

распла́чива|ться, юсь *impf. of* **⇒расплати́ться**

расплe|ска́ть, щу́, ~́щешь *pf.* (*of* **⇒~́скивать**) to spill.

распле|ска́ться, ~́щется *pf.* (*of* **⇒~́скиваться**) to spill.

расплёскива|ть(ся), ю, ет(ся) *impf. of* **⇒расплеска́ть(ся)**

распле|сти́, ту́, тёшь, *past* **~́л, ~ла́** *pf.* (*of* **⇒~та́ть**) (*верёвку*) to untwine, untwist; (*косу*) to undo.

распле|сти́сь, тётся, *past* **~́лся, ~ла́сь** *pf.* (*of* **⇒~та́ться**) (*о верёвке*) to untwine, untwist; (*о косе*) to come undone.

расплета́|ть(ся), ю, ет(ся) *impf. of* **⇒расплести́(сь)**

распло|ди́ть(ся), жу́, ди́т(ся) *pf. of* **⇒плоди́ть(ся)**

расплыва́|ться, ется *impf. of* **⇒расплы́ться**

расплы́вчат|ый (~, ~а) *adj.* (*рисунок*) blurred, indistinct; (*ответ*) vague.

расплы́|ться, вётся, *past* **~лся, ~ла́сь** *pf.* (*of* **⇒~ва́ться**) **1** (*о жидкости*) to run; **черни́ла ~лись** the ink has run; (*о фигурах*) to become blurred; (*о массе*) to disperse; (*уплыть*)

Р

to swim off. **2** (*coll.*) (*потолстеть*) to spread; to run to fat; **р. в улы́бку** to break into a smile.

расплю́щива|ть(ся), ю, ет(ся) *impf. of* ⇒**расплю́щить(ся)**

расплю́щ|ить, у, ишь *pf.* (*of* ⇒**~ивать**) to flatten out, hammer out.

расплю́щ|иться, ится *pf.* (*of* ⇒**~иваться**) to become flat.

распознава́|емый *pres. part. pass. of* ⇒**~ть** *and adj.* recognizable, identifiable.

распознава́ни|е, я *nt.* recognition, identification.

распозна|ва́ть, ю́, ёшь *impf. of* ⇒**~́ть**

распозна́|ть, ю, ешь *pf.* (*of* ⇒**~ва́ть**) to recognize, identify; **р. боле́знь** to diagnose an illness.

располага́|ть[1], ю *impf.* (+*i.*) to have at one's disposal, have available; **р. вре́менем** to have time available; **р. больши́ми сре́дствами** to dispose of ample means.

располага́|ть[2], ю *impf. of* ⇒**расположи́ть**

располага́|ться, юсь *impf. of* ⇒**расположи́ться[1]**

располага́|ющий *pres. part. act. of* ⇒**~ть** *and adj.* pleasant, prepossessing.

располз|а́ться, а́юсь *impf. of* ⇒**~ти́сь**

располз|ти́сь, у́сь, ёшься, *past* **~́ся, ~ла́сь** *pf.* (*of* ⇒**~а́ться**) **1** to crawl (away). **2** (*coll.*) (*об одежде*) to come unravelled; to tear, give at the seams. **3** (*coll.*) (*расплыться*) to become blurred. **4** (*sl.*) to put on weight.

расположе́ни|е, я *nt.*
1 (*предметов*) disposition, arrangement; **р. по кварти́рам** (*mil.*) billeting.
2 (*местоположение*) situation, location; **р. на ме́стности[1]** (*mil.*) location on the ground.
3 (*симпатия*) favour (*Br.*), favor (*US*); sympathies; **по́льзоваться чьим-н. ~ем** to enjoy s.o.'s favour (*Br.*), favor (*US*), to be liked by s.o.; **чу́вствовать к кому́-н. р.** to be favourably (*Br.*), favorably (*US*) disposed towards s.o.
4 (**к**+*d.*) (*наклонность*) disposition (to), inclination (to, for); tendency (to), penchant (for); **у неё р. к бронхи́ту** she has a tendency to bronchitis.
5: **р. (ду́ха)** disposition, mood, humour (*Br.*), humor (*US*); **быть в плохо́м ~и ду́ха** to be in a bad mood; **у меня́ нет ~я танцева́ть** I am not in the mood for dancing.

располо́жен|ный (~, ~а) *p.p.p. of* ⇒**расположи́ть** *and pred adj.*
1 (**к**+*d.*) (*питающий чувство симпатии*) well disposed (to, towards).
2 (**к**+*d. or* +*inf.*) (*склонный*) disposed (to), inclined (to); in the mood (for); **я не о́чень ~ сего́дня рабо́тать** I don't feel much like working today.

располож|и́ть, у́, ~́ишь *pf.* (*of* ⇒**располага́ть[2]**) **1** (*разместить*) to dispose, arrange, set out; **р. свои́ войска́** to station one's troops.
2 (*вызвать симпатию в ком-н.*) to win over, gain; **р. кого́-н. к себе́, в свою́ по́льзу** to gain s.o.'s favour (*Br.*), favor (*US*).

располож|и́ться[1], у́сь, ~́ишься *pf.* (*of* ⇒**располага́ться**) (*разместиться*) to take up position; to settle *or* compose o.s.; to make o.s. comfortable; **р. спать** to settle o.s. to sleep.

располож|и́ться[2], у́сь, ~́ишься *pf.* (+*inf.*; *obs.*) (*собраться*) to resolve, make up one's mind.

распо́рк|а, и *f.* (*tech.*) (*поперечина*) cross-bar; (*стойка*) strut; (*проставочный элемент*) spreader bar.

распор|о́ть, ю, ~́ешь *pf.* (*of* ⇒**поро́ть[1]** *and* **распа́рывать**) to unstitch, unpick.

распор|о́ться, ~́ется *pf.* (*of* ⇒**поро́ться** *and* **распа́рываться**) to come unstitched, come undone.

распоряди́тел|ь, я *m.* (*руководитель*) manager; (*вечера*) master of ceremonies.

распоряди́тель|ница, ницы *f. of* ⇒**~**

распоряди́тельност|ь, и *f.* good management; efficiency; **отсу́тствие ~и** mismanagement.

распоряди́тел|ьный (~ен, ~ьна) *adj.* capable; efficient; **р. челове́к** a good organizer.

распоря|ди́ться, жу́сь, ди́шься *pf.* (*of* ⇒**~жа́ться**) **1** (**о**+*p. or* +*inf.*) to order; to see (that); **я ~жу́сь возмести́ть вам расхо́ды** I will see that you are reimbursed for the expenses.
2 (+*i.*) to manage; to deal (with); **разреши́ть кому́-н. р. по своему́ усмотре́нию** to give s.o. a free hand; **как р. э́тими деньга́ми?** what is to be done with this money?

распоря́д|ок, ка *m.* order; routine; **пра́вила вну́треннего ~ка** (*в учреждении, на фабрике, и т.д.*) (office, factory, *etc.*) regulations.

распоряжа́|ться, юсь *impf.* **1** *impf. of* ⇒**распоряди́ться. 2** *impf. only* to give orders, be in charge; **р. как у себя́ до́ма** to behave as though the place belongs to one.

распоряже́ни|е, я *nt.* **1** (*приказ*) order; instruction, direction; **до осо́бого ~я** until further notice. **2**: **име́ть в своём ~и** to have at one's disposal.

распоя́|сать, шу, шешь *pf.* (*of* ⇒**~сывать**) to ungird.

распоя́|саться, шусь, шешься *pf.* (*of* ⇒**~сываться**) **1** to take off one's belt; to ungird o.s. **2** (*fig., coll., pej.*) (*стать распущенным*) to throw aside all restraint; to let o.s. go.

распоя́сыва|ть(ся), ю(сь) *impf. of* ⇒**распоя́сать(ся)**

распра́в|а, ы *f.* harsh punishment; reprisal; **крова́вая р.** massacre; **кула́чная р.** fist-law; **коро́ткая р.** short shrift; **у нас с ни́ми р. коротка́** we'll give them short shrift.

распра́в|ить, лю, ишь *pf.* (*of* ⇒**~ля́ть**) **1** (*выпрямить*) to straighten; to smooth out; **р. морщи́ны** to smooth out wrinkles. **2** (*вытянуть*) to spread, stretch; **р. кры́лья** to spread one's wings (*also fig.*).

распра́в|иться[1], ится *pf.* (*of* ⇒**~ля́ться**) (*выпрямиться*) to get smoothed out.

распра́в|иться[2], люсь, ишься *pf.* (*of* ⇒**~ля́ться**) (**с**+*i.*) (*произвести расправу*) to deal (with); **р. без суда́** to take the law into one's own hands; (*распорядиться*) to deal with, dispose of.

расправля́|ть(ся), ю(сь) *impf. of* ⇒**распра́вить(ся)**

распределе́ни|е, я *nt.* distribution; allocation, assignment; **р. нало́гов** assessment of taxes.

распредели́тел|ь, я *m.* **1** (*человек*) distributor. **2** (*устройство*) regulator; **р. зажига́ния** distributor.
3 (*учреждение*) distribution centre (*Br.*), center (*US*).

распредели́тельн|ый *adj.* distributive, distributing; **~ая доска́, р. щит** (*tech.*) switchboard; **р. вал** (*tech.*) camshaft; **~ая коро́бка** (*elec.*) switch box, junction box.

распредел|и́ть, ю́, и́шь *pf.* (*of* ⇒**~я́ть**) to distribute; to allocate, assign; **р. своё вре́мя** to allocate one's time.

распредел|и́ться, и́тся *pf.* (*of* ⇒**~я́ться**) to divide up, split up.

распредел|я́ть(ся), я́ю, я́ет(ся) *impf. of* ⇒**~и́ть(ся)**

распрекра́с|ный (~ен, ~на) *adj.* (*coll.*) beautiful, fine, splendid.

распрода|ва́ть, ю́, ёшь *impf. of* ⇒**~́ть**

распрода́ж|а, и *f.* sale; clearance sale.

распрода́ж|ный *adj. of* ⇒**~а**

распрода́|ть, м, шь, ст, ди́м, ди́те, ду́т, *past* **распро́дал, ~ла́, распро́дало** *pf.* (*of* ⇒**~ва́ть**) (*землю, вещи*) to sell off; (*билеты*) to sell out of; **биле́ты распро́даны** all the tickets are sold.

распростер|е́ть, *fut. tense not used, past* **~́, ~́ла** *pf.* (*of* ⇒**распростира́ть**) to stretch out, extend.

распростер|е́ться, *fut. tense not used, past* **~́ся, ~́лась** *pf.* (*of* ⇒**распростира́ться**) **1** to stretch o.s. out; to prostrate o.s. **2** (*fig.*) to spread.

распростёр|тый *p.p.p. of* ⇒**~е́ть** *and adj.* **1** (*руки*) outstretched; **встре́тить с ~тыми объя́тиями** to receive with outstretched arms. **2** (*тело*) prostrate, prone.

распростира́|ть(ся), ю(сь) *impf. of* ⇒**распростере́ть(ся)**

распро|сти́ться, щу́сь, сти́шься *pf.* (**с**+*i.*) to say goodbye to; **р. с мечто́й** to bid farewell to one's dream(s).

распростране́ни|е, я *nt.* (*слухов, заразы*) spreading; (*знания, идей*) dissemination; (*владений*) expansion; (*оружия*) proliferation; (*товаров*) distribution; **име́ть большо́е р.** to be widely practised (*Br.*), practiced (*US*).

распространённост|ь, и *f.* prevalence.

распростран|ённый *p.p.p. of* **⇒~и́ть** *and adj.* (*мнение*) widespread, prevalent; (*овощи*) common.

распространи́тел|ь, я *m.* (*слухов, знаний*) spreader, disseminator; (*книг, газет*) distributor.

распространи́тель|ница, ницы *f. of* **⇒~**

распространи́тельн|ый *adj.* extended; (excessively) wide; **~ое толкова́ние зако́на** a wide interpretation of a law.

распростран|и́ть, ю́, и́шь *pf.* (*of* **⇒~я́ть**) **1** (*слухи, заразу*) to spread; (*знания, информацию*) to disseminate; (*товары, книги*) to distribute; (*письмо, меморандум*) to circulate; (*владения*) to increase. **2** (*расширить*) to extend; **р. де́йствие зако́на на всех** to extend the application of a law to all. **3** (*запах*) to give off.

распростран|и́ться, ю́сь, и́шься *pf.* (*of* **⇒~я́ться**) **1** (*огонь, слухи, запах*) to spread; (*стать больше*) to extend; (*о законе*) to apply. **2** (**о**+*p.*; *coll.*) to enlarge (on), expatiate (on).

распростран|я́ть(ся), я́ю(сь) *impf. of* **⇒~и́ть(ся)**

распроща́|ться, юсь *pf.* (**с**+*i.*; *coll.*) = **распрости́ться**

ра́спр|я, и, *g. pl.* **~ей** *f.* feud, quarrel.

распряга́|ть(ся), ю, ет(ся) *impf. of* **⇒распря́чь(ся)**

распрям|и́ть, лю́, и́шь *pf.* (*of* **⇒~ля́ть**) (*проволоку*) to straighten, unbend; (*спину*) to straighten.

распрям|и́ться, лю́сь, и́шься *pf.* (*of* **⇒~ля́ться**) **1** to straighten o.s. up. **2** (*fig.*) (*стать увереннее*) to become more confident.

распрямля́|ть(ся), ю(сь) *impf. of* **⇒распрями́ть(ся)**

распря́|чь, гу́, жёшь, гу́т, *past* **~г, ~гла́** *pf.* (*of* **⇒~га́ть**) to unharness.

распря́|чься, жётся, гу́тся, *past* **~гся, ~гла́сь** *pf.* (*of* **⇒~га́ться**) to get unharnessed.

распуг|а́ть, а́ю *pf.* (*of* **⇒~́ивать**) (*coll.*) to scare away, frighten away.

распу́гива|ть, ю *impf. of* **⇒распуга́ть**

распуска́|ть(ся), ю(сь) *impf. of* **⇒распусти́ть(ся)**

распу|сти́ть, щу́, ~́стишь *pf.* (*of* **⇒~ска́ть**) **1** (*учеников*) to dismiss; (*расформировать*) to disband; **р. парла́мент** to dissolve parliament. **2** (*ремень, подпругу*) to loosen, let out; **р. во́лосы** to let one's hair down; **р. знамёна** to unfurl banners; **р. паруса́** to set sail. **3** (*fig.*) (*избаловать*) to allow to get out of hand; to spoil. **4** (*растворить*) to dissolve; (*растопить*) to melt. **5** (*coll.*) (*слухи*) to spread, put out. **6** (*свитер*) to unpick.

распу|сти́ться, щу́сь, ~́стишься *pf.* (*of* **⇒~ска́ться**) **1** (*bot.*) to open, blossom out, come out. **2** (*о завязках*) to come undone. **3** (*fig.*) (*о детях*) to become undisciplined, get out of hand, let o.s. go. **4** (*раствориться*) to dissolve; (*растопиться*) to melt.

распу́т|ать, аю *pf.* (*of* **⇒~ывать**) **1** (*узел*) to untangle, disentangle; to unravel. **2** (*животное*) to untie, loose. **3** (*fig.*) (*вопрос*) to disentangle, unravel; to puzzle out.

распу́т|аться, аюсь *pf.* (*of* **⇒~ываться**) **1** to get disentangled, come undone. **2** (*fig., coll.*) to get disentangled, be cleared up. **3** (**с**+*i.*; *coll.*) to rid o.s. (of), shake off.

распу́тиц|а, ы *f.* time (*during spring and autumn*) of bad roads.

распу́тник, а *m.* profligate, libertine.

распу́тни|ца, цы *f. of* **⇒~к**

распу́тнича|ть, ю *impf.* to lead a dissolute life.

распу́т|ный (~ен, ~на) *adj.* dissolute, dissipated, debauched.

распу́тств|о, а *nt.* dissipation, debauchery, profligacy.

распу́тыва|ть(ся), ю(сь) *impf. of* **⇒распу́тать(ся)**

распу́ть|е, я *nt.* crossroads; **быть на р.** (*fig.*) to be at the crossroads, be at the parting of the ways.

распух|а́ть, а́ю *impf. of* **⇒~́нуть**

распу́х|нуть, ну, нешь, *past* **~, ~ла** *pf.* (*of* **⇒~а́ть**) **1** (*о пальце*) to swell up. **2** (*о папке*) to bulge. **3** (*fig., coll.*) (*о штатах*) to swell in numbers, become inflated.

распуш|и́ть, у́, и́шь *pf. of* **⇒пуши́ть**

распу́щенност|ь, и *f.* **1** (*недисциплинированность*) lack of discipline. **2** (*безнравственность*) dissoluteness, dissipation.

распу́|щенный *p.p.p. of* **⇒~сти́ть** *and adj.* **1** (*недисциплинированный*) undisciplined; **р. ребёнок** spoiled child. **2** (*безнравственный*) dissolute, dissipated.

распыле́ни|е, я *nt.* **1** (*краски*) spraying. **2** (*энергии*) scattering; **р. средств** dissipation of resources.

распыли́тел|ь, я *m.* spray(er).

распыл|и́ть, ю́, и́шь *pf.* (*of* **⇒~я́ть**) **1** (*краску*) to spray. **2** (*fig.*) to scatter; **р. си́лы** to scatter one's forces.

распыл|и́ться, и́тся *pf.* (*of* **⇒~я́ться**) to disperse, to get scattered.

распыл|я́ть(ся), я́ю, я́ет(ся) *impf. of* **⇒~и́ть(ся)**

распя́лива|ть, ю *impf. of* **⇒распя́лить**

распя́л|ить, ю, ишь *pf.* (*of* **⇒~ивать**) to stretch (*on a frame*).

распя́ти|е, я *nt.* **1** (*действие*) crucifixion. **2** (*крест*) cross, crucifix.

расп|я́ть, ну́, нёшь *pf.* (*of* **⇒~ина́ть**) to crucify.

расса́д|а, ы *no pl., f.* seedlings.

расса|ди́ть, жу́, ~́дишь *pf.* (*of* **⇒~́живать**) **1** (*гостей*) to seat, offer seats. **2** (*посадить порознь*) to separate, seat separately. **3** (*растения*) to transplant, plant out.

расса́дк|а, и *f.* transplanting, planting out.

расса́дник, а *m.* **1** seed-plot. **2** (*fig.*) (*коррупции, инфекции*) hotbed, breeding-ground.

расса́жива|ть, ю *impf. of* **⇒рассади́ть**

расса́жива|ться, юсь *impf. of* **⇒рассе́сться[1]**

расса́сыва|ться, ю, ет(ся) *impf. of* **⇒рассоса́ться**

рассве|сти́, тёт, *past* **~ло́** *pf.* (*of* **⇒~та́ть**) to dawn; **уже́ ~ло́** it was already light.

рассве́т, а *m.* dawn, daybreak; (*fig.*) (*начало*) dawn.

рассвета́|ть, ет *impf. of* **⇒рассвести́; ~ет** day is breaking.

рассвирепе́|ть, ю *pf.* (*of* **⇒свирепе́ть**) to become savage; to turn nasty.

расседа́|ться, ется *impf. of* **⇒рассе́сться[2]**

расседл|а́ть, а́ю *pf.* (*of* **⇒~́ывать**) to unsaddle.

рассёдлыва|ть, ю *impf. of* **⇒рассёдла́ть**

рассе́ивани|е, я *nt.* dispersion; dispersal, scattering.

рассе́ива|ть(ся), ю(сь) *impf. of* **⇒рассе́ять(ся)**

рассека́|ть, ю *impf. of* **⇒рассе́чь**

рассекре́|тить, чу, тишь *pf.* (*of* **⇒~чивать**) to declassify.

рассекре́чива|ть, ю *impf. of* **⇒рассекре́тить**

расселе́ни|е, я *nt.* **1** settling (*in a new place*). **2** (*порознь*) separation; settling apart.

рассе́лин|а, ы *f.* cleft, fissure.

рассел|и́ть, ю́, и́шь *pf.* (*of* **⇒~я́ть**) **1** to settle (*in a new place*). **2** (*порознь*) to separate; to settle apart.

рассел|и́ться, ю́сь, и́шься *pf.* (*of* **⇒~я́ться**) **1** to settle (*in a new place*). **2** (*порознь*) to separate, settle separately.

рассел|я́ть(ся), я́ю(сь) *impf. of* **⇒~и́ть(ся)**

рассер|ди́ть, жу́, ~́дишь *pf.* to anger, make angry.

рассер|ди́ться, жу́сь, ~́дишься *pf.* (**на**+*a.*) to get, become angry (with).

рассе́р|женный *p.p.p. of* **⇒~ди́ть** *and adj.* angry.

рассерча́|ть, ю *pf.* (*coll.*) to get angry.

рас|се́сться[1], ся́дусь, ся́дешься, *past* **~се́лся** *pf.* (*of* **⇒~са́живаться**) **1** to take one's seat. **2** (*coll.*) (*развалиться*) to sprawl.

рас|се́сться[2], ся́дется, *past* **~се́лся** *pf.* (*of* **⇒~седа́ться**) to crack.

рассе́|чь, ку́, чёшь, ку́т, *past* **~к, ~кла́** *pf.* (*of* **⇒~ка́ть**) **1** (*разрубить*) to cut through; (*волну, небо*) to cleave. **2** (*поранить*) to cut (badly); **я ~к себе́ па́лец** I have cut my finger badly.

рассе́яни|е, я *nt.* diffusion; dispersion; **р. тепла́** (*phys.*) dissipation of heat; **р. све́та** (*phys.*) diffusion of light.

рассе́янно *adv.* absent-mindedly; (*смотреть*) vacantly.

рассе́янност|ь, и *f.*
1 (*разбросанность*) diffusion; dispersion; dissipation.
2 (*невнимательность*) absent-mindedness, distraction.

рассе́я|нный *p.p.p. of* ⇒**~ть** *and adj.*
1 diffused; dissipated; **р. свет** (*phys.*) diffused light. **2** scattered, dispersed; **~нное населе́ние** scattered population. **3** (*невнимательный*) absent-minded; **р. взгляд** vacant look.

рассе́|ять, ю, ешь *pf.* (*of* ⇒**~ивать**) **1** (*семена*) to sow broadcast, scatter. **2** (*fig.*) (*население*) to place (about), establish (about), dot (about). **3** (*неприятеля, толпу*) to disperse, scatter; (*fig.*) (*слухи; сомнения*) to dispel; (*горе, тоску*) to alleviate; (*человека*) to distract, cheer up.

рассе́|яться, юсь, ешься *pf.* (*of* ⇒**~иваться**) **1** to disperse; (*в беспорядке*) to scatter; (*о неприятном чувстве*) to pass; **толпа́ ~ялась** the crowd dispersed; **тума́н ~ялся** the fog cleared; **её го́ре ~ялось** her grief passed; **р. как дым** to vanish into thin air, into smoke. **2** (*развлечься*) to divert o.s., distract o.s.; **ему́ на́до р.** he needs a break.

расси|де́ться, жу́сь, ди́шься *pf.* (*of* ⇒**~́живаться**) (*coll.*) to sit for a long time; to sit around.

расси́жива|ться, юсь *impf. of* ⇒**рассиде́ться**

расска́з, а *m.* **1** story. **2** (*очевидца*) account.

расска|за́ть, жу́, ~́жешь *pf.* (*of* ⇒**~́зывать**) **1** (*+a. and d.*) to tell, relate (*sth. to s.o.*). **2** (**о**+*p.*) to tell of; **р. о де́тстве** to tell of one's childhood. **3**: **р., как всё произошло́** to tell how it all happened.

расска́зчик, а *m.* story-teller, narrator.

расска́зчи|ца, цы *f. of* ⇒**~к**

расска́зыва|ть, ю *impf. of* ⇒**рассказа́ть**

расслабева́|ть, ю *impf. of* ⇒**расслабе́ть**

расслабе́|ть, ю *pf.* (*of* ⇒**~ва́ть**) to grow weak; to tire.

рассла́б|ить, лю, ишь *pf.* (*of* ⇒**~ля́ть**) **1** to weaken. **2** (*сделать ненапряжённым*) to relax.

рассла́б|иться, люсь, ишься *pf.* (*of* ⇒**~ля́ться**) to relax.

рассла́б|ленный *p.p.p. of* ⇒**~ить** *and adj.* (*голос, организм*) weak; (*спокойный*) relaxed.

расслабля́|ть(ся), ю(сь) *impf. of* ⇒**рассла́бить(ся)**

рассла́б|нуть, ну, нешь *past* **~**, **~ла** *pf.* (*coll.*) = **~е́ть**

рассла́в|ить, лю, ишь *pf.* (*of* ⇒**~ля́ть**) (*coll.*) **1** (*obs.*) (*расхвалить*) to praise to the skies. **2** (*рассказать многим*) to shout from the house-tops.

расславля́|ть, ю *impf. of* ⇒**рассла́вить**

рассла́ива|ть(ся), ю, ет(ся) *impf. of* ⇒**расслои́ть(ся)**

рассле́довани|е, я *nt.* investigation; (*leg.*) inquiry; **произвести́ р.** (*+g.*) to hold an inquiry (into); **обще́ственное р.** public inquiry.

рассле́д|овать, ую *impf. and pf.* to investigate.

расслое́ни|е, я *nt.* stratification (*also fig.*); (*отслоение*) exfoliation.

рассло|и́ть, ю́, и́шь *pf.* (*of* ⇒**рассла́ивать**) to divide into layers, stratify (*also fig.*).

рассло|и́ться, и́тся *pf.* (*of* ⇒**рассла́иваться**) to become stratified (*also fig.*); (*отслоиться*) to exfoliate, flake off.

расслó|йк|а, и *f.* **1** stratification. **2** (*geol.*) stratum.

расслу́ша|ть, ю *pf.* (*obs.*) = **рассль́ышать**

рассль́ыш|ать, у, ишь *pf.* to catch; **я не ~ал вас** I didn't catch what you said.

рассма́тривани|е, я *nt.* (*картины*) examination, inspection.

рассма́трива|ть, ю *impf.* **1** *impf. of* ⇒**рассмотре́ть. 2** *impf. only* (*считать*) to regard (as), consider; **мы ~ем э́то как обма́н** we regard it as a fraud. **3** *impf. only* (*внимательно смотреть*) to scrutinize, examine.

рассмеш|и́ть, у́, и́шь *pf.* to make laugh.

рассме|я́ться, ю́сь, ёшься *pf.* to burst out laughing.

рассмотре́ни|е, я *nt.* examination, scrutiny; (*обсуждение*) consideration; **предста́вить на р.** to submit for consideration; **быть на ~и** to be under consideration.

рассмотр|е́ть, ю́, ~ишь *pf.* (*of* ⇒**рассма́тривать**) **1** (*различить*) to discern, make out; **мы с трудо́м ~е́ли на́дпись на па́мятнике** we had difficulty in making out the inscription on the monument. **2** (*обсудить*) to examine, consider; **р. заявле́ние** to consider an application.

расс|ова́ть, ую́, уёшь *pf.* (*of* ⇒**~о́вывать**) (*coll.*) to shove, stuff; **р. свой ве́щи по чемода́нам** to stuff one's things into suitcases.

рассо́выва|ть, ю *impf. of* ⇒**рассова́ть**

рассо́л, а *m.* brine.

рассо́льник, а *m.* rassolnik (*meat or fish soup with pickled cucumbers*).

рассо́р|ить, ю, ишь *pf.* to set at loggerheads.

рассор|и́ть, ю́, и́шь *pf.* (*coll.*) to drop (over); **р. оку́рки по́ полу** to litter the floor with cigarette-butts.

рассо́р|иться, юсь, ишься *pf.* (**с**+*i.*) to fall out (with).

рассортир|ова́ть, у́ю *pf.* (*of* ⇒**~о́вывать**) to sort out; (*по ассортименту*) to classify; (*по качеству*) to grade, sort.

рассортиро́вк|а, и *f.* sorting out; classification; grading.

рассортиро́выва|ть, ю *impf. of* ⇒**рассортирова́ть**

рассос|а́ться, ётся *pf.* (*of* ⇒**расса́сываться**) (*об опухоли*) to go down; (*о толпе*) to disperse.

рассо́х|нуться, нется, *past* **~ся**, **~лась** *pf.* (*of* ⇒**рассыха́ться**) to crack.

расспра́шива|ть, ю *impf. of* ⇒**расспроси́ть**

расспро́с, а *m.* (*действие*) questioning; (*pl.*) (*вопросы*) questions; **надое́сть ~ами** to pester with questions.

расспро|си́ть, шу́, ~́сишь *pf.* (*of* ⇒**расспра́шивать**) to question; (**о**+*p.*) (*узнать, спрашивая*) to find out.

рассредото́чени|е, я *nt.* (*mil.*) dispersion, dispersal.

рассредото́чива|ть, ю *impf. of* ⇒**рассредото́чить**

рассредото́ч|ить, у, ишь *pf.* (*of* ⇒**~ивать**) (*mil.*) to disperse.

рассро́чива|ть, ю *impf. of* ⇒**рассро́чить**

рассро́ч|ить, у, ишь *pf.* (*of* ⇒**~ивать**) to spread (*over a period*); **р. изда́ние энциклопе́дии на де́сять лет** to spread the publication of an encyclopedia over ten years.

рассро́чк|а, и *f.* instalment system; **в ~у** by, in instalments; **купи́ть с ~ой платежа́** to purchase by instalments.

расстава́ни|е, я *nt.* parting; **при ~и** on parting.

расста|ва́ться, ю́сь, ёшься *impf. of* ⇒**расста́ться**

расста́в|ить, лю, ишь *pf.* (*of* ⇒**~ля́ть**) **1** (*разместить*) (*книги, мебель*) to place, arrange; (*кадры, работников*) to place, position; **р. часовы́х** to post sentries; (*запятые*) to put, add. **2** (*раздвинуть*) to move apart; **р. но́ги** to stand with one's legs apart. **3** (*одежду*) to let out.

расста́вк|а, и *f.* (*одежды*) letting out.

расставля́|ть, ю *impf. of* ⇒**расста́вить**

расстано́вк|а, и *f.* **1** (*действие*) placing, arrangement; **р. зна́ков препина́ния** punctuation. **2** (*пауза*) pause; spacing; **говори́ть с ~ой** to speak slowly and deliberately.

расста́|ться, нусь, нешься *pf.* (*of* ⇒**~ва́ться**) (**с**+*i.*) **1** to part (with); **я ~лся с ней** I parted with her; **~немся друзья́ми** let us part friends; **я ~лся с родны́м го́родом мно́го лет наза́д** I left my home town many years ago. **2** (*с мечтой, с мыслью*) to give up. **3** (*уволить*) to part company (with).

расстега́|й, я *m.* open-topped pasty.

расстёгива|ть(ся), ю(сь) *impf. of* ⇒**расстегну́ть(ся)**

расстег|ну́ть, ну́, нёшь *pf.* (*of* ⇒**~́ивать**) to undo, unfasten.

расстег|ну́ться, ну́сь, нёшься *pf.* (*of* ⇒**~́иваться**) **1** (*об одежде, о предмете*) to come undone, become unfastened. **2** (*о человеке*) to undo one's coat, shirt, etc.; to undo one's buttons.

расстел|и́ть(ся), ю́, ~ет(ся), ~ишь(ся) *pf.* = **разостла́ть(ся)**

расстила́|ть, ю *impf. of* ⇒**разостла́ть**

расстила́|ться, ется *impf.* **1** *impf. of* ⇒**разостла́ться. 2** *impf. only* to extend, unfold; **перед нашими глазами ~лась величественная панорама гор** before our eyes unfolded a magnificent mountain panorama.

расстояни|е, я *nt.* distance; **на ~и** (*видеть*) at a distance; (*управлять*) from a distance; **на близком ~и** (**от**+*g.*) at a short distance (from), a short way away (from); **на далёком ~и** in the far distance, a great way off; **они живут на ~и двух миль от ближайшего города** they live two miles from the nearest town; **держать кого-н. на ~и** to keep s.o. at arm's length; **держаться на ~и** to keep one's distance.

расстраива|ть(ся), ю(сь) *impf. of* ⇨**расстроить(ся)**

расстрел, а *m.* **1** (*казнь*) execution (*by firing squad*); **приговорить к ~у** to sentence to be shot. **2** (*обстрел*) (+*g.*) shooting at; firing at, on.

расстрелива|ть, ю *impf. of* ⇨**расстрелять**

расстрельн|ый *adj.*: **~ая команда** firing squad.

расстрел|ять, яю *pf.* (*of* ⇨**~ивать**) **1** (*убить*) to shoot, execute by shooting. **2** (*танки*) to shoot at; (*демонстрацию*) to open fire on. **3** (*снаряды*) to use up (*in firing*).

расстриг|а, и *m.* unfrocked priest, unfrocked monk.

расстрига|ть, ю *impf. of* ⇨**расстричь**

расстри|чь, гу, жёшь, гут, *past* **~г, ~гла** *pf.* (*of* ⇨**~гать**) (*eccl.*) to unfrock.

расстро|енный *p.p.p. of* ⇨**~ить** *and adj.* (*ряды*) disordered; (*здоровье*) damaged, weak; (*нервы*) shattered; (*человек, вид*) upset; (*рояль*) out of tune.

расстро|ить, ю, ишь *pf.* (*of* ⇨**расстраивать**) **1** (*ряды*) to throw into disorder; (*здоровье, хозяйство*) to damage; (*планы*) to upset. **2** (*человека; желудок*) to upset. **3** (*mus.*) to put out of tune.

расстро|иться, юсь, ишься *pf.* (*of* ⇨**расстраиваться**) **1** (*о рядах*) to fall into disarray; (*о здоровье, хозяйстве*) to be damaged; (*о планах*) to fall through. **2** (**из-за**+*g.*) (*о человеке*) to be upset (over, about). **3** (*mus.*) to become out of tune.

расстройств|о, а *nt.* **1** disorder; confusion; **р. желудка** stomach upset; (*coll.*) diarrhoea (*Br.*), diarrhea (*US*); **р. пищеварения** indigestion; **нервное р.** nervous breakdown; **р. речи** speech defect; **внести р.** (**в**+*a.*), **привести в р.** to throw into confusion, disorganize; **дела пришли в р.** things are in disarray. **2** (*coll.*) upset; **привести в р.** to upset; **быть в ~е** to be upset.

расступ|аться, ается *impf. of* ⇨**~иться**

расступ|иться, ~ится *pf.* (*of* ⇨**~аться**) to part, make way; **толпа ~илась** the crowd parted.

расстыковк|а, и *f.* (*of space vehicles*) undocking.

рассудительност|ь, и *f.* reasonableness; good sense.

рассудител|ьный (~ен, ~ьна) *adj.* reasonable; sensible.

рассу|дить, жу, ~дишь *pf.* **1** (*людей*) to judge (between), arbitrate (between); **~дите нас** be our judge; settle our dispute; **р. спор** to settle a dispute. **2** (*решить*) to decide; **мы ~дили, что пришло время вернуться домой** we decided that the time had come to return home.

рассуд|ок, ка *m.* **1** (*способность*) reason; intellect; **голос ~ка** the voice of reason; **в полном ~ке** in full possession of one's faculties; **лишиться ~ка** to lose one's reason, go out of one's mind. **2** (*здравый смысл*) common sense, good sense.

рассудоч|ный (~ен, ~на) *adj.* rational.

рассужда|ть, ю *impf.* **1** (*мыслить*) to reason. **2** (**о**+*p.*, **на**+*a.*) (*обсуждать*) to discuss, debate; to argue (about); **р. на какую-н. тему** to discuss a topic.

рассуждени|е, я *nt.* **1** (*процесс*) reasoning. **2** (*usu. pl.*) (*обсуждение*) discussion, debate; argument; **без ~й** without argument, without arguing.

рассусолива|ть, ю *impf.* (*coll.*) (**о**+*p.*) to go on, yak on (about).

рассучива|ть(ся), ю, ет(ся) *impf. of* ⇨**рассучить(ся)**

рассуч|ить, у, ~ишь *pf.* (*of* ⇨**~ивать**) to untwist; to undo; **р. рукава** to roll one's sleeves down.

рассуч|иться, ~ится *pf.* (*of* ⇨**~иваться**) to untwist; to come undone.

рассчит|анный *p.p.p. of* ⇨**~ать** *and adj.* **1** calculated, deliberate; **~анная грубость** calculated rudeness. **2** (**на**+*a.*) intended (for), meant (for), designed (for); **книга, ~анная на широкого читателя** a book intended for the general public.

рассчит|ать, аю *pf.* (*of* ⇨**~ывать**) **1** (*стоимость, расходы*) to calculate; **он не ~ал своих сил** he miscalculated his strength. **2** (*уволить*) to dismiss, sack. **3** (*действия, поездку*) to plan.

рассчит|аться, аюсь *pf.* (*of* ⇨**~ываться**) (**с**+*i.*) to settle accounts (with); (*fig.*) to settle scores (with).

рассчитыва|ть, ю *impf.* **1** *impf. of* ⇨**рассчитать** *and* **расчесть. 2** *impf. only* (**на**+*a.*) (*предполагать*) to count (on, upon), reckon (on, upon); (+*inf.*) to expect (to), hope (to); **р. на многочисленную публику** to count on a large attendance; **мы ~ли кончить работу в этом году** we were hoping to finish the work this year. **3** *impf. only* (**на**+*a.*) (*полагаться*) to count (on, upon), rely (on, upon), depend (upon).

рассчитыва|ться, юсь *impf. of* ⇨**рассчитаться** *and* **расчесться**

рассыла|ть, ю *impf. of* ⇨**разослать**

рассылк|а, и *f.* distribution, dispatch.

рассыльн|ый *adj.*: **~ая книга** delivery book; *as n.* **р., ~ого** *m.* (*для почты*) courier, delivery man; (*для поручений*) errand-boy.

рассып|ать, лю, лешь *pf.* (*of* ⇨**~ать**) (*невольно*) to spill; (*разбросать*) to strew, scatter; (*распределить*) to distribute (*by pouring*).

рассып|аться, люсь, лешься *pf.* (*of* ⇨**~аться**) **1** (*о муке, о сахаре*) to spill; **монеты ~ались на полу** the coins spilt onto the floor; (*о толпе*) to scatter; (*о домах*) to be scattered; **волосы ~ались по её плечам** her hair fell loose over her shoulders. **2** (*о команде*) to spread out. **3** (*о стене, о хлебе*) to crumble; to disintegrate (*also fig.*). **4** (**в**+*p.*) to be profuse (in); **р. в благодарностях** to be profuse in the expression of thanks; **р. в похвалах** (+*d.*) to shower praises (upon).

рассып|ать(ся), аю(сь) *impf. of* ⇨**~ать(ся)**

рассыпн|ой *adj.* **1** (sold) loose; **~ые папиросы** cigarettes sold loose. **2**: **р. строй** (*mil.*) extended order.

рассыпчат|ый (~, ~а) *adj.* (*почва*) friable; (*каша*) fluffy; (*тесто, печенье*) crumbly.

рассыха|ться, ется *impf. of* ⇨**рассохнуться**

расталкива|ть, ю *impf. of* ⇨**растолкать**

растаплива|ть(ся), ю, ет(ся) *impf. of* ⇨**растопить(ся)**

растаптыва|ть, ю *impf. of* ⇨**растоптать**

растаск|ать, аю *pf.* (*of* ⇨**~ивать**) **1** (*унести по частям*) to take away, remove (*little by little, bit by bit*). **2** (*украсть*) to pilfer, filch.

растаскива|ть, ю *impf. of* ⇨**растаскать** *and* **растащить**

растас|овать, ую *pf.* (*of* ⇨**~овывать**) to shuffle (*cards*).

растасовыва|ть, ю *impf. of* ⇨**растасовать**

растафари *c.g. & adj. indecl.* Rastafarian; Rasta.

растачива|ть, ю *impf. of* ⇨**расточить**[2]

растащ|ить, у, ~ишь *pf.* (*of* ⇨**растаскивать**) **1** (*дерущихся*) to part, separate, drag apart. **2** = **растаскать**

раста|ять, ю, ешь *pf. of* ⇨**таять**

раствор[1]**, а** *m.* (extent of) opening, span; **р. двери** doorway; **р. циркуля** spread of a pair of compasses.

раствор[2]**, а** *m.* **1** (*chem.*) solution. **2** (*tech.*) (*строительный*) mortar; **заливочный р.** grout.

растворени|е, я *nt.* dissolving; dissolution.

растворимост|ь, и *f.* (*chem.*) solubility.

растворим|ый (~, ~а) *adj.* (*chem.*) soluble; **р. кофе** instant coffee.

растворител|ь, я *m.* (*chem.*) solvent.

раствор|ить[1]**, ю, ~ишь** *pf.* (*of* ⇨**~ять**) (*окно*) to open.

раствор|ить[2]**, ю, ишь** *pf.* (*of* ⇨**~ять**) (*соль*) to dissolve.

раствор|и́ться¹, ~и́тся *pf.* (*of* ⇒**~я́ться**) (*об окне*) to open.

раствор|и́ться², и́тся *pf.* (*of* ⇒**~я́ться**) (*о соли*) to dissolve; (*fig.*) (*исчезнуть*) to vanish.

раствор|я́ть(ся), я́ю, я́ет(ся) *impf. of* ⇒**~и́ть(ся)**

растека́|ться, юсь 1 *impf. of* ⇒**растéчься. 2** (*no pf.*) (*coll.*) (*говорить*) to go on, talk at length.

расте́ни|е, я *nt.* plant; **однолéтнее р.** annual; **многолéтнее р.** perennial; **ползу́чее р.** creeper.

растениево́д, а *m.* horticultur(al)ist, plant-grower.

растениево́дств|о, а *nt.* horticulture, plant-growing.

растере́ть, разотру́, разотрёшь, *past* **растёр, растёрла** *pf.* (*of* ⇒**растира́ть**) **1** to grind; **р. в порошо́к** to grind to powder. **2** (**по**+*d.*) (*мазь*) to rub (over), spread (over). **3** (*тело*) to rub, massage.

растере́ться, разотру́сь, разотрёшься, *past* **растёрся, растёрлась** *pf.* (*of* ⇒**растира́ться**) **1** (*о зёрнах*) to become powdered, turn into powder. **2** (+*i.*) (*обтереть себя*) to rub o.s. briskly (with).

растерз|анный *p.p.p. of* ⇒**~а́ть** *and adj.* dishevelled.

растерз|а́ть, а́ю *pf.* (*of* ⇒**~ывать**) **1** (*умертвить*) to tear to pieces. **2** (*fig., poet.*) (*измучить*) to lacerate; to harrow.

растерзыва|ть, ю *impf. of* ⇒**растерза́ть**

расте́рива|ть(ся), ю(сь) *impf. of* ⇒**растеря́ть(ся)**

расте́рянност|ь, и *f.* confusion, bewilderment, dismay; **он стоя́л в ~и** he stood there looking bewildered.

расте́р|янный *p.p.p. of* ⇒**~я́ть** *and adj.* confused, bewildered, dismayed.

растер|я́ть, я́ю *pf.* (*of* ⇒**~ивать**) to lose (*little by little*).

растер|я́ться, я́юсь *pf.* (*of* ⇒**~иваться**) **1** (*пропасть*) to get lost, go missing. **2** (*утратить самообладание*) to lose one's head, nerve; **он не ~я́лся пе́ред лицо́м опа́сности** he kept his head in the face of danger.

расте́|чься, чётся, ку́тся, *past* **~кся, ~кла́сь** *pf.* (*of* ⇒**~ка́ться**) **1** (*о воде*) to spill; (*о краске*) to run. **2** (*fig.*) (*об улыбке, о толпе, о синяке*) to spread.

раст|и́, у́, ёшь, *past* **рос, росла́** *impf.* (*of* ⇒**вы~**) **1** (*biol., bot.*) to grow; (*о детях*) to grow up; **он рос на Украи́не** he grew up in (the) Ukraine. **2** (*увеличиваться*) to grow, increase. **3** (*совершенствоваться*) to advance, develop; (*о специалисте*) to grow in stature.

растира́ни|е, я *nt.* **1** grinding. **2** (*med.*) massage.

растира́|ть(ся), ю(сь) *impf. of* ⇒**растере́ть(ся)**

расти́скива|ть, ю *impf. of* ⇒**расти́снуть**

расти́с|нуть, ну, нешь *pf.* (*of* ⇒**~кивать**) (*coll.*) to unclench.

расти́тельност|ь, и *f.* **1** (*растения*) vegetation. **2** (*волосы*) hair (*on face or body*).

расти́тельн|ый *adj.* vegetable; **~ое ма́сло** vegetable oil; **жить ~ой жи́знью** (*fig., iron.*) to vegetate.

ра|сти́ть, щу́, сти́шь *impf.* **1** (*детей*) to raise, bring up; (*кадры*) to nurture. **2** (*цветы*) to grow, cultivate; (*животных*) to rear; **р. бо́роду** to grow a beard. **3** (*талант*) to cultivate, nurture.

растлева́|ть, ю *impf. of* ⇒**растли́ть**

растле́ни|е, я *nt.* **1** (*малолетних*) defilement (*of minors*). **2** (*моральное*) corruption, depravity.

растле́н|ный (~, ~на) *adj.* corrupt, depraved.

растли́тел|ь, я *m.*: **р. малоле́тних дете́й** child molester.

растл|и́ть, ю́, и́шь *pf.* (*of* ⇒**~ева́ть**) **1** (*малолетних*) to defile (*minors*). **2** (*морально*) to corrupt, deprave.

растолка́|ть, ю *pf.* (*of* ⇒**раста́лкивать**) **1** (*толпу*) to push asunder, apart. **2** (*спящего*) to shake (*in order to awaken*).

растолкн|у́ть, у́, ёшь *pf.* (*coll.*) to push asunder, part forcibly.

растолк|ова́ть, у́ю *pf.* (*of* ⇒**~о́вывать**) to explain.

растолко́выва|ть, ю *impf. of* ⇒**растолкова́ть**

растол|о́чь, ку́, чёшь, ку́т, *past* **~о́к, ~окла́** *pf. of* ⇒**толо́чь**

растолсте́|ть, ю *pf.* to put on weight.

растоп|и́ть¹, лю́, ~ишь *pf.* (*of* ⇒**раста́пливать**) (*печь*) to light.

растоп|и́ть², лю́, ~ишь *pf.* (*of* ⇒**раста́пливать**) (*сало, лёд*) to melt.

растоп|и́ться¹, ~ится *pf.* (*of* ⇒**раста́пливаться**) (*о печи*) to begin to burn.

растоп|и́ться², ~ится *pf.* (*of* ⇒**раста́пливаться**) (*о сале*) to melt.

расто́пк|а, и *f.* **1** (*печи*) lighting, kindling. **2** (*collect.*) (*сучья*) kindling (wood).

растоп|та́ть, чу́, ~чешь *pf.* (*of* ⇒**раста́птывать**) to trample, stamp (on), crush (*also fig.*).

растопы́рива|ть, ю *impf. of* ⇒**растопы́рить**

растопы́р|ить, ю, ишь *pf.* (*of* ⇒**~ивать**) (*coll.*) to spread wide, open wide.

расторг|а́ть, а́ю *impf. of* ⇒**~нуть**

расто́рг|нуть, ну, нешь, *past* **~, ~ла** *pf.* (*of* ⇒**~а́ть**) (*контракт, договор*) to dissolve, annul, abrogate; **р. брак** to dissolve a marriage.

расторже́ни|е, я *nt.* dissolution, annulment, abrogation.

растормош|и́ть, у́, и́шь *pf.* (*coll.*) **1** (*спящего*) to shake (*in order to awaken*). **2** (*fig.*) to stir, rouse to activity.

расторо́п|ный (~ен, ~на) *adj.* (*coll.*) (*быстрый, ловкий*) quick, prompt, smart; (*деловой*) efficient.

расточ|а́ть, а́ю *pf.* (*of* ⇒**~и́ть¹**) **1** (*тратить*) to waste, squander, dissipate. **2** (*fig.*) to lavish, shower; **р. похвалы́** (+*d.*) to lavish praises (on, upon).

расточи́тел|ь, я *m.* squanderer, spendthrift.

расточи́тель|ница, ницы *f. of* ⇒**~**

расточи́тел|ьный (~ен, ~ьна) *adj.* extravagant, wasteful.

расточи́тельств|о, а *nt.* squandering.

расточ|и́ть¹, у́, и́шь *pf.* (*of* ⇒**~а́ть**)

расточ|и́ть², у́, ~ишь *pf.* (*of* ⇒**раста́чивать**) (*tech.*) to bore (out).

расто́чк|а, и *f.* (*tech.*) boring.

растрав|и́ть, лю́, ~ишь *pf.* (*of* ⇒**~ля́ть**) to irritate; **р. ра́ну** (*fig.*) to rub salt in a wound; **р. ста́рое го́ре** (*fig.*) to re-open an old wound.

растравля́|ть, ю *impf. of* ⇒**растрави́ть**

растранжи́р|ить, ю, ишь *pf. of* ⇒**транжи́рить**

растра́т|а, ы *f.* **1** (*денег, времени*) waste, squandering. **2** (*незаконная*) embezzlement. **3** (*растраченная сумма*) loss.

растра́|тить, чу, тишь *pf.* (*of* ⇒**~чивать**) **1** to waste, squander. **2** (*незаконно*) to embezzle.

растра́тчик, а *m.* embezzler.

растра́тчи|ца, цы *f. of* ⇒**~к**

растра́чива|ть, ю *impf. of* ⇒**растра́тить**

растрево́ж|ить, у, ишь *pf.* to alarm, agitate.

растрево́ж|иться, усь, ишься *pf.* to get the wind up.

растрезво́н|ить, ю, ишь *pf.* (**о**+*p.*) (*coll.*) to proclaim.

растрёп|а, ы *c.g.* (*coll.*) sloven, scruff.

растрёп|анный *p.p.p. of* ⇒**~а́ть** *and adj.* dishevelled (*Br.*), disheveled (*US*); tattered; **быть в ~анных чу́вствах** (*coll.*) to be agitated, worried.

растреп|а́ть, лю́, ~лешь *pf.* **1** (*волосы*) to mess up, tousle. **2** (*книгу*) to tatter, tear.

растреп|а́ться, ~лется *pf.* **1** (*о волосах*) to get messed up, get dishevelled. **2** (*о книге*) to get tattered, get torn.

растре́ск|аться, ается *pf.* (*of* ⇒**~иваться**) (*о земле*) to crack; (*о коже*) to chap.

растре́скива|ться, ется *impf. of* ⇒**растре́скаться**

растро́га|ть, ю *pf.* to move, touch; **р. кого́-н. до слёз** to move s.o. to tears.

растро́га|ться, юсь *pf.* to be (deeply) moved, touched.

растру́б, а *m.* funnel-shaped opening; (*музыкального инструмента*) bell; **брю́ки с ~ами** bell-bottomed trousers.

раструб|и́ть, лю, и́шь *pf.* (+*a. or* **о**+*p.*; *coll.*) to trumpet.

растряс|ти́, у́, ёшь, *past* **~, ~ла́** *pf.*

1 (*сено*) to strew. **2** (*coll.*) (*спящего*) to shake (*in order to awaken*). **3** (*impers.*) (*в машине*) to jolt about; **в маши́не нас растрясло́** we were jolted about in the car.

растуш|ева́ть, у́ю, у́ешь *pf.* (*of* **⇒~ёвывать**) to shade.

растушёвк|а, и *f.* **1** (*действие*) shading. **2** (*палочка*) stump (*for softening pencil-marks, etc., in drawing*).

растушёвыва|ть, ю *impf. of* **⇒растушева́ть**

растя́гива|ть(ся), ю(сь) *impf. of* **⇒растяну́ть(ся)**

растяже́ни|е, я *nt.* (*med.*) strain, sprain.

растяжи́мост|ь, и *f.* tensile strength.

растяжи́м|ый (~, ~а) *adj.* tensile; **~ое поня́тие** loose concept

растя́жк|а, и *f.* stretching, extension.

растя́нутост|ь, и *f.* long-windedness.

растя́н|утый *p.p.p. of* **⇒~уть** *and adj.* long-winded.

растя|ну́ть, ну́, ~́нешь *pf.* (*of* **⇒~́гивать**) **1** (*ковёр, скатерть*) to stretch, spread (out); (*лишить упругости*) to stretch; (*платежи*) to spread. **2** (*med.*) to strain, sprain; **р. му́скул** to pull a muscle; **р. свя́зку** to strain a ligament. **3** (*сделать слишком длинным*) to stretch out; (*fig.*) to protract, drag out; **р. расска́з** to drag out, spin out a story; **р. слова́** to drawl; (*встречу, удовольствие*) to prolong.

растя|ну́ться, ну́сь, ~́нешься *pf.* (*of* **⇒~́гиваться**) **1** to stretch (out); (*стать менее упругим*) to be stretched. **2** (*стать слишком длинным*) to stretch too far; (*fig.*) (*работа, собрание*) to drag on; **обсужде́ние его́ докла́да ~ну́лось на полтора́ часа́** discussion of his lecture dragged on for an hour and a half. **3** (*лечь*) to stretch o.s. out, sprawl.

растя́п|а, ы *c.g.* (*coll.*) bungler.

расфас|ова́ть, у́ю *pf.* (*of* **⇒~о́вывать**) to pack up, pre-pack.

расфасо́вк|а, и *f.* packing, pre-packing.

расфасо́выва|ть, ю *impf. of* **⇒расфасова́ть**

расформирова́ни|е, я *nt.* breaking up; (*mil.*) disbandment.

расформир|ова́ть, у́ю *pf.* (*of* **⇒~о́вывать**) (*отдел, организацию*) to break up; (*mil.*) to disband.

расформиро́выва|ть, ю *impf. of* **⇒расформирова́ть**

расфран|ти́ться, чу́сь, ти́шься *pf.* (*coll.*) to dress up.

расфуфы́рен|ный (~, ~а) *adj.* (*coll.*) overdressed.

расфуфы́р|иться, юсь, ишься *pf.* (*coll., pej.*) to dress flashily.

расха́жива|ть, ю *impf.* to walk, pace; **р. по ко́мнате** to pace up and down a room.

расхва́лива|ть, ю *impf. of* **⇒расхвали́ть**

расхвал|и́ть, ю́, ~́ишь *pf.* (*of* **⇒~́ивать**) to lavish, shower praise (on, upon).

расхва́рыва|ться, юсь *impf. of* **⇒расхвора́ться**

расхва́ста|ться, юсь *pf.* (**о**+*p.*; *coll.*) to boast extravagantly (of, about).

расхват|а́ть, а́ю *pf.* (*of* **⇒~́ывать**) to snatch, seize; (*товар*) to snap up.

расхва́тыва|ть, ю *impf. of* **⇒расхвата́ть**

расхвора́|ться, юсь *pf.* (*of* **⇒расхва́рываться**) (*coll.*) to fall ill.

расхити́тел|ь, я *m.* embezzler.

расхити́тель|ница, ницы *f. of* **⇒~**

расхи́|тить, щу, тишь *pf.* (*of* **⇒~ща́ть**) to embezzle, misappropriate.

расхища́|ть, ю *impf. of* **⇒расхи́тить**

расхище́ни|е, я *nt.* embezzlement, misappropriation.

расхлеб|а́ть, а́ю *pf.* (*of* **⇒~́ывать**) (*coll.*) **1** to eat up (*without leaving anything*). **2** (*fig.*) (*путаницу, дело*) to disentangle.

расхлёбыва|ть, ю *impf. of* **⇒расхлеба́ть; завари́л ка́шу, тепе́рь сам и ~й** (*coll.*) you got yourself into this mess, now get yourself out of it.

расхля́банност|ь, и *f.* (*coll.*) **1** looseness; instability. **2** (*fig.*) slackness; laxity, lack of discipline.

расхля́бан|ный (~, ~на) *adj.* (*coll.*) **1** (*дверь*) loose; (*движение, походка*) unstable. **2** (*fig.*) (*человек, поведение*) lax, undisciplined.

расхля́ба|ться, юсь *pf.* (*coll.*) **1** (*о колесе, гайке*) to come loose, work loose. **2** (*fig.*) (*о человеке, армии*) to go to pieces.

расхо́д, а *m.* **1** (*затрата*) expense; (*pl.*) expenses, outlay, cost; **госуда́рственные ~ы** public expenditure; **доро́жные ~ы** travel expenses; **накладны́е ~ы** overhead expenses, overheads; **де́ньги на карма́нные ~ы** pocket-money. **2** (*энергии*) consumption; **р. горю́чего** fuel consumption. **3** (*в бухгалтерии*) expenditure, outlay; **прихо́д и р.** income and expenditure; **списа́ть в р.** to write off; (*fig., coll.*) (*уничтожить*) to liquidate. **4**: **вы́вести/пусти́ть в р.** (*coll.*) to shoot.

расхо|ди́ться, жу́сь, ~́дишься *impf. of* **⇒разойти́сь**

расхо́д|ный *adj. of* **⇒~; ~ная кни́га** expenses book.

расхо́довани|е, я *nt.* (*денег*) spending, expenditure; (*потребление*) consumption; (*ресурсов*) use.

расхо́д|овать, ую *impf.* (*of* **⇒из~**) **1** (*деньги, время*) to spend, expend. **2** (*ресурсы*) to use (up), consume; **маши́на ~ует мно́го бензи́на** the car uses a lot of petrol (*Br.*), gas (*US*).

расхо́д|оваться, уюсь *impf.* (*of* **⇒из~**) **1** (*coll.*) (*тратить деньги*) to spend; to lay out money. **2** (*потребляться*) to be used (up), consumed.

расхожде́ни|е, я *nt.* (*лучей, дорог*) divergence; (*идейное*) difference; **р. во мне́ниях** difference of opinion; (*в тексте*) discrepancy.

расхо́жий *adj.* **1** (*coll.*) (*товар*) in great demand. **2** (*coll.*) (*одежда*) everyday. **3** (*истина, представление*) trite, commonplace.

расхола́жива|ть, ю *impf. of* **⇒расхолоди́ть**

расхоло|ди́ть, жу́, ди́шь *pf.* (*of* **⇒расхола́живать**) (*человека*) to damp the enthusiasm of; (*пыл, энтузиазм*) to damp.

расхо|те́ть, чу́, ~́чешь, ти́м, ти́те, тя́т *pf.* (+*g. or a. or inf.*; *coll.*) to no longer want; **я ~те́л ча́ю/суп** I no longer want any tea/soup; **я ~те́л спать** I am no longer sleepy.

расхо|те́ться, ~́чется *pf.* (*impers.*+*d.*; *coll.*) to no longer want; **мне ~те́лось есть** I no longer want to eat; **мне ~те́лось ча́ю** I no longer want any tea.

расхохо|та́ться, чу́сь, ~́чешься *pf.* to burst out laughing; to start roaring with laughter.

расхрабр|и́ться, ю́сь, и́шься *pf.* (*coll.*) to screw up one's courage, pluck up courage.

расцара́п|ать, аю *pf.* (*of* **⇒~ывать**) to scratch (all over).

расцара́п|аться, аюсь *pf.* (*of* **⇒~ываться**) to scratch o.s.

расцара́пыва|ть(ся), ю(сь) *impf. of* **⇒расцара́пать(ся)**

расцве|сти́, ту́, тёшь, *past* **~́л, ~ла́** *pf.* (*of* **⇒~та́ть**) (*цветок, девушка*) to bloom; to blossom (out) (*also fig.*); (*наука, искусство*) to flourish; **не дать чему́-н. р.** (*fig.*) to nip sth. in the bud; (*повеселеть*) to become radiant; **его́ лицо́ ~ло́ улы́бкой** his face was wreathed in smiles.

расцве́т, а *m.* bloom, blossoming (out); (*науки*) flourishing; flowering, heyday; **в ~е сил** in one's prime, in one's heyday.

расцвета́|ть, ю *impf. of* **⇒расцвести́**

расцве|ти́ть, чу́, ти́шь *pf.* (*of* **⇒~́чивать**) **1** (*раскрасить*) to paint in bright colours (*Br.*), colors (*US*). **2** (*украсить*) to deck, adorn.

расцве́тк|а, и *f.* colour (*Br.*), color (*US*) scheme; colours (*Br.*), colors (*US*).

расцве́чива|ть, ю *impf. of* **⇒расцвети́ть**

расцел|ова́ть, у́ю *pf.* to smother with kisses.

расцел|ова́ться, у́юсь *pf.* to exchange kisses.

расце́нива|ть, ю *impf. of* **⇒расцени́ть**

расце́нива|ться, ется *impf.* **1** to be regarded. **2** (*товар*) to be priced.

расцен|и́ть, ю́, ~́ишь *pf.* (*of* **⇒~́ивать**) **1** (*определить стоимость*) to assess, value; (*определить цену*) to price. **2** (*fig.*) (*талант*) to rate, assess; (*поступок, слова*) to regard; **его́ речь ~и́ли как провока́цию** his speech was regarded as provocation; **вы непра́вильно ~и́ли**

мой слова́ you misinterpreted my words.

расце́нк|а, и *f.* **1** (*действие*) valuation. **2** (*usu. pl.*) (*цена*) tariff, rates. **3** (*ведомость*) cost sheet.

расце́нщик, а *m.* appraiser, valuer.

расцеп|и́ть, лю́, ~́ишь *pf.* (*of* ⇒**~ля́ть**) (*вагоны*) to uncouple, unhook; (*драчунов*) to separate.

расцеп|и́ться, ~́ится *pf.* (*of* ⇒**~ля́ться**) to come uncoupled, come unhooked.

расцепле́ни|е, я *nt.* uncoupling, unhooking; disengaging.

расцепля́|ть(ся), ю, ет(ся) *impf. of* ⇒**расцепи́ть(ся)**

расчер|ти́ть, чу́, ~́тишь *pf.* (*of* ⇒**~́чивать**) to rule, line.

расче́рчива|ть, ю *impf. of* ⇒**расчерти́ть**

расче|са́ть, шу́, ~́шешь *pf.* (*of* ⇒**~́сывать**) **1** (*волосы*) to comb; (*лён, шерсть*) to card. **2** (*руку*) to scratch.

расче|са́ться, шу́сь, ~́шешься *pf.* (*of* ⇒**~́сываться**) (*coll.*) **1** (*расчесать волосы*) to comb one's hair. **2** (*расцарапаться*) to scratch o.s.

расчёск|а, и *f.* **1** (*действие*) combing. **2** (*гребёнка*) comb.

расче́сть, разочту́, разочтёшь, *past* **расчёл, разочла́** *pf.* (*of* ⇒**рассчи́тывать**) (*coll.*) **1** (*стоимость, расходы*) to calculate. **2** (*уволить*) to dismiss, sack.

расче́сться, разочту́сь, разочтёшься, *past* **расчёлся, разочла́сь** *pf.* (*of* ⇒**рассчи́тываться**) (*coll.*) (**с** + *i.*) to settle accounts (with).

расчёсыва|ть(ся), ю(сь) *impf. of* ⇒**расчеса́ть(ся)**

расчёт[1], а *m.* **1** (*стоимости*) calculation; (*смета*) statement; (*приблизительный*) estimate, reckoning; **из ~а** on the basis (of), at a rate (of); **из ~а три проце́нта годовы́х** at three per cent per annum; **приня́ть в р.** to take into account, consideration; **по мои́м ~ам** by my reckoning; **э́то не входи́ло в мои́ ~ы** I had not reckoned with that; **ошиби́ться в свои́х ~ах** to miscalculate; **в ~е на** (+*a.*) hoping for, reckoning on; **в ~е** +*inf.* hoping to. **2** (*coll.*) (*выгода*) gain, advantage; **нет ~а** (+*inf.*) it is not worth while, there is no point. **3** (**с** + *i.*) settling (with); (*оплата*) payment; **нали́чный р.** cash payment; **ба́нковские ~ы** bank transactions; **быть в ~е** (**с** + *i.*) to be quits (with), be even (with); **производи́ть ~ы** (**с** + *i.*) to settle accounts (with). **4** (*бережливость*) thrift, economy. **5** (*увольнение*) dismissal, discharge; **дать р.** (+*d.*) to dismiss, sack; **взять р.** to hand in one's notice.

расчёт[2], а *m.* (*mil.*) crew; **ору́дийный р.** gun crew.

расчётливост|ь, и *f.* thrift.

расчётлив|ый (~, ~а) *adj.* thrifty; careful.

расчётн|ый *adj.* **1** calculation, computation; **~ая оши́бка** error in computation; **~ая табли́ца** calculation table. **2** pay, accounts; **р. день** pay-day; **~ая кни́жка** pay-book; **р. отде́л** accounts department. **3** (*tech.*) rated, designed; **~ая мо́щность** rated capacity; **~ая ско́рость** rated speed.

расчи́сл|ить, ю, ишь *pf.* (*of* ⇒**~я́ть**) to calculate, reckon.

расчисл|я́ть, я́ю *impf. of* ⇒**~́ить**

расчи́|стить, щу, стишь *pf.* (*of* ⇒**~ща́ть**) to clear; **р. путь, доро́гу** (*fig.*) to pave the way.

расчи́|ститься, стится *pf.* (*of* ⇒**~ща́ться**) (*о небе*) to clear.

расчи́стк|а, и *f.* clearing.

расчиха́|ться, юсь *pf.* to sneeze repeatedly.

расчища́|ть(ся), ю, ет(ся) *impf. of* ⇒**расчи́стить(ся)**

расчлене́ни|е, я *nt.* breaking up, division.

расчлен|и́ть, ю́, и́шь *pf.* (*of* ⇒**~я́ть**) to break up, divide.

расчлен|я́ть, я́ю *impf. of* ⇒**~и́ть**

расчу́вств|оваться, уюсь *pf.* (*coll.*) to be deeply moved.

расчу́ха|ть, ю *pf.* (*coll.*) to nose out; (*fig.*) to sense; **он ~л, в чём де́ло** he sensed what was the matter.

расшал|и́ться, ю́сь, и́шься *pf.* to get up to mischief, start playing about.

расша́рк|аться, аюсь *pf.* (*of* ⇒**~иваться**) to bow, scraping one's feet; (*fig., coll.*) (**пе́ред** + *i.*) to bow and scrape (before).

расша́рким|ться, юсь *impf. of* ⇒**расша́ркаться**

расша́т|анный *p.p.p. of* ⇒**~а́ть** *and adj.* shaky; rickety; tottering; **~анные не́рвы** shattered nerves.

расшат|а́ть, а́ю *pf.* (*of* ⇒**~́ывать**) **1** to shake loose; to make rickety. **2** (*fig.*) (*дисциплину*) to undermine, impair; (*хозяйство*) to cripple; (*нервы, здоровье*) to damage.

расшат|а́ться, а́ется *pf.* (*of* ⇒**~́ываться**) **1** to get loose; to become rickety. **2** (*fig.*) (*дисциплина*) to be undermined; (*хозяйство*) to be crippled; (*нервы, здоровье*) to go to pieces, crack up.

расша́тыва|ть(ся), ю, ет(ся) *impf. of* ⇒**расшата́ть(ся)**

расшвы́рива|ть, ю *impf. of* ⇒**расшвыря́ть**

расшвыр|я́ть, я́ю *pf.* (*of* ⇒**~́ивать**) (*вещи; деньги*) to throw about, throw around.

расшеве́лива|ть, ю *impf. of* ⇒**расшевели́ть**

расшевел|и́ть, ю́, и́шь *pf.* (*of* ⇒**~́ивать**) to stir, shake; (*fig.*) (*стимулировать*) to stir, rouse.

расшевел|и́ться, ю́сь, и́шься *pf.* to begin to stir; (*fig.*) (*человек*) to rouse o.s.; (*чувства*) to be aroused.

расшиб|а́ть(ся), а́ю(сь) *impf. of* ⇒**расшиби́ть(ся)**

расшиб|и́ть, у́, ёшь, *past* **~́, ~́ла** *pf.* (*of* ⇒**~а́ть**) **1** (*ушибить*) to hurt; to knock, stub; **р. па́лец ноги́ об ка́мень** to stub one's toe on a rock. **2** (*coll.*) (*разбить*) to break up, smash to pieces.

расшиб|и́ться, у́сь, ёшься, *past* **~́ся, ~́лась** *pf.* (*of* ⇒**~а́ться**) **1** to hurt o.s., knock o.s. **2** (*coll.*) (*для приятеля*) to put o.s. out.

расшива́|ть, ю *impf. of* ⇒**расши́ть**

расшивно́й *adj.* embroidered.

расшире́ни|е, я *nt.* **1** (*отверстия*) widening; (*кругозора, знаний*) broadening. **2** (*производства*) expansion. **3** (*med.*) dilation, dilatation; **р. вен** varicose veins.

расши́р|енный *p.p.p. of* ⇒**~ить** *and adj.* (*отверстие*) widened; (*программа*) broadened, more extensive; (*заседание*) expanded; (*зрачки*) dilated.

расшири́тельн|ый *adj.* broad, extended; **~ое толкова́ние** broad interpretation.

расши́р|ить, ю, ишь *pf.* (*of* ⇒**~я́ть**) (*отверстие*) to widen; (*производство*) to expand; (*кругозор, знания*) to broaden; (*сферу влияния*) to extend.

расши́р|иться, ится *pf.* (*of* ⇒**~я́ться**) (*об отверстии*) to widen; (*о производстве, о знаниях*) to expand; (*о кругозоре*) to broaden; (*о зрачках*) to dilate.

расшир|я́ть(ся), я́ю, я́ет(ся) *impf. of* ⇒**~ить(ся)**

расши́ть[1], разошью́, разошьёшь *pf.* (*of* ⇒**расшива́ть**) (*украсить*) to embroider.

расши́ть[2], разошью́, разошьёшь *pf.* (*of* ⇒**расшива́ть**) (*распороть*) to undo, unpick.

расшифр|ова́ть, у́ю *pf.* (*of* ⇒**~о́вывать**) to decipher, decode; (*fig.*) (*угадать смысл*) to interpret; to figure out.

расшифро́вк|а, и *f.* deciphering, decoding; (*fig.*) interpretation.

расшифро́вщик, а *m.* code breaker.

расшифро́вщи|ца, цы *f. of* ⇒**~к**

расшифро́вывa|ть, ю *impf. of* ⇒**расшифрова́ть**

расшнур|ова́ть, у́ю *pf.* (*of* ⇒**~о́вывать**) to unlace.

расшнур|ова́ться, у́юсь *pf.* (*of* ⇒**~о́вываться**) **1** (*о ботинках*) to come unlaced, come undone. **2** (*о человеке*) to unlace o.s. (*from a corset, etc.*).

расшнуро́выва|ть(ся), ю(сь) *impf. of* ⇒**расшнурова́ть(ся)**

расшум|е́ться, лю́сь, и́шься *pf.* (*coll.*) to get noisy, kick up a din.

расще́др|иться, юсь, ишься *pf.* (*coll., also iron.*) to have a fit of generosity.

расще́лин|а, ы *f.* cleft, crevice.

расщёлкива|ть, ю *impf. of* ⇒**расщёлкнуть**

расщёлк|нуть, ну, нешь *pf.* (*of* ⇒**~ивать**) to crack open.

расще́п, а *m.* split.

расщеп|и́ть, лю́, и́шь *pf.* (*of* ⇒**~ля́ть**) **1** (*доску*) to split, splinter.

2 (*атом*) to split; (*вещество*) to decompose.

расщеп|и́ться, и́тся *pf.* (*of* ⇒**~ля́ться**) **1** to split, splinter. **2** (*атом*) to split; (*вещество*) to decompose.

расщепле́ни|е, я *nt.* **1** splitting, splintering. **2** (*phys.*) splitting, fission; (*chem.*) decomposition; **р. ядра́** nuclear fission.

расщепля́|ть(ся), ю, ет(ся) *impf. of* ⇒**расщепи́ть(ся)**

расщепля́|ющийся *pres. part. of* ⇒**~ться** *and adj.* (*phys.*) fissile, fissionable.

ратифика́ци|я, и *f.* ratification.

ратифици́р|овать, ую *impf. and pf.* to ratify.

ра́тник, а *m.* **1** (*arch.*) (*воин*) warrior. **2** (*obs.*) (*рядовой государственного ополчения*) militiaman.

ра́тный *adj.* (*poet.*) military, warlike; **р. по́двиг** feat of arms.

ра́т|овать, ую *impf.* (**за** + *a.*) to fight (for), advocate; (**про́тив** + *g.*) to fight (against), inveigh (against).

ра́туш|а, и *f.* **1** (*здание*) town hall. **2** (*орган*) town council.

рат|ь, и *f.* (*arch. or poet.*) **1** (*войско*) host, army. **2** (*война*) war; (*битва*) battle; **идти́ на р.** to go into battle.

ра́унд, а *m.* (*sport*) round; (*переговоров*) series, round.

ра́ут, а *m.* reception.

рафина́д, а *m.* lump sugar.

рафина́д|ный *adj. of* ⇒**~**; **р. заво́д** sugar refinery.

рафини́ровани|е, я *nt.* refinement, refining, purification.

рафини́рованност|ь, и *f.* refinement.

рафини́рова|нный *p.p.p. of* ⇒**~ть** *and adj.* refined.

рафини́р|овать, ую *impf. and pf.* to refine.

раха́т-луку́м, а *m.* Turkish delight.

рахи́т, а *m.* (*med.*) rickets.

рахи́тик, а *m.* person suffering from rickets.

рахити́|чка, чки *f. of* ⇒**рахи́тик**

рахити́чный *adj.* (*med.*) suffering from rickets, rickety.

раце́|я, и *f.* (*obs., coll.*) sermon, lecture.

рацио́н, а *m.* ration.

рационализа́тор, а *m.* rationalizer.

рационализа́тор|ский *adj. of* ⇒**~**; **~ское предложе́ние** proposal for improving production methods.

рационализа́ци|я, и *f.* rationalization, improvement.

рационализи́р|овать, ую *impf. and pf.* to rationalize, improve.

рационали́зм, а *m.* (*phil.*) rationalism.

рационали́ст, а *m.* rationalist.

рационалисти́ческий *adj.* rationalistic.

рационалисти́ч|ный (~ен, ~на) *adj.* rational.

рациона́льно *adv.* (*мыслить, поступать*) rationally; (*вести хозяйство*) efficiently; **р. испо́льзовать** to make efficient use (of).

рациона́л|ьный (~ен, ~ьна) *adj.* **1** (*поступок*) rational; (*использование средств*) efficient; **~ьная дие́та** balanced diet; **~ьное пита́ние** sound nutrition. **2** (*math.*) rational.

ра́ци|я, и *f.* (*на корабле, в здании*) radio set; (*небольшая переносная*) walkie-talkie.

ра́чий *adj. of* ⇒**рак; ра́чьи глаза́** goggle eyes.

рачи́тельност|ь, и *f.* (*старательность*) assiduity; (*бережность*) prudency.

рачи́тел|ьный (~ен, ~ьна) *adj.* (*старательный*) assiduous; (*бережный*) prudent.

рач|о́к, ка́ *m.* **1** *dim. of* ⇒**рак. 2** *pl.* ostracods.

ра́шпил|ь, я *m.* (*tech.*) rasp, rasp file.

рван|у́ть, у́, ёшь *pf.* **1** (*дёрнуть резко*) to jerk; to tug (at); **р. кого́-н. за рука́в** to tug s.o. by the sleeve. **2** (*машина*) to start (with a jerk); **вдруг ~у́л ве́тер** suddenly a wind got up. **3** (*coll.*) (*помчаться*) to dash off, shoot off. **4** (*coll.*) (*начать*) to begin; **орке́стр ~у́л марш** the orchestra struck up a march. **5** (*coll.*) (*взорвать*) to explode, blow up; **~у́ло в сосе́днем до́ме** there was an explosion in the next house.

рван|у́ться, у́сь, ёшься *pf.* to rush, dash, dart.

рва́н|ый *adj.* torn; lacerated; **~ые башмаки́** broken shoes; **~ая ра́на** (*med.*) laceration.

рван|ь, и *no pl., f.* **1** (*одежда*) rags. **2** (*coll.*) (*человек*) scoundrel, scamp; (*collect.*) riff-raff.

рвать[1]**, рву, рвёшь,** *past* **рвал, рвала́, рва́ло** *impf.* **1** (*одежду*) to tear (up); to rip; **р. в кло́чки** to tear to pieces; **р. на ча́сти** (*предмет*) to tear to pieces; (*человека*) to overburden; **р. письмо́** to tear up a letter; **р. на себе́ во́лосы** to tear one's hair; **р. и мета́ть** to rant and rave. **2** (*выдёргивать*) to pull out, tear out; **р. зу́бы** to pull out teeth; **р. из рук у кого́-н.** to snatch out of s.o.'s hands; **р. с ко́рнем** to uproot. **3** (*брать*) to pick, pluck; **р. цветы́** to pick flowers. **4** (*взрывать*) to blow up. **5** (*fig.*) (*прекратить*) to break off, sever; **р. отноше́ния с кем-н.** to break off relations with s.o.

рвать[2]**, рвёт,** *past* **рва́ло́** *impf.* (*of* ⇒**вы́рвать**[2]) (*impers.; coll.*) to vomit, throw up, be sick.

рва́|ться[1]**, рвётся,** *past* **~лся, ~ла́сь, ~ло́сь** *impf.* **1** (*об одежде*) to break; to tear; (*об отношениях*) to break up, be severed. **2** (*взрываться*) to burst, explode. **3** (*о сердце*) to break.

рва́|ться[2]**, рвусь, рвёшься,** *past* **~лся, ~ла́сь, ~ло́сь** *impf.* (*стремиться*) to strain (to, at); to be bursting (to); **р. в бой** to be bursting to go into action; **р. в дра́ку** to be spoiling for a fight; **р. в президе́нты** to strive to be president; **р. к вла́сти** to be hungry for power; **р. на свобо́ду** to be dying to be free; **р. с при́вязи** to strain at the leash.

рвач, а́ *m.* (*coll.*) self-seeker, grabber.

рва́ческий *adj.* (*coll.*) self-seeking, grabbing.

рва́честв|о, а *nt.* (*coll.*) self-seeking, grabbing.

рве́ни|е, я *nt.* zeal, enthusiasm.

рво́т|а, ы *f.* **1** (*действие*) vomiting. **2** (*масса*) vomit.

рво́тн|ый *adj.* emetic; **~ое сре́дство** (*also as n.* **~ое, ~ого** *nt.*) emetic.

рде|ть, ю *impf.* (*of sth. red*) to glow.

ре *nt. indecl.* (*mus.*) D.

реабилитацио́нный *adj.* rehabilitation.

реабилита́ци|я, и *f.* rehabilitation.

реабилити́р|овать, ую *impf. and pf.* to rehabilitate.

реабилити́р|оваться, уюсь *impf. and pf.* **1** to vindicate o.s. **2** *pass. of* ⇒**~овать**

реаге́нт, а *m.* (*chem.*) reagent.

реаги́р|овать, ую *impf.* (**на** + *a.*) **1** (*на свет*) to react (to). **2** (*pf.* **от~, про~**) (*на критику*) to react (to), respond (to).

реакти́в, а *m.* (*chem.*) reagent.

реакти́вност|ь, и *f.* (*physiol.*) reactivity.

реакти́вн|ый *adj.* **1** (*chem., phys.*) reactive. **2** (*tech., aeron.*) jet(-propelled); **р. дви́гатель** jet engine; **р. самолёт** jet-propelled aircraft, jet.

реа́ктор, а *m.* (*phys., tech.*) reactor; **р.-размножи́тель** breeder reactor, breeder plant.

реакционе́р, а *m.* (*pol.*) reactionary.

реакцио́н|ный (~ен, ~на) *adj.* (*pol.*) reactionary.

реа́кци|я, и *f.* (*chem., phys., pol.; fig.*) reaction; (*pol., collect.*) reactionaries.

реализа́ци|я, и *f.* (*планов*) realization; (*договора*) implementation; (*товаров*) sale, disposal.

реали́зм, а *m.* (*in var. senses*) realism.

реализо́ван|ный (~, ~а) *adj.* (*товар*) sold.

реализ|ова́ть, у́ю *impf. and pf.* (*планы*) to realize; (*договор*) to implement; (*товар*) to sell, dispose of; **р. це́нные бума́ги** to realize securities.

реализу́емый *adj.* (*товар*) marketable, saleable.

реали́ст, а *m.* realist.

реалисти́ческий *adj.* **1** (*искусство*) realist. **2** (*взгляд*) realistic.

реалисти́ч|ный (~ен, ~на) *adj.* = **~еский** 2

реали́ст|ка, ки *f. of* ⇒**~**

реа́ли|я, и *f.* realia.

реа́льност|ь, и *f.* **1** (*действительность*) reality. **2** (*осуществимость*) practicability, feasibility.

реа́л|ьный (~ен, ~ьна) *adj.* **1** (*действительный*) real; **~ьная действи́тельность** reality.

Р

2 (*осуществимый*) practicable, feasible, workable; **р. план** workable plan. **3** (*практический*) realistic; practical; **вести́ ~ьную поли́тику** to pursue a realistic policy.

реанимацио́нн|ый *adj.*: **~ое отделе́ние** intensive care unit, resuscitation unit.

реанима́ци|я, и *f.* resuscitation.

реаними́р|овать, ую *impf. and pf.* **1** (*человека*) to resuscitate. **2** (*fig.*) to revive.

ребён|ок, ка (*as pl.* **ребя́та, ребя́т** *and* **де́ти, дете́й)** *m.* child; (*младенец*) infant; **грудно́й р.** baby.

рёберный *adj.* (*anat.*) costal.

рebо́рд|а, ы *f.* (*eng.*) flange.

ребри́ст|ый (~, ~а) *adj.* **1** having prominent ribs. **2** (*tech.*) ribbed.

ребр|о́, а́, *pl.* **~̈а, рёбер, ~̈ам** *nt.* **1** (*anat., tech.*) rib; **пересчита́ть кому́-н. ~̈а** (*coll.*) to give s.o. a drubbing. **2** (*край*) edge; **поста́вить ~о́м** to place edgewise, place on its side; **поста́вить вопро́с ~о́м** to put a question point-blank.

ре́бус, а *m.* rebus; (*fig.*) riddle.

ребя́та, ребя́т *pl.* **1** (*sg.* **ребёнок** *m.*) children. **2** (*coll.*) (*парни*) boys, lads.

ребяти́ш|ки, ек, кам *no sg.* (*coll.*) children, kids.

ребя́ческий *adj.* **1** of a child, childish. **2** (*fig.*) (*поступок*) childish, infantile, puerile.

ребя́честв|о, а *nt.* childishness.

ребя́чий *adj.* (*coll.*) (*поступок*) childish.

ребя́ч|иться, усь, ишься *impf.* (*coll.*) to behave like a child, behave childishly.

рёв, а *m.* **1** roar; bellow, howl; **р. ве́тра** the howling of the wind. **2** (*coll.*) (*плач*) howl (*of a child, etc.*); **подня́ть р.** to raise a howl.

рев... *comb. form, abbr. of* ***революцио́нный***

ревальва́ци|я, и *f.* revaluation.

ревальви́р|овать, ую *impf. and pf.* to revalue.

рева́нш, а *m.* revenge; (*sport*) return match.

реванши́зм, а *m.* (*pol.*) revanchism.

реванши́ст, а *m.* (*pol.*) revanchist, revenge-seeker.

реве́н|ный *adj. of* ⇨**~ь**

реве́н|ь, я́ *m.* rhubarb.

рeverа́нс, а *m.* curts(e)y; **сде́лать р.** to curts(e)y; (*fig.*) (*usu. pl.*): **де́лать ~ы кому́-н.** to bow and scrape to s.o.

реверберáци|я, и *f.* (*tech.*) reverberation.

рев|е́ть, у́, ёшь *impf.* **1** to roar; to bellow, howl. **2** (*coll.*) (*плакать*) to howl; **ревмя́ р.** to set up a fearful howl.

ревизиони́зм, а *m.* (*pol.*) revisionism.

ревизиони́ст, а *m.* (*pol.*) revisionist.

ревизио́нн|ый *adj.*: **~ая коми́ссия** inspection commission; auditing commission.

реви́зи|я, и *f.* **1** (*учреждения*) inspection; (*бухгалтерская*) audit. **2** (*взглядов*) revision.

ревиз|ова́ть, у́ю *impf. and pf.* **1** (*pf. also* **об~**) (*учреждение*) to inspect; (*финансы*) to audit. **2** (*взгляды*) to revise.

ревизо́р, а *m.* inspector; (*финансов*) auditor.

ревмати́зм, а *m.* rheumatism; **суставно́й р.** rheumatic fever.

ревма́тик, а *m.* rheumatic.

ревмати́ческий *adj.* rheumatic.

ревмато́идный *adj.* rheumatoid; **р. артри́т** rheumatoid arthritis.

ревмато́лог, а *m.* rheumatologist.

ревматологи́ческий *adj.* rheumatological.

ревматоло́ги|я, и *f.* rheumatology.

рев|мя́ *see* ⇨**~е́ть**

ревни́в|ец, ца *m.* jealous person.

ревни́в|ица, ицы *f. of* ⇨**~ец**

ревни́в|ый (~, ~а) *adj.* jealous.

ревни́тел|ь, я *m.* (+*g.*) enthusiastic supporter (of), zealot.

ревни́тель|ница, ницы *f. of* ⇨**~**

ревн|ова́ть, у́ю *impf.* to be jealous; **р. кого́-н.** (**к**+*d.*) to be jealous because of s.o.'s attachment (to), begrudge s.o.'s attachment (to); **она́ ~ова́ла му́жа к его́ рабо́те** she was jealous of her husband's work.

ре́вност|ный (~ен, ~на) *adj.* zealous, fervent.

ре́вност|ь, и *f.* **1** jealousy. **2** (*obs.*) zeal, fervour (*Br.*), fervor (*US*).

револьве́р, а *m.* revolver.

револьве́р|ный *adj.* **1** *adj. of* ⇨**~**. **2** (*tech.*): **р. стано́к** capstan lathe.

револьве́рщик, а *m.* capstan, lathe operator.

революционе́р, а *m.* revolutionary.

революционе́р|ка, ки *f. of* ⇨**~**

революционизи́р|овать, ую *impf. and pf.* **1** (*людей*) to spread revolutionary ideas (among, in). **2** (*производство*) to revolutionize.

революционизи́р|оваться, уюсь *impf. and pf.* **1** (*о людях*) to become imbued with revolutionary ideas. **2** (*о технике*) to be revolutionized.

революцио́н|ный (~ен, ~на) *adj.* revolutionary.

револю́ци|я, и *f.* (*pol. and fig.*) revolution.

реву́н, а́ *m.* (*zool.; coll.*) howler.

ревю́ *nt. indecl.* revue.

рега́ли|и, й *pl.* (*sg.* **~я, ~и** *f.*) regalia.

рега́т|а, ы *f.* regatta.

ре́гби *nt. indecl.* Rugby (football), rugger.

рег|би́йный *adj. of* ⇨**~̈би**

регби́ст, а *m.* rugby-player.

ре́гги *nt. indecl.* = **рэ́ггей**

регенерати́вный *adj.* (*tech.*) regenerative.

регенера́ци|я, и *f.* (*tech.*) regeneration.

ре́гент, а *m.* **1** regent. **2** (*mus.*) precentor.

ре́гентств|о, а *nt.* regency.

регио́н, а *m.* region, area.

региона́льный *adj.* regional.

реги́стр, а *m.* register.

регистра́тор, а *m.* registrar; (*в поликлинике, в гостинице*) receptionist.

регистрату́р|а, ы *f.* records office, registry; (*в поликлинике*) reception desk.

регистра́ци|я, и *f.* registration; (*в гостинице*) reception desk.

регистри́р|овать, ую *impf. and pf.* (*pf. also* **за~**) to register, record.

регистри́р|оваться, уюсь *impf. and pf.* (*pf. also* **за~**) **1** to register (o.s.). **2** (*пожениться*) to register one's marriage. **3** *pass. of* ⇨**~овать**

регла́мент, а *m.* **1** (*правила*) regulations; standing orders. **2** (*время для речи*) time-limit.

регламента́ци|я, и *f.* regulation.

регламенти́р|овать, ую *impf. and pf.* to regulate.

регла́н, а *m.* raglan (*coat*).

регресси́в|ный (~ен, ~на) *adj.* regressive.

регресси́р|овать, ую *impf.* to regress.

регули́ровани|е, я *nt.* (*движения, цен*) regulation, control.

регули́р|овать, ую *impf.* **1** (*движение, цены*) to regulate; to control. **2** (*pf.* **у~**) (*отношения*) to normalize. **3** (*pf.* **от~**) to adjust; **р. мото́р** to tune an engine.

регулиро́вк|а, и *f.* adjustment.

регулиро́вщик, а *m.* traffic-controller; (*механизмов*) control man, regulator.

регулиро́вщи|ца, цы *f. of* ⇨**~к**

регуля́рност|ь, и *f.* regularity.

регуля́р|ный (~ен, ~на) *adj.* regular; **~ные войска́** regular troops, regulars.

регуля́тор, а *m.* (*tech.*) regulator; (*pl.*) controls (*on TV, etc.*).

ред. *abbr. of* **1** ***реда́ктор*** Ed., Editor. **2** ***реда́кция*** Editorial Office.

ред... *comb. form, abbr. of* ***редакцио́нный***

редакти́ровани|е, я *nt.* editing; **р. те́кста** (*в компьютерах*) word-processing.

редакти́р|овать, ую *impf.* **1** (*pf.* **от~**) (*рукопись*) to edit. **2** (*impf. only*) (*журнал*) to be editor of; to edit. **3** (*pf.* **с~**) (*формулировать*) to word.

реда́ктор, а *m.* **1** editor; **гла́вный р.** editor-in-chief. **2**: **р. те́кстов, те́кстовый р.** (*в компьютерах*) word-processor.

реда́кторский *adj.* editorial.

реда́кторств|о, а *nt.* editorship.

редакцио́нн|ый *adj.* editorial, editing; **~ая колле́гия** editorial board; **~ая коми́ссия** drafting committee; **~ая статья́** editorial.

реда́кци|я, и *f.* **1** (*работники*) editorial staff. **2** (*учреждение*) editorial office. **3** (*действие*) editing; **под ~ей** (+*g.*) edited (by). **4** (*формулировка*) wording. **5** (*вариант текста*) edition.

реде́|ть, ю *impf.* (*of* ⇨**по~**) to thin, thin out; **~ющие во́лосы** thinning hair.

реди́с, а *no pl., m.* radish(es).

реди́ск|а, и *f.* (*coll.*) radish(es).

ре́д|кий (~ок, ~ка́, ~ко) *adj.* **1** (*негустой*) thin, sparse; **~кие во́лосы** thin hair; **~кие зу́бы** widely spaced teeth; **р. лес** sparse wood. **2** (*необычный*) rare; uncommon, unusual; **~кая кни́га** rare book; **~кая красота́** rare beauty; **он — р. подража́тель** he is a rare mimic; **он челове́к ~кой доброты́** he is an unusually kind man; (*далеко не всякий*): **р. челове́к мо́жет э́то де́лать** not many people can do that. **3** (*гость, письмо*) occasional.

ре́дко *adv.* **1** (*не густо*) sparsely; far apart. **2** (*не часто*) rarely, seldom.

редколле́ги|я, и *f.* editorial board.

ре́дкост|ный (~ен, ~на) *adj.* rare; uncommon, exceptional.

ре́дкост|ь, и *f.* **1** (*населения*) thinness, sparseness. **2** (*книги*) rarity; **на р.** uncommonly; **на р. проница́тельный челове́к** a person of rare discernment; **не р., что** not uncommonly; **не р., что он проси́живает ночь за кни́гой** it is not unusual for him to sit up all night reading. **3** (*редкая вещь*) rarity, curiosity.

реду́ктор, а *m.* **1** (*tech.*) reducing gear. **2** (*chem.*) reducing agent.

реду́кци|я, и *f.* reduction.

реду́т, а *m.* (*mil., hist.*) redoubt.

ре́дьк|а, и *f.* radish(es); **надое́ло мне э́то ху́же го́рькой ~и** I am sick and tired of it.

рее́стр, а *m.* list, roll, register.

ре́|же *comp. of* ⇨**~дкий** *and* **~дко**

режи́м, а *m.* **1** (*pol.*) régime. **2** (*распорядок*) routine; procedure; (*med.*) regimen; (*станка*) mode of operation; **шко́льный р.** school routine; **р. пита́ния** diet; **р. безопа́сности** safety measures; **р. рабо́ты** mode of operation; **р. эконо́мии** policy of economy; **рабо́чий р.** operational conditions. **3** (*условия*) conditions; (*tech.*) operating conditions.

режи́мный *adj.* (*предприятие*) secret, classified; (*требования*) routine; (*показатели*) operational.

режиссёр, а *m.* (*в театре*) producer; (*в кино*) director.

режиссёр|ский *adj. of* ⇨**~**

режисси́р|овать, ую *impf.* (*в театре*) to produce, stage; (*в кино*) to direct.

режиссу́р|а, ы *f.* **1** (*деятельность, профессия*) producing, directing; profession of producer. **2** (*трактовка*) production, direction. **3** (*collect.*) (*режиссёры*) producers, directors.

ре́жущ|ий *pres. part. act. of* ⇨**ре́зать** *and adj.* cutting, sharp; **~ая кро́мка** cutting edge, blade; **р. уда́р** slash.

реза́к, а́ *m.* **1** (*нож*) chopper; pole-axe. **2** (*режущая часть машины*) cutter.

ре́зан|ый *adj.* **1** cut; **р. хлеб** cut loaf. **2** (*sport*) slice, sliced; **р. уда́р** slice.

ре́|зать, жу, жешь *impf.* **1** *impf. only* (*хлеб*) to cut; to slice. **2** *impf. only* (*med.*) to operate, open. **3** *impf. only* to cut (= *to have the power of cutting*); **э́ти но́жницы бо́льше не ~жут** these scissors do not cut any longer. **4** (*pf.* **за~**) (*убивать*) to kill; to slaughter; (*ножом*) to knife. **5** *impf. only* (**по** + *d.*) (*делать изображения*) to carve (on), engrave (on). **6** *impf. only* (*причинять боль*) to cut (into); to cause sharp pain; **реме́нь ~зал ему́ плечо́** the strap was cutting into his shoulder; **р. глаза́** to irritate the eyes; **р. слух** to grate upon the ears. **7** (*coll.*) (*говорить прямо*) to speak bluntly; **р. пра́вду в глаза́** to speak the truth boldly. **8** (*pf.* **с~**) (*coll.*) (*студента*) to fail. **9** (*pf.* **с~**) (*sport*) to slice, cut, chop.

ре́|заться, жусь, жешься *impf.* **1** (*pf.* **про~**) (*о зубах*) to come through; **у ребёнка уже́ ~жутся зу́бы** the child is already teething. **2** *impf. only* (*coll.*) (**в** + *a.*) (*играть*) to play furiously.

резв|и́ться, лю́сь, и́шься *impf.* to gambol, romp.

ре́звост|ь, и *f.* **1** playfulness, friskiness. **2** (*лошади*) speed.

ре́зв|ый (~, ~а́, ~о) *adj.* **1** playful, frisky. **2** (*лошадь*) fast.

резед|а́, ы́ *f.* (*bot.*) mignonette.

резе́рв, а *m.* (*mil., etc.*) reserve(s); **име́ть в ~е** to have in reserve; **перевести́ в р.** (*mil.*) to transfer to the reserve.

резерва́ци|я, и *f.* reservation.

резерви́р|овать, ую *impf. and pf.* (*pf. also* **за~**) to reserve, book.

резерви́ст, а *m.* (*mil.*) reservist.

резе́рвн|ый *adj.* (*mil. and fin.*) reserve; (*comput.*) back-up; **~ая ко́пия** back-up copy.

резервуа́р, а *m.* reservoir, tank.

рез|е́ц, ца́ *m.* **1** (*tech.*) cutter; cutting tool; (*скульптора*) chisel. **2** (*зуб*) incisor.

резиде́нт, а *m.* (*dipl., etc.*) **1** (*шпион*) secret agent (*operating in a foreign country*). **2** (*hist.*) (*представитель колониальной державы*) resident.

резиде́нци|я, и *f.* residence.

рези́н|а, ы *f.* (india-)rubber.

рези́нк|а, и *f.* **1** (*ластик*) rubber (*Br.*), eraser (*US*). **2** (*тесёмка*) (piece of) elastic. **3** (*вид вязки*) ribbing; **чулки́ в ~у** ribbed stockings. **4** (*coll.*) (*подвязка*) suspender (*Br.*), garter (*US*). **5** (*жвачка*) chewing-gum.

рези́нов|ый *adj.* rubber; **~ая промы́шленность** rubber industry; **~ая тесьма́, ле́нта** rubber band, elastic band.

рези́стор, а *m.* resistor.

ре́зк|а, и *f.* cutting.

ре́з|кий (~ок, ~ка́, ~ко) *adj.* (*ветер, слова, увеличение, движение, черты лица*) sharp; (*голос, свет, критика*) harsh; (*изменение, манера*) abrupt; **р. за́пах** strong smell.

ре́зкост|ь, и *f.* **1** (*свойство*) sharpness; harshness; abruptness. **2** (*usu. pl.*) sharp words, harsh words; **наговори́ть ~ей** to use harsh words.

резн|о́й *adj.* carved, fretted; **~а́я рабо́та** (*archit.*) carving, fretwork.

резн|я́, и́ *f.* slaughter, butchery, carnage.

резолюти́вн|ый *adj.* containing conclusions, containing a resolution; **в ~ой фо́рме** in the form of a resolution.

резолю́ци|я, и *f.* **1** (*решение*) resolution; **вы́нести, приня́ть ~ю** to pass, carry a resolution. **2** (*на документе*) instructions; **наложи́ть ~ю** to append instructions.

резо́н, а *m.* (*coll.*) reason, sense; **в э́том есть свой р.** there is a reason for (*or* some sense in) this; **нет ~а так поступа́ть** there's no reason to behave like that.

резона́нс, а *m.* **1** (*phys.*) resonance. **2** (*fig.*) echo, response; **выступле́ние име́ло широ́кий обще́ственный р.** the speech evoked a wide public response.

резонёр, а *m.* moralizer.

резонёрств|овать, ую *impf.* to moralize.

резони́р|овать, ую *impf.* (*о звуках*) to resound; (*о зале, о стенах*) to resonate; to be resonant.

резо́н|ный (~ен, ~на) *adj.* reasonable.

результа́т, а *m.* result; outcome; **дать ~ы** to yield results; **в ~е** (*в итоге*) in the end; (+*g.*) (*вследствие*) as a result (of).

результати́вный *adj.* successful.

ре́зус, а *m.* **1** (*обезьяна*) rhesus. **2** (*coll.*) rhesus factor.

ре́зус-фа́ктор, а *m.* rhesus factor.

ре́з|че *comp. of* ⇨**~кий, ~ко**

ре́зчик, а *m.* engraver, carver.

ре́зчи|ца, цы *f. of* ⇨**~к**

рез|ь, и *f.* (*в глазах*) sharp pain; (*в животе*) colic.

резьб|а́, ы *f.* **1** (*действие; рисунок*) carving. **2** (*tech.*) (*винта*) thread.

резюме́ *nt. indecl.* summary, résumé.

резюми́р|овать, ую *impf. and pf.* to sum up, summarize.

ре|й, я *m.* (*naut.*) yard.

рейд[1], а *m.* (*naut.*) road(s), roadstead; **стоя́ть на ~е** to lie at anchor.

рейд[2], а *m.* **1** (*mil.*) raid. **2** (*fig.*) (*милицейский*) raid.

ре́йк|а, и *f.* **1** (*плоская*) lath; (*бордюрная, стыковая*) strip. **2**: **зубча́тая р.** (*tech.*) rack. **3** (*геодезическая*) rod, pole.

Ре́йкьявик, а *m.* Reykjavik.

Рейн, а *m.* the Rhine (*river*).

рейнве́йн, а *m.* hock.

рейс, а *m.* (*автобуса*) trip, run; (*парохода*) voyage, passage; (*самолёта*) flight; **но́мер ~а** flight number; **да́льний р.** long-haul flight; **ча́ртерный р.** charter flight; **пе́рвый р.** maiden voyage.

ре́йсовый *adj.* (*автобус*) regular, operating on a set route.

рейсфе́дер, а *m.* mapping pen.

рейсши́н|а, ы *f.* T-square.

ре́йтинг, а *m.* (*популярность*) rating; (*классификация*) classification.

рейту́з|ы, ~ *no sg.* **1** (*для верховой езды*) (riding-)breeches. **2** (*трикотажные штаны*) leggings.

рейх, а *m.* Reich; **тре́тий р.** Third Reich.

река́, ре́ку́, реки́, *pl.* **ре́ки** *f.* river (*also fig.*); **ли́ться,** *etc.*, **реко́й** (*fig.*) to pour, flood.

ре́квием, а *m.* (*eccl. and mus.*) requiem.

реквизи́р|овать, ую *impf. and pf.* to requisition.

реквизи́т, а *m.* (*theatr.*) props.

реквизи́тор, а *m.* (*theatr.*) property-man.

реквизи́ци|я, и *f.* requisition, commandeering.

рекла́м|а, ы *f.* **1** (*товара, события*) advertising, publicity; **крикли́вая р.** hype. **2** (*объявление, телевизионная*) advertisement.

реклама́ци|я, и *f.* claim for replacement (*of defective goods, etc.*).

реклами́ровани|е, я *nt.* advertising, publicizing, publicity; **кампа́ния по ~ю** advertising/publicity campaign.

реклами́р|овать, ую *impf. and pf.* to advertise, publicize.

реклами́ст, а *m.* advertiser; (*создатель текста*) composer of advertisements, copywriter.

рекла́мный *adj.* (*агентство, кампания*) advertising; (*оповещательный*) publicity.

рекламода́тел|ь, я *m.* advertiser.

рекогносци́р|овать, ую *impf. and pf.* (*mil.*) to reconnoitre.

рекогносциро́вк|а, и *f.* (*mil.*) reconnaissance; reconnoitring.

рекогносциро́вочный *adj.* reconnaissance.

рекоменда́тельн|ый *adj.*: **р. о́тзыв** recommendation, testimonial; **~ое письмо́** letter of recommendation; **р. спи́сок книг** list of recommended books.

рекоменда́ци|я, и *f.* recommendation.

рекоменд|ова́ть, у́ю *impf. and pf.* **1** (*pf. also* **по~** *and* **от~**) (*предложить принять*) to recommend. **2** (*pf. also* **по~**) (+*d.* +*inf.*) (*советовать*) to recommend, advise; **я вам ~у́ю сходи́ть к врачу́** I recommend you to see a doctor. **3** (*pf. also* **от~**) (*obs.*) (*представить*) to introduce.

рекоменд|ова́ться, у́юсь *impf. and pf.* **1** (*pf. also* **от~**) (*при знакомстве*) to introduce o.s. **2** *pass. of* ⇒**~ова́ть; не ~у́ется** it is not recommended; it is not advisable.

реконструи́р|овать, ую *impf. and pf.* to reconstruct.

реконстру́кци|я, и *f.* reconstruction.

реко́рд, а *m.* record; **поби́ть р.** to break a record; **установи́ть р.** to set up, establish a record.

рекорди́ст, а *m.* (*agric.*) champion.

реко́рдный *adj.* record, record-breaking.

рекордсме́н, а *m.* record-holder; record-breaker; **р. ми́ра** world record-holder.

рекордсме́н|ка, ки *f. of* ⇒**~**

ре́крут, а *m.* (*hist.*) recruit (*in the army*).

рекру́т|ский *adj. of* ⇒**~; р. набо́р** recruiting, recruitment (*into the army*).

ректифика́ци|я, и *f.* (*tech.*) rectification.

ректифици́р|овать, ую *impf. and pf.* (*tech.*) to rectify.

ре́ктор, а *m.* principal.

ректора́т, а *m.* principal's office.

реле́ *nt. indecl.* (*tech.*) relay.

религиове́дени|е, я *nt.* religious studies.

религио́зност|ь, и *f.* (*обряда, учения*) religiosity; (*набожность*) piety, piousness.

религио́з|ный *adj.* **1** of religion, religious; **р. обря́д** religious ceremony; **~ное уче́ние** religious instruction. **2** (**~ен, ~на**) (*человек*) religious; pious.

рели́ги|я, и *f.* religion.

рели́кви|я, и *f.* relic; (*семейная*) heirloom.

рели́кт, а *m.* relic; survival.

рели́кт|овый *adj. of* ⇒**~;** surviving.

релье́ф, а *m.* (*art and geol.*) relief.

релье́фно *adv.* in relief; (*выраженный*) clearly; **р.-то́чечный шрифт** Braille (script).

релье́ф|ный (~ен, ~на) *adj.* relief, raised; (*ткань, обои*) embossed; **~ная ка́рта** relief map; (*fig.*) (*отчётливый*) clear-cut.

рельс, а, *m.* rail; **сойти́ с ~́ов** to be derailed, go off the rails; **поста́вить на ~́ы** (*fig.*) to launch; **на ~́ы** (+*g.*) towards; **перейти́ на ~́ы приватиза́ции** to move towards privatization.

ре́льс|овый *adj. of* ⇒**~; р. путь** railway, track.

релятиви́зм, а *m.* (*phil.*) relativism.

рема́рк|а, и *f.* **1** (*theatr.*) stage direction. **2** (*obs.*) (*отметка*) remark, note.

ремённ|ый *adj.* belt; **~ая переда́ча** (*tech.*) belt-drive.

рем|е́нь, ня́ *m.* (*пояс*) belt; (*для багажа*) strap; **р. безопа́сности** seat belt; **привязно́й р.** seat-belt; **приводно́й р.** drive belt.

ремёсленник, а *m.* **1** artisan, craftsman. **2** (*fig., pej.*) hack. **3** (*ученик ремесленного училища*) pupil of vocational school.

ремёсленни|ца, цы *f. of* ⇒**~к**

ремёсленнический *adj.* (*pej.*) hack-working, mechanical.

ремёсленничеств|о, а *nt.* **1** workmanship, craftsmanship. **2** (*fig., pej.*) hack-work.

ремёсленн|ый *adj.* **1** handicraft; trade; **~ое учи́лище** vocational school. **2** (*fig., pej.*) mechanical.

ремес|ло́, ла́, *pl.* **~́ла, ~́ел** *nt.* **1** handicraft; trade. **2** (*coll.*) (*профессия*) profession, trade.

ремеш|о́к, ка́ *m.* (small) strap.

реми́з, а *m.* (*cards*) fine; **поста́вить р.** to pay a fine.

ре́микс, а *m.* remix (*in sound recording*); **сде́лать р.** (+*g.*) to remix (*a recording*).

ремилитариза́ци|я, ую *f.* remilitarization.

ремилитаризи́р|овать, ую *impf. and pf.* to remilitarize.

ремилитариз|ова́ть, у́ю *impf. and pf.* to remilitarize.

реминисце́нци|я, и *f.* reminiscence; (*отголосок*) echo.

реми́сси|я, и *f.* remission.

ремо́нт, а *m.* repair(s); maintenance; (*здания*) refurbishment; (*мелкий*) redecoration; **капита́льный р.** overhaul, refit, major refurbishment, repairs; **космети́ческий р.** face-lift; **теку́щий р.** maintenance, routine repairs; **закры́т на р.** closed for repairs; **в ~е** under repair; **р. о́буви** shoe repair.

ремонти́р|овать, ую *impf. and pf.* (*pf. also* **от~**) (*чинить*) to repair; (*квартиру*) to refurbish, redecorate.

ремо́нтник, а *m.* repair man.

ремо́нт|ный *adj. of* ⇒**~; ~ная мастерска́я** repair shop; **р. рабо́чий** repair man; **~ные рабо́ты** repair/maintenance work.

ренега́т, а *m.* renegade.

ренега́тств|о, а *nt.* desertion; apostasy.

Ренесса́нс, а *m.* renaissance.

ренкло́д, а *m.* greengage.

renова́ци|я, и *f.* renovation.

ре́нт|а, ы *f.* **1** rent; **земе́льная р.** ground-rent. **2** (*проценты*) income (*from investments, etc.*); **ежего́дная р.** annuity.

рента́бельност|ь, и *f.* profitability.

рента́бел|ьный (~ен, ~ьна) *adj.* profitable, paying.

рентге́н, а *m.* (*просвечивание*) X-ray treatment, X-rays.

рентгениза́ци|я, и *f.* X-raying.

рентгенизи́р|овать, ую *impf. and pf.* to X-ray.

рентге́нов *adj.*: **~ы лучи́** X-rays.

рентге́новск|ий *adj.* X-ray; **~ие лучи́** X-rays; **р. сни́мок** X-ray photograph.

рентгеногра́мм|а, ы *f.* X-ray (photograph).

рентгеногра́фи|я, и *f.* radiography.

рентгено́лог, а *m.* radiologist.

рентгеноло́ги|я, и *f.* radiology.

рентгенотерапи́|я, и *f.* X-ray therapy.

Реомю́р, а *m.* Réaumur; **10° по ~у** 10° Réaumur.

реорганиза́ци|я, и *f.* reorganization.

реорганиз|ова́ть, у́ю *impf. and pf.* to reorganize.

реоста́т, а *m.* (*elec.*) rheostat.

ре́п|а, ы *f.* turnip; **дешёвле па́реной ~ы** (*coll.*) dirt-cheap; **про́ще па́реной ~ы** (*coll.*) very easy, a piece of cake.

репар|ацио́нный *adj. of* ⇒**~а́ция**

репара́ци|я, и *f.* reparation.

репатриа́нт, а *m.* repatriate.
репатриа́нт|ка, ки *f. of* ⇒~
репатриа́ци|я, и *f.* repatriation.
репатрии́р|овать, ую *impf. and pf.* to repatriate.
реп|е́й, ья́ *m.* (*coll.*) = **репе́йник**
репе́йник, а *m.* **1** (*bot.*) (*растение*) burdock; (*соцветие*) burdock flower, burr. **2** (*липучка*) Velcro.
репелле́нт, а *m.* insect repellent.
репе́р, а *m.* (*surveying*) bench-mark.
репертуа́р, а *m.* (*theatr. and fig.*) repertoire; **он в своём ~е** he is in his element.
репети́р|овать, ую *impf.* **1** (*pf.* **от~, про~,** *and* **с~**) (*theatr.*) to rehearse. **2** *impf. only* (*ученика*) to coach.
репети́тор, а *m.* tutor, coach.
репетицио́нный *adj.* rehearsal.
репети́ци|я, и *f.* rehearsal; **генера́льная р.** dress rehearsal.
ре́плик|а, и *f.* **1** (*возражение*) retort; (*ответ*) reply; (*враждебная*) heckling comment. **2** (*theatr.*) cue; **пода́ть ~у** to give the cue.
репол́ов, а *m.* (*zool.*) linnet.
репорта́ж, а *m.* (*деятельность*) reporting; (*сообщение*) report; **р. с ме́ста собы́тий** on-the-spot report.
репортёр, а *m.* reporter.
репресси́в|ный (~ен, ~на) *adj.* repressive.
репресси́р|овать, ую *impf. and pf.* to subject to repression.
репре́сси|я, и *f.* (*usu. pl.*) punitive measure.
репри́нт, а *m.* reprint.
репри́нтн|ый *adj.*: **~ое изда́ние** reprint.
репрогра́фи|я, и *f.* reprography.
репроду́ктор, а *m.* loud-speaker.
репроду́кци|я, и *f.* reproduction (*of a picture, etc.*).
репс, а *m.* (*text.*) rep(p), reps.
репти́ли|я, и *f.* **1** reptile. **2** (*pej.*) (*о человеке*) grovelling person.
репута́ци|я, и *f.* reputation; **по́льзоваться хоро́шей ~ей** to have a good reputation; **по́льзоваться ~ей** (+*g.*) to have a reputation (for); **заслужи́ть ~ю** to earn a reputation.
ре́пчатый *adj.* turnip-shaped; **р. лук** (common) onion.
ресни́ц|а, ы *f.* eyelash.
ресни́чк|а, и *f.* **1** *dim. of* ⇒**ресни́ца. 2** *pl.* (*biol.*) cilia.
ресни́чный *adj.* (*biol.*) ciliary.
респекта́бельност|ь, и *f.* respectability.
респекта́бел|ьный (~ен, ~ьна) *adj.* respectable.
респира́тор, а *m.* respirator.
респонде́нт, а *m.* respondent.
респу́блик|а, и *f.* republic.
республика́н|ец, ца *m.* republican.
республика́н|ка, ки *f. of* ⇒**~ец**
республика́нский *adj.* **1** republican. **2** (*hist.*) of (situated in, *etc.*) a constituent republic of the former USSR.
рессо́р|а, ы *f.* spring (*of vehicle*).
рессо́рный *adj.* spring; (*снабжённый рессорами*) sprung.
реставра́тор, а *m.* restorer.
реставра́ци|я, и *f.* restoration.
реставри́р|овать, ую *impf. and pf.* to restore.
рестора́н, а *m.* restaurant; **р. бы́строго обслу́живания** fast-food restaurant.
ресу́рс, а *m.* (*usu. pl.*) resource; **де́нежные ~ы** financial resources; **после́дний р.** the last resort; **приро́дные ~ы** natural resources.
рети́вост|ь, и *f.* zeal, eagerness.
рети́в|ый (~, ~а) *adj.* (*coll.*) zealous, eager.
рети́н|а, ы *f.* (*anat.*) retina.
ретир|ова́ться, у́юсь *impf. and pf.* (*coll.*) to retire, withdraw.
рето́рт|а, ы *f.* (*chem.*) retort.
ретрогра́д, а *m.* reactionary.
ретрогра́д|ный (~ен, ~на) *adj.* reactionary.
ретроспекти́в|а, ы *f.* retrospective.
ретроспекти́в|ный (~ен, ~на) *adj.* retrospective; **р. взгляд** backward glance.
ретушёр, а *m.* retoucher.
ретуши́р|овать, ую *impf. and pf.* (*pf. also* **от~**) to retouch.
ре́туш|ь, и *f.* retouching.
рефера́т, а *m.* **1** (*книги, статьи*) synopsis, abstract. **2** (*доклад*) paper, essay.
рефере́ндум, а *m.* referendum.
рефере́нт, а *m.* **1** (*диссертации, книги*) reader, reviewer. **2** (*консультант*) adviser.
рефери́ *m. indecl.* referee.
рефери́р|овать, ую *impf. and pf.* to abstract, summarize.
рефле́кс, а *m.* reflex; **усло́вный р., безусло́вный р.** conditioned, unconditioned reflex.
рефле́кси|я, и *f.* reflection; introspection.
рефлексотерапе́вт, а *m.* reflexologist.
рефлексотерапи́|я, и *f.* reflexology.
рефлекти́в|ный (~ен, ~на) *adj.* (*physiol.*) reflex.
рефле́ктор, а *m.* reflector.
рефле́кторный *adj.* (*physiol., astron.*) reflex.
рефо́рм|а, ы *f.* reform; **проводи́ть ~ы** to implement reforms.
реформа́тор, а *m.* reformer.
реформа́торский *adj.* reformative, reformatory.
реформа́тск|ий *adj. of* ⇒**Реформа́ция; ~ая це́рковь** Reformed Church.
Реформа́ци|я, и *f.* (*hist.*) Reformation.
реформи́р|овать, ую *impf. and pf.* to reform.
реформи́ст, а *m.* (*pol.*) reformist.
рефра́ктор, а *m.* (*phys., astron.*) refractor.
рефра́кци|я, и *f.* (*phys., astron.*) refraction.
рефре́н, а *m.* (*liter.*) refrain.
рефрижера́тор, а *m.* (*грузовик*) refrigerated lorry (*Br.*), truck (*US*); (*судно*) refrigerated ship.
рехн|у́ться, у́сь, ёшься *pf.* (*coll.*) to go mad, go off one's head.
рецензе́нт, а *m.* reviewer.
рецензи́р|овать, ую *impf.* (*of* ⇒**про~**) to review.
реце́нзи|я, и *f.* review; **р. на кни́гу, р. о кни́ге** book review.
реце́пт, а *m.* **1** (*med.*) prescription; **вы́писать р.** to write a prescription. **2** (*cul.*) recipe.
рециди́в, а *m.* **1** (*med., etc.*) recurrence; relapse. **2** (*leg.*) repetition (*of offence*).
рецидиви́зм, а *m.* (*leg.*) recidivism.
рецидиви́ст, а *m.* (*leg.*) recidivist.
рецидиви́ст|ка, ки *f. of* ⇒~
рециркули́р|овать, ую *impf. and pf.* to recycle.
рециркуля́ци|я, и *f.* recycling.
речево́й *adj.* speech; vocal; **р. аппара́т** vocal organs.
рече́ни|е, я *nt.* (*obs.*) set phrase; saying.
речи́ст|ый (~, ~а) *adj.* voluble, garrulous.
речитати́в, а *m.* (*mus.*) recitative.
ре́чк|а, и *f.* small river; rivulet.
речн|о́й *adj.* river; fluvial; **~ы́е пути́ сообще́ния** inland waterways; **~о́е судохо́дство** river navigation; **р. трамва́й** river bus, water bus.
реч|ь, и *f.* **1** (*способность*) speech; **дар ~и** faculty of speech, gift of speech. **2** (*произношение*) enunciation, speech, way of speaking; **горта́нная р.** guttural speech; **отчётливая р.** distinct enunciation. **3** (*стиль языка*) language; **делова́я р.** business language. **4** (*разговор*) conversation, talk; **о чём была́ р.?** what were they talking about?, what was it all about?; **р. идёт о том, где/как/когда́** *etc.* the question is where/how/when *etc.*; **не об э́том р.** that is not the point; **об э́том не мо́жет быть и ~и** that is out of the question; **завести́ р.** (**о**+*p.*) to lead, turn the conversation (towards); **о чём р.!** (*coll.*) of course!, sure! **5** (*выступление*) speech; address; **вступи́тельная р.** opening address; **торже́ственная р.** oration; **вы́ступить с ~ью** to make a speech. **6** (*gram.*) speech; **пряма́я р.** direct speech; **ко́свенная р.** indirect speech; **ча́сти ~и** parts of speech.
реш|а́ть(ся), а́ю(сь) *impf. of* ⇒**~и́ть(ся)**
реша́|ющий *pres. part. act. of* ⇒**~ть** *and adj.* decisive, deciding; **р. го́лос** casting vote; **р. фа́ктор** decisive factor.
реше́ни|е, я *nt.* **1** decision; **прийти́ к ~ю** to come to a decision; **приня́ть р.** to take a decision, make up one's mind. **2** (*суда, дирекции*) judg(e)ment; decision, verdict; **вы́нести р.** to deliver a judg(e)ment; to pass a resolution;

отмени́ть р. to revoke a decision; (*leg.*) to quash a sentence. **3** (*задачи*) solving; (*к задаче*) solution; answer; (*проблемы*) solution.

решётк|а, и *f.* **1** grating; (*оконная*) grille, railing; (*ограда*) railings; (*садовая*) trellis; (*перед камином*) fireguard; (*радиатора*) grille; **за ~ой** (*fig., coll.*) behind bars (= *in prison*); **посади́ть за ~у** to put behind bars. **2** (*в камине*) (fire-)grate. **3** (*в духовке*) rack, shelf. **4** (*obs.*) (*решка*) tail (*of coin*). **5**: **кристалли́ческая р.** crystal lattice.

решет|о́, а́, *pl.* **~́а** *nt.* sieve; **голова́ как р.** a head like a sieve; **чудеса́ в ~е́!** (*coll.*) what a remarkable thing!

решётчатый (*and* **решётчатый)** *adj.* lattice, latticed.

реши́мост|ь, и *f.* resolution, resoluteness.

реши́тельно *adv.* **1** (*твёрдо*) resolutely. **2** (*категорически*) decidedly, definitely; **р. отказа́ться** to refuse flatly; **я р. про́тив э́того прое́кта** I am definitely opposed to this scheme. **3** (*абсолютно*) absolutely; **э́то мне р. всё равно́** it makes absolutely no difference to me.

реши́тельност|ь, и *f.* resolution, determination.

реши́тел|ьный (~ен, ~ьна) *adj.* **1** (*твёрдый*) resolute, determined; decided; firm; **р. вид** resolute air; **~ьные ме́ры** strong measures, drastic measures; **р. тон** firm tone. **2** (*решающий*) decisive; crucial; **р. моме́нт** crucial point; **~ьная побе́да** sweeping victory. **3** (*coll.*) (*явный*) absolute, blatant; **р. дура́к** absolute fool.

реш|и́ть, у́, и́шь *pf.* (*of* **⇒~а́ть**) **1** (+*inf. or* +*a.*) to decide; **он ~и́л уе́хать** he decided to go away; **р. де́ло в чью-н. по́льзу** to decide a case in s.o.'s favour; **р. чью-н. у́часть** to decide s.o.'s fate. **2** (*найти ответ*) to solve; to settle; **р. зада́чу** to solve a problem; to accomplish a task.

реш|и́ться, у́сь, и́шься *pf.* (*of* **⇒~а́ться**) **1** (**на**+*a. or* +*inf.*) to make up one's mind (to), decide (to), resolve (to); to bring o.s. (to). **2** (*получить решение*) to be resolved; **спор ~и́лся в его́ по́льзу** the argument was resolved in his favour (*Br.*), favor (*US*).

ре́шк|а, и *f.* (*coll.*) tail (*of coin*); **орёл и́ли р.?** heads or tails?

ре́|я, и *f.* = **рей**

ре́|ять, ю, ешь *impf.* **1** (*о птице*) to soar, hover. **2** (*о флаге*) to flutter.

ржаве́|ть, ет *impf.* (*of* **⇒за~** *and* **по~**) to rust.

ржа́вост|ь, и *f.* rustiness.

ржа́вчин|а, ы *f.* **1** rust. **2** (*bot.*) mildew.

ржа́вый *adj.* rusty.

ржа́ни|е, я *nt.* neighing.

ржа́нк|а, и *f.* (*zool.*) plover.

ржано́й *adj.* rye.

рж|ать, у, ёшь *impf.* to neigh; (*coll.*) laugh loudly.

РИА *f. indecl.* (*abbr. of* ***Российское информационное агентство***) Russian News Agency.

Ривье́р|а, ы *f.* the Riviera.

Ри́г|а, и *f.* Riga.

ри́г|а, и *f.* threshing barn.

ридикю́л|ь, я *m.* (*obs.*) handbag.

ри́з|а, ы *f.* **1** (*eccl.*) chasuble. **2** (*на иконах*) riza. **3** (*obs., poet.*) (*платье*) garments.

ри́зниц|а, ы *f.* (*eccl.*) vestry, sacristy.

рикоше́т, а *m.* ricochet, rebound; **~ом** on the rebound (*also fig.*).

рикошети́р|овать, ую *impf.* to ricochet.

ри́кш|а, и *f.* rickshaw.

Рим, а *m.* Rome.

ри́млян|ин, ина, *pl.* **~е, ~** *m.* Roman.

ри́млян|ка, ки *f. of* **⇒~ин**

ри́мск|ий *adj.* Roman; **Па́па р.** the Pope; **р. нос** roman nose; **~ое пра́во** Roman law; **~ая свеча́** roman candle; **~ие ци́фры** roman numerals.

ринг, а *m.* (*sport*) ring.

ри́н|уться, усь, ешься *pf.* to dash, dart.

Ри́о-де-Жане́йро *m. indecl.* Rio de Janeiro.

рис, а *m.* rice.

рис. (*abbr. of* ***рису́нок***) fig., figure.

риск, а *m.* risk; **на свой (страх и) р.** at one's own risk, at one's peril; **с ~́ом (для**+*g.*) at the risk (of); **пойти́ на р.** to run risks, take chances; **р. — благоро́дное де́ло** (*prov.*) nothing venture, nothing gain.

рискн|у́ть, у́, ёшь *pf.* (+*inf.*) to take the risk (of), venture (to).

риско́ванност|ь, и *f.* riskiness.

риско́ван|ный (~, ~на) *adj.* **1** risky; **~ное предприя́тие** risky venture. **2** (*шутка, тема*) risqué.

риск|ова́ть, у́ю *impf.* **1** to run risks, take chances. **2** (+*i.*) to risk; (+*inf.*) to risk, take the risk (of); **р. голово́й** to risk one's neck; **ниче́м не р.** to run no risk; **р. опозда́ть на по́езд** to risk missing the train.

рисова́льный *adj.* drawing.

рисова́льщик, а *m.* graphic artist; **я о́чень плохо́й р.** I am no good at drawing.

рисова́ни|е, я *nt.* (*карандашом*) drawing; (*красками*) painting.

рис|ова́ть, у́ю *impf.* (*of* **⇒на~**) **1** (*карандашом*) to draw; (*красками*) to paint; **р. с нату́ры** to draw, paint from life. **2** (*fig.*) (*описывать*) to depict, paint, portray.

рис|ова́ться, у́юсь *impf.* **1** (*виднеться*) to be silhouetted; to appear. **2** (*pej.*) (*красоваться*) to pose, show off.

рисо́вк|а, и *f.* (*pej.*) posing, showing off.

ри́сов|ый *adj.* rice; **~ая ка́ша** rice pudding.

риста́лищ|е, а *nt.* (*obs.*) stadium; hippodrome.

рису́н|ок, ка *m.* (*изображение*) drawing; (*в книге*) illustration; (*в научной статье*) figure; (*на ткани*) pattern, design; (*контур*) outline; **акваре́льный р.** water-colour (*Br.*), water-color (*US*).

ритм, а *m.* (*музыки, сердца*) rhythm; (*работы, жизни*) pace.

ри́тмик|а, и *f.* **1** (*liter.*) rhythm system. **2** (*движения*) eurhythmics.

ритми́ческ|ий *adj.* rhythmic(al); **~ая гимна́стика** eurhythmics.

ритми́чност|ь, и *f.* rhythm.

ритми́ч|ный (~ен, ~на) *adj.* rhythmic(al); **~ная рабо́та** smooth functioning.

рито́рик|а, и *f.* rhetoric.

ритори́ческий *adj.* rhetorical.

ритуа́л, а *m.* ritual.

ритуа́льный *adj.* ritual.

риф, а *m.* reef; **кора́лловый р.** coral reef.

рифлён|ый *adj.* (*tech.*) grooved, fluted, corrugated; **~ое желе́зо** corrugated iron.

ри́фм|а, ы *f.* rhyme.

рифм|ова́ть, у́ю *impf.* (*of* **⇒с~**) **1** *no pf.* (*рифмоваться*) to rhyme. **2** (*слова*) to select in order to make rhyme.

рифм|ова́ться, у́ется *impf.* to rhyme.

рифмо́вк|а, и *f.* rhyming, rhyme system.

рифмоплёт, а *m.* (*pej.*) rhymer, rhymester.

рифф, а *m.* (*mus.*) riff.

рия́л, а *m.* riyal (*Saudi Arabian currency unit*).

р-н (*abbr. of* ***райо́н***) rayon, raion.

ро́б|а, ы *f.* working clothes, overalls.

ро́ббер, а *m.* (*cards*) rubber.

робе́|ть, ю *impf.* (*of* **⇒о~**) to be shy, timid; (*пугаться*) to be afraid, to quail.

ро́б|кий (~ок, ~ка́, ~ко) *adj.* timid, shy.

ро́бост|ь, и *f.* timidity, shyness.

ро́бот, а *m.* robot.

роботиза́ци|я, и *f.* robotization.

роботизи́р|овать, ую *impf. and pf.* to robotize.

робототе́хник|а, и *f.* robotics.

ро́бче *comp. of* **⇒ро́бкий**

ров, рва, о рве, во рву *m.* ditch; **крепостно́й р.** moat.

рове́сник, а *m.* person of the same age; **мы с ним ~и** we are of the same age; **р. револю́ции** person born in the same year as the revolution.

рове́сни|ца, цы *f. of* **⇒~к**

ро́вно *adv.* **1** (*равномерно*) regularly, evenly; **он к ней не р. ды́шит** (*coll.*) he fancies her. **2** (*точно*) exactly; **р. пять рубле́й** five roubles exactly; (*о времени*) sharp; **р. в час** at one o'clock sharp. **3** (*coll.*) (*совсем*) absolutely; **она́ р. ничего́ не зна́ет** she knows absolutely nothing. **4** (*as conj.*) (*coll.*) (*как будто, словно*) exactly like, just like.

ро́вност|ь, и *f.* (*пульса, дыхания*) regularity; (*дороги*) evenness; (*линии*) straightness; (*характера*) stability.

ро́в|ный (~ен, ~на́, ~но) *adj.* **1** (*дорога, поверхность*) flat, even, level; (*линия*) straight. **2** (*пульс*) regular; (*шаг, голос*) even; (*характер*) equable, stable. **3** (*одинаковый*) equal; **р. счёт** even account, exact money; **для ~ного счёта** to make it even; to bring to a round figure; **~ным счётом** exactly; **~ным счётом ничего́** (*coll.*) absolutely nothing.

ро́вня, ро́вни *c.g.* equal, match; **он ей не р.** he is not her equal, he is no match for her.

ровня́|ть, ю *impf.* (*of* ⇒**с~**) to even, level; **сровня́ть с землёй** to raze to the ground.

рог, а, *pl.* **~а́, ~о́в** *m.* **1** horn; (*олений*) antler; **р. изоби́лия** horn of plenty, cornucopia; **брать быка́ за ~а́** (*coll.*) to take the bull by the horns; **наста́вить ~а́** (+*d.*; *coll.*) to cuckold; **согну́ть в бара́ний р.** (*coll.*) to make knuckle under. **2** (*музыкальный инструмент*) bugle, horn; **альпи́йский р.** alpenhorn; **охо́тничий р.** hunting-horn.

рога́лик, а *m.* crescent-shaped roll, croissant.

рога́ст|ый (~, ~а) *adj.* (*coll.*) large-horned.

рога́тин|а, ы *f.* bear-spear.

рога́тк|а, и *f.* **1** (*на дороге*) roadblock; (*fig.*) obstacle; **ста́вить кому́-н. ~и** to put obstacles in s.o.'s way. **2** (*для стрельбы*) slingshot, catapult (*Br.*).

рога́т|ый (~, ~а) *adj.* **1** horned; **кру́пный р. скот** cattle; **ме́лкий р. скот** small cattle, sheep and goats. **2** (*coll.*) (*муж*) cuckolded.

рога́ч, а́ *m.* **1** (*олень*) stag. **2** (*жук*) stag-beetle.

рогови́ц|а, ы *f.* (*anat.*) cornea.

рогов|о́й *adj.* horn; horny; **~ы́е очки́** horn-rimmed spectacles; **~а́я оболо́чка гла́за** (*anat.*) cornea.

рого́ж|а, и *f.* bast, matting.

рого́з, а *m.* (*bot.*) reed mace.

рогоно́с|ец, ца *m.* (*coll.*, *joc.*) cuckold.

род, а, о ~е, в ~у́, *pl.* **~ы́, ~о́в** *m.* **1** family, kin, clan; **челове́ческий р.** mankind, human race; **без ~у, без пле́мени** without kith or kin **2** (*происхождение*) birth, origin, stock; (*поколение*) generation; **он ~ом из Ирла́ндии** he is an Irishman by birth, a native of Ireland; **из ~а в р.** from generation to generation; **ему́ на ~у́ напи́сано** (+*inf.*) he was preordained (to); **ей де́сять лет о́т ~у** she is ten years of age. **3** (*biol.*) genus. **4** (*сорт*) sort, kind; **р. во́йск** arm of the service; **вся́кого ~а** of all kinds, all kind of; **тако́го ~а** of such a kind, such; **в э́том ~е** of this sort; **что-то в э́том ~е** sth. of the kind; sth. to that effect; **в не́котором ~е** in some sort, to some extent; **в своём ~е** in one's own way; **своего́ ~а** a kind of; in one's own way; **он своего́ ~а ге́ний** he is a genius in his own way. **5** (*gram.*) gender; **же́нский р.** feminine (gender); **мужско́й р.** masculine (gender); **сре́дний р.** neuter (gender).

роддо́м, а *m.* (*abbr. of* **роди́льный дом**) maternity hospital.

родео́ *nt. indecl.* rodeo.

роди́льниц|а, ы *f.* woman recently confined.

роди́льн|ый *adj.*: **р. дом** maternity hospital; **~ое отделе́ние** maternity unit.

роди́м|ый *adj.* **1** (*город*) native. **2**: **~ое пятно́** birth-mark.

ро́дин|а, ы *f.* native land; home, homeland; **верну́ться на ~у** to return home; **тоска́ по ~е** home-sickness; **Испа́ния — р. фламе́нко** Spain is the home of the flamenco.

ро́динк|а, и *f.* birth-mark.

роди́тел|и, ей *no sg.* parents.

роди́тел|ь, я *m.* (*coll.*) father.

роди́тельниц|а, ы *f.* (*coll.*) mother.

роди́тельн|ый *adj.* (*gram.*) genitive; **в ~ом падеже́** in the genitive case.

роди́тельский *adj.* parental, parents'; paternal; **р. комите́т** parents' committee.

ро|ди́ть, жу́, ди́шь, *past* **~ди́л, ~ди́ла́, ~ди́ло** *impf. and pf.* **1** (*impf. also* **рожа́ть**) to bear, give birth (to); **в чём мать ~ди́ла** (*joc.*) in one's birthday suit. **2** (*impf. also* **рожда́ть**) (*fig.*) to give birth, rise (to); (*о почве*) to yield.

ро|ди́ться, жу́сь, ди́шься, *past* **~ди́лся́, ~ди́ла́сь, ~ди́ло́сь** *impf. and pf.* **1** (*impf. also* **рожда́ться**) to be born; **р. преподава́телем** to be a born teacher; (**у**+*g.*): **у неё ~ди́лась дочь** she had a daughter; **от пе́рвой жены́ у него́ ~ди́лся сын** he had a son by his first wife. **2** (*impf. also* **рожда́ться**) (*fig.*) (*мысль, план, город*) to arise, come into being. **3** (*произрастать*) to spring up, thrive; **кукуру́за у нас ~дила́сь хорошо́** we had a good maize-crop.

ро́дич, а *m.* (*coll.*) relation, relative.

родни́к, а́ *m.* spring; (*fig.*) (*сил, вдохновения*) source.

роднико́в|ый *adj. of* ⇒**родни́к**; **~ая вода́** spring water.

родн|и́ть, ю́, и́шь *impf.* (*of* ⇒**по~**) to make related, link.

родн|и́ться, ю́сь, и́шься *impf.* (*of* ⇒**по~**) (**с**+*i.*) to become related (with).

роднич|о́к[1]**, ка́** *m. dim. of* ⇒**родни́к**

роднич|о́к[2]**, ка́** *m.* (*anat.*) fontanel(le).

родн|о́й *adj.* **1** (*мать, брат, дядя*) related by blood; natural; **р. брат** one's brother (*opp. cousin, etc.*); *as n.* **~ы́е, ~ы́х** relations, relatives. **2** (*отечественный*) native; home; **~а́я страна́, ~а́я земля́** native land; **р. го́род** home town; **р. дом** one's own home; **р. язы́к** mother tongue. **3** (*в обращении*) (my) dear.

родн|я́, и́ *f.* **1** (*collect.*) (*родственники*) relatives, kinsfolk. **2** (*coll.*) (*родственник*) relative.

родови́тост|ь, и *f.* noble birth; high birth.

родови́т|ый (~, ~а) *adj.* of noble birth; high-born.

родов|о́й[1] *adj.* **1** (*ethnol.*) clan. **2** (*наследственный*) ancestral; **~о́е име́ние, ~о́е иму́щество** patrimony. **3** (*biol.*) generic. **4** (*gram.*) gender.

родов|о́й[2] *adj.* birth, labour (*Br.*), labor (*US*); **~ы́е схва́тки** contractions.

родовспомога́тельн|ый *adj.*: **~ое учрежде́ние** maternity home.

родовспоможе́ни|е, я *nt.* maternity care.

рододе́ндрон, а *m.* (*bot.*) rhododendron.

родонача́льник, а *m.* ancestor, forefather; (*fig.*) (*литературы*) father.

Ро́дос, а *m.* Rhodes.

родосло́вн|ая, ой *f.* genealogy, pedigree.

родосло́вн|ый *adj.* genealogical; **~ое де́рево** family tree.

ро́дственник, а *m.* relation, relative; **ближа́йший р.** next of kin; **бли́зкий р.** close relative; **да́льний р.** distant relative.

ро́дственни|ца, цы *f. of* ⇒**~к**

ро́дственност|ь, и *f.* **1** (*языков, народов, культур*) connection, tie. **2** (*характеров*) familiarity, intimacy.

ро́дствен|ный (~, ~на) *adj.* **1** kindred, related; **~ные отноше́ния** blood relations; **~ные свя́зи** kinship ties. **2** (*близкий*) kindred, related, allied; **~ные наро́ды** related peoples; **~ные языки́** cognate languages. **3** (*свойственный родственникам*) familiar, intimate.

родств|о́, а́ *nt.* **1** relationship, kinship (*also fig.*); **кро́вное р.** blood tie, consanguinity; **быть в ~е́** (**с**+*i.*) to be related (to). **2** (*collect., obs.*) (*родственники*) relations, relatives.

ро́д|ы, ов *no sg.* birth; childbirth; **в ~ах** in labour (*Br.*), labor (*US*); **стимуля́ция ~ов** induction (of labour).

ро́ж|а[1]**, и** *f.* (*coll.*) mug (=*face*); **ко́рчить, стро́ить ~и** to make faces.

ро́ж|а[2]**, и** *f.* (*med.*) erysipelas.

рожа́|ть, ю *impf. of* ⇒**роди́ть**

рожда́емост|ь, и *f.* birth-rate.

рожда́|ть(ся), ю(сь) *impf. of* ⇒**роди́ть(ся)**

рожде́ни|е, я *nt.* birth; **день ~я** birthday; **ме́сто ~я** birth-place; **глухо́й от ~я** deaf from birth; **по ~ю** by birth.

рождённый *p.p.p. of* ⇒**роди́ть**; (+*inf.*) born (to), destined (to).

рожде́ственск|ий *adj.* Christmas; **р. дед** Father Christmas, Santa Claus; **р. день** Christmas Day; **~ая ёлка** Christmas-tree; **р. обе́д** Christmas dinner; **~ое песнопе́ние** carol singing; **~ая пе́сня** carol; **р. пиро́г** Christmas cake; **р. пост** Advent; **р. пу́динг** Christmas pudding; **р. соче́льник** Christmas Eve.

Рождеств|о́, а́ *nt.* (*праздник*) Christmas; **на Р.** at Christmas(-time); **под Р.** on Christmas Eve; (*само рождение*) Nativity.

роже́ниц|а, ы *f.* woman in childbirth.

роже́чник, а *m.* horn-player; bugler.

рож|о́к, ка́ *m.* **1** (*животного*) small horn. **2** (*mus.*) horn; bugle; **англи́йский р.** cor anglais. **3** (*для тугоухих*) ear-

Р

trumpet. **4** (*для младенца*) feeding-bottle. **5** (*газовый*) (gas-)burner, (gas-)jet. **6** (*для одевания обуви*) shoe-horn.

рож|о́н, на́ *m.*: **лезть, идти́ на р.** (*coll.*) to kick against the pricks; **про́тив ~на́ пере́ть** (*coll.*) to swim against the tide; **како́го ещё ~на́ на́до?** (*coll.*) what the hell more do you need?

рожь, ржи *f.* rye.

ро́з|а, ы *f.* **1** (*цветок*) rose; (*растение*) rose-tree, rose-bush. **2** (*archit.*) rose-window. **3**: **р. ветро́в** wind rose.

роза́ри|й, я *m.* rosarium, rose-garden.

ро́звальн|и, ей *no sg.* rozvalni (*low, wide sledge*).

ро́з|га, ги, *g. pl.* **~ог** *f.* birch (rod); **наказа́ть ~гой** to birch.

ро́зговень|е, я *nt.* (*eccl.*) first meal after fast.

ро́здых, а *m.* (*coll.*) pause (*from work*), breather.

розе́тк|а, и *f.* **1** (*украшение*) rosette. **2** (*elec.*) socket; electric outlet. **3** (*для варенья*) jam-dish. **4** (*на свечке*) candle-ring (*ring on candlestick to collect wax*). **5** (*archit.*) rose-window.

розмари́н, а *m.* (*bot.*) rosemary.

ро́зниц|а, ы *f.* retail; **торгова́ть в ~у** to engage in retail trade; to retail.

ро́зничн|ый *adj.* retail; **р. торго́вец** retailer; **~ая цена́** retail price.

ро́зно *adv.* (*coll.*) apart, separately.

розн|ь, и *f.* **1** difference; **челове́к челове́ку р.** there are no two people alike; there are people and people. **2** (*вражда*) disagreement, dissension.

розова́т|ый (~, ~а) *adj.* pinkish.

розове́|ть, ю *impf.* (*of* ⇒**по~**) to turn pink.

розовощёкий *adj.* pink-cheeked, rosy-cheeked.

ро́зов|ый (~, ~а) *adj.* **1** *adj. of* ⇒**ро́за; ~ое де́рево** rosewood; **р. куст** rose-bush. **2** (*цвет*) pink, rose-coloured (*Br.*), -colored (*US*). **3** (*fig.*) rosy; **смотре́ть на что-н. сквозь ~ые очки́** to view sth. through rose-coloured spectacles (*Br.*), rose-colored glasses (*US*).

ро́зыгрыш, а *m.* **1** (*лотереи*) drawing. **2** (*sport*) (*решающая партия*) playing off (*of a cup-tie, etc.*). **3** (*sport*) (*ничья*) draw, drawn game. **4** (*шутка*) practical joke.

ро́зыск, а *m.* **1** (*разыскивание*) search. **2** (*leg.*) (*дознание*) inquiry; **Уголо́вный р.** Criminal Investigation Department (*Br.*), Federal Bureau of Investigation (*US*).

ро|и́ться, и́тся *impf.* to swarm; (*fig.*) (*о мыслях*) to crowd.

рой, ро́я, *pl.* **рои́** *m.* (*пчёл, комаров*) swarm.

рок¹, а *m.* (*судьба*) fate.

рок², а *m.* (*mus.*) rock; **тяжёлый р.** hard rock.

рок- *comb. form* rock.

рок-гру́пп|а, ы *f.* rock band.

ро́кер, а *m.* (*coll.*) rocker.

рок-звезд|а́, ы́ *pl.* **~ы, ~, ~ам** *f.* rock star.

рокир|ова́ть(ся), у́ю(сь) *impf. and pf.* (*chess*) to castle.

рокиро́вк|а, и *f.* (*chess*) castling.

рок-му́зык|а, и *f.* rock music.

рок-музыка́нт, а *m.* rock musician.

рок-н-ро́лл, а *m.* rock 'n' roll.

роков|о́й *adj.* **1** fateful; fated; **~а́я же́нщина** femme fatale. **2** (*имеющий тяжёлые последствия*) fatal.

рококо́ *nt. indecl.* rococo.

рок-о́пер|а, ы *f.* rock opera.

ро́кот, а *m.* roar, rumble.

роко|та́ть, чу́, ~чешь *impf.* to roar, rumble.

ро́лик, а *m.* **1** roller, castor. **2** (*elec.*) (porcelain) cleat. **3** *pl.* (*коньки*) roller skates. **4**: **рекла́мный р.** (*cin.*) advertisement; (*фильма*) trailer. **5** (*бумаги, плёнки*) roll.

ро́лик|овый *adj. of* ⇒**~; ~овая доска́** skateboard; **~овые коньки́** roller skates; **р. подши́пник** roller bearing.

роликодро́м, а *m.* roller-skating rink.

ро́лкер, а *m.* ro-ro (*roll-on roll-off*) ship.

ро́ллер, а *m.* scooter.

ро́ллинг, а *m.* **1** (*доска*) skateboard. **2** (*спорт*) skateboarding.

рол|ь, и, *pl.* **~и, ~е́й** *f.* (*theatr.*) role (*also fig.*); (*текст*) part; **в ~и** (+*g.*) in the role (of); **игра́ть р.** (+*g.*) to take the part (of), play, act; (*fig.*) to matter, count, be of importance; **э́то не игра́ет ~и** it is of no importance, it does not count; **войти́ в р.** to get into the part; **поменя́ться ~я́ми с ке́м-н.** to swap places with s.o.; **р. второ́го пла́на** support role.

ром, а *m.* rum.

рома́н, а *m.* **1** novel. **2** (*coll.*) (*любовная связь*) love affair; romance.

романи́ст¹, а *m.* novelist.

романи́ст², а *m.* Romance philologist.

романи́ст|ка, ки *f. of* ⇒**~¹,²**

рома́нс, а *m.* (*mus.*) romance.

рома́нск|ий *adj.* Romance; **р. стиль** (*archit.*) Romanesque; **~ие языки́** Romance languages.

романти́зм, а *m.* romanticism.

рома́нтик, а *m.* (*мечтатель*) romantic; (*художник, писатель*) romanticist.

рома́нтик|а, и *f.* romance.

романти́ческий *adj.* romantic.

романти́чност|ь, и *f.* romantic quality, nature.

романти́ч|ный (~ен, ~на) *adj.* = **~еский**

рома́шк|а, и *f.* (*bot. and pharm.*) camomile.

рома́шк|овый *adj. of* ⇒**~а; р. чай** camomile tea.

ромб, а *m.* (*math.*) rhomb(us); (*mil.*) diamond formation.

ромби́ческий *adj.* (*math.*) rhombic.

роме́йский *adj.* (*hist.*) Romaic, of East Rome.

ро́мовый *adj. of* ⇒**ром**

ромште́кс, а *m.* rump steak.

Ро́н|а, ы *f.* the Rhone (*river*).

ро́ндо *nt. indecl.* (*mus.*) rondo.

рондо́ *nt. indecl.* (*liter.*) rondeau, rondel.

роня́|ть, ю *impf.* (*of* ⇒**урони́ть**) **1** (*из рук*) to drop; (*голову, руки*) to let fall; (*книгу с полки*) to knock off; (*слова, замечания*) to say casually; **р. слёзы** to shed tears. **2** *impf. only* (*лишаться*) to shed; **р. ли́стья** to shed its leaves; **р. опере́ние** to moult. **3** (*fig.*) (*унижать*) to discredit; **р. себя́ в обще́ственном мне́нии** to drop in public estimation; **р. себя́ в чьих-н. глаза́х** to discredit o.s. in s.o.'s eyes; (*авторитет*) to lose.

ро́пот, а *m.* murmur, grumble.

роп|та́ть, щу́, ~щешь *impf.* (**на**+*a.*) to murmur, grumble (about).

рос, ~ла́ *see* ⇒**расти́**

рос|а́, ы́, *pl.* **~ы** *f.* dew.

роси́нк|а, и *f.* dewdrop.

роси́ст|ый (~, ~а) *adj.* dewy.

роско́ществ|о, а *nt.* **1** (*пристрастие*) extravagant taste. **2** (*излишество*) extravagance.

роско́шеств|овать, ую *impf.* to luxuriate, live in luxury.

роско́ш|ный (~ен, ~на) *adj.* **1** luxurious, sumptuous. **2** (*coll.*) (*замечательный*) luxuriant, splendid.

ро́скош|ь, и *f.* **1** (*излишества*) luxury; **жить в ~и** to live in luxury. **2** (*великолепие*) splendour (*Br.*), splendor (*US*). **3** (*природы*) luxuriance.

ро́слый *adj.* tall, strapping.

ро́сный¹ *adj.*: **р. ла́дан** benzoin, benjamin.

ро́с|ный² *adj. of* ⇒**~а́**

росома́х|а, и *f.* (*zool.*) wolverene, glutton.

ро́спис|ь, и *f.* **1** (*перечень*) list, inventory. **2** (*живопись*) painting; **р. стен** wall-painting(s), mural(s).

ро́спуск, а *m.* dismissal; (*mil.*) disbandment; **р. парла́мента** dissolution of Parliament; **р. на кани́кулы** breaking up for the holidays.

росси́йский *adj.* Russian.

Росси́|я, и *f.* Russia.

россия́н|ин, а, *pl.* **~е, ~** *m.* (*русский*) Russian; (*житель России*) Russian citizen.

россия́н|ка, ки *f. of* ⇒**~ин**

ро́сказн|и, ей *no sg.* (*coll.*) old wives' tale.

ро́ссып|ь, и *f.* **1** scattering; **грузи́ть зерно́ ~ью** to load grain loose. **2** (*pl.*; *min.*) deposit, placer.

рост, а *m.* **1** (*растений, городов, индустрии*) growth; (*fig.*) (*цен, преступности*) increase, rise. **2** (*вышина*) height, stature; **~ом** in height; **он ~ом с вас** he is (of) your height; **высо́кого ~а** tall; **во весь р.** full length; (*fig.*) in all its magnitude; **встать во весь р.** to stand upright, stand up straight; **э́то пальто́ мне не по ~у** this coat does not fit me. **3** (*одежды*) length. **4** (*прибыль*) interest; **отдава́ть де́ньги на р.** to lend money at interest.

ро́стбиф, а *m.* roast beef.

ростовщи́к, а́ *m.* usurer, money-lender.

ростовщи́|ца, цы *f. of* ⇒~к

ростовщи́ческий *adj.* usurious; (*грабительский*) predatory.

ростовщи́честв|о, а *nt.* usury, money-lending.

рост|о́к, ка́ *m.* shoot; **пусти́ть ~ки́** to sprout; (*pl.*, +*g.*) beginnings (of).

ро́счерк, а *m.* flourish; **одни́м ~ом пера́** with a stroke of the pen.

росянк|а, и *f.* (*bot.*) sundew.

рот, рта, о рте́, во рту́ *m.* mouth; **не брать в р.** (+*g.*) not to touch; **зажа́ть, заткну́ть р. кому́-н.** (*coll.*) to stop s.o.'s mouth, shut s.o. up; **смотре́ть в р. кому́-н.** (*coll.*) to hang on s.o.'s words; **говори́ть, не закрыва́я рта** to talk non-stop.

ро́т|а, ы *f.* (*mil.*) company.

ротапри́нт, а *m.* offset duplicator.

рота́тор, а *m.* duplicator, duplicating machine.

ротацио́нн|ый *adj.*: **~ая маши́на** (*typ.*) rotary press.

рота́ци|я, и *f.* **1** = **~о́нная маши́на. 2** rotation.

ротве́йлер, а *m.* Rottweiler.

ро́тмистр, а *m.* (*mil.*) captain (*of cavalry in tsarist Russian army*).

ро́т|ный *adj. of* ⇒**~а;** *as n.* **р., ~ного** *m.* company commander.

ротозе́|й, я *m.* (*coll.*) (*разиня*) scatter-brain; (*зевака*) idler.

ротозе́йств|о, а *nt.* (*coll.*) idleness.

рото́нд|а, ы *f.* **1** (*archit.*) rotunda. **2** (*накидка*) cloak.

ро́тор, а *m.* (*tech.*) rotor.

ро́хл|я, и, *g. pl.* **~ей** *c.g.* (*coll.*) dawdler.

ро́щ|а, и *f.* small wood, grove.

ро́щиц|а, ы *f. dim. of* ⇒**ро́ща**

рояли́ст, а *m.* royalist.

рояли́ст|ка, ки *f. of* ⇒~

рояли́стский *adj.* royalist.

роя́л|ь, я *m.* piano; grand piano; **кабине́тный р.** baby grand; **игра́ть на ~е** to play the piano.

РСФСР *f. indecl.* (*abbr. of* ***Росси́йская Сове́тская Федерати́вная Социалисти́ческая Респу́блика***) (*hist.*) RSFSR (*Russian Soviet Federal Socialist Republic*).

РТС *f. indecl.* (*abbr. of* ***ремо́нтно-техни́ческая ста́нция***) (*agric.*) repairs and engineering station.

рту́тный *adj.* mercury.

рту́т|ь, и *f.* mercury.

руба́к|а, и *m.* (*coll.*) fine swordsman.

руба́н|ок, ка *m.* (*tech.*) plane.

руба́х|а, и *f.* shirt; **р.-па́рень** (*coll.*) straightforward fellow.

руба́шк|а, и *f.* **1** shirt; **ни́жняя р., на́тельная р.** (*мужская*) undershirt; (*женская*) full-length slip; **ночна́я р.** (*мужская*) night-shirt; (*женская*) night-dress; **роди́ться в ~е** to be born with a silver spoon in one's mouth; **своя́ р. бли́же к те́лу** (*prov.*) charity begins at home. **2** (*игральной карты*) back.

рубе́ж, а́ *m.* **1** boundary, border(line); **уе́хать за р.** to go abroad; **жить за ~о́м** to live abroad; **р. веко́в** turn of the century. **2** (*mil.*) line; **р. ата́ки** assault position.

руб|е́ц¹, ца́ *m.* **1** (*от ран*) scar. **2** (*шов*) hem, seam.

руб|е́ц², ца́ *m.* (*cul.*) tripe.

руби́льник, а *m.* **1** (*elec.*) knife-switch. **2** (*sl.*) (*большой нос*) big nose, hooter.

руби́н, а *m.* ruby.

руби́новый *adj.* ruby.

руб|и́ть, лю́, ~ишь *impf.* **1** (*дерево*) to fell. **2** (*дрова*) to chop. **3** (*cul.*) to mince, chop up. **4** (*строить из брёвен*) to put up, erect. **5** (*уголь*) to mine, extract. **6** (*coll.*) (*говорить*) to say bluntly.

руб|и́ться, лю́сь, ~ишься *impf.* to fight (with cold steel).

ру́бищ|е, а *no pl., nt.* rags, tatters.

ру́бк|а¹, и *f.* **1** (*деревьев*) felling. **2** (*дров*) chopping. **3** (*cul.*) mincing, chopping up. **4** (*избы*) erection.

ру́бк|а², и *f.* (*naut.*) deck house; **боева́я р.** conning tower; **рулева́я р.** wheel-house.

рублёвк|а, и *f.* (*coll.*) one-rouble note.

рубл|ёвый *adj.* **1** *adj. of* ⇒**~ь. 2** one rouble (*in price*); (*coll.*) (*дешёвый*) cheap.

ру́блен|ый *adj.* **1** minced, chopped; **~ая капу́ста** chopped cabbage; **~ое мя́со** minced meat, hash; **~ые котле́ты** rissoles. **2** (*бревенчатый*) of logs; **~ая изба́** log hut, log cabin.

рубл|ь, я́ *m.* rouble; **биле́т сто́ит два ~я́** a ticket costs two roubles; **за р.** for one rouble; **сыру на сто ~е́й** a hundred roubles' worth of cheese.

ру́брик|а, и *f.* **1** (*заголовок*) rubric, heading. **2** (*раздел*) column.

рубц|ева́ться, у́ется *impf.* (*of* ⇒**за~**) to form a scar.

ру́бчат|ый (~, ~а) *adj.* ribbed.

ру́бчик, а *m.* **1** *dim. of* ⇒**рубе́ц¹**. **2** (*на ткани*) rib.

ру́ган|ь, и *f.* (*непристойная*) bad language, swearing, abuse; (*ссора*) row.

руга́тельн|ый *adj.* abusive; **~ые слова́** bad language, swear-words.

руга́тельств|о, а *nt.* abuse; (*непристойное*) swear-word.

руга́|ть, ю *impf.* **1** (*of* **вы́~, из~, об~, от~**) (*бранить*) to curse, swear (at), abuse. **2** (*of* **об~**) (*критиковать*) to tear to pieces.

руга́|ться, юсь *impf.* **1** to curse, swear, use bad language; **р. как изво́зчик** to swear like a trooper. **2** (**с**+*i.*) (*ссориться*) to quarrel (with), have a row (with).

ругн|у́ть(ся), у́(сь), ёшь(ся) *pf.* to swear.

руд|а́, ы́, *pl.* **~ы** *f.* ore; **желе́зная р.** iron-ore.

рудиме́нт, а *m.* rudiment.

рудимента́р|ный (~ен, ~на) *adj.* rudimentary.

рудни́к, а́ *m.* mine, pit.

руднико́вый *adj. of* ⇒**рудни́к**

рудни́|чный *adj. of* ⇒**~к; р. газ** fire-damp; **~чная сто́йка** pit prop; **~чная ла́мпа** miner's lamp.

ру́д|ный *adj. of* ⇒**~а́; ~ная жи́ла** vein.

рудоко́п, а *m.* miner.

рудоно́с|ный (~ен, ~на) *adj.* ore-bearing.

руже́йник, а *m.* gunsmith.

руже́йн|ый *adj. of* ⇒**ружьё; р. вы́стрел** rifle-shot; **р. ма́стер** armourer (*Br.*), armorer (*US*), gunsmith.

руж|ьё, ья́, *pl.* **~ья, ~ей, ~ьям** *nt.* (hand-)gun, rifle; **дробово́е р.** shot-gun; **противота́нковое р.** anti-tank rifle; **стать в р.** to fall in; **в р.!** (*mil. command*) to arms!; **быть под ~ьём** to be under arms; **призва́ть под р.** to call to arms.

руи́н|а, ы *f.* ruin (*usu. pl.*); **восста́ть из ~** to rise from the ashes.

рук|а́, и́, *a.* **~у,** *pl.* **~и, ~, ~а́м** *f.*

● **I. 1** (*кисть*) hand; (*от кисти до плеча*) arm; **пожа́ть ~у** (+*d.*) to shake hands (with); **~и вверх!** hands up!; **~а́ми не тро́гать!** please, do not touch!; **вести́ за́ ~у** to lead by the hand; **взя́ться за́ ~и** to join hands, link arms; **взять на́ ~и** to take in one's arms; **держа́ть на ~а́х** to hold in one's arms; **р. об ~у** hand in hand; **написа́ть от ~и** to write out by hand; **взять кого́-н. по́д ~у** to take s.o.'s arm; **идти́ с кем-н. по́д ~у** to walk arm in arm with s.o. **2** (*почерк*) hand, handwriting; (*подпись*) signature; **приложи́ть ~у** (*obs.*) to affix one's signature. **3** (*сторона*) side; **с ле́вой ~и́** on the left, to the left; **по пра́вую ~у** on the right, to the right. **4** *pl.* (*владение*) hands (*fig.* = *power, possession*); **взять в свои́ ~и** to take into one's own hands; **взять (себя́) в ~и** to take (o.s.) in hand; **держа́ть в свои́х ~а́х** to have in one's clutches; **попа́сться в ~и кому́-н.** to fall into s.o.'s hands; **прибра́ть к ~а́м** to appropriate; **быть в хоро́ших ~а́х** to be in good hands; **свобо́да ~** a free hand; **в со́бственные ~и** (*на конверте*) 'personal'. **5** (*fig.*) hand (*of person giving or receiving proposal of marriage*); **проси́ть ~и́ у кого́-н.** to ask s.o.'s hand in marriage. **6** (*fig.*) (*источник*) hand; source, authority; **из пе́рвых, вторы́х ~** at first, second hand; **узна́ть из ве́рных ~** to have on good authority.

● **II.** (*fig.; in var. senses*) hand; **переда́ть де́ло в чьи-н. ~и** to put a matter in s.o.'s hands; **сон в ~у** the dream has come true; **из ~ вон (пло́хо)** (*coll.*) thoroughly bad, quite useless; **вы́дать на́ ~и** to hand out; **име́ть на ~а́х** to have on one's hands; **умере́ть на чьих-н. ~а́х** to die in s.o.'s arms; **ма́стер на все ~и** Jack of all trades; **э́то бу́дет им на́ ~у** that will serve their purpose; it will be playing into their hands; **на́ ~у нечи́ст** (*coll.*) dishonest, underhand; **на ско́рую ~у** off-hand; **дать кому́-н. по ~а́м** (*coll.*) to give a rap over the knuckles; **уда́рить по ~а́м** to strike a bargain; **по ~а́м!** it's a bargain!, done!; **говори́ть кому́-н. по́д ~у** to distract s.o. by talking; **под ~о́й** at hand, to hand; **под пья́ную ~у** under the influence (of drink); **с ~ доло́й** off one's hands; **сбыть с ~** to get off one's hands; **э́то**

Р

тебе́ не сойдёт с ~ (*coll.*) you won't get away with it; **греть ~и (на + *p.*)** to make a good thing (out of); **э́то де́ло чужи́х ~** this is s.o. else's doing; **как ~о́й сня́ло** it has vanished as if by magic; **махну́ть ~о́й (на + *a.*)** to give up as lost; **наби́ть ~у** to get one's hand in; **наложи́ть на себя́ ~и** to lay hands on o.s.; **не поднима́ется р.** (+ *inf.*) one cannot bring o.s. (to); **приложи́ть ~у (к + *d.*)** to put one's hand (to), take a hand (in); **развяза́ть ~и** (+ *d.*) to give a free hand; **р. у него́ не дро́гнет** (+ *inf.*) he will not scruple (to); **~и у меня́ не дохо́дят до э́того** I've no time to do it; **~и прочь!** hands off!; **~о́й пода́ть** a stone's throw away; **умы́ть ~и (в + *p.*)** to wash one's hands (of); **у меня́ ~и че́шутся** (+ *inf.*) I'm itching (to).

рука́в, а́, *pl.* **~а́** *m.* **1** (*одежды*) sleeve; **спустя́ ~а́** (*coll.*) in a slipshod manner. **2** (*реки*) branch, arm. **3** (*tech.*) (*шланг*) hose; **пожа́рный р.** fire-hose.

рукави́ц|а, ы *f.* (*меховая*) mitten; (*рабочая*) gauntlet; **держа́ть в ежо́вых ~ах** to rule with a rod of iron.

рука́вчик, а *m.* **1** *dim. of* ⇒**рука́в.** **2** (*obs.*) (*манжета*) cuff.

руководи́тел|ь, я *m.* **1** (*учреждения, отдела*) head, manager; (*делегации, похода, восстания*) leader; **р. вы́сшего ра́нга** senior executive; **р. прое́кта** project manager; **кла́ссный р.** (*в школе*) form monitor. **2** (*воспитатель*) instructor; guide; **нау́чный руководи́тель** supervisor of studies.

руководи́тель|ница, ницы *f. of* ⇒~

руково|ди́ть, жу́, ди́шь *impf.* (+ *i.*) (*учреждением, отделом*) to be in charge of; to manage; (*походом, восстанием*) to lead; (*кружком, клубом*) to run; (*аспирантами*) to supervise; (*побуждать*) to govern; **его́ де́йствиями ~ди́т эгои́зм** his actions are governed by self-interest.

руково|ди́ться, жу́сь, ди́шься *impf.* (+ *i.*) to follow; to be guided (by).

руково́дств|о, а *nt.* **1** (*действие*) leadership; guidance; management. **2** (*стимул*) guiding principle, guide; **р. к де́йствию** guide to action. **3** (*книга*) handbook, guide, manual; **р. по эксплуата́ции** instructions for use. **4** (*collect.*) (*руководители*) (the) leadership, leaders; governing body.

руково́дств|оваться, уюсь *impf.* (+ *i.*) to follow; to be guided (by).

руковод|я́щий *pres. part. act. of* ⇒**~и́ть** *and adj.* leading; guiding; managing; (*старший*) high-level, senior; **р. рабо́тник** executive; **р. комите́т** steering committee.

рукоде́ли|е, я *nt.* **1** needlework. **2** (*pl.*) hand-made wares.

рукоде́льниц|а, ы *f.* needlewoman.

рукоде́льнича|ть, ю *impf.* to do needlework.

рукомо́йник, а *m.* wash-stand.

рукопа́шн|ая, ой *f.* hand-to-hand fight(-ing).

рукопа́шный *adj.* hand-to-hand.

рукопи́сный *adj.* (*текст*) handwritten; (*фонд*) manuscript; **р. па́мятник** written document.

ру́копис|ь, и *f.* manuscript.

рукоплеска́ни|е, я *nt.* applause, clapping.

рукопле|ска́ть, щу́, ~щешь *impf.* (+ *d.*) to applaud, clap.

рукопожа́ти|е, я *nt.* handshake.

рукотво́р|ный (~ен, ~на) *adj.* man-made, artificial.

рукоя́тк|а, и *f.* handle.

рула́д|а, ы *f.* (*mus.*) roulade, run.

рулев|о́й *adj. of* ⇒**руль; ~о́е колесо́** steering wheel; **~а́я коло́нка** steering column; **р. механи́зм, ~о́е устро́йство** steering gear; *as n.* **р., ~о́го** *m.* **1** (*на судне*) helmsman. **2** (*sport*) cox(swain).

рулёжк|а, и *f.* (*aeron.*) taxiing.

руле́т, а *m.* (*cul.*) **1** (*пирог*) roll; **мясно́й р.** meat loaf. **2** (*окорок без кости*) boned gammon.

руле́тк|а, и *f.* **1** (*для измерения*) tape-measure. **2** (*игра*) roulette.

рул|и́ть, ю́, и́шь *impf.* (*в машине, в лодке*) to steer; (*двигаться*) to taxi; to drive.

руло́н, а *m.* roll.

рул|ь, я́ *m.* (*судна*) rudder; helm (*also fig.*); (*автомобиля*) (steering-)wheel; (*велосипеда*) handle-bars; **стать за р.** to take the helm; **стоя́ть у ~я́** (*fig.*) to be at the helm.

румб, а *m.* (*naut.*) (compass) point.

ру́мпел|ь, я *m.* (*naut.*) tiller.

румы́н, а *m.* Romanian.

Румы́ни|я, и *f.* Romania.

румы́н|ка, ки *f. of* ⇒~

румы́нский *adj.* Romanian.

румя́н|а, ~ *no sg.* rouge; blusher.

румя́н|ец, ца *m.* (high) colour (*Br.*), color (*US*); flush; blush.

румя́н|ить, ю, ишь *impf.* **1** (*pf.* **раз~**) to redden (*also fig.*); to cause to glow. **2** (*pf.* **на~**) to rouge.

румя́н|иться, юсь, ишься *impf.* **1** (*pf.* **раз~**) to redden; to glow; to flush. **2** (*pf.* **на~**) to use rouge.

румя́н|ый (~, ~а) *adj.* rosy, ruddy.

ру́н|а, ы *f.* (*philol.*) rune.

руни́ческий *adj.* (*philol.*) runic.

рун|о́, а́, *pl.* **~а** *nt.* fleece; **золото́е р.** (*myth.*) the Golden Fleece.

ру́пи|я, и *f.* rupee.

ру́пор, а *m.* megaphone; loud hailer; (*fig.*) (*партии*) mouthpiece.

руса́к[1], а́ *m.* (*заяц*) (grey) hare.

руса́к[2], а́ *m.* (*coll.*) (*русский*) Russian.

руса́лк|а, и *f.* mermaid.

руса́чк|а, и *f. of* ⇒**руса́к[2]**

руси́зм, а *m.* (*ling.*) Russianism, Russ(ic)ism.

руси́ст, а *m.* Russianist.

руси́стик|а, и *f.* Russian studies.

руси́ст|ка, ки *f. of* ⇒~

русифика́тор, а *m.* Russifier, Russianizer.

русифика́ци|я, и *f.* Russification, Russianization.

русифици́р|овать, ую *impf. and pf.* to russify, russianize.

ру́сл|о, а, *g. pl.* **~** *nt.* **1** (river-)bed, channel; **измени́ть р. реки́** to change the course of a river. **2** (*fig.*) (*направление*) channel, course; **мои́ дела́ пошли́ по но́вому ~у** my affairs have taken a new turn; **войти́ в обы́чное р.** to resume the normal course; **в ~е** (+ *g.*) within the context of, in keeping with.

русоволо́с|ый (~, ~а) *adj.* having light-brown hair.

русофи́л, а *m.* Russophile.

русофи́л|ка, ки *f.* (*coll.*) *of* ⇒~

русофо́би|я, и *f.* Russophobia.

ру́сск|ая, ой *f.* **1** *f. of* ⇒**~ий** *as n.* **2** russkaya (*Russian folk-dance*).

ру́сск|ий *adj.* Russian (*also as n.* **р., ~ого** *m.*).

ру́с|ый (~, ~а) *adj.* light-brown.

Рус|ь, и́ *f.* (*hist.*) Rus, Russia.

руте́ни|й, я *m.* (*chem.*) ruthenium.

рути́н|а, ы *f.* (*pej.*) routine; rut.

рутинёр, а *m.* slave to routine, person in a rut.

рутинёр|ский *adj. of* ⇒**~; ~ские взгля́ды** rigid views.

рути́н|ный *adj. of* ⇒**~а**

Руфь, и *f.* (*bibl.*) Ruth.

ру́хлядь, и *f.* (*collect.*; *coll.*) junk.

ру́хн|уть, у, ешь *pf.* to crash down, tumble down, collapse; (*fig.*) (*планы, мечты*) to collapse, fall through.

руча́тельств|о, а *nt.* guarantee; **с ~ом** guaranteed.

руча́|ться, юсь *impf.* (*of* ⇒**поручи́ться**) **(за + *a.*)** to guarantee; to answer (for), vouch (for); **р. голово́й (за + *a.*)** to stake one's life (on); **я не могу́ за него́ р.** I cannot vouch for him.

руче|ёк, йка́ *m. dim. of* ⇒**руче́й**

руч|е́й, ья́ *m.* brook, stream; **~ьи́ слёз** floods of tears.

ру́чк|а, и *f.* **1** *dim. of* ⇒**рука́.** **2** (*двери, чайника*) handle; (*кресла, дивана*) arm; **р. две́ри** door-handle, door-knob; **дойти́ до ~и** (*fig., coll.*) to reach the end of one's tether. **3** (*для письма*) pen; **автомати́ческая р.** fountain-pen; **ша́риковая р.** ball-point pen.

ручн|о́й *adj.* **1** hand; (*управление*) manual; **~а́я грана́та** hand grenade; **~а́я кладь** hand luggage; **~а́я пила́** hand-saw; **~о́е полоте́нце** hand towel; **~а́я рабо́та** handwork; **~о́й рабо́ты** hand-made; **~а́я теле́жка** hand-cart; **р. труд** manual labour; **~ы́е часы́** wrist watch. **2** (*зверь, птица*) tame.

ру́ш|ить, у, ишь *impf.* (*здание*) to pull down; (*семью*) to wreck.

ру́ш|иться, ится *impf. and pf.* to fall down, collapse; (*fig.*) (*планы, надежды*) to collapse.

РФ *f. indecl.* (*abbr. of* ***Росси́йская Федера́ция***) Russian Federation.

ры́б|а, ы *f.* fish; (*pl., astron.*) Pisces; **ни р. ни мя́со** neither fish nor fowl; **чу́вствовать себя́ как р. в воде́** to feel in one's element; **как р. об лёд би́ться**

(*fig.*) to try to find a way out of a difficult situation.

рыбáк, á *m.* fisherman.

рыбáлк|а, и *f.* fishing; fishing trip; **идти́ на ~у** to go fishing.

ры́бар|ь, я (~я́) *m.* (*obs.*) = **рыбáк**

рыбá|цкий *adj. of* ⇒**~к; р. посёлок** fishing village.

рыбá|чий *adj. of* ⇒**~к; ~чья лóдка** fishing-boat.

рыбáч|ить, у, ишь *impf.* to fish.

рыбáчк|а, и *f.* **1** fisherwoman. **2** (*жена рыбака*) fisherman's wife.

рыбёшк|а, и *f.* (*coll.*) small fry.

ры́бий *adj.* fish; **р. жир** cod-liver oil.

ры́бин|а, ы *f.* (*coll.*) big fish.

рыбнадзóр, а *m.* fishing patrol.

ры́бн|ый *adj.* fish; **~ые консéрвы** tinned fish; **~ая лóвля** fishing; **р. магази́н** fish-shop, fishmonger's; **р. садóк** fish-pond.

рыбовóд, а *m.* fish-breeder.

рыбовóдств|о, а *nt.* fish-breeding.

рыбовóдческ|ий *adj.*: **~ая фéрма** fish farm.

рыбозавóд, а *m.* fish-factory; **плаву́чий р.** fish-factory ship.

рыбоконсéрвный *adj.*: **р. завóд** fish cannery.

рыболóв, а *m.* fisherman; angler.

рыболовéцкий *adj.* fishing.

рыболóвн|ый *adj.* fishing; **~ые принадлéжности, ~ая снасть** fishing tackle; **р. райóн** fishing-ground, fishery; **р. надзóр** fishing patrol.

рыболóвств|о, а *nt.* fishing (*as branch of economy*).

рыбопитóмник, а *m.* fish hatchery.

рыбопромы́шленност|ь, и *f.* fishing industry.

рыботоргóв|ец, ца *m.* fishmonger.

рыботоргóвк|а, и *f.* fishwife.

рыв|óк, кá *m.* **1** (*резкое движение*) jerk. **2** (*бегуна*) dash, spurt; (*в тяжёлой атлетике*) snatch. **3** (*в работе*) push, spurt.

рыгáнь|е, я *nt.* belching.

рыг|áть, áю *impf.* (*of* ⇒**~нýть**) to belch.

рыг|нýть, нý, нёшь *pf. of* ⇒**~áть**

рыдáни|е, я *nt.* sobbing.

рыдá|ть, ю *impf.* to sob.

рыдвáн, а *m.* (*hist.*) large coach.

рыжевáт|ый (~, ~а) *adj.* reddish; rust-coloured.

рыжевóлос|ый (~, ~а) *adj.* red-haired, ginger-haired.

рыжé|ть, ю *impf.* (*of* ⇒**по~**) to turn reddish.

ры́ж|ий (~, ~á, ~е) *adj.* **1** (*волосы*) red, ginger; (*человек*) red-haired, ginger-haired; (*лошадь*) chestnut. **2** *as n.* **р., ~его** *m.* (*coll.*) circus clown.

ры́жик, а *m.* saffron milk-cap (*mushroom*).

рык, а *m.* roar.

рыкá|ть, ю *impf.* to roar.

ры́л|о, а *nt.* **1** snout (*of pig, etc.*). **2** (*coll.*) (*лицо*) mug.

ры́льце, ьца, *g. pl.* **~ец** *nt.* **1** *dim. of* ⇒**~о; у негó р. в пухý** he has been at the jam-pot. **2** (*bot.*) stigma.

ры́нд|а¹, ы *f.* (*hist.*) rynda (*bodyguard of tsars in Muscovite period*).

ры́нд|а², ы *f.* ship's bell.

ры́н|ок, ка *m.* **1** market(-place). **2** (*econ.*) market; **внéшний р.** foreign market; **вну́тренний р.** domestic, internal market; **дéнежный р.** money market; **на ~ке** on the market.

ры́но|чный *adj. of* ⇒**~к; р. день** market-day; **~чная экономи́ка** market economy; **по ~чной цéне** at the market price.

рысáк, á *m.* trotter (*horse*).

ры́с|ий *adj.* lynx; **~ьи глазá** (*fig.*) lynx eyes.

рыси́ст|ый *adj.*: **~ые испытáния** trotting races; **~ая лóшадь** trotter.

рыс|и́ть, и́шь *impf.* to trot.

ры́|скать, щу, щешь *impf.* **1** (**по**+*d.*) (*в поисках*) to scour, ransack; **р. по кармáнам** to ransack one's pockets. **2** (*блуждать*) to rove, roam; **р. глазáми** to let one's eyes roam.

рысц|á, ы́ *f.* jog-trot; **éхать ~óй** to go at a jog-trot.

рыс|ь¹, и, о ~и, на ~и́ *f.* (*бег*) trot; **на ~я́х** at a trot.

рыс|ь², и *f.* (*животное*) lynx.

ры́сью *adv.* at a trot.

ры́твин|а, ы *f.* rut, groove.

рыть, рóю, рóешь *impf.* **1** (*яму, окопы*) to dig; (*картошку*) to dig up; **р. зéмлю копы́том** to paw the ground (*also fig.*). **2** (*в поисках*) to rummage, root about (in).

рыть|ё, я́ *nt.* digging.

ры́ться, рóюсь, рóешься *impf.* (**в**+*p.*) (*в земле*) to dig (in); (*fig.*) (*в мусоре, в чемодане*) to rummage (in); (*в книгах*) to root about (in).

рыхлé|ть, ю *impf.* (*of* ⇒**по~**) to become friable, crumbly.

рыхл|и́ть, ю́, и́шь *impf.* (*of* ⇒**вз~**) to break up, loosen; to make friable, crumbly.

ры́хл|ый (~, ~á, ~о) *adj.* **1** (*почва, камень*) friable, crumbly; (*снег*) loose. **2** (*fig.*) (*стиль*) loose. **3** (*fig.*) (*человек*) podgy (*Br.*), pudgy (*US*).

ры́цар|ский *adj.* **1** *adj. of* ⇒**~ь; р. поеди́нок** joust; **р. ромáн** tale of chivalry. **2** (*fig.*) chivalrous.

ры́царств|о, а *nt.* **1** (*collect.*; *hist.*) knights. **2** (*звание*) knighthood; **получи́ть р.** to receive a knighthood. **3** (*fig.*) (*благородство*) chivalry.

ры́цар|ь, я *m.* knight; **стрáнствующий р.** knight errant.

рычáг, á *m.* lever; (*fig.*) (*средство*) lever, means.

рычáни|е, я *nt.* growl, snarl.

рыч|áть, ý, и́шь *impf.* to growl, snarl.

рья́ност|ь, и *f.* zeal.

рья́н|ый (~, ~а) *adj.* zealous.

рэ́ггей *m. indecl.* reggae.

рэ́кет, а *m.* racket.

рэкети́р, а *m.* racketeer.

рэп, а *m.* rap (music).

рюкзáк, á *m.* rucksack; backpack.

рюкзáчник, а *m.* backpacker.

рю́мк|а, и *f.* (small) glass.

рю́мочк|а, и *f. dim. of* ⇒**рю́мка**

рю́шк|а, и *f.* frill.

рябé|ть, ет, еют *impf.* (*pf.* **по~**) (*о поверхности*) to become ruffled; (*о листьях*) to become speckled.

ряби́н|а¹, ы *f.* **1** (*дерево*) rowan-tree, mountain ash. **2** (*ягода*) rowan-berry.

ряби́н|а², ы *f.* (*coll.*) pockmark.

ряби́нник, а *m.* (*zool.*) fieldfare.

ряби́новк|а, и *f.* rowan-berry liqueur.

ряби́н|овый *adj. of* ⇒**~а¹**

ряб|и́ть, и́т *impf.* **1** to ripple. **2** (*impers.*): **у меня́ ~и́т в глазáх** I am dazzled.

ряб|óй (~, ~á, ~о) *adj.* **1** (*лицо*) pock-marked. **2** (*курица*) speckled.

ря́бчик, а *m.* (*zool.*) hazel-grouse.

ряб|ь, и *f.* **1** (*на воде*) ripple(s). **2** (*в глазах*) stars.

ря́вк|ать, аю *impf.* (*of* ⇒**~нуть**) (**на**+*a.*; *coll.*) to bellow (at), bark (at).

ря́вк|нуть, ну, нешь *pf. of* ⇒**~ать**

ряд, а, в ~е *and* **в ~ý,** *pl.* **~ы́, ~óв** *m.* **1** (*предметов, лиц*) row; **пéрвый р., послéдний р.** (*theatr.*) front row, back row; **р. за ~ом** row upon row; **из ~а вон выходя́щий** outstanding, extraordinary; **стоя́ть в однóм ~ý** (**с**+*i.*) to rank (with). **2** (*в армии, в партии*) file, rank; **в ~áх áрмии** in the ranks of the army; **в пéрвых ~áх** in the first ranks; (*fig.*) in the forefront. **3** (*серия*) series (*also math.*); (*совокупность*) number; **в цéлом ~е слу́чаев** in a number of cases. **4** (*ларьки*) stalls (*set out in a row*).

ря|ди́ть, жý, ~дишь *impf.* (+*i.*) to dress up (as), get up (as).

ря|ди́ться, жýсь, ~ди́шься *impf.* **1** (*coll.*) (*одеваться нарядно*) to dress up. **2** (+*i.*) (*одеваться в маскарадный костюм*) to dress up (as), disguise o.s. (as).

рядкóм *adv.* = **ря́дом**

рядов|óй *adj.* **1** (*член, работник, случай*) ordinary, common. **2** (*mil.*): **р. состáв** rank and file; men, other ranks; *as n.* **р., ~óго** *m.* private (soldier).

ря́дом *adv.* **1** alongside; (*о двух людях*) side by side; (**с**+*i.*) (*около*) next to; (*в сравнении с*) compared with; **он сиди́т р. с премьéр-мини́стром** he is sitting next to the Prime Minister. **2** (*поблизости*) near, close by, next door; **э́то совсéм р.** it is quite near, close; **он жил р. с пáрком** he lived next door to the park.

ря́дышком *adv.* (*coll.*) = **ря́дом**

ря́женк|а, и *f.* type of plain yogurt.

ря́жен|ый *adj.* in fancy dress; *as n.* **р., ~ого** *m.*; **~ая, ~ой** *f.* person in fancy dress.

ря́с|а, ы *f.* cassock.

ря́ск|а, и *f.* (*bot.*) duckweed.

ря́шк|а, и *f.* (*coll.*) mug (= *face*).

Р

Сс

С (*abbr. of* ***се́вер***) N, North.

с *prep.*

● **I.** + *g.* **1** from; off; **с ю́го-восто́ка** from the South-East; **с Кавка́за** from the Caucasus; **с головы́ до ног** from head to foot; **с пе́рвого взгля́да** at first sight; **по́шлина с табака́** duty from tobacco; **перево́д с ру́сского** translation from Russian; **верну́ться с рабо́ты** to return from work; **убра́ть посу́ду со стола́** to clear the things from the table; **упа́сть с ками́нной по́лки** to fall off the mantelpiece; **уста́ть с доро́ги** to be tired after a journey; **взять приме́р с кого́-н.** to follow s.o.'s example; **ско́лько с меня́?** how much do I owe?
2 (*по причине*) for, from, with; **с ра́дости** for joy; **со стыда́** for shame, with shame.
3 on, from; **с ле́вой стороны́ от желе́зной доро́ги** on the left-hand side of the railway; **с одно́й, с друго́й стороны́** on the one, on the other hand; **с како́й то́чки зре́ния?** from what point of view?
4 (*на основании*) with; **с разреше́ния дире́ктора шко́лы** with the headmaster's permission; **с ва́шего согла́сия** with your consent.
5 (*посредством*) by, with; **взять с бо́ю** to take by storm; **писа́ть с большо́й бу́квы** to write with a capital letter.
6 (*о времени*) from, since; as from; **с девяти́ (часо́в) до пяти́** from nine (o'clock) till five; **с де́тства** from childhood; **с утра́** since morning; **мы с ней не ви́делись с января́** I have not seen her since January; **они́ бу́дут в Москве́ с двадца́того числа́** they will be in Moscow from the twentieth; **с 1850 по 1900** from 1850 to 1900.

● **II.** + *a.* (*приблизительно*): **с год** about a year; **с ми́лю** about a mile; **с дом** the size of a house; **на́ша до́чка ро́стом с ва́шу** our daughter is about the same height as yours; **ма́льчик с па́льчик** Tom Thumb.

● **III.** + *i.* **1** with; and; **с удово́льствием** with pleasure; **мы с ва́ми** you and I; **он с сестро́й** he and his sister.
2 (*указывает на наличие чего-либо*): **хлеб с ма́слом** bread and butter; **челове́к со стра́нностями** peculiar person.
3 (*посредством*) by, on; **получи́ть с пе́рвой по́чтой** to receive by first post; **я прие́хал с пе́рвым по́ездом** I came on the first train.
4 (*при наступлении чего-либо*) with; **с года́ми** with the years; **с ка́ждым днём** every day.
5 (*относительно*) with (*or not translated*); **как у вас дела́ с рабо́той?** how is the work going?; **что с ва́ми?** what is the matter with you?; what's up?; **у неё пло́хо с се́рдцем** her heart is bad; **как у вас с деньга́ми?** how are you off for money?

с. *abbr. of* ***село́*** village.

с... (*also* **со...** *and* **съ...**) *vbl. pref. indicating* **1** *unification, movement from various sides to a point, as* **свари́ть** to weld. **2** *movement or action made in a downward direction, as* **спусти́ться** to descend. **3** *removal of sth. from somewhere, as* **сорва́ть** to tear off.

саа́ми *c.g. indecl.* Lapp, Laplander; **язы́к с.** Lapp, Lappish.

саа́мский *adj.* Lappish.

Саа́р, а *m.* the Saar (*river*).

сабанту́|й, я *m.* noisy merrymaking.

са́бельный *adj.* sabre (*Br.*), saber (*US*).

са́б|ля, ли, *g.pl.* **~ель** *f.* sabre (*Br.*), saber (*US*).

сабо́ *m. and nt. indecl.* clog.

сабота́ж, а *m.* sabotage.

сабота́жник, а *m.* saboteur.

сабота́жни|ца, цы *f. of* **⇒~к**

сабота́жнича|ть, ю *impf.* (*coll.*) to engage in sabotage.

саботи́р|овать, ую *impf. and pf.* to sabotage.

са́ван, а *m.* shroud, cerement; **сне́жный с.** blanket of snow.

сава́нн|а, ы *f.* (*geog.*) savannah.

савра́сый *adj.* (*о лошади*) light bay.

са́г|а, и *f.* saga.

сагити́р|овать, ую *pf. of* **⇒агити́ровать**

са́го *nt. indecl.* (*bot.*) sago.

са́го|вый *adj. of* **⇒~; ~вая ка́ша** sago pudding.

сад, а, о ~е, в ~у́, *pl.* **~ы** *m.* garden; **фрукто́вый с.** orchard; **зоологи́ческий с.** zoological gardens, zoo; **де́тский с.** kindergarten.

сада|ну́ть, ну́, нёшь *pf.* (*coll.*) to hit.

сади́зм, а *m.* sadism.

са́дик, а *m.* **1** (*small*) garden. **2** (*coll.*) (*детский сад*) kindergarten.

сади́ст, а *m.* sadist.

сади́ст|ка, ки *f. of* **⇒~**

сади́стский *adj.* sadistic.

са|ди́ть¹, жу́, ~дишь *impf.* (*of* **⇒по~**) (*coll.*) (*лук, огород*) to plant.

са|ди́ть², жу́, ~дишь *impf.* (*coll.*) (*употребляется вместо любого глагола для обозначения быстрого или энергического действия*): **он ~ит по доро́ге** he dashes along the road.

са|ди́ться, жу́сь, ди́шься *impf.* (*of* **⇒сесть**); **~ди́(те)сь!** (*polite request*) take a seat!

са́дн|ить, ит *impf.* (*impers.*; *coll.*) to smart, burn.

садо́вник, а *m.* gardener.

садо́вни|ца, цы *f. of* **⇒~к**

садово́д, а *m.* (*любитель*) gardener; (*специалист*) horticulturist.

садово́дств|о, а *nt.* (*хобби*) gardening; (*наука*) horticulture.

садово́дческий *adj.* horticultural.

сад|о́вый *adj.* **1** *adj. of* **⇒~.** **2** (*культурный*) garden, cultivated.

сад|о́к, ка́ *m.* place for keeping live creatures; **кро́личий с.** rabbit-hutch; **ры́бный с.** fish-pond.

садо-мазохи́зм, а *m.* sado-masochism.

са́ж|а, и *f.* soot.

сажа́|ть, ю *impf.* (*of* **⇒посади́ть**) **1** (*цветы*) to plant. **2** (*гостя*) to seat; (*помещать*) to set, put; (*предлагать сесть*) to offer a seat; **с. хлеб в печь** to put bread into the oven; **с. в тюрьму́** to put into prison, imprison, jail; **с. ку́рицу на я́йца** to set a hen on eggs; **с. под аре́ст** to put under arrest.

са́жен|ец, ца *m.* seedling; sapling.
сажён|ки, ок *no sg.* overarm stroke (*in swimming*).
саже́нный (and **сажённый)** *adj.* (*coll.*) huge, enormous.
са́женый *adj.* planted.
са́же́н|ь, и, *pl.* **~и, са́жен** *and* **саже́не́й** *f.* sazhen (*old Russian measure of length, equivalent to 2.13 metres*); **морска́я с.** Russian fathom (*1.83 metres*).
саза́н, а *m.* wild carp (*Cyprinus carpo*).
Сайго́н, а *m.* Saigon.
са́йк|а, и *f.* (*bread*) roll.
саквоя́ж, а *m.* travelling-bag (*Br.*), traveling-bag (*US*).
саке́ *nt. indecl.* sake (*Japanese drink*).
са́кл|я, и, *g. pl.* **~ей** *f.* saklya (*Caucasian mountain hut*).
сакрамента́л|ьный (~ен, ~ьна) *adj.* sacramental; sacred.
сакс, а *m.* (*hist.*) Saxon.
саксау́л, а *m.* (*bot.*) haloxylon.
саксо́н|ец, ца *m.* Saxon.
Саксо́ни|я, и *f.* Saxony.
саксо́нский *adj.* Saxon.
саксофо́н, а *m.* saxophone.
саксофони́ст, а *m.* saxophonist.
са́кур|а, ы *f.* Japanese flowering cherry.
сала́з|ки, ок *no sg.* hand sled, toboggan.
салама́ндр|а, ы *f.* salamander.
сала́т, а *m.* **1** (*растение*) lettuce. **2** (*кушанье*) salad.
сала́тник, а *m.* salad-dish, salad-bowl.
сала́тниц|а, ы *f.* = **сала́тник**
сала́т|ный *adj. of* ⇒**~**; **~ного цве́та** light green.
са́линг, а *m.* (*naut.*) cross-trees.
са́л|ить, ю, ишь *impf.* to grease.
са́л|ки, ок *pl.* (*sg.* **~ка, ~ки** *f.*) (*игра*) tag, touch.
са́л|о, а *nt.* **1** fat; (*топлёное свиное*) lard; (*нутряное*) suet; **ко́жное с.** sebum. **2** (*для свечей*) tallow. **3** (*мелкий лёд*) thin broken ice.
сало́н, а *m.* **1** (*для выставок; магазин*) salon; **автомоби́льный с.** motorcar showroom; **да́мский с.** beauty parlour (*Br.*), parlor (*US*). **2** (*самолёта, автобуса*) passenger section. **3** (*в отеле*) lounge; (*на пароходе*) saloon.
сало́н-ваго́н, а *m.* saloon car (*Br.*), parlor car (*US*).
сало́н|ный *adj. of* ⇒**~**; **~ные бесе́ды** small talk; **~ное воспита́ние** high society upbringing.
сало́п, а *m.* (*obs.*) (*woman's*) coat.
салфе́тк|а, и *f.* napkin.
Сальвадо́р, а *m.* El Salvador.
сальвадо́р|ец, ца *m.* Salvadorean.
сальвадо́р|ка, ки *f. of* ⇒**~ец**
сальвадо́рский *adj.* Salvadorean.
са́льдо *nt. indecl.* (*book-keeping*) balance.
сальмоне́лл|а, ы *f.* salmonella.
са́льник, а *m.* **1** (*anat.*) epiploon. **2** (*tech.*) stuffing box, (packing) gland.
са́льност|ь, и *f.* obscenity, bawdiness.
са́льн|ый *adj.* **1** tallow; **~ая свеча́** tallow candle. **2** (*anat.*) sebaceous; **~ая железа́** sebaceous gland. **3** (*жирный*) greasy. **4** (*непристойный*) obscene, bawdy.
са́льто(-морта́ле) *nt. indecl.* somersault.
салю́т, а *m.* (*mil., naut.*) salute.
салют|ова́ть, у́ю *impf. and pf.* (*pf. also* **от~**) (*+d.*) to salute.
саля́ми *f. indecl.* salami.
сам[1]**, самого́** *m.*; **сама́, само́й,** *a.* **самоё (**and **саму́)** *f.*; **~о́, самого́** *nt.*; *pl.* **са́ми, сами́х** *refl. pron.* (*я*) myself, (*ты, вы*) yourself, (*он*) himself, *etc.*; **с. по себе́** in itself, per se; (*без помощи*) by o.s., unassisted; **с. собо́й** of itself, of its own accord; **он с. не свой** he is not himself; **с. собо́ хозя́ин** one's own master; **она́ — сама́ доброта́** she is kindness itself.
сам[2]**, самого́** *m.* (*coll.*) (*глава*) boss, chief.
сама́н, а *m.* adobe.
сама́н|ный *adj. of* ⇒**~**; **с. кирпи́ч** adobe (brick).
самаритя́н|ин, ина, *pl.* **~е, ~** *m.* (*bibl., hist.*) Samaritan.
са́мб|а, ы *f.* samba.
са́мбо *nt. indecl.* (*abbr. of* ***самооборо́на без ору́жия***) unarmed combat.
самбу́к, а *m.* (*cul.*) mousse.
сам|е́ц, ца́ *m.* male (*of species*).
самизда́т, а *m.* (*coll.*) samizdat.
са́мк|а, и *f.* female (*of species*).
са́ммит, а *m.* (*pol.*) summit.
само... *comb. form* self-, auto-.
Само́а *nt. indecl.* Samoa.
самоана́лиз, а *m.* self-analysis, introspection.
самоа́н|ец, ца *m.* Samoan.
самоа́н|ка, ки *f. of* ⇒**~ец**
самоа́нский *adj.* Samoan.
самобичева́ни|е, я *nt.* **1** self-flagellation. **2** (*fig.*) self-reproach.
самобы́тност|ь, и *f.* originality.
самобы́т|ный (~ен, на) *adj.* original.
самова́р, а *m.* samovar.
самовла́сти|е, я *nt.* absolute power, despotism.
самовла́ст|ный (~ен, ~на) *adj.* despotic, autocratic.
самовлюблённост|ь, и *f.* narcissism.
самовлюблённый *adj.* narcissistic.
самовнуше́ни|е, я *nt.* auto-suggestion.
самовозгора́ни|е, я *nt.* spontaneous combustion.
самовозгора́|ться, ется *impf.* to ignite spontaneously.
самово́ли|е, я *nt.* licence.
самово́лк|а, и *f.* (*coll.*) absence without leave.
самово́л|ьный (~ен, ~ьна) *adj.* **1** (*человек*) wilful, self-willed. **2** (*отсутствие*) unauthorized; **~ьная отлу́чка** (*mil.*) absence without leave.
самовоспламене́ни|е, я *nt.* spontaneous ignition.
самовосхвале́ни|е, я *nt.* self-glorification.
самого́н, а *m.* home-made vodka, hooch, moonshine (*US*).
самого́н|ка, ки *f.* = **~**
самодви́жущийся *adj.* self-propelled.
самоде́йствующий *adj.* self-acting, automatic.
самоде́лк|а, и *f.* (*coll.*) home-made product.
самоде́л|ьный (~ен, ~ьна) *adj.* home-made.
самоде́льщик, а *m.* (*coll.*) do-it-yourselfer, DIY enthusiast.
самодержа́ви|е, я *nt.* autocracy.
самодержа́в|ный (~ен, ~на) *adj.* autocratic.
самоде́рж|ец, ца *m.* autocrat.
самоде́рж|ица, ицы *f. of* ⇒**~ец**
самоде́ятельност|ь, и *f.* **1** initiative, spontaneous action. **2** (*художественная деятельность*) amateur activities (*theatricals, music, etc.*); **ве́чер ~и** amateurs' night.
самоде́ятел|ьный (~ен, ~ьна) *adj.* **1** independent. **2** (*не профессиональный*) amateur. **3** (*econ.*) self-employed.
самодисципли́н|а, ы *f.* self-discipline.
самодовле́ющий *adj.* self-sufficient.
самодово́л|ьный (~ен, ~ьна) *adj.* self-satisfied, smug, complacent.
самодово́льств|о, а *nt.* self-satisfaction, smugness, complacency.
самодоста́точ|ный (~ен, ~на) *adj.* self-sufficient.
самоду́р, а *m.* petty tyrant.
самоду́рств|о, а *nt.* petty tyranny.
самозабве́ни|е, я *nt.* selflessness.
самозабве́н|ный (~ен, ~на) *adj.* selfless.
самозаводя́щийся *adj.* self-winding.
самозарожде́ни|е, я *nt.* (*biol.*) spontaneous generation.
самозаря́дный *adj.* self-loading.
самозащи́т|а, ы *f.* self-defence (*Br.*), self-defense (*US*).
самозва́н|ец, ца *m.* impostor, pretender.
самозва́н|ка, ки *f. of* ⇒**~ец**
самозва́нный *adj.* false, self-styled.
самозва́нств|о, а *nt.* imposture.
самока́т, а *m.* (*child's*) scooter.
самоконтро́л|ь, я *m.* self-control.
самокопа́ни|е, я *nt.* (*coll.*) self-analysis.
самокри́тик|а, и *f.* self-criticism.
самокрити́ч|ный (~ен, ~на) *adj.* self-critical.
самокру́тк|а, и *f.* (*coll.*) roll-up (*Br.*), roll-your-own.

С

самолёт, а *m.* (aero)plane (*Br.*), (air)plane (*US*); aircraft.

самолёт|ный *adj. of* ⇨~

самолётострое́ни|е, я *nt.* aircraft construction.

самоли́чно *adv.* (*coll.*) oneself; **сде́лать что-н. с.** to do sth. by o.s.; **я с. э́то ви́дел** I saw it with my own eyes.

самоли́ч|ный (~ен, ~на) *adj.* (*coll.*) personal; **~ное прису́тствие** attendance in person.

самолюби́в|ый (~, ~а) *adj.* proud, haughty.

самолю́би|е, я *nt.* pride, self-esteem; **ло́жное с.** false pride.

самомне́ни|е, я *nt.* conceit, self-importance; **он с больши́м ~ем** he has a high opinion of himself.

самонаблюде́ни|е, я *nt.* (*psych.*) introspection.

самонаводя́щийся *adj.* (*mil.*) (*снаряд*) homing; (*бомба*) smart.

самонаде́янност|ь, и *f.* conceit, arrogance.

самонаде́ян|ный (~, ~на) *adj.* conceited, arrogant.

самоназва́ни|е, я *nt.* native name, own name; **ро́мэни — с. цыга́н** 'Romany' is the gypsies' own name for themselves.

самообвине́ни|е, я *nt.* self-accusation.

самооблада́ни|е, я *nt.* self-control, self-possession, composure.

самообма́н, а *m.* self-deception.

самообольще́ни|е, я *nt.* self-deception; **пребыва́ть в ~и** to live in a fool's paradise.

самооборо́н|а, ы *f.* self-defence (*Br.*), self-defense (*US*).

самообразова́ни|е, я *nt.* self-education.

самообслу́живани|е, я *nt.* self-service.

самоокупа́емост|ь, и *f.* (*econ.*) self-sufficiency, ability to pay its way (*without subsidy*).

самоокупа́ющийся *adj.* (*econ.*) self-sufficient, paying its way.

самооплодотворе́ни|е, я *nt.* (*biol.*) self-fertilization.

самоопределе́ни|е, я *nt.* self-determination.

самоопредел|и́ться, ю́сь, и́шься *pf.* (*of* ⇨**~я́ться**) (*also pol.*) to define one's position.

самоопредел|я́ться, я́юсь *impf. of* ⇨**~и́ться**

самоопроки́дывающийся *adj.* self-tipping; **с. грузови́к** dumper truck (*Br.*), dump truck (*US*).

самоопыле́ни|е, я *nt.* (*bot.*) self-fertilization.

самоотверже́ни|е, я *nt.* = **самоотве́рженность**

самоотве́рженност|ь, и *f.* selflessness.

самоотве́ржен|ный (~, ~на) *adj.* selfless, self-sacrificing.

самоотво́д, а *m.* withdrawal (*of candidature*), refusal to accept (*nomination for an office, etc.*).

самоотрече́ни|е, я *nt.* self-denial, (self-)abnegation.

самооце́нк|а, и *f.* self-appraisal.

самоочеви́д|ный (~ен, ~на) *adj.* self-evident.

самопи́с|ец, ца *m.*: **бортово́й с.** (*aeron.*) flight recorder.

самопоже́ртвовани|е, я *nt.* self-sacrifice.

самопозна́ни|е, я *nt.* (*phil.*) self-knowledge.

самопроизво́льност|ь, и *f.* spontaneity

самопроизво́л|ьный (~ен, ~ьна) *adj.* spontaneous.

самопря́лк|а, и *f.* (treadle) spinning-wheel.

саморазгружа́ющ|ийся *adj.* self-unloading; **~аяся ба́ржа** hopper (-barge).

саморазоблаче́ни|е, я *nt.* self-exposure.

саморегули́рующий *adj.* self-regulating.

саморекла́м|а, ы *f.* self-advertisement.

саморо́д|ный (~ен, ~на) *adj.* (*min.*) native, virgin; (*талант*) natural.

саморо́д|ок, ка *m.* (*min.*) nugget; (*человек*) naturally talented person; a natural; **компози́тор-с.** born composer, natural composer.

самоса́д, а *m.* home-grown tobacco.

самоса́дочн|ый *adj.*: **~ая соль** lake-salt; **~ое о́зеро** salt lake.

самосва́л, а *m.* dump truck.

самосожже́ни|е, я *nt.* self-immolation.

самосозна́ни|е, я *nt.* self-awareness; **кла́ссовое с.** class consciousness.

самосохране́ни|е, я *nt.* self-preservation.

самости́йник, а *m.* Ukrainian separatist.

самости́|йный (~ен, ~йна) *adj.* (*liter.*) independent.

самостоя́тельно *adv.* independently; on one's own.

самостоя́тельност|ь, и *f.* independence.

самостоя́тел|ьный (~ен, ~ьна) *adj.* independent.

самостре́л[1], а *m.* (*hist.*) arbalest, cross-bow.

самостре́л[2], а *m.* **1** (*действие*) self-infliction of a wound (*designed to escape onerous military duty, etc.*). **2** (*coll.*) (*солдат*) soldier with self-inflicted wound.

самосу́д, а *m.* lynch law, mob law.

самотёк, а *m.* drift (*also fig.*); **пусти́ть де́ло на с.** to let things slide.

самотёком *adv.* **1** (*tech.*) by gravity. **2** (*стихийно*) haphazardly; of its own accord; **идти́ с.** to drift.

самоуби́йственный *adj.* suicidal (*also fig.*).

самоуби́йств|о, а *nt.* suicide; **поко́нчить жизнь ~ом** to commit suicide.

самоуби́йц|а, ы *c.g.* suicide (*victim*).

самоуваже́ни|е, я *nt.* self-esteem.

самоуве́ренност|ь, и *f.* self-confidence, self-assurance.

самоуве́рен|ный (~, ~на) *adj.* self-confident, self-assured.

самоуни(чи)же́ни|е, я *nt.* self-abasement, self-disparagement.

самоуправле́ни|е, я *nt.* self-government; **ме́стное с.** local government.

самоуправля́ющийся *adj.* self-governing.

самоупра́вно *adv.* arbitrarily; **поступа́ть с.** to take the law into one's own hands.

самоупра́в|ный (~ен, ~на) *adj.* arbitrary.

самоупра́вств|о, а *nt.* arbitrariness.

самоуспокое́ни|е, я *nt.* complacency.

самоуспоко́енност|ь, и *f.* = **самоуспокое́ние**

самоуста́навливающийся *adj.* (*tech.*) self-adjusting, self-aligning.

самоустран|и́ться, ю́сь, и́шься *pf.* (*of* ⇨**~я́ться**) (**от** + *g.*) to get out (of), dodge.

самоустран|я́ться, я́юсь *impf.* **1** *impf. of* ⇨**~и́ться. 2** *impf. only* (**от** + *g.*) to try to get out (of), try to dodge.

самоучи́тел|ь, я *m.* manual for self-tuition; **с. англи́йского языка́** teach-yourself English book.

самоу́чк|а, и *c.g.* self-taught person.

самохва́льств|о, а *nt.* self-advertisement.

самохо́дный *adj.* self-propelled.

самоцве́т, а *m.* semi-precious stone, gem.

самоцве́т|ный *adj.*: **с. ка́мень** = ~

самоце́л|ь, и *f.* end in itself.

самочи́н|ный (~ен, ~на) *adj.* arbitrary, unauthorized.

самочу́встви|е, я *nt.* general state; **у него́ плохо́е с.** he feels bad; **как ва́ше с.?** how are you (keeping)?

самура́|й, я *m.* samurai.

самши́т, а *m.* box(-tree).

са́м|ый *pron.* **1** (*in conjunction with nn., esp. denoting points of time or place, and with* **тот** *and* **э́тот**) the very, right; **в ~ое вре́мя** at the right time; **с ~ого нача́ла** from the very outset, right from the start; **с ~ого утра́** ever since the morning, since first thing; **в ~ом углу́** right in the corner; **до ~ого ве́рха** to the very top, right to the top; **до ~ого Владивосто́ка** right to, all the way to Vladivostok; **в с. раз** (*coll.*) just right; **в~ом де́ле** indeed; **в ~ом де́ле?** indeed?, really?; **на ~ом де́ле** actually, in (actual) fact; **тот с. челове́к, кото́рый**... the very man who ...; **на э́том ~ом ме́сте** on this very spot. **2**: **тот же с. (кото́рый, что); тако́й же с. (как)** the same (as); **э́тот же с.** the same. **3** *forms superl. of adjs.; also expr. superl.*

in conjunction with certain nn. denoting degree of quantity or quality; **с. глýпый** the stupidest, the most stupid; **~ые пустякú** the merest trifles; **погодúте ~ую мáлость!** wait just one moment!; just a second!

сан, а *m.* rank; office; **высóкий с.** high office; **духóвный с.** holy orders, the cloth; **быть посвящённым в духóвный с.** to be ordained.

сан... *comb. form, abbr. of* ***санитáрный***

санатóри|й, я *m.* sanatorium.

санатóр|ный *adj. of* ⇒**~ий; с. режúм** sanatorium regimen.

сангвúник, а *m.* sanguine person.

сангвинúческий *adj.* sanguine.

сандáл, а *m.* sandal-wood tree.

сандалéт|ы, ~ *no sg.* sandals.

сандáли|я, и *f.* sandal.

сандáловый *adj.* sandal-wood.

сáн|и, éй *no sg.* sledge (*Br.*), sled (*US*); sleigh; **éхать в, на ~я́х** to drive in a sleigh; (*спортивные*) toboggan.

санитáр, а *m.* hospital orderly; (*mil.*) medical orderly.

санитарú|я, и *f.* sanitation.

санитáр|ка, ки *f. of* ⇒**~**

санитáрн|ый *adj.* **1** (*связанный с медицинской службой*) medical; hospital; **~ая полевáя сýмка** (*mil.*) first-aid kit; **с. самолёт** ambulance plane; **~ая слýжба** health service, medical service; **~ое сýдно** hospital ship; **~ая часть** (*mil.*) medical unit. **2** (*связанный с санитарией*) sanitary; sanitation; **с. врач** sanitary inspector; **с. день** cleaning day; **~ые прáвила** sanitary regulations; **с. ýзел** lavatory; sanitary unit.

сáн|ки, ок *no sg.* **1** = **~и. 2** (*небольшие, ручные сани*) toboggan.

Санкт-Петербýрг, а *m.* St Petersburg.

санкт-петербýргский *adj.* St Petersburg.

санкционúр|овать, ую *impf. and pf.* to sanction.

сáнкци|я, и *f.* **1** sanction, approval. **2** *pl.* (*pol., econ.*) sanctions.

сáн|ный *adj. of* ⇒**~и; с. путь** sleigh-road.

сановúт|ый (~, ~а) *adj.* **1** (*человек*) high-ranking. **2** (*внешность*) imposing.

санóвник, а *m.* dignitary, high official.

санóв|ный (~ен, ~на) *adj.* high-ranking.

санскрúт, а *m.* Sanskrit.

санскрúтский *adj.* Sanskrit.

Сáнта-Клáус, Сáнта-Клáуса *m.* Santa Claus.

сантéхник, а *m.* plumber.

сантéхник|а, и *f.* plumbing equipment.

сантигрáмм, а *m.* centigram.

сантилúтр, а *m.* centilitre (*Br.*), centiliter (*US*).

сантúм, а *m.* centime.

сантимéнт|ы, ов *no sg.* (*coll.*) sentimentality; **развестú с.** to sentimentalize.

сантимéтр, а *m.* **1** centimetre (*Br.*), centimeter (*US*). **2** (*лента*) tape-measure.

санýз|ел, лá *m. see* ⇒**санитáрный**

Сан-Францúско *m. indecl.* San Francisco.

сап[1], а *m.* (*med.*) glanders.

сап[2], а *m.* (*coll.*) stertorous breathing.

сáп|а, ы *f.* (*mil.*) sap; **тúхой ~ой** (*coll.*) on the sly, on the quiet.

сапёр, а *m.* (*mil.*) sapper.

сапёр|ный *adj. of* ⇒**~; ~ные рабóты** field engineering.

сапóг, á, *g.pl.* **сапóг** *m.* boot.

сапóжник, а *m.* shoemaker, cobbler.

сапóжн|ый *adj.* boot, shoe; **~ая вáкса, с. крем** shoe-polish; **~ое ремеслó** shoemaking.

сапфúр, а *m.* sapphire.

сарабáнд|а, ы *f.* (*mus.*) saraband.

Сарáев|о, а *nt.* Sarajevo.

сарá|й, я *m.* **1** (*для дров, животных*) shed; (*для сена*) barn; **карéтный с.** coach-house. **2** (*fig., coll.*) (*о комнате*) tip.

саранч|á, ú *no pl., f.* locust(s).

сарафáн, а *m.* (*национальная женская одежда*) sarafan (*peasant women's sleeveless dress, buttoning in front*); (*платье*) pinafore dress (*Br.*), jumper (*US*).

сарацúн, а *m.* (*hist.*) Saracen.

сардéльк|а, и *f.* (*fat*) sausage (*of frankfurter type*).

сардúн|а, ы *f.* sardine, pilchard.

сардúн|ец, ца *m.* Sardinian.

Сардúни|я, и *f.* Sardinia.

сардúн|ка, ки *f.* = **~а**

сардúнский *adj.* Sardinian.

сардонúческий *adj.* sardonic.

сáрж|а, и *f.* (*text.*) serge.

саркáзм, а *m.* sarcasm.

саркастúческий *adj.* sarcastic.

саркофáг, а *m.* sarcophagus.

сары́ч, á *m.* (*zool.*) buzzard.

сатан|á, ы́ *m.* Satan.

сатанúзм, а *m.* satanism.

сатанúнский *adj.* satanic.

сатанúст, а *m.* satanist.

сателлúт, а *m.* (*astron.*; *fig.*) satellite.

сатúн, а *m.* (*text.*) sateen.

сатинéт, а *m.* (*text.*) satinet(te).

сатинúр|овать, ую *impf. and pf.* to satin.

сатúн|овый *adj. of* ⇒**~**

сатúр, а *m.* (*myth.*) satyr.

сатúр|а, ы *f.* satire.

сатúрик, а *m.* satirist.

сатирúческий *adj.* satirical.

сатрáп, а *m.* satrap.

сатурáтор, а *m.* soda-fountain.

сатурнáл|ии, ий *no sg.* (*hist.*) saturnalia.

саýдов|ец, ца *m.* Saudi.

саýдов|ка, ки *f. of* ⇒**~ец**

Саýдовск|ая Арáви|я, ~ой ~и *f.* Saudi Arabia.

саýдовский *adj.* Saudi.

сáун|а, ы *f.* sauna.

саундтрéк, а *m.* sound-track.

сафáри *nt. indecl.* safari; **«с.» зоопáрк** safari park.

сафья́н, а *m.* morocco (leather).

сафья́новый *adj.* morocco (leather).

Сахалúн, а *m.* Sakhalin.

сáхар, а (у) *m.* sugar.

Сахáр|а, ы *f.* the Sahara (*desert*).

сахарúн, а *m.* saccharin(e).

сáхарист|ый (~, ~а) *adj.* sugary; saccharine.

сáхар|ить, ю, ишь *impf.* (*of* ⇒**по~**) to sugar, sweeten.

сáхарниц|а, ы *f.* sugar-basin.

сáхар|ный *adj. of* ⇒**~**; (*fig.*) sugary; **~ная болéзнь** (*med.*) diabetes; **~ная глазýрь** icing; **~ная головá** sugar-loaf; **с. завóд** sugar-refinery; **с. песóк** granulated sugar; **~ная пýдра** icing sugar; **~ная свёкла** sugar-beet; **с. тростнúк** sugar-cane.

сахарóз|а, ы *f.* (*chem.*) sucrose.

сачк|овáть, ýю *impf.* (*coll.*) to loaf.

сач|óк[1], кá *m.* net; **с. для ры́бы** landing-net; **с. для бáбочек** butterfly-net.

сач|óк[2], кá *m.* (*coll.*) (*бездельник*) loafer.

сбáв|ить, лю, ишь *pf.* (*of* ⇒**~ля́ть**) (**с** + *g.*) to reduce; **с. в вéсе** to lose weight; **с. спéси комý-н.** (*coll.*) to take s.o. down a peg.

сбавля́|ть, ю *impf. of* ⇒**сбáвить**

сбалансúрованност|ь, и *f.* balance.

сбалансúр|овать, ую *pf. of* ⇒**балансúровать**

сбáлтыва|ть, ю *impf. of* ⇒**сболтáть**

сбéга|ть, ю *pf.* (**за** + *i.*; *coll.*) to run (for), run to fetch; **~й за дóктором!** run for a doctor!

сбегá|ть(ся), ю *impf. of* ⇒**сбежáть(ся)**

сбе|жáть, гý, жúшь, гýт *pf.* (*of* ⇒**~гáть**) **1** (**с** + *g.*) (*спуститься*) to run down (from); **с. с лéстницы** to run downstairs. **2** (*убежать*) to run away. **3** (**с** + *g.*; *fig.*) (*исчезнуть*) to disappear, vanish; **хмýрое выражéние ~жáло с егó лицá** the frown vanished from his face.

сбе|жáться, жúтся, гýтся *pf.* (*of* ⇒**~гáться**) to come running; to gather, collect.

сбер... *comb. form, abbr. of* ***сберегáтельный***

сбербáнк, а *m.* = **сберкáсса**

сберегáтельн|ый *adj.*: **~ая кáсса** savings bank; **~ая кнúжка** savings-bank book.

сберегá|ть, ю *impf. of* ⇒**сберéчь**

сбережéни|е, я *nt.* **1** (*действие*) (*денег*) saving; (*здоровья*) preservation; (*оружия*) care. **2** (*pl.*) (*деньги*) savings.

сберé|чь, гý, жёшь, гýт, *past* **~г,**

С

~гла́ *pf.* (*of* ⇒**~га́ть**) **1** (*время*) to save; (*семью*) to protect, look after; (*здоровье*) to preserve. **2** (*деньги*) to save, save up.

сберка́сс|а, ы *f.* savings bank.

сберкни́жк|а, и *f.* savings book.

сбива́лк|а, и *f.* (*coll., cul.*) (egg-)whisk.

сбива́|ть, ю *impf. of* ⇒**сбить**

сбива́|ться, юсь *impf.* **1** *impf. of* ⇒**сби́ться. 2** *impf. only* (**на** + *a.*) to resemble; to remind one (of).

сби́вчивост|ь, и *f.* inconsistency, contradictoriness.

сби́вчив|ый (~, ~а) *adj.* inconsistent, contradictory.

сби́т|ый *p.p.p. of* ⇒**~ь** *and adj.*: **~ые сли́вки** whipped cream.

сбить, собью́, собьёшь *pf.* (*of* ⇒**сбива́ть**) **1** (*ударом*) to bring down, knock down; (*с чего-либо*) to knock off, dislodge; (*птицу, самолёт*) to bring down, shoot down; **с. проти́вника с пози́ций** to dislodge the enemy from his positions; (*цену, температуру*) to bring down; **с. спесь с кого́-н.** to bring s.o. down a peg.
2 (*отклонить*) to put out; to distract; to deflect; **с. с та́кта** to throw out of time; **с. кого́-н. с то́лку** to confuse s.o.; **с. кого́-н. с доро́ги** to misdirect s.o.; **с. кого́-н. с пути́ и́стинного** (*fig.*) to lead s.o. astray.
3 (*каблуки, туфли*) to wear down.
4 (*составить*) to knock together; **с. я́щик из досо́к** to knock together a box out of planks.
5 (*impf. also* **бить**) (*масло*) to churn; (*сливки*) to beat up, whip, whisk.

сби́ться, собью́сь, собьёшься *pf.* (*of* ⇒**сбива́ться**) **1** (*сдвинуться с места*) to be dislodged; to slip; **у тебя́ шля́па сби́лась на́бок** your hat is crooked, skew-whiff; **с. с ног** (*coll.*) to be run off one's feet. **2** (*ошибиться*) to go wrong; **с. в вычисле́ниях** to be out in one's calculations; **с. в показа́ниях** to be inconsistent in one's testimony; **с. с доро́ги, с. с пути́** to lose one's way; to go astray (*also fig.*); **с. со счёта** to lose count; **с. с та́кта** to get out of time. **3** (*об обуви*) to become worn down. **4**: **с. в ку́чу, с. толпо́й** to bunch, huddle.

сближа́|ть(ся), ю(сь) *impf. of* ⇒**сбли́зить(ся)**

сближе́ние, я *nt.* **1** (*pol.*) rapprochement. **2** (*mil.*) approach, closing in. **3** (*дружба*) intimacy.

сбли́|зить, жу, зишь *pf.* (*of* ⇒**~жа́ть**) to bring together, draw together.

сбли́|зиться, жусь, зишься *pf.* (*of* ⇒**~жа́ться**) **1** (*об интересах*) to converge. **2** (**с** + *i.*) (*о людях*) to become close friends (with). **3** (*mil.*) to approach, close in.

сбо|й[1], я *m.* (*collect.*) head, legs, and entrails.

сбо|й[2], я *m.* (*перебой*) interruption; malfunction.

сбо́ку *adv.* from one side; on one side; **вид с.** side-view; **смотре́ть на кого́-н. с.** to look sideways at s.o.

сболта́|ть, ю *pf.* (*of* ⇒**сба́лтывать**) to stir up, shake up, mix up; **с. лека́рство** to shake (a bottle of) medicine.

сболтн|у́ть, у, ёшь *pf.* (*coll.*) to blurt out, let out.

сбор, а *m.* **1** (*действие*) collection; **с. урожа́я** harvest; **с. нало́гов** tax collection. **2** (*деньги*) dues; duty; (*выручка*) takings, returns; **ге́рбовый с.** stamp-duty; **порто́вый с.** harbour (*Br.*), harbor (*US*) dues; **тамо́женный с.** customs duty; **по́лный с.** (*theatr.*) full house; **де́лать хоро́шие ~ы** (*theatr.*) to play to full houses, get good box-office returns. **3** (*встреча*) assembly, gathering; **быть в ~е** to be assembled, be in session. **4** (*mil.*) assembly (= *signal to assemble*). **5** (*pl.*) (*приготовления*) preparations.

сбо́рищ|е, а *nt.* assemblage, mob.

сбо́рк|а, и *f.* **1** (*tech.*) assembling, assembly, erection. **2** (*на платье*) gather; **в ~ах, со ~ами** with gathers.

сбо́рник, а *m.* collection; anthology.

сбо́рн|ый *adj.* **1** (*дом*) prefabricated; (*мебель*) in kit form. **2** (*из разнородных частей*) mixed, combined; **~ая кома́нда** (*sport*) combined team, representative team. **3** (*mil.*) assembly; **с. пункт** assembly point.

сбо́рочный *adj.* (*tech.*) assembly; **с. конве́йер** assembly belt; **с. цех** assembly shop.

сбо́рчатый *adj.* gathered, with gathers.

сбо́рщик, а *m.* **1** collector; **с. нало́гов** tax-collector. **2** (*tech.*) assembler, fitter.

сбра́сыва|ть(ся), ю(сь) *impf. of* ⇒**сбро́сить(ся)**

сбре́нд|ить, ишь *pf.* (*coll.*)
1 (*струсить*) to get scared.
2 (*потерять рассудок*) to lose one's mind; to go mad.

сбрива́|ть, ю *impf. of* ⇒**сбрить**

сбрить, сбре́ю, сбре́ешь *pf.* (*of* ⇒**сбрива́ть**) to shave off.

сброд, а *no pl., m.* (*collect.*) riff-raff, rabble.

сбро́дн|ый *adj.* (*coll.*) assembled by chance; **~ая компа́ния** motley collection of people.

сброс, а *m.* **1** (*tech.*) overflow disposal (system). **2** (*бомб*) dropping; (*температуры*) reduction.

сбро́|сить, шу, сишь *pf.* (*of* ⇒**сбра́сывать**) **1** (*бросить вниз*) to throw down; to drop; **с. бо́мбы** to drop bombs; **с. на парашю́те** to drop by parachute. **2** (*скинуть*) to throw off (*also fig.*); (*кожу, листья*) to shed; **с. с себя́ одея́ло** to throw off a blanket; **с. и́го** to throw off the yoke; (*свергнуть*) to overthrow. **3** (*сбавить*) to reduce.
4 (*карты*) to throw away, discard.

сбро́|ситься, шусь, сишься *pf.* (*of* ⇒**сбра́сываться**) (**с** + *g.*) to leap (off, from).

сброшюр|ова́ть, у́ю *pf. of* ⇒**брошюрова́ть**

сбру́|я, и *f.* (*collect.*) harness.

сбыва́|ть(ся), ю, ет(ся) *impf. of* ⇒**сбы́ть(ся)**

сбыт, а *no pl., m.* (*econ., comm.*) sale; **ры́нок ~а** (seller's) market; **хоро́ший с.** good sales.

сбытово́й *adj.* (*econ., comm.*) selling, marketing.

сбы́тчик, а *m.*: **с. нарко́тиков** drug dealer *or* trafficker.

сбыть[1], сбу́ду, сбу́дешь, *past* **сбыл, сбыла́, сбы́ло** *pf.* (*of* ⇒**сбыва́ть**) **1** (*продать*) to sell, market. **2** (*coll.*) (*избавиться*) to get rid (of), rid o.s. (of); (*comm.*) to dump; **с. с рук** to get off one's hands.

сбыть[2], сбу́дет, *past* **сбыл, сбыла́, сбы́ло** *pf.* (*of* ⇒**сбыва́ть**) (*о поднявшейся воде*) to fall.

сбы́ться, сбу́дется, *past* **сбы́лся, сбыла́сь** *pf.* (*of* ⇒**сбыва́ться**) to come true, be realized.

СВ *pl. indecl.* (*abbr of* ***сре́дние во́лны***) MW (*medium wave*).

св. (*abbr. of* ***свято́й***) St, Saint.

сва́дебный *adj.* wedding; nuptial; **с. пода́рок** wedding present.

сва́д|ьба, ьбы, *g. pl.* **~еб** *f.* wedding; **справля́ть ~ьбу** to celebrate a wedding.

свайнобо́йный *adj.* pile-driving.

сва́йн|ый *adj.* pile; **~ые постро́йки** pile-dwellings.

сва́лива|ть(ся), ю(сь) *impf. of* **свали́ть(ся)**

свал|и́ть[1], ю́, ~ишь *pf.* (*of* ⇒**вали́ть[1]** *and* **~ивать**) **1** (*ударом*) to throw down, bring down; (*coll.*) (*свергнуть*) to overthrow; (*coll.*) (*о болезни*) to lay low. **2** (*дрова, уголь*) to heap up, pile up; **с. вину́** (**на** + *a.*) to dump the blame (on).

свал|и́ть[2], ~ит *pf.* (*coll.*) (*уменьшиться*) to sink, drop, fall, abate.

свал|и́ться, ю́сь, ~ишся *pf.* (*of* ⇒**вали́ться** *and* **~иваться**) to fall (down), collapse; **с. как снег на́ голову** to come like a bolt from the blue.

сва́лк|а, и *f.* **1** (*для мусора*) dump; scrap heap. **2** (*coll.*) (*драка*) scuffle, fight; **о́бщая с.** free-for-all, mêlée.

сваля́|ть, ю *pf. of* ⇒**валя́ть** 3, 4

сваля́|ться, ется *pf.* to get tangled.

сварга́н|ить, ю, ишь *pf. of* ⇒**варга́нить**

сва́рива|ть(ся), ю(сь) *impf. of* ⇒**свари́ть(ся)**

свар|и́ть, ю́, ~ишь *pf.* **1** *pf. of* ⇒**вари́ть. 2** (*impf.* **~ивать**) (*tech.*) to weld.

свар|и́ться, ю́сь, ~ишься *pf.* **1** *pf. of* ⇒**вари́ться. 2** (*impf.* **~иваться**) (*tech.*) to weld (together).

сва́рк|а, и *f.* (*tech.*) welding; **то́чечная с.** spot welding.

сварли́в|ый (~, ~а) *adj.* quarrelsome, shrewish.

сварно́й *adj.* (*tech.*) welded; **с. шов** welded joint.

сва́рочн|ый *adj.* (*tech.*) welding; **~ая горе́лка** welding torch, burner; **~ая сталь** wrought iron.

сва́рщик, а *m.* welder.

сва́стик|а, и *f.* swastika.

сват, а *m.* **1** matchmaker. **2** (*отец*

зятя) son-in-law's father; (*отец невестки*) daughter-in-law's father.

сва́та|ть, ю *impf.* (*of* ⇒**по~**) **1** (*pf. also* **со~**) (+*a. and d.*) to propose as husband; (*also* +*a. and* **за**+*a.*) to propose as wife; to (try to) marry off (to); to (try to) arrange a match (between); **ему́, за него́ ~ют вдову́** they are trying to arrange a match for him with a widow; they are trying to marry him off to a widow. **2** (*просить согласие на брак*) to ask in marriage.

сва́та|ться, юсь *impf.* (*of* ⇒**по~**) (**к**+*d. or* **за**+*a.*) to court; to ask, seek in marriage.

сва́ть|я, и *f.* (*мать зятя*) son-in-law's mother; (*мать невестки*) daughter-in-law's mother.

сва́х|а, и *f.* matchmaker.

сва́|я, и *f.* pile.

све́дени|е, я *nt.* **1** (*известие*) piece of information; (*pl.*) information, intelligence; **по полу́ченным ~ям** according to information received. **2** (*знание*) knowledge; attention, consideration, notice; **дойти́ до чьего́-н. ~я** to come to s.o.'s notice; **довести́ до чьего́-н. ~я** to bring to s.o.'s notice, inform s.o.; **приня́ть к ~ю** to take into consideration. **3** (*pl.*) (*познания*) knowledge; **у него́ обши́рные ~я по исто́рии Росси́и** he is very knowledgeable about the history of Russia.

сведе́ни|е, я *nt.* **1** (*расходов*) reduction; **с. счётов** settling of accounts. **2** (*пятна*) removal. **3** (*соединение*) bringing together. **4** (*med.*) contraction, cramp. **5** (*electronics*) mixing (*in sound recording*).

све́дущ|ий (~, ~а) *adj.* (**в**+*p.*) knowledgeable (about); (well-)versed (in).

свеж|ева́ть, у́ю *impf.* (*of* ⇒**о~**) to skin, dress.

свежезаморо́женный *adj.* fresh-frozen.

свежеиспечённый *adj.* newly-baked.

све́жест|ь, и *f.* freshness; (*прохлада*) coolness; **не пе́рвой ~и** (*coll.*) past its (*fig., joc.*; one's) best.

свеже́|ть, ю *impf.* (*of* ⇒**по~**) **1** to become cooler; (*о ветре*) to freshen (up), blow up. **2** (*о человеке*) to freshen up, acquire a glow of health.

све́ж|ий (~, ~а́, ~о́, ~и́) *adj.* fresh; **~ее бельё** clean underclothes; **с. ве́тер** fresh breeze; **на ~ем во́здухе** in the fresh air; **~ие но́вости** recent news; **со ~ими си́лами** with renewed strength; **с. цвет лица́** fresh complexion; **~о́ в па́мяти** fresh in one's memory; (*impers., as pred.*): **~о́** it is fresh, it is blowing up.

свез|ти́, у́, ёшь, *past* **~́, ~ла́** *pf.* (*of* ⇒**свози́ть**[1]) **1** (*отвезти*) to take, convey; **его́ ~ли́ в больни́цу** he has been taken to hospital. **2** (*вниз*) to take down. **3** (*увезти*) to take away, clear away.

свёкл|а, ы *f.* beet, beetroot (*Br.*); **кормова́я с.** mangel-wurzel; **са́харная с.** sugar-beet, white beet; **столо́вая с.** red beet.

свеклови́ц|а, ы *f.* sugar-beet.

свеклови́|чный *adj. of* ⇒**~ца; с. са́хар** beet-sugar.

свеклоса́харный *adj.* sugar-beet; beet-sugar.

свеко́льник, а *m.* **1** (*суп*) beetroot soup. **2** (*ботва*) beet tops.

свеко́льный *adj. of* ⇒**свёкла**

свёк|ор, ра *m.* father-in-law (*husband's father*).

свекро́в|ь, и *f.* mother-in-law (*husband's mother*).

сверб|ёж, ежа́ *m.* (*coll.*) itch, irritation.

сверб|е́ть, и́т *impf.* (*coll.*) to itch, irritate.

сверг|а́ть, а́ю *impf. of* ⇒**~́нуть**

све́рг|нуть, ну, нешь, *past* **~** *and* **~нул, ~ла** *pf.* (*of* ⇒**~а́ть**) to throw down, overthrow; **с. с престо́ла** to dethrone.

сверже́ни|е, я *nt.* overthrow.

све́р|зиться, жусь, зишься *pf.* (**с**+*g.*; *coll.*) to tumble (off, from).

све́р|ить, ю, ишь *pf.* (*of* ⇒**~я́ть**) (+*a.* **с**+*i.*) to check (sth. against sth.).

све́р|иться, юсь, ишься *pf.* (*of* ⇒**~я́ться**) (**с**+*i.*) to check (with).

све́рк|а, и *f.* collation.

сверка́ни|е, я *nt.* sparkling; glitter; glare; (*молнии*) flashing.

сверка́|ть, ю *impf.* to sparkle; to glitter; to gleam; (*о молнии*) to flash.

сверкн|у́ть, у́, ёшь *pf.* to flash (*also fig.*); **у меня́ в голове́ ~у́ла мысль** a thought flashed through my mind.

сверли́льный *adj.* (*tech.*) boring, drilling; **с. стано́к** boring machine, drilling machine, drill.

сверл|и́ть, ю́, и́шь *impf.* **1** (*tech.*) to bore, drill; **с. зуб** to drill a tooth. **2** (*о насекомых*) to bore through. **3** (*fig.*) (*о мыслях*) to nag (at), gnaw (at); **у меня́ ~и́т в у́хе** I have a nagging earache.

сверл|о́, а́, *pl.* **~́а** *nt.* (*tech.*) (*инструмент*) drill; (*пёрка*) drill bit.

сверл|я́щий *pres. part. act. of* ⇒**~и́ть** *and adj.*; **~я́щая боль** nagging, gnawing pain.

сверн|у́ть, у́, ёшь *pf.* (*of* ⇒**свёртывать** *and* **свора́чивать**) **1** to roll (up); **с. ковёр** to roll up the carpet; **с. сигаре́ту** to roll a cigarette; **с. паруса́** to furl sails; **с. ше́ю кому́-н.** to wring s.o.'s neck. **2** (*fig.*) (*сократить*) to reduce, contract, cut down. **3** (*повернуть*) to turn; **с. нале́во** to turn to the left; **с. с доро́ги** to turn off the road.

сверн|у́ться, у́сь, ёшься *pf.* (*of* ⇒**свёртываться**) **1** to roll up, curl up; to coil up; **с. клубко́м** to roll o.s. up into a ball. **2** (*о молоке*) to curdle; (*о крови*) to coagulate, clot. **3** (*fig.*) (*сократиться*) to contract.

сверста́|ть, ю *pf. of* ⇒**верста́ть**

све́рстник, а *m.* person of the same age; contemporary, peer; **мы с ним ~и** he and I are the same age.

свёрт|ок, ка *m.* package, parcel, bundle.

свёртывани|е, я *nt.* **1** rolling (up). **2** (*молока*) curdling; (*крови*) coagulation. **3** (*fig.*) (*сокращение*) reduction, cutting down; **с. произво́дства** production cuts.

свёртыва|ть(ся), ю(сь) *impf. of* ⇒**сверну́ть(ся)**

сверх *prep.*+*g.* **1** (*пиджака*) over, on top of; (*книги*) on top of. **2** (*нормы*) above, beyond; over and above; in excess of; **с. пла́на** in excess of the plan; **с. сил** beyond one's strength; **с. (вся́кого) ожида́ния** beyond (all) expectation; **с. всего́** on top of everything else; **с. того́** moreover, besides.

сверх... *comb. form* super-, supra-, extra-, over-, preter-.

сверхдержа́в|а, ы *f.* superpower.

сверхзвуково́й *adj.* (*phys., aeron.*) supersonic.

сверхмагистра́л|ь, и *f.*: **информацио́нная с.** information superhighway.

сверхмо́щный *adj.* (*tech.*) super-power, extra-high-power.

сверхно́в|ый *adj.*: **~ая (звезда́)** (*astron.*) super-nova.

сверхпла́новый *adj.* over and above the plan.

сверхпри́был|ь, и *f.* excess profit.

сверхпроводи́мост|ь, и *f.* (*phys.*) superconductivity.

сверхпроводни́к, а́ *m.* (*phys.*) superconductor.

сверхскоростно́й *adj.* super-high-speed.

сверхсме́тный *adj.* above-estimate, extra-budget.

сверхсро́чник, а *m.* = **сверхсрочнослу́жащий**

сверхсрочнослу́жащ|ий, его *m.* (*mil.*) man re-engaging after completion of statutory military service.

сверхсро́чн|ый *adj.* (*mil.*): **~ая слу́жба** additional service (*voluntarily undertaken after completion of statutory period*).

све́рху *adv.* **1** from above (*also fig.*); from the top; **с. до́низу** from top to bottom; **смотре́ть на кого́-н. с. вниз** (*fig.*) to look down on s.o. **2** (*на поверхности*) on the surface; on the top.

сверхуро́чн|ый *adj.* overtime; **~ая рабо́та** overtime; *as n.* **~ые, ~ых** (*payment for*) overtime.

сверхчелове́к, а *m.* superman.

сверхчелове́ческий *adj.* superhuman.

сверхчувстви́тел|ьный (~ен, ~ьна) *adj.* supersensitive.

сверхшта́тный *adj.* supernumerary.

сверхъесте́ствен|ный (~, ~на) *adj.* supernatural.

сверч|о́к, ка́ *m.* (*zool.*) cricket; **вся́к с. знай свой шесто́к** (*prov.*) the cobbler should stick to his last.

сверша́|ть(сь), ю, ет(ся) *impf.* = **соверша́ть(ся)**

сверш|и́ть(ся), у́, и́т(ся) *pf.* = **соверши́ть(ся)**

свер|я́ть(ся), я́ю(сь) *impf. of* ⇒**~́ить(ся)**

С

свес, а *m.* overhang.

свé|сить, шу, сишь *pf.* (*of* ⇒**~шивать**) **1** to let down, lower; **сидéть, ~сив нóги** to sit with one's legs dangling. **2** (*coll.*) (*взвесить*) to weigh.

свé|ситься, шусь, сишься *pf.* (*of* ⇒**~шиваться**) to lean over; to hang over; (*о ветвях*) to overhang; **с. чéрез перúла** to lean over the banisters.

све|стú, дý, дёшь, *past* **~л, ~лá** *pf.* (*of* ⇒**сводúть**[1]) **1** (*отвести*) to take; **с. детéй в шкóлу** to take the children to school; **с. в могúлу** to be the death (of). **2** (**с**+*g.*) (*спустить сверху вниз*) to take down (from, off); **с. когó-н. с пьедестáла** to take s.o. off his pedestal; **с. с умá** to drive mad.
3 (*удалить*) to take away; to lead off; **с. корóву с дорóги** to take a cow off the road; **с. разговóр на другýю тéму** to lead the conversation onto a different subject.
4 (*вывести*) to remove; **с. пятнó** to remove, get out a stain.
5 (*соединить; собрать*) to bring together; to put together; to unite; **с. стáрых друзéй** to bring old friends together; **судьбá ~лá их** fate threw them together; **с. дáнные в таблúцу** to tabulate data; **с. концы́ с концáми** to make (both) ends meet.
6: **с. дрýжбу** (**с**+*i.*), **с. знакóмство** (**с**+*i.*) (*coll.*) to make friends (with).
7 (**к**+*d. or* **на**+*a.*) (*довести*) to reduce (to), bring (to); **с. на нет** to bring to naught; **с. к сáмому необходúмому** to reduce to the barest essentials; **с. рассkáз к немнóгим словáм** to condense a story to a few words.
8 (*рисунок*) to trace, transfer.
9 (*о судороге*) to cramp, convulse; **у меня́ ~лó нóгу** I have cramp in my foot.
10 (*electronics*) to mix (*in sound recording*).

све|стúсь, дётся, *past* **~лся, ~лáсь** *pf.* (*of* ⇒**сводúться**) (**к**+*d. or* **на**+*a.*) to come (to), reduce (to); **с. на нет** to come to naught.

свет[1], **а** *m.* **1** light (*also fig.*); **лýнный с.** moonlight; **зажéчь с.** to turn the light on; **в ~е** (+*g.*) in the light (of); **представúть в невы́годном ~е** to represent in an unfavourable (*Br.*), unfavorable (*US*) light; **на ~ý** in the light; **при ~е** (+*g.*) by the light (of); **стоя́ть прóтив ~а** to stand in the light.
2 (*рассвет*) daybreak; **чем с.** first thing (in the morning); **чуть с.** at first light; **ни с., ни заря́** before dawn; (*iron.*) at the crack of dawn.

свéт[2], **а** *m.* **1** (*мир*) world (*also fig.*); **стáрый, нóвый с.** the Old, the New World; **тот с.** the next world; **конéц ~а** doomsday, the end of the world; **стрáны ~а** the cardinal points (*of the compass*); **произвестú на с.** to bring into the world; **(по)явúться на с.** to come into the world; **вы́пустить в с.** to bring out (= *to publish*); **ни за что на ~е** not for the world; **на чём с. стоúт** like hell; for all one is, was worth. **2** (*высшее общество*) society; **вы́сший с.** high society; **мóдный с.** the smart set.

светá|ть, ет *impf.*; (*impers.*): **~ет** it is dawning, it is getting light, day is breaking.

светёлк|а, и *f.* (*obs.*) small but very light upstairs room.

светúл|о, а *nt.* luminary (*also fig.*); **небéсные ~а** heavenly bodies.

светúльник, а *m.* lamp.

све|тúть, чý, ~тишь *impf.* **1** (*излучать свет*) to shine. **2** (+*d.*) to light the way (for); to shine a light (for).

све|тúться, чýсь, ~тишься *impf.* to shine, gleam; **в окнé ~тится огонёк** there is a light in the window.

светлéйший *adj.* (*obs.*) (his, her) Highness.

светлé|ть, ю *impf.* (*of* ⇒**по~**) to brighten (*also fig.*); (*о погоде*) to clear up, brighten up.

светлúц|а, ы *f.* (*obs.*) front room.

свéтло-... *comb. form* (*with names of colours*) light-; **светло-зелёный** light-green.

светловолóс|ый (~, ~а) *adj.* light-haired.

светлокóж|ий (~, ~а) *adj.* light-skinned.

свéтлост|ь, и *f.* **1** brightness (*also fig.*); lightness. **2**: **егó,** *etc.*, **с.** (*title of dukes and princes*) his, *etc.*, Grace.

свéт|лый (~ел, ~лá, ~лó) *adj.* **1** (*комната, волосы, краски*) light; (*день*) bright; **на ýлице ~лó** it is daylight. **2** (*fig.*) (*радостный*) bright, radiant, joyous; pure, unclouded; **~лое бýдущее** bright future; **~лой пáмяти** of blessed memory. **3** (*fig.*) (*проницательный*) lucid, clear; **он — ~лая головá** he has a lucid mind; **~лые минýты** lucid intervals. **4** (*eccl.*) Easter; **~лая недéля** Easter week.

светля́к, á *m.* glow-worm; fire-fly.

светов|óй *adj. of* ⇒**свет**[1]; **~áя волнá** light wave; **~áя реклáма** illuminated signs; **с. эффéкт** (*theatr.*) lighting effect.

светодиóд, а *m.* light-emitting diode, LED.

светозáр|ный (~ен, ~на) *adj.* (*poet.*) bright.

светозвукоспектáкл|ь, я *m.* son et lumière.

светокопировáльный *adj.* photocopying.

светокóпи|я, и *f.* photocopy.

светомаскирóвк|а, и *f.* black-out.

светонепроницáемый *adj.* light-proof.

светопреставлéни|е, я *nt.* **1** the end of the world, doomsday. **2** (*fig., coll.*) chaos.

светосигнализáци|я, и *f.* (*mil.*) lamp signalling (*Br.*), signaling (*US*).

светотéн|ь, и *f.* (*art*) chiaroscuro.

светотéхник|а, и *f.* lighting engineering.

светофúльтр, а *m.* light filter.

светофóр, а *m.* traffic lights.

свéточ, а *m.* **1** (*obs.*) torch, lamp. **2** (*fig.*) leading light, luminary; torch-bearer.

светочувствúтельност|ь, и *f.* photo-sensitivity; (*плёнки*) speed.

светочувствúтел|ьный (~ен, ~ьна) *adj.* photo-sensitive.

свéтск|ий *adj.* **1** society, fashionable; **~ая жизнь** high life; **с. человéк** man of the world. **2** (*манеры*) refined. **3** (*не церковный*) temporal, lay, secular; worldly; **~ая власть** temporal power.

свéтскост|ь, и *f.* good manners, good breeding.

свет|я́щийся *pres. part. of* ⇒**~úться** *and adj.* luminous, luminescent.

свеч|á, ú, *i.* **~óй,** *pl.* **~и, ~éй, ~áм** *f.* **1** candle. **2**: **зажигáтельная с., запáльная с.** spark plug. **3** (*единица*) candle-power; **лáмпочка в пятьдеся́т ~éй** lamp of fifty candle-power. **4** (*sport*) lob. **5** (*med.*) suppository.

свечéни|е, я *nt.* luminescence, fluorescence; phosphorescence.

свéчк|а, и *f.* **1** candle. **2** (*sport*) lob. **3** (*med.*) suppository.

свеч|нóй *adj. of* ⇒**~á**; **с. огáрок** candle-end.

свéша|ть, ю *pf.* to weigh.

свéша|ться, юсь *pf. of* ⇒**вéшаться**[2]

свéшива|ть(ся), ю(сь) *impf. of* ⇒**свéсить(ся)**

свивáльник, а *m.* (*obs.*) swaddling-clothes.

свивá|ть, ю *impf.* **1** *impf. of* ⇒**свить. 2** *impf. only* (*obs.*) (*ребёнка*) to swaddle.

свидáни|е, я *nt.* meeting; (*деловое*) appointment; (*влюблённых*) date; **назнáчить с.** (**на**+*a.*) to arrange a meeting (for), make an appointment (for), make a date (for); **до ~я!** good-bye!; **до скóрого ~я!** see you soon!

свидéтел|ь, я *m.* witness; **с. обвинéния, защúты** witness for the prosecution, for the defence (*Br.*), defense (*US*); **с. Иегóвы** Jehovah's Witness.

свидéтель|ница, ницы *f. of* ⇒**~**

свидéтель|ский *adj. of* ⇒**~**

свидéтельств|о, а *nt.* **1** evidence. **2** (*документ*) certificate; **с. о брáке** marriage certificate.

свидéтельств|овать, ую *impf.* **1** (**о**+*p. or* +*a. or* +**что**) (*leg.*) to give evidence (concerning); to testify. **2** (**о**+*p.*) (*подтверждать, доказывать*) to show, attest to, be evidence (of); **э́то письмó ~ует о егó бестáктности** this letter is evidence of his tactlessness. **3** (*pf.* **за~**) (*удостоверять подлинность*) to witness; to attest, certify; **с. кóпию** to certify a copy; **с. пóдпись** to witness a signature. **4** (*pf.* **о~**) (*осматривать*) to examine, inspect; **с. больнóго** to examine a patient.

сви|дéться, жусь, дишься *pf.* (**с**+*i.*; *coll.*) to meet; to see one another.

свинáр|ка, ки *f. of* ⇒ **~ь**

свинáрник, а *m.* pigsty.

свинáр|ня, ни, *g. pl.* **~ен** *f.* = **~ник**

свинáр|ь, я́ *m.* pig-tender.

свин|éц, цá *m.* lead.

свини́н|а, ы *f.* pork.

сви́н|ка¹, ки *f. dim. of* ⇒**~ья́; морска́я с.** guinea-pig.

сви́нк|а², и *f. (med.)* mumps.

свиново́д, а *m.* pig-breeder.

свиново́дств|о, а *nt.* pig-breeding.

свиново́д|ческий *adj. of* ⇒**~ство**

свин|о́й *adj. of* ⇒**~ья́; ~а́я ко́жа** pigskin; **~а́я котле́та** pork chop; **~о́е са́ло** lard.

свинома́тк|а, и *f.* sow.

свинопа́с, а *m. (obs.)* swineherd.

свинофе́рм|а, ы *f.* pig-farm, piggery.

сви́нский *adj. (coll.) (подлый)* swinish; *(грязный)* filthy.

сви́нств|о, а *nt. (coll.) (подлость)* swinishness; *(поступок)* swinish trick; *(грязь)* filth.

свин|ти́ть, чу́, ти́шь *pf. (of* ⇒**~чивать) 1** *(соединить)* to screw together. **2** *(гайку)* to unscrew.

сви́нтус, а *m. (coll., joc.)* swine, rogue.

свинцо́в|ый *adj.* lead; *(цвета свинца)* leaden; **~ые бели́ла** white lead; **с. блеск** *(min.)* galena; **~ая дробь** lead shot; **~ое отравле́ние** lead-poisoning; **с. су́рик** red lead.

сви́нчива|ть, ю *impf. of* ⇒**свинти́ть**

свин|ья́, ьи́, *pl.* **~ьи, ~е́й, ~ьям** *f.* **1** pig; *(самка)* sow; **морска́я с.** porpoise. **2** *(fig.) (человек)* swine; **подложи́ть ~ью́** *(+d.; coll.)* to play a dirty trick (on).

свире́л|ь, и *f.* (reed-)pipe.

свирепе́|ть, ю *impf.* to grow fierce, grow savage.

свире́пост|ь, и *f.* fierceness, ferocity.

свире́пств|овать, ую *impf.* to rage.

свире́п|ый (~, ~а) *adj.* fierce, ferocious.

свиристе́л|ь, я *m. (zool.)* waxwing.

свис|а́ть, а́ю *impf. (of* ⇒**~нуть)** to hang down.

сви́с|нуть, ну, нешь *pf. of* ⇒**~а́ть**

свист, а *m.* whistle; whistling.

сви|ста́ть, щу́, ~щешь *impf.* to whistle; **с. в свисто́к** to blow a whistle; **с. всех наве́рх** *(naut.)* to pipe all hands on deck.

сви|сте́ть, щу́, сти́шь *impf.* to whistle; **ищи́ ~щи́** *(coll.)* you can whistle for it.

сви́стн|уть, у, ешь *pf.* **1** to give a whistle. **2** *(coll.) (ударить)* to slap, smack. **3** *(coll.) (украсть)* to steal, snatch.

свист|о́к, ка́ *m.* whistle.

свистопля́ск|а, и *f. (coll.)* pandemonium, bedlam.

свисту́льк|а, и *f.* tin whistle.

свисту́н, а́ *m.* whistler.

сви́т|а, ы *f.* suite, retinue.

сви́тер, а *m.* sweater.

сви́т|ок, ка *m.* roll, scroll.

свить, совью́, совьёшь, *past* **свил, свила́, сви́ло** *pf. (of* ⇒**вить** *and* ⇒**свива́ть)** to twist, wind.

сви́ться, совью́сь, совьёшься, *past* **сви́лся, свила́сь** *pf. (of* ⇒**ви́ться)** to roll up, curl up, coil.

свихн|у́ть, у́, ёшь *pf.* to dislocate, sprain; **с. себе́ ше́ю** *(fig., coll.)* to come a cropper; **с. с ума́** to go off one's head.

свихн|у́ться, у́сь, ёшься *pf. (coll.)* **1** *(помешаться)* to go off one's head. **2**: **с. с пути́** to go astray, go off the rails.

свищ, а́ *m.* **1** *(в дереве)* knot hole. **2** *(med.)* fistula.

свия́з|ь, и *f. (zool.)* wigeon.

свобо́д|а, ы *f.* freedom, liberty; **с. во́ли** free will; **с. рук** a free hand; **с. сло́ва** freedom of speech; **с. собра́ний** freedom of assembly; **с. со́вести** liberty of conscience; **с. торго́вли** free trade; **вы́пустить на ~у** to set free; **предоста́вить по́лную ~у де́йствий** *(+d.)* to give a free hand; **на ~е** *(i) (на досуге)* at leisure, *(ii) (о преступнике)* at large.

свобо́дно *adv.* **1** *(без принуждения)* freely; *(с лёгкостью)* easily, with ease; **дыша́ть с.** to breathe freely; **она́ с. говори́т на пяти́ языка́х** she speaks five languages fluently. **2** *(просторно)* loose, loosely.

свобо́д|ный (~ен, ~на) *adj.* **1** free. **2** *(без помех)* free; easy; **с. до́ступ** easy access; **с. уда́р** *(sport)* free kick; **с. от недоста́тков** free from defects. **3** *(не занятый)* free; *(номер)* vacant; *(место)* spare; **~ное вре́мя** free time, time off; spare time; **~ное ме́сто** vacant seat, spare seat; **вы ~ны сего́дня ве́чером?** will you be free this evening? **4** *(поведение)* free(-and-easy). **5** *(одежда)* loose, loose-fitting; flowing. **6** *(chem.)* free, uncombined.

свободолюби́в|ый (~, ~а) *adj.* freedom-loving.

свободолю́би|е, я *nt.* love of freedom.

свободомы́сли|е, я *nt.* free-thinking.

свободомы́слящ|ий *adj.* free-thinking; *as n.* **с., ~его** *m.* free-thinker.

свод¹, а *m.* code; *(документов)* collection; **с. зако́нов** code of laws.

свод², а *m. (перекрытие)* arch, vault; **небе́сный с.** the firmament, the vault of heaven.

сво|ди́ть¹, жу́, ~дишь *impf. of* ⇒**свести́**

сво|ди́ть², жу́, ~дишь *pf. (отвести и привести обратно)* to take *(and bring back)*; **мы ~ди́ли дете́й в кино́** we took the children to the cinema.

сво|ди́ться, ~дится *impf. of* ⇒**свести́сь**

сво́дк|а, и *f.* summary; report; **с. пого́ды** weather forecast, weather report.

сво́дник, а *m.* procurer, pimp.

сво́дниц|а, ы *f.* procuress.

сво́днича|ть, ю *impf.* to procure, pimp.

сво́дничеств|о, а *nt.* procuring, pimping.

сво́дн|ый *adj.* **1** combined; collated; **~ая афи́ша теа́тров** theatre *(Br.)*, theater *(US)* guide *(bill listing all current productions)*; **с. отря́д** *(mil.)* combined force; **~ая табли́ца** summary table, index. **2** step-; **с. брат** step-brother.

сво́дн|я, и *f. (coll.)* procuress.

сво́дчатый *adj.* arched, vaulted.

своевла́ст|ный (~ен, ~на) *adj.* self-willed, wilful.

своево́ли|е, я *nt.* self-will, wilfulness.

своево́льнича|ть, ю *impf.* to be self-willed, be wilful.

своево́л|ьный (~ен, ~ьна) *adj.* self-willed, wilful.

своевре́менно *adv.* in good time; opportunely.

своевре́мен|ный (~ен, ~на) *adj.* timely, opportune.

своекоры́сти|е, я *nt.* self-interest.

своекоры́ст|ный (~ен, ~на) *adj.* self-seeking.

своенра́ви|е, я *nt.* wilfulness, capriciousness.

своенра́в|ный (~ен, ~на) *adj.* wilful, capricious.

своеобра́зи|е, я *nt.* originality; distinctiveness.

своеобра́з|ный (~ен, ~на) *adj.* original; peculiar, distinctive.

сво|зи́ть¹, жу́, ~зишь *impf. of* ⇒**свезти́**

сво|зи́ть², жу́, ~зишь *pf. (отвезти и привезти обратно)* to take *(and bring back)*; **мы ~зи́ли дете́й в цирк** we took the children to the circus.

свой *possessive adj.* one's (my, your, his, *etc., in accordance with subject of sentence or clause)*, one's own; **у них с. дом** they have a house of their own; **своё варе́нье** one's own, home-made jam; **свои́ войска́** friendly troops; **кри́кнуть не свои́м го́лосом** to give a frenzied scream; **умере́ть свое́й сме́ртью** to die a natural death; **в своё вре́мя** *(i)* at one time, in my, his, *etc.*, time, *(ii) (своевременно)* in due time, in due course; **в своём ро́де** in one's own way; **он не в своём уме́** he is not right in the head; **на свои́х (на) двои́х** on Shanks' mare, pony; **она́ сама́ не своя́** she is not herself; **он у нас с. челове́к** he's one of us; *as n.* **свои́** one's (own) people; **своё** one's own; **доби́ться своего́** to get one's own way; **получи́ть своё** to get one's own back.

сво́йственник, а *m.* relation *(or* relative) by marriage; **он мне с.** he is related to me by marriage.

сво́йственни|ца, цы *f. of* ⇒**~к**

сво́йствен|ный (~ *and* **~ен, ~на)** *adj. (+d.)* characteristic (of).

сво́йств|о, а *nt.* property, attribute, characteristic.

свойств|о́, а *nt.* relationship by marriage; **быть в ~е́ с кем-н.** to be related to s.o. by marriage.

свола́кива|ть, ю *impf. of* ⇒**своло́чь**

сволочно́й *adj. (coll.)* worthless, rubbishy.

сво́лоч|ь, и, *g. pl.* **~е́й** *f. (coll.)* **1** *(негодяй)* scum, swine. **2** *(collect.)* riff-raff, dregs.

С

сволó|чь, кý, чёшь, кýт, *past* **~к, ~клá** *pf.* (*of* **⇒сволáкивать**) (*coll.*) **1** to drag (off, down). **2** (*fig.*) (*украсть*) to steal.

свóр|а, ы *f.* **1** (*ремень*) leash. **2** (*пара*) pair (*of greyhounds*). **3** (*collect.*) pack (*of hounds*); (*fig.*) (*шайка*) gang.

сворáчива|ть, ю *impf. of* **⇒свернýть** *and* **своротúть**

свор|овáть, ýю *pf. of* **⇒воровáть**

своро|тúть, чý, ~́тишь *pf.* (*of* **⇒сворáчивать**) (*coll.*) **1** (*сдвинуть*) to dislodge, displace, shift. **2** (*свернуть*) to turn, swing (*also trans.*); **с. с дорóги** to turn off the road; **с. с умá** to go off one's head. **3** (*свихнуть*) to twist, dislocate; to break.

своя́к, á *m.* brother-in-law (*husband of wife's sister*).

своя́чениц|а, ы *f.* sister-in-law (*wife's sister*).

СВЧ-печ|ь, и *f.* (*abbr. of* ***сверхвысокочастóтная печь***) microwave (oven).

свык|áться, áюсь *impf. of* **⇒~́нуться**

свы́к|нуться, нусь, нешься, *past* **~ся, ~лась** *pf.* (*of* **~áться**) (*c*+*i.*) to get used (to).

свысокá *adv.* condescendingly; **обращáться с кем-н. с.** to talk down to, patronize s.o.

свы́ше 1 *adv.* from above; (*relig.*) from on high. **2** *prep.*+*g.* (*более*) over, more than; (*вне*) beyond; **с. ты́сячи самолётов учáствовало в налёте** over a thousand planes took part in the raid; **э́то с. мои́х сил** it is beyond me.

свя́з|анный *p.p.p. of* **⇒~áть** *and adj.* constrained; **~анная речь** halting utterance.

свя|зáть, жý, ~́жешь *pf.* (*of* **⇒вязáть** *and* **~зывать**) **1** to tie; to bind (*also fig.*); **с. по рукáм и ногáм** to bind hand and foot (*also fig.*); **с. свою́ судьбý** (*c*+*i.*) to throw in one's lot (with). **2** (*fig.*) (*соединить*) to connect, link; **быть (тéсно) ~́занным, ~́зано** (*c*+*i.*) to be (closely) connected (with), be bound up (with), be tied up (with). **3: (быть) ~́зано** (*c*+*i.*; *fig.*) to involve, entail; **э́то предприя́тие бýдет ~́зано с огрóмными расхóдами** this undertaking will involve huge expense. **4** (*установить связь*) to link, associate; **нéкоторые ~зáли эпидéмию с плохи́м водоснабжéнием** some connected the epidemic with the bad water-supply.

свя|зáться, жýсь, ~́жешься *pf.* (*of* **⇒~́зываться**) (*c*+*i.*) **1** to get in touch (with), communicate (with). **2** (*coll., pej.*) to get involved (with), get mixed up (with).

связи́ст, а *m.* **1** (*mil.*) signaller (*Br.*), signaler (*US*). **2** (*работник связи*) postal *and/or* telecommunications worker.

свя́зк|а, и *f.* **1** (*ключей*) bunch; (*книг, бумаг*) bundle. **2** (*anat.*) cord; ligament; **голосовы́е ~и** vocal cords. **3** (*gram.*) copula.

связн|óй *adj.* (*mil.*) liaison, communication; **с. самолёт** liaison aircraft; **~áя собáка** messenger dog; *as n.* **с., ~óго** *m.* messenger, runner, orderly.

свя́з|ный (~ен, ~на) *adj.* connected, coherent.

связýющий *adj.* connecting, linking.

свя́зыва|ть, ю *impf. of* **⇒связáть**

свя́зыва|ться, юсь *impf.* **1** *impf. of* **⇒связáться. 2** *impf. only* (*c*+*i.*) to have to do (with); **не ~йся с ни́ми** don't have anything to do with them.

связ|ь, и, о ~́и, в ~́и́ *f.* **1** (*отношение*) connection; **в ~́и с** (+*i.*) (*вследствие*) due to; owing to; (*по поводу*) in connection with; **в ~и с э́тим** in this connection. **2** (*тесное общение*) link, tie, bond; **дрýжеские ~́и** friendly relations, ties of friendship; **потеря́ть с.** (*c*+*i.*) to lose touch (with). **3** (*любовная*) liaison, relationship. **4** (*pl.*) (*близкое знакомство*) connections, contacts; **у негó мнóго ~́ей в Москвé** he has many influential connections in Moscow. **5** (*сообщение*) communication; **воздýшная с.** aerial communication; **с. по рáдио** radio communication; **с. с вóздухом** (*mil.*) ground-air communication. **6** (*sg. only*) (*почта, телефон*) (postal and tele-)communications; **Министéрство ~́и** Ministry of Communications; **отделéние ~́и** (branch) post office; **рабóтник ~́и** post office worker. **7** (*tech.*) tie, stay, brace, strut; (*elec.*) coupling.

святéйшеств|о, а *nt.*: **егó с.** (*title of Patriarchs and of the Pope*) His Holiness.

святéйший *adj.* most holy (*pertaining to the Patriarchs and synod of the Orthodox Church, also to the Pope*); **с. патриáрх** His Holiness the Patriarch.

святи́лищ|е, а *nt.* sanctuary.

святи́тел|ь, я *m.* prelate.

свя|ти́ть, чý, ти́шь *impf.* (*of* **⇒о~**) to consecrate; to bless.

Свя́т|ки, ок *no sg.* Christmas(-tide), Yuletide.

свя́то *adv.* piously; religiously; **с. берéчь** to treasure; **с. чтить** to hold sacred.

свят|óй (~, ~á, ~́о) *adj.* **1** (*священный*) holy; sacred (*also fig.*); **~áя водá** holy water; **с. долг** sacred duty; **с. дух** the Holy Ghost, the Holy Spirit; **~áя (недéля)** Holy Week. **2** (*человек*) saintly. **3** (*чувства*) pious. **4** *preceding name, or as n.* **с., ~óго** *m.*, **~áя, ~óй** *f.* saint; **причи́слить к ли́ку ~ы́х** (*eccl.*) to canonize.

свя́тост|ь, и *f.* holiness; sanctity.

святотáт|ец, ца *m.* person committing sacrilege.

святотáтственный *adj.* sacrilegious.

святотáтств|о, а *nt.* sacrilege.

святотáтств|овать, ую *impf.* to commit sacrilege.

свя́т|очный *adj. of* **⇒~ки; с. расскáз** Christmas tale.

святóш|а, и *c.g.* sanctimonious person.

свя́тц|ы, ев *no sg.* (church) calendar.

святы́н|я, и *f.* **1** (*eccl.*) (*предмет*) object of worship; (*место*) sacred place. **2** (*fig.*) (*предмет*) sacred object.

свящéнник, а *m.* priest (*of Orthodox Church*); clergyman.

свящéннический *adj.* priestly.

священнодéйстви|е, я *nt.* **1** religious rite. **2** (*fig.*) solemn performance (of ceremony, duties, *etc.*).

священнодéйств|овать, ую *impf.* **1** to perform a religious rite. **2** (*fig.*) to do sth. with solemnity, with pomp.

священнослужи́тел|ь, я *m.* clergyman (*priest or deacon*).

свящéн|ный (~ен, ~на) *adj.* holy; sacred (*also fig.*); **~ное писáние** Holy Writ, Scripture.

свящéнств|о, а *nt.* priesthood (*also collect.*).

с. г. (*abbr. of* ***сегó гóда***) of this year.

сгиб, а *m.* **1** bend. **2** (*anat.*) flexion.

сгибáем|ый (~, ~а) *adj.* flexible, pliable.

сгибá|ть(ся), ю(сь) *impf. of* **⇒согнýть(ся)**

сги́н|уть, у, ешь *pf.* (*coll.*) to disappear, vanish.

сглá|дить, жу, дишь *pf.* (*of* **⇒~живать**) **1** (*выровнять*) to smooth out. **2** (*fig.*) (*смягчить*) to smooth over, soften.

сглá|диться, дится *pf.* (*of* **⇒~живаться**) **1** (*выровняться*) to become smooth. **2** (*fig.*) (*смягчиться*) to be smoothed over, be softened.

сглáжива|ть(ся), ю, ет(ся) *impf. of* **⇒сглáдить(ся)**

сглаз, а (у) *m.* (*coll.*) the evil eye.

сглá|зить, жу, зишь *pf.* to put the evil eye (on, upon); (*fig., coll.*) to jinx; **чтóбы не с.!** touch wood!

сглуп|и́ть, лю́, и́шь *pf. of* **⇒глупи́ть**

сгнивá|ть, ю *impf. of* **⇒сгнить**

сгни|ть, ю́, ёшь *pf.* (*of* **⇒гнить** *and* **~вáть**) to rot, decay.

сгно|и́ть, ю́, и́шь *pf. of* **⇒гнои́ть**

сговáрива|ть(ся), ю(сь) *impf. of* **⇒сговори́ть(ся)**

сгóвор, а *m.* **1** (*usu. pej.*) (*соглашение*) agreement, compact, deal. **2** (*obs.*) (*помолвка*) betrothal.

сговор|и́ть, ю́, и́шь *pf.* (*of* **⇒сговáривать**) (*obs.*; *coll.*) to give consent to the marriage (of); to betroth.

сговор|и́ться, ю́сь, и́шься *pf.* (*of* **⇒сговáриваться**) (*c*+*i.*) **1** to arrange (with); **мы ~и́лись встрéтиться с ни́ми при вхóде в парк** we arranged to meet them at the entrance to the park. **2** (*достигнуть взаимного понимания в беседе*) to come to an arrangement (with), reach an understanding (with).

сговóрчивост|ь, и *f.* compliancy, tractability.

сговóрчив|ый, (~, ~а) *adj.* compliant, tractable.

сгон, а *m.* driving; herding, rounding-up.

сгóнк|а, и *f.* rafting, floating.

сгóнщик, а *m.* **1** (*коров*) herdsman, drover. **2** (*леса*) (lumber-)rafter.

сгоня́|ть, ю *impf. of* ⇒**согнáть**

сгорáни|е, я *nt.* combustion; **двúгатель внýтреннего ~я** internal-combustion engine.

сгор|áть, áю *impf.* **1** *impf. of* ⇒**~éть. 2** (**от**+*g.*; *fig.*) to be dying (of); **с. от сты́да, любопы́тства** to be dying of shame, curiosity.

сгóрб|ить(ся), лю(сь), ишь(ся) *pf. of* ⇒**гóрбить(ся)**

сгóрб|ленный *p.p.p. of* ⇒**~ить** *and adj.* crooked, bent; hunchbacked.

сгор|éть, ю́, и́шь *pf.* (*of* ⇒**~áть**) **1** to burn down; to be burnt out, down; **наш дом ~éл** our house was burnt down. **2** (*о топливе*) to be consumed, be used up. **3** (*fig., coll.*) (*потерять силы*) to burn o.s. out.

сгорячá *adv.* in the heat of the moment; in a fit of temper.

сгребá|ть, ю *impf. of* ⇒**сгрести́**

сгре|сти́, бý, бёшь, *past* **~̈б, ~блá** *pf.* (*of* ⇒**~бáть**) **1** (*собрать*) to rake up, rake together. **2** (**с**+*g.*) (*скинуть*) to shovel (off, from); **с. снег с кры́ши** to shovel snow off the roof.

сгруд|и́ться, и́тся *pf.* (*coll.*) to crowd, mill, bunch.

сгружá|ть, ю *impf. of* ⇒**сгрузи́ть**

сгру|зи́ть, жý, ~̃зишь *pf.* (*of* ⇒**~жáть**) to unload.

сгруппир|овáть(ся), ýю, ýет(ся) *pf. of* ⇒**группировáть(ся)**

сгрызá|ть, ю *impf. of* ⇒**сгры́зть**

сгры́з|ть, ý, ёшь, *past* **~, ~̃ла** *pf.* (*of* ⇒**~áть**) to chew (up).

сгуб|и́ть, лю́, ~̃ишь *pf.* (*coll.*) to ruin.

сгу|сти́ть, щý, сти́шь *pf.* (*of* ⇒**~щáть**) to thicken; (*конденсировать*) to condense; **с. крáски** (*fig.*) to lay it on thick.

сгу|сти́ться, сти́тся *pf.* (*of* ⇒**~щáться**) to thicken; (*конденсироваться*) to condense; (*о крови*) to clot.

сгýст|ок, ка *m.* clot; **с. крóви** clot of blood.

сгущá|ть(ся), ю, ет(ся) *impf. of* ⇒**сгусти́ть(ся)**

сгущéни|е, я *nt.* thickening; (*конденсация*) condensation; (*крови*) clotting.

сгу|щённый *p.p.p. of* ⇒**~сти́ть** *and adj.*; **~щённое молокó** condensed milk.

сдáбрива|ть, ю *impf. of* ⇒**сдóбрить**

сда|вáть, ю́, ёшь *impf. of* ⇒**сдать; с. экзáмен** to take, sit an examination.

сда|вáться¹, ю́сь, ёшься *impf. of* ⇒**~̃ться¹**

сда|вáться², ётся *impf.* (*impers., coll.*) it seems; **мне ~ётся** it seems to me; I think.

сдав|и́ть, лю́, ~̃ишь *pf.* (*of* ⇒**~̃ливать**) to squeeze.

сдáвлива|ть, ю *impf. of* ⇒**сдави́ть**

сдáточ|ный *adj.* delivery; **с. пункт** delivery point.

сдáтчик, а *m.* deliverer.

сдать, сдам, сдашь, сдаст, сдади́м, сдади́те, сдадýт, *past* **сдал, сдалá, сдáло** *pf.* (*of* ⇒**сдавáть**) **1** (*передать*) to hand over, pass; **с. делá преéмнику** to hand over to one's successor; **с. багáж на хранéние** to deposit one's luggage; **с. в архи́в** to deposit in the archives.
2 (*отдать внаём*) to let, let out, hire out; **с. в арéнду** to lease.
3 (*возвратить*) to give change; **с. пятьдеся́т копéек** to give fifty kopecks change.
4 (*уступить*) to surrender, yield, give up; **с. пéрвенство** (*sport*) to yield first place.
5 (*экзамен*) to pass (*an examination, examination subject, etc.*); **он сдал тóлько латы́нь** he only passed in Latin.
6 (*карты*) to deal (*cards*).
7 (*coll.*) (*о моторе, о сердце*) to give out; (*о морозе*) to abate; (*о старике, о здоровье*) to become weaker.

сдá|ться¹, мся, шься, стся, дúмся, дúтесь, дýтся, *past* **~лся, ~лáсь** *pf.* (*of* ⇒**~вáться¹**) to surrender, yield; (*chess*) to resign; **с. на прóсьбы** to yield to entreaties.

сдá|ться², *not used in fut.*, **~лся, ~лáсь** *pf.* (*coll.*) (*понадобиться*) to be necessary; **на что нам ~лúсь их совéты?** what need had we of advice from them?

сдáч|а, и *f.* **1** (*багажа*) handing over. **2** (*квартиры*) letting out, hiring out; **с. в арéнду** leasing. **3** (*города*) surrender. **4** (*деньги*) change; **три рубля́ ~и** three roubles change; **с. с рубля́** change from one rouble; **дать ~и** (+*d.*; *fig., coll.*) to give as good as one got. **5** (*cards*) deal; **вáша с.** it is your deal.

сдвáива|ть, ю *impf. of* ⇒**сдвои́ть**

сдвиг, а *m.* **1** displacement; (*geol.*) fault. **2** (*fig.*) (*улучшение*) change (for the better), improvement.

сдвигá|ть(ся), ю(сь) *impf. of* ⇒**сдви́нуть(ся)**

сдви́нут|ый *p.p.p. of* ⇒**~ь** *and adj.*; (*sl.*) (*сумасшедший*) crazy; **с. по фáзе** (*elec.*) out of phase; (*sl.*) crazy.

сдви́|нуть, ну, нешь *pf.* (*of* ⇒**~гáть**) **1** to shift, move, displace; **егó с мéста не ~нешь** he won't budge; **с. с мéста** (*fig.*) to get moving, set in motion. **2** (*соединить*) to move together, bring together; **с. брóви** to knit one's brows.

сдви́|нуться, нусь, нешься *pf.* (*of* ⇒**~гáться**) **1** to move, budge; **с. с мéста** (*fig.*) to progress; **дéло не ~нулось с мéста** no headway has been made. **2** (*вместе*) to come together. **3** (*sl.*) to go mad, crazy.

сдво|и́ть, ю́, и́шь *pf.* (*of* ⇒**сдвáивать**) to double.

сдéла|ть(ся), ю(сь) *pf. of* ⇒**дéлать(ся)**

сдéлк|а, и *f.* transaction, deal, bargain; **войти́ в ~у** (**с**+*i.*) to strike a bargain (with).

сдéльно *adv.* by the job.

сдéльн|ый *adj.* piecework; **~ая оплáта** payment by the piece, by the job; **~ая рабóта** piecework.

сдéльщик, а *m.* piece-worker.

сдéльщин|а, ы *f.* (*coll.*) piece-work.

сдéльщи|ца, цы *f. of* ⇒**~к**

сдёргива|ть, ю *impf. of* ⇒**сдёрнуть**

сдéржанно *adv.* with restraint, with reserve.

сдéржанност|ь, и *f.* restraint, reserve.

сдéржан|ный *p.p.p. of* ⇒**сдержáть** *and* (**~, ~на**) *adj.* restrained, reserved.

сдерж|áть, ý, ~̃ишь *pf.* (*of* ⇒**~̃ивать**) **1** to hold (back); (*неприятеля*) to hold in check, contain. **2** (*fig.*) (*чувства*) to keep back, restrain; **с. слёзы** to suppress tears. **3** (*обещание*) to keep; **с. слóво** to keep one's word.

сдерж|áться, ýсь, ~̃ишься *pf.* (*of* ⇒**~̃иваться**) to restrain o.s., contain o.s.; to check o.s.

сдéржива|ть(ся), ю(сь) *impf. of* ⇒**сдержáть(ся)**

сдёр|нуть, ну, нешь *pf.* (*of* ⇒**~гивать**) to pull off.

сдирá|ть, ю *impf. of* ⇒**содрáть**

сдóб|а, ы *f.* **1** (*cul.*) fat, sugar, eggs, *etc.* (*used in making dough*). **2** (*collect.*) (*изделия*) (fancy) buns.

сдóбный *adj.* (*cul.*) rich.

сдóбр|ить, ю, ишь *pf.* (*of* ⇒**сдáбривать**) (+*i.*) to flavour (*Br.*), flavor (*US*) (with), spice (with).

сдобровáть *only in phr.* **емý** *etc.*, **не с.** (*coll.*) it will be a bad look out for him, *etc.*

сдóхн|уть, у, ешь *pf.* (*of* ⇒**сдыхáть**) to die (*of cattle, also coll. of people*).

сдрéйф|ить, лю, ишь *pf. of* ⇒**дрéйфить**

сдруж|и́ть, ý, и́шь *pf.* to bring together, unite in friendship.

сдруж|и́ться, ýсь, и́шься *pf.* (**с**+*i.*) to become friends (with).

сдувá|ть, ю *impf. of* ⇒**сдуть**

сдýру *adv.* (*coll.*) stupidly; **он с. забы́л ключ дóма** he stupidly left his key at home.

сду|ть, ~̃ю, ~̃ешь *pf.* (*of* ⇒**~вáть**) **1** to blow away, blow off. **2** (**с**+*g. or* **у**+*g.*; *school sl.*) (*списать*) to crib (from).

сдыхá|ть, ю *impf. of* ⇒**сдóхнуть**

сё, сегó *pron.* this (*arch. exc. in certain set phrr.*; *see* ⇒**тот**).

сеáнс, а *m.* **1** (*представление*) performance, showing. **2** (*портретиста*) sitting; **написáть чей-н. портрéт в двенáдцать ~ов** to paint s.o.'s portrait in twelve sittings.

СЕАТО *nt. indecl.* SEATO (*abbr. of* South-East Asia Treaty Organization — *Организáция договóра Юго-Востóчной Áзии*).

себé¹ *see* ⇒**себя́**

себé² *particle* (*coll.*) *modifying v. or pron. and usu. containing hint of reproach*; **а они́ с. молчáли** and they just kept their

С

mouths shut; **ничего́ с.** not bad; **так с.** so-so.

себесто́имост|ь, и *f.* (*econ.*) cost (*of manufacture*); cost price; **прода́ть по ~и** to sell at cost price.

себя́, себе́, собо́й (собо́ю), о себе́ *refl. pron.* oneself; (*я*) myself, (*ты, вы*) yourself, (*он*) himself, *etc.*; **собо́ю** in appearance; **хоро́ш собо́ю** nice-looking; **прийти́ в с.** (**от**+*g.*) to get over; to come to one's senses; **не в себе́** not o.s.; **от с.** (*i*) away from o.s., outwards, (*ii*) (*лично, от своего имени*) for o.s., on one's own behalf; **рабо́та по себе́** work that suits one; **ка́к-то не по себе́** not quite o.s.; **он о́чень себе́ на уме́** he is very crafty; **чита́ть про с.** to read to o.s.; **у с.** at home, at one's (own) place.

себялю́б|ец, ца *m.* egoist.

себялюби́в|ый (~, ~а) *adj.* egoistical, selfish.

себялю́би|е, я *nt.* self-love, egoism.

сев, а *m.* sowing.

се́вер, а *m.* north.

се́вернее *adv.* (+*g.*) to the north (of).

се́верн|ый *adj.* north, northern; (*направление, ветер*) northerly; **с. оле́нь** reindeer; **С. по́люс** North Pole; **~ое сия́ние** northern lights, aurora borealis.

Се́верн|ый Ледови́т|ый океа́н, ~ого ~ого ~а *m.* the Arctic Ocean.

Се́верн|ый Поля́рн|ый круг, ~ого ~ого ~а *m.* the Arctic Circle.

североамерика́н|ец, ца *m.* North American.

североамерика́н|ка, ки *f. of* ⇨**~ец**

североамерика́нский *adj.* North American.

се́веро-восто́к, а *m.* north-east.

се́веро-восто́чный *adj.* north-east, north-eastern.

се́веро-за́пад, а *m.* north-west.

се́веро-за́падный *adj.* north-west, north-western.

североирла́ндский *adj.* Northern Irish.

северя́н|ин, ина, *pl.* **~е, ~** *m.* northerner.

севооборо́т, а *m.* rotation of crops.

севрю́г|а, и *f.* stellate sturgeon (*Acipenser stellatus*).

сегме́нт, а *m.* segment.

сегмента́ци|я, и *f.* segmentation.

сего́дня *adv.* today; **с. ве́чером** this evening, tonight; **не с.-за́втра** any day now.

сего́дня|шний *adj. of* ⇨**~**; **с. день** today; **~шняя газе́та** today's paper.

сегрега́ци|я, и *f.* segregation.

седа́лищ|е, а *nt.* (*anat.*) seat, buttocks.

седа́лищн|ый *adj.* (*anat.*) sciatic; **воспале́ние ~ого не́рва** (*med.*) sciatica.

седе́льник, а *m.* saddler.

седе́льн|ый *adj. of* ⇨**седло́**; **~ая лука́** saddle-bow.

седе́|ть, ю *impf.* (*of* ⇨**по~**) to go grey (*Br.*), gray (*US*).

седе́|ющий *pres. part. act. of* ⇨**~ть** *and adj.* grizzled, greying (*Br.*), graying (*US*).

седи́л|ь, я *m.* (*ling.*) cedilla.

седин|а́, ы́, *pl.* **~́ы, ~́** *f.* **1** grey (*Br.*), gray (*US*) hair(s). **2** (*в мехе*) grey (*Br.*), gray (*US*) streak.

седла́|ть, ю *impf.* (*of* ⇨**о~**) to saddle.

сед|ло́, ла́, *pl.* **~̈ла, ~̈ел** *nt.* saddle.

седлови́н|а, ы *f.* **1** (*в спине животного*) arch, saddle. **2** (*geog.*) col, saddle.

седоборо́д|ый (~) *adj.* grey-bearded (*Br.*), gray-bearded (*US*).

седовла́с|ый (~, ~а) *adj.* grey-haired (*Br.*), gray-haired (*US*).

седоволо́с|ый (~, ~а) *adj.* = **седовла́сый**

сед|о́й (~, ~а́, ~́о) *adj.* (*волосы*) grey (*Br.*), gray (*US*); (*человек*) grey-haired (*Br.*), gray-haired (*US*); (*fig.*): **~а́я старина́** hoary antiquity.

седо́к, а́ *m.* **1** (*пассажир*) fare. **2** (*всадник*) rider, horseman.

седьм|о́й *adj.* seventh; **быть на ~о́м не́бе** to be in the seventh heaven; **одна́ ~а́я** one seventh.

сеза́м, а *m.* (*bot.*) sesame; **с., откро́йся!** open sesame!

сезо́н, а *m.* season.

сезо́нник, а *m.* seasonal worker.

сезо́нни|ца, цы *f. of* ⇨**~к**

сезо́нн|ый *adj.* seasonal; **с. биле́т** season ticket; **~ые рабо́ты** seasonal work.

сей *m.*, **сия́** *f.*, **сие́** *nt.*, *pl.* **сии́** *pron.* this; **сию́ мину́ту** this (very) minute; at once, instantly; **сего́ го́да** of this year; **сего́ ме́сяца** (*abbr.* **с. м.**) of this month; **ва́ше письмо́ от 16-го с. м.** your letter of the 16th inst.; **до сих пор** up to now, till now, hitherto; **на с. раз** this time, for this once; **по с. день** to this day; **под сим ка́мнем поко́ится** here lies; **при сём прилага́ется** (there is) enclosed herewith; please find enclosed.

сейм, а *m.* (*in Poland*) the Sejm; (*hist.*) diet.

сейсми́ческий *adj.* seismic.

сейсмо́граф, а *m.* seismograph.

сейсмогра́фи|я, и *f.* seismography.

сейсмо́лог, а *m.* seismologist.

сейсмологи́ческий *adj.* seismological.

сейсмоло́ги|я, и *f.* seismology.

сейсмо́метр, а *m.* seismometer.

сейсмоопа́с|ный (~ен, ~на) *adj.* earthquake-prone.

сейсмосто́йкий *adj.* earthquake-proof.

сейф, а *m.* safe.

сейча́с *adv.* **1** (*теперь*) (right) now, at present, at the (present) moment; **они́ с. в Аме́рике** they are in America at present. **2** (*coll.*) (*только что*) just, just now; **она́ с. была́ здесь** she was here just now. **3** (*очень скоро*) presently, soon; **с. же** at once, immediately; **с.!** in a minute!; half a minute! **4** (*coll.*) (*сразу, с первого взгляда*) straight away, immediately; **с. ви́дно** it is immediately obvious. **5** (*coll.*) (*usu.* **с. же**) (*непосредственно*) immediately; **с. же за до́мом** immediately behind the house.

Сейше́льск|ие остров|а́, ~их ~о́в *no sg.* the Seychelles (*islands*).

сек. (*abbr. of* ***секу́нда***) sec., second(s).

сека́тор, а *m.* secateurs.

секве́стр, а *m.* (*leg.*) sequestration; **наложи́ть с.** (**на**+*a.*) to sequestrate.

секвестри́р|овать, ую *impf. and pf.* = **секвестрова́ть**

секвестр|ова́ть, у́ю *impf. and pf.* (*leg.*) to sequestrate.

секи́р|а, ы *f.* axe (*Br.*), ax (*US*).

секре́т[1]**, а** *m.* secret; **по ~у** confidentially, in confidence; **под больши́м ~ом** in strict confidence; **с. полишине́ля** open secret.

секре́т[2]**, а** *m.* (*physiol.*) secretion.

секретариа́т, а *m.* secretariat.

секрета́рский *adj.* secretarial; secretary's.

секрета́рств|овать, ую *impf.* to be a secretary, act as secretary.

секрета́р|ша, ши *f.* (*coll.*) *f. of* ⇨**~ь**

секрета́р|ь, я́ *m.* secretary; **ли́чный с.** private secretary, personal secretary; **генера́льный с.** secretary-general; **непреме́нный с.** (*hist.*) permanent secretary.

секре́тнича|ть, ю *impf.* (*coll.*) **1** (*держать что-н. в секрете*) to be secretive; to keep things secret. **2** (*разговаривать по секрету*) to converse in confidential tones.

секре́тно *adv.* secretly, in secret; (*надпись*) 'secret', 'confidential'; **соверше́нно с.** 'top secret'.

секре́тност|ь, и *f.* secrecy.

секре́т|ный (~ен, ~на) *adj.* secret; confidential; **с. замо́к** combination lock; **с. сотру́дник** secret agent, undercover agent.

секре́ци|я, и *f.* (*physiol.*) secretion.

секс, а *m.* sex; **с. вне бра́ка** extramarital sex.

сексапи́льност|ь, и *f.* sex appeal.

сексапи́л|ьный (~ен, ~ьна) *adj.* sexy.

сексо́лог, а *m.* sexologist.

сексоло́ги|я, и *f.* sexology.

сексо́т, а *m.* (*abbr. of* ***секре́тный сотру́дник***) secret agent, undercover agent.

се́кст|а, ы *f.* (*mus.*) sixth.

секста́нт, а *m.* sextant.

сексте́т, а *m.* (*mus.*) sextet.

сексуа́льност|ь, и *f.* sexuality.

сексуа́л|ьный (~ен, ~ьна) *adj.* sexual; (*эротичный*) sexy; **~ьное воспита́ние** sex education; **~ьное домога́тельство** sexual harassment; **~ьная жизнь** sex life.

се́кт|а, ы *f.* sect.

секта́нт, а *m.* sectarian; member of a sect.

секта́нтский *adj.* sectarian.

секта́нтств|о, а *nt.* sectarianism.

се́ктор, а, *pl.* **~ы, ~ов** *and* **~а́, ~о́в**

m. **1** (*math., mil.*) sector; **с. Га́за** the Gaza Strip. **2** (*отдел*) section, department; (*econ.*) sector; **госуда́рственный с. хозя́йства** State(-owned) sector of economy.

секуляриза́ци|я, и *f.* secularization.

секуляриз|ова́ть, у́ю *impf. and pf.* to secularize.

секу́нд|а, ы *f.* **1** (*единица времени*) second; **одну́ ~у!** just a moment! **2** (*mus., math.*) second.

секунда́нт, а *m.* (*in a duel or in boxing*) second.

секу́нд|ный *adj. of* ⇒**~а; ~ная стре́лка** second hand.

секундоме́р, а *m.* stop-watch.

секцио́нн|ая, ой *f.* dissection-room.

секцио́нный *adj.* sectional; modular.

се́кци|я, и *f.* section.

селадо́н, а *m.* (*obs.*) ladies' man, womanizer.

сел|ево́й *adj. of* ⇒**~ь**

селёдк|а, и *f.* herring.

селёдочниц|а, ы *f.* herring-dish.

селёд|очный *adj. of* ⇒**~ка**

селезёнк|а, и *f.* (*physiol.*) spleen.

се́лез|ень, ня *m.* drake.

селекти́вност|ь, и *f.* selectiveness; (*electronics*) selectivity.

селе́ктор, а *m.* intercom.

селе́кци|я, и *f.* (*agric.*) selective breeding.

селе́н, а *adj.* (*chem.*) selenium.

селе́ни|е, я *nt.* settlement.

селе́новый *adj.* (*chem.*) selenium, selenic.

сели́тр|а, ы *f.* (*chem.*) saltpetre (*Br.*), saltpeter (*US*); **кали́йная с.** potassium nitrate.

сели́тр|яный *adj. of* ⇒**~а; ~яная кислота́** nitric acid.

сел|и́ть, ю́ и́шь *impf.* (*of* ⇒**по~**) to settle.

сел|и́ться, ю́сь, и́шься *impf.* (*of* ⇒**по~**) to settle.

сел|о́, а́, *pl.* **~a** *nt.* village; **на ~е́** (*collect.*) in the country; **ни к ~у́, ни к го́роду** (*coll.*) for no reason at all; neither here nor there.

сел|ь, я *m.* (seasonal) mountain torrent.

сель... *comb. form, abbr. of* ***се́льский***

сельдере́|й, я *m.* celery.

сельд|ь, и, *pl.* **~и, ~е́й** *f.* herring; **как ~и в бо́чке** (*coll.*) like sardines.

сельќор, а *m.* (*abbr. of* ***се́льский корреспонде́нт***) rural correspondent.

сельпо́ *nt. indecl.* (*abbr. of* ***се́льское потреби́тельское о́бщество***) village (general) store, village shop.

се́льск|ий *adj.* **1** (*не городской*) country, rural; **~ая ме́стность** rural area; countryside; **~ое хозя́йство** agriculture, farming. **2** (*школа, улица*) village.

сельскохозя́йственный *adj.* agricultural, farming.

сельсове́т, а *m.* village soviet.

селян|и́н, и́на, *pl.* **~е, ~** *m.* peasant, villager.

селя́н|ка[1], ки *f. of* ⇒**~и́н**

селя́нк|а[2], и *f.* (*cul.*) hot-pot; **сбо́рная с.** (*fig.*) hotchpotch (*Br.*), hodgepodge (*US*).

сема́нтик|а, и *f.* **1** (*наука*) semantics. **2** (*значения слова*) meanings.

семанти́ческий *adj.* semantic.

семафо́р, а *m.* semaphore.

сёмг|а, и *f.* salmon.

семе́йн|ый *adj.* **1** family; domestic; **с. ве́чер** family party; **по ~ым обстоя́тельствам** for domestic reasons; **о́тпуск по ~ым обстоя́тельствам** (*mil.*) compassionate leave. **2** (*имеющий семью*) having a family; **с. челове́к** family man.

семе́йственност|ь, и *f.* **1** attachment to family life. **2** (*pej.*) nepotism.

семе́йственн|ый *adj.* **1** attached to family life. **2** (*fig., pej.*) nepotistic; **~ые отноше́ния** nepotism.

семе́йств|о, а *nt.* family.

семена́ *see* ⇒**се́мя**

семен|и́ть, ю́, и́шь *impf.* to mince (*of gait*).

семен|и́ться, и́тся *impf.* (*agric.*) to seed.

семенни́к, а́ *m.* **1** (*biol.*) testicle. **2** (*bot.*) pericarp.

семенн|о́й *adj.* **1** seed; **с. карто́фель** seed potato. **2** (*biol.*) seminal; **~а́я нить** spermatozoon.

семенов́одств|о, а *nt.* seed-growing.

семенов́од|ческий *adj. of* ⇒**~ство**

семёрк|а, и *f.* **1** (*цифра*) seven. **2** (*coll.*) (*автобус, трамвай*) number seven (*bus, tram, etc.*). **3**: **с. треф** *etc.* (*cards*) the seven of clubs, *etc.* **4** (*семь человек*) group of seven persons.

се́мер|о, ы́х *num.* (*collect.*) seven.

семе́стр, а *m.* term (*Br.*), semester (*US*).

се́меч|ко, ка, *pl.* **~ки, ~ек** *nt.* **1** *dim. of* ⇒**се́мя. 2** (*pl.*) sunflower seeds.

семидесятиле́ти|е, я *nt.* **1** (*срок*) seventy years. **2** (*годовщина*) seventieth anniversary; (*день рождения*) seventieth birthday.

семидесятиле́тний *adj.* **1** (*срок*) seventy-year, of seventy years. **2** (*человек*) seventy-year-old.

семидеся́т|ый *adj.* seventieth; **~ые го́ды** the seventies.

семикла́ссник, а *m.* seventh-form (*Br.*), seventh-grade (*US*) pupil.

семикла́ссни|ца, цы *f. of* ⇒**~к**

семикра́тный *adj.* sevenfold.

семиле́ти|е, я *nt.* **1** (*срок*) seven years; seven-year period. **2** (*годовщина*) seventh anniversary.

семиле́тк|а, и *f.* **1** (*hist.*) (*школа*) seven-year school. **2** (*econ.*) seven-year plan.

семиле́тний *adj.* **1** (*срок*) seven-year. **2** (*ребёнок*) seven-year-old.

семина́р, а *m.* seminar.

семинари́ст, а *m.* seminarist.

семина́ри|я, и *f.* seminary, training college; **духо́вная с.** theological college.

семина́р|ский *adj. of* ⇒**~** *and* **~ия**

семисо́тый *adj.* seven-hundredth.

семи́т, а *m.* Semite.

семити́ческий *adj.* Semitic.

семито́лог, а *m.* specialist in Semitic languages and cultures.

семитоло́ги|я, и *f.* study of Semitic languages and cultures.

семи́т|ский = **~и́ческий**

семиуго́льник *m.* (*math.*) heptagon.

семиуго́льный *adj.* heptagonal.

семнадцатиле́тний *adj.* **1** (*срок*) seventeen-year. **2** (*юноша*) seventeen-year-old.

семна́дцатый *adj.* seventeenth.

семна́дцат|ь, и *num.* seventeen.

сёмужий *adj.* salmon.

сем|ь, и́, ~ью́ *num.* seven.

се́мьдесят, семи́десяти, семью́десятью *num.* seventy.

семьсо́т, семисо́т, семиста́м, семьюста́ми, о семиста́х *num.* seven hundred.

се́мью *adv.* seven times.

сем|ья́, ьи́, *pl.* **~ьи ~е́й, ~ьям** *f.* family

семьяни́н, а, *pl.* **~ы** *m.* family man.

се́м|я, ени, *pl.* **~ена́, ~я́н, ~ена́м** *nt.* **1** (*bot. and fig.*) seed; **пойти́ в ~ена́** to go to seed, run to seed; **~ена́ раздо́ра** seeds of discord. **2** (*сперма*) semen, sperm.

семядо́л|я, и, *g. pl.* **~ей** *f.* (*bot.*) seed-lobe, cotyledon.

семяизверже́ни|е, я *nt.* = **семяизлия́ние**

семяизлия́ни|е, я *nt.* (*physiol.*) ejaculation.

семяпо́чк|а, и *f.* (*bot.*) seed-bud.

Се́н|а, ы *f.* the Seine (*river*).

сена́т, а *m.* senate.

сена́тор, а *m.* senator.

сена́торский *adj.* senatorial.

сена́т|ский *adj. of* ⇒**~**

сенберна́р, а *m.* St. Bernard (*dog*).

Сенега́л, а *m.* Senegal.

сенега́л|ец, ьца *m.* Senegalese.

сенега́л|ка, ки *f. of* ⇒**~ец**

сенега́льский *adj.* Senegalese.

се́н|и, е́й *no sg.* (entrance-)hall, vestibule.

сенни́к, а́ *m.* hay-mattress.

сенн|о́й[1] *adj.* hay; **~а́я лихора́дка** hay fever.

сен|но́й[2] *adj. of* ⇒**~и; ~на́я де́вушка** (*obs.*) maid.

се́н|о, а *nt.* hay.

сенова́л, а *m.* hay-loft, mow.

сеноко́с, а *m.* **1** (*действие*) haymaking. **2** (*время*) haymaking. **3** (*место*) hayfield.

сенокоси́лк|а, и *f.* (hay-)mowing machine.

сеноко́сный *adj.* haymaking.

С

сеноубо́рк|а, и *f.* hay harvesting, haymaking.
сенсацио́н|ный (~ен, ~на) *adj.* sensational.
сенса́ци|я, и *f.* sensation.
сенсо́рный *adj.* (*physiol.*) sensory.
сентенцио́зный *adj.* sententious.
сенте́нци|я, и *f.* maxim.
сентиментали́зм *m.* sentimentalism.
сентиментали́ст, а *m.* sentimentalist.
сентимента́льнича|ть, ю *impf.* **1** (*быть сентиментальным*) to be sentimental, sentimentalize. **2** (**с**+*i.*) (*обращаться с кем-н. чересчур мягко*) to be soft (with).
сентимента́льност|ь, и *f.* sentimentality.
сентимента́л|ьный (~ен, ~ьна) *adj.* sentimental.
сентя́бр|ь, я́ *m.* September.
сентя́брь|ский *adj. of* ⇨~
се́н|цы, цев *no sg., dim. of* ⇨~**и**
сен|ь, и, о ~**и, в** ~**и́** *f.* (*obs. or poet.*) canopy; **под** ~**ью** (+*g.*) under the protection (of).
сеньо́р, а *m.* señor.
сеньо́р|а, ы *f.* señora.
сеньори́т|а, ы *f.* señorita.
сепарати́в|ный (~ен, ~на) *adj.* (*pol.*) separatist.
сепарати́зм, а *m.* (*pol.*) separatism.
сепарати́ст, а *m.* (*pol.*) separatist.
сепара́тный *adj.* (*pol.*) separate; **с. ми́рный догово́р** separate peace treaty.
сепара́тор, а *m.* (*agric.*) separator.
се́пи|я, и *f.* **1** (*краска*) sepia. **2** (*рисунок*) sepia drawing; (*фотография*) sepia photograph.
се́псис, а *m.* (*med.*) septicaemia (*Br.*), septicemia (*US*).
септе́т, а *m.* (*mus.*) septet(te).
септи́ческий *adj.* (*med.*) septic.
се́р|а, ы *f.* **1** (*chem.*) sulphur (*Br.*), sulfur (*US*). **2** (*в ушах*) ear-wax.
сера́л|ь, я *m.* seraglio.
серб, а *m.* Serb, Serbian.
Се́рби|я, и *f.* Serbia.
се́рб|ка, ки *f. of* ⇨~
сербохорва́тский *adj.* = **сербскохорва́тский**
се́рбский *adj.* Serb, Serbian.
сербскохорва́тский *adj.* Serbo-Croat(ian); **с. язы́к** Serbo-Croat(ian).
серва́нт, а *m.* sideboard.
се́рвер, а *m.* (*comput.*) server.
серви́з, а *m.* service, set; **столо́вый с.** dinner service.
сервир|ова́ть, у́ю *impf. and pf.* **1**: **с. стол** to lay a table. **2** to serve; **с. за́втрак** to serve breakfast.
сервиро́вк|а, и *f.* **1** (*действие*) laying. **2** (*collect.*) table appointments (*crockery and table linen*).
се́рвис, а *m.* (consumer) service.
сервомото́р, а *m.* (*tech.*) servo-motor.
серде́чник[1]**, а** *m.* (*tech.*) core.
серде́чник[2]**, а** *m.* (*coll.*) **1** (*врач*) heart specialist. **2** (*больной*) sufferer from heart disease.
серде́чно-сосу́дистый *adj.* cardiovascular.
серде́чност|ь, и *f.* (*приёма*) cordiality; (*человека*) warmth.
серде́ч|ный (~ен, ~на) *adj.* **1** of the heart (*also fig.*); (*anat.*) cardiac; ~**ная боле́знь** heart disease; **с. припа́док** heart attack. **2** (*приём*) cordial; (*благодарность*) heartfelt, sincere; ~**ное согла́сие** (*hist.*) Entente cordiale. **3** (*человек*) warm, warm-hearted.
серди́т|ый (~, ~а) *adj.* (**на**+*a.*) angry (with, at, about), cross (with, about); irate.
сер|ди́ть, жу́, ~**дишь** *impf.* (*of* ⇨**рас**~) to anger, make angry.
сер|ди́ться, жу́сь, ~**дишься** *impf.* (*of* ⇨**рас**~) (**на**+*a.*) to be angry (with, at, about), be cross (with, about).
сердоболи|е, я *nt.* soft-heartedness.
сердобо́льнича|ть, ю *impf.* (*coll.*, *iron.*) to be (too) soft-hearted.
сердобо́л|ьный (~ен, ~ьна) *adj.* (*coll.*) soft-hearted.
сердоли́к, а *m.* (*min.*) carnelian.
се́рд|це, ца, *pl.* ~**ца́,** ~**е́ц** *nt.* heart; **золото́е с.** heart of gold; **в** ~**ца́х** in (a fit of) temper; **с глаз доло́й, из** ~**ца вон** (*prov.*) out of sight, out of mind; **приня́ть (бли́зко) к** ~**цу** to take to heart; **от всего́** ~**ца** from the bottom of one's heart, wholeheartedly; **у меня́ отлегло́ от** ~**ца** I felt relieved; **по́** ~**цу** (*coll.*) to one's liking; after one's own heart; **с замира́нием** ~**ца** with a sinking heart; **име́ть с.** (**на**+*a.*; *coll.*) to be cross (with); **с. боли́т** (+*inf.*) it pains one, one's heart bleeds; **у него́ не лежи́т с.** (**к**+*d.*) he has no inclination (to, for).
сердцебие́ни|е, я *nt.* palpitation; (*med.*) tachycardia.
сердцеве́д, а *m.* student of human nature, reader of the human heart.
сердцеви́д|ный (~ен, ~на) *adj.* heart-shaped.
сердцеви́н|а, ы *f.* (*плода, стебля*) core; (*событий*) heart.
сердцее́д, а *m.* (*coll.*) lady-killer.
сере́бреник, а *m.* = **сре́бреник**
серебрёный *adj.* silver-plated.
серебри́ст|ый (~, ~а) *adj.* silvery; **с. то́поль** silver poplar.
серебр|и́ть, ю́, и́шь *impf.* (*of* ⇨**по**~) **1** (*покрыть серебром*) to silver, silver-plate. **2** (*окрашивать в серебристый цвет*) to turn silver.
серебр|и́ться, и́тся *impf.* **1** (*становиться серебристым*) to turn silver, become silvery. **2** (*виднеться*) to show silver.
серебр|о́, а́ *nt.* **1** silver. **2** (*collect.*) silver; **столо́вое с.** silver, plate; **сда́ча** ~**о́м** change in silver.
сереброно́с|ный (~ен, ~на) *adj.* argentiferous.
сере́бряник, а *m.* silversmith.
сере́бряный *adj.* silver.
середи́н|а, ы *f.* middle, midst; **золота́я с.** the golden mean.
середи́нный *adj.* middle.
серёдк|а, и *f.* (*coll.*) middle, centre (*Br.*), center (*US*); **с. на полови́нку** neither one thing nor another.
середня́к, а́ *m.* **1** peasant of average means (*classified as intermediate between* **кула́к** *and* **бедня́к**). **2** (*fig., coll.*) middling person, undistinguished person.
серёжк|а, и *f.* **1** ear-ring. **2** (*bot.*) catkin.
серена́д|а, ы *f.* serenade.
сере́|ть, ю *impf.* **1** (*pf.* **по**~) (*становиться серым*) to turn grey, go grey (*Br.*), gray (*US*). **2** (*impf. only*) (*виднеться*) to show grey (*Br.*), gray (*US*).
сержа́нт, а *m.* sergeant.
сериа́л, а *m.* serial.
сери́йный *adj.* (*tech., econ.*) serial.
се́ри|я, и *f.* series; (*часть фильма*) part; **кинофи́льм в не́скольких** ~**ях** film in several parts.
сермя́г|а, и *f.* sermyaga (*coarse, undyed cloth or caftan of this material*).
се́рн|а, ы *f.* (*zool.*) chamois.
серни́стый *adj.* (*chem.*) sulphureous (*Br.*), sulfureous (*US*); sulphide (*Br.*), sulfide (*US*) (of); **с. аммо́ний** ammonium sulphide (*Br.*), sulfide (*US*).
серноки́сл|ый *adj.* (*chem.*) sulphate (*Br.*), sulfate (*US*) (of); ~**ая соль** sulphate (*Br.*), sulfate (*US*).
се́рн|ый *adj.* sulphuric (*Br.*), sulfuric (*US*); ~**ая кислота́** sulphuric acid; **с. цвет** flowers of sulphur.
серова́т|ый (~, ~а) *adj.* greyish (*Br.*), grayish (*US*).
сероводоро́д, а *m.* (*chem.*) hydrogen sulphide (*Br.*), sulfide (*US*).
сероглаз|ый (~, ~а) *adj.* grey-eyed (*Br.*), gray-eyed (*US*).
серп, а́ *m.* sickle; ~ **и мо́лот** hammer and sickle; **с. луны́** crescent moon.
серпанти́н, а *m.* **1** (*бумажная лента*) paper streamer. **2** (*дорога*) winding mountain road.
серпенти́н, а *m.* (*min.*) serpentine.
серпови́дный *adj.* crescent(-shaped).
сертифика́т, а *m.* certificate.
се́рум, а *m.* (*med.*) serum.
се́рфинг, а *m.* surfing.
сёрфинг = **се́рфинг**
серфинги́ст, а *m.* surfer.
серча́|ть, ю *impf.* (*of* ⇨**о**~) (*coll.*) to be angry, be cross.
се́р|ый (~, ~а́, ~о) *adj.* **1** grey (*Br.*), gray (*US*). **2** (*fig.*) (*бесцветный*) grey (*Br.*), gray (*US*); dull; drab; **с. день** grey day. **3** (*fig., coll.*) (*необразованный*) dull, dim.
серьг|а́, и́, *pl.* ~**и, серёг,** ~**а́м** *f.* ear-ring.
серьёзно *adv.* seriously; **с.?** seriously?; really?
серьёзност|ь, и *f.* seriousness.
серьёз|ный (~ен, ~на) *adj.* serious.
сессио́нный *adj.* sessional.
се́сси|я, и *f.* session, sitting.
сестр|а́, ы́, *pl.* ~**ы, сестёр,** ~**ам** *f.*

1 sister; **двою́родная с.** (first) cousin. **2**: **медици́нская с.** nurse.

сестрёнк|а, и *f.* little sister.

се́стрин *adj.* sister's.

сестри́ц|а, ы *f. affectionate form of* ⇒**сестра́**

сесть¹, ся́ду, ся́дешь, *past* **сел, се́ла** *pf.* (*of* ⇒**сади́ться**) **1** to sit down; **с. за стол** to sit down to table; **с. обе́дать** to sit down to dinner; **с. в ва́нну** to get into the bath; **с. рабо́тать** to get down to work; **с. в кало́шу, с. в лу́жу** (*coll.*) to get into a mess, into a fix. **2** (**в, на**+*a.*) to board, take; **с. на по́езд** to board a train; **с. на ло́шадь** to mount a horse. **3** (*о птице*) to alight, settle, perch; (*о самолёте*) to land. **4** (*о солнце, о луне*) to set. **5**: **с. в тюрьму́** to go to prison, jail.

сесть², ся́дет, *past* **сел** *pf.* (*of* ⇒**сади́ться**) (*о ткани*) to shrink.

сет, а *m.* (*sport*) set.

сетево́й *adj.* net, netting, mesh.

се́тк|а, и *f.* **1** net; (*для багажа*) (luggage) rack. **2** (*coll.*) (*сумка*) string-bag. **3** (*geog.*) grid; (*collect.*) co-ordinates. **4** (*radio*) grid. **5** (*тарифная*) scale (*of charges, etc.*).

се́т|овать, ую *impf.* (*of* ⇒**по~**) **1** (**на**+*a.*) to complain (of). **2** (**о**+*p.*) to lament, mourn.

се́точный *adj.* **1** net. **2** (*radio*) grid.

се́ттер, а *m.* setter (*dog*).

сетча́тк|а, и *f.* (*anat.*) retina.

се́тчат|ый *adj.* netted, network; reticular; **~ая ма́йка** string vest; **~ая оболо́чка гла́за** (*anat.*) retina.

сет|ь, и, о ~́и, в ~́и *and* **~и́,** *pl.* **~́и, ~е́й** *f.* **1** net (*also fig.*); **расста́вить ~́и кому́-н.** to set a trap for s.o. **2** (*система*) network; system; **лока́льная с.** (*comput.*) local area network, LAN. **3** (**Сеть**) the Net (*Internet*).

Сеу́л, а *m.* Seoul.

се́ч|а, и *f.* (*obs.*) battle.

сече́ни|е, я *nt.* section; **ке́сарево с.** Caesarean (*Br.*), Cesarean (*US*) (section); **попере́чное с.** cross section.

се́чк|а, и *f.* **1** (*нож*) chopper, vegetable knife. **2** (*нарубленная солома*) chopped straw, chaff.

сечь, секу́, сечёшь, секу́т, *past* **сек, секла́** *impf.* **1** (*impf. only*) (*рубить на части*) to cut to pieces. **2** (*pf.* **вы́~,** *past* **сек, се́кла**) (*бить*) to beat, flog.

се́|чься, чётся, ку́тся, *past* **~кся, ~кла́сь** *impf.* (*of* ⇒**по~**) (*о волосах*) to split; (*о тканях*) to cut.

се́ялк|а, и *f.* (*agric.*) sowing-machine, seed drill.

се́яльщик, а *m.* sower.

се́ян|ец, ца *m.* seedling.

се́ятел|ь, я *m.* sower (*also fig., rhet.*); (*fig.*) disseminator.

се́|ять, ю, ешь *impf.* (*of* ⇒**по~**) to sow (*also fig.*); **с. раздо́р** to sow the seeds of dissension.

сжа́л|иться, юсь, ишься *pf.* (**над**+*i.*) to take pity (on).

сжа́ти|е, я *nt.* **1** pressure; (*рукой*) grasp, grip. **2** (*жидкости, газа*) compression; **ка́мера ~я** compression chamber.

сжа́тост|ь, и *f.* **1** (*жидкости, газа*) compression. **2** (*краткость*) conciseness.

сжа́т|ый *p.p.p. of* ⇒**~ь¹** *and* **~ь²** *and adj.* **1** compressed (*air, gas*). **2** (*fig.*) condensed, concise.

сжать¹, сожму́, сожмёшь *pf.* (*of* ⇒**сжима́ть**) to squeeze; (*жидкость, газ*) to compress (*also fig.*); to grip; **с. гу́бы** to purse one's lips; **с. зу́бы** to grit one's teeth; **с. кулаки́** to clench one's fists; **с. в объя́тиях** to hug; **с. изложе́ние** to compress an exposition.

сжать², сожну́, сожнёшь *pf. of* ⇒**жать²**

сжа́|ться, сожму́сь, сожмёшься *pf.* (*of* ⇒**сжима́ться**) **1** (*о пальцах, о зубах*) to tighten, clench. **2** (*о теле*) to contract; **её душа́ ~лась** her heart sank.

сж|ева́ть, ую́, уёшь *pf.* to chew up.

сжечь, сожгу́, сожжёшь, сожгу́т, *past* **сжёг, сожгла́** *pf.* (*of* ⇒**жечь** *and* **сжига́ть**) to burn (up, down); (*в крематории*) to cremate; **с. свой корабли́** (*fig.*) to burn one's boats.

сжива́|ть(ся), ю(сь) *impf. of* ⇒**сжи́ть(ся)**

сжига́|ть, ю *impf. of* ⇒**сжечь**

сжи|ди́ть, жу́, ди́шь *pf.* (*of* ⇒**~жа́ть**) (*chem.*) to liquefy.

сжижа́|ть, ю *impf. of* ⇒**сжиди́ть**

сжиже́ни|е, я *nt.* (*chem.*) liquefaction.

сжи́женный *adj.* (*chem.*) liquefied.

сжима́емост|ь, и *f.* compressibility, condensability.

сжима́|ть(ся), ю(сь) *impf. of* ⇒**сжа́ть¹(ся)**

сжи|ть, ву́, вёшь, *past* **~л, ~ла́, ~́ло** *pf.* (*of* ⇒**~ва́ть**) (*coll.*) to force out; **с. со́ свету** to be the death (of).

сжи́|ться, ву́сь, вёшься, *past* **~лся, ~ла́сь** *pf.* (*of* ⇒**~ва́ться**) (**с**+*i.*) to get used (to), get accustomed (to); **с. с ро́лью** (*theatr.*) to get inside a part; to live a part.

сжу́льнича|ть, ю *pf. of* ⇒**жу́льничать**

сза́ди *adv. and prep.*+*g.* **1** *adv.* from behind; behind; from the end; from the rear; **вид с.** rear view; **тре́тий ваго́н с.** the third coach from the rear. **2** *prep.*+*g.* behind.

сзыва́|ть, ю *impf. of* ⇒**созва́ть**

си *nt. indecl.* (*mus.*) B.

сиа́мский *adj.* Siamese.

сибари́т, а *m.* sybarite.

сибари́тский *adj.* sybaritic.

сибари́тств|овать, ую *impf.* to lead the life of a sybarite.

сиби́рск|ий *adj.* Siberian; **~ая ко́шка** Persian cat; **~ая я́зва** (*med.*) anthrax.

Сиби́р|ь, и *f.* Siberia.

сибиря́к, а́ *m.* Siberian.

сибиря́|чка, чки *f. of* ⇒**~к**

сиве́|ть, ю *impf.* (*of* ⇒**по~**) to turn grey (*Br.*), gray (*US*).

си́вк|а, и *f.* dark grey (*Br.*), gray (*US*) (horse).

сивола́п|ый (~, ~а) *adj.* (*coll.*) rough, clumsy.

сиву́х|а, и *f.* impure vodka.

сиву́ч, а́ *m.* (*zool.*) Steller's sea lion.

си́в|ый (~, ~а́, ~о) *adj.* **1** (*лошадь*) grey (*Br.*), gray (*US*). **2** (*волосы*) grey (*Br.*), gray (*US*); (*седеющий*) greying (*Br.*), graying (*US*).

сиг, а́ *m.* whitefish.

сиган|у́ть, у́, ёшь *pf.* (*coll.*) to leap.

сига́р|а, ы *f.* cigar.

сигаре́т|а, ы *f.* cigarette.

сигаре́т|ный *adj. of* ⇒**~а**

сига́р|ный *adj. of* ⇒**~а**

сигна́л, а *m.* signal; **пожа́рный с.** fire-alarm; **с. бе́дствия** distress signal; **с. на трубе́** trumpet-call.

сигнализа́тор, а *m.* (*tech.*) signalling (*Br.*), signaling (*US*) apparatus.

сигнализа́ци|я, и *f.* **1** (*действие*) signalling (*Br.*), signaling (*US*). **2** (*устройство*) alarm system. **3** (*система*) signalling (*Br.*), signaling (*US*) system.

сигнализи́р|овать, ую *impf. and pf.* **1** (*pf. also* **про~**) to signal. **2** (+*a. or* **о**+*p.*; *fig.*) to give warning (of).

сигна́л|ить, ю, ишь *impf.* (*coll.*) to signal.

сигна́л|ьный *adj. of* ⇒**~; ~ьная бу́дка** signal-box.

сигна́льщик, а *m.* signal-man.

сигнату́р|а, ы *f.* **1** (*pharm.*) label. **2** (*typ.*) signature.

СИД *m.* (*indecl.*) (*abbr. of* ***светоизлуча́ющий дио́д***) LED (*light-emitting diode*).

сиде́лк|а, и *f.* (sick-)nurse.

сиде́ни|е, я *nt.* sitting.

си́д|ень, ня *m.* (*coll.*) stay-at-home; **сиде́ть ~нем** to be a stay-at-home.

сиде́нь|е, я *nt.* seat.

си|де́ть, жу́, ди́шь *impf.* **1** to sit; **с., поджа́в но́ги** to sit cross-legged; **с. верхо́м** to be on horseback; **с. на ко́рточках** to squat; **с. у мо́ря, ждать пого́ды** (*coll.*) to wait for sth. to turn up; **вот где ~ди́т кто-н., что-н.** (*coll.*) that's where all the trouble lies. **2** (*находиться*) to be; **с. (в тюрьме́)** to be in prison; **с. под аре́стом** to be under arrest; **с. без де́ла** to have nothing to do; **с. за кни́гой** to be (engaged in) reading; **с. на игле́** to do drugs. **3** (**на**+*p.*) (*об одежде*) to fit, sit (on).

сид|е́ться, и́тся *impf.* (*impers.*+*d.*): **ему́, *etc.*, не ~и́тся до́ма** he, *etc.*, can't bear staying at home; **ей не ~и́тся на ме́сте** she can't keep still.

Си́дне|й, я *m.* Sydney.

сидр, а *m.* cider.

сидя́ч|ий *adj.* **1** sitting; **в ~ей по́зе** in a sitting posture. **2** (*fig.*) sedentary; **с. о́браз жи́зни** sedentary life.

сие́ *see* ⇒**сей**

сие́н|а, ы *f.* sienna; **жжёная с.** burnt sienna.
сизиги́йный *adj.*: **с. прили́в** spring tide.
сизи́фов *adj.*: **~ труд** labour (*Br.*), labor (*US*) of Sisyphus.
си́з|ый (~, ~а́, ~о) *adj.* blue-grey (*Br.*), blue-gray (*US*).
сикомо́р, а *m.* (*bot.*) sycamore.
сикх, а *m.* Sikh.
си́кхский *adj.* Sikh.
си́л|а, ы *f.* **1** strength, force; **в ~у** (+*g.*) on the strength (of), by virtue (of), because (of); **быть в ~ах** (+*inf.*) to be able to, have the strength (to); **изо всех ~, что есть ~ы** with all one's might; **крича́ть изо всех ~** to shout at the top of one's voice; **от ~ы** (*coll.*) at most; **сверх ~, свы́ше ~, не по ~ам** beyond one's power(s); outside one's competence; **че́рез ~у** with the greatest of effort; **рабо́тать че́рез ~у** to work only with the greatest of effort; to force o.s. to work; **~ой** by force; **с по́мощью гру́бой ~ы** by brute force; **свои́ми ~ами** unaided; **~ою** (+*g. or* **в**+*a.*) to the strength (of); **с. во́ли** will-power; **с. ду́ха** strength of mind; **с. привы́чки** force of habit; **в ~у привы́чки** by force of habit. **2** (*phys., tech.*) force, power; **лошади́ная с.** horse-power; **подъёмная с.** (*aeron.*) lift; **с. све́та в свеча́х** candle-power; **с. тя́ги** tractive force; **с. тя́жести, с. притяже́ния** force of gravity. **3** (*leg. and fig.*) force; **име́ющий ~у** valid; **в ~е** in force, valid; **войти́, вступи́ть в ~у** to come into force, take effect; **оста́ться в ~е** to remain valid; (*fig.*) to hold good. **4** (*pl.*; *mil.*) forces; **вооружённые ~ы** armed forces; **вое́нно-возду́шные ~ы** air force(s); **сухопу́тные ~ы** land forces, ground forces. **5** (*coll.*) (*смысл*) point, essence; **с. в том, что** the crux of the matter is that. **6** (*coll.*) (*большое количество*) quantity, multitude.
сила́ч, а́ *m.* strong man.
силика́т, а *m.* (*min.*) silicate.
силико́н, а *m.* silicone.
си́л|иться, юсь, ишься *impf.* to try very hard, make efforts.
силко́м *adv.* (*coll.*) by (main) force.
силлаби́ческий *adj.* (*liter.*) syllabic.
Си́лли: о́стров|а́ С., ~о́в С. *no sg.* the Scilly Isles, the Isles of Scilly, the Scillies.
силлоги́зм, а *m.* (*phil.*) syllogism.
силов|о́й *adj.* power; **~о́е по́ле** (*phys.*) field of force; **с. про́вод** (*elec.*) power-line; **~а́я ста́нция** power-station; **~а́я устано́вка** power-plant; **~ы́е структу́ры** law enforcement agencies.
си́лой *adv.* (*coll.*) by force.
сил|о́к, ка́ *m.* snare.
силоме́р, а *m.* dynamometer.
си́лос, а *m.* (*agric.*) **1** (*сооружение*) silo. **2** (*корм*) silage.
силосова́ни|е, я *nt.* siloing.
силос|ова́ть, у́ю *impf. and pf.* to silo.
силури́йский *adj.* (*geol.*) Silurian.
силуэ́т, а *m.* silhouette.

си́льно *adv.* **1** strongly; violently; **с. ска́зано** that's going too far; that's putting it too strongly. **2** (*очень*) very much, greatly; badly; **с. нужда́ться в чём-н** to want sth. badly.
сильноде́йствующий *adj.* (*лекарство, яд*) potent, virulent; (*средство*) drastic.
си́л|ьный (~ен *and* ~ён, ~ьна́, ~ьно, ~ьны́) *adj.* strong; powerful; **~ьная во́ля** strong will; **с. до́вод** powerful argument; **с. дождь** heavy rain; **~ьное жела́ние** intense desire; **с. за́пах** strong smell; **с. моро́з** hard frost; **он не ~ён в языка́х** he is not good at languages; **~ьные ми́ра сего́** (*iron.*) influential, powerful people.
сильф, а *m.* (*myth.*) sylph.
сильфи́д|а, ы *f.* (*myth. and fig.*) sylph.
симбио́з, а *m.* (*biol.*) symbiosis.
си́мвол, а *m.* symbol; **с. ве́ры** (*relig.*) creed.
символиза́ци|я, и *f.* symbolization.
символизи́р|овать, ую *impf.* to symbolize.
символи́зм, а *m.* symbolism.
симво́лик|а, и *f.* symbolism.
символи́ст, а *m.* symbolist.
символи́ст|ка, ки *f. of* ⇒~
символи́ст|ский *adj. of* ⇒~
символи́ческий *adj.* symbolic(al).
символи́чност|ь, и *f.* symbolical character.
символи́ч|ный (~ен, ~на) *adj.* = **~еский**
симметри́ческий *adj.* symmetrical.
симметри́чност|ь, и *f.* symmetry.
симметри́ч|ный (~ен, ~на) *adj.* = **~еский**
симме́три́|я, и *f.* symmetry.
симпатизи́р|овать, ую *impf.* (+*d.*) **1** (*сочувствовать*) to be in sympathy (with), sympathize (with). **2** (*хорошо относиться*) to like, be fond of.
симпати́ческ|ий *adj.* (*physiol., etc.*) sympathetic; **~ая не́рвная систе́ма** sympathetic nervous system; **~ие черни́ла** invisible ink.
симпати́ч|ный (~ен, ~на) *adj.* (*человек*) nice, pleasant; (*лицо, голос, город*) attractive, pleasant.
симпа́ти|я, и *f.* (**к**+*d.*) liking, fondness (for); **чу́вствовать ~ю к кому́-н.** to take a liking to s.o., be drawn to s.o.
симпо́зиум, а *m.* symposium.
симпто́м, а *m.* symptom.
симптомати́ческий *adj.* **1** symptomatic. **2** (*med.*) eliminating symptoms, palliative.
симптомати́ч|ный (~ен, ~на) *adj.* = **~еский**
симули́р|овать, ую *impf. and pf.* to simulate, fake, sham.
симуля́нт, а *m.* faker; (*болезни*) malingerer.
симуля́ци|я, и *f.* simulation.
симфони́ческий *adj.* symphonic; **с. орке́стр** symphony orchestra.
симфо́ни|я, и *f.* symphony.
синаго́г|а, и *f.* synagogue.

Сина́|й, я *m.* Sinai.
синга́л, а *m.* Sin(g)halese.
синга́л|ец, ьца *m.* = **синга́л**
синга́л|ка, ки *f. of* ⇒~
синга́льский *adj.* Sin(g)halese.
Сингапу́р, а *m.* Singapore.
сингапу́р|ец, ца *m.* Singaporean.
сингапу́р|ка, ки *f. of* ⇒**~ец**
сингапу́рский *adj.* Singaporean.
синдика́т, а *m.* (*econ.*) syndicate.
синдици́р|овать, ую *impf. and pf.* (*econ.*) to syndicate.
синдро́м, а *m.* (*med.*) syndrome.
синев|а́, ы́ *f.* blue; **с. небе́с** the blue of the sky; **с. под глаза́ми** dark patches under the eyes.
синева́т|ый (~, ~а) *adj.* bluish.
синегла́з|ый (~, ~а) *adj.* blue-eyed.
сине́кдох|а, и *f.* (*liter.*) synecdoche.
синеку́р|а, ы *f.* sinecure.
сине́л|ь, и *f.* (*text.*) chenille.
сине́|ть, ю *impf.* **1** (*pf.* **по~**) (*становиться синим*) to turn blue, become blue. **2** (*impf. only*) (*виднеться*) to show blue.
си́н|ий (~ь, ~я́, ~е) *adj.* (dark) blue; **с. чуло́к** (*fig.*) blue-stocking.
сини́льн|ый *adj.*: **~ая кислота́** (*chem.*) prussic acid.
син|и́ть, ю́, и́шь *impf.* (*of* ⇒**по~**) **1** (*красить*) to paint blue. **2** (*бельё*) to blue.
сини́ц|а, ы *f.* tit (*bird*).
синкли́т, а *m.* (*joc.*) council, synod.
синко́п|а, ы *f.* **1** (*mus.*) syncopation. **2** (*ling.*) syncope.
синкопи́р|овать, ую *impf. and pf.* (*mus., ling.*) to syncopate.
синкрети́зм, а *m.* syncretism.
сино́д, а *m.* synod.
синода́льный *adj.* synodal.
сино́лог, а *m.* sinologist.
синоло́ги|я, и *f.* sinology.
сино́ним, а *m.* synonym.
синоними́ческий *adj.* synonymous.
синоними́ч|ный (~ен, ~на) *adj.* synonymous.
синоними́|я, и *f.* synonymy.
сино́птик, а *m.* weather forecaster.
сино́птик|а, и *f.* weather forecasting.
синопти́ческ|ий *adj.* synoptic; **~ая ка́рта** weather-chart.
си́нтаксис, а *m.* syntax.
синтакси́ческий *adj.* syntactical.
си́нтез, а *m.* synthesis.
синтеза́тор, а *m.* synthesizer.
синтези́р|овать, ую *impf. and pf.* to synthesize.
синте́тик|а, и *f.* (*collect.*) synthetic, synthetics.
синтети́ческий *adj.* synthetic.
си́нус[1], а *m.* (*math.*) sine.
си́нус[2], а *m.* (*anat.*) sinus.
синусо́ид|а, ы *f.* (*math.*) sinusoid.
синхрониза́ци|я, и *f.* synchronization.

синхронизи́р|овать, ую *impf. and pf.* to synchronize.

синхрони́зм, а *m.* synchronism.

синхрони́ст, а *m.* simultaneous interpreter.

синхрони́ческий *adj.* synchronic.

синхрони́|я, и *f.* synchrony.

синхро́нн|ый *adj.* synchronous; (*перевод*) simultaneous; **~ое пла́вание** synchronized swimming.

син|ь, и *f.* blue.

синьг|а́, и́ *f.* (*zool.*) common scoter.

си́ньк|а, и *f.* **1** (*для подкрашивания*) blue, blueing. **2** (*чертёж*) blueprint.

синьо́р, а *m.* signor.

синьо́р|а, ы *f.* signora.

синьори́н|а, ы *f.* signorina.

синю́х|а, и *f.* (*med.*) cyanosis.

синя́к, а́ *m.* bruise; **с. под гла́зом** black eye; **~и́ под глаза́ми** shadows, dark patches under the eyes; **изби́ть до ~о́в** to beat black and blue.

сиони́зм, а *m.* Zionism.

сиони́ст, а *m.* Zionist.

сиони́ст|ка, ки *f.* *of* ⇨**~**

сиони́стский *adj.* Zionist.

сип|е́ть, лю́, и́шь *impf.* **1** to speak in a hoarse voice. **2** (*impers.*) to be hoarse; **у него́ в го́рле ~и́т** he is hoarse.

си́пл|ый (~, ~а́, ~о) *adj.* hoarse, husky.

си́пн|уть, у, ешь, *past* **сип** *and* **~ул, си́пла** *impf.* (*coll.*) to become hoarse.

сипу́х|а, и *f.* (*zool.*) barn owl.

сире́н|а, ы *f.* siren.

сире́невый *adj.* lilac; lilac-coloured.

сире́н|ь, и *f.* lilac.

си́речь *particle* (*arch.*) that is to say.

сири́|ец, йца *m.* Syrian.

сири́|йка, йки *f.* *of* ⇨**~ец**

сири́йский *adj.* Syrian.

Си́ри|я, и *f.* Syria.

сиро́кко *m. indecl.* sirocco (*сухой ветер*).

сиро́п, а *m.* syrup.

сирот|а́, ы, *pl.* **~́ы** *c.g.* orphan; **каза́нская с.** (*fig., coll.*) person with 'hard luck story'.

сироте́|ть, ю *impf.* (*of* **о~**) to be orphaned.

сиротли́в|ый (~, ~а) *adj.* lonely.

сиро́т|ский *adj.* *of* ⇨**~а́; с. дом** orphanage; **~ская зима́** mild winter.

сиро́тств|о, а *nt.* orphanhood.

си́р|ый (~, ~а́, ~о) *adj.* (*obs.*) **1** orphaned. **2** (*fig.*) (*одинокий*) lonely.

систе́м|а, ы *f.* **1** system; **стать ~ой, войти́ в ~у** to become the rule; to become customary. **2** (*тип*) type; **пулемёт но́вой ~ы** machine-gun of a new type.

систематиза́ци|я, и *f.* systematization.

систематизи́р|овать, ую *impf. and pf.* to systematize, order.

системати́к|а, и *f.* **1** systematization. **2** (*biol.*) taxonomy.

системати́ческий *adj.* **1** systematic; methodical. **2** (*регулярный*) regular.

системати́чност|ь, и *f.* systematic character; system.

системати́ч|ный (~ен, ~на) *adj.* systematic; methodical.

систе́м|ный *adj.* *of* ⇨**~а; с. ана́лиз** systems analysis; **с. диск** system disk.

си́стол|а, ы *f.* (*med.*) systole.

си́с|ька, ьки, *g. pl.* **~ек** *f.* (*coll.*) nipple; tit.

си́т|ец, ца *m.* cotton (print); calico (print); chintz.

си́теч|ко, ка, *pl.* **~ки, ~ек** *nt. dim. of* ⇨**си́то; ча́йное с.** tea-strainer.

си́тник[1], а *m.* (*хлеб*) loaf made of sifted flour.

си́тник[2], а *m.* (*bot.*) rush.

си́т|о, а *nt.* sieve.

ситро́ *nt. indecl.* fruit-flavoured (*Br.*), -flavored (*US*) mineral water.

ситуа́ци|я, и *f.* situation.

си́т|цевый *adj.* *of* ⇨**~ец**

си́филис, а *m.* (*med.*) syphilis.

сифили́тик, а *m.* syphilitic.

сифилити́ческий *adj.* syphilitic.

сифо́н, а *m.* siphon.

сицили́|ец, йца *m.* Sicilian.

сицили́|йка, йки *f.* *of* ⇨**~ец**

сицили́йский *adj.* Sicilian.

Сици́ли|я, и *f.* Sicily.

сиюмину́т|ный (~ен, ~на) *adj.* present, current.

сия́ни|е, я *nt.* radiance; **се́верное с.** northern lights, aurora borealis.

сия́тельств|о, а *nt.*: **его́,** *etc.*, **с.** (*title of princes and counts*) his, *etc.*, Highness.

сия́|ть, ю *impf.* (*о солнце*) to shine; (*о человеке, от радости*) to beam; (*о лице, о красивой женщине*) to be radiant.

скабрёзност|ь, и *f.* obscenity; **говори́ть ~и** to use obscene language.

скабрёз|ный (~ен, ~на) *adj.* indecent, obscene.

сказ, а *m.* **1** (*coll.*) (*рассказ*) tale; **вот тебе́ и весь с.** (*coll.*) that's the long and the short of it. **2** (*в литературоведении*) skaz (= *first-person narrative*).

сказа́ни|е, я *nt.* story, tale, legend.

сказан|у́ть, у́, ёшь *pf.* (*coll.*) to blurt (out); **ну и ~у́л словцо́!** that's a fine thing to say!

ска|за́ть, жу́, ~́жешь *pf. of* ⇨**говори́ть; ~жи́(те)!** (*coll., iron.*) I say!; **как с.** how shall I put it?; **как с.!** it depends; **лу́чше с., верне́е с., точне́е с.** or rather; **не́чего с.!** well, I never!; **~́зано — сде́лано** (*coll.*) no sooner said than done; **ничего́ не ~́жешь, он прав** there is no denying it, he is right.

ска|за́ться[1], жу́сь, ~́жешься *pf.* (*of* ⇨**~́зываться**) (*coll.*) **1** (+*d.*) (*предупредить*) to inform; to give notice, give warning; **они́ уе́хали не ~за́вшись** they went away without (giving) warning. **2** (+*i.*) (*назваться*) to proclaim o.s.; **с. больны́м** to plead illness.

ска|за́ться[2], ~́жется *pf.* (*of* ⇨**~́зываться**) **1** (**на**+*p.*) to tell (on); **бомбёжка ~за́лась на её не́рвах** the bombing told on her nerves. **2** (**в**+*p.*) to be manifest (in); to be seen (in).

сказа́тел|ь, я *m.* folk-tale narrator, story-teller.

ска́зк|а, и *f.* **1** fairy-tale. **2** (*coll.*) (*ложь*) (tall) story, fib.

ска́зочник, а *m.* story-teller.

ска́зочни|ца, цы *f.* *of* ⇨**~к**

ска́зочн|ый *adj.* fairytale; (*необычайный*) fabulous, fantastic; **~ая страна́** fairyland; **~ое бога́тство** fabulous wealth.

сказу́ем|ое, ого *nt.* (*gram.*) predicate.

ска́зыва|ться, юсь *impf. of* ⇨**сказа́ться**

скак *m. only found in p. sg.*: **на всём ~у́** at full tilt.

скака́лк|а, и *f.* skipping-rope (*Br.*), jump rope (*US*).

ска|ка́ть, чу́, ~́чешь *impf.* **1** to skip, jump; **с. на одно́й ноге́** to hop. **2** (*о лошади, о всаднике*) to gallop. **3** (*coll.*) (*резко изменяться*) to fluctuate.

скаков|о́й *adj.* race, racing; **~а́я доро́жка** racecourse; **~а́я ло́шадь** racehorse.

скаку́н, а́ *m.* racehorse.

скал|а́, ы́, *pl.* **~́ы** *f.* rock face, crag; **(отве́сная) с.** cliff; **подво́дная с.** reef.

скаламбу́р|ить, ю, ишь *pf. of* ⇨**каламбу́рить**

скали́ст|ый (~, ~а) *adj.* rocky.

ска́л|ить, ю, ишь *impf.* (*of* ⇨**о~**); **с. зу́бы** to show one's teeth, bare one's teeth; (*impf. only*) (*fig. pej.*) to grin, laugh.

ска́л|иться, юсь, ишься *impf. of* ⇨**о~**

ска́лк|а, и *f.* **1** (*cul.*) rolling-pin. **2** (*для белья*) roller (*for ironing linen*).

скалола́з, а *m.* rock-climber.

скалола́зани|е, я *nt.* rock-climbing.

скалола́з|ка, ки *f.* *of* ⇨**~**

ска́лыва|ть, ю *impf. of* ⇨**сколо́ть**

скальки́р|овать, ую *pf. of* ⇨**кальки́ровать**

скалькули́р|овать, ую *pf. of* ⇨**калькули́ровать**

ска́льн|ый *adj.* (*geol.*) rock, rocky; **~ые рабо́ты** rock excavations.

скальп, а *m.* scalp.

ска́льпел|ь, я *m.* scalpel.

скальпи́р|овать, ую *impf. and pf.* (*pf. also* **о~**) to scalp.

скаме́ечк|а, и *f.* small bench; **с. для ног** footstool.

скаме́йк|а, и *f.* bench.

скам|ья́, ьи́, *pl.* **~́ьи, ~е́й** *f.* bench; **с. подсуди́мых** (*leg.*) the dock; **на шко́льной ~ье́** during one's schooldays; **со шко́льной ~ьи́** straight from school.

сканда́л, а *m.* **1** scandal. **2** (*ссора*) row, (rowdy) scene.

скандализи́р|овать, ую *impf. and pf.* to scandalize.

скандали́ст, а *m.* trouble-maker; rowdy.

сканда́л|ить, ю, ишь *impf.* **1** (*pf.*

на~) (*coll.*) (*безобразничать*) to brawl; to start a row. **2** (*pf.* **о~**) (*позорить*) to disgrace.

скандáл|иться, юсь, ишься *impf.* (*of* ⇨**о~**) to disgrace o.s.

скандáл|ьный (~ен, ~ьна) *adj.* **1** (*поведение*) scandalous. **2** (*coll.*) (*человек*) rowdy, quarrelsome. **3** scandal; **~ьная хрóника** scandal column, page (*of newspaper*).

скандинáв, а *m.* Scandinavian.

Скандинáви|я, и *f.* Scandinavia.

скандинáв|ка, ки *f. of* ⇨**~**

скандинáвский *adj.* Scandinavian.

скандúровани|е, я *nt.* (*liter.*) scansion.

скандúр|овать, ую *impf. and pf.* **1** (*стихи*) to declaim, recite (*stressing individual syllables of words*). **2** (*о толпе*) to chant.

скáнер, а *m.* (*comput., med.*) scanner.

сканúр|овать, ую *impf. and pf.* (*med., comput., TV*) to scan.

скáплива|ть(ся), ю, ет(ся) *impf. of* ⇨**скопúть(ся)**

скапý|ститься, щусь, стишься *pf.* (*sl.*) to croak, peg out (*Br.*).

скáпыва|ть, ю *impf.* (*of* ⇨**скопáть**) to shovel away, level with a spade.

скарабé|й, я *m.* (*жук*) scarab.

скарб, а *m.* (*coll.*) belongings; (one's) things; **со всем ~ом** bag and baggage.

скáред, а *m.* (*coll.*) stingy person, miser.

скáреднича|ть, ю *impf.* (*coll.*) to be stingy.

скáред|ный (~ен, ~на) *adj.* (*coll.*) stingy, miserly.

скарифицúр|овать, ую *impf.* (*agric.*) to scarify.

скарлатúн|а, ы *f.* (*med.*) scarlet fever.

скáрмлива|ть, ю *impf. of* ⇨**скормúть**

скат¹, а *m.* (*склон*) slope, incline; (*крыши*) pitch.

скат², а *m.* (*tech.*) (*колесо*) wheel; (*ось*) axle.

скат³, а *m.* (*zool.*) ray, skate.

скат|áть, áю *pf.* (*of* ⇨**~ывать**) to roll (up).

скáтерт|ь, и, *pl.* **~и, ~éй** *f.* tablecloth; **~ью дорóга!** (*coll.*) good riddance!

ска|тúть, чý, ~тишь *pf.* (*of* ⇨**~тывать**) to roll down.

ска|тúться, чýсь, ~тшься *pf.* (*of* ⇨**~тываться**) to roll down; **с. на лы́жах** to ski down; (*fig., pej.*) to slip, slide.

скáтк|а, и *f.* **1** (*mil.*) greatcoat roll. **2** (*действие*) rolling.

скáтыва|ть, ю *impf. of* ⇨**скатáть** *and* **скатúть**

скáтыва|ться, юсь *impf. of* ⇨**скатúться**

скáут, а *m.* (boy) scout.

скафáндр, а *m.* protective suit; (*водолаза*) diving suit; (*космонавта*) spacesuit.

скáчк|а, и *f.* **1** gallop, galloping. **2** (*pl.*) (*состязание*) horse-race; race meeting, the races; **с. с препя́тствиями** steeplechase.

скачкообрáз|ный (~ен, ~на) *adj.* spasmodic; uneven.

скач|óк, кá *m.* **1** jump, leap, bound; **~кáми** by leaps. **2** (*fig.*) (*цен, температуры*) leap.

скáшива|ть, ю *impf. of* ⇨**скосúть**

скáщива|ть, ю *impf. of* ⇨**скостúть**

СКВ *f. indecl.* (*abbr. of* ***свобóдно конвертúруемая валю́та***) hard currency, freely convertible currency.

сквáжин|а, ы *f.* slit, chink; **буровáя с.** (*tech.*) bore-hole; **замóчная с.** key-hole; **нефтянáя с.** oil-well.

сквáжист|ый (~, ~а) *adj.* porous.

сквалы́г|а, и *c.g.* (*coll.*) miser, skinflint.

сквер, а *m.* (*small*) public garden.

сквéрн|а, ы *no pl.* (*collect.; obs.*) pollution; filth.

сквéрно *adv.* badly; **с. чу́вствовать себя́** to feel bad, feel unwell; **с. поступúть с кем-н.** to treat s.o. badly.

сквернослóв, а *m.* foul-mouthed person.

сквернослóви|е, я *nt.* foul language.

сквернослóв|ить, лю, ишь *impf.* to use foul language.

сквéр|ный (~ен, ~нá, ~но) *adj.* (*человек, поступок*) nasty; (*погода, настроение*) foul, awful; (*impers.*): **мне ~но** I feel awful.

сквитá|ться, юсь *pf.* (**с** + *i.*; *coll.*) to settle accounts (with).

сквоз|úть, úт *impf.* **1** (*impers.*): **~úт** there is a draught (*Br.*), draft (*US*). **2** (*obs.*) (*пропускать свет*) to be transparent, show light through. **3** (*виднеться*) to show through, be seen through (*also fig.*); **синевá небéс ~úла меж ветвя́ми** the blue of the sky could be seen through the branches; **в егó словáх ~úла жáлость к себé** there was a hint of self-pity in his words.

сквозн|óй *adj.* **1** through; **с. вéтер** draught (*Br.*), draft (*US*); **~óе движéние** through traffic; **с. пóезд** through train. **2** (*рана, отверстие*) going right through. **3** (*просвечивающий*) transparent.

сквозня́к, á *m.* draught (*Br.*), draft (*US*).

сквозь *prep.* + *a.* through.

сквор|éц, цá *m.* starling.

скворéчник, а *m.* nesting-box (*for starlings*).

скворéч|ница, ницы *f.* = **~ник**

скворéч|ня, ни, *g. pl.* **~ен** *f.* = **~ник**

сквош, а *m.* (*sport*) squash.

скейтбóрд, а *m.* skateboard.

скейтбóрдинг, а *m.* skateboarding.

скелéт, а *m.* skeleton.

скéпсис, а *m.* scepticism (*Br.*), skepticism (*US*).

скéптик, а *m.* sceptic (*Br.*), skeptic (*US*).

скептицúзм, а *m.* scepticism (*Br.*), skepticism (*US*).

скептúческий *adj.* sceptical (*Br.*), skeptical (*US*).

скéрцо *nt. indecl.* (*mus.*) scherzo.

скéтинг-рúнг, а *m.* roller-skating rink.

скетч, а *m.* (*theatr.*) sketch.

скид|áть¹, áю *impf.* (*obs., coll.*) (*одежду*) to throw off.

скид|áть², áю *pf.* (*of* ⇨**~ывать²**) (*coll.*) to throw together, into a pile (*multiple objects*).

скúдк|а, и *f.* **1** reduction, discount; **со ~ой (в** + *a.*) with a reduction (of), at a discount (of). **2** (**на** + *a.*; *fig.*) allowance(s) (for); **сдéлать ~у на вóзраст** to make allowances for age.

скúдыва|ть¹, ю *impf. of* ⇨**скúнуть**

скúдыва|ть², ю *impf. of* ⇨**скидáть²**

скú|нуть, ну, нешь *pf.* (*of* ⇨**~дывать¹**) **1** (*coll.*) (*одежду*) to throw off, cast off; (*снег с крыши*) to throw down. **2** (*coll.*) (*в цене*) to knock off (*from price*).

скúпетр, а *m.* sceptre (*Br.*), scepter (*US*).

скипидáр, а *m.* turpentine.

скипидáр|ный *adj. of* ⇨**~**

скирд, á, *pl.* **~ы** *m.* stack, rick.

скирд|á, ы́, *pl.* **~ы, ~, ~áм** *f.* = **~**

скирд|овáть, ýю *impf.* (*of* ⇨**за~**) to stack.

скис|áть, áю *impf. of* ⇨**~нуть**

скúс|нуть, ну, нешь, *past* **~, ~ла** *pf.* (*of* ⇨**~áть**) to go sour, turn sour; (*fig.*) to lose heart.

скит, á, о ~é, в ~ý *m.* (*small and secluded*) monastery.

скитáл|ец, ьца *m.* wanderer.

скитáл|ица, ицы *f. of* ⇨**~ец**

скитáльческий *adj.* wandering.

скитá|ться, юсь *impf.* to wander.

скиф¹, а *m.* (*hist.*) Scythian.

скиф², а *m.* skiff.

скúфский *adj.* (*hist.*) Scythian.

склад¹, а *m.* **1** (*место*) storehouse; (*mil.*) depot; **тамóженный с.** bonded warehouse; **товáрный с.** warehouse. **2** (*запас*) store; **с. боеприпáсов** (*mil.*) ammunition dump.

склад², а *m.* **1** (*образ*) way; **с. умá** cast of mind, mentality. **2** (*coll.*): **ни ~у, ни лáду** neither rhyme nor reason.

склад³, а, *pl.* **~ы** *m.* (*слог*) syllable; **читáть по ~áм** to read haltingly, spell out.

склáд|ень, ня *m.* hinged icon.

складúр|овать, ую *impf. and pf.* to store.

склáдк|а, и *f.* **1** pleat, tuck; crease; **ю́бка в ~у** pleated skirt; **с. на брю́ках** trouser crease. **2** (*на коже*) wrinkle.

склáдно *adv.* smoothly, coherently.

складн|óй *adj.* folding, collapsible; **~áя кровáть** camp bed (*Br.*), cot (*US*); **с. нож** penknife.

склáд|ный (~ен, ~нá, ~но) *adj.* **1** (*coll.*) (*статный*) well-built. **2** (*coll.*) (*хорошо сделанный*) well-made. **3** (*речь*) well-rounded, coherent; **с. рассkáз** well-put-together story.

склáдочн|ый *adj.* storage; **~ое мéсто** store-room.

склад|ско́й *adj.* = **~очный**

скла́дчатый *adj.* (*geol.*) plicated, folded.

скла́дчин|а, ы *f.* clubbing, pooling; **устро́ить ~у** to club together; **купи́ть автомоби́ль в ~у** to club together to buy a car.

скла́дыва|ть(ся), ю(сь) *impf. of* **⇒сложи́ть(ся)**

скле́ива|ть(ся), ю, ет(ся) *impf. of* **⇒скле́ить(ся)**

скле́|ить, ю, ишь *pf.* (*of* **⇒~ивать**) to stick together; to glue together.

скле́|иться, ится *pf.* (*of* **⇒~иваться**) to stick together (*intrans.*).

скле́йк|а, и *f.* glueing together.

склеп, а *m.* burial vault, crypt.

склеп|а́ть, а́ю *pf.* (*of* **⇒~ывать**) to rivet.

склёпк|а, и *f.* riveting.

склёпыва|ть, ю *impf. of* **⇒склепа́ть**

склеро́з, а *m.* (*med.*) sclerosis; **рассе́янный с.** multiple sclerosis.

склероти́ческий *adj.* (*med.*) sclerotic.

скли́|кать, чу, чешь *pf. of* **⇒~ка́ть**

склик|а́ть, а́ю *impf.* (*of* **⇒~ать**) (*coll.*) to call together.

скло́к|а, и *f.* squabble; row.

склон, а *m.* slope; **на ~е лет** in one's declining years.

склоне́ни|е, я *nt.* **1** (*math.*) inclination; (*astron.*) declination. **2** (*gram.*) declension.

склон|и́ть, ю́, ~ишь *pf.* (*of* **⇒~я́ть**[1]) **1** to incline, bend, bow; **с. го́лову (пе́ред** + *i.*) (*fig.*) to bow one's head (to, before). **2** (*fig.*) (*убедить*) to talk (*s.o.*) over; to win over.

склон|и́ться, ю́сь, ~ишься *pf.* (*of* **⇒~я́ться**[1]) **1** to bend, bow. **2** (**к** + *d.*; *fig.*) to give in (to), yield (to).

скло́нност|ь, и *f.* (**к** + *d.*) (*к музыке, к живописи*) aptitude (for); (*к полноте, к меланхолии*) susceptibility (to), tendency (towards); (*к театру, к пиву*) liking, penchant (for).

скло́н|ный (~ен, ~на́, ~но) *adj.* (**к** + *d.*) (*к болезни*) prone, susceptible (to); (+ *inf.*) inclined (to); **он скло́нен к му́зыке** he has an aptitude for music.

склоня́|емый *pres. part. pass. of* **⇒~ть**[2] *and adj.* (*gram.*) declinable.

склон|я́ть[1]**, я́ю** *impf. of* **⇒~и́ть**

склон|я́ть[2]**, я́ю** *impf.* (*of* **⇒про~**) (*gram.*) to decline.

склон|я́ться[1]**, я́юсь** *impf. of* **⇒~и́ться**

склон|я́ться[2]**, я́ется** *impf.* (*gram.*) to be declined.

скло́чник, а *m.* (*coll.*) squabbler, trouble-maker.

скло́чни|ца, цы *f. of* **⇒~к**

скло́чнича|ть, ю *impf.* (*coll.*) to squabble; to cause rows.

скло́ч|ный (~ен, ~на) *adj.* (*coll.*) troublesome, argumentative.

скля́нк|а, и *f.* **1** (*сосуд*) phial; bottle. **2** (*naut.*) bell (= *one half-hour*); **шесть скля́нок** six bells.

скоб|а́, ы́, *pl.* **~ы, ~а́м** *f.* (*зажим*) clamp; (*изогнутая железная полоса*) staple.

ско́бел|ь, я *m.* adze, scraper(-knife), drawing-knife.

ско́бк|а, и *f.* **1** *dim. of* **⇒скоба́.** **2** (*знак*) bracket; *pl.* brackets, parentheses; **в ~ах** in brackets; (*fig.*) in parenthesis, by the way, incidentally.

скобл|и́ть, ю́, ~и́шь *impf.* to scrape; (*доску*) to plane.

ско́бочн|ый *adj. of* **⇒скоба́** *and* **ско́бка; ~ая маши́на** stapler, stapling machine.

скобян|о́й *adj.*: **с. това́р, ~ые изде́лия** hardware.

ско́в|анный 1 *p.p.p. of* **⇒~а́ть; с. льда́ми** ice-bound. **2** *adj.* (*движения, мысль*) constrained.

скова́|ть, скую́, скуёшь *pf.* (*of* **⇒ско́вывать**) **1** (*выковать*) to forge, hammer out. **2** (*соединить*) to weld together. **3** (*заковать*) to chain; to fetter (*also fig.*). **4** (*mil.*; *fig.*) to pin down. **5** (*о морозе, о льде*) to lock; **моро́з ~л ре́ку** the river was frozen over.

сковород|а́, ы́, *pl.* **ско́вороды, сковоро́д, ~а́м** *f.* frying-pan.

сковоро́дк|а, и *f.* (*coll.*) frying-pan.

ско́выва|ть, ю *impf. of* **⇒скова́ть**

сковы́рива|ть, ю *impf. of* **⇒сковырну́ть**

сковыр|ну́ть, ну́, нёшь *pf.* (*of* **⇒~ивать**) **1** to pick off, scratch off. **2** (*coll.*) (*свалить*) to knock over.

скок, а *m.* gallop; **во весь с.** at full gallop, at full tilt.

скола́чива|ть, ю *impf. of* **⇒сколоти́ть**

ско́л|ок, ка *m.* **1** chip. **2** (*fig.*) (*подобие*) copy.

сколо|ти́ть, чу́, ~тишь *pf.* (*of* **⇒скола́чивать**) **1** (*соединить*) to knock together; (*изготовить*) to knock up. **2** (*fig., coll.*) (*набрать*) to get together; to scrape together.

скол|о́ть[1]**, ю́, ~ешь** *pf.* (*of* **⇒ска́лывать**) (*снять*) to split off, chop off, knock off.

скол|о́ть[2]**, ю́, ~ешь** *pf.* (*of* **⇒ска́лывать**) (*соединить*) to pin together.

сколь *adv.* how.

скольже́ни|е, я *nt.* sliding, slipping.

сколь|зи́ть, жу́, зи́шь *impf.* (*плавно двигаться*) to slide; to glide; (*терять устойчивость*) to slip; **с. глаза́ми (по** + *d.*) to cast one's eye (over).

ско́льз|кий (~ок, ~ка́, ~ко) *adj.* slippery (*also fig.*); (*fig.*) tricky; sensitive, delicate, treacherous.

скользн|у́ть, у́, ёшь *pf.* to slide, slip; **с. в дверь** to slip through the door.

скольз|я́щий *pres. part. act. of* **⇒~и́ть** *and adj.* sliding; **~я́щая шкала́** sliding scale; **с. у́зел** slip-knot.

ско́лько *interrog. and rel. adv.* **1** (*денег, хлеба*) how much; (*книг, человек*) how many; **с. сто́ит?** how much does it cost?; **с. вам лет?** how old are you?; **с. вре́мени?** what time is it?; **с. лет, с. зим!** (*coll.*) it's been ages (since we met)! **2** = **наско́лько**

ско́лько-нибудь *adv.* any; **есть у вас при себе́ с.-н. де́нег?** have you any money on you?

скома́нд|овать, ую *pf. of* **⇒кома́ндовать**

скомбини́р|овать, ую *pf. of* **⇒комбини́ровать**

ско́мка|ть, ю *pf. of* **⇒ко́мкать**

скоморо́х, а *m.* **1** (*hist.*) skomorokh (*wandering minstrel-cum-clown*). **2** (*fig.*) buffoon, clown.

скоморо́шеств|о, а *nt.* buffoonery.

скоморо́шнича|ть, ю *impf.* to play the buffoon.

скомпили́р|овать, ую *pf. of* **⇒компили́ровать**

скомпон|ова́ть, у́ю *pf. of* **⇒компонова́ть**

скомпромети́р|овать, ую *pf. of* **⇒компромети́ровать**

сконструи́р|овать, ую *pf. of* **⇒конструи́ровать**

сконфу́|женный *p.p.p. of* **⇒~зить** *and adj.* confused, embarrassed, disconcerted.

сконфу́|зить(ся), жу(сь), зишь(ся) *pf. of* **⇒конфу́зить(ся)**

сконцентри́р|овать(ся), ую(сь) *pf. of* **⇒концентри́ровать(ся)**

сконча́|ться, юсь *pf.* to pass away (= *to die*).

скоопери́р|овать(ся), ую(сь) *pf. of* **⇒коопери́ровать(ся)**

скоп, а *m.* (*obs.*) pile, accumulation.

скоп|а́, ы *f.* (*zool.*) osprey.

скопа́|ть, ю *pf. of* **⇒ска́пывать**

скоп|е́ц, ца́ *m.* eunuch.

скопидо́м, а *m.* (*coll.*) hoarder, miser.

скопидо́мнича|ть, ю *impf.* (*coll.*) to be a hoarder, miser.

скопидо́мств|о, а *nt.* (*coll.*) hoarding; miserliness.

скопи́р|овать, ую *pf. of* **⇒копи́ровать**

скоп|и́ть[1]**, лю́, ~ишь** *pf.* (*of* **⇒ска́пливать**) (+ *a. or g.*) (*накопить*) to save (up); to amass, pile up.

скоп|и́ть[2]**, лю́, и́шь** *impf.* (*кастрировать*) to castrate.

скоп|и́ться, ~ится *pf.* (*of* **⇒ска́пливаться**) **1** to accumulate, pile up. **2** (*о людях*) to gather, collect.

ско́пищ|е, а *nt.* (*pej.*) crowd, throng.

скопле́ни|е, я *nt.* **1** (*действие*) accumulation. **2** (*народа*) crowd; (*предметов*) accumulation, mass.

скопн|и́ть, ю́, и́шь *pf. of* **⇒копни́ть**

ско́пом *adv.* (*coll.*) in a crowd, in a group, en masse.

скорб|е́ть, лю́, и́шь *impf.* (**о** + *p.*) to grieve (for, over), mourn (for, over), lament.

ско́рб|ный (~ен, ~на) *adj.* sorrowful, mournful.

скорб|ь, и, *pl.* **~и, ~е́й** *f.* sorrow, grief.

скор|е́е (*and* **~е́й) 1** *comp. of* ⇒**~ый** *and* **~о; как мо́жно с.** as soon as possible. **2** *adv.* rather, sooner; **с. всего́** most likely, most probably.

скорёж|иться, усь, ишься *pf. of* ⇒**корёжиться**

скорлуп|а́, ы́, *pl.* **~ы** *f.* shell; **с. оре́ха** nutshell; **замкну́ться в свою́ ~у́** to withdraw into one's shell.

скорм|и́ть, лю́, ~ишь *pf.* (*of* ⇒**ска́рмливать**) (+*d.*) to feed (to).

скорня́жн|ый *adj.*: **~ое де́ло** furriery; **с. това́р** furs.

скорня́к, а́ *m.* furrier.

ско́ро *adv.* **1** (*быстро*) quickly, fast. **2** (*вскоре*) soon; **с. весна́!** it will soon be spring!; **как с., коль с.** as soon as, as long as.

скоро́б|иться, ится *pf. of* ⇒**коро́биться**

скороговорк|а, и *f.* **1** (*быстрая речь*) rapid speech, patter. **2** (*придуманная фраза*) tongue-twister.

скоро́м|ный (~ен, ~на) *adj.* **1** (*пища*) forbidden to be consumed during fast; **~ное ма́сло** animal fat. **2** (*непристойный*) lewd.

скоропали́тел|ьный (~ен, ~ьна) *adj.* (*coll.*) hasty, rash.

скорописный *adj.* cursive.

ско́ропис|ь, и *f.* cursive (hand).

скороподъёмност|ь, и *f.* (*aeron.*) rate of climb.

скоропо́ртящийся *adj.* perishable.

скоропости́жн|ый *adj.*: **~ая смерть** sudden death.

скоропреходя́щий *adj.* transient, transitory.

скороспе́л|ый (~, ~а) *adj.* **1** early; fast-ripening. **2** (*fig., coll.*) (*непродуманный*) premature; hasty; **с. вы́вод** hasty conclusion.

скоростни́к, а́ *m.* high-speed worker.

скоростно́й *adj.* high-speed; **с. авто́бус** express bus.

скорострельный *adj.* rapid-firing.

ско́рост|ь, и, *pl.* **~и, ~е́й** *f.* **1** speed; velocity; rate; **дозво́ленная с. (езды́)** speed-limit; **со ~ью три́дцать миль в час** at thirty miles per hour; **с. подъёма** (*aeron.*) rate of climb; **с. све́та** velocity of light. **2**: **коро́бка ~е́й** (*tech.*) gear-box; **перейти́ на другу́ю с.** to change gear.

скоросшива́тел|ь, я *m.* ring binder.

скорота́|ть, ю *pf. of* ⇒**корота́ть**

скоротеч|ный (~ен, ~на) *adj.* transient, short-lived.

скорохо́д, а *m.* **1** fast runner; **конькобе́жец-с.** high-speed skater. **2** (*obs.*) (*слуга*) footman.

скорпио́н, а *m.* scorpion; **С.** Scorpio (*sign of zodiac*).

ско́рч|ить, у, ишь *pf. of* ⇒**ко́рчить**

ско́р|ый (~, ~а́, ~о) *adj.* **1** (*быстрый*) quick, fast; rapid; **с. по́езд** fast train; **~ая по́мощь** ambulance (service); **на ~ую ру́ку** off-hand, in rough-and-ready fashion. **2** (*близкий по времени*) near, forthcoming, impending; **в ~ом бу́дущем** in the near future; **в ~ом вре́мени** shortly, before long; **до ~ого (свида́ния)!** see you soon!

скос¹, а *m.* (*agric.*) mowing.

скос², а *m.* **1** (*горы, берега*) slope. **2** (*предмета*) slant, bevel.

ско|си́ть¹, шу́, ~сишь *pf.* (*of* ⇒**коси́ть¹** *and* **ска́шивать**) (*agric.*) to mow.

ско|си́ть², шу́, си́шь *pf.* (*of* ⇒**коси́ть²** *and* **ска́шивать**) (*глаза*) to squint.

ско|сти́ть, щу́, сти́шь *pf.* (*of* ⇒**ска́щивать**) (*coll.*) to knock off; **с. три рубля́ с цены́** to knock three roubles off the price.

скот, а́ *m.* **1** (*collect.*) cattle; livestock. **2** (*fig., coll.*) (*грубый человек*) swine, beast.

скоти́н|а, ы *f.* **1** (*collect.*) cattle; livestock. **2** (*also m.*) (*fig., coll.*) (*грубый человек*) swine, beast.

ско́тник, а *m.* herdsman; cowman.

ско́т|ный *adj. of* ⇒**~; с. двор** cattle-yard.

скотобо́|йня, йни, *g. pl.* **~ен** *f.* slaughter-house.

скотово́д, а *m.* cattle-breeder.

скотово́дств|о, а *nt.* cattle-breeding, cattle-raising.

скотово́дческий *adj.* cattle-breeding.

скотоло́жств|о, а *nt.* bestiality.

скотопромы́шленник, а *m.* cattle-dealer.

скотопромы́шленност|ь, и *f.* cattle-dealing, cattle-trade.

скотопромы́шленн|ый *adj. of* ⇒**~ость**

ско́тский *adj.* brutal, brutish, bestial.

скотств|о́, а́ *nt.* brutality, brutishness, bestiality.

скотч, а *m.* (*coll.*) adhesive tape; sellotape (*propr.*); (*виски*) Scotch (whisky).

скра́дыва|ть, ю *impf.* to conceal.

скра́|сить, шу, сишь *pf.* (*of* ⇒**~шивать**) (*fig.*) to relieve; **он мно́го чита́л, что́бы с. своё одино́чество** he read a lot to relieve his loneliness.

скра́шива|ть, ю *impf. of* ⇒**скра́сить**

скребни́ц|а, ы *f.* curry-comb.

скреб|о́к, ка́ *m.* scraper.

скре́жет, а *m.* (*металла*) grating, scraping; (*зубов*) gnashing.

скреже|та́ть, щу́, ~щешь *impf.* (*о металле*) to grate, scrape; **с. (зуба́ми)** to gnash one's teeth.

скре́п|а, ы *f.* **1** (*tech.*) tie, clamp, brace. **2** (*подпись*) counter-signature.

скре́пер, а *m.* (*tech.*) earth-moving machine.

скреп|и́ть, лю́, и́шь *pf.* (*of* ⇒**~ля́ть**) **1** (*соединить*) to fasten (together); (*tech.*) to clamp, brace; (*дружбу*) to cement; **~я́ се́рдце** reluctantly, grudgingly. **2** (*удостоверить*) to countersign, ratify.

скре́пк|а, и *f.* paper-clip.

скрепле́ни|е, я *nt.* **1** (*действие*) fastening; (*tech.*) clamping. **2** (*tech.*) (*скрепа*) tie, clamp.

скрепля́|ть, ю *impf. of* ⇒**скрепи́ть**

скре|сти́, бу́, бёшь, *past* **~б, ~бла́** *impf.* **1** (*о кошке, о ногтях*) to scratch, claw; (*дерево*) to sand; (*плиту*) to scour. **2** (*impers.; fig., coll.*) to nag; **у неё ~бло́ на се́рдце** she felt a nagging anxiety.

скре|сти́сь, бу́сь, бёшься, *past* **~бся, ~бла́сь** *impf.* to scratch, make a scratching noise.

скре|сти́ть, щу́, сти́шь *pf.* (*of* ⇒**~щивать**) **1** to cross; **с. мечи́, с. шпа́ги (с+*i.*)** to cross swords (with) (*also fig.*). **2** (*biol.*) to cross, interbreed.

скрест|и́ться, и́тся *pf.* (*of* ⇒**скре́щиваться**) **1** to cross; (*fig.*) to clash. **2** (*biol.*) to cross, interbreed.

скреще́ни|е, я *nt.* crossing; intersection.

скре́щивани|е, я *nt.* **1** crossing. **2** (*biol.*) crossing, interbreeding.

скре́щива|ть(ся), ю, ет(ся) *impf. of* ⇒**скрести́ть(ся)**

скрив|и́ть(ся), лю́(сь), и́шь(ся) *pf. of* ⇒**криви́ть(ся)**

скрижа́л|ь, и *f.* tablet, table (*with sacred text inscribed upon it*); **~и** (*fig., arch.*) annals.

скрип, а *m.* (*двери*) squeak, creak; (*снега*) crunch.

скрипа́ч, а́ *m.* violinist.

скрипа́ч|ка, ки *f. of* ⇒**~**

скрип|е́ть, лю́, и́шь *impf.* **1** (*о двери*) to squeak, creak; (*о снеге*) to crunch. **2** (*coll., joc.*) to scrape by.

скрипи́чный *adj.* violin; **с. ма́стер** violin-maker; **с. ключ** treble clef, G clef; **с. конце́рт** violin concerto.

скри́пк|а, и *f.* violin; **пе́рвая с.** first violin; (*fig., coll.*) first fiddle.

скри́пн|уть, у, ешь *pf.* to squeak, creak.

скрипу́чий *adj.* (*coll.*) squeaky, creaking; **с. го́лос** rasping voice; **с. снег** crunching snow.

скро|и́ть, ю́, и́шь *pf. of* ⇒**крои́ть**

скро́мник, а *m.* modest person.

скро́мни|ца, цы *f. of* ⇒**~к**

скро́мнича|ть, ю *impf.* to be overmodest.

скро́мност|ь, и *f.* modesty.

скро́м|ный (~ен, ~на́, ~но) *adj.* modest; **по моему́ ~ному мне́нию** in my humble opinion.

скрупулёзност|ь, и *f.* scrupulousness.

скрупулёз|ный (~ен, ~на) *adj.* scrupulous.

скру|ти́ть, чу́, ~тишь *pf.* (*of* ⇒**крути́ть** *and* **~чивать**) **1** (*верёвки*) to twist (together); (*папиросу*) to roll. **2** (*руки*) to bind, tie up. **3** (*о болезни, о жизни*) to lay low, bring down.

скру́чива|ть, ю *impf. of* ⇒**скрути́ть**

скрыва́|ть, ю *impf. of* ⇒**скрыть**

скрыва́|ться, юсь *impf.* **1** *impf. of*

⇨**скры́ться. 2** *impf. only* to lie in hiding; to lie low.

скры́тнича|ть, ю *impf.* (*coll.*) to be secretive.

скры́т|ный (~ен, ~на) *adj.* secretive.

скры́т|ый *p.p.p. of* ⇨**~ь** *and adj.* secret, concealed; **с. смысл** hidden meaning; **~ая теплота́** (*phys.*) latent heat.

скр|ыть, о́ю, о́ешь *pf.* (*of* ⇨**~ыва́ть**) (**от**+*g.*) to hide (from), conceal (from).

скр|ы́ться, о́юсь, о́ешься *pf.* (*of* ⇨**~ыва́ться**) (**от**+*g.*) **1** (*спрятаться*) to hide (o.s.) (from); (*о преступнике*) to go into hiding. **2** (*удалиться*) to steal away (from), escape, give the slip. **3** (*исчезнуть*) to disappear, vanish.

скрю́ч|ить, у, ишь *pf. of* ⇨**крю́чить**

скрю́ч|иться, усь, ишься *pf.* to bend (*intrans.*); (*о человеке*) to hunch o.s. up.

скря́г|а, и *c.g.* miser, skinflint.

скря́жнича|ть, ю *impf.* (*coll.*) to be a miser.

скуде́|ть, ю *impf.* (*of* ⇨**о~**) to grow scanty, run short; (+*i.*) to be short (of).

ску́д|ный (~ен, ~на́, ~но) *adj.* **1** (*средства, обед*) meagre (*Br.*), meager (*US*); (*урожай*) poor; (*знания, сведения*) scanty; (*растительность*) sparse. **2** (+*i.*) (*бедный*) poor (in).

ску́дост|ь, и *f.* scarcity; poverty.

скудоу́ми|е, я *nt.* feeble-mindedness.

скудоу́м|ный (~ен, ~на) *adj.* feeble-minded.

ску́к|а, и *f.* boredom, tedium; **кака́я с.!** what a bore!

скул|а́, ы́, *pl.* **~ы** *f.* cheek-bone.

скула́ст|ый (~, ~а) *adj.* with high cheek-bones.

скул|и́ть, ю́, и́шь *impf.* to whine, whimper (*also fig.*).

скулово́й *adj.* (*anat.*) malar.

ску́льптор, а *m.* sculptor.

скульпту́р|а, ы *f.* sculpture.

скульпту́рный *adj.* sculptural; (*fig.*) statuesque.

ску́мбри|я, и *f.* mackerel.

скунс, а *m.* skunk.

скуп|а́ть, а́ю *impf. of* ⇨**~и́ть**

скупердя́|й, я *m.* (*coll.*) miser, skinflint.

скуп|е́ц, ца́ *m.* miser, skinflint.

скуп|и́ть, лю́, ~ишь *pf.* (*of* ⇨**~а́ть**) to buy up.

скуп|и́ться, лю́сь, и́шься *impf.* (*of* ⇨**по~**) (+*inf. or* **на**+*a.*) to stint, grudge, skimp; to be sparing (of); **с. на де́ньги** to be close-fisted; **не с. на похвалы́** not to stint one's praise.

ску́пк|а, и *f.* buying up.

скуп|но́й *adj. of* ⇨**~ка**

ску́по *adv.* sparingly.

скуп|о́й (~, ~а́, ~о) *adj.* **1** stingy, miserly; **с. на слова́** sparing of words. **2** (*fig.*) (*недостаточный*) inadequate; **с. свет** inadequate illumination.

ску́пост|ь, и *f.* stinginess, miserliness.

ску́п|очный *adj. of* ⇨**~ка; с. магази́н** second-hand shop.

ску́пщик, а *m.* buyer(-up).

ску́тер, а, *pl.* **~а́** *m.* outboard-motor boat.

скуфе́йк|а, и *f. dim. of* ⇨**скуфья́**

скуфь|я́, и́ *f.* (*clerical*) skull-cap.

скуча́|ть, ю *impf.* **1** to be bored. **2** (**по**+*d. or* (*coll.*) *p.*) to miss, yearn (for).

ску́ченност|ь, и *f.* density, congestion; **с. населе́ния** overcrowding.

ску́ченный *adj.* dense, congested.

ску́чива|ть(ся), ю, ет(ся) *impf. of* ⇨**ску́чить(ся)**

ску́ч|ить, у, ишь *pf.* (*of* ⇨**~ивать**) to crowd (together).

ску́ч|иться, ится *pf.* (*of* ⇨**~иваться**) to flock, cluster; to crowd together.

ску́ч|ный (~ен, ~на́, ~но) *adj.* **1** (*книга*) boring, tedious, dull. **2** (*человек, взгляд*) bored; *as pred.* **мне,** *etc.,* **~но** I, *etc.*, am bored.

ску́ша|ть, ю *pf. of* ⇨**ку́шать**

слабе́|ть, ю *impf.* (*of* ⇨**о~**) (*о человеке*) to weaken, grow weak(er); (*о ветре*) to slacken, drop; (*о канате*) to slacken.

слабин|а́, ы́ *no pl., f.* **1** (*в верёвке*) slack. **2** (*coll.*) (*слабость*) weak spot, weak point.

слаби́тельн|ый *adj.* (*med.*) laxative; *as n.* **~ое, ~ого** *nt.* laxative.

сла́б|ить, ит *impf.* (*of* ⇨**про~**) **1** (*impers.*): **его́ ~ит** he has diarrhoea (*Br.*), diarrhea (*US*). **2** (*о лекарстве*) to purge, act as a laxative.

сла́б|нуть, ну, нешь, *past* **~, ~ла** *impf.* (*of* ⇨**о~**) (*coll.*) **1** (*о человеке, о здоровье*) to weaken, grow weak(er). **2** (*о канате*) to slacken, become slack.

слабоалкого́льный *adj.* low-alcohol.

слабово́ли|е, я *nt.* weak will.

слабово́л|ьный (~ен, ~ьна) *adj.* weak-willed.

слабогру́д|ый (~, ~а) *adj.* weak-chested.

слабоду́ши|е, я *nt.* faint-heartedness.

слабоду́ш|ный (~ен, ~на) *adj.* faint-hearted.

слабоне́рв|ный (~ен, ~на) *adj.* having weak nerves; nervous.

слабора́звитый *adj.* (*econ.*) under-developed.

слабоси́ли|е, я *nt.* weakness, feebleness, debility.

слабоси́л|ьный (~ен, ~ьна) *adj.* **1** weak, feeble. **2** (*tech.*) low-powered.

сла́бост|ь, и *f.* **1** weakness, feebleness; (*дисциплины*) slackness. **2** (**к**+*d.*) (*наклонность*) weakness (for).

слабото́чный *adj.* (*tech.*) low-current.

слабоу́ми|е, я *nt.* feeble-mindedness; **ста́рческое с.** senile dementia.

слабоу́м|ный (~ен, ~на) *adj.* feeble-minded.

слабохара́ктер|ный (~ен, ~на) *adj.* weak, weak-willed.

сла́б|ый (~, ~а́, ~о) *adj.* (*человек, характер, зрение, воля*) weak; (*голос*) feeble; (*верёвка*) slack, loose; (*ветер, боль, надежда*) slight; (*ученик, знания*) weak, poor; (*ребёнок, здоровье*) delicate; **~ое ме́сто** weak point; **с. пол** the weaker sex.

сла́в|а, ы *f.* **1** glory; fame; **во ~у** (+*g.*) to the glory (of); **на ~у** (*coll.*) wonderfully well, excellently; (*as int.*, +*d.*) hurrah (for)!; **с. Бо́гу** thank God, thank goodness. **2** (*репутация*) name, reputation; **до́брая с.** good name; **дурна́я с.** infamy. **3** (*coll.*) (*слухи*) rumour (*Br.*), rumor (*US*).

слави́ст, а *m.* Slavist.

слави́стик|а, и *f.* Slavonic studies.

слави́ст|ка, ки *f. of* ⇨**~**

сла́в|ить, лю, ишь *impf.* to glorify, sing the praises (of).

сла́в|иться, люсь, ишься *impf.* (+*i.*) to be famous (for), be renowned (for); to have a reputation (for).

сла́вк|а, и *f.* (*zool.*) warbler.

сла́в|ный (~ен, ~на́, ~но) *adj.* **1** glorious; famous, renowned. **2** (*coll.*) splendid; lovely; **с. ма́лый** nice chap.

славосло́ви|е, я *nt.* glorification, eulogy.

славосло́в|ить, лю, ишь *impf.* to eulogize, extol.

славяни́зм, а *m.* (*ling.*) **1** (*в неславянском языке*) Slavism, Slavicism. **2** (*в русском языке*) Slavonicism.

славян|и́н, и́на, *pl.* **~е, ~** *m.* Slav.

славя́н|ка, ки *f. of* ⇨**~и́н**

славянове́дени|е, я *nt.* Slavonic studies.

славянофи́л, а *m.* Slavophil(e).

славянофи́л|ьский *adj. of* ⇨**~** *and* **~ьство**

славянофи́льств|о, а *nt.* Slavophilism.

славя́нский *adj.* Slavonic; Slavic; Slav.

слага́ем|ое, ого *nt.* **1** (*math.*) item. **2** (*fig.*) component.

слага́|ть, ю *impf. of* ⇨**сложи́ть**

слад, а (у) *m., now only in phr.* **с ним,** *etc.*, **~у нет** (*coll.*) he, *etc.*, is unmanageable, is out of hand.

сла́ден|ький (~ек, ~ька) *adj.* (*coll.*) sweetish; (*fig.*) sugary, honeyed; **~ькая улы́бка** sugary smile.

сла́|дить, жу, дишь *pf.* (*of* ⇨**~живать**) **1** (*coll.*) (*устроить*) to arrange. **2** (**с**+*i.*) (*справиться*) to cope (with), handle; **он про́сто не мог с. с подчинёнными** he simply did not know how to handle his subordinates.

сла́д|кий (~ок, ~ка́, ~ко) *adj.* **1** sweet (*also fig.*); **~кое мя́со** (*cul.*) sweetbread; *as n.* **~кое, ~кого** *nt.* dessert. **2** (*fig., pej.*) sugary, honeyed.

сладкое́жк|а, и *c.g.* (*coll.*) (person with a) sweet tooth.

сладкозву́ч|ный (~ен, ~на) *adj.* (*obs.*) mellifluous.

сладкоречи́в|ый (~, ~а) *adj.* smooth-tongued.

сла́дост|ный (~ен, ~на) *adj.* sweet, delightful.

С

сладостра́сти|е, я *nt.* sensuality, voluptuousness.

сладостра́стник, а *m.* voluptuary.

сладостра́ст|ный (~ен, ~на) *adj.* sensual, voluptuous.

сла́дост|ь, и *f.* **1** sweetness. **2** (*pl.*) (*кондитерские изделия*) sweets, sweetmeats.

сла́женност|ь, и *f.* co-ordination, harmony, order.

сла́|женный *p.p.p. of* ⇨**~дить** *and adj.* (well-)coordinated, harmonious, orderly.

сла́жива|ть, ю *impf. of* ⇨**сла́дить**

сла́|зить, жу, зишь *pf.* (*coll.*) to go, climb; **с. в подва́л за дрова́ми** to go down to the cellar for logs.

слайд, а *m.* slide, transparency.

слайдопрое́ктор, а *m.* slide projector.

сла́лом, а *m.* (*sport*) slalom.

сла́н|ец, ца *m.* (*min.*) shale, schist; slate.

сла́нцевый *adj.* schistose; slate, slaty; shale; **с. пласт** schist.

сластён|а, ы *c.g.* (*coll.*) = **сладкое́жка**

сла|сти́ть, щу́, сти́шь *impf.* (*of* ⇨**по~**) to sweeten.

сластолю́б|ец, ца *m.* voluptuary.

сластолюби́в|ый (~, ~а) *adj.* sensual, voluptuous.

сластолю́би|е, я *nt.* sensuality, voluptuousness.

сласт|ь, и, *pl.* **~́и, ~е́й** *f.* **1** (*pl.*) (*кондитерские изделия*) sweets, sweetmeats. **2** (*fig.*) (*удовольствие*) delight, pleasure; **что за с. гуля́ть одному́?** what fun is there in going out alone?

слать, шлю, шлёшь *impf.* to send.

слаща́в|ый (~, ~а) *adj.* (*liter. and fig.*) sugary, sickly-sweet.

сла́ще *comp. of* ⇨**сла́дкий**

сле́ва *adv.* (**от**+*g.*) on the left (of), to the left (of); **с. напра́во** from left to right.

слег|а́, и́, *pl.* **~́и, ~, ~а́м** *f.* beam.

слегка́ *adv.* lightly, gently; (*немного*) slightly; **с. суту́литься** to stoop slightly; **с. гла́дить** to stroke gently.

след, а́ (у), *d.* **~у,** *i.* **~́ом,** *p.* **о ~́е, в/на ~́е/~у́** *pl.* **~ы́, ~о́в** *m.* **1** (*отпечаток*) track; (*ноги*) footprint, footstep; **верну́ться по свои́м ~а́м** to retrace one's steps; **замести́ свои́ ~ы́** to cover up one's tracks; **идти́ по чьим-н. ~а́м** (*fig.*) to follow in s.o.'s footsteps; **напа́сть на чей-н. ~** to get on s.o.'s trail. **2** (*fig.*) (*признак*) trace, sign, vestige; **~а́ нет его́** there is no trace of it; **~ы́ о́спы** pockmarks.

сле|ди́ть¹, жу́, ди́шь *impf.* (**за**+*i.*) **1** (*смотреть*) to watch; to follow; **с. глаза́ми за полётом мяча́** to follow (with one's eyes) the flight of a ball. **2** (*fig.*) to follow; to keep up (with); **с. за междунаро́дными собы́тиями** to keep up with international affairs. **3** (*заботиться*) to look after; to keep an eye (on); **с. за детьми́** to look after children; **с. за поря́дком** to keep order; **с. за тем, что́бы** to see to it that.

сле|ди́ть², жу́, ди́шь *impf.* (*of* ⇨**на~**) (**на**+*p.*) (*оставлять следы*) to mark; to leave traces (on), leave footprints (on).

сле́довани|е, я *nt.* movement, proceeding; **по́езд да́льнего ~я** long-distance train; **во вре́мя ~я по́езда** while the train is moving; **на всём пути́ ~я** all along the line, throughout the entire journey.

сле́довател|ь, я *m.* investigator.

сле́довательно *conj.* consequently, therefore, hence.

сле́д|овать¹, ую *impf.* (*of* ⇨**по~**) **1** (**за**+*i.*) to follow, go after; **с. за кем-н. по пята́м** to follow hard on s.o.'s heels. **2** (+*d.*) (*поступать подобно кому-н.*) to follow; **с. отцу́** to follow in one's father's footsteps. **3** (+*d.*) (*поступать согласно чему-н.*) to follow; to comply (with); **с. пра́вилам** to conform to the rules; **с. при́хоти** to follow a whim. **4** (*impf. only*) (**до**+*g.*, **в**+*a.*) (*отправляться*) to be bound (for); **э́тот по́езд ~ует в Варша́ву** this train is (bound) for Warsaw. **5** (*impf. only*) (*быть следствием*) to follow; to result; **из э́того ~ует, что мы оши́блись** it follows from this that we were mistaken.

сле́д|овать², ует *impf.* (*impers.*) **1** (+*d. and inf.*) (*нужно, должно*) ought, should; **вам ~ует обрати́ться к ре́ктору** you should approach the rector; **не ~ует забыва́ть** it should not be forgotten; **куда́ ~ует** to the proper quarter; **как и ~овало ожида́ть** as was to be expected; **как ~ует** as it should be, properly, well and truly. **2** (+*d. and* **с**+*g.*) (*причитаться*) to be owed, be owing; **ско́лько вам ~ует с меня́?** how much do I owe you?; **с вас ~ует де́сять рубле́й** you have ten roubles to pay.

сле́дом *adv.* (**за**+*i.*) immediately (after, behind); **идти́ с. за кем-н.** to follow s.o. close(ly).

следопы́т, а *m.* pathfinder, tracker.

сле́дств|енный *adj. of* ⇨**~ие;** investigatory; **~енная коми́ссия** committee of inquiry.

сле́дстви|е¹, я *nt.* (*результат*) consequence, result; **причи́на и с.** cause and effect.

сле́дстви|е², я *nt.* (*leg.*) (*расследование*) investigation; **суде́бное с.** inquest.

сле́дуем|ый *adj.* (+*d.*) due (to); **отда́ть ка́ждому ~ое** to give each his due.

сле́д|ующий *pres. part. act. of* ⇨**~овать** *and adj.* following, next; **на с. день** next day; **на ~ующей неде́ле** next week.

слеж|а́ться, и́тся *pf.* (*of* ⇨**~иваться**) (*о земле, о снеге*) to become compressed; (*об одежде*) to become creased.

слёжива|ться, ется *impf. of* ⇨**слежа́ться**

сле́жк|а, и *f.* surveillance; shadowing; **установи́ть ~у за кем-н.** to have s.o. shadowed.

слез|а́, ы́, *pl.* **~̈ы, ~̈, ~а́м** *f.* tear; **крокоди́ловы ~̈ы** crocodile tears; **довести́ до ~̈** to reduce to tears; **э́то до ~̈ оби́дно** it is enough to make one weep.

слеза́|ть, ю *impf. of* ⇨**слезть**

слез|и́ться, и́тся *impf.* to water; **её глаза́ ~и́лись** her eyes were watering.

слезли́в|ый (~, ~а) *adj.* **1** (*человек*) given to crying. **2** (*голос*) tearful.

слёзно *adv.* (*coll.*) tearfully, with tears in one's eyes; (*fig.*) humbly, plaintively.

слёзн|ый *adj.* **1** (*anat.*) lacrimal; **с. прото́к** tear duct. **2** (*fig., coll.*) humble, plaintive; **~ая про́сьба** humble petition.

слезоточи́в|ый (~, ~а) *adj.* **1** (*глаза*) tearful; (*coll.*) (*человек*) tearful, given to crying. **2** (*вызывающий слезотечение*) lachrymatory; **с. газ** tear-gas.

слезоточ|и́ть, и́т, а́т *impf.* (*о глазах*) to secrete tears.

слез|ть, у, ешь, *past* **~, ~ла** *pf.* (*of* ⇨**~а́ть**) (**с**+*g.*) **1** (*с дерева*) to come down (from), get down (from); (*с лошади, с велосипеда*) to get off; to dismount (from). **2** (*с автобуса, с трамвая*) to get off. **3** (*о краске, о коже*) to come off, peel.

сленг, а *m.* slang.

слеп|е́нь, ня́ *m.* gadfly, horse-fly.

слеп|е́ц, ца́ *m.* blind man.

слеп|и́ть¹, лю́, и́шь *impf.* to blind; to dazzle.

слеп|и́ть², лю́, ~́ишь *pf. of* ⇨**лепи́ть**

слеп|и́ть³, лю́, ~́ишь *pf.* (*of* ⇨**~ля́ть**) **1** (*соединить*) to stick together. **2** (*изготовить*) to make by sticking together.

слеп|и́ться, ~́ится *pf.* (*of* ⇨**~ля́ться**) to stick together.

слепля́|ть(ся), ю, ет(ся) *impf. of* ⇨**слепи́ть³(ся)**

сле́п|нуть, ну, нешь, *past* **~, ~ла** *and* **~нул, ~нула** *impf.* to go blind.

сле́по *adv.* blindly.

слеп|о́й (~, ~а́, ~́о) *adj.* blind (*also fig.*); **с. на оди́н глаз** blind in one eye; **~а́я кишка́** blind gut, caecum (*Br.*), cecum (*US*); **с. ме́тод машино́писи** touch-typing; *as n.* **с., ~о́го** *m.* blind person; (*pl., collect.*) the blind.

сле́п|ок, ка *m.* cast, copy.

слепот|а́, ы́ *f.* blindness (*also fig.*).

слепы́ш, а́ *m.* mole-rat.

слеса́рн|ый *adj.* metal-work, metal worker's; **~ое де́ло** metal work; **~ая (мастерска́я)** metal workshop.

сле́сар|ь, я, *pl.* **~и, ~ей** *and* **~я́, ~е́й** *m.* metal worker; (*специалист по замкам*) locksmith; (*специалист по починке*) repair man.

слёт, а *m.* **1** (*птиц*) flying together. **2** (*собрание*) gathering, meeting; rally.

слета́|ть¹, ю *pf.* **1** to fly (*there and back*). **2** (*fig., coll.*) (*сбегать*) to dash, nip.

слет|а́ть², а́ю *impf. of* ⇨**~е́ть**

слет|а́ться, а́ется *impf. of* ⇨**~е́ться**

сле|те́ть, чу́, ти́шь *pf.* (*of*

⇨~та́ть²) (**с**+*g*). **1** (*вниз*) to fly down (from). **2** (*coll.*) (*упасть*) to fall down, fall off; **с. с ло́шади** to fall from a horse. **3** (*улететь*) to fly away.
слет|е́ться, и́тся *pf.* (*of* **⇨~а́ться**) to fly together; (*о птицах*) to congregate.
слечь, сля́гу, сля́жешь, *past* **слёг, слегла́** *pf.* to take to one's bed.
слибера́льнича|ть, ю *pf. of* **⇨либера́льничать**
слив, а *m.* **1** (*действие*) discharge. **2** (*устройство*) drain.
сли́в|а, ы *f.* **1** (*плод*) plum. **2** (*дерево*) plum-tree.
слива́|ть(ся), ю(сь) *impf. of* **⇨слить(ся)**
сли́в|ки, ок *no sg.* cream (*also fig.*); **с. о́бщества** the cream of society.
сливн|о́й *adj.* overflow, waste; **~а́я труба́** overflow pipe.
сли́в|овый *adj. of* **⇨~а; с. джем** plum jam.
сли́вочник, а *m.* cream-jug.
сли́вочн|ый *adj.* cream; creamy; **~ое ма́сло** butter; **~ое моро́женое** vanilla ice-cream.
сливя́нк|а, и *f.* plum brandy.
сли|за́ть, жу́, ~́жешь *pf.* (*of* **⇨~́зывать**) to lick off.
слизи́ст|ый (~, ~а) *adj.* **1** slimy. **2** (*anat.*) mucous; **~ая оболо́чка** (*anat.*) mucous membrane.
слизня́к, а́ *m.* **1** slug. **2** (*pej., coll.*) (*о человеке*) pathetic person.
сли́зыва|ть, ю *impf. of* **⇨слиза́ть**
слиз|ь, и *f.* **1** slime. **2** (*anat.*) mucus.
слиня́|ть, ет *pf.* **1** (*о животных, о птицах*) to moult (*Br.*), molt (*US*). **2** (*coll.*) (*о красках*) to fade; (*fig.*) (*о человеке*) to slip away, disappear.
слип|а́ться, а́ется *impf. of* **⇨~́нуться**
слип|нуться, нется, *past* **~ся, ~лась** *pf.* (*of* **⇨~а́ться**) to stick together.
сли́тно *adv.* together; (*о написании слов*) as one word.
сли́тн|ый *adj.* united, continuous; **~ое написа́ние слов** omission of hyphen from words.
сли́т|ок, ка *m.* ingot, bar; **зо́лото в ~ках** gold bullion.
слить, солью́, сольёшь, *past* **слил, слила́, сли́ло** *pf.* (*of* **⇨слива́ть**) **1** (*вылить*) to pour out; (*отлить*) to pour off. **2** (*вместе*) to pour together; (*fig.*) to merge, amalgamate; **с. два конце́рна** to amalgamate two concerns.
сли́ться, солью́сь, сольёшься, *past* **сли́лся, слила́сь** *pf.* (*of* **⇨слива́ться**) **1** (*о ручьях*) to flow together. **2** (*fig.*) (*о голосах*) to blend, mingle; (*о концернах*) to merge, amalgamate.
слич|а́ть, а́ю *impf. of* **⇨~и́ть**
сличе́ни|е, я *nt.* checking.
сличи́тельн|ый *adj.* checking; **~ая ве́домость** check-list.
слич|и́ть, у́, и́шь *pf.* (*of* **⇨~а́ть**) (**с**+*i.*) to check (with, against).
сли́шком *adv.* too; (*перед глаголами*) too much; **э́то с.!** this is too much!
слия́ни|е, я *nt.* **1** (*рек*) confluence. **2** (*fig.*) (*голосов*) blending; merging; (*концернов*) amalgamation, merger.
слобод|а́, ы́, *pl.* **сло́боды, слобо́д, ~а́м** *f.* **1** (*hist.*) sloboda (*settlement exempted from normal State obligations*). **2** (*obs.*) (*пригород*) suburb.
слова́к, а *m.* Slovak.
Слова́ки|я, и *f.* Slovakia.
слова́рный *adj.* **1** lexical; **с. соста́в языка́** vocabulary; **с. фонд** word stock. **2** (*статья, работа*) lexicographic(al), dictionary.
слова́р|ь, я́ *m.* **1** (*книга*) dictionary; (*глоссарий*) glossary, vocabulary (*to particular text*). **2** (*collect.*) (*запас слов*) vocabulary.
слова́цкий *adj.* Slovak, Slovakian.
слова́|чка, чки *f. of* **⇨~к**
слове́н|е, ~ *no sg.* (*obs.*) the Slavs.
слове́н|ец, ца *m.* Slovene.
Слове́ни|я, и *f.* Slovenia.
слове́н|ка, ки *f. of* **⇨~ец**
слове́нский *adj.* Slovene, Slovenian.
слове́сник, а *m.* **1** (*филолог*) philologist. **2** (*преподаватель*) language and literature teacher.
слове́сност|ь, и *f.* literature.
слове́сный *adj.* verbal, oral; **с. прика́з** verbal order.
слове́ч|ко, ка, *pl.* **~ки, ~ек** *nt.*, (*coll.*) *dim. of* **⇨сло́во; мо́дное с.** buzz-word; **замо́лвить с. за кого́-н.** to put in a word for s.o.
сло́вник, а *m.* word-list (*for inclusion in a dictionary*).
сло́вно *conj.* **1** (*как будто*) as if. **2** (*как*) like, as.
сло́в|о, а, *pl.* **~а́** *nt.* **1** word; **други́ми ~а́ми** in other words; **одни́м ~ом** in a word; **с. в с.** word for word; **с. за́ с.** little by little; **к ~у (пришло́сь, сказа́ть)** by the way; **на ~а́х** (*i*) (*устно*) by word of mouth, (*ii*) (*только в разговоре*) empty words; **ве́рить на́ с. кому́-н. в чём-н.** to take s.o.'s word for sth.; **челове́к ~а** a man of his word; **сдержа́ть с.** to keep one's word; **игра́ ~** play on words; **~ нет** (*coll.*) it goes without saying; **~ нет, как тут ду́рно па́хнет** there is an indescribably nasty smell here. **2** (*речь*) speech, speaking; **дар ~а** talent for speaking; **свобо́да ~а** freedom of speech. **3** (*выступление*) speech, address; **заключи́тельное с.** concluding remarks; **надгро́бное с.** funeral oration; **дать, предоста́вить с.** (+*d.*) to give the floor, to call upon to speak. **4** (*liter.; hist.*) (*рассказ*) lay, tale.
словоблу́ди|е, я *nt.* (mere) verbiage, phrase-mongering.
словоизверже́ни|е, я *nt.* (*iron.*) spate of words.
словоизмене́ни|е, я *nt.* (*ling.*) inflection.
сло́вом *adv.* in a word, in short.
словообразова́ни|е, я *nt.* (*ling.*) word-formation.
словообразова́тельный *adj.* word-forming.
словоохо́тливост|ь, и *f.* talkativeness, loquacity.
словоохо́тлив|ый (~, ~а) *adj.* talkative, loquacious.
словопре́ни|е, я *nt.* (*obs.*) debate.
словопроизво́дный *adj.* (*ling.*) productive.
словопроизво́дств|о, а *nt.* (*ling.*) derivation.
словосочета́ни|е, я *nt.* combination of words; **усто́йчивое с.** set phrase.
словоупотребле́ни|е, я *nt.* use of words, usage.
словц|о́, а́ *nt.* (*coll.*) word; **для кра́сного ~а́** for effect.
слог¹, а, *pl.* **~́и, ~о́в** *m.* syllable.
слог², а *m.* (*стиль*) style.
слогово́й *adj.* syllabic.
слое́ни|е, я *nt.* stratification.
слоён|ый *adj.*: **~ое те́сто** puff-pastry.
сложе́ни|е, я *nt.* **1** (*чисел*) adding; (*песни*) composition; (*math.*) addition. **2** (*телосложение*) build, physique.
сло́ж|енный *p.p.p. of* **⇨~и́ть**
сложён|ный (~, ~а́) *adj.* formed, built; **хорошо́ с.** well built.
сложи́|вшийся *p.p. of* **⇨~ться; вполне́ с.** fully developed, fully formed; **в ~вшейся ситуа́ции** under the present circumstances.
слож|и́ть¹, у́, ~́ишь *pf.* **1** (*impf.* **скла́дывать**) (*положить вместе*) to put (together), lay (together); (*в кучу*) to pile, heap, stack; **с. свои́ ве́щи в сунду́к** to pack one's things in a trunk. **2** (*impf.* **скла́дывать**) (*числа*) to add (up). **3** (*impf.* **скла́дывать**) (*лист, платье*) to fold (up); **с. вдво́е** to fold in two; **с. ру́ки** to give up the struggle; **~а́ ру́ки** with arms folded; (*fig.*) idle. **4** (*impf.* **слага́ть**) (*сочинить*) to make up, compose.
слож|и́ть², у́, ~́ишь *pf.* **1** (*impf.* **скла́дывать**) (*сняв, положить*) to take off, put down, set down; **с. груз** to set down a load. **2** (*impf.* **слага́ть**) (**с**+*g.*; *fig.*) to relieve o.s. (of); **с. го́лову** (*rhet.*) to lay down one's life; **с. ору́жие** to lay down one's arms; **с. с себя́ обя́занности** to resign.
слож|и́ться¹, у́сь, ~́ишься *pf.* (*of* **⇨скла́дываться**) (**с**+*i.*) to club together (with); to pool one's resources.
слож|и́ться², у́сь, ~́ишься *pf.* (*of* **⇨скла́дываться**) (*о характере; об убеждении*) to form; (*об обстоятельствах*) to turn out; (*о ситуации*) to arise.
сложноподчинённ|ый *adj.*: **~ое предложе́ние** (*gram.*) complex sentence.
сложносочинённ|ый *adj.*: **~ое предложе́ние** (*gram.*) compound sentence.
сло́жност|ь, и *f.* complication; complexity; **в о́бщей ~и** all in all.
сло́ж|ный (~ен, ~на́, ~но) *adj.* **1** (*составной*) compound; complex; **~ное предложе́ние** (*gram.*) complex

С

sentence; **~ные проценты** compound interest; **~ное слово** compound (word); **~ное число** complex number.
2 (*трудный*) complicated, complex; (*узор, композиция*) intricate.

слоист|ый (~, ~а) *adj.* stratified; **~ые облака** strati.

сло|й, я, *pl.* **~и** *m.* layer; stratum (*also fig.*); **все ~и населения** all sections of the population.

слойк|а, и *f.* (*булочка*) puff.

слом, а *m.* demolition, breaking up; **пойти на с.** to be scrapped.

слома|ть(ся), ю, ет(ся) *pf. of* **⇒ломать(ся)**

слом|ить, лю, ~ишь *pf.* to break, smash; (*fig.*) to overcome; **~я голову** (*coll.*) like mad, at breakneck speed.

слом|иться, люсь, ~ишься *pf.* to break.

слон, а *m.* **1** elephant; **делать из мухи ~а** to make a mountain out of a mole-hill; **с. в посудной лавке** a bull in a china shop; **~а не приметить** to miss the point. **2** (*chess*) bishop.

слон|ёнок, ёнка, *pl.* **~ята, ~ят** *m.* elephant calf.

слоних|а, и *f.* she-elephant, cow-elephant.

слоновост|ь, и *f.* (*med.*) elephantiasis.

слонов|ый *adj. of* **⇒слон;** elephantine; **~ая болезнь = ~ость; ~ая кость** ivory.

слоня|ться, юсь *impf.* (*coll.*) to loiter about, mooch about (*Br.*).

слопа|ть, ю *pf. of* **⇒лопать**

слуг|а, и, *pl.* **~и, ~** *m.* servant.

служак|а, и *m.* (*coll.*) campaigner; old hand, veteran.

служанк|а, и *f.* maid.

служащ|ий, его *m.* white-collar worker, office worker.

служб|а, ы *f.* **1** service; (*работа*) work; employment; **действительная с.** (*mil.*) active service; **идти на ~у** to go to work; **быть на ~е у кого-н.** to work for s.o.; **по делам ~ы** on official business; **не в ~у, а в дружбу** (*coll.*) as a favour (*Br.*), favor (*US*). **2** (*специальная область работы*) (special) service; **с. пути** (*rail.*) track maintenance; **~ы тыла** (*mil.*) supply services.
3 (*богослужение*) church service.

служебн|ый *adj.* **1** *adj. of* **⇒служба;** office; official; work; **с. автомобиль** company car; **~ое время** office hours; **~ое дело** official business; **~ая поездка** business trip; **в ~ом порядке** in the line of duty; **с. путь** official channels; **с. стаж** length of service; **~ая характеристика** service record. **2** (*вспомогательный*) auxiliary; secondary; **~ое слово** (*gram.*) connective word.

служени|е, я *nt.* service, serving.

служител|ь, я *m.* **1** (*obs.*) (*слуга*) servant. **2** (*в музее*) attendant. **3**: **с. культа** priest, minister.

служитель|ница, ницы *f. of* **⇒~ 1, 2**

служ|ить, у, ~ишь *impf.* (*of* **⇒по~**)
1 (+*d.*) to serve, devote o.s. (to).
2 (+*i.*) (*работать*) to serve (as); to work (as), be employed (as), be; **с. в армии** to serve in the Army; **с. доказательством** (+*g.*) to serve as evidence (of).
3 *impf. only* (+*i. or* **для**+*g.*) (*функционировать*) to serve (for), do (for), be used (for); **гостиная ~ит нам и спальней** our sitting-room serves also as a bedroom.
4 (*быть полезным*) to be in use, do duty, serve; **мой старый плащ ещё ~ит** my old mac(k)intosh is still in use.
5 (*eccl.*) to celebrate; to conduct, officiate (at); **с. обедню** to celebrate mass.
6 *impf. only* (*о собаке*) to (sit up and) beg.

служк|а, и *m.* (*eccl.*) lay brother.

слукав|ить, лю, ишь *pf. of* **⇒лукавить**

слуп|ить, лю, ~ишь *pf. of* **⇒лупить**

слух, а *m.* **1** hearing; (*mus.*) ear; **абсолютный с.** perfect (*or* absolute) pitch; **играть по ~у, на с.** to play by ear; **она вся обратилась в с.** she was all ears. **2** (*известие*) rumour (*Br.*), rumor (*US*); **прошёл с., что** it was rumoured (*Br.*), rumored (*US*) that; **ни ~у ни духу (о**+*p.*) (*coll.*) not a word has been heard (of).

слухач, а *m.* monitor.

слухов|ой *adj.* acoustic, auditory, aural; **с. аппарат** hearing aid; **с. нерв** (*anat.*) auditory nerve; **~ое окно** dormer (-window); **с. рожок, ~ая трубка** ear-trumpet.

случа|й, я *m.* **1** case; **во всяком ~е** in any case, anyhow, anyway; **ни в коем ~е** in no circumstances; **в лучшем, худшем ~е** at best, at worst; **в противном ~е** otherwise; **в таком ~е** in that case; **в ~е чего** (*coll.*) if anything crops up; **на всякий с.** to be on the safe side, just in case; **на крайний с.** in case of special emergency; **по ~ю** (+*g.*) by reason (of), on account (of), on the occasion (of).
2 (*происшествие*) event, incident, occurrence; **несчастный с.** accident.
3 (*возможность*) opportunity, occasion, chance; **упустить удобный с.** to miss an opportunity; **при ~е** when an opportunity presents itself; **от ~я к ~ю** occasionally.
4 (*случайность*) chance.

случайно *adv.* **1** by chance, by accident, accidentally; **я с. подслушал их разговор** I happened to overhear their conversation. **2** (*как вводное слово*) by any chance; **вы, с., не видели моего зонтика?** have you by any chance seen my umbrella?

случайност|ь, и *f.* chance; **по счастливой ~и** by a lucky chance, by sheer luck.

случа|йный (~ен, ~йна) *adj.*
1 (*ошибка*) accidental; (*встреча, разговор*) chance; (*гость, удача*) unexpected. **2** (*расходы, поручения*) incidental; **с. заработок** casual earnings.

случ|ать, аю *impf. of* **⇒~ить**

случ|аться, ается *impf. of* **⇒~иться**

случ|ить, у, ишь *pf.* (*of* **⇒~ать**) (**с**+*i.*) to pair (with), mate (with).

случ|иться[1]**, ится** *pf.* (*of* **⇒~аться**) to pair, mate.

случ|иться[2]**, ится** *pf.* (*of* **⇒~аться**)
1 (*произойти*) to happen, come about; **что бы ни ~илось** whatever happens, come what may. **2** (*impers.;* +*d. and inf.*) to happen; **мне ~илось попасть в Москву** I happened to find myself in Moscow. **3** (*coll.*) (*оказаться*) to turn up, show up; **у меня как раз ~илось пять рублей** I happened to have just five roubles on me.

случк|а, и *f.* pairing, mating.

слушани|е, я *nt.* **1** hearing; **с. лекции** attendance at a lecture. **2** (*leg.*) hearing.

слушател|ь, я *m.* **1** listener; (*pl.; collect.*) audience. **2** (*студент*) student.

слушатель|ница, ницы *f. of* **⇒~**

слуша|ть, ю *impf.* (*of* **⇒по~**)
1 (*музыку, радио*) to listen (to); **с. лекцию** to attend a lecture; **~й(те)!** (*coll.*) listen!, look here!; **~ю!** at your service!; very good!; (*по телефону*) hello!
2 (*изучать*) to attend lectures (on), go to lectures (on). **3** (*слушаться*) to listen (to), obey. **4** (*leg.*) to hear.

слуша|ться, юсь *impf.* (*of* **⇒по~**)
1 (*человека*) to listen (to), obey; **~юсь!** (*mil.*) yes, sir! (*indicating readiness to carry out order*). **2** (*obs.*) (*советов*) to follow, heed, listen to.

слы|ть, ву, вёшь, *past* **~л, ~ла, ~ло** *impf.* (*of* **⇒про~**) (+*i. or* **за**+*a.*) to have a reputation (for), be said (to); **он ~вёт бездельником, за бездельника** he has a reputation for being an idler.

слыхать *no pres., impf.* **1** to hear; **что у вас с.?** (*coll.*) tell us what you have been up to!; **ничего не с.** nothing can be heard.
2 *as adv.* (*coll.*) apparently, it seems; **ты, с., пишешь новый роман** we hear you are writing a new novel.

слыш|ать, у, ишь *impf.* (*of* **⇒у~**)
1 to hear; **~ишь, ~ите** (*coll.*) do you hear? (*emph. command or direction*).
2 (*impf. only*) (*обладать слухом*) to have the sense of hearing; **не с.** to be hard of hearing. **3** (*coll.*) (*замечать*) to notice; to feel, sense; **с. запах** (*coll.*) to smell.

слыш|аться, ится *impf.* (*of* **⇒по~**) to be heard; to be audible.

слышимост|ь, и *f.* audibility.

слышим|ый (~, ~а) *adj.* audible.

слышно[1] *adv.* audibly.

слышно[2] *as pred., impers.* **1** one can hear; **было с., как она рыдала** one could hear her sobbing; **нам никого не было с.** we could not hear anyone.
2 (*coll.*): **что с.?** what news?, any news?; **о них ничего не с.** nothing has been heard of them. **3** (*coll.*) it is said, they say; **она, с., беременна** they say she is pregnant.

слыш|ный (~ен, ~на, ~но) *adj.* audible.

слюбиться *see* **⇒стерпеться**

слюд|а, ы *f.* mica.

слюдяной *adj.* mica.

слюн|а́, ы́ *f.* saliva.

слю́н|и, е́й *no sg.* (*coll.*) slobber, spittle; **пусти́ть с.** to slobber, dribble; **распусти́ть с.** (*coll.*) (*проявить нерешительность*) to dither; (*расплакаться*) to burst into tears.

слюн|и́ть, ю́, и́шь *impf.* **1** (*pf.* **по~**) (*папиросу*) to lick. **2** (*pf.* **за~**) (*пачкать*) to slobber over.

слю́н|ки, ок *no sg., dim. of* ⇒**~и; от э́того с. теку́т** it makes one's mouth water.

слюноотделе́ни|е, я *nt.* salivation.

слюнтя́|й, я *m.* (*coll.*) ditherer; cry-baby, whinger.

слюня́в|ить, лю, ишь *impf.* (*coll.*) = **слюни́ть**

слюня́вчик, а *m.* (*baby's*) bib.

слюня́вый *adj.* (*coll.*) **1** (*ребенок*) dribbling. **2** (*покрытый слюнями*) saliva-covered.

сля́кот|ный (~ен, ~на) *adj.* slushy.

сля́кот|ь, и *f.* slush.

см (*abbr. of* ***сантиме́тр***) cm, centimetre(s) (*Br.*), centimeter(s) (*US*).

с. м. (*abbr. of* ***сего́ ме́сяца***) (*comm.*) inst. (= *of the current month*).

см. (*abbr. of* ***смотри́***) see, *vide*.

сма́|зать, жу, жешь *pf.* (*of* ⇒**~зывать**) **1** to lubricate; to grease; **с. йо́дом** to paint with iodine. **2** (*fig., coll.*) (*дать взятку*) to grease the palm (of), grease the wheels (of). **3** (*размазать*) to smudge; (*стереть*) to rub off. **4** (*fig., coll.*) (*лишить чёткости*) to slur (over). **5** (*fig., coll.*) (*ударить*) to bash.

сма́|заться, жусь, жешься *pf.* (*of* ⇒**~зываться**) **1** to grease o.s. **2** (*о краске*) to become smudged; to come off.

сма́зк|а, и *f.* **1** (*действие*) lubrication; greasing. **2** (*вещество*) lubricant; grease.

смазли́в|ый (~, ~а) *adj.* (*coll.*) pretty.

сма́зочный *adj.* lubricating.

сма́зчик, а *m.* greaser.

сма́зывани|е, я *nt.* **1** lubrication; greasing. **2** (*fig.*) slurring over.

сма́зыва|ть(ся), ю(сь) *impf. of* ⇒**сма́зать(ся)**

смак, а *m.* (*coll.*) relish (*also fig.*); **со ~ом** with relish, with gusto.

смак|ова́ть, у́ю *impf.* (*coll.*) to savour (*Br.*), savor (*US*); to eat, drink with relish; to relish (*also fig.*).

сманеври́р|овать, ую *pf. of* ⇒**маневри́ровать**

сма́нива|ть, ю *impf. of* ⇒**смани́ть**

сман|и́ть, ю́, ~ишь *pf.* (*of* ⇒**~ивать**) to entice, lure.

смастер|и́ть, ю́, и́шь *pf. of* ⇒**мастери́ть**

сма́тыва|ть, ю *impf. of* ⇒**смота́ть**

сма́тыва|ться, юсь *impf. of* ⇒**смота́ться**

сма́хива|ть¹, ю *impf. of* ⇒**смахну́ть**

сма́хива|ть², ю *impf.* (**на**+*a.*; *coll.*) to look like, resemble.

смах|ну́ть, ну́, нёшь *pf.* (*of* ⇒**~ивать¹**) to brush (away, off), flick (away, off); **с. пыль** (**с**+*g.*) to dust.

сма́чива|ть, ю *impf. of* ⇒**смочи́ть**

сма́ч|ный (~ен, ~на́, ~но) *adj.* (*coll.*) **1** tasty. **2** (*fig., pej.*) fruity; **~ная ру́гань** colourful (*Br.*), colorful (*US*) language.

смеж|а́ть, а́ю *impf. of* ⇒**~и́ть**

смеж|и́ть, у́, и́шь *pf.* (*of* ⇒**~а́ть**) (*obs. or poet.*): **с. глаза́** to close one's eyes.

сме́жник, а *m.* factory producing parts for use by another.

сме́жност|ь, и *f.* contiguity.

сме́ж|ный (~ен, ~на) *adj.* (*комнаты, участки*) adjacent, adjoining; (*профессии, понятия*) related; **с. у́гол** (*math.*) adjacent angle.

смека́лист|ый (~, ~а) *adj.* (*coll.*) sharp, keen-witted.

смека́лк|а, и *f.* (*coll.*) native wit; nous; sharpness.

смек|а́ть, а́ю *impf.* (*of* ⇒**~ну́ть**) (*coll.*) to see the point (of), grasp; **~а́ешь, в чём де́ло?** do you get it?

смек|ну́ть, ну́, нёшь *pf. of* ⇒**~а́ть**

смеле́|ть, ю *impf.* (*of* ⇒**о~**) to grow bold(er).

сме́ло *adv.* **1** boldly. **2** (*с полной уверенностью*). confidently; **я могу́ с. сказа́ть** I can safely say.

сме́лост|ь, и *f.* boldness, audacity; **взять на себя́ с.** (+*inf.*) to take the liberty (of), make bold (to).

сме́л|ый (~, ~а́, ~о) *adj.* bold, audacious, daring.

смельча́к, а́ *m.* (*coll.*) bold spirit; dare-devil.

сме́н|а, ы *f.* **1** (*действие*) changing, change; (*замена*) replacement; **с. карау́ла** changing of the guard; **идти́ на ~у** (+*d.*) to come to take the place (of), come to relieve. **2** (*collect.*) replacements; successors; (*mil.*) relief; **гото́вить себе́ ~у** to prepare successors (*to take one's place, to take over*). **3** (*на заводе*) shift; **у́тренняя, дневна́я, вече́рняя с.** morning, day, night shift; **рабо́тать в три ~ы** to work in three shifts, work a three-shift system. **4** (*белья*) change.

смен|и́ть, ю́, ~ишь *pf.* (*of* ⇒**~я́ть¹**) **1** to change; (*работника*) to replace; (*mil.*) to relieve; **с. бельё** to change linen; **с. заве́дующего** to replace the manager; **с. карау́л** to relieve the guard; **с. ши́ны** to change tyres (*Br.*), tires (*US*); **с. гнев на ми́лость** to temper justice with mercy. **2** (*заместить*) to replace, relieve, succeed (s.o.).

смен|и́ться, ю́сь, ~ишься *pf.* (*of* ⇒**~я́ться**) **1** to hand over; (*mil.*) to be relieved; **с. с дежу́рства** to go off duty. **2** (+*i.*) to give way (to); **дневно́й зно́й ~и́лся прохла́дой ве́чера** the day's heat gave way to the coolness of evening.

сме́нност|ь, и *f.* shift system, shiftwork.

сме́нн|ый *adj.* **1** shift; **с. ма́стер** shift foreman; **~ая рабо́та** shift work. **2** (*tech.*) changeable; **~ое колесо́** spare wheel.

сме́нщик, а *m.* relief (worker); *pl.* (*collect.*) new shift.

сменя́|емый *pres. part. pass. of* ⇒**~ть¹** *and adj.* removable, changeable.

смен|я́ть¹, я́ю *impf. of* ⇒**~и́ть**

смен|я́ть², я́ю *pf.* (**на**+*a.*; *coll.*) to exchange (for).

смен|я́ться, я́юсь *impf. of* ⇒**смени́ться**

смер|де́ть, жу́, ди́шь *impf.* (*obs.*) to stink.

смерз|а́ться, а́ется *impf. of* ⇒**~нуться**

смёрз|нуться, нется, *past* **~ся, ~лась** *pf.* (*of* ⇒**~а́ться**) to freeze together.

сме́р|ить, ю, ишь *pf.* (*coll.*) to measure; **с. взгля́дом** to look (s.o.) up and down, measure at a glance.

смерк|а́ться, а́ется *impf.* (*of* ⇒**~нуться**) to get dark; **~а́лось** it was getting dark, twilight was falling.

сме́рк|нуться, нется *pf. of* ⇒**~а́ться**

смерте́льно *adv.* **1** mortally; **с. ра́ненный** mortally wounded. **2** (*coll.*) (*очень*) extremely, terribly; **с. уста́ть** to be dead tired.

смерте́л|ьный (~ен, ~ьна) *adj.* **1** (*борьба, враг*) mortal, deadly; **~ьная ра́на** fatal (*or* mortal) wound; **с. слу́чай** fatality; **с. уда́р** mortal blow. **2** (*coll., fig.*) (*сильный, крайний*) deadly, extreme.

сме́ртник, а *m.* prisoner sentenced to death.

сме́ртност|ь, и *f.* mortality, death-rate.

сме́рт|ный (~ен, ~на) *adj.* **1** mortal; *as n.* **с., ~ного** *m.* mortal; **просто́й с.** ordinary mortal. **2** deadly, death; **с. бой** mortal combat, fight to the death; **семь ~ных грехо́в** (*liter.*) the Seven Deadly Sins; **~ная казнь** capital punishment, death penalty; **с. пригово́р** death sentence; **с. час** last hour(s). **3** (*coll., fig.*) (*сильный, крайний*) deadly, extreme.

смертоно́с|ный (~ен, ~на) *adj.* mortal, fatal, lethal; **с. уда́р** mortal blow.

смертоуби́йств|о, а *nt.* (*obs.*) murder.

смерт|ь, и, *pl.* **~и, ~е́й** *f.* **1** death; **умере́ть голо́дной ~ью** to starve to death; **умере́ть свое́й ~ью** to die a natural death; **до́ ~и** (*fig., coll.*) to death; **я уста́л до́ ~и** I'm dead tired; **боро́ться не на жизнь, а на с.** to fight to the death; **быть при́ ~и** to be dying; **двум ~я́м не быва́ть, одно́й не минова́ть** you only die once. **2**: **с. как** *as adv.* (*coll.*) awfully, terribly; **ему́,** *etc.*, **с. как хо́чется** (+*inf.*) he, *etc.*, is dying (for).

смерч, а *m.* tornado.

смеси́тел|ь, я *m.* mixer; (*кран*) mixer tap (*Br.*).

сме|си́ть, шу́, ~сишь *pf. of* ⇒**меси́ть**

сме|сти́, ту́, тёшь, *past* **~л, ~ла́** *pf.* (*of* ⇒**~та́ть²**) **1** to sweep off, sweep away; **с. кро́шки со стола́** to sweep crumbs off the table; **с. с лица́ земли́** to wipe off the face of the earth. **2** (*метя, собрать*) to sweep into, together.

С

сме|сти́ть, щу́, сти́шь *pf.* (*of* ⇒~**ща́ть**) **1** to displace, remove; to shift, move. **2** (*fig.*) (*уволить*) to remove, dismiss.

сме|сти́ться, щу́сь, сти́шься *pf.* (*of* ⇒~**ща́ться**) to change position, become displaced.

смес|ь, и *f.* mixture; (*продукт*) blend.

сме́т|а, ы *f.* (*fin.*) estimate.

смета́н|а, ы *f.* sour cream.

смет|а́ть¹, а́ю *pf.* (*of* ⇒**мета́ть** *and* ~́**ывать**) to tack (together).

смета́|ть², ю *pf. of* ⇒**смести́**

смётк|а, и *f.* (*coll.*) quick-wittedness; gumption.

сме́тлив|ый (~, ~а) *adj.* quick (on the uptake).

сме́т|ный *adj. of* ⇒~**а; ~ные ассигно́вки** budget allowances.

смётыва|ть, ю *impf. of* ⇒**смета́ть¹**

сме|ть, ю *impf.* (*of* ⇒**по~**) to dare; to make bold; **не ~й(те)!** don't you dare!

смех, а (у) *m.* laughter; laugh; **разрази́ться ~́ом** to burst out laughing; **без ~́у** joking apart, in earnest; **в с., на́ с., ~́а ра́ди** for a joke, for fun, in jest; **и с. и грех** you can see the funny side of it; **нам не до ~́у** we are in no mood for laughter.

смехот|а́, ы́ *f.* (*coll.*) matter for laughter; **э́то пря́мо с.!** this is simply ludicrous!

смехотво́р|ный (~ен, ~на) *adj.* laughable, ludicrous.

сме́ш|анный *p.p.p. of* ⇒~**а́ть** *and adj.* mixed; combined; **~анное акционе́рное о́бщество** joint-stock company; **телефо́н ~анного по́льзования** party-line; **~анная поро́да** crossbreed.

смеш|а́ть, а́ю *pf.* (*of* ⇒**меша́ть²** *and* ~́**ивать**) **1** (**с**+*i.*) (*соединить*) to mix (with), blend (with). **2** (*перепутать, путать*) to mix up.

смеш|а́ться, а́юсь *pf.* (*of* ⇒~́**иваться**) **1** (*о красках*) to mix, blend; to mingle; **с. с толпо́й** to mingle in the crowd. **2** (*прийти в беспорядок; путаться*) to become confused, get mixed up.

смеше́ни|е, я *nt.* **1** (*смесь*) mixture. **2** (*путаница*) confusion, mixing up; **с. поня́тий** confusion of ideas.

сме́шива|ть(ся), ю(сь) *impf. of* ⇒**смеша́ть(ся)**

смеш|и́ть, у́, и́шь *impf.* (*of* ⇒**на~**) to make (s.o.) laugh.

смеш|но́й (~о́н, ~на́) *adj.* **1** funny; *as pred.*: **~но́** it is funny; **вам ~но́?** do you find it funny? **2** (*нелепый*) absurd, ridiculous, ludicrous; **до ~но́го** to the point of absurdity.

смеш|о́к, ка́ *m.* (*coll.*) chuckle; giggle.

смеща́|ть(ся), ю(сь) *impf. of* ⇒**смести́ть(ся)**

смеще́ни|е, я *nt.* **1** displacement; shift, removal. **2** (*увольнение*) dismissal.

сме|я́ться, ю́сь, ёшься *impf.* **1** to laugh; **с. шу́тке** to laugh at a joke; **~ётся тот, кто ~ётся после́дним** he who laughs last laughs longest. **2** (**над**+*i.*) to laugh (at), mock (at), make fun (of).

3 (*говорить в шутку*) to joke, say in jest.

СМИ *pl. indecl.* (*abbr. of* ***сре́дства ма́ссовой информа́ции***) mass media.

смил|оваться, уюсь *pf.* to have mercy, take pity.

смире́ни|е, я *nt.* humbleness, humility, meekness.

смире́нник, а *m.* humble person, meek person.

смире́нност|ь, и *f.* humility.

смире́н|ный (~, ~на) *adj.* humble, meek.

смири́тельн|ый *adj.*: **~ая руба́шка** straitjacket.

смир|и́ть, ю́, и́шь *pf.* (*of* ⇒~**я́ть**) to restrain, subdue.

смир|и́ться, ю́сь, и́шься *pf.* (*of* ⇒~**я́ться**) to submit; to resign o.s.

сми́рно *adv.* quietly; **с.!** (*mil. word of command*) attention!

сми́р|ный (~ен, ~на́, ~но) *adj.* quiet; submissive.

смир|я́ть(ся), я́ю(сь) *impf. of* ⇒~**и́ть(ся)**

см. на об. (*abbr. of* ***смотри́ на оборо́те***) PTO (= *please turn over*), see over.

смог, а *m.* smog.

смоделир|овать, ую *pf. of* ⇒**модели́ровать**

смо́кв|а, ы *f.* fig.

смо́кинг, а *m.* dinner-jacket.

смоко́вниц|а, ы *f.* fig-tree.

смол|а́, ы́, *pl.* ~́**ы** *f.* resin; (*дёготь*) pitch, tar.

смолёный *adj.* resined; tarred, pitched.

смоли́ст|ый (~, ~а) *adj.* resinous.

смол|и́ть, ю́, и́шь *impf.* (*of* ⇒**вы́~** *and* ⇒**о~**) to resin; to tar, pitch.

смолк|а́ть, а́ю *impf. of* ⇒~́**нуть**

смо́лк|нуть, ну, нешь, *past* **~, ~ла** *pf.* (*of* ⇒~**а́ть**) (*о голосе, о человеке*) to fall silent; (*о шуме*) to cease.

смо́лоду *adv.* from, in one's youth.

смоло|ти́ть, чу́, ~́тишь *pf. of* ⇒**молоти́ть**

смоло́ть, смелю́, сме́лешь *pf. of* ⇒**моло́ть**

смолч|а́ть, у́, и́шь *pf.* to hold one's tongue.

смоль *only in phr.* **чёрный как с.** jet-black.

смол|яно́й *adj. of* ⇒~**а́; (***волосы***)** jet-black.

смонти́р|овать, ую *pf. of* ⇒**монти́ровать**

сморгн|у́ть, у́, ёшь *pf.* (*coll.*): **гла́зом не с.** not to bat an eyelid.

сморка́|ть, ю *impf.* (*of* ⇒**вы́~**): **с. нос** to blow one's nose.

сморка́|ться, юсь *impf.* (*of* ⇒**вы́~**) to blow one's nose.

сморо́дин|а, ы *no pl., f.* **1** (*кустарник*) currant bush. **2** (*collect.*) (*ягоды*) currants; **кра́сная, чёрная с.** redcurrants, blackcurrants.

сморо́дин|ный *adj. of* ⇒~**а**

сморо́|зить, жу, зишь *pf.* (*coll.*) to blurt out.

сморч|о́к, ка́ *m.* morel (*mushroom*).

смо́рщ|енный *p.p.p. of* ⇒~**ить** *and adj.* wrinkled.

смо́рщ|ить(ся), у(сь), ишь(ся) *pf. of* ⇒**мо́рщить(ся)**

смота́|ть, ю *pf.* (*of* ⇒**сма́тывать**) to wind, reel; (*coll.*): **с. у́дочки** to take to one's heels, make off.

смота́|ться, юсь *pf.* (*of* ⇒**сма́тываться**) (*coll.*) **1** (*сходить*) to dash (there and back). **2** (*убраться*) to take to one's heels, make off.

смотр, а *m.* **1** (**на ~у́,** *pl.* **~ы**) review, inspection; **произвести́ с.** (+*d.*) to review, inspect. **2** (**на ~́е,** *pl.* **~́ы**) (*публичный показ*) public showing.

смотр|е́ть, ю́, ~́ишь *impf.* (*of* ⇒**по~**) **1** (**на**+*a.*, **в**+*a.*) to look (at); **с. в окно́** to look out of the window; **с. в глаза́, в лицо́** (+*d.*) to look in the face; **с. сквозь па́льцы** (**на**+*a.*; *coll.*) to turn a blind eye (to).
2 (*фильм, пьесу*) to see; (*фильм, телевидение*) to watch; (*книгу, журнал*) to look through.
3 (*больного*) to examine; (*войска*) to review, inspect.
4 (**за**+*i.*) to look (after); to be in charge (of), supervise; **с. за поря́дком** to keep order.
5 (**на**+*a.*; *coll.*) to follow the example (of).
6 *impf. only* (**в**+*a.*, **на**+*a.*) to look (on to, over); **о́кна в моей ко́мнате ~́ят в сад** my windows look on to the garden.
7 *impf. only* (+*i.*; *coll.*) to look (like); **он ~́ит простако́м** he looks a simple fellow.
8: **~й(те)!** mind!, take care!; **~и́те не опозда́йте!** mind you are not late!; **~и́те, что́бы на́шим гостя́м бы́ло удо́бно** see that our guests are comfortable.
9: **~я́ (где, как, *etc.*)** it depends (where, how, *etc.*); **~я́ (по**+*d.*) depending (on), in accordance (with).

смотр|е́ться, ю́сь, ~́ишься *impf.* (*of* ⇒**по~**) **1** to look at o.s.; **с. в зе́ркало** to look at o.s. in the mirror. **2** (*coll.*) (*хорошо выглядеть*) to look good.

смотри́тел|ь, я *m.* supervisor; (*в музее*) keeper, custodian.

смотри́тель|ница, ницы *f. of* ⇒~

смотров|о́й *adj.* **1** (*mil.*) review. **2**: **~о́е окно́** inspection window; **~о́е отве́рстие** sighting aperture (*of gun sight*); **~а́я щель** vision slit (*in tank*).

смоч|и́ть, у́, ~́ишь *pf.* (*of* ⇒**сма́чивать**) to damp, wet, moisten.

смо|чь, гу́, ~́жешь, *past* **~́г, ~гла́** *pf. of* ⇒**мочь¹**

смоше́ннича|ть, ю *pf. of* ⇒**моше́нничать**

смрад, а *m.* stink, stench.

смра́д|ный (~ен, ~на) *adj.* stinking.

смуглоли́ц|ый (~, ~а) *adj.* dark-complexioned.

сму́гл|ый (~, ~а́, ~о) *adj.* dark-complexioned.

сму́т|а, ы *f.* (*obs.*) disturbance, sedition; **се́ять ~у** to sow discord.

сму|ти́ть, щу́, ти́шь *pf.* (*of* ⇒**~ща́ть**) **1** (*поставить в неловкое положение*) to embarrass, confuse. **2** (*взволновать*) to disturb, trouble; **с. чей-н. поко́й** to disturb s.o.'s peace and quiet.

сму|ти́ться, щу́сь, ти́шься *pf.* (*of* ⇒**~ща́ться**) to be embarrassed, be confused.

сму́т|ный (~ен, ~на́, ~но) *adj.* **1** (*неопределённый*) vague; confused; **~ные воспомина́ния** dim recollections. **2** (*беспокойный*) disturbed, troubled; **~ное вре́мя** (*hist.*) Time of Troubles (*1605–13*).

смутья́н, а *m.* (*coll.*) trouble-maker.

смухл|ева́ть, ю́ю *pf. of* ⇒**мухлева́ть**

сму́шк|а, и *f.* astrakhan.

сму́шковый *adj.* astrakhan.

смуща́|ть(ся), ю(сь) *impf. of* ⇒**смути́ть(ся)**

смуще́ни|е, я *nt.* embarrassment, confusion.

сму|щённый *p.p.p. of* ⇒**~ти́ть** *and adj.* embarrassed, confused.

смыва́|ть(ся), ю(сь) *impf. of* ⇒**смы́ть(ся)**

смыка́|ть(ся), ю, ет(ся) *impf. of* ⇒**сомкну́ть(ся)**

смысл, а *m.* **1** sense, meaning; **прямо́й, перено́сный с.** literal, metaphorical sense; **в изве́стном ~е** in a sense; **в по́лном ~е сло́ва** in the true sense of the word; **в ~е** (+*g.*) as regards. **2** (*цель, разумное основание*) sense, point; **име́ть с.** to make sense; **нет никако́го ~а** (+*inf.*) there is no sense (in), there is no point (in). **3** (*разум*) (good) sense; **здра́вый с.** common sense.

смы́сл|ить, ю, ишь *impf.* (**в**+*p.*; *coll.*) to understand.

смыслов|о́й *adj. of* ⇒**смысл; ~ы́е отте́нки** shades of meaning.

смыть, смо́ю, смо́ешь *pf.* (*of* ⇒**смыва́ть**) **1** (*удалить*) to wash off; (*fig.*) to clear, wipe away; (*mil.*) to wipe out. **2** (*снести*) to wash away.

смы́ться, смо́юсь, смо́ешься *pf.* (*of* ⇒**смыва́ться**) **1** to wash off, come off. **2** (*fig., coll.*) (*уйти*) to slip away.

смы́чк|а, и *f.* union; linking.

смыч|ко́вый *adj. of* ⇒**~о́к**

смыч|о́к, ка́ *m.* (*mus.*) bow.

смышлён|ый (~, ~а) *adj.* (*coll.*) clever, bright.

смягч|а́ть(ся), а́ю(сь) *impf. of* ⇒**~и́ть(ся)**

смягча́|ющий *pres. part. act. of* ⇒**~ть; ~ющие вину́ обстоя́тельства** extenuating circumstances.

смягче́ни|е, я *nt.* **1** (*кожи, тона*) softening. **2** (*человека*) mollification; (*наказания*) mitigation; (*боли*) alleviation; (*вины*) extenuation. **3** (*ling.*) palatalization.

смягч|и́ть, у́, и́шь *pf.* (*of* ⇒**~а́ть**) **1** (*impf. also* **мягчи́ть**) (*кожу, тон*) to soften. **2** (*человека*) to mollify; (*боль*) to ease, alleviate; (*гнев*) to assuage; (*наказание*) to mitigate. **3** (*ling.*) to palatalize.

смягч|и́ться, у́сь, и́шься *pf.* (*of* ⇒**~а́ться**) **1** (*о коже, тоне, глазах*) to soften, become softer. **2** (*о человеке*) to be mollified; (*о боли, ветре, холоде, ситуации*) to ease (off).

смяте́ни|е, я *nt.* confusion, disarray; commotion.

смяте́н|ный (~, ~на) *adj.* (*obs.*) troubled, perturbed.

смять, сомну́, сомнёшь *pf.* (*of* ⇒**мять**) **1** to crumple; to rumple; **с. пла́тье** to crush a dress. **2** (*mil.*) to crush.

смя́ться, сомнётся *pf.* (*of* ⇒**мя́ться**[1]) to get creased; to get crumpled.

снаб|ди́ть, жу́, ди́шь *pf.* (*of* ⇒**~жа́ть**) (+*i.*) to supply (with), furnish (with), provide (with).

снабжа́|ть, ю *impf. of* ⇒**снабди́ть**

снабже́н|ец, ца *m.* supplier, provider.

снабже́ни|е, я *nt.* supply, supplying, provision.

снабже́н|ческий *adj. of* ⇒**~ие**

сна́доб|ье, ья, *g. pl.* **~ий** *nt.* (*coll.*) drug.

сна́йпер, а *m.* sniper; (*sport*) sharp-shooter.

снару́жи *adv.* on the outside; from (the) outside.

снаря́д, а *m.* **1** (*mil.*) projectile, missile; shell; **управля́емый с.** guided missile. **2** (*прибор*) contrivance, machine, gadget; **гимнасти́ческие ~ы** gymnastic apparatus.

снаря|ди́ть, жу́, ди́шь *pf.* (*of* ⇒**~жа́ть**) to equip, fit out.

снаря|ди́ться, жу́сь, ди́шься *pf.* (*of* ⇒**~жа́ться**) to equip o.s., get ready.

снаря́дн|ый *adj.* **1** (*mil.*) shell; ammunition. **2**: **~ая гимна́стика** (*sport*) apparatus work.

снаряжа́|ть(ся), ю(сь) *impf. of* ⇒**снаряди́ть(ся)**

снаряже́ни|е, я *nt.* equipment, outfit; **ко́нское с.** harness.

снаст|ь, и, *pl.* **~и, ~е́й** *f.* **1** (*collect.*) tackle, gear. **2** (*usu. pl.*) (*на судне*) rigging.

снача́ла *adv.* **1** (*прежде*) at first, at the beginning. **2** (*снова*) all over again.

сна́шива|ть, ю *impf. of* ⇒**сноси́ть**[1]

СНГ *nt. indecl.* (*abbr. of* ***Содру́жество незави́симых госуда́рств***) CIS (*Commonwealth of Independent States*).

снег, а, о ~е, в, на ~у́ *pl.* **~а́** *m.* snow; **идёт с.** it's snowing; **мо́крый с.** sleet; **как с. на́ голову** like a bolt from the blue.

снеги́р|ь, я́ *m.* bullfinch.

снегов|о́й *adj.* snow; **~а́я ли́ния** snow-line.

снегозадержа́ни|е, я *nt.* (*agric.*) retention of snow on fields (*as protection against drought and frost*).

снегозащи́тн|ый *adj.*: **~ое огражде́ние, с. щит** snow-fence.

снегоочисти́тел|ь, я *m.* snow-plough (*Br.*), snow-plow (*US*).

снегопа́д, а *m.* snow-fall.

снегосту́п|ы, ов *pl.* (*sport*) snow-shoes.

снегота́ялк|а, и *f.* snow-melter.

снегоубо́рочн|ый *adj.* snow-removal; **~ая маши́на** snow-plough (*Br.*), snow-plow (*US*).

снегохо́д, а *m.* snowmobile.

Снегу́рочк|а, и *f.* (*folklore*) Snow Maiden.

снеда́|ть, ю *impf.* to consume, gnaw.

сне́д|ь, и *f.* (*coll.*) food.

снежи́нк|а, и *f.* snow-flake.

сне́жн|ый *adj.* snow; snowy; **~ая ба́ба** snow man; **с. зано́с, с. сугро́б** snow-drift; **~ая зима́** snowy winter.

снеж|о́к, ка́ *m.* **1** light snow. **2** (*комок*) snowball; **игра́ть в ~ки́** to have a snowball fight.

снес|ти́[1]**, у́, ёшь,** *past* **~, ~ла́** *pf.* (*of* ⇒**сноси́ть**[3]) **1** (*отнести*) to take; **с. письмо́ на по́чту** to take a letter to the post. **2** (*вниз*) to fetch down, bring down; **с. сунду́к с чердака́** to fetch down a trunk from the attic. **3** (*usu. impers.*) (*о воде*) to carry away; (*о ветре*) to blow off, take off; **урага́ном ~ло́ кры́шу** a hurricane took the roof off. **4** (*разрушить*) to demolish, take down, pull down. **5** (*срезать*) to cut off, chop off; **с. го́лову кому́-н.** to chop s.o.'s head off. **6** (*cards*) to throw away.

снес|ти́[2]**, у́, ёшь** *pf.* (*of* ⇒**сноси́ть**[3]) (*в одно место*) to bring together, pile up.

снес|ти́[3]**, у́, ёшь** *pf.* (*of* ⇒**сноси́ть**[3]) (*стерпеть*) to bear, endure, suffer, stand, put up (with).

снес|ти́[4]**, у́, ёшь** *pf.* (*of* ⇒**нести́**[2]) to lay (eggs).

снес|ти́сь[1]**, у́сь, ёшься,** *past* **~ся, ~ла́сь** *pf.* (*of* ⇒**сноси́ться**) (**с**+*i.*) to communicate (with).

снес|ти́сь[2]**, ётся** *pf. of* ⇒**нести́сь**[2]

снет|о́к, ка́ *m.* (*fish*) smelt, sparling.

снижа́|ть(ся), ю(сь) *impf. of* ⇒**сни́зить(ся)**

сниже́ни|е, я *nt.* **1** lowering, reduction; **с. зарпла́ты** wage cut. **2** (*aeron.*) descent.

сни́|зить, жу, зишь *pf.* (*of* ⇒**~жа́ть**) **1** (*спустить ниже*) to bring down, lower. **2** (*цены*) to bring down, lower, reduce; **с. себесто́имость** to cut production costs; **с. по до́лжности** to reduce, demote.

сни́|зиться, жусь, зишься *pf.* (*of* ⇒**~жа́ться**) **1** (*спуститься ниже*) to descend, come down. **2** (*температура*) to fall, sink, come down; **це́ны ~зились** prices have come down.

снизо|йти́, йду́, йдёшь, *past* **~шёл, ~шла́** *pf.* (*of* ⇒**снисходи́ть**) (**к**+*d.*) to condescend (to); **с. к чьей-н. про́сьбе** to deign to grant s.o.'s request.

сни́зу *adv.* from below (*pol.; also fig.*); from the bottom; **с. вверх** upwards; **с. до́верху** from top to bottom; (*внизу*) at, on the bottom.

сни́к|нуть, ну, нешь *pf. of* ⇒**ни́кнуть**

С

снима́|ть(ся), ю(сь) *impf. of* ⇒**снять(ся)**

сни́м|ок, ка *m.* photograph, photo.

сни|ска́ть, щу́, ~щешь *pf.* (*of* ⇒**сни́скивать**) (*obs.*) to gain, get, win.

сни́скива|ть, ю *impf. of* ⇒**сниска́ть**

снисходи́тельност|ь, и *f.* **1** (*высокомерность*) condescension. **2** (*терпимость*) indulgence, tolerance, leniency.

снисходи́тел|ьный (~ен, ~ьна) *adj.* **1** (*высокомерный*) condescending. **2** (*не строгий*) indulgent, tolerant, lenient.

снисхо|ди́ть, жу́, ~дишь *impf. of* ⇒**снизойти́**

снисхожде́ни|е, я *nt.* indulgence, leniency.

сни́|ться, снюсь, сни́шься *impf.* (*of* ⇒**при~**) (+*d.*) to dream; **ей ~лось, что** she dreamed that; **мне ~лся лев** I dreamed about a lion.

сноб, а *m.* snob.

снобизм, а *m.* snobbery.

сно́ва *adv.* again, anew, afresh.

снова́ть, сную́, снуёшь *impf.* to scurry about, dash about.

сновиде́ни|е, я *nt.* dream.

сногсшиба́тел|ьный (~ен, ~ьна) *adj.* (*coll., joc.*) stunning.

сноп, а́ *m.* sheaf; **с. луче́й** shaft of light.

сноповяза́лк|а, и *f.* (*agric.*) binder.

сноро́ви́ст|ый (~, ~а) *adj.* (*coll.*) quick, smart, clever.

сноро́вк|а, и *f.* skill, knack.

снос[1], а *m.* **1** demolition, pulling down; **дом назна́чен на с.** the house is to be pulled down. **2** (*корабля*) drift.

снос[2], а (у) *m.*: **тако́й мате́рии ~у нет** this material won't wear out; **не знать ~у** to wear well.

сно́си: быть на ~ях (*coll.*) (*о беременной женщине*) to be near her time.

сно|си́ть[1], шу́, ~сишь *pf.* (*of* ⇒**сна́шивать**) to wear out.

сно|си́ть[2], шу́, ~сишь *pf.* (*coll.*) (*снести и принести*) to take (*and bring back*).

сно|си́ть[3], шу́, ~сишь *impf. of* ⇒**снести́[1,2,3]**

сно|си́ться, шу́сь, ~сишься *impf. of* ⇒**снести́сь[1]**

сно́ск|а, и *f.* footnote.

сно́сно *adv.* (*coll.*) tolerably, so-so.

сно́с|ный (~ен, ~на) *adj.* (*coll.*) tolerable; fair, reasonable.

снотво́р|ный (~ен, ~на) *adj.* soporific (*also fig.*); **~ное сре́дство** soporific; *as n.* **~ное, ~ного** *nt.* sleeping pill.

сноубо́рд, а *m.* snowboard.

сноубо́рдинг, а *m.* snowboarding.

снох|а́, и́, *pl.* **~и** *f.* (father's) daughter-in-law.

сноше́ни|е, я *nt.* (*usu. pl.*) relations, dealings; (*половой акт*) (sexual) intercourse; **дипломати́ческие ~я** diplomatic relations.

сну|ю́, ёшь *see* ⇒**снова́ть**

сню́ха|ться, юсь *pf.* (*coll.*) **1** to get to know one another by scent. **2** (*coll., pej.*) (*вступить в тайный сговор*) to come to terms, come to an understanding; (*вступить в любовную связь*) to have an affair.

сня́ти|е, я *nt.* **1** (*вниз*) taking down; **с. урожа́я** gathering in the harvest. **2** (*удаление, устранение*) removal; **с. запре́та** lifting of a ban; **с. с рабо́ты** dismissal, the sack. **3** (*изготовление*) taking, making; **с. ко́пии** copying.

снят|о́й *adj.*: **~о́е молоко́** skimmed milk.

сня́|ть, сниму́, сни́мешь, *past* **~л, ~ла́, ~ло** *pf.* (*of* ⇒**снима́ть**) **1** (*одежду, крышку*) to take off; (*вниз*) to take down; **с. шля́пу** to take one's hat off; **с. карти́ну** to take down a picture; **с. кора́бль с мели** to refloat a ship; **с. урожа́й** to gather in the harvest; **с. оса́ду** to raise a siege; **с. с себя́** to divest o.s. (of); **с. с себя́ отве́тственность** to decline responsibility. **2** (*устранить, отменить*) to remove; to withdraw, cancel; **с. запре́т** to lift a ban; **с. предложе́ние** to withdraw a motion; **с. с рабо́ты** to discharge, sack; **с. с учёта** to strike off the register; **с. с фро́нта** to withdraw from the front. **3** (*mil.*) (*выстрелом*) to pick off. **4** (*изготовить*) to take, make; to photograph, make a photograph (of); **с. ко́пию (с**+*g.*) to copy, make a copy (of); **с. ме́рку с кого́-н.** to take s.o.'s measurements; **с. план** to make a plan; **с. фильм** to shoot a film. **5** (*взять внаём*) to take, rent (*a house, etc.*); **с. в аре́нду** to take on lease. **6** (*sl.*) (*девушку*) to pick up, pull. **7** (*cards*) to cut.

сня́|ться, сниму́сь, сни́мешься, *past* **~лся, ~ла́сь** *pf.* (*of* ⇒**снима́ться**) **1** (*отделиться*) to come off. **2** (*отправиться*) to move off; **с. с я́коря** to weigh anchor; to get under way (*also fig.*). **3** (*фотографироваться*) to have one's photograph taken. **4** (*сыграть роль в фильме*) to play a part in a film.

со *prep.* = **с**

со... *vbl. pref.* = **с...**

соа́втор, а *m.* co-author.

соа́вторств|о, а *nt.* co-authorship.

соба́к|а, и *f.* dog; **дворо́вая с.** watchdog; **морска́я с.** dogfish; **охо́тничья с.** gun dog, hound; **с.-поводы́рь** guide-dog; **служе́бная с.** guard dog, patrol dog; **с.-ище́йка** bloodhound; **с. на се́не** dog in the manger; **уста́ть как с.** (*coll.*) to be dog-tired; **вот где с. зары́та!** so that's what it's all about!; **как ~ нере́занных** (+*g.*; *coll.*) any amount (of); **~у съесть (на**+*p.*; *coll.*) to know inside out.

собаково́д, а *m.* dog-breeder.

собаково́дств|о, а *nt.* dog-breeding.

соба́|чий *adj. of* ⇒**~ка; canine; ~чья жизнь** dog's life; **с. хо́лод** intense cold.

соба́чк|а[1], и *f.* little dog, doggie.

соба́чк|а[2], и *f.* **1** (*ружья*) trigger. **2** (*tech.*) catch, trip; (*храповика*) pawl.

соба́чник, а *m.* (*coll.*) dog-lover.

собезья́нннича|ть, ю *pf. of* ⇒**обезья́нничать**

СОБЕС, а *or* **собе́с, а** *m.* (*abbr. of* **(*отде́л*) *социа́льного обеспе́чения***) **1** social security. **2** (*учреждение*) social security department (*of local authority*).

собесе́дник, а *m.* interlocutor; **он — заба́вный с.** he is amusing company.

собесе́дни|ца, цы *f. of* ⇒**~к**

собесе́довани|е, я *nt.* conversation, discussion.

собира́тел|ь, я *m.* collector.

собира́тель|ница, ницы *f. of* ⇒**~**

собира́тельный *adj.* (*gram.*) collective.

собира́тельств|о, а *nt.* collecting.

собира́|ть, ю *impf. of* ⇒**собра́ть**

собира́|ться, юсь *impf.* **1** (*impf. of* ⇒**собра́ться**). **2** (+*inf.*) to intend (to), be about (to), be going (to); **я ~лся позвони́ть вам** I was going to ring you up.

собко́р, а *m.* (*abbr. of* ***со́бственный корреспонде́нт***) own correspondent.

соблаговол|и́ть, ю́, и́шь *pf.* (+*inf.*; *obs. or joc.*) to deign (to), condescend (to).

собла́зн, а *m.* temptation.

соблазни́тел|ь, я *m.* **1** tempter. **2** (*обольститель*) seducer.

соблазни́тельниц|а, ы *f.* temptress.

соблазни́тел|ьный (~ен, ~ьна) *adj.* tempting; alluring; (*женщина*) seductive.

соблазн|и́ть, ю́, и́шь *pf.* (*of* ⇒**~я́ть**) **1** (*прельстить*) to tempt. **2** (*обольстить*) to seduce.

соблазн|я́ть, я́ю *impf. of* ⇒**~и́ть**

соблюда́|ть, ю *impf. of* ⇒**соблюсти́**

соблюде́ни|е, я *nt.* observance; maintenance; **с. обы́чая** observance of a custom; **с. поря́дка** maintenance of order.

соблю|сти́, ду́, дёшь, *past* **~л, ~ла́** *pf.* (*of* ⇒**~да́ть**) (*диету*) to keep (to), stick to; (*порядок*) to maintain; to observe; **с. зако́н** to observe a law; **с. сро́ки** to keep to schedule.

собо́й *see* ⇒**себя́**

соболе́зновани|е, я *nt.* sympathy; (*pl.*) condolences.

соболе́зн|овать, ую *impf.* (+*d.*) to sympathize (with), commiserate (with).

собо́л|ий, ья, ье *adj. of* ⇒**со́боль; с. мех** sable.

соболи́ный *adj.* sable.

со́бол|ь, я, *pl.* **~я́, ~е́й** *and* **~и, ~ей** *m.* **1** sable. **2** (*pl.* **~я́, ~е́й**) (*мех*) sable (fur).

собо́р, а *m.* **1** (*hist.*) (*съезд*) council, synod, assembly; **вселе́нский с.** ecumenical council; **зе́мский с.** Assembly of the Land (*in Muscovite Russia*). **2** (*церковь*) cathedral.

собо́рност|ь, и *f.* collectivism; (*eccl., phil.*) conciliarism.

собо́р|ный *adj. of* ⇒**~**

собо́ровани|е, я *nt.* (*eccl.*) extreme unction.

собо́р|овать, ую *impf. and pf.* (*eccl.*) to administer extreme unction (to), anoint.

собо́р|оваться, уюсь *impf. and pf.* (*eccl.*) to receive extreme unction.

собо́ю = **собо́й,** *see* ⇒**себя́**

собра́ни|е, я *nt.* **1** (*заседание*) meeting, gathering; **о́бщее с.** general meeting; **с. правле́ния** board meeting. **2** (*государственный орган*) assembly; **учреди́тельное с.** constituent assembly. **3** (*коллекция*) collection; **с. зако́нов** code (of laws); **с. сочине́ний** collected works.

со́бр|анный *p.p.p. of* ⇒**~а́ть** *and adj.*; **с. челове́к** self-disciplined person.

собра́т, а, *pl.* **~ья, ~ьев** *m.* colleague; **с. по ору́жию** brother-in-arms.

собр|а́ть, соберу́, соберёшь, *past* **~а́л, ~ала́, ~а́ло** *pf.* (*of* ⇒**собира́ть**) **1** (*сведения*) to gather; (*книги, деньги*) to collect; (*цветы*) to pick. **2** (*людей*) to assemble, muster; to convene; **с. войска́** to muster troops; **с. всё своё му́жество** to muster up one's courage; **с. после́дние си́лы** to make a last effort. **3** (*tech.*) (*радиоприёмник*) to assemble. **4** (*голоса*) to obtain, poll (*stated number or percentage of votes*). **5** (*приготовить*) to prepare, make ready, equip; **с. кого́-н. в доро́гу** to equip s.o. for a journey; **с. на стол** to lay the table. **6** (*платье*) to gather, take in.

собр|а́ться, соберу́сь, соберёшься, *past* **~а́лся, ~ала́сь, ~а́ло́сь** *pf.* (*of* ⇒**собира́ться**) **1** (*сойтись*) to gather, assemble, muster; to be amassed. **2** (**в**+*a.*) (*приготовиться*) to prepare (for), make ready (for); **с. в го́сти** to get ready to go away (*to visit s.o.*). **3** (+*inf.*) (*решить*) to intend (to), be about (to), be going (to). **4** (**с**+*i., fig.*) (*привести силы*) to collect; **с. с ду́хом** to pluck up one's courage; **с. с мы́слями** to collect one's thoughts; **с. с си́лами** to summon up one's strength, brace o.s. **5**: **с. в комо́к** to hunch up.

со́бственник, а *m.* owner, proprietor; **земе́льный с.** landowner.

со́бственни|ца, цы *f. of* ⇒**~к**

со́бственнический *adj.* possessive.

со́бственно 1 *adv.* strictly; **с. говоря́** strictly speaking, as a matter of fact. **2** *particle* proper; **его́ не интересу́ет с. медици́на** he is not interested in medicine proper.

собственнору́чно *adv.* with one's own hand.

собственнору́чн|ый *adj.* done, made, written with one's own hand(s); **~ая по́дпись** autograph.

со́бственност|ь, и *f.* **1** (*имущество*) property. **2** (*владение*) possession, ownership; **приобрести́ в с.** to become the owner (of).

со́бственн|ый *adj.* **1** (*дом*) (one's) own; **~ыми глаза́ми** with one's own eyes; **в ~ые ру́ки** (*inscription on envelope, etc.*) 'personal'; **чу́вство ~ого досто́инства** self-respect; **~ой персо́ной** in person; **и́мя ~ое** (*gram.*) proper name. **2** (*настоящий*) true, proper; **в ~ом смы́сле** in the true sense. **3** (*tech.*) natural; internal; **~ое сопротивле́ние** internal resistance; **~ая ско́рость** actual speed.

собу́тыльник, а *m.* (*coll.*) drinking companion.

собы́ти|е, я *nt.* event; **теку́щие ~я** current affairs.

сов... *comb. form, abbr. of* **сове́тский**

сов|а́, ы, *pl.* **~ы** *f.* owl.

сова́ть, сую́, суёшь *impf.* (*of* ⇒**су́нуть**) to shove, thrust, poke; **с. ру́ки в карма́ны** to stick one's hands in one's pockets; **с. нос** (**в**+*a.*) (*coll.*) to poke one's nose (into), pry (into).

сова́ться, сую́сь, суёшься *impf.* (*of* ⇒**су́нуться**) (*coll.*) **1** to push, strain. **2** (**в**+*a.*; *fig.*) (*в чужие дела*) to butt (in); (*с советами*) to poke one's nose (into).

сов|ёнок, ёнка, *pl.* **~я́та, ~я́т** *m.* owlet.

соверш|а́ть(ся), а́ю, а́ет(ся) *impf. of* ⇒**~и́ть(ся)**

соверше́ни|е, я *nt.* (*подвига*) accomplishment; (*преступления*) perpetration; (*сделки*) conclusion.

соверше́нно *adv.* **1** (*превосходно*) perfectly. **2** (*совсем*) absolutely, utterly, completely, totally, perfectly; **с. ве́рно!** quite right!; perfectly true!

совершенноле́ти|е, я *nt.* majority; **дости́гнуть ~я** to come of age, attain one's majority.

совершенноле́тний *adj.* of age.

соверше́н|ный[1] (**~ен, ~на**) *adj.* **1** (*превосходный*) perfect. **2** (*coll.*) (*полный*) absolute, utter, complete, total, perfect; **с. идио́т** absolute idiot.

соверше́нный[2] *adj.* (*gram.*) perfective.

соверше́нств|о, а *nt.* perfection; **в ~е** perfectly, to perfection.

соверше́нств|овать, ую *impf.* (*of* ⇒**у~**) to perfect; to develop, improve.

соверше́нств|оваться, уюсь *impf.* (*of* ⇒**у~**) (**в**+*p.*) to perfect o.s. (in); to improve.

соверш|и́ть, у́, и́шь *pf.* (*of* ⇒**~а́ть**) **1** (*подвиг*) to accomplish, carry out; to perform; (*преступление*) to commit; **с. оши́бку** to make a mistake. **2** (*заключить*) to complete, conclude; **с. сде́лку** to complete a transaction, make a deal.

соверш|и́ться, и́тся *pf.* (*of* ⇒**~а́ться**) (*liter.*) **1** (*о событии*) to happen. **2** (*о подвиге*) to be accomplished; (*о сделке*) to be completed.

со́ве|стить, щу, стишь *impf.* to shame, put to shame.

со́ве|ститься, щусь, стишься *impf.* (*of* ⇒**по~**) (+*g. or inf.*; *obs.*) to be ashamed (of).

со́вестлив|ый (**~, ~а**) *adj.* conscientious.

со́вестно *as pred.* (+*d. and inf.*) to be ashamed; **ему́ бы́ло с.** he was ashamed; **как вам не с.!** you ought to be ashamed of yourself!

со́вест|ь, и *f.* conscience; **чи́стая, нечи́стая с.** clear, guilty conscience; **на ~и** on one's conscience; **со споко́йной ~ью** with a clear conscience; **по ~и** (**говоря́**) to be honest; **свобо́да ~и** freedom of worship; **рабо́тать на с.** to work conscientiously.

сове́т, а *m.* **1** advice; **проси́ть ~а** to ask for advice; (*leg.*) opinion. **2** (*совместное обсуждение*) discussion, council, conference; **вое́нный с.** council of war. **3** (*орган управления в СССР*) soviet. **4** (*административный орган*) council; **С. Безопа́сности** Security Council. **5** (*obs.*) (*согласие, дружба*) harmony, friendship.

сове́тник, а *m.* **1** adviser. **2** (*должность*) councillor.

сове́т|овать, ую *impf.* (*of* ⇒**по~**) (+*d.*) to advise.

сове́т|оваться, уюсь *impf.* (*of* ⇒**по~**) (**с**+*i.*) to consult, ask advice (of), seek advice (from).

сове́тск|ий *adj.* Soviet; **~ая власть** Soviet rule *or* power; **с. наро́д** the Soviet people.

Сове́тск|ий Сою́з, ~ого ~а *m.* the Soviet Union.

сове́тчик, а *m.* adviser, counsellor.

совеща́ни|е, я *nt.* conference, meeting; **с. на верха́х** summit conference.

совеща́тельный *adj.* consultative, deliberative.

совеща́|ться, юсь *impf.* **1** (**о**+*p.*) to deliberate (on, about). **2** (**с**+*i.*) to confer (with), consult.

сов|и́ный *adj. of* ⇒**~а́;** owlish.

совко́вый *adj.* (*sl., pej.*) Soviet.

совлада́|ть, ю *pf.* (**с**+*i.*; *coll.*) to control; **с. с собо́й** to control o.s.

совладе́л|ец, ьца *m.* joint owner, joint proprietor.

совладе́л|ица, ицы *f. of* ⇒**~ец**

совладе́ни|е, я *nt.* joint ownership.

совмести́мост|ь, и *f.* compatibility.

совмести́м|ый (**~, ~а**) *adj.* compatible.

совмести́тел|ь, я *m.* person having more than one job.

совмести́тельств|о, а *nt.* having more than one job; **рабо́тать по ~у** to have more than one job.

совме|сти́ть, щу́, сти́шь *pf.* (*of* ⇒**~ща́ть[2]**) to combine.

совме|сти́ться, сти́тся *pf.* (*of* ⇒**~ща́ться**) **1** (*совпасть*) to coincide. **2** (*оказаться одновременно существующим*) to be combined, combine.

совме́стно *adv.* in common, jointly.

совме́стн|ый *adj.* joint, combined; **~ые де́йствия** concerted action; **~ое обуче́ние** co-education; **~ое предприя́тие** joint venture; **~ая рабо́та** team-work.

совмеща́|ть[1], ю *impf.* to have more than one job.

C

совмещá|ть²(ся), ю, ет(ся) *impf. of* ⇒**совместúть(ся)**

совмещéни|е, я *nt.* combining.

совмúн, а *m.* (*abbr. of* ***совéт министров***) Council of Ministers.

сов|óк, кá *m.* **1** shovel, scoop; **садóвый с.** trowel; **с. для мýсора** dustpan. **2** (*sl.*) person with Soviet mentality.

совокуп|úть, лю, úшь *pf.* (*of* ⇒**~лять**) to combine, unite.

совокуп|úться, люсь, úшься *pf.* (*of* ⇒**~ляться**) (**с**+*i.*) to copulate (with).

совокуплéни|е, я *nt.* copulation.

совокупля́|ть(ся), ю(сь) *impf. of* ⇒**совокупúть(ся)**

совокýпно *adv.* in common, jointly.

совокýпност|ь, и *f.* aggregate, sum total; totality; **в ~и** in the aggregate; **по ~и** (+*g.*) on the basis (of).

совокýп|ный (~ен, ~на) *adj.* joint, combined, aggregate; **~ные усúлия** combined efforts.

совпадá|ть, ет *impf. of* ⇒**совпáсть**

совпадéни|е, я *nt.* coincidence.

совпá|сть, дёт, дýт *past* **~л** *pf.* (*of* ⇒**~дáть**) **1** (**с**+*i.*) (*произойти одновременно*) to coincide (with); **частúчно с.** to overlap. **2** (*оказаться общим*) to agree, concur, tally; **их показáния не ~ли** their evidence did not agree.

совратúтел|ь, я *m.* corrupter; (*женщин*) seducer.

совра|тúть, щý, тúшь *pf.* (*of* ⇒**~щáть**) (*соблазнить*) to lead astray; (*женщину*) to seduce.

совра|тúться, щýсь, тúшься *pf.* (*of* ⇒**~щáться**) to go astray.

совр|áть, ý, ёшь, *past* **~áл, ~алá, ~áло** *pf. of* ⇒**врать**

совращá|ть(ся), ю(сь) *impf. of* ⇒**совратúть(ся)**

совращéни|е, я *nt.* corrupting; (*женщины*) seducing, seduction.

совремéнник, а *m.* contemporary.

совремéнни|ца, цы *f. of* ⇒**~к**

совремéнност|ь, и *f.* **1** (*актуальность*) contemporaneity. **2** (*современная эпоха*) the present (time).

совремéн|ный (~ен, ~на) *adj.* **1** (+*d.*) (*относящийся к одному времени*) contemporaneous (with), of the time (of); **~ные Ивáну Грóзному понятия** ideas of the time of Ivan the Terrible. **2** (*относящийся к настоящему времени*) contemporary, present-day; (*человек*) modern; (*техника*) up-to-date, state-of-the-art; **~ная английская литератýра** modern English literature.

совсéм *adv.* quite, entirely, completely; **с. не** not at all, not in the least; **с. не то** nothing of the kind.

совхóз, а *m.* sovkhoz, State farm.

совхóз|ный *adj. of* ⇒**~**

согбéн|ный (~, ~на) *adj.* (*obs.*) bent, stooping.

соглáси|е, я *nt.* **1** (*разрешение*) consent; **с вáшего ~я** with your consent; **дать своё с.** to give one's consent. **2** (*единомыслие*) agreement; **в ~и** (**с**+*i.*) in accordance (with); **прийтú к ~ю** to come to an agreement. **3** (*единодушие*) harmony.

согласúтельн|ый *adj.* conciliatory; **~ая комиссия** conciliation commission.

согла|сúть, шý, сúшь *pf.* (*of* ⇒**~шáть**) to reconcile.

согла|сúться, шýсь, сúшься *pf.* (*of* ⇒**~шáться**) **1** (**на**+*a. or* +*inf.*) to consent (to), agree (to). **2** (**с**+*i.*) to agree (with).

соглáсно *adv.* **1** (*жить, петь*) in harmony. **2** *as prep.* (+*d. or* **с**+*i.*) in accordance (with); according (to); **с. договóру** in accordance with the treaty.

соглáсност|ь, и *f.* harmony, harmoniousness.

соглáс|ный¹ (~ен, ~на) *adj.* **1** (**на**+*a.*) agreeable (to); **онú нé были ~ны на нáши услóвия** they would not agree to our conditions. **2** (**с**+*i.*) in agreement (with), concordant (with); **быть ~ным** to agree (with); **~ен, ~на, ~ны?** do you agree? **3** (*хор, пение*) harmonious.

соглáс|ный² *adj.* (*gram.*) consonant(al); *as n.* **с., ~ого** *m.* consonant.

согласовáни|е, я *nt.* **1** (*действий*) co-ordination; (*разрешение*) agreement. **2** (*gram.*) agreement; **с. времён** sequence of tenses.

согласóванност|ь, и *f.* co-ordination; **с. во врéмени** synchronization.

согласóв|анный *p.p.p. of* ⇒**~áть** *and adj.* co-ordinated; **~анные дéйствия** concerted action; **с. текст** agreed text.

соглас|овáть, ýю *pf.* (*of* ⇒**~óвывать**) (**с**+*i.*) **1** to co-ordinate (with). **2**: **с. что-н. с кем-н.** to agree sth. with s.o., to come to an agreement with s.o. about sth. **3** (*gram.*) to make agree (with).

соглас|овáться, ýется *impf. and pf.* (**с**+*i.*) **1** to accord (with); to conform (to). **2** (*gram.*) to agree (with).

согласóвыва|ть, ю *impf. of* ⇒**согласовáть**

соглашáтел|ь, я *m.* (*pol.*; *pej.*) compromiser; appeaser.

соглашáтель|ский *adj. of* ⇒**~**; **~ская полúтика** policy of compromise, appeasement policy.

соглашáтельств|о, а *nt.* (*pol.*; *pej.*) compromise, appeasement.

соглашá|ть(ся), ю(сь) *impf. of* ⇒**согласúть(ся)**

соглашéни|е, я *nt.* **1** (*договорённость*) agreement, understanding. **2** (*договор*) agreement; **заключúть с.** to conclude an agreement.

соглядáта|й, я *m.* (*obs.*) spy.

согнá|ть¹, сгоню́, сгóнишь, *past* **~л, ~лá, ~ло** *pf.* (*of* ⇒**сгоня́ть**) (*удалить*) to drive away.

согнá|ть², сгоню́, сгóнишь, *past* **~л, ~лá, ~ло** *pf.* (*of* ⇒**сгоня́ть**) (*собрать*) to drive together, round up.

согн|ýть, ý, ёшь *pf.* (*of* ⇒**гнуть** *and* **сгибáть**) to bend, curve, crook.

согн|ýться, ýсь, ёшься *pf.* (*of* ⇒**гнýться** *and* **сгибáться**) to bend, bow (down).

согражданúн, а, *pl.* **сограждане, сограждан** *m.* fellow-citizen.

согревáни|е, я *nt.* warming, heating.

согревá|ть(ся), ю(сь) *impf. of* ⇒**согрéть(ся)**

согрé|ть, ю *pf.* (*of* ⇒**~вáть**) to warm, heat.

согрé|ться, юсь *pf.* (*of* ⇒**~вáться**) to get warm; to warm o.s.

согрешéни|е, я *nt.* sin, trespass.

согреш|úть, ý, úшь *pf.* (*of* ⇒**грешúть**) (**прóтив**+*g.*) to sin (against), trespass (against).

сóд|а, ы *f.* soda, sodium carbonate; **питьевáя с.** baking soda.

содéйстви|е, я *nt.* assistance, help.

содéйств|овать, ую *impf. and pf.* (*pf. also* **по~**) (+*d.*) to assist; to further; to contribute (to); **с. успéху предприя́тия** to contribute to the success of an undertaking.

содержáни|е, я *nt.* **1** (*семьи*) maintenance, upkeep; **(дéнежное) с.** allowance, financial support; **с. под арéстом** custody. **2** (*зарплата*) pay. **3** (*содержимое*) content; **кубúческое с.** volume; **с большúм ~ем** (+*g.*) rich (in). **4** (*сущность*) matter, substance; content; **фóрма и с.** form and content. **5** (*фабула*) content(s); plot (*of a novel, etc.*). **6** (*оглавление*) table of contents.

содержáнк|а, и *f.* (*obs.*) kept woman.

содержáтел|ь, я *m.* (*obs.*) owner, landlord.

содержáтель|ница, ницы *f. of* ⇒**~**

содержáтел|ьный (~ен, ~ьна) *adj.* rich in content; **~ьное письмó** interesting letter.

содерж|áть, ý, ~ишь *impf.* **1** (*семью*) to keep, maintain, support. **2** (*магазин*) to keep, have. **3** (**в**+*p.*) to keep (*in a given state*); **с. в исправности** to keep going, in working order; **с. в порядке** to keep in order; **с. под арéстом** to keep under arrest. **4** (*иметь в себе*) to contain; **егó перевóд ~ит мнóго ошúбок** his translation contains many mistakes.

содерж|áться, ýсь, ~ишься *impf.* **1** (*обеспечиваться*) to be kept, be maintained. **2** (*находиться*) to be kept, be; **с. под арéстом** to be under arrest. **3** (**в**+*p.*) (*заключаться*) to be contained (by); **в э́той рудé ~ится урáн** this ore contains uranium.

содержúм|ое, ого *nt.* contents.

содé|ять, ю, ешь *pf.* (*obs. or rhet.*) to commit, carry out.

содé|яться, ется *pf.* (*obs. or joc.*) to happen.

сóдов|ый *adj.* soda; **~ая водá** soda (water).

содóм, а *m.* (*coll.*) uproar, row; **поднять с.** to raise hell.

содоми́|я, и *f.* sodomy.

содра́|ть, сдеру́, сдерёшь, *past* **~л, ~ла́, ~ло** *pf.* (*of* ⇒**сдира́ть** *and* **драть**) **1** to tear off, strip off; **с. ко́жу** (**с**+*g.*) to skin, flay. **2** (*fig., coll.*) to fleece.

содрога́ни|е, я *nt.* shudder.

содрог|а́ться, а́юсь *impf. of* ⇒**~ну́ться**

содрог|ну́ться, ну́сь, нёшься *pf.* (*of* ⇒**~а́ться**) to shudder, shake, quake.

содру́жеств|о, а *nt.* **1** (*дружба*) concord; **рабо́тать в те́сном ~е** (**с**+*i.*) to work in close co-operation (with). **2** (*объединение*) community, commonwealth; **Брита́нское с. на́ций** the British Commonwealth.

со́евый *adj.* soya; **с. творо́г** tofu.

соедине́ни|е, я *nt.* **1** joining, combination. **2** (*tech.*) joint. **3** (*chem.*) compound. **4** (*mil.*) formation.

Соединённ|ое Королевств|о, ~ого ~а *nt.* United Kingdom.

Соединённ|ые Шта́т|ы (Аме́рики), ~ых ~ов (А.) *no sg.* United States (of America).

соедин|ённый *p.p.p. of* ⇒**~и́ть** *and adj.* united, joint.

соедини́тельн|ый *adj.* connecting; **~ая коро́бка** (*elec.*) junction box; **~ые ско́бки** (*typ.*) brace; **с. сою́з** (*gram.*) copulative conjunction; **~ая ткань** (*biol.*) connective tissue; **~ая тя́га** coupling rod.

соедин|и́ть, ю́, и́шь *pf.* (*of* ⇒**~я́ть**) **1** (*объединить*) to join, unite. **2** (*присоединить*) to connect, link; **с. по телефо́ну** to put through. **3** (*chem.*) to combine.

соедин|и́ться, ю́сь, и́шься *pf.* (*of* ⇒**~я́ться**) **1** to join, unite. **2** (*chem.*) to combine. **3** *pass. of* ⇒**~и́ть**

соедин|я́ть(ся), я́ю(сь) *impf. of* ⇒**~и́ть(ся)**

сожале́ни|е, я *nt.* **1** (**о**+*p.*) regret (for); **к ~ю** unfortunately. **2** (**к**+*d.*) pity (for).

сожале́|ть, ю *impf.* (**о**+*p. or* +**что**) to regret, deplore.

сожже́ни|е, я *nt.* burning; **с. на костре́** burning at the stake; **преда́ть ~ю** to commit to the flames.

сожи́тел|ь, я *m.* **1** (*по квартире*) flat-mate (*Br.*), room-mate (*US*). **2** (*любовник*) lover.

сожи́тель|ница, ницы *f. of* ⇒**~**

сожи́тельств|о, а *nt.* **1** living together, lodging together. **2** (*fig.*) (*интимные отношения*) sexual relations.

сожи́тельств|овать, ую *impf.* (**с**+*i.*) **1** to live (with), lodge (with); to live together. **2** (*fig.*) to have a sexual relationship (with).

сожр|а́ть, у́, ёшь, *past* **~а́л, ~ала́, ~а́ло** *pf. of* ⇒**жрать**

созва́нива|ться, юсь *impf. of* ⇒**созвони́ться**

созва́|ть, созову́, созовёшь, *past* **~л, ~ла́, ~ло** *pf.* **1** (*impf.* **созыва́ть** *and* **сзыва́ть**) (*гостей*) to gather; to invite. **2** (*impf.* **созыва́ть**) (*людей на совет*) to call (together), summon; (*митинг, парламент*) to convoke, convene.

созве́зди|е, я *nt.* constellation.

созвон|и́ться, ю́сь, и́шься *pf.* (*of* ⇒**созва́ниваться**) (**с**+*i.*; *coll.*) to speak on the telephone (to).

созву́чи|е, я *nt.* **1** (*mus.*) accord, consonance. **2** (*liter.*) assonance.

созву́ч|ный (~ен, ~на) *adj.* **1** harmonious. **2** (+*d.*) consonant (with), in keeping (with); **произведе́ние, ~ное эпо́хе** a work in keeping with the times.

созда|ва́ть(ся), ю́, ёт(ся) *impf. of* ⇒**~́ть(ся)**

созда́ни|е, я *nt.* **1** (*действие*) creation, making. **2** (*произведение*) creation, work. **3** (*существо*) creature.

созда́тел|ь, я *m.* **1** creator; (*организации*) founder; (*теории*) originator. **2** (*Бог*) the Creator.

созда́тель|ница, ницы *f. of* ⇒**~**

созда́|ть, м, шь, ст, ди́м, ди́те, ду́т, *past* **со́здал, ~ла́, со́здало** *pf.* (*of* ⇒**~ва́ть**) to create; (*организацию*) to found; (*теорию*) to originate; **с. впечатле́ние** to give the impression; **с. иллю́зию** to create an illusion.

созда́|ться, стся, ду́тся, *past* **~лся, ~ла́сь, ~ло́сь** *and* **~́лось** *pf.* (*of* ⇒**~ва́ться**) to be created; to arise; **созда́ло́сь неприя́тное положе́ние** a disagreeable situation arose; **у нас созда́ло́сь впечатле́ние, что** we gained the impression that.

созерца́ни|е, я *nt.* contemplation.

созерца́тел|ь, я *m.* contemplative person; observer.

созерца́тел|ьный (~ен, ~ьна) *adj.* contemplative.

созерца́|ть, ю *impf.* to contemplate.

созида́ни|е, я *nt.* creation.

созида́тел|ь, я *m.* creator.

созида́тел|ьный (~ен, ~ьна) *adj.* creative, constructive.

созида́|ть, ю *impf.* (*no pf.*) to build up.

созна|ва́ть, ю́, ёшь *impf.* **1** *impf. of* ⇒**~́ть. 2** to be conscious (of), realize; **я́сно с.** to be alive (to).

созна|ва́ться, ю́сь, ёшься *impf. of* ⇒**~́ться**

созна́ни|е, я *nt.* **1** consciousness; **кла́ссовое с.** class-consciousness; **потеря́ть с.** to lose consciousness; **прийти́ в с.** to regain, recover consciousness. **2** (*ошибки, вины*) recognition, acknowledgement; **с. до́лга** sense of duty.

созна́тельност|ь, и *f.* **1** awareness. **2** (*намеренность*) deliberateness.

созна́тел|ьный (~ен, ~ьна) *adj.* **1** conscious. **2** (*отношение*) intelligent. **3** (*намеренный*) deliberate.

созна́|ть, ю *pf.* (*of* ⇒**~ва́ть**) to recognize, acknowledge; **с. свою́ оши́бку** to recognize one's mistake.

созна́|ться, юсь *pf.* (*of* ⇒**~ва́ться**) (**в**+*p.*) (*в ошибке*) to admit (to); (*в преступлении*) to confess (to); (*leg.*) to plead guilty; **нельзя́ не с.** it must be admitted.

созорнича́|ть, ю *pf. of* ⇒**озорнича́ть**

созрева́|ть, ю *impf. of* ⇒**созре́ть**

созре́|ть, ю *pf.* (*of* ⇒**~ва́ть**) to ripen, mature.

созы́в, а *m.* calling, summoning.

созыва́|ть, ю *impf. of* ⇒**созва́ть**

соизво́л|ить, ю, ишь *pf.* (*of* ⇒**~я́ть**) (+*inf.*; *obs. or joc.*) to deign (to), be pleased (to).

соизвол|я́ть, я́ю *impf. of* ⇒**~́ить**

соизмери́мост|ь, и *f.* commensurability.

соизмери́м|ый (~, ~а) *adj.* commensurable.

соиска́ни|е, я *nt.* gaining; **диссерта́ция на с. до́кторской сте́пени** doctoral dissertation.

соиска́тел|ь, я *m.* (+*g.*) candidate (for).

со́йк|а, и, *g. pl.* **со́ек** *f.* (*zool.*) jay.

со|йти́[1], йду́, йдёшь, *past* **~шёл, ~шла́** *pf.* (*of* ⇒**сходи́ть**) **1** (*с лестницы, горы*) to go down, come down; (*с автобуса, поезда*) to get off; **с. с ло́шади** to dismount; **с. на не́т** to come to naught. **2** (*покинуть, уйти*) to leave; **с. с доро́ги** to get out of the way, step aside; **с. с ре́льсов** to come off the rails; **снег ~шёл** the snow has melted; **с. с ума́** to go mad, go off one's head. **3** (*о краске, о коже*) to come off.

со|йти́[2], йду́, йдёшь, *past* **~шёл, ~шла́** *pf.* (*of* ⇒**сходи́ть**) **1** (**за**+*a.*) to pass (for), be taken (for). **2** (*coll.*) (*пройти удачно*) to pass, go off; **~шло́ благополу́чно** it went off all right; **~йдёт и так** it will do as it is; **э́то ~шло́ ему́ с рук** he got away with it.

со|йти́сь, йду́сь, йдёшься, *past* **~шёлся, ~шла́сь** *pf.* (*of* ⇒**сходи́ться**) **1** (*встретиться*) to meet; to come together, gather. **2** (**с**+*i.*) (*подружиться*) to meet, take up (with), become friends (with); (*вступить в сожительство*) to become (*sexually*) intimate (with). **3** (+*i.*, **в**+*p. or* **на**+*p.*) (*договориться*) to agree (about); **с. в цене́** to agree about a price; **они́ не ~шли́сь хара́ктерами** they could not get on. **4** (*совпасть*) to agree, tally; **счета́ не ~шли́сь** the figures did not tally.

сок, а (у), о ~е, в *and* **на ~у́** *m.* juice; (*coll.*): **в (по́лном) ~у́** in the prime of life; **вари́ться в со́бственном ~у́** to keep o.s. to o.s.

соковыжима́лк|а, и *f.* juicer.

со́кол, а *m.* falcon (*also fig., rhet.*; *of air aces*); **гол как соко́л** (*coll.*) as poor as a church mouse.

соколи́н|ый *adj. of* ⇒**со́кол; ~ая охо́та** falconry.

соко́льник, а *m.* (*hist.*) falconer.

сократи́м|ый (~, ~а) *adj.* **1** (*math.*) able to be cancelled. **2** (*physiol.*) contractile.

сокра|ти́ть, щу́, ти́шь *pf.* (*of* ⇒**~ща́ть**) **1** (*статью, путь,*

С

рабочий день) to shorten. **2** (*расходы, штаты*) to reduce, cut down. **3** (*уволить*) to dismiss, discharge, lay off. **4** (*math.*) to cancel.

сокра|ти́ться, ти́тся *pf.* (*of* ⇒**~ща́ться**) **1** (*о днях*) to grow shorter. **2** (*о расходах*) to decrease. **3** (**на** + *a.*; *math.*) to be cancelled (by). **4** (*physiol.*) (*о мышцах*) to contract.

сокраща́|ть(ся), ю, ет(ся) *impf. of* ⇒**сократи́ть(ся)**

сокраще́ни|е, я *nt.* **1** (*рабочего дня*) shortening. **2** (*статьи*) abridgement; **с ~ями** abridged. **3** (*слова*) abbreviation. **4** (*штатов, вооружений*) reduction, cutting down. **5** (*math.*) cancellation. **6** (*physiol.*) contraction.

сокращённо *adv.* briefly; in abbreviated form.

сокра|щённый *p.p.p. of* ⇒**~ти́ть** *and adj.* brief; **~щённое сло́во** abbreviation, contraction.

сокрове́нност|ь, и *f.* secrecy.

сокрове́н|ный (~, ~на) *adj.* secret, concealed; **~ные мы́сли** innermost thoughts.

сокро́вищ|е, а *nt.* treasure; **ни за каки́е ~а** not for the world.

сокро́вищниц|а, ы *f.* treasure-house, treasure-trove (*also fig.*).

сокруш|а́ть, а́ю *impf. of* ⇒**~и́ть**

сокруша́|ться, юсь *impf.* (**о** + *p.*) to grieve (for, over); to be distressed (about).

сокруше́ни|е, я *nt.* **1** smashing, shattering. **2** (*obs.*) (*печаль*) grief, distress.

сокруш|ённый *p.p.p. of* ⇒**~и́ть** *and adj.* grief-stricken.

сокруши́тел|ьный (~ен, ~ьна) *adj.* shattering; **нанести́ с. уда́р** (+*d.*) to deal a crippling blow.

сокруш|и́ть, у́, и́шь *pf.* (*of* ⇒**~а́ть**) **1** (*уничтожить*) to shatter, smash. **2** (*fig.*) (*привести в отчаяние*) to shatter; to distress.

сокры́ти|е, я *nt.* concealment; **с. кра́деного** receiving of stolen goods.

сокр|ы́ть, о́ю, о́ешь *pf.* (*obs.*) to hide, conceal, cover up.

соку́рсник, а *m.* classmate.

соку́рсни|ца, цы *f. of* ⇒**~к**

со|лга́ть, лгу́, лжёшь, лгут, *past* **~лга́л, ~лгала́, ~лга́ло** *pf. of* ⇒**лгать**

солда́т, а, *g. pl.* **~** *m.* soldier; **служи́ть в ~ах** (*obs.*) to soldier, be a soldier.

солда́тик, а *m.* **1** *dim. of* ⇒**солда́т.** **2** toy soldier; **игра́ть в ~и** to play soldiers.

солда́тк|а, и *f.* soldier's wife.

солда́т|ский *adj. of* ⇒**~**

солда́тчин|а, ы *f.* (*obs.*) military service.

солдафо́н, а *m.* (*coll., pej.*) crude, loud-mouthed soldier.

солеваре́ни|е, я *nt.* salt production.

солева́р|енный (*and* **~ный)** *adj. of* ⇒**~е́ние; с. заво́д** salt-works.

солева́р|ня, ни, *g. pl.* **~ен** *f.* salt-works.

соле́ни|е, я *nt.* salting; pickling.

солено́ид, а *m.* (*elec.*) solenoid.

солён|ый *adj.* **1** salt; **~ое о́зеро** salt lake. **2** (**со́лон, солона́, со́лоно**) (*суп*) salty; **у меня́ во рту́ со́лоно** I have a salt taste in my mouth. **3** (*консервированный*) salted; pickled; **с. огуре́ц** pickled cucumber; *as n.* **~ое, ~ого** *nt.* salty food. **4** (*fig., coll.*) (*непристойный*) salty, spicy; **с. анекдо́т** spicy story. **5** (*short forms only*) (*fig.*): **ему́ со́лоно пришло́сь** he got it hot; **верну́ться не со́лоно хлеба́вши** to come home empty-handed.

соле́нь|е, я *nt.* salted food(s); pickles.

солеци́зм, а *m.* (*ling.*) solecism.

солидаризáци|я, и *f.* making common cause.

солидаризи́р|оваться, уюсь *impf. and pf.* (**с** + *i.*) to express one's solidarity (with), make common cause (with), identify o.s. (with).

солида́рност|ь, и *f.* solidarity; **из ~и** (**с** + *i.*) in sympathy (with).

солида́р|ный *adj.* **(~ен, ~на)** (**с** + *i.*) at one (with), in sympathy (with).

соли́д|ный (~ен, ~на) *adj.* **1** (*прочный*) solid, strong, sound; **~ные зна́ния** sound knowledge. **2** (*серьёзный*) solid, sound; (*надёжный*) reliable, respectable; **с. челове́к** a solid man; **с. журна́л** respectable magazine. **3** (*coll.*) (*значительный*) respectable, sizeable; **~ная су́мма** tidy sum. **4** (*немолодой*) middle-aged; **челове́к ~ных лет** a middle-aged man.

солипси́зм, а *m.* solipsism.

солипси́ст, а *m.* solipsist.

солипси́ческий *adj.* solipsistic.

соли́ст, а *m.* soloist.

соли́ст|ка, ки *f. of* ⇒**~**

солите́р, а *m.* (*min.*) solitaire (diamond).

солитёр, а *m.* tapeworm.

сол|и́ть, ю́, ~́ишь *impf.* (*of* ⇒**по~**) **1** (*суп*) to salt. **2** (*огурцы*) to pickle; **с. мя́со** to corn meat.

со́лк|а, и *f.* salting; pickling.

со́лнечн|ый *adj.* **1** sun; solar; **~ое затме́ние** solar eclipse; **с. луч** sunbeam; **~ая пане́ль** solar panel; **~ые пя́тна** (*astron.*) sun-spots; **с. свет** sunlight, sunshine; **~ая систе́ма** solar system; **~ое сплете́ние** (*anat.*) solar plexus; **с. уда́р** (*med.*) sunstroke; **~ые часы́** sun-dial. **2** (*день, погода*) sunny.

со́лнц|е, а *nt.* sun; **на с.** in the sun; **гре́ться на с.** to sun o.s., bask in the sun.

солнцезащи́тн|ый *adj.*: **с. крем** sun-cream; **~ые очки́** sun-glasses.

солнцепёк, а *m.*: **на ~е** right in the sun, in the full blaze of the sun.

солнцестоя́ни|е, я *nt.* solstice.

со́ло 1 *adv.* solo. **2** *n.*; *nt. indecl.* solo.

солов|е́й, ья́ *m.* nightingale.

solове́|ть, ю, ешь *impf.* (*of* ⇒**о~**) (*coll.*) to become drowsy.

соло́вый *adj.* light bay.

солов|ьи́ный *adj. of* ⇒**~е́й**

со́лод, а *m.* malt.

соло́дк|а, и *f.* liquorice.

солодо́венный *adj.*: **с. заво́д** malt-house.

солодо́вый *adj. of* ⇒**со́лод**

соло́м|а, ы *f.* straw; (*для крыши*) thatch; **крыть ~ой** to thatch.

соло́менн|ый *adj.* **1** straw; **~ая вдова́** grass widow; **~ая кры́ша** thatch, thatched roof; **~ая шля́па** straw hat. **2** (*светло-жёлтый*) straw-coloured (*Br.*), -colored (*US*).

соло́минк|а, и *f.* straw; **хвата́ться за ~у** to catch, clutch at straws.

соло́мк|а, и *f.* **1** *dim. of* ⇒**соло́ма.** **2** (*collect.*) (*для спичек*) matchwood. **3** (*collect.*) (*печенье*) stick-like biscuits.

соломоре́зк|а, и *f.* (*agric.*) chaff-cutter.

солони́н|а, ы *f.* salted beef, corned beef.

соло́нк|а, и *f.* salt-cellar.

со́лоно *see* ⇒**солёный**

солонча́к, а́ *m.* salt-marsh.

сол|ь¹, и, *pl.* **~́и, ~е́й** *f.* **1** salt; **го́рькая с.** Epsom salts; **ка́менная с.** rock-salt. **2** (*fig.*) (*рассказа*) point; **с. земли́** the salt of the earth; **вот в чём вся с.** that's the whole point; **мно́го ~́и съесть (с кем-н.)** to spend a long time together (with s.o.).

соль² *nt. indecl.* (*mus.*) G; **с.-дие́з** G sharp; **ключ с.** treble clef, G clef.

со́л|ьный 1 *adj. of* ⇒**~о; с. но́мер** solo; **~ьная па́ртия** solo part. **2** *adj. of* ⇒**~ь²; с. ключ** treble clef.

сольфе́джио *nt. indecl.* (*mus.*) solfeggio, sol-fa.

соля́нк|а, ~и *f.* solyanka (*a sharp-tasting Russian soup of vegetables and meat or fish*).

солян|о́й *adj.* salt, saline; **~ы́е ко́пи** salt-mines; **с. раство́р** saline solution, brine.

солянокислый *adj.* (*chem.*) hydrochloric.

соля́н|ый *adj.* (*chem.*): **~ая кислота́** hydrochloric acid.

соля́ри|й, я *m.* solarium.

сом, а́ *m.* catfish.

Сомали́ *nt. indecl.* Somalia.

сомали́|ец, йца *m.* Somali.

сомали́|йка, йки *f. of* ⇒**~ец**

сомали́йский *adj.* Somali.

сомати́ческий *adj.* somatic.

со́мкн|утый *p.p.p. of* ⇒**~у́ть** *and adj.*; **с. строй** (*mil.*) close order.

сомкн|у́ть, у́, ёшь *pf.* (*of* ⇒**смыка́ть**) to close; **с. глаза́** to close one's eyes; **с. ряды́** (*mil.*) to close the ranks.

сомкн|у́ться, ётся *pf.* (*of* ⇒**смыка́ться**) to close (up).

сомна́мбул|а, ы *c.g.* sleep-walker, somnambulist.

сомнамбули́зм, а *m.* sleep-walking, somnambulism.

сомнева́|ться, юсь *impf.* **1** (**в** + *p.*) to doubt; to question; **я не ~юсь в его́ че́стности** I do not question his integrity. **2** to worry; **мо́жете не с.** you need not worry.

сомне́ни|е, я *nt.* doubt; uncertainty; **без (вся́кого) ~я, вне ~я** without (any) doubt, beyond doubt.

сомни́тел|ьный (~ен, ~ьна) *adj.* **1** (*непроверенный*) doubtful, questionable; **~ьно** it is doubtful, it is open to question. **2** (*подозрительный*) dubious; equivocal; **с. комплиме́нт** dubious compliment; **~ьные дела́** shady dealings.

сомно́жител|ь, я *m.* (*math.*) factor.

сон, сна *m.* **1** sleep; **ве́чный с.** (*fig.*) eternal rest; **во сне, сквозь с.** in one's sleep; **со сна** half awake; **у меня́ сна ни в одно́м глазу́ нет** (*coll.*) I am not in the least sleepy. **2** (*сновидение*) dream; **ви́деть во сне** to dream, have a dream (about).

сона́т|а, ы *f.* (*mus.*) sonata.

сонати́н|а, ы *f.* (*mus.*) sonatina.

соне́т, а *m.* sonnet.

сонли́вост|ь, и *f.* sleepiness, drowsiness.

сонли́в|ый (~, ~а) *adj.* sleepy, drowsy.

сонм, а *m.* (*arch. or joc.*) assembly, throng.

со́нмищ|е, а *nt.* = **сонм**

со́нник, а *m.* book of dream interpretations.

со́нный *adj.* **1** sleepy, drowsy (*also fig.*); **~ая арте́рия** (*anat.*) carotid artery; **~ая боле́знь** (*med.*) (*i*) sleeping sickness (*morbus dormitivus*), (*ii*) sleepy sickness (*Br.*), sleeping sickness (*US*) (*encephalitis lethargica*); **~ое ца́рство** the land of Nod. **2** (*снотворный*) sleeping, soporific; **~ые ка́пли** sleeping-draught (*Br.*), -draft (*US*).

соно́рный *adj.* (*ling.*) sonant.

со́н|я, и *f. and c.g.* **1** *f.* (*грызун*) dormouse. **2** *c.g.* (*coll.*) (*человек*) sleepyhead.

сообража́|ть, ю *impf.* **1** *impf. of* **⇒сообрази́ть. 2** *impf. only* **хорошо́, пло́хо с.** to be quick, slow on the uptake.

соображе́ни|е, я *nt.* **1** (*суждение*) consideration, thought; **приня́ть в с.** to take into consideration. **2** (*понимание*) understanding, grasp. **3** (*причина*) consideration, reason; (*мысль*) notion, idea; **по фина́нсовым ~ям** for financial reasons; **вы́сказать свой ~я** to express one's views.

сообрази́тельност|ь, и *f.* quickness, quick-wittedness.

сообрази́тел|ьный (~ен, ~ьна) *adj.* quick-witted, quick, sharp, bright.

сообра|зи́ть, жу́, зи́шь *pf.* (*of* **⇒~жа́ть**) **1** (*взвесить*) to consider, ponder, think out; to weigh (the pros and cons of). **2** (*понять*) to understand, grasp. **3** (*coll.*) (*устроить*) to think up, arrange.

сообра́зно *adv.* (**с**+*i.*) in conformity (with).

сообра́зност|ь, и *f.* conformity.

сообра́з|ный (~ен, ~на) *adj.* (**с**+*i.*) in conformity (with); **э́то ни с чем не ~но** it makes no sense at all.

сообраз|ова́ть, у́ю *impf. and pf.* (**с**+*i.*) to make conform (to), adapt (to); **с. расхо́ды с дохо́дами** to adapt expenditure to income.

сообраз|ова́ться, у́юсь *impf. and pf.* (**с**+*i.*) to conform (to), adapt o.s. (to).

сообща́ *adv.* together, jointly.

сообщ|а́ть, а́ю *impf. of* **⇒~и́ть**

сообщ|а́ться, а́юсь *impf.* **1** *impf. of* **⇒~и́ться. 2** *impf. only* (**с**+*i.*) to communicate (with), be in communication (with).

сообще́ни|е, я *nt.* **1** (*известие*) communication, report; **сро́чное** *or* **э́кстренное с.** news flash; **по после́дним ~ям** according to latest reports. **2** (*связь*) communication; **прямо́е с.** through connection; **пути́ ~я** communications (*rail, road, canal, etc.*).

соо́бществ|о, а *nt.* (*международное, мировое*) community; **в ~е (с**+*i.*) in association (with), together (with).

сообщ|и́ть, у́, и́шь *pf.* (*of* **⇒~а́ть**) **1** (+*a. or* **о**+*p.*) (*уведомить*) to communicate, report, inform, announce; **с. после́дние изве́стия** to report the latest news. **2** (*придать*) to impart; **с. материа́лу огнеупо́рность** to make a material fireproof.

сообщ|и́ться, и́тся *pf.* (*of* **⇒~а́ться**) to be communicated.

соо́бщник, а *m.* accomplice; partner (*in crime*); (*leg.*) accessory.

соо́бщни|ца, цы *f. of* **⇒~к**

соо́бщничеств|о, а *nt.* complicity.

соору|ди́ть, жу́, ди́шь *pf.* (*of* **⇒~жа́ть**) **1** to build, erect. **2** (*coll.*) (*ужин, шалаш*) to make hastily; to knock up (*Br.*).

сооружа́|ть, ю *impf. of* **⇒сооруди́ть**

сооруже́ни|е, я *nt.* **1** (*действие*) building, erection. **2** (*постройка*) building, structure; **вое́нные ~я** military installations.

соотве́тственно *adv.* **1** accordingly. **2** (+*d. or* **с**+*i.*) according (to), in accordance (with), in conformity (with).

соотве́тствен|ный (~, ~на) *adj.* (+*d.*) corresponding (to).

соотве́тстви|е, я *nt.* accordance, conformity, correspondence; **в ~и (с**+*i.*) in accordance (with); **привести́ в с.** (**с**+*i.*) to bring into line (with).

соотве́тств|овать, ую *impf.* (+*d.*) to correspond (to, with), conform (to); **с. действи́тельности** to correspond to the facts; **с. тре́бованиям** to meet the requirements; **с. це́ли** to answer the purpose.

соотве́тств|ующий *pres. part. act. of* **⇒~овать** *and adj.* **1** (+*d.*) corresponding (to). **2** (*подходящий*) proper, appropriate; **поступа́ть ~ующим о́бразом** to act accordingly.

сооте́чественник, а *m.* compatriot, fellow-countryman.

сооте́чественни|ца, цы *f. of* **⇒~к**

соотнес|ти́, у́, ёшь, *past* **~, ~ла́** *pf.* (*of* **⇒соотноси́ть**) to correlate.

соотноси́тел|ьный (~ен, ~ьна) *adj.* correlative.

соотно|си́ть, шу́, ~сишь *impf. of* **⇒соотнести́**

соотно|си́ться, ~сится *impf.* to correspond.

соотноше́ни|е, я *nt.* correlation, ratio; **с. сил** correlation of forces, alignment of forces.

сопе́рник, а *m.* rival.

сопе́рни|ца, цы *f. of* **⇒~к**

сопе́рнича|ть, ю *impf.* to be rivals; (**с**+*i.*) to compete (with), vie (with).

сопе́рничеств|о, а *nt.* rivalry.

соп|е́ть, лю́, и́шь *impf.* to breathe heavily and noisily through the nose.

со́пк|а, и *f.* **1** (*гора*) hill. **2** (*на Дальнем Востоке, вулкан*) volcano.

соплеме́нник, а *m.* fellow-tribesman.

сопли́в|ый (~, ~а) *adj.* (*coll.*) snotty.

соп|ло́, а́, *pl.* **~ла, ~ел** *nt.* (*tech.*) nozzle.

сопл|я́, и́, *pl.* **~и, ~е́й** *f.* **1** (nose-)drip; (*pl.*) snivel, snot. **2** (*coll., pej.*) = **сопля́к**

сопля́к, а́ *m.* (*coll., pej.*) milksop.

сопостави́м|ый (~, ~а) *adj.* comparable.

сопоста́в|ить, лю, ишь *pf.* (*of* **⇒~ля́ть**) (**с**+*i.*) to compare (with).

сопоставле́ни|е, я *nt.* comparison.

сопоставля́|ть, ю *impf. of* **⇒сопоста́вить**

сопра́но *indecl.* (*mus.*) **1** *nt.* (*голос*) soprano (*voice*). **2** *f.* (*певица*) soprano (*singer*).

сопреде́л|ьный (~ен, ~ьна) *adj.* neighbouring (*Br.*), neighboring (*US*), contiguous; (*fig.*) (*родственный*) related.

сопре́|ть, ю *pf. of* **⇒преть**

соприкаса́|ться, юсь *impf.* (*of* **⇒соприкосну́ться**) (**с**+*i.*) **1** to adjoin, be contiguous (to). **2** (*fig.*) (*общаться*) to come into contact (with).

соприкоснове́ни|е, я *nt.* contiguity; (*mil. and fig.*) contact; **име́ть с.** (**с**+*i.*) to come into contact (with).

соприкосн|у́ться, у́сь, ёшься *pf. of* **⇒соприкаса́ться**

сопрvíча́стност|ь, и *f.* complicity, participation.

сопри́ча́ст|ный (~ен, ~на) *adj.*: **быть с.** (**к**+*d.*) to be implicated (in), be a participant (in).

сопроводи́тел|ь, я *m.* escort.

сопроводи́тельн|ый *adj.* accompanying; **~ое письмо́** covering letter.

сопрово|ди́ть, жу́, ди́шь *pf. of* **⇒~жда́ть**

сопровожда́|ть, ю *impf.* (*of* **⇒сопроводи́ть**) to accompany.

сопровожда́|ться, ется *impf.* (+*instr.*) to be accompanied (by).

сопровожде́ни|е, я *nt.* **1** (*действие*) accompanying, escort; **в ~и** (+*g.*) accompanied (by); escorted (by). **2** (*mus.*) accompaniment; **звуково́е с.** soundtrack.

сопротивле́ни|е, я *nt.* resistance,

С

opposition; (*phys., tech.*) strength; (*elec.*) resistance, impedance; **оказа́ть с.** to put up resistance; **идти́ по ли́нии наиме́ньшего ~я** to take the line of least resistance.

сопротивля́емост|ь, и *f.* capacity to resist; (*elec.*) resistivity.

сопротивля́|ться, юсь *impf.* (+*d.*) to resist, oppose.

сопряжё́н|ный (~, ~а́) *adj.* (**с**+*i.*) linked (with), attended (by), entailing; **ваш прое́кт ~ с больши́м ри́ском** your scheme entails great risk.

сопу́тств|овать, ую *impf.* (+*d.*) to accompany; **~ующие обстоя́тельства** attendant circumstances, concomitants.

сор, а *m.* litter, rubbish; **не выноси́ть ~а из избы́** not to wash one's dirty linen in public.

соразме́р|ить, ю, ишь *pf.* (*of* ⇒**~я́ть**) (**с**+*i.*) to make commensurate (with), balance (with).

соразме́рност|ь, и *f.* proportionality.

соразме́р|ный (~ен, ~на) *adj.* proportionate.

соразмер|я́ть, я́ю *impf. of* ⇒**~ить**

сора́тник, а *m.* comrade-in-arms.

сорван|е́ц, ца́ *m.* (*coll.*) (*о ребёнке*) a terror; (*о девочке*) tomboy.

сорв|а́ть, у́, ёшь, *past* **~а́л, ~ала́, ~а́ло** *pf.* (*of* ⇒**срыва́ть**[1]) **1** (*отделить*) to tear off, break off, tear away, tear down; (*цветок*) to pick, pluck; **с. ве́тку** to break off a branch. **2** (*coll.*) (*добиться*) to get, extract; **с. с кого́-н. улы́бку** to get a smile out of s.o. **3** (**на**+*p.*) (*выместить*) to vent (upon); **с. гнев на ком-н.** to vent one's anger upon s.o. **4** (*нарушить*) to wreck, ruin, spoil; **с. забасто́вку** to break a strike; **с. банк** (*cards*) to break the bank.

сорв|а́ться, у́сь, ёшься, *past* **~а́лся, ~ала́сь, ~а́ло́сь** *pf.* (*of* ⇒**срыва́ться**) **1** (*освободиться*) to break away, break loose; **с. с пе́тель** to come off its hinges; **с. с ме́ста** (*coll.*) to dart off; **с. с языка́** to escape one's lips. **2** (*упасть*) to fall, come down; **с. с колоко́льни** to fall from the belfry. **3** (*coll.*) (*не удаться*) to fall through.

сорвиголов|а́, ы́, *pl.* **сорвиго́ловы, сорвиголо́в, сорвиголова́м** *c.g.* (*coll.*) daredevil; desperado.

сорганиз|ова́ть, у́ю *pf. of* ⇒**организова́ть**

со́рго *nt. indecl.* (*bot.*) sorghum.

соревнова́ни|е, я *nt.* **1** (*sport*) competition, contest; event; **кома́ндное с.** team event; **отбо́рочные ~я** elimination contests; **с. на пе́рвенство ми́ра** world championship. **2** (*действие*) competition.

соревн|ова́ться, у́юсь *impf.* (**с**+*i.*) to compete (with, against).

соревн|у́ющийся *pres. part. of* ⇒**~ова́ться;** *as n.* **с., ~у́ющегося** *m.* competitor, contender.

соригина́льнича|ть, ю *pf. of* ⇒**оригина́льничать**

сори́нк|а, и *f.* mote; speck of dust.

сор|и́ть, ю́, и́шь *impf.* (*of* ⇒**на~**) (+*a. or i.*) to drop litter; to make a mess; **с. в ко́мнате оку́рками** to litter a room with cigarette butts; **с. деньга́ми** to throw one's money about.

со́рн|ый *adj.* **1** *adj. of* ⇒**сор; ~ое ведро́** refuse pail. **2**: **~ая трава́** weed; (*collect.*) weeds.

сорня́к, а́ *m.* weed.

соро́дич, а *m.* **1** (*родственник*) relative. **2** (*соотечественник*) fellow-countryman.

со́рок *all other cases* **а́,** *num.* forty; **с. ~о́в** (*coll., obs.*) a multitude, a great number.

соро́к|а, и *f.* magpie; **с. на хвосте́ принесла́** a little bird told me, us, *etc.*

сорокале́ти|е, я *nt.* **1** (*срок*) forty years. **2** (*годовщина*) fortieth anniversary; (*день рождения*) fortieth birthday.

сорокале́тний *adj.* **1** (*срок*) forty-year, of forty years. **2** (*человек*) forty-year-old.

сороков|о́й *adj.* fortieth; **~ы́е го́ды** the forties.

сороконо́жк|а, и *f.* centipede.

сорокопя́тк|а, и *f.* (*coll.*) single (record).

соро́чк|а, и *f.* **1** shirt; blouse; (*нижняя*) camisole; **ночна́я с.** (*мужская*) night-shirt; (*женская*) night-dress. **2** (*игральной карты*) reverse. **3** (*med.*) caul; **роди́ться в ~е** to be born with a silver spoon in one's mouth.

сорт, а, *pl.* **~а́** *m.* **1** (*качество*) grade, quality; **вы́сший с.** best quality; **пе́рвого ~а** first grade, first-rate. **2** (*разновидность*) sort, kind, variety.

сорти́р, а *m.* (*coll.*) loo.

сортир|ова́ть, у́ю *impf.* (*товар, уголь*) to sort, grade; (*корреспонденцию*) to sort; (*comput.*) to sort.

сортиро́вк|а, и *f.* sorting, grading.

сортиро́вочн|ый *adj.* sorting; *as n.* **~ая, ~ой** *f.* marshalling (*Br.*), marshaling (*US*) yard.

сортиро́вщик, а *m.* sorter.

сортиро́вщи|ца, цы *f. of* ⇒**~к**

со́ртност|ь, и *f.* grade, quality.

со́ртный *adj.* high-quality.

сортово́й *adj.* high-grade, high-quality.

соса́ни|е, я *nt.* sucking.

соса́тельный *adj.* sucking.

сос|а́ть, у́, ёшь *impf.* to suck.

сосва́та|ть, ю *pf. of* ⇒**сва́тать**

сосе́д, а, *pl.* **~и, ~ей** *m.* neighbour (*Br.*), neighbor (*US*); **с. по кварти́ре** flatmate (*Br.*), room-mate (*US*); **с. по купе́** (*rail.*) fellow passenger.

сосе́д|ить, ишь *impf.* (**с**+*i.*) to be adjacent (to), adjoin.

сосе́д|ка, ки *f. of* ⇒**~**

сосе́дн|ий *adj.* neighbouring (*Br.*), neighboring (*US*); adjacent, next; **с. дом** the house next door; **~яя ко́мната** the next room.

сосе́д|ский *adj. of* ⇒**~**

сосе́дств|о, а *nt.* neighbourhood (*Br.*), neighborhood (*US*); vicinity; **по ~у** (+*g.*) near, in the vicinity (of).

соси́ск|а, и *f.* sausage; (*варёная*) frankfurter.

со́ск|а, и *f.* **1** (*пустышка*) dummy. **2** (*на бутылке*) teat.

соска́блива|ть, ю *impf. of* ⇒**соскобли́ть**

соска́кива|ть, ю *impf. of* ⇒**соскочи́ть**

соска́льзыва|ть, ю *impf. of* ⇒**соскользну́ть**

соскобл|и́ть, ю́, ~и́шь *pf.* (*of* ⇒**соска́бливать**) to scrape off.

соско́к, а *m.* jump (down).

соскользн|у́ть, у́, ёшь *pf.* (*of* ⇒**соска́льзывать**) (*упасть*) to slip off, slide off; (*с горы*) to slide down.

соскоч|и́ть, у́, ~ишь *pf.* (*of* ⇒**соска́кивать**) **1** (*с трамвая, с коня*) to jump off, leap off; (*с дерева*) to jump down, leap down; **с. с крова́ти** to jump out of bed. **2** (*упасть*) to come off; **с. с пе́тель** to come off its hinges. **3** (**с**+*g.*; *coll.*) (*исчезнуть*) to disappear (from), leave; **хмель ~и́л с него́** he sobered up.

соскреба́|ть, ю *impf. of* ⇒**соскрести́**

соскре|сти́, бу́, бёшь, *past* **~б, ~бла́** *pf.* (*of* ⇒**~ба́ть**) to scrape away, off.

соску́ч|иться, усь, ишься *pf.* **1** (*почувствовать скуку*) to become bored. **2** (**по**+*p.*, *preceding sg. nn.*; **по**+*d.*, *preceding pl. nn.*) to miss; **с. по дере́вне** to miss the country; **с. по друзья́м** to miss one's friends.

сослага́тельный *adj.* (*gram.*) subjunctive.

со|сла́ть, шлю́, шлёшь *pf.* (*of* ⇒**ссыла́ть**) to exile, banish.

со|сла́ться, шлю́сь, шлёшься *pf.* (*of* ⇒**ссыла́ться**) (**на**+*a.*) **1** (*указать*) to refer (to), allude (to); (*процитировать*) to cite, quote. **2** (*оправдаться*) to plead; **с. на недомога́ние** to plead indisposition.

со́слепа *adv.* (*coll.*) due to poor sight.

со́слеп|у *adv.* = **~а**

сосло́ви|е, я *nt.* (social) class; **дворя́нское с.** the nobility; **духо́вное с.** the clergy; **купе́ческое с.** the merchants.

сосло́в|ный *adj. of* ⇒**~ие; с. предрассу́док** class prejudice.

сослужи́в|ец, ца *m.* colleague, fellow-employee.

сослужи́в|ица, ицы *f. of* ⇒**~ец**

сослуж|и́ть, у́, ~ишь *pf.*: **с. кому́-н. слу́жбу** to do s.o. a good turn; (*о вещи*) to stand s.o. in good stead.

сосн|а́, ы́, *pl.* **~ы, со́сен** *f.* pine (-tree).

сосно́вый *adj.* pine.

сосн|у́ть, у́, ёшь *pf.* (*coll.*) to have, take a nap.

сосня́к, а́ *m.* pine forest.

сос|о́к, ка́ *m.* nipple.

сосредото́чени|е, я *nt.* (*mil., etc.*) concentration.

сосредото́ченност|ь, и *f.* (degree of) concentration.

сосредото́ч|енный *p.p.p. of* ⇒**~ить** *and adj.* concentrated; **с. взгляд** fixed stare; **~енное внима́ние** rapt attention.

сосредото́чива|ть(ся), ю(сь) *impf. of* ⇒**сосредото́чить(ся)**

сосредото́ч|ить, у, ишь *pf.* (*of* ⇒**~ивать**) to concentrate; to focus; **с. внима́ние** (**на** + *p.*) to concentrate one's attention (on, upon).

сосредото́ч|иться, усь, ишься *pf.* (*of* ⇒**~иваться**) **1** (**на** + *p.*) to concentrate (on, upon). **2** *pass. of* ⇒**~ить**

соста́в, а *m.* **1** (*вещества*) composition, make-up; structure; **социа́льный с.** social structure; **хими́ческий с.** (*i*) (*совокупность частей*) chemical composition, (*ii*) (*само соединение*) chemical compound; **входи́ть в с.** (+*g.*) to form part (of); **с. преступле́ния** (*leg.*) corpus delicti. **2** (*коллектив людей*) staff, personnel; **ли́чный с.** personnel; **нали́чный с.** available personnel; **с. (актёров)** cast; (*mil.*) effectives; **офице́рский с.** the officers; **в по́лном ~е** with its full complement; in, at full strength; **в ~е** (+*g.*) numbering, consisting (of), amounting (to); **делега́ция в ~е тридцати́ челове́к** a delegation of thirty (persons); **входи́ть в с.** (+*g.*) to be a member (of); **войти́ в с.** (+*g.*) to become a member (of). **3** (*поезд*) train; **подвижно́й с.** rolling-stock.

состави́тел|ь, я *m.* compiler, author.

состави́тель|ница, ницы *f. of* ⇒**~**

соста́в|ить[1], лю, ишь *pf.* (*of* ⇒**~ля́ть**) **1** (*собрать, соединить*) to put together; **с. посу́ду** to stack crockery. **2** (*список, проект*) to make, draw up; to compile; to form, construct; **с. библиоте́ку** to form a library; **с. мне́ние** to form an opinion; **с. предложе́ние** to construct a sentence; **с. слова́рь** to compile a dictionary. **3** (*являться*) to be, constitute, make; **э́то не ~ит большо́го труда́** this will not constitute a lot of work. **4** (*образовать*) to form, make, amount to, total; **с. в сре́днем** to average; **расхо́ды ~или пятьсо́т фу́нтов** expenditure amounted to five hundred pounds. **5**: **с. себе́** to make (for o.s.); **с. себе́ и́мя** to make a name for o.s.

соста́в|ить[2], лю, ишь *pf.* (*of* ⇒**~ля́ть**) (*сверху вниз*) to take down, put down; **с. я́щик на пол** to put a drawer down on the floor.

соста́в|иться, ится *pf.* (*of* ⇒**~ля́ться**) to form, be formed, come into being.

составля́|ть(ся), ю, ет(ся) *impf. of* ⇒**соста́вить(ся)**

составн|о́й *adj.* **1** (*составленный из некоторых частей*) compound, composite; **~а́я кни́жная по́лка** sectional book-shelf. **2** (*входящий в состав чего-н.*) component; **~а́я часть** component, constituent.

соста́р|ить(ся), ю, ет(ся) *pf. of* ⇒**ста́рить(ся)**

состоя́ни|е, я *nt.* **1** state, condition; position; **в хоро́шем, плохо́м ~и** in good, bad condition; **быть в ~и войны́** (**с** + *i.*) to be at war (with); **быть в ~и** (+*inf.*) to be able (to), be in a position (to). **2** (*obs.*) (*социальное положение*) status; **гражда́нское с.** civil status. **3** (*имущество*) fortune; **нажи́ть с.** to make a fortune.

состоя́тельност|ь[1], и *f.* (*богатство*) wealth.

состоя́тельност|ь[2], и *f.* (*обоснованность*) justifiability, strength (*of an argument, etc.*).

состоя́тел|ьный[1] (~ен, ~ьна) *adj.* (*богатый*) well-off.

состоя́тел|ьный[2] (~ен, ~ьна) *adj.* (*обоснованный*) well-grounded.

состо|я́ть, ю́, и́шь *impf.* **1** (**из** + *g.*) to consist (of), comprise, be made up (of); **кварти́ра ~и́т из трёх ко́мнат** the flat consists of three rooms. **2** (**в** + *p.*) to consist (in), lie (in), be; **ра́зница ~и́т в том, что**... the difference is that.... **3** (*быть*) to be; **с. в па́ртии** to be a member of a party; **с. чле́ном о́бщества** to be a member of a society; **с. под судо́м** to be awaiting trial; **с. при посо́льстве** to be attached to the embassy.

состо|я́ться, и́тся *pf.* to take place; **визи́т не ~я́лся** the visit did not take place.

сострáгива|ть, ю *impf. of* ⇒**сострога́ть**

сострада́ни|е, я *nt.* compassion, sympathy.

сострада́тел|ьный (~ен, ~ьна) *adj.* compassionate, sympathetic.

сострада́|ть, ю *impf.* (+*d.*; *obs.*) to feel pity (for).

сострига́|ть, ю *impf. of* ⇒**состри́чь**

состр|и́ть, ю́, и́шь *pf. of* ⇒**остри́ть**

состри́|чь, гу́, жёшь, гу́т, *past* **~г, ~гла** *pf.* (*of* ⇒**~га́ть**) to shear, clip off.

сострога́|ть, ю *pf.* (*of* ⇒**сострáгивать**) to plane off.

сostро́|ить, ю, ишь *pf. of* ⇒**стро́ить** 3; **с. грима́су, с. ро́жу** (*coll.*) to make a face.

состря́па|ть, ю *pf. of* ⇒**стря́пать**

состык|ова́ть(ся), у́ю, у́ет(ся) *pf. of* ⇒**стыкова́ть(ся)**

состяза́ни|е, я *nt.* competition, contest; match; **с. в пла́вании** swimming contest; **с. по фехтова́нию** fencing match; **с. в остроу́мии** battle of wits.

состяза́|ться, юсь *impf.* (**с** + *i.*) to compete (with).

сосу́д, а *m.* vessel.

сосу́дистый *adj.* (*anat., biol.*) vascular.

сосу́льк|а, и *f.* icicle.

сосуществова́ни|е, я *nt.* co-existence.

сосуществ|ова́ть, у́ю *impf.* to co-exist.

сос|у́щий *pres. part. act. of* ⇒**~а́ть** *and adj.* (*zool.*) suctorial.

сосчита́|ть, ю *pf. of* ⇒**счита́ть**

сосчита́|ться, юсь *pf.* (**с** + *i.*) (*coll.*) to settle accounts (with), get even (with) (*also fig.*).

сотворе́ни|е, я *nt.* creation, making; **с. ми́ра** the creation of the world.

сотвор|и́ть, ю́, и́шь *pf. of* ⇒**твори́ть**

со́тенн|ая, ой *f.* (*coll.*) hundred-rouble note.

со́тенный *adj.* (*coll.*) worth a hundred roubles.

со́тк|а, и *f.* hundredth part.

сотк|а́ть, у́, ёшь, *past* **~а́л, ~ала́, ~а́ло** *pf. of* ⇒**ткать**

со́тник, а *m.* (*hist.*) sotnik (*lieutenant of Cossack troops*).

со́т|ня, ни, *g. pl.* **~ен** *f.* **1** (*сто*) a hundred (*esp. a hundred roubles*). **2** (*hist.*) sotnya, company (*mil. unit, originally of a hundred men*); **каза́чья с.** Cossack squadron.

сотова́рищ, а *m.* associate, partner.

сотови́д|ный (~ен, ~на) *adj.* honeycomb.

со́т|овый *adj.* **1** *adj. of* ⇒**~ы**; **с. мёд** comb-honey. **2** (*tech.*) honeycomb; **с. телефо́н** cellular phone, mobile phone.

сотрапе́зник, а *m.* (*obs.*) table-companion.

сотру́дник, а *m.* **1** (*коллега*) colleague. **2** (*служащий*) employee, worker; **нау́чный с.** research assistant; **с. посо́льства** embassy official. **3** (*газеты, журнала*) contributor.

сотру́дни|ца, цы *f. of* ⇒**~к**

сотру́днича|ть, ю *impf.* **1** (**с** + *i.*) to work (with). **2** (**в** + *p.*) to contribute (to); **с. в газе́те** to contribute to a newspaper; to work on a newspaper.

сотру́дничеств|о, а *nt.* collaboration, co-operation.

сотряс|а́ть(ся), а́ю(сь) *impf. of* ⇒**~ти́(сь)**

сотрясе́ни|е, я *nt.* shaking; **с. мо́зга** (*med.*) concussion.

сотряс|ти́, у́, ёшь, *past* **~, ~ла́** *pf.* (*of* ⇒**~а́ть**) to shake.

сотряс|ти́сь, у́сь, ёшься, *past* **~ся, ~ла́сь** *pf.* (*of* ⇒**~а́ться**) to shake, tremble.

со́т|ы, ов *no sg.* honeycombs; **мёд в ~ах** honey in combs.

со́т|ый *adj.* hundredth; **с. год** the year one hundred; *as n.* **~ая, ~ой** *f.* (a) hundredth.

со́ул, а *m.*: **(му́зыка) с.** soul music.

соумы́шленник, а *m.* accomplice.

со́ус, а *m.* sauce; (*мясной*) gravy; (*к салату*) dressing.

со́усник, а *m.* sauce-boat, gravy-boat.

соуча́ств|овать, ую *impf.* (**в** + *p.*) to participate (in), take part (in).

соуча́сти|е, я *nt.* complicity.

соуча́стник, а *m.* accomplice; **с. преступле́ния, с. в преступле́нии** (*leg.*) accessory to a crime.

соуча́стни|ца, цы *f. of* ⇒**~к**

С

соученик, а́ *m.* schoolmate, schoolfellow.

соучени́|ца, цы *f. of* ⇒~к

соф|а́, ы́, *pl.* ~ы *f.* sofa.

софи́зм, а *m.* sophism, sophistry.

софи́ст, а *m.* sophist.

софи́стик|а, и *f.* sophistry.

софисти́ческий *adj.* sophistic(al).

Софи́|я, и *f.* Sofia.

сох|а́, и́, *pl.* ~и *f.* (*wooden*) plough (*Br.*), plow (*US*).

соха́т|ый (~, ~а) *adj.* (*dial.*) with branching antlers; *as n.* **с., ~ого** *m.* elk, moose.

со́х|нуть, ну, нёшь, *past* ~, ~**ла** *impf.* **1** (*о белье*) to dry, get dry; (*о губах*) to become parched. **2** (*вянуть*) to wither; (*fig.*) (*от любви*) to pine. **3** (*coll.*) (*худеть*) to get thin.

сохране́ни|е, я *nt.* **1** preservation; conservation; (*попечение*) care, custody; **отда́ть кому́-н. на с.** to give into s.o.'s charge. **2** (*права*) retention; **о́тпуск с ~ем содержа́ния** holiday(s) with pay.

сохран|и́ть, ю, и́шь *pf.* (*of* ⇒~**я́ть**) **1** (*сберечь*) to preserve, keep; to keep safe; **с. ве́рность** (+*d.*) to remain faithful, loyal (to); **с. на па́мять** to keep as a souvenir. **2** (*не потерять*) to keep, retain, reserve; **с. хладнокро́вие** to keep cool; **с. за собо́й пра́во** to reserve the right; (*comput.*) to save.

сохран|и́ться, ю́сь, и́шься *pf.* (*of* ⇒~**я́ться**) **1** to remain (intact); to last out, hold out; **он хорошо́ ~и́лся** he is well preserved. **2** *pass. of* ⇒~**и́ть**

сохра́нно *adv.* safely, intact.

сохра́нност|ь, и *f.* safety, undamaged state; **в ~и** safe, intact.

сохра́н|ный (~ен, ~на) *adj.* safe; undamaged.

сохраня́емост|ь, и *f.* shelf-life.

сохран|я́ть(ся), я́ю(сь) *impf. of* ⇒~**и́ть(ся)**

соц... *comb. form, abbr. of*
1 ***социа́льный.***
2 ***социалисти́ческий***

соцбло́к, а *m.* Eastern bloc.

соцве́ти|е, я *nt.* (*bot.*) inflorescence.

социа́л-демокра́т, а *m.* social democrat.

социа́л-демократи́ческий *adj.* social democratic.

социа́л-демокра́ти|я, и *f.* social democracy.

социализа́ци|я, и *f.* socialization.

социализи́р|овать, ую *impf. and pf.* to socialize.

социали́зм, а *m.* socialism.

социали́ст, а *m.* socialist.

социалисти́ческий *adj.* socialist.

социали́ст|ка, ки *f. of* ⇒~

социали́ст-революционе́р, а *m.* (*hist.*) socialist revolutionary.

социа́льно-бытово́й *adj.* social, welfare.

социа́льно-экономи́ческий *adj.* socio-economic.

социа́льн|ый *adj.* social; **~ое обеспе́чение** social security; **~ое положе́ние** social status.

социо́лог, а *m.* sociologist.

социологи́ческий *adj.* sociological.

социоло́ги|я, и *f.* sociology.

соцреали́зм, а *m.* socialist realism.

соцстра́х, а *m.* (*abbr. of* ***социа́льное страхова́ние***) social insurance.

соч. (*abbr. of* ***сочине́ния***) works (*of creative artist*).

соче́льник, а *m.* (*eccl.*): **рожде́ственский с.** Christmas Eve; **креще́нский с.** Twelfth-night, eve of the Epiphany.

сочета́ни|е, я *nt.* combination.

сочета́|ть, ю *impf. and pf.* (**с**+*i.*) to combine (with).

сочета́|ться, юсь *impf. and pf.* **1** to combine; **в ней ~лся ум с красото́й** she combined intelligence and good looks. **2** (**с**+*i.*) (*гармонировать*) to harmonize (with), go (with); to match.

сочине́ни|е, я *nt.* **1** (*действие*) composing. **2** (*произведение*) work; **и́збранные ~я Го́голя** selected works of Gogol. **3** (*школьное*) composition, essay.

сочини́тел|ь, я *m.* **1** (*obs.*) (*писатель*) writer, author. **2** (*coll.*) (*выдумщик*) story-teller, fabricator.

сочини́тельный *adj.* (*gram.*) coordinating.

сочини́тельств|о, а *nt.* **1** (*obs.*) writing. **2** (*pej.*) scribbling, hack-writing. **3** (*coll.*) (*выдумывание*) fabrication.

сочин|и́ть, ю́, и́шь *pf.* (*of* ⇒~**я́ть**) **1** (*создать*) to compose (*a liter. or mus. work*); to write. **2** (*выдумать*) to make up, fabricate.

сочин|я́ть, я́ю *impf. of* ⇒~**и́ть**

соч|и́ть, у́, и́шь *impf.* to ooze (out), exude.

соч|и́ться, и́тся *impf.* to ooze (out), exude; **с. кро́вью** to bleed.

сочлене́ни|е, я *nt.* (*anat. and tech.*) articulation, joint, coupling.

сочлен|и́ть, ю́, и́шь *pf.* (*of* ⇒~**я́ть**) to join.

сочлен|я́ть, я́ю *impf. of* ⇒~**и́ть**

со́чност|ь, и *f.* juiciness, succulence.

со́ч|ный (~ен, ~на́, ~но) *adj.* **1** juicy (*also fig.*); succulent. **2** (*fig.*) (*краски*) rich; (*зелень*) lush; **с. го́лос** fruity voice; **~ная расти́тельность** lush vegetation.

сочу́вствен|ный (~, ~на) *adj.* sympathetic.

сочу́встви|е, я *nt.* sympathy; **вы́звать с.** to gain sympathy.

сочу́вств|овать, ую *impf.* (+*d.*) to sympathize (with), feel (for).

сочу́вств|ующий *pres. part. act. of* ⇒~**овать** *and adj.* sympathetic; *as n.* **с., ~ующего** *m.* sympathizer.

со́шк|а, и *f.* **1** *dim. of* ⇒**соха́; ме́лкая с.** (*coll.*) small fry. **2** (*mil.*) bipod.

сошни́к, а́ *m.* ploughshare (*Br.*), plowshare (*US*).

сощу́рива|ть(ся), ю(сь) *impf. of* ⇒**сощу́рить(ся)**

сощу́р|ить, ю, ишь *pf.* (*of* ⇒**щу́рить** *and* ~**ивать**); **с. глаза́** to screw up one's eyes.

сощу́р|иться, юсь, ишься *pf.* (*of* ⇒**щу́риться** *and* ~**иваться**) to screw up one's eyes.

сою́з[1], а *m.* **1** (*единение*) alliance, union; (*соглашение*) agreement; **заключи́ть с.** (**с**+*i.*) to conclude an alliance (with). **2** (*организация*) union; league; **профессиона́льный с.** trade union; **Сове́тский С.** the Soviet Union.

сою́з[2], а *m.* (*gram.*) conjunction.

сою́зк|а, и *f.* vamp (*of footwear*).

сою́зник, а *m.* ally.

сою́зни|ца, цы *f. of* ⇒~**к**

сою́знический *adj.* ally's.

сою́зн|ый[1] *adj.* **1** allied; **~ые держа́вы** allied powers; (*hist.*) the Allies. **2** (*бывшего СССР*) Union; **~ое гражда́нство** citizenship of the USSR.

сою́з|ный[2] *adj. of* ⇒~[2]

со́|я, и *f.* soya bean.

спаге́тти *nt. and pl. indecl.* spaghetti.

спад, а *m.* **1** (*econ.*) slump, recession. **2** (*ветра, шума*) abatement; **пойти́ на с.** to begin to abate.

спада́|ть, ет *impf. of* ⇒**спасть**

спазм, а *m.* spasm.

спа́зм|а, ы *f.* = ~

спа́ива|ть[1], ю *impf. of* ⇒**спои́ть**

спа́ива|ть[2], ю *impf. of* ⇒**спая́ть**

спа|й, я *m.* (*tech.*) (soldered) joint.

спа́йк|а, и *f.* **1** (*действие*) soldering; (*место соединения*) soldered joint. **2** (*fig.*) cohesion; union.

спал|и́ть, ю́, и́шь *pf. of* ⇒**пали́ть[1]**

спа́льник, а *m.* (*coll.*) sleeping-bag.

спа́льн|ый *adj.* sleeping; **с. ваго́н** sleeping-car; **~ое ме́сто** berth, bunk; **с. мешо́к** sleeping-bag.

спа́л|ьня, ьни, *g. pl.* ~**ен** *f.* **1** (*комната*) bedroom. **2** (*мебель*) bedroom suite.

спан|ьё, я́ *nt.* (*coll.*) sleep(ing).

спарашюти́р|овать, ую *pf. of* ⇒**парашюти́ровать**

спа́р|енный *p.p.p. of* ⇒~**ить** *and adj.* paired, coupled; **~енная устано́вка** (*mil.*) combination gun mount.

спа́рж|а, и *f.* asparagus.

спа́рива|ть(ся), ю(сь) *impf. of* ⇒**спа́рить(ся)**

спа́р|ить, ю, ишь *pf.* (*of* ⇒~**ивать**) **1** (*соединить*) to couple, link, connect. **2** (*животных*) to mate.

спа́р|иться, юсь, ишься *pf.* (*of* ⇒~**иваться**) **1** (*о животных*) to mate. **2** (*о рабочих*) to pair off (*to work together*).

Спа́рт|а, ы *f.* Sparta.

спартакиа́д|а, ы *f.* sports and/or athletics meeting.

спарта́н|ец, ца *m.* Spartan.

спарта́н|ка, ки *f. of* ⇒~**ец**

спарта́нский *adj.* Spartan.

спа́рхива|ть, ю *impf. of* ⇒**спорхну́ть**

спа́рыва|ть, ю *impf. of* ⇒**споро́ть**

Спас, а *m.* (*relig.*) the Saviour (*Br.*), Savior (*US*).

спаса́ни|е, я *nt.* rescuing, life-saving.

спаса́тел|ь, я *m.* **1** (*человек*) lifeguard; rescuer; (*pl.*) rescue party *or* team. **2** (*судно*) lifeboat.

спаса́тельн|ый *adj.* rescue, life-saving; **с. круг, с. по́яс** lifebelt; **~ая ло́дка** lifeboat.

спаса́|ть(ся), ю(сь) *impf. of* ⇒**спасти́(сь)**

спасе́ни|е, я *nt.* **1** (*действие*) rescuing, saving. **2** (*возможность спастись*) rescue, escape; (*relig.*) salvation.

спаси́бо *particle* thanks; thank you; **с. и на том** that's sth. at least, we must be thankful for small mercies; *as n.* thanks; **большо́е вам с.** thank you very much, many thanks; **сде́лать что-н. за (одно́) с.** (*coll.*) to do sth. for love.

спаси́тел|ь, я *m.* **1** rescuer. **2**: **С.** (*relig.*) the Saviour (*Br.*), Savior (*US*).

спаси́тел|ьный (~ен, ~ьна) *adj.* saving; **с. вы́ход, ~ьное сре́дство** means of escape.

спас|ова́ть, у́ю *pf. of* ⇒**пасова́ть[1]**

спас|ти́, у́, ёшь, *past* **~, ~ла́** *pf.* (*of* ⇒**~а́ть**) to save; to rescue; **с. положе́ние** to save the situation.

спас|ти́сь, у́сь, ёшься, *past* **~ся, ~ла́сь** *pf.* (*of* ⇒**~а́ться**) **1** to save o.s., escape. **2** (*relig.*) to be saved, save one's soul.

спа|сть, дёт *past* **~л** *pf.* (*of* ⇒**~да́ть**) **1** (**с**+*i.*) (*упасть вниз*) to fall down (from); **с. с го́лоса** (*coll.*) to lose one's voice; **с. с те́ла** (*coll.*) to lose weight. **2** (*о ветре, о шуме*) to abate.

спа|ть, сплю, спишь, *past* **~л, ~ла́, ~ло** *impf.* to sleep, be asleep; **с. мёртвым сном** to be fast asleep; **лечь с.** to go to bed; **пора́ с.** it is bedtime; **с. и ви́деть** to dream (of); **с. с** (+*i.*) to sleep with (*euph.*).

спа́|ться, спи́тся, *past* **~ло́сь** *impf.* (*impers.*, +*d.*): **мне не спи́тся** I cannot sleep; **ей пло́хо ~ло́сь** she did not sleep well.

спа́янност|ь, и *f.* cohesion, unity.

спа|я́ть, я́ю *pf.* (*of* ⇒**~ивать[2]**) **1** to solder together, weld. **2** (*fig.*) (*коллектив*) to weld together, unite.

СПБ, СПб (*abbr. of* ***Санкт-Петербу́рг***) St Petersburg.

спева́|ться, юсь *impf. of* ⇒**спе́ться**

спе́вк|а, и *f.* (choir) practice, rehearsal.

спека́|ться, ется *impf. of* ⇒**спе́чься**

спекта́кл|ь, я *m.* (*theatr.*) performance; show.

спектр, а *m.* spectrum.

спектра́льный *adj.* (*phys.*) spectral, spectrum.

спектроско́п, а *m.* (*phys.*) spectroscope.

спектроскопи́|я, и *f.* (*phys.*) spectroscopy.

спекули́р|овать, ую *impf.* **1** (+*i. or* **на**+*p.*) to speculate (in); to profiteer (in). **2** (**на**+*p.*; *fig.*) to exploit; to profit (by).

спекуля́нт, а *m.* speculator, profiteer.

спекуляти́вный *adj.* speculative.

спекуля́ци|я[1], и *f.* **1** (+*i.*, *or* **на**+*p.*) speculation (in); profiteering; **с. на иностра́нной валю́те** speculation in foreign currency. **2** (**на**+*p.*; *fig.*) exploitation (of).

спекуля́ци|я[2], и *f.* (*phil.*) speculation.

спелена́|ть, ю *pf. of* ⇒**пелена́ть**

спелео́лог, а *m.* **1** speleologist. **2**: (**спортсме́н-**)**с.** caver, potholer.

спелеологи́ческий *adj.* speleological.

спелеоло́ги|я, и *f.* speleology; potholing.

спе́л|ый (~, ~а́, ~о) *adj.* ripe.

сперва́ *adv.* (*coll.*) at first; first.

спе́реди *adv. and prep.*+*g.* in front (of); at the front, from the front.

спер|е́ть[1], сопрёт, *past* **~, ~ла** *pf.* (*of* ⇒**спира́ть**) (*coll.*) to press; **у меня́ дыха́нье ~ло** it took my breath away.

спер|е́ть[2], сопру́, сопрёшь, *past* **~, ~ла** *pf.* (*of* ⇒**пере́ть** 5) (*coll.*) to filch, pinch.

спе́рм|а, ы *f.* sperm.

сперматозо́ид, а *m.* (*biol.*) spermatozoon.

спермаце́т, а *m.* (*pharm.*) spermaceti.

спёр|тый *p.p.p. of* ⇒**~е́ть[1]** *and adj.* close, stuffy.

спеси́вост|ь, и *f.* arrogance, conceit, haughtiness, loftiness.

спеси́в|ый (~, ~а) *adj.* arrogant, conceited, haughty.

спес|ь, и *f.* arrogance, conceit, haughtiness; **сбить с. с кого́-н.** to take s.o. down a peg.

спе|ть[1], ет *impf.* to ripen.

спеть[2], спою́, споёшь *pf. of* ⇒**петь**

спе́ться, спою́сь, споёшься *pf.* **1** (*impf.* **спева́ться**) (*о хоре*) to achieve a unified sound. **2** *pf. only* (*coll.*) (*достичь согласия*) to get on, agree, see eye to eye.

спех, а (у) *m.* (*coll.*) hurry; **что за с.?** what's the hurry?; **мне не к ~у** I'm in no hurry.

спец, а́ *m.* (*coll.*) = **специали́ст**

спец... *comb. form, abbr. of* ***специа́льный***

специализа́ци|я, и *f.* specialization.

специализи́рова|нный *p.p.p. of* ⇒**~ть** *and adj.* specialized.

специализи́р|овать, ую *impf. and pf.* to assign a specialization (to); to earmark for a special role.

специализи́р|оваться, уюсь *impf. and pf.* (**в**+*p. or* **по**+*d.*) to specialize (in).

специали́ст, а *m.* (**в**+*p. or* **по**+*d.*) specialist (in), expert (in).

специали́ст|ка, ки *f. of* ⇒**~**

специа́льно *adv.* specially, especially.

специа́льност|ь, и *f.* **1** speciality, special interest. **2** (*профессия*) profession.

специа́л|ьный *adj.* **1** special; **с. корреспонде́нт** special correspondent; **со ~ьной це́лью** with the express purpose. **2** (**~ен, ~ьна**) specialist; **~ьное образова́ние** specialist education; **с. те́рмин** technical term.

специ́фик|а, и *f.* specific character.

спецификá|ци|я, и *f.* specification.

специфици́р|овать, ую *impf. and pf.* to specify.

специфи́ческий *adj.* specific.

спе́ци|я, и *f.* spice.

спецко́р, а *m.* (*abbr. of* ***специа́льный корреспонде́нт***) special correspondent.

спецку́рс, а *m.* special course.

спецна́з, а *m.* (*abbr. of* ***отря́д специа́льного назначе́ния***) special unit.

спецна́зов|ец, ца *m.* member of special unit.

спецо́вк|а, и *f.* (*coll.*) = **спецоде́жда**

спецоде́жд|а, ы *f.* working clothes, overalls.

спецслу́жб|а, ы *f.* special force.

спецхра́н, а *m.* (*abbr. of* ***специа́льное храни́лище***) restricted-access collection (*of politically sensitive materials*).

спецшко́л|а, ы *f.* special school.

спецэффе́кт, а *m.* special effect.

спе́|чься, чётся, ку́тся, *past* **~кся, ~кла́сь** *pf.* (*of* ⇒**~ка́ться**) **1** (*о крови*) to coagulate. **2** (*об угле*) to cake, clinker.

спе́шива|ть(ся), ю(сь) *impf. of* ⇒**спе́шить(ся)**

спе́ш|ить, у, ишь *pf.* (*of* ⇒**~ивать**) to dismount.

спеш|и́ть, у́, и́шь *impf.* (*of* ⇒**по~**) **1** to hurry, be in a hurry; to make haste; (**с**+*i.*) to hurry up (with); **с. домо́й** to be in a hurry to get home; **де́лать не ~а́** to do in leisurely style, take one's time over. **2** (*о часах*) to be fast.

спе́ш|иться, усь, ишься *pf.* (*of* ⇒**~иваться**) to dismount.

спе́шк|а, и *f.* hurry, rush.

спе́шност|ь, и *f.* hurry, haste.

спе́ш|ный (~ен, ~на) *adj.* urgent, pressing; **с. зака́з** rush order; **~ное письмо́** express letter; **~ная по́чта** express delivery.

спива́|ться, юсь *impf. of* ⇒**спи́ться**

СПИД, а *m.* (*abbr. of* ***синдро́м приобретённого имму́нного дефици́та***) (*med.*) AIDS (*acquired immune deficiency syndrome*).

спидве́|й, я *m.* speedway (racing).

спидо́метр, а *m.* speedometer.

спи́кер, а *m.* (*parl.*) speaker.

спики́р|овать, ую *pf. of* ⇒**пики́ровать**

спи́лива|ть, ю *impf. of* ⇒**спили́ть**

спил|и́ть, ю́, ~ишь *pf.* (*of*

С

⇒**~ива́ть**) (*дерево*) to saw down; (*сук, верхушку*) to saw off.

спин|а́, ы́, *a.* **~у,** *pl.* **~ы** *f.* back; **за ~о́й у кого́-н.** (*fig.*) behind s.o.'s back; **гнуть ~у (пе́ред**+*i.*) to cringe (to), kowtow (to); **нож в ~у, уда́р в ~у** (*fig.*) stab in the back; **узна́ть на со́бственной ~е́** to learn from (one's own) bitter experience.

спи́нк|а, и *f.* **1** *dim. of* ⇒**спина́.** **2** back (*of article of furniture or clothing*).

спи́ннинг, а *m.* (*sport*) **1** (*техника*) spinning (*fishing technique*). **2** (*снасть*) spinner.

спинно́й *adj.* spinal; **с. мозг** spinal cord; **с. хребе́т** spinal column.

спинномозгов|о́й *adj.*: **~а́я жи́дкость** (*anat.*) spinal fluid.

спира́л|ь, и *f.* spiral; (*противозачаточное средство*) coil.

спира́льный *adj.* spiral, helical.

спира́|ть, ет *impf. of* ⇒**сопере́ть**[1]

спири́т, а *m.* spiritualist.

спири́т|ка, ки *f. of* ⇒**~**

спирити́зм, а *m.* spiritualism.

спирити́ческий *adj.* spiritualistic; **с. сеа́нс** seance.

спирт, а *m.* alcohol, spirit(s); **безво́дный с.** absolute alcohol; **древе́сный с.** wood alcohol.

спиртн|о́й *adj.* alcoholic, spirituous; **~ы́е напи́тки** alcoholic drinks, spirits; *as n.* **~о́е, ~о́го** *nt.* = **~ы́е напи́тки**

спирто́вк|а, и *f.* spirit-lamp.

спиртово́й *adj.* alcoholic, spirituous; **с. заво́д** distillery.

спи|са́ть, шу́, ~шешь *pf.* (*of* ⇒**~сывать**) **1** (**с**+*i.*) to copy from. **2** (**у**+*g.*) to copy (off), crib (off). **3** (*оборудование*) to write off. **4**: **с. с корабля́** (*naut.*) to discharge (*from a ship*).

спи|са́ться, шу́сь, ~шешься *pf.* (*of* ⇒**~сываться**) (**с**+*i.*) **1** to write to; to exchange letters (with). **2**: **с. с корабля́** (*naut.*) to leave ship.

спи́с|ок, ка *m.* **1** (*рукописная копия*) manuscript copy. **2** (*письменный перечень*) list; roll; **с. избира́телей** electoral roll; **с. уби́тых и ра́неных** casualty list; **с. ли́чного соста́ва** (*mil.*) muster-roll. **3**: **послужно́й с.** service record.

спи́сыва|ть(ся), ю(сь) *impf. of* ⇒**списа́ть(ся)**

спито́й *adj.* (*coll.*; *of hot beverages*) weak.

спи́|ться, сопью́сь, сопьёшься, *past* **~лся, ~ла́сь** *pf.* (*of* ⇒**~ва́ться**) to become a drunkard, take to drink.

спи́хива|ть, ю *impf. of* ⇒**спихну́ть**

спих|ну́ть, ну́, нёшь *pf.* (*of* ⇒**~ивать**) to push aside, shove aside; (*вниз*) to push down.

спи́ц|а, ы *f.* **1** (*для вязания*) knitting needle. **2** (*колеса*) spoke; **после́дняя с. в колесни́це** minor cog in the machine.

спич, а *m.* speech, address.

спи́чечниц|а, ы *f.* **1** (*футляр*) match-box case. **2** (*подставка*) match-box stand.

спи́ч|ечный *adj. of* ⇒**~ка; ~ечная коро́бка** match-box.

спи́чк|а, и *f.* match.

сплав[1]**, а** *m.* (*tech.*) alloy.

сплав[2]**, а** *m.* (*леса*) (timber) floating.

спла́в|ить[1]**, лю, ишь** *pf.* (*of* ⇒**~ля́ть**) (*tech.*) to alloy, melt, fuse.

спла́в|ить[2]**, лю, ишь** *pf.* (*of* ⇒**~ля́ть**) **1** (*лес*) to float (*timber*); to raft. **2** (*coll.*) (*избавиться*) to get rid of.

спла́в|иться, ится *pf.* (*of* ⇒**~ля́ться**) to fuse together, coalesce.

сплавля́|ть(ся), ю, ет(ся) *impf. of* ⇒**спла́вить(ся)**

сплани́р|овать, ую *pf. of* ⇒**плани́ровать**[2]

спла́чива|ть(ся), ю, ет(ся) *impf. of* ⇒**сплоти́ть(ся)**

сплёвыва|ть, ю *impf. of* ⇒**сплю́нуть**

сплёскива|ть, ю *impf. of* ⇒**сплесну́ть**

сплес|ну́ть, ну́, нёшь *pf.* (*of* ⇒**~кивать**) to splash (down).

спле|сти́, ту́, тёшь, *past* **~л, ~ла́** *pf.* (*of* ⇒**плести́** *and* **~та́ть**) to weave, plait, interlace.

сплета́|ть, ю *impf. of* ⇒**сплести́**

сплете́ни|е, я *nt.* **1** interlacing; **с. лжи** tissue of lies; **с. обстоя́тельств** combination of circumstances. **2** (*anat.*) plexus.

спле́тник, а *m.* gossip, scandalmonger.

спле́тниц|а, ы *f. of* ⇒**спле́тник**

спле́тнича|ть, ю *impf.* to gossip.

спле́т|ня, ни, *g. pl.* **~ен** *f.* gossip; piece of scandal.

сплеча́ *adv.* **1** (*ударить*) straight from the shoulder. **2** (*fig., coll.*) (*решать*) on the spur of the moment.

спло|ти́ть, чу́, ти́шь *pf.* (*of* ⇒**спла́чивать**) **1** to join. **2** (*fig.*) to unite, rally; **с. ряды́** to close the ranks.

спло|ти́ться, ти́тся *pf.* (*of* ⇒**спла́чиваться**) to unite, rally; to close the ranks.

сплох|ова́ть, у́ю *pf.* (*coll.*) to make a blunder.

сплочённост|ь, и *f.* cohesion, unity.

спло|чённый *p.p.p. of* ⇒**~ти́ть** *and adj.* **1** (*сомкнутый друг с другом*) unbroken. **2** (*единодушный*) united, firm; **~чённые ряды́** serried ranks.

сплоша́|ть, ю *pf. of* ⇒**плоша́ть**

сплошн|о́й *adj.* **1** unbroken, continuous; **с. лес** dense forest; **~а́я ма́сса** solid mass. **2** (*всеобщий*) complete; **~а́я гра́мотность** universal literacy. **3** (*coll.*) (*чрезвычайный*) sheer, complete and utter; **с. восто́рг** sheer joy; **~а́я чепуха́** utter rubbish.

сплошь *adv.* **1** (*по всей поверхности*) all over; **её но́ги бы́ли с. покры́ты комари́ными уку́сами** her legs were covered all over with gnat bites; **с. и (да) ря́дом** (*coll.*) nearly always; pretty often. **2** (*coll.*) (*целиком*) completely, entirely; (*без исключения*) without exception; (*исключительно*) only, exclusively.

сплут|ова́ть, у́ю *pf. of* ⇒**плутова́ть**

сплыва́|ть(ся), ет(ся) *impf. of* ⇒**сплы́ть(ся)**

сплы|ть, вёт, *past* **~л, ~ла́, ~ло** *pf.* (*of* ⇒**~ва́ть**) (*coll.*) **1** (*уплыть*) to be carried away (*by a current of water, by a flood*); **бы́ло да ~ло** it was a short-lived joy; it's all over. **2** (*стечь*) to overflow, run over.

сплы|ться, вётся, *past* **~лся, ~ла́сь** *pf.* (*of* ⇒**~ва́ться**) (*coll.*) to run (together), merge, blend.

сплю́н|уть, у, ешь *pf.* (*of* ⇒**сплёвывать**) **1** (*плюнуть*) to spit. **2** (*coll.*) (*косточку*) to spit out.

сплю́сн|уть, у, ешь *pf.* = **сплю́щить**

сплю́щива|ть(ся), ю, ет(ся) *impf. of* ⇒**сплю́щить(ся)**

сплю́щ|ить, у, ишь *pf.* (*of* ⇒**плю́щить** *and* **~ивать**) to flatten.

сплю́щ|иться, ится *pf.* (*of* ⇒**~иваться**) to become flat.

спля|са́ть, шу́, ~шешь *pf.* to dance.

сподви́жник, а *m.* (*rhet.*) associate; comrade-in-arms.

сподо́б|ить, ит *pf.* (*impers.*+*inf.*; *obs. or joc.*) to manage (to), come (to); **как э́то тебя́ ~ило упа́сть в реку́?** how did you manage to fall in the river?

сподо́б|иться, люсь, ишься *pf.* (+*g. or* +*inf.*; *coll., joc.*) to have the honour (*Br.*), honor (*US*) (of, to).

сподру́ч|ный (~ен, ~на) *adj.* (*coll.*) easy; convenient, handy.

спозара́нку *adv.* (*coll.*) very early (in the morning).

спо|и́ть, ю́, и́шь *pf.* (*of* ⇒**спа́ивать**[1]) (*coll.*) **1** (*дать выпить*) to give to drink. **2** (*поить до опьянения*) to get drunk; (*сделать пьяницей*) to make a drunkard (of).

споко́|йный (~ен, ~йна) *adj.* **1** quiet; calm, tranquil; **~йное мо́ре** calm sea; **с. о́браз жи́зни** quiet life; **~йная со́весть** clear conscience; **~йная улы́бка** serene smile; **бу́дьте ~йны!** don't worry!, rest assured!; **~йной но́чи!** good night! **2** (*человек*) quiet, composed. **3** (*кресло, обувь*) comfortable.

споко́йстви|е, я *nt.* **1** (*покой*) quiet, tranquillity; calm. **2** (*порядок*) order; **наруше́ние обще́ственного ~я** breach of the peace. **3** (*душевное*) composure, serenity; **с. ду́ха** peace of mind.

споко́н: с. ве́ку, с. веко́в (*coll.*) from time immemorial.

спола́скива|ть, ю *impf. of* ⇒**сполосну́ть**

сполз|а́ть, а́ю *impf. of* ⇒**~ти́**

сполз|ти́, у́, ёшь, *past* **~, ~ла́** *pf.* (*of* ⇒**~а́ть**) **1** (**с**+*g.*) to climb down (from). **2** (*о шапке*) to slip down. **3** (**в**+*a.*, **к**+*d.*; *fig., coll.*) (*оказаться на ложном пути*) to slip (into).

сполна́ *adv.* completely, in full; **де́ньги полу́чены с.** 'money received in full'.

сполосн|у́ть, у́, ёшь *pf.* (*of* ⇒**спола́скивать**) to rinse (out).

спо́ло́х|и, ов *no sg.* (*dial.*) **1** (*северное*

сияние) northern lights. **2** (*зарница*) lightning.

сподé|й, я *m.* (*liter.*) spondee.

спóнсор, а *m.* sponsor, backer.

спóнсорств|о, а *nt.* sponsorship.

спонтáнност|ь, и *f.* spontaneity.

спонтáнный *adj.* spontaneous.

спор, а *m.* **1** argument; controversy; debate; **затéять с.** to start an argument; **~у нет** undoubtedly; there's no denying. **2** (*leg.*) dispute.

спóр|а, ы *f.* (*biol.*) spore.

спорадúческий *adj.* sporadic.

спóр|ить, ю, ишь *impf.* (*of* ⇒**по~**) (**о**+*p.*) **1** to argue (about); to dispute (about), debate; **о вкýсах не ~ят** tastes differ. **2** (*leg.*) (**о**+*p.*, **за**+*a.*) to dispute; **с. о наслéдстве** to dispute a legacy. **3** (*держать пари*) to bet (on), have a bet (on).

спóр|иться, ится *impf.* (*coll.*) to succeed, go well; **у негó всё ~ится** he never puts a foot wrong.

спóр|ный (~ен, ~на) *adj.* debatable, questionable; disputed, at issue; **с. вопрóс** moot point, vexed question; **~ное наслéдство** disputed legacy.

спор|óть, ю, ~ешь *pf.* (*of* ⇒**спáрывать**) to unstitch, take off (*by cutting stitches*).

спорт, а *m.* sport; **автомобúльный с.** motor sports; **кóнный с.** equestrianism.

спортзáл, а *m.* sports hall.

спортúвн|ый *adj.* (*инвентарь, комментатор*) sports; (*человек, фигура*) sporty; (*одежда*) casual; **с. зал** gymnasium; **с. кóмплекс** sports centre (*Br.*), center (*US*); **~ая площáдка** sports ground, playing-field; **~ое пóле** playing-field; **из ~ого интерéса** (*pej.*) just for the sake of it.

спортсмéн, а *m.* sportsman.

спортсмéнк|а, и *f.* sportswoman.

спорхн|ýть, ý, ёшь *pf.* (*of* ⇒**спáрхивать**) to flutter off; to flutter away.

спóрщик, а *m.* debater, wrangler.

спóрщи|ца, цы *f. of* ⇒**~к**

спóр|ый (~, ~á, ~о) *adj.* (*coll.*) successful; **~ая рабóта** good work.

спорынь|я́, ú *f.* (*bot.*) ergot, spur.

спóсоб, а *m.* way, method; means; **такúм ~ом** in this way; **слéдующим ~ом** as follows.

спосóбност|ь, и *f.* **1** (*usu. pl.*; **к**+*d.*) (*талант*) ability (for), talent (for), aptitude (for); **человéк с большúми ~ями** person of great abilities; **с. к языкáм** talent for languages, linguistic ability. **2** (*умение*) capacity; **покупáтельная с.** purchasing power; **пропускнáя с.** capacity.

спосóб|ный (~ен, ~на) *adj.* **1** (*талантливый*) able, talented, clever; **с. к математúке** good at mathematics. **2** (**на**+*a. or* +*inf.*) capable (of), able (to); **онú ~ны на всё** they are capable of anything.

спосóбств|овать, ую *impf.* (*of* ⇒**по~**) (+*d.*) **1** (*помогать*) to assist. **2** (*служить средством*) to be conducive (to), further, promote.

споткн|ýться, ýсь, ёшься *pf.* (*of* ⇒**спотыкáться**) **1** (**о**+*a.*) to stumble (against, over). **2** (**на**+*p. or* **о**+*a.*; *fig., coll.*) to get stuck (on). **3** (*coll.*) (*оступиться*) to slip up.

спотыкá|ться, юсь *impf. of* ⇒**споткнýться**

спохва|тúться, чýсь, ~тишься *pf.* (*of* ⇒**~тываться**) (*coll.*) to remember suddenly, think suddenly.

спохвáтыва|ться, юсь *impf. of* ⇒**спохватúться**

спрáва *adv.* (**от**+*g.*) on the right (of), to the right (of).

справедлúвост|ь, и *f.* **1** justice; fairness; **по ~и говоря́** in (all) fairness, by rights; **отдáть с.** (+*d.*) to do justice (to); **поступáть по ~и** to act fairly. **2** (*правильность*) truth, correctness.

справедлúв|ый (~, ~а) *adj.* **1** just; fair; **с. судья́** impartial judge; **~ая войнá** just war. **2** (*правильный*) justified, true, correct; **нáши подозрéния оказáлись ~ыми** our suspicions proved to be justified.

спрáв|ить[1], лю, ишь *pf.* (*of* ⇒**~ля́ть**) (*coll.*) to celebrate; **с. свáдьбу** to celebrate one's wedding.

спрáв|ить[2], лю, ишь *pf.* (*of* ⇒**~ля́ть**) (**себé**; *coll.*) (*приобрести*) to get, procure, acquire.

спрáв|иться[1], люсь, ишься *pf.* (*of* ⇒**~ля́ться**) (**с**+*i.*) **1** (*с работой, с детьми*) to cope (with), manage. **2** (*с противником*) to deal (with), get the better (of); **я с ним ~люсь!** I'll deal with him! **3** (*с волнением, со страхом*) to control.

спрáв|иться[2], люсь, ишься *pf.* (*of* ⇒**~ля́ться**) (**о**+*p.*) to ask (about), inquire (about); **с. в словарé** to consult a dictionary.

спрáвк|а, и *f.* **1** (*сведение*) information; **навестú ~у** (**о**+*p.*) to inquire (about); **обратúться за ~ой** to apply for information. **2** (*документ*) certificate; **с. с мéста рабóты** document confirming that one works at a place.

справля́|ть(ся), ю(сь) *impf. of* ⇒**спрáвить(ся)**

спрáв|ный (~ен, ~на) *adj.* (*coll.*) in good condition.

спрáвочник, а *m.* reference book, handbook, guide; **телефóнный с.** telephone directory.

спрáвочн|ый *adj.* inquiry, information; **~ая** directory enquiries (*Br.*), directory assistance (*US*); **~ое бюрó, с. стол** inquiries office, information bureau; **~ая кнúга** = **~ик**

спрáшива|ть, ю *impf. of* ⇒**спросúть**

спрáшива|ться, юсь *impf.* **1** *impf. of* ⇒**спросúться. 2** *impf. only* **~ется** the question is, arises.

спресс|овáть, ýю *pf. of* ⇒**прессовáть**

спринт, а *m.* (*sport*) sprint.

спрúнтер, а *m.* (*sport*) sprinter.

спринц|евáть, ýю *impf.* to syringe.

спринцóвк|а, и *f.* **1** (*действие*) syringing. **2** (*прибор*) syringe.

спровá|дить, жу, дишь *pf.* (*of* ⇒**~живать**) (*coll.*) to show out, show the door, send on his way.

спровáжива|ть, ю *impf. of* ⇒**спровáдить**

спровоцúр|овать, ую *pf. of* ⇒**провоцúровать**

спроектúр|овать, ую *pf. of* ⇒**проектúровать[1]**

спрос, а *m.* **1** (*econ.*) demand; (**на**+*a.*) demand (for), run (on); **с. и предложéние** supply and demand; **пóльзоваться большúм ~ом** to be much in demand. **2** (**с**+*g.*) demands on; **с негó нет ~у** nobody expects anything from him. **3**: **без ~а (~у)** (*coll.*) without permission.

спро|сúть, шý, ~сишь *pf.* (*of* ⇒**спрáшивать**) **1** (**о**+*p.*) (*осведомиться*) to ask (about), inquire (about); **с. дорóгу** to ask the way. **2** (+*a. or g.*) (*попросить*) to ask (for); (*пожелать видеть*) to ask to see, desire to speak (to); **с. совéта** to ask (for) advice; **~сúте хозя́йку** ask to see the landlady. **3** (**с**+*g.*) (*призвать к ответу*) to make answer (for), make responsible (for). **4** (**с**+*g.*) (*потребовать*) to demand (from).

спро|сúться, шýсь, ~сишься *pf.* (*of* ⇒**спрáшиваться**) **1** (+*g. or* **у**+*g.*) to ask permission (of). **2** (*impers.*): **~сится с негó**, *etc.*, he, *etc.*, will be answerable.

спросóнок *adv.* (*coll.*) being only half-awake.

спростá *adv.* (*coll.*) without reflection; off the reel.

спрут, а *m.* octopus.

спры́гива|ть, ю *impf. of* ⇒**спры́гнуть**

спры́г|нуть, ну, нешь *pf.* (*of* ⇒**~ивать**) (**с**+*g.*) to jump off; to jump down (from).

спры́скива|ть, ю *impf. of* ⇒**спры́снуть**

спры́с|нуть, ну, нешь *pf.* (*of* ⇒**~кивать**) **1** to sprinkle. **2** (*coll.*) (*отпраздновать*) to celebrate, drink (to).

спрягá|ть[1], ю *impf.* (*of* ⇒**про~**) (*gram.*) to conjugate.

спрягá|ть[2], ю *impf. of* ⇒**спрячь**

спрягá|ться, ется *impf.* (*gram.*) to conjugate, be conjugated.

спряжéни|е, я *nt.* (*gram.*) conjugation.

спря|сть, дý, дёшь, *past* **~л, ~лá, ~ло** *pf. of* ⇒**прясть**

спря́|тать(ся), чу(сь), чешь(ся) *pf. of* ⇒**пря́тать(ся)**

спря|чь, гý, жёшь, гýт, *past* **~г, ~глá** *pf.* (*of* ⇒**~гáть[2]**) to harness together.

спýгива|ть, ю *impf. of* ⇒**спугнýть**

спуг|нýть, нý, нёшь *pf.* (*of* ⇒**~ивать**) to frighten off, scare off.

спуд, а *m.* (*arch.*) bushel; *now only used in phrr.* (*i*) **под ~ом** under a bushel; **держáть под ~ом** (*fig.*) to hide under a bushel, keep back; (*ii*) **из-под ~а** from

С

hiding; **вы́тащить, извле́чь из-под ~а** to put to use.

спуск, а *m.* **1** (*флага*) lowering; **с. корабля́** launch(ing). **2** (*с высоты*) descent, descending. **3** (*воды*) release; draining. **4** (*откос*) slope, descent. **5** (*оружия*) trigger. **6** (*coll.*) (*пощада*) quarter; **не дава́ть ~у** (+*d.*) to give no quarter, not let off.

спуска́|ть, ю *impf. of* ⇒**спусти́ть; не с. глаз** (**с**+*g.*) not to take one's eyes (off); not to let out of one's sight.

спуска́|ться, юсь *impf. of* ⇒**спусти́ться**

спускн|о́й *adj.* drain; **~а́я труба́** drain-pipe.

спусково́й *adj.* trigger; **с. крючо́к** trigger; **с. механи́зм** trigger mechanism.

спу|сти́ть, щу́, ~стишь *pf.* (*of* ⇒**~ска́ть**) **1** (*флаг, занавеску*) to let down, lower; **с. кора́бль (на́ воду)** to launch a ship; **~стя́ рукава́** (*coll.*) in a slipshod fashion, carelessly; **с. с ле́стницы** (*fig., coll.*) to kick downstairs. **2** (*освободить*) to let go, let loose, release; **с. куро́к** to pull, release the trigger; **с. затво́р** (*phot.*) to release the shutter; **с. пе́тлю** to drop a stitch; **с. соба́ку с при́вязи** to unleash a dog.
3 (*воду, воздух*) to let out; **с. во́ду в туале́те** to flush a lavatory.
4 (*директиву, указание*) to send down, send out.
5 (*о шине*) to go down.
6 (*coll.*) (*простить*) to pardon, let off, let go.
7 (*coll.*) (*потерять в весе*) to lose (*weight*).
8 (*coll.*) (*деньги*) to throw away, squander.

спу|сти́ться, щу́сь, ~стишься *pf.* (*of* ⇒**~ска́ться**) to descend; to come down, go down; (*вниз по течению*) to go downstream; (*о мраке*) to fall; **с. с ле́стницы** to come downstairs; **~сти́лась мгла** a mist came down; **на её чулке́ ~сти́лась пе́тля** she has laddered her stocking.

спустя́ *prep.*+*a.* after; later; **с. год** after a year, a year later.

спу́та|ть(ся), ю(сь) *pf. of* ⇒**пу́тать(ся)**

спу́тник, а *m.* **1** (*человек*) (travelling (*Br.*), traveling (*US*)) companion; **с. жи́зни** husband. **2** (*обстоятельство*) concomitant. **3** (*astron.*) satellite; **с. свя́зи** communications satellite; **иску́сственный с. Земли́** artificial earth satellite, sputnik.

спу́тников|ый *adj.*: **~ая связь** satellite link; **~ое телеви́дение** satellite television.

спу́тни|ца, цы *f. of* ⇒**~к 1**; **с. жи́зни** wife.

спу́щенный *p.p.p. of* ⇒**спусти́ть** *and adj.* (*of a flag*) at half-mast.

спья́на *adv.* in a state of drunkenness, in one's cups.

спья́н|у *adv.* = **~а**

спя́|тить, чу, тишь *pf.*: **с. (с ума́)** (*coll.*) to go nuts, go off one's rocker.

спя́чк|а, и *f.* **1** (*животных*) hibernation. **2** (*coll.*) (*сонливое состояние*) sleepiness, lethargy.

ср. (*abbr. of* ***сравни́***) cf., compare.

сраба́тыва|ть(ся), ю(сь) *impf. of* ⇒**срабо́тать(ся)**

срабо́танност|ь[1], и *f.* (*согласованность*) harmony in work, harmonious team-work.

срабо́танност|ь[2], и *f.* (*изношенность*) wear.

срабо́танный *adj.* (*износившийся*) worn (out).

срабо́та|ть, ю *pf.* (*of* ⇒**сраба́тывать**) **1** (*машина, сигнализация*) to work. **2** (*coll.*) (*изготовить*) to make.

срабо́та|ться[1], юсь *pf.* (*of* ⇒**сраба́тываться**) (*коллектив*) to achieve harmony in work, work well together.

срабо́та|ться[2], ется *pf.* (*of* ⇒**сраба́тываться**) (*износиться*) to wear out.

сравне́ни|е, я *nt.* **1** comparison; **по ~ю, в ~и** (**с**+*i.*) by, in comparison (with), compared (with); **вне ~я** beyond comparison; **не идёт (ни) в (како́е) с.** (**с**+*i.*) it cannot be compared (with). **2** (*liter.*) simile.

сра́внива|ть, ю *impf. of* ⇒**сравни́ть** *and* **сравня́ть**

сравни́тельно *adv.* **1** (**с**+*i.*) by, in comparison (with). **2**: **с. недорого́й/хоро́ший** comparatively cheap/good.

сравни́тельн|ый *adj.* comparative; **~ая сте́пень** (*gram.*) comparative (degree).

сравн|и́ть, ю́, и́шь *pf.* (*of* ⇒**~ивать**) (**с**+*i.*) to compare (to, with); (*уподобить*) to liken (to).

сравн|и́ться, ю́сь, и́шься *pf.* (**с**+*i.*) to compare (with), come up (to), touch.

сравн|я́ть, я́ю *pf.* (*of* ⇒**равня́ть** *and* **~ивать**) to make even; **с. счёт** (*sport*) to equalize, bring the score level.

сравня́|ться, юсь *pf.* (**с**+*i.*) to become equal (with).

сража́|ть, ю *impf. of* ⇒**срази́ть**

сража́|ться, юсь *impf.* (*of* ⇒**срази́ться**) **1** (**с**+*i.*) to fight; to join battle (with). **2** (**в**+*a.*) (*coll.*) to play.

сраже́ни|е, я *nt.* battle, engagement.

сра|зи́ть, жу́, зи́шь *pf.* (*of* ⇒**~жа́ть**) **1** (*убить*) to slay. **2** (*fig.*) to overwhelm, crush; **её ~зи́ла весть о катастро́фе** she was crushed by the news of the disaster.

сра|зи́ться, жу́сь, зи́шься *pf. of* ⇒**~жа́ться**

сра́зу *adv.* **1** (*в один приём*) (all) at once. **2** (*немедленно*) straight away, immediately. **3** (*рядом*) right, just; **с. о́коло до́ма** right next to the house.

срам, а *m.* (*coll.*) shame; **како́й с.!** for shame!

срам|и́ть, лю́, и́шь *impf.* (*of* ⇒**о~**) (*coll.*) to shame, put to shame.

срам|и́ться, лю́сь, и́шься *impf.* (*of* ⇒**о~**) (*coll.*) to disgrace o.s.

срамни́к, а́ *m.* (*coll.*) shameless person.

срамни́|ца, цы *f. of* ⇒**~к**

срамно́й *adj.* (*coll.*) indecent.

срамот|а́, ы́ *f.* (*coll.*) shame.

сраста́ни|е, я *nt.* (*костей*) knitting.

сраст|а́ться, а́ется *impf. of* ⇒**~и́сь**

сраст|и́сь, ётся, *past* **сро́сся, сросла́сь** *pf.* (*of* ⇒**~а́ться**) **1** (*о корнях*) to grow together; (*о костях*) to knit. **2** (*fig.*) (**с**+*i.*) (*соединиться*) to merge (with); (*привыкнуть*) to get used to.

сра|сти́ть, щу́, сти́шь *pf.* (*of* ⇒**~щивать**) **1** (*заставить срастись*) to join. **2** (*концы канаты*) to splice.

ср|ать, у, ёшь *impf.* (*of* ⇒**насра́ть**) (*vulg.*) to shit.

сраще́ни|е, я *nt.* (*костей*) knitting.

сра́щивани|е, я *nt.* **1** joining; splicing. **2** (*fig.*) fusion, merging.

сра́щива|ть, ю *impf. of* ⇒**срасти́ть**

сре́бреник, а *m.* silver coin, piece of silver; **прода́ть за три́дцать ~ов** to sell for thirty pieces of silver.

сребролю́б|ец, ца *m.* (*obs.*) money-grubber.

сребролю́би|е, я *nt.* (*obs.*) greed for money.

сребронос́|ный (~ен, ~на) *adj.* argentiferous.

сред|а́[1], ы́, *a.* **~у́,** *pl.* **~ы** *f.* **1** (*природная*) environment, surroundings; **окружа́ющая с.** the environment; (*социальная*) environment, milieu; **худо́жественная с.** artistic circles, milieu; (*biol.*) habitat; **в ~е́** (+*g.*) among; **в на́шей ~е́** in our midst, among us. **2** (*phys.*) medium.

сред|а́[2], ы́, *a.* **~у,** *pl.* **~ы, ~а́м** *f.* (*день недели*) Wednesday; **в ~у** on Wednesday.

средакти́р|овать, ую *pf. of* ⇒**редакти́ровать**

среди́ *prep.*+*g.* **1** (*в числе*) among; amidst; **с. них** among them, in their midst. **2** (*посредине*) in the middle (of); **с. бе́ла дня** in broad daylight.

Средизе́мн|ое мо́р|е, ~ого ~я *nt.* the Mediterranean (Sea).

средиземномо́рский *adj.* Mediterranean.

среди́н|а, ы *f.* middle.

среди́нный *adj.* middle.

сре́дне *adv.* (*coll.*) middling, so-so.

среднеазиа́тский *adj.* central Asian.

среднеангли́йский *adj.*: **с. язы́к** Middle English.

средневеко́вый *adj.* medieval.

средневеко́вь|е, я *nt.* the Middle Ages.

среднево́лновый *adj.* medium-wave.

среднегодово́й *adj.* average annual.

среднеме́сячный *adj.* average monthly.

среднесу́точный *adj.* average daily.

сре́дн|ий *adj.* **1** (*комната, проход*) middle; (*рост*) medium; **~ие века́** the Middle Ages; **~их лет** middle-aged; **с.**

пáлец middle finger; **~его рóста** of medium height. **2** (*в среднем*) mean, average; **~ее врéмя** mean time; **с. зáработок** average earnings; **~яя ошибка** standard deviation; *as n.* **~ее, ~его** *nt.* mean, average; **в ~ем** on average; **вы́ше ~его** above (the) average. **3** (*посредственный*) middling, average; **~ие способности** average abilities; **ни́же ~его** below average. **4** (*школа, образование*) secondary. **5**: **с. род** (*gram.*) neuter (gender).

средостéни|е, я *nt.* **1** (*anat.*) mediastinum. **2** (*fig.*) (*преграда*) partition, barrier.

средотóчи|е, я *nt.* focus, centre (*Br.*), center (*US*) point.

срéдств|о, а *nt.* **1** means; facilities; **~а мáссовой информáции** mass media; **~а передвижéния** means of conveyance; **~а сообщéния** means of communication; **пусти́ть в ход все ~а** to move heaven and earth. **2** (**от**+*g.*) remedy (for); **с. от кáшля** cough medicine, sth. for a cough; **с. от насекóмых** insect repellent; **с. от потéния** antiperspirant. **3** (*pl.*) (*деньги, капитал*) resources; funds; **~а к существовáнию** livelihood. **4** (*pl.*) (*состояние*) means; **человéк со ~ами** man of means; **жить не по ~ам** to live beyond one's means.

средь *prep.*+*g.* = **среди́**

срез, а *m.* **1** cut; microscopic section. **2** (*tech.*) shear, shearing. **3** (*sport*) slice, slicing.

срé|зать, жу, жешь *pf.* **1** (*impf.* **~зáть**) (*ветку*) to cut off; **с. ýгол** (*fig.*) to cut off a corner; **с. на экзáмене** (*school sl.*) to fail an exam. **2** (*кредиты, фонды*) to cut, reduce. **3** (*говорящего*) to cut short. **4** (*impf.* **рéзать**) (*sport*) to slice, cut, chop.

срезá|ть, ю *impf. of* ⇒**срéзать**

срé|заться, жусь, жешься *pf.* (*of* ⇒**~зáться**) (*school sl.*) to fail.

срезá|ться, юсь *impf. of* ⇒**срéзаться**

срепети́р|овать, ую *pf. of* ⇒**репети́ровать**

срéтени|е, я *nt.* **1** (*arch. or poet.*) meeting. **2**: **С.** (*eccl.*) Candlemas Day; Feast of the Purification.

срис|овáть, ýю *pf.* (*of* ⇒**~óвывать**) to copy.

сриcóвыва|ть, ю *impf. of* ⇒**срисовáть**

срифм|овáть, ýю *pf. of* ⇒**рифмовáть** 2

сровня́|ть, ю *pf. of* ⇒**ровня́ть**

сродни́ *adv.* akin; **быть, приходи́ться с.** (+*d.*) to be akin, related (to).

сродн|и́ть, ю́, и́шь *pf.* (**с**+*i.*) to bring close (to).

сродн|и́ться, ю́сь, и́шься *pf.* (**с**+*i.*) (*сблизиться*) to become close (to); (*свыкнуться*) to get used (to).

срóд|ный (~ен, ~на) *adj.* (+*d. or* **с**+*i.*) related (to); similar (to).

сродств|ó, á *nt.* relationship, affinity.

срóду *adj.* (*coll.*) in one's life; never.

срок, а (у) *m.* **1** (*промежуток времени*) time, period; term; **мéсячный с.** period of one month; **в кратчáйший с.** in the shortest possible time; **с. дéйствия** period of validity; **с. полномóчий** term of office; **с. рабóты** life (*of machine, etc.*); **продли́ть с. ви́зы** to extend a visa; **~ом на** (+*a.*) for a period of; **~óм до трёх мéсяцев** within three months; **дáй(те) с.** (*coll.*) wait a minute!, give us time!; **ни óтдыху, ни ~ý не давáть** (+*d.*) to give no peace. **2** (*дата*) date; **крáйний с.** closing date; **с. платежá** date of payment; **с. хранéния** shelf life; **пропусти́ть с. платежá** to fail to pay by the date fixed; **в укáзанный с., к установлéнному ~ý** by the date fixed, by a specified date; **в с., к ~ý** in time, to time.

срóчно *adv.* urgently; quickly.

срóчност|ь, и *f.* urgency; hurry; **что за с.?** what's the hurry?

срóч|ный (~ен, ~нá, ~но) *adj.* **1** (*сообщение, заказ*) urgent. **2** (*ссуда, вклад*) fixed-term; for a fixed period; **~ная слýжба** (*mil.*) service for a fixed period.

сруб, а *m.* **1** felling; **на с.** for timber. **2** (*избы, колодца*) frame(work), shell.

сруб|áть, áю *impf. of* ⇒**~и́ть**

сруб|и́ть, лю́, ~ишь *pf.* (*of* ⇒**~áть**) **1** (*рубить*) to fell, cut down. **2** (*построить*) to build (*of logs*).

срыв, а *m.* **1** (*плана, работы*) disruption; **с. переговóров** break-down of talks; **с. рабóты** stoppage. **2** (*со скалы*) fall. **3** (*неудача*) failure. **4** (*обрыв*) precipice.

сры́вá|ть[1], ю *impf. of* ⇒**сорвáть**

срывá|ть[2], ю *impf. of* ⇒**срыть**

срывá|ться, юсь *impf. of* ⇒**сорвáться**

срыть, срóю, срóешь *pf.* (*of* ⇒**срывáть[2]**) to raze, level to the ground.

ся́ряду *adv.* (*coll.*) running; **два рáза с.** twice running.

ссáдин|а, ы *f.* scratch, abrasion.

сса|ди́ть[1], жý, ~дишь *pf.* (*of* ⇒**~живáть**) (*coll.*) (*поцарапать*) to scratch.

сса|ди́ть[2], жý, ~дишь *pf.* (*of* ⇒**~живáть**) **1** (*помочь сойти*) to help down; **с. когó-н. с лóшади** to help s.o. down from a horse. **2** (*заставить выйти*) to put off, make get off (*from public transport*).

ссáжива|ть, ю *impf. of* ⇒**ссади́ть**

сс|ать, у, ишь, *3rd pers. pl.* **ут** *impf.* (*of* ⇒**поссáть**) (*vulg.*) to piss.

ссóр|а, ы *f.* **1** quarrel; **они́ в ~е (друг с дрýгом)** they have fallen out; **онá в ~е с сестрóй** she's fallen out with her sister. **2** (*перебранка*) slanging-match.

ссóр|ить, ю, ишь *impf.* (*of* ⇒**по~**) to cause to quarrel, cause to fall out.

ссóр|иться, юсь, ишься *impf.* (*of* ⇒**по~**) (**с**+*i.*) to quarrel (with), fall out (with).

ссóх|нуться, нется, *past* **~ся, ~лась** *pf.* (*of* ⇒**ссыхáться**) **1** (*сжаться*) to shrink, shrivel, warp. **2** (*затвердеть*) to harden out, dry out.

ССР *f. indecl.* (*abbr. of* ***Совéтская Социалисти́ческая Респýблика***) (*hist.*) Soviet Socialist Republic.

СССР *m. indecl.* (*abbr. of* ***Союз Совéтских Социалисти́ческих Респýблик***) (*hist.*) USSR (*Union of Soviet Socialist Republics*).

ссýд|а, ы *f.* loan; **бáнковская с.** bank loan; **беспроцéнтная с.** interest-free loan; **с. под залóг** secured loan.

ссу|ди́ть, жý, ~дишь *pf.* (*of* ⇒**~жáть**) (+*a. and i. or* +*d. and a.*) to lend, loan.

ссýд|ный *adj. of* ⇒**~а; с. процéнт** interest on a loan.

ссужá|ть, ю *impf. of* ⇒**ссуди́ть**

ссутýл|ить(ся), ю(сь), ишь(ся) *pf. of* ⇒**сутýлить(ся)**

ссуч|и́ть, ý, ~ишь *pf. of* ⇒**сучи́ть**

ссылá|ть(ся), ю(сь) *impf. of* ⇒**сослáть(ся)**

ссы́лк|а[1], и *f.* exile, banishment.

ссы́лк|а[2], и *f.* (**на**+*a.*) (*указание*) reference (to); (*comput.*) link.

ссы́л|очный *adj. of* ⇒**~ка[2]**; **~очное примечáние** reference note.

ссы́льн|ый, ого *m.* exile.

ссып|áть, áю *impf. of* ⇒**~ать**

ссы́п|ать, лю, лешь *pf.* (*of* ⇒**~áть**) to pour.

ссыпнóй *adj.*: **с. пункт** grain-collecting station.

ссыхá|ться, ется *impf. of* ⇒**ссóхнуться**

ст. *abbr. of* **1** ***статья́*** Art., Article (*of law, etc.*). **2** ***столéтие*** C, century.

стабилизáтор, а *m.* (*tech.*) stabilizer; (*aeron.*) tail-plane.

стабилизáци|я, и *f.* stabilization.

стабилизи́р|овать, ую *impf. and pf.* to stabilize.

стабилизи́р|оваться, уется *impf. and pf.* to become stable.

стабилиз|овáть(ся), ýю, ует(ся) *impf. and pf.* = **~и́ровать(ся)**

стаби́льност|ь, и *f.* stability.

стаби́л|ьный (~ен, ~ьна) *adj.* stable, firm; **с. учéбник** standard text-book.

стáв|ень, ня, *g. pl.* **~ней** *m.* shutter (*on window*).

стáв|ить, лю, ишь *impf.* (*of* ⇒**по~**) **1** (*помещать*) to put, place, set; (*что-н. вертикальное*) to stand; **с. цветы́ в вáзу** to put flowers in a vase; **с. буты́лки в ряд** to stand bottles in a row; **с. диáгноз** to diagnose; **с. рекóрд** to set up, create a record; **с. тóчку** to put a full stop; **с. часы́** to set a clock; **с. самовáр** to put a samovar on; **с. в заслýгу что-н. комý-н.** to credit s.o. with sth.; **с. в извéстность** to notify; **с. под вопрóс** to call into question; **с. в винý что-н. комý-н.** to accuse s.o. of sth.; **с. в упрёк что-н. комý-н.** to reproach s.o. for sth.; **с. когó-н. в нелóвкое положéние** to put s.o. in an awkward position; **с. в тупи́к** to nonplus; **с. за прáвило** to make it a rule; **с. когó-н. на мéсто** to put s.o. in his

place; **его́ ни во что не ста́вят** he is not respected.
2 (*сооружать*) to put up, erect; (*устанавливать*) to install; **с. па́мятник** to erect a monument; **с. телефо́н** to install the telephone.
3 (*назначать*) to put in, install; **с. но́вого гла́вного инжене́ра** to put in a new chief engineer.
4 (*накладывать*) to apply, put on; **с. горчи́чник** to apply a mustard plaster; **с. кому́-н. термо́метр** to take s.o.'s temperature.
5 (*вопрос, проблему*) to put, present; (*пьесу*) to put on, stage.
6 (**на**+*a.*) (*в игре*) to place, stake (*money on*); **с. на ло́шадь** to back a horse.

ста́вк|а[1], и *f.* **1** (*fin.*) rate; **с. зарпла́ты** wage rate; **~и нало́га** tax rates; **проце́нтная с.** interest rate. **2** (*в играх*) stake; **де́лать ~у** (**на**+*a.*) to stake (on); (*fig.*) to count (on), gamble (on).

ста́вк|а[2], и *f.* (*mil.*) headquarters; **с. главнокома́ндующего** General Headquarters.

ста́вк|а[3], и *f.*: **о́чная с.** (*leg.*) confrontation.

ста́вленник, а *m.* protégé.

ста́вленни|ца, цы *f.* protégée.

ста́в|ня, ни, *g. pl.* **~ен** *f.* = **ста́вень**

стагна́ци|я, и *f.* (*econ.*) stagnation.

стадиа́льный *adj.* taking place by stages.

стадио́н, а *m.* stadium.

ста́ди|я, и *f.* stage.

ста́дност|ь, и *f.* herd instinct, gregariousness.

ста́дный *adj.* (*животное*) gregarious; **с. инсти́нкт** herd instinct.

ста́д|о, а, *pl.* **~а́** *nt.* herd; flock.

стаж, а *m.* **1** (*трудовой*) length of service. **2**: (**испыта́тельный**) **с.** probation; **проходи́ть с.** to work on probation.

стажёр, а *m.* **1** (*проходящий испытательный срок*) probationer. **2** (*студент*) stazher (*student on special course not leading to degree*); exchange student.

стажи́рова́ть, стажи́рую *impf.* = **стажи́рова́ться**

стажи́рова́ться, стажи́руюсь *impf.* **1** (*проходить испытательный срок*) to work on probation. **2** (*о студенте*) to attend a special course; to be an exchange student.

стажиро́вк|а, и *f.* **1** (*испытательный срок*) probationary period. **2** (*студента*) period as a stazher; period as an exchange student.

ста́ива|ть, ет *impf. of* **⇒ста́ять**

ста́йер, а *m.* (*sport*) long-distance runner.

стака́н, а *m.* glass, tumbler; (*пластмассовый*) beaker; **бума́жный с.** paper cup.

стакка́то *nt. indecl. & adv.* (*mus.*) staccato.

сталагми́т, а *m.* stalagmite.

сталакти́т, а *m.* stalactite.

сталева́р, а *m.* steel founder.

сталелите́йный *adj.*: **с. заво́д** steel mill, steel works.

сталелите́йщик, а *m.* steel founder.

сталепрока́тный *adj.*: **с. заво́д, с. стан** steel-rolling mill.

сталини́зм, а *m.* Stalinism.

сталини́ст, а *m.* Stalinist.

сталини́ст|ка, ки *f. of* **⇒~**

ста́линск|ий *adj.* Stalin's, of Stalin; **~ая пре́мия** (*hist.*) Stalin Prize.

ста́лкива|ть(ся), ю(сь) *impf. of* **⇒столкну́ть(ся)**

ста́ло быть *see* **⇒стать[2]** 5

стал|ь, и *f.* steel; **нержаве́ющая с.** stainless steel.

стальн|о́й *adj.* steel; **~о́го цве́та** steel-blue; **с. взгляд** cold, unfriendly look; **~а́я во́ля** iron will; **с. го́лос** firm voice; **~ы́е не́рвы** nerves of steel.

Стамбу́л, а *m.* Istanbul.

стаме́ск|а, и *f.* (*tech.*) chisel.

стан[1], а *m.* (*человека*) figure, torso.

стан[2], а *m.* (*лагерь*) camp (*also fig.*); **в ~е врага́** in the enemy's camp.

стан[3], а *m.* (*tech.*) mill; **прока́тный с.** steel-rolling mill.

станда́рт, а *m.* **1** standard; **по ~у** according to the standard; **отвеча́ть/соотве́тствовать ~у** to conform to a standard. **2** (*fig.*) (*шаблон*) cliché, stereotype.

стандартиза́ци|я, и *f.* **1** standardization. **2** (*fig.*) (*личности*) stereotyping.

стандартиз|ова́ть, у́ю *impf. and pf.* to standardize.

станда́рт|ный (~ен, ~на) *adj.* standard.

стани́н|а, ы *f.* (*tech.*) mounting, bed (plate).

стани́ол|ь, я *m.* tin foil.

стани́ц|а[1], ы *f.* (*селение*) stanitsa (*large Cossack village*).

стани́ц|а[2], ы *f.* (*obs.*) (*стая*) flock.

станко́в|ый *adj.* **1** *adj. of* **⇒стано́к; с. пулемёт** (*mil.*) heavy machine-gun. **2**: **~ая жи́вопись** easel (*opp. mural*) painting.

станкострое́ни|е, я *nt.* machine-tool construction.

станов|и́ться, лю́сь, ~ишься *impf. of* **⇒стать**

стано́вищ|е, а *nt.* stopping place.

становле́ни|е, я *nt.* (*идей, характера, государства*) formation; **в проце́ссе ~я** in the making.

станово́й *adj.*: **с. хребе́т** (*fig.*) backbone.

стан|о́к[1], ка́ *m.* **1** (*tech.*) machine-tool, machine; **печа́тный с.** printing-press; **столя́рный с.** joiner's bench; **тка́цкий с.** loom; **тока́рный с.** lathe; **сверли́льный с.** drill, drilling machine. **2** (*mil.*) mount, mounting. **3** (*для холста*) frame; (*балетный*) barre.

стан|о́к[2], ка́ *m.* (*стойло*) stall (*for one horse*).

стано́чник, а *m.* machine operator, machine minder.

стано́чни|ца, цы *f. of* **⇒~к**

станс, а *m.* (*liter.*) stanza.

станцио́нный *adj. of* **⇒ста́нция; с. зал** waiting-room.

ста́нци|я, и *f.* station; **авто́бусная с.** bus station; **гидроэлектри́ческая с.** hydro-electric power station; **железнодоро́жная с.** railway (*Br.*), railroad (*US*) station; **телефо́нная с.** telephone exchange; **с. метро́** underground (*Br.*), subway (*US*) station.

ста́пел|ь, я, *pl.* **~я́** *and* **~и** *m.* (*naut.*) slipway, slip(s), stocks; **на ~е, на ~ях** on the stocks.

ста́плива|ть, ю *impf. of* **⇒стопи́ть**

ста́птыва|ть(ся), ю, ет(ся) *impf. of* **⇒стопта́ть(ся)**

стара́ни|е, я *nt.* (*усилие*) effort; (*прилежание*) diligence; **приложи́ть с.** to make an effort; **приложи́ть все ~я** to do one's best; **при всём ~и не смогу́ прийти́** however hard I try I won't be able to come.

стара́тел|ь, я *m.* gold prospector, gold-digger.

стара́тельност|ь, и *f.* application, assiduity, diligence.

стара́тел|ьный (~ен, ~ьна) *adj.* assiduous, diligent.

стара́|ться, юсь *impf.* (*of* **⇒по~**) **1** (*усердствовать*) to try; to apply o.s.; **с. изо всех сил** to do one's utmost. **2** (+*inf.*) (*стремиться*) to try, endeavour; **я ~юсь помо́чь ему́** I'm trying to help him.

стар|е́е *comp. of* **⇒~ый**

старе́йшин|а, ы *m.* (*hist., ethnol.*) elder.

старе́ни|е, я *nt.* aging.

старе́|ть, ю *impf.* **1** (*pf.* **по~**) (*человек*) to grow old, age. **2** (*pf.* **у~**) (*идея, машина*) to become obsolete.

ста́р|ец, ца *m.* **1** (*старик*) elder; (venerable) old man. **2** (*монах*) elderly monk.

стари́к, а́ *m.* old man; **глубо́кий с.** very old man; **~и́** old people.

старика́н, а *m.* (*coll.*) old fellow.

старико́вский *adj.* (*фигура*) old man's; (*привычки*) old people's.

ста́рин|а, ы *f.* (*liter.*) bylina.

старин|а́[1], ы́ *f.* **1** antiquity, olden times; **в ~у́** in olden times, in days of old; **предме́т ~ы́** antique; **тряхну́ть ~о́й** to do sth. like in the good old days. **2** (*collect.*) (*предметы*) antiques.

старин|а́[2], ы́ *m.* (*coll.*) (*старик*) old fellow, old chap (*Br.*).

стари́нк|а, и *f.* (*coll.*) old fashion, old custom(s); **по ~е** in the old fashion, in the old way.

стари́нный *adj.* **1** (*книга, обычай*) ancient, old; (*мебель, фарфор*) antique. **2** (*друг*) old, of long standing.

ста́р|ить, ю, ишь *impf.* (*of* **⇒со~**) to age.

ста́р|иться, юсь, ишься *impf.* (*of* **⇒со~**) to age; to grow old.

ста́риц|а[1], ы *f.* (*реки*) old bed.

ста́риц|а[2], ы *f.* (*монахиня*) elderly nun.

старич|о́к, ка́ *m.* little old man.

старове́р, а *m.* (*relig.*) Old Believer.
старове́р|ка, ки *f. of* ⇒~
старове́р|ский *adj. of* ⇒~
староверств|о, а *nt.* Old Belief.
старода́вний *adj.* ancient.
старожи́л, а *m.* old inhabitant, old resident.
старозаве́т|ный (~ен, ~на) *adj.* **1** (*человек*) old-fashioned, conservative; (*предание*) ancient. **2** (*pej.*) (*взгляды*) old, antiquated.
старомо́д|ный (~ен, ~на) *adj.* old-fashioned; out-of-date.
старообра́з|ный (~ен, на) *adj.* old-looking.
старообря́д|ец, ца *m.* (*relig.*) Old Believer.
старообря́д|ческий *adj. of* ⇒**~ец** *and* **~чество**
старообря́дчеств|о, а *nt.* (*relig.*) Old Belief.
старору́сский *adj.* old Russian.
старосве́тский *adj.* old-world; old-fashioned.
старославя́нский *adj.* (*ling.*) Old Church Slavonic.
ста́рост|а, ы *m.* head; **се́льский с.** (*hist.*) village headman, elder; **церко́вный с.** churchwarden; **с. кла́сса** (*in school*) form prefect, monitor.
ста́рост|ь, и *f.* old age; **на ~и лет, под с.** in one's old age.
старт, а *m.* **1** (*sport, fig.*) start; **взять с.** (*спортсмен*) to start; (*начать делать*) to begin, commence; **дать с.** to start; **на с.!** on your marks! **2** (*aeron.*) take-off.
ста́ртер, а *m.* (*tech.*) starter.
стартёр, а *m.* (*sport*) starter.
старт|ова́ть, у́ю *impf. and pf.* **1** (*sport*) to start. **2** (*aeron.*) to take off. **3** (*отправляться*) to start out; to depart. **4** (*начинаться*) to begin, commence.
ста́ртовый *adj.* starting.
стару́х|а, и *f.* old woman, old lady; **глубо́кая с.** very old woman.
стару́|шечий *adj. of* ⇒**~ха;** old-womanish.
стару́шк|а, и *f.* (little) old lady, old woman.
ста́рческий *adj.* old person's; **с. во́зраст** old age; **с. мара́зм** senility.
ста́рше *comp. of* ⇒**ста́рый;** (*взрослее*): **она́ с. меня́ на три го́да** she is three years older than me; (*выше*): **он ста́рше меня́ по зва́нию** he is senior to me in rank.
старшекла́ссник, а *m.* senior (pupil).
старшекла́ссни|ца, цы *f. of* ⇒**~к**
старшеку́рсник, а *m.* senior student.
старшеку́рсни|ца, цы *f. of* ⇒**~к**
ста́рш|ий *adj.* **1** (*более старый*) elder, older; **с. брат** older brother; **~ее поколе́ние** older generation; *as n.* **~ие, ~их** (one's) elders, grown-ups; **слу́шаться ~их** to obey one's elders. **2** (*самый старый*) oldest, eldest. **3** (*по служебному положению*) senior, superior; (*в названиях*) chief, head; **с. врач** head physician; **~ая медсестра́** senior nurse, sister (*Br.*); *as n.* **с., ~его** *m.* chief; (*mil.*) man in charge. **4** (*высший*) senior, upper, higher; **~ая ка́рта** higher card; **с. класс** (*in school*) higher form (*Br.*), senior grade (*US*).
старшин|а́, ы́, *pl.* **~ы, ~** *m.* **1** (*mil.*) sergeant-major; (*naut.*) petty officer. **2** (*hist.*) leader, senior representative; **с. прися́жных заседа́телей** foreman of the jury.
старшинств|о́, а́ *nt.* seniority; **по ~у́** by seniority.
ста́р|ый (~, ~а́, ~о́) *adj.* old; **с. стиль** the Old Style (*of the Julian calendar*); **~ая де́ва** old maid, spinster; **по ~ой па́мяти** for old times' sake; from force of habit; *as n.* **~ые, ~ых** the old, old people; **~ое, ~ого** *nt.* the old, the past.
стар|ьё, я *nt.* (*collect.*; *coll.*) old things, old clothes; (*давно известное*) old stuff; (*старики*) old people.
старьёвщик, а *m.* old-clothes dealer; junk dealer.
ста́скива|ть, ю *impf. of* ⇒**стащи́ть**
стас|ова́ть, у́ю *pf. of* ⇒**тасова́ть**
ста́тик|а, и *f.* **1** statics. **2** (*неподвижность*) stasis.
стати́ст, а *m.* (*theatr.*) extra.
стати́стик, а *m.* statistician.
стати́стик|а, и *f.* statistics.
статисти́ческий *adj.* statistical.
стати́ческий *adj.* static.
ста́т|ный (~ен, ~на) *adj.* stately.
ста́тор, а *m.* (*tech.*) stator.
ста́точн|ый *adj.*: **~ое ли де́ло?** (*obs.*) is it possible?
статс-да́м|а, ы *f.* (*hist.*) lady-in-waiting.
ста́тский *adj.* **1** (*obs.*) = **шта́тский. 2** (*hist.*; *as part of titles of ranks in tsarist Russian civil service*) State; **с. сове́тник** Councillor of State.
статс-секрета́р|ь, я *m.* (*должностное лицо*) Secretary of State.
ста́тус, а *m.* status.
ста́тус-кво́ *m. indecl.* status quo.
стату́т, а *m.* statute.
статуэ́тк|а, и *f.* statuette, figurine.
ста́ту|я, и *f.* statue.
стать[1], ста́ну, ста́нешь *pf.* (*of* ⇒**станови́ться**) **1** (*встать*) to stand; **с. на коле́ни** to kneel; **с. в о́чередь** to queue (up) (*Br.*), stand in line (*US*); **с. на о́чередь** to join the waiting list; **с. в по́зу** to strike an attitude; **с. на цы́почки** to stand on tip-toe; (*начать бороться*) to stand up for; **с. на чью-н. сто́рону** to take s.o.'s side, stand up for s.o.; **с. на защи́ту угнетённых** to stand up for the oppressed. **2** (*расположиться*) to take up position; **с. ла́герем** to camp, encamp; **с. в карау́л** to mount guard; **с. на рабо́ту** to start work; **с. на я́корь** to anchor. **3** (*остановиться*) to stop, come to a halt; **мои́ часы́ ста́ли** my watch has stopped; **река́ ста́ла** the river has frozen over; **за чем ста́ло де́ло?** (*coll.*) what's holding things up? **4** (**в**+*a.*; *coll.*) (*стоить*) to cost; **телеви́зор стал в 100 рубле́й** the television cost 100 roubles; **во что бы то ни ста́ло** at any price, at all costs.
стать[2], ста́ну, ста́нешь *pf.* (*of* ⇒**станови́ться**) **1** (+*inf.*) (*начать*) to begin (to), start; **она́ ста́ла говори́ть** she began talking. **2** (+*i.*) (*сделаться*) to become, get, grow; **он стал машини́стом** he became an engine-driver; **ста́ло темно́** it got dark; **ей ста́ло лу́чше** she was better; she had got better; **мне ста́ло интере́сно/стра́шно** I became interested/afraid; **мне ста́ло тру́дно** it got difficult for me. **3** (**с**+*i.*) (*случиться*) to become (of), happen (to); **что с ни́ми ста́ло?** what has become of them? **4**: **не с.** (*impers.*+*g.*) (*умереть*) to die; **её отца́ давно́ не ста́ло** her father passed away long ago; (*исчезнуть*) to disappear, go; **дере́вьев не ста́ло** all the trees have gone; **сил не ста́ло у него́** all his energy has gone. **5**: **ста́ло быть** (*coll.*) consequently, therefore. **6** (*impers.*; *coll.*) (*хватать*) to suffice; **с него́ э́то ста́нет** it is what one might expect of him.
стат|ь[3], и, *pl.* **~и, ~е́й** *f.* **1** (*телосложение*) figure, build; (*pl.*) (*лошади*) points. **2** (*характер*) character, type; **быть под с.** (+*d.*) to be (well) matched (with).
стат|ь[4], и *f.* (*obs.*) (*надобность*) need, necessity; **с како́й ~и?** why?, whatever for?
ста́|ться, нется *pf.* (*coll.*) to happen, become; **что с на́ми ~нется?** what will become of us?; **вполне́ мо́жет с.** it is quite possible; **с него́ ста́нется** it is what one might expect from him.
стат|ья́, ьи́, *g. pl.* **~е́й** *f.* **1** (*газетная, научная*) article; **передова́я с.** leading article, leader, editorial. **2** (*закона, договора*) clause; (*финансого документа*) item; (*в словаре*) entry; **расхо́дная с.** debit item. **3** (*coll.*) (*дело*) matter, job; **э́то осо́бая с.** this is a separate matter; **по всем ~ья́м** (*coll.*) in all respects; completely. **4** (*naut.*) class, rating; **матро́с пе́рвой ~ьи́** able seaman. **5** (*pl.*) (*лошади*) points. **6** (*coll.*) (*наказание*) conviction.
стафилоко́кк, а *m.* (*med.*, *biol.*) staphylococcus.
стаха́нов|ец, ца *m.* (*hist.*) Stakhanovite.
стаха́нов|ка, ки *f. of* ⇒**~ец**
стаха́новский *adj.* (*hist.*) Stakhanovite.
стациона́р, а *m.* permanent establishment; (*лечебный*) hospital.
стациона́рн|ый *adj.* **1** stationary; **с. объе́кт** (*mil.*) stationary target. **2** permanent, fixed; **~ая библиоте́ка** permanent library. **3** (*больничный*) hospital; **с. больно́й** in-patient; **~ое лече́ние** hospitalization.
ста́чечник, а *m.* striker.
ста́чечни|ца, цы *f. of* ⇒**~к**
ста́ч|ечный *adj. of* ⇒**~ка**
ста́чива|ть, ю *impf. of* ⇒**сточи́ть**
ста́чк|а, и *f.* (*забастовка*) strike.

С

стащ|и́ть, у́, ~́ишь *pf.* (*of* ⇒**ста́скивать**) **1** (*сапоги*) to pull off; (*тащa, доставить*) to drag. **2** (*coll.*) (*украсть*) to pinch (*Br.*), swipe.

ста́|я, и *f.* (*птиц*) flock; (*рыб*) school, shoal; (*волков*) pack.

ста́|ять, ет *pf.* (*of* ⇒**~ивать**) to melt.

ствол, а́ *m.* **1** (*дерева*) trunk. **2** (*оружия*) barrel; (*само оружие*) gun. **3** (*mining*) shaft.

створ, а *m.* = **~ка**

ство́рк|а, и *f.* (*двери, зеркала*) leaf, fold; (*ворот, ставней*) half, side.

створо́ж|иться, ится *pf.* to curdle.

ство́рчатый *adj.* (*дверь*) folding; (*раковина*) valved.

стеари́н, а *m.* stearin.

стеари́н|овый *adj. of* ⇒**~**; **~овая свеча́** stearin candle.

сте́бел|ь, ля, *pl.* **~ли, ~ле́й** *m.* stem, stalk.

стёганк|а, и *f.* (*coll.*) quilted jacket.

стёган|ый *adj.* quilted; **~ое одея́ло** quilt.

стега́|ть[1], ю *impf.* (*of* ⇒**от~** *and* **стегну́ть**) (*хлестать*) to whip, lash.

стега́|ть[2], ю *impf.* (*of* ⇒**вы́~**) (*одеяло*) to quilt.

стег|ну́ть, ну́, нёшь *pf. of* ⇒**~а́ть[1]**

стёжк|а[1], и *f.* (*действие*) quilting; (*шов*) stitch.

стёжк|а[2], и *f.* (*coll.*) (*дорожка*) path.

стеж|о́к, ка́ *m.* stitch.

стез|я́, и́, *g. pl.* **~е́й** *f.* (*rhet.*) path, way.

стека́|ть(ся), ет(ся) *impf. of* ⇒**сте́чь(ся)**

стеклене́|ть, ет *impf.* (*of* ⇒**о~**) to become glassy; (*fig.*) (*о глазах*) to glaze over.

стекл|и́ть, ю́, и́шь *impf.* (*of* **за~, о~**) to glaze.

стек|ло́, ла́, *pl.* **~́ла, ~́ол** *nt.* glass; (*collect.*) glassware; **око́нное с.** window-pane; **лобово́е, ветрово́е с.** windscreen (*Br.*), windshield (*US*); **~́ла для очко́в** lenses (*for spectacles*).

стеклова́т|а, ы *f.* glass wool.

стеклови́д|ный (~ен, ~на) *adj.* glassy; vitreous.

стекловолокн|о́, а́ *nt.* fibreglass (*Br.*), fiberglass (*US*).

стеклоду́в, а *m.* glass-blower.

стеклоду́вный *adj.* glass-blowing.

стеклоочисти́тел|ь, я *m.* windscreen (*Br.*), windshield (*US*) wiper.

стеклоре́з, а *m.* (*инструмент*) glass cutter.

стеклота́р|а, ы *f.* glass containers.

стёклыш|ко, ка, *pl.* **~ки, ~ек, ~кам** *nt.* **1** *dim. of* ⇒**стекло́**. **2** (*кусочек стекла*) piece of glass. **3**: **как с.** (*безупречно чист*) squeaky clean; (*трезвый*) sober.

стекля́нн|ый *adj.* **1** glass; **~ая бума́га** glass-paper; **~ые изде́лия** glassware; (*окно, дверь*) glazed; **~ое волокно́** fibreglass (*Br.*), fiberglass (*US*). **2** (*fig.*) (*взгляд, глаза*) glassy.

стекля́рус, а *m.* (*collect.*) bugles (*tube-shaped glass beads*).

стекля́шк|а, и *f.* (*coll.*) piece of glass.

стеко́льный *adj.* glass; **с. заво́д** glass-works, glass-factory.

стеко́льщик, а *m.* glazier.

сте́л|а, ы *f.* obelisk.

стел|и́ть, ю́, ~́ешь *impf.* **1** (*pf.* **по~**) to spread; **с. посте́ль** to make a bed; **с. ска́терть** to lay a table-cloth. **2** (*pf.* **на~**) (*паркет, пол*) to lay.

стел|и́ться, ю́сь, ~́ешься *impf.* **1** (*распространяться*) to spread, creep. **2** (*pf.* **по~**) (*стелить себе постель*) to make one's bed, get ready for bed.

стелла́ж, а́ *m.* **1** (*полки*) shelves. **2** (*для лыж, для вёсел*) rack, stand.

сте́льк|а, и *f.* insole, sock; **пьян в ~у, как с.** (*coll.*) drunk as a lord.

сте́льная *adj.*: **с. коро́ва** calver, in-calf cow.

стемне́|ть, ет *pf. of* ⇒**темне́ть**

стен|а́, ы́, *a.* **~́у,** *pl.* **~́ы,** *d.* **~а́м** *f.* wall (*also fig.*); **жить с. в ~́у (с** + *i.*) to live right on top (of); **жить/сиде́ть в четырёх ~а́х** to sit at home, be isolated; **в ~а́х** (+*g.*) inside, within the precincts (of); **как о́б ~у горо́х** (*coll.*) pointless, useless.

стена́|ть, ю *impf.* (*obs.*) to groan, moan.

стенгазе́т|а, ы *f.* (*abbr. of* ***стенна́я газе́та***) wall newspaper.

стенд, а *m.* **1** (*на выставке*) stand (*Br.*), booth (*US*). **2** (*для испытаний*) test bed. **3** (*для стрельбы*) rifle range.

сте́нк|а, и *f.* **1** (*стена*) wall; **гимнасти́ческая с.** wall-bars. **2** (*ящика, кастрюли*) side; (*желудка*) wall. **3** (*мебель*) wall unit. **4**: **ста́вить к ~е** (*coll.*) to shoot (*execute*).

стенн|о́й *adj.* wall; **~а́я жи́вопись** mural painting.

стеноби́тный *adj.*: **с. тара́н** battering-ram.

стенограмм|а, ы *f.* shorthand report.

стено́граф, а *m.* stenographer.

стенографи́р|овать, ую *impf. and pf.* (*pf. also* **за~**) to take down in shorthand.

стенографи́ст, а *m.* = **стено́граф**

стенографи́ст|ка, ки *f. of* ⇒**~**

стенографи́ческий *adj.* stenographic, shorthand.

стеногра́фи|я, и *f.* stenography, shorthand.

стенокарди́|я, и *f.* angina (pectoris).

стенопи́с|ец, ца *m.* mural painter.

сте́нопис|ь, и *f.* mural (painting).

сте́ньг|а, и *f.* (*naut.*) topmast.

степе́н|ный (~ен, ~на) *adj.* **1** staid, steady. **2** (*coll.*) (*немолодой*) middle-aged.

сте́пен|ь, и, *g. pl.* **~е́й** *f.* **1** degree, extent; **в вы́сшей ~и** in the highest degree; **до изве́стной ~и, до не́которой ~и** to some extent, to a certain extent; **~и сравне́ния** (*gram.*) degrees of comparison; **ожо́г пе́рвой ~и** first-degree burn. **2** (*math.*) power; **возвести́ в тре́тью с.** to raise to the third power. **3** (*звание*) (academic) degree; (*разряд*) class; **дипло́м пе́рвой ~и** first-class degree; **с. бакала́вра** bachelor's degree; **учёная с. до́ктора нау́к** doctorate.

сте́плер, а *m.* stapler.

степ|но́й *adj. of* ⇒**~ь**

степ|ь, и, о ~́и, в ~и́, *pl.* **~́и, ~е́й** *f.* steppe.

сте́рв|а, ы *f.* (*vulg.; as term of abuse*) bastard, shit; (*о женщине*) bitch.

стервене́|ть, ю *impf.* (*of* ⇒**о~**) (*coll.*) to get mad.

стерв|е́ц, еца́ *m.* = **~́а**

стервя́тник, а *m.* carrion-crow.

сте́рео *nt. indecl.* stereo (*record-player, cassette player*).

стерео... *comb. form* stereo-.

стереозвуча́ни|е, я *nt.* stereo (sound).

стереокино́ *nt. indecl.* stereoscopic cinema.

стереоме́три|я, и *f.* stereometry, solid geometry.

стереосисте́м|а, ы *f.* stereo (system).

стереоско́п, а *m.* stereoscope.

стереоскопи́ческий *adj.* stereoscopic.

стереоти́п, а *m.* stereotype.

стереоти́пн|ый *adj.* **1** (*копия, издание*) stereotype. **2** (*fig.*) (*ответ, поведение*) stereotypical, stereotyped; **~ая фра́за** stock phrase.

стереофони́ческий *adj.* stereophonic.

стереохи́ми|я, и *f.* stereochemistry.

стер|е́ть, сотру́, сотрёшь, *past* **~́, ~ла** *pf.* (*of* ⇒**стира́ть[1]**) **1** (*рисунок*) to rub out, erase; (*comput.*) to delete; (*пыль, пот*) to wipe off; **с. с лица́ земли́** to wipe off the face of the earth. **2** (*ногу*) to rub sore. **3** (*в порошок*) to grind (down).

стер|е́ться, сотрётся, *past* **~́ся, ~́лась** *pf.* (*of* ⇒**стира́ться[1]**) **1** (*о надписи, о краске*) to rub off; (*fig.*) (*забыться*) to fade; **с. в па́мяти** to fade from one's memory. **2** (*о подошвах, о пальцах*) to become worn down.

стере́|чь, гу́, жёшь, гу́т, *past* **~́г, ~гла́** *impf.* **1** (*вещи, стадо*) to guard, watch (over). **2** (*ждать появления*) to lie in wait (for).

сте́рж|ень, ня *m.* **1** (*tech.*) pivot; shank, rod; **поршнево́й с.** piston rod. **2** (*fig.*) (*основа*) core.

стержнево́й *adj.* pivoted; **с. вопро́с** key question.

стерилиза́тор, а *m.* sterilizer.

стерилиза́ци|я, и *f.* sterilization.

стерилиз|ова́ть, у́ю *impf. and pf.* to sterilize.

стери́льност|ь, и *f.* sterility.

стери́л|ьный (~ен, ~ьна) *adj.* sterile; (*не загрязнённый*) germ-free.

сте́рлинг, а *m.* (*fin.*) sterling; **фунт ~ов** pound sterling.

сте́рлинг|овый *adj. of* ⇒**~**; **~ая зо́на** sterling area.

сте́рляд|ь, и *f.* (*zool.*) sterlet.

стерн|ь, и *f.* **1** (*жнивьё*) harvest-field. **2** (*collect.*) (*остатки стеблей*) stubble.

стерн|я́, и́ *f.* = **∼ь**

стеро́ид, а *m.* steroid.

стерп|е́ть, лю́, ∼́ишь *pf.* to bear, suffer, endure.

стерп|е́ться, лю́сь, ∼́ишься *pf.* (**с** + *i.*; *coll.*) to get used (to), accept; **∼́ится — слю́бится** you will like it when you get used to it.

стёр|тый *p.p.p. of* ⇒**∼е́ть** *and adj.* (*надпись, монета*) worn, faded; (*fig.*) (*очертание*) faint; (*фраза*) hackneyed.

сте|са́ть, шу́, ∼́ешь *pf.* (*of* ⇒**стёсывать**) **1** (*удалить*) to plane off. **2** (*обровнять*) to plane.

стесне́ни|е, я *nt.* (*ограничение*) constraint; (*смущение*) shyness, timidness; **без(о) вся́ких ∼й** quite uninhibitedly.

стесн|ённый *p.p.p. of* ⇒**∼и́ть** *and adj.* **∼ённые обстоя́тельства** straitened circumstances; **∼ённое дыха́ние** constricted, laboured (*Br.*), labored (*US*) breathing; **с ∼ённым се́рдцем** with a heavy heart.

стесни́тельност|ь, и *f.* (*застенчивость*) shyness; awkwardness.

стесни́тел|ьный (∼ен, ∼ьна) *adj.* **1** (*застенчивый*) shy; awkward. **2** (*obs.*) (*условия*) straitened.

стесн|и́ть, ю́, и́шь *pf.* (*of* ⇒**∼я́ть**) **1** (*в расходах, в поведении, свободу*) to constrain; (*проход*) to hamper; (*в поведении*) to inhibit. **2** (*горло, грудь*) to constrict. **3** (*потеснить*) to inconvenience.

стесн|и́ться, ю́сь, и́шься *pf.* (*of* ⇒**тесни́ться**) **1** (*о людях*) to crowd together. **2** (*о дыхании*) to become constricted; (*impers.*): **∼и́лось в груди́** his/her, *etc.* chest became constricted.

стесн|я́ть, я́ю *impf. of* ⇒**∼и́ть**

стесня́|ться, юсь *impf.* (*of* ⇒**по∼**) (+ *inf.*) to feel too shy (to), be ashamed (to); (+ *g.*) to feel shy (before, of); **не ∼йтесь!** don't be shy!; **не с. в сре́дствах** to use any means possible; **не с. в выраже́ниях** to not mince one's words; **ниче́м не с.** to stop at nothing.

стёсыва|ть, ю *impf. of* ⇒**стеса́ть**

стетоско́п, а *m.* (*med.*) stethoscope.

стече́ни|е, я *nt.* (*рек*) confluence; **с. наро́да** assembly, gathering; **при большо́м ∼и наро́да** with lots of people present; **с. обстоя́тельств** coincidence.

сте|чь, чёт, ку́т, *past* **∼́к, ∼кла́** *pf.* (*of* ⇒**∼ка́ть**) to flow down.

сте́|чься, чётся, ку́тся, *past* **∼́кся, ∼кла́сь** *pf.* (*of* ⇒**∼ка́ться**) to flow together; (*о людях*) to gather, assemble.

сти́бр|ить, ю, ишь *pf.* (*coll.*) to pinch (*Br.*), snaffle.

стивидо́р, а *m.* stevedore.

стил|ево́й *adj. of* ⇒**∼ь**; **∼евы́е катего́рии** stylistic categories.

стиле́т, а *m.* (*кинжал*) stiletto (*dagger*).

стилиза́ци|я, и *f.* stylization.

стилиз|ова́ть, у́ю *impf. and pf.* to stylize.

стили́ст, а *m.* **1** (*мастер стиля*) stylist. **2** (*гримёр*) make-up artist.

стили́стик|а, и *f.* (*study of*) style, stylistics.

стилисти́ческий *adj.* stylistic.

стил|ь, я *m.* style; **но́вый с.** New Style (*Gregorian calendar*); **ста́рый с.** Old Style (*Julian calendar*); **он в своём ∼е** he is his usual self.

сти́л|ьный (∼ен, ∼ьна) *adj.* stylish; **∼ьная ме́бель** period furniture.

стиля́г|а, и *c.g.* slave to fashion.

сти́мул, а *m.* incentive, stimulus.

стимули́ровани|е, я *nt.* stimulation, encouragement.

стимули́р|овать, ую *impf. and pf.* to stimulate, encourage.

стимуля́ци|я, и *f.* stimulation; **с. ро́дов** (*med.*) induction.

стипендиа́т, а *m.* grant-aided student, scholarship holder.

стипе́нди|я, и *f.* grant, scholarship.

стипль-чёз, а *m.* steeplechase.

стира́льн|ый *adj.* washing; **∼ая маши́на** washing machine; **с. порошо́к** washing powder.

стира́|ть[1]**, ю** *impf. of* ⇒**стере́ть**

стира́|ть[2]**, ю** *impf.* (*of* ⇒**вы́∼**) to wash, launder.

стира́|ться[1]**, ется** *impf. of* ⇒**стере́ться**

стира́|ться[2]**, ется** *impf.* to wash; **хорошо́ с.** to wash well.

сти́рк|а, и *f.* washing, laundering; **отда́ть в ∼у** to send to the wash, send to the laundry.

сти́скива|ть, ю *impf. of* ⇒**сти́снуть**

сти́с|нуть, ну, нешь *pf.* (*of* ⇒**∼кивать**) to squeeze; **с. зу́бы** to clench one's teeth; **с. в объя́тиях** to hug.

стих[1]**, а́** *m.* **1** verse. **2** (*pl.*) verses; poetry.

стих[2] *m. indecl.* (*coll.*) (*настроение*) mood; **на него́ угрю́мый с. нашёл** he was in a gloomy mood.

стих[3] *see* ⇒**∼нуть**

стиха́р|ь, я́ *m.* (*eccl.*) surplice.

стих|а́ть, а́ю *impf. of* ⇒**∼нуть**

стихи́йност|ь, и *f.* spontaneity.

стихи́|йный (∼ен, ∼йна) *adj.* **1** elemental; **∼йное бе́дствие** natural disaster. **2** (*fig.*) (*протест*) spontaneous, uncontrolled.

стихи́|я, и *f.* element; **борьба́ со ∼ями** struggle with the elements; **быть в свое́й ∼и** to be in one's element; (*fig.*) (*общественной жизни*) natural force.

сти́х|нуть, ну, нешь, *past* **∼, ∼ла** *pf.* (*of* ⇒**∼а́ть**) (*шум, ветер, дождь*) to abate, subside, die down; (*человек*) to calm down.

стихоплёт, а *m.* (*coll.*) rhymester, versifier.

стихосложе́ни|е, я *nt.* versification; (*размер*) metre (*Br.*), meter (*US*).

стихотворе́ни|е, я *nt.* poem.

стихотво́р|ец, ца *m.* poet.

стихотво́рный *adj.* in verse form; **с. разме́р** metre (*Br.*), meter (*US*).

стихотво́рчеств|о, а *nt.* poetry-writing.

стиш|о́к, ка́ *m.* (*coll.*) verse, rhyme.

стлать, стелю́, сте́лешь *impf.* (*of* ⇒**по∼**) = **стели́ть**

стла́ться, сте́лется *impf.* = **стели́ться** 1

сто, ста, *pl.* **ста, сот, стам, ста́ми, стах** *num.* hundred; **не́сколько сот рубле́й** several hundred roubles; **на все сто** (*coll.*) in first-rate fashion; **я сто раз тебе́ говори́л** (*coll.*) I've told you a hundred times.

стог, а, *pl.* **∼а́** *m.* (*agric.*) stack, rick.

стоеро́сов|ый *adj. only in phrr.* (*coll.*): **дуби́на ∼ая!, дура́к (болва́н) с.!** damned fool!

сто́ик, а *m.* (*phil. and fig.*) stoic.

сто́имост|ь, и *f.* **1** (*цена*) cost; **с. перево́зки** carriage; **с. прое́зда** fare; **с. по по́чте** postage; **с. жи́зни** cost of living; **о́бщей ∼ью в** (+ *a.*) to a total value of. **2** (*econ.*) (*ценность*) value; **доба́вленная с.** added value; **менова́я с.** exchange value; **номина́льная с.** face value; **приба́вочная с.** surplus value.

сто́|ить, ю, ишь *impf.* **1** to cost (*also fig.*); **ско́лько ∼ит э́то пла́тье?** how much is this dress?; **до́рого с.** to cost dear; **э́то ему́ ничего́ не ∼ило** it cost him nothing.
2 (+ *g.*) (*заслуживать*) to be worth; to deserve; **он её не ∼ит** he doesn't deserve her; **чего́ ∼ят его́ обеща́ния?** his promises are worth nothing; **чего́ ∼ит его́ после́дний фильм!** his last film was very good!; (*impers.*): **∼ит** it is worth while; **∼ит посмотре́ть э́тот фильм** this film is worth seeing; **об э́том ∼ит поду́мать** it's worth thinking about; **не ∼ит того́** (*coll.*) it is not worth while; **не ∼ит (благода́рности)** don't mention it, you're welcome.
3: **∼ит то́лько** (*impers.* + *inf.*) one has only (to); **∼ит то́лько упомяну́ть её и́мя, (как) он вы́йдет из себя́** you have only to mention her name for him to fly off the handle.

стоици́зм, а *m.* (*phil. and fig.*) stoicism.

стои́ческий *adj.* (*phil.*) stoic; (*fig.*) stoical.

сто́йбищ|е, а *nt.* nomad camp; (*животных*) stopping place, resting place.

сто́йк|а, и *f.* **1** (*sport*) stand, stance; **с. на рука́х** hand-stand; **стоя́ть по ∼е сми́рно/во́льно** to stand to attention/at ease. **2** (*hunting*) set; **сде́лать ∼у** to point. **3** (*tech.*) support, prop; (*ворот*) bar. **4** (*прилавок*) bar, counter. **5** (*воротник*) stand-up collar.

сто́|йкий (∼ек, ∼йка́, ∼йко) *adj.* **1** firm, stable; (*chem.*) stable; (*запах*) persistent. **2** (*fig.*) (*характер*) stable; steadfast, staunch, steady.

сто́йкост|ь, и *f.* **1** (*постоянство качеств*) stability; (*к воздействию*) resistance; (*к износу*) durability. **2** (*fig.*) (*характера*) steadfastness, staunchness, firmness.

сто́йл|о, а *nt.* stall.

сто́йло|вый *adj. of* ⇒**∼**; **∼вое**

С

содержа́ние скота́ keeping cattle stalled.

стоймя́ *adv.* upright.

сток, а *m.* **1** (*действие*) flow; drainage, outflow. **2** (*место, устройство*) drain, gutter; sewer.

Стокго́льм, а *m.* Stockholm.

стокра́т *adv.* a hundred times.

стокра́тный *adj.* hundredfold.

сто́л, а́ *m.* **1** (*предмет мебели*) table; **пи́сьменный с.** desk; **сесть за с.** to sit down to table; **за ~о́м** at table. **2** (*питание*) board; (*кухня*) cooking, cuisine; **ры́бный с.** fish diet; **«шве́дский» с.** smorgasbord; **с. и кварти́ра** board and lodging. **3** (*отделение*) department; office; **с. нахо́док** lost property office. **4** (*hist.*) (*престол*) throne.

столб, а́ *m.* post, pole, pillar, column; **телегра́фный с.** telegraph pole; (*fig.*) (*дыма, пыли*) cloud; **стоя́ть ~о́м** (*coll.*) to stand rooted to the ground.

столбене́|ть, ю *impf.* (*of* ⇒**о~**) (*coll.*) to be rooted to the ground.

столб|е́ц, ца́ *m.* **1** (*в газете, словаре*) column. **2** (*pl.*) (*свиток*) parchment roll.

сто́лбик, а *m.* **1** *dim. of* ⇒**столб;** (*в газете*) column; **рту́тный с.** mercury column. **2** (*bot.*) style.

столбня́к, а́ *m.* **1** (*med.*) tetanus. **2** (*coll.*) stupor; **на неё нашёл с.** she was in a stupor.

столбов|о́й *adj. of* ⇒**столб;** (*hist.*) hereditary; (*fig., coll.*) main, chief; **~а́я доро́га** high road, highway (*also fig.*).

столе́ти|е, я *nt.* **1** (*век*) century. **2** (*годовщина*) centenary.

столе́тн|ий *adj.* **1** hundred-year; **~яя война́** the Hundred Years' War. **2** (*дуб, старец*) hundred-year-old; **~яя годовщи́на** centenary.

столе́тник, а *m.* (*bot.*) agave.

сто́л|ик, а *m. dim. of* ⇒**~ 1; ни́зкий с.** coffee table.

столи́ц|а, ы *f.* capital; metropolis.

столи́|чный *adj. of* ⇒**~ца; с. го́род** capital (city).

столкнове́ни|е, я *nt.* (*автомобилей*) collision; (*mil. and fig.*) clash; **вооружённое с.** armed conflict, hostilities; **с. интере́сов** clash of interests.

столкн|у́ть, у́, ёшь *pf.* (*of* ⇒**ста́лкивать**) **1** (*сбросить, сдвинуть*) to push off; **с. ло́дку в во́ду** to push a boat off (into the water). **2** (*сблизить*) to cause to collide; to knock together. **3** (*о случае, об обстоятельствах*) to bring together.

столкн|у́ться, у́сь, ёшься *pf.* (*of* ⇒**ста́лкиваться**) **1** (**с**+*i.*) to collide (with) (*also fig.*); (*вступить в конфликт*) to clash (with), conflict (with). **2** (**с**+*i.*; *fig.*) (*встретиться*) to run (into), bump (into); **с. со ста́рым ученико́м** to bump into an old pupil; (*с трудностями, с равнодушием*) to encounter.

столк|ова́ться, у́юсь *pf.* (*of* ⇒**~о́вываться**) (**с**+*i.*; *coll.*) to come to an agreement (with).

столко́выва|ться, юсь *impf. of* ⇒**столкова́ться**

стол|ова́ться, у́юсь *impf.* to have meals.

столо́в|ая, ой *f.* (*в доме*) dining-room; (*в армии*) mess; (*на работе*) canteen, cafeteria; (*общественная*) cafeteria.

столо́в|ый *adj.* table; **~ое вино́** table wine; **~ая ло́жка** table-spoon; **с. прибо́р** cover; **~ое серебро́** (*collect.*) silver, plate; **с. серви́з** dinner service; **~ая соль** table-salt.

столонача́льник, а *m.* head of a 'desk' (*in civil service*).

стол|о́чь, ку́, чёшь, ку́т, *past* **~о́к, ~кла́** *pf.* (*of* ⇒**толо́чь**) to pound, grind.

столп, а́ *m.* (*arch. or fig.*) pillar, column; **~ы́ о́бщества** pillars of society.

столп|и́ться, и́тся *pf.* to crowd.

столпотворе́ни|е, я *nt.* chaos, pandemonium.

столь *adv.* so; **э́то не с. ва́жно** it is of no particular importance.

сто́лько *adv.* (*неисчисляемые*) so much; (*исчисляемые*) so many; **с. любви́/де́нег** so much love/money; **с. домо́в** so many houses; **нельзя́ с. рабо́тать** you should not work so much; **с. ..., ско́лько** as much ... as; **не с. ... ско́лько** not so much ... as.

сто́лько-то *adv.* (*о неисчисляемом количестве*) so much; (*об исчисляемом количестве*) so many.

столя́р, а́ *m.* joiner.

столя́рнича|ть, ю *impf.* to do carpentry.

столя́рн|ый *adj.* joiner's; **~ое де́ло** joinery.

стомато́лог, а *m.* dental surgeon.

стоматологи́ческий *adj.* dental.

стоматоло́ги|я, и *f.* dentistry.

стометро́вк|а, и *f.* (*sport*) (*coll.*) the hundred metres (*Br.*), meters (*US*).

стон, а *m.* moan, groan.

стон|а́ть, у́, ~ешь *and* **~а́ю, ~а́ешь** *impf.* to moan, groan (*also fig.*).

стоп *int.* stop!; **сигна́л с.** stop signal.

стоп|а́[1], ы́ *f.* **1** (*pl.* **~ы́**) (*нога*) foot (*also fig.*); **напра́вить свои́ ~ы** to direct, bend one's steps; **идти́ по чьим-н. ~а́м** to follow in s.o.'s footsteps. **2** (*pl.* **~ы**) (*liter.*) foot.

стоп|а́[2], ы́, *pl.* **~ы** *f.* **1** (*единица счёта бумаги*) ream. **2** (*куча*) pile, heap.

стоп|а́[3], ы́, *pl.* **~ы** *f.* (*obs.*) (*для вина*) winebowl.

стоп|и́ть, лю́, ~ишь *pf.* (*of* ⇒**ста́пливать**) to use up (*fuel, by burning*).

сто́пк|а[1], и *f.* (*куча*) pile, heap.

сто́пк|а[2], и *f.* (*стаканчик*) small glass.

стоп-кра́н, а *m.* emergency cord (*on train*).

сто́пор, а *m.* (*tech.*) stop, catch, locking device.

сто́пор|ить, ю, ишь *impf.* (*tech.*) to stop; (*fig., coll.*) to bring to a standstill, halt.

сто́пор|иться, ится *impf.* (*coll.*) to come to a standstill, halt.

сто́пор|ный *adj. of* ⇒**~; с. кран** stopcock; **с. механи́зм** stop gear, locking device.

стопроце́нтный *adj.* hundred per cent.

стоп-сигна́л, а *m.* brake-light (*on car*).

стоп|та́ть, чу́, ~чешь *pf.* (*of* ⇒**ста́птывать**) **1** (*обувь*) to wear down. **2** (*coll.*) (*вытоптать*) to trample.

стоп|та́ться, ~чется *pf.* (*of* ⇒**ста́птываться**) to wear down, be worn down (*of footwear*).

сторг|ова́ть(ся), у́ю(сь) *pf. of* ⇒**торгова́ть(ся)**

стори́цею *adv.* (*obs.*) a hundredfold; **возда́ть с.** (+*d.*) to repay with interest; to reward handsomely.

сто́рож, а, *pl.* **~а́, ~е́й** *m.* watchman, guard.

сторожев|о́й *adj.* watch; **~а́я бу́дка** sentry-box; **~а́я вы́шка** watch-tower; **с. кора́бль** escort vessel; **с. пост** sentry post; **~а́я соба́ка** watch-dog.

сторож|и́ть, у́, и́шь *impf.* **1** (*дом, стадо*) to guard, watch, keep watch (over). **2** (*зверя*) to lie in wait (for).

сторо́жк|а, и *f.* lodge.

сторон|а́, ы́, *a.* **сто́рону,** *pl.* **сто́роны, сторо́н, ~а́м** *f.* **1** side; (*направление*) direction; **в сто́рону** (+*g.*) in the direction of; **со ~ы́** (+*g.*) from the direction of; **в сто́рону** (*theatr.*) aside; **шу́тки в сто́рону** (*coll.*) joking aside; **в сто́рону, в ~е́** aside; **держа́ться в ~е́** to keep aloof; **на ~е́** (*coll.*) (*в другом месте*) elsewhere, not on the spot; **продава́ть на́ сторону** to sell on the black market; **по ту сто́рону** (+*g.*) across, on the other side (of); **пра́вая/ле́вая с.** right/left hand side; **с пра́вой, с ле́вой ~ы́** on the right, left side; **с мое́й ~ы́** for my part; **э́то о́чень любе́зно с ва́шей ~ы́** it is very kind of you; **наблюда́ть со ~ы́** to observe from the outside; **со ~ы́** (+*g.*) (*indicating line of descent*) on the side of; **дед со ~ы́ ма́тери** maternal grandfather; **с одно́й ~ы́..., с друго́й ~ы́** on the one hand ..., on the other hand; **узна́ть ~о́й** to find out indirectly. **2** (*в споре*) side, party; **вы на чьей ~е́?** whose side are you on?; **взять чью-н. сто́рону** to take s.o.'s part, side with s.o.; **вражду́ющие сто́роны** warring parties; **тре́тья с.** third party. **3** (*страна*) land, place; parts; **на чужо́й ~е́** in foreign parts. **4** (*элемент, свойство*) aspect, side; **с како́й бы ~ы́ ни посмотре́ть** whichever way you look at it.

сторон|и́ться, ю́сь, ~ишься *impf.* (*of* ⇒**по~**) **1** to stand aside, make way. **2** *no pf.* (+*g.*) (*избегать*) to shun, avoid.

сторо́нний *adj.* **1** (*посторонний*) strange, foreign; **с. наблюда́тель** detached observer. **2** (*влияние, взгляд*) outside.

сторо́нник, а *m.* supporter, advocate; **с. ми́ра** peace campaigner.

сторо́нни|ца, цы *f. of* ⇒**~к**

стоск|овáться, ýюсь *pf.* (**по**+*p. or* **о**+*p.*) to miss, pine (for), yearn (for).

сточ|úть, ý, ~ишь *pf.* (*of* ⇒**стáчивать**) to grind off.

стóчн|ый *adj.* sewage, drainage; **~ые вóды** sewage; **~ая трубá** drainpipe.

стошн|úть, úт *pf.* (*impers.*) to be sick, vomit; **меня́ ~úло** I was sick.

стóя *adv.* standing up.

стоя́к, á *m.* **1** (*брус*) post, upright. **2** (*водопроводный*) vertical pipe, rising pipe. **3** (*печной*) chimney.

стоя́лый *adj.* (*вода*) stagnant; (*воздух*) stale; (*конь*) old.

стоя́ни|е, я *nt.* standing.

стоя́нк|а, и *f.* **1** (*остановка*) stop; (*автомобилей*) parking; **«с. запрещенá!»** 'no parking!'; **во врéмя ~и (пóезда) на стáнции** while the train is standing at a station. **2** (*место остановки*) stopping place; (*автомобилей*) parking area; (*судов*) moorage; **автомобúльная с.** car park (*Br.*), parking lot (*US*); **с. таксú** taxi-rank. **3** (*archaeol.*) site.

сто|я́ть, ю́, úшь *impf.* **1** to stand; **с. в óчереди** to stand in a queue; **с. на колéнях** to kneel; **с. на четверéньках** to be on all fours; **крéпко с. на ногáх** (*fig.*) to stand firm. **2** (*находиться*) to be, be situated, lie; **селó ~úт на возвы́шенности** the village is situated on rising ground; **стакáны ~я́т в шкафý** the glasses are in the cupboard; **кнúги ~я́т на пóлке** the books are on the shelf; **чáйник ~úт на плитé** the kettle is on the stove; **с. во главé** (+*g.*) to be at the head (of), head; **с. на я́коре** to be at anchor; **с. у влáсти** to be in power, be in office; **с. у руля́** to be at the helm. **3** (*быть*) to be; to continue; **~úт морóз** there is a frost; **~я́ла хорóшая погóда** the weather continued fine; **~я́ло начáло декабря́** it was the beginning of December; **áкции ~я́т высокó** shares continue high. **4** (*жить*) to stay, put up; (*mil.*) to be stationed; **с. лáгерем** to be encamped. **5** (**за**+*a.*) (*защищать*) to stand up (for); (**на**+*p.*) (*настаивать*) to insist (on); **с. на своём** to refuse to give in; **с. на чьей-н. тóчке зрéния** to share s.o.'s point of view. **6** (*не двигаться*) to have stopped; to have come to a halt, come to a standstill; **мой часы́ ~я́т** my watch has stopped; **рабóта ~úт** work has come to a standstill; **~й(те)!** stop!; halt! **7** (*не портиться*) to keep; **óвощи ~я́т недéлю** vegetables keep for a week.

стоя́ч|ий *adj.* **1** standing; upright; **с. воротничóк** stand-up collar; **~ая лáмпа** standard lamp; **~ая трубá** stand-pipe. **2** (*вода, воздух*) stagnant.

стó|ящий *pres. part. act. of* ⇒**~ить** *and adj.* (*человек*) deserving, worthy; (*дело, книга, предложение*) worth-while.

стр. *abbr. of* **1** ***странúца*** p., page. **2** ***странúцы*** pp., pages.

страв|úть, лю́, ~ишь *pf.* (*of* ⇒**~ливать** *and* **~ля́ть**) (*натравить*) to set on (*to fight*).

стрáвлива|ть, ю *impf. of* ⇒**стравúть**

стравля́|ть, ю *impf.* = **стрáвливать**

стрáгива|ть(ся), ю(сь) *impf. of* ⇒**стрóнуть(ся)**

страд|á, ы́, *pl.* **~ы** *f.* hard work at harvest-time; (*fig.*) toil, hard work.

страдáл|ец, ьца *m.* sufferer.

страдáл|ица, ицы *f. of* ⇒**~ец**

страдáльческ|ий *adj.* full of suffering; **с. вид** an air of suffering, a martyr's air; **~ая жизнь** life of suffering.

страдáни|е, я *nt.* suffering.

страдáтельный *adj.* (*gram.*) passive; **с. залóг** passive voice; **~ое причáстие** passive participle.

страдá|ть, ю *and* (*arch.*) **стрáжду, стрáждешь** *impf.* **1** *impf. only* (+*i.*) to suffer (from); to be subject (to); **с. бессóнницей** to suffer from insomnia; **онá мнóго ~ла** she suffered a lot. **2** *impf. only* (**от**+*g.*) to suffer (from), be in pain (with); **с. от зубнóй бóли** to have (a) toothache; **с. от любвú** to be in love. **3** *impf. only* **с. за когó-н.** (*сочувствовать*) to feel for s.o. **4** *impf. only* (**по**+*d.*; *coll.*) (*тосковать*) to miss; to long (for), pine (for). **5** (*pf.* **по~**) to suffer; **с. за вéру** to suffer for one's faith; **с. от зáсухи** to suffer from the drought; **с. по своéй винé** to suffer through one's own fault. **6** *impf. only* (*быть плохим*) to be weak, be poor; **у неё ~ет пáмять** she has a poor memory.

стрáд|ный *adj. of* ⇒**~á**; **~ная порá** busy period.

страж, а *m.* **1** (*rhet.*) guard, custodian; **с. поря́дка** (*iron.*) arm of the law. **2**: **с. мúра** peacekeeper.

стрáж|а, и *f.* guard, watch; **быть, стоя́ть на ~е** (+*g.*) to guard; **под ~ей** under arrest, in custody; **взять, заключúть под ~у** to take into custody.

стрáждущ|ий *pres. part. act.* (*obs.*) *of* ⇒**страдáть**; **~ее человéчество** suffering humanity.

стрáжник, а *m.* **1** (*hist.*) (*полицейский*) police constable (*in rural areas*). **2** (*obs.*): **береговóй с.** coastguard; **леснóй с.** forest warden.

страз, а *m.* paste (*jewel*).

стран|á, ы́, *pl.* **~ы** *f.* **1** country; land. **2**: **с. свéта** cardinal point (*of compass*).

странúц|а, ы *f.* page (*also comput., fig., rhet.*); (*истории, жизни*) chapter.

странúчк|а, и *f.* = **странúца**

стрáнник, а *m.* wanderer (*esp.* religious pilgrim).

стрáнниц|а, ы *f. of* ⇒**стрáнник**

стрáнно *adv.* **1** strangely, in a strange way. **2** *as pred.* (*необычно*) it is strange; (*непонятно*) funny, odd, queer; **как э́то ни с.** strangely enough; **мне э́то с.** I find it strange; **мне с., что** I find it strange that.

стрáнност|ь, и *f.* **1** strangeness. **2** (*странная манера*) oddity, eccentricity; **за ним водúлись ~и** he was an odd person.

стрáн|ный (~ен, ~нá, ~но) *adj.* (*необычный*) strange; (*непонятный*) funny, odd; **~ное дéло** (*как вводное слово*) funnily enough, strangely enough; **~ное дéло!** that's strange!, that's funny!

странові́дени|е, я *nt.* regional studies.

стрáнстви|е, я *nt.* wandering, travelling (*Br.*), traveling (*US*).

стрáнствовани|е, я *nt.* wandering, travelling (*Br.*), traveling (*US*).

стрáнств|овать, ую *impf.* to wander, travel; **с. по свéту** to wander the earth; to travel the world.

стрáнств|ующий *pres. part. act. of* ⇒**~овать** *and adj.*; **с. актёр** strolling player; **с. ры́царь** knight-errant; **с. цирк** travelling (*Br.*), traveling (*US*) circus.

Стрáсбург, а *m.* Strasbourg.

стрáстно *adv.* passionately.

страстн|óй *adj.* of Holy Week; **С~áя недéля** Holy Week; **С~áя пя́тница** Good Friday; **С. четвéрг** Maundy Thursday.

стрáстност|ь, и *f.* passion.

стрáст|ный (~ен, ~нá, ~но) *adj.* (*речь, поцелуй, человек*) passionate; (*сторонник, поклонник*) ardent.

страстоцвéт, а *m.* passion flower.

страст|ь[1]**, и,** *g. pl.* **~éй** *f.* **1** (**к**+*d.*) passion (for); **до ~и** (*coll.*) passionately; **со ~ью** with passion, fervour (*Br.*), fervor (*US*); **~и кипя́т** passions are running high. **2**: **~и Христóвы** (*relig.*) the Passion; **Стрáсти по Матфéю** (*title of oratorio*) St Matthew Passion. **3** (*coll.*) (*ужас*) horror; **расскáзывать (про) вся́кие ~и** to recount all manner of horrors.

страсть[2] *adv.* (*coll.*) **1**: **с. (как, какóй)** (*очень*) awfully, frightfully; **мне с. как хóчется увúдеть э́тот фильм** I want awfully to see this film. **2** *as pred.* (*очень много*) an awful lot, a terrific number; **дéнег у негó — с.** he's got an awful lot of money.

стратагéм|а, ы *f.* stratagem.

стратéг, а *m.* strategist.

стратегúческий *adj.* strategic.

стратéги|я, и *f.* strategy.

стратификáци|я, и *f.* stratification.

стратосфéр|а, ы *f.* stratosphere.

стратосфéрный *adj.* stratospheric.

стрáус, а *m.* ostrich.

стрáус|овый *adj. of* ⇒**~**; **~овое перó** ostrich feather.

страх[1]**, а** *m.* **1** fear; (*сильный*) terror; **с. накáзания** fear of punishment; **с. за ребёнка** fear for one's child; **не знать ~а** to know no fear; **со ~у** from fear; **с. Бóжий** the fear of God; **с. пéред неизвéстностью** fear of the unknown; **под ~ом смéрти** on pain of death. **2** (*pl.*) (*ужасные события*) terrors. **3** (*ответственность*) risk, responsibility; **на свой с. (и риск)** at one's own risk.

страх[2] *adv.* (*coll.*): **с. (как)** (*очень*) terribly; **им с. (как) хóчется побывáть во Фрáнции** they want terribly to go to France.

С

страх... *comb. form, abbr. of* ***страховóй***

страхкáсс|а, ы *f.* insurance office.

страховáни|е, я *nt.* insurance; **с. автомобиля** motor insurance; **госудáрственное с.** national insurance; **с. жи́зни** life insurance; **с. от огня́** fire insurance; **с. от несчáстных слу́чаев** personal accident insurance.

страховáтел|ь, я *m.* the insured (*person, etc.*).

страх|овáть, у́ю *impf.* (*pf.* **за~**) (**от**+*g.*) to insure (against); **с. себя́** (**от**+*g.*, *fig.*) to insure (against), safeguard o.s. (against).

страх|овáться, у́юсь *impf.* (*of* ⇒**за~**) (**от**+*g.*) to insure o.s. (against) (*also fig.*).

страхóвк|а, и *f.* **1** insurance. **2** (*fig., coll.*): **для ~и** as a safeguard.

страховóй *adj.* insurance; **с. пóлис** insurance policy.

страхóвщик, а *m.* insurer.

страши́л|а, ы *c.g.* = **страши́лище**

страши́лищ|е, а *m. and nt.* fright (*object inspiring fear*); (*coll.*) (*некрасивый человек*) monster; scarecrow.

страш|и́ть, у́, и́шь *impf.* to frighten, scare.

страш|и́ться, у́сь, и́шься *impf.* (+*g.*) to be afraid (of), fear.

стрáшно *adv.* **1** terribly, awfully; **с. испугáться** to get a terrible fright; **с. обрáдоваться** to be awfully glad; **мне с. хóчется поéхать** I am terribly keen to go. **2** *as pred.* it is terrible; it is terrifying; **мне с.** I am terrified; **мне с.** (+*inf.*) I am terrified to do sth.; **с. поду́мать, что...** it is awful to think that ...; **с. поду́мать!** it is an awful thought!

стрáш|ный (~ен, ~нá, ~но) *adj.* (*очень плохой*) terrible, awful, dreadful; (*вызывающий страх*) terrifying, frightening; **с. расскáз** terrifying story; **с. сон** bad dream; **с. беспоря́док** (*coll.*) awful, dreadful mess; **с. шум** (*coll.*) awful din; **С. суд** the Day of Judgement, Doomsday; **ничегó ~ного** it doesn't matter.

стращá|ть, ю *impf.* (*of* ⇒**по~**) (*coll.*) to frighten, scare.

стрéж|ень, ня *m.* channel, main stream (*of river*).

стрекáч, á *m. now only in phr.* **(за)дáть ~á** (*coll.*) to take to one's heels, run for it.

стрекоз|á, ы́, *pl.* **~ы** *f.* **1** dragon-fly. **2** (*ребёнок*) fidget.

стрéкот, а *m.* (*кузнечиков*) chirr; (*fig.*) rattle, chatter (*of machine-guns, etc.*).

стрекотáни|е, я *nt.* chirring; (*fig.*) rattle, chatter.

стреко|тáть, чу́, ~чешь *impf.* (*о кузнечиках*) to chirr; (*fig.*) (*болтать*) to rattle, chatter.

стрел|á, ы́, *pl.* **~ы** *f.* **1** arrow (*also fig.*); (*fig.*) shaft, dart; **пусти́ть ~у́** to shoot an arrow; **мчáться ~óй** to fly like an arrow. **2** (*bot.*) shaft. **3** (*крана*) arm. **4** (*поезд*) express (train). **5**: **с. мóста** cantilever.

стрел|éц, ьцá *m.* **1** (*hist.*) strelets (*member of military corps in Muscovite Russia in the 16th and 17th centuries*). **2 С.** (*astron.*) Sagittarius (*constellation*).

стрéлк|а, и *f.* **1** pointer, indicator; (*часов*) hand; (*компаса*) needle. **2** (*знак*) arrow (*on diagram, etc.*). **3** (*rail.*) point(s) (*Br.*), switch (*US*); **перевести́ ~у** to change the points. **4** (*geog.*) spit. **5** (*стебель*) shoot, blade (*of grass, etc.*). **6** (*sl.*) (*свидание*) meeting, appointment.

стрелкóв|ый *adj.* **1** rifle, shooting; **~ое мастерствó** marksmanship; **~ое ору́жие** small arms; **с. спорт** shooting; **с. тир** rifle range. **2** (*mil.*) rifle, infantry; **с. батальóн** infantry battalion; **~ые войскá** infantry.

стреловид|ный (~ен, ~на) *adj.* arrow-shaped.

стрел|óк, кá *m.* **1** shot; **иску́сный с., отли́чный с.** good shot. **2** (*mil.*) rifleman; (*в самолёте, в танке*) gunner.

стрéлочник, а *m.* (*rail.*) signalman, (*US*) switchman; **с. виновáт** (*iron.*) the little man is always blamed.

стрéлочниц|а, ы *f. of* ⇒**стрéлочник**

стрéл|очный *adj. of* ⇒**~ка** 3

стрельб|á, ы́, *pl.* **~ы** *f.* shooting, firing; **ружéйная с.** small arms fire; **учéбная с.** firing practice.

стрéльбищ|е, а *nt.* shooting range, target range.

стрельн|у́ть, у́, ёшь *pf.* (*coll.*) **1** to fire a shot. **2** (*impers.*): **у меня́ ~у́ло в у́хе** I had a stab of pain in my ear. **3** (*убегать*) to rush away. **4** (*sl.*) (*сигареты*) to cadge (*Br.*), bum (*US*).

стрéльчат|ый *adj.* **1** (*archit.*) lancet. **2** arched, pointed; **~ые брóви** arched eyebrows.

стрéлян|ый *adj.* **1** (*дичь*) shot (*opp. killed by strangling*). **2** (*солдат*) who has been under fire; **с. воробéй/~ая пти́ца** (*coll.*) old hand. **3** (*гильза*) used, fired, spent.

стреля́|ть, ю *impf.* **1** (**в**+*a. or* **по**+*d.*) to shoot (at), fire (at); **хорошó с.** to be a good shot; **с. из револьвéра, из ружья́** to fire a revolver, a gun; **с. в цель** to shoot at a target; **с. по самолёту** to fire at an aeroplane (*Br.*), airplane (*US*); **с. глазáми** (*coll.*) to shoot glances (at); to make eyes (at). **2** (*убивать*) to shoot; **с. куропáток** to go partridge-shooting. **3** (*sl.*) to cadge (*Br.*), bum (*US*). **4** (*impers.*) (*о боли*) to have a shooting pain. **5** (*мотор, дрова*) to crack.

стреля́|ться, юсь *impf.* **1** (*самоубийца*) to shoot o.s. **2** (**с**+*i.*) (*на дуэли*) to fight a duel (with firearms) (with).

стремглáв *adv.* headlong.

стрем|еннóй *adj.* = **~я́нный**

стреми́тел|ьный (~ен, ~ьна) *adj.* (*полёт, бег*) swift, headlong; (*рост, развитие*) rapid; (*человек*) energetic; (*ручей, поток*) fast-flowing.

стрем|и́ться, лю́сь, и́шься *impf.* **1** (*устремиться*) to rush. **2** (**к**+*d.*) (*добиваться*) to strive (for), seek, aspire (to); (+*inf.*) to strive (to), try (to); **с. к совершéнству** to strive for perfection. **3** (**в, на**+*a.*) (*желать попасть*) to want to go (to); **с. в Росси́ю/на рóдину/в университéт** to want to go to Russia/ one's homeland/university.

стремлéни|е, я *nt.* (**к**+*d.*) striving (for), aspiration (to).

стремни́н|а, ы *f.* **1** (*в реке*) rapids. **2** (*obs.*) (*обрыв*) precipice.

стремни́ст|ый (~, ~а) *adj.* (*obs.*) steep, precipitous.

стрёмный *adj.* (*sl.*) dodgy, dangerous.

стрéм|я, *g., d. and p.* **~ени,** *i.* **~енем,** *pl.* **~енá, ~я́н, ~енáм** *nt.* stirrup.

стремя́нк|а, и *f.* step-ladder, steps.

стремя́нн|ый *adj. of* ⇒**стрéмя;** *as n.* (*hist.*) **с., ~ого** *m.* groom.

стренóж|ить, у, ишь *pf. of* ⇒**тренóжить**

стрéпет, а *m.* (*zool.*) little bustard.

стрептокóкк, а *m.* (*biol., med.*) streptococcus.

стрептокóкк|овый *adj. of* ⇒**~**

стрептомици́н, а *m.* (*med.*) streptomycin.

стресс, а *m.* (*psych.*) stress.

стрéссовый *adj.* (*положение*) stressful; (*состояние*) stressed.

стрех|á, и́, *pl.* **~и** *f.* eaves.

стреч|óк, кá *m. now only in phr.* **(за)дáть ~кá** (*coll.*) to take to one's heels, run for it.

стригáльн|ый *adj.*: **~ая маши́на** (*text.*) cloth-shearing machine.

стригáльщик, а *m.* (*text. and agric.*) shearer.

стригáльщиц|а, ы *f. of* ⇒**стригáльщик**

стригу́н, á *m.* yearling (foal).

стригун|óк, кá *m.* = **стригу́н**

стригу́щий *pres. part. act. of* ⇒**стричь; с. лишáй** (*med.*) ring-worm.

стриж, á *m.* (*zool.*) swift.

стри́женый *adj.* **1** (*человек*) short-haired, close-cropped. **2** (*волосы*) short; (*овца*) sheared; (*дерево*) clipped.

стри́жк|а, и *f.* **1** (*действие*) hair-cutting; shearing; clipping. **2** (*причёска*) haircut, hair-style.

стрипти́з, а *m.* striptease.

стриптизёр, а *m.* (*male*) stripper.

стриптизёр|ша, ши *f.* (*female*) stripper.

стрихни́н, а *m.* (*med.*) strychnine.

стри|чь, гу́, жёшь, гу́т, *past* **~г, ~гла** *impf.* (*of* ⇒**о~**) **1** (*волосы, ногти, кусты*) to cut, clip. **2**: **с. когó-н.** to cut s.o.'s hair; **с. овéц** to shear sheep; **с. пу́деля** to clip a poodle; **с. всех под одну́ гребёнку** to treat all alike; **с. купóны** to live on interest from one's investments.

стри́|чься, гу́сь, жёшься, гу́тся, *past* **~гся, ~глась** *impf.* (*of* ⇒**о~**) **1** to cut one's hair; to have one's hair cut. **2** (*носить короткие волосы*) to wear one's hair short.

стробоскóп, а *m.* (*phys.*) stroboscope.

стробоскопи́ческий *adj.* stroboscopic.

строгáл|ь, я́ *m.* (*coll.*) = **~ьщик**

строга́льный *adj.* (*tech.*): **с. стано́к** planing machine.

строга́льщик, а *m.* plane operator, planer.

строга́|ть, ю *impf.* (*of* ⇒**вы́~**) (*tech.*) to plane, shave.

стро́г|ий (~, ~á, ~о) *adj.* (*начальник, правила, диета*) strict; (*наказание, причёска*) severe; **~ие ме́ры** strong measures; **с. пригово́р** severe sentence; **под ~им секре́том** in strict confidence; **в ~ом смы́сле сло́ва** in the strict sense of the word; **с. стиль** severe, austere style; **~ие черты́ лица́** regular features.

стро́го *adv.* strictly; severely; **с. говоря́** strictly speaking; **«с. воспреща́ется»** 'strictly forbidden'.

стро́го-на́строго *adv.* (*coll.*) very strictly.

стро́гост|ь, и *f.* **1** strictness; severity. **2** (*pl.*) (*coll.*) (*меры*) strong measures.

строеви́к, á *m.* combatant soldier.

строево́й[1] *adj.* (*употребляемый на постройки*) building; **с. лес** timber forest; (*collect.*) timber.

строев|о́й[2] *adj.* (*mil.*) **1** combatant, line; **с. офице́р** officer serving in line; **~а́я слу́жба** (front-)line service, combatant service; **~а́я часть** line unit. **2** drill; **~а́я подгото́вка** drill; **с. шаг** goose-step.

строе́ни|е, я *nt.* **1** (*здание*) building, structure. **2** (*структура*) structure, composition.

строжа́йший *superl. of* ⇒**стро́гий**

стро́же *comp. of* ⇒**стро́гий** *and* **стро́го**

строи́тел|ь, я *m.* **1** builder, constructor. **2** (*fig.*) creator.

строи́тельн|ый *adj.* building, construction; **~ая брига́да** construction team; **~ая площа́дка** building site; **с. раство́р** lime mortar.

строи́тельств|о, а *nt.* **1** (*процесс*) building, construction (*also fig.*); **доро́жное с.** road-building; **жили́щное с.** house-building; **хозя́йственное с.** building up of the economy. **2** (*место*) building site, construction project. **3** (*fig.*) (*организация*) organization, structuring.

стро́|ить, ю, ишь *impf.* **1** (*pf.* **по~**) (*здание, дорогу, мост, плотину*) to build, construct; (*корабль, танк*) to build.
2 (*pf.* **по~**) (*новую жизнь, общество, счастье*) to create, build.
3 (*pf.* **по~**) (*фигуры, фразы, мысли*) to construct; to formulate; **с. многоуго́льник** to construct a polygon; **с. у́гол** to plot an angle; **с. фра́зу** to construct a sentence; **с. мысль** to formulate a thought.
4 (*pf.* **со~**) (*in phrr. denoting facial expressions, etc.*) to make; **с. гла́зки** to make eyes; **с. грима́сы, с. ро́жу** to make, pull faces; **с. из себя́ дурака́** to make a fool of o.s.
5 (*pf.* **по~**) (**на** + *p.*) (*обосновывать*) to base (on); **с. расчёт на** (+ *p.*) to base one's calculations on; **с. отноше́ния на дове́рии** to base relations on trust.
6 (*pf.* **по~**) (*планы, догадки*) to make; **с. гипоте́зу** to advance a hypothesis.
7 (*pf.* **по~**) (*ставить строй*) to draw up, form (up).

стро́|иться, юсь, ишься *impf.* (*of* ⇒**по~**) **1** (*строить себе дом*) to build (*a house, etc.*) for o.s. **2** (*mil.*) to draw up, form up; **стро́йся!** (*mil.*) fall in! **3** *pass. of* ⇒**~ить**

стро|й[1]**, ~я, о ~е, в ~е,** *pl.* **~и, ~ев** *m.* **1** (*система*) system, order; **обще́ственный с.** social system; **феода́льный с.** feudal system. **2** (*предложения, языка*) structure. **3** (*mus.*) pitch.

стро|й[2]**, ~я, о ~е, в ~ю́,** *pl.* **~и́, ~ёв** *m.* **1** (*mil., naut., aeron.*) (*порядок*) formation; **со́мкнутый с.** close order; **расчленённый с.** deployed formation; **с. фро́нта** (*naut.*) line abreast; **в ко́нном ~ю́** mounted; **в пе́шем ~ю́** dismounted. **2** (*mil.*) (*шеренга, часть*) unit in formation; **пе́ред ~ем** in front of the ranks. **3** (*mil. and fig.*) (*действующий состав*) service, commission; **ввести́ в с.** to put into commission; (*машину*) to put into operation; **вы́вести из ~я** to disable; to put out of action; **вступи́ть в с.** to come into service, come into operation; **вы́йти из ~я** to be disabled; to become unserviceable; (*машина*) to break down; **оста́ться в ~ю́** (*mil.*) to remain in the ranks; (*fig.*) to remain at one's post.

строй... *comb. form, abbr. of* ***строи́тельный***

стро́йк|а, и *f.* **1** (*действие*) building, construction. **2** (*место*) building-site.

стройматериа́л|ы, ов *no sg.* building materials.

стро́йност|ь, и *f.* **1** (*фигуры*) proportion. **2** (*пения*) harmony; (*доклада*) balance; (*рядов*) order.

стро́|йный (~ен, ~йна́, ~йно) *adj.* **1** (*фигура*) well-proportioned; shapely. **2** (*пение*) harmonious; (*ряды*) orderly; (*фраза, доклад*) well-constructed.

строк|á, и́, *pl.* **~и, ~, ~áм** *f.* line; (*comput.*) string; **с. в ~у́** line by line; **нача́ть с кра́сной/но́вой ~и́** to begin a new paragraph; **чита́ть ме́жду ~** to read between the lines.

стро́н|уть, у, ешь *pf.* (*of* ⇒**стра́гивать**) (*coll.*) to move out, shift.

стро́н|уться, усь, ешься *pf.* (*of* ⇒**стра́гиваться**) (*coll.*) to start moving.

стро́нци|й, я *m.* (*chem.*) strontium.

строп, а *m.* sling (rope); (*парашюта*) shroud line.

стропи́л|о, а *nt.* rafter, beam.

строптúв|ец, ца *m.* obstinate person.

строптúвост|ь, и *f.* obstinacy.

строптúв|ый (~, ~а) *adj.* obstinate.

строф|á, ы́, *pl.* **~ы, ~, ~áм** *f.* (*liter.*) stanza, strophe.

строфи́ческий *adj.* (*liter.*) strophic.

строчёный *adj.* stitched.

строч|и́ть, у́, ~ишь *impf.* **1** (*pf.* **про~**) (*шить*) to stitch. **2** (*pf.* **на~**) (*coll.*) (*писать*) to scribble, dash off. **3** *no pf.* (*coll.*) (*стрелять*) to bang away (*with automatic weapons*).

стро́чк|а[1]**, и** *f.* (*шов*) stitch.

стро́чк|а[2]**, и** *f.* = **строка́**

строчн|о́й *adj.*: **~áя бу́ква** small letter, lower-case letter; **писа́ть со ~о́й бу́квы** to write a small letter.

струбци́н|а, ы *f.* (*tech.*) (screw) clamp, cramp.

струга́|ть, ю *impf.* (*of* ⇒**вы́~**) = **строга́ть**

струг, а *m.* (*tech.*) plane.

стру́жк|а, и *f.* shaving, filing; **снять ~у с кого́-н.** (*sl.*) to tear s.o. off a strip.

стру|и́ть, и́т *impf.* to pour, shed.

стру|и́ться, и́тся *impf.* to stream, flow.

стру́йный *adj.*: **с. при́нтер** inkjet printer.

структу́р|а, ы *f.* structure; **вла́стные ~ы** power structures.

структурали́зм, а *m.* structuralism.

структурали́ст, а *m.* structuralist.

структу́рный *adj.* structural.

струн|á, ы́, *pl.* **~ы** *f.* **1** (*скрипки, ракетки*) string. **2** (*черта*): **сла́бая с.** weak point; **чувстви́тельная с.** sensitive spot.

стру́н|ка, ки *f. dim. of* ⇒**~á**; **вы́тянуться в ~ку, стать в ~ку** to stand at attention; **ходи́ть по ~ке** (**у** + *g.*, **пе́ред** + *i.*) to be at the beck and call (of), dance attendance (on).

стру́нник, а *m.* string player.

стру́нный *adj.* (*mus.*): **с. инструме́нт** stringed instrument; **с. орке́стр** string orchestra.

струп, а, *pl.* **~ья, ~ьев** *m.* scab.

стру́|сить, шу, сишь *pf. of* ⇒**тру́сить**

стручко́в|ый *adj.* leguminous; **~ая фасо́ль** runner beans (*Br.*), string beans; **с. пе́рец** chilli pepper, capsicum; **с. горо́шек** peas in the pod.

струч|о́к, кá *m.* pod.

стру|я́, и́, *pl.* **~и** *f.* **1** (*воды*) jet, spurt, stream; (*света*) stream; (*воздуха*) stream, current; **бить ~ёй** to spurt. **2** (*fig.*) spirit; impetus; **внести́ све́жую ~ю́ в рабо́ту** to give the work fresh impetus; **попа́сть в ~ю́** (*coll.*) to fit in.

стря́па|ть, ю *impf.* (*of* ⇒**со~**) (*coll.*) to cook; (*fig.*) (*сочинять*) to cook up, concoct.

стряпн|я́, и́ *f.* (*coll.*) cooking; (*fig., pej.*) concoction.

стряпу́х|а, и *f.* (*coll.*) cook.

стряс|áть, áю *impf. of* ⇒**~ти́**

стряс|ти́, у́, ёшь, *past* **~, ~лá** *pf.* (*of* ⇒**~áть**) to shake off.

стряс|ти́сь, ётся, *past* **~ся, ~лáсь** *pf.* (**над, с** + *i.*; *coll.*) to befall; **бедá ~лáсь с нáми** a disaster befell us; **что с тобо́й ~ло́сь?** what's the matter with you?

стря́хива|ть, ю *impf. of* ⇒**стряхну́ть**

стрях|ну́ть, ну́, нёшь *pf.* (*of* ⇒**~ивать**) to shake off.

ст. ст. (*abbr. of* ***ста́рый стиль***) OS, Old Style (*of calendar*).

студене́|ть, ет *impf.* to thicken, gel; (*coll.*) (*вода*) to freeze.

студени́ст|ый (~, ~а) *adj.* jelly-like.

студе́нт, а *m.* student, undergraduate; **с.-ме́дик** medical student; **с.-юри́ст** law student.

студе́нт|ка, ки *f. of* ⇒~

студе́нческ|ий *adj. of* ⇒**студе́нт; с. биле́т** student card; **~ое общежи́тие** student hostel (*Br.*), student dormitory (*US*).

студе́нчеств|о, а *nt.* **1** (*collect.*) (*студенты*) students. **2** (*время*) student days.

студёны|й (~, ~а) *adj.* (*coll.*) very cold, freezing.

сту́д|ень, ня *m.* galantine; aspic.

студи́|ец, йца *m.* (*coll.*) student (*of art school, drama school, music school, etc.*).

студи́|йка, йки *f. of* ⇒**~ец**

студи́йный *adj. of* ⇒**сту́дия**

сту|ди́ть, жу́, ~дишь *impf.* (*of* ⇒**о~**) to cool.

сту́ди|я, и *f.* **1** (*живописца; телестудия*) studio; **с. звукоза́писи** recording studio. **2** (*школа*) (*art, drama, music, etc.*) school.

сту́ж|а, и *f.* severe cold, hard frost.

стук¹, а *m.* (*в дверь*) knock; (*сердца*) thump; (*пишущей машинки*) clatter; (*падающего предмета*) thud; **с. в дверь** knock at the door; **с. колёс** rumble of wheels; **входи́ть без ~а** to enter without knocking.

стук² (*coll.*) *as pred.* = **~нул**

сту́к|ать(ся), аю(сь) *impf. of* ⇒**~нуть(ся)**

стука́ч, а́ *m.* (*sl.*) stool-pigeon (= *informer*).

сту́к|нуть, ну, нешь *pf.* (*of* ⇒**~ать**) **1** (**в** + *a. or* **по** + *d.*) to knock; to bang; **с. в дверь** to knock, bang at (on) the door; **с. кулако́м по́ столу** to bang one's fist on the table. **2** (*ударить*) to bang, hit, strike; **с. кого́-н. по спине́** to bang s.o. on the back; **часы́ ~нули де́сять** (*coll.*) the clock struck ten. **3** (*coll.*) (*убить*) to kill. **4** (*coll.*) (*наступить*) to begin; **~нул но́вый год** the new year began. **5** *pf. only* (*impers.* + *d.*; *coll.*) (*исполниться*): **ему́ ско́ро ~нет пятьдеся́т** he will soon hit fifty. **6** (*coll.*): **ему́ вдруг ~нуло в го́лову, что...** it suddenly occurred to him that . . . **7** (*coll.*) (**на** + *a.*) (*донести*) to denounce.

сту́к|нуться, нусь, нешься *pf.* (*of* ⇒**~аться**) (**о** + *a.*) to bang o.s. (against), bump o.s. (against).

стукотн|я́, и́ *f.* (*coll.*) knocking, banging, tapping.

стул, а, *pl.* **~ья, ~ьев** *m.* **1** chair; **сиде́ть ме́жду двух ~ьев** to fall between two stools. **2** (*med.*) stool.

стульча́к, а́ *m.* (lavatory) seat.

сту́льчик, а *m.* small chair.

сту́п|а, ы *f.* mortar.

ступ|а́ть, а́ю *impf. of* ⇒**~и́ть; ~а́й(те) сюда́!** come here!; **~а́й(те)!** be off!, clear out!

ступе́нчатый *adj.* stepped, graduated, graded; (*процесс*) gradual.

ступ|е́нь, е́ни *f.* **1** (*g. pl.* **~е́ней**) (*лестницы*) step; (*стремянки*) rung. **2** (*g. pl.* **~ене́й**) (*этап*) stage; (*разряд*) grade; (*уровень*) level; (*mus.*) degree (*of scale*); (*ракеты*) stage.

ступе́нь|ка, ки *f.* = **~ 1**

ступ|и́ть, лю́, ~ишь *pf.* (*of* ⇒**~а́ть**) to step; to tread; **тяжело́ с.** to tread heavily; **с. че́рез поро́г** to cross the threshold.

ступи́ц|а, ы *f.* hub (*of a wheel*).

сту́пк|а, и *f.* small mortar.

ступн|я́, и́, *pl.* **~и́, ~е́й** *f.* **1** (*стопа*) foot. **2** (*подошва*) sole.

сту́пор, а *m.* stupor.

стуч|а́ть, у́, и́шь *impf.* **1** (*pf.* **по~**) to knock; to bang; to rap; (*о зубах*) to chatter. **2** *no pf.* (*сердце*) to thump, pound; *impers.*: **(у неё) ~а́ло в голове́** her head was throbbing. **3** (*pf.* **на~**) (*sl.*) (**на** + *a.*) (*доносить*) to report (*s.o.*).

стуч|а́ться, у́сь, и́шься *impf.* (*of* ⇒**по~**) (**в** + *a.*) to knock (at); **с. в дверь** to knock at the door (*also fig.*); **с. к сосе́ду** to knock at a neighbour's (*Br.*), neighbor's (*US*) door.

стуш|ева́ться¹, у́юсь *pf.* (*of* ⇒**~ёвываться**) **1** (*сделаться менее отчётливым*) to fade away, shade off. **2** (*coll.*) (*незаметно удалиться*) to retire into the background; to efface o.s.

стуш|ева́ться², у́юсь *pf. of* ⇒**тушева́ться**

стушёвыва|ться, юсь *impf. of* ⇒**стушева́ться¹**

стыд, а́ *m.* shame; **к на́шему ~у́** to our shame; **у него́ ни ~а́, ни со́вести** he knows no shame.

сты|ди́ть, жу́, ди́шь *impf.* (*of* ⇒**при~**) to shame, put to shame.

сты|ди́ться, жу́сь, ди́шься *impf.* (*of* ⇒**по~**) (+ *g.*) to be ashamed (of); (+ *inf.*) to be ashamed (to); **~ди́сь!** you should be ashamed of yourself!

стыдли́в|ый (~, ~а) *adj.* bashful.

сты́дно *as pred.* it is a shame; **ему́,** *etc.*, **с.** he, *etc.*, is ashamed; **как тебе́ не с.!** you ought to be ashamed of yourself!

сты́дный *adj.* shameful.

стык, а *m.* **1** (*tech.*) joint, junction. **2** (*fig.*) junction, meeting-point; **с. доро́г** road junction; **на ~е двух веко́в** at the turn of the century.

стык|ова́ть, у́ю *impf.* (*of* ⇒**со~**) (*tech.*) to join.

стык|ова́ться, у́ется *impf.* (*of* ⇒**со~**) (*tech.*) to join (*intrans.*); (*о космических кораблях*) to dock.

стыко́вк|а, и *f.* (*космических кораблей*) docking.

стыков|о́й *adj. of* ⇒**стык 1**; (*rail.*): **~а́я накла́дка** fish-plate; **~о́е соедине́ние, с. шов** butt-weld, butt-joint.

сты́н|уть, у, ешь, *past* **стыл, сты́ла** *impf.* **1** (*pf.* **о~**) (*становиться холодным*) to cool, get cool. **2** (*мёрзнуть*) to become frozen over. **3** (*fig.*): **кровь ~ет в жи́лах** one's blood runs cold.

стыть = **сты́нуть**

сты́чк|а, и *f.* **1** (*бой*) skirmish. **2** (*coll.*) (*ссора*) squabble.

стю́ард, а *m.* steward.

стюарде́сс|а, ы *f.* stewardess.

стяг, а *m.* (*rhet.*) banner.

стя́гива|ть(ся), ю(сь) *impf. of* ⇒**стяну́ть(ся)**

стяжа́тел|ь, я *m.* money-grubber.

стяжа́тель|ница, ницы *f. of* ⇒**~**

стяжа́тел|ьный (~ен, ~ьна) *adj.* greedy, grasping.

стяжа́|ть, ю *impf. and pf.* **1** (*приобретать*) to gain, win. **2** (*impf. only*) (*добиваться*) to seek, court; **с. сла́ву** to court fame.

стя|ну́ть¹, ну́, ~нешь *pf.* (*of* ⇒**~гивать**) **1** to tighten; **с. на себе́ по́яс** to tighten one's belt. **2** (*войска, силы*) to gather, assemble (*trans.*). **3** (*impers., coll.*) to have cramp; **у меня́ ~ну́ло но́гу** I have cramp in my leg.

стя|ну́ть², ну́, ~нешь *pf.* (*of* ⇒**~гивать**) **1** (*перчатки, сапоги*) to pull off; **с. чемода́н с маши́ны** to pull the suitcase out of the car. **2** (*coll.*) (*украсть*) to pinch (*Br.*), steal.

стя|ну́ться, ну́сь, ~нешься *pf.* (*of* ⇒**~гиваться**) **1** to tighten (*intrans.*). **2** (*туго подпоясаться*) to gird o.s. tightly. **3** (*войска, демонстранты*) to gather, assemble (*intrans.*).

суахи́ли *m. indecl.* Swahili.

субаре́нд|а, ы *f.* sub-lease.

субарендо́тор, а *m.* sub-tenant.

суббо́т|а, ы *f.* Saturday; **Вели́кая с.** Holy Saturday.

суббо́т|ний *adj. of* ⇒**~а; в ~ние и воскре́сные дни** at weekends.

суббо́тник, а *m.* subbotnik (*in former USSR, voluntary unpaid work on days off, originally esp. on Saturdays*).

субве́нци|я, и *f.* grant, subsidy, subvention.

субконтине́нт, а *m.* subcontinent.

сублима́т, а *m.* (*chem.*) sublimate.

сублима́ци|я, и *f.* (*chem., psych.*) sublimation.

сублими́р|овать, ую *impf. and pf.* (*chem., psych.*) to sublimate.

субмари́н|а, ы *f.* (*naut.*) submarine.

субордина́ци|я, и *f.* (system of) seniority; subordination.

субподря́д, а *m.* subcontract.

субподря́дчик, а *m.* subcontractor.

субсиди́р|овать, ую *impf. and pf.* to subsidize.

субси́ди|я, и *f.* subsidy.

субста́нци|я, и *f.* (*phil.*) substance.

субстра́т, а *m.* substratum.

субти́льност|ь, и *f.* delicateness; frailty.

субти́л|ьный (~ен, ~ьна) *adj.* (*coll.*) delicate; frail.

субти́тр, а *m.* subtitle (*in film*).

субтро́пик|и, ов *no sg.* subtropics.

субтропи́ческий *adj.* subtropical.

субъе́кт, а *m.* **1** (*phil., gram.*) subject; (*phil.*) the self, the ego. **2** (*med., leg.*) subject. **3** (*coll.*) (*человек*) fellow, character, type; **подозри́тельный с.** suspicious character.

субъективи́зм, а *m.* **1** (*phil.*) subjectivism. **2** (*субъективность*) subjectivity.

субъективи́ст, а *m.* (*phil.*) subjectivist.

субъекти́вност|ь, и *f.* subjectivity.

субъекти́в|ный (~ен, ~на) *adj.* subjective.

субъе́кт|ный *adj. of* ⇒**~**

сувени́р, а *m.* souvenir.

сувере́н, а *m.* (*pol., leg.*) sovereign.

суверените́т, а *m.* (*pol., leg.*) sovereignty.

сувере́нный *adj.* (*pol., leg.*) sovereign.

сугли́нистый *adj.* loamy.

сугли́н|ок, ка *m.* loam, loamy soil.

сугро́б, а *m.* snow-drift.

сугу́бо *adv.* especially, particularly.

сугу́б|ый (~, ~а) *adj.* **1** (*obs.*) (*двойной*) double, two-fold. **2** (*особенный*) especial, particular.

суд, а́ *m.* **1** court, law-court; **зал ~а́** court-room; **заседа́ние ~а́** sitting of the court; **на ~е́** in court. **2** (*разбирательство*) trial, legal proceedings; **вы́звать в с.** to summons, subpoena; **пода́ть в с. на кого́-н.** to bring an action against s.o.; **отда́ть под с., преда́ть ~у́** to prosecute; **быть под ~о́м** to be on trial; **на тебя́ и ~а́ нет** no one can blame you; **с. прися́жных** jury. **3** (*collect.*) (*судьи*) the judges; the bench. **4** (*мнение*) judgement, verdict; **с. исто́рии** verdict of history; **на нет и ~а́ нет** if you can't (do it), you can't (do it); if it can't be done, it can't be done.

суда́к, а́ *m.* pike-perch (*fish*).

Суда́н, а *m.* (the) Sudan.

суда́н|ец, ца *m.* Sudanese.

суда́н|ка, ки *f. of* ⇒**~ец**

суда́нский *adj.* Sudanese.

суда́рын|я, и *f.* (*obs.; mode of address*) madam, ma'am.

су́дар|ь, я *m.* (*obs.; mode of address*) sir.

суда́ч|ить, у, ишь *impf.* (*coll.*) to gossip, tittle-tattle.

суде́бник, а *m.* (*hist.*) code of laws.

суде́бн|ый *adj.* judicial; legal; forensic; **~ые изде́ржки/расхо́ды** (*legal*) costs; **с. исполни́тель** bailiff, officer of the court; **~ая медици́на** forensic medicine; **~ая оши́бка** miscarriage of justice; **~ое разбира́тельство** legal proceedings, hearing of a case; **~ое реше́ние** court decision, court order; **с. сле́дователь** investigator; coroner; **~ое сле́дствие** investigation in court, inquest.

суде́йск|ий *adj.* **1** (*leg.*) judge's; **~ая колле́гия** the bench. **2** (*sport*) referee's, umpire's; **с. свисто́к** referee's whistle.

суде́йств|о, а *nt.* (*sport*) refereeing, umpiring.

суди́лищ|е, а *nt.* (*pej.*) mock trial.

суди́мост|ь, и *f.* (*leg.*) conviction(s); **снять с кого́-н. с.** to expunge s.o.'s previous convictions.

су|ди́ть, жу́, ~́дишь *impf.* **1** (**о**+*p.*) (*составлять мнение*) to judge; to form an opinion (about, on); **наско́лько мы могли́ с.** as far as we could judge; **~ди́те са́ми** judge for yourself; **~́дя (по**+*d.*) judging (by), to judge (from); **~́дя по всему́** to all appearances. **2** (*leg.*) (**за**+*a.*) (*преступника*) to try (for). **3** (*осуждать*) to judge, pass judgement (upon); **не ~ди́те их стро́го** don't be hard on them. **4** (*sport*) to referee; (*в крикете, теннисе*) to umpire. **5** (*also pf.*) (*предназначать*) to predestine, preordain; **но Бог ~ди́л ино́е** but God decreed a different fate.

су|ди́ться, жу́сь, ~́дишься *impf.* (**с**+*i.*) to sue.

су́д|но¹, на, *pl.* **~а́, ~о́в** *nt.* vessel; **с. на возду́шной поду́шке** hovercraft; **с. на подво́дных кры́льях** hydrofoil.

су́д|но², на, *pl.* **~на, ~ен** *nt.* chamber-pot; **подкладно́е с.** bed-pan.

су́дный *adj.* (*obs.*) **1** court; judicial. **2**: **С. день** (*relig.*) Day of Judgement.

судове́рф|ь, и *f.* shipyard.

судовладе́л|ец, ьца *m.* shipowner.

судоводи́тел|ь, я *m.* navigator.

судовожде́ни|е, я *nt.* navigation.

судов|о́й *adj.* ship's; marine; **с. журна́л** logbook; **~а́я кома́нда** ship's crew; **~о́е свиде́тельство** ship's certificate of registry.

судоговоре́ни|е, я *nt.* (*leg.*) pleading(s).

суд|о́к, ка́ *m.* **1** (*соусник*) sauce-boat, gravy-boat. **2** (*для уксуса, перца*) cruet (-stand). **3** (*usu. pl.*) (*для переноски пищи*) set of dishes.

судомо́йк|а, и *f.* scullery maid, washer-up.

судопроизво́дств|о, а *nt.* legal proceedings; **арбитра́жное с.** arbitration proceedings.

судоремо́нт, а *m.* ship repair.

судоремо́нт|ный *adj. of* ⇒**~**

су́дорог|а, и *f.* cramp, convulsion, spasm.

су́дорож|ный (~ен, ~на) *adj.* convulsive; (*сборы*) frantic.

судостро́ени|е, я *nt.* shipbuilding.

судострои́тел|ь, я *m.* shipbuilder, shipwright.

судострои́тельный *adj.* shipbuilding.

судоустро́йств|о, а *nt.* judicial system.

судохо́д|ный (~ен, ~на) *adj.* **1** navigable; **с. кана́л** shipping canal. **2**: **~ная компа́ния** shipping company.

судохо́дств|о, а *nt.* navigation, shipping.

суд|ьба́, ьбы́, *pl.* **~́ьбы, ~́еб, ~́ьбам** *f.* fate, fortune; (*будущее*) destiny; (*история существования*) story; **благодари́ть ~ьбу́** to thank one's lucky stars; **искуша́ть ~ьбу́** to tempt fate; **избра́нник ~ьбы́** fortunate person; **каки́ми ~ьба́ми?** (*coll.*) fancy meeting you here!; how did you get here?; **не с. нам** (+*inf.*) we are not fated (to).

судьби́н|а, ы *f.* (*folk., poet.*) fate, lot.

суд|ья́, ьи́, *pl.* **~́ьи, ~е́й, ~́ьям** *m.* **1** judge; **трете́йский с.** arbitrator; **я вам не с.** who am I to judge you? **2** (*sport*) referee; (*в крикете, теннисе*) umpire; **с. на ли́нии** linesman.

су́д|я *see* ⇒**~и́ть**

суеве́ри|е, я *nt.* superstition.

суеве́р|ный (~ен, ~на) *adj.* superstitious.

суесло́ви|е, я *nt.* (*obs.*) idle talk.

сует|а́, ы́ *f.* **1** (*тщетность*) vanity; **с. сует** vanity of vanities. **2** (*хлопоты*) bustle, fuss.

суе|ти́ться, чу́сь, ти́шься *impf.* to bustle, fuss.

суетли́в|ый (~, ~а) *adj.* fussy, bustling.

су́етност|ь, и *f.* vanity.

су́ет|ный (~ен, ~на) *adj.* vain, empty.

суетн|я́, и́ *f.* (*coll.*) fuss, bustle.

сужде́ни|е, я *nt.* (*мнение*) opinion; (*в логике*) judgement.

суждён|ный (~, ~а́) *p.p.p. of* ⇒**суди́ть; нам бы́ло ~о́ встре́титься** we were fated to meet.

су́жен|ая, ой *f.* (*folk poet.*) intended (*bride*).

су́жен|ый, ого *m.* (*folk poet.*) intended (*bridegroom*).

су́жива|ть(ся), ю, ет(ся) *impf. of* ⇒**су́зить(ся)**

су́|зить, жу, зишь *pf.* (*of* ⇒**~живать**) to narrow (*trans.*); (*платье*) to take in.

су́|зиться, зится *pf.* (*of* ⇒**~живаться**) to narrow (*intrans.*), get narrow; to taper.

сук, а́, о ~е́, на ~у́, *pl.* **~и́, ~о́в** *and* **су́чья, су́чьев** *m.* **1** bough; **руби́ть с., на кото́ром сиди́шь** to be your own worst enemy. **2** (*в бревне, в доске*) knot.

су́к|а, и *f.* bitch (*also as term of abuse*).

су́к|ин *adj. of* ⇒**~а; с. сын** (*as term of abuse*) son of a bitch.

сук|но́, на́, *pl.* **~́на, ~́он** *nt.* (heavy, coarse) cloth; **положи́ть под с.** (*fig.*) to shelve.

суконова́льн|ый *adj.* fulling; **~ая гли́на** fuller's earth.

сукова́т|ый (~, ~а) *adj.* with many twigs; (*of planks*) knotty.

суко́нк|а, и *f.* piece of cloth, rag.

суко́нн|ый *adj.* **1** cloth; **~ая фа́брика** cloth mill. **2** (*fig.*) (*язык, речь*) dull, hackneyed, clichéed.

су́кровиц|а, ы *f.* **1** (*physiol.*) lymph, serum. **2** (*в язве, в нарыве*) pus.

сул|и́ть, ю́, и́шь *impf.* (*of* ⇒**по~**) to promise; **с. золоты́е го́ры** to promise the earth; **э́то не ~и́т ничего́ хоро́шего** this does not bode well.

султа́н¹, а *m.* (*титул*) sultan.

султа́н², а *m.* (*перьев; огня*) plume.

султана́т, а *m.* sultanate.

султа́н|ский *adj. of* ⇒**~¹**

сульфа́т, а *m.* (*chem.*) sulphate (*Br.*), sulfate (*US*).

сульфи́д, а *m.* (*chem.*) sulphide (*Br.*), sulfide (*US*).

С

сум|á, ы́ *f.* bag, pouch; **ходи́ть с ~óй** to beg, go a-begging.

сумасбрóд, а *m.* madcap.

сумасбрó|дить, жу, дишь *impf.* (*coll.*) to behave wildly, extravagantly.

сумасбрóд|ка, ки *f. of* ⇒~

сумасбрóднича|ть, ю *impf.* (*coll.*) = **сумасбрóдить**

сумасбрóд|ный (~ен, ~на) *adj.* wild, extravagant.

сумасбрóдств|о, а *nt.* wild, extravagant behaviour (*Br.*), behavior (*US*).

сумасшéдш|ий *adj.* **1** mad; *as n.* **с., ~его** *m.* madman, lunatic; **~ая, ~ей** *f.* madwoman; **бу́йный с.** raving, violent lunatic; **объяви́ть когó-н. ~им** to certify s.o. **2**: **с. дом** (*coll.*) lunatic asylum, madhouse. **3** (*fig.*) mad, lunatic; **~ая скóрость** lunatic speed; **э́то бу́дет стóить ~их дéнег** it will cost the earth.

сумасшéстви|е, я *nt.* madness, lunacy; **до ~я** (*coll.*) extremely, terribly; **я устáл до ~я** I'm terribly tired.

сумасшéств|овать, ую *impf.* (*coll.*) to act like a madman.

суматóх|а, и *f.* confusion, chaos, turmoil.

суматóшлив|ый (~, ~а) *adj.* (*coll.*) given to fussing, fussy.

суматóш|ный (~ен, ~на) *adj.* (*человек*) fussy; (*день, подготовка*) chaotic.

Сумáтр|а, ы *f.* Sumatra.

суматри́йский *adj.* Sumatran.

сумбу́р, а *m.* confusion, chaos.

сумбу́р|ный (~ен, ~на) *adj.* confused, chaotic.

су́меречный *adj.* twilight, dusk.

су́мер|ки, ек *no sg.* twilight, dusk.

су́мернича|ть, ю *impf.* (*coll.*) to sit in the twilight.

сумé|ть, ю *pf.* (+*inf.*) to be able (to), manage (to).

су́мк|а, и *f.* **1** bag; **хозя́йственная с.** shopping bag. **2** (*biol.*) pouch.

су́мм|а, ы *f.* sum; **кру́пные ~ы** large sums (of money); **óбщая/пóлная с.** sum total; (*количество*) amount; **с. к получéнию** amount due; **с. к перенóсу** amount carried forward; **в ~е** all in all.

суммáр|ный (~ен, ~на) *adj.* **1** (*количество*) total. **2** (*обзор*) summary.

сумми́р|овать, ую *impf. and pf.* **1** (*складывать*) to add up. **2** (*обобщать*) to summarize; to sum up.

су́мнича|ть, ю *pf. of* ⇒**у́мничать**

сумня́ся, сумня́шеся *see* ⇒**ничтóже**

су́мочк|а, и *f.* (*дамская*) handbag.

су́мрак, а *m.* dusk, twilight.

су́мрач|ный (~ен, ~на) *adj.* gloomy (*also fig.*).

су́мчатый *adj.* (*zool.*) marsupial.

сумя́тиц|а, ы *f.* confusion, chaos.

сунду́к, á *m.* trunk, box, chest.

су́н|уть(ся), у(сь), ешь(ся) *pf. of* ⇒**совáть(ся)**

суп, а, *pl.* **~ы́** *m.* soup.

суперарби́тр, а *m.* chief arbitrator.

суперзвезд|á, ы́, *pl.* **~́ы, ~́, ~́ам** *f.* superstar.

супермáркет, а *m.* supermarket.

суперме́н, а *m.* superman.

суперoблóжк|а, и *f.* dust-cover, jacket (*of book*).

суперфосфáт, а *m.* (*chem.*) superphosphate.

су́пес|ь, и *f.* sandy soil, sandy loam.

су́п|ить, лю, ишь *impf.* (*of* ⇒**на~**): **с. брóви** to knit one's brows, frown.

су́п|иться, люсь, ишься *impf.* (*of* ⇒**на~**) = **су́пить брóви**

су́пниц|а, ы *f.* soup tureen.

супов|óй *adj. of* ⇒**суп; ~áя лóжка** soup ladle; **~áя ми́ска** soup plate, bowl.

супостáт, а *m.* (*arch., or rhet.*) adversary, foe.

супроти́в (*coll.*) **1** *prep.*+*g.* against. **2** *adv. and prep.*+*g.* opposite.

супроти́в|ный *adj.* (*coll.*): **~ная стенá** the opposite wall, the wall opposite.

супру́г, а *m.* **1** husband, spouse. **2** (*pl.*) (*муж и жена*) husband and wife, married couple.

супру́г|а, и *f.* wife, spouse.

супру́жеский *adj.* (*чета, жизнь*) married; (*верность, счастье*) marital.

супру́жеств|о, а *nt.* matrimony, wedlock.

супру́жник, а *m.* (*coll.*) husband, hubby.

супру́жниц|а, ы *f.* (*coll.*) wife.

сургу́ч, á *m.* sealing-wax.

surди́нк|а, и *f.* (*mus.*) mute; **под ~у** (*coll.*) (*тайком*) on the quiet; (*тихо*) quietly.

сурéпиц|а, ы *f.* (*bot.*) **1** rape. **2** (*сорное растение*) charlock.

сурéпк|а, и *f.* = **сурéпица** 2

сурéп|ный *adj. of* ⇒**~ица; ~ное мáсло** rape oil.

су́рик, а *m.* (*chem.*) red lead.

сурóвост|ь, и *f.* severity, sternness.

сурó|вый (~, ~а) *adj.* **1** (*взгляд, критика*) severe, stern; (*зима, жизнь, приговор*) harsh; (*красота, воспитание*) austere. **2** (*ткань*) coarse.

сур|óк, кá *m.* marmot; **спать как с.** to sleep like a log.

суррогáт, а *m.* surrogate, substitute.

суррогáтн|ый *adj.* surrogate, substitute, ersatz; **~ая мать** surrogate mother.

сурьм|á, ы́ *f.* (*chem.*) antimony.

сурьм|и́ть, лю́, и́шь *impf.* (*of* ⇒**на~**) (*obs.*) to dye, darken (*hair, eye-brows, etc.*).

сурьм|и́ться, лю́сь, и́шься *impf.* (*of* ⇒**на~**) (*obs.*) to dye, darken one's hair, eye-brows, *etc.*

сусáльн|ый *adj.* **1** tinsel; **~ое зóлото** gold leaf. **2** (*fig., coll.*) (*слащавый*) sugary.

су́слик, а *m.* (*zool.*) ground squirrel, gopher (*US*).

су́сл|о, а *nt.* **1**: **виногрáдное с.** must; **пивнóе с.** wort. **2** (*сок винограда*) grape-juice.

суспéнзи|я, и *f.* (*chem.*) suspension.

суспензóри|й, я *m.* (*sport*) jock-strap.

сустáв, а *m.* (*anat.*) joint.

суставнóй *adj. of* ⇒**сустáв**

сутáн|а, ы *f.* soutane.

сутенёр, а *m.* pimp, ponce.

су́т|ки, ок *no sg.* twenty-four hours; twenty-four-hour period; **цéлые с.** for days and nights.

су́толок|а, и *f.* commotion, hubbub; **предпрáздничная с.** pre-holiday rush.

су́точн|ый *adj.* twenty-four-hour; daily; round-the-clock; **~ые дéньги** per diem subsistence allowance; *as n.* **~ые, ~ых** = **~ые дéньги**

суту́л|ить, ю, ишь *impf.* (*of* ⇒**с~**) to stoop.

суту́л|иться, юсь, ишься *impf.* (*of* ⇒**с~**) to stoop.

суту́лост|ь, и *f.*: **с. фигу́ры** round shoulders, stoop.

суту́л|ый (~, ~а) *adj.* round-shouldered, stooping.

сут|ь[1], и *f.* essence; **с. дéла** the heart, crux of the matter; **вни́кнуть в с. вопрóса** to get to the heart of the matter; **по ~́и дéла** as a matter of fact, in point of fact.

сут|ь[2] (*arch.*) **1** *3rd pers. pl. pres. of* ⇒**быть** is, are; **э́то не с. вáжно** this is not so important. **2** (*перед перечислением; следующие*) are as follows.

сутя́г|а, и *c.g.* (*coll., obs.*) = **сутя́жник**

сутя́жник, а *m.* litigious person.

сутя́жнича|ть, ю *impf.* to engage in (malicious) litigation.

сутя́жничеств|о, а *nt.* malicious litigation.

сутя́жн|ый *adj.* litigious; **~ое дéло** malicious litigation.

суфлé *nt. indecl.* (*cul.*) soufflé.

суфлёр, а *m.* (*theatr.*) prompter.

суфлёр|ский *adj. of* ⇒**~; ~ская бу́дка** prompt-box.

суфли́р|овать, ую *impf.* (+*d.*) (*theatr.*) to prompt.

суфражи́зм, а *m.* suffragette movement.

суфражи́стк|а, и *f.* suffragette.

су́ффикс, а *m.* (*gram.*) suffix.

сухáрниц|а, ы *f.* biscuit dish.

сухáр|ь, я́ *m.* **1** rusk. **2** (*fig., coll.*) cold, detached, unemotional person.

сух|áя, óй *f.* (*sport*) whitewash (*Br.*), shutout (*US*) (*game in which loser fails to score a single point*); **сдéлать ~у́ю комý-н.** to whitewash s.o. (*Br.*), shut s.o. out (*US*).

сухмéн|ь, и *f.* (*dial.*) **1** (*погода*) dry weather, drought. **2** (*почва*) dry soil.

су́хо *adv.* **1** coldly; **нас при́няли с.** we were received coldly. **2** *as pred.* it is dry; **на у́лице с.** it is dry out of doors; **у меня́ в гóрле с.** my throat is parched.

суховáт|ый (~, ~а) *adj.* dryish.

суховé|й, я *m.* hot dry wind.

сухогру́з, а *m.* bulk carrier.

сухогру́зн|ый *adj.*: **~ое су́дно** bulk carrier.

сухожи́ли|е, я *nt.* (*anat.*) tendon, sinew.

сух|о́й (~, ~а́, ~о) *adj.* **1** dry; **~и́е дрова́** dry firewood; **~о́е ру́сло реки́** dried-up river-bed; **~и́м путём** by land, overland; **вы́йти ~и́м из воды́** to come out unscathed. **2** (*хлеб*) dry; (*фрукты*) dried; **~о́е молоко́** dried milk. **3** (*кожа*) dried-up; (*рука*) withered; (*худощавый*) lean. **4** (*без влаги, без жидкости*) dry; **с. док** dry-dock; **с. ка́шель** dry cough; **с. лёд** dry ice; **~а́я мо́лния** summer lightning; **с. элеме́нт** (*elec.*) dry pile. **5** (*fig.*) (*скучный*) dry; (*не выразительный*) dreary. **6** (*fig.*) (*холодный*) chilly, cold; **с. приём** chilly reception. **7** (*sport*): **с. счёт** = **суха́я. 8**: **с. зако́н** prohibition.

сухомя́тк|а, и *f.* (*coll.*) dry food (*without any beverage*).

сухопа́р|ый (~, ~а) *adj.* (*coll.*) lean, spare.

сухопу́тн|ый *adj.* land (*opp. marine, air*); **~ые си́лы** (*mil.*) ground forces.

сухосто́|й, я *m.* (*collect.*) dead standing trees.

су́хост|ь, и *f.* **1** dryness; (*почвы*) aridity. **2** (*fig.*) chilliness, coldness.

сухот|а́, ы́ *f.* **1** (*ощущение сухости*) dryness; **у меня́ в го́рле с.** my throat is parched. **2** (*сушь*) dry spell (*of weather*). **3** (*folk poet.*; *dial.*) (*тоска*) longing, yearning.

сухофру́кт|ы, ов *no sg.* dried fruits.

сухоща́в|ый (~, ~а) *adj.* lean.

сухоя́дени|е, я *nt.* dry food.

сучёный *adj.* twisted.

суч|и́ть, у́, ~ишь *impf.* (*of* ⇒**с~**) **1** to twist, spin. **2** (*cul.*) to roll out (*dough*).

су́чк|а, и *f.* = **су́ка**

сучкова́т|ый (~, ~а) *adj.* knotty; gnarled.

суч|о́к, ка́ *m.* **1** (*ветка*) twig. **2** (*в древесине*) knot (*in wood*); **без ~ка́, без задо́ринки** (*coll.*) without a hitch.

су́ш|а, и *f.* (dry) land (*opp. sea*); **по ~е** by land.

су́ше *comp. of* ⇒**сухо́й** *and* **су́хо**

суше́ни|е, я *nt.* drying.

сушёный *adj.* dried.

суши́лк|а, и *f.* **1** (*устройство*) drying apparatus, dryer; **напо́льная с.** clothes horse. **2** (*помещение*) drying-room. **3** (*cul.*) drying rack.

суши́льный *adj.* (*tech.*) drying.

суши́л|ьня, ьни, *g. pl.* **~ен** *f.* drying-room.

суш|и́ть, у́, ~ишь *impf.* (*of* ⇒**вы́~**) to dry (out); (*fig.*) (*изводить*) to waste, eat away; (*делать суровым*) to harden.

суш|и́ться, у́сь, ~ишься *impf.* (*of* ⇒**вы́~**) to dry (out); (*человек*) to get dry.

су́шк|а, и *f.* **1** drying. **2** (*cul.*) dry (*ring-shaped*) cracker.

суш|ь, и *f.* **1** (*пора*) dry spell (*of weather*). **2** (*место на земле*) dry place. **3** (*хворост*) dry twigs.

суще́ствен|ный (~, ~на) *adj.* (*черта, разница*) essential; (*роль, значение*) vital; (*крупный*) substantial; (*вопрос*) important; **~ная попра́вка** important amendment.

существи́тельн|ое *adj.*: **и́мя с.** (*or as n.* **с., ~ого** *nt.*) noun, substantive; **с. же́нского/мужско́го/сре́днего ро́да** feminine/masculine/neuter noun.

существ|о́, а́ *nt.* **1** (*сущность*) essence; **по ~у́** (*говоря*) in essence, essentially; **говори́ть по ~у́** to speak to the point; **не по ~у́** off the point, beside the point; **всё моё с.** my whole being. **2** (*живая особь*) being, creature; **люби́мое с.** loved one.

существова́ни|е, я *nt.* existence; **сре́дства к ~ю** livelihood; **отрави́ть кому́-н. (всё) с.** to make s.o.'s life a misery; **прекрати́ть с.** to cease to exist; **борьба́ за с.** struggle for survival.

существ|ова́ть, у́ю *impf.* to exist; (+*i. or* **на**+*a.*) to live on; **он ~у́ет на случа́йные за́работки** he lives on casual earnings; **он ~у́ет уро́ками** he lives by giving lessons.

су́щ|ий *adj.* **1** (*obs.*) (*существующий*) existing. **2** (*coll.*) (*правда*) absolute; utter; **с. ад** absolute hell; **~ая ерунда́** utter rubbish; **э́то/он ~ее наказа́ние** it/he is the bane of my life.

су́щност|ь, и *f.* essence; **в ~и (говоря́)** in essence, essentially.

Суэ́ц, а *m.* Suez.

Суэ́цк|ий кана́л, ~ого ~а *m.* the Suez Canal.

сфабрик|ова́ть, у́ю *pf. of* ⇒**фабрикова́ть**

сфа́гнум, а *m.* (*bot.*) sphagnum, bog-moss.

сфальц|ева́ть, у́ю *pf. of* ⇒**фальцева́ть**

сфальши́в|ить, лю, ишь *pf. of* ⇒**фальши́вить**

сфантази́р|овать, ую *pf. of* ⇒**фантази́ровать**

сфе́р|а, ы *f.* **1** sphere; **с. влия́ния** (*pol.*) sphere of influence; **вы́сшие ~ы** highest circles. **2** (*mil.*) zone, area; **с. огня́** zone of fire.

сфери́ческий *adj.* spherical.

сферо́ид, а *m.* (*math.*) spheroid.

сфероида́льный *adj.* (*math.*) spheroidal.

сфинкс, а *m.* sphinx.

сфи́нктер, а *m.* (*anat.*) sphincter.

сфокуси́р|овать(ся), ую(сь) *pf. of* ⇒**фокуси́ровать(ся)**

сформир|ова́ть(ся), у́ю(сь) *pf. of* ⇒**формирова́ть(ся)**

сформ|ова́ть, у́ю *pf. of* ⇒**формова́ть**

сформули́р|овать, ую *pf. of* ⇒**формули́ровать**

сфотографи́р|овать(ся), ую(сь) *pf. of* ⇒**фотографи́ровать(ся)**

с.-х. (*abbr. of* **сельскохозя́йственный**) agricultural.

схва|ти́ть, чу́, ~тишь *pf.* **1** *pf. of* ⇒**хвата́ть**[1]. **2** (*impf.* **~тывать**) (*coll.*) (*простуду*) to catch. **3** (*impf.* **~тывать**) (*coll.*) (*мысль*) to grasp, comprehend; **с. смысл** to grasp the meaning, catch on. **4** (*impf.* **~тывать**) (*tech.*) (*скрепить*) to clamp together. **5** *no impf.* (*в рисунке, фотографии*) to capture; **он ~ти́л настрое́ние** he captured the mood.

схва|ти́ться, чу́сь, ~тишься *pf.* **1** *pf. of* ⇒**хвата́ться. 2** (*impf.* **~тываться**) (**с**+*i.*) to grapple (with), come to grips (with) (*also fig.*).

схва́тк|а, и *f.* skirmish, fight; (*в спорте*) fight; (*в споре*) clash; **рукопа́шная с.** hand-to-hand fight.

схва́т|ки, ок *no sg.* contractions (*of muscles*); spasms; **родовы́е с.** labour (*Br.*), labor (*US*).

схва́тыва|ть(ся), ю(сь) *impf. of* ⇒**схвати́ть(ся)**

схе́м|а, ы *f.* **1** (*чертёж*) diagram, chart; **с. метро́** metro map. **2** (*сочинения*) sketch, outline, plan; **с. рома́на** plan of a novel. **3** (*elec., radio*) circuit.

схематизи́р|овать, ую *impf. and pf.* to present in sketchy form, (over-)simplify.

схемати́зм, а *m.* sketchiness, (over-)simplification.

схемати́ческий *adj.* **1** (*изображение*) diagrammatic, schematic. **2** (*изложение*) sketchy, (over-)simplified.

схемати́ч|ный (~ен, ~на) *adj.* sketchy, (over-)simplified.

схи́зм|а, ы *f.* (*eccl.*) schism.

схи́м|а, ы *f.* (*eccl.*) schema (*strictest monastic rule in Orthodox Church*).

схи́мник, а *m.* (*eccl.*) monk having taken vows of schema.

схи́мниц|а, ы *f.* (*eccl.*) nun having taken vows of schema.

схитр|и́ть, ю́, и́шь *pf. of* ⇒**хитри́ть**

схлестн|у́ться, у́сь, ёшься *pf.* (*coll.*) (*в споре*) to clash, lock together.

схлоп|ота́ть, очу́, о́чешь *pf.* (*coll.*) to get.

схлы́н|уть, ет *pf.* **1** (*о волнах*) to break and flow back. **2** (*о толпе*) to break up; to dwindle. **3** (*о чувствах*) to subside.

сход[1]**, а** *m.* **1** (*с автобуса*) coming off, alighting. **2** (*с горы*) descent.

сход[2]**, а** *m.* (*собрание*) gathering, assembly.

схо|ди́ть[1]**, жу́, ~дишь** *impf. of* ⇒**сойти́**

схо|ди́ть[2]**, жу́, ~дишь** *pf.* to go (*and come back*); (**за**+*i.*) to go to fetch; **с. посмотре́ть** to go to see; **~ди́ за врачо́м!** go and fetch a doctor!

схо|ди́ться, жу́сь, ~дишься *impf. of* ⇒**сойти́сь**

схо́дк|а, и *f.* gathering, assembly.

схо́дн|и, ей *pl.* (*sg.* **~я, ~и** *f.*) gangway, gang-plank.

схо́д|ный (~ен, ~на́, ~но) *adj.*

С

1 (**с**+*i.*) (*похожий*) similar (to). **2** (*coll.*) (*цена*) reasonable, fair.

схо́дств|о, а *nt.* likeness, similarity, resemblance; **вне́шнее с.** similarity in appearance.

схо́дств|овать, ую *impf.* (**с**+*i.*; *obs.*) to resemble.

схо́жест|ь, и *f.* (*coll.*) likeness, similarity.

схо́ж|ий (~, ~а) *adj.* (*coll.*) (**с**+*i.*) similar (to).

схола́стик|а, и *f.* scholasticism.

схоласти́ческий *adj.* scholastic (*of scholasticism*).

схорон|и́ть(ся), ю́(сь), ~́ишь(ся) *pf.* *of* ⇨**хорони́ть(ся)**

сца́па|ть, ю *pf.* (*coll.*) to grab, catch hold (of).

сцара́п|ать, аю *pf.* (*of* ⇨**~ывать**) to scratch off.

сцара́пыва|ть, ю *impf.* *of* ⇨**сцара́пать**

сце|ди́ть, жу́, ~́дишь *pf.* (*of* ⇨**~́живать**) to pour off, decant; (*через сито, марлю*) to strain off.

сце́жива|ть, ю *impf.* *of* ⇨**сцеди́ть**

сцементи́р|овать, ую *pf.* *of* ⇨**цементи́ровать**

сце́н|а, ы *f.* **1** (*подмостки*) stage (*also fig.*); **ста́вить на ~е** to stage; **сойти́ со ~ы** to go off the scene, make one's exit (*also fig.*). **2** (*эпизод, происшествие*) scene. **3** (*coll.*) scene; **устро́ить ~у** to make a scene.

сцена́ри|й, я *m.* **1** (*фильма, передачи*) scenario, script. **2** (*детальный план*) plan, programme (*Br.*), program (*US*). **3** (*fig.*) (*вариант*) scenario.

сценари́ст, а *m.* script-writer.

сценари́ст|ка, ки *f.* *of* ⇨**~**

сцени́ческ|ий *adj.* stage; **~ое иску́сство** dramatic art; **~ая рема́рка** stage direction.

сцени́ч|ный (~ен, ~на) *adj.* suitable for the theatre (*Br.*), theater (*US*), effective on the stage.

сце́нк|а, и *f.* **1** *dim.* *of* ⇨**сце́на.** **2** (*из жизни*) scene.

сцено́граф, а *m.* (*theatr.*) set designer.

сценогра́фи|я, и *f.* set design.

сцеп, а *m.* **1** (*приспособление*) coupling; drawbar. **2** (*несколько машин, сцепленных вместе*) chain (*of two or more goods trucks, etc., coupled together*).

сцеп|и́ть, лю́, ~́ишь *pf.* (*of* ⇨**~ля́ть**) **1** (*вагоны, кузова*) to couple. **2** (*пальцы*) to clasp.

сцеп|и́ться, лю́сь, ~́ишься *pf.* (*of* ⇨**~ля́ться**) **1** (*вагоны, детали*) to be coupled; (*ветки*) to be intertwined; to intertwine; (*частицы*) to stick together. **2** (**с**+*i.*; *coll.*) (*начать драться*) to grapple (with).

сце́пк|а, и *f.* (*действие*) coupling.

сцепле́ни|е, я *nt.* **1** (*действие*) coupling. **2** (*tech.*) clutch; **выключе́ние ~я** clutch release; (*клеток, вещества*) cohesion. **3** (*fig.*) (*совокупность*) accumulation; **с. обстоя́тельств** chain of events.

сцепля́|ть(ся), ю(сь) *impf.* *of* ⇨**сцепи́ть(ся)**

сцепно́й *adj.* (*tech.*) coupling.

сце́пщик, а *m.* (*rail.*) shunter.

сча́лива|ть, ю *impf.* *of* ⇨**сча́лить**

сча́л|ить, ю, ишь *pf.* (*of* ⇨**~ивать**) to lash together.

счастли́в|ец, ца *m.* lucky man.

счастли́виц|а, ы *f.* lucky woman.

счастли́вчик, а *m.* (*coll.*) = **счастли́вец**

сча́стливо *adv.* (*жить, улыбаться*) happily; **с. отде́латься** (**от**+*g.*) to have a lucky escape (from); **счастли́во (остава́ться)!** good luck!

счастли́в|ый (сча́стлив, ~а) *adj.* **1** (*лицо, детство, человек*) happy; **с. коне́ц** happy end. **2** (*игрок, случай, день*) lucky; **у неё ~ая рука́** she brings luck. **3**: **~ого пути́!** bon voyage!

сча́сть|е, я *nt.* **1** (*чувство*) happiness; **жела́ю вам с.** I wish you happiness. **2** (*удача*) luck, good fortune; **к ~ю, на с., по ~ю** luckily, fortunately; **на на́ше с.** luckily for us; **попыта́ть ~я** to try one's luck; **име́ть с.** (+*inf.*) to have the good fortune to; (*как формула вежливости*) to be honoured (*Br.*), honored (*US*) to; **твоё с.(, что)** you were lucky (that); **како́е с., что…** how fortunate that ….

счесть, сочту́, сочтёшь, *past* **счёл, сочла́** *impf.* *of* ⇨**счита́ть**[1]; **не с.** (+*g.*) countless (numbers of); **у него́ друзе́й не с.** he has countless (numbers of) friends; **там бы́ло люде́й не с.** there were countless (numbers of) people there.

сче́сться, сочту́сь, сочтёшься, *past* **счёлся, сочла́сь** *pf.* *of* ⇨**счита́ться**[1]

счёт, а (у), *pl.* **~ы** *and* **~а́** *m.* **1** *sg. only* (*действие*) counting, calculation, reckoning; **вести́ с.** (+*d.*) to keep count (of); **потеря́ть с.** (+*d.*) to lose count (of); **он не в с.** he does not count; **в два ~а** in a jiffy, in a trice; **без ~у, ~у нет** countless. **2** *sg. only* (*sport*) score; **со ~ом 2:1** with a score of 2–1. **3** (*pl.* **~а́**) (*в ресторане, за газ, за телефон*) bill; (*накладная*) invoice; **пода́ть с.** to present a bill; **уплати́ть по ~у** to pay the bill. **4** (*pl.* **~а́**) (*в банке*) account; **откры́ть с.** to open an account; **за с.** (+*g.*) at the expense (of); **на с.** on account; **на с.** (+*g.*) to the account (of). **5** (*fig.*) account, expense; **в с.** (+*g.*) on the strength (of); **в коне́чном ~е, в после́днем ~е** in the end; **за с.** (+*g.*) at the expense (of); owing (to); **на свой с.** on one's own account; **приня́ть на свой с.** to take (sth.) personally; **на чужо́й с.** at others' expense; **на э́тот с.** in this respect; **быть на хоро́шем, дурно́м ~у́** to be in good, bad (repute); to stand well, badly; **име́ть на своём ~у́** to have to one's credit; **отнести́ за с.** (+*g.*) to put (sth.) down to. **6** **~ы** (*no sg.*; *fig.*) (*претензии*) accounts, score(s); **ста́рые ~ы** old scores; **свести́ ~ы** (**с**+*i.*) to settle a score (with), get even (with); **сбро́сить со счето́в** to ignore. **7** *see* ⇨**~ы**[1]

счётн|ый *adj.* **1** (*служащий для счёта*) counting, calculating; **~ая коми́ссия** vote counting committee; **~ая лине́йка** slide-rule; **~ая маши́на** calculator, calculating machine. **2** (*относящийся к счетоводству*) accounts, accounting; **Счётная пала́та** National Audit Office; **с. рабо́тник** accounts clerk; **~ая часть** accounts department.

счетово́д, а *m.* accountant; accounts clerk.

счетово́дн|ый *adj.* accounting; **~ая кни́га** account book.

счетово́дств|о, а *nt.* accounting.

счётчик[1]**, а** *m.* (*человек*) counter.

счётчик[2]**, а** *m.* (*прибор*) meter; counter; **га́зовый с.** gas meter; **с. километра́жа** milometer (*Br.*), odometer (*US*); **с. магни́тной ле́нты** tape counter.

счётчиц|а, ы *f.* *of* ⇨**счётчик**[1]

счёт|ы[1]**, ов** *no sg.* abacus.

счёт|ы[2] *see* ⇨**~** 6

счисле́ни|е, я *nt.* **1** counting; **систе́ма ~я** (*math.*) scale of notation. **2**: **с. пути́** (*naut.*) dead reckoning.

счи́|стить, щу, стишь *pf.* (*of* ⇨**~ща́ть**) to clean off.

счи́|ститься, стится *pf.* (*of* ⇨**~ща́ться**) (*о грязи*) to come off.

счита́лк|а, и *f.* counting rhyme.

счи́тан|ный (~, ~а) *p.p.p.* *of* ⇨**счита́ть** *and adj.*; **остаю́тся ~ные дни** (**до**+*g.*) one can count the days (until); there are only a few days left (until); **~ное коли́чество** (*денег*) very little; (*предметов*) very few.

счита́|ть[1]**, ю** *impf.* (*of* ⇨**счесть**) **1** (*pf. also* **со~**) to count; **с. де́ньги** to count money; **с. на па́льцах** to count on one's fingers; **с. до ста** to count up to a hundred; **с. дни, мину́ты** to count the days, minutes; **не ~я** not counting. **2** (+*i.* *or* **за**+*a.*) to count, consider, think; to regard (as); **я ~ю его́ надёжным наблюда́телем, я ~ю его́ за надёжного наблюда́теля** I consider him a reliable observer; **с. необходи́мым/ну́жным, с. за ну́жное** to consider it necessary; **с. за сча́стье** to count it one's good fortune; **с. кого́-н. отве́тственным** to hold s.o. responsible. **3** **(что)** to consider (that), hold (that); **они́ ~ют, что я не в состоя́нии об э́том суди́ть** they consider that I am not in a position to be a judge of this; **я ~ю, что он интере́сный челове́к** I consider him an interesting person; I regard him as an interesting person.

счит|а́ть[2]**, а́ю** *pf.* (*of* ⇨**~́ывать**) (**с**+*i.*) (*сверить*) to compare (with), check (against); (*показания прибора*) to read; (*comput.*) to read.

счита́|ться[1]**, юсь** *impf.* (*of* ⇨**сче́сться**) (**с**+*i.*) (*расплачиваться*) to settle accounts (with) (*also fig.*).

счита́|ться[2]**, юсь** *impf.* (*no pf.*) **1** (+*i.*) to be considered, be thought, be reputed; to be regarded (as); **он ~ется первокла́ссным специали́стом** he is considered a first-rate specialist; **~ется, что...** it is considered that .... **2** (**с**+*i.*) (*принимать в расчёт*) to consider, take into consideration; to take into account, reckon (with); **он всегда́ ~лся с моим мне́нием** he always took my opinion into consideration; **он ~ется со своими колле́гами** he has consideration for his colleagues; **он ни с кем не ~ется** he has no consideration for anyone; **с шéфом ещё нáдо с.** the boss has still to be reckoned with.

счи́тк|а, и *f.* **1** comparison, checking; **с. гра́нок с ру́кописью** comparison of proofs with manuscript. **2** (*theatr.*) reading (*of a part in a play*).

счи́тыва|ть, ю *impf. of* ⇒**счита́ть**[2]

счища́|ть(ся), ю, ет(ся) *impf. of* ⇒**счи́стить(ся)**

США *no sg., indecl.* (*abbr. of* ***Соединённые Шта́ты Аме́рики***) USA (*United States of America*).

сшиб|а́ть(ся), а́ю(сь) *impf. of* ⇒**~и́ть(ся)**

сшиб|и́ть, у́, ёшь, *past* **~, ~ла** *pf.* (*of* ⇒**~а́ть**) (*coll.*) to knock off; **с. с ног** to knock down, knock over; **с. с кого́-н. спесь** to take s.o. down a peg.

сшиб|и́ться, у́сь, ёшься, *past* **~ся, ~лась** *pf.* (*of* ⇒**~а́ться**) (*coll.*) to collide; to come to blows.

сшива́|ть, ю *impf. of* ⇒**сшить**

сшить, сошью́, сошьёшь *pf.* **1** *pf. of* ⇒**шить. 2** (*impf.* **сшива́ть**) to sew together; (*med.*) to suture.

съ... *vbl. pref.* = **с...**

съеда́|ть, ю *impf.* to eat (up).

съеде́ни|е, я *nt., only in phr.* **отда́ть на с.** (+*d.*) (*fig.*) to put at the mercy (of).

съедо́б|ный (~ен, ~на) *adj.* edible.

съёжива|ться, юсь *impf. of* ⇒**съёжиться**

съёж|иться, усь, ишься *pf.* (*of* ⇒**ёжиться** *and* **~иваться**) (*в комочек*; *от холода*) to huddle up; (*о листьях, о лице*) to shrivel up; (*о ткани*) to shrink.

съезд[1]**, а** *m.* **1** (*собрание*) congress; conference, convention. **2** (*прибытие*) arrival, gathering.

съезд[2]**, а** *m.* (*спуск*) descent.

съе́з|дить, жу, дишь *pf.* **1** to go (*and come back*); **как ты ~дила?** how was your trip? **2** (*coll.*) (+*d.*) (*ударить*) to bash.

съе́здовский *adj.* congress.

съезжа́|ть(ся), ю(сь) *impf. of* ⇒**съе́хать(ся)**

съе́зж|ая, ей *f.* (*obs.*) cell (*in police station*)

съе́зж|ий *adj.* (*obs.*) of assembly; **~ая изба́** assembly house.

съел *see* ⇒**съесть**

съём, а *m.* removal.

съёмк|а, и *f.* **1** (*удаление*) removal. **2** (*местности*) survey, surveying; plotting. **3** (*usu. pl.*) (*фильма*) shooting. **4** (*копии, плана*) making.

съёмный *adj.* detachable, removable.

съём|очный *adj. of* ⇒**~ка; ~очная гру́ппа** film-crew; **~очная площа́дка** film-set; **~очные рабо́ты** surveying.

съёмщик, а *m.* tenant.

съёмщиц|а, ы *f. of* ⇒**съёмщик**

съестн|о́й *adj.* food; **~ы́е припа́сы** food supplies, provisions; *as n.* **~о́е, ~о́го** *nt.* food.

съе|сть, м, шь, ст, ди́м, ди́те, дя́т, *past* **~л, ~ла** *pf. of* ⇒**есть**[1]; **с. соба́ку** (**на**+*p.*; *coll.*) to have at one's finger-tips, know inside out.

съе́|хать, ду, дешь *pf.* (*of* ⇒**~зжа́ть**) **1** (*спуститься*) to go down, come down. **2**: **с. на́ берег** (*naut.*) to go ashore. **3** (*с квартиры*) to move out. **4** (*fig., coll.*) (*двинуться с места*) to come down, slip; **у тебя́ ~хал га́лстук на́бок** your tie is on one side. **5** (*свернуть*) to turn.

съе́|хаться, дусь, дешься *pf.* (*of* ⇒**~зжа́ться**) **1** (*встретиться*) to meet. **2** (*собраться*) to arrive, gather, assemble.

съехи́днича|ть, ю *pf. of* ⇒**ехи́дничать**

съязв|и́ть, лю́, и́шь *pf. of* ⇒**язви́ть**

сы́воротк|а, и *f.* **1** whey. **2** (*biol., med.*) serum.

сы́гранност|ь, и *f.* team-work.

сыгра́|ть, ю *pf. of* ⇒**игра́ть; с. шу́тку** (**с**+*i.*) to play a practical joke (on).

сыгра́|ться, юсь *pf.* (*of* ⇒**сы́грываться**) to play well together.

сы́грыва|ться, юсь *impf. of* ⇒**сыгра́ться**

сы́змала *adv.* (*coll.*) since childhood.

сы́знова *adv.* (*coll.*) anew, afresh; **нача́ть с.** to make a fresh start, begin all over again.

сымпровизи́р|овать, ую *pf. of* ⇒**импровизи́ровать**

сын, а, *pl.* **~овья́, ~ове́й** *and* **~ы́, ~о́в** *m.* **1** (*pl.* **~овья́**) son. **2** (*pl.* **~ы́**) (*fig., rhet.*) son, child; **с. своего́ вре́мени** child, product of one's time.

сыни́шк|а, и *m.* (*coll.*) *dim. of* ⇒**сын**

сыно́вний *adj.* filial.

сын|о́к, ка́ *m. dim. of* ⇒**~**; (*as mode of address*) sonny.

сы́п|ать, лю, лешь *impf.* **1** to pour. **2** (+*a. or i.*; *fig., coll.*) to pour forth; **с. жа́лобами** to pour forth complaints; **с. деньга́ми** to squander money.

сы́п|аться, лется *impf.* **1** (*о чём-н. мелком*) to fall; (*о сыпучем*) to pour out; (*разбегаться*) to scatter; **мука́ ~алась из мешка́** flour poured out of the bag. **2** (*coll.*) (*о звуках*) to pour forth (*intrans.*), rain down; **уда́ры ~ались гра́дом** blows were raining down, falling thick and fast. **3** (*о штукатурке*) to flake off. **4** (*о ткани*) to fray out.

сыпно́й *adj.*: **с. тиф** (*med.*) typhus, spotted fever.

сыпня́к, а́ *m.* (*coll.*) = **сыпно́й тиф**

сыпу́ч|ий (~, ~а) *adj.* friable, free-flowing; **с. грунт** shifting ground; **с. песо́к** quicksand; **~ие тела́** dry substances; **ме́ры ~их тел** dry measures.

сып|ь, и *f.* (*med.*) rash, eruption.

сыр, а, *pl.* **~ы́** *m.* cheese; **как с. в ма́сле ката́ться** (*coll.*) to live on the fat of the land.

сыр-бо́р *now only in phr.* **вот отку́да с. загоре́лся** (*coll.*) that was the spark that set the forest on fire.

сыре́|ть, ю *impf.* (*of* ⇒**от~**) to become damp.

сыр|е́ц, ца́ *m.* product in raw state; **кирпи́ч-с.** adobe; **хло́пок-с.** raw cotton; **шёлк-с.** raw silk.

сы́рник, а *m.* curd fritter.

сы́р|ный *adj. of* ⇒**~; ~ная неде́ля** (*obs.*) Shrovetide.

сы́ро *as predicate* it is damp.

сырова́р, а *m.* cheese-maker.

сыроваре́ни|е, я *nt.* cheese-making.

сырова́т|ый (~, ~а) *adj.* **1** (*климат*) dampish. **2** (*банан*) not quite ripe. **3** (*cul.*) (*мясо*) underdone, undercooked.

сыроде́л, а *m.* cheese-maker.

сыроде́льный *adj.* cheese-processing.

сыроéжк|а, и *f.* russula (*mushroom*).

сыр|о́й (~, ~а́, ~о) *adj.* **1** (*влажный*) damp; (*лето, день*) wet. **2** (*овощи, тесто*) raw, uncooked; **~а́я вода́** unboiled water; **~о́е мя́со** raw meat. **3** (*незрелый*) green, unripe. **4** (*необработанный*) raw; (*рассказ, план*) unfinished, unrefined; **~ы́е материа́лы** raw materials. **5** (*coll.*) (*тучный*) fat, podgy.

сыр|о́к, ка́ *m.* (*творожный*) curd cheese; **пла́вленый с.** processed cheese.

сыромя́тн|ый *adj.*: **~ая ко́жа** rawhide.

сы́ромят|ь, и *f.* rawhide.

сы́рост|ь, и *f.* dampness, humidity.

сырь|ё, я́ *no pl., nt.* raw material(s).

сырьев|о́й *adj. of* **сырьё; ~а́я ба́за** raw material supply.

сырьём *adv.* (*coll.*) raw; **есть морко́вь с.** to eat carrots raw.

сыск, а *m.* investigation, detection (*of criminals*).

сыска́ть, щу́, ~щешь *pf.* (*coll.*) to find.

сыска́ться, щу́сь, ~щешься *pf.* (*coll.*) to be found.

сыск|но́й *adj. of* ⇒**~; ~на́я поли́ция** criminal investigation department.

сыте́|ть, ю *impf.* (*coll.*) to become fuller.

сы́тно *adv.* well; **с. поза́втракать** to have a good breakfast.

сы́т|ный (~ен, ~на́, ~но) *adj.* (*обед*) substantial, copious; (*пирог*) filling, rich; (*питательный*) nourishing.

сы́тост|ь, и *f.* satiety, repletion.

сы́т|ый (~, ~а́, ~о) *adj.* **1** satisfied, full; **спаси́бо, я ~** thank you, I am full. **2** (*смех, улыбка*) satisfied. **3** (*откормленный*) well-fed. **4** (*fig.*) (+*i.*) (*пресыщенный*) fed up with; **я ~ по го́рло** I'm fed up to the back teech (with).

сыч, а́ *m.* little owl (*Athene noctua*);

С

(*человек*) gloomy unsociable person, loner; **~о́м сиде́ть** (*coll.*) to look glum.

сычу́жин|а, ы *f.* rennet.

сы́щик, а *m.* detective.

Сье́рра-Лео́не *indecl.* Sierra Leone.

СЭВ, а *m.* (*hist.*) (*abbr. of* ***Сове́т экономи́ческой взаимопо́мощи***) COMECON (*Council for Mutual Economic Assistance*).

сэконо́м|ить, лю, ишь *pf. of* **⇒эконо́мить**

сэр, а *m.* sir.

сюда́ *adv.* here, hither.

сюже́т, а *m.* (*картины, симфонии*) subject; (*романа*) plot; (*coll.*) (*беседы*) topic.

сюже́т|ный *adj. of* **⇒~**

сюзере́н, а *m.* (*hist.*) suzerain.

сюзере́н|ный *adj. of* **⇒~**

сюи́т|а, ы *f.* (*mus.*) suite.

сюрпри́з, а *m.* surprise.

сюрреали́зм, а *m.* surrealism.

сюрреали́ст, а *m.* surrealist.

сюрреалисти́ческий *adj.* surrealist.

сюрту́к, а́ *m.* frock-coat.

сюсю́кань|е, я *nt.* **1** (*в речи*) lisping. **2** (*в обращении*) indulgence, fussing over.

сюсю́ка|ть, ю *impf.* **1** (*в речи*) to lisp. **2** (*потворствовать*) to indulge, fuss over.

сяк *adv.* (*coll.*): **и так и с.**, *see* **⇒так**

сяко́й *see* **⇒тако́й-сяко́й**

сям *adv.*: **и там и с., ни там ни с.**, *see* **⇒там**

Tт

т (*abbr. of* ***тонна***) t., ton(s), tonne(s).

т. *abbr. of* **1** ***товарищ*** Comrade. **2** ***том*** vol., volume.

табак, а́ (у́) *m.* **1** (*растение*) tobacco-plant. **2** (*листья*) tobacco; **нюхательный т.** snuff; **дело — т.!** (*coll.*) things are in a bad way.

табака́ *indecl., only in phr.* (*cul.*): **цыплёнок т.** chicken tabak (*chicken flattened and grilled on charcoal*).

табаке́рк|а, и *f.* snuff-box.

табаково́д, а *m.* tobacco-grower.

табаково́дств|о, а *nt.* tobacco-growing.

табаково́д|ческий *adj. of* **⇒∼ство**

таба́чный *adj.* tobacco; **т. кисе́т** tobacco-pouch.

та́бел|ь, я *m.* **1** (*график*) table, chart; **т. о ра́нгах** (*hist.*) Table of Ranks (*introduced by Peter the Great*). **2** (*на заводе*) time-board. **3** (*номерок*) number (*removed on arrival at work and replaced on leaving*). **4** (*в школе*) report (*Br.*), report card (*US*).

та́бель|ный *adj. of* **⇒∼; ∼ная доска́** time-board; **∼ные часы́** time-clock.

та́бельщик, а *m.* timekeeper.

та́бельщиц|а, ы *f. of* **⇒та́бельщик**

табле́тк|а, и *f.* tablet, pill; **т. аспири́на** an aspirin.

табли́ц|а, ы *f.* table; (*рисунков, чертежей*) plate; **т. умноже́ния** multiplication table; **∼ы логари́фмов** logarithm tables; **т. Менделе́ева** (*chem.*) periodic table; **т. прили́вов** tide table; **электро́нная т.** (*comput.*) spreadsheet; **т. вы́игрышей** prize-list; **т. (ро́зыгрыша) пе́рвенства** (*sport*) (score-)table; **внести́ в ∼у** to tabulate.

табли́чный *adj.* tabular.

табло́ *indec., nt.* (*на вокзале*) indicator (board) (*Br.*), indicator panel; (*sport*) scoreboard.

табло́ид, а *m.* tabloid (newspaper).

табло́ид|ный *adj. of* **⇒∼; ∼ная пре́сса** tabloid press, the tabloids.

табльдо́т, а *m.* table d'hôte.

та́бор, а *m.* **1** (*лагерь*) camp. **2** (*группа цыган*) band of gypsies.

та́бор|ный *adj.* **1** *adj. of* **⇒∼.** **2** gypsy.

табу́ *nt. indecl.* taboo.

табу́н, а́ *m.* herd (*usu. of horses*).

табу́нщик, а *m.* herdsman.

табуре́т, а *m.* = **∼ка**

табуре́т|ка, ки *f.* stool.

таве́рн|а, ы *f.* tavern, inn.

та́волг|а, и *f.* (*bot.*) meadow-sweet.

таво́т, а *m.* (*tech.*) axle grease, lubricating grease.

таврёный *adj.* branded.

тавр|и́ть, ю́, и́шь *impf.* (*of* **⇒за∼**) to brand.

тавр|о́, а́, *pl.* **∼́а, ∼, ∼а́м** *nt.* brand (*on cattle, etc.*).

тавро́|вый *adj.* **1** *adj. of* **⇒∼.** **2** (*tech.*) T-shaped; **∼вая ба́лка** T-beam.

тавтологи́ческий *adj.* tautological.

тавтоло́ги|я, и *f.* tautology.

тага́н, а́ *m.* trivet.

таджи́к, а *m.* Tadjik.

Таджикиста́н, а *m.* Tadjikistan.

таджи́кский *adj.* Tadjik.

таджи́|чка, чки *f. of* **⇒∼к**

таёжник, а *m.* taiga dweller.

таёжни|ца, цы *f. of* **⇒∼к**

таёжный *adj. of* **⇒тайга́**

таз¹, а, в ∼у́, *pl.* **∼ы́** *m.* bowl.

таз², а, в ∼е *and* **в ∼у́,** *pl.* **∼ы́** *m.* (*anat.*) pelvis.

тазобе́дренный *adj.* (*anat.*) hip; **т. суста́в** hip joint.

та́зовый *adj.* (*anat.*) pelvic.

Таила́нд, а *m.* Thailand.

таила́нд|ец, ца *m.* Thai.

таила́нд|ка, ки *f. of* **⇒∼ец**

таи́нственност|ь, и *f.* mystery.

таи́нствен|ный (∼, ∼на) *adj.* **1** (*место, шорох*) mysterious; (*человек*) enigmatic. **2** (*цель*) secret. **3** (*вид*) secretive.

та́инств|о, а *nt.* **1** (*relig.*) sacrament. **2** (*obs.*) mystery, secret.

Таи́ти *m. indecl.* Tahiti.

та|и́ть, ю́, и́шь *impf.* (*горе*) to hide, conceal; (*злобу*) to harbour (*Br.*), harbor (*US*); **т. зло́бу (про́тив)** to harbour a grudge (against); **не́чего/что греха́ т.** it must be admitted, we must admit.

та|и́ться, ю́сь, и́шься *impf.* **1** (*coll.*) (*скрываться*) to be (in) hiding, lurk. **2** (*fig.*) (*иметься*) to lurk, be lurking; **что за э́тим ∼и́тся?** what lies behind this? **3** (*coll.*) (*скрывать что-н.*) to hold back (= *to decline to reveal*).

таитя́н|ин, ина, *pl.* **∼е, ∼** *m.* Tahitian.

таитя́н|ка, ки *f. of* **⇒∼ин**

таитя́нский *adj.* Tahitian.

Тайбэ́|й, я *m.* Taipei.

Тайва́н|ь, я *m.* Taiwan.

тайва́нский *adj.* Taiwanese.

тайг|а́, и́ *f.* (*geog.*) taiga.

тайко́м *adv.* in secret, surreptitiously; on the quiet; behind s.o.'s back.

тайм, а *m.* (*sport*) half, period (*of game*).

тайм-а́ут, а *m.* (*sport*) time-out.

таймен|ь, я *m.* salmon-trout.

та́йн|а, ы *f.* **1** (*то, что непонятно*) mystery. **2** (*секрет*) secret; **держа́ть в ∼е** to keep secret, keep dark; **храни́ть ∼у** to keep a secret; **не т., что** it is no secret that.

тайни́к, а́ *m.* hiding-place; **в ∼а́х души́** in the inmost recesses of the heart.

та́йнопис|ь, и *f.* secret writing.

та́йн|ый *adj.* secret; clandestine; **т. аге́нт** undercover agent; **∼ое голосова́ние** secret ballot; **т. коммуни́ст** crypto-Communist; **т. сове́т** (*hist.*) Privy Council.

та́йский *adj.* Thai.

тайфу́н, а *m.* typhoon.

так 1 *adv.* (*таким образом*) so; thus, in this way, like this; in such a way; **т. мно́го** so many; **мы сде́лали т.** this is what we did, we did as follows; **т. бы (и)**... (*coll.*) (*выражает сильное желание сделать что-н.*) how I, *etc.*, should like ...; **т. во́т** (*выражает продолжение повествования после отступления*) and so, so then; **т. же** in the same way; **т. и**

быть (*coll.*) all right, right you are; **т. и есть** (*coll.*) so it is; **т. и зна́й(те)** (*expr. warning*; *coll.*) get this clear; **т. ему́** *etc.*, **и на́до** serves him, *etc.*, right; **т. и́ли ина́че** whatever happens, one way or another; **т. называ́емый** so-called; **т. себе́** so-so, middling; **т. сказа́ть** so to speak; **за т.** (*coll.*) for nothing; **и т.** even so; as it is; **и т. да́лее** and so on, and so forth; **и т. и сяк** this way and that; **когда́ т.** (*coll.*) if so; **(не) т. ли?** isn't it so?
2 *adv.* (*как следует*) as it should be; **не т.** amiss, wrong; **т. ли я говорю́?** am I right?; **что́-то бы́ло не совсе́м т.** sth. was not quite right.
3 *adv.* (*без специальных средств*; *без последствий*) just like that; **боле́знь не пройдёт т.** the illness will not pass just like that; **т. ему́ э́то не пройдёт** he won't get away with it like that.
4 *adv.*: **т. (то́лько), про́сто т.** for no special reason, for no reason in particular; just for fun.
5 *particle* (*в репликах*) nothing in particular, nothing special; **что тебе́ не понра́вилось там? — т., о́бщее положе́ние** what did you not like there? — Nothing in particular, just the set-up in general.
6: **т. и** (*as emph. particle*) simply, just; **её глаза́ т. и сверка́ли гне́вом** her eyes were simply blazing with anger.
7 *conj.* (*тогда*) then (*or not translated*); **ты не спро́сишь его́, т. я спрошу́** if you won't ask him, then I will; **е́хать, т. е́хать** if we are going, let's go; **не сего́дня, т. за́втра** if not today, then tomorrow.
8 *conj.* so; **т. вы зна́ете друг дру́га?** so you know one another?
9: **т. как** *conj.* as, since.
10 *affirmative or emph. particle* (*да*) yes; **т. то́чно** (*mil.*) yes.
11: **т. что** so; **т. что́бы** so that.

такела́ж, а *m.* **1** (*naut.*) rigging. **2** (*для подъёма грузов*) lifting tackle.

такела́жник, а *m.* rigger, scaffolder.

такела́жн|ый *adj.* **1** (*naut.*) rigging. **2** scaffolding; **~ые рабо́ты** erection of scaffolding.

та́кже *adv.* also, too, as well; (*after neg.*) or, nor.

-таки *particle* (*coll.*) however, though; **всё-т.** nevertheless; **опя́ть-т.** again.

тако́в *m.*, **~а́** *f.*, **~о́** *nt.*, *pl.* **~ы́,** *pron.* such; **все они́ ~ы́** they are all the same; **и был т.** (*coll.*) and that was the last we saw of him.

таков|о́й *adj.* **1** (*obs.*) such; **е́сли ~ы́е име́ются** if any. **2**: **как т.** as such.

тако́вский *adj.* (*coll.*) of such a kind.

так|о́й *pron.* **1** such; so; **т. же** the same; **он т. до́брый!** he is such a kind man; **~о́е пальто́ мне ну́жно** I need a coat like that; **~и́м о́бразом** thus, in this way; **в ~о́м слу́чае** in that case; **до ~о́й сте́пени** to such an extent. **2** (*coll.*) (*известного рода*) a kind of; **бли́нчик т.** a kind of pancake. **3**: **кто он т.?** who is he?; **что э́то ~о́е?** what is this?; **что ~о́е** what's that?; what did you say?; **куда́ ~о́е он пошёл?** (*coll.*) wherever has he gone?

тако́й-сяко́й *pron.* (*coll.*) (a) so-and-so.

тако́й-то *pron.* so-and-so; such-and-such.

та́кс|а¹, ы *f.* (*установленная расценка*) set rate; **по чёрной ~е** at the black-market rate.

та́кс|а², ы *f.* (*собака*) dachshund.

такса́ци|я, и *f.* price-fixing; valuation.

такси́ *nt. indecl.* taxi.

таксидерми́ст, а *m.* taxidermist.

таксидерми́|я, и *f.* taxidermy.

та́ксик, а *m. dim. of* ⇒**та́кса²**

такси́р|овать, ую *impf. and pf.* to fix the price (of), price.

такси́ст, а *m.* taxi-driver.

таксо́метр, а *m.* (taxi)meter; 'clock'.

таксомото́р, а *m.* taxi.

таксомото́р|ный *adj. of* ⇒**~**; **т. парк** (*стоянка*) taxi depot; (*совокупность машин*) fleet of taxis.

таксофо́н, а *m.* payphone.

так-ся́к *adv. as pred.* (*coll.*) it is tolerable, it is passable.

такт¹, а *m.* **1** (*mus.*, *etc.*) (*ритм*) time; **отбива́ть т.** to beat time; **в т.** in time; (*в нотах*) bar. **2** (*tech.*) stroke (*of engine*).

такт², а *m.* (*тактичность*) tact.

та́к-таки *particle* (*coll.*) after all; really.

та́ктик, а *m.* tactician.

та́ктик|а, и *f.* tactics.

такти́ческий *adj.* tactical.

такти́чност|ь, и *f.* tact.

такти́ч|ный (~ен, ~на) *adj.* tactful.

та́к-то *adv.* (*coll.*) so; **он не т. скро́мен** he's not all that humble; **т. так** that's as it may be.

та́кт|овый *adj. of* ⇒**~¹**; **~овая черта́** bar.

тала́н, а *m.* (*folklore*) luck, good fortune.

тала́нт, а *m.* **1** (*дарование*) talent, gift(s). **2** (*человек*) gifted person.

тала́нтливост|ь, и *f.* talent, gifts.

тала́нтлив|ый (~, ~а) *adj.* talented, gifted.

та́л|и, ей *no sg.* block and tackle.

талидоми́д, а *m.* (*pharm.*) thalidomide.

талисма́н, а *m.* talisman, charm, mascot.

та́ли|я¹, и *f.* waist; **пла́тье в ~ю** dress fitting at the waist; **обня́ть кого́-н. за ~ю** to put one's arm round s.o.'s waist.

та́ли|я², и *f.* (*две колоды*) two packs of playing cards.

Та́ллин(н), а *m.* Tallin(n).

талму́д, а *m.* (*relig.*) Talmud.

талмуди́стский *adj.* Talmudistic; (*fig.*) doctrinaire.

талмуди́ческий = **талмуди́стский**

тало́н, а *m.* (*на бензин*) coupon; (*чека*) stub; **т. на обе́д** luncheon voucher (*Br.*); **поса́дочный т.** boarding pass.

тало́нчик, а *m. dim. of* ⇒**тало́н**

та́лреп, а *m.* (*naut.*) lanyard.

та́л|ый *adj.* thawed, melted; **~ая вода́** water from melted snow.

тальк, а *m.* (*минерал*) talc; (*косметический*) talcum powder.

та́льк|овый *adj. of* ⇒**~**

тальни́к, а́ *m.* willow.

там *adv.* **1** there; **т. же** in the same place; (*при ссылках*) ibidem; **и т. и сям** here, there and everywhere. **2** (*coll.*) (*потом*) later, by and by. **3** *as particle* (*coll.*) (*выражает сомнение, пренебрежение*): **вся́кие т. глу́пости говори́т** he talks all kinds of nonsense.

тамад|а́, ы́ *m.* master of ceremonies, toast-master.

та́мбур¹, а *m.* **1** (*вестибюль*) lobby. **2** (*железнодорожного вагона*) platform (*of railway carriage*).

та́мбур², а *m.* (*вышивание*) chain-stitch.

тамбу́р, а *m.* (*mus.*) tamboura.

тамбури́н, а *m.* **1** (*бубен*) tambourine. **2** (*барабан*) tambourin.

тамбурмажо́р, а *m.* (*mil.*; *obs.*) drum major.

та́мбур|ный *adj. of* ⇒**~²**; **т. шов** chain-stitch.

тамизда́т, а *m.* (*coll.*) 'tamizdat' (*publication abroad*).

тами́л, а *m.* Tamil.

тами́л|ка, ки *f. of* ⇒**~**

тами́льский *adj.* Tamil.

тамо́женник, а *m.* customs official.

тамо́женн|ый *adj.* customs; **~ые по́шлины, ~ые сбо́ры** customs (*duties*).

тамо́жн|я, и *f.* custom-house.

та́мошн|ий *adj.* (*coll.*) of that place; **~ие жи́тели** the local inhabitants.

тампо́н, а *m.* (*med.*) tampon; **гигиени́ческий т.** tampon (*used during menstruation*).

тампони́р|овать, ую *impf. and pf.* (*med.*) to tampon, plug.

тамта́м, а *m.* tom-tom.

та́нгенс, а *m.* (*math.*) tangent.

тангенциа́льный *adj.* (*math.*) tangential.

та́нго *nt. indecl.* tango.

та́нде́м, а *m.* tandem; **велосипе́д-т.** tandem.

та́н|ец, ца *m.* **1** (*искусство*) dance; dancing; **уро́ки ~цев** dancing lessons; **т. живота́** belly-dance. **2** (*pl.*) (*вечер*) a dance, dancing; **пойти́ на ~цы** to go to a dance, go dancing.

Танже́р, а *m.* Tangier.

танзани́йский *adj.* Tanzanian.

Танза́ни|я, и *f.* Tanzania.

тани́н, а *m.* tannin.

танк¹, а *m.* (*mil.*) tank.

танк², а *m.* container (*for transportation of liquids*).

та́нкер, а *m.* (*naut.*) tanker.

танке́тк|а¹, и *f.* (*mil.*) small tank.

танке́тк|а², и *f.* (*coll.*) (*туфля, подошва*) wedge.

танки́ст, а *m.* member of tank crew.

та́нковый *adj.* tank, armoured (*Br.*), armored (*US*).

танкодро́м, а *m.* tank training area.

танк-парово́з, а *m.* (*rail.*) tank (engine).

тантье́м|а, ы *f.* bonus.

танцева́льн|ый *adj.* dance, dancing; **т. ве́чер** a dance, party with dancing; **~ая площа́дка** dance floor.
танц|ева́ть, у́ю *impf.* to dance.
танцкла́сс, а *m.* (*obs.*) school of dancing; dancing-classes.
танцме́йстер, а *m.* (*obs.*) dancing-master.
танцо́вщик, а *m.* (ballet) dancer.
танцо́вщиц|а, ы *f. of* ⇒**танцо́вщик**
танцо́р, а *m.* dancer.
танцо́рк|а, и *f. of* ⇒**танцо́р**
танцу́льк|а, и *f.* (*coll.*) dance, hop.
тапёр, а *m.* ballroom pianist.
тапёрш|а, и *f. of* ⇒**тапёр**
тапио́к|а, и *f.* tapioca.
тапи́р, а *m.* tapir.
та́пк|а, и *f.* (*coll.*) slipper.
та́почк|а, и *f.* slipper; **спорти́вная т.** sports shoe, plimsoll (*Br.*), sneaker (*US*).
та́р|а, ы *f.* packing, packaging.
тараба́н|ить, ю, ишь *impf.* (*coll.*) to clatter.
тараба́рск|ий *adj.* incomprehensible; **~ая гра́мота** (*coll.*) double Dutch.
тараба́рщин|а, ы *f.* (*coll.*) double Dutch, gibberish.
тарака́н, а *m.* cockroach.
тарака́н|ий *adj. of* ⇒**~**
тара́н, а *m.* (*mil.*) **1** ram; ramming. **2** (*hist.*) battering ram.
тара́н|ить, ю, ишь *impf.* (*of* ⇒**про~**) to ram.
таранта́с, а *m.* tarantass (*springless carriage*).
таранте́лл|а, ы *f.* tarantella.
таран|ти́ть, чу́, ти́шь *impf.* (*coll.*) to jabber, natter.
тара́нтул, а *m.* tarantula.
тара́н|ь, и *f.* sea-roach (*Rutilus rutilus Heckeli*).
тарара́м, а *m.* (*coll.*) row, racket, hullabaloo.
тарара́х|ать, аю *impf. of* ⇒**~нуть**
тарара́х|нуть, ну, нешь *pf.* (*of* ⇒**~ать**) (*coll.*) to bang; to crash.
тарата́йк|а, и *f.* cabriolet, gig.
тарато́р|а, ы *c.g.* (*coll.*) chatterbox, gabbler.
тарато́р|ить, ю, ишь *impf.* (*coll.*) to jabber; to gabble.
тарах|те́ть, чу́, ти́шь *impf.* (*coll.*) to rattle, rumble.
тара́щ|ить, у, ишь *impf.* (*of* ⇒**вы́~**): **т. глаза́** (**на**+*a.*) to goggle (at).
тарбага́н, а *m.* Siberian marmot.
таре́лк|а, и *f.* **1** plate; **глубо́кая т.** soup-plate; **быть/чу́вствовать себя́ в свое́й ~е** to be in one's element; **быть/чу́вствовать себя́ не в свое́й ~е** (*i*) (*плохо себя чувствовать*) to be not quite o.s., (*ii*) (*чувствовать себя неловко*) to feel uncomfortable. **2** (*tech.*) plate, disc; (*coll.*) (*TV*) (satellite) dish. **3** (*pl.*) (*mus.*) cymbals.
таре́л|очный *adj. of* ⇒**~ка; ~очная ми́на** (*mil.*) flat anti-tank mine.
таре́льчатый *adj.* (*tech.*) plate, disc; **т. то́рмоз** disc brake.
тари́ф, а *m.* tariff, rate.
тарифика́ци|я, и *f.* tariffing.
тарифици́р|овать, ую *impf. and pf.* to tariff.
тари́ф|ный *adj. of* ⇒**~**
тартарары́: провали́ться в т. (*coll.*) I'll be damned.
тарти́нк|а, и *f.* slice of bread and butter.
та́ры-ба́ры *pl. indecl.* (*coll.*) tittle-tattle.
таска́|ть, ю *impf.* (*indet. of* ⇒**тащи́ть**) **1** *see* ⇒**тащи́ть. 2** (*pf.* **от~**) (*coll.*) (*трепать*) to pull (*as punishment*); **т. кого́-н. за́ во́лосы** to pull s.o.'s hair. **3** (*coll.*) (*носить*) to wear.
таска́|ться, юсь *impf.* (*indet. of* ⇒**тащи́ться**) **1** *see* ⇒**тащи́ться. 2** (*coll., pej.*) to roam about; to hang about.
тасмани́|ец, йца *m.* Tasmanian.
тасмани́|йка, йки *f. of* ⇒**~ец**
Тасма́ни|я, и *f.* Tasmania.
тасма́нский *adj.* Tasmanian.
тас|ова́ть, у́ю *impf.* (*of* ⇒**с~**) to shuffle (*cards in a pack*).
тaсо́вк|а, и *f.* shuffle, shuffling (*of playing cards*).
ТАСС *m.* (*indecl.*) (*abbr. of* ***Телегра́фное аге́нтство Сове́тского Сою́за***) TASS (*Telegraph Agency of the Soviet Union*).
тата́р|ин, ина, *pl.* **~ы, ~** *m.* Ta(r)tar.
тата́р|ка, ки *f. of* ⇒**~ин**
тата́рский *adj.* Ta(r)tar.
татуи́р|овать, ую *impf. and pf.* to tattoo.
татуи́р|оваться, уюсь *impf. and pf.* to tattoo o.s.; to have o.s. tattooed.
татуиро́вк|а, и *f.* tattooing.
тат|ь, я *m.* (*arch.*) thief, robber.
тафт|а́, ы́ *f.* taffeta.
тахикарди́|я, и *f.* (*med.*) tachycardia.
Та́хо *f. indecl.* the Tagus (*river*).
тахо́метр, а *m.* tachometer.
тахт|а́, ы́ *f.* ottoman.
тача́нк|а, и *f.* cart (*used in Ukraine and Caucasus*).
тача́|ть, ю *impf.* (*of* ⇒**вы́~**) to stitch.
та́чк|а, и *f.* wheelbarrow.
Ташке́нт, а *m.* Tashkent.
тащ|и́ть, у́, ~ишь *impf.* (*det. of* ⇒**таска́ть**) **1** (*тянуть*) to pull; (*что-н. тяжёлое*) to drag, lug; (*нести*) to carry. **2** (*coll.*) (*вести*) to take; (*fig.*) (*заставлять пойти куда-н.*) to drag off; **т. кого́-н. в кино́** to drag s.o. off to the cinema. **3** (*извлекать*) to pull out. **4** (*coll.*) (*украсть*) to pinch (*Br.*), swipe.
тащ|и́ться, у́сь, ~ишься *impf.* (*det. of* ⇒**таска́ться**) **1** (*идти с трудом*) to drag o.s. along; (*медленно ехать*) to trundle along; (*за кем-н.*) to trail along. **2** (*о подоле*) to drag, trail. **3** (**от**+*g.*) (*sl.*) to be crazy about.
та́яни|е, я *nt.* thaw, thawing.
та́|ять, ю, ешь *impf.* (*of* ⇒**рас~**) **1** to melt; to thaw; **~ет** it is thawing. **2** (*fig.*) (*исчезать*) to melt away, dwindle, wane; **на́ши запа́сы ~ют** our stocks are dwindling; **его́ си́лы ~яли** his strength was ebbing. **3** (**от**+*g.*; *fig.*) (*от любви*) to melt (with), languish (with). **4** (*impf. only*) (*чахнуть*) to waste away.
Тбили́си *m. indecl.* Tbilisi.
твар|ь, и *f.* creature; (*collect.*) creatures; all creation (*also pej.*); (*подлый человек*) swine.
тверде́ни|е, я *nt.* hardening.
тверде́|ть, ю *impf.* to harden, become hard.
твер|ди́ть, жу́, ди́шь *impf.* **1** (+*a. or* **о**+*p.*) to repeat, say over and over again. **2** (*запомнить*) to memorize, learn by rote.
твёрдо *adv.* firmly; (*знать, выучить*) thoroughly.
твердока́менный *adj.* (*rhet.*) steadfast, staunch.
твердоло́б|ый (~, ~а) *adj.* **1** thick-skulled. **2** (*pol.*) diehard.
твёрдост|ь, и *f.* hardness; (*fig.*) firmness.
твёрд|ый (~, ~а́, ~о) *adj.* **1** (*не мягкий*) hard. **2** (*крепкий*) firm; (*не жидкий*) solid; **т. грунт** firm soil; **т. переплёт** stiff binding; **~ое те́ло** (*phys., chem.*) solid; **фи́зика ~ого те́ла** solid state physics. **3** (*fig.*) (*непоколебимый*) firm; (*установленный*) stable; (*стойкий*) steadfast; **~ое зада́ние** specified task; **~ые зна́ния** sound knowledge; **~ое реше́ние** firm decision; **т. срок** fixed time-limit; **~ые це́ны** stable, fixed prices. **4** (*ling.*) hard; **т. знак** hard sign (*name of Russian letter* 'ъ').
тверды́н|я, и *f.* stronghold (*also fig.*).
тверд|ь, и *f.* (*arch.*): **т. земна́я** the earth; **т. небе́сная** the firmament, the heavens.
твид, а *m.* tweed.
тви́д|овый *adj. of* ⇒**~**
тво|й, его́ *m.*, **~я́, ~е́й** *f.*, **~ё, ~его́** *nt.*, *pl.* **~и́, ~и́х** *possessive pron.* (*при существительном*) your; (*без существительного*) yours; **~его́** (*after comp. adv.; coll.*) than you; **я зна́ю лу́чше ~его́** I know better than you; *as n.* **~и́, ~и́х** your people.
творе́ни|е, я *nt.* **1** (*произведение*) creation; work. **2** (*существо*) creature, being.
твор|е́ц, ца́ *m.* creator.
твори́тельный *adj.*: **т. паде́ж** (*gram.*) instrumental case.
твор|и́ть, ю́, и́шь *impf.* (*of* ⇒**со~**) **1** (*создавать*) to create. **2** (*делать*) to do; to make; **т. добро́** to do good; **т. чудеса́** to work wonders.
твор|и́ться, и́тся *impf.* (*coll.*) to happen, go on; **что тут ~и́тся?** what is going on here?
творо́г, а́ *and* **тво́рог, а** *m.* curd cheese; **со́евый т.** tofu.
творо́жник, а *m.* curd pancake.
творо́жный *adj.* curd; **т. сыро́к** curd cheese.
тво́рческ|ий *adj.* creative; **~ая си́ла** creative power, creativeness; **т. путь Толсто́го** Tolstoy's career as a writer.

тво́рчеств|о, а *nt.* **1** creation; creative work. **2** (*collect.*) works.

ТВЧ *nt. indecl.* (*abbr. of* ***телеви́дение высо́кой чёткости***) HDTV (*high-definition television*).

т. е. (*abbr. of* ***то есть***) i.e., that is, viz.

теа́тр, а *m.* **1** theatre (*Br.*), theater (*US*); **т. вое́нных де́йствий** (*mil.*) theatre of operations. **2** (*fig.*) the stage. **3** (*collect.*) (the) plays; **т. Шекспи́ра** the plays of Shakespeare.

театра́л, а *m.* theatre-goer (*Br.*), theater-goer (*US*).

театрализа́ци|я, и *f.* adaptation for the stage.

театрализ|ова́ть, у́ю *impf. and pf.* to adapt for the stage.

театра́л|ка, ки *f. of* ⇨~

театра́л|ьный (~ен, ~ьна) *adj.* **1** theatre (*Br.*), theater (*US*); theatrical; **т. зал** auditorium; **~ьная ка́сса** box-office; **~ьная шко́ла** drama school. **2** (*fig.*) (*жест, поза*) theatrical.

театрове́д, а *m.* expert on the theatre (*Br.*), theater (*US*).

театрове́дени|е, я *nt.* theatre studies (*Br.*), theater studies (*US*).

тевто́н, а *m.* Teuton.

тевто́нский *adj.* Teutonic.

Тегера́н, а *m.* Teh(e)ran.

Те́жу *f. indecl.* = **Та́хо**

теза́урус, а *m.* thesaurus.

те́зис, а *m.* thesis, proposition; **вы́двинуть т.** to advance a thesis.

тёзк|а, и *c.g.* namesake.

тезоимени́тств|о, а *nt.* (*obs.*) name-day (*esp. of member of Tsar's family*).

теи́зм, а *m.* theism.

теи́ст, а *m.* theist.

теисти́ческий *adj.* theistic.

текст, а *m.* **1** text. **2** (*песни*) words; (*оперы*) libretto.

тексти́л|ь, я *no pl., m.* (*collect.*) textiles.

тексти́льный *adj.* textile.

тексти́льщик, а *m.* textile worker.

тексти́льщи|ца, цы *f. of* ⇨~к

те́кст|овый *adj. of* ⇨~; **т. реда́ктор** text editor; **т. проце́ссор** word processor.

тексто́лог, а *m.* textual critic.

текстоло́ги|я, и *f.* textual criticism.

текстуа́л|ьный (~ен, ~ьна) *adj.* **1** (*дословный*) verbatim, word-for-word. **2** (*philol.*) textual.

текто́ник|а, и *f.* (*geol.*) tectonics.

тектони́ческий *adj.* (*geol.*) tectonic.

теку́чест|ь, и *f.* **1** (*phys.*) fluidity. **2** fluctuation, instability; **т. рабо́чей си́лы** fluctuation of manpower.

теку́ч|ий (~, ~а) *adj.* **1** (*phys.*) fluid. **2** fluctuating, unstable.

теку́щ|ий *pres. part. act. of* ⇨**течь** *and adj.* **1** current; of the present moment; **в ~ем году́** in the current year; **~ие собы́тия** current events, current affairs; **т. счёт** current account (*Br.*), checking account (*US*). **2** (*повседневный*) routine, ordinary; **т. ремо́нт** routine repairs.

тел. (*abbr. of* ***телефо́н***) tel., telephone.

теле... *comb. form* tele-.

телеавтома́т, а *m.* video games machine.

телевеща́ни|е, я *nt.* television broadcasting.

телеви́дени|е, я *nt.* television, TV; **за́мкнутое т.** closed-circuit TV.

телевизио́нный *adj.* television.

телевизио́нщик, а *m.* (*coll.*) TV person.

телеви́зор, а *m.* television set.

телеви́зор|ный *adj. of* ⇨~

теле́г|а, и *f.* cart, wagon.

телегра́мм|а, ы *f.* telegram.

телегра́ф, а *m.* **1** (*система*) telegraph. **2** (*учреждение*) telegraph office.

телеграфи́р|овать, ую *impf. and pf.* to telegraph, wire.

телеграфи́ст, а *m.* telegraphist.

телеграфи́ст|ка, ки *f. of* ⇨~

телеграфи́|я, и *f.* telegraphy.

телегра́фн|ый *adj.* telegraph; telegraphic; **~ое аге́нтство** news agency; **~ая ле́нта** ticker-tape; **т. стиль** telegraphese; **т. столб** telegraph-pole.

теле́жк|а, и *f.* **1** *dim. of* ⇨**теле́га**. **2** (*багажный; в универсаме*) trolley (*Br.*), cart (*US*).

теле́|жный *adj. of* ⇨~**га**; **~жное колесо́** cartwheel.

тележурна́л, а *m.* current affairs programme (*on TV*).

телезри́тел|ь, я *m.* (television) viewer.

телеигр|а́, ы́ *f.* game show.

телеизмере́ни|е, я *nt.* telemetry.

теле́к, а *m.* = **те́лик**

телека́мер|а, ы *f.* television camera.

телекана́л, а *m.* television channel.

телекине́з, а *m.* telekinesis.

телекоммуника́ци|и, й *f. pl.* telecommunications.

телекоммуникаци|о́нный *adj. of* ⇨~**и**

телекомпа́ни|я, и *f.* television company.

телеконфере́нци|я, и *f.* teleconference.

те́лекс, а *m.* telex.

телемарафо́н, а *m.*: (**благотвори́тельный**) **т.** telethon.

телеметри́ческий *adj.* telemetric.

телеметри́|я, и *f.* telemetry.

телемо́ст, а *m.* satellite (TV) link-up.

тел|ёнок, ёнка, *pl.* **~я́та, ~я́т** *m.* calf.

телеобъекти́в, а *m.* (*phot.*) telephoto lens.

телеологи́ческий *adj.* teleological.

телеоло́ги|я, и *f.* teleology.

телеопера́тор, а *m.* TV cameraman.

телепа́т, а *m.* telepathic person, telepath.

телепати́ческий *adj.* telepathic.

телепа́ти|я, и *f.* telepathy.

телепереда́ч|а, и *f.* television programme (*Br.*), program (*US*); **пряма́я т.** live television coverage.

телес|а́, теле́с, ~а́м *no sg.* (*coll., joc.*) frame (*of a stout person*).

телеско́п, а *m.* telescope.

телескопи́ческий *adj.* telescopic.

теле́сн|ый *adj.* **1** bodily; corporal; physical; **~ое наказа́ние** corporal punishment; **~ого цве́та** flesh-coloured (*Br.*), flesh-colored (*US*). **2** (*земной*) corporeal.

телесту́ди|я, и *f.* television studio.

телесуфлёр, а *m.* teleprompter, Autocue (*propr.*).

телете́кст, а *m.* teletext.

телеуправле́ни|е, я *nt.* remote control.

телефа́кс, а *m.* (tele)fax (machine).

телефика́ци|я, и *f.* equipping with television.

телефо́н, а *m.* **1** telephone; **позвони́ть по ~у** (+*d.*) to telephone, phone, ring up (*Br.*); **вы́зов по ~у** telephone call; **т.-автома́т** public telephone, call-box (*Br.*); **т.-отве́тчик** answerphone. **2** (*coll.*) (*номер*) telephone number.

телефони́р|овать, ую *impf. and pf.* to telephone.

телефони́ст, а *m.* telephone operator, telephonist.

телефони́ст|ка, ки *f. of* ⇨~

телефо́н|ный *adj. of* ⇨~; **~ная кни́га** telephone directory; **~ная ста́нция** telephone exchange.

телефоногра́мм|а, ы *f.* telephoned telegram.

тел|е́ц, ьца́ *m.* **1** (*obs.*) calf. **2**: **Т.** (*astron.*) Taurus.

телеце́нтр, а *m.* television centre (*Br.*), center (*US*).

телешпарга́лк|а, и *f.* Autocue (*propr.*), 'idiot board'.

те́лик, а *m.* (*coll.*) (the) telly (*Br.*), (the) TV.

тел|и́ться, ~и́тся *impf.* (*of* ⇨**о**~) to calve.

тёлк|а, и *f.* **1** heifer. **2** (*sl.*) (*девушка*) bird (*Br.*), chick.

теллу́р, а *m.* (*chem.*) tellurium.

те́л|о, а, *pl.* **~а́, ~, ~а́м** *nt.* body; (*coll.*): **быть в ~е** to be stout; **войти́ в т.** to put on weight; **спасть с ~а** to grow thin; **держа́ть в чёрном ~е** to ill-treat.

телогре́йк|а, и *f.* body warmer.

телодвиже́ни|е, я *nt.* movement, motion.

тел|о́к, ка́ *m.* (*coll.*) calf.

телосложе́ни|е, я *nt.* build, frame.

телохрани́тел|ь, я *m.* bodyguard.

Тель-Ави́в, а *m.* Tel Aviv.

те́льник, а *m.* = **тельня́шка**

тельня́шк|а, и *f.* (*coll.*) (*sailor's*) striped vest.

теля́тин|а, ы *f.* veal.

теля́тник, а *m.* calf-house.

теля́ч|ий *adj.* **1** *adj. of* ⇨**телёнок**; **~ья ко́жа** calf(skin). **2** (*cul.*) veal. **3**: **т.**

восторг (*coll.*) foolish raptures; **~ьи нéжности** (*coll.*) sloppy sentimentality.

тем 1 *i. sg. m. and nt., d. pl. of* ⇒**тот.** **2** *conj.* (so much) the; **чем вы́ше, т. лу́чше** the taller, the better; **т. лу́чше** so much the better; **т. бо́лее, что** especially as; **т. не мéнее** none the less, nevertheless; **т. сáмым** thus, thereby.

тéм|а, ы *f.* **1** subject, topic, theme; **перейти́ к друго́й ~е** to change the subject. **2** (*mus.*) theme; **т. с вариáциями** theme and variations.

темáтик|а, и *f.* (*collect.*) subject-matter.

темати́ческий *adj.* **1** *adj. of* ⇒**темáтика; т. план** plan of subject-matter (*e.g. of forthcoming publications*). **2** (*mus.*) thematic.

тембр, а *m.* timbre.

тéмен|ь, и *f.* (*coll.*) darkness.

Тéмз|а, ы *f.* the Thames (*river*).

тéми *i. pl. of* ⇒**тот**

темнé|ть, ю *impf.* **1** (*pf.* **по~**) to grow *or* become dark; to darken. **2** (*pf.* **с~**): **~ет** (*impers.*) it gets dark; it is getting dark. **3** (*impf. only*) (*видне́ться*) to show up darkly.

темн|и́ть, ю́, и́шь *impf.* (*комнату*) to darken; (*изложение*) to obscure; (*coll.*) (*путать*) to be deliberately obscure.

темни́ц|а, ы *f.* (*obs.*) dungeon.

темно́ *as pred.* it is dark; **у меня́ в глазáх стáло т.** everything went dark before my eyes.

темно... *comb. form* dark-.

тёмно-... *comb. form* (*with names of colours*) dark-; **тёмно-си́ний** dark-blue, navy-blue.

темноволо́с|ый (~, ~а) *adj.* dark-haired.

темноко́ж|ий (~, ~а) *adj.* dark-skinned, swarthy.

темнот|á, ы́ *f.* **1** dark, darkness; **в ~é** in the dark; **до ~ы́** before dark; **с ~о́й** under cover of dark(ness). **2** (*coll.*) (*невежество*) ignorance.

тём|ный (~ен, ~нá, ~но́) *adj.* **1** dark; **~ное пятно́** (*fig.*) dark stain, blemish; **~нá водá во о́блацех** the matter is wrapped in mystery. **2** (*неясный*) obscure, vague; **~ное пятно́** obscure place. **3** (*мрачный*) gloomy, sombre (*Br.*), somber (*US*). **4** (*подозрительный*) shady, suspicious; **~ное дéло** shady business. **5** (*невежественный*) ignorant.

темп, а *m.* **1** (*mus.*) tempo. **2** (*fig.*) tempo; rate, speed, pace; **в тéмпе** (*coll.*) quickly; **замéдлить т.** to slacken one's pace; **уско́рить т.** to accelerate.

тéмпер|а, ы *f.* **1** (*краска*) distemper. **2** (*картина*) tempera.

темперáмент, а *m.* temperament; **человéк с ~ом** spirited person.

темперáмент|ный (~ен, ~на) *adj.* energetic; spirited.

температу́р|а, ы *f.* **1** temperature; **т. кипéния** boiling-point; **т. замерзáния** freezing-point; **мéрить кому́-н. ~у** to take s.o.'s temperature. **2** (*coll.*) (heightened) temperature; **у него́ т.** he's got a temperature.

температу́р|ить, ю, ишь *impf.* (*coll.*) to have a temperature.

температу́р|ный *adj. of* ⇒**~а**

темперáци|я, и *f.* (*mus.*) temperament.

темпери́р|овать, ую *impf. and pf.* (*mus.*) to temper.

тем|ь, и *f.* (*coll.*) dark, darkness.

тéм|я, ени *no pl., nt.* crown, top of the head.

тенденцио́зност|ь, и *f.* tendentiousness.

тенденцио́з|ный (~ен, ~на) *adj.* (*pej.*) tendentious, biased.

тендéнци|я, и *f.* **1** (**к**+*d.*) tendency (to, towards); **у него́ т.** (**к**+*d.*) he has a tendency (to), he tends (to). **2** (*pej.*) bias; **с ~ей** tendentious, biased.

тéндер, а *m.* **1** (*rail.*) tender. **2** (*naut.*) cutter. **3** (*comm.*) tender, bid.

тенев|о́й *adj.* shady (*also fig.*); **т. кабинéт** (*pol.*) shadow cabinet; **~áя сторонá** shady side; (*fig.*) bad side, seamy side; **~ая эконо́мика** shadow economy.

тенелюби́в|ый (~, ~а) *adj.* (*bot.*) shade-loving.

Тенери́фе *m. indecl.* Tenerife.

тенёт|а, ~ *no sg.* snare.

тени́ст|ый (~, ~а) *adj.* shady.

тéннис, а *m.* tennis.

теннис́ист, а *m.* tennis-player.

теннис́ист|ка, ки *f. of* ⇒**~**

тéннисk|а, и *f.* (*coll.*) tennis shirt, polo shirt.

тéннисн|ый *adj.* tennis; **т. корт, ~ая площáдка** tennis-court.

тéнор, а, *pl.* **~á, ~о́в** *m.* (*mus.*) tenor.

теноро́вый *adj. of* ⇒**тéнор**

тент, а *m.* awning.

тен|ь, и, в ~и́, *pl.* **~и, ~éй** *f.* **1** (*тенистое место*) shade; **сидéть в ~и́** to sit in the shade; **держáться в ~и́** (*fig.*) to keep in the background. **2** (*тёмное отражение*) shadow; **давáть т.** to cast a shadow; **от негó остáлась однá т.** he is but a shadow of his former self; **навести́ т.** (*coll.*) to confuse the issue. **3** (*призрак*) shadow, ghost; **блéден, как т.** pale as a ghost. **4** (*fig.*) (*малейшая доля*) shadow, atom; **нет ни ~и сомнéния** there is not a shadow of doubt; **в егó расскáзе нет ни ~и прáвды** there is not an atom of truth in his story. **5** (*подозрение*) suspicion; **бро́сить т. на когó-н.** to cast suspicion on s.o.

теодоли́т, а *m.* theodolite.

теократи́ческий *adj.* theocratic.

теокрáти|я, и *f.* theocracy.

теологи́ческий *adj.* theological.

теоло́ги|я, и *f.* theology.

теорéм|а, ы *f.* theorem.

теоретизи́р|овать, ую *impf.* to theorize.

теорéтик, а *m.* theorist.

теорети́ческий *adj.* theoretical.

теорети́ч|ный (~ен, ~на) *adj.* (*pej.*) theoretical, abstract, abstruse.

тео́ри|я, и *f.* theory.

теософи́ческий *adj.* theosophical.

теосо́фи|я, и *f.* theosophy.

тепéрешн|ий *adj.* (*coll.*) present; **~ие лю́ди** people (of) today; **в ~ее врéмя** at the present time, nowadays.

тепéрь *adv.* now; nowadays, today.

тёпленьк|ий *adj.* (*coll.*) (nice and) warm; **~ое местéчко** cushy job.

теплé|ть, ет *impf.* (*of* ⇒**по~**) to get warm.

тéпл|иться, ится *impf.* to flicker, glimmer (*also fig.*); **~ится надéжда** there is still a glimmer of hope.

тепли́ц|а, ы *f.* greenhouse, hothouse.

тепли́|чный *adj. of* ⇒**~ца; ~чное растéние** hothouse plant (*also fig.*).

тепло́[1] *adv.* **1** warmly. **2** *as pred.* it is warm.

тепл|о́[2]**, á** *nt.* heat; warmth; **дéсять грáдусов ~á** ten degrees (*Celsius*) above zero.

теплово́з, а *m.* diesel locomotive.

теплово́зный *adj.* diesel.

теплов|о́й *adj.* heat; thermal; **~áя едини́ца** thermal unit; **т. удáр** (*med.*) heat stroke; **~áя энéргия** thermal energy.

теплоёмкост|ь, и *f.* (*phys.*) thermal capacity; **удéльная т.** specific heat.

теплокро́вный *adj.* (*zool.*) warm-blooded.

теплолюби́в|ый (~, ~а) *adj.* (*bot.*) heat-loving.

тепломéр, а *m.* (*phys.*) calorimeter.

теплообмéн, а *m.* (*phys.*) heat exchange.

теплопрово́д, а *m.* hot-water system.

теплопрово́дност|ь, и *f.* heat conductivity.

теплопрово́дный *adj.* heat-conducting.

теплосто́|йкий (~ек, ~йка) *adj.* heat-proof, heat-resistant.

теплот|á, ы́ *f.* **1** (*phys.*) heat; **едини́ца ~ы́** thermal unit. **2** warmth (*also fig.*); **душéвная т.** warm-heartedness.

теплотво́рност|ь, и *f.* (*phys.*) heating value, calorific value.

теплотво́рн|ый *adj.* (*phys.*) calorific; **~ая спосо́бность** calorific value.

теплотéхник, а *m.* heating engineer.

теплотéхник|а, и *f.* heating engineering.

теплохо́д, а *m.* motor ship.

теплоцентрáл|ь, и *f.* heating plant.

теплу́шк|а, и *f.* (*coll.*) heated goods van (*for transportation of human beings*).

тёп|лый (~ел, ~лá, ~ло́, ~лы) *adj.* **1** warm; **~лая одéжда** warm clothing; **~лые крáски** warm colours; **~лое местéчко** (*coll.*) cushy job. **2** (*дача, изба*) warmed, heated. **3** (*fig.*) warm, cordial; affectionate; **т. приём** warm welcome. **4** (*слова*) heartfelt.

теплы́н|ь, и *f.* (*coll.*) warm weather.

тепля́к, á *m.* temporary heated enclosure on building site.

терáкт, а *m.* act of terrorism, terrorist act.

Т

терапе́вт, а *m.* therapist.
терапевти́ческий *adj.* therapeutic.
терапи́|я, и *f.* therapy; **интенси́вная т.** intensive care.
тератоло́ги|я, и *f.* (*biol.*) teratology.
те́рби|й, я *m.* (*chem.*) terbium.
тереби́льщик, а *m.* flax-puller.
тереб|и́ть, лю́, и́шь *impf.* **1** (*дёргать*) to pull (at), tug (at). **2**: **т. лён** to pull flax. **3** (*fig., coll.*) (*вопросами*) to pester, bother.
те́рем, а, *pl.* **~а́** *m.* (*hist.*) (tower)-chamber; tower.
тере́ть, тру, трёшь, *past* **тёр, тёрла** *impf.* **1** (*глаза; грязное место*) to rub. **2** (*сыр*) to grate. **3** (*об обуви*) to rub, chafe.
тере́ться, трусь, трёшься, *past* **тёрся, тёрлась** *impf.* **1** to rub o.s.; (**о, обо** + *a.*) to rub (against). **2** (*fig., coll.*) (**о́коло** + *g.*) to hang (about, round). **3** (*fig., coll.*) (**среди́** + *g.*) to mix (with), hobnob (with).
терза́|ть, ю *impf.* **1** (*добычу*) to tear to pieces. **2** (*мучить*) to torment, torture.
терза́|ться, юсь *impf.* (+ *i.*) to suffer; to be tormented (by).
тёрк|а, и *f.* (*cul.*) grater.
те́рмин, а *m.* term.
термина́л, а *m.* (*comput.*) terminal.
терминологи́ческий *adj.* terminological.
терминоло́ги|я, и *f.* terminology.
терми́т, а *m.* (*zool.*) termite.
терми́ческий *adj.* (*phys., tech.*) thermal.
термобигуди́ *no sg. indecl.* heated hair rollers.
термодина́мик|а, и *f.* thermodynamics.
термодинами́ческий *adj.* thermodynamic.
термо́метр, а *m.* thermometer; **поста́вить т. кому́-н.** to take s.o.'s temperature.
термообрабо́тк|а, и *f.* (*tech.*) heat treatment, thermal treatment.
термопа́р|а, ы *f.* (*phys.*) thermocouple.
те́рмос, а *m.* thermos (flask) (*propr.*).
термоста́т, а *m.* thermostat.
термоэлектри́ческий *adj.* thermoelectrical.
термоя́дерный *adj.* thermonuclear.
те́рм|ы, ~ *no sg.* (*hist.*) thermae, (hot) baths.
тёрн, а *m.* (*bot.*) **1** (*куст*) blackthorn. **2** (*плод*) sloe(s).
те́рни|е, я *nt.* (*obs.*) **1** (*растение*) prickly plant. **2** (*колючка*) prickle, thorn.
терни́ст|ый (~, ~а) *adj.* (*obs.*) thorny, prickly; **т. путь** (*fig.*) difficult path.
терно́вник, а *m.* (*bot.*) blackthorn.
терно́в|ый *adj.* **1** *adj. of* ⇒**тёрн** *and* **~ник. 2** thorny, prickly; **т. вене́ц** crown of thorns.
тернosли́|в, а *m.* damson.
тернosли́в|а, ы *f.* = **тернosли́в**
терпели́вост|ь, и *f.* patience.
терпели́в|ый (~, ~а) *adj.* patient.
терпе́ни|е, я *nt.* patience; **вы́вести из ~я** to exasperate; **вы́йти из ~я** to lose patience.
терпенти́н, а *m.* turpentine.
терпенти́н|ный *adj. of* ⇒**~**
терпенти́н|овый *adj.* = **~ный**
терп|е́ть, лю́, ~́ишь *impf.* **1** (*pf.* **по~**) (*испытывать*) to suffer, undergo; **т. пораже́ние** to suffer a defeat. **2** (*стойко переносить*) to bear, endure, stand; **мы не могли́ бо́льше т. тако́го хо́лода** we could bear the cold no longer. **3** (*запастись терпением*) to have patience. **4** (*допускать*) to tolerate, suffer, put up (with); **не (мочь) т.** to be unable to bear, endure, stand; **т. не могу́** I can't stand it; I hate it; **вре́мя ~́ит** there is plenty of time; **вре́мя не ~́ит** there is no time to be lost; **де́ло не ~́ит** the matter is urgent; **де́ло не ~́ит отлaга́тельства** the matter brooks no delay.
терп|е́ться, ~́ится *impf.* (*impers.*): **ему́,** *etc.*, **не ~́ится** (+ *inf.*) he, *etc.*, is impatient (to).
терпи́мост|ь, и *f.* tolerance; indulgence.
терпи́м|ый (~, ~а) *adj.* **1** (*характер, человек*) tolerant; indulgent, forbearing. **2** (*условия*) tolerable, bearable, supportable.
те́рп|кий (~ок, ~ка́) *adj.* astringent; tart, sharp.
те́рпкост|ь, и *f.* astringency; tartness, sharpness.
террако́т|а, ы *f.* terracotta.
террако́т|овый *adj. of* ⇒**~а**
терра́ри|й, я *m.* terrarium.
терра́риум, а *m.* = **терра́рий**
терра́с|а, ы *f.* terrace.
террасир|овать, ую *impf. and pf.* to terrace.
территориа́льный *adj.* territorial.
террито́ри|я, и *f.* territory, confines; area.
терро́р, а *m.* terror.
терроризи́р|овать, ую *impf. and pf.* to terrorize.
террори́зм, а *m.* terrorism.
террориз|ова́ть, у́ю *impf. and pf.* = **~и́ровать**
террори́ст, а *m.* terrorist.
террористи́ческий *adj.* terrorist.
террори́ст|ка, ки *f. of* ⇒**~**
тёрт|ый (~, ~а) *p.p.p. of* ⇒**тере́ть** *and adj.* (*full form only*) **1** (*сыр*) grated. **2** (*fig., coll.*) (*бывалый*) hardened, experienced; **т. кала́ч** old stager, old hand.
те́рци|я, и *f.* (*mus.*) mediant; third; **больша́я т.** major third; **ма́лая т.** minor third.
терье́р, а *m.* terrier (*dog*).
теря́|ть, ю *impf.* (*of* ⇒**по~**) to lose; **т. наде́жду** to lose hope; **не т. головы́** to keep one's head; **т. си́лу** to become invalid; **т. по́чву под нога́ми** to feel the ground slipping away from under one's feet; **т. вре́мя на что-н.** to waste time on sth.; **т. в ве́се** to lose weight; **т. в чьём-н. мне́нии** to sink in s.o.'s estimation; **не т. из ви́ду** to keep in sight; (*fig.*) to remember, bear in mind; **нам не́чего т.** we have nothing to lose.
теря́|ться, юсь *impf.* (*of* ⇒**по~**) **1** to be lost; to get lost; (*исчезать*) to disappear. **2** (*становиться слабее*) to fail, decline, weaken; **па́мять у него́ ~ется** his memory is failing, is going. **3** (*лишаться самообладания*) to become flustered; **~юсь, ума́ не приложу́** I am at my wits' end. **4**: **т. в дога́дках, т. в предположе́ниях** to be lost in conjecture.
тёс, а (у) *m.* (*collect.*) boards, planks.
теса́к, а́ *m.* cutlass.
те|са́ть, шу́, ~́шешь *impf.* to cut, hew.
тесёмк|а, и *f.* = **тесьма́**
тесём|очный *adj. of* ⇒**~ка**
тесёмчатый *adj.* tape-like; **т. глист** tape-worm.
теси́н|а, ы *f.* board, plank.
тес|ло́, ла́, *pl.* **~́ла, ~ел** *nt.* adze (*Br.*), adz (*US*).
тесни́н|а, ы *f.* gorge, ravine.
тесн|и́ть, ю́, и́шь *impf.* **1** (*pf.* **по~**) (*в толпе*) to press, crowd. **2** (*сжимать*) to squeeze, constrict; (*об одежде*) to be too tight; **мне грудь ~и́т** I have a tightness in my chest; my chest feels tight.
тесн|и́ться, ю́сь, и́шься *impf.* **1** (*pf.* **по~**) (*пробираться*) to press through, push a way through. **2** (*pf.* **с~**) (*толпиться*) to crowd, cluster, jostle one another (*also fig.*; *of thoughts, etc.*).
те́сно *adv.* **1** closely (*also fig.*); tightly; narrowly; **быть т. свя́зано (с** + *i.*) to be closely linked (with). **2** *as pred.* it is crowded; it is (too) tight; **в трамва́е бы́ло о́чень т.** the tram was very crowded; **мне т. под мы́шками** it feels tight in the arm-pits.
тесно́т|а́, ы́ *f.* **1** (*свойство*) crowded state; narrowness; tightness; closeness. **2** (*недостаток места*) crush, squash; **жить в ~е́** to live cooped up; **в ~е́, да не в оби́де** the more the merrier.
те́с|ный (~ен, ~на́, ~но) *adj.* **1** (*непросторный*) crowded, cramped; **мир ~ен!** it's a small world. **2** (*узкий*) narrow; **т. прохо́д** narrow passage. **3** (*пиджак*) (too) tight. **4** (*сплочённый*) close, compact; **~ные ряды́** close ranks. **5** (*fig.*) (*близкий*) close, tight; **~ная дру́жба** close friendship.
тесо́вый *adj.* board, plank.
тест, а *m.* test.
тести́р|овать, ую *impf. and pf.* to test.
те́ст|о, а *nt.* dough; pastry; **т. для блино́в** batter.
тестостеро́н, а *m.* testosterone.
тест|ь, я *m.* father-in-law (*wife's father*).
тесьм|а́, ы́ *f.* tape, ribbon, lace, braid (*as adornment or for tying sth.*).
тётеньк|а, и *f.* (*affectionate form of* ⇒**тётя,** *also used by children in addressing an unknown woman*) aunty.
те́терев, а, *pl.* **~а́, ~о́в** *m.* (*zool.*) black grouse.
тетеревя́тник, а *m.* goshawk.

тетёрк|а, и *f.* grey-hen (*fem. of black grouse*).

тетéр|я, и *f.* **1** (*dial.*) = **тéтерев. 2** (*coll., joc.*) (*о человеке*) chap, fellow; **ленúвая т.** lazybones; **сóнная т.** sleepyhead.

тетив|á, ы́ *f.* bowstring.

тётк|а, и *f.* **1** aunt. **2** (*coll.*) (*о пожилой женщине*) old dear.

тетрáд|ка, ки *f.* = **~ь**

тетрáд|ь, и *f.* **1** exercise book (*Br.*), notebook; **т. для рисовáния** drawing-book; sketch-book. **2**: **т. пúсчей бумáги** packet of notepaper.

тетраэ́др, а *m.* (*math.*) tetrahedron.

тётушк|а, и *f.* (*affectionate form of* ***тётка***) aunty.

тёт|я, и, *g. pl.* **~ей** *f.* **1** aunt. **2** (*знакомая немолодая женщина; в сочетании с именем собственным*) auntie. **3** (*coll.*) (*женщина*) lady.

тéфтел|и, ей *no sg.* (*cul.*) meat-balls.

тех *g., a., p. pl. of* **⇒тот**

тех... *comb. form, abbr. of* ***технúческий***

техмúнимум, а *m.* required minimum of technical knowledge.

технáр|ь, я́ *m.* service engineer; 'techie'.

тéхник, а *m.* technician.

тéхник|а, и *f.* **1** technology. **2** (*приёмы исполнения*) technique, art; **это — дéло ~и** it is a matter of technique; **овладéть ~ой** to master the art. **3** (*collect.*) (*машины*) machinery; technical devices; **т. безопáсности** safety devices.

тéхникум, а *m.* technical college.

техни́чески *adv.* technically.

технúческ|ий *adj.* **1** technical; **~ие нáуки** engineering sciences; **т. персонáл** technical staff; **т. редáктор,** *see* **⇒техрéд; т. тéрмин** technical term; **~ие услóвия** specifications. **2** (*mil*) maintenance; **~ое обслýживание** maintenance. **3**: **~ие культýры** (*agric.*) industrial crops. **4** (*вспомогательный*) assistant; **т. сотрýдник** junior member of staff.

техни́ч|ный (~ен, ~на) *adj.* technically good.

тéхно *nt. indecl.* (*mus.*) techno.

технокрáт, а *m.* technocrat.

технократúческий *adj.* technocratic.

технóлог, а *m.* technologist; production engineer.

технологи́ческий *adj.* technological.

технолóги|я, и *f.* technology; **высокослóжная т.** high technology.

технорýк, а *m.* (*abbr. of* ***технúческий руководúтель***) technical director.

техосмóтр, а *m.* (*abbr. of* ***технúческий осмóтр***) check-up (*of motor vehicle*), MOT (*Br.*); **листóк ~а** ≈ MOT (*Ministry of Transport*) certificate (*of roadworthiness*).

техрéд, а *m.* (*abbr. of* ***технúческий редáктор***) technical editor, copy editor.

течéни|е, я *nt.* **1** (*поток*) flow. **2** (*fig.*) course; **с ~ем врéмени** in the course of time, in time. **3** (*ток, струя*) current, stream (*also fig.*); **по ~ю, прóтив ~я** with the stream, against the stream (*also fig.*). **4** (*fig.*) (*направление*) trend, tendency. **5**: **в т.** (+*g.*) during, in the course (of).

тéчк|а, и *f.* heat (*in animals*).

теч|ь[1]**, и** *f.* leak; **дать т.** to spring a leak; **задéлать т.** to stop a leak.

течь[2]**, текý, течёшь, текýт,** *past* **тёк, теклá** *impf.* **1** to flow (*also fig.*); to stream; (*fig.*) (*о времени*) to pass; **у тебя́ кровь течёт и́з носу** your nose is bleeding; **у негó и́з носу течёт** his nose is running; **у меня́ слю́нки теклú** my mouth was watering. **2** (*иметь течь*) to leak, be leaky.

тéш|ить, у, ишь *impf.* (*of* **⇒по~**) **1** (*развлекать*) to amuse, entertain. **2** (*удовлетворять*) to gratify, please.

тéш|иться, усь, ишься *impf.* (*of* **⇒по~**) **1** (+*i.*) to amuse o.s. (with), play (with). **2** (**над**+*i.*) to make fun (of).

тёщ|а, и *f.* mother-in-law (*wife's mother*).

тиáр|а, ы *f.* tiara.

Тибéт, а *m.* Tibet.

тибéт|ец, ца *m.* Tibetan.

тибéт|ка, ки *f. of* **⇒~ец**

тибéтский *adj.* Tibetan.

Тибр, а *m.* the Tiber (*river*).

тúг|ель, ля *m.* (*tech.*) crucible.

Тигр, а *m.* the Tigris (*river*).

тигр, а *m.* tiger.

тигр|ёнок, ёнка, *pl.* **~я́та, ~я́т** *m.* tiger cub.

тигрúц|а, ы *f.* tigress.

тигрóв|ый *adj. of* **⇒тигр; ~ая шкýра** tiger-skin.

тик[1]**, а** *m.* (*med.*) tic.

тик[2]**, а** *m.* (*ткань*) tick, ticking (*material*).

тик[3]**, а** *m.* (*bot.*) teak.

тúкань|е, я *nt.* tick, ticking (*of a clock*).

тúка|ть, ю *impf.* (*coll.*) to tick.

тúковый[1] *adj. of* **⇒тик**[2]

тúковый[2] *adj. of* **⇒тик**[3]

тик-тáк *onomat.* tick-tock.

тúльд|а, ы *f.* (*typ.*) tilde, swung dash.

тимиáн, а *m.* = **тимья́н**

тимофéевк|а, и *f.* (*bot.*) timothy-grass.

тимпáн, а *m.* **1** (*mus.*) timbrel. **2** (*archit.*) tympanum.

тимья́н, а *m.* (*bot.*) thyme.

тúн|а, ы *no pl., f.* slime, mud; mire (*also fig.*).

тúнист|ый (~, ~а) *adj.* slimy, muddy.

тинктýр|а, ы *f.* tincture.

тип, а *m.* **1** type; model. **2** (*coll.*) (*человек*) fellow, character; **стрáнный т.** odd character.

типáж, á *m.* (*liter., art*) type.

типизáци|я, и *f.* typification.

типизúр|овать, ую *impf. and pf.* to typify.

типúческий *adj.* typical.

типúчност|ь, и *f.* typicalness, typical nature.

типúч|ный (~ен, ~на) *adj.* typical.

типов|óй *adj.* model; standard; **~áя модéль** standard model; **~óе издéлие** standard product.

типóграф, а *m.* printer.

типогрáфи|я, и *f.* printing-house, press.

типогрáфск|ий *adj.* typographical; **~ое искýсство** typography.

типологúческий *adj.* typological.

типолóги|я, и *f.* typology.

типýн, á *m.* pip (*disease of birds*); **т. тебé на язы́к!** keep your trap shut!

тир, а *m.* shooting-range; shooting gallery.

тирáд|а, ы *f.* tirade.

тирáж, á *m.* **1** drawing (*of loan or lottery*); **вы́йти в т.** to be drawn; (*fig.*) to retire from the scene, take a back seat. **2** (*количество экземпляров*) circulation; edition; print run; **т. э́той газéты полторá миллиóна** this newspaper has a circulation of a million and a half; **т. в сто ты́сяч экземпля́ров** an edition of a hundred thousand copies.

тирáн, а *m.* tyrant.

тирáн|ить, ю, ишь *impf.* to tyrannize (over), torment.

тиранúческий *adj.* tyrannical.

тиранú|я, и *f.* (*hist. and fig.*) tyranny.

тирáнств|о, а *nt.* tyranny.

тирáнств|овать, ую *impf.* (**над**+*i.*) to tyrannize (over).

тирé *nt. indecl.* dash.

тир|овáть, ýю *impf.* (*naut.*) to pitch, tar.

Тирóл|ь, я *m.* the Tyrol, the Tirol.

тирóльский *adj.* Tyrolese, Tyrolean.

тис, а *m.* yew(-tree).

тúска|ть, ю *impf.* (*of* **⇒тúснуть**) to press, squeeze.

тиск|ú, óв *no sg.* (*tech.*) vice (*Br.*), vise (*US*); **зажáть в т.** to grip in a vice; **в ~áх** (+*g.*) in the grip (of).

тиснéни|е, я *nt.* **1** (*действие*) stamping, printing. **2** (*изображение*) imprint; design.

тиснёный *adj.* stamped, printed; **т. шрифт** raised (Braille) type.

тúс|нуть, ну, нешь *pf. of* **⇒~кать**

тúс|овый *adj. of* **⇒~**

титáн[1]**, а** *m.* (*myth. and fig.*) titan.

титáн[2]**, а** *m.* (*chem.*) titanium.

титáн[3]**, а** *m.* (*кипятильник*) boiler.

титанúческий *adj.* titanic.

титáн|овый *adj. of* **⇒~**[2]; (*chem.*) titanic.

титр, а *m.* (*cin.*) title, credit.

титровáни|е, я *nt.* (*chem.*) titration.

титр|овáть, ýю *impf. and pf.* (*chem.*) to titrate.

тúтул, а *m.* **1** title. **2** (*страница*) title-page.

титулóв|анный *p.p.p. of* **⇒~áть** *and adj.* titled.

титул|овáть, ýю *impf. and pf.* to style, call by one's title.

тúтул|ьный *adj. of* **⇒~; т. лист** title-page.

титуля́рный *adj.*: **т. совéтник** (*hist.*) titular counsellor (*civil servant of 9th grade in tsarist Russia*).

Т

тиф, а *m.* typhus; **брюшно́й т.** typhoid (fever); **сыпно́й т.** typhus.

тифо́зн|ый *adj.* typhus; typhoid; **~ая лихора́дка** typhoid fever; *as n.* **т., ~ого** *m.* typhus patient.

ти́х|ий (~, ~а́, ~о) *adj.* **1** quiet; (*звук*) low, soft; (*мягкий*) gentle; (*слабый*) faint; **т. го́лос** low voice. **2** (*бесшумный*) silent, noiseless; still; **~ая ночь** still night. **3** (*fig.*) (*спокойный*) quiet, calm; gentle; still; **~ая жизнь** quiet life; **т. нрав** gentle disposition; **~ая пого́да** calm weather; **в ~ом о́муте че́рти во́дятся** (*prov.*) still waters run deep. **4** (*медленный*) slow, slow-moving; **т. ход** slow speed, slow pace.

Ти́х|ий океа́н, ~ого ~а *m.* the Pacific Ocean; the Pacific.

ти́хо¹ *adv.* **1** (*негромко*) quietly; softly, gently; **т. постуча́ть** to knock gently. **2** (*бесшумно*) silently, noiselessly. **3** (*fig.*) (*спокойно*) quietly, calmly; still; **сиде́ть т.** to sit still; **т.** gently!, careful! **4** (*медленно*) slowly; **дела́ иду́т т.** things are slack.

ти́хо² *as pred.* **1** it is quiet, there is not a sound; **ста́ло т.** it became quiet. **2** (*fig.*) it is quiet; it is calm; **на душе́ у меня́ ста́ло т.** my mind is at rest. **3** (*comm.*) it is slack.

тихомо́лком *adv.* (*coll.*) quietly, without a sound.

тихо́нько *adv.* (*coll.*) quietly; softly, gently.

тихо́н|я, и, *g. pl.* **~ей** *c.g.* demure person.

тихоокеа́нский *adj.* Pacific.

тихохо́д, а *m.* (*zool.*) sloth.

тихохо́д|ный (~ен, ~на) *adj.* slow.

ти́ше 1 *comp. of* **⇨ти́хий** *and* **ти́хо.** **2**: **т.!** (*i*) (*молчать!*) (be) quiet!, silence!, (*ii*) (*осторожнее!*) gently!; careful!

тишин|а́, ы́ *f.* quiet, silence; stillness; **нару́шить ~у́** to break the silence; **соблюда́ть ~у́** to keep quiet.

тишко́м *adv.* (*coll.*) quietly; imperceptibly.

тиш|ь, и, в ~и́ *f.* quiet, silence; stillness; **т. да гладь** peace and quiet.

т. к. (*abbr. of* ***так как***) as, since.

тка́н|евый *adj. of* **⇨~ь** 1, 2

тка́ный *adj.* woven.

ткан|ь, и *f.* **1** fabric, cloth; **льняны́е ~и** linen(s); **шёлковые ~и** silks. **2** (*anat.*) tissue. **3** (*fig.*) (*основа*) substance, essence; **т. расска́за** gist of a story.

ткань|ё, я́ *nt.* **1** (*действие*) weaving. **2** (*collect.*) (*изделия*) woven fabrics, cloth.

тканьёвый *adj.* woven.

ткать, тку, ткёшь, *past* **ткал, ткала́, тка́ло** *impf.* (*of* **⇨со~**) to weave; **т. паути́ну** to spin a web.

тка́цк|ий *adj.* weaver's, weaving; **~ое де́ло** weaving; **т. стано́к** loom; **т. челно́к** shuttle.

ткач, а́ *m.* weaver.

тка́честв|о, а *nt.* weaving.

ткачи́х|а, и *f. of* **⇨ткач**

ткн|у́ть(ся), у́(сь), ёшь(ся) *pf. of* **⇨ты́кать(ся)**

тлен, а *m.* decay.

тле́ни|е, я *nt.* **1** (*гниение*) decay, decomposition, putrefaction. **2** (*горение*) smouldering (*Br.*), smoldering (*US*).

тле́н|ный (~ен, ~на) *adj.* liable to decay.

тлетво́р|ный (~ен, ~на) *adj.* **1** putrid. **2** (*fig.*) (*вредный*) pernicious, noxious.

тле́|ть, ет *impf.* **1** (*гнить*) to rot, decay, decompose. **2** (*гореть*) to smoulder (*Br.*) smolder (*US*) (*also fig.*); **ещё ~ет наде́жда** there is still a glimmer of hope.

тле́|ться, ется *impf.* to smoulder (*Br.*), smolder (*US*).

тл|я, и, *g. pl.* **~ей** *f.* aphid.

тмин, а *m.* **1** (*растение*) caraway. **2** (*collect.*) (*семена*) caraway-seeds.

тми́н|ный *adj. of* **⇨~; ~ная во́дка** kümmel.

то¹ *pron.* (*nom. and a. sg. nt. of* **⇨тот**) that; **то, что...** the fact that ...; **то, что́** that which; **то был, была́, бы́ло** that was; **то бы́ли** those were; **то́ есть** that is (to say); **то бишь** that is to say; **то ли де́ло** (*coll.*) what a difference, how different (= *how much better*); **а то,** *see* **⇨а; (да) и то** and that, at that.

то² *conj.* **1** (*in apodosis of conditional sentence*) then (*or not translated*); **е́сли вас там не бу́дет, то и я не пойду́** if you won't be there, (then) I shan't go either. **2**: **то..., то** now ..., now; **то тут, то там** now here, now there. **3**: **не то..., не то** either ... or; whether ... or; half ..., half; **не то по глу́пости, не то по зло́бе** either through stupidity or through malice; **не то удивле́ние, не то доса́да** half surprise, half annoyance. **4**: **не то, что́бы..., но** it is not, it was not that ... (but); **не то, что́бы я не хоте́л слу́шать радиопереда́чу, но я про́сто забы́л о ней** it was not that I did not want to hear the broadcast: I simply forgot about it. **5**: **то и де́ло, то и знай** (*coll.*) time and again; perpetually.

-то¹ *emph. particle* (*in coll. Russian oft. merely adds familiar tone*) just, precisely, exactly (*or not translated*); **в то́м-то и де́ло** that's just it; **чего́ же ва́м-то боя́ться?** what have *you* to be afraid of?

-то² *particle forming indef. prons and advs.* (**кто́-то, како́й-то, когда́-то,** *etc.*).

т. о. (*abbr. of* ***таки́м о́бразом***) thus, in this way.

тобо́й, тобо́ю *i. of* **⇨ты**

тов. (*abbr. of* ***това́рищ***) Comrade.

това́р, а *m.* (*collect. or in pl.*) goods; wares; (*sing.*) article; product, commodity; **~ы широ́кого потребле́ния** consumer goods.

това́рищ, а *m.* **1** comrade; (*друг*) friend; (*коллега*) colleague; **т. де́тства** childhood friend; **т. по несча́стью** fellow-sufferer, companion in distress; **т. по ору́жию** comrade-in-arms; **т. по рабо́те** colleague; workmate; **т. по шко́ле** school-friend. **2** (*при советской власти, обращение к гражданину*) Comrade. **3** (*человек*) person; **э́тот т. прие́хал из Москвы́** this man has come from Moscow.

това́рищеск|ий *adj.* **1** comradely; friendly; **с ~им приве́том** (*epistolary formula*) with fraternal greetings. **2** (*sport*) friendly, unofficial; **~ое состяза́ние, ~ая встре́ча** friendly (match).

това́риществ|о, а *nt.* **1** comradeship, camaraderie; **чу́вство ~а** feeling of solidarity. **2** (*компания*) company; (*объединение*) association, society; **т. на пая́х** joint-stock company.

това́рк|а, и *f.* (*coll., obs.*) friend.

това́рност|ь, и *f.* (*econ.*) marketability.

това́рн|ый *adj.* **1** goods (*Br.*), freight; **т. знак** trade mark; **т. склад** warehouse. **2** (*rail.*) goods (*Br.*), freight; **т. ваго́н** goods truck (*Br.*), freight car; **т. соста́в** goods train (*Br.*), freight train. **3** (*econ.*) commodity; **~ая проду́кция** commodity output. **4** (*econ.*) marketable; **~ое зерно́** marketable grain.

товарове́д, а *m.* commodity researcher.

товарове́дени|е, я *nt.* commodity research.

товарообме́н, а *m.* (*econ.*) barter.

товарооборо́т, а *m.* commodity turnover.

товароотправи́тел|ь, я *m.* consignor.

товарополуча́тел|ь, я *m.* consignee.

то́г|а, и *f.* (*hist.*) toga.

тогда́ 1 *adv.* (*в то время; в таком случае*) then (= (*i*) at that time, (*ii*) in that case). **2**: **когда́..., т.** (*conj.*) when; **когда́ решу́сь, т. тебе́ напишу́** I will write to you when I have decided. **3**: **т. как** (*conj.*) whereas, while.

тогда́шний *adj.* (*coll.*) of that time; the then.

того́¹ *int.* (*для заполнения паузы*) er ..., um ....

того́² *as pred.* you know (*coll., euph.* = (*i*) (*ненормален*) abnormal, simple, (*ii*) (*пьян*) drunk, (*iii*) (*неважен*) mediocre); **к десяти́ часа́м он был совсе́м т.** by ten o'clock he was completely — you know.

того́³ *g. sg. m. and nt. of* **⇨тот**

тожде́ственност|ь, и *f.* identity.

тожде́ствен|ный (~, ~на) *adj.* identical, one and the same.

то́ждеств|о, а *nt.* identity.

то́же¹ *adv.* also, as well, too.

то́же² *particle* (*coll., iron.*) (*выражает недоверчивое или отрицательное отношение*): **ты т. хоро́ш!** you're a fine one, I must say; **т. знато́к нашёлся!** since when is he an expert!

тоже́ственност|ь, и *f.* = **тожде́ственность**

тоже́ствен|ный (~, ~на) *adj.* = **тожде́ственный**

то́жеств|о, а *nt.* = **то́ждество**

ток¹, а *m.* (*elec.*) current; **т. высо́кого напряже́ния** (*elec.*) high-tension current; **переме́нный т.** alternating current; **постоя́нный т.** direct current.

ток², а, о ~е, на ~у́, *pl.* **~а́, ~о́в** *m.*

(*где токуют птицы*) (*birds'*) mating-place.

ток³, а, о ~е́, на ~у́, *pl.* **~а́** *and* **~и, ~о́в** *m.* (*для молотьбы зерна*) threshing-floor.

ток⁴, а *m.* (*головной убор*) toque.

тока́рный *adj.* (*tech.*) turning; **т. стано́к** lathe; **т. цех** turning shop.

то́кар|ь, я, *pl.* **~и** *and* **~я** *m.* turner, lathe operator.

То́кио *m. indecl.* Tokyo.

токка́т|а, ы *f.* (*mus.*) toccata.

ток|ова́ть, у́ет *impf.* (*of birds*) to utter the mating-call.

токоприёмник, а *m.* (*elec.*) current collector, trolley (*of electric locomotive, trolleybus, etc.*).

токсикологи́ческий *adj.* toxicological.

токсиколо́ги|я, и *f.* toxicology.

токсикома́н, а *m.* glue sniffer, solvent abuser.

токсикома́ни|я, и *f.* glue sniffing, solvent abuse.

токси́н, а *m.* (*med.*) toxin.

токси́ческий *adj.* toxic.

ток-шо́у *nt. indecl.* talk show.

толера́нтност|ь, и *f.* tolerance.

толера́нтный *adj.* tolerant.

толи́к|а, и *f.* (*coll.*): **ма́лая т., не́которая т.** a little, a small quantity; a few.

толк¹, а (у) *m.* **1** (*смысл*) sense; understanding; **бе́з ~у** senselessly; **с ~ом** sensibly, intelligently; **сбить с ~у** to confuse; **взять в т.** (*coll.*) to understand, grasp, get; **от него́ ~у не добьёшься** you'll get no sense out of him. **2** (*coll.*) (*польза*) use, profit; **из э́того не вы́йдет ~у** nothing will come of it; **понима́ть, знать т. (в** + *p.*) to know what one is talking about (in). **3** (*секта*) persuasion (= *sect, grouping*).

толк² *as pred.* (*coll.*) = **~ну́л**

толка́тел|ь, я *m.*: **т. ядра́** (*sport*) shot-putter.

толк|а́ть, а́ю *impf.* (*of* ⇒**~ну́ть**) **1** to push, shove; (*нечаянно*) to jog; **т. ло́ктем** to nudge. **2** (*sport*): **т. шта́нгу** to weight-lift; **т. ядро́** to put the shot. **3** (**на** + *a.*) (*побуждать*) to push (into), incite (to).

толк|а́ться, а́юсь *impf.* **1** (*impf. only*) (*толкать друг друга*) to push (one another). **2** (*pf.* **~ну́ться**): **т. в дверь** to knock on the door. **3** (*pf.* **~ну́ться**) (**к** + *d.*) (*пытаться увидеть*) to try to see, try to get access (to). **4** (*impf. only*) (*coll.*) (*слоняться*) to knock about.

толка́ч, а́ *m.* (*coll.*) pusher, go-getter, fixer (*in industrial enterprises*).

то́лк|и, ов *pl.* talk; rumours (*Br.*), rumors (*US*), gossip; **иду́т т. о том, что** it is said that, it is rumoured (*Br.*), rumored (*US*) that.

толк|ну́ть, ну́, нёшь *pf. of* ⇒**~а́ть**

толк|ну́ться, ну́сь, нёшься *pf. of* ⇒**~а́ться** 2, 3

толкова́ни|е, я *nt.* **1** interpretation. **2** (*pl.*) commentary.

толкова́тел|ь, я *m.* interpreter, commentator.

толк|ова́ть, у́ю *impf.* **1** to interpret; **ло́жно т. чьи-н. слова́** to misinterpret, misconstrue s.o.'s words. **2** (+*d.*; *coll.*) (*объяснять*) to explain (to). **3** (*coll.*) (*говорить*) to talk; to say; **т. де́ло** to talk sense; **~у́ют, бу́дто** people say that, they say that.

толко́в|ый (~, ~а) *adj.* **1** (*человек*) intelligent, sensible. **2** (*объяснение*) intelligible, clear. **3**: **т. слова́рь** defining dictionary.

то́лком *adv.* (*coll.*) plainly, clearly.

толкотн|я́, и́ *f.* (*coll.*) crush, scrum, squash.

тол|ку́, ку́т *see* ⇒**~о́чь**

толку́чий *adj.*: **т. ры́нок** (*coll.*) flea market.

толку́ч|ка, ки *f.* (*coll.*) **1** crush, scrum, squash. **2** = **~ий ры́нок**

толма́ч, а́ *m.* (*obs.*) interpreter.

толокн|о́, а́ *nt.* oat flour.

толокня́нк|а, и *f.* (*bot.*) bearberry (*Arctostaphylos*).

толок|о́нный *adj. of* ⇒**~но́; т. лоб** blockhead.

тол|о́чь, ку́, чёшь, ку́т, *past* **~о́к, ~кла́** *impf.* (*of* ⇒**рас~** *and* **с~**) to pound, crush; **т. во́ду в сту́пе** to beat the air, mill the wind.

тол|о́чься, ку́сь, чёшься, ку́тся, *past* **~о́кся, ~кла́сь** *impf.* (*coll.*) to knock about; to gad about; (*fig.*) to swarm.

толп|а́, ы́, *pl.* **~ы** *f.* crowd; throng; multitude.

толп|и́ться, и́тся *impf.* to crowd; to throng.

толсте́нный *adj.* (*coll.*) very fat.

толсте́|ть, ю *impf.* (*of* ⇒**по~**) to grow fat; to put on weight.

толст|и́ть, и́т *impf.* (*coll.*) to make (look) fat; **хлеб о́чень ~и́т** bread is very fattening; **шу́ба её о́чень ~и́ла** the fur coat made her look very fat.

толстобрю́х|ий (~, ~а) *adj.* (*coll.*) fat-bellied.

толсто́вк|а, и *f.* **1** (*мужская блуза*) tolstovka (*long belted blouse*). **2** (*coll.*) sweatshirt.

толстогу́б|ый (~, ~а) *adj.* thick-lipped.

толстоко́ж|ий (~, ~а) *adj.* **1** thick-skinned (*also fig.*). **2** (*zool.*): **~ее живо́тное** pachyderm.

толстомо́рдый *adj.* (*coll.*) fat-faced.

толстопу́з|ый (~, ~а) *adj.* pot-bellied (*hist., esp. as term of abuse applied to merchants*).

толстосте́нный *adj.* (*tech.*) thick-walled.

толстосу́м, а *m.* (*obs., coll.*) money-bags.

толсту́х|а, и *f.* (*coll.*) (*женщина*) fat woman; (*девушка*) fat girl.

толсту́шк|а, и *f. affectionate form of* ⇒**толсту́ха**

то́лст|ый (~, ~а́, ~о) *adj.* **1** (*человек*) fat; **т. нос** big nose. **2** (*книга, бумага, слой*) thick; (*ткань*) heavy; **т. про́вод** heavy-gauge wire; **~ая кишка́** (*anat.*) large intestine.

толстя́к, а́ *m.* (*мужчина*) fat man; (*мальчик*) fat boy.

толче́ни|е, я *nt.* pounding, crushing.

толчёный *adj.* pounded, crushed; (*миндаль*) ground.

тол|чёт *see* ⇒**~о́чь**

толче|я́¹, и́ *f.* (*coll.*) (*толкотня*) crush, scrum, squash.

толче|я́², и́ *f.* (*tech.*) mill.

толч|о́к¹, ка́ *m.* **1** (*толкающий удар*) push, shove; (*sport*) put. **2** (*при езде*) jolt, bump; (*при землетрясении*) (earthquake) shock, tremor. **3** (*fig.*) (*побуждение*) push, shove; stimulus; **дать т. эконо́мике** to kick-start the economy. **4** (*coll.*) (*унитаз*) lavatory bowl.

толч|о́к², ка́ *m.* (*coll.*) = **толку́чий ры́нок**

то́лщ|а, и *f.* **1** thickness; **т. сне́га** depth of snow. **2**: **в ~е наро́да** in the (thick of the) people.

то́лще *comp. of* ⇒**то́лстый**

толщин|а́, ы́ *f.* **1** (*человека*) fatness, corpulence. **2** (*бревна, слоя*) thickness.

тол|ь, я *m.* (tarred) roofing paper.

то́лько 1 *adv.* only; solely; alone; just; **не т. . ., но и** not only . . ., but also; **поду́май(те) т.!** just think!; **т. и всего́, да и т.** (*coll.*) that's all; **т. что не** (*coll.*) the only thing lacking (is, was); **не т. что** (*coll.*) not to mention, let alone; **т. за после́дние пять лет. . .** in the last five years alone . . . .
2: **т. что** (*adv. and conj.*) just, only just; **он т. что позвони́л** he has just rung up. **3** *conj.* (+ **как, лишь**) as soon as; one has only to . . .; **т. ска́жешь, я уйду́** you have only to say (the word) and I will go. **4** *conj.* only, but; **с удово́льствием, т. не сего́дня** with pleasure, only not today. **5**: **т. бы** (+*inf.*) (*particle*) if only; **т. бы получи́ть о нём ве́сточку** if only we could hear news of him. **6** *particle intensifying interrog. prons. and advs.*: **заче́м т.?** why on earth?, whatever for?; **где т. они́ не быва́ли?** where have they *not* been?

то́лько-то́лько *adv.* (*coll.*) only just.

том, а, *pl.* **~а́, ~о́в** *m.* volume.

томага́вк, а *m.* tomahawk.

тома́т, а *m.* **1** tomato. **2** (*пюре*) tomato purée.

тома́тный *adj.* tomato; **т. сок** tomato juice.

то́мик, а *m. dim. of* ⇒**том**

томи́тел|ьный (~ен, ~ьна) *adj.* (*скучный*) tedious; wearing; (*утомительный*) tiring, exhausting; (*гнетущий*) oppressive; (*мучительный*) agonizing, painful.

том|и́ть, лю́, и́шь *impf.* (*of* ⇒**ис~**) **1** to tire, wear out, weary; (*мучить*) to torment; (*вопросами*) to wear down; **т. в тюрьме́** to leave to languish in prison; **меня́ ~и́т жа́жда** I am parched. **2** (*cul.*) to stew; to braise.

том|и́ться, лю́сь, и́шься *impf.* (*of* ⇒**ис~**) (*страдать*) to suffer; (*голодом, ожиданием*) to be tormented by; (*испытывать чувство тоски*) to languish, pine; **т. в тюрьме́** to languish in prison.

Т

томле́ни|е, я *nt.* **1** (*страдание*) suffering, anguish. **2** (*тоска*) languor.

то́мност|ь, и *f.* languor.

то́м|ный (~ен, ~на́) *adj.* languid, languorous.

тон, а, *pl.* **~ы** *and* **~а́** *m.* **1** (*pl.* **~ы**) (*mus. and fig.*) tone; **~ом вы́ше, ни́же** a tone higher, lower; **хоро́ший, дурно́й т.** good, bad form; **зада́ть т.** to set the tone; **перемени́ть т.** to change one's tone; **попа́сть в т.** to hit the right note. **2** (*pl.* **~а́**) (*краски, цвета*) tone, tint.

тона́льност|ь, и *f.* (*mus.*) key.

то́ненький *adj.* thin; slender, slim.

то́нер, а *m.* toner.

тонзилли́т, а *m.* tonsillitis.

тонзу́р|а, ы *f.* tonsure.

тонизи́р|овать, ую *impf. and pf.* (*physiol.*) to tone up.

то́ник, а *m.* tonic (water).

то́ник|а, и *f.* (*mus.*) tonic, keynote.

тони́ческий[1] *adj.* (*mus., liter.*) tonic.

тони́ческий[2] *adj.* (*physiol., med*) tonic.

то́н|кий (~ок, ~ка́, ~ко) *adj.* **1** (*слой*) thin; (*фигура*) slim; **т. ло́мтик** thin slice; **~кая кишка́** (*anat.*) small intestine. **2** (*изысканный*) fine; delicate; refined; **~кое бельё** fine linen; **т. за́пах** delicate perfume; **~кая рабо́та** fine workmanship; **~кие черты́ лица́** refined features; (*не грубый*) subtle, fine; **~кая лесть** subtle flattery; **т. намёк** gentle hint; **~кое разли́чие** subtle, fine distinction. **3** (*звук*) high, squeaky. **4** (*fig.*) (*проницательный, умный*) shrewd, subtle, penetrating; **т. знато́к** connoisseur; **т. кри́тик** shrewd critic. **5** (*зрение, слух*) keen. **6**: **т. сон** light sleep.

то́нко *adv.* **1** (*резать*) thinly. **2** (*чувствовать*) subtly, delicately, finely.

тонковолокни́ст|ый (~, ~а) *adj.* fine-fibred (*Br.*), fine-fibered (*US*).

тонкоко́ж|ий (~, ~а) *adj.* thin-skinned.

то́нкост|ь, и *f.* **1** thinness; (*фигуры*) slimness. **2** (*ткани, работы*) fineness. **3** (*ума*) subtlety. **4** (*мелкая подробность*) nice point, subtle point; **до ~ей** to a nicety; **вдава́ться в ~и** to split hairs.

то́нн|а, ы *f.* metric ton, tonne; (*sl.*) 1000 roubles; grand (*sl.*).

тонна́ж, а *m.* tonnage.

тонне́л|ь, я *m.* = **тунне́ль**

то́нус, а *m.* (*physiol., med.*) tone; **жи́зненный т.** vitality.

тон|у́ть, у́, ~ешь *impf.* **1** (*pf.* **по~**) (*о судне*) to sink, go down. **2** (*pf.* **у~**) (*о человеке*) to drown. **3** (*pf.* **у~**) (**в**+*p.*) to sink (in); to be lost (in); to be hidden (in, by); **т. в поду́шках** to sink in the pillows; **т. в дела́х** to be up to one's eyes in work; **надгро́бный па́мятник ~ет в высо́кой траве́** the tomb-stone is hidden by the long grass.

то́ньше *comp. of* ⇒**то́нкий** *and* **то́нко**

то́н|я, и *f.* **1** (*место*) fishery, fishing-ground. **2** (*улов*) haul (*of fish*).

топа́з, а *m.* (*min.*) topaz.

топа́з|овый *adj. of* ⇒**~**

то́п|ать, аю *impf.* (*pf.* **~нуть**) to stamp; **т. нога́ми** to stamp one's feet.

топинамбу́р, а *m.* Jerusalem artichoke.

топ|и́ть[1]**, лю́, ~ишь** *impf.* **1** (*камин*) to stoke (*a boiler, stove, etc.*). **2** (*помещение*) to heat.

топ|и́ть[2]**, лю́, ~ишь** *impf.* **1** (*воск*) to melt (down), render. **2**: **т. молоко́** to bake milk.

топ|и́ть[3]**, лю́, ~ишь** *impf.* **1** (*pf.* **по~**) (*корабль*) to sink. **2** (*pf.* **у~**) (*человека*) to drown; (*fig., coll.*) to wreck, ruin; **т. го́ре в вине́** to drown one's sorrows in drink.

топ|и́ться[1]**, ~ится** *impf.* (*о камине*) to burn, be alight.

топ|и́ться[2]**, ~ится** *impf.* **1** (*о воске*) to melt. **2** *pass of* ⇒**~и́ть**[2]

топ|и́ться[3]**, люсь, ~ишься** *impf.* (*of* ⇒**у~**) (*о человеке*) to drown o.s.

то́пк|а[1]**, и** *f.* **1** (*камина*) stoking. **2** (*помещения*) heating. **3** (*часть печи*) furnace; (*rail.*) fire-box.

то́пк|а[2]**, и** *f.* (*воска*) melting (down).

то́п|кий (~ок, ~ка́, ~ко) *adj.* boggy, marshy, swampy.

топлён|ый *adj.* melted; **~ое молоко́** baked milk.

то́плив|ный *adj. of* ⇒**~о**; **~ная нефть** fuel oil.

то́плив|о, а *nt.* fuel; **жи́дкое т.** fuel oil; **твёрдое т.** solid fuel.

топ-моде́л|ь, и *f.* top model.

то́п|нуть, ну, нешь *pf. of* ⇒**~ать**

топо́граф, а *m.* topographer.

топографи́ческий *adj.* topographical.

топогра́фи|я, и *f.* topography.

то́пол|евый *adj. of* ⇒**~ь**

то́пол|ь, я, *pl.* **~и** *and* **~я́** *m.* poplar.

топони́ми|ка, ки *f.* (*collect.*) place-names (*of a region*).

топони́ми|я, и *f.* toponymy.

топо́р, а́ *m.* axe (*Br.*), ax (*US*).

топо́рик, а *m.* hatchet.

топори́щ|е[1]**, а** *nt.* axe-handle (*Br.*), ax-handle (*US*).

топори́щ|е[2]**, а** *nt.* large axe (*Br.*), ax (*US*).

топо́р|ный (~ен, ~на) *adj.* (*работа*) clumsy, crude; (*человек*) uncouth.

топо́рщ|ить, ит *impf.* (*coll.*) to make stand on end.

топо́рщ|иться, ится *impf.* (*coll.*) **1** (*о волосах*) to stand on end, bristle. **2** (*о ёже*) to bristle; (*о птице*) to puff up its feathers. **3** (*об одежде*) to stick out, pucker. **4** (*упорствовать*) to be stubborn.

то́пот, а *m.* tramp; **ко́нский т.** clatter of horses' hoofs.

топо|та́ть, чу́, ~чешь *impf.* (*coll.*) to stamp; (*о лошадях*) to clatter.

то́почн|ый *adj.* furnace; **~ая коро́бка** fire-box.

то́псел|ь, я *m.* (*naut.*) topsail.

топ|та́ть, чу́, ~чешь *impf.* **1** (*траву*) to trample (down). **2** (*пол*) to make dirty (*with one's feet*). **3** (*виноград*) to trample out; **т. гли́ну** to knead clay.

топ|та́ться, чу́сь, ~чешься *impf.* **1** to shift from one foot to the other; **т. на ме́сте** to mark time (*also fig.*). **2** (*ходить туда и сюда*) to walk about aimlessly.

топ-топ *onomat.* pitter-patter.

топча́к, а́ *m.* treadmill.

топча́н, а́ *m.* trestle-bed.

топ|ь, и *f.* bog, marsh, swamp.

то́р|а, ы *f.* (*relig.*) Torah, Pentateuch.

то́рб|а, ы *f.* bag; **носи́ться (с**+*i.*) **как (дура́к) с пи́саной ~ой** (*coll.*) to make a great song and dance (about).

торг[1]**, а, о ~е, на ~у́,** *pl.* **~и́** *m.* **1** (*действие*) trading; bargaining, haggling. **2** (*obs.*) (*рынок*) market. **3** (*pl.*) (*аукцион*) auction; **прода́ть с ~о́в** to sell by auction. **4** (*pl.*) (*заявка на подряд*) tender.

торг[2]**, а** *m.* (*abbr. of* ***торго́вая организа́ция***) trading organization.

торг... *comb. form, abbr. of* ***торго́вый***

...торг *comb. form, abbr. of* **1** ***торг***[2]. **2** ***торго́вля***

торга́ш, а́ *m.* (*pej.*) **1** (*торговец*) (small) tradesman. **2** (*fig.*) mercenary person.

торга́ш|еский *adj. of* ⇒**~**

торга́шеств|о, а *nt.* mercenariness.

торг|ова́ть, у́ю *impf.* **1** (*impf. only*) (+*i.*) to trade (in), deal (in), sell. **2** (*impf. only*) (*о магазине*) to be open. **3** (*pf.* **с~**) (*coll.*) (*прицениваться*) to bargain (for).

торг|ова́ться, у́юсь *impf.* **1** (*pf.* **с~**) (**с**+*i.*) to bargain (with), haggle (with). **2** (*impf. only*) (*coll.*) (*спорить*) to argue.

торго́в|ец, ца *m.* merchant; dealer; tradesman; **т. нарко́тиками** drug trafficker *or* pusher.

торго́вк|а, и *f.* (female) stall-holder; (woman) street-trader.

торго́вл|я, и *f.* trade, commerce; **посы́лочная т.** mail-order.

торго́во-посы́лочн|ый *adj.*: **~ая фи́рма** mail-order firm.

торго́в|ый *adj.* trade, commercial; **т. бала́нс** balance of trade; **т. дом** firm; **~ая пала́та** chamber of commerce; **т. представи́тель** trade representative; **~ая то́чка** shop; **~ое су́дно** merchant ship; **т. флот** merchant navy.

торгпре́д, а *m.* (*abbr. of* ***торго́вый представи́тель***) trade representative.

торгпре́дств|о, а *nt.* (*abbr. of* ***торго́вое представи́тельство***) trade delegation.

торгфло́т, а *m.* merchant navy.

тореадо́р, а *m.* toreador.

тор|е́ц, ца́ *m.* **1** (*балки, доски*) butt-end, face. **2** (*для мощения улиц*) wooden paving-block. **3** (*мостовая*) pavement (*Br.*), sidewalk (*US*) of wooden blocks.

торже́ственност|ь, и *f.* solemnity.

торже́ствен|ный (~, ~на) *adj.* **1** ceremonial; (*праздничный*) festive;

gala; **т. день** red-letter day.
2 (*серьёзный*) solemn.
торжеств|о́, а́ *nt.* **1** celebration; (*pl.*) (*празднество*) festivities, rejoicings.
2 (*победа*) triumph (= *victory*).
3 (*радость*) triumph, exultation; **сказа́ть с ~о́м** to say triumphantly; to say gloatingly.
торжеств|ова́ть, у́ю *impf.* **1** to celebrate; **т. побе́ду** to celebrate a victory; (*fig.*) (*радоваться*) to rejoice.
2 (**над** + *i.*) to triumph (over); to exult (over).
торжеств|у́ющий *pres. part. act. of* ⇒**~ова́ть** *and adj.* triumphant, exultant.
то́ри *m. indecl.* (*pol.*) Tory.
торма́шк|и: вверх т., вверх ~ами (*coll.*) (*кувырком*) head over heels; (*в беспорядке*) upside down, topsy-turvy.
торможе́ни|е, я *nt.* **1** (*tech.*) braking.
2 (*psych.*) inhibition.
то́рмоз, а *m.* **1** (*pl.* **~а́**) brake. **2** (*pl.* **~ы**) (*fig.*) (*помеха*) hindrance, obstacle.
тормо|зи́ть, жу́, зи́шь *impf.* (*of* ⇒**за~**) **1** (*tech.*) to brake, apply the brake (to). **2** (*fig.*) (*замедлить*) to hamper, impede. **3** (*psych.*) to inhibit.
тормозн|о́й *adj.* (*tech.*) brake, braking; **т. башма́к** brake-shoe; **~а́я ракéта** retro-rocket.
тормош|и́ть, у́, и́шь *impf.* (*coll.*) **1** (*дёргать*) to pull (at), tug (at). **2** (*fig.*) (*вопросами*) to pester, plague.
то́рн|ый *adj.* smooth, even; **пойти́ по ~ой доро́ге** (*fig.*) to stick to the beaten track.
торова́т|ый (~, ~а) *adj.* (*coll.*) liberal, generous.
тороп|и́ть, лю́, ~ишь *impf.* (*of* ⇒**по~**) **1** to hurry, hasten; to press; **меня́ ~ят с оконча́нием рабо́ты** I am being pressed to finish my work.
2 (*события*) to precipitate.
тороп|и́ться, лю́сь, ~ишься *impf.* (*of* ⇒**по~**) to hurry, be in a hurry, hasten.
торопли́во *adv.* hurriedly, hastily; in a hurry.
торопли́вост|ь, и *f.* hurry, haste.
торопли́в|ый (~, ~а) *adj.* hurried, hasty.
торопы́г|а, и *c.g.* (*coll.*) person always in a hurry.
торо́с, а *m.* ice-hummock.
торо́сист|ый (~, ~а) *adj.* hummocky; **т. лёд** pack ice.
торпе́д|а, ы *f.* torpedo.
торпеди́р|овать, ую *impf. and pf.* to torpedo.
торпе́дн|ый *adj. of* ⇒**~а; т. аппара́т** torpedo-tube; **т. ка́тер** motor torpedo boat (*abbr.* MTB).
торс, а *m.* trunk; torso.
торт, а *m.* cake.
торф, а *m.* peat.
торфоразрабо́т|ки, ок *no sg.* peatbog.
торфяни́к, а́ *m.* **1** (*болото*) peatbog.
2 (*рабочий*) peat-cutter.
торфяни́ст|ый (~, ~а) *adj.* peaty.
торфян|о́й *adj.* peat; **~о́е боло́то** peatbog.
торц|ева́ть, у́ю *impf.* to pave with wood blocks.
торцо́в|ый *adj. of* ⇒**торе́ц; ~ая мостова́я** wood pavement (*Br.*), sidewalk (*US*).
торч|а́ть, у́, и́шь *impf.* **1** (*вверх*) to stick up; (*в сторону*) to stick out; (*о волосах*) to stand on end. **2** (*coll.*) to hang about; **т. пе́ред чьи́ми-н. глаза́ми** to be under s.o.'s feet; **он ~и́т це́лый день у бра́та** he hangs about at his brother's all day.
торчко́м *adv.* (*coll.*) on end, sticking up.
торч|мя́ *adv.* (*sl.*) = **~ко́м**
торше́р, а *m.* standard lamp.
тоск|а́, и́ *f.* **1** (*уныние*) melancholy; (*тревога*) anguish; **у неё т. на се́рдце** she is sick at heart; **т. любви́** pangs of love. **2** (*скука*) ennui, boredom; **одна́ т., сплошна́я т.** a frightful bore. **3** (**по** + *d. or p.*) longing (for); yearning (for), nostalgia (for); **т. по ро́дине** home-sickness.
тоскли́в|ый (~, ~а) *adj.*
1 (*настроение*) melancholy; depressed, miserable. **2** (*погода, город*) dull, dreary, depressing.
тоск|ова́ть, у́ю *impf.* **1** to be melancholy, be depressed, be miserable.
2 (**по** + *d. or p.*) to long (for), yearn (for), pine (for), miss.
тост[1], а *m.* toast; **провозгласи́ть, предложи́ть, т.** (**за** + *a.*) to toast, drink (to); to propose a toast (to).
тост[2], а *m.* (*хлеб*) piece of toast; **т. с сы́ром** Welsh rarebit.
то́стер, а *m.* toaster.
тот *m.*, **та** *f.*, **то** *nt.*, *pl.* **те,** *pron.* **1** (*opp.* **э́тот**) that; (*pl.*) those; **мне бо́льше нра́вится та карти́на** I like that picture better; **в тот раз** on that occasion; **в то вре́мя** then, at that time, in those days; **в том слу́чае** in that case.
2 (*opp.* **э́тот**) the former; (*replacing 3rd pers. sg. pron.*) he; she; it; **я пе́редал корректу́ру профе́ссору, тот до́лжен был вам верну́ть её** I passed the proofs on to the professor, he was supposed to return them to you.
3 (*opp.* **э́тот**) (*другой*) the other; the opposite; **на той стороне́** on the other side; **по ту сто́рону** (+*g.*) beyond, on the other side (of).
4 (*opp.* **сей** *in certain set phrr.*) that, the other; **то да сё** one thing and another; **ни то ни сё** neither one thing nor another; **поговори́ть о том, о сём** to talk about this and that; **ни с того́ ни с сего́** for no reason at all.
5 (*opp.* **друго́й, ино́й**) the one; **и тот, и друго́й** both; **ни тот, ни друго́й** neither; **не тот, так друго́й** if not one, then the other.
6: **тот... , (кото́рый)** the ... (which); **тот, (кто)** the one (who), the person (who); **тот фильм, кото́рый вы ви́дели вчера́** the film (which) you saw yesterday; **тот факт, что** the fact that (*see also* ⇒**то[1]**).
7: **тот (же), тот (же) са́мый** the same; **одно́ и то же** one and the same thing, the same thing over again; **в то же са́мое вре́мя** at the same time, on the other hand; **он тепе́рь не тот** he is not the man he was.
8 (*такой, какой нужен*) the right; **не тот** the wrong; **э́то не та дверь** that's the wrong door; **э́то тот но́мер?** is this the (right) room?
9 +*preps. forms the following conjs.*: **для того́, что́бы** in order that, in order to; **до того́, что** (*i*) (*так долго, что*) until, (*ii*) (*до такой степени*) to such an extent that; **ме́жду тем, как** whereas; **несмотря́ на то, что** in spite of the fact that; **пе́ред тем, как** before; **по́сле того́, как** after; **по ме́ре того́, как** in proportion as; **с тем, что́бы** (*i*) (*чтобы*) in order to, with a view to, (*ii*) (*при условии, что*) on condition that, provided that.
10 *forms part of var. adv. phrr. and particles* (*see also* ⇒**то[1]**): **вме́сте с тем** at the same time; **к тому́ же** moreover; **кро́ме того́** besides; **ме́жду тем, тем вре́менем** meanwhile; **со всем тем** notwithstanding all this; **тем са́мым** hereby; **тому́ наза́д** ago; **и тому́ подо́бное (и т. п.)** and so forth; **того́ и гляди́** any minute now; before you know where you are; **и без того́** as it is.
тотализа́тор, а *m.* tote, totalizator.
тоталитари́зм, а *m.* (*pol.*) totalitarianism.
тоталита́рный *adj.* (*pol.*) totalitarian.
тота́льный *adj.* total.
тоте́м, а *m.* totem.
тотеми́зм, а *m.* totemism.
то́-то *particle* (*coll.*) **1** *emph. point of utterance*: **(вот) то́-то, (вот) то́-то и оно́, (вот) то́-то и есть** that's just it; precisely, exactly. **2** (*как*): **то́-то прекра́сно!** there, isn't that lovely!
3 (*вот, видите!*): **ну, то́-то же!** there you are; well, what did I tell you!
то́тчас *adv.* at once; immediately (*also of spatial relations*).
точёный *adj.* **1** (*острый*) sharpened.
2 (*tech.*) turned. **3** (*fig.*) (*о фигуре*) finely-moulded (*Br.*), finely-molded (*US*); (*о чертах лица*) chiselled (*Br.*), chiseled (*US*).
то́чечн|ый *adj.* **1** consisting of points; **~ая ли́ния** dotted line. **2**: **~ая сва́рка** (*tech.*) spot welding.
точи́лк|а, и *f.* (*coll.*) (*для ножей*) steel, knife-sharpener; (*для карандашей*) pencil-sharpener.
точи́л|о, а *nt.* whetstone, grindstone.
точи́льный *adj.* grinding, sharpening; **т. ка́мень** whetstone, grindstone; **т. материа́л** abrasive; **т. реме́нь** strop.
точи́льщик, а *m.* knife-grinder.
точ|и́ть[1], у́, ~ишь *impf.* **1** (*pf* **на~**) (*нож, карандаш*) to sharpen; **т. зу́бы на кого́-н.** to have a grudge against s.o.
2 (*impf. only*) (*на токарном станке*) to turn.
точ|и́ть[2], у́, ~ишь *impf.* (*прогрызать*) to eat away, gnaw away; to corrode; (*fig.*) (*терзать*) to gnaw (at), prey (upon).
то́чк|а[1], и *f.* **1** spot, dot; **бе́лое пла́тье в ро́зовых ~ах** white dress with pink spots; 'i' **с ~ой** *name of letter* 'i' *in old Russian orthography*; **ста́вить ~и на(д) 'и'** to dot one's 'i's' (and cross one's 't's').

Т

2 (*gram.*) full stop; **т. с запято́й** semicolon; **поста́вить ~у** to place a full stop; (*fig.*) to finish, come to the end. **3** (*mus.*) dot. **4** (*math., phys., tech.*) point; **т. опо́ры** fulcrum, point of support; (*fig.*) rallying-point; **мёртвая т.** dead point, dead centre; (*fig.*) standstill; **дойти́ до мёртвой ~и** to come to a standstill, to a full stop. **5** (*mil.*) point; **т. попада́ния** point of impact; **т. наво́дки** aiming point; **т. прице́ливания** point of aim. **6**: **т. замерза́ния, кипе́ния, плавле́ния** freezing, boiling, melting point. **7** (*fig.*) point; **т. зре́ния** point of view; **т. соприкоснове́ния** point of contact; **горя́чая т.** trouble spot; **т. в ~у** (*coll.*) exactly; to the letter, word for word; **попа́сть в (са́мую) ~у** (*coll.*) to hit the nail on the head; **до ~и** (*coll.*) to the limit, to the extreme point; **дойти́ до ~и** (*coll.*) to come to the end of one's tether.

то́чк|а², и *f.* **1** (*ножа*) sharpening. **2** (*на токарном станке*) turning.

то́чно¹ *adv.* **1** exactly, precisely; (*пунктуально*) punctually; **т. переписа́ть** to make an exact copy; **приходи́те, пожа́луйста, т. в час** please, come at one o'clock sharp. **2**: **т. так** just so, exactly, precisely; **т. тако́й (же)** just the same. **3** (*действительно*) indeed.

то́чно² *particle* (*coll.*) (*да*) yes; (*верно*) true; **так т.** (*in mil. parlance*) yes.

то́чно³ *conj.* as though, as if; like; **он там стоя́л т. окамене́лый** he stood there as if turned to stone.

то́чност|ь, и *f.* exactness; precision; accuracy; punctuality; **в ~и** exactly, precisely; accurately; to the letter; **вы́числить с ~ью до...** to calculate to within ...; **с ~ью часово́го механи́зма** like clockwork.

то́ч|ный (~ен, ~на́, ~но) *adj.* exact, precise; accurate; (*пунктуальный*) punctual; **~ная бомбардиро́вка** precision bombing; **~ные нау́ки** exact sciences; **т. перево́д** accurate translation; **т. прибо́р** precision instrument; **т. челове́к** punctual person.

то́чь-в-то́чь *adv.* (*coll.*) exactly; (*слово в слово*) word for word; **он — т.-в-т. оте́ц** he is the spitting image of his father.

тошн|и́ть, и́т *impf.* (*impers.*): **меня́,** *etc.*, **~и́т** I, *etc.*, feel sick; **меня́ от э́того ~и́т** (*fig.*) it makes me sick, it sickens me.

то́шно *as pred.* (*coll.*) **1**: **мне,** *etc.*, **т.** I, *etc.*, feel sick; (*fig.*) I, *etc.*, feel wretched, awful. **2** (+*inf.*) (*противно*) it is sickening, it makes one sick, it is nauseating.

тошнот|а́, ы́ *f.* sickness, nausea (*also fig.*); **испы́тывать ~у́** to feel sick; **у́тренняя т.** morning sickness.

тошнотво́р|ный (~ен, ~на) *adj.* sickening, nauseating (*also fig.*).

то́ш|ный (~ен, ~на́, ~но) *adj.* (*coll.*) **1** (*докучный*) tiresome, tedious. **2** (*отвратительный*) sickening, nauseating.

тоща́|ть, ю *impf.* (*of* ⇒**о~**) (*coll.*) to become thin.

то́щ|ий (~, ~а́, ~е) *adj.* **1** (*исхудалый*) gaunt, emaciated; skinny. **2** (*пустой*) empty; **на т. желу́док** on an empty stomach; **т. карма́н** (*fig.*) empty pocket. **3** (*скудный*) poor (= *with low content of some substance*); **~ее мя́со** lean meat; **~ая по́чва** poor soil.

тпру *int.* (*to horses*) whoa!

трав|а́, ы́, *pl.* **~́ы** *f.* grass; (*кухонная, лекарственная*) herb; **морска́я т.** sea-weed; **со́рная т.** weed; **хоть т. не расти́** (*coll.*) (everything else) can go to hell.

травести́ *nt. indecl.* (*theatr.*) travesty (*cross-dressing*).

трави́нк|а, и *f.* blade of grass.

трав|и́ть¹, лю́, ~́ишь *impf.* **1** (*pf.* **вы́~**) (*тараканов*) to exterminate, destroy (*by poisoning*). **2** (*coll.*) (*организм, сознание*) to poison. **3** (*pf.* **вы́~**) (*узоры*) to etch. **4** (*pf.* **по~**) (*о скоте*) to trample down; to damage (*crops, etc.*). **5** (*pf.* **за~**) (*дичь*) to hunt; (*fig.*) to persecute, torment.

трав|и́ть², лю́, ~́ишь *impf.* (*of* ⇒**по~**) **1** (*naut.*) (*канат*) to pay out. **2** (*sl.*) (*рассказы, анекдоты*) to tell; **переста́нь т.!** stop telling stories!, stop lying!

трав|и́ться, лю́сь, ~́ишься *impf.* (*coll.*) to poison o.s.

тра́в|ка, ки *f. dim of* ⇒**~а́**; (*sl.*) (*марихуана*) grass, dope.

травле́ни|е, я *nt.* (*узоров*) etching.

тра́вленый¹ *adj.* (*узор*) etched.

тра́вленый² *adj.* (*зверь*) hunted; **т. зверь** (*fig., coll.*) old hand.

тра́вл|я, и *f.* hunting; (*fig.*) persecution, tormenting.

тра́вм|а, ы *f.* (*med.*) (*психическая*) trauma; (*физическая*) injury.

травмати́зм, а *m.* (*med.*) traumatism; (*collect.*) injuries; **произво́дственный т.** industrial injuries.

травмати́ческий *adj.* (*med., psych.*) traumatic.

травматологи́ческ|ий *adj.*: **~ое отделе́ние** casualty department; **т. пункт** first aid room.

тра́вник¹, а *m.* (*coll.*) herbalist.

тра́вник², а *m.* (*zool.*) redshank.

травни́к, а *m.* **1** (*obs.*) (*настойка*) herb-tea. **2** (*hist.*) (*книга*) herbal. **3** (*obs.*) (*гербарий*) herbarium.

тра́вни|ца, цы *f. of* ⇒**~к¹**

травокоси́лк|а, и *f.* lawn mower.

траволече́ни|е, я *nt.* herbal medicine.

травосе́яни|е, я *nt.* fodder-grass cultivation.

травосто́|й, я *m.* (*collect.*; *agric.*) grass, herbage.

травоя́дный *adj.* herbivorous.

травяни́ст|ый (~, ~а) *adj.* **1** (*растение*) herbaceous. **2** (*луг*) grassy. **3** (*coll.*) (*безвкусный*) tasteless, insipid.

травян|о́й *adj.* **1** grass; herbaceous; **т. покро́в** grass, herbage; **~ы́е расте́ния** grasses, herbs; **~ы́е уго́дья** grasslands. **2** grassy; **т. за́пах** grassy smell; **т. цвет** grass-green. **3**: **~а́я насто́йка** herb-tea.

трагеди́йный *adj.* (*theatr.*) tragic.

траге́ди|я, и *f.* tragedy.

траги́зм, а *m.* tragic element.

тра́гик, а *m.* **1** (*актёр*) tragic actor. **2** (*автор*) tragedian.

трагикоме́ди|я, и *f.* tragicomedy.

трагикоми́ческий *adj.* tragicomic.

траги́ческ|ий *adj.* tragic; **т. актёр** tragic actor; **~ое зре́лище** tragic sight.

траги́чност|ь, и *f.* tragedy, tragic nature.

траги́ч|ный (~ен, ~на) *adj.* tragic.

традицио́нност|ь, и *f.* traditional character.

традицио́н|ный (~ен, ~на) *adj.* traditional.

тради́ци|я, и *f.* tradition.

траекто́ри|я, и *f.* trajectory.

тракт, а *m.* **1** (*дорога*) high road, highway; **желу́дочно-кише́чный т.** (*anat.*) alimentary canal. **2** (*маршрут*) route.

тракта́т, а *m.* **1** (*сочинение*) treatise. **2** (*договор*) treaty.

тракти́р, а *m.* (*obs.*) inn, eating-house.

тракти́р|ный *adj. of* ⇒**~**

тракти́рщик, а *m.* (*obs.*) innkeeper.

тракти́рщи|ца, цы *f. of* ⇒**~к**

тракт|ова́ть, у́ю *impf.* **1** (+*a.* or **о**+*p.*) (*вопрос*) to treat, discuss. **2** (*роль*) to interpret (*a part in a play, etc.*).

тракт|ова́ться, у́ется *impf.* to be treated, be discussed; **о чём ~у́ется в э́том рома́не?** what is the subject of this novel?

тракто́вк|а, и *f.* treatment; interpretation.

тра́ктор, а *m.* tractor; **т. на гу́сеничном ходу́, гу́сеничный т.** caterpillar tractor.

трактори́ст, а *m.* tractor driver.

трактори́ст|ка, ки *f. of* ⇒**~**

тра́ктор|ный *adj. of* ⇒**~**; **на ~ной тя́ге** tractor-drawn.

тракторострое́ни|е, я *nt.* tractor-making.

тракторострои́тельный *adj.*: **т. заво́д** tractor works.

трал, а *m.* **1** trawl. **2** (*mil.*) mine-sweep.

тра́лени|е, я *nt.* **1** trawling. **2** (*mil.*) mine-sweeping.

тра́л|ить, ю, ишь *impf.* **1** to trawl. **2** (*mil.*) to sweep.

тра́ловый *adj.* **1** trawling; **т. лов** trawling. **2** (*mil.*) mine-sweeping.

тра́льщик, а *m.* **1** trawler. **2** (*mil.*) mine-sweeper.

трамб|ова́ть, у́ю *impf.* to ram, tamp.

трамбо́вк|а, и *f.* **1** (*действие*) ramming, tamping. **2** (*машина*) rammer, beetle.

трамва́|й, я *m.* tram (*Br.*), streetcar (*US*); **речно́й т.** river bus.

трамва́й|ный *adj. of* ⇒**~**; **~ные ре́льсы** tram-lines.

трамва́йщик, а *m.* tram worker.

трамва́йщи|ца, цы *f. of* ⇒**~к**

трампа́рк, а *m.* **1** (*место стоянки*) tram depot. **2** (*трамвайный состав*) tram fleet.

трампли́н, а *m.* (*sport and fig.*) spring-board; (*лыжный*) ski-jump.

транжи́р, а *m.* (*coll.*) spendthrift.

транжи́р|а, ы *c.g.* = ~

транжи́р|ить, ю, ишь *impf.* (*of* ⇨**рас~**) (*coll.*) to blow, squander.

транжи́р|ка, ки *f. of* ⇨~

транзи́стор, а *m.* transistor.

транзи́т, а *m.* transit; **пойти́ ~ом** to go as transit goods.

транзи́т|ный *adj. of* ⇨~; **~ная ви́за** transit visa.

транквилиза́тор, а *m.* tranquillizer (*Br.*), tranquilizer (*US*).

транс, а *m.* trance.

транс... *pref.* trans-.

трансаге́нтств|о, а *nt.* (*abbr. of* ***тра́нспортное аге́нтство***) removal company.

трансатланти́ческий *adj.* transatlantic.

Трансильва́ни|я, и *f.* Transylvania.

транскриби́р|овать, ую *impf. and pf.* to transcribe.

транскри́пци|я, и *f.* transcription.

трансли́р|овать, ую *impf. and pf.* to broadcast; to relay.

транслитера́ци|я, и *f.* transliteration.

трансляцио́нный *adj.* broadcasting.

трансля́ци|я, и *f.* (*действие*) transmission, broadcasting; (*передача*) broadcast.

трансмисс|ио́нный *adj. of* ⇨**~ия**

трансми́сси|я, и *f.* (*tech.*) transmission.

транснациона́льный *adj.* transnational.

транспара́нт, а *m.* **1** (*разлинованный лист*) black-lined paper (*placed under unruled writing-paper*). **2** (*знамя*) banner.

транспланта́ци|я, и *f.* (*med.*) transplantation.

транспози́ци|я, и *f.* (*mus.*) transposition.

транспони́р|овать, ую *impf. and pf.* (*mus.*) to transpose.

транспониро́вк|а, и *f.* (*mus.*) transposition.

тра́нспорт, а *m.* **1** (*система перевозки*) transport; **обще́ственный т.** public transport. **2** (*перевозка*) transportation, conveyance. **3** (*партия грузов*) consignment. **4** (*mil.*) train, transport. **5** (*naut.*) supply ship; troopship.

транспо́рт, а *m.* (*book-keeping*) carrying forward.

транспорта́бел|ьный (~ен, ~ьна) *adj.* transportable, mobile.

транспортёр, а *m.* **1** (*tech.*) conveyor. **2** (*mil.*) carrier.

транспорти́р, а *m.* protractor.

транспорти́ровать[1]**, ую** *impf. and pf.* to transport.

транспорти́р|овать[2]**, ую** *impf. and pf.* (*book-keeping*) to carry forward.

транспортиро́вк|а, и *f.* transport, transportation.

тра́нспортник, а *m.* **1** (*работник*) transport worker. **2** (*самолёт*) transport plane.

тра́нспортни|ца, цы *f. of* ⇨**~к**

тра́нспорт|ный *adj. of* ⇨~

транссексуа́л, а *m.* transsexual.

транссиби́рск|ий *adj.* Trans-Siberian; **~ая магистра́ль** the Trans-Siberian Railway.

трансформа́тор[1]**, а** *m.* (*elec.*) transformer.

трансформа́тор[2]**, а** *m.* **1** (*актёр*) quick-change actor. **2** (*фокусник*) conjuror, illusionist.

трансформа́ци|я, и *f.* transformation.

трансформи́р|овать, ую *impf. and pf.* to transform.

трансцендента́л|ьный (~ен, ~ьна) *adj.* (*phil.*) transcendental.

трансценде́нт|ный (~ен, ~на) *adj.* (*phil.*) transcendent; (*math.*) transcendental.

транш, а *m.* (*fin.*) tranche.

транше́|йный *adj. of* ⇨**~я**

транше́|я, и *f.* (*mil.*) trench.

трап, а *m.* (*naut.*) ladder; (*aeron.*) gangway.

тра́пе́з|а, ы *f.* **1** (*общий стол*) dining-table (*esp. in a monastery*). **2** (*еда*) meal; **дели́ть ~у (с** + *i.*) to share a meal (with). **3** (*трапезная*) refectory.

тра́пез|ный *adj. of* ⇨**~а;** *as n.* **~ная, ~ной** *f.* refectory.

трапе́ци|я, и *f.* **1** (*math.*) trapezium. **2** (*цирковая*) trapeze.

тра́сс|а, ы *f.* **1** (*трубопровода, метро*) route, course; **возду́шная т.** airway. **2** (*дорога*) main road, highway (*US*). **3** (*пули, ракеты*) path.

трасса́нт, а *m.* (*fin.*) drawer.

трасса́т, а *m.* (*fin.*) drawee.

трасси́р|овать, ую *impf. and pf.* to mark out, trace.

трасси́р|ующий *pres. part. act. of* ⇨**~овать** *and adj.* (*mil.*) tracer; **~ующая пу́ля** tracer bullet.

тра́т|а, ы *f.* expenditure; **пуста́я т. вре́мени** waste of time.

тра́|тить, чу, тишь *impf.* (*of* ⇨**ис~** *and* **по~**) to spend, expend, use up; (*понапрасну*) to waste.

тра́|титься, чусь, тишься *impf.* (*of* ⇨**ис~** *and* **по~**) (**на** + *a.*; *coll.*) to spend one's money (on).

тра́улер, а *m.* trawler.

тра́ур, а *m.* mourning.

тра́урн|ый *adj.* **1** mourning; funeral; **т. марш** funeral march; **~ое ше́ствие** funeral procession. **2** (*скорбный*) mournful, sorrowful; funereal.

трафаре́т, а *m.* **1** stencil. **2** (*fig.*) stereotyped pattern; cliché; **мы́слить по ~у** to think along conventional lines.

трафаре́тност|ь, и *f.* conventionality; stereotyped character.

трафаре́т|ный *adj.* **1** stencilled; **т. рису́нок** stencil drawing. **2 (~ен, ~на)** (*fig.*) conventional, stereotyped; (*фраза*) hackneyed.

тра́ф|ить, лю, ишь *impf.* (*coll.*) to please, oblige.

трах *int.* bang! (*also as pred.* = **~нул**)

тра́х|ать, аю *impf. of* ⇨**~нуть**

тра́х|аться, аюсь *impf. of* ⇨**~нуться**

трахеотоми́|я, и *f.* (*med.*) tracheotomy.

трахе́|я, и *f.* (*anat.*) trachea, windpipe.

тра́х|нуть, ну, нешь *pf.* (*of* ⇨**~ать**) (*coll.*) **1** to bang, crash; **т. кого́-н. по спине́** to bang s.o. on the back; **т. из ружья́** to loose off with a gun. **2** (*vulg.*) to screw, hump.

тра́х|нуться, нусь, нешься *pf.* (*of* ⇨**~аться**) **1** to bang, crash; **т. голово́й о кося́к** to bang one's head on the door. **2** (*vulg.*) to screw, hump.

трахо́м|а, ы *f.* (*med.*) trachoma.

тре́б|а, ы *f.* occasional religious rite (*christening, marriage, funeral, etc.*).

тре́бник, а *m.* prayer-book.

тре́бовани|е, я *nt.* **1** (*действие*) demand, request; **по ~ю** on demand, by request; **остано́вка по ~ю** request stop; **по ~ю суда́** by order of the court. **2** (*настоятельная просьба*) demand; (*притязание*) claim; **согласи́ться на чьи-н. ~я** to agree to s.o.'s demands; **вы́двинуть т.** to put in a claim. **3** (*usu. pl.*) (*условие*) requirement, condition; **отвеча́ть, соотве́тствовать ~ям** to meet requirements. **4** (*pl.*) (*запросы*) aspirations; needs. **5** (*документ*) requisition, order; **т. на то́пливо** fuel requisition.

тре́бовател|ьный (~ен, ~ьна) *adj.* (*зритель, тон*) demanding; (*учитель, руководитель*) exacting.

тре́б|овать, ую *impf.* (*of* ⇨**по~**) **1** (+*g. or* +**что́бы**) to demand, require; **т. извине́ния у кого́-н.** to demand an apology from s.o.; **они́ ~уют, что́бы мы извини́лись** they demand that we apologize. **2** (*impf. only*) (+*g.* **от**+*g.*) to expect (from), ask (of); **т. сочу́вствия от му́жа** to expect sympathy from one's husband; **вы ~уете сли́шком мно́го от ва́ших ученико́в** you expect too much from your pupils. **3** (*pf.* **по~**) (+*g.*) (*нуждаться*) to require, need, call (for); **т. неме́дленного реше́ния** to require an immediate decision. **4** (*вызывать*) to send for, call, summon.

тре́б|оваться, уется *impf.* (*of* ⇨**по~**) to be needed, be required; **на э́то ~уется мно́го вре́мени** it takes a lot of time; **что и ~овалось доказа́ть** Q.E.D. (*abbr. of* quod erat demonstrandum); **фи́рме ~уется бухга́лтер** the company seeks an accountant.

требух|а́, и́ *no pl., f.* entrails; (*cul.*) offal, tripe.

трево́г|а, и *f.* **1** (*беспокойство*) alarm, anxiety. **2** (*сигнал*) alarm; **возду́шная т.** air-raid warning; **бить ~у** to sound the alarm (*also fig.*); **подня́ть ~у** to raise the alarm.

трево́ж|ить, у, ишь *impf.* **1** (*pf.* **вс~**) to alarm; to worry. **2** (*pf.* **по~**)

(*мешать*) to disturb, interrupt; **нас всё врéмя ~ат посети́тели** we are continually disturbed by callers. **3**: **т. рáну** to re-open a wound.

тревóж|иться, усь, ишься *impf.* **1** (*pf.* **вс~**) to worry, be alarmed, be uneasy. **2** (*pf.* **по~**) to trouble o.s., put o.s. out; **не ~ьтесь!** don't bother (yourself)!

тревóж|ный (~ен, ~на) *adj.* **1** (*полный тревоги*) anxious, uneasy, troubled. **2** (*вызывающий тревогу*) alarming, disturbing; **~ные вéсти** alarming reports. **3** (*предупреждающий*) alarm; **т. звонóк** alarm (bell).

треволнéни|е, я *nt.* (*now coll., joc.*) agitation, disquiet.

треглáвый *adj.* **1** with three cupolas. **2** (*poet.*) three-headed.

тред-юниóн, а *m.* trade union.

тред-юниони́зм, а *m.* trade-unionism.

тред-юниони́ст, а *m.* trade unionist.

трéзвенник, а *m.* teetotaller, abstainer.

трéзвенническ|ий *adj.* temperance; **~ое движéние** temperance movement.

трезвé|ть, ю *impf.* (*of* ⇒**о~**) to sober (up), become sober.

трезвóн, а *m.* **1** peal (of bells). **2** (*coll.*) (*толки*) rumours (*Br.*), rumors (*US*), gossip. **3** (*coll.*) (*переполох*) row, fuss; **подня́ть т., задáть ~у** to kick up a row.

трезвóн|ить, ю, ишь *impf.* **1** (*о колоколах*) to ring (a peal). **2** (*fig.*) (**о** + *p.*; *coll.*) to trumpet; **т. по всемý гóроду** to proclaim from the housetops. **3** (*о телефоне*) to ring.

трéзвост|ь, и *f.* **1** soberness, sobriety (*also fig.*); **т. умá** cool-headedness. **2** (*воздержанность*) abstinence; temperance.

трезвýчи|е, я *nt.* (*mus.*) triad.

трéзв|ый (~, ~á, ~о) *adj.* **1** sober (*also fig.*); **имéть т. взгляд на собы́тия** to take a sober view of events; **человéк ~ого умá** sober-minded person. **2** (*воздержанный*) teetotal, abstinent.

трезýб|ец, ца *m.* trident.

трéйдер, а *m.* trader (*in stocks and shares*).

трéйлер, а *m.* **1** (*прицеп*) trailer. **2** (*домик*) caravan (*Br.*), trailer (*US*).

трек, а *m.* (*sport*) track.

трекбóл, а *m.* (*comput.*) trackball.

трекля́тый *adj.* (*coll.*) accursed.

трел|ь, и *f.* (*mus.*) trill, shake; (*птицы*) warble.

трелья́ж, а *m.* **1** (*решётка*) trellis. **2** (*зеркало*) three-leaved mirror.

трéмоло *nt. indecl.* (*mus.*) tremolo.

тренáж, а *m.* training.

тренажёр, а *m.* training apparatus; **гребнóй т.** rowing machine; **лётный т.** flight simulator.

трéнер, а *m.* (*sport*) trainer, coach; **т. по тéннису/футбóлу** tennis/football coach.

трéнзел|ь, я, *pl.* **~и** *and* **~я́** *m.* snaffle.

трéни|е, я *nt.* **1** friction, rubbing. **2** (*pl.*) (*fig.*) friction.

тренир|овáть, ýю *impf.* (*of* ⇒**на~**) to train, coach; (*память*) to train.

тренир|овáться, ýюсь *impf.* (*of* ⇒**на~**) to train o.s., coach o.s.; to be in training.

трениро́вк|а, и *f.* training, coaching.

трениро́вочный *adj.* training; practice; **т. костю́м** tracksuit.

тренóг|а, и *f.* tripod.

тренóгий *adj.* three-legged.

тренóж|ить, у, ишь *impf.* (*of* ⇒**с~**) to hobble.

тренóжник, а *m.* tripod.

трéнька|ть, ю *impf.* (*coll.*) (*на гитаре*) to strum.

трёп, а *m.* (*coll.*) idle chatter.

трепáк, á *m.* trepak (*Russian folk-dance*).

трепáл|о, а *nt.* (*tech.*) swingle, scutcher.

трепанáци|я, и *f.* (*med.*) trepanation.

трепáнг, а *m.* (*zool.*) trepang.

трепани́р|овать, ую *impf. and pf.* (*med.*) to trepan.

трёпаный *adj.* **1** (*лён*) scutched. **2** (*одежда, книга*) torn, tattered. **3** (*волосы*) dishevelled (*Br.*), disheveled (*US*).

треп|áть, лю́, ~лешь *impf.* **1** (*impf. only*) (*лён*) to scutch, swingle. **2** (*pf.* **по~**) to pull about; (*о ветре*) to blow about; **т. когó-н. за вóлосы** to pull s.o.'s hair; **т. чьи-н. вóлосы** to tousle s.o.'s hair; **т. языкóм** (*coll.*) to prattle; **т. чьи-н. нéрвы** to get on s.o.'s nerves; **егó ~лет лихорáдка** he is feverish; **т. чьё-н. и́мя** to bandy s.o.'s name about. **3** (*pf.* **по~, ис~**) (*книгу*) to tear; (*одежду, обувь*) to wear out. **4** (*pf.* **по~**) (*по плечу*) to pat.

треп|áться, лю́сь, ~лешься *impf.* **1** (*pf.* **по~, ис~**) (*о книге*) to tear; (*об одежде*) to wear out. **2** (*impf. only*) (*о флагах*) to flutter; (*о волосах*) to blow about. **3** (*pf.* **по~**) (*coll., pej.*) (*околачиваться*) to hang out. **4** (*pf.* **по~**) (*coll.*) = **трепáть языкóм**

трепáч, á *m.* (*coll.*) prattler.

трéпет, а *m.* (*дрожь*) trembling, quivering; (*сердца*) palpitation; (*страх*) trepidation, terror; (*волнение*) agitation; (*уважительность*) awe; **быть в ~е** to be a-tremble, be in a dither.

трепе|тáть, щý, ~щешь *impf.* **1** (*дрожать*) to tremble, quiver. **2** (*fig.*) (*испытывать волнение*) to tremble; to thrill; **т. от востóрга** to thrill with joy; **т. при мы́сли** (**о** + *p.*) to tremble at the thought (of). **3** (**пéред** + *i. or* (*obs.*) + *a.*; *fig.*) (*испытывать страх*) to tremble (before).

трéпетный *adj.* **1** trembling; (*свет*) flickering. **2** (*улыбка, ожидание*) anxious. **3** (*робкий*) timid.

трёпк|а, и *f.* **1** (*льна*) scutching. **2** (*coll.*) (*выговор*) dressing-down, scolding. **3**: **т. нéрвов** nervous strain.

трепыхá|ться, юсь *impf.* (*coll.*) to flutter, quiver; (*волноваться*) to fuss, panic.

треск, а *m.* **1** crack; crackle, crackling; **т. ружéйных вы́стрелов** crackle of gun-fire; **т. огня́** crackling of a fire; **т. мотóра** popping of an engine; **с ~ом провали́ться** (*fig., coll.*) to be a flop. **2** (*fig., coll.*) (*шумиха*) noise, fuss.

треск|á, и́ *f.* cod.

трéска|ть, ю *impf.* (*coll.*) to guzzle.

трéска|ться[1], ется *impf.* (*of* ⇒**по~**) to crack; to chap.

трéска|ться[2], юсь *impf. of* ⇒**трéснуться**

треск|óвый *adj. of* ⇒**~á; т. жир** cod-liver oil.

трескотн|я́, и́ *f.* (*coll.*) **1** (*выстрелов*) crackle; (*огня*) crackling; (*кузнечиков*) chirring. **2** (*fig.*) (*болтовня*) chatter.

трескýч|ий (~, ~а) *adj.* **1** (*pej.*) (*речь, слова*) highfalutin(g), high-flown. **2**: **т. морóз** hard frost.

трéснут|ый (~, ~а) *adj.* (*coll.*) cracked.

трéсн|уть, у, ешь *pf.* **1** (*о ветке*) to snap. **2** (*о стакане, коже*) to crack; (*лопнуть*) to burst; (*fig., coll.*) (*провалиться*) to flop; **хоть ~и** (*coll.*) for the life of me. **3** (+ *i.* **по** + *d. or* + *a.* **по** + *d.*; *coll.*) to bring down with a crash (on); to hit, bang; **т. кулакóм по столý** to bang one's fist on the table.

трéс|нуться, нусь, нешься *pf.* (*of* ⇒**~каться[2]**) (+ *i.* **о** + *a.*; *coll.*) to bang (against); **т. головóй о дверь** to bang one's head against the door.

трест, а *m.* (*econ.*) trust; (*строительный*) company.

третéйский *adj.* arbitration; **т. суд** arbitration tribunal; **т. судья́** arbitrator.

трéт|ий, ья, ье *adj.* **1** third; **т. нóмер** number three; **полови́на ~ьего** half past two; **в ~ьем часý** between two and three; **~ьего дня** the day before yesterday; **~ье лицó** (*gram.*) third person; **т. мир** Third World; **~ий сорт** (*fig.*) third rate; **~ья сторонá** third party. **2** *as n.* **~ье, ~ьего** *nt.* sweet, dessert.

трети́р|овать, ую *impf.* to slight.

трети́чный *adj.* (*geol., chem., etc.*) tertiary, ternary.

трет|ь, и, *pl.* **~и, ~éй** *f.* third.

третьеклáссник, а *m.* third-former (*Br.*), third-grader (*US*).

третьеклáсснн|ца, цы *f. of* ⇒**~к**

третьеклáссный *adj.* third-class (*also fig.*).

третьесóртный *adj.* third-rate.

третьестепéнный *adj.* **1** (*малозначительный*) insignificant. **2** (*посредственный*) third-rate.

треугóлк|а, и *f.* cocked hat.

треугóльник, а *m.* triangle.

треугóльный *adj.* three-cornered, triangular.

трéф|а, ы *f.* (*cards*) **1** *see* ⇒**~ы.** **2** (*coll.*) a club.

трéфóвый *adj.* (*cards*) of clubs.

трéф|ы, ~ *pl.* (*sg.* **~а, ~ы** *f.*) (*cards*) clubs; **дáма ~** queen of clubs.

трёх... *comb. form* three-, tri-.

трёхвалéнтный *adj.* (*chem.*) trivalent.

трёхгоди́чный *adj.* three-year.

трёхгодова́лый *adj.* three-year-old.
трёхголо́с(н)ый *adj.* (*mus.*) three-part.
трёхгра́нный *adj.* three-edged; (*math.*) trihedral.
трёхдне́вный *adj.* three-day.
трёхзна́чный *adj.* three-digit, three-figure.
трёхколёсный *adj.* three-wheeled; **т. велосипе́д** tricycle.
трёхле́ти|е, я *nt.* **1** (*срок*) period of three years. **2** (*годовщина*) third anniversary.
трёхле́тний *adj.* **1** (*срок*) three-year. **2** (*ребёнок*) three-year-old.
трёхме́рный *adj.* three-dimensional.
трёхме́стный *adj.* three-seater.
трёхме́сячный *adj.* **1** (*срок*) three-month; (*издание*) quarterly. **2** (*ребёнок*) three-month-old.
трёхнеде́льный *adj.* **1** (*срок*) three-week. **2** (*ребёнок*) three-week-old.
трёхпо́ль|е, я *nt.* (*agric.*) three-field system.
трёхпо́ль|ный *adj. of* ⇨**~е**
трёхра́зовый *adj.* (*питание*) three times a day; (*талон*) valid for three occasions.
трёхсло́йный *adj.* three-ply.
трёхсотле́ти|е, я *nt.* **1** (*срок*) three hundred years. **2** (*годовщина*) tercentenary.
трёхсотле́тний *adj.* **1** (*срок*) of three hundred years. **2** (*годовщина*) tercentennial.
трёхсо́тый *adj.* three-hundredth.
трёхсторо́нний *adj.* **1** three-sided; (*math.*) trilateral. **2** (*договор*) tripartite, trilateral.
трёхфа́зный *adj.* (*elec.*) three-phase.
трёхцве́тный *adj.* three-coloured (*Br.*), three-colored (*US*); tricolour(ed) (*Br.*), tricolor(ed) (*US*).
трёхчасово́й *adj.* **1** (*экзамен*) three-hour. **2** (*поезд*) three o'clock.
трёхъязы́чный *adj.* trilingual.
трёхэта́жный *adj.* three-storey (*Br.*), three-story (*US*).
трёшк|а, и *f.* (*coll.*) three-rouble note.
трещ|а́ть, у́, и́шь *impf.* **1** (*о льде*) to crack; **у меня́ голова́ ~и́т** I have a splitting headache; **т. по всем швам** (*fig.*) to go to pieces. **2** (*о дровах*) to crackle; (*о мебели*) to creak; (*о кузнечиках*) to chirr; **~а́т моро́зы** there is a hard frost. **3** (*coll.*) (*тараторить*) to jabber, chatter.
тре́щин|а, ы *f.* crack, split (*also fig.*); **дать ~у** to crack, split; (*fig.*) to show signs of cracking.
трещо́тк|а, и *f. and c.g.* **1** *f.* rattle. **2** *c.g.* (*fig., coll.*) chatterbox.
три, трёх, трём, тремя́, о трёх *num.* three.
триа́д|а, ы *f.* triad.
триангуля́ци|я, и *f.* (*math., geod.*) triangulation.
триа́совый *adj.* (*geol.*) Triassic.
трибу́н, а *m.* (*hist. or rhet.*) tribune.
трибу́н|а, ы *f.* **1** platform, rostrum. **2** (*на стадионах*) stand.
трибуна́л, а *m.* tribunal; **вое́нный т.** military tribunal.
тривиа́льност|ь, и *f.* triviality, banality.
тривиа́л|ьный (~ен, ~ьна) *adj.* trivial, banal; (*пошлый*) trite.
тригонометри́ческий *adj.* trigonometric(al).
тригономе́три|я, и *f.* trigonometry.
тридевя́т|ый *adj.*: **в ~ом ца́рстве** = **за три́девять земе́ль**
три́девять: **за т. земе́ль** (*in legends and fig., coll.*) at the other end of the world.
тридцатиле́ти|е, я *nt.* **1** (*срок*) thirty years. **2** (*годовщина*) thirtieth anniversary.
тридцатиле́тний *adj.* **1** (*срок*) thirty-year. **2** (*человек*) thirty-year-old.
тридца́т|ый *adj.* thirtieth; **~ые го́ды** the thirties.
три́дцат|ь, и́, *i.* **ью** *num.* thirty.
три́жды *adv.* three times, thrice.
тризм, а *m.* (*med.*) lockjaw, trismus.
три́зн|а, ы *f.* (*обряд*) funeral service; (*угощение*) funeral feast.
трико́ *nt. indecl.* **1** (*ткань*) tricot. **2** (*леотард*) leotard. **3** (*нижние штаны*) pants.
трико́вый *adj.* tricot.
трикота́ж, а *m.* **1** (*из шерсти*) jersey; (*из хлопка*) cotton jersey. **2** (*collect.*) (*изделия*) knitted wear, knitted garments.
трикота́жн|ый *adj.* (*шерстяной*) jersey; (*из хлопка*) knitted; **~ые изде́лия** knitted wear; **~ая фа́брика** knitted goods factory.
триктра́к, а *m.* backgammon.
трили́стник, а *m.* (*bot.*) trefoil.
три́ллер, а *m.* thriller.
триллио́н, а *m.* trillion.
трило́ги|я, и *f.* trilogy.
тримара́н, а *m.* (*трёхкорпусное судно*) trimaran.
триме́стр, а *m.* term (*at educational establishment*).
тринадцатиле́тний *adj.* **1** (*срок*) thirteen year. **2** (*ребёнок*) thirteen-year-old.
трина́дцатый *adj.* thirteenth.
трина́дцат|ь, и *num.* thirteen.
три́о *nt. indecl.* (*mus.*) trio.
трио́д, а *m.* (*electronics*) triode.
трио́л|ь, и *f.* (*mus.*) triplet.
Три́поли *m. indecl.* Tripoli.
три́ппер, а *m.* (*med.*) gonorrhoea (*Br.*), gonorrhea (*US*).
три́птих, а *m.* triptych.
три́ста, трёхсо́т, трёмста́м, тремяста́ми, трёхста́х *num.* three hundred.
трито́н, а *m.* (*zool.*) newt.
триумвира́т, а *m.* triumvirate.
триу́мф, а *m.* triumph; **с ~ом** triumphantly, in triumph.
триумфа́льн|ый *adj.* triumphal; **~ая а́рка** triumphal arch.
триумфа́тор, а *m.* victor.
тро́гател|ьный (~ен, ~ьна) *adj.* touching; moving, affecting.
тро́га|ть[1], ю *impf.* (*of* ⇨**тро́нуть**) **1** (*прикасаться*) to touch. **2** (*беспокоить*) to disturb, trouble; **не ~й его́!** don't disturb him!; leave him alone! **3** (*волновать*) to touch, move, affect; **т. до слёз** to move to tears.
тро́га|ть[2], ю *impf.* (*of* ⇨**тро́нуть**) (*coll.*) to start; **ну ~й!** go ahead!; get going!
тро́га|ться[1], юсь *impf.* (*of* ⇨**тро́нуться[1]**) to be touched, be moved, be affected.
тро́га|ться[2], юсь *impf. of* ⇨**тро́нуться[2]**
троглоди́т, а *m.* troglodyte (*also fig. of a person*).
тро́е, трои́х *num.* (*preceding m. nn. denoting living beings and pluralia tantum*) three; **т. су́ток** seventy-two hours, three days and three nights; **т. но́жниц** three pairs of scissors; **т. друзе́й** three friends; **т. брюк** three pairs of trousers.
троебо́рь|е, я *nt.* (*sport*) triathlon.
троекра́тный *adj.* (*вызов*) thrice-repeated; (*чемпион*) three-times; (*штраф*) trebled.
троепе́рсти|е, я *nt.* (*eccl.*) making the sign of the cross with three fingers.
тро́ечник, а *m.* mediocre student.
тро́ечный *adj.* mediocre.
Тро́иц|а, ы *f.* **1** (*theol.*) Trinity. **2** (*eccl.*) Trinity; Whitsun(day). **3** (*coll.*) trio.
Тро́ицын *adj.*: **Т. день** Trinity; Whitsun(day).
тро́йк|а, и *f.* **1** (*цифра*) three. **2** (*отметка*) three (*out of five*). **3** (*cards*) three. **4** (*упряжка*) troika. **5** (*костюм*) three-piece suit. **6** (*coll.*) (*автобус, трамвай*) No. 3 (*bus, tram, etc.*). **7** (*три человека*) threesome.
тройни́к, а́ *m.* **1** (*elec.*) three-way adaptor. **2** (*tech.*) T-joint, T-pipe, T-bend.
тройн|о́й *adj.* triple, threefold, treble; **т. кана́т** three-ply rope; **т. прыжо́к** triple jump; **в ~о́м разме́ре** threefold, treble.
тро́йн|я, и *f.* triplets.
тро́йственный *adj.* triple; (*соглашение*) tripartite.
тройча́тк|а, и *f.* (*coll.*) mild painkiller (*consisting of three ingredients*).
тролле́йбус, а *m.* trolleybus.
тролле́йбус|ный *adj. of* ⇨**~**
тромб, а *m.* (*med.*) clot of blood.
тромбо́з, а *m.* (*med.*) thrombosis.
тромбо́н, а *m.* trombone.
тромбони́ст, а *m.* trombonist.
трон, а *m.* throne.
тро́н|ный *adj. of* ⇨**~**; **т. зал** throne-room; (*parl.*): **~ная речь** King's *or* Queen's speech.
тро́|нуть, ну, нешь *pf. of* ⇨**~гать**
тро́|нуться[1], нусь, нешься *pf.* **1** *pf. of* ⇨**~гаться[1]**. **2** (*pf. only*) (*fig., coll.*) to be touched (= *to lose one's mind*); **он немно́го ~нулся** he is a bit touched, he is a bit cracked.
тро́|нуться[2], нусь, нешься *pf.* (*of*

⇨~**гаться²**) **1** (*двинуться с места*) to start, set out; **т. с ме́ста** to make a move, get going; **по́езд ~нулся** the train started; **лёд ~нулся** the ice has begun to break (*also fig.*). **2** (*coll.*) (*испортиться*) to go bad.

троп, а *m.* (*liter.*) trope.

троп|а́, ы́, *pl.* **~ы, ~, ~а́м** *f.* path.

тропа́р|ь, я́ *m.* (*eccl.*) anthem (*for festival or saint's day*); troparion.

тро́пик, а *m.* (*geog.*) **1** tropic; **т. Ра́ка** tropic of Cancer; **т. Козеро́га** tropic of Capricorn. **2** (*pl.*) the tropics.

тропи́нк|а, и *f.* path.

тропи́ческ|ий *adj.* tropical; **~ая лихора́дка** jungle fever; **т. по́яс** torrid zone.

тропосфе́р|а, ы *f.* (*meteor.*) troposphere.

трос, а *m.* rope, cable, hawser.

трости́нк|а, и *f.* thin reed.

тростни́к, а́ *m.* reed; **са́харный т.** sugar-cane.

тростнико́вый *adj.* reed; **т. са́хар** cane-sugar.

тро́сточк|а, и *f.* = **трость**

трост|ь, и, *pl.* **~и, ~е́й** *f.* cane, walking-stick.

троти́л, а *m.* (*chem., mil.*) trinitrotoluene (*abbr.* TNT).

тротуа́р, а *m.* pavement.

трофе́|й, я *m.* trophy (*also fig.*); (*pl.*) spoils of war, booty.

трофе́йный *adj.* (*mil.*) captured.

трохеи́ческий *adj.* (*liter.*) trochaic.

трохе́|й, я *m.* (*liter.*) trochee.

троцки́зм, а *m.* Trotskyism.

троцки́ст, а *m.* Trotskyite, Trotskyist.

троцки́ст|ка, ки *f. of* ⇨~

троцки́стский *adj.* Trotskyite, Trotskyist.

трою́родн|ый *adj.*: **т. брат, ~ая сестра́** second cousin; **т. племя́нник** second cousin once removed (*son of second cousin*).

тро́який *adj.* threefold, triple.

тро́яко *adv.* in three (different) ways.

троя́нский *adj.*: **т. конь** Trojan horse.

труб|а́, ы́, *pl.* **~ы** *f.* **1** pipe; **т. орга́на** organ-pipe; **водопрово́дная т.** water pipe; **водосто́чная т.** drainpipe; **канализацио́нная т.** sewage pipe; **подзо́рная т.** telescope. **2** (*дымовая, заводская*) chimney; (*парохода*) funnel, smoke-stack. **3** (*mus.*) trumpet; **игра́ть на ~е́** to play the trumpet. **4** (*anat.*) tube; duct. **5** (*беда, гибель*): **де́ло т.** (*coll.*) things are in a bad way; it's a wash-out; **вы́лететь в ~у́** (*coll.*) to go bust; **пусти́ть в ~у́** to blow, squander.

трубаду́р, а *m.* troubadour.

труба́ч, а́ *m.* trumpeter, trumpet-player.

труб|и́ть, лю́, и́шь *impf.* **1** (**в**+*a.*; *mus.*) to blow. **2** (*о трубах*) to sound; to blare. **3** (*давать сигнал*) to sound (*by blast of trumpet, etc.*); **т. сбор** (*mil.*) to sound assembly. **4** (**о**+*p.*; *coll.*) (*разглашать*) to trumpet, proclaim from the housetops.

тру́бк|а, и *f.* **1** tube; pipe; (*свёрток*) roll; **сверну́ть ~ой** to roll up. **2** (*курительная*) (tobacco-)pipe; **наби́ть ~у** to fill a pipe. **3** (*зажигательная*) fuse (*Br.*), fuze (*US*). **4** (*телефона*) receiver; **взять, подня́ть ~у** to answer the phone.

трубкозу́б, а *m.* (*zool.*) aardvark.

тру́бный *adj.* trumpet; **т. сигна́л** trumpet-call.

труболите́йный *adj.* pipe-casting, tube-casting.

трубопрово́д, а *m.* pipe-line.

трубопрока́тный *adj.* (*tech.*) tube-rolling.

трубочи́ст, а *m.* chimney-sweep.

тру́бочный *adj. of* ⇨**тру́бка; т. таба́к** pipe tobacco.

тру́бчатый *adj.* tubular.

труве́р, а *m.* (*hist., liter.*) trouvère.

труд, а́ *m.* **1** (*работа*) labour (*Br.*), labor (*US*), work. **2** (*трудность*) difficulty, trouble; **взять на себя́ т., дать себе́ т.** (+*inf.*) to take the trouble (to); **не сто́ит ~а́** it is not worth the trouble; **с ~о́м** with difficulty; **без ~а́** without difficulty. **3** (*произведение*) (scholarly) work; (*pl.*) (*издание*) transactions.

тру|ди́ться, жу́сь, ~дишься *impf.* (**над**+*i.*) to toil (over), labour (*Br.*), labor (*US*) (over), work (on); **не ~ди́тесь!** (please) don't trouble.

тру́дно *as pred.* it is hard, it is difficult; **т. сказа́ть** it is hard to say; **мне т.** I find it difficult; **мне т. суди́ть** it is hard for me to tell; **э́ту кни́гу т. чита́ть** this book is difficult to read; **ему́ т. прихо́дится** he has a hard time.

трудновоспиту́ем|ый (~, ~а) *adj.* **т. ребёнок** difficult child.

труднодосту́п|ный (~ен, ~на) *adj.* difficult to gain access to.

труднопроходи́м|ый (~, ~а) *adj.* difficult (to traverse).

тру́дност|ь, и *f.* difficulty; (*препятствие*) obstacle.

тру́д|ный (~ен, ~на́, ~но) *adj.* **1** difficult, hard; (*изнурительный*) arduous; **в ~ную мину́ту** in a time of need. **2** (*человек*) difficult, awkward. **3** (*случай*) serious, grave; **т. больно́й** seriously ill patient.

трудов|о́й *adj.* **1** labour (*Br.*), labor (*US*), work; **т. день** working day; **~ое законода́тельство** labour (*Br.*), labor (*US*) legislation; **~а́я кни́жка** work-book, work record; **т. коллекти́в** work force; **~ы́е отноше́ния** working relations; **т. стаж** length of service. **2** (*работающий*) working; living on one's own earnings; **т. наро́д** working people. **3** (*полученный трудом*) earned; hard-earned.

трудого́лик, а *m.* (*coll.*) workaholic.

трудод|е́нь, ня́ *m.* (*hist.*) work-day (*unit of payment on collective farms*).

трудоём|кий (~ок, ~ка) *adj.* labour-intensive (*Br.*), labor-intensive (*US*).

трудолюби́в|ый (~, ~а) *adj.* hard-working, industrious.

трудолю́би|е, я *nt.* industry; liking for hard work.

трудосберега́ющий *adj.* labour-saving (*Br.*), labor-saving (*US*).

трудоспосо́бност|ь, и *f.* ability to work.

трудоспосо́б|ный (~ен, ~на) *adj.* able-bodied; capable of working.

трудотерапи́|я, и *f.* occupational therapy.

трудоустра́ива|ть, ю *impf. of* ⇨**трудоустро́ить**

трудоустро́|ить, ю, ишь *pf.* (*of* ⇨**трудоустра́ивать**) to find employment for, place in a job.

трудоустро́йств|о, а *nt.* placement in a job.

труд|я́щийся *pres. part. of* ⇨**~и́ться** *and adj.* working; *as n.* **~я́щиеся, ~я́щихся** working people, the workers.

тру́женик, а *m.* (*многоработающий*) toiler; (+*g.*) worker, employee.

тру́жени|ца, цы *f. of* ⇨**~к**

тру́жени|ческий *adj. of* ⇨**~к; ~ческая жизнь** life of toil.

трун|и́ть, ю́, и́шь *impf.* (**над**+*i.*; *coll.*) to make fun (of), mock.

труп, а *m.* dead body, corpse; (*животного*) carcass; **то́лько че́рез мой т.** over my dead body.

тру́п|ный *adj. of* ⇨~; **т. за́пах** putrid smell; **~ное разложе́ние** putrefaction; **т. яд** ptomaine.

тру́пп|а, ы *f.* company.

трус, а *m.* coward; **~а пра́здновать** (*coll.*) to show the white feather.

тру́сик|и, ов *no sg.* **1** (*шорты*) shorts. **2** (*плавки*) swimming trunks. **3** (*бельё*) (under)pants; (*женские*) knickers (*Br.*), panties.

тру́|сить, шу, сишь *impf.* (*of* ⇨**с~**) **1** to be a coward; to get cold feet. **2** (**пе́ред**+*i. or* +*a.*) to be afraid (of), be frightened (of).

тру|си́ть¹, шу́, си́шь *impf.* (*сыпать*) to shake out, scatter.

тру|си́ть², шу́, си́шь *impf.* (*бежать рысцой*) to trot, jog.

труси́х|а, и *f.* (*coll.*) *of* ⇨**трус**

трусли́в|ый (~, ~а) *adj.* cowardly.

тру́сост|ь, и *f.* cowardice.

трусц|а́, ы́ *f.* (*coll.*) jog-trot; **бег ~о́й** (*sport*) jogging.

трус|ы́, о́в *no sg.* = **~ики**

трут, а *m.* tinder.

тру́т|ень, ня *m.* (*zool.*) drone; (*fig.*) parasite.

трутови́к, а́ *m.* polyporus, tree-fungus.

трух|а́, и́ *f.* dust (*of rotted wood*); (*fig.*) (*о чём-н. никчёмном*) rubbish.

трухля́в|ый (~, ~а) *adj.* mouldering (*Br.*), moldering (*US*); rotten.

трущо́б|а, ы *f.* **1** (*заросшее место*) overgrown place (*in forest, etc.*). **2** (*fig.*) (*глушь*) hole, out-of-the-way place. **3** (*жильё, район*) slum.

трын-трава́ *as pred.* (+*d.*; *coll.*) it makes no odds; it's all the same; **ему́ т.** it's all the same to him.

трюи́зм, а *m.* truism.

трюк, а *m.* **1** (*акробатический*) feat; (*каскадёра*) stunt; **рекла́мный т.**

advertising gimmick. **2** (*fig., pej.*) (*проделка*) trick.

трюка́ч, á *m.* **1** stuntman. **2** (*мошенник*) trickster.

трюка́чес|кий *adj. of* **⇒~тво; т. приём** crafty trick, stunt.

трюка́честв|о, а *nt.* (*pej.*) craft, wiliness.

трю́к|овый *adj. of* **⇒~ 1; т. но́мер** turn.

трюм, а *m.* (*naut.*) hold.

трю́м|ный *adj. of* **⇒~; ~ная вода́** bilge-water.

трюмо́ *nt. indecl.* cheval-glass, pier-glass.

трю́фел|ь, я, *pl.* **~и, ~е́й** *m.* truffle.

тряпи́чник, а *m.* (*obs.*) ragman; rag-picker.

тряпи́чный *adj.* **1** (*куклы, коврик*) rag. **2** (*coll., pej.*) (*бесхарактерный*) soft, spineless.

тря́пк|а, и *f.* **1** rag; (*для пыли*) duster. **2** (*pl., coll.*) (*одежда*) finery, clothes. **3** (*coll., pej.*) (*человек*) milksop, spineless creature.

тряпь|ё, я́ *nt.* (*collect.*) rags.

трясин|а, ы *f.* quagmire.

тря́ск|а, и *f.* shaking, jolting.

тря́с|кий (~ок, ~ка) *adj.* **1** (*вагон*) shaky, jolty. **2** (*дорога*) bumpy.

трясогу́зк|а, и *f.* (*zool.*) wagtail.

тряс|ти́, у́, ёшь, *past* **~, ~ла́** *impf.* **1** to shake; **т. кому́-н. ру́ку** to shake s.o.'s hand. **2** (*ковёр; крошки*) to shake out. **3** (*о дрожи*) to cause to shake, cause to shiver (*usu. impers.*); **его́ ~ла́ лихора́дка** he was in the grip of a fever; **её ~по́ от стра́ха** she was trembling with fear. **4** (+*i.*) (*головой, кулаком*) to shake; **т. гри́вой** to toss its mane. **5** (*о вагоне*) to jolt, be jolty; (*impers.*): **в авто́бусе ~ёт** the bus is jolting.

тряс|ти́сь, у́сь, ёшься, *past* **~ся, ~ла́сь** *impf.* **1** to shake; to tremble, shiver; **т. от сме́ха** to shake with laughter; **т. от хо́лода** to shiver with cold. **2** (**за**+*a.*) (*опасаться*) to worry about. **3** (**пе́ред**+*i.*) (*бояться*) to tremble before, dread. **4** (*coll.*) (*ехать*) to bump along, jog along; (*в машине, поезде*) to be jolted. **5** (**над**+*i.*; *coll.*) (*бояться потерять*) to watch (over) (= *to fear to lose*); **они́ ~у́тся над ка́ждой копе́йкой** they watch every penny; (*оберегать*) to dote (up)on.

тряхн|у́ть, у́, ёшь *pf.* **1** to shake; (*в машине*) to give a jolt. **2**: **т. старино́й** (*coll.*) to hark back to the (good) old days; **т. мо́лодостью** (*coll.*) to behave as if one were still young. **3** (+*i.*; *coll.*) (*деньгами, кошельком*) to make free (with).

тсс *int.* ssh!; (s)hush!

тт. *abbr. of* **1** ***това́рищи*** Comrades. **2** ***тома́*** vols; volumes.

туале́т, а *m.* **1** (*наряд*) dress; attire. **2** (*одевание*) toilet, dressing; **соверша́ть т.** to make one's toilet, dress. **3** (*столик*) dressing-table. **4** (*уборная*) lavatory, toilet.

туале́т|ный *adj. of* **⇒~; ~ная бума́га** toilet-paper; **~ное мы́ло** toilet-soap; **~ные принадле́жности** toiletries; **т. сто́лик** dressing-table.

ту́б|а[1]**, ы** *f.* (*mus.*) tuba.

ту́б|а[2]**, ы** *f.* (*большой тюбик*) tube.

туберкулёз, а *m.* tuberculosis; **т. лёгких** pulmonary tuberculosis, consumption.

туберкулёз|ный *adj. of* **⇒~; т. больно́й** tubercular (patient); *as n.* **т., ~ного** *m.* = **т. больно́й**

тубеpо́з|а, ы *f.* (*bot.*) tuberose.

ту́го *adv.* **1** tight(ly), taut; **т. наби́ть чемода́н** to pack a suitcase tight. **2** (*с трудом*) with difficulty; **т. продвига́ться вперёд** to make slow progress. **3** *as pred.* (*о трудностях*) it's hard, it's difficult; **мне т. прихо́дится** I'm having a rough time; (**с**+*i.*) to be hard-pressed for; **с деньга́ми у нас т.** we are hard-pressed for money.

тугоду́м, а *m.* (*coll.*) slow-witted person, blockhead.

туг|о́й (~, ~á, ~о) *adj.* **1** (*узел, воротничок*) tight; (*струна, пружина*) taut. **2** (*плотно набитый*) tightly-filled; **т. кошелёк** tightly-stuffed purse. **3** (*о способностях; о темпах*) slow. **4**: **т. на́ ухо** hard of hearing. **5** (*fig., coll.*) (**на**+*a.*) (*несклонный*) disinclined, unresponsive. **6** (*fig., coll.*) (*трудный*) difficult.

тугопла́в|кий (~ок, ~ка) *adj* (*tech.*) refractory.

туда́ *adv.* there; (*в ту сторону*) that way; (*куда нужно*) to the right place; **т. и обра́тно** there and back; **биле́т т. и обра́тно** return ticket; **не т.!** not that way!; **ни т. ни сюда́** neither one way nor the other; **то т., то сюда́** back and forth; **вы не т. попа́ли** (*по телефону*) you have got the wrong number; **т. ему́ и доро́га** (*coll.*) it serves him right.

туда́-сюда́ *adv.* (*coll.*) **1** hither and thither. **2** *as pred.* (*сносно*) it will do, it will pass muster.

ту́|евый *adj. of* **⇒~я**

ту́же *comp. of* **⇒туго́й** *and* **ту́го**

туж|и́ть, у́, ~ишь *impf.* (**о, по**+*p.*; *coll.*) to grieve (for).

ту́ж|иться, усь, ишься *impf.* (*coll.*) to make an effort.

тужу́рк|а, и *f.* (*man's*) double-breasted jacket.

туз, á *m.* **1** (*cards*) ace; **ходи́ть ~ом** to play an ace. **2** (*coll.*) bigwig; big shot.

тузе́м|ец, ца *m.* native.

тузе́м|ка, ки *f. of* **⇒~ец**

тузе́мный *adj.* native, indigenous.

ту|зи́ть, жу́, зи́шь *impf.* (*of* **⇒от~**) (*coll.*) to punch; to pummel.

ту́к|ать, аю *impf.* (*of* **⇒~нуть**) (*coll.*) to tap, knock.

ту́к|нуть, ну, нешь *pf. of* **⇒~ать**

тук-ту́к *int.* (*coll.*) rat-tat (*also as pred.*).

ту́ловищ|е, а *nt.* trunk; torso.

тулу́п, а *m.* sheepskin coat.

тул|ья́, ьи́, *g. pl.* **~е́й** *f.* crown (*of headgear*).

тума́к, á *m.* (*coll.*) cuff, punch.

тума́н, а *m.* fog; mist, haze; (*дыма, пыли*) haze; (*в голове*) fog, haze; **как в ~е** in a daze.

тума́н|ить, ит *impf.* to dim, cloud, obscure (*also fig.*).

тума́н|иться, ится *impf.* **1** to grow misty; to become enveloped in mist. **2** (*fig., coll.*) (*о сознании*) to be in a fog; (*о лице*) to cloud over.

тума́нно *as pred.* it is foggy, it is misty; **в голове́ у него́ бы́ло т.** his mind was in a fog.

тума́нност|ь, и *f.* **1** fog, mist. **2** (*astron.*) nebula. **3** (*неясность*) haziness, obscurity.

тума́н|ный (~ен, ~на) *adj.* **1** foggy; misty; hazy; **~ная полоса́** fog patch. **2** (*fig.*) (*тусклый*) dull, lacklustre (*Br.*), lackluster (*US*). **3** (*fig.*) (*неясный*) hazy, obscure, vague. **4** (*obs.*): **~ные карти́ны** (magic) lantern slides.

ту́мб|а, ы *f.* **1** (*столб*) bollard. **2** (*подставка*) pedestal. **3** (*афишная*) advertisement hoarding (*of cylindrical shape*). **4** (*fig., joc.*) (*о человеке*) lump.

ту́мблер, а *m.* toggle (switch).

ту́мбочк|а, и *f.* **1** bedside table, night table (*US*). **2** *dim. of* **⇒ту́мба**

ту́ндр|а, ы *f.* (*geog.*) tundra.

ту́ндр|овый *adj. of* **⇒~а**

тун|е́ц, ца́ *m.* tunny(-fish).

туне́яд|ец, ца *m.* parasite, sponger.

туне́ядств|о, а *nt.* parasitism, sponging.

туни́к|а, и *f.* **1** (*в Древнем Риме*) tunic. **2** (*танцовщицы*) ballerina's dress.

Туни́с, а *m.* **1** (*страна*) Tunisia. **2** (*город*) Tunis.

туни́с|ец, ца *m.* Tunisian.

туни́с|ка, ки *f. of* **⇒~ец**

туни́сский *adj.* Tunisian.

тунне́л|ь, я *m.* tunnel; (*пешеходный*) subway.

тунне́ль|ный *adj. of* **⇒~**

тупе́|ть, ю *impf.* (*of* **⇒о~**) (*о ноже*) to become blunt; (*об уме, взгляде*) to grow dull; (*о человеке*) to become stupid.

ту́пик, а *m.* (*zool.*) puffin.

тупи́к, á *m.* **1** blind alley, cul-de-sac. **2** (*rail.*) siding. **3** (*fig.*) (*безвыходное положение*) impasse, deadlock; **зайти́ в т.** to reach a deadlock. **4**: **поста́вить в т.** to stump, nonplus; **стать в т.** to be stumped, be nonplussed, be at a loss.

тупико́вый *adj.* (*ситуация*) dead-end; (*станция*) at the end of the line.

туп|и́ть, лю́, ~ишь *impf.* (*pf.* **ис~**) to blunt.

туп|и́ться, ~ится *impf.* (*pf.* **ис~**) to become blunt.

тупи́ц|а, ы *c.g.* (*coll.*) dolt, blockhead, dimwit.

тупоголо́в|ый (~, ~а) *adj.* (*coll.*) dim-witted.

туп|о́й (~, ~á, ~о) *adj.* **1** (*нож*) blunt. **2**: **т. у́гол** (*math.*) obtuse angle. **3** (*fig.*) (*боль, чувство*) dull. **4** (*fig.*) (*взгляд, улыбка*) vacant, stupid. **5** (*fig.*) (*человек, ум*) dull, obtuse; slow; dim. **6** (*fig.*) blind; (*безропотный*) unquestioning; **~а́я поко́рность** blind submission.

ту́пост|ь, и *f.* **1** (*ножа*) bluntness. **2** (*fig.*) (*взгляда*) vacancy. **3** (*fig.*) (*ума*) dullness, slowness.

тупоу́ми|е, я *nt.* dullness, obtuseness.

Т

тупоу́м|ный (~ен, ~на) *adj.* dull, obtuse.

тур[1], а *m.* **1** (*танца*) turn (*in a dance*). **2** (*турнира, выборов*) round. **3** (*артиста*) tour.

тур[2], а *m.* (*zool.*) **1** (*вымерший дикий бык*) aurochs. **2** (*козёл*) Caucasian goat (*Capra caucasia*).

тур|а́, ы́ *f.* (*chess*) castle, rook.

тураге́нт, а *m.* travel agent.

тураге́нтств|о, а *nt.* travel agency.

турба́з|а, ы *f.* tourist centre (*Br.*), center (*US*).

турби́н|а, ы *f.* (*tech.*) turbine.

турби́нный *adj.* turbine.

турбовинтово́й *adj.* (*tech., aeron.*) turbo-prop.

турбово́з, а *m.* turbine locomotive.

турбогенера́тор, а *m.* (*tech.*) turbo-alternator.

турбореакти́вный *adj.* (*tech., aeron.*) turbo-jet.

туре́цк|ий *adj.* Turkish; **т. бараба́н** bass drum; **~ие бобы́** haricot beans; **т. горо́х** chick pea; **т. язы́к** Turkish, the Turkish language.

тури́зм, а *m.* (*путешествия*) tourism; (*спорт*) hiking; **во́дный т.** boating; **го́рный т.** mountain walking.

тури́ст, а *m.* tourist; (*в походах*) hiker.

туристи́ческ|ий *adj.* tourist; **~ое аге́нтство** travel agency; **т. похо́д** hiking tour.

тури́ст|ка, ки *f. of* ⇒**~**

тури́стск|ий *adj.* tourist; **~ая ба́за** tourist centre (*Br.*), center (*US*).

тур|и́ть, ю, и́шь *impf.* (*coll.*) to throw out, chuck out.

туркме́н, а, *g. pl.* **т.** *m.* Turkmen.

Туркмениста́н, а *m.* Turkmenistan.

туркме́н|ка, ки *f. of* ⇒**~**

туркме́нский *adj.* Turkmen.

ту́рман, а *m.* tumbler-pigeon.

турне́ *nt. indecl.* tour (*esp. of artistes or sportsmen*).

турне́пс, а *m.* turnip.

турни́к, а́ *m.* (*sport*) horizontal bar.

турнике́т, а *m.* **1** turnstile. **2** (*med.*) tourniquet.

турни́р, а *m.* tournament (*at chess, etc., also hist.*).

турн|у́ть, у́, ёшь *pf.* (*coll.*) to chuck out.

турню́р, а *m.* bustle.

ту́р|ок, ка, *g. pl.* **т.** *m.* Turk.

турпа́н, а *m.* (*zool.*) scoter.

туру́с|ы, ов *no sg.* (*coll.*) idle gossip.

турухта́н, а *m.* (*zool.*) ruff (*Philomachus pugnax*).

Ту́рци|я, и *f.* Turkey.

тур|ча́нка, ча́нки *f. of* ⇒**~ок**

ту́скл|ый (~, ~а́, ~о) *adj.* **1** (*свет*) dim, dull; (*стекло*) opaque; (*металл*) tarnished; (*краска, лак*) matt. **2** (*fig.*) (*взгляд, глаза; стиль*) dull, lacklustre (*Br.*), lackluster (*US*).

тусќне|ть, ет *impf.* (*of* ⇒**по~**) **1** (*о свете*) to grow dim; (*о красках, взгляде*) to become dull; (*о металле, зеркале*) to tarnish; (*о таланте, стиле*) to lose its lustre (*Br.*), luster (*US*). **2** (**пе́ред** + *i.*; *fig.*) to pale (before, by the side of).

тус|ова́ться, у́юсь *impf.* (*coll.*) to get together, meet, hang out.

тусо́вк|а, и *f.* (*coll.*) get-together; (*место*) meeting place, hang-out.

тусо́в|очный *adj. of* ⇒**~ка**

тусо́вщик, а *m.* (*sl.*) party-goer, good-timer.

тусо́вщи|ца, цы *f. of* ⇒**~к**

тут *adv.* **1** here; **кто т.?** who's there?; **и всё т.** (*coll.*) and that's it, and that was that; **т. как т.** (*coll.*) there he is, there they are. **2** (*о времени*) now; **т. же** there and then.

ту́т|а, ы *f.* mulberry (tree).

ту́товник, а *m.* **1** mulberry (tree). **2** mulberry grove.

ту́тов|ый *adj.* mulberry; **~ое де́рево** mulberry (tree); **т. шелкопря́д** silkworm.

ту́т-то *adv.* (*coll.*) **1** right here. **2** (*о времени*) there and then. **3**: **не т.-то бы́ло!** nothing of the sort!; far from it!

туф, а *m.* (*geol., min.*) tufa; tuff.

ту́фл|я, и *f.* shoe.

туфт|а́, ы́ *f.* (*sl.*) rubbish, garbage, crap.

туфт|о́вый *adj. of* ⇒**~а́**

ту́хл|ый (~, ~а́, ~о) *adj.* rotten, bad.

тухля́тин|а, ы *f.* (*coll.*) rotten food.

ту́х|нуть[1], нет, *past* **~, ~ла** *impf.* (*of* ⇒**по~**) (*огонь*) to go out; (*взгляд, глаза*) to become dull.

ту́х|нуть[2], нет, *past* **~, ~ла** *impf.* (*загнивать*) to go bad, become rotten.

ту́ч|а, и *f.* **1** (rain) cloud; storm cloud (*also fig.*); **не из ~и гром** a bolt from the blue; **~и собрали́сь, нави́сли** (**над** + *i.*) (*fig.*) the clouds are gathering (over); **он сего́дня как т.** he is in a black mood today. **2** (*пыли*) cloud; (*мух*) swarm.

ту́чк|а, и *f. dim. of* ⇒**ту́ча**

тучне́|ть, ю *impf.* (*of* ⇒**по~**) **1** (*о человеке*) to grow stout, grow fat. **2** (*о почве*) to become fertile.

ту́чност|ь, и *f.* **1** (*человека*) fatness, stoutness, obesity, corpulence. **2** (*почвы*) richness, fertility.

ту́ч|ный (~ен, ~на́, ~но) *adj.* **1** (*человек*) stout, obese, corpulent. **2** (*почва*) rich, fertile. **3** (*трава, луг*) succulent.

туш, а *m.* (*mus.*) flourish.

ту́ш|а, и *f.* **1** carcass. **2** (*fig., coll.*) (*человек*) hulk.

туше́ *nt. indecl.* **1** (*mus.*) touch. **2** (*fencing*) touché.

туш|ева́ть, у́ю *impf.* (*of* ⇒**за~**) **1** to shade. **2** (*fig.*) (*скрывать*) to conceal, disguise.

туш|ева́ться, у́юсь *impf.* (*of* ⇒**с~**) to get embarrassed.

тушёвк|а, и *f.* shading.

тушёнк|а, и *f.* (*coll.*) tinned meat (*Br.*), canned meat (*US*).

тушёный *adj.* (*cul.*) braised, stewed.

туш|и́ть[1], у́, ~́ишь *impf.* (*of* ⇒**по~**) **1** (*лампу, пожар*) to extinguish, put out. **2** (*fig.*) (*возбуждение, интерес*) to suppress, stifle, quell.

туш|и́ть[2], у́, ~́ишь *impf.* (*cul.*) to braise, stew.

тушка́нчик, а *m.* jerboa.

туш|ь, и *f.* Indian ink; **т. (для ресни́ц)** mascara.

ту́|я, и *f.* (*bot.*) thuya.

т/ф (*abbr. of* ***телефи́льм***) television film.

т/х (*abbr. of* ***теплохо́д***) steamship.

т.ч.: в ~ (*abbr. of* ***в том числе́***) incl., including.

тчк (*abbr. of* ***то́чка***) stop (*in telegram*).

тща́ни|е, я *nt.* (*obs.*) zeal, assiduity.

тща́тельност|ь, и *f.* thoroughness; care.

тща́тел|ьный (~ен, ~ьна) *adj.* thorough, careful; painstaking.

тщеду́ши|е, я *nt.* feebleness, frailty.

тщеду́ш|ный (~ен, ~на) *adj.* feeble, frail, weak.

тщесла́ви|е, я *nt.* vanity, vainglory.

тщесла́в|ный (~ен, ~на) *adj.* vain, vainglorious.

тщет|а́, ы́ *f.* futility, vanity.

тще́тно *adv.* vainly, in vain.

тще́тност|ь, и *f.* futility, vanity.

тще́т|ный (~ен, ~на) *adj.* vain, futile; unavailing.

тщ|и́ться, усь, и́шься *impf.* (+ *inf.*; *obs.*) to endeavour (*Br.*), endeavor (*US*), struggle (to).

ты, тебя́, тебе́, тобо́й (*and* **тобо́ю**), **о тебе́** *2nd pers. sg. pers. pron.* you; **быть 'на ты'** (**с** + *i*), **говори́ть 'ты'** (+ *d*) to be on familiar terms (with); (*для обобщения*) one, you; **ситуа́ция така́я сло́жная — ты не зна́ешь, что де́лать** it is a difficult situation — one doesn't know what to do; (*для усиления*): **ах ты, как стра́нно!** oh, how strange!

ты́|кать[1], чу, чешь *impf.* (*of* ⇒**ткнуть**) **1** (+ *i.* **в** + *a. or* + *a.* **в** + *a.*) to stick (into) (*also fig.*); to poke (into); to prod; to jab (into); **т. була́вкой во что-н.** to stick a pin into sth.; **т. па́лкой** to prod with a stick; **т. ко́лья в зе́млю** to stick stakes into the ground; **т. (свой) нос** (**в** + *a.*; *fig., pej.*) to stick, poke one's nose (into); **т. в нос кому́-н. чем-н.** (*fig., coll.*) to cast sth. in s.o.'s teeth; **т. кого́-н. но́сом во что-н.** (*fig., coll.*) to rub s.o.'s nose in sth. **2**: **т. па́льцем** (**на** + *a.*; *coll.*) to point (at), poke one's finger (at).

тыка|ть[2], ю *impf.* (*coll.*) to address as 'ты'; be on familiar terms (with).

ты́|каться, чусь, чешься *impf.* (*of* ⇒**ткну́ться**) (*coll.*) **1** (**в** + *a.*) to knock (against, into). **2** (*суетливо двигаться*) to rush about, fuss about.

ты́кв|а, ы *f.* pumpkin, gourd.

ты́кв|енный *adj. of* ⇒**~а**

тыл, а, о ~́е, в ~у́, *pl.* **~ы́** *m.* **1** back, rear. **2** (*mil.*) rear; home front; **напа́сть с ~́а** to attack in the rear. **3** (*pl.; mil.*) (*вспомогательные части*) rear services, rear organizations. **4** (*вся страна*) the (whole) country (*opp. front or frontier areas*), the interior.

тылови́к, á *m.* (*mil.*) man serving in the rear.

тылов|о́й *adj.* (*mil.*) rear; **~а́я часть** service element (*of unit*); **т. го́спиталь** base hospital.

ты́льн|ый *adj.* **1** back, rear; **~ая пове́рхность руки́** back of the hand. **2** (*mil.*) rear.

тын, а *m.* paling; palisade, stockade.

тыс. (*abbr. of* ***ты́сяча***) thousand.

ты́сяч|а, и, *i.* **~ей** *and* **~ью** *num. and n., f.* thousand; **в ~у раз** a thousand times (*also fig.*); **~и люде́й** thousands of people.

тысячеле́ти|е, я *nt.* **1** (*срок*) a thousand years; millennium. **2** (*годовщина*) thousandth anniversary.

тысячеле́тний *adj.* **1** (*период, годовщина*) thousand-year; millennial. **2** (*здание*) thousand-year-old.

ты́сячн|ый *adj.* **1** thousandth; *as n.* **~ая, ~ой** *f.* thousandth. **2** (*толпа, стадо*) of many thousands. **3** (*coll.*) (*шуба*) worth a thousand, many thousand roubles.

тычи́нк|а, и *f.* (*bot.*) stamen.

тыч|о́к, ка́ *m.* (*coll.*) **1** (*предмет*) sharp object sticking up. **2** (*удар*) hit, prod, jab.

тьм|а[1]**, ы** *no pl., f.* (*мрак*) darkness (*also fig.* = *ignorance*).

тьм|а[2]**, ы,** *g. pl.* **тем** *f.* (*coll.*) (*множество*) host, multitude; **т.-тьму́щая** countless multitudes.

тьфу *int.* (*coll.*) pah!; **т. про́пасть!** confound it!

тюбете́йк|а, и tyubeteyka (*embroidered skull-cap worn in Central Asia*).

тю́бик, а *m.* tube (*of toothpaste, etc.*).

ТЮЗ, а *m.* (*abbr. of* ***теа́тр ю́ного зри́теля***) youth theatre (*Br.*), theater (*US*).

тюк, á *m.* bale, package.

тю́к|ать, аю *impf.* (*of* ⇒**~нуть**) (*coll.*) to chop, hack.

тю́к|нуть, ну, нешь *pf. of* ⇒**~ать**

тю́левый *adj.* (*text.*) tulle.

тюле́невый *adj.* sealskin.

тюле́н|ий *adj. of* ⇒**~ь**

тюле́н|ь, я *m.* **1** (*zool.*) seal. **2** (*fig., coll.*) clumsy clot.

тюл|ь, я *m.* (*text.*) tulle.

тюльпа́н, а *m.* tulip.

тюльпа́н|ный *adj. of* ⇒**~**; **~ное де́рево** tulip-tree.

тюни́к, а *m.* (*obs.*) overskirt.

тюрба́н, а *m.* turban.

тюр|е́мный *adj. of* ⇒**~ьма́**; **~е́мное заключе́ние** imprisonment; **т. смотри́тель** (*obs.*) prison governor.

тюре́мщик, а *m.* (*coll.*) jailer; (*fig.*) (*угнетатель*) oppressor.

тю́ркский *adj.* (*ethnol., ling.*) Turkic.

тюр|ьма́, ьмы́, *pl.* **~ьмы, ~ем** *f.* **1** prison; jail; **заключи́ть, посади́ть в ~ьму́** to put into prison, jail; **сиде́ть в ~ьме́** to be in prison. **2** (*пребывание в тюрьме*) imprisonment.

тю́тельк|а, и *f.*: **т. в ~у** (*coll.*) to a T.

тю́тька|ться, юсь *impf.* (**с**+*i.*; *coll., pej.*) to nursemaid.

тю-тю́ *as pred.* (*coll., joc.*) it's all gone; we've (you've, they've) had it.

тютю́н, á *m.* (*dial.*) shag (tobacco).

тюфя́к, á *m.* **1** mattress (*filled with straw, hay, etc.*). **2** (*fig., coll.*) (*о человеке*) drip, wimp.

тя́вк|ать, аю *impf.* (*of* ⇒**~нуть**) to yap, yelp.

тя́вк|нуть, ну, нешь *pf. of* ⇒**~ать**

тяг, у *m.*: **дать, зада́ть ~у** (*coll.*) to take to one's heels.

тя́г|а, и *f.* **1** (*действие*) pulling; (*наземного транспорта*) traction; **на ко́нной ~е** horse-drawn. **2** (*collect.*) locomotives. **3** (*от воздушного транспорта*) thrust; (*стержень рычага*) rod. **4** (*в печи*) draught (*Br.*), draft (*US*); **регуля́тор ~и** damper. **5** (**к**+*d.*; *fig.*) (*влечение*) pull (towards), attraction (towards); (*стремление*) thirst (for), craving (for); (*склонность*) inclination (to, for); **т. к зна́ниям** thirst for knowledge.

тяга́|ться, юсь *impf.* (*of* ⇒**по~**) (**с**+*i.*) (*coll.*) to contend (with), vie (with), compete (with).

тяга́ч, á *m.* tractor (*for pulling train of trailers*).

тя́гл|о[1]**, а** *nt.* (*collect.*) (*рабочий скот*) draught (*Br.*), draft (*US*) animals.

тя́гл|о[2]**, а,** *g. pl.* **тя́гол** *nt.* (*hist.*) **1** (*налог*) tax. **2** (*семья*) household (*as unit for tax assessment*). **3** (*крепостная повинность*) dues (*corvée, quit-rent, etc.*). **4** (*участок земли*) strip of land (*worked by one household*).

тя́гловый[1] *adj.* = **тя́глый**

тя́гловый[2] *adj.* (*hist.*) taxed, liable to tax.

тя́глый *adj.* draught (*Br.*), draft (*US*) (*of cattle*).

тя́гов|ый *adj.* traction, tractive; **т. крюк** towing hook; **т. сте́ржень** drawbar; **~ая си́ла** tractive force.

тя́гост|ный (~ен, ~на) *adj.* **1** (*тяжёлый*) burdensome, onerous. **2** (*мучительный*) painful, distressing; **~ное зре́лище** painful spectacle.

тя́гост|ь, и *f.* **1** weight, burden; **быть кому́-н. в т.** to be a burden to s.o., weigh on s.o. **2** (*coll.*) (*усталость*) fatigue.

тягот|á, ы́, *pl.* **тя́готы** *f.* weight, burden.

тяготе́ни|е, я *nt.* **1** (*phys.*) gravity, gravitation; **зако́н (всеми́рного) ~я** law of gravity. **2** (**к**+*d.*) attraction (towards), taste (for); inclination (to, for); **т. к детекти́вам** taste for detective stories.

тяготе́|ть, ю *impf.* **1** (**к**+*d.*) (*phys.*) to gravitate (towards). **2** (**к**+*d.*) (*fig.*) to gravitate (towards), be drawn (by, towards), be attracted (by, towards). **3** (**над**+*i.*) to hang (over), threaten.

тяго|ти́ть, щу́, ти́шь *impf.* (*обременять*) to burden, be a burden (on, to); (*о мыслях, об обязанностях*) to lie heavy (on), oppress.

тяго|ти́ться, щу́сь, ти́шься *impf.* (+*i.*) to be weighed down, oppressed (by).

тягу́чест|ь, и *f.* **1** (*металла*) malleability. **2** (*жидкости*) viscosity.

тягу́ч|ий (~, ~а) *adj.* **1** (*металл*) malleable. **2** (*жидкость*) viscous. **3** (*fig.*) (*речь*) slow, leisurely, unhurried.

тягча́йш|ий *superl. of* ⇒**тя́жкий; ~ее преступле́ние** grave crime.

тя́жб|а, ы *f.* **1** (*судебное дело*) (civil) suit, lawsuit; litigation. **2** (*fig., coll.*) competition, rivalry.

тяжел|е́е *comp. of* ⇒**~ый** *and* **~о́**

тяжеле́|ть, ю *impf.* **1** (*становиться тяжелее*) to become heavier; (*толстеть*) to put on weight. **2** (*о глазах*) to become heavy with sleep.

тяжело́[1] *adv.* **1** heavily. **2** (*серьёзно*) seriously, gravely. **т. больно́й** seriously ill. **3** (*с трудом*) with difficulty.

тяжело́[2] *as pred.* **1** (*при поднятии*) it is heavy; (*трудно*) it is hard; **мне т. ходи́ть пешко́м** it's hard for me to walk; (*мучительно*) it is painful, it is distressing; **мне т. ду́мать об э́том** it's painful for me to think about it. **2**: **ему́,** *etc.*, **т.** (*о настроении*) he, *etc.*, feels miserable, wretched.

тяжелоатле́т, а *m.* (*штангист*) weight-lifter.

тяжелове́с, а *m.* (*sport*) heavyweight.

тяжелове́с|ный (~ен, ~на) *adj.* **1** heavily-loaded; **т. соста́в** heavy goods train. **2** (*fig., pej.*) (*стиль, язык*) heavy, ponderous, heavy-handed.

тяжелово́з, а *m.* **1** (*лошадь*) heavy draught-horse (*Br.*), draft-horse (*US*). **2** (*грузовик*) heavy lorry (*Br.*), truck (*US*).

тяжелоду́м, а *m.* (*coll.*) slow-witted person.

тяжёл|ый (~, ~а́) *adj.* **1** heavy; **т. чемода́н** heavy suitcase; **~ая артилле́рия** heavy artillery; **~ая атле́тика** (*sport*) weight-lifting; **спортсме́н ~ого ве́са** heavyweight; **~ое дыха́ние** heavy breathing; **~ая промы́шленность** heavy industry. **2** (*доставляющий беспокойство, неприятность*): **т. во́здух** close air; **т. за́пах** oppressive, strong smell; **~ая пи́ща** heavy, indigestible food. **3** (*трудный*) hard, difficult; **~ая зада́ча** hard task; **~ые ро́ды** difficult confinement. **4** (*медленный*) slow; **т. ум** slow brain, wits. **5** (*суровый*) heavy, severe; **~ые поте́ри** heavy casualties; **~ое наказа́ние** severe punishment; **т. уда́р** severe blow. **6** (*серьёзный*) serious, grave, bad; **~ое ране́ние** serious injury; **т. больно́й** seriously ill patient. **7** (*горестный*) heavy, hard, painful; **с ~ым се́рдцем** with a heavy heart; **~ое чу́вство** heavy heart; misgivings; **~ые времена́** hard times; **~ая обя́занность** painful duty; **т. день** bad, hard day. **8** (*характер*) difficult. **9** (*стиль*) heavy, ponderous, unwieldy.

тя́жест|ь, и *f.* **1** (*phys.*) gravity; **центр ~и** centre of gravity (*also fig.*). **2** (*тяжёлый предмет*) weight, heavy object; **подня́тие ~ей** (*sport*) weight-lifting. **3** (*вес*) weight, heaviness; **вся т.**

чего́-н. (*fig.*) the whole weight, the brunt of sth.; **т. ули́к** weight of evidence.
4 (*трудность*) difficulty.
5 (*суровость*) heaviness, severity.
6 (*что-н. обременительное*) burden.

тя́ж|кий (~ек, ~ка́, ~ко) *adj.*
1 (*fig.*) (*доля, судьба*) heavy, hard.
2 (*суровый*) severe; (*серьёзный*) serious, grave; **~кая боле́знь** dangerous illness; **~кое преступле́ние** grave crime, felony; **т. уда́р** severe blow.
3: **пусти́ться во все ~кие** (*coll.*) (*о пороках*) to plunge into dissipation.

тяжкоду́м, а *m.* (*coll.*) slow-witted person, blockhead.

тя́жущийся *adj.* litigant.

тян|у́ть, у́, ~́ешь *impf.* **1** (*невод*) to pull, draw; to haul; to drag; **т. на букси́ре** to tow; **т. кого́-н. за рука́в** to tug at s.o.'s sleeve; (*руку, шею*) to stretch out; **т. ру́ку к**+*d.* to reach out for, towards; **кто тебя́ ~у́л за язы́к?** who made you speak up?
2 (*tech.*) (*проволоку*) to draw.
3 (*прокладывать*) to lay; **т. телефо́нную ли́нию** to lay a telephone cable.
4: **т. жре́бий** to draw lots.
5 (*fig.*) (*влечь*) to draw, attract; **меня́,** *etc.* **~́ет** I, *etc.* long, I, *etc.* want; **его́ ~́ет домо́й** he wants to go home; **меня́ ~́ет ко сну** I feel sleepy; **меня́ ~́ет купа́ться** I'm dying for a swim.
6 (*произносить*) to drawl, drag out; **т. слова́** to drawl; **т. но́ту** to sustain a note.
7 (*медлить*) to drag out, protract, delay; **т. с отве́том** to delay one's answer.
8 (*весить*) to weigh (*intrans.*).
9 (*всасывать*) to draw up; to take in, suck in; **т. в себя́ во́здух** to inhale deeply; **т. че́рез соло́минку** to suck through a straw.
10 (**из, с**+*g.*) to extract (from); to extort (from); **т. все си́лы из кого́-н.** to exhaust all the strength from s.o.
11 (*о трубе*) to draw; **пе́чь пло́хо ~́ет** the stove is not drawing well.
12 (*распространяться*) *impers.*, +*i.*: **из-под две́ри ~́ет хо́лодом** there is a draught (*Br.*), draft (*US*) coming under the door; **с поле́й ~у́ло за́пахом се́на** a smell of hay wafted from the fields.
13 (*usu. impers.*) (*причинять боль*) to press, be tight; **~́ет в плеча́х** it feels tight in the shoulders.
14 (*coll.*) (*работу, обязанности*) to carry out (*with difficulty or unwillingly*).
15 (*убеждать идти*) to drag; **никто́ тебя́ си́лой не тяну́л** nobody forced you to go.
16 (*вымогать*) to extort.
17 (*coll.*) (**на**+*a.*) (*соответствовать*) to measure up; **он не ~ет на дире́ктора** he won't make a director.

тян|у́ться, у́сь, ~́ешься *impf.* **1** (*о резине*) to stretch. **2** (*pf.* **по~**) (*о человеке*) to stretch out, stretch o.s. **3** (*о равнине*) to stretch, extend; **тайга́ ~́ется на со́тни киломе́тров** the taiga stretches for hundreds of kilometres (*Br.*), kilometers (*US*). **4** (*о времени*) to drag on; to hang heavy. **5** (*coll.*) (*о запасах*) to last out, hold out. **6** (**к**+*d.*) (*к матери*) to reach (for), reach out (for); (*к славе*) to strive (after). **7** (**за**+*i.*; *fig., coll.*) (*стремиться сравняться*) to try to keep up (with), try to equal. **8** (*двигаться один за другим*) to move one after the other. **9** (*о дыме, запахе*) to drift.

тяну́чк|а, и *f.* toffee, caramel.

тя́н|ущий *pres. part. act. of* ⇒**~у́ть** *and adj.*; **~ущая боль** nagging, persistent pain.

тя́п|ать, а́ю *impf.* (*of* ⇒**~нуть**) (*coll.*) (*ударить*) to hit; (*топором*) to chop (at), hack (at).

тя́пк|а, и *f.* **1** (*для рубки*) chopper.
2 (*мотыга*) hoe.

тяп-ля́п *adv. or as pred.* (*coll.*) anyhow (*of careless work*).

тя́п|нуть, ну, нешь *pf.* **1** *pf. of* ⇒**~ать. 2** (*украсть*) to pinch (*Br.*), steal. **3** (*укусить*) to bite. **4** (*выпить*) to knock back.

тя́т|я, и *m.* (*dial.*) dad, daddy.

У у

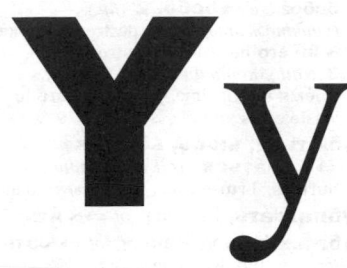

у[1] *int.* (*выражает угрозу, страх, одобрение, удивление*) oh!

у[2] *prep.* +*g.* **1** (*возле*) by; at; **у окна́** by the window; **у воро́т** at the gate; **у руля́** at the wheel; **у станка́** at the work-bench; **у це́ли** at one's destination; **у фи́ниша** at the finishing post; **у мо́ря** by the sea; **у вла́сти** in power.
2 (*обозначает место действия*) at; with (*oft.* = *French 'chez'*); **у нас** (*i*) (*в доме*) at our place, with us, (*ii*) (*в стране*) in our country; **у себя́** at one's (own) place, at home; **я был у парикма́хера** I was at the hairdresser's; **она́ учи́лась у знамени́того скрипача́** she was taught by a celebrated violinist.
3 (*обозначает принадлежность*): **у меня́ боли́т зуб** my tooth aches; **у пере́днего колеса́ ло́пнула ши́на** there is a puncture in the front wheel; **у неё больна́ мать** her mother is ill.
4 (*указывает на источник*) from, of; **я за́нял де́сять рубле́й у сосе́да** I borrowed ten roubles from a neighbour (*Br.*), neighbor (*US*); **попроси́те у него́ кни́гу** ask him to let you have the book.
5 (*обозначает владельца*): **у меня́**, *etc.*, I, *etc.*, have; **у них есть великоле́пный дог** they have a magnificent Great Dane; **у вас радиоприёмник есть?** do you have a radio?; **у меня́ к вам ма́ленькая про́сьба** I have a small favour (*Br.*), favor (*US*) to ask of you.

у... *vbl. pref. indicating* **1** *movement away from a place, as* **улете́ть** to fly away. **2** *insertion in sth., as* **умести́ть** to put in. **3** *covering of sth. all over, as* **усе́ять** to strew. **4** *reduction, curtailment, etc., as* **уба́вить** to reduce. **5** *achievement of aim sought, as* **уговори́ть** to persuade; *with adj. roots forms vv. expr. comp. degree, as* **уско́рить** to accelerate.

уа́йт-спири́т, а *m.* white spirit.

уба́в|ить, лю, ишь *pf.* (*of* ⇒**~ля́ть**) **1** (+*a. or g.*) (*жалованье, цену*) to reduce, lower; **у. ход** to reduce speed; **у. рука́в** to shorten a sleeve. **2** (*coll.*): **у. в ве́се** to lose weight.

уба́в|иться, ится *pf.* (*of* **~ля́ться**) to diminish, decrease; **дни ~ились** the days are shorter; **воды́ ~илось** the water(-level) has fallen.

убавля́|ть(ся), ю, ет(ся) *impf. of* ⇒**уба́вить(ся)**

убаю́к|ать, аю *pf.* (*of* ⇒**~ивать**) to lull (*also fig.*).

убаю́кива|ть, ю *impf. of* ⇒**убаю́кать**

убега́|ть, ю *impf. of* ⇒**убежа́ть**

убеди́тельност|ь, и *f.* persuasiveness, cogency.

убеди́тел|ьный (~ен, ~ьна) *adj.* **1** convincing, persuasive; **быть ~ьным** to be convincing, carry conviction. **2** (*сильный*) pressing; earnest; **~ьная про́сьба** pressing request, earnest entreaty.

убе|ди́ть, *1st pers. sg. not used,* **ди́шь** *pf.* (*of* ⇒**~жда́ть**) **1** (**в** + *p.*) to convince (of). **2** (+*inf.*) (*уговорить*) to persuade (to), prevail on (to).

убе|ди́ться, *1st pers. sg. not used,* **ди́шься** *pf.* (*of* ⇒**~жда́ться**) (**в** + *p.*) to satisfy o.s. (of); to be convinced (of); **мы ~ди́лись в необходи́мости рефо́рм** we are convinced of the need for reform; **он ~ди́лся, что э́то тру́дно** he is convinced that it is difficult; **я сама́ ~ди́лась, како́й он плохо́й челове́к** I have seen for myself what a bad person he is.

убе|жа́ть, гу́, жи́шь, гу́т *pf.* (*of* ⇒**~га́ть**) **1** (*удалиться бегом*) to run away, run off. **2** (*спастись бегством*) to escape, flee. **3** (*coll.*) (*о жидкости*) to boil over.

убежда́|ть(ся), ю(сь) *impf. of* ⇒**убеди́ть(ся)**

убежде́ни|е, я *nt.* **1** (*действие*) persuasion; **путём ~я** by means of persuasion. **2** (*мнение*) conviction, belief; **э́то проти́вно мои́м ~ям** it's against my convictions.

убеждённо *adv.* with conviction.

убеждённост|ь, и *f.* conviction.

убеждён|ный *p.p.p. of* ⇒**убеди́ть** *and adj.* **1** (**~, ~а́**) (**в** + *p.*) convinced (of), persuaded (of); **я в э́том соверше́нно ~** I am absolutely convinced of this. **2** (**~, ~на**) (*тон*) assured. **3** (*no short form*) (*непоколебимый*) convinced, confirmed; staunch; **у. пацифи́ст** convinced pacifist; **у. сторо́нник** staunch supporter.

убе́жищ|е, а *nt.* **1** (*защита*) refuge, asylum; **полити́ческое ~е** political asylum; **иска́ть ~а** to seek refuge, asylum; **пра́во ~а** a right of asylum; **нало́говое у.** tax haven. **2** (*укрытие*) shelter; (*mil.*) dug-out.

убел|ённый *p.p.p. of* ⇒**~и́ть; у. седино́й, седи́нами** hoary with age.

убел|и́ть, ю, и́шь *pf.* to whiten.

уберега́|ть(ся), ю(сь) *impf. of* ⇒**убере́чь(ся)**

убере́|чь, гу́, жёшь, гу́т, *past* **~г, ~гла́** *pf.* (*of* ⇒**~га́ть**) (**от** + *g.*) to protect (against), guard (against), keep safe (from), preserve (from).

убере́|чься, гу́сь, жёшься, гу́тся, *past* **~гся, ~гла́сь** *pf.* (*of* ⇒**~га́ться**) (**от** + *g.*) to protect o.s. (against), guard (*intrans.*) (against).

убива́|ть, ю *impf. of* ⇒**уби́ть**

убива́|ться, юсь *impf.* **1** (*impf. only*) (**о** + *p.*; *coll.*) to grieve (over); (*работая*) to kill oneself. **2** *impf. of* ⇒**уби́ться**

уби́йствен|ный (~, ~на) *adj.* **1** (*obs.*) death-dealing; **~ная стрела́** deadly arrow. **2** (*fig., coll.*) (*жара, голод*) unbearable, killing, murderous; (*известие, результат, взгляд, критика*) devastating.

уби́йств|о, а *nt.* killing; (*с обдуманным замыслом*) murder; (*политическое*) assassination.

уби́йц|а, ы *c.g.* killer; murderer; assassin.

убира́|ть(ся), ю(сь) *impf. of* ⇒**убра́ть(ся); ~йся!** clear off!, beat it!, hop it!

убира́|ющийся *pres. part. of* ⇒**~ться; ~ющееся шасси́** (*aeron.*) retractable undercarriage.

уби́т|ый (~, ~а) 1 *p.p.p. of* ⇒**~ь; неприя́тель потеря́л две ты́сячи ~ыми** the enemy lost two thousand killed; *as n.* **у., ~ого** *m.* dead man; (*жертва преступления*) murdered man; (*при аварии*) fatality; **спать как у.** to sleep like a log; **ходи́ть, как у.** to be dazed (with grief, *etc.*). **2** *adj.* (*fig.*) (*подавленный*) crushed, broken.

уб|и́ть, ью́, ьёшь *pf.* (*of* ⇒**~ива́ть**) **1** to kill; (*предумышленно*) to murder; (*с политическим мотивом*) to assassinate; **хоть ~е́й** (*coll.*) for the life of me; **у. бобра́** *see* ⇒**бобр. 2** (*fig.*) (*уничтожить*) to kill, destroy; **её отка́з ~и́л его́** her refusal destroyed him. **3** (*coll.*) (*потратить*) to waste; **у. вре́мя** to kill time; **у. мо́лодость** to waste one's youth.

уб|и́ться, ью́сь, ьёшься *pf.* (*of* ⇒**~ива́ться**) (*coll.*) (*ушибиться*) to hurt o.s., bruise o.s.; (*разбиться*) to die.

ублаж|а́ть, а́ю *impf. of* ⇒**~и́ть**

ублаж|и́ть, у́, и́шь *pf.* (*of* ⇒**~а́ть**) (*coll.*) to indulge; to gratify.

ублю́д|ок, ка *m.* mongrel; (*о человеке*) bastard.

убо́г|ий (~, ~а) *adj.* (*с увечьем*) crippled; (*нищенский*) poverty-stricken, beggarly (*also fig.*); (*жилище*) wretched, squalid; (*мысль, работа*) pathetic, dismal; *as n.* **у., ~ого** *m.* (*калека*) cripple.

убо́гост|ь, и *f.* poverty (*also fig.*); (*жилища*) wretchedness, squalor.

убо́жеств|о, а *nt.* **1** (*obs.*) (*увечье*) physical disability; infirmity. **2** (*fig.*) (*нужда*) poverty; (*мысли, работы*) mediocrity; **у. иде́й** poverty of ideas.

убо́|й, я *m.* slaughter (*of livestock*); **корми́ть на у.** to fatten (*livestock*); (*fig.*) to feed up, stuff with food.

убо́йност|ь, и *f.* (*mil.*) effectiveness, destructive power (*of missile, weapon*).

убо́йн|ый *adj.* **1**: **у. скот** livestock for slaughter; **у. пункт** slaughterhouse. **2** (*mil.*) killing, destructive, lethal; **~ая мо́щность** destructive power.

убо́р, а *m.* **1** (*одежда*) dress, attire. **2**: **головно́й у.** headgear.

убо́рист|ый (~, ~а) *adj.* close, small (*of handwriting, etc.*).

убо́рк|а, и *f.* **1** (*урожая*) harvesting; (*хлопка, ягод*) picking. **2** (*помещения*) clearing up, tidying up.

убо́рн|ая, ой *f.* **1** (*theatr.*) dressing-room. **2** (*туалет*) lavatory; toilet.

убо́рочн|ый *adj.* harvest(ing); **~ая маши́на** harvester.

убо́рщик, а *m.* cleaner.

убо́рщи|ца, цы *f. of* ⇒**~к**

убра́нств|о, а *nt.* (*меблировка*) furnishings; (*украшения*) decoration; (*poet.*) attire.

убра́|ть, уберу́, уберёшь, *past* **~л, ~ла́, ~ло** *pf.* (*of* ⇒**убира́ть**) **1** (*унести*) to remove, take away; **у. со стола́** to clear the table. **2** (*fig., coll.*) (*выгнать*) to kick out; (*убить*) to kill, take out. **3** (*прятать куда-н.*) to put away; to store; **у. я́корь** to stow the anchor. **4** (*урожай*) to harvest. **5** (*привести в порядок*) to clear up, tidy up; **у. посте́ль** to make the bed. **6** (*украсить*) to decorate, adorn.

убра́|ться, уберу́сь, уберёшься, *past* **~лся, ~ла́сь, ~ло́сь** *pf.* (*of* ⇒**убира́ться**) **1** (*coll.*) to clear up, tidy up, clean up. **2** (*obs. or poet.*) (*нарядиться*) to attire o.s. **3** (*coll.*) (*уйти*) to clear off, beat it.

убыва́|ть, ю *impf. of* ⇒**убы́ть**

у́был|ь, и *f.* **1** diminution, decrease; (*воды*) subsidence; **идти́ на у.** to decrease; (*о воде*) to subside. **2** (*mil.*) (*потери*) losses, casualties.

убы́стр|и́ть, ю́, и́шь *pf.* (*of* ⇒**~я́ть**) to speed up; to hasten.

убыстр|я́ть, я́ю *impf. of* ⇒**~и́ть**

убы́т|ок, ка *m.* **1** loss; **терпе́ть, нести́ ~ки** to incur losses; **в у., с ~ком** at a loss; **быть в ~ке** to lose, be down. **2** (*pl.*) (*возмещение*) damages; **взыска́ть ~ки** to claim damages.

убы́точно *adv.* at a loss.

убы́точ|ный (~ен, ~на) *adj.* unprofitable; **~ная торго́вля** trading at a loss.

убы́ть, убу́ду, убу́дешь, *past* **у́был, убыла́, у́было** *pf.* (*of* ⇒**убыва́ть**) **1** to decrease, diminish; (*о воде*) to subside, fall, go down; (*о луне*) to wane (*also fig.*). **2 тебя́**, *etc.*, **не убу́дет (от**+*g.*; *coll.*) you, *etc.*, won't be any the worse (for). **3** (*выбыть*) to go away, leave; **у. в командиро́вку** to go away on business; **у. по боле́зни** to go sick.

уважа́|емый *pres. part. pass. of* ⇒**~ть** *and adj.* respected; (*в письме*) dear.

уважа́|ть, ю *impf.* to respect, esteem.

уваже́ни|е, я *nt.* (**к**+*d.*) respect, esteem (for); **внуша́ть у.** to command respect; **по́льзоваться ~ем** to be held in respect; **из ~я (к**+*d.*) out of respect (for); **с ~ем** (*в письме*) yours sincerely.

уважи́тельност|ь, и *f.* **1** (*причины*) validity. **2** (*к старшим*) respectfulness.

уважи́тел|ьный (~ен, ~ьна) *adj.* **1** (*основательный*) valid; **~ьная причи́на** valid cause, good reason. **2** (*почтительный*) respectful, deferential.

ува́ж|ить, у, ишь *pf.* (*coll.*) **1** (*просьбу*) to comply (with), grant. **2** (*чувство*) to indulge, gratify; (*человека*) to indulge; to humour (*Br.*), humor (*US*).

у́вал|ень, ьня *m.* (*coll.*) clumsy oaf, clodhopper.

ува́рива|ться, ется *impf. of* ⇒**увари́ться**

увар|и́ться, ~ится *pf.* (*of* ⇒**~иваться**) (*coll.*) **1** (*свариться*) to be thoroughly cooked. **2** (*уменьшиться от варки*) to boil away.

уведоми́тельн|ый *adj.*: **~ое письмо́** letter of advice, notice.

уве́дом|ить, лю, ишь *pf.* (*of* ⇒**~ля́ть**) to inform, notify.

уведомле́ни|е, я *nt.* notification; (*документ*) letter of advice.

уведомля́|ть, ю *impf. of* ⇒**уве́домить**

увез|ти́, у́, ёшь, *past* **~, ~ла́** *pf.* (*of* ⇒**увози́ть**) **1** to take (away); (*с собой*) to take with one. **2** (*похитить*) to abduct, kidnap.

увекове́чива|ть, ю *impf. of* ⇒**увекове́чить**

увекове́ч|ить, у, ишь *pf.* (*of* ⇒**~ивать**) **1** (*героев*) to immortalize. **2** (*порядок, систему*) to perpetuate.

увеличе́ни|е, я *nt.* **1** (*зарплаты*) increase; (*температуры*) rise. **2** (*изображения*) magnification; (*phot.*) (*снимка*) enlargement.

увели́чива|ть(ся), ю, ет(ся) *impf. of* ⇒**увели́чить(ся)**

увеличи́тельн|ый *adj.* magnifying; **~ое стекло́** magnifying glass; **у. аппара́т** (*phot.*) enlarger.

увели́ч|ить, у, ишь *pf.* (*of* ⇒**~ивать**) **1** (*в количестве, в объёме*) to increase. **2** (*изображение*) to magnify; (*phot.*) to enlarge.

увели́ч|иться, ится *pf.* (*of* ⇒**~иваться**) to increase, grow, rise.

увенч|а́ть, а́ю *pf.* (*of* ⇒**венча́ть** 1, 2 *and* **~ивать**) to crown.

увенч|а́ться, а́ется *pf.* (*of* ⇒**~иваться**) (+*i.*; *fig.*) to be crowned (with); **у. успе́хом** to be crowned with success.

уве́нчива|ть(ся), ю, ет(ся) *impf. of* ⇒**увенча́ть(ся)**

увере́ни|е, я *nt.* assurance.

уве́ренно *adv.* confidently, with confidence.

уве́ренност|ь, и *f.* **1** (*шага, голоса*) confidence; **у. в себе́** self-confidence. **2** (*убеждённость*) (**в**+*p.*) confidence (in), certainty (of); **мо́жно с ~ью сказа́ть** one can say with confidence, it is safe to say; **я был в по́лной ~и, что пойдёт дождь** I was quite certain that it would rain.

уве́рен|ный (~, ~на) *adj.* **1** (*твёрдый*) confident, sure; **~ная рука́** sure hand. **2** *as pred.* **(~, ~а)** (*убеждённый*) (**в**+*p.*) confident (in), sure (of), certain (of); **быть ~ным** to be sure, be certain; **бу́дь(те) ~(ы)!** you may be sure; you may rely on it; **он ~ в себе́** he is self-confident; **я ~а в нём** I have confidence in him.

уве́р|ить, ю, ишь *pf.* (*of* ⇒**~я́ть**) to assure; (*убедить*) to convince, persuade.

уве́р|иться, юсь, ишься *pf.* (*of* ⇒**~я́ться**) to assure o.s., satisfy o.s.

увер|ну́ться, ну́сь, нёшься *pf.* (*of* ⇒**~тываться**) (**от**+*g.*) to dodge; to evade (*also fig.*); **у. от прямо́го отве́та** to avoid giving a direct answer.

уве́р|овать, ую *pf.* (**в**+*a.*) to come to believe (in).

увёртк|а, и *f.* dodge, trick, evasion.

увёртлив|ый (~, ~а) *adj.* evasive, shifty.

увёртыва|ться, юсь *impf. of* ⇒**уверну́ться**

увертю́р|а, ы *f.* (*mus.*) overture.

увер|я́ть(ся), я́ю(сь) *impf. of* ⇒**~ить(ся)**

увеселе́ни|е, я *nt.* entertainment, amusement.

увесели́тельн|ый *adj.* pleasure, entertainment; **~ая пое́здка** pleasure-trip, jaunt.

увесел|и́ть, ю́, и́шь *pf.* (*of* ⇒**~я́ть**) to entertain, amuse.

увесел|я́ть, я́ю *impf. of* ⇒**~и́ть**

уве́сист|ый (~, ~а) *adj.* (*том*) weighty; **у. уда́р** (*coll.*) heavy blow.

уве|сти́, ду́, дёшь, *past* **~̀л, ~ла́** *pf.* (*of* ⇒**уводи́ть**) **1** to take (away); (*с собой*) to take with one. **2** (*coll.*) (*украсть*) to steal, nick (*Br.*).

уве́ч|ить, у, ишь *impf.* to maim, mutilate.

уве́чн|ый *adj.* maimed, mutilated; *as n.* **у., ~ого** *m.*, **~ая, ~ой** *f.* cripple.

уве́чь|е, я *nt.* (*действие*) maiming, mutilation; (*само повреждение*) (serious) injury; **нанести́ у. кому́-н.** to maim, injure s.o.

уве́ш|ать, аю *pf.* (*of* ⇒**~ивать**) to cover (*with objects suspended*); **у. сте́ну карти́нами** to cover a wall with pictures.

уве́шива|ть, ю *impf. of* ⇒**уве́шать**

увеща́ни|е, я *nt.* exhortation, admonition.

увеща́|ть, ю *impf.* to exhort, admonish.

увещева́ни|е, я *nt.* = **увеща́ние**

увещева́|ть, ю *impf.* (*obs.*) = **увеща́ть**

увива́|ть, ю *impf. of* ⇒**уви́ть**

увива́|ться, юсь *impf.* (**за** + *i.*; *coll.*, *pej.*) to hang round.

увида́|ть, ю *pf.* (*of* ⇒**вида́ть**) (*coll.*) to see.

увида́|ться, юсь *pf.* (*coll.*) to see one another; (**с** + *i.*) to see s.o.; to meet s.o.

уви́|деть, жу, дишь *pf.* **1** *pf. of* ⇒**ви́деть; ~дим** we'll see. **2** to catch sight of.

уви́|деться, жусь, дишься *pf. of* ⇒**ви́деться**

уви́лива|ть, ю *impf.* (**от** + *g.*) **1** *impf. of* ⇒**увильну́ть. 2** (*impf. only*) to try to get out (of).

увильн|у́ть, у́, ёшь *pf.* (*of* ⇒**уви́ливать**) (**от** + *g.*; *coll.*) **1** to dodge. **2** (*fig.*) (*от ответственности, от налогов*) to evade; to get out (of); **у. от отве́та** to get out of replying.

ув|и́ть, ью, ьёшь, *past* **~и́л, ~ила́, ~и́ло** *pf.* (*of* ⇒**~ива́ть**) to twine all over.

увлажни́тел|ь, я *m.*: **у. во́здуха** humidifier.

увлажн|и́ть, ю́, и́шь *pf.* (*of* ⇒**~я́ть**) to moisten, damp, wet.

увлажн|и́ться, и́тся *pf.* (*of* ⇒**~я́ться**) to become moist, damp, wet.

увлажн|я́ть(ся), я́ю, я́ет(ся) *impf. of* ⇒**~и́ть(ся)**

увлажня́ющий *adj.*: **у. крем** moisturizer, moisturizing cream.

увлека́тел|ьный (~ен, ~ьна) *adj.* fascinating; absorbing.

увлека́|ть(ся), ю(сь) *impf. of* ⇒**увле́чь(ся)**

увлече́ни|е, я *nt.* **1** (*воодушевление*) animation. **2** (+ *i.*) (*большой интерес*) passion (for); enthusiasm (for); (*влюблённость*) crush (on). **3** (*предмет любви*) (object of) passion; **планери́зм — его́ у.** gliding is his passion; he is mad about gliding; **ста́рое у.** old flame.

увлечённост|ь, и *f.* enthusiasm.

увлечён|ный (~, ~на) *adj.* enthusiastic.

увле́|чь, ку́, чёшь, ку́т, *past* **~̀к, ~кла́** *pf.* (*of* ⇒**~ка́ть**) **1** (*увести*) to carry along. **2** (*fig.*) (*о работе*) to carry away, distract. **3** (*восхитить*) to captivate, fascinate. **4** (*соблазнить*) to entice, allure.

увле́|чься, ку́сь, чёшься, ку́тся, *past* **~̀кся, ~кла́сь** *pf.* (*of* ⇒**~ка́ться**) (+ *i.*) **1** (*забыться*) to be carried away (by); (*заинтересоваться*) to become keen (on); **ора́тор ~̀кся** the speaker got carried away. **2** (*влюбиться*) to become enamoured (*Br.*), enamored (*US*) (of), become keen (on), fall (for).

уво́д, а *m.* **1** taking away; **у. войск** withdrawal of troops. **2** (*coll.*) (*кража*) carrying off; lifting (= *stealing*).

уво|ди́ть, жу́, ~̀дишь *impf. of* ⇒**увести́**

уво́з, а *m.* (*coll.*) (*человека*) abduction; (*кража*) carrying off; lifting (= *stealing*).

уво|зи́ть, жу́, ~̀зишь *pf. of* ⇒**увезти́**

увола́кива|ть, ю *impf. of* ⇒**уволо́чь**

уво́л|ить, ю, ишь *pf.* (*of* ⇒**~ьня́ть**) **1** (*с работы*) to dismiss; to sack; (*mil.*) to discharge; **у. в отста́вку** to retire, pension off; **у. в запа́с** (*mil.*) to transfer to the reserve. **2** (*pf. only*) (**от** + *g.*; *obs.*) to spare; **~ьте нас от подро́бностей** spare us the details.

уво́л|иться, юсь, ишься *pf.* (*of* ⇒**~ьня́ться**) (*уйти*) to resign; (*mil.*) to get one's discharge; **у. в отста́вку** to retire.

уволо́|чь, оку́, очёшь, оку́т, *past* **~о́к, ~окла́** *pf.* (*of* ⇒**~а́кивать**) (*coll.*) **1** (*утащить*) to drag away; **е́ле но́ги у.** to have a narrow escape. **2** (*украсть*) to make off with.

увольне́ни|е, я *nt.* dismissal; (*mil.*) discharge; (*на пенсию*) retiring, pensioning off.

увольни́тельн|ый *adj.* discharge, dismissal; **у. биле́т, ~ая запи́ска** (*mil.*) leave-pass.

увольня́|ть(ся), ю(сь) *impf. of* ⇒**уво́лить(ся)**

увор|ова́ть, у́ю *pf.* (*coll.*) to pinch (*Br.*), swipe.

уврач|ева́ть, у́ю *pf. of* ⇒**врачева́ть**

увы́ *int.* alas!

увяда́|ть, ю *impf. of* ⇒**увя́нуть**

увя|за́ть[1], жу́, ~̀жешь *pf.* (*of* ⇒**~̀зывать**) **1** (*вещи, тюк*) to tie up. **2** (*согласовать*) to co-ordinate.

увяз|а́ть[2], а́ю *impf. of* ⇒**~̀нуть**

увя|за́ться, жу́сь, ~̀жешься *pf.* (*of* ⇒**~̀зываться**) (*coll.*) **1** (*упаковать свои вещи*) to pack. **2** (**за** + *i.*) to tag along (behind), follow closely.

увя́зк|а, и *f.* **1** (*вещей*) tying up, roping, strapping. **2** (*согласованность*) co-ordination.

увя́з|нуть, ну, нешь, *past* **~, ~ла** *pf.* (*of* ⇒**~а́ть[2]**) (**в** + *p.*) to get stuck (in); to get bogged down (in) (*also fig.*).

увя́зыва|ть, ю *impf. of* ⇒**увяза́ть[1]**

увя́зыва|ться, юсь *impf. of* ⇒**увяза́ться**

увя́|нуть, ну, нешь *pf.* (*of* ⇒**~да́ть**) to fade, wither (*also fig.*).

угад|а́ть[1], а́ю *pf.* (*of* ⇒**~̀ывать**) to guess (right), divine; (*желания*) to anticipate.

угад|а́ть[2], а́ю *pf.* (**в** + *a.*; *coll.*) to get (into), fall (into); (*попасть*) to hit.

уга́дыва|ть, ю *impf. of* ⇒**угада́ть[1]**

Уга́нд|а, ы *f.* Uganda.

уганди́|ец, йца *m.* Ugandan.

уганди́|йка, йки *f. of* ⇒**~ец**

уганди́йский *adj.* Ugandan.

уга́р, а *m.* **1** (*газ*) carbon monoxide fumes. **2** (*отравление*) carbon monoxide poisoning; **у них у.** they are suffering from carbon monoxide poisoning. **3** (*fig.*) (*упоение*) ecstasy, intoxication; **пья́ный у.** drunken stupor; **в ~е** (+ *g.*) carried away (by).

уга́рный *adj.* full of (monoxide) fumes; (*tech.*): **у. газ** coal-gas, carbon monoxide.

угаса́ни|е, я *nt.* (*пламени*) dying down; (*сил*) fading, ebbing.

угас|а́ть, а́ет *impf.* **1** *impf. of* ⇒**~̀нуть. 2** (*impf. only*) (*огонь*) to die down; **си́лы у него́ ~а́ли** his strength was fading, ebbing.

уга́с|нуть, нет, *past* **~, ~ла** *pf.* (*of* ⇒**~а́ть**) (*пламя, свеча*) to go out; (*звук*) to die away; (*чувство*) to be extinguished; (*человек*) to die.

углево́д, а *m.* (*chem.*) carbohydrate.

углеводоро́д, а *m.* (*chem.*) hydrocarbon.

угледо́быч|а, и *f.* coal extraction.

углежже́ни|е, я *nt.* charcoal burning.

углежо́г, а *m.* charcoal-burner.

углекислот|а́, ы́ *f.* (*chem.*) carbon dioxide.

углеки́слый *adj.* (*chem.*) carbonate (of); **у. газ** carbon dioxide; **у. аммо́ний** ammonium carbonate.

углеко́п, а *m.* (*obs.*) coal-miner, collier.

углено́сный *adj.* rich in coal.

углепромы́шленност|ь, и *f.* coal-mining, coal industry.

углеро́д, а *m.* (*chem.*) carbon.

углеро́дист|ый *adj.* (*chem.*) carbon; carbide (of); **~ое желе́зо** iron carbide.

углова́т|ый (~, ~а) *adj.* **1** angular. **2** (*fig.*, *coll.*) (*неловкий*) awkward.

углов|о́й *adj.* **1** (*math.*, *phys.*, *tech.*) angle; angular; **~а́я ско́рость** angular velocity; **~а́я частота́** angular frequency. **2** (*на углу*) corner; **у. дом** corner house; **у. уда́р** (*sport*) corner; *as n.* **у., ~о́го** *m.* (*sport*) corner; **пода́ть у.** to take a corner.

угломе́р, а *m.* (*tech.*) goniometer, protractor, clinometer.

углуб|и́ть, лю́, и́шь *pf.* (*of* ⇒**~ля́ть**) **1** (*яму*) to deepen, make deeper. **2** (*поместить глубоко, глубже*) to drive in deep, sink deeper. **3** (*fig.*) to deepen, extend; **у. свои́ зна́ния** to deepen one's knowledge.

углуб|и́ться, лю́сь, и́шься *pf.* (*of*

⇒~ля́ться) **1** (*яма*) to deepen, become deeper. **2** (*fig.*) (*о знаниях*) to deepen, become deeper; (*о противоречиях*) to become intensified. **3** (в+*a.*) (*в лес*) to go deep (into); (*в воспоминания*) to become absorbed in, lose o.s. in; (*в историю*) to delve deeply (into) (*also fig.*); **у. в ко́рень веще́й** to go to the root of the matter. **4** (в+*a.*; *fig.*) (*в чтение*) to become absorbed (in); **у. в кни́гу** to become absorbed in a book; **у. в себя́** to become introspective.

углубле́ни|е, я *nt.* **1** deepening. **2** (*fig.*) deepening, extending; intensification; **для ~я свои́х зна́ний** in order to deepen one's knowledge. **3** (*geog.*) hollow, depression, dip.

углубл|ённый (~ён, ~ена́) *adj.* **1** (*работа, изучение*) intensive; (*интерес*) profound. **2** (в+*a.*) absorbed (in).

углубля́|ть(ся), ю(сь) *impf. of* ⇒**углуби́ть(ся)**

угля|де́ть, жу́, ди́шь *pf.* (*coll.*) **1** (*увидеть*) to spot. **2** (за+*i.*) (*уберечь*) to look after; **не у.** (за+*i.*) to fail to take proper care (of).

угна́|ть, угоню́, уго́нишь, *past* **~л, ~ла́, ~ло** *pf.* (*of* ⇒**угоня́ть**) **1** (*скот*) to drive away, off. **2** (*coll.*) (*украсть*) to steal; (*самолёт*) to hijack.

угна́|ться, угоню́сь, уго́нишься, *past* **~лся, ~ла́сь, ~ло́сь** *pf.* (за+*i.*) to keep pace (with); to keep up (with) (*also fig.*).

угнезд|и́ться, и́шься *pf.* (*coll.*) to nestle.

угнета́тел|ь, я *m.* oppressor.

угнета́тельский *adj.* oppressive.

угнета́|ть, ю *impf.* **1** (*жестоко притеснять*) to oppress. **2** (*удручать*) to depress, dispirit.

угнете́ни|е, я *nt.* **1** (*притеснение*) oppression. **2** (*угнетённость*) depression; **быть в ~и** to be depressed.

угнетённост|ь, и *f.* depression, low spirits; (*нации*) oppression.

угнетённ|ый *adj.* **1** (*притесняемый*) oppressed. **2** (*удручённый*) depressed; **быть в ~ом состоя́нии** to be depressed, be in low spirits.

угова́рива|ть, ю *impf.* **1** *impf. of* ⇒**уговори́ть. 2** (*impf. only*) to try to persuade, urge.

угова́рива|ться, юсь *impf. of* ⇒**уговори́ться**

угово́р, а *m.* **1** persuasion; **подда́ться на ~ы** to give in to persuasion. **2** (*соглашение*) agreement, compact; **с ~ом...** on condition...; with the proviso ...; **тако́го ~а не́ было** we did not agree on that.

уговор|и́ть, ю, и́шь *pf.* (*of* ⇒**угова́ривать**) (+*inf.*) to persuade (to); to talk (into).

уговор|и́ться, ю́сь, и́шься *pf.* (*of* ⇒**угова́риваться**) (+*inf.*) to arrange (to), agree (to).

уго́д|а, ы *f.*: **в ~у** (+*d.*) to please.

уго|ди́ть¹, жу́, ди́шь *pf.* (*of* ⇒**~жда́ть**) (+*d. or* на+*a.*) (*удовлетворить*) to please, oblige.

уго|ди́ть², жу́, ди́шь *pf.* (*coll.*) **1** (в+*a.*) (*попасть*) to fall (into), get (into); (*при падении*) to bang (against); **у. в западню́** to fall into a trap; **у. в тюрьму́** to land up in prison. **2** (+*d.* в+*a.*) (*о выстреле, об ударе*) to hit (in, on), get (in, on); **у. кому́-н. в глаз ка́мнем** to hit s.o. in the eye with a stone.

уго́длив|ый (~, ~а) *adj.* obsequious.

уго́дник, а *m.* **1** (*coll.*) person anxious to please; **да́мский у.** ladies' man. **2** (*relig.*): **(свято́й) у.** saint.

уго́днича|ть, ю *impf.* (**пе́ред**+*i.*; *coll.*) to fawn (on).

уго́дничеств|о, а *nt.* subservience, servility.

уго́дно 1 *as pred.* (+*d.*) **что вам у.?** what would you like?, what can I do for you?; **не у. ли вам** (+*inf.*) would you like to; **там есть всё, что у.** there is everything there one could wish for; **как вам у.** as you like; please yourself; **ско́лько душе́ у.** to one's heart's content. **2** *particle forming indef. prons. and advs.*: **кто у.** anyone (you like), whoever you like; **что у.** anything (you like); whatever you like; **ско́лько у.** as much as you like; any amount; **когда́ у.** any time.

уго́д|ный (~ен, ~на) *adj.* (+*d.*) pleasing, welcome (to).

уго́д|ье, ья, *g. pl.* **~ий** *nt.* object or area of economic significance; **лесны́е ~ья** forests; **полевы́е ~ья** arable land; **ры́бные ~ья** fishing-ground.

угожда́|ть, ю *impf. of* ⇒**угоди́ть¹**

у́г|ол, ла́, об ~ле́, в ~лу́ *m.* **1** (**в ~ле́**) (*math., phys.*) angle; **у. зре́ния** (*fig.*) point of view; **под ~ло́м** (в+*a.*) at an angle (of); **под прямы́м ~ло́м** at right angles. **2** (*улицы, стола, комнаты*) corner; **в ~лу́** in the corner; **на ~лу́** at the corner; **за ~ло́м** round the corner; **из-за ~ла́** (from) round the corner; (*fig.*) on the sly, behind s.o.'s back; **сре́зать у.** to cut off a corner; **загна́ть кого́-н. в у.** to corner s.o. **3** (*часть комнаты, сдаваемая внаём*) part of a room. **4** (*место, где можно жить*) place; **име́ть свой у.** to have a place of one's own; **глухо́й у., медве́жий у.** remote part, godforsaken spot.

угол|ёк, ька́ *m.* small piece of coal.

уголо́вник, а *m.* criminal.

уголо́вн|ый *adj.* criminal; **~ое де́ло** criminal case; **у. ко́декс** criminal code; **~ое пра́во** criminal law; **~ое преступле́ние** crime, felony; **у. престу́пник** criminal; **у. ро́зыск** Criminal Investigation Department.

угол|о́к, ка́ *m. dim. of* ⇒**у́гол;** corner; **у. приро́ды** nature study corner; **живо́й у.** pets' corner; **кра́сный у.** recreation and reading room.

у́голь, угля́ *m.* **1** (*pl.* **у́гли, угле́й**) coal; **ка́менный у.** coal; **бу́рый у.** lignite; **древе́сный у.** charcoal. **2** (*pl.* **у́гли, у́гле́й** *and* **у́гля, у́глев**) (*кусок горючей древесины*) a coal; piece of coal; **сиде́ть как на у́глях** to be on thorns. **3** (*art*) charcoal.

уго́льник, а *m.* set square.

у́гольн|ый *adj.* **1** coal; **у. бассе́йн** coal-field; **у. райо́н** coal-mining area. **2** carbon; **~ая дугова́я ла́мпа** carbon arc lamp. **3** (*chem.*) carbonic; **~ая кислота́** carbonic acid.

у́гольщик, а *m.* **1** (*шахтёр*) coal-miner, collier. **2** (*углежог*) charcoal-burner.

угомо́н, а (у) *m.* (*coll.*) peace (and quiet); **на них ~у нет** they give one no peace; **не знать ~у** to have no peace.

угомон|и́ть, ю, и́шь *pf.* (*coll.*) to calm.

угомон|и́ться, ю́сь, и́шься *pf.* (*coll.*) to calm down.

уго́н, а *m.* **1** (*людей*) driving away. **2** (*велосипеда*) stealing; (*самолёта*) hijacking; **у. маши́ны** car theft.

уго́нщик, а *m.* thief; (*самолёта*) hijacker; **у. маши́ны** car thief; **у.-лиха́ч** joyrider.

угоня́|ть, ю *impf. of* ⇒**угна́ть**

угора́зд|ить, ит *pf.* (+*inf.*, *usu. impers.*; *coll.*) to urge, make; **как э́то его́ ~ило жени́ться на ней?** what on earth made him marry her?

угор|а́ть, а́ю *impf. of* ⇒**~е́ть**

угоре́лый *adj.* **1** (*obs.*) poisoned by fumes. **2**: **как у.** like a madman, like one possessed.

угор|е́ть¹, ю́, и́шь *pf.* (*of* ⇒**~а́ть**) **1** (*отравиться*) to be poisoned by fumes, get carbon monoxide poisoning. **2** (*coll.*) (*одуреть*) to be mad, be crazy; **что ты, ~е́л?** are you out of your mind?

угор|е́ть², ю́, и́шь *pf.* (*of* ⇒**~а́ть**) (*уменьшиться*) to burn away, burn down.

у́г|орь¹, ря́ *m.* (*рыба*) eel; **живо́й как у.** as lively as a cricket.

у́г|орь², ря́ *m.* (*на коже*) blackhead.

уго|сти́ть, щу́, сти́шь *pf.* (*of* ⇒**~ща́ть**) (+*i.*) to entertain (to), treat (to); **у. кого́-н. обе́дом** to treat s.o. to dinner.

угото́ван|ный *p.p.p. as pred. adj.* (*rhet.*) prepared, in store; **им ~о све́тлое бу́дущее** a splendid future is in store for them.

угото́в|ить, лю, ишь *pf.* (*obs.*) to prepare.

угоща́|ть, ю *impf. of* ⇒**угости́ть**

угоще́ни|е, я *nt.* **1** (+*i.*) entertaining (to, with), treating (to). **2** (*то, чем угощают*) refreshments; fare.

угрева́т|ый (~, ~а) *adj.* covered with blackheads; pimply.

угро́б|ить, лю, ишь *pf.* (*sl.*) **1** (*убить*) to do in. **2** (*fig.*) (*загубить*) to ruin, wreck; **у. чью-н. репута́цию** to ruin s.o.'s reputation.

угрожа́|ть, ю *impf.* (+*d. and i.*) to threaten (with); **он ~л ему́ тюрьмо́й** he threatened him with prison; **ему́ ~ет разоре́ние** he is in danger of bankruptcy; **ему́ ~ет опа́сность** he is in danger; **нам ничего́ не ~ет** we are in no danger; **ситуа́ция ~ет войно́й** the situation carries the threat of war.

угрожа́|ющий *pres. part. act. of* ⇒**~ть** *and adj.* threatening, menacing; **~ющее положе́ние** perilous situation.

угро́з|а, ы *f.* threat, menace; **под ~ой**

(+*g.*) under threat (of); **поста́вить под ~у** to threaten, endanger, jeopardize.

угро́зыск, а *m.* (*abbr. of* **уголо́вный ро́зыск**) Criminal Investigation Department (*abbr.* CID).

угро́ха|ть, ю *pf.* (*sl.*) to blow (*money, savings*).

угрызе́ни|е, я *nt.* pangs; **~я со́вести** remorse; **чу́вствовать, испы́тывать ~я со́вести** to feel pangs of conscience.

угрю́м|ый (~, ~а) *adj.* (*человек*) sullen, morose, gloomy; (*местность, пейзаж*) gloomy.

уда́в, а *m.* (*zool.*) boa, boa constrictor.

уда|ва́ться, ётся *impf. of* ⇒**~́ться**

удав|и́ть, лю́, ~́ишь *pf.* to strangle.

удавле́ни|е, я *nt.* strangling, strangulation.

уда́вленник, а *m.* (*coll.*) (*тот, кто повесился*) person who has hanged himself; (*тот, кого удушили*) victim of strangling.

удале́ни|е, я *nt.* **1** (*устранение*) removal; **у. аппе́ндикса** appendectomy; **у. зу́ба** extraction of a tooth. **2** (*изгнание*) sending away; **у. с по́ля** (*sport*) sending off the field. **3** (*от берега*) moving off.

удалённост|ь, и *f.* remoteness, distance.

удал|ённый *p.p.p. of* ⇒**~и́ть** *and adj.* remote.

удал|е́ц, ьца́ *m.* daring person.

удал|и́ть, ю́, и́шь *pf.* (*of* ⇒**~я́ть**) **1** (*отдалить*) to take away, move away. **2** (*убрать, устранить*) to remove; **у. зуб** to extract a tooth. **3** (*заставить уйти*) to remove, send away; (*от дел, от обязанностей*) to remove; **у. с рабо́ты** to dismiss, sack; **у. с по́ля** (*sport*) to send off (the field).

удал|и́ться, ю́сь, и́шься *pf.* (*of* ⇒**~я́ться**) **1** (*отдалиться*) to move off, move away. **2** (*уйти*) to leave, withdraw, retire; **у. на поко́й** to retire to a quiet life; **у. от о́бщества** to withdraw from society.

удал|о́й (уда́л, ~а́, уда́ло) *adj.* daring, bold.

у́дал|ь, и *f.* daring, boldness.

удальств|о́, а́ *nt.* (*coll.*) = **у́даль**

удал|я́ть(ся), я́ю(сь) *impf. of* ⇒**~и́ть(ся)**

уда́р, а *m.* **1** (*рукой, палкой, топором*) blow; (*ногой*) kick; (*ножом*) stab; **одни́м ~ом** at one stroke; **нанести́ у. кому́-н.** to strike s.o. a blow; **у. в спи́ну** (*fig.*) stab in the back; **у. гро́ма** thunder-clap; (*неприятность*) blow; **у. по самолю́бию** a blow to one's pride; **у. судьбы́** a stroke of bad luck. **2** (*колокола*) stroke. **3** (*mil.*) blow; attack; thrust; **у. с во́здуха** air strike; **под ~ом** exposed (to attack). **4**: **быть в ~е** (*coll.*) to be in good form; to be on the ball. **5** (*med.*) (*кровоизлияние в мозг*) stroke; (*сердца, пульса*) beat; **со́лнечный у.** sun-stroke. **6** (*sport*) shot, hit, stroke.

ударе́ни|е, я *nt.* **1** (*ling.*) stress, accent; (*fig.*) stress, emphasis; **поста́вить у.** to stress, accent; **сде́лать у. (на**+*p. or* **на**+*a.*) to stress, emphasize. **2** (*знак*) stress(-mark).

уда́р|енный *p.p.p. of* ⇒**~ить** *and adj.* (*ling.*) stressed, accented.

уда́р|ить, ю, ишь *pf.* (*of* ⇒**~я́ть**) **1** (+*a.* **по**+*d. or* **в**+*a.*) (*нанести удар*) to strike; to hit; **у. кого́-н. по лицу́** to slap s.o.'s face; **у. кулако́м по́ столу** to bang on the table with one's fist; **пу́ля ~ила в сте́ну** the bullet hit the wall. **2** (**в**+*a. or* +*a.*) (*дать сигнал*) to strike; to sound; to beat; **у. в бараба́н** to beat a drum; **у. в наба́т, у. трево́гу** to sound the alarm; **часы́ ~или по́лночь** the clock struck midnight. **3** (*раздаться*) to sound; **~ил гром** there was a clap of thunder; (*фонтан, пар*) to gush; (*подействовать резко*): **в глаза́ ~ил я́ркий свет** a bright light struck his eyes; **вино́ ~ило в го́лову** the wine went to my head; **кровь ~ила в го́лову** blood rushed to my head. **4** (**на**+*a. or* **по**+*d.*) (*mil.*) to attack. **5** (**по**+*d.*) to strike (at); to combat; **у. по кумовству́** to combat nepotism; **у. по карма́ну** (*coll.*) to hit one's pocket, set one back. **6** (*coll.*) (*о погоде*) to strike; to set in; **ну и моро́зец ~ил** the frosts have really set in. **7**: **у. по рука́м** to strike a bargain. **8**: **па́лец о па́лец не у.** (*coll.*) not to raise, lift a finger. **9**: **старика́ ~ил парали́ч** the old man had a stroke.

уда́р|иться, юсь, ишься *pf.* (*of* ⇒**~я́ться**) **1** (**о**+*a. or* **в**+*a.*) to strike (against), hit. **2** (**в**+*a. or* +*inf.*) to break (into); **у. в бе́гство, у. бежа́ть** to break into a run; **у. в слёзы** to burst into tears. **3** (**в**+*a.*) (*пристраститься*) to become addicted (to), become keen (on). **4**: **у. в кра́йность** to go to an extreme; **у. из одно́й кра́йности в другу́ю** to go from one extreme to another.

уда́рник[1], а *m.* (*hist.*) (*работник*) shock-worker, udarnik.

уда́рник[2], а *m.* (*ружья*) striker, firing pin; (*детонатора*) plunger.

уда́рник[3], а *m.* (*mus.*) percussionist; (*в рок группе*) drummer.

уда́рниц|а, ы *f. of* ⇒**уда́рник[1]**

уда́рн|ый *adj.* **1** (*tech. and mil.*) percussive; percussion; **у. ка́псюль** percussion cap; **~ая сва́рка** percussive welding; **~ая си́ла** striking power, force of impact. **2** (*mus.*) percussion. **3** (*mil.*) striking, shock; **~ая гру́ппа** striking force; **~ые ча́сти** shock troops. **4** (*передовой*) shock(-working); **~ая рабо́та** shock work; **~ые те́мпы** accelerated tempo (*of work*). **5** (*срочный*) urgent; **~ое зада́ние** urgent task, rush job. **6** (*гласный*) stressed.

удар|я́ть(ся), я́ю(сь) *impf. of* ⇒**~́ить(ся)**

уда́|ться, стся, ду́тся, *past* **~лся, ~ла́сь** *pf.* (*of* ⇒**~ва́ться**) **1** (*получиться*) to be successful, work (well), succeed; **опера́ция ~ла́сь** the operation was a success; **рабо́та не ~ла́сь** the work did not turn out well; **перегово́ры не ~ли́сь** the talks were a failure, did not succeed; **ему́ всё ~ётся** he succeeds in everything he does. **2** (*impers.* +*d. and inf.*) to succeed, manage; **мне не ~ло́сь написа́ть статью́ во́время** I did not manage to write the article on time.

уда́ч|а, и *f.* success; (*везение*) good luck, good fortune; **жела́ть ~и** to wish good luck; **им всегда́ у.** they are always lucky.

уда́чливост|ь, и *f.* success, luck.

уда́члив|ый (~, ~а) *adj.* successful, lucky.

уда́чник, а *m.* (*coll.*) lucky person.

уда́ч|ный (~ен, ~на) *adj.* **1** (*успешный*) successful. **2** (*хороший*) felicitous, apt, good; **у. перево́д** felicitous translation; **у. оборо́т** apt turn of phrase; **у. вы́бор** happy choice.

удва́ива|ть, ю *impf. of* ⇒**удво́ить**

удвое́ни|е, я *nt.* doubling, redoubling.

удво́|енный *p.p.p. of* ⇒**~ить** *and adj.* doubled, redoubled.

удво́|ить, ю, ишь *pf.* (*of* ⇒**удва́ивать**) (*увеличить вдвое*) to double; (*букву*) to double; (*значительно увеличить*) to redouble; **у. свои́ уси́лия** to redouble one's efforts.

уде́л, а *m.* lot, destiny; **доста́ться в у. кому́-н.** to fall to one's lot.

удел|и́ть, ю́, и́шь *pf.* (*of* ⇒**~я́ть**) to give, spare, devote; **у. вре́мя чему́-н.** to spare the time for sth.

уде́льн|ый[1] *adj.* (*phys.*) specific; **у. вес** specific gravity; (*fig.*) (*доля*) proportion, share; **~ая мо́щность** horse power per pound of weight.

уде́льный[2] *adj.* (*hist.*) appanage; **у. князь** appanage prince (*in Kievan Russia*).

удел|я́ть, я́ю *impf. of* ⇒**~и́ть**

у́держ, у *m.*: **без ~у** (*coll.*) uncontrollably, without restraint; **пла́кать без ~у** to weep uncontrollably; **~у нет ему́, на него́** (*coll.*) there's no holding him; **~у не знать** (*coll.*) to know no bounds.

удержа́ни|е, я *nt.* **1** keeping, holding, retention. **2** (*вычет*) deduction; **у. из зарпла́ты** money stopped from wages; **у. нало́гов** deduction of taxes.

удерж|а́ть, у́, ~́ишь *pf.* (*of* ⇒**~́ивать**) **1** (*не выпустить*) to hold, hold on to, not let go. **2** (*сохранить*) to keep, retain; **у. своё ме́сто в чемпиона́те** to retain one's place in a championship competition; **у. в па́мяти** to retain in one's memory. **3** (*не отпустить; не дать сделать*) to hold back, keep back, restrain; **у. лошаде́й** to hold horses back; **у. кого́-н. от опроме́тчивого посту́пка** to restrain s.o. from a headstrong action. **4** (*подавить*) to keep down, suppress; **у. слёзы** to stifle one's tears. **5** (*вычесть*) to deduct, keep back; **у. из зарпла́ты** to stop from wages.

удерж|а́ться, у́сь, ~́ишься *pf.* (*of* ⇒**~́иваться**) **1** (*не отступить*) to hold one's ground, hold out; to stand firm; **у. на нога́х** to remain on one's feet. **2** (**от**+*g.*) to keep (from), refrain (from); **у. от собла́зна** to resist a temptation; **мы не могли́ у. от сме́ха** we couldn't help laughing.

Y

удéржива|ть(ся), ю(сь) *impf. of* **⇒удержáть(ся)**

удесятер|и́ть, ю́, и́шь *pf.* (*of* **⇒~я́ть**) to increase tenfold.

удесятер|и́ться, и́тся *pf.* (*of* **⇒~я́ться**) to increase (*intrans.*) tenfold.

удесятер|я́ть(ся), я́ю, я́ет(ся) *impf. of* **⇒~и́ть(ся)**

удешев|и́ть, лю́, и́шь *pf.* (*of* **⇒~ля́ть**) to reduce the price (of).

удешев|и́ться, и́тся *pf.* (*of* **⇒~ля́ться**) to become cheaper.

удешевлéни|е, я *nt.* reduction of prices.

удешевля́|ть(ся), ю, ет(ся) *impf. of* **⇒удешеви́ть(ся)**

удиви́тельно *adv.* **1** astonishingly, surprisingly. **2** (*чудесно*) wonderfully, marvellously (*Br.*), marvelously (*US*). **3** (*очень*) very, extremely. **4** (*as pred.*) it is astonishing, it is surprising, it is amazing; (*странно*) it is funny; **у., что** it is surprising that; **мне у., что** I am surprised that; **у., как он сдéлал э́то** I wonder how he did it; **не у., что** no wonder that.

удиви́тел|ьный (~ен, ~ьна) *adj.* **1** astonishing, surprising, amazing. **2** (*чудесный*) wonderful, marvellous (*Br.*), marvelous (*US*).

удив|и́ть, лю́, и́шь *pf.* (*of* **⇒~ля́ть**) to astonish, surprise, amaze.

удив|и́ться, лю́сь, и́шься *pf.* (*of* **⇒~ля́ться**) (+*d.*) to be astonished (at), be surprised (at); to marvel (at).

удивлéни|е, я *nt.* astonishment, surprise, amazement; **к моему́ вели́кому ~ю** to my great surprise; **на у.** (*coll.*) excellent(ly), splendid(ly); **приём вы́шел на у.** the reception went off splendidly; **хоро́ший на у.** surprisingly good.

удивля́|ть(ся), ю(сь) *impf. of* **⇒удиви́ть(ся)**

удил|á, уди́л, ~áм *no sg.* bit; **закуси́ть у.** to take the bit between one's teeth (*also fig.*).

уди́лищ|е, а *nt.* fishing-rod.

уди́льн|ый *adj.*: **~ые принадлéжности** fishing tackle.

уди́льщик, а *m.* angler.

уди́льщиц|а, ы *f. of* **⇒уди́льщик**

удирá|ть, ю *impf. of* **⇒удрáть**

уди́ть, ужу́, у́дишь *impf.*: **у. (ры́бу)** to fish, angle.

уди́ться, у́дится *impf.* (*of fish*) to bite.

удлинéни|е, я *nt.* lengthening; **у. сро́ка** extension (of time).

удлини́тел|ь, я *m.* extension lead.

удлин|и́ть, ю́, и́шь *pf.* (*of* **⇒~я́ть**) to lengthen; (*срок*) to extend, prolong.

удлин|и́ться, и́тся *pf.* (*of* **⇒~я́ться**) (*о тенях*) to become longer; (*о сроке*) to be extended, be prolonged.

удлин|я́ть(ся), я́ю, я́ет(ся) *impf. of* **⇒~и́ть(ся)**

удму́рт, а *m.* Udmurt.

удму́рт|ка, ки *f. of* **⇒~**

удму́ртский *adj.* Udmurt.

удо́бно[1] *adv.* **1** (*сидеть*) comfortably. **2** (*расположить*) conveniently.

удо́бно[2] *as pred.* **1** (+*d.*) (*хорошо*) to feel, be comfortable; to be at one's ease; **нам здесь вполнé у.** we are very comfortable here. **2** (+*d.*) (*подходит*) it is convenient (for), it suits; **у. ли вам приéхать срáзу?** is it convenient for you to come at once? **3** (*прилично*) it is proper, it is in order; **у. ли задáть такóй вопро́с?** is it proper to ask such a question?

удо́б|ный (~ен, ~на) *adj.* **1** (*кресло, туфли*) comfortable; (*уютный*) cosy. **2** (*подходящий*) convenient, suitable, opportune; **в ~ное для вас врéмя** at your convenience; **по́льзоваться ~ным слу́чаем** (+*inf.*) to take an opportunity (to do sth.). **3** (*приличный*) proper, in order.

удобовари́м|ый (~, ~а) *adj.* digestible.

удобоисполни́м|ый (~, ~а) *adj.* easy to carry out; **~ая про́сьба** a simple request.

удобочитáем|ый (~, ~а) *adj.* easy to read; legible.

удобрéни|е, я *nt.* (*agric.*) **1** (*действие*) fertilization; (*навозом*) manuring. **2** (*вещество*) fertilizer; (*навоз*) manure.

удо́бр|ить, ю, ишь *pf.* (*of* **⇒~я́ть**) to fertilize.

удобр|я́ть, я́ю *impf. of* **⇒~ить**

удо́бств|о, а *nt.* **1** (*одежды*) comfort. **2** (*употребления*) convenience; **кварти́ра со всéми ~ами** flat with all (modern) conveniences.

удовлетворéни|е, я *nt.* satisfaction, gratification; **трéбовать ~я у когó-н.** to demand satisfaction from s.o.; **отмечáть с ~ем** to note with satisfaction.

удовлетворённо *adv.* (*улыбаться, сказать*) with satisfaction.

удовлетворённост|ь, и *f.* satisfaction, contentment.

удовлетвор|ённый *p.p.p. of* **⇒~и́ть** *and adj.* (+*i.*) satisfied, contented (with).

удовлетвори́тельно 1 *adv.* satisfactorily. **2** *n.; nt. indecl.* (*отметка*) 'satisfactory', 'fair' (*as school mark*).

удовлетвори́тел|ьный (~ен, ~ьна) *adj.* satisfactory.

удовлетвор|и́ть, ю́, и́шь *pf.* (*of* **⇒~я́ть**) **1** to satisfy; to comply (with); **у. запро́сы** to satisfy requirements; **у. про́сьбу** to comply with a request. **2** (+*d.*) to answer, meet; **у. трéбованиям** to answer requirements. **3** (+*i.*) (*снабдить*) to supply (with), furnish (with).

удовлетвор|и́ться, ю́сь, и́шься *pf.* (*of* **⇒~я́ться**) (+*i.*) to content o.s. (with), be satisfied (with).

удовлетвор|я́ть(ся), я́ю(сь) *impf. of* **⇒~и́ть(ся)**

удово́льстви|е, я *nt.* **1** (*sg. only*) pleasure; **достáвить у.** (+*d.*) to give pleasure; **с ~ем!** with pleasure! **2** (*забава*) amusement; **жить в своё у.** to live a life of leisure; **дорогóе у.** (*coll.*) it doesn't come cheap.

удово́льств|оваться, уюсь *pf. of* **⇒дово́льствоваться**

удо́д, а *m.* (*zool.*) hoopoe.

удо́|й, я *m.* **1** (*количество молока*) yield of milk. **2** (*доение*) milking.

удо́йлив|ый (~, ~а) *adj.* yielding much milk; **~ая корóва** good milker.

удо́йност|ь, и *f.* (*количество молока*) yield of milk; (*способность коровы*) milking capacity.

удо́й|ный *adj.* **1** *adj. of* **⇒~**. **2** = **~ливый**

удорожáни|е, я *nt.* rise in price(s).

удорож|áть, áю *impf. of* **⇒~и́ть**

удорож|и́ть, у́, и́шь *pf.* (*of* **⇒~áть**) to raise the price (of).

удостáива|ть(ся), ю(сь) *impf. of* **⇒удосто́ить(ся)**

удостоверéни|е, я *nt.* **1** (*действие*) certification, attestation; **в у.** (+*g.*) in witness (of). **2** (*документ*) certificate; **у. ли́чности** identity card, ID; **у. прáва вождéния автомоби́ля** driving licence (*Br.*), driver's license (*US*); **у. о смéрти** death certificate.

удостовéр|ить, ю, ишь *pf.* (*of* **⇒~я́ть**) to certify, attest, witness; **у. по́дпись** to witness a signature.

удостовéр|иться, юсь, ишься *pf.* (*of* **⇒~я́ться**) (**в**+*p.*) to make sure (of); to assure o.s. (of).

удостовер|я́ть(ся), я́ю(сь) *impf. of* **⇒~ить(ся)**

удосто́|ить, ю, ишь *pf.* (*of* **⇒удостáивать**) **1** (+*a. and g.*) (*звания, степени*) to award (to), confer (on); **у. когó-н. Но́белевской прéмии** to award s.o. a Nobel prize. **2** (+*i.*; *usu. iron.*) (*вниманием*) to favour (*Br.*), favor (*US*) (with); to deign to give; **у. улы́бкой** to favour with a smile; **он не ~ил нас отвéтом** he did not deign to give us an answer.

удосто́|иться, юсь, ишься *pf.* (*of* **⇒удостáиваться**) (+*g.*) **1** (*награды*) to receive, be awarded. **2** (*usu. iron.*) (*улыбки*) to be favoured (*Br.*), favored (*US*) (with).

удосу́жива|ться, юсь *impf. of* **⇒удосу́житься**

удосу́ж|иться, усь, ишься *pf.* (*of* **⇒~иваться**) (+*inf.*; *coll.*) to find time (to); to manage.

удочер|и́ть, ю́, и́шь *pf.* (*of* **⇒~я́ть**) to adopt (*as a daughter*).

удочер|я́ть, я́ю *impf. of* **⇒~и́ть**

у́дочк|а, и *f.* (fishing-)rod (*also in fig., coll. phrr.*); **заки́нуть ~у** to cast a line; to put a line out (= *to try to discover sth.*); **поймáть, поддéть на ~у** to catch out; **попáсться на ~у** to swallow the bait.

удрá|ть, удеру́, удерёшь, *past* **~л, ~лá, ~ло** *pf.* (*of* **⇒удирáть**) (*coll.*) to make off; to do a bunk (*Br.*).

удруж|и́ть, у́, и́шь *pf.* (+*d.*; *coll.*) to do a good turn (*also iron.* = *to do a bad turn*).

удруч|áть, áю *impf. of* **⇒~и́ть**

удручённост|ь, и *f.* depression, despondency.

удруч|и́ть, у́, и́шь *pf.* (*of* ⇒**~а́ть**) to depress, dispirit.
уду́м|ать, аю *pf.* (*of* ⇒**~ывать**) (*coll.*) to think up.
уду́мыва|ть, ю *impf. of* ⇒**уду́мать**
удуш|а́ть, а́ю *impf. of* ⇒**~и́ть**
удуше́ни|е, я *nt.* suffocation.
удуш|и́ть, у́, ~ишь *pf.* (*of* ⇒**~а́ть**) (*человека*) to suffocate, smother; (*свободу*) to stifle.
уду́шлив|ый (~, ~а) *adj.* suffocating; **~ая жара́** stifling heat.
уду́шь|е, я *nt.* breathlessness, shortness of breath.
уедине́ни|е, я *nt.* solitude; seclusion.
уединённост|ь, и *f.* solitariness, seclusion.
уединён|ный (~, ~на) *adj.* solitary, secluded.
уедин|и́ть, ю́, и́шь *pf.* (*of* ⇒**~я́ть**) to seclude, set apart.
уедин|и́ться, ю́сь, и́шься *pf.* (*of* ⇒**~я́ться**) (**от**+*g.*) to retire (from), withdraw (from); to go off (by o.s.); **у. в свою́ ко́мнату** to retire to one's room.
уедин|я́ть(ся), я́ю(сь) *impf. of* ⇒**~и́ть(ся)**
уе́зд, а *m.* (*hist.*) uyezd (*administrative unit*).
уе́зд|ный *adj. of* ⇒**~; у. го́род** chief town of uyezd.
уезжа́|ть, ю *impf. of* ⇒**уе́хать**
УЕФА́ *m. indecl.* UEFA (*Union of European Football Associations*).
уе́хать, уе́ду, уе́дешь, *imper.* **уезжа́й(те)** *pf.* (*of* ⇒**уезжа́ть**) to go away, leave, depart.
уж[1], **а́** *m.* grass-snake.
уж[2] **1** *adv.* = **уже́. 2** *emph. particle* (*coll.*) (*безусловно*) to be sure, indeed, certainly; **уж он узна́ет** he is sure to find out. **3** *particle emph. certain prons. and advs.* (*очень*) very; **э́то не так уж сло́жно** it's not so very complicated.
ужа́л|ить, ю, ишь *pf. of* ⇒**жа́лить**
ужа́рива|ться, ется *impf. of* ⇒**ужа́риться**
ужа́р|иться, ится *pf.* (*of* ⇒**~иваться**) (*coll.*) to shrink (during cooking).
у́жас, а *m.* **1** (*чувство страха*) horror, terror; **прийти́ в у.** to be horrified; **привести́ в у.** to horrify; **внуши́ть у.** (+*d.*) to inspire with horror, horrify; **навести́ у.** (**на**+*a.*) to instil terror (into); **к моему́ ~у** to my horror. **2** (*usu. pl.*) (*предмет страха*) horror; **~ы го́лода** the horrors of famine. **3** *as pred.* (*coll.*) it is awful, it is terrible; **у. что тако́е** it's terrible; **ти́хий у.** horror of horrors; **како́й у.!** how awful! **4**: **у. (как)** *as adv.* (*coll.*) awfully, terribly; **у. как гро́мко** awfully loud.
ужас|а́ть(ся), а́ю(сь) *impf. of* ⇒**~ну́ть(ся)**
ужаса́ющий *adj.* awful, terrible.
ужа́сно[1] *adv.* **1** horribly, terribly; **у. себя́ чу́вствовать** to feel awful. **2** (*coll.*) (*чрезвычайно*) awfully, terribly; **он у. пло́хо игра́ет** he plays terribly badly.
ужа́сно[2] *as pred.* (*coll.*) it is awful, it is terrible; **как у.!** how awful!
ужас|ну́ть, ну́, нёшь *pf.* (*of* ⇒**~а́ть**) to horrify, terrify.
ужас|ну́ться, ну́сь, нёшься *pf.* (*of* ⇒**~а́ться**) to be horrified, be terrified.
ужа́с|ный (~ен, ~на) *adj.* awful, terrible; **у. вид** awful sight; **у. на́сморк** awful cold.
ужа́стик, а *m.* (*coll.*) **1** (*фильм*) horror film. **2** (*usu. pl.*) (*ужас*) horror.
у́же *comp. of* ⇒**у́зкий, у́зко**
уже́ 1 *adv.* already; now; by now; **у. не** no longer; **они́ у. прие́хали** they are here already; **он, должно́ быть, у. уе́хал** he must have gone by now; **она́ у. не ребёнок** she is no longer a child. **2** *emph. particle* = **уж; э́то у. друго́е де́ло** that's quite a different matter.
уже́ли, уже́ль *adv.* (*obs.*) = **неуже́ли**
уже́ни|е, я *nt.* fishing, angling.
ужесточа́|ть, ю *impf. of* ⇒**ужесточи́ть**
ужесточ|и́ть, у́, и́шь *pf.* (*of* ⇒**~а́ть**) to make more severe.
ужива́|ться, юсь *impf. of* ⇒**ужи́ться**
ужи́вчив|ый (~, ~а) *adj.* (*человек*) easy to get on with; (*характер*) gregarious.
ужи́мк|а, и *f.* grimace.
у́жин, а *m.* supper.
у́жина|ть, ю *impf.* (*of* ⇒**по~**) to have supper.
ужи́|ться, ву́сь, вёшься, *past* **~лся, ~ла́сь** *pf.* (*of* ⇒**~ва́ться**) **1** (**с**+*i.*) to get on (with); **мы с ней так и не ~ли́сь** she and I simply couldn't get on. **2** (*привыкнуть*) to settle (down).
ужо́ *adv.* (*coll.*) **1** (*потом*) later, by and by. **2** (*как угроза*): **у. тебе́!** just you wait!; **я тебя́ у. проучу́!** just you wait — I'll show you!
узаконе́ни|е, я *nt.* **1** (*действие*) legalization; (*fig.*) legitimization. **2** (*obs.*) (*закон*) statute.
узако́н|енный *p.p.p. of* ⇒**~ить** *and adj.* established.
узако́нива|ть, ю *impf. of* ⇒**узако́нить**
узако́н|ить, ю, ишь *pf.* (*of* ⇒**~ивать**) (*придать законную силу*) to legalize; (*fig.*) (*сделать приемлемым*) to legitimize.
узбе́к, а *m.* Uzbek.
Узбекиста́н, а *m.* Uzbekistan.
узбе́кский *adj.* Uzbek.
узбе́|чка, чки *f. of* ⇒**~к**
узд|а́, ы́, *pl.* **~ы** *f.* bridle (*also fig.*); **держа́ть в ~е́** to keep in check, restrain.
узде́чк|а, и *f.* bridle.
уздцы́: под у. by the bridle.
у́з|ел, ла́ *m.* **1** (*на верёвке*) knot (*also fig.*); (*мера скорости*) knot; **завяза́ть у.** to tie a knot; **завяза́ть ~ло́м** to knot; **у. противоре́чий** knot of contradictions. **2** (*место пересечения*) junction; (*центр*) centre (*Br.*), center (*US*); **у. доро́г** road junction; **промы́шленный у.** industrial centre (*Br.*), center (*US*); **телефо́нный у.** telephone exchange; **у. сопротивле́ния** (*mil.*) centre of resistance. **3**: **не́рвный у.** (*anat.*) nerve-centre (*Br.*), -center (*US*); ganglion. **4** (*bot.*) node. **5** (*tech.*) (*часть механизма*) group, assembly. **6** (*свёрток*) bundle, pack.
узел|о́к, ка́ *m.* **1** small knot. **2** (*bot.*) nodule. **3** (*свёрток*) small bundle.
у́з|кий (~ок, ~ка́, ~ко) *adj.* **1** narrow; **~кое ме́сто** (*fig.*) bottleneck. **2** (*об одежде*) tight. **3** (*fig.*) (*ограниченный*) narrow, limited; **у. круг друзе́й** narrow circle of friends; **~кая специа́льность** narrow specialism, specialized field; **в ~ком смы́сле сло́ва** in the narrow sense of the word. **4** (*fig.*) (*односторонний*) narrow; **у. ум** narrow mind; **у. челове́к** narrow-minded person.
узкова́т|ый (~, ~а) *adj.* rather narrow; (*об одежде*) rather tight.
узкоколе́йный *adj.* narrow-gauge.
узколо́б|ый (~, ~а) *adj.* (*fig.*) narrow-minded.
узлова́т|ый (~, ~а) *adj.* knotty; gnarled.
узлов|о́й *adj.* **1** junction; **~а́я ста́нция** (*rail.*) junction. **2** (*основной*) main, key; **у. вопро́с** key, central question.
узна|ва́ть, ю́, ёшь *impf. of* ⇒**~́ть**
узна́|ть, ю *pf.* (*of* ⇒**~ва́ть**) **1** (*старого друга, свою машину*) to recognize. **2** (*нужду, любовь*) to get to know; to become familiar with. **3** (*новости*) to learn, hear; (*обнаружить*) to find out; **я ~л о его́ прие́зде из газе́т** I learnt of his arrival from the newspapers; **я ~л, что он прие́хал** I found out that he had arrived; **мы ~ли о подро́бностях намно́го по́зже** we found out the details much later; **он ~л, как всё произошло́ от поли́ции** he found out how it had all happened from the police.
у́зник, а *m.* (*rhet.*) prisoner.
у́зниц|а, ы *f. of* ⇒**у́зник**
узо́р, а *m.* pattern, design.
узо́р|ный *adj.* **1** *adj. of* ⇒**~. 2** decorated with a pattern, design.
узо́рчат|ый (~, ~а) *adj.* decorated with a pattern, design.
у́зост|ь, и *f.* narrowness (*also fig.*); (*одежды*) tightness.
узр|е́ть, ю́, ~ишь *pf.* **1** *pf. of* ⇒**зреть**[2]. **2** (*усмотреть*) to see; to take (as).
узурпа́тор, а *m.* usurper.
узурпа́ци|я, и *f.* usurpation.
узурпи́р|овать, ую *impf. and pf.* to usurp.
у́зус, а *m.* (*ling.*) usage.
у́з|ы, ~ *no sg.* (*fig.*) bonds, ties.
уике́нд, а *m.* weekend.
уикэ́нд, а *m.* = **уике́нд**
уйгу́р, а *m.* Uighur.
уйгу́р|ка, ки *f. of* ⇒**~**
уйгу́рский *adj.* Uighur.
уй|ду́, дёшь *see* ⇒**~ти́**
у́йм|а, ы *f.* (+*g.*) (*coll.*) lots (of), masses (of).

уйм|у́, ёшь *see* ⇒**уня́ть**

уй|ти́, ду́, дёшь, *past* **ушёл, ушла́** *pf.* (*of* ⇒**уходи́ть**) **1** (*покинуть место*) to go away, go off, leave; (**из, от, с**+*g.*) to leave; **у. из ко́мнаты** to leave the room; **у. домо́й** to go (off) home; **у. в монасты́рь** to go into a monastery; **мне на́до у.** I must leave; **у. ни с чем** to leave empty-handed; **так мы далеко́ не ~дём** this won't get us far; **э́то не ~дёт** it won't go away; it can wait. **2** (**от, из**+*g.*) (*спастись, избавиться*) to escape (from), get away (from); to evade. **3** (**от, из, с**+*g.*) (*перестать заниматься чем-н.*) to retire (from), give up; **он ушёл из фи́рмы** he left the company; **она́ ушла́ с рабо́ты** she left her job; **у. из поли́тики** to retire from politics; **у. (из жи́зни)** to pass away (= *to die*); **у. со сце́ны** to quit the stage. **4** (**в**+*a.*) (*погрузиться*) to sink (into); (*fig.*) to bury o.s. (in); **студе́нт ушёл в кни́ги** the student buried himself in his books; **у. в себя́** to retire into one's shell. **5** (**на**+*a.*) (*израсходоваться*) to be used, be spent; **на пол ушло́ мно́го де́рева** a lot of wood was used on the floor; **на кни́гу ушёл год** a year was spent on the book; **на дом ушло́ де́сять ты́сяч** ten thousand was spent on the house. **6** (*о времени, об эпохе*) to pass away, slip away. **7** (*coll.*) (*о жидкости*) to boil over. **8**: **у. (вперёд)** (*о часах*) to gain, be fast.

ука́з, а *m.* **1** decree; edict, ukase; **изда́ть у.** to issue a decree. **2** *as pred.* (+*d.*, *coll.*): **ты мне не у.** I'm not obliged to do as *you* say.

указа́ни|е, я *nt.* **1** (*действие*) indication, pointing out. **2** (*инструкция*) instructions, directions; **дать ~я** to give instructions.

ука́з|анный *p.p.p. of* ⇒**~а́ть** *and adj.* fixed, appointed; **на ~анном ме́сте** at the place appointed.

указа́тел|ь, я *m.* **1** (*прибор, стрелка*) indicator; (*надпись*) sign; (*comput.*) cursor; **доро́жный у.** road sign; **у. оборо́тов** (*tech.*) revolution counter; **у. у́ровня воды́** water gauge. **2** (*справочный список*) index; **у. со́бственных имён** index of proper names. **3** (*справочная книга*) guide, directory.

указа́тельн|ый *adj.* **1** indicating; **~ая стре́лка** pointer; **у. па́лец** index finger; **у. знак** road sign. **2**: **~ое местоиме́ние** (*gram.*) demonstrative pronoun.

ука|за́ть, жу́, ~жешь *pf.* (*of* ⇒**~зывать**) **1** (*дорогу*) to show; (*адрес, день*) to indicate. **2** (**на**+*a.*) (*жестом*) to point (at, to); (*fig.*) (*на ошибку, на недостаток*) to point out; (*свидетельствовать*) to point to; to indicate, suggest; **но́вые откры́тия ~зывают на прису́тствие воды́ на Ма́рсе** new data point to the presence of water on Mars; **его́ поведе́ние ~зывает на то, что он чу́вствует себя́ винова́тым** his behaviour (*Br.*), behavior (*US*) suggests that he feels guilty. **3** (*дать совет*) to explain; to give directions.

ука́зк|а, и *f.* **1** (*палочка*) pointer. **2** (*coll., pej.*) (*приказ*) orders; **по чужо́й ~е** at s.o. else's bidding.

указу́ющий *adj.*: **у. перст** gesture of authority; authoritative instruction.

ука́зчик, а *m.* (*coll.*) person who gives orders; **ты нам не у.** you can't give us orders.

ука́зыва|ть, ю 1 *impf. of* ⇒**указа́ть. 2** *no pf.* (*свидетельствовать*) (**на**+*a.*) to indicate; **ци́фры ~ют на то, что пробле́ма остаётся** the figures indicate that there is still a problem.

ука́лыва|ть(ся), ю(сь) *impf. of* ⇒**уколо́ть(ся)**

укат|а́ть, а́ю *pf.* (*of* ⇒**~ывать**[1]) **1** to roll (out); **у. доро́гу** (*катком*) to roll a road; (*ездой*) to make a road smooth. **2** (*coll.*) (*утомить*) to wear out, tire out.

укат|а́ться, а́ется *pf.* (*of* ⇒**~ываться**[1]) (*о дороге*) to become smooth.

ука|ти́ть, чу́, ~тишь *pf.* (*of* ⇒**~тывать**[2]) **1** (*бочку*) to roll away; (*велосипед*) to wheel away. **2** (*coll.*) (*уехать*) to go off.

ука|ти́ться, ~тится *pf.* (*of* ⇒**~тываться**[2]) to roll away (*intrans.*).

ука́тыва|ть(ся)[1]**, ю, ет(ся)** *impf. of* ⇒**уката́ть(ся)**

ука́тыва|ть(ся)[2]**, ю, ет(ся)** *impf. of* ⇒**укати́ть(ся)**

укач|а́ть, а́ю *pf.* (*of* ⇒**~ивать**) **1** (*до сна*) to rock to sleep. **2** (*о море, о езде*) to make sick; (*impers.*): **меня́ ~а́ло на парохо́де** I was (sea-)sick on the boat.

ука́чива|ть, ю *impf. of* ⇒**укача́ть**

УКВ (*abbr. of* ***ультракоро́ткие во́лны***) VHF (*very high frequency*) waveband.

укип|а́ть, а́ет *impf. of* ⇒**~е́ть**

укип|е́ть, и́т *pf.* (*of* ⇒**~а́ть**) (*coll.*) to boil away.

укла́д, а *m.* structure; **у. жи́зни** style of life; **обще́ственно-экономи́ческий у.** social and economic structure.

укла́дк|а, и *f.* **1** (*вещей, чемодана*) packing; (*в штабеля*) stacking; (*в груду*) piling. **2** (*фундамента, рельсов*) laying. **3** (*причёска*) styling.

укла́дчик, а *m.* **1** (*вещей*) packer. **2** (*рельсов*) layer.

укла́дыва|ть, ю *impf. of* ⇒**уложи́ть**

укла́дыва|ться[1]**, юсь,** *impf. of* ⇒**уложи́ться; э́то не ~ется в голове́** it is hard to take it in; it doesn't make sense; **э́то собы́тие не ~ется в (обы́чные) ра́мки** this event is out of the ordinary.

укла́дыва|ться[2]**, юсь,** *impf. of* ⇒**уле́чься**

укле́йк|а, и *f.* (*zool.*) bleak.

укло́н, а *m.* **1** slope; (*градиент*) gradient; **под у.** downhill; **кати́ться под у.** (*fig.*) to go downhill. **2** (*fig.*) (*направленность*) bias; **шко́ла с математи́ческим ~ом** school with a mathematical bias. **3** (*отклонение*) deviation.

уклоне́ни|е, я *nt.* (*от плана*) deviation; (*от обязанностей*) evasion; (*от удара*) dodging; **у. от те́мы** digression; **у. от вое́нной слу́жбы** evasion of military service.

уклони́зм, а *m.* (*pol.*) deviationism.

уклони́ст, а *m.* (*pol.*) deviationist.

уклон|и́ться, ю́сь, ~ишься *pf.* (*of* ⇒**~я́ться**) **1** (**от**+*g.*) (*избежать*) to avoid; to evade; **у. от встре́чи** to avoid a meeting; **у. от отве́тственностей** to evade responsibilities; **у. от уда́ра** to dodge a blow; **у. от прямо́го отве́та** to avoid giving a direct answer. **2** (*от пути, курса*) to deviate; **у. от те́мы** to digress.

укло́нчив|ый (~, ~а) *adj.* evasive.

уклон|я́ться, я́юсь *impf. of* ⇒**~и́ться**

уклю́чин|а, ы *f.* rowlock.

укоко́ш|ить, у, ишь *pf.* (*sl.*) to bump off.

уко́л, а *m.* **1** (*булавкой*) prick. **2** (*fig.*) (*что-н. обидное*) jibe. **3** (*med.*) injection, 'jab'.

укол|о́ть, ю́, ~ешь *pf.* (*of* ⇒**ука́лывать** *and* **коло́ть**) **1** (*булавкой, шилом*) to prick. **2** (*fig.*) (*обидеть*) to sting, wound; **у. чьё-н. самолю́бие** to wound s.o.'s pride. **3** (*coll.*) (*лекарство, наркотики*) to inject.

укол|о́ться, ю́сь, ~ешься *pf.* (*of* ⇒**ука́лываться**) **1** (*булавкой, шилом*) to prick o.s. **2** (*coll.*) (*о наркомане, о больном*) to inject o.s.

укомплектова́ни|е, я *nt.* bringing up to strength.

укомплекто́в|анный *p.p.p. of* ⇒**~а́ть** *and adj.* complete, at full strength.

укомплект|ова́ть, у́ю *pf.* (*of* ⇒**комплектова́ть** *and* **~о́вывать**) **1** (*оборудование*) to complete; (*добавить людей*) to bring up to (full) strength; (*набрать людей*) to man. **2** (+*a. and i.*) (*снабдить*) to equip (with), furnish (with).

укомплекто́выва|ть, ю *impf. of* ⇒**укомплектова́ть**

уко́р, а *m.* reproach; **ста́вить что-н. в у. кому́-н.** to reproach s.o. with sth.; **~ы со́вести** pangs of conscience.

укора́чива|ть, ю *impf. of* ⇒**укороти́ть**

укорене́ни|е, я *nt.* **1** (*взглядов*) implanting, inculcation. **2** (*черенков, привычек*) taking root, striking root.

укорен|и́ть, ю́, и́шь *pf.* (*of* ⇒**~я́ть**) to implant, inculcate.

укорен|и́ться, и́тся *pf.* (*of* ⇒**~я́ться**) to take, strike root (*also fig.*).

укорен|я́ть(ся), я́ю, я́ет(ся) *impf. of* ⇒**~и́ть(ся)**

укори́зн|а, ы *f.* reproach.

укори́зненный *adj.* reproachful.

укор|и́ть, ю́, и́шь *pf.* (*of* ⇒**~я́ть**) (+*a. and* **в**+*p.*) to reproach (with).

укоро|ти́ть, чу́, ти́шь *pf.* (*of* ⇒**укора́чивать**) to shorten.

укор|я́ть, я́ю *impf. of* ⇒**~и́ть**

укóс, а *m.* hay-harvest, hay crop.
укрáдкой *adv.* stealthily, furtively.
Украи́н|а, ы *f.* (the) Ukraine.
украи́н|ец, ца *m.* Ukrainian.
украи́н|ка, ки *f. of* **⇒~ец**
украи́нский *adj.* Ukrainian.
укрá|сить, шу, сишь *pf.* (*of* **⇒~шáть**) (*дом, комнату*) to decorate; (*ёлку*) to decorate (*Br.*), trim (*US*); (*речь, стиль*) to embellish; (*жизнь*) to enrich.
укрá|ситься, шусь, сишься *pf.* (*of* **⇒~шáться**) **1** (*улица, комната*) to be decorated; (*человек*) to adorn o.s. **2** (*речь*) to be embellished; (*жизнь*) to be enriched.
укрá|сть, ду́, дёшь, *past* **~л** *pf.* (*of* **⇒красть**) to steal.
украшá|ть(ся), ю(сь) *impf. of* **⇒укрáсить(ся)**
украшéни|е, я *nt.* **1** (*действие*) decorating, decoration. **2** (*предмет*) decoration, ornament; (*ювелирное*) jewellery. **3** (*гордость*) pride; (*выставки*) centrepiece (*Br.*), centerpiece (*US*).
укреп|и́ть, лю́, и́шь *pf.* (*of* **⇒~ля́ть**) **1** (*стены, ограду, мускулы*) to strengthen. **2** (*mil.*) to fortify. **3** (*fig.*) (*убеждение, любовь, власть, положение, семью*) to strengthen; **у. дисципли́ну** to tighten up discipline.
укреп|и́ться, лю́сь, и́шься *pf.* (*of* **⇒~ля́ться**) **1** to become stronger. **2** (*mil.*) to fortify one's position. **3** (*fig.*) (*дисциплина, власть*) to become firmly established; **за ним ~и́лась репутáция справедли́вого человéка** he has earned the reputation of being a fair person; **у. в убеждéнии** to be confirmed in one's belief; **у. в намéрении** (+*inf.*) to become determined to do sth.
укреплéни|е, я *nt.* **1** strengthening. **2** (*mil.*) fortification; **ли́ния ~й** fortification line.
укреп|лённый *p.p.p. of* **⇒~и́ть** *and adj.* (*mil.*) fortified.
укрепля́|ть(ся), ю(сь) *impf. of* **⇒укрепи́ть(ся)**
укрóм|ный (~ен, ~на) *adj.* secluded; sheltered.
укрóп, а *m.* (*bot.*) dill (*Anethum graveolens*).
укроти́тел|ь, я *m.* (animal-)tamer.
укроти́тель|ница, ницы *f. of* **⇒~**
укро|ти́ть, щу́, ти́шь *pf.* (*of* **⇒~щáть**) **1** (*зверя*) to tame. **2** (*чувство*) to curb; **у. свои́ стрáсти** to curb one's passions.
укро|ти́ться, щу́сь, ти́шься *pf.* (*of* **⇒~щáться**) **1** (*о животном*) to become tame. **2** (*о гневе*) to calm down, die down.
укрощá|ть(ся), ю(сь) *impf. of* **⇒укроти́ть(ся)**
укрощéни|е, я *nt.* taming.
укрупнéни|е, я *nt.* enlargement, extension; (*объединение*) amalgamation (*of small firms, etc.*).
укрупн|и́ть, ю́, и́шь *pf.* (*of* **⇒~я́ть**) to enlarge, extend; (*объединить*) to amalgamate.
укрупн|я́ть, я́ю *impf. of* **⇒~и́ть**
укрывáтел|ь, я *m.* (*leg.*) concealer, harbourer (*Br.*), harborer (*US*); **у. крáденого** receiver (of stolen goods).
укрывáтельств|о, а *nt.* (*leg.*) concealment, harbouring (*Br.*), harboring (*US*); **у. крáденого** receiving (of stolen goods).
укрывá|ть(ся), ю(сь) *impf. of* **⇒укры́ть(ся)**
укры́ти|е, я *nt.* (*mil., etc.*) cover, concealment; shelter; **у. от огня́** cover (from fire).
укр|ы́ть, óю, óешь *pf.* (*of* **⇒~ывáть**) **1** (*ноги, поля*) to cover (up). **2** (*преступника*) to conceal, harbour (*Br.*), harbor (*US*); (*беженца*) to give shelter; (*краденое*) to receive (*stolen goods*); **у. от дождя́** to give shelter from the rain.
укр|ы́ться, óюсь, óешься *pf.* (*of* **⇒~ывáться**) **1** (*одеялом*) to cover o.s. (up). **2** (*от дождя*) to take cover; to seek shelter. **3** (*остаться незаметным*) to escape notice; **э́то от меня́ не ~ы́лось** it has not escaped my notice.
у́ксус, а (у) *m.* vinegar.
у́ксусник, а *m.* vinegar-cruet.
у́ксусниц|а, ы *f.* = **у́ксусник**
уксуснокúсл|ый *adj.* (*chem.*) acetate (of); **~ая соль** acetate.
у́ксусн|ый *adj.* **1** *adj. of* **⇒у́ксус. 2** acetic; **~ая кислотá** acetic acid.
уку́поривa|ть, ю *impf. of* **⇒уку́порить**
уку́пор|ить, ю, ишь *pf.* (*of* **⇒~ивать**) to cork (up).
уку́порк|а, и *f.* corking.
уку́с, а *m.* bite; (*насекомого*) sting.
уку|си́ть, шу́, ~сишь *pf.* to bite; (*о насекомом*) to sting; **какáя му́ха егó ~си́ла?** (*coll.*) what's bitten him?; what's got into him?
уку́т|ать, аю *pf.* (*of* **⇒~ывать**) (+*i. or* **в**+*a.*) to wrap up (in).
уку́т|аться, аюсь *pf.* (*of* **⇒~ываться**) (+*i. or* **в**+*a.*) to wrap o.s. up (in).
уку́тывa|ть(ся), ю(сь) *impf. of* **⇒уку́тать(ся)**
ул. (*abbr. of* **у́лица**) St., Street; Rd., Road.
улáвливa|ть, ю *impf. of* **⇒улови́ть**
улá|дить, жу, дишь *pf.* (*of* **⇒~живать**) (*спорный вопрос, дело, недоразумение*) to settle, resolve.
улá|диться, дится *pf.* (*of* **⇒~живаться**) to be settled, resolved.
улáживa|ть(ся), ю, ет(ся) *impf. of* **⇒улáдить(ся)**
улáмывa|ть, ю *impf. of* **⇒уломáть**
улáн, а, *g. pl.* **~ов** (*and in collect. sense* **улáн**) *m.* (*mil.*) uhlan; lancer.
Улáн-Бáтор, а *m.* Ulan-Bator.
улеж|áть, у́, и́шь *pf.* (*coll.*) to lie down.
у́л|ей, ья *m.* (bee)hive.
улепет|ну́ть, ну́, нёшь *pf. of* **⇒~ывать**
улепётывa|ть, ю *impf.* (*of* **⇒улепетну́ть**) (*coll.*) to make off, bolt; **~й!** hop it! (*Br.*), skedaddle!
уле|сти́ть, щу́, сти́шь *pf.* (*of* **⇒~щáть**) (*coll.*) to butter up, chat up.
улёт, а *m.* (*sl.*) high, buzz; **в ~е** on a high.
улет|áть, áю *impf. of* **⇒~éть**
уле|тéть, чу́, ти́шь *pf.* (*of* **⇒~тáть**) **1** (*о птице*) to fly (away); (*о самолёте, о человеке*) to leave (*by air*); **делегáция ~тéла в Лóндон вчерá** the delegation left for London yesterday (*sc. by air*). **2** (*fig.*) (*о времени*) to fly by; (*о чувствах*) to vanish.
улету́чивa|ться, юсь *impf. of* **⇒улету́читься**
улету́ч|иться, усь, ишься *pf.* (*of* **⇒~иваться**) **1** (*жидкость*) to evaporate. **2** (*coll.*) (*исчезнуть*) to vanish, disappear.
ул|éчься, я́гусь, я́жешься, я́гутся, *past* **~ёгся, ~еглáсь** *pf.* **1** (*impf.* **уклáдываться**[2]) (*лечь*) to lie down. **2** (*impf.* **уклáдываться**[2]) (*уместиться*) to find room (*to lie down*). **3** (*о пыли*) to settle. **4** (*fig.*) (*успокоиться*) to subside; to calm down; **вéтер ~ёгся** the wind dropped.
улещá|ть, ю *impf. of* **⇒улести́ть**
улизн|у́ть, у́, ёшь *pf.* (*coll.*) to slip away, steal away.
ули́к|а, и *f.* (piece of) evidence; **кóсвенная у.** circumstantial evidence; **прямáя у.** hard evidence; **прóтив негó нет никаки́х ули́к** there is no evidence against him.
ули́тк|а, и *f.* (*zool.*) snail.
у́лиц|а, ы *f.* street; **на ~е** (*i*) in the street, (*ii*) (*вне дома*) out (of doors), outside; **с ~ы** from out of doors; **человéк с ~ы** total stranger.
улич|áть, áю *impf. of* **⇒~и́ть**
улич|и́ть, у́, и́шь *pf.* (*of* **⇒~áть**) (+*a. and* **в**+*p.*) to expose (as); **егó ~и́ли в крáже/обмáне** he was exposed as a thief/fraud.
у́личный *adj.* street.
улóв, а *m.* catch (*of fish*).
улови́м|ый *adj.* (*разница, запах*) perceptible; (*звук*) audible; **едвá/чуть/éле ~ая рáзница** a barely perceptible difference.
улов|и́ть, лю́, ~ишь *pf.* (*of* **⇒улáвливать**) **1** (*tech.*) to catch, pick up (*a sound wave, etc.*). **2** (*заметить*) to detect, perceive; (*смысл, связь*) to grasp, understand. **3** (*coll.*) (*возможность*) to seize; (*подходящий момент*) to find.
улóвк|а, и *f.* trick, ruse.
уложéни|е, я *nt.* (*leg.*) code (*esp. hist., of the Russian Law Code of 1649*).
улож|и́ть, у́, ~ишь *pf.* (*of* **⇒уклáдывать**) **1** (*положить*) to lay; (*положить спать*) to put to bed; **у. в постéль** to put to bed. **2** (*чемодан, вещи*) to pack; (*в груду*) to pile, stack. **3** (+*i.*) (*покрыть*) to cover (with), lay (with). **4** (*рельсы*) to lay. **5** (*волосы*) to style. **6** (*pf. only*) (*coll.*) (*убить*) to dispatch. **7** (**в**+*a.*) (*уместить*) to fit in;

у. рабо́ту в срок to fit the work into the time available.

улож|и́ться, у́сь, ~́ишься *pf.* (*of* ⇒**укла́дываться**[1]) **1** (*упаковать вещи*) to pack (up). **2** (**в** + *a.*) (*уместиться*) to go (in), fit (in); **шу́ба не ~́ится в э́тот чемода́н** a fur coat won't go into that case. **3** (**в** + *a.*) (*в пределы*) to keep (within), confine o.s. (to); **у. в полчаса́** to confine o.s. to half an hour; **у. в сме́ту** to keep within the estimate. **4**: **у. в голове́, в созна́ии** to sink in, go in.

улома́|ть, ю *pf.* (*of* ⇒**ула́мывать**) (*coll.*) to talk round; (+*inf.*) to talk into, prevail upon (to).

у́лочк|а, и *f. dim. of* ⇒**у́лица**

улуч|а́ть, а́ю *impf. of* ⇒**~и́ть**

улуч|и́ть, у́, и́шь *pf.* (*of* ⇒**~а́ть**) (*coll.*) to find, seize, catch; **у. моме́нт для разгово́ра** to find a moment for a talk; **у. удо́бный слу́чай** to seize an opportunity.

улучш|а́ть(ся), а́ю(сь) *impf. of* ⇒**~́ить(ся)**

улучше́ни|е, я *nt.* improvement.

улу́чш|ить, у, ишь *pf.* (*of* ⇒**~а́ть**) to improve.

улу́чш|иться, усь, ишься *pf.* (*of* ⇒**~а́ться**) to improve.

улыб|а́ться, а́юсь *impf.* (*of* ⇒**~ну́ться**) **1** (+*d.*) to smile (at); **она́ мне ~ну́лась** she smiled at me. **2** (+*d.*; *fig.*) (*о жизни, о судьбе*) to smile (upon). **3** (*impf. only*) (+*d.*; *coll.*) (*нравиться*) to attract, appeal to; **зада́ча э́та мне во́все не ~а́ется** this task doesn't appeal to me at all.

улы́бк|а, и *f.* smile.

улыб|ну́ться, ну́сь, нёшься *pf.* **1** *pf. of* ⇒**~а́ться. 2** (*fig., coll.*) (*не достаться*) to fail to materialize; to fall through; (*исчезнуть*) to vanish; **на́ша но́вая кварти́ра ~ну́лась** our new flat failed to materialize.

улы́бчив|ый (~, ~а) *adj.* (*coll.*) smiling; happy.

ультимати́в|ный (~ен, ~на) *adj.* categorical, having the nature of an ultimatum; **в ~ной фо́рме** as an ultimatum.

ультима́тум, а *m.* ultimatum.

ультра... *comb. form* ultra-.

ультразву́к, а *m.* ultrasound.

ультразвуково́й *adj.* (*phys.*) ultrasonic.

ультракоро́тк|ий *adj.* (*radio*) ultra-short; **~ие во́лны, у. диапазо́н** VHF (*abbr. of* very high frequency) waveband.

ультрамари́н, а *m.* ultramarine.

ультрафиоле́товый *adj.* ultra-violet.

улюлю́ка|ть, ю *impf.* **1** (*при травле зверей*) to halloo. **2** (*coll.*) (*издеваться*) to whoop.

ум, а́ *m.* mind, intellect; wits; **склад ~а́** mentality; **~а́ не приложу́** (*coll.*) it's beyond me; I give up; **у меня́ ум за ра́зум захо́дит** (*coll.*) I am at my wits' end; **быть без ~а́** (**от** + *g.*) to be out of one's mind (about), be mad, crazy (about); (**счита́ть**, *etc.*) **в ~е́** (to count, *etc.*) in one's head; **в ~е́ ли ты?** (*coll.*) are you in your right mind?; **и в ~е́ у меня́ не́ было** (*coll.*) the thought never even entered my head; **взя́ться за ум** to come to one's senses; **прийти́ на ум** (+*d.*) to occur to one, cross one's mind; **быть на ~е́** (*coll.*) to be on one's mind; **от большо́го ~а́** (*coll., iron.*) in one's infinite wisdom; **свести́ с ~а́** to drive mad; (*fig.*) (*очаровать*) to send wild; **сойти́ с ~а́** to go mad; (**по** + *d., fig.*) to go crazy (about); **с ~о́м** (*coll.*) sensibly, intelligently; **с ~а́ сойти́!** (*coll.*) incredible, brilliant!

умале́ни|е, я *nt.* belittling, disparagement.

умал|и́ть, ю́, и́шь *pf.* (*of* ⇒**~я́ть**) to belittle, disparage.

умалишённ|ый *adj.* mad, mentally ill; *as n.* **у., ~ого** *m.*; **~ая, ~ой** *f.* madman; madwoman; **дом ~ых** mental hospital.

ума́лчива|ть, ю *impf. of* ⇒**умолча́ть**

умал|я́ть, я́ю *impf. of* ⇒**~и́ть**

ума́слива|ть, ю *impf. of* ⇒**ума́слить**

ума́сл|ить, ю, ишь *pf.* (*of* ⇒**~ивать**) (*coll.*) to butter up.

ума́|ять, ю *pf.* (*coll.*) to tire out.

у́мбр|а, ы *f.* umber.

уме́л|ец, ьца *m.* skilled craftsman.

уме́лый *adj.* able, skilful (*Br.*), skillful (*US*).

уме́ни|е, я *nt.* ability, skill.

уменьша́ем|ое, ого *nt.* (*math.*) minuend.

уменьш|а́ть(ся), а́ю(сь) *impf. of* ⇒**~́ить(ся)**

уменьше́ни|е, я *nt.* reduction, diminution, decrease; **у. ско́рости** deceleration.

уменьши́тельн|ый *adj.* **1** diminishing. **2** (*gram.*) diminutive. **3**: **~ое и́мя** pet name (*as* Kolya *for* Nikolai).

уме́ньш|ить, ~́у, ~́ишь *pf.* (*of* ⇒**~а́ть**) to reduce, decrease; **у. ход** to reduce speed; **у. це́ны** to reduce prices.

уме́ньш|иться, ~́усь, ~́ишься *pf.* (*of* ⇒**~а́ться**) to diminish, decrease; to abate.

уме́ренност|ь, и *f.* (*взглядов, политики*) moderateness; (*в расходах*) moderation.

уме́р|енный *p.p.p. of* ⇒**~ить** *and adj.* **1** (**~ен, ~енна**) moderate (*pol.*; *also fig.*); **у. аппети́т** moderate appetite; **~енная поли́тика** moderate policy. **2** (*geog., meteor.*) temperate; moderate; **у. по́яс** temperate zone.

умер|е́ть, умру́, умрёшь, *past* **у́мер, ~ла́, у́мерло** *pf.* (*of* ⇒**умира́ть**) to die; **у. есте́ственной, наси́льственной сме́ртью** to die a natural, a violent death.

уме́р|ить, ю, ишь *pf.* (*of* ⇒**~я́ть**) (*требования*) to moderate; (*гнев*) to restrain.

умер|тви́ть, щвлю́, тви́шь *pf.* (*of* ⇒**~щвля́ть**) to kill, destroy (*also fig.*).

умерщвле́ни|е, я *nt.* killing, destruction (*also fig.*).

умерщвля́|ть, ю *impf. of* ⇒**умертви́ть**

умер|я́ть, я́ю *impf. of* ⇒**~́ить**

уме|сти́ть, щу́, сти́шь *pf.* (*of* ⇒**~ща́ть**) to fit, find room (for).

уме|сти́ться, щу́сь, сти́шься *pf.* (*of* ⇒**~ща́ться**) to go in, fit in, find room.

уме́стно[1] *adv.* appropriately; opportunely.

уме́стно[2] *as pred.* it is appropriate, it is in order, it is not out of place.

уме́ст|ный (~ен, ~на) *adj.* appropriate; pertinent; (*сделанный вовремя*) opportune, timely; **у. вопро́с** pertinent question; **ва́ше предложе́ние вполне́ ~но** your suggestion is quite in order.

уме́|ть, ю *impf.* (+*inf.*) to be able (to), know how (to); **она́ ~ет ката́ться на конька́х** she can skate; **он ~ет жить** he knows how to live; **она́ не ~ет притворя́ться** she is incapable of pretending.

умеща́|ть(ся), ю(сь) *impf. of* ⇒**умести́ть(ся)**

уме́ючи *adv.* (*coll.*) skilfully (*Br.*), skillfully (*US*).

умиле́ни|е, я *nt.* emotion; tenderness; **прийти́ в у.** to be moved; **лить слёзы ~я** to weep with emotion.

умили́тел|ьный (~ен, ~ьна) *adj.* moving, touching, affecting.

умил|и́ть, ю́, и́шь *pf.* (*of* ⇒**~я́ть**) to move, touch.

умил|и́ться, ю́сь, и́шься *pf.* (*of* ⇒**~я́ться**) to be moved, be touched.

умилосе́рд|ить, ишь *pf.* to propitiate, mollify.

уми́лостив|ить, лю, ишь *pf.* = **умилосе́рдить**

уми́л|ьный (~ен, ~ьна) *adj.* **1** (*нежный*) touching; **~ьное ли́чико** sweet face. **2** (*pej.*) (*льстивый*) ingratiating, smarmy.

умил|я́ть(ся), я́ю(сь) *impf. of* ⇒**~и́ть(ся)**

умина́|ть, ю *impf. of* ⇒**умя́ть**

умира́ни|е, я *nt.* dying.

умира́|ть, ю *impf.* **1** *impf. of* ⇒**умере́ть. 2** (*fig.*) (*очень хотеть*) to be dying to; **~ю, как хочу́ спать** I'm dying to have a sleep; **хочу́ есть — про́сто ~ю** I'm dying for something to eat; (**от** + *g.*) to be dying of; **у. от ску́ки** to be dying of boredom; to be bored to death.

умир|и́ть, ю́, и́шь *pf.* (*of* ⇒**~я́ть**) to pacify.

умиротворе́ни|е, я *nt.* **1** (*недовольных*) pacification; (*агрессора*) appeasement; (*души*) bringing of peace (to). **2** (*спокойствие*) peace, tranquillity (*Br.*), tranquility (*US*).

умиротворён|ный (~, ~на) *adj.* tranquil; contented.

умиротвори́тел|ь, я *m.* peacemaker.

умиротвор|и́ть, ю́, и́шь *pf.* (*of* ⇒**~я́ть**) (*недовольных, враждующих*) to pacify; (*агрессора*) to appease; (*душу*) to bring peace to.

умиротвор|и́ться, ю́сь, и́шься

pf. (*of* ⇒~я́ться) (*недовольные*) to calm down, be pacified; (*враждующие*) to be reconciled.

умиротвор|я́ть(ся), я́ю(сь) *impf. of* ⇒~и́ть(ся)

умир|я́ть, я́ю *impf. of* ⇒~и́ть

умля́ут, а *m.* (*ling.*) umlaut.

умн|е́е *comp. of* ⇒~ый *and* ~о

умне́|ть, ю *impf.* (*of* ⇒по~) to grow wiser.

у́мник, а *m.* (*coll.*) **1** (*о мальчике*) good boy; (*о человеке*) clever person. **2** (*iron.*) know-all, smart alec.

у́мниц|а, ы *f. and c.g.* (*coll.*) **1** *f.* (*о девочке*) good girl. **2** *c.g.* (*о человеке*) clever person.

у́мнича|ть, ю *impf.* (*of* ⇒с~) (*coll.*) **1** (*iron.*) (*выказывать ум*) to show off one's intelligence. **2** (*pej.*) (*мудрить*) to try to be clever.

у́мно¹ *adv.* cleverly, wisely; (*разумно*) sensibly.

у́мно² *as pred.* it is wise; it is sensible.

умнож|а́ть(ся), а́ю, ает(ся) *impf. of* ⇒~́ить(ся)

умноже́ни|е, я *nt.* **1** increase, rise. **2** (*math.*) multiplication.

умно́ж|ить, у, ишь *pf.* (*of* ⇒мно́жить *and* ~а́ть) **1** to increase, augment. **2** (*math.*) to multiply.

умно́ж|иться, ится *pf.* (*of* ⇒мно́житься *and* ~а́ться) to increase, multiply (*intrans.*).

у́м|ный (~ён, ~на́, ~но) *adj.* (*человек*) clever, wise, intelligent; (*лицо, глаза, книга*) intelligent; (*разумный*) sensible.

умозаключ|а́ть, а́ю *impf. of* ⇒~и́ть

умозаключе́ни|е, я *nt.* deduction; conclusion.

умозаключ|и́ть, у́, и́шь *pf.* (*of* ⇒~а́ть) to deduce; to conclude.

умозре́ни|е, я *nt.* (*phil.*) speculation.

умозри́тел|ьный (~ен, ~ьна) *adj.* (*phil.*) speculative; (*отвлечённый*) abstract.

умоисступле́ни|е, я *nt.* delirium; **де́йствовать в ~и** to act while the balance of one's mind is disturbed.

умол|и́ть, ю́, и́шь *pf.* (*of* ⇒~я́ть) to prevail upon.

у́молк: **без ~у** (*to talk, etc.*) unceasingly, incessantly.

умолк|а́ть, а́ю *impf. of* ⇒~́нуть

умо́лк|нуть, ну, нешь, *past* ~, **~ла** *pf.* (*of* ⇒~а́ть) (*о человеке*) to fall silent; (*о звуках*) to cease, stop; (*о славе*) to fade.

умоло́т, а *m.* (*agric.*) yield (*of threshed grain*).

умолча́ни|е, я *nt.* **1** passing over in silence, failure to mention, suppression, hushing up. **2** (*comput.*): **по ~ю** default; **шрифт по ~ю** default font; **значе́ния, устана́вливаемые по ~ю** default setting.

умолча́|ть, ю *pf.* (*of* ⇒ума́лчивать) (**о** + *p.*) to pass over in silence, fail to mention, suppress, hush up; **нельзя́ у. о** (+*p.*) one must mention.

умол|я́ть, я́ю *impf.* **1** *impf. of* ⇒~и́ть. **2** to entreat, implore.

умоля́ющий *adj.* imploring, pleading, suppliant.

умонастрое́ни|е, я *nt.* mentality.

умопомеша́тельств|о, а *nt.* derangement of mind.

умопомраче́ни|е, я *nt.* derangement of mind; fit of insanity; **до ~я** (*coll.*) stupendously, tremendously.

умопомрачи́тел|ьный (~ен, ~ьна) *adj.* stupendous, tremendous, terrific.

умо́р|а, ы *f. as pred.* (*coll.*) it's hilarious; it's a scream.

умори́тел|ьный (~ен, ~ьна) *adj.* (*coll.*) hilarious.

умор|и́ть, ю́, и́шь *pf.* (*of* ⇒мори́ть¹) (*coll.*) **1** (*погубить*) to kill; (*fig.*) to be the death (of); **у. кого́-н. со́ смеху** to make s.o. die of laughing. **2** (*утомить*) to tire out, exhaust.

умор|и́ться, ю́сь, и́шься *pf.* (*coll.*) to become exhausted.

у́мственн|о *adv. of* ⇒~ый; **у. отста́лый** retarded, backward.

у́мственный *adj.* mental, intellectual; **у. бага́ж** mental equipment, store of knowledge.

у́мствовани|е, я *nt.* (*pej.*) theorizing, philosophizing.

у́мств|овать, ую *impf.* (*pej.*) to theorize, philosophize.

умудрё|нный (~, ~а́) *adj.*: **у. о́пытом** experienced.

умудр|и́ть, ю́, и́шь *pf.* (*of* ⇒~я́ть) to teach, make wiser.

умудр|и́ться, ю́сь, и́шься *pf.* (*of* ⇒~я́ться) (*coll.*) to contrive, manage (*also, iron., to do sth. which might easily have been avoided*); **как ты ~и́лся туда́ попа́сть?** how on earth did you get there?

умудр|я́ть(ся), я́ю(сь) *impf. of* ⇒~и́ть(ся)

умч|а́ть, у́, и́шь *pf.* to whirl, hurtle away.

умч|а́ться, у́сь, и́шься *pf.* **1** to whirl, hurtle away (*intrans.*). **2** (*fig.*) (*время, детство*) to fly away.

умыва́льн|ая, ой *f.* wash-room.

умыва́льник, а *m.* wash-basin.

умыва́льный *adj.* wash, washing.

умыва́|ть(ся), ю(сь) *impf. of* ⇒умы́ть(ся)

умыка́|ть, ю *impf. of* ⇒умыкну́ть

умык|ну́ть, ну́, нёшь *pf.* (*of* ⇒~а́ть) (*coll.*) (*девушку*) to abduct; (*вещь*) to steal, pinch (*Br.*).

у́мыс|ел, ла *m.* design, intention; **со злым ~лом** with malicious intent.

умы́сл|ить, ю, ишь *pf.* (*of* ⇒умышля́ть) (*obs.*) (+*inf.*) to intend, design; (+*a.*) to plan, plot.

ум|ы́ть, о́ю, о́ешь *pf.* (*of* ⇒~ыва́ть) to wash; **у. ру́ки** to wash one's hands (*also fig.*).

ум|ы́ться, о́юсь, о́ешься *pf.* (*of* ⇒~ыва́ться) to wash (o.s.).

умы́шленно *adv.* purposely, intentionally.

умы́|шленный *p.p.p. of* ⇒~слить *and adj.* intentional, deliberate; (*убийство*) premeditated.

умышля́|ть, ю *impf. of* ⇒умы́слить

умягч|а́ть, а́ю *impf. of* ⇒~и́ть

умягч|и́ть, у́, и́шь *pf.* (*of* ⇒~а́ть) (*obs.*) to soften; (*fig.*) to mollify.

умя́ть, умну́, умнёшь *pf.* (*of* ⇒умина́ть) **1** (*хлеб*) to knead well. **2** (*coll.*) (*уплотнить*) to press down; (*ногами*) to tread down. **3** (*coll.*) (*съесть*) to stuff down.

унава́живать = **унаво́живать**

унаво́жива|ть, ю *impf. of* ⇒унаво́зить

унаво́|зить, жу, зишь *pf.* (*of* ⇒наво́зить *and* ~живать) to manure.

унасле́д|овать, ую *pf. of* ⇒насле́довать 1

унди́н|а, ы *f.* undine, water-sprite.

унес|ти́, у́, ёшь, *past* ~́, **~ла́** *pf.* (*of* ⇒уноси́ть) **1** (*уходя, взять с собой*) to take away; **е́ле/едва́ но́ги у.** to escape by the skin of one's teeth. **2** (*coll.*) (*украсть*) to walk off with, make off with. **3** (*о воде, о ветре*) to carry away, remove; (*impers.*): **ло́дку ~ло́ тече́нием** the boat was carried away by the current; **куда́ его́ опя́ть ~ло́?** where has he disappeared to again? **4** (*fig.*) (*о мыслях, о мечтах*) to carry (*in thought*). **5** (*fig.*) (*жизнь, здоровье*) to claim; **война́ ~ла́ мно́го жи́зней** the war claimed many lives.

унес|ти́сь, у́сь, ёшься, *past* ~́ся, **~ла́сь** *pf.* (*of* ⇒уноси́ться) **1** (*поезд, машина*) to speed away; (*тучи*) to be whisked away. **2** (*fig.*) (*миновать*) to fly away, fly by; **го́ды ~ли́сь** the years flew by. **3** (*fig.*) (*в мыслях, в мечтах*) to be carried away.

униа́т, а *m.* (*relig.*) member of Uniat(e) Church.

униа́тский *adj.* (*relig.*) Uniat(e).

универма́г, а *m.* (*abbr. of* ***универса́льный магази́н***) department store.

универса́л, а *m.* **1** (*работник*) all-round craftsman; (*спортсмен*) all-rounder. **2** (*coll.*) (*машина*) estate car (*Br.*), station wagon (*US*).

универса́л|ьный (~ен, ~ьна) *adj.* **1** universal; **у. магази́н** department store; **~ьные зна́ния** encyclopaedic (*Br.*), encyclopedic (*US*) knowledge. **2** (*разносторонний*) many-sided; versatile; **~ьное образова́ние** all-round education; **у. челове́к** versatile person; all-rounder. **3** (*tech.*) multi-purpose, all-purpose. **у. ключ** universal wrench; **~ьное пита́ние** (*elec.*) mains-or-battery power supply.

универса́м, а *m.* (*abbr. of* ***универса́льный магази́н самообслу́живания***) supermarket.

университе́т, а *m.* university; **поступи́ть в у.** to enter, start university; **око́нчить у.** to graduate (from a university).

университе́т|ский *adj. of* ⇒~

У

унижа́|ть(ся), ю(сь) *impf. of* ⇒**уни́зить(ся)**

униже́ни|е, я *nt.* humiliation, degradation, abasement.

уни́жен|ный *p.p.p. of* ⇒**уни́зить** *and adj.* **(~, ~на)** (*просьба*) humble; (*человек*) humiliated; (*взгляд, тон*) abject.

унижённ|ый (~, ~на) *adj.* (*obs.*) oppressed, degraded.

уни|за́ть, жу́, ~жешь *pf.* (*of* ⇒**~зывать**) (+*i.*) to cover (with), stud (with).

унизи́тел|ьный (~ен, ~ьна) *adj.* humiliating, degrading.

уни́|зить, жу, зишь *pf.* (*of* ⇒**~жа́ть**) to humiliate; to degrade.

уни́|зиться, жусь, зишься *pf.* (*of* ⇒**~жа́ться**) to demean o.s.; **у. до лжи/про́сьбы/шантажа́** to stoop to lying/asking/blackmail.

уни́зыва|ть, ю *impf. of* ⇒**униза́ть**

уника́л|ьный (~ен, ~ьна) *adj.* unique.

у́никум, а *m.* unique object; (*о человеке*) unique person.

унима́|ть(ся), ю(сь) *impf. of* ⇒**уня́ть(ся)**

унисо́н, а *m.* (*mus.*) unison; **петь в у.** to sing in unison; **в у.** (**с**+*i.*) (*fig.*) in unison, in concert (with).

унита́з, а *m.* toilet (bowl).

унифика́ци|я, и *f.* standardization.

унифици́р|овать, ую *impf. and pf.* to standardize.

унифо́рм|а, ы *f.* **1** (*одежда*) uniform. **2** (*collect.*) (*в цирке*) circus staff (*in the ring*).

униформи́ст, а *m.* circus hand (*in the ring*).

уничижа́|ть, ю *impf.* to disparage.

уничиже́ни|е, я *nt.* disparaging, disparagement.

уничижи́тел|ьный (~ен, ~ьна) *adj.* **1** disparaging. **2** (*gram.*) pejorative.

уничтож|а́ть, а́ю *impf. of* ⇒**~ить**

уничтожа́|ющий *pres. part. act. of* ⇒**~ть** *and adj.* (*огонь*) devastating, destructive; **у. взгляд** withering look; **~ющее замеча́ние** scathing comment; **~ющая кри́тика** scathing critique.

уничтоже́ни|е, я *nt.* **1** destruction, annihilation. **2** (*упразднение*) abolition, elimination.

уничто́ж|ить, у, ишь *pf.* (*of* ⇒**~а́ть**) **1** to destroy; (*врага*) to annihilate; (*насекомых*) to exterminate; **у. си́лы проти́вника** to wipe out the enemy's forces. **2** (*упразднить*) to abolish; to do away with; **у. крепостно́е пра́во** to abolish serfdom. **3** (*fig.*) (*унизить*) to crush, tear to shreds (*with an argument, etc.*).

у́ни|я, и *f.* (*hist., eccl.*) union.

уно́с, а *m.* taking away, carrying away.

уно|си́ть(ся), шу́(сь), ~сишь(ся) *impf. of* ⇒**унести́(сь)**

у́нтер, а *m.* (*coll.*) = **~-офице́р**

у́нтер-офице́р, а *m.* non-commissioned officer (*abbr.* NCO).

унт|ы́, о́в *pl.* (*sg.* **~, ~а́** *m.*) (*and* **у́нт|ы, ~,** *sg.* **~а, ~ы** *f.*) high boots (*of inverted pelt or deerskin*).

у́нци|я, и *f.* ounce (*measure*).

унывá|ть, ю *impf.* to be depressed, be dejected, be downhearted; **не ~й!** cheer up!

уны́л|ый (~, ~а) *adj.* **1** (*человек*) despondent, downcast. **2** (*мысль, взгляд*) melancholy, doleful, cheerless.

уны́ни|е, я *nt.* despondency, depression; **впасть в у.** to become downhearted, depressed; **навести́ у. на** (+*a.*) to depress.

уня́|ть, уйму́, уймёшь, *past* **~л, ~ла́, ~ло** *pf.* (*of* ⇒**унима́ть**) **1** (*успокоить*) to calm, soothe, pacify. **2** (*боль, кровотечение, слёзы*) to stop; **у. пожа́р** to stop a fire. **3** (*чувства*) to suppress.

уня́|ться, уйму́сь, уймёшься, *past* **~лся, ~ла́сь** *pf.* (*of* ⇒**унима́ться**) **1** (*успокоиться*) to calm down. **2** (*ветер, буря*) to abate, die down; (*боль, обида*) to die down; **кровотече́ние ~ло́сь** the bleeding has stopped.

упа́вший *adj.* (*голос*) weak (*from emotion or fear*).

упа́д: до ~у to the point of exhaustion, till one drops.

упада́|ть, ю *impf.* (*obs.*) to fall.

упа́д|ок, ка *m.* decline; **у. ду́ха** depression; **у. сил** breakdown.

упа́дочнический *adj.* decadent.

упа́дочничеств|о, а *nt.* decadence.

упа́доч|ный (~ен, ~на) *adj.* **1** (*искусство*) decadent. **2** depressive; **~ное настрое́ние** depression.

упак|ова́ть, у́ю *pf.* (*of* ⇒**пакова́ть** *and* **~о́вывать**) to pack (up).

упако́вк|а, и *f.* **1** (*действие*) packing, packaging. **2** (*материал*) packing, packaging; (*пакет*) package.

упако́вочный *adj.* packing.

упако́вщик, а *m.* packer.

упако́вщи|ца, цы *f. of* ⇒**~к**

упако́выва|ть, ю *impf. of* ⇒**упакова́ть**

упа́рива|ть, ю *impf. of* ⇒**упа́рить**

упа́р|ить, ю, ишь *pf.* (*of* ⇒**~ивать**) to boil down, concentrate.

упас|ти́, у́, ёшь, *past* **~, ~ла́** *pf.* (*coll.*) to save, preserve; **~й Бог, Бо́же ~й** (*i*) (*предостережение*) God preserve you!; heaven help you!, (*ii*) (*отрицание*) God forbid!

упа́|сть, ду́, дёшь, *past* **~л** *pf.* (*of* ⇒**па́дать** 1) to fall.

упёк *see* ⇒**упе́чь**

упека́|ть, ю *impf. of* ⇒**упе́чь**

упер|е́ть, упру́, упрёшь, *past* **~, ~ла** *pf.* (*of* ⇒**упира́ть**) **1** (*a.* **в**+*a.*) to rest (against), prop (against), lean (against); **у. ле́стницу в сте́ну** to rest a ladder against the wall; **у. глаза́, взгляд в кого́-н.** (*coll.*) to fasten one's gaze upon s.o. **2** (*sl.*) (*украсть*) to pinch (*Br.*), swipe.

упер|е́ться, упру́сь, упрёшься, *past* **~ся, ~лась** *pf.* (*of* ⇒**упира́ться**) **1** (+*i.* **в**+*a.*) to rest (against), prop (against), lean (against); **у. ло́ктем в стол** to rest one's elbow on the table; **у. нога́ми в зе́млю** to dig one's heels in the ground. **2** (**в**+*a.*; *coll.*) (*натолкнуться*) to come up (against), bump (into). **3** (*coll., fig.*) (*не согласиться*) to dig one's heels in; (**на**+*p.*) (*настоять*) to insist on; **он ~ся на своём** he refuses to budge.

упе́|чь, ку́, чёшь, ку́т, *past* **~к, ~кла́** *pf.* (*of* ⇒**~ка́ть**) **1** (*хлеб*) to bake thoroughly. **2** (*coll.*) (*отправить*) to send, banish (*against one's will*); **у. под суд** to drag into court, through the courts; **у. в тюрьму́** to lock up (*in prison*).

упива́|ться, юсь *impf. of* ⇒**упи́ться**

упира́|ть, ю *impf.* **1** *impf. of* ⇒**упере́ть. 2** (*impf. only*) (**на**+*a.*; *coll.*) to stress, insist (on).

упира́|ться, юсь *impf.* **1** *impf. of* ⇒**упере́ться. 2** (*impf. only*) (**в**+*a.*) (*сопротивляться*) to come up (against), be held up (by), be stuck (on account of); **прое́кт экспеди́ции ~ется в недоста́ток де́нег** the plan for an expedition is held up for want of funds.

упи|са́ть[1], шу́, ~шешь *pf.* (*of* ⇒**~сывать**) (*текст*) to get in, fit in; **у. всё письмо́ на одно́й страни́це** to get the whole letter on one page.

упи|са́ть[2], шу́, ~шешь *pf.* (*of* ⇒**~сывать**) (*coll.*) (*съесть*) to get through, consume.

упи|са́ться, ~шется *pf.* (*of* ⇒**~сываться**) (*о тексте*) to go in, fit in.

упи́сыва|ть(ся), ю, ет(ся) *impf. of* ⇒**уписа́ть(ся)**

упи́тан|ный *p.p.p. of* ⇒**упита́ть** *and adj.* **(~, ~на)** well-fed; (*толстый*) plump.

упит|а́ть, а́ю *pf.* (*of* ⇒**~ывать**) to fatten (up).

упи́тыва|ть, ю *impf. of* ⇒**упита́ть**

упи́|ться, упью́сь, упьёшься, *past* **~лся, ~ла́сь** *pf.* (*of* ⇒**~ва́ться**) (+*i.*) **1** (*coll.*) to get drunk (on). **2** (*fig.*) to revel (in), be intoxicated (by).

упла́т|а, ы *f.* payment, paying; **в ~у** on account, in payment; **подлежа́щий ~е** payable.

упла|ти́ть, чу́, ~тишь *pf.* (*of* ⇒**~чивать**) to pay; **у. по счёту** to pay a bill, settle an account.

упла́чива|ть, ю *impf. of* ⇒**уплати́ть**

упле|сти́, ту́, тёшь, *past* **~л, ~ла́** *pf.* (*of* ⇒**~та́ть**) (*coll.*) to tuck in (to).

уплета́|ть, ю *impf. of* ⇒**уплести́**

уплотне́ни|е, я *nt.* **1** compression; **у. кварти́ры** reduction of space per person in living accommodation; **у. рабо́чего дня** tightening up of time-schedules to increase amount of work done. **2** (*med.*) lump (*under skin*).

уплотн|и́ть, ю́, и́шь *pf.* (*of* ⇒**~я́ть**) (*почву, грунт*) to compress; **у. кварти́ру** to reduce space per person in living accommodation; **у. рабо́чий день** to plan the working day to increase amount of work done.

уплотн|и́ться, ю́сь, и́шься *pf.* (*of* ⇒**~я́ться**) **1** (*med.*) to harden. **2** (*о жильцах*) to be packed in more densely. **3** (*стать плотным*) to be compressed; to condense, thicken. **4** (*о рабочем дне*) to be tightened up.

уплотн|я́ть(ся), я́ю(сь) *impf. of* ⇒**~и́ть(ся)**

уплыва́|ть, ю *impf. of* ⇒**уплы́ть**

уплы́|ть, ву́, вёшь, *past* **~л, ~ла́, ~ло** *pf.* (*of* ⇒**~ва́ть**) **1** (*вплавь*) to swim away; (*о кораблях*) to sail away; (*о вещах*) to float away. **2** (*fig., coll.*) (*миновать*) to pass; **нема́ло вре́мени ~ло** much water has flowed under the bridge. **3** (*fig., coll.*) (*исчезнуть*) to vanish, ebb; **наде́жда ~ла́** hope faded.

упова́ни|е, я *nt.* (*obs.*) hope.

упова́|ть, ю *impf.* (**на**+*a.*) to put one's trust (in); (+*inf.*) to hope to.

уподо́б|ить, лю, ишь *pf.* (*of* ⇒**~ля́ть**) to liken.

уподо́б|иться, люсь, ишься *pf.* (*of* ⇒**~ля́ться**) (+*d.*) to become like.

уподобле́ни|е, я *nt.* likening, comparison.

уподобля́|ть(ся), ю(сь) *impf. of* ⇒**уподо́бить(ся)**

упое́ни|е, я *nt.* ecstasy, rapture, thrill; **с ~ем** ecstatically.

упо|ённый (~ён, ~ена́) *adj.* (+*i.*) intoxicated (with), thrilled (by), in raptures (about, over); **~ён успе́хом** intoxicated with success.

упоител|ьный (~ен, ~ьна) *adj.* intoxicating, ravishing.

упокое́ни|е, я *nt.* rest, repose; **ме́сто ~я** resting-place (= *grave*).

упоко́|ить, ю, ишь *pf.* (*obs.*) to lay to rest (= *to bury*).

упоко́|иться, юсь, ишься *pf.* (*obs.*) to find repose; to find one's resting-place (= *to be buried*).

упоко́|й, я *m.* repose.

уполз|а́ть, а́ю *impf. of* ⇒**~ти́**

уполз|ти́, у́, ёшь, *past* **~̆, ~ла́** *pf.* (*of* ⇒**~а́ть**) to creep, crawl away.

уполномо́ч|енный *p.p.p. of* ⇒**~ить;** *as n.* **у., ~енного** *m.* plenipotentiary, representative, person authorized.

уполномо́чива|ть, ю *impf. of* ⇒**уполномо́чить**

уполномо́чи|е, я *nt.* authorization; **подписа́ть докуме́нт по ~ю кого́-н.** to sign a document on s.o.'s authority.

уполномо́ч|ить, у, ишь *pf.* (*of* ⇒**~ивать**) (**на**+*a.*) to authorize, empower.

упомина́ни|е, я *nt.* mentioning; (**о**+*p.*) mention (of).

упомина́|ть, ю *impf. of* ⇒**упомяну́ть**

упо́мн|ить, ю, ишь *pf.* (*coll.*) to remember.

упомян|у́ть, у́, ~̆ешь *pf.* (*of* ⇒**упомина́ть**) (+*a.* *or* **о**+*p.*) to mention, refer (to).

упо́р, а *m.* **1** rest, prop, support; (*tech.*) stay, brace. **2**: **в у.** (*mil.*) point-blank (*also fig.*); **сказа́ть кому́-н. в у.** to tell s.o. point-blank, flat(ly); **смотре́ть на кого́-н. в у.** to stare straight at s.o.; **в у. не ви́деть кого́-н.** (*coll.*) to ignore s.o. completely. **3**: **сде́лать у.** (**на**+*a.* *or* *p.*) to lay stress (on).

упо́р|ный (~ен, ~на) *adj.* **1** (*упрямый*) stubborn, obstinate; (*настойчивый*) persistent; sustained; **у. ка́шель** persistent cough; **~ная оборо́на** sustained defence (*Br.*), defense (*US*). **2** (*tech.*) supporting; **у. като́к** bogie wheel.

упо́рств|о, а *nt.* (*упрямство*) stubbornness, obstinacy; (*настойчивость*) persistence.

упо́рств|овать, ую *impf.* to be stubborn, unyielding; (**в**+*p.*) to persist (in).

упорхн|у́ть, у́, ёшь *pf.* to fly, flit away.

упоря́дочива|ть(ся), ю, ет(ся) *impf. of* ⇒**упоря́дочить(ся)**

упоря́доч|ить, у, ишь *pf.* (*of* ⇒**~ивать**) to regulate, put in (good) order, set to rights.

упоря́доч|иться, ится *pf.* (*of* ⇒**~иваться**) to come right.

употреби́тельност|ь, и *f.* (frequency of) use.

употреби́тел|ьный (~ен, ~ьна) *adj.* (widely-)used; common, usual.

употреб|и́ть, лю́, и́шь *pf.* (*of* ⇒**~ля́ть**) to use; to make use (of); **у. все уси́лия** to make every effort, do one's utmost; **у. чьё-н. дове́рие во зло** to abuse s.o.'s confidence.

употребле́ни|е, я *nt.* use; (*применение*) application; **спо́соб ~я** directions for use; **для вну́треннего ~я** to be taken internally; **вы́йти из ~я** to go out of use, fall into disuse.

употребля́|ть, ю *impf. of* ⇒**употреби́ть**

упра́в|а, ы *f.* **1** (*coll.*) justice, satisfaction; **иска́ть ~ы на кого́-н.** to seek justice in the case of s.o.; **найти́ на кого́-н. ~у** to obtain satisfaction from s.o. **2** (*hist.*) office, board.

управдо́м, а *m.* (*abbr. of* ***управля́ющий до́мом, дома́ми***) house-manager.

управи́тел|ь, я *m.* (*obs.*) manager, bailiff, steward.

упра́в|иться, люсь, ишься *pf.* (*of* ⇒**~ля́ться**) (**с**+*i.*; *coll.*) **1** (*с работой*) to cope (with), manage. **2** (*с противником*) to deal (with) (= *to get the better of*).

управле́ни|е, я *nt.* **1** management, administration; direction; **у. госуда́рством** government; **орке́стр под ~ем Мрави́нского** orchestra conducted by Mravinsky. **2** (*tech.*) control; (*автомобилем*) driving; (*самолётом*) piloting; (*кораблём*) steering; **у. на расстоя́нии** remote control; **у. по ра́дио** radio control; **теря́ть у.** to get out of control. **3** (*деятельность органов власти*) government; **о́рганы ме́стного ~я** local government organs. **4** (*учреждение*) administration, authority, directorate, board, office; **Статисти́ческое у.** Statistics Office; (*здание*) head office. **5** (*tech.*) (*совокупность приборов*) controls; (*рулевое*) steering; **щит ~я** control panel. **6** (*gram.*) government.

управле́н|ческий *adj. of* ⇒**~ие** 3, 4; administrative; **у. аппара́т** (*учреждение*) government apparatus; (*люди*) administrative personnel.

управл|я́емый *pres. part. pass. of* ⇒**~я́ть** *and adj.* **у. снаря́д** guided missile.

управля́|ть, ю *impf.* (+*i.*) **1** (*учреждением*) to manage, administer, direct, run; (*оркестром, хором*) to conduct; (*страной*) to govern; to be in charge (of); **у. канцеля́рией** to manage an office. **2** (*tech.*) (*машиной*) to control, operate; (*автомобилем*) to drive; (*самолётом*) to pilot; (*кораблём*) to steer; **у. су́дном** (*naut.*) to navigate a vessel. **3** (*gram.*) to govern.

управля́|ться, юсь *impf. of* ⇒**упра́виться**

управл|я́ющий *pres. part. act. of* ⇒**~я́ть** *and adj.* control, controlling; **у. вал** (*tech.*) camshaft; *as n.* **у., ~я́ющего** *m.* (*в учреждении*) manager; (*в имении*) manager, steward, bailiff (*Br.*); **у. по́ртом** harbour (*Br.*), harbor (*US*) master.

упражне́ни|е, я *nt.* (*сил, мышц*) exercising; (*голоса, на рояле*) practising (*Br.*), practicing (*US*); (*гимнастическое, музыкальное*) exercise.

упражня́|ть, ю *impf.* to exercise, train; **у. му́скулы** to exercise one's muscles; **у. па́мять** to train one's memory.

упражня́|ться, юсь *impf.* (**в**+*p.*, **на**+*p.*, **с**+*i.*) to practise (*Br.*), practice (*US*), train (at).

упраздне́ни|е, я *nt.* abolition.

упраздн|и́ть, ю́, и́шь *pf.* (*of* ⇒**~я́ть**) to abolish.

упраздн|я́ть, я́ю *impf. of* ⇒**~и́ть**

упра́шива|ть, ю *impf. of* ⇒**упроси́ть**

упрева́|ть, ю *impf. of* ⇒**упре́ть**

упре|ди́ть, жу́, ди́шь *pf.* (*of* ⇒**~жда́ть**) **1** (*coll.*) (*предупредить*) to warn. **2** (*опередить*) to forestall, anticipate.

упрежда́|ть, ю *impf. of* ⇒**упреди́ть**

упрежда́ющий *adj.* (*mil.*) pre-emptive; **у. уда́р** pre-emptive strike.

упрежде́ни|е, я *nt.* (*mil.*) range correction, lead (*for firing at moving target*).

упрёк, а *m.* reproach; **бро́сить у. кому́-н.** to reproach s.o.; **ста́вить кому́-н. что-н. в у.** to hold sth. against s.o.

упрек|а́ть, а́ю *impf.* (*of* ⇒**~ну́ть**) (**в**+*p.*) to reproach (for); to accuse (of).

упрек|ну́ть, ну́, нёшь *pf. of* ⇒**~а́ть**

упре́|ть, ю *pf.* (*of* ⇒**~ва́ть**) (*coll.*) **1** (*о мясе*) to be well stewed. **2** (*о человеке*) to be covered with sweat.

упро|си́ть, шу́, ~̆сишь *pf.* (*of* ⇒**упра́шивать**) **1** (*настойчиво просить*) to beg, entreat. **2** (*pf. only*) (*убедить сделать что-н.*) to prevail upon.

У

упро|сти́ть, щу́, сти́шь *pf.* (*of* ⇒**~ща́ть**) **1** to simplify; (**до**+*g.*) to reduce (to). **2** (*pej.*) to oversimplify.

упро|сти́ться, сти́тся *pf.* (*of* ⇒**~ща́ться**) to become simpler, be simplified.

упро́чени|е, я *nt.* strengthening, consolidation.

упро́чива|ть(ся), ю(сь) *impf. of* ⇒**упро́чить(ся)**

упро́ч|ить, у, ишь *pf.* (*of* ⇒**~ивать**) **1** to strengthen, consolidate; to establish firmly. **2** (**за**+*i.*) to ensure; **его́ Пе́рвая симфо́ния ~ила за ним репута́цию выдаю́щегося компози́тора** his First Symphony ensured his reputation as an outstanding composer.

упро́ч|иться, усь, ишься *pf.* (*of* ⇒**~иваться**) **1** to be strengthened, consolidated; to be firmly established; **на́ше положе́ние ~илось** our position is firmly established. **2** (*упрочить своё положение*) to establish o.s. (firmly), settle o.s. **3** (**за**+*i.*) to be ensured; to become firmly attached (to); **за ним ~илась сла́ва хоро́шего учи́теля** his name as a good teacher was made; **про́звище ~илось за ней** the nickname stuck to her.

упроща́|ть(ся), ю, ет(ся) *impf. of* ⇒**упрости́ть(ся)**

упроще́ни|е, я *nt.* simplification.

упрощённост|ь, и *f.* **1** simplified character. **2** (*pej.*) (*примитивная*) oversimplification.

упро|щённый *p.p.p. of* ⇒**~сти́ть** *and adj.* **1** simplified. **2** (*pej.*) (*примитивный*) oversimplified.

упроще́нческий *adj.* (*pej.*) oversimplified.

упроще́нчеств|о, а *nt.* (*pej.*) oversimplification.

упру́г|ий (~, ~а) *adj.* elastic, resilient; **~ая похо́дка** springy gait.

упру́гост|ь, и *f.* elasticity, resilience; (*походки*) spring.

упру́|же *comp. of* ⇒**~гий, ~го**

упря́жк|а, и *f.* **1** team, relay (*of horses, dogs, etc.*). **2** (*упряжь*) harness, gear.

упряжн|о́й *adj.* draught (*Br.*), draft (*US*); **~а́я ло́шадь** draught-horse (*Br.*), draft-horse (*US*), carriage-horse; **~а́я тя́га** draw-bar.

у́пряж|ь, и *f.* harness, gear.

упря́м|ец, ца *m.* obstinate person.

упря́м|иться, люсь, ишься *impf.* to be obstinate; (**в**+*p.*) to persist (in).

упря́миц|а, ы *f. of* ⇒**упря́мец**

упря́мств|о, а *nt.* obstinacy, stubbornness.

упря́мств|овать, ую *impf.* = **упря́миться**

упря́м|ый (~, ~а) *adj.* **1** (*неуступчивый*) obstinate, stubborn; **фа́кты — упря́мая вещь** you can't ignore facts. **2** (*настойчивый*) persistent.

упря́|тать, чу, чешь *pf.* (*of* ⇒**~тывать**) **1** (*спрятать*) to hide, conceal. **2** (*fig., coll.*) (*убрать*) to put away; (*услать*) to banish; **у. в тюрьму́** to lock up.

упря́|таться, чусь, чешься *pf.* (*of* ⇒**~тываться**) (*coll.*) to hide (*intrans.*).

упря́тыва|ть(ся), ю(сь) *impf. of* ⇒**упря́тать(ся)**

упуска́|ть, ю *impf. of* ⇒**упусти́ть**

упу|сти́ть, щу́, ~стишь *pf.* (*of* ⇒**~ска́ть**) **1** (*из рук*) to let go, let slip, let fall; **у. пово́дья** to let the reins go; (*отпустить*) to let go; (*не заметить*) to miss. **2** (*fig.*) (*пропустить*) to let go, let slip; to miss; to lose; **у. возмо́жность, слу́чай** to miss an opportunity; **у. из виду** to overlook, fail to take account (of); **у. вре́мя** to let the moment pass. **3** (*fig.*) (*подростка, дисциплину*) to be too lax with.

упуще́ни|е, я *nt.* omission; (careless) slip; negligence; **у. по слу́жбе** neglect of duty, dereliction of duty.

упы́р|ь, я́ *m.* (*coll.*) vampire; ghoul; bloodsucker.

ура́ *int.* hurrah!; hurray! (*exclamation (i) expr. exultation or approbation, (ii) of troops going in to attack*); **на у.** (*i*) (*mil.*) by storm, (*ii*) (*iron.*) by luck (= *without due preparation*), (*iii*) (*с энтузиазмом*) with enthusiasm.

ура́- *comb. form* blind, unthinking (*e.g.* **ура́-патриоти́зм, а** *m.* jingoism).

уравне́ни|е, я *nt.* **1** (*в правах*) equalization. **2** (*math.*) equation; **у. пе́рвой сте́пени** simple equation.

ура́внива|ть¹, ю *impf. of* ⇒**уравня́ть**

ура́внива|ть², ю *impf. of* ⇒**уровня́ть**

уравни́ловк|а, и *f.* (*coll., pej.*) unjustified egalitarianism; **у. в опла́те труда́** wage-levelling (*Br.*), -leveling (*US*).

уравни́тельный *adj.* equalizing, levelling (*Br.*), leveling (*US*).

уравнове́|сить, шу, сишь *pf.* (*of* ⇒**~шивать**) **1** to balance. **2** (*fig.*) to counterbalance, offset.

уравнове́шенност|ь, и *f.* (*fig.*) balance, steadiness, composure.

уравнове́|шенный *p.p.p. of* ⇒**~сить** *and adj.* (*fig.*) balanced, steady, composed.

уравнове́шивани|е, я *nt.* balancing.

уравнове́шива|ть, ю *impf. of* ⇒**уравнове́сить**

уравня́|ть, ю *pf.* (*of* ⇒**ура́внивать¹**) to equalize, make equal, make level.

урага́н, а *m.* hurricane; (*fig.*) (*событий*) storm.

урага́н|ный *adj. of* ⇒**~; у. ого́нь** (*mil.*) drum-fire.

уразумева́|ть, ю *impf. of* ⇒**уразуме́ть**

уразуме́|ть, ю *pf.* (*of* ⇒**~ва́ть**) to comprehend.

Ура́л, а *m.* the Urals.

ура́льский *adj.* (*geog.*) Ural(s).

ура́н, а *m.* **1** **У.** (*astron.*) Uranus. **2** (*chem.*) uranium.

уранини́т, а *m.* (*min.*) uraninite, pitchblende.

ура́новый *adj.* uranium.

урбаниза́ци|я, и *f.* urbanization.

урбанизи́р|овать, ую *impf. and pf.* to urbanize.

урв|а́ть, у́, ёшь, *past* **~а́л, ~ала́, ~а́ло** *pf.* (*of* ⇒**урыва́ть**) (*coll.*) to snatch (*also fig.*), grab; **у. мину́ту-две для бесе́ды** to snatch a minute or two for a chat.

урв|а́ться, у́сь, ёшься, *past* **~а́лся, ~ала́сь, ~а́ло́сь** *pf.* (*of* ⇒**урыва́ться**) (*coll.*) to break loose; (*fig.*) to get away, snatch a free minute.

урду́ *m. indecl.* Urdu (*language*).

урегули́ровани|е, я *nt.* normalization; settlement.

урегули́р|овать, ую *pf.* (*of* ⇒**регули́ровать**) (*отношения*) to normalize; (*вопрос, спор*) to settle.

уре́|зать, жу, жешь *pf.* (*of* ⇒**~за́ть** *and* **~зывать**) **1** (*coll.*) (*края*) to cut off; to shorten. **2** (*бюджет*) to cut down, reduce; (*права*) to reduce; **у. шта́ты** to cut down the staff.

урез|а́ть, а́ю *impf. of* ⇒**~ать**

урезо́нива|ть, ю *impf. of* ⇒**урезо́нить**

урезо́н|ить, ю, ишь *pf.* (*of* ⇒**~ивать**) (*coll.*) to make to see reason, bring to reason.

уре́зыва|ть, ю *impf.* = **уреза́ть**

уреми́|я, и *f.* (*med.*) uraemia (*Br.*), uremia (*US*).

уре́тр|а, ы *f.* (*anat.*) urethra.

уретри́т, а *m.* (*med.*) urethritis.

у́рк|а, и *c.g.* (*prison sl.*) 'urka' (*criminal serving time, as opposed to political prisoner*).

у́рн|а, ы *f.* **1** (*для праха*) urn. **2**: **избира́тельная у.** ballot-box. **3** (*для мусора*) refuse bin (*Br.*), garbage can (*US*).

у́ров|ень, ня *m.* **1** level; (*fig.*) standard; **у. мо́ря** sea level; **высота́ над ~нем мо́ря** altitude above sea level; **в у.** (**с**+*i.*) (*i*) level (with); flush (with), (*ii*) (*fig.*) abreast (of), in pace (with); **на ~не земли́** at ground level; **быть на ~не** (*coll.*) to be up to standard; **у. жи́зни** standard of living. **2** (*tech.*) (*прибор*) level, gauge.

уровня́|ть, ю *pf.* (*of* ⇒**ура́внивать²**) to level, make even.

уро́д, а *m.* **1** freak, monster. **2** (*некрасивый человек*) ugly person; **нра́вственный у.** depraved person.

уро́дин|а, ы *c.g.* (*coll.*) = **уро́д**

уро|ди́ть, жу́, ди́шь *pf.* (*coll.*) to bear, bring forth.

уро|ди́ться, жу́сь, ди́шься *pf.* **1** (*о злаках*) to ripen; (*о человеке*) to be born. **2** (**в**+*a.*; *coll.*) (*в мать, в отца*) to take after.

уро́дливост|ь, и *f.* **1** (*недостаток*) deformity. **2** (*некрасивость*) ugliness.

уро́длив|ый (~, ~а) *adj.* **1** (*с уродством*) deformed, misshapen. **2** (*некрасивый*) ugly. **3** (*fig.*) (*плохой, ненормальный*) bad; abnormal; faulty; distorted; **~ое воспита́ние** bad upbringing; **у. перево́д** faulty translation.

уро́д|овать, ую *impf.* (*of* ⇒**из~**) **1** (*калечить*) to deform, disfigure, mutilate. **2** (*делать некрасивым*) to make ugly. **3** (*fig.*) (*искажать*) to distort.

уро́д|ский *adj.* (*coll.*) **1** *adj. of* ⇒**~. 2** distorted.

уро́дств|о, а *nt.* **1** (*физический недостаток*) deformity; disfigurement. **2** (*некрасивость*) ugliness. **3** (*fig.*) (*ненормальность*) abnormality.

урожа́|й, я *m.* **1** harvest; crop; **собра́ть у.** to gather in the harvest. **2** (*хороший сбор*) bumper crop, abundance (*also fig., coll.*); **урожа́й на** (+*a.*) a bumper crop of.

урожа́йност|ь, и *f.* productivity (*of crops*), yield.

урожа́|йный (~ен, ~йна) *adj.* **1** *adj. of* ⇒**~й. 2** producing high yield, productive; **у. год** good year (*for a crop*).

урождённ|ый *adj.*: **~ая** (*before maiden name*) née.

уроже́н|ец, ца *m.* (+*g.*) native (of).

уроже́н|ка, ки *f. of* ⇒**~ец**

уро́к, а *m.* **1** lesson (*also fig.*); **брать ~и** (+*g.*) to have, take lessons (in); **дава́ть ~и** (+*g.*) to give lessons (in); **препода́ть кому́-н. у.** (*fig.*) to teach s.o. a lesson; **дать кому́-н. у., послужи́ть ~ом кому́-н.** to serve as a lesson to s.o. **2** (*задание*) homework; **зада́ть у.** to set homework; **сде́лать, пригото́вить ~и** to do one's homework.

уро́лог, а *m.* (*med.*) urologist.

урологи́ческий *adj.* (*med.*) urological.

уроло́ги|я, и *f.* (*med.*) urology.

уро́н, а *no pl., m.* (*ущерб*) damages, losses; (*люди*) casualties; **нанести́ у.** to inflict casualties; **понести́ у.** to suffer losses.

урон|и́ть, ю́, ~́ишь *pf. of* ⇒**роня́ть**

уро́чищ|е, а *nt.* (*geog.*) **1** (*граница*) natural boundary. **2** (*местность*) isolated terrain feature (*e.g. wood in swamp country*).

уро́чный *adj.* fixed, agreed.

уругва́|ец, йца *m.* Uruguayan.

Уругва́|й, я *m.* Uruguay.

уругва́|йка, йки *f. of* ⇒**~ец**

уругва́йский *adj.* Uruguayan.

урча́ни|е, я *nt.* rumbling; (*собаки*) growling.

урч|а́ть, у́, и́шь *impf.* to rumble; (*о собаке*) to growl.

урыва́|ть(ся), ю(сь) *impf. of* ⇒**урва́ть(ся)**

уры́вками *adv.* (*coll.*) in snatches, by fits and starts.

урю́к, а (у) *no pl., m.* (*collect.*) dried apricots.

урю́к|овый *adj. of* ⇒**~**

уря́дник, а *m.* **1** (*в казачьих войсках*) Cossack NCO (= *non-commissioned officer*). **2** (*hist.*) (*в полиции*) village constable.

ус, а *m.* **1** (*see also* ⇒**~ы́**) (*человека*) moustache hair (*Br.*), mustache hair (*US*); **и в ус (себе́) не дуть** (*coll.*) not to give a damn; **мота́ть (себе́) на ус** (*coll.*) to take good note (of). **2** (*животного*) whisker. **3** (*насекомого*) antenna, feeler. **4** (*bot.*) tendril; (*злака*) awn. **5**: **кито́вый ус** whalebone.

уса́д|ебный *adj. of* ⇒**~ьба;** (*постройки, земля*) estate; **у. быт** life of the country gentry.

уса|ди́ть, жу́, ~́дишь *pf.* (*of* ⇒**~́живать**) **1** (*помочь усесться*) to seat, help sit down; (*заставить усесться*) to make sit down; **у. в тюрьму́** (*coll.*) to throw into jail. **2** (**за**+*a. or* +*inf.*) to sit (*s.o.*) down; **у. за уро́ки** to sit (*s.o.*) down to his/her lessons; **у. за пиани́но** to sit (*s.o.*) down at the piano. **3** (+*i.*) to plant (with).

уса́дк|а, и *f.* shrinking; shrinkage; contraction.

уса́дьб|а, ы, *g. pl.* **уса́деб** *f.* **1** (*hist.*) (*помещика*) country estate; country seat. **2** (*фермы*) farmstead.

уса́жива|ть, ю *impf. of* ⇒**усади́ть**

уса́жива|ться, юсь *impf. of* ⇒**усе́сться**

уса́т|ый (~, ~а) *adj.* **1** (*человек*) moustached (*Br.*), mustached (*US*); with a big moustache (*Br.*), mustache (*US*). **2** (*животное*) whiskered.

уса́ч, а́ *m.* **1** (*coll.*) man with a (big) moustache (*Br.*), mustache (*US*). **2** (*рыба*) barbel (*fish*). **3** (*жук*) Capricorn beetle (*Agapanthia dahli*).

усва́ива|ть, ю *impf. of* ⇒**усво́ить**

усвое́ни|е, я *nt.* (*привычки*) adoption; (*урока*) mastering; (*пищи*) assimilation.

усво́|ить, ю, ишь *pf.* (*of* ⇒**усва́ивать**) **1** (*привычку*) to adopt, acquire; to imitate. **2** (*урок*) to master; to assimilate; **у. пра́вила доро́жного движе́ния** to master the traffic regulations. **3** (*пищу*) to assimilate.

усвоя́емост|ь, и *f.* **1** comprehensibility; **хоро́шая у.** ease of comprehension, easiness. **2** (*chem.*) assimilability.

усе́ива|ть, ю *impf. of* ⇒**усе́ять**

усека́|ть, ю *impf. of* ⇒**усе́чь**

усе́рди|е, я *nt.* zeal; diligence.

усе́рд|ный (~ен, ~на) *adj.* diligent, painstaking.

усе́рдств|овать, ую *impf.* to be zealous; to take pains.

усе́|сться, уся́дусь, уся́дешься, *past* **~лся, ~лась** *pf.* (*of* ⇒**уса́живаться**) **1** to take a seat; to settle (down). **2** (**за**+*a. or* +*inf.*) to set (to), settle down (to); **у. за ка́рты** to settle down to (a game of) cards.

усеч|ённый *p.p.p. of* ⇒**~́ь** *and adj.* (*math.*) truncated.

усе́|чь, ку́, чёшь, ку́т, *past* **~́к, ~кла́** *pf.* (*of* ⇒**~ка́ть**) **1** (*укоротить*) to cut off, truncate. **2** (*coll.*) (*понять*) to understand, get.

усе́|ять, ю, ешь *pf.* (*of* ⇒**~ивать**) (+*i.*) **1** (*засеять*) to sow (with). **2** (*покрыть*) to cover (with), dot (with), stud (with), strew (with); **лицо́, ~янное весну́шками** face covered with freckles.

уси|де́ть, жу́, ди́шь *pf.* **1** (*остаться сидеть*) to keep one's place, remain sitting; **он так волнова́лся, что е́ле ~де́л** he was so excited that he could hardly sit still. **2** (*coll.*) (*удержаться на каком-н. месте*) to stay around in a place. **3** (*sl.*) (*съесть*) to guzzle; (*выпить*) to knock back.

уси́дчивост|ь, и *f.* assiduity.

уси́дчив|ый (~, ~а) *adj.* assiduous; painstaking.

у́сик, а *m.* **1** (*pl.*) small moustache (*Br.*), mustache (*US*). **2** (*bot.*) tendril; (*злака*) awn; (*клубники*) runner. **3** (*zool.*) antenna, feeler.

усиле́ни|е, я *nt.* **1** (*контроля*) strengthening; (*охраны, прочности*) reinforcement. **2** (*работы*) intensification; (*проблем*) aggravation; (*radio*) amplification.

уси́л|енный *p.p.p. of* ⇒**~ить** *and adj.* **1** (*охрана*) reinforced; **~енное пита́ние** high-calorie diet. **2** (*внимание, скорость*) intensified, increased. **3** (*настойчивый*) persistent, urgent; **~енные про́сьбы** earnest entreaties.

уси́лива|ть, ю *impf. of* ⇒**уси́лить**

уси́лива|ться, юсь *impf.* **1** *impf. of* ⇒**уси́литься. 2** (+*inf.*; *obs.*) to try (to).

уси́ли|е, я *nt.* effort; exertion; **приложи́ть все ~я** to make every effort, spare no effort; **сде́лать у. над собо́й** to make an effort.

усили́тел|ь, я *m.* amplifier.

усили́тельный *adj.* amplifying.

уси́л|ить, ю, ишь *pf.* (*of* ⇒**~ивать**) **1** (*войска, конструкцию*) to strengthen, reinforce. **2** (*наблюдение, волнение*) to intensify, increase, heighten; (*звук*) to amplify.

уси́л|иться, ится *pf.* (*of* ⇒**~иваться**) (*ветер, чувство*) to become stronger; (*дождь, боль*) to intensify, increase (*intrans.*); (*звук*) to grow louder.

уска|ка́ть, чу́, ~́чешь *pf.* **1** (*о зайце*) to bound away; (*coll.*) (*о человеке*) to run off. **2** (*о лошади; на лошади*) to gallop off.

ускольз|а́ть, а́ю *impf. of* ⇒**~ну́ть**

ускольз|ну́ть, ну́, нёшь *pf.* (*of* ⇒**~а́ть**) **1** (*из рук*) to slip out; (*из-под ног*) to slip away. **2** (*fig., coll.*) (*о человеке*) to slip off, steal away. **3** (*fig.*) (**от**+*g.*) to disappear; to escape; **у. от внима́ния** to escape one's notice. **4** (**от**+*g.*; *coll.*) to evade, avoid; **у. от пря́мого отве́та** to avoid giving a direct answer.

ускоре́ни|е, я *nt.* acceleration; speeding up.

уско́р|енный *p.p.p. of* ⇒**~ить** *and adj.* (*темп*) accelerated; (*развитие*) rapid; (*курс*) crash.

ускори́тел|ь, я *m.* (*tech.*) accelerator.

уско́р|ить, ю, ишь *pf.* (*of* ⇒**~я́ть**) **1** (*убыстрить*) to quicken; to speed up, accelerate; **у. шаг** to quicken one's pace. **2** (*приблизить*) to hasten; (*смерть, что-н. плохое*) to precipitate.

уско́р|иться, ится *pf.* (*of* ⇒**~я́ться**) **1** (*шаги*) to quicken; (*ход механизма*) to accelerate. **2** (*выздоровление, отъезд*) to be speeded up.

ускор|я́ть, я́ю *impf. of* ⇒**~́ить**

Y

ускор|я́ться, я́ется *impf. of* ⇒**~иться**

усла́влива|ться, юсь *impf. of* ⇒**усло́виться**

усла́д|а, ы *f.* (*obs.*) joy, delight.

услади́тел|ьный (~ен, ~ьна) *adj.* (*obs.*) pleasing, delightful.

усла|ди́ть, жу́, ди́шь *pf.* (*of* ⇒**~жда́ть**) (*obs. or poet.*) **1** to delight, charm. **2** (*облегчить*) to soften, mitigate.

усла|ди́ться, жу́сь, ди́шься *pf.* (*of* ⇒**~жда́ться**) (+*i.*; *obs. or poet.*) to delight (in).

услажда́|ть(ся), ю(сь) *impf. of* ⇒**услади́ть(ся)**

усла|сти́ть, щу́, сти́шь *pf.* (*of* ⇒**~ща́ть**) to sweeten.

усла́ть, ушлю́, ушлёшь *pf.* (*of* ⇒**усыла́ть**) (*с поручением*) to send, dispatch; (*в тюрьму, на каторгу*) to banish, send away.

услаща́|ть, ю *impf. of* ⇒**усласти́ть**

усле|ди́ть, жу́, ди́шь *pf.* (**за**+*i.*) **1** (*за ребёнком*) to keep an eye (on), mind. **2** (*за ходом разговора*) to follow.

усло́ви|е, я *nt.* **1** (*требование*) condition; stipulation, proviso; **поста́вить ~ем** to make it a condition, stipulate; **под ~ем, что; при ~и, что; с ~ем, что** on condition that, provided that, providing. **2** (*obs.*) (*договор*) agreement; **заключи́ть у.** to conclude an agreement. **3** (*pl.*) (*правила, обстоятельства*) conditions; **пого́дные ~я** weather conditions; **~я приёма** (*radio*) reception; **при про́чих ра́вных ~ях** other things being equal; **все ~я** (*coll.*) everything necessary.

усло́в|иться, люсь, ишься *pf.* (*of* ⇒**усла́вливаться**) (**о**+*p.*) to agree, settle (on); (+*inf.*) to agree (to); to arrange, make arrangements (to); **мы ~ились о ме́сте свида́ния** we agreed on a meeting-place.

усло́вленный *adj.* agreed; **в у. час** at the hour agreed.

усло́влива|ться, юсь = **усла́вливаться**

усло́вно *adv.* (*как принято*) conventionally; (*с условием*) conditionally; **его́ приговори́ли/осуди́ли у.** he was given a suspended sentence.

усло́вност|ь, и *f.* **1** (*условный характер*) conditional character. **2** (*норма поведения*) convention, conventionality.

усло́в|ный *adj.* **1** (*принятый*) conventional; (*знак, жест*) agreed, prearranged. **2 (~ен, ~на)** (*с условием*) conditional; **у. пригово́р** (*leg.*) suspended sentence; **~ное согла́сие** conditional consent. **3 (~ен, ~на)** (*относительный*) relative. **4** (*воображаемый*) imaginary. **5** (*gram.*) conditional. **6**: **у. рефле́кс** (*physiol.*) conditioned reflex.

усложне́ни|е, я *nt.* complication.

усложн|ённый *p.p.p. of* ⇒**~и́ть** *and adj.* complicated.

усложн|и́ть, ю́, и́шь *pf.* (*of* ⇒**~я́ть**) to complicate.

усложн|и́ться, и́тся *pf.* (*of* ⇒**~я́ться**) to become complicated.

усложн|я́ть, я́ю *impf. of* ⇒**~и́ть**

усложн|я́ться, я́ется *impf. of* ⇒**~и́ться**

услу́г|а, и *f.* **1** service; favour (*Br.*), favor (*US*), good turn; **до́брые ~и** (*dipl.*) good offices; **оказа́ть ~у кому́-н.** to do s.o. a service; **предложи́ть свой ~и** to offer one's services; **к ва́шим ~ам** at your service. **2** (*pl.*) service(s); **коммуна́льные ~и** public utilities.

услуже́ни|е, я *nt.* (*obs.*) service; **быть в ~и (у**+*g.*) to be in service (with); (*fig.*; *iron.*) to be a lackey (of).

услу́жива|ть, ю *impf.* (*obs.*) to serve, act as a servant.

услуж|и́ть, у́, ~ишь *pf.* (*of* ⇒**~ивать**) (+*d.*) to do a service, good turn.

услу́жлив|ый (~, ~а) *adj.* obliging.

услыха́ть = **услы́шать**

услы́ш|ать, у, ишь *pf. of* ⇒**слы́шать**

усма́трива|ть, ю *impf. of* ⇒**усмотре́ть**

усмех|а́ться, а́юсь *impf. of* ⇒**~ну́ться**

усмех|ну́ться, ну́сь, нёшься *pf.* (*of* ⇒**~а́ться**) to smirk; to grin.

усме́шк|а, и *f.* smirk, grin.

усмире́ни|е, я *nt.* (*мятежа*) suppression, putting down; (*агрессора*) pacification; (*зверя*) taming.

усмир|и́ть, ю́, и́шь *pf.* (*of* ⇒**~я́ть**) **1** (*успокоить*) to pacify; to calm, quieten; (*укротить*) to tame (*also fig.*). **2** (*мятеж*) to suppress, put down.

усмир|я́ть, я́ю *impf. of* ⇒**~и́ть**

усмотре́ни|е, я *nt.* discretion, judgement; **де́йствовать по своему́ ~ю** to use one's own discretion; **мы оста́вили э́то на ва́ше у.** we left it to your discretion.

усмотр|е́ть, ю́, ~ишь *pf.* (*of* ⇒**усма́тривать**) **1** (**за**+*i.*) (*coll.*) (*уследить*) to keep an eye (on). **2** (*увидеть*) to perceive, observe. **3** (**в**+*p.*) (*принять*) to see (in); to regard (as), interpret (as); **у. угро́зу в заявле́нии** to interpret the statement as a threat.

усна|сти́ть, щу́, сти́шь *pf.* (*of* ⇒**~ща́ть**) (+*i.*) to stuff (with), lard (with); **у. речь ци́фрами** to stuff a speech with figures.

усноща́|ть, ю *impf. of* ⇒**усласти́ть**

усн|у́ть, у́, ёшь *pf.* to go to sleep, fall asleep (*also fig.*); **у. ве́чным сном, наве́ки** (*rhet.*) to pass on to one's eternal rest.

усо́биц|а, ы *f.* (*hist.*) internal strife.

усоверше́нствовани|е, я *nt.* **1** (*действие*) improvement, refinement; (*usu. pl.*) (*изменения*) improvements, refinements. **2**: **ку́рсы ~я** advanced training courses.

усоверше́нствов|анный *p.p.p. of* ⇒**~ать** *and adj.* (*модель, двигатель*) improved.

усоверше́нств|овать(ся), ую(сь) *pf. of* ⇒**соверше́нствовать(ся)**

усо́ве|стить, щу, стишь *pf.* (*of* ⇒**~щивать**) to appeal to the conscience (of); to make ashamed.

усо́ве|ститься, щусь, стишься *pf.* (*of* ⇒**~щиваться**) to be sorry, be conscience-stricken.

усо́вещива|ть(ся), ю(сь) *impf. of* ⇒**усо́вестить(ся)**

усомн|и́ться, ю́сь, и́шься *pf.* (**в**+*p.*) to doubt.

усо́пш|ий *adj.* deceased; *as n.* **у., ~его** *m.*, **~ая, ~ей** *f.* the deceased.

усо́х|нуть, ну, нешь, *past* **~, ~ла** *pf.* (*of* ⇒**усыха́ть**) to dry up, dry out; (*о человеке*) to wither.

успева́емост|ь, и *f.* progress (*in studies*).

успева́|ть, ю *impf.* **1** *impf. of* ⇒**успе́ть. 2** (*impf. only*) (**в**+*p. or* **по**+*d.*) to make progress (in), get on well (in, at) (*studies*).

успе́ется *impers., pf.* (*coll.*) there's plenty of time.

успе́ни|е, я *nt.* (*eccl.*) **1** death, passing. **2 У.** (Feast of) the Dormition, Assumption (of the Virgin).

успе́н|ский *adj. of* ⇒**~ие** 2

успе́|ть, ю *pf.* (*of* ⇒**~ва́ть**) **1** to have time; to manage; **у. написа́ть** to have time to write; **у. на заседа́ние** to be in time for the meeting; **у. к по́езду** to manage to catch the train; **не ~л вы́йти из до́ма, как пошёл дождь** no sooner had I left the house than it started to rain. **2** (*obs.*) (**в**+*p.*) (*достигнуть успеха*) to succeed (in), be successful (in), excel (in).

успе́х, а *m.* **1** success; **име́ть большо́й у.** to be a great success; **по́льзоваться ~ом** to be a success; **по́льзоваться ~ом у кого́-н.** to be successful with s.o.; **с тем же ~ом** equally well, with the same result; **с ~ом** successfully. **2** (*pl.*) success, progress; **как ва́ши ~и?** how are you getting on?; **де́лать ~и (в**+*p.*) to make progress (in).

успе́шно *adv.* successfully.

успе́шност|ь, и *f.* success.

успе́ш|ный (~ен, ~на) *adj.* successful.

успока́ива|ть(ся), ю(сь) *impf. of* ⇒**успоко́ить(ся)**

успока́ив|ающий *pres. part. act. of* ⇒**~ать** *and adj.* (*тон*) soothing, calming; (*действие*) sedative; **~ающее сре́дство** sedative.

успокое́ни|е, я *nt.* **1** (*действие*) calming, quieting, soothing; (*med.*) sedation. **2** (*состояние*) calm; peace, tranquillity.

успоко́енност|ь, и *f.* **1** calmness; tranquillity. **2** (*pej.*) (*беспечность*) complacency.

успокои́тел|ьный (~ен, ~ьна) *adj.* calming, soothing; reassuring; *as n.* **~ьное, ~ьного** *nt.* sedative.

успоко́|ить, ю, ишь *pf.* (*of* ⇒**успока́ивать**) **1** to calm; (*убедить не тревожиться*) to reassure, set one's mind at rest. **2** (*боль*) to assuage, deaden; **у. чьи-н. подозре́ния** to still s.o.'s suspicions. **3** (*усмирить, заставляя повиноваться*) to reduce to order, control; **у. дете́й** to make children be quiet.

успоко́|иться, юсь, ишься *pf.* (*of* ⇒**успока́иваться**) **1** (*о человеке*) to calm down; to compose o.s. **2** (*стать пассивным*) to be satisfied; **у. на дости́гнутом** to rest content with what has been achieved. **3** (*о боли*) to abate; (*о море*) to become still; (*о ветре*) to drop.

уст|а́, ~, ~а́м *no sg.* (*obs. or poet.*) mouth, lips; **вложи́ть в чьи-н. у.** (*fig.*) to put into s.o.'s mouth; **из ~ в у.** by word of mouth; **узна́ть из пе́рвых, вторы́х ~** to learn at first, second hand; **э́то у всех на ~а́х** everyone's talking about it; **твои́ми бы ~а́ми мёд пить** if only you were right.

уста́в, а *m.* regulations, rules, statutes; (*mil.*) service regulations; (*в монастыре*) rule; **у. университе́та** university statutes; **У. ООН** UN Charter.

уста|ва́ть, ю́, ёшь *impf. of* ⇒**~́ть; не ~ва́я** (*as adv.*) incessantly, tirelessly.

уста́в|ить, лю, ишь *pf.* (*of* ⇒**~ля́ть**) **1** (*разместить*) to set, arrange, dispose; **у. ме́бель в ко́мнате** to arrange furniture about the room. **2** (+*i.*) (*занять*) to cover (with), fill (with), pile (with); **у. стол буты́лками** to cover a table with bottles; **у. по́лку кни́гами** to fill, cram a shelf with books. **3** (*coll.*) (**глаза́,** *etc.* **на**+*a.*) to direct, fix (one's gaze, *etc.*, upon).

уста́в|иться, люсь, ишься *pf.* (*of* ⇒**~ля́ться**) **1** (*поместиться*) to find room, go in. **2** (+*i.*) (*стать заставленным*) to become crammed, cluttered (with). **3** (*coll.*) (**в, на**+*a.*) to fix one's gaze (upon), stare (at).

уставля́|ть(ся), ю(сь) *impf. of* ⇒**уста́вить(ся)**

уста́вный *adj.* regulation, statutory, prescribed.

уста́лост|ь, и *f.* fatigue, tiredness, weariness; **у. мета́лла** (*tech.*) metal fatigue.

уста́лый *adj.* tired, weary, fatigued.

у́стал|ь, и *f.* = **~́ость; без ~и** tirelessly, unceasingly.

устана́влива|ть(ся), ю, ет(ся) *impf. of* ⇒**установи́ть(ся)**

установ|и́ть, лю́, ~́ишь *pf.* (*of* ⇒**устана́вливать**) **1** (*поставить, поместить*) to place, put, set up; (*оборудование, механизм*) to install, mount, rig up; (*памятник*) to put up. **2** (*показание, личину*) to adjust, regulate, set (to, by); **у. часы́ по ра́дио** to set one's watch by the radio. **3** (*власть, контакт*) to establish, institute; **у. связь** (**с**+*i.*; *mil.*) to establish communication (with). **4** (*назначить*) to fix, prescribe, establish; **у. гра́фик** to fix the schedule. **5** (*добиться*) to secure, obtain; **у. тишину́** to secure quiet. **6** (*обнаружить, выяснить*) to establish, determine; to ascertain; **у. причи́ну ава́рии** to establish the cause of a crash.

установ|и́ться, ~́ится *pf.* (*of* ⇒**устана́вливаться**) **1** (*наступить*) to be established; to set in; **~и́лся поря́док** a procedure was established; **~и́лся обы́чай** it has become a custom; **пого́да ~и́лась** the weather has become settled. **2** (*о характере, взглядах*) to be formed, mature.

устано́вк|а, и *f.* **1** (*действие*) placing, setting up, arrangement; (*оборудования*) installation; (*величины*) setting. **2** (*часов*) adjustment, setting. **3** (*tech.*) (*механизм, приспособление*) installation; (*comput.*) set-up. **4** (*цель*) aim, purpose; **име́ть ~у** (**на**+*a.*) to aim (at). **5** (*директива*) directions, directive.

установле́ни|е, я *nt.* establishment; (*определение*) determination.

устано́в|ленный *p.p.p. of* ⇒**~и́ть** *and adj.* established, fixed, prescribed, regulation; **в ~ленном поря́дке** in prescribed manner.

устано́в|очный *adj.* **1** (*tech.*) *adj. of* ⇒**~ка 1, 2; у. винт** adjusting screw. **2** *adj. of* ⇒**~ка 5; у. вопро́с** fundamental question.

устано́вщик, а *m.* fitter, mounter; (*mil.*) (instrument) setter.

устарева́|ть, ю *impf. of* ⇒**устаре́ть**

устаре́|вший *past. part. act. of* ⇒**~ть** *and adj.* obsolete.

устаре́лый *adj.* obsolete; antiquated, out of date.

устаре́|ть, ю *pf.* (*of* ⇒**~ва́ть**) to become obsolete; to become antiquated, out of date.

уста́|ть, ну, нешь *pf.* (*of* ⇒**~ва́ть**) to become tired; **я ~л** I am tired; **мы ~ли с доро́ги** we're tired from the journey; **студе́нт ~л чита́ть** the student was tired from reading.

устерега́|ть, ю *impf. of* ⇒**устере́чь**

устере́|чь, гу́, жёшь, гу́т, *past* **~̈г, ~гла́** *pf.* (*of* ⇒**~га́ть**) (**от**+*g.*; *coll.*) to guard (against).

устила́|ть, ю *impf. of* ⇒**устла́ть**

устла́ть, устелю́, усте́лешь *pf.* (*of* ⇒**устила́ть**) (+*i.*) to cover (with); (*плитами, камнями*) to pave (with).

у́стно *adv.* orally, by word of mouth.

у́стн|ый *adj.* verbal, oral; **~ое обеща́ние** verbal promise; **~ая речь** spoken language; **у. экза́мен** oral (examination).

усто́|й[1], я *m.* **1** (*tech.*) (*моста*) abutment, buttress, pier. **2** (*опора*) foundation, support. **3** (*pl.*; *fig.*) (*основы*) foundations, bases.

усто́|й[2], я *m.* (*coll.*) (*на поверхности жидкости*) thickened layer on surface of liquid; **у. молока́** cream.

усто́йчивост|ь, и *f.* (*опоры*) stability, steadiness; (*веры*) firmness.

усто́йчив|ый (~, ~а) *adj.* (*опора, плот*) stable, steady; (*вера, принцип*) firm; **~ая валю́та** stable currency; **~ая пого́да** settled weather.

усто|я́ть, ю́, и́шь *pf.* **1** (*не упасть*) to keep one's balance, remain standing; **у. на нога́х** to keep one's balance. **2** (*fig.*) (*в споре*) to stand one's ground. **3** (*не поддаться*) to resist, hold out; **у. пе́ред собла́зном** to resist a temptation; **у. про́тив проти́вника** to hold out against an opponent.

усто|я́ться, и́тся *pf.* **1** (*о жидкостях*) to settle. **2** (*о пиве, о тесте*) to have stood (*sufficient time*). **3** (*о взглядах*) to become fixed, become permanent.

устра́ива|ть(ся), ю(сь) *impf. of* ⇒**устро́ить(ся)**

устране́ни|е, я *nt.* removal; (*уничтожение*) elimination.

устран|и́ть, ю́, и́шь *pf.* (*of* ⇒**~я́ть**) **1** (*убрать в сторону*) to remove; **у. прегра́ды** to remove obstacles; (*уничтожить*) to eliminate. **2** (*уволить*) to remove (*from office*), dismiss.

устран|и́ться, ю́сь, и́шься *pf.* (*of* ⇒**~я́ться**) to resign, retire, withdraw.

устран|я́ть(ся), я́ю(сь) *impf. of* ⇒**~и́ть(ся)**

устраш|а́ть(ся), а́ю(сь) *impf. of* ⇒**~и́ть(ся)**

устраша́|ющий *pres. part. act. of* ⇒**~ть** *and adj.* frightening, appalling.

устраше́ни|е, я *nt.* **1** (*действие*) frightening; **сре́дство ~я** (*mil., pol.*) deterrent. **2** (*состояние*) fright, fear.

устраш|и́ть, у́, и́шь *pf.* (*of* ⇒**~а́ть**) to frighten, scare.

устраш|и́ться, у́сь, и́шься *pf.* (*of* ⇒**~а́ться**) (+*g.*) to be afraid, be scared (of).

устрем|и́ть, лю́, и́шь *pf.* (*of* ⇒**~ля́ть**) (**на**+*a.*) to direct (to, at); **у. глаза́ на что-н.** to fasten one's gaze upon sth.

устрем|и́ться, лю́сь, и́шься *pf.* (*of* ⇒**~ля́ться**) **1** (**на**+*a.*) (*направиться*) to rush (upon, at); to head (for). **2** (**на**+*a.*; **к**+*d.*) (*сосредоточиться*) to be directed (at, towards), be fixed (upon), be concentrated (on); (*о человеке*) to concentrate (on).

устремле́ни|е, я *nt.* **1** (*порыв*) rush. **2** (*желание*) striving, aspiration.

устремлённост|ь, и *f.* aspiration.

устремля́|ть(ся), ю(сь) *impf. of* ⇒**устреми́ть(ся)**

у́стриц|а, ы *f.* oyster.

у́стри|чный *adj. of* ⇒**~ца**

устрое́ни|е, я *nt.* arranging, organization.

устро́ител|ь, я *m.* organizer.

устро́итель|ница, ницы *f. of* ⇒**~**

устро́|ить, ю, ишь *pf.* (*of* ⇒**устра́ивать**) **1** (*изготовить, соорудить*) to make, construct. **2** (*концерт*) to arrange, organize; (*школу*) to establish. **3** (*вызвать*) to make, cause, create; **у. сканда́л** to make a scene; **я ~ил так, что она́ не узна́ла** I arranged things so that she didn't find out. **4** (*наладить*) to settle, order, put in (good) order; **у. свои́ дела́** to put one's affairs in order. **5** (*поместить*) to place, fix up; **у. кого́-н. на рабо́ту** to fix s.o. up with work; (*coll.*) (*достать*) to get (hold of); **она́ всегда́ мо́жет у. биле́т на бале́т** she can always get hold of a ticket for the

У

ballet.
6 (*impers.*; *coll.*) (*оказаться удобным*) to suit, be convenient (to, for).

устро́|иться, юсь, ишься *pf.* (*of* ⇒**устра́иваться**) **1** (*прийти в порядок*) to work out (well).
2 (*наладить свои дела*) to manage, get by. **3** (*расположиться*) to settle down, get settled; **они́ ~ились в гости́ницу** they got settled into the hotel. **4** (*на работу*) to get (*a job*); **он ~ился на желе́зную доро́гу проводнико́м** he has got a job on the railway as a conductor.

устро́йств|о, а *nt.* **1** (*концерта*) arrangement, organization; (*на работу*) getting (*of work*); (*в новой квартире*) settling down. **2** (*расположение, конструкция*) construction; layout; (*tech.*) working principle(s). **3** (*прибор*) apparatus, device; **запомина́ющее у.** (*comput.*) storage (device), memory; **постоя́нное запомина́ющее у.** (*comput.*) ROM (*read-only memory*).
4 (*порядок, строй*) structure, system; **общественное у.** social structure.

усту́п, а *m.* **1** (*в стене, скале*) shelf, ledge; (*agric.*) terrace. **2** (*mil.*) echelon formation (*of artillery*).

уступ|а́ть, а́ю *impf. of* ⇒**~и́ть**

уступи́тельный *adj.* (*gram.*) concessive.

уступ|и́ть, лю́, ~́ишь *pf.* (*of* ⇒**~а́ть**) **1** (*+d.*) (*в пользу другого*) to let have, give up (to); to cede (to); **у. кому́-н. ме́сто** to give up one's place to s.o.; **у. доро́гу** (*+d.*) to make way (for), let pass.
2 (*+d.*) (*покориться*) to yield (to), give in (to); **у. кому́-н. в спо́ре** to give in to s.o.'s argument.
3 (*+d.*) (*быть хуже кого-н., чего-н.*) to be inferior (to); **как расска́зчик он никому́ не ~́ит** as a story-teller he is second to none.
4 (*coll.*) (*продать дешевле*) to let have (= *to sell*); **он ~и́л ей кни́гу за 100 рубле́й** he let her have the book for 100 roubles.
5 (*coll.*) (*сумму*) to take off, knock off; **он ~и́л 10 рубле́й** he knocked off ten roubles.

усту́пк|а, и *f.* **1** concession, compromise; **сде́лать ~и** to make concessions, compromise. **2** (*в цене*) reduction, discount.

усту́пчат|ый (~, ~а) *adj.* stepped, terraced.

усту́пчивост|ь, и *f.* pliancy; compliance.

усту́пчив|ый (~, ~а) *adj.* pliant, pliable; compliant.

усты|ди́ть, жу́, ди́шь *pf.* to shame, put to shame.

усты|ди́ться, жу́сь, ди́шься *pf.* (*+g.*) to be ashamed (of); to feel embarrassed (for).

у́сть|е, я, *g. pl.* **~ев** *nt.* **1** (*реки*) mouth, estuary. **2** (*шахты, трубы*) mouth, orifice.

усугу́б|ить, ~́лю, ~́ишь *pf.* (*of* ⇒**~ля́ть**) to increase; to intensify; to aggravate.

усугубля́|ть, ю *impf. of* ⇒**усугу́бить**

усугубл|я́ющий *pres. part. act. of* ⇒**~я́ть** *and adj.*: **~я́ющие обстоя́тельства** (*leg.*) aggravating circumstances.

усу́шк|а, и *f.* (*comm.*) wastage, loss of weight (*through drying*).

ус|ы́, о́в *pl.* (*sg.* **ус, а** *m.*) moustache (*Br.*), mustache (*US*) (*see also* ⇒**ус**); **мы,** *etc.* **са́ми с ~а́ми** (*coll.*) we, *etc.*, weren't born yesterday.

усыла́|ть, ю *impf. of* ⇒**усла́ть**

усынов|и́ть, лю́, и́шь *pf.* (*of* ⇒**~ля́ть**) to adopt (*as a son*).

усыновле́ни|е, я *nt.* adoption.

усыновля́|ть, ю *impf. of* ⇒**усынови́ть**

усыпа́льниц|а, ы *f.* burial-vault.

усы́п|ать, лю, лешь *pf.* (*of* ⇒**~а́ть**) (*+i.*) to strew (with), scatter (with); (*покрыть*) to cover (with).

усып|а́ть, а́ю *impf. of* ⇒**~́ать**

усыпи́тел|ьный (~ен, ~ьна) *adj.* soporific (*also fig.*).

усып|и́ть, лю́, и́шь *pf.* (*of* ⇒**~ля́ть**) **1** (*перед операцией*) to put to sleep; (*пением, чтением*) to lull to sleep. **2** (*fig.*) (*подозрения*) to lull; (*внимание*) to weaken, undermine; **у. со́весть** to lull one's conscience; **у. боль** to deaden pain. **3** (*больную собаку*) to put to sleep.

усыпле́ни|е, я *nt.* putting to sleep; lulling (to sleep).

усыпля́|ть, ю *impf. of* ⇒**усыпи́ть**

усыха́|ть, ю *impf. of* ⇒**усо́хнуть**

ута́ива|ть, ю *impf. of* ⇒**утаи́ть**

ута|и́ть, ю́, и́шь *pf.* (*of* ⇒**~́ивать**) **1** (*скрыть*) to conceal; (*умолчать*) to keep to o.s., keep secret. **2** (*присвоить*) to appropriate.

ута́йк|а, и *f.* (*coll.*) **1** (*истины*) concealment; **без ~и** frankly, openly.
2 (*денег*) appropriation.

ута́птыва|ть, ю *impf. of* ⇒**утопта́ть**

ута́скива|ть, ю *impf. of* ⇒**утащи́ть**

утащ|и́ть, у́, ~́ишь *pf.* (*of* ⇒**ута́скивать**) **1** to drag away, off (*also fig.*); **у. кого́-н. в кино́** (*coll.*) to drag s.o. off to the cinema. **2** (*coll.*) (*украсть*) to steal, pinch (*Br.*).

у́твар|ь, и *no pl.*, *f.* (*collect.*) utensils, equipment.

утверди́тел|ьный (~ен, ~ьна) *adj.* affirmative.

утвер|ди́ть, жу́, ди́шь *pf.* (*of* ⇒**~жда́ть**) **1** (*диктатуру, правила*) to establish (*securely, firmly*). **2** (**в** *+p.*) (*убедить*) to confirm (in); **у. в како́м-н. мне́нии** to confirm in some opinion.
3 (*санкционировать*) to approve; to confirm; (*договор*) to ratify; **у. пове́стку дня** to approve an agenda; **у. в до́лжности** to confirm in a job.

утвер|ди́ться, жу́сь, ди́шься *pf.* (*of* ⇒**~жда́ться**) **1** (*укрепиться*) to gain a foothold, gain a firm hold (*also fig.*); (*порядок, режим*) to become firmly established. **2** (**в** *+p.*) (*поверить*) to be confirmed in (*one's resolve, etc.*); **у. в мы́сли** to become firmly convinced.
3 (**за** *+i.*) (*о репутации*): **за ним ~ди́лась репута́ция хоро́шего инжене́ра** he gained a reputation for being a good engineer.

утвержда́|ть, ю *impf.* **1** *impf. of* ⇒**утверди́ть**. **2** (*impf. only*) to assert, maintain; (*без доказательства*) to claim, allege; **учи́тель ~л необходи́мость регуля́рной рабо́ты** the teacher maintained that regular work was necessary; **свиде́тель ~л, что ви́дел подозрева́емого о́коло окна́** the witness claimed to have seen the suspect by the window.

утвержда́|ться, юсь *impf. of* ⇒**утверди́ться**

утвержде́ни|е, я *nt.*
1 (*высказывание*) assertion; claim, allegation. **2** (*санкционирование*) approval; confirmation; (*договора*) ratification; (*leg.*) (*завещания*) probate.
3 (*диктатуры, порядка*) establishment.

утека́|ть, ю *impf. of* ⇒**уте́чь**

ут|ёнок, ёнка, *pl.* **~я́та, ~я́т** *m.* duckling.

утепле́ни|е, я *nt.* insulation.

утепл|ённый *p.p.p. of* ⇒**~и́ть** *and adj.* (*дом*) insulated; (*плащ*) lined.

утепли́тел|ь, я *m.* (*tech.*) insulating material.

утепл|и́ть, ю́, и́шь *pf.* (*of* ⇒**~я́ть**) to insulate.

утепл|я́ть, я́ю *impf. of* ⇒**~и́ть**

утер|е́ть, утру́, утрёшь, *past* **~́, ~́ла** *pf.* (*of* ⇒**утира́ть**) to wipe (off); to wipe dry; **у. пот со лба** to wipe the sweat off one's brow; **у. кому́-н. нос** (*coll.*) to score off s.o.

утер|е́ться, утру́сь, утрёшься, *past* **~́ся, ~́лась** *pf.* (*of* ⇒**утира́ться**) to wipe o.s.; to dry o.s.

утерп|е́ть, лю́, ~́ишь *pf.* to restrain o.s.

уте́р|я, и *f.* loss.

утеря́|ть, ю *pf.* to lose.

утёс, а *m.* cliff, crag.

утёсист|ый (~, ~а) *adj.* steep, precipitous.

уте́х|а, и *f.* (*coll.*) **1** (*удовольствие*) pleasure; delight; **для ~и** for fun.
2 (*утешение*) comfort, consolation.

уте́чк|а, и *f.* (*жидкости, информации*) leak, leakage; (*убыль*) loss, wastage, dissipation; **у. га́за** gas escape; **«у. мозго́в»** brain drain.

уте́|чь, ку́, чёшь, ку́т, *past* **~́к, ~кла́** *pf.* (*of* ⇒**~ка́ть**) **1** to flow away; to leak; (*о газе*) to escape; **мно́го воды́ ~кло́** (*fig.*) much water has flowed under the bridge. **2** (*о времени*) to pass, go by.
3 (*coll.*) (*убежать*) to run away.

утеш|а́ть(ся), а́ю(сь) *impf. of* ⇒**~́ить(ся)**

утеше́ни|е, я *nt.* comfort, consolation.

утеши́тел|ь, я *m.* comforter.

утеши́тель|ница, ницы *f. of* ⇒**~**

утеши́тел|ьный (~ен, ~ьна) *adj.* comforting, consoling.

уте́ш|ить, у, ишь *pf.* (*of* ⇒**~а́ть**) to comfort, console.

уте́ш|иться, усь, ишься *pf.* (*of*

⇨~а́ться) **1** to console o.s. **2** (+*i.*) (*мыслью, событием*) to take comfort (in).

утилизацио́нный *adj.*: **у. заво́д** salvage factory, by-products factory; **у. цех** salvage department.

утилиза́ци|я, и *f.* **1** utilization. **2** (*повторное использование*) recycling.

утилизи́р|овать, ую *impf. and pf.* to utilize; (*повторно*) to recycle.

ути́лит|а, ы *f.* (*comput.*) utility.

утилитари́зм, а *m.* utilitarianism.

утилита́рност|ь, и *f.* utilitarian attitude.

утилита́рный *adj.* (*подход*) utilitarian; (*знания*) practical.

ути́л|ь, я *no pl., m.* (*collect.*) scrap, recyclable waste.

ути́ль|ный *adj. of* **⇨~; ~ное желе́зо** scrap iron.

утильсырь|ё, я́ *no pl., nt.* (*collect.*) = **ути́ль**

ути́ный *adj. of* **⇨у́тка** 1

утира́льник, а *m.* (*coll.*) hand-towel.

утира́|ть(ся), ю(сь) *impf. of* **⇨утере́ть(ся)**

утих|а́ть, а́ю *impf. of* **⇨~нуть**

ути́х|нуть, ну, нешь, *past* **~, ~ла** *pf.* (*of* **⇨~а́ть**) **1** (*о месте*) to become quiet, still; (*о звуках*) to cease, die away. **2** (*о буре, о боли*) to abate, subside; (*о ветре*) to drop; (*о споре*) to die down. **3** (*о человеке*) to become calm, calm down.

утихоми́рива|ть(ся), ю(сь) *impf. of* **⇨утихоми́рить(ся)**

утихоми́р|ить, ю, ишь *pf.* (*of* **⇨~ивать**) to calm down; to pacify, placate.

утихоми́р|иться, юсь, ишься *pf.* (*of* **⇨~иваться**) to calm down; to abate, subside.

у́тк|а, и *f.* **1** duck. **2** (*ложный слух*) canard, false report; **пусти́ть ~у** to start a canard. **3** (*сосуд*) bedpan.

уткн|у́ть, у́, ёшь *pf.* (*coll.*) to bury; to fix; **у. нос в кни́гу** to bury o.s. in a book; **у. глаза́** (**в**+*a.*) to fix one's gaze (upon).

уткн|у́ться, у́сь, ёшься *pf.* (**в**+*a.*; *coll.*) **1** to bury o.s. (in), one's head (in); **у. в рабо́ту** to bury o.s. in one's work; **у. в газе́ту** to bury one's head in a newspaper. **2** (*натолкнуться*) to bump (into); **ло́дка ~у́лась в бе́рег** the boat bumped into the bank.

утконо́с, а *m.* (*zool.*) duck-billed platypus.

утле́гар|ь, я *m.* (*naut.*) jib-boom.

у́тлый *adj.* **1** (*ненадёжный*) frail; unsound. **2** (*убогий*) poor, wretched.

ут|о́к, ка́ *m.* (*text.*) woof, weft.

утол|и́ть, ю́, и́шь *pf.* (*of* **⇨~я́ть**) **1** (*жажду*) to quench, slake; (*голод, любопытство*) to satisfy. **2** (*боль*) to relieve, alleviate.

утол|сти́ть, щу́, сти́шь *pf.* (*of* **⇨~ща́ть**) to thicken, make thicker.

утол|сти́ться, сти́тся *pf.* (*of* **⇨~ща́ться**) to become thicker.

утолща́|ть(ся), ю, ет(ся) *impf. of* **⇨утолсти́ть(ся)**

утолще́ни|е, я *nt.* **1** (*действие*) thickening. **2** (*место*) bulge.

утол|щённый *p.p.p. of* **⇨~сти́ть** *and adj.* reinforced.

утол|я́ть, я́ю *impf. of* **⇨~и́ть**

утоми́тел|ьный (~ен, ~ьна) *adj.* **1** (*утомляющий*) wearisome, tiring, fatiguing. **2** (*скучный*) tiresome; tedious.

утом|и́ть, лю́, и́шь *pf.* (*of* **⇨~ля́ть**) to tire, weary, fatigue.

утом|и́ться, лю́сь, и́шься *pf.* (*of* **⇨~ля́ться**) to get tired.

утомле́ни|е, я *nt.* tiredness, weariness, fatigue.

утом|лённый *p.p.p. of* **⇨~и́ть** *and adj.* tired, weary, fatigued.

утомля́|ть(ся), ю(сь) *impf. of* **⇨утоми́ть(ся)**

утон|у́ть, у́, ~ешь *pf.* (*of* **⇨тону́ть** *and* **утопа́ть**) **1** (*погибнуть*) to drown, be drowned; (*оказаться под водой*) to sink. **2** (**в**+*p.*; *fig.*) to be lost (in).

утонч|а́ть(ся), а́ю, а́ет(ся) *impf. of* **⇨~и́ть(ся)**

утончённост|ь, и *f.* refinement.

утонч|ённый *p.p.p. of* **⇨~и́ть** *and adj.* refined; exquisite, subtle.

утонч|и́ть, у́, и́шь *pf.* (*of* **⇨~а́ть**) **1** to make thinner. **2** (*fig.*) (*вкус, потребности*) to refine, make refined.

утонч|и́ться, и́тся *pf.* (*of* **⇨~а́ться**) **1** to become thinner. **2** (*fig.*) (*о вкусах*) to become refined.

утопа́|ть, ю *impf.* **1** *impf. of* **⇨утону́ть. 2** (*impf. only*) (**в**+*p.*; *fig.*) (*в зелени*) to be covered (in); (*в роскоши, в богатстве*) to wallow (in).

утопа́ющ|ий *pres. part. act. of* **⇨утопа́ть;** *as n.* **~ий, ~его** drowning person.

утопи́зм, а *m.* Utopianism.

утопи́ст, а *m.* Utopian.

утоп|и́ть, лю́, ~ишь *pf.* (*of* **⇨топи́ть**) **1** (*человека, животного*) to drown. **2** (*fig., coll.*) (*погубить*) to ruin. **3** (*сделать едва видным*) to bury, embed.

утоп|и́ться, лю́сь, ~ишься *pf.* (*of* **⇨топи́ться**) to drown o.s.

утопи́ческий *adj.* Utopian.

уто́пи|я, и *f.* Utopia.

уто́пленник, а *m.* drowned man.

уто́пленниц|а, ы *f. of* **⇨уто́пленник**

утоп|та́ть, чу́, ~чешь *pf.* (*of* **⇨ута́птывать**) to trample down, pound.

у́точк|а, и *f. dim. of* **⇨у́тка; ходи́ть ~ой** to waddle along.

уточне́ни|е, я *nt.* clarification, elaboration; **внести́ ~е в что-н.** to elaborate on sth.

уточн|и́ть, ю́, и́шь *pf.* (*of* **⇨~я́ть**) to make more precise, clarify; to elaborate.

уточн|я́ть, я́ю *impf. of* **⇨~и́ть**

утра́ива|ть, ю *impf. of* **⇨утро́ить**

утрамб|ова́ть, у́ю *pf.* (*of* **⇨~о́вывать**) to ram, tamp (*road material, etc.*).

утрамб|ова́ться, у́ется *pf.* (*of* **⇨~о́вываться**) to become flat, level (*also fig.*).

утрамбо́выва|ть(ся), ю, ет(ся) *impf. of* **⇨утрамбова́ть(ся)**

утра́т|а, ы *f.* loss; **у. трудоспосо́бности** disablement.

утра́|тить, чу, тишь *pf.* (*of* **⇨~чивать**) to lose.

утра́чива|ть, ю *impf. of* **⇨утра́тить**

у́тренний *adj.* morning, early.

у́тренник, а *m.* **1** (*мороз*) morning frost. **2** (*представление*) morning performance, matinée.

у́трен|я, и *f.* (*eccl.*) matins.

у́тречком *adv.* (*coll.*) in the morning.

утри́р|овать, ую *impf. and pf.* to exaggerate.

утриро́вк|а, и *f.* exaggeration.

у́тр|о, а (до ~а́, с ~а́), *d.* **у (к ~у́),** *pl.* **~а, ~, ~ам (по ~а́м)** *nt.* morning; **в семь часо́в ~а́** at 7 a.m.; **на сле́дующее у.** the next morning; **с ~а́** early in the morning; **с ~а́ до ве́чера** from morn till night; **до́брое у.!** good morning!

утро́б|а, ы *f.* **1** womb; **в ~е ма́тери** in the womb. **2** (*coll.*) (*живот*) belly; **ненасы́тная у.** greedy guts.

утро́бный *adj.* **1** uterine, foetal (*Br.*), fetal (*US*); **у. плод** foetus (*Br.*), fetus (*US*). **2** (*о звуках*) deep, hollow; **у. смех** belly-laugh.

утро́|ить, ю, ишь *pf.* (*of* **⇨утра́ивать**) to treble.

у́тром *adv.* in the morning; **сего́дня у.** this morning.

утружда́|ть, ю *impf.* to trouble; **у. кого́-н. про́сьбами** to trouble s.o. with requests.

утружда́|ться, юсь *impf.* (*coll.*) to trouble o.s., take trouble.

утряс|а́ть(ся), а́ю, а́ет(ся) *impf. of* **⇨~ти́(сь)**

утряс|ти́, у́, ёшь *pf.* (*of* **⇨~а́ть**) (*coll.*) **1** (*уладить*) to settle; **у. вопро́с** to have a matter out. **2** (*муку, мешок*) to shake down. **3** (*человека*) to tire, make drowsy.

утряс|ти́сь, ётся, у́тся *pf. of* **⇨~а́ться** (*coll.*) (*дело, проблема*) to sort itself out; **всё ~ётся** everything will be sorted out.

утучн|и́ть, ю́, и́шь *pf.* (*of* **⇨~я́ть**) (*obs.*) **1** (*скот*) to fatten. **2** (*землю*) to enrich, manure.

утучн|я́ть, я́ю *impf. of* **⇨~и́ть**

уты́к|ать, аю *pf.* (*of* **⇨~а́ть** *and* **~ивать**) (*coll.*) **1** (*воткнуть*) to stick (in) all over. **2** (*забить*) to stop up, caulk.

утык|а́ть, а́ю *impf. of* **⇨~ать**

уты́кива|ть, ю *impf.* = **утыка́ть**

утю́г, а́ *m.* (*flat*) iron.

утю́ж|ить, у, ишь *impf.* (*of* **⇨вы́~**) **1** (*брюки*) to iron, press. **2** (*асфальт*) to smooth.

утю́жк|а, и *f.* ironing, pressing.

утя́гива|ть, ю *impf. of* **⇨утяну́ть**

утяжел|и́ть, ю́, и́шь *pf.* (*of* **⇨~я́ть**)

(*о весе*) to make heavier, increase the weight (of); (*о стиле*) to make awkward, cumbersome.

утяжел|я́ть, я́ю, я́ешь *impf. of* **⇒~и́ть**

утян|у́ть, у́, ~́ешь *pf.* (*of* **⇒утя́гивать**) (*coll.*) **1** (*утащить*) to drag away, off. **2** (*украсть*) to steal, pinch (*Br.*).

утя́тин|а, ы *f.* (*cul.*) duck.

уф *int.* (*expr.* (*i*) *relief*, (*ii*) *fatigue, physical discomfort, etc.*) ooh!; gosh!; phew!; **уф, жа́рко!** phew, it's hot!

уфо́лог, а *m.* ufologist.

уфоло́ги|я, и *f.* ufology.

ух *int.* (*expr. various strong feelings*) ooh!; gosh!

ух|á, и́ *f.* ukha (*fish-soup*).

уха́б, а *m.* pot-hole, pit (*in road*).

уха́бист|ый (~, ~а) *adj.* full of pot-holes; bumpy.

ухажёр, а *m.* (*coll.*) ladies' man; (*поклонник*) admirer.

уха́живани|е, я *nt.* courting.

уха́жива|ть, ю *impf.* (**за**+*i.*) **1** (*за больным*) to nurse, tend; (*за животными, растениями*) to look after. **2** (*за женщиной*) to court; to pay court (to), make advances (to). **3** (*вести себя угодливо*) to make up (to).

у́хань|е, я *nt.* (*филина*) hooting; (*орудий*) banging; (*людей*) shouts.

у́харский *adj.* (*coll.*) dashing; rakish.

у́харств|о, а *nt.* (*coll.*) bravado.

у́хар|ь, я *m.* (*coll.*) dashing fellow.

у́ха|ть(ся), ю(сь) *impf. of* **⇒у́хнуть(ся)**

ухва́т, а *m.* **1** oven fork. **2** (*tech.*) clip.

ухва|ти́ть, чу́, ~́тишь *pf.* **1** (*схватить*) to lay hold (of); (*захватить для себя*) to seize, grab. **2** (*fig., coll.*) (*понять*) to grasp.

ухва|ти́ться, чу́сь, ~́тишься *pf.* (**за**+*a.*) **1** to grasp, lay hold (of); **у. за ве́тку** to grasp a branch. **2** (*fig., coll.*) (*за возможность*) to seize; to jump (at); **у. за предложе́ние** to jump at an offer; (*за мысль, за человека*) to latch on to.

ухва́тк|а, и *f.* (*coll.*) **1** (*ловкость*) skill; trick. **2** (*usu. pl.*) (*манера*) manner.

ухитр|и́ться, ю́сь, и́шься *pf.* (*of* **⇒~я́ться**) (+*inf.*) to manage (to), contrive (to).

ухитр|я́ться, я́юсь *impf. of* **⇒~и́ться**

ухищре́ни|е, я *nt.* trick, dodge.

ухищрён|ный (~, ~на) *adj.* cunning, artful.

ухищря́|ться, юсь *impf.* to contrive; to resort to contrivance.

ухло́п|ать, аю *pf.* (*of* **⇒~ывать**) (*coll.*) **1** (*убить*) to kill. **2** (*истратить*) to squander.

ухло́пыва|ть, ю *impf. of* **⇒ухло́пать**

ухмы́лк|а, и *f.* (*coll.*) smirk, grin.

ухмыльн|у́ться, у́сь, ёшься *pf.* (*of* **⇒ухмыля́ться**) (*coll.*) to smirk, grin.

ухмыл|я́ться, я́юсь *impf. of* **⇒~ьну́ться**

у́хн|уть, у, ешь *pf.* (*of* **⇒у́хать**) (*coll.*) **1** (*от удивления, боли, удовольствия*) to cry out; (*о совах*) to hoot. **2** (*раздаться*) to crash, bang, rumble; **вдруг ~ул гром** there was a sudden crash of thunder. **3** (*упасть*) to fall; to come a cropper (*also fig.*). **4** (*fig.*) (*утратиться*) to go to waste. **5** (*уронить*) to drop; (*бросить*) to throw. **6** (*истратить*) to squander. **7** (*с силой ударить*) to bang, slap; **у. кулако́м по столу́** to bang one's fist on the table.

у́хн|уться, усь, ешься *pf.* (*of* **⇒у́хаться**) (*coll.*) to fall with a bang.

у́х|о, а, *pl.* **у́ши, уше́й** *nt.* **1** ear; **у́ши вя́нут (от**+*g.*) (*coll.*) it makes one sick to hear; **и ~ом не вести́** not to listen (= *to pay no heed*); **кра́ем ~а слу́шать** to listen with half an ear; **прожужжа́ть, прокрича́ть кому́-н. у́ши** to talk s.o.'s head off; **у. в у. (с**+*i.*) level (with), alongside; **дать кому́-н. в у.** (*coll.*) to box s.o.'s ear; **во все у́ши слу́шать** to be all ears; **пропусти́ть ми́мо уше́й** (*coll.*) to turn a deaf ear (to), pay no heed (to); **говори́ть кому́-н. на́ у.** to have a word in s.o.'s ear, have a private word with s.o.; **по́ уши** (*в долгах*) up to one's ears *or* eyes (*in debt, etc.*); (*влюблённый*) head over heels (*in love, etc.*). **2** (*шапки*) ear-flap. **3** (*tech.*) ear, lug.

уховёртк|а, и *f.* (*zool.*) earwig.

ухо́д[1], а *m.* (*из комнаты; с работы*) leaving; (*с должности*) resignation; (*на пенсию*) retirement; (*поезда*) departure; (*с собрания; в монастырь*) withdrawal.

ухо́д[2], а *m.* (**за**+*i.*) (*за больным, садом*) looking after; care (of); (*за машиной*) maintenance; (*за зданием*) upkeep.

ухо|ди́ть[1], жу́, ~́дишь *impf.* **1** *impf. of* **⇒уйти́. 2** *impf. only* (*простираться*) to stretch, extend.

ухо|ди́ть[2], жу́, ~́дишь *pf.* (*coll.*) **1** (*изнурить*) to wear out, tire out. **2** (*убить*) to do in.

ухо|ди́ться, жу́сь, ~́дишься *pf.* (*coll.*) **1** (*устать*) to be worn out, be tired out. **2** (*успокоиться*) to calm down.

ухо́жен|ный (~, ~а) *adj.* well-looked-after, well-cared-for.

ухудш|а́ть(ся), а́ю, а́ет(ся) *impf. of* **⇒~ить(ся)**

ухудше́ни|е, я *nt.* worsening, deterioration.

уху́дш|енный *p.p.p. of* **⇒~ить** *and adj.* inferior.

уху́дш|ить, у, ишь *pf.* (*of* **⇒~а́ть**) to make worse, worsen.

уху́дш|иться, ится *pf.* (*of* **⇒~а́ться**) to become worse, worsen, deteriorate (*intrans.*).

уцеле́|ть, ю *pf.* (*остаться целым*) to remain intact, escape destruction; (*остаться живым*) to remain alive, survive.

уцен|ённый *p.p.p. of* **⇒~и́ть** *and adj.* reduced(-price).

уце́нива|ть, ю *impf. of* **⇒уцени́ть**

уцен|и́ть, ю́, ~́ишь *pf.* (*of* **⇒~́ивать**) to reduce the price (of).

уце́нк|а, и *f.* price reduction.

уцеп|и́ть, лю́, ~́ишь *pf.* (*coll.*) to catch hold (of), grasp, seize.

уцеп|и́ться, лю́сь, ~́ишься *pf.* (**за**+*a.*) **1** to catch hold (of), grasp, seize. **2** (*fig., coll.*) (*за предложение, за мысль*) to jump (at).

уча́ств|овать, ую *impf.* **1** (**в**+*p.*) to take part (in), participate (in). **2** (**в**+*p.*) (*иметь долю*) to have a share (in), have shares (in); **у. в акционе́рном о́бществе** to have shares in a (joint-stock) company; **у. в при́былях** to have a share in the profits.

уча́ств|ующий *pres. part. act. of* **⇒~овать;** *as n.* **у., ~ующего** *m.* participant.

уча́сти|е, я *nt.* **1** taking part, participation; **у. в при́былях** profit-sharing; **при ~и, с ~ем** (+*g.*) with the participation (of), with assistance (of), featuring; **принима́ть у. (в**+*p.*) to take part (in), participate (in). **2** (*сочувствие*) sympathy, concern; **принима́ть у. в ко́м-н.** to display concern for s.o.

уча|сти́ть, щу́, сти́шь *pf.* (*of* **⇒~ща́ть**) (*посещения*) to make more frequent; (*шаг*) to quicken.

участ|и́ться, и́тся *pf.* (*of* **⇒учаща́ться**) (*удары грома*) to become more frequent; (*шаг, пульс*) to quicken.

участко́в|ый *adj. of* **⇒уча́сток; у. врач** general practitioner, GP; family doctor; **у. инспе́ктор** divisional inspector (*of police*); *as n.* **у., ~ого** *m.* (*coll.*) = **у. инспе́ктор.**

уча́стлив|ый (~, ~а) *adj.* sympathetic.

уча́стник, а *m.* (+*g.*) participant (in), member (of); **~и перегово́ров** negotiating parties; **~и соглаше́ния** parties to the agreement; **у. состяза́ния** competitor; **у. литерату́рного кружка́** member of a literary society; **у. торго́в** bidder.

уча́ст|ок, ка *m.* **1** (*земли*) plot, strip; lot, parcel. **2** (*площади, стены, дороги*) part, section, portion; length (*of road, etc.*); (*rail.*) division. **3** (*mil.*) (*часть фронта*) sector (*area occupied by one regiment of Army*); area, zone; **у. гла́вного уда́ра** area of main strike; **у. проры́ва** breakthrough area. **4** (*в административном делении*) district, area, zone (*as administrative unit*); **избира́тельный у.** (*i*) (*подразделение*) electoral district, ward, (*ii*) (*здание*) polling station. **5** (*fig.*) (*сфера деятельности*) field, sphere. **6** (*hist.*) (*i*) (*подразделение*) police division, district, (*ii*) (*здание*) police-station.

у́част|ь, и *f.* lot, fate.

учаща́|ть(ся), ю, ет(ся) *impf. of* **⇒участи́ть(ся)**

уча|щённый *p.p.p. of* **⇒~сти́ть** *and adj.* quickened; faster; **у. пульс** quickened pulse.

уча́щ|ийся *pres. part. of* **⇒учи́ться;** *as n.* **у., ~егося** *m.* student; (*школы*) pupil.

учёб|а, ы *f.* **1** studies; studying, learning; **за ~ой** at one's studies. **2** (*подготовка*) training.

учёбник, а *m.* text-book.

учёбно... *comb. form, abbr. of* **учёбный**

учёбн|ый *adj.* **1** educational; school; **у. год** academic year, school year; **~ое заведе́ние** educational institution; **у. план** curriculum; **заве́дующий ~ой ча́стью** director of studies. **2** (*mil.*) training, practice; **у. патро́н** dummy cartridge (*used in training*); **~ое по́ле** training ground; **~ая стрельба́** practice shoot; **~ое су́дно** training ship.

уче́ни|е, я *nt.* **1** learning; studies; (*ремеслу*) apprenticeship; **отда́ть в у.** (+*d.*) to apprentice (to). **2** (*преподавание*) teaching, instruction. **3** (*mil.*) exercise; (*pl.*) training. **4** (*система взглядов*) teaching, doctrine.

учени́к, а́ *m.* **1** (*школы*) pupil. **2** (*в ремесле*) apprentice. **3** (*последователь*) disciple, follower.

учени́ц|а, ы *f. of* ⇒**учени́к**

учени́|ческий *adj.* **1** *adj. of* ⇒**~к.** **2** (*работа*) primitive.

учени́честв|о, а *nt.* **1** period spent as a pupil, student; student years, school years. **2** (*ремеслу*) apprenticeship.

учёност|ь, и *f.* learning, erudition (*also iron.*).

учён|ый (~, ~а) *adj.* **1** (*человек*) learned, erudite; (*coll.*) educated. **2** (*научный*) scholarly; academic; **~ая статья́** scholarly article; **~ая сте́пень** higher (university) degree (*PhD or higher*). **3** *in titles of certain academic posts and institutions*: **у. секрета́рь** academic secretary; **у. сове́т** academic council. **4** (*животное*) trained, performing. **5** *as n.* **у., ~ого** *m.* scholar; (*в университете*) academic; (*в области естественных наук*) scientist.

уч|е́сть, учту́, учтёшь, *past* **~ёл, ~ла́** *pf.* (*of* ⇒**~и́тывать**) **1** (*обстоятельства*) to take into account, consideration. **2** (*товары*) to take stock (of), make an inventory (of). **3** (*fin.*) (*вексель*) to discount.

учёт, а *m.* **1** (*действие*) accounting; **бухга́лтерский у.** accounting, book-keeping; (*товаров*) stock-taking, inventory-making; (*определение*) calculation; **вести́ у.** (+*g.*) to take stock (of); **веде́ние ~а** record-keeping; (*запись*) record. **2** (*обстоятельств*) taking into account; **без ~а** (+*g.*) disregarding. **3** (*регистрация*) registration; **взять на у.** to register; **встать, стать на у.** to be registered; **снять с ~а** to strike off the register, take off the books. **4** (*fin.*) (*векселей*) discount, discounting.

учетвер|и́ть, ю́, и́шь *pf.* (*of* ⇒**~я́ть**) to quadruple.

учетвер|я́ть, я́ю *impf. of* ⇒**~и́ть**

учётно-медици́нск|ий *adj.*: **~ая ка́рточка** medical record, medical card.

учётн|ый *adj.* **1** registration; **~ая ка́рточка** registration form; **~ая кни́га** records book; **~ое отделе́ние** records section. **2** (*fin.*) discount; **у. проце́нт, ~ая ста́вка ба́нковского проце́нта** bank rate.

учи́лищ|е, а *nt.* school, college (*institution providing specialist instruction at secondary level*); **вое́нное у.** military school; **ремесленное у.** trade school.

учин|и́ть, ю́, и́шь *pf.* (*of* ⇒**~я́ть**) to make, cause; **у. сканда́л кому́-н.** to make a scene.

учин|я́ть, я́ю *impf. of* ⇒**~и́ть**

учи́тел|ь, я *m.* **1** (*pl.* **~я́**) teacher. **2** (*pl.* **~и**) (*fig.*) teacher, master (= *authority*).

учи́тельниц|а, ы *f. of* ⇒**учи́тель**

учи́тель|ский *adj. of* ⇒**~**; *as n.* **~ская, ~ской** *f.* teachers' common room, staff (common) room.

учи́тельств|овать, ую *impf.* to teach, work as a teacher.

учи́тыва|ть, ю *impf. of* ⇒**уче́сть**

уч|и́ть, у́, ~ишь *impf.* **1** (*pf.* **вы́~, на~** *and* **об~**) (+*a. and d. or* +*inf.*) (*преподавать*) to teach; **у. кого́-н. неме́цкому языку́** to teach s.o. German; **у. игра́ть на скри́пке** to teach to play the violin. **2** *no pf.* (*быть учителем*) to be a teacher. **3** (**что**) (*о теории*) to teach (that), say (that). **4** (*pf.* **вы́~**) (+*a.*) (*усваивать, запоминать*) to learn; to memorize.

уч|и́ться, у́сь, ~ишься *impf.* **1** (*pf.* **вы́~, на~** *and* **об~**) (+*d. or* +*inf.*) to learn, study. **2** (*быть студентом*) to be a student; **у. в шко́ле** to go to, be at school. **3** (**на кого́-н.**; *coll.*) to study (to be, to become), learn (to be); **он ~ится на перево́дчика** he is studying to be an interpreter.

учреди́тел|ь, я *m.* founder.

учреди́тель|ница, ницы *f. of* ⇒**~**

учреди́тельн|ый *adj.* constituent; **~ое собра́ние** (*pol.*) constituent assembly.

учре|ди́ть, жу́, ди́шь *pf.* (*of* ⇒**~жда́ть**) (*основать*) to found, establish, set up; (*ввести*) to introduce, institute.

учрежда́|ть, ю *impf. of* ⇒**учреди́ть**

учрежде́ни|е, я *nt.* **1** (*школы, организации*) founding, establishment, setting up, (*ордена*) introduction. **2** (*заведение*) establishment, institution.

учти́вост|ь, и *f.* civility, courtesy.

учти́в|ый (~, ~а) *adj.* civil, courteous.

учуд|и́ть, и́шь *pf. of* ⇒**чуди́ть**

учу́|ять, ю, ешь *pf.* (*coll.*) to smell, nose out; (*fig.*) (*издёвку, подвох*) to sense.

уша́нк|а, и *f.* (*coll.*) cap with ear-flaps.

уша́ст|ый (~, ~а) *adj.* (*coll.*) big-eared.

уша́т, а *m.* tub (*carried on pole slung through handles*); **вы́лить на кого́-н. у. гря́зи** to insult s.o.

у́ши *see* ⇒**у́хо**

уши́б, а *m.* injury; bruise.

ушиб|а́ть(ся), а́ю(сь) *impf. of* ⇒**~и́ть(ся)**

ушиб|и́ть, у́, ёшь, *past* **~, ~ла** *pf.* (*of* ⇒**~а́ть**) **1** to injure (*by knocking*); (*до синяка*) to bruise. **2** (*fig., coll.*) to hurt, bruise.

ушиб|и́ться, у́сь, ёшься, *past* **~ся, ~лась** *pf.* (*of* ⇒**~а́ться**) to hurt o.s., give o.s. a knock; to bruise o.s.

ушива́|ть, ю *impf. of* ⇒**уши́ть**

уш|и́ть, ью́, ьёшь *pf.* (*of* ⇒**~ива́ть**) (*dressmaking*) to take in.

у́шк|о, а, *pl.* **~и, у́шек** *nt. dim. of* ⇒**у́хо; у него́ ~и на маку́шке** he is on the qui-vive.

ушк|о́, а́, *pl.* **~и́, ~о́в** *nt.* **1** (*tech.*) eye, lug. **2** (*сапога*) tab, tag. **3** (*в иголке*) eye. **4** (*pl.*) (*cul.*) pasta (*in small shapes*).

у́шлый *adj.* (*coll.*) smart, shrewd.

ушни́к, а́ *m.* (*coll.*) ear doctor.

ушн|о́й *adj.* ear; **~а́я боль** ear-ache; **у. врач** ear-specialist; **~а́я ра́ковина** (*anat.*) auricle.

уще́лист|ый (~, ~а) *adj.* abounding in ravines.

уще́л|ье, ья, *g. pl.* **~ий** *nt.* ravine, gorge.

ущем|и́ть, лю́, и́шь *pf.* (*of* ⇒**~ля́ть**) **1** to pinch, jam; **у. па́лец две́рью** to pinch one's finger in the door. **2** (*fig.*) (*стеснить*) to limit; to encroach (upon). **3** (*fig.*) (*оскорбить*) to wound, hurt; **у. чьё-н. самолю́бие** to hurt s.o.'s pride.

ущемле́ни|е, я *nt.* **1** (*пальца*) pinching, jamming. **2** (*fig.*) (*прав*) limitation. **3** (*fig.*) (*самолюбия*) wounding, hurting.

ущем|лённый *p.p.p. of* ⇒**~и́ть** *and adj.* (*fig.*) (*самолюбие*) wounded, hurt; (*права*) limited.

ущемля́|ть, ю *impf. of* ⇒**ущеми́ть**

уще́рб, а *m.* **1** (*убыток*) detriment; loss; (*вред*) damage, injury; **без ~а** (**для**+*g.*) without prejudice (to); **в у.** (+*d.*) to the detriment (of), to the prejudice (of). **2** (*спад*) weakening, decline. **3**: **на ~е** (*о луне*) on the wane; (*fig.*) (*слава*) on the decline; (*характер, психика*) defective, abnormal.

ущерблённый *adj.* **1** (*луна*) waning. **2** (*самолюбие*) wounded, hurt.

уще́рбност|ь, и *f.* **1** (*луны, таланта*) waning. **2** (*психики*) defectiveness, abnormality.

уще́рб|ный (~ен, ~на) *adj.* **1** (*луна*) waning. **2** (*психика*) warped, abnormal.

ущипн|у́ть, у́, ёшь *pf.* to pinch, tweak.

Уэ́льс, а *m.* Wales.

уэ́льс|ец, ца *m.* Welshman.

уэ́льский *adj.* Welsh.

ую́т, а *m.* comfort, cosiness (*Br.*), coziness (*US*).

ую́т|ный (~ен, ~на) *adj.* cosy (*Br.*), cozy (*US*), comfortable.

уязви́м|ый (~, ~а) *adj.* vulnerable (*also fig.*); **~ое ме́сто** (*fig.*) weak spot, sensitive spot.

уязв|и́ть, лю́, и́шь *pf.* (*of* ⇒**~ля́ть**) to wound, hurt.

уязвля́|ть, ю *impf. of* ⇒**уязви́ть**

уясне́ни|е, я *nt.* clarification.

уясн|и́ть, ю́, и́шь *pf.* (*of* ⇒**~я́ть**) (**себе́, для себя́**) to comprehend.

уясн|я́ть, я́ю *impf. of* ⇒**~и́ть**

Фф

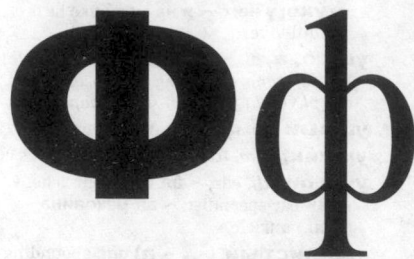

фа *nt. indecl. (mus.)* F.
фаб... *comb. form, abbr. of* ***фабри́чный***
фа́брик|а, и *f.* factory; (*бумажная*) mill.
фа́брика-ку́хня, фа́брики-ку́хни *f. (hist.) (large-scale)* canteen, municipal restaurant.
фабрика́нт, а *m.* manufacturer, factory-owner, mill-owner; (*слухов*) fabricator.
фабрика́т, а *m.* finished product.
фабрика́ци|я, и *f.* fabrication (*also fig.*).
фабрик|ова́ть, у́ю *impf.* **1** *(obs.)* (*изготовить*) to manufacture, make. **2** (*pf.* **с~**) *(fig.)* to fabricate.
фабри́чно-заводско́й (*and* **ф.-заво́дский**) *adj.* factory, works, industrial.
фабри́чн|ый *adj.* **1** factory; manufacturing; **ф. го́род** manufacturing town; **~ая ма́рка** trade mark; **~ое произво́дство** manufacturing; *as n.* **ф., ~ого** *m.*, **~ая, ~ой** *f. (obs.)* factory worker. **2** (*произведённый на фабрике*) factory-made.
фа́бул|а, ы *f. (liter.)* plot, story.
фавн, а *m. (myth.)* faun.
фаво́р, а *m. (obs.)*: **быть в ~е (у)** to be in favour *(Br.)*, favor *(US)* (with); **быть не в ~е у кого́-н.** to be in s.o.'s bad books.
фавори́т, а *m.* favourite *(Br.)*, favorite *(US)* (*also sport*).
фаворити́зм, а *m.* favouritism *(Br.)*, favoritism *(US)*.
фавори́т|ка, ки *f. of* **⇒~**
фаго́т, а *m. (mus.)* bassoon.
фаготи́ст, а *m.* bassoon-player.
фа́з|а, ы *f.* phase; stage.
фаза́н, а *m.* pheasant.
фаза́н|ий *adj. of* **⇒~**
фа́зис, а *m.* phase.
фазотро́н, а *m. (phys.)* synchro-cyclotron.
файл, а *m. (comput.)* file.
фа́йл|овый *adj. of* **⇒~; ф. се́рвер** file server.
файл-се́рвер, а *m. (comput.)* file server.
...фа́к *comb. form, abbr. of* **факульте́т**
фа́кел, а *m.* torch, flare.
фа́кел|ьный *adj. of* **⇒~; ~ьное ше́ствие** torch-light procession.
фа́кельщик, а *m.* **1** torch-bearer. **2** *(fig., pej.)* incendiary, fire-bug.
фа́кельщи|ца, цы *f. of* **⇒~к** 1
факи́р, а *m.* fakir.
фа́кс, а *m.* fax; **посла́ть по ~у** to fax.
факси́миле *indecl.* **1** *adj.* **2** *n.; nt.* facsimile.
факс|ими́льный *adj. of* **⇒~ими́ле; ф. аппара́т** fax (machine).
факт, а *m.* fact; **соверши́вшийся ф.** fait accompli; **факт, что** *(coll.)* it is a fact that; **ф. остаётся ~ом** the fact remains.
факти́чески *adv.* in fact, actually; practically, virtually, to all intents and purposes.
факти́ческ|ий *adj.* actual; real; virtual; **~ие да́нные** the facts.
факти́ч|ный (~ен, ~на) *adj.* factual.
фактогра́фи|я, и *f.* factual account.
фа́ктор, а *m.* factor.
факто́ри|я, и *f.* trading station.
факту́р|а, ы *f.* **1** (*своеобразие художественной техники*) manner of execution; (*строение материала*) texture. **2** *(comm.)* invoice, bill.
факту́р|ный *adj. of* **⇒~а**
факультати́в, а *m.* optional course.
факультати́в|ный (~ен, ~на) *adj.* optional.
факульте́т, а *m.* faculty, department.
факульте́т|ский *adj. of* **⇒~**
фал, а *m. (naut.)* halyard.
фала́нг|а, и *f.* **1** *(hist.)* phalanx. **2** *(anat.)* phalanx, phalange.
фа́лд|а, ы *f.* tail, skirt (*of coat*).
фа́лин|ь, я *m. (naut.)* painter.
фалли́ческий *adj.* phallic.
фалло́пиев *adj.*: **~а труба́** *(med.)* Fallopian tube.
фа́ллос, а *m.* phallus.
фальсифика́тор *m.* falsifier.
фальсифика́ци|я, и *f.* **1** (*подделывание*) falsification. **2** (*изменение качества*) adulteration. **3** (*поддельный предмет*) forgery, fake, counterfeit.
фальсифици́р|овать, ую *impf. and pf.* **1** (*историю*) to falsify. **2** (*вино*) to adulterate.
фальста́рт, а *m.* false start.
фальц, а *m.* **1** (*загиб, шов на месте соединения металлических листов*) fold, seam. **2** (*печатного листа*) fold. **3** (*паз*) groove, rebate.
фальц|ева́ть, у́ю *impf.* (*of* **⇒с~**) **1** (*металлические листы*) to seam. **2** (*печатный лист*) to fold, crease. **3** (*пазить*) to groove, rebate.
фальце́т, а *m. (mus.)* falsetto.
фальшбо́рт, а *m. (naut.)* bulwark, rails.
фальши́в|ить, лю, ишь *impf.* **1** to be a hypocrite; to act insincerely. **2** (*pf.* **с~**) *(mus.)* (*петь*) to sing out of tune; (*играть*) to play out of tune.
фальши́вк|а, и *f. (coll.)* forged document.
фальшивомоне́тчик, а *m.* counterfeiter.
фальши́в|ый (~, ~а) *adj.* **1** (*зубы, волосы*) false; (*документ*) forged, fake; (*жемчуг*) artificial, imitation. **2** (*неискренний*) false; insincere; **ф. комплиме́нт** insincere compliment; **попа́сть в ~ое положе́ние** to put o.s. into a false position. **3** *(mus.)* out of tune.
фальшки́л|ь, я *m. (naut.)* false keel.
фальш|ь, и *f.* **1** (*обман*) deception, trickery. **2** (*неискренность*) falsity; insincerity. **3** *(mus.)* (*пение*) singing out of tune; (*игра*) playing out of tune.
фами́ли|я, и *f.* **1** surname; **двойна́я ф.** double-barrelled *(Br.)*, -barreled *(US)* surname. **2** (*род*) family, kin.
фами́льный *adj.* family.
фамилья́рнича|ть, ю *impf. (coll.)* to be over-familiar.

фамилья́рност|ь, и *f.* over-familiarity.

фамилья́р|ный (~ен, ~на) *adj.* over-familiar; unceremonious.

фанабе́ри|я, и *f. (coll.)* arrogance, bumptiousness.

фана́т, а *m. (coll.)* freak, fan, devotée; **музыка́льный ф.** music freak.

фанати́зм, а *m.* fanaticism.

фана́тик, а *m.* fanatic.

фанати́ческий *adj.* fanatical.

фанати́ч|ный (~ен, ~на) *adj.* fanatic(al).

фана́т|ка, ки *f. of* ⇒**~; groupie.

фане́р|а, ы *f.* **1** *(для облицовки)* veneer. **2** *(древесный материал)* plywood. **3** *(mus. sl., pej.) (фонограмма)* pre-recorded soundtrack; **петь под ~у** to mime, lip-sync.

фане́р|ный *adj. of* ⇒**~а**

фа́нз|а́, ~́ы *f.* fanza *(peasant dwelling in China or Korea).*

фант, а *m.* forfeit; **игра́ть в ~́ы** to play forfeits.

фантазёр, а *m.* dreamer, visionary.

фантази́р|овать, ую *impf.* **1** *impf. only (мечтать)* to dream, indulge in fantasies. **2** *(pf.* **с~**) *(выдумывать)* to make up, dream up. **3** *impf. only (импровизировать)* to improvise *(on piano, etc.).*

фанта́зи|я, и *f.* **1** *(воображение)* fantasy; imagination; **бога́тая ф.** fertile imagination. **2** *(мечта)* fantasy, fancy; **предава́ться ~ям** to indulge in fantasies. **3** *(выдумка)* fabrication. **4** *(coll.) (прихоть)* fancy, whim. **5** *(mus.)* fantasia.

фантасмаго́ри|я, и *f.* phantasmagoria.

фанта́ст, а *m.* **1** *(фантазёр)* dreamer, visionary. **2** *(писатель, художник)* writer, artist treating the fantastic.

фанта́стик|а, и *f.* **1** *(народных сказок)* the fantastic element. **2** *(collect., liter.)* fantasy; **нау́чная ф.** science fiction; sci-fi. **3** *(coll.) (нечто нереальное)* a fantastic thing.

фантасти́ческий *adj.* **1** *(пейзаж, освещение)* fantastic, fabulous, unreal; *(новость, нахал)* fantastic, incredible. **2** *(литература)* fantasy.

фантасти́ч|ный (~ен, ~на) *adj.* = **~еский**

фа́нтик, а *m.* sweet wrapper.

фанто́м, а *m.* phantom.

фанфа́р|а, ы *f. (mus.)* **1** *(инструмент)* bugle. **2** *(торжественная фраза)* fanfare.

фанфаро́н, а *m. (coll.)* braggart.

фанфаро́н|ить, ю, ишь *impf. (coll.)* to brag.

фанфаро́нств|о, а *nt. (coll.)* bragging.

ФАО *f. indecl.* FAO *(abbr. of* Food and Agriculture Organization — *Продовольственная и сельскохозяйственная организация Объединённых Наций).*

фа́р|а, ы *f.* headlight; **поса́дочные ~ы** landing lights.

фара́д|а, ы *f. (elec.)* farad.

фарао́н, а *m.* **1** *(hist.)* Pharaoh. **2** *(игра)* faro *(card-game).*

фарва́тер, а *m. (naut.)* fairway, channel; **плыть, быть в чьём-н. ~е** *(fig.)* to follow s.o.'s lead, side with s.o.

Фаренге́йт, а *m.* Fahrenheit (thermometer); **80° по ~у** 80° Fahrenheit.

фаре́р|ец, ца *m.* Faeroese, Faeroe Islander.

фаре́р|ка, ки *f. of* ⇒**~ец**

Фаре́рск|ие острова́, ~их ~о́в *no sg.* the Faeroe Islands; the Faeroes.

фаре́рский *adj.* Faeroese.

фаринги́т, а *m. (med.)* pharyngitis.

фарисе́|й, я *m.* Pharisee *(also fig.).*

фарисе́йский *adj.* pharisaical *(also fig.).*

фарисе́йств|о, а *nt.* pharisaism.

фарисе́йств|овать, ую *impf.* to act pharisaically.

фармазо́н, а *m. (coll., obs.)* freemason.

фармако́лог, а *m.* pharmacologist.

фармакологи́ческий *adj.* pharmacological.

фармаколо́ги|я, и *f.* pharmacology.

фармакопе́|я, и *f.* pharmacopoeia.

фармаце́вт, а *m.* pharmacist.

фармаце́втик|а, и *f.* pharmaceutics.

фармацевти́ческий *adj.* pharmaceutical.

фармаци́|я, и *f.* pharmacy.

фарс, а *m. (theatr.)* farce *(also fig.).*

фарт, а *m. (sl.)* luck.

фарт|и́ть, и́т *impf. (of* ⇒**по~**) *(impers.+d.; sl.)* to be in luck, be lucky; **нам пофарти́ло** we were in luck.

фарто́вый *adj. (sl.)* **1** lucky. **2** *(очень хороший)* fine.

фа́ртук, а *m.* apron.

фарфо́р, а *m.* **1** *(материал)* porcelain, china. **2** *(collect.) (посуда)* china.

фарфо́р|овый *adj. of* ⇒**~; ~овая гли́на** china clay.

фарцо́вщик, а *m. (sl.)* black-marketeer.

фарш, а *m. (cul.)* force-meat; stuffing; *(мясной)* minced meat.

фарширо́в|анный *p.p.p. of* ⇒**~а́ть** *and adj. (cul.)* stuffed.

фаршир|ова́ть, у́ю *impf. (of* ⇒**за~**) *(cul.)* to stuff.

фас, а *m.* front, façade; **в ф.** full face.

фаса́д, а *m.* façade, front.

фа́ск|а, и *f. (tech.)* face, facet; (bevel) edge.

фас|ова́ть, у́ю *impf. (comm.)* to prepack.

фасо́вк|а, и *f. (comm.)* prepacking.

фасо́вочный *adj. (comm.)* (pre)packing, packaging.

фасо́л|евый *adj. of* ⇒**~ь**

фасо́л|ь, и *f.* **1** *(растение)* bean plant. **2** *(collect.) (плод)* beans.

фасо́н, а *m.* **1** *(покрой, образец)* cut; style; **не ф.** *(coll.)* it's not done. **2** *(coll.) (стиль)* style. **3** *(coll.) (форс)* swank, showing off; **держа́ть ф.** to swank, show off.

фасо́нист|ый (~, ~а) *adj. (coll.)* fashionable, stylish.

фасо́нный *adj. (tech.)* fashioned, shaped.

фат, а *m.* fop.

фат|а́, ы *f. (bridal)* veil.

фатали́зм, а *m.* fatalism.

фатали́ст, а *m.* fatalist.

фаталисти́ческий *adj.* **1** *(взгляды, мысли)* fatalistic. **2** *(гибельный)* fatal.

фатали́ст|ка, ки *f. of* ⇒**~**

фата́льност|ь, и *f.* fatality, fate.

фата́л|ьный (~ен, ~ьна) *adj.* **1** *(совпадение)* fateful; *(последствия)* fatal. **2** *(вид, наружность)* resigned (to one's fate).

фатова́т|ый (~, ~а) *adj.* foppish.

фа́тум, а *m.* fate.

фа́ун|а, ы *f.* fauna.

фаши́зм, а *m.* Fascism.

фаши́н|а, ы *f.* fascine, faggot.

фаши́ст, а *m.* Fascist.

фаши́ст|ка, ки *f. of* ⇒**~**

фаши́стский *adj.* Fascist.

фаэто́н, а *m.* phaeton.

фая́нс, а *m.* faience, glazed earthenware.

фая́нс|овый *adj. of* ⇒**~**

ФБР *nt. indecl. (abbr. of* ***Федера́льное бюро́ рассле́дований****)* FBI *(Federal Bureau of Investigation).*

февра́л|ь, я́ *m.* February.

февра́ль|ский *adj. of* ⇒**~**

федерали́зм, а *m.* federalism.

федерали́ст, а *m.* federalist.

федера́льный *adj.* federal.

федерати́вный *adj.* federative, federal.

федера́ци|я, и *f.* federation.

феери́ческий *adj.* **1** *(theatr.)* (based on a) fairytale. **2** *(сказочный)* fairy-like; magical.

фее́ри|я, и *f.* **1** *(theatr.)* extravaganza. **2** *(сказочное зрелище)* magical sight.

фейерве́рк, а *m.* **1** firework(s). **2** *(событие)* firework display.

фейерве́ркер, а *m. (hist.)* bombardier.

фека́л|ии, ий *pl. (sg.* **~ия, ~ии** *f.)* faeces *(Br.)*, feces *(US).*

фека́льный *adj.* faecal *(Br.)*, fecal *(US).*

фелла́х, а *m.* fellah.

фельдма́ршал, а *m.* field-marshal.

фельдфе́бел|ь, я *m. (hist.)* sergeant-major.

фе́льдшер, а, *pl.* **~а́** *m.* medical assistant.

фельдшери́ц|а, ы *f. of* ⇒**фе́льдшер**

фе́льдшер|ский *adj. of* ⇒**~**

фельдъе́гер|ский *adj. of* ⇒**~ь; ~ская связь** communication by courier.

фельдъе́гер|ь, я *m. (hist.)* courier, special messenger.

Ф

фельетóн, а *m.* satirical article.

фельетонúст, а *m.* composer of satirical articles.

фельетóн|ный *adj. of* ⇒~

фелю́г|а, и *f.* (*naut.*) felucca.

феминúзм, а *m.* feminism.

феминúст, а *m.* feminist.

феминúст|ка, ки *f. of* ⇒~

феминúстский *adj.* feminist.

фен, а *m.* (hair-)drier.

фéникс, а *m.* (*mythol.*) phoenix (*Br.*), phenix (*US*).

фенóл, а *m.* (*chem.*) phenol.

фенóмен, а *m.* (*явление*) phenomenon; (*событие, человек*) marvel.

феноменалúзм, а *m.* (*phil.*) phenomenalism.

феноменáл|ьный (~ен, ~ьна) *adj.* phenomenal.

феноменолóги|я, и *f.* (*phil.*) phenomenology.

фéнхел|ь, я *m.* (*bot.*) fennel.

фéн|я, и *f.* (*sl.*) thieves' slang.

феóд, а *m.* (*hist.*) feud, fief.

феодáл, а *m.* (*hist.*) feudal lord.

феодалúзм, а *m.* feudalism.

феодáльный *adj.* feudal.

фéрз|евый *adj. of* ⇒**~ь**

ферз|ь, я́, *pl.* **~ú, ~éй** *m.* (*chess*) queen.

фéрм|а[1]**, ы** *f.* farm.

фéрм|а[2]**, ы** *f.* (*tech.*) girder.

фермáт|а, ы *f.* (*mus.*) fermata.

фéрм|енный[1] *adj. of* ⇒**~а**[1]

фéрм|енный[2] *adj. of* ⇒**~а**[2]; lattice.

фермéнт, а *m.* (*biol., chem.*) enzyme.

ферментáци|я, и *f.* fermentation.

ферментúр|овать, ую *impf.* to ferment.

фéрмер, а *m.* farmer.

фéрмер|ский *adj. of* ⇒~; **ф. дом** farm-house.

фéрмерств|о, а *nt.* **1** (*private*) farming. **2** (*collect.*) farmers.

фéрмер|ша, ши *f.* (*coll.*) **1** *f. of* ⇒~. **2** (*жена фермера*) farmer's wife.

фéрм|овый *adj. of* ⇒**~а**[2]

фермуáр, а *m.* (*obs.*) **1** (*застёжка*) clasp. **2** (*ожерелье*) necklace.

ферросплáв, а *m.* ferro-alloy.

ферт, а *m.* **1** old name of letter **'ф'**; **~ом стоя́ть** to stand with arms akimbo. **2** (*coll.*) (*франт*) fop; smug person; **~ом глядéть** to look smug; **~ом ходúть** to strut about.

фес, а *m.* (*and* **фéск|а, и** *f.*) fez.

фестивáл|ь, я *m.* festival.

фестóн, а *m.* scallops (*decoration on fabrics*).

фетúш, а *m.* fetish.

фетишизúр|овать, ую *impf.* to make a fetish (of).

фетишúзм, а *m.* fetishism.

фетишúст, а *m.* fetishist.

фетр, а *m.* felt.

фéтр|овый *adj. of* ⇒~

фефёл|а, ы *c.g.* (*coll.*) clumsy person.

фехтовáльный *adj.* fencing.

фехтовáльщик, а *m.* fencer; **ф. рапúрой** foil fencer; **ф. шпáгой** épée fencer.

фехтовáльщи|ца, цы *f. of* ⇒**~к**

фехтовáни|е, я *nt.* fencing.

фехт|овáть, у́ю, *impf.* to fence.

фешенéбел|ьный (~ен, ~ьна) *adj.* fashionable.

фé|я, и *f.* fairy.

фи *int.* ugh!; pah!

фиáлк|а, и *f.* violet.

фиáлк|овый *adj. of* ⇒**~а**

фиáско *nt. indecl.* fiasco, failure; **потерпéть ф.** to be a flop.

фибергла́с, а *m.* fibreglass (*Br.*), fiberglass (*US*).

фибергла́с|овый *adj. of* ⇒~

фúбр|а, ы *f.* (*obs., anat., bot.*) fibre (*Br.*), fiber (*US*) (*also fig.*); **всéми ~ами душú** in every fibre (of one's being).

фибрóзный *adj.* (*anat., bot.*) fibrous.

фибрóм|а, ы *f.* (*med.*) fibroma.

фúг|а, и *f.* **1** (*дерево*) fig(-tree); (*плод*) fig. **2** (*coll.*) = **ку́киш**

фúгли-мúгли, фúглей-мúглей *no sg.* (*coll.*) tricks.

фигля́р, а *m.* **1** (*obs.*) (*акробат*) (circus) acrobat; (*фокусник*) conjuror. **2** (*шут*) buffoon.

фигля́р|ить, ю, ишь *impf.* (*coll.*) to act the buffoon.

фигля́рнича|ть, ю *impf.* = **фигля́рить**

фигн|я́, ú *f.* (*sl.*) rubbish.

фúг|овый *adj. of* ⇒**~а 1**; **ф. листóк** fig leaf.

фигóвый *adj.* (*coll.*) rubbishy, inferior, worthless.

фигу́р|а, ы *f.* **1** figure. **2** (*в картах*) court-card (*Br.*), face card (*US*). **3** (*в шахматах*) piece, chess-man (*excluding pawns*).

фигурáл|ьный (~ен, ~ьна) *adj.* figurative, metaphorical.

фигурúр|овать, ую *impf.* to figure, appear.

фигурúст, а *m.* figure skater.

фигурúст|ка, ки *f. of* ⇒~

фигу́р|ка, ки *f.* **1** *dim. of* ⇒**~а.** **2** (*статуэтка*) figurine, statuette.

фигу́рн|ый *adj.* **1** figured; ornamented. **2**: **~ое катáние (на конькáх)** figure skating; **ф. пилотáж** aerobatics.

Фúджи *nt. indecl.* Fiji.

фиджú|ец, йца *m.* Fijian.

фиджú|йка, йки *f. of* ⇒**~ец**

фиджúйский *adj.* Fijian.

фúжм|ы, ~ *no sg.* farthingale.

физ... *comb. form, abbr. of* ***физúческий***

фúзик, а *m.* physicist.

фúзик|а, и *f.* physics.

физиóлог, а *m.* physiologist.

физиологúческий *adj.* physiological.

физиолóги|я, и *f.* physiology.

физионóми|я, и *f.* (*coll.*) face; physiognomy (*also joc.*).

физиотерапéвт, а *m.* physiotherapist.

физиотерапú|я, и *f.* physiotherapy.

физúческ|ий *adj.* **1** physical; **~ая культу́ра** physical training, gymnastics; **ф. труд** manual labour (*Br.*), labor (*US*). **2** *adj. of* ⇒**фúзика; ф. кабинéт** physics laboratory.

физкульту́р|а, ы *f.* physical training (*abbr.* PT); physical education (*abbr.* PE); **урóк ~ы** PE lesson; **лечéбная ф.** exercise therapy.

физкульту́рник, а *m.* athlete, sportsman.

физкульту́рни|ца, цы *f. of* ⇒**~к**

физкульту́рн|ый *adj.* gymnastic; athletic, sports; **ф. зал** gymnasium; **~ая подготóвка** physical training.

фикс: идéя ~ idée fixe.

фиксáж, а *m.* (*phot.*) fixing solution, fixer.

фиксатúв, а *m.* (*art*) fixative.

фиксáтор, а *m.* (*tech.*) **1** stop; index pin. **2** (*раствор*) fixing solution.

фиксатуáр, а *m.* hair-grease.

фиксáци|я, и *f.* fixing.

фиксúр|овать, ую *impf. and pf.* (*pf. also* **за~**) **1** (*регистрировать*) to record (*in writing, etc.*). **2** (*устанавливать*) to fix; **ф. день встрéчи** to fix a date to meet, make a date. **3** (*внимание, взгляд*) to fix, direct. **4** (*закреплять в определённом положении*) to fix in place. **5** (*phot., chem.*) to fix.

фиктúв|ный (~ен, ~на) *adj.* fictitious; **ф. брак** marriage of convenience.

фúкус, а *m.* (*bot.*) ficus; rubber plant.

фúкци|я, и *f.* fiction.

филантрóп, а *m.* philanthropist.

филантропúческий *adj.* philanthropic.

филантрóпи|я, и *f.* philanthropy.

филантрóп|ка, ки *f. of* ⇒~

филармóни|я, и *f.* philharmonic society; (*зал*) concert hall.

филателúст, а *m.* philatelist, stamp collector.

филателúст|ка, ки *f. of* ⇒~

филателú|я, и *f.* philately.

филé[1] *nt. indecl.* (*cul.*) **1** (*мясо высшего сорта*) sirloin. **2** (*кусок мяса или рыбы без костей*) fillet.

филé[2] *nt. indecl.* (*вышивка*) drawn-thread work.

филёнк|а, и *f.* panel, slat.

филёр, а *m.* (*obs.*) detective, sleuth.

филиáл, а *m.* branch (*of a business, organization*).

филиáл|ьный *adj. of* ⇒~; **~ьное отделéние** branch (office).

филигрáнный *adj.* **1** filigree. **2** (*fig.*) (*очень тщательный*) meticulous.

филигрáн|ь, и *f.* **1** filigree. **2** (*водяной знак*) water-mark.

фúлин, а *m.* eagle owl (*Bubo bubo*).

фили́ппик|а, и *f.* philippic.
филиппи́н|ец, ца *m.* Filipino.
филиппи́н|ка, ки *f. of* ⇒**~ец**
филиппи́нский *adj.* Philippine; Filipino.
Филиппи́н|ы, ~ *no sg.* the Philippines.
фили́стер, а *m.* philistine.
фили́стер|ский *adj. of* ⇒**~**
фили́стерств|о, а *nt.* philistinism.
фило́лог, а *m.* philologist.
филологи́ческий *adj.* philological.
филоло́ги|я, и *f.* philology.
фило́н, а *m.* (*coll.*) idler, loafer.
фило́н|ить, ю, ишь *impf.* (*coll.*) to idle, loaf.
фило́соф, а *m.* philosopher.
филосо́фи|я, и *f.* philosophy.
филосо́фский *adj.* philosophic(al).
филосо́фств|овать, ую *impf.* to philosophize.
филфа́к, а *m.* (*abbr. of* ***филологи́ческий факульте́т***) faculty of philology.
фильм, а *m.* (*cin.*) film; **приключе́нческий ф.** thriller.
фильмоте́к|а, и *f.* film library.
фильтр, а *m.* filter.
фильтра́ци|я, и *f.* filtration.
фильтрова́льный *adj.*: **ф. насо́с** filter pump.
фильтр|ова́ть, у́ю *impf.* (*of* ⇒**про~**) **1** to filter. **2** (*fig., coll.*) screen, check.
фимиа́м, а *m.* incense; **кури́ть ф.** (+*d.*) to praise to the skies, sing the praises (of).
фин... *comb. form, abbr. of* ***фина́нсовый***
фина́л, а *m.* **1** (*спектакля*) finale. **2** (*sport*) final.
финали́ст, а *m.* finalist.
финали́ст|ка, ки *f. of* ⇒**~**
фина́льный *adj.* final; **ф. акко́рд** (*mus.*) final chord; **ф. матч** (*sport*) final.
финанси́р|овать, ую *impf. and pf.* to finance.
финанси́ст, а *m.*
1 (*предприниматель*) financier.
2 (*специалист по финансовым наукам*) financial expert.
фина́нсовый *adj.* financial; **ф. год** fiscal year; **ф. отде́л** finance department.
фина́нс|ы, ов *no sg.* **1** finance(s). **2** (*coll.*) (*деньги*) money.
фи́ник, а *m.* date (*fruit*).
финики́йский *adj.* Phoenician.
фи́ник|овый *adj. of* ⇒**~**; **~овая па́льма** date-palm.
фининспе́ктор, а *m.* inspector of finance(s).
фини́фтевый *adj.* enamelled (*Br.*), enameled (*US*).
фини́фт|ь, и *f.* enamel.
фини́фт|яный *adj.* = **~евый**
фи́ниш, а *m.* (*sport*)
1 (*заключительная часть состязания*) finish; (*конечный пункт*) finishing post.
2 (*расстояние перед конечным пунктом*) final lap.
финиши́р|овать, ую *impf. and pf.* (*sport*) to finish, come in.
фи́ниш|ный *adj. of* ⇒**~**; **~ная ле́нточка** finishing tape; **~ная пряма́я** home straight.
фи́нк|а[1]**, и** *f. of* ⇒**финн**
фи́нк|а[2]**, и** *f.* (*нож*) Finnish knife.
Финля́нди|я, и *f.* Finland.
финля́ндский *adj.* Finnish.
финн, а *m.* Finn.
фи́нно-уго́рский *adj.* (*ling.*) Finno-Ugric.
фи́нский *adj.* Finnish; **ф. зали́в** Gulf of Finland.
финт, а *m.* (*sport*) feint.
фин|ти́ть, чу́, ти́шь *impf.* (*coll.*) to be crafty, resort to ruses.
финтифлю́шк|а, и *f.* (*coll.*)
1 (*украшение*) bauble, bagatelle. **2** (*pl.*) (*нелепые слова, поступки*) nonsense.
3 (*женщина*) flibbertigibbet.
фиоле́товый *adj.* violet.
фио́рд, а *m.* (*geog.*) fiord, fjord.
фиориту́р|а, ы *f.* (*mus.*) fioritura, (*vocal*) grace-note.
фи́рм|а, ы *f.* (*econ.*) firm.
фи́рм|енный *adj. of* ⇒**~а**; **~енная этике́тка** proprietary label; **ф. бланк** letterhead.
фисгармо́ни|я, и *f.* (*mus.*) harmonium.
фиска́л, а *m.* (*coll.*) tell-tale, informer.
фиска́л|ить, ю, ишь *impf.* (*coll.*) to tell tales, be an informer.
фиска́льный *adj.* (*leg.*) fiscal.
фиста́шк|а, и *f.* (*дерево*) pistachio (-tree); (*орех*) pistachio (nut).
фиста́шков|ый *adj.* **1** pistachio; **ф. лак** mastic varnish; **~ая смола́** mastic. **2** (*цвет*) pistachio-green.
фи́стул|а́[1]**, ы-ы́** *f.* (*med.*) fistula.
фистул|а́[2]**, ы́** *f.* **1** (*mus.*) pipe, flute. **2** (*голос*) falsetto.
фити́л|ь, я́ *m.* (*лампы, свечи*) wick; (*для воспламенения зарядов*) fuse.
фитю́льк|а, и *f.* (*coll.*) little thing.
фи́ф|а, ы *f.* bimbo, flibbertigibbet (*coll.*).
фи́шк|а, и *f.* **1** (*в играх*) counter, chip. **2** (*sl.*) (*лицо*) face.
флаг, а *m.* flag; **под ~ом** (+*g.*) (*i*) flying the flag (of), (*ii*) (*fig.*) under the guise (of).
фла́гман, а *m.* (*naut.*)
1 (*командующий*) flag-officer.
2 (*корабль*) flag-ship.
фла́гман|ский *adj. of* ⇒**~**; **ф. кора́бль** = **~** 2
флагшто́к, а *m.* flagstaff.
фла́жный *adj.* flag.
флаж|о́к, ка́ *m.* (*small*) flag; (*для сигнализации*) signal flag.
флажоле́т, а *m.* (*mus.*) (*инструмент*) flageolet; (*нота*) harmonic.
флако́н, а *m.* (scent-)bottle.
флама́нд|ец, ца *m.* Fleming.
флама́нд|ка, ки *f. of* ⇒**~ец**
флама́ндский *adj.* Flemish.
флам́енко *nt. indecl.* flamenco.
флами́нго *m. indecl.* flamingo.
фланг, а *m.* (*mil.*) flank.
фланго́вый *adj.* (*mil.*) flank; **ф. охва́т** flanking movement.
флане́левый *adj.* flannel.
флане́л|ь, и *f.* flannel.
фланёр, а *m.* flâneur, idler.
фла́н|ец, ца *m.* (*tech.*) flange.
флани́р|овать, ую *impf.* (*coll.*) to wander aimlessly; to mooch (*Br.*).
фланки́р|овать, ую *impf. and pf.* (*mil.*) to flank.
фла́н|цевый *adj. of* ⇒**~ец**
фла́тов|ый *adj.*: **~ая бума́га** (*typ.*) flat paper.
флегм|а, ы *f.* **1** (*невозмутимость*) phlegm. **2** (*coll.*) (*человек*) phlegmatic person.
флегма́тик, а *m.* phlegmatic person.
флегмати́ч|ный (~ен, ~на) *adj.* phlegmatic.
фле́йт|а, ы *f.* flute.
флейти́ст, а *m.* flautist.
флейти́ст|ка, ки *f. of* ⇒**~**
фле́йт|овый *adj. of* ⇒**~а**
фле́кси|я, и *f.* (*ling.*) inflection.
флекти́вный *adj.* (*ling.*) inflected.
флёр, а *m.* crêpe.
флибустье́р, а *m.* freebooter.
фли́гел|ь, я, *pl.* **~я́, ~е́й** *m.*
1 (*пристройка*) wing (*of building*).
2 (*отдельное здание*) outbuilding.
фли́гель-адъюта́нт, а *m.* (*hist.*) aide-de-camp.
флирт, а *m.* flirtation.
флирт|ова́ть, у́ю *impf.* (**с**+*i.*) to flirt (with).
флокс, а *m.* phlox.
флома́стер, а *m.* felt-tip pen.
фло́р|а, ы *f.* flora.
флоренти́йский *adj.* Florentine.
Флоре́нци|я, и *f.* Florence.
Флори́д|а, ы *f.* Florida.
флот, а *m.* **1** fleet; **вое́нно-морско́й ф.** navy. **2**: **возду́шный ф.** (air) fleet.
флоти́ли|я, и *f.* flotilla.
фло́тск|ий *adj.* naval; *as n.* **ф., ~ого** *m.* sailor.
флэт, а *m.* (*sl.*) flat, 'pad'.
флюга́рк|а, и *f.* **1** (*naut.*) (*флажок*) pennant; (*дощечка*) distinguishing plate (*of boat*). **2** (*флюгер*) weather-vane.
флю́гер, а, *pl.* **~а́** *m.* weather-vane.
флюи́д|ы, ов *pl.* (*sg.* **~, ~а** *m.*) ectoplasm; (*fig.*) emanations.
флюоресце́нци|я, и *f.* fluorescence.
флюоресци́р|овать, ует *impf.* (*phys.*) to fluoresce; **~ующий** fluorescent.
флюс[1]**, а,** *pl.* **~ы** *m.* (*med.*) gumboil.
флюс[2]**, а,** *pl.* **~ы́** *m.* (*tech.*) flux.
фля́г|а, и *f.* **1** flask; (*mil.*) water bottle. **2** (*для молока*) churn.
фля́жк|а, и *f. dim. of* ⇒**фля́га**
...фо́ *comb. form, abbr. of* ***фина́нсовый отде́л***

Ф

фо́би|я, и *f.* phobia.
фойе́ *nt. indecl.* foyer.
фок, а *m.* (*naut.*) **1** (*парус*) foresail. **2** (*фок-мачта*) foremast.
фок- *pref.* (*naut.*) fore-.
фока́льный *adj.* (*phys.*) focal.
фок-ма́чт|а, ы *f.* (*naut.*) foremast.
фокстерье́р, а *m.* fox-terrier.
фокстро́т, а *m.* foxtrot.
фо́кус¹, а *m.* (*phys.*) focus (*also fig.*).
фо́кус², а *m.* **1** (*трюк*) (conjuring) trick; **пока́зывать ~ы** to do conjuring tricks. **2** (*fig.*) (*проделка*) trick, secret (*of mechanism, etc.*); **в то́м-то и ф.** that's the whole point; that's just it. **3** (*coll.*) (*каприз*) whim, caprice.
фокуси́р|овать, ую *impf.* (*of* ⇒**с~**) (*phys.*) to focus; (*fig.*) (**на** + *p.*) to focus (on).
фокуси́р|оваться, уюсь *impf.* (*of* ⇒**с~**) (**на** + *p.*) to focus (on), be focussed (on).
фо́кусник, а *m.* conjurer, juggler.
фо́куснича|ть, ю *impf.* (*coll.*) to play tricks.
фо́кусный *adj.* (*phys.*) focal.
фолиа́нт, а *m.* folio.
Фолкле́ндск|ие остров|а́, ~их ~о́в *no sg.* the Falkland Islands; the Falklands.
фолли́кул, а *m.* (*anat.*) follicle.
фольг|а́, и́ *f.* foil.
фолькло́р, а *m.* folklore.
фольклори́ст, а *m.* folklorist.
фо́мк|а, и *f.* (*coll.*) jemmy.
фон, а *m.* **1** background (*also fig.*). **2** (*помехи*) background noise.
фона́рик, а *m.* small lamp; torch (*Br.*), flash-light (*US*).
фона́р|ный *adj. of* ⇒**~ь; ф. столб** lamppost.
фона́рщик, а *m.* (*obs.*) lamplighter.
фона́р|ь, я́ *m.* **1** (*с ручкой*) lantern; (*уличный*) lamp; light. **2** (*archit.*) light; (*на крыше*) skylight. **3** (*coll.*) (*синяк*) black eye.
фонд, а *m.* **1** (*fin.*) fund; stock, reserves, resources; **валю́тный ф.** currency reserves; **земе́льный ф.** available land; **золото́й ф.** gold reserves; **о́бщий ф.** pool. **2** (*pl.*) (*fin.*) (*ценные бумаги*) stocks; (*fig., obs.*) stock. **3** (*организация*) fund, foundation (*in former USSR, organization serving as channel for State subsidies*). **4** (*архив*) archive.
фо́нд|овый *adj. of* ⇒**~; ~овая би́ржа** stock exchange.
фоне́м|а, ы *f.* (*ling.*) phoneme.
фонендоско́п, а *m.* (*med.*) phonendoscope.
фоне́тик|а, и *f.* phonetics.
фонети́ст, а *m.* phonetician.
фонети́ческий *adj.* phonetic.
фо́н|овый *adj. of* ⇒**~**
фонограмм|а, ы *f.* soundtrack; **спеть под ~у** to mime to a recording.
фоно́граф, а *m.* phonograph.
фоноло́ги|я, и *f.* phonemics.
фоноте́к|а, и *f.* sound archive, audio library.

фонта́н, а *m.* fountain; (*fig.*) stream; **нефтяно́й ф.** oil gusher; **бить ~ом** to gush forth.
фонтани́р|овать, ует *impf.* to gush forth.
фо́р|а, ы *f.*: **дать ~у** (+*d.*) to give a start (*in a game*); (*fig., coll.*) to be much better than.
фо́рвард, а *m.* (*sport*) forward.
фордеви́нд, а *m.* (*naut.*) following wind; **идти́ на ф.** to run before the wind.
форе́йтор, а *m.* (*obs.*) postilion.
форе́л|ь, и *f.* trout.
фо́рзац, а *m.* fly-leaf (*of a book*).
фо́ринт, а *m.* forint (*Hungarian currency unit*).
фо́рм|а, ы *f.* **1** form; **по ~е, … по содержа́нию** in form, … in content. **2** (*для печенья*) cake tin; shape. **3** (*tech.*) (*внешнее очертание*) mould (*Br.*), mold (*US*), cast; **отли́ть в ~у** to mould (*Br.*), mold (*US*), cast. **4** (*одежда*) uniform. **5**: **быть в ~е** (*coll.*) to be in (good) form. **6** (*pl., coll.*) (*фигура*) contours (*of human body*).
формали́зм, а *m.* formalism.
формали́н, а *m.* formalin.
формали́ст, а *m.* formalist.
формали́стик|а, и *f.* formalities.
формальдеги́д, а *m.* (*chem.*) formaldehyde.
форма́льност|ь, и *f.* formality.
форма́л|ьный (~ен, ~ьна) *adj.* formal.
форма́т, а *m.* format.
формати́р|овать, ую *impf. and pf.* (*comput.*) to format.
форма́ци|я, и *f.* **1** (*структура*) structure; (*стадия развития*) stage (of development). **2** (*система взглядов*) mentality. **3** (*geol.*) formation.
фо́рменный *adj.* **1** (*платье, фуражка*) uniform. **2** (*obs.*) (*формальный*) formal. **3** (*coll.*) (*настоящий*) proper, regular, positive.
формирова́ни|е, я *nt.* **1** (*действие*) forming; organizing. **2** (*mil.*) (*воинская часть*) unit, formation.
формир|ова́ть, у́ю *impf.* (*of* ⇒**с~**) to form; to organize; **ф. хара́ктер** to form character; **ф. батальо́н** to raise a battalion.
формир|ова́ться, у́юсь *impf.* (*of* ⇒**с~**) **1** to form, develop (*intrans.*). **2** *pass. of* ⇒**~ова́ть**
форм|ова́ть, у́ю *impf.* (*of* ⇒**с~**) to form, shape; to model; (*tech.*) to mould (*Br.*), mold (*US*), cast.
формо́вк|а, и *f.* forming, shaping; (*tech.*) moulding (*Br.*), molding (*US*), casting.
фо́рмул|а, ы *f.* formula; formulation.
формули́р|овать, ую *impf. and pf.* (*pf. also* **с~**) to formulate.
формулиро́вк|а, и *f.* **1** formulation. **2** (*сформулированная мысль*) wording.
формуля́р, а *m.* **1** (*obs.*) (*послужной список*) record of service. **2** (*tech.*) logbook (*of installation, machine, etc.*). **3** (*в библиотеке*) (*книги*) card (*card in book recording its details*); (*читателя*) record card (*card for each reader, recording details of books loaned*).

форпо́ст, а *m.* (*mil.*) advanced post; outpost (*also fig.*).
форс, а (у) *m.* (*coll.*) swank; **для ~а** to show off; **сбить кому́-н. ф.** to take s.o. down a peg.
форси́ров|анный *p.p.p. of* ⇒**~ать** *and adj.* forced; accelerated; **ф. марш** forced march.
форси́р|овать, ую *impf. and pf.* **1** to force; to speed up. **2** (*mil.*) to force (*a crossing of*).
фор|си́ть, шу́, си́шь *impf.* (*coll.*) to show off.
форс-мажо́р, а *m.* force majeure.
форсу́нк|а, и *f.* (*tech.*) fuel injector.
форт, а, о ~е, в ~у́, *pl.* **~ы** *m.* (*mil.*) fort.
фо́ртел|ь, я *m.* (*coll.*) trick, stunt.
фортепья́нный *adj.* piano; **ф. конце́рт** piano concerto.
фортепья́но *nt. indecl.* piano.
фортификацио́нный *adj.* fortification.
фортифика́ци|я, и *f.* fortification.
фо́рточк|а, и *f.* fortochka (*small hinged pane for ventilation in window of Russian houses*).
фо́рум, а *m.* forum.
форшла́г, а *m.* (*mus.*) grace-note.
форшма́к, а́ *m.* (*cul.*) forshmak (*baked hashed meat or herring with sliced potatoes and onions*).
форште́в|ень, ня *m.* (*naut.*) stem.
фосге́н, а *m.* (*chem.*) phosgene.
фосфа́т, а *m.* (*chem.*) phosphate.
фо́сфор, а *m.* (*chem.*) phosphorus.
фосфоресце́нци|я, и *f.* phosphorescence.
фосфоресци́р|овать, ую *impf.* to phosphoresce; **~ующий** phosphorescent; luminous.
фосфори́ческий *adj.* phosphoric.
фосфорноки́слый *adj.* (*chem.*) phosphate (*of*).
фо́сфорный *adj.* (*chem.*) phosphorous, phosphoric.
фо́то *nt. indecl.* (*coll.*) photo.
фото... *comb. form* photo-.
фотоальбо́м, а *m.* photograph album.
фотоаппара́т, а *m.* camera.
фотобума́г|а, и *f.* photographic paper.
фотогени́ч|ный (~ен, ~на) *adj.* photogenic.
фото́граф, а *m.* photographer.
фотографи́р|овать, ую *impf.* (*of* ⇒**с~**) to photograph.
фотографи́р|оваться, уюсь *impf.* (*of* ⇒**с~**) to be photographed, have one's photo taken.
фотографи́ческий *adj.* photographic.
фотогра́фи|я, и *f.* **1** (*получение изображений*) photography. **2** (*снимок*) photograph. **3** (*мастерская*) photographer's studio.
фотожурнали́зм, а *m.* photojournalism.

фотожурнали́ст, а *m.* photojournalist.
фотожурнали́ст|ка, ки *f. of* ⇒~
фотока́рточк|а, и *f.* photograph.
фотокомпозицио́нный *adj.*: **ф. портре́т** photofit.
фотокопирова́льный *adj.*: **ф. аппара́т** photocopier.
фотоко́пи|я, и *f.* photocopy.
фотокорреспонде́нт, а *m.* press photographer.
фотолюби́тел|ь, я *m.* amateur photographer.
фото́н, а *m.* (*phys.*) photon.
фотонабо́р, а *m.* photo typesetting.
фотонабо́рный *adj.*: **ф. аппара́т** phototypesetter; photo–typesetting machine.
фотообъекти́в, а *m.* (camera) lens.
фотоохо́т|а, ы *f.* wildlife photography.
фотоохо́тник, а *m.* wildlife photographer.
фоторепорта́ж, а *m.* picture story.
фоторепортёр, а *m.* photojournalist.
фото-ро́бот, а *m.* identikit (*propr.*) (picture).
фотоси́нтез, а *m.* (*bot.*) photosynthesis.
фототе́к|а, и *f.* photograph library.
фотоувеличи́тел|ь, я *m.* photographic enlarger.
фотофи́ниш, а *m.* (*sport*) photofinish.
фотохро́ник|а, и *f.* news in pictures.
фотоэлеме́нт, а *m.* (*elec.*) photoelectric cell.
фо́фан, а *m.* (*coll.*) dim-wit.
фрагме́нт, а *m.* fragment; detail (*of painting, etc.*); **ф. фи́льма** film clip.
фрагмента́р|ный (~ен, ~на) *adj.* fragmentary.
фра́ер, а *m.* (*sl.*) trendy chap, guy.
фра́з|а, ы *f.* **1** (*предложение*) sentence. **2** (*выражение*) phrase.
фразеологи́зм, а *m.* (*ling.*) idiom, idiomatic expression.
фразеологи́ческий *adj.* phraseological; **ф. оборо́т** idiom.
фразеоло́ги|я, и *f.* **1** phraseology. **2** (*пустословие*) mere verbiage.
фразёр, а *m.* phrase-monger.
фрази́р|овать, ую *impf.* (*mus.*) to phrase.
фрак, а *m.* tail-coat, tails.
фракцио́нный *adj.* (*pol.*) fractional; factional.
фра́кци|я, и *f.* (*pol.*) fraction; faction, group.
фраму́г|а, и *f.* transom.
франк, а *m.* franc.
франки́р|овать, ую *impf. and pf.* to frank (*a letter*).
франкмасо́н, а *m.* freemason.
фра́нко- *comb. form* (*comm.*) free, prepaid; **ф.-борт, ф.-су́дно** free on board.
франкоязы́чный *adj.* francophone.
фра́нкский *adj.* (*hist.*) Frankish.
франт, а *m.* dandy.
фран|ти́ть, чу́, ти́шь *impf.* (*coll.*) to play the dandy, dress foppishly.
франти́х|а, и *f. of* ⇒**франт**
франтова́т|ый (~, ~а) *adj.* (*coll.*) dandyish.
франтовско́й *adj.* dandyish.
франтовств|о́, а́ *nt.* dandyism.
Фра́нци|я, и *f.* France.
францу́женк|а, и *f.* Frenchwoman.
францу́з, а *m.* Frenchman.
францу́зский *adj.* French.
фраппи́р|овать, ую *impf. and pf.* (*obs.*) to shock.
фрахт, а *m.* freight.
фрахт|ова́ть, у́ю *impf.* (*of* ⇒**за~**) to charter.
фра́чный *adj. of* ⇒**фрак**
ФРГ *f. indecl.* (*abbr. of* ***Федерати́вная Респу́блика Герма́нии***) (*hist.*) FRG (*Federal Republic of Germany*).
фрега́т, а *m.* **1** (*naut.*) frigate. **2** (*zool.*) frigate-bird.
фрез|а́, ы́ *f.* (*tech.*) milling cutter.
фре́зерный *adj.* (*tech.*) milling; **ф. стано́к** milling machine.
фрезер|ова́ть, у́ю *impf. and pf.* (*tech.*) to mill, cut.
фрезеро́вщик, а *m.* milling-machine operator.
фре́йлин|а, ы *f.* (*hist.*) lady-in-waiting.
френо́лог, а *m.* phrenologist.
френологи́ческий *adj.* phrenological.
френоло́ги|я, и *f.* phrenology.
френч, а *m.* service jacket.
фре́ск|а, и *f.* fresco.
фриво́льност|ь, и *f.* frivolity.
фриво́л|ьный (~ен, ~ьна) *adj.* frivolous.
фриги́д|ный (~ен, ~на) *adj.* (*med.*) frigid.
фриз, а *m.* (*archit.*) frieze.
фрикаде́льк|а, и *f.* (*мясная*) meat-ball; (*рыбная*) fish-ball (*in soup*).
фрикасе́ *nt. indecl.* fricassee.
фрикати́вный *adj.* (*ling.*) fricative.
фрикцио́н, а *m.* (*tech.*) friction clutch.
фронт, а, *pl.* **~ы́** *m.* (*mil., meteor.; fig.*) front; **на два ~а** on two fronts; **стать во ф.** to stand to attention.
фронта́льный *adj.* frontal.
фронтиспи́с, а *m.* (*archit., typ.*) frontispiece.
фронтови́к, а́ *m.* front-line soldier.
фронтов|о́й *adj.* (*mil.*) front(-line); **~ы́е пи́сьма** letters from the front.
фронто́н, а *m.* (*archit.*) pediment.
фрукт, а *m.* **1** fruit. **2** (*pl.*) fruit (*collect.*).
фрукто́вый *adj.* fruit; **ф. нож** fruit knife; **ф. сад** orchard.
фр|я, и *f.* (*coll., pej.*) personage.
ФСБ *f. indecl.* (*abbr. of* ***Федера́льная слу́жба безопа́сности***) Federal Security Service.
фтор, а *m.* (*chem.*) fluorine.
фтори́д, а *m.* fluoride.
фтори́ровани|е, я *nt.* (*med.*) fluoridation.
фто́ристый *adj.* fluorine; fluoride (of).
фу *int.* **1** (*выражает презрение, отвращение*) ugh! **2** (*выражает усталость*) oh!; ooh! **3**: **фу́ ты** (*выражает удивление, досаду*) my word!; my goodness!
фу́г|а, и *f.* (*mus.*) fugue.
фуга́н|ок, ка *m.* (*tech.*) smoothing-plane.
фуга́с, а *m.* (*mil.*) landmine.
фуга́ск|а, и *f.* (*coll.*) **1** (*фугас*) landmine. **2** (*авиабомба*) high-explosive bomb.
фуга́с|ный *adj.* **1** *adj. of* ⇒**~.** **2** high-explosive; **~ная бо́мба** high-explosive bomb.
фуг|ова́ть, у́ю *impf.* (*tech.*) to joint, mortise.
фужéр, а *m.* tall wineglass.
фу́к|ать, аю *impf. of* ⇒**~нуть**
фу́к|нуть, ну, нешь *pf.* (*of* ⇒**~ать**) (*coll.*) **1** (*дунуть*) to blow; (*задуть*) to blow out. **2** (*в шашках*) to huff.
фу́кси|я, и *f.* fuchsia.
фуля́р, а *m.* (*text.*) foulard.
фунда́мент, а *m.* foundation, base (*also fig.*).
фундаментали́зм, а *m.* fundamentalism.
фундаментали́ст, а *m.* fundamentalist.
фундамента́л|ьный (~ен, ~ьна) *adj.* **1** (*прочный*) solid, sound; (*основательный*) thorough(-going). **2** (*основной, главный*) main, basic; **~ьная библиоте́ка** main library.
фунда́мент|ный *adj. of* ⇒**~**
фуникулёр, а *m.* funicular (railway).
функциона́льн|ый *adj.* functional **~ая кла́виша** (*comput.*) function key.
фунциони́р|овать, ую *impf.* to function.
фу́нкци|я, и *f.* function.
фунт[1], а *m.* **1** (*obs.*) (*старая русская мера*) pound (*equivalent to 409.5 grams*). **2** (*английская мера*) pound (*equivalent to 453.6 grams*).
фунт[2], а *m.* (*fin.*): **ф. (сте́рлингов)** pound (sterling).
фу́нтик, а *m.* (*cone-shaped*) paper bag.
фу́р|а, ы *f.* (baggage-)wagon.
фура́ж, а́ *m.* forage, fodder.
фуражиро́вк|а, и *f.* (*mil.*) foraging.
фура́жк|а, и *f.* peak-cap; (*mil.*) service cap.
фура́ж|ный *adj. of* ⇒**~; ~ное зерно́** fodder grain.
фурго́н, а *m.* **1** (*автомобиль*) van. **2** (*крытая повозка*) covered wagon.
фу́ри|я, и *f.* **1** (*myth.*) Fury. **2** (*fig.*) shrew, virago.
фурниту́р|а, ы *f.* accessories.
фуро́р, а *m.* furore.
фуру́нкул, а *m.* (*med.*) furuncle, boil.
фуршéт *see* ⇒**а-ля фуршéт**
фут, а *m.* foot (*measure of length*).
футбо́л, а *m.* football (*Br.*), soccer.

Ф

футболи́ст, а *m.* football-player (*Br.*), soccer-player.

футбо́лк|а, и *f.* T-shirt.

футбо́л|ьный *adj. of* ⇨~; **~ьные бу́тсы** football boots; **ф. мяч** football.

футеро́вк|а, и *f.* (*tech.*) (brick-)lining, fettling.

футля́р, а *m.* case; **ф. для очко́в** spectacle-case; **ф. для скри́пки** violin-case.

фу́товый *adj.* one-foot.

футури́зм, а *m.* futurism.

футури́ст, а *m.* futurist.

футуристи́ческий *adj.* futuristic.

футуро́лог, а *m.* futurologist.

футурологи́ческий *adj.* futurological.

футуроло́ги|я, и *f.* futurology.

фуфа́йк|а, и *f.* jersey.

фуфл|о́, а́ *nt.* (*sl.*) rubbish, garbage, crap.

фуфу́: **на ф.** (*coll.*) anyhow, carelessly.

фы́рк|ать, аю *impf.* (*of* ⇨**~нуть**)
1 (*о животном; о машине*) to snort.
2 (*fig., coll.*) (*смеяться*) to chuckle.
3 (*fig., coll.*) (*брюзжать*) to grouse.

фы́рк|нуть, ну, нешь *pf. of* ⇨**~ать**

фьорд = **фио́рд**

фью́черс|ы, ов *pl.* (*comm.*) futures.

фюзеля́ж, а *m.* (*aeron.*) fuselage.

Хх

хаба́р, а *m.* (*and* **~а́, ~ы́** *f.*) (*coll., obs.*) bribe.

хавро́нь|я, и *f.* (*coll.*) sow.

ха́живать *pres. tense not used, impf.* (*coll.*) *freq. of* ⇒**ходи́ть**

хайл|о́, а́, *pl.* **~а** *nt.* (*sl.*) gob.

ха́кер, а *m.* (*comput.*) hacker.

ха́ки *indecl.* **1** *adj.* khaki. **2** *n.*; *nt.* khaki.

хала́т, а *m.* **1** (*домашний*) dressing-gown; (*купальный*) bathrobe. **2** (*рабочий*) overall; **до́кторский х.** doctor's smock. **3** (*восточный*) robe.

хала́тност|ь, и *f.* carelessness, negligence.

хала́т|ный *adj.* **1** *adj. of* ⇒**~.** **2** **(~ен, ~на)** careless, negligent.

халв|а́, ы *f.* (*cul.*) halva.

хали́ф, а *m.* (*hist.*) caliph.

халифа́т, а *m.* (*hist.*) caliphate.

халту́р|а, ы *f.* (*coll.*) **1** (*collect.*) (*небрежная работа*) poor-quality work. **2** (*работа*) work done on the side; (*деньги*) money earned on the side.

халту́р|ить, ю, ишь *impf.* (*coll.*) **1** (*небрежно работать*) to turn out poor work. **2** (*зарабатывать на стороне*) to moonlight; to make money on the side.

халту́р|ный *adj. of* ⇒**~а**

халту́рщик, а *m.* (*coll.*) **1** (*том, кто работает небрежно*) poor worker, hack. **2** (*том, кто зарабатывает на стороне*) moonlighter.

халу́п|а, ы *f.* peasant house (*in Ukraine and Byelorussia*).

халцедо́н, а *m.* (*min.*) chalcedony.

халя́в|а, ы *f.*: **на ~у** (*sl.*) free of charge; for free.

халя́вщик, а *m.* (*sl.*) scrounger, layabout.

хам, а *m.* (*coll.*) boor, lout.

хамелео́н, а *m.* chameleon (*also fig.*).

хам|и́ть, лю́, и́шь *impf.* (*pf.* **на~**) (*+d.*) to be rude (to).

хамс|а́, ы́ *f.* khamsa (*small fish of anchovy family*).

ха́мский *adj.* (*coll.*) boorish, loutish.

ха́мств|о, а *nt.* (*coll.*) boorishness, loutishness.

хан, а *m.* khan.

хандр|а́, ы́ *f.* depression.

хандр|и́ть, ю́, и́шь *impf.* to be depressed.

ханж|а́, и́, *g. pl.* **~е́й** *c.g.* sanctimonious person; hypocrite.

ха́нжеск|ий (*and* ~о́й) *adj.* sanctimonious; hypocritical.

ханжеств|о́, а́ *nt.* sanctimoniousness; hypocrisy.

ханж|и́ть, у́, и́шь *impf.* (*coll.*) to display sanctimoniousness; to play the hypocrite.

Хано́|й, я *m.* Hanoi.

ха́нств|о, а *nt.* khanate.

ханты *c.g. indecl.* Khanty (*formerly Ostyak(s), inhabitant(s) of Khanty-Mansi National Region*).

ханы́г|а, и *m.* (*sl.*) drunkard.

хао́с, а *m.* chaos.

хаоти́ческий *adj.* chaotic.

хаоти́чност|ь, и *f.* chaotic character; state of chaos.

хаоти́ч|ный (~ен, ~на) *adj.* = **~еский**

ха́п|ать, аю *impf. of* ⇒**~нуть**

ха́п|нуть, ну, нешь *pf.* (*of* ⇒**~ать**) (*coll.*) **1** (*хватать*) to seize, grab. **2** (*fig.*) (*украсть*) to nab, pinch (*Br.*).

хапу́г|а, и *c.g.* (*coll.*) thief.

хараки́ри *nt. indecl.* hara-kiri; **сде́лать себе́ х.** to commit hara-kiri.

хара́ктер, а *m.* **1** (*человека*) character, personality, nature, disposition (*of a human being*); **они́ не сошли́сь ~ами** they could not get on (together); **э́то не в его́ ~е** it's not like him. **2** (*твёрдый характер*) (strong) character; **челове́к с ~ом** determined person, strong character. **3** (*свойство*) character, nature, type; **х. рабо́ты** type of work.

характериз|ова́ть, у́ю *impf. and pf.* (*pf. also* **о~**) **1** (*описывать*) to describe. **2** (*быть характерным*) to characterize, be characteristic (of).

характериз|ова́ться, у́юсь *impf.* (*+i.*) to be characterized (by).

характери́стик|а, и *f.* **1** (*описание*) description. **2** (*отзыв*) reference; **х. с ме́ста пре́жней рабо́ты** reference from former place of work.

характе́рно *as pred.* it is characteristic; it is typical.

хара́ктерный *adj.* (*coll.*) stubborn, strong-willed; temperamental.

характе́р|ный (~ен, ~на) *adj.* **1** (*свойственный*) characteristic; typical; **э́то для него́ ~но** it is typical of him. **2** (*своеобразный*) distinctive. **3** (*theatr.*) character; **х. актёр** character actor.

хариджа́н, а *m.* untouchable.

хари́зм|а, ы *f.* charisma.

харизмати́ческий *adj.* charismatic.

ха́риус, а *m.* (*zool.*) grayling.

ха́рканы|е, я *nt.* (*coll.*) expectoration.

ха́рк|ать, аю *impf.* (*of* ⇒**~нуть**) (*coll.*) to spit, expectorate; **х. кро́вью** to spit blood.

ха́рк|нуть, ну, нешь *pf. of* ⇒**~ать**

ха́рти|я, и *f.* charter.

харче́вн|я, и *f.* (*obs.*) eating-house.

харч|и́, е́й *pl.* (*sg.* **~,** **~а** *m.*) (*coll.*) grub.

харчо́ *nt. indecl.* kharcho (*Caucasian mutton soup*).

ха́р|я, и *f.* (*sl.*) mug (= *face*).

хаси́дский *adj.* (*relig.*) Hasidic.

ха́т|а, ы *f.* **1** peasant house (*in Southern Russia, Ukraine, and Byelorussia*); **моя́ х. с кра́ю** it's no concern of mine; that's your, their, *etc.*, funeral. **2** (*sl.*) 'pad'.

ха-(ха)-ха́ *onomat.* ha ha.

ха́хал|ь, я *m.* (*sl.*) fancy man.

ха́|ять, ю, ешь *impf.* (*of* ⇒**о~**) (*coll.*) to run down, knock (*fig.*).

хвал|а́, ы́ *f.* praise; **х. Бо́гу!** thank God!

хвале́б|ный (~ен, ~на) *adj.* laudatory, eulogistic.

хвалёный *adj.* (*iron.*) much-vaunted, celebrated.

хвал|и́ть, ю́, ~ишь *impf.* (*of* ⇒**по~**) to praise.

хвал|и́ться, ю́сь, ~ишься *impf.* (*of* ⇒**по~**) (+*i.*) to boast (of).

хва́ста|ть, ю *impf.* = **~ся**

хва́ста|ться, юсь *impf.* (*of* ⇒**по~**) (+*i.*) to boast (of).

хвастли́в|ый (~, ~а) *adj.* boastful.

хвастовств|о́, а́ *nt.* boasting, bragging.

хвасту́н, а́ *m.* (*coll.*) boaster, braggart.

хват, а *m.* (*coll.*) dashing blade.

хват|а́ть¹, а́ю *impf.* (*of* ⇒**~и́ть¹** *and* **схвати́ть**) **1** to snatch, seize, catch hold (of); to grab, grasp; **х. что попа́ло** to grab whatever comes to hand. **2** (*impf. only*) (*coll.*) (*о рыбе*) to bite. **3** (*impf. only*) (*coll.*) (*вора*) to pick up.

хват|а́ть², а́ет *impf.* (*of* ⇒**~и́ть²**) *impers.* **1** (+*g.*) (*быть достаточным*) to suffice, be sufficient, enough; to last out; **у меня́**, *etc.*, **не ~а́ет** I, *etc.*, am short (of); **вре́мени не ~а́ло** there was not enough time; **у нас не ~а́ет де́нег** we have not enough money; **э́того ещё не ~а́ло!** that's all we, *etc.* need! **2** (+*g.* **на**+*a.*) to be up to, be capable (of); **его́ не ~а́ет на тако́й посту́пок** he is not capable of such an act.

хват|а́ться, а́юсь *impf.* (*of* ⇒**~и́ться** *and* **схвати́ться**) (**за**+*a.*) **1** to snatch (at), catch (at), pluck (at); **х. за соло́минку** to clutch at straws. **2** (*приниматься*) to start doing, take up, try out.

хва|ти́ть¹, чу́, ~тишь *pf.* (*coll.*) **1** *pf. of* ⇒**~та́ть¹**. **2** (*выпить*) to drink up, knock back; **х. ли́шнего** to have one too many. **3** (*испытать*) to suffer, endure. **4** (*сделать что-н. сверх меры*) to stick one's neck out; (*сказать лишнее*) to blurt out; **х. че́рез край** to go too far. **5** (*ударить*) to strike; to hit; **его́ ~ти́л уда́р** he has had a stroke; (*impers.*): **посе́вы хвати́ло моро́зом** the frost hit the crops. **6** (*песню*) to strike up, start up.

хват|и́ть², ~ит *pf.* (*of* ⇒**~а́ть²**); **~ит!** that will do!; that's enough!; **с меня́ ~ит!** I've had enough!; **~ит тебе́ хны́кать!** that's enough of your whining!

хва|ти́ться, чу́сь, ~тишься *pf.* **1** *pf. of* ⇒**~та́ться**. **2** (+*g.*; *coll.*) to miss, notice the absence (of); **по́здно ~ти́лись!** you thought of it too late!

хва́тк|а, и *f.* **1** grasp, grip. **2** (*coll.*) (*ловкость*) skill.

хва́т|кий (~ок, ~ка́, ~ко) *adj.* (*coll.*) **1** (*руки*) strong. **2** (*fig.*) (*глаз, ум*) keen.

хвать (*coll.*) *used in place of various forms of* ⇒**хвати́ть¹** *and* **хвати́ться** 2 (*also as int.*); **я х. его́ за воротни́к** I grabbed him by the collar; **я чуть бы́ло не сел на по́езд, а — х.! — биле́та нет** I was just about to get on the train when suddenly I found I had not got my ticket.

хво́йн|ый *adj.* **1** *adj. of* ⇒**хво́я; х. покро́в** covering of (pine) needles; **х. дёготь** pine-tar. **2** (*дерево*) coniferous; *as n.* **~ые, ~ых** (*bot.*) conifers.

хвора́|ть, ю *impf.* (*coll.*) to be ill (*Br.*), sick (*US*).

хво́рост, а (у) *m.* (*collect.*) **1** brushwood. **2** (*cul.*) (pastry) straws, twiglets.

хворости́н|а, ы *f.* stick, switch (*for driving cattle, etc.*).

хво́рост|ь, и *f.* (*coll.*) illness, ailment.

хворостяно́й *adj. of* ⇒**хво́рост** 1

хво́р|ый (~, ~а́, ~о) *adj.* (*coll.*) ill (*Br.*), sick (*US*).

хвор|ь, и *f.* (*coll.*) illness, ailment.

хвост, а́ *m.* **1** tail (*also fig.*); **маха́ть ~о́м** to wag one's tail; **задра́ть х.** to get on one's high horse; **поджа́ть х.** to draw in one's horns; **показа́ть х.** (*coll.*) to show a clean pair of heels; **наступи́ть на х. кому́-н.** (*coll.*) to tread on s.o.'s toes. **2** (*fig.*) (*задняя часть*) tail, rear, tail-end; **х. по́езда** rear of train; **быть, плести́сь в ~е́** to get behind, lag behind. **3** (*coll.*) (*платья*) train. **4** (*coll.*) (*очередь*) queue (*Br.*), line (*US*); **х. за хле́бом** bread queue.

хвоста́т|ый (~, ~а) *adj.* **1** (*имеющий хвост*) having a tail; caudate. **2** (*с большим хвостом*) having a large tail.

хво́стик, а *m. dim. of* ⇒**хвост;** (*причёска*) pony-tail; **с ~ом** (*coll.*) and a little more; **сто с ~ом** (*coll.*) a hundred odd.

хвостов|о́й *adj. of* ⇒**хвост; х. ого́нь** (*aeron.*) tail light; **~о́е опере́ние** (*aeron.*) tail unit.

хвощ, а́ *m.* (*bot.*) horse-tail, mare's tail (*Equisetum*).

хво́|я, и *f.* **1** needle(s) (*of conifer*). **2** (*collect.*) (*ветви*) branches (*of conifer*).

хек, а *m.* (*zool.*) whiting.

Хе́льсинки *m. indecl.* Helsinki.

хер, ~а́ *m.* (*vulg.*) = **хуй**

хе́рес, а (у) *m.* sherry.

херн|я́, и́ *f.* (*vulg.*) = **хуйня́**

херуви́м, а *m.* cherub.

херуви́м|ский *adj.* **1** *adj. of* ⇒**~.** **2** (*coll.*) cherubic.

хе́ттский *adj.* (*hist. and ling.*) Hittite.

хиба́р|а, ы *f.* (*coll.*) shack, hovel.

хиба́р|ка, ки *f. dim. of* ⇒**~а**

хи́жин|а, ы *f.* shack, hut.

хиле́|ть, ю *impf.* (*of* ⇒**за~**) (*coll.*) to become weak, sickly.

хи́л|ый (~, ~а́, ~о) *adj.* weak, sickly; puny.

хим... *comb. form, abbr. of* ***хими́ческий***

химе́р|а, ы *f.* **1** chimera. **2** (*archit.*) gargoyle.

химери́ческий *adj.* chimerical.

хи́мик, а *m.* chemist.

химика́л|ии, ий *no sg.* chemicals.

химика́т|ы, ов *pl.* (*sg.* **~, ~а** *m.*) = **химика́лии**

химиотерапи́|я, и *f.* chemotherapy.

хими́ческ|ий *adj.* **1** chemical; **~ая война́** chemical warfare; **х. каранда́ш** indelible pencil; **~ие препара́ты** chemicals; **~ая чи́стка (оде́жды)** dry-cleaning; **х. элеме́нт** chemical element. **2** chemistry; **х. кабине́т** chemistry laboratory.

хи́ми|я, и *f.* chemistry.

химчи́стк|а, и *f.* **1** (*действие*) dry-cleaning. **2** (*мастерская*) dry-cleaner's.

хи́нди *m. indecl.* Hindi (*language*).

хини́н, а *m.* quinine.

хи́нн|ый *adj.* cinchona; **~ое де́рево** cinchona (*tree*).

хиппа́р|ь, я́ *m.* (*sl.*) weirdo.

хи́ппи *c.g. indecl.* hippie.

хипп|ова́ть, у́ю *impf.* (*coll.*) to be, live like, dress like, a hippy.

хиппо́вый *adj.* (*coll.*) hippy.

хире́|ть, ю *impf.* (*of* ⇒**за~**) to grow sickly; (*о растениях*) to wither; (*fig.*) to decay.

хирома́нт, а *m.* palmist.

хирома́нти|я, и *f.* palmistry.

хиропра́ктик, а *m.* chiropractor.

Хиро́сим|а, ы *f.* Hiroshima.

хиру́рг, а *m.* surgeon.

хирурги́ческ|ий *adj.* surgical; **~ие но́жницы** forceps; **~ая сестра́** theatre nurse (*Br.*), theater nurse (*US*).

хирурги́|я, и *f.* surgery.

хит, а *m.* (*mus.*) hit.

хит-пара́д, а *m.* (*mus.*) the charts.

хитре́ц, а́ *m.* cunning person; (*coll.*) slyboots.

хитрец|а́, ы́ *f.* (*coll.*) cunning, guile.

хитри́нк|а, и *f.* = **хитреца́**

хитр|и́ть, ю́, и́шь *impf.* (*of* ⇒**с~**) to use cunning, guile; to dissemble.

хитросплете́ни|е, я *nt.* **1** (*уловка*) cunning trick, stratagem. **2** (*pl.*) (*вычурное изложение мыслей*) fanciful construction; hair-splitting.

хитросплетённый *adj.* intricate, contrived.

хи́трост|ь, и *f.* **1** (*свойство*) cunning, guile, craft, wiles. **2** (*уловка*) ruse, stratagem. **3** (*coll.*) ingenuity, subtlety.

хитроу́ми|е, я *nt.* cunning; resourcefulness.

хитроу́м|ный (~ен, ~на) *adj.* **1** (*изобретательный*) cunning; resourceful. **2** (*сложный*) intricate, complicated.

хи́т|рый (~ёр, ~ра́, ~ро) *adj.* **1** (*лукавый*) cunning, sly, crafty. **2** (*coll.*) (*изобретательный*) skilful, resourceful. **3** (*coll.*) (*замысловатый*) intricate, subtle; complicated.

хихи́к|ать, аю *impf.* (*of* ⇒**~нуть**) to giggle, snigger.

хихи́к|нуть, ну, нешь *pf. of* ⇒**~ать**

хище́ни|е, я *nt.* theft; embezzlement, misappropriation.

хи́щник, а *m.* **1** predator; (*животное*) beast of prey; (*птица*) bird of prey. **2** (*fig.*) (*человек*) predator.

хи́щнический *adj.* **1** *adj. of* ⇒**хи́щник.** **2** (*fig.*) predatory, rapacious.

хи́щничеств|о, а *nt.* **1** preying. **2** (*fig.*) predatorines, rapaciousness.

хи́щ|ный (~ен, ~на) *adj.* **1** predatory; **~ные зве́ри, пти́цы** beasts, birds of prey. **2** (*fig.*) rapacious, grasping.

хлад, а *m.* (*obs. or poet.*) cold.

хладнокро́ви|е, я *nt.* composure, sang-froid.

хладнокро́в|ный (~ен, ~на) *adj.* cool, composed; (*жестокий*) cold-blooded.

хла́д|ный (~ен, ~на) *adj.* (*obs. or poet.*) cold.

хлам, а *m.* (*collect.*) rubbish, trash.

хлами́д|а, ы *f.* **1** (*hist.*) chlamys. **2** (*coll.*) long, loose-fitting garment.

хлеб, а, *pl.* **~ы** *and* **~á** *m.* **1** (*sg. only*) bread (*also fig.*); **отби́ть х. у кого́-н.** to take the bread out of s.o.'s mouth. **2** (*pl.* **~ы**) (*буханка*) loaf. **3** (*pl.* **~á**) (*семена злаков*) bread-grain; (*pl.*) (*злаки*) corn, crops; cereals.

хлеба́|ть, ю *impf.* to gulp (down).

хле́б|ец, ца *m.* small loaf.

хле́бниц|а, ы *f.* (*тарелка*) bread-plate, (*коробка*) bread-basket.

хлебн|у́ть, у́, ёшь *pf.* (*coll.*) **1** (*выпить*) to drink down. **2** (+*g.*) (*перенести*) to go through, endure, experience.

хле́бн|ый *adj.* **1** *adj. of* ⇒**хлеб 1; ~ые дро́жжи** baker's yeast; **х. магази́н** baker's shop; **~ое де́рево** bread-fruit tree. **2** *adj. of* ⇒**хлеб** 3; **х. амба́р** granary; **~ые зла́ки** bread-grains, cereals; **х. спирт** grain alcohol. **3** (*урожайный*) rich (*in grain*); abundant; grain-producing. **4** (*coll.*) (*выгодный*) lucrative, profitable.

хлёбов|о, а *nt.* (*coll.*) gruel.

хлебозаво́д, а *m.* bread-baking plant, bakery.

хлебо|заготови́тельный *adj. of* ⇒**~загото́вка**

хлебозаготóвк|а, и *f.* (State) grain procurement.

хлеб|о́к, ка́ *m.* (*coll.*) mouthful (*of liquid*).

хлебопа́шеств|о, а *nt.* (*obs.*) tillage, cultivation, arable farming.

хлебопа́ш|ец, ца *m.* (*obs.*) tiller of the soil.

хлебопа́шный *adj.* ploughing (*Br.*), plowing (*US*); arable.

хлебопёк, а *m.* baker.

хлебопека́рн|я, и *f.* bakery, bake-house.

хлеборо́б, а *m.* peasant (engaged in arable farming).

хлеборо́д|ный (~ен, ~на) *adj.* rich (in grain crops), abundant; **х. год** good year (for grain crops).

хлебосо́л, а *m.* hospitable person.

хлебосо́л|ьный (~ен, ~ьна) *adj.* hospitable.

хлебосо́льств|о, а *nt.* hospitality.

хлеботорго́в|ец, ца *m.* corn-merchant, grain-merchant.

хлеботорго́вл|я, и *f.* corn-trade.

хлебоубо́рк|а, и *f.* (corn-)harvest.

хлебоубо́рочный *adj.* harvest(ing); **х. комба́йн** combine harvester.

хле́б-со́ль, хле́ба-со́ли bread and salt (*offered to guest as symbol of hospitality*); hospitality.

хлев, а, в ~е *or* **в ~у́,** *pl.* **~á** *m.* cow-shed; (*fig., coll.*) pig-sty.

хлестако́вщин|а, ы *f.* shameless bragging (*in the manner of Khlestakov, hero of N.V. Gogol's comedy* 'The Government Inspector').

хле|ста́ть, щу́, ~щешь *impf.* (*of* ⇒**~стну́ть**) **1** (+*a. or* **по**+*d.*) to lash; to whip. **2** (*о дожде*) to lash (down), beat (down), pour; to stream, gush. **3** (*coll.*) (*пить в большом количестве*) to swill.

хлёст|кий (~ок, ~ка́, ~ко) *adj.* **1** (*ветер*) biting. **2** (*fig.*) (*замечание*) biting, scathing. **3** (*fig.*) (*звук*) sharp.

хлест|ну́ть, ну́, нёшь *pf. of* ⇒**~а́ть**

хлёст|че *comp. of* ⇒**~кий**

хли́па|ть, ю *impf.* (*coll.*) to sob.

хли́п|кий (~ок, ~ка́, ~ко) *adj.* (*coll.*) **1** (*стол, мост*) rickety. **2** (*fig.*) (*человек, здоровье*) weak, fragile. **3** (*суп*) watery, slushy.

хлобы|ста́ть, щу́, ~щешь *impf.* (*of* ⇒**~стну́ть**) (*coll.*) to lash.

хлобыст|ну́ть, ну́, нёшь *inst. pf. of* ⇒**~а́ть**

хлоп *int.* bang! (*as pred.; stands for pres. and past tenses of* ⇒**~ать, ~нуть** *and* **~аться**).

хло́па|ть, ю *impf.* (*of* ⇒**хло́пнуть**) **1** (+*i. or* **по**+*d.*) to bang; to slap; **х. кали́ткой** to bang the gate; **х. кого́-н. по спине́** to slap s.o. on the back; **х. глаза́ми/уша́ми** (*coll.*) (*i*) (*бессмысленно смотреть*) to look blank, (*ii*) (*не знать, что сказать в ответ*) to be at a loss what to say. **2**: **х. (в ладо́ши)** (+*d.*) to clap, applaud. **3** (*coll.*) (*раздаваться*) to go bang, explode. **4** (*coll.*) (*пить залпом*) to knock back.

хло́па|ться, юсь *impf.* (*of* ⇒**хло́пнуться**) (*coll.*) to flop down.

хло́п|ец, ца *m.* (*coll.*) lad.

хлопково́д, а *m.* cotton-grower.

хлопково́дств|о, а *nt.* cotton-growing.

хлопково́дческий *adj.* cotton-growing.

хло́пков|ый *adj.* cotton; **~ое ма́сло** cotton-seed oil.

хлопкопряди́льный *adj.* cotton-spinning.

хлопкоро́б, а *m.* cotton-grower.

хлопкоубо́рочный *adj.* cotton-picking.

хло́п|нуть(ся), ну(сь), нешь(ся) *pf. of* ⇒**~ать(ся)**

хло́п|ок, ка *m.* cotton; **х.-сыре́ц** raw cotton.

хлоп|о́к, ка́ *m.* **1** (*в ладоши*) clap. **2** (*выстрела*) bang.

хлопо|та́ть, чу́, ~чешь *impf.* (*of* ⇒**по~**) **1** (*impf. only*) (*быть в хлопотах*) to busy o.s.; to bustle about, toil. **2** (**о**+*p. or* +**что́бы**) (*беспокоиться*) to make efforts; to take trouble, go to pains; to solicit, petition (for). **3** (**за**+*a. or* **о**+*p.*) (*стараться помочь кому-н.*) to plead (for), make efforts on behalf (of).

хлопотли́в|ый (~, ~а) *adj.* **1** (*дело*) troublesome, bothersome. **2** (*человек*) busy, bustling.

хло́пот|ный (~ен, ~на) *adj.* (*coll.*) onerous, exacting.

хлопотн|я́, и́ *f.* (*coll.*) efforts, labour (*Br.*), labor (*US*), toil.

хлопоту́н, а́ *m.* (*coll.*) busy, restless person.

хло́пот|ы, хлопо́т, ~ам *no sg.* **1** (*занятия по дому, по работе*) jobs, chores; (*заботы*) trouble. **2** (**о**+*p.*) (*старания добиться чего-н.*) efforts (on behalf of, for); pains.

хлопу́шк|а, и *f.* **1** (*для мух*) fly-swatter. **2** (*ёлочная игрушка*) (Christmas) cracker. **3** (*cin.*) clapperboard. **4** (*bot.*) catchfly (*Silene venosa*).

хлопча́тк|а, и *f.* (*coll.*) cotton (*fabric*).

хлопча́тник, а *m.* cotton(-plant).

хлопчатобума́жный *adj.* cotton.

хло́пчик, а *m.* (*coll. or dial.*) boy.

хлопьеви́д|ный (~ен, ~на) *adj.* flaky, flocculent.

хло́пь|я, ев *no sg.* flakes (*of snow, etc., or as component of name of certain cereal foods*); **кукуру́зные х., пшени́чные х.** corn flakes.

хлор, а *m.* (*chem.*) chlorine.

хлори́р|овать, ую *impf. and pf.* to chlorinate.

хло́ристый *adj.* (*chem.*) chlorine; chloride (of); **х. водоро́д** hydrogen chloride.

хло́рк|а, и *f.* (*coll.*) bleaching powder.

хло́р|ный *adj. of* ⇒**~**

хлоро́з, а *m.* (*bot. and med.*) chlorosis.

хлорофи́лл, а *m.* (*bot.*) chlorophyll.

хлорофо́рм, а *m.* chloroform.

хлы́н|уть, у, ешь *pf.* **1** (*о крови, дожде*) to gush, pour. **2** (*fig.*) to pour, rush, surge; **на пло́щадь ~ула толпа́ наро́ду** a crowd poured into the square.

хлыст[1]**, а́** *m.* (*прут*) whip, switch.

хлыст[2]**, а́** *m.* (*последователь религиозного секта*) Khlyst (*member of sect*).

хлыщ, а́ *m.* (*coll.*) fop.

хлю́па|ть, ю *impf.* (*coll.*) **1** (*грязи*) to squelch; **х. по грязи́** to squelch through the mud. **2** (*плача, всхлипывать*) to snivel; **х. но́сом** to sniff.

хлю́пик, а *m.* (*coll.*) sniveller (*Br.*), sniveler (*US*), milksop.

хлю́п|кий (~ок, ~ка́, ~ко) *adj.* (*coll.*) **1** (*топкий*) soggy. **2** (*шаткий*) rickety. **3** (*fig.*) (*хилый*) frail, feeble.

хлюст[1]**, а́** *m.* (*coll.*) smart Alec.

хлюст[2]**, а́** *m.* (*obs., coll.*) suit (*in a hand at cards*).

хляб|ь, и *f.* **1** (*poet.*) (*бездна*) abyss; **~и небе́сные разве́рзлись** (*joc.*) the heavens opened. **2** (*coll.*) (*грязь*) mud, muddy ground.

хля́стик, а *m.* half-belt (*on back of coat*).

хмелево́дств|о, а *nt.* hop-growing.

хмел|ёк, ька́ *m. dim. of* ⇒**~ь; под ~ько́м** tipsy, tight.

хмеле́|ть, ю *impf.* (*of* ⇒**за~** *and* **о~**) to become tipsy, get tight.

Х

хмел|ь, я *m.* **1** (*bot.*) (*семена*) hops; (*растение*) hop-plant. **2 (о ~е, во ~ю́)** (*состояние*) drunkenness, tipsiness; **под ~ем, во ~ю́**, tipsy, tight.

хмел|ьно́й (~ён, ~ьна́) *adj.* **1** (*пьяный*) drunken, tipsy. **2** (*пьянящий*) intoxicating; *as n.* **~ьно́е, ~ьно́го** *nt.* intoxicating liquor, alcohol.

хму́р|ить, ю, ишь *impf.* (*of* ⇒**на~**) **х. лицо́** to frown; **х. бро́ви** to knit one's brows.

хму́р|иться, юсь, ишься *impf.* (*of* ⇒**на~**) **1** (*хмурить брови*) to frown. **2** (*о погоде, о дне*) to become gloomy. **3** (*о небе*) to be overcast, cloudy.

хму́рост|ь, и *f.* **1** (*человека*) gloom. **2** (*неба*) cloudiness.

хму́р|ый (~, ~а́, ~о) *adj.* **1** (*человек*) gloomy, sullen. **2** (*небо, день*) overcast, cloudy; **х. день** dull day.

хмыка|ть, ю *impf.* (*coll.*) to hem (*expr. surprise, annoyance, doubt, etc.*).

хн|а, ы *f.* henna.

хны́ка|ть, ю (*and* **хны́ч|у, ешь**) *impf.* (*coll.*) to whimper, snivel; (*fig.*) to whine.

хо́бби *nt. indecl.* hobby.

хо́бот, а *m.* (*zool.*) trunk, proboscis.

хобот|о́к, ка́ *m.* proboscis (*of insects*).

ход, а (у), о ~е, в (на) ~е *and* **~у́** *m.* **1 (в ~е, на ~у́)** motion, movement, travel, going; speed, pace; **три часа́ ~у** three hours' walk; **за́дний х.** backing, reversing; **ма́лый х., ти́хий х.** slow speed; **по́лный х.** full speed; **по́лный х.!** full speed ahead!; **по́лным ~ом** (*fig.*) in full swing; **свобо́дный х.** free-wheeling, coasting; **дать х.** (+*d.*) to set in motion, set going; **не дать ~у кому́-н.** not to give s.o. a chance, hold s.o. back; **идти́ свои́м ~ом** (*i*) (*о человеке*) to travel under one's own steam, (*ii*) (*о болезни*) to take its course; **пойти́ в х.** to come to be widely used; **пусти́ть в х.** to start, set in motion, set going (*also fig.*), put into service; **быть в ~у́** to be in demand, be in vogue; **на ~у́** (*i*) (*двигаясь*) on the move, without halting, (*ii*) (*в действии*) in motion, in operation; **на по́лном ~у́** at full speed; **с ~у** (*coll.*) straight off. **2** (*eccl.*) procession. **3 (в, на ~е)** (*fig.*) (*развитие*) course, progress; **х. мы́слей** train of thought; **х. собы́тий** course of events. **4 (в ~е, на ~е** *and* **~у́)** (*tech.*) work, operation, running; **на холосто́м ~у́** idling. **5 (в, на ~е;** *pl.* **~ы́)** (*tech.*) stroke (*of piston*). **6 (на ~е;** *pl.* **~ы́)** (*в шахматах*) move; (*в картах*) lead; **х. бе́лых** white's move. **7 (в ~е;** *pl.* **~ы́)** (*fig.*) move, gambit; **ло́вкий х.** shrewd move. **8 (в ~е** *and* **~у́;** *pl.* **~ы)** (*вход*) entrance (*to building*); **знать все ~ы и вы́ходы** to know all the ins and outs. **9 (в, на ~е** *and* **~у́;** *pl.* **~ы́, ~о́в)** (*путь*) passage(way), thoroughfare. **10 (в, на ~у́;** *pl.* **~ы** *and* **~а́, ~о́в)** (*tech.*) wheel-base; runners (*of sledge*); **гу́сеничный х.** caterpillar tracks.

хода́та|й, я *m.* intercessor, mediator.

хода́тайств|о, а *nt.* **1** (*действие*) petitioning; entreaty, pleading. **2** (*просьба*) petition; application.

хода́тайств|овать, ую *impf.* (*of* ⇒**по~**) **1 (о**+*p.*) to petition (for); to apply (for). **2 (за**+*a.*) to intercede (for), plead (on behalf of).

хо́дик|и, ов *no sg.* (*coll.*) wall clock (*worked by weights*).

хо|ди́ть, жу́, ~дишь *impf.* **1** (*передвигаться, шагая*) to (be able to) walk. **2** (*indet. of* ⇒**идти́**) to go (*on foot*); **х. в кино́** to go to the cinema; **х. в ата́ку** to go into the attack; **х. под па́русом** to go sailing. **3** (*о поездах*) to run. **4** (*о слухах, о новостях*) to pass, go round; **х. из рук в ру́ки, по рука́м** to pass from hand to hand. **5** (*cards*) to lead, play; (*chess, etc.*) to move; **х. с пик** to lead a spade; **х. ферзём** to move one's queen. **6** (*indet. only*) **(за**+*i.*) (*ухаживать*) to look after, take care of, tend. **7** (*шататься*) to sway, shake, wobble. **8 (в**+*p.*) (*носить*) to wear.

хо́д|кий (~ок, ~ка́, ~ко) *adj.* (*coll.*) **1** (*конь, машина*) fast. **2** (*товар*) popular, in great demand; **~кое выраже́ние** popular phrase.

ходов|о́й *adj.* **1** (*tech.*) running, working; **~о́е вре́мя** working time; **~ы́е испыта́ния** running tests; **х. механи́зм** running gear. **2** (*coll.*) (*популярный*) popular; current; **х. анекдо́т** (currently) popular story.

ходо́к, а́ *m.* **1** walker. **2: быть ~о́м (куда́-н.)** (*coll.*) to make regular visits (to). **3** (*obs.*) (*посланец*) envoy. **4 (на**+*a.*; **по**+*d.*) (*coll.*) (*ловкий человек*) person clever (at).

ходу́л|и, ей *pl.* (*sg.* **~я, ~и** *f.*) stilts.

ходу́л|ьный (~ен, ~ьна) *adj.* stilted; pompous.

ходу́н, а́ *m. now only in phr.* **~о́м ходи́ть** (*coll.*) to shake.

ходун|о́к, ка́ *m.* baby walker.

ходьб|а́, ы *f.* walking; **це́рковь нахо́дится в пяти́ мину́тах ~ы отсю́да** the church is five minutes' walk from here.

ходя́ч|ий *adj.* **1** walking; able to walk. **2** (*fig., coll., iron.*) the personification (of); **~ая доброде́тель** virtue personified. **3** (*употребительный*) popular; current; **~ее выраже́ние** current phrase.

хожде́ни|е, я *nt.* **1** walking; going; **х. по му́кам** (*fig.*) (going through) purgatory. **2: име́ть х.** to be in circulation.

хоз... *comb. form, abbr. of* ***хозя́йственный***

...хоз *comb. form, abbr. of* ***хозя́йство***

хозрасчёт, а *m.* (*econ.*) operation on a self-supporting basis; self-financing.

хозрасчёт|ный *adj. of* ⇒**~**

хозя́|ин, ина, *pl.* **~ева, ~ев** *m.* **1** (*владелец*) owner, proprietor. **2** (*своей судьбы; в доме*) master; (*предприятия*) boss. **3** (*по отношению к жильцу*) landlord. **4** (*по отношению к гостям*) host; **~ева по́ля** (*sport*) the home team. **5: хоро́ший, плохо́й х.** good, bad manager. **6** (*coll.*) (*муж*) husband. **7** (*biol.*) host.

хозя́йк|а, и, *g. pl.* **хозя́ек** *f.* **1** (*владелица*) owner, proprietress. **2** (*своей судьбы; в доме*) mistress. **3** (*по отношению к жильцу*) landlady. **4** (*по отношению к гостям*) hostess. **5** (*coll.*) (*жена*) wife.

хозя́йнича|ть, ю *impf.* **1** to manage, be in charge. **2** (*по дому*) to keep house. **3** (*pej.*) to lord it; to throw one's weight about.

хозя́йский *adj.* **1** *adj. of* ⇒**хозя́ин. 2** (*тон, глаз*) solicitous, careful. **3** (*pej.*) proprietary; imperious.

хозя́йственник, а *m.* economic planner.

хозя́йствен|ный (~, ~на) *adj.* **1** economic, of the economy; **~ная жизнь страны́** the country's economy. **2: х. расчёт** *see* ⇒**хозрасчёт. 3** (*товары, инвентарь*) household; home management. **4** (*экономный*) economical, thrifty.

хозя́йств|о, а *nt.* **1** (*экономика*) economy; **се́льское х.** agriculture; **дома́шнее х.** housekeeping; **вести́ х.** to manage, carry on management. **2** (*оборудование*) equipment. **3** (*agric.*) farm, holding. **4** (*работы по дому*) housekeeping; **хлопота́ть по ~у** to be busy about the house.

хозя́йств|овать, ую *impf.* to manage, carry on management.

хозя́йчик, а *m.* (*coll., pej.*) small proprietor.

хоккеи́ст, а *m.* hockey-player.

хоккеи́ст|ка, ки *f. of* ⇒**~**

хокке́|й, я *m.* hockey; **х. с мячо́м, ру́сский х.** bandy; **х. с ша́йбой** ice hockey; **ко́нный х.** polo.

хокке́й|ный *adj. of* ⇒**~; ~ная клю́шка** hockey-stick.

хо́лдинг-компа́ни|я, и *f.* holding company.

хо́леный *adj.* well-groomed.

холёный *adj.* = **хо́леный**

холе́р|а, ы *f.* (*med.*) cholera.

холе́рик, а *m.* choleric person.

холери́ческий *adj.* choleric.

холе́р|ный *adj. of* ⇒**~а; х. вибрио́н** cholera bacillus.

холестери́н, а *m.* cholesterol.

хо́л|ить, ю, ишь *impf.* to tend, care for.

хо́лк|а, и *f.* withers; **намы́лить ~у кому́-н.** (*fig., coll.*) to give s.o. a dressing-down.

холл, а *m.* hall, vestibule, foyer.

холм, а́ *m.* hill.

холми́ст|ый (~, ~а) *adj.* hilly.

хо́лод, а (у), *pl.* **~а́, ~о́в** *m.* **1** cold; coldness (*also fig.*); **ди́кий х.** bitter cold. **2** (*pl.*) cold (spell of) weather.

холода́|ть, ю *impf.* **1** (*pf.* **по~;** *impers.*) (*становиться холоднее*) to become cold, turn cold. **2** (*coll.*) (*страдать от холода*) to endure cold.

холоде́|ть, ю *impf.* (*of* ⇒**по~**) to grow cold; (*impers.*) to turn cold.

холод|е́ц, ца́ *m.* (*cul.*) meat *or* fish in jelly.

холоди́льник, а *m.* refrigerator; ваго́н-х. refrigerator van; двухсекцио́нный х. fridge-freezer.

холоди́льн|ый *adj.* refrigeration; ~ая устано́вка cold storage plant.

холо|ди́ть, жу́, ди́шь *impf.* **1** (*pf.* на~) (*coll.*) (*делать холодным*) to cool. **2** (*вызывать ощущение холода*) to cause a cold sensation (*also impers.*).

хо́лодно[1] *adv.* (*fig.*) coldly.

хо́лодно[2] *as pred.* it is cold; мне, *etc.*, х. I, *etc.*, am cold, feel cold.

холоднова́т|ый (~, ~а) *adj.* rather cold, chilly.

холоднокро́вный *adj.* (*zool.*) cold-blooded.

хо́лодност|ь, и *f.* coldness.

холо́д|ный (хо́лоден, ~на́, хо́лодно) *adj.* **1** cold; х. ве́тер cold wind; х. отве́т cold reply; х. по́яс (*geog.*) frigid zone; ~ная война́ cold war; ~ное ору́жие side-arms, cold steel; *as n.* ~ная, ~ной *f.* (*obs., coll.*) 'the cooler' (= *place of detention*). **2** (*одежда*) light, thin.

холод|о́к, ка́ *m.* **1** (*холод*) coolness, chill (*also fig.*). **2** (*ветерок*) cool breeze. **3** (*прохладное место*) cool place. **4** (*время суток*) cool of the day.

холодосто́|йкий (~ек, ~йка) *adj.* (*agric.*) cold-resistant.

холо́п, а *m.* **1** (*hist.*) villein, serf. **2** (*fig., pej.*) lackey.

холо́п|ский *adj.* **1** *adj. of* ⇒~. **2** servile.

холо́пств|о, а *nt.* **1** (*hist.*) villeinage. **2** (*fig., pej.*) servility.

холо́пств|овать, ую *impf.* to display servility.

холостёж|ь, и *f.* (*collect.*) (*coll.*) bachelors.

холо|сти́ть, щу́, сти́шь *impf.* to castrate, geld.

холост|о́й (хо́лост, ~а́) *adj.* **1** unmarried, single; bachelor. **2** (*tech.*) idle, free-running; на ~о́м ходу́ idling. **3** (*mil.*) blank, dummy; х. патро́н blank cartridge.

холостя́к, а́ *m.* bachelor.

холостя́|цкий *adj. of* ⇒~к

холоще́ни|е, я *nt.* castration, gelding.

холощёный *adj.* castrated, gelded.

холст, а́ *m.* **1** (*ткань*) coarse linen, canvas, burlap. **2** (*art*) canvas.

холсти́н|а, ы *f.* **1** = холст. **2** (*кусок холста*) piece of linen, canvas, burlap.

холсти́нк|а, и *f.* (*text.*) gingham.

холу́|й, я́ *m.* (*obs. and fig., pej.*) lackey.

холщо́вый *adj. of* холст 1

хо́л|я, и *f.* (*coll.*) care, attention; жить в ~е to be well cared for.

хо́мо са́пиенс *nt. indecl.* homo sapiens.

хому́т, а́ *m.* **1** (*на лошади*) collar; (*fig.*) burden. **2** (*tech.*) clamp, ring.

хомя́к, а́ *m.* hamster.

хор, а, *pl.* **~ы** (*and* ~ы́) *m.* **1** choir. **2** (*mus. and fig.*) chorus; ~ом all together. *See also* ⇒ хо́ры

хора́л, а *m.* chorale.

хорва́т, а *m.* Croat.

Хорва́ти|я, и *f.* Croatia.

хорва́т|ка, ки *f. of* ⇒~

хорва́тский *adj.* Croatian, Croat.

хо́рд|а, ы *f.* **1** (*math.*) chord. **2** (*biol.*) notochord.

хо́рд|овый *adj. of* ⇒~а 2; *as n.* ~овые, ~овых (*zool.*) chordata.

хоре́|й, я *m.* (*liter.*) trochee.

хор|ёк, ька́ *m.* polecat, ferret.

хорео́граф, а *m.* choreographer.

хореографи́ческий *adj.* choreographic.

хореогра́фи|я, и *f.* choreography.

хоре́|я, и *f.* (*med.*) chorea, St Vitus' dance.

хори́ст, а *m.* member of a choir, chorister.

хори́ст|ка, ки *f. of* ⇒~

хорме́йстер, а *m.* choirmaster.

хорово́д, а *m.* round dance (*traditional Slavonic folk dance*).

хорово́|диться, жусь, дишься *impf.* (с + *i.*) (*coll.*) **1** (*заниматься чем-н.*) to be occupied (with), take up one's time (with). **2** (*крутить*) to carry on (with) (= *to have a sexual liaison*).

хорово́й *adj.* choral.

хоро́м|ы, ~ *no sg.* (*obs. or joc.*) mansion.

хорон|и́ть, ю́, ~ишь *impf.* (*of* ⇒по~) (*pf. also* за~ *and* с~) to bury (*also fig.*).

хорон|и́ться, ю́сь, ~ишься *impf.* (*of* ⇒с~) (*coll.*) to hide, conceal o.s.

хорохо́р|иться, юсь, ишься *impf.* (*coll.*) to swagger; to boast.

хоро́шенький *adj.* pretty, nice (*also iron.*).

хороше́нько *adv.* (*coll.*) properly, thoroughly, well and truly.

хороше́|ть, ю *impf.* (*of* ⇒по~) to grow prettier.

хоро́ш|ий (~, ~а́, ~о́) *adj.* **1** good. **2** (*приятный*) nice. **3** (*short forms*) (*красивый*) pretty, good-looking.

хорошо́[1] **1** *adv.* well; nicely. **2** *particle* (*выражает согласие*) all right!; OK! **3** *n.*; *nt. indecl.* (*отметка*) good (*mark*).

хорошо́[2] *as pred.* it is good; it is nice; х., что вы успе́ли прие́хать it is good that you managed to come; им х. — ведь у них своя́ маши́на it is all right for them, they have a car of their own.

хору́гв|ь, и *f.* **1** (*mil.*; *obs.*) ensign, standard. **2** (*eccl.*) banner.

хо́р|ы, ~ *and* ~ов *pl.* (*musicians'*) gallery.

хор|ь, я́ *m.* = хорёк

хор|ько́вый *adj. of* ⇒~ёк

хо́спис, а *m.* hospice.

хо́т-до́г, а *m.* hot dog.

хоте́ни|е, я *nt.* (*coll.*) desire, wish.

хоте́|ть, хочу́, хо́чешь, хо́чет, хоти́м, хоти́те, хотя́т *impf.* (*of* ⇒за~) (+*g.*, *inf. or* что́бы) to want, desire; я ~л бы I should like; х. пить to be thirsty; х. сказа́ть to mean; е́сли хоти́те if you like (*also* = *perhaps*).

хоте́|ться, хо́чется *impf.* (*of* ⇒за~) (*impers.* + *d.*) to want; мне хо́чется I want; мне ~лось бы I should like.

хоть *conj. and particle* **1** *conj.* (*хотя*) although. **2** *conj.* (*даже если*) even if (*esp. in set phrr.*); у него́ де́нег х. отбавля́й he has more than enough money; х. убе́й, не скажу́ I couldn't tell you to save my life; х. бы и так (*coll.*) even so, even at that. **3** *particle* (*also* х. бы) (*по крайней мере*) at least, if only; ты бы посмотре́л х. на мину́точку you should take a look, if only for a minute. **4** *particle* (*coll.*) (*например*) for example, even; вот х. его́ семиле́тняя сестрёнка, и та догада́лась why, even his little seven-year-old sister had guessed it. **5**: х. бы if only. **6** + *rel. pron. forms indef. pron.*: х. кто anyone; х. где anywhere, everywhere; х. куда́ (*as pred.*; *coll.*) first-rate, terrific. **7**: х. бы что (+ *d.*; *coll.*) it does not bother.

хотя́ *conj.* **1** although, though. **2**: х. бы even if. **3** *as particle*: х. бы if only; э́то я́вствует х. бы из заключи́тельной фра́зы его́ ре́чи this is evident if only from the final sentence of his speech.

хохла́т|ый (~, ~а) *adj.* crested, tufted.

хо́хл|иться, юсь, ишься *impf. of* ⇒на~

хо́хм|а, ы *f.* (*coll.*) joke, quip, gag.

хох|о́л, ла́ *m.* **1** crest; topknot, tuft of hair. **2** (*joc.*) Ukrainian.

хо́хот, а *m.* guffaw, loud laugh.

хохо|та́ть, чу́, ~чешь *impf.* to guffaw, laugh loudly.

хохоту́н, а́ *m.* (*coll.*) laugher, joker.

Хошими́н, а *m.* Ho Chi Minh City.

храбре́|ть, ю *impf.* (*of* ⇒по~) (*coll.*) to grow brave, braver.

храбре́ц, а́ *m.* brave person.

храбр|и́ться, ю́сь, и́шься *impf.* (*coll.*) to try to appear brave.

хра́брост|ь, и *f.* bravery, courage.

хра́бр|ый (~, ~а́, ~о) *adj.* brave, courageous.

храм, а *m.* temple, church, place of worship.

храм|ово́й *adj. of* ⇒~; х. пра́здник patronal festival.

хране́ни|е, я *nt.* keeping, custody; storage, conservation; ка́мера ~я left luggage office (*Br.*), baggage room (*US*); сдать на х. to deposit for safekeeping.

храни́лищ|е, а *nt.* storehouse, depository.

храни́тел|ь, я *m.* **1** keeper, custodian; (*fig.*) repository. **2** (*музея*) curator.

хран|и́ть, ю́, и́шь *impf.* (*старые письма, деньги в банке*) to keep; (*традиции, доброе имя*) to preserve; (*молчание, гордый вид*) to maintain; х. в та́йне to keep secret.

храни́т|ься, ~ся *impf.* **1** (*находиться*) to be, be kept. **2** (*быть в сохранности*) to be preserved.

храп, а *m.* snore; snoring.

храп|е́ть, лю́, и́шь *impf.* **1** to snore. **2** (*о животном*) to snort.

храпови́к, а́ *m.* (*tech.*) ratchet.

храпови́цк|ий: *only in phr.* **зада́ть ~ого** (*coll.*) to fall fast asleep (*and snore*).

храпово́й *adj.* (*tech.*) ratchet; **х. механи́зм** ratchet gear.

хреб|е́т, та́ *m.* **1** (*anat.*) spine, spinal column; (*fig., coll.*) (*спина*) back. **2** (*горная цепь*) (mountain) range; ridge; (*fig.*) crest, peak.

хреб|то́вый *adj. of* ⇒**~е́т**

хрен, а (у) *m.* horseradish; **говя́дина под ~ом** roast beef with horseradish sauce; **х. ре́дьки не сла́ще** it's six of one to half a dozen of the other; **ста́рый х.** (*fig., coll.*) old fogey, old sod; **х. с** (+*i.*) (*coll.*) to hell (with); **ни ~а́** (*vulg.*) bugger all.

хрен|о́вый *adj. of* ⇒**~**; (*vulg.*) rotten, lousy.

хрестомат|и́йный *adj. of* ⇒**~ия**; (*fig.*) well-known; **х. слу́чай** textbook case.

хрестома́ти|я, и *f.* reader (= *selections of literature, etc. for study*).

хризанте́м|а, ы *f.* chrysanthemum.

хрип, а *m.* wheeze, wheezing sound.

хрип|е́ть, лю́, и́шь *impf.* to wheeze.

хрипли́в|ый (~, ~а) *adj.* (*coll.*) (rather) hoarse.

хри́пл|ый (~, ~а́, ~о) *adj.* hoarse; wheezy.

хри́п|нуть, ну, нешь, *past* **~, ~ла** *impf.* (*of* ⇒**о~**) to become hoarse, lose one's voice.

хрипот|а́, ы́ *f.* hoarseness.

хрипотц|а́, ы́ *f.* (*coll.*) slight hoarseness.

христи|ани́н, ани́на, *pl.* **~а́не, ~а́н** *m.* Christian.

христиа́н|ка, ки *f. of* ⇒**~и́н**

христиа́нский *adj.* Christian; **привести́ в х. вид, прида́ть** (+*d.*) **х. вид** (*joc.*) to give an air of respectability.

христиа́нств|о, а *nt.* **1** Christianity. **2** (*collect.*) Christendom.

Христо́с, Христа́ *m.* Christ.

христо́с|оваться, уюсь *impf.* (*of* ⇒**по~**) to exchange a triple kiss (*as Easter salutation*).

хром[1]**, а** *m.* (*chem.*) chromium, chrome.

хром[2]**, а** *m.* (*сорт кожи*) box-calf.

хромати́зм, а *m.* **1** (*phys.*) chromatic aberration. **2** (*mus.*) chromaticism.

хромат|и́ческий *adj. of* ⇒**~и́зм**; **~и́ческая га́мма** (*mus.*) chromatic scale.

хрома́|ть, ю *impf.* **1** to limp, be lame. **2** (*fig., coll.*) (*иметь недостатки*) to be weak; **арифме́тика у тебя́ ~ет** your arithmetic is very shaky; **х. на о́бе ноги́** to be in a poor way.

хроме́|ть, ю *impf.* (*of* ⇒**о~**) to go lame.

хроми́р|овать, ую *impf. and pf.* to chromium-plate.

хро́м|истый *adj. of* ⇒**~**[1]

хро́мовый[1] *adj.* (*chem.*) chromium, chromic.

хро́м|овый[2] *adj. of* ⇒**~**[2]

хром|о́й (~, ~а́, ~о) *adj.* **1** lame, limping; **х. на ле́вую но́гу** lame in the left leg; *as n.* **х., ~о́го** *m.*; **~а́я, ~о́й** *f.* lame man, woman. **2** (*coll.*) (*нога*) lame. **3** (*fig., coll.*) (*стол*) shaky.

хромоно́г|ий (~, ~а) *adj.* lame, limping.

хромоно́жк|а, и *c.g.* (*coll.*) lame person.

хромосо́м|а, ы *f.* (*biol.*) chromosome.

хромот|а́, ы́ *f.* lameness.

хро́ник, а *m.* (*coll.*) chronic invalid.

хро́ник|а, и *f.* **1** (*летопись*) chronicle. **2** (*в газете*) news items. **3** (*cin.*) newsreel.

хроника́льный *adj. of* ⇒**хро́ника** **2, 3**; **х. фильм** = **хро́ника 3**

хроникёр, а *m.* news reporter.

хрони́ческий *adj.* chronic.

хроно́граф[1]**, а** *m.* (*hist.*) chronicle.

хроно́граф[2]**, а** *m.* (*прибор*) stopwatch.

хронологи́ческий *adj.* chronological.

хроноло́ги|я, и *f.* chronology.

хроно́метр, а *m.* chronometer.

хронометра́ж, а *m.* time study, time-keeping.

хронометражи́ст, а *m.* time study specialist, timekeeper.

хру́п|кий (~ок, ~ка́, ~ко) *adj.* **1** (*стекло*) fragile, brittle. **2** (*fig.*) (*здоровье, ребёнок*) fragile, frail; delicate.

хру́пкост|ь, и *f.* **1** fragility, brittleness. **2** (*fig.*) fragility, frailness.

хруст, а *m.* crunch; crunching sound.

хруста́лик, а *m.* (*anat.*) lens (*of the eye*).

хруста́л|ь, я́ *m.* cut glass, crystal; **го́рный х.** rock crystal.

хруста́льный *adj.* **1** cut glass, crystal. **2** (*fig.*) crystal-clear.

хру|сте́ть, щу́, сти́шь *impf.* (*of* ⇒**~стнуть**) to crunch.

хру́ст|нуть, ну, нешь *pf. of* ⇒**~е́ть**

хруст|я́щий *pres. part. of* ⇒**~е́ть** *and adj.*; **х. карто́фель** potato crisps (*Br.*), chips (*US*).

хрущ, а́ *m.* cockchafer, may bug.

хрыч, а́ *m.*: **ста́рый х.** (*coll.*) old sod, old fogey.

хрычо́вк|а, и *f.*: **ста́рая х.** (*coll.*) old hag, old bag.

хрю́кань|е, я *nt.* grunting.

хрю́к|ать, аю *impf.* (*of* ⇒**~нуть**) to grunt.

хрю́к|нуть, ну, нешь *pf.* (*of* ⇒**~ать**) to give a grunt.

хряк, а́ *m.* hog.

хря́стн|уть, у, ешь *pf.* (*coll.*) **1** (*треснуть*) to snap (off). **2** (*человека*) to bash.

хрящ, а́ *m.* (*anat.*) cartilage, gristle.

хрящева́т|ый (~, ~а) *adj.* cartilaginous, gristly.

хрящ|ево́й *adj. of* ⇒**~**

Хуанхэ́ *f. indecl.* the Yellow River.

худ|е́е *comp. of* ⇒**~о́й**[1,3]

худе́|ть, ю *impf.* (*of* ⇒**по~**) to grow thin, lose weight.

ху́д|о[1]**, а** *nt.* harm, ill, evil; **нет ~а без добра́** every cloud has a silver lining.

ху́до[2] *adv.* ill, badly.

ху́до[3] *as pred.* (*impers.* + *d.*): **ему́,** *etc.*, **х.** (*i*) (*о физическом состоянии*) he, *etc.*, feels poorly, unwell, (*ii*) (*о душевном состоянии*) he, *etc.*, is in a bad way; he, *etc.*, is having a bad time.

худоб|а́, ы́ *f.* thinness, leanness.

худо́жественност|ь, и *f.* artistry, artistic merit.

худо́жествен|ный (~, ~на) *adj.* **1** of art, of the arts; **~ная литерату́ра** fiction; **~ная самоде́ятельность** amateur art (and dramatic) activities, amateur theatricals; **х. фильм** feature film; **~ная шко́ла** art school. **2** (*красивый*) artistic; tasteful.

худо́жеств|о, а *nt.* **1** art; *pl.* (*obs.*) the arts; **Акаде́мия ~** Academy of Arts. **2** (*coll.*) (*проделка*) trick, escapade.

худо́жник, а *m.* artist; **х. по костю́мам/све́те** costume/lighting designer.

худо́жни|ца, цы *f. of* ⇒**~к**

худ|о́й[1] **(~, ~а́, ~о)** *adj.* (*не толстый*) thin, lean.

худ|о́й[2] **(~, ~а́, ~о)** *adj.* (*плохой*) bad; **на х. коне́ц** if the worst comes to the worst; **не говоря́ ~о́го сло́ва** (*coll.*) without a word, without warning.

худ|о́й[3] **(~, ~а́, ~о)** *adj.* (*coll.*) (*дырявый*) in holes, full of holes.

худоща́вост|ь, и *f.* thinness, leanness.

худоща́в|ый (~, ~а) *adj.* thin, lean.

ху́д|ший *superl. of* ⇒**~о́й**[2] *and* **плохо́й**; (the) worst.

хуёвин|а, ы *f.* (*vulg.*) = **хуйня́**

ху|ёвый *adj. of* ⇒**~й**; (*vulg.*) shitty, crap(py).

ху́|же *comp. of* ⇒**~до́й**[2] *and* **~до**[2]**, плохо́й** *and* **пло́хо**; worse.

хуй, ху́я *m.* (*vulg.*) prick, cock (= *penis*); **ни ху́я** (*vulg.*) fuck all.

хуйн|я́, и́ *f.* (*vulg.*) (a load of) bollocks, crap.

хул|а́, ы́ *f.* (verbal) abuse.

хулига́н, а *m.* hooligan.

хулига́н|ить, ю, ишь *impf.* to act like a hooligan.

хулига́н|ский *adj. of* ⇒**~**

хулига́нств|о, а *nt.* hooliganism.

хулига́нствующ|ий *adj.* marauding, rampaging; **~ая молодёжь** young louts.

хули́тел|ьный (~ен, ~ьна) *adj.* abusive.

хул|и́ть, ю́, и́шь *impf.* to abuse, criticize.

ху́нт|а, ы *f.* (*pol.*) junta.

хурм|а́, ы́ *f.* (*bot.*) persimmon, sharon fruit (*Diospyros*).

ху́тор, а, *pl.* **~а́** *m.* **1** (*ферма*) farm; farmstead. **2** (*посёлок*) village (*in Ukraine and Southern Russia*).

хуторск|о́й *adj. of* ⇒**ху́тор**; **~о́е хозя́йство** individual (*as opp. to collective or State*) farm.

хуторя́н|ин, ина, *pl.* **~е, ~** *m.*
1 (*владелец хутора*) farmer.
2 (*житель хутора*) villager.

хуторя́н|ка, ки *f. of* ⇒**~ин**

хэ́ппи-энд, а *m.* happy ending.

Цц

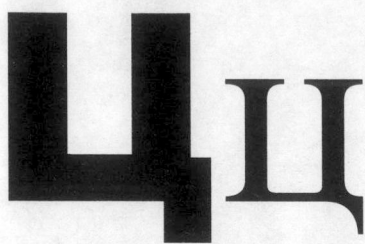

ц. (*abbr. of* **це́нтнер**) q., quintal(s).

ЦАП *m. indecl.* (*abbr. of* **цифро-ана́логовый преобразова́тель**) DAC (*digital to analogue converter*).

цап *as pred.* (*coll.*) = **~́нул**

ца́п|ать, аю *impf.* (*of* ⇒**~нуть**) to snatch, grab.

ца́п|аться, аюсь *impf.* (*coll.*) **1** to scratch one another. **2** (*pf.* **по~**) (*fig.*) to bicker, squabble.

ца́п|ля, ли, *g. pl.* **~ель** *f.* heron.

ца́п|нуть, ну, нешь *pf. of* ⇒**~ать**

цап-цара́п *as pred.* (*coll.*) he, *etc.*, grabbed, made a grab.

цара́п|ать, аю *impf.* **1** (*pf.* **о~** *and* **~нуть**) to scratch. **2** (*coll.*) (*писать*) to scribble.

цара́па|ться, юсь *impf.* **1** to scratch (*intrans.*); (*друг друга*) to scratch one another. **2** (*карабкаться*) to scramble (along).

цара́пин|а, ы *f.* scratch; abrasion.

цара́п|нуть, ну, нешь *pf. of* ⇒**~ать**

царе́вич, а *m.* tsarevich (*son of a tsar*).

царе́в|на, ны, *g. pl.* **~ен** *f.* tsarevna (*daughter of a tsar*).

царедво́р|ец, ца *m.* (*obs.*) courtier.

цар|ёк, ька́ *m.* princeling, ruler.

цареуби́йств|о, а *nt.* regicide (*action*).

цареуби́йц|а, ы *c.g.* regicide (*agent*).

цари́зм, а *m.* tsarism.

цари́стский *adj.* tsarist.

цар|и́ть, ю́, и́шь *impf.* **1** (*obs.*) (*быть царём*) to be tsar. **2** (*первенствовать*) to hold sway, reign supreme. **3** (*fig.*) (*господствовать*) to reign, prevail; **~и́ла тишина́** silence reigned.

цари́ц|а, ы *f.* **1** (*жена царя*) tsarina. **2** (*fig.*) queen.

ца́рск|ий *adj.* **1** tsar's, of the tsar; royal; **ц. двор** tsar's court; **~ая во́дка** aqua regia; **~ие врата́** (*eccl.*) royal gates (*central doors in iconostasis in Orthodox churches*). **2** (*pol.*) tsarist. **3** (*fig.*) regal, kingly; **~ая ро́скошь** regal splendour (*Br.*), splendor (*US*).

ца́рствен|ный (~, ~на) *adj.* regal, kingly.

ца́рств|о, а *nt.* **1** (*государство*) kingdom, realm. **2** (*царствование*) reign. **3** (*fig.*) (*область деятельности*) realm, domain; **живо́тное ц.** animal kingdom; **со́нное ц.** land of Nod.

ца́рствовани|е, я *nt.* reign; **в ц.** (+*g.*) during the reign (of).

ца́рств|овать, ую *impf.* to reign (*also fig.*).

цар|ь, я́ *m.* **1** tsar; **он с ~ём (без ~я́) в голове́** (*coll.*) he is wise (stupid). **2** (*fig.*) king, ruler.

ца́ц|а, ы *f.* (*coll.*) big-head.

ца́цка|ться, юсь *impf.* (**с кем-н.**; *coll.*) to make a fuss (of s.o.).

цве|сти́, ту́, тёшь, *past* **~̈л, ~ла́, ~ло́** *impf.* **1** to flower, bloom, blossom (*also fig.*); **ц. здоро́вьем** to be radiant with health. **2** (*fig.*) to prosper, flourish.

цвет¹, а, *pl.* **~а́** *m.* (*окраска*) colour (*Br.*), color (*US*); **ц. лица́** complexion.

цвет², а *m.* **1** (*pl.* **~ы́**) (*coll.*) (*цветок*) flower. **2** (*fig.*) (*лучшая часть*) flower, cream, pick. **3** (*расцвет*) blossoming; (*fig.*) prime; **в цвету́** in blossom; **дать ц.** to blossom, flower; **во ~́е сил** in one's prime; at the height of one's powers. **4** (*collect.*) (*цветы на растении*) blossom.

цвета́ст|ый (~, ~а) *adj.* (*coll.*) colourful (*Br.*), colorful (*US*); (*pej.*) gaudy, garish.

цвете́ни|е, я *nt.* (*bot.*) flowering, blossoming.

цве́т|ень, ня *m.* (*coll.*) pollen.

цвети́ст|ый (~, ~а) *adj.* **1** (*покрытый цветами*) flower-covered. **2** (*красочный*) colourful (*Br.*), colorful (*US*). **3** (*fig.*) flowery, florid.

цветко́в|ый *adj.*: **~ые расте́ния** (*bot.*) flowering plants.

цветни́к, а́ *m.* flower-bed.

цветн|о́й *adj.* **1** coloured (*Br.*), colored (*US*); colour (*Br.*), color (*US*); **~о́е стекло́** stained glass; **~а́я капу́ста** cauliflower; **~ое телеви́дение** colour (*Br.*), color (*US*) television; *as n.* **ц., ~о́го** *m.* coloured (*Br.*), colored (*US*) person. **2** (*tech.*) non-ferrous.

цветово́д, а *m.* flower-grower.

цветово́дств|о, а *nt.* flower-growing, floriculture.

цветов|о́й *adj. of* ⇒**цвет¹**; **~а́я га́мма** colour (*Br.*), color (*US*) spectrum.

цвет|о́к, ка́, *pl.* **~ы́, ~о́в** *m.* flower; (*pl. also* **~ки́, ~ко́в**) (*орган размножения*) flower.

цветому́зык|а, и *f.* son et lumière.

цветоно́жк|а, и *f.* (*bot.*) peduncle.

цвето́ч|ек, ка *m. dim. of* ⇒**цвето́к**

цвето́чник, а *m.* flower-seller.

цвето́чни|ца, цы *f. of* ⇒**~к**

цвето́чн|ый *adj. of* ⇒**цвето́к; ~ая клу́мба** flower-bed; **ц. магази́н** flower-shop, florist's.

цвету́щий *pres. part. act. of* ⇒**цвести́** *and adj.* **1** (*растение*) flowering, blossoming, blooming; (*здоровье, юноша*) blooming. **2** (*fig.*) (*страна*) prosperous, flourishing.

цеди́лк|а, и *f.* (*coll.*) strainer, filter.

цеди́льн|ый *adj.* filter, filtering; **~ая бума́га** filter paper.

це|ди́ть, жу́, ~́дишь *impf.* **1** (*через сито*) to strain, filter. **2** (*вино*) to decant. **3** (*coll.*) (*говорить*) to say (through clenched teeth).

це́др|а, ы *f.* (dried) lemon *or* orange peel.

це́зи|й, я *m.* (*chem.*) caesium (*Br.*), cesium (*US*).

цезу́р|а, ы *f.* (*liter.*) caesura.

цейтно́т, а *m.*: **находи́ться в ~е** to be in time-trouble (*at chess*).

цейхга́уз, а *m.* (*mil.*; *obs*) armoury (*Br.*), armory (*US*), stores.

целе́бност|ь, и *f.* curative, healing properties.

целе́б|ный (~ен, ~на) *adj.* curative, healing, medicinal.

цел|ево́й *adj.* **1** *adj. of* ⇒**~ь. 2** having a special purpose; **~евы́е сбо́ры** funds earmarked for a special purpose. **3** (*постройка*) special.

целенапра́вленност|ь, и *f.* purposefulness, single-mindedness.

целенапра́влен|ный (~, ~на) *adj.* purposeful, single-minded.

целесообра́зност|ь, и *f.* expediency.

целесообра́з|ный (~ен, ~на) *adj.* expedient.

целеустремлённост|ь, и *f.* purposefulness.

целеустремлён|ный (~, ~на) *adj.* purposeful.

целико́м *adv.* **1** (*в целом виде*) whole; **проглоти́ть ц.** to swallow whole. **2** (*полностью*) wholly, entirely; **ц. и по́лностью** utterly and completely.

целин|а́, ы́ *f.* virgin lands, virgin soil.

цели́н|ный *adj. of* ⇨**~а́; ~ные зе́мли** virgin lands.

целител|ьный (~ен, ~ьна) *adj.* curative, healing, medicinal.

це́л|ить, ю, ишь *impf.* (*of* ⇨**на~**) to take aim; (**в**+*a.*) to aim (at).

цел|и́ть, ю́, и́шь *impf.* (*obs.*) to heal, cure.

це́л|иться, юсь, ишься *impf.* (*of* ⇨**на~**) = **~ить**

целлофа́н, а *m.* cellophane.

целлофа́н|овый *adj. of* ⇨**~**

целлуло́ид, а *m.* celluloid.

целлуло́ид|ный *adj. of* ⇨**~**

целлюло́з|а, ы *f.* cellulose.

цело́ва́льник, а *m.* **1** (*hist.*) (*сборщик подати*) tax collector. **2** (*obs.*) (*хозяин трактира*) inn-keeper, publican.

цел|ова́ть, у́ю *impf.* (*of* ⇨**по~**) to kiss.

цел|ова́ться, у́юсь *impf.* (*of* ⇨**по~**) to kiss (one another).

це́л|ое, ого *nt.* **1** whole. **2** (*math.*) integer.

целому́дрен|ный (~, ~на) *adj.* chaste.

целому́дри|е, я *nt.* chastity.

це́лостност|ь, и *f.* integrity.

це́лост|ный (~ен, ~на) *adj.* integrated; complete.

це́лост|ь, и *f.* **1** (*неповреждённое состояние*) safety; **в ~и и сохра́нности** intact. **2** (*единство*) unity.

це́л|ый *adj.* **1** (*полный*) whole, entire; **~ая но́та** (*mus.*) semibreve (*Br.*), whole note (*US*); **~ое число́** whole number, integer; **в ~ом** as a whole; **по ~ым неде́лям** for weeks on end. **2 (~, ~а́, ~о)** (*неповреждённый*) safe, intact; **~ и невреди́м** safe and sound.

цел|ь, и *f.* **1** (*мишень*) target; **бить в ц., попа́сть в ц.** to hit the target; **бить ми́мо ~и** to miss. **2** (*предмет стремления*) aim, object, goal, end, purpose; **с ~ью** (+*inf.*) with the object (of), in order (to); **отвеча́ть ~и** to answer the purpose; **пресле́довать ц.** to pursue a goal.

це́льност|ь, и *f.* wholeness, integrity.

це́л|ьный *adj.* **1** (*из одного куска*) of one piece, solid. **2 (~ен, ~ьна́, ~ьно)** (*целостный*) entire, integral; single. **3** (*неразбавленный*) undiluted. **4** (*coll.*) = **~ый**

Це́льси|й, я *m.* Celsius, centigrade (thermometer); **10° по ~ю** 10° Celsius.

цеме́нт, а *m.* cement.

цемента́ци|я, и *f.* (*tech.*) **1** (*скважин, трещин*) cementing **2** (*железа, стали; горных пород*) case-hardening, cementation. **3** (*fig.*) cementing.

цементи́р|овать, ую *impf. and pf.* (*pf. also* **с~**) **1** (*tech.*) (*заполнить цементом*) to cement; (*железо; горные породы*) to case-harden, cement. **2** (*fig.*) to cement.

цеме́нт|ный *adj. of* ⇨**~**

цен|а́, ы́, *a.* **~у,** *pl.* **~ы** *f.* **1** price, cost; **~о́ю** (+*g.*) at the price (of), at the cost (of); **любо́й ~о́й** at any cost; **э́тому ~ы́ нет** it is invaluable; **э́то в ~е́** (*i*) it is very costly, (*ii*) it is rated highly, highly prized. **2** (*fig.*) (*значение*) worth, value; **знать ~у** (+*d.*) to know the worth (of); **знать себе́ ~у** to be self-assured, self-possessed, to know one's own value.

ценз, а *m.* qualification, requirement.

це́нз|овый *adj. of* ⇨**~**

це́нзор, а *m.* censor.

цензу́р|а, ы *f.* censorship.

цензу́р|ный *adj.* **1** *adj. of* ⇨**~а. 2 (~ен, ~на)** decent, printable.

цени́тел|ь, я *m.* judge, connoisseur, expert.

цени́тель|ница, ницы *f. of* ⇨**~**

цен|и́ть, ю́, ~ишь *impf.* **1** (*coll.*) (*назначать цену чего-н.*) to fix a price for; (*fig.*) to assess, evaluate. **2** (*признавать ценность кого-чего-н.*) to value, appreciate; **высоко́ ц.** to rate highly.

це́нник, а *m.* (*список*) price-list; (*бирка*) price-tag.

це́нност|ь, и *f.* **1** (*цена, стоимость*) price, value. **2** (*fig.*) (*значение*) value, importance. **3** (*pl.*) (*предметы*) valuables; (*моральные, духовные*) values.

це́н|ный (~ен, ~на) *adj.* **1** (*с обозначенной ценой*) containing valuables; representing a stated value; **~ная бандеро́ль** registered postal packet; **~ные бума́ги** (*fin.*) securities. **2** (*дорогой*) valuable, costly; **~ная вещь** valuable object. **3** (*fig.*) (*важный*) valuable; precious; important; **ц. докуме́нт** important document; **ц. пода́рок** treasured gift.

цент, а *m.* cent (*unit of currency*).

це́нтнер, а *m.* quintal (= *100 kilograms*).

центр, а *m.* centre (*Br.*), center (*US*).

централиза́ци|я, и *f.* centralization.

централи́зм, а *m.* (*pol.*) centralism.

централиз|ова́ть, у́ю *impf. and pf.* to centralize.

центра́льн|ый *adj.* central; **~ые газе́ты** national newspapers; **ц. напада́ющий** (*sport*) centre forward; **~ое отопле́ние** central heating.

центри́зм, а *m.* centrism.

центри́р|овать, ую *impf. and pf.* (*tech.*) to centre (*Br.*), center (*US*).

центри́ст, а *m.* centrist.

центрифу́г|а, и *f.* **1** (*tech.*) centrifuge. **2** (*для белья*) spin dryer.

центробе́жный *adj.* centrifugal.

центров|о́й *adj.* (*tech.*) central, centre (*Br.*), center (*US*); *as n.* **с., ~о́го** (*sport*) centre (*Br.*), center (*US*).

центростреми́тельный *adj.* centripetal.

цеп, а́ *m.* (*agric.*) flail.

цепене́|ть, ю *impf.* (*of* ⇨**о~**) to freeze, be rooted to the spot (*from cold or from strong emotion*).

це́п|кий (~ок, ~ка́, ~ко) *adj.* **1** (*руки, когти*) tenacious, strong (*also fig.*). **2** (*почва, грязь*) sticky, tacky, loamy. **3** (*coll.*) (*упорный*) obstinate, persistent, strong-willed.

це́пкост|ь, и *f.* **1** tenacity, strength. **2** (*coll.*) (*упорство*) obstinacy, persistence.

цепля́|ть, ю *impf.* (*coll.*) **1** (**за**+*a.*) to hang on to, cling to. **2** (*задевать чем-н. загнутым*) to hook. **3** (*прицеплять*) to hook on (to); to attach (to).

цепля́|ться, юсь *impf.* **1** (**за**+*a.*) (*зацепляться*) to hang on to, cling to. **2** (**за**+*a.*; *coll.*) (*стремиться удержать, сохранить что-н.*) to cling (to); to stick (to). **3** (**к**+*d.*, **за**+*a.*; *coll.*) (*придираться*) to pick (on) (= *to carp at, complain of*).

цеп|но́й *adj. of* ⇨**~ь; ~на́я соба́ка** watchdog, house-dog; **~но́е колесо́** sprocket wheel; **~на́я реа́кция** (*chem., phys.*; *fig.*) chain reaction.

цепо́чк|а, и *f.* **1** (small) chain. **2** (*ряд*) file, series; **идти́ ~ой** to walk in file.

цеп|ь, и, о ~и, на ~и́, *pl.* **~и, ~е́й** *f.* **1** chain; (*pl.*) chains (= *fetters*; *also fig.*); **посади́ть на́ ц.** to chain (up), shackle. **2** (*гор, островов*) chain. **3** (*mil.*) line, file. **4** (*fig.*) (*ряд*) series, succession; **ц. катастро́ф** succession of disasters. **5** (*elec.*) circuit.

Це́рбер, а *m.* (*myth.*; *fig.*) Cerberus.

церемониа́л, а *m.* ceremonial, ritual.

церемониа́л|ьный *adj.* **1** *adj. of* ⇨**~. 2** solemn, ceremonial; **ц. марш** (*mil.*) march-past.

церемо́н|иться, юсь *impf.* (*of* ⇨**по~**) **1** to stand upon ceremony. **2** (**с**+*i.*) to treat excessively considerately.

церемо́ни|я, и *f.* **1** ceremony. **2** (*pl.*) (*стеснение*) ceremony (*pej.*), exaggerated observation of convention, etiquette.

церемо́н|ный (~ен, ~на) *adj.* ceremonious.

церко́вник, а *m.* churchman, clergyman.

церковноприхо́дский *adj.* (*eccl.*) parish.

церковнославя́нский *adj.* (*ling.*) Church Slavonic.

церковнослужи́тел|ь, я *m.* church officer (*sexton, etc.*).

церко́вный *adj.* church; **ц. ста́роста** churchwarden; **ц. сто́рож** sexton.

це́рк|овь, ви, *i.* **~овью,** *pl.* **~ви, ~ве́й, ~ва́м** *f.* church.

Ц

цесаре́вич, а *m.* cesarevitch, crown prince.

цеса́рк|а, и *f.* guinea-fowl.

цех, а, в ~е *and* (*coll.*) **в ~у́,** *pl.* **~и** *and* (*coll.*) **~а́** *m.* **1** (*на заводе*) shop, section. **2** (*hist.*) guild.

цех|ово́й *adj. of* ⇨~

цеце́ *f. indecl.* tsetse (fly).

циа́н, а *m.* (*chem.*) cyanogen.

циа́нистый *adj.* (*chem.*) cyanogen; cyanide (of); **ц. ка́лий** potassium cyanide.

циа́новый *adj.* (*chem.*) cyanic.

циано́з, а *m.* (*med.*) cyanosis.

цивилиза́тор, а *m.* (*usu. iron.*) civilizer.

цивилиза́ци|я, и *f.* civilization.

цивилизо́в|анный *p.p.p. of* ⇨**~а́ть** *and adj.* civilized.

цивилиз|ова́ть, у́ю *impf. and pf.* to civilize.

цига́рк|а, и *f.* (*coll.*) hand-rolled cigarette.

циге́йк|а, и *f.* beaver lamb.

циге́йковый *adj.* beaver-lamb.

циду́лк|а, и *f.* (*coll., obs*) note.

цика́д|а, ы *f.* cicada.

цикл, а *m.* cycle; (*лекций, концертов*) series.

циклaméн, а *m.* cyclamen.

цикл|ева́ть, ю́ю *impf.* (*of* ⇨**от~**) to spokeshave, smooth.

цикли́ческий *adj.* cyclic(al).

цикли́ч|ный (~ен, ~на) *adj.* = **~еский**

цикло́н, а *m.* (*meteor.*) cyclone.

циклони́ческий *adj.* (*meteor.*) cyclonic.

циклопи́ческий *adj.* (*archit.*) cyclopean.

циклотро́н, а *m.* (*phys.*) cyclotron.

ци́кл|я, и *f.* (*tech.*) spokeshave, scraper.

цико́ри|й, я *m.* chicory.

цико́р|ный *adj. of* ⇨**~ий**

ци́ку́т|а, ы *f.* (*bot.*) water hemlock (*Cicuta virosa*).

цили́ндр, а *m.* **1** cylinder. **2** (*шляпа*) top hat.

цилиндри́ческий *adj.* cylindrical.

цимбали́ст, а *m.* cymbalist.

цимба́л|ы, ~ *no sg.* (*mus.*) cymbals.

цинг|а́, и́ *f.* (*med.*) scurvy.

цинг|о́тный *adj. of* ⇨**~а́;** scorbutic.

цини́зм, а *m.* cynicism.

ци́ник, а *m.* cynic.

цини́ческий *adj.* cynical.

цини́ч|ный (~ен, ~на) *adj.* cynical.

цинк, а *m.* (*chem.*) zinc.

ци́нковый *adj.* zinc.

цино́вк|а, и *f.* mat.

цирк, а *m.* circus.

цирка́ч, а́ *m.* (*coll.*) circus artiste.

цирка́чес|кий *adj. of* ⇨**~тво**

цирка́честв|о, а *nt.* (*fig., pej.*) playing to the gallery, exhibitionism.

цирка́ч|ка, ки *f. of* ⇨~

цирк|ово́й *adj. of* ⇨~

цирко́ни|й, я *m.* (*chem.*) zirconium.

циркули́р|овать, ую *impf.* **1** (*о жидкостях*) to circulate; **~овали слу́хи** rumours (*Br.*), rumors (*US*) were circulating. **2** (*coll.*) (*ходить*) to pass, go to and fro.

ци́ркул|ь, я *m.* (pair of) compasses; dividers.

ци́ркуль|ный *adj. of* ⇨~

циркуля́р, а *m.* (*official*) circular.

циркуля́рн|ый¹ *adj.* circulated; **~ое письмо́** circular (letter).

циркуля́рн|ый² *adj.* (*имеющий форму окружности*) circular; **~ая пила́** circular saw.

циркуляцио́нный *adj.* (*tech.*) circulating, circulation.

циркуля́ци|я, и *f.* circulation.

цирро́з, а *m.* (*med.*) cirrhosis.

цирю́льник, а *m.* (*obs.*) barber.

цирю́л|ьня, ьни, *g. pl.* **~ен** *f.* (*obs.*) barber's shop.

цисте́рн|а, ы *f.* (*резервуар*) cistern, tank; (*вагон*) tank car; (*автомобиль*) tanker.

цисти́т, а *m.* cystitis.

цитаде́л|ь, и *f.* citadel; (*fig.*) bulwark, stronghold.

цита́т|а, ы *f.* quotation.

цити́р|овать, ую *impf.* (*of* ⇨**про~**) to quote.

цитоло́ги|я, и *f.* (*biol.*) cytology.

ци́тр|а, ы *f.* (*mus.*) zither.

ци́трус, а *m.* citrus.

ци́трус|овый *adj. of* ⇨**~;** *as n.* **~овые, ~овых** citrus plants.

циферблáт, а *m.* dial; (*часов*) face.

цифи́р|ь, и *f.* (*obs.*) **1** (*collect.*) (*цифры*) figures. **2** (*счисление*) counting, calculation; (*арифметика*) arithmetic.

ци́фр|а, ы *f.* **1** figure; digit, number, numeral. **2** (*pl.*) (*данные*) figures.

ци́фро-ана́логовый *adj.*: **ц. преобразова́тель** digital to analogue converter.

цифров|о́й *adj.* **1** numerical. **2** (*electronics, comput.*) digital; **~а́я за́пись** digital recording.

ЦК *m. indecl.* (*abbr. of* ***Центра́льный Комите́т***) Central Committee.

цо́к|ать¹, аю *impf.* (*of* ⇨**~нуть**) (*о подковах*) to clatter; **ц. языко́м** to tut(-tut).

цо́к|ать², аю *impf.* (*о произношении*) to pronounce **ч** as **ц** (*as in some North Russian dialects*).

цо́к|нуть, ну *pf. of* ⇨**~ать¹**

цо́кол|ь, я *m.* **1** (*archit.*) socle, plinth, pedestal. **2** (*elec.*) cap (*metal extremity of light bulb which is fitted into socket*).

цо́коль|ный *adj. of* ⇨**~; ц. эта́ж** ground floor.

цо́кот, а *m.* clatter.

цоко|та́ть, чу́, ~чешь *impf.* (*coll.*) to clatter.

ЦП *m. indecl.* (*abbr. of* ***центра́льный проце́ссор***) CPU (*central processing unit*).

ЦРУ *nt. indecl.* (*abbr. of* ***Центра́льное разве́дывательное управле́ние***) CIA (*Central Intelligence Agency*).

цуг, а *m.* (*of horses harnessed tandem or in pairs*) team.

цу́гом *adv.* tandem (*of horses in harness*).

цука́т, а *m.* candied peel.

ЦУМ, а *m.* (*abbr. of* ***центра́льный универса́льный магази́н***) Central Department Store.

цыга́н, а, *pl.* **~е, ~** (*obs.* **~ы, ~ов**) *m.* Gypsy.

цыга́н|ка, ки *f. of* ⇨~

цыга́нский *adj.* Gypsy.

цы́к|ать, аю *impf.* (*of* ⇨**~нуть**) (**на кого́-н.**; *coll.*) to shout at; to silence.

цы́к|нуть, ну *pf. of* ⇨**~ать**

цы́пк|а, и *f.* (*coll.*) chicken, chick (*also used as affectionate mode of address to women*).

цы́п|ки, ок *pl.* (*sg.* **~ка, ~ки** *f.*) (*coll.*) red spots (*on hands, etc.*).

цыпл|ёнок, ёнка, *pl.* **~я́та, ~я́т** *m.* chick(en).

цыпл|я́чий *adj. of* ⇨**~ёнок**

цы́почк|и: **на ц., на ~ах** on tiptoe.

цыц *int.* (*coll.*) (s)hush!

цэрэу́шник, а *m.* (*coll.*) CIA (*Central Intelligence Agency*) agent.

Цю́рих, а *m.* Zurich.

Чч

ч. (*abbr. of* **час**) hour; o'clock.

чаба́н, а́ *m.* shepherd.

чаба́н|ский *adj. of* ⇨**~**

ча́бер, ра *and* **чабёр, ра́** *m.* (*bot., cul.*) savory.

чабре́ц, а́ *m.* (*bot., cul.*) thyme.

ча́вк|ать, аю *impf.* (*of* ⇨**~нуть**) **1** (*во время еды*) to champ; to munch noisily. **2** (*по грязи*) to tramp; to squelch.

ча́вк|нуть, ну, нешь *pf. of* ⇨**~ать**

чад, а (у), о ~́е, в ~ý *m.* **1** fumes. **2** (*fig.*) intoxication.

ча|ди́ть, жу́, ди́шь *impf.* (*of* ⇨**на~**) to smoke, emit fumes.

ча́д|ный (~ен, ~на, ~но) *adj.* **1** smoky, smoke-laden; **~но** (*as pred.*) it is smoky, full of smoke. **2** (*fig.*) (*одурманенный*) doped, drugged, stupefied; (*дурманящий*) stupefying.

ча́д|о, а *nt.* **1** (*obs. or joc.*) child, offspring, progeny. **2** (*fig.*) child, product, creature; **ч. двадца́того ве́ка** product of the twentieth century.

чадолюби́в|ый (~, ~а) *adj.* (*obs. or joc.*) fond of one's child(ren).

чадр|а́, ы́ *f.* chador (*worn by Moslem women*).

чаёвник, а *m.* (*coll.*) tea-drinker (*person partial to tea-drinking*).

чаёвнича|ть, ю *impf.* (*coll.*) to drink tea, indulge in tea-drinking.

чаево́д, а *m.* tea-grower.

чаево́дств|о, а *nt.* tea-growing.

чаево́д|ческий *adj. of* ⇨**~ство**

чаев|ы́е, ы́х *no sg.* tip, gratuity.

ча|ёк, ~йка́ (ý) *m.* = **чай**

чаепи́ти|е, я *nt.* tea-drinking.

чаинк|а, и *f.* tea-leaf.

ча|й¹, я (ю), *pl.* **~и́, ~ёв** *m.* **1** tea; **шипо́вниковый ч.** rose-hip tea. **2** tea (-drinking); **за ~́ем, за ча́шкой ~́я** over (a cup of) tea. **3**: **дать** (+*d.*) **на ч.** to tip.

чай² *as adv.* (*coll.*) **1** (*вероятно*) probably, maybe; no doubt; **вам тут, ч., ску́чно** you must find it dull here. **2** (*ведь*) after all, for.

ча́йк|а, и, *g. pl.* **ча́ек** *f.* (sea-)gull.

ча́йн|ая, ой *f.* tea-room, tea-shop.

ча́йник, а *m.* **1** (*для заварки*) teapot; (*для кипячения воды*) kettle. **2** (*sl.*) (*идиот*) stupid person, idiot.

ча́йниц|а, ы *f.* tea-caddy.

ча́йн|ый *adj.* tea; **ч. куст** tea-plant; **~ая ло́жка** tea-spoon; **~ая ча́шка** teacup.

чайхан|а́, ы́ *f.* chaikhana (*tea-drinking establishment in Central Asia*).

ча́л|ить, ю, ишь *impf.* (*naut.*) to tie up, moor.

ча́лк|а, и *f.* (*naut.*) tie-rope, mooring rope.

чалм|а́, ы́ *f.* turban.

ча́лый *adj.* roan.

чан, а, в ~́е *or* **в ~ý,** *pl.* **~ы́** *m.* vat, tub, tank.

ча́р|а, ы *f.* (*folk poet.*) cup, goblet.

ча́р|ка, ки *f.* = **~а**

чар|ова́ть, ýю *impf.* (*fig.*) to charm, captivate, enchant.

чароде́|й, я *m.* sorcerer, magician (*also fig.*).

чароде́йк|а, и *f.* sorceress.

чароде́йств|о, а *nt.* sorcery, magic.

ча́ртер, а *m.* charter.

ча́ртерный *adj.*: **ч. рейс** (*aeron.*) charter flight.

ча́р|ы, ~ *no sg.* magic, charms (*also fig.*).

час, а, о ~́е, в ~ý *and* **в ~́е,** *pl.* **~ы́** *m.* **1** hour (*also fig.*); **че́тверть ~а́** a quarter of an hour; **ч. о́т ~у** with every passing hour; **с ~́у на ч.** at any moment; **в до́брый ч.!** good luck!

2 (*время по часам*): *g. sg.* **~а́** (*after numerals 2, 3, 4*) o'clock; **час** one o'clock; **два ~а́** two o'clock; **во второ́м ~ý** between one and two (o'clock); **кото́рый ч.?** what is the time?

3 (*usu. pl.*) (*время*) hours, time, period; **ч. пик, ~ы́ пик** rush hour; **~ы́ заня́тий** working hours; **«золоты́е ~ы́»** prime (*television viewing*) time.

4: **~ы́** (*mil.*) guard-duty; **стоя́ть на ~а́х** to stand guard.

5: **~ы́** (*eccl.*) (canonical) hours.

часа́ми *adv.* for hours.

часо́в|ня, ни, *g. pl.* **~ен** *f.* chapel.

часов|о́й¹, о́го *m.* sentry, guard.

часов|о́й² *adj.* (*of* ⇨**час**) **1** (*подолжающийся один час*) of one hour's duration; **ч. переры́в** one hour's interval. **2** (*по часам*) (measured) by the hour; **~а́я опла́та** payment by the hour; **ч. по́яс** time zone. **3** (*поезд, самолёт*) one o'clock.

часов|о́й³ *adj. of* ⇨**часы́; ч. магази́н** watch shop, watchmaker's, watch repair shop; **~ы́х дел ма́стер** watchmaker; **ч. механи́зм** clockwork; **~а́я стре́лка** clock hand, hour hand; **по ~о́й стре́лке** clockwise.

часовщи́к, а́ *m.* watchmaker.

ча́сом *adv.* (*coll.*) **1** (*иногда*) sometimes, at times. **2** (*случайно*) by chance, by the way.

часосло́в, а *m.* (*eccl.*) Book of Hours.

часте́нько *adv.* (*coll.*) quite often, fairly often.

ча|сти́ть, щý, сти́шь *impf.* (*coll.*) to do sth. (*делать что-н.*) *or* speak (*говорить*) rapidly, hurriedly.

части́ц|а, ы *f.* **1** small part, element. **2** (*phys.*) particle. **3** (*gram.*) particle.

части́чно *adv.* partly, partially.

части́ч|ный (~ен, ~на) *adj.* partial.

ча́стник, а *m.* (*coll.*) private trader.

частновладе́льческий *adj.* privately-owned.

ча́стн|ое, ого *nt.* (*math.*) quotient.

частнособственни́ческий *adj.* private-ownership.

ча́стност|ь, и *f.* detail; **в ~и** in particular.

ча́стн|ый *adj.* **1** (*личный*) private, personal; **~ым о́бразом** privately. **2** (*econ.*) private, privately-owned; **~ая со́бственность** private property. **3** (*отдельный, особый*) particular, individual; *as n.* **~ое, ~ого** *nt.* the particular.

ча́сто *adv.* often, frequently.

частоко́л, а *m.* fence, paling; palisade.

частот|а́, ы́, *pl.* **~́ы** *f.* frequency.

частóт|ный *adj.* (*tech.*) *of* ⇨**~а́**

частýшк|а, и *f.* chastushka (*two-line or*

four-line rhymed poem or ditty on some topical or humorous theme).

ча́ст|ый (~, ~а́, ~о) *adj.* **1** frequent; **он у нас ч. гость** he is a frequent visitor at our house. **2** (*густой*) close (together); dense, thick; **ч. гре́бень** fine-tooth comb; **~ые дере́вни** villages close together; **ч. дождь** steady rain; **~ое си́то** fine sieve. **3** (*быстрый*) quick, rapid; **ч. ого́нь** (*mil.*) rapid fire.

част|ь, и, *pl.* **~и, ~е́й** *f.* **1** part; portion; **~и ре́чи** (*gram.*) parts of speech; **разобра́ть на ~и** to take to pieces, dismantle; **бо́льшей ~ью, по бо́льшей ~и** for the most part, mostly. **2** (*отдел*) section, department. **3** (*область*) sphere, field; **э́то не по моє́й ~и** this is not my province; **по ~и** (+*g.*) in connection (with). **4** (*coll.*) (*доля*) share. **5** (*mil.*) unit.

ча́стью *adv.* partly, in part.

час|ы́[1]**, о́в** *no sg.* clock, watch.

часы́[2] *see* ⇒**час** 4, 5

ча́тни *nt. indecl.* chutney.

ча́хл|ый (~, ~а) *adj.* **1** (*растительность*) stunted; poor. **2** (*человек*) weakly, sickly, puny.

ча́х|нуть, ну, нешь, *past* **~, ~ла** *impf.* (*of* ⇒**за~**) **1** (*о растительности*) to wither away. **2** (*о человеке*) to become weak, (go into a) decline; (*fig.*) to become exhausted.

чахо́тк|а, и *f.* (*coll.*) consumption.

чахо́точный *adj.* (*coll.*) **1** consumptive. **2** (*жалкий*) poor, sorry, feeble.

ча-ча-ча́ *nt. indecl.* the cha-cha (*dance*).

ча́ш|а, и *f.* cup, bowl (*also fig.*); (*eccl.*) chalice; **ч. весо́в** scale, pan; **ч. на́шего терпе́ния перепо́лнилась** our patience is/was exhausted.

чашели́стик, а *m.* (*bot.*) sepal.

ча́шечк|а, и *f.* **1** *dim. of* ⇒**ча́шка. 2** (*bot.*) calyx.

ча́шк|а, и *f.* **1** (*для питья*) cup. **2**: **ч. весо́в** pan (*of scales*). **3**: **(коле́нная) ч.** knee-cap. **4** (*tech.*) housing.

ча́шник, а *m.* (*hist.*) cellarer.

ча́щ|а, и *f.* thicket.

ча́ще *comp. of* ⇒**ча́стый** *and* **ча́сто** more often, more frequently; **ч. всего́** most often, mostly.

ча́яни|е, я *nt.* expectation; aspiration; **па́че ~я, сверх ~я** unexpectedly, contrary to expectation.

ча́|ять, ю, ешь *impf.* (*obs. or coll.*) **1** (*думать*) to think, suppose. **2** (+*g. or inf.*) (*ожидать*) to hope (for), expect.

чва́н|иться, юсь, ишься *impf.* to boast.

чванли́вост|ь, и *f.* boastfulness, arrogance.

чванли́в|ый (~, ~а) *adj.* boastful, arrogant.

чва́нный *adj.* conceited, arrogant.

чва́нств|о, а *nt.* conceit, arrogance.

чебура́хн|уть, у, ешь *pf.* (*coll.*) to crash down (*trans.*).

чебура́хн|уться, усь, ешься *pf.* (*coll.*) to crash down (*intrans.*).

чебуре́к, а *m.* cheburek (*kind of lamb pasty eaten in the Crimea and the Caucasus*).

чебуре́чн|ая, ой *f.* stall selling chebureki.

чего́[1] *interrog. adv.* (*coll.*) why? what for?

чего́[2] *g. of* ⇒**что**

чей, чья, чьё *interrog. and rel. pron.* whose.

че́й-либо *pron.* anyone's.

че́й-нибудь *pron.* anyone's.

че́й-то *pron.* someone's.

чек, а *m.* **1** (*банковский*) cheque (*Br.*), check (*US*); **вы́писать ч.** to write a cheque (*Br.*), check (*US*). **2** (*с указанием суммы, которую следует уплатить*) chit; (*удостоверяющий, что товар оплачен*) receipt.

чек|а́, и́ *f.* pin, linchpin, cotter-pin.

Чек|а́ *f. indecl. or* (*coll.*) *g.* **~и́** *f.* (*coll.*) (*hist.*) Cheka (*abbr. of* ***Чрезвыча́йная коми́ссия по борьбе́ с контрреволю́цией и сабота́жем*** *the Soviet state security organ, 1918–1922*).

чека́н, а *m.* **1** (*штемпель*) stamp, die. **2** (*zool.*) chat; **лугово́й ч.** whinchat; **черноголо́вый ч.** stonechat.

чека́н|ить, ю, ишь *impf.* **1** (*pf.* **вы́~, от~**) (*монету*) to mint, coin; (*надпись, узор*) to engrave, emboss, chase. **2** (*pf.* **от~**) (*отчетливо делать что-н.*) to do, make with precision; **ч. слова́** to enunciate one's words clearly; **ч. шаг** to measure one's pace, step out.

чека́нк|а, и *f.* **1** (*монеты*) coining, minting; (*надписи, узора*) engraving, embossing, chasing. **2** (*рельефное изображение*) stamp, engraving, relief work (*in metal*).

чека́нн|ый *adj.* **1** (*цех*) engraving, embossing; **~ая рабо́та** = **чека́нка** 2. **2** (*пистолет, браслет*) engraved, embossed, chased. **3** (*fig.*) precise, expressive, sharp.

чека́нщик, а *m.* coiner; stamper, engraver; caulker.

чеки́ст, а *m.* (state) security officer; (*hist.*) Chekist, Cheka agent (*see also* ⇒**Чека́**).

чекме́н|ь, я́ *m.* (cloth) jacket.

че́к|овый *adj. of* ⇒**~**; **~овая кни́жка** cheque book (*Br.*), check book (*US*).

челе́ст|а, ы *f.* (*mus.*) celesta.

чёлк|а, и *f.* fringe (*Br.*), bangs (*US*); (*лошади*) forelock.

чёлн, а́, *pl.* **~ы́,** *or* **~ы** *m.* dug-out (canoe).

челно́к, а́ *m.* **1** = **чёлн. 2** (*в ткацком станке, швейной машине*) shuttle. **3** (*sl.*) small trader (*going to another region or abroad to buy things to resell at home*).

челно́|чный *adj. of* ⇒**~к** 2; **ч. полёт** (*aeron.*) shuttle flight; **~чная диплома́тия** shuttle diplomacy.

чел|о́[1]**, а́** *nt.* (*obs.*) (*лоб*) forehead, brow; **бить ~о́м кому́-н.** (*hist. or iron.*) (*i*) (*при встрече*) to bow to s.o., (*ii*) (*просить*) to petition s.o., (*iii*) (*благодарить*) to offer s.o. humble thanks.

чел|о́[2]**, а́,** *pl.* **~а** *nt.* (*tech.*) (*печи*) stoking hole.

челоби́тн|ая, ой *f.* (*hist.*) petition.

челоби́тчик, а *m.* (*hist.*) petitioner.

челоби́ть|е, я *nt.* (*hist.*) **1** (*низкий поклон*) low bow. **2** (*челобитная*) petition.

челове́к, а, *pl.* **лю́ди** (*g. pl., etc.,* **челове́к, ~ам, ~ами, о ~ах** *only in comb. with nums.*) *m.* man, person, human being.

челове́ко-де́нь, ч.-дня́ *m.* (*econ.*) man-day.

человеколюби́в|ый (~, ~а) *adj.* philanthropic.

человеколю́би|е, я *nt.* philanthropy, love of fellow-men.

человеконенави́стник, а *m.* misanthrope.

человеконенави́стнический *adj.* misanthropic.

человеконенави́стничеств|о, а *nt.* misanthropy.

человекообра́з|ный (~ен, ~на) *adj.* anthropomorphous; (*zool.*) anthropoid.

человекоподо́б|ный (~ен, ~на) *adj.* humanoid.

челове́ко-ча́с, а *m.* (*econ.*) man-hour.

челове́ч|ек, ка *m.* little man, little person.

челове́ческий *adj.* **1** (*относящийся к человеку*) human. **2** (*гуманный*) humane.

челове́честв|о, а *nt.* humanity, mankind.

челове́|чий *adj. of* ⇒**~к**

челове́чин|а, ы *c.g. and f.* (*coll.*) **1** *c.g.* (*человек*) person, human being. **2** *f.* (*мясо человека*) human flesh (*as meat*).

челове́чност|ь, и *f.* humaneness, humanity.

челове́ч|ный (~ен, ~на) *adj.* humane.

челюстно́й *adj.* jaw; (*anat.*) maxillary.

че́люст|ь, и *f.* **1** jaw, jaw-bone. **2** (*зубной протез*) denture, set of false teeth.

че́ляд|ь, и *f.* (*collect.; hist.*) servants, retainers; (*fig.*) underlings.

чем *conj.* **1** than. **2** (+*comp.*): **ч.…, тем…** the more …, the more …; **ч. скоре́е, тем лу́чше** the sooner, the better. **3** (+*inf.*) rather than, instead of; **чем писа́ть, ты бы лу́чше позвони́л** you'd do better to ring up rather than write.

чембу́р, а *m.* halter.

чемери́ц|а, ы *f.* false hellebore.

чемода́н, а *m.* suitcase.

чемпио́н, а *m.* champion.

чемпиона́т, а *m.* championship.

чемпио́н|ка, ки *f. of* ⇒**~**

чемпио́нств|о, а *nt.* champion's title.

чепе́ *nt. indecl.* (*abbr. of* ***чрезвыча́йное происше́ствие***) incident, emergency, disaster.

чеп|е́ц, ца́ *m.* (*woman's*) cap.

чепра́к, а́ *m.* saddle-cloth.

чепух|а́, и́ *f.* (*coll.*) **1** (*вздор*) nonsense, rubbish. **2** (*незначительное дело*) a trifle, trifling matter; (*пустяки*) trivialities. **3** (*незначительное количество*) trifling amount.

чепухо́вый *adj.* (*coll.*) **1** (*рассказы*) nonsensical. **2** (*услуга*) trifling; trivial; insignificant.

че́пчик, а *m.* **1** = **чепе́ц.** **2** (*младенца*) bonnet.

червеобра́з|ный (~ен, ~на) *adj.* vermiform, vermicular; **ч. отро́сток** (*anat.*) appendix.

че́рв|и[1], е́й *and* **~ы, ~** *pl.* (*sg.* **~а, ~ы** *f.*) (*в картах*) hearts; **коро́ль ~е́й** king of hearts.

че́рв|и[2] *pl. of* ⇒**~ь**

черви́ве|ть, ет *impf.* (*of* ⇒**о~**) to become worm-eaten.

черви́в|ый (~, ~а) *adj.* worm-eaten.

черв|о́вый *adj. of* ⇒**~и[1]**

черво́н|ец, ца *m.* **1** (*hist.*) chervonets (*gold coin of 3, 5, or 10 roubles' denomination; or 10 rouble bank-note in circulation 1922–47*). **2** (*coll.*) ten roubles.

черво́нн|ый[1] *adj.* **1** (*obs. or dial.*) (*красный*) red, scarlet; **~ое зо́лото** pure gold (*as having a reddish tint*). **2** *adj. of* ⇒**черво́нец** 1

черв|о́нный[2] *adj. of* ⇒**~и[1]**; **ч. туз** ace of hearts.

червото́чин|а, ы *f.* **1** worm-hole. **2** (*fig.*) (*испорченность*) rottenness.

черв|ь, я́, *pl.* **~и, ~е́й** *m.* **1** worm; maggot. **2** (*fig.*) nagging feeling; **его́ то́чит ч. сомне́ния** he is nagged by doubts.

червя́к, а́ *m.* **1** = **червь.** **2** (*tech.*) worm.

червя́чн|ый *adj. of* ⇒**червя́к** 2; **~ое колесо́, ~ая шестерня́** worm wheel.

червяч|о́к, ка́ *m. dim. of* ⇒**червя́к** 1; **замори́ть ~ка́** (*coll.*) to have a bite to eat.

черда́к, а́ *m.* attic, loft.

черда́|чный *adj. of* ⇒**~к**

черёд, а́, о ~е́, в ~у́ *m.* **1** turn; **идти́ свои́м ~о́м** to take its course. **2** (*coll.*) (*ряд*) queue (*Br.*), line (*US*).

черед|а́[1], ы́ *f.* **1** (*obs.*) = **черёд** 1. **2** (*событий*) sequence. **3** (*людей*) file (*of people*).

черед|а́[2], ы́ *f.* (*bot.*) bur-marigold (*Bidens*).

чередова́ни|е, я *nt.* alternation, interchange, rotation.

чеpед|ова́ть, у́ю *impf.* (**с** + *i.*) to alternate (with).

черед|ова́ться, у́юсь *impf.* to alternate; to take turns.

чередо́м *adv.* (*coll.*) properly.

че́рез *prep.* + *a.* **1** (*улицу, забор*) across; over; (*лес, окно*) through. **2** (*о пунктах следовании*) via. **3** (*посредством*) through; **ч. печа́ть** through the press; **ч. перево́дчика** through an interpreter. **4** (*coll.*) (*из-за чего-н.*) through; **ч. боле́знь** through illness. **5** (*по прошествии*) in; **ч. полчаса́** in half an hour's time; **я верну́сь ч. год** I shall be back in a year's time. **6** (*минуя какое-н. пространство*) after; (further) on; **ч. три киломе́тра** three kilometres (further) on. **7** (*повторяя в регулярные промежутки*): **принима́ть ч. час по столо́вой ло́жке** to take one tablespoonful every hour; **ч. ка́ждые три страни́цы** every three pages; **дежу́рить ч. день** to be on duty every other day, on alternate days; **печа́тать ч. строку́** to double-space.

черёмух|а, и *f.* bird cherry (*Padus*).

черёмух|овый *adj. of* ⇒**~а**

черен|о́к, ка́ *m.* **1** (*рукоятка*) handle, haft (*of implement*). **2** (*hort.*) graft, cutting.

че́реп, а, *pl.* **~а́** *m.* skull, cranium.

черепа́х|а, и *f.* **1** tortoise; (*морская*) turtle; **ползти́ как ч.** to go at a snail's pace. **2** (*панцирь*) tortoise-shell.

черепа́ховый *adj.* (*суп*) turtle; (*очки*) tortoise-shell.

черепа́|ший *adj.* **1** *adj. of* ⇒**~ха** 1. **2** (*fig.*) very slow.

черепи́ц|а, ы *f.* tile; (*collect.*) tiles.

черепи́чный *adj.* tile; tiled.

черепн|о́й *adj. of* ⇒**че́реп**; **~а́я коро́бка** cranium.

череп|о́к, ка́ *m.* broken piece of pottery.

чересчу́р *adv.* too; (*перед глаголом*) too much.

чере́шн|евый *adj. of* ⇒**~я**

чере́шн|я, и *f.* cherry(-tree) (*Cerasus avium*).

черка́|ть, ю (*and* **чёрка|ть, ю**) *impf.* (*coll.*) to cross out, cross through.

черке́с, а *m.* Circassian.

черке́ск|а, и *f.* Circassian coat (*long, narrow, collar-less coat worn by Caucasian highlanders*).

черке́сский *adj.* Circassian.

черке́шенк|а, и *f. of* ⇒**черке́с**

черкн|у́ть, у́, ёшь *pf.* (*coll.*) **1** (*провести черту по чему-н.*) to make, leave a line on. **2** (*написать*) to dash off, scribble.

черне́|ть, ю *impf.* **1** (*pf.* **по~**) (*становиться чёрным*) to turn black, grow black. **2** (*виднеться*) to show up black.

черни́к|а, и *f.* bilberry (*Vaccinium myrtillus*).

черни́л|а, ~ *no sg.* ink.

черни́льниц|а, ы *f.* ink-pot, ink-well.

черни́л|ьный *adj. of* ⇒**~а**; **ч. каранда́ш** indelible pencil.

черн|и́ть, ю́, и́шь *impf.* **1** (*pf.* **за~** *and* **на~**) (*делать чёрным*) to blacken, paint black. **2** (*pf.* **о~**) (*fig.*) (*порочить*) to blacken, slander. **3** (*воронить*) to burnish.

чернобу́рк|а, и *f.* (*coll.*) silver fox (fur).

чернобы́льник, а *m.* (*bot.*) mugwort.

чернови́к, а́ *m.* rough copy, draft.

чернов|о́й *adj.* **1** rough, draft; preparatory. **2**: **~а́я рабо́та** (*coll.*) heavy, rough, dirty work.

черноволо́с|ый (~, ~а) *adj.* black-haired.

черногла́з|ый (~, ~а) *adj.* black-eyed.

черного́р|ец, ца *m.* Montenegrin.

Черного́ри|я, и *f.* Montenegro.

черного́р|ка, ки *f. of* ⇒**~ец**

черного́рский *adj.* Montenegrin.

чернозём, а *m.* (*agric., geol.*) chernozem, black earth.

чернозём|ный *adj. of* ⇒**~**

чернозо́бик, а *m.* (*zool.*) dunlin.

черноко́ж|ий (~, ~а) *adj.* black; *as n.* **ч., ~его** *m.* negro, black (man).

черномаз|ый (~, ~а) *adj.* (*coll.*) swarthy.

черномо́р|ец, ца *m.* sailor of Black Sea fleet.

черномо́рский *adj.* Black Sea.

чернорабо́ч|ий, его *m.* unskilled labourer (*Br.*), laborer (*US*).

чернослив, а (у) *m.* (*collect.*) prunes.

черносморо́динный *adj.* blackcurrant.

черносо́тен|ец, ца *m.* (*hist.*) member of 'Black Hundred' (*name of armed monarchist anti-Semitic groups in Russia, active 1905—7*); (*fig.*) extreme reactionary, chauvinist.

чернот|а́, ы́ *f.* blackness (*also fig.*); darkness.

черну́х|а, и *f.* (*sl.*) presentation of the darker side of life (*in films, books, etc.*); gratuitous sex and violence.

чёр|ный (~ен, ~на́, ~но́) *adj.* **1** black; **ч. ры́нок** black market; **(отложи́ть на) ч. день** (to put by for) a rainy day; **~ное де́рево** ebony; **~ное зо́лото** 'black gold' (= *oil*); **ч. наро́д** (*hist.*) common people; **держа́ть в ~ном те́ле** to ill-treat; **~ным по бе́лому** in black and white; (*чернокожий*) black; *as n.* **ч., ~ного** *m.* negro, black (man). **2** (*задний*) back; **ч. ход** back entrance, back door. **3** (*о работе*) (*тяжёлый*) heavy; (*неквалифицированный*) unskilled. **4** (*fig.*) (*мысли, дни*) gloomy, melancholy.

черн|ь[1], и *f.* (*люди*) mob, common people.

черн|ь[2], и *f.* (*гравировка*) niello; black enamel.

черпа́к, а́ *m.* scoop; bucket; grab.

черпа́лк|а, и *f.* scoop; ladle.

че́рп|ать, аю *impf.* (*of* ⇒**~ну́ть**) **1** to draw (up); to scoop; to ladle. **2** (*fig.*) (*извлекать*) to extract, derive, draw.

черп|ну́ть, ну́, нёшь *pf. of* ⇒**~ать**

черстве́|ть, ю *impf.* **1** (*pf.* **за~**) (*о хлебе*) to become stale. **2** (*pf.* **о~**) (*о душе*) to grow hardened, become hard (*fig.*).

чёрств|ый (~, ~а́, ~о) *adj.* **1** stale. **2** (*fig.*) (*бездушный*) hard, callous.

чёрт, а, *pl.* **че́рти, ~е́й** *m.* devil; **ч. (его́) возьми́!** the devil take it!; **ч. его́ зна́ет!** the devil only knows!; **до ~а** hellishly; **на кой ч.?** why the hell?; **~а с два** like hell!; **у ~а на рога́х, на кули́чках** at the back of beyond.

черт|а́, ы́ *f.* **1** (*линия*) line; **провести́**

Ч

~у́ to draw a line; **подвести́ ~у́ (под)** (*fig.*) to draw a line (under), put an end (to), dispose (of). **2** (*граница*) boundary; **ч. осе́длости** (*hist.*) the (Jewish) Pale. **3** (*свойство*) trait, characteristic; **~ы́ лица́** features; **в о́бщих ~а́х** in general outline.

чертёж, а́ *m.* draft, drawing, sketch.

чертёжник, а *m.* draughtsman (*Br.*), draftsman (*US*).

чертёжн|ый *adj.* drawing; **~ая доска́** drawing board.

чертён|ок, ка, *pl.* **~я́та, ~я́т** *m.* (*coll.*) imp.

чер|ти́ть¹, чу́, ~́тишь *impf.* (*of* ⇒**на~**) (*карту*) to draw; (*план*) to draw up.

чер|ти́ть², чу́, ти́шь *impf.* (*coll.*) (*кутить*) to go on a binge, on the booze.

чёртов *adj.* **1** devil's; **~а дю́жина** baker's dozen. **2** (*coll.*) devilish, hellish.

черто́вк|а, и *f.* she-devil; (*как бранное слово*) bitch.

черто́вский *adj.* (*coll.*) devilish, damnable.

чертовщи́н|а, ы *f.* **1** (*collect.*) (*черти*) devils, demons. **2** (*fig., coll.*) (*нечто невероятное, нелепое*) devilry; idiocy.

черто́г, а *m.* (*obs.*) hall, mansion.

чертополо́х, а *m.* thistle.

чёрточк|а, и *f.* **1** *dim. of* ⇒**черта́ 1. 2** (*дефис*) hyphen.

чертых|а́ться, а́юсь *impf.* (*of* ⇒**~ну́ться**) (*coll.*) to swear.

чертых|ну́ться, ну́сь, нёшься *pf. of* ⇒**~а́ться**

черче́ни|е, я *nt.* drawing; sketching.

чеса́лк|а, и *f.* (*text.*) comb, combing machine.

чеса́льный *adj.* (*text.*) combing, carding.

чёсаный *adj.* (*text.*) combed, carded.

че|са́ть, шу́, ~́шешь *impf.* (*of* ⇒**по~**) **1** to scratch; **ч. заты́лок, в заты́лке** to scratch one's head (*also fig.*); **ч. язы́к** to wag one's tongue. **2** (*coll.*) (*волосы*) to comb (*hair*). **3** (*text.*) to comb, card.

че|са́ться, шу́сь, ~́шешься *impf.* (*of* ⇒**по~**) **1** to scratch o.s. **2** (*impf. only*) (*об ощущении зуда*) to itch; **ру́ки у него́** *etc.* **~́шутся** (+*inf.*) he is, *etc.*, itching to .... **3** (*coll.*) (*причесываться*) to comb one's hair.

чесно́к, а́ (у́) *m.* garlic.

чесно́|чный *adj. of* ⇒**~к**

чесо́тк|а, и *f.* (*med.*) scabies; (*у животных*) mange.

че́ствовани|е, я *nt.* **(кого́-н.)** celebration (in honour (*Br.*), honor (*US*) of s.o.).

че́ств|овать, ую *impf.* to honour (*Br.*), honor (*US*); to pay tribute to.

че|сти́ть, щу́, сти́шь *impf.* (*coll.*) to abuse.

честн|о́й *adj.* (*obs.*) **1** (*eccl.*) sanctified, sainted; saintly; **мать ~а́я!** (*coll.*) my sainted aunt! **2** (*достойный*) worthy, honoured (*Br.*), honored (*US*).

че́стност|ь, и *f.* honesty, integrity.

че́ст|ный (~ен, ~на́, ~но) *adj.* honest; (*справедливый*) fair; **~ное сло́во!** honestly, truly!

честолю́б|ец, ца *m.* ambitious person.

честолюби́в|ый (~, ~а) *adj.* ambitious.

честолю́би|е, я *nt.* ambition.

че́ст|ь, и *f.* honour (*Br.*), honor (*US*); **в ч.** (+*g.*) in honour (*Br.*), honor (*US*) (of); **по ~́и сказа́ть** to say in all honesty; **отда́ть ч.** (+*d.*) to salute; **проси́ть ~́ью** to urge; **пора́ и ч. знать** (*coll.*) it is time we were going; **ч. ~́ью** (*coll.*) fittingly, properly; **ч. и ме́сто!** (*coll., obs.*) please be seated!

чесуч|а́, и́ *f.* tussore.

чесуч|о́вый *adj. of* ⇒**~а́**

чёт, а *m.* even number.

чет|а́, ы́ *f.* pair, couple; **счастли́вая ч.** (the) happy couple; **не ч. кому́-н.** no match for s.o.

четве́рг, а́ *m.* Thursday.

четвере́ньк|и (*coll.*): **на ч., на ~ах** on all fours, on one's hands and knees; **стать на ч.** to go down on all fours.

четвери́к, а́ *m.* chetverik (*old Russian dry measure, equivalent to 26.239 litres*).

четвёрк|а, и *f.* (*coll.*) **1** (*цифр*) number '4'. **2** (*coll.*) (*автобус, трамвай*) No. 4. **3** (*отметка*) 'four' (*as school mark—out of five, hence* = 'good'). **4** (*cards*) four. **5** (*упряжка*) team of four horses. **6** (*группа людей*) foursome.

четверно́й *adj.* fourfold, quadruple.

четверн|я́, и́ *f.* **1** team of four horses. **2** (*дети*) quadruplets.

че́твер|о, ы́х *num.* four; **нас бы́ло ч.** there were four of us.

четвероклáссник, а *m.* fourth-former (*Br.*), fourth-grader (*US*).

четвероклáссни|ца, цы *f. of* ⇒**~к**

четвероно́г|ий *adj.* four-legged; *as n.* **~ое, ~ого** *nt.* quadruped.

четверости́ши|е, я *nt.* (*liter.*) quatrain.

четверта́к, а́ *m.* **1** (*obs.*) 25 copecks. **2** (*sl.*) 25 roubles.

четверти́нк|а, и *f.* (*coll.*) quarter-litre (*Br.*), -liter (*US*) bottle (*of vodka or wine*).

четверти́чный *adj.* (*geol.*) Quaternary.

четвертн|о́й *adj.* quarter; **~а́я но́та** (*mus.*) crotchet (*Br.*), quarter note (*US*).

четверт|ова́ть, у́ю *impf. and pf.* (*hist.*) to quarter (*as means of execution*).

четвёртый *adj.* fourth.

че́тверт|ь, и, *g. pl.* **~е́й** *f.* **1** (*четвёртая часть целого*) quarter. **2** (*четверть часа*) quarter (of an hour); **без ~и час** a quarter to one; **ч. деся́того** a quarter past nine. **3** (*учебного года*) term. **4** (*mus.*) crotchet (*Br.*), quarter note (*US*).

четвертьфина́л, а *m.* (*sport*) quarter-final.

чёт|ки, ок *no sg.* (*eccl.*) rosary.

чёт|кий (~ок, ~ка́, ~ко) *adj.* **1** precise; clear-cut; **~кое движе́ние** precise movement. **2** (*изложение*) clear, well-defined; (*почерк*) legible; (*звук*) plain, distinct; (*речь*) articulate.

чёткост|ь, и *f.* **1** (*движения*) precision, preciseness. **2** (*изложения*) clarity, clearness; (*почерка*) legibility; (*звука*) distinctness.

чётный *adj.* even (*of numbers*).

четы́р|е, ёх, ём, ьмя́, о ~ёх *num.* four.

четы́режды *adv.* four times.

четы́р|еста, ёхсо́т, ёмста́м, ьмяста́ми, о ~ёхста́х *num.* four hundred.

четырёх... *comb. form* four-, quadri-, tetra-.

четырёхгоди́чный *adj.* four-year.

четырёхголо́сный *adj.* (*mus.*) four-part.

четырёхгра́нник, а *m.* (*math.*) tetrahedron.

четырёхгра́нный *adj.* (*math.*) tetrahedral.

четырёхдоро́жечный *adj.* four-track (*of tape recorder*).

четырёхкра́тный *adj.* fourfold.

четырёхле́ти|е, я *nt.* **1** (*срок*) four-year period. **2** (*годовщина*) fourth anniversary.

четырёхле́тний *adj.* **1** (*срок*) four years', of four years' duration. **2** (*ребёнок*) four-year-old.

четырёхме́стный *adj.* four-seater.

четырёхме́сячный *adj.* **1** (*срок*) four-month, four months', of four months' duration. **2** (*ребёнок*) four-month-old.

четырёхсотле́ти|е, я *nt.* **1** (*срок*) four hundred years. **2** (*годовщина*) quatercentenary.

четырёхсотле́тний *adj.* **1** (*история*) four hundred years', of four hundred years' duration. **2** (*юбилей*) quatercentenary.

четырёхсо́тый *adj.* fourhundredth.

черырёхсто́пный *adj.* (*liter.*) tetrameter.

четырёхсторо́нний *adj.* **1** (*math.*) quadrilateral. **2** (*pol., etc.*) (*пакт*) quadripartite.

четырёхта́ктный *adj.* **1** (*tech.*) four-stroke. **2** (*mus.*) four-beat.

четырёхуго́льник, а *m.* quadrangle.

четырёхуго́льный *adj.* quadrangular.

четырёхчасово́й *adj.* **1** (*промежуток*) four hours', of four hours' duration. **2** (*поезд*) four o'clock.

четы́рнадцатый *adj.* fourteenth.

четы́рнадцат|ь, и *num.* fourteen.

чех, а *m.* Czech.

чехард|а́, ы́ *f.* (*игра*) leap-frog; (*fig.*) reshuffle.

Че́хи|я, и *f.* Czech Republic.

чехл|и́ть, ю́, и́шь *impf.* (*of* ⇒**за~**) to cover.

чех|о́л, ла́ *m.* **1** (*подушки, кресла*) cover; (*контрабаса*) case. **2** (*род нижней одежды*) under-dress (*worn under see-through garment*).

Чехослова́ки|я, и *f.* (*hist.*) Czechoslovakia.

чехослова́цкий *adj.* (*hist.*) Czechoslovak.

чечеви́ц|а, ы *f.* lentil; (*collect.*) lentils.

чечеви́|чный *adj. of* ⇒**~ца; прода́ть за ~чную похлёбку** to sell for a mess of pottage.

чече́н|ец, ца *m.* Chechen.

чече́н|ка, ки *f. of* ⇒**~ец**

чече́нский *adj.* Chechen.

чечётк|а, и *f.* chechotka (*kind of tap-dance*).

Чечн|я́, и́ *f.* Chechnya.

че́шк|а, и *f. of* ⇒**чех**

че́шский *adj.* Czech.

чешу́йк|а, и *f.* scale (*of fish*).

чешу́йчат|ый *adj.* scaly; *as n.* **~ые, ~ых** *pl.* (*zool.*) Squamata.

чешу|я́, и́ *no pl., f.* (*zool.*) scales.

чи́бис, а *m.* (*zool.*) lapwing.

чиж, а́ *m.* (*zool.*) siskin.

чи́жик, а *m.* **1** = **чиж. 2**: **~и** (*игра*) tip-cat (*children's game*).

чи́к|ать, аю *impf.* (*of* ⇒**~нуть**) to click; (*о часах*) to tick.

чи́к|нуть, ну, нешь *pf. of* ⇒**~ать**

Чи́ли *nt. indecl.* Chile.

чили́|ец, йца *m.* Chilean.

чили́|йка, йки *f. of* ⇒**~ец**

чили́йский *adj.* Chilean.

чин, а, *pl.* **~ы́** *m.* **1** (*разряд*) rank; **быть в ~а́х** to hold, be of high rank. **2** (*чиновник*) official. **3** (*порядок*) rite, ceremony; **ч. ~ом** properly, fittingly; **без ~о́в** without ceremony.

чина́р, а *m.* plane (tree).

чина́р|а, ы *f.* = **~**

чинёный *adj.* (*coll.*) old, patched (*of clothing, etc.*).

чин|и́ть¹, ю́, ~ишь *impf.* (*of* ⇒**по~**) (*обувь, велосипед*) to repair, mend.

чин|и́ть², ю́, ~ишь *impf.* (*of* ⇒**о~**) (*карандаш*) to sharpen.

чин|и́ть³, ю́, и́шь *impf.* (*создавать*) to carry out, execute; to cause; **ч. препя́тствия** (+*d.*) to impede; **ч. распра́ву** to carry out reprisals.

чин|и́ться, ю́сь, и́шься *impf.* (*obs.*) (*скромничать*) to stand on ceremony, hold back, be shy.

чи́нност|ь, и *f.* decorum, propriety, orderliness.

чи́н|ный (~ен, ~на́, ~но) *adj.* decorous, proper, orderly.

чино́вник, а *m.* **1** (*hist.*) (*служащий*) official, functionary. **2** (*pej.*) (*бюрократ*) bureaucrat.

чино́вни|ческий *adj.* **1** *adj. of* ⇒**~к. 2** (*pej.*) bureaucratic.

чино́вничеств|о, а *nt.* **1** (*collect.*) officials, officialdom. **2** (*pej.*) red tape.

чино́внич|ий *adj.* = **~еский**

чину́ш|а, и *m.* (*pej.*) bureaucrat.

чип, а *m.* (micro)chip.

чи́пс|ы, ов *no sg.* (*coll.*) (potato) crisps (*Br.*), chips (*US*).

чи́р|ей, ья *m.* (*coll.*) boil.

чи́рик, а *m.* (*sl.*) 10 roubles.

чири́ка|ть, ю *impf.* to chirp, twitter.

чири́кн|уть, у, ешь *pf.* to give a chirp.

чи́рк|ать, аю *impf.* (*of* ⇒**~нуть**) (+*i.*) (**по** + *d.*) to strike sharply (against, on); **ч. спи́чкой** to strike a match.

чи́рк|нуть, ну, нешь *pf. of* ⇒**~ать**

чир|о́к, ка́ *m.* (*zool.*) teal.

чи́сленност|ь, и *f.* numbers; **ч. населе́ния** population size; (*mil.*) strength.

чи́сленный *adj.* numerical.

числи́тел|ь, я *m.* (*math.*) numerator.

числи́тельн|ое, ого *nt.* (*gram.*) numeral.

числи́тельн|ый *adj.*: **и́мя ~ое** (*gram.*) numeral.

чи́сл|ить, ю, ишь *impf.* to count, reckon.

чи́сл|иться, юсь, ишься *impf.* **1** to be (*in context of calculation or official records*); **в на́шей дере́вне ~ится три́ста жи́телей** there are three hundred inhabitants in our village; **ч. в о́тпуску** to be (recorded as) on leave; **он ~ится в ко́нкурсе** his name is down for the competition. **2** (+*i.*) to be officially, be on paper; **он ещё ~ился заве́дующим отде́лом, а все обя́занности исполня́ли его́ замести́тели** he was still head of the department on paper, but all the duties were being performed by his deputies. **3** (**за** + *i.*) to be attributed (to), have; **за ним ~ится мно́го недоста́тков** he has many failings.

чис|ло́, ла́, *pl.* **~̆ла, ~̆ел** *nt.* **1** number; **тео́рия ~̆ел** number theory; **~ло́м** in number; **без ~ла́** without number, in great numbers; **в ~ле́** (+*g.*) among; **в том ~ле́** including. **2** (*дата*) date, day (*of month*); **како́е сего́дня ч.?** what is the date today?; **како́го ~ла́ вы уезжа́ете?** what is the date of your departure, which day are you leaving?; **без ~ла́** undated; **поме́тить (за́дним) ~ло́м** to date (antedate). **3** (*gram.*) number; **еди́нственное, мно́жественное ч.** singular, plural.

числово́й *adj.* numerical.

чисти́лищ|е, а *nt.* (*relig.*) purgatory.

чи́стильщик, а *m.* cleaner; **ч. сапо́г** bootblack.

чи́|стить, щу, стишь *impf.* **1** (*pf.* **по~, вы́~**) to clean; **(щёткой)** to brush; **ч. посу́ду** to wash dishes, wash up; **ч. трубу́** to sweep a chimney. **2** (*pf.* **по~, вы́~**) (*дорожки*) to clear; (*канал*) to dredge. **3** (*pf.* **о~**) (*овощи, фрукты*) to peel; (*орехи*) to shell; (*рыбу*) to clean. **4** (*pf.* **по~**) (*pol.*) to purge. **5** (*coll.*) (*грабить*) to clean out (= *to rob*).

чи́|ститься, щусь, стишься *impf.* **1** (*pf.* **по~, вы́~**) to clean o.s. (up). **2** *pass. of* ⇒**~стить**

чи́стк|а, и *f.* **1** cleaning; **отда́ть в ~у** to have cleaned, send to be cleaned. **2** (*pol.*) purge; **этни́ческая ч.** ethnic cleansing.

чи́сто¹ *as pred.* it is clean.

чи́ст|о² *adv.* **1** *adv. of* ⇒**~ый; ч.-на́чисто** spotlessly clean. **2** (*совершенно*) purely, merely; completely; **я ч. случа́йно его́ нашёл** it was by mere chance that I found it. **3** *as conj.* (*coll.*) just like, just as if.

чистови́к, а́ *m.* (*coll.*) fair copy.

чистово́й *adj.* fair, clean; **ч. экземпля́р** fair copy.

чистога́н, а *m.* (*coll.*) cash, ready money.

чистокро́в|ный (~ен, ~на) *adj.* thoroughbred.

чистописа́ни|е, я *nt.* calligraphy.

чистопло́т|ный (~ен, ~на) *adj.* **1** clean; (*опрятный*) neat, tidy. **2** (*fig.*) (*порядочный*) decent, upright.

чистоплю́|й, я *m.* (*coll.*) sissy; fastidious person.

чистопоро́д|ный (~ен, ~на) *adj.* thoroughbred.

чистопро́бный *adj.* pure (*of gold or silver*).

чистосерде́ч|ие, ия *nt.* = **~ность**

чистосерде́чност|ь, и *f.* frankness, sincerity, candour (*Br.*), candor (*US*).

чистосерде́ч|ный (~ен, ~на) *adj.* frank, sincere, candid.

чистот|а́, ы́ *f.* **1** cleanliness; (*опрятность*) neatness, tidiness. **2** (*безупречность*; *отсутствие примесей*) purity.

чистоте́л, а *m.* (*bot.*) greater celandine.

чи́ст|ый (~, ~а́, ~о) *adj.* **1** clean; (*опрятный*) neat, tidy; (*голос, речь*) pure; **экологи́чески ч.** eco-friendly. **2** (*fig.*) (*безупречный*) pure, unsullied; **от ~ого се́рдца, с ~ой со́вестью** with a clear conscience. **3** (*без примесей*) pure; undiluted, neat; **~ое зо́лото, ~ая шерсть** pure gold, wool; **ч. спирт** pure, neat alcohol; **~ой воды́** (*min.*) of the first water; (*fig.*) pure, first-class; **вы́вести на ~ую во́ду** to expose, unmask; **за ~ые де́ньги** for cash. **4** (*открытый*) clear; open; **~ое не́бо** clear sky; **на ~ом во́здухе** in the open air; **ч. лист** blank sheet. **5** (*fin., etc.*) net, clear; **~ая при́быль** clear profit. **6** (*coll.*) (*сущий*) pure, utter; sheer; complete, absolute; **ч. вздор** utter nonsense; **~ая случа́йность** pure chance.

чистю́л|я, и *c.g.* (*coll.*) person with passion for cleanliness *or* tidiness.

чита́|емый *pres. part. pass. of* ⇒**~ть** *and adj.* widely-read, popular.

чита́льн|ый *adj.*: **ч. зал** = **~я**

чита́л|ьня, ьни, *g. pl.* **~ен** *f.* reading-room.

чита́тел|ь, я *m.* reader.

чита́тель|ница, ницы *f. of* ⇒**~**

чита́тель|ский *adj. of* ⇒**~**

чита́|ть, ю *impf.* (*of* ⇒**про~, проче́сть**) **1** to read; **ч. с губ** to lip-read. **2**: **ч. ле́кцию** to give a lecture; **ч. стихи́** to recite poetry; **ч. кому́-н. наставле́ния, нравоуче́ния** to lecture s.o.

чита́|ться, ется *impf.* **1** *pass. of* ⇒**~ть. 2**: **ч. легко́** to be easy to read; **ч. с интере́сом** to be interesting to read; **по́дпись ~ется с трудо́м** it's difficult to read the signature. **3** (*fig.*) (*быть видным*) to be visible, be discernible. **4** (*impers.*): **мне,** *etc.*, **не ~ется** I, *etc.*, don't feel like reading.

Ч

чи́тк|а, и *f.* **1** reading (*usu. of documents, etc., by a group*). **2** (*theatr.*) (first) reading, read-through.

чих, а *m.* (*coll.*) sneeze; (*as int.*) atishoo, achoo!

чиха́нь|е, я *nt.* sneezing.

чих|а́ть, а́ю *impf.* (*of* ⇒**~ну́ть**) **1** to sneeze. **2** (**на** + *a.*; *coll.*) to scorn; **ч. мне на него́!** I don't give a damn for him!

чих|ну́ть, ну́, нёшь *pf. of* ⇒**~а́ть**

чи́ще *comp. of* ⇒**чи́стый, чи́сто**

ЧК = **Чека́**

член, а *m.* **1** member; (*академик*) Fellow; **ч.-корреспонде́нт** corresponding member (*of an Academy*); Associate (*of learned body*); **ч. Королéвского о́бщества** Fellow of the Royal Society; FRS. **2** (*math.*) term; (*gram.*) part (*of sentence*). **3** (*конечность*) limb; (*половой*) penis. **4** (*gram.*) article.

члене́ни|е, я *nt.* articulation.

членистоно́г|ие, их *n. pl.* (*zool.*) Arthropoda.

член|и́ть, ю́, и́шь *impf.* (*of* ⇒**рас~**) to divide into parts, articulate.

членовреди́тельств|о, а *nt.* maiming, mutilation; (*самому себе*) self-mutilation.

членоразде́л|ьный (~ен, ~ьна) *adj.* articulate.

чле́н|ский *adj. of* ⇒**~**; **~ские взно́сы** membership fees, dues.

чле́нств|о, а *nt.* membership.

ЧМ *f. indecl.* (*abbr. of* ***часто́тная модуля́ция***) FM (*frequency modulation*).

чмо́к|ать, аю *impf.* (*of* ⇒**~нуть**) **1** to smack one's lips. **2** (*coll.*) (*целовать*) to give a smacking kiss. **3** (*о грязи*) to squelch.

чмо́к|нуть, ну, нешь *pf. of* ⇒**~ать**

чо́кань|е, я *nt.* clinking of glasses.

чо́к|аться, аюсь *impf.* (*of* ⇒**~нуться**) to clink glasses (*when drinking toasts*).

чо́кнутый *adj.* odd, crazy.

чо́к|нуться, нусь, нешься *pf. of* ⇒**~аться**

чо́порност|ь, и *f.* primness; standoffishness.

чо́пор|ный (~ен, ~на) *adj.* prim; stuck-up; standoffish.

чо́хом *adv.* (*coll.*) wholesale.

ЧП = **чепе́**

чрева́т|ый (~, ~а) *adj.* (+*i.*) fraught (with).

чре́в|о, а *nt.* (*rhet., fig.*) belly; womb.

чревовеща́ни|е, я *nt.* ventriloquy.

чревовеща́тел|ь, я *m.* ventriloquist.

чревовеща́тель|ница, ницы *f. of* ⇒**~**

чревоуго́ди|е, я *nt.* gluttony.

чревоуго́дник, а *m.* glutton, gourmand.

чревоуго́дни|ца, цы *f. of* ⇒**~к**

черед|а́, ы́ *f.* (*obs., poet.*) turn, succession.

чрез = **че́рез**

чрезвыча́йно *adv.* extremely, extraordinarily.

чрезвыча́|йный (~ен, ~йна) *adj.* **1** extraordinary. **2** (*экстренный*) special, emergency; **~йные ме́ры** emergency measures; **~йное положе́ние** state of emergency; **ч. и полномо́чный посо́л** ambassador extraordinary and plenipotentiary.

чрезме́рно *adv.* excessively, to excess.

чрезме́р|ный (~ен, ~на) *adj.* excessive, inordinate.

чре́сл|а, ~ *no sg.* (*arch. or poet.*) hips, loins.

чте́ни|е, я *nt.* **1** reading; **ч. карт** map-reading; **ч. ле́кций** lecturing; **ч. с губ** lip-reading. **2** (*читаемый текст*) reading-matter.

чтец, а́ *m.* reader; (*артист*) reciter.

чти́в|о, а *nt.* (*coll., pej.*) reading-matter.

чтить, чту, чтишь, чтят (*and* **чтут**) *impf.* to honour (*Br.*), honor (*US*).

чти́ц|а, ы *f. of* ⇒**чтец**

что[1], чего́, чему́, о чём *interrog. pron.* **1** what?; **что с тобо́й?** what's the matter (with you)?; **что де́лать, что поде́лаешь?** it can't be helped; **для чего́?** why?, what … for?; **к чему́?** why?; **с чего́?** why?; on what grounds?; **что ты (вы)!** (*expr. surprise, fear, etc.*) you don't mean to say so!; **что ему́** *etc.* **до…?** what does it matter to him, *etc.*? **2** (*как*) how?; **что сего́дня На́дя?** how is Nadya today? **3** (*почему*) why?; **что вы не пьёте?** why aren't you drinking? **4** (*coll.*) (*сколько*) how much?; **что сто́ит?** how much does it cost?

что[2] (*sometimes printed* **что́**) *rel. pron.* which, that; (*coll.*) (*который*) who; **я зна́ю, что вы име́ете в виду́** I know what you mean; **па́рень, что стоя́л ря́дом со мной** the fellow (who was) standing next to me; **он всё молча́л, что для него́ не характе́рно** he said nothing the whole time, which is unlike him.

что[3] (*coll.*) = **что́-нибудь; е́сли что случи́тся** if anything happens.

что[4] as far as; **что есть мо́чи** with all one's might; **что до, что каса́ется** (+*g.*) as for, with regard (to), as far as … is concerned.

что[5] *conj.* that; **то, что…** the fact that ….

чтоб = **что́бы**

что́бы *conj.* **1** (*выражает цель*) in order to, in order that; **ч.… не** lest. **2** (that); **я никогда́ не вида́л, ч. он яви́лся пья́ным на рабо́ту** I have never seen him turn up drunk for work; **сомнева́юсь, ч. вам э́то понра́вилось** I doubt whether you will like it; **он хо́чет, ч. она́ пришла́ в шесть часо́в** he wants her to come at 6 o'clock. **3** (*as particle*) (*выражает требование, пожелание*): **ч. я тебя́ бо́льше не ви́дел!** may I never see your face again!

что ж (*coll.*) (*выражает признание чего-н.*) yes; all right; right you are.

что за (*coll.*) **1** (*interrog.*) what? what sort of … ?; **что э́то за пти́ца?** what sort of bird is that? **2** (*int.*): **что за день!** what a (marvellous) day!; **что за ерунда́!** what (utter) nonsense!

что ли (*coll.*) (*выражает неуверенность*): **пора́ нам идти́, что ли?** perhaps we should be going?; **позвони́ть тебе́, что ли?** do you want me to ring you, then?

что́-либо, чего́-либо *indef. pron.* anything.

что ни *indef. pron.*: **что ни день** every day, not a day passes but …; **что ни говори́** say what you like; **во что бы то ни ста́ло** at whatever cost.

что́-нибудь, чего́-нибудь *indef. pron.* anything.

что́-то[1], чего́-то *indef. pron.* something.

что́-то[2] *adv.* (*coll.*) **1** (*несколько*) somewhat, slightly; **на слу́шателей его́ выступле́ние произвело́ что́-то не о́чень прия́тное впечатле́ние** his speech made a somewhat disagreeable impression on the audience. **2** (*почему-то*) somehow, for no obvious reason; **что́-то мне не хо́чется идти́** I don't feel like going for some reason.

чу *int.* hark!

чуб, а, *pl.* **~ы́** *m.* forelock.

чуба́рый *adj.* (*of a horse's coat*) dappled.

чубу́к, а́ *m.* (*стержень трубки*) stem (*of smoking pipe*); (*трубка*) chibouk.

чува́к, а́ *m.* (*sl.*) guy, fellow.

чува́ш, а (*and* **а́**), *pl.* **~и, ~ей** (*and* **~и́, ~е́й**) *m.* Chuvash.

чува́ш|ка, ки *f. of* ⇒**~**

чува́шский *adj.* Chuvash.

чуви́х|а, и *f.* (*sl.*) girlfriend.

чу́вственност|ь, и *f.* sensuality.

чу́вствен|ный *adj.* **1 (~, ~на)** sensual. **2** (*phil.*) perceptible; **~ное восприя́тие** perception.

чувстви́тельност|ь, и *f.* **1** (*кожи, прибора, человека*) sensitivity, sensitiveness; (*плёнки*) speed. **2** (*сентиментальность*) sentimentality. **3** (*сердца*) tenderness.

чувстви́тел|ьный (~ен, ~ьна) *adj.* **1** (*место тела, прибор, человек*) sensitive. **2** (*толчок, расход*) perceptible. **3** (*стихи, музыка*) sentimental. **4** (*сердце*) tender.

чу́вств|о, а *nt.* **1** (*physiol.*) sense; **ч. вку́са** sense of taste; **о́рганы ~** senses, organs of sense; **обма́н ~** delusion. **2** (*sg. or pl.*) (*сознание*) senses; **без ~** unconscious; **лиши́ться ~, упа́сть без ~** to faint, lose consciousness; **привести́ в ч.** to bring round; **прийти́ в ч.** to come round, regain consciousness, come to one's senses. **3** (*ощущение*) feeling; sense; **ч. ло́ктя** feeling of comradeship, of solidarity; **ч. ю́мора** sense of humour (*Br.*), humor (*US*); **пита́ть к кому́-н. не́жные ~а** to have a soft spot for s.o.

чу́вств|овать, ую *impf.* (*of* ⇒**по~**) **1** to feel, sense; **ч. себя́** to feel (*intrans.*); **ч. го́лод** to feel hungry; **дава́ть себя́ ч.** to make itself felt; **как вы себя́ ~уете?** how do you feel? **2** (*уметь воспринимать*) to appreciate, have a feeling (for) (*music, etc.*).

чу́вств|оваться, уется *impf.* **1** to

be perceptible; to make itself felt. **2** *pass. of* ⇨**~овать**

чувя́к|и, ов *pl.* (*sg.* **~**, **~а** *m.*) slippers (*worn mainly in the Caucasus and Crimea*).

чугу́н, а́ *m.* **1** (*сплав*) cast iron. **2** (*сосуд*) cast-iron pot, vessel.

чугу́нный *adj.* cast-iron (*also fig.*).

чугунолите́йный *adj.*: **ч. заво́д** iron foundry.

чуда́к, а́ *m.* eccentric, crank.

чуда́ческий *adj.* eccentric.

чуда́честв|о, а *nt.* eccentricity, crankiness.

чуда́ч|ить, у, ишь *impf.* (*coll.*) = **чуди́ть**

чуда́чк|а, и *f. of* ⇨**чуда́к**

чуде́с|ный (~ен, ~на) *adj.* **1** (*сверхъестественный*) miraculous; **~ное исцеле́ние** miraculous healing. **2** (*чудный*) marvellous (*Br.*), marvelous (*US*), wonderful.

чуд|и́ть, *1st pers. not used,* **и́шь** *impf.* (*of* ⇨**у~**) (*coll.*) **1** (*вести себя странно*) to behave eccentrically, oddly. **2** (*дурачиться*) to clown, act the fool.

чу́д|иться, ится *impf.* (*of* ⇨**по~** *and* **при~**) (*coll.*) to seem.

чуд|но́й (~ён, ~на́, ~но́) *adj.* strange, odd; **~но́** (*as pred.*) it is strange, it is odd.

чу́д|ный (~ен, ~на) *adj.* marvellous (*Br.*), marvelous (*US*), wonderful, lovely; **~но** *as pred.* it is marvellous (*Br.*), marvelous (*US*), wonderful, lovely.

чу́д|о, а, *pl.* **~еса́, ~е́с** *nt.* **1** (*сверхъестественное явление*) miracle. **2** (*нечто поразительное*) wonder, marvel; **~еса́ те́хники** wonders of technology; **~еса́ в решете́** (*coll.*) *said of sth. unusual or absurd*; **ч. как** *as adv.* marvellously (*Br.*), marvelously (*US*); **ч., что...** *as pred.* it is a marvel that ....

чудо́вищ|е, а *nt.* monster; **лохне́сское ч.** Loch Ness monster.

чудо́вищ|ный (~ен, ~на) *adj.* **1** monstrous (*also fig., pej.*). **2** (*огромный*) enormous.

чудоде́|й, я *m.* **1** (*obs.*) miracle-worker. **2** (*coll.*) crank.

чудоде́йствен|ный (~, ~на) *adj.* miracle-working; miraculous; **~ное лека́рство** wonder drug.

чу́дом *adv.* miraculously; **ч. спасти́сь** to be saved by a miracle.

чудотво́р|ец, ца *m.* miracle-worker.

чудотво́р|ный (~ен, ~на) *adj.* miracle-working; (*fig.*) marvellous (*Br.*), marvelous (*US*).

чужа́к, а́ *m.* (*coll.*) stranger; (*pej.*) alien, interloper.

чужан|и́н, и́на, *pl.* **~е, ~** *m.* (*folk poet. or coll.*) stranger.

чужби́н|а, ы *f.* foreign land, country.

чужда́|ться, юсь *impf.* (+*g.*) (*друзей*) to shun, avoid; (*славы*) to stand aloof (from), remain unaffected (by).

чу́жд|ый (~, ~а́, ~о) *adj.* **1** (+*d.*) (*идеология, взгляды*) alien (to); extraneous. **2** (+*g.*) (*лишенный*) free (from), devoid (of); **он ~ зло́бы** he is devoid of malice.

чужезе́м|ец, ца *m.* (*obs.*) foreigner, stranger.

чужезе́мный *adj.* (*obs.*) foreign.

чужеро́д|ный (~ен, ~на) *adj.* alien, foreign.

чужестра́н|ец, ца *m.* (*obs.*) = **чужезе́мец**

чужестра́нный *adj.* (*obs.*) = **чужезе́мный**

чужея́д|ный (~ен, ~на) *adj.* (*bot.*) parasitic.

чуж|о́й *adj.* **1** (*не свой*) s.o. else's, another's, others'; **на ч. счёт** at s.o. else's expense; **с ~и́х слов** at second-hand; *as n.* **~о́е, ~о́го** *nt.* s.o. else's belongings. **2** (*посторонний*) strange, alien; foreign; **~и́е края́ = ~би́на; попа́сть в ~и́е ру́ки** to fall into strange hands; *as n.* **ч., ~о́го** *m.* stranger.

чуко́тский *adj.* Chukchi.

чу́кч|а, и *m.* Chukchi (man).

чук|ча́нка, ча́нки *f. of* ⇨**~ча**

чула́н, а *m.* **1** (*для вещей*) store-room, lumber room. **2** (*для продуктов*) larder.

чул|о́к, ка́, *g. pl.* **ч.** *m.* stocking.

чуло́чно-носо́чн|ый *adj.*: **~ые изде́лия** hosiery.

чуло́чный *adj. of* ⇨**чуло́к**

чум|а́, ы *f.* plague.

чума́з|ый (~, ~а) *adj.* (*coll.*) grubby, dirty.

чуми́чк|а, и *f.* **1** (*dial.*) (*ложка*) ladle. **2** (*coll., obs.*) (*служанка*) servant-girl. **3** (*coll.*) (*замарашка*) slut, slattern.

чум|но́й *adj. of* ⇨**~а́;** plague-stricken; (*sl.*) crazy, mad.

чумово́й *adj.* (*sl.*) (*одурелый*) crazy, mad; (*отличный*) great, terrific.

чу́н|и, ей *pl.* (*sg.* **~я, ~и** *f.*) (*dial.*) **1** (*верёвочные лапти*) rope shoes. **2** (*галоши*) galoshes.

чупри́н|а, ы *f.* (*dial.*) = **чуб**

чур *int.* (*coll.*) keep away!; mind out!; **ч. меня́** (*in children's games, etc.*) keep away from me!

чура́|ться, юсь *impf.* (+*g.*; *coll.*) to shun, avoid, steer clear (of).

чурба́н, а *m.* **1** block, log. **2** (*coll.*) (*тупой человек*) blockhead.

чу́рк|а, и *f.* block, lump.

чу́т|кий (~ок, ~ка́, ~ко) *adj.* **1** keen, sharp; **ч. нюх** keen sense of smell; **~кая соба́ка** keen-nosed dog; **ч. сон** light sleep. **2** (*fig.*) (*отзывчивый*) sensitive; sympathetic; tactful.

чу́ткост|ь, и *f.* **1** (*слуха*) keenness, sharpness. **2** (*отзывчивость*) sensitivity; sympathetic attitude; tactfulness.

чуто́к *adv.* (*coll.*) a little.

чу́точк|а, и *f.*: **ни ~и** (*coll.*) not in the least.

чу́точку *adv.* (*coll.*) a little bit.

чу́точный *adj.* (*coll.*) tiny.

чу́т|че *comp. of* ⇨**~кий**

чуть (*coll.*) **1** *adv.* (*едва*) hardly, scarcely; just; **ч. (бы́ло) не, ч. ли не** almost, nearly. **2** *adv.* (*немного*) (just) a little, very slightly. **3** *conj.* (*как только*) as soon as; **ч. свет** at daybreak, at first light; **ч. что** at the slightest provocation.

чуть|ё, я *nt.* **1** (*у животных*) scent. **2** (*fig.*) (*способность*) flair, feeling (for).

чуть-чу́ть *adv.* (*coll.*) a tiny bit; **ч.-ч. не = чуть не.**

чу́чел|о, а *nt.* **1** (*животное*) stuffed animal. **2** (*пугало*) scarecrow (*also fig.*).

чу́шк|а, и *f.* **1** (*coll.*) (*свинья*) piglet. **2** (*tech.*) (*слиток металла*) pig, ingot, bar.

чуш|ь, и *f.* (*coll.*) nonsense.

чу́|ять, ю, ешь *impf.* to scent, smell; (*fig.*) to sense, feel.

чу́|яться, ется *impf.* (*impers.*) to make itself felt.

Ч

Шш

ша́баш, а *m.* (*relig.*) sabbath; **ш. ведьм** witches' sabbath; (*fig.*) orgy.

шаба́ш, а *m. as pred.* that's enough!; that'll do!

шаба́ш|ить, у, ишь *impf.* (*coll.*) (*trans. and intrans.*) to stop (work); to knock off.

шаба́шник, а *m.* (*coll., pej.*) moonlighter.

шаба́шнича|ть, ю *impf.* (*coll., pej.*) to moonlight.

ша́бер, а *m.* (*tech.*) scraper.

шабло́н, а *m.* **1** (*tech.*) template, pattern; (*форма*) mould (*Br.*), mold (*US*). **2** (*fig., pej.*) cliché; routine; **рабо́тать по ~у** to work by rote, work mechanically.

шабло́нност|ь, и *f.* triteness, banality.

шабло́н|ный *adj.* **1** *adj. of* ⇨**~.** **2 (~ен, ~на)** trite, banal.

ша́вк|а, и *f.* (*coll.*) (small) dog.

шаг, а (у) (*after numerals 2, 3, 4* **~а́**) **о ~е, в (на) ~у́,** *pl.* **~и́, ~о́в** *m.* step (*also fig.*); (*походка*) pace; (*большой*) stride; **ш. на ме́сте** marking time; **ни ~у да́льше!** stay where you are!; **идти́ бы́стрыми ~а́ми** make rapid strides; **~у ступи́ть нельзя́ (не даю́т)** one can't do anything; **заме́длить ш.** to slow down; **приба́вить ~у** to quicken one's pace; **в двух ~а́х, в не́скольких ~а́х** a stone's throw away; **у́зки в ~у́** (*of cut of trousers*) tight in the seat; **на ка́ждом ~у́** everywhere, at every turn, continually; **с пе́рвого ~у** (*obs.*) from the outset.

шаг|а́ть, а́ю *impf.* (*of* ⇨**~ну́ть**) **1** (*ступать*) to step; (*ходить*) to walk; (*большими шагами*) to stride; (*мерными шагами*) to pace. **2** (*coll.*) (*идти*) to go, come.

шага́|ющий *pres. part. act. of* ⇨**~ть; ш. экскава́тор** self-propelled excavator.

шаги́стик|а, и *f.* (*pej.*) square-bashing.

шаг|ну́ть, ну́, нёшь *pf.* (*of* ⇨**~а́ть**) to take a step; (*fig.*) to make progress; **ш. нельзя́ (не даю́т)** one can't do anything, there's no scope for action.

ша́гом *adv.* at a walk, at a walking pace; slowly; **ш. марш!** (*mil. word of command*) quick march!

шагоме́р, а *m.* pedometer.

шагре́н|евый *adj. of* ⇨**~ь**

шагре́н|ь, и *f.* shagreen.

шажко́м *adv.* (*coll.*) taking short steps.

шаж|о́к, ка́ *m., dim. of* ⇨**шаг**

ша́йб|а, ы *f.* **1** (*tech.*) washer. **2** (*sport*) puck; **хокке́й с ~ой** ice hockey.

ша́йк|а[1]**, и,** *g. pl.* **ша́ек** *f.* (*сосуд*) tub.

ша́йк|а[2]**, и,** *g. pl.* **ша́ек** *f.* (*банда*) gang, band.

шайта́н, а *m.* (*in Muslim theology*) Shaitan, the Devil; (*coll.*) (*чёрт*) devil.

шака́л, а *m.* jackal.

шала́нд|а, ы *f.* (*flat-bottomed*) barge, lighter.

шала́ш, а́ *m.* (*hunter's or fisherman's*) cabin (*made of branches and straw, etc.*).

шалашо́вк|а, и *f.* (*sl.*) tart, prostitute.

шале́|ть, ю *impf.* (*of* ⇨**о~**) (*coll.*) to go crazy.

шал|и́ть, ю́, и́шь *impf.* to be naughty; to play up, play tricks (*also of inanimate objects*); **~и́шь!** (*as rebuke*) don't try that on!, you're joking!

шаловли́в|ый (~, ~а) *adj.* **1** (*ребёнок*) naughty, mischievous. **2** (*тон, стихи*) playful, mischievous.

шалопа́|й, я *m.* (*coll.*) idler, skiver.

ша́лост|ь, и *f.* prank; (*pl.*) mischief.

шалу́н, а́ *m.* naughty child.

шалу́н|ья, ьи *f. of* ⇨**~**

шалфе́|й, я *m.* (*bot.*) sage.

ша́л|ый (~, ~а) *adj.* (*coll.*) mad, crazy.

шал|ь, и *f.* shawl.

шальн|о́й *adj.* mad, crazy; wild; **~ы́е де́ньги** easy money; **~а́я пу́ля** stray bullet.

шама́н, а *m.* (*relig.*) shaman.

шама́нств|о, а *nt.* (*relig.*) shamanism.

ша́ма|ть, ю *impf.* (*sl.*) to eat.

ша́мка|ть, ю *impf.* to mumble.

шамо́вк|а, и *f.* (*sl.*) grub (*food*).

шампа́нск|ое, ого *nt.* champagne.

шампиньо́н, а *m.* field mushroom (*Agaricus campestris* or *Psalliota campestris*).

шампу́н|ь, я *m.* shampoo.

шампу́р, а *m.* skewer.

шанда́л, а *m.* (*obs.*) candlestick.

шанкр, а *m.* (*med.*) chancre.

шанс, а *m.* chance; **име́ть мно́го ~ов, бо́льшие ~ы (на** + *a.*) to have a good chance (of).

шансо́н, а *m.* ballad.

шансоне́тк|а, и *f.* **1** (*песенка*) (music-hall) song. **2** (*певица*) singer (*in music-hall or café chantant*).

шансонье́ *m. indecl.* balladeer; singer-songwriter.

шанта́ж, а́ *m.* blackmail.

шантажи́р|овать, ую *impf.* to blackmail.

шантажи́ст, а *m.* blackmailer.

шантажи́ст|ка, ки *f. of* ⇨**~**

шантрап|а́, ы́ *c.g.* (*coll.*) worthless individual; (*collect.*) scum, riff-raff.

Шанха́|й, я *m.* Shanghai.

ша́пк|а, и *f.* **1** hat, cap; **академи́ческая ш.** mortarboard; **дать по ~е** (+*d.*; *coll.*) (*i*) (*ударить*) to hit, strike, (*ii*) (*уволить*) to sack, fire; **получи́ть по ~е** (*coll.*) to be reprimanded; **по Се́ньке ш.** he's got his deserts. **2** (*заголовок*) banner headline(s).

ша́почк|а, и *f. dim. of* ⇨**ша́пка**

ша́почн|ый *adj. of* ⇨**ша́пка; ~ое знако́мство** nodding acquaintance; **прийти́ к ~ому разбо́ру** (*fig., coll.*) to miss the bus *or* boat.

шар, а (*after numerals 2, 3, 4* **~а́**), *pl.* **~ы́** *m.* **1** (*math.*) sphere; **земно́й ш.** the Earth, globe. **2** (*шаровидный предмет*) spherical object, ball; **возду́шный ш.** balloon; **хоть ~о́м покати́** completely empty.

шара́д|а, ы *f.* charade.

шара́х|ать, аю *impf.* (*of* ⇨**~нуть**) (*coll.*) (*ударить*) to strike; (*выстрелить*) to shoot.

шара́х|аться, аюсь *impf.* (*of* ⇨**~нуться**) (*coll.*) **1** (*о лошади*) to shy; (*о толпе*) to start (up); (*бросаться*) to rush, dash. **2** (**о** + *a.*) to hit, strike.

шара́х|нуть(ся), ну(сь), нешь(ся) *pf. of* ⇨**~ать(ся)**

шарж, а *m.* caricature, cartoon.
шаржи́р|овать, ую *impf.* to caricature.
ша́рик, а *m. dim. of* ⇒**шар; (кровяно́й) ш.** (blood) corpuscle; (*ру́чка*) biro (*propr.*), ball-point (pen).
ша́рик|овый *adj. of* ⇒**~; ~овая (авто)ру́чка** ball-point pen; **ш. подши́пник** (*tech.*) ball-bearing.
шарикоподши́пник, а *m.* (*tech.*) ball-bearing.
шарикоподши́пник|овый *adj. of* ⇒**~**
ша́р|ить, ю, ишь *impf.* (**в**+*p. or* **по**+*d.*) (*искать ощупью*) to grope about, feel, fumble (in, through); (*о прожекторе*) to sweep (*in order to locate a target*).
ша́ркань|е, я *nt.* shuffling (*of the feet or footwear*).
ша́рк|ать, аю *impf.* (*of* ⇒**~нуть**) **1** (+*i.*) to shuffle. **2** (**ного́й;** *obs.*) to click one's heels. **3** (*coll.*) (*ударять*) to hit, strike.
ша́рк|нуть, ну, нешь *pf. of* ⇒**~ать**
шарлата́н, а *m.* charlatan, fraud; quack.
шарлата́н|ка, ки *f. of* ⇒**~**
шарлата́н|ский *adj. of* ⇒**~**
шарлата́нств|о, а *nt.* charlatanism.
шарло́тк|а, и *f.* (*cul.*) charlotte.
шарм, а *m.* charm.
шарма́нк|а, и *f.* barrel-organ, street organ.
шарма́нщик, а *m.* organ-grinder.
шарни́р, а *m.* (*tech.*) hinge, joint; **на ~ах** hinged; **быть как на ~ах** (*fig.*) to be on edge, be restless, fidget.
шарни́р|ный *adj. of* ⇒**~**
шарова́р|ы, ~ *no sg.* baggy trousers (*as worn by certain Eastern peoples, or for certain sports*).
шарови́д|ный (~ен, ~на) *adj.* spherical, globe-shaped.
шар|ово́й *adj. of* ⇒**~; globular; ш. кла́пан** ball-cock; **ш. шарни́р** ball and socket joint.
шаромы́г|а, и *c.g.* (*coll.*) parasite; rogue, scoundrel.
шаромы́жник, а *m.* = **шаромы́га**
шарообра́з|ный (~ен, ~на) *adj.* spherical.
шарф, а *m.* scarf.
шасси́ *nt. indecl.* **1** (*автомобиля*) chassis. **2** (*aeron.*) undercarriage.
ша́ста|ть, ю *impf.* (*coll.*) to roam, hang about.
шата́ни|е, я *nt.* **1** (*качание*) swaying, reeling. **2** (*ходьба без цели*) roaming, wandering. **3** (*fig.*) (*колебание*) vacillation; instability.
шата́|ть, ю *impf.* to rock, shake.
шата́|ться, юсь *impf.* **1** (*intrans.*) (*о человеке, вагоне*) to rock, sway, reel. **2** (*о гвозде*) to be, come loose; (*о стуле, заборе*) to wobble, be unsteady. **3** (*coll.*) (*бродить*) to roam; to loaf, lounge about.
шата́|ющийся *pres. part. of* ⇒**~ться** *and adj.* loose (*of a screw, tooth, etc.*).
шате́н, а *m.* person with auburn hair.
шате́н|ка, ки *f. of* ⇒**~**
шат|ёр, ра́ *m.* tent, marquee.
ша́ти|я, и *f.* (*coll., pej.*) gang, crowd, 'mob'.
ша́т|кий (~ок, ~ка) *adj.* **1** (*стол*) unsteady; shaky; (*гайка*) loose. **2** (*fig.*) unstable, insecure, shaky; unreliable; vacillating; **ш. в убежде́ниях** lacking the courage of one's convictions.
ша́ткост|ь, и *f.* **1** unsteadiness; shakiness. **2** (*fig.*) instability; precariousness.
шатро́в|ый *adj. of* ⇒**шатёр; ~ая кры́ша** hipped roof.
шату́н¹, а́ *m.* (*tech.*) connecting rod.
шату́н², а́ *m.* (*coll.*) loafer, idler.
ша́фер, а, *pl.* **~а́** *m.* best man (*at wedding*).
шафра́н, а *m.* (*bot.*) saffron.
шафра́н|ный *adj. of* ⇒**~**
шах¹, а *m.* (*монарх*) Shah.
шах², а *m.* (*chess*) check; **ш. и мат** checkmate.
шахмати́ст, а *m.* chess-player.
шахмати́ст|ка, ки *f. of* ⇒**~**
ша́хматн|ый *adj.* **1** chess; **~ая доска́** chess-board; **~ая па́ртия** game of chess. **2** (*с квадратами клеток*) check(ed); chequered (*Br.*), checkered (*US*); **~ая ска́терть** check table-cloth; **ш. флажо́к** chequered flag; **в ~ом поря́дке** staggered.
ша́хмат|ы, ~ *no sg.* **1** (*игра*) chess. **2** (*фигуры*) chessmen.
ша́хт|а, ы *f.* **1** (*горная выработка*) mine, pit. **2** (*tech.*) (*вертикальная полость*) shaft.
шахтёр, а *m.* miner.
шахтёр|ский *adj. of* ⇒**~**
ша́хт|ный *adj. of* ⇒**~а; ш. ствол** pit-shaft.
ша́хт|овый *adj. of* ⇒**~а**
ша́шечниц|а, ы *f.* draught-board (*Br.*), checker-board (*US*); chess-board.
ша́шк|а¹, и *f.* (*взрывчатка*) charge (*of explosive*).
ша́шк|а², и *f.* **1** (*в игре*) draught, draughtsman (*Br.*), checker (*US*) (*piece in game of draughts*). **2** (*pl.*) (*игра*) draughts (*Br.*), checkers (*US*).
ша́шк|а³, и *f.* (*оружие*) sabre (*Br.*), saber (*US*), cavalry sword.
шашлы́к, а́ *m.* (*cul.*) shashlik, kebab.
шашлы́чн|ая, ой *f.* shashlik-house.
ша́шн|и, ей *no sg.* (*coll., pej.*) **1** (*проделки*) tricks. **2** (*любовные*) amorous intrigues; affair; **завести́ ш. с** (+*i.*) to take up with.
шва *g. sg. of* ⇒**шов**
шва́бр|а, ы *f.* mop, swab.
шваль, и *f.* (*coll.*) **1** (*collect.*) rubbish, junk. **2** (*о человеке*) good-for-nothing.
шва́ркн|уть, у, ешь *pf.* (*coll.*) to hurl.
шварто́в, а *m.* (*naut.*) hawser, mooring line; **отда́ть ~ы** to cast off.
швартов|а́ть, у́ю *impf.* (*of* ⇒**при~, о~**) (*naut.*) to moor.
швартов|а́ться, у́юсь *impf.* (*of* ⇒**при~, о~**) (*naut.*) to moor, make fast.
швед, а *m.* Swede.
шве́д|ка, ки *f. of* ⇒**~**
шве́дский *adj.* Swedish.
швейник, а *m.* clothing industry worker.
швейни|ца, цы *f. of* ⇒**~к**
швейн|ый *adj.* sewing; **~ая маши́на** sewing-machine; **~ая фа́брика** garment factory.
швейца́р, а *m.* porter, commissionaire.
швейца́р|ец, ца *m.* Swiss.
Швейца́ри|я, и *f.* Switzerland.
швейца́р|ка, ки *f. of* ⇒**~ец**
швейца́рск|ая, ой *f.* porter's lodge.
швейца́рский *adj.* Swiss.
швец, а́ *m.* (*obs.*) tailor; **и ш., и жнец, и в ду́ду игре́ц** (*fig.*) jack of all trades.
Шве́ци|я, и *f.* Sweden.
шве|я́, и́ *f.* seamstress.
швор|ень, ня *m.* = **шкво́рень**
швыр|ну́ть, ну́, нёшь *pf. of* ⇒**~я́ть**
швыр|о́к, ка́ *m.* **1** (*бросок*) throw. **2** (*collect.*) (*поленья*) logs, firewood. **3** (*движущаяся мишень*) (*moving*) practice target.
швыр|я́ть, я́ю *impf.* (*of* ⇒**~ну́ть**) (+*a. or i.*; *coll.*) to throw, fling, chuck, hurl; **ш. де́ньги (*or* деньга́ми)** to throw one's money about.
швыря́|ться, юсь *impf.* (*coll.*) (+*i.*) **1** (*камнями*) to throw, fling, hurl (at one another). **2** (*пренебрегать*) to make light (of), trifle (with).
шевел|и́ть, ю́, и́шь *impf.* (*of* ⇒**~ьну́ть** *and* **по~**) **1** (*переворачивать*) to turn over. **2** (+*i.*) (*слегка сдвигать*) to move, stir; **ш. мозга́ми** (*coll., joc.*) to use one's brains.
шевел|и́ться, ю́сь, и́шься *impf.* (*of* ⇒**~ьну́ться** *and* **по~**) **1** (*слегка сдвигаться*) to move, stir; **у него́ ~я́тся де́ньги** (*coll.*) he has a tidy bank balance. **2** (*fig.*) (*о надежде, сомнениях*) to stir. **3: ~и́сь; ~и́тесь!** (*coll.*) get a move on!; get cracking!
шевел|ьну́ть, ьну́, ьнёшь *pf.* (*of* ⇒**~и́ть**); **па́льцем не ш.** not to lift a finger.
шевел|ьну́ться, ьну́сь, ьнёшься *pf. of* ⇒**~и́ться**
шевелю́р|а, ы *f.* (head of) hair.
шевио́т, а *m.* (*text.*) cheviot (*cloth*).
шевио́т|овый *adj. of* ⇒**~**
шевро́ *nt. indecl.* kid (*leather*).
шевро́|вый *adj. of* ⇒**~**
шевро́н, а *m.* (*mil.*) long-service stripe.
шеде́вр, а *m.* masterpiece.
шезло́нг, а *m.* deck-chair; lounger.
ше́йк|а, и, *g. pl.* **ше́ек** *f.* **1** *dim. of* ⇒**ше́я. 2** (*узкая часть чего-н.*) neck; (*tech.*) pin, journal; **ш. ги́льзы** cartridge neck; **ш. ре́льса** web (*of rail*). **3** (*anat.*) cervix.
ше́йный *adj. of* ⇒**ше́я;** (*anat.*) cervical.
шейх, а *m.* sheikh.

шёл *see* ⇒**идтú**

шéлест, а *m.* rustle, rustling.

шелест|éть *1st pers. not used,* **úшь** *impf.* to rustle.

шёлк, а (у), о ~е, на (в) ~ý, *pl.* **~á** *m.* silk; **ш.-сырéц** raw silk; **в долгý как в ~ý** up to the eyes in debt.

шелковúнк|а, и *f.* silk thread.

шелковúст|ый (~, ~а) *adj.* silky.

шелковúц|а, ы *f.* mulberry (tree).

шелковú|чный *adj. of* ⇒**~ца; ш. червь** silk-worm.

шелковóд, а *m.* silkworm breeder.

шелководóдств|о, а *nt.* silkworm breeding, sericulture.

шелковóд|ческий *adj. of* ⇒**~ство**

шёлковый *adj.* **1** silk. **2** (*fig., coll.*) (*кроткий*) meek, docile.

шёлкогрáфи|я, и *f.* silk-screen printing.

шелкопря́д, а *m.* silkworm.

шёлкопрядéни|е, я *nt.* silk-spinning.

шёлкопряд|úльный *adj. of* ⇒**~éние**

шёлкоткáцкий *adj.* silk-weaving.

шелохн|ýть, ý, ёшь *pf.* to stir, agitate.

шелохн|ýться, ýсь, ёшься *pf.* to stir, move.

шелудúв|ый (~, ~а) *adj.* (*coll.*) mangy.

шелух|á, ú *f.* (*плодов, овощей*) skin; peel; (*гороха*) pod.

шелуш|úть, ý, úшь *impf.* to shell.

шелуш|úться, úтся *impf.* to peel (off).

шéльм|а, ы *c.g.* (*coll.*) rascal, scoundrel.

шельмовáт|ый (~, ~а) *adj.* (*coll.*) rascally, sly, wily.

шельм|овáть, ýю *impf.* (*of* ⇒**о~**) (*coll.*) to blacken (*fig.*); to defame.

шельф, а *m.* (*geog.*) shelf.

шемя́кин *adj., only in phr.* **ш. суд** unjust trial.

шепеля́в|ить, лю, ишь *impf.* to lisp.

шепеля́в|ый (~, ~а) *adj.* lisping.

шеп|нýть, нý, нёшь *pf. of* ⇒**~тáть**

шёпот, а *m.* whisper (*also fig.*).

шёпотом *adv.* in a whisper.

шептал|á, ы́ *f.* (*collect.*) (*абрикосы*) dried apricots; (*персики*) dried peaches.

шеп|тáть, чý, ~чешь *impf.* (*of* ⇒**~нýть**) to whisper.

шеп|тáться, чýсь, ~чешься *impf.* to whisper, converse in whispers.

шептýн, á *m.* (*coll.*) **1** whisperer. **2** (*fig.*) (*сплетник*) tell-tale, informer.

шербéт, а *m.* (*восточный напиток*) sherbet; (*кондитерское изделие*) sweet confection containing fruit, nuts, *etc.*

шерéнг|а, и *f.* **1** (*mil.*) rank; file, column. **2** (*fig.*) line, row.

шерúф, а *m.* sheriff.

шероховáтост|ь, и *f.* roughness (*also fig.*); (*неровность*) unevenness.

шероховáт|ый (~, ~а) *adj.* rough (*also fig.*); (*неровный*) uneven.

шерсте... *comb. form* wool-.

шерстúнк|а, и *f.* strand of wool.

шерстúст|ый (~, ~а) *adj.* woolly (*Br.*), wooly (*US*), fleecy.

шерст|úть, úт *impf.* to irritate, tickle (*of a garment*).

шерсто... *comb. form* wool-.

шерстопрядéни|е, я *nt.* wool-spinning.

шерстопряд|úльный *adj. of* ⇒**~éние**

шерсточесáльный *adj.* wool-carding.

шерст|ь, и, *pl.* **~и, ~éй** *f.* **1** (*на животных*) hair; **глáдить когó-н. прóтив ~и** (*fig.*) to rub s.o. up the wrong way. **2** (*волокно*) wool.

шерстянóй *adj.* wool, woollen (*Br.*), woolen (*US*).

шерхéбел|ь, я *m.* (*tech.*) rough plane.

шершáве|ть, ет *impf.* to become rough.

шершáв|ый (~, ~а) *adj.* rough.

шéрш|ень, ня *m.* hornet.

шест, á *m.* pole.

шéстви|е, я *nt.* procession.

шéств|овать, ую *impf.* to walk (*as in procession*); to process.

шестерёнк|а, и *f. dim. of* ⇒**шестерня**

шестерён|очный *adj. of* ⇒**~ка; ~очная корóбка** gear-box.

шестёрк|а, и *f.* **1** (*цифра*) figure '6'. **2** (*coll.*) (*автобус, трамвай*) number six (*bus, tram, etc.*). **3: ш. треф** *etc.* (*cards*) the six of clubs, *etc.* **4** (*шесть человек*) group of six persons. **5** (*лодка*) six-oar boat. **6** (*упряжка*) team of six horses. **7** (*sl.*) (*подчинённый*) slave, skivvy (*Br.*), gofer.

шестернóй *adj.* sixfold, sextuple.

шестер|ня́, нú, *g. pl.* **~ён** *f.* (*tech.*) gear (wheel), cogwheel, pinion.

шéстер|о, ы́х *collect. num.* six.

шести... *comb. form* six-.

шестигрáнник, а *m.* (*math.*) hexahedron.

шестидесятилéти|е, я *nt.* **1** (*срок*) sixty years, sixty-year period. **2** (*годовщина*) sixtieth anniversary.

шестидесятилéтний *adj.* **1** (*срок*) of sixty years, sixty-year. **2** (*человек*) sixty-year-old.

шестидеся́тник, а *m.* 'man of the sixties' (*progressive social literary, or artistic figure of 1860s or 1960s*).

шестидеся́тый *adj.* sixtieth.

шестиклáссник, а *m.* sixth-former (*Br.*), sixth-grader (*US*).

шестиклáссни|ца, цы *f. of* ⇒**~к**

шестисотлéти|е, я *nt.* **1** (*срок*) six hundred years. **2** (*годовщина*) six hundredth anniversary, sexcentenary.

шестисóтый *adj.* six-hundredth.

шестиугóльник, а *m.* (*math.*) hexagon.

шестиугóльный *adj.* hexagonal.

шестичасовóй *adj.* **1** (*срок*) lasting six hours. **2** (*coll.*) (*поезд*) six o'clock.

шестнадцати... *comb. form* sixteen-.

шестнадцатилéтний *adj.* **1** (*срок*) of sixteen years, sixteen-year. **2** (*мальчик*) sixteen-year-old.

шестнáдцат|ый *adj.* sixteenth; **~ая нóта** (*mus.*) semiquaver (*Br.*), sixteenth note (*US*).

шестнáдцат|ь, и *num.* sixteen.

шестовúк, á *m.* (*sport*) pole-vaulter.

шест|óй *adj.* sixth; **однá ~áя** one sixth.

шест|óк, кá *m.* **1** (*в печи*) hearth. **2** (*насест*) roost.

шест|ь, ú, ью *num.* six.

шестьдеся́т, шестúдесяти, шестью́десятью, о шестúдесяти *num.* sixty.

шест|ьсóт, ~исóт, ~истáм, ~ьюстáми, о ~истáх *num.* six hundred.

шéстью *adv.* six times.

Шетлáндск|ие óстров|á, ~их ~óв *no sg.* the Shetland Islands; the Shetlands.

шеф, а *m.* **1** (*coll.*) (*начальник*) boss, chief. **2** (*покровитель*) patron, sponsor.

шеф-пóвар, а, *pl.* **~á, ~óв** *m.* chef.

шéф|ский *adj. of* ⇒**~ство**

шéфств|о, а *nt.* patronage, sponsorship; **взять ш. (над+*i.*)** to take under one's patronage.

шéфств|овать, ую *impf.* **(над+*i.*)** to act as patron, sponsor (to).

шé|я, и *f.* neck; **бросáться на ~ю комý-н.** to throw one's arms around s.o.'s neck; **на своЮ ~ю** (*coll.*) to one's own detriment; **бить по ~я́м** (*coll.*) to beat up; **прогнáть, вы́толкать когó-н. в ~ю, в три ~и** (*coll.*) to throw s.o. out on his ear; **сидéть на ~е у когó-н.** (*coll.*) to live off s.o.

шибá|ть, ю *impf.* (*coll.*) to hit (*also, impers., of smells, etc.*).

шúб|кий (~ок, ~кá, ~ко) *adj.* (*coll.*) fast, quick.

шúбк|о *adv.* (*coll.*) **1** *adv. of* ⇒**~ий. 2** (*ударить*) hard; (*любить, скучать*) much, very; **ш. испугáться** to be scared stiff.

шúб|че *comp. of* ⇒**~кий** *and* **~ко**

шúворот, а *m.* (*coll.*): **за ш.** by the collar, by the scruff of the neck; **ш.-навы́ворот** (*adv.*) topsy-turvy, upside down.

шúзик, а *m.* (*sl., pej.*) crackpot, freak.

шизофрéник, а *m.* (*med.*) schizophrenic.

шизофрéни|я, и *f.* (*med.*) schizophrenia.

шиúт, а *m.* Shiite; **мусульмáнин-ш.** Shiite Muslim.

шиúтский *adj.* Shiite.

шик, а (у) *m.* stylishness; style.

шикáрно *as pred.* it is splendid, magnificent.

шикáр|ный (~ен, ~на) *adj.* (*coll.*) chic, smart, stylish.

шúк|ать, аю *impf.* (*of* ⇒**~нуть**) (*coll.*) **1** (**на+*a.***) to hush (*by crying 'sh'*). **2** (**+*d.***) (*в знак неодобрения*) to hiss (at), boo, catcall.

шúк|нуть, ну, нешь *pf. of* ⇒**~ать**

шик|нýть, ну, нёшь *pf. of* ⇒**~овáть**

шик|овáть, ýю *impf.* (*of* ⇒**~нýть**) (+*i. or intrans.*; *coll.*) to show off.

шúл|о, а, *pl.* **~ья, ~ьев** *nt.* awl.

шилохвóст|ь, и *f.* (*zool.*) pintail.

шимпанзé *m. indecl.* chimpanzee.

шúн|а, ы *f.* **1** tyre (*Br.*), tire (*US*). **2** (*med.*) splint.

шинéл|ь, и *f.* greatcoat.

шинéль|ный *adj. of* ⇒**~**

шинкáр|ка, ки *f. of* ⇒**~ь**

шинкáр|ь, я *m.* (*obs.*) tavern-keeper, publican.

шинк|овáть, ýю *impf.* (*cul.*) to shred, chop.

шúн|ный *adj. of* ⇒**~а; ш. завóд** tyre factory (*Br.*), tire factory (*US*).

шин|óк, кá *m.* (*obs.*) tavern.

шиншúлл|а, ы *f.* chinchilla.

шип[1], á *m.* **1** (*bot.*) thorn. **2** (*на спортивной обуви*) spike; (*на ботинках альпиниста*) crampon. **3** (*tech.*) tenon; **ш. и гнездó** mortise and tenon.

шип[2], а *m.* (*coll.*) (*звук*) hissing (sound).

шипéни|е, я *nt.* hissing; sizzling; sputtering.

шип|éть, лю, úшь *impf.* **1** (*о змее*) to hiss; (*при жаренье*) to sizzle; (*о напитке*) to fizz. **2** (*от злости*) to hiss; (*ворчать*) to grumble.

шипóвник, а *m.* (*bot.*) dogrose; (*плод*) hip(s).

шипýчий *adj.* (*вино*) sparkling; (*напиток, пиво, вода*) fizzy.

шипýчк|а, и *f.* (*coll.*) fizzy drink.

шип|ящий *pres. part. act. of* ⇒**~éть** *and adj.* (*ling.*) sibilant.

шúр|е *comp. of* ⇒**~óкий** *and* **~óкó; ш. шаг,** *see* ⇒**шаг**

ширин|á, ы *f.* width, breadth; (*колеи*) gauge (*of railway track*).

ширúнк|а, и *f.* (*coll.*) fly (*of trousers*).

шúр|ить, ю, ишь *impf.* to extend, expand.

шúр|иться, ится *impf.* to spread, expand (*intrans.*).

шúрм|а, ы *f.* screen (*also fig.*).

ширóк|ий (~, ~á, ~ó, *pl.* **~ú)** *adj.* **1** wide, broad (*also fig.*), **~ая колея** (*rail.*) broad gauge; **в ~ом смысле** in a broad sense. **2** (*fig.*) big, extensive, general; **~ие плáны** big plans; **~ие мáссы** the general public; **ш. читáтель** the average reader, the general reading public; **товáры ~ого потреблéния** (*econ.*) consumer goods; **жить на ~ую нóгу** to live in grand style.

широкó *adv.* **1** wide, widely, broadly (*also fig.*); **ш. раскрúть глазá** to open one's eyes wide; **ш. толковáть** to interpret loosely. **2** (*в широком масштабе*) extensively, on a large scale.

широко... *comb. form* wide-, broad-.

широковещáни|е, я *nt.* (*radio*) broadcasting.

широковещáтельный *adj.* **1** broadcasting. **2** (*pej.*) (*реклама, манифест*) promising much, extravagant.

ширококолéйный *adj.* (*rail.*) broad-gauge.

ширококóст|ный (~ен, ~на) *adj.* big-boned.

широкоплéч|ий (~, ~а) *adj.* broad-shouldered.

широкопóлый *adj.* (*шляпа*) wide-brimmed; (*сюртук*) full-skirted.

широкоэкрáнный *adj.* wide-screen.

широт|á, ы, *pl.* **~ы, ~** *f.* **1** width, breadth; **ш. взглядов** broad-mindedness. **2** (*geog.*) latitude.

ширóтный *adj.* (*geog.*) latitudinal, of latitude.

ширóчайший *superl. of* ⇒**ширóкий**

широчéнный *adj.* (*coll.*) very wide, broad.

ширпотрéб, а *m.* (*collect.*) mass-market goods.

ширпотрéбный *adj.* mass-market

шир|ь, и *f.* (*wide*) expanse; **во всю ш.** to full width; (*fig.*) to the full extent.

ширя́|ться, юсь *impf.* (*of* ⇒**на~**) (*sl.*) to shoot up (*inject drugs*).

шúто-крúто *adv.* (*coll.*): **всё ш.-к.** it's all being kept dark.

шúт|ый *p.p.p. of* ⇒**~ь** *and adj.* embroidered.

шить, шью, шьёшь *impf.* (*of* ⇒**с~**) **1** to sew. **2** (*изготовлять*) to make (*by sewing*); **ш. себé что-н.** to have sth. made. **3** (*impf. only*) (*вышивать*) to embroider.

шить|ё, я́ *nt.* **1** sewing, needlework; **лоскýтное ш.** patchwork. **2** (*вышивание*) embroidering; (*вышивка*) embroidery.

шúфер, а *m.* slate.

шúфер|ный *adj. of* ⇒**~**

шифóн, а *m.* (*text.*) chiffon.

шифоньéрк|а, и *f.* chest of drawers.

шифр, а *m.* **1** cipher; code. **2** (*библиотечный*) pressmark (*Br.*), call number (*US*).

шифровáльщик, а *m.* cipher clerk.

шифрóв|анный *p.p.p. of* ⇒**~áть** *and adj.* (in) cipher.

шифр|овáть, ýю *impf.* (*of* ⇒**за~**) to encipher.

шифрóвк|а, и *f.* **1** (*действие*) enciphering. **2** (*coll.*) (*шифрованная запись*) coded message.

шиш, á *m.* (*coll.*) **1** (*vulg.*) = **кукúш. 2** (*ничего*) nothing; **ни ~á** damn all.

шишáк, á *m.* (*hist.*) spiked helmet.

шúшк|а, и *f.* **1** (*bot.*) cone. **2** (*бугорок*) bump; lump. **3** (*coll., joc.*) (*важный человек*) big-wig.

шишковáт|ый (~, ~а) *adj.* knobbly; bumpy.

шишковúд|ный (~ен, ~на) *adj.* cone-shaped.

шишконóсный *adj.* (*bot.*) coniferous.

шкал|á, ы́, *pl.* **~ы** *f.* (*зарплаты, термометра*) scale; (*приёмника*) dial.

шкáлик, а *m.* (*obs.*) **1** (*мера*) shkalik (*unit of liquid volume, 0.06 litres*). **2** (*посуда*) bottle or glass (*containing above measure*).

шкáнц|ы, ев *no sg.* (*naut.*) quarterdeck.

шкатýлк|а, и *f.* box, casket, case.

шкаф, а, о ~е, в ~ý, *pl.* **~ы́** *m.* cupboard; (*платяной*) wardrobe; (*кухонный*) dresser; **книжный ш.** bookcase (*with doors*); **несгорáемый ш.** safe.

шкáфчик, а *m.* closet, locker.

шквал, а *nt.* squall; (*fig.*) (*огня, возмущения*) burst.

шквáлистый *adj.* squally.

шквальный *adj.* squally; **ш. огóнь** (*mil.*) heavy fire.

шквáр|ки, ок *pl.* (*sg.* **~ка, ~ки** *f.*) (*cul.*) crackling.

шквóр|ень, ня *m.* (*tech.*) kingpin.

шкет, а *m.* (*sl.*) boy, lad.

шкив, а, *pl.* **~ы́** *m.* (*tech.*) pulley.

шкúпер, а, *pl.* **~ы** *and* **~á** *m.* (*naut.*) skipper, master.

шкóд|а, ы *f.* (*coll.*) **1** (*вред*) harm, damage. **2** (*проделка*) trick, mischief.

шкодлúв|ый (~, ~а) *adj.* (*coll.*) **1** (*вредный*) harmful. **2** (*озорной*) mischievous.

шкóл|а, ы *f.* **1** (*учреждение*) school; **ходúть в ~у** to go to school; **окóнчить ~у** to leave school; **ш.-интернáт** boarding school. **2** (*выучка*) schooling, training.

шкóл|ить, ю, ишь *impf.* (*of* ⇒**вы́~**) (*coll.*) to train, discipline.

шкóльник, а *m.* schoolboy.

шкóльниц|а, ы *f.* schoolgirl.

шкóльнический *adj.* schoolboy(ish).

шкóльничеств|о, а *nt.* schoolboyish behaviour (*Br.*), behavior (*US*), schoolboy tricks.

шкóльн|ый *adj.* school; **ш. вóзраст** school age; **со ~ой скамьú** since one's schooldays.

школя́рств|о, а *nt.* scholasticism, pedantry.

шкот, а *m.* (*naut.*) sheet.

шкóт|овый *adj. of* ⇒**~; ш. ýзел** sheet bend.

шкýр|а, ы *f.* skin (*also fig.*), hide, pelt; **быть в чьей-н. ~е** to be in s.o.'s shoes; **драть ~у (с когó-н.)** to fleece s.o.; **дрожáть за свою ~у** to be concerned for one's own skin; **чýвствовать что-н. на своéй ~е** to know what sth. feels like.

шкýрк|а, и *f.* **1** (*шкура*) skin. **2** (*coll.*) (*плода*) rind. **3** (*бумага*) emery paper, sandpaper.

шкýрник, а *m.* (*coll., pej.*) selfish person, self-seeker.

шкýрный *adj.* (*pej.*) selfish, self-seeking.

шла *see* ⇒**идтú**

шлагбáум, а *m.* barrier (*of swing-beam type, at road or rail crossing*).

шлак, а *m.* slag; clinker.

шлакобетóн, а *m.* (*материал*) breezeblock (*Br.*), cinderblock (*US*).

шлакобетóн|ный *adj. of* ⇒**~; ~ блок** breeze block (*Br.*), cinder block (*US*).

шлакоблóк, а *m.* breeze block (*Br.*), cinder block (*US*).

шлáк|овый *adj. of* ⇒**~**

шланг, а *m.* hose.

шлáф|ор, а *m.* = **~рóк**

шлафро́к, а *m.* (*obs.*) housecoat, dressing-gown.

шлейф, а *m.* train (*of dress*).

шлем[1], а *m.* helmet; **вя́заный ш.** balaclava; **защи́тный ш.** (*on building site, etc.*) hard hat.

шлем[2], а *m.* (*cards*) slam; **большо́й, ма́лый ш.** grand, small slam.

шлёпан|цы, цев *pl.* (*sg.* **~ец, ~ца** *m.*) slippers.

шлёп|ать, аю *impf.* (*of* ⇨**~нуть**) **1** (*ударять*) to smack, spank. **2** (*coll.*) (*ходить*) to shuffle; to tramp; (*по воде*) to splash.

шлёп|аться, аюсь *impf.* (*of* ⇨**~нуться**) (*coll.*) to fall with a plop, thud.

шлёп|нуть(ся), ну(сь), нешь(ся) *pf. of* ⇨**~ать(ся)**

шлеп|о́к, ка́ *m.* smack, slap.

шле|я́, и́ *f.* breech-band, breast-band (*part of harness*).

шли[1] *see* ⇨**идти́**

шли[2] *see* ⇨**слать**

шлифова́льный *adj.* (*tech.*) polishing; grinding; **ш. материа́л** abrasive(s); **ш. стано́к** grinding-machine.

шлифова́ни|е, я *nt.* (*tech.*) polishing; grinding.

шлиф|ова́ть, у́ю *impf.* (*of* ⇨**от~**) **1** (*tech.*) to polish; to grind. **2** (*fig.*) (*совершенствовать*) to polish, perfect.

шлифо́вк|а, и *f.* (*tech.*) **1** (*действие*) polishing; grinding. **2** (*результат*) polish (*result of action*).

шли́хт|а, ы *f.* (*tech.*) size.

шлихт|ова́ть, у́ю *impf.* (*tech.*) to size, dress.

шло *see* ⇨**идти́**

шлюз, а *m.* lock, sluice, floodgate.

шлюз|ово́й *adj. of* ⇨**~**

шлюпба́лк|а, и *f.* (*naut.*) davit.

шлю́пк|а, и *f.* launch, boat; **спаса́тельная ш.** lifeboat.

шлю́х|а, и *f.* (*vulg.*) streetwalker, tart.

шля́гер, а *m.* (*mus.*) hit.

шля́п|а, ы *f. and c.g.* **1** *f.* hat; **де́ло в ~е** (*coll.*) it's in the bag. **2** *c.g.* (*coll., pej.*) duffer.

шля́пк|а, и *f.* **1** (*woman's*) hat. **2** (*гвоздя*) head (*of nail, etc.*); (*гриба*) cap.

шля́пник, а *m.* milliner, hatter.

шля́п|ный *adj. of* ⇨**~а**

шля́|ться, юсь *impf.* (*coll.*) to loaf about.

шляхе́т|ский *adj. of* ⇨**~ство** *and* **шля́хта**

шляхе́тств|о, а *nt.* = **шля́хта**

шля́хт|а, ы *f.* (*hist.*) szlachta (*Polish gentry*).

шля́хтич, а *m.* (*hist.*) member of szlachta.

шляхтя́нк|а, и *f. of* ⇨**шля́хтич**

шмат, а *m.* (*coll.*) sound bite.

шмат|о́к, ка́ *m.* (*coll.*) bit, piece.

шмел|ь, я́ *m.* bumble-bee.

шмона́|ть, ю *impf.* (*sl.*) to frisk.

шмо́т|ки, ок *no sg.* (*coll.*) clothes.

шмуцти́тул, а *m.* (*typ.*) half-title.

шмы́г|ать, аю *impf.* (*of* ⇨**~ну́ть**) (*coll.*) **1** (+*i.*) (*ногами, туфлями*) to scrape; (*щеткой*) to brush; **ш. но́сом** to sniff. **2** (*быстро двигаться*) to rush around; to scurry.

шмыг|ну́ть, ну́, нёшь *pf.* (*coll.*) **1** *inst. pf. of* ⇨**~́ать. 2** (*быстро убежать*) to dart, nip, sneak (*in order to escape notice*).

шмя́к|ать, аю *impf.* (*of* ⇨**~нуть**) (*coll.*) to drop with a thud.

шмя́к|нуть, ну, нешь *pf. of* ⇨**~ать**

шнапс, а *m.* schnapps.

шнит(т)-лу́к, а *m.* (*bot.*) chive.

шни́цел|ь, я *m.* (*cul.*) schnitzel.

шнур, а́ *m.* **1** (*верёвка*) cord; lace. **2** (*electr.*) flex, cable.

шнур|ова́ть, у́ю *impf.* **1** (*pf.* **за~**) (*ботинки*) to lace up. **2** (*pf.* **про~**) (*листы*) to tie (*leaves of a document, etc.*).

шнур|ова́ться, у́юсь *impf.* (*of* ⇨**за~**) **1** to lace o.s. up. **2** *pass. of* ⇨**~ова́ть**

шнуро́вк|а, и *f.* lacing, tying.

шнур|о́к, ка́ *m.* lace.

шныр|ну́ть, ну́, нёшь *pf. of* ⇨**~я́ть**

шныр|я́ть, я́ю *impf.* (*of* ⇨**~ну́ть**) (*coll.*) to dart about.

шов, шва *m.* **1** (*швейный*) seam; **без шва** seamless; **треща́ть по всем швам** (*fig.*) to burst at the seams, fall to pieces. **2** (*в вышивании*) stitch. **3** (*хирургический*) stitch, suture; **наложи́ть, снять швы** to put in, remove stitches. **4** (*tech.*) (*место соединения*) joint, seam, junction.

шовини́зм, а *m.* chauvinism.

шовини́ст, а *m.* chauvinist.

шовинисти́ческий *adj.* chauvinistic.

шовини́ст|ка, ки *f. of* ⇨**~**

шок, а *m.* (*med., fig.*) shock.

шоки́р|овать, ую *impf.* to shock.

шо́ков|ый *adj.*: **~ая терапи́я** shock therapy.

шокола́д, а *m.* chocolate.

шокола́дк|а, и *f.* (*coll.*) (*плитка шоколада*) bar of chocolate; (*конфета*) a chocolate (sweet).

шокола́д|ный *adj.* **1** *adj. of* ⇨**~. 2** (*коричневый*) chocolate-coloured (*Br.*), -colored (*US*).

шо́мпол, а, *pl.* **~а́** *m.* (*mil.*) **1** (*для чистки*) cleaning rod. **2** (*obs.*) (*для забивания заряда*) ramrod.

шо́рник, а *m.* saddler, harness-maker.

шо́рн|ый *adj.* harness; **~ая мастерска́я** = **~я**

шо́рн|я, и *f.* saddler's shop, harness-maker's.

шо́рох, а *m.* rustle.

шо́рт|ы, ~ *no sg.* shorts.

шо́р|ы, ~ *no sg.* blinkers (*also fig.*).

шоссе́ *nt. indecl.* highway; surfaced road.

шоссе́|йный *adj. of* ⇨**~; ~йная доро́га** = **~**

шосси́р|овать, ую *impf. and pf.* to surface (*a road*).

шотла́нд|ец, ца *m.* Scotsman, Scot.

Шотла́нди|я, и *f.* Scotland; **Но́вая Ш.** Nova Scotia.

шотла́нд|ка[1], ки *f. of* ⇨**~ец**

шотла́нд|ка[2], ки *f.* (*text.*) tartan, plaid.

шотла́ндский *adj.* Scottish, Scots.

шо́у *nt. indecl.* show.

шо́у-би́знес, а *m.* show business.

шофёр, а *m.* driver; (*персональный*) chauffeur.

шофёр|ский *adj. of* ⇨**~; ~ское свиде́тельство, ~ские права́** driving licence (*Br.*), driver's license (*US*).

шпа́г|а, и *f.* sword; (*sport*) épée; **обнажи́ть ~у** to draw one's sword; **скрести́ть ~и** to cross swords (*also fig.*).

шпага́т, а *m.* **1** string, cord; (*agric.*) binder twine. **2** (*в гимнастике*) the splits.

шпагоглота́тел|ь, я *m.* sword-swallower.

шпакл|ева́ть, ю́ю, ю́ешь *impf.* (*of* ⇨**за~**) to fill, putty, stop (*holes*); (*naut.*) to caulk.

шпаклёвк|а, и *f.* **1** (*действие*) filling, puttying, stopping up. **2** (*вещество*) putty, filler.

шпа́л|а, ы *f.* (*rail.*) sleeper (*Br.*), cross tie (*US*).

шпале́р|а, ы *f.* **1** (*решётка*) trellis, lattice-work. **2** (*ряд деревьев, кустов*) hedge, line of trees (*lining road*). **3** (*mil.*) line (*of soldiers along ceremonial route*); **стоя́ть ~ами** to line the route. **4** *pl.* (*obs.*) (*обои*) wall-paper.

шпан|а́, ы́ *f.* (*coll.*) hooligan; (*also collect.*) rabble.

шпанго́ут, а *m.* (*tech.*) (*самолёта*) frame; (*судна*) ribs.

шпарга́лк|а, и *f.* (*coll.*) crib sheet (*in school*).

шпа́р|ить, ю, ишь *impf.* (*coll.*) **1** (*pf.* **о~**) (*обливать кипятком*) to scald, pour boiling water on. **2** (*делать, говорить быстро, энергично*) to do, say, *etc.*, in a rush, energetically.

шпат, а *m.* (*min.*) spar; **полево́й ш.** feldspar.

шпа́тел|ь, я *m.* **1** (*tech., art*) palette-knife. **2** (*med.*) spatula.

шпа́ци|я, и *f.* (*typ.*) space.

шпен|ёк, ька́ *m.* pin, peg, prong.

шпига́т, а *m.* (*naut.*) scupper.

шпиг|ова́ть, у́ю *impf.* (*of* ⇨**на~**) **1** (*cul.*) to lard. **2** (*coll.*): **ш. кого́-н. чем-н.** to cram sth. into s.o.'s head.

шпик[1], а (у) *m.* (*cul.*) (*сало*) lard.

шпик[2], а́ *m.* (*coll.*) (*сыщик*) secret agent; detective.

шпил|ь, я *m.* **1** spire, steeple. **2** (*naut.*) capstan.

шпи́льк|а, и *f.* **1** (*для волос*) hairpin; (*для шляпы*) hat-pin. **2** (*tech.*) (*стержень*) peg, dowel; (*гвоздик*) tack, brad. **3** (*fig.*) (*замечание*) caustic remark; **подпусти́ть ~и (кому́-н.)** to get at, have a dig at (s.o.). **4** (*каблук*) stiletto.

шпина́т, а *m.* spinach.

шпингале́т, а *m.* **1** catch, latch (*of door or window*). **2** (*coll.*) (*мальчишка*) urchin, boy.

шпио́н, а *m.* spy.

шпиона́ж, а *m.* espionage.

шпио́н|ить, ю, ишь *impf.* (**за**+*i.*) to spy (on).

шпио́н|ка, ки *f. of* ⇒~

шпио́н|ский *adj. of* ⇒~

шпиц¹, а *m.* (*obs.*) (*шпиль*) spire, steeple.

шпиц², а *m.* (*собака*) Pomeranian (*dog*).

шпон, а *m.* (*typ.*) lead.

шпо́нк|а, и *f.* (*tech.*) bushing key, dowel.

шпо́р|а, ы *f.* spur; **дать ~ы** (+*d.*) to spur on.

шприц, а *m.* (*med.*) syringe.

шпро́т|ы, ~ *pl.* (*sg.* **~а, ~ы** *f. and* **~, ~а** *m.*) sprats.

шпу́льк|а, и *f.* spool, bobbin.

шпунт, а́ *m.* (*tech.*) groove, tongue, rabbet.

шпур, а *m.* (*min.*) blast-hole, bore-hole.

шпыня́|ть, ю *impf.* (*coll.*) to needle, nag.

шрам, а *m.* scar.

шрапне́л|ь, и *f.* shrapnel.

Шри-Ла́нк|а, и *f.* Sri Lanka.

шрифт, а, *pl.* **~ы́** *m.* type, type face; (*comput.*) font.

штаб, а, *pl.* **~ы́** *m.* (*mil.*) (*лица*) staff; (*место*) headquarters.

шта́бел|ь, я, *pl.* **~я́, ~е́й** *m.* stack, pile.

штаби́ст, а *m.* (*coll.*) staff officer.

штаб-кварти́р|а, ы *f.* (*mil.*) headquarters.

штабни́к, а́ *m.* (*coll.*) staff officer.

штаб|но́й *adj. of* ⇒~

штаб-офице́р, а *m.* (*mil., hist.*) field officer.

штабс-капита́н, а *m.* (*mil., hist.*) staff-captain (*rank between lieutenant and captain*).

штаг, а *m.* (*naut.*) stay.

штаке́тник, а *m.* (*забор*) fence; (*планки*) fencing.

шталме́йстер, а *m.* (*hist.*) equerry.

штамп, а *m.* **1** (*tech.*) (*форма*) die, punch. **2** (*печать*) stamp. **3** (*fig., pej.*) (*банальность*) cliché, stock phrase.

штампова́льный *adj.* (*tech.*) punching, stamping.

штампо́в|анный *p.p.p. of* ⇒**~а́ть** *and adj.* **1** (*tech.*) punched, stamped. **2** (*fig.*) (*банальный*) trite, hackneyed.

штамп|ова́ть, у́ю *impf.* **1** (*tech.*) (*детали*) to punch, press. **2** (*бланки*) to stamp, die. **3** (*fig.*) (*стихи*) to churn out; (*решения*) to rubber-stamp.

штампо́вк|а, и *f.* **1** (*tech.*) (*деталей*) punching. **2** (*бланков*) (die-)stamping.

штампо́вщик, а *m.* puncher; stamp operator.

шта́нг|а, и *f.* **1** (*tech.*) bar, rod, beam. **2** (*sport*) (*стержень с тяжестями*) weight. **3** (*sport*) (*ворот*) goal-post.

штангенци́ркул|ь, я *m.* (*tech.*) sliding callipers (*Br.*), calipers (*US*), slide gauge.

штанги́ст, а *m.* (*sport*) weight-lifter.

штанда́рт, а *m.* (*obs.*) standard.

штани́н|а, ы *f.* (*coll.*) trouser-leg.

штани́ш|ки, ек *no sg., dim. of* ⇒**штаны́**

штан|ы́, о́в *no sg.* trousers, breeches.

шта́пел|ь, я *m.* (*text.*) staple.

шта́пельный *adj.* (*text.*) staple.

штат¹, а *m.* state; **Соединённые ~ы Аме́рики** United States of America.

штат², а *m.* (*sg. or pl.*) **1** (*сотрудники*) staff; **зачи́слить в ш.** to take on the staff. **2** (*usu. pl.*) (*положение*) regulations.

штати́в, а *m.* tripod, base, support, stand.

шта́т|ный *adj. of* ⇒**~²**; **~ная до́лжность** established post; **ш. рабо́тник** permanent member of staff.

шта́тск|ий *adj.* civilian; **~ое (пла́тье)** civilian clothes, civvies, mufti; *as n.* **ш., ~ого** *m.* civilian.

ште́ккер, а *m.* jack plug.

штемпел|ева́ть, ю́ю, ю́ешь *impf.* (*of* ⇒**за~**) to stamp.

ште́мпел|ь, я, *pl.* **~я́** *m.* stamp; **почто́вый ш.** postmark.

ште́мпель|ный *adj. of* ⇒~

ште́псел|ь, я, *pl.* **~я́** *m.* (*electr.*) (*вилка*) plug; (*coll.*) (*розетка*) socket.

ште́псель|ный *adj. of* ⇒~; **~ная ви́лка** plug; **~ная розе́тка** socket.

штибле́т|ы, ~ *pl.* (*sg.* **~а, ~ы** *f.*) (*lace-up*) boots, shoes.

штил|ево́й *adj. of* ⇒**~ь**

штил|ь, я *m.* (*naut.*) calm.

штифт, а́ *m.* (*tech.*) (joint-)pin, dowel.

шток, а *m.* (*tech.*) (coupling) rod; **ш. по́ршня** piston rod.

штокро́з|а, ы *f.* (*bot.*) hollyhock.

што́льн|я, и, *g. pl.* **што́лен** *f.* (*mining*) gallery.

што́пальный *adj.* darning.

што́па|ть, ю *impf.* (*of* ⇒**за~**) to darn.

што́пк|а, и *f.* **1** (*действие*) darning. **2** (*нитки*) darning thread, wool. **3** (*coll.*) (*заштопанное место*) darn.

што́пор, а *m.* **1** corkscrew. **2** (*aeron.*) spin.

што́р|а, ы *f.* blind.

шторм, а *m.* (*naut.*) strong gale (*wind force 9*).

шторм|ова́ть, у́ет *impf.* (*naut.*) to ride out a storm.

штормо́вк|а, и *f.* anorak; parka.

шторм|ово́й *adj. of* ⇒~; **ве́тер ~ово́й си́лы** gale-force wind; **ш. костю́м** weatherproof clothing; **~ова́я пого́да** stormy weather; **~ово́е предупрежде́ние** storm warning.

што́р|ный *adj. of* ⇒**~а**

штоф¹, а *m.* (*мера, бутылка*) shtof (*old Russian liquid measure, (1.23 litres), or bottle of this measure*).

штоф², а *m.* (*text.*) damask, brocade.

што́ф|ный¹ *adj. of* ⇒**~¹**; **~ная ла́вка** drinking-shop.

што́ф|ный² *adj. of* ⇒**~²**

штраф, а *m.* fine; **взима́ть ш.** (**с**+*g.*) to fine; **наложи́ть ш.** to impose a fine.

штрафба́т, а *m.* (*abbr. of* ***штрафно́й батальо́н***) (*mil.*) penal battalion.

штрафни́к, а́ *m.* (*coll.*) **1** soldier in the 'glasshouse'. **2** (*sport*) player who has been sent off.

штраф|но́й *adj.* **1** *adj. of* ⇒**~.** **2** penal, penalty; **ш. батальо́н** (*mil.*) penal battalion; **~на́я площа́дка** (*sport*) penalty area; **ш. уда́р** (*sport*) penalty kick.

штраф|ова́ть, у́ю *impf.* (*of* ⇒**о~**) to fine.

штрейкбре́хер, а *m.* strike-breaker, blackleg.

штрейкбре́херств|о, а *nt.* strike-breaking, blacklegging.

штрек, а *m.* (*mining*) drift.

штрих, а́ *m.* **1** (*черта*) stroke (*in drawing*). **2** (*fig.*) (*частность*) feature, trait.

штрих-ко́д, а *m.* bar-code.

штрих|ова́ть, у́ю *impf.* (*of* ⇒**за~**) to shade, hatch.

штрих|ово́й *adj. of* ⇒~; **ш. рису́нок** line drawing.

штуди́р|овать, ую *impf.* (*of* ⇒**про~**) to study.

шту́к|а, и *f.* **1** (*отдельный предмет*) item, one of a kind (*oft. not translated*); **по рублю́ ш.** one rouble each; **пять ~ яи́ц** five eggs; **я возьму́ шесть ~** I'll have six (*of item in question*). **2** (*coll.*) (*вещь*) thing; **вот так ш.!** well I'll be damned! **3** (*coll.*) (*проделка*) trick; **сыгра́ть ~у** to play a trick.

штука́р|ь, я́ *m.* (*coll.*) joker; rogue.

штукату́р, а *m.* plasterer.

штукату́р|ить, ю, ишь *impf.* (*of* ⇒**о~** *and* **от~**) to plaster.

штукату́рк|а, и *f.* **1** (*действие*) plastering. **2** (*раствор*) plaster. **3** (*слой раствора*) stucco.

штукату́р|ный *adj. of* ⇒**~ка**

штуко́вин|а, ы *f.* (*coll.*) thingumajig, thingummy; gizmo.

штурва́л, а *m.* steering-wheel; controls; **стоя́ть за ~ом** to be at the wheel, helm, controls.

штурва́л|ьный *adj. of* ⇒~; *as n.* **ш., ~ьного** *m.* helmsman, pilot.

штурм, а *m.* (*mil.*) storm, assault.

шту́рман, а, *pl.* **~ы** *and* **~а́** *m.* (*naut., aeron.*) navigator.

штурм|ова́ть, у́ю *impf.* to storm, assault.

штурмови́к, а́ *m.* (*самолёт*) low-flying attack aircraft; (*человек*) storm-trooper.

штурмо́вк|а, и *f.* low-flying air attack.

штурм|ово́й *adj. of* ⇒~ *and* **~о́вка; ~ова́я авиа́ция** ground support aircraft; **~ова́я ле́стница** (*hist.*) scaling ladder; **~ова́я ло́дка** assault craft; **~ова́я полоса́** assault course; **ш. самолёт** = **~ови́к**

штурмовщи́н|а, ы *f.* (*pej.*) rushed work, production spurt.

шту́чн|ый *adj.* (by the) piece; **ш. пол** parquet floor; **~ая рабо́та** piece-work;

Ш

ш. това́р goods sold by the piece (*and not by weight*).

штык, а́ *m.* bayonet; **идти́ в ~и́** to fight at bayonet point; **встре́тить, приня́ть в ~и́** (*fig.*) to give a hostile reception (to), oppose adamantly.

штык|ово́й *adj. of* ⇒**~**; **ш. уда́р** bayonet thrust.

штыр|ь, я́ *m.* (*tech.*) pin, dowel.

шу́б|а, ы *f.* fur coat.

шуг|а́, и́ *f.* sludge ice.

шуг|а́ть, а́ю *impf.* (*of* ⇒**~ну́ть**) (*coll.*) to scare off.

шуг|ну́ть, ну́, нёшь *pf. of* ⇒**~а́ть**

шу́лер, а, *pl.* **~а́** *m.* card-sharper, cheat.

шу́лер|ский *adj. of* ⇒**~**

шу́лерств|о, а *nt.* card-sharping, sharp practice.

шум, а (у) *m.* **1** (*звуки*) noise. **2** (*coll.*) (*брань, скандал*) din, uproar, racket; **подня́ть ш.** to kick up a racket. **3** (*fig.*) (*оживлённое обсуждение*) sensation, stir. **4** (*med.*) murmur; **ш. се́рдца** cardiac murmur.

шум|е́ть, лю́, и́шь *impf.* **1** (*издавать шум*) to make a noise. **2** (*coll.*) (*браниться, кричать*) to row, wrangle. **3** (*fig.*) (*оживлённо обсуждать*) to make a stir, fuss; to cause a sensation, stir.

шуми́х|а, и *f.* (*coll.*) sensation, stir.

шумли́в|ый (~, ~а) *adj.* noisy.

шу́м|ный (~ен, ~на́, ~но) *adj.* **1** noisy; loud. **2** (*fig.*) sensational.

шумови́к, а́ *m.* (*theatr.*) sound effects man.

шумо́вк|а, и *f.* (*cul.*) perforated spoon, straining ladle.

шум|ово́й *adj. of* ⇒**~**; **ш. орке́стр** percussion band; **~овы́е эффе́кты** sound effects.

шум|о́к, ка́ *m.* (*coll.*) noise; **под ш.** on the quiet.

шу́р|ин, ина, *pl.* **~ья́, ~ьёв** *m.* brother-in-law (*wife's brother*).

шур|ова́ть, у́ю *impf.* to stoke, poke (*a furnace*).

шуру́п, а *m.* (*tech.*) screw.

шурф, а *m.* (*mining*) prospecting shaft.

шурш|а́ть, у́, и́шь *impf.* to rustle (*also* + *i.*, *trans.*).

шу́ры-му́ры *pl. indecl.* (*coll.*) love affair(s).

шу́ст|рый (~ёр, ~ра́, ~ро) *adj.* (*coll.*) smart, bright, sharp.

шут, а́ *m.* **1** (*hist.*) (*при дворе*) fool, jester. **2** (*fig.*) (*паяц*) fool, buffoon, clown; **разыгра́ть ~а́** to play the fool. **3** (*coll.*) (*чёрт*) devil; **на кой ш.?, како́го ~а?** why the devil?

шу|ти́ть, чу́, ~тишь *impf.* (*of* ⇒**по~**) **1** to joke, jest; **я же не ~чу́** but I'm not joking; **чем чёрт не ~тит!** (*coll.*) we can but see (what will happen)! **2** (**с** + *i.*) (*несерьёзно относиться*) to play (with), trifle (with); **ш. с огнём** to play with fire. **3** (**над** + *i.*) (*смеяться*) to laugh (at), make fun (of).

шути́х|а, и *f.* **1** *f. of* ⇒**шут.** **2** (*ракета*) firecracker, rocket.

шу́тк|а, и *f.* **1** joke, jest; **не ш.** it's no joke; **ш. (ли)** + *inf.* it's not so easy, it's no laughing matter (to); **с ней ~и пло́хи** she is not to be trifled with; **~и в сто́рону, ~и прочь** let's get down to business; **без шу́ток** joking apart; **сказа́ть в ~у** to say as a joke; **не на ~у** in earnest. **2** (*проделка*) trick; **сыгра́ть ~у (с** + *i.*) to play a trick (on). **3** (*theatr.*) farce.

шутли́в|ый (~, ~а) *adj.* **1** (*человек, характер*) joky. **2** (*тон, замечание*) joking, light-hearted, humorous. **3** (*рассказ, песня*) humorous.

шутни́к, а́ *m.* joker, wag.

шут|овско́й *adj. of* ⇒**~**; **ш. колпа́к** fool's cap; **~овски́е вы́ходки** clowning, buffoonery.

шутовств|о́, а́ *nt.* buffoonery.

шу́точ|ный (~ен, ~на) *adj.* **1** (*рассказ, стихи*) humorous. **2** (*вопрос, тон*) joking, light-hearted. **3**: **де́ло не ~ное** it's no joke, no laughing matter.

шут|я́ *pres. ger. of* ⇒**~и́ть** *and adv.* **1** (*легко*) easily, lightly; **ш. отде́латься** to get off lightly. **2** (*в шутку*) for fun, in jest; **не ш.** in earnest.

шу́шер|а, ы *f.* (*coll.*) riff-raff.

шушу́ка|ться, юсь *impf.* (*coll.*) to whisper; (*fig.*) to gossip.

шхе́р|ный *adj. of* ⇒**~ы**

шхе́р|ы, ~ *no sg.* (*geog.*) skerries.

шху́н|а, ы *f.* schooner.

ш-ш *int.* ssh!; (s)hush!

Щщ

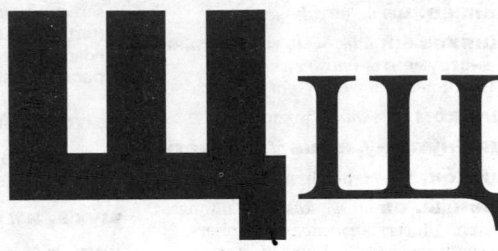

щаве́л|евый *adj.* **1** *adj. of* ⇒**~ь. 2** (*chem.*) oxalic; **~евая кислота́** oxalic acid.

щаве́л|ь, я́ *m.* (*bot.*) sorrel (*Rumex*).

ща|ди́ть, жу́, ди́шь *impf.* (*of* ⇒**по~**) to spare; to have mercy (on); **щ. чьи-н. чу́вства** to spare s.o.'s feelings; **не щ. враго́в** to give one's enemies no quarter.

щебёнк|а, и *f.* = **щебень**

ще́б|ень, ня *m.* **1** crushed stone, ballast (*as road surfacing*). **2** (*geol.*) detritus.

ще́бет, а *m.* twitter, chirp.

щебета́ни|е, я *nt.* twittering, chirping.

щебе|та́ть, чу́, ́чешь *impf.* to twitter, chirp.

щегл|ёнок, ёнка, *pl.* **~я́та, ~я́т** *m.* young goldfinch.

щег|о́л, ла́ *m.* goldfinch.

щеголева́т|ый (~, ~а) *adj.* foppish, dandified.

щёгол|ь, я *m.* fop, dandy.

щегол|ьну́ть, ьну́, ьнёшь *pf. of* ⇒**~я́ть** 3

щегольско́й *adj.* foppish, dandified.

щегольств|о́, а́ *nt.* foppishness, dandyism.

щегол|я́ть, я́ю *impf.* **1** (*щегольски одеваться*) to dress ultra-fashionably. **2** (**в**+*p.*; *coll.*) (*в новом платье*) to strut around in; to sport. **3** (*pf.* **~ьну́ть**) (+*i.*; *coll.*) (*своими знаниями*) to show off, parade, flaunt.

ще́дрост|ь, и *f.* generosity.

щедро́т|ы, ~ *pl.* (*sg.* **~а, ~ы** *f.*) (*obs.*) munificence; **подари́ть от свои́х ~** (*iron.*) to donate generously.

ще́др|ый (~, ~а́, ~о) *adj.* generous; (**на**+*a.*) lavish with, in.

щек|а́, и́, *a.* **́~у,** *pl.* **́~и, ́~, ~а́м** *f.* cheek; **уда́рить кого́-н. по ~е́** to slap s.o.'s face; **упи́сывать, уплета́ть за обе ́~и** (*coll.*) to eat ravenously, guzzle.

щеко́лд|а, ы *f.* latch; catch.

щеко|та́ть, чу́, ́чешь *impf.* (*of* ⇒**по~**) **1** to tickle (*also fig.*). **2** (*impers.*): **у меня́ в го́рле,** *etc.*, **́~чет** I have a tickle in my throat, *etc.*

щеко́тк|а, и *f.* tickling; **боя́ться ~и** to be ticklish.

щекотли́в|ый (~, ~а) *adj.* delicate, sensitive; **~ая те́ма** delicate subject.

щеко́тно *as pred.* (*impers.*; +*i.*) it tickles.

щел|ево́й *adj.* **1** *adj. of* ⇒**~ь. 2** = **~и́нный**

щели́нный *adj.* (*ling.*) fricative.

щели́ст|ый (~, ~а) *adj.* (*coll.*) full of chinks.

щёлк, а *m.* snap, crack.

щёлк|а, и *f.* chink.

щёлканы|е, я *nt.* **1** (*по лбу*) flicking. **2** (*звук*) clicking, snapping, cracking, popping. **3** (*птичье*) trilling (*of some birds*).

щёлк|ать, аю *impf.* (*of* ⇒**~нуть**) **1** (*человека*) to flick. **2** (+*i.*) (*производить звук*) to click, snap, crack; (*comput.*) to click; **два́жды ~** to double-click; **щ. затво́ром** to click the shutter (*of a camera*); **щ. па́льцами** to snap one's fingers; **щ. кнуто́м** to crack a whip. **3** (*impf. only*) (*орехи*) to crack. **4** (*impf. only*) (*о птице*) to trill.

щёлк|нуть, ну, нешь *pf. of* ⇒**~ать**

щелкопёр, а *m.* (*obs., pej.*) scribbler, hack.

щёлок, а *m.* alkaline solution, lye.

щелочно́й *adj.* (*chem.*) alkaline.

щёлочност|ь, и *f.* (*chem.*) alkalinity.

щёлоч|ь, и, *pl.* **~и, ~е́й** *f.* (*chem.*) alkali.

щелч|о́к, ка́ *m.* **1** (*удар*) flick (of the fingers). **2** (*fig., coll.*) (*оскорбление*) insult, slight.

щел|ь, и, *pl.* **́~и, ~е́й** *f.* **1** crack; chink; slit; (*в автомате*) slot. **2** (*mil.*) slit trench. **3**: **голосова́я щ.** (*anat.*) glottis.

щем|и́ть, и́т *impf.* **1** (*кожу*) to pinch. **2** (*ныть, болеть*) to ache, hurt (*also impers.*); **~и́т в боку́** my *etc.* side is aching. **3** (*сердце, душу*) to oppress, grieve (*also impers.*).

щем|я́щий *pres. part. act. of* ⇒**~и́ть** *and adj.* **1** aching, nagging; **~я́щая боль** ache. **2** (*fig.*) painful, oppressive.

щен|и́ться, и́тся *impf.* (*of* ⇒**о~**) to whelp, cub.

щен|о́к, ка́, *pl.* **~ки́, ~ко́в** *and* **~я́та, ~я́т** *m.* puppy, pup (*also fig.*); whelp, cub.

щеп|а́, ы́, *pl.* **́~ы, ~, ~а́м** *f.* (*wood*) splinter, chip; (*collect.*) kindling.

щеп|а́ть, лю́, ́~лешь *impf.* to chip, chop (*wood*).

щепети́л|ьный (~ен, ~ьна) *adj.* **1** (*человек*) punctilious; (over-)scrupulous. **2** (*вопрос*) delicate.

ще́пк|а, и *f.* = **щепа́; худо́й как щ.** thin as a rake; **лес ру́бят — ~и летя́т** (*prov.*) you can't make omelettes without breaking eggs.

щепо́т|ка, ки *f.* = **щёпо́ть**

щёпо́т|ь, и *f.* pinch (*of salt, snuff, etc.*).

щерба́т|ый (~, ~а) *adj.* **1** dented; chipped. **2** (*coll.*) (*лицо*) pock-marked. **3** (*coll.*) (*рот*) gap-toothed.

щерби́н|а, ы *f.* **1** indentation; gap, hole. **2** (*на коже*) pock-mark.

ще́р|ить, ю, ишь *impf.* (*of* ⇒**о~**) **1** (*зубы*) to bare. **2** (*шерсть*) to bristle.

ще́р|иться, юсь, ишься *impf.* (*of* ⇒**о~**) **1** (*оскаливать зубы*) to bare one's teeth. **2** (*щетиниться*) to bristle (*also fig.*).

щети́н|а, ы *f.* bristle; (*coll.*) (*борода*) stubble.

щети́нист|ый (~, ~а) *adj.* bristly, bristling; (*coll.*) (*щёки*) stubble-covered.

щети́н|иться, ится *impf.* (*of* ⇒**о~**) to bristle (*also fig.*).

щётк|а, и *f.* **1** brush; **зубна́я щ.** toothbrush; **щ. для воло́с** hairbrush. **2** (*у лошади*) fetlock.

щёт|очный *adj. of* ⇒**~ка**

щёчный *adj. of* ⇒**щека́**

щи, щей, щам, ща́ми, о щах *no sg.* shchi (*cabbage soup*); **попа́сть как кур во́ щи** to get into hot water.

щи́колотк|а, и *f.* ankle.

щип|а́ть, лю́, ́~лешь *impf.* **1** (*pf.* **~ну́ть**) (*защемлять до боли*) to pinch, nip, tweak. **2** (*impf. only*) (*о морозе*) to sting, bite; (*о горчице*) to burn. **3** (*impf. only*) (*съедать*) to nibble, munch, browse (on), pick (at). **4** (*pf.* **об~** *and* **о~**) (*птицу*) to pluck.

щип|а́ться, лю́сь, ~лешься *impf.* (*coll.*) **1** (*иметь повадку щипать*) to nip, pinch. **2** (*щипать друг друга*) to pinch each other.

щип|е́ц, ца́ *m.* (*archit.*) gable.

щипко́в|ый *adj.*: **~ые музыка́льные инструме́нты** (*mus.*) stringed instruments played by plucking.

щипко́м *adv.* (*mus.*) pizzicato.

щип|ну́ть, ну́, нёшь *pf. of* **⇒~а́ть** 1

щип|о́к, ка́ *m.* pinch, nip, tweak.

щипц|ы́, о́в *no sg.* (*каминные*) tongs; (*tech.*) pincers; (*плоскогубцы*) pliers; (*хирургические*) forceps; **щ. для зави́вки воло́с** curling-tongs; **щ. для са́хара** sugar-tongs.

щи́пчик|и, ов *no sg.* tweezers.

щит, а́ *m.* **1** shield; **живо́й щ.** human shield; **подня́ть на щ.** to extol, eulogize; **верну́ться на ~е́** to suffer defeat; **верну́ться со ~о́м** to be triumphant, victorious. **2** (*ограждение*) shield, screen. **3** (*шлюза*) sluice-gate. **4** (*zool.*) (tortoise-)shell. **5** (*рекламный*) (display) board. **6** (*tech.*) (*пульт*) panel; **распредели́тельный щ.** switchboard.

щитови́дный *adj.* (*anat.*) thyroid.

щит|о́к, ка́ *m.* **1** *dim. of* **⇒~** 2—6; (*у машины*) dashboard. **2** (*sport*) shin-pad.

щу́к|а, и *f.* pike (*fish*).

щуп, а *m.* (*tech.*) **1** probe, probing instrument. **2** (*coll.*) (*уровнемер*) dipstick.

щу́пальц|е, а, *g. pl.* **щу́палец** *nt.* (*zool.*) tentacle; antenna.

щу́па|ть, ю *impf.* (*of* **⇒по~**) to feel (for), touch; (*fig.*; *coll.*) to size up, suss out; **щ. глаза́ми** to scan; **щ. пульс** (*med.*) to feel the pulse.

щу́пл|ый (~, ~а́, ~о) *adj.* weak, puny, frail.

щур[1], а *m.* (*ethnol.*) ancestor.

щур[2], а́ *m.* (*zool.*) pine grosbeak.

щу́р|ить, ю, ишь *impf.* (*of* **⇒со~**); **щ. глаза́** = **~иться**

щу́р|иться, юсь, ишься *impf.* (*of* **⇒со~**) **1** to screw up one's eyes. **2** (*о глазах*) to narrow.

щу́рк|а, и *f.* (*zool.*) bee-eater.

щу́|чий *adj. of* **⇒~ка; как по ~чьему веле́нью** as if of its own volition; as if by magic.

Ээ

эбéновый *adj.* ebony.
эбони́т, а *m.* vulcanite, ebonite.
э́ва[1] *particle* (*coll. or dial.*) (*вон*) over there.
э́ва[2] *int.* (*coll.*) **1** (*выражает удивление*) what's that!; you don't mean to say so! **2** (*выражает несогласие*) nonsense!
эвакуацио́нный *adj. of* ⇒**эвакуа́ция; э. пункт** evacuation centre (*Br.*), center (*US*); **э. райо́н** evacuation area.
эвакуа́ци|я, и *f.* evacuation.
эвакуи́ров|анный *p.p.p. of* ⇒**~ать;** *as n.* **э., ~анного** *m.*, **~анная, ~анной** *f.* evacuee.
эвакуи́р|овать, ую *impf. and pf.* to evacuate (*trans.*).
эвакуи́р|оваться, уюсь *impf. and pf.* to be evacuated.
эвентуа́л|ьный (~ен, ~ьна) *adj.* possible.
Эвере́ст, а *m.* (Mt.) Everest.
эвкали́пт, а *m.* (*bot.*) eucalyptus.
эвкали́пт|овый *adj. of* ⇒**~; ~овое ма́сло** eucalyptus oil.
ЭВМ *f. indecl.* (*abbr. of* ***электро́нно-вычисли́тельная маши́на***) computer; **больша́я Э.** mainframe computer; **сверхбольша́я Э., су́пер-Э.** supercomputer; **персона́льная Э.** personal computer.
эволюциони́р|овать, ую *impf. and pf.* to evolve.
эволюциони́ст, а *m.* evolutionist.
эволюцио́нн|ый *adj.* evolutionary; **~ое уче́ние** (*biol.*) doctrine of evolution.
эволю́ци|я, и *f.* evolution.
эвристи́ческий *adj.* heuristic.
эвфеми́зм, а *m.* euphemism.
эвфемисти́ческий *adj.* euphemistic.
эвфони́ческий *adj.* euphonious.
эвфони́|я, и *f.* euphony.
эгалита́рный *adj.* egalitarian.
Эге́йск|ое мо́р|е, ~ого ~я *nt.* the Aegean Sea; the Aegean.
эги́д|а, ы *f.* aegis; **под ~ой** (*+g.*) under the aegis (of).
эгои́зм, а *m.* egoism, selfishness.
эгои́ст, а *m.* egoist.
эгоисти́ческий *adj.* egoistic, selfish.
эгоисти́ч|ный (~ен, ~на) *adj.* = **~еский**
эгои́ст|ка, ки *f. of* ⇒**~**
эготи́зм, а *m.* egotism.
эгоцентри́ст, а *m.* egocentric person.
эгоцентри́ст|ка, ки *f. of* ⇒**~**
эгоцентри́ческий *adj.* egocentric.
эгоцентри́ч|ный (~ен, ~на) *adj.* = **эгоцентри́ческий**
э́дак(ий) = **э́так(ий)**
эдельве́йс, а *m.* (*bot.*) edelweiss.
Эде́м, а *m.* (*bibl.*) Eden.
эде́мский *adj. of* ↪**Эде́м; сад Э.** the Garden of Eden.
Э́динбург, а *m.* Edinburgh.
эди́пов *adj.*: **э. ко́мплекс** (*psych.*) Oedipus complex.
эзо́пов *adj.* = **~ский**
эзо́повский *adj.* Aesopian; **э. язы́к** 'Aesopian language' (*esp. of allegorical language used by Russian non-conformist publicists to conceal anti-régime sentiments*).
эй *int.* hey!
Э́йре *nt. indecl.* Eire.
эйтана́зи|я, и *f.* euthanasia.
эйфори́|я, и *f.* euphoria
эк (*and* **э́ко, э́ка**) *particle* (*coll.*) *expr. surprise, indignation, etc.*, my goodness!
Эквадо́р, а *m.* Ecuador.
эквадо́р|ец, ца *m.* Ecuadorian.
эквадо́р|ка, ки *f. of* ⇒**~ец**
эквадо́рский *adj.* Ecuadorian.
эква́тор, а *m.* equator.
экваториа́льный *adj.* equatorial.
эквивале́нт, а *m.* equivalent.
эквивале́нтност|ь, и *f.* equivalence.
эквивале́нт|ный (~ен, ~на) *adj.* equivalent.
эквилибри́ст, а *m.* tightrope-walker.
эквилибри́стик|а, и *f.* tightrope-walking (*also fig.*).
экз. (*abbr. of* ***экземпля́р***) copy.
экзальта́ци|я, и *f.* exaltation; excitement.
экзальтиро́ван|ный (~, ~на) *adj.* in a state of exaltation, excited.
экза́мен, а *m.* examination; **держа́ть, сдава́ть э.** to take, sit an examination; **вы́держать, сдать э.** to pass an examination; **провали́ться на ~е** to fail an examination; **э. на вожде́ние** driving test.
экзамена́тор, а *m.* examiner.
экзамен|ацио́нный *adj. of* ⇒**экза́мен; э. биле́т** examination paper; **~ацио́нная се́ссия** examination period, exams.
экзамен|ова́ть, у́ю *impf.* (*of* ⇒**про~**) to examine.
экзамен|ова́ться, у́юсь *impf.* (*of* ⇒**про~**) to go in for an examination; to be examined.
экзамен|у́ющийся *pres. part. of* ⇒**~ова́ться;** *as n.* **э., ~у́ющегося** *m.* examinee.
экзеку́ци|я, и *f.* (*obs.*) **1** (*телесное наказание*) corporal punishment. **2** (*исполнение приговора*) execution (*of an order, etc.*).
экзе́м|а, ы *f.* (*med.*) eczema.
экземпля́р, а *m.* **1** copy; **в двух, трёх ~ах** in duplicate, in triplicate; **переписа́ть в двух ~ах** to make two copies; **резе́рвный э.** (*comput.*) backup (copy). **2** (*животного, растения*) specimen, example.
экзистенциали́зм, а *m.* existentialism.
экзистенциали́ст, а *m.* existentialist.
экзистенциа́л|ьный (~ен, ~ьна) *adj.* existential.
экзо́тик|а, и *f.* exotica, exotic objects.
экзоти́ческий *adj.* exotic.
экиво́к|и, ов *pl.* (*sg.* **~, ~а** *m.*) ambiguities, quibbling, evasion; **говори́ть без ~ов** to call a spade a spade.
э́кий *pron.* (*coll.*) what (a).
экипа́ж[1], **а** *m.* (*повозка*) carriage.

экипа́ж[2], **а** *m.* (*команда*) crew (*of ship, aircraft, tank*).

экипир|ова́ть, у́ю *impf. and pf.* to equip.

экипиро́вк|а, и *f.* **1** (*действие*) equipping. **2** (*снаряжение*) equipment.

э́ккер, а *m.* (*geod.*) cross-staff (*instrument for erecting a perpendicular*).

эклекти́зм, а *m.* eclecticism.

экле́ктик, а *m.* eclectic.

эклекти́ч|ный (~ен, ~на) *adj.* eclectic.

экле́р, а *m.* éclair.

экли́птик|а, и *f.* (*astron.*) ecliptic.

эклóг|а, и *f.* (*liter.*) eclogue.

э́ко *see* ⇨**эк**

эко... *comb. form* eco-.

эко́лог, а *m.* ecologist.

экологи́ческий *adj.* ecological.

эколо́ги|я, и *f.* ecology.

эконо́м, а *m.* (*obs.*) **1** (*заведующий хозяйством*) steward, housekeeper. **2** (*экономист*) economist. **3** (*obs.*) (*бережливый человек*) thrifty person.

экономе́трик|а, и *f.* econometrics.

эконо́мик|а, и *f.* **1** (*наука*) economics. **2** (*страны*) economy; **ры́ночная э.** market economy.

экономи́ст, а *m.* economist.

эконо́м|ить, лю, ишь *impf.* (*of* ⇨**с~**) **1** (*деньги, силы*) to use sparingly, husband; to save. **2** (**на**+*p.*) to economize (on), save (on).

экономи́ческ|ий *adj.* economic; **э. райо́н** economic region; **э. журна́л** economics journal; **~ая ско́рость** cruising speed.

экономи́ч|ный (~ен, ~на) *adj.* economical.

эконо́ми|я, и *f.* **1** economy, saving; **режи́м ~и** economy effort; **соблюда́ть ~ю** to economize. **2**: **полити́ческая э.** political economy.

эконо́мк|а, и *f.* housekeeper.

эконо́мнича|ть, ю *impf.* (*coll.*) to be (excessively) economical.

эконо́м|ный (~ен, ~на) *adj.* economical; careful, thrifty.

экосисте́м|а, ы *f.* ecosystem.

экоци́д, а *m.* ecocide.

экра́н, а *m.* **1** (*cin., TV, comput.*) screen. **2** (*fig.*) (*киноискусство*) screen. **3** (*phys., tech.*) screen, shield, shade.

экраниза́ци|я, и *f.* (*cin.*) filming, screening; (*романа*) film adaptation.

экранизи́р|овать, ую *impf. and pf.* (*cin.*) to film, screen; (*роман*) to adapt for the screen.

экрани́р|овать, ую *impf. and pf.* (*tech.*) to screen, shield.

экра́нн|ый *adj.* (*comput.*) on-screen; **~ая гра́фика** on-screen graphics; **э. реда́ктор** screen editor.

экс-... *pref.* ex-.

эксгума́ци|я, и *f.* exhumation.

экскава́тор, а *m.* (*tech.*) excavator, earth-moving machine.

экскава́торщик, а *m.* excavator operator.

эксклюзи́вный *adj.* exclusive.

экскреме́нт|ы, ов *no sg.* excrement.

э́кскурс, а *m.* excursus, digression.

экскурса́нт, а *m.* tourist; participant in (conducted) tour *or* excursion.

экскурса́нт|ка, ки *f. of* ⇨**~**

экскурс|ио́нный *adj. of* ⇨**~ия**

экску́рси|я, и *f.* **1** (*поездка*) excursion, (conducted) tour, trip. **2** (*группа*) tourist group, excursion party.

экскурсово́д, а *m.* guide.

экслибрис, а *m.* book-plate.

экспанси́в|ный (~ен, ~на) *adj.* effusive.

экспансиони́зм, а *m.* (*pol.*) expansionism.

экспа́нси|я, и *f.* (*pol.*) expansion.

экспатриа́нт, а *m.* expatriate.

экспатриа́нт|ка, ки *f. of* ⇨**~**

экспеди́р|овать, ую *impf. and pf.* to dispatch.

экспеди́тор, а *m.* forwarding agent, shipping clerk.

экспедицио́нный *adj.* **1** (*относящийся к отправке*) dispatch, forwarding. **2** (*относящийся к поездке*) expeditionary.

экспеди́ци|я, и *f.* **1** (*действие*) dispatch, forwarding. **2** (*учреждение*) dispatch office. **3** (*поездка*) expedition.

экспериме́нт, а *m.* experiment.

эксперимента́льный *adj.* experimental.

эксперимента́тор, а *m.* experimenter.

эксперименти́р|овать, ую *impf.* (**над, с**+*i.*) to experiment (on, with).

экспе́рт, а *m.* expert.

эксперти́з|а, ы *f.* (*leg., med.*) **1** (*expert*) examination, expert opinion; **э. на СПИД** AIDS test; **произвести́ ~у** to make an examination. **2** (*комиссия*) commission of experts.

экспе́рт|ный *adj. of* ⇨**~**; **~ная коми́ссия** commission of experts.

эксплуата́тор, а *m.* exploiter.

эксплуатац|ио́нный *adj. of* ⇨**~ия** 2; **~ио́нные ка́чества** operating characteristics; **~ио́нные расхо́ды** running costs; **~ио́нные усло́вия** working conditions.

эксплуата́ци|я, и *f.* **1** (*pol.; pej.*) exploitation. **2** (*природных богатств*) exploitation; (*средств производства*) utilization; (*машин*) operation, running; **сдать в ~ю** to commission, put into operation.

эксплуати́р|овать, ую *impf.* **1** (*pol.; pej.*) to exploit. **2** (*природные богатства*) to exploit; (*машины*) to operate, run, work.

экспози́ци|я, и *f.* **1** (*музейная*) display. **2** (*liter., mus.*) exposition. **3** (*phot.*) exposure.

экспона́т, а *m.* exhibit.

экспоне́нт, а *m.* **1** exhibitor. **2** (*math.*) = **экспоне́нта**

экспоне́нт|а, ы *f.* (*math.*) exponent.

экспоненциа́льный *adj.* (*math.*) exponential.

экспони́р|овать, ую *impf. and pf.* **1** to exhibit. **2** (*phot.*) to expose.

экспоно́метр, а *m.* (*phot.*) exposure meter.

э́кспорт, а *m.* export.

экспортёр, а *m.* exporter.

экспорти́р|овать, ую *impf. and pf.* to export.

э́кспорт|ный *adj. of* ⇨**~**

экспре́сс, а *m.* express (*train, motor coach, etc.*).

экспресси́в|ный (~ен, ~на) *adj.* expressive.

экспрессиони́зм, а *m.* expressionism.

экспрессиони́ст, а *m.* expressionist.

экспрессиони́ст|ка, ки *f. of* ⇨**~**

экспрессиони́стский *adj.* expressionist, expressionistic.

экспре́сси|я, и *f.* expression.

экспре́сс|ный *adj. of* ⇨**~**

экспро́мт, а *m.* improvisation; (*mus.*) impromptu.

экспро́мтом *adv.* **1** impromptu; **петь, игра́ть,** *etc.*, **э.** to improvise. **2** (*coll.*) (*внезапно*) without warning.

экспроприа́тор, а *m.* expropriator.

экспроприа́ци|я, и *f.* expropriation.

экспроприи́р|овать, ую *impf. and pf.* to expropriate.

экста́з, а *m.* ecstasy.

э́кстази *nt. indecl.* ecstasy (*the drug*); E.

экстенси́в|ный (~ен, ~на) *adj.* extensive.

эксте́рн, а *m.* external student; **око́нчить университе́т ~ом** to take an external degree.

экстерна́т, а *m.* external studies.

экстерриториа́льност|ь, и *f.* extraterritoriality.

экстерриториа́л|ьный (~ен, ~ьна) *adj.* extraterritorial.

экстерье́р, а *m.* outward appearance, form (*of an animal*).

экстрава́га́нт|ный (~ен, ~на) *adj.* eccentric, bizarre.

экстраве́рт, а *m.* extrovert.

экстраги́р|овать, ую *impf. and pf.* (*chem., med.*) to extract.

экстради́ци|я, и *f.* (*leg.*) extradition.

экстра́кт, а *m.* **1** (*cul.*) extract. **2** (*резюме*) résumé.

экстра́кци|я, и *f.* (*chem., med.*) extraction.

экстраордина́р|ный (~ен, ~на) *adj.* extraordinary.

экстрасе́нс, а *m.* psychic.

экстрасенсо́р|ный (~ен, ~на) *adj.* extrasensory.

экстрема́л|ьный (~ен, ~ьна) *adj.* extreme.

экстреми́зм, а *m.* extremism.

экстреми́ст, а *m.* extremist.

экстреми́стский *adj.* extremist.

э́кстрен|ный (~, ~на) *adj.*

1 (*срочный*) urgent; emergency; **э. вы́зов** urgent summons; **в ~ном слу́чае** in case of emergency. **2** (*чрезвычайный*) extra, special; **~ное заседа́ние** extraordinary session; **~ное изда́ние** special edition.

эксце́нтрик[1], **а** *m.* **1** (*клоун*) clown. **2** (*obs.*) (*человек*) eccentric.

эксце́нтрик[2], **а** *m.* (*tech.*) cam.

эксце́нтрик|а, и *f.* clowning.

эксцентриситéт, а *m.* (*tech.*) eccentricity.

эксцентри́ческий *adj.* **1** = **эксцентри́чный. 2** (*tech.*) eccentric, off-centre (*Br.*), off-center (*US*).

эксцентри́чност|ь, и *f.* eccentricity.

эксцентри́ч|ный (~ен, ~на) *adj.* eccentric.

эксцéсс, а *m.* excess.

экумени́ческий *adj.* ecumenical.

экю́ *m. and nt. indecl.* écu.

эла́стик, а *m.* stretchy fabric.

эласти́чност|ь, и *f.* elasticity.

эласти́ч|ный (~ен, ~на) *adj.* **1** elastic (*also fig.*); **~ные брю́ки** stretch pants. **2** (*fig.*) springy, resilient.

элева́тор, а *m.* **1** (*agric.*) grain store (*Br.*), elevator (*US*). **2** (*tech.*) hoist.

элега́нтност|ь, и *f.* elegance.

элега́нт|ный (~ен, ~на) *adj.* elegant, smart.

элеги́ческий *adj.* (*liter.*, *mus.*) elegiac.

элеги́ч|ный (~ен, ~на) *adj.* melancholy.

эле́ги|я, и *f.* (*liter.*, *mus.*) elegy.

электриза́ци|я, и *f.* (*phys.*, *med.*) electrification; treatment by electric charge(s).

электриз|ова́ть, у́ю *impf.* (*of* **⇒на~**) **1** (*phys.*, *med.*) to electrify, subject to electric charge(s). **2** (*fig.*) to electrify.

эле́ктрик, а *m.* electrician.

электри́к *adj. indecl.* electric blue.

электрифика́ци|я, и *f.* electrification.

электрифици́р|овать, ую *impf. and pf.* (*tech.*) to electrify.

электри́ческий *adj.* electric(al).

электри́честв|о, а *nt.* **1** electricity. **2** (*освещение*) electric light; **заже́чь э.** to turn on the light.

электри́чк|а, и *f.* (*coll.*) (suburban) electric train.

электро... *comb. form* electro-, electric.

электробытов|о́й *adj.* electrical; **~ы́е прибо́ры** (electrical) household appliances.

электрово́з, а *m.* electric locomotive.

электрогита́р|а, ы *f.* electric guitar.

электро́д, а *m.* (*phys.*) electrode.

электродви́гател|ь, я *m.* electric motor.

электродви́жущий *adj.* (*phys.*) electromotive.

электродина́мик|а, и *f.* electrodynamics.

электродугов|о́й *adj.*: **~а́я сва́рка** arc welding.

электроёмкост|ь, и *f.* (*phys.*) capacity.

электрока́р, а *m.* electric vehicle, float (*Br.*).

электрокардиостимуля́тор, а *m.* (*med.*) pacemaker (*device*).

электрола́мп|а, ы *f.* electric light bulb.

электролече́ни|е, я *nt.* (*med.*) electrical treatment.

электро́лиз, а *m.* (*phys.*) electrolysis.

электромагни́т, а *m.* electromagnet.

электромагни́тный *adj.* electromagnetic.

электромоби́л|ь, я *m.* electric car.

электромонтёр, а *m.* electrician.

электро́н, а *m.* (*phys.*) electron.

электро́ник|а, и *f.* electronics.

электро́нно... *comb. form* electronic-; **~-лучева́я тру́бка** cathode ray tube.

электро́н|ный *adj.* **1** *adj. of* **⇒~; ~ная ла́мпа** electron tube; **э. микроско́п** electron microscope. **2** electronic; **~ная вычисли́тельная маши́на** computer; **~ная по́чта** electronic mail, email (*the system*); **~ное письмо́** email letter; **~ные пи́сьма** email (*letters*); **э. а́дрес** email address; **~ная табли́ца** spreadsheet.

электро́нщик, а *m.* electronics engineer.

электропереда́ч|а, и *f.* electricity transmission.

электропе́ч|ь, и *f.* electric furnace.

электропли́тк|а, и *f.* (electric) hotplate.

электропо́езд, а *m.* electric train.

электрополоте́нц|е, а *nt.* hand-drier.

электропribо́р, а *m.* electrical appliance.

электропро́вод, а *m.* electricity cable.

электропрово́дк|а, и *f.* electric wiring.

электросва́рк|а, и *f.* electric welding.

электросилов|о́й *adj.* electric power.

электроста́нци|я, и *f.* power station.

электроте́хник, а *m.* electrical engineer.

электроте́хник|а, и *f.* electrical engineering.

электротех|ни́ческий *adj. of* **⇒~ника**

электрохими́ческий *adj.* electrochemical.

электроцентра́л|ь, и *f.* electric power plant.

электроча́йник, а *m.* electric kettle.

электроэне́рги|я, и *f.* electric power.

элеме́нт, а *m.* **1** (*компонент, доля*) element; **э. изображе́ния** (*comput.*) pixel. **2** (*coll.*) (*человек*) type, character; **подозри́тельный э.** suspicious type. **3** (*chem.*) element. **4** (*electr.*) cell, battery; **сухо́й э.** dry cell; **рабо́тать от ~ов** to be battery-operated.

элемента́р|ный (~ен, ~на) *adj.* elementary.

элеро́н, а *m.* (*aeron.*) aileron.

эликси́р, а *m.* elixir.

эли́т|а, ы *f.* **1** (*collect.*; *agric.*) best specimens; **э. карто́феля** highest-quality potatoes. **2** élite.

элита́р|ный (~ен, ~на) *adj.* élite; (*pej.*) élitist.

эли́тный *adj.* best-quality.

э́ллин, а *m.* ancient Greek, Hellene.

э́ллинг, а *m.* **1** (*naut.*) slipway. **2** (*aeron.*) shed, hangar.

эллини́ст, а *m.* Hellenist.

эллинисти́ческий *adj.* (*hist.*) Hellenistic.

э́ллин|ка, ки *f. of* **⇒~**

э́ллинский *adj.* ancient Greek, Hellenic.

э́ллипс, а *m.* **1** (*math.*) ellipse. **2** (*ling.*) ellipsis.

э́ллипс|ис, а *m.* (*ling.*) ellipsis.

эллипти́ческий *adj.* **1** (*math.*) elliptic(al). **2** (*ling.*) elliptical.

эл|ь, я *m.* ale.

Э́льб|а, ы *f.* **1** (*остров*) Elba. **2** (*река*) the Elbe.

эльф, а *m.* elf.

эма́левый *adj.* enamel.

эмалиро́в|анный *p.p.p. of* **⇒~а́ть** *and adj.* enamelled (*Br.*), enameled (*US*); **~анная посу́да** enamel ware.

эмалир|ова́ть, у́ю *impf.* to enamel.

эмалиро́вк|а, и *f.* **1** (*действие*) enamelling (*Br.*), enameling (*US*). **2** (*слой эмали*) enamel.

эма́л|ь, и *f.* enamel.

эмана́ци|я, и *f.* emanation.

эмансипа́ци|я, и *f.* emancipation; **боре́ц за ~ю же́нщин** women's liberationist; women's libber.

эмансипи́р|овать, ую *impf. and pf.* to emancipate.

эмба́рго *nt. indecl.* (*econ.*) embargo; **наложи́ть э.** (**на** + *a.*) to embargo, place an embargo (on).

эмбле́м|а, ы *f.* **1** emblem. **2** (*mil.*) insignia.

эмболи́|я, и *f.* (*med.*) embolism.

эмбрио́лог, а *m.* embryologist.

эмбриоло́ги|я, и *f.* embryology.

эмбрио́н, а *m.* (*biol.*) embryo.

эмбриона́льный *adj.* (*biol.*) embryonic.

эмигра́нт, а *m.* émigré, emigrant.

эмигра́нт|ка, ки *f. of* **⇒~**

эмигра́нт|ский *adj. of* **⇒~**

эмигра|цио́нный *adj. of* **⇒~ция**

эмигра́ци|я, и *f.* **1** emigration. **2** (*collect.*) emigration, emigrés.

эмигри́р|овать, ую *impf. and pf.* to emigrate.

эми́р, а *m.* emir.

эмира́т, а *m.* emirate.

эмисса́р, а *m.* emissary.

эмисс|ио́нный *adj. of* **⇒~ия**

эми́сси|я, и *f.* (*fin.*) issuing.

эмоциона́л|ьный (~ен, ~ьна) *adj.* emotional.

Э

эмо́ци|я, и *f.* emotion.

эмпире́|й, я *m.* empyrean; **вита́ть в ~ях** to have one's head in the clouds.

эмпири́зм, а *m.* empiricism.

эмпи́рик, а *m.* empiricist.

эмпири́ческий *adj.* (*phil.*) empirical.

эмпири́ч|ный (~ен, ~на) *adj.* = **~еский**

э́му *m. indecl.* emu.

эму́льси|я, и *f.* emulsion.

эмфа́з|а, ы *f.* (*ling.*) emphasis.

эмфати́ческий *adj.* (*ling.*) emphatic.

эндокри́нн|ый *adj.* (*physiol.*) endocrine; **~ые же́лезы** endocrine glands.

эндокрино́лог, а *m.* endocrinologist.

эндокриноло́ги|я, и *f.* endocrinology.

э́ндшпил|ь, я *m.* (*chess*) end-game.

энерге́тик, а *m.* energy specialist.

энерге́тик|а, и *f.* energy sector (of the economy), power industry.

энергет|и́ческий *adj. of* ⇨**~ика**

энерги́ч|ный (~ен, ~на) *adj.* energetic, vigorous, forceful.

эне́рги|я, и *f.* **1** (*phys.*) energy; power; **затра́та ~и** energy consumption; **растра́та ~и** energy loss; **э. ве́тра** wind power. **2** (*fig.*) energy; vigour (*Br.*), vigor (*US*), effort.

энерго... *comb. form* power-.

энергоёмкий *adj.* power-consuming.

энергосисте́м|а, ы *f.* power (supply) system.

энкли́тик|а, и *f.* (*ling.*) enclitic.

энклити́ческий *adj.* (*ling.*) enclitic.

э́нн|ый *adj.* (*expr. indefinite quantity, size, duration of time, etc.*): **в э. раз** for the nth time; **в ~ой сте́пени** to the nth degree; **~ое коли́чество вре́мени** any number of hours.

э́нский *adj.* (*used to designate sth. that cannot be identified for reasons of security*) ... 'X'; a certain ... (that shall remain nameless); **э. заво́д** factory 'X'.

энтомо́лог, а *m.* entomologist.

энтомологи́ческий *adj.* entomological.

энтомоло́ги|я, и *f.* entomology.

энтропи́|я, и *f.* (*phys.*) entropy.

энтузиа́зм, а *m.* enthusiasm.

энтузиа́ст, а *m.* (+*g.*) enthusiast (about, for), devotee (of); **э. футбо́ла** football enthusiast.

энцефали́т, а *m.* (*med.*) encephalitis.

энцефалопати́|я, и *f.* (*med.*): **бы́чья губкови́дная э.** bovine spongiform encephalopathy (*abbr.* BSE).

энци́клик|а, и *f.* (*eccl.*) encyclical.

энциклопеди́зм, а *m.* encyclopedic learning.

энциклопеди́ст, а *m.* person of encyclopedic learning.

энциклопеди́ческий *adj.* encyclopedic; **э. слова́рь** encyclopedia; **э. ум** encyclopedic brain.

энциклопе́ди|я, и *f.* encyclopedia; **ходя́чая э.** (*joc.*) walking encyclopedia.

эо́лов *adj.*: **~а а́рфа** Aeolian harp.

эоце́н, а *m.* (*geol.*) Eocene period.

эпиго́н, а *m.* (*pej.*) imitator, unoriginal follower.

эпиго́н|ский *adj. of* ⇨**~**

эпиго́нств|о, а *nt.* (*pej.*) imitation.

эпигра́мм|а, ы *f.* epigram.

эпи́граф, а *m.* epigraph.

эпиде́ми|я, и *f.* epidemic.

эпиде́рмис, а *m.* (*biol.*) epidermis.

эпизо́д, а *m.* episode.

эпизоди́ческий *adj.* episodic; occasional, sporadic.

э́пик, а *m.* epic poet.

э́пик|а, и *f.* epic poetry.

эпикуре́|ец, йца *m.* epicurean.

эпикуре́йский *adj.* epicurean.

эпикуре́йств|о, а *nt.* epicureanism.

эпиле́пси|я, и *f.* (*med.*) epilepsy.

эпиле́птик, а *m.* epileptic.

эпилепти́ческий *adj.* epileptic.

эпило́г, а *m.* epilogue (*Br.*), epilog (*US*).

эпистоля́рный *adj.* epistolary.

эпита́фи|я, и *f.* epitaph.

эпите́ли|й, я *m.* epithelium.

эпи́тет, а *m.* epithet.

эпице́нтр, а *m.* (*geol.*) epicentre (*Br.*), epicenter (*US*).

эпици́кл, а *m.* (*math.*) epicycle.

эпи́ческий *adj.* epic.

эполе́т|ы, ~ *pl.* (*sg.* **~а, ~ы** *f.*) epaulettes.

эпони́м, а *m.* eponym.

эпони́мный *adj.* eponymous.

эпопе́|я, и *f.* (*liter. or fig.*) epic.

э́пос, а *m.* epic literature.

эпо́х|а, и *f.* epoch, age, era.

эпоха́льный *adj.* epoch-making.

эпю́р, а *m.* diagram, drawing.

э́р|а, ы *f.* era; **до на́шей ~ы** BC (*before Christ*); **на́шей ~ы** AD (*Anno Domini*).

эрг, а *m.* erg (*unit of work*).

эргоно́мик|а, и *f.* ergonomics.

эргономи́ст, а *m.* ergonomist.

эргономи́ческий *adj.* ergonomic.

эрдельтерье́р, а *m.* Airedale.

эре́кци|я, и *f.* (*physiol.*) erection.

эрза́ц, а *m.* ersatz, substitute.

Эритре́|я, и *f.* Eritrea.

эритроци́т, а *m.* (*physiol.*) erythrocyte, red corpuscle.

э́ркер, а *m.* (*archit.*) oriel (window).

эроге́нн|ый *adj.* erogenous; **~ые зо́ны** erogenous zones.

эро́зи|я, и *f.* erosion.

эроти́зм, а *m.* eroticism.

эро́тик|а, и *f.* **1** (*чувственность*) sensuality. **2** (*collect.*) (*литература*) erotica.

эроти́ческий *adj.* erotic, sensual.

эроти́ч|ный (~ен, ~на) *adj.* = **~еский**

эротома́н, а *m.* erotomaniac, sex maniac.

эротома́ни|я, и *f.* erotomania.

Эр-Рия́д, а *m.* Riyadh.

эрсте́д, а *m.* oersted (*unit of magnetism*).

эруди́рован|ный (~, ~на) *adj.* erudite.

эруди́т, а *m.* polymath.

эруди́ци|я, и *f.* erudition.

эрцге́рцог, а *m.* archduke.

эрцгерцоги́н|я, и *f.* archduchess.

эрцге́рцогств|о, а *nt.* archduchy, archdukedom.

эска́др|а, ы *f.* (*naut.*) squadron.

эска́др|енный *adj. of* ⇨**~а; э. бронено́сец** (*obs.*) battleship; **э. миноно́сец** destroyer.

эскадри́л|ьный *adj. of* ⇨**~ья**

эскадри́л|ья, ьи, *g. pl.* **~ий** *f.* (*aeron.*) squadron.

эскадро́н, а *m.* (*mil.*) (*cavalry*) squadron, troop.

эскадро́н|ный *adj. of* ⇨**~**

эскала́тор, а *m.* escalator.

эскала́ци|я, и *f.* (*mil.*) escalation.

эскало́п, а *m.* (*cul.*) escalope.

эска́рп, а *m.* (*mil.*) scarp, escarpment.

эски́з, а *m.* (*к картине*) sketch, study; (*к роману*) draft, outline.

эски́з|ный *adj. of* ⇨**~; э. чертёж** draft, outline sketch.

эскимо́ *nt. indecl.* ice cream covered in chocolate, choc ice (*Br.*).

эскимо́с, а *m.* Eskimo, Inuit.

эскимо́с|ка, ки *f. of* ⇨**~**

эскимо́сский *adj.* Eskimo, Inuit.

эско́рт, а *m.* (*mil.*) escort.

эскорти́р|овать, ую *impf. and pf.* (*mil.*) to escort.

эсми́н|ец, ца *m.* (*abbr. of* ***эска́дренный миноно́сец***) (*naut.*) destroyer.

эспадро́н, а *m.* (*fencing*) cutting-sword, back-sword.

эспаньо́лк|а, и *f.* imperial (*beard*).

эспарце́т, а *m.* (*bot.*) sainfoin.

эспера́нто *m. & nt. indecl.* Esperanto.

эссе́ *nt. indecl.* essay.

эссе́нци|я, и *f.* essence.

эстака́д|а, ы *f.* **1** (*на железной дороге*) viaduct. **2** (*на шоссе*) flyover (*Br.*), overpass. **3** (*naut.*) (*для причала*) pier. **4** (*naut.*) (*заграждение*) boom (*of harbour*).

эстака́д|ный *adj. of* ⇨**~а; ~ная желе́зная доро́га** elevated railway.

эста́мп, а *m.* (*art*) print, engraving.

эстафе́т|а, ы *f.* **1** (*sport*) relay race. **2** (*палочка*) baton (*in relay race*); **приня́ть у кого́-н. ~у** (*fig.*) to carry on s.o.'s work, maintain s.o.'s tradition. **3** (*obs.*) mail (*carried by relays of horsemen*).

эсте́т, а *m.* aesthete.

эстети́зм, а *m.* aestheticism.

эсте́тик|а, и *f.* **1** aesthetics. **2** (*художественность*) design; **промы́шленная э.** industrial design.

эстети́ческий *adj.* aesthetic.

эстети́ч|ный (~ен, ~на) *adj.* aesthetic.

эсте́т|ский *adj. of* ⇨**~**

эсте́тств|о, а *nt.* aestheticism.

эсто́н|ец, ца *m.* Estonian.

Эсто́ни|я, и *f.* Estonia.

эсто́н|ка, ки *f. of* ⇨**~ец**

эсто́нский *adj.* Estonian.

эстраго́н, а *m.* (*bot.*) tarragon.

эстра́д|а, ы *f.* **1** stage, platform; **вы́йти на ~у** to come on stage. **2** (*представление*) variety; **арти́ст ~ы** variety performer, artiste.

эстра́д|ный *adj. of* ⇨**~а; э. конце́рт** variety show; **~ная му́зыка** popular music.

эстроге́н, а *m.* oestrogen (*Br.*), estrogen (*US*).

эстуа́ри|й, я *m.* estuary.

эсэнго́вский *adj.* (*coll.*) CIS (*Commonwealth of Independent States*).

эсэ́сов|ец, ца *m.* (*hist.*) SS (*Schutz-Staffel*) man.

эсэ́совский *adj.* (*hist.*) SS (*Schutz-Staffel*).

эта́ж, а́ *m.* storey (*Br.*), story (*US*), floor; **пе́рвый, второ́й**, *etc.*, **э.** ground floor, first floor, *etc.* (*Br.*), first floor, second floor, *etc.* (*US*).

этаже́рк|а, и *f.* bookcase, shelves.

эта́жност|ь, и *f.* number of storeys (*Br.*), stories (*US*).

э́так *adv.* (*coll.*) **1** (*так*) so, thus; **мо́жно э́то сде́лать и так и э.** you can do it like this or like that. **2** (*примерно*) about, approximately.

э́такий *pron.* (*coll.*) such (a), what (a).

этало́н, а *m.* standard (*of weights and measures*); (*fig.*) (*мерило*) bench-mark.

эта́н, а *m.* (*chem.*) ethane.

эта́п, а *m.* **1** (*стадия*) stage, phase. **2** (*sport*) lap. **3** (*пункт для ночлега*) halting-place, stage (*for troops; formerly, for groups of deported convicts in transit*); **отпра́вить по ~у, ~ом** to transport, deport (*under guard*).

эта́пник, а *m.* (*hist.*) convict in transit.

эта́п|ный *adj. of* ⇨**~; ~ное собы́тие** (*fig.*) landmark, turning-point; **отпра́вить ~ным поря́дком** (*hist.*) to transport, deport (*under guard*).

э́тик|а, и *f.* ethics.

этике́т, а *m.* etiquette.

этике́тк|а, и *f.* label.

эти́л, а *m.* (*chem.*) ethyl.

этиле́н, а *m.* (*chem.*) ethylene.

эти́л|овый *adj. of* ⇨**~; э. спирт** ethyl alcohol.

этимо́лог, а *m.* etymologist.

этимологи́ческий *adj.* etymological.

этимоло́ги|я, и *f.* etymology; **наро́дная э.** popular etymology.

эти́ческий *adj. of* ⇨**э́тика**

эти́ч|ный (~ен, ~на) *adj.* othical.

этни́ческий *adj.* ethnic.

этно́граф, а *m.* ethnographer, social anthropologist.

этнографи́ческий *adj.* ethnographic(al).

этногра́фи|я, и *f.* ethnography, social anthropology.

э́то[1] *see* ⇨**э́тот**

э́то[2] *emph. particle* (*coll.*); **куда́ э. он де́лся?** wherever has he got to?; **что э. ты не гото́в?** why on earth aren't you ready?; **э. вы спра́шивали?** was it *you* who was asking?

э́то[3] *pron.* (*as n.*) this (is), that (is); **э. наш дом** this is our house; **э. вам помо́жет** this will help you; **э. ве́рно** that is true; **не в ~м де́ло** that's not the point; **об ~м я вам пото́м расскажу́** I will tell you about it later; **э. я ви́жу** so I can see.

это́лог, а *m.* ethologist.

этологи́ческий *adj.* ethological.

этоло́ги|я, и *f.* ethology.

э́тот, э́та, э́то, *pl.* **э́ти** *pron.* this (these); *as n.* (*i*) this one, (*ii*) (*последнее из названных лиц*) the latter.

этру́ск, а *m.* Etruscan.

этру́сский *adj.* Etruscan.

этю́д, а *m.* **1** (*art, liter.*) study, sketch. **2** (*mus.*) étude. **3** (*mus.*) (*упражнение*) exercise; (*chess*) problem.

эфеме́р|ный (~ен, ~на) *adj.* ephemeral.

эфе́с, а *m.* hilt, handle (*of sword, sabre, etc.*).

эфио́п, а *m.* Ethiopian.

Эфио́пи|я, и *f.* Ethiopia.

эфио́п|ка, ки *f. of* ⇨**~**

эфио́пский *adj.* Ethiopian.

эфи́р, а *m.* **1** ether; (*fig.*) air; **вре́мя в ~е** air time; **передава́ть в э.** to put on the air, broadcast; **прямо́й э.** live broadcast. **2** (*chem.*) ether; **просто́й э.** ether; **сло́жный э.** ester.

эфи́р|ный (~ен, ~на) *adj.* **1** othereal **2** (*chem.*) ether, ester; **~ное ма́сло** essential oil.

эффе́кт, а *m.* **1** effect, impact; **произвести́ э.** (**на** + *a.*) to have an effect (on), make an impression (on); **парнико́вый** *or* **тепли́чный э.** greenhouse effect. **2** (*econ.*) result, consequences. **3** (*pl.*) (*theatr.*) effects; **шумовы́е ~ы** sound effects.

эффекти́в|ный (~ен, ~на) *adj.* effective, efficacious.

эффе́кт|ный (~ен, ~на) *adj.* effective, striking; eye-catching.

эх *int. expr. regret, reproval, amazement, etc.*; eh!; oh!

эхма́ *int.* = **эх**

э́х|о, а *nt.* echo.

эхоло́т, а *m.* (*naut.*) sonic depth finder, echo sounder.

эшафо́т, а *m.* scaffold; **взойти́ на э.** to mount the scaffold.

эшело́н, а *m.* **1** (*mil.*) echelon. **2** (*поезд*) special train. **3** (*верхний слой*) echelon.

эшелони́р|овать, ую *impf. and pf.* (*mil.*) to echelon.

эякуля́ци|я, и *f.* (*physiol.*) ejaculation.

Э

Юю

Ю (*abbr. of* ***юг***) S, South.
юа́н|ь, я *m.* yuan (*Chinese currency unit*).
ЮАР *f. indecl.* (*abbr. of* ***Южно-Африка́нская Респу́блика***) Republic of South Africa.
юа́ров|ец, ца *m.* South African.
юа́ровский *adj.* South African.
юбиле́|й, я *m.* **1** (*годовщина*) anniversary; jubilee. **2** (*празднование*) anniversary celebrations.
юбиле́й|ный *adj. of* ⇒~
юбиля́р, а *m.* person (*or* institution) whose anniversary is celebrated.
ю́бк|а, и *f.* skirt; **шотла́ндская ю.** kilt; **ю.-брю́ки** culottes; **держа́ться за чью-н. ~у** to cling to s.o.'s apron-strings.
ю́бочк|а, и *f.* short skirt.
ю́бочник, а *m.* (*coll.*) womanizer.
ю́б|очный *adj. of* ⇒**~ка**
ювели́р, а *m.* jeweller (*Br.*), jeweler (*US*).
ювели́р|ный *adj.* **1** *adj. of* ⇒**~; ~ные изде́лия** gold and silver ware, jewellery (*Br.*), jewelry (*US*); **ю. магази́н** jeweller's (*Br.*), jeweler's (*US*). **2** (*fig.*) (*тщательный*) fine, intricate.
юг, а *m.* south; the South (*of Russia, etc.*); **на ю́ге** in the south; **к ю́гу от** to the south of.
ю́го-восто́к, а *m.* south-east.
ю́го-восто́чный *adj.* south-east(ern).
ю́го-за́пад, а *m.* south-west.
ю́го-за́падный *adj.* south-west(ern).
югосла́в, а *m.* Yugoslav.
Югосла́ви|я, и *f.* Yugoslavia.
югосла́в|ка, ки *f. of* ⇒~
югосла́вский *adj.* Yugoslav.
юдо́л|ь, и *f.* (*arch.*) valley; **ю. пла́ча, ю. печа́ли, земна́я ю.** 'vale of tears'.
юдофо́б, а *m.* anti-Semite.
юдофо́бств|о, а *nt.* anti-Semitism.
ю́жа́н|ин, ина, *pl.* **~е, ~** *m.* southerner.
ю́жн|ее *comp. of* ⇒**~ый; ю. Ло́ндона** to the south of London.
южноамерика́н|ец, ца *m.* South American.
южноамерика́н|ка, ки *f. of* ⇒**~ец**
южноамерика́нский *adj.* South American.
южноафрика́н|ец, ца *m.* South African.
южноафрика́н|ка, ки *f. of* ⇒**~ец**
Ю́жно-Африка́нск|ая Респу́блик|а, ~ой ~и *f.* Republic of South Africa.
южноафрика́нский *adj.* South African.
ю́жный *adj.* south, southern; **Ю́жная А́фрика** South Africa; **Ю. по́люс** South Pole; **Ю. поля́рный круг** antarctic circle; **ю. темпера́мент** (*fig.*) southern temperament.
Ю́жн|ый океа́н, ~ого ~а *m.* the Antarctic Ocean.
ю́зом *adv.* skidding, in a skid.
ю́кк|а, и *f.* (*bot.*) yucca.
юл|а́, ы́ 1 *f.* (*игрушка*) top (*child's toy*). **2** *m.* & *f.* (*coll.*) (*о человеке*) fidget. **3** *f.* (*zool.*) woodlark.
юл|и́ть, ю́, и́шь *impf.* (*coll.*) **1** (*суетиться*) to fuss, fidget. **2** (**пе́ред** + *i.*) (*лебезить*) to play up (to). **3** (*хитрить*) to be evasive.
ю́мор, а *m.* humour (*Br.*), humor (*US*); **чу́вство ~а** a sense of humour (*Br.*), humor (*US*).
юморе́ск|а, и *f.* (*mus., liter.*) humoresque.
юмори́ст, а *m.* humorist.
юмори́стик|а, и *f.* (*collect.*) humour (*Br.*), humor (*US*).
юмористи́ческий *adj.* humorous, comic, funny.
юмори́ст|ка, ки *f. of* ⇒~
ю́нг|а, и *m.* cabin boy; sea cadet.
ЮНЕ́СКО *f. indecl.* UNESCO (*abbr. of* United Nations Educational, Scientific and Cultural Organization — *Организа́ция Объединённых На́ций по вопро́сам образова́ния, нау́ки и культу́ры*).
юн|е́ц, ца́ *m.* (*coll.*) youth.
юнио́р, а *m.* (*sport*) junior.
юнио́р|ка, ки *f. of* ⇒~
ЮНИСЕ́Ф *m. indecl.* UNICEF (*abbr. of* United Nations International Children's Emergency Fund — *Де́тский фонд Организа́ции Объединённых На́ций*).
ю́нкер, а *m.* (*hist.*) **1** (*pl.* **~а́, ~о́в**) (*воспитанник*) cadet. **2** (*pl.* **~ы, ~ов**) (*дворянин*) Junker (*Prussian landowner*).
ю́нкер|ский *adj. of* ⇒~
ю́ност|ь, и *f.* youth (*age*).
ю́нош|а, и *m.* youth (*person*).
ю́ношеский *adj.* youthful.
ю́ношеств|о, а *nt.* **1** (*юность*) youth (*age*). **2** (*collect.*) youth, young people.
ю́н|ый (~, ~а́, ~о) *adj.* **1** young; **теа́тр ~ого зри́теля** young people's theatre (*Br.*), theater (*US*). **2** (*свойственный молодости*) youthful.
юпи́тер, а *m.* floodlight.
юр, а *m. only in phr.* **на ~у́** (*i*) (*на открытом месте*) in a high, exposed place, (*ii*) (*fig.*) (*на виду у всех*) in the limelight, in the forefront.
ю́р|а, ы *f.* (*geol.*) Jurassic period.
юриди́ческ|ий *adj.* legal, juridical; **~ая консульта́ция** legal advice office; **~ое лицо́** corporation; **~ие нау́ки** jurisprudence, law; **ю. факульте́т** faculty of law.
юрисди́кци|я, и *f.* jurisdiction.
юриско́нсульт, а *m.* legal adviser.
юриспруде́нци|я, и *f.* jurisprudence, law (*as academic discipline*).
юри́ст, а *m.* legal expert, lawyer.
ю́р|кий (~ок, ~ка́, ~ко) *adj.* **1** quick-moving, brisk. **2** (*fig., coll.*) clever, sharp, smart.
юркн|у́ть, у́, ёшь *pf.* to scamper away, dart away, plunge.
юро́див|ый *adj.* **1** crazy, simple, touched. **2** *as n.* **ю., ~ого** *m.* holy fool (*idiot believed to possess divine gift of prophecy*).
юро́дств|о, а *nt.* **1** craziness, idiocy. **2** (*поступок*) idiotic action.
юро́дств|овать, ую *impf.* to behave like an idiot.
ю́рский *adj.* (*geol.*) Jurassic.

ю́рт|а, ы *f.* yurt (*nomad's tent in Central Asia*).

Ю́рьев *adj.*: **Ю. день** St George's Day; **вот тебе́ и Ю. день!** here's a how d'ye do!

юс, а, *pl.* **~ы́** *m.* (*ling.*) yus (*name of two letters originally representing nasal vowels in Old Church Slavonic*); **юс большо́й** large 'yus'; **юс ма́лый** little 'yus'.

юстир|ова́ть, у́ю *impf. and pf.* to adjust, regulate (*instruments*).

юсти́ци|я, и *f.* justice.

ют, а *m.* (*naut.*) quarter-deck.

ю|ти́ться, чу́сь, ти́шься *impf.* to huddle (together); (*иметь пристанище*) to take shelter.

ю́фт|евый *adj. of* A**~ь**

юфт|ь, и *f.* yuft, Russia leather.

юфт|яно́й = **~евый**

Я я

я, меня́, мне, мной (мно́ю), обо мне 1 *pers. pron.* I (me); **я не я** (*coll.*) it's nothing to do with me; **(я) не я бу́ду, е́сли не добью́сь от него́ извине́ния** I'll damn well see that I get an apology from him. **2** *n.; nt. indecl.* the self, the ego; **второ́е я** alter ego.

я́бед|а, ы *f. and c.g.* **1** *f.* (*obs.*) (*клевета*) slander. **2** *c.g.* = **~ник**

я́бедник, а *m.* (*coll.*) informer, tell-tale.

я́беднича|ть, ю *impf.* (*of* ⇒**на~**) (**на**+*a.*; *coll.*) to inform (on), tell tales (about).

я́блок|о, а, *pl.* **~и, ~** *nt.* apple; **глазно́е я.** eyeball; **в ~ах** (*о масти животного*) dappled; **я. раздо́ра** bone of contention; **~у не́где упа́сть** there isn't room to swing a cat.

я́блон|евый *adj. of* ⇒**~я; я. цвет** apple blossom.

я́блон|ный *adj.* = **~евый**

я́блон|я, и *f.* apple-tree.

я́блочк|о, а *nt.* **1** *dim. of* ⇒**я́блоко. 2** (*на мишени*) bull's eye.

я́бло|чный *adj. of* ⇒**~ко**

Я́в|а, ы *f.* Java.

ява́н|ец, ца *m.* Javan(ese).

ява́н|ка, ки *f. of* ⇒**~ец**

ява́нский *adj.* Javan; Javanese.

яв|и́ть, лю́, ~́ишь *pf.* (*of* ⇒**~ля́ть**) to show, display; **я. (собо́й) приме́р** (+*g.*) to give an example (of), display.

яв|и́ться, лю́сь, ~́ишься *pf.* (*of* ⇒**~ля́ться**) **1** (*прийти по вызову*) to appear, present o.s.; to report; **я. в суд** to appear before the court; **я. на слу́жбу** to report for duty; **я. с пови́нной** to give o.s. up. **2** (*прибыть*) to turn up, arrive, show up. **3** (*возникнуть*) to arise, occur; **у меня́ появи́лась блестя́щая мысль** I had a brilliant idea; **~и́лся удо́бный слу́чай** a suitable opportunity presented itself.

я́вк|а, и *f.* **1** (*присутствие*) appearance, attendance; **я. в суд** appearance in court. **2** (*место*) secret rendezvous; (*знак*) signal for secret rendezvous.

явле́ни|е, я *nt.* **1** phenomenon; (*событие*) occurrence; **стихи́йное я.** natural calamity. **2** (*theatr.*) scene.

явле́нный *adj.* (*relig.*) appearing miraculously (*esp. of icons*).

явля́|ть, ю *impf. of* ⇒**яви́ть**

явля́|ться, юсь *impf.* **1** *impf. of* ⇒**яви́ться. 2** (*impf. only*) (+*i.*) (*быть*) to be; to represent; **э́то ~ется кощу́нством** this is blasphemy.

я́вно[1] *adv.* manifestly, patently; obviously.

я́вно[2] *as pred.* it is manifest, patent; it is obvious.

я́в|ный (~ен, ~на) *adj.* **1** (*открытый*) manifest, patent; overt. **2** (*очевидный*) obvious.

я́вор, а *m.* sycamore (*tree*).

я́вор|овый *adj. of* ⇒**~**

я́вочн|ый *adj.* **1** *adj. of* ⇒**я́вка** 2; **~ая кварти́ра** secret rendezvous. **2** (*mil.*) reporting, recruiting; **я. пункт** reporting point (*for conscripts*); **я. уча́сток** recruiting office. **3**: **~ым поря́дком** on the spur of the moment, without prior arrangement.

я́вствен|ный (~, ~на) *adj.* clear, distinct.

я́вств|овать, ует *impf.* to be clear, apparent, obvious; to follow (*logically*).

яв|ь, и *f.* reality.

ягдта́ш, а *m.* game-bag.

я́гел|ь, я *m.* (*bot.*) reindeer moss.

ягн|ёнок, ёнка, *pl.* **~я́та, ~я́т** *m.* lamb.

ягн|и́ться, и́тся *impf.* (*of* ⇒**о~**) to lamb.

ягня́тник, а *m.* (*zool.*) lammergeyer.

я́год|а, ы *f.* berry; (*collect.*) soft fruit; **ви́нная я.** dried fig; **пойти́ по ~ы** to go berry-picking; **одного́ по́ля я.** soul-mate.

я́годиц|а, ы *f.* buttock.

я́годи|чный *adj. of* ⇒**~ца**

я́годник, а *m.* **1** (*место*) berry plantation. **2** (*растение*) berry bush. **3** (*coll.*) (*человек*) berry-picker.

я́год|ный *adj. of* ⇒**~а**

ягуа́р, а *m.* jaguar.

яд, а (у) *m.* poison; venom (*also fig.*).

я́дерн|ый *adj.* **1** (*phys.*) nuclear; **~ое расщепле́ние** nuclear fission; **я. реа́ктор** nuclear reactor; **~ая фи́зика** nuclear physics. **2** *adj. of* ⇒**ядро́**

я́дерщик, а *m.* (*coll.*) nuclear scientist.

ядови́т|ый (~, ~а) *adj.* **1** poisonous; toxic; **я. газ** poison gas; **~ая змея́** poisonous snake. **2** (*fig.*) (*человек, замечание*) venomous, malicious.

ядохимика́т, а *m.* (*agric.*) (chemical) pesticide.

ядрён|ый (~, ~а) *adj.* (*coll.*) **1** (*орех*) having a large kernel; (*сочный*) juicy; (*напиток*) strong, hearty. **2** (*fig.*) (*человек*) healthy, vigorous. **3** (*fig.*) (*воздух*) fresh, bracing; (*мороз*) hard.

ядр|о́, а́, *pl.* **~́а, я́дер, ~́ам** *nt.* **1** (*ореха*) kernel; (*древесины, Земли*) core. **2** (*phys., biol.*) nucleus. **3** (*основная группа*) main body (*of a unit, group*). **4** (*hist., mil.*) ball, shot. **5** (*sport*) shot; **толка́ние ~а́** putting the shot.

я́зв|а, ы *f.* **1** ulcer, sore; **я. желу́дка** stomach ulcer. **2** (*fig.*) (*вред*) plague, curse. **3** (*fig., coll.*) (*человек*) malicious person; (*подонки*) scum.

я́звенн|ый *adj.* ulcerous; **~ая боле́знь** stomach ulcer.

я́звин|а, ы *f.* **1** (*coll.*) (*выбоина*) indentation, pit. **2** (*obs.*) (*язва*) ulcer.

язви́тел|ьный (~ен, ~ьна) *adj.* caustic, biting, sarcastic.

язв|и́ть, лю́, и́шь *impf.* (*of* ⇒**съ~**) **1** (*obs.*) (*причинять боль кому-н.*) to wound; to sting. **2** (*говорить язвительно*) to speak, say sarcastically; **я. на чей-н. счёт** to be sarcastic at s.o.'s expense.

язы́к[1]**, а́,** *pl.* **~и́** *m.* **1** (*anat.*) tongue; **у него́ я. без косте́й** he is too fond of talking; **у него́ что на уме́, то и на ~е́** (*coll.*) he cannot keep his thoughts to himself; **держа́ть я. за зуба́ми, придержа́ть я.** to hold one's tongue; **прикуси́ть я.** (*coll.*) to shut up; **я. у него́ хорошо́ подве́шен** (*coll.*) he has a glib tongue; **распусти́ть я.** (*coll.*) to talk too glibly; **дёргать, тяну́ть кого́-н. за я.** (*coll.*) to make s.o. talk; **сорвало́сь с ~а́** (*fig.*) it slipped out; **лиши́ться ~а́** (*fig.*) to

lose one's tongue; **я. у меня́ не поверну́лся э́то сказа́ть** (*coll.*) I could not bring myself to say it; **чеса́ть, болта́ть ~о́м** (*coll.*) to natter, blather; **я. у меня́ чеса́лся** (*coll.*) I was itching to speak; **я. проглоти́шь** (*coll.*) it makes one's mouth water.
2 (*cul.*) tongue; **копчёный я.** smoked tongue.
3 (*колокола*) clapper.
4 (*mil.*; *coll.*) prisoner who will talk (*will provide information when interrogated*).
5: **морско́й я.** (*zool.*) sole.

язы́к², а́, *pl.* **~и́**, *m.* (*речь*) language (*also fig.*); **владе́ть мно́гими ~а́ми** to know many languages; **говори́ть на ло́маном ру́сском ~е́** to talk in broken Russian; **найти́ о́бщий я.** (*fig.*) to find a common language.

языка́ст|ый (~, ~а) *adj.* (*coll.*) sharp-tongued.

языкове́д, а *m.* linguist, specialist in linguistics.

языкове́дени|е, я *nt.* linguistics.

языкове́д|ческий *adj. of* ⇨**~ение**

языково́й *adj.* linguistic.

языко́вый *adj.* **1** (*anat.*) tongue, lingual. **2** (*cul.*) tongue.

языкозна́ни|е, я *nt.* linguistics.

язы́ческий *adj.* heathen, pagan.

язы́честв|о, а *nt.* heathenism, paganism.

языч|ко́вый *adj. of* ⇨**~о́к; я. инструме́нт** (*mus.*) reed instrument.

язы́чник, а *m.* heathen, pagan.

язы́чни|ца, цы *f. of* ⇨**~к**

язы́|чный *adj. of* ⇨**~к¹ 1**

языч|о́к, ка́ *m.* **1** (*anat.*) uvula. **2** (*mus.*) reed. **3** (*боти́нка*) tongue; (*замка́*) catch. **4** *dim. of* ⇨**язы́к**

яз|ь, я́ *m.* ide (*fish of carp family*).

я́ичк|о, а *pl.* **~и** *nt.* **1** (*anat.*) testicle. **2** *dim. of* ⇨**яйцо́**

яи́чник, а *m.* (*anat.*) ovary.

яи́чниц|а, ы *f.* (*cul.*) fried eggs (*also* **я.-глазу́нья**); **я.-болту́нья** scrambled eggs.

яи́чн|ый *adj. of* ⇨**яйцо́; я. бело́к** white of eggs; **я. желто́к** yolk of egg; **я. порошо́к** dried egg(s); **~ая скорлупа́** egg-shell.

яйцеви́д|ный (~ен, ~на) *adj.* egg-shaped, oval.

яйцево́д, а *m.* (*anat.*) oviduct.

яйцекле́тк|а, и *f.* (*biol.*) ovule.

яйцеро́дный *adj.* (*zool.*) oviparous.

яйц|о́, а́, *pl.* **~а, яи́ц, ~ам** *nt.* **1** egg; (*biol.*) ovum; **нести́ ~а** to lay eggs; **я. всмя́тку** soft-boiled, lightly-boiled egg; **я. вкруту́ю** hard-boiled egg; **я. в мешо́чек** medium-boiled egg. **2** (*pl., coll.*) (*у мужчи́ны*) balls, nuts (= *testicles*).

як, а *m.* yak.

якоби́н|ец, ца *m.* (*hist., pol.*) Jacobin.

якоби́н|ский *adj. of* ⇨**~ец**

я́кобы 1 *conj.* (*expr. doubt about validity of another's statement*) (*что*) that; **говоря́т, я. он у́мер** they say (= *they claim*) that he has died. **2** *conj.* (*как бу́дто*) as if, as though; **он вообрази́л, я. его́ произвели́ в генера́лы** he imagined he had been made a general. **3** *particle* (*мни́мо*) supposedly, allegedly; **мы посмотре́ли э́ту я. стра́шную карти́ну** we have seen this supposedly terrifying film.

я́кор|ный *adj. of* ⇨**~ь; ~ная лебёдка** capstan; **~ное ме́сто, ~ная стоя́нка** anchorage.

я́кор|ь, я, *pl.* **~я́, ~е́й** *m.* **1** (*naut.*) anchor; **я. спасе́ния** (*fig.*) sheet-anchor; **стать на я.** to anchor; **бро́сить я.** to cast, drop anchor; **стоя́ть на ~е** to ride at anchor; **сня́ться с ~я** to weigh anchor. **2** (*electr.*) armature; rotor.

яку́т, а *m.* Yakut.

яку́т|ка, ки *f. of* ⇨**~**

яку́тский *adj.* Yakut.

якша́|ться, юсь *impf.* (**с** + *i.*; *coll.*) to consort (with), hobnob (with).

ял, а *m.* yawl.

я́лик, а *m.* skiff, dinghy; yawl.

я́лове|ть, ет *impf.* to be barren, dry (*of cows*).

я́ловый *adj.* barren, dry (*of cows*).

Я́лт|а, ы *f.* Yalta.

я́м|а, ы *f.* **1** pit, hole; **возду́шная я.** air pocket; **выгребна́я я.** cesspit; **оркестро́вая я.** orchestra pit; **у́гольная я.** coal bunker; **рыть кому́-н. ~у** (*fig.*) to lay a trap for s.o. **2** (*coll.*) (*впа́дина*) hollow. **3** (*obs.*) (*тюрьма́*) prison.

яма́|ец, йца *m.* Jamaican.

Яма́йк|а, и *f.* Jamaica.

яма́йский *adj.* Jamaican; **я. ром** Jamaica rum.

ямб, а *m.* (*liter.*) iambus, iambic verse.

ямби́ческий *adj.* iambic.

я́мк|а, и *f. dim. of* ⇨**я́ма; я. на щека́х** dimple.

ямщи́к, а́ *m.* coachman.

янва́р|ский *adj. of* ⇨**~ь**

янва́р|ь, я́ *m.* January.

я́нки *m. indecl.* Yankee.

янта́рный *adj.* amber.

янта́р|ь, я́ *m.* amber.

Янцзы́ *f. indecl.* the Yangtze (*river*).

янычáр, а *m.* (*hist.*) janissary.

япо́н|ец, ца *m.* Japanese.

Япо́ни|я, и *f.* Japan.

япо́н|ка, ки *f. of* ⇨**~ец**

япо́нский *adj.* Japanese; **я. лак** japan.

яр, а, о ~е, на ~у́ *m.* **1** (*крутой бе́рег*) steep bank; (*склон овра́га*) slope (*of ravine*). **2** (*овра́г*) ravine.

ярд, а *m.* yard (*measure*).

яре́мн|ый *adj. of* ⇨**ярмо́; ~ая ве́на** (*anat.*) jugular vein.

яр|и́ться, ю́сь, и́шься *impf.* (*obs., coll.*) to rage, be in a fury.

я́рк|а, и *f.* young ewe (*up to first lambing*).

я́р|кий (~ок, ~ка́, ~ко) *adj.* **1** bright (*of light, colours, etc.*). **2** (*fig.*) (*впечатля́ющий*) colourful (*Br.*), colorful (*US*), striking; (*живо́й*) vivid, graphic; **~кая карти́на** graphic picture; **я. приме́р** striking, glaring example. **3** (*fig.*) (*блестя́щий*) brilliant, outstanding; impressive; **~кая речь** brilliant speech; **я. тала́нт** outstanding talent.

я́ркост|ь, и *f.* **1** brightness. **2** (*fig.*) (*жи́вость*) vividness. **3** (*блеск*) brilliance.

ярлы́к, а́ *m.* **1** label, tag. **2** (*fig.*) label; **прикле́ить я. кому́-н.** to pin a label on s.o.

я́рмарк|а, и *f.* (trade) fair.

я́рмар|очный *adj. of* ⇨**~ка**

ярм|о́, а́, *pl.* **~а** *nt.* yoke (*also fig.*); **сбро́сить с себя́ я.** (*fig.*) to cast off the yoke.

яровиза́ци|я, и *f.* (*agric.*) vernalization.

яровизи́р|овать, ую *impf. and pf.* (*agric.*) to vernalize.

яров|о́й *adj.* (*agric.*) spring; **~а́я пшени́ца** spring wheat; *as n.* **~о́е, ~о́го** *nt.* spring crop.

я́рост|ный (~ен, ~на) *adj.* furious, fierce, savage.

я́рост|ь, и *f.* fury, rage.

я́рус, а *m.* **1** (*theatr.*) circle. **2** (*ряд*) tier.

я́рус|ный *adj.* **1** *adj. of* ⇨**~. 2** (*в ви́де я́русов*) tiered; stepped; graduated.

ярча́йший *superl. of* ⇨**я́ркий**

я́р|че *comp. of* ⇨**~кий**

я́р|ый (~, ~а) *adj.* **1** (*я́ростный*) furious, raging; violent. **2** (*рья́ный*) passionate, fervent.

я́рь-медя́нка, я́ри-медя́нки *f.* (*chem.*) verdigris.

я́с|ельный *adj. of* ⇨**~ли**

я́сен|евый *adj. of* ⇨**~ь**

я́сен|ь, я *m.* ash-tree.

я́сл|и, ей *no sg.* **1** (*корму́шка*) manger, crib (*for cattle*). **2** (*де́тские*) crèche (*Br.*), day nursery.

ясне́|ть, ет *impf.* to become clear(er).

я́сн|о¹ *adv. of* ⇨**~ый**

я́сно² *as pred.* **1** (*о пого́де*) it is fine. **2** (*fig.*) it is clear. **3** (*as affirmative particle*) (*да; по́нял*) yes, of course.

ясновиде́ни|е, я *nt.* clairvoyance.

ясновид|е́ц, ца *m.* clairvoyant.

ясновидя́щий *adj.* (*also as n.*) clairvoyant.

я́сност|ь, и *f.* (*но́чи, не́ба*) clearness; (*со́лнца, пого́ды*) brightness; (*зву́ка*) distinctness; (*ду́ха*) serenity; (*fig.*) (*вопро́са*) clarity; (*ре́чи, ума́*) lucidity, preciseness; **внести́ я. во что-н.** to clarify sth.

я́с|ный (~ен, ~на́, ~но) *adj.* **1** (*ночь, не́бо*) clear; (*со́лнце, ме́сяц*) bright; (*пого́да*) fine; **гром средь ~ного не́ба** a bolt from the blue. **2** (*звук, да́льний бе́рег*) distinct. **3** (*глаза́, сча́стье*) serene. **4** (*fig.*) (*вопро́с, наме́рение*) clear, plain; **сде́лать ~ным** to make it clear; **~ное де́ло** of course. **5** (*ум, изложе́ние*) lucid; precise, logical.

я́ств|а, ~ *pl.* (*sg.* **~о, ~а** *nt.*) viands, victuals.

я́стреб, а, *pl.* **~а́** *and* **~ы** *m.* hawk.

ястреби́н|ый *adj. of* ⇨**я́стреб; ~ая охо́та** falconry; **с ~ым взгля́дом** hawk-eyed; **я. нос** hawk nose.

Я

ястреб|óк, ка́ *m.* **1** *dim. of* **⇒я́стреб. 2** (*coll.*) (*самолёт*) fighter (*plane*).

ятага́н, а *m.* yataghan, scimitar.

ят|ь, я *m.* yat' (*name of old Russian letter* **'Ѣ'**, *replaced by* **'е'** *in 1918*); **на я.** (*coll.*) first-class; splendid(ly).

я́хонт, а *m.*: **(кра́сный) я.** ruby; **(си́ний) я.** sapphire.

я́хонт|овый *adj. of* **⇒~**

я́хт|а, ы *f.* yacht.

яхт-клу́б, а *m.* yacht club.

яхтсме́н, а *m.* yachtsman.

яхтсме́нк|а, и *f.* yachtswoman.

яче́ист|ый (~, ~а) *adj.* cellular, porous.

яче́йк|а, и, *g. pl.* **яче́ек** *f.* **1** (*biol.*, *pol.*) cell. **2** (*mil.*) foxhole; slit trench.

яче|я́, и́ *f.* (*biol.*) cell.

я́чий *adj. of* **⇒як**

ячме́н|ный *adj. of* **⇒~ь¹**; **~ное зерно́** barley-corn; **я. отва́р** barley-water; **я. са́хар** barley-sugar.

ячме́н|ь¹, я́ *m.* (*злак*) barley.

ячме́н|ь², я́ *m.* (*на глазу*) sty (*in the eye*).

я́чнев|ый *adj.*: **~ая крупа́** fine-ground barley.

я́шм|а, ы *f.* (*min.*) jasper.

я́шм|овый *adj. of* **⇒~а**

я́щериц|а, ы *f.* lizard.

я́щик, а *m.* **1** box; (*большой*) chest; (*coll.*, *joc.*) (*телевизор*) the box (= *television*); **откла́дывать в до́лгий я.** (*fig.*) to shelve, put off. **2** (*выдвижной*) drawer. **3** (*fig.*) (*номерное учреждение*) hush-hush institution (*designated by post-office box number*).

я́щи|чный *adj. of* **⇒~к**

я́щур, а *m.* foot-and-mouth disease.

я́щур|ный *adj.* **1** *adj. of* **⇒~. 2** infected with foot-and-mouth disease.

Aa

A^{1} /eɪ/ *letter*: **from ~ to Z** от нача́ла до конца́; **he knows the subject from ~ to Z** он зна́ет э́тот предме́т доскона́льно; **~ road** магистра́льная доро́га, магистра́ль; **A1** *adj.* (*coll.*) первокла́ссный; **A-bomb** а́томная бо́мба.

A^{2} /eɪ/ *n.* **1** (*mus.*) ля (*nt. indecl.*); **she reached top ~** она́ взяла́ ве́рхнее ля. **2** (*acad. mark*) «отли́чно», пятёрка; **he got an ~ in physics** он получи́л «отли́чно» *or* пятёрку по фи́зике.

a /ə/, /eɪ/, **an** /æn/, /ən/ *indef. art.* **1** *not usu. translated*: **it's an elephant** э́то слон.
2 (**~** *certain*): **~ Mr. Smith rang** звони́л не́кий господи́н Смит; **in ~ sense** в како́м-то смы́сле; **an old friend of mine** оди́н мой ста́рый знако́мый.
3 (*one*; *the same*): **all of ~ size** все одного́ разме́ра; все одина́ковой величины́.
4 (*distributive, in each*) в + *a.*; **twice ~ week** два ра́за в неде́лю; **10 miles an hour** де́сять миль в час; (*for each*) за + *a.*; **10p ~ pound** 10 пе́нсов за фунт; (*to each*): **he gave out £5 ~ person** он вы́дал ка́ждому по пять фу́нтов; (*from each*) с + *g.*; **they charged £1 ~ head** они́ взя́ли по фу́нту с челове́ка.

AA (*abbr. of* ***Automobile Association***) (*Br.*) Автомоби́льная ассоциа́ция.

AAA (*abbr. of* ***American Automobile Association***) (*US*) Америка́нская автомоби́льная ассоциа́ция.

aardvark /ˈɑːdvɑːk/ *n.* трубкозу́б.

aback /əˈbæk/ *adv.*: **we were taken ~ by the news** но́вость нас порази́ла; **I was taken ~ by his audacity** я растеря́лся от его́ на́глости.

abacus /ˈæbəkəs/ *n.* (*pl.* **~es**) счёт|ы (*pl., g.* -ов).

abandon /əˈbænd(ə)n/ *n.* самозабве́ние; **with ~** самозабве́нно.
● *v.t.* **1** (*forsake, desert*) пок|ида́ть, -и́нуть; ост|авля́ть, -а́вить; **he ~ed his wife** он оста́вил свою́ жену́; **~ ship!** поки́нуть кора́бль! **2** (*renounce*) отка́з|ываться, -а́ться от + *g.*; **we must ~ the idea** мы должны́ отказа́ться от э́той иде́и; **they had ~ed all hope** они́ оста́вили вся́кую наде́жду.
3 (*discontinue*) прекра|ща́ть, -ти́ть; **the search was ~ed** по́иски бы́ли прекращены́. **4** (*surrender*) ост|авля́ть, -а́вить; **the town was ~ed to the enemy** го́род был оста́влен врагу́; **she ~ed herself to grief** она́ предала́сь своему́ го́рю.

abandoned /əˈbænd(ə)nd/ *adj.* **1** (*forsaken, deserted*) оста́вленный, поки́нутый; **an ~ child** бро́шенный ребёнок. **2** (*profligate*) распу́тный.

abandonment /əˈbændənmənt/ *n.* **1** (*of a belief, lawsuit, right*) отка́з (от + *g.*). **2** (*neglect*) забро́шенность. **3** (*of a project*) прекраще́ние. **4**: **~ of a ship** ухо́д с корабля́.

abase /əˈbeɪs/ *v.t.* ун|ижа́ть, -и́зить.

abasement /əˈbeɪsmənt/ *n.* униже́ние.

abash /əˈbæʃ/ *v.t.* сму|ща́ть, -ти́ть; **she felt ~ed** она́ была́ смущена́.

abate /əˈbeɪt/ *v.i.* (*diminish*) ум|еньша́ться, -е́ньшиться; (*weaken*) ослаб|ева́ть, -е́ть; (*of storm, epidemic etc.*) ут|иха́ть, -и́хнуть.

abatement /əˈbeɪtmənt/ *n.* **1** (*reduction*) уменьше́ние; (*mitigation*) смягче́ние; (*weakening*) ослабле́ние; (*lowering*) сниже́ние; **noise ~** сниже́ние у́ровня шу́ма; (*of storm etc.*) затиха́ние. **2** (*deduction*) ски́дка. **3** (*leg.*) аннули́рование, отме́на.

abattoir /ˈæbəˌtwɑː(r)/ *n.* скотобо́йня.

abbess /ˈæbɪs/ *n.* аббати́са.

abbey /ˈæbɪ/ *n.* (*pl.* **~s**) абба́тство.

abbot /ˈæbət/ *n.* абба́т.

abbreviate /əˈbriːvɪˌeɪt/ *v.t.* сокра|ща́ть, -ти́ть; **'ampere' is ~d to A** «ампе́р» сокращённо обознача́ется че́рез «А»; **~d** сокращённый.

abbreviation /əˌbriːvɪˈeɪʃ(ə)n/ *n.* сокраще́ние, аббревиату́ра.

ABC^{1} /ˌeɪbiːˈsiː/ *n.* (*alphabet*) алфави́т, а́збука; **it's as easy as ~** э́то (про́сто) как два́жды два — четы́ре; (*reading primer*) буква́рь (*m.*); а́збука; (*fig., rudiments*) а́збука; осно́вы (*f. pl.*).

ABC^{2} (*abbr. of* ***American Broadcasting Company***) (*US*) Эй-би-си́ (*nt. indecl.*).

abdicate /ˈæbdɪˌkeɪt/ *v.t.* отка́з|ываться, -а́ться от + *g.*; **~ the throne** (*also* **~** *v.i.*) отр|ека́ться, -е́чься от престо́ла.

abdication /ˌæbdɪˈkeɪʃ(ə)n/ *n.* отка́з (*от чего*); отрече́ние (от престо́ла).

abdomen /ˈæbdəmən/ *n.* брюшна́я по́лость; живо́т.

abdominal /æbˈdɒmɪn(ə)l/ *adj.* брюшно́й; **~ pain** боль в животе́; **~ wound** ране́ние в живо́т.

abduct /əbˈdʌkt/ *v.t.* пох|ища́ть, -и́тить.

abduction /əbˈdʌkʃ(ə)n/ *n.* похище́ние.

abductor /əbˈdʌktə(r)/ *n.* похити́тель (*m.*).

aberrant /əˈberənt/ *adj.* анорма́льный.

aberration /ˌæbəˈreɪʃ(ə)n/ *n.* **1** (*error of judgement or conduct*) заблужде́ние; **mental ~** помраче́ние рассу́дка. **2** (*deviation*) отклоне́ние от но́рмы, аберра́ция.

abet /əˈbet/ *v.t.* (**abetted, abetting**) подстрека́ть (*impf.*) к + *d.*; **he was ~ted by X** его́ посо́бником был X; **~ s.o. in a crime** соде́йствовать (*impf.*) кому́-н. в соверше́нии преступле́ния; **~ a crime** соде́йствовать (*impf.*) преступле́нию.

abettor /əˈbetə(r)/ *n.* посо́бник.

abeyance /əˈbeɪəns/ *n.*: **in ~** приостано́вленный; **the matter is in ~** де́ло вре́менно приостано́влено.

abhor /əbˈhɔː(r)/ *v.t.* (**abhorred, abhorring**) пита́ть (*impf.*) (*or* испы́т|ывать, -а́ть) омерзе́ние, отвраще́ние к + *d.*; **nature ~s a vacuum** приро́да не те́рпит пустоты́.

abhorrence /əbˈhɒrəns/ *n.* омерзе́ние, отвраще́ние; **hold in ~; have an ~ of** пита́ть (*impf.*) отвраще́ние к + *d.*

abhorrent /əbˈhɒrənt/ *adj.* омерзи́тельный, отврати́тельный; **the very idea is ~ to me** мне проти́вно да́же ду́мать об э́том.

abidance /ə'baɪdəns/ *n.*: **~ by the rules** соблюде́ние пра́вил.

abide /ə'baɪd/ *v.t.* терпе́ть (*impf.*); выноси́ть (*impf.*); **I cannot ~ him** я не могу́ терпе́ть его́.

● *v.i.* **1** (*remain*) пребыва́ть (*impf.*). **2**: **~ by** (*comply with*) соблю|да́ть, -сти́; приде́рживаться (*impf.*) + *g.*; **~ by the law** соблюда́ть (*impf.*) зако́н.

abiding /ə'baɪdɪŋ/ *adj.* постоя́нный, неизме́нный.

ability /ə'bɪlɪtɪ/ *n.* **1** (*capacity in general*) спосо́бность; **to the best of one's ~** по ме́ре спосо́бностей; **he shows an ~ for music** он проявля́ет музыка́льные спосо́бности; (*knowing how*) уме́ние; (*mental competence*) спосо́бность; **a man of ~** спосо́бный челове́к. **2** (*pl., gifts*) спосо́бности (*f. pl.*); **natural ~** врождённые спосо́бности.

abject /'æbdʒekt/ *adj.* (*humble*) уни́женный; **an ~ apology** уни́женная мольба́ о проще́нии; (*craven*): **~ fear** малоду́шный страх; (*despicable*) презре́нный; (*pitiful, wretched*) жа́лкий; **in ~ poverty** в кра́йней нищете́.

abject|ion /əb'dʒekʃ(ə)n/, **-ness** /'æbdʒektnɪs/ *nn.* униже́ние; уни́женность.

abjuration /,æbdʒʊ'reɪʃ(ə)n/ *n.* (кля́твенное) отрече́ние; отка́з (*от чего*).

abjure /əb'dʒʊə(r)/ *v.t.* (*renounce on oath*) кля́твенно отр|ека́ться, -е́чься от + *g.*; (*forswear*) отр|ека́ться, -е́чься от + *g.*; отка́з|ываться, -а́ться от + *g.*

ablative /'æblətɪv/ *n.* аблати́в, отложи́тельный/твори́тельный паде́ж; **~ absolute** аблати́в абсолю́тный.

● *adj.* аблати́вный.

ablaze /ə'bleɪz/ *pred. adj.*: **to be ~** пыла́ть, полыха́ть (*both impf.*); **the fire was soon ~** ого́нь вско́ре полыха́л; **the buildings were ~** зда́ния полыха́ли *or* пыла́ли; **her cheeks were ~ with anger** её щёки пыла́ли гне́вом; **streets ~ with light** зали́тые огня́ми у́лицы.

● *adv.*: **set a house ~** подж|ига́ть, -е́чь дом.

able /'eɪb(ə)l/ *adj.* (**abler, ablest**) **1**: **be ~ to** мочь, с-; быть в состоя́нии; **will you be ~ to come?** вы смо́жете прийти́?; (*have the strength or power to*): **he was not ~ to walk any farther** он был не в си́лах (*or* не в состоя́нии) идти́ да́льше; (*know how to*) уме́ть (*impf.*); **he is ~ to swim** он уме́ет пла́вать. **2** (*skilful*) уме́лый; (*capable*) спосо́бный; **~ seaman** матро́с пе́рвого кла́сса.

● *cpd.* **~-bodied** *adj.* здоро́вый, кре́пкий; (*mil.*) го́дный к вое́нной слу́жбе.

ablution /ə'blu:ʃ(ə)n/ *n.* (*usu. pl., act of washing o.s.*) обмове́ние; **perform one's ~s** соверш|а́ть, -и́ть обмове́ние.

abnegate /'æbnɪ,geɪt/ *v.t.* (*renounce*) отр|ека́ться, -е́чься от + *g.*; (*deny o.s.*) отка́з|ывать, -а́ть себе́ в + *p.*

abnegation /,æbnɪ'geɪʃ(ə)n/ *n.* (*renunciation*) отка́з, отрече́ние (*от чего*); (*self-sacrifice*) самоотрече́ние.

abnormal /æb'nɔ:m(ə)l/ *adj.* ненорма́льный; (*deviating from type*) анома́льный.

abnormality /,æbnɔ:'mælɪtɪ/ *n.* ненорма́льность; анома́лия.

aboard /ə'bɔ:d/ *adv.* **1** (*on a ship or aircraft*) на борту́; (*on a train*) в по́езде. **2** (*on to a ship or aircraft*) на́ борт; (*on to a train*) в по́езд; **all ~!** поса́дка зака́нчивается!; (*rail.*) по ваго́нам!; **go ~** сади́ться, сесть (*a ship, train* на кора́бль, на по́езд; *a plane* в самолёт); **take ~** взять (*pf.*) на́ борт.

● *prep.*: **~ ship** на борт(у́) корабля́.

abode /ə'bəʊd/ *n.* (*dwelling-place*) жили́ще; **of no fixed ~** без постоя́нного местожи́тельства.

abolish /ə'bɒlɪʃ/ *v.t.* отмен|я́ть, -и́ть.

abolition /,æbə'lɪʃ(ə)n/ *n.* отме́на; **the ~ of capital punishment** отме́на сме́ртной ка́зни.

abolitionism /,æbə'lɪʃənɪz(ə)m/ *n.* аболициони́зм.

abolitionist /,æbə'lɪʃənɪst/ *n.* аболициони́ст.

abominable /ə'bɒmɪnəb(ə)l/ *adj.* отврати́тельный, ме́рзкий; **the food was ~** еда́ была́ отврати́тельная, корми́ли отврати́тельно; **the A~ Snowman** сне́жный челове́к, йе́ти (*m. indecl.*).

abominate /ə'bɒmɪ,neɪt/ *v.t.* пита́ть (*impf.*) отвраще́ние к + *d.*, омерзе́ние к + *d.*

abomination /ə,bɒmɪ'neɪʃ(ə)n/ *n.* (*detestation*) отвраще́ние, омерзе́ние; (*detestable thing*) ме́рзость; **this building is an ~** э́то зда́ние — ме́рзость.

aboriginal /,æbə'rɪdʒɪn(ə)l/ *n.* = **aborigine**

● *adj.* тузе́мный, коренно́й; (*primitive*) первобы́тный.

aborigine /,æbə'rɪdʒɪnɪ/ *n.* тузе́м|ец (*fem.* -ка); абориге́н; коренно́й жи́тель.

abort /ə'bɔ:t/ *v.t.* **1** (*carry out abortion of*): **she should have had the baby ~ed** она́ должна́ была́ сде́лать або́рт. **2** (*fig., terminate or cancel prematurely*) приостан|а́вливать, -ови́ть.

● *v.i.* **1** (*of a person*) выки́дывать, вы́кинуть. **2** (*fig., come to nothing*) срыва́ться, сорва́ться.

abortion /ə'bɔ:ʃ(ə)n/ *n.* **1** (*miscarriage*) або́рт, вы́кидыш; **backstreet ~** подпо́льный або́рт; **get, have an ~** (*by surgery*) де́лать, с- або́рт; **she had an ~** она́ сде́лала або́рт. **2** (*freak*) уро́д. **3** (*failure*) неуда́ча. **4** (*discontinuation*) прекраще́ние.

abortionist /ə'bɔ:ʃənɪst/ *n.* подпо́льный акуше́р.

abortive /ə'bɔ:tɪv/ *adj.* (*fig.*) мертворождённый, неуда́вшийся.

abound /ə'baʊnd/ *v.i.* **1** (*exist in large numbers or quantities*) быть в изоби́лии; изоби́ловать (*impf.*). **2**: **~ in** (*be rich in*) изоби́ловать (*impf.*) + *i.*; **the country ~s in oil** страна́ бога́та не́фтью; **~ with** (*teem with*) кише́ть (*impf.*) + *i.*

about /ə'baʊt/ *adv.* **1** (*here and there*): **don't leave your clothes ~** не оставля́йте свое́й оде́жды где попа́ло. **2** (*in the vicinity; in circulation*) вокру́г, круго́м; **there are a lot of soldiers ~** круго́м мно́го солда́т; **is he anywhere ~?** он где́-нибудь здесь?; **there are rumours** (*Br.*), **rumors** (*US*) **~** хо́дят слу́хи; **up and ~** на нога́х; **she is too ill to get ~** она́ так больна́, что не мо́жет выходи́ть. **3** (*to face the other way*): **~ turn!** (*mil.*) круго́м!; (*alternately*): **turn and turn ~** по о́череди. **4** (*almost*) почти́; **that's ~ right** приме́рно так; **dinner is ~ ready** обе́д почти́ гото́в; **it's ~ time we went** нам пора́ идти́; **and ~ time too!** давно́ пора́! **5** (*approximately*) о́коло + *g.*; приблизи́тельно; **~ 3 o'clock** о́коло трёх часо́в; **he is ~ your height** он приблизи́тельно ва́шего ро́ста; **it costs ~ 100 roubles** э́то сто́ит о́коло ста рубле́й; **~ a kilogram in weight** ве́сом о́коло килогра́мма; **in ~ half an hour** приме́рно че́рез полчаса́. **6**: **~ to** (*ready to, just going to*): **he was ~ to leave when I arrived** он собира́лся уходи́ть, когда́ я пришёл; **I was ~ to say** я собира́лся сказа́ть; **the train is ~ to leave** по́езд сейча́с тро́нется; **I was just ~ to do so** я как раз собира́лся э́то сде́лать. **7** *For phrasal vv. with* **~**, *see relevant v. entries.*

● *prep.* **1** (*around; near*) вокру́г + *g.*; **the people ~ him** окружа́ющие его́ лю́ди; **somewhere ~ here** где́-то здесь; **he looked ~ him** он огляде́лся вокру́г; **I have no money ~ me** у меня́ нет при себе́ де́нег. **2** (*at or to var. places, in*) по + *d.*; **walk ~ the streets** ходи́ть (*indet.*) по у́лицам. **3** (*fig., in*) в + *p.*; **there was no vanity ~ him** в нём не́ было тщесла́вия. **4** (*concerning*) о + *p.*; насчёт + *g.*; относи́тельно + *g.*; **what are you talking ~?** о чём вы говори́те?; **what ~ dinner?** как насчёт обе́да?; **how ~ a game of cards?** не сыгра́ть ли нам в ка́рты?; **what is it all ~?** в чём де́ло?; **he has called ~ the rent** он зашёл насчёт квартпла́ты; **she is mad ~ him** она́ без ума́ от него́; **much ado ~ nothing** мно́го шу́ма из ничего́; **there is no doubt ~ it** в э́том нет сомне́ния. **5** (*engaged in*): **be ~ one's business** занима́ться (*impf.*) свои́ми дела́ми.

● *cpds.* **~-face, ~-turn** *nn.* (*lit.*) поворо́т круго́м; (*fig.*) ре́зкий поворо́т.

above /ə'bʌv/ *n.*: **the ~** вышеска́занное; вышеупомя́нутое.

● *adj.* (**~-mentioned**) вышеупомя́нутый; (*foregoing*) предыду́щий.

● *adv.* **1** (*overhead; upstairs*) наверху́; **we live in the flat ~** мы живём в кварти́ре этажо́м вы́ше; (*expr. motion*) наве́рх; **from ~** све́рху. **2** (*higher up*) вы́ше. **3** (*in text, speech etc.*) вы́ше; ра́нее.

● *prep.* **1** (*over; higher than*) над + *i.*; **his**

voice was heard ~ the noise его́ го́лос перекрыва́л шум.
2 (*more than*) свы́ше + *g.*; **~ 30 tons** свы́ше 30 тонн.
3 (*fig.*): **~ me in rank** вы́ше меня́ чи́ном; **~ all praise** вы́ше вся́ких похва́л; **he is ~ such base actions** он не спосо́бен на таки́е по́длости; **~ suspicion** вне подозре́ния; **he is getting ~ himself** он начина́ет зазнава́ться; **he is not ~ cheating at cards** он позволя́ет себе́ жу́льничать в ка́ртах; **~ all** пре́жде всего́; са́мое гла́вное; **over and ~** вдоба́вок к + *d.*; **this is ~ my head** э́то вы́ше моего́ понима́ния.
● *cpds.* **~-board** *adj.* (*honourable*) че́стный; (*open, frank*) откры́тый; **~-mentioned** *adj.* вышеупомя́нутый; **~-named** *adj.* вышена́званный.

abracadabra /ˌæbrəkəˈdæbrə/ *n.* абракада́бра.

abrade /əˈbreɪd/ *v.t.* (*skin etc.*) сдира́ть, содра́ть; (*bark*) об|дира́ть, -одра́ть.

abrasion /əˈbreɪʒ(ə)n/ *n.* (*rubbing off*) истира́ние; (*wounded area of skin*) сса́дина.

abrasive /əˈbreɪsɪv/ *n.* абрази́в, абрази́вный материа́л.
● *adj.* абрази́вный; (*fig.*) ре́зкий, колю́чий; **an ~ personality** ре́зкий хара́ктер.

abreast /əˈbrest/ *adv.* в ряд, на одно́й ли́нии; **three ~** по́ трое в ряд; (*fig.*): **~ of events** в ку́рсе собы́тий.

abridge /əˈbrɪdʒ/ *v.t.* **1** (*shorten*) сокра|ща́ть, -ти́ть; **an ~d version** сокращённый вариа́нт. **2** (*curtail*) ограни́чи|вать, -ть.

abridgement /əˈbrɪdʒmənt/ *n.* (*shortening*) сокраще́ние; (*curtailment*) ограниче́ние; (*shortened version of a book*) сокращённое изда́ние; (*summary*) аннота́ция.

abroad /əˈbrɔːd/ *adv.* за грани́цей, за рубежо́м; (*motion*) за грани́цу, за рубе́ж; **from ~** из-за грани́цы, из-за рубежа́; (*fig., in circulation*): **there are rumours** (*Br.*), **rumors** (*US*) **~** хо́дят слу́хи.

abrogate /ˈæbrəˌgeɪt/ *v.t.* отмен|я́ть, -и́ть.

abrogation /ˌæbrəˈgeɪʃ(ə)n/ *n.* отме́на.

abrupt /əˈbrʌpt/ *adj.* **1** (*disconnected*) отры́вистый. **2** (*brusque*) ре́зкий. **3** (*sudden*) внеза́пный. **4** (*steep, precipitous*) круто́й, обры́вистый.

abruptness /əˈbrʌptnɪs/ *n.* отры́вистость; ре́зкость; внеза́пность; крутизна́.

abscess /ˈæbsɪs/ *n.* абсце́сс.

abscond /əbˈskɒnd/ *v.i.* скр|ыва́ться, -ы́ться; **he ~ed with the takings** он с вы́ручкой скры́лся.

abseil /ˈæbseɪl/ *n.* спуск на верёвке.
● *v.i.* спус|ка́ться, -ти́ться на верёвке.

absence /ˈæbs(ə)ns/ *n.* отсу́тствие; **in his ~** в его́ отсу́тствие; **leave of ~** о́тпуск; **~ of mind** рассе́янность; (*lack*): **in the ~ of evidence** за недоста́точностью ули́к.

absent¹ /ˈæbs(ə)nt/ *adj.* **1** (*not present*) отсу́тствующий; **~ without leave** в самово́льной отлу́чке; **be ~** отсу́тствовать (*impf.*); **he was ~ from school** он отсу́тствовал в шко́ле. **2** (*abstracted*) рассе́янный.
● *cpds.* **~-minded** *adj.* рассе́янный; **~-mindedness** *n.* рассе́янность.

absent² /əbˈsent/ *v.t.*: **~ o.s.** отлуч|а́ться, -и́ться.

absentee /ˌæbsənˈtiː/ *n.* отсу́тствующий; **there were six ~s** отсу́тствовало шесть челове́к; бы́ло шесть отсу́тствующих; **~ landlord** владе́лец, сдаю́щий свою́ со́бственность и живу́щий в друго́м ме́сте.

absenteeism /ˌæbsənˈtiːɪz(ə)m/ *n.* (*from work, school*) прогу́л; (*from voting*) абсенте́изм.

absinth(e) /ˈæbsɪnθ/ *n.* (*liqueur*) абсе́нт, полы́нная во́дка.

absolute /ˈæbsəˌluːt/, /ˌljuːt/ *n.* (*phil.*: **the A~**) абсолю́т.
● *adj.* (*perfect*): **~ beauty** соверше́нная красота́; (*pure*): **~ alcohol** чи́стый спирт; (*unconditional*): **~ monarchy** абсолю́тная мона́рхия; (*consummate*): **an ~ ruffian** зако́нченный, абсолю́тный негодя́й; (*indubitable*): **~ proof** несомне́нное, абсолю́тное доказа́тельство; (*gram.*): **~ construction** абсолю́тная констру́кция.

absolutely /ˈæbsəˌluːtlɪ/, /-ˌljuːtlɪ/ *adv.* **1** (*completely*) абсолю́тно; соверше́нно; (*unquestionably*) безусло́вно. **2**: **~!** (*expr. agreement*) безусло́вно/коне́чно!

absolution /ˌæbsəˈluːʃ(ə)n/, /-ˈljuːʃ(ə)n/ *n.* (*forgiveness*) проще́ние; (*eccl.*) отпуще́ние грехо́в.

absolutism /ˈæbsəluːˌtɪz(ə)m/, /-ljuːˌtɪz(ə)m/ *n.* абсолюти́зм.

absolutist /ˈæbsəˌluːtɪst/, /-ˌljuːtɪst/ *n.* абсолюти́ст.
● *adj.* абсолюти́стский.

absolve /əbˈzɒlv/ *v.t.* (*of blame*) призн|ава́ть, -а́ть невино́вным; **he was ~d of all blame** он был при́знан по́лностью невино́вным; (*of sins*) отпус|ка́ть, -ти́ть грехи́ + *d.*; **his sins were ~d** он получи́л отпуще́ние грехо́в; (*of obligation*) освобо|жда́ть, -ди́ть.

absorb /əbˈsɔːb/, /-ˈzɔːb/ *v.t.* **1** (*soak up*) впи́т|ывать, -а́ть. **2** (*fig.*): **~ knowledge** впи́т|ывать, -а́ть зна́ния. **3** (*engross*) погло|ща́ть, -ти́ть; **his business ~s him** он поглощён свои́ми дела́ми; **he was ~ed in reading** он был погружён в чте́ние. **4** (*shock, vibration etc.*) амортизи́ровать (*impf., pf.*).

absorbability /əbˌsɔːbəˈbɪlɪtɪ/, /-ˌzɔːbəˈbɪlɪtɪ/ *n.* поглоща́емость.

absorbable /əbˈsɔːbəb(ə)l/, /-ˈzɔːbəb(ə)l/ *adj.* поглоща́емый.

absorbency /əbˈsɔːbənsɪ/, /-ˈzɔːbənsɪ/ *n.* впи́тывающая спосо́бность.

absorbent /əbˈsɔːbənt/, /-ˈzɔːbənt/ *adj.* вса́сывающий, поглоща́ющий; **~ cotton** (*US*) (гигроскопи́ческая) ва́та.

absorbing /əbˈsɔːbɪŋ/, /-ˈzɔːbɪŋ/ *adj.* (*engrossing*) захва́тывающий.

absorption /əbˈsɔːpʃ(ə)n/, /-ˈzɔːpʃ(ə)n/ *n.* **1** (*soaking up*) впи́тывание. **2** (*engrossment*): **his ~ in his studies** его́ погружённость в заня́тия.

abstain /əbˈsteɪn/ *v.i.* возде́рж|иваться, -а́ться; **he ~ed (from drinking) on principle** он возде́рживался (от спиртно́го) из при́нципа; **the Opposition decided to ~ (from voting)** оппози́ция реши́ла воздержа́ться (от голосова́ния).

abstainer /əbˈsteɪnə(r)/ *n.* (*from drinking*) тре́звенник, непью́щий; (*from voting*) воздержа́вшийся.

abstemious /æbˈstiːmɪəs/ *adj.* возде́ржанный.

abstemiousness /æbˈstiːmɪəsnɪs/ *n.* возде́ржанность.

abstention /əbˈstenʃ(ə)n/ *n.* воздержа́ние (от + *g.*); **the resolution was passed with three ~s** резолю́ция была́ принята́ при трёх воздержа́вшихся.

abstinence /ˈæbstɪnəns/ *n.* воздержа́ние (от + *g.*); (*moderation*) уме́ренность.

abstinent /ˈæbstɪnənt/ *adj.* (*of person*) возде́ржанный; (*not taking alcohol*) непью́щий.

abstract¹ /ˈæbstrækt/ *n.* (*summary*) резюме́ (*indecl.*); (*of dissertation*) рефера́т; **in the ~** абстра́ктно, отвлечённо.
● *adj.* абстра́ктный, отвлечённый; **~ noun** абстра́ктное, отвлечённое и́мя/существи́тельное; **~ art** абстра́ктное иску́сство; **~ artist** абстракциони́ст; **~ expressionism** абстра́ктный экспрессиони́зм.

abstract² /əbˈstrækt/ *v.t.* **1** (*remove, separate*) отдел|я́ть, -и́ть; (*coll., make away with*) утащи́ть (*pf.*). **2** (*divert, e.g. attention*) отвл|ека́ть, -е́чь. **3** (*summarize*) резюми́ровать (*impf., pf.*). **4** (*consider ~ly*) абстраги́ровать (*impf., pf.*).

abstracted /əbˈstræktɪd/ *adj.* заду́мавшийся, рассе́янный.

abstraction /əbˈstrækʃ(ə)n/ *n.* **1** (*withdrawal, removal*) отделе́ние. **2** (*process of thought or idea*) отвлече́ние; абстраги́рование. **3** (*absence of mind*) рассе́янность.

abstruse /əbˈstruːs/ *adj.* замыслова́тый, мудрёный.

abstruseness /əbˈstruːsnɪs/ *n.* замыслова́тость.

absurd /əbˈsɜːd/ *adj.* неле́пый, абсу́рдный; **the Theatre of the A~** теа́тр абсу́рда; **don't be ~!** како́й вздор!; не смеши́те люде́й!; **you look ~ in that hat** в э́той шля́пе у вас неле́пый вид; **he was ~ly generous** он был до абсу́рда щедр.

absurdity /əbˈsɜːdɪtɪ/ *n.* неле́пость, абсу́рд, абсу́рдность; **reduce to ~** дов|оди́ть, -ести́ до абсу́рда.

ABTA /ˈæbtə/ (*abbr. of* ***Association of British Travel Agents***) (*Br.*) Ассоциа́ция брита́нских туристи́ческих аге́нтств.

abundance /əˈbʌnd(ə)ns/ *n.* (*plenty*) изоби́лие; **there was food in ~** еды́ было вдо́воль; (*affluence*): **live in ~** жить в доста́тке; (*superfluity*) избы́ток.

abundant /ə'bʌnd(ə)nt/ *adj.* (из)оби́льный (*чем*); **there is ~ proof** доказа́тельств бо́льше чем доста́точно; **be ~** изоби́ловать (*impf.*); **~ly clear** преде́льно я́сно.

abuse¹ /ə'bju:s/ *n.* **1** (*misuse*) злоупотребле́ние; **~ of confidence** злоупотребле́ние дове́рием; **child ~** (*sexual*) сексуа́льное наси́лие над ребёнком; (*physical*) физи́ческое наси́лие над ребёнком; **drug ~** злоупотребле́ние нарко́тиками; **human rights ~** наруше́ние прав челове́ка; **sexual ~** сексуа́льное уси́лие. **2** (*reviling*) брань; издева́тельство; **term of ~** оскорбле́ние; **he heaped/showered ~ on me** он осы́пал меня́ бра́нью.

abuse² /ə'bju:z/ *v.t.* **1** (*misuse*) злоупотреб|ля́ть, -и́ть + *i.* **2** (*revile*) руга́ть (*impf.*); оскорб|ля́ть, -и́ть.

abusive /ə'bju:sɪv/ *adj.* **1** (*insulting*) оскорби́тельный; (*using curses*) бра́нный, руга́тельный; **~ language** брань, ру́гань. **2** (*cruel*) жесто́кий.

abusiveness /ə'bju:sɪvnɪs/ *n.* оскорби́тельность, брань, ру́гань.

abut /ə'bʌt/ *v.i.* (**abutted, abutting**): **~ on** (*border on*) прилега́ть (*impf.*) к + *d.*; примыка́ть (*impf.*) к + *d.*; (*lean against*) уп|ира́ться, -ере́ться в + *a.*

abutment /ə'bʌtmənt/ *n.* **1** (*junction*) стык. **2** (*part of structure*) пята́; контрфо́рс.

abysmal /ə'bɪzm(ə)l/ *adj.* (*awful*) ужа́сный; **the concert was ~** конце́рт был ужа́сный; (*extreme*): **~ ignorance** кра́йнее неве́жество.

abyss /ə'bɪs/ *n.* бе́здна, про́пасть.

AC (*abbr. of* ***alternating current***) переме́нный ток.

a/c /ə'kaʊnt/ *n.* (*abbr. of* ***account***) счёт.

acacia /ə'keɪʃə/ *n.* ака́ция; **false ~** бе́лая ака́ция.

academia /ˌækə'di:mɪə/ *n.* учёный, нау́чный мир.

academic /ˌækə'demɪk/ *n.* учёный, нау́чный рабо́тник.

● *adj.* академи́ческий, нау́чный; (*unpractical*) академи́чный; нереа́льный.

academician /əˌkædə'mɪʃ(ə)n/ *n.* акаде́мик.

academicism /ˌækə'demɪˌsɪz(ə)m/ *n.* академи́чность.

academy /ə'kædəmɪ/ *n.* акаде́мия; (*police, military, etc.*) учи́лище; (*in Scotland*) сре́дняя шко́ла; **~ of fine arts** акаде́мия изя́щных иску́сств; **military ~** вое́нное учи́лище.

acanthus /ə'kænθəs/ *n.* ака́нт.

a cappella /ˌæ kə'pelə/ *adj. & adv.* (*mus.*) а капе́лла.

accede /æk'si:d/ *v.i.* **1** (*agree, assent*) согла|ша́ться, -си́ться (с + *i.*). **2**: **~ to** (*grant*): **~ to a request** удовлетвор|я́ть, -и́ть про́сьбу; (*take up, enter upon*) вступ|а́ть, -и́ть в + *a.*; **~ to the throne** всходи́ть, взойти́ на престо́л.

accelerate /ək'seləˌreɪt/ *v.t. & i.* уск|оря́ть(ся), -о́рить(ся); (*motoring*) наб|ира́ть, -ра́ть ско́рость.

acceleration /əkˌselə'reɪʃ(ə)n/ *n.* ускоре́ние; **the car has good ~** у автомоби́ля хоро́ший разго́н.

accelerator /ək'seləˌreɪtə(r)/ *n.* (*of car*) акселера́тор; (*phys., etc.*) ускори́тель (*m.*); (*chem.*) катализа́тор.

accent¹ /'æks(ə)nt/, /-sent/ *n.* **1** (*orthographical sign; emphasis*) ударе́ние; акце́нт. **2** (*mode of speech*) акце́нт; **he speaks with a slight ~** он говори́т с лёгким акце́нтом.

accent² /æk'sent/ *v.t.* **1** (*emphasize in speech or fig.*) де́лать, с- ударе́ние/акце́нт на + *p.*; акценти́ровать (*impf.*). **2** (*put written ~s on*) ста́вить, по- ударе́ние на + *a.*

accentuate /æk'sentjʊˌeɪt/ *v.t.* (*lit.*) = **accent²**; (*fig.*) акценти́ровать (*impf.*); подч|ёркивать, -еркну́ть; **the difference was ~d** ра́зница была́ подчёркнута.

accentuation /ækˌsentjʊ'eɪʃ(ə)n/ *n.* ударе́ние; акцентуа́ция; (*fig.*) акценти́рование; подчёркивание.

accept /ək'sept/ *v.t.* **1** (*agree to receive*) прин|има́ть, -я́ть; **he refused to ~ a tip** он не при́нял чаевы́е; **he was ~ed as one of the group** его́ при́няли как своего́. **2** (*recognize, admit*) призн|ава́ть, -а́ть; **you must ~ this fact** вы должны́ смири́ться с э́тим фа́ктом; **I ~ that it may take time** я призна́ю, что для э́того потре́буется вре́мя; **it is an ~ed fact** э́то общепри́знанный факт. **3** (*comm.*) акцептова́ть (*impf., pf.*).

acceptability /əkˌseptə'bɪlɪtɪ/ *n.* прие́млемость.

acceptable /ək'septəb(ə)l/ *adj.* прие́млемый.

acceptance /ək'sept(ə)ns/ *n.* (*willing receipt*) приня́тие; (*approval*) одобре́ние; **his words found ~** его́ слова́ вы́звали одобре́ние; (*comm.*) акце́пт.

access /'ækses/ *n.* **1** (*to person, thing*) до́ступ (к + *d.*); **you may have ~ to my library** вы мо́жете по́льзоваться мое́й библиоте́кой; **easy of ~** (*of places or persons*) досту́пный; (*means of approach; way in*) подхо́д (к + *d.*); **~ road** подъездно́й путь; **~ time** (*comput.*) вре́мя до́ступа. **2** (*attack, outburst*) при́ступ, вспы́шка.

● *v.t.* (*comput.*): **~ data** осуществ|ля́ть,-и́ть до́ступ к да́нным.

accessary /ək'sesərɪ/ = **accessory** *n.* 1

accessibility /əkˌsesɪ'bɪlɪtɪ/ *n.* досту́пность.

accessible /ək'sesɪb(ə)l/ *adj.* досту́пный.

accession /ək'seʃ(ə)n/ *n.* **1** (*attaining*) вступле́ние; **~ to an office** вступле́ние в до́лжность; **~ to power** прихо́д к вла́сти; **~ to the throne** вступле́ние на престо́л; (*committal*): **~ to a treaty** присоедине́ние к догово́ру. **2** (*of book into library etc.*) поступле́ние.

● *v.t.* вн|оси́ть, -ести́ в катало́г.

accessory /ək'sesərɪ/ *n.* **1** (*leg., also* **accessary**) соуча́стник; **~ to a crime** соуча́стник преступле́ния; **~ before/after the fact** соуча́стник до/по́сле фа́кта преступле́ния. **2** (*pl., ancillary parts*) принадле́жности (*f. pl.*); (*of clothing*) аксессуа́ры (*m. pl.*).

● *adj.* вспомога́тельный; дополни́тельный.

accident /'æksɪd(ə)nt/ *n.* **1** (*chance*) слу́чай, случа́йность; **by ~** случа́йно; **by (sheer) ~** (чи́сто) случа́йно; **it was no ~ that he was present** его́ прису́тствие не́ было случа́йным. **2** (*unintentional action*): **I'm sorry, it was an ~** прости́те, я неча́янно. **3** (*mishap*) несча́стный слу́чай; (*rail.*) круше́ние, ава́рия; **car ~** автомоби́льная катастро́фа, автокатастро́фа, ава́рия; **road ~** доро́жно-тра́нспортное происше́ствие; **~s in the home** бытовы́е несча́стные слу́чаи; **~ insurance** страхова́ние от несча́стных слу́чаев; **he had an ~** он попа́л в ава́рию.

● *cpd.* **~-prone** *adj.* невезу́чий.

accidental /ˌæksɪ'dent(ə)l/ *n.* (*mus.*) случа́йный знак альтера́ции.

● *adj.* **1** (*chance*) случа́йный; **~ death** смерть в результа́те несча́стного слу́чая. **2** (*incidental*) побо́чный.

acclaim /ə'kleɪm/ *n.* (*public recognition*) призна́ние; (*welcome*) приве́тствие; (*applause*) ова́ция.

● *v.t.* (*praise publicly*): **he was ~ed** он получи́л призна́ние; (*welcome*) приве́тствовать (*impf.*); (*hail*) провозгла|ша́ть, -си́ть; **he was ~ed king** его́ провозгласи́ли королём; (*applaud*) бу́рно аплоди́ровать (*impf.*) + *d.*

acclamation /ˌæklə'meɪʃ(ə)n/ *n.* (*public recognition*) призна́ние; (*loud approval*) шу́мное одобре́ние; (*enthusiasm*) энтузиа́зм; (*pl., shouts of welcome or applause*) приве́тственные во́згласы (*m. pl.*); **his books won the ~ of critics** его́ кни́ги вы́звали шу́мное одобре́ние кри́тиков.

acclimate /ə'klaɪmət/ (*US*) = **acclimatize**

acclimation /æklaɪ'meɪʃ(ə)n/ (*US*) = **acclimatization**

acclimatization /əˌklaɪmətaɪ'zeɪʃ(ə)n/ *n.* акклиматиза́ция.

acclimatize /ə'klaɪməˌtaɪz/ *v.t. & i.* акклиматизи́ровать(ся) (*impf., pf.*).

acclivity /ə'klɪvɪtɪ/ *n.* подъём.

accolade /'ækəˌleɪd/, /-'leɪd/ *n.* (*praise*) похвала́; (*reward*) награ́да.

accommodat|e /ə'kɒməˌdeɪt/ *v.t.* **1** (*house*) разме|ща́ть, -сти́ть; (*single person*) поме|ща́ть, -сти́ть; предост|авля́ть, -а́вить жильё + *d.* **2** (*hold, seat*) вме|ща́ть, -сти́ть; **the car will ~e 6 persons** маши́на вмеща́ет шесть челове́к; **a hall ~ing 500** зал на 500 челове́к. **3** (*oblige*) ока́з|ывать, -а́ть услу́гу + *d.* **4** (*equip*) снаб|жа́ть, -ди́ть (*кого чем*). **5** (*adapt*) приспос|обля́ть, -о́бить; **she ~ed herself to circumstances** она приспосо́билась к обстоя́тельствам.

accommodating /əˈkɒməˌdeɪtɪŋ/ *adj.* сговóрчивый, услýжливый.

accommodation /əˌkɒməˈdeɪʃ(ə)n/ *n.* **1** (*lodgings*) жильё; **can you provide a night's ~?** мóжно останoвиться у вас нá ночь?; **hotel ~ is scarce** гостúного жилья́ не хватáет; **~ address** (*Br.*) áдрес до востребования. **2** (*adaptation*) приспособлéние. **3** (*settlement*) соглашéние. **4** (*convenience*) удóбство; **~ ladder** забóртный трап.

accompaniment /əˈkʌmpənɪmənt/ *n.* **1** (*accompanying*) сопровождéние. **2** (*mus.*) аккомпанемéнт; **to the ~ of a grand piano** под аккомпанемéнт роя́ля; (*fig.*): **he spoke to the ~ of laughter** егó речь то и дéло прерывáл смех.

accompanist /əˈkʌmpənɪst/ *n.* (*mus.*) аккомпаниáтор.

accompan|y /əˈkʌmpənɪ/ *v.t.* **1** (*lit., go or be with; fig., occur with*) сопровождáть (*impf.*); **~ied by friends** в сопровождéнии друзéй; (*lit. and fig., attend*) сопýтствовать (*impf.*) + *d.*; **many illnesses are ~ied by fever** жар сопýтствует мнóгим болéзням; (*escort*): **may I ~y you home?** разрешúте проводúть вас домóй? **2** (*fig., supplement*) сопрово|ждáть, -дúть (*что чем*); **your offer must be ~ied by a letter** вáше предложéние необходúмо сопроводúть письмóм. **3** (*mus.*) аккомпанúровать (*impf.*) + *d.*

accomplice /əˈkʌmplɪs/, /-ˈkɒm-/ *n.* соучáстни|к (*fem.* -ца); сообщни|к (*fem.* -ца).

accomplish /əˈkʌmplɪʃ/, /əˈkɒm-/ *v.t.* (*complete*) заверш|áть, -úть; (*fulfil, perform*) выполня́ть, вы́полнить; соверш|áть, -úть.

accomplished /əˈkʌmplɪʃt/, /əˈkɒm-/ *adj.* **1** (*completed*) завершённый, совершённый; **an ~ fact** соверши́вшийся факт. **2** (*skilled, experienced*) совершéнный, искýсный. **3** (*cultivated*) культýрный. **4** (*egregious*): **an ~ liar** закóнченный лгун.

accomplishment /əˈkʌmplɪʃmənt/, /əˈkɒm-/ *n.* завершéние; выполнéние; (*achievement*) достижéние; (*skill*) умéние; **a man of many ~s** разносторóнний человéк.

accord /əˈkɔːd/ *n.* **1** (*agreement*) соглáсие, соглашéние; **with one ~** единодýшно; **be in ~ with** быть соглáсным с + *i.*; быть в соглáсии с + *i.* **2** (*volition*): **of one's own ~** по сóбственному желáнию, по сóбственной вóле; **the door opened of its own ~** дверь открылась самá.

● *v.t.* предост|авля́ть, -áвить (*что комy*); **he was ~ed the necessary facilities** емý предостáвили всё необходúмое; **he was ~ed a hero's welcome** егó встрéтили как герóя.

● *v.i.*: **~ with** быть в соглáсии с + *i.*; согласóв|ываться, -áться с + *i.*

accordance /əˈkɔːd(ə)ns/ *n.* соответствие; **in ~ with** в соотвéтствии с + *i.*, соглáсно + *d.*

according /əˈkɔːdɪŋ/ *adv.*: **~ as** соотвéтственно + *d.*; **~ as your work is good or bad** в завúсимости от кáчества вáшей рабóты; **~ to** (*in keeping or conformity with*) соглáсно + *d.*; **~ to the laws** соглáсно закóнам; (*in a manner or degree consistent with; corresponding to*) сообрáзно + *d.*, сообрáзно с + *i.*; **books arranged ~ to authors** кнúги, размещённые по áвторам; (*depending on*): **~ to circumstances** в завúсимости от обстоя́тельств; (*on the authority or information of*) по + *d.*, соглáсно + *d.*; по мнéнию/словáм/сообщéнию + *g.*; **the Gospel ~ to St. Mark** Евáнгелие от Мáрка.

accordingly /əˈkɔːdɪŋlɪ/ *adv.* **1** (*as circumstances suggest*) соотвéтственно. **2** (*therefore*) поэ́тому; такúм óбразом.

accordion /əˈkɔːdɪən/ *n.* аккордеóн.

accordionist /əˈkɔːdɪənɪst/ *n.* аккордеонúст.

accost /əˈkɒst/ *v.t.* прист|авáть, -áть к + *d.* (с разговóрами).

account /əˈkaʊnt/ *n.* **1** (*comm.*) счёт (*pl.* -á); **current ~** текýщий счёт; **deposit ~** депозúтный счёт; **joint ~** óбщий счёт; **~ book** счётная/бухгáлтерская кнúга; **do the ~s** подв|одúть, -естú счетá; **keep ~s** вестú (*det.*) счетá; **open an ~** откр|ывáть, -ы́ть счёт; **settle an ~** оплá|чивать, -тúть счёт; **render an ~** предст|авля́ть, -áвить счёт; **put these goods down to my ~** запишúте э́ти товáры на мой счёт; **balance, square ~s** св|одúть, -естú счетá; подв|одúть, -естú балáнс; (*fig.*): **settle ~s with s.o.** (*take revenge*) сводúть, свестú счёты с кем-н. **2** (*purpose; benefit*) пóльза; вы́года; **turn something to (good) ~** извл|екáть, -éчь пóльзу из чегó-н. **3** (*statement, report*) отчёт; (*description*) описáние; **by his own ~** по егó сóбственным словáм; **by all ~s** сýдя по всемý; **call to ~** приз|ывáть, -вáть (*кого*) к отвéту; **give a good ~ of o.s.** (*perform well*) хорошó покáзывать, показáть себя́. **4** (*estimation, consideration*) расчёт; **take into ~, take ~ of** уч|úтывать, -éсть; прин|имáть, -я́ть в расчёт; **leave out of ~, take no ~ of** не прин|имáть, -я́ть в расчёт; не уч|úтывать, -éсть; **a man of no ~** незначúтельный/ничтóжный человéк. **5** (*reason, cause*): **on ~ of** (*for the sake of*) рáди + *g.*; (*because of*) из-за + *g.*; (*in consequence of*) по причúне + *g.*; (*as a result of*) вслéдствие + *g.*; **on no ~** ни в кóем слýчае.

● *v.t.* (*consider*) сч|итáть, -éсть.

● *v.i.* **~ for**: (*lit., fig., give a reckoning of*) отчúт|ываться, -áться в + *p.*; да|вáть, -ть отчёт в + *p.*; **he had to ~ for his expenses** он дóлжен был отчитáться в свойх расхóдах; (*fig., answer for*) отв|ечáть, -éтить за + *a.*; **is everyone ~ed for?** никогó не забы́ли?; (*explain*) объясн|я́ть, -úть; **how do you ~ for being late?** как вы объясняéте своё опоздáние?; **there's no ~ing for tastes** о вкýсах не спóрят; (*be reason for*) явля́ться (*impf.*) причúной + *g.*; (*comprise*) сост|авля́ть, -áвить; **women ~ for about 60% of our audiences** жéнщины составля́ют óколо 60% нáшей аудитóрии; (*dispose of*): **our company ~ed for 60 of the enemy** на счетý нáшей рóты 60 неприя́тельских солдáт.

accountability /əˌkaʊntəˈbɪlɪtɪ/ *n.* ответственность; (*for money*) подотчётность.

accountable /əˈkaʊntəb(ə)l/ *adj.* ответственный; **I shall hold you ~** я возложý ответственность на вас; **he is ~ to me** он отчúтывается пéредо мной; **he is not ~ for his actions** он не отвечáет за свой постýпки.

accountancy /əˈkaʊntənsɪ/ *n.* бухгалтéрия, счетовóдство.

accountant /əˈkaʊnt(ə)nt/ *n.* бухгáлтер, счетовóд.

accounting /əˈkaʊntɪŋ/ *n.* (*profession*) бухгáлтерское дéло.

accouterments /əˈkuːtəmənts/ (*US*) = **accoutrements**

accoutrements /əˈkuːtrəmənts/, /-təmənts/ *n.* снаряжéние.

accredit /əˈkredɪt/ *v.t.* (**accredited, accrediting**) **1** (*appoint as ambassador*) аккредитовáть (*impf., pf.*). **2** (*credit*) выдавáть, вы́дать кредúт + *d.*

accreditation /əˌkredɪˈteɪʃ(ə)n/ *n.* аккредитовáние.

accredited /əˈkredɪtɪd/ *adj.* (*officially recognized*) аккредитóванный; (*generally accepted*) прúзнанный.

accrete /əˈkriːt/ *v.i.* (*grow together*) сраст|áться, -úсь; (*grow around*) обраст|áть, -ú.

accretion /əˈkriːʃ(ə)n/ *n.* приращéние, прирóст.

accrue /əˈkruː/ *v.i.* (**accrues, accrued, accruing**) **1** (*accumulate*) нараст|áть, -ú; **~d interest** нарóсшие процéнты (*m. pl.*). **2** (*come about*): **certain advantages will ~ from this** э́то даст определённые преимýщества. **3**: **~ to** (*fall to the lot of*) дост|авáться, -áться + *d.*

accumulate /əˈkjuːmjʊˌleɪt/ *v.t.* нак|áпливать, -опúть; соб|ирáть, -рáть; **~d experience** накóпленный óпыт; **he ~d a fine library** он собрáл хорóшую библиотéку.

● *v.i.* нак|áпливаться, -опúться; ск|áпливаться, -опúться; **~d dividend** накóпленные дивидéнды; **dust ~s** пыль скáпливается.

accumulation /əˌkjuːmjʊˈleɪʃ(ə)n/ *n.* **1** (*piling up, amassing*) накоплéние; (*gathering together*) собрáние. **2** (*mass*): **an ~ of dust/snow** скоплéние пы́ли/снéга.

accumulative /əˈkjuːmjʊlətɪv/ *adj.* (*growing by addition*) нарастáющий; (*cumulative*) кумулятúвный.

accumulator /əˈkjuːmjʊˌleɪtə(r)/ *n.* (*amasser*) стяжáтель (*m.*); (*Br., elec.*) аккумуля́тор, аккумуля́торная батарéя.

accuracy /ˈækjʊrəsɪ/ *n.* тóчность; (*of aim or shot*) мéткость.

accurate /ˈækjʊrət/ *adj.* (*of persons,*

statements, instruments etc.) то́чный; ~ **to 6 places of decimals** с то́чностью до одно́й миллио́нной; (*of aim or shot*) ме́ткий.

accursed /əˈkɜːsɪd/, /əˈkɜːst/ *adj.* про́клятый.

accusation /ˌækjuːˈzeɪʃ(ə)n/ *n.* обвине́ние; **bring an ~ against** выдвига́ть, вы́двинуть обвине́ние про́тив + *g.*

accusative /əˈkjuːzətɪv/ *n.* вини́тельный паде́ж.

● *adj.* вини́тельный.

accusator|ial /əˌkjuːzəˈtɔːrɪəl/, **-y** /əˈkjuːzətərɪ/ *adjs.* обвини́тельный.

accuse /əˈkjuːz/ *v.t.* обвин|я́ть, -и́ть; **he was ~d of stealing** его́ обвини́ли в кра́же.

accused /əˈkjuːzd/ *n.*: **the ~** обвиня́емый, подсуди́мый.

accuser /əˈkjuːzə(r)/ *n.* обвини́тель (*m.*).

accusing /əˈkjuːzɪŋ/ *adj.* укори́зненный, обвиня́ющий.

accustom /əˈkʌstəm/ *v.t.* приуч|а́ть, -и́ть (**to**: к + *d.*); **~ o.s., become ~ed** прив|ыка́ть, -ы́кнуть (**to**: к + *d.*); **I am not ~ed to such language** я не привы́к к таки́м выраже́ниям; **he was ~ed to ride every morning** он име́л привы́чку/обыкнове́ние е́здить верхо́м ка́ждое у́тро.

accustomed /əˈkʌstəmd/ *adj.* (*usual*) обы́чный, привы́чный.

ace /eɪs/ *n.* **1** (*single pip on dice, cards, dominoes*) очко́. **2** (*card*) туз; **he has an ~ up his sleeve** у него́ есть ко́зырь про запа́с. **3** (*pilot, champion sportsman etc.*) ас. **4**: **within an ~ of** на волосо́к от + *g.*

● *adj.* (*coll.*) (перво)кла́ссный.

acerbic /əˈsɜːbɪk/ *adj.* (*astringent*) те́рпкий; (*of speech, manner etc.*) язви́тельный.

acerbity /əˈsɜːbɪtɪ/ *n.* те́рпкость; язви́тельность.

acetate /ˈæsɪˌteɪt/ *n.* ацета́т; уксуснокі́слая соль.

acetic /əˈsiːtɪk/ *adj.* у́ксусный; **~ acid** у́ксусная кислота́.

acetone /ˈæsɪˌtəʊn/ *n.* ацето́н.

acetylene /əˈsetɪˌliːn/ *n.* ацетиле́н; **~ welding** ацетиле́новая сва́рка.

ach|e /eɪk/ *n.* боль.

● *v.i.* боле́ть (*impf.*); ныть (*impf.*); **my head ~es** у меня́ боли́т голова́; **an ~ing tooth** больно́й зуб; **my bones ~e** у меня́ но́ют ко́сти; **my heart ~es** у меня́ се́рдце боли́т; **my heart ~es for him** у меня́ душа́ боли́т за него́; **I ~e to see him** я жа́жду уви́деть его́.

achievable /əˈtʃiːvəb(ə)l/ *adj.* достижи́мый.

achieve /əˈtʃiːv/ *v.t.* **1** (*attain*) дост|ига́ть, -и́чь + *g.*; добива́ться, доби́ться + *g.* **2** (*carry out*) выполня́ть, вы́полнить.

achievement /əˈtʃiːvmənt/ *n.* (*attainment*) достиже́ние; (*carrying out*) выполне́ние; (*success*) достиже́ние, завоева́ние.

Achilles /əˈkɪliːz/ *n.* Ахилле́с; **~' heel** ахилле́сова пята́; **~ tendon** ахи́ллово сухожи́лие.

acid /ˈæsɪd/ *n.* кислота́; **~ rain** кисло́тный дождь; **~ test** (*fig.*) про́бный ка́мень.

● *adj.* (*lit. and fig.*) ки́слый.

acidify /əˈsɪdɪˌfaɪ/ *v.t. & i.* (*chem.*) подкисл|я́ть(ся), -и́ть(ся); (*make, become sour*) окисл|я́ть(ся), -и́ть(ся).

acidity /əˈsɪdɪtɪ/ *n.* кисло́тность.

ack-ack /ˈækˈæk/ *n.* (*mil. sl.*) **1** (*gun*) зени́тка. **2** (*gunfire*) зени́тный ого́нь. **3** (*attr.*): **~ battalion** зени́тный дивизио́н.

acknowledge /əkˈnɒlɪdʒ/ *v.t.* **1** (*recognize*; *admit*) призн|ава́ть, -а́ть; **he refused to ~ defeat** он отказа́лся призна́ть пораже́ние; **he was ~d as (*or* to be) the champion** его́ призна́ли чемпио́ном. **2** (*confirm receipt of*; *reply to*): **~ a letter** подтвер|жда́ть, -ди́ть получе́ние письма́; **~ a greeting** отвеча́ть, отве́тить на приве́тствие. **3** (*indicate recognition of*): **he did not even ~ me as we passed** он прошёл ми́мо и да́же не поздоро́вался. **4** (*express thanks for*) выража́ть, вы́разить призна́тельность за + *a.*

acknowledg(e)ment /əkˈnɒlɪdʒmənt/ *n.* **1** (*recognition, admission*) призна́ние. **2** (*confirmation*) подтвержде́ние. **3** (*reward*): **this is in ~ of your kindness** э́то в призна́тельность за ва́шу доброту́.

acme /ˈækmɪ/ *n.* верх, верши́на.

acmeism /ˈækmɪˌɪz(ə)m/ *n.* (*liter.*) акмеи́зм.

acmeist /ˈækmɪˌɪst/ *n.* (*liter.*) акмеи́ст (*fem.* -ка).

acne /ˈæknɪ/ *n.* угри́ (*m. pl.*).

acolyte /ˈækəˌlaɪt/ *n.* церко́вный слу́жка; (*fig.*) сподви́жник.

aconite /ˈækəˌnaɪt/ *n.* (*bot.*) акони́т, боре́ц; (*drug*) акони́т.

acorn /ˈeɪkɔːn/ *n.* жёлудь (*m.*).

acoustic /əˈkuːstɪk/ *adj.* акусти́ческий; звуково́й; **~ coupler** акусти́ческий соедини́тель; **an ~ guitar** класси́ческая гита́ра.

acoustics /əˈkuːstɪks/ *n.* (*science*; *acoustic properties*) аку́стика.

acquaint /əˈkweɪnt/ *v.t.* знако́мить, по-; **I ~ed him with the facts** я ознако́мил его́ с фа́ктами; **he soon got ~ed with the situation** он бы́стро ознако́мился с положе́нием дел; **be ~ed with s.o.** быть знако́мым с кем-н.

acquaintance /əˈkweɪnt(ə)ns/ *n.* знако́мство; **make the ~ of** знако́миться, по- с + *i.*; **strike up an ~** зав|оди́ть, -ести́ знако́мство; **for old ~' sake** по ста́рой дру́жбе/па́мяти; (*person*) знако́мый; **an ~ of mine** оди́н мой знако́мый.

acquaintanceship /əˈkweɪnt(ə)nsʃɪp/ *n.* знако́мство.

acquiesce /ˌækwɪˈes/ *v.i.* (*agree tacitly*) согла|ша́ться, -си́ться; **~ in** (*accept*) примир|я́ться, -и́ться с + *i.*

acquiescence /ˌækwɪˈesəns/ *n.* (*agreement*) согла́сие; (*tractability*) усту́пчивость.

acquiescent /ˌækwɪˈesənt/ *adj.* усту́пчивый.

acquire /əˈkwaɪə(r)/ *v.t.* приобре|та́ть, -сти́; **~ a habit** усв|а́ивать, -о́ить себе́/приобре|та́ть, -сти́ привы́чку; **~ a language** овлад|ева́ть, -е́ть языко́м; **~ a reputation** приобре|та́ть, -сти́ репута́цию; **asparagus is an ~d taste** к спа́рже на́до привы́кнуть.

acquisition /ˌækwɪˈzɪʃ(ə)n/ *n.* приобрете́ние; **the ~ of knowledge** приобрете́ние зна́ний; **the ~ of language** овладе́ние языко́м; **the library's new ~s** но́вые библиоте́чные поступле́ния.

acquisitive /əˈkwɪzɪtɪv/ *adj.* стяжа́тельский.

acquisitiveness /əˈkwɪzɪtɪvnɪs/ *n.* стяжа́тельство.

acquit /əˈkwɪt/ *v.t.* (**acquitted, acquitting**) **1** (*declare not guilty*) опра́вд|ывать, -а́ть; **he was ~ted of murder** его́ призна́ли нев́ино́вным в уби́йстве. **2**: **~ o.s. well** хорошо́ проя́в|ля́ть, -и́ть себя́. **3**: **~ o.s. of** (*discharge*) **a duty** выполня́ть, вы́полнить долг. **4** (*pay*): **~ a debt** распл|а́чиваться, -ати́ться (по счёту).

acquittal /əˈkwɪt(ə)l/ *n.* (*in court of law*) оправда́ние; (*of duty etc.*) выполне́ние; (*of debt etc.*) освобожде́ние.

acre /ˈeɪkə(r)/ *n.* акр; **broad ~s** обши́рные зе́мли (*f. pl.*).

acreage /ˈeɪkərɪdʒ/ *n.* пло́щадь земли́ в а́крах.

acrid /ˈækrɪd/ *adj.* е́дкий (*lit., fig.*).

acrimonious /ˌækrɪˈməʊnɪəs/ *adj.* ожесточённый, го́рький.

acrimon|iousness /ˌækrɪˈməʊnɪəsnɪs/, **-y** /ˈækrɪmənɪ/ *nn.* ожесточённость.

acrobat /ˈækrəˌbæt/ *n.* акроба́т.

acrobatic /ˌækrəˈbætɪk/ *adj.* акробати́ческий.

acrobatics /ˌækrəˈbætɪks/ *n.* акроба́тика.

acronym /ˈækrənɪm/ *n.* аббревиату́ра, акро́ним.

acropolis /əˈkrɒpəlɪs/ *n.* акро́поль (*m.*).

across /əˈkrɒs/ *adv.* **1** (*athwart, crosswise*) поперёк; (*in crosswords*) по горизонта́ли. **2** (*on the other side*) на той стороне́; **he must be ~ by now** он, должно́ быть, уже́ на той стороне́. **3** (*to the other side*) на ту сто́рону. **4** (*in width*): **the river here is more than six miles ~** ширина́ реки́ здесь бо́льше шести́ миль; **a beam 2 feet ~** бревно́ толщино́й в два фу́та.

● *prep.* **1** (*from one side of to the other*) че́рез + *a.*, *sometimes omitted with vv. compounded with* пере. . .; **he went ~ the street** он перешёл у́лицу; **they were talking ~ the table** они́ разгова́ривали че́рез стол; **they were talking ~ me** они́ разгова́ривали че́рез мою́ го́лову. **2** (*over the surface of*) по + *d.*; **he drew a line ~ the page** он провёл черту́ на

страни́це; **clouds travelled ~ the sky** облака́ плы́ли по не́бу; **he hit me ~ the face** он уда́рил меня́ по лицу́; **~ country** напрями́к; **~ the board** (*fig.*) для всех; во всех слу́чаях.
3 (*athwart*) поперёк + *g.*; **she lay ~ the bed** она́ лежа́ла поперёк крова́ти; **with his arms ~ his breast** скрести́в ру́ки на груди́.
4 (*on the other side of*) на той стороне́ + *g.*, по ту сто́рону + *g.*; **he lives ~ (the street) from the park** он живёт напро́тив па́рка; **our friends ~ the ocean** на́ши друзья́ за океа́ном; **~ the table from him** про́тив него́ за столо́м.
● *cpd.* **~-the-board** *adj.* всео́бщий, всеобъе́млющий, по всем катего́риям; **an ~-the-board pay increase** всео́бщее увеличе́ние зарпла́ты; **an ~-the-board agreement** всеобъе́млющее соглаше́ние.

acrostic /ə'krɒstɪk/ *n.* акрости́х.

acrylic /ə'krɪlɪk/ *n.* акри́л.
● *adj.* акри́ловый.

act /ækt/ *n.* **1** (*action*) посту́пок; (*feat*) по́двиг; **~ of God** стихи́йное бе́дствие; **catch in the ~** пойма́ть (*pf.*) на ме́сте преступле́ния; **he was in the ~ of putting on his hat** он как раз надева́л шля́пу; **an ~ of kindness** до́брое де́ло.
2 (*document*) акт, докуме́нт; **~ of sale** акт о прода́же; (*proof*): **~ of confidence** зало́г/проявле́ние дове́рия.
3 (*law*) акт, зако́н; **~ of Parliament** акт парла́мента, парла́ментский акт; **he was prosecuted under the ~** его́ привлекли́ к суду́ в соотве́тствии с э́тим зако́ном.
4 (*of drama*) де́йствие; **a 3-~ play** пье́са в трёх де́йствиях.
5 (*performance*) но́мер; **circus ~** цирково́й но́мер; (*fig., coll.*): **put on an ~** притвор|я́ться, -и́ться.
● *v.t.* игра́ть (*impf.*); **~ a part** (*lit., fig.*) игра́ть роль; **~ Hamlet** игра́ть Га́млета; **~ the fool** валя́ть (*impf.*) дурака́; **~ a play** игра́ть, разыгра́ть (*or* да|ва́ть, -ть) пье́су.
● *v.i.* **1** (*behave*) поступ|а́ть, -и́ть; вести́ (*det.*) себя́; (*take action, intervene*) прин|има́ть, -я́ть ме́ры; **~ on advice** сле́довать, по- сове́ту; **~ (up)on an order** де́йствовать (*impf.*) по прика́зу; **it is time to ~** пора́ де́йствовать; **he ~s rich** (*coll.*) он разы́грывает из себя́ богача́.
2 (*serve, function*) де́йствовать (*impf.*); **~ for s.o.** де́йствовать от и́мени кого́-л.; **~ against s.o.** выступа́ть, вы́ступить про́тив кого́-н.; **he is ~ing as interpreter** он выступа́ет в ро́ли перево́дчика.
3 (*have or take effect*) де́йствовать, по- (**on**: на + *a.*); **the medicine will ~ immediately** лека́рство поде́йствует сра́зу.
4 (*theatr.*) игра́ть (*impf.*); **he wants to ~** он хо́чет игра́ть на сце́не.
● *with advs.* **~ out** *v.t.* разы́гр|ывать, -а́ть; **~ up** *v.i.* (*coll., misbehave*) шали́ть (*impf.*); (*give trouble*): **my car has been ~ing up** моя́ маши́на барахли́т.

acting /'æktɪŋ/ *n.* (*theatr.*) игра́; (*as skill*) актёрское мастерство́; **the ~ profession** актёрская профе́ссия.
● *adj.* (*doing duty temporarily*): **~ manager** исполня́ющий обя́занности (*abbr.* и.о.) заве́дующего.

action /'ækʃ(ə)n/ *n.* **1** (*acting; activity; effect*) де́йствие; **in ~** в де́йствии; **come into ~** вступ|а́ть, -и́ть в де́йствие; **bring into ~** вв|оди́ть, -ести́ в де́йствие; **put out of ~** выводи́ть, вы́вести из стро́я; **out of ~** него́дный к употребле́нию; **take ~** прин|има́ть, -я́ть ме́ры; **what we need is some ~** нам ну́жно де́йствовать; **~ replay** (*Br., TV*) повто́р.
2 (*deed*) посту́пок; **a man of ~** челове́к де́ла; **~s speak louder than words** дела́ говоря́т са́ми за себя́.
3 (*conduct*) поведе́ние; **line of ~** ли́ния поведе́ния.
4 (*functioning*): **the ~ of the heart** де́ятельность се́рдца; (*of a piano*) меха́ника.
5 (*physical movement*) движе́ние.
6 (*theatr.*): **the ~ takes place in London** де́йствие происхо́дит в Ло́ндоне.
7 (*leg.*) иск, суде́бное де́ло; **~ for damages** иск о взыска́нии убы́тков; **bring an ~ against** предъяв|ля́ть, -и́ть иск к + *d.*
8 (*mil.*) бой, де́йствие; **killed in ~** па́вший, уби́тый в бою́; **go into ~** вступ|а́ть, -и́ть в бой; **~ stations** (*Br.*) боевы́е посты́.

actionable /'ækʃənəb(ə)l/ *adj.*: **his words are ~** его́ слова́ даю́т основа́ния для суде́бного и́ска.

activate /'æktɪ,veɪt/ *v.t.* (*make operative*) прив|оди́ть, -ести́ в де́йствие; активизи́ровать (*impf., pf.*); (*chem., biol.*) активи́ровать (*impf., pf.*).

activation /,æktɪ'veɪʃ(ə)n/ *n.* приведе́ние в де́йствие; активиза́ция; (*chem., biol.*) актива́ция.

active /'æktɪv/ *adj.* **1** (*lively; energetic; displaying activity*) акти́вный, де́ятельный; **he is old but still ~** несмотря́ на во́зраст, он всё ещё акти́вен/бодр; **take an ~ interest in** проявл|я́ть, -и́ть живо́й интере́с к + *d.*; **an ~ brain** живо́й/де́ятельный ум; **an ~ volcano** де́йствующий вулка́н.
2 (*gram.*) действи́тельный. **3** (*phys., chem.*) акти́вный. **4** (*mil.*): **on ~ service** на действи́тельной слу́жбе; **~ division** боева́я диви́зия.

activist /'æktɪvɪst/ *n.* активи́ст (*fem.* -ка).

activit|y /æk'tɪvɪtɪ/ *n.* **1** (*being active; exertion of energy*) акти́вность; (*comm.*): **~y in the market** оживле́ние на ры́нке. **2** (*usu. pl., pursuit, sphere of action; doings*) де́ятельность; **he indulged in various ~ies** он занима́лся са́мой разли́чной де́ятельностью.

actor /'æktə(r)/ *n.* актёр.

actress /'æktrɪs/ *n.* актри́са.

actual /'æktʃʊəl/, /'æktjʊəl/ *adj.* (*real*) действи́тельный; факти́ческий; (*genuine*) по́длинный; (*existing*) существу́ющий; (*current*) настоя́щий, теку́щий; **in ~ fact** в действи́тельности; **those were his ~ words** э́то его́ по́длинные слова́; **~ time of arrival** факти́ческое вре́мя прибы́тия; **the ~ state of affairs** действи́тельное положе́ние дел; **~ strength** (*mil.*) ли́чный соста́в.

actuality /,æktʃʊ'ælɪtɪ/, /,æktjʊ-/ *n.* действи́тельность; **in ~** в действи́тельности; (*reality*) реа́льность; (*pl., existing conditions*) по́длинные усло́вия.

actualize /'æktʃʊəlaɪz/, /'æktjʊəlaɪz/ *v.t.* реализова́ть (*impf., pf.*).

actually /'æktʃʊəlɪ/ *adv.* **1** (*really; in fact*) действи́тельно; на (са́мом) де́ле; (*in expansion or correction of former statement*) в/на са́мом де́ле; (*in sense 'to tell the truth'*) со́бственно (говоря́).
2 (*even*) да́же.

actuarial /,æktʃʊ'eərɪəl/ *adj.* актуа́рный

actuary /'æktʃʊərɪ/ *n.* актуа́рий.

actuate /'æktʃʊ,eɪt/ *v.t.* **1** (*bring into action*) прив|оди́ть, -ести́ в де́йствие.
2 (*motivate*) побу|жда́ть, -ди́ть.

acuity /ə'kju:ɪtɪ/ *n.* (*lit., fig.*) острота́.

acumen /'ækjʊmən/, /ə'kju:mən/ *n.* (*judgement*) сообрази́тельность; (*penetration*) проница́тельность; **business ~** делова́я хва́тка.

acupressure /'ækju:,preʃə(r)/ *n.* то́чечный масса́ж.

acupuncture /'ækju:,pʌŋktʃə(r)/ *n.* акупункту́ра, иглоука́лывание.

acupuncturist /'ækju:,pʌŋktʃərɪst/ *n.* иглотерапе́вт.

acute /ə'kju:t/ *adj.* (**acuter, acutest**) (*in var. senses*) о́стрый; **~ angle** о́стрый у́гол; **~ shortage** о́страя нехва́тка; **~ sense of smell** то́нкое обоня́ние; **~ accent** аку́т.

acuteness /ə'kju:tnɪs/ *n.* острота́.

AD (*abbr. of* ***Anno Domini***) н.э. (на́шей э́ры).

ad /æd/ (*coll.*) = **advertisement**

adage /'ædɪdʒ/ *n.* погово́рка.

adagio /ə'dɑ:ʒɪəʊ/ *n., adj. & adv.* (*pl.* **~s**) ада́жио (*indecl.*).

Adam /'ædəm/ *n.* Ада́м; **~'s apple** ада́мово я́блоко, кады́к; **I don't know him from ~** я его́ никогда́ в глаза́ не ви́дел.

adamant /'ædəmənt/ *adj.* (*fig.*) непрекло́нный.

adapt /ə'dæpt/ *v.t.* **1** приспос|обля́ть, -о́бить; **he soon ~ed himself to the new situation** он бы́стро приспосо́бился к но́вой ситуа́ции.
2 (*text, book*) адапти́ровать (*impf., pf.*); **~ for the stage** инсцени́ровать (*impf., pf.*).
● *v.i.* приспос|обля́ться, -о́биться; адапти́роваться (*impf., pf.*).

adaptability /ə,dæptə'bɪlɪtɪ/ *n.* приспособля́емость; (*of person*): **he showed ~** он прояви́л уме́ние приспособля́ться.

adaptable /ə'dæptəb(ə)l/ *adj.* приспособля́емый; (*of person*) легко́ приспоса́бливающийся.

adaptation /,ædæp'teɪʃ(ə)n/ *n.* приспособле́ние; (*of book etc.*) адапта́ция; (*for stage*) инсцениро́вка.

adapt|er, -or /ə'dæptə(r)/ *nn.* **1** (*of book etc.*) áвтор адаптáции. **2** (*tech.*) адáптер.

ADC 1 (*abbr. of* ***aide-de-camp***) адъютáнт. **2** (*abbr. of* ***analog to digital converter***) АЦП (анáлого-цифровóй преобразовáтель).

add /æd/ *v.t.* **1** (*make an addition of*) приб|авля́ть, -áвить; **you must ~ water** нáдо прибáвить воды́; **~ sugar to tea** положи́ть (*pf.*) сáхар в чай; **~ salt to** подс|áливать, -оли́ть; **~ed to this is the fact that ...** к э́тому нýжно прибáвить/добáвить тот факт, что...; (*build on*) пристр|áивать, -óить; (*impart*): **~ lustre** (*Br.*), **luster** (*US*) **to** прид|авáть, -áть блеск + *d.*
2 (*say in addition*) доб|авля́ть, -áвить; **I have nothing to ~** мне нéчего добáвить; **what can I ~?** что ещё я могý сказáть?
3 (*math.*) склáдывать, сложи́ть; **~ two and (or to) three!** сложи́те два и три!

● *v.i.* **1**: **~ to** (*increase, enlarge*) увели́чи|вать, -ть; уси́ли|вать, -ть; (*knowledge etc.*) углуб|ля́ть, -и́ть; **this will ~ to the expense** э́то увели́чит расхóды; **to ~ to our difficulties it was getting dark** в доверше́ние ко всемý начинáло темнéть.
2 (*perform addition*) *see* ⇒ **~ up** *v.i.*

● *with advs.* **~ in** *v.t.* включ|áть, -и́ть; **~ on** *v.t.* приб|авля́ть, -áвить; доб|авля́ть, -áвить; **the tip was ~ed on to the bill** чаевы́е бы́ли включены́ в счёт; (*build on*): **the porch was ~ed on later** крыльцó пристрóили пóзже; **~ together** *v.t.* склáдывать, сложи́ть; **~ up** *v.t.* (*find sum of*) подсч|и́тывать, -итáть; подытóжи|вать, -ть; *v.i.* (*perform addition*): **you can't ~ up!** вы не умéете считáть!; (*total*): **it ~s up to 50** э́то составля́ет в сýмме 50; (*coll.*): **it ~s up to this, that ...** э́то свóдится к томý, что...; **it doesn't ~ up** (*make sense*) концы́ не схóдятся.

● *cpds.* **~ing-machine** *n.* счётная маши́на; арифмóметр; **~-ons** *n. pl.* (*comput.*) дополни́тельный встрóенный ресýрс.

addend|um /ə'dendəm/ *n.* (*pl.* **~a**) приложéние, дополнéние.

adder /'ædə(r)/ *n.* (*snake*) гадю́ка.

addict[1] /'ædɪkt/ *n.*: **(drug ~)** наркомáн (*fem.* -ка); **smoking ~** стрáстный кури́льщик; **theatre** (*Br.*), **theater** (*US*) **~** завзя́тый театрáл.

addict[2] /ə'dɪkt/ *v.t.*: **be, become ~ed to** пристрасти́ться (*pf.*) к + *d.*; **he became ~ed to drugs** он пристрасти́лся к наркóтикам; **he is ~ed to reading** он читáет запóем.

addiction /ə'dɪkʃ(ə)n/ *n.* пристрáстие (*to* к + *d.*); **~ to drugs** наркомáния.

addictive /ə'dɪktɪv/ *adj.* вырабáтывающий привыкáние.

Addis Ababa /'ædɪs 'æbəbə/ *n.* Адди́с-Абéба.

addition /ə'dɪʃ(ə)n/ *n.* **1** (*act of adding; thing added*) прибавлéние; добавлéние; **an ~ to the family** прибавлéние семéйства; **a useful ~ to the staff** полéзное пополнéние штáта; **in ~ to** в дополнéние к + *d.*; **in ~** (*as well*) вдобáвок; (*moreover*) к томý же. **2** (*math.*) сложéние.

additional /ə'dɪʃən(ə)l/ *adj.* добáвочный, дополни́тельный; **~ charge** доплáта.

additive /'ædɪtɪv/ *n.* добáвка, добавлéние.

addle /'æd(ə)l/ *adj.*: **an ~(d) egg** тýхлое яйцó.

● *v.t.* (*confuse*) пýтать, за-.

● *v.i.* (*of an egg*) тýхнуть, про-.

● *cpd.* **~-brained** *adj.* пýтаный.

address /ə'dres/ *n.* **1** (*of letter etc.; place of residence*) áдрес; **the parcel was sent to the wrong ~** посы́лку напрáвили не по томý áдресу; **~ book** (*also comput.*) записнáя кни́жка; **what is your ~?** какóй у вас áдрес? **2** (*discourse*) обращéние; **make (or deliver) an ~** выступáть, вы́ступить с обращéнием. **3**: **form of ~** фóрма обращéния.

● *v.t.* **1** (*a letter*) адресовáть (*impf., pf.*). **2** (*speak to*) обра|щáться, -ти́ться к + *d.*; **he ~ed the meeting** он обрати́лся к собрáвшимся. **3** (*direct*): **~ one's remarks to** адресовáть свои́ замечáния + *d.*

addressee /,ædre'si:/ *n.* адресáт.

adduce /ə'dju:s/ *v.t.* прив|оди́ть, -ести́ (как доказáтельство).

adenoids /'ædɪ,nɔɪdz/ *n.* аденóиды (*m. pl.*); **he had his ~ out** емý удали́ли аденóиды.

adept /'ædept/, /ə'dept/ *n.* мáстер.

● *adj.* умéлый; **he is ~ at finding excuses** он мáстер находи́ть оправдáния.

adeptness /'ædeptnɪs/, /ə'deptnɪs/ *n.* умéние.

adequacy /'ædɪkwəsɪ/ *n.* достáточность; адеквáтность; компетéнтность.

adequate /'ædɪkwət/ *adj.* **1** (*sufficient*) достáточный; **a salary ~ to support a family** зарплáта, достáточная для содержáния семьи́. **2** (*suitable*) адеквáтный; **he is ~ to his post** он справля́ется с рабóтой; **his thoughts could not find ~ expression** он не мог как слéдует вы́разить свои́ мы́сли. **3** (*of person, capable*) компетéнтный.

adhere /əd'hɪə(r)/ *v.i.* (*lit.*) прил|ипáть, -и́пнуть (к + *d.*); (*fig.*): **~ to an opinion** придéрживаться (*impf.*) мнéния (*g. sg.*); **~ to a promise** сдéрживать, сдержáть обещáние; **~ to a programme** (*Br.*), **program** (*US*) слéдовать (*impf.*) прогрáмме.

adherence /əd'hɪərəns/ *n.* (*lit.*) прилипáние; (*fig.*) привéрженность.

adherent /əd'hɪərənt/ *n.* привéрженец.

adhesion /əd'hi:ʒ(ə)n/ *n.* (*lit.*) прилипáние; склéивание; (*fig.*) прéданность.

adhesive /əd'hi:sɪv/ *n.* клéй; клéйкое веществó.

● *adj.* ли́пкий; (*sticky*) клéйкий; **~ tape** клéйкая лéнта, липýчка (*coll.*), скотч; (*US, med.*) лейкоплáстырь (*m.*), ли́пкий плáстырь.

ad hoc /æd 'hɒk/ *adv.* для дáнного слýчая; (*attr.*) специáльный; **~ committee** врéменный комитéт.

adieu /ə'dju:/ *n.* (*pl.* **~s** *or* **~x** /ə'dju:z/) прощáние; **bid ~ to** (*also fig.*) про|щáться, -сти́ться с + *i.*; (*coll.*) распро|щáться, -сти́ться с + *i.*; **make one's ~s** про|щáться, -сти́ться.

● *int.* прощáй(те).

ad infinitum /æd ,ɪnfɪ'naɪtəm/ *adv.* до бесконéчности.

adipose /'ædɪ,pəʊz/ *adj.* жи́рный; **~ tissue** жировáя ткань.

adjacent /ə'dʒeɪs(ə)nt/ *adj.* (*geom.*): **~ angles** смéжные углы́; (*neighbouring*) совéдний; смéжный; **~ to** примыкáющий к + *d.*; **our house is ~ to the school** наш дом примыкáет к шкóле.

adjectival /,ædʒɪk'taɪv(ə)l/ *adj.* адъекти́вный.

adjective /'ædʒɪktɪv/ *n.* (и́мя) прилагáтельное.

adjoin /ə'dʒɔɪn/ *v.t.* примыкáть (*impf.*) к + *d.*; прилегáть (*impf.*) к + *d.*

● *v.i.* примыкáть (*impf.*), прилегáть (*impf.*); **the two houses ~** э́ти два дóма примыкáют друг к дрýгу; **~ing rooms** смéжные кóмнаты; **in the ~ing house** в совéднем дóме.

adjourn /ə'dʒɜ:n/ *v.t.* (*postpone*) от|клáдывать, -ложи́ть; **the meeting was ~ed till Monday** заседáние бы́ло отлóжено до понедéльника; (*break off*): **they ~ed the meeting till 2 o'clock** они́ объяви́ли переры́в в заседáнии до двух часóв.

● *v.i.* **1** (*suspend proceedings*) закр|ывáть, -ы́ть заседáние; (*disperse*) ра|сходи́ться, -зойти́сь; **Parliament has ~ed for the summer** парлáмент распýщен на лéто. **2** (*coll., move*): **shall we ~ to the dining-room?** перейдём в столóвую?

adjournment /ə'dʒɜ:nmənt/ *n.* (*postponement*) отсрóчка; (*dispersal*) рóспуск; (*break in proceedings*) переры́в.

adjudge /ə'dʒʌdʒ/ *v.t.* **1** (*pronounce*): **~ s.o. guilty** призн|авáть, -áть когó-н. винóвным; **~ s.o. bankrupt** объяв|ля́ть, -и́ть когó-н. банкрóтом. **2** (*award judicially*) прису|ждáть, -ди́ть (*что комý*).

adjudicate /ə'dʒu:dɪ,keɪt/ *v.t.* (*a claim*) рассм|áтривать, -отрéть.

● *v.i.* суди́ть (*impf.*).

adjudication /ə,dʒu:dɪ'keɪʃ(ə)n/ *n.* (*judgement*) судéбное/арбитрáжное решéние.

adjudicator /ə'dʒu:dɪ,keɪtə(r)/ *n.* арби́тр; (*judge*) судья́ (*m.*).

adjunct /'ædʒʌŋkt/ *n.* (*appendage*) приложéние; (*addition*) дополнéние; (*gram.*) обстоя́тельство.

adjuration /,ædʒʊə'reɪʃ(ə)n/ *n.* заклинáние; мольбá.

adjure /ə'dʒʊə(r)/ *v.t.* заклинáть (*impf.*); умоля́ть (*impf.*).

adjust /ə'dʒʌst/ *v.t.* **1** (*arrange; put right or straight*) прив|оди́ть, -ести́ в поря́док; попр|авля́ть, -áвить; **he ~ed**

his tie он поправи́л га́лстук; (*mechanism*) регули́ровать, от-; нала́|живать, -дить. **2** (*fit, adapt*) приг|оня́ть, -на́ть; под|гоня́ть, -огна́ть; **you must ~ your expenditure to your income** вы должны́ соразмеря́ть свои́ расхо́ды с дохо́дами; **~ (o.s.) to** приспос|обля́ться, -о́биться к + *d.*; **well-~ed** (*of person*) уравнове́шенный.

adjustable /əˈdʒʌstəb(ə)l/ *adj.* регули́руемый; подвижно́й; **~ spanner** разводно́й (га́ечный) ключ; **the shelves of the bookcase are ~** по́лки в э́том кни́жном шкафу́ переставля́ются.

adjustment /əˈdʒʌstmənt/ *n.* (*regulation*) регул|и́рование, -иро́вка; (*correction*) исправле́ние, попра́вка; (*fitting*) приго́нка; (*adaptation*) приспособле́ние.

adjutant /ˈædʒʊt(ə)nt/ *n.* (*mil.*) адъюта́нт.

● *cpd.* **~-general** *n.* генера́л-адъюта́нт.

ad lib /æd ˈlɪb/ *adv.* (*without preparation*) экспро́мтом; (*as much as desired*) ско́лько уго́дно.

ad-lib /æd ˈlɪb/ (*coll.*) *n.* экспро́мт; **his speech was full of ~s** в свое́й ре́чи он мно́го импровизи́ровал.

● *v.i.* (**ad-libbed, ad-libbing**) говори́ть (*impf.*) экспро́мтом.

adman /ˈædmæn/ *n.* (*coll.*) реклами́ст.

administer /ədˈmɪnɪstə(r)/ *v.t.* **1** (*manage, govern*) управля́ть (*impf.*) + *i.*; заве́довать (*impf.*) + *i.* **2**: **~ a blow** нан|оси́ть, -ести́ уда́р (*кому*); **~ medicine** да|ва́ть, -ть лека́рство; **~ an oath to s.o.** прив|оди́ть, -ести́ кого́-н. к прися́ге; **the priest ~ed the sacrament of marriage** свяще́нник соверши́л обря́д венча́ния.

administration /əd,mɪnɪˈstreɪʃ(ə)n/ *n.* **1** (*management*) управле́ние; **letters of ~** пра́во на распоряже́ние иму́ществом. **2** (*of public affairs*) администра́ция; **the A~** администра́ция, прави́тельство; **during the Kennedy ~** при администра́ции Ке́ннеди. **3**: **~ of justice** отправле́ние правосу́дия. **4** (*putting into effect*): **~ of punishment** примене́ние наказа́ния. **5**: **~ of an oath** приведе́ние к прися́ге. **6**: **~ of a sacrament** соверше́ние обря́да.

administrative /ədˈmɪnɪstrətɪv/ *adj.* администрати́вный, организацио́нный; **~ ability** администрати́вные спосо́бности.

administrator /ədˈmɪnɪ,streɪtə(r)/ *n.* администра́тор; (*of an estate*) распоряди́тель (*m.*).

admirable /ˈædmərəb(ə)l/ *adj.* замеча́тельный, прекра́сный.

admiral /ˈædmər(ə)l/ *n.* адмира́л.

Admiralty /ˈædmərəltɪ/ *n.* адмиралте́йство.

admiration /,ædmɪˈreɪʃ(ə)n/ *n.* восхище́ние, восто́рг; **be, win the ~ of all** вызыва́ть, вы́звать всео́бщее восхище́ние; **fill with ~** прив|оди́ть, -ести́ в восто́рг/восхище́ние; **lost in ~** вне себя́ от восто́рга.

admir|e /ədˈmaɪə(r)/ *v.t.* (*view with pleasure*) любова́ться (*impf.*) + *i.* (*or* на + *a.*); **she was ~ing the sunrise** она́ любова́лась восхо́дом со́лнца; **he ~ed himself in the mirror** он любова́лся собо́й (*or* на себя́) в зе́ркало; (*respect*) восхи|ща́ться, -ти́ться + *i.*; восторга́ться (*impf.*) + *i.*; (*speak or think highly of*): **I forgot to ~e her dress** я забы́л похвали́ть её пла́тье; **~ing glances** восхищённые взгля́ды.

admirer /ədˈmaɪərə(r)/ *n.* покло́нни|к (*fem.* -ца); **I am an ~ of Picasso** я покло́нник Пика́ссо.

admissibility /əd,mɪsɪˈbɪlɪtɪ/ *n.* прие́млемость, допусти́мость.

admissible /ədˈmɪsɪb(ə)l/ *adj.* прие́млемый, допусти́мый.

admission /ədˈmɪʃ(ə)n/ *n.* **1** (*permitted entry or access*) вход; до́ступ; **~ by ticket** вход по биле́там; **~ free** вход беспла́тный; **no ~** вход воспреща́ется; нет вхо́да; **he was refused ~** его́ не впусти́ли; **~ charge** входна́я пла́та. **2** (*acknowledgement*) призна́ние; **he made an ~ of guilt** он призна́л свою́ вину́; **on his own ~** по его́ со́бственному призна́нию.

admit /ədˈmɪt/ *v.t.* & *i.* (**admitted, admitting**) **1** (*allow, accept*) допус|ка́ть, -ти́ть; призн|ава́ть, -а́ть; **he was ~ted to the examination** его́ допусти́ли к экза́мену; **I ~ that this is true** допуска́ю, что э́то ве́рно; **the matter ~s of no delay** де́ло не те́рпит отлага́тельства; **you must ~ he is right** вы должны́ призна́ть, что он прав. **2** (*let in*) впус|ка́ть, -ти́ть; (*to organization*) прин|има́ть, -я́ть; **the public are not ~ted to the gardens** э́тот парк закры́т для широ́кой пу́блики; **he was ~ted to the Party** его́ при́няли в па́ртию; **this ticket ~s one (person)** э́то биле́т на одно́ лицо́; **children are not ~ted** де́тям вход воспрещён. **3** (*confess*) призн|ава́ть, -а́ть; **he ~s his guilt** он признаёт свою́ вину́; **~ to feeling ashamed** призн|ава́ться, -а́ться, что сты́дно; **~ to a crime** созн|ава́ться, -а́ться в преступле́нии.

admittance /ədˈmɪt(ə)ns/ *n.* (*entry*) вход; **no ~!** вход запрещён/воспрещён!; **gain ~** получи́ть (*pf.*) разреше́ние на вход; (*access*) до́ступ.

admittedly /ədˈmɪtɪdlɪ/ *adv.* пра́вда; призна́ться.

admixture /ædˈmɪkstʃə(r)/ *n.* (*mixing*) сме́шивание; (*addition*) при́месь.

admonish /ədˈmɒnɪʃ/ *v.t.* **1** (*reprove*) де́лать, с- внуше́ние/замеча́ние + *d.*; **the boys were ~ed for being late** ма́льчикам сде́лали замеча́ние за опозда́ние. **2** (*exhort*) увещева́ть (*impf.*); наст|авля́ть, -а́вить.

admoni|shment /ədˈmɒnɪʃmənt/, **-tion** /,ædməˈnɪʃ(ə)n/ *nn.* (*reproof*) внуше́ние, замеча́ние; (*exhortation*) увещева́ние, наставле́ние.

admonitory /ədˈmɒnɪtərɪ/ *adj.* предостерега́ющий.

ad nauseam /æd ˈnɔːzɪ,æm/, /ˈnɔːsɪ,æm/ *adv.* до тошноты́.

ado /əˈduː/ *n.* (*fuss*) суета́; **without further ~** без дальне́йших церемо́ний; **much ~ about nothing** мно́го шу́ма из ничего́.

adobe /əˈdəʊbɪ/, /əˈdəʊb/ *n.* кирпи́ч-сыре́ц; **an ~ hut** глинobи́тная хи́жина.

adolescence /,ædəˈlesəns/ *n.* о́трочество.

adolescent /,ædəˈles(ə)nt/ *n.* подро́сток.

● *adj.* подро́стко́вый.

Adonis /əˈdəʊnɪs/ *n.* (*myth., fig.*) Адо́нис.

adopt /əˈdɒpt/ *v.t.* **1** (*a son*) усынов|ля́ть, -и́ть; (*a daughter*) удочер|я́ть, -и́ть; **~ed child** приёмный ребёнок, приёмыш (*coll.*). **2** (*acquire*) усв|а́ивать, -о́ить; **she is ~ing good habits** она́ усва́ивает хоро́шие привы́чки; **he is ~ing bad habits** он подхва́тывает дурны́е привы́чки. **3** (*accept*) прин|има́ть, -я́ть; **the resolution was ~ed** резолю́ция была́ принята́; (*take over*) перен|има́ть, -я́ть; **his methods should be ~ed** сле́дует переня́ть его́ ме́тоды; (*take up*) зан|има́ть, -я́ть; **he ~ed a condescending attitude** он стал держа́ться снисходи́тельно. **4** (*ling., borrow*) заи́мствовать (*impf., pf.*); **words ~ed from the French** слова́, заи́мствованные из францу́зского языка́. **5** (*Br., choose*) выбира́ть, вы́брать; **he was ~ed as candidate** его́ вы́двинули в кандида́ты.

adoption /əˈdɒpʃ(ə)n/ *n.* **1** усыновле́ние; удочере́ние. **2** усвое́ние. **3** приня́тие. **4** заи́мствование. **5** вы́бор; **the country of his ~** его́ второ́е оте́чество.

adoptive /əˈdɒptɪv/ *adj.* приёмный; **~ parent** усынови́тель (*fem.* -ница).

adorable /əˈdɔːrəb(ə)l/ *adj.* преле́стный, восхити́тельный.

adoration /,ædəˈreɪʃ(ə)n/ *n.* обожа́ние.

ador|e /əˈdɔː(r)/ *v.t.* (*worship*) обожа́ть; поклоня́ться (*impf.*) + *d.*; **her ~ing husband** обожа́ющий её муж; (*coll., love*): **the baby ~es being tickled** ребёнок обожа́ет, когда́ его́ щeко́чут.

adorer /əˈdɔːrə(r)/ *n.* покло́нни|к (*fem.* -ца); обожа́тель (*fem.* -ница) (*coll.*).

adorn /əˈdɔːn/ *v.t.* (*lit., fig.*) укр|аша́ть, -а́сить.

adornment /əˈdɔːnmənt/ *n.* украше́ние.

adrenal /əˈdriːn(ə)l/ *adj.* надпо́чечный; **~ glands** надпо́чечные же́лезы (*f. pl.*).

adrenalin /əˈdrenəlɪn/ *n.* адренали́н.

Adriatic /,eɪdrɪˈætɪk/ *n.*: **the ~ (Sea)** Адриати́ческое мо́ре.

adrift /əˈdrɪft/ *pred. adj.* & *adv.* (*of a boat or its crew*): **go ~** дрейфова́ть (*impf.*); **cut ~** (*v.t.*) пус|ка́ть, -ти́ть; **they were ~ on the open sea** они́ дрейфова́ли в откры́том мо́ре; (*fig.*): **he was all ~** он был сбит с то́лку.

adroit /əˈdrɔɪt/ *adj.* (*dexterous*) ло́вкий; (*skilful*) иску́сный.

adroitness /əˈdrɔɪtnɪs/ *n.* ло́вкость; иску́сность.

adulation /ˌædjʊˈleɪʃ(ə)n/ *n.* низкопоклóнство, лесть.

adult /əˈdʌlt/, /ˈædʌlt/ *n.* & *adj.* **1** взрóслый; ~ **education** обучéние взрóслых. **2** (*mature*) зрéлый.

adulterate /əˈdʌltəˌreɪt/ *v.t.* (*debase*) пóртить, ис-; (*dilute*) разб|авля́ть, -áвить.

adulteration /əˌdʌltəˈreɪʃ(ə)n/ *n.* пóрча; разбавлéние.

adulterer /əˈdʌltərə(r)/ *n.* невéрный супрýг.

adulteress /əˈdʌltərɪs/ *n.* невéрная супрýга.

adulterous /əˈdʌltərəs/ *adj.* невéрный.

adultery /əˈdʌltərɪ/ *n.* адюльтéр, прелюбодея́ние; **to commit** ~ соверш|áть, -и́ть прелюбодея́ние.

adulthood /ˈædʌlthʊd/, /əˈdʌlthʊd/ *n.* зрéлость; (*of men*) возмужáлость.

adumbrate /ˈædʌmˌbreɪt/ *v.t.* **1** (*sketch out*) набр|áсывать, -осáть. **2** (*foreshadow*) предвещáть (*impf.*).

advance /ədˈvɑːns/ *n.* **1** (*forward move*) продвижéние; (*mil.: also*) наступлéние; **we made an** ~ **of 10 miles** мы продви́нулись на 10 миль; (*approach, onset*): **the** ~ **of old age** наступлéние стáрости; (*pl., overtures to a person*): **make** ~**s to** заи́грывать (*impf.*) с + *i.* **2** (*progress*) прогрéсс; (*in rank, social position etc.*) продвижéние; ~**s of science** прогрéсс наýки; ~**s of civilization** достижéния (*nt. pl.*) цивилизáции; **the country has made great** ~**s** странá добилáсь бóльших успéхов. **3** (*increase*) повышéние; **an** ~ **on his original offer** надбáвка к первоначáльному предложéнию; **any** ~ **on £5?** 5 фýнтов — кто бóльше? **4** (*loan*) ссýда; (*payment beforehand*) авáнс; **an** ~ **on salary** авáнс под зарплáту; **the bank made me an** ~ банк вы́дал мне авáнс. **5**: **in** ~ (*in front*) вперёд; (*beforehand*) зарáнее; **in** ~ **of** впереди́ + *g.*; **he expects to be paid in** ~ он ожидáет, что емý заплáтят вперёд. **6** (*attr.*): ~ **booking** предвари́тельный закáз; ~ **copy** (*of book*) сигнáльный экземпля́р; ~ **copy of a speech** предвари́тельный текст рéчи; ~ **guard** авангáрд; **I had** ~ **knowledge of this** я знал об э́том зарáнее; ~ **payment** авáнсовый платёж.

● *v.t.* **1** (*move forward*) продв|игáть, -и́нуть; **he** ~**d his troops to the frontier** он продви́нул войскá к грани́це. **2** (*fig., put forward*): ~ **an opinion** выскáзывать, вы́сказать мнéние; ~ **a proposal** выдвигáть, вы́двинуть предложéние. **3** (*fig., further*): ~ **s.o.'s interests** содéйствовать (*impf.*) чьим-н. интерéсам; служи́ть, по- чьим-н. интерéсам; **he did this to** ~ **his own interests** он сдéлал э́то рáди сóбственной вы́годы. **4** (*of payment*) плати́ть, за- авáнсом; (*lend*) ссу|жáть, -ди́ть. **5** (*bring forward; make earlier*): ~ **the date of** переноси́ть, перенести́ на бóлее рáнний срок.

● *v.i.* **1** (*move forward*) продв|игáться, -и́нуться; ~ **on** наступáть (*impf.*) на + *a.* **2** (*progress*) разв|ивáться, -и́ться; дéлать, с- успéхи; ~ **in knowledge** углуб|ля́ть, -и́ть знáния. **3** (*increase*) пов|ышáться, -ы́ситься.

advanced /ədˈvɑːnst/ *adj.* **1** (*far on*): ~ **age, years** преклóнный вóзраст; **in an** ~ **state of decomposition** в крáйней стáдии разложéния; **he is very** ~ **for his years** он óчень рáзвит для свои́х лет. **2** (*opp. elementary*): **an** ~ **course** курс для продви́нутого этáпа (обучéния); ~ **algebra** вы́сшая áлгебра. **3** (*progressive*) передовóй.

advancement /ədˈvɑːnsmənt/ *n.* (*moving forward*) продвижéние; (*promotion*) продвижéние по слýжбе; (*progress*) прогрéсс.

advantage /ədˈvɑːntɪdʒ/ *n.* **1** (*superiority; more favourable or superior position*) преимýщество, достóинство; **this method has the** ~ **that ...** преимýщество э́того мéтода состои́т в том, что...; **have an** ~ **over, have the** ~ **of** имéть (*impf.*) преимýщество пéред + *i.*; **gain, win an** ~ **over** брать, взять верх над + *i.* **2** (*profit, benefit*) вы́года, пóльза; **it is to your** ~ **to sell** вам бýдет вы́годно продáть; **gain** ~ **from** извл|екáть, -éчь вы́году (*or* пóльзу) из + *g.*; **turn something to** ~ обра|щáть, -ти́ть что-н. себé на пóльзу; **take** ~ **of something** воспóльзоваться (*pf.*) чем-н.; (*abuse*) злоупотреб|ля́ть, -и́ть чем-н.; **take** ~ **of s.o.** эксплуати́ровать (*impf.*); **use to** ~ вы́годно испóльзовать (*impf., pf.*); **you may learn something to your** ~ вы мóжете узнáть/почерпнýть для себя́ чтó-то полéзное; **the picture can be seen to better** ~ **from here** отсю́да карти́на смóтрится лýчше. **3** (*tennis*): ~ **in/out** «бóльше»/«мéньше».

● *v.t.* (*favour*) благоприя́тствовать (*impf.*) + *d.*; (*give* ~ *to*) да|вáть, -ть преимýщество + *d.*; (*further*) продв|игáть, -и́нуть.

advantageous /ˌædvənˈteɪdʒəs/ *adj.* (*favourable*) благоприя́тный; (*profitable*) вы́годный.

advent /ˈædvent/ *n.* **1** (*arrival*) прибы́тие. **2** (*appearance; occurrence*) появлéние. **3** (**A**~: *eccl.*) рождéственский пост.

Adventist /ˈædventɪst/ *n.* адвенти́ст (*fem.* -ка); **Seventh-day A**~ адвенти́ст седьмóго дня.

adventitious /ˌædvenˈtɪʃəs/ *adj.* (*accidental*) случáйный.

adventure /ədˈventʃə(r)/ *n.* (*exciting incident or episode*) приключéние; **a life of** ~ жизнь, пóлная приключéний; (*risky or irresponsible activity*) авантю́ра; ~ **story** приключéнческий ромáн.

adventurer /ədˈventʃərə(r)/ *n.* (*seeker of adventure*) искáтель (*m.*) приключéний; (*speculator*) авантюри́ст.

adventuress /ədˈventʃərɪs/ *n.* авантюри́стка.

adventurism /ədˈventʃəˌrɪz(ə)m/ *n.* авантюри́зм.

adventurist /ədˈventʃərɪst/ *n.* авантюри́ст.

adventurous /ədˈventʃərəs/ *adj.* **1** (*of person*) смéлый; (*enterprising*) предприи́мчивый. **2** (*of actions*) рискóванный, авантю́рный; (*dangerous*) рискóванный.

adventurousness /ədˈventʃərəsnɪs/ *n.* смéлость; предприи́мчивость.

adverb /ˈædvɜːb/ *n.* нарéчие.

adverbial /ədˈvɜːbɪəl/ *adj.* нарéчный, адвербиáльный.

adversary /ˈædvəsərɪ/ *n.* проти́вник.

adverse /ˈædvɜːs/ *adj.* (*unfavourable*) неблагоприя́тный; **it is** ~ **to our interests** э́то противорéчит нáшим интерéсам; (*harmful*) врéдный; ~ **winds** встрéчные, проти́вные вéтры (*m. pl.*).

adversity /ədˈvɜːsɪtɪ/ *n.* бедá, несчáстье; **show courage in, under** ~ проявля́ть, прояви́ть мýжество в бедé; **companions in** ~ товáрищи по несчáстью.

advert /ˈædvɜːt/ (*Br. coll.*) = **advertisement**

advertise /ˈædvəˌtaɪz/ *v.t.* (*boost, publicize*) реклами́ровать (*impf., pf.*); (*in newspaper*) да|вáть, -ть (*or* поме|щáть, -сти́ть) объявлéние о + *p.*; **I shall** ~ **my house for sale in the Times** я дам объявлéние о продáже дóма в «Таймс»; **even if you don't like him you needn't** ~ **the fact** дáже éсли он вам неприя́тен, не слéдует э́то афиши́ровать.

● *v.i.*: **she** ~**d for a secretary** онá далá объявлéние о вакáнсии секретаря́.

advertisement /ədˈvɜːtɪsmənt/, /-tɪzmənt/ *n.* реклáма; (*classified advertisement*) объявлéние; **his behaviour** (*Br.*), **behavior** (*US*) **is a poor** ~ **for the school** егó поведéние — плохáя реклáма для шкóлы.

advertiser /ˈædvəˌtaɪzə(r)/ *n.* рекламодáтель (*m.*).

advertising /ˈædvəˌtaɪzɪŋ/ *n.* реклами́рование; ~ **agent** реклáмный агéнт; **Smith is in the** ~ **business** Смит реклами́ст *or* рабóтает в реклáме.

advice /ədˈvaɪs/ *n.* **1** (*also* **piece of** ~) совéт; **give s.o. a piece, word of** ~ совéтовать, по- комý-н.; **seek s.o.'s** ~ совéтоваться, по- с кем-н.; **take legal** ~ обра|щáться, -ти́ться за совéтом к юри́сту; консульти́роваться, про- с юри́стом; **take, follow s.o.'s** ~ слéдовать, по- чьемý-н. совéту. **2** (*information*) сообщéние. **3** (*comm.: notification*) извещéние; **shipping** ~ извещéние об отгрýзке; **letter of** ~ ави́зо (*indecl.*).

advisability /ədˌvaɪzəˈbɪlɪtɪ/ *n.* целесообрáзность.

advisable /ədˈvaɪzəb(ə)l/ *adj.* целесообрáзный; **it may be** ~ **to wait** стóит, навéрное, подождáть.

advise /ədˈvaɪz/ *v.t.* **1** (*counsel*) совéтовать, по- + *d.*; рекомендовáть

(*impf., pf.*) + *d.*; **what do you ~ (me to do)?** что вы мне совéтуете дéлать?; **the doctor ~d complete rest** врач рекомендовáл пóлный óтдых; **I have been ~d not to smoke** мне посовéтовали не курить; **you would be well ~d to go** вам стóило бы пойти; **you would be better ~d to stay at home** разýмнее бы́ло бы остáться дóма; **I ~d him against going** я посовéтовал емý не ходить тудá; **an ill-~d move** необдýманный шаг; (*give professional advice to*) консультировать, про-.
2 (*comm.: notify*) изве|щáть, -стить (*кого о чём*); **please ~ me of receipt** увéдомите меня о получéнии.
● *v.i.*: **he ~d against marriage** он совéтовал не вступáть в брак; **doctors ~ against smoking** врачи рекомендýют не курить.

advisedly /əd'vaɪzɪdlɪ/ *adv.* намéренно.

advis|er, -or /əd'vaɪzə(r)/ *nn.* совéтник; (*professional*) консультáнт; **legal ~** юрискóнсульт; **medical ~** врач.

advisory /əd'vaɪzərɪ/ *adj.* совещáтельный, консультативный; **in an ~ capacity** в кáчестве совéтника; **~ committee** консультативный *or* совещáтельный комитéт.

advocacy /'ædvəkəsɪ/ *n.* (*support*) поддéржка; **he was well known for his ~ of penal reform** он был хорошó извéстен как сторóнник репóрмы пенитенциáрной систéмы; (*work of an advocate*) адвокатýра.

advocate[1] /'ædvəkət/ *n.* **1** (*defender*) защитник; (*supporter*) сторóнни|к (*fem.* -ца). **2** (*lawyer*) адвокáт; **Lord A~** (*Sc.*) Генерáльный прокурóр; **devil's ~** (*fig.*) «адвокáт дьявола».

advocate[2] /'ædvə,keɪt/ *v.t.* (*speak in favour of*) выступáть, вы́ступить за + *a.*; (*advise, recommend*) совéтовать, по-; рекомендовáть (*impf., pf.*).

adze /ædʒ/ (*US* **adz**) *n.* теслó (*род топора*).

Aegean /i:'dʒi:ən/ *n.*: **the ~** Эгéйское мóре.

aegis /'i:dʒɪs/ *n.*: **under the ~ of** под эгидой + *g.*

aeolian /i:'əʊlɪən/ *adj.*: **~ harp** Эóлова áрфа.

aeon /'i:ɒn/ *n.* (*geol.*) э́ра; (*fig.*) (цéлая) вéчность.

aerate /'eəreɪt/ *v.t.* провéтр|ивать, -ить.

aeration /,eə'reɪʃ(ə)n/ *n.* провéтривание; (*of the soil*) аэрáция.

aerial /'eərɪəl/ *n.* антéнна.
● *adj.* (*lit., fig.*) воздýшный; **~ photography** аэрофотосъёмка.

aero- /'eərəʊ/ *comb. form*: **~club** аэроклýб; **~engine** (*Br.*) авиамотóр, авиациóнный двигатель.

aerobatics /,eərə'bætɪks/ *n.* вы́сший/ фигýрный пилотáж.

aerobic /eə'rəʊbɪk/ *adj.* аэрóбный.

aerobics /eə'rəʊbɪks/ *n.* аэрóбика.

aerodrome /'eərə,drəʊm/ *n.* (*Br.*) аэродрóм.

aerodynamic /,eərəʊdaɪ'næmɪk/ *adj.* аэродинамический.

aerodynamics /,eərəʊdaɪ'næmɪks/ *n.* аэродинáмика.

aerofoil /'eərə,fɔɪl/ *n.* (*Br.*) (*wing*) крылó; (*wing shape or design*) прóфиль (*m.*) крылá.

aerogramme /'eərə,græm/ (*US* **aerogram**) *n.* авиаписьмó.

aerolite /'eərə,laɪt/ *n.* аэролит.

aeronaut /,eərəʊ'nɔ:t/ *n.* аэронáвт; воздухоплáватель (*m.*).

aeronautic(al) /,eərəʊ'nɔ:tɪk(ə)l/ *adj.* аэронавигациóнный, авиациóнный.

aeronautics /,eərəʊ'nɔ:tɪks/ *n.* аэронáвтика.

aeroplane /'eərə,pleɪn/ *n.* (*Br.*) самолёт, аэроплáн.

aerosol /'eərə,sɒl/ *n.* аэрозóль (*m.*).

aerospace /'eərəʊ,speɪs/ *n.* воздýшно-космическое прострáнство.
● *adj.* аэрокосмический.

aesthete /'i:sθi:t/ (*US also* **esthete**) *n.* эстéт.

aesthetic /i:s'θetɪk/ (*US also* **esthetic**) *adj.* эстетический.

aestheticism /i:s'θetɪ,sɪz(ə)m/ (*US also* **estheticism**) *n.* эстетизм.

aesthetics /i:s'θetɪks/ (*US also* **esthetics**) *n.* эстéтика.

aetiology /,i:tɪ'ɒlədʒɪ/ (*US* **etiology**) *n.* этиолóгия.

afar /ə'fɑ:(r)/ *adv.* вдалекé; **from ~** издали, издалекá.

affability /,æfə'bɪlɪtɪ/ *n.* привéтливость; любéзность.

affable /'æfəb(ə)l/ *adj.* привéтливый; любéзный.

affair /ə'feə(r)/ *n.* **1** (*business, matter*) дéло; **that's my ~** э́то моё дéло; **he asked me to look after his ~s** он попросил меня проследить за егó делáми; **~s of state** государственные делá; **~s of the heart** сердéчные делá; **Ministry of Foreign A~s** министéрство инострáнных дел; **man of ~s** деловóй человéк. **2** (*also* **love ~**) любóвная связь; ромáн; **they are having an ~** у них ромáн. **3** (*coll.*) (*event*) собы́тие; (*object; thing*) штýка.

affect[1] /ə'fekt/ *v.t.* **1** (*act on*) дéйствовать, по- на + *a.*; влиять, по- на + *a.*; **the climate ~ed his health** климат повлиял на егó здорóвье.
2 (*concern*) касáться, коснýться + *g.*; затрáгивать, затрóнуть; **everyone is ~ed by the rise in prices** повышéние цен затрáгивает всех. **3** (*touch emotionally*) трó|гать, -нуть; волновáть, вз-; **he was ~ed by the news** э́то извéстие на негó óчень подéйствовало; **an ~ing sight** волнýющее зрéлище. **4** (*of disease*): **the lung is ~ed** лёгкое поражéно; **several hundred cattle were ~ed** пострадáло нéсколько сот гóлов скотá.

affect[2] /ə'fekt/ *v.t.* (*assume pretentiously*): **he affects a northern accent** он говорит с дéланным сéверным акцéнтом; (*pretend*): **~ indifference** прики|дываться, -нуться равнодýшным; **he ~ed not to hear me** он притворился, что не слы́шит меня.

affectation /,æfek'teɪʃ(ə)n/ *n.* **1** (*pretence*) притвóрство. **2** (*unnatural behaviour*) аффектáция. **3** (*of language or style*) искýсственность.

affected /ə'fektɪd/ *adj.* (*person, behaviour*) жемáнный, неестéственный; (*feigned*) притвóрный.

affection /ə'fekʃ(ə)n/ *n.* привязанность (**for**: к + *d.*); любóвь; **I feel ~ for him** я к немý привязан.

affectionate /ə'fekʃənət/ *adj.* нéжный.

affective /ə'fektɪv/ *adj.* эмоционáльный.

affiance /ə'faɪəns/ *v.t.* (*arch.*): **they were ~d** они бы́ли обручены́.

affidavit /,æfɪ'deɪvɪt/ *n.* аффидáвит, пи́сьменное показáние под присягой; **make, swear an ~** да|вáть, -ть показáние под присягой.

affiliate /ə'fɪlɪ,eɪt/ *v.t.* **1** (*join, attach*) присоедин|ять, -ить (**to**: к + *d.*); **~d company** дочéрняя компáния.
2 (*adopt as member*) прин|имáть, -ять в члéны.
● *v.i.* присоедин|яться, -иться (**with**: к + *d.*).

affiliation /ə,fɪlɪ'eɪʃ(ə)n/ *n.* **1** присоединéние. **2** принятие в члéны. **3** (*connection*) связь.

affinity /ə'fɪnɪtɪ/ *n.* **1** (*resemblance*) схóдство; (*relationship*) рóдство; (*connection*) связь; (*closeness*) бли́зость; **there is a close ~ between these languages** э́ти языки óчень близки. **2** (*liking, attraction*) влечéние, склóнность.

affirm /ə'fɜ:m/ *v.t.* (*assert*) утвер|ждáть, -дить; (*leg.: make an ~ation*) торжéственно заяв|лять, -ить (вмéсто присяги).

affirmation /,æfə'meɪʃ(ə)n/ *n.* утверждéние; (*leg.*) торжéственное заявлéние; (*confirmation*) подтверждéние.

affirmative /ə'fɜ:mətɪv/ *n.*: **he answered in the ~** он отвéтил утвердительно.
● *adj.* утвердительный.

affix[1] /'æfɪks/ *n.* (*gram.*) áффикс.

affix[2] /ə'fɪks/ *v.t.* прикреп|лять, -ить (*что к чему*); **~ one's signature** стáвить, по- пóдпись; **~ a seal/stamp** при|клáдывать, -ложить печáть/ штéмпель (*m.*); **~ a postage stamp** приклéи|вать, -ть мáрку.

afflict /ə'flɪkt/ *v.t.* **1** (*distress: of misfortune etc.*) пост|игáть, -ичь (*or* -игнуть); **he was ~ed by a great misfortune** егó постигло большóе несчáстье; (*grieve*) огорч|áть -ить.
2 (*pass.: suffer from*): **be ~ed with** страдáть (*impf.*) + *i.*; **he is ~ed with rheumatism** он страдáет ревматизмом; **the ~ed** стрáждущие (*pl.*).

affliction /ə'flɪkʃ(ə)n/ *n.* (*grief*) гóре; (*misfortune*) несчáстье; бéдствие;

(*illness*) болéзнь; **the ~s of old age** стáрческие нéмощи (*f. pl.*).

affluence /ˈæfluəns/ *n.* (*wealth*) богáтство; (*plenty*) изобилие.

affluent /ˈæfluənt/ *adj.* богáтый; **~ society** óбщество изобилия.

afford /əˈfɔːd/ *v.t.* **1** (*with* **can**, *expr. possibility*): **I can't ~ all these books** все э́ти кни́ги мне не по кармáну; **he can ~ to laugh** он мóжет позвóлить себé смея́ться; **they can ~ a new car** они́ мóгут позвóлить себé нóвую маши́ну; **I can't ~ it** э́то мне не по кармáну; я не могý позвóлить себé э́то; **I can't ~ the time** мне нéкогда.
2 (*yield*; *supply*; *give*) предост|авля́ть, -áвить; да|вáть, -ть; **it will ~ me an opportunity to speak to her** э́то предостáвит *or* даст мне возмóжность поговори́ть с ней; **it ~s me great pleasure** э́то доставля́ет мне большóе удовóльствие; **the hill ~ed a fine view** с холмá открывáлся прекрáсный вид.

afforest /əˈfɒrɪst/, /æ-/ *v.t.* зас|áживать, -ади́ть лéсом; облеси́ть (*pf.*).

afforestation /əˌfɒrɪˈsteɪʃ(ə)n/ *n.* лесонасаждéние, облесéние.

affray /əˈfreɪ/ *n.* дрáка; скандáл; **they were charged with causing an ~** их обвини́ли в том, что они́ затéяли дрáку.

affront /əˈfrʌnt/ *n.* оскорблéние; **it was an ~ to his pride** э́то оскорбля́ло егó гóрдость.
● *v.t.* **1** (*insult*) оскорб|ля́ть, -и́ть.
2 (*confront*) смотрéть (*impf.*) в лицó + *d.*

Afghan /ˈæfgæn/ *n.* афгáн|ец (*fem.* -ка); (*~ hound*) афгáнская борзáя.
● *adj.* афгáнский.

Afghanistan /æfˈgænɪˌstɑːn/, /-stæn/ *n.* Афганистáн.

aficionado /əˌfɪsjəˈnɑːdəʊ/ *n.* (*pl.* **~s**) поклóнни|к (*fem.* -ца).

afield /əˈfiːld/ *adv.*: **far ~** вдалекé, вдали́; (*expr. motion*) вдаль.

afire /əˈfaɪə(r)/ *pred. adj. & adv.*: **the house was ~** дом был охвáчен огнём; **set something ~** подж|игáть, -éчь что-н.; (*fig.*): **he was ~ with enthusiasm** он пылáл энтузиáзмом.

aflame /əˈfleɪm/ *pred. adj. & adv.*: **his clothes were ~** егó одéжда загорéлась; (*fig.*): **~ with passion** пылáя стрáстью; **the woods were ~ with colour** лесá горéли рáзными крáсками.

afloat /əˈfləʊt/ *pred. adj. & adv.*
1 (*floating on water*) на водé; (*in sailing order*) на плавý; **get a ship ~** (*after grounding*) сн|имáть, -я́ть корáбль с мéли; **they had been ~ for several days** они́ плы́ли нéсколько дней.
2 (*at sea*) в мóре; **life ~** жизнь на водé/мóре. **3** (*fig., in circulation*): **various rumours** (*Br.*), **rumors** (*US*) **were ~** ходи́ли рáзные слýхи; (*comm.*) в обращéнии. **4 keep ~** (*fig., solvent*) (*v.t.*): **they kept the newspaper ~** они́ поддéрживали существовáние газéты; (*v.i.*) быть свобóдным от долгóв; не залезáть в долги́.

aflutter /əˈflʌtə(r)/ *pred. adj. & adv.* трепéщущий; (*fig.*) взволнóванный; **the news set her heart ~** от э́того извéстия у неё затрепетáло сéрдце.

afoot /əˈfʊt/ *pred. adj. & adv.* (*in progress or preparation*): **there is a plan ~** готóвится план; **there is something ~** чтó-то затевáется.

afore- /əˈfɔː(r)/ *comb. form*: **~mentioned** *adj.* вышеупомя́нутый; **~named** *adj.* вышенáзванный; **~said** *adj.* вышескáзанный; **malice ~thought** злой ýмысел.

a fortiori /ˌeɪ fɔːtɪˈɔːraɪ/ *adv.* тем бóлее.

afraid /əˈfreɪd/ *pred. adj.* испýганный; **be ~ of** боя́ться (*impf.*) + *g.*; **don't be ~** не бóйтесь!; **make s.o. ~** пугáть, ис- когó-н.; **I'm ~ he will die** бою́сь, что он умрёт; **I'm ~ of waking him** (*that I may wake him*) я бою́сь егó разбуди́ть; (*of the consequences*) я бою́сь егó буди́ть; **I'm ~ he is out** к сожалéнию, егó нет.

afresh /əˈfreʃ/ *adv.* зáново.

Africa /ˈæfrɪkə/ *n.* Áфрика.

African /ˈæfrɪkən/ *n.* африкáн|ец (*fem.* -ка).
● *adj.* африкáнский.
● *cpd.* **~ American** *n.* америкáнский негр (*fem.* америкáнская негритя́нка); *adj.* афро-америкáнский.

Afrikaans /ˌæfrɪˈkɑːns/ *n.* (язы́к) африкáанс.

Afrikaner /ˌæfrɪˈkɑːnə(r)/ *n.* жи́тель Ю́жно-Африкáнской Респýблики голлáндского происхождéния; африкáнер.

Afro /ˈæfrəʊ/ *n.* (*pl.* **Afros**) (*hairstyle*) причёска «áфро».
● *adj.*: **an ~ hair-do** причёска «áфро».

Afro- /ˈæfrəʊ/ *comb. form* áфро-. . .

Afro-American /ˌæfrəʊəˈmerɪkən/ = **African American**

Afro-Caribbean /ˌæfrəʊkærɪˈbiːən/, /-kəˈrɪbɪən/ *adj.* афро-кари́бский.
● *n.* афро-кари́б (*fem.* -ка).

aft /ɑːft/ *adv.* (*naut.*) на кормé; **fore and ~** от нóса к кормé.

after /ˈɑːftə(r)/ *adj.* **1** (*subsequent*) послéдующий; **in ~ years** в послéдующие гóды.
2 (*rear*) зáдний; (*naut.*) кормовóй; **~ deck** ют.
● *adv.* **1** (*subsequently*; *then*) потóм, затéм; **soon ~** вскóре пóсле э́того.
2 (*later*) позднéе, пóзже; **3 days ~** спустя́ три дня.
3 (*in consequence*) вспослéдствии.
4 (*Br. coll., as n. in pl.*) слáдкое; **what's for ~s?** что у нас на слáдкое?
● *prep.* **1** (*in expressions of time*) пóсле + *g.*; за + *i.*; чéрез + *a.*; спустя́ + *a.*; **~ dinner** пóсле обéда; **~ you!** тóлько пóсле вас!; **~ that** потóм, затéм; **the day ~ tomorrow** послезáвтра; **the day ~ the invitation** на слéдующий день пóсле приглашéния; **I am tired ~ my journey** я устáл с дорóги; **the week ~ next** недéля пóсле слéдующей; (*in adv. sense*) чéрез две недéли; **they met ~ 10 years** они́ встрéтились чéрез дéсять лет; **~ passing his exams, he ...** сдав экзáмены, он. . .; пóсле тогó, как он сдал экзáмены, он. . .; **he wrote that ~ receiving my letter** он написáл э́то, ужé получи́в моё письмó; он написáл э́то пóсле тогó, как он получи́л моё письмó; **~ midday** пóсле полýдня, зá полдень; **~ midnight** зá полночь, пóсле полýночи; **it's ~ 6 (o'clock)** ужé седьмóй час; (*in sequence*): **day ~ day** день за днём; **one ~ another** оди́н за други́м; **~ what he has done I shall never trust him again** пóсле тогó, что он сдéлал, я никогдá бóльше не бýду емý вéрить; (*in spite of*) несмотря́ на + *a.*; **~ all my care** в отвéт на все мои́ забóты; **~ all** (*in the end*) в конéчном счёте; в концé концóв; (*nevertheless*) всё-таки; **he's your brother, ~ all** ведь он ваш брат; **not so bad ~ all** не так уж плóхо.
2 (*in expressions of place*) за + *i.*; **shut the door ~ you** закрóйте за собóй дверь; **run ~ s.o.** бежáть за кем-н.; **he climbed up ~ Ivan** он влез (вслед) за Ивáном; **we shouted ~ him** мы кричáли емý вслед/вдогóнку.
3 (*in search of*; *trying to get*): **the police are ~ him** егó разы́скивает поли́ция; **he likes going ~ the girls** он бéгает за дéвушками; **what is he ~?** на что он мéтит?; что он замышля́ет?; **he is ~ your money** он мéтит на вáши дéньги.
4 (*in accordance with*) по + *d.*, соглáсно + *d.*; **a man ~ my own heart** человéк мне по душé; **~ a fashion** кóе-как; **he paints ~ a fashion** он в своём рóде худóжник; **named ~** нáзванный по + *d.* (*or* в честь + *g.*); **he takes ~ his father** он похóж на отцá; **a portrait ~ Van Dyck** портрéт в манéре Ван-Дéйка.
● *conj.* пóсле тогó как; **I arrived ~ he had left** я пришёл пóсле тогó, как он ушёл.
● *cpds.* **~birth** *n.* послéд; **~burner** *n.* дожигáтель (*m.*); **~-care** *n.* ухóд за выздорáвливающим; **~-dinner** *adj.* послеобéденный; **~-effect** *n.* послéдствие; **~glow** *n.* вечéрняя заря́; **~life** *n.* загрóбная жизнь; **~math** *n.* отáва; (*fig.*) послéдствия (*nt. pl.*); **~most** *adj.* сáмый зáдний; крáйний к кормé; **~noon** *n.* послеполýденное врéмя; **in the ~noon** днём; пóсле обéда; пополýдни; во вторóй полови́не дня; **at 3 in the ~noon** в три часá дня; **it is a beautiful ~noon** какóй прекрáсный день!; **good ~noon!** (*in greeting*) дóбрый день!; (*in leave-taking*) до свидáния; (*attr.*): **~noon nap** послеобéденный сон; **~shave** *n.* лосьóн пóсле бритья́; **~shock** *n.* повтóрные толчки́; **~taste** *n.* при́вкус; **~thought** *n.* запоздáлая мысль.

afterward /ˈɑːftəwəd/ *adv.* (*US*) = **afterwards**

afterwards /ˈɑːftəwədz/ *adv.* (*then*) потóм; (*subsequently*) вспослéдствии; (*later*) пóзже; **(a) long (time) ~** горáздо пóзже; **I only heard of it ~** я тóлько потóм услы́шал об э́том.

again /əˈgeɪn/, /əˈgen/ *adv.* **1** (*expr. repetition*) опя́ть, снóва; (*afresh, anew*) вновь; (*once more*) ещё раз; (*with certain vv.*) *by use of pref.* пере. . .; **read ~**

перечит|ывать, -ать; **open ~** вновь откр|ывать, -ыть; **say ~** повтор|ять, -ить; **start ~** (*v.t.*) возобнов|лять, -ить; (*v.i.*) нач|инать, -ать снова; **she married ~** она снова вышла замуж; **what's his name ~?** как, вы сказали, его фамилия?; **~ and ~** снова и снова; **time and (time) ~, over and over ~** то и дело; **now and ~** время от времени; **once ~** ещё раз; **he did his work over ~** он переделал работу.
2 (*with neg.: any more*) больше; **never ~** никогда больше; **don't do it ~!** больше этого не делай!
3 (*in addition*): **as far ~** вдвое дальше; **as much ~** ещё столько же; **half as much ~** (в) полтора раза больше.
4 (*expr. return to original state or position*): **back ~** обратно; **get something back ~** получ|ать, -ить что-н. обратно; **you'll soon be well ~** вы скоро поправитесь; **he is himself ~** он пришёл в себя.
5 (*moreover; besides*) к тому же; кроме того; (*on the other hand*) с другой стороны.

against /ə'geɪnst/, /ə'genst/ *prep.* **1** (*in opposition to*) против + *g.*; **I have nothing ~ it** я ничего не имею против этого; **I was ~ his going** я был против того, чтобы он шёл туда; **I acted ~ my will** я действовал против своей воли; **swim ~ the current** (*lit., fig.*) плыть (*impf.*) против течения; **they were working ~ time** они работали наперегонки со временем; **~ the rules** не по правилам; **fight, struggle ~** бороться (*impf.*) против + *g.* (*or* с + *i.*); **the battle ~ drunkenness** борьба с пьянством; **speak ~** (*oppose*) выступать, выступить против + *g.*
2 (*in spite of*) вопреки + *d.*; **~ reason** вопреки рассудку; **~ my better judgement** вопреки голосу рассудка.
3 (*to the disfavour of*): **her age is ~ her** возраст её подводит.
4 (*to oppose or combat*) на + *a.*; **march ~ the enemy** наступать (*impf.*) на врага.
5 (*to withstand*) от + *g.*; **a shelter ~ the storm** убежище от бури; **defend o.s. ~ the enemy** защищаться (*impf.*) от врага.
6 (*in readiness for, anticipation of*): **~ a rainy day** на чёрный день; **they bought provisions ~ the winter** они купили провизию на зиму.
7 (*compared with*): **3 deaths this year ~ 20 last year** три смерти в этом году против двадцати в прошлом.
8 (*in contrast with*): **it shows up ~ a dark background** это выделяется на тёмном фоне.
9 (*in collision with*) о + *a.*; **knock ~ something** ударяться, удариться о что-н.; **he banged his head ~ a stone** он ударился головой о камень.
10 (*into contact with*) к + *d.*; **he moved the chair ~ the wall** он придвинул стул к стене; **he stood leaning ~ the wall** он стоял, прислонившись к стене.
11 (*facing*): **over ~ the church** напротив церкви; **he held the photograph ~ the light** он поднёс фотографию к свету; **we are up ~ strong competition** у нас сильная конкуренция; **he is up ~ it** ему приходится тяжко; ≈ он прижат к стене.

agape /ə'geɪp/ *pred. adj. & adv.* разинув рот.

agate /'ægət/ *n.* агат; (*attr.*) агатовый.

agave /ə'geɪvɪ/ *n.* столетник, агава.

age /eɪdʒ/ *n.* **1** (*time of life*) возраст; **what ~ is he?** какого он возраста?; (*expecting exact answer*) сколько ему лет?; **he is 40 years of ~** ему сорок лет; **he and I are the same ~** мы с ним одного возраста *or* ровесники; **when I was your ~** когда я был в вашем возрасте; **a man (of) your ~** человек вашего возраста; **at his ~ he should be more careful** в его возрасте *or* годы надо быть более осторожным; **he is at an ~ (***or* **has reached an ~) when ...** он достиг возраста, когда...; **she doesn't look her ~** она выглядит моложе своих лет; **at an early ~** в раннем возрасте; **a man in middle ~** мужчина средних лет; **he took up tennis in middle ~** он занялся теннисом в солидном возрасте; **be your ~!** (*coll.*) ведите себя как взрослый человек!; **over ~** старше положенного возраста; **~ of consent** брачный возраст; **~ of discretion** возраст, с которого человек считается ответственным за свои поступки; (*of inanimate objects*): **what is the ~ of this house?** сколько лет этому дому?
2 (*majority*): **be of ~** быть совершеннолетним; **come of ~** дост|игать, -ичь совершеннолетия; **he is under ~** он несовершеннолетний.
3 (*old ~*) старость; **his back was bent with ~** он согнулся от старости; **he lived to a ripe (old) ~** он дожил до преклонных лет.
4 (*period*) период; (*century*) век; **Ice A~** ледниковый период; **Stone A~** каменный век; **golden ~** золотой век; **the Middle A~s** средние века; **the ~ we live in** наш век; (*coll., often pl., long time*): **it took an ~ to get there** мы добирались туда целую вечность; **the bus left ~s ago** автобус ушёл давным-давно; **we have not seen each other for ~s** мы не виделись целую вечность.
● *v.t.* (*pres. part.* **ageing, aging**) старить, со-; **worries have ~d him** заботы его состарили; (*of wine*) выдерживать, выдержать.
● *v.i.* (*pres. part.* **ageing, aging**) (*of person*) стареть, по-; стариться, со-; (*of thing*) стареть, у-.
● *cpds.* **~-bracket, ~-group** *nn.* возрастная группа; **~-limit** *n.* предельный возраст; **~-long** *adj.* вечный, вековечный; **~-old** *adj.* вековой, (старо)давний.

aged[1] /eɪdʒd/ *adj.* (*of the age of*): **~ six** шести лет.

aged[2] /'eɪdʒɪd/ *adj.* (*very old*) престарелый.
● *n.* : **the ~** пожилые люди, престарелые.

ag(e)ing /'eɪdʒɪŋ/ *n.* старение.
● *adj.* стареющий.

ageism /'eɪdʒɪz(ə)m/ *n.* дискриминация по возрасту.

ageist /'eɪdʒɪst/ *n.* сторонник дискриминации по возрасту.
● *adj.* дискриминирующий по возрасту.

ageless /'eɪdʒlɪs/ *adj.* (*always young*) нестареющий; (*eternal*) вечный.

agency /'eɪdʒənsɪ/ *n.* **1** (*action*) действие; (*instrumentality*) посредство; **by the ~ of** при посредстве + *g.*; посредством + *g.*; через + *a.* **2** (*force*): **an invisible ~** незримая сила.
3 (*comm.*) агентство; **employment ~** агентство по найму; **news ~** информационное агентство; **travel ~** туристическое агентство, бюро (*indecl.*) путешествий.
4 (*organization*): **government ~** правительственное учреждение.
5 (*representation*): **sole ~** единственное представительство.

agenda /ə'dʒendə/ *n.* повестка дня; **it is on the ~** это стоит на повестке дня; **put on the ~** ставить, по- на повестку дня.

agent /'eɪdʒ(ə)nt/ *n.* **1** (*person acting for others*) агент; (*representative*) представитель (*m.*); **commission ~** (*Br.*) комиссионер; **forwarding ~** экспедитор. **2** (*chem.*) агент; средство; **chemical ~** реактив, реагент.
3 (*gram.*) деятель (*m.*).

agent provocateur /ˌɑːʒɑ̃ prəˌvɒkə'tɜː(r)/ *n.* (*pl.* ***agents provocateurs*** *pronunc. same*) провокатор.

agglomerate[1] /ə'glɒmərət/ *n.* (*geol.*) агломерат, скопление.

agglomerate[2] /ə'glɒməˌreɪt/ *v.t. & i.* (*gather*) соб|ирать(ся), -рать(ся); (*mass*) ск|апливать(ся), -опить(ся).

agglomeration /əˌglɒmə'reɪʃ(ə)n/ *n.* скопление.

agglutinative /ə'gluːtɪnətɪv/ *adj.* (*ling.*) агглютинативный.

aggrandize /ə'grændaɪz/ *v.t.* увеличи|вать, -ть; расш|ирять, -ирить.

aggrandizement /ə'grændɪzmənt/ *n.* увеличение; расширение.

aggravat|e /'ægrəˌveɪt/ *v.t.* **1** (*make worse*) усугуб|лять, -ить; (*pain*) обостр|ять, -ить. **2** (*coll., exasperate*) раздраж|ать, -ить.

aggravation /ˌægrə'veɪʃ(ə)n/ *n.*
1 усугубление; обострение.
2 раздражение.

aggregate[1] /'ægrɪgət/ *n.* **1** (*total, mass*) совокупность; **in the ~** в совокупности. **2** (*phys.*) скопление.
3 (*ingredient of concrete*) заполнитель (*m.*) (бетона).
● *adj.* (*total*) совокупный; **~ membership** общее число членов.

aggregate[2] /'ægrɪˌgeɪt/ *v.t.* **1** (*collect into a mass*) соб|ирать, -рать в целое. **2** (*amount to*) сост|авлять, -авить; состоять (*impf.*) (в общей сложности) из + *g.*
● *v.i.* (*collect or come together*) соб|ираться, -раться.

aggregation /ˌægrɪ'geɪʃ(ə)n/ *n.*
1 (*collecting together*) сбор, собирание; (*collection of persons or things*)

скопле́ние, конгломера́т. **2** (*phys.*) скопле́ние; (*mass*) ма́сса.

aggression /əˈgreʃ(ə)n/ *n.* агре́ссия.

aggressive /əˈgresɪv/ *adj.* агресси́вный; **an ~ salesman** напо́ристый аге́нт по прода́же.

aggressiveness /əˈgresɪvnɪs/ *n.* агресси́вность.

aggressor /əˈgresə(r)/ *n.* агре́ссор.

aggrieve /əˈgriːv/ *v.t.* огорч|а́ть, -и́ть; **be ~d; feel (o.s.) ~d** быть огорчённым; огорч|а́ться, -и́ться.

aghast /əˈgɑːst/ *pred. adj.* (*terrified*) в у́жасе (*от чего*); (*amazed*) потрясённый.

agile /ˈædʒaɪl/ *adj.* прово́рный; **an ~ mind** живо́й ум.

agility /əˈdʒɪlɪtɪ/ *n.* прово́рство; **~ of mind** жи́вость ума́.

aging /ˈeɪdʒɪŋ/ = **ag(e)ing**

agitate /ˈædʒɪˌteɪt/ *v.t.* **1** (*excite*) волнова́ть, вз-; **be ~d about something** волнова́ться (*impf.*) из-за чего́-н.; **in an ~d voice** взволно́ванным го́лосом; (*arouse*) возбу|жда́ть, -ди́ть. **2** (*liquids*) взб|а́лтывать, -олта́ть.

● *v.i.* агити́ровать (*impf.*) (*for, against*: за + *a.*, про́тив + *g.*).

agitation /ˌædʒɪˈteɪʃ(ə)n/ *n.* **1** (*disturbance*) волне́ние; **in a state of ~** взволно́ванный. **2** (*of liquids*) взба́лтывание. **3** (*pol.*) агита́ция.

agitator /ˈædʒɪˌteɪtə(r)/ *n.* **1** (*pol.*) агита́тор. **2** (*apparatus*) смеси́тель (*m.*); меша́лка (*coll.*).

aglow /əˈgləʊ/ *pred. adj.* (*lit.*): **be ~** пыла́ть (*impf.*); (*red-hot*) раскалённый до́красна́; (*fig.*): **his face was ~** он раскрасне́лся; **~ with pleasure** раскрасне́вшийся от удово́льствия.

AGM (*abbr. of* ***Annual General Meeting***) (*Br.*) ежего́дное о́бщее собра́ние.

agnostic /ægˈnɒstɪk/ *n.* агно́стик.

● *adj.* агности́ческий.

agnosticism /ægˈnɒstɪˌsɪz(ə)m/ *n.* агностици́зм.

ago /əˈgəʊ/ *adv.* тому́ наза́д; **long ~** давно́; **not long ~** неда́вно; **it was longer ~ than I thought** э́то бы́ло (ещё) ра́ньше, чем я ду́мал.

agog /əˈgɒg/ *pred. adj.*: **she was ~ with excitement** она́ была́ вне себя́ от волне́ния.

● *adv.*: **he listened ~** он слу́шал, затаи́в дыха́ние.

agoniz|e /ˈægəˌnaɪz/ *v.t.* му́чить (*impf.*); **~ed, ~ing shrieks** отча́янные во́пли (*m. pl.*).

● *v.i.* **1** (*suffer agony*) терза́ться (*impf.*); му́читься (*impf.*). **2** (*fig.*): **he ~ed over his speech** он му́чился над свое́й ре́чью.

agon|y /ˈægənɪ/ *n.* (*torment*) муче́ние, страда́ние; (*pains of death*) аго́ния; **in his last ~y** в предсме́ртной аго́нии; **suffer ~ies** терза́ться (*impf.*); **I was in ~y** я о́чень страда́л; я му́чился от бо́ли; **~y column** (*Br.*) по́чта дове́рия.

agoraphobia /ˌægərəˈfəʊbɪə/ *n.* агорафо́бия, боя́знь простра́нства.

agoraphobic /ˌægərəˈfəʊbɪk/ *adj.* страда́ющий агорафо́бией.

agrarian /əˈgreərɪən/ *adj.* агра́рный.

agree /əˈgriː/ *v.t.* (**agrees, agreed, agreeing**) (*Br.*) **1** (*reach agreement on*) согласо́в|ывать, -а́ть (*что с кем*). **2** (*accept as correct*) утвер|жда́ть, -ди́ть; прин|има́ть, -я́ть.

● *v.i.* (**agrees, agreed, agreeing**) **1** (*concur; be of like opinion*) согла|ша́ться, -си́ться (*с кем*) (*used mainly for past and future*); **I quite ~ with you** я соверше́нно с ва́ми согла́сен; **we are ~d on this** мы в э́том согла́сны; **those two will never ~** э́ти дво́е никогда́ не договоря́тся. **2** (*reach agreement; make common decision*): **we ~d to go together** мы договори́лись е́хать вме́сте; **~ on a price** догова́риваться, договори́ться о цене́; **let us ~ to differ** оста́немся ка́ждый при своём мне́нии. **3** (*consent*) согла|ша́ться, -си́ться (*на что*) (*used mainly for past and future*). **4** (*accept*): **I ~ that it was wrong** согла́сен, что э́то бы́ло непра́вильно; **~ with** (*accept as correct or right*): **I don't ~ with his policy** я не согла́сен с его́ поли́тикой; **I don't ~ with keeping children up late** я про́тив того́, что́бы укла́дывать дете́й спать по́здно. **5**: **~ with** (*suit*) под|ходи́ть, -ойти́ + *d.*; годи́ться (*impf.*) + *d.*; **oysters don't ~ with me** от у́стриц мне быва́ет пло́хо. **6** (*conform; tally*): **the adjective ~s with the noun** прилага́тельное согласу́ется с существи́тельным; **his story ~s with mine** его́ расска́з схо́дится с мои́м.

agreeabl|e /əˈgriːəb(ə)l/ *adj.* **1** (*pleasant*) прия́тный; **he was ~y surprised** он был прия́тно удивлён; **make o.s. ~e to** стара́ться (*impf.*) угоди́ть + *d.* **2** (*acceptable*): **if that is ~e to you** е́сли вас э́то устра́ивает. **3** (*prepared to agree*): **be ~e to something** согла|ша́ться, -си́ться на что-н.

agreement /əˈgriːmənt/ *n.* **1** (*consent*) согла́сие; **by mutual ~** по взаи́мному согла́сию; **be in ~ with** согла|ша́ться, -си́ться с + *i.* **2** (*treaty*) соглаше́ние, догово́р; **come to an ~** при|ходи́ть, -йти́ к соглаше́нию; **enter into an ~ with** заключ|а́ть, -и́ть соглаше́ние/догово́р с + *i.* **3** (*gram.*) согласова́ние.

agricultural /ˌægrɪˈkʌltʃər(ə)l/ *adj.* сельскохозя́йственный.

agricultur(al)ist /ˌægrɪˈkʌltʃər(əl)ɪst/ *n.* земледе́лец.

agriculture /ˈægrɪˌkʌltʃə(r)/ *n.* се́льское хозя́йство.

agrimony /ˈægrɪmənɪ/ *n.* репе́йник, репе́й.

agrochemical /ˌægrəʊˈkemɪk(ə)l/ *n.* агрохимика́т.

● *adj.* агрохими́ческий.

agronomist /əˈgrɒnəmɪst/ *n.* агроно́м.

agronomy /əˈgrɒnəmɪ/ *n.* агроно́мия.

aground /əˈgraʊnd/ *pred. adj. & adv.*: **the ship was ~** кора́бль сиде́л на мели́; **run ~** (*v.i.*) сади́ться, сесть на мель.

ague /ˈeɪgjuː/ *n.* лихора́дочный озно́б.

ah /ɑː/ *int.* ах!; а!

aha /ɑːˈhɑː/, /əˈhɑː/ *int.* ага́!

ahead /əˈhed/ *adv.* впереди́; (*expr. motion*) вперёд; **he was ten yards ~ of us** он был на де́сять я́рдов впереди́ нас; **be, get ~ of** опере|жа́ть, -ди́ть; **move ~** продвига́ться, продви́нуться вперёд; **go ~!** (ну) дава́йте!; **things are going ~** дела́ иду́т; **~ of time** досро́чно; **look ~** (*fig.*) смотре́ть (*impf.*) вперёд; **in the days ~** в бу́дущем.

ahem /əˈhəm/, /əˈhem/ *int.* гм!

ahoy /əˈhɔɪ/ *int.*: **~ there!, ship ~!** эй, на корабле́/су́дне!; **land ~!** земля́!

AI 1 (*abbr. of* ***Artificial Intelligence***) иску́сственный интелле́кт. **2** (*abbr. of* ***artificial insemination***) иску́сственное оплодотворе́ние.

aid /eɪd/ *n.* **1** (*help, assistance*) по́мощь; (*support*) подде́ржка; **first ~** пе́рвая по́мощь; **~ agency** организа́ция по оказа́нию по́мощи; **~ worker** рабо́тн|ик (*fem.* -ица) организа́ции по оказа́нию по́мощи; **with, by the ~ of** при по́мощи + *g.*; **call on s.o.'s ~** приб|ега́ть, -е́гнуть к чьей-н. по́мощи; **go to s.o.'s ~** при|ходи́ть, -йти́ кому́-н. на по́мощь; **mutual ~** взаимопо́мощь; **in ~ of** в по́мощь + *d.*; **what is the collection in ~ of?** на что собира́ют де́ньги?; **what is this in ~ of?** (*Br. coll.*) к чему́ э́то?; **an ~ to digestion** сре́дство, спосо́бствующее пищеваре́нию. **2** (*appliance*) посо́бие; **visual ~s** нагля́дные посо́бия.

● *v.t.* (*help*) пом|ога́ть, -о́чь + *d.*; (*promote*) спосо́бствовать (*impf.*) + *d.*; **~ing and abetting** посо́бничество и подстрека́тельство.

aide /eɪd/ *n.* помо́щни|к (*fem.* -ца).

● *cpds.* **~-de-camp** *n.* адъюта́нт; **~-memoire** *n.* па́мятная запи́ска.

AIDS /eɪdz/ *n.* (*abbr. of* ***acquired immune deficiency syndrome***) СПИД (синдро́м приобретённого имму́нного дефици́та); **an ~ sufferer** страда́ющ|ий (*fem.* -ая) СПИДом; **an ~ vaccine** вакци́на про́тив СПИДа.

aigrette /ˈeɪgret/, /eɪˈgret/ *n.* (*plume*) султа́н, плюма́ж.

aiguillette /ˌeɪgwɪˈlet/ *n.* аксельба́нт.

aikido /aɪˈkiːdəʊ/ *n.* айки́до.

ail /eɪl/ *v.t.*: **what ~s him?** (*arch.*) чем он хвора́ет?

● *v.i.*: **he is always ~ing** он постоя́нно хвора́ет.

aileron /ˈeɪləˌrɒn/ *n.* элеро́н.

ailing /ˈeɪlɪŋ/ *adj.* больно́й; **an ~ economy** больна́я эконо́мика.

ailment /ˈeɪlmənt/ *n.* неду́г, хворь.

aim /eɪm/ *n.* **1** (*purpose*) цель; **with the ~ of** с це́лью + *g.*; **what is the ~ of these questions?** к чему́ э́ти вопро́сы? **2** (*of a gun, etc.*) прице́л; **take ~ at** прице́л|иваться, -иться в + *a.*; **miss one's ~** не попада́ть, попа́сть в цель; **is your ~ good?** у вас хоро́ший глаз?

● *v.t.* нав|оди́ть, -ести́; ~ **a rifle at** нав|оди́ть, -ести́ *or* напр|авля́ть, -а́вить винто́вку на + *a.*; ~ **a stone at** це́литься, на- ка́мнем в + *a.*; ~ **a blow at** зама́х|иваться, -ну́ться на + *a.*; (*fig.*): ~ **one's remarks at** предназн|ача́ть, -а́чить свои́ замеча́ния + *d.*

● *v.i.* це́лить (*impf.*); ~ **at** (*with rifle*) прице́л|иваться, -иться в + *a.*; (*fig.*): ~ **at** (*aspire to*) це́литься, на- на + *a.*; стреми́ться (*impf.*) к + *d.*; **he ~ed at becoming (or to become) a doctor** он поста́вил себе це́лью стать врачо́м; ~ **high** высоко́ ме́тить (*impf.*); **what are you ~ing at?** что вы име́ете в виду́; ~ **for** напр|авля́ться, -а́виться в/на + *a.*; **he ~ed for the tree** он напра́вился к де́реву.

aimless /ˈeɪmlɪs/ *adj.* бесце́льный.

aimlessness /ˈeɪmlɪsnɪs/ *n.* бесце́льность.

air /eə(r)/ *n.* **1** (*lit.*) во́здух; **stale ~** ду́шный *or* тяжёлый во́здух; **get some fresh ~** подыша́ть (*pf.*) све́жим во́здухом; **in the open ~** на откры́том во́здухе; **let some ~ into a room** прове́три|вать, -ть ко́мнату; **let the ~ out of** (*balloon, tyre*) выпуска́ть, вы́пустить во́здух из + *g.*; **take the ~** прогу́л|иваться, -я́ться; **take to the ~** взлет|а́ть, -е́ть; **into the ~** в во́здух, вверх; **travel by ~** лета́ть (*impf.*) (самолётом); **a change of ~** переме́на обстано́вки; ~ **current** возду́шное тече́ние; ~ **pollution** загрязне́ние во́здуха.
2 (*in fig. phrr.*): **a plan is in the ~** гото́вится план; **the question was left in the ~** вопро́с пови́с в во́здухе; **clear the ~** разря|жа́ть, -ди́ть атмосфе́ру; **hot ~** (*coll.*) хвастовство́, пустозво́нство; **he vanished into thin ~** его́ и след просты́л; **live on ~** пита́ться (*impf.*) во́здухом; **castles in the ~** возду́шные за́мки; **he was walking on ~** он ног под собо́й не чу́ял; **with his, her head in the ~** задра́в нос.
3 (*appearance, manner*) (*of person*) вид; (*of place*) дух; **there was a general ~ of desolation** во всём чу́вствовалось запусте́ние; **with a triumphant ~** с торжеству́ющим ви́дом; **~s and graces** мане́рность; **put on (or give o.s.) ~s** задава́ться, ва́жничать (*both impf.*).
4 (*mus., song*) пе́сня; (*tune*) моти́в.
5 (*radio, TV*): **the programme** (*Br.*), **program** (*US*) **is on the ~** програ́мма в эфи́ре; **go on the ~** выходи́ть, вы́йти в эфи́р; **go off the ~** (*of station*) зак|а́нчивать, -о́нчить переда́чу.
6 (*attr., pert. to aviation*) возду́шный; авиацио́нный, авиа...; (*mil.*) вое́нно-возду́шный; ~ **base** авиаба́за; ~ **corridor** возду́шный коридо́р; ~ **crash** авиакатастро́фа; ~ **display** возду́шный пара́д; ~ **force** вое́нно-возду́шные си́лы; ~ **hostess** (*Br.*) бортпроводни́ца, стюарде́сса; **A~ Marshal** ма́ршал авиа́ции; ~ **show** авиасало́н; ~ **terminal** аэровокза́л; ~ **ticket** авиабиле́т.

● *v.t.* **1** (*ventilate*) прове́три|вать, -ть; (*Br., dry*) суши́ть, вы-.
2 (*fig.*) (*opinions, feelings*) выска́зывать, вы́сказать; ~ **one's knowledge** выставля́ть, вы́ставить напока́з свои́ зна́ния.

● *v.i.* про|су́шивать, -суши́ть; **she hung the clothes out to ~** она́ разве́сила ве́щи для просу́шки.

● *cpds.* **~bag** *n.* авари́йная предохрани́тельная поду́шка; **~-bed** *n.* (*Br.*) надувно́й матра́ц; **~borne** *adj.* (*landed by ~*) возду́шно-деса́нтный; (*in the air*): **we were ~borne at 9 o'clock** мы бы́ли в во́здухе в 9 ч.; **~-brake** *n.* возду́шный то́рмоз; **~-brick** *n.* (*Br.*) пустоте́лый кирпи́ч; **~bus** *n.* аэро́бус; **~-conditioned** *adj.* с кондициони́рованным во́здухом; **~-conditioner** *n.* кондиционе́р (во́здуха); **~-conditioning** *n.* кондициони́рование во́здуха; **~-cooled** *adj.* охлажда́емый во́здухом; **~craft** *n.* самолёт, (*collect.*) самолёты, авиа́ция; **~craft-carrier** *n.* авиано́сец; **~craftman** *n.* рядово́й авиа́ции; **~crew** *n.* экипа́ж; **~-cushion** *n.* надувна́я поду́шка; **~-dried** *adj.* воздушносухо́й, возду́шной су́шки; **~drome** *n.* (*US*) = **aerodrome; ~-drop** *n.* (*of troops*) возду́шный деса́нт; (*of supplies*) сбра́сывание гру́за с самолёта; **~-duct** *n.* воздухопрово́д; **~field** *n.* лётное по́ле; **~flow** *n.* возду́шный пото́к; **~foil** *n.* (*US*) = **aerofoil; ~-frame** *n.* ко́рпус самолёта; **~-freighter** *n.* грузово́й самолёт; **~-gauge** *n.* возду́шный мано́метр; **~gun** *n.* духово́е ружьё; **~lane** *n.* возду́шный коридо́р; **~-letter** *n.* авиаписьмо́; **~lift** *n.* возду́шная перебро́ска; *v.t.* перебр|а́сывать, -о́сить (*or* перев|ози́ть, -езти́) по во́здуху; **~line** *n.* (*company*) авиакомпа́ния; (*route*) авиали́ния, авиатра́сса; **~-liner** *n.* авиала́йнер, возду́шный ла́йнер; **~-lock** *n.* (*stoppage*) возду́шная про́бка; **~mail** *n.* авиапо́чта; **~man** *n.* лётчик; **~plane** *n.* (*US*) = **aeroplane; ~-pocket** *n.* (*aeron.*) возду́шная я́ма, (*tech.*) возду́шный мешо́к, га́зовый пузы́рь; **~port** *n.* аэропо́рт; **~-power** *n.* возду́шная мощь; **~-pump** *n.* возду́шный насо́с; **~-raid** *n.* возду́шный налёт; **~-raid alert, warning** возду́шная трево́га; **~-raid shelter** бомбоубе́жище; **~-raid warden** уполномо́ченный по противовозду́шной оборо́не; **~-rifle** *n.* пневмати́ческая винто́вка; **~screw** *n.* (*Br.*) (возду́шный) винт; пропе́ллер; **~-sea rescue** *n.* спаса́тельные опера́ции (*f. pl.*), проводи́мые самолётами на мо́ре; **~ship** *n.* возду́шный кора́бль, дирижа́бль (*m.*); **~sick** *adj.*: **I was ~sick** меня́ укача́ло в самолёте; **~sickness** *n.* возду́шная боле́знь; **~space** *n.* возду́шное простра́нство; **~speed** *n.* возду́шная ско́рость; **~stream** *n.* возду́шный пото́к; **~strip** *n.* взлётно-поса́дочная полоса́; **~tight** *adj.* гермети́ческий; ~ **time** *n.* вре́мя в эфи́ре; **~-to-air** *adj.*: **~-to-air missile** раке́та «во́здух — во́здух»; **~-to-ground** *adj.*: **~-to-ground missile** раке́та «во́здух — земля́»; **~-traffic control** *n.* авиадиспе́тчерская слу́жба; **~-traffic controller** *n.* авиадиспе́тчер; **~waves** *n.* радиоволны́; **~way** *n.* (*route*) возду́шная тра́сса; **~woman** *n.* лётчица; **~worthiness** *n.* го́дность к полётам, лётная го́дность; **~worthy** *adj.* го́дный к полётам.

Airedale /ˈeədeɪl/ *n.* эрдельтерье́р.

airer /ˈeərə(r)/ *n.* (*Br.*) суши́лка.

airily /ˈeərɪlɪ/ *adv.* небре́жно, с лёгкостью.

airiness /ˈeərɪnɪs/ *n.* (*freshness*) све́жесть; (*lightness*) возду́шность; (*fig., of manner*) беспе́чность.

airing /ˈeərɪŋ/ *n.* **1** (*admission of air*) прове́тривание; ~ **cupboard** (*Br.*) суши́льный шкаф. **2** (*fig.*): **give one's views an ~** выска́зывать, вы́сказать свои́ взгля́ды.

airless /ˈeəlɪs/ *adj.* (*stuffy*) ду́шный; (*still*) безве́тренный.

airlessness /ˈeəlɪsnɪs/ *n.* духота́, безве́трие.

airy /ˈeərɪ/ *adj.* (**airier, airiest**)
1 (*well-ventilated*) све́жий; (*spacious*) просто́рный. **2** (*light in movement etc.*) возду́шный; **an ~ dress** возду́шное пла́тье. **3** (*superficial; light-hearted*) ве́треный, беспе́чный.

● *cpd.* **~-fairy** *adj.* (*coll., pej.*) прожектёрский; **~-fairy scheme** проже́кт.

aisle /aɪl/ *n.* боково́й неф; (*in theatre etc.*) прохо́д.

ajar /əˈdʒɑː(r)/ *pred. adj.* приоткры́тый.

aka (*abbr. of* **also known as**) изве́стный та́кже под и́менем.

akimbo /əˈkɪmbəʊ/ *adv.* подбоче́нясь; **stand with arms ~** подбоче́ниться (*pf.*) *or* стоя́ть (*impf.*) подбоче́нясь.

akin /əˈkɪn/ *pred. adj. & adv.* (*related*) ро́дственный; ~ **to** сродни́ + *d.*

à la /ˈɑː lɑː/ *prep.* а-ля́.

alabaster /ˈæləˌbɑːstə(r)/, /-ˌbæstə(r)/, /ˌæləˈb-/ *n.* алеба́стр; (*attr.*) алеба́стровый.

à la carte /ˌɑː lɑː ˈkɑːt/ *adv.* порцио́нно, на зака́з.

alacrity /əˈlækrɪtɪ/ *n.* (*liveliness*) жи́вость; (*zeal*) рве́ние.

à la mode /ˌɑː lɑː ˈməʊd/ *adj. & adv.* мо́дный; по мо́де.

alarm /əˈlɑːm/ *n.* **1** (*warning; warning signal*) трево́га; **false ~** ло́жная трево́га; **give, raise, sound the ~** подн|има́ть, -я́ть трево́гу; **fire ~** пожа́рная трево́га. **2** (**~-clock**) буди́льник; **I set the ~ for 6** я поста́вил буди́льник на 6 часо́в.
3 (*fright*): **he ran away in ~** он убежа́л в испу́ге.

● *v.t.* трево́жить; **to be ~ed** трево́житься, вс-; **don't be ~ed** не трево́жьтесь; **~ing news** трево́жные но́вости (*f. pl.*); **there's nothing to be ~ed about** не сто́ит трево́житься; нет по́вода для трево́ги.

alarming /əˈlɑːmɪŋ/ *adj.* трево́жный.

alarmist /əˈlɑːmɪst/ *n.* паникёр (*fem.* -ша).

alas /əˈlæs/, /əˈlɑːs/ *int.* увы́!

Alaska /əˈlæskə/ *n.* Аля́ска; **in ~** на Аля́ске.

Alaskan /əˈlæskən/ *n.* аля́скин|ец (*fem.* -ка).

● *adj.* аля́скинский.

alb /ælb/ *n.* стиха́рь (*m.*).

Albania /ælˈbeɪnɪə/ *n.* Алба́ния.

Albanian /ælˈbeɪnɪən/ *n.* **1** (*person*) алба́н|ец (*fem.* -ка). **2** (*language*) алба́нский язы́к.

● *adj.* алба́нский.

albatross /ˈælbəˌtrɒs/ *n.* альбатро́с.

albeit /ɔːlˈbiːɪt/ *conj.* пусть (и), хотя́ и.

albinism /ˈælbɪˌnɪz(ə)m/ *n.* альбини́зм.

albino /ælˈbiːnəʊ/ *n.* (*pl.* **~s**) альбино́с (*fem.* -ка); **an ~ rabbit** кро́лик-альбино́с.

album /ˈælbəm/ *n.* (*book*; *recordings*) альбо́м.

albumen /ˈælbjʊmɪn/ *n.* (*white of egg*) яи́чный бело́к; (*chem.*) альбуми́н; (*biol.*) бело́к.

alchemist /ˈælkəmɪst/ *n.* алхи́мик.

alchemy /ˈælkəmɪ/ *n.* алхи́мия.

alcohol /ˈælkəˌhɒl/ *n.* (*chem.*) алкого́ль (*m.*); (*spirit*) спирт.

● *cpd.* **~-free** *adj.* безалкого́льный.

alcoholic /ˌælkəˈhɒlɪk/ *n.* алкого́лик.

● *adj.* алкого́льный; **~ beverages** спиртно́е; спиртны́е напи́тки (*m. pl.*).

alcoholism /ˈælkəhɒˌlɪz(ə)m/ *n.* алкоголи́зм.

alcove /ˈælkəʊv/ *n.* альков, ни́ша.

alder /ˈɔːldə(r)/ *n.* ольха́ (чёрная).

alderman /ˈɔːldəmən/ *n.* (*US*) член муниципалите́та.

ale /eɪl/ *n.* эль (*m.*); (*beer*) пи́во.

● *cpd.* **~-house** *n.* пивна́я.

alert /əˈlɜːt/ *n.* **1** (*alarm*) трево́га; **give the ~** поднима́ть, подня́ть трево́гу. **2**: **on the ~** наготове; **keep s.o. on the ~** держа́ть (*impf.*) кого́-н. в гото́вности.

● *adj.* (*vigilant*) чу́ткий; (*lively*) живо́й.

● *v.t.* прив|оди́ть, -ести́ в состоя́ние гото́вности; **~ s.o. to a situation** предупре|жда́ть, -ди́ть кого́-н. о созда́вшейся обстано́вке.

alertness /əˈlɜːtnɪs/ *n.* чу́ткость; жи́вость.

Aleutians /əˈluːʃənz/ *n.*: **the ~** Алеу́тские острова́ (*m. pl.*).

A level /ˈeɪ levəl/ *n.* (*Br.*) экза́мен по програ́мме сре́дней шко́лы на повы́шенном у́ровне; **he has three ~s** он сдал три предме́та на повы́шенном у́ровне.

Alexandria /ˌælɪgˈzɑːndrɪə/, /-ˈzændrɪə/ *n.* Александри́я.

Alexandrine /ˌælɪgˈzændraɪn/ *n.* александри́йский стих.

alfalfa /ælˈfælfə/ *n.* люце́рна.

alfresco /ælˈfreskəʊ/ *adv.* на откры́том во́здухе.

alga /ˈælgə/ *n.* (*pl.* **algae** /ˈældʒiː/, /ˈælgiː/) морска́я во́доросль.

algebra /ˈældʒɪbrə/ *n.* а́лгебра.

algebraic /ˌældʒɪˈbreɪɪk/ *adj.* алгебраи́ческий.

Algeria /ælˈdʒɪərɪə/ *n.* Алжи́р.

Algerian /ælˈdʒɪərɪən/ *n.* алжи́р|ец (*fem.* -ка).

● *adj.* алжи́рский.

Algiers /ælˈdʒɪəz/ *n.* Алжи́р.

algorithm /ˈælgəˌrɪð(ə)m/ *n.* алгори́тм.

alias /ˈeɪlɪəs/ *n.* кли́чка, про́звище; вы́мышленное и́мя?; (*comput.*) псевдони́м; **the thief had several ~es** у во́ра бы́ло не́сколько кли́чек; **his ~ was ...** он называ́л себя́...; **he travelled** (*Br.*), **traveled** (*US*) **under an ~** он путеше́ствовал под вы́мышленным и́менем.

● *adv.*: **Jones, ~ Robinson** Джо́нс, он же Ро́бинсон.

alibi /ˈælɪˌbaɪ/ *n.* (*pl.* **~s**) **1** (*plea or proof of being elsewhere*) а́либи (*nt. indecl.*); **establish an ~** устан|а́вливать, -ови́ть а́либи; **produce an ~** предст|авля́ть, -а́вить а́либи. **2** (*coll.*, *excuse*) отгово́рка.

alien /ˈeɪlɪən/ *n.* иностра́н|ец (*fem.* -ка); (*extra-terrestrial*) инопланетя́н|ин (*fem.* -ка).

● *adj.* **1** (*foreign*) иностра́нный; (*extra-terrestrial*) инопланетный. **2**: **~ to** чу́ждый + *d.*

alienable /ˈeɪlɪənəb(ə)l/ *adj.* (*leg.*) отчужда́емый.

alienate /ˈeɪlɪəˌneɪt/ *v.t.* **1** (*estrange, antagonize*) отвра|ща́ть, -ти́ть; отчужда́ть (*impf.*). **2** (*leg.*) отчужда́ть (*impf.*).

alienation /ˌeɪlɪəˈneɪʃ(ə)n/ *n.* (*alienating*) отчужде́ние; (*being alienated*) отчуждённость.

alight[1] /əˈlaɪt/ *pred. adj.* & *adv.* **1** (*on fire*) горя́щий, в огне́; **catch ~** загор|а́ться, -е́ться; **set ~** заж|ига́ть, -е́чь; **is your cigarette ~?** у вас сигаре́та гори́т? **2** (*illuminated*) освещённый. **3** (*fig.*): **eyes ~ with happiness** глаза́, сия́ющие сча́стьем.

alight[2] /əˈlaɪt/ *v.i.* (**alighted**) **1** (*Br.*, *dismount from horse or vehicle*) сходи́ть, сойти́ (с + *g.*). **2** (*come to earth*: *of birds etc.*) сади́ться, сесть; (*of an aircraft*) приземл|я́ться, -и́ться.

align /əˈlaɪn/ *v.t.* выра́внивать, вы́ровнять; **~ o.s. with s.o.** станови́ться, стать на чью-н. сто́рону.

alignment /əˈlaɪnmənt/ *n.* выра́внивание; **out of ~** неро́вно, не в ряд; (*arrangement*) расстано́вка; **~ with** (*adherence to*) присоедине́ние к + *d.*

alike /əˈlaɪk/ *pred. adj.* (*similar*) (*people*) похо́жий (на + *a.*); (*objects*) схо́жий (с + *i.*); **they are very much ~** они́ о́чень похо́жи друг на дру́га; (*as one*) одина́ковый; **all things are ~ to him** ему́ всё одно́.

● *adv.* одина́ково; **treat everyone ~** обраща́ться (*impf.*) со все́ми одина́ково; **winter and summer ~** как зимо́й, так и ле́том.

aliment /ˈælɪmənt/ *n.* пи́ща.

alimentary /ˌælɪˈmentərɪ/ *adj.* (*of food*): **~ products** пищевы́е проду́кты; (*digestive*): **~ canal, tract** пищевари́тельный тракт.

alimentation /ˌælɪmenˈteɪʃ(ə)n/ *n.* (*nourishment*) пита́ние.

alimony /ˈælɪmənɪ/ *n.* (*leg.*) алиме́нт|ы (*pl.*, *g.* -ов).

alive /əˈlaɪv/ *pred. adj.* & *adv.* **1** (*living*) живо́й; в живы́х; **who is the greatest man ~?** кто са́мый вели́кий из живу́щих люде́й?; **buried ~** за́живо похоро́ненный; **~ and kicking** жив-здоро́в (*coll.*); **more dead than ~** е́ле живо́й; **he was kept ~ with drugs** его́ подде́рживали лека́рствами. **2** (*alert*): **be ~ to the danger** сознава́ть (*impf.*) опа́сность; быть начеку́; **look ~!** живе́е! **3** (*infested*): **the bed was ~ with fleas** крова́ть кише́ла блоха́ми.

alkali /ˈælkəˌlaɪ/ *n.* (*pl.* **~s**) щёлочь; (*attr.*) щелочно́й.

alkaline /ˈælkəˌlaɪn/ *adj.* щелочно́й.

alkaloid /ˈælkəˌlɔɪd/ *n.* (*chem.*) алкало́ид.

all /ɔːl/ *n.*: **he staked his ~** он поста́вил на ка́рту всё.

● *pron.* (*everybody*) все; (*everything*) всё; **~ of us** мы все; **it cost ~ of £10** э́то сто́ило це́лых 10 фу́нтов; **the score is 2 ~** счёт 2:2; **it was ~ I could do not to ...** я едва́ сдержа́лся, что́бы не...; **~ but** (*almost*) почти́, чуть не; **he ~ but died** он чуть бы́ло не у́мер; **~ but a few died** почти́ все у́мерли; **~ in the day's work** де́ло привы́чное; **~ in good time** всё в своё вре́мя; **~ in ~** (*in general*) в о́бщем и це́лом; **it's ~ one to me** мне всё равно́; **that's ~ very well, but ...** всё э́то прекра́сно, но...; *see also* ⇨**well**[2]; **above ~** пре́жде всего́; **after ~** в конце́ концо́в; в коне́чном счёте; **after ~, I did warn you!** я ведь предупрежда́л вас; **he came after ~** он всё же пришёл; **any card at ~** люба́я ка́рта; **not at ~** совсе́м/во́все не; наско́лько, ничу́ть; **'Thank you.' — 'Not at ~!'** «Спаси́бо.» — «Не́ за что!»; **he has no money at ~** у него́ совсе́м нет де́нег; **you have eaten nothing at ~** вы ничего́ не е́ли; **for ~ I care, he may drown** по мне, пусть хоть уто́нет; **for ~ I know he may be dead** отку́да/почём я зна́ю, мо́жет, он и у́мер; **once and for ~** раз и навсегда́; **in ~; ~ told** в це́лом; всего́.

● *adj.* весь; (*every*) вся́кий; **~ his life** всю свою́ жизнь; **~ day long** весь день; **~ the time** всё вре́мя; **at ~ times** в любо́е вре́мя; всегда́; **at ~ costs** любо́й цено́й; во что бы то ни ста́ло; **beyond ~ doubt** без/вне вся́кого сомне́ния; **by ~ accounts** су́дя по всему́; **for ~ his wealth** несмотря́ на всё его́ бога́тство; **for ~ that** всё-таки; **for ~ time** навсегда́; **of ~ the cheek!** кака́я на́глость!; **you of ~ people** кто-кто, а уж вы-то; **on ~ fours** на четвере́ньках; **with ~ respect** при всём уваже́нии; ... **and ~ that** и так да́лее; и про́чее; **it's not ~ that hard** (*coll.*), **not as hard as ~ that** э́то не так уж тру́дно; **he's very clever and ~ that, but ...** он о́чень умён и всё тако́е, но...

● *adv.* (*quite*) совсе́м, соверше́нно;

целико́м; ~ **dressed up** наряди́вшись; разряди́вшись в пух и прах; **she was (dressed) ~ in black** она́ была́ оде́та во всё чёрное; **I got ~ excited** я разволнова́лся; **he was ~ ready to go** он был гото́в идти́; **~ along the road** всю доро́гу; на всём пути́; **I knew it ~ along** я всегда́ э́то знал; **~ around** повсю́ду, круго́м; **~ at once** соверше́нно внеза́пно; вдруг; **she lived ~ by herself** она́ жила́ совсе́м одна́; **she did it ~ by herself** она́ сде́лала э́то сама́; **I am ~ ears** я обрати́лся в слух; **I'm ~ for it** я целико́м и по́лностью за; **~ in** (*exhausted*) вы́бившийся из сил; (*inclusive of everything*) включа́я всё; **he went ~ out to win** он сде́лал всё для побе́ды; **~ over the room** по всей ко́мнате; **~ the world over** по всему́ ми́ру; **it's ~ over now** всё ко́нчено; с э́тим поко́нчено; **~ over again** (всё) сно́ва; **he was ~ over her** (*coll.*) он ей прохо́ду не дава́л; **that's him ~ over** э́то так на него́ похо́же; **~ the rage** после́дний крик мо́ды; **~ right!** ла́дно!, хорошо́!; **how are you? — ~ right!;** как дела́? — ничего́!; **is the coffee ~ right?** ну, как ко́фе, ничего́?; **the film was ~ right** фильм был неплохо́й; **are you ~ right?** вы чу́вствуете себя́ норма́льно?; **I'm ~ right now** сейча́с у меня́ всё хорошо́; (*safe*): **we got back ~ right** мы верну́лись благополу́чно; (*in good order*) в поря́дке; (*implying threat*): **~ right, you wait!** ну хорошо́ же, погоди́те!; **~ the better** тем лу́чше; **~ the same** (*however*) всё-таки; **if it's ~ the same to you** е́сли вам всё равно́; **he's not ~ there** у него́ не все до́ма; **~ too soon** сли́шком ско́ро; **you're ~ wrong** вы соверше́нно не пра́вы.

● *cpds.* **~-American** *adj.* чи́сто америка́нский; **~-clear** *n.* отбо́й (трево́ги); **sound the ~-clear** дава́ть, дать отбо́й; **~-embracing** *adj.* всеобъе́млющий; **~-important** *adj.* чрезвыча́йно ва́жный; **~-in** *adj.* (*Br.*): **~-in price** цена́, включа́ющая всё; **~-in wrestling** во́льная борьба́; **~-night** *adj.*: **~-night session** заседа́ние, продолжа́ющееся всю ночь; **~-out** *adj.*: **an ~-out effort** максима́льное уси́лие; **~-party** *adj.* общепарти́йный; **~-powerful** *adj.* всемогу́щий, всеси́льный; **~-purpose** *adj.* универса́льный; **~-round** *adj.*: **~-round sportsman, ~-rounder** (*Br.*) разносторо́нний спортсме́н; **~-Russian** *adj.* всеросси́йский; **~-seeing** *adj.* всеви́дящий; **~spice** *n.* души́стый/ яма́йский пе́рец; **~-star** *adj.*: **with an ~-star cast** с уча́стием звёзд; **~-time** *adj.*: **at an ~-time low** на небыва́ло ни́зком у́ровне; **~-time record** непревзойдённый реко́рд; **~-up** *adj.*: **~-up weight** (*Br., aeron.*) по́лный полётный вес; **~-weather** *adj.* всепого́дный.

Allah /'ælə/ *n.* Алла́х.

allay /ə'leɪ/ *v.t.* (*doubts, suspicions*) рассе́|ивать, -ять; (*fears*) разве́|ивать, -ять; **~ pain** ун|има́ть, -я́ть боль; **~ thirst/hunger** утол|я́ть, -и́ть жа́жду/ го́лод.

allegation /ˌælɪ'geɪʃ(ə)n/ *n.* заявле́ние, утвержде́ние; **~s of corruption were brought against him** его́ обвини́ли в корру́пции.

allege /ə'ledʒ/ *v.t.* утвержда́ть (*impf.*); **he ~d ill health** он сосла́лся на нездоро́вье; **words ~d to have been spoken by him** слова́, припи́сываемые ему́; **he is ~d to have died** его́ счита́ют уме́ршим; **an ~d murderer** подозрева́емый в уби́йстве.

allegedly /ə'ledʒɪdlɪ/ *adv.* бу́дто бы, я́кобы.

allegiance /ə'li:dʒ(ə)ns/ *n.* (*loyalty*) ве́рность; (*devotion*) пре́данность; **owe ~ to the queen** быть по́дданным короле́вы.

allegorical /ˌælɪ'gɒrɪk(ə)l/ *adj.* аллегори́ческий.

allegory /'ælɪgərɪ/ *n.* аллего́рия.

allegretto /ˌælɪ'gretəʊ/ *n., adj. & adv.* (*pl.* **~s**) аллегре́тто (*indecl.*).

allegro /ə'leɪgrəʊ/, /ə'leg-/ *n., adj. & adv.* (*pl.* **~s**) алле́гро (*indecl.*).

alleluia /ˌælɪ'lu:jə/ *n. & int.* аллилу́йя.

allergen /'ælədʒ(ə)n/ *n.* аллерге́н.

allergic /ə'lɜ:dʒɪk/ *adj.* аллерги́ческий; **I'm ~ to strawberries** у меня́ аллерги́я на клубни́ку.

allergy /'ælədʒɪ/ *n.* аллерги́я.

alleviate /ə'li:vɪˌeɪt/ *v.t.* (*relieve, lighten*) облегч|а́ть, -и́ть; (*mitigate, soften*) смягч|а́ть, -и́ть.

alleviation /əˌli:vɪ'eɪʃ(ə)n/ *n.* облегче́ние; смягче́ние.

alley /'ælɪ/ *n.* (*pl.* **~s**) **1** (*narrow street*) переу́лок; **blind ~** тупи́к; **~ cat** бездо́мная ко́шка; **that's right up my ~** (*coll.*) э́то как раз по мое́й ча́сти. **2** (*walk, avenue*) алле́я.

alliance /ə'laɪəns/ *n.* сою́з; (*pol.*)алья́нс; **marriage ~** бра́чный сою́з; брак; **Holy A~** (*hist.*) Свяще́нный Сою́з.

allied /'ælaɪd/ *adj.* (*joined by alliance*) сою́зный; (*related*) ро́дственный; **~ sciences** сме́жные нау́ки; **a bird ~ to the ostrich** пти́ца из отря́да стра́усов; (*closely connected*) сме́жный, схо́дный.

alligator /'ælɪˌgeɪtə(r)/ *n.* аллига́тор; **~ pear** (*US*) авока́до (*indecl.*).

alliteration /əˌlɪtə'reɪʃ(ə)n/ *n.* аллитера́ция.

alliterative /ə'lɪtərətɪv/ *adj.* аллитери́рующий.

allocate /'æləˌkeɪt/ *v.t.* (*fin.: allot, earmark*) выделя́ть, вы́делить; (*money*) ассигнова́ть (*impf., pf.*); (*distribute*) разме|ща́ть, -сти́ть; (*assign*) назн|ача́ть, -а́чить.

allocation /ˌælə'keɪʃ(ə)n/ *n.* (*allocating*) выделе́ние; ассигнова́ние; размеще́ние; назначе́ние; (*portion*) до́ля; (*sum allocated*) ассигнова́ние.

allot /ə'lɒt/ *v.t.* (**allotted, allotting**) (*distribute*) распредел|я́ть, -и́ть; (*assign*) назн|ача́ть, -а́чить; (*award*) прису|жда́ть, -ди́ть; **~ a task** да|ва́ть, -ть зада́ние.

allotment /ə'lɒtmənt/ *n.* **1** (*in vbl. senses*) распределе́ние; назначе́ние; присужде́ние. **2** (*Br., plot of land*) (земе́льный) уча́сток.

allow /ə'laʊ/ *v.t.* **1** (*permit*) позв|оля́ть, -о́лить; разреш|а́ть, -и́ть; **~ me!** разреши́те!; **he was ~ed to smoke** ему́ позво́лили кури́ть; **I will not ~ you to be deceived** я не допущу́, что́бы вас обману́ли; **~ no discussion** запре|ща́ть, -ти́ть вся́кое обсужде́ние; **smoking is not ~ed** кури́ть воспреща́ется; **no dogs ~ed** вход с соба́ками воспрещён. **2** (*grant, provide*) да|ва́ть, -ть; предост|авля́ть, -а́вить; допус|ка́ть, -ти́ть; **I ~ed him a free hand** я предоста́вил ему́ свобо́ду де́йствий; **at the end of the 6 months ~ed** в конце́ предоста́вленных шести́ ме́сяцев; **~ discount** предост|авля́ть, -а́вить ски́дку. **3** (*admit*) допус|ка́ть, -ти́ть; (*recognize*) призн|ава́ть, -а́ть; **his claim was allowed** его́ тре́бование бы́ло при́нято.

● *v.i.* **1 ~ for** (*take into account*) уч|и́тывать, -е́сть; **~ing for casualties** учи́тывая возмо́жные поте́ри; **not ~ing for expenses** не принима́я в расчёт изде́ржек; **~ £50 for emergencies** выделя́ть, вы́делить 50 фу́нтов на чрезвыча́йный слу́чай; **~ for his being ill** принима́ть, приня́ть во внима́ние то, что он бо́лен; **~ for shrinkage** де́лать, с- до́пуск на уса́дку. **2 ~ of**: **his tone ~ed of no reply** его́ тон не допуска́л возраже́ний.

allowable /ə'laʊəb(ə)l/ *adj.* допусти́мый, допуска́емый.

allowance /ə'laʊəns/ *n.* **1** (*amount provided*): **monthly ~** ме́сячное посо́бие; **family ~** посо́бие на семью́; **make s.o. an ~** назнача́ть, назна́чить содержа́ние кому́-н.; (*mil.*) дово́льствие. **2** (*discount*) ски́дка; **~ for cash** ски́дка за платёж нали́чными. **3** (*concession*): **we will make an ~ in your case** мы сде́лаем для вас исключе́ние; **make ~(s) for** уч|и́тывать, -е́сть; прин|има́ть, -я́ть во внима́ние. **4** (*tech.*) до́пуск; **shrinkage ~** до́пуск на уса́дку; (*correction*): **~ for wind** попра́вка на ве́тер.

alloy /'ælɔɪ/, /ə'lɔɪ/ *n.* сплав.

● *v.t.* спл|авля́ть, -а́вить; (*fig., becloud*) омрач|а́ть, -и́ть.

allud|e /ə'lu:d/, /ə'lju:d/ *v.i.*: **~ to** ссыла́ться, сосла́ться на + *a.*; упом|ина́ть, -яну́ть; (*mean*): **what are you ~ing to?** на что вы намека́ете?

allure /ə'ljʊə(r)/ *n.* привлека́тельность, пре́лесть.

● *v.t.* (*entice, attract*) зама́н|ивать, -и́ть; (*charm*) завл|ека́ть, -е́чь; очаро́|вывать, -а́ть.

allurement /ə'ljʊəmənt/ *n.* (*enticement*) привлече́ние; (*charm*) привлека́тельность, пре́лесть.

alluring /ə'ljʊərɪŋ/ *adj.* зама́нчивый; очарова́тельный.

allusion /ə'lu:ʒ(ə)n/, /ə'lju:-/ *n.* намёк; ссы́лка; **make an ~ to** ссыла́ться, сосла́ться на + *a.*

allusive /ə'lu:sɪv/, /ə'lju:-/ *adj.* содержа́щий намёк; намека́ющий.

alluvia /ə'lu:vɪə/ *pl. of* ⇒**alluvium**

alluvial /ə'lu:vɪəl/ *adj.* аллювиа́льный; **~ deposit** ро́ссыпь.

alluvi|um /ə'lu:vɪəm/ *n.* (*pl.* **~a** *or* **~ums**) аллю́вий.

ally¹ /'ælaɪ/ *n.* сою́зник.

all|y² /ə'laɪ/ *v.t.* (*connect*) соедин|я́ть, -и́ть; **~ied to** (*of things*) соединённый с + *i.*, свя́занный с + *i.*; **to be ~ied to, with** (*of nations*) быть в сою́зе с + *i.*; **~y o.s. with** вступ|а́ть, -и́ть в сою́з с + *i.*

Alma-Ata /ˌælməə'tɑ:/ *n.* Алма́-Ата́.

Alma Mater /ˌælmə 'mɑ:tə(r)/, /'meɪtə(r)/ *n.* а́льма-ма́тер (*f. indecl.*).

almanac /'ɔ:lməˌnæk/, /'ɒl-/ *n.* альмана́х.

Almaty /æl'mɑ:tɪ/ *n.* Алма́ты (*m. indecl.*).

almighty /ɔ:l'maɪtɪ/ *n.*: **the A~** Всемогу́щий, Всевы́шний.

● *adj.* всемогу́щий; (*coll., great*): **an ~ blow** мо́щный уда́р; **we had an ~ row** у нас был ужа́сный сканда́л.

almond /'ɑ:mənd/ *n.* минда́ль (*m.*); **a smell of ~s** за́пах миндаля́.

● *adj.* минда́льный.

almost /'ɔ:lməʊst/ *adv.* почти́; (*with vv.*) почти́, чуть не, едва́ не.

alms /ɑ:mz/ *n.* ми́лостыня; **give ~** подава́ть, пода́ть ми́лостыню.

● *cpds.* **~giving** *n.* разда́ча ми́лостыни; **~house** *n.* богаде́льня.

aloe /'æləʊ/ *n.* ало́э (*nt. indecl.*); **(bitter) ~s** ало́э, сабу́р.

aloft /ə'lɒft/ *adv.* наверху́; (*of motion*) наве́рх; (*naut.*) на ма́рсе; (*aeron.*) в во́здухе.

alone /ə'ləʊn/ *adj.* **1** (*by o.s., itself*) оди́н; еди́нственный; **he came ~** он пришёл оди́н; **you can't move the piano ~** вы оди́н не смо́жете сдви́нуть роя́ль; **not by bread ~** не хле́бом еди́ным.
2 (... *and no other*(*s*)): **in the month of June ~** то́лько в ию́не ме́сяце; **she and I are ~ (together)** мы с ней вдвоём/одни́; (*pred.*: *the only one*(*s*)): **he was ~ opposing the suggestion** он оди́н был про́тив предложе́ния; **we are not ~ in thinking so** не то́лько мы так ду́маем.
3 let, leave ~: his parents left him ~ all day роди́тели оста́вили его́ на це́лый день одного́; **I should leave the dog ~** я бы оста́вил соба́ку в поко́е; **let well ~!** от добра́ добра́ не и́щут; **let ~** (*coll.*) не говоря́ уже́ о + *p.*

along /ə'lɒŋ/ *adv.* **1** (*on; forward*): **move ~** продв|ига́ться, -и́нуться; **move ~, please!** проходи́те/продвига́йтесь, пожа́луйста!; **come ~!** пошли́!; **a few doors ~ from the station** в не́скольких шага́х от вокза́ла; **get ~ with** ла́дить с + *i.*; уж|ива́ться, -и́ться с + *i.*; **they do not get ~** они́ не ла́дят; **get ~ with you!** (*go away*) проходи́те!; (*expr. disbelief*) бро́сьте.
2 (*denoting accompaniment*): **come ~ with me** пойдёмте/иди́те со мной; **he brought a book ~** он принёс с собо́й кни́гу.
3 (*over there; over here*): **he went ~ to the exhibition** он пошёл на вы́ставку; **he'll be ~ in 10 minutes** он бу́дет че́рез де́сять мину́т.
4: **all ~** (*the whole time*) всё вре́мя; **I said so all ~** я э́то всегда́ говори́л; **I knew it all ~** я э́то знал с са́мого нача́ла.

● *prep.* вдоль + *g.*; по + *d.*; **she was walking ~ the river** она́ шла вдоль реки́; **they sailed ~ the river** они́ плы́ли по реке́.

● *cpd.* **~shore** *adv.* вдоль бе́рега.

alongside /əlɒŋ'saɪd/ *adv.* (*naut.*) борт о́ борт; **come ~** прист|ава́ть, -а́ть (к + *d.*); (*in general*) ря́дом, сбо́ку; **we stopped and the police car drew up ~** мы останови́лись, и подъе́хавшая полице́йская маши́на вста́ла ря́дом.

● *prep.* (*also* **~ of**) ря́дом с + *i.*; у + *g.*; **they were walking ~ us** они́ шли ря́дом с на́ми; **~ the quay** у при́стани; **come ~ a ship/wharf** прист|ава́ть, -а́ть к кораблю́/прича́лу; (*compared with*) в сравне́нии с + *i.*

aloof /ə'lu:f/ *adj.* сде́ржанный, отчуждённый.

● *adv.*: **keep, hold ~** держа́ться (*impf.*) в стороне́.

aloofness /ə'lu:fnɪs/ *n.* сде́ржанность, отчуждённость.

aloud /ə'laʊd/ *adv.* вслух; **read ~** чита́ть вслух; **she wept ~** она́ пла́кала навзры́д.

alp /ælp/ *n.*: **the A~s** А́льп|ы (*pl., g.* —).

alpaca /æl'pækə/ *n.* (*animal*) альпака́ (*c.g. indecl.*); (*fabric*) альпака́ (*nt. indecl.*).

alpha /'ælfə/ *n.* а́льфа; **~ particle** а́льфа-части́ца; **~ plus** (*Br., examination mark*) «отли́чно».

alphabet /'ælfəˌbet/ *n.* алфави́т, а́збука.

alphabetical /ˌælfə'betɪk(ə)l/ *adj.* алфави́тный; **in ~ order** в алфави́тном поря́дке.

alphanumeric /ˌælfənju:'merɪk/ *adj.* алфави́тно-цифрово́й.

alpine /'ælpaɪn/ *adj.* альпи́йский.

alpinist /'ælpɪnɪst/ *n.* альпини́ст.

already /ɔ:l'redɪ/ *adv.* уже́.

Alsatian /æl'seɪʃ(ə)n/ *n.* (*Br.*) неме́цкая овча́рка.

also /'ɔ:lsəʊ/ *adv.* то́же; та́кже; (*moreover*) к тому́ же; **not only ... but ~** ... не то́лько..., но и...

● *cpd.* **~-ran** *n.* неуда́чник.

altar /'ɔ:ltə(r)/, /'ɒl-/ *n.* престо́л; (*in fig. uses*) алта́рь (*m.*); **high ~** гла́вный престо́л; **lead to the ~** вести́ (*det.*) под вене́ц; (*pagan*) алта́рь, же́ртвенник.

● *cpds.* **~-piece** *n.* запресто́льный о́браз; **~-rail** *n.* огра́да алтаря́; **~-screen** *n.* (*in Russian church*) иконоста́с.

alter /'ɔ:ltə(r)/, /'ɒl-/ *v.t. & i.* меня́ть(ся) (*impf.*); измен|я́ть(ся), -и́ть(ся); **~ for the worse** изменя́ться, измени́ться к ху́дшему; **he has ~ed towards her** он перемени́лся к ней; (*re-make*) переде́л|ывать, -ать; **the dress needs ~ing** э́то пла́тье на́до переде́лать.

alterable /'ɔ:ltərəb(ə)l/, /'ɒl-/ *adj.* изменя́емый.

alteration /ˌɔ:ltə'reɪʃ(ə)n/, /'ɒl-/ *n.* (*change*) измене́ние; (*replacement*) переме́на; (*re-making e.g. of clothes*) переде́лка; (*re-building*) перестро́йка, реконстру́кция; **the theatre** (*Br.*), **theater** (*US*) **is under ~** теа́тр под реконстру́кцией.

altercation /ˌɔ:ltə'keɪʃ(ə)n/, /ˌɒl-/ *n.* ссо́ра, перебра́нка.

alter ego /ˌæltər 'i:gəʊ/, /'egəʊ/ *n.* (*pl.* ***alter egos***) второ́е «я», «а́льтер э́го» (*indecl.*).

alternate¹ /ɔ:l'tɜ:nət/, /ɒl-/ *n.* (*US*) замести́тель (*m.*).

alternate² /ɔ:l'tɜ:nət/, /ɒl-/ *adj.*
1 (*taking turns*) чередую́щийся; **on ~ Saturdays** ка́ждую втору́ю суббо́ту; **~ly** попереме́нно. **2** (*US, alternative*) альтернати́вный. **3** (*math.*): **~ angles** противолежа́щие углы́.

alternat|e³ /'ɔ:ltəˌneɪt/, /'ɒl-/ *v.t. & i.* чередова́ть(ся) (*impf.*); перемежа́ть(ся) (*impf.*); **~e work and rest** чередова́ть труд с о́тдыхом; **~ing current** переме́нный ток.

alternation /ˌɔ:ltə'neɪʃ(ə)n/, /ˌɒl-/ *n.* чередова́ние; **the ~ of day and night** сме́на дня и но́чи.

alternative /ɔ:l'tɜ:nətɪv/, /ɒl-/ *n.* альтернати́ва; **there is no ~** друго́го вы́бора нет.

● *adj.* альтернати́вный; **~ medicine** альтернати́вная медици́на; **an ~ proposal** встре́чное предложе́ние; **~ technology** альтернати́вная техноло́гия; **we have several ~ plans** у нас есть не́сколько альтернати́вных пла́нов.

alternatively /ɔ:l'tɜ:nətɪvlɪ/, /ɒl-/ *adv.* (*indicating choice*): **a £5 fine, ~ one month's imprisonment** штраф 5 фу́нтов и́ли оди́н ме́сяц тюре́много заключе́ния.

alternator /'ɔ:ltəˌneɪtə(r)/, /'ɒl-/ *n.* (*elec.*) генера́тор переме́нного то́ка.

although /ɔ:l'ðəʊ/ *conj.* хотя́; (*despite the fact that*) несмотря́ на то, что; **~ ill, he came** несмотря́ на боле́знь, он пришёл; **~ young, he is experienced** он хоть и молодо́й, но о́пытный.

altimeter /'æltɪˌmi:tə(r)/ *n.* альтиме́тр; высотоме́р.

altitude /'æltɪˌtju:d/ *n.* (*of flight*) высота́; (*of a place*) высота́ над у́ровнем мо́ря; **they flew at an ~ of 10,000 metres** они́ лете́ли на высоте́ 10 000 ме́тров; **~ sickness** го́рная боле́знь.

alto /'æltəʊ/ *n.* (*pl.* **altos**) альт; (*attr.*) альто́вый.

altogether /ˌɔ:ltə'geðə(r)/ *adv.*
1 (*entirely*) вполне́; соверше́нно; **he is not ~ pleased with the result** он не вполне́ дово́лен результа́том; **it is ~ out of the question** э́то соверше́нно исключено́; (*completely*) совсе́м. **2** (*in all, in general; as a whole*) в це́лом, в о́бщем; всего́; **how much is that ~?** ско́лько всего́?

altruism /'æltru:ˌɪz(ə)m/ *n.* альтруи́зм.

altruist /'æltru:ɪst/ *n.* альтруи́ст.

altruistic /ˌæltruːˈɪstɪk/ *adj.* альтруисти́ческий.

alum /ˈæləm/ *n.* квасц|ы́ (*pl., g.* -о́в).

alumin|ium (*US* **-um**) /ˌæljʊˈmɪnɪəm:/, /əˈluːmɪnəm/ *n.* алюми́ний.

alumna /əˈlʌmnə/ *n.* (*pl.* **alumnae** /-niː/) (бы́вшая) учени́ца; (*of a university*) (бы́вшая) студе́нтка.

alumnus /əˈlʌmnəs/ *n.* (*pl.* **alumni** /-niː/) (бы́вший) учени́к; (*of a university*) (бы́вший) студе́нт.

always /ˈɔːlweɪz/ *adv.* всегда́; (*constantly*) постоя́нно, всё вре́мя; **he is ~ after money** он всегда́/постоя́нно ду́мает о деньга́х; **~ the same old thing** всё одно́ и то же; **this child is ~ crying** этот ребёнок все вре́мя пла́чет; **there is ~ Mr Smith** на худо́й коне́ц всегда́ есть ми́стер Смит.

Alzheimer's disease /ˈæltsˌhaɪməz/ *n.* боле́знь Альцге́ймера.

am /æm/, /əm/ *1st pers. sing. pres. of* ⇨**be**

a.m. (*abbr. of* ***ante meridiem***) утра́; (*in the morning*) у́тром; **6 ~** шесть часо́в утра́; **Sunday a.m.** в воскресе́нье у́тром.

amalgam /əˈmælgəm/ *n.* амальга́ма; (*fig.*) смесь.

amalgamate /əˈmælgəˌmeɪt/ *v.t. & i.* (*of metals*) амальгами́ровать(ся) (*impf., pf.*); (*fig., unite*) объедин|я́ть(ся), -и́ть(ся); (*companies*) слива́ть(ся), сли́ть(ся).

amalgamation /əˌmælgəˈmeɪʃ(ə)n/ *n.* амальгами́рование; объедине́ние; (*of companies*) слия́ние.

amanuensis /əˌmænjuːˈensɪs/ *n.* (*pl.* **amanuenses** /-siːz/) ли́чный секрета́рь.

amass /əˈmæs/ *v.t.* накоп|ля́ть, -и́ть.

amateur /ˈæmətə(r)/ *n.* люби́тель (*m.*); (*pej.*) дилета́нт; (*attr.*) люби́тельский; **~ theatricals** театра́льная самоде́ятельность, люби́тельский теа́тр; **~ sport** люби́тельский спорт.

amateurish /ˈæmətərɪʃ/ *adj.* дилета́нтский, непрофессиона́льный.

amatory /ˈæmətərɪ/ *adj.* любо́вный.

amaz|e /əˈmeɪz/ *v.t.* изум|ля́ть, -и́ть; **be ~ed at** изум|ля́ться, -и́ться + *d.*; **~ing** изуми́тельный, удиви́тельный.

amazement /əˈmeɪzmənt/ *n.* изумле́ние; **he looked at me in ~** он посмотре́л на меня́ с изумле́нием; **to everyone's ~** ко всео́бщему изумле́нию.

Amazon /ˈæməz(ə)n/ *n.* (*myth., fig.*) амазо́нка; (*river*) Амазо́нка.

ambassador /æmˈbæsədə(r)/ *n.* посо́л; (*representative*) представи́тель (*m.*).

ambassadorial /ˌæmbæsəˈdɔːrɪəl/ *adj.* посо́льский.

amber /ˈæmbə(r)/ *n.* **1** (*resin*) янта́рь (*m.*). **2** (*colour*) янта́рный цвет, цвет янтаря́; **he crossed on the ~ (traffic light)** он прое́хал на жёлтый свет.

ambergris /ˈæmbəgrɪs/, /-ˌgriːs/ *n.* се́рая а́мбра.

ambidexterity /ˌæmbɪdekˈsterɪtɪ/ *n.* одина́ковое владе́ние обе́ими рука́ми.

ambidext(e)rous /ˌæmbɪˈdekstrəs/ *adj.* одина́ково владе́ющий обе́ими рука́ми.

ambience /ˈæmbɪəns/ *n.* среда́; атмосфе́ра.

ambient /ˈæmbɪənt/ *adj.* окружа́ющий; **~ temperature** температу́ра окружа́ющего во́здуха.

ambiguity /ˌæmbɪˈgjuːɪtɪ/ *n.* двусмы́сленность; нея́сность.

ambiguous /æmˈbɪgjʊəs/ *adj.* двусмы́сленный; нея́сный.

ambit /ˈæmbɪt/ *n.* (*bounds, limits*) грани́цы (*f. pl.*); **within the ~ of** в преде́лах + *g.*

ambition /æmˈbɪʃ(ə)n/ *n.* (*desire for distinction*) честолю́бие, амби́ция; (*aspiration*) стремле́ние; **her great ~ is to be a dancer** её заве́тная мечта́ — стать танцо́вщицей.

ambitious /æmˈbɪʃəs/ *adj.* честолюби́вый; амбицио́зный; **he is too ~** он сли́шком мно́гого хо́чет; **an ~ attempt** сме́лая попы́тка; **an ~ plan** грандио́зный план.

ambivalence /æmˈbɪvələns/ *n.* дво́йственность.

ambivalent /æmˈbɪvələnt/ *adj.* дво́йственный.

amble /ˈæmb(ə)l/ *n.* (*horse's pace*) и́ноходь; (*easy gait*) лёгкая похо́дка.

● *v.i.* (*of horse*) идти́ (*det.*) и́ноходью; (*of person*) идти́ (*det.*) лёгкой похо́дкой.

ambrosia /æmˈbrəʊzɪə/, /-ʒjə/ *n.* амбро́зия.

ambulance /ˈæmbjʊləns/ *n.* маши́на ско́рой по́мощи; (*mil.*): **field ~** полево́й го́спиталь; **~ station** (*where first aid is given*) медици́нский пункт; (*where ambulances are kept*) ста́нция ско́рой по́мощи; **call an ~!** вы́зовите ско́рую по́мощь!

ambulant /ˈæmbjʊlənt/ *adj.*: **~ patient** ходя́чий больно́й; **~ treatment** амбулато́рное лече́ние.

ambush /ˈæmbʊʃ/ *n.* заса́да; **lay an ~** устр|а́ивать, -о́ить заса́ду; **lie in ~** сиде́ть (*impf.*) в заса́де; **run into an ~** поп|ада́ть, -а́сть в заса́ду.

● *v.t.* нап|ада́ть, -а́сть на (*кого*) из заса́ды.

ameba /əˈmiːbə/ (*US*) = **amoeba**

ameliorate /əˈmiːlɪəˌreɪt/ *v.t. & i.* ул|учша́ть(ся), -у́чшить(ся).

amelioration /əˌmiːlɪəˈreɪʃ(ə)n/ *n.* улучше́ние.

amen /ɑːˈmen/, /eɪ-/ *int.* ами́нь.

amenability /əˌmiːnəˈbɪlɪtɪ/ *n.* пода́тливость.

amenable /əˈmiːnəb(ə)l/ *adj.* (*tractable*) пода́тливый, послу́шный; (*responsive*) поддаю́щийся (*чему*); **~ to reason** досту́пный го́лосу ра́зума.

amend /əˈmend/ *v.t.* **1** (*correct*) испр|авля́ть, -а́вить; (*improve*) ул|учша́ть, -у́чшить. **2** (*make changes to*) вн|оси́ть, -ести́ поправки/добавле́ния в + *a.*; **an ~ed law** зако́н с (при́нятыми к нему́) попра́вками.

amendment /əˈmendmənt/ *n.* **1** (*reform*) исправле́ние. **2** (*of document etc.*) попра́вка; **make an ~ to** вн|оси́ть, -ести́ попра́вку в + *a.*

amends /əˈmendz/ *n.* возмеще́ние; исправле́ние; **make ~ to s.o.** загла́|живать, -дить вину́ пе́ред + *i.* (*за что*); **he made ~ for his rudeness** он загла́дил свою́ гру́бость.

amenit|y /əˈmiːnɪtɪ/, /əˈmenɪtɪ/ *n.* (*usu. in pl.*) (*comforts*) удо́бства (*nt. pl.*); (*pleasures*) удово́льствия (*nt. pl.*).

America /əˈmerɪkə/ *n.* Аме́рика.

American /əˈmerɪkən/ *n.* америка́н|ец (*fem.* -ка).

● *adj.* америка́нский; **~ English** америка́нский вариа́нт англи́йского языка́; **~ Indian** америка́нск|ий инде́ец (*fem.* -ая индиа́нка).

Americanism /əˈmerɪkəˌnɪz(ə)m/ *n.* американи́зм.

Americanize /əˈmerɪkəˌnaɪz/ *v.t.* американизи́ровать (*impf., pf.*).

amethyst /ˈæmɪθɪst/ *n.* амети́ст; (*attr.*) амети́стовый.

Amharic /æmˈhærɪk/ *n.* амха́рский язы́к.

● *adj.* амха́рский.

amiability /ˌeɪmɪəˈbɪlɪtɪ/ *n.* приве́тливость; доброду́шие.

amiable /ˈeɪmɪəb(ə)l/ *adj.* приве́тливый; доброду́шный.

amicability /ˌæmɪkəˈbɪlɪtɪ/ *n.* дружелю́бие.

amicable /ˈæmɪkəb(ə)l/ *adj.* дружелю́бный; (*agreement, separation*) дру́жеский; (*divorce*) ми́рный.

amid(st) /əˈmɪdst/ *prep.* среди́ + *g.*

● *cpd.* **~ships** *adv.* посереди́не корабля́; **the torpedo hit us ~** торпе́да попа́ла в са́мый центр на́шего корабля́.

amino acid /əˌmiːnəʊˈæsɪd/ *n.* аминокислота́.

amiss /əˈmɪs/ *pred. adj.* непра́вильный; **something is ~** что́-то нела́дно; **what's ~?** в чём де́ло?

● *adv.* **1** (*wrongly*) непра́вильно; **take ~** (*take offence at*) об|ижа́ться, -и́деться на + *a.* **2** (*out of place*) некста́ти.

amity /ˈæmɪtɪ/ *n.* дру́жеские отноше́ния; дру́жба.

ammeter /ˈæmɪtə(r)/ *n.* ампермéтр.

ammonia /əˈməʊnɪə/ *n.* (*gas*) аммиа́к; (*attr.*) аммиа́чный; (*solution; spirit of ~*) нашаты́рный спирт.

ammoniac /əˈməʊnɪˌæk/ *adj.* аммиа́чный; **sal ~** нашаты́рь (*m.*).

ammonium /əˈməʊnɪəm/ *n.* аммо́ний; **~ chloride** нашаты́рь (*m.*), хло́ристый аммо́ний; **~ nitrate** аммони́йная сели́тра.

ammunition /ˌæmjʊˈnɪʃ(ə)n/ *n.* боевы́е припа́сы, боеприпа́сы (*m. pl.*); **~ belt** патро́нная ле́нта, патронта́ш; **~ dump, store** склад боеприпа́сов; (*fig.*): **this article will provide the ~ I need** э́та статья́ даст мне в ру́ки необходи́мое ору́жие.

amnesia /æmˈniːzɪə/ *n.* амнези́я.

amnesiac /æmˈniːzɪˌæk/ *adj.* страда́ющий амнези́ей.

amnesty /ˈæmnɪstɪ/ *n.* амни́стия.

● *v.t.* амнисти́ровать (*impf., pf.*); да|ва́ть, -ть амни́стию + *d.*

amniocentesis /ˌæmnɪəʊsenˈtiːsɪs/ *n.* про́ба амниоти́ческой жи́дкости.

amoeba /əˈmiːbə/ (*US also* **ameba**) *n.* (*pl.* **amoebas** *or* **amoebae** /-biː/) амёба.

am|ok /əˈmɒk/, **-uck** /əˈmʌk/ *adv.*: **run ~** бу́йствовать (*impf.*); беси́ться (*impf.*).

among /əˈmʌŋ/ *prep.* **1** (*between*) ме́жду + *i.*; **conversation ~ friends** разгово́р ме́жду друзья́ми; **they hadn't £5 ~ them** у них на всех не́ было и пяти́ фу́нтов.
2 (*in the midst of*) среди́ + *g.*; ме́жду + *g.*; **~ the trees** среди́ дере́вьев; **~ those present** среди́/в числе́ прису́тствующих; (*into the midst of*): **he fell ~ thieves** он попа́лся разбо́йникам; (*shared by*) у + *g.*; **there was a legend ~ the Greeks** у гре́ков существова́ла леге́нда; (*from the midst of*): **a great leader rose ~ them** из их среды́ вы́шел вели́кий ли́дер.
3 (*expr. one of a number*) из + *g.*; **Leeds is ~ the biggest towns in England** Лидс — оди́н из са́мых больши́х городо́в А́нглии; Лидс вхо́дит в число́ са́мых больши́х городо́в А́нглии; **he was numbered ~ the dead** его́ включи́ли в число́ поги́бших.

amongst /əˈmʌŋst/ (*Br.*) = **among**

amoral /eɪˈmɒr(ə)l/ *adj.* амора́льный.

amorous /ˈæmərəs/ *adj.* (*inclined to love*) влю́бчивый; (*in love*) влюблённый; **an ~ look** влюблённый взгляд; (*pert. to love*) любо́вный.

amorousness /ˈæmərəsnɪs/ *n.* влю́бчивость; влюблённость.

amorphous /əˈmɔːfəs/ *adj.* (*shapeless*) бесфо́рменный; (*chem. etc.*) амо́рфный.

amortization /əˌmɔːtaɪˈzeɪʃ(ə)n/ *n.* (*of debt*) амортиза́ция.

amortize /əˈmɔːtaɪz/ *v.t.* амортизи́ровать (*impf.*, *pf.*).

Amos /ˈeɪmɒs/ *n.* (*bibl.*) Амо́с.

amount /əˈmaʊnt/ *n.* **1** (*sum*) су́мма; **to the ~ of** на су́мму в + *a.*
2 (*quantity*) коли́чество; **he spent any ~ of money** он истра́тил ку́чу де́нег; **we have any ~ of books** у нас полно́/ку́ча книг.
● *v.i.*: **~ to** (*add up to*) сост|авля́ть, -а́вить + *g.*; дост|ига́ть, -и́чь + *g.*; **his income does not ~ to £500 a year** его́ дохо́д не достига́ет пятисо́т фу́нтов в год; **the expenses ~ to £600** расхо́ды составля́ют шестьсо́т фу́нтов; **an invoice ~ing to £100** счёт на су́мму в сто фу́нтов; (*be equivalent to*) быть ра́вным/равноси́льным + *d.*; **these conditions ~ to a refusal** э́ти усло́вия равноси́льны отка́зу; **it ~s to the same thing** э́то сво́дится всё к тому́ же; **~ to very little, not ~ to much** быть незначи́тельным; **the difference does not ~ to much** ра́зница невелика́; **he will never ~ to much** из него́ никогда́ ничего́ пу́тного не вы́йдет; (*signify*): **what does it ~ to?** к чему́ э́то сво́дится?

amour /əˈmʊə(r)/ *n.* (*affair*) любо́вная интри́га; (*lover*) любо́вни|к (*fem.* -ца).

amour-propre /ˌæˌmʊə ˈprɒpr/ *n.* самолю́бие.

amp¹ /æmp/ *n.* (*abbr. of* **ampere**) A (ампе́р).

amp² /æmp/ *n.* (*abbr. of* **amplifier**) (*coll.*) усили́тель (*m.*).

ampere /ˈæmpeə(r)/ *n.* ампе́р.

ampersand /ˈæmpəˌsænd/ *n.* знак «&».

amphetamine /æmˈfetəmɪn/ *n.* амфетами́н.

amphibia /æmˈfɪbɪə/ *n.* земново́дные (*nt. pl.*); амфи́бии (*f. pl.*).

amphibian /æmˈfɪbɪən/ *n.* **1** (*animal*) земново́дное; амфи́бия. **2** (*mil.*) (*aircraft*) самолёт-амфи́бия; (*tank*) танк-амфи́бия; (*car*) пла́вающий автомоби́ль.
● *adj.* = **amphibious**

amphibi|ous /æmˈfɪbɪəs/, **-an** /æmˈfɪbɪən/ *adjs.* земново́дный; (*mil.*) пла́вающий; -амфи́бия (*as suff.*); **~ assault** морско́й деса́нт.

amphitheatre /ˈæmfɪˌθɪətə(r)/ (*US* **amphitheater**) *n.* амфитеа́тр.

ample /ˈæmp(ə)l/ *adj.* (**ampler, amplest**) (*sufficient*) доста́точный; **we have ~ time** у нас доста́точно вре́мени; (*spacious*) просто́рный; широ́кий; (*extensive*) простра́нный; (*abundant*) оби́льный.

ampleness /ˈæmpəlnɪs/ *n.* (*sufficiency*) доста́точность; (*of clothes etc.*) просто́рность; (*abundance*) оби́лие.

amplification /ˌæmplɪfɪˈkeɪʃ(ə)n/ *n.* (*expansion, extension*) расшире́ние; (*of sound, radio signal etc.*) усиле́ние.

amplifier /ˈæmplɪˌfaɪə(r)/ *n.* усили́тель (*m.*).

amplify /ˈæmplɪˌfaɪ/ *v.t.* (*expand, extend*) расш|иря́ть, -и́рить; **~ a theme** разв|ива́ть, -и́ть те́му; (*of sound, radio signal etc.*) уси́ли|вать, -ть.

amplitude /ˈæmplɪˌtjuːd/ *n.* (*width*) широта́, разма́х; (*spaciousness*) просто́р; (*phys., elec.*) амплиту́да.

amply /ˈæmplɪ/ *adv.* (*sufficiently*) доста́точно; (*fully*) вполне́; оби́льно.

ampoule /ˈæmpuːl/ (*US also* **ampul(e)** /-pjuːl/) *n.* а́мпула.

amputate /ˈæmpjʊˌteɪt/ *v.t.* ампути́ровать (*impf.*, *pf.*); отн|има́ть, -я́ть; **his left leg was ~d** ему́ ампути́ровали/о́тняли ле́вую но́гу.

amputation /ˌæmpjʊˈteɪʃ(ə)n/ *n.* ампута́ция.

Amsterdam /ˌæmstəˈdæm/ *n.* Амстерда́м.

amuck /əˈmʌk/ = **amok**

amulet /ˈæmjʊlɪt/ *n.* амуле́т.

amus|e /əˈmjuːz/ *v.t.* (*entertain, divert*) развл|ека́ть, -е́чь; забавля́ть (*impf.*); (*make laugh*) смеши́ть (*impf.*); позаба́вить (*pf.*); **an ~ing little hat** заба́вная шля́пка; **I don't find that ~ing** я не ви́жу в э́том ничего́ смешно́го.

amusement /əˈmjuːzmənt/ *n.*
1 (*diversion*) развлече́ние, заба́ва; **I play the piano for my own ~** я игра́ю на фортепья́но для со́бственного удово́льствия; **the town has few ~s** в э́том го́роде ма́ло развлече́ний; (*Br., fairground ride etc.*) аттракцио́н; **~ arcade** (*Br.*) павильо́н с игровы́ми аппара́тами; **~ park** парк с аттракцио́нами; лу́на-па́рк.
2 (*tendency to laughter*): **to everyone's ~ the clown fell over** ко всео́бщему удово́льствию кло́ун упа́л; **it afforded me great ~** э́то меня́ о́чень позаба́вило.

anachronism /əˈnækrəˌnɪz(ə)m/ *n.* анахрони́зм.

anachronistic /əˌnækrəˈnɪstɪk/ *adj.* анахрони́ческий.

anacoluth|on /ˌænəkəˈluːθɒn/ *n.* (*pl.* **~a** /-θə/) анаколу́ф.

anaconda /ˌænəˈkɒndə/ *n.* анако́нда.

anaemia /əˈniːmɪə/ (*US* **anemia**) *n.* малокро́вие, анеми́я.

anaemic /əˈniːmɪk/ (*US* **anemic**) *adj.* малокро́вный, анеми́чный.

anaesthesia /ˌænɪsˈθiːzɪə/ (*US* **anesthesia**) *n.* анестези́я; обезбо́ливание.

anaesthetic /ˌænɪsˈθetɪk/ (*US* **anesthetic**) *n.* анестези́рующее сре́дство; анесте́тик; **general/local ~** о́бщий/ме́стный нарко́з; **under ~** под нарко́зом.
● *adj.* анестези́рующий; обезбо́ливающий.

anaesthetist /əˈniːsθətɪst/ (*US* **anesthetist**) *n.* анестезио́лог.

anaesthetize /əˈniːsθəˌtaɪz/ (*US* **anesthetize**) *v.t.* анестези́ровать (*impf.*, *pf.*).

anagram /ˈænəˌɡræm/ *n.* анагра́мма.

anal /ˈeɪn(ə)l/ *adj.* заднепрохо́дный, ана́льный.

analgesia /ˌænælˈdʒiːzɪə/, /-sɪə/ *n.* анальгези́я.

analgesic /ˌænælˈdʒiːsɪk/, /-zɪk/ *adj.* болеутоля́ющий.

analog /ˈænəˌlɒɡ/ (*US*) = **analogue**

analogical /ˌænəˈlɒdʒɪk(ə)l/ *adj.* аналоги́ческий.

analogous /əˈnæləɡəs/ *adj.* аналоги́чный.

analogue /ˈænəˌlɒɡ/ (*US also* **analog**) *n.* ана́лог; **~ to digital converter** ана́лого-цифрово́й преобразова́тель.
● *adj.* ана́логовый.

analogy /əˈnælədʒɪ/ *n.* анало́гия; схо́дство; **by ~ with** по анало́гии с + *i.*

analysable /ˈænəˌlaɪzəb(ə)l/ (*US* **analyzable**) *adj.* поддаю́щийся ана́лизу.

analyse /ˈænəˌlaɪz/ (*US* **analyze**) *v.t.* анализи́ровать (*impf.*, *pf.*); (*gram.*) раз|бира́ть, -обра́ть; (*psych.*) подв|ерга́ть, -е́ргнуть психоана́лизу.

analysis /əˈnælɪsɪs/ *n.* (*pl.* **analyses** /-siːz/) ана́лиз; (*gram.*) разбо́р; **in the last ~** в коне́чном счёте; (*psycho~*) психоана́лиз.

analyst /ˈænəlɪst/ *n.* анали́тик; (*political*) коммента́тор; (*psych.*) психоанали́тик.

analytic(al) /ˌænəˈlɪtɪk(ə)l/ *adj.* аналити́ческий.

analyzable /ˈænəˌlaɪzəb(ə)l/ (*US*) = **analysable**

analyze /ˈænəˌlaɪz/ (*US*) = **analyse**

anapaest /ˈænəˌpiːst/ (*US* **anapest**) *n.* ана́пест.

anarchic(al) /əˈnɑːkɪk/, /əˈnɑːkɪk(ə)l/ *adj.* анархи́ческий.

anarchism /ˈænəˌkɪz(ə)m/ *n.* анархи́зм.

anarchist /ˈænəkɪst/ *n.* анархи́ст (*fem.* -ка).

● *adj.* анархи́стский.

anarchy /ˈænəkɪ/ *n.* ана́рхия.

anathema /əˈnæθəmə/ *n.* (*pl.* **~s**) (*hated thing*) ана́фема; **it's ~ to me** для меня́ э́то ана́фема; (*excommunication*) ана́фема; отлуче́ние от це́ркви.

anathematize /əˈnæθəməˌtaɪz/ *v.t.* пред|ава́ть, -а́ть ана́феме; (*curse*) прокл|ина́ть, -я́сть.

anatomical /ˌænəˈtɒmɪk(ə)l/ *adj.* анатоми́ческий.

anatomist /əˈnætəmɪst/ *n.* ана́том.

anatomize /əˈnætəˌmaɪz/ *v.t.* **1** (*dissect*) анатоми́ровать (*impf.*, *pf.*). **2** (*analyse*) подв|ерга́ть, -е́ргнуть разбо́ру.

anatomy /əˈnætəmɪ/ *n.* **1** (*science*) анато́мия. **2** (*analysis*) разбо́р; ана́лиз. **3** (*joc.*) (*body*) те́ло; **I ache in every part of my ~** у меня́ боли́т всё те́ло.

ANC (*abbr. of* ***African National Congress***) АНК (Африка́нский национа́льный конгре́сс).

ancestor /ˈænsestə(r)/ *n.* пре́док.

ancestral /ænˈsestr(ə)l/ *adj.* родово́й; **~ home** родово́е име́ние.

ancestress /ˈænsestrɪs/ *n.* прароди́тельница.

ancestry /ˈænsestrɪ/ *n.* (*lineage*) родосло́вная, происхожде́ние; **he comes of distinguished ~** он благоро́дного происхожде́ния.

anchor /ˈæŋkə(r)/ *n.* я́корь (*m.*); **cast, drop ~** бр|оса́ть, -о́сить я́корь; **lie, ride at ~** стоя́ть на я́коре; **weigh ~** сн|има́ться, -я́ться с я́коря.

● *v.t.* ста́вить, по- на я́корь; (*fig.*, *secure*) закреп|ля́ть, -и́ть.

● *v.i.* (*of vessel*) ста|нови́ться, -ть на я́корь; (*of crew*: *cast* **~**) бр|оса́ть, -о́сить я́корь.

anchorage /ˈæŋkərɪdʒ/ *n.* (*anchoring-place*) я́корная стоя́нка; (*dues*) я́корный сбор.

anchorite /ˈæŋkəˌraɪt/ *n.* отше́льник.

anchorman /ˈæŋkəmən/ *n.* (*TV, radio*) веду́щий.

anchovy /ˈæntʃəvɪ/, /ænˈtʃəʊvɪ/ *n.* анчо́ус.

ancient /ˈeɪnʃ(ə)nt/ *n.*: **the ~s** дре́вние наро́ды (*m. pl.*); (*writers*) анти́чные писа́тели (*m. pl.*).

● *adj.* дре́вний; анти́чный; (*very old*) стари́нный; веково́й; **~ history** дре́вняя исто́рия; **that's ~ history!** э́то ста́рая исто́рия; **~ monument** (*Br.*) па́мятник старины́; **an ~ castle** стари́нный за́мок.

ancillary /ænˈsɪlərɪ/ *adj.* (*auxiliary*) вспомога́тельный; (*subordinate*) подчинённый.

and /ænd/, /ənd/ *conj.* **1** (*connecting words or clauses*) и; (*in addition*) и, да; (*with certain closely linked pairs, esp. of persons*) с + *i.*; **bread ~ butter** хлеб с ма́слом; **the doctor ~ his wife came** пришли́ до́ктор с жено́й; **you ~ I** мы с ва́ми; (*with nums. denoting addition*) и; плюс; **2 ~ 2 are 4** два и два — четы́ре; (*to form cpd. num.*) *omitted*: **260** две́сти шестьдеся́т; (*with following fraction*) с + *i.*; **4½** четы́ре с полови́ной.
2 (*intensive*): **he ran ~ ran** он всё бежа́л и бежа́л; **better ~ better** всё лу́чше (и лу́чше); **they talked for hours ~ hours** они́ разгова́ривали часа́ми; **the plain stretched for miles ~ miles** равни́на простира́лась на мно́го миль.
3 (*in order to*) *omitted before inf.*: **try ~ find out** постара́йтесь узна́ть; **wait ~ see!** погоди́те — ещё уви́дите!
4 (*expr. consequence*): **move, ~ I shoot!** одно́ движе́ние, и я стреля́ю.
5 (*in contrast*) а; **I shall go, ~ you stay here** я пойду́, а вы остава́йтесь здесь.
6 (*emph.*) к тому́ же; и прито́м; **he speaks English, ~ very well too** он говори́т по-англи́йски, и прито́м о́чень хорошо́.

Andalusia /ˌændəˈluːzɪə/ *n.* Андалу́зия.

andante /ænˈdæntɪ/ *n.*, *adj. and adv.* анда́нте (*indecl.*).

Andes /ˈændiːz/ *n.* А́нд|ы (*pl.*, *g.* —).

androgynous /ænˈdrɒdʒɪnəs/ *adj.* двупо́лый; (*bot.*) обоепо́лый.

android /ˈændrɔɪd/ *n.* андро́ид.

anecdotal /ˌænɪkˈdəʊt(ə)l/ *adj.* анекдоти́ческий.

anecdote /ˈænɪkˌdəʊt/ *n.* исто́рия; (*joke*) анекдо́т.

anemia /əˈniːmɪə/ (*US*) = **anaemia**

anemic /əˈniːmɪk/ (*US*) = **anaemic**

anemone /əˈnemənɪ/ *n.* анемо́н; (*windflower, wood-~*) ве́треница; **sea ~** морско́й анемо́н; акти́ния.

aneroid /ˈænəˌrɔɪd/ *n.* & *adj.* (**~ barometer**) (баро́метр-)анеро́ид.

anesthesia /ˌænɪsˈθiːzɪə/ (*US*) = **anaesthesia**

anesthetic /ˌænɪsˈθetɪk/ (*US*) = **anaesthetic**

anesthetist /əˈniːsθətɪst/ (*US*) = **anaesthetist**

anesthetize /əˈniːsθəˌtaɪz/ (*US*) = **anaesthetize**

anew /əˈnjuː/ *adj.* (*again*) сно́ва; (*in a different way*) за́ново, по-но́вому.

angel /ˈeɪndʒ(ə)l/ *n.* (*lit.*, *fig.*) а́нгел; **guardian ~** а́нгел-храни́тель; **~ of darkness** а́нгел тьмы; **good/bad ~** до́брый/злой ге́ний.

angelic /ænˈdʒelɪk/ *adj.* а́нгельский.

angelica /ænˈdʒelɪkə/ *n.* дя́гиль (*m.*).

anger /ˈæŋgə(r)/ *n.* гнев; **I said it in ~** я сказа́л э́то в гне́ве.

● *v.t.* серди́ть, рас-; разгне́вать (*pf.*).

angina /ænˈdʒaɪnə/ *n.* (*also* **~ pectoris** /ˈpektərɪs/) стенокарди́я, грудна́я жа́ба.

angle[1] /ˈæŋg(ə)l/ *n.* у́гол; **acute ~** о́стрый у́гол; **obtuse ~** тупо́й у́гол; **right ~** прямо́й у́гол; **at an ~ of 30°** под угло́м в три́дцать гра́дусов; **the house stands at an ~ to the street** дом стои́т под угло́м к у́лице; **at right ~s** под прямы́м угло́м; **~ of incidence** у́гол паде́ния; (*fig.*, *viewpoint*) то́чка зре́ния, подхо́д; **one must consider all ~s of a question** на́до уче́сть все аспе́кты вопро́са; **we examined the matter from every ~** мы рассмотре́ли вопро́с со всех то́чек зре́ния.

● *v.t.* ста́вить, по- под угло́м; **he ~d the lamp to shine on his book** он поста́вил ла́мпу так, что́бы свет па́дал на кни́гу; (*fig.*): **the news was ~d** но́вости бы́ли по́даны тенденцио́зно.

● *cpd.* **~-iron** *n.* углово́е желе́зо.

angl|e[2] /ˈæŋg(ə)l/ *v.i.* (*fish*) уди́ть (*impf.*) ры́бу; **~e for trout** уди́ть форе́ль; **yesterday we went ~ing** вчера́ мы е́здили на рыба́лку; (*fig.*): **~e for compliments** напра́шиваться (*impf.*) на комплиме́нты.

angler /ˈæŋglə(r)/ *n.* рыбо́лов.

Anglican /ˈæŋglɪkən/ *n.* англика́н|ец (*fem.* -ка).

● *adj.* англика́нский.

Anglicanism /ˈæŋglɪkənɪz(ə)m/ *n.* англика́нство.

Anglicism /ˈæŋglɪˌsɪz(ə)m/ *n.* англици́зм.

Anglicize /ˈæŋglɪˌsaɪz/ *v.t.* англизи́ровать (*impf.*, *pf.*).

angling /ˈæŋglɪŋ/ *n.* (спорти́вное) рыболо́вство.

Anglo- /ˈæŋgləʊ/ *comb. form* англо...; англо-...

Anglomania /ˌæŋgləʊˈmeɪnɪə/ *n.* англома́ния.

Anglomaniac /ˌæŋgləʊˈmeɪnɪˌæk/ *n.* англома́н (*fem.* -ка).

Anglophile /ˈæŋgləʊˌfaɪl/ *n.* англофи́л.

● *adj.* англофи́льский.

Anglophilia /ˌæŋgləʊˈfɪlɪə/ *n.* англофили́я.

Anglophobe /ˈæŋgləʊˌfəʊb/ *n.* англофо́б.

Anglophobia /ˌæŋgləʊˈfəʊbɪə/ *n.* англофо́бия.

anglophone /ˈæŋgləʊˌfəʊn/ *adj.* англоязы́чный.

Anglo-Saxon /ˌæŋgləʊˈsæks(ə)n/ *n.* **1** (*racial type*) англоса́кс; чистокро́вный англича́нин. **2** (*language*) англосаксо́нский/древнеангли́йский язы́к.

● *adj.* англосаксо́нский, древнеангли́йский.

Angola /æŋˈgəʊlə/ *n.* Анго́ла.

Angolan /æŋˈgəʊlən/ *n.* анго́л|ец (*fem.* -ка).

● *adj.* анго́льский.

angora /æŋˈgɔːrə/ *n.* (*cloth*) анго́рская шерсть.

● *adj.* анго́рский.

angry /ˈæŋgrɪ/ *adj.* (**angrier, angriest**) серди́тый, разгне́ванный; **be ~ with** серди́ться/гне́ваться (*both impf.*) на + *a.* (**over, about something**: за что-н.); **get ~ with** рассерди́ться/разгне́ваться (*both pf.*) на + *a.*; **make ~** серди́ть, рас-; **I was ~ with him for going** я рассерди́лся на него́ за то, что он пошёл; (*annoyed*):

he is ~ about the delay он раздражён опозда́нием; **she got extremely ~** она́ была́ в гне́ве; она́ была́ о́чень серди́та.

angst /æŋst/ *n.* страх; трево́жное состоя́ние.

anguish /'æŋgwɪʃ/ *n.* муче́ние; му́ка; страда́ние; (*pain*) боль; **a look of ~, an ~ed look** му́ченический/страда́льческий взгляд.

angular /'æŋgjʊlə(r)/ *adj.* **1** (*forming or pert. to an angle*) углово́й; **~ velocity** углова́я ско́рость. **2** (*having angles*) углова́тый; **an ~ face** лицо́ с ре́зкими черта́ми. **3** (*of person, thin, bony*) худо́й, костля́вый.

angularity /ˌæŋgjʊ'lærɪtɪ/ *n.* углова́тость; худоба́; костля́вость.

anhydride /æn'haɪdraɪd/ *n.* (*chem.*) ангидри́д.

aniline /'ænɪˌli:n/, /-lɪn/, /-ˌlaɪn/ *n.* анили́н.

● *adj.* анили́новый.

animadversion /ˌænɪmæd'vɜ:ʃ(ə)n/ *n.* (*censure*) порица́ние; (*observation*) замеча́ние.

animadvert /ˌænɪmæd'vɜ:t/ *v.i.*: **~ on** (*censure*) порица́ть (*impf.*); (*comment on*) де́лать, с- замеча́ние по по́воду +*g.*

animal /'ænɪm(ə)l/ *n.* живо́тное; **domestic ~s** дома́шние живо́тные; **farm ~s** живо́тные, кото́рых разво́дят на фе́рме; **wild ~** зверь (*m.*), ди́кое живо́тное.

● *adj.* живо́тный; **the ~ kingdom** живо́тное ца́рство; **~ husbandry** животново́дство; **~ needs** есте́ственные потре́бности; **~ desires** пло́тские жела́ния; **~ spirits** жизнера́достность.

animate[1] /'ænɪmət/ *adj.* (*living*) живо́й; **an ~ noun** одушевлённое (и́мя) существи́тельное; (*lively*) оживлённый.

animate[2] /'ænɪˌmeɪt/ *v.t.* (*enliven*) ожив|ля́ть, -и́ть; (*give life to*) вдохну́ть (*pf.*) жизнь в +*a.*; (*inspire, actuate*) вдохнов|ля́ть, -и́ть; (во)одушев|ля́ть, -и́ть; **become ~d** ожив|ля́ться, -и́ться; **~d cartoon** мультипликацио́нный фильм, анима́ция.

animation /ˌænɪ'meɪʃ(ə)n/ *n.* (*liveliness*) оживле́ние; (*enthusiasm*) воодушевле́ние; (*cin.*) мультиплика́ция, анима́ция.

animator /'ænɪˌmeɪtə(r)/ *n.* (*cin.*) (худо́жник-)мультиплика́тор.

animosity /ˌænɪ'mɒsɪtɪ/ *n.* (*hostility*) вражде́бность; **feel ~ against** пита́ть (*impf.*) вражду́ к +*d.*

animus /'ænɪməs/ *n.* **1** (*spirit: atmosphere*) дух; атмосфе́ра. **2** (*animosity*) вражде́бность.

aniseed /'ænɪˌsi:d/ *n.* ани́с; ани́совое се́мя.

anisette /ˌænɪ'zet/ *n.* ани́совый ликёр.

Ankara /'æŋkərə/ *n.* Анкара́ (*m.*).

ankle /'æŋk(ə)l/ *n.* лоды́жка, щи́колотка.

● *cpds.* **~-boot** *n.* боти́нок; **~-deep** *adj.*: **~-deep in mud** по щи́колотку в грязи́; **~-length** *adj.*: **~-length dress** пла́тье по щи́колотку; **~-socks** *n. pl.* носки́ (*m. pl.*).

anklet /'æŋklɪt/ *n.* (*ornament*) ножно́й брасле́т.

annalist /'ænəlɪst/ *n.* летопи́сец.

annals /'æn(ə)lz/ *n.* анна́л|ы (*pl., g.* -ов); ле́топись.

anneal /ə'ni:l/ *v.t.* отж|ига́ть, -е́чь; (*fig.*) закал|я́ть, -и́ть.

annealing /ə'ni:lɪŋ/ *n.* о́тжиг; **~ furnace** печь для о́тжига.

annex[1] /'æneks/ *n.* (*to document*) приложе́ние; (*to a building*) пристро́йка, фли́гель (*m.*); (*separate building*) фли́гель (*m.*).

annex[2] /æ'neks/, /ə'n-/ *v.t.* присоедин|я́ть, -и́ть; прил|ага́ть, -ожи́ть; (*territory etc.*) аннекси́ровать (*impf., pf.*).

annexation /ˌænek'seɪʃ(ə)n/ *n.* присоедине́ние; анне́ксия, аннекси́рование.

annexationist /ˌænek'seɪʃ(ə)nɪst/ *adj.* захва́тнический.

annexe /'æneks/ (*Br.*) = **annex**[1]

annihilat|e /ə'naɪəˌleɪt/, /ə'naɪl-/ *v.t.* (*destroy*) уничт|ожа́ть, -о́жить; (*extirpate*) истреб|ля́ть, -и́ть.

annihilation /əˌnaɪə'leɪʃ(ə)n/, /əˌnaɪl-/ *n.* уничтоже́ние; истребле́ние.

anniversary /ˌænɪ'vɜ:sərɪ/ *n.* годовщи́на; **on his fifth wedding ~** в пя́тую годовщи́ну его́ сва́дьбы; **40th ~** сорокова́я годовщи́на, сорокале́тие.

● *adj.*: **~ edition** юбиле́йное изда́ние.

Anno Domini /ˌænəʊ 'dɒmɪˌnaɪ/ *adv.* на́шей э́ры (*abbr.* н.э.); **AD 400** 400 г. на́шей э́ры.

annotate /'ænəʊˌteɪt/, /'ænəˌteɪt/ *v.t.* снаб|жа́ть, -ди́ть коммента́риями *or* примеча́ниями; **~d text** текст с коммента́риями *or* примеча́ниями.

annotation /ˌænəʊ'teɪʃ(ə)n/, /ˌænə'teɪʃ(ə)n/ *n.* (*annotating*) комменти́рование; (*added note*) коммента́рий, примеча́ние.

announce /ə'naʊns/ *v.t.* (*state; declare*) объяв|ля́ть, -и́ть (*что or о чём*); заяв|ля́ть, -и́ть (*что or о чём or relative clause*); **he ~d his intention to be present** он объяви́л о своём наме́рении прису́тствовать; **the verdict was ~d yesterday** пригово́р был объя́влен вчера́; (*notify, tell*) сообщ|а́ть, -и́ть (*о чём кому*); **he ~d the results of his researches** он сообщи́л о результа́тах свои́х иссле́дований; **the footman ~d the guests as they arrived** лаке́й докла́дывал о прибы́тии госте́й.

announcement /ə'naʊnsmənt/ *n.* объявле́ние, заявле́ние; **put an ~ in the newspaper** поме|ща́ть, -сти́ть объявле́ние в газе́те; (*written notification*) извеще́ние; (*on radio etc.*) сообще́ние; **the ~ of his death was made at 4 o'clock** о его́ сме́рти сообщи́ли в 4 часа́.

announcer /ə'naʊnsə(r)/ *n.* (*on radio etc.*) ди́ктор; (*of stage entertainment*) конферансье́ (*m. indecl.*).

annoy /ə'nɔɪ/ *v.t.* (*vex*) доса|жда́ть, -ди́ть +*d.*; (*irritate*) раздража́ть (*impf.*); де́йствовать (*impf.*) на не́рвы +*d.*; (*pester*) докуча́ть (*impf.*) +*d.*; **I was ~ed with him** я был на него́ серди́т.

annoyance /ə'nɔɪəns/ *n.* раздраже́ние; (*cause of ~*) доса́да, неприя́тность.

annoying /ə'nɔɪɪŋ/ *adj.* доса́дный; **how ~!** кака́я доса́да!, как доса́дно!; **an ~ person** невозмо́жный челове́к.

annual /'ænjʊəl/ *n.* **1** (*publication*) ежего́дник. **2** (*plant*) одноле́тнее расте́ние, одноле́тник.

● *adj.* **1** (*happening once a year*) ежего́дный; **~ fair** ежего́дная я́рмарка; **~ general meeting** (*Br.*) ежего́дное о́бщее собра́ние. **2** (*pert. to whole year*) годово́й; **~ income** годово́й дохо́д; **~ report** годово́й отчёт. **3** (*bot., lasting for one year*) одноле́тний.

annually /'ænjʊəlɪ/ *adv.* ежего́дно.

annuity /ə'nju:ɪtɪ/ *n.* ежего́дная ре́нта; аннуите́т; **life ~** пожи́зненная ре́нта.

annul /ə'nʌl/ *v.t.* (**annulled, annulling**) аннули́ровать (*impf., pf.*); отмен|я́ть, -и́ть; **the marriage was ~led** брак был при́знан недействи́тельным.

annular /'ænjʊlə(r)/ *adj.* кольцеобра́зный, кольцево́й.

annulment /ə'nʌlmənt/ *n.* аннули́рование, отме́на.

Annunciation /əˌnʌnsɪ'eɪʃ(ə)n/ *n.* (*relig.*) Благове́щение.

anode /'ænəʊd/ *n.* ано́д; (*attr.*) ано́дный.

anodyne /'ænəˌdaɪn/ *n.* (*pain-killer*) болеутоля́ющее сре́дство.

● *adj.* (*fig.*) безоби́дный.

anoint /ə'nɔɪnt/ *v.t.* пома́з|ывать, -ать; **he was ~ed king** его́ пома́зали на ца́рство.

anomalous /ə'nɒmələs/ *adj.* анома́льный.

anomaly /ə'nɒməlɪ/ *n.* анома́лия.

anon /ə'nɒn/ *adv.* ско́ро, вско́ре; **see you ~!** пока́!

anonymity /ˌænə'nɪmɪtɪ/ *n.* анони́мность.

anonymous /ə'nɒnɪməs/ *adj.* анони́мный; безымя́нный; **~ letter, ~ telephone call** анони́мка.

anorak /'ænəˌræk/ *n.* анора́к, ку́ртка с капюшо́ном.

anorexia /ˌænə'reksɪə/ *n.* анор́ексия.

anorexic /ˌænə'reksɪk/ *n.* больн|о́й (*fem.* -а́я) анор́ексией.

● *adj.* страда́ющий анор́ексией.

another /ə'nʌðə(r)/ *pron. & adj.* **1** (*additional*) ещё; **~ cup of tea?** ещё ча́шку ча́я?; **will you have ~ (drink)?** хоти́те ещё вы́пить? **have ~ go!** попыта́йтесь ещё раз!; **in ~ 10 years** ещё че́рез де́сять лет; **and ~ thing** и вот ещё что; **not ~ word!** ни сло́ва бо́льше!; **without ~ word** не говоря́ бо́льше ни сло́ва; **ask me ~!** (*coll.*) почём я зна́ю? **2** (*similar*): **such ~ as I** подо́бный мне; **~ Tolstoy** второ́й Толсто́й. **3** (*different*) друго́й; **~ time**

в другóй раз; **that's ~ matter altogether** э́то совсéм другóе дéло; **one way or ~** так и́ли ина́че. **4**: **one ~** (*refl.*) *see* ⇒**one**

answer /ˈɑːnsə(r)/ *n.* **1** (*reply*) отвéт; **what was his ~?** что он отвéтил?; **in ~ to your letter** в отвéт на Ва́ше письмó; **by way of ~** в отвéт; (*retort*) возражéние; (*defence*): **he has a complete ~ to the charges** он мóжет опровéргнуть все обвинéния.
2 (*solution*) отвéт; решéние; **there is no simple ~ to the problem** проблéму реши́ть нелегкó; **he thinks he knows all the ~s** он дýмает, что он ужé всё пости́г.
● *v.t.* **1** (*reply to*) отв|еча́ть, -éтить (*комý, на что*); **the question was not ~ed** вопрóс оста́лся без отвéта; **~ the door** откр|ыва́ть, -ы́ть дверь; **~ the door-bell** (*or* **a knock at the door**) откр|ыва́ть, -ы́ть (дверь) на звонóк (*or* на стук); **~ the telephone** под|ходи́ть, -ойти́ к телефóну; отвеча́ть, отвéтить на телефóнные звонки́.
2 (*fulfil*): **~ requirements** отвеча́ть (*impf.*) трéбованиям; **~ the purpose** соотвéтствовать (*impf.*) цéли.
3 (*correspond to*): **he ~s the description exactly** он тóчно соотвéтствует описа́нию.
4 (*refute*): **~ a charge** опров|ерга́ть, -éргнуть обвинéние.
5 (*solve*) реш|а́ть, -и́ть.
6 (*satisfy, grant*): **our prayers were ~ed** на́ши моли́твы бы́ли услы́шаны.
● *v.i.* **1** (*reply*) отв|еча́ть, -éтить.
2 (*respond; react*): **the dog ~s to the name of Rex** собáка отзывáется на кли́чку Рекс.
3: **~ for** (*vouch, accept responsibility for*) руча́ться, поручи́ться за + *a.*; **I will ~ for his honesty** я руча́юсь за егó чéстность; (*suffer, bear responsibility for*): **you will ~ for your words** вы отвéтите за э́ти словá; **he has much to ~ for** он за мнóгое в отвéте.
4 (*give an account*): **I ~ to no one** я никомý не обя́зан отчи́тываться.
5: **~ back** дерзи́ть, на-.
● *cpd.* **~phone** /ˈɑːnsəˌfəʊn/ *n.* (*Br.*) автоотвéтчик.

answerable /ˈɑːnsərəb(ə)l/ *adj.*
1 (*responsible*) отвéтственный (*перед кем за что*); **you are ~ to me for your conduct** вы несёте передо мнóй отвéтственность за свои́ постýпки.
2 (*capable of being answered*): **the charges are ~** э́ти обвинéния мóжно опровéргнуть.

answering /ˈɑːnsərɪŋ/ *adj.*: **~ machine** автоотвéтчик.

ant /ænt/ *n.* муравéй; (*attr.*) муравьи́ный.
● *cpds.* **~-bear** *n.* трубкозýб; гига́нтский муравьéд; **~-eater** *n.* муравьéд; **~-hill, ~-heap** *nn.* муравéйник.

antacid /æntˈæsɪd/ *n.* срéдство, нейтрализýющее кислотý; антаци́дное срéдство.

antagonism /ænˈtægəˌnɪz(ə)m/ *n.* антагони́зм.

antagonist /ænˈtægənɪst/ *n.* антагони́ст; (*adversary*) проти́вник.

antagonistic /ænˌtægəˈnɪstɪk/ *adj.* антагонисти́ческий.

antagonize /ænˈtægəˌnaɪz/ *v.t.* вызыва́ть, вы́звать чьё-н. отчуждéние; отчужда́ть (*impf.*).

Antarctic /æntˈɑːktɪk/ *n.*: **the ~** Антáрктика.
● *adj.* антаркти́ческий; **~ Circle** Ю́жный поля́рный круг; **~ Ocean** Антаркти́ческий океáн.

Antarctica /æntˈɑːktɪkə/ *n.* Антаркти́да.

ante /ˈæntɪ/ *n.* (*stake*) стáвка; **raise the ~** пов|ыша́ть, -ы́сить стáвку.

antecedent /ˌæntɪˈsiːd(ə)nt/ *n.*
1 (*preceding thing or circumstance*) предыдýщее. **2** (*gram.*) слóво, к котóрому отнóсится послéдующее местоимéние (чáще всегó относи́тельное). **3** (*pl., the past*) прóшлое; (*past life*) прóшлая жизнь; (*ancestors*) прéдки.
● *adj.* предшéствующий, предыдýщий.

antechamber /ˈæntɪˌtʃeɪmbə(r)/ *n.* прихóжая, перéдняя.

antedate /ˌæntɪˈdeɪt/ *v.t.* **1** (*put earlier date on*) пом|еча́ть, -éтить за́дним числóм. **2** (*precede*) предшéствовать (*impf.*) + *d.*

antediluvian /ˌæntɪdɪˈluːvɪən/, /-ˈljuːvɪən/ *adj.* (*lit., fig.*) допотóпный.

antelope /ˈæntɪˌləʊp/ *n.* (*pl.* **~** *or* **~s**) антилóпа.

antenatal /ˌæntɪˈneɪt(ə)l/ *adj.* (*Br.*) (*care*) дородовóй; **~ clinic** жéнская консультáция.

antenna /ænˈtenə/ *n.* (*pl.* **antennae** /-niː/) (*radio*) антéнна; (*of insect*) ýсик.

anterior /ænˈtɪərɪə(r)/ *adj.* (*of place*) перéдний; (*of time*) предшéствующий.

ante-room /ˈæntɪˌruːm/, /-ˌrʊm/ *n.* перéдняя, прихóжая.

anthem /ˈænθəm/ *n.* (*choral*) хорáл; (*rousing song*) гимн; **national ~** госудáрственный гимн.

anther /ˈænθə(r)/ *n.* пы́льник.

anthologist /ænˈθɒlədʒɪst/ *n.* состави́тель (*m.*) антолóгии.

anthology /ænˈθɒlədʒɪ/ *n.* антолóгия.

anthracite /ˈænθrəˌsaɪt/ *n.* антраци́т.

anthrax /ˈænθræks/ *n.* сиби́рская я́зва.

anthropocentric /ˌænθrəpəʊˈsentrɪk/ *adj.* антропоцентри́ческий.

anthropoid /ˈænθrəˌpɔɪd/ *n.* антропóид.
● *adj.* человекообрáзный, антропóидный.

anthropological /ˌænθrəpəˈlɒdʒɪk(ə)l/ *adj.* антропологи́ческий.

anthropologist /ˌænθrəˈpɒlədʒɪst/ *n.* (*biological*) антропóлог; **social ~** этнóграф.

anthropology /ˌænθrəˈpɒlədʒɪ/ *n.* (*biological*) антрополóгия; **social ~** этногрáфия.

anthropomorphic /ˌænθrəpəˈmɔːfɪk/ *adj.* антропоморфи́ческий.

anthropomorphism /ˌænθrəpəˈmɔːfɪz(ə)m/ *n.* антропоморфи́зм.

anti- /ˈæntɪ/ *pref.* анти..., противо...

anti-aircraft /ˌæntɪˈeəkrɑːft/ *adj.* зени́тный, противовоздýшный; **~ artillery** зени́тная артиллéрия; **~ defence** (*Br.*), **defense** (*US*) противовоздýшная оборóна (*abbr.* ПВО).

anti-ballistic /ˌæntɪbəˈlɪstɪk/ *adj.* = **anti-missile**

antibiotic /ˌæntɪbaɪˈɒtɪk/ *n.* антибиóтик.
● *adj.* антибиоти́ческий.

antibody /ˈæntɪˌbɒdɪ/ *n.* антитéло.

Antichrist /ˈæntɪˌkraɪst/ *n.* анти́христ.

anticipate /ænˈtɪsɪˌpeɪt/ *v.t.* **1** (*precede*) опере|жа́ть, -ди́ть. **2** (*foresee*) предви́деть (*impf.*); предчýвствовать (*impf.*); (*expect*) ожида́ть (*impf.*); (*with pleasure*) предвку|ша́ть, -си́ть.
3 (*forestall*) предвосх|ища́ть, -и́тить; предупре|жда́ть, -ди́ть; **he ~d my wishes** он предупреди́л мои́ желáния; **the general ~d the enemy's attack** генерáл предупреди́л неприя́тельское наступлéние.

anticipation /ænˌtɪsɪˈpeɪʃ(ə)n/ *n.*
1 (*looking forward to*) ожидáние; **in ~ of your early reply** в ожидáнии вáшего скóрого отвéта; **thanking you in ~** (*as formula in letter*) зарáнее благодáрный.
2 (*foreseeing*) предви́дение, предвосхищéние; **in ~ of a cold winter** предви́дя холóдную зи́му; **~ of events** предвосхищéние собы́тий.
3 (*foretasting*) предвкушéние; **half the pleasure lies in the ~** предвкушéние — э́то ужé полови́на удовóльствия.

anticipatory /ænˈtɪsɪˌpeɪtərɪ/ *adj.* (*full of expectation*) пóлный ожидáний; **he smiled with ~ pleasure** он улыбнýлся, предвкушáя удовóльствие; (*forestalling*) предупреди́тельный, предупреждáющий.

anticlerical /ˌæntɪˈklerɪk(ə)l/ *adj.* антиклерикáльный.

anticlericalism /ˌæntɪˈklerɪk(ə)lɪz(ə)m/ *n.* антиклерикали́зм.

anticlimactic /ˌæntɪklaɪˈmæktɪk/ *adj.* не опрáвдывающий ожидáний.

anticlimax /ˌæntɪˈklaɪmæks/ *n.* (рéзкий) спад (интерéса *и т.п.*); разочаровáние.

anticlockwise /ˌæntɪˈklɒkwaɪz/ *adj.* & *adv.* (*Br.*) прóтив часовóй стрéлки.

anti-Communist /ˌæntɪˈkɒmjʊnɪst/ *n.* проти́вник коммуни́зма.
● *adj.* антикоммунисти́ческий.

antics /ˈæntɪks/ *n. pl.* (*physical*) кривля́нье, ужи́мки (*f. pl.*); (*behaviour*) продéлки (*f. pl.*).

anticyclone /ˌæntɪˈsaɪkləʊn/ *n.* антициклóн.

antidepressant /ˌæntɪdɪˈpres(ə)nt/ *n.* антидепрессáнт.

antidote /ˈæntɪˌdəʊt/ *n.* противоя́дие, антидóт.

antifreeze /ˈæntɪˌfriːz/ *n.* антифри́з.

anti-hero /ˈæntɪˌhɪərəʊ/ *n.* антигерóй.

antihistamine /ˌæntɪˈhɪstəˌmiːn/ *n.* антигистами́н.

antiknock /ˈæntɪˌnɒk/ *n.* антидетона́тор.

Antilles /ænˈtɪliːz/ *n.*: **the ~** Анти́льские острова́ (*m. pl.*).

antimacassar /ˌæntɪməˈkæsə(r)/ *n.* салфе́тка.

anti-missile /ˌæntɪˈmɪsaɪl/ *adj.* противораке́тный; **~ missile** противораке́тный снаря́д, противораке́та.

antimony /ˈæntɪmənɪ/ *n.* сурьма́; (*attr.*) сурьмя́ный.

antipathetic /ˌæntɪpəˈθetɪk/ *adj.* антипати́чный, вражде́бный.

antipathy /ænˈtɪpəθɪ/ *n.* антипа́тия; **have, feel an ~ to, against, for** испы́тывать (*impf.*) антипа́тию к + *d.*

anti-personnel /ˌæntɪˌpɜːsəˈnel/ *adj.* противопехо́тный; **~ weapon** противопехо́тное ору́жие; **~** (*fragmentation*) **bomb** оско́лочная бо́мба.

antiperspirant /ˌæntɪˈpɜːspɪrənt/ *n.* сре́дство от поте́ния, антиперспира́нт.

Antipodean /ænˌtɪpəˈdiːən/ *adj.* (*geog.*) относя́щийся к Австра́лии и Но́вой Зела́ндии.

● *n.* антипо́д, жи́тель Австра́лии или Но́вой Зела́ндии.

Antipodes /ænˈtɪpəˌdiːz/ *n.* регио́н Австра́лии и Но́вой Зела́ндии.

antipyretic /ˌæntɪpaɪˈretɪk/ *n.* жаропонижа́ющее (сре́дство).

● *adj.* жаропонижа́ющий.

antiquarian /ˌæntɪˈkweərɪən/ *n.* антиква́р.

● *adj.* антиква́рный; **~ bookshop** букинисти́ческий магази́н.

antiquary /ˈæntɪkwərɪ/ *n.* антиква́р.

antiquated /ˈæntɪˌkweɪtɪd/ *adj.* (*obsolete*) устаре́лый; (*old-fashioned*) старомо́дный.

antique /ænˈtiːk/ *n.* антиква́рная вещь; **~ dealer** антиква́р; **~ shop** антиква́рный магази́н.

● *adj.* (*vase, table*) антиква́рный; (*ancient*) дре́вний, стари́нный; (*pert. to ancient, esp. classical times*) анти́чный.

antiquity /ænˈtɪkwɪtɪ/ *n.* (*great age; olden times*) дре́вность; (*classical times*) анти́чность; (*pl., ancient objects*) антиквариа́т.

antirrhinum /ˌæntɪˈraɪnəm/ *n.* льви́ный зев.

anti-Semite /ˌæntɪˈsiːmaɪt/ *n.* антисеми́т (*fem.* -ка).

anti-Semitic /ˌæntɪsɪˈmɪtɪk/ *adj.* антисеми́тский.

anti-Semitism /ˌæntɪˈsemɪˌtɪz(ə)m/ *n.* антисемити́зм.

antisepsis /ˌæntɪˈsepsɪs/ *n.* антисе́птика.

antiseptic /ˌæntɪˈseptɪk/ *n.* антисе́птик.

● *adj.* антисепти́ческий.

anti-social /ˌæntɪˈsəʊʃ(ə)l/ *adj.* антиобще́ственный.

anti-Soviet /ˌæntɪˈsəʊvɪət/ *adj.* антисове́тский.

anti-submarine /ˌæntɪsʌbməˈriːn/ *adj.* противоло́дочный.

anti-tank /ˌæntɪˈtæŋk/ *adj.* противота́нковый.

anti-tetanus /ˌæntɪˈtetənəs/ *adj.*: **~ injection** противостолбня́чный уко́л.

anti-theft /ˌæntɪˈθeft/ *adj.*: **~ device** (*on car*) противоуго́нное устро́йство.

antithesis /ænˈtɪθɪsɪs/ *n.* (*pl.* **antitheses** /-ˌsiːz/) (*contrast of opposite ideas*) антите́за; (*contrast*) контра́ст; (*opposite*) противополо́жность; **he is the ~ of his brother** он по́лная противополо́жность своему́ бра́ту.

antithetic(al) /ˌæntɪˈθetɪk(ə)l/ *adj.* противополо́жный; антитети́ческий.

anti-vivisectionist /ˌæntɪˌvɪvɪˈsekʃəˌnɪst/ *n.* проти́вник вивисе́кции.

anti-war /ˌæntɪˈwɔː(r)/ *adj.* антивое́нный.

antler /ˈæntlə(r)/ *n.* оле́ний рог.

antonym /ˈæntənɪm/ *n.* анто́ним.

antrum /ˈæntrəm/ *n.* (*pl.* **antra**) по́лость.

anus /ˈeɪnəs/ *n.* за́дний прохо́д, а́нус.

anvil /ˈænvɪl/ *n.* накова́льня.

anxiety /æŋˈzaɪətɪ/ *n.* **1** (*uneasiness*) беспоко́йство; (*alarm*) трево́га; **cause ~ to** трево́жить, вс-; **be full of ~** беспоко́иться, трево́житься (*both impf.*); **feel ~ for, over** беспоко́иться (*impf.*) о + *p.*; трево́житься (*impf.*) о + *p.* **2** (*desire; keenness*) жела́ние/стремле́ние + *inf.* **3** (*pl., cares, worries*) забо́ты (*f. pl.*).

anxious /ˈæŋkʃəs/ *adj.* **1** (*worried, uneasy*) озабо́ченный; **be ~ about, for, over** трево́житься (*impf.*) за + *a.*; беспоко́иться (*impf.*) о + *p.*; **I am ~ for his safety** я беспоко́юсь, как бы с ним чего́ не случи́лось. **2** (*causing anxiety*) трево́жный, беспоко́йный; **he gave me some ~ moments** он доста́вил мне не́сколько трево́жных мину́т. **3** (*keen, desirous*): **I am ~ to see him** мне о́чень хо́чется его́ ви́деть.

any /ˈenɪ/ *pron.* **1** (*in interrog. or conditional sentences*) (*animates*) кто́-нибудь; (*inanimates*) что́-нибудь; **if ~ of them should see him** е́сли кто́-нибудь из них уви́дит его́. **2** (*in neg. sentences*) (*with animates*) никто́; (*with inanimates*) ничто́; ни оди́н; **I don't like ~ of these actors** мне не нра́вится никто́/ни оди́н из э́тих арти́стов; **he never spoke to ~ of our friends** он не говори́л ни с кем из на́ших друзе́й; **I looked for the books but couldn't find ~** я иска́л кни́ги, но не нашёл ни одно́й; **I offered him food but he didn't want ~** я предложи́л ему́ пое́сть, но он ничего́ не хоте́л. **3** (*in affirmative sentences*) любо́й; **take ~ of these books** возьми́те любу́ю/любы́е из э́тих книг. **4**: **he has little money, if ~** у него́ де́нег ма́ло, а то и во́все нет.

● *adj.* **1** (*in interrog. or conditional sentences*) *untranslated*: **have you ~ children?** у вас есть де́ти?; **have you ~ matches?** (*request*) нет ли у вас спи́чек?; **were there ~ Russians there?** ру́сские там бы́ли?; **is there ~ news?** есть каки́е-нибудь но́вости?; (*no matter what*) любо́й, како́й уго́дно. **2** (*in neg. sentences*): **we haven't ~ milk** у нас нет молока́; **haven't you ~ cigarettes?** ра́зве у вас нет сигаре́т?; (*not ~ at all, not a single*) никако́й, ни оди́н; **there wasn't ~ hope** никако́й наде́жды не́ было; **there isn't ~ man who would ...** нет тако́го челове́ка, кото́рый бы. . .; (*with* **hardly**, *vv. of prevention etc.*): **there is hardly ~ doubt** нет почти́ никако́го сомне́ния; **without ~ doubt** без вся́кого сомне́ния; **they stopped us from scoring ~ goals** они́ не да́ли нам заби́ть ни одного́ гола́. **3** (*no matter which*) любо́й; **at ~ time** в любо́е вре́мя; **~ excuse will do** любо́й предло́г подойдёт; (*every*) любо́й, вся́кий; **in ~ case** во вся́ком слу́чае; **~ student knows this** э́то зна́ет любо́й студе́нт; **~ amount** *see* ⇒**amount; ~ man, ~ person = ~body, ~one.**

● *adv.* **1** (*in interrog. or conditional sentences*) *untranslated or* ско́лько-нибудь; **do you want ~ more tea?** хоти́те ещё ча́ю?; **if you stay here ~ longer** е́сли вы ещё хоть немно́го заде́ржитесь здесь. **2** (*in neg. sentences*) *untranslated or* ниско́лько; ничу́ть; **I can't go ~ farther** я не могу́ идти́ да́льше; **he doesn't live here ~ more, longer** он здесь бо́льше не живёт; **I am not ~ better** мне ничу́ть не лу́чше; **he did not get ~ nearer** он ниско́лько не прибли́зился. **3** (*US, at all*): **it didn't snow ~ yesterday** вчера́ сне́га во́все не́ было; **that didn't help us ~** э́то нам ниско́лько не помогло́.

anybody /ˈenɪˌbɒdɪ/, **anyone** /ˈenɪˌwʌn/ *n. & pron.* **1** (*in interrog. or conditional sentences*) кто́-нибудь; кто́-либо; **did you meet ~?** вы кого́-нибудь встре́тили?; **if ~ rings, don't answer** е́сли кто позвони́т, не отвеча́йте; **is this ~'s seat?** э́то ме́сто за́нято?; **is ~ hurt?** кто́-нибудь ра́нен? **2** (*in neg. sentences*) никто́; **I didn't speak to ~** я ни с кем не говори́л. **3** (*~ at all; no matter who*) вся́кий, любо́й; **~ will tell you** любо́й/вся́кий вам ска́жет; **~ who says that is a liar** кто бы э́то ни сказа́л, он лжёц; **~ but you** кто уго́дно, то́лько не вы; **~ else** кто́-нибудь ещё; **he speaks better than ~** он говори́т лу́чше всех (*or* лу́чше, чем кто́-либо); **there was hardly ~ there** там почти́ никого́ не́ было; **he loved her more than ~** он люби́л её бо́льше всех; **he's a scholar if ~ is** е́сли кто учёный, так э́то он. **4** (*person of note*): **everyone who was ~ was invited** пригласи́ли всех, кто что́-то из себя́ представля́л.

anyhow /ˈenɪˌhaʊ/ *adv.* **1** (*haphazardly; carelessly*) ко́е-как; ка́к-нибудь; **the work was done ~** рабо́та была́ сде́лана ко́е-как. **2** (*anyway, in any case*) во вся́ком слу́чае; так или и́наче; (*nevertheless*) всё равно́, всё же; **I shall go ~** я всё равно́ пойду́.

anyone /'enɪ,wʌn/ = **anybody**

anything /'enɪθɪŋ/ *n. & pron.* **1** (*in interrog. or conditional sentences*) что́-нибудь; что́-либо; что; **is there ~ I can get for you?** вам что́-нибудь принести́?; **can I do ~ to help?** я могу́ че́м-нибудь помо́чь?; **have you ~ to say?** у вас (*or* вам) есть, что сказа́ть?; **did you see ~ of him in London?** вы ви́делись с ним в Ло́ндоне?; **better, if ~** вро́де бы лу́чше.
2 (*in neg. sentences*) ничто́; **I haven't ~ to say to that** мне не́чего сказа́ть на э́то.
3 (*everything*) всё; **I'd give ~ to see him again** я о́тдал бы всё, что́бы уви́деть его́ опя́ть; **we were left without ~** мы оста́лись без ничего́; **more, better than ~** бо́льше всего́.
4 (~ *at all*, ~ *you please*) что уго́дно; **it's as simple as ~** э́то про́ще просто́го.
5 (*whatever*): **I will do ~ you suggest** я сде́лаю всё, что вы ска́жете.
6: **~ but** отню́дь не/совсе́м не; **he is ~ but a genius** он совсе́м не ге́ний; **it is ~ but** (*far from*) **clear** э́то далеко́ не я́сно.
7: **like ~** да ещё как; **he worked like ~** он рабо́тал изо всех сил; **it's raining like ~** льёт как из ведра́.

anyway /'enɪ,weɪ/ = **anyhow** 2

anywhere /'enɪ,weə(r)/ *adv.* **1** (*in interrog. and conditional sentences*) где́-нибудь; где́-либо; (*of motion*) куда́-нибудь; куда́-либо; **is there a chemist's ~?** здесь есть апте́ка где́-нибудь?; **have you ~ to stay?** у вас есть где останови́ться? **2** (*in neg. sentences*) нигде́; (*of motion*) никуда́; **we haven't been ~ for ages** мы уже́ це́лую ве́чность нигде́ не́ были. **3** (*in any place at all*; *everywhere*) где уго́дно; везде́; (по)всю́ду; **it is miles from ~** э́то у чёрта на кули́чках; **he earns ~ from 200 to 300 pounds a month** он зараба́тывает не ме́ньше двухсо́т-трёхсот фу́нтов в ме́сяц; **it isn't ~ near finished** э́то ещё далеко́ не зако́нчено.

AOB (*abbr. of* ***any other business***) (*Br.*) ра́зное.

aorist /'eərɪst/ *n.* ао́рист.
● *adj.* (*also* **aoristic**) аористи́ческий.

aorta /eɪ'ɔ:tə/ *n.* (*pl.* **~s**) ао́рта.

apace /ə'peɪs/ *adv.* (*liter.*) бы́стро.

Apache /ə'pætʃɪ/ *n.* (*pl.* ~ *or* **~s**) апа́ч.

apart /ə'pɑ:t/ *adv.* **1** (*position*) в стороне́; (*motion*) в сто́рону; **he held himself ~** он держа́лся в стороне́; **his height set him ~** он выделя́лся свои́м ро́стом; **joking ~** шу́тки в сто́рону; **~ from** (*with the exception of*) за исключе́нием +*g.*; кро́ме +*g.*; (*other than*; *besides*) кро́ме/поми́мо +*g.*
2 (*separate(ly)*; *asunder*) отде́льно; **the dish came ~ in her hands** таре́лка слома́лась у неё в рука́х; **they lived ~ for 2 years** они́ жи́ли два го́да врозь; **the baby pulled its rattle ~** ребёнок разлома́л погрему́шку на ча́сти; **they took the machine ~** они́ разобра́ли маши́ну на ча́сти; **I could not tell them ~** я не мог их различи́ть/отличи́ть; **with one's feet wide ~** расста́вив но́ги.
3 (*distant*): **the houses are a mile ~** дома́ нахо́дятся в ми́ле друг от дру́га.

apartheid /ə'pɑ:teɪt/ *n.* апартеи́д.

apartment /ə'pɑ:tmənt/ *n.* **1** (*room*) ко́мната. **2**: **the royal ~s** короле́вские апартаме́нты (*m. pl.*). **3** (*US*) кварти́ра; **~ block/house** многокварти́рный дом.

apathetic /,æpə'θetɪk/ *adj.* апати́чный.

apathy /'æpəθɪ/ *n.* апа́тия.

apatite /'æpə,taɪt/ *n.* (*min.*) апати́т.

APC (*abbr. of* ***armoured personnel carrier***) БТР, бронетранспортёр.

ape /eɪp/ *n.* (*lit., fig.*) обезья́на.
● *v.t.* (*imitate*) подража́ть (*impf.*) +*d.*
● *cpd.* **~-like** *adj.* обезьяноподо́бный.

Apennines /'æpə,naɪnz/ *n.* Апенни́н|ы (*pl., g.* —).

aperient /ə'pɪərɪənt/ *n.* слаби́тельное (сре́дство).
● *adj.* слаби́тельный.

aperitif /ə,perɪ'ti:f/, /ə'pe-/ *n.* аперити́в.

aperture /'æpə,tjʊə(r)/ *n.* отве́рстие; (*opt.*) аперту́ра; (*phot.*) диафра́гма.

apex /'eɪpeks/ *n.* (*pl.* **apexes** *or* **apices**) (*lit., fig.*) верши́на, верх.

aphasia /ə'feɪzɪə/ *n.* (*med.*) афа́зия.

apheli|on /æp'hi:lɪən/, /ə'fi:lɪən/ *n.* (*astron.*) (*pl.* **~a**) афе́лий.

apheresis /ə'fɪərɪsɪs/ *n.* (*phon.*) афере́зис.

aphid /'eɪfɪd/ *n.* тля.

aphorism /'æfə,rɪz(ə)m/ *n.* афори́зм.

aphoristic /,æfə'rɪstɪk/ *adj.* афористи́ческий.

aphrodisiac /,æfrə'dɪzɪ,æk/ *n.* сре́дство, уси́ливающее полово́е влече́ние.
● *adj.* уси́ливающий полово́е влече́ние.

apiarist /'eɪpɪərɪst/ *n.* пчелово́д.

apiary /'eɪpɪərɪ/ *n.* па́сека, пче́льник.

apices /'eɪpɪ,si:z/ *pl. of* ⇒**apex**

apiculture /'eɪpɪ,kʌltʃə(r)/ *n.* пчелово́дство.

apiece /ə'pi:s/ *adv.* **1** (*of thing*): **I sell books for a dollar ~** я продаю́ кни́ги по до́ллару (за ка́ждую). **2** (*of person*): **we had £10 ~** у ка́ждого из нас бы́ло по де́сять фу́нтов; у нас бы́ло по де́сять фу́нтов на челове́ка; **the dinner cost £30 ~** обе́д сто́ил по три́дцать фу́нтов с ка́ждого; **they scored two goals ~** ка́ждый из них заби́л по два го́ла.

aplenty /ə'plentɪ/ *adv.* (*arch.*) в изоби́лии.

aplomb /ə'plɒm/ *n.* апло́мб.

apocalypse /ə'pɒkəlɪps/ *n.* апока́липсис.

apocalyptic /ə,pɒkə'lɪptɪk/ *adj.* апокалипти́ческий.

Apocrypha /ə'pɒkrɪfə/ *n.* апо́крифы (*m. pl.*).

apocryphal /ə'pɒkrɪf(ə)l/ *adj.* **1** (*bibl.*) апокрифи́ческий. **2** (*of doubtful authenticity*) недостове́рный.

apogee /'æpə,dʒi:/ *n.* (*lit., fig.*) апоге́й.

apolitical /,eɪpə'lɪtɪk(ə)l/ *adj.* аполити́чный.

apologetic /ə,pɒlə'dʒetɪk/ *adj.* извиня́ющийся; **he was very ~** он о́чень извиня́лся; **an ~ smile** винова́тая улы́бка.

apologetics /ə,pɒlə'dʒetɪks/ *n.* апологе́тика.

apologia /,æpə'ləʊdʒɪə/ *n.* аполо́гия.

apologist /ə'pɒlədʒɪst/ *n.* апологе́т, защи́тник.

apologize /ə'pɒlə,dʒaɪz/ *v.i.* извин|я́ться, -и́ться (*перед кем за что*).

apolog|y /ə'pɒlədʒɪ/ *n.* **1** (*expression of regret*) извине́ние; **make, offer an ~y to s.o. for something** прин|оси́ть, -ести́ извине́ния кому́-н. за что-н.; **please accept my ~ies** прими́те мои́ извине́ния; **they sent their ~ies** они́ переда́ли свои́ извине́ния. **2** (*poor substitute*): **this ~y for a dinner** э́тот го́ре-обе́д.

apoplectic /,æpə'plektɪk/ *adj.* (*pert. to apoplexy*): **an ~ fit** апоплекси́ческий уда́р; (*coll.*): **~ with rage** в бе́шеном припа́дке.

apoplexy /'æpə,pleksɪ/ *n.* апопле́ксия; (*stroke*) инсу́льт, кровоизлия́ние в мозг.

apostasy /ə'pɒstəsɪ/ *n.* (*abandonment or loss of faith, principles etc.*) отсту́пничество; (*desertion of cause or party*) ренега́тство; (*betrayal*) изме́на.

apostate /ə'pɒsteɪt/ *n.* отсту́пник; ренега́т.
● *adj.* отсту́пнический.

a posteriori /,eɪ pɒ,sterɪ'ɔ:raɪ/ *adj.* апостерио́рный; осно́ванный на о́пыте.
● *adv.* апостерио́ри; из о́пыта.

apostle /ə'pɒs(ə)l/ *n.* апо́стол.

apostolic /,æpə'stɒlɪk/ *adj.*: **~ succession** апо́стольское насле́дование; **A~ See** па́пский престо́л.

apostrophe /ə'pɒstrəfɪ/ *n.* (*rhetoric*) апостро́фа; (*gram.*) апостро́ф.

apostrophize /ə'pɒstrəfaɪz/ *v.t.* обра|ща́ться, -ти́ться к+*d.*

apothecary /ə'pɒθəkərɪ/ *n.* (*arch.*) апте́карь (*m.*); **~'s weight** апте́карский вес.

apotheosis /ə,pɒθɪ'əʊsɪs/ *n.* (*pl.* **apotheoses** /-si:z/) (*lit., fig.*) апофео́з.

appal /ə'pɔ:l/ *v.t.* (*US also* **appall; appalled, appalling**) ужас|а́ть, -ну́ть; устраш|а́ть, -и́ть; **we were ~led at the sight** мы ужасну́лись (*or* пришли́ в у́жас) при ви́де э́того; **I was ~led at the cost** цена́ меня́ ужасну́ла.

Appalachians /,æpə'leɪtʃɪənz/ *n.* Аппала́ч|и (*pl., g.* -ей).

appall /ə'pɔ:l/ (*US*) = **appal**

appalling /ə'pɔ:lɪŋ/ *adj.* ужа́сный, жу́ткий.

apparatus /,æpə'reɪtəs/, /'æp-/ *n.* **1** (*instrument; appliance*) прибо́р, инструме́нт. **2** (*in laboratory*) аппарату́ра; обору́дование. **3** (*gymnastic*) снаря́ды (*m. pl.*). **4** (*set of* *institutions*) аппара́т; **~ of government** прави́тельственный аппара́т.

apparel /əˈpær(ə)l/ *n.* одея́ние, наря́д.

apparent /əˈpærənt/ *adj.* **1** (*visible*) ви́димый. **2** (*plain, obvious*) очеви́дный; я́вный; **heir ~** зако́нный/прямо́й насле́дник; **be ~** быть я́вным/очеви́дным; **become ~** обнару́жи|ваться, -ться. **3** (*seeming*) ка́жущийся, мни́мый.

apparently /əˈpærəntlɪ/ *adv.* **1** (*clearly*) очеви́дно, я́вно. **2** (*seemingly*) по-ви́димому; вероя́тно; (как) бу́дто; **~ he's the local doctor** он по-ви́димому/вероя́тно зде́шний врач; **~ he was here yesterday** по-ви́димому/вероя́тно он был здесь вчера́.

apparition /ˌæpəˈrɪʃ(ə)n/ *n.* **1** (*manifestation, esp. of ghost*) (по)явле́ние. **2** (*ghost*) привиде́ние, виде́ние, при́зрак.

appeal /əˈpiːl/ *n.* **1** (*earnest request, plea*) обраще́ние (с про́сьбой); (*official*) воззва́ние; (*call*) призы́в; **an ~ to public opinion** обраще́ние к обще́ственному мне́нию; **an ~ on behalf of the Red Cross** обраще́ние от и́мени Кра́сного Креста́; **an ~ for support** про́сьба о подде́ржке; **an ~ for silence** про́сьба соблюда́ть тишину́.
2 (*reference to higher authority*) апелля́ция, обжа́лование; **court of ~** апелляцио́нный суд; **supreme court of ~** кассацио́нный суд; **an ~ to the referee** обраще́ние к судье́.
3 (*attraction*) привлека́тельность; **this life has little ~ for me** э́та жизнь меня́ ма́ло привлека́ет.

● *v.i.* **1** (*make earnest request*) обра|ща́ться, -ти́ться (*to* к + *d.*; *for* за + *a.*) **he ~ed to us for help** он обрати́лся к нам за по́мощью; **she ~ed to him for mercy** она́ моли́ла его́ о милосе́рдии; **I ~ to you to support them** я призыва́ю вас поддержа́ть их; (*address o.s. to*) апелли́ровать (*impf., pf.*); **he ~ed to the common sense of the people** он апелли́ровал к здра́вому смы́слу наро́да.
2 (*leg.*) апелли́ровать (*impf., pf.*); под|ава́ть, -а́ть апелля́цию; обжа́ловать (*pf.*) пригово́р.
3: **~ to** (*attract*) привлека́ть (*impf.*); нра́виться (*impf.*) + *d.*

appealing /əˈpiːlɪŋ/ *adj.* (*imploring*) умоля́ющий; (*attractive*) привлека́тельный.

appear /əˈpɪə(r)/ *v.i.* **1** (*become visible; coll.: arrive*) появ|ля́ться, -и́ться; (*of qualities etc.*) прояв|ля́ться, -и́ться.
2 (*present o.s.*) выступа́ть, вы́ступить; **~ in court** предст|ава́ть, -а́ть пе́ред судо́м; (*of actor*) игра́ть (*impf.*) на сце́не; снима́ться, сня́ться в кино́; (*make an entrance on stage*) выходи́ть, вы́йти на сце́ну; (*of book*) выходи́ть, вы́йти (в свет); быть и́зданным.
3 (*seem*) каза́ться, по-; (*follow as inference*) сле́довать (*impf.*); (*be manifest*) я́вствовать (*impf.*); **it ~s strange to me** мне э́то ка́жется стра́нным; **strange as it may ~** как бы стра́нно э́то ни показа́лось; **he ~s to have left** он, ка́жется, уе́хал.
4 (*turn out*) ока́з|ываться, -а́ться; **if it ~s that this is so** е́сли ока́жется, что э́то так; **it ~s his wife is a Swede** ока́зывается, его́ жена́ шве́дка.

appearance /əˈpɪərəns/ *n.* **1** (*act of appearing*) появле́ние; (*in public*) выступле́ние; **make (*or* put in) an ~** пока́з|ываться, -а́ться; появ|ля́ться, -и́ться; **his ~ as Hamlet** его́ выступле́ние в ро́ли Га́млета; **make one's first ~** дебюти́ровать (*impf., pf.*); **~ in court** я́вка в суд; (*of a book*) вы́ход в свет; появле́ние.
2 (*look, aspect*) (*of thing*) вид; (*of person*) нару́жность, вне́шность; **a pleasing ~** прия́тный вид; **~s are deceptive** нару́жность обма́нчива; **judge by ~(s)** суди́ть (*impf.*) по вне́шнему ви́ду; **in ~** на вид; по ви́ду; **to, by all ~s** по всем при́знакам; су́дя по всему́.
3 (*semblance*) вид, ви́димость; **keep up ~s** соблюда́ть (*impf.*) ви́димость прили́чия; **for ~'s sake** для ви́димости; напока́з.

appease /əˈpiːz/ *v.t.* (*one's conscience*) успок|а́ивать, -о́ить; (*person*) умиротвор|я́ть, -и́ть; (*appetites, passions*) утол|я́ть, -и́ть.

appeasement /əˈpiːzmənt/ *n.* **1** успокое́ние; умиротворе́ние. **2** (*of hunger, desire etc.*) утоле́ние.

appeaser /əˈpiːzə(r)/ *n.* умиротвори́тель (*m.*).

appellant /əˈpelənt/ *n.* апелля́нт.

appellation /ˌæpəˈleɪʃ(ə)n/ *n.* назва́ние.

append /əˈpend/ *v.t.* **1** (*fasten*) прикреп|ля́ть, -и́ть; **a label was ~ed to the parcel** к посы́лке был прикреплён ярлы́к; (*hang on*) подве́|шивать, -сить.
2 (*add, in writing etc.*) прил|ага́ть, -ожи́ть; приб|авля́ть, -а́вить; **he ~ed a report to the letter** он приложи́л докла́д к письму́; **notes ~ed to the chapter** примеча́ния к главе́; **they wish to ~ a clause to the treaty** они́ хотя́т доба́вить статью́ к догово́ру.

appendage /əˈpendɪdʒ/ *n.* (*anat.*) отро́сток, прида́ток; (*fig.*) прида́ток.

appendectomy /ˌæpenˈdektəmɪ/ *n.* удале́ние аппе́ндикса.

appendices /əˈpendɪˌsiːz/ *pl. of* ⇒**appendix**

appendicitis /əˌpendɪˈsaɪtɪs/ *n.* аппендици́т.

appendi|x /əˈpendɪks/ *n.* (*pl.* **~ces** *or* **~xes**) **1** (*anat.*) аппе́ндикс. **2** (*of a book, document, etc.*) приложе́ние.

appertain /ˌæpəˈteɪn/ *v.i.* (*relate*) относи́ться (*impf.*) (к + *d.*); **the chapters ~ing to his childhood** гла́вы, относя́щиеся к его́ де́тству; (*be appropriate*) соотве́тствовать (*impf.*); **the duties ~ing to his office** обя́занности, соотве́тствующие его́ до́лжности.

appetite /ˈæpɪˌtaɪt/ *n.* **1** (*for food*) аппети́т; **I have lost my ~** у меня́ пропа́л аппети́т. **2** (*natural desire*) потре́бность; **sexual ~** полово́е влече́ние; (*thirst*) жа́жда; **~ for revenge** жа́жда ме́сти; (*inclination*) влече́ние, скло́нность (к + *d.*); **he had no ~ for the task** у него́ се́рдце не лежа́ло к э́той рабо́те.

appetizer /ˈæpɪˌtaɪzə(r)/ *n.* (*aperitif*) аперити́в; (*hors d'oeuvre*) заку́ска.

appetizing /ˈæpɪˌtaɪzɪŋ/ *adj.* аппети́тный.

applaud /əˈplɔːd/ *v.t.* (*also v.i., clap*) аплоди́ровать (*impf.*) + *d.*; (*praise*) приве́тствовать (*impf.*); од|обря́ть, -о́брить.

applause /əˈplɔːz/ *n.* аплодисме́нты (*m. pl.*); рукоплеска́ния (*nt. pl.*); **a roar of ~** гром аплодисме́нтов; **loud ~** бу́рные аплодисме́нты; (*fig., approval*): **he won the ~ of all** он завоева́л всео́бщее одобре́ние.

apple /ˈæp(ə)l/ *n.* я́блоко; **she was the ~ of her father's eye** оте́ц души́ в ней не ча́ял.

● *cpds.* **~-blossom** *n.* я́блоневый цвет; **~-cart** *n.*: **upset the ~-cart** (*fig.*) спу́тать (*pf.*) ка́рты; **~-core** *n.* сердцеви́на я́блока; **~-juice** *n.* я́блочный сок; **~-orchard** *n.* я́блоневый сад; **~-pie** *n.* я́блочный пиро́г; **in ~-pie order** в по́лном поря́дке; **~-sauce** *n.* я́блочное пюре́ (*indecl.*); **~-tree** *n.* я́блоня.

appliance /əˈplaɪəns/ *n.* **1** (*act of applying*) примене́ние. **2** (*instrument*) прибо́р, приспособле́ние; **dental ~** проте́з; **domestic ~** бытово́й прибо́р; **electric ~** эле́ктроприбо́р.

applicable /ˈæplɪkəb(ə)l/, /əˈplɪkəb(ə)l/ *adj.* примени́мый; (*appropriate*) подходя́щий; **the rule is not ~ to this case** пра́вило неприме́нимо к э́тому слу́чаю.

applicant /ˈæplɪkənt/ *n.* кандида́т, претенде́нт; **~ for a job** кандида́т, претенде́нт на до́лжность.

application /ˌæplɪˈkeɪʃ(ə)n/ *n.* **1** (*applying; putting on to a surface*) прикла́дывание; наложе́ние; **~ of paint** наложе́ние кра́ски.
2 (*employment; use*) примене́ние; приложе́ние. **3** (*diligence*) прилежа́ние; (*concentration*) сосредото́ченность. **4** (*request*) (*for work*) заявле́ние; (*for a grant*) зая́вка; (*for permission*) проше́ние; **~ form** бланк заявле́ния; **~ for payment** тре́бование упла́ты; **prices are sent on ~** расце́нки высыла́ются по тре́бованию; **there were twenty ~s for the job** на э́то ме́сто бы́ло по́дано два́дцать заявле́ний; **make (*or* put in) an ~** под|ава́ть, -а́ть заявле́ние.
5 (*comput.*) (*also* **~ program**) прикладна́я програ́мма; приложе́ние.

applied /əˈplaɪd/ *adj.*: **~ sciences** прикладны́е нау́ки.

appliqué /æˈpliːkeɪ/ *n.* апплика́ция.

appl|y /əˈplaɪ/ *v.t.* **1** (*lay, put on*) при|кла́дывать, -ложи́ть; (*dressing, plaster*) накла́дывать, наложи́ть; (*paint, cream*) наноси́ть, нанести́; **the doctor ~ied a plaster to his chest** врач наложи́л ему́ пла́стырь на грудь; **~y the liniment twice a day** мазь наноси́ть два́жды в день.
2 (*bring into action*) прил|ага́ть, -ожи́ть; **~y the brakes** тормози́ть, за-.
3 (*make use of*) примен|я́ть, -и́ть; **he**

~ied his knowledge well он хорошо́ примени́л свои́ зна́ния; **it is easy if you ~y your mind to it** э́то легко́, е́сли хороше́нько поду́мать.
4: **~y o.s. to** зан|има́ться, -я́ться + *i.*
● *v.i.*: **~y for** (*a job, grant, pass*) подава́ть, пода́ть заявле́ние на + *a.*; **~y to** (*concern; relate to*) относи́ться (*impf.*) к + *d.*; (*approach, request*) обра|ща́ться, -ти́ться к + *d.*; **I ~ied to him for permission** я обрати́лся к нему́ за разреше́нием.

appoint /ə'pɔɪnt/ *v.t.* **1** (*fix*) назн|ача́ть, -а́чить; определ|я́ть, -и́ть; **at the ~ed time** в назна́ченное вре́мя. **2** (*nominate*) назн|ача́ть, -а́чить; **he was ~ed ambassador** он был назна́чен посло́м; **they ~ed him to the post** они́ назна́чили его́ на э́ту до́лжность. **3** (*equip*): **well ~ed** хорошо́ оснащённый.

appointee /ə,pɔɪn'tiː/ *n.* назна́ченное лицо́.

appointment /ə'pɔɪntmənt/ *n.* **1** (*act of appointing*) назначе́ние; **by ~ to Her Majesty the Queen** поставщи́к Её Вели́чества. **2** (*office*) до́лжность; **permanent ~** шта́тная до́лжность; **hold an ~** занима́ть (*impf.*) до́лжность. **3** (*at doctor's etc.*): **to make an ~ with** запи́|сываться, -са́ться на приём к + *d.*; полу|ча́ть, -чи́ть назначе́ние к + *d.*; **I have an ~ with my dentist for 4 o'clock** я запи́сан на приём к зубно́му врачу́ в четы́ре часа́; (*business*) встре́ча; **she was late for the ~** она́ опозда́ла на встре́чу; **make an ~ to meet s.o.** назнача́ть, назна́чить встре́чу с кем-н.; **he could not keep his ~** он не смог прийти́ на встре́чу. **4** (*pl., fittings*) оснаще́ние.

apportion /ə'pɔːʃ(ə)n/ *v.t.* распредел|я́ть, -и́ть; раздел|я́ть, -и́ть.

apportionment /ə'pɔːʃənmənt/ *n.* распределе́ние, разделе́ние.

apposite /'æpəzɪt/ *adj.* (*suitable*) подходя́щий; (*to the point*) уме́стный; уда́чный.

appositeness /'æpəzɪtnɪs/ *n.* уме́стность.

apposition /,æpə'zɪʃ(ə)n/ *n.* (*gram.*) приложе́ние; аппози́ция; **noun in ~** приложе́ние.

appraisal /ə'preɪz(ə)l/ *n.* оце́нка; (*of performance, of a worker*) аттеста́ция.

appraise /ə'preɪz/ *v.t.* оце́н|ивать, -и́ть; (*work, a worker*) аттестова́ть (*impf., pf.*).

appraiser /ə'preɪzə(r)/ *n.* оце́нщик.

appreciable /ə'priːʃəb(ə)l/ *adj.* (*perceptible*) заме́тный; (*considerable*) значи́тельный.

appreciate /ə'priːʃɪ,eɪt/, /-sɪ,eɪt/ *v.t.* **1** (*value*) оц|е́нивать, -ени́ть; цени́ть (*impf.*); **we ~ your help** мы це́ним ва́шу по́мощь. **2** (*understand*) пон|има́ть, -я́ть; (*take into account*) прин|има́ть, -я́ть во внима́ние; **I don't think you ~ my difficulties** вы, ка́жется, не понима́ете мои́х затрудне́ний. **3** (*enjoy*): **he doesn't ~ French cooking** он не признаёт францу́зскую ку́хню; (*through understanding*): **he has learnt to ~ music** он научи́лся понима́ть и цени́ть му́зыку.
● *v.i.* (*rise in value*) пов|ыша́ться, -ы́ситься; **furniture has ~d in value** ме́бель повы́силась в цене́/сто́имости.

appreciation /ə,priːʃɪ'eɪʃ(ə)n/, /ə,priːs-/ *n.* **1** (*estimation, judgement*) оце́нка. **2** (*critique*) оце́нка. **3** (*understanding*) понима́ние, призна́ние досто́инств. **4** (*rise in value*) повыше́ние в цене́/сто́имости. **5** (*gratitude*) призна́тельность; **in ~ of your kindness** в знак призна́тельности за ва́шу любе́зность.

appreciative /ə'priːʃətɪv/ *adj.* **1** (*perceptive of merit*): **an ~ audience** понима́ющая аудито́рия. **2** (*grateful*) благода́рный, призна́тельный (за + *a*).

apprehend /,æprɪ'hend/ *v.t.* **1** (*understand*) уясн|я́ть, -и́ть. **2** (*arrest*) аресто́в|ывать, -а́ть; заде́рж|ивать, -а́ть.

apprehension /,æprɪ'henʃ(ə)n/ *n.* **1** (*understanding*) уясне́ние. **2** (*fear*) опасе́ние. **3** (*arrest*) аре́ст, задержа́ние.

apprehensive /,æprɪ'hensɪv/ *adj.* озабо́ченный; беспоко́йный; по́лный трево́ги; **I am ~ for you** я опаса́юсь за вас.

apprentice /ə'prentɪs/ *n.* подмасте́рье (*m.*).
● *v.t.* отд|ава́ть, -а́ть в уче́ние подмасте́рья; **he was ~d to a tailor** его́ о́тдали в подмасте́рья к портно́му.

apprenticeship /ə'prentɪsʃɪp/ *n.* уче́ние, учени́чество; **serve one's ~** про|ходи́ть, -йти́ обуче́ние; (*fig.*) овладе́ть (*pf.*) ремесло́м/мастерство́м.

apprise /ə'praɪz/ *v.t.* изве|ща́ть, -сти́ть.

approach /ə'prəʊtʃ/ *n.* **1** (*drawing near; advance*) приближе́ние; наступле́ние; **at our ~** при на́шем приближе́нии; как/когда́ мы подошли́. **2** (*fig.*) подхо́д; **his ~ to the subject** его́ подхо́д к предме́ту. **3** (*way, passage*) подхо́д; **the ~ to the river** подхо́д к реке́. **4** (*access*) по́дступ; **the ~es to the town** по́дступы к го́роду; **easy of ~** (*lit., fig.*) (легко)досту́пный. **5** (*fig., overture*) предложе́ние; **they made unofficial ~es** они́ де́лали неофициа́льные предложе́ния.
● *v.t.* **1** (*come near to*) прибл|ижа́ться, -и́зиться к + *d.*; (*come up to — on foot*) под|ходи́ть, -ойти́ к + *d.*; (*come up to — by riding*) подъ|езжа́ть, -е́хать к + *d.*; (*fig.*): **he ~ed the subject in a light-hearted way** он подошёл к вопро́су несерьёзно/легкомы́сленно; **he is difficult to ~** к нему́ тру́дно подступи́ться. **2** (*make overtures to*) обра|ща́ться, -ти́ться к + *d.*; **the beggar ~ed him for money** ни́щий попроси́л у него́ де́нег. **3** (*approximate to*) прибл|ижа́ться, -и́зиться к + *d.*; **no one can ~ him for style** по сти́лю никто́ не мо́жет с ним сравни́ться.
● *v.i.* прибл|ижа́ться, -и́зиться; под|ходи́ть, -ойти́; подъ|езжа́ть, -е́хать.

approachable /ə'prəʊtʃəb(ə)l/ *adj.* досту́пный.

approaching /ə'prəʊtʃɪŋ/ *adj.* приближа́ющийся; **the ~ storm** надвига́ющаяся бу́ря.

approbation /,æprə'beɪʃ(ə)n/ *n.* одобре́ние.

approbatory /'æprə,beɪtərɪ/ *adj.* одобри́тельный.

appropriate[1] /ə'prəʊprɪət/ *adj.* соотве́тствующий; **remarks ~ to the occasion** соотве́тствующие слу́чаю замеча́ния; (*suitable*) подходя́щий; **clothing ~ for hot weather** оде́жда, подходя́щая для жа́ркой пого́ды; (*to the point*) уме́стный.

appropriate[2] /ə'prəʊprɪ,eɪt/ *v.t.* **1** (*devote to special purpose*) предназн|ача́ть, -а́чить; (*funds*) ассигнова́ть (*impf., pf.*). **2** (*take possession of*) присв|а́ивать, -о́ить.

appropriation /ə,prəʊprɪ'eɪʃ(ə)n/ *n.* **1** назначе́ние; ассигнова́ние. **2** присвое́ние.

approval /ə'pruːv(ə)l/ *n.* одобре́ние; (*confirmation*) утвержде́ние; (*consent*) согла́сие; (*sanction*) апроба́ция; **meet with ~** получ|а́ть, -и́ть одобре́ние; **on ~** на про́бу.

approv|e /ə'pruːv/ *v.t.* од|обря́ть, -о́брить; (*confirm*) утвер|жда́ть, -ди́ть; **the report was ~ed** отчёт был утверждён.
● *v.i.*: **~e of** од|обря́ть, -о́брить; **an ~ing glance** одобри́тельный взгляд.

approximate[1] /ə'prɒksɪmət/ *adj.* приблизи́тельный.

approximate[2] /ə'prɒksɪ,meɪt/ *v.t.* **1** (*bring near*) прибл|ижа́ть, -и́зить (*что к чему*). **2** (*come near to*) прибл|ижа́ться, -и́зиться к + *d.*
● *v.i.*: **~ to** прибл|ижа́ться, -и́зиться к + *d.*

approximation /ə,prɒksɪ'meɪʃ(ə)n/ *n.* приближе́ние; **this is an ~ to the truth** э́то бли́зко к и́стине.

appurtenance /ə'pɜːtɪnəns/ *n.* (*accessory*) принадле́жность; (*appendage*) прида́ток.

apricot /'eɪprɪ,kɒt/ *n.* (*fruit or tree*) абрико́с; **~ jam** абрико́совый джем.

April /'eɪprɪl/, /'eɪpr(ə)l/ *n.* апре́ль (*m.*); **this ~** в апре́ле э́того го́да; **~ fool** первоапре́льский дурачо́к; **~ Fool!** пе́рвое апре́ля — никому́ не ве́рю! **~ fool's day** пе́рвое апре́ля.
● *adj.* апре́льский; **~ shower** внеза́пный дождь.

a priori /,eɪ praɪ'ɔːraɪ/ *adj.* априо́рный.
● *adv.* априо́ри.

apron /'eɪprən/ *n.* **1** (*garment*) пере́дник; фа́ртук. **2** (*theatr.*) авансце́на. **3** (*aeron.*) площа́дка пе́ред анга́ром.
● *cpd.* **~-strings** *n. pl.*: **he is tied to his mother's ~-strings** он ма́менькин сыно́к.

apropos /'æprə,pəʊ/, /-'pəʊ/ *adj. & adv.* (*appropriate*) уме́стн|ый, -о; (*timely*) своевре́менн|ый, -о; (*by the way*) ктáти, мéжду прóчим; **~ of** по пóводу *+g.*

apse /æps/ *n.* апсúда.

apt /æpt/ *adj.* **1** (*suitable*) подходя́щий; (*apposite*) умéстный, удáчный. **2** (*intelligent*) спосóбный. **3**: **~ to** склóнный к *+d.*; **he is ~ to fall asleep** он склóнен засыпáть.

aptitude /ˈæptɪˌtju:d/ *n.* (*capacity*) спосóбность; **~ for work** работоспосóбность; **~ test** провéрка спосóбностей; (*propensity*): **~ for** склóнность к *+d.*

aptness /ˈæptnɪs/ *n.* (*suitability*) пригóдность; (*appositeness*) умéстность; (*intelligence*) спосóбность; (*inclination*) склóнность.

aqua /ˈækwə/ *n.* (*colour*) цвет морскóй волны́.

aqualung /ˈækwəˌlʌŋ/ *n.* аквалáнг.

aquamarine /ˌækwəməˈri:n/ *n.* (*min.*) аквамарúн; (*colour*) аквамарúновый цвет.

● *adj.* аквамарúновый; зеленовáто-голубóй.

aquaplane /ˈækwəˌpleɪn/ *n.* аквапла́н.

● *v.i.* катáться (*indet.*) на акваплáне.

aquaria /əˈkweərɪə/ *pl. of* ⇒**aquarium**

aquari|um /əˈkweərɪəm/ *n.* (*pl.* **~a** *or* **~ums**) аквáриум.

Aquarius /əˈkweərɪəs/ *n.* Водолéй; **she's (an) Aquarius** онá — Водолéй.

aquatic /əˈkwætɪk/ *adj.* (*of plant or animal*) водянóй; (*of bird*) водоплáвающий; (*of sport*) вóдный.

aquatics /əˈkwætɪks/ *n.* вóдный спорт.

aquatint /ˈækwətɪnt/ *n.* (*art*) акватúнта.

aqua vitae /ˌækwə ˈvi:taɪ/ *n.* спирт, алкогóль (*m.*).

aqueduct /ˈækwɪˌdʌkt/ *n.* акведýк.

aqueous /ˈeɪkwɪəs/ *adj.* вóдный; (*watery*) водянúстый; **~ solution** вóдный раствóр; **~ humour** (*Br.*), **humor** (*US*) водянúстая влáга (глáза).

aquiline /ˈækwɪˌlaɪn/ *adj.* орлúный.

aquiver /əˈkwɪvə(r)/ *pred. adj.* дрожá; **her hands were ~ with excitement** от волнéния у неё дрожáли рýки.

Arab /ˈærəb/ *n.* **1** (*person*) арáб (*fem.* -ка). **2** (*horse*) арáбская лóшадь.

● *adj.* арáбский; **the ~ League** Лúга арáбских стран.

arabesque /ˌærəˈbesk/ *n.* арабéска.

Arabia /əˈreɪbɪə/ *n.* Арáвия.

Arabian /əˈreɪbɪən/ *n.* жúтель Аравúйского полуострова.

● *adj.* аравúйский; **the ~ Nights** Ты́сяча и однá ночь.

Arabic /ˈærəbɪk/ *n.* арáбский язы́к; **in ~** по-арáбски.

● *adj.* арáбский; **a~ numerals** арáбские цúфры.

Arabist /ˈærəbɪst/ *n.* арабúст.

arable /ˈærəb(ə)l/ *n.* пáхотная землá.

● *adj.* пáхотный; **~ farming** землелéлие.

Aramaic /ˌærəˈmeɪɪk/ *n.* арамéйский язы́к.

● *adj.* арамéйский.

arbiter /ˈɑ:bɪtə(r)/ *n.* **1** (*judge*) арбúтр; **~ of fashion** законодáтель (*m.*) мод. **2** (*third party*) трéтейский судья́; посрéдник.

arbitrariness /ˈɑ:bɪtrərɪnɪs/ *n.* произвóл; произвóльность.

arbitrary /ˈɑ:bɪtrərɪ/ *adj.* (*random, capricious, dictatorial*) произвóльный.

arbitrate /ˈɑ:bɪˌtreɪt/ *v.t.* (*decide*) реш|áть, -úть трéтейским судóм; (*refer to arbitration*) перед|авáть, -áть в арбитрáж.

● *v.i.* (*act as arbiter*) быть арбúтром; быть трéтейским судьёй.

arbitration /ˌɑ:bɪˈtreɪʃ(ə)n/ *n.* арбитрáж; трéтейский суд; **refer, submit to ~** перед|авáть, -áть в арбитрáж; (*attr.*) арбитрáжный, трéтейский; **~ clause** арбитрáжная оговóрка.

arbitrator /ˈɑ:bɪˌtreɪtə(r)/ *n.* трéтейский судья́; арбúтр.

arbor /ˈɑ:bə(r)/ (*US*) = **arbour**

arboreal /ɑ:ˈbɔ:rɪəl/ *adj.* древéсный.

arboret|um /ˌɑ:bəˈri:təm/ *n.* (*pl.* **~ums** *or* **~a**) дендрáрий, арборéтум.

arboriculture /ˈɑ:bərɪˌkʌltʃə(r)/ *n.* лесовóдство.

arbour /ˈɑ:bə(r)/ (*US* **arbor**) *n.* бесéдка.

arbutus /ɑ:ˈbju:təs/ *n.* землянúчное дéрево.

arc /ɑ:k/ *n.* дугá.

● *cpds.* **~-lamp** *n.* дуговáя лáмпа; **~-light** *n.* дуговóй свет; **~-welder** *n.* электросвáрщик; **~-welding** *n.* электродуговáя свáрка.

arcade /ɑ:ˈkeɪd/ *n.* (*covered passage*) аркáда; (*with shops*) пассáж.

Arcadian /ɑ:ˈkeɪdɪən/ *adj.* аркáдский; (*idyllic*) идиллúческий.

arcana /ɑ:ˈkeɪnə/ *n.* тáйны (*f. pl.*), таúнственность.

arcane /ɑ:ˈkeɪn/ *adj.* таúнственный, тáйный.

arch[1] /ɑ:tʃ/ *n.* (*curved shape*) áрка; (**~ed** *roof; vault*) свод; **~es of a bridge** пролёты мостá; **~ of the foot** свод стопы́; **he suffers from fallen ~es** у негó плоскостóпие.

● *v.t.* (*part of the body*) выгибáть, вы́гнуть; **the cat ~ed its back** кóшка вы́гнула спúну; **she ~ed her eyebrows** онá вскúнула брóви.

● *v.i.* (*form an* **~**) выгибáться, вы́гнуться.

● *cpd.* **~way** *n.* свóдчатый прохóд.

arch[2] /ɑ:tʃ/ *adj.* лукáвый, игрúвый.

arch- /ɑ:tʃ/ *comb. form* архи...; глáвный.

archaeological /ˌɑ:kɪəˈlɒdʒɪk(ə)l/ (*US also* **archeological**) *adj.* археологúческий.

archaeologist /ˌɑ:kɪˈɒlədʒɪst/ (*US also* **archeologist**) *n.* археóлог.

archaeology /ˌɑ:kɪˈɒlədʒɪ/ (*US also* **archeology**) *n.* археолóгия.

archaic /ɑ:ˈkeɪɪk/ *adj.* архаúчный; устарéвший.

archaism /ˈɑ:keɪˌɪz(ə)m/ *n.* архаúзм.

archangel /ˈɑ:kˌeɪndʒ(ə)l/ *n.* архáнгел.

archbishop /ɑ:tʃˈbɪʃəp/ *n.* архиепúскоп.

archbishopric /ɑ:tʃˈbɪʃəprɪk/ *n.* **1** (*office*) архиепúскопство. **2** (*district*) архиепúскопская епáрхия.

archdeacon /ɑ:tʃˈdi:kən/ *n.* архидья́кон.

archdiocese /ɑ:tʃˈdaɪəsɪs/ = **archbishopric** 2

archduchess /ɑ:tʃˈdʌtʃɪs/ *n.* эрцгерцогúня.

archduchy /ɑ:tʃˈdʌtʃɪ/ *n.* эрцгéрцогство.

archduke /ɑ:tʃˈdju:k/ *n.* эрцгéрцог.

arched /ɑ:tʃt/ *adj.* **1** (*furnished with, consisting of, arches*) áрочный, свóдчатый. **2** (*bent, curved*) изóгнутый.

arch-enemy /ɑ:tʃˈenəmɪ/ *n.* закля́тый враг.

archeological /ˌɑ:kɪəˈlɒdʒɪk(ə)l/ (*US*) = **archaeological**

archeologist /ˌɑ:kɪˈɒlədʒɪst/ (*US*) = **archaeologist**

archeology /ˌɑ:kɪˈɒlədʒɪ/ (*US*) = **archaeology**

archer /ˈɑ:tʃə(r)/ *n.* лýчни|к (*fem.* -ца); стрелóк из лýка.

archery /ˈɑ:tʃərɪ/ *n.* стрельбá из лýка; **~ range** лукодрóм.

archetypal /ˌɑ:kɪˈtaɪp(ə)l/ *adj.* (*typical*) типúчный.

archetype /ˈɑ:kɪˌtaɪp/ *n.* прототúп.

archimandrite /ˌɑ:kɪˈmændraɪt/ *n.* архимандрúт.

Archimedean /ˌɑ:kɪˈmi:dɪən/ *adj.*: **~ screw** архимéдов винт.

Archimedes /ˌɑ:kɪˈmi:di:z/ *n.* Архимéд; **~' principle** закóн Архимéда.

archipelago /ˌɑ:kɪˈpeləˌgəʊ/ *n.* (*pl.* **~s** *or* **~es**) архипелáг.

architect /ˈɑ:kɪˌtekt/ *n.* архитéктор; **naval ~** корабéльный инженéр; (*fig.*) áвтор, творéц.

architectonic /ˌɑ:kɪtekˈtɒnɪk/ *adj.* архитектонúческий.

architectonics /ˌɑ:kɪtekˈtɒnɪks/ *n.* архитектóника.

architectural /ˌɑ:kɪˈtektʃər(ə)l/ *adj.* архитектýрный; строúтельный.

architecture /ˈɑ:kɪˌtektʃə(r)/ *n.* (*science, style*) архитектýра; (*fig., structure, construction*) построéние, структýра.

architrave /ˈɑ:kɪˌtreɪv/ *n.* (*archit.*) архитрáв.

archival /ɑ:ˈkaɪv(ə)l/ *adj.* архúвный.

archive /ˈɑ:kaɪv/ *n.* (*also pl.; also comput.*) архúв.

● *v.t.* помe|щáть, -стúть в архúв; архивúровать (*impf., pf.*).

archivist /ˈɑ:kɪvɪst/ *n.* архивáриус.

archness /ˈɑ:tʃnɪs/ *n.* лукáвство.

arctic /ˈɑ:ktɪk/ *n.*: **the A~** Áрктика.

● *adj.* арктúческий; **A~ Circle** Сéверный поля́рный круг; **A~ Ocean** Сéверный Ледовúтый океáн; (*very cold*) ледянóй, студёный.

ardent /ˈɑ:d(ə)nt/ *adj.* (*fervent*) горя́чий,

пылкий; (*passionate*) стра́стный; (*zealous*) ре́вностный.

ardour /ˈɑːdə(r)/ (*US* **ardor**) *n.* жар, пыл, рве́ние.

arduous /ˈɑːdjʊəs/ *adj.* (*difficult*) тя́жкий; тяжёлый; **an ~ ascent** тру́дный подъём; **an ~ road** тяжёлая доро́га.

arduousness /ˈɑːdjʊəsnɪs/ *n.* тру́дность.

are /ɑː/, /ə/ *2nd pers. sing. pres. and pl. pres. of* ⇨**be**

area /ˈeərɪə/ *n.* **1** (*measurement*) пло́щадь; **what is the ~ of this triangle?** какова́ пло́щадь э́того треуго́льника?; **a room 12 square metres** (*Br.*), **meters** (*US*) **in ~** ко́мната пло́щадью в 12 $м^2$. **2** (*defined or designated space*) пло́щадь; **the ~ under cultivation** посевна́я пло́щадь; **landing ~** поса́дочная площа́дка; **training ~** полиго́н; (*expanse*) простра́нство; **vast ~s of forest** огро́мные лесны́е простра́нства; (*portion*) уча́сток; **a small ~ of skin was affected** был поражён небольшо́й уча́сток ко́жи. **3** (*region, tract, zone*) райо́н, край, зо́на; **residential ~** жило́й райо́н; **depressed ~** райо́н экономи́ческой депре́ссии; **wheat-growing ~** пло́щадь под пшени́цей; **sterling ~** сте́рлинговая зо́на; **~ (***regional***) studies** странове́дение. **4** (*scope, range*) разма́х; (*sphere*) о́бласть, сфе́ра; **in the ~ of research** в сфе́ре иссле́дования; **broad ~s of agreement** соглаше́ние по широ́кому кру́гу вопро́сов.

arena /əˈriːnə/ *n.* (*lit., fig.*) аре́на; **he entered the political ~** он вступи́л на полити́ческую аре́ну.

arête /æˈret/ *n.* о́стрый гре́бень горы́.

argentiferous /ˌɑːdʒənˈtɪfərəs/ *adj.* сереброно́сный.

Argentina /ˌɑːdʒənˈtiːnə/ *n.* (*also* **the Argentine**) Аргенти́на.

Argentin|e /ˈɑːdʒənˌtaɪn/, /-ˌtiːn/, **-ian** /ˌɑːdʒənˈtɪnɪən/ *n.* аргенти́н|ец (*fem.* -ка).

● *adj.* аргенти́нский.

argon /ˈɑːgɒn/ *n.* арго́н.

argot /ˈɑːgəʊ/ *n.* арго́ (*indecl.*), жарго́н.

arguable /ˈɑːgjʊəb(ə)l/ *adj.* **1** (*open to argument*) спо́рный. **2** (*demonstrable by argument*) доказу́емый; **it is ~ that ...** есть основа́ния полага́ть, что...; мо́жно утвержда́ть, что...

argue /ˈɑːgjuː/ *v.t.* (**argues, argued, arguing**) **1** (*discuss*) обсу|жда́ть, -ди́ть; (*debate*) дебати́ровать (*impf.*); спо́рить (*impf.*) о + *p.*; **let's not ~ the point** дава́йте об э́том не спо́рить. **2** (*contend*) дока́зывать (*impf.*); **he ~d that the money should be shared** он дока́зывал, что де́ньги сле́дует раздели́ть; **it was ~d that ...** утвержда́лось, что... **3** (*speak in support of*) дока́зывать (*impf.*), отста́ивать (*impf.*); **he ~d his case eloquently** он красноречи́во отста́ивал свою́ то́чку зре́ния. **4**: **~ s.o. into something** убе|жда́ть, -ди́ть (*кого в чём-н.*); **he ~d me into accepting the decision** он убеди́л меня́ приня́ть реше́ние; **~ s.o. out of something** отгов|а́ривать, -ори́ть (*кого от чего-н.*).

● *v.i.* **1** (*debate; disagree; quarrel*) спо́рить (*impf.*); препира́ться (*impf.*); (*object*) возража́ть (*impf.*); **get dressed and don't ~!** одева́йся — и не спорь!; **they ~d over who should drive** они́ спо́рили, кому́ вести́ маши́ну. **2** (*give reasons*) прив|оди́ть, -ести́ до́воды, выступа́ть, вы́ступить (**against**: про́тив + *g.*; **for, in favour of**: в по́льзу + *g.*, за + *a.*).

● *with advs.*: **~ away** осп|а́ривать, -о́рить; **one cannot ~ away the fact that ...** невозмо́жно оспо́рить тот факт, что...; **~ out: let's ~ the matter out** дава́йте обсу́дим вопро́с доскона́льно.

argument /ˈɑːgjʊmənt/ *n.* **1** (*reason*) аргуме́нт; до́вод; **it's an ~ for staying at home** э́то до́вод в по́льзу того́, что́бы оста́ться до́ма. **2** (*process of reasoning*) аргумента́ция; **the ~ ran as follows** аргумента́ция была́ такова́. **3** (*discussion, debate*) спор; **a heated ~ took place** разгоре́лся жа́ркий спор; **who won the ~?** кто победи́л в спо́ре?; **a matter of ~** спо́рный вопро́с; **have an ~ over, about** спо́рить (*impf.*) о + *p.*

argumentation /ˌɑːgjʊmenˈteɪʃ(ə)n/ *n.* (*reasoning*) аргумента́ция; (*debate*) спор.

argumentative /ˌɑːgjʊˈmentətɪv/ *adj.* сварли́вый.

argy-bargy /ˌɑːdʒɪˈbɑːdʒɪ/ *n.* (*Br. coll.*) перепа́лка.

aria /ˈɑːrɪə/ *n.* а́рия.

arid /ˈærɪd/ *adj.* (*of soil etc.*) сухо́й, пересо́хший; (*of climate; lit., fig.*) (*dry*) сухо́й; (*barren*) беспло́дный.

aridity /əˈrɪdɪtɪ/ *n.* (*lit.*) засу́шливость; (*lit., fig.*) су́хость; беспло́дность.

Aries /ˈeəriːz/ *n.* (*pl.* **~**) Ове́н; **she's (an) Aries** она́ — Ове́н.

aright /əˈraɪt/ *adv.* пра́вильно.

arise /əˈraɪz/ *v.i.* (*past* **arose**; *p.p.* **arisen** /əˈrɪz(ə)n/) **1** (*lit., get up; stand up*) вст|ава́ть, -а́ть; (*lit., fig., rise*) восст|ава́ть, -а́ть; (*from the dead*) воскр|еса́ть, -е́снуть. **2** (*fig., come into being*) возн|ика́ть, -и́кнуть; **if the need should ~** е́сли возни́кнет необходи́мость; **the question arose** возни́к вопро́с; **a shout arose from the crowd** из толпы́ разда́лся крик.

aristocracy /ˌærɪˈstɒkrəsɪ/ *n.* аристокра́тия.

aristocrat /ˈærɪstəˌkræt/ *n.* аристокра́т.

aristocratic /ˌærɪstəˈkrætɪk/ *adj.* аристократи́ческий.

arithmetic /əˈrɪθmətɪk/ *n.* арифме́тика.

arithmetical /əˌrɪθˈmetɪk(ə)l/ *adj.* арифмети́ческий.

ark /ɑːk/ *n.* ковче́г; **Noah's ~** Но́ев ковче́г; **A~ of the Covenant** ковче́г заве́та.

arm¹ /ɑːm/ *n.* **1** (*of person*) рука́; **with a book under his ~** с кни́гой под мы́шкой; **he offered her his ~** он предложи́л ей ру́ку; **within ~'s reach** под руко́й; **he broke his ~** он слома́л ру́ку; **he kept me at ~'s length** он держа́л меня́ на расстоя́нии; **~ in ~** рука́ в руке́, по́д руку; **twist s.o.'s ~** (*fig., coerce*) выкру́чивать, вы́крутить ру́ки кому́-н.; **with open ~s** (*lit., fig.*) с распростёртыми объя́тиями; **fold one's ~s** сложи́ть (*pf.*) ру́ки; **infant in ~s** младе́нец; **take s.o. in one's ~s** заключ|а́ть, -и́ть кого́-н. в объя́тия; **he gathered the books (up) in his ~s** он собра́л кни́ги в оха́пку. **2** (*of object*): **~ of a garment** рука́в; **~ of a chair** ру́чка кре́сла; **~ of the sea** зали́в; **~ of a crane** стрела́. **3** (*of organization*) подразделе́ние. **4** (*fig., reach*): **the (long) ~ of the law** (кара́ющая) рука́ зако́на.

● *cpds.* **~band** *n.* нарука́вная повя́зка; **~chair** *n.* кре́сло; **~-hole** *n.* про́йма; **~pit** *n.* подмы́шка; **under one's ~pit** (*position*) под мы́шкой; (*motion*) под мы́шку; **~-rest** *n.* подлоко́тник.

arm² /ɑːm/ *n.* **1** (*mil., force*): **air ~** вое́нно-возду́шные си́лы (*f. pl.*). **2** (*pl., weapons*) ору́жие; **small ~s** стрелко́вое ору́жие; **~s race** го́нка вооруже́ний; **under ~s** под ружьём; **take up ~s** бра́ться, взя́ться за ору́жие; **bear ~s** носи́ть (*impf.*) ору́жие; **lay down one's ~s** (*lit., fig.*) скла́дывать, сложи́ть ору́жие; **they were up in ~s** (*fig.*) они́ взбунтова́лись. **3** (*her.*): **(coat of) ~s** герб.

● *v.t.* вооруж|а́ть, -и́ть; (*equip*) снаб|жа́ть, -ди́ть; **~ o.s.** (*lit., fig.*) вооруж|а́ться, -и́ться; **~ed forces** вооружённые си́лы.

● *v.i.* вооруж|а́ться, -и́ться.

armada /ɑːˈmɑːdə/ *n.* арма́да.

armadillo /ˌɑːməˈdɪləʊ/ *n.* (*pl.* **~s**) армади́лл; броненосец.

Armageddon /ˌɑːməˈged(ə)n/ *n.* (*fig.*) реша́ющее сраже́ние.

armament /ˈɑːməmənt/ *n.* (*also pl., weapons; military equipment*) вооруже́ние; **~ factory** вое́нный заво́д.

armature /ˈɑːməˌtjʊə(r)/ *n.* (*elec.*) я́корь (*m.*), броня́ (ка́беля).

Armenia /ɑːˈmiːnɪə/ *n.* Арме́ния.

Armenian /ɑːˈmiːnɪən/ *n.* **1** (*person*) арм|яни́н (*fem.* -я́нка). **2** (*language*) армя́нский язы́к.

● *adj.* армя́нский.

armful /ˈɑːmfʊl/ *n.* оха́пка.

armistice /ˈɑːmɪstɪs/ *n.* переми́рие.

armless /ˈɑːmlɪs/ *adj.* безру́кий.

armlet /ˈɑːmlɪt/ *n.* (*band*) нарука́вная повя́зка; нарука́вник.

armor /ˈɑːmə(r)/ (*US*) = **armour**

armored /ˈɑːməd/ (*US*) = **armoured**

armorer /ˈɑːmərə(r)/ (*US*) = **armourer**

armorial /ɑːˈmɔːrɪəl/ *adj.* геральди́ческий, ге́рбовый; **~ bearings** герб.

armory /ˈɑːmərɪ/ (*US*) = **armoury**

armour /ˈɑːmə(r)/ (*US* **armor**) *n.* (*for*

body) доспе́хи (*m. pl.*); **he wore (a suit of) ~** он был в доспе́хах; (*of plant or animal*) па́нцирь (*m.*); (*of vehicle, ship etc.*) броня́; (*coll., armoured vehicles*) бронете́хника.

● *v.t.* брони́ровать (*impf., pf.*).

● *cpds.* **~-bearer** *n.* оруженóсец; **~-clad, ~-plated** *adjs.* брони́рованный; **~-plate** *n.* броневáя плитá.

armoured /ˈɑːməd/ (*US* **armored**) *adj.* брони́рованный, броненóсный; **~ car** бронеавтомоби́ль (*m.*), бронемаши́на; **~ column** бронетáнковая колóнна; **~ concrete** железобетóн; **~ corps** тáнковый кóрпус; **~ cruiser** броненóсный крéйсер; **~ division** тáнковая диви́зия; **~ glass** бронестеклó, арми́рованное стеклó; **~ train** бронепóезд.

armourer /ˈɑːmərə(r)/ (*US* **armorer**) *n.* оружéйник, оружéйный мáстер.

armoury /ˈɑːmərɪ/ (*US* **armory**) *n.* арсенáл.

army /ˈɑːmɪ/ *n.* áрмия; **he served in the regular ~** он служи́л в регуля́рных частя́х; **join the ~** вступ|áть, -и́ть в áрмию; **~ command** комáндование áрмии; **Salvation A~** Áрмия спасéния; (*fig., large number*) áрмия; мнóжество; (*attr.*) армéйский; **~ chaplain** капеллáн, армéйский свящéнник; **~ corps** армéйский кóрпус; **~ general** генерáл áрмии.

arnica /ˈɑːnɪkə/ *n.* áрника.

aroma /əˈrəʊmə/ *n.* аромáт.

aromatherapy /əˌrəʊməˈθerəpɪ/ *n.* ароматерапи́я.

aromatic /ˌærəˈmætɪk/ *adj.* (*smell*) аромáтный; (*substance*) ароматúческий.

arose /əˈrəʊz/ *past of* ⇒**arise**

around /əˈraʊnd/ (*see also* ⇒**round**) *adv.* вокру́г; кругóм; **all ~** повсю́ду; **from all ~** отовсю́ду; **for miles ~** на ми́ли вокру́г; **they were standing ~** они́ стоя́ли поблúзости; **hang ~** болтáться (*impf.*); **he's been ~** (*coll.*) он видáл ви́ды; он человéк бывáлый; **he travels ~** он мнóго путешéствует; **computers have been ~ for quite a long time** компью́теры извéстны довóльно дóлгое врéмя; **this singer has been ~ for 30 years** э́тот певéц ужé 30 лет поёт.

● *prep.* **1** (*encircling*) вокру́г + *g.*; кругóм + *g.*; **they stood ~ the table** они́ стоя́ли вокру́г столá; **the path goes ~ the garden** дорóжка огибáет сад; **his arm was ~ her waist** он обнимáл её за тáлию.
2 (*over*): **he walked ~ the town** он броди́л по гóроду; **he looked ~ the house** он осмотрéл дом.
3 (*in the vicinity of*) óколо + *g.*
4 (*in var. parts of*): **the child played ~ the house** ребёнок игрáл по всему́ дóму; **he stayed ~ the house** он не выходи́л из дóму.
5 (*approximately*) óколо + *g.*; приблизи́тельно.

arousal /əˈraʊz(ə)l/ *n.* пробуждéние.

arouse /əˈraʊz/ *v.t.* (*awaken from sleep*) буди́ть, раз-; (*fig.*) пробу|ждáть, -ди́ть; возбу|ждáть, -ди́ть; **his interest was ~d** у негó пробуди́лся интерéс; **my suspicions were ~d** у меня́ возни́кли подозрéния; **she ~d everyone's sympathy** онá вы́звала у всех сочу́вствие; (*stimulate sexually*) возбу|ждáть, -ди́ть.

arpeggio /ɑːˈpedʒɪəʊ/ *n.* (*pl.* **~s**) арпéджио (*indecl.*).

arrack /ˈærək/ *n.* арáк; ри́совая вóдка.

arraign /əˈreɪn/ *v.t.* (*bring to trial*) привл|екáть, -éчь к суду́; (*accuse*) обвин|я́ть, -и́ть.

arraignment /əˈreɪnmənt/ *n.* привлечéние к суду́; обвинéние.

arrang|e /əˈreɪndʒ/ *v.t.* **1** (*put in order*) прив|оди́ть, -ести́ в поря́док; **she was ~ing flowers** онá расставля́ла цветы́; **I must ~e my hair** мне нáдо сдéлать причёску.
2 (*put in a certain order; group*) распол|агáть, -ожи́ть; расст|авля́ть, -áвить; **~ed in alphabetical order** располóженный в алфави́тном поря́дке; **he ~ed books on the shelves** он расстáвил кни́ги по пóлкам; (*draw up in line*) выстрáивать, вы́строить.
3 (*settle*) улá|живать, -дить.
4 (*organize*) устр|áивать, -óить; организóв|ывать, -áть; (*prepare; plan in advance*) подгот|áвливать, -óвить; организóв|ывать, -áть; налá|живать, -дить; **it was an ~ed marriage** их сосвáтали.
5 (*mus.*) аранжи́ровать (*impf., pf.*).

● *v.i.* догов|áриваться, -ори́ться; усл|áвливаться, -óвиться; **I ~ed with my friend to go to a concert** мы с дру́гом договори́лись пойти́ на концéрт; **I have ~ed for somebody to meet him at the station** я распоряди́лся, чтóбы егó встрéтили на стáнции.

arrangement /əˈreɪndʒmənt/ *n.* **1** (*setting in order*) приведéние в поря́док. **2** (*specific order*) расположéние. **3** (*pl., planning, preparation*) мéры (*f. pl.*), приготовлéния (*nt. pl.*); **make ~s for** организóв|ывать, -áть; устр|áивать, -óить. **4** (*agreement, understanding*) соглашéние, договорённость; **they came to an ~** они́ пришли́ к соглашéнию/договорённости; **we made ~s to meet** мы договори́лись встрéтиться. **5** (*mus.*) аранжирóвка.

arranger /əˈreɪndʒə(r)/ *n.* (*mus.*) аранжирóвщик.

arrant /ˈærənt/ *adj.* (*liter.*) (*thief, coward*) отъя́вленный; (*rudeness, hypocrisy*) су́щий; **~ nonsense** су́щий вздор; **an ~ fool** наби́тый дурáк.

array /əˈreɪ/ *n.* **1** (*order*): **in battle ~** в боевóм поря́дке. **2** (*display*) мнóжество. **3** (*dress, apparel*) облачéние, одея́ние.

● *v.t.* **1** (*place in order or line*) выстрáивать, вы́строить; **the troops were ~ed for battle** войскá бы́ли вы́строены в боевóм поря́дке. **2** (*set out, display*) выставля́ть, вы́ставить. **3** (*adorn*) укр|ашáть, -áсить; **she was ~ed in all her finery** онá облачи́лась в сáмое лу́чшее; (*deck out, dress*) од|евáть, -éть.

arrears /əˈrɪəz/ *n.* (*of payment*) задóлженность; просрóчка; **~ of rent** задóлженность по квартплáте; **fall into ~** (*of person*) просрóчи|вать, -ть платёж.

arrest /əˈrest/ *n.* **1** (*seizure; leg. apprehension*) арéст; **place under ~** сажáть, посади́ть под арéст; **be under ~** сидéть (*impf.*) под арéстом; **you are under ~!** вы арестóваны; **he was put under ~** егó арестовáли; **the police made several ~s** поли́ция произвелá нéсколько арéстов. **2** (*stoppage*): **cardiac ~** (*med.*) остановка сéрдца.

● *v.t.* **1** (*apprehend*) арестóв|ывать, -áть; (*fig., seize*): **~ s.o.'s attention** прикóв|ывать, -áть чьё-н. внимáние. **2** (*check*) задéрж|ивать, -áть; **~ed development** замéдленное разви́тие; (*stop*) приостан|áвливать, -ови́ть; **inflation has been ~ed** инфля́ция приостанóвлена.

arresting /əˈrestɪŋ/ *adj.* (*striking*) захвáтывающий; прикóвывающий внимáние.

arrhythmic /eɪˈrɪðmɪk/ *adj.* аритми́чный.

arrière-pensée /ˌærjerpɑ̃ˈseɪ/ *n.* зáдняя мысль.

arrival /əˈraɪv(ə)l/ *n.* **1** (*act or moment of arriving*) прибы́тие; **on his ~** по егó прибы́тии; **on the ~ of the train** по прибы́тии пóезда; **'to await ~'** «остáвить до прибы́тия адресáта»; (*of person etc. on foot*) прихóд; (*of person by vehicle*) приéзд; (*by air*) прилёт.
2 (*person or thing*): **new ~** нóвое пополнéние; (*baby*) новорождённый.
3: **~ at a decision** принятие решéния; **~ at an agreement** достижéние соглашéния.

arrive /əˈraɪv/ *v.i.* **1** (*reach destination*) приб|ывáть, -ы́ть; (*of persons on foot; also fig.*) при|ходи́ть, -йти́; (*by land transport*) при|езжáть, -éхать; (*by air*) прилет|áть, -éть. **2**: **~ at a decision/conclusion** приходи́ть, прийти́ к решéнию/заключéнию. **3** (*of time*) наступ|áть, -и́ть.

arrogance /ˈærəgəns/ *n.* высокомéрие, надмéнность.

arrogant /ˈærəgənt/ *adj.* высокомéрный, надмéнный.

arrogate /ˈærəˌgeɪt/ *v.t.* (*claim*) присв|áивать, -óить себé; **he ~d to himself the right** он присвóил себé прáво.

arrogation /ˌærəˈgeɪʃ(ə)n/ *n.* необоснóванная претéнзия, присвоéние.

arrow /ˈærəʊ/ *n.* стрелá; (*as symbol or indicator*) стрéлка.

● *cpds.* **~-head** *n.* наконéчник/остриё стрелы́; **~root** *n.* (*cul.*) аррору́т; **~-shaped** *adj.* стрелови́дный.

arse /ɑːs/ (*US* **ass**) *n.* (*vulg.*) жóпа (*vulg.*), зáдница (*vulg.*).

● *cpds.* **~-hole** *n.* (*person*) засрáн|ец (*fem.* -ка); **~-licker** *n.* жополи́з.

arsenal /ˈɑːsən(ə)l/ *n.* (*lit., fig.*) арсенáл.

arsenic /ˈɑːsənɪk/ *n.* мышья́к.

● *adj.* (*also* **~al**) мышьяко́вый.

arson /ˈɑːs(ə)n/ *n.* поджо́г.

arsonist /ˈɑːsənɪst/ *n.* поджига́тель (*m.*) (*fem.* -ница).

art /ɑːt/ *n.* **1** (*skill, craft*) иску́сство; **the ~ of war** вое́нное иску́сство; **a work of ~** произведе́ние иску́сства; **mechanical, useful ~s** ремёсла (*nt. pl.*); **black ~** чёрная ма́гия. **2** (*esp. pl.*) (*device, trick*) уло́вки (*f. pl.*); **there's an ~ to making an omelette** пригото́вить омле́т — то́же иску́сство. **3** (*decorative*) иску́сство; **fine ~s** изя́щные/изобрази́тельные иску́сства; **applied ~s** прикладны́е иску́сства; **~ deco** ар деко́; **~ nouveau** стиль моде́рн; **he prefers ~ to music** он предпочита́ет изобрази́тельное иску́сство му́зыке; **~ school** худо́жественное учи́лище; **~ gallery** карти́нная галере́я; **~ critic** искусствове́д. **4** (*pl., humanities*) гуманита́рные нау́ки (*f. pl.*); **Bachelor of Arts** бакала́вр гуманита́рных нау́к.

● *cpd.* **~work** *n.* иллюстрати́вный материа́л.

artefact, artifact /ˈɑːtɪˌfækt/ *nn.* худо́жественное изде́лие; поде́лка.

artel /ɑːˈtel/ *n.* арте́ль.

arterial /ɑːˈtɪərɪəl/ *adj.* **1** (*anat.*) артериа́льный. **2**: **~ road** магистра́льная доро́га; магистра́ль.

arteriosclerosis /ɑːˌtɪərɪəʊsklɪəˈrəʊsɪs/ *n.* артериосклеро́з.

artery /ˈɑːtərɪ/ *n.* (*anat.*) арте́рия; (*road*) магистра́ль.

artesian /ɑːˈtiːzɪən/, /-ʒ(ə)n/ *adj.* артезиа́нский.

artful /ˈɑːtfʊl/ *adj.* хи́трый.

artfulness /ˈɑːtfʊlnɪs/ *n.* хи́трость.

arthritic /ɑːˈθrɪtɪk/ *n.* больн|о́й (*fem.* -а́я) артри́том.

● *adj.* артри́тный; **an ~ old woman** стару́ха, страда́ющая артри́том.

arthritis /ɑːˈθraɪtɪs/ *n.* артри́т.

Arthurian /ɑːˈθjʊrɪən/ *adj.*: **~ romances** рома́ны Арту́рова ци́кла.

artichoke /ˈɑːtɪˌtʃəʊk/ *n.* артишо́к; **Jerusalem ~** земляна́я гру́ша.

article /ˈɑːtɪk(ə)l/ *n.* **1** (*item*) предме́т; (*manufactured*) изде́лие; **~ of clothing** предме́т оде́жды; **~ of food** пищево́й проду́кт; (*of trade*) това́р; **consumer ~s** потреби́тельские това́ры (*m. pl.*). **2** (*clause etc. of document*) статья́; пункт, пара́граф; **~ of faith** догма́т ве́ры. **3** (*piece of writing*) статья́; **leading ~** передова́я статья́. **4** (*gram.*): **(in)definite ~** (не)определённый арти́кль. **5** (*pl., period of training*) срок учени́чества.

articulate[1] /ɑːˈtɪkjʊlət/ *adj.* (*of speech*) членоразде́льный; (*of thoughts*) отчётливый; (*of person*) чётко выража́ющий свои́ мы́сли.

articulate[2] /ɑːˈtɪkjʊˌleɪt/ *v.t.* **1** (*ideas*) я́сно выража́ть, вы́разить; (*speech*) отчётливо произн|оси́ть, -ести́. **2** (*connect by joints*) свя́з|ывать, -а́ть; соедин|я́ть, -и́ть; **~d lorry** (*Br.*) грузови́к с прице́пом; автопо́езд.

● *v.i.*: **he ~s well** у него́ хоро́шая артикуля́ция.

articulation /ɑːˌtɪkjʊˈleɪʃ(ə)n/ *n.* (*of ideas*) я́сное выраже́ние; (*of speech*) артикуля́ция; произноше́ние; (*jointing*) сочлене́ние.

artifact /ˈɑːtɪˌfækt/ = **artefact**

artifice /ˈɑːtɪfɪs/ *n.* хи́трость.

artificial /ˌɑːtɪˈfɪʃ(ə)l/ *adj.* (*not natural*) иску́сственный; **~ respiration** иску́сственное дыха́ние; **~ insemination** иску́сственное оплодотворе́ние; **~ intelligence** иску́сственный интелле́кт; (*feigned*) притво́рный.

artificiality /ˌɑːtɪfɪʃɪˈælɪtɪ/ *n.* иску́сственность.

artillery /ɑːˈtɪlərɪ/ *n.* артилле́рия; (*attr.*) артиллери́йский.

● *cpd.* **~man** *n.* артиллери́ст.

artiness /ˈɑːtɪnɪs/ *n.* (*coll.*) прете́нзия, претенцио́зность.

artisan /ˌɑːtɪˈzæn/, /ˈɑː-/ *n.* ремéсленн|ик (*fem.* -ица).

artist /ˈɑːtɪst/ *n.* **1** (*practiser of art*) худо́жн|ик (*fem.* -ица). **2** (*performer*) арти́ст (*fem.* -ка).

artiste /ɑːˈtiːst/ *n.* (эстра́дный) арти́ст; (*fem.*) (эстра́дная) арти́стка.

artistic /ɑːˈtɪstɪk/ *adj.* (*person*) худо́жественный; (*character, appearance*) артисти́ческий; (*work*) артисти́ческий, артисти́чный.

artistry /ˈɑːtɪstrɪ/ *n.* артисти́чность, мастерство́.

artless /ˈɑːtlɪs/ *adj.* (*unskilled*) неиску́сный; (*ingenuous*) простоду́шный; (*natural*) безыску́сственный.

artlessness /ˈɑːtlɪsnɪs/ *n.* неиску́сность; простоду́шие; безыску́сственность.

arty /ˈɑːtɪ/ *adj.* (**artier, artiest**) (*coll.*) вы́чурный; претенцио́зно-боге́мный; **~-farty** *adj.* претенцио́зный.

arum /ˈeərəm/ *n.* (*bot.*) а́рум, аро́нник; **~ lily** (*Br.*) ка́лла.

Aryan /ˈeərɪən/ *n.* ари́|ец (*fem.* -йка).

● *adj.* ари́йский.

as /æz/, /əz/ *pron.* кото́рый; **such men ~ knew him** те, кото́рые зна́ли его́.

● *adv. & conj.* **1** (*expr. comparison or conformity*) как; **~ I was saying** как я говори́л; **~ follows** сле́дующим о́бразом; **such countries ~ Spain** таки́е стра́ны, как Испа́ния; **the same ~ ...** то же са́мое, что. . .; **~ heavy ~ lead** тяжёлый, как свине́ц; **he is ~ clever ~ she** он так же умён, как она́; **he is ~ kind ~ he is rich** он и добр, и бога́т; **I am ~ tall ~ he** я тако́го же ро́ста, как и он; **walk ~ fast ~ you can** иди́те как мо́жно быстре́е; **~ quickly ~ possible** как мо́жно скоре́е; **just ~** так же, как; **~ usual** как всегда́; **we are late ~ it is** мы и так опа́здываем; **~ things are, you cannot go** положе́ние дел таково́, что вы не мо́жете идти́; **he is tall, ~ are his brothers** как и его́ бра́тья, он высо́кого ро́ста; **he pictured the room ~ it would be** он представля́л себе́, како́й бу́дет ко́мната; **~ it were** так сказа́ть; как бы; **~ you were!** (*mil.*) отста́вить!; **he arranged matters so ~ to suit everyone** он организова́л всё так, что́бы э́то всех устра́ивало; **~ a man sows, so shall he reap** что посе́ешь, то и пожнёшь; **he was not so foolish ~ to say ...** он был не так глуп, что́бы сказа́ть. . .; **so ~ to** (*expr. purpose*) что́бы; (*expr. manner*) так, что́бы; **that's ~ may be** поло́жим; мо́жет быть и так; **~ well ~ may be** как мо́жно лу́чше. **2** (*expr. capacity or category*) как; **I regard him ~ a fool** я счита́ю его́ дурако́м; **his appointment ~ colonel** присвое́ние ему́ зва́ния полко́вника; **~ your guardian, I ...** как ваш опеку́н, я. . .; **he appeared ~ Hamlet** он вы́ступил в ро́ли Га́млета; **~ a rule** как пра́вило; **I said it ~ a joke** я сказа́л э́то в шу́тку; **I recognized him ~ the new tenant** я узна́л в нём но́вого жильца́. **3** (*concessive*): **young** (*US* **~ young**) **~ I am** хоть я и мо́лод; **much ~ I should like to** как бы мне ни хоте́лось; **try ~ he would** как он ни стара́лся. **4** (*temporal*) когда́; пока́, в то вре́мя как; **(just) ~ I reached the door** когда́ я подошёл к две́ри; **~ I was going** пока́ я шёл. **5** (*causative*) так как, поско́льку; **~ you are ready, let us begin** поско́льку вы уже́ гото́вы, дава́йте начнём. **6** (*in proportion* **~**) по ме́ре того́, как. **7** (*var.*): **~ far ~ I know** наско́лько мне изве́стно; **he walked ~ far ~ the station** он дошёл до ста́нции; **~ far back ~ 1920** ещё/уже́ в 1920 году́; **~ for you** что каса́ется вас; **~ from January** (*Br.*) начина́я с января́; **the work is ~ good ~ done** рабо́та всё равно́ что сде́лана; **he was ~ good ~ his word** он сдержа́л своё сло́во; **be so good ~ to tell me** бу́дьте добры́, скажи́те мне; **~ if** бу́дто (бы); как бу́дто (бы); **he made ~ if to go** он собра́лся бы́ло уходи́ть; **it is not ~ if I was poor** не то, что́бы я был бе́ден; **I will stay ~ long ~ you want me** я пробу́ду (сто́лько), ско́лько вы захоти́те; **keep it ~ long ~ you like** держи́те э́то (сто́лько), ско́лько вам уго́дно; **~ much ~ ...** сто́лько, ско́лько. . .; **~ much ~ to say** как бы говоря́; **I thought ~ much!** так я и ду́мал!; **no one so much ~ looked at us** на нас никто́ да́же не посмотре́л; **~ of this moment** в да́нный моме́нт; **~ regards** что каса́ется + *g.*; относи́тельно + *g.*; **~ soon ~** как то́лько; **I would just ~ soon go** я предпочёл бы пойти́; **the drawings ~ such** рису́нки как таковы́е/са́ми по себе́; **~ though** бу́дто (бы); как бу́дто (бы); **~ to** (*regarding*) что каса́ется + *g.*; **he enquired ~ to the date** он спра́вился о да́те; **he said nothing ~ to when he would come** он ничего́ не сказа́л насчёт того́, когда́ он придёт; **~ well** (*in addition*) та́кже, то́же; **he came ~ well ~ John** и он, и Джон пришли́; **you might ~ well help me** вы могли́ бы мне помо́чь; **it is just ~ well you came** хорошо́, что вы пришли́; **~ yet** ещё; до сих пор.

a.s.a.p. (*abbr. of* ***as soon as possible***) как мо́жно скоре́е.

asbestos /æz'bestɒs/, /æs-/ *n.* асбе́ст; (*attr.*) асбе́стовый.

ascend /ə'send/ *v.t.* подн|има́ться, -я́ться по + *d.* (*or* на + *a.*); **he ~ed the stairs/the mountain** он подня́лся по ле́стнице/на го́ру; **~ the throne** всходи́ть, взойти́ на престо́л.

● *v.i.* подн|има́ться, -я́ться; восходи́ть (*impf.*); **in ~ing order of magnitude** по возраста́ющей сте́пени ва́жности/зна́чимости.

ascend|ancy, -ency /ə'send(ə)nsɪ/ *nn.* власть, госпо́дство; **gain, obtain ~ over** доб|ива́ться, -и́ться вла́сти/госпо́дства над + *i.*

ascendant /ə'send(ə)nt/ *n.*: **his star is in the ~** его́ звезда́ восхо́дит.

● *adj.* (*rising*) восходя́щий; (*predominant*) госпо́дствующий.

ascendency /ə'send(ə)nsɪ/ = **ascendancy**

ascension /ə'senʃ(ə)n/ *n.* (*act of ascending*) восхожде́ние; (*relig.*) **the A~** Вознесе́ние; **A~ Island** о́стров Вознесе́ния.

ascent /ə'sent/ *n.* **1** (*rise in ground; slope*) подъём. **2** (*act of climbing or rising*) восхожде́ние, подъём; **~ of a mountain** восхожде́ние на́ гору; **they made the ~ in 5 hours** они́ соверши́ли восхожде́ние за пять часо́в.

ascertain /,æsə'teɪn/ *v.t.* устан|а́вливать, -ови́ть; выясня́ть, вы́яснить.

ascertainable /,æsə'teɪnəb(ə)l/ *adj.*: **it is ~** э́то мо́жно установи́ть.

ascetic /ə'setɪk/ *n.* аске́т.

● *adj.* аскети́ческий.

asceticism /ə'setɪ,sɪz(ə)m/ *n.* аскети́зм.

ASCII /'æskɪ/ (*abbr. of* ***American Standard Code for Information Interchange***) Америка́нский станда́ртный код для обме́на информа́цией.

ascorbic /ə'skɔ:bɪk/ *adj.* аскорби́новый.

ascribable /ə'skraɪbəb(ə)l/ *adj.* припи́сываемый.

ascribe /ə'skraɪb/ *v.t.* припи́с|ывать, -а́ть (**to** + *d.*).

asexual /eɪ'seksjʊəl/, /æ-/ *adj.* беспо́лый.

ash[1] /æʃ/ *n.* (*bot.*) я́сень (*m.*); (*attr.*) я́сеневый.

ash[2] /æʃ/ *n.* **1** (*also pl.*) зола́; пе́пел; **he took the ~es out of the stove** он вы́греб золу́ из пе́чки; **this coal makes a lot of ~** от э́того угля́ мно́го золы́; **cigarette ~** пе́пел; **they burnt the town to ~es** они́ сожгли́ го́род дотла́; **A~ Wednesday** пе́рвый день Вели́кого поста́. **2** (*pl., human remains*) прах; (*fig.*): **his hopes turned to ~es** его́ наде́жды ру́хнули.

● *cpds.* **~-blond** *n.* пе́пельная блонди́нка; **~-box, ~-pan** *nn.* зо́льник; я́щик для золы́; **~-can** *n.* (*US*) му́сорный я́щик; **~tray** *n.* пе́пельница.

ashamed /ə'ʃeɪmd/ *adj.* присты́женный; **I am, feel ~** мне сты́дно; **be ~ of** стыди́ться (*impf.*) + *g.*; **be, feel ~ for s.o.** стыди́ться за кого́-н.; **there's nothing to be ~ of in that** в э́том нет ничего́ посты́дного; **you ought to be ~ of yourself** как вам не сты́дно!

ash|en /'æʃ(ə)n/, **-y** /'æʃɪ/ *adjs.* (*ash-coloured*) пе́пельный; (*pale*) ме́ртвенно-бле́дный.

Ashgabat /'æʃgə,bæt/, **Ashkhabad** /,æʃkə'bæd/ *nn.* Ашхаба́д.

ashore /ə'ʃɔ:(r)/ *adv.* (*position*) на берегу́; (*motion*) на бе́рег; **go ~** сходи́ть, сойти́ на бе́рег; **put ~** выса́живать, вы́садить на бе́рег.

ashy /'æʃɪ/ = **ashen**

Asia /'eɪʃə/, /-ʒə/ *n.* А́зия; **~ Minor** Ма́лая А́зия.

Asia|n /'eɪʃ(ə)n/, /-ʒ(ə)n/ *n.* азиа́т (*fem.* -ка).

● *adj.* азиа́тский.

Asiatic /,eɪʃɪ'ætɪk/, /,eɪz-/ *adj.* азиа́тский.

aside /ə'saɪd/ *n.* ре́плика в сто́рону.

● *adv.* (*place*) в стороне́; (*motion*) в сто́рону; (*in reserve*) отде́льно, в резе́рве; **joking ~** кро́ме шу́ток, шу́тки в сто́рону; **~ from** (*US*) за исключе́нием + *g.*; кро́ме + *g.*; **take s.o. ~** отв|оди́ть, -ести́ кого́-н. в сто́рону; **set, put ~** (*reserve*) от|кла́дывать, -ложи́ть.

asinine /'æsɪ,naɪn/ *adj.* (*lit., fig.*) осли́ный.

ask /ɑ:sk/ *v.t.* **1** (*enquire*) спр|а́шивать, -оси́ть (*что у кого or кого о чём*); **he was ~ed his name** у него́ спроси́ли фами́лию; **he ~ed me the time** он спроси́л меня́, кото́рый час; **if you ~ me ...** е́сли хоти́те знать моё мне́ние, то...; **I ~ you!** скажи́те, пожа́луйста! **2** (*pose*): **~ a question** зад|ава́ть, -а́ть вопро́с. **3** (*request permission*): **he ~ed to leave the room** он попроси́л разреше́ния вы́йти из ко́мнаты; **he went off without ~ing** он ушёл не спро́сясь. **4** (*request*) проси́ть, по- (*что у кого or кого о чём*); **may I ~ you a favour** (*Br.*), **favor** (*US*)? мо́жно попроси́ть вас об одолже́нии?; **I ~ed him to do it** я попроси́л его́ сде́лать э́то; (*require*) тре́бовать, по- + *g.*; **the society ~s obedience of its members** о́бщество тре́бует от свои́х чле́нов подчине́ния; **if it's not too much to ~** е́сли э́то вас не затрудни́т; *see also* ⇨**asking.** **5** (*charge*) проси́ть, за-; **he ~ed a high price** он запроси́л высо́кую це́ну; **what is he ~ing for his car?** ско́лько он про́сит за свою́ маши́ну?; **~ing price** запра́шиваемая цена́. **6** (*invite*) звать, по-; пригла|ша́ть, -си́ть; **have you been ~ed?** вас (по)зва́ли?; **why don't you ~ him in?** почему́ вы не пригласи́те его́ войти́?; **~ a girl out** пригла|ша́ть, -си́ть де́вушку на свида́ние; **we have been ~ed out to dinner** нас позва́ли на у́жин.

● *v.i.* **1** (*make enquiries*) спра́шивать, спроси́ть (о + *p.*); справля́ться, спра́виться (о + *p.*); **I am going to the station to ~ about the trains** я иду́ на вокза́л узна́ть расписа́ние поездо́в; **she ~ed after your health** она́ справля́лась о ва́шем здоро́вье; (**~** *to see*): **I ~ed for Mr. Smith** я спроси́л г-на Сми́та. **2** (*make a request*) проси́ть, по-; **~ for help** проси́ть, по- о по́мощи; **he ~ed him for a pencil** он попроси́л у него́ каранда́ш; **he ~ed for advice** он попроси́л сове́та; **~ for trouble** (*coll.*) напра́шиваться на неприя́тности.

askance /ə'skæns/, /-'skɑ:ns/ *adv.* (*lit., fig.*) ко́со, и́скоса; **he looked at me ~** он посмотре́л на меня́ и́скоса.

askew /ə'skju:/ *adv.* кри́во, ко́со; **you have hung the picture ~** вы пове́сили карти́ну ко́со.

asking /'ɑ:skɪŋ/ *n.*: **it is yours for the ~** вам сто́ит то́лько попроси́ть; **food was there for the ~** еды́ там бы́ло ско́лько уго́дно.

aslant /ə'slɑ:nt/ *adv.* на́искось, ко́со.

asleep /ə'sli:p/ *pred. adj.* спя́щий; **he was sound, fast ~** он спал кре́пким сном; **fall ~** зас|ыпа́ть, -ну́ть; **my leg is ~** я отсиде́л но́гу; (*fig., mentally*) тупо́й, со́нный.

asp /æsp/ *n.* а́спид.

asparagus /ə'spærəgəs/ *n.* спа́ржа; **~ bed** гря́дка со спа́ржей; **~ tips** спа́ржевые голо́вки.

aspect /'æspekt/ *n.* **1** (*look, appearance; expression*) вид, выраже́ние. **2** (*fig., facet; mode of presentation*) аспе́кт, сторона́; (*point of view*) то́чка зре́ния; **have you considered the question in all its ~s?** вы рассмотре́ли вопро́с со всех то́чек зре́ния? **3** (*outlook*) вид; (*side facing a certain direction*) сторона́; **my house has a north ~** мой дом смо́трит на се́вер. **4** (*gram.*) вид.

aspen /'æspən/ *n.* оси́на; (*attr.*) оси́новый.

aspergill|um /,æspə'dʒɪləm/ *n.* (*pl.* **~a** *or* **~ums**) (*eccl.*) кропи́ло.

asperity /ə'sperɪtɪ/ *n.* (*roughness*) неро́вность; (*severity*) суро́вость; (*sharpness*) ре́зкость.

aspersion /ə'spɜ:ʃ(ə)n/ *n.* (*slur*) клевета́; **cast ~s** возв|оди́ть, -ести́ клевету́ на + *a.*; клевета́ть (*impf.*) на + *a.*

asphalt /'æsfælt/ *n.* асфа́льт; (*attr.*) асфа́льтовый.

● *v.t.* асфальти́ровать (*impf., pf.*), за- (*pf.*).

asphodel /'æsfə,del/ *n.* асфоде́ль (*m.*).

asphyxia /æs'fɪksɪə/ *n.* уду́шье; асфи́ксия.

asphyxiate /æs'fɪksɪ,eɪt/ *v.t.* вызыва́ть, вы́звать уду́шье у + *g.*; (*suffocate*) души́ть, за-; **be ~d** зад|ыха́ться, -охну́ться.

asphyxiation /æs,fɪksɪ'eɪʃ(ə)n/ *n.* уду́шье.

aspic /'æspɪk/ *n.* заливно́е; **veal in ~** заливна́я теля́тина.

aspidistra /,æspɪ'dɪstrə/ *n.* (*bot.*) аспиди́стра.

aspirant /'æspɪrənt/, /ə'spaɪərənt/ *n.* претенде́нт.

aspirate¹ /'æspərət/ *n.* аспира́т; придыха́тельный согла́сный звук.

aspirate² /'æspə,reɪt/ *v.t.* произн|оси́ть, -ести́ с придыха́нием.

aspiration /,æspɪ'reɪʃ(ə)n/ *n.* **1** (*desire*) стремле́ние; **his ~s to, for fame** его́ стремле́ние к сла́ве. **2** (*phon.*) придыха́ние.

aspirator /'æspɪ,reɪtə(r)/ *n.* аспира́тор.

aspir|e /ə'spaɪə(r)/ *v.i.* стреми́ться (*impf.*); **he ~es to be a leader** он стреми́тся стать ли́дером.

aspirin /'æsprɪn/ *n.* (*pl.* ~ *or* **~s**) аспири́н; (*tablet*) табле́тка аспири́на.

aspiring /ə'spaɪərɪŋ/ *adj.*: **~ young musicians** честолюби́вые молоды́е музыка́нты.

ass¹ /æs/ (*donkey, lit., fig.*) осёл; **~'s** *or* **~es'** (*as adj.*) осли́ный; **he made an ~ of himself** он сваля́л дурака́; **he was made an ~ of** он оста́лся в дурака́х.

ass² /æs/ (*US vulg.*) = **arse**

assagai /'æsə,gaɪ/ = **assegai**

assail /ə'seɪl/ *v.t.* (*lit., fig.*) нап|ада́ть, -а́сть на + *a.*; атакова́ть (*impf., pf.*); **I was ~ed by doubts** меня́ одолева́ли сомне́ния; **~ with criticism** обру́ши|ваться, -ться с кри́тикой на + *a.*; **~ with questions** зас|ыпа́ть, -ы́пать вопро́сами.

assailable /ə'seɪləb(ə)l/ *adj.* откры́тый для нападе́ния; (*vulnerable*) уязви́мый.

assailant /ə'seɪlənt/ *n.* напада́ющ|ий (*fem.* -ая).

assassin /ə'sæsɪn/ *n.* уби́йца (*c.g.*).

assassinate /ə'sæsɪ,neɪt/ *v.t.* уб|ива́ть, -и́ть (по полити́ческим моти́вам).

assassination /ə,sæsɪ'neɪʃ(ə)n/ *n.* уби́йство по полити́ческим моти́вам; (*fig.*): **character ~** подры́в репута́ции.

assault /ə'sɔ:lt/, /ə'sɒlt/ *n.* (*in general*) нападе́ние; (*mil.*) ата́ка, штурм, при́ступ; **carry, take by ~** брать, взять шту́рмом/при́ступом; **mount an ~** предприн|има́ть, -я́ть ата́ку; **airborne ~** вы́садка возду́шного деса́нта; **~ troops** штурмовы́е ча́сти; **~ boat, craft** деса́нтный ка́тер; штурмова́я ло́дка; (*leg.*): **~ and battery** оскорбле́ние де́йствием; **indecent ~** оскорбле́ние де́йствием на сексуа́льной по́чве; **sexual ~** сексуа́льное посяга́тельство.

● *v.t.* нап|ада́ть, -а́сть на + *a.*; (*mil.*) атакова́ть (*impf., pf.*); (*storm*) штурмова́ть (*impf.*); (*leg.*) оскорб|ля́ть, -и́ть де́йствием.

assay /ə'seɪ/, /'æseɪ/ *n.* (*test*) испыта́ние; (*analysis*) ана́лиз.

● *v.t.* (*test*) испы́т|ывать, -а́ть; (*analyse*) анализи́ровать (*impf., pf.*).

ass|egai /'æsɪ,gaɪ/, **-agai** *nn.* дро́тик.

assemblage /ə'semblɪdʒ/ *n.* **1** (*also* **assembly**: *bringing or coming together*) собира́ние, сбор. **2** (*collection*) собра́ние, скопле́ние. **3** (*putting together*) сбо́рка.

assemble /ə'semb(ə)l/ *v.t.* (*gather together*) соб|ира́ть, -ра́ть; (*call together*) соз|ыва́ть, -ва́ть; (*tech., fit together*) монти́ровать, с-.

● *v.i.* соб|ира́ться, -ра́ться.

assembly /ə'semblɪ/ *n.* **1** (*assembling*): = **assemblage** *n.* 1. **2** (*company of persons*) собра́ние; (*school*) **~ hall** а́ктовый зал; **unlawful ~** незако́нное сбо́рище. **3** (*pol.*) собра́ние; ассамбле́я. **4** (*mil.*) сбор; **~ area** райо́н сбо́ра. **5** (*of machine parts*) сбо́рка; **~ line** сбо́рочный конве́йер; **~ shop** сбо́рочный цех; **~ worker** сбо́рщик.

assent /ə'sent/ *n.* согла́сие; **the Royal ~** короле́вская са́нкция.

● *v.i.* согла|ша́ться, -си́ться (*с чем or на что*).

assert /ə'sɜ:t/ *v.t.* **1** (*declare; affirm*) утвер|жда́ть, -ди́ть; заяв|ля́ть, -и́ть. **2** (*stand up for*) отст|а́ивать, -оя́ть; **~ one's rights** отст|а́ивать, -оя́ть свои́ права́; **~ o.s.** самоутвер|жда́ться, -ди́ться.

assertion /ə'sɜ:ʃ(ə)n/ *n.* **1** (*statement*) утвержде́ние. **2** (*defence*) отста́ивание.

assertive /ə'sɜ:tɪv/ *adj.* (*self-assured*) самоуве́ренный; (*dogmatic*) догмати́ческий; (*insistent*) насто́йчивый.

assess /ə'ses/ *v.t.* **1** (*estimate value of; appraise; also fig.*) оце́н|ивать, -и́ть. **2** (*determine amount of*) определ|я́ть, -и́ть су́мму/разме́р + *g.*; **damages were ~ed at £10,000** убы́тки оцени́ли в 10 000 фу́нтов.

assessment /ə'sesmənt/ *n.* (*valuation*) оце́нка; (*for taxation*) определе́ние; (*sum to be levied*) су́мма обложе́ния.

assessor /ə'sesə(r)/ *n.* **1** (*of taxes, property etc.*) нало́говый чино́вник. **2** (*leg., adviser*) экспе́рт(-консульта́нт).

asset /'æset/ *n.* **1** (*advantage; useful quality*) це́нность; **knowledge of French is an ~ in this job** зна́ние францу́зского языка́ осо́бенно це́нно для э́той рабо́ты. **2** (*pl., fin.: possessions with money value*) акти́вы; (*on balance sheet*): **~s and liabilities** акти́в и пасси́в; **current ~s** теку́щие акти́вы; **fixed ~s** недви́жимое иму́щество; **liquid ~s** ликви́дные акти́вы; **personal ~s** ли́чное/дви́жимое иму́щество.

asseverate /ə'sevə,reɪt/ *v.t.* торже́ственно заяв|ля́ть, -и́ть.

asseveration /ə,sevə'reɪʃ(ə)n/ *n.* торже́ственное заявле́ние.

assiduity /,æsɪ'dju:ɪtɪ/ *n.* прилежа́ние; усе́рдие.

assiduous /ə'sɪdjʊəs/ *adj.* приле́жный; усе́рдный.

assign /ə'saɪn/ *v.t.* **1** (*task*) возл|ага́ть, -ожи́ть; пору|ча́ть, -чи́ть; (*person*) назн|ача́ть, -а́чить; (*resources*) предназн|ача́ть, -а́чить; **the task was ~ed to me** на меня́ возложи́ли зада́чу. **2** (*ascribe*) припи́с|ывать, -а́ть; **they could ~ no cause to the fire** они́ не могли́ установи́ть причи́ну пожа́ра. **3** (*leg., transfer*) перед|ава́ть, -а́ть; переуступ|а́ть, -и́ть.

assignable /ə'saɪnəb(ə)l/ *adj.* припи́сываемый.

assignation /,æsɪg'neɪʃ(ə)n/ *n.* **1** (*of person*) назначе́ние; (*of resources*) предназначе́ние; (*of task*) поруче́ние. **2** (*illicit meeting*) та́йное свида́ние. **3** (*leg., transfer*) переда́ча, переусту́пка.

assignee /,æsaɪ'ni:/ *n.* **1** (*person empowered to act for another*) уполномо́ченный. **2** (*leg.*) правопрее́мник.

assignment /ə'saɪnmənt/ *n.* **1** (*allotment*) (*of person*) назначе́ние; (*of resources*) предназначе́ние; (*of task*) поруче́ние. **2** (*task, duty*) поруче́ние; зада́ние; (*involving journey*) командиро́вка, (*schoolwork*) зада́ние. **3** (*fin., transfer*) переда́ча, переусту́пка.

assimilate /ə'sɪmɪ,leɪt/ *v.t.* (*absorb by digestion etc., and fig.*) ассимили́ровать (*impf., pf.*); усв|а́ивать, -о́ить; **the immigrants were quickly ~d** иммигра́нты бы́стро ассимили́ровались; **new ideas take time to be ~d** но́вые иде́и привива́ются не сра́зу.

● *v.i.* ассимили́роваться (*impf., pf.*).

assimilation /ə,sɪmɪ'leɪʃ(ə)n/ *n.* (*physiol., ling.*) ассимиля́ция; (*of knowledge etc.*) усвое́ние.

assist /ə'sɪst/ *v.t.* (*help*) пом|ога́ть, -о́чь + *d.*; (*cooperate with*) соде́йствовать (*impf., pf.*) + *d.*; **she was ~ed to her feet by a passer-by** прохо́жий помо́г ей подня́ться на́ ноги.

● *v.i.* (*take part*) прин|има́ть, -я́ть уча́стие; (*be present*) прису́тствовать (*impf.*).

assistance /ə'sɪstəns/ *n.* по́мощь; соде́йствие; **he rendered valuable ~** он оказа́л це́нную по́мощь; **can you come to my ~?** вы мо́жете мне помо́чь?; **may I be of ~?** могу́ я че́м-нибудь помо́чь?

assistant /ə'sɪst(ə)nt/ *n.* помо́щни|к (*fem.* -ца); ассисте́нт (*fem.* -ка); **~ manager** замести́тель заве́дующего; **~ professor** ≈ доце́нт; (*Br., in shop*) продав|е́ц (*fem.* -щи́ца).

assize /ə'saɪz/ *n.* (*usu. pl.*) суде́бное заседа́ние; выездна́я се́ссия суда́ присяжных.

associate¹ /ə'səʊʃɪət/, /-sɪət/ *n.* **1** (*colleague*) колле́га (*c.g.*), това́рищ; (*in business*) партнёр; **his ~s in crime** его́ соо́бщники в преступле́нии. **2** (*of a society*) член о́бщества.

● *adj.* (*closely connected*) свя́занный; (*united*) объединённый; **~ member** непо́лный член; (*of Academy of Sciences*) член-корреспонде́нт; **~ editor** помо́щник реда́ктора.

associate² /ə'səʊʃɪ,eɪt/, /-sɪ,eɪt/ *v.t.* соедин|я́ть, -и́ть; свя́з|ывать, -а́ть; (*esp. psych.*) ассоции́ровать (*impf., pf.*); **his name was ~d with the cause of reform** его́ и́мя ассоции́ровалось с реформа́торской де́ятельностью; **~ o.s. with** присоедин|я́ться, -и́ться к + *d.*

● *v.i.* води́ться (*impf.*), обща́ться (*impf.*) (*with* с + *i.*).

association /əˌsəʊsɪˈeɪʃ(ə)n/ *n.* **1** (*uniting; joining*) объедине́ние; соедине́ние. **2** (*consorting*) обще́ние. **3** (*connection; bond*) связь; ассоциа́ция; **~ of ideas** мы́сленная ассоциа́ция. **4** (*group*) ассоциа́ция, о́бщество; (*union*) сою́з; **~ football** футбо́л.

assonance /ˈæsənəns/ *n.* ассона́нс; непо́лная ри́фма.

assorted /əˈsɔːtɪd/ *adj.* (*varied*) разнообра́зный; **~ chocolates** шокола́дный набо́р; (шокола́дное) ассорти́ (*indecl.*); (*matched*): **an ill-~ couple** неподходя́щая па́ра.

assortment /əˈsɔːtmənt/ *n.* (*mixture*) ассортиме́нт; (*set*) набо́р; **an ~ of books** вы́бор книг.

assuage /əˈsweɪdʒ/ *v.t.* (*soothe*) успок|а́ивать, -о́ить; (*alleviate*) смягч|а́ть, -и́ть; (*appetite etc.*) утол|я́ть, -и́ть.

assum|e /əˈsjuːm/ *v.t.* **1** (*take on*) прин|има́ть, -я́ть; **he ~ed command** он при́нял кома́ндование; **I ~e full responsibility** я принима́ю на себя́ по́лную отве́тственность; **~e control of** брать, взять на себя́ управле́ние/руково́дство + *i.* **2** (*feign*) напус|ка́ть, -ти́ть на себя́; **he ~ed a new name** он взял себе́ но́вое и́мя; **he went under an ~ed name** он был изве́стен под вы́мышленным и́менем; **she ~ed an air of indifference** она́ напусти́ла на себя́ равноду́шный вид. **3** (*suppose*) предпол|ага́ть, -ожи́ть; допус|ка́ть, -ти́ть; **let us ~e that ...** допу́стим, что. . .; **~ing that ...** при усло́вии, что. . ..

assumption /əˈsʌmpʃ(ə)n/ *n.* **1** (*taking on*) приня́тие (на себя́); **his ~ of power** его́ прихо́д к вла́сти. **2** (*pretence*): **~ of indifference** притво́рное равноду́шие. **3** (*supposition*) предположе́ние; допуще́ние; **on the ~ that ...** исходя́ из того́, что. . .; е́сли допусти́ть, что. . .; **you are making a dangerous ~** вы де́лаете опа́сное предположе́ние. **4** (*eccl.*): **the A~** Успе́ние.

assurance /əˈʃʊərəns/ *n.* **1** (*act of assuring; promise; guarantee*) завере́ние, увере́ние; **have I your ~ of this?** вы мо́жете за э́то поручи́ться?; **I give you my ~ that you will get the money** могу́ вас заве́рить, что вы полу́чите де́ньги. **2** (*confidence*) уве́ренность (в себе́). **3** (*Br., insurance*) страхова́ние; **life ~ company** о́бщество по страхова́нию жи́зни.

assure /əˈʃʊə(r)/ *v.t.* **1** (*ensure*) обеспе́чи|вать, -ть; **~ o.s. of something** обеспе́чи|вать, -ть себе́ что-н.; **he is ~d of a steady income** ему́ обеспе́чен постоя́нный дохо́д. **2** (*assert confidently*) ув|еря́ть, -е́рить; зав|еря́ть, -е́рить; **I can ~ you of this** (я) могу́ вас в э́том уве́рить; **you may rest ~d that ...** мо́жете быть уве́рены, что. . ..

assuredly /əˈʃʊərɪdlɪ/ *adv.* несомне́нно.

Assyria /əˈsɪrɪə/ *n.* Асси́рия.

aster /ˈæstə(r)/ *n.* а́стра.

asterisk /ˈæstərɪsk/ *n.* звёздочка.

● *v.t.* отм|еча́ть, -е́тить звёздочкой.

astern /əˈstɜːn/ *adv.* (*behind ship*) за кормо́й; (*on ship*) на корме́; (*of motion*) наза́д; **full speed ~** по́лный ход наза́д; **~ of** позади́ + *g.* (*or* за кормо́й + *g.*).

asteroid /ˈæstəˌrɔɪd/ *n.* астеро́ид.

asthma /ˈæsmə/ *n.* а́стма.

asthmatic /æsˈmætɪk/ *n.* астма́тик.

● *adj.* (*pertaining to asthma*) астмати́ческий; (*suffering from asthma*) страда́ющий а́стмой.

astigmatic /ˌæstɪgˈmætɪk/ *adj.* астигмати́ческий.

astigmatism /əˈstɪgməˌtɪz(ə)m/ *n.* астигмати́зм.

astir /əˈstɜː(r)/ *pred. adj.* (*out of bed*) на нога́х; (*agog*) взбудора́женный.

astonish /əˈstɒnɪʃ/ *v.t.* пора|жа́ть, -зи́ть; изум|ля́ть, -и́ть; **be ~ed at** пора|жа́ться, -зи́ться + *d.*; изум|ля́ться, -и́ться + *d.*; **I was ~ed to learn ...** я порази́лся, узна́в. . .; **his success was ~ing** он име́л порази́тельный успе́х.

astonishment /əˈstɒnɪʃmənt/ *n.* изумле́ние; **he cried out in ~** он вскри́кнул от изумле́ния; **to my ~** к моему́ изумле́нию.

astound /əˈstaʊnd/ *v.t.* изум|ля́ть, -и́ть; пора|жа́ть, -зи́ть; **he had an ~ing memory** у него́ была́ порази́тельная па́мять; **I was ~ed at the difference** меня́ порази́ла ра́зница.

astraddle /əˈstræd(ə)l/ *adv.* широко́ расста́вив но́ги.

● *prep.*: **~ a motorbike** верхо́м на мотоци́кле.

astrakhan /ˌæstrəˈkæn/ *n.* (*lambskin*) кара́куль (*m.*); (*attr.*) кара́кулевый.

astral /ˈæstr(ə)l/ *adj.* звёздный; астра́льный; **~ body** астра́льное те́ло.

astray /əˈstreɪ/ *pred. adj. & adv.*: **go ~** (*lit., miss one's way*) заблуди́ться (*pf.*); (*fig.*) сб|ива́ться, -и́ться с пути́; **lead ~** (*fig.*) сб|ива́ть, -ить с пути́ (и́стинного).

astride /əˈstraɪd/ *adv.* (*on animal*) верхо́м; (*with legs apart*) расста́вив но́ги.

● *prep.*: **~ a horse** верхо́м на ло́шади; **~ his father's knee** на коле́нях у отца́.

astringency /əˈstrɪndʒ(ə)nsɪ/ *n.* вя́жущее сво́йство; (*fig.*) суро́вость.

astringent /əˈstrɪndʒ(ə)nt/ *n.* вя́жущее сре́дство.

● *adj.* вя́жущий; (*fig.*) суро́вый.

astrolabe /ˈæstrəˌleɪb/ *n.* астроля́бия.

astrologer /əˈstrɒlədʒə(r)/ *n.* астро́лог.

astrological /ˌæstrəˈlɒdʒɪk(ə)l/ *adj.* астрологи́ческий.

astrology /əˈstrɒlədʒɪ/ *n.* астроло́гия.

astronaut /ˈæstrəˌnɔːt/ *n.* астрона́вт, космона́вт.

astronautics /ˌæstrəˈnɔːtɪks/ *n.* астрона́втика, космона́втика.

astronomer /əˈstrɒnəmə(r)/ *n.* астроно́м.

astronomical /ˌæstrəˈnɒmɪk(ə)l/ *adj.* (*lit., fig.*) астрономи́ческий.

astronomy /əˈstrɒnəmɪ/ *n.* астроно́мия.

astrophysicist /ˌæstrəʊˈfɪzɪsɪst/ *n.* астрофи́зик.

astrophysics /ˌæstrəʊˈfɪzɪks/ *n.* астрофи́зика.

astute /əˈstjuːt/ *adj.* **1** (*shrewd*) проница́тельный. **2** (*cunning, smart*) хва́ткий, ло́вкий.

astuteness /əˈstjuːtnɪs/ *n.* **1** проница́тельность. **2** хва́ткость, ло́вкость.

asunder /əˈsʌndə(r)/ *adv.* **1** (*separated*) по́рознь, врозь; (*far apart*) далеко́ друг от дру́га. **2** (*into pieces*) на куски́, на ча́сти; **tear ~** (*lit.*) раз|рыва́ть, -орва́ть на ча́сти; (*fig., of persons*) разлуч|а́ть, -и́ть.

asylum /əˈsaɪləm/ *n.* **1** (*sanctuary*) прию́т; (*place of refuge*) убе́жище; **political ~** полити́ческое убе́жище. **2** (*mental home*) сумасше́дший дом.

asymmetrical /ˌeɪsɪˈmetrɪk(ə)l/, /ˌæsɪˈmetrɪk(ə)l/ *adj.* асимметри́ческий.

asymmetry /eɪˈsɪmɪtrɪ/, /æˈsɪmɪtrɪ/ *n.* асимметри́я.

asymptote /ˈæsɪmpˌtəʊt/, /ˈæsɪmˌtəʊt/ *n.* асимпто́та.

at /æt/, *unstressed* /ət/ *prep.* **1** (*denoting place*) в/на + *p.*; (*near, by*) у + *g.*, при + *p.*; **~ the university** в университе́те; **~ No. 10** в до́ме (но́мер) де́сять; **~ home** до́ма; **~ sea** (*lit.*) в мо́ре; **~ school** в шко́ле; **~ the station** на вокза́ле/ста́нции; **~ the corner** на углу́; **~ the fork in the road** на разви́лке доро́г; **~ the concert** на конце́рте; **~ that distance** на э́том расстоя́нии; **~ hand** под руко́й; **~ the piano** у роя́ля; за роя́лем; **~ the helm** у руля́; **~ my aunt's** у мое́й тётки; **~ table** за столо́м; **~ his feet** у его́ ног; **~ the gates** у воро́т; **~ Court** при дворе́; **a translator ~ the UN** перево́дчик при ООН. **2** (*denoting motion or direction; lit., fig.*): **he tapped ~ the window** он постуча́л в окно́; **he sat down ~ the table** он сел за стол; **she fell ~ his feet** она́ упа́ла к его́ нога́м; **he arrived ~ the station** он при́был на ста́нцию; **he went in ~ this door** он вошёл в/че́рез э́ту дверь; **throw a stone ~** броса́ть, бро́сить ка́мень/ка́мнем в + *a.* **3** (*denoting time or order*): **~ night** но́чью; **~ present** в настоя́щее вре́мя; **~ 2 o'clock** в два часа́; **~ half-past 2** в полови́не тре́тьего; **~ any moment** в любо́й моме́нт; **~ (the age of) 15** (в во́зрасте) пятна́дцати лет; **~ his death** в моме́нт его́ сме́рти; **~ the first attempt** с пе́рвой попы́тки; **~ intervals** с переры́вами; **~ his signal** по его́ сигна́лу; **~ Easter** на Па́сху; **~ dawn** на заре́; на рассве́те; **~ twilight** в су́мерки; **~ midday** в по́лдень; **~ that time** в э́то вре́мя; **~ what hour?** в кото́ром часу́?; **~ the beginning** в нача́ле; **~ first** снача́ла; **he began ~ the beginning** он на́чал снача́ла; **~ parting** при расстава́нии. **4** (*of activity, state, manner, rate etc.*): **~ work** на рабо́те; за рабо́той; **good ~ languages** спосо́бный к языка́м; **~ war** в состоя́нии войны́; **~ peace** в

ми́ре; ~ **a gallop** гало́пом; ~ **one blow** одни́м уда́ром; ~ **a sitting** в оди́н присе́ст; ~ **60 m.p.h.** со ско́ростью шестьдеся́т миль в час; ~ **full speed** на по́лной ско́рости; ~ **my expense** за мой счёт; **estimate** ~ оце́нивать, оцени́ть в + *a.*; ~ **best** в лу́чшем слу́чае; ~ **least** по кра́йней ме́ре; ~ **most** са́мое бо́льшее; ~ **your own risk** на ваш/свой страх и риск; ~ **all** вообще́; (*with neg.*) совсе́м; ~ **your service** к ва́шим услу́гам; ~ **my request** по мое́й про́сьбе; ~ **that** (*moreover*) к тому́ же; ~ **first sight** с пе́рвого взгля́да; ~ **a reduced price** по сни́женной цене́; ~ **fivepence a pound** по пять пе́нсов за фунт; ~ **a high rate of interest** под больши́е проце́нты; ~ **a high remuneration** за большо́е вознагражде́ние.
5 (*of cause*): **be impatient** ~ **the delay** волнова́ться (*impf.*) из-за заде́ржки; **delighted** ~ в восто́рге от + *g.*; **he was amazed** ~ **what he heard** он был поражён услы́шанным; **he was angry** ~ **this suggestion** э́то предложе́ние его́ рассерди́ло.
● *cpd.* ~**-home** *n.* приём госте́й, зва́ный ве́чер.

atavism /ˈætəˌvɪz(ə)m/ *n.* атави́зм.

atavistic /ˌætəˈvɪstɪk/ *adj.* атависти́ческий.

ate /et/, /eɪt/ *past of* ⇨**eat**

atelier /əˈtelɪˌeɪ/, /ˈætəˌljeɪ/ *n.* ателье́ (*indecl.*).

atheism /ˈeɪθɪˌɪz(ə)m/ *n.* атеи́зм, безбо́жие.

atheist /ˈeɪθɪɪst/ *n.* атеи́ст (*fem.* -ка).

atheistic /ˌeɪθɪˈɪstɪk/ *adj.* атеисти́ческий.

Athens /ˈæθɪnz/ *n.* Афи́н|ы (*pl., g.* —).

atherosclerosis /ˌæθəˌrəʊsklɪəˈrəʊsɪs/ *n.* атероскле́ро́з.

athlete /ˈæθliːt/ *n.* спортсме́н (*fem.* -ка); ~**'s foot** грибко́вое заболева́ние ног.

athletic /æθˈletɪk/ *adj.* атлети́ческий.

athletics /æθˈletɪks/ *n.* атле́тика.

athwart /əˈθwɔːt/ *adv.* ко́со, попере́к.
● *prep.* попере́к + *g.*; че́рез + *a.*; (*fig., in opposition to*) вопреки́ + *d.*

atishoo /əˈtɪʃuː/ *int.* (*coll.*) апчхи́.

Atlantic /ətˈlæntɪk/ *n.* Атланти́ческий океа́н; **North** ~ **Treaty Organization (NATO)** Североатланти́ческий сою́з (НАТО).
● *adj.* атланти́ческий.

Atlas /ˈætləs/ *n.*: ~ **mountains** Атла́сские го́ры (*f. pl.*).

atlas /ˈætləs/ *n.* а́тлас.

atmosphere /ˈætməsˌfɪə(r)/ *n.* (*lit., fig.*) атмосфе́ра; (*fig.*) обстано́вка.

atmospheric /ˌætməsˈferɪk/ *adj.* атмосфе́рный.

atmospherics /ˌætməsˈferɪks/ *n.* атмосфе́рные поме́хи (*f. pl.*).

atoll /ˈætɒl/ *n.* ато́лл.

atom /ˈætəm/ *n.* а́том; **split the** ~ расщеп|ля́ть, -и́ть а́том; ~ **bomb** а́томная бо́мба; (*fig.*): **not an** ~ **of strength** ни ка́пли си́лы.

atomic /əˈtɒmɪk/ *adj.* а́томный; ~ **bomb** а́томная бо́мба; ~ **energy, power** а́томная эне́ргия; ~ **number** а́томное число́; ~ **pile/reactor** а́томный котёл/реа́ктор; ~ **warfare** а́томная война́; ~ **weight** а́томный вес.

atomization /ˌætəmaɪˈzeɪʃ(ə)n/ *n.* (*of liquid*) распыле́ние; (*of solid*) измельче́ние.

atomize /ˈætəˌmaɪz/ *v.t.* распыл|я́ть, -и́ть; измельч|а́ть, -и́ть.

atomizer /ˈætəˌmaɪzə(r)/ *n.* (*spray*) пульвериза́тор, распыли́тель (*m.*).

atonal /eɪˈtəʊn(ə)l/, /ə-/ *adj.* атона́льный.

atone /əˈtəʊn/ *v.i.*: ~ **for** искуп|а́ть, -и́ть; **he** ~**d for his crimes** он искупи́л свои́ преступле́ния.

atonement /əˈtəʊnmənt/ *n.* искупле́ние; **Day of A**~ Су́дный день.

atop /əˈtɒp/ *adv. & prep.* наверху́; на верши́не (+ *g.*).

atremble /əˈtremb(ə)l/ *adv.* дрожа́.

atrium /ˈeɪtrɪəm/ *n.* (*pl.* **atriums** *or* **atria**) а́триум.

atrocious /əˈtrəʊʃəs/ *adj.* (*brutal, wicked*) злоде́йский, зве́рский; (*very bad*) ужа́сный.

atrocit|y /əˈtrɒsɪtɪ/ *n.* злодея́ние, зве́рство; **many** ~**ies were committed** бы́ло совершено́ мно́го зверств; (*hideous object*) у́жас.

atroph|y /ˈætrəfɪ/ *n.* атрофи́я.
● *v.t. & i.* атрофи́ровать(ся) (*impf., pf.*); ~**ied muscles** атрофи́рованные му́скулы.

atropine /ˈætrəˌpiːn/, /-pɪn/ *n.* атропи́н.

attaboy /ˈætəˌbɔɪ/ *int.* (*coll.*) молоде́ц!

attach /əˈtætʃ/ *v.t.* **1** (*fasten*) прикреп|ля́ть, -и́ть; (*by tying*) привя́з|ывать, -а́ть; (*by sticking*) прикле́и|вать, -ть; (*document, letter*) прилага́ть, приложи́ть; ~ **a seal** прилага́ть, приложи́ть печа́ть; **the** ~**ed document** прилага́емый докуме́нт.
2 (*fig., of person*) присоедин|я́ть, -и́ть; (*appoint*) назн|ача́ть, -а́чить.
3: ~ **o.s. to** присоедин|я́ться, -и́ться к + *d.*
4 (*assign*) прид|ава́ть, -а́ть; (*ascribe*) припи́с|ывать, -а́ть; **he** ~**es much importance to this visit** он придаёт большо́е значе́ние э́тому визи́ту; ~ **blame to** возл|ага́ть, -ожи́ть вину́ на + *a.*
5 (*of affection*): **she is very** ~**ed to her brother** она́ о́чень привя́зана к своему́ бра́ту; **I am** ~**ed to this necklace** э́то ожере́лье мне о́чень до́рого.
● *v.i.*: ~ **to** (*inhere in*): **the responsibility that** ~**es to this position** отве́тственность, свя́занная с э́той до́лжностью; **no blame/suspicion** ~**es to him** на него́ не па́дает вина́/подозре́ние.

attaché /əˈtæʃeɪ/ *n.* атташе́ (*m. indecl.*); **cultural** ~ атташе́ по вопро́сам культу́ры; **military** ~ вое́нный атташе́; ~ **case** диплома́т.

attachment /əˈtætʃmənt/ *n.* **1** (*action*) прикрепле́ние, привя́зывание, прикле́ивание; (*part attached*) приста́вка; (*comput.*) (*document*) приложе́ние. **2** (*affection*) привя́занность; **form an** ~ **for** привя́зываться, привяза́ться к + *d.*; (*devotion*) пре́данность. **3** (*leg.*): ~ **of property** наложе́ние аре́ста на иму́щество.

attack /əˈtæk/ *n.* **1** нападе́ние; (*mil.*) ата́ка, нападе́ние; **make an** ~ **on** атакова́ть (*impf., pf.*); **we went into the** ~ мы пошли́ в ата́ку; **our troops were under** ~ на́ши войска́ бы́ли атако́ваны.
2 (*fig., criticism*) напа́д|ки (*pl., g.* -ок); **you will be open to** ~ **on all sides** вас бу́дут атакова́ть со всех сторо́н.
3 (*of illness*) при́ступ; припа́док; **he had a heart** ~ с ним случи́лся серде́чный при́ступ.
4 (*mus.*) ата́ка.
● *v.t.* **1** (*lit., fig.*) нап|ада́ть, -а́сть на + *a.*; атакова́ть (*impf., pf.*); обру́ши|ваться, -ться на + *a.*; **he was** ~**ed by a lion** на него́ напа́л лев; **he was** ~**ed in the press** его́ атакова́ли в печа́ти.
2 (*of illness*) пора|жа́ть, -зи́ть.
3 (*harm*) повре|жда́ть, -ди́ть + *d.*; (*of chemical action*) разъ|еда́ть, -е́сть.
4 (*a task etc.*) набр|а́сываться, -о́ситься на + *a.*
● *v.i.*: **the enemy** ~**ed** враг бро́сился/пошёл в ата́ку.

attacker /əˈtækə(r)/ *n.* напада́ющий; (*mil.*) атаку́ющий.

attain /əˈteɪn/ *v.t.* (*also* ~ **to**) (*reach; gain; accomplish*) дост|ига́ть, -и́гнуть (*or* -и́чь) + *g.*; доб|ива́ться, -и́ться + *g.*; **our ends were** ~**ed** мы доби́лись своего́.

attainable /əˈteɪnəb(ə)l/ *adj.* достижи́мый.

attainment /əˈteɪnmənt/ *n.* (*attaining*) достиже́ние; (*acquisition*) приобрете́ние; (*accomplishment*): **linguistic** ~**s** лингвисти́ческие позна́ния.

attar /ˈætɑː(r)/ *n.*: ~ **of roses** ро́зовое ма́сло.

attempt /əˈtempt/ *n.* **1** (*endeavour*) попы́тка; **they made no** ~ **to escape** они́ не сде́лали попы́тки убежа́ть; **at the first** ~ с пе́рвой попы́тки.
2 (*assault*) покуше́ние; **an** ~ **was made on his life** покуша́лись на его́ жизнь; **an** ~ **will be made on Everest this summer** э́тим ле́том бу́дет сде́лана попы́тка подня́ться на Эвере́ст. **3** ~ **at**: **her** ~ **at producing a meal** плод её кулина́рных поту́г.
● *v.t.* (*try; try to do*) пыта́ться, по-; ~**ed theft** попы́тка воровства́; **he was charged with** ~**ed murder** его́ обвини́ли в покуше́нии на жизнь.

attend /əˈtend/ *v.t.* **1** (*be present at*) прису́тствовать (*impf.*) на + *p.*; **the concert was well** ~**ed** на конце́рте бы́ло мно́го пу́блики; ~ **school** посеща́ть (*impf.*) шко́лу.
2 (*lit., fig.; accompany*) сопровожда́ть (*impf.*); **he** ~**ed the queen** он сопровожда́л короле́ву; **the venture was** ~**ed with risk** предприя́тие бы́ло сопряжено́ с ри́ском.

3 (*serve professionally*) уха́живать (*impf.*) за + *i.*; **three nurses ~ed him** за ним уха́живали три медсестры́; **he was ~ed by Dr. Smith** его́ лечи́л до́ктор Смит.

● *v.i.* **1** (*be present*) прису́тствовать (*impf.*).
2 (*direct one's mind*) удел|я́ть, -и́ть внима́ние + *d.*; обра|ща́ть, -ти́ть внима́ние на + *a.*; (*listen carefully*): **~ to what I am saying** слу́шайте меня́ внима́тельно; **you are not ~ing** вы не слу́шаете.
3: **~ to** (*take care of, look after*) следи́ть (*impf.*) за + *i.*; забо́титься, по- о + *p.*; (*deal with*) зан|има́ться, -я́ться + *i.*; **he ~s to the education of his own children** он сам занима́ется образова́нием свои́х дете́й; **she ~ed to the children** она́ присма́тривала за детьми́; **~ to one's duties** исполня́ть (*impf.*) свои́ обя́занности; **~ to one's correspondence** занима́ться (*impf.*) свое́й перепи́ской; **~ to s.o.'s needs** забо́титься, по- о чьих-н. ну́ждах; **are you being ~ed to?** (*in shop*) вас (уже́) обслу́живают?; **I have things to ~ to** у меня́ есть дела́.

attendance /əˈtend(ə)ns/ *n.* **1** (*presence*) прису́тствие; (*number of visits or of those present*) посеща́емость; **there was a high, large ~ at church today** сего́дня в це́ркви бы́ло мно́го наро́ду; (*body of persons present*) аудито́рия, пу́блика. **2**: **in ~** (*present*) прису́тствующий; **the police were not in ~** поли́ция отсу́тствовала; (*accompanying*): **the queen with the prince in ~** короле́ва в сопровожде́нии при́нца. **3** (*service to*) обслу́живание; **he dances ~ on her** он хо́дит перед не́ю на за́дних ла́пках.

attendant /əˈtend(ə)nt/ *n.* (*servant*) слуга́ (*m.*); (*in museum, car park*) служи́тель (*m.*); (*one who waits upon another*) обслу́живающее лицо́; (*one who accompanies another*) сопровожда́ющее лицо́; **medical ~** врач.

● *adj.* (*circumstances, problems*) сопу́тствующий; (*nurse, aide*) сопровожда́ющий; (*present*) прису́тствующий; (*serving*) обслу́живающий.

attender /əˈtendə(r)/ *n.*: **he is a regular ~ at church** он регуля́рно хо́дит в це́рковь.

attention /əˈtenʃ(ə)n/ *n.* **1** (*heed*) внима́ние; **pay, give ~ to** обра|ща́ть, -ти́ть внима́ние на + *a.*; **pay, devote much/little ~ to** удел|я́ть, -и́ть мно́го/ма́ло внима́ния + *d.*; **pay ~!** бу́дьте внима́тельны!; **direct, draw ~ to** привл|ека́ть, -е́чь внима́ние к + *d.*; **(for the) ~ (of)** (*on letters etc.*) на рассмотре́ние + *g.* **2** (*mil. command*) сми́рно!; (*posture*): **stand to ~** стоя́ть (*impf.*) сми́рно; **he came to ~** он при́нял сто́йку сми́рно. **3** (*care*) ухо́д; **he was given immediate medical ~** ему́ была́ ока́зана неме́дленная медици́нская по́мощь. **4** (*courtesy*) внима́ние, внима́тельность; (*thoughtfulness*) забо́тливость.

attentive /əˈtentɪv/ *adj.* **1** (*heedful*) внима́тельный; **~ to detail** внима́тельный к дета́лям
2 (*thoughtful, solicitous*) забо́тливый.

attentiveness /əˈtentɪvnɪs/ *n.* внима́тельность; забо́тливость.

attenuate /əˈtenjʊˌeɪt/ *v.t.* (*weaken*) ослабля́ть, осла́бить.

attenuation /əˌtenjʊˈeɪʃ(ə)n/ *n.* ослабле́ние.

attest /əˈtest/ *v.t.* (*certify*) удостов|еря́ть, -е́рить; (*bear witness to*) свиде́тельствовать, за-; (*confirm*) подтвер|жда́ть, -ди́ть.

● *v.i.*: **~ to** свиде́тельствовать (*impf.*) о + *p.*

attestation /ˌæteˈsteɪʃ(ə)n/ *n.* засвиде́тельствование, удостовере́ние, подтвержде́ние.

attic /ˈætɪk/ *n.* манса́рда, черда́к.

attire /əˈtaɪə(r)/ *n.* облаче́ние, одея́ние; **in night ~** в ночно́м облаче́нии.

● *v.t.* (*dress*) облач|а́ть, -и́ть; од|ева́ть, -е́ть; **she was ~d in white** она́ была́ вся в бе́лом.

attitude /ˈætɪˌtjuːd/ *n.* **1** (*pose*) по́за; **strike an ~** прин|има́ть, -я́ть по́зу.
2 (*fig., disposition*) отноше́ние; **~ of mind** склад ума́; **what is your ~ to this book?** как вы отно́ситесь к э́той кни́ге?; **that is an odd ~ to take up** э́то стра́нный подхо́д.

attn. /əˈtenʃ(ə)n/ *n.* (*abbr. of* ***for the attention of***) внима́нию (+ *g.*).

attorney /əˈtɜːnɪ/ *n.* (*pl.* **~s**) (*US, lawyer*) адвока́т; (*person appointed to act for another*) пове́ренный; **power of ~** дове́ренность; **A~ General** мини́стр юсти́ции.

attract /əˈtrækt/ *v.t.* **1** (*of physical forces*) притя́|гивать, -ну́ть; (*fig.*) привл|ека́ть, -е́чь (к себе́); **can you ~ the waiter's attention?** вы мо́жете привле́чь внима́ние официа́нта?; **his manner ~ed a good deal of criticism** его́ мане́ра держа́ть себя́ вызыва́ла нема́ло нарека́ний. **2** (*captivate*) влечь (*impf.*), притя́гивать (*impf.*); **he found himself ~ed to her** он почу́вствовал, что увлечён е́ю; **I am not ~ed by the idea** меня́ э́та иде́я не привлека́ет.

attraction /əˈtrækʃ(ə)n/ *n.* **1** (*phys.*) притяже́ние, тяготе́ние. **2** (*charm, allure*) привлека́тельность; **the ~s of a big city** собла́зны большо́го го́рода.
3 (*thing of interest*) достопримеча́тельность; (*amusement*) аттракцио́н.

attractive /əˈtræktɪv/ *adj.* **1** (*phys.*): **~ force** си́ла притяже́ния. **2** (*fig.*) привлека́тельный; притяга́тельный; **an ~ dress** ми́лое/симпати́чное пла́тье.

attractiveness /əˈtræktɪvnɪs/ *n.* привлека́тельность.

attributable /əˈtrɪbjʊtəb(ə)l/ *adj.*: **his illness is ~ to drink** его́ боле́знь объясня́ется пья́нством.

attribute[1] /ˈætrɪˌbjuːt/ *n.* **1** (*quality*) сво́йство; (*characteristic*) при́знак, характе́рная черта́. **2** (*accompanying feature, emblem*) атрибу́т. **3** (*gram.*) определе́ние; атрибу́т.

attribute[2] /əˈtrɪbjuːt/ *v.t.*: **~ something to** (*work of art, quality*) припи́с|ывать, -а́ть что-н. + *d.*; (*event, result*) отн|оси́ть, -ести́ что-н. к + *d.*

attribution /ˌætrɪˈbjuːʃ(ə)n/ *n.* (*ascription*) припи́сывание; отнесе́ние.

attributive /əˈtrɪbjʊtɪv/ *adj.* определи́тельный; атрибути́вный.

attrition /əˈtrɪʃ(ə)n/ *n.* тре́ние; истира́ние; (*fig.*) истоще́ние; измо́р; **war of ~** война́ на истоще́ние.

attune /əˈtjuːn/ *v.t.* (*lit., fig.*) настр|а́ивать, -о́ить.

atypical /eɪˈtɪpɪk(ə)l/ *adj.* нетипи́чный.

aubergine /ˈəʊbəˌʒiːn/ *n.* (*Br.*) баклажа́н.

auburn /ˈɔːbən/ *adj.* тёмно-ры́жий.

au courant /ˌəʊ kuːˈrɑ̃/ *pred. adj.* в ку́рсе (*чего*).

auction /ˈɔːkʃ(ə)n/ *n.* аукцио́н; **~ room** аукцио́нный зал; **~ sale** аукцио́н; **put up for ~** выставля́ть, вы́ставить на аукцио́н; прод|ава́ть, -а́ть с молотка́; **the house is for sale by ~** дом продаётся с аукцио́на.

● *v.t.* (*also* **~ off**) прод|ава́ть, -а́ть с аукцио́на.

auctioneer /ˌɔːkʃəˈnɪə(r)/ *n.* аукциони́ст.

audacious /ɔːˈdeɪʃəs/ *adj.* (*bold*) сме́лый; (*daring*) отва́жный; (*impudent*) де́рзкий.

audacity /ɔːˈdæsɪtɪ/ *n.* сме́лость; отва́га; де́рзость.

audibility /ˌɔːdɪˈbɪlɪtɪ/ *n.* слы́шимость; вня́тность.

audible /ˈɔːdɪb(ə)l/ *adj.* слы́шимый, слы́шный; (*distinct*) вня́тный.

audience /ˈɔːdɪəns/ *n.* **1** (*listeners*) аудито́рия; слу́шатели (*m. pl.*); (*spectators*) зри́тели (*m. pl.*); пу́блика; **a captive ~** зри́тели/слу́шатели понево́ле; **~ participation** уча́стие аудито́рии. **2** (*hearing*; *interview*) аудие́нция; **he requested an ~ of the queen** он попроси́л аудие́нцию у короле́вы.

audio cassette /ˈɔːdɪəʊ kəˈset/ *n.* аудиокассе́та.

audiotape /ˈɔːdɪəʊˌteɪp/ *n.* (*cassette*) аудиоплёнка.

audiotypist /ˌɔːdɪəʊˈtaɪpɪst/ *n.* фономашини́стка.

audio-visual /ˌɔːdɪəʊˈvɪʒjʊəl/ *adj.* а́удио-визуа́льный.

audit /ˈɔːdɪt/ *n.* реви́зия, ауди́т.

● *v.t.* (**audited, auditing**) пров|еря́ть, -е́рить отчётность + *g.*; ревизова́ть (*impf., pf.*).

audition /ɔːˈdɪʃ(ə)n/ *n.* (*listening*) слу́шание; (*theatr.*) прослу́шивание, про́ба.

● *v.t.* прослу́ш|ивать, -ать.

auditor /ˈɔːdɪtə(r)/ *n.* бухга́лтер-ревизо́р; ауди́тор.

auditori|um /ˌɔːdɪˈtɔːrɪəm/ *n.* (*pl.* **~ums** *or* **~a** /-rɪə/) (*where audience sits*) зри́тельный зал; (*public building*) аудито́рия, зал.

auditory /ˈɔːdɪtərɪ/ *adj.* слухово́й.

au fait /əʊ ˈfeɪ/ *pred. adj.* в ку́рсе;

осведомлённый; **~ with the situation** в ку́рсе дел.

auger /'ɔ:gə(r)/ *n.* сверло́; (*woodworking tool*) бура́в.

augment /ɔ:g'ment/ *v.t.* приумн|ожа́ть, -о́жить; увели́чи|вать, -ть; **~ed interval** (*mus.*) увели́ченный интерва́л.

● *v.i.* увели́чи|ваться, -ться; уси́ли|ваться, -тся.

augmentation /,ɔ:gmen'teɪʃ(ə)n/ *n.* увеличе́ние; прираще́ние.

augmentative /ɔ:g'mentətɪv/ *adj.* (*gram.*) увеличи́тельный.

augur /'ɔ:gə(r)/ *n.* (*hist.*) авгу́р.

● *v.t.* (*portend*) предвеща́ть (*impf.*).

● *v.i.* (*of things*) служи́ть (*impf.*) предзнаменова́нием (+*g.*); **the exam results ~ well for his future** результа́ты его́ экза́менов — хоро́шая зая́вка на бу́дущее.

augury /'ɔ:gjərɪ/ *n.* (*divination*) предсказа́ние; (*omen; sign*) предзнаменова́ние.

August /'ɔ:gəst/ *n.* а́вгуст; (*attr.*) а́вгустовский.

august /ɔ:'gʌst/ *adj.* вели́чественный.

augustness /ɔ:'gʌstnɪs/ *n.* вели́чественность.

auk /ɔ:k/ *n.* гага́рка.

aunt /ɑ:nt/ *n.* тётя, тётка.

aunt|ie, -y /'ɑ:ntɪ/ *nn.* тётушка, тётенька.

au pair /əʊ 'peə(r)/ *n.* ≈ ня́ня-иностра́нка.

aura /'ɔ:rə/ *n.* (*pl.* **aurae** /-ri:/ *or* **auras**) (*emanation; med.*) а́ура; (*atmosphere*) атмосфе́ра; **there is an ~ of tranquillity about him** от него́ ве́ет споко́йствием.

aural /'ɔ:r(ə)l/ *adj.* (*pert. to hearing*) слухово́й; **~ly** на слух; (*pert. to the ear*) ушно́й.

aureole /'ɔ:rɪ,əʊl/ *n.* (*halo*) орео́л; (*crown*) ве́нчик.

au revoir /əʊ rə'vwɑ:(r)/ *int.* до свида́нья.

auricle /'ɔ:rɪk(ə)l/ *n.* (*of ear*) нару́жное у́хо; (*of heart*) предсе́рдие.

aurochs /'ɔ:rɒks/, /'aʊrɒks/ *n.* (*pl.* ~) зубр.

aurora /ɔ:'rɔ:rə/ *n.* (*pl.* **auroras** *or* **aurorae** /-ri:/) **1** (*poet., dawn*) авро́ра, у́тренняя заря́. **2** (*atmospheric phenomenon*): **~ borealis/australis** се́верное/ю́жное сия́ние.

Auschwitz /'aʊʃvɪts/ *n.* Осве́нцим.

auscultation /,ɔ:skəl'teɪʃ(ə)n/ *n.* (*med.*) выслу́шивание, аускульта́ция.

auspices /'ɔ:spɪsɪz/ *n.* **1** (*omens*) предзнаменова́ния (*nt. pl.*); **under favourable ~** при благоприя́тных усло́виях. **2** (*patronage*) покрови́тельство; эги́да; **under UN ~** под эги́дой ООН.

auspicious /ɔ:'spɪʃəs/ *adj.* благоприя́тный; **on this ~ day** в э́тот знамена́тельный день.

Aussie /'ɒzɪ/, /'ɒsɪ/ (*coll.*) = **Australian**

austere /ɒ'stɪə(r)/, /ɔ:'stɪə(r)/ *adj.* (**austerer, austerest**) (*lit., fig.*) стро́гий, суро́вый.

austerity /ɒ'sterɪtɪ/, /ɔ:'sterɪtɪ/ *n.* стро́гость, суро́вость; (*economy*) стро́гая эконо́мия.

Australasia /,ɒstrə'leɪʒə/, /-ʃə/ *n.* Австра́лия и Океа́ния; Австра́лия и Но́вая Зела́ндия.

Australia /ɒ'streɪlɪə/ *n.* Австра́лия.

Australian /ɒ'streɪlɪən/ *n.* австрали́|ец (*fem.* -йка).

● *adj.* австрали́йский.

Austria /'ɒstrɪə/ *n.* А́встрия.

Austria-Hungary /,ɒstrɪə'hʌŋgərɪ/ *n.* А́встро-Ве́нгрия.

Austrian /'ɒstrɪən/ *n.* австри́|ец (*fem.* -йка).

● *adj.* австри́йский.

Austro-Hungarian /,ɒstrəʊhʌŋ'geərɪən/ *adj.* а́встро-венге́рский.

authentic /ɔ:'θentɪk/ *adj.* (*genuine*) по́длинный.

authenticate /ɔ:'θentɪ,keɪt/ *v.t.* удостов|еря́ть, -е́рить по́длинность +*g.*

authentication /ɔ:,θentɪ'keɪʃ(ə)n/ *n.* установле́ние/удостовере́ние по́длинности (*чего*).

authenticity /,ɔ:θen'tɪsɪtɪ/ *n.* по́длинность.

author[1] /'ɔ:θə(r)/ *n.* **1** (*of specific work*) а́втор; (*writer in general*) писа́тель (*m.*) (*fem.* -ница). **2** (*of plan*) а́втор.

author[2] /'ɔ:θə(r)/ *v.t.* писа́ть, на-.

authoritarian /ɔ:,θɒrɪ'teərɪən/ *adj.* авторита́рный, деспоти́ческий.

authoritative /ɔ:'θɒrɪtətɪv/ *adj.* авторите́тный.

authority /ɔ:'θɒrɪtɪ/ *n.* **1** (*power; right*) власть; (*legal*) полномо́чие; **~ to sign** пра́во по́дписи; **who is in ~ here?** кто здесь гла́вный/нача́льник?; **published by ~ of parliament** опублико́ванный по ука́зу парла́мента; **on one's own ~** на свою́ отве́тственность; **I did it on his ~** я э́то сде́лал по его́ поруче́нию; **who gave you ~ over me?** кто вам дал пра́во мне прика́зывать? **2** (*usu. pl.: public bodies*) вла́сти (*f. pl.*); о́рганы (*m. pl.*) вла́сти; **the Atomic Energy A~** Управле́ние по а́томной эне́ргии; **he is always getting into trouble with ~** у него́ всё вре́мя неприя́тности с властя́ми. **3** (*influence, weight*) авторите́т; **carry, have ~** по́льзоваться (*impf.*) авторите́том; **he speaks with ~** он говори́т авторите́тно/внуши́тельно (*or* со зна́нием де́ла). **4** (*source*) достове́рный исто́чник; **I have it on good ~** я э́то зна́ю из достове́рного исто́чника; **what is your ~ for saying so?** на основа́нии чего́ вы э́то говори́те? **5** (*expert*): **he is an ~ on Greek** он кру́пный специали́ст по гре́ческому языку́.

authorization /,ɔ:θəraɪ'zeɪʃ(ə)n/ *n.* (*authorizing*) уполномо́чивание; (*sanction*) разреше́ние; са́нкция.

authorize /'ɔ:θə,raɪz/ *v.t.* **1** (*give authority to*) уполномо́чи|вать, -ть. **2** (*permit; sanction*) разреш|а́ть, -и́ть; дозв|оля́ть, -о́лить; санкциони́ровать (*impf., pf.*); **~d expenditure** утверждённые расхо́ды; **~d translation** авторизо́ванный перево́д.

authorship /'ɔ:θəʃɪp/ *n.* а́вторство; **a manuscript of doubtful ~** ру́копись, а́втор кото́рой то́чно не устано́влен.

autism /'ɔ:tɪz(ə)m/ *n.* аути́зм.

autistic /ɔ:'tɪstɪk/ *adj.* аутисти́ческий.

auto /'ɔ:təʊ/ *n.* (*pl.* **~s**) (*US coll.*) авто́.

autobiographer /,ɔ:təʊbaɪ'ɒgrəfə(r)/ *n.* автобио́граф.

autobiographical /,ɔ:təʊ,baɪə'græfɪk(ə)l/ *adj.* автобиографи́ческий.

autobiography /,ɔ:təʊbaɪ'ɒgrəfɪ/ *n.* автобиогра́фия.

autochthonous /ɔ:'tɒkθ(ə)nəs/ *adj.* автохто́нный.

autocracy /ɔ:'tɒkrəsɪ/ *n.* самодержа́вие, автокра́тия.

autocrat /'ɔ:tə,kræt/ *n.* самоде́ржец, автокра́т.

autocratic /,ɔ:tə'krætɪk/ *adj.* самодержа́вный, автократи́ческий; (*dictatorial*) деспоти́ческий.

autocross /'ɔ:təʊ,krɒs/ *n.* автокро́сс.

autocue /'ɔ:təʊ,kju:/ *n.* (*Br., propr.*) автосуфлёр.

autodidact /'ɔ:təʊ,daɪdækt/ *n.* самоу́чка; автодида́кт.

autog|iro, -yro /,ɔ:təʊ'dʒaɪərəʊ/ *nn.* (*pl.* **~s**) автожи́р.

autograph /'ɔ:tə,grɑ:f/ *n.* авто́граф.

● *v.t.* надпи́с|ывать, -а́ть; **~ed copy** экземпля́р с авто́графом.

autoimmune /,ɔ:təʊɪ'mju:n/ *adj.* аутоиммýнный.

automata /ɔ:'tɒmətə/ *pl. of* ⇒**automaton**

automate /'ɔ:tə,meɪt/ *v.t.* автоматизи́ровать (*impf., pf.*).

automated /'ɔ:tə,meɪtɪd/ *adj.* автоматизи́рованный.

automatic /,ɔ:tə'mætɪk/ *n.* (*firearm*) автомати́ческое ору́жие.

● *adj.* автомати́ческий; **~ pilot** автопило́т; **~ pistol** самозаря́дный пистоле́т; **~ machine** автома́т.

automation /,ɔ:tə'meɪʃ(ə)n/ *n.* автоматиза́ция.

automat|on /ɔ:'tɒmət(ə)n/ *n.* (*pl.* **~a** *or* **~ons**) автома́т.

automobile /'ɔ:təmə,bi:l/ *n.* автомоби́ль (*m.*); (*attr.*) автомоби́льный.

autonomous /ɔ:'tɒnəməs/ *adj.* автоно́мный.

autonomy /ɔ:'tɒnəmɪ/ *n.* автоно́мия, самоуправле́ние.

autopilot /'ɔ:təʊ,paɪlət/ *n.* автопило́т.

autopsy /'ɔ:tɒpsɪ/, /ɔ:'tɒpsɪ/ *n.* вскры́тие тру́па, ауто́псия.

auto-suggestion /,ɔ:təʊsə'dʒestʃ(ə)n/ *n.* самовнуше́ние.

autumn /'ɔ:təm/ *n.* о́сень; **in ~** о́сенью; (*attr.*) осе́нний; **~ crocus** лугово́й шафра́н.

autumnal /ɔː'tʌmn(ə)l/ *adj.* осе́нний.

auxiliary /ɔːg'zɪljərɪ/ *n.* (*assistant*) помо́щник; (*gram.*, **~ verb**) вспомога́тельный глаго́л; (*mil.*) солда́т вспомога́тельных во́йск; (*pl.*) вспомога́тельные войска́.

● *adj.* (*helpful; supporting*) вспомога́тельный; (*additional*) доба́вочный; (*in reserve*) запасно́й.

avail /ə'veɪl/ *n.* (*use*) по́льза; **his entreaties were of no ~** его́ мольбы́ бы́ли безуспе́шны; **his intervention was of little ~** от его́ вмеша́тельства бы́ло ма́ло по́льзы; **to no ~** напра́сно.

● *v.t.* **1** (*benefit*) быть поле́зным/вы́годным +*d.*; **our efforts ~ed us nothing** на́ши уси́лия ни к чему́ не привели́. **2**: **~ o.s. of** воспо́льзоваться (*pf.*) +*i.*

availability /ə,veɪlə'bɪlɪtɪ/ *n.* (*presence*) нали́чие; (*accessibility*) досту́пность.

available /ə'veɪləb(ə)l/ *adj.* (*product*) име́ющийся в прода́же, досту́пный; **it is not ~ in your size** ва́шего разме́ра нет; **drinks were ~ all day** напи́тки продава́лись це́лый день; (*information*): **the information was not ~** информа́ция была́ недосту́пна; (*person*) свобо́дный; **are you ~ tomorrow?** вы свобо́дны за́втра?; **she's not ~** она́ занята́; **if there is money ~** е́сли есть де́ньги (в нали́чии); **he used every ~ argument** он испо́льзовал все досту́пные аргуме́нты; **make ~** предост|авля́ть, -а́вить.

avalanche /'ævə,lɑːntʃ/ *n.* (*lit., fig.*) лави́на.

avant-garde /,ævɑ̃'gɑːd/ *n.* авангарди́сты; (*attr.*) авангарди́стский.

avarice /'ævərɪs/ *n.* жа́дность.

avaricious /,ævə'rɪʃəs/ *adj.* жа́дный.

Av(e). /'ævə,njuː/ *n.* (*abbr. of* **avenue**) пр. (проспе́кт).

avenge /ə'vendʒ/ *v.t.* мстить, ото- за +*a.*; **she ~d her friend** она́ отомсти́ла за дру́га; **he ~d his father's death on the murderer** (*or* **he ~d himself on the murderer for his father's death**) он отомсти́л уби́йце за смерть своего́ отца́.

avenger /ə'vendʒə(r)/ *n.* мсти́тель (*m.*).

avenue /'ævə,njuː/ *n.* **1** (*tree-lined road*) алле́я; (*wide street*) проспе́кт. **2** (*fig., approach, way*) путь (*m.*); **~ to fame** путь к сла́ве; **explore every ~** испо́льзовать (*impf., pf.*) все пути́/кана́лы.

aver /ə'vɜː(r)/ *v.t.* (**averred, averring**) утвер|жда́ть, -ди́ть.

average /'ævərɪdʒ/ *n.* (*mean*) сре́днее число́; **strike an ~** выводи́ть, вы́вести сре́днее число́; (*norm*) сре́днее; **above/below ~** вы́ше/ни́же сре́днего; **on (an, the) ~** в сре́днем.

● *adj.* сре́дний; **the ~ age of the class is 12** сре́дний во́зраст кла́сса — двена́дцать лет; **the ~ man** сре́дний челове́к.

● *v.t. & i.* **1** (*find the ~ of*) выводи́ть, вы́вести сре́днее число́ +*g.*; **his salary, when ~d, was £2,000 a month** его́ сре́дняя зарпла́та соста́вила 2 000 фу́нтов в ме́сяц.
2 (*amount to on ~*): **my expenses ~ £10 a day** мои́ расхо́ды составля́ют в сре́днем де́сять фу́нтов в день; (*do on ~*): **he ~s 6 hours' work a day** он рабо́тает в сре́днем шесть часо́в в день; **we ~d sixty on the motorway** мы де́лали на автостра́де в сре́днем шестьдеся́т миль в час; **it ~s out in the end** к концу́ э́то всё ура́внивается.

averse /ə'vɜːs/ *pred. adj.*: **~ to** нерасполо́женный к +*d.*; **he is ~ to coming** ему́ не хо́чется приходи́ть; **I am not ~ to a good dinner** я не прочь хорошо́ пообе́дать.

aversion /ə'vɜːʃ(ə)n/ *n.* (*dislike*) отвраще́ние, антипа́тия; **have an ~ to** пита́ть (*impf.*) отвраще́ние к +*d.*; **cats are my (pet) ~** я терпе́ть не могу́ ко́шек.

avert /ə'vɜːt/ *v.t.* **1** (*turn aside*): **~ one's glance, eyes** отв|оди́ть, -ести́ взгляд; **~ one's thoughts** отвл|ека́ть, -е́чь мы́сли. **2** (*ward off*) предотвра|ща́ть, -ти́ть; **the danger has been ~ed** опа́сность предотврати́ли.

aviary /'eɪvɪərɪ/ *n.* пти́чник.

aviation /,eɪvɪ'eɪʃ(ə)n/ *n.* авиа́ция; (*attr.*) авиацио́нный; **~ spirit** авиабензи́н.

aviator /'eɪvɪ,eɪtə(r)/ *n.* авиа́тор.

aviculture /'eɪvɪ,kʌltʃə(r)/ *n.* птицево́дство.

avid /'ævɪd/ *adj.* жа́дный, а́лчный; **he was ~ to hear the results** он жа́ждал узна́ть результа́ты.

avidity /ə'vɪdɪtɪ/ *n.* жа́дность, а́лчность.

avionics /,eɪvɪ'ɒnɪks/ *n.* авиацио́нная электро́ника.

avocado /,ævə'kɑːdəʊ/ *n.* (*pl.* **~s**) (**~** *pear*) авока́до (*indecl.*).

avocation /,ævə'keɪʃ(ə)n/ *n.* побо́чное заня́тие.

avocet /'ævə,set/ *n.* шилоклю́вка.

avoid /ə'vɔɪd/ *v.t.* (*drive round*) объезжа́ть, объе́хать; **the car ~ed a pedestrian** маши́на объе́хала пешехо́да; (*escape, evade*) избе|га́ть, -жа́ть +*g.*; **I could not ~ meeting him** я не мог избежа́ть встре́чи с ним; (*shun*) сторони́ться (*impf.*) +*g.*; **he ~s all his old friends** он сторо́нится всех свои́х ста́рых друзе́й; (*refrain from*) уклон|я́ться, -и́ться от +*g.*; **she ~ed a direct answer** она́ уклони́лась от прямо́го отве́та.

avoidable /ə'vɔɪdəb(ə)l/ *adj.*: **delays are ~** заде́ржек мо́жно избежа́ть; **without ~ delay** без нену́жных/изли́шних заде́ржек.

avoidance /ə'vɔɪd(ə)ns/ *n.* (*of an issue*) уклоне́ние; **~ of strong drink** воздержа́ние от употребле́ния спиртно́го; **tax ~** *see* ⇒**tax**

avow /ə'vaʊ/ *v.t.* призн|ава́ть, -а́ть; **he is an ~ed racist** он открове́нный раси́ст; **it was his ~ed intent to emigrate** он откры́то выража́л наме́рение эмигри́ровать; **~edly** по со́бственному призна́нию.

avowal /ə'vaʊ(ə)l/ *n.* призна́ние.

avuncular /ə'vʌŋkjʊlə(r)/ *adj.* дя́дин; (*manner, tone*) оте́ческий; (*person*) дружелю́бный.

await /ə'weɪt/ *v.t.* ожида́ть (*impf.*) +*g.*; **~ing your reply** в ожида́нии ва́шего отве́та.

awake /ə'weɪk/ *pred. adj.* **1**: **are you ~ or asleep?** вы спи́те и́ли нет?; **is he ~ yet?** он просну́лся?; **I've been ~ all night** я не сомкну́л глаз всю ночь; **he lay ~ thinking** он лежа́л без сна и ду́мал; **she stayed ~ till her husband came home** она́ не засыпа́ла, пока́ муж не верну́лся домо́й; **the baby was wide ~** у ребёнка сна не́ было ни в одно́м глазу́.
2 (*fig., vigilant, alert*) бди́тельный; начеку́; **we must be ~ to the possibility of defeat** пораже́ние возмо́жно, и мы не должны́ закрыва́ть на э́то глаза́.

● *v.t.* (*past* **awoke;** *p.p.* **awoken**) **1** (*rouse from sleep*) буди́ть, раз-; **I was awoken by the song of birds** меня́ разбуди́ло пе́ние птиц.
2 (*fig., inspire*) = **awaken 2.**

● *v.i.* (*past* **awoke;** *p.p.* **awoken**) **1** (*wake from sleep*) прос|ыпа́ться, -ну́ться; **he awoke to find himself famous** нау́тро он просну́лся знамени́тым.
2: **~ to** (*fig., realize*) осозн|ава́ть, -а́ть; **he awoke to the fact that ...** он осозна́л тот факт, что. . . .

awaken /ə'weɪkən/ *v.t.* **1** (*lit.*) = **awake** *v.t.* 1. **2** (*fig., arouse, inspire*) пробу|жда́ть, -ди́ть; **his father's death ~ed him to** (*or* **~ed in him**) **a sense of responsibility** смерть отца́ пробуди́ла в нём чу́вство отве́тственности.

awakening /ə'weɪkənɪŋ/ *n.* пробужде́ние; **a rude ~** (*fig.*) го́рькое разочарова́ние.

award /ə'wɔːd/ *n.* (*act of ~ing*) присужде́ние; (*prize*) награ́да, приз.

● *v.t.* прису|жда́ть, -ди́ть (*что кому*); награ|жда́ть, -ди́ть (*кого чем*); **he was ~ed a medal** его́ награди́ли меда́лью.

aware /ə'weə(r)/ *pred. adj.*: **be ~ of** сознава́ть (*impf.*); (*realize*) осозн|ава́ть, -а́ть; **I am well ~ of the dangers** я вполне́ сознаю́ все опа́сности; **he became ~ of someone following him** он почу́вствовал, что за ним следя́т; **I was not ~ of that** я э́того не знал; **you are probably ~ that ...** вам, вероя́тно, изве́стно, что. . .; **I passed him without being ~ of it** я прошёл ми́мо, не заме́тив его́.

awareness /ə'weənɪs/ *n.* созна́ние.

awash /ə'wɒʃ/ *pred. adj.* омы́тый водо́й; **the place was ~ with champagne** шампа́нское лило́сь реко́й.

away /ə'weɪ/ *adv.* **1** (*at a distance*): **the shops are ten minutes' walk ~** магази́ны нахо́дятся в десяти́ мину́тах ходьбы́ отсю́да; **the sea is only 5 miles ~ from our villa** мо́ре всего́ в пяти́ ми́лях от на́шей ви́ллы; **her mother lived half an hour ~ by bus** её мать жила́ в получа́се езды́ на авто́бусе.
2 (*not present or near*): **he is ~** он в

отъе́зде; **he was ~ on leave** он был в о́тпуске; **how long have you been ~?** ско́лько (вре́мени) вас не́ было?; **we shall be ~ in July** в ию́ле нас не бу́дет; **our team are playing ~ (from home)** на́ша кома́нда игра́ет на вы́езде *or* на чужо́м по́ле; **hold it ~ from the light** держи́те э́то пода́льше от све́та.
3 (*fig., of time or degree*): **the wedding is three weeks ~** до сва́дьбы (оста́лось) три неде́ли; **far and ~ the best** наилу́чший.
4 (*expr. continuance*): **he works ~** он рабо́тает не перестава́я; **he was talking ~ to himself** он всё вре́мя сам с собо́й разгова́ривал; **all the time the clock was ticking ~** всё э́то вре́мя часы́ ти́кали, не перестава́я.
5 (*with imper.*): **You have some questions? Ask ~, then!** У вас есть вопро́сы? Ну, спра́шивайте!
6: **right, straight ~** сейча́с; неме́дленно.
7: **~ with him!** доло́й его́!; **~ with you!** убира́йтесь!

awe /ɔː/ *n.* благогове́ние, тре́пет; **he stands in ~ of his teacher** он благогове́ет пе́ред учи́телем.
● *v.t.* внуш|а́ть, -и́ть (*кому*) благогове́ние/тре́пет.
● *cpds.* **~-inspiring** *adj.* внуша́ющий благогове́ние; **~-struck** *adj.* испо́лненный благогове́нием.

awesome /ˈɔːsəm/ *adj.* устраша́ющий.

awful /ˈɔːfʊl/ *adj.* (*terrible; also coll.: very bad, great etc.*) ужа́сный, стра́шный; **it's an ~ shame** ужа́сно доса́дно; **an ~ lot** ужа́сно мно́го.

awfully /ˈɔːfəlɪ/, /-flɪ/ *adv.* ужа́сно; **~ nice** стра́шно ми́лый; **thanks ~** огро́мное вам спаси́бо; **I'm ~ sorry** прости́те, ра́ди Бо́га.

awhile /əˈwaɪl/ *adv.* а не́которое вре́мя; **I shan't be ready to leave yet ~** я не смогу́ пое́хать сра́зу.

awkward /ˈɔːkwəd/ *adj.* **1** (*clumsy*) неуклю́жий, нело́вкий.
2 (*inconvenient, uncomfortable*) неудо́бный. **3** (*difficult*): **an ~ problem** ка́верзная пробле́ма; **an ~ turning** тру́дный поворо́т. **4** (*embarrassing*): **an ~ silence** нело́вкое молча́ние.
5 (*Br., of person, hard to manage*) тру́дный; **he's being ~ (about it)** он чини́т препя́тствия.

awkwardness /ˈɔːkwədnɪs/ *n.* неуклю́жесть, нело́вкость; неудо́бство.

awl /ɔːl/ *n.* ши́ло.

awning /ˈɔːnɪŋ/ *n.* наве́с; тент.

awoke /əˈwəʊk/ *past of* ⇒**awake**

awoken /əˈwəʊk(ə)n/ *p.p. of* ⇒**awake**

AWOL /ˈeɪwɒl/ *pred. adj.* (*abbr. of* ***absent without leave***) в самово́льной отлу́чке.

awry /əˈraɪ/ *pred. adj.* криво́й; (*distorted*) искажённый.
● *adv.* ко́со; (*on, to one side*) на́бок; **your tie is all ~** ваш га́лстук съе́хал на́бок; (*fig.*): **things went ~** дела́ пошли́ скве́рно.

axe (*US also* **ax**) /æks/ *n.* **1** (*tool*) топо́р; **I have no ~ to grind** (*fig.*) у меня́ нет коры́стных побужде́ний. **2** (*coll.: reduction of expenditure*) уре́зывание.
● *v.t.* (**axing**) (*fig.*) (*reduce: budget, expenditure, staff*) уре́з|ывать, -ать; (*project*) заруб|а́ть, -и́ть; **many workers have been ~d** уво́лено мно́го рабо́чих.

axes /ˈæksiːz/ *pl. of* ⇒**axis**

axial /ˈæksɪəl/ *adj.* осево́й.

axillary /ækˈsɪlərɪ/ *adj.* подмы́шечный.

axiom /ˈæksɪəm/ *n.* аксио́ма.

axiomatic /ˌæksɪəˈmætɪk/ *adj.* аксиомати́чный.

axis /ˈæksɪs/ *n.* (*pl.* **axes**) ось, вал; **the A~ (powers)** (*hist.*) Ось «Берли́н—Рим».

axle /ˈæks(ə)l/ *n.* ось.

ayatollah /ˌaɪəˈtɒlə/ *n.* аятолла́ (*m.*).

ay(e) /aɪ/ *n.* (*affirmative vote*) го́лос «за»; **the ~s have it** большинство́ за.
● *int.* да; есть; **~, ~, Sir!** есть!

aye-aye /ˈaɪaɪ/ *n.* (*zool.*) а́йе-а́йе (*m. indecl.*).

azalea /əˈzeɪlɪə/ *n.* аза́лия.

Azerbaijan /ˌæzəbaɪˈdʒɑːn/ *n.* Азербайджа́н.

Azerbaijani /ˌæzəbaɪˈdʒɑːnɪ/ *n.* (*pl.* **~s**) (*person*) азербайджа́н|ец (*fem.* -ка); (*language*) азербайджа́нский язы́к.
● *adj.* азербайджа́нский.

azimuth /ˈæzɪməθ/ *n.* а́зимут.

Azores /əˈzɔːz/ *n.*: **the ~** Азо́рские острова́ (*m. pl.*).

Azov /ˈɑːzɒv/ *n.*: **Sea of ~** Азо́вское мо́ре.

Aztec /ˈæztek/ *n.* ацте́к.
● *adj.* ацте́кский.

azure /ˈæʒə(r)/, /-zjə(r)/, /ˈeɪ / *n.* лазу́рь.
● *adj.* лазу́рный, голубо́й.

Bb

B /biː/ *n.* **1** (*mus.*) си (*nt. indecl.*). **2** (*acad. mark*) «хорошо́», четвёрка; **she got a ~ in arithmetic** она́ получи́ла «хорошо́» *or* четвёрку по арифме́тике.

BA (*abbr. of* ***Bachelor of Arts***) бакала́вр гуманита́рных нау́к; **he has a ~ in Russian** он име́ет сте́пень бакала́вра по ру́сскому языку́.

baa /bɑː/ *n.* бле́яние.

● *v.i.* (**baas, baaed** *or* **baa'd**) бле́ять (*impf.*).

babble /ˈbæb(ə)l/ *n.* (*imperfect speech*) ле́пет; (*idle talk*) болтовня́; (*of water etc.*) журча́ние.

● *v.t. & i.* (*speak inarticulately*) болта́ть (*impf.*); лепета́ть (*impf.*); (*utter trivialities*) болта́ть (*impf.*); (*let out secrets*) выба́лтывать, вы́болтать; проб|а́лтываться, -олта́ться; **babbling brook** журча́щий ручеёк.

babbler /ˈbæbl(ə)r/ *n.* болту́н (*fem.* -нья).

babe /beɪb/ *n.* (*lit., fig.*) младе́нец; (*US sl.*) де́вушка.

babel /ˈbeɪb(ə)l/ *n.* **1**: **the tower of B~** вавило́нская ба́шня. **2** (*fig.*) вавило́нское столпотворе́ние.

baboon /bəˈbuːn/ *n.* бабуи́н, павиа́н.

baby /ˈbeɪbɪ/ *n.* **1** младе́нец; **the ~ of the family** мла́дший в семье́; **empty out the baby with the bathwater** (*fig.*) вме́сте с водо́й вы́плеснуть (*pf.*) и ребёнка; **they left me holding the ~** (*fig.*) мне пришло́сь за них отдува́ться. **2** (*of animals etc.*) детёныш. **3** (*coll., sweetheart*) де́тка. **4** (*attr.*): **~ elephant** слонёнок; **~ grand (piano)** кабине́тный роя́ль.

● *v.t.* обраща́ться (*impf.*) (*с кем*) как с младе́нцем.

● *cpds.* **~-carriage** *n.* (*US*) де́тская коля́ска; **~-sit** *v.i.* присма́тривать (*impf.*) за детьми́ в отсу́тствие роди́телей; **~-sitter** *n.* приходя́щая ня́ня; **~-sitting** *n.* присмо́тр за детьми́; **~-snatcher** *n.* похити́тель(ница) дете́й; **~-talk** *n.* де́тский язы́к, де́тский ле́пет; (*by adults*) сюсю́канье.

babyhood /ˈbeɪbɪhʊd/ *n.* младе́нчество.

babyish /ˈbeɪbɪɪʃ/ *adj.* де́тский, ребя́ческий.

Babylon /ˈbæbɪlən/ *n.* Вавило́н.

Babylonian /ˌbæbɪˈləʊnɪən/ *adj.* вавило́нский.

baccalaureate /ˌbækəˈlɔːrɪət/ *n.* сте́пень бакала́вра.

baccarat /ˈbækəˌrɑː/ *n.* баккара́ (*nt. indecl.*).

Bacchanalia /ˌbækəˈneɪlɪə/ *n.* вакхана́лия.

Bacchanalian /ˌbækəˈneɪlɪən/ *adj.* вакхи́ческий, вакхана́льный.

Bacchante /bəˈkæntɪ/ *n.* вакха́нка.

Bacchic /ˈbækɪk/ *adj.* вакхи́ческий.

Bacchus /ˈbækəs/ *n.* Вакх, Ба́хус.

bachelor /ˈbætʃələ(r)/ *n.* **1** холостя́к; **~ girl** «холостя́чка»; **~ pad** (*coll.*) холостя́цкая кварти́ра; **~ party** (*US*) мальчи́шник. **2** (*acad.*) бакала́вр.

bachelorhood /ˈbætʃələ(r)hʊd/ *n.* холостя́цкая/холостя́я жизнь.

bacil|lus /bəˈsɪləs/ *n.* (*pl.* **~li** /-laɪ/, /-liː/) баци́лла.

back /bæk/ *n.* **1** (*part of body*) спина́; **~ to ~** спино́й к спине́; **break one's ~** переломи́ть (*pf.*) спинно́й хребе́т; **he fell on his ~** он упа́л на́ спину; **turn one's ~ on** (*lit.*) отв|ора́чиваться, -ерну́ться от + *g.*; (*fig.*) пок|ида́ть, -и́нуть; **as soon as my ~ was turned** не успе́л я отверну́ться.
2 (*fig. uses*): **behind my ~** за мое́й спино́й; **on one's ~** (*as burden*) на ше́е; **put s.o.'s ~ up** рассерди́ть (*pf.*) кого́-н.; **break the ~ of a task** одоле́ть (*pf.*) трудне́йшую часть зада́ния; **see the ~ of** (*get rid of*) отде́латься (*pf.*) от + *g.*; **with one's ~ against the wall** припёртый к сте́нке; **put one's ~ into something** вложи́ть (*pf.*) все си́лы во что-н.
3 (*of chair, dress*) спи́нка; (*of playing card*) руба́шка.
4 (*other side, rear*): **~ of an envelope** обра́тная сторона́ конве́рта; **~ of one's head** заты́лок; **~ of one's hand** ты́льная сторона́ руки́; **know something like the ~ of one's hand** знать (*impf.*) что-н. как свой пять па́льцев; **~ of one's leg** нога́ сза́ди; икра́; **at the ~ of the house** в за́дней ча́сти до́ма; (*behind it*) позади́ до́ма; **at the ~ of one's mind** подсозна́тельно; в глубине́ души́; **at the ~ of the book** в конце́ кни́ги; **at the ~ of beyond** на краю́ све́та; **the ~ of a car** за́дняя часть автомоби́ля.
5 (*sport*): **full ~** защи́тник, бек.
6 (*attr.*; *see also cpds. as separate headwords*): **~ door** чёрный ход; **~ seat** за́днее сиде́нье; **~ stairs** чёрная ле́стница; **~ street** глуха́я у́лица.

● *adv.* **1** (*to or at the rear*) наза́д, сза́ди; **~ and forth** взад и вперёд; **hold the crowd ~** сде́рживать (*impf.*) толпу́; **sit ~ in one's chair** отки́нуться (*pf.*) на спи́нку сту́ла; усе́сться (*pf.*) глу́бже; **keep ~ the truth** скрыва́ть (*impf.*) пра́вду; **(in) ~ of** (*US*) позади́ + *g.*; **~ from the road** в стороне́ от доро́ги.
2 (*returning to former position etc.*) обра́тно; **he is ~ again** он сно́ва здесь; **we shall be ~ before dark** мы вернёмся за́светло; **pay s.o. ~** отпла́|чивать, -ти́ть кому́-н.; **hit ~** уд|аря́ть, -а́рить в отве́т; (*coll.*) дать (*pf.*) сда́чи (*кому*); **get one's own ~** отплати́ть (*pf.*) (*кому*).
3 (*ago*) тому́ наза́д; **~ in 1930** ещё в 1930 году́.

● *v.t.* **1** (*move backwards*) дви́гать, -нуть наза́д (*or* в обра́тном направле́нии); **she ~ed the car into the garage** она́ въе́хала за́дним хо́дом в гара́ж.
2 (*support; also* **~ up**) подде́рж|ивать, -а́ть; **~** (*bet on*) **a horse** ста́вить, по- на ло́шадь.
3 (*finance*) финанси́ровать (*impf., pf.*).
4 (*line*) покр|ыва́ть, -ы́ть; **~ed with sheet-iron** кры́тый листовы́м желе́зом.
5 (*mus.*) аккомпани́ровать (*impf.*) + *d.*
6 (*form ~ of*) примыка́ть (*impf.*) сза́ди; быть фо́ном (*чего*); **the lake is ~ed by mountains** сза́ди к о́зеру примыка́ют го́ры.
7 ~ up (*comput.*) резерви́ровать (*impf., pf.*).

● *v.i.* **1** (*move backwards*) пя́титься, по-;

B

(*of motor car*) идти́ (*det.*) за́дним хо́дом; **the car ~ed into a side street** маши́на въе́хала за́дним хо́дом в переу́лок. **2** **~ down (from)** отступ|а́ться, -и́ться (*от чего*); **~ out (of)** уклон|я́ться, -и́ться (*от чего*).

backache /ˈbækeɪk/ *n.* боль в спине́/поясни́це.

backbencher /ˈbækˈbentʃə(r)/ *n.* (*Br.*) заднескаме́ечник, рядово́й член парла́мента.

backbite /ˈbækbaɪt/ *v.t. & i.* злосло́вить (*impf.*) (*о ком*).

backbiting /ˈbækˌbaɪtɪŋ/ *n.* злосло́вие.

backbone /ˈbækbəʊn/ *n.* **1** спинно́й хребе́т, позвоно́чник. **2** (*basis*) осно́ва; (*substance*) суть; (*support*) опо́ра; (*strength of character*) твёрдость хара́ктера.

back-chat /ˈbæktʃæt/ *n.* (*Br.*) де́рзкий отве́т, де́рзость.

back|cloth /ˈbækklɒθ/ (*Br.*), **-drop** *nn.* за́дник.

backcomb /ˈbækkəʊm/ *v.t.* (*Br.*) нач|ёсывать, -еса́ть.

back-date /bækˈdeɪt/ *v.t.* (*letter*) пом|еча́ть, -е́тить за́дним число́м; (*pay*) пров|оди́ть, -ести́ за́дним число́м.

backdoor /ˈbækdɔː(r)/ *adj.* (*fig.*) закули́сный, та́йный.

backdrop /ˈbækdrɒp/ *n.* **1**: **against the ~ of crisis** на фо́не кри́зиса. **2** = **backcloth**

back-end /ˈbækend/ *n.* (*rear part*) за́дняя часть; (*coll., buttocks*) зад, за́дница; (*of period of time*) коне́ц.

backer /ˈbækə(r)/ *n.* ока́зывающий подде́ржку; субсиди́рующий.

backfire /ˈbækfaɪə(r)/ *v.t.* да|ва́ть, -ть обра́тную вспы́шку; (*fig.*) прив|оди́ть, -ести́ к обра́тным результа́там.

backgammon /ˈbækˌgæmən/ *n.* трикгра́к (*игра*).

background /ˈbækgraʊnd/ *n.* **1** за́дний план, фон; (*attr.*) фо́новый; **in the ~ of the picture** на за́днем пла́не карти́ны; **on a dark ~** на тёмном фо́не; **keep in the ~** (*fig.*) держа́ть(ся) (*impf.*) в тени́. **2** (*of person*) ≈ происхожде́ние; образова́ние; о́пыт. **3** (*to a situation*) предысто́рия. **4**: **~ music** музыка́льное сопровожде́ние/оформле́ние.

backhand /ˈbækhænd/ *n.* (*sport*: **~ stroke**) уда́р сле́ва.

backhanded /bækˈhændɪd/ *adj.* сде́ланный ты́льной стороно́й руки́; (*fig.*) сомни́тельный, двусмы́сленный.

backhander /ˈbækˌhændə(r)/ *n.* (*Br., bribe*) взя́тка, бакши́ш.

backing /ˈbækɪŋ/ *n.* **1** (*assistance*) подде́ржка; (*subsidy*) субсиди́рование. **2** (*of cloth*) подкла́дка; (*covering*) покры́тие. **3** (*mus.*) аккомпанеме́нт.

backlash /ˈbæklæʃ/ *n.* (*fig.*) реа́кция.

backlight /ˈbæklaɪt/ *v.t.* (*phot.*) осве|ща́ть, -ти́ть контражу́рным све́том; (*comput.*): **backlit LCD screen** жидкокристалли́ческий экра́н с подсве́ткой.

backlog /ˈbæklɒg/ *n.* за́лежи (*f. pl.*) накопи́вшейся рабо́ты.

backpack /ˈbækpæk/ *n.* рюкза́к.

backpacker /ˈbækpækə(r)/ *n.* челове́к путеше́ствующий с рюкзако́м.

back-pedal /ˈbækped(ə)l/ *v.i.* крути́ть (*impf.*) педа́ли наза́д; (*fig.*) пойти́ (*pf.*) на попя́тный/попя́тную.

backside /bækˈsaɪd/, /ˈbæk-/ *n.* (*coll., buttocks*) зад, за́дница.

back-slapper /ˈbækˌslæpə(r)/ *n.* руба́ха-па́рень (*m.*).

back-slapping /ˈbækˌslæpɪŋ/ *n.* похло́пывание по спине́; панибра́тство.

● *adj.* панибра́тский.

backslide /ˈbækslaɪd/ *v.t.* вновь подда́ться (*pf.*) искуше́нию; верну́ться (*pf.*) к дурны́м привы́чкам.

backslider /ˈbækˌslaɪdə(r)/ *n.* ≈ отсту́пник; верну́вшийся к дурны́м привы́чкам.

back-spacer /ˈbækˌspeɪsə(r)/ *n.* (*on typewriter*) обра́тный реги́стр; кла́виша «обра́тный ход».

backstage /ˈbæksteɪdʒ/ *adj.* (*also fig.*) закули́сный.

● *adv.* за кули́сами.

backstairs /ˈbæksteəz/ *adj.* (*fig.*) та́йный, закули́сный.

backstreet /ˈbækstriːt/ *adj.* (*illicit*) подпо́льный.

backstroke /ˈbækstrəʊk/ *n.* пла́вание на спине́.

back-track /ˈbæktræk/ *v.i.* идти́ (*det.*) за́дним хо́дом; пя́титься, по-; (*fig.*) идти́ (*det.*) на попя́тный/попя́тную.

back-up /ˈbækʌp/ *n.* (*comput.*) резе́рвная ко́пия.

● *adj.* запасно́й; (*comput.*) резе́рвный.

backward /ˈbækwəd/ *adj.* **1** (*towards the back*) обра́тный; **a ~ glance** взгля́д наза́д. **2** (*lagging*) отста́лый; **~ children** у́мственно отста́лые де́ти; **~ country** отста́лая страна́. **3** (*reluctant*) ме́длящий.

● *adv.*: *see next entry.*

backward(s) /ˈbækwədz/ *adv.* (*in backward direction*) наза́д; (*in opposite direction*) в обра́тном направле́нии; (*in reverse order*) в обра́тном поря́дке; **sit ~ on a horse** сиде́ть (*impf.*) на ло́шади за́дом наперёд; **walk ~** пя́титься, по-; **~ and forwards** взад и вперёд; туда́ и обра́тно; туда́-сюда́; **know something ~** знать (*impf.*) что-н. от ко́рки до ко́рки; **lean over ~ to do something** (*fig.*) из ко́жи вон лезть (*pf.*), что́бы сде́лать что-н.

backward-looking /ˈbækwədˈlʊkɪŋ/ *adj.* (*fig.*) отста́лый, ретрогра́дный.

backwardness /ˈbækwədnɪs/ *n.* отста́лость; (*disinclination*) неохо́та.

backwash /ˈbækwɒʃ/ *n.* обра́тный пото́к; (*fig.*) о́тзвук, след.

backwater /ˈbækˌwɔːtə(r)/ *n.* за́водь; (*fig.*) боло́то, ти́хая за́водь.

backwoods /ˈbækwʊdz/ *n.* (лесна́я) глушь.

backwoodsman /ˈbækˌwʊdzmən/ *n.* (*US*) обита́тель (*m.*) лесно́й глуши́; дереве́нщина (*c.g.*).

backyard /bækˈjɑːd/ *n.* **1** (*Br.*) за́дний двор. **2** (*US*) за́дний са́дик.

bacon /ˈbeɪkən/ *n.* бе́кон; **~ and eggs** яи́чница с бе́коном; (*fig.*): **save one's ~** спа|са́ть, -сти́ свою́ шку́ру.

bacteria /bækˈtɪərɪə/ *pl. of* ⇒**bacterium**

bacterial /bækˈtɪərɪəl/ *adj.* бактери́йный.

bacteriological /bækˌtɪərɪəˈlɒdʒɪk(ə)l/ *adj.* бактериологи́ческий; **~ warfare** бактериологи́ческая война́.

bacteriology /bækˌtɪərɪˈɒlədʒɪ/ *n.* бактериоло́гия.

bacteri|um /bækˈtɪərɪəm/ *n.* (*pl.* **~a**) бакте́рия.

bad /bæd/ *n.* (*evil*) дурно́е, плохо́е; ху́до.

● *adj.* (**worse, worst**) **1** плохо́й, дурно́й, скве́рный; **not ~!** непло́хо!; **things went from ~ to worse** дела́ шли всё ху́же и ху́же; **too ~!** о́чень жаль!; **it is too ~ of him** э́то о́чень некраси́во с его́ стороны́; **a ~ light** (*to read in*) сла́бый свет.
2 (*morally bad*) плохо́й, дурно́й; **it is ~ to steal** ворова́ть (*impf.*) ду́рно/пло́хо; **a ~ name** дурна́я репута́ция.
3 (*spoilt*) испо́рченный; **go ~** по́ртиться, ис-.
4 (*severe*) си́льный; **I caught a ~ cold** я си́льно простуди́лся; **a ~ wound** тяжёлая ра́на.
5 (*harmful*) вре́дный; **coffee is ~ for him** ко́фе ему́ вре́ден; **smoking is ~ for one** куре́ние вре́дно для здоро́вья.
6 (*of health*) больно́й; **I feel ~** я чу́вствую себя́ пло́хо.
7 (*var.*): **a ~ mistake** гру́бая оши́бка; **a ~ debt** безнадёжный долг; **a ~ lot, hat** (*coll.*) дрянь-челове́к; **~ language** ру́гань; **~ taste** безвку́сица.

● *cpds.* **~-mannered** *adj.* невоспи́танный; **~-tempered** *adj.* раздражи́тельный.

baddie /ˈbædɪ/ *n.* (*coll.*) злоде́й; плохо́й дя́дя.

bade /beɪd bæd/ *arch. past of* ⇒**bid**

badge /bædʒ/ *n.* значо́к; (*fig.*) си́мвол.

badger /ˈbædʒə(r)/ *n.* барсу́к.

● *v.t.* (*coll.*) трави́ть (*impf.*); **~ s.o. for something** пристава́ть (*impf.*) к кому́-н. с про́сьбой о чём-н.

badinage /ˈbædɪˌnɑːʒ/ *n.* подшу́чивание.

badly /ˈbædlɪ/ *adv.* (**worse, worst**) **1** (*not well*) пло́хо. **2** (*very much*) о́чень; си́льно; (*urgently*) сро́чно. **3**: **~ off** в нужде́.

badminton /ˈbædmɪnt(ə)n/ *n.* бадминто́н.

badness /ˈbædnɪs/ *n.* (*evil*) дурно́е, плохо́е; (*poor quality*) него́дность; (*depravity*) поро́чность; **the ~ of the weather** плоха́я пого́да, нена́стье, непого́да.

baffle¹ /ˈbæf(ə)l/ *n.* (*tech.*) экра́н, щит.

● *cpd.* **~-plate** *n.* отража́тельная плита́.

baffle² /ˈbæf(ə)l/ *v.t.* (*perplex*) сби|ва́ть,

-ть с то́лку; озада́чи|вать, -ть; **the police are ~d** поли́ция не зна́ет, что де́лать.

baffling /ˈbæf(ə)lɪŋ/ *adj.* сбива́ющий с то́лку; ста́вящий в тупи́к; зага́дочный.

bag /bæg/ *n.* **1** су́мка; (*small ~, hand ~*) су́мочка; (*paper ~, plastic ~*) паке́т; **shopping ~** хозя́йственная су́мка.
2 (*large ~, sack*) мешо́к.
3 (*luggage*) чемода́н; **pack one's ~s** упакова́ться (*pf.*); **~ and baggage** со все́ми пожи́тками.
4 (*game shot by sportsman*) добы́ча.
5: **by diplomatic ~** дипломати́ческой по́чтой.
6 (*pl., Br. coll., plenty*): **~s of room** полно́ ме́ста; **~ of money** мешки́ (*m. pl.*) де́нег.
7 (*var.*): **in the ~** (*coll., assured*) ≈ уже́ в карма́не; **~s under the eyes** мешки́ под глаза́ми; **a ~ of bones** (*fig.*) ко́жа да ко́сти; **old ~** (*sl., pej., woman*) ста́рая хрычо́вка; **What's your ~?** (*sl.*) что вас интересу́ет *or* колы́шет?; **classical music isn't my ~** класси́ческая му́зыка меня́ не колы́шет.
● *v.t.* (**bagged, bagging**) **1** (*put in bag*) класть, положи́ть в мешо́к, паке́т.
2 (*shoot down*): **~ game** бить (*impf.*) дичь; **~ an aircraft** сбить (*pf.*) самолёт.
3: **he ~ged the best seat** он за́нял лу́чшее ме́сто; **~s I first!** (*Br.*) чур я пе́рвый! (*coll.*).
● *v.i.* (**bagged, bagging**): **his trousers ~ at the knees** его́ брю́ки пузы́рятся на коле́нях.
● *cpds.* **~pipe(s)** *n.* волы́нка; **~piper** *n.* волы́нщик.

bagatelle /ˌbægəˈtel/ *n.* пустя́к.

baggage /ˈbægɪdʒ/ *n.* **1** бага́ж. **2** (*mil.*) вози́мое иму́щество. **3** (*saucy girl*) наха́лка; озорни́ца. **4** (*attr.*) бага́жный; (*mil.*) вещево́й; **~ car** (*US*) бага́жный ваго́н; **~ room** (*US*) ка́мера хране́ния; **~ train** вещево́й обо́з.

bagginess /ˈbægɪnɪs/ *n.* мешкова́тость.

baggy /ˈbægɪ/ *adj.* (**baggier, baggiest**) мешкова́тый.

Baghdad /bægˈdæd/ *n.* Багда́д; (*attr.*) багда́дский.

bah /bɑː/ *int.* ба!

Bahamas /bəˈhɑːməz/ *n.*: **the ~** Бага́мские острова́ (*m. pl.*).

Bahrain /bɑːˈreɪn/ *n.* Бахре́йн.

bail[1] /beɪl/ *n.* **1** (*pledge*) зало́г; поручи́тельство; **release on ~** отпус|ка́ть, -ти́ть на пору́ки.
2 (*person*) поручи́тель (*m.*); **stand, go ~ for s.o.** поручи́ться (*pf.*) за кого́-н.
● *v.t.*: **~ s.o. out** брать, взять кого́-н. на пору́ки.

bail[2], **bale** /beɪl/ *vv.t.* (*also* **~ out**) выче́рпывать, вы́черпать (*воду из лодки*).
● *v.i.*: **~ out** (*aeron.*) выбра́сываться, вы́броситься с парашю́том.

bailiff /ˈbeɪlɪf/ *n.* **1** (*leg.*) суде́бный при́став; бе́йлиф. **2** (*Br., steward*) управля́ющий.

bairn /beən/ *n.* (*Sc.*) дитя́ (*nt.*), ребёнок.

bait /beɪt/ *n.* (*hunting*) прима́нка; (*fishing*) наса́дка, нажи́вка; **live ~** живе́ц; (*fig.*) прима́нка; **rise to the ~** (*lit., fig.*) попа́сться (*pf.*) на у́дочку.
● *v.t.* **1** (*attach ~ to*) наса́|живать, -ди́ть нажи́вку на + *a.* **2** (*entice*) прима́н|ивать, -и́ть. **3** (*tease*) пресле́довать (*impf.*), изводи́ть (*impf.*).

baize /beɪz/ *n.* ба́йка; **green ~** зелёное сукно́.

bake /beɪk/ *v.t.* печь, с-; (*of bricks*) обж|ига́ть, -е́чь.
● *v.i.* пе́чься; **I'm baking** (*coll.*) я умира́ю от жары́; **baking powder, soda** пека́рный порошо́к; со́да (для пече́ния); разрыхли́тель (*m.*); **baking sheet, tray** про́тивень.

bakelite /ˈbeɪkəˌlaɪt/ *n.* бакели́т.

baker /ˈbeɪkə(r)/ *n.* пе́карь (*m.*); (*in charge of ~'s shop*) бу́лочник; **~'s dozen** чёртова дю́жина.

bakery /ˈbeɪkərɪ/ *n.* пека́рня; (*shop*) бу́лочная.

Baku /bæˈkuː/ *n.* Баку́ (*m. indecl.*).

Balaclava /ˌbæləˈklɑːvə/ *n.*: **~ helmet** вя́заный шлем.

balalaika /ˌbæləˈlaɪkə/ *n.* балала́йка.

balance /ˈbæləns/ *n.* **1** (*machine*) вес|ы́ (*pl., g.* -о́в); **spring ~** пружи́нные весы́.
2 (*equilibrium*) равнове́сие; **lose one's ~** (*fig.*) теря́ть, по- душе́вное равнове́сие; **hang in the ~** висе́ть (*impf.*) на волоске́; **catch s.o. off ~** засти́гнуть (*pf.*) кого́-н. врасплох.
3 (*counterbalance*) противове́с.
4 (*bookkeeping*) бала́нс; са́льдо (*indecl.*); **~ sheet** бухга́лтерский бала́нс; **~ of payments** платёжный бала́нс; **~ of trade** торго́вый бала́нс; **on ~** в ито́ге, в коне́чном счёте.
5 (*relative volume of sound*) бала́нс.
● *v.t.* **1** (*lit.*): **he ~d a pole on his chin** он баланси́ровал шест на подборо́дке.
2 (*make equal*) уравнове́|шивать, -сить.
3 (*weigh one thing against another*) взве́|шивать, -сить; сопо|ставля́ть, -ста́вить (*что с чем*).
4 (*comm.*) баланси́ровать, с/за-; **~ the books** забаланси́ровать (*pf.*) бухга́лтерские кни́ги.
● *v.i.* (*of accounts*) сходи́ться (*impf.*); (*be in equilibrium*) баланси́ровать (*impf.*).
● *cpd.* **~-wheel** *n.* ма́ятник.

balanced /ˈbælənsd/ *adj.* (*of person*) уравнове́шенный; **~ judgement** проду́манное сужде́ние; **~ diet** сбаланси́рованная/рациона́льная дие́та.

balcony /ˈbælkənɪ/ *n.* балко́н.

bald /bɔːld/ *adj.* **1** лы́сый, плеши́вый; **as ~ as a coot** (*coll.*) го́лый, как коле́но; **~ patch** лы́сина, плешь.
2 (*bare*) го́лый; **~ tyre** (*Br.*), **tire** (*US*) изно́шенная покры́шка.
3 (*unadorned*) неприкра́шенный, прямо́й.
● *cpds.* **~-head, ~-pate** *nn.* лы́сый (челове́к); **~-headed** *adj.* лы́сый, плеши́вый.

baldachin /ˈbɔːldəkɪn/ *n.* балдахи́н.

balderdash /ˈbɔːldəˌdæʃ/ *n.* галиматья́.

balding /ˈbɔːldɪŋ/ *adj.* лысе́ющий.

baldness /ˈbɔːldnɪs/ *n.* плеши́вость.

bale[1] /beɪl/ *n.* (*of hay*) тюк; (*of cotton*) ки́па.
● *v.t.* (*hay*) прессова́ть, с-; (*cotton*) упако́в|ывать, -а́ть в ки́пы; тюкова́ть (*impf.*).

bale[2] /beɪl/ *v.i.* (*Br.*) = **bail**[2]

baleful /ˈbeɪlfʊl/ *adj.* злове́щий.

balk, baulk /bɔːlk/ *vv.t.* (*hinder*) меша́ть, по- (*кому, чему, в чём*); (*frustrate*) расстр|а́ивать, -о́ить; **~ s.o. of his prey** лиши́ть (*pf.*) кого́-н. добы́чи; **he was ~ed of his desires** его́ жела́ния не осуществи́лись.
● *v.i.* **1** (*of horses*) арта́читься, за- (*при чём*). **2**: **he ~ed at the expense** таки́е расхо́ды его́ испуга́ли; (*hesitate*) колеба́ться (*impf.*).

Balkan /ˈbɔːlkən/ *n.*: **the ~s** Балка́н|ы (*pl., g.* —); Балка́нский полуо́стров.
● *adj.* балка́нский.

ball[1] /bɔːl/ *n.* (*dance*) бал; **give a ~** устр|а́ивать, -о́ить бал; **fancy-dress ~** маскара́д.
● *cpds.* **~-dress** *n.* ба́льное пла́тье; **~room** *n.* танцева́льный зал.

ball[2] /bɔːl/ *n.* **1** (*sphere*) шар; **billiard ~** билья́рдный шар. **2** (*in football, rugby, tennis*) мяч; (*in golf, table tennis*) мя́чик; **play ~** игра́ть (*impf.*) в мяч. **3** (*of wool*) клубо́к. **4** (*for cannon*) ядро́.
5 (*of thumb, foot*) поду́шечка. **6** (*pl., vulg.*) (*testicles*) я́йца (*nt. pl.*); (*Br., nonsense*) чепуха́; **make a ~s of** напорта́чить (*pf.*). **7** (*tech.*): **~ and socket** шарово́й шарни́р. **8** (*var. fig. uses*): **on the ~** сметли́вый, (*coll.*) расторо́пный; **get on the ~** смекну́ть (*pf.*); **keep the ~ rolling** (*in conversation*) подде́рж|ивать, -а́ть разгово́р; **set the ~ rolling** (*start sth.*) пус|ка́ть, -ти́ть что-н. в ход.
● *cpds.* **~-bearing** *n.* шарикоподши́пник; **~-cock** *n.* шарово́й кла́пан; **~-park** *adj.*: **a ~-park figure** приме́рная ци́фра; **~-point** (*pen*) *n.* ша́риковая ру́чка, ша́рик.

ballad /ˈbæləd/ *n.* балла́да.

ballade /bæˈlɑːd/ *n.* балла́да.

balladeer /ˌbæləˈdɪə(r)/ *n.* шансонье́ (*m. indecl.*).

balladry /ˈbælədrɪ/ *n.* балла́ды (*f. pl.*).

ballast /ˈbæləst/ *n.* балла́ст.
● *v.t.* грузи́ть, на- балла́стом.

ballerina /ˌbæləˈriːnə/ *n.* балери́на.

ballet /ˈbæleɪ/ *n.* бале́т.
● *cpds.* **~-dancer** *n.* арти́ст (*fem.* -ка) бале́та; **~-master** *n.* балетме́йстер.

ballistic /bəˈlɪstɪk/ *adj.* баллисти́ческий; **~ missile** баллисти́ческий снаря́д.

ballistics /bəˈlɪstɪks/ *n.* баллисти́ка.

ballon d'essai /bæˌlɔ̃ deˈseɪ/ *n.* (*pl.* ***ballons d'essai*** *pronunc. same*) про́бный шар.

balloon /bəˈluːn/ *n.* аэроста́т; (*also child's*) возду́шный шар; (*in comic strip,* *etc.*) ова́л; **barrage ~** аэроста́т загражде́ния.

● *v.i.* (*fly in ~*) лета́ть (*indet.*) на возду́шном ша́ре.

balloonist /bəˈluːnɪst/ *n.* воздухопла́ватель (*m.*), аэрона́вт.

ballot /ˈbælət/ *n.* (*~-paper*) избира́тельный бюллете́нь; (*vote*) баллотиро́вка; **put a question to the ~, take a ~** ста́вить, по- вопро́с на голосова́ние; (*number of votes*) коли́чество по́данных голосо́в.

● *v.i.* (**balloted, balloting**) (*vote*) голосова́ть (*impf.*).

● *v.t.* (**balloted, balloting**) пров|оди́ть, -ести́ голосова́ние ме́жду + *i.*

● *cpds.* **~-box** *n.* избира́тельная у́рна; **~ paper** *n.* (*Br.*) избира́тельный бюллете́нь.

ballyhoo /ˌbælɪˈhuː/ *n.* (*coll.*) шуми́ха.

balm /bɑːm/ *n.* (*exudation, fragrance; also fig.*) бальза́м; (*ointment*) бальза́м, болеутоля́ющее сре́дство.

balmy /ˈbɑːmɪ/ *adj.* (**balmier, balmiest**) **1** (*fragrant*) арома́тный. **2** (*soft*) мя́гкий; (*of wind*) не́жный.

baloney /bəˈləʊnɪ/ *n.* (*sl.*) ерунда́.

balsa /ˈbɒlsə/, /ˈbɔːl-/ *n.* (*also* **~ wood**) ба́льза, ба́льзовое де́рево.

balsam /ˈbɒlsəm/, /ˈbɔːl-/ *n.* бальза́м.

Baltic /ˈbɔːltɪk/, /ˈbɒl-/ *n.*: **the ~** Балти́йское мо́ре.

● *adj.* балти́йский; прибалти́йский; **~ states** прибалти́йские госуда́рства, Приба́лтика.

baluster /ˈbæləstə(r)/ *n.* баля́сина.

balustrade /ˌbæləˈstreɪd/ *n.* балюстра́да.

bamboo /bæmˈbuː/ *n.* бамбу́к; (*attr.*) бамбу́ковый.

bamboozle /bæmˈbuːz(ə)l/ *v.t.* (*coll.*) околпа́чи|вать, -ть; одура́чи|вать, -ть; над|ува́ть, -у́ть.

ban /bæn/ *n.* (*prohibition*) запреще́ние, запре́т.

● *v.t.* (**banned, banning**) запре|ща́ть, -ти́ть.

banal /bəˈnɑːl/ *adj.* бана́льный.

banality /bəˈnælɪtɪ/ *n.* бана́льность; (*remark*) бана́льное замеча́ние.

banana /bəˈnɑːnə/ *n.* бана́н; (*pl. coll.: mad*) **he's ~s** у него́ кры́ша пое́хала; **to go ~s** чо́кнуться (*pf.*), сдви́нуться (*pf.*); **to drive ~s** дов|оди́ть, -ести́ до сумасше́ствия.

band[1] /bænd/ *n.* **1** (*braid*) тесьма́; (*for decoration*) ле́нта; (*on barrel*) о́бруч, обо́д; **rubber ~** рези́нка. **2** (*strip*) полоса́; **a plate with a blue ~ round it** таре́лка с голубы́м ободко́м. **3** (*radio*): **frequency ~** полоса́ часто́т.

● *cpds.* **~box** *n.* карто́нка для шляп; **~-saw** *n.* ле́нточная пила́.

band[2] /bænd/ *n.* (*company*) гру́ппа; (*detachment*) отря́д; (*gang*) ба́нда, ша́йка; (*mus.*) орке́стр; **jazz ~** джаз-ба́нд, джаз-орке́стр.

● *v.t. & i.* **~ together** объедин|я́ться, -и́ться.

● *cpds.* **~master** *n.* капельме́йстер; **~sman** *n.* оркестра́нт; **~stand** *n.* эстра́да для орке́стра.

bandage /ˈbændɪdʒ/ *n.* бинт; (*blindfold*) повя́зка.

● *v.t.* бинтова́ть, за-; перевя́з|ывать, -а́ть.

Band-Aid /ˈbændeɪd/ *n.* (*US, propr.*) пла́стырь (*m.*).

bandan(n)a /bænˈdænə/ *n.* цветно́й плато́к.

bandeau /ˈbændəʊ/, /-ˈdəʊ/ *n.* (*pl.* **~x** /-dəʊz/) (*hair-ribbon*) ле́нта для воло́с.

banderole /ˌbændəˈrəʊl/ *n.* вы́мпел.

bandit /ˈbændɪt/ *n.* разбо́йник, банди́т.

banditry /ˈbændɪtrɪ/ *n.* бандити́зм.

bandol|eer, -ier /ˌbændəˈlɪə(r)/ *n.* нагру́дный патронта́ш.

bandy[1] /ˈbændɪ/ *adj.* (**bandier, bandiest**) криво́й.

● *cpd.* **~-legged** *adj.* кривоно́гий.

band|y[2] /ˈbændɪ/ *v.t.*: **have one's name ~ied about** быть предме́том то́лков; **~y words** перебра́сываться (*impf.*) слова́ми.

bane /beɪn/ *n.* прокля́тие; **it is the ~ of my life** э́то отравля́ет мне жизнь.

baneful /ˈbeɪnfʊl/ *adj.* па́губный, губи́тельный.

bang /bæŋ/ *n.* **1** (*blow*) уда́р. **2** (*crash*) гро́хот; стук. **3** (*sound of a gun*) вы́стрел; (*of explosion*) взрыв. **4** (*coll.*): **go with a ~** (*succeed*) про|ходи́ть, -йти́ блестя́ще.

● *v.t.* (*strike, thump*) уд|ара́ть, -а́рить; (*at the door etc.*) ст|уча́ть, -у́кнуть + *a.*; **~ a drum** уда́рить (*pf.*) в бараба́н; **~ one's fist on the table** сту́кнуть (*pf.*) кулако́м по столу́; **~ the door** хло́пнуть (*pf.*) две́рью; **~ the lid down** захло́пнуть (*pf.*) кры́шку; **~ the box down on the floor** гро́хнуть (*pf.*) я́щик на́ пол.

● *v.i.* (*of door, window etc.; also* **~ to**) захло́пнуться (*pf.*); **the door is ~ing** дверь хло́пает; (*of person*): **~ at the door** стуча́ть/колоти́ть (*impf.*) в дверь.

● *adv.* **1**: **go ~** (*of gun*) ба́хнуть (*pf.*); **~ went £100** раз! — и ста фу́нтов как не быва́ло. **2** (*suddenly*) вдруг; (*Br., just, exactly*) пря́мо; как раз; **~ on** (*Br. coll.*) как раз, в аккура́т.

● *int.* бац!; бах!

banger /ˈbæŋə(r)/ *n.* (*Br., coll.*) (*sausage*) соси́ска; (*car*) драндуле́т.

Bangkok /bæŋˈkɒk/ *n.* Бангко́к.

Bangladesh /ˌbæŋgləˈdeʃ/, /ˌbʌŋg-/ *n.* Бангладе́ш.

Bangladeshi /ˌbæŋgləˈdeʃɪ/, /ˌbʌŋg-/ *n.* (*pl.* **~** *or* **~s**) бангладе́ш|ец (*fem.* -ка).

● *adj.* бангладе́шский.

bangle /ˈbæŋg(ə)l/ *n.* брасле́т.

bangs /bæŋz/ *n. pl.* (*US*) чёлка.

banish /ˈbænɪʃ/ *v.t.* (*exile*) высыла́ть, вы́слать; (*dismiss*) прог|оня́ть, -на́ть; изг|оня́ть, -на́ть; (*from one's mind*) от|гоня́ть, -огна́ть.

banishment /ˈbænɪʃmənt/ *n.* вы́сылка, ссы́лка; изгна́ние.

banisters /ˈbænɪstəz/ *n.* пери́л|а (*pl., g.* —).

banjo /ˈbændʒəʊ/ *n.* (*pl.* **~s** *or* **~es**) ба́нджо (*indecl.*).

banjoist /ˈbændʒəʊɪst/ *n.* игро́к на ба́нджо.

bank[1] /bæŋk/ *n.* **1** (*of river*) бе́рег. **2** (*under-water shelf*) ба́нка. **3**: **~ of clouds** гряда́ облако́в; **~ of fog** полоса́ тума́на; (*of snow*) зано́с, сугро́б; **~s of earth** земляны́е валы́. **4** (*embankment*) на́сыпь.

● *v.t.* **1**: **~ (up) a fire** подде́рж|ивать, -а́ть ого́нь. **2** (*aeron.*) крени́ть, на-.

● *v.i.* **1** (*also* **~ up**, *of snow etc.*) образо́в|ывать, -а́ть зано́сы. **2** (*aeron.*) накрен|я́ться, -и́ться.

bank[2] /bæŋk/ *n.* (*tier of oars*) ряд вёсел; (*row of keys*) ряд клавиату́ры

bank[3] /bæŋk/ *n.* **1** (*fin.*) банк; **~ account** ба́нковский счёт; **B~ of England** Англи́йский банк; **~ rate** учётная ста́вка; **clearing ~** кли́ринговый банк; **savings ~** сберега́тельная ка́сса, сберка́сса. **2** (*at cards etc.*) банк; **break the ~** сорва́ть (*pf.*) банк. **3**: **blood ~** до́норский пункт. **4** (*attr.*) ба́нковый, ба́нковский; **~ book** ба́нковская кни́жка; **~ card** ба́нковская креди́тная ка́рта; **~ clerk** ба́нковский слу́жащий; **~ holiday** ≈ пра́здничный день; **~ loan** ба́нковская ссу́да; **~ manager** управля́ющий ба́нком.

● *v.t.* (*put into ~*) класть, положи́ть в банк.

● *v.i.* (*keep money in ~*) держа́ть (*impf.*) де́ньги в ба́нке; (*at cards*) мета́ть (*impf.*) банк; **~ on** (*fig., rely on*) пол|ага́ться, -ожи́ться на + *a.*; де́лать, с- ста́вку на + *a.*

● *cpd.* **~-note** *n.* банкно́т.

banker /ˈbæŋkə(r)/ *n.* банки́р; (*at cards*) банкомёт.

banking /ˈbæŋkɪŋ/ *n.* (*aeron.*) крен; (*fin.*) ба́нковое де́ло.

bankroll /ˈbæŋkrəʊl/ *n.* (*US*) де́нежные сре́дства.

● *v.t.* финанси́ровать (*impf., pf.*).

bankrupt /ˈbæŋkrʌpt/ *n.* банкро́т, несостоя́тельный должни́к.

● *adj.* (*also fig.*) обанкро́тившийся; несостоя́тельный; **go ~** обанкро́титься (*pf.*).

● *v.t.* де́лать, с- несостоя́тельным; дов|оди́ть, -ести́ до банкро́тства.

bankruptcy /ˈbæŋkˌrʌptsɪ/ *n.* банкро́тство, несостоя́тельность; **file a declaration of ~** официа́льно объяв|ля́ть, -и́ть себя́ несостоя́тельным; **B~ Court** суд по дела́м несостоя́тельных должнико́в.

banner /ˈbænə(r)/ *n.* (*lit., fig.*) зна́мя (*nt. pl.*); (*flag*) флаг; (*poet.*) стяг; (*with slogan*) плака́т; **~ headlines** кру́пные заголо́вки.

banns /bænz/ *n.* оглаше́ние (предстоя́щего бра́ка); **ask, call, read the ~** огла|ша́ть, -си́ть имена́ жениха́ и неве́сты.

banquet /ˈbæŋkwɪt/ *n.* пир; (*formal*) банке́т.

● *v.i.* (**banqueted, banqueting**) пирова́ть (*impf.*).

banquette /bæŋ'ket/ *n.* (*seat*) банке́тка.

bantam /'bæntəm/ *n.* (*fowl*) бента́мка.

● *cpd.* **~-weight** *n.* боксёр легча́йшего ве́са.

banter /'bæntə(r)/ *n.* подшу́чивание, подтру́нивание.

● *v.i.* шути́ть, по-.

banyan /'bænɪən/, /-jən/ *n.* (*bot.*) баньян.

baobab /'beɪəʊˌbæb/ *n.* баоба́б.

baptism /'bæptɪz(ə)m/ *n.* креще́ние; **~ of fire** боево́е креще́ние.

baptismal /bæp'tɪzm(ə)l/ *adj.* крести́льный; **~ name** и́мя при креще́нии.

Baptist /'bæptɪst/ *n.* **1**: **St John the B~** Иоа́нн Крести́тель (*m.*). **2** (*member of sect*) бапти́ст (*fem.* -ка).

baptist(e)ry /'bæptɪstərɪ/ *n.* (*eccl.*) баптисте́рий.

baptize /bæp'taɪz/ *v.t.* крести́ть, о́-; нар|ека́ть, -е́чь; **he was ~d Peter** он был наречён Петро́м.

bar[1] /bɑ:(r)/ *n.* **1** (*strip, flat piece*) полоса́; (*ingot*) сли́ток; (*lever*) ва́га; **parallel ~s** паралле́льные бру́сья (*m. pl.*); **horizontal ~** перекла́дина; (*rod, pole*) шта́нга; (*of chocolate*) пли́тка; (*of soap*) кусо́к. **2** (*bolt*) затво́р, засо́в. **3** (*obstacle*) прегра́да; препя́тствие; **colour** (*Br.*), **color** (*US*) **~** цветно́й барье́р; **~ to marriage** препя́тствие к вступле́нию в брак. **4** (*usu. pl.*) решётка; **behind ~s** за решёткой. **5** (*naut.*) бар, о́тмель. **6** (*mus.*) такт.

● *v.t.* (**barred, barring**) (*bolt, lock*) зап|ира́ть, -ере́ть на засо́в; (*obstruct*) прегра|жда́ть, -ди́ть; (*close*) закр|ыва́ть, -ы́ть; загор|а́живать, -оди́ть; (*exclude*) исключ|а́ть, -и́ть; (*prohibit*) запре|ща́ть, -ти́ть; **~ o.s. in** зап|ира́ться, -ере́ться; **~ s.o. out** не впус|ка́ть, -ти́ть кого́-н.; **soldiers ~red the way** солда́ты загороди́ли доро́гу.

● *cpd.* **~-code** *n.* штрих-ко́д.

bar[2] /bɑ:(r)/ *n.* (*legal profession*) адвокату́ра; **read for the ~** гото́виться (*impf.*) к адвокату́ре; **he was called to the ~** (*Br.*) он получи́л пра́во адвока́тской пра́ктики; **be at the ~** быть адвока́том; **prisoner at the ~** обвиня́емый (на скамье́ подсуди́мых).

bar[3] /bɑ:(r)/ *n.* (*room*) бар, буфе́т; (*counter*) прила́вок; **snack ~** заку́сочная.

● *cpds.* **~fly** *n.* выпиво́ха (*c.g., coll.*); **~maid** *n.* буфе́тчица, официа́нтка в пивно́й, ба́рменша; **~man, ~-tender** *nn.* буфе́тчик, ба́рмен.

bar[4] /bɑ:(r)/ *n.* (*unit of pressure*) бар.

bar[5] /bɑ:(r)/ *prep.* (*Br. coll., excluding*) исключа́я, не счита́я; **~ none** без исключе́ния; **it's all over ~ the shouting** (*fig.*) ко́нчен бал.

barb /bɑ:b/ *n.* **1** (*fish's feeler*) у́сик. **2** (*sting, spike*) колю́чка. **3** (*of arrow, fish-hook etc.*) зубе́ц. **4** (*cutting remark*) ко́лкость.

Barbados /bɑ:'beɪdɒs/ *n.* Барба́дос.

barbarian /bɑ:'beərɪən/ *n.* ва́рвар.

● *adj.* ва́рварский.

barbaric /bɑ:'bærɪk/ *adj.* ва́рварский.

barbarism /'bɑ:bəˌrɪz(ə)m/ *n.* ва́рварство; (*ling.*) варвари́зм.

barbarity /bɑ:'bærɪtɪ/ *n.* ва́рварство.

barbarous /'bɑ:bərəs/ *adj.* ва́рварский; (*cruel*) бесчелове́чный.

Barbary ape /'bɑ:bərɪ/ *n.* (*zool.*) маго́т.

barbecue /'bɑ:bɪˌkju:/ *n.* (*party*) пи́кник, где подаю́т мя́со, зажа́ренное на ве́ртеле, жаро́вне.

● *v.t.* (**barbecues, barbecued, barbecuing**) жа́рить, за- на ве́ртеле, жаро́вне.

barbed /bɑ:bd/ *adj.* **1** колю́чий; име́ющий колю́чки/шипы́; **~ wire** колю́чая про́волока. **2**: **a ~ remark** ко́лкое замеча́ние.

barber /'bɑ:bə(r)/ *n.* парикма́хер; **~'s shop** парикма́херская.

barberry /'bɑ:bərɪ/ *n.* барбари́с.

barbiturate /bɑ:'bɪtjʊrət/, /-ˌreɪt/ *n.* барбитура́т.

barcarol(l)e /'bɑ:kəˌrəʊl/ *n.* (*mus.*) баркаро́ла.

bard /bɑ:d/ *n.* бард.

bardic /'bɑ:dɪk/ *adj.*: **~ poetry** поэ́зия ба́рдов.

bare /beə(r)/ *adj.* **1** (*naked, not covered*) го́лый, наго́й; обнажённый; **with one's ~ hands** го́лыми рука́ми; **~ feet** босы́е но́ги; **~ shoulders** обнажённые пле́чи; **with ~ head** с непокры́той голово́й; **~ trees** го́лые дере́вья; **lay ~** (*fig.*) вскры|ва́ть, -ть; раскр|ыва́ть, -ы́ть.
2 (*threadbare*) поно́шенный.
3 (*empty*) пусто́й; **the room was ~ of furniture** в ко́мнате не́ было ме́бели.
4 (*unadorned*) просто́й, неприкра́шенный.
5 (*slight, mere*) мале́йший; **a ~ majority** о́чень незначи́тельное большинство́; **~ necessities of life** насу́щные потре́бности жи́зни; **they made a ~ £100** они́ едва́ набра́ли сто фу́нтов; **at the ~ mention of** при одно́м упомина́нии о + *p.*
6 (*elec.*) го́лый, неизоли́рованный.

● *v.t.* обнаж|а́ть, -и́ть; огол|я́ть, -и́ть; **~ one's head** обнаж|а́ть, -и́ть го́лову; **~ one's teeth** ска́лить, о- зу́бы; **~ one's heart** изли́ть (*pf.*) ду́шу.

● *cpds.* **~back** *adv.* без седла́; **~faced** *adj.* (*fig.*) на́глый, бессты́дный; **~foot** *adj.* босо́й; *adv.* босико́м; **~footed** *adj.* босо́й, босоно́гий; **~headed** *adj.* простоволо́сый, с непокры́той голово́й; **~legged** *adj.* с го́лыми нога́ми.

barely /'beəlɪ/ *adv.* (*simply*) то́лько, про́сто; (*scarcely*) едва́; **I have ~ enough money** мне едва́ хва́тит де́нег.

bareness /beə(r)nɪs/ *n.* (*lack of covering*) нагота́, неприкры́тость; (*unadorned state*) простота́, неприкра́шенность; (*poorness*) бе́дность, ску́дость.

Barents Sea /'bærənts/ *n.* Ба́ренцево мо́ре.

bargain /'bɑ:gɪn/ *n.* **1** (*deal*) сде́лка, соглаше́ние; **good/bad ~** вы́годная/невы́годная сде́лка; **make, strike, drive a ~** заключ|а́ть, -и́ть сде́лку; **he drives a hard ~** он неусту́пчив; **it's a ~!** по рука́м!; **into the ~** в прида́чу. **2** (*thing cheaply acquired*) вы́годная поку́пка; **~ sale** (дешёвая) распрода́жа; **~ price** распрода́жная цена́.

● *v.t.*: **~ away** променя́ть (*pf.*) (*что на что*).

● *v.i.* торгова́ться, с-; (*agree*) догов|а́риваться, -ори́ться; **~ for** (*expect*) ожида́ть (*impf.*); **it was more than I ~ed for** на э́то я не рассчи́тывал.

● *cpd.* **~-hunter** *n.* охо́тник за дешеви́зной.

bargainer /'bɑ:gɪnə(r)/ *n.*: **he is a hard ~** он упо́рно торгу́ется.

bargaining /'bɑ:gɪnɪŋ/ *n.*: **pay ~** перегово́ры о зарпла́те.

barge /bɑ:dʒ/ *n.* ба́ржа.

● *v.i.* (*coll.*): **~ about** носи́ться (*impf.*), мета́ться (*impf.*); **~ into, against** налет|а́ть, -е́ть на + *a.*; наск|а́кивать, -очи́ть на + *a.*; **~ in** (*intrude*) ввал|иваться, -и́ться.

● *cpd.* **~-pole** *n.* ба́ржевый баго́р; **I wouldn't touch it with a ~-pole** (*Br. coll.*) я не подойду́ к э́тому и на вы́стрел.

bargee /bɑ:'dʒi:/ *n.* (*Br.*) ба́рочник.

baritone /'bærɪˌtəʊn/ *n.* (*voice, singer*) барито́н.

● *adj.* баритона́льный.

barium /'beərɪəm/ *n.* ба́рий.

bark[1] /bɑ:k/ *n.* (*of tree etc.*) кора́.

● *v.t.* (*strip of ~*) окор|я́ть, -и́ть; сдира́ть, содра́ть кору́ + *g.*; **~ one's shins** об|дира́ть, -одра́ть себе́ но́ги.

bark[2], **barque** /bɑ:k/ *nn.* (*vessel*) барк.

bark[3] /bɑ:k/ *n.* (*of dog*) лай; **his ~ is worse than his bite** ≈ он гро́зен лишь на слова́х.

● *v.t.*: **~ out** (*e.g. an order*) ря́вк|ать, -нуть.

● *v.t.* (*of dog etc.*) ла́ять (*impf.*) (**at**: на + *a.*); **~ up the wrong tree** (*fig.*) обра|ща́ться, -ти́ться не по а́дресу.

barley /'bɑ:lɪ/ *n.* ячме́нь (*m.*); **pearl ~** перло́вая крупа́.

● *cpds.* **~-mow** *n.* (*Br.*) скирда́ ячменя́; **~-sugar** *n.* леденцы́ (*m. pl.*); **~-water** *n.* ячме́нный отва́р.

bar mitzvah /bɑ: 'mɪtzvə/ *n.* бар-ми́цва.

barmy /'bɑ:mɪ/ *adj.* (**barmier, barmiest**) (*Br. coll., silly*) чо́кнутый, тро́нутый; **go ~** тро́нуться (*pf.*); спя́тить (*pf.*) (с ума́).

barn /bɑ:n/ *n.* амба́р, сара́й; (*threshing-floor*) гумно́; (*fig., comfortless building*) сара́й.

● *cpds.* **~-owl** *n.* сипу́ха; **~stormer** *n.* (*coll.*) бродя́чий актёр.

barnacle /'bɑ:nək(ə)l/ *n.* **1** (*on ship's bottom*) морска́я у́точка. **2**: **~ goose** белощёкая каза́рка.

barney /ˈbɑːnɪ/ *n.* (*pl.* **~s**) (*Br. sl.*) перебра́нка.

barometer /bəˈrɒmɪtə(r)/ *n.* баро́метр.

barometric /ˌbærəʊˈmetrɪk/ *adj.* барометри́ческий.

baron /ˈbærən/ *n.* баро́н; (*industrial leader*) магна́т.

baroness /ˈbærənɪs/ *n.* барон́есса.

baronet /ˈbærənɪt/ *n.* бароне́т.

baronial /bəˈrəʊnɪəl/ *adj.* баро́нский; (*fig.*) ба́рский.

barony /ˈbærənɪ/ *n.* (*title*) баро́нство; (*domain*) владе́ния (*nt. pl.*) баро́на.

baroque /bəˈrɒk/ *n.* баро́кко (*indecl.*).

● *adj.* баро́чный.

barque /bɑːk/ = **bark²**

barrack¹ /ˈbærək/ *n.* (*usu. pl.*) каза́рма; **confinement to ~s** каза́рменный аре́ст.

● *v.t.* (*lodge in ~s*) разме|ща́ть, -сти́ть в каза́рмах.

● *cpd.* **~-square** *n.* (*Br.*) каза́рменный плац.

barrack² /ˈbærək/ *v.i.* (*Br. coll.*) (*jeer at*) гро́мко высме́ивать (*impf.*); **~ for** подба́дривать (*impf.*) кри́ками.

barracuda /ˌbærəˈkuːdə/ *n.* (*zool.*) (*pl.* **~** *or* **~s**) барраку́да.

barrage /ˈbærɑːʒ/ *n.* **1** (*Br.*) (*in watercourse*) запру́да; (*dam*) плоти́на. **2** (*mil.*) загражде́ние; (*gunfire*) огнево́й вал; (*fig.*): **a ~ of questions** град/шквал вопро́сов.

barrel /ˈbær(ə)l/ *n.* **1** бо́чка. **2** (*of firearm*) ствол, (*muzzle*) ду́ло; (*of fountain pen*) резервуа́р. **3** (*measure*) ба́ррель (*m.*).

● *cpd.* **~-organ** *n.* шарма́нка.

barren /ˈbærən/ *adj.* (**barrener, barrenest**) (*of woman*) беспло́дная; (*of plants, trees etc.*) беспло́дный, неплодоно́сный; **~ land** то́щая/неплодоро́дная/беспло́дная земля́; (*fig.*) беспло́дный.

barrenness /ˈbærənnɪs/ *n.* (*of woman*) беспло́дие; (*of trees, plants*) неплодоно́сность; (*of land*) беспло́дность; неплодоро́дность; (*fig.*) беспло́дность.

barricade /ˌbærɪˈkeɪd/ *n.* баррика́да.

● *v.t.* баррикади́ровать, за-; **~ o.s. in** забаррикади́роваться (*pf.*).

barrier /ˈbærɪə(r)/ *n.* барье́р; **Great B~ Reef** Большо́й Барье́рный риф; **language ~** языково́й барье́р; **sound ~** звуково́й барье́р; (*dividing-line*) прегра́да; (*obstacle*) поме́ха, прегра́да.

barring /ˈbɑːrɪŋ/ *prep.* за исключе́нием + *g.*

barrister /ˈbærɪstə(r)/ *n.* (*Br.*) адвока́т.

barrow¹ /ˈbærəʊ/ *n.* (*archaeol.*) курга́н, моги́льный холм.

barrow² /ˈbærəʊ/ *n.* (*Br., hand-~*) ручна́я теле́жка; (*wheel~*) та́чка.

● *cpd.* **~-boy** (*Br.*) *n.* лото́чник.

barter /ˈbɑːtə(r)/ *n.* ме́на, менова́я торго́вля, ба́ртер.

● *v.t.* обме́н|ивать, -я́ть (*что на что*).

● *v.i.* обме́н|иваться, -я́ться + *i.*; меня́ться (*impf.*) + *i.*

barterer /ˈbɑːtərə(r)/ *n.* производя́щий товарообме́н.

basal /ˈbeɪs(ə)l/ *adj.* основно́й, лежа́щий в осно́ве.

basalt /ˈbæsɔːlt/ *n.* база́льт; (*attr.*) база́льтовый.

bascule /ˈbæskjuːl/ *n.*: **~ bridge** подъёмный мост.

base¹ /beɪs/ *n.* **1** (*of wall, column etc.*) фунда́мент, пьедеста́л, основа́ние, ба́зис. **2** (*fig., basis; also math.*) основа́ние. **3** (*chem.*) основа́ние. **4** (*gram.*) осно́ва. **5** (*mil. etc.*) ба́за; **~ camp** ба́за; **~ hospital** ба́зовый го́спиталь; **~ of operations** операцио́нная ба́за, плацда́рм; **supply ~** ба́за снабже́ния. **6**: **get to first ~** (*fig.*) доби́ться (*pf.*) пе́рвого успе́ха.

● *v.t.* осно́в|ывать, -а́ть; **~ one's hopes on** возл|ага́ть, -ожи́ть наде́жды на + *a.*; **the legend is ~d on fact** в осно́ве э́той леге́нды лежа́т действи́тельные собы́тия.

● *cpds.* **~ball** *n.* бейсбо́л; **~line** *n.* (*sport*) ли́ния пода́чи.

base² /beɪs/ *adj.* ни́зкий, ни́зменный, по́длый; **~ metal** неблагоро́дный мета́лл.

baseless /ˈbeɪslɪs/ *adj.* необосно́ванный.

basement /ˈbeɪsmənt/ *n.* подва́л; (*attr.*) подва́льный.

baseness /ˈbeɪsnɪs/ *n.* ни́зость, ни́зменность.

bases /ˈbeɪsiːz/ *pl. of* ⇒**basis**

bash /bæʃ/ (*coll.*) *n.* (*Br., attempt*) попы́тка; **have a ~** попыта́ться, попро́бовать; (*party*) гуля́нка, выпиво́н; (*bang*): **give s.o. a ~ on the head** тра́хнуть (*pf.*) кому́-н. башку́ (*coll.*).

● *v.t.* тра́хнуть (*pf.*); **~ s.o.'s head against a wall** тра́хнуть (*pf.*) кого́-н. башко́й об сте́ну (*coll.*); **~ s.o.'s head in** прошиби́ть (*pf.*) кому́-н. башку́ (*coll.*).

bashful /ˈbæʃfʊl/ *adj.* засте́нчивый.

bashfulness /ˈbæʃfʊlnɪs/ *n.* засте́нчивость.

-bashing¹ /ˈbæʃɪŋ/ *comb. form n.* **gay-~** избие́ние гомосексуали́стов; **union-~** ущемле́ние профсою́зов.

● *adj.* анти…; **union-~ legislation** антипрофсою́зные зако́ны.

bashing² /ˈbæʃɪŋ/ *n.* (*thrashing*) взбу́чка, лупцо́вка (*coll.*).

Bashkir /bæʃˈkɪə(r)/ *n.* башки́р (*fem.* -ка).

● *adj.* башки́рский.

BASIC¹ /ˈbeɪsɪk/ *n.* (*comput.*) Бе́йсик.

basic² /ˈbeɪsɪk/ *adj.* основно́й.

basically /ˈbeɪsɪkəlɪ/ *adv.* в основно́м.

basil /ˈbæz(ə)l/ *n.* бази́лик.

basilica /bəˈzɪlɪkə/ *n.* бази́лика.

basilisk /ˈbæzɪlɪsk/ *n.* васили́ск.

basin /ˈbeɪs(ə)n/ *n.* **1** (*for food*) ми́ска; (*washbasin*) умыва́льник, ра́ковина. **2** (*of dock, river*) бассе́йн; **tidal ~** прили́вный бассе́йн. **3** (*bay*) бу́хта.

basis /ˈbeɪsɪs/ *n.* (*pl.* **bases**) осно́ва, ба́зис; **~ of negotiations** осно́ва для перегово́ров; **on the ~ of** на осно́ве + *g.*; **on this ~** на э́том основа́нии; **lay the ~ for** заложи́ть (*pf.*) осно́ву + *g.*

bask /bɑːsk/ *v.i.* гре́ться (*impf.*) (**in the sun**: на со́лнце); (*fig.*): **~ in glory** купа́ться (*impf.*) в луча́х сла́вы.

basket /ˈbɑːskɪt/ *n.* корзи́на, корзи́нка; **clothes, laundry ~** корзи́на для гря́зного белья́; **shopping ~** корзи́на/корзи́нка для поку́пок.

● *cpds.* **~-ball** *n.* баскетбо́л; **~-work** *n.* = **basketry**

basket|ry /ˈbɑːskɪtrɪ/, **-work** /ˈbɑːskɪtˌwɜːk/ *nn.* плете́ние; (*product*) плетёные изде́лия (*nt. pl.*).

Basle /bɑːl/ *n.* Ба́зель (*m.*).

Basque /bɑːsk/ *n.* баск (*fem.* баско́нка).

● *adj.* ба́скский.

bas-relief /ˌbɑː rɪˈliːf/ *n.* барелье́ф.

bass¹ /bæs/ *n.* (*pl.* **~** *or* **~es**) (*zool.*) ка́менный о́кунь.

bass² /beɪs/ *n.* (*mus.*) бас.

● *adj.* басо́вый; **he has a ~ voice** у него́ бас; **~ drum** туре́цкий бараба́н; **~-guitar** бас-гита́ра; **~-guitarist** бас-гитари́ст.

basset /ˈbæsɪt/ *n.* (*also* **~-hound**) ба́с(с)ет (*порода собак*).

bassist /ˈbeɪsɪst/ *n.* (*double bass player*) контрабаси́ст; (*bass-guitarist*) бас-гитари́ст.

bassoon /bəˈsuːn/ *n.* фаго́т.

bassoonist /bəˈsuːnɪst/ *n.* фаготи́ст.

basswood /ˈbæswʊd/ *n.* (*bot.*) ли́па америка́нская.

bast /bæst/ *n.* луб, лы́ко; (*attr.*) лубяно́й, лы́ковый; **~ mat** рого́жа; **~ shoe** ла́поть (*m.*).

bastard /ˈbɑːstəd/, /ˈbæ-/ *n.* **1** (*child*) внебра́чный ребёнок. **2** (*as term of abuse etc.*) мерза́вец; **poor ~** несча́стный ублю́док; **lucky ~** везу́чий дья́вол. **3** (*attr.*): **~ French** испо́рченный францу́зский язы́к.

bastardize /ˈbɑːstəˌdaɪz/ *v.t.* (*debase*) по́ртить, ис-; иска|жа́ть, -зи́ть.

bastardy /ˈbɑːstədɪ/ *n.* незаконнорождённость.

baste¹ /beɪst/ *v.t.* (*stitch*) смёт|ывать, -а́ть; сши|ва́ть, -ть на живу́ю ни́тку.

baste² /beɪst/ *v.t.* (*cul.*) пол|ива́ть, -и́ть (*жаркое*).

bastion /ˈbæstɪən/ *n.* бастио́н.

bat¹ /bæt/ *n.* (*zool.*) лету́чая мышь; **blind as a ~** соверше́нно слепо́й; **like a ~ out of hell** о́чень бы́стро, внеза́пно.

bat² /bæt/ *n.* (*at games*) бита́, лапта́; (*fig.*): **off one's own ~** (*Br.*) по со́бственному почи́ну; самостоя́тельно; **right off the ~** (*US*) с ме́ста в карье́р.

● *v.t.* (**batted, batting**) бить (*impf.*) (*or* уд|аря́ть, -а́рить) бито́й/лапто́й.

bat³ /bæt/ *v.t.* (**batted, batting**): **he did not ~ an eyelid** (*paid no attention*) он и гла́зом не моргну́л.

bat⁴ /bæt/ (*coll.*) *v.i.* (**batted, batting**): **~ along** нести́сь (*impf.*), мча́ться (*impf.*).

batch /bætʃ/ *n.* **1** (*of bread*) вы́печка.

2 (*of pottery etc.*) па́ртия.
3 (*consignment, collection*) ку́чка, па́чка; гру́ппа; **~ of letters** па́чка пи́сем; **~ processing** (*comput.*) паке́тная обрабо́тка.

bated /ˈbeɪtɪd/: **with ~ breath** затаи́в дыха́ние.

bath /bɑːθ/ *n.* ва́нна; (*steam* **~**) ба́ня; **take, have a ~** прин|има́ть, -я́ть ва́нну; купа́ться, вы́-/ис-; **run me a ~!** напусти́те мне ва́нну!; **swimming ~(s)** пла́вательный бассе́йн; **~chair** инвали́дное кре́сло.
● *v.t. & i.* купа́ть(ся), вы́/ис-.
● *cpds.* **~-attendant** *n.* ба́нщик; **~-house** *n.* купа́льня, ба́ня; **~-mat** *n.* ко́врик для ва́нной; **~robe** *n.* купа́льный хала́т; **~room** *n.* ва́нная (ко́мната); **~-salts** *n.* аромати́ческие со́ли для ва́нны; **~-towel** *n.* купа́льное полоте́нце; **~-tub** *n.* ва́нна.

bathe /beɪð/ *n.* купа́ние; **go for a ~** искупа́ться (*pf.*).
● *v.t.* **1** (*one's face etc.*) мыть, по-; обм|ыва́ть, -ы́ть; **~ one's eyes, a wound** пром|ыва́ть, -ы́ть глаза́/ра́ну. **2**: **he was ~d in sweat** он облива́лся по́том; **a face ~d in tears** лицо́, за́литое слеза́ми. **3** (*of light, warmth*) зал|ива́ть, -и́ть.
● *v.i.* купа́ться, вы́-/ис-.

bather /ˈbeɪðə(r)/ *n.* купа́льщи|к (*fem.* -ца).

bathing /ˈbeɪðɪŋ/ *n.* купа́ние.
● *cpds.* **~-cabin** *n.* каби́на для переодева́ния; **~-cap** *n.* купа́льная ша́почка; **~-costume** (*Br.*) **~-suit** (*US*) *nn.* купа́льный костю́м, купа́льник; **~-trunks** *n. pl.* пла́в|ки (*pl., g.* -ок).

bathos /ˈbeɪθɒs/ *n.* перехо́д от высо́кого к коми́ческому.

batik /bəˈtiːk/, /ˈbætɪk/ *n.* бати́к; (*attr.*) бати́ковый.

batiste /bæˈtiːst/ *n.* бати́ст; (*attr.*) бати́стовый.

batman /ˈbætmən/ *n.* денщи́к, ордина́рец.

baton /ˈbæt(ə)n/ *n.* **1** (*staff of office*) жезл. **2** (*mus.*) дирижёрская па́лочка. **3** (*sport*) эстафе́тная па́лочка. **4** (*Br., policeman's*) дуби́нка.

batsman /ˈbætsmən/ *n.* игро́к с бито́й; отбива́ющий мяч.

battalion /bəˈtæljən/ *n.* батальо́н; **labour ~** строи́тельный батальо́н.

batten /ˈbæt(ə)n/ *n.* ре́йка, пла́нка.
● *v.t.*: **~ down** (*naut.*) задра́и|вать, -ть.

batter¹ /ˈbætə(r)/ *n.* (*cul.*) взби́тое те́сто.

batter² /ˈbætə(r)/ *n.* (*US*) = **batsman**

batter³ /ˈbætə(r)/ *v.t. & i.* **1** (*beat*) колоти́ть, по-; дуба́сить, от-; громи́ть, раз-; **~ a wall down** разру́шить (*pf.*) сте́ну; **hostel for ~ed wives** убе́жище для же́нщин страда́ющих от физи́ческого наси́лия в семье́; **~ing-ram** тара́н. **2** (*knock about*): **a ~ed old car/hat** потрёпанная ста́рая маши́на/шля́па.

battery /ˈbætərɪ/ *n.* **1** (*beating*): **assault and ~** (*leg.*) побо́|и (*pl., g.* -ев); оскорбле́ние де́йствием. **2** (*group of guns*) батаре́я; (*artillery unit*) дивизио́н. **3** (*elec.*) (*in car*) батаре́я; (*in torch*) батаре́йка. **4**: **~ farming** (*Br.*) выра́щивание живо́тных в инкуба́торах; **~ hens** (*Br.*) инкуба́торные ку́ры.
● *cpds.* **~-farmed** *adj.* выращенный в инкуба́торе; **~-operated** *adj.* на батаре́ях; с батаре́йным пита́нием.

batting /ˈbætɪŋ/ *n.* (*cotton fibre*) вати́н.

battle /ˈbæt(ə)l/ *n.* би́тва, сраже́ние, бой; (*struggle*) борьба́; **drawn ~** безрезульта́тный бой; **pitched ~** сраже́ние; **~ royal** побо́ище; **join ~** вступи́ть (*pf.*) в бой; **give ~** дать (*pf.*) бой; **do ~** сража́ться (*impf.*); **order of ~** боево́й поря́док; **~ of Britain** би́тва за А́нглию; **~ of Waterloo** сраже́ние при Ватерло́о; **~ of Stalingrad** би́тва под Сталингра́дом; **~ of Borodino** Бороди́нское сраже́ние; **the ~ is ours** побе́да за на́ми; **fight a losing ~** вести́ (*det.*) безнадёжную борьбу́; **fight s.o.'s ~s for him** лезть (*det.*) в дра́ку за кого́-н.; **fight one's own ~s** постоя́ть (*pf.*) за себя́; **half the ~** (*fig.*) зало́г успе́ха, полде́ла.
● *v.i.* боро́ться (*impf.*); сража́ться (*impf.*).
● *cpds.* **~-array** *n.* боево́й поря́док; **~-axe** *n.* алеба́рда; (*fig., termagant*) бой-ба́ба; **~-cry** *n.* боево́й клич; (*fig.*) ло́зунг; **~-dress** *n.* похо́дная фо́рма; **~field, ~-ground** *nn.* по́ле сраже́ния/бо́я; **~-scarred** *adj.* изра́ненный в боя́х; **~ scene** *n.* (*art*) бата́льная сце́на; **~ship** *n.* лине́йный кора́бль, линко́р.

battlement /ˈbæt(ə)lmənt/ *n.* зубча́тая стена́.

batty /ˈbætɪ/ *adj.* (**battier, battiest**) чо́кнутый, тро́нутый (*coll.*).

bauble /ˈbɔːb(ə)l/ *n.* (*on Christmas tree*) ёлочный шар; (*trinket*) безделу́шка.

baud /bəʊd/, /bɔːd/ *n.* (*pl.* **~** *or* **~s**) (*comput.*) бод.

baulk /bɔːlk/, /bɔːk/ = **balk**

bauxite /ˈbɔːksaɪt/ *n.* бокси́т.

Bavaria /bəˈveərɪə/ *n.* Бава́рия.

Bavarian /bəˈveərɪən/ *adj.* бава́рский.

bawd|iness /ˈbɔːdɪnɪs/ *n.* непристо́йность, похa'бщина.

bawdy /ˈbɔːdɪ/ *adj.* (**bawdier, bawdiest**) непристо́йный, поха́бный.

bawl /bɔːl/ *v.t. & i.* ора́ть (*impf.*); выкри́кивать, вы́крикнуть; **~ at s.o.** ора́ть на кого́-н.; **~ s.o. out** (*coll.*) наора́ть (*pf.*) на кого́-н.

bay¹ /beɪ/ *n.* (*bot.*) лавр; (*attr.*) лавро́вый.
● *cpds.* **~-leaf** *n.* лавро́вый лист; **~-tree** *n.* лавр, ла́вровое де́рево.

bay² /beɪ/ *n.* (*geog.*) зали́в, бу́хта; **B~ of Biscay** Биска́йский зали́в.

bay³ /beɪ/ *n.* **1** (*of wall*) пролёт, пане́ль. **2** (*window recess*) ни́ша; **~ window** э́ркер, фона́рь (*m.*). **3**: **sick ~** (*naut.*) судово́й лазаре́т. **4** (*aeron.*): **bomb ~** бо́мбовый отсе́к.

bay⁴ /beɪ/ *n.* **1** (*bark*) лай. **2** (*fig. uses*): **keep s.o. at ~** держа́ть (*impf.*) кого́-н. на расстоя́нии; **keep the enemy at ~** сде́рживать (*impf.*) неприя́теля.
● *v.t. & i.* ла́ять (*impf.*); залива́ться (*impf.*) ла́ем; выть (*impf.*); **~ (at) the moon** выть на луну́.

bay⁵ /beɪ/ *n.* (*horse*) гнеда́я (ло́шадь).
● *adj.* гнедо́й.

bayonet /ˈbeɪəˌnet/ *n.* штык; **hold s.o. at ~ point** держа́ть кого́-н. на штыка́х.
● *v.t.* (**bayoneted, bayoneting**) коло́ть, за- штыко́м.

bazaar /bəˈzɑː(r)/ *n.* база́р.

bazooka /bəˈzuːkə/ *n.* противота́нковый гранатомёт.

BBC (*abbr. of* ***British Broadcasting Corporation***) Би-Би-Си́ (*nt. indecl.*); **~ English** нормати́вный англи́йский язы́к.

BC (*abbr. of* ***before Christ***) до н.э. (до на́шей э́ры), до рождества́ Христо́ва.

be /biː/, /bɪ/ *v.i.* (*sing. pres.* **am, are, is;** *pl. pres.* **are;** *1st and 3rd person sing. past* **was;** *2nd person sing. past and pl. past* **were;** *pres. subjunctive* **be;** *past subjunctive* **were;** *pres. part.* **being;** *p.p.* **been**) **1** быть (*impf.*); (*exist*) существова́ть (*impf.*); (*as copula in the present tense, usu. omitted or expr. by dash*): **the world is round** земля́ кру́глая; **that is a dog** э́то соба́ка. **2** (*more emphatic uses*): **an order is an order** прика́з есть прика́з; **there is a God** Бог есть; **we should love people as they are** ну́жно люби́ть люде́й таки́ми, каки́е они́ есть; **there are books on all subjects** име́ются кни́ги по всем те́мам. **3** (*expr. frequency*) быва́ть (*impf.*); **he is in London every Tuesday** он быва́ет в Ло́ндоне по вто́рникам; **there is no smoke without fire** нет ды́ма без огня́. **4** (*more formally, with complement*) явля́ться (*impf.*) + *i.*; представля́ть (*impf.*) собо́й; (*of membership etc.*) состоя́ть (*impf.*) + *i.* **5** (*expr. present continuous*): **she is crying** она́ пла́чет. **6** (*of place, time, cost etc.*): **it is a mile away** э́то в ми́ле отсю́да; **where is the office?** где нахо́дится бюро́?; **he is 21 today** ему́ сего́дня исполня́ется два́дцать оди́н год; **it is 25 pence a yard** э́то сто́ит два́дцать пять пе́нсов за ярд; (*of person or obj. in a certain position*) стоя́ть, лежа́ть, сиде́ть (*acc. to sense*; *all impf.*); **the books are on the floor** кни́ги лежа́т на полу́; **the books are on the shelf** кни́ги стоя́т на по́лке; **the ship is at anchor** кора́бль стои́т на я́коре; **Paris is on the Seine** Пари́ж стои́т на Се́не; **he is in hospital** он лежи́т в больни́це; **he is in prison** он (сиди́т) в тюрьме́; **I was at home all day** я сиде́л до́ма весь день; (*of continuing states*): **the weather was settled** пого́да стоя́ла хоро́шая; **the heat was unbearable** жара́ стоя́ла невыноси́мая; **prices are high** це́ны сохраня́ются высо́кие. **7** (*become*): **what are you going to ~ when you grow up?** кем ты ста́нешь/бу́дешь, когда́ вы́растешь? **8** (*behave, act a part*): **you are ~ing silly**

вы ведёте себя глу́по; **am I ~ing a bore?** я вам надое́л?
9 (*take place, happen*): **there is a party next door** в сосе́днем до́ме идёт вечери́нка; **the meeting is** (*will be*) **on Friday** заседа́ние состои́тся в пя́тницу.
10 (*exist, live*): **he is no more** его́ бо́льше нет; **the government that was** тогда́шнее прави́тельство; **the greatest man that ever was** велича́йший из когда́-либо жи́вших люде́й.
11 (*remain*): **let him ~!** оста́вьте его́!; **don't ~ too long!** не заде́рживайтесь!
12 (*expr. motion*): **he is off to London** он уезжа́ет в Ло́ндон; **the dog was after him** за ним гнала́сь соба́ка; **has the postman been?** по́чта уже́ была́?
13 (*expr. pass.*): **the house is ~ing built** дом стро́ится; **I am told** мне сказа́ли.
14 (*uses of pres. part. and gerund*): **~ing a doctor, he knew what to do** бу́дучи врачо́м, он знал, что де́лать; **for the time ~ing** пока́ что, на вре́мя; **he is far from ~ing an expert** он далеко́ не специали́ст.
15 (*with* **at**): **what are you at?** что вы хоти́те?; что вы де́лаете?
16 (*with* **for**): **I am for tariff reform** я за тари́фную рефо́рму.
17 (*with* **to**): **I am to inform you** я до́лжен сообщи́ть вам; **he is to ~ married today** он сего́дня же́нится; **you are not to do that** вам нельзя́ (*or* не сле́дует) э́то де́лать; **how was I to know?** как же я мог знать?; **the book is not to ~ found** э́той кни́ги нигде́ не найти́; **when am I to ~ there?** когда́ мне на́до быть там?; **it is to ~ hoped that ...** на́до наде́яться, что...; **he met the woman he was to marry** (*i.e. later married*) он встре́тил же́нщину, на кото́рой впосле́дствии жени́лся; **it is not to ~** э́тому не суждено́ соверши́ться (*or* не быва́ть); **his wife to ~** его́ бу́дущая жена́.
18 (*var.*): **~ it so! so ~ it!** быть по сему́!; **how are you?** как пожива́ете?; **~ that as it may** как бы то ни́ было; **how is it that ...?** как э́то так, что...?; **what is that to me?** что мне до э́того?; **as you were!** (*mil.*) отста́вить!
● *cpd.* **~-all** *n.* (*also* **~-all and end-all**) суть; коне́ц и нача́ло всего́.
● *See also* ⇨**being**

beach /bi:tʃ/ *n.* пляж; (*seashore*) взмо́рье.
● *v.t.* (*run ashore*) посади́ть (*pf.*) на мель; (*haul up*) выта́скивать, вы́тащить на бе́рег.
● *cpds.* **~-head** *n.* (*mil.*) примо́рский/берегово́й плацда́рм; **~-wear** *n.* пля́жная оде́жда.

beacon /'bi:kən/ *n.* (*signal light, fire*) сигна́льный ого́нь; (*lighthouse*) мая́к; (*buoy*) ба́кен; (*signal tower*) сигна́льная ба́шня; (*Br., at crossing*) знак пешехо́дного перехо́да.

bead /bi:d/ *n.* **1** бу́син(к)а, би́серина; **glass ~s** би́сер; **pearl ~s** жемчу́жины (*f. pl.*); **string of ~s** бу́сы (*pl. g.* —). **2** (*drop of liquid*) ка́пля.

beading /'bi:dɪŋ/ *n.* (*archit.*) орна́мент в ви́де бус.

beady /'bi:dɪ/ *adj.* (**beadier, beadiest**): **~ eyes** глаза́-бу́синки.

beagle /'bi:g(ə)l/ *n.* бигль (*m.*) (*порода гончих*).

beak /bi:k/ *n.* клюв.

beaker /'bi:k(ə)r/ *n.* (*Br., for drinking*) пластма́ссовый стака́н (с но́сиком); (*in laboratory*) мензу́рка.

beam[1] /bi:m/ *n.* **1** (*of timber etc.*) брус, ба́лка, перекла́дина. **2** (*naut.*) бимс; **broad in the ~** (*lit.*) с широ́кими би́мсами; (*fig., coll.*) толстоза́дый; **the ship was on her ~ ends** кора́бль лежа́л на боку́; **he was on his ~ ends** (*fig.*) он был в тяжёлом положе́нии.
3 (*of scales*) коромы́сло.

beam[2] /bi:m/ *n.* **1** (*ray*) луч; (*of particles etc.*) пучо́к луче́й; (*as radio signal*) радиосигна́л. **2** (*smile*) сия́ющая улы́бка. **3** (*of car's headlights*) свет; **full ~** (*Br.*), **high ~s** (*US*) да́льний свет; **low ~s** (*US*) бли́жний свет.
● *v.t.* напр|авля́ть, -а́вить (сигна́л).
● *v.i.* (*shine*) свети́ть (*impf.*), сия́ть (*impf.*); (*smile broadly*) сия́ть улы́бкой; **she ~ed with delight** она́ сия́ла от ра́дости.

beaming /'bi:mɪŋ/ *adj.* сия́ющий.

bean /bi:n/ *n.* **1** боб; **broad ~s** бобы́ (*m. pl.*); **French ~s** фасо́ль; **string ~s** зелёная фасо́ль. **2** (*coll., coin*) грош; **I haven't a ~** у меня́ нет ни гроша́.
3 (*coll. uses*): **spill the ~s** проболта́ться (*pf.*); **full of ~s** по́лный задо́ра.
● *cpds.* **~-feast** *n.* (*Br.*) пиру́шка, пир горо́й; **~-pod** *n.* бобо́вый стручо́к; **~-stalk** *n.* сте́бель (*m.*) бобо́вого расте́ния.

bear[1] /beə(r)/ *n.* **1** (*zool., also fig.*) медве́дь (*m.*); **she-~** медве́дица; **~ cub** медвежо́нок; **Teddy ~** ми́шка.
2 (*astron.*) **Great/Little B~** Больша́я/Ма́лая Медве́дица. **3** (*econ.*) спекуля́нт, игра́ющий на пониже́ние.
● *cpds.* **~-baiting** *n.* медве́жья тра́вля; **~-garden** *n.* (*fig.*) (шу́мное) сбо́рище, база́р; **~-skin** *n.* (*lit.*) медве́жья шку́ра; (*headgear*) мехово́й ки́вер.

bear[2] /beə(r)/ *v.t.* (*past* **bore;** *p.p.* **borne, born**) **1** (*carry*) носи́ть (*indet.*), нести́, по- (*det.*); **~ arms** носи́ть ору́жие; **~ one's head high** высоко́ нести́/держа́ть (*impf.*) го́лову; **~ in mind** име́ть (*impf.*) в виду́; **~ tales** разноси́ть (*impf.*) спле́тни.
2: **~ o.s.** (*behave*) держа́ться (*impf.*).
3 (*show, have*): **the document ~s your signature** на докуме́нте есть ва́ша по́дпись; **a monument ~ing an inscription** па́мятник с на́дписью; **~ a resemblance to** име́ть (*impf.*) схо́дство с + *i.*; **~ the marks of ill-treatment** нести́ (*det.*) на себе́ следы́ дурно́го обраще́ния.
4 (*harbour*): **~ ill-will** пита́ть (*impf.*) дурны́е чу́вства.
5 (*provide*): **~ false witness** лжесвиде́тельствовать (*impf.*); **~ s.o. company** соста́вить (*pf.*) компа́нию кому́-н.
6 (*sustain, support*): **the ice will ~ his weight** лёд вы́держит его́; **~ responsibility/expense/a loss** нести́ (*det.*) отве́тственность/расхо́ды/убы́тки.
7 (*endure, tolerate*) терпе́ть, с-; выноси́ть, вы́нести; сн|оси́ть, -ести́; **I cannot ~ him** я его́ не выношу́; **grin and ~ it** (*coll.*) му́жественно переноси́ть (*impf.*) страда́ния/неприя́тности.
8 (*be fit for, capable of*): **the joke ~s repeating** э́тот анекдо́т мо́жно повтори́ть ещё раз; **~ comparison** выде́рживать (*impf.*) сравне́ние.
9 (*press, push*): **he was borne backwards by the crowd** он был отти́снут толпо́й наза́д.
10 (*give birth to*): **she bore him a son** она родила́ ему́ сы́на; **be born** роди́ться (*impf., pf.*); **a man born in 1919** челове́к 1919 го́да рожде́ния; **he was born with a talent for music** у него́ от рожде́ния (был) тала́нт к му́зыке.
11 (*yield*): **trees/efforts ~ fruit** дере́вья/уси́лия прино́сят плоды́; **the bonds ~ 5% interest** облига́ции прино́сят пять проце́нтов дохо́да.
● *v.i.* (*past* **bore;** *p.p.* **borne, born**)
1 (*of direction*): **the road ~s to the right** доро́га идёт впра́во.
2 (*exert pressure, affect*): **bring one's energy to ~ on** напра́вить (*pf.*) эне́ргию на + *a.*; **taxation ~s on all classes** налогообложе́ние распространя́ется на все́ кла́ссы; **this ~s on our problem** э́то отно́сится к на́шей пробле́ме; **~ with** терпе́ть (*impf.*), переноси́ть (*impf.*); относи́ться (*impf.*) терпи́мо к + *d.*
● *with advs.*: **~ away** *v.t.* ун|оси́ть, -ести́; **he was borne away (by his feelings)** он был увлечён; **~ down**: **~ down upon s.o.** (*swoop etc.*) устрем|ля́ться, -и́ться на кого́-н.; **~ out** *v.t.* (*carry out*) выноси́ть, вы́нести; (*confirm*) подтвер|жда́ть, -ди́ть; подкреп|ля́ть, -и́ть; **~ up** *v.i.* (*endure*) держа́ться (*impf.*).

bearable /'beərəb(ə)l/ *adj.* терпи́мый, сно́сный.

beard /bɪəd/ *n.* **1** борода́; **grow a ~** расти́ть, от- бо́роду. **2** (*of animal*) боро́дка. **3** (*bot.*) ость.
● *v.t.* бр|оса́ть, -о́сить вы́зов + *d.*; **~ the lion in his den** (*fig.*) лезть (*impf.*) в ло́гово зве́ря.

bearded /'bɪədɪd/ *adj.* борода́тый; (*bot.*) ости́стый.

beardless /'bɪədlɪs/ *adj.* безборо́дый; (*youthful*) безу́сый.

bearer /'beərə(r)/ *n.* (*one who carries*) несу́щий, нося́щий; **~ of good news** до́брый ве́стник; (*of letter*) пода́тель (*m.*); (*of a cheque*) предъяви́тель (*m.*); (*of title*) носи́тель (*m.*).

bearing /'beərɪŋ/ *n.* **1** (*carrying*) ноше́ние. **2** (*behaviour*) поведе́ние; (*deportment*) мане́ра держа́ться.
3 (*relevance*) отноше́ние (к + *d.*).
4 (*direction*) пе́ленг, румб, а́зимут; **take a compass ~** опреде́л|я́ть, -и́ть магни́тный а́зимут (*or* ко́мпасный пе́ленг); **find, get, take one's ~s** опреде́л|я́ть, -и́ть своё местонахожде́ние/положе́ние; ориенти́роваться (*impf., pf.*); **lose one's ~s** потеря́ть (*pf.*)

ориентиро́вку. **5** (*tech.*) опо́ра; **roller ~** ро́ликовый подши́пник. **6** (*pl., her.*) деви́з.

bearish /ˈbeərɪʃ/ *adj.* **1** (*rough*) медве́жий, гру́бый. **2** (*on stock exchange*) понизи́тельный.

beast /biːst/ *n.* **1** (*animal*) живо́тное; (*wild animal*) зверь (*m.*); (*pl., cattle*) рога́тый скот; **~ of burden** вью́чное живо́тное. **2** (*savage person*) зверь; (*nasty person*) скот, скоти́на (*c.g.*).

beastliness /ˈbiːstlɪnɪs/ *n.* отврати́тельность.

beastly /ˈbiːstlɪ/ *adj.* (**beastlier, beastliest**) (*unpleasant*) отврати́тельный; **~ weather** ужа́сная пого́да; **a ~ headache** мéрзкая/гну́сная головна́я боль.

beat[1] /biːt/ *n.* **1** (*of drum*) бой; (*of heart*) бие́ние; (*rhythm*) ритм; (*mus.*) такт. **2** (*policeman's*) райо́н обхо́да; **be on the ~** соверша́ть (*impf.*) обхо́д.

● *v.t.* (*past* **beat;** *p.p.* **beaten**) **1** (*strike*) бить, по-; уд|аря́ть, -а́рить; колоти́ть, по-; **~ s.o. black and blue** исколоти́ть (*pf.*) кого́-н.; изби́ть (*pf.*) кого́-н. до синяко́в (*or* до полусме́рти); **~ one's breast** бить (*impf.*) себя́ в грудь; **~ a carpet** выкола́чивать, вы́колотить (*or* выбива́ть, вы́бить) ковёр; **~ a drum** бить (*impf.*) в бараба́н; **~ eggs** взби|ва́ть, -ть я́йца; **~ one's head against a wall** (*lit., fig.*) би́ться (*impf.*) голово́й о сте́нку; **~ a path through the forest** протори́ть (*pf.*) тропи́нку че́рез лес; **~ a retreat** (*lit., fig.*) бить (*impf.*) отбо́й; (*fig.*) идти́ (*det.*) на попя́тную; **~ a steak** отб|ива́ть, -и́ть бифште́кс; **he ~ the table with his fists** он колоти́л кулака́ми по столу́; **~ time** отбива́ть (*impf.*) такт; **the bird ~s its wings** пти́ца бьёт кры́льями; **~ it!** (*sl.*) кати́сь!; **~ the dust out of something** выбива́ть, вы́бить пыль из чего́-н.; **~ a stick into the ground** вбить (*pf.*) па́лку в зе́млю; **~ something into s.o.'s head** вкол|а́чивать, -оти́ть (*or* вби|ва́ть, -ть) что-н. кому́-н. в го́лову.
2 (*defeat, surpass*) поб|ива́ть, -и́ть; разб|ива́ть, -и́ть; побе|жда́ть, -ди́ть; одéрж|ивать, -а́ть побе́ду над + *i.*; **the liberal-democrats ~ the conservatives** либера́л-демокра́ты победи́ли консерва́торов; **he ~ me at chess** он обыгра́л меня́ в ша́хматы; **he always ~s me at golf** он всегда́ вы́игрывает, когда́ мы игра́ем в гольф; **these armies have never been ~en** э́ти а́рмии не зна́ли пораже́ния; **he ~ the record** он поби́л реко́рд; **that ~s all (*or* the band)** (*coll.*) э́то превосхо́дит всё; **it ~s me how he does it** (*coll.*) убе́й Бог, е́сли я понима́ю, как ему́ э́то удаётся; **can you ~ it?** (*coll.*) как вам э́то нра́вится?; **I'll ~ you to the top of the hill** я быстре́е вас доберу́сь до верши́ны холма́.

● *v.i.* (*past* **beat;** *p.p.* **beaten**)**: his heart is ~ing** его́ се́рдце бьётся; **he heard drums ~ing** он слы́шал бараба́нный бой; **the rain ~ against the windows** дождь стуча́л в о́кна; **~ about the bush** (*fig.*) ходи́ть (*indet.*) вокру́г да о́коло; **~ at, on a door** колоти́ть (*impf.*) в дверь.

● *with advs.*: **~ back** *v.t.* отб|ива́ть, -и́ть; **~ down** *v.t.*: **the rain ~ down the corn** дождь поби́л хлеба́; **he ~ down the price** он сбил це́ну; он доби́лся ски́дки; **he ~ me down** он заста́вил меня́ уступи́ть в цене́; **he ~ down all opposition** он подави́л вся́кое сопротивле́ние; *v.i.*: **the sun ~ down on us** со́лнце нещáдно пали́ло нас; **~ in** *v.t.*: **~ a door in** вы́ломать (*pf.*) дверь; **~ off** *v.t.*: **~ off an attack** отб|ива́ть, -и́ть ата́ку; **~ out** *v.t.*: **~ out a fire** зат|а́птывать, -опта́ть ого́нь; **~ out gold** кова́ть, вы- зо́лото; **~ out a path** проб|ива́ть, -и́ть; (*or* протор|я́ть, -и́ть) тропи́нку; **~ out a rhythm** отбива́ть (*impf.*) ритм; **~ s.o.'s brains out** вышиба́ть, вы́шибить мозги́ кому́-н.; **~ up** *v.t.*: **~ up eggs/cream** взби|ва́ть, -ть я́йца/сли́вки; **~ s.o. up** изб|ива́ть, -и́ть кого́-н.

● *See also* ⇒**beaten**

beat[2] /biːt/ *adj.* (*coll., tired*): **dead ~** смерте́льно уста́лый.

beat[3] /biːt/ (*coll.*) *n.*: **the ~ generation** поколе́ние би́тников.

beaten /ˈbiːt(ə)n/ *adj.* би́тый, поби́тый, изби́тый; (*conquered*) разби́тый; **off the ~ track** не по проторённой доро́жке.

beatific /ˌbiːəˈtɪfɪk/ *adj.* **1** (*making blessed*) благослове́нный. **2**: **a ~ smile** блаже́нная улы́бка.

beatification /biːˌætɪfɪˈkeɪʃ(ə)n/ *n.* причисле́ние к ли́ку блаже́нных.

beatify /biːˈætɪˌfaɪ/ *v.t.* (*eccl.*) ≈ канонизи́ровать (*impf. pf.*).

beating /ˈbiːtɪŋ/ *n.* **1** (*of heart*) бие́ние. **2** (*thrashing*) битьё, по́рка; **give s.o. a good ~** отлупи́ть (*pf.*) кого́-н.; **the boy deserves a ~** ма́льчик заслу́живает по́рки. **3** (*defeat*) разгро́м, пораже́ние; **they gave the enemy a thorough ~** врагу́ от них здо́рово доста́лось.

beatitude /biːˈætɪˌtjuːd/ *n.* **1** (*blessedness*) блаже́нство. **2** (*bibl.*): **the B~s** за́поведи (*f. pl.*) блаже́нства.

beat(nik) /ˈbiːtnɪk/ *n.* (*sl.*) би́тник.

beau /bəʊ/ *n.* (*pl.* **~x** *or* **~s**) ухажёр, покло́нник.

Beaufort scale /ˈbəʊfət/ *n.* бофо́ртова шкала́.

beau monde /bəʊ ˈmɒnd/ *n.* бомо́нд, вы́сший свет.

beauteous /ˈbjuːtɪəs/ *adj.* прекра́сный.

beautician /bjuːˈtɪʃ(ə)n/ *n.* космето́лог, космети́чка.

beautiful /ˈbjuːtɪˌfʊl/ *adj.* краси́вый; (*excellent*) прекра́сный; **~ly warm** необыкнове́нно тепло́.

beautify /ˈbjuːtɪˌfaɪ/ *v.t.* укр|аша́ть, -а́сить.

beauty /ˈbjuːtɪ/ *n.* **1** (*quality*) красота́; **~ is skin-deep** красота́ недолгове́чна; **~ contest** ко́нкурс красоты́; **~ parlour** космети́ческий кабине́т; **~ queen** короле́ва красоты́; **~ sleep** сон до полу́ночи, ра́нний сон (*перед балом и т.д.*); **~ spot** (*Br., place*) живопи́сная ме́стность; (*on face*) му́шка. **2** (*woman*) краса́вица; **B~ and the Beast** краса́вица и чудо́вище; **she's no ~** она́ совсе́м не краса́вица. **3** (*excellence, fine specimen*): **that's the ~ of it** в э́том-то вся пре́лесть; **his car is a ~** у него́ прекра́сная маши́на.

beaux /bəʊz/, /bəʊ/ *pl. of* ⇒**beau**

beaver /ˈbiːvə(r)/ *n.* (*pl.* **~** *or* **~s**) **1** (*zool.*) бобр; **eager ~** (*coll.*) хлопоту́н. **2** (*fur*) бобёр; (*hat*) бобро́вая ша́пка.

● *v.i.* (*coll., toil*) вка́лывать (*impf.*).

bebop /ˈbiːbɒp/ *n.* (*mus.*) бибо́п (*род джазовой музыки*).

becalm /bɪˈkɑːm/ *v.t.*: **be ~ed** (*naut.*) штилева́ть (*impf.*); заштил|ева́ть, -е́ть; **a ~ed ship** заштиле́вший кора́бль.

became /bɪˈkeɪm/ *past of* ⇒**become**

because /bɪˈkɒz/ *conj.* потому́ что; (*since*) так как; **all the more ~** тем бо́лее, что; **~ of** из-за + *g.*, (*thanks to*) благодаря́ + *d.*

béchamel /ˈbeʃəˌmel/ *n.* (*cul.*) бешаме́ль.

beck /bek/ *n.*: **be at s.o.'s ~ and call** быть у кого́-н. на побегу́шках.

beckon /ˈbekən/ *v.t. & i.* мани́ть, по-; заз|ыва́ть, -ва́ть; **I ~ed (to) him to approach** я помани́л его́ к себе́; **he ~ed them in** он зазва́л их внутрь.

becloud /bɪˈklaʊd/ *v.t.* завол|а́кивать, -о́чь; **tears ~ed his eyes** его́ глаза́ заволокло́ слеза́ми; (*of the mind*) затума́ни|вать, -ть.

become /bɪˈkʌm/ *v.t.* (*past* **became;** *p.p.* **become**) (*befit*) годи́ться, подоба́ть, прили́чествовать (*кому*); **it doesn't ~ you to complain** вам не к лицу́ жа́ловаться; (*look well on*) идти́ (*det.*); **the dress ~s you** э́то пла́тье вам идёт; *see also* ⇒**becoming**

● *v.i.* (*past* **became;** *p.p.* **become**) (*come to be*) ста|нови́ться, -ть + *i.*; *often expr. by v. in* ...еть; **~ pale** побледне́ть; **~ rich** разбогате́ть; **~ smaller** уме́ньшиться (*all pf.*); **what became of him?** что с ним ста́лось?; **he became a waiter** он стал официа́нтом; **the weather became worse** пого́да испо́ртилась.

becoming /bɪˈkʌmɪŋ/ *adj.* (*proper*) подоба́ющий, прили́чествующий; (*of dress etc.*) (иду́щий) к лицу́; **she is ~ly dressed** она́ оде́та к лицу́; **she wore a ~ hat** шля́пка ей о́чень шла.

bed /bed/ *n.* **1** (*esp. bedstead*) крова́ть; (*esp. bedding*) посте́ль; (*in hospital*) ко́йка; (*dog's etc. bedding*) подсти́лка; **single/double ~** односпа́льная/двуспа́льная крова́ть; **twin ~s** па́рные крова́ти; **go to ~** ложи́ться, лечь спать; (*in sexual sense*) переспа́ть (*pf.*) (*с кем*); **put to ~** укла́дывать, уложи́ть спать; **send to ~** отпр|авля́ть, -а́вить (*or* от|сыла́ть, -осла́ть) спать; **get into ~** ложи́ться, лечь в посте́ль/крова́ть; **get out of ~** вста|ва́ть, -ть с посте́ли/крова́ти; **get out of ~ on the wrong side** (*fig.*) встать (*pf.*) с ле́вой ноги́; **make a ~** (*arrange for sleep*) стлать, по- (*or* стели́ть, по-) посте́ль; (*tidy after sleep*) заст|ила́ть, -ла́ть (*or* уб|ира́ть, -ра́ть) посте́ль; **as you make your ~, so you must lie on it** что посе́ешь, то и пожнёшь; **take to**

one's ~ слечь (*pf.*); **die in one's ~** умере́ть (*pf.*) свое́й сме́ртью; **early to ~ and early to rise** (*prov.*) кто ра́но встаёт, тому́ Бог подаёт; **out of ~** (*up, recovered*) на нога́х.
2 (*base, bottom*): (*of concrete etc.*) основа́ние, фунда́мент; (*of rock, clay etc.*) пласт, слой; (*of a road*) полотно́; (*of the sea*) морско́е дно; (*of a river*) речно́е ру́сло, ло́же реки́.
3 (*place of cultivation*): **~ of flowers** клу́мба; **~ of nettles** за́росль крапи́вы; **~ of potatoes** карто́фельная гря́дка.

● *v.t.* (**bedded, bedding**) **1** (*of flowers; also* **~ out**) сажа́ть, посади́ть; выса́живать, вы́садить.
2: **~ a horse** стлать, по- подсти́лку для ло́шади.

● *v.i.* (**bedded, bedding**): **~ down** распол|ага́ться, -ожи́ться на ночле́г; (*cohabit*) сожи́тельствовать (*impf.*).

● *cpds.* **~ and breakfast** (*guest-house*) ма́ленькая гости́ница; (*terms*) ночле́г и за́втрак; **~bug** *n.* клоп; **~clothes** *n. pl.* посте́ль; посте́льные принадле́жности (*f. pl.*); **~-cover** *n.* покрыва́ло; **~-head** *n.* (*Br.*) изголо́вье; **~-jacket** *n.* ночна́я ко́фта; **~-linen** *n.* посте́льное бельё; **~-pan** *n.* подкладно́е су́дно; **~post** *n.* сто́лбик крова́ти; **between you and me and the ~post** (*coll.*) стро́го ме́жду на́ми; **~ridden** *adj.* прико́ванный к посте́ли; **~rock** *n.* коренна́я поро́да; (*fig.*) осно́ва; **~room** *n.* спа́льня; **~room farce** альќовный фарс; **~room slippers** дома́шние ту́фли, та́почки (*f. pl.*); **~side** *n.*: **keep books at one's ~side** держа́ть (*impf.*) кни́ги на ночно́м сто́лике; **watch at s.o.'s ~side** уха́живать (*impf.*) за больны́м; сиде́ть (*impf.*) у посте́ли больно́го; **a good ~side manner** уме́лый подхо́д к больно́му, враче́бный такт; **~side table** ту́мбочка, ночно́й сто́лик; **~-sitter, ~-sitting-room** *nn.* (*Br.*) однокомна́тная кварти́ра; **~sore** *n.* проле́жень (*m.*); **~spread** *n.* покрыва́ло; **~stead** *n.* крова́ть; о́стов, стано́к крова́ти; **~time** *n.* вре́мя ложи́ться/идти́ спать; **my ~time is at 11** я ложу́сь спать в оди́ннадцать часо́в; **~time story** ска́зка, расска́з на сон гряду́щий.

B.Ed. (*abbr. of* ***Bachelor of Education***) бакала́вр педагоги́ческих нау́к.

bedaub /bɪ'dɔ:b/ *v.t.* ма́зать, за-.

bedding /'bedɪŋ/ *n.* (*bedclothes*) посте́ль; посте́льные принадле́жности (*f. pl.*).

bedeck /bɪ'dek/ *v.t.* укр|аша́ть, -а́сить.

bedevil /bɪ'dev(ə)l/ *v.t.* (**bedevilled, bedevilling;** *US* **bedeviled, bedeviling**) (*confuse*) спу́т|ывать, -ать; вн|оси́ть, -ести́ неразбери́ху в + *a.*

bedevilment /bɪ'dev(ə)lmənt/ *n.* (*confusion*) неразбери́ха, пу́таница.

bedew /bɪ'dju:/ *v.t.* оро|ша́ть, -си́ть; обры́зг|ивать, -ать.

bedizen /bɪ'daɪz(ə)n/, /-'dɪz(ə)n/ *v.t.* разря|жа́ть, -ди́ть.

bedlam /'bedləm/ *n.* (*fig.*) бедла́м.

Bed(o)uin /'bedʊɪn/ *n.* (*pl.* **~**) бедуи́н (*fem.* -ка).

● *adj.* бедуи́нский.

bedraggled /bɪ'dræg(ə)ld/ *adj.* забры́зганный.

bee /bi:/ *n.* пчела́; **have a ~ in one's bonnet** быть поме́шанным (*на чём*).

● *cpds.* **~hive** *n.* у́лей; **~-keeper** *n.* пчелово́д; **~-keeping** *n.* пчелово́дство; **~-line** *n.* пряма́я; **make a ~-line for** стрело́й помча́ться (*pf.*) к + *d.*; **~swax** *n.* пчели́ный воск.

beech /bi:tʃ/ *n.* бук.

● *cpd.* **~mast** *n.* бу́ковый оре́шек.

beef[1] /bi:f/ *n.* (*meat*) говя́дина; (*fig., energy*) си́ла, эне́ргия.

● *v.t.*: **~ up** (*coll., strengthen, increase*) укреп|ля́ть, -и́ть.

● *cpds.* **~burger** *n.* ру́бленый бифште́кс; **~eater** *n.* солда́т охра́ны ло́ндонского Та́уэра; **~steak** *n.* бифште́кс; **~-tea** (*Br.*) *n.* кре́пкий бульо́н.

beef[2] /bi:f/ *v.i.* (*sl., complain*) стона́ть (*impf.*).

beefy /'bi:fɪ/ *adj.* (**beefier, beefiest**) (*like beef*) мяси́стый; (*muscular*) мускули́стый.

been /bi:n bɪn/ *p.p. of* ⇒**be**

beep /bi:p/ *n.* гудо́к.

● *v.i.* гуде́ть, про-.

beer /bɪə(r)/ *n.* пи́во.

beery /'bɪərɪ/ *adj.* (**beerier, beeriest**) (*smelling of beer*) отдаю́щий пи́вом; **he has ~ breath** от него́ несёт/рази́т пи́вом.

beet /bi:t/ *n.* свёкла; (*sugar* **~**) са́харная свёкла, свеклови́ца.

● *cpd.* **~root** *n.* (*Br.*) свёкла, бура́к; **he blushed as red as a ~root** он покрасне́л как рак.

beetle[1] /'bi:t(ə)l/ *n.* (*zool.*) жук.

beetle[2] /'bi:t(ə)l/ *n.* (*tool*) кува́лда, трамбо́вка.

beetle[3] /'bi:t(ə)l/ *adj.*: **~ brows** нави́сшие бро́ви (*f. pl.*).

● *v.i.* нав|иса́ть, -и́снуть.

● *cpd.* **~-browed** *adj.* с нави́сшими бровя́ми.

beetle[4] /'bi:t(ə)l/ *v.i.*: **~ off!** кати́сь! (*sl.*).

beeves /bi:vz/ *pl. of* ⇒**beef**

befall /bɪ'fɔ:l/ *v.t. & i.* (*past* **befell** /bɪ'fel/; *p.p.* **befallen** /bɪ'fɔ:lən/) (*liter.*) приключ|а́ться, -и́ться (с + *i.*); пост|ига́ть, -и́гнуть (*кого/что*); **what has ~en him?** что с ним ста́ло?

befit /bɪ'fɪt/ *v.t.* (**befitted, befitting**) под|ходи́ть, -ойти́ + *d.*

befog /bɪ'fɒg/ *v.t.* (**befogged, befogging**) (*lit., fig.*) затума́ни|вать, -ть.

before /bɪ'fɔ:(r)/ *adv.* **1** (*sooner, previously*) ра́ньше; **six weeks ~** шестью́ неде́лями ра́ньше; **18 years ~** 18 лет наза́д.
2 (*of place*) впереди́.

● *prep.* **1** (*of time*) пе́ред + *i.*; **~ leaving** пе́ред отъе́здом; (*earlier than*) до + *g.*; **~ the war** до войны́; **since ~ the war** с довое́нного вре́мени; **long ~ that** задо́лго до э́того; **~ now** пре́жде; **the week ~ last** позапро́шлая неде́ля; **don't come ~ I call you** не приходи́те, пока́ я вас не позову́.
2 (*rather than*) скоре́е чем; **he would die ~ lying** он скоре́е умрёт, чем солжёт.
3 (*of place*) пе́ред + *i.*; впереди́ + *g.*; **your whole life is ~ you** у вас вся жизнь впереди́; **~ the court** пе́ред судо́м; **~ witnesses** при свиде́телях; **~ my eyes** на мои́х глаза́х; **~ God** пе́ред Бо́гом.
4 (*fig., ahead of*): **he is ~ me in class** он впереди́ меня́ в кла́ссе.
5 (*naut.*): **~ the wind** по ве́тру.

● *conj.* (*earlier than*) ра́ньше чем; (*immediately* **~**) пре́жде/пе́ред тем, как; (*at a previous time*) до того́ как; **do it ~ you forget** сде́лайте э́то, пока́ не забы́ли; **it will be years ~ we meet** пройду́т го́ды, пока́ мы встре́тимся; **just ~ you arrived** пе́ред са́мым ва́шим прихо́дом.

● *cpds.* **~hand** *adv.* зара́нее; **~-mentioned** *adj.* вышеупомя́нутый; **~-tax** *adj.* начи́сленный до упла́ты нало́гов.

befoul /bɪ'faʊl/ *v.t.* па́чкать, за-.

befriend /bɪ'frend/ *v.t.* дру́жески отн|оси́ться, -ести́сь к + *d.*; помога́ть (*impf.*) + *d.*

befuddle /bɪ'fʌd(ə)l/ *v.t.* одурма́ни|вать, -ть.

beg /beg/ *v.t.* (**begged, begging**) проси́ть, по-; умоля́ть (*impf.*); **~ money of s.o.** проси́ть (*impf.*) у кого́-н. де́нег; **~ s.o. to do something** умоля́ть (*impf.*) кого́-н. сде́лать что-н.; **~ a favour** (*Br.*), **favor** (*US*) **of s.o.** проси́ть, по- кого́-н. о любе́зности; **they ~ged to come with us** они́ умоля́ли нас взять их с собо́й.

● *v.i.* (**begged, begging**) **1** (*ask for charity*) проси́ть подая́ния, ни́щенствовать, (*coll.*) побира́ться (*all impf.*); **~ from door to door** побира́ться по двора́м; **~ging letter** проси́тельное письмо́.
2: **~ for something** умол|я́ть, -и́ть о + *p.*; выпра́шивать, вы́просить что-н.; **~ for mercy** моли́ть (*impf.*) о поща́де; проси́ть (*impf.*) поща́ды; **I ~ of you not to go** я умоля́ю вас не ходи́ть; **~ off** (*excuse o.s.*) отпр|а́шиваться, -о́ситься.
3 (*of a dog*) служи́ть (*impf.*).
4: **the cakes are going ~ging** пирожки́ зря пропада́ют.

began /bɪ'gæn/ *past of* ⇒**begin**

beget /bɪ'get/ *v.t.* (**begetting;** *past* **begot;** *arch.* **begat;** *p.p.* **begotten**) (*lit., fig.*) поро|жда́ть, -ди́ть.

beggar /'begə(r)/ *n.* **1** ни́щий; **~ woman** ни́щенка; **~s cannot be choosers** ни́щий не выбира́ет.
2 (*fellow*) па́рень (*m.*), ма́лый; **poor ~** бедня́га (*m.*), бе́дный ма́лый; **little ~s** малыши́ (*m. pl.*).

● *v.t.*: **it ~s description** э́то не поддаётся описа́нию.

beggarly /ˈbegəlɪ/ *adj.* ни́щенский, жа́лкий.

beggary /ˈbegərɪ/ *n.* нищета́, ни́щенство.

begin /bɪˈgɪn/ *v.t.* (**beginning;** *past* **began;** *p.p.* **begun**) нач|ина́ть, -а́ть; **he began English** он на́чал изуча́ть англи́йский язы́к; **he began the meeting** он откры́л собра́ние; **he began (on) another bottle** он поча́л но́вую буты́лку; **I began to think she would not come** я поду́мал бы́ло, что она́ не придёт; (*often translated by* за-): **~ to sing** запе́ть (*pf.*); **he began to cry** он запла́кал.

● *v.i.* (**beginning;** *past* **began;** *p.p.* **begun**) нач|ина́ть(ся), -а́ть(ся); **he began at the beginning** он на́чал с са́мого нача́ла; **the meeting began** собра́ние начало́сь; **before winter ~s** до нача́ла зимы́; до того́ как начнётся зима́; **he began as a reporter** он на́чал свою́ карье́ру с рабо́ты репортёра; **to ~ with** во-пе́рвых.

beginner /bɪˈgɪnə(r)/ *n.* начина́ющий.

beginning /bɪˈgɪnɪŋ/ *n.* нача́ло; (*source*) исто́чник; **at the ~ of April** в нача́ле (*or* в пе́рвых чи́слах) апре́ля; **make a ~** нача́ть (*pf.*).

begone /bɪˈgɒn/ *v.i.*: (*arch.*) **~!** прочь!

begonia /bɪˈgəʊnjə/ *n.* бего́ния.

begot /bɪˈgɒt/ *past of* ⇒**beget**

begotten /bɪˈgɒt(ə)n/ *p.p. of* ⇒**beget**

begrime /bɪˈgraɪm/ *v.t.* па́чкать, вы́-; грязни́ть, за-.

begrudge /bɪˈgrʌdʒ/ *v.t.* зави́довать, по- (*кому чему*); **I ~ the time** мне жаль вре́мени; **they ~d him his food** они́ укоря́ли/попрека́ли его́ куско́м хле́ба.

beguile /bɪˈgaɪl/ *v.t.* **1** (*charm*) очаро́в|ыва́ть, -а́ть. **2** (*delude*) завл|ека́ть, -е́чь; **they ~d him into giving them his money** они́ (обма́ном) вы́удили у него́ де́ньги.

begun /bɪˈgʌn/ *p.p. of* ⇒**begin**

behalf /bɪˈhɑːf/ *n.*: **on/in my ~** от моего́ и́мени/лица́; ра́ди меня́; в мои́х интере́сах, в мою́ по́льзу; **he is going on our ~** он идёт за нас; **plead on s.o.'s ~** выступа́ть (*impf.*) в защи́ту кого́-н.

behave /bɪˈheɪv/ *v.i.* **1** (*of person*) вести́ (*det.*) себя́, держа́ться (*impf.*); **~ well, ~ o.s.** вести́ себя́ хорошо́; **~ badly** пло́хо поступ|а́ть, -и́ть; **~ (well *etc.*) towards s.o.** (хорошо́) относи́ться (*impf.*) к кому́-н. **2** (*of thing*): **my bicycle ~s well** мой велосипе́д хорошо́ слу́жит; **how does this metal ~ under stress?** как ведёт себя́ э́тот мета́лл под давле́нием?

behaviour /bɪˈheɪvjə(r)/ (*US* **behavior**) *n.* **1** (*conduct*) поведе́ние; отноше́ние (*к кому*), обраще́ние (*с кем*); **be on one's best ~** вести́ (*det.*) себя́ безупре́чно. **2**: **the ~ of steel under stress** поведе́ние ста́ли под давле́нием.

behavioural /bɪˈheɪvjər(ə)l/ (*US* **behavioral**) *adj.* поведе́нческий.

behaviourism /bɪˈheɪvjəˌrɪz(ə)m/ (*US* **behaviorism**) *n.* бихевиори́зм.

behead /bɪˈhed/ *v.t.* обезгла́в|ливать, -ить.

beheld /bɪˈheld/ *past and p.p. of* ⇒**behold**

behemoth /bɪˈhiːmɒθ/ *n.* чу́дище; (*bibl.*) бегемо́т.

behest /bɪˈhest/ *n.* (*liter.*) повеле́ние.

behind /bɪˈhaɪnd/ *n.* (*coll.*) зад, за́дница.

● *adv.* сза́ди, позади́; **a long way ~** далеко́ позади́; **from ~** сза́ди; **he is ~ in his studies** он отста́л в учёбе; **he is ~ with his payments** он запа́здывает с упла́той.

● *prep.* (*expr. place*) за + *i.*; (*expr. motion*) за + *a.*; (*more emphatic*) сза́ди, позади́ + *g.*; (*after*) по́сле + *g.*; **from ~** из-за + *g.*; **he walked (just) ~ me** он шёл сле́дом за мной; **what is ~ it all?** что стои́т за всем э́тим?; **he has the army ~ him** его́ подде́рживает а́рмия; **he left debts ~ him** он оста́вил по́сле себя́ долги́; **he put the idea ~ him** он бро́сил э́ту мысль; **the country is ~ its neighbours** страна́ отста́ла от свои́х сосе́дей.

● *cpd.* **~hand** *adj. & adv.*: **he is ~hand in his work** он запусти́л рабо́ту; **I am ~hand with the rent** я задолжа́л за кварти́ру.

behold /bɪˈhəʊld/ *v.t.* (*past and p.p.* **beheld**) (*arch.*) узре́ть (*pf.*); **lo and ~!** о чу́до!

beholden /bɪˈhəʊld(ə)n/ *pred. adj.* обя́зан, призна́телен.

beholder /bɪˈhəʊldə(r)/ *n.* очеви́дец; **beauty is in the eye of the ~** у ка́ждого своё представле́ние о красоте́.

behove /bɪˈhəʊv/ (*US* **behoove** /bɪˈhuːv/) *v.t.* (*liter.*): **it ~s you to work** вам надлежи́т рабо́тать; **it ill ~s him to complain** ему́ не к лицу́ жа́ловаться.

beige /beɪʒ/ *adj.* беж (*indecl.*), бе́жевый.

Beijing /beɪˈdʒɪŋ/ *n.* Пеки́н.

being /ˈbiːɪŋ/ *n.* **1** (*existence*) бытие́, существова́ние; **come into ~** возн|ика́ть, -и́кнуть; **call, bring into ~** вы́звать (*pf.*) к жи́зни. **2** (*creature, person*) существо́; **human ~** челове́к; **the Supreme B~** Всевы́шний. **3** (*nature*) существо́.

Beirut /beɪˈruːt/ *n.* Бе́йру́т.

bejewelled /bɪˈdʒuːəld/ (*US* **bejeweled**) *adj.* разукра́шенный драгоце́нностями.

belabour /bɪˈleɪbə(r)/ (*US* **belabor**) *v.t.* (*thrash*) взду́ть (*pf.*); изб|ива́ть, -и́ть; (*over-emphasize*): **~ the obvious** дока́зывать (*impf.*) очеви́дное.

Belarus /beləˈrʌs/ *n.* Белару́сь.

belated /bɪˈleɪtɪd/ *adj.* запозда́лый.

belch /beltʃ/ *n.* отры́жка; **give a ~** рыгну́ть (*pf.*); (*of smoke etc.*) столб.

● *v.t.* (*smoke etc.*; *also* **~ forth, out**) выбра́сывать, вы́бросить; (*lava*) изв|ерга́ть, -е́ргнуть.

● *v.i.* рыг|а́ть, -ну́ть.

beleaguer /bɪˈliːgə(r)/ *v.t.* оса|жда́ть, -ди́ть.

belfry /ˈbelfrɪ/ *n.* колоко́льня.

Belgian /ˈbeldʒ(ə)n/ *n.* бельги́|ец (*fem.* -йка).

● *adj.* бельги́йский.

Belgium /ˈbeldʒəm/ *n.* Бе́льгия.

Belgrade /belˈgreɪd/ *n.* Белгра́д.

belie /bɪˈlaɪ/ *v.t.* (**belying**) (*contradict*) противоре́чить (*impf.*) + *d.*; (*disappoint*): **our hopes were ~d** на́ши наде́жды не оправда́лись.

belief /bɪˈliːf/ *n.* **1** (*trust*) ве́ра (в + *a.*); дове́рие (к + *d.*). **2** (*acceptance as true*; *thing believed*) ве́ра, ве́рование; **entertain the ~ that** пита́ть (*impf.*) уве́ренность в том, что; **to the best of my ~** по моему́ убежде́нию; **he has a strong ~ in education** он глубоко́ убеждён в необходи́мости образова́ния; **beyond ~** невероя́тно, непостижи́мо; **the ~s of the Christian church** ве́рования/вероуче́ния (*nt. pl.*) христиа́нской це́ркви; **strange ~s** стра́нные пове́рья (*nt. pl.*).

believable /bɪˈliːvəb(ə)l/ *adj.* правдоподо́бный.

believe /bɪˈliːv/ *v.t.* ве́рить, по- (*кому, во что*); ду́мать (*impf.*); **I ~ so** ду́маю, что э́то так; мне так ка́жется; **~ one's eyes** ве́рить, по- свои́м глаза́м; **~ it or not; would you ~ it?** хоти́те ве́рьте, хоти́те — нет; **~ me** мо́жете мне пове́рить; **I ~ him to be honest** я счита́ю его́ че́стным челове́ком; **make ~** де́лать вид, притворя́ться (*impf.*).

● *v.i.* ве́рить (*impf.*); (*esp. relig.*) ве́ровать (*impf.*); **~ in God** ве́рить (*impf.*) в Бо́га; **~ in a remedy** ве́рить (*impf.*) в како́е-н. лека́рство; **~ in s.o.** ве́рить (*impf.*) в кого́-н.; име́ть (*impf.*) дове́рие к кому́-н.; **I ~ in taking exercise** я ве́рю в по́льзу заря́дки.

believer /bɪˈliːvə(r)/ *n.* **1** (*relig.*) ве́рующий. **2** (*advocate*) сторо́нни|к (*fem.* -ца) + *g.*; **~ in discipline** сторо́нник дисципли́ны.

belittle /bɪˈlɪt(ə)l/ *v.t.* преум|еньша́ть, -е́ньшить; умал|я́ть, -и́ть; **~ o.s.** уничижа́ться (*impf.*).

bell /bel/ *n.* **1** ко́локол; (*smaller*) колоко́льчик; (*of door, telephone, bicycle etc.*) звоно́к; **ring the ~** звони́ть (*impf.*) в звоно́к/ко́локол; **that rings a ~** (*fig., coll.*) да, я что́-то припомина́ю; **answer the ~** откры́ть (*pf.*) дверь; яви́ться (*pf.*) на зов; **clear as a ~** чи́стый как звон колоко́льчика; **sound as a ~** в полне́йшем поря́дке. **2** (*naut.*) ры́нда; **ring the ~s** бить (*impf.*) скля́нки. **3** (*of flower*) ча́шечка.

● *cpds.* **~-bottomed** *adj.*: **~-bottomed trousers** брю́ки-клёш, брю́ки с растру́бом; **~boy** *n.* (*US*) коридо́рный; **~-captain** *n.* (*US*) ста́рший коридо́рный; **~-founder** *n.* колоко́льник, колоко́льный ма́стер; **~-foundry** *n.* колоко́льная мастерска́я; **~-glass** *n.* стекля́нный колпа́к; **~hop** (*US*) = **~boy; ~-jar** *n.* стекля́нный колпа́к; **~-push** *n.* (*Br.*) кно́пка звонка́; **~ringer** *n.* звона́рь (*m.*); **~-tent** *n.* кру́глая пала́тка.

belladonna /ˌbeləˈdɒnə/ *n.* (*plant, drug*) белладо́нна.

belle /bel/ *n.* красáвица; **the ~ of the ball** цари́ца бáла.

belles-lettres /bel 'letr/ *n.* беллетри́стика.

belletristic /ˌbelə'trɪstɪk/ *adj.* беллетристи́ческий.

bellicose /'belɪˌkəʊz/ *adj.* вои́нственный.

bellicosity /'belɪ'kɒsɪtɪ/ *n.* вои́нственность.

belligerency /bɪ'lɪdʒərənsɪ/ *n.* состоя́ние войны́; (*aggressiveness*) вои́нственность, агресси́вность.

belligerent /bɪ'lɪdʒərənt/ *n.* вою́ющая сторонá.

● *adj.* (*waging war*) вою́ющий; (*aggressive*) вои́нственный, задúристый.

bellow /'beləʊ/ *n.* (*of animal*) мычáние; (*of sea, storm*) рёв.

● *v.t.* (*also* ~ **forth, out**) орáть (*impf.*).

● *v.i.* **1** (*of animal*) мычáть, про-; ревéть (*impf.*). **2** (*shout*) орáть (*impf.*); (*roar with pain*) ревéть (*impf.*), орáть (*impf.*); (*of thunder, cannon etc.*) гремéть (*impf.*), грóхот|ать, -нýть.

bellows /'beləʊz/ *n.* мехи́ (*m. pl.*).

belly /'belɪ/ *n.* **1** живóт, (*coll.*) брю́хо; **pot ~** тóлстое брю́хо; пýзо; **~ dancer** исполни́тельница тáнца животá; **he has fire in his ~** он пóлон огня́. **2** (*of ship etc.*) дни́ще; (*of violin etc.*) дéка.

● *v.t.* (*of wind*): **~ (out) a sail** над|увáть, -ýть пáрус.

● *v.i.* (*of sail*) нап|олня́ться, -óлниться.

● *cpds.* **~-ache** *n.* боль в живот́е; *v.i.* (*sl.*) стонáть, хны́кать, ныть (*all impf.*); **~-band** *n.* подпрýга; **~ button** *n.* (*coll.*) пупóк; **~-flop** *n.* (*coll.*) удáр живот́ом (*при прыжке в воду*); **~-landing** *n.* (*aeron.*) посáдка на «брю́хо» (*coll.*).

bellyful /'belɪfʊl/ *n.*: **he has had his ~ of it** он сыт по гóрло э́тим.

belong /bɪ'lɒŋ/ *v.i.* **1**: **~ to** (*be the property of*) принадлежáть (*impf.*) + *d.*; (*be a member of*) состоя́ть (*impf.*) в + *p.*; (*befit, appertain*): **it ~s to me to decide** мне решáть; **that ~s to my duties** э́то вхóдит в мои́ обя́занности. **2** (*of place*): **these books ~ here** э́ти кни́ги стоя́т здесь; э́ти кни́ги отсю́да; **I ~ here** (*was born here*) я рóдом отсю́да; (*live here*) я отсю́да; я здéшний; (*am rightly placed here*) я здесь на мéсте; **this ~s under 'Science'** э́то отнóсится к раздéлу «Нау́ка».

belongings /bɪ'lɒŋɪŋz/ *n.* вéщи (*f. pl.*) пожи́тк|и (*pl., g.* -ов).

Belorussia /ˌbeləʊ'rʌʃə/, **-n** /ˌbeləʊ'rʌʃ(ə)n/ = **Byelorussia, -n**

beloved /bɪ'lʌvɪd/, *pred. also* /-lʌvd/ *n.* возлю́бленн|ый (*fem.* -ая); **dearly ~!** (*to congregation*) возлю́бленные чáда!

● *adj.* возлю́бленный, люби́мый.

below /bɪ'ləʊ/ *adv.* (*of place*) внизý; (*of motion*) вниз; (*in text etc.*) ни́же; **from ~** сни́зу; **go ~** (*naut.*) спусти́ться (*pf.*) вниз.

● *prep.* (*of place*) под + *i.*; (*of motion*) под + *a.*; (*lower, downstream*) ни́же + *g.*; **~ 60** молóже шести́десяти; **~ £10** дешéвле/мéньше десяти́ фýнтов; **he is ~ average height** он ни́же срéднего рóста.

belt /belt/ *n.* **1** (*of leather*) ремéнь (*m.*); (*of linen etc.*) пóяс (*pl.* -á); (*mil.*) патрóнная лéнта; **hit below the ~** удáрить (*pf.*) ни́же пóяса; **tighten one's ~** (*fig.*) затянýть (*pf.*) потýже ремéнь; **seat ~** привязнóй ремéнь, ремéнь безопáсности. **2** (*zone*) пóяс, полосá; **cotton ~** хлóпковый пóяс. **3** (*tech.*) (приводнóй) ремéнь.

● *v.t.* **1** (*fasten*): **~ on a sword** опоя́с|ываться, -аться мечóм. **2** (*coll., thrash*) порóть, вы́-. **3**: **~ out a song** горлáнить (*impf.*) пéсню.

beluga /bə'lu:gə/ *n.* белýга.

belvedere /'belvɪˌdɪə(r)/ *n.* бельведéр.

belying /bɪ'laɪɪŋ/ *pres. part. of* ⇒**belie**

bemoan /bɪ'məʊn/ *v.t.* оплáк|ивать, -ать.

bemuse /bɪ'mju:z/ *v.t.* ошелом|ля́ть, -и́ть.

bench /bentʃ/ *n.* **1** (*seat*) скамья́, лáвка. **2** (*work-table*) верстáк, станóк. **3** (*judges*) сýдьи (*m. pl.*), судéйская коллéгия.

● *cpd.* **~-mark** *n.* эталóн, стандáрт; **~-mark test** эталóнный тест.

bend /bend/ *n.* **1** (*curve*) изги́б; (*in road*) поворóт; (*in river*) излýчина; **~ of the arm** локтевóй сгиб руки́; **round the ~** (*coll.*) свихнýвшийся. **2**: **the ~s** (*disease*) кессóнная болéзнь.

● *v.t.* (*past and p.p.* **bent**) **1** (*twist, incline*): **~ a branch** гнуть, при- вéтку; **~ an iron bar** из|гибáть, -огнýть желéзный брус; **the storm bent the tree to the ground** бýря пригнýла дéрево к землé; **a bent pin** сóгнутая булáвка; **the axle is bent** ось погнýлась; **~ a bow** сгибáть, согнýть лук; **on ~ed knee** преклони́в колéна; **knees ~!** колéни согнýть!; **~ one's head over a book** склон|я́ться, -и́ться над кни́гой; **~ s.o. to one's will** подчин|я́ть, -и́ть когó-н. своéй вóле. **2** (*direct*): **~ one's steps homewards** напрáвить (*pf.*) стопы́ к дóму; **all eyes were bent on him** все взóры бы́ли напрáвлены на негó; **he is bent on learning English** он твёрдо реши́л изучи́ть англи́йский язы́к; **he is bent on mischief** он тóлько и дýмает, как бы набедокýрить.

● *v.i.* (*past and p.p.* **bent**): **the river ~s here** рекá здесь изгибáется; **the trees bent in the wind** дерéвья гнýлись на ветрý; **~ at the knees** сгибáться, согнýться в колéнях; **~ over one's desk** сгибáться, согнýться над столóм; **~ before s.o.'s will** склон|я́ться, -и́ться пéред чьей-н. вóлей; **~ forward** наклон|я́ться, -и́ться (вперёд); **~ over backwards** (*fig.*) ≈ из кóжи вон лезть.

● *with advs.*: **~ back** *v.t.* (*e.g. a finger*) оття́|гивать, -нýть назáд; **~ down** *v.t.* наг|ибáть, -нýть; сгибáть, согнýть; преклон|я́ть, -и́ть; *v.i.* (*also* **~ over**) наг|ибáться, -нýться; перег|ибáться, -нýться.

bender /'bendə(r)/ *n.* (*sl.*) кутёж; **go on a ~** загуля́ть (*pf.*).

beneath /bɪ'ni:θ/ *adv.* внизý.

● *prep.* (*of place*) под + *i.*; (*of motion*) под + *a.*; (*lower than*) ни́же + *g.*; **~ criticism** ни́же вся́кой крити́ки; **marry ~ one** соверши́ть (*pf.*) мезалья́нс; заключи́ть (*pf.*) нерáвный брак; **it is ~ you to complain** жáловаться — недостóйно вас; **it is ~ contempt** э́то не заслýживает ничегó, крóме презрéния.

Benedictine /ˌbenɪ'dɪktɪn/, *in sense* 2 /-ˌti:n/ *n.* **1** (*monk*) бенедикти́нец; (*nun*) бенедикти́нка. **2** (*liqueur*) бенедикти́н.

● *adj.* бенедикти́нский.

benediction /ˌbenɪ'dɪkʃ(ə)n/ *n.* благословéние.

benefaction /ˌbenɪ'fækʃ(ə)n/ *n.* (*kind act*) благодея́ние; (*donation*) пожéртвование.

benefactor /'benɪˌfæktə(r)/ *n.* (*one who confers benefit*) благодéтель (*m.*); (*donor*) благотвори́тель (*m.*).

benefactress /'benɪˌfæktrɪs/ *n.* благодéтельница; благотвори́тельница.

benefice /'benɪfɪs/ *n.* бенефи́ций.

beneficence /bɪ'nefɪsəns/ *n.* благодея́ние; благотвори́тельность.

beneficent /bɪ'nefɪs(ə)nt/ *adj.* благотвори́тельный.

beneficial /ˌbenɪ'fɪʃ(ə)l/ *adj.* благотвóрный, полéзный, вы́годный. **mutually ~** взаимовы́годный.

beneficiary /ˌbenɪ'fɪʃərɪ/ *n.* (*leg.*) бенефициáрий.

benefit /'benɪfɪt/ *n.* **1** (*advantage*) пóльза, вы́года, преимýщество; **for the ~ of the poor** в пóльзу бéдных; **for the ~ of mankind** на блáго человéчества; **give s.o. the ~ of one's advice** помóчь (*pf.*) комý-н. совéтом; **I gave him the ~ of the doubt** я емý повéрил (на э́тот раз); **reap the ~ of** пожинáть (*impf.*) плоды́ + *g.*; **she wore a new dress for his ~** онá надéла нóвое плáтье рáди негó. **2** (*favour*) благодея́ние; **confer ~s on** окáзывать (*impf.*) благодея́ния + *d.* **3** (*grant*) пособие; **child ~** пособие на детéй; **invalidity ~** пособие по инвали́дности; **maternity ~** пособие по берéменности и рóдам; **unemployment ~** пособие по безрабóтице. **4**: **~ concert** благотвори́тельный концéрт.

● *v.t.* (**benefited, benefiting;** *US* **benefitted, benefitting**) прин|оси́ть, -ести́ пóльзу + *d.*, идти́ (*det.*) на пóльзу + *d.*; (*of health*) прин|оси́ть, -ести́ пóльзу + *d.*

● *v.i.* (**benefited, benefiting;** *US* **benefitted, benefitting**) извл|екáть, -éчь пóльзу (из + *g.*); **you will ~ by a holiday** óтдых пойдёт вам на пóльзу.

Benelux /'benɪˌlʌks/ *n.* Бенилю́кс.

benevolence /bɪ'nevələns/ *n.* благожелáтельность, доброжелáтельность.

benevolent /bɪ'nevələnt/ *adj.*

благожела́тельный, доброжела́тельный.

benighted /bɪˈnaɪtɪd/ *adj.* засти́гнутый но́чью; (*fig.*) тёмный; обскура́нтский.

benign /bɪˈnaɪn/ *adj.* (*of person*) добросерде́чный; (*of climate*) благотво́рный; (*med.*) доброка́чественный.

benignity /bɪˈnɪgnɪtɪ/ *n.* добросерде́чие, великоду́шие.

bent /bent/ *n.* (*inclination*) скло́нность; (*aptitude*) накло́нность; **to the top of one's ~** в по́лное своё удово́льствие.

● *adj.* (*Br. coll.*) (*corrupt*) нече́стный, извращённый, прода́жный; (*homosexual*) гомосексуа́льный.

● *also p.p. of* ⇒**bend,** *q.v.*

benz|ene /ˈbenziːn/, **-ol** /ˈbenzɒl/ *nn.* бензо́л.

benzine /ˈbenziːn/ *n.* бензи́н.

benzol /ˈbenzɒl/ = **benzene**

bequeath /bɪˈkwiːð/ *v.t.* завеща́ть (*impf.*, *pf.*); (*fig.*) оста́вить (*pf.*).

bequest /bɪˈkwest/ *n.* (*object*) вещь, оста́вленная в насле́дство; (*as part of museum collection*) фонд, посме́ртный дар; (*act*) завеща́тельный отка́з иму́щества; **make a ~ of** завеща́ть (*impf.*, *pf.*).

berate /bɪˈreɪt/ *v.t.* брани́ть (*impf.*).

bereave /bɪˈriːv/ *v.t.*: **a ~d husband** неда́вно овдове́вший муж; **the ~d** (*pl.*) ро́дственники поко́йного.

bereavement /bɪˈriːvmənt/ *n.* тяжёлая утра́та/поте́ря.

bereft /bɪˈreft/ *adj.* (*lonely*) одино́кий; **~ of hope** лишённый наде́жды.

beret /ˈbereɪ/ *n.* бере́т.

beriberi /ˌberɪˈberɪ/ *n.* бе́ри-бе́ри (*f. indecl.*).

Bering Sea /ˈberɪŋ/ *n.* Бе́рингово мо́ре.

berk /bɜːk/ *n.* (*Br. sl.*) болва́н.

Berlin /bɜːˈlɪn/ *n.* Берли́н.

Bermuda /bəˈmjuːdə/ *n.*: (*also* **the ~s**) Берму́дские острова́ (*m. pl.*); **~ shorts** шо́рты-берму́ды; **~ Triangle** Берму́дский треуго́льник.

Berne /bɜːn/ *n.* Берн.

berry /ˈberɪ/ *n.* я́года.

berserk /bəˈsɜːk/, /-ˈzɜːk/ *n.*: **go ~** разъяри́ться (*pf.*), обезу́меть (*pf.*).

berth /bɜːθ/ *n.* **1** (*place at wharf*) при́стань, прича́л. **2**: **give a ship a wide ~** держа́ться на доста́точном расстоя́нии от корабля́; **give s.o. a wide ~** (*fig.*) обходи́ть (*impf.*) кого́-н. стороно́й (*or* за версту́). **3** (*sleeping-place on ship*) ко́йка; (*on train*) спа́льное ме́сто.

● *v.t.* **1** (*moor*) ста́вить (*impf.*) к прича́лу; **~ing-place** ме́сто стоя́нки. **2** (*give sleeping-room to*) предост|авля́ть, -а́вить спа́льное ме́сто + *d.*

● *v.i.* (*of ship*) прича́ли|вать, -ть.

beryl /ˈberɪl/ *n.* бери́лл; (*attr.*) бери́лловый.

beryllium /bəˈrɪlɪəm/ *n.* бери́ллий.

beseech /bɪˈsiːtʃ/ *v.t.* (*past and p.p.* **besought** *or* **beseeched**) умол|я́ть, -и́ть; моли́ть (*impf.*).

beset /bɪˈset/ *v.t.* (**besetting;** *past and p.p.* **beset**) окруж|а́ть, -и́ть; оса|жда́ть, -ди́ть.

beside /bɪˈsaɪd/ *prep.* **1** (*alongside*) ря́дом с + *i.*; (*near*) о́коло + *g.*, у + *g.* **2** (*compared with*) по сравне́нию с + *i.*; пе́ред + *i.*; **~ him all novelists are insignificant** по сравне́нию с ним все романи́сты ничего́ не сто́ят; **set ~** поста́вить (*pf.*) ря́дом с + *i.* **3** (*wide of*) ми́мо + *g.*; **that is ~ the point** э́то к де́лу не отно́сится. **4**: **~ o.s.** вне себя́. **5** (*as well as*) кро́ме + *g.*

besides /bɪˈsaɪdz/ *adv.* сверх того́; кро́ме того́.

● *prep.* кро́ме + *g.*

besiege /bɪˈsiːdʒ/ *v.t.* (*lit.*, *fig.*) оса|жда́ть, -ди́ть.

besmear /bɪˈsmɪə(r)/ *v.t.* заса́ли|вать, -ть; выма́зывать, вы́мазать.

besmirch /bɪˈsmɜːtʃ/ *v.t.* па́чкать, вы́-; (*fig.*) поро́чить, о-.

besom /ˈbiːz(ə)m/ *n.* метла́, ве́ник.

besotted /bɪˈsɒtɪd/ *adj.* одурма́ненный.

besought /bɪˈsɔːt/ *past and p.p. of* ⇒**beseech**

bespangle /bɪˈspæŋg(ə)l/ *v.t.* ос|ыпа́ть, -ы́пать блёстками; **a ~d sky** усе́янное звёздами не́бо.

bespatter /bɪˈspætə(r)/ *v.t.* забры́зг|ивать, -ать.

bespeak /bɪˈspiːk/ *v.t.* (*past* **bespoke;** *p.p.* **bespoken**) (*order*) зака́з|ывать, -а́ть; (*reveal*) свиде́тельствовать, говори́ть (*both impf.*) о.

bespectacled /bɪˈspektək(ə)ld/ *adj.* в очка́х.

bespoke /bɪˈspəʊk/ *adj.* (*Br.*) сде́ланный на зака́з; **~ tailor** портно́й, рабо́тающий на зака́з.

bespoken /bɪˈspəʊkən/ *p.p. of* ⇒**bespeak**

besprinkle /bɪˈsprɪŋk(ə)l/ *v.t.* (*with liquid*) обры́зг|ивать, -ать; (*with powder etc.*) обс|ыпа́ть, -ы́пать.

Bessarabia /ˌbesəˈreɪbɪə/ *n.* Бессара́бия.

best /best/ *n.* (**~** *performance*) лу́чший результа́т; *see also adj.*

● *adj.* лу́чший; **the ~ way to the station** са́мый лу́чший путь к ста́нции; **we are the ~ of friends** мы бли́зкие друзья́; **at ~** в лу́чшем слу́чае; **I did it for the ~** я де́лал э́то с лу́чшими наме́рениями; **get the ~ of it** взять (*pf.*) верх; **do one's ~** сде́лать (*pf.*) всё возмо́жное; **I know what is ~ for him** я лу́чше зна́ю, что ему́ ну́жно; **to the ~ of one's ability** в ме́ру свои́х сил/спосо́бностей; **to the ~ of my knowledge** наско́лько мне изве́стно; **in the ~ of health** в до́бром здра́вии; **give s.o. ~** (*Br.*) призна́ть (*pf.*) чьё-н. превосхо́дство; **all the ~!** всего́ наилу́чшего!; **hope for the ~** наде́яться (*impf.*) на лу́чшее; **turn out for the ~** оберну́ться (*pf.*) к лу́чшему; **may the ~ man win** пусть победи́т сильне́йший; **~ pupil** пе́рвый учени́к; **~ quality** вы́сший сорт; (*greater*): **the ~ part of a week** бо́льшая часть неде́ли; **I waited for the ~ part of an hour** я ждал почти́ це́лый час; **~ man** (*at wedding*) ша́фер.

● *adv.* лу́чше всего́; **he works ~** (*better than others*) он рабо́тает лу́чше всех; **I work ~ in the evening** мне лу́чше всего́ рабо́тается по вечера́м; **you know ~** вам лу́чше знать; **I had ~ tell him** мне бы сле́довало сказа́ть ему́; **do as you think ~** де́лайте, как вам ка́жется лу́чше; **which town did you like ~?** како́й го́род вам бо́льше всего́ понра́вился?; **I liked her ~ (of all)** она́ мне понра́вилась бо́льше всех; **it is ~ forgotten** лу́чше всего́ забы́ть об э́том.

● *v.t.* брать, взять верх над + *i.*

● *cpds.* **~-dressed** *adj.* са́мый элега́нтный; **~-looking** *adj.* са́мый краси́вый; **~-seller** *n.* (*book*) бестсе́ллер; (*Br.*, *author*) а́втор бестсе́ллера; **~-selling** *adj.* хо́дкий.

bestial /ˈbestɪəl/ *adj.* звери́ный; (*brutish*) зве́рский; (*depraved*) ско́тский.

bestiality /ˌbestɪˈælɪtɪ/ *n.* (*brutishness*) зве́рство; (*depravity*) ско́тство; (*leg.*) скотоло́жество.

bestir /bɪˈstɜː(r)/ *v.t.* (**bestirred, bestirring**): **~ o.s.** встряхну́ться (*pf.*).

bestow /bɪˈstəʊ/ *v.t.* (*confer*): **~ gifts on s.o.** ода́р|ивать, -и́ть кого́-н.; **he ~ed a fortune on his nephew** он переда́л племя́ннику це́лое состоя́ние; **~ a title on s.o.** присв|а́ивать, -о́ить кому́-н. ти́тул; **~ honours** (*Br.*), **honors** (*US*) возд|ава́ть, -а́ть по́чести.

bestowal /bɪˈstəʊəl/ *n.* **1** (*donation*) дар. **2**: **~ of a title** присвое́ние ти́тула; **~ of honours** воздая́ние по́честей.

bestrew /bɪˈstruː/ *v.t.* (*p.p.* **bestrewed** *or* **bestrewn** /-ˈstruːn/) ус|ыпа́ть, -ы́пать.

bestride /bɪˈstraɪd/ *v.t.* (*past* **bestrode** /-ˈstrəʊd/; *p.p.* **bestridden** /-ˈstrɪd(ə)n/) (*a chair, fence etc.*) осёдл|ывать, -а́ть; **~ a horse** сиде́ть (*impf.*) верхо́м.

bet /bet/ *n.* пари́ (*nt. indecl.*), ста́вка; **make, lay a ~** держа́ть (*impf.*) пари́; **accept a ~** идти́ (*det.*) на пари́; **the grey is the best ~ to win** се́рый/се́рко име́ет бо́льше всех ша́нсов на вы́игрыш; **your best ~ is to go there** вам лу́чше всего́ пойти́ туда́.

● *v.t. & i.* (**betting;** *past and p.p.* **bet** *or* **betted**) держа́ть (*impf.*) пари́; би́ться, по- об закла́д; **he ~ £5 on a horse** он поста́вил 5 фу́нтов на ло́шадь; **he ~ me £10 I wouldn't do it** он поспо́рил со мной на 10 фу́нтов, что я не сде́лаю э́того; **I ~ he doesn't turn up** держу́ пари́, что он не придёт; **you ~ (your life)!** (*coll.*) ещё бы!; ещё как!

beta /ˈbiːtə/ *n.*: **~ blocker** (*pharm.*) бе́та-блока́тор; **~ particle** бе́та-части́ца; **~ rays** бе́та-лучи́.

betake /bɪˈteɪk/ *v.t.* (*past* **betook;** *p.p.* **betaken** /bɪˈteɪk(ə)n/): **~ o.s. to** (*a place*) отпр|авля́ться, -а́виться к + *d.*

betel /ˈbiːt(ə)l/ *n.* бе́тель (*m.*).

● *cpd.* **~-nut** *n.* аре́ковое се́мя.

B

bête noire /beɪt 'nwɑ:(r)/ *n.* (*pl.* ***bêtes noires*** *pronunc. same*): **he is my ~** он мне ненави́стен.

Bethlehem /'beθlɪˌhem/ *n.* Вифлее́м.

betide /bɪ'taɪd/ (*arch.*) *v.t.*: **woe ~ you** го́ре вам!

betimes /bɪ'taɪmz/ *adv.* (*in good time*) своевре́менно; (*early*) ра́но.

betoken /bɪ'təʊkən/ *v.t.* (*indicate*) ука́з|ывать, -а́ть на + *a.*; (*signify*) означа́ть (*impf.*).

betony /'betənɪ/ *n.* (*bot.*) бу́квица.

betook /bɪ'tʊk/ *past of* ⇒**betake**

betray /bɪ'treɪ/ *v.t.* **1** (*abandon treacherously*) измен|я́ть, -и́ть + *d.*; пред|ава́ть, -а́ть. **2**: **~ s.o.'s hopes** обману́ть (*pf.*) чьи-н. наде́жды; **~ s.o.'s trust** обману́ть чьё-н. дове́рие; не оправда́ть (*pf.*) чьего́-н. дове́рия. **3** (*disclose, evince*) выдава́ть, вы́дать; **his accent ~ed him** его́ вы́дало произноше́ние; **~ official secrets** выдава́ть, вы́дать госуда́рственные та́йны; **~ surprise** выража́ть, вы́разить удивле́ние.

betrayal /bɪ'treɪəl/ *n.* (*treachery*) преда́тельство, изме́на; (*disclosure*) вы́дача; (*disappointment*) обма́н; **the ~ of his hopes** круше́ние его́ наде́жд.

betrayer /bɪ'treɪə(r)/ *n.* преда́тель (*m.*); изме́нник.

betroth /bɪ'trəʊð/ *v.t.* (*liter.*) обруч|а́ть, -и́ть; помо́лвить (*pf.*); **she is ~ed to him** она́ с ним обручена́/помо́лвлена.

betrothal /bɪ'trəʊðəl/ *n.* обруче́ние, помо́лвка.

bett|er[1], **-or** /'betə(r)/ *nn.* (*one who bets*) держа́щий пари́, понтёр.

better[2] /'betə(r)/ *adj.* лу́чший, лу́чше; **~ still** ещё лу́чше; **all the ~** тем лу́чше; **I hoped for ~ things** я наде́ялся на лу́чшее; **it is ~ that you go** вам бы лу́чше уйти́; **(one's) ~ half** дража́йшая полови́на; **get ~** ул|учша́ться, -у́чшиться; (*in health*) попр|авля́ться, -а́виться; **things are getting ~** дела́ иду́т лу́чше; **go one ~ than s.o.** превзойти́ (*pf.*) кого́-н.; **get the ~ of s.o.** взять (*pf.*) верх над кем-н.; превзойти́ (*pf.*) кого́-н.; **he got the ~ of his anger** он превозмо́г/преодоле́л свой гнев; **a change for the ~** переме́на к лу́чшему; **for ~, for worse** на го́ре и ра́дость; **you will be the ~ for a holiday** о́тдых пойдёт вам на по́льзу; **he is no ~ than a fool** он по́просту дура́к; **appeal to s.o.'s ~ feelings** взыва́ть (*impf.*) к чьим-н. лу́чшим чу́вствам; **the ~ part of a day** бо́льшая часть дня; **one's ~s** вышестоя́щие ли́ца.

● *adv.* лу́чше; (*more*) бо́льше; **~ and ~** всё лу́чше и лу́чше; **the more the ~** чем бо́льше, тем лу́чше; **you had ~ stay here** вам бы лу́чше оста́ться здесь; **I thought ~ of it** я разду́мал/переду́мал; **~ off** бо́лее состоя́тельный.

● *v.t.* **1** (*improve*) ул|учша́ть, -у́чшить; **he ~ed himself** он продви́нулся. **2** (*improve on*) превзойти́ (*pf.*).

betterment /'betəmənt/ *n.* улучше́ние, соверше́нствование.

betting /'betɪŋ/ *n.*: **what's the ~ he marries her?** (*Br.*) на ско́лько спо́рим, что он на ней же́нится?

● *adj.*: **he is not a ~ man** он челове́к не аза́ртный; **~ shop** (*Br.*) букме́керская конто́ра.

bettor /'betə(r)/ = **better**[1]

between /bɪ'twi:n/ *adv.*: **I attended the two lectures and had lunch in ~** я посети́л две ле́кции и пообе́дал в переры́ве.

● *prep.* ме́жду + *g. or i.*; **~ you and me** ме́жду на́ми; **(in) ~ times** вре́мя от вре́мени; **~ two and three months** от двух до трёх ме́сяцев; **choose ~ the two** выбира́ть, вы́брать одно́ из двух; **~ now and then** к тому́ вре́мени; **they scored 150 ~ them** они́ набра́ли сто пятьдеся́т очко́в вме́сте; **we have only a pound ~ us** у нас на двои́х всего́ оди́н фунт; **we bought a car ~ us** мы сообща́ купи́ли маши́ну.

betwixt /bɪ'twɪkst/ *adv.*: **~ and between** ни то ни сё.

bevel /'bev(ə)l/ *n.* (*tool*) ма́лка; (*surface*) скос; **~ edge** фацёт; **~ gear** кони́ческая зубча́тая переда́ча.

● *v.t.* (**bevelled, bevelling;** *US* **beveled, beveling**) ск|а́шивать, -оси́ть.

beverage /'bevərɪdʒ/ *n.* напи́ток.

bevy /'bevɪ/ *n.* (*of people*) гру́ппа; (*of birds*) ста́я.

bewail /bɪ'weɪl/ *v.t.* опла́к|ивать, -ать.

beware /bɪ'weə(r)/ *v.t. & i.* остер|ега́ться, -е́чься (*impf.*) + *g.*; **~ lest you fall** осторо́жно, а то упадёте; **~ of the dog** осторо́жно, зла́я соба́ка.

bewilder /bɪ'wɪldə(r)/ *v.t.* сби|ва́ть, -ть с то́лку; прив|оди́ть, -ести́ в замеша́тельство; **~ed** смущённый, озада́ченный.

bewilderment /bɪ'wɪldəmənt/ *n.* замеша́тельство, озада́ченность.

bewitch /bɪ'wɪtʃ/ *v.t.* (*put spell on*) околдо́в|ывать, -а́ть; (*delight*) очаро́в|ывать, -а́ть.

bewitching /bɪ'wɪtʃɪŋ/ *adj.* чару́ющий.

beyond /bɪ'jɒnd/ *n.*: **he lives at the back of ~** он живёт на краю́ све́та.

● *adv.* вдали́; вдаль.

● *prep.* (*of place*) за + *i.*; (*of motion*) за + *a.*; (*later than*) по́сле + *g.*; **~ doubt** вне сомне́ния; **~ dispute** бесспо́рно; **~ my comprehension** вы́ше моего́ понима́ния; **~ my powers** не в мои́х си́лах; **~ belief** невероя́тно; **~ expression** невырази́мо; **~ my expectations** сверх мои́х ожида́ний; **succeed ~ one's hopes** да́же не ожида́ть (*impf.*) тако́го успе́ха; **this is ~ a joke** здесь уже́ не до шу́ток; **live ~ one's income** жить (*impf.*) не по сре́дствам; **~ measure** сверх ме́ры, чрезме́рно; **~ hope** безнадёжно; **~ cure** неизлечи́мый; **go ~ one's duty** сде́лать (*pf.*) бо́льше, чем обя́зан.

biannual /baɪ'ænjʊəl/ *adj.* выходя́щий два́жды в год; полугодово́й.

bias /'baɪəs/ *n.* **1** предрассу́док, предвзя́тое отноше́ние (*к чему*); (*favourable prejudice*) пристра́стие (к + *d.*); (*adverse*) предубежде́ние (про́тив + *g.*). **2** (*of material*): **cut on the ~** крои́ть, с- по косо́й ли́нии (*or* по диагона́ли).

● *v.t.* (**biased, biasing; biassed, biassing**) (*influence*) склон|я́ть, -и́ть; (*prejudice*) предубе|жда́ть, -ди́ть; **~ s.o. against an idea** настр|а́ивать, -о́ить кого́-н. про́тив како́й-н. иде́и; **a ~(s)ed opinion** предвзя́тое мне́ние.

biathlete /baɪ'æθli:t/ *n.* биатлони́ст (*fem.* -ка).

biathlon /baɪ'æθlən/ *n.* биатло́н.

bib /bɪb/ *n.* (де́тский) нагру́дник, слюня́вчик (*coll.*); **best ~ and tucker** (*joc.*) лу́чший наря́д, лу́чшее одея́ние.

Bible /'baɪb(ə)l/ *n.* Би́блия; (*fig.*) би́блия.

biblical /'bɪblɪk(ə)l/ *adj.* библе́йский.

bibliographer /ˌbɪblɪ'ɒgrəfə(r)/ *n.* библио́граф.

bibliographic(al) /ˌbɪblɪə'græfɪk(ə)l/ *adj.* библиографи́ческий.

bibliography /ˌbɪblɪ'ɒgrəfɪ/ *n.* библиогра́фия; (*list of works referred to*) спи́сок испо́льзованной литерату́ры.

bibliophile /'bɪblɪəʊˌfaɪl/ *n.* библиофи́л.

bibulous /'bɪbjʊləs/ *adj.* пья́нствующий, выпива́ющий.

bicameral /baɪ'kæmər(ə)l/ *adj.* двухпала́тный.

bicarbonate /baɪ'kɑ:bənɪt/ *n.* двууглеки́слая соль; **~ of soda** питьева́я со́да.

bicentenary /ˌbaɪsen'ti:nərɪ/ *n.* двухсотле́тие.

● *adj.* двухсотле́тний.

bicentennial /ˌbaɪsen'tenɪəl/ *n.* двухсотле́тие.

● *adj.* (*occurring every 200 years*) повторя́ющийся ка́ждые две́сти лет.

biceps /'baɪseps/ *n.* (*pl.* **~**) би́цепс.

bicker /'bɪkə(r)/ *v.t.* (*squabble*) перебра́ниваться (*impf.*), препира́ться (*impf.*).

bicycle /'baɪsɪk(ə)l/ *n.* велосипе́д.

● *v.i.* е́здить (*indet.*), е́хать, по- (*det.*) на велосипе́де.

bicyclist /'baɪsɪklɪst/ *n.* велосипеди́ст.

bid /bɪd/ *n.* **1** (*at auction*) зая́вка; предложе́ние цены́; **make a higher ~** сде́лать (*pf.*) надба́вку. **2** (*tender*) зая́вка. **3** (*claim, demand*) зая́вка (на + *a.*); претензия. **4** (*attempt*) ста́вка; попы́тка; **make a ~ for power** сде́лать (*pf.*) ста́вку на захва́т вла́сти. **5** (*at cards*) зая́вка.

● *v.t. & i.* (**bidding;** *past* **bid;** *arch.* **bade;** *p.p.* **bid;** *arch.* **bidden**) **1** (*at auction*) предл|ага́ть, -ожи́ть це́ну (*за что*); **~ against s.o.** наб|авля́ть, -а́вить це́ну про́тив кого́-н. **2** (*at cards*) объяв|ля́ть, -и́ть. **3** (*tender*): **~ for a contract** де́лать, с- зая́вку на контра́кт. **4** (*liter., order*): **~ him come in!** вели́те ему́ войти́!; **do as you are ~(den)!** де́лай как ска́зано! **5** (*liter., say*): **~ s.o. farewell** про|ща́ться, -сти́ться с кем-н.; **~ s.o. welcome** приве́тствовать (*impf.*) кого́-н.; **~ s.o. goodnight** пожела́ть (*pf.*) поко́йной но́чи кому́-н.

biddable /ˈbɪdəb(ə)l/ *adj.* послу́шный.

bidden /ˈbɪd(ə)n/ *arch. p.p. of* ⇒**bid**

bidder /ˈbɪdə(r)/ *n.* покупщи́к; (*at auction*) аукционе́р; **the highest ~** предложи́вший наивы́сшую це́ну.

bidding /ˈbɪdɪŋ/ *n.* **1** (*at auction*) предложе́ние цены́; **the ~ was brisk** надба́вки сле́довали одна́ за друго́й. **2** (*command*): **do s.o.'s ~** исп|олня́ть, -о́лнить чьи-н. приказа́ния. **3** (*at cards*) объявле́ние.

bide /baɪd/ *v.t.*: **~ one's time** ждать (*impf.*) благоприя́тного слу́чая.

bidet /ˈbiːdeɪ/ *n.* биде́ (*indecl.*).

biennial /baɪˈenɪəl/ *n.* (*bot.*) двуле́тник.

● *adj.* двухле́тний.

bier /bɪə(r)/ *n.* катафа́лк.

biff /bɪf/ (*coll.*) *n.*: **a ~ on the nose** уда́р по́ носу.

● *v.t.*: **~ s.o. in the eye** дать (*pf.*) кому́-н. в глаз.

bifocal /baɪˈfəʊk(ə)l/ *adj.* двухфо́кусный, бифока́льный; **~ spectacles** (*also* **~s**) бифока́льные очки́.

bifurcate /ˈbaɪfəˌkeɪt/ *v.t. & i.* разветв|ля́ть(ся), -и́ть(ся); (*of road, river: also*) раздв|а́иваться, -ои́ться; **a ~d tail** раздво́енный хвост.

bifurcation /ˌbaɪfəˈkeɪʃ(ə)n/ *n.* разветвле́ние.

big /bɪg/ *adj.* (**bigger, biggest**) (*in size*) большо́й, кру́пный; (*great*) кру́пный, вели́кий; (*extensive*) обши́рный; (*intense*) си́льный; (*tall*) высо́кий; (*adult*) взро́слый; (*magnanimous*) великоду́шный; (*important*) ва́жный; **a ~ man** (*in stature*) кру́пный мужчи́на; (*in importance*) кру́пная фигу́ра; **a ~ voice** си́льный го́лос; **a ~ landowner** кру́пный землевладе́лец; **these boots are too ~ for me** э́ти сапоги́ мне велики́; **~ (capital) letters** прописны́е бу́квы; **a ~ fire** си́льный/большо́й пожа́р; **as ~ as** величино́й в + *a.*; **~ words** гро́мкие слова́; **talk ~** хва́статься (*impf.*); **think ~** мы́слить (*impf.*) сме́ло/де́рзко; **a ~ noise** (*person*) ши́шка (*coll.*); **my ~ brother** мой ста́рший брат; **Big Dipper** (*Br.*) америка́нские го́ры; (*US*) Больша́я Медве́дица; **in a ~ way** с широ́ким разма́хом; **~ wheel** колесо́ обозре́ния; **a ~ name** (*celebrity*) знамени́тость.

● *cpds.* **~ end** *n.* (*tech.*) больша́я (кривоши́пная) голо́вка (шатуна́); **~-headed** *adj.* (*conceited*) зазна́вшийся; возомни́вший о себе́; **~-hearted** *adj.* великоду́шный; **~wig** *n.* ши́шка (*coll.*).

bigamist /ˈbɪgəmɪst/ *n.* (*man*) двоеже́нец; (*woman*) двуму́жница.

bigamous /ˈbɪgəməs/ *adj.* бигами́ческий, двубра́чный; име́ющий/име́ющая двух жён/муже́й.

bigamy /ˈbɪgəmɪ/ *n.* бига́мия; (*of man*) двоежёнство; (*of woman*) двоему́жие, двуму́жие.

bight /baɪt/ *n.* (*bay*) бу́хта; (*in rope*) шлаг.

bigness /ˈbɪgnɪs/ *n.* величина́.

bigot /ˈbɪgət/ *n.* фана́тик.

bigoted /ˈbɪgətɪd/ *adj.* фанати́ческий, фанати́чный.

bigotry /ˈbɪgətrɪ/ *n.* фанати́зм.

bijou /ˈbiːʒuː/ *adj.* ма́ленький и изя́щный.

bike /baɪk/ *n.* **1** (*coll.*) = **bicycle.** **2** (*motorcycle*) мотоци́кл.

● *v.i.* е́здить (*indet.*) на мотоци́кле.

biker /ˈbaɪkə(r)/ *n.* мотоцикли́ст (*fem.* -ка).

bikini /bɪˈkiːnɪ/ *n.* бики́ни (*nt. indecl.*).

bilabial /baɪˈleɪbɪəl/ *adj.* билабиа́льный.

bilateral /baɪˈlætər(ə)l/ *adj.* двусторо́нний.

bilberry /ˈbɪlbərɪ/ *n.* черни́ка (*collect.*); я́года черни́ки.

bile /baɪl/ *n.* жёлчь; (*fig.*) жёлчность.

● *cpd.* **~-duct** *n.* жёлчный прото́к.

bilge /bɪldʒ/ *n.* **1** (*of ship*) дни́ще; дно трю́ма. **2** (*coll.*) чепуха́.

● *cpd.* **~-water** *n.* трю́мная вода́.

bilingual /baɪˈlɪŋgw(ə)l/ *adj.* двуязы́чный.

bilingualism /baɪˈlɪŋgw(ə)lɪz(ə)m/ *n.* двуязы́чие.

bilious /ˈbɪljəs/ *adj.* **1** жёлчный; **a ~ headache** мигре́нь. **2** (*fig.*) жёлчный, раздражи́тельный.

biliousness /ˈbɪljəsnɪs/ *n.* жёлчность, раздражи́тельность.

bilk /bɪlk/ *v.t.*: **~ s.o. of something** наду́ть (*pf.*) (*coll.*) кого́-н. на что-н.; **he ~ed me of £1,000** он наду́л меня́ на ты́сячу фу́нтов.

bill[1] /bɪl/ *n.* **1** (*beak*) клюв. **2** (*promontory*) мыс.

● *v.i.*: **~ and coo** милова́ться (*impf.*), воркова́ть (*impf.*).

bill[2] /bɪl/ *n.* (*also* **~hook**) садо́вый нож.

bill[3] /bɪl/ *n.* **1** (*parl.*) законопрое́кт, билль (*m.*). **2** (*certificate*): **clean ~ of health** каранти́нное свиде́тельство. **3** (*comm.*) счёт (*pl.* -а́); **~ of exchange** ве́ксель (*m.*); **~ of lading** накладна́я, коносаме́нт; **pay a ~, foot the ~** заплати́ть (*pf.*) по счёту; опла́|чивать, -ти́ть счёт; **run up a ~** набра́ть (*pf.*) мно́го в долг, мно́го задолжа́ть (*pf.*). **4** (*advertisement*): **~ of fare** меню́ (*nt. indecl.*); **theatre** (*Br.*), **theater** (*US*) **~** театра́льная афи́ша; **stick no ~s** (*as notice*) наклéивать объявле́ния воспреща́ется; **fill the ~** (*satisfy requirements*) отвеча́ть (*impf.*) всем тре́бованиям. **5** (*US, banknote*) банкно́та; **dollar ~** до́лларовый биле́т.

● *v.t.* **1** (*announce*) объяв|ля́ть, -и́ть; **he was ~ed to appear in 'Hamlet'** объяви́ли, что он бу́дет игра́ть в «Га́млете»; **get top ~ing** быть помещённым на афи́ше на пе́рвом ме́сте. **2** (*charge*): **~ me for the goods** пришли́те мне счёт за това́ры.

● *cpds.* **~board** *n.* доска́ объявле́ний; **~fold** *n.* (*US*) бума́жник; **~-poster, ~-sticker** *nn.* раскле́йщик афи́ш.

billet /ˈbɪlɪt/ *n.* **1** (*order for* **~ing**) о́рдер на посто́й. **2** (*place of lodging*) помеще́ние для посто́я; **be in ~s** быть на посто́е.

● *v.t.* (**billeted, billeting**) (*assign to* **~**) расквартиро́в|ывать, -а́ть; назн|ача́ть, -а́чить (*or* ста́вить, по-) на посто́й (**on s.o.**: к кому́-н.).

billiard|s /ˈbɪljədz/ *n.* билья́рд.

● *cpds.* **~-ball** *n.* бильярдный шар; **~-cue** *n.* кий; **~-table** *n.* билья́рд, билья́рдный стол.

billion /ˈbɪljən/ *n.* (*pl.* **~s** *or, with numeral or qualifying word,* **~**) (*thousand million*) миллиа́рд; (*Br., million million*) биллио́н.

billionaire /ˌbɪljəˈneə(r)/ *n.* миллиарде́р.

billow /ˈbɪləʊ/ *n.* вал.

● *v.i.* (*of smoke*) вздыма́ться (*impf.*); (*of fabric*) над|ува́ться, -у́ться.

billy /ˈbɪlɪ/ *n.* (*also* **~can**) жестяно́й (похо́дный) котело́к.

billy-goat /ˈbɪlɪˌgəʊt/ *n.* козёл.

bimbo /ˈbɪmbəʊ/ *n.* (*pl.* **~s**) фи́ф(очк)а.

bimetallic /ˌbaɪmɪˈtælɪk/ *adj.* биметалли́ческий.

bimonthly /baɪˈmʌnθlɪ/ *adj.* **1** (*fortnightly*) выходя́щий (*и т.п.*) два ра́за в ме́сяц. **2** (*two-monthly*) выходя́щий (*и т.п.*) раз в два ме́сяца.

● *adv.* **1** два ра́за в ме́сяц. **2** раз в два ме́сяца.

bin /bɪn/ *n.* (*for corn*) закро́м, ларь (*m.*); (*Br., for ashes, dust*) му́сорное ведро́.

binary /ˈbaɪnərɪ/ *adj.* (*math.*) двои́чный.

bind /baɪnd/ *n.* (*coll., nuisance*) ску́ка, доку́ка.

● *v.t.* (*past and p.p.* **bound**) **1** (*tie, fasten*) свя́з|ывать, -а́ть; **~ on one's skis** привя́з|ывать, -а́ть лы́жи; **~ up one's hair** подвя́з|ывать, -а́ть во́лосы; **~ up a wound** перевя́з|ывать, -а́ть ра́ну; **~ s.o. to a stake** привя́з|ывать, -а́ть кого́-н. к столбу́ (для сожже́ния); **~ together** свя́з|ывать, -а́ть. **2** (*secure*): **~ the edge of a carpet** закреп|ля́ть, -и́ть край ковра́. **3** (*books etc.*) перепле|та́ть, -сти́. **4** (*hold firmly*): **frost ~s the soil** моро́з ско́вывает зе́млю; **~ gravel with tar** скреп|ля́ть, -и́ть щёбень дёгтем. **5** (*oblige, exact promise*) обя́з|ывать, -а́ть; **~ s.o. to secrecy** обя́з|ывать, -а́ть кого́-н. храни́ть та́йну; **I am bound to say** я до́лжен сказа́ть; **I'll be bound** уве́рен; вот уви́дишь; **~ o.s.** обяза́ться (*pf.*); **~ over** (*leg.*) обя́з|ывать, -а́ть; **~ s.o. (as an) apprentice** отд|ава́ть, -а́ть кого́-н. учи́ться ремеслу́. *See also* ⇒**binding, bound**[3]

● *cpd.* **~weed** *n.* вьюно́к.

binder /ˈbaɪndə(r)/ *n.* **1** (*book* **~**) переплётчик. **2** (*substance*) свя́зывающее вещество́. **3** (*agric.*) сноповяза́лка. **4** (*cover for magazines etc.*) па́пка.

binding /ˈbaɪndɪŋ/ *n.* (*of book*) переплёт; (*braid etc.*) обши́вка.
● *adj.* обя́зывающий; име́ющий обяза́тельную си́лу; **make it ~ on s.o. to do something** обя́з|ывать, -а́ть кого́-н. сде́лать что-н.

binge /bɪndʒ/ *n.* (*sl.*) кутёж; пья́нка; **go on the ~** закути́ть, запи́ть (*both pf.*).

bingo /ˈbɪŋgəʊ/ *n.* лото́ (*indecl.*).

binoculars /bɪˈnɒkjʊləz/ *n.* бино́кль (*m.*).

binomial /baɪˈnəʊmɪəl/ *adj.* двучле́нный, биномиа́льный; **the ~ theorem** бино́м Нью́тона.

biochemical /ˌbaɪəʊˈkemɪk(ə)l/ *adj.* биохими́ческий.

biochemist /ˌbaɪəʊˈkemɪst/ *n.* биохи́мик.

biochemistry /ˌbaɪəʊˈkemɪstrɪ/ *n.* биохи́мия.

biocide /ˈbaɪəʊsaɪd/ *n.* биоци́д.

biodegradable /ˌbaɪəʊdɪˈgreɪdəb(ə)l/ *adj.* подве́рженный биологи́ческому разложе́нию.

biodiversity /ˌbaɪəʊdaɪˈvɜːsɪtɪ/ *n.* биологи́ческое разнообра́зие.

bioengineering /ˌbaɪəʊˌendʒɪˈnɪərɪŋ/ *n.* биоинжене́рия.

biogenic /ˌbaɪəʊˈdʒenɪk/ *adj.* биоге́нный.

biographer /baɪˈɒgrəfə(r)/ *n.* био́граф.

biographic(al) /ˌbaɪəˈgræfɪk(ə)l/ *adj.* биографи́ческий.

biography /baɪˈɒgrəfɪ/ *n.* биогра́фия.

biological /ˌbaɪəˈlɒdʒɪk(ə)l/ *adj.* биологи́ческий; **~ clock** биологи́ческие часы́; **~ warfare** бактериологи́ческая война́.

biologist /baɪˈɒlədʒɪst/ *n.* био́лог.

biology /baɪˈɒlədʒɪ/ *n.* биоло́гия.

biomedical /ˌbaɪəʊˈmedɪk(ə)l/ *adj.*: **~ research** биомедици́нские иссле́дования.

bionic /baɪˈɒnɪk/ *adj.* биони́ческий.

biophysical /ˌbaɪəʊˈfɪzɪkəl/ *adj.* биофизи́ческий.

biophysicist /ˌbaɪəʊˈfɪzɪsɪst/ *n.* биофи́зик.

biophysics /ˌbaɪəʊˈfɪzɪks/ *n.* биофи́зика.

biopsy /ˈbaɪɒpsɪ/ *n.* (*med.*) биопси́я.

biorhythm /ˈbaɪəʊrɪð(ə)m/ *n.* биори́тм.

biosphere /ˈbaɪəʊˌsfɪə(r)/ *n.* биосфе́ра.

biotechnology /ˌbaɪəʊtekˈnɒlədʒɪ/ *n.* биотехноло́гия.

bipartisan /ˌbaɪpɑːtɪˈzæn/, /baɪˈpɑːtɪz(ə)n/ *adj.* двухпарти́йный.

bipartite /baɪˈpɑːtaɪt/ *adj.* (*divided into two parts*) состоя́щий из двух часте́й; (*shared by two parties*) двусторо́нний.

biped /ˈbaɪped/ *n.* двуно́гое.

biplane /ˈbaɪpleɪn/ *n.* (*aeron.*) бипла́н.

bipolar /baɪˈpəʊlə(r)/ *adj.* двухпо́лярный, биполя́рный.

bipolarity /ˌbaɪpəʊˈlærɪtɪ/ *n.* двухполя́рность, биполя́рность.

birch /bɜːtʃ/ *n.* **1** (*tree*) берёза; (*attr.*) берёзовый. **2** (*rod*) ро́зга.
● *v.t.* сечь, вы́-.

bird /bɜːd/ *n.* **1** пти́ца; **~ of prey** хи́щная пти́ца; **~ of passage** перелётная пти́ца; **game ~** дичь; **hen ~** са́мка; **~ life** пти́чий мир; **~ of paradise** ра́йская пти́ца; **~'s eye view** вид с (высоты́) пти́чьего полёта; о́бщая перспекти́ва; **the ~ has flown** улете́ла пти́чка; **a ~ in the hand is worth two in the bush** лу́чше сини́ца в ру́ки, чем жура́вль в не́бе; **~s of a feather flock together** рыба́к рыбака́ ви́дит издалека́; **kill two ~s with one stone** уби́ть (*pf.*) двух за́йцев одни́м вы́стрелом; **the early ~ catches the worm** кто ра́но встаёт, тому́ Бог подаёт; **a little ~ told me** ≈ слу́хом земля́ по́лнится; **an early ~** ра́нняя пта́шка; **night ~** (*fig.*) ночно́й гуля́ка; **give an actor the ~** (*Br. sl.*) освиста́ть (*pf.*) актёра.
2 (*of person*): **he's a queer ~** он стра́нный тип; он чуда́к; **he's a wise old ~** он стре́ляный вороб́ей; он тёртый кала́ч.
3 (*Br. sl., girl*) деви́ца.
● *cpds.* **~-brain** *n.* (*fig.*) кури́ные мо́зги (*m. pl.*); **~-cage** *n.* кле́тка для птиц; **~-call** *n.* пти́чий крик; **~-fancier** *n.* люби́тель (*m.*) птиц; **~-lime** *n.* пти́чий клей; **~-seed** *n.* пти́чий корм; **~'s nest** *n.* пти́чье гнездо́; **~-table** *n.* (*Br.*) корму́шка для птиц; **~-watcher** *n.* орнито́лог-люби́тель (*m.*).

Biro /ˈbaɪərəʊ/ *n.* (*pl.* **~s**) (*Br. propr.*) ша́риковая ру́чка, ша́рик.

birth /bɜːθ/ *n.* **1** (*being born*) рожде́ние; (*giving birth*) ро́ды *pl.*; **he weighed 7lbs. at ~** он ве́сил 7 фу́нтов при рожде́нии; **give ~ to** роди́ть (*impf.*, *pf.*), рожа́ть (*impf.*); (*fig.*) произвести́ (*pf.*) на свет; породи́ть (*pf.*); **premature ~** преждевре́менные ро́ды (*pl., g.* -ов); **since ~** с рожде́ния; о́т роду; **still ~** рожде́ние мёртвого ребёнка; **there are more ~s than deaths** рожда́емость превыша́ет сме́ртность; **~ certificate** свиде́тельство о рожде́нии; **~ control** регули́рование рожда́емости; (*contraception*) противозача́точные ме́ры (*f. pl.*).
2 (*descent*): **an Englishman by ~** англича́нин по происхожде́нию; **of noble ~** благоро́дного происхожде́ния.
3 (*fig.*): **~ of an idea** зарожде́ние мы́сли/иде́и; **new ~** второ́е рожде́ние.
● *cpds.* **~day** *n.* день рожде́ния; рожде́ние; **~day present** пода́рок ко дню рожде́ния; **~day cake** ≈ имени́нный пиро́г; **in one's ~day suit** (*joc.*) в чём мать родила́; **~mark** *n.* роди́мое пятно́; **~place** *n.* ме́сто рожде́ния; ро́дина; **~rate** *n.* рожда́емость; **a fall in the ~rate** паде́ние рожда́емости; **~right** *n.* пра́во первоpо́дства; пра́во по рожде́нию.

Biscay /ˈbɪskeɪ/ *n.*: **Bay of ~** Биска́йский зали́в.

biscuit /ˈbɪskɪt/ *n.* (*Br.*) пече́нье; (*US*) ≈ бу́лочка; **ship's ~** галёта; **take the ~** (*coll.*) превосходи́ть (*impf.*) всё.

bisect /baɪˈsekt/ *v.t.* дели́ть, раз- попола́м.

bisection /baɪˈsekʃ(ə)n/ *n.* деле́ние попола́м.

bisector /baɪˈsektə(r)/ *n.* биссектри́са.

bisexual /baɪˈseksjʊəl/ *adj.* (*having organs of both sexes*) двупо́лый, гермафроди́тный; (*attracted by both sexes*) бисексуа́льный.

bishop /ˈbɪʃəp/ *n.* (*eccl.*) епи́скоп; (*chess*) слон.

bishopric /ˈbɪʃəprɪk/ *n.* (*office*) епи́скопство; (*diocese*) епа́рхия.

bismuth /ˈbɪzməθ/ *n.* (*chem.*) ви́смут.

bison /ˈbaɪs(ə)n/ *n.* (*pl.* **~**) бизо́н.

bistro /ˈbiːstrəʊ/ *n.* (*pl.* **~s**) бистро́ (*indecl.*).

bit[1] /bɪt/ *n.* **1** кусо́к, кусо́чек; **a ~ of paper** листо́к бума́ги; **a nice ~ of furniture** краси́вый предме́т ме́бели; **come to ~s** развали́ться (*pf.*) на куски́; **eat up every ~** съесть (*pf.*) всё подчисту́ю (*or* без оста́тка); **that's only a ~ of what he spends** э́то лишь ма́лая толи́ка того́, что он тра́тит.
2 (*abstr. uses*): **a ~ of news** но́вость; **a ~ of advice** сове́т; **I am a ~ late** я немно́го опозда́л; **not a ~ of it!** (*Br.*) ниско́лько!; ничу́ть!; ничу́ть не быва́ло!; **wait a ~!** подожди́те чуть-чуть!; **a good ~ older** значи́тельно ста́рше; **~ by ~** ма́ло-пома́лу; **not a ~ of use** никако́й по́льзы, никако́го про́ку; **every ~ as good** так же хоро́ш; ниско́лько не ху́же; **a ~ of a coward** трусова́тый; **a nasty ~ of work** (*person*) проти́вная осо́ба; **do one's ~** вноси́ть, внести́ свою́ ле́пту; **it will take a ~ of doing** э́то бу́дет нелегко́ сде́лать; **~ part** (*theatr.*) ма́ленькая роль; **~ player** (*theatr.*) актёр на эпизоди́ческих роля́х.

bit[2] /bɪt/ *n.* (*comput.*) бит.
● *cpd.* **~-mapped** *adj.* (*comput.*) би́товый.

bit[3] /bɪt/ *n.* **1** (*of drill*) коро́нка, сверло́, бур; (*of plane*) ле́звие. **2** (*of bridle*) уд|ила́ (*pl., g.* -и́л); мундшту́к; **take the ~ between one's teeth** (*fig.*) закуси́ть (*pf.*) удила́.

bit[4] /bɪt/ *past of* ⇒**bite**

bitch /bɪtʃ/ *n.* **1** (*of dog*) су́ка; (*of fox*) лиси́ца; (*of wolf*) волчи́ца. **2** (*coll., spiteful woman*) сте́рва; (*promiscuous woman*) су́ка.
● *v.i.*: **~ about one's colleagues** поро́чить, о- колле́г.

bitchiness /ˈbɪtʃɪnɪs/ *n.* (*coll.*) стервóзность.

bitchy /ˈbɪtʃɪ/ *adj.* (**bitchier, bitchiest**) (*coll.*) стерво́зный.

bite /baɪt/ *n.* **1** (*act of biting*) куса́ние; **eat something at one ~** съесть (*pf.*) что-н. зара́з.
2 (*mouthful*): **I haven't had a ~ to eat** у меня́ куска́ во рту́ не́ было; **have a ~ of food** перекуси́ть (*pf.*), закуси́ть (*pf.*).
3 (*wound caused by biting*) уку́с; **snake ~** зме́иный уку́с.
4 (*of fish*) клёв; **I have been fishing all day and haven't had a ~** весь день

сижу́, а ры́ба не клюёт.
5 (*grip, hold*) захва́тывание, зажа́тие; **this screw has a good ~** э́тот болт кре́пит надёжно.
6 (*sharpness, pungency*): **there is a ~ in the air** моро́з пощи́пывает.
● *v.t.* (*past* **bit;** *p.p.* **bitten**) **1** куса́ть, укуси́ть; **he bit the apple** он откуси́л я́блоко; **the dog bit him in the leg** соба́ка укуси́ла его́ за́ ногу; **a piece was bitten from the apple** я́блоко бы́ло надку́сано; **he was bitten by midges** его́ искуса́ли комары́.
2 (*fig.*): **what's biting him?** что его́ гло́жет?; **~ off more than one can chew** ≈ де́ло не по плечу́; **~ s.o.'s head off** откуси́ть (*pf.*) кому́-н. го́лову; **~ back a remark** прикуси́ть (*pf.*) язы́к; **he was bitten by this craze** он зарази́лся э́тим увлече́нием; **~ the dust** быть пове́рженным; **once bitten, twice shy** пу́ганая воро́на куста́ бои́тся; обжёгшись на молоке́, бу́дешь дуть и на́ воду.
● *v.i.* (*past* **bit;** *p.p.* **bitten**): **does your dog ~?** ва́ша соба́ка куса́ется?; **the fish won't ~** ры́ба не клюёт; **~ into something** вгр|ыза́ться, -ы́зться во что-н.; **acid ~s into metal** кислота́ разъеда́ет мета́лл.

biting /ˈbaɪtɪŋ/ *adj.* куса́ющий; (*of wind, cold*) ре́зкий; (*of satire*) е́дкий, язви́тельный.

bitten /ˈbɪt(ə)n/ *p.p. of* ⇒**bite**

bitter /ˈbɪtə(r)/ *adj.* (*lit., fig.*) го́рький; **a ~ wind** ре́зкий ве́тер; **~ conflict** о́стрый конфли́кт; **~ enemy** зле́йший/закля́тый враг; **to the ~ end** до са́мого конца́.
● *n.* (*Br.*) го́рькое пи́во.
● *adv.*: **~ cold** ужа́сно хо́лодно.
● *cpd.* **~-sweet** *adj.* горькова́то-сла́дкий.

bittern /ˈbɪt(ə)n/ *n.* выпь.

bitty /ˈbɪtɪ/ *adj.* (**bittier, bittiest**) (*coll.*) **1** (*Br.*) неодноро́дный, бессвя́зный. **2** (*US*) кро́хотный.

bitumen /ˈbɪtjʊmɪn/ *n.* би́тум; асфа́льт.

bituminous /bɪˈtju:mɪnəs/ *adj.* би́тумный, асфа́льтовый.

bivalve /ˈbaɪvælv/ *n.* двуство́рчатый моллю́ск.

bivouac /ˈbɪvʊˌæk/ *n.* бива́к.
● *v.i.* (**bivouacked, bivouacking**) распол|ага́ться, -ожи́ться бивако́м.

bi-weekly /baɪˈwi:klɪ/ *adj.*
1 (*fortnightly*) двухнеде́льный; выходя́щий (*и т.п.*) ра́з в две неде́ли.
2 (*twice a week*) выходя́щий (*и т.п.*) два ра́за в неде́лю.
● *adv.* **1** раз в две неде́ли. **2** два ра́за в неде́лю.

biz /bɪz/ (*sl.*) = **business**

bizarre /bɪˈzɑ:(r)/ *adj.* чудно́й, дико́винный.

blab /blæb/ *v.t.* (**blabbed, blabbing**) (*also* **~ out**) выба́лтывать, вы́болтать; разб|а́лтывать, -олта́ть.
● *v.i.* (**blabbed, blabbing**) болта́ть (*impf.*).

blabber /ˈblæbə(r)/ *n.* болту́н; пустоме́ля (*c.g.*).

black /blæk/ *n.* **1** (*colour*) чернота́, чёрное; **dress in ~** одева́ться (*impf.*) в чёрное; **be in the ~** не име́ть долго́в.
2 (*soot etc.*): **you have some ~ on your sleeve** у вас что-то чёрное на рукаве́.
3 (*negro*) чёрный, черноко́жий; негр, (*fem.*) -итя́нка.
4 (*fig.*): **two ~s don't make a white** злом зла не попра́вишь; **swear ~ is white** называ́ть (*impf.*) чёрное бе́лым.
● *adj.* **1** (*colour*) чёрный; **as ~ as ink** (*etc.*) чёрный как смоль; **a ~ eye** подби́тый глаз.
2 (*fig.*): **a ~ deed** чёрное де́ло; **he is not as ~ as he is painted** он не так плох, как его́ изобража́ют; **a ~ heart** чёрная душа́; **~ despair** безысхо́дное отча́яние.
3 (*negro*) чёрный; **~ man** чёрный, черноко́жий; **B~ Power** «Власть чёрным».
4 (*var.*): **~ and tan** чёрно-ры́жий; **~ and white** чёрно-бе́лый; **in ~ and white** (*in writing*) чёрным по бе́лому; **he beat him ~ and blue** он изби́л его́ до полусме́рти; **~ art** чёрная ма́гия; **I am in his ~ books** я у него́ на плохо́м счету́; **~ bread** чёрный/ржано́й хлеб; **~ coffee** чёрный ко́фе; **~ earth** чернозём; **~ frost** моро́з без и́нея; треску́чий моро́з; **~ hole** (*astron.*) чёрная дыра́; **~ ice** гололе́дица; **~ Maria** чёрный во́рон (*coll.*); **it is a ~ mark against him** э́то его́ поро́чит; **~ economy** тенева́я эконо́мика; **~ market** чёрный ры́нок; **B~ Sea** Чёрное мо́ре.
● *v.t.* **1** (*paint black*) кра́сить (*impf.*) в чёрное; (*boots etc.*) ва́ксить, на-; **~ one's face** кра́сить, вы- лицо́ чёрным; **~ s.o.'s eye** подб|ива́ть, -и́ть кому́-н. глаз.
2 (*Br., boycott*) бойкоти́ровать (*impf., pf.*), внести́ в чёрный спи́сок.
3: **~ out** (*text*) выма́рывать, вы́марать; (*light*) затемн|я́ть, -и́ть.
● *v.i.*: **~ out** (*lose consciousness*) теря́ть, по- созна́ние.
● *cpds.* **~ball** *v.t.* забаллоти́ровать (*pf.*); **~-beetle** *n.* (*Br.*) чёрный тарака́н; **~berry** *n.* ежеви́ка (*collect*); я́года ежеви́ки; **~bird** *n.* чёрный дрозд; **~board** *n.* кла́ссная доска́; **~cap** *n.* черноголо́вка; **~cock** *n.* те́терев; **~currant** *n.* чёрная сморо́дина; **~guard** *n.* негодя́й; **~head** *n.* у́горь (*m.*); **~-hearted** *adj.* зло́бный; **~jack** *n.* (*US, bludgeon*) дуби́нка; **~-lead** *n.* графи́т; **~leg** *n.* (*Br.*) штрейкбре́хер; **~-list** *v.t.* вн|оси́ть, -ести́ в чёрный спи́сок; **~mail** *n.* шанта́ж, вымога́тельство; *v.t.* шантажи́ровать (*impf.*); **~mailer** *n.* шантажи́ст, вымога́тель (*m.*); **~-marketeer** *n.* спекуля́нт, фарцо́вщик; **~out** *n.* (*in wartime*) затемне́ние; (*electricity failure*) обесто́чка; (*loss of consciousness or awareness*) поте́ря созна́ния; *v.t.* затемн|я́ть, -и́ть; **~shirt** *n.* чернорuба́шечник; **~smith** *n.* кузне́ц; **~thorn** *n.* (*plant*) тёрн; **~ tie** *n.* (*bow-tie*) чёрный га́лстук-ба́бочка; (*evening dress*) стро́гий вече́рний костю́м; **a ~ tie reception** официа́льный приём.

blacken /ˈblækən/ *v.t.* **1** (*paint black*) кра́сить, по- в чёрное; (*boots etc.*) ва́ксить, на-. **2** (*soil, dirty*) грязни́ть, за-. **3** (*reputation*) черни́ть, о-.
● *v.i.* черне́ть, по-.

blacking /ˈblækɪŋ/ *n.* (*for boots etc.*) ва́кса, чёрный крем для о́буви.

blackish /ˈblækɪʃ/ *adj.* темнова́тый.

blackness /ˈblæknɪs/ *n.* чернота́; (*darkness*) темнота́; (*gloominess*) мра́чность.

bladder /ˈblædə(r)/ *n.* (*anat., bot.*) пузы́рь (*m.*); (*in ball etc.*) ка́мера; (*in seaweed*) пузырёк.

blade /bleɪd/ *n.* **1** (*of knife etc.*) ле́звие. **2** (*of oar etc.*) ло́пасть, лопа́тка. **3** (*of grass etc.*) были́нка, стебелёк. **4** (*fig., sword*) клино́к.

blame /bleɪm/ *n.* (*censure*) порица́ние; осужде́ние; (*fault*) вина́; **his conduct was free from ~** его́ поведе́ние бы́ло безупре́чным; **the ~ is mine** я винова́т; **lay, put the ~ on s.o.** возложи́ть (*pf.*) вину́ на кого́-н.; **bear, take the ~** приня́ть (*pf.*) на себя́ вину́/отве́тственность; **where does the ~ lie?** кто винова́т?
● *v.t.* порица́ть (*impf.*); вини́ть (*impf.*); осу|жда́ть, -ди́ть (*кого за что*); **he was ~d for the mistake** вину́ за оши́бку возложи́ли на него́; **he cannot be ~d for it** он не винова́т в э́том; **he has only himself to ~** он мо́жет вини́ть то́лько себя́; **I am in no way to ~** мне не́ в чем упрекну́ть себя́; **he is entirely to ~** э́то по́лностью его́ вина́; **~ something on s.o.** взва́л|ивать, -и́ть вину́ за что-н. на кого́-н.
● *cpds.* **~worthiness** *n.* предосуди́тельность; **~worthy** *adj.* предосуди́тельный.

blameable /ˈbleɪməb(ə)l/ *adj.* предосуди́тельный.

blameless /ˈbleɪmlɪs/ *adj.* безупре́чный; неви́нный.

blanch /blɑ:ntʃ/ *v.t.* бели́ть, вы́-; **~ed almonds** бланширо́ванный минда́ль.
● *v.i.* (*go pale*) беле́ть, по-.

blancmange /bləˈmɒndʒ/ *n.* (*cul.*) бланманже́ (*indecl.*).

bland /blænd/ *adj.* (*mild*) мя́гкий; (*insipid*) пре́сный.

blandishment /ˈblændɪʃmənt/ *n.* (*usu. pl.*) обха́живание, лесть.

blank /blæŋk/ *n.* **1** (*empty space*) про́пуск; (*fig.*): **fill in the ~s in one's education** воспо́лнить (*pf.*) пробе́лы в своём образова́нии; **my mind is a ~ on this subject** у меня́ э́то вы́летело из головы́.
2 (*in lottery*): **draw a ~** вы́тянуть (*pf.*) пусто́й биле́т; (*fig.*) иска́ть (*impf.*) беспло́дно/напра́сно.
3 (*US, form*) бланк.
● *adj.* **1** (*empty*): **a ~ sheet of paper** пусто́й лист бума́ги; **a ~ cheque** незапо́лненный чек; (*fig.*) карт-бла́нш; **a ~ space** про́пуск; пусто́е ме́сто; **~ cartridge** холосто́й патро́н.
2 (*bare, plain*): **a ~ wall** глуха́я стена́; **we are up against a ~ wall** (*fig.*) мы упёрлись в глуху́ю сте́ну; **~ verse** бе́лый стих.

B

3 (*fig.*): **my memory is ~** ничего́ не по́мню; **~ despair** по́лное отча́яние; **look ~** (*of person*) вы́глядеть (*impf.*) расте́рянным; **the future looks ~** бу́дущее ничего́ не сули́т.

blanket /ˈblæŋkɪt/ *n.* одея́ло; (*horse-cloth*) попо́на; **~ of fog** пелена́ тума́на; **~ of smoke** пелена́ ды́ма; **the hills lay under a ~ of snow** холмы́ бы́ли покры́ты сло́ем сне́га (*or* бы́ли под снегови́м покрыва́лом); **wet ~** (*fig., of person*) кисля́й; **~ instructions** о́бщие указа́ния.
● *v.t.* (**blanketed, blanketing**) (*cover*) оку́т|ывать, -ать; (*stifle, hush up*) зам|ина́ть, -я́ть.

blankly /ˈblæŋklɪ/ *adv.* (*without expression*) бессмы́сленно, ту́по; (*categorically*) реши́тельно, наотре́з.

blankness /ˈblæŋknɪs/ *n.* пустота́, пробе́л; **the ~ of his countenance** отсу́тствие како́го бы то ни́ было выраже́ния на его́ лице́.

blare /bleə(r)/ *n.* рёв.
● *v.t.*: **~ out** труби́ть, про-; **the band ~d out a waltz** орке́стр гря́нул вальс.
● *v.i.* труби́ть, про-; реве́ть (*impf.*); **the fanfare ~d forth** гря́нули фанфа́ры.

blarney /ˈblɑːnɪ/ *n.* загова́ривание зубо́в.
● *v.t. & i.* (**~s, ~ed**) загов|а́ривать, -ори́ть зу́бы (*кому*).

blasé /ˈblɑːzeɪ/ *adj.* пресы́щенный (жи́знью).

blaspheme /blæsˈfiːm/ *v.t.* (*revile*) поноси́ть (*impf.*), хули́ть (*impf.*).
● *v.i.* богоху́льствовать (*impf.*), богоху́льничать (*impf.*).

blasphemer /blæsˈfiːmə(r)/ *n.* богоху́льник.

blasphemous /ˈblæsfiməs/ *adj.* богоху́льный.

blasphemy /ˈblæsfəmɪ/ *n.* богоху́льство.

blast /blɑːst/ *n.* **1**: **~ of wind** поры́в ве́тра; **~ of hot air** волна́ горя́чего во́здуха. **2** (*from explosion*) взрыв; **~ wave** взрывна́я волна́. **3**: **at full ~** (*fig.*) в по́лном разга́ре; по́лным хо́дом. **4** (*of an instrument*): **~ on a whistle** свисто́к; **give three ~s on the horn** три́жды протруби́ть (*pf.*) в рог.
● *v.t.* **1** (*explode rocks etc.*) вз|рыва́ть, -орва́ть. **2** (*shrivel*): **frost ~ed the plants** моро́з поби́л расте́ния; (*hopes*) разру́шить (*pf.*). **3** (*curse*): **~ it!** прокля́тие!; пропади́ всё пропадо́м; **~ you!** чтоб тебя́ разорва́ло!; чтоб ты ло́пнул!
● *v.i.*: **~ off** (*rocketry*) взлет|а́ть, -е́ть; стартова́ть (*impf., pf.*).
● *cpds.* **~-furnace** *n.* до́мна, до́менная печь; **~-off** *n.* взлёт; моме́нт ста́рта.

blasted /ˈblɑːstɪd/ *adj.* **1**: **~ heath** го́лая пу́стошь. **2** (*cursed*) прокля́тый.

blasting /ˈblɑːstɪŋ/ *n.* (*of rocks etc.*) подрывны́е рабо́ты (*f. pl.*).

blatancy /ˈbleɪt(ə)nsɪ/ *n.* крикли́вость; беззасте́нчивость, бессты́дство.

blatant /ˈbleɪt(ə)nt/ *adj.* крикли́вый; бессты́дный; (*flagrant*) я́вный, вопию́щий.

blather /ˈblæðə(r)/ *n.* болтовня́.
● *v.i.* (*also* **blether**) болта́ть (*impf.*).

blaz|e[1] /bleɪz/ *n.* **1** (*of fire*) пла́мя (*nt.*); **burst into a ~e** запыла́ть (*pf.*). **2** (*of colour, light*) я́ркость; **the garden was a ~e of colour** (*Br.*), **color** (*US*) сад пыла́л я́ркими кра́сками. **3** (*conflagration*) пожа́р. **4** (*fig.*): **~e of publicity** шу́мная рекла́ма. **5** (*expletive*): **go to ~es** иди́/убира́йся к чёрту/дья́волу!; **what the ~es do you want?** како́го чёрта вам на́до?; **run like ~es** нести́сь, по- (*det.*) сломя́ го́лову.
● *v.t.*: **~e the news abroad** раструби́ть (*pf.*) но́вость.
● *v.i.*: **a fire was ~ing in the hearth** в ками́не пыла́л ого́нь; **the building was ~ing** зда́ние полыха́ло; **he was ~ing with anger** он пыла́л гне́вом.
● *with advs.*: **~e away** *v.i.* (*with rifle etc.*) вести́ (*det.*) ого́нь, (*coll.*) пали́ть (*impf.*); (*work vigorously*) рабо́тать (*impf.*) вовсю́; **~e up** *v.i.* (*lit., fig.*) вспы́хивать, -ы́хнуть.

blaze[2] /bleɪz/ *n.* (*mark on horse*) звёздочка; (*on tree*) ме́тка.
● *v.t.*: **~ a trail** про|кла́дывать, -ложи́ть путь.

blazer /ˈbleɪzə(r)/ *n.* ≈ ку́ртка, пиджа́к, бле́йзер.

blazing /ˈbleɪzɪŋ/ *adj.* **1** (*of fire*) пыла́ющий. **2** (*of light*) сверка́ющий, сия́ющий. **3**: **he was in a ~ fury** он пыла́л я́ростью. **4** (*coll., expletive*): **what's the ~ hurry?** како́го чёрта торопи́ться?; что за спе́шка, чёрт побери́?

blazon /ˈbleɪz(ə)n/ *n.* (*her.*) герб; описа́ние ге́рба.
● *v.t.* (*broadcast*) разгла|ша́ть, -си́ть.

bleach /bliːtʃ/ *n.* (**~ing agent**) отбе́ливатель (*m.*), отбе́льное/отбе́ливающее вещество́; (*chloride of lime*) хло́рная и́звесть.
● *v.t.* бели́ть (*impf.*); отбе́л|ивать, -и́ть; (*hair*) обесцве́|чивать, -тить; **the sun ~ed the curtains** занаве́ски вы́горели на со́лнце.
● *v.i.* беле́ть (*impf.*).

bleachers /ˈbliːtʃəz/ *n. pl.* (*US*) дешёвые места́ (на стадио́не).

bleak[1] /bliːk/ *n.* (*zool.*) укле́йка.

bleak[2] /bliːk/ *adj.* уны́лый, безра́достный; (*gloomy*) мра́чный; **a ~ hillside** откры́тый ветра́м склон холма́.

bleakness /ˈbliːknɪs/ *n.* уны́лость, мра́чность.

bleary /ˈblɪərɪ/ *adj.* (**blearier, bleariest**) (*of eyes*) затума́ненный, му́тный.

bleary-eyed /blɪə(r)/ *adj.* с затума́ненными/му́тными глаза́ми.

bleat /bliːt/ *n.* бле́яние, мыча́ние.
● *v.t. & i.* мыча́ть (*impf.*), бле́ять (*impf.*).

bleed /bliːd/ *v.t.* (*past and p.p.* **bled** /bled/) пус|ка́ть, -ти́ть кровь +*d.*; (*drain*) опорожн|я́ть, -и́ть; **~ s.o.** (*for money*) об|ира́ть, -обра́ть кого́-н.; **~ s.o. white** (*fig.*) обескро́в|ливать -ить кого́-н.; **~ a tree** подта́чивать (*impf.*) де́рево.
● *v.i.* (*past and p.p.* **bled** /bled/) (*of person*) ист|ека́ть, -е́чь кро́вью; (*of wound*) кровоточи́ть (*impf.*); **his nose is ~ing** у него́ кровь идёт но́сом; **he bled to death** он у́мер от поте́ри кро́ви; **my heart ~s for him** у меня́ се́рдце кро́вью облива́ется за него́.

bleeder /ˈbliːdə(r)/ *n.* (*Br. vulg., blighter*) па́рень (*m.*), тип.

bleeding /ˈbliːdɪŋ/ *n.* кровотече́ние (*from the nose*: из́ носу).
● *adj.* кровоточа́щий, истека́ющий кро́вью; (*Br. vulg., blasted*) прокля́тый, чёртов.

bleep /bliːp/ *n.* сигна́л;
● *v.i.* сигна́лить, про-.
● *v.t.* (*summon*) вызыва́ть, вы́звать сигна́лом.

bleeper /ˈbliːpə(r)/ *n.* (*Br.*) миниатю́рный приёмник для вы́зова на связь; пе́йджер.

blemish /ˈblemɪʃ/ *n.* (*defect*) недоста́ток, изъя́н; (*stain*) пятно́; **his name is without ~** у него́ незапя́тнанная репута́ция.
● *v.t.* пятна́ть, за-.

blench /blentʃ/ *v.i.* уклон|я́ться, -и́ться (*от чего*); отступ|а́ть, -и́ть (*перед чем*).

blend /blend/ *n.* смесь; (*of colours*) сочета́ние.
● *v.t.* сме́ш|ивать, -а́ть; (*colours, ideas*) сочета́ть (*impf.*).
● *v.i.* сме́ш|иваться, -а́ться; (*of colours, ideas*) сочета́ться (*impf.*); гармони́ровать (*impf.*); (*of sounds, waters*) сл|ива́ться, -и́ться; **these teas do not ~ well** из э́тих двух сорто́в ча́я хоро́шей сме́си не получа́ется.

blender /ˈblendə(r)/ *n.* (*cul.*) смеси́тель (*m.*), ми́ксер.

bless /bles/ *v.t.* (*past and p.p.* **blessed;** *poet.* **blest**) **1** (*relig.*) благослов|ля́ть, -и́ть; **~ me!, ~ my soul!** Го́споди, поми́луй!; **(God) ~ you!** дай вам Бог здоро́вья; (*after sneeze*) бу́дьте здоро́вы!; **well I'm ~ed!** Бо́же мой!; Го́споди, поми́луй!; **I'm ~ed, blest if I know** ей-Бо́гу, не зна́ю. **2** (*prosper, favour*): **he was ~ed with good health** Бог награди́л его́ здоро́вьем; **~ed are the poor in spirit** блаже́нны ни́щие ду́хом.

blessed /ˈblesɪd/, /blest/ *adj.* **1** (*holy*) благослове́нный; **the B~ Virgin** Пресвята́я Де́ва, Богоро́дица. **2** (*happy*) блаже́нный, благослове́нный. **3** (*coll.*): **not a ~ drop of rain** ни еди́ной ка́пли дождя́.

blessedness /ˈblesɪdnɪs/ *n.* блаже́нство.

blessing /ˈblesɪŋ/ *n.* **1** благослове́ние; **give, pronounce a ~ upon** благослов|ля́ть, -и́ть; **with God's ~** с Бо́жьего благослове́ния; **with official ~** с благослове́ния нача́льства. **2**: **the ~s of civilization** бла́га цивилиза́ции; **it is a ~ in disguise** ≈ не́ было бы сча́стья, да несча́стье помогло́!; **what**

a ~ that he came! какóе счáстье, что он пришёл!

blest /blest/ *poet. past and p.p. of* ⇒**bless**

blether /ˈbleðə(r)/ = **blather**

blew /bluː/ *past of* ⇒**blow**[1]

blight /blaɪt/ *n.* **1** (*disease*) головня́; ржа. **2**: **it cast a ~ on her youth** э́то омрачи́ло её ю́ность.

● *v.t.* **1** пора|жáть, -зи́ть ржой. **2**: **~ s.o.'s hopes** разр|ушáть, -у́шить чьи-н. надéжды; (*career, plans*) погуби́ть (*pf.*).

blighted /ˈblaɪtəd/ *adj.* (*of plants*) поги́бший; поражённый ржой; (*of plans etc.*) погу́бленный.

blighter /ˈblaɪtə(r)/ *n.* (*Br. coll., fellow*) пáрень (*m.*), тип.

blimey /ˈblaɪmɪ/ *int.* (*Br. vulg.*) чтоб мне провали́ться!

blind /blaɪnd/ *n.* **1** (*screen*) штóра, стáвень (*m.*); **Venetian ~** жалюзи́ (*nt. indecl.*); (*Br., awning*) марки́за, тент. **2** (*mil.*) дымовáя завéса. **3** (*ruse*) улóвка; **his generosity is only a ~** егó щéдрость — тóлько ши́рма. **4** (*Br. coll., spree*) пья́нка.

● *adj.* **1** слепóй; **the ~** (*as n.*) слепы́е, слепцы́ (*m. pl.*); **as ~ as a bat** слепáя ку́рица; **~ in one eye** слепóй на оди́н глаз; кривóй; **go ~** слéпнуть, о-; **~ spot** слепóе пятнó; (*fig.*) пробéл; **~ man's buff** жму́р|ки (*pl., g.* -ок); **he is ~ to his opportunities** он не ви́дит свои́х возмóжностей; **turn a ~ eye to something** закр|ывáть, -ы́ть глазá на что-н. **2** (*concealed*): **a ~ corner** непросмáтривающийся поворóт; **a ~ date** (*coll.*) свидáние с незнакóмым/незнакóмой. **3** (*closed up*): **a ~ alley** (*lit., fig.*) тупи́к. **4**: **he didn't take a ~ bit of notice** (*coll.*) он э́то абсолю́тно проигнори́ровал.

● *adv.*: **fly ~** летáть (*indet.*) по прибóрам; **~ drunk** мертвéцки пья́ный; **sign a document ~** подпи́с|ывать, -áть докумéнт не читáя; **go it ~** дéйствовать (*impf.*) втёмную/вслепу́ю.

● *v.t.* **1** ослеп|ля́ть, -и́ть (*also fig.*); (*temporarily*) слепи́ть (*impf.*); **he was ~ed, went ~ in the left eye** он ослéп на лéвый глаз. **2** (*block, obstruct*) затемн|я́ть, -и́ть.

● *cpd.* **~fold** *adv.* с завя́занными глазáми; (*recklessly*) вслепу́ю; *v.t.* завя́з|ывать, -áть глазá + *d.*

blinders /ˈblaɪndəz/ (*US*) = **blinkers**

blindly /ˈblaɪndlɪ/ *adv.* (*gropingly*) óщупью; (*recklessly*) слéпо.

blindness /ˈblaɪndnɪs/ *n.* слепотá; (*fig.*) слепотá, ослеплéние.

blink /blɪŋk/ *n.* (*of eye*) моргáние, мигáние; (*of light*) мерцáние; прóблеск; **be on the ~** (*coll.*) барахли́ть (*impf.*).

● *v.t. & i.* (*of person*) миг|áть, -ну́ть; морг|áть, -ну́ть; (*of light*) мерцáть (*impf.*); **~ at** (*fig., ignore*) закр|ывáть, -ы́ть глазá на + *a.*

blinkers /ˈblɪŋkəz/ *n.* (*Br.*) шóр|ы (*pl., g.* —) (*also fig.*); нагля́зники (*m. pl.*).

blip /blɪp/ *n.* (*on screen*) отражённый и́мпульс.

bliss /blɪs/ *n.* блажéнство.

blissful /ˈblɪsfʊl/ *adj.* блажéнный.

blister /ˈblɪstə(r)/ *n.* (*on skin*) волды́рь (*m.*); (*on paint*) пузы́рь (*m.*).

● *v.t.* вызывáть, вы́звать волдыри́/пузыри́ на + *p.*

● *v.i.* покр|ывáться, -ы́ться волдыря́ми/пузыря́ми.

blithering /ˈblɪðərɪŋ/ *adj.* (*coll.*): **a ~ idiot** закóнченный иди́от.

blithe(some) /ˈblaɪð(səm)/ *adj.* жизнерáдостный, беспéчный.

blitz /blɪts/ *n.* бомбёжка.

● *v.t.* разбомби́ть (*pf.*).

blitzkrieg /ˈblɪtskriːg/ *n.* блицкри́г; мóлниенóсная войнá.

blizzard /ˈblɪzəd/ *n.* бурáн, вью́га.

bloated /ˈbləʊtɪd/ *adj.* (*swollen*) разду́тый, разду́вшийся; **he is ~ with pride** егó распирáет от гóрдости.

bloater /ˈbləʊtə(r)/ *n.* копчёная сельдь.

blob /blɒb/ *n.* (*small mass*) кáпля; шáрик; (*spot of colour*) кля́кса; (*coll., zero*) нуль (*m.*).

bloc /blɒk/ *n.* блок.

block /blɒk/ *n.* **1** (*of wood*) чурбáн, колóда; (*of stone, marble*) глы́ба; **children's ~s** ку́бики (*m. pl.*). **2** (*for execution*) плáха. **3** (*of houses*) квартáл; (*of shares, tickets etc.*) пáчка; **~ of flats** (*Br.*) многокварти́рный дом. **4** (*for lifting*: *also* **~ and tackle**) блок, лебёдка. **5** (*typ.*): **~ capitals** печáтные бу́квы. **6** (*obstruction*): **~ in a pipe** заку́порка/засорéние трубы́; (*fig.*): **mental ~** у́мственное торможéние. **7**: **~ booking** группов́ой закáз; **~ vote** (*Br.*) представи́тельное голосовáние.

● *v.t.* **1** (*obstruct physically*): **roads ~ed by snow** дорóги, занесённые снéгом; **~ (up) an entrance** загор|áживать, -оди́ть вход; **mud ~ed the pipe** грязь заби́ла трубу́; **the sink is ~ed** рáковина засори́лась; **~ s.o.'s way** прегра|ждáть, -ди́ть кому́-н. путь. **2** (*fig.*): **~ the enemy's plan** срывáть, сорвáть плáны неприя́теля. **3**: **~ in, out** (*sketch*) набр|áсывать, -осáть.

● *cpds.* **~buster** *n.* (*coll.*) боеви́к; **~head** *n.* болвáн, тупи́ца (*c.g.*); **~house** *n.* блокгáуз.

blockade /blɒˈkeɪd/ *n.* блокáда; **raise a ~** снять (*pf.*) блокáду; **run a ~** прорвáть (*pf.*) блокáду.

● *v.t.* блоки́ровать (*impf., pf.*).

bloke /bləʊk/ *n.* (*Br. coll.*) тип; пáрень (*m.*).

blond(e) /blɒnd/ *n.* блонди́н (*fem.* -ка).

● *adj.* белоку́рый, свéтлый.

blood /blʌd/ *n.* **1** кровь; **the ~ rushed to his head** кровь брóсилась/удáрила емý в гóлову; **hands covered with ~** ру́ки в крови́; **sweat ~** рабóтать (*impf.*) до кровáвого пóта; **taste ~** вку|шáть, -си́ть крóви; **you cannot get ~ out of a stone** ≈ кáменное сéрдце не разжáлобишь. **2** (*attr.*): **~ bank** дóнорский пункт; **~ clot** сгу́сток крóви; тромб; **~ donor** дóнор; **~ group** гру́ппа крóви; **~ orange** королёк; **~ plasma** плáзма; **~ sports** охóта; **~ test** анáлиз крóви; (*for paternity*) исслéдование крóви; **~ transfusion** переливáние крóви; *see also cpds.* **3** (*var. fig. uses*): **it made my ~ boil** э́то меня́ взбеси́ло; **his ~ ran cold** кровь сты́ла/леденéла у негó в жи́лах; **in cold ~** хладнокрóвно; **his ~ is up** он взбешён; **we need new ~** нам нужны́ нóвые си́лы; **there is bad ~ between them** они́ врáждуют. **4** (*lineage, kinship*): **blue ~** голубáя кровь; **~ is thicker than water** кровь не води́ца.

● *cpds.* **~-and-thunder** *adj.* (*story etc.*) пóлный у́жасов; **~-bath** *n.* кровáвая бáня; **~-brother** *n.* побрати́м; **~-count** *n.* анáлиз крóви; **~curdling** *adj.* леденя́щий кровь; **a ~curdling sight** зрéлище, от котóрого сты́нет кровь в жи́лах; **~-heat** *n.* температу́ра человéческого тéла; **~hound** *n.* ищéйка; **~-letting** *n.* (*med.*) кровопускáние; (*bloodshed*) кровопроли́тие; **~-lust** *n.* жáжда крóви; **~-poisoning** *n.* заражéние крóви; **~-pressure** *n.* кровянóе давлéние; **~-red** *adj.* кровавокрáсный; **~-relation** *n.* крóвный рóдственник; **~-relationship** *n.* крóвное родствó; **~shed** *n.* кровопроли́тие; **~shot** *adj.* нáлитый крóвью; **~stain** *n.* кровáвое пятнó; **~stained** *adj.* запáчканный крóвью; **~stained hands** ру́ки в крови́; **~stock** *n.* чистокрóвные лóшади (*f. pl.*); **~stone** *n.* гелиотрóп, кровáвик; **~stream** *n.* ток крóви; **~sucker** *n.* (*insect*) насекóмое-кровосóс; (*leech*) пия́вка; (*fig.*) кровопи́йца (*c.g.*), кровосóс; **~thirstiness** *n.* кровожáдность; **~thirsty** *adj.* кровожáдный; **~-vessel** *n.* кровенóсный сосу́д; **he burst a ~vessel** у негó лóпнул кровенóсный сосу́д; **~worm** *n.* крáсный червь.

bloodily /ˈblʌdɪlɪ/ *adv.* с проли́тием крóви.

bloodless /ˈblʌdlɪs/ *adj.* бескрóвный; (*insipid*) безжи́зненный.

bloodlessness /ˈblʌdlɪsnɪs/ *n.* (*insipidity*) безжи́зненность.

bloody /ˈblʌdɪ/ *adj.* (**bloodier, bloodiest**) **1** кровáвый; (*smeared with blood*) окровáвленный; **give s.o. a ~ nose** разби́ть (*pf.*) кому́-н. нос в кровь. **2** (*Br., expletive*): **a ~ liar** отчáянный лгун; **stop that ~ row!** прекрати́те э́тот чёртов скандáл!; **not a ~ thing** ни чертá/хренá; **no ~ fear!; not ~ likely!** чёрта с два!; фиг-то!

● *adv.* (*sl.*): **~ awful** чертóвский; сквéрный, дряннóй.

● *v.t.* окровáвить (*pf.*).

● *cpds.* **~-minded** *adj.* (*Br. coll., obstructive*) зловрéдный, неуслу́жливый; **~-mindedness** *n.* (*Br.*) зловрéдность.

bloom /bluːm/ *n.* **1** (*flower*) цвет; цветы́

(*m. pl.*); (*single flower*) цвето́к; **in ~** в цвету́; **burst into ~** расцве|та́ть, -сти́. **2** (*prime*) расцве́т; **in the ~ of youth** в расцве́те ю́ности. **3** (*on cheeks*) румя́нец. **4** (*down*) пушо́к.

● *v.i.* **1** цвести́ (*impf.*); (*come into ~*) расцве|та́ть, -сти́; **finish ~ing** отцве|та́ть, -сти́. **2** (*fig.*): **~ into something** расцвести́ (*pf.*) и преврати́ться (*pf.*) во что-н.

bloomer /'blu:mə(r)/ *n.* **1** (*Br.*) (*coll., mistake*) про́мах; (*in speech*) оговорка; **make a ~** де́лать, с- про́мах; огов|а́риваться, -ори́ться. **2** (*pl.*) (*undergarment*) пантало́н|ы (*pl., g.* —).

blooming[1] /'blu:mɪŋ/ *n.* (*metall.*) блю́минг; **~ mill** обжимно́й стан, блю́минг.

blooming[2] /'blu:mɪŋ/ *adj.* (*flowering, flourishing*) цвету́щий; (*Br., expletive*): **a ~ fool** наби́тый дура́к.

blossom /'blɒsəm/ *n.* цвет, цвете́ние; **in ~** в цвету́; **come into ~** расцве|та́ть, -сти́.

● *v.i.* цвести́ (*impf.*); **finish ~ing** отцве|та́ть, -сти́; (*fig.*): **he ~ed into a statesman** он вы́рос в госуда́рственного де́ятеля.

blot /blɒt/ *n.* (*on paper*) кля́кса; (*blemish*) пятно́; **it is a ~ on the landscape** э́то по́ртит вид/пейза́ж; (*fig.*): **without a ~ on one's character** с незапя́тнанной репута́цией.

● *v.t. & i.* (**blotted, blotting**) **1** (*smudge*) па́чкать, за-; ста́вить, по- кля́ксу. **2** (*dry*) промок|а́ть, -ну́ть; **~ting-paper** промока́тельная бума́га, (*coll.*) промока́шка. **3** (*sully*) пятна́ть, за-; **~ one's copybook** (*Br. fig.*) пятна́ть, за- свою́ репута́цию.

● *with adv.*: **~ out** *v.t.* выма́рывать, вы́марать; (*from one's memory*) изгла́|живать, -дить (*or* ст|ира́ть, -ере́ть) из па́мяти; (*a view*) закр|ыва́ть, -ы́ть; заслон|я́ть, -и́ть.

blotch /blɒtʃ/ *n.* пятно́; (*of ink*) кля́кса.

blotchy /'blɒtʃɪ/ *adj.* (**blotchier, blotchiest**) в пя́тнах.

blotter /'blɒtə(r)/ *n.* бюва́р.

blotto /'blɒtəʊ/ *adj.* (*sl.*) пья́ный в сте́льку.

blouse /blaʊz/ *n.* (*workman's*) блу́за; (*woman's*) ко́фточка, блу́зка.

blow[1] /bləʊ/ *n.* (*of air, wind*) дунове́ние, поры́в; **give your nose a good ~!** вы́сморкайся хороше́нько (*or* как сле́дует); **let's go out for a ~** (*of fresh air*) пойдём подыша́ть све́жим во́здухом.

● *v.t.* (*past* **blew;** *p.p.* **blown**) **1** дуть, ду́нуть; **~ a horn** дуть, ду́нуть в рог; труби́ть (*impf.*); **~ a whistle** свисте́ть, за- в свисто́к; дава́ть, дать свисто́к; **~ one's nose** сморк|а́ться, -ну́ться; **~ the dust off a book** сду|ва́ть, -ть пыль с кни́ги; **~ s.o. a kiss** пос|ыла́ть, -ла́ть кому́-н. возду́шный поцелу́й; **~ glass** выдува́ть (*impf.*) стекло́; **~ bubbles** пуска́ть (*impf.*) пузыри́; **~ one's own trumpet** (*fig.*) хвали́ться, похваля́ться (*both impf.*); **~ the gaff** (*Br., fig.*) пробо|а́лтываться, -олта́ться.

2 (*of wind*): **the wind ~s the rain against the windows** ве́тер с дождём бьёт по о́кнам; **the ship was ~n off course** кора́бль снесло́ с ку́рса; **the wind blew the papers out of my hand** ве́тер вы́рвал бума́ги у меня́ из рук; **he was ~n ashore** его́ вы́несло на бе́рег; **we were ~n out to sea** нас унесло́ в мо́ре.

3 (*with bellows*): **he blew the fire** он разду́л ого́нь.

4 (*elec.*): **~ a fuse** переж|ига́ть, -е́чь про́бку.

5 (*coll., spend*) угро́хать (*pf.*) (*sl.*); **~ £45 on a dinner** проса́|живать, -ди́ть (*coll.*) 45 фу́нтов на обе́д.

6 (*Br. coll., curse*): **I'm ~ed if I know** ей-Бо́гу, не зна́ю; **well, I'm ~ed!** так та́к!; во́т-те ра́з!

● *v.i.* (*past* **blew;** *p.p.* **blown**) **1** (*of wind or person*) дуть, по-, ду́нуть; **it is ~ing hard** си́льно ду́ет; о́чень ве́трено; **~ hot and cold** (*fig.*) помину́тно меня́ть (*impf.*) мне́ние.

2 (*of thing*): **the door blew open** дверь распахну́лась; **dust blew into the room** пыль налете́ла в ко́мнату; **the whistle blew** разда́лся свисто́к; гудо́к загуде́л; **the fuse blew** про́бка перегоре́ла.

● *with advs.*: **~ about** *v.t.*: **the wind blew her hair about** ве́тер развева́л её во́лосы; *v.i.*: **the leaves blew about** носи́лись ли́стья; **~ away** *v.t. & i.* ун|оси́ть(ся), -ести́(сь); **~ down** *v.t.* вали́ть, по-; **he was blown down from the roof** его́ снесло́ с кры́ши; *v.i.*: **the tree blew down** бу́ря повали́ла де́рево; **~ in** *v.t.*: **the gale blew the windows in** урага́ном разби́ло о́кна; *v.i.*: **the wind blows in through the door** ве́тер ду́ет в дверь; **~ off** *v.t.*: **the wind blew his hat off** ве́тер сорва́л с него́ шля́пу; *v.i.*: **his hat blew off** у него́ слете́ла шля́па; **~ out** *v.t.*: **he blew the candle out** он заду́л свечу́; **~ out one's cheeks** над|ува́ть, -у́ть щёки; **~ one's brains out** пусти́ть (*pf.*) себе́ пу́лю в лоб; **the bomb blew out the doors** от взры́ва бо́мбы вы́летели две́ри; *v.i.*: **the candle blew out** свеча́ пога́сла; **the tyre blew out** ши́на ло́пнула; **~ over** *v.t.*: **he was blown over by the wind** его́ свали́ло с ног ве́тром; *v.i.*: **the storm blew over** бу́ря ути́хла; **the scandal blew over** сканда́л улёгся/зати́х; **~ up** *v.t.*: **~ up a bridge** взрыва́ть, взорва́ть мост; **~ up a tyre** над|ува́ть, -у́ть ши́ну; **~ up a photograph** увели́чи|вать, -ть фотогра́фию; **blown up by pride** разду́тый го́рдостью; **the boss blew him up** (*coll.*) нача́льник сде́лал ему́ разно́с; *v.i.*: **the mine blew up** ми́на взорвала́сь; **a storm blew up** разыгра́лся шторм.

● *cpds.* **~-fly** *n.* мясна́я му́ха; **~-hole** *n.* (*of whale*) ды́хало; (*opening in ice*) отве́рстие; (*in tunnel*) вентиляцио́нное отве́рстие; **~-job** *n.* (*vulg. sl.*) мине́т, отсо́с; **~-lamp** *n.* (*Br.*) пая́льная ла́мпа; **~-out** *n.* (*of tyre*) разры́в; (*oil*) фонта́н (не́фти); (*coll., feast*) кутёж, пиру́шка; **~pipe** *n.* (*tool*) пая́льная тру́бка; **~-torch** *n.* пая́льная ла́мпа; **~-up** *n.* (*explosion, outburst*) взрыв, вспы́шка; (*phot.*) увеличе́ние.

blow[2] /bləʊ/ *n.* (*lit., fig.: stroke*) уда́р; **deliver, deal, strike a ~** нан|оси́ть, -ести́ уда́р; **at a ~** одни́м уда́ром; **strike a ~ at s.o.** нан|оси́ть, -ести́ уда́р кому́-н.; **strike a ~ for** (*fig.*) вступи́ться (*pf.*) за + *a.*; **they came to ~s** они́ подрали́сь; де́ло дошло́ до рукопа́шной; **without striking a ~** без дра́ки; **her death was a ~ to us** её смерть была́ уда́ром для нас; **it was a ~ to our hopes** э́то разби́ло на́ши наде́жды.

blowing-up /ˌbləʊɪŋ'ʌp/ *n.* (*explosion*) взрыв; (*coll., reprimand*) разно́с.

blowsy /'blaʊzɪ/ *adj.* (**blowsier, blowsiest**): **a ~ woman** растрёпанная же́нщина.

blowy /'bləʊɪ/ *adj.* (**blowier, blowiest**) ве́треный.

blowzy /'blaʊzɪ/ (**blowzier, blowziest**) = **blowsy**

blub /blʌb/ *v.i.* (**blubbed, blubbing**) (*coll.*) реве́ть (*impf.*).

blubber[1] /'blʌbə(r)/ *n.* (*whale-fat*) во́рвань.

blubber[2] /'blʌbə(r)/ *v.t. & i.* реве́ть (*impf.*), рыда́ть (*impf.*).

bludgeon /'blʌdʒ(ə)n/ *n.* дуби́нка.

● *v.t.* бить (*impf.*) дуби́нкой; (*fig.*) принужда́ть (*impf.*).

blue /blu:/ *n.* **1** (*colour*) синева́, голубизна́; **navy ~** тёмно-си́ний цвет.

2 (*sky*): **out of the ~** (*fig.*) ни с того́ ни с сего́; **he arrived out of the ~** он нагря́нул неожи́данно; **like a bolt from the ~** (*fig.*) как гром среди́ я́сного не́ба.

3 (*sea*) (си́нее) мо́ре.

4: **the ~s** (*coll.*) тоска́, уны́ние, хандра́; **have the ~s** хандри́ть (*impf.*); **give s.o. the ~s** нав|оди́ть, -ести́ тоску́ на кого́-н.

5: **~s** (*mus.*) блюз.

● *adj.* (**bluer, bluest**) **1** (*colour*) (*dark*) си́ний; (*light*) голубо́й; **her hands were ~ with cold** её ру́ки посине́ли от хо́лода; **his arms are ~ (with bruises)** у него́ все ру́ки в синяка́х; **he shouted till he was ~ in the face** он крича́л до изнеможе́ния, посине́ния; **once in a ~ moon** раз в сто лет; **scream ~ murder** крича́ть (*impf.*) во всю гло́тку/(*coll.*) ива́новскую; **~ baby** (*med.*) синю́шный младе́нец; **~ blood** голуба́я кровь; **~ book** «си́няя кни́га» (*сборник официальных документов*); **~ funk** (*coll.*) пани́ческий страх; **B~ Peter** флаг отплы́тия; **~ water** откры́тое мо́ре.

2 (*coll., sad*): **feel ~** хандри́ть (*impf.*); **look ~** (*of person*) вы́глядеть (*impf.*) уны́лым; **things look ~** дела́ обстоя́т скве́рно.

3 (*coll., obscene*) скабрёзный.

● *cpds.* **~bell** *n.* (*wild hyacinth*) ди́кий/лесно́й гиаци́нт; (*campanula*) колоко́льчик; (*scilla*) проле́ска; **~bird** *n.* синешейка; **~-blooded** *adj.* голубо́й кро́ви; **~bottle** *n.* мясна́я му́ха; **~-collar worker** *n.* произво́дственный рабо́чий; **~-eyed** *adj.* синегла́зый, голубогла́зый; **~-eyed boy** (*Br. iron.*) люби́мчик, люби́мец; **~-grey** *adj.* си́зый, си́зо-голубо́й; **~-pencil** *v.t.* (*abridge*) сокра|ща́ть, -ти́ть; (*erase*) вычёркивать, вы́черкнуть; **~print** *n.* (*phot.*) светоко́пия, си́нька; (*fig.*) намётка; **~stocking** *n.* (*fig.*) си́ний чуло́к, учёная же́нщина; **~ tit** *n.* си́няя сини́ца.

blueness /ˈbluːnɪs/ *n.* синева́; голубизна́.

bluff[1] /blʌf/ *n.* (*headland*) утёс.
● *adj.* (*of cliffs etc.*) обры́вистый, отве́сный; (*of person*) грубова́то-доброду́шный; прямоду́шный.

bluff[2] /blʌf/ *n.* блеф; **call s.o.'s ~** заставля́ть, заста́вить кого́-н. раскры́ть ка́рты.
● *v.t. & i.* блефова́ть (*impf.*); втира́ть (*impf.*) очки́ +*d.*; пуска́ть (*impf.*) пыль в глаза́ +*d.*

bluish /ˈbluːɪʃ/ *adj.* (*dark*) синева́тый; (*light*) голубова́тый.

blunder /ˈblʌndə(r)/ *n.* оши́бка, оплО́шность.
● *v.i.* блужда́ть (*impf.*); (*grope*) о́щупью пробира́ться/дви́гаться (*impf.*); **~ into a table** натыка́ться, наткну́ться на стол; **~ upon the facts** натыка́ться, наткну́ться на фа́кты; **~ through one's work** де́лать (*impf.*) рабо́ту ко́е-как.

blunderbuss /ˈblʌndəˌbʌs/ *n.* (*mil.*) мушкето́н.

blundering /ˈblʌndərɪŋ/ *adj.* (*clumsy*) нескла́дный; (*tactless*) беста́ктный.

blunt /blʌnt/ *adj.* (*not sharp*) тупо́й; **a ~ pencil** неотто́ченный каранда́ш; (*plain-spoken*) прямо́й.
● *v.t.* тупи́ть (*impf.*); **~ a needle** притуп|ля́ть, -и́ть иглу́; **~ a knife/scissors** затуп|ля́ть, -и́ть нож/но́жницы; (*feelings etc.*) притуп|ля́ть, -и́ть; **~ s.o.'s intelligence** притуп|ля́ть, -и́ть чьё-н. восприя́тие; **~ s.o.'s anger** ум|еря́ть, -е́рить чей-н. гнев.

bluntness /ˈblʌntnɪs/ *n.* (*lit.*) ту́пость; (*frankness*) прямота́.

blur /blɜː(r)/ *n.* (*confused effect*) ды́мка; **she saw him through a ~ of tears** она́ ви́дела его́ сквозь ды́мку слёз; **the village is now only a ~ in my mind** об э́той дере́вне у меня́ оста́лись лишь сму́тные воспомина́ния.
● *v.t.* (**blurred, blurring**) (*make indistinct*) сма́з|ывать, -ать; **rain ~s the windows** дождь затума́нивает о́кна; (*fig.*) затума́ни|вать, -ть; затемн|я́ть, -и́ть.

blurb /blɜːb/ *n.* (*coll.*) (изда́тельская) аннота́ция.

blurry /ˈblɜːrɪ/ *adj.* (**blurrier, blurriest**) затума́ненный.

blurt /blɜːt/ *v.t.*: **~ out** выпа́ливать, вы́палить.

blush /blʌʃ/ *n.* **1** кра́ска; **spare s.o.'s ~es** щади́ть, по- чью-н. стыдли́вость; **a ~ rose to her cheeks** кра́ска залила́ её щёки. **2** (*glow*) румя́нец. **3**: **at first ~** с пе́рвого взгля́да.
● *v.i.* красне́ть, по-; зарде́ться (*pf.*); **~ to the roots of one's hair** красне́ть, по- до корне́й воло́с; **~ crimson** зарде́ться (*pf.*); **I ~ to suggest** мне со́вестно предположи́ть.

blusher /ˈblʌʃə(r)/ *n.* (*cosmetic*) румя́на.

blushing /ˈblʌʃɪŋ/ *adj.* (*modest*) застéнчивый, стыдли́вый; **a ~ bride** стыдли́вая неве́ста.

bluster /ˈblʌstə(r)/ *n.* (*of storm*) рёв; (*of person*) гро́мкие слова́, угро́зы (*f. pl.*).
● *v.i.* (*of storm*) реве́ть (*impf.*); (*of person*) расшуме́ться (*pf.*), разбушева́ться (*pf.*).

blusterer /ˈblʌstərə(r)/ *n.* забия́ка (*c.g.*).

BO (*abbr. of* **body odour**) за́пах по́та.

bo /bəʊ/ = **boo** *int.* 2

boa /ˈbəʊə/ *n.* (*zool.*) боа́ (*m. indecl.*); **~ constrictor** уда́в; (*wrap*) боа́ (*nt. indecl.*).

boar /bɔː(r)/ *n.* каба́н.

board /bɔːd/ *n.* **1** (*piece of wood*) доска́ (*also for chess etc.*); **bed of ~s** на́р|ы (*pl., g.* —); **~ game** насто́льная игра́.
2 (*pl., theatr.*) подмо́стк|и (*pl., g.* -ов); **go on the ~s** пойти́ (*pf.*) на сце́ну; **tread the ~s** игра́ть (*impf.*) на сце́не.
3 (*pl., cover of book*) переплёт; **cloth ~s** коленко́ровый переплёт.
4 (*food*) стол; **~ and lodging, bed and ~** кварти́ра и стол; пансио́н; **full ~** по́лный пансио́н.
5 (*table*): **above ~** (*fig.*) в откры́тую, че́стно; **sweep the ~** (*at cards*) заб|ира́ть, -ра́ть все ста́вки.
6 (*council*) правле́ние; **~ of enquiry** коми́ссия по рассле́дованию; **~ of directors** правле́ние дире́кторов.
7 (*naut. etc.*): **on ~** на борту́; **come, go on ~ a ship/aircraft** сади́ться, сесть на кора́бль/самолёт; (*comm.*): **free on ~ (f.o.b.)** фра́нко борт (фоб); **go by the ~** (*fig.*) быть вы́брошенным за́ борт.
8 (*for electronic circuit*) пла́та.
● *v.t.* **1** (*cover with ~s; also* **~ up**) обш|ива́ть, -и́ть (*or* покр|ыва́ть, -ы́ть) до́сками.
2: **~ a ship** (*go on ~*) сади́ться, сесть на кора́бль; (*attack*) брать, взять кора́бль на аборда́ж.
3: **~ s.o. out** (*find quarters for*) пом|еща́ть, -сти́ть кого́-н. на по́лный пансио́н.
● *v.i.* (*reside*) жить (*impf.*) на по́лном пансио́не; (*at school*) жить в шко́ле-интерна́те.
● *cpds.* **~-room** *n.* зал заседа́ний сове́та дире́кторов; **~walk** *n.* доща́тый насти́л.

boarder /ˈbɔːdə(r)/ *n.* (*lodger*) жиле́ц, постоя́лец; **take in ~s** брать (*impf.*) жильцо́в; (*at school*) учени́|к (*fem.* -ца), живу́щий в шко́ле-интерна́те.

boarding /ˈbɔːdɪŋ/ *n.* **1** (*boards*) обши́вка до́сками. **2** (*naut.*) аборда́ж; (*aeron.*) поса́дка.
● *cpds.* **~-card, ~-pass** *nn.* поса́дочный биле́т; **~-house** *n.* пансио́н; **~-school** *n.* шко́ла-интерна́т.

boast /bəʊst/ *n.* хвастовство́; (*coll.*) похвальба́; **an empty ~** пусто́е хвастовство́; **their ~ is that . . .** они́ похваля́ются тем, что. . .; (*person or thing ~ed of*) го́рдость, предме́т го́рдости.
● *v.t. & i.* **1** (**~ of**) хва́стать(ся), по- +*i.*; хвали́ться (*or* похваля́ться), по- +*i.*; **it is nothing to ~ of** похва́статься не́чем.
2 (*possess*) горди́ться (*impf.*) +*i.*

boaster /ˈbəʊstə(r)/ *n.* хвасту́н (*fem.* -ья).

boastful /ˈbəʊstfʊl/ *adj.* хвастли́вый.

boastfulness /ˈbəʊstfʊlnɪs/ *n.* хвастли́вость.

boat /bəʊt/ *n.* (*small, rowing ~*) ло́дка, шлю́пка; (*vessel*) су́дно; (*large ~*) кора́бль (*m.*), парохо́д; **in the same ~** (*fig.*) в одина́ковом положе́нии; **burn one's ~s** (*fig.*) сжечь (*pf.*) (свои́) корабли́; **miss the ~** (*fig.*) прозева́ть (*pf.*) слу́чай.
● *v.i.* (*go ~ing*) ката́ться (*indet.*) на ло́дке.
● *cpds.* **~-deck** *n.* шлю́почная па́луба; **~-hook** *n.* баго́р; **~house** *n.* э́ллинг; **~man** *n.* ло́дочник; **~-race** *n.* состяза́ния (*nt. pl.*) по гре́бле; **~swain** *n.* бо́цман; **~-train** *n.* по́езд, согласо́ванный с парохо́дным расписа́нием.

boater /ˈbəʊtə(r)/ *n.* соло́менная шля́па.

bob[1] /bɒb/ *n.* **1** (*weight*) подве́сок; (*on fishing-line*) поплаво́к; (*on pendulum*) ги́ря. **2** (*hair-style*) коро́ткая стри́жка; (*horse's tail*) подстри́женный хвост.
● *v.t.* (**bobbed, bobbing**) (*of hair*) ко́ротко стричь (*impf.*); остр|ига́ть, -и́чь.
● *cpd.* **~tail** *n.* (*of horse or dog*) обре́занный хвост, ку́цый хвост.

bob[2] /bɒb/ *n.* (*jerk, e.g. of the head*) киво́к; (*curtsey*) приседа́ние, рева́ранс.
● *v.i.* (**bobbed, bobbing**) **1** (*move up and down*) подпры́г|ивать, -нуть; подск|а́кивать, -очи́ть; **~ up** выска́кивать, вы́скочить. **2** (*curtsey*) прис|еда́ть, -е́сть; **she ~bed him a curtsey** она́ присе́ла в рева́рансе пе́ред ним.

bob[3] /bɒb/ *n.* (*pl.* **~**) (*Br. coll., shilling*) ши́ллинг.

bob[4] /bɒb/ *n.*: **~'s your uncle** (*Br. coll.*) всё в поря́дке; де́ло сде́лано.

bobbin /ˈbɒbɪn/ *n.* (*reel, spool*) кату́шка, шпу́лька; (*for raising latch*) рычажо́к.

bobbinet /ˈbɒbɪˌnet/ *n.* маши́нное кру́жево.

bobble /ˈbɒb(ə)l/ *n.* помпо́н(чик).

bobby /ˈbɒbɪ/ *n.* (*Br. coll.*) полисме́н.

bobby-socks /ˈbɒbɪ ˌsɒks/ *n.* (*US*) коро́ткие носки́ (*m. pl.*).

bobby-soxer /ˈbɒbɪˌsɒksə(r)/ *n.* (*US*) де́вочка-подро́сток.

bobolink /ˈbɒbəlɪŋk/ *n.* (*zool.*) ри́совый тупиа́л.

bob-sled /ˈbɒbsled/ (*US*), **bob-sleigh** /ˈbɒbsleɪ/ (*Br.*) *nn.* бо́бслей.

bobstay /ˈbɒbsteɪ/ *n.* (*naut.*) ватершта́г.

Boche /bɒʃ/ *n.* (*sl.*) бош (*неме́цкий солда́т*).

bode /bəʊd/ *v.t. & i.*: **~ ill/well** предвеща́ть/сули́ть (*impf.*) недо́брое/хоро́шее; **it ~s no good** э́то не предвеща́ет ничего́ хоро́шего.

B

bodega /bəʊ'di:gə/ *n.* ви́нный погребо́к.

bodice /'bɒdɪs/ *n.* корса́ж, лиф.

bodiless /'bɒdɪlɪs/ *adj.* бестеле́сный.

bodily /'bɒdɪlɪ/ *adj.* теле́сный, физи́ческий; ~ **harm** физи́ческое уве́чье/поврежде́ние.

● *adv.*: **he was carried ~ to the doors** его́ на рука́х вы́несли к дверя́м; **the house was moved ~** дом был передви́нут целико́м.

bodkin /'bɒdkɪn/ *n.* дли́нная тупа́я игла́; ши́ло.

body /'bɒdɪ/ *n.* **1** (*of person or animal*) те́ло; (*dim., e.g. baby's*) те́льце; (*build*) телосложе́ние; ~ **odour** (*US* **odor**) за́пах по́та; ~ **scanner** ска́нер; **strong in ~** физи́чески си́льный; **keep ~ and soul together** своди́ть (*impf.*) концы́ с конца́ми; **he is ours ~ and soul** он пре́дан нам душо́й и те́лом.
2 (*trunk*) ту́ловище, торс; **he was wounded in the ~** его́ ра́нили в ко́рпус.
3 (*dead person*) мёртвое те́ло; уби́т|ый (*fem.* -ая); ~ **bag** похоро́нный мешо́к.
4 (*main portion*): **the ~ of a hall/building** гла́вная часть за́ла/зда́ния; (*of ship*) ко́рпус; (*of car*) ку́зов; (*of aircraft*) фюзеля́ж; **the ~ of his supporters** все его́ сторо́нники; (*of letter, book*) основна́я часть.
5 (*quantity, aggregate*) ма́сса, гру́ппа; **a large ~ of facts** ма́сса фа́ктов; ~ **of evidence** совоку́пность доказа́тельств.
6 (*group, institution, system*): **governing ~** о́рган управле́ния; **legislative ~** законода́тельный о́рган; **learned ~** учёное о́бщество; **public ~** обще́ственная организа́ция; **the ~ politic** госуда́рство; **in a ~** в по́лном соста́ве.
7 (*object*) те́ло; **the heavenly bodies** небе́сные тела́; **foreign ~** иноро́дное те́ло.
8 (*strength, consistency*) консисте́нция, вя́зкость.

● *v.t.*: ~ **forth** (*give shape to*) вопло|ща́ть, -ти́ть; прид|ава́ть, -а́ть фо́рму + *d.*

● *cpds.* **~-blow** *n.* (*lit.*) уда́р в ко́рпус; (*fig.*) сокруши́тельный уда́р; **~-builder** *n.* (*person*) культури́ст; (*apparatus*) экспанде́р; **~-building** *n.* культури́зм; **~guard** *n.* (*group*) ли́чная охра́на; (*individual*) телохрани́тель (*m.*); ~ **shop** *n.* (*US*) кузовно́й цех; **~-snatcher** *n.* похити́тель (*m.*) тру́пов; **~-stocking** *n.* трико́ (*indecl.*); **~warmer** *n.* телогре́йка; **~work** *n.* (*of vehicle*) ку́зов.

Boer /'bəʊə(r)/, /bʊə(r)/ *n.* бур.

● *adj.* бу́рский; ~ **War** а́нгло-бу́рская война́.

boffin /'bɒfɪn/ *n.* (*Br. coll.*) техни́ческий экспе́рт, (*coll.*) до́ка (*m.*).

bog /bɒg/ *n.* **1** боло́то, тряси́на. **2** (*Br. sl., latrine*) отхо́жее ме́сто.

● *v.t.* (**bogged, bogging**): **get ~ged down** (*fig.*) вя́знуть, за-, у-.

bogeyman /'bəʊgɪ,mæn/ = **bogyman**

boggle /'bɒg(ə)l/ *v.i.* отша́т|ываться, -ну́ться; отпря́|дывать, -нуть; **the mind ~s** уму́ непостижи́мо.

boggy /'bɒgɪ/ *adj.* (**boggier, boggiest**) боло́тистый.

bogie /'bəʊgɪ/ *n.* (*Br., rail.*) двухо́сная теле́жка.

bogus /'bəʊgəs/ *adj.* фикти́вный, притво́рный.

bog|yman, -eyman /'bəʊgɪ,mæn/ *n.* (*bugbear*) бу́ка, пу́гало.

Bohemia /bəʊ'hi:mɪə/ *n.* (*geog.*) Боге́мия.

Bohemian /bəʊ'hi:mɪən/ *n.* (*native of Bohemia*) боге́м|ец (*fem.* -ка); чех (*fem.* че́шка); (*artist etc.*) представи́тель (*fem.* -ница) боге́мы.

● *adj.* (*geog.*) боге́мский; (*fig.*) боге́мный.

boil[1] /bɔɪl/ *n.* (*swelling*) нары́в, чи́рей.

boil[2] /bɔɪl/ *n.* (*state of ~ing*) кипе́ние; **come to the ~** вскипе́ть (*pf.*), закипе́ть (*pf.*); **bring to the ~** довести́ (*pf.*) до кипе́ния; вскипяти́ть (*pf.*); **be on, at the ~** кипе́ть (*impf.*); **go off the ~** переста́ть (*pf.*) кипе́ть.

● *v.t.*: ~ **water** кипяти́ть, вс- во́ду; ~ **fish/an egg** вари́ть, с- ры́бу/яйцо́; ~ **laundry** кипяти́ть (*impf.*) бельё.

● *v.i.*: **the water is ~ing** вода́ кипи́т; **the egg has ~ed** яйцо́ свари́лось; **the kettle has ~ed dry** ча́йник совсе́м вы́кипел; ~ **with indignation** кипе́ть (*impf.*) от негодова́ния (*or* негодова́нием).

● *with advs.*: **~away** *v.i.*: **the kettle was ~ing away** ча́йник кипе́л вовсю́; **the water ~ed away** вода́ вы́кипела; **~down** *v.t.* (*lit.*) выпа́ривать; вы́парить; (*abridge*) сж|има́ть, -а́ть; *v.i.*: **it ~s down to this, that** . . . э́то сво́дится к тому́, что. . .; ~ **over** *v.i.* (*lit.*) уходи́ть, уйти́ (*or* убе|га́ть, -жа́ть) че́рез край; **the milk ~ed over** молоко́ убежа́ло; (*fig., with rage*) вскипе́ть (*pf.*); **he was ~ing over** всё в нём кипе́ло; ~ **up** *v.t.* вскипяти́ть (*pf.*); *v.i.* вскип|а́ть, -е́ть.

boiler /'bɔɪlə(r)/ *n.* **1** (*vessel*) кипяти́льный котёл, бо́йлер; (*of steam engine*) парово́й котёл; (*for domestic heating*) котёл отопле́ния; бо́йлер; (*for laundry*) бак. **2** (*Br., chicken*) ку́рица для ва́рки.

● *cpds.* **~-house** *n.* котéльная; **~-maker** *n.* коте́льщик; **~-suit** *n.* (*Br.*) комбинезо́н.

boiling /'bɔɪlɪŋ/ *n.* кипе́ние, кипяче́ние, ва́рка.

● *adj.* (*also of waves etc.*) кипя́щий; ~ **water** кипято́к; ~ **hot** горя́чий, как кипято́к; **a ~ hot day** зно́йный день.

● *cpd.* **~-point** *n.* то́чка кипе́ния.

boisterous /'bɔɪstərəs/ *adj.* бу́йный, шумли́вый.

boisterousness /'bɔɪstərəsnɪs/ *n.* бу́йность, шумли́вость.

bold /bəʊld/ *n.* (*typ.*) жи́рный шрифт.

● *adj.* **1** сме́лый, отва́жный; **grow ~** смеле́ть, о-; **make so ~ as to** осме́ли|ваться, -ться; **make ~ with something** во́льно обраща́ться (*impf.*) с чем-н.; (*impudent*) наха́льный; **as ~ as brass** бессты́жий. **2** (*prominent*): **a ~ headland** ре́зко оче́рченный мыс. **3** (*clear*) чёткий, отчётливый. **4**: ~ **strokes** (*in painting*) широ́кие мазки́.

● *cpds.* **~-face** *n.* (*typ.*) жи́рный шрифт; **~-faced** *adj.* (*impudent*) на́глый, бессты́жий; (*of type*) жи́рный.

boldness /'bəʊldnɪs/ *n.* сме́лость, отва́жность; (*impudence*) на́глость.

bole /bəʊl/ *n.* ствол.

bolero /bəʊ'leərəʊ/, /'bɒlərəʊ/ *n.* (*pl.* **~s**) (*dance, jacket*) болеро́ (*indecl.*).

boletus /bəʊ'li:təs/ *n.* мохови́к; **edible ~** бе́лый гриб, борови́к.

bolide /'bəʊlaɪd/ *n.* (*astron.*) боли́д.

Bolivia /bəl'ɪvɪə/ *n.* Боли́вия.

Bolivian /bəl'ɪvɪən/ *n.* боливи́|ец (*fem.* -йка).

● *adj.* боливи́йский.

boll /bəʊl/ *n.* семенна́я коро́бочка.

● *cpd.* **~-weevil** *n.* долгоно́сик.

bollard /'bɒlɑ:d/ *n.* (*on ship or quay*) пал; (*Br., on traffic island*) ту́мба.

bollock /'bɒlək/ *n.* (*Br. vulg.*) (*testicle*) яйцо́; *pl.* (*nonsense*) херня́, бредя́тина; **to talk ~s** бздеть (*impf.*); **~s!** ни хуя́!, ни фига́!

bollocking /'bɒləkɪŋ/ *n.* (*Br. vulg.*) взъёбка; **give s.o. a ~** дава́ть, дать (+ *d.*) взъёбку.

boloney /bə'ləʊnɪ/ *n.* (*sl.*) чепуха́, ерунда́.

Bolshevi|k /'bɒlʃəvɪk/, **-st** /'bɒlʃəvɪst/ *nn.* большеви́|к (*fem.* -чка).

● *adj.* большеви́стский.

Bolshevism /'bɒlʃə,vɪz(ə)m/ *n.* большеви́зм.

bolsh|ie, -y /'bɒlʃɪ/ *adj.* (*Br. sl.*) (*mutinous*) стропти́вый.

bolster /'bəʊlstə(r)/ *n.* ва́лик; (*fig.*) опо́ра.

● *v.t.* (*prop; also fig.*) подп|ира́ть, -ере́ть.

bolt[1] /bəʊlt/ *n.* **1** (*on door etc.*) засо́в, задви́жка. **2** (*screw*) болт. **3** (*arrow*): **he has shot his ~** (*fig.*) он исче́рпал все свои́ возмо́жности. **4** (*thunderbolt*) уда́р гро́ма; (*lightning ~*) мо́лния. **5** (*of cloth*) руло́н.

● *adv.*: ~ **upright** пря́мо; вытяну́вшись.

● *v.t.*: ~ **the door** зап|ира́ть, -ере́ть дверь на засо́в/задви́жку.

● *v.i.*: **the door ~s on the inside** дверь запира́ется изнутри́.

bolt[2] /bəʊlt/ *n.* (*escape*): **make a ~ for it** удра́ть (*pf.*); дать (*pf.*) стрекача́.

● *v.t.* (*gulp down*) глота́ть, проглоти́ть.

● *v.i.* (*of horse*) понести́ (*pf.*); (*of person*) ри́нуться (*pf.*), помча́ться (*pf.*), удра́ть (*pf.*).

● *cpd.* **~-hole** *n.* (*Br.*) заго́н; (*fig.*) прибе́жище.

bolus /'bəʊləs/ *n.* (*pl.* **boluses**) пилю́ля.

bomb /bɒm/ *n.* бо́мба; (*mortar ~*) ми́на; (*shell*) снаря́д; **incendiary ~** зажига́тельная бо́мба; **neutron ~** нейтро́нная бо́мба; **drop a ~** сбро́сить (*pf.*) бо́мбу; ~ **disposal** обезвре́живание неразорва́вшихся бомб; (*fig.*) **to cost a ~** (*Br.*) сто́ить (*impf.*) бе́шеных де́нег.

● *v.t. & i.* бомби́ть, раз-.

● *with adv.*: **~ out** *v.t.* (*a building*) разбомби́ть (*pf.*).

● *cpds.* **~-bay** *n.* бо́мбовый отсе́к; **~-proof** *adj.* бомбосто́йкий; **~shell** *n.* артиллери́йский снаря́д; **the news came as a ~shell to them** весть их как гро́мом порази́ла; **~-shelter** *n.* бомбоубе́жище; **~-site** *n.* разбомблённый уча́сток.

bombard /bɒm'bɑːd/ *v.t.* **1** бомби́ть, раз-; бомбардирова́ть (*impf.*); обстре́л|ивать, -я́ть. **2** (*fig.*): **~ s.o. with rotten eggs** забр|а́сывать, -оса́ть кого́-н. ту́хлыми я́йцами; **~ s.o. with abuse** ос|ыпа́ть, -ы́пать кого́-н. оскорбле́ниями; **~ s.o. with questions** бомбардирова́ть (*impf.*) кого́-н. вопро́сами.

bombardier /ˌbɒmbə'dɪə(r)/ *n.* бомбарди́р.

bombardment /bɒm'bɑːdmənt/ *n.* бомбардиро́вка, бомбёжка; (*with shells*) артиллери́йский обстре́л.

bombast /'bɒmbæst/ *n.* высокопа́рность, напы́щенность.

bombastic /bɒm'bæstɪk/ *adj.* высокопа́рный, напы́щенный.

bomber /'bɒmə(r)/ *n.* (*aircraft*) бомбардиро́вщик; (*person*) бомбомета́тель (*m.*).

bombing /'bɒmɪŋ/ *n.* бомбомета́ние, бомбардиро́вка; **precision ~** прице́льное бомбомета́ние.

bona fide /ˌbəʊnə 'faɪdɪ/ *adj.* добросо́вестный, че́стный.

● *adv.* че́стно; без обма́на.

bona fides /ˌbəʊnə 'faɪdiːz/ *n.* че́стное наме́рение; че́стность.

bonanza /bə'nænzə/ *n.* (*coll.*) золото́е дно.

bond /bɒnd/ *n.* **1** (*link*) связь; **love of music was a ~ between us** нас свя́зывала любо́вь к му́зыке. **2** (*shackle*): **in ~s** в око́вах; в заключе́нии; **burst one's ~s** разорва́ть (*pf.*) око́вы. **3** (*obligation*) гара́нтия; **his word is as good as his ~** на его́ сло́во мо́жно положи́ться. **4** (*fin.*) облига́ция; (*pl.*) бо́ны (*f. pl.*); **premium ~s** вы́игрышные облига́ции. **5** (*comm.*): **goods in ~** това́ры, не опла́ченные по́шлиной.

● *v.t.* **1** (*of bricks*) сцеп|ля́ть, -и́ть; свя́з|ывать, -а́ть. **2** (*comm.*): **~ed warehouse** тамо́женный склад.

● *cpds.* **~holder** *n.* держа́тель (*m.*) облига́ций; **~sman** *n.* крепостно́й; (*guarantor*) поручи́тель (*m.*); **~swoman** *n.* крепостна́я.

bondage /'bɒndɪdʒ/ *n.* нево́ля; закрепоще́ние.

bone /bəʊn/ *n.* **1** кость; **drenched to the ~** промо́кший до косте́й; **he is all skin and ~** он ко́жа да ко́сти; **I feel in my ~s that ...** чу́ет моё се́рдце, что...; **near the ~** (*coll.*) риско́ванный; **cut costs to the ~** сокра|ща́ть, -ти́ть расхо́ды до преде́ла; **the bare ~s** (*of a subject*) элемента́рные поня́тия/зна́ния; **make no ~s about something** не церемо́ниться (*impf.*) с чем-н.; **he made no ~s about telling me ...** он не постесня́лся сказа́ть мне...; **~ of contention** я́блоко раздо́ра; **I have a ~ to pick with you** у меня́ к вам прете́нзия; **take a fish off the ~** отдел|я́ть, -и́ть ры́бу от косте́й. **2** (*substance*) кость; **buttons made of ~** костяны́е пу́говицы; **~ china** твёрдый англи́йский фарфо́р.

● *v.t.*: **~ fish/meat** отдел|я́ть, -и́ть ры́бу/мя́со от косте́й.

● *v.i.*: **~ up on** (*coll.*) зубри́ть, вы́-.

● *cpds.* **~-dry** *adj.* соверше́нно сухо́й; **~-idle** *adj.* ужа́сно лени́вый; **he is ~idle** он безде́льник/лентя́й; **~meal** *n.* костяна́я мука́.

boneless /'bəʊnlɪs/ *adj.* беско́стный.

boner /'bəʊnə(r)/ *n.* (*US sl.*) про́мах, оплóшность; **pull a ~** дать (*pf.*) ма́ху (*coll.*).

bonfire /'bɒnˌfaɪə(r)/ *n.* костёр.

bonhomie /ˌbɒnɒ'miː/ *n.* доброду́шие.

bonhomous /'bɒnəməs/ *adj.* (*coll.*) доброду́шный.

bon mot /bɔ̃ 'məʊ/, /bɒn-/ *n.* (*pl.* ***bons mots***) остро́та, ме́ткое слове́чко.

bonk /bɒnk/ *v.t.* (*coll.*) (*hit*) уд|аря́ть, -а́рить; **he ~ed his head** он уда́рился голово́й; (*Br. vulg.*) тра́х|ать, -нуть.

● *v.i.* (*Br. vulg.*) тра́х|аться, -нуться.

bonkers /'bɒŋkəz/ *adj.* (*coll.*): **he's ~** он чо́кнутый; он с приве́том.

bonnet /'bɒnɪt/ *n.* **1** (*woman's hat*) ка́пор; чепе́ц, че́пчик. **2** (*Br., of car*) капо́т.

bonny /'bɒnɪ/ *adj.* (**bonnier, bonniest**) (*Sc.*) (*comely*) хоро́шенький; (*healthy*): **a ~ baby** кре́пкий ребёнок.

bons mots /bɔ̃ 'məʊ/, /bɒn 'məʊ/, /'məʊz/ *pl. of* ***bon mot***

bonus /'bəʊnəs/ *n.* пре́мия, премиа́льные (*pl.*); (*fig.*) доба́вочное преиму́щество.

bon vivant /bɔ̃ viː'vɑ̃/ *n.* (*pl.* **bon vivants** *or* **bons vivants** *pronunc. same*) бонвива́н.

bony /'bəʊnɪ/ *adj.* (**bonier, boniest**) **1** (*of, like bone*) костяно́й. **2** (*of person*) костяно́й, кости́стый; **~ fingers** костля́вые па́льцы. **3** (*having many bones*): **~ fish** кости́стая ры́ба.

boo /buː/ *n.* ши́канье.

● *v.t.* (**boos, booed**) освист|ывать, -а́ть; ши́кать (*impf.*) +*d.*; **~ an actor off the stage** ши́каньем прогна́ть (*pf.*) актёра со сце́ны.

● *v.i.* (**boos, booed**) улюлю́кать (*impf.*).

● *int.* **1** (*expr. disapproval*) фу!; у-у! **2** (*used to startle*) у-у!

boob /buːb/ *n.* **1** (*US coll., simpleton*) простофи́ля (*c.g.*), дурале́й. **2** (*Br. coll., mistake*) прома́шка. **3** (*pl., sl., breasts*) буфера́ (*m. pl.*).

● *v.i.* (*Br. coll.*) оплоша́ть (*pf.*); дать (*pf.*) прома́шку.

booby /'buːbɪ/ *n.* дурачо́к, дурале́й.

● *cpd.* **~-trap** *n.* (*mil.*) ми́на-ловýшка; *v.t.* устан|а́вливать, -ови́ть ми́ны-ловýшки в/на +*p.*

boogie-woogie /ˌbuːgɪ'wuːgɪ/ *n.* бу́ги-ву́ги (*nt. indecl.*).

boohoo /ˌbuː'huː/ *v.i.* (**boohoos, boohooed**) реве́ть (*impf.*).

● *int.* у-у-у!

book /bʊk/ *n.* **1** кни́га; (*small*) кни́жка; **the B~ of Genesis** Кни́га Бытия́; **it is a closed ~ to me** э́то для меня́ кни́га за семью́ печа́тями; **read s.o. like a ~** ви́деть (*impf.*) кого́-н. насквóзь; **he is an open ~** он весь как на ладо́ни; **go by the ~** сле́довать (*impf.*) предписа́нию/пра́вилам. **2** (*set*): **~ of tickets/needles** па́чка биле́тов/иго́лок; **~ of matches/stamps** кни́жечка спи́чек/ма́рок. **3** (*account*): **he is on the firm's ~s** (*an employee*) он в шта́те э́той фи́рмы; **keep the ~s** вести́ (*det.*) бухга́лтерские/счётные кни́ги; **~ value** сто́имость по торго́вым кни́гам; **in s.o.'s good/bad ~s** на хоро́шем/плохо́м счету́ у кого́-н.; **bring s.o. to ~** призва́ть (*pf.*) кого́-н. к отве́ту; посчита́ться (*pf.*) с кем-н.; **that suits my ~** (*Br.*) э́то меня́ устра́ивает.

● *v.t.* **1** (*enter in ~ or list*) зан|оси́ть, -ести в кни́гу; регистри́ровать, за-. **2** (*ticket, table, taxi*) зака́з|ывать, -а́ть; (*hotel room, seat*) брони́ровать, за-; **~ one's passage** покупа́ть, купи́ть биле́т на парохо́д; **speculators ~ed up all the seats** спекуля́нты скупи́ли все биле́ты; **I am ~ed (up) on Wednesday** я (по́лностью) за́нят в сре́ду; **~ s.o. in at a hotel** брони́ровать, за- для кого́-н. но́мер в гости́нице.

● *v.i.*: **he ~ed in/out last night** он въе́хал/вы́ехал вчера́ ве́чером.

● *cpds.* **~binder** *n.* переплётчик; **~binding** *n.* переплётное де́ло; **~case** *n.* кни́жный шкаф; (*open-fronted*) кни́жные по́лки (*f. pl.*); **~-club** *n.* клуб книголю́бов; **~-ends** *n. pl.* подста́вки (*f. pl.*) для книг; **~-jacket** *n.* суперобло́жка; **~keeper** *n.* бухга́лтер, счетово́д; **~keeping** *n.* бухгалте́рия, счетово́дство; **~-learned** *adj.* кни́жный; **~-learning** *n.* кни́жность; кни́жные зна́ния; **~-lover** *n.* кни́жник, книголю́б; **~maker** *n.* букме́кер; **~mark** *n.* (*also comput.*) закла́дка; **~plate** *n.* экслибри́с; **~-rest** *n.* (*Br.*) (насто́льная) подста́вка для книг; **~seller** *n.* торго́вец кни́гами; **second-hand ~seller** букини́ст; **~selling** *n.* книготорго́вля; **~shelf** *n.* кни́жная по́лка; **~shop, ~store** (*US*) *nn.* кни́жный магази́н; **~stall** *n.* кни́жный кио́ск; **~worm** *n.* (*lit., fig.*) кни́жный червь.

bookie /'bʊkɪ/ (*coll.*) = **bookmaker**

booking /'bʊkɪŋ/ *n.* зака́з; **advance ~** предвари́тельный зака́з.

● *cpds.* **~-clerk** *n.* (*Br.*) касси́р; **~-office** *n.* (*Br.*) биле́тная ка́сса.

bookish /'bʊkɪʃ/ *adj.* (*literary, studious*) кни́жный; (*pedantic*) педанти́чный.

bookishness /ˈbʊkɪʃnɪs/ *n.* кни́жность; педанти́чность.

booklet /ˈbʊklɪt/ *n.* брошю́ра, букле́т.

Boolean /ˈbuːlɪən/ *adj.* (*comput.*) бу́лев, логи́ческий; **~ algebra** бу́лева а́лгебра, а́лгебра ло́гики; **~ operator** знак бу́левой опера́ции, знак логи́ческой опера́ции.

boom¹ /buːm/ *n.* (*naut., spar*) утле́гарь (*m.*); (*barrier*) плаву́чий бон.

boom² /buːm/ *n.* (*of gun, thunder, waves*) гул, ро́кот; (*of voice*) гул; **supersonic ~** сверхзвуково́й хлопо́к.

● *v.t. & i.* (*of gun*) бу́хать (*impf.*), грохота́ть (*impf.*); (*of thunder*) глу́хо грохота́ть (*impf.*); (*of waves*) рокота́ть (*impf.*); (*of bittern*) выть (*impf.*), у́хать (*impf.*); **the clock ~ed out the hour** часы́ гу́лко проби́ли час.

● *int.* бум!; бух!

boom³ /buːm/ *n.* (*comm.*) бум, оживле́ние; **~ town** бы́стро расту́щий го́род.

● *v.i.*: **business is ~ing** де́ло процвета́ет.

boomerang /ˈbuːməˌræŋ/ *n.* бумера́нг.

● *v.i.* (*fig.*): **his plan ~ed** его́ зате́я обрати́лась про́тив него́.

boon¹ /buːn/ *n.* (*advantage*) бла́го.

boon² /buːn/ *adj.*: **~ companion** до́брый прия́тель.

boor /ˈbʊə(r)/ *n.* (*coarse person*) хам, мужи́к.

boorish /ˈbʊərɪʃ/ *adj.* ха́мский, мужи́цкий.

boorishness /ˈbʊərɪʃnɪs/ *n.* ха́мство, мужикова́тость.

boost /buːst/ *n.* (*increase*) увеличе́ние; (*stimulus*) толчо́к, сти́мул; **give a ~ to the economy** стимули́ровать (*impf., pf.*) эконо́мику.

● *v.t.* (*increase*) увели́чи|вать, -ть; **~ s.o.'s reputation** создава́ть (*impf.*) кому́-н. репута́цию.

booster /ˈbuːstə(r)/ *n.* **1** (*elec.*) побуди́тель (*m.*), усили́тель (*m.*). **2**: **~ rocket** раке́тный ускори́тель; **~ injection** (*med.*) повто́рная приви́вка.

boot¹ /buːt/ *n.* **1** (*footwear*) боти́нок, башма́к; (*knee-length*) сапо́г; **riding ~** (высо́кий) сапо́г; **football ~s** бу́тсы (*f. pl.*); **he is too big for his ~s** он зазна́лся; **the ~ is on the other foot** (*Br.*) тепе́рь уж всё наоборо́т; **my heart was in my ~s** у меня́ душа́ в пя́тки ушла́; **you bet your ~s!** (*coll.*) бу́дьте уве́рены!
2 (*Br., pl. as sg. n., hotel servant*) коридо́рный.
3 (*dismissal*): **give s.o. the ~** вы́турить (*pf.*) (*coll.*) кого́-н. (с рабо́ты); **get the ~** вы́лететь (*pf.*) (*coll.*) (с рабо́ты).
4 (*Br., of a car*) бага́жник.

● *v.t.*: **~ s.o. in the face** съе́здить (*pf.*) (*coll.*) кому́-н. по физионо́мии; **~ s.o. out of his job** вы́турить (*pf.*) (*coll.*) кого́-н.; (*comput.*) загру|жа́ть, -зи́ть.

● *cpds.* **~black** *n.* чисти́льщик сапо́г; **~lace** *n.* шнуро́к для боти́нок; **~leg** *adj.* (*fig.*): **~leg whisky** контраба́ндное ви́ски; **~legger** *n.* самого́нщик; **~licker** *n.* (*coll.*) лизоблю́д, подхали́м; **~maker** *n.* сапо́жник; **~-polish** *n.* ва́кса; **~strap** *n.* ушко́; **pull o.s. up by one's own ~straps** (*fig.*) спасти́ (*pf.*) себя́ со́бственными рука́ми.

boot² /buːt/ *n.*: **to ~** в прида́чу.

bootee /buːˈtiː/ *n.* (*woman's*) да́мский боти́нок; (*child's*) пине́тка; вя́заный башмачо́к.

booth /buːð/, /buːθ/ *n.* (*for telephoning*) бу́дка; (*stall*) пала́тка, ларёк; (*for staging shows*) балага́н; (*in restaurant*) каби́нка; (*for listening to recordings*) каби́нка; (*polling-~*) каби́на для голосова́ния; (*US, exhibition stand*) стенд, щит.

booty /ˈbuːtɪ/ *n.* добы́ча.

booze /buːz/ *n.* вы́пивка; попо́йка; **go on the ~** запи́ть (*pf.*); **be on the ~** пья́нствовать (*impf.*).

● *v.i.* пья́нствовать (*impf.*), выпива́ть (*impf.*).

● *cpd.* **~-up** *n.* попо́йка.

boozer /ˈbuːzə(r)/ *n.* (*person*) выпиво́ха (*c.g.*); (*Br., pub*) забега́ловка.

boozy /ˈbuːzɪ/ *adj.* (**boozier, booziest**) (*of an event*) пья́ный; (*fond of drinking*) выпива́ющий, пью́щий; **a ~ type** люби́тель (*m.*) подда́ть (*coll.*).

boracic /bəˈræsɪk/ *adj.* бо́рный.

borage /ˈbɒrɪdʒ/ *n.* огуре́чник, бура́чник.

borax /ˈbɔːræks/ *n.* бура́; (*attr.*) бо́рный.

bordello /bɔːˈdeləʊ/ *n.* (*pl.* **~s**) (*US*) борде́ль (*m.*).

border /ˈbɔːdə(r)/ *n.* **1** (*side, edging*): **~ of a lake** бе́рег о́зера; (*of a sheet of paper*) кайма́; (*of a handkerchief*) каёмка; **a ~ of tulips** бордю́р из тюльпа́нов; **herbaceous ~** бордю́р из многоле́тних цвето́в.
2 (*frontier*) грани́ца; (*fig.*) грань; **~ incidents** пограни́чные инциде́нты; **~ post** пограни́чная заста́ва.

● *v.t.*: **the garden is ~ed by a stream** сад ограни́чен ручьём; вокру́г са́да протека́ет руче́й; **our garden ~s his field** наш сад грани́чит с его́ по́лем.

● *v.i.*: **these countries ~ on one another** э́ти стра́ны грани́чат друг с дру́гом; **this ~s on fanaticism** э́то грани́чит с фанати́змом.

● *cpd.* **~line** *n.* грани́ца; (*fig.*) грань; (*demarcation line*) демаркацио́нная ли́ния; **a ~line case** промежу́точный слу́чай.

borderer /ˈbɔːdərə(r)/ *n.* жи́тель (*m.*) пограни́чного райо́на.

bore¹ /bɔː(r)/ *n.* (*of tube, pipe*) расто́ченное отве́рстие; (*calibre*) кали́бр, кана́л ствола́.

● *v.t.* сверли́ть, про-; бури́ть, про-; **~ a hole** сверли́ть, про- дыру́.

● *v.i.* бури́ть (*impf.*); **~ for oil** бури́ть (*impf.*) в по́исках не́фти.

● *cpd.* **~-hole** *n.* бурова́я сква́жина.

bore² /bɔː(r)/ *n.* (*person*) ску́чный челове́к; зану́да (*c.g.*); (*thing*) (что-н.) надое́дливое; **what a ~!** кака́я тоска́!; кака́я ску́ка!

● *v.t.* надо|еда́ть, -е́сть + *d.*; **~ s.o. to death, tears** надо|еда́ть, -е́сть кому́-н. до́ смерти. *See also* ⇒**bored**

bore³ /bɔː(r)/ *n.* (*tidal wave*) бор; напо́р волн в у́стье реки́.

bore⁴ /bɔː(r)/ *past of* ⇒**bear²**

boreal /ˈbɔːrɪəl/ *adj.* се́верный, бореа́льный.

bored /ˈbɔːd/ *adj.* скуча́ющий; **I am ~** мне ску́чно; **in a ~ voice** ску́чным/скуча́ющим го́лосом; **I am ~ with him** он мне надое́л.

boredom /ˈbɔːdəm/ *n.* ску́ка, тоска́.

boric /ˈbɔːrɪk/ *adj.* бо́рный.

boring /ˈbɔːrɪŋ/ *adj.* (*tedious*) ску́чный, надое́дливый.

born /bɔːn/ *adj.* **1**: **a ~ poet/fool** прирождённый поэ́т/дура́к. **2**: **be ~** роди́ться (*pf.*); **he was ~ with a silver spoon in his mouth** он роди́лся в соро́чке; **I wasn't ~ yesterday** я не вчера́ роди́лся. **3**: **in all my ~ days** за всю мою́ жизнь.

borne /bɔːn/ *p.p. of* ⇒**bear²**

Borneo /ˈbɔːnɪˌəʊ/ *n.* Борне́о (*indecl.*).

boron /ˈbɔːrɒn/ *n.* бор.

borough /ˈbʌrə/ *n.* (*town*) го́род; (*section of town*) райо́н; **parliamentary ~** го́род, предста́вленный в парла́менте.

borrow /ˈbɒrəʊ/ *v.t. & i.* **1** (*take for a time*) брать, взять на вре́мя; заи́мствовать, по-; зан|има́ть, -я́ть (*also math.*); (*money*) брать, взять взаймы́; **he is always ~ing** он постоя́нно берёт взаймы́ (*or* в долг); **~ an idea from s.o.** заи́мствовать (*impf., pf.*) у кого́-н. иде́ю; **wear ~ed clothes** носи́ть (*impf.*) что-н. с чужо́го плеча́. **2** (*ling.*) заи́мствовать (*impf.*).

borrowing /ˈbɒrəʊɪŋ/ *n.*
1 одолжи́вание; **~ is a bad habit** брать взаймы́ — плоха́я привы́чка.
2 (*ling.*) заи́мствование.

bor(t)sch /bɔːʃ/ *n.* борщ.

borzoi /ˈbɔːzɔɪ/ *n.* ру́сская борза́я.

Bosnia /ˈbɒznɪə/ *n.* Бо́сния.

Bosnia–Herzegovina /ˈbɒznɪə ˌhɜːtsɪgəˈviːnə/ *n.* (*also* **Bosnia and Herzegovina**) Бо́сния и Герцегови́на.

bosom /ˈbʊz(ə)m/ *n.* **1** (*breast*) грудь; (*of clothing*) лиф. **2** (*fig.*) се́рдце, душа́; **~ friend** закады́чный друг; **in one's (own) ~** в глубине́ души́; **in the ~ of one's family** в ло́не семьи́; **the ~ of the church** ло́но це́ркви.

Bosp(h)orus /ˈbɒspərəs/ *n.* Босфо́р.

boss¹ /bɒs/ *n.* (*protuberance*) ши́шка; (*of shield*) умбо́н; (*archit.*) орна́мент в места́х пересече́ний ба́лок.

boss² /bɒs/ *n.* (*master*) босс, хозя́ин, нача́льник.

● *v.t.*: **~ s.o. about** кома́ндовать (*impf.*) кем-н.

boss-eyed /ˈbɒsaɪd/ *adj.* (*Br.*) криво́й, косо́й, косогла́зый.

bossy /ˈbɒsɪ/ *adj.* (**bossier, bossiest**) (*overbearing*) команди́рский.

botanical /bəˈtænɪk(ə)l/ *adj.* ботани́ческий.

botanist /ˈbɒtənɪst/ *n.* бота́ник.

botany /ˈbɒtənɪ/ *n.* бота́ника.

botch /bɒtʃ/ *v.t.* (*bungle*) зава́л|ивать, -и́ть; по́ртить, ис-; (*patch roughly*) зала́т|ывать, -а́ть; **~ up an essay** состря́пать (*pf.*) статее́чку.

botcher /ˈbɒtʃə(r)/ *n.* (*bungler*) порта́ч, «сапо́жник».

both /bəʊθ/ *pron. & adj.* о́ба (*m., nt.*), о́бе (*f.*); и тот и друго́й; **~ sledges** о́бе па́ры сане́й; **~ of us** мы о́ба; **of ~ sexes** обо́его по́ла; **you cannot have it ~ ways** выбира́йте одно́ из двух.

● *adv.*: **~ ... and ...** и... и...; **he is ~ tired and hungry** он уста́л и к тому́ же го́лоден; **I am fond of music, ~ ancient and modern** я люблю́ му́зыку, как ста́рую, так и совреме́нную; **my sister and I ~ helped him** мы о́ба помогли́ ему́, и я, и сестра́.

bother /ˈbɒðə(r)/ *n.* беспоко́йство; хлоп|оты (*pl., g.* -о́т); возня́; **I had no ~ finding the book** я нашёл кни́гу без труда́.

● *v.t.* (*disturb*) беспоко́ить, по-; трево́жить, по-; (*importune*) надоеда́ть (*impf.*) + *d.*; **~ one's head** трево́житься (*impf.*); **~ (it)!** (*Br.*) чёрт возьми́!; **he is always ~ing me to lend him money** он ве́чно пристаёт ко мне с про́сьбой одолжи́ть ему́ де́нег; **I can't be ~ed** мне лень, мне недосу́г.

● *v.i.* беспоко́иться, по-; **don't ~ to make tea** не вози́тесь с ча́ем.

bothersome /ˈbɒðəsəm/ *adj.* доса́дный, надое́дливый.

bottle /ˈbɒt(ə)l/ *n.* **1** буты́лка; (*Br., for infants*) рожо́к; **over a ~ of wine** за буты́лкой вина́; **bring up a child on the ~** вска́рмливать (*impf.*) ребёнка иску́сственно; **hot-water ~** гре́лка. **2** (*fig.*): **he is fond of the ~** он прикла́дывается к буты́лке; **take to the ~** пристрасти́ться (*pf.*) к буты́лке. **3** (*Br. coll., courage*) сме́лость.

● *v.t.* (*put in ~s*) разл|ива́ть, -и́ть по буты́лкам; **~d in Moscow** моско́вского разли́ва; **~ fruit** (*Br.*) консерви́ровать (*impf., pf.*) фру́кты; **~ up** (*conceal*) скры|ва́ть, -ть; (*restrain*) сдерж|ивать, -а́ть; **~ up one's feelings** скры|ва́ть, -ть свои́ чу́вства.

● *cpds.* **~-fed** *adj.* иску́сственно вско́рмленный; **~-green** *n.* буты́лочный цвет; *adj.* буты́лочного цве́та; буты́лочно-зелёный; **~neck** *n.* (*fig.*) зато́р; про́бка; у́зкое ме́сто; **~-nosed** *adj.* толстоно́сый; **~-nosed dolphin** афали́на; **~-nosed whale** бутылконо́с; **~-opener** *n.* открыва́лка (*coll.*); **~-party** *n.* (*Br.*) ≈ пиру́шка в скла́дчину; **~-top** *n.* колпачо́к на буты́лку.

bottled /ˈbɒt(ə)ld/ *adj.*: **~ beer** буты́лочное пи́во.

bottom /ˈbɒtəm/ *n.* **1** (*lowest part*) дно; (*of mountain*) подно́жие, подо́шва; (*of page*) низ, коне́ц; (*of stairs*) низ, основа́ние; **~ shelf** ни́жняя по́лка; (*of coat*) подо́л; **false ~** двойно́е дно; **~ up(wards)** вверх дном; **~s up!** пей до дна!; **at the ~ of the class** отстаю́щий в кла́ссе.
2 (*further end*): **at the ~ of the bed** в нога́х крова́ти; **~ (end) of the table** ни́жний коне́ц стола́; **~ of the garden** за́дняя часть са́да; **~ of the street** коне́ц у́лицы.
3 (*of sea*) дно; **send to the ~** пус|ка́ть, -ти́ть на дно; топи́ть, по-.
4 (*of a chair*) сиде́нье.
5 (*Br., anat.*) зад; за́дняя часть; за́днее ме́сто.
6 (*of ship*) дни́ще.
7 (*fig.*): **~ line** (*final total*) ито́г; (*crux of the matter*) суть де́ла; **from the ~ of my heart** из глубины́ души́; от всего́ се́рдца; **get to the ~ of something** доб|ира́ться, -ра́ться до су́ти чего́-н.; **he was at the ~ of it** за э́тим стоя́л он; **knock the ~ out of a scheme** сорва́ть (*pf.*) план; **prices touched (rock-)~** це́ны дости́гли са́мого ни́зкого у́ровня; **he came ~ in algebra** он был после́дним по а́лгебре.

bottomless /ˈbɒtəmlɪs/ *adj.* бездо́нный; **~ pit** бездо́нная я́ма; (*hell*) ад, преиспо́дняя; (*immeasurable*) безграни́чный, беспреде́льный.

bottommost /ˈbɒtəm,məʊst/ *adj.* са́мый ни́жний.

botulism /ˈbɒtjʊ,lɪz(ə)m/ *n.* ботули́зм.

boudoir /ˈbu:dwɑ:(r)/ *n.* будуа́р.

bougainvillaea /,bu:gənˈvɪlɪə/ *n.* (*bot.*) бугенви́лия.

bough /baʊ/ *n.* сук.

bought /bɔ:t/ *past and p.p. of* ⇒**buy**

bouillon /bu:ˈjɔ̃/, /ˈbu:jɒn/ *n.* бульо́н.

boulder /ˈbəʊldə(r)/ *n.* валу́н.

boulevard /ˈbu:lə,vɑ:d/, /ˈbu:lvɑ:(r)/ *n.* бульва́р.

bounce /baʊns/ *n.* (*of ball*) подпры́гивание, отско́к.

● *v.t.* (*eject*) вы́ки́дывать, вы́кинуть; (*US coll., dismiss from a job*) выгоня́ть, вы́гнать; **~ a ball** бить (*impf.*) мячо́м о́б пол (о зе́млю, об сте́нку *и т.п.*); **~ s.o. into a decision** (*Br.*) подт|а́лкивать, -олкну́ть кого́-н. приня́ть реше́ние.

● *v.i.* (*of ball etc.*) отск|а́кивать, -очи́ть; подпры́г|ивать, -нуть; (*coll., of cheque*) верну́ться (*pf.*); (*of person*): **~ into a room** влете́ть (*pf.*) в ко́мнату; **~ out of a room** вы́скочить (*pf.*) из ко́мнаты; **~ back** (*fig.*) бы́стро опра́виться.

bouncer /ˈbaʊnsə(r)/ *n.* (*chucker-out*) вышиба́ла (*m.*).

bouncing /ˈbaʊnsɪŋ/ *adj.* **1** (*of ball*) пры́гающий, подпры́гивающий. **2** (*healthy*) здоро́вый; (*lively*) живо́й.

bouncy /ˈbaʊnsɪ/ *adj.* (**bouncier, bounciest**) (*lit., resilient*) упру́гий; (*in manner*) энерги́чный, живо́й.

● *cpd.* **~ castle** *n.* надувно́й за́мок.

bound[1] /baʊnd/ *n.* (*usu. pl., limit*) грани́ца, преде́л; **set ~s to something** ста́вить, по- преде́л чему́-н.; ограни́чи|вать, -ть что-н.; **know no ~s** не знать (*impf.*) грани́ц; **beyond the ~s of reason** за преде́лами разу́много; **keep something within ~s** держа́ть (*impf.*) что-н. в определённых грани́цах; **within the ~s of possibility** в преде́лах возмо́жного; **the town is out of ~s to troops** вход в го́род солда́там воспрещён.

● *v.t.* (*limit*) ограни́чи|вать, -ть.

bound[2] /baʊnd/ *n.* (*jump*) прыжо́к; скачо́к; **by leaps and ~s** гало́пом; не по дням, а по часа́м; **at a ~** одни́м прыжко́м; (*bounce*) отско́к.

● *v.i.* пры́г|ать, -нуть; скак|а́ть, -ну́ть; **~ over a ditch** переск|а́кивать, -очи́ть че́рез кана́ву; **he ~ed off to fetch the book** он подпры́гнул, что́бы доста́ть кни́гу; **her heart ~ed with joy** её се́рдце (за)би́лось от ра́дости.

bound[3] /baʊnd/ *adj.* **1** (*connected*) свя́занный; **this is ~ up with politics** э́то свя́зано с поли́тикой.
2 (*absorbed*): **he is ~ up in his work** он поглощён рабо́той; **she is ~ up in her son** она́ по́лностью занята́ сы́ном.
3 (*certain*): **he is ~ to win** он непреме́нно вы́играет; **I'll be ~** я уве́рен; го́лову положу́, что...
4 (*obliged*): **you are not ~ to go** вам не обяза́тельно идти́. **5** (*of book*) переплетённый; в переплёте. **6** (*en route*): **the ship is ~ for New York** парохо́д направля́ется в Нью-Йо́рк; **where are you ~ for?** куда́ вы направля́етесь?; **homeward ~** направля́ющийся на ро́дину.

boundary /ˈbaʊndərɪ/, /-drɪ/ *n.* (*of a field etc.*) грани́ца, рубе́ж; (*fig.*) преде́л; (*attr.*) пограни́чный.

boundless /ˈbaʊndlɪs/ *adj.* безграни́чный, беспреде́льный.

boundlessness /ˈbaʊndlɪsnɪs/ *n.* безграни́чность, беспреде́льность.

bounteous /ˈbaʊntɪəs/ *adj.* (*generous*) ще́дрый; (*plentiful*) оби́льный.

bountiful /ˈbaʊntɪ,fʊl/ *adj.* ще́дрый; оби́льный.

bounty /ˈbaʊntɪ/ *n.* **1** (*generosity*) ще́дрость, щедро́ты (*f. pl.*). **2** (*reward*) пре́мия, вознагражде́ние.

bouquet /bu:ˈkeɪ/, /bəʊ-/ *n.* (*of flowers, wine*) буке́т.

bourbon /ˈbɜ:bən/, /ˈbʊə-/ *n.* (*whisky*) бурбо́н, бе́рбон.

bourgeois /ˈbʊəʒwɑ:/ *n.* (*pl.* **~**) буржуа́ (*m. indecl.*); **she is a ~** она́ меща́нка.

● *adj.* буржуа́зный.

bourgeoisie /,bʊəʒwɑ:ˈzi:/ *n.* буржуази́я.

bout /baʊt/ *n.* **1** (*at games*) бой, встре́ча, схва́тка; **fencing ~** бой в фехтова́нии; **wrestling ~** схва́тка в борьбе́; **have a ~ with** схва́т|ываться, -и́ться с + *i.* **2** (*of illness*) при́ступ. **3** (*drinking-~*) запо́й.

boutique /bu:ˈti:k/ *n.* (небольшо́й) мо́дный магази́н; бути́к.

bovine /ˈbəʊvaɪn/ *adj.* (*zool.*) быча́чий, бы́чий; (*fig.*) тупо́й.

bow[1] /bəʊ/ *n.* **1** (*weapon*) лук; **draw a ~** натя́|гивать, -ну́ть тетиву́ лу́ка. **2** (*rainbow*) ра́дуга. **3** (*of violin etc.*) смычо́к. **4** (*knot*) бант; **tie a ~** завя́з|ывать, -а́ть бант; **tie something in a ~** завя́з|ывать, -а́ть что-н. ба́нтиком.

● *v.i.* (*of violinist*) владе́ть (*impf.*) смычко́м.

● *cpds.* **~-head** *n.* гренла́ндский/поля́рный кит; **~-legged** *adj.*

B

кривоно́гий; **~-legs** *n. pl.* кривы́е но́ги (*f. pl.*); **~-line** *n.* (*rope*) були́нь (*m.*); (*knot*) бесе́дочный у́зел; **~man** *n.* (*archer*) лу́чник; **~-saw** *n.* лучко́вая пила́; **~shot** *n.*: **within a ~shot of** на расстоя́нии полёта стрелы́ от + *g.*; **~string** *n.* тетива́; **~-tie** *n.* (га́лстук-)ба́бочка; **~-window** *n.* э́ркер.

bow² /baʊ/ *n.* (*salutation*) покло́н; **make a deep/low ~** ни́зко кла́няться, поклони́ться.

● *v.t.* **1** (*bend*): **~ one's head** склон|я́ть, -и́ть го́лову; **the wind ~ed the trees** ве́тер гнул/клони́л дере́вья; **~ed down by grief** сло́мленный го́рем. **2** (*express by ~ing*): **~ one's thanks** благодари́ть покло́ном.

● *v.i.* **1** (*salute*) кла́няться, поклони́ться; **~ and scrape** расша́ркиваться (*перед кем-н.*); **~ down** (*worship*) преклон|я́ться, -и́ться (пе́ред + *i.*); **~ out** (= *retire*): **~ out of politics** распрости́ться (*pf.*) с поли́тикой. **2** (*defer*) склон|я́ться, -и́ться (**to, before**: перед + *i.*); **~ to fate** смир|я́ться, -и́ться с судьбо́й.

bow³ /baʊ/ *n.* (*naut.*) нос; **on the ~** на носовы́х курсовы́х угла́х; **cross s.o.'s ~s** (*fig.*) перебе|га́ть, -жа́ть кому́-н. доро́гу.

bowdlerization /ˌbaʊdləraɪˈzeɪʃ(ə)n/ *n.* выхола́щивание; изъя́тие нежела́тельных мест (*в книге*).

bowdlerize /ˈbaʊdləˌraɪz/ *v.t.* выхола́щивать, вы́холостить.

bowel /ˈbaʊəl/ *n.* **1** кишка́; **have a ~ movement** име́ть (*impf.*) стул; испражня́ться; **are your ~s regular?** регуля́рно ли де́йствует у вас кише́чник?; **castor oil is good for moving your ~s** касто́рка хорошо́ сла́бит. **2**: **~s of the earth** не́др|а (*pl., g.* —) земли́.

bower /ˈbaʊə(r)/ *n.* (*arbour*) бесе́дка.

● *cpd.* **~-bird** *n.* бесе́дочница, шала́шник.

bowie-knife /ˈbəʊɪ/ *n.* дли́нный охо́тничий нож.

bowing /ˈbəʊɪŋ/ *n.* (*mus.*) владе́ние смычко́м.

bowl¹ /bəʊl/ *n.* **1** (*vessel*) ча́ша, ва́за, ми́ска; **crystal ~** хруста́льная ва́за; **wooden ~** деревя́нная ми́ска. **2** (*of pipe*) ча́шечка; (*of spoon*) углубле́ние.

bowl² /bəʊl/ *n.* (*ball*) ке́гельный шар; **play ~s** игра́ть (*impf.*) в ке́гли/шары́.

● *v.t.* (*roll*) ката́ть (*indet.*), кати́ть, по-; **~ a hoop** гоня́ть (*indet.*), гнать о́бруч; **~ over** (*lit.*) сшиб|а́ть, -и́ть; (*fig.*); **he was ~ed over by her** она́ срази́ла его́; **he was ~ed over by the news** он был ошара́шен/ошеломлён э́тим изве́стием.

● *v.i.* **1** (*cricket*) под|ава́ть, -а́ть мяч. **2**: **~ along** бы́стро кати́ться. **3** (*play bowls*) игра́ть (*impf.*) в ке́гли/шары́; **~ing-alley** кегельба́н; **~ing-green** лужа́йка для игры́ в шары́.

bowler¹ /ˈbəʊlə(r)/ *n.* (*at games*) подаю́щий/броса́ющий мяч.

bowler² /ˈbəʊlə(r)/ *n.* (**~ hat**) котело́к.

bowser /ˈbaʊzə(r)/ *n.* (*propr.*) бензозапра́вщик.

bowsprit /ˈbəʊsprɪt/ *n.* (*naut.*) бушпри́т.

bow-wow /ˈbaʊwaʊ/, /-ˈwaʊ/ *n.* (*bark*) гав-га́в; (*coll., dog*) соба́чка.

● *int.* гав-га́в!

box¹ /bɒks/ *n.* (*bot.*) (*also* **~wood**) самши́т.

box² /bɒks/ *n.* **1** (*receptacle*) коро́бка, я́щик; **letter-~** (*Br.*), **mail~** (*US*) почто́вый я́щик; **PO** (*abbr. of* ***post office***) **box** абонеме́нтный я́щик; **~ number** но́мер абонеме́нтного я́щика; **cardboard ~** карто́нка. **2**: **Christmas ~** (*Br.*) рожде́ственский пода́рок. **3** (*hist., driver's seat*) ко́зл|ы (*pl., g.* -ел). **4** (*theatr.*) ло́жа. **5** (*Br. coll., television*) я́щик, те́лик. **6** (*for horse*) сто́йло; **loose ~** широ́кое сто́йло. **7** (*witness-~*) ме́сто для свиде́телей; **be in the ~** свиде́тельствовать (*impf.*); **put s.o. in the ~** вы́звать (*pf.*) кого́-н. в ка́честве свиде́теля. **8** (*typ.*) ра́мка.

● *v.t.* **1** класть, положи́ть в коро́бку/я́щик. **2**: **~ the compass** (*name points*) наз|ыва́ть, -ва́ть все ру́мбы ко́мпаса. **3** **~ in, up** (*confine*) сти́с|кивать, -нуть; вти́с|кивать, -нуть; запи́х|ивать, -а́ть; **~ed in** сти́снутый, зажа́тый.

● *cpds.* **~-board** *n.* коро́бочный карто́н; **~-calf** *n.* бокс; хро́мовая теля́чья ко́жа; **~-camera** *n.* я́щичный фотоаппара́т; **~-car** *n.* (*US, rail.*) това́рный ваго́н; **~-kite** *n.* коро́бчатый возду́шный змей; **~-office** *n.* (театра́льная) ка́сса; **~-pleat** *n.* бантова́я скла́дка; **~-pleated** *adj.* в бантову́ю скла́дку; **~room** *n.* (*Br.*) кладова́я; **~-seat** *n.* (*theatr.*) ме́сто в ло́же.

box³ /bɒks/ *n.*: **~ on the ear** оплеу́ха.

● *v.t.*: **~ s.o.'s ears** да|ва́ть, -ть кому́-н. оплеу́ху (*or* по́ уху).

● *v.i.* (*sport*) бокси́ровать (*impf.*).

boxer /ˈbɒksə(r)/ *n.* (*sportsman; dog*) боксёр; **~ shorts** боксёрские трусы́.

boxful /ˈbɒksfʊl/ *n.* я́щик, коро́бка (*чего*).

boxing /ˈbɒksɪŋ/ *n.* (*sport*) бокс.

● *cpd.* **~-glove** *n.* боксёрская перча́тка.

Boxing Day /ˈbɒksɪŋ/ *n.* (*Br.*) второ́й день Рождества́.

boy /bɔɪ/ *n.* **1** (*child*) ма́льчик; **I knew him as** (*when I was*) **a ~** я знал его́, когда́ я был ребёнком; (*when he was*) я знал его́ ма́льчиком; **~ scout** бойска́ут. **2** (*son*) сын. **3**: **grocer's** (*etc.*) **~** ма́льчик в бакале́йной (*и т.п.*) ла́вке. **4**: **old ~** старина́ (*m.*), стари́к; **~s!** ребя́та (*m. pl.*); **oh ~!** (*coll.*) здо́рово! вот э́то да́!

● *cpd.* **~-friend** *n.* ≈ (*её*) па́рень (*m.*), молодо́й челове́к.

boyar /ˈbɔɪə/ *n.* боя́рин; (*attr.*) боя́рский.

boycott /ˈbɔɪkɒt/ *n.* бойко́т.

● *v.t.* бойкоти́ровать (*impf., pf.*).

boyhood /ˈbɔɪhʊd/ *n.* о́трочество.

boyish /ˈbɔɪɪʃ/ *adj.* мальчи́шеский.

boyishness /ˈbɔɪɪʃnɪs/ *n.* мальчи́шество.

bra /brɑː/ *n.* (*pl.* **bras**) (*coll.*) ли́фчик, бюстга́льтер.

brace /breɪs/ *n.* **1** (*support*) подпо́рка, распо́рка; (*clasp*) скре́па; (*in building*) связь, подко́с, скоба́. **2** (*naut.*) брас. **3**: **~s** (*Br., for trousers*) подтя́ж|ки (*pl. g.* -ек), по́моч|и (*pl., g.* -е́й). **4** (*typ., bracket*) фигу́рная ско́бка. **5** (*pl.* **~**) (*pair*) па́ра. **6**: **~ and bit** коловоро́т, пёрка. **7** (*dentistry etc.*) ши́на.

● *v.t.* **1** (*make fast*) скреп|ля́ть, -и́ть; подкреп|ля́ть, -и́ть; (*support*) подп|ира́ть, -ере́ть; **he ~d himself against the wall** он опёрся о стéну. **2** (*of nerves*) укреп|ля́ть, -и́ть; **he ~d himself to do it** он собра́лся с ду́хом сде́лать э́то.

bracelet /ˈbreɪslɪt/ *n.* брасле́т; (*pl., sl., handcuffs*) нару́чники (*m. pl.*).

bracer /ˈbreɪsə(r)/ *n.* (*pick-me-up*) рю́мка для сме́лости.

bracing /ˈbreɪsɪŋ/ *adj.* бодря́щий, укрепля́ющий.

bracken /ˈbrækən/ *n.* орля́к; (*collect.*) па́поротник.

bracket /ˈbrækɪt/ *n.* **1** (*support*) кронште́йн; (*lamp-~*) ла́мповый кронште́йн; бра (*nt. indecl.*). **2** (*shelf*) по́лочка на кронште́йнах. **3** (*typ.*) ско́бка; **square/round ~** квадра́тная/кру́глая ско́бка; **open/close ~s** откры́ть/закры́ть (*pf.*) ско́бки. **4** (*fig.*): **the higher income ~s** гру́ппа населе́ния с бо́лее высо́кими дохо́дами.

● *v.t.* (**bracketed, bracketing**) **1** (*enclose in ~s*) заключ|а́ть, -и́ть в ско́бки. **2** (*link with a ~*) соедин|я́ть, -и́ть ско́бкой; (*fig.*): **do not ~ me with him** не ста́вьте меня́ с ним на одну́ до́ску; **A and B were ~ed for first prize** пе́рвую пре́мию раздели́ли ме́жду А и Б. **3** (*mil.*) захва́т|ывать, -и́ть в ви́лку.

● *cpd.* **~-lamp** *n.* ла́мпа на кронште́йне.

brackish /ˈbrækɪʃ/ *adj.* солонова́тый.

bradawl /ˈbrædɔːl/ *n.* ши́ло.

brag /bræɡ/ *n.* хвастовство́.

● *v.i.* (**bragged, bragging**) хва́стать(ся), по- (*чем*).

braggart /ˈbræɡət/ *n.* хвасту́н.

bragging /ˈbræɡɪŋ/ *n.* хвастовство́.

Brahmin /ˈbrɑːmɪn/ *n.* брами́н, брахма́н.

Brahminism /ˈbrɑːmɪnɪz(ə)m/ *n.* брахмани́зм.

braid /breɪd/ *n.* (*of hair*) коса́; (*band, ribbon*) тесьма́; (*cord-like fabric*) галу́н; **gold ~** золото́й галу́н.

● *v.t.* (*interweave*) плести́, с-; (*arrange in braids*) запле|та́ть, -сти́; (*edge with braid*) обш|ива́ть, -и́ть тесьмо́й.

Braille /breɪl/ *n.* шрифт Бра́йля; **read ~** чита́ть (*impf.*) по Бра́йлю.

brain /breɪn/ *n.* **1** (*anat.*) мозг; (*pl., cul.*) мозги́; **~ tumour** (*Br.*), **tumor** (*US*) о́пухоль мо́зга; **~ death** сме́рть (головно́го) мо́зга; **blow one's ~s out**

пус|ка́ть, -ти́ть себе́ пу́лю в лоб. **2** (*intellect*): **overtax one's ~** перенапряга́ть (*impf.*) свой мозги́; **rack one's ~s** лома́ть (*impf.*) го́лову (над + *i.*); **pick people's ~s** испо́льзовать (*impf.*, *pf.*) чужи́е мы́сли; присва́ивать (*impf.*) чужи́е иде́и; **use one's ~s** шевели́ть (*impf.*) мозга́ми; **he has that tune on the ~** э́тот моти́в нейдёт у него́ из головы́; **~s trust** (*Br.*) мозгово́й трест; **the best ~s in the country** лу́чшие го́ловы в стране́; **he's the ~s of the family** он са́мый башкови́тый/мозгови́тый в семье́; **a great ~** (*person*) све́тлая голова́.

● *v.t.* размозжи́ть (*pf.*) го́лову + *d.*

● *cpds.* **~-child** *n.* де́тище/плод ра́зума/воображе́ния; **~ drain** *n.* «уте́чка мозго́в»; **~storm** *n.* (*coll.*, *moment of madness*) припа́док безу́мия; (*US*, *clever idea*) блестя́щая иде́я; **~storming session** *n.* коллекти́вное обсужде́ние пробле́м; **~-wash** *v.t.* пром|ыва́ть, -ы́ть мозги́ + *d.*; **~-washing** *n.* промыва́ние мозго́в; **~wave** *n.*: **he had a ~wave** ему́ пришла́ счастли́вая мысль; его́ осени́ла иде́я; **~-work** *n.* у́мственная де́ятельность/рабо́та; **~-worker** *n.* рабо́тник у́мственного труда́.

brainless /ˈbreɪnlɪs/ *adj.* безмо́зглый, пустоголо́вый.

brainlessness /ˈbreɪnlɪsnɪs/ *n.* безмо́зглость, пустоголо́вость.

brainy /ˈbreɪnɪ/ *adj.* (**brainier, brainiest**) (*coll.*) башкови́тый, мозгови́тый.

braise /breɪz/ *v.t.* туши́ть (*impf.*).

brake[1] /breɪk/ *n.* (*thicket*) ча́ща, за́росль.

brake[2] /breɪk/ *n.* (*on vehicle*) то́рмоз (*pl.* -а́); **put on the ~** тормози́ть, за-; (*fig.*) **put a ~ on s.o's enthusiasm** ум|еря́ть, -е́рить чей-н. пыл.

● *v.t.* & *i.* тормози́ть, за-; **braking distance** тормозно́й путь; **braking power** мо́щность торможе́ния.

● *cpds.* **~-drum** *n.* тормозно́й бараба́н; **~-fluid** *n.* тормозна́я жи́дкость; **~-light** *n.* фона́рь (*m.*) сигна́ла торможе́ния (*or* стоп-сигна́ла); **~-shoe** *n.* тормозно́й башма́к; **~-van** *n.* (*Br.*) тормозно́й ваго́н.

bramble /ˈbræmb(ə)l/ *n.* ежеви́ка.

bran /bræn/ *n.* о́труб|и (*pl.*, *g.* -е́й).

branch /brɑːntʃ/ *n.* (*of tree*) ветвь; ве́тка; (*of river*) рука́в; (*of road*) ответвле́ние; (*of family*, *genus*) ли́ния, ветвь; (*of railway line*) ве́тка; (*comm.*) филиа́л, отделе́ние; **~ office** филиа́льное отделе́ние, филиа́л; (*of knowledge*, *subject*, *industry*) о́трасль; **the Slavonic ~ of the Indo-European languages** славя́нская ветвь индоевропе́йских языко́в.

● *v.i.* (*of plants*): **~ forth, out** разветв|ля́ться, -и́ться; раски́|дывать, -нуть ве́тви; (*of organization*): **~ out** разветв|ля́ться, -и́ться; (*of person*): **~ out in a new direction** расш|иря́ть, -и́рить де́ятельность в но́вом направле́нии; (*of road or rail.*, *also* **~ off**) разветв|ля́ться, -и́ться; ответв|ля́ться, -и́ться; (*of river*) разветв|ля́ться, -и́ться; раздел|я́ться, -и́ться на рукава́.

brand /brænd/ *n.* **1** (*piece of burning wood*) головня́, голове́шка. **2** (*mark of ~ing*, *also fig.*) клеймо́, тавро́, печа́ть. **3** (*trade-mark*) фабри́чная ма́рка; фабри́чное клеймо́. **4** (*species of goods*) сорт, ма́рка; **~ name** фи́рменное назва́ние.

● *v.t.* **1** (*cattle etc.*) таври́ть, за-; клейми́ть, за-; **~ing-iron** клеймо́. **2** (*fig.*, *imprint*): **~ something on s.o.'s memory** запечатле́ть (*pf.*) что-н. в чьей-н. па́мяти. **3** (*stigmatize*) клейми́ть, за-. **4** (*comm.*): **~ed goods** това́ры с фабри́чным клеймо́м.

● *cpd.* **~-new** *adj.* соверше́нно но́вый, с иго́лочки.

brandish /ˈbrændɪʃ/ *v.t.* разма́хивать (*impf.*) + *i.*

brandy /ˈbrændɪ/ *n.* конья́к; бре́нди (*nt. indecl.*).

brant /ˈbrænt/ (*US*) = **brent**

brash /bræʃ/ *adj.* наха́льный, наглова́тый, де́рзкий.

brashness /bræʃnɪs/ *n.* наха́льство, де́рзость.

brass /brɑːs/ *n.* **1** (*metal*) лату́нь, жёлтая медь; **~ plate** ме́дная доще́чка (на две́ри); **the top ~** (*sl.*) вы́сшее нача́льство; **get down to ~ tacks** доходи́ть, дойти́ до су́ти де́ла; **it is not worth a ~ farthing** э́то ло́маного гроша́ не сто́ит. **2** (*also* **~-ware**) лату́нные/ме́дные изде́лия. **3** (*mus.*): **the ~** духовы́е инструме́нты (*m. pl.*); медь; **~ band** духово́й орке́стр. **4** (*Br. sl.*, *money*) деньга́ (*coll.*). **5** (*sl.*, *impudence*) наха́льство.

brasserie /ˈbræsərɪ/ *n.* пивна́я.

brassière /ˈbræzɪə(r)/, /-sɪˌeə(r)/ *n.* ли́фчик, бюстга́льтер.

brassy /ˈbrɑːsɪ/ *adj.* (**brassier, brassiest**) (*of colour*) ме́дный; (*of sound*) металли́ческий; (*coarse*, *impudent*) наха́льный.

brat /bræt/ *n.* щено́к, (*coll.*) сопля́к.

bravado /brəˈvɑːdəʊ/ *n.* брава́да; **out of ~** из жела́ния порисова́ться.

brave /breɪv/ *n.* (*American Indian warrior*) инде́йский во́ин.

● *adj.* (*courageous*) хра́брый, сме́лый; (*bold*) де́рзкий; (*fearless*, *intrepid*) бесстра́шный, му́жественный, отва́жный.

● *v.t.* (*danger etc.*) бр|оса́ть, -о́сить вы́зов + *d.*; **~ the storm** боро́ться (*impf.*) с бу́рей; **~ publicity** не боя́ться (*impf.*) гла́сности.

bravery /ˈbreɪvərɪ/ *n.* (*courage*) хра́брость, сме́лость.

bravo /brɑːˈvəʊ/ *int.* бра́во!

bravura /brəˈvʊərə/, /-ˈvjʊərə/ *n.* (*mus.*) браву́рность; (*attr.*) браву́рный.

brawl /brɔːl/ *n.* сканда́л.

● *v.i.* сканда́лить (*impf.*).

brawn /brɔːn/ *n.* (*Br.*, *meat*) зельц; (*fig.*) му́скулы (*m. pl.*).

brawny /ˈbrɔːnɪ/ *adj.* (**brawnier, brawniest**) мускули́стый.

bray /breɪ/ *n.* рёв.

● *v.i.* реве́ть (*impf.*).

braze /breɪz/ *v.t.* (*solder*) пая́ть (*impf.*) твёрдым припо́ем.

brazen /ˈbreɪz(ə)n/ *adj.* ме́дный, бро́нзовый; (*fig.*, *shameless*) на́глый, бессты́дный.

● *v.t.*: **~ something out** на́гло выкру́чиваться, вы́крутиться из чего́-н.

brazier /ˈbreɪzɪə(r)/, /-ʒə(r)/ *n.* (*worker*) ме́дник; (*pan*) жаро́вня.

Brazil /brəˈzɪl/ *n.* Брази́лия; **~ nut** америка́нский оре́х; **~ wood** цезальпи́ния, фернамбу́к.

Brazilian /brəˈzɪljən/ *n.* брази́л|ец (*fem.* -ья́нка).

● *adj.* брази́льский.

breach /briːtʃ/ *n.* **1** (*violation*, *interruption*) наруше́ние; **~ of duty** невыполне́ние обяза́тельств; **~ of trust** злоупотребле́ние дове́рием; **~ of good manners** наруше́ние пра́вил поведе́ния. **2** (*gap*) проло́м, брешь; **step into the ~** (*fig.*) при|ходи́ть, -йти на по́мощь. **3** (*quarrel*) ссо́ра, разры́в; **heal the ~** класть, положи́ть коне́ц ссо́ре; мири́ться, по-.

● *v.t.* прор|ыва́ть, -ва́ть.

bread /bred/ *n.* хлеб; (*sl.*, *money*) деньга́; **brown ~** се́рый хлеб; **loaf of ~** бато́н, буха́нка; **~ and butter** (*fig.*) хлеб с ма́слом; **daily ~** (*lit.*, *fig.*) хлеб насу́щный; **take the ~ out of s.o.'s mouth** лиш|а́ть, -и́ть кого́-н. куска́ хле́ба; **be on ~ and water** сиде́ть (*impf.*) на хле́бе и воде́; **he knows which side his ~ is buttered on** он зна́ет свою́ вы́году; **half a loaf is better than no ~** лу́чше немно́го, чем ничего́; на безры́бье и рак ры́ба; **~ and circuses** хлеб и зре́лища.

● *cpds.* **~-and-butter** *adj.* насу́щный; **~-and-butter issues** насу́щные пробле́мы; **~-basket** *n.* (*sl.*) брю́хо; **~-bin** *n.* (*Br.*) хле́бница; **~-board** *n.* хле́бная доска́; **~-crumb** *n.* кро́шка; (*pl.*, *cul.*) толчёные сухари́ (*m. pl.*); **~-fruit** *n.* плод хле́бного де́рева; **~-fruit tree** хле́бное де́рево; **~-knife** *n.* хле́бный нож; **~line** *n.*: **on the ~line** (*Br.*) в тяжёлом материа́льном положе́нии; **~-sauce** *n.* хле́бный со́ус; **~winner** *n.* корми́лец.

breadth /bredθ/ *n.* **1** (*width*) ширина́; **he missed by a hair's ~** он был на волосо́к от це́ли. **2** (*fig.*): **~ of mind** широта́ ума́.

breadth|ways /ˈbredθweɪz/, **-wise** /ˈbredθwaɪz/ *advs.* в ширину́.

break /breɪk/ *n.* **1** (*broken place*, *gap*) тре́щина, разры́в; **~ in the clouds** (*fig.*) луч наде́жды.
2: **~ of day** рассве́т.
3 (*interval*) переры́в, па́уза; (*rest*) переды́шка; **give him a ~!** оста́вь его́ в поко́е!
4 (*change*) переме́на; **the trip made a pleasant ~** пое́здка внесла́ прия́тное разнообра́зие; (*in voice at puberty*) ло́мка.
5 (*of bouncing ball*) отско́к в сто́рону.
6 (*coll.*, *opportunity*) возмо́жность; **lucky ~** счастли́вый слу́чай.
7 (*escape*): **prison ~** побе́г из тюрьмы́.

● *v.t.* (*past* **broke,** *p.p.* **broken;** *see also* ⇨**broken**) **1** (*fracture, divide, destroy*) ломáть, с-; (*glass, china*) бить (*or* разбивáть), раз-; **he broke his leg** он сломáл нóгу; **she broke the plate in two** тарéлка у неё разбилась пополáм; **~ something in pieces** разл|áмывать, -омáть что-н. на куски́; **~ a piece off something** отл|áмывать, -омáть (*or* -оми́ть) кусóк от чегó-н.; **he broke the seal** он сломáл печáть; **~ the ice** (*lit., fig.*) ломáть, с- лёд; **~ the skin** прор|ывáть, -вáть кóжу; **~ s.o.'s head (open)** прол|áмывать, -оми́ть комý-н. чéреп; **~ s.o.'s nose** раз|бивáть, -би́ть комý-н. нос.
2 (*fig.*): **~ new ground** про|клáдывать, -ложи́ть нóвые пути́; **~ cover** выходи́ть, вы́йти из укры́тия; **~ camp** сн|имáться, -я́ться с лáгеря; **~ the bank** (*gambling*) срывáть, сорвáть банк; **~ a record** побивáть, поби́ть рекóрд; **~** (*defeat*) **a strike** срывáть, сорвáть забастóвку; **~ wind** (*fart*) пердéть, пёрнуть; пóртить, ис- вóздух; **~** (*into*) **a five-pound note** размéн|ивать, -я́ть пятифунтóвую бумáжку; **~ s.o.'s heart** разб|ивать, -и́ть комý-н. сéрдце; **~ s.o.'s spirit** сломи́ть (*pf.*) когó-н.; **~ a spell** разр|ушáть, -ýшить чáры; **~ the back of a task** одол|евáть, -éть труднéйшую часть задáния; **he was broken by the failure of his business** егó сломи́ла неудáча в дéле.
3 (*tame*): **~ a horse to harness** приуч|áть, -и́ть лóшадь к ýпряжи.
4 (*disaccustom*): **~ s.o. of a habit** отуч|áть, -и́ть когó-н. от привы́чки.
5 (*convey*): **~ the news** сообщ|áть, -и́ть (неприя́тные) нóвости.
6 (*weaken*): **~ a blow** смягч|áть, -и́ть удáр; **~ a fall** осл|аблять, -áбить си́лу падéния.
7 (*violate, e.g. the law, a promise*) нар|ушáть, -ýшить; **~ a secret** разгл|ашáть, -аси́ть тáйну; **~ a cypher** расшифрóв|ывать, -áть код.
8 (*interrupt, put an end to*): **~ silence** нар|ушáть, -ýшить молчáние; **~ one's journey** прер|ывáть, -вáть путешéствие; **~ a fast** прекра|щáть, -ти́ть пост; **~ a circuit** (*elec.*) прер|ывáть, -вáть ток.
9 (*destroy uniformity or completeness of*): **~ a set of books** разрóзни|вáть, -ть компле́кт книг; **~ ranks** выходи́ть, вы́йти из стрóя; **~** (*refuse to join*) **a strike** быть штрéйкбрéхером.

● *v.i.* (*past* **broke,** *p.p.* **broken**)
1 (*fracture, divide, disperse*) ломáться, с-; обл|áмываться, -омáться; (*of glass, china*) би́ться (*or* разбивáться), раз-; (*of rope etc.*) об|рывáться, -орвáться; лóпаться, лóпнуть; (*of ice*) трещáть, трéснуть; **~ in two** ломáться, с- пополáм; **~ in pieces** разл|áмываться, -омáться на куски́; **the door broke open** дверь поддалáсь, распахнýлась; **the waves ~ on the beach** вóлны бью́тся о бéрег; **the clouds broke** тýчи рассéялись.
2 (*fig.*): **his heart broke** он был (совершéнно) уби́т; **their spirit broke** они́ пáли дýхом; **~ing-point** предéл.
3 (*burst, dawn*): **the blister/bubble broke** волды́рь/пузы́рь лóпнул; **day broke** забрéзжил день; рассвелó; **the storm broke** разрази́лась грозá; **the news broke at 5 o'clock** об э́том стáло извéстно в 5 часóв; **a cry broke from his lips** крик сорвáлся с егó уст.
4 (*change*): **his voice broke** (*puberty*) у негó сломáлся гóлос; (*emotion*) егó гóлос дрóгнул/сорвáлся; **the weather broke** погóда испóртилась.
5 (*var.*): **~ even** ост|авáться, -áться при свои́х; **we broke for lunch** мы сдéлали переры́в на обéд.

● *with preps.*: **burglars broke into the house** граби́тели ворвáлись в дом; **the house was broken into** в дóме произошёл грабёж со взлóмом; **~ into song** затя́|гивать, -нýть пéсню; запéть (*pf.*); **~ into a trot** пусти́ться (*pf.*) ры́сью; **~ into laughter** рассмея́ться (*pf.*); **~ into a £5 note** размéн|ивать, -я́ть пятифунтóвую бумáжку; **~ into the publishing world** проб|ивáться, -и́ться в издáтельский мир; **cattle broke through the fence** скот прорвáлся чéрез забóр; **~ through s.o.'s reserve** поборóть (*pf.*) чью-н. застéнчивость; **the sun broke through the cloud** сóлнце проби́лось сквозь тýчи; **he broke with her** он порвáл с ней; **~ with old habits** покóнчить (*pf.*) со стáрыми привы́чками.

● *with advs.*: **~ away** *v.i.*: **~ away from one's gaolers** вырывáться, вы́рваться из рук тюрéмщиков; **~ away from old habits** откáз|ываться, -áться от стáрых привы́чек; покóнчить (*pf.*) со стáрыми привы́чками; **~ away from a group** отк|áлываться, -олóться от грýппы; **~ down** *v.t.*: **~ down a door** вылáмывать, вы́ломать дверь; **~ down resistance** сломи́ть (*pf.*) сопротивлéние; **~ down expenditure** разб|ивáть, -и́ть расхóды по статья́м; *v.i.*: **the bridge broke down** мост рýхнул; **negotiations broke down** переговóры сорвáлись; **the car broke down** маши́на сломáлась; **he broke down** он не вы́держал; **his health broke down** егó здорóвье пошатнýлось; **the argument ~s down** дóвод окáзывается несостоя́тельным; **~ forth** *v.i.* вырывáться, вы́рваться вперёд; **~ in** *v.t.*: **~ in a door** вл|áмываться, -оми́ться в дверь; **~ in a horse** выезжáть, вы́ездить лóшадь; **~ in a new pair of shoes** разн|áшивать, -оси́ть нóвые тýфли; *v.i.*: **~ in on a conversation** вмéш|иваться, -áться в разговóр; **~ off** *v.t.*: **~ off a twig** отл|áмывать, -оми́ть вéточку; **~ off relations** пор|ывáть, -вáть отношéния (с+*i.*); **~ off an engagement** раст|оргáть, -óргнуть помóлвку; *v.i.*: **the nib broke off** кóнчик перá отломи́лся; **he broke off** (*speaking*) он замолчáл; **~ open** *v.t.*: **~ open a chest** взл|áмывать, -омáть сундýк; **~ out** *v.i.*: **the prisoner broke out** заключённый сбежáл; **fire broke out** вспы́хнул пожáр; **war broke out** разрази́лась/вспы́хнула войнá; **his face broke out in pimples** на егó лицé вы́сыпали прыщи́; **~ up** *v.t.*: **~ up the ground** взры|вáть, -ть зéмлю; **~ up furniture** переломáть (*pf.*) мéбель; **~ up a meeting** прекра|щáть, -ти́ть собрáние; **~ it up!** (*coll., desist*) кончáйте; **~ up a family** (*separate*) разб|ивáть, -и́ть семью́; (*cause to quarrel*) вн|оси́ть, -ести́ разлáд в семью́; *v.i.* **school ~s up tomorrow** (*Br.*) учáщихся зáвтра распускáют на кани́кулы; **she broke up with her boyfriend** онá разошлáсь с дрýгом; **the crowd broke up** толпá разошлáсь; **the fine weather is ~ing up** погóда пóртится.

● *cpds.* **~away** *n.* (*secession*) отко́л, отделéние; **a ~away faction** отколóвшаяся фрáкция; (*sport*) отры́в; **~down** *n.* (*mechanical*) полóмка; **~down van** (*Br.*) авари́йный грузови́к; маши́на техни́ческой пóмощи; (*of health*) расстрóйство; упáдок сил; **nervous ~down** нéрвное расстрóйство; (*of negotiations etc.*) срыв; (*analysis*) подразделéние, разби́вка; **~-in** *n.* (*raid*) взлом; **~neck** *adj.*: **~neck speed** головокружи́тельная скóрость; **~-out** *n.* (*escape*) побéг; **~through** *n.* (*mil.*) проры́в; (*fig., e.g. in science*) скачóк, перелóм, проры́в; **~-up** *n.* развáл, распáд; (*of school, assembly*) рóспуск; (*of friendship*) разры́в; **~water** *n.* волнолóм, волнорéз.

breakable /ˈbreɪkəb(ə)l/ *adj.* лóмкий, хрýпкий.

breakage /ˈbreɪkɪdʒ/ *n.* (*break*) полóмка; (*pl., broken articles*) бой, полóмка.

break-dancer /ˈbreɪkdɑːnsə(r)/ *n.* брéйкер.

break-dancing /ˈbreɪkdɑːnsɪŋ/ *n.* брейк.

breaker /ˈbreɪkə(r)/ *n.* (*wave*) вал, бурýн.

breakfast /ˈbrekfəst/ *n.* зáвтрак; **have ~** зáвтракать, по-; **~ food** (*cereal*) корнфлéкс.
● *v.i.* зáвтракать, по-.

bream /briːm/ *n.* (*pl.* **~**) лещ.

breast /brest/ *n.* **1** грудь; **give a child the ~** да|вáть, -ть ребёнку грудь; **child at the ~** груднóй ребёнок.
2 (*fig.*) грудь, душá; **~beating** биéние себя́ в грудь; покáзнóе раскáяние; **make a clean ~ of something** чистосердéчно созн|авáться, -áться в чём-н. **3**: (*cul.*): **~ of lamb** барáнья груди́нка.
● *v.t.*: **~ the waves** расс|екáть, -éчь вóлны.
● *cpds.* **~bone** *n.* груднáя кость, груди́на; **~-fed** *adj.* вскóрмленный грýдью; **~-feeding** *n.* кормлéние грýдью; **~plate** *n.* (*armour*) нагрýдник; **~-pocket** *n.* нагрýдный кармáн; **~-stroke** *n.* брасс; **do the ~-stroke** плáвать (*indet.*), плыть (*det.*) брáссом; **~work** *n.* брýствер.

breath /breθ/ *n.* дыхáние; (*single ~*) вздох; **draw ~** дышáть (*impf.*); **he drew, took a deep ~** он сдéлал глубóкий вздох; **he drew his last ~** он испусти́л послéдний вздох; **lose one's ~** зад|ыхáться, -охнýться; **take ~** перев|оди́ть, -ести́ дух; отд|ыхáть,

-охну́ть; **out of ~** задыха́ясь; **recover one's ~** отдыша́ться (*pf.*); перев|оди́ть, -ести́ дух; **bad ~** дурно́й за́пах изо рта; **waste one's ~** говори́ть (*impf.*) на ве́тер; **catch, hold one's ~** зата́|ивать, -и́ть дыха́ние; **take s.o.'s ~ away** захва́т|ывать, -и́ть дух у кого́-н.; **with bated ~** зата́ив дыха́ние; **under one's ~** о́чень ти́хо; **in the same ~** еди́ным/одни́м ду́хом; **there is not a ~ of air** не́чем дыша́ть; **get a ~ of air** подыша́ть (*pf.*) све́жим во́здухом; **it was so cold we could see our ~** бы́ло так хо́лодно, что у нас пар шёл изо рта.

● *cpd.* **~-taking** *adj.* захва́тывающий.

breathalyse /ˈbreθəlaɪz/ (*US* **breathalyze**) *v.t.* проверя́ть, прове́рить на алкого́ль.

breathalyser /ˈbreθəˌlaɪzə(r)/ (*US propr.* **Breathalyzer**) *n.* алкоме́тр, алкого́льно-респира́торная тру́бка.

breathe /bri:ð/ *v.t.* **1**: **~ fresh air** дыша́ть (*impf.*) све́жим во́здухом; **~ one's last** испусти́ть (*pf.*) дух (*or* после́дний вздох). **2**: **~ new life into** вд|ыха́ть, -охну́ть но́вую жизнь в + *a.* **3** (*utter softly*): **he ~d these words** он произнёс э́ти слова́ полушёпотом; **~ a sigh** изд|ава́ть, -а́ть вздох; **don't ~ a word!** ни сло́ва бо́льше!; не пророни́те ни сло́ва!

● *v.i.* дыша́ть (*impf.*); (*fig.*): **~ again, freely** вздохну́ть (*pf.*) с облегче́нием (*or* свобо́дно); **give me a chance to ~** да́йте мне вздохну́ть.

breather /ˈbri:ðə(r)/ *n.* переды́шка; **it's time for a ~** пора́ сде́лать переды́шку (*or* передохну́ть).

breathing /ˈbri:ðɪŋ/ *n.* дыха́ние; **his ~ is heavy** он тяжело́ ды́шит.

● *cpd.* **~-space** *n.* переды́шка.

breathless /ˈbreθlɪs/ *adj.* (*panting*) задыха́ющийся, запыха́вшийся; **~ speed** захва́тывающая дух ско́рость; **~ silence** напряжённая тишина́.

breathy /ˈbreθɪ/ *adj.* (**breathier, breathiest**) с придыха́нием.

bred /bred/ *past and p.p. of* ⇒**breed**

breech /bri:tʃ/ *n.* **1** (*pl., knee-***~es**) пантало́н|ы (*pl., g.* —); (*riding-***~es**) бри́дж|и (*pl., g.* -ей). **2** (*of a gun*) казённая часть. **3**: **~ delivery, presentation** (*med.*) яго́дичное предлежа́ние плода́.

● *cpds.* **~-block** *n.* (*mil.*) затво́р; **~-loader** *n.* (*mil.*) ору́жие, заряжа́ющееся с казённой ча́сти; **~-loading** *adj.* заряжа́ющийся с казённой ча́сти.

breed /bri:d/ *n.* поро́да; **men of the same ~** лю́ди одного́ то́лка.

● *v.t.* (*past and p.p.* **bred**) **1** (*engender, cause*) поро|жда́ть, -ди́ть. **2** (*animals*) раз|води́ть, -вести́.

● *v.i.* (*past and p.p.* **bred**) размножа́ться, размно́житься; плоди́ться, рас-; **~ true** да|ва́ть, -ть поро́дистый припло́д.

breeder /ˈbri:də(r)/ *n.* **1** (*animal*) производи́тель (*m.*); **elephants are slow ~s** слоны́ размножа́ются ме́дленно. **2** (*stock-*~) животново́д, скотово́д; **he is a ~ of horses** он разво́дит лошаде́й. **3**: **~ reactor** (*phys.*) реа́ктор-размножи́тель (*m.*).

breeding /ˈbri:dɪŋ/ *n.* **1** (*by animals*) размноже́ние; **~ season** пери́од размноже́ния; **~ stock** племенно́й скот. **2** (*by stock-breeders*) разведе́ние. **3** (*manners etc.*) воспи́танность; **man of good ~** хорошо́ воспи́танный челове́к.

● *cpd.* **~-ground** *n.* (*fig.*) расса́дник, оча́г.

breeze /bri:z/ *n.* (*wind*) ветеро́к; бриз; **moderate/strong ~** уме́ренный/си́льный ве́тер; **sea/land ~** морско́й/берегово́й бриз.

● *v.i.*: **~ in/out** (*coll.*) влете́ть/вы́лететь (*pf.*).

breeze block /bri:z/ *n.* (*Br., brick*) шлакобето́нный блок; (**breezeblock**: *material*) шлакобето́н.

breezy /ˈbri:zɪ/ *adj.* (**breezier, breeziest**) (*of weather*) све́жий; (*of locality*) обдува́емый ветра́ми; (*fig., of person*) живо́й, беззабо́тный.

brent /brent/, (*US*) **brant** /brænt/ *nn.* (*zool.; also* **~-goose**) чёрная каза́рка.

brethren /ˈbreðrɪn/ *n.* собра́тья (*m. pl.*); бра́тия (*f. sg.*).

breviary /ˈbri:vɪərɪ/ *n.* тре́бник.

brevity /ˈbrevɪtɪ/ *n.* кра́ткость.

brew /bru:/ *n.* (*amount brewed: of beer*) ва́рка; (*of tea*) зава́рка; (*beverage*) сва́ренный напи́ток, (*pej.*) ва́рево.

● *v.t.* (*beer*) вари́ть, с-; (*tea*) зава́р|ивать, -и́ть.

● *v.i.* **1** (*of tea etc.*) зава́р|иваться, -и́ться. **2**: **a storm is ~ing** (*lit.*) собира́ется гроза́; (*lit. and fig.*) гроза́ надвига́ется; **there's trouble ~ing** быть беде́.

brewer /ˈbru:ə(r)/ *n.* пивова́р.

brewery /ˈbru:ərɪ/ *n.* пивова́ренный заво́д; пивова́рня.

briar[1] /ˈbraɪə(r)/ *n.* (*prickly bush; also* **sweet briar**) шипо́вник.

● *cpd.* **~-rose** *n.* шипо́вник.

briar[2] /ˈbraɪə(r)/ *n.* (*heather*) ве́реск, э́рика; (**~ pipe**) тру́бка из ко́рня э́рики.

bribe /braɪb/ *n.* взя́тка, по́дкуп.

● *v.t.* да|ва́ть, -ть взя́тку + *d.*; подкуп|а́ть, -и́ть; **~ s.o. to silence** взя́ткой заст|авля́ть, -а́вить кого́-н. молча́ть; **~ s.o. to do something** по́дкупом доб|ива́ться, -и́ться чего́-н. от кого́-н.

brib(e)able /ˈbraɪbəb(ə)l/ *adj.* подкупно́й, прода́жный.

bribery /ˈbraɪbərɪ/ *n.* взя́точничество.

bric-à-brac /ˈbrɪkəˌbræk/ *n.* старьё; безделу́шки (*f. pl.*).

brick /brɪk/ *n.* **1** кирпи́ч; **~s** (*collect.*) кирпи́ч; (*attr.*) кирпи́чный; **like a ton of ~s** изо всей си́лы; **drop a ~** (*Br.*) ля́пнуть (*pf.*) (*coll.*); **like a cat on hot ~s** (*Br.*) как на горя́чих у́глях; **make ~s without straw** би́ться (*impf.*) над чем-н. по́пусту. **2** (*Br., toy*): **~s** ку́бики (*m. pl.*). **3** (*of ice-cream*) брике́т.

● *v.t.*: **~ up** за|кла́дывать, -ложи́ть кирпича́ми.

● *cpds.* **~bat** *n.* обло́мок кирпича́; (*fig.*) нелéстный о́тзыв; **~-dust** *n.* кирпи́чная мука́; **~layer** *n.* ка́менщик; **~-red** *adj.* кирпи́чно-кра́сный; **~work** *n.* кирпи́чная кла́дка.

bridal /ˈbraɪd(ə)l/ *adj.* сва́дебный.

bride /braɪd/ *n.* неве́ста; (*after wedding*) молода́я, новобра́чная.

● *cpds.* **~groom** *n.* жени́х; (*after wedding*) новобра́чный; **~smaid** *n.* подру́жка неве́сты.

bridge[1] /brɪdʒ/ *n.* **1** мост (*also in dentistry*); **suspension ~** вися́чий мост; **throw a ~ over a river** навести́/переброси́ть (*pf.*) мост через ре́ку; **we'll cross that ~ when we come to it** не́чего зара́нее волнова́ться/трево́житься. **2** (*naut.*) капита́нский мо́стик. **3** (*of nose*) перено́сица. **4** (*of violin*) кобы́лка. **5** (*elec.*) шунт; электроизмери́тельный мост; **Wheatstone ~** мо́стик сопротивле́ния.

● *v.t.*: **~ a river** нав|оди́ть, -ести́ мост че́рез ре́ку; (*join by bridging*) соедин|я́ть, -и́ть мосто́м; (*fig.*): **~ a gap** зап|олня́ть, -о́лнить пробе́л.

● *cpds.* **~head** *n.* плацда́рм (*also fig.*); предмо́стное укрепле́ние; **~work** *n.* постро́йка/наво́дка моста́; (*dentistry*) мост, мо́стик.

bridge[2] /brɪdʒ/ *n.* (*game*) бридж.

bridle /ˈbraɪd(ə)l/ *n.* узда́, узде́чка.

● *v.t.* (*of horse, also* **~ in**) взнузд|ывать, -а́ть; (*fig.*) обузд|ывать, -а́ть.

● *v.i.* (*fig.*) зад|ира́ть, -ра́ть нос.

● *cpds.* **~-path, ~-way** (*Br.*) *nn.* верхова́я тропа́.

brief /bri:f/ *n.* **1** (*lawyer's*) изложе́ние де́ла; **hold a ~ for s.o.** (*Br.*) вести́ (*det.*) чьё-н. де́ло в суде́; **he has plenty of ~s** он име́ет мно́го клие́нтов; (*fig.*): **I hold no ~ for smoking** я отню́дь не сторо́нник куре́ния. **2** (*Br.*) (*mil. etc., instructions*) инстру́кция. **3** (*pl., coll., underpants*) трус|ы́ (*pl., g.* -о́в).

● *adj.* (*of duration*) коро́ткий, недо́лгий; (*concise*) кра́ткий, сжа́тый; **in ~** вкра́тце.

● *v.t.* **1**: **~ a lawyer** (*Br.*) поруч|а́ть, -и́ть адвока́ту веде́ние де́ла. **2** (*mil. etc.*) инструкти́ровать (*impf., pf.*).

● *cpd.* **~-case** *n.* портфе́ль (*m.*).

briefing /ˈbri:fɪŋ/ *n.* (*also* **~ meeting**) инструкта́ж; (*press*) бри́финг.

briefless /ˈbri:flɪs/ *adj.* (*Br., of lawyer*) не име́ющий клие́нтов.

briefly /ˈbri:flɪ/ *adv.* кра́тко, сжа́то; **the point is ~ that** . . . говоря́ вкра́тце, де́ло в том, что. . . .

briefness /ˈbri:fnɪs/ *n.* кра́ткость; (*conciseness*) сжа́тость.

brier[1,2] /ˈbraɪə(r)/ = **briar**[1,2]

Brig. /ˌbrɪgəˈdɪə(r)/ *n.* (*abbr. of* ***Brigadier***) брига́дный генера́л.

brig /brɪg/ *n.* бриг.

brigade /brɪˈgeɪd/ *n.* брига́да; **fire ~** пожа́рная кома́нда; **~ major** нача́льник

B

оперативно-разведывательного отделения штаба бригады.

brigadier /ˌbrɪɡəˈdɪə(r)/ *n.* (*also* **~-general**) бригадный генерал.

brigand /ˈbrɪɡənd/ *n.* разбойник.

brigandage /ˈbrɪɡəndɪdʒ/ *n.* разбой.

brigantine /ˈbrɪɡənˌtiːn/ *n.* бригантина.

bright /braɪt/ *adj.* **1** (*clear, shining*) яркий, светлый; **a ~ day** ясный день; **~ red** ярко-красный; **the sun shines ~** солнце светит ярко; **a ~ room** светлая комната. **2** (*cheerful*): **~ faces** весёлые лица; **look on the ~ side** смотреть (*impf.*) на вещи оптимистически; **he came ~ and early** он ранёхонько явился. **3** (*clever*): **a ~ girl** толковая девочка; **a ~ idea** блестящая мысль.

brighten /ˈbraɪt(ə)n/ *v.t.* (*also* **~ up**): (*polish*) полировать, от-; (*enliven*) ожив|лять, -ить; подб|адривать (*or* -одрять), -одрить.

● *v.i.* (*also* **~ up**): **the weather ~ed** погода прояснилась; **his face ~ed** его лицо просветлело; **things are ~ing up** дела улучшаются.

brightness /ˈbraɪtnɪs/ *n.* (*lustre*) яркость; (*cheer*) весёлость; (*cleverness*) блеск, смышлёность.

Bright's disease /braɪts/ *n.* нефрит, брайтова болезнь.

brill[1] /brɪl/ *n.* камбала, ромб.

brill[2] /brɪl/ *adj.* (*abbr. of* **brilliant**) (*Br. coll.*) балдёжный, потрясный; **~!** блеск!; класс!; **the film is ~** фильм — блеск!

brilliance /ˈbrɪlɪəns/ *n.* (*brightness*) яркость; (*magnificence*) великолепие, блеск; (*intelligence*) блеск (ума); блестящие способности (*f. pl.*).

brilliant /ˈbrɪlɪənt/ *n.* (*diamond*) бриллиант.

● *adj.* (*lit., fig.*) сверкающий, блестящий; (*Br. coll., excellent*) замечательный.

brim /brɪm/ *n.* край; **fill a glass to the ~** нап|олнять, -олнить стакан до краёв; (*of hat*) поля (*nt. pl.*).

● *v.i.* (**brimmed, brimming**) (*of vessel*) нап|олняться, -олниться до краёв; **a ~ming cup** наполненная до краёв чаша; **~ over** перел|иваться, -иться через край; (*fig.*): **she was ~ming over with the news** её распирало желание рассказать новости.

● *cpd.* **~-full** *adj.* полный до краёв.

brimstone /ˈbrɪmstəʊn/ *n.* самородная сера.

brindle(d) /ˈbrɪnd(ə)ld/ *adj.* коричневый с полосами/пятнами.

brine /braɪn/ *n.* рассол.

bring /brɪŋ/ *v.t.* (*past and p.p.* **brought**) **1** (*cause to come, deliver*): (*a thing*) прин|осить, -ести; (*a person*) прив|одить, -ести; (*thing or person, by vehicle*) прив|озить, -езти; **he brought an umbrella** он захватил с собой зонтик; **~ s.o. into the world** произвести (*pf.*) кого-н. на свет; **it brought tears to my eyes** это вызвало у меня слёзы; **spring ~s warm weather** с весной приходит тепло; **~ a ship into harbour** вв|одить, -ести корабль в гавань; **~ into action, effect, play** прив|одить, -ести в действие; **~ to light** выявлять, выявить; **~ to pass** осуществ|лять, -ить; **~ to mind** прив|одить, -ести на ум; нап|оминать, -омнить; **~ to an end** зак|анчивать, -ончить; заверш|ать, -ить; **~ pressure to bear on** оказ|ывать, -ать давление на + *a.*; **~ s.o. to his senses** (*lit.*) прив|одить, -ести кого-н. в сознание; (*fig.*) образум|ливать, -ить кого-н.; **~ a misfortune upon o.s.** навл|екать, -ечь на себя беду.

2 (*yield*): **this ~s me (in) £500 a year** это приносит мне 500 фунтов в год; **the harvest will not ~ much** урожай не будет большим.

3 (*induce*): **I could not ~ him to agree** я не мог убедить его дать согласие; **I cannot ~ myself to do it** я не могу заставить себя сделать это.

4 (*leg.*): **~ an action against s.o.** возбу|ждать, -дить дело против кого-н.; **~ a charge** выдвигать, выдвинуть обвинение.

● *with advs.*: **~ about** *v.t.* (*cause*) вызывать, вызвать; произв|одить, -ести; **~ a ship about** пов|орачивать, -ернуть корабль; **~ back** *v.t.* прин|осить, -ести (*or* прив|одить, -ести) назад; **they brought back the news that** ... они вернулись с новостью, будто...; **it ~s back the past** это напоминает (*or* приводит на память) былое; **~ s.o. back to health** возвращать, вернуть кому-н. здоровье; **~ down** *v.t.* (*a tree*) сруб|ать, -ить; валить, по-; (*an aircraft*) сби|вать, -ть; (*a bird*) подстрел|ивать, -ить; **~ down the house** (*fig.*) вызывать, вызвать гром аплодисментов; **~ prices down** сн|ижать, -изить цены; **he brought his fist down on the table** он стукнул кулаком по столу; **~ down s.o.'s wrath on s.o.** навл|екать, -ечь на кого-н. чей-н. гнев; **~ forth** *v.t.* (*give birth to*) произв|одить, -ести; **his speech brought forth protests** его речь вызвала протесты; **~ forward** *v.t.*: **~ a chair forward** выдвигать, выдвинуть стул; **~ forward a proposal** выдвигать, выдвинуть предложение; (*advance date of*) перен|осить, -ести на более ранний срок; (*bookkeeping*) делать, с- перенос счёта на следующую страницу; **~ in** *v.t.* вн|осить, -ести; вв|одить, -ести; **~ in a verdict** выносить, вынести вердикт; **~ off** *v.t.*: **~ off a manoeuvre** (*Br.*), **maneuver** (*US*) успешно заверш|ать, -ить операцию; **~ on** *v.t.*: **this brought on a bad cold** это вызвало сильный насморк; **the sun is ~ing on the plants** солнце способствует развитию растений; **~ out** *v.t.* выносить, вынести; выводить, вывести; (*make evident*) выявлять, выявить; (*publish*) выпускать, выпустить; (*launch into society*) вывозить, вывезти в свет; **the curtains ~ out the green in the carpet** занавески оттеняют зелень ковра; **the sun ~s out the roses** розы распускаются под солнечными лучами; **~ over** *v.t.* (*convert, convince*) переубе|ждать, -дить; **~ round** *v.t.* (*deliver*) прив|озить, -езти; дост|авлять, -авить; (*restore to consciousness*) прив|одить, -ести в себя; (*persuade*) убе|ждать, -дить; **he brought the conversation round to politics** он перевёл разговор на политику; **~ through** *v.t.*: **the doctors brought him through** доктора вытянули его; **~ to** *v.t.* (*restore to consciousness*) прив|одить, -ести в сознание/себя; (*a ship*) остан|авливать, -овить; **~ together** *v.t.* (*assemble*) соб|ирать, -рать; св|одить, -ести вместе; (*reconcile*) примир|ять, -ить; **~ up** *v.t.* (*carry up*) прин|осить, -ести наверх; (*educate*) воспит|ывать, -ать; **I was brought up to believe that** ... мне с детства внушали, что...; (*vomit*): **he brought up his dinner** его вырвало после обеда; **~ up a subject** подн|имать, -ять вопрос; зав|одить, -ести разговор о чём-н.; **~ up the rear** замыкать, замкнуть колонну/шествие.

brink /brɪŋk/ *n.* край (*also fig.*); **on the ~ of despair** на грани отчаяния; **he was on the ~ of tears** он едва сдерживал слёзы; **we were on the ~ of a great discovery** мы вплотную подошли к великому открытию.

● *cpd.* **~manship** *n.* балансирование на грани войны.

briny /ˈbraɪnɪ/ *adj.* солёный; **the ~** (*Br. coll.*) море.

brio /ˈbriːəʊ/ *n.* живость.

briquette /brɪˈket/ *n.* брикет.

brisk /brɪsk/ *adj.* (*of movement*) скорый; (*of air, wind*) свежий; **~ demand** большой спрос; **~ trade** оживлённая торговля.

brisket /ˈbrɪskɪt/ *n.* грудинка.

bris|ling /ˈbrɪzlɪŋ/, /ˈbrɪs-/ *n.* (*pl.* **~** *or* **~s**) шпрот.

bristle /ˈbrɪs(ə)l/ *n.* щетина.

● *v.i.* (*of hair*) стоять (*impf.*) дыбом; встать (*pf.*) дыбом; (*of animal, also fig., of person*) ощетини|ваться, -ться; **the cat ~d** шерсть у кошки поднялась дыбом; **~ with bayonets** ощетиниваться (*impf.*) штыками.

bristly /ˈbrɪslɪ/ *adj.* щетинистый.

Brit /brɪt/ *n.* (*coll.*) = **Briton 1**

Britain /ˈbrɪt(ə)n/ *n.* Англия, Британия; (*also* **Great ~**) Великобритания.

Briticism /ˈbrɪtɪˌsɪz(ə)m/ *n.* англицизм.

British /ˈbrɪtɪʃ/ *n.*: **the ~** англичане, британцы (*both m. pl.*).

● *adj.* британский (*also of ancient Britons*); великобританский, английский; **~ Empire** Британская империя; **~ Commonwealth of Nations** Британское Содружество Наций; **~ Isles** Британские острова; **~ English** британский вариант английского языка.

Briton /ˈbrɪt(ə)n/ *n.* **1** (*native or inhabitant of Great Britain*) британ|ец (*fem.* -ка); англичан|ин (*fem.* -ка). **2** (*ancient*) бритт.

Brittany /ˈbrɪtənɪ/ *n.* Бретань.

brittle /ˈbrɪt(ə)l/ *adj.* ло́мкий, хру́пкий.

brittleness /ˈbrɪt(ə)lnɪs/ *n.* ло́мкость, хру́пкость.

broach /brəʊtʃ/ *v.t.* (*pierce*) прот|ыка́ть, -кну́ть; (*start consuming*) поча́ть, откры́ть (*both pf.*); (*discussion*) откр|ыва́ть, -ы́ть; **~ a subject** подн|има́ть, -я́ть вопро́с.

broad /brɔ:d/ *n.* (*US coll.*) девчо́нка.

● *adj.* **1** (*wide*) широ́кий; **the river is 50 feet ~** ширина́ реки́ 50 фу́тов; **it's as ~ as it's long** то же на́ то же выхо́дит. **2** (*extensive*): **~ lands** обши́рные зе́мли. **3**: **in ~ daylight** средь бе́ла дня. **4** (*decided*): **a ~ hint** то́лстый намёк; **a ~ accent** си́льный акце́нт. **5** (*approximate*): **a ~ definition** о́бщее определе́ние; **in ~ outline** в о́бщих черта́х. **6** (*tolerant*): **he takes a ~ view** у него́ широ́кий взгля́д на ве́щи. **7** (*coarse*): **a ~ joke** гру́бая шу́тка.

● *adv.*: **~ awake** вполне́ просну́вшийся.

● *cpds.* **~ bean** *n.* фасо́ль; **~cast** *n.* трансля́ция; (*radio*) радиопереда́ча, (*TV*) телепереда́ча; *v.t.* (*agric.*) се́ять, по- вразбро́с; (*radio, TV*) трансли́ровать (*impf., pf.*); перед|ава́ть, -а́ть по ра́дио, телеви́дению; (*spread, of news etc.*) распростран|я́ть, -и́ть; *v.i.* (*radio, TV*) вести́ (*det.*) радиопереда́чу, телепереда́чу; выступа́ть, вы́ступить по ра́дио, телеви́дению; **~caster** *n.* (*radio*) радиожурнали́ст, (*TV*) тележурнали́ст; **~casting** *n.* (*radio*) радиовеща́ние, (*TV*) телевеща́ние; трансля́ция; **~cloth** *n.* то́нкое сукно́; **~-gauge** *adj.* ширококоле́йный; **~-minded** *adj.* широ́ких взгля́дов; **~-mindedness** *n.* широта́ взгля́дов; **~sheet** *n.* газе́та большо́го форма́та; **~side** *n.* (*side of ship*) (надво́дный) борт; **be ~side on to something** стоя́ть (*impf.*) бо́ртом к чему́-н.; **fire a ~side** дать (*pf.*) бортово́й залп; (*fig., vbl. onslaught*) обру́шиться (*pf.*) с ре́зкими напа́дками; **~sword** *n.* пала́ш; **~tail** *n.* каракульча́; **~ways, ~wise** *advs.* вширь; в ширину́; попере́к.

broaden /ˈbrɔ:d(ə)n/ *v.t. & i.* (*lit., fig.*) расш|иря́ть(ся), -и́рить(ся).

broadly /ˈbrɔ:dlɪ/ *adv.* (*in the main*) в основно́м; **~ speaking** вообще́ говоря́.

broadness /ˈbrɔ:dnɪs/ *n.* ширина́.

brocade /brəˈkeɪd/, /brəʊ-/ *n.* парча́.

● *v.t.*: **a ~d gown** парчо́вый наря́д.

broccoli /ˈbrɒkəlɪ/ *n.* бро́кколи (*nt. indecl.*); капу́ста спа́ржевая.

brochure /ˈbrəʊʃə(r)/, /brəʊˈʃjʊə(r)/ *n.* брошю́ра.

brogue /brəʊg/ *n.* (*shoe*) башма́к; (*accent*) провинциа́льный акце́нт.

broil /brɔɪl/ *v.t.* (*US, cul.*) жа́рить, за- на откры́том огне́.

● *v.i.* (*cul.*) жа́риться, за- *etc. as above*; (*fig., be roasted*) жа́риться (*impf.*); **a ~ing hot day** зно́йный день.

broiler /ˈbrɔɪlə(r)/ *n.* **1** (*chicken*) бро́йлер. **2** (*US, grill*) гриль (*m.*).

broke /brəʊk/ *adj.* (*coll.*) разори́вшийся, безде́нежный; **stony ~** без гроша́.

broken /ˈbrəʊkən/ *adj.* **1**: **a ~ leg** сло́манная нога́; **~ English** ло́маный англи́йский язы́к. **2** (**~-down**): **a ~ marriage** расстро́енный брак; **a ~ home** разби́тая семья́. **3** (*crushed*): **a ~ man** сло́мленный челове́к. **4** (*rough*): **~ ground** пересечённая ме́стность. **5** (*interrupted*): **~ sleep** пре́рванный сон. **6** (**~ in**: *of a horse*) вы́езженный, объе́зженный.

● *cpds.* **~-down** *adj.* (*of wall*) полуразру́шенный; (*of health*) подо́рванный; (*of person*) надло́мленный; (*morally*) сло́мленный; (*of machine*) сло́манный; **~-hearted** *adj.* с разби́тым се́рдцем.

broker /ˈbrəʊkə(r)/ *n.* (*of shares etc.*) ма́клер, бро́кер; (*go-between*) посре́дник; **marriage ~** сват.

brokerage /ˈbrəʊkərɪdʒ/ *n.* (*business*) ма́клерство; (*commission*) курта́ж; комиссио́нное вознагражде́ние.

broking /ˈbrəʊkɪŋ/ *n.* (*Br.*) ма́клерство, посре́дничество.

brolly /ˈbrɒlɪ/ *n.* (*Br. coll.*) = **umbrella** *n.* 1

bromide /ˈbrəʊmaɪd/ *n.* (*chem.*) броми́д; (*fig., coll.*) бана́льность.

bromine /ˈbrəʊmi:n/ *n.* бром.

bronch|i /ˈbrɒŋkaɪ/, **-ia** /ˈbrɒŋkɪə/ *nn.* (*anat.*) бро́нхи (*m. pl.*).

bronchial /ˈbrɒŋkɪəl/ *adj.* бронхиа́льный.

bronchitis /brɒŋˈkaɪtɪs/ *n.* бронхи́т.

bronco /ˈbrɒŋkəʊ/ *n.* (*pl.* **~s**) полуди́кая ло́шадь.

brontosaurus /ˌbrɒntəˈsɔ:rəs/ *n.* бронтоза́вр.

bronze /brɒnz/ *n.* бро́нза; (*article*) бро́нза, изде́лие из бро́нзы; (*attr.*) бро́нзовый.

● *v.t.* бронзи́ровать (*impf., pf.*); (*tan*) покр|ыва́ть, -ы́ть зага́ром; **~d cheeks** загоре́лые щёки.

brooch /brəʊtʃ/ *n.* брошь.

brood /bru:d/ *n.* вы́водок; (*of children, also*) пото́мство.

● *v.i.* **1** (*of bird*) сиде́ть (*impf.*) на я́йцах. **2**: **~ over one's plans** вына́шивать (*impf.*) пла́ны; **~ over an insult** копи́ть (*impf.*) в себе́ оби́ду. **3** (*of night, clouds etc.*) нав|иса́ть, -и́снуть.

● *cpds.* **~-hen** *n.* насе́дка; **~-mare** *n.* племенна́я кобы́ла.

broody /ˈbru:dɪ/ *adj.* (**broodier, broodiest**) **1** (*thoughtful*) заду́мчивый; (*morose*) угрю́мый. **2**: **a ~ hen** (хоро́шая) насе́дка. **3** (*of a woman*): **she's feeling ~** в ней просну́лся матери́нский инсти́нкт.

brook[1] /brʊk/ *n.* (*stream*) руче́й.

brook[2] /brʊk/ *v.t.* (*liter.*): **this ~s no delay** э́то не те́рпит отлага́тельства.

brooklet /ˈbrʊklɪt/ *n.* ручеёк.

broom /bru:m/ *n.* **1** (*bot.*) раки́тник. **2** (*implement*) метла́; (*besom*) ве́ник.

● *cpd.* **~stick** *n.* метлови́ще; (*witch's*) помело́.

Bros. /ˈbrʌðəz/ *n.* (*abbr. of* ***Brother(s)***) Бра́тья (*в названии фирмы*).

broth /brɒθ/ *n.* мясно́й бульо́н; **Scotch ~** перло́вый суп.

brothel /ˈbrɒθ(ə)l/ *n.* публи́чный дом.

brother /ˈbrʌðə(r)/ *n.* **1** (*also relig.*) брат; **own, full ~** родно́й брат; **half ~** сво́дный брат; **the Ivanov ~s** бра́тья Ивано́вы. **2** (*fig.*): **~ in arms** собра́т по ору́жию. **3** (*eccl.*): **lay ~** послу́шник.

● *cpd.* **~-in-law** *n.* (*sister's husband*) зять (*m.*); (*wife's ~*) шу́рин; (*husband's ~*) де́верь (*m.*); (*wife's sister's husband*) своя́к.

brotherhood /ˈbrʌðəˌhʊd/ *n.* (*kinship*) бра́тство; (*comradeship*) бра́тские отноше́ния; (*association, community*) содру́жество.

brotherliness /ˈbrʌðəlmɪs/ *n.* бра́тское отноше́ние.

brotherly /ˈbrʌðəlɪ/ *adj.* бра́тский.

brought /brɔ:t/ *past and p.p. of* ⇒**bring**

brouhaha /ˈbru:hɑ:ˌhɑ:/ *n.* шуми́ха (*coll.*).

brow /braʊ/ *n.* (*eye ~*) бровь; **knit one's ~s** хму́рить, на- бро́ви; (*forehead*) лоб, чело́; (*of hill*) гре́бень (*m.*); **over the ~ of the hill** за гре́бнем холма́.

● *cpd.* **~beat** *v.t.* наг|оня́ть, -на́ть страх на + *a.*; запу́г|ивать, -а́ть.

brown /braʊn/ *n.* (*colour*) кори́чневый цвет; **he was dressed in ~** он был оде́т в кори́чневое.

● *adj.* **1** кори́чневый; (*grey-~*) бу́рый; **light-~** све́тло-кори́чневый; **~ shoes** кори́чневые ту́фли; **~ eyes** ка́рие глаза́; **~ hair** кашта́новые во́лосы; **~ bear** бу́рый медве́дь; **~ bread** се́рый хлеб; **~ sugar** кори́чневый са́хар; **~ paper** обёрточная бума́га; **~ coal** бу́рый у́голь. **2** (*fig.*): **in a ~ study** в глубо́ком разду́мье. **3** (*toasted*) поджа́ренный, подрумя́ненный. **4** (*tanned*) загоре́лый; **as ~ as a berry** чёрный, как га́лка; **he returned from his holidays quite ~** он верну́лся из о́тпуска тёмным от зага́ра. **5** (*dark-skinned*) сму́глый.

● *v.t.* (*roast, toast*) поджа́ри|вать, -ть; (*tan*) опал|я́ть, -и́ть; **he is ~ed off** ему́ всё осточерте́ло (*sl.*).

● *cpds.* **~-eyed** *adj.* с ка́рими глаза́ми; **~-haired** *adj.* с тёмно-ру́сыми волоса́ми.

brownie /ˈbraʊnɪ/ *n.* (*goblin*) домово́й.

Browning /ˈbraʊnɪŋ/ *n.* (*pistol*) бра́унинг.

brownish /ˈbraʊnɪʃ/ *adj.* коричнева́тый.

browse /braʊz/ *v.i.* щипа́ть (*impf.*) траву́; пасти́сь (*impf.*); (*fig.*): **~ through a book** просм|а́тривать, -отре́ть кни́гу; **~ in a bookshop** ры́ться (*impf.*) в кни́гах в кни́жном магази́не.

browser /ˈbraʊzə(r)/ *n.* (*comput.*) бро́узер.

brr /bɜ:/ *int.* брр-р-р!

Bruges /ˈbru:ʒ/ *n.* Брю́гге (*m. indecl.*).

bruise /bru:z/ *n.* синя́к, кровоподтёк; (*of fruit*) помя́тость.

● *v.t.* подст|авля́ть, -а́вить синя́к + *d.*; (*fruit*) помя́ть, поби́ть (*both pf.*); **I ~d my shoulder** я уши́б плечо́; **this apple is ~d** э́то я́блоко поби́то; **~ s.o.'s feelings** ра́нить (*impf., pf.*) чьи-н. чу́вства.

● *v.i.* (*of person*) ушиб|а́ться, -и́ться; **she ~s easily** её чуть тронь — и она́ покрыва́ется синяка́ми; (*of fruit*) помя́ться, поби́ться (*both pf.*).

bruiser /'bru:zə(r)/ *n.* (*prizefighter*) боре́ц; боксёр; (*thug*) хулига́н.

Brunei /bru:'naɪ/ *n.* Бруне́й.

brunette /bru:'net/ *n.* брюне́тка.

● *adj.* тёмный, темноволо́сый.

brunt /brʌnt/ *n.* гла́вный уда́р; **bear the ~ of the work** выноси́ть, вы́нести всю тя́жесть рабо́ты.

brush /brʌʃ/ *n.* **1** (*brushwood*) куста́рник, хво́рост.
2 (*for sweeping*) щётка; (*painter's*) кисть.
3 (*fox's tail*) труба́.
4 (*skirmish, tiff*) сты́чка.
5 (*brushing*) чи́стка; **give something a good ~** хорошо́ почи́стить (*pf.*) что-н.

● *v.t.* (*clean*) чи́стить, по-; **~ mud off a coat** счища́ть, счи́стить грязь с пальто́; (*touch slightly*): **the twigs ~ed my cheek** ве́тки легко́ косну́лись мое́й щеки́.

● *v.i.*: **~ against something** слегка́ каса́ться, косну́ться чего́-н.; **~ past s.o.** прон|оси́ться, -ести́сь ми́мо кого́-н.

● *with advs.*: **~ aside** *v.t.*: **~ aside difficulties** отме|та́ть, -сти́ тру́дности; **~ away** *v.t.*: **~ away a fly** сма́хивать, смахну́ть му́ху; **~ off** *v.i.*: **the mud will ~ off** грязь счи́стится/отчи́стится; **~ out** *v.t.*: **~ out a room** подме|та́ть, -сти́ ко́мнату; **~ out one's hair** причеса́ть (*pf.*) щёткой во́лосы; **~ out** (*obliterate*) **part of a picture** зама́зывать, замаза́ть часть карти́ны; **~ up** *v.t.*: **~ up crumbs** сме|та́ть, -сти́ кро́шки; **~ up one's French** освеж|а́ть, -и́ть в па́мяти францу́зский; *v.i.*: **~ up on a subject** освеж|а́ть, -и́ть зна́ния по како́му-н. предме́ту.

● *cpds.* **~-down** *n.*: **give s.o. a ~-down** почи́стить (*pf.*) кого́-н.; **give a horse a ~-down** вы́чистить (*pf.*) коня́; **have a ~-down** почи́ститься (*pf.*); **~-off** *n.*: **give s.o. the ~-off** (*coll.*) отряхну́ть (*pf.*) кого́-н.; **~-up** *n.* (*Br.*): **have a wash and ~-up** приводи́ть, привести́ себя́ в поря́док; **~wood** *n.* хво́рост, вале́жник; **~work** *n.* живопи́сная мане́ра, мане́ра письма́.

brusque /brʊsk/, /bru:sk/, /brʌsk/ *adj.* ре́зкий.

brusqueness /'brʊsknɪs/, /bru:sknɪs/, /brʌsknɪs/ *n.* ре́зкость.

Brussels /'brʌs(ə)lz/ *n.* Брюссе́ль (*m.*); **~ sprouts** брюссе́льская капу́ста.

brutal /'bru:t(ə)l/ *adj.* (*rough*) гру́бый; (*cruel*) жесто́кий.

brutality /bru:'tælɪtɪ/ *n.* гру́бость; жесто́кость; (*cruel act*) зве́рство.

brutalization /ˌbru:təlaɪ'zeɪʃ(ə)n/ *n.* огрубле́ние, ожесточе́ние.

brutalize /'bru:təˌlaɪz/ *v.t.* ожесточ|а́ть, -и́ть; огруб|ля́ть, -и́ть.

brute /bru:t/ *n.* (*animal*) живо́тное, зверь (*m.*); (*person*) скоти́на (*c.g.*).

● *adj.*: **~ strength, force** гру́бая, физи́ческая си́ла.

brutish /'bru:tɪʃ/ *adj.* гру́бый, бесчу́вственный; (*coarse*) ско́тский, живо́тный; (*stupid*) тупо́й.

bryony /'braɪənɪ/ *n.* (*bot.*) пересту́пень (*m.*), брио́ния.

B.Sc. (*abbr. of* ***Bachelor of Science***) бакала́вр (есте́ственных) нау́к; **he has a ~ in physics** он бакала́вр физи́ческих нау́к.

BSE (*abbr. of* ***bovine spongiform encephalopathy***) бы́чья губкови́дная энцефалопа́тия.

BST (*abbr. of* ***British Summer Time***) Брита́нское ле́тнее вре́мя.

bubble /'bʌb(ə)l/ *n.* **1** пузы́рь (*m.*); (*of air, gas in liquid*) пузырёк; (*in glass*) пузырёк во́здуха; **~ bath** пе́на для ва́нны; **blow ~s** пус|ка́ть, -ти́ть пузыри́; **prick a, the ~** (*lit.*) прот|ыка́ть, -кну́ть пузы́рь; (*fig.*) док|а́зывать, -аза́ть пустоту́/никчёмность чего́-н. **2** (*gurgle*) бу́льканье.

● *v.i.* (*of water*) пузы́риться (*impf.*), кипе́ть (*impf.*); (*of a fountain*) кипе́ть (*impf.*); **~ up** бить (*impf.*) ключо́м; бу́лькать (*impf.*); **~ (over) with laughter** залива́ться (*impf.*) сме́хом; **he ~s (over) with high spirits** из него́ так и бры́зжет весе́лье.

bubbly /'bʌblɪ/ *n.* (*coll., champagne*) шипу́чка, шампа́нское.

● *adj.* (**bubblier, bubbliest**) (*of wine*) шипу́чий, пе́нящийся; (*of person*) живо́й.

bubonic /bju:'bɒnɪk/ *adj.* бубо́нный; **~ plague** бубо́нная чума́.

buccaneer /ˌbʌkə'nɪə(r)/ *n.* пира́т.

Bucharest /ˌbu:kə'rest/ *n.* Бухаре́ст.

buck[1] /bʌk/ *n.* **1** (*male deer*) оле́нь (*m.*). **2** (*male animal*) саме́ц; **~ rabbit** саме́ц кро́лика. **3** (*coll., dollar*) до́ллар; **big ~s** ку́ча де́нег. **4**: **pass the ~** (*coll.*) снима́ть, снять с себя́ отве́тственность.

● *cpds.* **~shot** *n.* кру́пная дробь; **~skin** *n.* оле́нья (*or* лоси́ная) ко́жа; (*pl.*) ко́жаные штан|ы́ (*pl., g.* -о́в); лоси́ны (*f. pl.*); **~thorn** *n.* круши́на; **~-tooth** *n.* выступа́ющий зуб.

buck[2] /bʌk/ *v.t.* **1**: **the horse ~ed him off** ло́шадь сбро́сила его́. **2**: **~ s.o. up** (*cheer*) подбодри́ть/встряхну́ть (*pf.*) кого́-н.; **~ things up** (*hasten*) подт|а́лкивать, -олкну́ть де́ло.

● *v.i.* **1** (*of horse*) брыка́ться (*impf.*); (*of engine*) трясти́сь (*impf.*). **2**: **~ against fate** проти́виться (*impf.*) судьбе́. **3**: **~ up** (*coll.*) (*cheer up*) подбодри́ться, оживи́ться (*both pf.*); (*get a move on*) пошеве́ливаться (*impf.*).

bucket /'bʌkɪt/ *n.* **1** ведро́; **the rain came down in ~s** дождь лил как из ведра́; **kick the ~** сыгра́ть (*pf.*) в я́щик (*sl.*). **2** (*of dredger*) черпа́к, ковш; (*of water-wheel*) ло́пасть. **3**: **~ seat** чашеобра́зное сиде́нье.

● *v.i.* (**bucketed, bucketing**) (*ride jerkily*) дви́гаться (*impf.*) рывка́ми; (*Br., rain*): **it's ~ing down** льёт как из ведра́.

bucketful /'bʌkɪtfʊl/ *n.* ведро́.

buckle /'bʌk(ə)l/ *n.* пря́жка.

● *v.t.* **1** (*coat, shoe*) застёг|ивать, -ну́ть; **~ on one's sword** пристёг|ивать, -ну́ть меч. **2** (*wheel*) гнуть, по-; деформи́ровать (*impf., pf.*).

● *v.i.* **1** (*of coat, shoe*) застёг|иваться, -ну́ться. **2**: **~ down to a task, ~ to** прин|има́ться, -я́ться за де́ло. **3** (*of wheel*) гну́ться, по-; деформи́роваться (*impf., pf.*). **4** (*of legs, knees*) под|гиба́ться, -огну́ться.

buckram /'bʌkrəm/ *n.* клеёнка; (*attr.*) клеёнчатый.

buckwheat /'bʌkwi:t/ *n.* греча́ха, (*coll.*) гре́чка; (*attr.*) грechи́шный, (*cooked*) гре́чневый.

bucolic /bju:'kɒlɪk/ *adj.* букoли́ческий.

bud /bʌd/ *n.* по́чка; (*flower not fully opened*) буто́н; **the trees are in ~** на дере́вьях появи́лись по́чки; **nip something in the ~** уничт|ожа́ть, -о́жить что-н. в заро́дыше.

● *v.i.* (**budded, budding**) (*of plant*) покр|ыва́ться, -ы́ться по́чками; (*fig.*) распус|ка́ться, -ти́ться; расцве|та́ть, -сти́.

Budapest /ˌbju:də'pest/ *n.* Будапе́шт.

Buddha /'bʊdə/ *n.* Бу́дда (*m.*).

Buddhism /'bʊdɪz(ə)m/ *n.* будди́зм.

Buddhist /'bʊdɪst/ *n.* будди́ст.

● *adj.* (*also* **~ic**) будди́йский.

buddleia /'bʌdlɪə/ *n.* будле́я.

buddy /'bʌdɪ/ *n.* (*US coll.*) дружи́ще (*m.*), прия́тель (*m.*).

budge /bʌdʒ/ *v.t.*: **I cannot ~ this rock** я не могу́ сдви́нуть э́тот ка́мень.

● *v.i.*: **he never ~d the whole time** за всё вре́мя он не пошевельну́лся; **the bookcase won't ~ an inch** кни́жный шкаф невозмо́жно с ме́ста сдви́нуть.

budgerigar /'bʌdʒərɪˌgɑ:(r)/ *n.* волни́стый попуга́йчик.

budget /'bʌdʒɪt/ *n.* бюдже́т.

● *v.t. & i.* (**budgeted, budgeting**): **~ (funds) for a project** ассигнова́ть (*impf., pf.*) определённую су́мму на прое́кт.

budgetary /'bʌdʒɪtərɪ/ *adj.* бюдже́тный.

budgie /'bʌdʒɪ/ (*coll.*) = **budgerigar**

Buenos Aires /'bweɪnɒs 'aɪrɪz/ *n.* Буэ́нос-А́йрес.

buff /bʌf/ *n.* (*ox-hide*) быча́чья ко́жа; (*buffalo-hide*) бу́йволовая ко́жа; (*coll., human skin*): **in the ~** нагишо́м; (*colour*) тёмно-жёлтый цвет.

● *adj.* тёмно-жёлтый.

● *v.t.* (*metal*) полирова́ть, от- ко́жей; (*leather*) размягч|а́ть, -и́ть.

buffalo /'bʌfəˌləʊ/ *n.* (*pl.* **~** *or* **~es**) (*wild ox*) бу́йвол; (*bison*) бизо́н.

buffer /'bʌfə(r)/ *n.* (*rail., comput.*) бу́фер; (*fig.*): **~ state** бу́ферное госуда́рство.

buffet[1] /ˈbʌfɪt/ *n.* (*blow*) уда́р, шлепо́к.
● *v.t.* (**buffeted, buffeting**) уд|аря́ть, -а́рить в + *a.*; **they were ~ed by waves** их швыря́ло по волна́м; **they were ~ed by the crowd** их затолка́ла толпа́.

buffet[2] /ˈbʊfeɪ/, /ˈbʌfeɪ/ *n.* (*sideboard*) буфе́т, серва́нт; (*refreshment bar*) буфе́т; (*supper, reception*) а-ля фурше́т.

buffeting /ˈbʌfɪtɪŋ/ *n.* битьё.

buffoon /bəˈfu:n/ *n.* шут, фигля́р.

buffoonery /bəˈfu:nərɪ/ *n.* шутовство́, фигля́рство.

bug /bʌg/ *n.* (*bedbug*) клоп; (*any small insect*) бука́шка, жучо́к; (*coll., germ*) зара́за; (*error*) оши́бка; (*concealed microphone*) подслу́шивающее устро́йство, жучо́к (*coll.*); (*craze*) пове́трие; **he's got the travelling ~** он поме́шан на путеше́ствиях.
● *v.t.* (**bugged, bugging**): **the room was ~ged** (*coll.*) в ко́мнате бы́ли устано́влены подслу́шивающие устро́йства; **the conversation was ~ged** разгово́р подслу́шивали; (*coll., annoy*) раздраж|а́ть, -и́ть.
● *cpd.* **~-eyed** *adj.* с выпученными глаза́ми.

bugaboo /ˈbʌgəˌbu:/ *n.* (*US*) бу́ка, пу́гало.

bugbear /ˈbʌgbeə(r)/ *n.* (*bogy*) бу́ка, пу́гало; (*object of aversion*) жу́пел; (*problem*) пробле́ма.

bugger /ˈbʌgə(r)/ (*Br. vulg.*) *n.* (*sodomite*) содоми́т; (*as term of abuse*) сво́лочь; **poor ~** несча́стный.
● *v.t.* **1** (*commit sodomy with*) занима́ться (*impf.*) содоми́ей с + *i.* **2** (*vulg. uses*): **~ s.o. about** трави́ть, за- кого́-н.; **~ something up** искове́ркать/запоро́ть (*pf., sl.*) что-н.; **I'm ~ed if I know** чёрта с два, е́сли я зна́ю; **~ all** ни шиша́; ни хрена́; **~ (it)!** чёрт возьми́! **~ them!** да хрен с ни́ми!
● *v.i.*: **~ off!** (*vulg.*) прова́ливай!; убира́йся!

buggery /ˈbʌgərɪ/ *n.* содоми́я.

buggy /ˈbʌgɪ/ *n.* (**baby ~**) лёгкая де́тская коля́ска; (*beach, dune etc.*) ба́гги (*indecl.*).

bugle[1] /ˈbju:g(ə)l/ *n.* горн.
● *cpd.* **~-call** *n.* сигна́л го́рна.

bugle[2] /ˈbju:g(ə)l/ *n.* (*bead*) стекля́рус.

bugler /ˈbju:glə(r)/ *n.* горни́ст.

bugloss /ˈbju:glɒs/ *n.* volovи́к.

build /bɪld/ *n.* (*structure*) констру́кция; фо́рма; (*of human body*) телосложе́ние; **a man of powerful ~** челове́к могу́чего сложе́ния.
● *v.t.* (*past and p.p.* **built**) **1** стро́ить, по-; выстра́ивать, вы́строить; **~ a nest** вить, с- гнездо́; **~ a fire** (*in the open*) разв|оди́ть, -ести́ костёр.
2: **a well-built man** хорошо́ сложённый челове́к.
3 (*fig.*): **~ a new world** созд|ава́ть, -а́ть но́вый мир; **he is not built that way** он сде́лан из друго́го те́ста.
4 (*base*): **~ one's hopes on something** стро́ить, по- наде́жды на чём-н.
● *v.i.* (*past and p.p.* **built**): **I shan't ~ if I can find a suitable house** я не бу́ду стро́иться, е́сли найду́ подходя́щий дом.
● *with advs.*: **~ in** *v.t.*: (*insert into structure*) вмонти́ровать (*pf.*); *see also* ⇒**built-in; ~ on** *v.t.*: **~ a wing on to a house** пристр|а́ивать, -о́ить крыло́ к до́му; **~ up** *v.t.*: **~ s.o. up** (*in health*) укреп|ля́ть, -и́ть кому́-н. здоро́вье; (*in prestige*) популяризи́ровать (*impf., pf.*) кого́-н.; созд|ава́ть, -а́ть и́мя кому́-н.; **~ up a theory** стро́ить, по- тео́рию; **~ up a business** созд|ава́ть, -а́ть де́ло; *v.i.*: **work has built up over the past year** накопи́лось мно́го рабо́ты за после́дний год; **our forces are ~ing up** на́ши си́лы расту́т (*see also* ⇒**built-up**).
● *cpd.* **~-up** *n.* (*accumulation*) скопле́ние; рост, разви́тие, развёртывание; (*coll., boosting*) популяриза́ция, созда́ние и́мени; **arms ~-up** нара́щивание вооруже́ний; **publicity ~-up** рекла́мная кампа́ния.

builder /ˈbɪldə(r)/ *n.* строи́тель (*m.*); (*housing contractor*) подря́дчик.

building /ˈbɪldɪŋ/ *n.* **1** (*structure*) зда́ние, постро́йка, строе́ние; (*large edifice*) сооруже́ние; (*premises*) помеще́ние. **2** (*activity*) (по)стро́йка; (*esp. large-scale*) строи́тельство; **~ of socialism** построе́ние/строи́тельство социали́зма; **~ of schools/houses** шко́льное/жили́щное строи́тельство; **~ materials** строи́тельные материа́лы, стройматериа́лы; **~ land** земля́ под постро́йку; **~ site** стро́йка; **~ society** (*Br.*) (жили́щно-) строи́тельное о́бщество.

built /bɪlt/ *past and p.p. of* ⇒**build**

built-in /bɪlt/ *adj.*: **a ~ cupboard** встро́енный/стенно́й шкаф; **he has a ~ resistance to this argument** он органи́чески не мо́жет согласи́ться с э́тим аргуме́нтом.

built-up /bɪlt/ *adj.*: **~ area** застро́енный райо́н.

bulb /bʌlb/ *n.* (*bot., anat.*) лу́ковица; (*of lamp*) ла́мпочка.

bulbous /ˈbʌlbəs/ *adj.* лу́ковичный; луковицеобра́зный; **a ~ nose** нос карто́шкой.

Bulgaria /bʌlˈgeərɪə/ *n.* Болга́рия.

Bulgarian /bʌlˈgeərɪən/ *n.* (*person*) болга́р|ин (*fem.* -ка); (*language*) болга́рский язы́к; **Old ~** старославя́нский язы́к.
● *adj.* болга́рский.

bulg|e /bʌldʒ/ *n.* (*swelling*) вы́пуклость; (*temporary increase*) вре́менное увеличе́ние.
● *v.i.* (*swell*) выпя́чиваться, вы́пятиться; (*of wall*) выступа́ть (*impf.*); выдава́ться (*impf.*); (*of bag etc.*) над|ува́ться, -у́ться; разд|ува́ться, -у́ться; **his pockets were ~ing with apples** его карма́ны оттопы́ривались от я́блок.

bulimia /bʊˈlɪmɪə/ *n.* булими́я.

bulimic /bʊˈlɪmɪk/ *adj.* страда́ющий булими́ей.

bulk /bʌlk/ *n.* **1** (*size, mass, volume*) величина́, ма́сса, объём; **in ~** (*not packaged*) без упако́вки. **2** (*in large quantities*): **~ purchase** поку́пка гурто́м; ма́ссовая заку́пка; **~ buying** о́птовые заку́пки. **3** (*greater part*) основна́я ма́сса/часть.
● *v.t.*: **~ out** (*enlarge*) увели́чи|вать, -ть.
● *v.i.*: **~ large** зан|има́ть, -я́ть ва́жное ме́сто.
● *cpds.* **~-carrier** *n.* сухогру́з, ба́лкер; **~head** *n.* перебо́рка, перегоро́дка.

bulky /ˈbʌlkɪ/ *adj.* (**bulkier, bulkiest**) (*large*) объёмистый; (*unwieldy*) громо́здкий.

bull[1] /bʊl/ *n.* **1** (*ox*) бык; (*buffalo*) бу́йвол; (*elephant, whale etc.*) саме́ц; (*fig.*): **~ in a china shop** слон в посу́дной ла́вке; **take the ~ by the horns** взять (*pf.*) быка́ за рога́; **go at something like a ~ at a gate** лезть/пере́ть (*impf.*) напроло́м.
2 (*astron.*) Теле́ц.
3 (*Br.*, **~'s eye**) я́блоко мише́ни.
4 (*comm.*) спекуля́нт, игра́ющий на повыше́ние.
5 (*sl., nonsense*) неле́пость.
● *cpds.* **~dog** *n.* бульдо́г; **~dog tenacity** бульдо́жья хва́тка; **~doze** *v.t.* (*clear with ~dozer*) расч|ища́ть, -и́стить бульдо́зером; **~doze s.o. into doing something** прин|ужда́ть, -у́дить кого́-н. сде́лать что-н.; **~dozer** *n.* бульдо́зер; **~fight, ~fighting** *nn.* бой быко́в; **~fighter** *n.* тореадо́р; **~finch** *n.* снеги́рь (*m.*); **~frog** *n.* лягу́шка-бык; **~-ring** *n.* аре́на для бо́я быко́в; **~'s-eye** *n.* (*of target*) я́блоко; **hit the ~'s-eye** (*fig.*) поп|ада́ть, -а́сть в цель; **~-terrier** *n.* бультерье́р.

bull[2] /bʊl/ *n.* (*edict*) бу́лла.

bull[3] /bʊl/ *n.*: **Irish ~** неле́пость, неле́пица.

bullet /ˈbʊlɪt/ *n.* пу́ля; **put a ~ through s.o.** вса́|живать, -ди́ть в кого́-н. пу́лю.
● *cpds.* **~-headed** *adj.* круглоголо́вый; **~-hole** *n.* пулево́е отве́рстие; **~-proof** *adj.* пуленепробива́емый; **~-proof vest** бронежиле́т.

bulletin /ˈbʊlɪtɪn/ *n.* (*periodical; official statement*) бюллете́нь (*m.*); (*news report*) бюллете́нь (*m.*), вы́пуск, сообще́ние.

bullion /ˈbʊlɪən/ *n.*: **gold ~** зо́лото в сли́тках.

bullish /ˈbʊlɪʃ/ *adj.* (*optimistic*) оптимисти́ческий; (*comm.*): **a ~ market** повыша́ющийся ры́нок; **~ speculators** спекуля́нты на повыше́ние цен.

bullock /ˈbʊlək/ *n.* вол.

bullshit /ˈbʊlʃɪt/ *n.* (*vulg.*) брехня́, бредя́тина, херня́; **don't give me that ~!** не пори́ херню́!
● *v.i.* (*vulg.*) бреха́ть (*impf.*).

bullshitter /ˈbʊlʃɪtə(r)/ *n.* (*vulg.*) брехло́, бреху́н.

bully[1] /ˈbʊlɪ/ *n.* громи́ла (*m.*), задира (*c.g.*).
● *v.t.* запу́г|ивать, -а́ть; **~ s.o. into doing something** запу́гиванием заст|авля́ть, -а́вить кого́-н. сде́лать что-н.
● *v.i.*: **~ off** (*at hockey*) скре́|щивать, -сти́ть клю́шки.

bully[2] /ˈbʊlɪ/ *adj.* (*coll.*): **~ for you!** молоде́ц!

bullyboy /ˈbʊlɪbɔɪ/ *n.* громи́ла (*m.*), задира (*c.g.*).

bulrush /ˈbʊlrʌʃ/ *n.* камы́ш.

bulwark /ˈbʊlwək/ *n.* (*rampart*) вал, бастио́н; (*mole, breakwater*) мол; (*naut., usu. pl.*) фальшбо́рт; (*fig.*): **~ of freedom** оплот свобо́ды.

bum /bʌm/ *n.* (*coll.*) **1** (*Br., buttocks*) зад, за́дница. **2** (*US, loafer*) ло́дырь (*m.*), (*vagrant*) бродя́га (*m.*); **give s.o. the ~'s rush** выгоня́ть, вы́гнать кого́-н. взаше́й.

● *adj.* дрянно́й.

● *v.t.* (**bummed, bumming**) (*sl., cadge, scrounge*) кля́нчить, вы́-.

● *v.i.* (**bummed, bumming**): **~ around** шата́ться (*impf.*).

● *cpd.* **~bag** *n.* (*Br. coll.*) поясно́й кошелёк.

bumble /ˈbʌmb(ə)l/ *v.i.*: **~ about** идти́ (*det.*) неуве́ренно/спотыка́ясь.

bumble-bee /ˈbʌmb(ə)lˌbiː/ *n.* шмель (*m.*).

bumbling /ˈbʌmblɪŋ/ *adj.* неуклю́жий, неуме́лый.

bum|f, -ph /bʌmf/ *n.* (*Br., papers*) бума́жки (*f. pl.*).

bump /bʌmp/ *n.* **1** (*thump*) глухо́й уда́р; **he landed with a ~ on the floor** он шлёпнулся/гро́хнулся на́ пол; (*collision*) толчо́к. **2** (*swelling, protuberance*) ши́шка. **3** (*air pocket*) возду́шная я́ма; (*in a road*) уха́б, бугор.

● *adv.*: **he went ~ into the door** он так и вре́зался в дверь.

● *v.t.* уд|аря́ть, -а́рить; ушиб|а́ть, -и́ть; **I ~ed my knee as I fell** я ушиб коле́но при паде́нии; **the car ~ed the one in front** маши́на сту́кнулась о другу́ю, стоя́вшую/ше́дшую впереди́; **I ~ed the table and spilt the ink** я толкну́л стол и проли́л черни́ла; **~ off** (*kill*) уб|ира́ть, -ра́ть (*sl.*).

● *v.i.*: **~ against a tree** уда́риться (*pf.*) о де́рево; наскочи́ть/наткну́ться (*pf.*) на де́рево; **my head ~ed against the beam** я уда́рился голово́й о ба́лку; **~ along** (*in cart etc.*) трясти́сь (*impf.*); **he ~ed into a lamp-post** он наткну́лся на фона́рный столб; **his car ~ed into ours** его́ маши́на вре́залась в на́шу; **I ~ed into him in London** я наткну́лся на него́ в Ло́ндоне.

bumper /ˈbʌmpə(r)/ *n.* **1** (*of car*) ба́мпер. **2**: **~ crop** небыва́лый/неви́данный урожа́й.

bumph /bʌmf/ = **bumf**

bumpkin /ˈbʌmpkɪn/ *n.* мужла́н.

bumptious /ˈbʌmpʃəs/ *adj.* самоуве́ренный, зазна́вшийся.

bumptiousness /ˈbʌmpʃəsnɪs/ *n.* самоуве́ренность, зазна́йство.

bumpy /ˈbʌmpɪ/ *adj.* (**bumpier, bumpiest**) (*of road*) уха́бистый, тря́ский; **we had a ~ journey** нас трясло́ всю доро́гу; **a ~ flight** ≈ болта́нка.

bun /bʌn/ *n.* **1** (*cul.*) бу́лочка, плю́шка. **2** (*of hair*) пучо́к.

bunch /bʌntʃ/ *n.* **1** (*of flowers*) буке́т; (*of grapes*) кисть, гроздь; (*of bananas*) гроздь; **~ of keys** свя́зка ключе́й. **2** (*coll., group*) компа́ния, гру́ппа; **the best of the ~** лу́чший среди́ них.

● *v.t.* (*also* **~ together**) соб|ира́ть, -ра́ть в гру́ппу, пучо́к; **~ up** (*dress etc.*) соб|ира́ть, -ра́ть (пла́тье) в сбо́рки.

● *v.i.*: **~ together** ск|а́пливаться, -опи́ться; (*of people*) сб|ива́ться, -и́ться в ку́чу; **~ up** (*of dress etc.*) собра́ться (*impf.*) в сбо́рки.

bundle /ˈbʌnd(ə)l/ *n.* **1** (*of clothes etc.*) у́зел; (*of sticks*) вяза́нка; (*of hay*) оха́пка. **2** (*packet*) паке́т. **3**: **she is a ~ of nerves** она́ комо́к не́рвов.

● *v.t.* **1**: **~ up** свя́з|ывать, -а́ть в у́зел/вяза́нку; **~ up one's hair** соб|ира́ть, -ра́ть во́лосы в пучо́к. **2** (*shove*) запи́х|ивать, -а́ть; **~ s.o. into a room** вта́лкивать, втолкну́ть кого́-н. в ко́мнату; **~ off** спрова́|живать, -дить; выprова́живать, вы́проводить.

bung /bʌŋ/ *n.* заты́чка, вту́лка.

● *v.t.* **1** (*cask etc.*) зат|ыка́ть, -кну́ть; закупо́ри|вать, -ть; **the sink is ~ed up** ра́ковина засори́лась; **my nose is ~ed up** у меня́ зало́жен нос. **2** (*Br. sl., throw*) швыр|я́ть, -ну́ть.

bungalow /ˈbʌŋgəˌləʊ/ *n.* бу́нгало (*indecl.*); одноэта́жный дом.

bungle /ˈbʌŋg(ə)l/ *v.t.* по́ртить, на-; пу́тать, с-.

bungler /ˈbʌŋglə(r)/ *n.* портa̍ч, «сапо́жник».

bunion /ˈbʌnjən/ *n.* о́пухоль/ши́шка на ноге́.

bunk[1] /bʌŋk/ *n.* (*sleeping-berth*) ко́йка; **~ bed** двухъя́русная крова́ть.

bunk[2] /bʌŋk/ (*Br.*) *n.*: **do a ~** (за)д|ава́ть, -а́ть дра́ла/тя́гу (*coll.*).

● *v.i.* см|ыва́ться, -ы́ться; **~ off** (*coll.*): **to ~ off lessons/school** прогу́ливать, прогуля́ть уро́ки, сачкова́ть (*impf.*).

bunker /ˈbʌŋkə(r)/ *n.* (*ship's*) бу́нкер; (*underground shelter*) блинда́ж; (*golf*) я́ма.

bunkum /ˈbʌŋkəm/ *n.* (*coll.*) чушь, пустосло́вие.

bunny /ˈbʌnɪ/ *n.* (*coll.*) кро́лик, за́йчик.

Bunsen burner /ˈbʌns(ə)n/ *n.* бу́нзеновская горе́лка.

bunting[1] /ˈbʌntɪŋ/ *n.* (*zool.*) овся́нка; **snow ~** пу́ночка.

bunting[2] /ˈbʌntɪŋ/ *n.* (*cloth*) фла́жная мате́рия; (*naut.*) флагду́к; (*fig., flags*) фла́ги (*m. pl.*).

buoy /bɔɪ/ *n.* буй, ба́кен; **mooring-~** швартóвная бо́чка; (*life-~*) спаса́тельный буй/круг.

● *v.t.* (*mark with ~s*) обст|авля́ть, -а́вить буя́ми; **~ up** (*lit.*) подде́рж|ивать, -а́ть на пове́рхности; (*fig., support*) подде́рж|ивать, -а́ть; (*cheer up*) подб|а́дривать, -одри́ть.

buoyancy /ˈbɔɪənsɪ/ *n.* плаву́честь; (*fig.*) жизнера́достность; оживле́ние.

buoyant /ˈbɔɪənt/ *adj.* плаву́чий; (*of person*) жизнера́достный; (*of hopes, market*) оживлённый; (*of prices*) повыша́тельный.

bur, burr /bɜː(r)/ *n.* репе́й, репе́йник.

burden /ˈbɜːd(ə)n/ *n.* (*load*) но́ша, груз; (*fig.*) бре́мя (*nt.*); обу́за; **beast of ~** вью́чное живо́тное; **~ of taxation** бре́мя нало́гов; **~ of proof** бре́мя доказывания/доказа́тельства; **become a ~ on s.o.** станови́ться, стать в тя́гость (*or* обу́зой) кому́-н.

● *v.t.* (*load*) нагру|жа́ть, -зи́ть; (*fig.*) обремен|я́ть, -и́ть; **~ s.o. with expenses** взва́л|ивать, -и́ть на кого́-н. расхо́ды.

burdensome /ˈbɜːd(ə)nsəm/ *adj.* обремени́тельный, тя́гостный.

burdock /ˈbɜːdɒk/ *n.* лопу́х.

bureau /ˈbjʊərəʊ/ *n.* (*pl.* **~x** *or* **~s**) (*Br., desk*) бюро́ (*indecl.*), конто́рка; (*US, chest*) комо́д; (*office*) бюро́; **information ~** спра́вочное бюро́; **employment ~** бюро́ по на́йму; **marriage ~** бра́чное бюро́; **~ de change** разме́нная конто́ра, обме́нный пункт.

bureaucracy /bjʊəˈrɒkrəsɪ/ *n.* бюрокра́тия.

bureaucrat /ˈbjʊərəˌkræt/, /-rəʊˌkræt/ *n.* бюрокра́т, чино́вник.

bureaucratic /bjʊərəˈkrætɪk/, /-rəʊˈkrætɪk/ *adj.* бюрократи́ческий.

bureaux /ˈbjʊərəʊz/ *pl. of* ⇒**bureau**

burette /bjʊəˈret/ (*US also* **buret**) *n.* бюре́тка.

burgeon /ˈbɜːdʒ(ə)n/ *v.i.* да|ва́ть, -ть по́чки; распус|ка́ться, -ти́ться.

burger /ˈbɜːgə(r)/ *n.* котле́та; **~ bar** га́мбургерная, котле́тная.

burgher /ˈbɜːgə(r)/ *n.* бю́ргер, горожа́нин.

burglar /ˈbɜːglə(r)/ *n.* граби́тель (*m.*), взло́мщик; **cat ~** граби́тель, проника́ющий в до́м че́рез окно́.

burglarize /ˈbɜːgləˌraɪz/ (*US*) = **burgle** *v.t.*

burglary /ˈbɜːglərɪ/ *n.* грабёж; кра́жа со взло́мом.

burgle /ˈbɜːg(ə)l/ *v.t.*: гра́бить, о-.

● *v.i.* соверш|а́ть, -и́ть кра́жу со взло́мом.

burgomaster /ˈbɜːgəˌmɑːstə(r)/ *n.* бургоми́стр.

burgundy /ˈbɜːgəndɪ/ *n.* (*wine*) бургу́ндское (вино́).

burial /ˈberɪəl/ *n.* (*interment*) погребе́ние, захороне́ние; (*funeral*) по́хор|оны (*pl., g.* -он); **~ service** заупоко́йная слу́жба.

● *cpds.* **~-ground** *n.* кла́дбище, пого́ст; (*archaeol.*) моги́льник; **~-mound** *n.* курга́н; **~-place** *n.* ме́сто погребе́ния.

burin /ˈbjʊərɪn/ *n.* резе́ц гравёра.

burlap /ˈbɜːlæp/ *n.* дерю́га.

burlesque /bɜːˈlesk/ *n.* (*parody*) бурле́ск.

● *adj.* бурле́скный, фа́рсовый, пароди́йный.

● *v.t.* (**burlesques, burlesqued, burlesquing**) пароди́ровать (*impf., pf.*).

burly /ˈbɜːlɪ/ *adj.* (**burlier, burliest**) здорове́нный, дю́жий.

Burma /ˈbɜːmə/ *n.* Би́рма.

burn[1] /bɜːn/ *n.* (*injury*) ожо́г;

first-degree ~s ожо́ги пе́рвой сте́пени.

● *v.t.* (*past and p.p.* **burnt** *or* **burned**) **1** (*sting*) жечь, с-; (*destroy by fire*) сж|ига́ть, -ечь; **~ o.s.** обж|ига́ться, -е́чься; **~ one's fingers** (*lit.*) обж|ига́ть, -е́чь себе́ па́льцы; (*fig.*) обж|ига́ться, -е́чься (*на чём*); **~ a hole in something** прож|ига́ть, -е́чь дыру́ в чём-н.; **the meat is ~t** мя́со сгоре́ло/подгоре́ло; **a ~t taste/smell** вкус/за́пах горе́лого; **he was ~t all over** на нём живо́го ме́ста не оста́лось от ожо́гов; **she was ~t at the stake** её сожгли́ на костре́; **the ship ~s oil** кора́бль рабо́тает на жи́дком то́пливе; **acid ~s the carpet** кислота́ прожига́ет ковёр; **pepper ~s one's mouth** от пе́рца жжёт во рту; **~ paint off a wall** сжига́ть, сжечь кра́ску со стены́.
2 (*bricks, charcoal etc.*) обж|ига́ть, -е́чь.
3 (*tan*) опал|я́ть, -и́ть; обж|ига́ть, -е́чь.
4 (*fig.*): **~ one's boats** сже́чь (*pf.*) свои́ корабли́; **~ the candle at both ends** безрассу́дно расхо́довать (*impf.*) си́лы; **~ the midnight oil** заси́|живаться, -де́ться за рабо́той за́ полночь; **he has money to ~** у него́ де́нег ку́ры не клюю́т; **money ~s a hole in his pocket** де́ньги у него́ не де́ржатся.

● *v.i.* (*past and p.p.* **burnt** *or* **burned**) горе́ть (*impf.*) (*also fig.*): **the house is ~ing** дом гори́т; в до́ме пожа́р; **the lamp is ~ing low** ла́мпа догора́ет; **acid ~s into metal** кислота́ разъеда́ет мета́лл; **he ~t with fever** он был в жару́; он горе́л в лихора́дке; **he ~t with shame/curiosity** он сгора́л от стыда́/любопы́тства; **he ~t with passion** он пыла́л стра́стью; **he ~t with anger** он кипе́л от зло́сти.

● *with advs.*: **~ down** *v.t.* сж|ига́ть, -ечь; *v.i.*: **the house ~t down** дом сгоре́л дотла́; **the fire ~t down** костёр догоре́л; **~ out** *v.t.*: **the house was ~t out** дом сгоре́л дотла́; **the fire ~t itself out** пожа́р/костёр догоре́л и загло́х; **~ o.s. out** (*fig.*) сгоре́ть (*pf.*); **~ out a fuse** (*elec.*) переж|ига́ть, -е́чь про́бку; *v.i.*: **the fire ~t out** ого́нь поту́х; костёр загло́х; **~ up** *v.i.*: **make the fire ~ up** разж|ига́ть, -е́чь пе́чку/ками́н.

burn² /bɜ:n/ *n.* (*Sc., stream*) руче́й, пото́к.

burner /ˈbɜ:nə(r)/ *n.* (*of stove etc.*) горе́лка, конфо́рка; **to put on the back burner** отодв|ига́ть, -и́нуть на за́дний план.

burning /ˈbɜ:nɪŋ/ *n.* горе́ние; обжига́ние, о́бжиг.

● *adj.* (*of fever*) сжига́ющий; (*of shame*) жгу́чий; (*of zeal*) нейстовый.

burnish /ˈbɜ:nɪʃ/ *v.t.* полирова́ть, от-.

burnous /bɜ:ˈnu:s/ *n.* бурну́с.

burnt /bɜ:nt/ *past and p.p. of* ⇒**burn¹**

burp /bɜ:p/ (*coll.*) *n.* отры́жка, рыга́ние.

● *v.t.*: **~ a baby** да|ва́ть, -ть ребёнку отрыгну́ть.

● *v.i.* рыг|а́ть, -ну́ть.

burr¹ /bɜ:(r)/ *n.* (*in speech*) карта́вость; **speak with a ~** карта́вить (*impf.*).

burr² /bɜ:(r)/ *n.* (*on metal*) заусе́нец, грат.

burr³ /bɜ:(r)/ *n.* (*bot.*) = **bur**

burrow /ˈbʌrəʊ/ *n.* нора́.

● *v.t.*: **~ a hole** рыть, вы́- нору́.

● *v.i.* (*of rabbit/mole*) рыть, вы́- нору́/ходы́; **~ among archives** ры́ться (*impf.*) в архи́вах.

bursar /ˈbɜ:sə/ *n.* (*Br., treasurer*) казначе́й.

bursary /ˈbɜ:sərɪ/ *n.* (*Br.*) (*office*) канцеля́рия казначе́я; (*grant*) стипе́ндия.

burst /bɜ:st/ *n.* взрыв; разры́в; **the ~ of a shell** разры́в снаря́да; **a ~ of energy** вспы́шка/взрыв эне́ргии; **work in sudden ~s** рабо́тать (*impf.*) рывка́ми; **~ of applause** взрыв аплодисме́нтов; **~ of anger** вспы́шка гне́ва; взрыв негодова́ния; **~ of tears** внеза́пный пото́к слёз; **~ of machine-gun fire** пулемётная о́чередь.

● *v.t.* (*past and p.p.* **burst**) (*e.g. a shell. tyre, balloon, blood-vessel*) раз|рыва́ть, -орва́ть; **the river ~ its banks** река́ вы́шла из берего́в; **~ one's bonds** разорва́ть (*pf.*) свои́ око́вы; **~ one's sides with laughing** надорва́ть (*pf.*) живо́т от сме́ха; **~ a door open** расп|а́хивать, -ахну́ть дверь.

● *v.i.* (*past and p.p.* **burst**): **the shell ~** снаря́д разорва́лся; **the balloon ~** возду́шный шар ло́пнул; **the bubble ~** пузы́рь ло́пнул; **the granaries are ~ing** закрома́ ло́мятся; **the dam ~** плоти́ну прорва́ло; **full to ~ing** по́лный до отка́за; **he is ~ing with health** он пы́шет здоро́вьем; **~ with laughter** расхохота́ться (*pf.*); **he was ~ing with pride** его́ распира́ло от го́рдости; **I was ~ing to tell her** мне не терпе́лось сказа́ть ей; **the door ~ open** дверь распахну́лась.

● *with preps.*: **~ into bloom** распус|ка́ться, -ти́ться, расцве|та́ть, -сти́; **~ into song** запе́ть (*pf.*); **~ into tears** разрыда́ться (*pf.*); **~ into a room** врыва́ться, ворва́ться в ко́мнату; **~ into flame(s)** вспы́х|ивать, -нуть; **oil ~ out of the ground** из земли́ заби́ла нефть; **the sun ~ through the clouds** со́лнце прорва́лось сквозь ту́чи; **shouts ~ upon our ears** внеза́пно нас оглуши́ли кри́ки; **the truth ~ upon him** его́ вдруг осени́ло; **the news ~ upon the world** э́та но́вость потрясла́ мир.

● *with advs.*: **~ in** *v.i.* (*interrupt*) вме́ш|иваться, -а́ться; **he ~ in upon us** он ворва́лся к нам; **~ out** *v.i.* (*exclaim*) вы́палить (*pf.*); **~ out laughing** расхохота́ться (*pf.*).

bur|y /ˈberɪ/ *v.t.* **1** (*inter*) хорони́ть, по-; погре|ба́ть, -сти́; **he is dead and ~ied** его́ нет в живы́х; **he ~ied** (*lost by death*) **all his relatives** он похорони́л всех свои́х родны́х. **2** (*hide in earth*) зар|ыва́ть, -ы́ть; зак|а́пывать, -опа́ть. **3** (*remove from view*): **~y one's face in one's hands** закр|ыва́ть, -ы́ть лицо́ рука́ми; **~y o.s. in one's books** зар|ыва́ться, -ы́ться в кни́ги; **~y o.s. in the country** хорони́ть, по- себя́ в дере́вне; **~ying-ground** = **burial-ground**

Buryat /buəˈjɑ:t/ *n.* (*person*) буря́т (*fem.* -ка).

● *adj.* буря́тский.

bus /bʌs/ *n.* (*pl.* **buses** *or US* **busses**) авто́бус; **miss the ~** (*fig.*) упус|ка́ть, -ти́ть слу́чай.

● *v.i.* (**buses** *or* **busses, bussed, bussing**) е́хать (*det.*) авто́бусом.

● *v.t.* (**buses** *or* **busses, bussed, bussing**) перев|ози́ть, -езти́ на авто́бусе.

● *cpds.* **~-conductor** *n.* конду́ктор авто́буса; **~-conductress** *n.* же́нщина-конду́ктор; **~-driver** *n.* води́тель (*m.*)/шофёр авто́буса; **~man** *n.*: **~man's holiday** пра́здник, похо́жий на бу́дни; **~-shelter** *n.* автопавильо́н; **~-station** *n.* авто́бусная ста́нция; **~-stop** *n.* авто́бусная остано́вка; **~-ticket** *n.* авто́бусный биле́т.

busby /ˈbʌzbɪ/ *n.* гуса́рский ки́вер.

bush /bʊʃ/ *n.* (*shrub*) куст; (*thicket*) куста́рник; (*wild land*) некультиви́рованная земля́; **~ telegraph** бы́строе распростране́ние слу́хов; ≈ молва́.

bushed /bʊʃt/ *adj.* (*coll.*) вы́мотанный.

bushel /ˈbʊʃ(ə)l/ *n.* бу́шель (*m.*); **hide one's light under a ~** быть изли́шне скро́мным.

bushing /ˈbʊʃɪŋ/ *n.* вту́лка, вкла́дыш.

bushy /ˈbʊʃɪ/ *adj.* (**bushier, bushiest**) (*covered with bush*) покры́тый куста́рником; (*of beard etc.*) густо́й; (*of plant*) кусти́стый; (*of tail*) пуши́стый.

busily /ˈbɪzɪlɪ/ *adv.* делови́то; энерги́чно.

business /ˈbɪznɪs/ *n.* **1** (*task, affair*) де́ло; **he made it his ~ to find out** . . . он счёл свои́м до́лгом узна́ть. . .; **what is your ~ here?** что вам здесь на́до?; **it is none of your ~** э́то не ва́ше де́ло; э́то вас не каса́ется; **mind your own ~** не вме́шивайтесь/су́йтесь не в своё де́ло; **it is his ~ to keep a record** его́ обя́занность — вести́ за́писи; **you have no ~ to say that** не вам э́то говори́ть; **funny, monkey ~** нечи́стое де́ло; штý́чки (*f. pl.*); **I am sick of the whole ~** мне вся э́та исто́рия надое́ла; **'any other ~'** (*on agenda*) «Ра́зное».
2 (*trouble*): **what a ~ it is!** кака́я возня́/исто́рия!; **make a great ~ of something** преувели́чивать (*impf.*) значе́ние чего́-н.
3 (*serious purpose, work*): **he means ~** он име́ет серьёзные наме́рения; **get down to ~** бра́ться, взя́ться за де́ло.
4 (*comm. etc.*): **~ of the day, meeting** пове́стка дня; **~ hours, hours of ~** (*of an office*) часы́ приёма/заня́тий/рабо́ты; **~ year** хозя́йственный год; **~ card** визи́тка, визи́тная ка́рточка; **~ before pleasure** де́лу вре́мя, поте́хе час; сде́лал де́ло — гуля́й сме́ло; **he is in the wool ~** он занима́ется торго́влей ше́рстью; **big ~** большо́й би́знес; **~ as usual** фи́рма рабо́тает как обы́чно; **set up in ~** нач|ина́ть, -а́ть торго́вое де́ло; **go into ~**

заня́ться (*pf.*) комме́рцией; **~ is ~** де́ло есть де́ло; **on ~** по де́лу; **put s.o. out of ~** разор|я́ть, -и́ть кого́-н.; **do ~ with s.o.** вести́ (*det.*) дела́ с кем-н.; **lose ~** теря́ть, по- клие́нтов; **talk ~** говори́ть (*impf.*) по де́лу/существу́; **~ is slow/brisk** дела́ иду́т вя́ло/хорошо́; **~ deal, piece of ~** сде́лка. **5** (*establishment*) фи́рма, предприя́тие; про́мысел; (*office*) конто́ра.

● *cpds.* **~-like** *adj.* делово́й, практи́чный; **~man** *n.* коммерса́нт, бизнесме́н, деле́ц; **~woman** *n.* бизнесме́нка.

busker /ˈbʌskə(r)/ *n.* у́личный музыка́нт.

busses /ˈbʌsɪz/ *US pl. of* ⇒**bus**

bust¹ /bʌst/ *n.* (*sculpture*; *bosom*) бюст; (*upper part of body*) грудь.

bust² /bʌst/ (*coll.*) *v.t.* (*past and p.p.* **busted** *or* **bust**) (*break*) раскол|а́чивать, -оти́ть; **~ up** разб|ива́ть, -и́ть; (*sl., arrest*) аресто́в|ывать, -а́ть; (*sl., police raid*) соверш|а́ть, -и́ть налёт на + *a.*

● *v.i.* (*past and p.p.* **busted** *or* **bust**) (*also* **go ~**) раскол|а́чиваться, -оти́ться; **~ up** разб|ива́ться, -и́ться; **the business went ~** де́ло ло́пнуло.

● *cpd.* **~-up** *n.* (*Br., quarrel*) раздо́р, разла́д.

bustard /ˈbʌstəd/ *n.* дрофа́.

bustle¹ /ˈbʌs(ə)l/ *n.* (*on skirt*) турню́р.

bustle² /ˈbʌs(ə)l/ *n.* (*activity*) сумато́ха, суета́.

● *v.i.* (*also* **~ about**) суети́ться, тормоши́ться (*both impf.*).

bustling /ˈbʌslɪŋ/ *n.* суета́; суетли́вость.

● *adj.* суетли́вый, суетя́щийся; **a ~ city** оживлённый го́род.

busy /ˈbɪzɪ/ *adj.* (**busier, busiest**) **1** (*occupied*) за́нятый; **I had a ~ day** мой день был о́чень загру́жен; я был за́нят весь день; **he was ~ packing** он был за́нят упако́вкой; **keep s.o. ~** зан|има́ть (*impf.*) кого́-н. (*чем-н.*); **the line is ~** (*US*) но́мер за́нят. **2** (*habitually unresting*) занято́й. **3**: **a ~ street** шу́мная/оживлённая у́лица. **4**: **a ~ pattern** вычурный узо́р.

● *v.t.*: **~ o.s.** зан|има́ться, -я́ться.

● *cpd.* **~body** *n.* доку́чливый/назо́йливый челове́к.

busyness /ˈbɪzɪnɪs/ *n.* за́нятость.

but /bʌt/ *n.*: **(~ me) no ~s** никаки́х «но»; без вся́ких «но».

● *adv.* (*liter.*): (*only*) всего́ (лишь); **we can ~ try** попы́тка — не пы́тка.

● *prep. & conj.* (*except*): **no one ~ me** никто́, кро́ме меня́; **she is anything ~ beautiful** она́ далеко́ не краса́вица; **he all ~ failed** он то́лько что не провали́лся; **nothing remains ~ to thank her** остаётся то́лько поблагодари́ть её; **he had no choice ~ to go there** ему́ не остава́лось ничего́ друго́го, кроме как пойти́ туда́; **not a day passes ~ there is some trouble** не прохо́дит и дня без неприя́тностей; **next door ~ one** че́рез одну́ дверь; **the last ~ one** предпосле́дний; **~ for me he would have stayed** е́сли бы не я, он бы оста́лся; **she would have fallen ~ that I caught her** она́ бы упа́ла, е́сли бы я не подхвати́л её; **he cannot ~ agree** ему́ остаётся то́лько согласи́ться; **I do not doubt ~ that he is honest** я не сомнева́юсь в его́ че́стности; **I cannot help ~ think** . . . я не могу́ не ду́мать, что. . . .

● *conj.* (*adversative*) но; (*less emphatic*) а; **~ yet, then, again** но всё же; но опя́ть-таки.

butane /ˈbju:teɪn/, /bju:ˈteɪn/ *n.* бута́н.

butch /bʊtʃ/ *adj.* му́жественный (*о мужчине*), мужепо́добная (*о женщине*).

butcher /ˈbʊtʃə(r)/ *n.* **1** (*tradesman*) мясни́к; **~'s (shop)** мясна́я ла́вка, мясно́й магази́н. **2** (*murderer*) пала́ч.

● *v.t.* (*cattle*) забива́ть (*impf.*); (*people*) истреб|ля́ть, -и́ть; выреза́ть, вы́резать.

● *cpd.* **~-bird** *n.* сорокопу́т.

butchery /ˈbʊtʃərɪ/ *n.* (*trade*) торго́вля мя́сом; (*massacre*) резня́.

butler /ˈbʌtlə(r)/ *n.* дворе́цкий.

butt¹ /bʌt/ *n.* (*cask*) бо́чка.

butt² /bʌt/ (*fig., target*): **a ~ for ridicule** мише́нь для насме́шек.

butt³ /bʌt/ *n.* (*of rifle*) прикла́д; (*of tree*) ко́мель (*m.*); (*of cigarette*) оку́рок; (*US coll., buttocks*) зад, за́дница.

● *v.i.*: **~ up against, up to** прилега́ть (*impf.*) к + *d.*

● *cpd.* **~-end** *n.* (*remainder*) оста́ток; (*thick end*) утолщённый коне́ц.

butt⁴ /bʌt/ *n.* (*blow with the head*) уда́р голово́й.

● *v.t.* бода́ть, за-; **~ s.o. in the stomach** ударя́ть, уда́рить кого́-н. голово́й в живо́т.

● *v.i.*: **~ in** (*interrupt*) встр|ева́ть, -ять; вмéш|иваться, -а́ться; **~ into a conversation** встрять/вмеша́ться/влезть (*pf.*) в разгово́р.

butter /ˈbʌtə(r)/ *n.* ма́сло; **melted ~** топлёное ма́сло; **fry something in ~** жа́рить, под- что-н. на ма́сле; **she looks as if ~ wouldn't melt in her mouth** на вид она́ ти́ше воды́.

● *v.t.* нама́з|ывать, -ать ма́слом; (*a dish*) сма́з|ывать, -ать ма́слом; **~ up** (*fig.*) льсти́ть, по- + *d.*; ума́сл|ивать, -ить.

● *cpds.* **~-bean** *n.* боб (кароли́нский); **~cup** *n.* лю́тик; **~-dish** *n.* маслёнка; **~-fingered** *adj.* растя́пистый; **~-fingers** *n.* размазня́ (*c.g.*), растя́па (*c.g.*); **~-knife** *n.* нож для ма́сла; **~milk** *n.* па́хта, па́хтанье.

butterfly /ˈbʌtəˌflaɪ/ *n.* **1** ба́бочка; **I have butterflies in my stomach** у меня́ се́рдце ёкает. **2** (*fig., flighty person*) мотылёк. **3**: **~ nut** (*tech.*) бара́шек; **~ stroke** (*swimming*) баттерфля́й.

buttery /ˈbʌtərɪ/ *n.* (*Br.*) кладова́я.

● *adj.* ма́сленый; маслянистый, в ма́сле.

buttocks /ˈbʌtəks/ *n.* я́годицы (*f. pl.*).

button /ˈbʌt(ə)n/ *n.* **1** пу́говица. **2** (*knob*) кно́пка; **press a ~** наж|има́ть, -а́ть кно́пку. **3** (*US, badge*) значо́к. **4**: **~ mushroom** ме́лкий гриб.

● *v.t.* (*also* **~ up**) застёг|ивать, -ну́ть; **~ up a child** застёг|ивать, -ну́ть оде́жду на ребёнке; **~ one's lip** (*sl.*) держа́ть (*impf.*) язы́к за зуба́ми.

● *v.i.* застёг|иваться, -ну́ться; **the dress ~s up the back** пла́тье застёгивается на спине́.

● *cpd.* **~hole** *n.* петля́, петли́ца; (*Br., flower*) бутонье́рка; *v.t.* (*fig.*) заде́рж|ивать, -а́ть разгово́ром.

buttress /ˈbʌtrɪs/ *n.* (*archit.*) контрфо́рс; (*fig.*) опо́ра, подде́ржка; **flying ~** аркбута́н, а́рочный контрфо́рс.

● *v.t.* (*archit.*) подп|ира́ть, -ере́ть контрфо́рсом; (*fig.*) укреп|ля́ть, -и́ть; подкреп|ля́ть, -и́ть; служи́ть (*impf.*) опо́рой + *d.*

buxom /ˈbʌksəm/ *adj.* (*of woman*) полногру́дая.

buy /baɪ/ *n.*: **a good ~** вы́годная поку́пка.

● *v.t.* (**buys, buying;** *past and p.p.* **bought**) **1** покупа́ть, купи́ть; **money cannot ~ happiness** сча́стья не ку́пишь; **the victory was dearly bought** побе́да доста́лась дорого́й цено́й; **~ s.o. a drink** ста́вить, по- кому́-н. вы́пивку. **2** (*bribe*) подкуп|а́ть, -и́ть.

● *with advs.*: **~ back** *v.t.* сно́ва купи́ть (*pf.*) (*проданное*); **~ in** *v.t.* (*Br., stock up with*) закуп|а́ть, -и́ть; (*at auction*) выкупа́ть, вы́купить; **~ off** *v.t.* откуп|а́ться, -и́ться (*от кого*); **~ out** *v.t.*: **~ s.o. out** выкупа́ть, вы́купить чью-н. до́лю; **~ o.s. out of the army** откуп|а́ться, -и́ться от вое́нной слу́жбы; **~ up** *v.t.* скуп|а́ть, -и́ть.

● *cpd.* **~-out** *n.* (*comm.*) вы́куп.

buyer /ˈbaɪə(r)/ *n.* **1** покупа́тель (*m.*); **~'s market** ры́ночная конъюнкту́ра, вы́годная для покупа́телей. **2** (*firm's agent*) заку́пщи|к (*fem.* -ца).

buzz /bʌz/ *n.* **1** (*of bee etc.*) жужжа́ние; (*of talk*) гул, жужжа́ние. **2**: **give s.o. a ~** (*ring*) звя́кнуть (*pf.*) кому́-н. (*coll.*).

● *v.t.* (*summon with buzzer*) звони́ть , по-; вызыва́ть, вы́звать сигна́лом.

● *v.i.* **1** (*of insect, projectile*) жужжа́ть (*impf.*); (*of place, people*) гуде́ть (*impf.*); **my ears were ~ing** у меня́ гуде́ло в уша́х. **2**: **~ off!** (*sl.*) убира́йся!; прова́ливай!

● *cpds.* **~-saw** *n.* (*US*) циркуля́рная пила́; **~-word** *n.* мо́дное слове́чко.

buzzard /ˈbʌzəd/ *n.* сары́ч, каню́к; (*US, turkey vulture*) гриф-инде́йка.

buzzer /ˈbʌzə(r)/ *n.* (*elec.*) зу́ммер.

by /baɪ/ *adv.* (*near*) побли́зости; (*alongside*) ря́дом; (*past*) ми́мо; **the days went ~** дни шли за дня́ми; **~ and large** в це́лом.

● *prep.* **1** (*near, close to*): **sit ~ the fire(side)** сиде́ть (*impf.*) у ками́на; **I was going ~ the house** я шёл ми́мо до́ма; **she sat ~ the sick man** она́ сиде́ла у посте́ли больно́го; **~ o.s.** (*alone*) (соверше́нно) оди́н/одна́; (*unaided*) сам/сама́, самостоя́тельно; **he played billiards ~ himself** он игра́л в билья́рд сам с собо́й; **~ and ~** вско́ре; сейча́с; **side ~ side** ря́дом; **pass ~ s.o.** про|ходи́ть, -йти́ ми́мо

кого́-н.; **a path ~ the river** доро́жка у/вдоль реки́; **~ the ~; ~ the way** кста́ти.
2 (*along, via*): **~ land and sea** по су́ше и по мо́рю; **~ the nearest road** ближа́йшей доро́гой; **we travelled ~ (way of) Paris** мы е́хали че́рез Пари́ж; **~ water** по воде́; во́дным путём.
3 (*during*): **~ day/night** днём/но́чью; **~ daylight** при дневно́м све́те.
4 (*of time-limit*): **~ Thursday** к четвергу́; **~ then** к тому́ вре́мени; **~ now** тепе́рь; **he should know ~ now** пора́ бы уж ему́ знать.
5 (*manner, means or agency*) *often expr. by i. case*; (**~** *means of*) при по́мощи +*g.*; **lead ~ the hand** вести́ (*det.*) за́ руку; **~ the name of George** по и́мени Гео́ргий; **have children ~ s.o.** име́ть (*impf.*) дете́й от кого́-н.; **a Frenchman ~ blood** францу́з по происхожде́нию; **pull up ~ the roots** выта́скивать, вы́тащить с ко́рнем; **a book ~ Tolstoy** кни́га Толсто́го; **know ~ experience** знать (*impf.*) по о́пыту; **~ Article 5 of the treaty** согла́сно 5 (пя́той) статье́ догово́ра; **~ my watch** по мои́м часа́м; **~ rail** по желе́зной доро́ге; **~ the one o'clock train** (с) часовы́м по́ездом; **~ taxi** на/в такси́; **die ~ drowning** утону́ть (*pf.*); **work ~ electric light** рабо́тать при электри́ческом све́те; **~ law** по зако́ну; **~ radio** по ра́дио; **~ no means** ни в ко́ем слу́чае; **hang ~ a thread** висе́ть (*impf.*) на волоске́; **~ post** по́чтой, по по́чте; **~ the morning post** (с) у́тренней по́чтой; **~ telephone** по телефо́ну; **~ nature/profession/invitation** по приро́де/профе́ссии/приглаше́нию; **cautious ~ nature** осторо́жный от приро́ды; **sold ~ auction** про́дан с торго́в/молотка́; **a letter written ~ hand** письмо́, напи́санное от руки́; **~ means of** при по́мощи +*g.*; **I knew ~ his eyes that he was afraid** я по́нял по его́ глаза́м, что он бои́тся; **he led her ~ the hand** он вёл её за́ руку; **he held the horse ~ the bridle** он держа́л ло́шадь под уздцы́; **what is meant ~ this word?** что означа́ет э́то сло́во?
6 (*of rate or measurement*): **pay ~ the day** плати́ть (*impf.*) подённо; **~ degrees** постепе́нно; **little ~ little** ма́ло-пома́лу; **bread came down in price ~ 5 copecks** хлеб подешеве́л на пять копе́ек; **he missed ~ a foot** он промахну́лся на (це́лый) фут; **better ~ far** намно́го лу́чше; **sell something ~ the yard** прод|ава́ть, -а́ть что-н. на я́рды; **tomatoes are sold ~ weight, ~ the pound** помидо́ры продаю́тся на вес/фу́нты; **~ the dozen** дю́жинами; **one ~ one** оди́н за други́м; по одному́, поодино́чке; **day ~ day** день за днём; **we divide thirty ~ five** де́лим 30 на́ 5; **a room 13 feet ~ 12** ко́мната трина́дцать фу́тов на двена́дцать; **they discussed the report paragraph ~ paragraph** они́ обсуди́ли докла́д пункт за пу́нктом.
7: **~ God!** кляну́сь Бо́гом!

bye /baɪ/ *n.*: **draw a ~** (*sport*) быть свобо́дным от игры́.

bye-bye /ˈbaɪbaɪ/, /bəˈbaɪ/ *int.* (*good-bye*) пока́!; всего́ хоро́шего!

bye-law /ˈbaɪlɔː/ = **by-law**

by-election /ˈbaɪɪˌlekʃ(ə)n/ *n.* (*Br.*) дополни́тельные вы́боры (*m. pl.*).

Byelorussia /ˌbjeləʊˈrʌʃə/ *n.* Белору́ссия.

Byelorussian /ˌbjeləʊˈrʌʃ(ə)n/ *n.* (*person*) белору́с (*fem.* -ка); (*language*) белору́сский язы́к.
● *adj.* белору́сский.

bygone /ˈbaɪgɒn/ *n.* (*usu. pl.*): **let ~s be ~s** что бы́ло, то прошло́.
● *adj.* проше́дший, мину́вший; **in ~ days** в давно́ мину́вшие времена́.

by-law, bye-law /ˈbaɪlɔː/ *n.* (*Br.*) распоряже́ние, постановле́ние (ме́стной вла́сти).

by-line /ˈbaɪlaɪn/ *n.* (*journ.*) по́дпись а́втора.

by-pass /ˈbaɪpɑːs/ *n.* объе́зд, обхо́д; обхо́дный путь; (*med.*) шунт; **heart ~** корона́рное шунти́рование.
● *v.t.* об|ходи́ть, -ойти́ (*also fig.*).

by-product /ˈbaɪˌprɒdʌkt/ *n.* побо́чный проду́кт.

byre /ˈbaɪə(r)/ *n.* (*Br.*) хлев, коро́вник.

by-road /ˈbaɪrəʊd/ *n.* бокова́я доро́га.

bystander /ˈbaɪˌstændə(r)/ *n.* зри́тель (*m.*); прохо́жий.

byte /baɪt/ *n.* (*comput.*) байт.

byway /ˈbaɪweɪ/ *n.* бокова́я доро́га, боково́й путь; (*fig.*): **~s of learning** забро́шенные уголки́ (*m. pl.*) нау́ки/зна́ния.

byword /ˈbaɪwɜːd/ *n.*: **a ~ for iniquity** олицетворе́ние несправедли́вости.

by-your-leave /ˌbaɪjɔːˈliːv/ *n.*: **without (so much as) a ~** не спрося́сь.

Byzantine /bɪˈzæntaɪn/, /baɪ-/, /ˈbɪzənˌtiːn/, /ˈbɪzənˌtaɪn/ *adj.* (*lit., fig.*) византи́йский; **~ Empire** Византи́я, византи́йская импе́рия.

Byzantium /bɪˈzæntɪəm/ *n.* (*city*) Виза́нтий.

Cc

C¹ /siː/ *n.* **1** (*mus.*) до (*indecl.*). **2** (*acad. mark*) «удовлетвори́тельно», тро́йка; **she got a ~ in maths** она получи́ла «удовлетвори́тельно» *or* тро́йку по матема́тике.

C² (*abbr. of* ***Celsius*** /ˈselsɪəs/ *or* ***centigrade*** /ˈsentɪˌgreɪd/) (шкала́) Це́льсия; **20°C** 20°Ц (гра́дусов Це́льсия (*or* по Це́льсию)).

c. *abbr. of* **1** ***century*** /ˈsentʃərɪ/, /-tjʊrɪ/ в. (век); ст. (столе́тие). **2** ***circa*** /ˈsɜːkə/ ок. (о́коло). **3** ***cent(s)*** /sent(s)/ це́нт.

CAB (*abbr. of* ***Citizens' Advice Bureau***) Бюро́ консульта́ции населе́ния.

cab /kæb/ *n.* **1** (*taxi*) такси́ (*nt. indecl.*); кеб; **go by ~** е́хать (*det.*) на такси́. **2** (*of lorry etc.*) каби́на води́теля.

● *cpds.* **~-driver, ~man** *nn.* шофёр такси́; **~-rank, ~-stand** *nn.* стоя́нка такси́.

cabal /kəˈbæl/ *n.* полити́ческая кли́ка.

cabaret /ˈkæbəˌreɪ/ *n.* (*place*) кабаре́ (*indecl.*); (*entertainment*) кабаре́, эстра́дное представле́ние.

cabbage /ˈkæbɪdʒ/ *n.* капу́ста; **~ butterfly** капу́стница; **~-head** коча́н капу́сты.

cab(b)alistic /ˌkæbəˈlɪstɪk/ *adj.* кабалисти́ческий.

cabby /ˈkæbɪ/ *n.* (*coll.*) таксист.

caber /ˈkeɪbə(r)/ *n.* (*sport*): **tossing the ~** мета́ние ствола́.

cabin /ˈkæbɪn/ *n.* каби́на; (*dwelling*) хи́жина; (*in ship etc.*) каю́та; **~ class** каю́тный класс; (*of aeroplane*) каби́на; **~ boy** каю́т-ю́нга (*m.*).

cabinet /ˈkæbɪnɪt/ *n.* **1** (*piece of furniture*) го́рка, шкаф; **filing ~** картоте́чный шкаф; **medicine ~** апте́чка. **2** (*of radio set etc.*) ко́рпус. **3** (*pol.*) кабине́т (мини́стров); **~ crisis** прави́тельственный кри́зис; **~ minister** член кабине́та; **shadow ~** «тенево́й кабине́т».

● *cpd.* **~-maker** *n.* краснодере́вец.

cable /ˈkeɪb(ə)l/ *n.* **1** (*rope*) кана́т, трос. **2** (*wire*) ка́бель (*m.*); **~ car** ваго́н подвесно́й доро́ги; фуникулёр; **~ railway** кана́тная/подвесна́я доро́га; фуникулёр; **~ TV** ка́бельное телеви́дение. **3** (*telegram*) телегра́мма.

● *v.t.*: **he cabled his congratulations** он посла́л поздрави́тельную телегра́мму.

● *v.i.* телеграфи́ровать (*impf., pf.*).

cablegram /ˈkeɪb(ə)lˌgræm/ *n.* каблогра́мма, телегра́мма.

caboodle /kəˈbuːd(ə)l/ *n.* (*sl.*): **the whole ~** (*of people*) вся ора́ва/компа́ния; (*of things*) всё хозя́йство.

cabriolet /ˌkæbrɪəʊˈleɪ/ *n.* (*carriage*) кабриоле́т; (*motor-car*) автомоби́ль (*m.*) с откидны́м ве́рхом.

cacao /kəˈkɑːəʊ/, /-ˈkeɪəʊ/ *n.* (*pl.* **~s**) кака́о (*indecl.*).

cache /kæʃ/ *n.* тайни́к, та́йный склад.

● *v.t.* пря́тать, с- в тайнике́.

cachet /ˈkæʃeɪ/ *n.* **1** (*prestige*) прести́ж; (*mark of distinction*) печа́ть. **2** (*med.*) ка́псула.

cackle /ˈkæk(ə)l/ *n.* куда́хтанье; (*fig., chatter*) трескотня́, болтовня́; **cut the ~!** дово́льно треща́ть!; (*laugh*) хихи́канье.

● *v.t. & i.* (*of geese, of a person*) гого́тать (*impf.*); (*of hens*) куда́хтать (*impf.*).

cacophonous /kəˈkɒfənəs/ *adj.* какофони́ческий, какофони́чный.

cacophony /kəˈkɒfənɪ/ *n.* какофо́ния.

cactus /ˈkæktəs/ *n.* (*pl.* **cacti** /-taɪ/ *or* **cactuses**) ка́ктус.

CAD (*abbr. of* ***computer-aided design***) автоматизи́рованное проекти́рование.

cad /kæd/ *n.* хам.

cadaver /kəˈdeɪvə(r)/, /-ˈdɑːvə(r)/ *n.* труп.

cadaverous /kəˈdævərəs/ *adj.* мёртвенно-бле́дный.

caddie /ˈkædɪ/ *n.* носи́льщик клю́шек (*в гольфе*).

caddish /ˈkædɪʃ/ *adj.* ни́зкий, ха́мский.

caddishness /ˈkædɪʃnɪs/ *n.* ни́зость, ха́мство.

caddy /ˈkædɪ/ *n.* ча́йница.

cadence /ˈkeɪd(ə)ns/ *n.* каде́нция; (*rhythm*) ритм; (*rise and fall of voice*) модуля́ция.

cadenza /kəˈdenzə/ *n.* каде́нция.

cadet /kəˈdet/ *n.* (*mil.*) каде́т, курса́нт; **~ corps** каде́тский ко́рпус.

cadge /kædʒ/ *v.t. & i.* попроша́йничать (*impf.*); жить, по- на чужо́й счёт; (*get by sponging*) выкля́нчивать, вы́клянчить; (*coll.*) стрел|я́ть, -ьну́ть (*что у кого*).

cadger /ˈkædʒə(r)/ *n.* попроша́йка (*c.g.*), прихлеба́тель (*m.*), нахле́бник.

cadmium /ˈkædmɪəm/ *n.* ка́дмий.

cadre /ˈkɑːdə(r)/, /ˈkɑːdrə/ *n.* (*mil. etc.*) ка́дровый соста́в; (*pl., key personnel*) ка́дры (*m. pl.*).

caduceus /kəˈdjuːsɪəs/ *n.* (*pl.* **caducei** /-sɪˌaɪ/) кадуце́й.

caec|um /ˈsiːkəm/ (*US* **cecum**) *n.* (*pl.* **~a**) слепа́я кишка́.

Caesarean /sɪˈzeərɪən/ (*US also* **Cesarean**) *adj.* це́зарев, ке́сарев; **~ birth, operation** ке́сарево сече́ние.

caesium /ˈsiːzɪəm/ (*US* **cesium**) *n.* це́зий.

caesura /sɪˈzjʊərə/ *n.* (*pl.* **~s**) цезу́ра.

café /ˈkæfeɪ/, /ˈkæfɪ/ *n.* кафе́ (*indecl.*).

cafeteria /ˌkæfɪˈtɪərɪə/ *n.* кафете́рий.

caffeine /ˈkæfiːn/ *n.* кофеи́н.

c|aftan, k- /ˈkæftæn/ *n.* кафта́н.

cage /keɪdʒ/ *n.* (*for animals etc.*) кле́тка; (*of lift etc.*) каби́на.

● *v.t.* сажа́ть, посади́ть в кле́тку; **a ~d lion** лев в кле́тке.

cag(e)y /ˈkeɪdʒɪ/ *adj.* (**cagier, cagiest**) (*coll.*) скры́тный.

caginess /ˈkeɪdʒɪnɪs/ *n.* скры́тность.

cagoule /kəˈguːl/ *n.* кагу́ль (*m.*), водонепроница́емая ку́ртка.

cagy /ˈkeɪdʒɪ/ = **cag(e)y**

cahoots /kəˈhuːts/ *n.* (*sl.*): **in ~ with s.o.** в сго́воре с кем-н.

Cainozoic /ˌkaɪnəʊˈzəʊɪk/ *adj.* кайнозо́йский.

cairn /keən/ *n.* пирами́да из гру́бого ка́мня.

Cairo /ˈkaɪrəʊ/ *n.* Каи́р.

caisson /ˈkeɪs(ə)n/, /kəˈsuːn/ *n.*

(*ammunition chest*) заря́дный я́щик; (*underwater chamber*) кессо́н.

cajole /kəˈdʒəʊl/ *v.t.* обха́живать (*impf.*); уле|ща́ть, -сти́ть.

cajolery /kəˈdʒəʊlərɪ/ *n.* лесть; обха́живание.

cake /keɪk/ *n.* **1** (*sponge* **~**) кекс; **fruit ~** кекс с изю́мом; (*with cream*) торт; (*small fancy* **~**) пиро́жное; **~ shop** конди́терская. **2** (*flat piece*) брусо́к, пли́тка; **~ of soap** кусо́к мы́ла. **3** (*fig.*): **a piece of ~** (*coll.*) пустяко́вое де́ло; **they sell like hot ~s** э́то раскупа́ется нарасхва́т; **that takes the ~!** (*coll.*) да́льше е́хать не́куда!; **you can't have your ~ and eat it** оди́н пиро́г два ра́за не съешь.

● *v.t.*: **his shoes were ~d with mud** его́ боти́нки бы́ли облёплены гря́зью.

● *cpds.* **~-mix** *n.* порошо́к (*or* брике́т) для ке́кса, пу́динга *и m.n.*; **~-mixer** *n.* ми́ксер; **~-walk** *n.* (*dance*) кекуо́к; (*fig., easy task*) па́ра пустяко́в.

calabrese /ˌkæləˈbriːz/ *n.* спа́ржевая капу́ста.

calamitous /kəˈlæmɪtəs/ *adj.* бе́дственный, па́губный.

calamity /kəˈlæmɪtɪ/ *n.* бе́дствие.

calceolaria /ˌkælsɪəˈleərɪə/ *n.* (*bot.*) кошельки́ (*m. pl.*).

calcification /ˌkælsɪfɪˈkeɪʃ(ə)n/ *n.* обызвествле́ние.

calcify /ˈkælsɪˌfaɪ/ *v.t. & i.* обызвеств|ля́ть(ся), -и́ть(ся).

calcination /ˌkælsɪˈneɪʃ(ə)n/ *n.* кальцина́ция, о́бжиг, прока́ливание.

calcine /ˈkælsɪn/, /-saɪn/ *v.t. & i.* кальцини́ровать(ся) (*impf., pf.*); обж|ига́ть(ся), -е́чь(ся); прока́л|ивать(ся), -и́ть(ся).

calcite /ˈkælsaɪt/ *n.* (*min.*) кальци́т.

calcium /ˈkælsɪəm/ *n.* ка́льций; **~ chloride** хло́ристый ка́льций.

calculability /ˌkælkjʊləˈbɪlɪtɪ/ *n.* исчисли́мость.

calculable /ˈkælkjʊləb(ə)l/ *adj.* исчисли́мый.

calculat|e /ˈkælkjʊˌleɪt/ *v.t.* **1** (*compute*) вычисля́ть, вы́числить; рассчи́т|ывать, -а́ть; высчи́тывать, вы́считать; **he ~ed the date of the eclipse** он вы́числил день затме́ния; **a ~ing machine** счётная маши́на, арифмо́метр. **2** (*estimate*) рассчи́т|ывать, -а́ть; калькули́ровать, с-; **I ~ed that he would act in this way** я рассчи́тывал, что он посту́пит и́менно так. **3** (*plan*): **a ~ed insult** наме́ренное оскорбле́ние; **a ~ed risk** обду́манный риск. **4** (*past part.: intended*): **that is ~ed to offend him** э́то рассчи́тано на то, что́бы его́ оби́деть.

● *v.i.* (*rely*) рассчи́тывать (*impf.*) (на + *a.*); **we cannot ~e upon fine weather** мы не мо́жем рассчи́тывать на хоро́шую пого́ду.

calculating /ˈkælkjʊˌleɪtɪŋ/ *adj.* (*of person*) расчётливый, себе́ на уме́.

calculation /ˌkælkjʊˈleɪʃ(ə)n/ *n.* **1** (*mathematical*) вычисле́ние. **2** (*planning, forecast*) расчёт; **my ~s were at fault** мои́ расчёты оказа́лись оши́бочными. **3** (*estimate*) калькуля́ция.

calculator /ˈkælkjʊˌleɪtə(r)/ *n.* калькуля́тор.

calcu|lus /ˈkælkjʊləs/ *n.* (*math.*) (*pl.* **~luses**) исчисле́ние; (*med.*) (*pl.* **~li** /-ˌlaɪ/, /-ˌliː/) ка́мень (*m.*).

Calcutta /kælˈkʌtə/ *n.* Кальку́тта.

calendar /ˈkælɪndə(r)/ *n.* календа́рь; **~ month** календа́рный ме́сяц.

calender /ˈkælɪndə(r)/ *n.* (*machine*) кала́ндр.

● *v.t.* (*press cloth*) каландри́ровать (*impf.*); лощи́ть, на-.

calends /ˈkælendz/ (*also* **kalends**) *n.* (*hist.*) кале́нд|ы (*pl., g.* —).

calf¹ /kɑːf/ *n.* (*pl.* **calves**) **1** (*of cattle*) телёнок; **a cow in ~** сте́льная коро́ва; (*of seal, whale etc.*) детёныш. **2** (*leather*) теля́чья ко́жа; опо́ек; **bound in ~** переплетённый в теля́чью ко́жу.

● *cpds.* **~-love** *n.* ю́ношеское увлече́ние; **~skin** *n.* опо́ек; теля́чья ко́жа.

calf² /kɑːf/ *n.* (*pl.* **calves**) (*of leg*) икра́.

caliber /ˈkælɪbə(r)/ (*US*) = **calibre**

calibrate /ˈkælɪˌbreɪt/ *v.t.* калиброва́ть (*impf.*), градуи́ровать (*impf., pf.*).

calibration /ˌkælɪˈbreɪʃ(ə)n/ *n.* калибро́вка.

calibre /ˈkælɪbə(r)/ (*US* **caliber**) *n.* (*lit., fig.*) кали́бр.

calico /ˈkælɪˌkəʊ/ *n.* (*pl.* **~es** *or US also* **~s**) (*Br.*) митка́ль (*m.*); (*US*) си́тец.

California /ˌkælɪˈfɔːnɪə/ *n.* Калифо́рния.

Californian /ˌkælɪˈfɔːnɪən/ *n.* калифорни́|ец (*fem.* -йка).

● *adj.* калифорни́йский.

calipers /ˈkælɪpəz/ = **callipers**

caliph /ˈkeɪlɪf/, /ˈkæl-/ *n.* кали́ф, хали́ф.

caliphate /ˈkeɪlɪˌfeɪt/ *n.* халифа́т.

calisthenics /ˌkælɪsˈθenɪks/ (*US*) = **callisthenics**

calk /kɔːk/ (*US*) = **caulk**

call /kɔːl/ *n.* **1** (*cry, shout*) зов, о́клик; **I heard a ~ for help** я услы́шал крик о по́мощи; **they came at my ~** они́ пришли́ на мой зов. **2** (*of bird*) крик; (*of bugle*) зов, сигна́л. **3** (*message*): **telephone ~** вы́зов по телефо́ну; телефо́нный звоно́к; **he took the ~ in his study** он подошёл к телефо́ну в своём кабине́те. **4** (*visit*): **pay a ~** нан|оси́ть, -ести́ визи́т; **he returned my ~** он нанёс мне отве́тный визи́т; **port of ~** порт захо́да. **5** (*invitation, summons, demand*) зов, клич, призы́в; **the ~ of the sea** зов мо́ря; **the doctor is on ~** врач на вы́зове; **he answered his country's ~** он откли́кнулся на призы́в свое́й ро́дины; **I have many ~s on my time** у меня́ почти́ нет свобо́дного вре́мени. **6** (*need*): **there is no ~ for him to worry** ему́ не́чего волнова́ться. **7** (*at cards*) объявле́ние игры́.

● *v.t.* **1** (*name, designate*) наз|ыва́ть, -ва́ть; **he is ~ed John** его́ зову́т Джон; **he ~s himself a colonel** он называ́ет себя́ полко́вником; **~ s.o. names** об|зыва́ть, -озва́ть кого́-н.; **we have nothing we can ~ our own** у нас нет ничего́, что мы могли́ бы счита́ть свои́м; **I ~ that a shame** я счита́ю э́то посты́дным; **let's ~ it £5** сойдёмся на пяти́ фу́нтах; **~ a halt** объяв|ля́ть, -и́ть переры́в/остано́вку; **~ the roll** де́лать, с- перекли́чку; **~ a strike** приз|ыва́ть, -ва́ть к забасто́вке. **2** (*summon, arouse attention of*): **~ a doctor/taxi!** вы́зовите врача́/такси́!; **duty ~s** долг вели́т; **~ me at 6** разбуди́те меня́ в 6 часо́в; **(this is) London ~ing** говори́т Ло́ндон; *for sense 'telephone' see* ⇒**~ up.** **3** (*announce*): **the case is ~ed for Tuesday** слу́шание де́ла назна́чено на вто́рник; **~ a meeting** соз|ыва́ть, -ва́ть собра́ние. **4** (*var. idioms*): **~ into question** ста́вить, по- под сомне́ние; **~ to mind** вызыва́ть, вы́звать в па́мяти; **~ into being** вызыва́ть, вы́звать к жи́зни; **~ attention to** обра|ща́ть, -ти́ть (*чьё-н.*) внима́ние на + *a.*; **~ into play** прив|оди́ть, -ести́ в де́йствие; **~ to witness** приз|ыва́ть, -ва́ть в свиде́тели; **~ to order** приз|ыва́ть, -ва́ть к поря́дку.

● *v.i.* **1** (*cry, shout*) звать, по-; окл|ика́ть, -и́кнуть; **I heard someone ~** я слы́шал, как кто́-то позва́л; **I ~ed to him** я окли́кнул его́. **2** (*pay a visit*) за|ходи́ть, -йти́; **I ~ed on him** я зашёл к нему́; **the ship ~ed at Naples** парохо́д зашёл в Неа́поль; **the train ~s at every station** по́езд остана́вливается на ка́ждой ста́нции; **the butcher ~ed** мясни́к заходи́л. **3**: **~ for** (*pick up*): **I ~ed for him at 6** я зашёл за ним в 6 часо́в; **to be ~ed for** до востре́бования; (*demand*): **the situation ~s for courage** обстоя́тельства тре́буют му́жества; **they ~ed for his resignation** они́ тре́бовали его́ отста́вки. **4**: **~ on, upon** (*require*): **I ~ on you to keep your promise** я призыва́ю вас сдержа́ть своё обеща́ние; (*appeal to*): **I ~ed on him for help** я призва́л его́ на по́мощь; (*invite*) предл|ага́ть, -ожи́ть (*что кому*); **I ~ on Mr. Grey to speak** я предоставля́ю сло́во г-ну Гре́ю; **I feel ~ed on to reply** я чу́вствую, что до́лжен отве́тить.

● *with advs.*: **~ away** *v.t.* от|зыва́ть, -озва́ть; **~ back** *v.t. & i.* (*answer*) откл|ика́ться, -и́кнуться (на + *a.*); (*on telephone*) позвони́ть (*pf.*) сно́ва (+ *d.*); перезв|а́нивать, -они́ть; **~ down** *v.t.*: **~ down curses on s.o.'s head** приз|ыва́ть, -ва́ть прокля́тия на чью-н. го́лову; **~ forth** *v.t.* (*lit., fig.*) вызыва́ть, вы́звать; **~ in** *v.t.* (*books*) тре́бовать, за- наза́д; (*currency*) из|ыма́ть, -ъя́ть из обраще́ния; (*a specialist*) вызыва́ть, вы́звать; **~ off** *v.t.* (*e.g. a dog*) от|зыва́ть, -озва́ть; (*cancel*) отмен|я́ть, -и́ть; **~ out** *v.t.* (*announce*) выклика́ть, вы́кликнуть; (*summon away*) от|зыва́ть, -озва́ть; (*workers, on strike*) приз|ыва́ть, -ва́ть (к + *d.*); (*doctor*) вызыва́ть, вы́звать; (*to a duel*) вызыва́ть, вы́звать; *v.i.* выклика́ть, вы́кликнуть;

выкри́кивать, вы́крикнуть; **~ over** *v.t.* (*summon*): **I ~ ed him over** я подозва́л его́; **~ up** *v.t.* (*telephone*) звони́ть, по- (*кому*) по телефо́ну; (*evoke*) вызыва́ть, вы́звать; (*for mil. service*) приз|ыва́ть, -ва́ть.

● *cpds.* **~-box** *n.* (*Br.*) телефо́нная бу́дка; **~-boy** *n.* ма́льчик, вызыва́ющий актёров на сце́ну; **~-girl** *n.* проститу́тка, приходя́щая по вы́зову; **~-sign** *n.* (*radio*) позывно́й (сигна́л); **~up** *n.* (*mil.*) призы́в.

calla /ˈkælə/ *n.*: **~ lily** (*US*) ка́лла.

caller /ˈkɔːlə(r)/ *n.* (*visitor*) посети́тель (*fem.* -ница); (*telephone*) позвони́вший (по телефо́ну).

calligrapher /kəˈlɪgrəfə(r)/ *n.* каллигра́ф.

calligraphic /ˌkælɪˈgræfɪk/ *adj.* каллиграфи́ческий.

calligraphy /kəˈlɪgrəfɪ/ *n.* каллигра́фия.

calling /ˈkɔːlɪŋ/ *n.* (*summoning*) созы́в; (*profession, occupation*) призва́ние; **~ card** (*US*) визи́тная ка́рточка.

callipers /ˈkælɪpəz/ *n.* (*math.*) кронци́ркуль.

callisthenics /ˌkælɪsˈθenɪks/ (*US* **calisthenics**) *n.* ритми́ческая гимна́стика, ри́тмика; пласти́ческая гимна́стика.

callous /ˈkæləs/ *n.* = **callus**

● *adj.* (*of skin*) огрубе́лый, мозо́листый; (*fig.*) чёрствый.

callousness /ˈkæləsnɪs/ *n.* чёрствость.

callow /ˈkæləʊ/ *adj.* (*unfledged*; *also fig.*) неопери́вшийся.

callus /ˈkæləs/ *n.* ко́стная мозо́ль.

calm /kɑːm/ *n.* споко́йствие, тишина́; **a dead ~** мёртвая тишина́; (*at sea*) штиль (*m.*), безве́трие.

● *adj.* споко́йный.

● *v.t.* & *i.* (*also* **calm down**) успок|а́ивать(ся), -о́ить(ся).

calmness /ˈkɑːmnɪs/ *n.* споко́йствие, тишина́, поко́й.

caloric /ˈkælərɪk/ *adj.* (*US*) теплово́й, терми́ческий.

calorie /ˈkælərɪ/ *n.* кало́рия.

calorific /ˌkæləˈrɪfɪk/ *adj.* (*Br.*) теплово́й, теплотво́рный; калори́йный; **~ value** теплотво́рная спосо́бность; калори́йность.

calorimeter /ˌkæləˈrɪmɪtə(r)/ *n.* калори́метр.

calque /kælk/ *n.* (*ling.*) ка́лька.

calumniate /kəˈlʌmnɪˌeɪt/ *v.t.* клевета́ть, на- на + *a.*; оклевета́ть (*pf.*).

calumniator /kəˈlʌmnɪˌeɪtə(r)/ *n.* клеветни́к.

calumnious /kəˈlʌmnɪəs/ *adj.* клеветни́ческий.

calumny /ˈkæləmnɪ/ *n.* клевета́.

Calvary /ˈkælvərɪ/ *n.* (*place*) Голго́фа.

calve /kɑːv/ *v.i.* тели́ться, о-.

calves /kɑːvz/ *pl. of* ⇨**calf**[1], **calf**[2]

Calvinism /ˈkælvɪˌnɪz(ə)m/ *n.* кальвини́зм.

Calvinist /ˈkælvɪˌnɪst/ *n.* кальвини́ст.

Calvinistic /ˌkælvɪˈnɪstɪk/ *adj.* кальвини́стский.

calyces /ˈkeɪlɪˌsiːz/, /ˈkæ-/ *pl. of* ⇨**calyx**

calypso /kəˈlɪpsəʊ/ *n.* (*pl.* **~s**) кали́псо (*indecl.*).

caly|x /ˈkeɪlɪks/, /ˈkæl-/ *n.* (*pl.* **~ces** *or* **~xes**) (*bot.*) ча́шечка; (*anat.*) чашеви́дная по́лость.

cam /kæm/ *n.* (*tech.*) кулачо́к, копи́р, па́лец.

● *cpd.* **~shaft** *n.* кулачко́вый вал.

camaraderie /ˌkæməˈrɑːdərɪ/ *n.* това́рищеские отноше́ния.

camber /ˈkæmbə(r)/ *n.* вы́пуклость; (*of road*) попере́чный укло́н.

● *v.t.* & *i.* выгиба́ть(ся), вы́гнуть(ся).

Cambodia /kæmˈbəʊdɪə/ *n.* Камбо́джа.

Cambodian /kæmˈbəʊdɪən/ *n.* (*person*) камбоджи́|ец (*fem.* -йка).

● *adj.* камбоджи́йский.

Cambrian /ˈkæmbrɪən/ *adj.* кембри́йский.

cambric /ˈkæmbrɪk/ *n.* бати́ст.

Cambridge /ˈkeɪmbrɪdʒ/ *n.* Ке́мбридж; (*attr.*) ке́мбриджский.

camcorder /ˈkæmˌkɔːdə(r)/ *n.* камко́рдер.

came /keɪm/ *past of* ⇨**come**

camel /ˈkæm(ə)l/ *n.* верблю́д; **Arabian ~** дромаде́р, одного́рбый верблю́д; **Bactrian ~** бактриа́н, двуго́рбый верблю́д; **the last straw breaks the ~'s back** после́дняя ка́пля переполня́ет ча́шу.

● *cpds.* **~-driver** *n.* пого́нщик верблю́дов; **~-hair** *adj.*: **~-hair coat** пальто́ из верблю́жьей ше́рсти.

camel(l)ia /kəˈmiːlɪə/ *n.* каме́лия.

cameo /ˈkæmɪˌəʊ/ *n.* (*pl.* **~s**) каме́я; (*fig.*) скетч, эссе́ (*indecl.*), винье́тка; **~ role** эпизоди́ческая роль.

camera /ˈkæmrə/, /-ərə/ *n.* **1** (*phot.*) фотоаппара́т. **2**: **in ~** (*leg.*) при закры́тых дверя́х.

● *cpd.* **~man** *n.* (*cin.*) (кино)опера́тор; (*TV*) (теле)опера́тор.

camomile /ˈkæməˌmaɪl/ *n.* рома́шка.

camouflage /ˈkæməˌflɑːʒ/ *n.* камуфля́ж; (*also fig.*) маскиро́вка.

● *v.t.* (*lit., fig.*) маскирова́ть, за-.

camp[1] /kæmp/ *n.* ла́герь (*m.*; *pl. in mil. etc. sense* лагеря́, *in pol. sense* ла́гери); бива́к; **pitch ~** расположи́ться/стать (*both pf.*) ла́герем; **break, strike ~** сн|има́ться, -я́ться с ла́геря; **he has a foot in both ~s** ≈ он слу́жит и на́шим и ва́шим.

● *v.i.* разб|ива́ть, -и́ть ла́герь; распол|ага́ться, -ожи́ться ла́герем; **go ~ing** отпр|авля́ться, -а́виться в (туристи́ческий) похо́д; жить (*impf.*) в пала́тках; **~ out** спать (*impf.*) на откры́том во́здухе; **~(ing) site** ке́мпинг, турба́за.

● *cpds.* **~-bed** *n.* (*Br.*) похо́дная крова́ть, раскладу́шка; **~-chair, ~-stool** *nn.* складно́й стул; **~-fire** *n.* бива́чный костёр.

camp[2] /kæmp/ *n.* (*coll., affected behaviour*) аффекта́ция, мане́рность, кэмп.

● *adj.* аффекти́рованный, мане́рный; (*effeminate*) женоподо́бный.

● *v.t.*: **~ up** переигр|ывать, -а́ть.

campaign /kæmˈpeɪn/ *n.* похо́д; (*lit., fig.*) кампа́ния.

● *v.i.* уча́ствовать (*impf.*) в похо́де; (*fig.*) вести́ (*det.*) кампа́нию.

campaigner /kæmˈpeɪnə(r)/ *n.* уча́стник кампа́нии; боре́ц; **old ~** ста́рый вoя́ка; **peace ~** боре́ц за мир.

campanile /ˌkæmpəˈniːlɪ/ *n.* колоко́льня.

campanologist /ˌkæmpəˈnɒlədʒɪst/ *n.* звона́рь (*m.*).

campanula /kæmˈpænjʊlə/ *n.* (*bot.*) колоко́льчик.

camper /ˈkæmpə(r)/ *n.* (*person*) ночу́ющий на откры́том во́здухе; тури́ст, живу́щий в пала́тке; (*vehicle*) жило́й/тури́стский автоприце́п.

camphor /ˈkæmfə(r)/ *n.* камфара́.

camphorate /ˈkæmfəˌreɪt/ *v.t.*: **~d oil** камфа́рное ма́сло.

camping /ˈkæmpɪŋ/ *n.* ке́мпинг.

● *cpd.* **~-ground** *n.* террито́рия ке́мпинга.

Campuchea /ˌkæmpʊˈtʃɪə/ *n.* Кампучи́я.

campus /ˈkæmpəs/ *n.* (*pl.* **~es**) университе́тский городо́к; (*attr.*) университе́тский, студе́нческий.

can[1] /kæn/ *n.* **1** (*for liquids*) бидо́н; **milk-~** моло́чный бидо́н. **2** (*for food etc.*) (консе́рвная) ба́нка; **a ~ of beer/peaches** ба́нка пи́ва/пе́рсиков. **3**: **carry the ~** (*Br. sl.*) отдува́ться (*impf.*) (*за кого/что*); **open a ~ of worms** навл|ека́ть, -е́чь на себя́ ку́чу неприя́тностей.

● *v.t.* (**canned, canning**) консерви́ровать (*impf., pf.*); **~ned food** консе́рв|ы (*pl., g.* -ов); **~ned vegetables** овощны́е консе́рвы; **~ned music** му́зыка в за́писи, фонogра́мма.

● *cpd.* **~-opener** *n.* консе́рвный ключ/нож.

can[2] /kæn/ *v.i.* (*3rd pers. sing. pres.* **can;** *past* **could**) (*expr. ability or permission*) мочь (*impf.*); (*expr. capability*) уме́ть (*impf.*); **I ~ speak French** я уме́ю говори́ть по-францу́зски; **I ~ see him** я ви́жу его́; **I ~ understand that** я понима́ю (*or* могу́ поня́ть) э́то; **I could have laughed for joy** я гото́в был смея́ться от ра́дости; **I ~not but feel that** ... я не могу́ не чу́вствовать, что...; **one ~ hardly blame him** едва́ ли мо́жно вини́ть его́; **~ it be true?** неуже́ли э́то пра́вда?; **he is as happy as ~ be** он абсолю́тно сча́стлив; **as soon as you ~** как то́лько смо́жете; как мо́жно скоре́е; **we ~ but try** мо́жно всё-таки попыта́ться; **he ~ be very trying** он мо́жет доня́ть кого́ уго́дно.

Canada /ˈkænədə/ *n.* Кана́да.

Canadian /kə'neɪdɪən/ *n.* (*person*) канáд|ец (*fem.* -ка).

● *adj.* канáдский.

canal /kə'næl/ *n.* **1** (*channel through land*) канáл; **~ boat** сýдно для канáлов. **2** (*anat.*) канáл, прохóд; **alimentary ~** пищеварúтельный тракт.

canalization /ˌkænəlaɪ'zeɪʃ(ə)n/ *n.* сооружéние канáлов.

canalize /'kænəˌlaɪz/ *v.t.* напр|авлять, -áвить (*реку*) в канáлы; (*fig.*) напр|авлять, -áвить по определённому рýслу.

canapé /'kænəpɪ/, /-ˌpeɪ/ *n.* канапé (*nt. indecl.*); лóмтик поджáренного хлéба с холóдным мя́сом *и т.д.*; закýска.

canard /kə'nɑːd/, /'kænɑːd/ *n.* лóжный слух, (газéтная) ýтка.

canary /kə'neərɪ/ *n.* канарéйка; **C~ Islands** Канáрские островá.

● *cpd.* **~-yellow** *n.* канарéечный цвет.

Canberra /'kænbərə/ *n.* Канбéрра.

cancan /'kænkæn/ *n.* канкáн.

cancel /'kæns(ə)l/ *n.* (*cancelling*) отмéна; (*on postage stamps*) погашéние.

● *v.t.* (**cancelled, cancelling;** *US also* **canceled, canceling**) **1** (*cross out*) вычёркивать, вычеркнуть. **2** (*countermand*) отмен|я́ть, -úть; аннулúровать (*impf., pf.*). **3** (*nullify*) св|одúть, -естú на нет.

● *v.i.*: **these items ~ out** э́ти пýнкты свóдят друг дрýга на нет.

cancellation /ˌkænsə'leɪʃ(ə)n/ *n.* отмéна, аннулúрование; погашéние; вычёркивание.

cancer /'kænsə(r)/ *n.* **1** (*astron.*) Рак; **Tropic of C~** трóпик Рáка. **2** (*med.*) рак. **3** (*fig.*) я́зва.

cancerous /'kænsərəs/ *adj.* (*med.*) рáковый; (*fig.*) разъедáющий.

candelabr|a /ˌkændɪ'lɑːbrə/ (*also* **-um**) /ˌkændɪ'lɑːbrəm/ *n.* (*pl.* **~a** *or* **~as;** *US also* **~ums**) канделя́бр.

candid /'kændɪd/ *adj.* (*frank*) úскренний, откровéнный; (*unbiased*) беспристрáстный.

candidacy /'kændɪdəsɪ/ *n.* кандидатýра.

candidate /'kændɪdət/, /-ˌdeɪt/ *n.* кандидáт.

candidature /'kændɪdətjə(r)/ *n.* (*Br.*) кандидатýра.

candle /'kænd(ə)l/ *n.* свечá; **the game is not worth the ~** игрá не стóит свеч; **burn the ~ at both ends** ≈ трудúться (*impf.*) от зарú до зарú; **she is not fit to hold a ~ to him** онá емý в подмётки не годúтся.

● *cpds.* **~-light** *n.* свет свечú/свечéй; свечнóе освещéние; **~-power** *n.* (*elec.*) сúла свéта в свечáх; **~stick** *n.* подсвéчник.

Candlemas /'kænd(ə)lməs/, /-ˌmæs/ *n.* Срéтение (Госпóдне).

candour /'kændə(r)/ (*US* **candor**) *n.* откровéнность, úскренность; беспристрáстность.

candy /'kændɪ/ *n.* (*Br.*) леденцы́ (*m. pl.*), карамéль; (*US*) конфéты, слáсти (*f. pl.*); **~ store** (*US*) кондúтерская; **piece of ~** (*US*) конфéта.

● *v.t.*: **candied fruit(s)** засáхаренные фрýкты.

candyfloss /'kændɪˌflɒs/ *n.* (*Br.*) сáхарная вáта.

cane /keɪn/ *n.* **1** (*bot.*) камы́ш, тростни́к; **~ chair** плетёное крéсло, плетёный стул. **2** (*walking-stick*) трость, пáлка. **3** (*for punishment*) рóзга; **the boy got the ~** мáльчика наказáли рóзгой.

● *v.t.* **1**: **~ a chair** плестú, с- крéсло из камышá. **2**: **~ a pupil** накáз|ывать, -áть ученикá рóзгой.

● *cpd.* **~-sugar** *n.* тростникóвый сáхар.

canine /'keɪnaɪn/, /'kæn-/ *adj.* собáчий; **~ tooth** клык.

caning /'keɪnɪŋ/ *n.* (*punishment*) наказáние рóзгой.

canister /'kænɪstə(r)/ *n.* бáнка, корóбка.

● *cpd.* **~-shot** *n.* картéчь.

canker /'kæŋkə(r)/ *n.* (*US, med.*) я́зва; (*fig.*) я́зва; (*agric.*) рак растéний; некрóз плодóвых дерéвьев.

● *cpd.* **~-worm** *n.* плодóвый червь.

cankerous /'kæŋkərəs/ *adj.* разъедáющий.

cannabis /'kænəbɪs/ *n.* гаши́ш.

cannery /'kænərɪ/ *n.* консéрвный завóд.

cannibal /'kænɪb(ə)l/ *n.* каннибáл, людоéд.

● *adj.* каннибáльский, людоéдский.

cannibalism /'kænɪbəˌlɪz(ə)m/ *n.* каннибали́зм, людоéдство.

cannibalistic /ˌkænɪbə'lɪstɪk/ *adj.* каннибáльский, людоéдский.

cannibalize /'kænɪbəˌlaɪz/ *v.t.* (*mil. etc.*): **~ a car** сн|имáть, -ять гóдные детáли с неисправной маши́ны; «разд|евáть, -éть».

canniness /'kænɪnɪs/ *n.* хи́трость, осторóжность.

canning /'kænɪŋ/ *n.* консерви́рование.

● *cpd.* **~-factory** *n.* консéрвный завóд.

cannon /'kænən/ *n.* **1** (*pl. usu.* **~**) (*gun*) пýшка, орýдие. **2** (*artillery*) артиллéрия. **3** (*Br., at billiards: also US* **carom**) карамбóль (*m.*).

● *v.i.* (*Br.*) (*collide*) ст|áлкиваться, -олкнýться; (*at billiards*) сдéлать (*pf.*) карамбóль.

● *cpds.* **~-ball** *n.* пýшечное ядрó; **~-fodder** *n.* пýшечное мя́со.

cannonade /ˌkænə'neɪd/ *n.* канонáда, орýдийный огóнь.

canny /'kænɪ/ *adj.* (**cannier, canniest**) (*shrewd, cautious*) хи́трый, осторóжный.

canoe /kə'nuː/ *n.* канóэ (*nt. indecl.*), челнóк; **paddle one's own ~** (*fig.*) идтú (*det.*) свои́м путём.

● *v.i.* (**canoes, canoed, canoeing**) плыть (*det.*) в челнокé (*or* на канóэ).

canoeist /kə'nuːɪst/ *n.* канои́ст.

canon /'kænən/ *n.* **1** (*church decree*) канóн; **~ law** канони́ческое прáво. **2** (*criterion*) прáвило. **3** (*body of writings*) канóн. **4** (*list of saints*) святцы (*pl., g.* -ев). **5** (*priest*) канóник. **6** (*mus.*) канóн.

canonical /kə'nɒnɪk(ə)l/ *adj.* канони́ческий.

canonicity /ˌkænə'nɪsɪtɪ/ *n.* канони́чность.

canonist /'kænənɪst/ *n.* канони́ст.

canonization /kænəˌnaɪ'zeɪʃ(ə)n/ *n.* канонизáция.

canonize /'kænəˌnaɪz/ *v.t.* (*recognize as a saint*) канонизи́ровать (*impf., pf.*).

canonry /'kænənrɪ/ *n.* дóлжность канóника.

canoodle /kə'nuːd(ə)l/ *v.t.* (*coll.*) нéжничать (*impf.*).

canopy /'kænəpɪ/ *n.* **1** (*covering over bed etc.*) балдахи́н, пóлог. **2** (*of parachute*) кýпол. **3** (*fig.*) пóлог, покрóв.

cant¹ /kænt/ *n.* (*insincere talk*) хáнжество; (*jargon*): **thieves' ~** воровскóй жаргóн; блатнáя мýзыка.

● *v.i.* лицемéрить (*impf.*), ханжи́ть (*impf.*); **a ~ing hypocrite** лицемéр и ханжá.

cant² /kænt/ *v.t.* (*incline, tilt*) наклон|я́ть, -и́ть.

● *v.i.* наклон|я́ться, -и́ться.

cantabile /kæn'tɑːbɪlɪ/ *adv.* (*mus.*) кантáбиле.

cantaloup(e) /'kæntəˌluːp/ *n.* канталýпа; (мýскусная) ды́ня.

cantankerous /kæn'tæŋkərəs/ *adj.* сварли́вый.

cantankerousness /kæn'tæŋkərəsnɪs/ *n.* сварли́вость.

cantata /kæn'tɑːtə/ *n.* кантáта.

canteen /kæn'tiːn/ *n.* **1** (*eating-place*) столóвая. **2** (*water-container*) фля́га. **3** (*Br., case of cutlery*) (похóдный) я́щик со столóвыми принадлéжностями.

canter /'kæntə(r)/ *n.* лёгкий галóп.

● *v.i.* éхать (*impf.*) лёгким галóпом.

canticle /'kæntɪk(ə)l/ *n.* песнь, гимн, кант.

cantilever /'kæntɪˌliːvə(r)/ *n.* консóль, кронштéйн, укóсина; **~ bridge** консóльный мост.

canto /'kæntəʊ/ *n.* (*pl.* **~s**) песнь.

canton /'kæntɒn/ *n.* **1** (*Swiss etc.*) кантóн. **2** (*in shield or flag*) прáвый вéрхний ýгол.

cantonal /'kæntən(ə)l/, /kæn'tɒn(ə)l/ *adj.* кантонáльный.

Cantonese /ˌkæntə'niːz/ *n.* (*dialect*) кантóнский диалéкт (китáйского языкá).

cantonment /kæn'tuːnmənt/ *n.* (*mil., station*) лáгерь (*m.*), воéнный городóк.

cantor /'kæntɔː(r)/ *n.* (*choir-leader*) рéгент (хóра); (*in synagogue*) кáнтор.

canvas /'kænvəs/ *n.* **1** (*cloth*) холст; паруси́на, брезéнт; **under ~** (*in camp*) в палáтках; (*with sails spread*) под парусáми. **2** (*for painting*) холст. **3** (*fig., picture*) полотнó, холст. **4** (*attr.*) холщóвый; брезéнтовый, паруси́новый; **a ~ bag** холщóвый мешóк.

canvass /ˈkænvəs/ *n.* (*for votes*) предвы́борная агита́ция.

● *v.t. & i.*: ~ **a constituency** вести́ (*det.*) предвы́борную агита́цию в избира́тельном о́круге; ~ **opinions** соб|ира́ть, -ра́ть мне́ния.

canvasser /ˈkænvəsə(r)/ *n.* агита́тор.

canyon /ˈkænjən/ *n.* каньо́н; глубо́кое уще́лье.

caoutchouc /ˈkaʊtʃʊk/ *n.* каучу́к.

CAP (*abbr. of* ***Common Agricultural Policy***) О́бщая сельскохозя́йственная поли́тика.

cap /kæp/ *n.* **1** (*worker's*) ке́пка; (*of uniform, incl. school*) фура́жка; (*without peak*) ша́пка; **dunce's** ~ дура́цкий колпа́к; **fool's** ~ шутовско́й колпа́к; (*lady's, servant's or nurse's*) чепе́ц; (*baby's*) че́пчик. **2** (*of mountain*) верши́на, верху́шка. **3** (*of bottle*) кры́шка; (*of pen*) колпачо́к; **percussion** ~ писто́н, ка́псюль (*m.*). **4** (*Br., contraceptive device*) колпачо́к. **5** (*fig.*): **he came to us** ~ **in hand** он яви́лся к нам со смире́нным ви́дом; **if the** ~ **fits, wear it** принима́йте э́то на свой счёт, е́сли хоти́те; ≈ на во́ре ша́пка гори́т; **he put on his thinking** ~ он заду́мался.

● *v.t.* (**capped, capping**) **1** (*cover, seal*) закр|ыва́ть, -ы́ть. **2** (*excel*) прев|осходи́ть, -зойти́; (*a joke etc.*) перещеголя́ть (*pf.*); **to** ~ **our misfortunes** в доверше́ние на́ших злоключе́ний. **3**: **mountains** ~**ped with snow** го́ры уве́нчаны снегово́й ша́пкой. **4** (*Br., sport*) прин|има́ть, -я́ть в соста́в кома́нды.

capability /ˌkeɪpəˈbɪlɪtɪ/ *n.* спосо́бность, возмо́жность.

capable /ˈkeɪpəb(ə)l/ *adj.* **1** (*gifted*) спосо́бный. **2** (~ *of*) спосо́бный на + *a.*; **he is** ~ **of telling lies** он спосо́бен солга́ть. **3** (*susceptible*) поддаю́щийся; **the situation is** ~ **of improvement** положе́ние мо́жно испра́вить.

capacious /kəˈpeɪʃəs/ *adj.* просто́рный.

capaciousness /kəˈpeɪʃəsnɪs/ *n.* просто́рность.

capacity /kəˈpæsɪtɪ/ *n.* **1** (*ability to hold*) вмести́мость; **measure of** ~ ме́ра объёма; **the hall's seating** ~ **is 500** вмести́мость за́ла — пятьсо́т мест; **the room was filled to** ~ ко́мната была́ запо́лнена до отка́за; **play to** ~ (*theatr.*) де́лать (*impf.*) по́лные сбо́ры. **2** (*of engine*) (наибо́льшая) мо́щность, нагру́зка; (*of ship*) вмести́мость; **to work at, to** ~ рабо́тать (*impf.*) в по́лную си́лу. **3** (*fig.*): **he has little** ~ **for happiness** он не со́здан для сча́стья. **4** (*position, character*): **in my** ~ **as critic** как кри́тик; в ро́ли/ка́честве кри́тика; **I have come in the** ~ **of a friend** я пришёл как друг; **legal** ~ правоспосо́бность. **5** (*elec.*) электри́ческая ёмкость.

caparison /kəˈpærɪs(ə)n/ *n.* попо́на, чепра́к.

● *v.t.* покр|ыва́ть, -ы́ть попо́ной/чепрако́м.

cape[1] /keɪp/ *n.* (*garment*) наки́дка, плащ.

cape[2] /keɪp/ (*geog.*) мыс; **the C**~ **(of Good Hope)** мыс До́брой Наде́жды.

caper[1] /ˈkeɪpə(r)/ *n.* (*pl., cul.*) ка́персы (*m. pl.*).

caper[2] /ˈkeɪpə(r)/ *n.* (*leap*) прыжо́к.

● *v.i.* (*also* **cut** ~**s**) скака́ть (*impf.*).

capercail|lie /ˌkæpəˈkeɪlɪ/, **-zie** /ˌkæpəˈkeɪlzɪ/ *nn.* глуха́рь (*m.*).

capillary /kəˈpɪlərɪ/ *adj.* капилля́рный; ~ **action** капилля́рное притяже́ние, капилля́рность.

capital /ˈkæpɪt(ə)l/ *n.* **1** (*principal city*) столи́ца; (*attr.*) столи́чный. **2** (*upper-case letter*) прописна́я/загла́вная бу́ква; **block** ~**s** прописны́е печа́тные бу́квы; **small** ~**s** капите́ль. **3** (*wealth*) капита́л; **circulating** ~ оборо́тный капита́л; **fixed** ~ основно́й капита́л; **loan** ~ ссу́дный капита́л; **paid-up** ~ опла́ченный акционе́рный капита́л; ~ **and interest** основна́я су́мма и наро́сшие проце́нты. **4** (*fig., advantage*) вы́игрыш, капита́л; **he made** ~ **out of our mistakes** он нажи́лся на на́ших оши́бках. **5** (*employers*) капита́л; ~ **and labour** (*Br.*), **labor** (*US*) труд и капита́л. **6** (*archit.*) капите́ль.

● *adj.* **1** (*major*) гла́вный, основно́й. **2** (*excellent*) капита́льный, превосхо́дный. **3** (*involving death penalty*): **a** ~ **offence** (*Br.*), **offense** (*US*) преступле́ние, кара́емое сме́ртью; ~ **punishment** сме́ртная казнь. **4** (*econ.*): ~ **goods** сре́дства произво́дства; ~ **expenditure** капита́льные затра́ты; ~ **assets** основны́е сре́дства; ~ **gains tax** нало́г на дохо́ды от приро́ста капита́ла. **5** (*upper-case*) прописно́й, загла́вный, большо́й.

capitalism /ˈkæpɪtəˌlɪz(ə)m/ *n.* капитали́зм.

capitalist /ˈkæpɪtəlɪst/ *n.* капитали́ст.

capitalistic /ˌkæpɪtəˈlɪstɪk/ *adj.* капиталисти́ческий.

capitalization /ˌkæpɪtəlaɪˈzeɪʃ(ə)n/ *n.* **1** (*writing with capital letter*) письмо́ прописны́ми бу́квами; заме́на строчны́х букв прописны́ми. **2** (*econ.*) капитализа́ция.

capitalize /ˈkæpɪtəˌlaɪz/ *v.t. & i.* **1** (*write with capital letter*) писа́ть, на- прописны́ми бу́квами. **2** (*econ.*) капитализи́ровать (*impf., pf.*). **3** (*fig.*) наж|ива́ться, -и́ться; ~ **on s.o.'s misfortune** извл|ека́ть, -е́чь вы́году из чьего́-н. несча́стья.

capitation /ˌkæpɪˈteɪʃ(ə)n/ *n.* поголо́вное исчисле́ние; ~ **grant** о́тпуск де́нежных сумм по числу́ люде́й.

capitulate /kəˈpɪtjʊˌleɪt/ *v.t.* капитули́ровать (*impf., pf.*).

capitulation /kəˌpɪtjʊˈleɪʃ(ə)n/ *n.* (*surrender*) капитуля́ция.

capon /ˈkeɪpən/ *n.* каплу́н.

cappuccino /ˌkæpʊˈtʃiːnəʊ/ *n.* (*pl.* ~**s**) ко́фе (*m. indecl.*) «капучи́н».

capriccio /kəˈprɪtʃɪəʊ/ *n.* (*pl.* ~**s**) капри́чч(и)о (*indecl.*).

caprice /kəˈpriːs/ *n.* при́хоть, капри́з, причу́да.

capricious /kəˈprɪʃəs/ *adj.* прихотли́вый, капри́зный.

capriciousness /kəˈprɪʃəsnɪs/ *n.* непостоя́нство; капри́зность.

Capricorn /ˈkæprɪˌkɔːn/ *n.* Козеро́г; **Tropic of** ~ тро́пик Козеро́га.

capsicum /ˈkæpsɪkəm/ *n.* стручко́вый пе́рец.

capsize /kæpˈsaɪz/ *v.t. & i.* опроки́|дывать(ся), -нуть(ся).

capstan /ˈkæpst(ə)n/ *n.* кабеста́н.

capsule /ˈkæpsjuːl/ *n.* **1** (*bot.*) семенна́я коро́бочка. **2** (*med.*) ка́псула. **3** (*metal cap*) кры́шка, колпачо́к. **4** (*for space travel*) ка́псула, отсе́к. **5** (*fig.*): ~ **biography** кра́ткая биогра́фия.

Capt. /ˈkæptɪn/ *n.* (*abbr. of* ***Captain***) кап. (капита́н).

captain /ˈkæptɪn/ *n.* **1** (*leader*) руководи́тель (*m.*); ~ **of industry** промы́шленный магна́т; (*head of team*) капита́н кома́нды. **2** (*army rank*) капита́н. **3** (*naval rank*) капита́н пе́рвого ра́нга; команди́р корабля́.

● *v.i.* руководи́ть (*impf.*); вести́ (*det.*); быть капита́ном + *g.*

captaincy /ˈkæptɪnsɪ/ *n.* зва́ние/до́лжность капита́на.

caption /ˈkæpʃ(ə)n/ *n.* (*title, words accompanying picture*) по́дпись к карти́нке; (*film subtitle*) титр.

captious /ˈkæpʃəs/ *adj.* приди́рчивый.

captiousness /ˈkæpʃəsnɪs/ *n.* приди́рчивость.

captivate /ˈkæptɪˌveɪt/ *v.t.* плен|я́ть, -и́ть; очаро́в|ывать, -а́ть.

captivating /ˈkæptɪˌveɪtɪŋ/ *adj.* плени́тельный, чару́ющий.

captive /ˈkæptɪv/ *n.* пле́нник, пле́нный; **take** ~ брать, взять в плен; **hold** ~ держа́ть (*impf.*) в плену́.

● *adj.* пле́нный; ~ **audience** слу́шатели (*m. pl.*) понево́ле.

captivity /kæpˈtɪvɪtɪ/ *n.* плен, плене́ние.

captor /ˈkæptə(r)/, /-tɔː(r)/ *n.* захвати́вший в плен; взя́вший приз.

capture /ˈkæptʃə(r)/ *n.* (*action*) пои́мка, захва́т; (*thing* ~**d**) добы́ча.

● *v.t.* брать, взять в плен; захва́т|ывать, -и́ть; ~ **s.o.'s attention** прико́в|ывать, -а́ть чьё-н. внима́ние.

Capuchin /ˈkæpjuːtʃɪn/ *n.* (*friar; monkey*) капуци́н.

capybara /ˌkæpɪˈbɑːrə/ *n.* водосви́нка.

car /kɑː(r)/ *n.* **1** (*motor vehicle*) (легково́й) автомоби́ль, маши́на; ~ **boot sale** (*Br.*) прода́жа (пря́мо) из бага́жника; ~ **pool** автоба́за предприя́тия (*or* учрежде́ния). **2** (*rail vehicle*) ваго́н; **dining-**~ ваго́н-рестора́н; **sleeping-**~ спа́льный ваго́н; **Pullman** ~ пу́льмановский ваго́н.

● *cpds.* ~ **coat** *n.* полупальто́ (*indecl.*); ~**-driver** *n.* шофёр; ~**-ferry** *n.*

автопаро́м; **~-hire** *n.* прока́т автомоби́лей; **~-park** *n.* (*Br.*) па́ркинг, автостоя́нка; **~phone** *n.* автотелефо́н; **~-port** *n.* наве́с для автомоби́ля; **~-race** *n.* автого́нка; **~-sick** *adj.*: **he was ~-sick** его́ укача́ло в маши́не.

caracul, karakul /ˈkærəˌkʊl/ *n.* кара́куль (*m.*).

carafe /kəˈræf/, /-rɑːf/ *n.* графи́н.

caramel /ˈkærəˌmel/ *n.* (*burnt sugar*) караме́ль; (*sweetmeat*) караме́ль, караме́лька.

● *adj.* (*~-coloured*) све́тло-кори́чневый.

carapace /ˈkærəˌpeɪs/ *n.* щито́к (*черепахи и т.п.*).

carat /ˈkærət/ (*US also* **karat**) *n.* кара́т.

caravan /ˈkærəˌvæn/ *n.* (*group travelling together*) карава́н; (*Gypsy's*) фурго́н, кры́тая теле́га; (*Br., trailer*) жило́й/тури́стский автоприце́п.

● *v.i.* (**caravanned, caravanning**) (*Br.*): **go ~ning** путеше́ствовать (*impf.*) в до́ме-автоприце́пе.

caravanner /ˈkærəvænə(r)/ *n.* (*Br.*) путеше́ствующий с автоприце́пом.

caravanserai /ˌkærəˈvænsərɪ/, /-ˌraɪ/ *n.* карава́н-сара́й.

caraway /ˈkærəˌweɪ/ *n.* тмин; **~ seed** тми́нное се́мя.

carbide /ˈkɑːbaɪd/ *n.* карби́д; **calcium ~** карби́д ка́льция.

carbine /ˈkɑːbaɪn/ *n.* караби́н.

carbohydrate /ˌkɑːbəˈhaɪdreɪt/ *n.* углево́д.

carbolic /kɑːˈbɒlɪk/ *adj.* карбо́ловый.

carbon /ˈkɑːbən/ *n.* **1** (*element*) углеро́д; **~ monoxide** уга́рный газ; **~ dioxide** двуо́кись углеро́да, углекислота́, углеки́слый газ; **~ dating** (радио)углеро́дный ана́лиз. **2** (*elec.*) у́голь (*m.*); у́гольный электро́д. **3** (*~-paper*) копирова́льная бума́га, копи́рка; **~ copy** (*lit.*) ко́пия под копи́рку; (*fig.*) (то́чная) ко́пия.

carbonaceous /ˌkɑːbəˈneɪʃəs/ *adj.* углеро́дистый.

carbonic /kɑːˈbɒnɪk/ *adj.* у́гольный, углеро́дный, углеро́дистый; **~ acid** углекислота́.

carboniferous /ˌkɑːbəˈnɪfərəs/ *adj.* углено́сный; каменноуго́льный.

carbonization /ˌkɑːbənaɪˈzeɪʃ(ə)n/ *n.* обу́гливание, карбониза́ция.

carbonize /ˈkɑːbəˌnaɪz/ *v.t.* **1** (*convert into carbon*) карбонизи́ровать (*impf., pf.*). **2** (*apply carbon black to*) покр|ыва́ть, -ы́ть углём. **3** (*char*) обу́гли|вать, -ть; коксова́ть (*impf.*).

carborundum /ˌkɑːbəˈrʌndəm/ *n.* карбору́нд.

carboy /ˈkɑːbɔɪ/ *n.* оплетённая буты́ль.

carbuncle /ˈkɑːbʌŋk(ə)l/ *n.* (*jewel; med.*) карбу́нкул.

carburettor /ˌkɑːbjʊˈretə(r)/, /ˌkɑːbə-/ (*US* **carburetor**) *n.* карбюра́тор.

carcass /ˈkɑːkəs/ *n.* **1** (*of animal*) ту́ша; **~ meat** (*Br.*) парно́е мя́со. **2** (*of building, ship etc.*) карка́с, о́стов, ко́рпус.

carcinogen /kɑːˈsɪnədʒ(ə)n/ *n.* канцероге́нное вещество́.

carcinogenic /ˌkɑːsɪnəˈdʒenɪk/ *adj.* канцероге́нный.

carcinoma /ˌkɑːsɪˈnəʊmə/ *n.* (*pl.* **~ta** *or* **~s**) карцино́ма, ра́ковое новообразова́ние.

card[1] /kɑːd/ *n.* **1** (*material*) карто́н; (*piece of pasteboard*) ка́рточка; (*postcard*) откры́тка; **calling ~, visiting ~** визи́тная ка́рточка; **Party ~** парти́йный биле́т; **invitation ~** пригласи́тельный биле́т; **Christmas ~** рожде́ственская откры́тка; **birthday ~** поздрави́тельная ка́рточка/откры́тка ко дню рожде́ния; **identity ~** удостовере́ние ли́чности.
2 (*playing-~*) игра́льная ка́рта; **play ~s** игра́ть, сыгра́ть в ка́рты; **play a ~** пойти́ (*pf.*) с (како́й-н.) ка́рты; **house of ~s** (*lit., fig.*) ка́рточный до́мик; **I won £5 at ~s** я вы́играл в ка́рты 5 фу́нтов.
3 (*in libraries etc.*) катало́жная ка́рточка; **~s** (*Br., documents of employment*) учётная ка́рточка; **give s.o. his ~s** (*dismiss him*) уво́лить (*pf.*) кого́-н.
4 (*comput.*) пла́та.
5 (*fig.*): **he put his ~s on the table** он раскры́л свои́ ка́рты; **I have a ~ up my sleeve** (*Br.*) у меня́ есть в запа́се ко́зырь; **he holds all the ~s** у него́ все ко́зыри на рука́х; **he plays his ~s well** он уме́ло испо́льзует обстоя́тельства; **it is on the ~s that we shall go** возмо́жно, что мы пойдём.

● *cpds.* **~-carrying** *adj.* зарегистри́рованный, состоя́щий в организа́ции; **~-index** *n.* картоте́ка; *v.t.* (*enter on ~s*) зан|оси́ть, -ести́ в картоте́ку; каталогизи́ровать (*impf., pf.*); **~-party** *n.* ве́чер за ка́ртами; **~-player** *n.* игро́к в ка́рты; картёжник; **~-playing** *n.* игра́ в ка́рты; **~-sharper** *n.* шу́лер; **~-table** *n.* ло́мберный стол.

card[2] /kɑːd/ *n.* (*for wool*) ка́рда, чеса́лка.

● *v.t.* чеса́ть, по-; проч|ёсывать, -еса́ть; кардова́ть (*impf.*); **~ing-machine** кардочеса́льная маши́на.

cardam|om, -um /ˈkɑːdəməm/ *n.* кардамо́н.

cardboard /ˈkɑːdbɔːd/ *n.* карто́н; **~ box** карто́нная коро́бка.

carder /ˈkɑːdə(r)/ *n.* (*person*) чеса́льщи|к (*fem.* -ца); ворси́льщи|к (*fem.* -ца); (*machine*) ка́рдная маши́на.

cardiac /ˈkɑːdɪˌæk/ *adj.* серде́чный; **~ arrest** остано́вка се́рдца.

cardigan /ˈkɑːdɪgən/ *n.* шерстяна́я ко́фта; кардига́н; (*man's*) вя́заная ку́ртка.

cardinal /ˈkɑːdɪn(ə)l/ *n.* (*eccl., zool.*) кардина́л.

● *adj.* (*principal*) кардина́льный; **~ number** коли́чественное числи́тельное; **~ point** страна́ све́та; **a matter of ~ importance** де́ло чрезвыча́йной ва́жности.

cardiogram /ˈkɑːdɪəʊˌgræm/ *n.* кардиогра́мма.

cardiological /ˌkɑːdɪəˈlɒdʒɪk(ə)l/ *adj.* кардиологи́ческий.

cardiologist /ˌkɑːdɪˈɒlədʒɪst/ *n.* кардио́лог.

cardiology /ˌkɑːdɪˈɒlədʒɪ/ *n.* кардиоло́гия.

cardiovascular /ˌkɑːdɪəʊˈvæskjʊlə(r)/ *adj.* серде́чно-сосу́дистый.

care /keə(r)/ *n.* **1** (*serious attention, caution*) осторо́жность; **he works with ~** он стара́тельно рабо́тает; **handle this with ~** обраща́йтесь с э́тим осторо́жно; **take ~ you don't fall** смотри́те, не упади́те; **have a ~!** береги́тесь!
2 (*charge, responsibility*) забо́та, попече́ние; **he is under the doctor's ~** он нахо́дится под наблюде́нием врача́; **the child is in my ~** ребёнок на моём попече́нии; **take a child into ~** (*Br.*) взять (*pf.*) ребёнка в систе́му госуда́рственного призре́ния; **Mr Smith, ~ of Mr Jones** г-ну Джо́нсу для г-на Сми́та (*or* для переда́чи г-ну Сми́ту); **that will take ~ of** (*meet*) **our needs** э́то обеспе́чит нас необходи́мым.
3 (*anxiety*): **free from ~** свобо́дный от забо́т; не зна́ющий забо́т, беззабо́тный.

● *v.i.* **1** (*feel concern or anxiety*): **I don't ~ what they say** мне всё равно́, что они́ ска́жут; **he doesn't ~ a bit** ему́ наплева́ть (*coll.*); **who ~s?** не всё ли равно́?; **I couldn't ~ less** (*coll.*) мне-то что?; мне наплева́ть; **he can go for all I ~** по мне он мо́жет идти́; **not that I ~** не то, что́бы меня́ э́то волнова́ло/трево́жило/беспоко́ило; **that's all he ~s about** он бо́льше ниче́м не интересу́ется.
2 (*feel inclination*): **would you ~ for a walk?** не хоти́те ли пойти́ погуля́ть?; **I don't ~ for asparagus** я не люблю́ спа́ржу; **I knew she ~d for him** я знал, что он ей нра́вится (*or* что она́ неравноду́шна к нему́); **you might ~ to look at this letter** вам, мо́жет быть, бу́дет интере́сно взгляну́ть на э́то письмо́.
3 (*look after*): **he is well ~d for** за ним хоро́ший ухо́д.

● *cpds.* **~free** *adj.* беззабо́тный; **~-laden** *adj.* обременённый забо́тами; **~taker** *n.* сто́рож, смотри́тель (*m.*) зда́ния; **~taker government** вре́менное прави́тельство; **~worn** *adj.* изму́ченный забо́тами.

careen /kəˈriːn/ *v.t.* кренгова́ть (*impf.*), килева́ть (*impf.*).

● *v.i.* (*heel over*) крени́ться (*impf.*); (*US, career*) нести́сь, по- (*det.*).

career /kəˈrɪə(r)/ *n.* **1** (*life story*) жи́зненный путь. **2** (*profession*) карье́ра, профе́ссия; **~s open to women** профе́ссии, досту́пные же́нщинам; **~ diplomat(ist)** профессиона́льный диплома́т; **~s teacher** (*at school*) консульта́нт по профессиона́льной ориента́ции.

● *v.i.* нести́сь, по- (*det.*); мча́ться (*impf.*).

careerism /kəˈrɪərˌɪz(ə)m/ *n.* карьери́зм.

careerist /kəˈrɪərɪst/ *n.* карьерист.
● *adj.* карьеристский.

careful /ˈkeəfʊl/ *adj.* **1** (*attentive*) осторожный; заботливый, внимательный; **be ~ not to fall** будьте осторожны, не упадите; **he is ~ with his money** он не тратит денег зря. **2** (*of work etc.*) тщательный, аккуратный.

carefulness /ˈkeəfʊlnɪs/ *n.* осторожность; заботливость, внимательность; тщательность, аккуратность.

careless /ˈkeəlɪs/ *adj.* (*thoughtless*) неосторожный, неосмотрительный; **a ~ driver** неосторожный водитель; **a ~ mistake** ошибка по невнимательности; (*negligent*) небрежный; (*carefree, unconcerned*) беззаботный, беспечный; **~ of danger** не думающий об опасности.

carelessness /ˈkeəlɪsnɪs/ *n.* небрежность, неосторожность; (*negligence*) неосмотрительность.

carer /ˈkeərə(r)/ *n.* (*Br.*) человек, ухаживающий за ребёнком, больным, инвалидом *и т.д.*

caress /kəˈres/ *n.* ласка.
● *v.t.* ласкать (*impf.*).

caressing /kəˈresɪŋ/ *adj.* ласкающий, ласковый.

caret /ˈkærət/ *n.* знак вставки.

cargo /ˈkɑːgəʊ/ *n.* (*pl.* **~es** *or* **~s**) груз; **~ ship, boat** торговое/грузовое судно.

Caribbean /ˌkærɪˈbiːən/, /kəˈrɪbɪən/ *adj.* кар(а)ибский; (*as n.*): **the ~ (Sea)** Кар(а)ибское море; (*region*) страны (*fem. pl.*) бассейна Кар(а)ибского моря.

caribou /ˈkærɪˌbuː/ *n.* (*pl.* **~**) карибу (*m. indecl.*), канадский олень.

caricature /ˈkærɪkətjʊə(r)/ *n.* карикатура; (*fig., also*) искажение.
● *v.t.* изобра|жать, -зить в карикатурном виде.

caricaturist /ˈkærɪkəˌtjʊərɪst/ *n.* карикатурист (*fem.* -ка).

caries /ˈkeəriːz/, /-rɪˌiːz/ *n.* (*pl.* **~**) кариес.

carillon /kəˈrɪljən/, /ˈkærɪljən/ *n.* подбор колоколов; перезвон.

caring /ˈkeərɪŋ/ *adj.* заботливый.

carious /ˈkeərɪəs/ *adj.* кариозный.

carmine /ˈkɑːmaɪn/ *n.* кармин.
● *adj.* карминный.

carnage /ˈkɑːnɪdʒ/ *n.* бойня.

carnal /ˈkɑːn(ə)l/ *adj.* (*sensual*) плотский, телесный; (*sexual*) половой.

carnation /kɑːˈneɪʃ(ə)n/ *n.* гвоздика.

carnelian /kɑːˈniːlɪən/ *n.* сердолик.

carnival /ˈkɑːnɪv(ə)l/ *n.* (*merrymaking*) карнавал; (*Shrovetide*) масленица.

carnivore /ˈkɑːnɪˌvɔː(r)/ *n.* плотоядное/хищное животное.

carnivorous /kɑːˈnɪvərəs/ *adj.* плотоядный.

carob /ˈkærəb/ *n.* (*tree*) рожковое дерево; (*bean*) сладкий рожок.

carol /ˈkær(ə)l/ *n.* (*song*) песня; (*Xmas song*) рождественский гимн, рождественская песня.
● *v.t. & i.* (**carolled, carolling;** *US* **caroled, caroling**) восп|евать, -еть.
● *cpd.* **~-singing** *n.* рождественское песнопение.

carom /ˈkærəm/ (*US*) = **cannon** *n.* 3 *& v.i.*

carotid /kəˈrɒtɪd/ *adj.*: **~ artery** сонная артерия.

carousal /kəˈraʊzəl/ *n.* пирушка, попойка.

carouse /kəˈraʊz/ *v.i.* бражничать (*impf.*).

carousel /ˌkærəˈsel/, /-ˈzel/ *n.* (*roundabout*) карусель.

carouser /kəˈraʊzə(r)/ *n.* гуляка (*c.g.*), кутила (*m.*).

carp[1] /kɑːp/ *n.* (*pl.* **~**) (*zool.*) карп.

carp[2] /kɑːp/ *v.i.* придираться (*impf.*) (**at**: к + *d.*); **~ing criticism** придирчивая критика.

Carpathians /kɑːˈpeɪθɪəns/ *n.* Карпат|ы (*pl., g.* —).

carpenter /ˈkɑːpɪntə(r)/ *n.* плотник.

carpentry /ˈkɑːpɪntrɪ/ *n.* (*occupation*) плотничество, плотницкое дело; (*product*) плотничьи изделия (*nt. pl.*).

carpet /ˈkɑːpɪt/ *n.* ковёр; **be on the ~** (*reprimanded*) получ|ать, -ить нагоняй/взбучку (*coll.*); **~ bombing** бомбометание по площади; **~ slippers** тёплые тапочки.
● *v.t.* (**carpeted, carpeting**) покр|ывать, -ыть ковром; уст|илать, -лать коврами; (*Br., reprimand*) да|вать, -ть нагоняй/взбучку + *d.*; вызывать, вызвать на ковёр (*coll.*).
● *cpds.* **~-bag** *n.* саквояж; **~-sweeper** *n.* щётка для ковра.

carpeting /ˈkɑːpɪtɪŋ/ *n.* **1** (*carpet material*) ковровая ткань; **felt ~** половой настил на войлочной подкладке; (*covering with carpets*) устилание/покрывание коврами. **2** (*Br., reprimand*) разнос, нагоняй.

carpus /ˈkɑːpəs/ *n.* (*pl.* **carpi** /-paɪ/) запястье.

carrel /ˈkær(ə)l/ *n.* отсек (*в библиотеке*).

carriage /ˈkærɪdʒ/ *n.* **1** (*road vehicle*) экипаж, карета, коляска. **2** (*Br., rail car*) пассажирский вагон. **3** (*Br., transport of goods*) перевозка, доставка; **~ forward** стоимость перевозки за счёт покупателя. **4** (*manner of standing or walking*) осанка; манера держаться. **5** (*gun-~*) лафет. **6** (*of typewriter etc.*) каретка.
● *cpd.* **~way** *n.* (*Br.*) проезжая часть дороги.

carrier /ˈkærɪə(r)/ *n.* **1** (*transport agent*) транспортёр. **2** (*receptacle or support for luggage etc.*) багажник; **~ bag** (*Br.*) сумка для покупок. **3** (*of disease*) бациллоноситель (*m.*), вирусоноситель (*m.*). **4** (*vehicle, ship etc.*) транспортное средство. **5** (*aircraft-~*) авианосец. **6**: **~ pigeon** почтовый голубь.

carrion /ˈkærɪən/ *n.* падаль, мертвечина; **~ crow** ворона чёрная.

carrot /ˈkærət/ *n.* морковка; (*pl., collect.*) морковь; **~ and stick policy** политика кнута и пряника.

carroty /ˈkærətɪ/ *adj.* рыжеватый, рыжеволосый.

carry /ˈkærɪ/ *v.t.* **1** (*bear, transport*) носить, нести; (*of or by vehicle*) возить (*indet.*), везти (*det.*); пере|возить, -везти; **ships ~ goods** корабли перевозят товары; **this bicycle has carried me 500 miles** на этом велосипеде я проехал 500 миль; **pipes ~ water** вода идёт по трубам; **wires ~ sound** звук передаётся по проводам; **pillars ~ an arch** колонны поддерживают арку; **what weight will the bridge ~?** на какой вес рассчитан этот мост?; **he carries himself well** он хорошо держится; **the police carried him off to prison** полиция увезла его в тюрьму; **~ing trade** транспортное дело.
2 (*have on or about one*): **I always ~ an umbrella (money) with me** у меня всегда с собой зонтик (всегда деньги при себе); **the police ~ arms** полиция вооружена; **~ figures in one's head** держать (*impf.*) цифры в голове; **this crime carries a heavy penalty** это преступление влечёт за собой тяжёлое наказание.
3 (*fig.*): **~ into effect** осуществ|лять, -ить; **his voice carries weight** с его мнением считаются; **the argument carries conviction** этот аргумент убедителен; **he carries modesty too far** он излишне скромен; **~ the day** одерж|ивать, -ать победу; **he carried his audience with him** он увлёк своих слушателей; **the bill was carried** законопроект был принят.
4 (*include*): **the book carries many tables** книга содержит много таблиц; **the newspaper carried this report** газета поместила это сообщение.
5 (*fin., comm.*): **the loan carries interest** заём приносит проценты/доход; **the shop carries hardware** этот магазин торгует скобяными товарами.
6 (*math.*): **put down 6 and ~ 1** записать (*pf.*) 6 и держать (*impf.*) в уме один; **'~ 1'** «один в уме».
● *v.i.*: **the shot carried 200 yards** снаряд пролетел 200 ярдов; **his voice carries well** у него звучный голос.
● *with advs.*: **~ away** *v.t.* (*lit.*) ун|осить, -ести; **the masts were carried away by the storm** бурей унесло мачты; (*fig.*): **he was carried away by his feelings** он оказался во власти чувств; он увлёкся; **~ back** *v.t.* (*lit.*) прин|осить, -ести обратно; (*fig.*): **the incident carried me back to my schooldays** этот случай перенёс меня обратно в мои школьные годы; **~ forward, over** *vv.t.* (*transfer*) перен|осить, -ести; **~ off** *v.t.* (*remove*) ун|осить, -ести; **death carried off several of them** нескольких из них унесла смерть; **he carried the situation off well** он хорошо вышел из положения; **~ on** *v.t.* (*conduct, perform*): **~ on a conversation/business** вести (*det.*) разговор/дело; *v.i.* (*continue*)

прод|олжа́ть, -о́лжить; **~ on with your work** продолжа́йте рабо́ту; (*talk, behave excitedly*) волнова́ться (*impf.*); проявля́ть (*impf.*) несде́ржанность; **don't ~ on so!** не распаля́йтесь так!; **~ out** *v.t.* (*lit.*) выноси́ть, вы́нести; (*execute*) выполня́ть, вы́полнить; **~ through** *v.t.* (*bring out of difficulties*) выводи́ть, вы́вести из затрудне́ний.

● *cpds.* **~-all** *n.* (*US*) вещево́й мешо́к; **~-cot** *n.* (*Br.*) перено́сная де́тская крова́тка.

carrying(s)-on /ˈkærɪŋ(z)ˈɒn/ *n.* (*to-do*) сумато́ха, суета́; (*coll., flirtation*) ша́шн|и (*pl., g.* -ей); шу́ры-му́ры (*pl. indecl.*).

cart /kɑːt/ *n.* двуко́лка, теле́жка; **put the ~ before the horse** (*fig.*) де́лать, с- (*что-н.*) ши́ворот-навы́ворот.

● *v.t.* (*carry in* **~**) вози́ть (*indet.*) в теле́жке; **~ away** отв|ози́ть, -езти́; ув|ози́ть, -езти́; (*coll., carry*) тащи́ть (*impf.*).

● *cpds.* **~-horse** *n.* (*Br.*) ломова́я ло́шадь; **~-load** *n.* воз, теле́га (*чего*); **~-road, ~-track** *nn.* просёлочная доро́га; **~wheel** *n.* колесо́ теле́ги; **turn ~wheels** кувырк|а́ться, -ну́ться колесо́м; **~wright** *n.* теле́жный ма́стер.

cartage /ˈkɑːtɪdʒ/ *n.* (*transport*) (гужево́й) тра́нспорт; (*charge*) сто́имость (гужево́й) перево́зки.

carte blanche /kɑːt ˈblɑ̃ʃ/ *n.* карт-бла́нш (*indecl.*).

cartel /kɑːˈtel/ *n.* (*comm.*) карте́ль (*m.*).

cartelize /ˈkɑːtəˌlaɪz/ *v.t.* объедин|я́ть, -и́ть в карте́ли.

carter /ˈkɑːtə(r)/ *n.* во́зчик.

Cartesian /kɑːˈtiːzjən/, /-ʒ(ə)n/ *adj.* картезиа́нский.

cartful /ˈkɑːtfʊl/ *n.* воз, теле́га (*чего*).

Carthage /ˈkɑːθɪdʒ/ *n.* Карфаге́н.

Carthaginian /ˌkɑːθəˈdʒɪnɪən/ *n.* карфаге́ня́н|ин (*fem.* -ка).

● *adj.* карфаге́нский, пуни́ческий.

cartilage /ˈkɑːtɪlɪdʒ/ *n.* хря́щ.

cartilaginous /ˌkɑːtɪˈlædʒɪnəs/ *adj.* хрящево́й.

cartographer /kɑːˈtɒgrəfə(r)/ *n.* карто́граф.

cartographic(al) /kɑːtəˈgræfɪk(ə)l/ *adj.* картографи́ческий.

cartography /kɑːˈtɒgrəfɪ/ *n.* картогра́фия.

cartomancy /ˈkɑːtəˌmænsɪ/ *n.* гада́ние на ка́ртах.

carton /ˈkɑːt(ə)n/ *n.* (*container*) карто́нка; блок.

cartoon /kɑːˈtuːn/ *n.* (*in fine arts*) карто́н; (*in newspaper*) карикату́ра; (*film*) мультиплика́ция, мультфи́льм; (*comic strip*) ко́микс.

cartoonist /kɑːˈtuːnɪst/ *n.* карикатури́ст; (*film*) мультиплика́тор.

cartridge /ˈkɑːtrɪdʒ/ *n.* (*mil.*) патро́н; **blank ~** холосто́й патро́н; (*for printer*) ка́ртридж; (*for camera*) кассе́та.

● *cpds.* **~-belt** *n.* патронта́ш; патро́нная ле́нта; **~-case** *n.* патро́нная ги́льза; **~-paper** *n.* пло́тная бума́га (*для рисования и т.п.*).

carv|e /kɑːv/ *v.t.* (*cut*) ре́зать (*impf.*); выреза́ть, вы́резать; (*shape by cutting*): **~e a statue out of wood** выреза́ть, вы́резать ста́тую из де́рева; **he ~ed his initials** он вы́резал свои́ инициа́лы; **he ~ed out a career for himself** он сде́лал карье́ру; **~e meat** ре́зать, на- мя́со; **~ing-fork/knife** ви́лка/нож для нареза́ния мя́са.

● *with adv.*: **~e up** *v.t.* (*fig., of wealth etc.*) раздел|я́ть, -и́ть.

● *cpd.* **~e-up** *n.* (*Br. fig.*) делёж.

carver /ˈkɑːvə(r)/ *n.* (*person*) ре́зчик; (*knife*) нож для нареза́ния мя́са.

carving /ˈkɑːvɪŋ/ *n.* (*object*) резна́я рабо́та, резьба́.

caryatid /ˌkærɪˈætɪd/ *n.* (*pl.* **~es** /-iːz/ *or* **~s**) кариати́да.

cascade /kæsˈkeɪd/ *n.* каска́д; водопа́д.

● *v.i.* па́дать/ниспада́ть (*both impf.*) каска́дом.

case[1] /keɪs/ *n.* **1** (*instance, circumstances*) слу́чай, обстоя́тельство, де́ло; **it is (not) the ~ that** ... де́ло обстои́т (не) так, что...; (не) ве́рно, что...; **such being the ~** поско́льку э́то так; поско́льку де́ло обстои́т таки́м о́бразом; **that alters the ~** э́то меня́ет де́ло; **a ~ in point** приме́р; **a hard ~** (*difficult point to decide*) тру́дный слу́чай/вопро́с; (*hardened criminal*) закорене́лый престу́пник; **in that ~** в тако́м/э́том слу́чае; **in any ~** во вся́ком слу́чае; **as the ~ may be** как полу́чится; в зави́симости от обстоя́тельств; **in ~ of fire** (*if fire breaks out*) в слу́чае пожа́ра; **in the ~ of Mr Smith** что каса́ется г-на Сми́та; в отноше́нии г-на Сми́та.
2 (*med.*) слу́чай, заболева́ние; больно́й, ра́неный; **there were five ~s of influenza** бы́ло пять слу́чаев гри́ппа; **the worst ~s were taken to hospital** наибо́лее тяжело́ больны́х/ра́неных отвезли́ в больни́цу; **~ history** исто́рия боле́зни; **stretcher ~** носи́лочный больно́й (*or* ра́неный); **mental ~** душевнобольно́й.
3 (*hypothesis*): **put the ~ that** ... предполо́жим, что...; **take an umbrella in ~ it rains (*or* in ~ of rain)** возьми́те зо́нтик на слу́чай дождя́; **just in ~** на вся́кий слу́чай.
4 (*leg.*) суде́бное де́ло; **try a ~** раз|бира́ть, -обра́ть де́ло в суде́; **leading ~** суде́бный прецеде́нт; **~ law** прецеде́нтное пра́во.
5 (*sum of arguments*): **he makes out a good ~ for the change** его́ до́воды о необходи́мости переме́н убеди́тельны.
6 (*gram.*) паде́ж.

case[2] /keɪs/ *n.* **1** (*container*) я́щик, ларе́ц, коро́бка; (*for spectacles etc.*) футля́р; (*Br., suitcase*) чемода́н; **glass ~** витри́на. **2** (*typ.*) набо́рная ка́сса; **lower ~** ка́сса строчны́х ли́тер; строчны́е бу́квы (*f. pl.*).

● *cpds.* **~-harden** *v.t.* (*lit.*) цементи́ровать (*impf., pf.*); **~-hardened** *adj.* (*fig.*) зачерстве́вший, загрубе́лый; **~-shot** *n.* карте́чь.

casein /ˈkeɪsɪɪn/, /ˈkeɪsiːn/ *n.* казеи́н.

casemate /ˈkeɪsmeɪt/ *n.* эска́рповая галере́я; казема́т.

casement /ˈkeɪsmənt/ *n.* (*frame*) ство́рчатый око́нный переплёт; (*window*) ство́рчатое окно́.

cash /kæʃ/ *n.* (*ready money; also* **hard ~**) нали́чные (де́н|ьги, *pl., g.* -ег); **on a ~ basis** за нали́чные; за нали́чный расчёт; **~ on delivery** нало́женным платежо́м; **discount for ~** (*payment*) ски́дка за нали́чный расчёт; **out of ~** не при деньга́х; **petty ~** ме́лкие су́ммы (*f. pl.*); ка́сса для ме́лких расхо́дов; **~ desk** (*Br.*) ка́сса; **~ dispenser** (*Br.*), **~ machine** банкома́т, де́нежный автома́т; **~ flow** движе́ние де́нежной нали́чности; **~ register** ка́ссовый аппара́т, ка́сса.

● *v.t.*: **~ a cheque (*Br.*), check (*US*)** получ|а́ть, -и́ть де́ньги по че́ку; **~ in** получ|а́ть, -и́ть де́ньги по + *d.*

● *v.i.*: **~ in on** (*fig.*) воспо́льзоваться (*pf.*) + *i.*

cashcard /ˈkæʃkɑːd/ *n.* (*Br.*) ка́рточка для банкома́та.

cashew /ˈkæʃuː/, /kæˈʃuː/ *n.* анака́рд, оре́х ке́шью (*indecl.*).

cashier[1] /kæˈʃɪə(r)/ *n.* касси́р.

cashier[2] /kæˈʃɪə(r)/ *v.t.* ув|ольня́ть, -о́лить со слу́жбы.

cashmere /ˈkæʃmɪə(r)/ *n.* кашеми́р; (*attr.*) кашеми́ровый.

cashpoint /ˈkæʃpɔɪnt/ *n.* (*Br.*) банкома́т, де́нежный автома́т.

casino /kəˈsiːnəʊ/ *n.* (*pl.* **~s**) казино́ (*indecl.*).

cask /kɑːsk/ *n.* бо́чка, бочо́нок.

casket /ˈkɑːskɪt/ *n.* шкату́лка; (*US, coffin*) гроб.

Caspian /ˈkæspɪən/ *n.*: **the ~ (Sea)** Каспи́йское мо́ре.

casque /kæsk/ *n.* (*poet.*) шлем, ка́ска.

cassation /kəˈseɪʃ(ə)n/ *n.* касса́ция; **court of ~** кассацио́нный суд.

cassava /kəˈsɑːvə/ *n.* маниóк(а).

casserole /ˈkæsəˌrəʊl/ *n.* (*container*) кастрю́ля для туше́ния; (*food*) рагу́ (*indecl.*).

cassette /kæˈset/, /kə-/ *n.* кассе́та; **~ player** пле́ер; **~ recorder** кассе́тный магнитофо́н.

cassia /ˈkæsɪə/, /ˈkæʃə/ *n.* ка́ссия.

cassock /ˈkæsək/ *n.* ря́са, сута́на.

cast /kɑːst/ *n.* **1** (*act of throwing*) броса́ние, мета́ние, бросо́к.
2 (*mould*) фо́рма для отли́вки; (*moulded object*): **plaster ~** ги́псовый сле́пок.
3 (*theatr.*) соста́в актёров; спи́сок исполни́телей.
4: **~ of mind** склад ума́/мы́слей.
5 (*squint*) косогла́зие.

● *v.t.* (*past and p.p.* **~**) **1** (*throw*) бр|оса́ть, -о́сить; кида́ть, ки́нуть; **the snake ~s its skin** змея́ меня́ет ко́жу; **his horse ~ a shoe** его́ ло́шадь потеря́ла подко́ву.

C

2 (*fig.*): **~ a vote** проголосова́ть (*pf.*); отда́ть (*pf.*) го́лос; **~ lots** тяну́ть/броса́ть/кида́ть (*all impf.*) жре́бий; **~ doubt on** подв|ерга́ть, -е́ргнуть сомне́нию; **~ a gloom on the proceedings** омрач|а́ть, -и́ть происходя́щее; **~ an eye on, over** бро́сить (*pf.*) взгля́д на + *a.*; оки́нуть (*pf.*) взгля́дом; **~ a spell (up)on** околд|о́вывать, -ова́ть; **~ing vote** реша́ющий го́лос.
3 (*pour, form in a mould*) отл|ива́ть, -и́ть; **~ iron** чугу́н.
4 (*theatr.*): **~ a play** распредел|я́ть, -и́ть ро́ли в пье́се; **he was ~ for the part of Hamlet** ему́ была́ пору́чена роль Га́млета.

● *with advs.*: **~ about** *v.i.*: **~ about for** разы́скивать, изы́скивать (*both impf.*); **~ away** *v.t.* (*reject*) отбр|а́сывать, -о́сить; **he was ~ away on a desert island** он был вы́брошен на необита́емый о́стров; **~ down** *v.t.* (*depress*) угнета́ть (*impf.*); подав|ля́ть, -и́ть; **~ off** *v.t.* (*abandon*) бр|оса́ть, -о́сить; сбр|а́сывать, -о́сить; *v.i.* (*naut.*) отва́л|ивать, -и́ть; **~ out** *v.t.* выгоня́ть, вы́гнать; изг|оня́ть, -на́ть.

● *cpds.* **~away** *n.* & *adj.* потерпе́вший кораблекруше́ние; **~-iron** *adj.* чугу́нный; (*fig.*) стально́й, желе́зный; несгиба́емый, непреклонный; **~-off** *n.* & *adj.*: **~-off clothing** обно́ск|и (*pl.*, *g.* -ов), старьё.

castanets /ˌkæstəˈnets/ *n.* кастанье́ты (*f. pl.*).

caste /kɑːst/ *n.* ка́ста; **lose ~** (*fig.*) утра́|чивать, -тить положе́ние в о́бществе.

castellated /ˈkæstəˌleɪtɪd/ *adj.* (*battlemented*) зу́бчатый.

caster /ˈkɑːstə(r)/ = **castor**[1]

castigate /ˈkæstɪˌgeɪt/ *v.t.* бичева́ть (*impf.*).

castigation /ˌkæstɪˈgeɪʃ(ə)n/ *n.* бичева́ние.

casting /ˈkɑːstɪŋ/ *n.* **1** (*tech.*) (*process*) литьё, отли́вка; (*product*) отли́вка. **2** (*theatr.*) распределе́ние роле́й.

castle /ˈkɑːs(ə)l/ *n.* за́мок; **~s in Spain** возду́шные за́мки; (*at chess*) ладья́, тура́.

● *v.i.* (*at chess*) рокирова́ться (*impf.*, *pf.*).

cast|or[1], **-er** /ˈkɑːstə(r)/ *nn.* **1** (*wheel on furniture*) ро́лик. **2**: **~ sugar** (*Br.*) са́харный песо́к.

castor[2] /ˈkɑːstə(r)/ *n.*: **~ oil** касто́ровое ма́сло, касто́рка.

castrate /kæˈstreɪt/ *v.t.* кастри́ровать (*impf.*, *pf.*).

castrati /kæˈstrɑːtɪ/ *pl. of* ⇒**castrato**

castration /kæˈstreɪʃ(ə)n/ *n.* кастра́ция.

castrat|o /kæˈstrɑːtəʊ/ *n.* (*pl.* **~i**) кастра́т.

casual /ˈkæʒʊəl/, /-zjʊəl/ *adj.* **1** (*chance, occasional*) случа́йный; **a ~ meeting** случа́йная встре́ча; **~ labourer** (*Br.*), **laborer** (*US*) рабо́чий, живу́щий на случа́йные за́работки. **2** (*careless*) небре́жный, беспе́чный; (*familiar*) развя́зный; **clothes for ~ wear** проста́я/бу́дничная оде́жда. **3** (*freelance*) внешта́тный.

casualness /ˈkæʒʊəlnɪs/, /-zjʊəlnɪs/ *n.* случа́йность; небре́жность, беспе́чность, развя́зность.

casualty /ˈkæʒʊəltɪ/, /ˈkæzjʊ-/ *n.* **1** (*accident*) несча́стный слу́чай. **2** (*person*) пострада́вший от несча́стного слу́чая; (*mil.*) (*injured*) ра́неный; (*killed*) уби́тый; **~ department** (*Br.*) травматологи́ческое отделе́ние; **~ list** спи́сок уби́тых и ра́неных; **~ ward** (*Br.*) пала́та ско́рой по́мощи. **3** (*fig., victim*) же́ртва.

casuist /ˈkæʒjuːɪst/, /ˈkæʒʊɪst/ *n.* казуи́ст.

casuistic(al) /kæʒjuːˈɪstɪk(ə)l/, /kæʒʊˈɪstɪk(ə)l/ *adj.* казуисти́ческий.

casuistry /ˈkæzjʊɪstrɪ/ *n.* казуи́стика.

casus belli /ˌkɑːzəs ˈbelɪ/, /ˌkeɪsəs/ *n.* ка́зус бе́лли, по́вод к войне́.

cat /kæt/ *n.* **1** ко́шка; **tom ~** кот; **wild ~** ди́кая ко́шка; (*pl.*, *felines*) коша́чьи (*pl.*, *g.* -х), ко́шки (*f. pl.*).
2 (*fig.*, *spiteful woman*) ехи́дная же́нщина.
3: **~ o'nine tails** ко́шка (*плеть*).
4 (*idioms and provs.*): **let the ~ out of the bag** проб|а́лтываться, -олта́ться; выба́лтывать, вы́болтать секре́т; **lead a ~-and-dog life** жить (*impf.*) как ко́шка с соба́кой; **there's no(t) room to swing a ~** я́блоку не́где упа́сть; поверну́ться не́где; **it's raining ~s and dogs** дождь льёт как из ведра́; **a ~ may look at a king** за просмо́тр де́нег не беру́т; **like a ~ on hot bricks** (*Br.*) (*or* **on a hot tin roof**) как на у́гольях/иго́лках; **there are more ways than one to kill a ~** свет не кли́ном сошёлся; **when the ~'s away the mice will play** без кота́ мыша́м раздо́лье; **grin like a Cheshire ~** ухмыл|я́ться, -ьну́ться во весь рот; **curiosity killed the ~** любопы́тство до добра́ не дово́дит; **~'s pyjamas** (*US*), **whiskers** (*sl.*) что на́до; пе́рвый сорт.

● *cpds.* **~call** *n.* освисты́вание; **~fish** *n.* сом, со́мик; **~ flap** *n.* коша́чья две́рца; **~-like** *adj.* коша́чий; **with ~-like tread** неслы́шной по́ступью; **~mint, ~nip** *nn.* кото́вник; коша́чья мя́та; **~-nap** *v.i.* вздремну́ть (*pf.*); **~'s-eye** *n.* (*gem*) коша́чий глаз; **~'s-paw** *n.* (*dupe*) ору́дие в чужи́х рука́х; (*breeze*) лёгкий бриз; **~-suit** *n.* (*Br.*) «ко́шечка» (комбинезо́н в обтя́жку); **~walk** *n.* рабо́чие мостк|и́ (*pl.*, *g.* -о́в); (*in fashion-house*) помо́ст, «язы́к», эстра́да.

catachresis /ˌkætəˈkriːsɪs/ *n.* (*pl.* **catachreses** /-siːz/) катахре́за.

cataclysm /ˈkætəˌklɪz(ə)m/ *n.* катаклизм.

cataclysmic /ˌkætəˈklɪzmɪk/ *adj.* катастрофи́ческий.

catacomb /ˈkætəˌkuːm/, /-ˌkəʊm/ *n.* катако́мба.

catafalque /ˈkætəˌfælk/ *n.* катафа́лк.

Catalan /ˈkætəlæn/ *n.* (*person*) катало́н|ец (*fem.* -ка); (*language*) катала́нский язы́к.

● *adj.* катало́нский; (*of language*) катала́нский.

catalepsy /ˈkætəˌlepsɪ/ *n.* катале́псия.

cataleptic /ˌkætəˈleptɪk/ *adj.* каталепти́ческий.

catalogue /ˈkætəˌlɒg/ (*US* **catalog**) *n.* катало́г.

● *v.t.* (**catalogues, catalogued, cataloguing;** *US* **catalogs, cataloged, cataloging**) каталогизи́ровать (*impf.*, *pf.*).

cataloguer /ˈkætəˌlɒgə(r)/ (*US* **cataloger**) *n.* каталогиза́тор.

Catalonia /ˌkætəˈləʊnɪə/ *n.* Катало́ния.

catalysis /kəˈtælɪsɪs/ *n.* (*pl.* **catalyses** /-siːz/) ката́лиз.

catalyst /ˈkætəlɪst/ *n.* катализа́тор.

catalytic /ˌkætəˈlɪtɪk/ *adj.* каталити́ческий; **~ converter** каталити́ческий нейтрализа́тор.

catamaran /ˌkætəməˈræn/ *n.* катамара́н.

catamite /ˈkætəˌmaɪt/ *n.* ма́льчик-педера́ст.

catapult /ˈkætəˌpʌlt/ *n.* (*Br.*, *toy*) рога́тка; (*hist.*, *aeron.*) катапу́льта.

● *v.t.* выбра́сывать, вы́бросить катапу́льтой; катапульти́ровать (*impf.*, *pf.*).

cataract /ˈkætəˌrækt/ *n.* (*waterfall*) водопа́д; (*med.*) катара́кта.

catarrh /kəˈtɑː(r)/ *n.* ката́р.

catastrophe /kəˈtæstrəfɪ/ *n.* катастро́фа; **natural ~** стихи́йное бе́дствие.

catastrophic /ˌkætəˈstrɒfɪk/ *adj.* катастрофи́ческий.

catch /kætʃ/ *n.* **1** (*act of catching*) поимка, захва́т; **play ~** игра́ть (*impf.*) в са́лки.
2 (*amount caught*) уло́в, добы́ча.
3 (*prize*): **she is a good ~ for somebody** она́ — ви́дная па́ртия для кого́-нибудь.
4 (*trap*) уло́вка, лову́шка; **there must be a ~ in it** здесь есть како́й-то подво́х; **a ~ question** ка́верзный вопро́с.
5 (*device for fastening etc.*) щеко́лда, защёлка, шпингале́т.
6 (*mus.*) ро́ндо.

● *v.t.* & *i.* (*past and p.p.* **caught**) **1** (*seize*) лови́ть, пойма́ть; хвата́ть, схвати́ть; **he caught the ball** он пойма́л мяч; **~ a fish** пойма́ть (*pf.*) ры́бу; **~ a fugitive** пойма́ть (*pf.*) беглеца́; **she caught hold of him** она́ схвати́ла его́; **~ at** хвата́ться, схвати́ться за + *a.*
2 (*of entanglement, fastening etc.*): **her dress caught on a nail; the nail caught her dress** она́ зацепи́лась пла́тьем за гвоздь; **I caught my finger in the door** я прищеми́л себе́ па́лец две́рью; **the door doesn't ~** дверь не запира́ется; **the car was caught between two trams** автомоби́ль оказа́лся зажа́тым ме́жду двумя́ трамва́ями; **he caught his foot** у него́ застря́ла нога́.
3 (*intercept, detect*): **I caught him stealing** я заста́л его́, когда́ он крал; **I caught him as he was leaving the house** я заста́л/захвати́л его́ как раз, когда́ он выходи́л из дому; **I was caught by the rain** я попа́л под дождь; дождь захвати́л меня́; **we were caught**

in the storm нас застигла бу́ря.
4 (*be in time for*): **~ a train** поспе́ть (*pf.*) к по́езду; **he caught the post** он успе́л отпра́вить письмо́ с э́той по́чтой.
5 (*fig.*) пойма́ть, улови́ть, схвати́ть (*all pf.*); **~ s.o.'s words** расслы́шать (*pf.*) чьи-н. слова́; **I didn't ~ what you said** я прослу́шал, что вы сказа́ли; **~ s.o.'s meaning** улови́ть (*pf.*) чью-н. мысль; **~ one's breath** затаи́ть (*pf.*) дыха́ние; **~ s.o.'s eye** привле́чь (*pf.*) чьё-н. внима́ние; **~ fire, alight** загоре́ться (*pf.*); **~ a glimpse of** уви́деть (*pf.*) ме́льком; **~ hold of** схвати́ть, улови́ть (*both pf.*).
6 (*be hit by*): **he caught it on the forehead** он получи́л уда́р в лоб (*or* по́ лбу); **this side of the house ~es the east wind** с э́той стороны́ в дом ду́ет восто́чный ве́тер; (*of punishment*): **you'll ~ it!** тебе́ доста́нется/попадёт.
7 (*be infected by*; *lit., fig.*) схвати́ть, получи́ть (*both pf.*); **he caught a fever** он схвати́л лихора́дку; **~ cold** простуди́ться (*pf.*); **he was caught with the general enthusiasm** его́ захвати́л/увлёк о́бщий энтузиа́зм.
● *with advs.*: **~ on** *v.i.*: **the fashion did not ~ on** э́та мо́да не привила́сь; **I don't ~ on** (*coll.*) я не понима́ю; я не схва́тываю; **~ out** *v.t.* (*Br.*): **he was caught out in a mistake** его́ пойма́ли на оши́бке; **~ up** *v.t. & i.* (*pick up quickly*) подхва́т|ывать, -и́ть; **he caught the others up; he caught up with the others** он догна́л остальны́х; **I must ~ up on my work** я запусти́л рабо́ту — тепе́рь на́до нагоня́ть; **this paper got caught up with the others** э́та бума́га затеря́лась среди́ остальны́х; **the police caught up with, on him** поли́ция его́ насти́гла.
● *cpds.* **~-all** *n.*: **a ~-all expression** всеобъе́млющая формулиро́вка; **~penny** *adj.* показно́й; рассчи́танный на дешёвый успе́х; **~-phrase, ~word** *nn.* мо́дное выраже́ние, слове́чко; **~-22 situation** *n.* безвы́ходное положе́ние.

catching /ˈkætʃɪŋ/ *adj.* (*of disease*) зара́зный; (*fig.*) зарази́тельный.

catchment /ˈkætʃmənt/ *n.*: **~ area** (*geog.*) бассе́йн реки́; водосбо́рная пло́щадь; (*of school etc.*) микрорайо́н, обслу́живаемый шко́лой *и т.п.*

catchy /ˈkætʃɪ/ (**catchier, catchiest**) *adj.* (*of tune etc.*) легко́ запомина́ющийся, прили́пчивый.

catechism /ˈkætɪˌkɪz(ə)m/ *n.* катехи́зис.

catechize /ˈkætɪˌkaɪz/ *v.t.* (*teach catechism to*) обуча́ть (*impf.*) катехи́зису; (*fig.*) допра́шивать (*impf.*).

catechumen /ˌkætɪˈkjuːmən/ *n.* (*relig.*) оглашённый.

categorical /ˌkætɪˈgɒrɪk(ə)l/ *adj.* категори́ческий.

categorize /ˈkætɪgəˌraɪz/ *v.t.* распредел|я́ть, -и́ть по катего́риям.

category /ˈkætɪgərɪ/ *n.* катего́рия.

cater /ˈkeɪtə(r)/ *v.i.*: **~ for** (*Br.*) пост|авля́ть, -а́вить прови́зию для + *g.*; (*fig.*) обслу́ж|ивать, -и́ть; **~ to** уго|жда́ть, -ди́ть (*кому*); (*tastes*) удовлетвор|я́ть, -и́ть; **the ~ing trade** рестора́нное де́ло.

cater-cornered /ˈkætəˌkɔːnəd/ *adj.* (*US*) диагона́льный.

caterer /ˈkeɪtərə(r)/ *n.* поставщи́к прови́зии; (*pl., company*) фи́рма, обслу́живающая банке́ты, сва́дьбы *и т.п.*

caterpillar /ˈkætəˌpɪlə(r)/ *n.* (*zool., tech.*) гу́сеница; (*attr.*) гу́сеничный.

caterwaul /ˈkætəˌwɔːl/ *n.* коша́чий конце́рт.
● *v.i.* задава́ть (*impf.*) коша́чий конце́рт.

catgut /ˈkætgʌt/ *n.* кетгу́т, кише́чная струна́.

catharsis /kəˈθɑːsɪs/ *n.* (*pl.* **catharses** /-siːz/) (*med.*) очище́ние желу́дка; (*fig.*) ка́тарсис.

cathartic /kəˈθɑːtɪk/ *adj.* (*med.*) слаби́тельный; (*fig.*) очища́ющий.

cathedral /kəˈθiːdr(ə)l/ *n.* (кафедра́льный) собо́р.

catheter /ˈkæθɪtə(r)/ *n.* кате́тер.

cathode /ˈkæθəʊd/ *n.* като́д; **~ rays** като́дные лучи́; **~ ray tube** электро́нно-лучева́я тру́бка.

catholic /ˈkæθəlɪk/, /ˈkæθlɪk/ *n.* като́л|ик (*fem.* -и́чка).
● *adj.* (*relig.*) католи́ческий; **Roman ~** ри́мско-католи́ческий; (*liberal*): **a man of ~ tastes** челове́к широ́ких вку́сов.

Catholicism /kəˈθɒlɪˌsɪz(ə)m/ *n.* католици́зм, католи́чество.

catholicity /ˌkæθəˈlɪsɪtɪ/ *n.* (*liberality*) широта́ интере́сов.

catkin /ˈkætkɪn/ *n.* серёжка.

Catseye /ˈkætsaɪ/ *n.* (*Br., propr., reflector*) катафо́т.

catsup /ˈkætsəp/ *n.* (*US*) = **ketchup**

cattiness /ˈkætɪnɪs/ *n.* ехи́дность.

cattle /ˈkæt(ə)l/ *n.* (*livestock*) скот, скоти́на; (*bovines*) кру́пный рога́тый скот; (*fig., pej.*) скот, скоти́на.
● *cpds.* **~-dealer** *n.* скотопромы́шленник; **~-truck** *n.* ваго́н для перево́зки скота́.

catty /ˈkætɪ/ *adj.* (**cattier, cattiest**) ехи́дный.

Caucasian /kɔːˈkeɪʒ(ə)n/, /-ˈkeɪzɪən/ *n.* (*of Caucasus*) кавка́з|ец (*fem.* -ка); (*of white race*) челове́к бе́лой ра́сы.
● *adj.* кавка́зский.

Caucasus /ˈkɔːkəsəs/ *n.* Кавка́з.

caucus /ˈkɔːkəs/ *n.* (*pl.* **~es**) фракцио́нное совеща́ние.

caudal /ˈkɔːd(ə)l/ *adj.* хвостови́дный, кауда́льный, хвостово́й.

caught /kɔːt/ *past and p.p. of* ⇨**catch**

caul /kɔːl/ *n.* (*membrane*) во́дная оболо́чка плода́; соро́чка.

cauldron /ˈkɔːldrən/ *n.* котёл.

cauliflower /ˈkɒlɪˌflaʊə(r)/ *n.* цветна́я капу́ста.

caulk /kɔːk/ (*US also* **calk**) *v.t.* конопа́тить, за-.

causal /ˈkɔːz(ə)l/ *adj.* казуа́льный, причи́нный.

causality /kɔːˈzælɪtɪ/ *n.* казуа́льность, причи́нность; причи́нная связь.

causation /kɔːˈzeɪʃ(ə)n/ *n.* причине́ние; причи́нность; причи́нная связь.

cause /kɔːz/ *n.* **1** (*that which ~s*) причи́на, по́вод. **2** (*need*) причи́на, основа́ние; **there is no ~ for alarm** нет основа́ний/причи́н для беспоко́йства. **3** (*purpose, objective*): **the workers' ~** де́ло трудя́щихся; рабо́чее де́ло; **make common ~ with s.o.** объедин|я́ться, -и́ться с кем-н. ра́ди о́бщего де́ла; **he pleaded his ~** он защища́л своё де́ло; **a lost ~** прои́гранное де́ло.
● *v.t.* вызыва́ть, вы́звать; **~ a disturbance** вызыва́ть, вы́звать беспоря́дки; **~ s.o. trouble (*or* a loss)** причин|я́ть, и́ть кому́-н. беспоко́йство/убы́тки; **what ~d the accident?** от чего́ произошёл несча́стный слу́чай?; **he ~d them to be put to death** он повеле́л уби́ть их.

cause célèbre /ˌkɔːz seˈlebr/ *n.* (*pl.* ***causes célèbres*** *pronunc. same*) гро́мкий/сканда́льный проце́сс.

causeless /ˈkɔːzlɪs/ *adj.* беспричи́нный, необосно́ванный.

causeway /ˈkɔːzweɪ/ *n.* да́мба; гать; мощёная доро́га.

caustic /ˈkɔːstɪk/ *adj.* каусти́ческий; **~ soda** е́дкий натр; (*fig.*) е́дкий, ко́лкий, язви́тельный.

cauter|ization /ˌkɔːtəraɪˈzeɪʃ(ə)n/, **-y** /ˈkɔːtərɪ/ *nn.* прижига́ние.

cauterize /ˈkɔːtəˌraɪz/ *v.t.* (*med.*) приж|ига́ть, -е́чь; (*fig.*) очерств|ля́ть, -и́ть.

caution /ˈkɔːʃ(ə)n/ *n.* **1** (*prudence*) осторо́жность; **with ~** осторо́жно, с осторо́жностью. **2** (*Br., warning*) предостереже́ние, предосторо́жность; **C~!** (*as notice*) Внима́ние!; Осторо́жно!; **he was let off with a ~** (*leg.*) его́ отпусти́ли с предупрежде́нием. **3**: **~ money** (*Br.*) зало́г.
● *v.t.* предостер|ега́ть, -е́чь.

cautionary /ˈkɔːʃənərɪ/ *adj.* предостерега́ющий.

cautious /ˈkɔːʃəs/ *adj.* осторо́жный, осмотри́тельный.

cautiousness /ˈkɔːʃəsnɪs/ *n.* осторо́жность, осмотри́тельность.

cavalcade /ˌkævəlˈkeɪd/ *n.* кавалька́да.

cavalier /ˌkævəˈlɪə(r)/ *n.* (*gallant; royalist*) кавале́р.
● *adj.* бесцеремо́нный, надме́нный.

cavalry /ˈkævəlrɪ/ *n.* кавале́рия, ко́нница; **two hundred ~** две́сти ко́нников; **a ~ charge** кавалери́йская ата́ка.
● *cpd.* **~man** *n.* кавалери́ст.

cave[1] /keɪv/ *n.* пеще́ра.
● *cpds.* **~-dweller, ~-man** *nn.* (*lit., fig.*) пеще́рный челове́к, троглоди́т; **~-painting** *n.* пеще́рная жи́вопись.

cave[2] /keɪv/ *v.i.*: **~ in** (*lit.*) прова́л|иваться, -и́ться; прода́в|ливаться, -и́ться; (*fig.*) сд|ава́ться, -а́ться.

caveat /'kævɪ,æt/ *n.* предостереже́ние.
caver /'keɪvə(r)/ *n.* спелео́лог.
cavern /'kæv(ə)n/ *n.* грот, пеще́ра.
cavernous /'kæv(ə)nəs/ *adj.* пеще́ристый; (*of voice*) глубо́кий.
caviar(e) /'kævɪ,ɑ:(r)/, /,kævɪ'ɑ:(r)/ *n.* икра́.
cavil /'kævɪl/ *n.* приди́рка.
● *v.i.* (**cavilled, cavilling;** *US* **caviled, caviling**)**: ~ at** прид|ира́ться, -ра́ться к + *d.*
cavity /'kævɪtɪ/ *n.* по́лость, впа́дина; (*in tooth*) дупло́.
cavort /kə'vɔ:t/ *v.i.* скака́ть (*impf.*).
caw /'kɔ:/ *n.* ка́рканье.
● *v.t. & i.* ка́рк|ать -нуть.
cayenne /keɪ'en/ *n.*: **~ pepper** кайе́нский пе́рец.
cayman /'keɪmən/ *n.* кайма́н.
CBE (*abbr. of* ***Commander of the Order of the British Empire***) кавале́р о́рдена Брита́нской импе́рии.
CD (*abbr. of* ***compact disk***) компа́кт-ди́ск; **~-player** прои́грыватель (*m.*) для компа́кт-ди́сков.
CD-ROM (*abbr. of* ***compact disk — read-only memory***) компа́кт-ди́ск ПЗУ; **~ drive** дисково́д компа́кт-ди́сков ПЗУ.
cease /si:s/ *n.*: **without ~** непреста́нно, не перестава́я.
● *v.t.* прекра|ща́ть, -ти́ть; перест|ава́ть, -а́ть; **~ talking** прекрати́ть (*pf.*) разгово́р; замолча́ть (*pf.*); **~ fire/payment** прекрати́ть (*pf.*) ого́нь/платежи́.
● *v.i.* прекра|ща́ться, -ти́ться.
● *cpd.* **~-fire** *n.* прекраще́ние огня́.
ceaseless /'si:slɪs/ *adj.* непреста́нный, непреры́вный.
cecum /'si:kəm/ (*US*) = **caecum**
cedar /'si:də(r)/ *n.* кедр; (*attr.*) кедро́вый; **~ forest** кедро́вник.
cede /si:d/ *v.t.* сда|ва́ть, -а́ть; уступ|а́ть, -и́ть.
cedilla /sɪ'dɪlə/ *n.* седи́ль (*m.*).
ceilidh /'keɪlɪ/ *n.* вечери́нка с шотла́ндской или ирла́ндской наро́дной му́зыкой и та́нцами.
ceiling /'si:lɪŋ/ *n.* (*lit., fig.*) потоло́к; (*fig.*) максима́льный у́ровень; **~ price** максима́льная цена́; **hit the ~** (*fig., fly into a rage*) рассвирепе́ть (*pf.*); на́ стену лезть (*impf.*).
celandine /'selən,daɪn/ *n.* (*also* **greater ~**) чистоте́л.
celebrant /'selɪbrənt/ *n.* свяще́нник, отправля́ющий церко́вную слу́жбу.
celebrate /'selɪ,breɪt/ *v.t. & i.* **1** (*mark an occasion*) пра́здновать, от-. **2** (*praise*) просл|авля́ть, -а́вить. **3** (*relig.*) отпр|авля́ть, -а́вить (церко́вную слу́жбу). **4**: **~ a marriage** соверш|а́ть, -и́ть обря́д бракосочета́ния.
celebrated /'selɪ,breɪtɪd/ *adj.* просла́вленный, знамени́тый.
celebration /selɪ'breɪʃ(ə)n/ *n.* пра́зднование, торжества́ (*nt. pl.*), прославле́ние; **this calls for a ~** э́то сле́дует отпра́здновать/отме́тить; (*of marriage*) соверше́ние.
celebratory /selɪ'breɪtərɪ/ *adj.* пра́здничный, торже́ственный.
celebrity /sɪ'lebrɪtɪ/ *n.* (*fame*) знамени́тость, изве́стность; (*person*) знамени́тость.
celeriac /sɪ'lerɪ,æk/ *n.* (корнево́й) сельдере́й.
celerity /sɪ'lerɪtɪ/ *n.* быстрота́.
celery /'selərɪ/ *n.* (листово́й) сельдере́й.
celestial /sɪ'lestɪəl/ *adj.* (*astron., fig.*) небе́сный; **~ globe** гло́бус звёздного не́ба.
celibacy /'selɪbəsɪ/ *n.* безбра́чие сексуа́льное воздержа́ние.
celibate /'selɪbət/ *adj.* безбра́чный, да́вший обе́т безбра́чия.
● *n.* да́вший обе́т безбра́чия.
cell /sel/ *n.* **1** (*in prison*) ка́мера; **condemned ~** ка́мера сме́ртников; **padded ~** пала́та, оби́тая во́йлоком. **2** (*in monastery*) ке́лья. **3** (*of honeycomb*) ячея́, яче́йка. **4** (*elec.*) элеме́нт. **5** (*biol.*) кле́тка. **6** (*pol.*) яче́йка.
● *cpds.* **~-mate** *n.* сока́мерник; **~phone** *n.* со́товый телефо́н.
cellar /'selə(r)/ *n.* по́греб, подва́л; **he keeps a good ~** у него́ хоро́ший запа́с вин.
cellarer /'selərə(r)/ *n.* ке́ларь (*m.*).
cellist /'tʃelɪst/ *n.* виолончели́ст (*fem.* -ка).
cello /'tʃeləʊ/ *n.* (*pl.* **~s**) виолонче́ль.
cellophane /'selə,feɪn/ *n.* целлофа́н; (*attr.*) целлофа́новый.
cellular /'seljʊlə(r)/ *adj.* кле́точный, яче́истый; **~ phone** со́товый телефо́н; **~ tissue** (*anat.*) клетча́тка.
celluloid /'seljʊ,lɔɪd/ *n.* целлуло́ид; (*attr.*) целлуло́идный.
cellulose /'seljʊ,ləʊz/, /-,ləʊs/ *n.* (*chem.*) целлюло́за; клетча́тка.
Celt /kelt/, /selt/ *n.* кельт.
Celtic /'keltɪk/, /'seltɪk/ *adj.* ке́льтский.
cement /sɪ'ment/ *n.* цеме́нт; (*attr.*) цеме́нтный.
● *v.t.* цементи́ровать (*impf., pf.*); (*fig.*): **~ relations** упро́ч|ивать, -ить отноше́ния; укреп|ля́ть, -и́ть свя́зи.
● *cpd.* **~-mixer** *n.* бетономеша́лка.
cemetery /'semɪtərɪ/ *n.* кла́дбище.
cenotaph /'senə,tɑ:f/ *n.* кенота́ф; па́мятник поги́бшим солда́там.
cense /sens/ *v.t.* кади́ть (*impf.*) ла́даном.
censer /'sensə(r)/ *n.* кади́ло.
censor /'sensə(r)/ *n.* це́нзор.
● *v.t.* цензурова́ть (*impf., pf.*); подв|ерга́ть, -е́ргнуть цензу́ре.
censorial /sen'sɔ:rɪəl/ *adj.* це́нзорский, цензу́рный.
censorious /sen'sɔ:rɪəs/ *adj.* сверхкрити́чный, приди́рчивый.
censoriousness /sen'sɔ:rɪəsnɪs/ *n.* крити́чность, приди́рчивость.
censorship /'sensərʃɪp/ *n.* цензу́ра.
censure /'sensjə(r)/ *n.* кри́тика, осужде́ние, порица́ние; **pass a vote of ~** вы́нести (*pf.*) во́тум недове́рия.
● *v.t.* критикова́ть (*impf.*); осу|жда́ть, -ди́ть; порица́ть (*impf.*).
census /'sensəs/ *n.* (*pl.* **~es**) пе́репись (населе́ния); **take a ~** произв|оди́ть, -ести́ пе́репись (населе́ния).
cent /sent/ *n.* **1** (*coin*) цент; (*fig.*): **it is not worth a ~** э́то гроша́ ло́маного не сто́ит. **2**: **per ~** проце́нт.
centaur /'sentɔ:(r)/ *n.* кента́вр.
centenarian /,sentɪ'neərɪən/ *n.* челове́к, дости́гший столе́тнего во́зраста.
● *adj.* столе́тний.
centen|ary /sen'ti:nərɪ/ (*Br.*), **-nial** /sen'tenɪəl/ (*US*) *n.* (*100th anniversary*) столе́тие.
● *adj.* столе́тний.
center /'sentə(r)/ (*US*) = **centre**
centigrade /'sentɪ,greɪd/ *adj.*: **~ thermometer** термо́метр Це́льсия; **20° ~** 20 гра́дусов Це́льсия (*or* по Це́льсию).
centigram(me) /'sentɪ,græm/ *n.* сантигра́мм.
centilitre /'sentɪ,li:tə(r)/ (*US* **centiliter**) *n.* сантили́тр.
centime /'sɑ̃ti:m/ *n.* санти́м.
centimetre /'sentɪ,mi:tə(r)/ (*US* **centimeter**) *n.* сантиме́тр.
centipede /'sentɪ,pi:d/ *n.* многоно́жка.
central /'sentr(ə)l/ *adj.* **1** (*pert. to a centre*) центра́льный; **C~ America** Центра́льная Аме́рика; **~ Asia** Сре́дняя А́зия; **~ European** среднеевропе́йский; **~ bank** центра́льный банк; **~ processing unit** центра́льный проце́ссор; **the house is very ~** дом нахо́дится в са́мом це́нтре го́рода. **2** (*principal*) центра́льный, гла́вный; **the ~ figure in the story** гла́вный персона́ж расска́за.
centralism /'sentrə,lɪz(ə)m/ *n.* централи́зм.
centralist /'sentrəlɪst/ *n.* сторо́нник централи́зма.
centralization /,sentrəlaɪ'zeɪʃ(ə)n/ *n.* централиза́ция.
centralize /'sentrə,laɪz/ *v.t.* централизова́ть (*impf., pf.*).
centre /'sentə(r)/ (*US* **center**) *n.* **1** (*middle point or section*) центр; (*of a chocolate*) начи́нка; **~ of gravity** центр тя́жести; **dead ~** мёртвая то́чка. **2** (*fig., key-point*): **~ of attraction** центр внима́ния; **~ of commerce** комме́рческий центр; **shopping ~** торго́вый центр; **gardening ~** (*shop*) «всё для садо́вника»; **cultural ~** культу́рный центр. **3** (*pol.*) центр. **4** (*attr.*) центра́льный.
● *v.t.* **1** (*fix in central position*) поме|ща́ть, -сти́ть в це́нтре. **2** (*fig.*) сосредото́чи|вать, -ть; концентри́ровать, с-; **~ one's thoughts on** сосредото́чить (*pf.*) мы́сли на + *p.*
● *v.i.* сосредото́чи|ваться, -ться; концентри́роваться, с-; **our thoughts**

~ on наши мысли сосредоточены на (+*p.*); **the discussion ~d round this point** дискуссия сосредоточилась вокруг этого вопроса.

● *cpds.* **~-bit** *n.* центровое сверло; **~board** *n.* (*naut.*) выдвижной киль; **~-forward** *n.* (*sport*) центральный нападающий; **~-half** *n.* центральный полузащитник; **~piece** *n.* орнаментальная ваза в середине стола; (*fig.*) главное украшение; **~-right** *adj.* (*pol.*) правоцентристский.

centrifugal /ˌsentrɪˈfjuːg(ə)l/, /senˈtrɪfjʊg(ə)l/ *adj.* центробежный.

centrifuge /ˈsentrɪˌfjuːdʒ/ *n.* центрифуга.

centripetal /senˈtrɪpɪt(ə)l/ *adj.* центростремительный.

centrism /ˈsentrɪz(ə)m/ *n.* центризм.

centrist /ˈsentrɪst/ *n.* центрист.

centuple /ˈsentjʊp(ə)l/ *n.* стократный размер.

● *adj.* стократный.

centurion /senˈtjʊərɪən/ *n.* центурион.

century /ˈsentʃərɪ/, /-tjʊrɪ/ *n.* (*100 years*) столетие, век; **~ plant** столетник; (*set of 100*) сотня.

CEO (*abbr. of* ***chief executive officer***) Глава исполнительной власти.

cephalic /sɪˈfælɪk/, /ke-/ *adj.* головной.

cephalopod /ˈsefələˌpɒd/ *n.* головоногий моллюск.

ceramic /sɪˈræmɪk/ *adj.* керамический.

ceramicist /sɪˈræmɪsɪst/ *n.* керамист.

ceramics /sɪˈræmɪks/ *n.* керамика.

cereal /ˈsɪərɪəl/ *n.* хлебный злак; **(breakfast) ~** хлопья (к завтраку) (*корнфлекс и т.п.*).

● *adj.* хлебный, зерновой.

cerebel|lum /ˌserɪˈbeləm/ *n.* (*pl.* **~lums** *or* **~la**) мозжечок.

cerebra /ˈserɪbrə/ *pl. of* ⇒**cerebrum**

cerebral /ˈserɪbr(ə)l/ *adj.* **1** (*of the brain*) мозговой, церебральный; **~ haemorrhage** (*Br.*), **hemorrhage** (*US*) кровоизлияние в мозг. **2** (*intellectual*) умозрительный, интеллектуальный; **he is a ~ person** он живёт рассудком.

cerebrum /ˈserɪbrəm/ *n.* (*pl.* **cerebra**) головной мозг.

cerecloth /ˈsɪəklɒθ/ *n.* саван.

ceremonial /ˌserɪˈməʊnɪəl/ *n.* (*relig. rites*) церемониал, обряд, ритуал.

● *adj.* церемониальный, обрядовый; **~ dress** парадная форма одежды.

ceremonious /ˌserɪˈməʊnɪəs/ *adj.* церемонный.

ceremoniousness /ˌserɪˈməʊnɪəsnɪs/ *n.* церемонность.

ceremony /ˈserɪmənɪ/ *n.* (*rite*) обряд, церемония; **wedding ~** венчание; обряд венчания; (*formal behaviour*) церемонность; **stand (up)on ~** церемониться (*impf.*); наст|аивать, -оять на соблюдении формальностей; **without ~** без церемоний.

cerise /səˈriːz/, /-ˈriːs/ *adj.* светло-вишнёвый.

cert /sɜːt/ *n.* (*Br. sl.*): **a (dead) ~** верное дело.

certain /ˈsɜːt(ə)n/, /-tɪn/ *adj.* **1** (*undoubted*) несомненный; **I cannot say for ~** я не могу сказать наверняка; **make ~ of** (*ascertain*) удостов|еряться, -ериться в чём-н.; (*ensure possession of*) обеспечи|вать, -ть; **he faced ~ death** ему угрожала верная смерть; **he is ~ to succeed** он наверняка/несомненно преуспеет. **2** (*confident*) уверенный; **he is ~ of success** он уверен в успехе; **I am ~ he will come** я уверен, что он придёт. **3** (*definite but unspecified*) известный, некоторый; один; **a ~ person** некто, некое лицо; **in a ~ town** в одном городе; **a ~ Mr Jones** некий г. Джоунс; **a ~ type of people** люди известного рода; **under ~ conditions** при известных условиях; **a ~ (*some*) pleasure** некоторое удовольствие.

certainly /ˈsɜːtənlɪ/, /-tɪnlɪ/ *adv.* (*without doubt*) несомненно, наверняка, наверно; (*expr. obedience or consent*) конечно, безусловно; **'May we go?' — '~ not!'** «Можно нам идти?» — «Ни в коем случае!».

certainty /ˈsɜːtəntɪ/, /-tɪntɪ/ *n.* **1** (*being certainly true*) несомненность. **2** (*certain fact*) несомненный факт; **for a ~** наверняка. **3** (*confidence*) уверенность. **4** (*accuracy*): **I cannot say with ~** не могу определённо сказать.

certifiable /ˌsɜːtɪˈfaɪəb(ə)l/, /ˈsɜːt-/ *adj.* (*lunatic*) душевнобольной.

certificate /səˈtɪfɪkət/ *n.* удостоверение, свидетельство, сертификат; **~ of health** медицинское свидетельство; **birth ~** свидетельство о рождении, метрика; **marriage ~** свидетельство о браке.

● *v.t.*: **a ~d teacher** учитель (*m.*) (*fem.* -ница) с дипломом.

certification /ˌsɜːtɪfɪˈkeɪʃ(ə)n/ *n.* удостоверение.

certify /ˈsɜːtɪˌfaɪ/ *v.t.* **1** (*attest*) удостов|ерять, -ерить; зав|ерять, -ерить; **this is to ~ that** ... настоящим удостоверяется, что.... **2** (*declare insane*) призн|авать, -ать душевнобольным.

certitude /ˈsɜːtɪˌtjuːd/ *n.* уверенность; несомненность.

cerulean /səˈruːlɪən/ *adj.* небесно-голубой.

cervical /sɜːˈvaɪk(ə)l/, /ˈsɜːvɪk(ə)l/ *adj.* шейный; **~ smear** (*Br.*) мазок с шейки матки.

cervix /ˈsɜːvɪks/ *n.* (*pl.* **cervices** /-ˌsiːz/) шея; (*of womb*) шейка (матки).

Cesarean /sɪˈzeərɪən/ (*US*) = **Caesarean**

cesium /ˈsiːzɪəm/ (*US*) = **caesium**

cessation /seˈseɪʃ(ə)n/ *n.* прекращение, остановка; **~ of hostilities** прекращение военных действий.

cession /ˈseʃ(ə)n/ *n.* уступка, передача.

cess|pit /ˈsespɪt/, **-pool** /ˈsespuːl/ *nn.* выгребная/помойная/сточная яма; (*fig.*) помойная яма, клоака.

cetacean /sɪˈteɪʃ(ə)n/ *n.* животное из семейства китовых.

ceteris paribus /ˌsetərɪs ˈpærɪˌbʊs/ *adv.* при прочих равных условиях.

cf. (*abbr. of Latin* ***confer*** = ***compare with***) ср., сравни.

CFCs (*abbr. of* ***chloro-fluorocarbons***) хлорированные фторуглероды.

cha-cha /ˈtʃɑːtʃɑː/ *n.* ча-ча-ча (*nt. indecl.*).

chafe /tʃeɪf/ *n.* (**~*d place***) ссадина.

● *v.t.* (*rub*) тереть (*impf.*); (*make sore*) нат|ирать, -ереть; **the collar ~d his neck** воротник натёр ему шею.

● *v.i.* нат|ираться, -ереться; **her skin ~s easily** у неё кожа легко воспаляется; **he ~d at the delay** отсрочка раздражала его.

chaff /tʃɑːf/ *n.* **1** (*husks*) мякина. **2** (*banter*) подшучивание.

● *v.t.* подшу|чивать, -тить над + *i.*

● *cpd.* **~-cutter** *n.* соломорезка.

chaffinch /ˈtʃæfɪntʃ/ *n.* зяблик.

chafing-dish /ˈtʃeɪfɪŋ/ *n.* жаровня.

chagrin /ˈʃægrɪn/, /ʃəˈgriːn/ *n.* огорчение, досада.

● *v.t.* огорч|ать, -ить.

chain /tʃeɪn/ *n.* цепь; цепочка; **mountain ~** горная цепь; (*pl., fetters*) цепи (*f. pl.*), оков|ы (*pl., g.* —); (*fig.*): **~ of events/consequences** цепь событий/последствий; **~ reaction** цепная реакция.

● *v.t.* прико́в|ывать, -ать цепью; **the dog is ~ed up** собака посажена на цепь.

● *cpds.* **~-gang** *n.* группа заключённых, скованных общей цепью; **~-mail** *n.* кольчуга; **~-smoke** *v.t.* курить (*impf.*) одну сигарету за другой; **~-smoker** *n.* заядлый курильщик, табакоман; **~-stitch** *n.* тамбурная строчка; **~-store** *n.* однотипный фирменный магазин.

chair /tʃeə(r)/ *n.* **1** стул; **take a ~!** садитесь! **2** (**~*manship***) председательство; **Mr X took/left the ~** г-н X занял/покинул председательское место. **3** (**~*man***) председатель (*m.*); **Madam C~man!** госпожа председатель! **4** (*professorship*) кафедра; **he holds the ~ of physics** он заведует кафедрой физики.

● *v.t.* (*preside over*) председательствовать (*impf.*) на + *p.*

● *cpds.* **~-lift** *n.* подвесной подъёмник; **~man, ~-person** *nn.* = **chair** 3; **~manship** *n.* председательство; обязанности (*f. pl.*) председателя.

chaise longue /ʃeɪz ˈlɒŋg/ *n.* (*pl.* ***chaise longues*** *or* ***chaises longues*** *pronunc. same*) шезлонг.

chalcedony /kælˈsedənɪ/ *n.* (*min.*) халцедон.

chalet /ˈʃæleɪ/ *n.* шале (*indecl.*).

chalice /ˈtʃælɪs/ *n.* (*goblet*) кубок, чаша; (*eccl.*) потир.

chalk /tʃɔ:k/ *n.* **1** (*material*) мел; (*attr.*) мелово́й. **2** (*piece of* ~) мел, мело́к. **3** (*fig.*): **not by a long** ~ (*Br.*) отню́дь нет; далеко́ не; **as different as** ~ **from cheese** (*Br.*) похо́же, как гвоздь на панихи́ду.

● *v.t.* (*write or mark with* ~) писа́ть, на- (*or* отм|еча́ть, -е́тить) ме́лом; (*whiten with* ~) бели́ть, по-; ~ **out** (*sketch*) набр|а́сывать, -оса́ть; ~ **up** (*register*) отм|еча́ть, -е́тить.

chalky /ˈtʃɔ:kɪ/ *adj.* (**chalkier, chalkiest**) (*like chalk*) мелово́й; (*containing chalk*) известко́вый.

challenge /ˈtʃælɪndʒ/ *n.* (*to a race etc.*) вы́зов; ~ **cup** переходя́щий ку́бок; (*sentry's*) о́клик; (*fig.*): **this task was a** ~ **to his ingenuity** э́та зада́ча потре́бовала от него́ большо́й изобрета́тельности.

● *v.t.* вызыва́ть, вы́звать; (*dispute*) оспа́ривать (*impf.*); ~ **a juryman** отв|оди́ть, -ести́ прися́жного; ~ **s.o. to a race/duel** вызыва́ть, вы́звать кого́-н. на состяза́ние/дуэ́ль; **I** ~ **you to deny it** попро́буйте опрове́ргнуть э́то; **he** ~**d my right to attend** он возража́л про́тив моего́ прису́тствия.

challenger /ˈtʃælɪndʒə(r)/ *n.* претенде́нт (*fem.* -ка).

challenging /ˈtʃælɪndʒɪŋ/ *adj.* (*of opportunity etc.*) тру́дный, но интере́сный.

chamber /ˈtʃeɪmbə(r)/ *n.* **1** (*room*) ко́мната; (*pl., apartment*) кварти́ра; (*pl., Br., rooms of barrister(s)*) адвока́тская конто́ра; (*judge's room*) ка́мера, кабине́т судьи́; ~ **of horrors** зал у́жасов; **bridal** ~ спа́льня новобра́чных; ~ **music** ка́мерная му́зыка. **2** (*hall, e.g. of parliament*) зал, за́ла. **3** (*official body*) пала́та; **C**~ **of Commerce** торго́вая пала́та; ~ **of deputies** пала́та депута́тов. **4** (*of revolver*) патро́нник.

● *cpds.* ~**maid** *n.* го́рничная; ~**-pot** *n.* ночно́й горшо́к.

chamberlain /ˈtʃeɪmbəlɪn/ *n.* камерге́р, мажордо́м.

chameleon /kəˈmi:lɪən/ *n.* (*lit., fig.*) хамелео́н.

chamfer /ˈtʃæmfə(r)/ *n.* ско́шенная кро́мка.

● *v.t.* ска́шивать, скоси́ть.

chamois /ˈʃæmwɑ:/, *sense* 2 *also* /ˈʃæmɪ/ *n.* **1** (*pl.* ~ /-wɑ:z/) (*zool.*) се́рна. **2** (*pl.* ~ /-mɪz/, /-wɑ:z/) (~*-leather*) за́мша.

champ[1] /tʃæmp/ *n.* (*chewing action or noise*) ча́вканье.

● *v.t. & i.* (*chew noisily*) ча́вкать (*impf.*); (*bite on*): ~ **the bit** грызть (*impf.*) удила́; (*fig.*): **he was** ~**ing to start** он рва́лся в путь.

champ[2] /tʃæmp/ (*coll.*) = **champion** 2

champagne /ʃæmˈpeɪn/ *n.* шампа́нское; (*colour*) бле́дно-па́левый цвет.

champion /ˈtʃæmpɪən/ *n.* **1** (*defender*) побо́рни|к, защи́тни|к (*fem.* -ца); боре́ц; **a** ~ **of women's rights** побо́рник же́нского равнопра́вия. **2** (*prize-winning person or thing*) чемпио́н (*fem., coll.* -ка); **a** ~ **chess-player** чемпио́н по ша́хматам.

championship /ˈtʃæmpɪənʃɪp/ *n.* (*advocacy*) защи́та; (*sport*) чемпио́нство, чемпиона́т, пе́рвенство.

chance /tʃɑ:ns/ *n.* **1** (*casual occurrence*) слу́чай, случа́йность; **by** ~ случа́йно; **he left it to** ~ он оста́вил э́то на во́лю слу́чая; **game of** ~ аза́ртная игра́. **2** (*possibility, likelihood, opportunity*) шанс, возмо́жность; **I went there on the** ~ **of seeing him** я пошёл туда́, наде́ясь его́ уви́деть; **the** ~**s are that he will come** все ша́нсы за то, что он придёт; **I had no** ~ **of winning** у меня́ не́ было никаки́х ша́нсов на успе́х; **he stands a good** ~ **of winning** он име́ет все ша́нсы на успе́х; **now is your** ~ вот ваш шанс; де́ло за ва́ми; **the** ~ **of a lifetime** раз в жи́зни предста́вившийся слу́чай; **a fat** ~ **he has!** куда́ уж ему́ (*coll.*); **he hasn't a dog's** ~ у него́ нет никаки́х ша́нсов; **a** ~ **companion** случа́йный попу́тчик.

● *v.t.*: **let's** ~ **it** рискнём!

● *v.i.* (*happen*) случ|а́ться, -и́ться; **I** ~**d to see him** мне довело́сь уви́деть его́; **he** ~**d upon the book** ему́ попала́сь э́та кни́га.

chancel /ˈtʃɑ:ns(ə)l/ *n.* алта́рь (*m.*).

chancellery /ˈtʃɑ:nsələrɪ/ *n.* канцеля́рия.

chancellor /ˈtʃɑ:nsələ(r)/ *n.* ка́нцлер; (*of university*) ре́ктор; **C**~ **of the Exchequer** ка́нцлер казначе́йства, мини́стр фина́нсов.

chancellorship /ˈtʃɑ:nsələˌʃɪp/ *n.* зва́ние ка́нцлера, ка́нцлерство.

chancery /ˈtʃɑ:nsərɪ/ *n.* **1** (*leg.*) ка́нцлерский суд; **in** ~ (*fig.*) в тиска́х. **2** (*Br., of embassy*) канцеля́рия.

chancre /ˈʃæŋkə(r)/ *n.* твёрдый шанкр.

chancy /ˈtʃɑ:nsɪ/ *adj.* (**chancier, chanciest**) (*coll.*) риско́ванный.

chandelier /ˌʃændɪˈlɪə(r)/ *n.* лю́стра.

chandler /ˈtʃɑ:ndlə(r)/ *n.* москате́льщик.

change /tʃeɪndʒ/ *n.* **1** (*alteration*) измене́ние; (*substitution*) переме́на; ~ **of air, scene** переме́на обстано́вки; ~ **of life** (*med.*) кли́макс; **for a** ~ для разнообра́зия; ~ **of heart** измене́ние наме́рений; **a** ~ **for the better** переме́на к лу́чшему. **2** (*spare set*) сме́на; **he took a** ~ **of linen with him** он взял с собо́й сме́ну белья́. **3** (*money*) ме́лкие де́н|ьги (*pl., g.* -ег); ме́лочь; (*returned as balance*) сда́ча; **have you** ~ **for a pound?** мо́жете ли вы разменя́ть фунт? **4** (*of trains etc.*) переса́дка; **no** ~ **for Oxford** в О́ксфорд без переса́дки. **5** (*of bells*) перезво́н, трезво́н; **ring (the)** ~**s** (*lit.*) вызва́нивать (*impf.*) на колокола́х; (*fig.*) тверди́ть (*impf.*) на все лады́ одно́ и то же.

● *v.t.* **1** (*alter, replace*) меня́ть, по-; **she** ~**d her address** она́ перее́хала на друго́е ме́сто; ~ **(one's) clothes** переод|ева́ться, -е́ться; смен|я́ть, -и́ть оде́жду; ~ **one's shoes** переоб|ува́ться, -у́ться; **the snake** ~**s its skin** змея́ меня́ет ко́жу; ~ **colour** (*Br.*), **color** (*US*) (*turn pale*) бледне́ть, по-; измени́ться (*pf.*) в лице́; (*blush*) красне́ть, по-; ~ **one's mind** разду́м|ывать, -ать; переду́м|ывать, -ать; ~ **one's tune** (*fig.*) запе́ть (*pf.*) на друго́й лад (*or* по-друго́му); ~ **hands** (*of a property*) пере|ходи́ть, -йти́ из рук в ру́ки; ~ **sides** пере|ходи́ть, -йти́ на другу́ю сто́рону (*or* в друго́й ла́герь); ~ **trains** перес|а́живаться, -е́сть на друго́й по́езд; ~ **gear** меня́ть, по- ско́рость; переключ|а́ть, -и́ть ско́рость/переда́чу; ~ **the subject** смени́ть/перемени́ть (*pf.*) те́му разгово́ра. **2** (*re-clothe etc.*): ~ **a child** переод|ева́ть, -е́ть ребёнка; (*of baby*) перепел|ёнывать, -ена́ть; ~ **a bed** меня́ть, по- посте́льное бельё. **3** (*money*): ~ **a pound note** разменя́ть (*pf.*) фу́нтовую бума́жку; ~ **francs into pounds** обменя́ть (*pf.*) фра́нки на фу́нты сте́рлингов. **4** (*exchange*): ~ **a book** обменя́ть (*pf.*) кни́гу; ~ **places with s.o.** (*lit.*) поменя́ться (*pf.*) места́ми с кем-н.; ~**ing of the guard** сме́на карау́ла.

● *v.i.* **1**: **he has** ~**d a lot** он си́льно измени́лся/перемени́лся; **caterpillars** ~ **into butterflies** гу́сеницы превраща́ются в ба́бочек; **we** ~**d to central heating** мы перешли́ на центра́льное отопле́ние; **his expression** ~**d** он измени́лся/перемени́лся в лице́; **the weather** ~**d to rain** пого́да перемени́лась, и пошёл дождь; **the wind** ~**d** ве́тер перемени́лся. **2** (*rail.*) перес|а́живаться, -е́сть; **all** ~**!** коне́чная остано́вка!; переса́дка, по́езд да́льше не пойдёт! **3** (*clothing*): ~ **for dinner** переод|ева́ться, -е́ться к у́жину.

● *with advs.*: ~ **down** *v.i.* (*Br., motoring*) переключ|а́ть, -и́ть на ни́жнюю ско́рость; ~ **over** *v.i.*: **the railways** ~**d over to electricity** желе́зные доро́ги перешли́ на электри́чество/электроэне́ргию; ~ **up** *v.i.* (*Br., motoring*) переключ|а́ть, -и́ть на вы́сшую ско́рость.

● *cpd.* ~**-over** *n.*: ~**-over to electricity** перехо́д на электроэне́ргию; (*of leader etc.*) сме́на.

changeab|ility /ˌtʃeɪndʒəˈbɪlɪtɪ/, **-leness** /ˈtʃeɪndʒəb(ə)lnɪs/ *nn.* переме́нчивость; изме́нчивость.

changeable /ˈtʃeɪndʒəb(ə)l/ *adj.*: ~ **weather** изме́нчивая пого́да; (*of person*) изме́нчивый, непостоя́нный.

changeless /ˈtʃeɪndʒlɪs/ *adj.* неизме́нный.

changing-room /ˈtʃeɪndʒɪŋˌru:m/ *n.* (*sport*) раздева́лка; (*Br., in shop*) приме́рочная.

channel /ˈtʃæn(ə)l/ *n.* **1** (*strait*) проли́в, кана́л; **the English C**~ Ла-Ма́нш; **the C**~ **Islands** Норма́ндские острова́; **C**~ **tunnel** тонне́ль под Ла-Ма́ншем; (*branch, arm of waterway*) рука́в. **2** (*bed of a stream*) ру́сло. **3** (*deeper part of a waterway*) фарва́тер.

4 (*fig.*): **through the usual ~s** обы́чным путём; **~ of information** исто́чник информа́ции.
5 (*television*) кана́л.
● *v.t.* (**channelled, channelling;** *US* **channeled, channeling**) (*make a ~ in*) пров|оди́ть, -ести́ кана́л в + *p.*; (*cause to flow*): **the river ~led its way through the rocks** река́ проложи́ла себе́ путь че́рез ска́лы; (*fig.*): **we ~led the information to him** мы переда́ли ему́ э́ти све́дения; **his energies are ~led into sport** вся его́ эне́ргия ухо́дит на спорт.
● *with adv.*: **~ off** *v.t.* отв|оди́ть, -ести́.

chant /tʃɑ:nt/ *n.* песнь; (*eccl.*) пе́ние.
● *v.t.* восп|ева́ть, -е́ть.
● *v.i.* петь (*impf.*).

chantry /'tʃɑ:ntrɪ/ *n.* (*chapel*) часо́вня.

chaos /'keɪɒs/ *n.* хао́с.

chaotic /keɪ'ɒtɪk/ *adj.* хаоти́ческий, хаоти́чный.

chap[1] /tʃæp/ *v.t.* (**chapped, chapping**) произв|оди́ть, -ести́ тре́щину в + *p.*; **~ped hands** потре́скавшиеся ру́ки.

chap[2] (*also* **chappie**) /tʃæp/ *n.* (*Br. coll., fellow*) па́рень (*m.*), ма́лый; **a good ~** сла́вный ма́лый; **old ~** старина́ (*m.*).

chapel /'tʃæp(ə)l/ *n.* **1** (*small church*) часо́вня, моле́льня; (*Catholic*) капе́лла.
2 (*part of church*) приде́л с алтарём.
3 (*Br., trade union branch*) отделе́ние профсою́за (печа́тников).

chaperon(e) /'ʃæpə,rəʊn/ *n.* компаньо́нка.
● *v.t.* сопрово|жда́ть, -ди́ть.

chaplain /'tʃæplɪn/ *n.* капелла́н, свяще́нник.

chaplaincy /'tʃæplɪnsɪ/ *n.* до́лжность капелла́на.

chaplet /'tʃæplɪt/ *n.* (*wreath*) вено́к; (*necklace*) ожере́лье; (*rosary*) чёт|ки (*pl., g.* -ок).

chappie /'tʃæpɪ/ = **chap**[2]

chapter /'tʃæptə(r)/ *n.* **1** (*of book*) глава́; **~ and verse** (*fig.*) то́чная ссы́лка; **~ of accidents** череда́ неуда́ч.
2 (*of clergy*) собра́ние кано́ников (*or* чле́нов мона́шеского о́рдена).
● *cpd.* **~-house** *n.* дом капи́тула.

char[1] /tʃɑ:(r)/ *v.t.* (**charred, charring**) (*burn*) обу́гли|вать, -ть.
● *v.i.* (**charred, charring**) обу́гли|ваться, -ться.

char[2] /tʃɑ:(r)/ *n.* (*Br. coll.*) = **~woman**
● *v.t.* (**charred, charring**) (*coll., perform housework*) уб|ира́ть, -ра́ть помеще́ние подённо.
● *cpds.* **~lady, ~woman** *nn.* (подённая) убо́рщица.

character /'kærɪktə(r)/ *n.* **1** (*nature*) сво́йство, ка́чество; **a book of that ~** кни́га тако́го ро́да.
2 (*personal qualities*) хара́ктер; **a man of ~** челове́к с си́льным хара́ктером; **he lacks ~** он бесхара́ктерный челове́к; **an interesting ~** интере́сный челове́к; **his remark was in (*or* out of) ~** э́то замеча́ние бы́ло вполне́ (*or* не) в его́ ду́хе/сти́ле.
3 (*well-known person*): **a public ~** обще́ственный де́ятель.
4 (*eccentric or distinctive person*): **she is quite a ~** она́ оригина́льная ли́чность; **a weird ~** стра́нный субъе́кт; **a ~ actor** характе́рный актёр.
5 (*fictional*) геро́й, тип, о́браз, персона́ж; **in the ~ of Hamlet** в о́бразе Га́млета.
6 (*reputation*) репута́ция; **~ assassination** подры́в репута́ции.
7 (*letter, graphic symbol*) бу́ква, ли́тера, знак; **Chinese ~s** кита́йские иеро́глифы (*m. pl.*); **Runic ~s** руни́ческое письмо́.

characteristic /,kærɪktə'rɪstɪk/ *n.* характе́рная черта́, сво́йство, осо́бенность; (*math.*) характери́стика.
● *adj.* характе́рный, типи́чный; **it is ~ of him** э́то характе́рно для него́.

characterization /,kærɪktəraɪ'zeɪʃ(ə)n/ *n.* **1** (*description*) характери́стика. **2** (*by author or actor*) созда́ние о́браза; тракто́вка.

characterize /'kærɪktə,raɪz/ *v.t.* **1** (*describe*) (о)характеризова́ть (*impf., pf.*); **~ s.o. as a liar** охарактеризова́ть кого́-н. как лгуна́. **2** (*distinguish*) отлич|а́ть, -и́ть; **he is ~d by honesty** он отлича́ется свое́й че́стностью.

characterless /'kærɪktəlɪs/ *adj.* (*undistinguished*) бесхара́ктерный, зауря́дный.

charade /ʃə'rɑ:d/ *n.* шара́да.

charcoal /'tʃɑ:kəʊl/ *n.* древе́сный у́голь; **a ~ drawing** рису́нок у́глем.
● *cpds.* **~-burner** *n.* у́гольщик; **~-grey** *n. & adj.* тёмно-се́рый, пе́пельный (цвет).

charcuterie /ʃɑ:'ku:tərɪ/ *n.* магази́н мясно́й кулина́рии.

charge /tʃɑ:dʒ/ *n.* **1** (*load*) нагру́зка, груз.
2 (*for gun etc.*) заря́д.
3 (*elec.*) заря́д, заряжа́ние; **the battery is on ~** батаре́я заряжа́ется.
4 (*her.*) эмбле́ма, деви́з.
5 (*expense*) цена́, расхо́ды (*m. pl.*); **what is the ~?** ско́лько э́то сто́ит?; **his ~s are reasonable** его́ це́ны вполне́ уме́ренные; **a ~ account** счёт в магази́не; **~ card** креди́тная ка́рточка; **at his own ~** на его́/свой со́бственный счёт; **free of ~** беспла́тно.
6 (*duty, care*): **the child is in my ~** э́тот ребёнок на моём попече́нии; **I am in ~ here** я здесь гла́вный; я здесь за ста́ршего; **she's in ~ of the hospital** она́ возглавля́ет больни́цу; **take ~ of a business** взять (*pf.*) на себя́ руково́дство де́лом.
7 (*person entrusted*): **the nurse took her ~s for a walk** ня́ня повела́ свои́х пито́мцев на прогу́лку.
8 (*instructions*) предписа́ние.
9 (*accusation*) обвине́ние; **bring a ~ against s.o.** выдвига́ть, вы́двинуть обвине́ние про́тив кого́-н.; **he pleaded guilty to the ~ of speeding** он призна́л себя́ вино́вным в превыше́нии ско́рости.
10 (*attack*) нападе́ние, ата́ка; **return to the ~** (*fig.*) возобнови́ть (*pf.*) ата́ку.
● *v.t.* **1** (*load, fill*) нагру|жа́ть, -зи́ть; **~ your glasses!** напо́лните свои́ бока́лы!; (*elec.*) заря|жа́ть, -ди́ть.
2 (*make responsible*): **he was ~d with an important mission** ему́ бы́ло пору́чено ва́жное зада́ние.
3 (*instruct*): **I ~ you to obey him** я тре́бую, что́бы вы повинова́лись ему́; **the judge ~d the jury** судья́ напу́тствовал прися́жных.
4 (*accuse*) обвин|я́ть, -и́ть; **he is ~d with murder** его́ обвиня́ют в уби́йстве.
5 (*debit*): **~ the amount/goods to me** запиши́те су́мму/това́ры на мой счёт; **his estate was ~d with the debt; the debt was ~d to his estate** за его́ име́нием чи́слился долг; **tax is ~d on the proceeds of the sale** дохо́ды с прода́жи подлежа́т обложе́нию нало́гом.
6 (*ask price*): **he ~d £5 for the book** он запроси́л 5 фу́нтов за э́ту кни́гу.
7 (*also v.i.; attack*): **the troops ~d the enemy** войска́ атакова́ли неприя́теля; **he ~d at me** он набро́сился на меня́.
● *cpds.* **~-nurse** *n.* (*Br.*) ста́ршая медсестра́ отделе́ния; **~-sheet** *n.* (*Br.*) полице́йский протоко́л.

chargeable /'tʃɑ:dʒəb(ə)l/ *adj.* **1**: **~** (*to be debited*) **to** относи́мый за счёт + *g.*; **the expense is ~ to him** э́тот расхо́д сле́дует отнести́ на его́ счёт. **2** (*liable to be accused*): **he is ~ with theft** он мо́жет быть обвинён в кра́же.

chargé d'affaires /,ʃɑ:ʒeɪ dæ'feə(r)/ *n.* (*pl.* **chargés** *pronunc. same*) пове́ренный в дела́х.

charger /'tʃɑ:dʒə(r)/ *n.* (*horse*) строева́я ло́шадь; боево́й конь.

chariness /'tʃernəs/ *n.* осторо́жность; сде́ржанность.

chariot /'tʃærɪət/ *n.* колесни́ца.

charioteer /,tʃærɪə'tɪə(r)/ *n.* возни́ца (*m.*).

charisma /kə'rɪzmə/ *n.* хари́зма, обая́ние.

charismatic /,kærɪz'mætɪk/ *adj.* харизмати́ческий, обая́тельный.

charitable /'tʃærɪtəb(ə)l/ *adj.* (*in judgement etc.*) ми́лостивый, снисходи́тельный; **it would be ~ to suppose that he was drunk** в лу́чшем слу́чае мо́жно предположи́ть, что он был пьян; (*in almsgiving*) благотвори́тельный.

charity /'tʃærɪtɪ/ *n.* **1** (*kindness*) любо́вь к бли́жнему; **~ begins at home** ≈ кто ду́мает о родны́х, не забу́дет и чужи́х; **he lives on ~** он живёт ми́лостыней. **2** (*indulgence*) милосе́рдие; снисхожде́ние.
3 (*almsgiving*) благотвори́тельность; ми́лостыня; **give, dispense ~** под|ава́ть, -а́ть ми́лостыню.
4 (*institution*) благотвори́тельная организа́ция; **~ concert** благотвори́тельный конце́рт.

charlatan /'ʃɑ:lət(ə)n/ *n.* шарлата́н.

charlatanism /'ʃɑ:lətən,ɪz(ə)m/ *n.* шарлата́нство.

charm /tʃɑ:m/ *n.* **1** (*attraction*) обая́ние, очарова́ние, очарова́тельность, шарм; **her ~s** её пре́лести (*f. pl.*). **2** (*spell*) ча́р|ы (*pl., g.* —); **under a ~** заколдо́ванный; очаро́ванный; **it worked like a ~** э́то оказа́ло маги́ческое де́йствие. **3** (*talisman*) амуле́т.

● *v.t.* **1** (*attract, delight*) очаро́в|ывать, -а́ть. **2** (*use magic on*) чарова́ть (*impf.*); зачаро́в|ывать, -а́ть; **he bears a ~ed life** он как бы неуязви́м; его́ Бог храни́т.

● *cpd.* **~ bracelet** *n.* брасле́т с брелка́ми.

charmer /ˈtʃɑːmə(r)/ *n.* **1** (*beauty*) чаровни́ца, чаро́дейка. **2** (*charming person*) обая́тельный/очарова́тельный челове́к.

charming /ˈtʃɑːmɪŋ/ *adj.* очарова́тельный, обая́тельный, чару́ющий.

chart /tʃɑːt/ *n.* **1** (*nautical map*) морска́я ка́рта; (*record*) табли́ца, гра́фик; **weather ~** синопти́ческая ка́рта; **temperature ~** температу́рный гра́фик. **2** (*pl., hit parade*) хит-пара́д.

● *v.t.* черти́ть, на- ка́рту +*g.*; нан|оси́ть, -ести́ на ка́рту; **~ an ocean** черти́ть, на- ка́рту океа́на; **~ s.o.'s progress** де́лать, с- диагра́мму чьего́-н. продвиже́ния; **~ a course of action** нам|еча́ть, -е́тить план де́йствий.

charter /ˈtʃɑːtə(r)/ *n.* **1** (*grant of rights*) ха́ртия, гра́мота. **2** (*of society*): **C~ of the United Nations** Уста́в ООН; **~ member** член-основа́тель (*m.*) организа́ции. **3** (*hire*) фрахто́вка, наём; **~ flight** ча́ртерный рейс.

● *v.t.* **1** (*grant diploma etc. to*) дарова́ть (*impf., pf.*) ха́ртию/привиле́гию +*d.*; **~ed accountant** (*Br.*) бухга́лтер-экспе́рт, аудито́р. **2** (*provide on hire*) сд|ава́ть, -ать внаём по ча́ртеру. **3** (*procure on hire*) фрахтова́ть, за-.

● *cpd.* **~-party** *n.* фрахто́вый контра́кт, ча́ртер-па́ртия.

charterer /ˈtʃɑːtərə(r)/ *n.* (*person providing on hire*) фрахто́вщик; (*person receiving*) фрахтова́тель (*m.*).

chartreuse /ʃɑːˈtrɜːz/ *n.* (*liqueur*) шартре́з.

chary /ˈtʃeərɪ/ *adj.* (**charier, chariest**) осторо́жный, сде́ржанный; **he is ~ of praise** он скуп на похвалу́; **I shall be ~ of going there** я два́жды поду́маю, пре́жде чем пойти́ туда́.

chase[1] /tʃeɪs/ *n.* **1** (*act of chasing*) пого́ня; **give ~ to** погна́ться (*pf.*) за+*i.*; пусти́ться (*pf.*) вдого́нку за+*i.*; **in ~ of** в пого́не за+*i.*; **wild goose ~** напра́сная пого́ня. **2**: **the ~** (*hunting*) охо́та.

● *v.t.* гоня́ться (*indet.*), гна́ться (*det.*) за+*i.*; **~ away** отгоня́ть, отогна́ть; **~ out** выгоня́ть, вы́гнать; **he owes us a reply — please ~ him up** (*coll.*) мы ждём его́ отве́та — потороми́те-ка его́!

● *v.i.* (*rush*) бе́гать (*indet.*); бежа́ть (*det.*), по-; **~ after** гна́ться, по- за+*i.*; охо́титься (*impf.*) за+*i.*

chase[2] /tʃeɪs/ *v.t.* (*engrave*) гравирова́ть, вы́-.

chaser /ˈtʃeɪsə(r)/ *n.* **1** (*pursuer*) пресле́дователь (*m.*). **2** (*gun at bow or stern*) судово́е ору́дие. **3** (*drink*) стака́н спиртно́го по́сле пи́ва *и т.п.*

chasm /ˈkæz(ə)m/ *n.* бе́здна, про́пасть (*also fig.*).

chassis /ˈʃæsɪ/ *n.* (*pl.* **~** /-sɪz/) шасси́ (*nt. indecl.*).

chaste /tʃeɪst/ *adj.* целому́дренный.

chasten /ˈtʃeɪs(ə)n/ *v.t.* (*punish, subdue*) смир|я́ть, -и́ть; **the rebuke had a ~ing effect** упрёк поде́йствовал отрезвля́юще.

chastise /tʃæsˈtaɪz/ *v.t.* нака́з|ывать, -а́ть; кара́ть, по-.

chastisement /tʃæsˈtaɪzmənt/ *n.* наказа́ние.

chastity /ˈtʃæstɪtɪ/ *n.* целому́дрие.

chasuble /ˈtʃæzjʊb(ə)l/ *n.* ри́за.

chat /tʃæt/ *n.* болтовня́, бесе́да; **~ show** (*Br.*) бесе́да/интервью́ (*nt. indecl.*) со знамени́тостями.

● *v.t.* (**chatted, chatting**): **~ s.o. up** (*Br. coll.*) заи́грывать (*impf.*) с кем-н.

● *v.i.* (**chatted, chatting**) болта́ть, по-; бесе́довать, по-.

château /ˈʃætəʊ/ *n.* (*pl.* **~x** *pronunc. same or* /-təʊz/) за́мок.

chattel /ˈtʃæt(ə)l/ *n.* дви́жимое иму́щество; **goods and ~s** всё иму́щество; **he treated his wife like a ~** он обраща́лся с жено́й, как с принадлежа́щей ему́ ве́щью.

chatter /ˈtʃætə(r)/ *n.* **1** (*talk*) болтовня́, трескотня́. **2** (*of birds*) щебета́ние; (*of monkeys etc.*) вереща́ние.

● *v.i.* **1** болта́ть, тарато́рить (*both impf.*). **2** щебета́ть, треща́ть, вереща́ть (*impf.*). **3**: **his teeth are ~ing** у него́ стуча́т зу́бы.

● *cpd.* **~box** *n.* болту́н (*fem.* -ья); трещо́тка (*c.g.*).

chatterer /ˈtʃætərə(r)/ *n.* болту́н (*fem.* -ья).

chattiness /ˈtʃætɪnɪs/ *n.* болтли́вость.

chatty /ˈtʃætɪ/ *adj.* (**chattier, chattiest**) болтли́вый, говорли́вый; (*style*) разгово́рный.

chauffeur /ˈʃəʊfə(r)/, /-ˈfɜː(r)/ *n.* (персона́льный) шофёр.

chauffeuse /ʃəʊˈfɜːz/ *n.* же́нщина-шофёр.

chauvinism /ˈʃəʊvɪˌnɪz(ə)m/ *n.* шовини́зм.

chauvinist /ˈʃəʊvɪnɪst/ *n.* шовини́ст (*fem.* -ка); **male ~** сторо́нник дискримина́ции же́нщин.

chauvinistic /ʃəʊvɪˈnɪstɪk/ *adj.* шовинисти́ческий.

cheap /tʃiːp/ *adj.* **1** (*low in price*) дешёвый; **I bought it ~** я дёшево это купи́л; **~ and nasty** (*Br.*) дёшево да гни́ло; **~ at the price** вполне́ прили́чно за таку́ю це́ну; **dirt ~** деше́вле па́реной ре́пы; грошо́вый; **on the ~** по дешёвке. **2** (*facile, tawdry, petty, vulgar*): **~ flattery** дешёвая лесть; **a ~ remark** по́шлое замеча́ние. **3**: **I feel ~** (*ashamed*) я чу́вствую себя́ дешёвкой.

● *cpd.* **~jack** *n.* разно́счик дешёвых това́ров.

cheapen /ˈtʃiːpən/ *v.t.* (*make cheap*) удешев|ля́ть, -и́ть; де́лать, с- деше́вле; (*degrade*) ун|ижа́ть, -и́зить; **~ o.s.** (*fig.*) роня́ть (*impf.*) себя́.

cheapness /ˈtʃiːpnɪs/ *n.* дешеви́зна.

cheat /tʃiːt/ *n.* (*person*) обма́нщик, плут, жу́лик; (*thing, action*) обма́н, плутовство́, жу́льничество.

● *v.t.* & *i.* обм|а́нывать, -ану́ть; плутова́ть, на-/с-; **~ s.o. out of something** обма́ном лиши́ть кого́-н. чего́-н.; **~ at cards** жу́льничать, с- в ка́ртах; плутова́ть, на-/с- в ка́ртах.

Chechen /ˈtʃetʃen/ *n.* чече́н|ец (*fem.* -ка).

● *adj.* чече́нский.

Chechnya /tʃetʃˈnjɑː/ *n.* Чечня́.

check[1] /tʃek/ *n.* **1** (*restraint*) заде́ржка; **wind acts as a ~ upon speed** ве́тер замедля́ет ско́рость; **keep a ~ on your temper** сде́рживайте свой нрав; **they held the enemy in ~** они́ сде́рживали проти́вника. **2** (*verification*) контро́ль (*m.*); прове́рка; **keep a ~ on his expenses** держа́ть под контро́лем его́ расхо́ды. **3** (*US, for hat, luggage etc.*) номеро́к; квита́нция. **4** (*at chess*) шах. **5** (*US, at cards etc.*) фи́шка, ма́рка. **6** (*US*) = **cheque.** **7** (*US*) = **bill.** **8** (*US, tick*) га́лочка.

● *v.t.* **1** (*restrain*) сде́рж|ивать, -а́ть; **he ~ed himself from speaking** он сдержа́лся и промолча́л; **the car ~ed its speed** автомоби́ль заме́длил ско́рость. **2** (*stop*) остан|а́вливать, -ови́ть; зад|е́рживать, -ержа́ть. **3** (*rebuke*) проб|ира́ть, -ра́ть. **4** (*verify*) контроли́ровать, про-; пров|еря́ть, -е́рить. **5** (*US, deposit, of luggage etc.*) сд|ава́ть, -а́ть. **6** (*at chess*) объяв|ля́ть, -и́ть шах +*d.* **7** (*US, tick*) отм|еча́ть, -е́тить га́лочкой.

● *v.i.* **1** (*pause*) остан|а́вливаться, -ови́ться. **2**: **~ on** = **~ up.** **3**: **~** (*accord*) **with** совп|ада́ть, -а́сть с+*i.*

● *with advs.*: **~ in** *v.i.* (*at hotel*) регистри́роваться, за-; *v.t.* (*baggage*) сд|ава́ть, -ать; **~ out** *v.i.* (*from hotel*) выпи́сываться, вы́писаться; **~ up** *v.i.*: **~ up on something** пров|еря́ть, -е́рить что-н.

● *cpds.* **~-list** *n.* контро́льный спи́сок, пе́речень (*m.*); **~out** *n.* ка́сса; **~-point, ~-post** *nn.* контро́льный пункт; **~room** *n.* (*US*) гардеро́бная; **~-up** *n.* прове́рка; (техни́ческий/медици́нский) осмо́тр; (*of motor vehicle*) техосмо́тр.

● *int.*: **~!** (*US, coll.*) то́чно!; (*at chess*) шах!

check[2] /tʃek/ *n.* (*pattern*) кле́тка; (*attr., also* **~ed**) кле́тчатый.

checker /'tʃekə(r)/ (*US*) = **chequer**

checkers /'tʃekəz/ *n.* (*US*) ша́ш|ки (*pl.*, *g.* -ек).

checkmate /'tʃekmeɪt/ *n.* шах и мат; (*fig.*) мат.

● *v.t.* де́лать, с- мат +*d.*; (*fig.*) нанести́ (*pf.*) по́лное пораже́ние +*d.*

cheek /tʃi:k/ *n.* **1** (*part of face*) щека́; (*dim., e.g. baby's*) щёчка; **~ by jowl** бок о бок; **turn the other ~** подст|авля́ть, -а́вить другу́ю щёку. **2** (*buttock*) полови́нка (за́да), ягоди́ца. **3** (*impudence*) на́глость; **he had the ~ to say . . .** у него́ хвати́ло на́глости сказа́ть. . . .

● *v.t.* (*coll.*) дерзи́ть, на- +*d.*

● *cpd.* **~-bone** *n.* скула́.

cheekiness /'tʃi:kɪnɪs/ *n.* на́глость, наха́льство.

cheeky /'tʃi:kɪ/ *adj.* (**cheekier, cheekiest**) наха́льный.

cheep /tʃi:p/ *n.* писк.

● *v.t. & i.* пища́ть, пи́скнуть.

cheer /tʃɪə(r)/ *n.* **1** (*comfort*): **words of ~** ободря́ющие/подба́дривающие слова́; **be of good ~!** не унывайте! **2** (*food*) угоще́ние; **good ~** пир горо́й. **3** (*shout*): **three ~s for our visitors!** троекра́тное ура́ на́шим гостя́м!; **~s!** (*as toast*) (за) ва́ше здоро́вье! **4** *pl., as int.* (*Br. coll.*) спаси́бо.

● *v.t.* **1** (*comfort, encourage*) подбодр|я́ть, -и́ть; ободр|я́ть, -и́ть; **his visit ~ed (up) the patient** его́ посеще́ние подбодри́ло больно́го; **~ing news** прия́тная но́вость. **2** (*acclaim*) приве́тствовать (*impf.*); **the spectators ~ed the team** зри́тели кри́ками подба́дривали кома́нду.

● *v.i.* (*utter ~s*) изд|ава́ть, -а́ть восто́рженные кри́ки.

● *with adv.*: **~ up** *v.t. & i.* ободр|я́ть(ся), -и́ть(ся); *v.i.* повеселе́ть (*pf.*); **~ up!** не унывайте!

● *cpd.* **~-leader** *n.* заводи́ла (*c.g.*).

cheerful /'tʃɪəfʊl/ *adj.* весёлый, ра́достный; **a ~ room** весёлая/све́тлая ко́мната.

cheer|fulness /'tʃɪəfʊlnɪs/, **-iness** /'tʃɪərɪnɪs/ *nn.* весёлость, ра́достность.

cheerio /,tʃɪrɪ'əʊ/ *int.* (*Br. coll.*) всего́ хоро́шего!; всего́!

cheerless /'tʃɪəlɪs/ *adj.* уны́лый.

cheerlessness /'tʃɪəlɪsnɪs/ *n.* уны́лость.

cheery /'tʃɪərɪ/ *adj.* (**cheerier, cheeriest**) весёлый, ра́достный.

cheese[1] /tʃi:z/ *n.* сыр; **ripe ~** вы́держанный сыр; **~ straw** (*cul.*) соло́мка с сы́ром.

● *cpds.* **~burger** *n.* чизбу́ргер; **~cake** *n.* ватру́шка; **~cloth** *n.* ма́рля; **~-paring** *n.* крохобо́рство; *adj.* крохобо́рский, крохобо́рческий.

cheese[2] /tʃi:z/ *v.t.* (*sl.*): **he is ~d off** (*Br., fed up*) ему́ всё осточерте́ло.

cheesy /'tʃi:zɪ/ *adj.* (**cheesier, cheesiest**) **1** (*like cheese*) сы́рный. **2** (*sl., shabby, scruffy*) дешёвый.

cheetah /'tʃi:tə/ *n.* гепа́рд.

chef /ʃef/ *n.* шеф-по́вар.

chemical /'kemɪk(ə)l/ *n.* хими́ческий проду́кт; (*pl.*) химика́ли|и (*pl., g.* -й); химика́ты (*m. pl.*).

● *adj.* хими́ческий; **~ warfare** хими́ческая война́.

chemise /ʃə'mi:z/ *n.* же́нская соро́чка/руба́шка.

chemist /'kemɪst/ *n.* **1** (*scientist*) хи́мик. **2** (*Br., pharmacist*) апте́карь (*m.*); **~'s shop** (*Br.*) апте́ка.

chemistry /'kemɪstrɪ/ *n.* хи́мия.

chemotherapy /,ki:mə'θerəpɪ/ *n.* химиотерапи́я.

chenille /ʃə'ni:l/ *n.* (*yarn*) сине́ль; (*fabric*) шени́ль.

che|que /tʃek/ (*US* **-ck**) *n.* чек; **he made the ~ out to me** он вы́писал чек на моё и́мя; **blank ~** незапо́лненный чек; (*fig.*) карт-бланш; **crossed ~** кроссиро́ванный чек; **traveller's** (*Br.*), **traveler's** (*US*) **~** тури́стский чек; **draw a ~ on a bank for £100** вы́писать (*pf.*) чек на банк на су́мму в 100 фу́нтов.

● *cpds.* **~-book** *n.* че́ковая кни́жка; **~-stub** *n.* корешо́к че́ковой кни́жки.

chequer /'tʃekə(r)/ (*US* **checker**) *n.* (*pl., check or mixed pattern*) узо́р в кле́тку.

● *v.t.* (*mark in ~s*) графи́ть, раз- в кле́тку; **~ed flag** клетча́тый, ша́хматный флажо́к; **~ed career** (*fig.*) бу́рная жизнь; жизнь, по́лная переме́н.

cherish /'tʃerɪʃ/ *v.t.* **1** (*love, care for*) не́жно люби́ть (*impf.*); леле́ять (*impf.*). **2** (*of hopes etc.*) леле́ять (*impf.*); дорожи́ть (*impf.*) +*i.*

Cherokee /'tʃerəkɪ/ *n.* черок|е́з(ец) (*fem.* -е́зка).

● *adj.* черокéзский.

cheroot /ʃə'ru:t/ *n.* сига́ра с обре́занными конца́ми.

cherry /'tʃerɪ/ *n.* (*fruit*) ви́шня; чере́шня; (*tree*) ви́шня, вишнёвое де́рево; **~ brandy** че́рри-бре́нди (*indecl.*), вишнёвый ликёр; **~ orchard** вишнёвый сад.

● *cpds.* **~-blossom** *n.* вишнёвый цвет; **~-pie** *n.* (*cul.*) пиро́г с ви́шнями; **~-stone** *n.* вишнёвая ко́сточка.

cherub /'tʃerəb/ *n.* (*pl.* **~im**) (*relig., art*) херуви́м; (*fig., child*) херуви́мчик, а́нгел.

cherubic /tʃɪ'ru:bɪk/ *adj.* херуви́мский, ангелоподо́бный, а́нгельский.

cherubim /'tʃerəbɪm/ *pl. of* ⇒**cherub**

chervil /'tʃɜ:vɪl/ *n.* (*bot.*) ке́рвель (*m.*).

chess /tʃes/ *n.* ша́хмат|ы (*pl., g.* —).

● *cpds.* **~-board** *n.* ша́хматная доска́; **~-man** *n.* ша́хматная фигу́ра; **~-player** *n.* шахмати́ст (*fem.* -ка).

chest /tʃest/ *n.* **1** (*furniture*) сунду́к; **~ of drawers** комо́д; **medicine ~** апте́чка. **2** (*Br., treasury, funds*) казна́. **3** (*anat.*) грудна́я кле́тка; грудь; **get something off one's ~** облегчи́ть (*pf.*) ду́шу; **~ cold, cold in the ~** просту́да.

chestnut /'tʃesnʌt/ *n.* **1** (*tree, fruit*) кашта́н. **2** (*stale anecdote*) анекдо́т с бородо́й. **3** (*horse*) гнеда́я ло́шадь. **4** (*attr., of colour*) кашта́новый.

chesty /'tʃestɪ/ *adj.* (**chestier, chestiest**) (*Br., of cold*) грудно́й.

cheval-glass /ʃə'væl/ *n.* психе́ (*indecl.*).

chevron /'ʃevrən/ *n.* шевро́н.

chew /tʃu:/ *v.t. & i.* жева́ть (*impf.*); **~ the cud** жева́ть жва́чку; **~ upon, ~ over** (*fig.*) пережёвывать (*impf.*); **~ the rag, fat** (*coll.*) болта́ть (*impf.*) о том и сём; перемыва́ть (*impf.*) ко́сточки; **~ing-gum** жева́тельная рези́нка.

chewy /'tʃu:ɪ/ *adj.* (**chewier, chewiest**) (*coll.*) тягу́чий.

chiaroscuro /kɪ,ɑ:rə'skʊərəʊ/ *n.* светоте́нь.

chic /ʃi:k/ *n.* элега́нтность, шик.

● *adj.* (**chic-er, chic-est**) элега́нтный, шика́рный.

chicane(ry) /ʃɪ'keɪnə(rɪ)/ *n.* крючкотво́рство.

chick /tʃɪk/ *n.* птене́ц; цыплёнок; (*child*) дитя́ (*nt.*); (*sl., girl*) цы́почка.

● *cpds.* **~peas** *n.* (*bot.*) туре́цкий горо́х; **~weed** *n.* (*bot.*) мокри́ца, мокри́чник.

chicken /'tʃɪkɪn/ *n.* цыплёнок; (*as food*) куря́тина, цыплёнок, ку́рица; **don't count your ~s before they are hatched** цыпля́т по о́сени счита́ют; (*fig., coward*) трус.

● *cpds.* **~-feed** *n.* (*fig.*) пустяки́ (*m. pl.*); **~-hearted, ~-livered** *adjs.* трусли́вый, малоду́шный; **~-pox** *n.* ветряна́я о́спа; **~-run** *n.* заго́н для кур.

chicory /'tʃɪkərɪ/ *n.* (*bot.*) цико́рий (полево́й).

chide /tʃaɪd/ *v.t.* попрек|а́ть, -ну́ть; брани́ть, вы́-.

chief /tʃi:f/ *n.* **1** (*leader, ruler*) вождь (*m.*), глава́ (*m.*); **~ of state** глава́ госуда́рства. **2** (*boss, senior official*) шеф, нача́льник; **C~ of Staff** нача́льник шта́ба.

● *adj.* **1** (*most important*) гла́вный, основно́й, важне́йший. **2** (*senior*) гла́вный, ста́рший; **C~ Justice** верхо́вный судья́; председа́тель (*m.*) верхо́вного суда́; **~ constable** (*Br.*) нача́льник поли́ции.

chiefdom /'tʃi:fdəm/ *n.* (*position*) главе́нство; (*territory*) террито́рия под управле́нием вождя́ пле́мени.

chiefly /'tʃi:flɪ/ *adv.* гла́вным о́бразом; в пе́рвую о́чередь.

chieftain /'tʃi:ft(ə)n/ *n.* вождь (*m.*), атама́н.

chieftaincy /'tʃi:ftənsɪ/ *n.* положе́ние вождя́/атама́на/главаря́.

chiffon /'ʃɪfɒn/ *n.* шифо́н.

chiffonier /,ʃɪfə'nɪə(r)/ *n.* шифонье́рка.

chignon /'ʃi:njɔ̃/ *n.* шиньо́н.

chihuahua /tʃɪ'wɑ:wə/ *n.* чихуа́хуа (*indecl.*).

chilblain /'tʃɪlbleɪn/ *n.* обморо́женное ме́сто.

child /tʃaɪld/ *n.* (*pl.* **children**) дитя́ (*nt.*), ребёнок; **~ren of Israel** (*bibl.*) израильтя́не (*m. pl.*); сыны́ (*m. pl.*)

Изра́илевы; **~ of nature** дитя́ приро́ды; **~'s play** (*fig.*) де́тские игру́шки; **with ~** бере́менная, в положе́нии; **I am a ~ in these matters** я ма́ло смы́слю в э́том; **from a ~** с де́тства;**~ molester** растли́тель (*m.*) малоле́тних (дете́й); **~ labour** (*Br.*), **labor** (*US*) де́тский труд; **~ welfare** охра́на младе́нчества.

● *cpds.* **~-bearing** *n.* деторожде́ние; **of ~-bearing age** детоpо́дного во́зраста; **~birth** *n.* ро́д|ы (*pl., g.* -ов); **natural ~birth** ро́ды в есте́ственных усло́виях; **she died in ~birth** она́ умерла́ от ро́дов; **~-minder** *n.* (*Br.*) ня́ня; **~-minding** *n.* присмо́тр за детьми́.

childhood /'tʃaɪldhʊd/ *n.* де́тство; **second ~** второ́е де́тство.

childish /'tʃaɪldɪʃ/ *adj.* де́тский, ребя́ческий.

childishness /'tʃaɪldɪʃnɪs/ *n.* де́тскость, ребя́чество.

childless /'tʃaɪldlɪs/ *adj.* безде́тный.

childlike /'tʃaɪldlaɪk/ *adj.* де́тский, младе́нческий.

children /'tʃɪldr(ə)n/ *pl. of* ⇒**child**

Chile /'tʃɪlɪ/ *n.* Чи́ли (*nt. indecl.*).

Chilean /'tʃɪlɪən/ *n.* чили́|ец (*fem.* -йка).

● *adj.* чили́йский.

chill /tʃɪl/ *n.* **1** (*physical*) хо́лод; **there is a ~ in the air** прохла́дно; холода́ет; **take the ~ off wine** подогре́ть (*pf.*) вино́. **2** (*fig.*) хо́лод; расхола́живание; **this cast a ~ over the proceedings** э́то всё омрачи́ло. **3** (*med.*) просту́да; **catch a ~** просту|жа́ться, -ди́ться.

● *adj.* холо́дный; расхола́живающий.

● *v.t.* (*lit.*) охлаж|да́ть, -ди́ть; студи́ть, о-; осту|жа́ть, -ди́ть; (*fig.*) осту|жа́ть, -ди́ть.

● *v.i.*: **~ out** (*coll.*) рассл|абля́ться, -а́биться.

chilli /'tʃɪlɪ/ *n.* (*pl.* **chillies**) кра́сный стручко́вый пе́рец.

chilliness /'tʃɪlɪnɪs/ *n.* (*lit.*) хо́лод; зя́бкость; (*fig.*) хо́лодность, су́хость.

chilly /'tʃɪlɪ/ *adj.* (**chillier, chilliest**) холо́дный; (*sensitive to cold*) зя́бкий; (*fig.*) холо́дный, сухо́й.

chime /tʃaɪm/ *n.* (*set of bells*) подбо́р колоколо́в; (*sound*) перезво́н.

● *v.t.*: **the clock ~d midnight** часы́ про́били по́лночь; **the clock ~s the quarters** часы́ отбива́ют ка́ждую че́тверть ча́са.

● *v.i.* трезво́нить (*impf.*); (*fig., harmonize*) гармонизи́ровать (*impf., pf.*) (c + *i.*); **~ in** (*interject*) ввёртывать, вверну́ть слове́чко.

chimera /kaɪ'mɪərə/, /kɪ-/ *n.* химе́ра.

chimerical /lɪ'merɪk(ə)l/ *adj.* химери́ческий.

chimney /'tʃɪmnɪ/ *n.* **1** труба́, дымохо́д; **he smokes like a ~** он дыми́т, как паро́воз. **2** (*for lamp*) ла́мповое стекло́. **3** (*mountaineering*) труба́, расще́лина.

● *cpds.* **~-piece** *n.* (*Br.*) ками́нная доска́/по́лочка; **~-pot** *n.* колпа́к дымово́й трубы́; **~-stack** *n.* дымова́я труба́; **~-sweep** *n.* трубочи́ст.

chimpanzee /,tʃɪmpən'zi:/ *n.* шимпанзе́ (*m. indecl.*).

chin /tʃɪn/ *n.* подборо́док; **double ~** двойно́й подборо́док; **(keep your) ~ up!** (*fig.*) не уныва́й(те)!; не́чего нос ве́шать!; **take it on the ~** (*fig.*) вы́нести (*pf.*) уда́р.

● *cpds.* **~-strap** *n.* подборо́дочный реме́нь; **~-wag** (*Br. coll.*) *n.* трепотня́; *v.i.* трепа́ться (*impf.*); чеса́ть, по- языки́.

China /'tʃaɪnə/ *n.* Кита́й.

● *cpd.* **~town** *n.* кита́йский кварта́л.

china /'tʃaɪnə/ *n.* фарфо́р.

● *cpds.* **~-clay** *n.* каоли́н, фарфо́ровая гли́на; **~-closet, ~-cupboard** *nn.* буфе́т, серва́нт; **~ware** *n.* фарфо́р, фарфо́ровые изде́лия.

chinchilla /tʃɪn'tʃɪlə/ *n.* шинши́лла; (*fur*) шинши́лловый мех.

chine /tʃaɪn/ *n.* (*anat.*) спинно́й хребе́т; (*mountain ridge*) го́рная гряда́; (*ravine*) уще́лье.

Chinese /tʃaɪ'ni:z/ *n.* (*pl.* **~**) (*person*) кит|а́ец (*fem.* -ая́нка); (*language*) кита́йский язы́к.

● *adj.* кита́йский; **~ lantern** лампио́н, кита́йский фона́рик.

chink[1] /tʃɪŋk/ *n.* (*crevice*) щель.

chink[2] /tʃɪŋk/ *n.* (*sound*) звя́канье.

● *v.i.* звя́к|ать, -нуть.

chinoiserie /ʃi:n'wɑ:zərɪ/ *n.* (*art*) кита́йский стиль; кита́йские ве́щи (*f. pl.*).

chintz /tʃɪnts/ *n.* си́тец; (*attr.*) си́тцевый.

chintzy /'tʃɪntsɪ/ *adj.* (**chintzier, chintziest**) си́тцевый; (*fig.*) меща́нский, по́шлый.

chip /tʃɪp/ *n.* **1** (*of wood*) щепа́, ще́пка; стру́жка; (*of stone*) обло́мок; (*of china*) оско́лок.

2 (*fig.*): **he is a ~ off the old block** он вы́литый оте́ц; он весь в отца́; **he has a ~ on his shoulder** он де́ржится вызыва́юще.

3: **the cup has a ~** на ча́шке щерби́на.

4 (*pl., food*) (*Br.*) карто́фель-соло́мка; карто́фель-фри́; (*US*) хрустя́щий карто́фель; чи́пс|ы (*pl., g.* -ов) (*coll.*).

5 (*at games*) фи́шка, ма́рка; **bargaining ~** (*fig.*) ко́зырь (*m.*) (в запа́се).

6 (*in microelectronics*) чип, микросхе́ма.

● *v.t.* (**chipped, chipping**) струга́ть, вы́стругать; отк|а́лывать, -оло́ть; отб|ива́ть, -и́ть; обб|ива́ть, -и́ть; **~ paint off a ship** соск|а́бливать, -обли́ть кра́ску с корабля́; **the plates have ~ped edges** у таре́лок отби́тые/ щерба́тые края́; **~ potatoes** (*Br.*) то́нко нар|еза́ть, -е́зать карто́фель.

● *v.i.* (**chipped, chipping**)

1 отк|а́лываться, -оло́ться; отб|ива́ться, -и́ться; обб|ива́ться, -и́ться.

2: **~ in** (*coll.*) вме́ш|иваться, -а́ться; влез|а́ть, -ть (в разгово́р).

● *cpd.* **~board** *n.* фиброли́т; (*attr.*) фиброли́товый.

chipmunk /'tʃɪpmʌŋk/ *n.* бурунду́к.

chipper /'tʃɪpə(r)/ *adj.* (*coll.*) бо́дрый.

chiropodist /kɪ'rɒpədɪst/ *n.* специали́ст (*fem.* -ка) по лече́нию заболева́ний стопы́; мозо́льный опера́тор.

chiropody /kɪ'rɒpədɪ/ *n.* лече́ние заболева́ний стопы́.

chiropractor /'kaɪərəʊ,præktə(r)/ *n.* хиропра́ктик.

chirp /tʃɜ:p/ *n.* чири́канье, щебета́ние.

● *v.t. & i.* чири́кать (*impf.*); щебета́ть (*impf.*).

chirpiness /'tʃɜ:pɪnɪs/ *n.* (*coll.*) бо́дрость.

chirpy /'tʃɜpɪ/ *adj.* (**chirpier, chirpiest**) (*coll.*) бо́дрый.

chirr /tʃɜ:(r)/ *n.* стрекота́ние; трескотня́, треск.

● *v.i.* стрекота́ть (*impf.*); треща́ть (*impf.*).

chirrup /'tʃɪrəp/ *n.* ще́бет, щебета́ние.

● *v.i.* (**chirruped, chirruping**) щебета́ть (*impf.*).

chisel /'tʃɪz(ə)l/ *n.* (*sculptor's*) резе́ц; (*carpenter's*) долото́, стаме́ска; (*stonemason's*) зуби́ло.

● *v.t.* (**chiselled, chiselling;** *US* **chiseled, chiseling**) **1** вая́ть, из-; высека́ть, вы́сечь; **finely ~led features** точёные черты́ лица́. **2** (*US sl., cheat*) над|ува́ть, -у́ть.

chiseller /'tʃɪzlə(r)/ *n.* (*US sl., cheat*) жу́лик, моше́нник.

chit /tʃɪt/ *n.* (*note*) запи́ска.

chit-chat /'tʃɪttʃæt/ *n.* болтовня́, пересу́д|ы (*pl., g.* -ов).

● *v.i.* (**chit-chatted, chit-chatting**) болта́ть (*impf.*); суда́чить (*impf.*).

chivalrous /'ʃɪvəlrəs/ *adj.* ры́царский.

chivalry /'ʃɪvəlrɪ/ *n.* ры́царство; ры́царское поведе́ние.

chive /tʃaɪv/ *n.* лук-ре́занец.

chivvy /'tʃɪvɪ/ *v.t.* (*Br. coll.*) гоня́ть (*impf.*).

chloric /'klɔ:rɪk/ *adj.*: **~ acid** хлорнова́тая кислота́.

chloride /'klɔ:raɪd/ *n.* хлори́д; **~ of lime** хло́рная и́звесть; **sodium ~** хло́ристый на́трий.

chlorinate /'klɔ:rɪ,neɪt/ *v.t.* хлори́ровать (*impf., pf.*).

chlorination /,klɔ:rɪ'neɪʃ(ə)n/ *n.* хлори́рование.

chlorine /'klɔ:ri:n/ *n.* хлор.

chloroform /'klɒrə,fɔ:m/, /'klɔ:rə-/ *n.* хлорофо́рм.

● *v.t.* хлороформи́ровать (*impf., pf.*).

chlorophyll /'klɒrəfɪl/ *n.* хлорофи́л.

choc-ice /tʃɒk/ *n.* (*Br.*) моро́женое в шокола́де; эскимо́ (*indecl.*).

chock /tʃɒk/ *n.* клин; подпо́рка; тормозна́я коло́дка.

● *v.t.* (*Br., support*) подп|ира́ть, -ере́ть; (*drive a wedge under*) под|кла́дывать, -ложи́ть клин под + *a.*; **~ up** (*fig.*) загромозди́ть (*pf.*).

● *cpds.* **~-a-block** *adj.*

загромождённый; **~-full** *adj.* битко́м наби́тый.

chocolate /'tʃɒkələt/, /'tʃɒklət/ *n.* **1** шокола́д (*also drink*); (*~-coated sweet*) шокола́дная конфе́та; **~ bar** шокола́дный бато́нчик; **~ biscuit** шокола́дное пече́нье. **2** (*attr., colour*) шокола́дный.

choice /tʃɔɪs/ *n.* **1** (*act or power of choosing*) вы́бор, отбо́р; **Hobson's ~** вы́бор понево́ле; ≈ не́ из чего вы́брать; **I have no ~ but to . . .** у меня́ нет друго́го вы́бора, кро́ме как (*+inf.*); **the girl of his ~** его́ избра́нница; **for ~** предпочти́тельно; **take your ~!** выбира́йте! **2** (*thing chosen*) вы́бор; **this is my ~** я выбира́ю э́то; вот мой вы́бор. **3** (*variety*) вы́бор; **the shop has a large ~ of hats** в магази́не широ́кий ассортиме́нт головны́х убо́ров.

● *adj.* отбо́рный.

choiceness /'tʃɔɪsnɪs/ *n.* отбо́рность.

choir /'kwaɪə(r)/ *n.* (*singers*) хор; (*part of church*) хо́ры (*m. pl.*), кли́рос.

● *cpds.* **~boy** *n.* пе́вчий; **~master** *n.* хорме́йстер.

choke /tʃəʊk/ *n.* (*in car*) возду́шная заслóнка; дрóссель (*m.*).

● *v.t.* **1** (*throttle*) души́ть, за-; **~ the life out of s.o.** вы́шибить (*pf.*) дух из кого́-н.; **anger ~d him** его́ души́л гнев. **2** (*block*) заку́пор|ивать, -ить; засор|я́ть, -и́ть; **the drain is ~d** сток засори́лся; **the garden is ~d with weeds** сорняки́ заглуши́ли сад. **3**: **he ~d back his anger** он сдержа́л свой гнев; **he ~d off enquiries** он отде́лался от расспро́сов; **he ~d down his food** он с трудо́м проглоти́л еду́.

● *v.i.* зад|ыха́ться, -охну́ться; **he ~d on a plum-stone** он подави́лся сли́вовой ко́сточкой; **he spoke with a choking voice** он говори́л прерыва́ющимся го́лосом.

choker /'tʃəʊkə(r)/ *n.* коро́ткое ожере́лье, колье́ (*indecl.*).

choky /'tʃəʊkɪ/ *adj.* (**chokier, chokiest**): **I felt ~ with emotion** я задыха́лся от волне́ния.

cholera /'kɒlərə/ *n.* холе́ра.

choleric /'kɒlərɪk/ *adj.* холери́ческий.

cholesterol /kə'lestə,rɒl/ *n.* холестери́н.

choose /tʃu:z/ *v.t.* (*past* **chose**; *p.p.* **chosen**) выбира́ть, вы́брать; изб|ира́ть, -ра́ть; **there are five to ~ from** мо́жно выбира́ть из пяти́; **there is little to ~ between them** оди́н друго́го сто́ит; **the chosen people, race** и́збранный наро́д; **I cannot ~ but obey** я вы́нужден повинова́ться; **he was chosen king** его́ вы́брали/избра́ли королём; **I chose to remain** я предпочёл оста́ться.

● *v.i.* (*past* **chose**; *p.p.* **chosen**): **pick and ~** (*fig.*) быть разбо́рчивым.

choos(e)y /'tʃu:zɪ/ *adj.* (**choosier, choosiest**) разбо́рчивый.

chop[1] /tʃɒp/ *n.* **1** (*cut*) ру́бящий уда́р. **2** (*of meat*) отбивна́я котле́та. **3**: **get the ~** (*Br., be dismissed*) вы́лететь (*pf.*) (с рабо́ты) (*coll.*).

● *v.t.* (**chopped, chopping**) руби́ть (*impf.*); (*cut*) нар|еза́ть, -е́зать; кроши́ть (*impf.*); **~ up** нар|еза́ть, -е́зать; **~ a branch off a tree** сруби́ть (*pf.*) ве́тку с де́рева; **~ a way through the bushes** проруб|а́ть, -и́ть доро́гу че́рез кусты́; **~ a tree down** руби́ть, с- де́рево.

chop[2] /tʃɒp/ *n.* (*jaw*): **lick one's ~s** обли́з|ываться, -а́ться.

chop[3] /tʃɒp/ *v.i.* (**chopped, chopping**): **~ and change** (*Br.*) постоя́нно меня́ть свои́ взгля́ды.

chopper /'tʃɒpə(r)/ *n.* (*Br., implement*) нож, коса́рь (*m.*); (*sl., helicopter*) вертолёт.

choppy /'tʃɒpɪ/ *adj.* (**choppier, choppiest**) (*of sea*) неспоко́йный.

chopstick /'tʃɒpstɪk/ *n.* па́лочка для еды́.

chop-suey /tʃɒp'su:ɪ/ *n.* кита́йское рагу́ (*indecl.*).

choral /'kɔ:r(ə)l/ *adj.* хорово́й.

chorale /kɔ:'rɑ:l/ *n.* хора́л.

chord /kɔ:d/ *n.* **1** (*string of harp etc.*) струна́; **strike a ~** (*fig., remind of sth.*) вы́звать (*pf.*) о́тклик. **2** (*anat.*): **vocal ~s** голосовы́е свя́зки (*f. pl.*); **spinal ~** спинно́й мозг. **3** (*mus.*) акко́рд. **4** (*geom.*) хо́рда.

chore /tʃɔ:(r)/ *n.* (*odd job*) случа́йная рабо́та; (*heavy task*) бре́мя (*nt.*); **household ~s** дома́шняя рабо́та.

choreographer /,kɒrɪ'ɒgrəfə(r)/ *n.* балетме́йстер, хорео́граф.

choreographic /,kɒrɪəg'ræfɪk/ *adj.* хореографи́ческий.

choreography /,kɒrɪ'ɒgrəfɪ/ *n.* хореогра́фия.

chorister /'kɒrɪstə(r)/ *n.* хори́ст (*fem.* -ка).

chortle /'tʃɔ:t(ə)l/ *v.i.* фы́ркать (*impf.*); дави́ться (*impf.*) от сме́ха.

chorus /'kɔ:rəs/ *n.* (*pl.* **~es**) **1** (*singers; also in anc. drama*) хор; **in ~** (*lit., fig.*) хо́ром; **~ of approval** хвале́бный хор. **2** (*refrain*) припе́в, рефре́н.

● *v.t. & i.* (**chorused, chorusing**) петь, с- (*or* произн|оси́ть, -ести́) хо́ром.

● *cpd.* **~-girl** *n.* хори́стка.

chose /tʃəʊz/ *past of* ⇒**choose**

chosen /'tʃəʊz(ə)n/ *p.p. of* ⇒**choose**

chough /tʃʌf/ *n.* (*zool.*) клуши́ца.

chowder /'tʃaʊdə(r)/ *n.* ≈ ры́бный суп.

Christ /kraɪst/ *n.* **1** Христо́с; **the ~ child** младе́нец Иису́с; **before ~** до на́шей э́ры (*abbr.* до н.э.). **2** *as int.* Бо́же (мой)!; Го́споди!

christen /'krɪs(ə)n/ *v.t.* **1** крести́ть (*impf., pf.*); **he was ~ed John** ему́ при креще́нии да́ли и́мя Джон; его́ нарекли́ Джо́ном. **2** (*fig.*) окрести́ть (*pf.*); да|ва́ть, -ть и́мя +*d.*

Christendom /'krɪsəndəm/ *n.* христиа́нский мир.

christening /'krɪs(ə)nɪŋ/ *n.* крести́н|ы (*pl., g.* —); креще́ние.

Christian /'krɪstɪən/, /'krɪstʃ(ə)n/ *n.* христи|ани́н (*fem.* -а́нка).

● *adj.* христиа́нский; **~ burial** по́хороны по церко́вному обря́ду; **~ era** христиа́нская э́ра; **~ name** и́мя (*nt.*) (*в противополо́жность фами́лии*); **~ Science** «христиа́нская нау́ка».

Christianity /,krɪstɪ'ænɪtɪ/ *n.* христиа́нство.

Christmas /'krɪsməs/ *n.* (*pl.* **~es**) Рождество́; **~ box** (*Br.*), **present** рожде́ственский пода́рок; **~ cake** (*Br.*) рожде́ственский пиро́г; **~ card** рожде́ственская откры́тка; **~ day** пе́рвый день Рождества́; **~ eve** кану́н Рождества́; **Father ~** дед-моро́з; **at ~** на Рождество́; **~ pudding** (*Br.*) рожде́ственский пу́динг; **~ rose** моро́зник чёрный; **~ tree** рожде́ственская ёлка.

● *cpds.* **~-time, ~-tide** *nn.* свя́т|ки (*pl., g.* -ок).

chromatic /krə'mætɪk/ *adj.* **1** (*pert. to colour*) цветно́й. **2** (*mus.*) хромати́ческий.

chrome /krəʊm/ *n.* **1** (*chem.*) хром. **2** (*pigment, also* **~ yellow**) хром; жёлтый цвет.

chromium /'krəʊmɪəm/ *n.* хром.

● *cpds.* **~-plated** *adj.* хроми́рованный; **~-plating** *n.* хроми́рование, хромиро́вка.

chromosome /'krəʊmə,səʊm/ *n.* хромосо́ма.

chronic /'krɒnɪk/ *adj.* **1** (*med.*) хрони́ческий. **2** (*fig., incessant*) хрони́ческий, постоя́нный. **3** (*Br. coll., very bad*) ужа́сный.

chronicle /'krɒnɪk(ə)l/ *n.* хро́ника, ле́топись; **C~s** (*book of Bible*) Паралипоменóн.

● *v.t.* вести́ (*det.*) хро́нику +*g.*

chronicler /'krɒnɪklə(r)/ *n.* летопи́сец, исто́рик.

chronograph /'krɒnə,grɑ:f/, /'krəʊnə-/, /-,græf/ *n.* хроно́граф.

chronological /,krɒnə'lɒdʒɪk(ə)l/ *adj.* хронологи́ческий.

chronology /krə'nɒlədʒɪ/ *n.* хроноло́гия; (*table*) хронологи́ческая табли́ца.

chronometer /krə'nɒmɪtə(r)/ *n.* хроно́метр.

chronometry /krə'nɒmɪtrɪ/ *n.* хронометра́ж.

chrysali|s /'krɪsəlɪs/ *n.* (*pl.* **~ses** *or* **~des** /krɪ'sælɪ,di:z/) ку́колка.

chrysanthemum /krɪ'sænθəməm/ *n.* хризанте́ма.

chub /tʃʌb/ *n.* гола́вль (*m.*).

chubby /'tʃʌbɪ/ *adj.* (**chubbier, chubbiest**) то́лстенький, пу́хленький.

chuck /tʃʌk/ *v.t.* **1**: **~ s.o. under the chin** потрепа́ть (*pf.*) кого́-н. по подборо́дку. **2** (*coll., throw*) швыр|я́ть, -ну́ть. **3** (*coll., give up*) бр|оса́ть, -о́сить; **~ it!** бро́сьте!

● *with advs.*: (*coll.*): **~ away** *v.t.* (*lit.*) выбра́сывать, вы́бросить; (*fig.*): **~ away a chance** упусти́ть (*pf.*) слу́чай; **~ out** *v.t.* (*thing or person*) вы́кинуть (*pf.*); вышвырнуть (*pf.*); **~ up** *v.t.* (*give up*) бр|оса́ть, -о́сить.

chucker-out /ˈtʃʌkə(r)/ *n.* (*Br. coll.*) вышиба́ла (*m.*).

chuckle /ˈtʃʌk(ə)l/ *n.* сда́вленный смешо́к, смех.

● *v.i.* фы́ркать (*impf.*) от сме́ха, посме́иваться (*impf.*).

chuffed /tʃʌft/ *adj.* (*Br. coll.*) дово́льный.

chug /tʃʌg/ *v.i.* (**chugged, chugging**): **the boat ~ged past** ло́дка пропыхте́ла ми́мо.

chum /tʃʌm/ *n.* прия́тель (*m.*), дружо́к.

● *v.i.* дружи́ть (*impf.*) (c + *i.*); **~ up with s.o.** сдружи́ться (*pf.*) с кем-н.

chumminess /ˈtʃʌmɪnɪs/ *n.* дружелю́бие, общи́тельность.

chummy /ˈtʃʌmɪ/ *adj.* (**chummier, chummiest**) дружелю́бный, общи́тельный.

chump /tʃʌmp/ *n.* (*log; blockhead*) чурба́н; **he is off his ~** (*Br.*) он рехну́лся/спя́тил (*coll.*); **~ chop** (*Br.*) филе́йный кусо́к.

chunk /tʃʌŋk/ *n.* то́лстый кусо́к/ломо́ть (*m.*); куси́ще (*m.*).

chunky /ˈtʃʌŋkɪ/ *adj.* (**chunkier, chunkiest**) (*person*) корена́стый; (*jumper*) то́лстый.

church /tʃɜːtʃ/ *n.* **1** (*institution*) це́рковь; (*building*) це́рковь (*esp. Orthodox*), храм; **go to ~** (*regularly*) ходи́ть (*indet.*) в це́рковь; (*attend a service*) пойти́ (*pf.*) в це́рковь; **poor as a ~ mouse** бе́ден, как церко́вная мышь; **C~ of England/Scotland** англика́нская/пресвитериа́нская це́рковь; **C~ of Rome** ри́мско-католи́ческая це́рковь; **~ parade** построе́ние на моли́тву; **C~ Slavonic** церковнославя́нский (язы́к). **2** (*holy orders*): **he entered the ~** он при́нял духо́вный сан.

● *cpds.* **~goer** *n.*: **he is a regular ~goer** он регуля́рно хо́дит в це́рковь; **~going** *n.* посеще́ние це́ркви; **~man** *n.* церко́вник, ве́рующий; **~warden** *n.* кти́тор, церко́вный ста́роста; **~yard** *n.* пого́ст, кла́дбище при це́ркви.

churl /tʃɜːl/ *n.* хам, мужи́к.

churlish /ˈtʃɜːlɪʃ/ *adj.* ха́мский, гру́бый.

churlishness /ˈtʃɜːlɪʃnɪs/ *n.* ха́мство, гру́бость.

churn /tʃɜːn/ *n.* (*tub*) маслобо́йка; (*Br., can*) бидо́н.

● *v.t.*: **~ butter** сби|ва́ть, -ть ма́сло; (*fig.*): **he ~s out novels** он печёт рома́ны (как блины́); **the propeller ~ed up the waves** винт взвихри́л во́лны.

churr /tʃɜː(r)/ *n.* стрекота́ние, трескотня́.

● *v.i.* стрекота́ть, треща́ть (*both impf.*).

chute /ʃuːt/ *n.* (*slide, slope*) жёлоб, спуск; (*for amusement*) гора́, го́рка; (*for rubbish*) мусоропрово́д.

chutney /ˈtʃʌtnɪ/ *n.* ча́тни (*nt. indecl.*).

CIA (*abbr. of* ***Central Intelligence Agency***) ЦРУ (Центра́льное разве́дывательное управле́ние).

cica|da /sɪˈkɑːdə/, /-ˈkeɪdə/, **-la** /sɪˈkɑːlə/ *n.* (*zool.*) цика́да.

cicatrice /ˈsɪkətrɪs/ *n.* шрам, рубе́ц.

cicatrize /ˈsɪkəˌtraɪz/ *v.t.* зажив|ля́ть, -и́ть.

● *v.i.* зарубц|о́вываться, -ева́ться.

cicely /ˈsɪsəlɪ/ *n.* (*bot.*) (*also* **sweet ~**) испа́нский ке́рвель (*m.*).

Cicero /ˈsɪsəˌrəʊ/ *n.* Цицеро́н.

ciceron|e /ˌtʃɪtʃəˈrəʊnɪ/, /ˌsɪsəˈrəʊnɪ/ *n.* (*pl.* **~i** *pronunc. same*) гид, чичеро́не (*m. indecl.*).

CID (*abbr. of* ***Criminal Investigation Department***) уголо́вный ро́зыск, угро́зыск.

cider /ˈsaɪdə(r)/ *n.* сидр.

● *cpd.* **~-press** *n.* я́блочный пресс.

c.i.f. (*abbr. of* ***cost, insurance and freight***) сиф.

cigar /sɪˈgɑː(r)/ *n.* сига́ра.

● *cpds.* **~-case** *n.* сига́рочница; **~-holder** *n.* мундшту́к.

cigarette /ˌsɪgəˈret/ *n.* сигаре́та; (*of Russian type*) папиро́са.

● *cpds.* **~-case** *n.* портсига́р; **~-end** (*Br.*), **~-stub** *nn.* оку́рок; **~-holder** *n.* мундшту́к; **~-lighter** *n.* зажига́лка; **~-paper** *n.* папиро́сная бума́га.

C.-in-C. (*abbr. of* ***Commander-in-Chief***) главко́м (главнокома́ндующий).

cinch /sɪntʃ/ *n.* (*sl.*) (*sure thing*) де́ло ве́рное; (*easy task*) лёгкое де́ло.

cinchona /sɪŋˈkəʊnə/ *n.* хи́нное де́рево.

cinder /ˈsɪndə(r)/ *n.*: (*pl.*) шлак, зола́, пе́пел; **burn something to a ~** сжечь (*pf.*) что-н. дотла́; **~ path, track** (бегова́я) га́ревая доро́жка.

Cinderella /ˌsɪndəˈrelə/ *n.* Зо́лушка; **education is the ~ of our system** образова́ние — са́мая забро́шенная о́бласть на́шего о́бщества.

cine-camera /ˈsɪnɪ-/ *n.* киноаппара́т.

cine-film /ˈsɪnɪ-/ *n.* (*Br.*) киноплёнка.

cinema /ˈsɪnɪˌmɑː/, /-mə/ *n.* (*art*) кино́ (*indecl.*), кинематогра́фия; (*place*) кино́ (*indecl.*), кинотеа́тр.

cinematic /ˌsɪnɪˈmætɪk/ *adj.* кинематографи́ческий.

cinematographer /ˌsɪnɪməˈtɒgrəfə(r)/ *n.* кинематографи́ст.

cinematographic /sɪnɪˌmætəˈgræfɪk/ *adj.* кинематографи́ческий.

cinematography /ˌsɪnɪməˈtɒgrəfɪ/ *n.* кинематогра́фия.

cine-projector /ˈsɪnɪ/ *n.* (*Br.*) кинопроекцио́нный аппара́т.

cineraria /ˌsɪnəˈreərɪə/ *n.* пе́пельник, цинера́рия.

cinerary /ˈsɪnərərɪ/ *adj.*: **~ urn** у́рна с пра́хом.

cinnabar /ˈsɪnəˌbɑː(r)/ *n.* (*min., chem.*) ки́новарь.

cinnamon /ˈsɪnəmən/ *n.* кори́ца; (*colour*) све́тло-кори́чневый цвет.

cinquefoil /ˈsɪŋkfɔɪl/ *n.* (*bot.*) лапча́тка; (*archit.*) пятили́стник.

ci|pher /ˈsaɪfə(r)/, **cy-** *nn.* **1** (*figure 0*) нуль, ноль (*both m.*). **2** (*fig., nonentity*) ничто́жество, нуль. **3** (*monogram*) моногра́мма, ве́нзель (*m.*). **4** (*secret writing*) шифр, код; **message in ~, ~ message** (за)шифро́ванное сообще́ние.

● *v.t.* шифрова́ть, за-.

circa /ˈsɜːkə/ *prep.* приблизи́тельно; о́коло + *g.*

circadian /sɜːˈkeɪdɪən/ *adj.*: **~ rhythm** су́точный ритм.

Circassian /sɜːˈkæsɪən/ *n.* черке́|с (*fem.* -шенка).

● *adj.* черке́сский.

circle /ˈsɜːk(ə)l/ *n.* **1** (*math., fig.*) круг, окру́жность; **a ~ of trees** кольцо́ дере́вьев; **they stood in a ~** они́ ста́ли в кру́г; они́ стоя́ли кольцо́м; **square the ~** (*fig.*) найти́ (*pf.*) квадрату́ру кру́га; **great ~** ортодро́мия; **great ~ sailing** пла́вание по дуге́ большо́го кру́га; **Arctic/Antarctic ~** Се́верный/Ю́жный поля́рный круг; **vicious ~** поро́чный круг; **go round in a ~** (*fig., e.g. argument*) возвраща́ться (*impf.*) к исхо́дной то́чке; **run round in ~s** (*fig.*) носи́ться (*impf.*) без то́лку. **2** (*theatr.*): **dress ~** бельэта́ж; **upper ~** балко́н. **3** (*of seasons etc.*) цикл; по́лный оборо́т; **come full ~** описа́ть (*pf.*) по́лный круг; заверши́ть (*pf.*) цикл.

● *v.t.*: **the earth ~s the sun** земля́ враща́ется вокру́г со́лнца; **he ~d the misspelt words** он обвёл кружка́ми непра́вильно напи́санные слова́.

● *v.i.*: **the hawk ~d** я́стреб кружи́лся (*or* опи́сывал круги́); **the news ~d round** но́вость распространи́лась повсю́ду.

circuit /ˈsɜːkɪt/ *n.* **1** (*distance, journey round*): **the ~ of the walls is 3 miles** окру́жность стен 3 ми́ли; **he made a ~ of the camp** он обошёл ла́герь; (*detour*) окружно́й путь, объе́зд. **2** (*itinerary*) маршру́т. **3** (*leg.*) суде́бный круг. **4** (*elec.*) цепь; схе́ма; **integrated ~** интегра́льная схе́ма; **short ~** коро́ткое замыка́ние; **~ board** монта́жная пла́та; **~ breaker** автомати́ческий выключа́тель; **closed-~ television** ка́бельное телеви́дение (по за́мкнутому кана́лу).

● *v.t. & i.* об|ходи́ть, -ойти́ (*or* враща́ться) (вокру́г + *g.*).

circuitous /sɜːˈkjuːɪtəs/ *adj.* кру́жный, око́льный.

circular /ˈsɜːkjʊlə(r)/ *n.* (*letter etc.*) циркуля́р; (*commercial*) рекла́мный проспе́кт.

● *adj.* кругово́й; (*round in shape*) кру́глый, кругообра́зный; **~ saw** кру́глая/циркуля́рная пила́; **~ road** (*round a town*) окружна́я доро́га; **~ letter** циркуля́рное письмо́.

circularize /ˈsɜːkjʊləˌraɪz/ *v.t.* ра|ссыла́ть, -зосла́ть циркуля́ры + *d.*

circulate /ˈsɜːkjʊˌleɪt/ *v.t.* (*put about, e.g. rumour*) распростран|я́ть, -и́ть; перед|ава́ть, -а́ть; (*pass round, e.g. port*) передава́ть (*impf.*) по кру́гу.

● *v.i.* циркули́ровать (*impf., pf.*); **blood ~s through the body** кровь циркули́рует в те́ле; **she ~d among the guests** она́ обходи́ла госте́й.

circulation /ˌsɜːkjʊˈleɪʃ(ə)n/ *n.* **1** (*of blood*) кровообраще́ние; (*of air*) циркуля́ция. **2** (*of banknotes etc.*) обраще́ние. **3**: **Smith is back in ~** Смит верну́лся к свое́й обы́чной жи́зни. **4** (*of newspaper etc.*) тира́ж; **this paper has a ~ of 5,000** у э́той газе́ты тира́ж 5 000.

circumcise /'sɜːkəm,saɪz/ *v.t.* соверш|а́ть, -и́ть обре́зание + *d.*

circumcision /,sɜːkəm'sɪʒ(ə)n/ *n.* обре́зание.

circumference /sɜː'kʌmfərəns/ *n.* окру́жность.

circumflex /'sɜːkəm,fleks/ *n.* (**~** *accent*) циркумфле́кс, знак облегчённого ударе́ния.

circumlocution /,sɜːkəmlə'kjuːʃ(ə)n/ *n.* многосло́вие, околи́чности (*f. pl.*).

circumnavigate /,sɜːkəm'nævɪ,geɪt/ *v.t.* пла́вать (*indet.*) вокру́г + *g.*; **Drake ~d the globe** Дрейк соверши́л кругосве́тное пла́вание.

circumnavigation /,sɜːkəmnævɪ'geɪʃ(ə)n/ *n.* кругосве́тное пла́вание.

circumpolar /,sɜːkəm'pəʊlə(r)/ *adj.* (*geog.*) околопо́люсный; (*astron.*) околополя́рный.

circumscribe /'sɜːkəm,skraɪb/ *v.t.* (*draw line round*) опи́с|ывать, -а́ть; (*fig., restrict*) ста́вить, по- преде́л + *d.*; ограни́чи|вать, -ть.

circumscription /,sɜːkəm'skrɪpʃ(ə)n/ *n.* (*restriction*) ограниче́ние, преде́л.

circumspect /'sɜːkəm,spekt/ *adj.* осмотри́тельный.

circumspection /,sɜːkəm'spekʃ(ə)n/ *n.* осмотри́тельность.

circumstance /'sɜːkəmst(ə)ns/ *n.* **1** (*fact, detail*) обстоя́тельство, усло́вие; **in, under the ~s** в да́нных усло́виях/обстоя́тельствах; **in, under no ~s** ни при каки́х усло́виях/обстоя́тельствах; **extenuating ~s** смягча́ющие обстоя́тельства. **2** (*condition of life*) материа́льное положе́ние; **in easy ~s** в хоро́шем материа́льном положе́нии. **3** (*ceremony*) церемо́ния, торже́ственность.

circumstantial /,sɜːkəm'stænʃ(ə)l/ *adj.*: **~ evidence** ко́свенные ули́ки (*f. pl.*).

circumvent /,sɜːkəm'vent/ *v.t.* об|ходи́ть, -ойти́; (*outwit, cheat*) перехитри́ть (*pf.*).

circumvention /,sɜːkəm'venʃ(ə)n/ *n.* (*deception*) обма́н.

circus /'sɜːkəs/ *n.* (*pl.* **~es**) **1** (*also hist.*) цирк; (*fig.*) балага́н. **2** (*Br., intersection of streets*) (кру́глая) пло́щадь.

cirrhosis /sɪ'rəʊsɪs/ *n.* цирро́з.

cirri /'sɪraɪ/ *pl. of* ⇒**cirrus**

cirro-cumulus /,sɪrəʊ'kjuːmjʊləs/ *n.* пе́ристо-кучевы́е облака́.

cirr|us /'sɪrəs/ *n.* (*pl.* **~i**) (*clouds*) пе́ристые облака́.

CIS (*abbr. of* ***Commonwealth of Independent States***) СНГ (Содру́жество незави́симых госуда́рств); (*attr., coll.*) эсэнго́вский.

cissy /'sɪsɪ/ = **sissy**

cistern /'sɪst(ə)n/ *n.* цисте́рна, бак.

citadel /'sɪtəd(ə)l/, /-,del/ *n.* (*lit., fig.*) цитаде́ль.

citation /saɪ'teɪʃ(ə)n/ *n.* **1** (*US, summons*) вы́зов. **2** (*quotation*) цита́ция, цити́рование. **3** (*for bravery*) упомина́ние в прика́зе.

cite /saɪt/ *v.t.* **1** (*US, summon*) вызыва́ть, вы́звать. **2** (*quote*) цити́ровать, про-. **3** (*for bravery*) отм|еча́ть, -е́тить в прика́зе.

citizen /'sɪtɪz(ə)n/ *n.* гражд|ани́н (*fem.* -а́нка); **French ~** францу́зский граждани́н; (*of city*) жи́тель (*fem.* -ница); **private ~** ча́стное лицо́.

citizenry /'sɪtɪzənrɪ/ *n.* гра́ждане (*m. pl.*), населе́ние.

citizenship /'sɪtɪzənʃɪp/ *n.* (*nationality*) гражда́нство, по́дданство.

citric /'sɪtrɪk/ *adj.* лимо́нный; **~ acid** лимо́нная кислота́.

citrus /'sɪtrəs/ *n.* (*pl.* **~es**) ци́трус; **~ fruit** ци́трусовые (*m. pl.*).

city /'sɪtɪ/ *n.* го́род; (*of London*) Си́ти (*nt. indecl.*); **~ centre** (*Br.*), **center** (*US*) центр го́рода; **~ council** городско́й сове́т; **~ fathers** отцы́ го́рода; **~ hall** ра́туша; **~ state** (*hist.*) го́род-госуда́рство, по́лис.

civet /'sɪvɪt/ *n.* (*also* **~-cat**) виве́рра.

civic /'sɪvɪk/ *adj.* гражда́нский; **~ activity** обще́ственная де́ятельность; **~ virtue** гражда́нская доброде́тель.

civics /'sɪvɪks/ *n.* осно́вы (*f. pl.*) гражда́нственности.

civil /'sɪv(ə)l/, /-ɪl/ *adj.* **1** (*pert. to a community*): **~ war** гражда́нская война́; **~ rights** гражда́нские права́; **~ marriage** гражда́нский брак; **~ servant** госуда́рственный слу́жащий, чино́вник; **~ service** госуда́рственная слу́жба; **~ law** гражда́нское пра́во; **~ engineer** инжене́р-строи́тель (*m.*). **2** (*civilian*) гражда́нский, шта́тский; **~ defence** (*Br.*), **defense** (*US*) гражда́нская оборо́на. **3** (*polite*) ве́жливый, любе́зный.

civilian /sɪ'vɪlɪən/ *n.* & *adj.* шта́тский; **~ population** ми́рные жи́тели; **what did you do in ~ life?** чем вы занима́лись до а́рмии?

civility /sɪ'vɪlɪtɪ/ *n.* ве́жливость, любе́зность; (*pl.*) любе́зности (*f. pl.*).

civilization /,sɪvɪlaɪ'zeɪʃ(ə)n/ *n.* цивилиза́ция; **deeds that horrified ~** дея́ния, ужасну́вшие цивилизо́ванный мир.

civilize /'sɪvɪ,laɪz/ *v.t.* цивилизова́ть (*impf., pf.*).

civvies /'sɪvɪz/ *n.* (*coll.*) шта́тская оде́жда; **in ~** в шта́тском.

clack /klæk/ *n.* (*sharp sound*) треск, щёлканье, стук; (*talk*) трескотня́.

● *v.i.* (*lit., fig.*) треща́ть, щёлкать (*both impf.*); **tongues were ~ing** языки́ болта́ли.

clad[1] /klæd/ *v.t.* (**cladding;** *past and p.p.* **cladded** *or* **clad**) покр|ыва́ть, -ы́ть.

clad[2] /klæd/ *archaic or literary past and p.p. of* ⇒**clothe**

cladding /'klædɪŋ/ *n.* покры́тие.

claim /kleɪm/ *n.* **1** (*assertion of right*) притяза́ние; **lay ~ to something** предъявл|я́ть, -и́ть прете́нзии на что-н.; претендова́ть (*impf.*) на что-н.; **file (*or* put in) a ~ for damages** предъяви́ть (*pf.*) иск о возмеще́нии убы́тков; **stake out a ~** (*fig.*) закреп|ля́ть, -и́ть своё пра́во (*на что*). **2** (*assertion*) утвержде́ние, заявле́ние. **3** (*demand*) тре́бование; (*just demand*): **you have no ~ on my sympathies** вы не заслу́живаете моего́ сочу́вствия.

● *v.t.* **1** (*demand*) тре́бовать, по- + *g.*; **where do I ~ my baggage?** где здесь выдаю́т бага́ж?; **does anyone ~ this umbrella?** есть ли владе́лец у э́того зо́нтика? **2** (*assert as fact*) утвер|жда́ть, -ди́ть; **he ~s to own the land** он заявля́ет, что э́та земля́ принадлежи́т ему́; **he ~s to have done the work alone** он утвержда́ет, что сде́лал рабо́ту сам. **3** (*of things*) тре́бовать, по- + *g.*; **this matter ~s attention** э́тот вопро́с заслу́живает внима́ния.

claimant /'kleɪmənt/ *n.* претенде́нт (*fem.* -ка) (*на что*).

clairvoyance /kleə'vɔɪəns/ *n.* ясновиде́ние.

clairvoyant /kleə'vɔɪənt/ *n.* ясновид|ец (*fem.* -ица).

clam /klæm/ *n.* (*shellfish*) двуство́рчатый морско́й моллю́ск; **he shut up like a ~** (*fig.*) он как воды́ в рот набра́л.

● *v.i.* (**clammed, clamming**) (*US, gather* **~s**) собира́ть (*impf.*) моллю́сков; **~ up** (*coll.*) уходи́ть, уйти́ в себя́.

clamber /'klæmbə(r)/ *v.i.* кара́бкаться, вс- (*на что*).

clamminess /'klæmɪnɪs/ *n.* ли́пкость.

clammy /'klæmɪ/ *adj.* (**clammier, clammiest**) холо́дный и ли́пкий.

clamorous /'klæmərəs/ *adj.* шу́мный, шумли́вый.

clamour /'klæmə(r)/ (*US* **clamor**) *n.* шум, кри́ки (*m. pl.*).

● *v.i.* шуме́ть (*impf.*), крича́ть (*impf.*).

clamp /klæmp/ *n.* (*implement*) зажи́м, скоба́.

● *v.t.* заж|има́ть, -а́ть; скреп|ля́ть, -и́ть.

● *v.i.*: **~ down on** (*fig., suppress*) заж|има́ть, -а́ть; приж|има́ть, -а́ть; прин|има́ть, -я́ть стро́гие ме́ры про́тив + *g.*

● *cpd.* **~down** *n.* стро́гий запре́т, стро́гие ме́ры (*против чего*).

clan /klæn/ *n.* клан, род.

clandestine /klæn'destɪn/ *adj.* та́йный, подпо́льный.

clang /'klæŋ/ *n.* лязг, звон.

● *v.t.* & *i.* ля́зг|ать, -нуть; звене́ть (*impf.*); **the tram-driver ~ed his bell** вагоновожа́тый гро́мко звони́л в звоно́к.

clanger /'klæŋə(r)/ *n.* (*Br.*): **he dropped a ~** (*sl.*) он допусти́л опо́шлость; он дал ма́ху (*coll.*).

clangorous /'klæŋgərəs/ *adj.* ля́згающий.

clangour /ˈklæŋgə(r)/ (*US* **clangor**) *n.* звон, ля́зганье.

clank /klæŋk/ *n.* звон, лязг, бряца́ние.
● *v.t. & i.* ля́зг|ать, -нуть; бряца́ть (*impf.*); греме́ть (*impf.*); **the ghost ~ed its chains** привиде́ние ля́згало/греме́ло цепя́ми.

clannish /ˈklænɪʃ/ *adj.* держа́щийся своего́ кла́на (*or* свое́й гру́ппы).

clansman /ˈklænzmən/ *n.* член кла́на/ ро́да.

clap¹ /klæp/ *n.* (*of thunder*) уда́р; (*of applause*) хлопо́к, хло́панье; **let's give him a ~!** похло́паем ему́!; (*slap*) хлопо́к; **a ~ on the back** хлопо́к по спине́.
● *v.t.* (**clapped, clapping**) **1** (*strike, slap*) хло́п|ать, -нуть; **he ~ped me on the back** он хло́пнул меня́ по спине́; **~ one's hands** хло́п|ать, -нуть в ладо́ши.
2 (*coll., put*): **~ s.o. in prison** упе́чь (*pf.*) кого́-н. в тюрьму́; **~ duties on goods** обложи́ть (*pf.*) това́ры по́шлиной; **~ handcuffs on s.o.** наде́ть (*pf.*) нару́чники на кого́-н.; **I have not ~ped eyes on him since then** с тех пор я ни ра́зу его́ не ви́дел.
3 (*applaud*) аплоди́ровать (*impf.*) + *d.*; рукоплеска́ть (*impf.*) + *d.*
● *v.i.* (**clapped, clapping**) хло́пать (*impf.*); аплоди́ровать (*impf.*); рукоплеска́ть (*impf.*).
● *cpds.* **~board** *n.* (*US*) клёпка; дра́нка, гонт; **~trap** *n.* трескýчая фра́за, болтовня́.

clap² /klæp/ *n.* (*vulg., gonorrhoea*) три́ппер.

clapper /ˈklæpə(r)/ *n.* (*of bell*) язы́к; **go like the ~s** (*Br.*) мча́ться (*impf.*) как угоре́лый.

claque /klæk/, /klɑːk/ *n.* кла́ка.

claret /ˈklærət/ *n.* кларе́т; бордо́ (*indecl.*).
● *cpd.* **~-coloured** (*Br.*), **-colored** (*US*) *adj.* цве́та бордо́; бордо́вый.

clarification /ˌklærɪfɪˈkeɪʃ(ə)n/ *n.* проясне́ние, разъясне́ние; (*of liquid*) очище́ние.

clarify /ˈklærɪˌfaɪ/ *v.t.* вн|оси́ть, -ести́ я́сность в + *a.*; разъясн|я́ть, -и́ть; **~ one's mind about something** уясни́ть (*pf.*) себе́ что-н.; (*butter etc.*) оч|ища́ть, -и́стить.

clarinet /ˌklærɪˈnet/ *n.* кларне́т.

clarinettist /ˌklærɪˈnetɪst/ *n.* кларнети́ст (*fem.* -ка).

clarion /ˈklærɪən/ *n.* рог, рожо́к; **~ call** (*fig.*) призы́вный звук; боево́й клич.

clarity /ˈklærɪtɪ/ *n.* я́сность.

clash /klæʃ/ *n.* **1** (*sound*) гул, лязг, звон. **2** (*conflict*): **I had a ~ with him** у меня́ бы́ло с ним столкнове́ние; **~ of views** расхожде́ние во взгля́дах; **~ of colours** (*Br.*), **colors** (*US*) дисгармо́ния цвето́в; (*inconvenient coincidence*) совпаде́ние по вре́мени.
● *v.t.*: **he ~ed the cymbals** он уда́рил в цимба́лы.
● *v.i.* **1** (*sound*): **the cymbals ~ed** зазвене́ли цимба́лы. **2** (*conflict*): **the armies ~ed** а́рмии столкну́лись; **my interests ~ with his** у нас с ним ста́лкиваются интере́сы; (*coincide inconveniently*): **the two concerts ~** о́ба конце́рта совпада́ют по вре́мени; **the colours ~** э́ти цвета́ не гармони́руют друг с дру́гом.

clasp /klɑːsp/ *n.* **1** (*fastener*) пря́жка, застёжка. **2** (*grip, handshake*) пожа́тие, сжа́тие, объя́тие.
● *v.t.*: **~ a bracelet round one's wrist** застёг|ивать, -ну́ть на руке́ брасле́т; **~ one's hands** сплести́ (*pf.*) па́льцы; **~ s.o. by the hand** сж|има́ть, -ать кому́-н. ру́ку; **they were ~ed in each other's arms** они́ заключи́ли друг дру́га в объя́тия; **~ hands with s.o.** (*fig.*) пожа́ть (*pf.*) ру́ку кому́-н.
● *v.i.*: **the necklace won't ~** ожере́лье не застёгивается.
● *cpd.* **~-knife** *n.* складно́й нож.

class /klɑːs/ *n.* **1** (*group, category*) класс, разря́д; (*railway etc.*): **he went first ~** он е́хал пе́рвым кла́ссом; (*fig.*): **he is not in the same ~ as X** ему́ о́чень далеко́ до X; (*biol.*) класс.
2 (*social*) класс; **lower ~(es)** ни́зшие кла́ссы; **middle ~** буржуази́я; сре́дние слои́ о́бщества; **upper ~(es)** вы́сшие кла́ссы, аристокра́тия; **~ conflict** кла́ссовые конфли́кты; **~ war** кла́ссовая борьба́.
3 (*scholastic*) класс; **he is top of the ~** он пе́рвый учени́к в кла́ссе; (*period of instruction*): **a mathematics ~** уро́к матема́тики; **Mr X is taking the ~** г-н X ведёт заня́тия; **he attended ~es in French** он посеща́л заня́тия по францу́зскому языку́; (*US*): **the ~ of 1955** вы́пуск 1955 го́да.
4 (*mil.*): **the ~ of 1960** набо́р 1960 го́да.
5 (*distinction*) класс, шик.
● *v.t.* классифици́ровать (*impf., pf.*); **the ship is ~ed A1** су́дну присвоен пе́рвый класс; **you cannot ~ him with the Romantics** его́ нельзя́ отнести́ к рома́нтикам.
● *v.i.*: **those who ~ as believers** те, кото́рые счита́ются ве́рующими.
● *cpds.* **~-conscious** *adj.* кла́ссово-созна́тельный; **~-consciousness** *n.* кла́ссовое созна́ние; **~fellow, ~mate** *nn.* однокла́ссни|к (*fem.* -ца); **~room** *n.* кла́ссная ко́мната, класс.

classic /ˈklæsɪk/ *n.* **1** (*writer etc.*) кла́ссик. **2** (*book etc.*) класси́ческое произведе́ние. **3** (*ancient writer*) кла́ссик, анти́чный а́втор; **the ~s** кла́ссика, класси́ческая литерату́ра. **4** (*pl., studies*): **he studied ~s** он изуча́л класси́ческую филоло́гию.
● *adj.* класси́ческий.

classical /ˈklæsɪk(ə)l/ *adj.* класси́ческий; **~ scholar** кла́ссик.

classicism /ˈklæsɪˌsɪz(ə)m/ *n.* классици́зм; (*classical scholarship*) изуче́ние класси́ческой филоло́гии.

classicist /ˈklæsɪsɪst/ *n.* классици́ст.

classifiable /ˈklæsɪˌfaɪəb(ə)l/ *adj.* поддаю́щийся классифика́ции.

classification /ˌklæsɪfɪˈkeɪʃ(ə)n/ *n.* классифика́ция.

classifier /ˈklæsɪˌfaɪə(r)/ *n.* классифика́тор.

classif|y /ˈklæsɪˌfaɪ/ *v.t.* классифици́ровать (*impf., pf.*); **~ied** (*secret*) засекре́ченный; **~ied ad** темати́ческое объявле́ние.

classless /ˈklɑːslɪs/ *adj.* бескла́ссовый.

classlessness /ˈklɑːslɪsnɪs/ *n.* бескла́ссовость.

classy /ˈklɑːsɪ/ *adj.* (**classier, classiest**) сти́льный (*coll.*).

clatter /ˈklætə(r)/ *n.* **1** (*of metal*) гро́хот; (*of hoofs, plates, cutlery etc.*) стук, звон, звя́канье. **2** (*chatter, noise*) трескотня́.
● *v.t.* стуча́ть, греме́ть, звя́кать (*all impf.*).
● *v.i.* греме́ть; грохота́ть (*both impf.*); **the plates came ~ing down** таре́лки с гро́хотом полете́ли на́ пол.

clause /klɔːz/ *n.* **1** (*gram.*) предложе́ние; **main ~** гла́вное предложе́ние; **subordinate ~** прида́точное предложе́ние. **2** (*leg.*) статья́; пункт; кла́узула, огово́рка; **escape ~** пункт, предусма́тривающий отка́з от взя́того обяза́тельства.

claustrophobia /ˌklɔːstrəˈfəʊbɪə/ *n.* боя́знь за́мкнутого простра́нства; клаустрофо́бия.

claustrophobic /ˌklɔːstrəˈfəʊbɪk/ *adj.* клаустрофоби́чный; вызыва́ющий клаустрофо́бию; **I'm ~** я страда́ю клаустрофо́бией.

clave /kleɪv/ *archaic past of* ⇒**cleave²**

clavichord /ˈklævɪˌkɔːd/ *n.* клавико́рд|ы (*pl., g.* -ов).

clavicle /ˈklævɪk(ə)l/ *n.* ключи́ца.

claw /klɔː/ *n.* (*of animal, bird*) ко́готь (*m.*); (*of crustacean*) клешня́; **get one's ~s into something** вцеп|ля́ться, -и́ться когтя́ми во что-н.; (*of machinery*) кула́к, ла́па, кле́щ|и (*pl., g.* -ей).
● *v.t. & i.* цара́пать(ся); рвать когтя́ми; когти́ть (*all impf.*); **the cat ~ed at the door** ко́шка цара́палась в дверь; **~ one's way to the top** (*fig.*) вскара́бкаться (*pf.*) наве́рх.
● *cpd.* **~-hammer** *n.* молото́к с гвоздодёром.

clay /kleɪ/ *n.* гли́на; **~ soil** гли́нистая по́чва; **~ pigeon** летя́щая таре́лочка (*в тире*); **~ pipe** гли́няная тру́бка; **an idol with feet of ~** коло́сс на гли́няных нога́х.

clayey /ˈkleɪɪ/ *adj.* гли́нистый.

claymore /ˈkleɪmɔː(r)/ *n.* (*hist., broadsword*) пала́ш.

clean /kliːn/ *n.* (*Br.*) чи́стка, убо́рка; **he gave the table a good ~** он хороше́нько вы́тер стол.
● *adj.* **1** (*not dirty*) чи́стый; **wash something ~** до́чиста вы́мыть (*pf.*) что-н.; **keep a room ~** содержа́ть (*impf.*) ко́мнату в чистоте́.
2 (*fresh*): **a ~ sheet of paper** чи́стый лист бума́ги; **a ~ copy** (*of draft*) чистови́к, белови́к.
3 (*pure, unblemished*) чи́стый, незапя́тнанный; **a ~ driving licence**

(*Br.*), ~ **record** (*US*) чи́стые права́.
4 (*neat, smooth*): ~ **lines** чёткие очерта́ния; чи́стые ли́нии; **a ~ cut** ро́вный разре́з.
5 (*fig.*): **my hands are ~** я невино́вен; **make a ~ sweep of** подчи́стить под метёлку; **he showed a ~ pair of heels** у него́ пя́тки засверка́ли; **come ~** (*coll., confess or vouchsafe the truth*) созна́ться (*pf.*).

● *adv.*: **I ~ forgot** я на́чисто забы́л; **the bullet went ~ through his shoulder** пу́ля проби́ла его́ плечо́ навы́лет.

● *v.t.* чи́стить (*impf.; for forms of pf. see examples*); ~ **one's teeth** чи́стить, по- зу́бы; ~ **a suit** чи́стить, вы́-/по- костю́м; ~ **streets** уб|ира́ть, -ра́ть у́лицы; ~ **a car** мыть, вы́- маши́ну; ~ **a window** прот|ира́ть, -ере́ть окно́; ~ **a rifle** проч|ища́ть, -и́стить ружьё; **~ing fluid** жи́дкость для выведе́ния пя́тен; **he had his suit ~ed** он отда́л костю́м в чи́стку.

● *v.i.* чи́ститься (*impf.*); **the sink ~s easily** ра́ковина хорошо́ мо́ется; **~ing day** (*in hostels, shops etc.*) санита́рный день.

● *with advs.*: ~ **down** *v.t.* сч|ища́ть, -и́стить; сме|та́ть, -сти́; ~ **out** *v.t.*: ~ **out a room** убра́ть (*pf.*) ко́мнату; ~ **out a car** чи́стить, вы́- маши́ну; **he was ~ed out** (*fig.*) его́ обчи́стили; ~ **up** *v.t.*: ~ **o.s. up** прив|оди́ть, -ести́ себя́ в поря́док; ~ **up a city** (*fig.*) почи́стить (*pf.*) го́род; *v.i.*: **they ~ed up after the picnic** они́ убра́ли за собо́й по́сле пикника́.

● *cpds.* **~-cut** *adj.* ре́зко оче́рченный; **~-cut features** чёткие черты́ лица́; (*fig.*) я́сный, я́вный, отчётливый; **~-limbed** *adj.* стро́йный; **~-living** *adj.* целому́дренный, чи́стый; **~-out** *n.* чи́стка, убо́рка; **~-shaven** *adj.* чи́сто вы́бритый; **~-up** *n.* (*lit.*) чи́стка; (*fig.*) чи́стка, очи́стка; приведе́ние в поря́док.

cleaner /ˈkli:nə(r)/ *n.* (*person*) убо́рщи|к (*fem.* -ца); чи́стильщи|к (*fem.* -ца); **he sent the suit to the ~'s** он отда́л костю́м в чи́стку; (*tool, machine*) очисти́тель (*m.*); (*substance*) мо́ющее сре́дство; очисти́тель (*m.*).

cleanliness /ˈklenlınıs/ *n.* чистота́.

cleanness /ˈkli:nnıs/ *n.* чистота́.

cleans|e /klenz/ *v.t.* оч|ища́ть, -и́стить; **~ing cream** очища́ющий крем; **~ing department** (*Br.*) санита́рное управле́ние; **ethnic ~ing** этни́ческая чи́стка.

cleanser /ˈklenzə(r)/ *n.* сре́дство для очи́стки ко́жи.

clear /klıə(r)/ *adj.* **1** (*easy to see*) я́сный, отчётливый; (*evident*) я́вный, очеви́дный.
2 (*bright, unclouded*) я́ркий, я́сный; **a ~ sky** я́сное не́бо; **on a ~ day** в пого́жий день.
3 (*transparent*) прозра́чный.
4 (*of sound*) чи́стый, отчётливый.
5 (*intelligible, certain*): **make something ~ to s.o.** объясн|я́ть, -и́ть что-н. кому́-н.; **make o.s. ~** объясн|я́ться, -и́ться; **I am not ~ what he wants** мне нея́сно, чего́ он хо́чет; **as ~ as day, crystal ~** я́сно как день; преде́льно я́сно; ~ **as mud** (*coll.*) соверше́нно нея́сно.
6 (*safe, free, unencumbered*) свобо́дный; **the field is ~ of trees** на по́ле нет дере́вьев; **the river is ~ of ice** река́ освободи́лась ото льда́; **the 'all ~'** отбо́й (*воздушной тревоги*); **~ of debt** свобо́дный от долго́в; **~ of suspicion** вне подозре́ний; **my conscience is ~** моя́ со́весть чиста́; ~ **profit** чи́стая при́быль; **three ~ days** це́лых три дня; **keep a ~ head** сохраня́ть (*impf.*) я́сный ум.
7: **in the ~** (*free from suspicion, out of trouble*) чи́стый.

● *adv.*: **he spoke loud and ~** он говори́л гро́мко и я́сно; **stand ~ of the gates** стоя́ть (*impf.*) в стороне́ от воро́т; **get ~ of** от|ходи́ть, -ойти́ в сто́рону от + *g.*; **keep ~ of** держа́ться (*impf.*) в стороне́ от + *g.*; остер|ега́ться, -е́чься + *g.*; избе|га́ть, -жа́ть + *g.*

● *v.t.* **1** (*make ~, empty*) оч|ища́ть, -и́стить; **the streets were ~ed of snow** у́лицы очи́стили от сне́га; ~ **land** расч|ища́ть, -и́стить зе́млю; **he ~ed his desk** он убра́л свой стол; **she ~ed the table** она́ убрала́ со стола́; **our talk ~ed the air** наш разгово́р разряди́л атмосфе́ру; ~ **o.s. (of a charge)** оправда́ться (*pf.*); опрове́ргнуть (*pf.*) обвине́ние; **he was ~ed for security** его́ засекре́тили; ~ **s.o.'s mind of doubt** рассе́|ивать, -ять чьи-н. сомне́ния; **to ~ one's conscience** для очи́стки со́вести; **he ~ed his throat** он отка́шлялся; ~ **something out of the way** уб|ира́ть, -ра́ть что-н. с доро́ги; отодв|ига́ть, -и́нуть что-н.; **he ~ed the things out of the drawer** он освободи́л я́щик; **he ~ed the children out of the garden** он вы́гнал дете́й из са́да.
2 (*jump over; get past*): **the horse ~ed the hedge** ло́шадь взяла́ барье́р; **the car ~ed the gate** автомоби́ль прошёл в воро́та.
3 (*make profit of*): **we ~ed £50** мы получи́ли 50 фу́нтов при́были; **we just ~ed expenses** нам удало́сь лишь покры́ть расхо́ды.
4: ~ **an account** опла́|чивать, -ти́ть счёт; ~ **a debt** погаси́ть (*pf.*) долг.

● *v.i.*: *cf.* ⇒ ~ **up; his brow ~ed** его́ лицо́ проясни́лось.

● *with advs.*: ~ **away** *v.t.* уб|ира́ть, -ра́ть; *v.i.* (*disperse*) рассе́|иваться, -яться; ~ **off** *v.i.* (*coll., go away*) уб|ира́ться, -ра́ться; ~ **off!** убира́йтесь!; ~ **out** *v.t.*: **she ~ed out the cupboard** она́ очи́стила шкаф; (*fig., make destitute*) обчи́стить (*pf.*); *v.i.* (*coll., go away*) убра́ться (*pf.*); ~ **up** *v.t.* (*tidy, remove*) уб|ира́ть, -ра́ть; ~ **up a mystery** распу́тать (*pf.*) та́йну; *v.i.*: **the weather ~ed up** пого́да проясни́лась; **please ~ up after you** бу́дьте добры́, убери́те за собо́й.

● *cpds.* **~-cut** *adj.* (*fig.*) чёткий; **~-headed** *adj.* толко́вый, у́мный; **~-headedness** *n.* толко́вость; **~-sighted** *adj.* проница́тельный, дальнови́дный; **~-sightedness** *n.* проница́тельность, дальнови́дность; **~way** *n.* (*Br.*) скоростна́я автостра́да.

clearance /ˈklıərəns/ *n.* **1** (*removal of obstruction etc.*) очи́стка, расчи́стка; ~ **sale** распрода́жа. **2** (*free space*) зазо́р; промежу́ток; **the barge had a ~ of 2 feet** кана́л был на 2 фу́та ши́ре ба́ржи. **3** (*customs*) очи́стка от тамо́женных по́шлин. **4**: **security ~** до́пуск к секре́тной рабо́те; **medical ~** свиде́тельство о го́дности по здоро́вью.

clearing /ˈklıərıŋ/ *n.* **1** (*glade*) про́сека, поля́на. **2** (*fin.*) кли́ринг; ~ **agreement** кли́ринговое соглаше́ние; ~ **house** расчётная пала́та.

clearly /ˈklıəlı/ *adv.* (*distinctly*) я́сно; (*evidently*) очеви́дно, коне́чно; **it is too dark to see ~** сли́шком темно́, что́бы разгляде́ть; ~ **he is wrong** я́сно, что он непра́в.

clearness /ˈklıənıs/ *n.* я́сность, очеви́дность.

cleat /kli:t/ *n.* **1** (*strip of wood on gangway etc.*) пла́нка, ре́йка. **2** (*fitting for attachment of rope*) крепи́тельная у́тка/пла́нка. **3** (*on sole or heel of shoe*) ско́бка, гвоздь (*m.*).

cleavage /ˈkli:vıdʒ/ *n.* **1** (*splitting*) расщепле́ние, раска́лывание. **2** (*fig., discord*) расхожде́ние, раско́л. **3** (*of bosom*) «ручеёк», ложби́нка бю́ста.

cleave[1] /kli:v/ *v.t.* (*past* **clove** *or* **cleft** *or* **cleaved;** *p.p.* **cloven** *or* **cleft** *or* **cleaved**) **1** (*split*) раск|а́лывать, -оло́ть; расс|ека́ть, -е́чь. **2** (*fig.*): **he ~d his way through the crowd** он проти́снулся че́рез толпу́. **3**: **cleft palate** (*med.*) во́лчья пасть; **cloven hoof** раздво́енное копы́то; **cloven-footed, -hooved** парнокопы́тный; **show the cloven hoof** (*fig.*) обнару́жить свою́ кова́рную приро́ду; **he is in a cleft stick** (*Br.*) он зажа́т в тиски́; он в тупике́.

● *v.i.* (*past* **clove** *or* **cleft** *or* **cleaved;** *p.p.* **cloven** *or* **cleft** *or* **cleaved**) раск|а́лываться, -оло́ться; **the wood ~s easily** э́то де́рево легко́ ко́лется.

cleave[2] /kli:v/ *v.i.* (*past* **cleaved** *or archaic* **clave**) (*adhere*) прил|ипа́ть, -и́пнуть; **his tongue ~d to the roof of his mouth** у него́ язы́к к горта́ни прили́п; **he ~s to his friends** он пре́дан свои́м друзья́м.

cleaver /ˈkli:və(r)/ *n.* нож мясника́.

clef /klef/ *n.* ключ; **treble ~** скрипи́чный ключ; **bass ~** басо́вый ключ.

cleft[1] /kleft/ *n.* тре́щина, рассе́лина.

cleft[2] /kleft/ *adj.* = **cleave**[1] 3

clematis /ˈklemətıs/, /kləˈmeıtıs/ *n.* клема́тис, ломоно́с.

clemency /ˈklemənsı/ *n.* (*of person*) милосе́рдие; **the defence** (*Br.*), **defense** (*US*) **lawyer appealed for ~** защи́тник проси́л снисхожде́ния; (*of weather*) мя́гкость.

clement /ˈklemənt/ *adj.* (*of person*) милосе́рдный, ми́лостивый; (*of weather*) мя́гкий.

clench /klentʃ/ *v.t.*: ~ **one's teeth**

сти́с|кивать, -нуть зу́бы; **~ one's fist** сж|има́ть, -ать кулаки́; **~ something in one's hands** сж|има́ть, -ать что-н. в рука́х.

clergy /ˈklɜːdʒɪ/ *n.* духове́нство, клир.
● *cpd.* **~man** *n.* духо́вное лицо́; (*Protestant*) па́стор.

cleric /ˈklerɪk/ *n.* церко́вник, духо́вное лицо́.

clerical /ˈklerɪk(ə)l/ *adj.* **1** (*of clergy*) клерика́льный; **~ collar** па́сторский воротни́к. **2** (*of clerks*) канцеля́рский, конто́рский; **~ error** канцеля́рская оши́бка.

clericalism /ˈklerɪk(ə),lɪz(ə)m/ *n.* клерикали́зм.

clerk /klɑːk/ *n.* **1** (*person in charge of correspondence*) секрета́рь (*m.*), письмоводи́тель (*m.*); **bank ~** ба́нковский слу́жащий. **2** (*official*) слу́жащий, чино́вник; (*of court*) регистра́тор. **3** (*US, shop assistant*) продаве́ц; (*US, hotel receptionist*) (дежу́рный) администра́тор. **4**: **~ of the works** (*Br.*) производи́тель (*m.*) рабо́т; проpа́б.
● *v.i.* (*work as ~*) выполня́ть (*impf.*) конто́рскую рабо́ту.

clever /ˈklevə(r)/ *adj.* (**cleverer, cleverest**) у́мный, сообрази́тельный; (*skilful*) ло́вкий; **he is ~ at arithmetic** он спосо́бен к арифме́тике; **he is ~ with his fingers** у него́ уме́лые ру́ки; **he was too ~ for us** он перехитри́л нас; **~ clogs/Dick** (*Br. coll.*) у́мник.
● *cpd.* **~-~** *adj.* (*coll.*) у́мничающий.

cleverness /ˈklevənɪs/ *n.* ум, одарённость; (*skill*) ло́вкость, уме́ние.

cliché /ˈkliːʃeɪ/ *n.* (*fig.*) клише́ (*indecl.*), штамп.
● *cpd.* **~-ridden** *adj.* по́лный клише́/шта́мпов.

click /klɪk/ *n.* щёлканье, щёлк, щелчо́к.
● *v.t.* щёлк|ать, -нуть +*i.*; прищёлк|ивать, -нуть +*i.*; (*comput.*): **~ a button** наж|има́ть, -а́ть на кно́пку; **he ~ed his tongue** он (при)щёлкнул языко́м; **he ~ed his heels** он щёлкнул каблука́ми.
● *v.i.* щёлк|ать, -нуть; **the door ~ed shut** дверь защёлкнулась; (*comput.*): **~ on an icon** щёлк|ать, -нуть (мы́шкой) на ико́нку; (*coll., hit it off*) пола́дить (*pf.*), сойти́сь (*pf.*) (*с кем*).

client /ˈklaɪənt/ *n.* клие́нт.

clientele /,kliːɒnˈtel/ *n.* клиенту́ра.

cliff /klɪf/ *n.* утёс, скала́.
● *cpd.* **~hanger** *n.* (*coll.*) захва́тывающий расска́з/рома́н/фильм.

climacteric /klaɪˈmæktərɪk/, /,klaɪmækˈterɪk/ *n.* климакте́рий; (*age*) климактери́ческий во́зраст.
● *adj.* климактери́ческий, крити́ческий.

climactic /klaɪˈmæktɪk/ *adj.* кульминацио́нный.

climate /ˈklaɪmɪt/ *n.* кли́мат; (*fig.*) атмосфе́ра; **~ of opinion** состоя́ние обще́ственного мне́ния.

climatic /,klaɪˈmætɪk/ *adj.* климати́ческий.

climax /ˈklaɪmæks/ *n.* кульмина́ция; (*orgasm*) орга́зм.
● *v.t.* (*top off, crown*) довести́ (*pf.*) до кульмина́ции.
● *v.i.* (*culminate*) кульмини́ровать (*impf., pf.*); дойти́ (*pf.*) до кульмина́ции.

climb /klaɪm/ *n.* подъём, восхожде́ние; **it was a long ~ to the top** подъём на верши́ну был до́лгим.
● *v.t.* вл|еза́ть, -езть на + *a.*
● *v.i.* ла́зить (*indet.*), лезть (*det.*); подн|има́ться, -я́ться; **~ up a tree** влез|а́ть, -ть на де́рево; **~ over a wall** перел|еза́ть, -е́зть че́рез сте́ну; **~ down a ladder** слез|а́ть, -ть с ле́стницы; **~ on to a table** зал|еза́ть, -е́зть на стол; **the sun/aircraft ~ed slowly** со́лнце/самолёт ме́дленно поднима́лось/поднима́лся; **~ down** (*lit.*) слез|а́ть, -ть; (*fig.*) отступ|а́ть, -и́ть.
● *cpd.* **~-down** *n.* (*fig.*) отступле́ние, усту́пка.

climber /ˈklaɪmə(r)/ *n.* (*person*) альпини́ст (*fem.* -ка); (*fig.*) карьери́ст (*fem.* -ка); (*plant*) выю́щееся расте́ние.

climbing /ˈklaɪmɪŋ/ *n.* (*mountaineering*) альпини́зм.
● *cpd.* **~-irons** *n. pl.* шипы́ (*m. pl.*) на альпини́стской о́буви; три́кон|и (*pl., g.* -ей).

clime /klaɪm/ *n.* (*poet., region*) край, сторона́.

clinch /klɪntʃ/ *n.* захва́т; (*in boxing*) клинч, захва́т; (*embrace*) кре́пкое объя́тие.
● *v.t.* (*make fast*) закл|ёпывать, -епа́ть; (*fig.*): **~ an argument** заверши́ть (*pf.*) спор; **~ a bargain** закрепи́ть (*pf.*) сде́лку.

clincher /ˈklɪntʃ(ə)r/ *n.* (*coll., decisive remark etc.*) реша́ющий до́вод.

cling /klɪŋ/ *v.i.* (*past and p.p.* **clung**) (*adhere*) цепля́ться (*impf.*) (за + *a.*); льну́ть (*impf.*) (к + *d.*); (*fig.*): **he clung to his possessions** он цепля́лся за своё иму́щество; **they clung together** они́ держа́лись вме́сте; **the child clung to its mother** ребёнок льнул к ма́тери; **a ~ing dress** облега́ющее пла́тье; **a ~ing person** привя́зчивый челове́к.

clinic /ˈklɪnɪk/ *n.* кли́ника.

clinical /ˈklɪnɪk(ə)l/ *adj.* **1** клини́ческий; **~ record** исто́рия боле́зни; **~ thermometer** медици́нский термо́метр. **2** (*fig.*) бесстра́стный.

clinician /klɪˈnɪʃ(ə)n/ *n.* клиници́ст.

clink[1] /klɪŋk/ *n.* звон.
● *v.t.* звене́ть (*impf.*) + *i.*; **~ glasses with s.o.** чо́к|аться, -нуться с кем-н.
● *v.i.* звене́ть (*impf.*); чо́к|аться, -нуться.

clink[2] /klɪŋk/ *n.* (*prison*) куту́зка, катала́жка (*sl.*).

clinker /ˈklɪŋkə(r)/ *n.* (*brick*) кли́нкер; (*pl., slag*) шлак.

clinker-built /ˈklɪŋkə,bɪlt/ *adj.* обши́тый внакро́й.

clip[1] /klɪp/ *n.* **1** (*slide-on ~*) скре́пка; (*grip-~*) зажи́м, зажи́мка. **2** (*brooch*) брошь. **3** (*of cartridges*) обо́йма. **4** (*for hair*) зако́лка.
● *v.t.* (**clipped, clipping**) заж|има́ть, -а́ть; скреп|ля́ть, -и́ть; **~ a paper to a board** прикреп|ля́ть, -и́ть бума́гу к доске́.
● *cpds.* **~board** *n.* доска́ с зажи́мом для бума́ги; **~-on** *adj.* пристёгивающийся, прикрепля́ющийся.

clip[2] /klɪp/ *n.* **1** (*shearing*) стри́жка. **2** (*coll., blow*): **a ~ on the jaw** уда́р по скуле́. **3** (*coll., speed*): **at a fast ~** бы́стрым хо́дом. **4** (*cin.*) отры́вок из фи́льма; клип.
● *v.t.* (**clipped, clipping**) **1** (*cut*): **~ a hedge** подстр|ига́ть, -и́чь живу́ю и́згородь; **~ a bird's wings** подр|еза́ть, -е́зать пти́це кры́лья; **~ s.o.'s wings** (*fig.*) подре́зать (*pf.*) кому́-н. кры́лышки; **~ an article out of a newspaper** выреза́ть, вы́резать статью́ из газе́ты; **~ tickets** (*Br.*) проб|ива́ть, -и́ть (*or* компости́ровать, про-) биле́ты. **2** (*hit*): **~ s.o. on the jaw** съе́здить (*pf.*) кому́-н. по физионо́мии (*coll.*).

clipper /ˈklɪpə(r)/ *n.* **1** (*pl., for hair*) маши́нка для стри́жки воло́с; (*pl., for nails*) куса́ч|ки (*pl., g.* -ек). **2** (*naut.*) кли́пер.

clipping /ˈklɪpɪŋ/ *n.* (*from newspaper*) вы́резка; (*pl., bits cut off*) обре́зки (*m. pl.*).

clique /kliːk/ *n.* кли́ка.

clitoris /ˈklɪtərɪs/, /ˈklaɪ-/ *n.* кли́тор.

cloak /kləʊk/ *n.* (*garment*) плащ, ма́нтия; **~-and-dagger stories** расска́зы о шпио́нах; (*covering*): **a ~ of snow** сне́жный покро́в; **under the ~ of darkness** под покро́вом темноты́; (*fig., pretext*) ма́ска.
● *v.t.* (*fig.*) прикр|ыва́ть, -ы́ть; скр|ыва́ть, -ыть.
● *cpd.* **~room** *n.* (*for clothes*) гардеро́б, раздева́льня; (*for luggage*) ка́мера хране́ния; (*Br., lavatory*) убо́рная.

clobber /ˈklɒbə(r)/ *n.* (*Br. sl., gear*) барахло́.
● *v.t.* (*sl., beat*) лупи́ть, от-; лупцева́ть, от- (*both coll.*).

cloche /klɒʃ/, /kləʊʃ/ *n.* (*for plants*) стекля́нный колпа́к.

clock /klɒk/ *n.* час|ы́ (*pl., g.* -о́в); (*taximeter*) таксо́метр; (*milometer*) счётчик (про́йденного пути́); **he works round the ~** он рабо́тает кру́глые су́тки; **put the ~ forward** ста́вить, по- часы́ вперёд; **put the ~ back** (*lit.*) отв|оди́ть, -ести́ часы́ наза́д; (*fig.*) поверну́ть (*pf.*) вре́мя вспять.
● *v.t.* (*time*) хронометри́ровать (*impf., pf.*); (*register*): **she ~ed 11 seconds in this race** она́ показа́ла 11 секу́нд в э́том забе́ге.
● *v.i.*: **~ in, on** (*Br.*) отм|еча́ться, -е́титься по прихо́де на рабо́ту; **~ out, off** (*Br.*) отм|еча́ться, -е́титься при ухо́де с рабо́ты.
● *cpds.* **~-face** *n.* цифербла́т; **~-maker** *n.* часовщи́к; **~-watch** *v.i.* стара́ться (*impf.*) не перерабо́тать;

~watcher *n.* нерадивый работник; **~work** *n.* часовой механизм; **~work toy** заводная игрушка; **the ceremony went like ~work** церемония шла без сучка, без задоринки.

clockwise /'klɒkwaɪz/ *adj. & adv.* (движущийся) по часовой стрелке.

clod /klɒd/ *n.* ком, глыба.

● *cpd.* **~-hopper** *n.* болван, деревенщина (*c.g.*); (*pl., shoes*) тяжёлые башмаки.

clog[1] /klɒg/ *n.* (*shoe*) башмак на деревянной подошве; сабо (*indecl.*).

clog[2] /klɒg/ *v.t.* (**clogged, clogging**) (*lit., fig.*) засор|ять, -ить; **the sink is ~ged** раковина засорилась.

cloister /'klɔɪstə(r)/ *n.* (*covered walk*) аркада.

● *v.t.* (*fig.*): **he led a ~ed life** он вёл уединённую жизнь.

clone /kləʊn/ *n.* клон.

● *v.t.* размн|ожать, -ожить вегетативным путём; клонировать (*impf., pf.*).

clop /klɒp/ *n.* (*of hoofs*) цоканье, цокот.

close[1] /kləʊs/ *n.* (*Br.*) (*street*) тупик; (*cathedral precinct*) соборная площадь.

● *adj.* **1** (*near*) близкий; **he fired at ~ range** он стрелял (*or* выстрелил) с близкого расстояния; **~ combat** ближний бой; рукопашный бой; **~ contact** тесное общение; **at ~ quarters** на близком расстоянии; **in ~ proximity** в непосредственной близости; **~ competition** острая конкуренция; **he had a ~ shave, call** он был на волосок от гибели *и т.д.*; **~ resemblance** большое сходство.
2 (*intimate*) близкий; **a ~ friend** близкий друг; **his sister was very ~ to him** они с сестрой были очень близки.
3 (*serried, compact*): **~ writing** убористый почерк; **~ texture** плотная ткань; **in ~ order** (*mil.*) сомкнутым строем; **~ column** (*mil.*) сомкнутая колонна; **~ reasoning** безукоризненная аргументация.
4 (*strict, attentive*): **keep a ~ watch on s.o.** тщательно следить (*impf.*) за кем-н.; **~ examination** тщательное обследование; **~ attention** пристальное внимание; **~ confinement** строгая изоляция; **the suit is a ~ fit** этот костюм хорошо сидит; **a ~ translation** точный перевод; **a ~ observer** внимательный наблюдатель.
5 (*restricted*) закрытый; **~ season** время, когда охота запрещена.
6 (*of games etc.*): **a ~ contest** упорная борьба; состязание с почти равными шансами.
7 (*stingy*) скупой, прижимистый.
8 (*reticent, secret*) скрытный; **he is ~ about his affairs** он держит свои дела в секрете.
9 (*stuffy*) (*of air*) душный, спёртый; (*of weather*) душный, тяжёлый.
10 (*phon.*): **a ~ vowel** узкий/закрытый гласный.

● *adv.*: **he lives ~ to, by the church** он живёт поблизости от церкви; **keep ~ to me** не отходите от меня; **it was ~ upon midnight** близилась полночь; **~ upon 500 boys** почти 500 мальчиков; **follow ~ behind s.o.** следовать (*impf.*) непосредственно за кем-н.; **stand ~ against the wall** стоять (*impf.*) вплотную к стене; **cut one's hair ~** коротко подстр|игаться, -ичься; **come ~r together** (*fig.*) сбл|ижаться, -изиться; **sail ~ to the wind** (*lit.*) идти (*det.*) круто к ветру; (*fig.*) ходить (*indet.*) по острию (ножа).

● *cpds.* **~-cropped** *adj.* коротко остриженный; **~-fisted** *adj.* прижимистый, скупой; **~-fistedness** *n.* прижимистость, скупость; **~-fitting** *adj.* облегающий; **~-grained** *adj.* (*of wood*) мелковолокнистый; **~-set** *adj.* близко поставленный; **~-up** *n.* (*cin.*) крупный план.

close[2] /kləʊz/ *n.* (*end*) конец; **at ~ of day** в конце дня; на исходе дня; **~ of play** конец игры; **at the ~ of the nineteenth century** в конце девятнадцатого столетия; **bring to a ~** заверш|ать, -ить, зак|анчивать, -ончить; **the day reached its ~** день кончился; **the meeting drew to a ~** собрание подошло к концу.

● *v.t.* **1** (*shut*) закр|ывать, -ыть; **~ a gap** зап|олнять, -олнить пробел; **~ a knife** складывать, сложить нож; **~ one's hand** сж|имать, -ать руку в кулак; **~ one's lips** смыкать, сомкнуть губы; **~d shop** предприятие, нанимающее только членов профсоюза; **'road ~d'** «проезд закрыт»; **the museum is ~d** музей не работает.
2 (*end, complete, settle*): **~ a meeting** закр|ывать, -ыть собрание; **~ a deal** заключ|ать, -ить сделку; **the closing scene of the play** заключительная сцена пьесы; **the closing date is December 1** последний срок — первое декабря.
3: **~ the ranks** смыкать, сомкнуть ряды.

● *v.i.* **1** (*shut*) закр|ываться, -ыться; **the door ~d** дверь закрылась; **flowers ~ at night** ночью цветы закрываются; **the theatres** (*Br.*), **theaters** (*US*) **~d** театры закрылись; **closing day** выходной день.
2 (*cease*): **the performance ~d last night** вчера пьеса шла в последний раз; **he ~d with this remark** он закончил этим замечанием.
3 (*come closer*) сбл|ижаться, -изиться; прибл|ижаться, -изиться; **the soldiers ~d up** солдаты сомкнули ряды.

● *with advs.*: **~ down** *v.t.* закр|ывать, -ыть; *v.i.* (*e.g. of a factory*) закр|ываться, -ыться; (*Br., broadcasting*) зак|анчивать, -ончить передачу; **~ in** *v.i.*: **the days are closing in** дни укорачиваются (*or* становятся короче); **the darkness ~d in on us** нас окутала темнота; **the enemy ~d in upon us** неприятель подступил вплотную; **~ up** *v.t. & i.* закр|ывать(ся), -ыть(ся).

● *cpd.* **~-down** *n.* (*Br., broadcasting*) окончание.

closely /'kləʊslɪ/ *adv.*: **it ~ resembles pork** это очень напоминает свинину; (*attentively*) внимательно; **watch ~** пристально следить (*impf.*) за + *i.*; **~ printed** убористо напечатанный; **~ connected** тесно/прочно связанный; **we worked ~ together** мы работали в тесном сотрудничестве; **they questioned him ~** его подробно расспросили.

closeness /'kləʊsnɪs/ *n.* (*proximity, resemblance; intimacy*) близость; (*of texture etc.*) плотность; (*of reasoning etc.*) безукоризненность; тщательность; (*attentiveness*) пристальность; (*reticence*) скрытность; (*parsimony*) прижимистость, скупость; (*of air etc.*) духота, спёртость.

closet /'klɒzɪt/ *n.* (*US, cupboard*) шкаф; **china ~** буфет.

● *v.t.* (**closeted, closeting**) зап|ирать, -ереть; **he was ~ed with his solicitor** он совещался со своим адвокатом наедине.

closure /'kləʊʒə(r)/ *n.* **1** (*closing*) закрытие. **2** (*parl., also* (*US*) **cloture**) прекращение прений.

clot /klɒt/ *n.* (*of blood etc.*) сгусток, комок; (*Br. sl., stupid person*) болван, тупица (*c.g.*).

● *v.i.* (**clotted, clotting**) свёр|тываться, -нуться; сгу|щаться, -ститься; **~ted blood** запёкшаяся кровь; **~ted cream** (*Br.*) густые топлёные сливки.

cloth /klɒθ/ *n.* **1** (*material*) ткань, материя; **bound in ~** в матерчатом переплёте. **2** (*piece of ~*) тряпка; (*table ~*) скатерть; (*Br., for drying dishes*) полотенце. **3**: **the ~** (*clerical profession*) духовный сан; (*clergy*) духовенство. **4**: **a ~ cap** (*Br.*) (матерчатая) кепка.

clothe /kləʊð/ *v.t.* (*past and p.p.* **clothed** *or archaic or literary* **clad**) од|евать, -еть; **~ o.s.** (*acquire clothing*) приодеться (*pf.*).

clothes /kləʊðz/ *n.* платье, одежда; **evening ~** вечернее платье; (*bed ~*) постельное бельё; **in plain ~** (*out of uniform*) в штатском (платье).

● *cpds.* **~-basket** *n.* корзина для белья; **~-brush** *n.* платяная щётка; **~-horse** *n.* напольная сушилка; **~-line** *n.* верёвка для белья; **~-moth** *n.* моль; **~-peg** (*Br.*), **~-pin** (*US*) *nn.* прищепка.

clothier /'kləʊðɪə(r)/ *n.* торговец мужской одеждой.

clothing /'kləʊðɪŋ/ *n.* одежда.

cloture /'kləʊtʃə(r)/, /-tjʊə(r)/ = ⇒**closure** 2

cloud /klaʊd/ *n.* **1** (*in the sky*) облако; туча; **every ~ has a silver lining** нет худа без добра; **~ cuckoo land** мир фантазий. **2** (*of smoke*) клубы (*m. pl.*); (*of dust*) облако. **3** (*of unhappiness etc.*): **this cast a ~ over our meeting** это омрачило нашу встречу; **under a ~** (*fig.*) в немилости.

● *v.t.* покр|ывать, -ыть облаками; (*fig.*) омрач|ать, -ить; **eyes ~ed with tears** глаза, затуманенные слезами; **his troubles ~ed his mind** несчастья помутили его рассудок.

● *v.i.* омрач|аться, -иться;

покр|ыва́ться, -ы́ться облака́ми/ту́чами; нахму́ри|ваться, -ться; **the sky ~ed over, up** (*US*) не́бо затяну́ло облака́ми/ту́чами; **his brow ~ed** он нахму́рил бро́ви.

● *cpds.* **~berry** *n.* моро́шка; **~burst** *n.* ли́вень (*m.*).

cloudiness /'klaʊdɪnɪs/ *n.* о́блачность; (*fig.*) тума́нность, нея́сность.

cloudless /'klaʊdlɪs/ *adj.* безо́блачный.

cloudlessness /'klaʊdlɪsnɪs/ *n.* безо́блачность.

cloudy /'klaʊdɪ/ *adj.* (**cloudier, cloudiest**) о́блачный; (*of liquid etc.*) му́тный; (*fig., of ideas*) тума́нный.

clout /klaʊt/ *n.* (*coll., blow*) затре́щина, оплеу́ха; (*coll., influence*) влия́ние.

● *v.t.* (*coll., hit*) тре́снуть (*pf.*).

clove[1] /kləʊv/ *n.* (*section of bulb*) зубо́к; **a ~ of garlic** зубо́к чеснока́.

clove[2] /kləʊv/ *n.* (*aromatic*) гвозди́ка; **oil of ~s** гвозди́чное ма́сло.

● *cpds.* **~-gillyflower, ~-pink** *nn.* гвозди́ка садо́вая.

clove[3] /kləʊv/ *n.* (*naut.*): **~ hitch** вы́бленочный у́зел.

clove[4] /kləʊv/ *past of* ⇒**cleave**[1]

cloven /'kləʊv(ə)n/ = **cleave**[1] 3

clover /'kləʊvə(r)/ *n.* кле́вер; **we are in ~** у нас не жизнь, а ма́сленица; мы живём припева́ючи; **four-leaved ~** четырёхли́стный кле́вер.

clown /klaʊn/ *n.* (*at circus*) кло́ун; (*ludicrous person*) шут; (*boor*) неве́жа (*c.g.*).

● *v.i.* стро́ить (*impf.*) из себя́ шута́.

clowning /'klaʊnɪŋ/ *n.* шутовство́, пая́сничанье.

clownish /'klaʊnɪʃ/ *adj.* кло́унский, шутовско́й.

cloy /klɔɪ/ *v.t.* прес|ыща́ть, -ы́тить; **too much honey ~s the palate** сли́шком мно́го мёда притупля́ет вкус.

● *v.i.* надо|еда́ть, -е́сть.

cloying /'klɔɪɪŋ/ *adj.* при́торный.

club[1] /klʌb/ *n.* (*weapon*) дуби́нка; (*at golf*) клю́шка; (*pl., at cards*) тре́фы (*f. pl.*); **Indian ~** булава́.

● *v.t.* (**clubbed, clubbing**) бить (*impf.*) дуби́нкой; **he was ~bed to death** его́ заби́ли дуби́нками на́смерть.

● *cpds.* **~-foot** *n.* изуро́дованная ступня́; **~-footed** *adj.* с изуро́дованной ступнёй; косола́пый.

club[2] /klʌb/ *n.* (*society, building*) клуб.

● *v.i.* (**clubbed, clubbing**) скла́дываться, сложи́ться; устр|а́ивать, -о́ить скла́дчину; **they ~bed together to pay the fine** они́ сложи́лись и уплати́ли штраф; **they go out ~bing every night** они́ ка́ждый ве́чер хо́дят на та́нцы.

● *cpds.* **~ car** *n.* (*US*) пассажи́рский ваго́н с ба́ром; **~-house** *n.* клуб, помеще́ние клу́ба; **~ sandwich** *n.* многосло́йный бутербро́д с мя́сом, сала́том, майоне́зом *и т.п.*

clubbable /'klʌbəb(ə)l/ *adj.* общи́тельный.

cluck /klʌk/ *n.* куда́хтанье, клохта́нье.

● *v.i.* куда́хтать, клохта́ть (*both impf.*).

clue /klu:/ *n.* ключ, нить; (*for crossword*) определе́ние; **the police found a ~** поли́ция нашла́ ули́ку; **the ~ to this mystery** ключ к разга́дке э́той та́йны; **I haven't a ~** (*coll.*) поня́тия не име́ю.

clueless /'klu:lɪs/ *adj.* (*coll.*) бестолко́вый; не в ку́рсе; без поня́тия.

clump[1] /klʌmp/ *n.* (*cluster*) гру́ппа, ку́па.

● *v.t.* сажа́ть, посади́ть гру́ппами; соб|ира́ть, -ра́ть в ку́чу.

clump[2] /klʌmp/ *n.* (*heavy tread*) то́пот.

● *v.i.* (*tread heavily*) то́пать (*impf.*).

clumsiness /'klʌmzɪnɪs/ *n.* неуклю́жесть, нело́вкость.

clumsy /'klʌmzɪ/ *adj.* (**clumsier, clumsiest**) неуклю́жий, нело́вкий.

clung /klʌŋ/ *past and p.p. of* ⇒**cling**

cluster /'klʌstə(r)/ *n.* (*of people, stars*) скопле́ние; (*of grapes*) гроздь, кисть; (*of flowers*) кисть; (*of bees*) рой; (*of trees*) ку́па; **consonant ~s** скопле́ния (*nt. pl.*) согла́сных.

● *v.t.*: **~ed column** (*archit.*) пучко́вая коло́нна.

● *v.i.* (*of plants*) расти́ (*impf.*) пучка́ми; (*of people*) соб|ира́ться, -ра́ться гру́ппами; **roses ~ed round the window** ро́зы разросли́сь под окно́м; **the children ~ed round the teacher** де́ти столпи́лись вокру́г учи́теля.

● *cpd.* **~ bomb** *n.* кассе́тная бо́мба.

clutch[1] /klʌtʃ/ *n.* **1** (*act of ~ing*) сжа́тие, захва́т, схва́тывание; **make a ~ at something** схвати́ть/захвати́ть (*pf.*) что-н. **2** (*pl., grasp*) ла́пы (*f. pl.*), ко́гти (*m. pl.*); **they fell into his ~es** (*fig.*) они́ попа́ли к нему́ в ла́пы. **3** (*of car*) сцепле́ние; **let in the ~** отпусти́ть сцепле́ние; **the ~ is out** сцепле́ние вы́ключено; **the ~ slips** сцепле́ние проска́льзывает/пробуксо́вывает; **~ pedal** педа́ль сцепле́ния.

● *v.t. & i.* хвата́ться, схвати́ться (за + *a.*); сж|има́ть, -ать; **he ~ed (at) the rope** он ухвати́лся за верёвку; **he ~ed the toy to his chest** он прижа́л игру́шку к груди́; **a drowning man will ~ at a straw** утопа́ющий за соло́минку хвата́ется.

clutch[2] /klʌtʃ/ *n.* (*of eggs*) я́йца (*nt. pl.*) под насе́дкой; (*brood*) вы́водок.

clutter /'klʌtə(r)/ *n.* (*confused mess*) сумато́ха, суета́; (*untidiness*) хао́с, беспоря́док; **the room is in a ~** в ко́мнате хао́с.

● *v.t.* (*also* **~ up**) загромо|жда́ть, -зди́ть.

cm. /'sentɪ,mi:tə(r)(z)/ *n.* (*abbr. of* ***centimetre(s)***) см. (сантиме́тр).

CMEA (*abbr.*) = **Comecon**

CND (*abbr. of* ***Campaign for Nuclear Disarmament***) Кампа́ния за я́дерное разоруже́ние.

CO (*abbr. of* ***Commanding Officer***) команди́р.

Co. /kəʊ/ *n.* (*abbr. of* ***company***) Ко (компа́ния).

c/o (*abbr. of* ***care of***) че́рез; **John Smith c/o David Green** Дэ́виду Гри́ну для переда́чи Джо́ну Сми́ту.

coach[1] /kəʊtʃ/ *n.* **1** (*horse-drawn*) каре́та, экипа́ж. **2** (*railway*) пассажи́рский ваго́н. **3** (*Br., motor-bus*) (тури́стский междугоро́дный) авто́бус.

● *cpds.* **~-house** *n.* каре́тный сара́й; **~man** *n.* ку́чер; **~-party** *n.* экскурса́нты (*m. pl.*) (*на автобусе*); **~-tour** *n.* авто́бусная экску́рсия.

coach[2] /kəʊtʃ/ *n.* (*tutor*) репети́тор; (*trainer*) тре́нер.

● *v.t.* репети́ровать (*impf.*); (*train*) тренирова́ть, на-; (*prepare for questioning, e.g. a witness*) ната́скивать, натаска́ть.

coagulant /kəʊ'ægjʊlənt/ *n.* коагуля́нт.

coagulate /kəʊ'ægjʊ,leɪt/ *v.t.* сгу|ща́ть, -сти́ть; коагули́ровать (*impf., pf.*); свёртывать, сверну́ть.

● *v.i.* коагули́роваться (*impf., pf.*); свёртываться, сверну́ться.

coagulation /,kəʊægjʊ'leɪʃ(ə)n/ *n.* коагуля́ция, свёртывание.

coal /kəʊl/ *n.* (*mineral*) ка́менный у́голь; (*Br., piece of* **~**) у́голь (*m.*); уголёк; **~s** у́гли (*m. pl.*); **a live ~** горя́щий уголёк; (*fig.*): **carry ~s to Newcastle** е́хать (*det.*) в Ту́лу со свои́м самова́ром; **haul s.o. over the ~s** да|ва́ть, -ть нагоня́й кому́-н.

● *cpds.* **~-black** *adj.* (*e.g. hair*) чёрный как смоль; **~-cellar** *n.* подва́л для хране́ния угля́; **~-dust** *n.* у́гольная пыль; **~-face** *n.* забо́й; **~-field** *n.* каменноуго́льный бассе́йн; **~-gas** *n.* каменноуго́льный/свети́льный газ; **~-mine, ~-pit** *nn.* у́гольная ша́хта; **~-miner** *n.* шахтёр; **~-scuttle** *n.* ведёрко для угля́; **~-seam** *n.* у́гольный пласт; **~-tar** *n.* каменноуго́льная смола́; дёготь (*m.*).

coalesce /,kəʊə'les/ *v.i.* соедин|я́ться, -и́ться; объедин|я́ться, -и́ться.

coalescence /,kəʊə'lesəns/ *n.* соедине́ние, объедине́ние.

coalition /,kəʊə'lɪʃ(ə)n/ *n.* (*pol.*) коали́ция; (*attr.*) коалицио́нный.

coarse /kɔ:s/ *adj.* (*of material*) гру́бый; (*of sand, sugar*) кру́пный; **~ fish** (*Br.*) ры́ба просты́х сорто́в; **~ manners** гру́бые/вульга́рные мане́ры; **a ~ skin** гру́бая ко́жа.

● *cpd.* **~-grained** *adj.* (*lit.*) крупнозерни́стый; (*fig.*) гру́бый, неотёсанный.

coarsen /'kɔ:s(ə)n/ *v.t.* де́лать, с- гру́бым.

● *v.i.* грубе́ть, о-.

coarseness /'kɔ:snɪs/ *n.* (*lit.*) гру́бость; (*fig.*) гру́бость, вульга́рность.

coast /kəʊst/ *n.* (*sea-*~) морско́й бе́рег; побере́жье; **the ~ is clear** (*fig.*) путь свобо́ден.

● *v.i.* (*bicycle downhill*) кати́ться (*impf.*) на велосипе́де с горы́.

● *cpds.* **~guard** *n.* (*officer*) член (тамо́женной) берегово́й стра́жи; (*collect.*) берегова́я стра́жа; **~line** *n.* берегова́я ли́ния.

coastal /'kəʊstəl/ *adj.* берегово́й,

прибре́жный; ~ **traffic** кабота́жное пла́вание; ~ **command** берегова́я охра́на; ~ **waters** прибре́жные во́ды (*f. pl.*); взмо́рье.

coaster /ˈkəʊstə(r)/ *n.* (*ship*) кабота́жное су́дно; (*stand for decanter or glass*) подно́с, подста́вка.

coat /kəʊt/ *n.* **1** (*overcoat*) пальто́ (*indecl.*); (*man's jacket*) пиджа́к; (*woman's jacket*) жаке́т; ~ **of arms** герб; ~ **of mail** кольчу́га; (*fig.*): **you must cut your ~ according to your cloth** по одёжке протя́гивай но́жки. **2** (*of animal*) шерсть, мех. **3** (*of paint etc.*) слой; **this wall needs a ~ of paint** э́ту стену́ на́до покра́сить.

● *v.t.* покр|ыва́ть, -ы́ть; облиц|о́вывать, -ева́ть; **the pill is ~ed with sugar** пилю́ля в са́харной оболо́чке; **he ~ed the wall with whitewash** он побели́л сте́ну; **his tongue is ~ed** у него́ обло́жен язы́к.

● *cpds.* **~-hanger** *n.* ве́шалка; **~-tails** *n. pl.* фа́лды (*f. pl.*) фра́ка.

coating /ˈkəʊtɪŋ/ *n.* (*layer*) слой.

co-author /ˌkəʊˈɔːθə(r)/ *n.* соа́втор.

● *v.t.* писа́ть, на- в соа́вторстве.

coax /kəʊks/ *v.t.* угов|а́ривать, -ори́ть; зад|а́бривать, -о́брить; **he ~ed the child to take its medicine** он уговори́л ребёнка приня́ть лека́рство; **he ~ed the fire to burn** он до́лго вози́лся, пока́ не разжёг ого́нь.

coaxial /kəʊˈæksɪəl/ *adj.* (*tech.*): ~ **cable** коаксиа́льный ка́бель.

cob /kɒb/ *n.* **1** (*swan*) ле́бедь-саме́ц. **2** (*horse*) невысо́кая корена́стая ло́шадь. **3** (*nut*) оре́х. **4** (*of maize*) поча́ток; **corn on the ~** поча́ток кукуру́зы.

cobalt /ˈkəʊbɔːlt/, /-bɒlt/ *n.* (*chem.*) ко́бальт; (*pigment*) ко́бальтовая синь.

cobber /ˈkɒbə(r)/ *n.* (*Austral.*) ко́реш (*coll.*).

cobble /ˈkɒb(ə)l/ *n.* (*also* **~-stone(s)**) булы́жник.

● *v.t.* (*pave*) мости́ть, за-/вы- булы́жником.

cobbler /ˈkɒblə(r)/ *n.* (*shoemaker*) сапо́жник; **the ~ should stick to his last** всяк сверчо́к знай свой шесто́к.

COBOL /ˈkəʊbɒl/ *n.* (*comput.*) КОБО́Л.

cobra /ˈkəʊbrə/, /ˈkɒbrə/ *n.* ко́бра; очко́вая змея́.

cobweb /ˈkɒbweb/ *n.* паути́на.

coca /ˈkəʊkə/ *n.* ко́ка.

Coca-Cola /ˌkəʊkəˈkəʊlə/ *n.* (*propr.*) ко́ка-ко́ла.

cocaine /kəˈkeɪn/, /kəʊ-/ *n.* кокаи́н.

coccy|x /ˈkɒksɪks/ (*pl.* **~ges** /-ˌdʒiːz/ *or* **~xes**) *n.* ко́пчик.

cochineal /ˈkɒtʃɪˌniːl/, /-ˈniːl/ *n.* (*red dye*) кошени́ль.

cock[1] /kɒk/ *n.* **1** (*male domestic fowl*) пету́х. **2** (*male bird*) пету́х, саме́ц.

● *v.t.*: ~ **up** (*Br. sl.*) пу́тать, на-; порта́чить, на-.

● *cpds.* **~-a-doodle-doo** *n.* кукареку́ (*nt. indecl.*); **~-and-bull** *adj.*: **~-and-bull story** вздор, небыли́ца; **~chafer** *n.* ма́йский жук, хрущ; **~-crow** *n.* рассве́т; **before ~-crow** до петухо́в; **~-fighting** *n.* петуши́ные бои́ (*m. pl.*); **~pit** *n.* аре́на для петуши́ного бо́я; (*aeron.*) каби́на; (*fig.*) аре́на борьбы́; **~roach** *n.* тарака́н; **~scomb** *n.* (*crest of ~*) петуши́ный гре́бень; **~sure** *adj.* самоуве́ренный; **~sureness** *n.* самоуве́ренность; **~tail** *n.* (*drink*) кокте́йль (*m.*); **~tail dress** коро́ткое выходно́е пла́тье; **~tail party** кокте́йль (*m.*); **~-up** *n.* (*Br. sl.*) неразбери́ха, пу́таница; **make a ~-up of something** пу́тать, на-; порта́чить, на-.

cock[2] /kɒk/ *n.* **1** (*tap*) кран. **2** (*lever in gun*) куро́к; **at half ~** (*lit.*) на пе́рвом взво́де; (*fig.*): **the scheme went off at half ~** план сорва́лся; **at full ~** со взведённым курко́м. **3** (*vulg., penis*) хуй. **4** (*Br. sl., nonsense*) вздор.

cock[3] /kɒk/ *v.t.* **1** (*stick up etc.*): ~ **one's hat** зал|а́мывать, -оми́ть ша́пку набекре́нь; **the horse ~ed (up) its ears** ло́шадь насторожи́ла у́ши; **he ~ed an eye at me** он подмигну́л мне; ~ **one's nose (or a snook) at s.o.** пок|а́зывать, -аза́ть нос кому́-н.; **~ed hat** треуго́лка; **knock s.o. into a ~ed hat** вы́сыпать кому́-н. по пе́рвое число́. **2** (*of gun*) взв|оди́ть, -ести́ куро́к +*g.*

● *cpd.* **~-eyed** *adj.* (*squinting*) косогла́зый, косо́й; (*askew*) косо́й; (*drunk*) косо́й; (*absurd*) дура́цкий.

cockade /kɒˈkeɪd/ *n.* кока́рда.

cock-a-hoop /ˌkɒkəˈhuːp/ *adj.* хвастли́вый и самодово́льный.

cockatoo /ˌkɒkəˈtuː/ *n.* какаду́ (*m. indecl.*).

cockatrice /ˈkɒkətrɪs/, /-ˌtraɪs/ *n.* василиск.

cocker /ˈkɒkə(r)/ *n.* (*also* **~ spaniel**) ко́кер-спание́ль (*m.*).

cockerel /ˈkɒkər(ə)l/ *n.* петушо́к.

cockiness /ˈkɒkɪnɪs/ *n.* бо́йкость, наха́льство.

cockle[1] /ˈkɒk(ə)l/ *n.* (*plant*) (*corncockle*) ку́коль (*m.*); (*ryegrass*) плеве́л.

cockle[2] /ˈkɒk(ə)l/ *n.* **1** (*shellfish*) сердцеви́дка, съедо́бный моллю́ск. **2**: **it warms the ~s of one's heart** э́то согрева́ет ду́шу.

cockney /ˈkɒknɪ/ *n. & adj.* ко́кни (*c.g. indecl.*); ~ **accent** акце́нт ко́кни.

cocky /ˈkɒkɪ/ *adj.* (**cockier, cockiest**) наха́льный; разбитно́й.

coco /ˈkəʊkəʊ/ *n.* (*pl.* **~s**) (*also* **~ palm**) коко́совая па́льма.

● *cpd.* **~nut** *n.* коко́с, коко́совый оре́х; **~nut butter, oil** коко́совое ма́сло; **~nut matting** цино́вка из коко́сового волокна́.

cocoa /ˈkəʊkəʊ/ *n.* (*powder or drink*) кака́о (*indecl.*); (*attr.*) кака́овый; ~ **bean** боб кака́о.

cocoon /kəˈkuːn/ *n.* ко́кон.

COD (*abbr. of* ***cash on delivery***) упла́та при доста́вке; нало́женный платёж.

cod /kɒd/ *n.* (*pl.* ~) (*also* **~fish**) треска́.

● *cpd.* **~-liver oil** *n.* ры́бий жир.

coda /ˈkəʊdə/ *n.* (*mus.*) ко́да.

coddle /ˈkɒd(ə)l/ *v.t.* не́жить (*or* изне́живать), из-.

code /kəʊd/ *n.* (*of laws*) ко́декс; свод зако́нов; (*of conduct*) ко́декс; но́рмы (*f. pl.*); (*set of symbols, cipher*) код; **Morse ~** код/а́збука Мо́рзе.

● *v.t.* (*encode*) коди́ровать (*impf., pf.*); шифрова́ть, за- по ко́ду.

co-defendant /ˌkəʊdɪˈfendənt/ *n.* (*leg.*) соотве́тчик.

codeine /ˈkəʊdiːn/ *n.* кодеи́н.

codex /ˈkəʊdeks/ *n.* (*pl.* **codices** *or* **codexes**) ко́декс; стари́нная ру́копись.

codger /ˈkɒdʒə(r)/ *n.* (*coll.*) чуда́к.

codices /ˈkəʊdɪˌsiːz/, /ˈkɒd-/ *pl. of* ⇒**codex**

codicil /ˈkəʊdɪsɪl/, /ˈkɒd-/ *n.* дополни́тельное распоряже́ние к завеща́нию.

codification /ˌkəʊdɪfɪˈkeɪʃ(ə)n/ *n.* кодифика́ция.

codify /ˈkəʊdɪˌfaɪ/, /ˈkɒd-/ *v.t.* кодифици́ровать (*impf., pf*).

codpiece /ˈkɒdpiːs/ *n.* (*hist.*) гу́льфик.

codswallop /ˈkɒdzˌwɒləp/ *n.* (*Br. coll.*) ерунда́ (на по́стном ма́сле), бред соба́чий.

co-ed /ˈkəʊed/, /kəʊˈed/ *n.* (*US, coll.*) учени́ца сме́шанной шко́лы; студе́нтка (*уче́бного заведе́ния для лиц обо́его по́ла*).

co-education /ˌkəʊedjuːˈkeɪʃ(ə)n/ *n.* совме́стное обуче́ние.

co-educational /ˌkəʊedjuːˈkeɪʃ(ə)nəl/ *adj.* совме́стного обуче́ния; **this college is ~** в э́том ко́лледже совме́стное обуче́ние.

coefficient /ˌkəʊɪˈfɪʃ(ə)nt/ *n.* коэффицие́нт.

coerce /kəʊˈɜːs/ *v.t.* прин|ужда́ть, -у́дить; ~ **into silence** заст|авля́ть, -а́вить молча́ть.

coercion /kəʊˈɜːʃ(ə)n/ *n.* принужде́ние; **he paid under ~** он заплати́л под давле́нием; его́ прину́дили заплати́ть.

coercive /kəʊˈɜːsɪv/ *adj.* принуди́тельный.

coeval /kəʊˈiːv(ə)l/ *n.* све́рстни|к; совреме́нни|к (*fem.* -ца).

● *adj.* одного́ во́зраста (с+*i.*); совреме́нный (+*d.*).

coexist /ˌkəʊɪgˈzɪst/ *v.i.* сосуществова́ть (*impf.*).

coexistence /ˌkəʊɪgˈzɪstəns/ *n.* сосуществова́ние.

coexistent /ˌkəʊɪgˈzɪstənt/ *adj.* сосуществу́ющий.

coextensive /ˌkəʊɪkˈstensɪv/ *adj.* одина́ковой протяжённости во вре́мени (*or* в простра́нстве).

C. of E. (*abbr. of* ***Church of England***) Англика́нская це́рковь.

coffee /ˈkɒfɪ/ *n.* ко́фе (*m. indecl.*); **two ~s** два ко́фе; ко́фе два ра́за; **black ~** чёрный ко́фе; **white ~** ко́фе с молоко́м; **ground ~** мо́лотый ко́фе; **Turkish ~** ко́фе по-туре́цки; ~ **ice cream** кофе́йное моро́женое; **instant ~** раствори́мый ко́фе.

● *cpds.* **~-bar** *n.* буфе́т; **~-bean** *n.* (*on

tree) кофе́йный боб; (*as product*) кофе́йное зерно́; (*pl.*) ко́фе в зёрнах; **~-break** *n.* переры́в на ко́фе; **~-cup** *n.* кофе́йная ча́шка; **~-grinder, ~-mill** *nn.* кофе́йница, кофе́йная ме́льница, кофемо́лка; **~-grounds** *n. pl.* кофе́йная гу́ща; **~-house** *n.* кафе́ (*indecl.*); **~-maker** *n.* кофева́рка; **~-pot** *n.* кофе́йник; **~-table** *n.* кофе́йный/журна́льный сто́лик.

coffer /ˈkɒfə(r)/ *n.* **1** (*chest*) сунду́к; (*pl., fig., funds*) казна́. **2** (*in ceiling*) кессо́н.

coffin /ˈkɒfɪn/ *n.* гроб; **drive a nail into s.o.'s ~** вбить гвоздь в чей-н. гроб.

cog /kɒg/ *n.* зуб (*pl.* -ья); зубе́ц; вы́ступ; **a ~ in the machine** (*fig.*) ви́нтик, ме́лкая со́шка; **~ railway** зу́бчатая желе́зная доро́га.

● *cpd.* **~-wheel** *n.* зу́бчатое колесо́.

cogency /ˈkəʊdʒənsɪ/ *n.* убеди́тельность.

cogent /ˈkəʊdʒ(ə)nt/ *adj.* убеди́тельный.

cogitate /ˈkɒdʒɪˌteɪt/ *v.i.* размышля́ть (*impf.*) (*о чём or над чем*).

cogitation /ˌkɒdʒɪˈteɪʃ(ə)n/ *n.* размышле́ние, обду́мывание.

cognac /ˈkɒnjæk/ *n.* конья́к.

cognate /ˈkɒgneɪt/ *adj.* ро́дственный.

cognition /kɒgˈnɪʃ(ə)n/ *n.* позна́ние; зна́ние.

cognitive /ˈkɒgnɪtɪv/ *adj.* познава́тельный.

cognizance /ˈkɒgnɪz(ə)ns/, /ˈkɒn-/ *n.* зна́ние, узнава́ние; **take ~ of** обра|ща́ть, -ти́ть внима́ние на + *a.*; прин|има́ть, -я́ть к све́дению.

cognizant /ˈkɒgnɪz(ə)nt/, /ˈkɒn-/ *adj.* зна́ющий, осведомлённый.

cognoscen|te /ˌkɒnjəˈʃentɪ/ *n.* (*pl.* ***~ti*** *pronunc. same*) знато́к, цени́тель (*m.*).

cohabit /kəʊˈhæbɪt/ *v.t.* (**cohabited, cohabiting**) сожи́тельствова́ть (*impf.*).

cohabitation /ˌkəʊhæbɪˈteɪʃ(ə)n/ *n.* (внебра́чное) сожи́тельство.

cohere /kəʊˈhɪə(r)/ *v.t.* (*stick, together*) сцеп|ля́ться, -и́ться; быть соединённым/объединённым; (*fig., be consistent*) быть свя́зным.

coherence /kəʊˈhɪərəns/ *n.* свя́зность, после́довательность; членоразде́льность.

coherent /kəʊˈhɪərənt/ *adj.* свя́зный, после́довательный; членоразде́льный.

cohesion /kəʊˈhiːʒ(ə)n/ *n.* сцепле́ние; сплочённость.

cohesive /kəʊˈhiːsɪv/ *adj.* спосо́бный к сцепле́нию; связу́ющий; (*united*) сплочённый.

cohesiveness /kəʊˈhiːsɪvnɪs/ *n.* спосо́бность к сцепле́нию; сплочённость.

cohort /ˈkəʊhɔːt/ *n.* кого́рта.

coiffure /kwɑːˈfjʊə(r)/ *n.* приче́ска.

coil¹ /kɔɪl/ *n.* **1** (*of rope, snake etc.*) вито́к; кольцо́. **2** (*elec.*) кату́шка. **3** (*contraceptive device*) спира́ль.

● *v.t. & i.* (*also* **~ up**) свёртывать(ся), сверну́ть(ся) кольцо́м (*or* в кольцо́).

coil² /kɔɪl/ *n.* (*arch., trouble, fuss*) суета́.

coin /kɔɪn/ *n.* моне́та; **spin, toss a ~** игра́ть (*impf.*) в орля́нку; подки́|дывать, -нуть моне́тку.

● *v.t.* чека́нить (*impf.*) (*моне́ты*); **~ a phrase** созд|ава́ть, -а́ть выраже́ние; **he is ~ing money** (*fig., Br.*) он гребёт/загреба́ет де́ньги лопа́той.

● *cpds.* **~-box** *n.* моне́тник (*автома́та*); (*Br., telephone*) телефо́н-автома́т; **~-operated** *adj.* моне́тный.

coinage /ˈkɔɪnɪdʒ/ *n.* **1** (*monetary system*) моне́тная систе́ма; **decimal ~** десяти́чная де́нежная систе́ма. **2** (*inventing*) созда́ние (слов); **a word of his own ~** со́зданное/пу́щенное им сло́во. **3** (*coined word*) неологи́зм.

coincide /ˌkəʊɪnˈsaɪd/ *v.i.* (*also math.*) совп|ада́ть, -а́сть.

coincidence /kəʊˈɪnsɪd(ə)ns/ *n.* **1** (*fact of coinciding*) совпаде́ние. **2** (*curious chance*) совпаде́ние, стече́ние обстоя́тельств.

coincident /kəʊˈɪnsɪd(ə)nt/ *adj.* совпада́ющий.

coincidental /kəʊˌɪnsɪˈdent(ə)l/ *adj.* случа́йный.

coiner /ˈkɔɪnə(r)/ *n.* **1** (*stamper of money*) чека́нщик моне́т, моне́тчик. **2** (*counterfeiter*) фальшивомоне́тчик. **3** (*inventor*) вы́думщик, сочини́тель (*m.*).

coir /ˈkɔɪə(r)/ *n.* койр, коко́совое волокно́.

coital /ˈkəʊɪtəl/ *adj.* относя́щийся к совокупле́нию.

coit|ion /kəʊˈɪʃ(ə)n/, **-us** /ˈkəʊɪtəs/ *nn.* совокупле́ние, полово́й акт, ко́итус.

Coke /kəʊk/ *n.* (*propr.*) «Ко́ка-ко́ла», «Ко́ла».

coke¹ /kəʊk/ *n.* кокс; **~ oven** коксова́льная печь.

● *v.t.* коксова́ть (*impf.*); **coking coal** коксу́ющийся у́голь.

coke² /kəʊk/ *n.* (*sl., cocaine*) кока́ин.

Col. /ˈkɜːn(ə)l/ *n.* (*abbr. of* **Colonel**) полк. (полко́вник).

col /kɒl/ *n.* перева́л.

colander /ˈkʌləndə(r)/ *n.* дуршла́г.

colchicum /ˈkɒltʃɪkəm/, /ˈkɒlkɪ-/ *n.* (*bot.*) безвре́менник.

cold /kəʊld/ *n.* **1** хо́лод; **he was left out in the ~** (*fig.*) им пренебрегли́; он оста́лся за бо́ртом. **2** (*illness*) просту́да; **catch (a) ~** просту|жа́ться, -ди́ться; схв|а́тывать, -ати́ть на́сморк; **~ in the head** на́сморк; **~ in the chest** просту́да; **~ sore** лихора́дка.

● *adj.* **1** (*at low temperature*) холо́дный; **I am, feel ~** мне хо́лодно. **2** (*fig.*): **throw ~ water on s.o.'s plan** окати́ть уша́том холо́дной воды́ кого́-н.; **in ~ blood** хладнокро́вно; **~ steel** холо́дное ору́жие; **~ war** холо́дная война́; **get ~ feet** (*fig., coll.*) тру́сить, с-; **it makes one's blood run ~** от э́того кровь сты́нет/леденеет в жи́лах. **3** (*unfeeling*): **a ~ person** холо́дный челове́к; **~ facts** го́лые фа́кты; **~ comfort** сла́бое утеше́ние; **the idea leaves me ~** э́та мысль меня́ не волну́ет. **4** (*of scent*) сла́бый, осты́вший.

● *cpds.* **~-blooded** *adj.* (*of reptile, fish*) холоднокро́вный; (*fig.*) бесчу́вственный, безжа́лостный; **~-bloodedness** *n.* бесчу́вственность, безжа́лостность; **~-hearted** *adj.* бессерде́чный; **~-heartedness** *n.* бессерде́чность; **~-shoulder** *v.t.* ока́з|ывать, -а́ть кому́-н. холо́дный приём.

coldish /ˈkəʊldɪʃ/ *adj.* холоднова́тый.

coldness /ˈkəʊldnɪs/ *n.* (*of temperature*) хо́лод; (*of character etc.*) хо́лодность.

coleoptera /ˌkɒlɪˈɒptərə/ *n.* жесткокры́лые (*nt. pl.*).

coleslaw /ˈkəʊlslɔː/ *n.* капу́стный сала́т.

colic /ˈkɒlɪk/ *n.* ко́лик|и (*pl., g.* —).

colicky /ˈkɒlɪkɪ/ *adj.* страда́ющий ко́ликами.

colitis /kəˈlaɪtɪs/ *n.* коли́т.

collaborate /kəˈlæbəˌreɪt/ *v.i.* сотру́дничать (*impf.*).

collaboration /kəˌlæbəˈreɪʃ(ə)n/ *n.* сотру́дничество.

collaborator /kəˈlæbəˌreɪtə(r)/ *n.* сотру́дник; (*with enemy*) коллаборациони́ст.

collage /ˈkɒlɑːʒ/, /kəˈlɑːʒ/ *n.* колла́ж.

collapse /kəˈlæps/ *n.* (*of a building etc.*) обва́л, паде́ние, обру́шение; (*of hopes etc.*) круше́ние; (*of resistance etc.*) разва́л, крах; (*med.*) колла́пс, упа́док сил, изнеможе́ние; **nervous ~** не́рвное истоще́ние.

● *v.t.* (*e.g. a telescope*) скла́дывать, сложи́ть.

● *v.i.* (*of a building etc.*) обва́л|иваться, -и́ться; ру́хнуть (*pf.*); (*of person*) вали́ться, с-; сва́ливаться, свали́ться; **the house ~d** дом ру́хнул/обвали́лся; **this table ~s** (*folds up*) э́тот стол скла́дывается; **the plan ~d** план ру́хнул.

collapsible /kəˈlæpsɪb(ə)l/ *adj.* складно́й, разбо́рный.

collar /ˈkɒlə(r)/ *n.* **1** (*of garment*) воротни́к; (*detachable*) воротничо́к; **hot under the ~** (*fig., excited, vexed*) рассе́рженный, рассвирепе́вший. **2** (*of dog*) оше́йник; (*of horse*) хому́т.

● *v.t.* (*seize*) схва́т|ывать, -и́ть за во́рот/ши́ворот; (*coll., appropriate*) стяну́ть (*pf.*).

● *cpds.* **~-bone** *n.* (*anat.*) ключи́ца; **~-stud** *n.* за́понка (для воротника́).

collate /kəˈleɪt/ *v.t.* (*e.g. texts*) слич|а́ть, -и́ть; сопост|авля́ть, -а́вить.

collateral /kəˈlætər(ə)l/ *adj.* побо́чный, дополни́тельный; **~ security** дополни́тельное обеспе́чение.

collation /kəˈleɪʃ(ə)n/ *n.* (*collating*) сличе́ние, сопоставле́ние; (*meal*) заку́ска.

colleague /ˈkɒliːg/ *n.* колле́га (*c.g.*); сослужи́в|ец (*fem.* -ица).

collect[1] /ˈkɒlekt/ *n.* (*prayer*) кра́ткая моли́тва.

collect[2] /kəˈlekt/ *v.t.* **1** (*gather together*) соб|ира́ть, -ра́ть; **~ed works** (по́лное) собра́ние сочине́ний. **2** (*of debts, taxes*) соб|ира́ть, -ра́ть; получ|а́ть, -и́ть; **the telegram was sent ~** (*US*) телегра́мма была́ вы́слана нало́женным платежо́м. **3** (*of stamps etc.*) коллекциони́ровать (*impf.*). **4** (*fetch*) заб|ира́ть, -ра́ть; за|ходи́ть, -йти́ за + *i.*; **he ~ed the children from school** он забра́л дете́й из шко́лы. **5** (*keep in hand*): **~ o.s.** брать, взять себя́ в ру́ки; **~ one's thoughts** соб|ира́ться, -ра́ться с мы́слями.

● *v.i.* соб|ира́ться, -ра́ться; **a crowd ~ed** собрала́сь толпа́; **dust ~s** пыль ска́пливается.

collected /kəˈlektɪd/ *adj.* (*calm*) со́бранный; споко́йный.

collection /kəˈlekʃ(ə)n/ *n.* (*of valuables etc.*) колле́кция; (*accumulation*) скопле́ние; (*church etc.*) сбор, собира́ние; (*of mail*) вы́емка.

collective /kəˈlektɪv/ *n.* (*co-operative unit*) коллекти́в.

● *adj.* коллекти́вный; **~ farm** колхо́з; **~ farmer** колхо́зни|к (*fem.* -ца); (*gram.*): **~ noun** собира́тельное существи́тельное.

collectivism /kəˈlektɪˌvɪz(ə)m/ *n.* коллективи́зм.

collectivist /kəˈlektɪvɪst/ *n.* коллективи́ст.

● *adj.* коллективи́стский.

collectivity /kəˌlekˈtɪvɪtɪ/ *n.* коллекти́вность.

collectivization /kəˌlektɪvaɪˈzeɪʃ(ə)n/ *n.* коллективиза́ция.

collectivize /kəˈlektɪˌvaɪz/ *v.t.* коллективизи́ровать (*impf., pf.*).

collector /kəˈlektə(r)/ *n.* (*of stamps etc.*) коллекционе́р; **a ~'s piece** ре́дкий/уника́льный экземпля́р; (*of taxes, debts*) сбо́рщик; (*of tickets*) контролёр.

colleen /kɒˈliːn/ *n.* (ирла́ндская) де́вушка.

college /ˈkɒlɪdʒ/ *n.* **1** (*school*) колле́дж. **2** (*university*) университе́т; институ́т; вы́сшее уче́бное заведе́ние (*abbr.* вуз); **a ~ education** университе́тское образова́ние. **3** (*within university*) университе́тский колле́дж. **4** (*body of colleagues*) колле́гия; **~ of cardinals** колле́гия кардина́лов; **~ of arms** геральди́ческая пала́та.

collegial /kəˈliːdʒ(ə)l/ *adj.* **1** (*of college*) университе́тский. **2** (*involving shared responsibility*) коллегиа́льный.

collegian /kəˈliːdʒ(ə)n/ *n.* (*member of college*) член колле́джа.

collegiate /kəˈliːdʒət/ *adj.* **1** (*of college*) университе́тский. **2** (*of students*) студе́нческий.

collide /kəˈlaɪd/ *v.i.* ст|а́лкиваться, -олкну́ться.

collie /ˈkɒlɪ/ *n.* ко́лли (*c.g. indecl.*), шотла́ндская овча́рка.

collier /ˈkɒlɪə(r)/ *n.* (*miner*) углеко́п; (*ship*) углево́з, у́гольщик.

colliery /ˈkɒlɪərɪ/ *n.* каменноуго́льная ша́хта.

collision /kəˈlɪʒ(ə)n/ *n.* столкнове́ние; (*fig.*) колли́зия, столкнове́ние; **come into ~ with** ст|а́лкиваться, -олкну́ться с + *i.*; **~ course** пу́ть, на кото́ром неизбе́жно столкнове́ние.

collocate /ˈkɒləˌkeɪt/ *v.t.* распол|ага́ть, -ожи́ть; расстан|а́вливать, -ови́ть.

collocation /ˌkɒləˈkeɪʃ(ə)n/ *n.* расположе́ние, расстано́вка.

collodion /kəˈləʊdɪən/ *n.* колло́дий.

colloid /ˈkɒlɔɪd/ *n.* (*chem.*) коллои́д.

colloidal /kəˈlɔɪd(ə)l/ *adj.* (*chem.*) колло́идный.

colloquial /kəˈləʊkwɪəl/ *adj.* разгово́рный.

colloquialism /kəˈləʊkwɪəˌlɪz(ə)m/ *n.* разгово́рное выраже́ние/сло́во.

colloquy /ˈkɒləkwɪ/ *n.* собесе́дование.

collusion /kəˈluːʒ(ə)n/, /-ˈljuːʒ(ə)n/ *n.* сго́вор; **act in ~** де́йствовать (*impf.*) по сго́вору.

collusive /kəˈluːsɪv/ *adj.* соверше́нный по сго́вору.

collywobbles /ˈkɒlɪˌwɒb(ə)lz/ *n.* (*coll.*) урча́ние в животе́.

Cologne /kəˈləʊn/ *n.* Кёльн.

Colombia /kəˈlɒmbɪə/ *n.* Колу́мбия.

Colombian /kəˈlɒmbɪən/ *n.* колумби́|ец (*fem.* -йка).

● *adj.* колумби́йский.

Colombo /kəˈlʌmbəʊ/ *n.* Коло́мбо (*m. indecl.*).

colon[1] /ˈkəʊlən/, /-lɒn/ *n.* (*anat.*) то́лстая/ободо́чная кишка́.

colon[2] /ˈkəʊlən/, /-lɒn/ *n.* (*gram.*) двоето́чие.

colonel /ˈkɜːn(ə)l/ *n.* полко́вник.

● *cpds.* **~-general** *n.* генера́л-полко́вник; **~-in-chief** *n.* шеф полка́.

colonial /kəˈləʊnɪəl/ *n.* жи́тель (*fem.* -ница) коло́нии.

● *adj.* колониа́льный.

colonialism /kəˈləʊnɪəˌlɪz(ə)m/ *n.* колониали́зм.

colonialist /kəˈləʊnɪəlɪst/ *n.* колониали́ст.

● *adj.* колониали́стский.

colonic /kəˈlɒnɪk/ *adj.* (*anat.*) относя́щийся к то́лстой кишке́.

colonist /ˈkɒlənɪst/ *n.* колони́ст (*fem.* -ка); (*settler*) поселе́н|ец (*fem.* -ка).

colonization /ˌkɒləˌnaɪˈzeɪʃ(ə)n/ *n.* колониза́ция.

colonize /ˈkɒləˌnaɪz/ *v.t.* колонизова́ть, колонизи́ровать (*both impf., pf.*); (*settle in*) засел|я́ть, -и́ть.

colonizer /ˈkɒləˌnaɪzə(r)/ *n.* колониза́тор.

colonnade /ˌkɒləˈneɪd/ *n.* колонна́да.

colony /ˈkɒlənɪ/ *n.* коло́ния.

colophon /ˈkɒləˌfɒn/, /-fən/ *n.* колофо́н.

color /ˈkʌlə(r)/ *etc. US* = **colour** *etc.*

Colorado beetle /ˌkɒləˈrɑːdəʊ/ *n.* колора́дский/карто́фельный жук.

coloration /ˌkʌləˈreɪʃ(ə)n/ *n.* (*putting on colour*) окра́шивание; (*varied colour*) окра́ска, раскра́ска, расцве́тка.

coloratura /ˌkɒlərəˈtʊərə/ *n.* колорату́ра; **~ soprano** колорату́рное сопра́но.

colorimeter /ˌkɒləˈrɪmɪtə(r)/, /ˌkʌl-/ *n.* колори́метр, цветоме́р.

colossal /kəˈlɒs(ə)l/ *adj.* колосса́льный, грома́дный.

colos|sus /kəˈlɒsəs/ *n.* (*pl.* **~si** /-saɪ/ *or* **~suses**) коло́сс.

colour /ˈkʌlə(r)/ (*US* **color**) *n.* **1** (*lit.*) цвет; (*of horses*) масть; **primary ~s** основны́е цвета́; **secondary ~s** составны́е цвета́; **complementary ~s** дополни́тельные цвета́; **change ~** (*lit.*) меня́ть, по- цвет; (*fig.*) бледне́ть, по-/красне́ть, по-; **the film is in ~** э́то цветно́й фильм; **what ~ are his eyes?** како́го цве́та у него́ глаза́?; **~ code** цветово́й код; **~ film** цветна́я плёнка; **~ scheme** цветова́я га́мма; **~ television** цветно́е телеви́дение; (*pl., of team*) фо́рма; **what are their ~s?** в како́й фо́рме они́ игра́ют?
2 (*of face*) цвет лица́; румя́нец; **she has very little ~** у неё бле́дное лицо́; **lose ~** бледне́ть, по-; **he has a high ~** он о́чень румя́ный; **off ~** (*out of sorts*) не в фо́рме.
3 (*pl., paints*) кра́ски; **water ~s** акваре́ль; **oil ~s** ма́сляные кра́ски; ма́сло; **paint something in bright ~s** (*fig.*) рисова́ть, на- что-н. я́ркими кра́сками; **see something in its true ~s** (*fig.*) ви́деть, у- что-н. в и́стинном све́те.
4 (*semblance, probability*): **this fact lent ~ to his tale** э́тот факт прида́л не́которое правдоподо́бие его́ расска́зу; **under ~ of** под ви́дом/предло́гом + *g.*
5 (*liveliness*): **his style lacks ~** его́ сти́лю недостаёт кра́сочности; **local ~** ме́стный колори́т.
6 (*pl., Br. flag; also fig.*): **regimental ~s** полково́е зна́мя; **sail under false ~s** плыть (*det.*) под чужи́м фла́гом; выдава́ть, вы́дать себя́ за друго́го; **pass an examination with flying ~s** сдать (*pf.*) экза́мен с бле́ском; **nail one's ~s to the mast** не отступ|а́ться, -и́ться от свои́х убежде́ний; **show one's true ~s** предст|ава́ть, -а́ть в и́стинном све́те.
7 (*of race*): **a person of ~** представи́тель (*m.*) небе́лой ра́сы.

● *v.t.* **1** (*paint, endow with ~*) кра́сить, по-; окра́|шивать, -сить; **she wants the walls ~ed green** она́ хо́чет покра́сить сте́ны в зелёный цвет.
2 (*embellish*) приукра́|шивать, -сить; **a highly ~ed story** си́льно приукра́шенный расска́з.
3 (*imbue*): **his action was ~ed by envy** его́ посту́пок был отча́сти продикто́ван за́вистью. *See also* ⇒**coloured**

● *v.i.* **1** (*take on ~*): **the leaves ~ in autumn** о́сенью ли́стья меня́ют свой цвет.
2 (*blush*) красне́ть, по-.

● *cpds.* **~-bar** *n.* ра́ссовый барье́р; **~-blind** *adj.* страда́ющий дальтони́змом; **~-blind person** не

C

различа́ющий цвето́в, дальто́ник; **~-blindness** *n.* неспосо́бность различа́ть цвета́, дальтони́зм; **~ code** *v.t.* коди́ровать (*impf., pf.*) по цве́ту; **~-fast** *adj.* цветосто́йкий; **~-printing** *n.* хромоти́пия, многокра́сочная печа́ть; **~-sergeant** *n.* сержа́нт-знамёнщик; **~-wash** *n.* клеева́я кра́ска; *v.t.* кра́сить, по- клеево́й кра́ской.

colourant /ˈkʌlərənt/ (*US* **colorant**) краси́тель (*m.*), пигме́нт.

coloured /ˈkʌləd/ (*US* **colored**) *adj.* цветно́й; **~ pencil** цветно́й каранда́ш; **~ plate** (*illustration*) цветна́я иллюстра́ция; **~ print** цветна́я гравю́ра; (*offens., of race*): **~ people** цветны́е (*pl.*).

colourful /ˈkʌləˌfʊl/ (*US* **colorful**) *adj.* кра́сочный, я́ркий; **a ~ personality** я́ркая/колори́тная ли́чность.

colouring /ˈkʌlərɪŋ/ (*US* **coloring**) *n.* окра́ска; **protective ~** защи́тная окра́ска; (*complexion*) цвет лица́; (*substance*) краси́тель (*m.*); (*of a picture*) кра́ски (*f. pl.*); **~ book** (*for children*) альбо́м для раскра́шивания.

● *adj.* кра́сящий; **~ matter** кра́сящее вещество́.

colourist /ˈkʌlərɪst/ (*US* **colorist**) *n.* колори́ст.

colourless /ˈkʌləlɪs/ (*US* **colorless**) *adj.* (*lit., fig.*) бесцве́тный.

Colt /kəʊlt/ *n.* (*propr.*) (*~ revolver*) кольт.

colt /kəʊlt/ *n.* (*young horse*) жеребёнок.

coltish /ˈkəʊltɪʃ/ *adj.* (*lively*) живо́й, игри́вый.

columbarium /ˌkɒləmˈbeərɪəm/ *n.* (*in crematorium*) колумба́рий.

columbine /ˈkɒləmˌbaɪn/ *n.* водосбо́р.

column /ˈkɒləm/ *n.* **1** (*pillar*) коло́нна. **2** (*vertical object or mass*) столб; **~ of smoke** столб ды́ма; **spinal ~** позвоно́чный столб; **mercury ~** рту́тный сто́лбик. **3** (*in book etc.*) столбе́ц; **in the ~s of the Times** на страни́цах «Та́ймса». **4** (*regular feature in newspaper*): **weekly ~** еженеде́льная коло́нка/ру́брика. **5** (*of figures*) сто́лбик, столбе́ц, коло́нка. **6** (*mil. etc.*) коло́нна; **~ of ships** коло́нна корабле́й; **close ~** со́мкнутая коло́нна; **in ~** в коло́нне; **fifth ~** (*fig.*) пя́тая коло́нна.

columnist /ˈkɒləmnɪst/, /-mɪst/ *n.* обозрева́тель (*fem.* -ница).

coma /ˈkəʊmə/ *n.* (*pl.* **~s**) ко́ма.

comatose /ˈkəʊməˌtəʊz/ *adj.* комато́зный; **he is ~** он в ко́ме.

comb /kəʊm/ *n.* **1** (*for ~ing hair*) расчёска, гребёнка, гребешо́к; (*as adornment*) гре́бень (*m.*). **2** (*of bird*) гребешо́к, гре́бень (*m.*).

● *v.t.* **1** (*hair etc.*) чеса́ть (*impf.*); расчёс|ывать, -а́ть; причёс|ывать, -а́ть; (*horse*) чи́стить, вы- скребни́цей; (*wool, flax etc.*) чеса́ть (*impf.*); трепа́ть (*impf.*). **2** (*fig., search*) прочёс|ывать, -а́ть; **the police ~ed the city** поли́ция прочеса́ла весь го́род.

combat /ˈkɒmbæt/, /ˈkʌm-/ *n.* бой; **single ~** единобо́рство, поеди́нок; **mortal ~** сме́ртный бой; (*mil.*): **~ fatigue** котýзия, боева́я психи́ческая тра́вма; **~ zone** зо́на боевы́х де́йствий.

● *v.t.* (**combated, combating**) боро́ться (*impf.*) с + *i.* (*or* про́тив + *g.*).

● *v.i.* (**combated, combating**) боро́ться; сража́ться (*both impf.*).

combatant /ˈkɒmbət(ə)nt/, /ˈkʌm-/ *n.* бое́ц; вою́ющая сторона́.

● *adj.* бо́рющийся; сража́ющийся.

combative /ˈkɒmbətɪv/, /ˈkʌm-/ *adj.* боево́й, задиристый.

combativeness /ˈkɒmbətɪvnɪs/, /ˈkʌm-/ *n.* задиристость.

combe /kuːm/ = **coomb**

comber /ˈkəʊmə(r)/ *n.* (*machine*) гребнечеса́льная маши́на; (*wave*) вал, больша́я волна́.

combination /ˌkɒmbɪˈneɪʃ(ə)n/ *n.* **1** (*combining*) сочета́ние, комбина́ция; **in ~ with** в сочета́нии с + *i.* **2** (*of a safe*) ко́довая комбина́ция; **~ lock** секре́тный замо́к.

combinatorics /ˌkɒmbɪnəˈtɒrɪks/ *n.* (*math.*) комбинато́рика.

combine[1] /ˈkɒmbaɪn/ *n.* **1** (*group of persons*) объедине́ние; (*group of concerns*) комбина́т, синдика́т. **2** (*also* **~ harvester**) комба́йн.

combine[2] /kəmˈbaɪn/ *v.t.* сочета́ть (*impf.*); объедин|я́ть, -и́ть; комбини́ровать, с-; **~ forces** объедин|я́ть, -и́ть (*or* соедин|я́ть, -и́ть) си́лы; **he ~s business with pleasure** он сочета́ет прия́тное с поле́зным; **~d operations** (*mil.*) общевойскова́я опера́ция.

combings /ˈkəʊmɪŋz/ *n.* (*tech.*) гребенны́е очи́стки (*f. pl.*).

combo /ˈkɒmbəʊ/ *n.* (*pl.* **~s**) (*coll.*) небольшо́й анса́мбль; **jazz-~** джаз-анса́мбль (*m.*).

combust /kəmˈbʌst/ *v.t.* сж|ига́ть, -ечь.

combustible /kəmˈbʌstɪb(ə)l/ *adj.* горю́чий.

combustion /kəmˈbʌstʃ(ə)n/ *n.* воспламене́ние; сгора́ние; **spontaneous ~** самовоспламене́ние; **internal ~ engine** дви́гатель вну́треннего сгора́ния.

come /kʌm/ *v.i.* (*past* **came;** *p.p.* **come**) **1** (*move near, arrive*) при|ходи́ть, -йти́; приб|ыва́ть, -ы́ть; при|езжа́ть, -е́хать; **~ and see us!** приходи́те/заходи́те к нам!; **he came running** он прибежа́л; **he has ~ a hundred miles** он прие́хал за сто миль; **he was long in coming** он до́лго не появля́лся; **he came near to falling** он чуть не упа́л; **~ along!** пойдёмте!; **~ into the house!** заходи́те/зайди́те в дом!

2 (*of inanimate things; lit., fig.*): **the dress ~s to her knees** пла́тье дохо́дит ей до коле́н; **the sunshine came streaming into the room** лучи́ со́лнца лили́сь в ко́мнату; **dinner came** по́дали обе́д; **a parcel has ~** полу́чена посы́лка; **the feeling ~s and goes** э́то чу́вство то появля́ется, то исчеза́ет; **easy ~, easy go** легко́ на́жито, легко́ про́жито; **no work has ~ his way** никака́я рабо́та ему́ не попада́лась; **these shirts ~ in three sizes** э́ти руба́шки быва́ют трёх разме́ров; **it came as a shock to me** э́то бы́ло для меня́ уда́ром; **it came into my head** э́то пришло́ мне в го́лову; **the water came to the boil** вода́ закипе́ла; **the solution came to me** я (вдруг) нашёл реше́ние; **what are we coming to?** до чего́ мы до́жили?; **when it came to 6 o'clock** когда́ вре́мя подошло́ к 6 часа́м; **she takes things as they ~** она́ споко́йно отно́сится ко всему́, что бы ни случи́лось.

3 (*fig. uses with 'to': see also relevant nn.*): **~ to a decision** при|ходи́ть, -йти́ к реше́нию; **~ to blows** до|ходи́ть, -йти́ до рукопа́шной; **~ to terms** при|ходи́ть, -йти́ к соглаше́нию; **~ to light** обнару́жи|ваться, -ться; стать (*pf.*) очеви́дным; **~ to one's senses** образу́м|ливаться, -иться.

4 (*fig. uses with 'into': see also relevant nn.*): **the trees have ~ into leaf** на дере́вьях распусти́лись ли́стья; **he has ~ into a fortune** он получи́л большо́е насле́дство; **he came into his own** он доби́лся призна́ния/своего́; **they came into sight** они́ появи́лись; **the party came into power** па́ртия пришла́ к вла́сти.

5 (*occur, happen*) случа́ться, быва́ть (*both impf.*); **Christmas ~s once a year** Рождество́ быва́ет раз в году́; **who ~s next?** кто сле́дующий; **it ~s on page 20** э́то на двадца́той страни́це; **no harm will ~ to you** с ва́ми ничего́ не случи́тся; **he had it coming to him** ему́ сле́довало э́того ожида́ть; **how ~ he was late?** как э́то получи́лось, что он опозда́л?; **how did you ~ to meet him?** как случи́лось, что вы с ним встре́тились?; **that ~s of grumbling** всё э́то из-за ворча́ния; **no good will ~ of it** ничего́ хоро́шего из э́того не вы́йдет; **in years to ~** в после́дующие го́ды; в бу́дущем; **~ what may** будь что бу́дет; **how ~?** (*coll.*) э́то почему́ же?; как так?

6 (*amount, result*): **the bill ~s to £5** счёт равня́ется пяти́ фу́нтам; **it ~s to this, that** ... де́ло сво́дится к тому́, что...; **it ~s to the same thing** получа́ется то же са́мое; **if it ~s to that** е́сли уж на то пошло́; **his plans came to nothing** из его́ пла́нов ничего́ не вы́шло; **he is no good when it ~s to talking** когда́ ну́жно говори́ть, он теря́ется.

7 (*become, prove to be*): **his dreams came true** его́ мечты́ осуществи́лись/сбыли́сь; **it ~s naturally to him** ему́ э́то легко́ даётся; **his shoelace came undone** у него́ шнуро́к развяза́лся; **it all came right in the end** всё ко́нчилось благополу́чно; **~ clean** (*sl., confess*) выкла́дывать, вы́ложить всё.

8 (*fig., find o.s. in a position*): **I have ~ to see that he is right** я убеди́лся, что он прав; **how did you ~ to do that?** как вас угоразди́ло так поступи́ть?

9 (*of person, originate*) прои|сходи́ть, -зойти́; **he ~s from Scotland** он уроже́нец Шотла́ндии; **she ~s of a noble family** она́ происхо́дит из зна́тной семьи́.

10 (*coll. uses*): **it will be 5 years ago ~ Christmas that . . .** на Рождество́ бу́дет пять лет с тех пор, как. . .; **~ off it!** (*desist*) отста́нь!; конча́й!; переста́нь!
11 (*imper., fig.*): **~, ~!** (*expostulatory*) ну! ну!; ну, что вы!; **~, tell me what you know** ну́-ка, расскажи́те мне, что вы зна́ете.
12 (*Br. coll., have orgasm*) конча́ть, ко́нчить.

● *with preps.* (*see also* 3 *and* 4 *above*): **~ across** (*traverse*) пере|ходи́ть, -йти́ че́рез + *a.*; (*encounter*) нат|а́лкиваться, -олкну́ться на + *a.*; нат|ыка́ться, -кну́ться на + *a.*; **~ after** (*follow*) сле́довать, по- за + *i.*; **~ at** (*reach*): **the truth is hard to ~ at** до пра́вды тру́дно добра́ться; (*attack*): **the dog came at me** соба́ка набро́силась на меня́; **~ before** (*precede*): **dukes ~ before earls** ге́рцоги стоя́т вы́ше гра́фов; (*appear before*): **he came before the court** он предста́л пе́ред судо́м; **~ by** (*obtain*) дост|ава́ть, -а́ть; **~ for** (*attack*): **he came for us with a stick** он набро́сился на нас с па́лкой; **~ from: wine ~s from grapes** вино́ получа́ется из виногра́да; **a sob came from her throat** из её груди́ вы́рвалось рыда́ние; **~ into: he came into a large estate** ему́ доста́лось большо́е име́ние; **~ off** (*lit.*): **~ off the grass!** сойди́те с травы́; (*become detached from*): **a button came off my coat** от моего́ пальто́ оторвала́сь пу́говица; (*Br., fall off*): **she came off her bicycle** она́ упа́ла с велосипе́да; **~ on: he came on to me for £5** (*coll.*) он потре́бовал от меня́ пять фу́нтов; **~ out of** (*lit.*): **he came out of the house** он вы́шел из до́ма; **~ over** (*lit.*): **a cloud came over the sky** ту́чи затяну́ли не́бо; (*fig.*): **what came over you?** что на вас нашло́?; **~ round: he came round the corner** он поверну́л за́ угол; **~ through: he came through both wars** он прошёл о́бе войны́; **~ under: what heading does this ~ under?** к како́й ру́брике э́то отно́сится; **he came under her influence** он попа́л под её влия́ние; **~ upon** (*find*) напа́сть (*pf.*) на + *a.*; нат|а́лкиваться, -олкну́ться на + *a.*; **fear came upon us** на нас напа́л страх.

● *with advs.*: **~ about** *v.i.* (*happen*) прои|сходи́ть, -зойти́; **~ across (as)** показа́ться (*pf.*) (+ *i.*); **~ again** *v.i.*: **~ again?** (*coll., what did you say?*) ну́-ка повтори́!; скажи́ сно́ва!; **~ apart** *v.i.* (*unfastened*) ра|сходи́ться, -зойти́сь; разва́л|иваться, -и́ться на ча́сти; **~ around** (*US*) = **~ round; ~ away** *v.i.* (*become detached*) отл|а́мываться, -ома́ться *or* -оми́ться (*om* + *g.*); **~ back** *v.i.* (*return*) возвра|ща́ться, -ти́ться; верну́ться (*pf.*); **his name came back to me** я вспо́мнил его́ и́мя; (*retort*) возра|жа́ть, -зи́ть; **~ by** *v.i.* (*pass by*) минова́ть (*impf., pf.*); про|ходи́ть, -йти́ ми́мо; **~ down** *v.i.*: **he came down off the ladder** он спусти́лся с ле́стницы; **her hair ~s down to her waist** у неё во́лосы дохо́дят до по́яса; (*of prices*) па́дать, упа́сть; (*fig.*): **he has ~ down in the world** он опусти́лся; **the story has ~ down to us** до нас дошла́ э́та исто́рия; (*coll.*): **the master came down on the boy for cheating** учи́тель напусти́лся на ма́льчика за спи́сывание; **he came down with influenza** он слёг с гри́ппом; **~ forward** *v.i.* (*present o.s. as candidate*) выдвига́ть, вы́двинуть свою́ кандидату́ру; (*offer one's services*) предл|ага́ть, -ожи́ть свои́ услу́ги; (*become available*) поступ|а́ть, -и́ть; **~ in** *v.i.* (*lit.*) входи́ть, войти́; **~ in!** (*to s.o. knocking*) войди́те; **the tide came in** наступи́л прили́в; **short skirts came in** коро́ткие ю́бки вошли́ в мо́ду; **his horse came in first** его́ ло́шадь пришла́ пе́рвой; **the Conservatives came in** консерва́торы победи́ли на вы́борах; **information came in** поступи́ли све́дения; **the money is coming in well** де́ньги поступа́ют хорошо́; **~ in, please!** (*radio etc.*) пожа́луйста, начина́йте!; **where do I ~ in?** како́е э́то име́ет ко мне отноше́ние?; что я получу́ с э́того?; **it came in handy** э́то пригоди́лось; **he came in for a thrashing** ему́ всы́пали; **~ off** *v.i.* (*become detached*) отва́л|иваться, -и́ться; **the table-leg came off** у стола́ отвали́лась но́жка; **lipstick ~s off on glasses** губна́я пома́да остаётся на стака́нах; (*happen, succeed*): **the marriage came off** брак состоя́лся; **the experiment came off** о́пыт уда́лся; **he came off best** он вы́шел победи́телем; (**~** *off duty*): **he ~s off at 10** он ухо́дит со слу́жбы в 10; **~ on** *v.i.* (*follow*) сле́довать (*impf.*); **he came on later** он появи́лся поздне́е; **~ on!** (*impatient*) ну!; ну-же; **~ on! I'll race you** дава́йте побежи́м наперегонки́!; (*progress*) де́лать (*impf.*) успе́хи; **the garden is coming on well** в саду́ всё хорошо́ растёт; (*start, set in*): **it came on to rain** начался́ дождь; **I have a cold coming on** у меня́ начина́ется просту́да; (*of actor; appear*) появ|ля́ться, -и́ться; выходи́ть, вы́йти на сце́ну; (*of play; be performed*): **the play ~s on next week** пье́са бу́дет предста́влена на сле́дующей неде́ле; **~ out** *v.i.* (*lit.*) выходи́ть, вы́йти; **the sun came out** со́лнце появи́лось/вы́глянуло; **the flowers came out** цветы́ распусти́лись; (*become known, appear*): **the news came out** но́вость ста́ла изве́стной; **the book came out** кни́га вы́шла; **the paper ~s out on Thursday** э́та газе́та выхо́дит по четверга́м; **he came out well in the photograph** он хорошо́ вы́шел на фотогра́фии; **all his arrogance came out** вся его́ спесь вы́шла нару́жу; (*disappear*): **the stains came out** пя́тна сошли́; **the colour** (*Br.*), **color** (*US*) **came out** (*faded*) кра́ска вы́цвела/полиня́ла/поблёкла; (*of results*): **the sum came out** зада́ча получи́лась; **he came out first in the exam** он был лу́чшим на э́том экза́мене; (*declare o.s.*): **he came out against the plan** он вы́ступил про́тив пла́на; **the total came out at 700** о́бщий ито́г оказа́лся ра́вным 700; (*Br., make début in society*) дебюти́ровать (*impf., pf*); (*publicly acknowledge one's homosexuality*) откры́то призн|ава́ть, -а́ть свою́ гомосексуа́льность; (*Br., go on strike*) забастова́ть (*pf.*); выходи́ть, вы́йти на забасто́вку; **he came out with the truth** он рассказа́л всю пра́вду; **he came out with an oath** он вы́ругался; **she came out in a rash** (*Br.*) она́ покры́лась сы́пью; **~ over** *v.i.*: **they came over to England** они́ прие́хали в А́нглию; **he came over to our side** он перешёл на на́шу сто́рону; **he came over dizzy** (*Br. coll.*) у него́ закружи́лась голова́; **~ round** *v.i.* (*make detour*): **we came round by the fields** мы пришли́ кру́жным путём че́рез поля́; (*make trip*): **~ round and see us!** заходи́те к нам!; (*recur*): **Christmas will soon ~ round** ско́ро (насту́пит) Рождество́; (*change mind*): **he came round to my view** он пришёл-таки к мое́й то́чке зре́ния; (*yield*): **she'll ~ round** (*Br.*) она́ усту́пит/согласи́тся; (*recover consciousness*) при|ходи́ть, -йти́ в себя́; очну́ться (*pf.*); **~ through** *v.i.* (*survive experience*) пережи́ть (*pf.*); **he came through without a scratch** он вы́шел из э́той исто́рии без еди́ной цара́пины; (*teleph.*): **the call came through at 3 o'clock** разгово́р состоя́лся в 3 часа́; **~ to** *v.i.* (*recover one's senses*) при|ходи́ть, -йти́ в себя́; очну́ться (*pf.*); **~ up** *v.i.*: **the sun came up** со́лнце взошло́; **the seeds came up** семена́ взошли́; **he came up to London** он прие́хал в Ло́ндон; **he came up to me** он подошёл ко мне; **the water came up to my waist** вода́ доходи́ла мне до по́яса; **the question came up** встал вопро́с; **the case ~s up tomorrow** э́то де́ло разбира́ется за́втра; **the book came up to my expectations** кни́га оправда́ла мои́ ожида́ния; **he came up against a difficulty** он натолкну́лся на тру́дности; **he came up with a suggestion** он внёс предложе́ние.

● *cpds.* **~back** *n.* (*retort*) возраже́ние; (*return*) возвраще́ние; **~-down** *n.* униже́ние; разочарова́ние; **~-hither** *adj.* (*coll.*): **a ~-hither look** завлека́ющий взгляд; **~-uppance** *n.* (*coll.*): **he got his ~-uppance** он получи́л по заслу́гам.

Comecon /ˈkɒmɪˌkɒn/ *n.* (*abbr. of* ***Council for Mutual Economic Assistance***) СЭВ (Сове́т экономи́ческой взаимопо́мощи).

comedian /kəˈmiːdɪən/ *n.* ко́мик.

comedienne /kəˌmiːdɪˈen/ *n.* коми́ческая актри́са.

comedy /ˈkɒmɪdɪ/ *n.* коме́дия.

comeliness /ˈkʌmlɪnɪs/ *n.* милови́дность.

comely /ˈkʌmlɪ/ *adj.* (**comelier, comeliest**) милови́дный.

comer /ˈkʌmə(r)/ *n.*: **the first ~** прише́дший пе́рвым; **he will fight all ~s** гото́в дра́ться с кем уго́дно.

comestible /kəˈmestɪb(ə)l/ *n.* (*usu. pl.*) съестны́е припа́с|ы (*pl., g.* -ов).
● *adj.* съестно́й.

comet /ˈkɒmɪt/ *n.* коме́та.

comfort /ˈkʌmfət/ *n.* **1** (*physical ease*) комфо́рт; удо́бства (*nt. pl.*); **he lives in ~** он живёт, не ве́дая нужды́; **~ station** (*US*) обще́ственная убо́рная.

C

2 (*relief of suffering*) утешéние, отрáда; **cold ~** слáбое утешéние. **3** (*thing that brings ~*) утешéние, успокоéние; **his letters are a ~** егó пи́сьма — большóе утешéние.

● *v.t.* ут|ешáть, -éшить; успок|áивать, -óить.

comfortabl|e /'kʌmftəb(ə)l/, /-fətəb(ə)l/ *adj.* удóбный, ую́тный, комфортáбельный, комфóртный; **I am ~e here** мне здесь удóбно; **the car holds six people ~y** э́та маши́на свобóдно вмещáет шесть человéк; **he makes a ~e living** он прили́чно зарабáтывает; **he is ~y off** он живёт в достáтке.

comforter /'kʌmfətə(r)/ *n.* **1** (*person*) утеши́тель. **2** (*Br., teat*) сóска, пусты́шка. **3** (*US, quilt*) стёганое одея́ло.

comforting /'kʌmfətɪŋ/ *adj.* утеши́тельный, успокои́тельный; **it is ~ to know that ...** утеши́тельно знать, что. . . .

comfortless /'kʌmfətlɪs/ *adj.* неую́тный; безрáдостный; **a ~ room** неую́тная кóмната.

comic /'kɒmɪk/ *n.* **1** (*coll., comedian*) кóмик, юмори́ст. **2** (*magazine*) кóмикс; (*pl., US, ~ strips*) кóмиксы (*m. pl.*).

● *adj.* коми́ческий, юмористи́ческий; **~ book** кни́жка кóмиксов; **~ strip** кóмикс.

comical /'kɒmɪk(ə)l/ *adj.* коми́чный, смешнóй.

coming /'kʌmɪŋ/ *n.* приéзд, прихóд; **the Second C~** вторóе пришéствие (Христá); **~ and going** движéние взад-вперёд.

● *adj.* бу́дущий, наступáющий; **the ~ week** бу́дущая недéля.

Comintern /'kɒmɪn,tɜ:n/ *n.* (*hist., abbr. of* ***Communist International,*** *1914–43*) Коминтéрн.

comity /'kɒmɪtɪ/ *n.* вéжливость; **~ of nations** взаи́мное призна́ние закóнов и обы́чаев рáзными стрáнами.

comma /'kɒmə/ *n.* запятáя; **inverted ~s** кавы́ч|ки (*pl., g.* -ек).

command /kə'mɑ:nd/ *n.* **1** (*order; also comput.*) комáнда; **at the word of ~** по комáнде.
2 (*authority*) комáндование; **he is in ~ of the army** он комáндует áрмией; **he took ~** он при́нял комáндование.
3 (*control*) контрóль (*m.*); **~ of the air** госпóдство в вóздухе; **~ of one's emotions** владéние свои́ми чу́вствами.
4 (*knowledge, ability to use*): **she has a good ~ of French** онá хорошó владéет францу́зским языкóм; **she has a great ~ of language** онá прекрáсно владéет слóвом.
5 (*mil.*) комáндование; **High C~** верхóвное комáндование; (*attr.*) комáндный; **~ module** комáндный отсéк; **~ post** комáндный пункт, КП.

● *v.t. & i.* **1** (*give orders to*) прикáз|ывать, -áть + *d.*; **he ~ed his men to fire** он приказáл свои́м солдáтам откры́ть огóнь.
2 (*have authority over*) комáндовать (*impf.*) + *i.*
3 (*be able to use or enjoy*) располагáть (*impf.*) + *i.*; **he ~s great sums of money** в егó распоряжéнии кру́пные дéнежные срéдства; **he ~s respect** он внушáет к себé уважéние.
4 (*of things*): **this article ~s a high price** э́тот товáр продаётся по высóкой ценé; **the window ~s a fine view** из oкнá открывáется прекрáсный вид.

commandant /,kɒmən'dænt/, /'kɒm-/ *n.* комендáнт.

commandeer /,kɒmən'dɪə(r)/ *v.t.* реквизи́ровать (*impf., pf.*).

commander /kə'mɑ:ndə(r)/ *n.* команди́р, комáндующий; **C~-in-Chief** главнокомáндующий; (*naval rank*) капитáн трéтьего рáнга.

commanding /kə'mɑ:ndɪŋ/ *adj.* (*in command*) комáндующий; **~ officer** команди́р; **a ~ tone** повели́тельный тон; **~ heights** комáндные высóты; **a ~ presence** внуши́тельная осáнка.

commandment /kə'mɑ:ndmənt/ *n.*: **the Ten C~s** дéсять зáповедей.

commando /kə'mɑ:ndəʊ/ *n.* (*pl.* **~s**) (*force*) десáнтно-диверсиóнный отря́д; (*person*) солдáт десáнтно-диверсиóнного отря́да.

commemorate /kə'memə,reɪt/ *v.t.* (*celebrate memory of*) отм|ечáть, -éтить (*годовщину, событие*); ознамен|óвывать, -овáть; (*be in memory of*): **this monument ~s the victory** э́тот пáмятник воздви́гнут в честь побéды.

commemoration /kə,memə'reɪʃ(ə)n/ *n.* ознаменовáние (*годовщины, события*).

commemorative /kə'memərətɪv/ *adj.* пáмятный, мемориáльный.

commence /kə'mens/ *v.t. & i.* нач|инáть(ся), -áть(ся).

commencement /kə'mensmənt/ *n.* начáло; (*US, acad.*) áктовый день; торжéственное вручéние диплóмов.

commend /kə'mend/ *v.t.* **1** (*entrust*) вв|ерять, -éрить; поруч|áть, -и́ть; **he ~ed his soul to God** он посвяти́л себя́ Бóгу. **2** (*praise*) хвали́ть, по-.
3 (*recommend*) рекомендовáть (*impf., pf.*); **the book does not ~ itself to me** э́та кни́га меня́ не привлекáет.

commendable /kə'mendəb(ə)l/ *adj.* похвáльный.

commendation /,kɒmen'deɪʃ(ə)n/ *n.* похвалá, рекомендáция.

commendatory /kə'mendətərɪ/ *adj.* (*of a trust*) довери́тельный; (*of praise*) похвáльный.

commensurable /kə'menʃərəb(ə)l/, /-sjərəb(ə)l/ *adj.* соизмери́мый.

commensurate /kə'menʃərət/, /-sjərət/ *adj.* размéрный.

comment /'kɒment/ *n.* замечáние, комментáрий; óтзыв, óтклик; **her behaviour** (*Br.*), **behavior** (*US*) **aroused ~** её поведéние вы́звало тóлки.

● *v.t. & i.* комменти́ровать (*impf., pf.*); толковáть (*impf.*); дéлать, с- замечáния; **he ~ed on the book** он вы́сказал своё мнéние об э́той кни́ге.

commentary /'kɒməntərɪ/ *n.* комментáрий.

commentator /'kɒmən,teɪtə(r)/ *n.* (*textual*) комментáтор, толковáтель (*m.*); (*radio etc.*) комментáтор, обозревáтель (*m.*); **sports ~** спорти́вный комментáтор.

commerce /'kɒmɜ:s/ *n.* коммéрция, торгóвля; **Chamber of C~** Торгóвая палáта.

commercial /kə'mɜ:ʃ(ə)l/ *n.* (*coll., TV advertisement*) реклáмная передáча.

● *adj.* коммéрческий, торгóвый; **~ traveller** (*Br*) коммивояжёр; **~ television** коммéрческое телеви́дение; **~ vehicle** грузовáя маши́на.

commercialism /kə'mɜ:ʃ(ə),lɪz(ə)m/ *n.* меркантили́зм.

commercialize /kə'mɜ:ʃə,laɪz/ *n.* стáвить, по- на коммéрческую оснóву; вн|оси́ть, -ести́ коммéрческий дух в + *a.*

commingle /kə'mɪŋg(ə)l/ *v.t. & i.* смéш|ивать(ся), -áть(ся).

commiserate /kə'mɪzə,reɪt/ *v.i.* (*feel sympathy*) сочу́вствовать (*impf.*) (**with**: *кому*); (*express sympathy*) выражáть, вы́разить соболéзнование (**with**: *кому*).

commiseration /kə,mɪzə'reɪʃ(ə)n/ *n.* сочу́вствие, соболéзнование.

commissar /'kɒmɪ,sɑ:(r)/ *n.* комиссáр.

commissariat /,kɒmɪ'seərɪət/, /-'særɪ,æt/ *n.* **1** (*office of commissar*) комиссариáт. **2** (*mil.*) интендáнтство.

commissary /'kɒmɪsərɪ/, /kə'mɪs-/ *n.* **1** (*deputy*) уполномóченный. **2** (*US, mil. store*) воéнный магази́н; (*restaurant*) столóвая.

commission /kə'mɪʃ(ə)n/ *n.*
1 (*authorization*) полномóчие; **he went beyond his ~** он превы́сил свои́ полномóчия.
2 (*errand*) поручéние; **I carried out some ~s for him** я вы́полнил нéсколько егó поручéний; (*order for work of art*) закáз.
3 (*action*) совершéние; **the ~ of a crime** совершéние преступлéния; **sin of ~** грех дея́нием.
4 (*comm.*) комиссиóнн|ые (*pl., g.* -ых); **he sells goods on ~** он продаёт товáры за комиссиóнное вознаграждéние.
5 (*officer's*) патéнт на офицéрский чин.
6 (*committee*) коми́ссия; (*commissariat*) комиссариáт; **high ~** верхóвный комиссариáт.
7: **in ~** (*fit for action*) в испрáвности; в готóвности; **a ship in ~** корáбль, готóвый к плáванию; **out of ~** (*out of active service*) в резéрве; не в строю́; (*out of working order*) в неиспрáвности.

● *v.t.* поруч|áть, -и́ть (*что кому*); **he ~ed me to buy this** он поручи́л мне купи́ть э́то; **he ~ed a portrait from the artist** он заказáл худóжнику портрéт; **the ship was ~ed** корáбль был введён в строй; **a ~ed officer** офицéр; **he was ~ed from the ranks** он был произведён в офицéры из рядовы́х.

commissionaire /kəˌmɪʃəˈneə(r)/ *n.* (*Br.*) швейца́р.

commissioner /kəˈmɪʃənə(r)/ *n.* член коми́ссия; комисса́р; **high ~** верхо́вный комисса́р.

commit /kəˈmɪt/ *v.t.* (**committed, committing**) **1** (*perform*) соверш|а́ть, -и́ть. **2** (*entrust, consign*): **~ s.o. for trial** пред|ава́ть, -а́ть кого́-н. суду́; **~ to paper** изл|ага́ть, -ожи́ть на бума́ге; **~ to memory** зау́ч|ивать, -и́ть; **~ to the flames** пред|ава́ть, -а́ть огню́. **3** (*engage*): **he ~ted himself to helping her** он взя́лся помо́чь ей; **he would not ~ himself** он уклони́лся от чёткого отве́та; он не хоте́л свя́зывать себя́ конкре́тными обяза́тельствами. **4**: **~ troops to battle** вв|оди́ть, -ести́ (*or* бр|оса́ть, -о́сить) войска́ в бой. **5**: **a ~ted writer** иде́йный писа́тель.

commitment /kəˈmɪtmənt/ *n.* (*obligation*) обяза́тельство; **~ to a cause** пре́данность де́лу.

committal /kəˈmɪt(ə)l/ *n.*: **~ for trial** преда́ние суду́.

committee /kəˈmɪtɪ/ *n.* (*body of persons*) комите́т, коми́ссия; **steering ~** организацио́нный/руководя́щий комите́т.

commode /kəˈməʊd/ *n.* (*chest of drawers*) комо́д; (*for chamber-pot*) стульча́к для ночно́го горшка́.

commodious /kəˈməʊdɪəs/ *adj.* просто́рный, удо́бный.

commodity /kəˈmɒdɪtɪ/ *n.* това́р, предме́т потребле́ния; (*attr.*) това́рный.

commodore /ˈkɒməˌdɔː(r)/ *n.* (*in navy or merchant marine*) коммодо́р, капита́н пе́рвого ра́нга; (*of yacht club*) командо́р.

common /ˈkɒmən/ *n.* **1** (*land*) пусты́рь (*m.*), вы́гон. **2** (*something usual or shared*): **they have some tastes in ~** у них есть о́бщие вку́сы; **in ~ with most Englishmen, he is fond of sport** как и большинство́ англича́н, он лю́бит спорт.

● *adj.* (**commoner, commonest**) **1** (*belonging to more than one, general*) о́бщий; **it is ~ ground between us that** . . . мы согла́сны в том, что. . .; **it is ~ knowledge that** . . . общеизве́стно, что. . .. **2** (*belonging to the public or a specific group*): **~ land** obще́ственная земля́; **~ law** о́бщее/обы́чное/некодифици́рованное пра́во; **C~ Market** О́бщий ры́нок; **he has the ~ touch** он со все́ми нахо́дит о́бщий язы́к. **3** (*ordinary, usual*) обы́чный, обы́денный, обыкнове́нный; **~ honesty** проста́я/элемента́рная че́стность; **the ~ man** обыкнове́нный/просто́й челове́к; **the ~ people** (просто́й) наро́д; **~ sense** здра́вый смысл; **~ salt** пова́ренная соль; **~ or garden** (*coll.*) обыкнове́нный; **a ~ (or garden** *Br.*) **impostor** обма́нщик, каки́х мно́го. **4** (*vulgar*) вульга́рный, по́шлый. **5** (*math.*): **~ logarithm** десяти́чный логари́фм. **6** (*gram.*): **~ gender** о́бщий род; **~ noun** и́мя нарица́тельное. **7** (*mus.*): **~ time** просто́й такт.

● *cpds.* **~-law** *adj.*: **~-law marriage** незарегистри́рованный брак; **~-law wife** сожи́тельница; **~place** *n.* бана́льность; *adj.* бана́льный; **~-room** *n.* (*Br.*) (*senior*) учи́тельская, профе́ссорская; (*junior*) студе́нческая ко́мната о́тдыха; **~-sense** *adj.* здра́вый, разу́мный.

commonalty /ˈkɒmənəltɪ/ *n.* (*the common people*) простонаро́дье; (просто́й) наро́д.

commoner /ˈkɒmənə(r)/ *n.* недворяни́н, челове́к незна́тного происхожде́ния.

commonly /ˈkɒmənlɪ/ *adv.* (*usually*) обы́чно, обыкнове́нно.

commonness /ˈkɒmənnɪs/ *n.* (*frequency*) обы́чность, обы́денность; (*vulgarity*) вульга́рность, по́шлость.

commons /ˈkɒmənz/ *n.* (*common people*) простонаро́дье; **(House of) C~** пала́та о́бщин.

commonsensical /ˌkɒmənˈsensɪk(ə)l/ *adj.* здра́вый, разу́мный.

commonwealth /ˈkɒmənˌwelθ/ *n.* **the British C~** брита́нское Содру́жество (на́ций); **C~ of Independent States** Содру́жество незави́симых госуда́рств.

commotion /kəˈməʊʃ(ə)n/ *n.* волне́ние, возня́.

communal /ˈkɒmjʊn(ə)l/ *adj.* obще́ственный, коммуна́льный; **~ flat** коммуна́льная кварти́ра.

commune[1] /ˈkɒmjuːn/ *n.* (*administrative unit*) общи́на, комму́на; (*Russian hist., peasant ~*) мир; **the Paris C~** Пари́жская Комму́на.

commune[2] /kəˈmjuːn/ *v.i.* обща́ться (*impf.*) (с + *i.*); быть в те́сном обще́нии (с + *i.*); **~ with nature** обща́ться с приро́дой.

communicable /kəˈmjuːnɪkəb(ə)l/ *adj.* передаю́щийся; **a ~ disease** зара́зная боле́знь.

communicant /kəˈmjuːnɪkənt/ *n.* (*relig.*) прича́стни|к (*fem.* -ца).

communicate /kəˈmjuːnɪˌkeɪt/ *v.t.* сообщ|а́ть, -и́ть; (*a disease, also*) перед|ава́ть, -а́ть.

● *v.i.* свя́з|ываться, -а́ться; сообщ|а́ть, -и́ть (*кому о чём*); **~ with s.o.** обща́ться (*impf.*) с кем-н.; сн|оси́ться, -ести́сь с кем-н.; **the rooms ~** э́ти ко́мнаты сообща́ются; (*relig.*) прича|ща́ться, -сти́ться.

communication /kəˌmjuːnɪˈkeɪʃ(ə)n/ *n.* **1** (*act of communicating*) обще́ние; связь, сообще́ние, коммуника́ция; **language is a means of ~** язы́к — сре́дство обще́ния; **get into ~ with s.o.** устан|а́вливать, -ови́ть связь с кем-н.; **lack of ~** (*understanding*) отсу́тствие взаимопонима́ния. **2** (*message*) сообще́ние. **3** (*means of ~*) сре́дства свя́зи/сообще́ния; (*pl.: roads, railways etc.*) пути́ (*m. pl.*) сообще́ния. **4** (*mil.*): **lines of ~** коммуника́ции.

communicative /kəˈmjuːnɪkətɪv/ *adj.* общи́тельный, разгово́рчивый.

communion /kəˈmjuːnɪən/ *n.* **1** (*intercourse*) обще́ние; **~ with nature** обще́ние с приро́дой. **2** (*sacrament*) прича́стие.

communiqué /kəˈmjuːnɪˌkeɪ/ *n.* коммюнике́ (*indecl.*).

communism /ˈkɒmjʊˌnɪz(ə)m/ *n.* коммуни́зм.

communist /ˈkɒmjʊnɪst/ *n.* коммуни́ст (*fem.* -ка).

● *adj.* (*also* **-ic**) коммунисти́ческий.

community /kəˈmjuːnɪtɪ/ *n.* **1** (*commonness; joint ownership*): **~ of interest** о́бщность интере́сов. **2** (*society*) о́бщество. **3** (*pol., social etc. group*) общи́на, гру́ппа населе́ния.

commutation /ˌkɒmjuːˈteɪʃ(ə)n/ *n.* **1** (*commuting*) заме́на (одного́ ви́да платежа́ други́м). **2** (*leg., of sentence*) смягче́ние пригово́ра.

commutator /ˈkɒmjuːˌteɪtə(r)/ *n.* (*elec.*) колле́ктор, переключа́тель (*m.*), коммута́тор.

commute /kəˈmjuːt/ *v.t.* замен|я́ть, -и́ть; (*leg.*) смягч|а́ть, -и́ть (*приговор*).

● *v.i.* (*to work*) е́здить (*indet.*) ка́ждый день на значи́тельное расстоя́ние на рабо́ту.

commuter /kəˈmjuːtə(r)/ *n.* (*traveller*) челове́к, кото́рый регуля́рно е́здит на рабо́ту (*на пригородном транспорте*).

compact[1] /ˈkɒmpækt/ *n.* (*pact*) соглаше́ние, догово́р.

compact[2] /ˈkɒmpækt/ *n.* (*cosmetic case*) пу́дреница.

compact[3] /kəmˈpækt/ *adj.* (*closely packed*) компа́ктный; (*tense, concise*) сжа́тый, компа́ктный; **~ disk** /ˈkɒmpækt/ компа́кт-ди́ск; **~ disk player** прои́грыватель (*m.*) для компа́кт-ди́сков.

● *v.t.* (*press together*) сж|има́ть, -ать; сти́с|кивать, -нуть; уплотн|я́ть, -и́ть.

compactness /kəmˈpæktnɪs/ *n.* компа́ктность, сжа́тость.

companion[1] /kəmˈpænjən/ *n.* **1** (*person who accompanies*) спу́тни|к (*fem.* -ца); **my ~ on the journey** мой попу́тчик; **~ in adversity** това́рищ по несча́стью; **~ in crime** соуча́стник преступле́ния; **he is an excellent ~** с ним мо́жно отли́чно провести́ вре́мя. **2** (*object matching another*) па́ра; (*attr.*) па́рный; **~ volume** сопроводи́тельный том. **3** (*woman paid to keep another company*) компаньо́нка. **4** (*member of order*): **C~ of the Bath** кавале́р о́рдена Ба́ни. **5** (*handbook*) спра́вочник, спу́тник; **the Gardener's C~** спра́вочник садо́вника.

companion[2] /kəmˈpænjən/ *n.* (*naut.: also* **~-way, ~-ladder**) сходно́й трап.

companionable /kəmˈpænjənəb(ə)l/ *adj.* общи́тельный, (*coll.*) компане́йский.

companionship /kəmˈpænjənʃɪp/ *n.* дру́жеское обще́ние; дру́жеские отноше́ния.

company /ˈkʌmpənɪ/ *n.*
1 (*companionship*): **I was glad of his ~** я был рад его́ обществу; **keep, bear s.o. ~** сост|авля́ть, -а́вить кому́-н. компа́нию; **part ~** расст|ава́ться, -а́ться; **we parted ~** на́ши пути́ разошли́сь; **in ~ with** совме́стно с+*i.*; **he is good ~** с ним хорошо́; с ним не соску́чишься.
2 (*associates, guests*): **we have ~ this evening** у нас сего́дня бу́дут го́сти; **present ~ excepted** не упомина́я прису́тствующих; о прису́тствующих не говоря́т; **two's ~ (but three is none)** где двое, там тре́тий ли́шний.
3 (*commercial firm*) това́рищество, компа́ния; **Jones and Company (***abbr.* **Co.)** Джо́унз и компа́ния (*abbr.* Ко); **~ car** служе́бная маши́на.
4 (*theatr.*) тру́ппа.
5 (*naut.*) кома́нда, экипа́ж; **ship's ~** экипа́ж су́дна.
6 (*mil.*) ро́та; **~ officer** мла́дший офице́р; **~ sergeant major** старшина́ ро́ты.

comparable /ˈkɒmpərəb(ə)l/ *adj.* сравни́мый.

comparative /kəmˈpærətɪv/ *adj.*
1 (*proceeding by comparison*) сравни́тельный. **2** (*relative*) относи́тельный; **he is a ~ newcomer** он здесь сравни́тельно неда́вно.
3 (*gram.*) сравни́тельный; (*as n.*): **'better' is the ~ of 'good'** «лу́чший» — сравни́тельная сте́пень от прилага́тельного «хоро́ший».

compare /kəmˈpeə(r)/ *n.* (*liter.*): **beyond ~** вне вся́кого сравне́ния.
● *v.t.* **1** (*assess degree of similarity*) сра́вн|ивать, -и́ть; слич|а́ть, -и́ть; **~ notes with s.o.** обме́н|иваться, -я́ться впечатле́ниями с кем-н. **2** (*assert similarity of*) сра́вн|ивать, -и́ть; **he is not to be ~d with his father** ему́ далеко́ до отца́.
● *v.i.* сра́вн|иваться, -и́ться; **he ~s favourably** (*Br.*), **favorably** (*US*) **with his predecessor** он вы́годно отлича́ется от своего́ предше́ственника.

comparison /kəmˈpærɪs(ə)n/ *n.* сравне́ние; **make a ~** пров|оди́ть, -ести́ сравне́ние; **there is no ~ between them** их нельзя́ сра́внивать; **in, by ~ with** по сравне́нию с+*i.*; (*gram.*): **degrees of ~** сте́пени сравне́ния.

compartment /kəmˈpɑːtmənt/ *n.* (*railway*) купе́ (*indecl.*); (*of ship*) отсе́к.

compartmentalize /ˌkɒmpɑːtˈmentəˌlaɪz/ *v.t.* раздроб|ля́ть, -и́ть.

compass /ˈkʌmpəs/ *n.* **1** (*mariner's*) ко́мпас; (*surveying ~*) буссо́ль; **points of the ~** стра́ны све́та. **2** (*geom., also* **pair of ~es**) ци́ркуль (*m.*). **3** (*extent, range*): **~ of a voice** диапазо́н го́лоса; **within the ~ of a lifetime** в преде́лах одно́й жи́зни; **beyond my ~** вне моего́ понима́ния; вне мои́х возмо́жностей.

compassion /kəmˈpæʃ(ə)n/ *n.* сострада́ние; **show ~ to s.o.** проявл|я́ть, -и́ть сострада́ние к кому́-н.

compassionate /kəmˈpæʃənət/ *adj.* сострада́тельный; **~ leave** о́тпуск по семе́йным обстоя́тельствам.

compatibility /kəmˌpætəˈbɪlɪtɪ/ *n.* совмести́мость.

compatible /kəmˈpætəb(ə)l/ *adj.* совмести́мый.

compatriot /kəmˈpætrɪət/ *n.* соотéчественник.

compel /kəmˈpel/ *v.t.* (**compelled, compelling**) заст|авля́ть, -а́вить; прин|ужда́ть, -у́дить; **~ attention** прико́в|ывать, -а́ть внима́ние.

compelling /kəmˈpelɪŋ/ *adj.* непреодоли́мый, неотрази́мый; (*fascinating*) захва́тывающий.

compendia /kəmˈpendɪə/ *pl. of* ⇒**compendium**

compendious /kəmˈpendɪəs/ *adj.* конспекти́вный.

compendi|um /kəmˈpendɪəm/ *n.* (*pl.* **~ums** *or* **~a**) компе́ндиум, консп́ект; **~ of games** (*Br.*) игроте́ка.

compensate /ˈkɒmpenˌseɪt/ *v.t. & i.* компенси́ровать (*impf., pf.*) (*кому что*); **he was ~d for his injuries** он получи́л компенса́цию за свои́ уве́чья; (*tech.*) компенси́ровать (*impf., pf.*).

compensation /ˌkɒmpenˈseɪʃ(ə)n/ *n.* компенса́ция (*also psych.*); **pay ~** выпла́чивать, вы́платить компенса́цию; **in ~ for the loss** в компенса́цию за понесённые убы́тки; (*tech.*) компенса́ция.

compensatory /-ˈpensətərɪ/, /-ˈseɪtərɪ/ *adj.* компенси́рующий (*also psych.*); компенсацио́нный.

compère /ˈkɒmpeə(r)/ *n.* (*Br.*) (*theatr.*) конферансье́ (*m. indecl.*); (*radio, TV*) веду́щий.
● *v.t. & i.* конфери́ровать (*impf., pf.*).

compete /kəmˈpiːt/ *v.i.* (*vie*) конкури́ровать (*impf.*); сопе́рничать (*impf.*); **~ with, against s.o. for something** конкури́ровать (*impf.*) с кем-н. из-за чего́-н.; (*in sport*) состяза́ться (*impf.*).

competenc|e /ˈkɒmpɪt(ə)ns/, **-y** /ˈkɒmpɪtənsɪ/ *nn.* (*ability, authority*) уме́ние, компете́нтность.

competent /ˈkɒmpɪt(ə)nt/ *adj.* компете́нтный.

competition /ˌkɒmpəˈtɪʃ(ə)n/ *n.*
1 (*rivalry*) сопе́рничество, конкуре́нция; **they are in ~ with us** они́ конкури́руют с на́ми. **2** (*contest*) состяза́ние, соревнова́ние.
3 (*examination*) ко́нкурс; ко́нкурсный экза́мен.

competitive /kəmˈpetɪtɪv/ *adj.* (*person*) честолюби́вый; **~ examination** ко́нкурсный экза́мен; **~ prices** конкурентоспосо́бные це́ны; **~ spirit** боево́й дух.

competitiveness /kəmˈpetɪtɪvnɪs/ *n.* (*of person*) дух сопе́рничества; (*of prices*) конкурентоспосо́бность.

competitor /kəmˈpetɪtə(r)/ *n.* конкуре́нт.

compilation /ˌkɒmpɪˈleɪʃ(ə)n/ *n.* (*act*) собира́ние, компили́рование; (*result*) сбо́рник, собра́ние, компиля́ция.

compile /kəmˈpaɪl/ *v.t.* соб|ира́ть, -ра́ть; сост|авля́ть, -а́вить; компили́ровать (*impf., pf.*).

compiler /kəmˈpaɪlə(r)/ *n.* состави́тель (*m.*); компиля́тор.

complacency /kəmˈpleɪsənsɪ/ *n.* самодово́льство.

complacent /kəmˈpleɪs(ə)nt/ *adj.* самодово́льный.

complain /kəmˈpleɪn/ *v.i.* **1** (*express dissatisfaction*) жа́ловаться, по-. **2** (*to an authority*) под|ава́ть, -а́ть жа́лобу (на+*a.*); жа́ловаться, по- (на+*a.*).
3: **he ~s of frequent headaches** он жа́луется на ча́стые головны́е бо́ли.

complainant /kəmˈpleɪnənt/ *n.* (*leg.*) жа́лобщик, исте́ц.

complainer /kəmˈpleɪnə(r)/ *n.* ны́тик (*c.g.*).

complaint /kəmˈpleɪnt/ *n.* жа́лоба; причи́на недово́льства; **lodge, make a ~** под|ава́ть, -а́ть жа́лобу; (*ailment*) неду́г, боле́знь.

complaisance /kəmˈpleɪzəns/ *n.* обходи́тельность, услу́жливость.

complaisant /kəmˈpleɪz(ə)nt/ *adj.* обходи́тельный, услу́жливый.

complement /ˈkɒmplɪmənt/ *n.* **1** (*that which completes*) дополне́ние.
2 (*muster*) ли́чный соста́в, по́лный компле́кт. **3** (*gram.*) дополне́ние.
● *v.t.* доп|олня́ть, -о́лнить.

complementary /ˌkɒmplɪˈmentərɪ/ *adj.* дополни́тельный; **~ medicine** альтернати́вная медици́на.

complete /kəmˈpliːt/ *adj.* **1** (*whole*) по́лный; **~ edition** по́лное изда́ние; **car ~ with tyres** (*Br.*), **tires** (*US*) автомоби́ль, снабжённый ши́нами.
2 (*finished*) зако́нченный, завершённый; **when will the work be ~?** когда́ бу́дет завершён э́тот труд?
3 (*thorough*) соверше́нный; **he is a ~ stranger to me** он мне соверше́нно не знако́м; **a ~ surprise** по́лная/соверше́нная неожи́данность.
● *v.t.* зак|а́нчивать, -о́нчить; заверш|а́ть, -и́ть; (*fill in*) зап|олня́ть, -о́лнить.

completely /kəmˈpliːtlɪ/ *adv.* соверше́нно, по́лностью.

completeness /kəmˈpliːtnɪs/ *n.* полнота́; зако́нченность.

completion /kəmˈpliːʃ(ə)n/ *n.* заверше́ние, оконча́ние; (*of a form*) заполне́ние.

complex /ˈkɒmpleks/ *n.* (*abstr. or physical whole, also psych.*) ко́мплекс.
● *adj.* сло́жный, ко́мплексный; (*gram.*): **~ sentence** сложноподчинённое предложе́ние.

complexion /kəmˈplekʃ(ə)n/ *n.* **1** (*of face*) цвет лица́. **2** (*character, aspect*) вид, аспе́кт; **that puts a different ~ on the matter** э́то представля́ет де́ло в ино́м све́те.

complexity /kəmˈpleksɪtɪ/ *n.* сло́жность.

compliance /kəmˈplaɪəns/ *n.* усту́пчивость, пода́тливость, послуша́ние; **in ~ with his orders** согла́сно его́ прика́зам.

compliant /kəm'plaɪənt/ *adj.* усту́пчивый, пода́тливый.

complicate /'kɒmplɪˌkeɪt/ *v.t.* осложн|я́ть, -и́ть; усложн|я́ть, -и́ть.

complicated /'kɒmplɪˌkeɪtɪd/ *adj.* сло́жный.

complication /ˌkɒmplɪ'keɪʃ(ə)n/ *n.* (*complexity*) сло́жность; (*complicating circumstance*) осложне́ние; (*med.*): **~s set in** после́довали осложне́ния.

complicity /kəm'plɪsɪtɪ/ *n.* соуча́стие.

compliment /'kɒmplɪmənt/ *n.* **1** (*praise*) комплиме́нт; похвала́; **a back-handed ~** сомни́тельный комплиме́нт. **2** (*pl., greetings*) приве́т, поздравле́ние; **~s of the season** нового́дние (*и т.п.*) поздравле́ния; **with the author's ~s** с наилу́чшими пожела́ниями от а́втора.

● *v.t.* говори́ть (*impf.*) комплиме́нты + *d.* (*по поводу чего*); хвали́ть, по- (за + *a.*).

complimentary /ˌkɒmplɪ'mentərɪ/ *adj.* **1** (*laudatory*) похва́льный, ле́стный. **2**: **~ copy** (*of book*) беспла́тный экземпля́р; **~ ticket** контрама́рка, пригласи́тельный биле́т.

compline /'kɒmplɪn/, /-plaɪn/ *n.* повече́рие.

comply /kəm'plaɪ/ *v.i.*: **~ with** уступ|а́ть, -и́ть (+ *d.*); слу́шаться, по- (+ *g.*); подчин|я́ться, -и́ться (+ *d.*).

component /kəm'pəʊnənt/ *n.* компоне́нт; составна́я часть; дета́ль.

● *adj.* составно́й, составля́ющий.

comport /kəm'pɔːt/ *v.t. & i.*: **~ o.s.** держа́ться (*impf.*); вести́ (*det.*) себя́.

comportment /kəm'pɔːtmənt/ *n.* мане́ра держа́ться; поведе́ние.

compose /kəm'pəʊz/ *v.t. & i.* **1** (*make up, constitute*) сост|авля́ть, -а́вить; компонова́ть, с-; **the party was ~d of teachers** гру́ппа состоя́ла из учителе́й. **2** (*liter., mus.*) сочин|я́ть, -и́ть; **~ a picture** сост|авля́ть, -а́вить компози́цию карти́ны. **3** (*control, assuage*): **~ o.s.** успок|а́иваться, -о́иться; **a ~d manner** сде́ржанная мане́ра. **4** (*typ.*) наб|ира́ть, -ра́ть.

composedly /kəm'pəʊzɪdlɪ/ *adv.* сде́ржанно, споко́йно.

composer /kəm'pəʊzə(r)/ *n.* (*mus.*) компози́тор.

composite /'kɒmpəzɪt/, /-ˌzaɪt/ *n.* составно́й предме́т.

● *adj.* составно́й; (*bot.*) сложноцве́тный; (*math.*) сло́жный.

composition /ˌkɒmpə'zɪʃ(ə)n/ *n.* **1** (*act or art of composing*) сочине́ние, составле́ние; **a work of his own ~** произведе́ние его́ со́бственного сочине́ния. **2** (*liter. or mus. work*) произведе́ние, сочине́ние. **3** (*school exercise*) сочине́ние. **4** (*arrangement*) компози́ция, расстано́вка. **5** (*make-up*) соста́в; **~ of the soil** соста́в по́чвы. **6** (*artificial substance*) смесь, соедине́ние, спла́в. **7** (*typ.*) набо́р.

compositor /kəm'pɒzɪtə(r)/ *n.* набо́рщик.

compos mentis /ˌkɒmpɒs 'mentɪs/ *adj.* в здра́вом уме́.

compost /'kɒmpɒst/ *n.* компо́ст.

● *v.t.* (*make into ~*) гото́вить (*impf.*) компо́ст из + *g.*; (*treat with ~*) уд|обря́ть, -о́брить компо́стом.

composure /kəm'pəʊʒə(r)/ *n.* споко́йствие.

compote /'kɒmpəʊt/, /-pɒt/ *n.* компо́т.

compound[1] /'kɒmpaʊnd/ *n.* (*enclosure*) огоро́женное ме́сто.

compound[2] /'kɒmpaʊnd/ *n.* (*mixture*) смесь; (*gram.*) сло́жное сло́во; (*chem.*) соедине́ние.

● *adj.* составно́й, сло́жный; **~ interest** сло́жные проце́нты; **~ fracture** осложнённый перело́м.

compound[3] /kəm'paʊnd/ *v.t.* **1** (*mix, combine*) сме́ш|ивать, -а́ть; соедин|я́ть, -и́ть; **a dish ~ed of many ingredients** блю́до, пригото́вленное из мно́гих составны́х часте́й. **2** (*aggravate*) отягча́ть (*impf.*).

comprehend /ˌkɒmprɪ'hend/ *v.t.* (*understand*) пон|има́ть, -я́ть; пост|ига́ть, -и́гнуть.

comprehensible /ˌkɒmprɪ'hensɪb(ə)l/ *adj.* поня́тный, постижи́мый.

comprehension /ˌkɒmprɪ'henʃ(ə)n/ *n.* (*understanding*) понима́ние, постиже́ние.

comprehensive /ˌkɒmprɪ'hensɪv/ *adj.* (*of wide scope*) всеобъе́млющий, исче́рпывающий; **~ school** (*Br.*) общеобразова́тельная шко́ла со ста́ршими кла́ссами.

comprehensiveness /ˌkɒmprɪ'hensɪvnɪs/ *n.* всеобъе́млемость; широта́ охва́та.

compress[1] /'kɒmpres/ *n.* (*to relieve inflammation*) компре́сс.

compress[2] /kəm'pres/ *v.t.* (*physically*) сж|има́ть, -ать; сда́в|ливать, -и́ть; **~ed air** сжа́тый во́здух; (*make more concise*) сж|има́ть, -ать; сокра|ща́ть, -ти́ть.

compressible /kəm'presɪb(ə)l/ *adj.* сжима́ющийся.

compression /kəm'preʃ(ə)n/ *n.* (*lit.*) сжа́тие, сда́вливание; (*fig.*) сжа́тие, сокраще́ние; (*tech., comput.*) компре́ссия.

compressor /kəm'presə(r)/ *n.* компре́ссор.

comprise /kəm'praɪz/ *v.t.* включ|а́ть, -и́ть в себя́; состоя́ть (*impf.*) из + *g.*

compromise /'kɒmprəˌmaɪz/ *n.* компроми́сс.

● *v.t.* (*expose to discredit*) компромети́ровать; (*endanger*) ста́вить, по- под угро́зу.

● *v.i.* пойти́ (*pf.*) на компроми́сс; (*reach ~*) при|ходи́ть, -йти́ к компроми́ссу.

comptroller /kən'trəʊlə(r)/ = **controller**

compulsion /kəm'pʌlʃ(ə)n/ *n.* принужде́ние; **on, under ~** по принужде́нию.

compulsive /kəm'pʌlsɪv/ *adj.* (*irresistible*) непреодоли́мый; (*inveterate*) зая́длый; **a ~ liar** патологи́ческий враль.

compulsoriness /kəm'pʌlsərɪnɪs/ *n.* обяза́тельность.

compulsory /kəm'pʌlsərɪ/ *adj.* обяза́тельный, принуди́тельный; **~ measures** принуди́тельные ме́ры; **~ military service** во́инская пови́нность.

compunction /kəm'pʌŋkʃ(ə)n/ *n.* угрызе́ния (*nt. pl.*) со́вести; раска́яние; **without ~** без сожале́ния.

computable /ˌkɒm'pjuːtəb(ə)l/, /'kɒm-/ *adj.* исчисли́мый.

computation /ˌkɒmpjuː'teɪʃ(ə)n/ *n.* вычисле́ние.

compute /kəm'pjuːt/ *v.t. & i.* вычисля́ть, вы́числить.

computer /kəm'pjuːtə(r)/ *n.* (*person*) счётчик; (*machine*) электро́нно-вычисли́тельная маши́на (*abbr.* ЭВМ); компью́тер; **IBM-compatible ~** ИБМ-совмести́мый компью́тер; **laptop ~** портати́вный компью́тер; **~ dating** подбо́р супру́гов с по́мощью ЭВМ; (*coll.*) «электро́нная сва́ха»; **~ game** компью́терная игра́; **~ graphics** компью́терная гра́фика; **~ literate** владе́ющий основны́ми компью́терными на́выками; **~ programmer** программи́ст (*fem.* -ка); **~ programming** программи́рование; **~ science** вычисли́тельная те́хника.

● *cpds.* **~-aided design** *n.* автоматизи́рованное проекти́рование; **~-aided learning** *n.* маши́нное обуче́ние; **~-assisted** *adj.* автоматизи́рованный.

computerization /kəmˌpjuːtəraɪ'zeɪʃ(ə)n/ *n.* компьютериза́ция.

computerize /kəm'pjuːtəˌraɪz/ *v.t.* компьютеризова́ть (*impf., pf.*); осна|ща́ть, -сти́ть компью́терами.

comrade /'kɒmreɪd/, /-rɪd/ *n.* това́рищ; **~-in-arms** сора́тник.

comradely /'kɒmreɪdlɪ/, /-rɪdlɪ/ *adj.* това́рищеский.

comradeship /'kɒmreɪdʃɪp/, /-rɪdʃɪp/ *n.* това́рищество.

con[1] /kɒn/ *see* ⇒**pro**[1]

con[2] /kɒn/ *v.t.* (**conned, conning**) (*sl., dupe*) над|ува́ть, -у́ть; **~ man** моше́нник, жу́лик.

concatenation /kɒnˌkætɪ'neɪʃ(ə)n/ *n.* сцепле́ние, связь; **~ of circumstances** стече́ние обстоя́тельств.

concave /'kɒnkeɪv/ *adj.* во́гнутый.

concavity /kɒn'kævɪtɪ/ *n.* во́гнутость.

concavo-concave /kɒnˌkeɪvəʊ'kɒnkeɪv/ *adj.* двояково́гнутый.

concavo-convex /kɒnˌkeɪvəʊ'kɒnveks/ *adj.* во́гнуто-вы́пуклый.

conceal /kən'siːl/ *v.t.* скр|ыва́ть, -ы́ть; (*keep secret*) ута́|ивать, -и́ть.

concealment /kən'siːlmənt/ *n.* сокры́тие, ута́ивание; **he remained in ~** он продолжа́л скрыва́ться.

concede /kən'siːd/ *v.t.* уступ|а́ть, -и́ть;

~ a point уступ|áть, -и́ть по одномý пýнкту; **the candidate ~d the election** кандидáт признáл себя́ побеждённым на вы́борах; (*sport*): **he ~d ten points to his opponent** он дал своемý проти́внику фóру в дéсять очкóв.

conceit /kən'si:t/ *n.* (*vanity*) самомнéние, самонадéянность, тщеслáвие, зазнáйство.

conceited /kən'si:tɪd/ *adj.* самонадéянный, зазнáвшийся.

conceivabl|e /kən'si:vəb(ə)l/ *adj.* мы́слимый, постижи́мый; **he may ~y be right** не исключенó, что он прáв.

conceive /kən'si:v/ *v.t.* **1** (*form in the mind, imagine*) задýм|ывать, -ать; **~ a dislike for** невзлюби́ть (*pf.*), **I ~ that there may be difficulties** я допускáю, что мóгут встрéтиться трýдности. **2** (*formulate*) выражáть, вы́разить; **a letter ~d in simple language** письмó, напи́санное прóстым языкóм. **3** (*become pregnant with*) зач|инáть, -áть; **she ~d a child** онá зачалá ребёнка.

● *v.i.* зач|инáть, -áть, заберéменеть (*pf.*).

concentrate /'kɒnsən,treɪt/ *n.* (*of product*) концентрáт.

● *v.t.* **1** (*bring together, focus*) сосредотóчи|вать, -ть; концентри́ровать, с-. **2** (*increase strength of*) концентри́ровать, с-; **a ~d solution** концентри́рованный раствóр; **~d food** концентрáты (*m. pl.*).

● *v.i.* сосредотóчи|ваться, -ться; концентри́роваться, с-; **he ~d on his work** он сосредотóчился на своéй рабóте.

concentration /,kɒnsən'treɪʃ(ə)n/ *n.* **1** (*chem.*) концентрáция, крéпость. **2** (*of troops etc.*) сосредотóчение, концентрáция; **~ camp** концентрациóнный лáгерь, концлáгерь (*m.*). **3** (*of attention etc.*) сосредотóченность.

concentric /kən'sentrɪk/ *adj.* концентри́ческий.

concept /'kɒnsept/ *n.* поня́тие, концéпция.

conception /kən'sepʃ(ə)n/ *n.* **1** (*notion*) концéпция, поня́тие; **I have no ~ of what he means** поня́тия не имéю, что он хóчет э́тим сказáть. **2** (*physiol.*) зачáтие; **Immaculate C~** непорóчное зачáтие.

conceptual /kən'septjʊəl/ *adj.* концептуáльный.

conceptualism /kən'septjʊə,lɪz(ə)m/ *n.* концептуали́зм.

concern /kən'sɜ:n/ *n.* **1** (*affair*) отношéние, касáтельство; **it is no ~ of mine** э́то меня́ не касáется. **2** (*business*) концéрн, предприя́тие; **a going ~** дéйствующее предприя́тие. **3** (*share*) учáстие, интерéс; **he has a ~ in the enterprise** он учáствует в э́том предприя́тии. **4** (*importance*) вáжность; значи́тельность; **it is a matter of ~ to us all** э́то дéло большóй вáжности для нас всех. **5** (*anxiety*) беспокóйство.

● *v.t.* **1** (*have to do with*) касáться (*impf.*) + *g.*; **~ed** (*involved*) заинтересóванный; **I am not ~ed** э́то меня́ не касáется; **as far as that is ~ed** что касáется э́того; **the parties ~ed** заинтересóванные стóроны; **to whom it may ~** тем, когó э́то касáется. **2** (*cause anxiety to*) беспокóить (*impf.*); **~ed** (*anxious*) озабóченный, обеспокóенный; **I am ~ed about the future** меня́ беспокóит бýдущее; **I am ~ed that he should be heard** я заинтересóван в том, чтóбы егó вы́слушали.

concerning /kən'sɜ:nɪŋ/ *prep.* относи́тельно + *g.*; касáтельно + *g.*; к вопрóсу о + *p.*

concert /'kɒnsət/ *n.* **1** (*agreement*) соглáсие, соглашéние; **he acted in ~ with his colleague** он дéйствовал сообщá со свои́м коллéгой. **2** (*entertainment*) концéрт.

● *cpds.* **~-goer** *n.* люби́тель (*m.*) концéртов; **~-hall** *n.* концéртный зал.

concerted /kən'sɜ:tɪd/ *adj.* совмéстный; **a ~ effort to eradicate poverty** совмéстные уси́лия, напрáвленные на уничтожéние бéдности; **he made a ~ effort to improve the results** он сконцентри́ровал все свои́ уси́лия, чтóбы улучши́ть результáты.

concerti /kən'tʃeətɪ/, /-'tʃɜ:tɪ/ *pl. of* ⇒**concerto**

concertina /,kɒnsə'ti:nə/ *n.* концерти́но, гармóника.

concert|o /kən'tʃeətəʊ/, /-'tʃɜ:təʊ/ *n.* (*pl.* **~os** *or* **~i**) концéрт; **piano ~** концéрт для фортепиáно.

concession /kən'seʃ(ə)n/ *n.* **1** (*yielding; thing yielded*) устýпка; **I did it as a ~ to his feelings** я сдéлал э́то, щадя́ егó чýвства; **as a special ~** идя́ навстрéчу. **2** (*mining etc.*) концéссия. **3** (*preferential rate*) льгóта; (*reduction*) ски́дка.

concessionaire /kən,seʃə'neə(r)/ *n.* концессионéр.

concessionary /kən'seʃ(ə)nərɪ/ *adj.* концессиóнный.

concessive /kən'sesɪv/ *adj.* (*gram.*) уступи́тельный.

conch /kɒŋk/, /kɒntʃ/ *n.* (*pl.* **~s** /kɒŋks/ *or* **~es** /'kɒntʃɪz/) **1** (*shellfish*) моллю́ск. **2** (*shell*) рáковина. **3** (*archit.*) апси́да.

concierge /,kɔ̃sɪ'eəʒ/, /,kɒn-/ *n.* консьéрж (*fem.* -ка).

conciliate /kən'sɪlɪ,eɪt/ *v.t.* (*win over*) распол|агáть, -ожи́ть к себé; (*reconcile*) примир|я́ть, -и́ть.

conciliation /kən,sɪlɪ'eɪʃ(ə)n/ *n.* примирéние.

conciliator /kən'sɪlɪ,eɪtə(r)/ *n.* миротвóрец; посрéдник.

conciliatory /kən'sɪlɪətərɪ/ *adj.* примири́тельный.

concise /kən'saɪs/ *adj.* крáткий, сжáтый.

concis|eness /kən'saɪsnɪs/, **-ion** /kən'sɪʒ(ə)n/ *nn.* крáткость, сжáтость.

conclave /'kɒnkleɪv/ *n.* конклáв; (*fig.*) тáйное совещáние.

conclud|e /kən'klu:d/ *v.t.* **1** (*terminate*) зак|áнчивать, -óнчить; заверш|áть, -и́ть; **to ~e** в заключéние; **~ing** заключи́тельный, завершáющий; (*session etc.*) закр|ывáть, -ы́ть. **2** (*agreement etc.*) заключ|áть, -и́ть. **3** (*infer*) дéлать, с- вы́вод, что...; при|ходи́ть, -йти́ к вы́воду, что....

● *v.i.* (*end*) зак|áнчиваться, -óнчиться; **he ~ed by saying** в заключéние он сказáл.

conclusion /kən'klu:ʒ(ə)n/ *n.* **1** (*end*) окончáние, заключéние, завершéние; **bring to a ~** заверш|áть, -и́ть; дов|оди́ть, ести́ до концá; **in ~** в заключéние. **2** (*of agreement etc.*) заключéние. **3** (*inference*) вы́вод, заключéние; **he jumps to ~s** он дéлает поспéшные вы́воды. **4**: **it was a foregone ~ that he would win** бы́ло предрешенó, что он победи́т.

conclusive /kən'klu:sɪv/ *adj.* решáющий, окончáтельный, убеди́тельный.

conclusiveness /kən'klu:sɪvnɪs/ *n.* окончáтельность, убеди́тельность.

concoct /kən'kɒkt/ *v.t.* (*of drink etc.*) стря́пать, со-; готóвить, при-/с-; (*of story etc.*) стря́пать, со-; сочин|я́ть, -и́ть.

concoction /kən'kɒkʃ(ə)n/ *n.* (*drink etc.*) смесь; (*invention of story*) сочинéние, придýмывание; (*story invented*) вы́думка.

concomitant /kən'kɒmɪt(ə)nt/ *adj.* сопýтствующий.

concord /'kɒnkɔ:d/, /'kɒŋ-/ *n.* соглáсие, соглашéние.

concordance /kən'kɔ:d(ə)ns/, /kəŋ-/ *n.* (*agreement*) соглáсие; (*vocabulary*) указáтель (*библейских изречений и т.п.*).

concordant /kən'kɔ:d(ə)nt/ *adj.* соглáсный, согласýющийся (*both* c + *i.*); (*mus.*) гармони́чный.

concordat /kən'kɔ:dæt/ *n.* конкордáт.

concourse /'kɒnkɔ:s/, /'kɒŋ-/ *n.* (*coming together*) стечéние; (*of railway station*) вестибю́ль (*m.*) вокзáла.

concrete[1] /'kɒnkri:t/, /'kɒŋ-/ *n.* (*building material*) бетóн; **reinforced ~** железобетóн; **~ jungle** бетóнные джýнгл|и (*pl., g.* -ей).

● *v.t.* бетони́ровать (*impf., pf.*).

● *cpd.* **~-mixer** *n.* бетономешáлка.

concrete[2] /'kɒnkri:t/, /'kɒŋ-/ *adj.* конкрéтный; **in the ~** реáльно.

concretion /kən'kri:ʃ(ə)n/ *n.* сращéние, срóсшаяся мáсса; (*med.*) кáмни (*m. pl.*), конкремéнты (*m. pl.*).

concubine /'kɒŋkjʊ,baɪn/ *n.* налóжница.

concur /kən'kɜ:(r)/ *v.i.* (**concurred, concurring**) **1** (*of circumstance etc.*) совп|адáть, -áсть; сходи́ться, сойти́сь. **2** (*agree, consent*) согла|шáться, -си́ться (c + *i.*).

concurrence /kən'kʌr(ə)ns/ *n.* (*of things*) совпадéние, стечéние; (*agreement, consent*) соглáсие.

concurrent /kən'kʌrənt/ *adj.* (*simultaneous, agreeing*) совпада́ющий; (*math.*) сходя́щийся, встреча́ющийся; **∼ly** одновре́ме́нно.

concuss /kən'kʌs/ *v.t.* (*med.*) вызыва́ть, вы́звать сотрясе́ние мо́зга у + *g.*

concussion /kən'kʌʃ(ə)n/ *n.* (*med.*) сотрясе́ние мо́зга.

condemn /kən'dem/ *v.t.* осу|жда́ть, -ди́ть; пригов|а́ривать, -ори́ть; (*blame*) порица́ть (*impf.*); **he was ∼ed to life imprisonment** он был приговорён к пожи́зненному заключе́нию; **∼ed cell** (*Br.*) ка́мера сме́ртника; (*declare unfit for use*) призн|ава́ть, -а́ть неприго́дным; **the building was ∼ed** зда́ние бы́ло при́знано неприго́дным для жилья́; (*doom*) обр|ека́ть, -е́чь; **he was ∼ed to silence** он был обречён на молча́ние.

condemnation /ˌkɒndem'neɪʃ(ə)n/ *n.* осужде́ние; порица́ние; (*of building*) призна́ние него́дным.

condemnatory /ˌkɒndem'neɪtərɪ/ *adj.* осужда́ющий.

condensation /ˌkɒnden'seɪʃ(ə)n/ *n.* (*phys.*) конденса́ция, сгуще́ние, уплотне́ние; (*liquefaction*) сжиже́ние; (*abridgement*) сокраще́ние.

condense /kən'dens/ *v.t.* **1** (*phys.*) конденси́ровать (*impf., pf.*); сгу|ща́ть, -сти́ть; сжи|жа́ть, -ди́ть; **∼d milk** сгущённое молоко́. **2** (*fig.*): **a ∼d account of events** сжа́тый отчёт о собы́тиях.

● *v.i.* (*phys.*) конденси́роваться (*impf., pf.*).

condenser /kən'densə(r)/ *n.* (*tech.*) конденса́тор.

condescend /ˌkɒndɪ'send/ *v.i.* сни|сходи́ть, -зойти́.

condescending /ˌkɒndɪ'sendɪŋ/ *adj.* снисходи́тельный.

condescension /ˌkɒndɪ'senʃ(ə)n/ *n.* снисхожде́ние, снисходи́тельность.

condiment /'kɒndɪmənt/ *n.* припра́ва.

condition /kən'dɪʃ(ə)n/ *n.* **1** (*state*) состоя́ние, положе́ние; **he is in no ∼ to travel** он не в состоя́нии путеше́ствовать. **2** (*fitness*): **the athlete is out of ∼** спортсме́н не в фо́рме. **3** (*pl., circumstances*) усло́вия; обстоя́тельства (*both nt. pl.*). **4** (*requisite, stipulation*) усло́вие; **on ∼ that** ... при усло́вии, что...; **on no ∼** ни при каки́х усло́виях. **5** (*status in life*) положе́ние.

● *v.t.* **1** (*determine, govern*) обусло́в|ливать, -ить; **∼ed reflex** усло́вный рефле́кс. **2** (*of athletes*) тренирова́ть, на-. **3** (*indoctrinate*) приуч|а́ть, -и́ть; **he was ∼ed to obey unquestioningly** его́ приучи́ли беспрекосло́вно подчиня́ться.

conditional /kən'dɪʃən(ə)l/ *adj.* усло́вный, обусло́вленный; **my agreement is ∼ on his coming** я согла́сен при усло́вии, что он придёт; (*gram.*): **the ∼ (mood)** усло́вное наклоне́ние.

conditioner /kən'dɪʃənə(r)/ *n.* (*for hair*) бальза́м для воло́с, кондиционе́р.

condole /kən'dəʊl/ *v.i.* соболе́зновать (*impf.*) (+*d.*); выража́ть, вы́разить соболе́знование.

condolence /kən'dəʊləns/ *n.* (*also pl.*) соболе́знование.

condom /'kɒndɒm/ *n.* презервати́в, кондо́м.

condominium /ˌkɒndə'mɪnɪəm/ *n.* кондоми́ниум.

condone /kən'dəʊn/ *v.t.* про|ща́ть, -сти́ть; смотре́ть (*impf.*) сквозь па́льцы на + *a.*

condor /'kɒndɔː(r)/ *n.* (*zool.*) ко́ндор.

conduce /kən'djuːs/ *v.i.* спосо́бствовать (*impf.*) (+*d.*).

conducive /kən'djuːsɪv/ *adj.* спосо́бствующий; **health is ∼ to happiness** здоро́вье — помо́щник сча́стью.

conduct[1] /'kɒndʌkt/ *n.* **1** (*behaviour*) поведе́ние. **2** (*manner of ∼ing*) веде́ние. **3**: **safe ∼** гара́нтия неприкоснове́нности, охра́нная гра́мота.

conduct[2] /kən'dʌkt/ *v.t.* **1** (*lead, guide*) води́ть (*indet.*), вести́ (*det.*); руководи́ть (*impf.*) +*i.*; **a ∼ed tour** экску́рсия/осмо́тр с ги́дом. **2** (*manage*) вести́ (*det.*); **he ∼s his affairs well** он хорошо́ ведёт свои́ дела́; **∼ an experiment** ста́вить, по- о́пыт; **∼ o.s.** вести́ себя́, держа́ться (*impf.*). **3** (*mus., also v.i.*) дирижи́ровать (*impf.*) (+*i.*). **4** (*phys.*) проводи́ть (*impf.*).

conductance /kən'dʌkt(ə)ns/ *n.* (*tech.*) акти́вная проводи́мость.

conduction /kən'dʌkʃ(ə)n/ *n.* (*tech.*) проводи́мость, конду́кция; **∼ of heat** теплопрово́дность.

conductive /kən'dʌktɪv/ *adj.* (*tech.*) проводя́щий.

conductivity /ˌkɒndʌk'tɪvɪtɪ/ *n.* (*tech.*) (уде́льная) проводи́мость; электропрово́дность.

conductor /kən'dʌktə(r)/ *n.* **1** (*mus.*) дирижёр. **2** (*of bus, tram*) конду́ктор; (*US, of train*) проводни́к. **3** (*phys.*) проводни́к.

conductorship /kən'dʌktəʃɪp/ *n.* (*mus.*) дирижёрство.

conductress /kən'dʌktrɪs/ *n.* (*of bus, tram*) же́нщина-конду́ктор; (*US, of train*) проводни́ца.

conduit /'kɒndɪt/, /-djʊɪt/ *n.* трубопрово́д; водопрово́дная труба́; (*elec.*) изоляцио́нная тру́бка.

cone /kəʊn/ *n.* **1** (*geom.*) ко́нус. **2** (*bot.*) ши́шка. **3** (*for ice-cream*) ва́фельная тру́бочка.

● *cpd.* **∼-shaped** *adj.* конусообра́зный.

coney /'kəʊnɪ/ = **cony**

confabulate /kən'fæbjʊˌleɪt/ *v.i.* бесе́довать (*impf.*).

confabulation /kənˌfæbjʊ'leɪʃ(ə)n/ *n.* обсужде́ние, собесе́дование.

confection /kən'fekʃ(ə)n/ *n.* (*sweetmeat*) сла́дост|и (*pl., g.* -ей), конфе́т|ы (*pl., g.* —).

confectioner /kən'fekʃənə(r)/ *n.* конди́тер.

confectionery /kən'fekʃənərɪ/ *n.* (*wares*) конди́терские изде́лия; (*shop*) конди́терская.

Confederacy /kən'fedərəsɪ/ *n.* (*hist.*) Конфедера́ция.

confederate /kən'fedərət/ *n.* соо́бщник, сою́зник; (*conjurer's*) посо́бник.

● *adj.* сою́зный; (*US hist.*) конфедерати́вный.

confederation /kənˌfedə'reɪʃ(ə)n/ *n.* сою́з; федера́ция; конфедера́ция.

confer[1] /kən'fɜː(r)/ *v.t.* (**conferred, conferring**) (*grant*) (**on s.o.** +*d.*) присв|а́ивать, -о́ить; прису|жда́ть, -ди́ть; дарова́ть (*impf.*); **∼ a degree** (*acad.*) прису|жда́ть, -ди́ть учёную сте́пень; **∼ a title** присв|а́ивать, -о́ить ти́тул; **∼ a favour** (*Br.*), **favor** (*US*) ок|а́зывать, -аза́ть услу́гу.

confer[2] /kən'fɜː(r)/ *v.i.* (**conferred, conferring**) (*consult*) совеща́ться (*impf.*) (с + *i.*); сове́товаться, по- (с + *i.*).

conference /'kɒnfərəns/ *n.* конфере́нция, совеща́ние; **he is in ∼** он на совеща́нии.

● *cpds.* **∼ hall** *n.* конфере́нц-за́л; **∼-table** *n.* стол для заседа́ний; стол перегово́ров.

conferment /kən'fɜːmənt/ *n.* присвое́ние, присужде́ние.

confess /kən'fes/ *v.t. & i.* **1** призн|ава́ть, -а́ть; призн|ава́ться, -а́ться (*or* созн|ава́ться, -а́ться) (в чём); **I ∼ I haven't read it** призна́юсь, я э́того не чита́л; **he ∼ed to the crime** он призна́лся в преступле́нии; **a ∼ed murderer** созна́вшийся уби́йца. **2** (*eccl.*) (*hear confession of*) испове́д|овать, -ать; (**∼ one's sins**) испове́д|оваться, -аться.

confession /kən'feʃ(ə)n/ *n.* **1** (*avowal*) призна́ние, созна́ние. **2** (*profession of faith*) испове́дание. **3** (*denomination*) вероиспове́дание. **4** (*to a priest*) и́споведь.

confessional /kən'feʃən(ə)l/ *n.* исповеда́льня.

● *adj.* исповеда́льный.

confessor /kən'fesə(r)/ *n.* (*priest*) испове́дник, духовни́к.

confetti /kən'fetɪ/ *n.* конфетти́ (*nt. indecl.*).

confidant, -e /ˌkɒnfɪ'dænt/, /'kɒn-/ *nn.* напе́рсни|к (*fem.* -ца); дове́ренное лицо́.

confide /kən'faɪd/ *v.t.* **1** (*entrust*) поруч|а́ть, -и́ть; вв|еря́ть, -е́рить. **2** (*impart*) сообщ|а́ть, -и́ть; пов|еря́ть, -е́рить; вв|еря́ть, -е́рить; **he ∼d his secret to me** он дове́рил мне свою́ та́йну.

● *v.i.*: **∼ in** (*impart secrets to*) дели́ться, по- (*своими планами и т.п.*) + *i.*

confidence /'kɒnfɪd(ə)ns/ *n.* **1** (*confiding of secrets*) дове́рие; **I tell you this in ∼** я говорю́ вам э́то конфиденциа́льно (*or* по секре́ту); **take s.o. into one's ∼** дов|еря́ть, -е́рить кому́-н. свои́ та́йны. **2** (*secret*)

C

та́йна; конфиденциа́льное сообще́ние. **3** (*trust*): **I have ~ in him** я уве́рен в нём; я ве́рю в него́; **he enjoys her ~** он по́льзуется её дове́рием; **he gained her ~** он завоева́л её дове́рие. **4** (*certainty, assurance*) уве́ренность; самоуве́ренность; **he spoke with ~** он говори́л с уве́ренностью. **5**: **~ trick** моше́нничество; **~ trickster** моше́нник.

confident /'kɒnfɪd(ə)nt/ *adj.* уве́ренный; **I am ~ of success** я уве́рен в успе́хе; (*self-confident*) самоуве́ренный.

confidential /,kɒnfɪ'denʃ(ə)l/ *adj.* конфиденциа́льный, секре́тный; **a ~ tone** довери́тельный тон.

confidentiality /,kɒnfɪ,denʃɪ'ælɪtɪ/ *n.* конфиденциа́льность.

configuration /kən,fɪgjʊ'reɪʃ(ə)n/, /-gə'reɪʃ(ə)n/ *n.* конфигура́ция.

confine¹ /'kɒnfaɪn/ *n.* (*usu. pl.*) грани́цы (*f. pl.*), преде́лы (*m. pl.*).

confine² /kən'faɪn/ *v.t.* ограни́чи|вать, -ть; заключ|а́ть, -и́ть; **a bird ~d in a cage** пти́ца, поса́женная в кле́тку; **~ yourself to the subject** приде́рживайтесь те́мы; **be ~d** (*of childbirth*) разреш|а́ться, -и́ться от бре́мени, ро|жа́ть, -ди́ть.

confinement /kən'faɪnmənt/ *n.* **1** (*restriction*) ограниче́ние. **2** (*imprisonment*) заключе́ние; **solitary ~** одино́чное заключе́ние. **3** (*childbirth*) ро́д|ы (*pl., g.* -ов); **she had a difficult ~** у неё бы́ли тяжёлые ро́ды.

confirm /kən'fɜ:m/ *v.t.* **1** (*strengthen, e.g. power*) подтвер|жда́ть, -ди́ть; подкреп|ля́ть, -и́ть. **2** (*establish as certain*) утвер|жда́ть, -ди́ть; подтвер|жда́ть, -ди́ть; **the report is ~ed** сообще́ние подтвержда́ется; **his appointment was ~ed** его́ назначе́ние бы́ло утверждено́. **3** (*of person*): **I was ~ed in this belief by the fact that ...** меня́ укрепи́л в э́том убежде́нии тот фа́кт, что...; **a ~ed drunkard** го́рький пья́ница; **a ~ed bachelor** убеждённый холостя́к. **4** (*relig.*) конфирмова́ть (*impf., pf.*).

confirmation /,kɒnfə'meɪʃ(ə)n/ *n.* **1** (*of report etc.*) подтвержде́ние, утвержде́ние. **2** (*relig.*) конфирма́ция.

confiscate /'kɒnfɪ,skeɪt/ *v.t.* конфискова́ть (*impf., pf.*).

confiscation /,kɒnfɪ'skeɪʃ(ə)n/ *n.* конфиска́ция.

conflagration /,kɒnflə'greɪʃ(ə)n/ *n.* большо́й пожа́р.

conflate /kən'fleɪt/ *v.t.* объедин|я́ть, -и́ть (*ра́зные вариа́нты те́кста и т.п.*).

conflation /kən'fleɪʃ(ə)n/ *n.* соедине́ние/объедине́ние ра́зных вариа́нтов те́кста.

conflict¹ /'kɒnflɪkt/ *n.* конфли́кт, противоре́чие; **~ of jurisdiction** колли́зия прав.

conflict² /kən'flɪkt/ *v.t.* быть в конфли́кте (с+*i.*); противоре́чить (*impf.*) (+*d.*).

confluence /'kɒnfluəns/ *n.* слия́ние; **at the ~ of two rivers** при слия́нии двух рек.

confluent /'kɒnfluənt/ *adj.* слива́ющийся.

conform /kən'fɔ:m/ *v.i.* (*adapt*) приспос|а́бливаться, -о́биться (к+*d.*); (*comply*) подчин|я́ться, -и́ться (+*d.*).

conformation /,kɒnfɔ:'meɪʃ(ə)n/ *n.* структу́ра, устро́йство.

conformism /kən'fɔ:mɪz(ə)m/ *n.* конформи́зм.

conformist /kən'fɔ:mɪst/ *n.* конформи́ст.

conformity /kən'fɔ:mɪtɪ/ *n.* (*correspondence, accordance*) соотве́тствие; (*compliance*) подчине́ние; (*conformism*) конформи́зм.

confound /kən'faʊnd/ *v.t.* **1** (*amaze*) пора|жа́ть, -зи́ть; потряс|а́ть, -ти́. **2** (*confuse*) сме́ш|ивать, -а́ть; спу́т|ывать, -ать. **3** (*as expletive*): **~ it!** чёрт возьми́!; **he is a ~ed nuisance** он ужа́сно доку́члив.

confront /kən'frʌnt/ *v.t.* **1** (*bring face to face*) ста́вить, по- лицо́м к лицу́ (с+*i.*). **2** (*face*) смотре́ть (*impf.*) в лицо́ +*d.*; встр|еча́ть, -е́тить; **many difficulties ~ed us** мы столкну́лись со мно́гими тру́дностями.

confrontation /,kɒnfrʌn'teɪʃ(ə)n/ *n.* конфронта́ция.

confuse /kən'fju:z/ *v.t.* **1** (*throw into confusion*) смущ|а́ть, -ти́ть; прив|оди́ть, -ести́ в замеша́тельство; **his question ~d me** его́ вопро́с смути́л меня́; **the situation is ~d** положе́ние запу́танное. **2** (*mistake*) спу́т|ывать, -ать; сме́ш|ивать, -а́ть; **he ~d Austria with Australia** он спу́тал А́встрию с Австра́лией.

confusion /kən'fju:ʒ(ə)n/ *n.* смуще́ние, замеша́тельство; (*mix-up*) пу́таница, беспоря́док.

confutation /,kɒnfju:'teɪʃ(ə)n/ *n.* опроверже́ние.

confute /kən'fju:t/ *v.t.* опров|ерга́ть, -е́ргнуть.

congeal /kən'dʒi:l/ *v.t.* замор|а́живать, -о́зить; сгу|ща́ть, -сти́ть.

● *v.i.* свёр|тываться, -ну́ться; сгу|ща́ться, -сти́ться; заст|ыва́ть, -ы́ть.

congenial /kən'dʒi:nɪəl/ *adj.* бли́зкий по ду́ху; **a ~ companion** прия́тный спу́тник; **a ~ climate** благоприя́тный кли́мат; **~ employment** рабо́та по душе́.

congeniality /kən,dʒi:nɪ'ælɪtɪ/ *n.* конгениа́льность; духо́вная бли́зость.

congenital /kən'dʒenɪt(ə)l/ *adj.*: **~ defect** врождённый дефе́кт; **~ idiot** идио́т от рожде́ния.

conger /'kɒŋgə(r)/ (*also* **~ eel**) морско́й у́горь.

congeries /kən'dʒɪəri:z/, /-'dʒerɪ,i:z/ *n.* (*pl.* **~**) ку́ча, гру́да.

congested /kən'dʒestɪd/ *adj.* перенаселённый; перегру́женный; (*of street*) запру́женный; (*med.*) перепо́лненный кро́вью; засто́йный.

congestion /kən'dʒestʃ(ə)n/ *n.* перенаселённость; перегру́женность; (*med.*) гипереми́я, засто́й.

conglomerate¹ /kən'glɒmərət/ *n.* конгломера́т (*also geol.*).

● *adj.* конгломера́тный.

conglomerate² /kən'glɒmə,reɪt/ *v.t. & i.* соб|ира́ть(ся), -ра́ть(ся); ск|а́пливать(ся), -опи́ться.

conglomeration /kən,glɒmə'reɪʃ(ə)n/ *n.* конгломера́т.

Congo /'kɒŋgəʊ/ *n.* Ко́нго (*indecl.*).

Congolese /,kɒŋgə'li:z/ *n.* (*person*) конголе́з|ец (*fem.* -ка).

● *adj.* конголе́зский.

congratulate /kən'grætjʊ,leɪt/ *v.t.* поздр|авля́ть, -а́вить (*кого с чем*).

congratulation /kən,grætjʊ'leɪʃ(ə)n/ *n.* поздравле́ние; **~s!** поздравля́ю!; **letter of ~** поздрави́тельное письмо́.

congratulatory /kən'grætjʊlətərɪ/ *adj.* поздрави́тельный.

congregate /'kɒŋgrɪ,geɪt/ *v.t.* соб|ира́ть, -ра́ть.

● *v.i.* соб|ира́ться, -ра́ться; сходи́ться, сойти́сь.

congregation /,kɒŋgrɪ'geɪʃ(ə)n/ *n.* (*assembly*) собра́ние; (*in church*) прихожа́не (*m. pl.*), па́ства.

congress /'kɒŋgres/ *n.* **1** (*organized meeting*) конгре́сс, съезд. **2** (*pol., hist.*) конгре́сс; **C~** (*US*) конгре́сс США; **C~ of Vienna** Ве́нский конгре́сс.

● *cpds.* **~man** *n.* член конгре́сса, конгрессме́н; **~woman** *n.* же́нщина-член конгре́сса.

congruence /'kɒŋgrʊəns/ *n.* согласо́ванность, соотве́тствие.

congruent /'kɒŋgrʊənt/ *adj.* соотве́тствующий, подходя́щий; (*geom.*) конгру-э́нтный.

congruity /,kɒŋ'gru:ɪtɪ/ *n.* соотве́тствие.

congruous /'kɒŋgrʊəs/ *adj.* соотве́тствующий, подходя́щий.

conic /'kɒnɪk/ *adj.* кони́ческий, ко́нусный; **~ section** кони́ческое сече́ние.

conical /'kɒnɪk(ə)l/ *adj.* кони́ческий, ко́нусный.

conifer /'kɒnɪfə(r)/, /'kəʊn-/ *n.* хво́йное де́рево.

coniferous /kə'nɪfərəs/ *adj.* хво́йный, шишконо́сный.

conjectural /kən'dʒektʃər(ə)l/ *adj.* предположи́тельный.

conjecture /kən'dʒektʃə(r)/ *n.* предположе́ние, дога́дка.

● *v.t. & i.* предпол|ага́ть, -ожи́ть; гада́ть (*impf.*).

conjoin /kən'dʒɔɪn/ *v.t. & i.* соедин|я́ть(ся), -и́ть(ся); сочета́ть(ся) (*impf., pf.*).

conjoint /kən'dʒɔɪnt/ *adj.* соединённый, объединённый.

conjugal /'kɒndʒʊg(ə)l/ *adj.* супру́жеский, бра́чный; **~ rights** супру́жеские права́.

conjugate /'kɒndʒʊ,geɪt/ *v.t.* спряга́ть, про-.

conjugation /ˌkɒndʒʊˈgeɪʃ(ə)n/ *n.* спряже́ние.

conjunction /kənˈdʒʌŋkʃ(ə)n/ *n.* **1** (*union*) соедине́ние, связь; **in ~ with** совме́стно/сообща́ с+*i.*; **~ of circumstances** стече́ние обстоя́тельств; **~ of events** совпаде́ние собы́тий. **2** (*gram.*) сою́з.

conjunctivitis /kənˌdʒʌŋktɪˈvaɪtɪs/ *n.* конъюнктиви́т.

conjuncture /kənˈdʒʌŋktʃə(r)/ *n.* конъюнкту́ра; стече́ние обстоя́тельств.

conjur|e /ˈkʌndʒə(r)/ *v.t. & i.* **1** (*evoke by magic spell*) вызыва́ть, вы́звать. **2** (*fig.*): **~e up** вызыва́ть, вы́звать в воображе́нии; **his is a name to ~e with** он влия́тельное лицо́; его́ и́мя име́ет волше́бную си́лу. **3** (*perform tricks*) пока́з|ывать, -а́ть фо́кусы; **he ~ed a rabbit out of a hat** он извлёк из шля́пы за́йца; **~ing trick** фо́кус.

conjur|er, -or /ˈkʌndʒərə(r)/ *nn.* фо́кусник, заклина́тель (*m.*).

conk /kɒŋk/ *v.i.* (*usu.* **~ out**) (*break down*) гло́хнуть, за-; (*die*) заг|иба́ться, -ну́ться (*sl.*).

conker /ˈkɒŋkə(r)/ *n.* (*Br.*) ко́нский кашта́н.

connect /kəˈnekt/ *v.t.* (*join*) соедин|я́ть, -и́ть; свя́з|ывать, -а́ть; **the towns are ~ed by railway** э́ти города́ соединены́ желе́зной доро́гой; **please ~ me with the hospital** пожа́луйста, соедини́те меня́ с больни́цей; **what firm are you ~ed with?** с како́й фи́рмой вы свя́заны?; **he is well ~ed** у него́ хоро́шие свя́зи; **~ up** подключ|а́ть, -и́ть; (*associate*) свя́з|ывать, -а́ть; ассоции́ровать (*impf., pf.*); **I ~ him with music** его́ и́мя ассоции́руется у меня́ с му́зыкой.

● *v.i.* соедин|я́ться, -и́ться; свя́з|ываться, -а́ться; **the train ~s with the one from London** э́тот по́езд согласо́ван по расписа́нию с ло́ндонским по́ездом.

connecting-rod /kəˈnektɪŋ/ *n.* шату́н, тя́га.

connection /kəˈnekʃ(ə)n/ *n.* **1** (*joining up, installation*) соедине́ние, связь. **2** (*fig., link*) связь; **in this ~** в э́той свя́зи. **3** (*of transport*) согласо́ванность расписа́ния; **the train runs in ~ with the ferry** расписа́ние поездо́в и паро́мов согласо́вано; **I missed my ~** я не успе́л сде́лать переса́дку. **4** (*association*) связь; **he formed a ~ with her** он установи́л с ней связь. **5** (*teleph.*): **the ~ was bad** телефо́н пло́хо рабо́тал. **6** (*tech.*): **a loose ~ in the engine** сла́бый конта́кт в электросисте́ме дви́гателя.

connective /kəˈnektɪv/ *adj.* соедини́тельный, связу́ющий.

connexion /kəˈnekʃ(ə)n/ (*Br.*) = **connection**

conning-tower /ˈkɒnɪŋ/ *n.* (*naut.*) боева́я ру́бка.

connivance /kəˈnaɪv(ə)ns/ *n.* потво́рство, попусти́тельство.

connive /kəˈnaɪv/ *v.i.*: **~ at** потво́рствовать (*impf.*) +*d.*; попусти́тельствовать (*impf.*) +*d.*

connoisseur /ˌkɒnəˈsɜː(r)/ *n.* знато́к, цени́тель (*m.*).

connotation /ˌkɒnəˈteɪʃ(ə)n/ *n.* побо́чное значе́ние; ассоциа́ция, коннота́ция.

connote /kəˈnəʊt/ *v.t.* означа́ть (*impf.*).

connubial /kəˈnjuːbɪəl/ *adj.* супру́жеский, бра́чный.

conquer /ˈkɒŋkə(r)/ *v.t. & i.* (*overcome; obtain by conquest*) завоё|вывать, -а́ть; покор|я́ть, -и́ть; **~ one's feelings** совлада́ть (*pf.*) со свои́ми чу́вствами.

conqueror /ˈkɒŋkərə(r)/ *n.* завоева́тель (*m.*).

conquest /ˈkɒŋkwest/ *n.* (*action*) завоева́ние; (*territory*) завоёванная террито́рия; завоева́ния (*pl.*); (*person whose affection has been won*) побе́да.

conquistador /kɒnˈkwɪstəˌdɔː(r)/ *n.* (*pl.* **~es** /-ˈdɔːreɪz/ *or* **~s**) конкистадо́р.

consanguineous /ˌkɒnsæŋˈgwɪnɪəs/ *adj.* единокро́вный, ро́дственный.

consanguinity /ˌkɒnsæŋˈgwɪnɪtɪ/ *n.* единокро́вность, родство́.

conscience /ˈkɒnʃ(ə)ns/ *n.* со́весть; **good, clear ~** чи́стая со́весть; **bad, guilty ~** нечи́стая со́весть; **for ~ sake** для успокое́ния/очи́стки со́вести; **he has many sins on his ~** у него́ на со́вести мно́го грехо́в; **have you no ~?** как то́лько у вас со́вести хвата́ет?; **in all ~** по со́вести говоря́.

● *cpd.* **~-stricken** *adj.* испы́тывающий угрызе́ния со́вести.

conscienceless /ˈkɒnʃ(ə)nslɪs/ *adj.* бессо́вестный.

conscientious /ˌkɒnʃɪˈenʃəs/ *adj.* созна́тельный, добросо́вестный, со́вестливый; **~ work** добросо́вестная рабо́та; **~ objector** отка́зывающийся от вое́нной слу́жбы по убежде́нию.

conscientiousness /ˌkɒnʃɪˈenʃəsnɪs/ *n.* созна́тельность, добросо́вестность, со́вестливость.

conscious /ˈkɒnʃəs/ *adj.* **1** (*physically aware*) сознаю́щий, ощуща́ющий; **he was ~ to the last** он был в созна́нии до после́дней мину́ты; **~ of pain** чу́вствующий боль; **I was ~ of what I was doing** я де́йствовал созна́тельно. **2** (*mentally aware*) сознаю́щий, понима́ющий; **I was ~ of having offended him** я сознава́л, что оскорби́л его́. **3** (*realized*) сознаю́щий, созна́тельный; **with ~ superiority** с созна́нием своего́ превосхо́дства; **a ~ effort** созна́тельное уси́лие. **4** (*self-~*) стеснённый. **5** (*as suff.*): **class-~** кла́ссово созна́тельный; **security-~** бди́тельный.

consciousness /ˈkɒnʃəsnɪs/ *n.* **1** (*physical*) созна́ние; **he lost ~** он потеря́л созна́ние; **she regained ~** она́ пришла́ в себя́/созна́ние. **2** (*mental*) созна́тельность.

conscript[1] /ˈkɒnskrɪpt/ *n.* новобра́нец, призывни́к.

● *adj.* при́званный на вое́нную слу́жбу; **~ soldiers** солда́ты-призывники́.

conscript[2] /kənˈskrɪpt/ *v.t.* приз|ыва́ть, -ва́ть на вое́нную слу́жбу.

conscription /kənˈskrɪpʃ(ə)n/ *n.* во́инская пови́нность; (*call-up*) призы́в на вое́нную слу́жбу.

consecrate /ˈkɒnsɪˌkreɪt/ *v.t.* освя|ща́ть, -ти́ть; посвя|ща́ть, -ти́ть.

consecration /ˌkɒnsɪˈkreɪʃ(ə)n/ *n.* освяще́ние; посвяще́ние.

consecutive /kənˈsekjʊtɪv/ *adj.* после́довательный; **(on) five ~ days** пять дней подря́д.

consensus /kənˈsensəs/ *n.* согла́сие, единоду́шие; (*pol.*) консе́нсус.

consent /kənˈsent/ *n.* согла́сие; **with one ~** единоду́шно, с о́бщего согла́сия; **age of ~** во́зраст с кото́рого челове́к правомо́чен дава́ть согла́сие на половы́е отноше́ния.

● *v.i.* согла|ша́ться, -си́ться; да|ва́ть, -ть согла́сие.

consequence /ˈkɒnsɪkwəns/ *n.* **1** (*result*) сле́дствие, после́дствие; **you must take the ~s of your acts** вам придётся отвеча́ть за после́дствия ва́ших посту́пков; **in ~ of** всле́дствие+*g.*; в результа́те +*g.* **2** (*importance*) ва́жность, значе́ние; **a man of ~** влия́тельный/большо́й челове́к; **it is of no ~** э́то не име́ет значе́ния.

consequent /ˈkɒnsɪkwənt/ *adj.* явля́ющийся результа́том (*чего*); сле́дующий/вытека́ющий (*из чего*).

consequential /ˌkɒnsɪˈkwenʃ(ə)l/ *adj.* **1** (*consequent*) сле́дующий/вытека́ющий (*из чего*). **2** (*important*) ва́жный, значи́тельный.

consequently /ˈkɒnsɪˌkwentlɪ/ *adv.* сле́довательно, зна́чит, (*coll.*) ста́ло быть.

conservancy /kənˈsɜːvənsɪ/ *n.* (*preservation*) охра́на (приро́ды).

conservation /ˌkɒnsəˈveɪʃ(ə)n/ *n.* сохране́ние, охра́на; **~ area** запове́дник; **~ of energy** (*phys.*) сохране́ние эне́ргии.

conservationist /ˌkɒnsəˈveɪʃənɪst/ *n.* боре́ц за охра́ну приро́ды.

conservatism /kənˈsɜːvətɪz(ə)m/ *n.* консервати́зм.

conservative /kənˈsɜːvətɪv/ *n.* консерва́тор.

● *adj.* консервати́вный; **a ~ estimate** скро́мный/уме́ренный подсчёт.

conservatoire /kənˈsɜːvəˌtwɑː(r)/ *n.* консервато́рия.

conservatory /kənˈsɜːvətərɪ/ *n.* **1** (*Br., room*) застеклённая вера́нда; оранжере́я. **2** (*US, mus.*) консервато́рия.

conserve /kənˈsɜːv/, *n. only also* /ˈkɒnsɜːv/ *n.* (*preserved fruit*) варе́нье.

● *v.t.* (*fruit*) консерви́ровать, за-; (*protect*) сохран|я́ть, -и́ть; сбер|ега́ть, -е́чь; **~ one's strength** бере́чь (*impf.*) свои́ си́лы.

consider /kənˈsɪdə(r)/ *v.t. & i.* рассм|а́тривать, -отре́ть; счита́ть (*impf.*); **we are ~ing going to Canada** мы поду́мываем о пое́здке в Кана́ду; **~ yourself under arrest** счита́йте, что вы арестóваны; **he is ~ed clever** егó считáют ýмным; он считáется ýмным; (*make allowance for*) считáться (*impf.*) с + *i.*; прин|имáть, -я́ть во внимáние; **we must ~ his feelings** мы должны́ считáться с егó чýвствами; **all things ~ed** приня́в всё во внимáние.

considerable /kən'sɪdərəb(ə)l/ *adj.* значи́тельный.

considerate /kən'sɪdərət/ *adj.* внимáтельный, забóтливый.

considerateness /kən'sɪdərətnɪs/ *n.* внимáние, внимáтельность, забóтливость.

consideration /kən,sɪdə'reɪʃ(ə)n/ *n.* **1** (*reflection*) рассмотрéние; **take into ~** прин|имáть, -я́ть во внимáние; **leave out of ~** упус|кáть, -ти́ть из ви́ду; не прин|имáть, -я́ть во внимáние; **the matter is under ~** дéло рассмáтривается. **2** (*making allowance*): **in ~ of his youth** принимáя во внимáние егó мóлодость; **he showed ~ for my feelings** он считáлся с моими чýвствами; он щади́л мои́ чýвства. **3** (*reason, factor*) соображéние; **time is an important ~** врéмя — вáжный фáктор; **money is no ~** дéньги не имéют значéния. **4** (*requital*) вознаграждéние; (*leg.*) встрéчное удовлетворéние.

considering /kən'sɪdərɪŋ/ *adv. & prep.* учи́тывая; принимáя во внимáние; **that is not so bad, ~** (*coll.*) в óбщем э́то не так уж плóхо.

consign /kən'saɪn/ *v.t.* (*send*) пос|ылáть, -лáть; (*condemn*) обр|екáть, -éчь; (*entrust*) поруч|áть, -и́ть; вруч|áть, -и́ть; (*hand over*) перед|авáть, -áть; **his body was ~ed to the earth** егó тéло бы́ло прéдано землé.

consignee /,kɒnsaɪ'ni:/ *n.* грýзополучáтель (*m.*).

consignment /kən'saɪnmənt/ *n.* (*act of consigning*) отпрáвка; (*goods*) груз, пáртия товáра.

consignor /kən'saɪnə(r)/ *n.* грузоотправи́тель (*m.*).

consist /kən'sɪst/ *v.i.*: **~ of** состоя́ть (*impf.*) из + *g.*; заключáться (*impf.*) в + *p.*; **the committee ~s of nine members** комитéт состои́т из девяти́ человéк; **~ in**: **his task ~s in defining work norms** егó рабóта состои́т в определéнии норм вырáботки.

consistency /kən'sɪstənsɪ/ *n.* **1** (*of mixture etc.; also* **consistence**) консистéнция. **2** (*adherence to logic or principle*) послéдовательность; постоя́нство.

consistent /kən'sɪst(ə)nt/ *adj.* (*of argument etc.*) послéдовательный; **this fact is ~ with his having written the book** э́тот факт не противорéчит томý, что он явля́ется áвтором э́той кни́ги; (*of person*) послéдовательный.

consolable /kən'səʊləb(ə)l/ *adj.* утеши́мый.

consolation /,kɒnsə'leɪʃ(ə)n/ *n.* утешéние, отрáда; **it is a ~ that he is here** утеши́тельно знать, что он здесь; **~ prize** утеши́тельный приз.

consolatory /kən'sɒlətərɪ/ *adj.* утеши́тельный.

console[1] /'kɒnsəʊl/ *n.* **1** (*bracket*) консóль, кронштéйн; **~ table** пристéнный стол/стóлик. **2** (*panel*) пульт управлéния. **3** (*cabinet*) кóрпус, шкáфчик (*радиоприёмника и т.п.*).

console[2] /kən'səʊl/ *v.t.* ут|ешáть, -éшить.

consolidate /kən'sɒlɪ,deɪt/ *v.t.* укреп|ля́ть, -и́ть; консолиди́ровать (*impf., pf.*); **C~d Fund** консолиди́рованный фонд.

● *v.i.* укреп|ля́ться, -и́ться; консолиди́роваться (*impf., pf.*).

consolidation /kən,sɒlɪ'deɪʃ(ə)n/ *n.* консолидáция; укреплéние.

consols /'kɒnsɒlz/ *n.* консолиди́рованная рéнта.

consommé /kən'sɒmeɪ/ *n.* консомé (*indecl.*), бульóн.

consonance /'kɒnsənəns/ *n.* (*agreement*) соглáсие; (*mus.*) консонáнс.

consonant /'kɒnsənənt/ *n.* (*phon.*) соглáсный (звук), консонáнт.

● *adj.* (*in accord*) соглáсный, созвýчный.

consonantal /,kɒnsə'nænt(ə)l/ *adj.* (*phon.*) консонáнтный.

consort[1] /'kɒnsɔ:t/ *n.* **1** (*spouse*) консóрт, супрýг (*fem.* -а); **Prince C~** принц-консóрт. **2** (*ship*) сопровождáющий корáбль.

consort[2] /kən'sɔ:t/ *v.t.* (*associate*) общáться (*impf.*).

consorti|um /kən'sɔ:tɪəm/ *n.* (*pl.* **~a** *or* **~ums**) консóрциум.

conspectus /kən'spektəs/ *n.* конспéкт, обзóр.

conspicuous /kən'spɪkjʊəs/ *adj.* замéтный; бросáющийся в глазá; **he was ~ by his absence** егó отсýтствие бросáлось в глазá.

conspiracy /kən'spɪrəsɪ/ *n.* зáговор; конспирáция.

conspirator /kən'spɪrətə(r)/ *n.* заговóрщик; конспирáтор.

conspiratorial /kən,spɪrə'tɔ:rɪəl/ *adj.* заговóрщический, конспирáторский.

conspire /kən'spaɪə(r)/ *v.t. & i.* устр|áивать, -óить зáговор; сгов|áриваться, -ори́ться; **events ~d against him** собы́тия склáдывались прóтив негó.

constable /'kʌnstəb(ə)l/ *n.* (*Br., policeman*) полицéйский; **Chief C~** начáльник поли́ции.

constabulary /kən'stæbjʊlərɪ/ *n.* (*Br.*) поли́ция.

● *adj.* полицéйский.

constancy /'kɒnstənsɪ/ *n.* постоя́нство; неизмéнность.

constant /'kɒnst(ə)nt/ *n.* (*math., phys.*) констáнта.

● *adj.* постоя́нный; (*faithful*) неизмéнный.

Constantinople /,kɒnstæntɪ'nəʊp(ə)l/ *n.* (*hist.*) Константинóполь (*m.*).

constantly /'kɒnst(ə)ntlɪ/ *adj.* (*continuously*) постоя́нно; (*frequently*) вéчно.

constellation /,kɒnstə'leɪʃ(ə)n/ *n.* созвéздие, констелля́ция.

consternation /,kɒnstə'neɪʃ(ə)n/ *n.* смятéние, ýжас.

constipate /'kɒnstɪ,peɪt/ *v.t.* (*med.*) вызывáть, вы́звать запóр у + *g.*; **he is ~d** у негó запóр.

constipation /,kɒnstɪ'peɪʃ(ə)n/ *n.* запóр.

constituency /kən'stɪtjʊənsɪ/ *n.* избирáтельный óкруг.

constituent /kən'stɪtjʊənt/ *n.* (*elector*) избирáтель (*fem.* -ница); (*element*) составнáя часть.

● *adj.* составля́ющий часть цéлого; (*pol.*) избирáющий; **~ assembly** учреди́тельное собрáние.

constitute /'kɒnstɪ,tju:t/ *v.t.* (*make up*) сост|авля́ть, -áвить; (*set up*) учре|ждáть, -ди́ть; устан|áвливать, -ови́ть.

constitution /,kɒnstɪ'tju:ʃ(ə)n/ *n.* **1** (*make-up*) строéние, структýра; **the ~ of one's mind** склад умá. **2** (*of body*) (тело)сложéние. **3** (*pol.*) конститýция.

constitutional /,kɒnstɪ'tju:ʃən(ə)l/ *n.* (*walk*) моциóн, прогýлка.

● *adj.* (*of body*) органи́ческий, конституционáльный; (*pol.*) конституциóнный.

constitutionalism /,kɒnstɪ'tju:ʃənə,lɪz(ə)m/ *n.* конституционали́зм.

constitutive /'kɒnstɪ,tju:tɪv/ *adj.* учреди́тельный, существéнный.

constrain /kən'streɪn/ *v.t.* (*force*) прин|уждáть, -ýдить; заст|авля́ть, -áвить; вынуждáть, вы́нудить; (*restrict*) ограни́чи|вать, -ть; **~ed** (*embarrassed*) стеснённый.

constraint /kən'streɪnt/ *n.* (*compulsion*) принуждéние, давлéние; (*restriction*) ограничéние; (*repression of feelings*) скóванность.

constrict /kən'strɪkt/ *v.t.* сж|имáть, -ать; сужáть, сýзить; **a ~ed outlook** ограни́ченный кругозóр.

constriction /kən'strɪkʃ(ə)n/ *n.* сжáтие, сужéние; **I feel a ~ in the chest** я чýвствую стеснéние в груди́.

constrictive /kən'strɪktɪv/ *adj.* сжимáющий, сужáющий.

construct /kən'strʌkt/ *v.t.* конструи́ровать (*impf., pf.*); (*also gram., geom.*) стрóить, по-.

construction /kən'strʌkʃ(ə)n/ *n.* **1** (*act or method of constructing*) построéние, строи́тельство, стрóйка; (*thing constructed*) пострóйка, сооружéние; **the road is under ~** дорóга стрóится; **a car of solid ~** маши́на прóчной констрýкции. **2** (*interpretation*) истолковáние; **he put a wrong ~ on my words** он непрáвильно истолковáл мои́ словá. **3** (*gram.*) констрýкция.

constructional /kən'strʌkʃ(ə)nəl/ *adj.* структýрный; (*pert. to building*) строи́тельный.

constructive /kən'strʌktɪv/ *adj.* (*pert. to construction; helpful*) конструкти́вный; (*implicit*) подразумевáемый; **a ~ denial** кóсвенный откáз.

constructor /kən'strʌktə(r)/ *n.* констру́ктор; строи́тель (*m.*).

construe /kən'stru:/ *v.t.* (**construes, construed, construing**) (*interpret*) истолко́в|ывать, -а́ть.

consul /'kɒns(ə)l/ *n.* ко́нсул.

● *cpd.* **~-general** *n.* генера́льный ко́нсул.

consular /'kɒnsjʊlə(r)/ *adj.* ко́нсульский.

consulate /'kɒnsjʊlət/ *n.* (*also hist.*) ко́нсульство.

consulship /'kɒns(ə)lʃɪp/ *n.* до́лжность ко́нсула.

consult /kən'sʌlt/ *v.t.* **1** (*refer to*): **~ a book** спр|авля́ться, -а́виться в кни́ге; **~ one's watch** посмотре́ть (*pf.*) на часы́; **~ a lawyer** сове́товаться, по- с юри́стом. **2** (*take account of*): **~ s.o.'s interests** прин|има́ть, -я́ть во внима́ние чьи-н. интере́сы.

● *v.i.* сове́товаться, по- (с + *i.*); **~ with s.o.** консульти́роваться (*impf., pf.*) с кем-н.; совеща́ться (*impf.*) с кем-н.; **~ing physician** (врач-)консульта́нт; **~ing hours** приёмные часы́; **~ing room** кабине́т (врача́).

consultant /kən'sʌlt(ə)nt/ *n.* консульта́нт.

● *adj.* консульти́рующий.

consultation /,kɒnsəl'teɪʃ(ə)n/ *n.* консульта́ция; **he acted in ~ with me** он де́йствовал, сове́туясь со мной.

consultative /,kən'sʌltətɪv/ *adj.* консультати́вный, совеща́тельный.

consumable /kən'sju:məb(ə)l/ *adj.* (*edible*) съедо́бный.

consume /kən'sju:m/ *v.t.* **1** (*eat or drink*) съ|еда́ть, -есть; погло|ща́ть, -ти́ть. **2** (*use up*) потреб|ля́ть, -и́ть; расхо́доваться, из-. **3** (*destroy*) истреб|ля́ть, -и́ть; **the fire ~d the huts** пожа́р уничто́жил лачу́ги. **4**: **he was ~d with envy/curiosity** его́ снеда́ла за́висть; его́ снеда́ло любопы́тство.

consumer /kən'sju:mə(r)/ *n.* потреби́тель (*m.*); **~ goods** потреби́тельские това́ры; **~ society** о́бщество потребле́ния.

consumerism /kən'sju:mə,rɪz(ə)m/ *n.* потреби́тельство.

consummate¹ /kən'sʌmɪt/, /'kɒnsəmɪt/ *adj.* соверше́нный, зако́нченный; **a ~ artist** блестя́щий худо́жник; **~ skill** зако́нченное мастерство́.

consummate² /'kɒnsə,meɪt/ *v.t.* (*e.g. happiness*) заверш|а́ть, -и́ть; (*marriage*) осуществ|ля́ть, -и́ть (*брачные отношения*).

consummation /,kɒnsə'meɪʃ(ə)n/ *n.* (*completion, achievement*) заверше́ние, осуществле́ние; (*of marriage*) осуществле́ние.

consumption /kən'sʌmpʃ(ə)n/ *n.* **1** (*eating etc.*) потребле́ние, поглоще́ние; **the ~ of beer has gone up** потребле́ние пи́ва вы́росло *or* увели́чилось. **2** (*using up*) потребле́ние. **3** (*med.*) чахо́тка, туберкулёз.

consumptive /kən'sʌmptɪv/ *n. & adj.* (*med.*) чахо́точный, туберкулёзный (больно́й).

contact /'kɒntækt/ *n.* **1** (*lit., fig.*) конта́кт, соприкоснове́ние; **bring, come into ~ with** установи́ть (*pf.*) конта́кт с + *i.*; прийти́ (*pf.*) в соприкоснове́ние с + *i.*; войти́ (*pf.*) в конта́кт с + *i.*; **keep in ~ with** подде́рживать (*impf.*) связь с + *i.*; **our troops are in ~ with the enemy** на́ши войска́ вошли́ в соприкоснове́ние с проти́вником; **make/break ~** (*elec.*) включи́ть/вы́ключить (*both pf.*) ток; **~ lenses** конта́ктные ли́нзы. **2** (*of person*): **he made useful ~s** он завяза́л поле́зные знако́мства/свя́зи; **who is your ~ in that office?** к кому́ вы обы́чно обраща́етесь в э́том учрежде́нии?; **~ man** аге́нт.

● *v.t.* (*coll.*) связа́ться (*pf.*) с + *i.*

contagion /kən'teɪdʒ(ə)n/ *n.* зара́за, инфе́кция.

contagious /kən'teɪdʒəs/ *adj.* зара́зный, инфекцио́нный; **laughter is ~** смех зарази́телен.

contain /kən'teɪn/ *v.t.* **1** (*hold within itself*) содержа́ть (*impf.*) в себе́; **the newspaper ~s interesting reports** в газе́те есть/име́ются интере́сные сообще́ния. **2** (*comprise*) содержа́ть (*impf.*); состоя́ть (*impf.*) из + *g.*; **a gallon ~s eight pints** в галло́не во́семь пинт. **3** (*be capable of holding*) вмеща́ть (*impf.*); **how much does this bottle ~?** ско́лько вмеща́ет э́та буты́лка?; какова́ ёмкость э́той буты́лки? **4** (*control*) сде́рж|ивать, -а́ть; **he could not ~ his enthusiasm** он не мог сдержа́ть своего́ восто́рга; **~ yourself!** возьми́те себя́ в ру́ки!; владе́йте собо́й! **5** (*hold in check*) сде́рж|ивать, -а́ть; **our forces ~ed the enemy** на́ши войска́ сде́рживали проти́вника.

container /kən'teɪnə(r)/ *n.* **1** (*receptacle*) сосу́д. **2** (*for transport*) конте́йнер; **~ ship/truck** контейнерово́з.

containment /kən'teɪnmənt/ *n.* (*of enemy forces etc.*) сде́рживание.

contaminate /kən'tæmɪ,neɪt/ *v.t.* зара|жа́ть, -зи́ть; загрязн|я́ть, -и́ть.

contamination /kən,tæmɪ'neɪʃ(ə)n/ *v.t.* зараже́ние, загрязне́ние.

contemplate /'kɒntəm,pleɪt/ *v.t.* **1** (*gaze at*) созерца́ть (*impf.*); при́стально рассма́тривать (*impf.*). **2** (*view mentally*) рассма́тривать (*impf.*); созерца́ть (*impf*). **3** (*envisage, plan*) обду́м|ывать, -ать; заду́м|ывать, -ать; зам|ышля́ть, -ы́слить.

contemplation /,kɒntəm'pleɪʃ(ə)n/ *n.* созерца́ние, размышле́ние, обду́мывание.

contemplative /kən'templətɪv/ *adj.* созерца́тельный.

contemporaneity /kən,tempərə'ni:ɪtɪ/ *n.* совреме́нность, одновре́ме́нность.

contemporaneous /kən,tempə'reɪnɪəs/ *adj.* совреме́нный, одновре́ме́нный.

contemporary /kən'tempərərɪ/ *n.* совреме́нни|к, све́рстни|к (*fem.* -ца).

● *adj.* совреме́нный; **~ history** нове́йшая исто́рия.

contempt /kən'tempt/ *n.* презре́ние; **have ~ for** презира́ть (*impf.*); **in ~ of rules** невзира́я на пра́вила; **~ of court** оскорбле́ние суда́.

contemptible /kən'temptɪb(ə)l/ *adj.* презре́нный.

contemptuous /kən'temptjʊəs/ *adj.* презри́тельный.

contend /kən'tend/ *v.t.* утвержда́ть (*impf.*).

● *v.i.* (*fight*) боро́ться (*impf.*) (**with**: с + *i.*; **for**: за + *a.*); (*compete*) состяза́ться (*impf.*); сопе́рничать (*impf.*); **~ for a prize** боро́ться (*impf.*) за приз; оспа́ривать (*impf.*) приз; **~ing interests** противополо́жные интере́сы.

contender /kən'tendə(r)/ *n.* сопе́рни|к (*fem.* -ца), претенде́нт (*fem.* -ка).

content¹ /'kɒntent/ *n.* (*lit., fig.*) содержа́ние; **the sugar ~ of beet** содержа́ние са́хара в свёкле; (*pl.*) содержи́мое; **(table of) ~s** оглавле́ние.

content² /kən'tent/ *n.*: **to one's heart's ~** в своё удово́льствие, вво́лю, всласть.

● *adj.* дово́льный.

● *v.t.* удовлетвор|я́ть, -и́ть; **~ o.s.** дово́льствоваться (*impf.*); **a ~ed look** дово́льный вид.

contention /kən'tenʃ(ə)n/ *n.* (*strife*) спор, раздо́р; (*assertion*) утвержде́ние.

contentious /kən'tenʃəs/ *adj.* вздо́рный, задири́стый.

contentment /kən'tentmənt/ *n.* удовлетворённость, дово́льство.

contest /'kɒntest:/ *v. only* /kən'test/ *n.* ко́нкурс, состяза́ние; **beauty ~** ко́нкурс красоты́.

● *v.t. & i.* **1** (*dispute*) осп|а́ривать, -о́рить. **2** (*contend for*) отст|а́ивать, -оя́ть; боро́ться (*impf.*) за + *a.*; **the enemy ~ed every inch of ground** враг отста́ивал ка́ждую пядь земли́; **he ~ed the election** он боро́лся на вы́борах.

contestable /kən'testəb(ə)l/ *adj.* спо́рный, оспа́риваемый.

contestant /kən'test(ə)nt/ *n.* конкуре́нт (*fem.* -ка), уча́стни|к (*fem.* -ца) состяза́ния.

context /'kɒntekst/ *n.* (*textual*) конте́кст; (*connection*) связь; **in the ~ of today's America** в усло́виях совреме́нной Аме́рики.

contiguity /,kɒntɪ'gju:ɪtɪ/ *n.* сме́жность, соприкоснове́ние.

contiguous /kən'tɪgjʊəs/ *adj.* сме́жный, соприкаса́ющийся, прилега́ющий.

continence /'kɒntɪnəns/ *n.* сде́ржанность; воздержа́ние.

continent¹ /'kɒntɪnənt/ *n.* контине́нт, матери́к; **the C~** (*Europe*) (континента́льная) Евро́па; **the five ~s** пять контине́нтов.

continent² /'kɒntɪnənt/ *adj.* сде́ржанный, возде́ржанный.

continental /,kɒntɪ'nent(ə)l/ *n.*

(*inhabitant of Europe*) жи́тель (*m.*) европе́йского контине́нта; европе́|ец (*fem.* -йка).

● *adj.* континента́льный; **~ quilt** (*Br.*) стёганое одея́ло; **~ shelf** материко́вая о́тмель; **C~ breakfast** лёгкий у́тренний за́втрак.

contingency /kən'tɪndʒənsɪ/ *n.* **1** (*uncertainty*) случа́йность, слу́чай. **2** (*possible event*) возмо́жное обстоя́тельство; **~ plan** вариа́нт пла́на; альтернати́вный план.

contingent /kən'tɪndʒ(ə)nt/ *n.* (*mil.*) континге́нт.

● *adj.* случа́йный; возмо́жный.

continua /kən'tɪnjʊə/ *pl. of* ⇒**continuum**

continual /kən'tɪnjʊəl/ *adj.* постоя́нный, беспреры́вный, беспреста́нный.

continuance /kən'tɪnjʊəns/ *n.* продолжи́тельность, продолже́ние; (*e.g. in office*) пребыва́ние.

continuation /kən,tɪnjʊ'eɪʃ(ə)n/ *n.* продолже́ние; возобновле́ние.

continue /kən'tɪnju:/ *v.t.* (**continues, continued, continuing**) прод|олжа́ть, -о́лжить; **'to be ~d'** (*of story etc.*) продолже́ние сле́дует; **~d on p. 15** (смотри́) продолже́ние на стр. 15; **~d from p. 2** (смотри́) нача́ло на стр. 2.

● *v.i.* (**continues, continued, continuing**) прод|олжа́ться, -о́лжиться; **the wet weather ~s** сыра́я пого́да де́ржится; **if you ~ (to be) obstinate** е́сли вы бу́дете по-пре́жнему упо́рствовать.

continuity /,kɒntɪ'nju:ɪtɪ/ *n.* непреры́вность, неразры́вность, беспреры́вность; **~ girl** (*cin.*) монта́жница.

continuous /kən'tɪnjʊəs/ *adj.* непреры́вный, неразры́вный, беспреры́вный; (*gram.*) дли́тельный.

continu|um /kən'tɪnjʊəm/ *n.* (*pl.* **~a**) конти́нуум.

contort /kən'tɔ:t/ *v.t.* иска|жа́ть, -зи́ть; искрив|ля́ть, -и́ть.

contortion /kən'tɔ:ʃ(ə)n/ *n.* искаже́ние; искривле́ние.

contortionist /kən'tɔ:ʃənɪst/ *n.* челове́к-змея́.

contour /'kɒntʊə(r)/ *n.* ко́нтур; **~ line** горизонта́ль; **~ map** гипсометри́ческая ка́рта.

● *v.t.* (*a map*) вычё́рчивать, вы́чертить в горизонта́лях; (*a road*) нан|оси́ть, -ести́ ко́нтур *+g.*

contraband /'kɒntrə,bænd/ *n.* контраба́нда; **~ of war** вое́нная контраба́нда; **~ goods** контраба́ндные това́ры.

contrabandist /'kɒntrə,bændɪst/ *n.* контрабанди́ст.

contraception /,kɒntrə'sepʃ(ə)n/ *n.* предупрежде́ние бере́менности; примене́ние противозача́точных средств.

contraceptive /,kɒntrə'septɪv/ *n.* противозача́точное сре́дство.

● *adj.* противозача́точный.

contract[1] /'kɒntrækt/ *n.* (*agreement*) контра́кт, догово́р; **marriage ~** бра́чный контра́кт; **breach of ~** наруше́ние догово́ра/контра́кта; **~ bridge** бридж-контра́кт; **~ killer** ки́ллер, наёмный уби́йца; **~ killing** заказно́е уби́йство.

contract[2] /kən'trækt/ *v.t.* (*conclude*) заключ|а́ть, -и́ть (*догово́р/контра́кт*); **~ a marriage** вступи́ть (*pf.*) в брак; (*incur*): **~ an illness** заболе́ть (*pf.*); **~ debts** влезть (*pf.*) в долги́; наде́лать (*pf.*) долго́в.

● *v.i.* (*agree*) прин|има́ть, -я́ть на себя́ обяза́тельство; **he ~ed to build a bridge** он подряди́лся вы́строить мост; **~ing parties** (*dipl.*) догова́ривающиеся сто́роны (*f. pl.*); **~ out** (*Br.*) отказа́ться (*pf.*) от уча́стия в (*чём*); вы́йти (*pf.*) из де́ла.

contract[3] /kən'trækt/ *v.t.* (*shorten*) сокра|ща́ть, -ти́ть; (*tighten*) сж|има́ть, -ать; **~ one's brow** нахму́рить/намо́рщить (*pf.*) лоб; (*reduce*) сокра|ща́ть, -ти́ть.

● *v.i.* (*shorten*) сокра|ща́ться, -ти́ться; **metal ~s** мета́лл сжима́ется; (*tighten*) сж|има́ться, -а́ться; (*grow smaller*) сокра|ща́ться, -ти́ться.

contraction /kən'trækʃ(ə)n/ *n.* **1** (*shortening*) сокраще́ние, суже́ние; (*short form*) стяжённая фо́рма, контракту́ра. **2** (*of metal*) сжа́тие; (*of muscle etc.*) сокраще́ние, уса́дка. **3** (*of illness*) заболева́ние (*чем*).

contractor /kən'træktə(r)/ *n.* (*person*) подря́дчик.

contractual /kən'træktjʊəl/ *adj.* догово́рный.

contradict /,kɒntrə'dɪkt/ *v.t.* противоре́чить (*impf.*) *+d.*; (*rumours etc.*) опров|ерга́ть, -е́ргнуть.

contradiction /,kɒntrə'dɪkʃ(ə)n/ *n.* противоре́чие, опроверже́ние; **~ in terms** логи́ческая несообра́зность.

contradictory /,kɒntrə'dɪktərɪ/ *adj.* противоречи́вый.

contradistinction /,kɒntrədɪ'stɪŋkʃ(ə)n/ *n.* противопоставле́ние, противополо́жность; **in ~ to** в отли́чие от *+g.*

contra-indicated /,kɒntrə'ɪndɪ,keɪtɪd/ *adj.* (*med.*) противопока́занный.

contra-indication /,kɒntrə,ɪndɪ'keɪʃ(ə)n/ *n.* (*med.*) противопоказа́ние.

contralto /kən'træltəʊ/ *n.* (*pl.* **~s**) (*voice, singer*) контра́льто (*nt. & f., indecl.*).

contraption /kən'træpʃ(ə)n/ *n.* (*coll.*) приспособле́ние.

contrapuntal /,kɒntrə'pʌnt(ə)l/ *adj.* (*mus.*) контрапункти́ческий, контрапу́нктный.

contrariness /'kɒntrərɪnɪs/ *n.* (*coll., perversity*) своево́лие, своенра́вность, своенра́вие.

contrariwise /kən'treərɪ,waɪz/ *adj.* с друго́й стороны́; наоборо́т.

contrary[1] /'kɒntrərɪ/ *n.* противополо́жность; противополо́жное, обра́тное; **on, quite the ~** (как раз) наоборо́т; **to the ~** в обра́тном смы́сле; **I have heard nothing to the ~** у меня́ нет основа́ния сомнева́ться в э́том; **unless I hear to the ~** е́сли я не услы́шу чего́-нибудь ино́го/противополо́жного; **there is no evidence to the ~** нет доказа́тельств проти́вного/обра́тного.

● *adj.* противополо́жный, проти́вный, обра́тный; **~ winds** проти́вные ве́тры; **~ information** противополо́жные сообще́ния.

● *adv.*: **he acted ~ to the rules** он поступи́л про́тив пра́вил; **~ to my expectations** вопреки́ мои́м ожида́ниям.

contrary[2] /kən'treərɪ/ *adj.* (*coll.*) своево́льный, своенра́вный.

contrast /'kɒntrɑ:st/ *n.* контра́ст; противополо́жность; (*tech., TV etc.*) контра́стность; **in ~ to** в противополо́жность *+d.*; **by ~ with** по сравне́нию с *+i.*

● *v.t.* противопост|авля́ть, -а́вить; сопост|авля́ть, -а́вить.

● *v.i.* контрасти́ровать (*impf., pf.*); **the colours** (*Br.*), **colors** (*US*) **~ well** э́ти цвета́ создаю́т хоро́ший контра́ст; **his words ~ with his behaviour** (*Br.*), **behavior** (*US*) его́ слова́ противоре́чат его́ поведе́нию.

contravene /,kɒntrə'vi:n/ *v.t.* противоре́чить (*impf.*) *+d.*; **he ~d the law** он нару́шил зако́н.

contravention /,kɒntrə'venʃ(ə)n/ *n.* наруше́ние; **in ~ of** в наруше́ние *+g.*

contretemps /'kɔ:ntrə,tɑ̃/ *n.* (*pl.* **~** /-tɑ̃z/) неприя́тность; непредви́денное препя́тствие.

contribute /kən'trɪbju:t/ *v.t.* (*money etc.*) же́ртвовать, по-; **he ~d £5** он внёс 5 фу́нтов; **he ~d new information** он сообщи́л но́вые све́дения.

● *v.i.* соде́йствовать (*impf.*) *+d.*; спосо́бствовать (*impf.*) *+d.*; **it ~d to his ruin** э́то яви́лось одно́й из причи́н его́ разоре́ния; **he ~s to our magazine** он пи́шет для на́шего журна́ла.

contribution /,kɒntrɪ'bju:ʃ(ə)n/ *n.*: **a ~ of £5** поже́ртвование/взнос в пять фу́нтов; **his ~ to our success** его́ вклад в наш успе́х; (*to a periodical etc.*) статья́, заме́тка.

contributor /kən'trɪbjʊtə(r)/ *n.* (*writer*) (постоя́нный) сотру́дник; (*of funds*) же́ртвователь (*m.*).

contributory /kən'trɪbjʊtərɪ/ *adj.* соде́йствующий, спосо́бствующий; **~ negligence** встре́чная вина́, вина́ потерпе́вшего; **a ~ pension scheme** (*Br.*) пенсио́нная систе́ма, осно́ванная на отчисле́ниях из за́работка рабо́тающих.

contrite /'kɒntraɪt/, /kən'traɪt/ *adj.* сокруша́ющийся, ка́ющийся.

contrition /kən'trɪʃ(ə)n/ *n.* сокруше́ние, раска́яние, покая́ние.

contrivance /kən'traɪv(ə)ns/ *n.* (*skill*) изобрета́тельность; (*device*) приспособле́ние, изобрете́ние.

contrive /kən'traɪv/ *v.t.* (*devise*) заду́м|ывать, -ать; изобре|та́ть, -сти; (*succeed*) изловчи́ться (*pf.*); **he ~d to**

offend everybody он ухитри́лся всех оби́деть; **~d** (*artificial*) иску́сственный.

control /kən'trəʊl/ *n.* **1** (*power to direct etc.*) управле́ние, регули́рование; **he lost ~ of the car** он потеря́л управле́ние автомоби́лем; **he is in ~ of the situation** он хозя́ин положе́ния; **the situation is under ~** ситуа́ция нормализова́лась/нахо́дится под контро́лем; **the children are out of ~** де́ти не слу́шаются; **traffic ~** регули́рование у́личного движе́ния; **remote ~** дистанцио́нное управле́ние. **2** (*means of regulating*) контро́ль (*m.*); **government ~s** госуда́рственный контро́ль; **birth ~** регули́рование рожда́емости. **3** (*pl., of a machine etc.*) рычаги́ (*m. pl.*) управле́ния; **volume ~** регуля́тор гро́мкости/усиле́ния. **4**: **~ experiment** контро́льный о́пыт; **~ panel** прибо́рная доска́; пульт управле́ния; **~ room** пункт управле́ния; **~ tower** (*aeron.*) контро́льно-диспе́тчерский пункт.
● *v.t.* (**controlled, controlling**) **1** (*master, regulate*) контроли́ровать (*impf.*); регули́ровать (*impf., pf.*); держа́ть (*impf.*) в повинове́нии; **~ children** держа́ть (*impf.*) дете́й в послуша́нии; **~ one's temper** владе́ть (*impf.*) собо́й; **~ prices** регули́ровать це́ны. **2** (*verify*) контроли́ровать, про-.

controllable /kən'trəʊləb(ə)l/ *adj.* регули́руемый, контроли́руемый, управля́емый.

controller /kən'trəʊlə(r)/ *n.* контролёр, инспе́ктор; (*comput.*) контро́ллер.

controversial /ˌkɒntrə'vɜːʃ(ə)l/ *adj.* спо́рный, полеми́ческий; **a ~ subject** предме́т, вызыва́ющий поле́мику/спо́ры.

controversy /'kɒntrəˌvɜːsɪ/ *n.* поле́мика, спор.

controvert /'kɒntrəˌvɜːt/, /-'vɜːt/ *v.t.* противоре́чить (*impf.*) + *d.*

contuse /kən'tjuːz/ *v.t.* конту́зить (*pf.*).

contusion /kən'tjuːʃ(ə)n/, /-ʒ(ə)n/ *n.* конту́зия, ушиб.

conundrum /kə'nʌndrəm/ *n.* зага́дка, головоло́мка.

conurbation /ˌkɒnɜː'beɪʃ(ə)n/ *n.* конурба́ция, городска́я агломера́ция.

convalesce /ˌkɒnvə'les/ *v.i.* выздора́вливать (*impf.*).

convalescence /ˌkɒnvə'lesəns/ *n.* выздоровле́ние.

convalescent /ˌkɒnvə'les(ə)nt/ *n.* выздора́вливающий.
● *adj.* (*of patient*) выздора́вливающий, поправля́ющийся; **~ home** санато́рий для выздора́вливающих.

convection /kən'vekʃ(ə)n/ *n.* конве́кция.

convector /kən'vektə(r)/ *n.* конве́ктор.

convene /kən'viːn/ *v.t.* (*people*) соб|ира́ть, -ра́ть; (*meeting*) соз|ыва́ть, -ва́ть.
● *v.i.* соб|ира́ться, -ра́ться.

conven|er, -or /kən'viːnə(r)/ *nn.* организа́тор/инициа́тор собра́ния.

convenience /kən'viːnɪəns/ *n.* **1** удо́бство; **marriage of ~** брак по расчёту; **at your ~** когда́ вам бу́дет удо́бно; **having the railway close by is a ~** удо́бно жить вблизи́ от желе́зной доро́ги; **~ foods** пищевы́е полуфабрика́ты. **2** (*appliance*) удо́бства (*nt. pl.*); **all modern ~s** все удо́бства. **3**: **public ~** (*Br.*) обще́ственная убо́рная.

convenient /kən'viːnɪənt/ *adj.* удо́бный, подходя́щий; **if it is ~ for you** е́сли вам удо́бно; **the station is ~ly near** до ста́нции — руко́й пода́ть.

convenor /kən'viːnə(r)/ = **convener**

convent /'kɒnv(ə)nt/, /-vent/ *n.* (же́нский) монасты́рь; **she entered a ~** она́ постри́глась в мона́хини.

convention /kən'venʃ(ə)n/ *n.* **1** (*congress*) съезд. **2** (*treaty*) конве́нция. **3** (*custom*) обы́чай, усло́вность.

conventional /kən'venʃən(ə)l/ *adj.* обы́чный, традицио́нный; **a ~ greeting** (обще)при́нятое приве́тствие; **~ sign** усло́вный знак; **~ armaments** вооруже́ние обы́чного ти́па; **a ~ person** челове́к, кото́рый приде́рживается усло́вностей; (*banal*) станда́ртный; **~ war** война́ с примене́нием обы́чных вооруже́ний.

conventionality /kənˌvenʃə'nælɪtɪ/ *n.* усло́вность.

converge /kən'vɜːdʒ/ *v.i.* сходи́ться, сойти́сь; (*math.*) стреми́ться (*impf.*) к преде́лу; **the armies ~d on the city** а́рмии прибли́зились к го́роду.

convergence /kən'vɜːdʒəns/ *n.* сходи́мость, конверге́нция.

convergent /kən'vɜːdʒ(ə)nt/ *adj.* сходя́щийся в одно́й то́чке.

conversant /kən'vɜːs(ə)nt/, /'kɒnvəs(ə)nt/ *adj.* знако́мый (с + *i.*), осведомлённый (в + *p.*).

conversation /ˌkɒnvə'seɪʃ(ə)n/ *n.* разгово́р, бесе́да, речь; **~s** (*e.g. dipl.*) перегово́ры (*pl., g.* -ов); **make ~** вести́/подде́рживать (*impf.*) пусто́й разгово́р; **~ piece** жа́нровая карти́на.

conversational /ˌkɒnvə'seɪʃən(ə)l/ *adj.* (*pert. to conversation*) разгово́рный; (*talkative*) разгово́рчивый.

conversationalist /ˌkɒnvə'seɪʃənəlɪst/ *n.* (интере́сный) собесе́дник.

converse[1] /'kɒnvɜːs/ *n.* (*logic, math.*) обра́тное положе́ние; обра́тная теоре́ма.

converse[2] /kən'vɜːs/ *v.i.* (*talk*) бесе́довать (*impf.*), разгова́ривать (*impf.*).

conversely /'kɒnvɜːslɪ/, /kən'vɜːslɪ/ *adv.* наоборо́т.

conversion /kən'vɜːʃ(ə)n/ *n.* **1** (*transformation*) превраще́ние, перехо́д; **~ of cream into butter** сбива́ние сли́вок в ма́сло. **2** (*relig. etc.*) обраще́ние (в + *a.*); **there were many ~s to Islam** мно́гие при́няли исла́м. **3** (*math.*) преобразова́ние, перево́д; **~ of pounds into dollars** перево́д фу́нтов в до́ллары; обме́н фу́нтов на до́ллары. **4** (*appropriation*) обраще́ние в свою́ по́льзу; **~ of funds to one's own use** присвое́ние фо́ндов. **5** (*fin., of stocks etc.*) конве́рсия.

convert[1] /'kɒnvɜːt/ *n.* (ново)обращённый; **he is a ~ to Buddhism** он перешёл в будди́зм.

convert[2] /kən'vɜːt/ *v.t.* **1** (*change*) превра|ща́ть, -ти́ть; **the house was ~ed into flats** дом был разби́т на кварти́ры. **2** (*relig. etc.*) обра|ща́ть, -ти́ть; **I ~ed him to my view** я убеди́л его́ приня́ть мою́ то́чку зре́ния. **3** (*math.*) пере|води́ть, -вести́; **~ pounds into francs** перевести́ (*pf.*) фу́нты сте́рлингов во фра́нки. **4** (*appropriate*) обра|ща́ть, -ти́ть в свою́ по́льзу.
● *v.i.*: **he ~ed to Buddhism** он обрати́лся в будди́зм; он при́нял будди́стскую ве́ру.

converter /kən'vɜːtə(r)/ *n.* (*elec.*) преобразова́тель (*m.*).

convertibility /kənˌvɜːtɪ'bɪlɪtɪ/ *n.* (*fin.*) обрати́мость.

convertible /kən'vɜːtɪb(ə)l/ *n.* (*car*) автомоби́ль (*m.*) с откидны́м/открыва́ющимся ве́рхом.
● *adj.* обрати́мый, конверти́руемый; **~ currency** конверти́руемая валю́та.

convex /'kɒnveks/ *adj.* вы́пуклый, вы́гнутый.

convexity /kɒn'veksɪtɪ/ *n.* вы́пуклость, вы́гнутость.

convey /kən'veɪ/ *v.t.* **1** (*carry, transmit*) перев|ози́ть, -езти́; перепр|авля́ть, -а́вить; **pipes ~ water** вода́ доставля́ется по тру́бам. **2** (*impart*) перед|ава́ть, -а́ть; **the words ~ nothing to me** э́ти слова́ мне ничего́ не говоря́т; **~ my greetings to him** переда́йте ему́ приве́т от меня́. **3** (*leg.*) перед|ава́ть, -а́ть (*имущество, права*).

conveyance /kən'veɪəns/ *n.* (*transmission*) перево́зка, переда́ча; (*vehicle*) тра́нспортное сре́дство.

conveyancer /kən'veɪənsə(r)/ *n.* (*leg.*) нота́риус, веду́щий дела́ по переда́че иму́щества.

conveyancing /kən'veɪənsɪŋ/ *n.* (*leg.*) составле́ние нотариа́льных а́ктов о переда́че иму́щества.

conveyer /kən'veɪə(r)/ *n.* конве́йер, транспортёр; **~ belt** конве́йерная ле́нта; ле́нточный транспортёр.

convict[1] /'kɒnvɪkt/ *n.* осуждённый, ка́торжник.

convict[2] /kən'vɪkt/ *v.t.* (*leg.*) осу|жда́ть, -ди́ть (*в чём*).

conviction /kən'vɪkʃ(ə)n/ *n.* **1** (*leg.*) осужде́ние; (*previous*) суди́мость. **2** (*settled opinion*) убежде́ние, убеждённость. **3** (*persuasive force*) убежде́ние; **these arguments carry ~** э́ти аргуме́нты убеди́тельны; **he spoke without ~** он говори́л без убежде́ния.

convince /kən'vɪns/ *v.t.* убе|жда́ть, -ди́ть; **she ~d me that she was right** она́ убеди́ла меня́ в свое́й правоте́.

convincing /kən'vɪnsɪŋ/ *adj.* убеди́тельный.

convivial /kən'vɪvɪəl/ *adj.* (*of person*) компане́йский, весёлый; (*of evening etc.*) весёлый.

conviviality /kən,vɪvɪ'ælɪtɪ/ *n.* весёлость, весе́лье.

convocation /,kɒnvə'keɪʃ(ə)n/ *n.* созы́в, собра́ние.

convoke /kən'vəʊk/ *v.t.* соз|ыва́ть, -ва́ть.

convoluted /'kɒnvə,lu:tɪd/ *adj.* зави́тый, изо́гнутый; (*fig.*) запу́танный.

convolution /,kɒnvə'lu:ʃ(ə)n/ *n.* изо́гнутость; **the ~s of his argument** запу́танность его́ аргуме́нтов.

convolvulus /kən'vɒlvjʊləs/ *n.* (*pl.* **~es**) вьюно́к.

convoy /'kɒnvɔɪ/ *n.* конво́й; тра́нспортная коло́нна с конво́ем; **the ships sailed under ~** корабли́ шли под охра́ной конво́я.

● *v.t.* конвои́ровать (*impf.*).

convulse /kən'vʌls/ *v.t.* сотряс|а́ть, -ти́; потряс|а́ть, -ти́; **country ~d by war** страна́, потрясённая войно́й; **he was ~d with laughter** он ко́рчился от сме́ха.

convulsion /kən'vʌlʃ(ə)n/ *n.* сотрясе́ние; (*fig.*) потрясе́ние; (*pl., med.*) конву́льсия, су́дорога; (*of laughter*) су́дорожный смех.

convulsive /kən'vʌlsɪv/ *adj.* конвульси́вный, су́дорожный.

con|y, -ey /'kəʊnɪ/ *nn.* (*fur*) кро́лик; кро́личий мех.

coo /ku:/ *n.* воркова́нье.

● *v.t.* & *i.* (**coos, cooed**) воркова́ть (*impf.*).

cooee /'ku:i:/ *int.* ау́!

cook /kʊk/ *n.* (*male*) по́вар; (*on shipboard*) кок; (*fem.*) куха́рка; **too many ~s spoil the broth** ≈ у семи́ ня́нек дитя́ без гла́зу.

● *v.t.* вари́ть, с-; стря́пать, со-; гото́вить, с-/при-; **~ one's own meals** гото́вить самому́; **~ accounts** (*coll.*) подде́л|ывать, -ать счета́; **~ up a story** (*coll.*) состря́пать (*pf.*) исто́рию; **~ s.o.'s goose** угро́бить (*pf.*) кого́-н. (*coll.*).

● *v.i.* вари́ться, с-; гото́виться, при-; **these apples ~ well** э́ти я́блоки хорошо́ пеку́тся; **what's ~ing?** (*coll.*) что тут затева́ется?

● *cpds.* **~-book** *n.* = **cookery-book; ~-house** *n.* похо́дная ку́хня; (*on ship*) ка́мбуз.

cooker /'kʊkə(r)/ *n.* (*Br.*) (*stove*) плита́; печь; (*apple*) я́блоко для запека́ния.

cookery /'kʊkərɪ/ *n.* кулина́рия, стряпня́.

● *cpd.* **~-book** (*Br.*) (*also* **cook-book**) *n.* пова́ренная кни́га.

cookie /'kʊkɪ/ *n.* (*US, small cake*) пече́нье.

cooking /'kʊkɪŋ/ *n.* (*cuisine*) ку́хня.

● *adj.* столо́вый, ку́хонный; **~ apple** я́блоко для запека́ния, гото́вки.

cool /ku:l/ *n.* **1** прохла́да; **in the ~ of the evening** в вече́рней прохла́де. **2**: **lose one's ~** (*coll.*) вы́йти (*pf.*) из себя́, потеря́ть (*pf.*) самооблада́ние.

● *adj.* **1** (*lit.*) прохла́дный, све́жий. **2** (*unexcited*) хладнокро́вный, невозмути́мый. **3** (*impudent*) на́глый, беззасте́нчивый. **4** (*unenthusiastic*) прохла́дный, холо́дный; **they gave him a ~ reception** они́ его́ встре́тили с холодко́м.

● *v.t.* охла|жда́ть, -ди́ть; осту|жа́ть, -ди́ть; освеж|а́ть, -и́ть; **rain ~ed the air** по́сле дождя́ ста́ло прохла́дно.

● *v.i.* охла|жда́ться, -ди́ться; освеж|а́ться, -и́ться; ост|ыва́ть, -ы́ть; **his anger ~ed** его́ гнев осты́л; **~ down, off** ост|ыва́ть, -ы́ть; **~ing-off period** пери́од обду́мывания и перегово́ров.

● *cpds.* **~-headed** *adj.* уравнове́шенный, споко́йный; **~-headedness** *n.* уравнове́шенность, споко́йствие.

coolant /'ku:lənt/ *n.* охлади́тель (*m.*).

cooler /'ku:lə(r)/ *n.* (*vessel*) ведёрко для охлажде́ния; (*sl., prison cell*) ка́мера, ка́рцер.

coolie /'ku:lɪ/ *n.* (*unskilled labourer in some Asian countries*) ку́ли (*m. indecl.*).

coolness /'ku:lnɪs/ *n.* прохла́да, хо́лод; (*of manner*) холодо́к, хо́лодность; (*estrangement*) охлажде́ние; (*impudence*) беззасте́нчивость.

coomb, combe /ku:m/ *nn.* (*Br.*) ложби́на, овра́г.

coop /ku:p/ *n.* куря́тник.

● *v.t.* сажа́ть, посади́ть в кле́тку; **~ up, in** (*fig.*) держа́ть (*impf.*) взаперти́.

co-op /'kəʊɒp/ *n.* (*coll.*) кооперати́вный магази́н.

cooper /'ku:pə(r)/ *n.* бонда́рь (*m.*), боча́р.

co-operate /kəʊ'ɒpə,reɪt/ *v.i.* сотру́дничать (*impf.*); коопери́роваться (*impf., pf.*).

co-operation /kəʊ,ɒpə'reɪʃ(ə)n/ *n.* сотру́дничество, коопера́ция.

co-operative /kəʊ'ɒpərətɪv/ *n.* кооперати́в; (*pl., collect.*) коопера́ция.

● *adj.* кооперати́вный; (*helpful*) гото́вый к сотру́дничеству.

co-opt /kəʊ'ɒpt/ *v.t.* коопти́ровать (*impf., pf.*).

co-option /kəʊ'ɒpʃ(ə)n/ *n.* коопта́ция.

co-ordinate /kəʊ'ɔ:dɪnət/ *v. only* /kəʊ'ɔ:dɪ,neɪt/ *n.* (*math.*) координа́та; (*pl.*) о́си (*f. pl.*) координа́т.

● *adj.* координи́рованный; ра́вный по значе́нию.

● *v.t.* координи́ровать (*impf., pf.*).

co-ordination /kəʊ,ɔ:dɪ'neɪʃ(ə)n/ *n.* координа́ция.

coot /ku:t/ *n.* лысу́ха; **he is as bald as a ~** у него́ голова́ го́лая, как коле́нка.

cop /kɒp/ *n.* **1** (*sl., policeman*) полице́йский, мильто́н (*sl.*); **~s and robbers** (*game*) сы́щики и во́ры (*m. pl.*). **2**: **not much ~** (*Br. sl.*) не фонта́н.

● *v.t.* (**copped, copping**) (*catch, arrest*) задержа́ть, арестова́ть (*both pf.*); **~ it** (*Br.*) (*get into trouble*): **you'll ~ it** ты у меня́ полу́чишь.

co-partner /kəʊ'pɑ:tnə(r)/ *n.* компаньо́н, уча́стник в при́былях.

co-partnership /kəʊ'pɑ:tnəʃɪp/ *n.* това́рищество, уча́стие в при́былях.

cope[1] /kəʊp/ *n.* (*vestment*) ри́за; (*fig., canopy*) свод.

cope[2] /kəʊp/ *v.i.* спр|авля́ться, -а́виться (с + *i.*).

copeck (*also* **kope(c)k**) /'kəʊpek/, /'kɒpek/ *n.* копе́йка.

Copenhagen /,kəʊpən'heɪgən/ *n.* Копенга́ген.

Copernican /kə'pɜ:nɪkən/ *adj.*: **~ system** систе́ма Копе́рника.

copier /'kɒpɪə(r)/ *n.* (*person*) перепи́счик; (*imitator*) подража́тель (*fem.* -ница); (*machine*) мно́жительный аппара́т.

co-pilot /'kəʊ,paɪlət/ *n.* второ́й пило́т.

coping /'kəʊpɪŋ/ *n.* парапе́тная плита́.

● *cpd.* **~-stone** *n.* карни́зный/ парапе́тный ка́мень.

copious /'kəʊpɪəs/ *adj.* оби́льный.

copiousness /'kəʊpɪəsnɪs/ *n.* оби́лие.

copper[1] /'kɒpə(r)/ *n.* **1** (*metal*) медь; **~ wire** ме́дная про́волока; (**~ coin**) (*Br. coll.*) медя́к. **2** (*vessel*) ме́дный котёл.

● *v.t.* покр|ыва́ть, -ы́ть ме́дью.

● *cpds.* **~-bottomed** *adj.* обши́тый ме́дью; (*fig., Br. coll.*) надёжный, ве́рный; **a ~-bottomed excuse** желе́зный предло́г; **~head** *n.* щитомо́рдник; **~plate** *n.* ме́дная гравирова́льная доска́; (*engraving*) о́ттиск с ме́дной гравирова́льной доски́; **~plate handwriting** каллиграфи́ческий по́черк; **~-smith** *n.* ме́дник, коте́льщик.

copper[2] /'kɒpə(r)/ *n.* (*Br. sl., policeman*) полице́йский, мильто́н (*sl.*)

coppery /'kɒpərɪ/ *adj.* ме́дного цве́та.

coppice /'kɒpɪs/, **copse** /kɒps/ *nn.* подле́сок, ро́щица.

copra /'kɒprə/ *n.* ко́пра, сушёное ядро́ коко́сового оре́ха.

copse /kɒps/ = **coppice**

copula /'kɒpjʊlə/ *n.* (*pl.* **~s**) свя́зка.

copulate /'kɒpjʊ,leɪt/ *v.i.* совокуп|ля́ться, -и́ться.

copulation /,kɒpjʊ'leɪʃ(ə)n/ *n.* совокупле́ние.

copulative /'kɒpjʊlətɪv/ *adj.* (*gram.*) соедини́тельный.

copy /'kɒpɪ/ *n.* **1** (*imitation, version*) ко́пия, ру́копись; **fair, clean ~** белови́к, чистови́к; **rough ~** чернови́к.
2 (*of book etc.*) экземпля́р.
3 (*for printer*) текст, материа́л; **advertising ~** текст рекла́много объявле́ния.

● *v.t.* & *i.* перепи́с|ывать, -а́ть; копи́ровать, с-; (*imitate*) подража́ть (*impf.*) + *d.*; **~ out a letter** переписа́ть (*pf.*) письмо́; **he copied in the examination** он спи́сывал на экза́мене.

● *cpds.* **~-book** *n.* тетра́дь; **blot one's ~-book** (*fig.*) замара́ть (*pf.*) свою́ репута́цию; **~-cat** *n.* (*coll.*) подража́тель (*fem.* -ница); обезья́на; **~-editor** *n.* техни́ческий реда́ктор (*abbr.* техре́д); **~right** *n.* а́вторское пра́во; *adj.* охраня́емый а́вторским пра́вом; **this book is (in) ~right** на э́ту кни́гу распространя́ется а́вторское пра́во; *v.t.* обеспе́чи|вать, -ть а́вторское пра́во на + *a.*; **~-typist** *n.* машини́стка-перепи́счица; **~writer** *n.* рекла́мист (*fem.* -ка).

copyist /ˈkɒpɪɪst/ *n.* перепи́счик, копиро́вщик.

coquetry /ˈkɒkɪtrɪ/, /ˈkəʊk-/ *n.* коке́тство.

coquette /kɒˈket/, /kəˈket/ *n.* коке́тка.

coquettish /kɒˈketɪʃ/, /kəˈketɪʃ/ *adj.* коке́тливый.

cor /kɔ:(r)/ *int.* (*Br. sl.*) Го́споди!; Бо́же мой!

coral /ˈkɒr(ə)l/ *n.* кора́лл; (*attr., also fig.*) кора́лловый.

cor anglais /kɔ:r ˈɒŋgleɪ/, /ɑ̃ˈgleɪ/ *n.* (*pl.* **cors anglais** *pronunc. same*) англи́йский рожо́к.

corbel /ˈkɔ:b(ə)l/ *n.* поясо́к, вы́ступ.

cord /kɔ:d/ *n.* (*rope, string*) верёвка, бечёвка; (*flex*) шнур; **spinal ~** спинно́й мозг; **vocal ~s** голосовы́е свя́зки (*f. pl.*).

● *v.t.* свя́з|ывать, -а́ть верёвкой; **~ed** (*ribbed*) в ру́бчик; ру́бчатый.

cordage /ˈkɔ:dɪdʒ/ *n.* (*naut.*) такела́ж; сна́сти (*pl., g.* -е́й).

cordial /ˈkɔ:dɪəl/ *n.* (*Br.*) подслащённый напи́ток.

● *adj.* (*friendly*) серде́чный, раду́шный.

cordiality /ˌkɔ:dɪˈælɪtɪ/ *n.* серде́чность, раду́шие.

cordite /ˈkɔ:daɪt/ *n.* корди́т (*бездымный порох*).

cordless /ˈkɔ:dlɪs/ *adj.* беспроводно́й, бесшнурово́й; **~ telephone** радиотелефо́н.

cordon /ˈkɔ:d(ə)n/ *n.* (*of police etc.*) кордо́н.

● *v.t.* (*also* **~ off**) оцеп|ля́ть, -и́ть.

cordon bleu /ˌkɔ:dɒn ˈblɜ:/, /ˌkɔ:dɔ̃/ *adj.* первокла́ссный.

corduroy /ˈkɔ:dəˌrɔɪ/, /-djʊˌrɔɪ/ *n.* вельве́т; ру́бчатый плис; (*pl.,* **~** *trousers*) вельве́товые брю́к|и (*pl., g.* —).

core /kɔ:(r)/ *n.* **1** (*of fruit*) сердцеви́на; (*fig.*) центр, ядро́, суть; **rotten at the ~** насквозь прогни́вший. **English to the ~** англича́нин до мо́зга косте́й; **this is the ~ of his argument** э́то — суть его́ аргуме́нта; **~ of a problem** суть пробле́мы; **hard ~** (*attr.*) закорене́лый, отча́янный. **2** (*elec.*) жи́ла ка́беля; (*of nuclear reactor*) акти́вная зо́на.

● *v.t.* выреза́ть, вы́резать сердцеви́ну + *g.*

co-religionist /ˌkəʊrɪˈlɪdʒənɪst/ *n.* единове́р|ец (*fem.* -ка).

co-respondent /ˌkəʊrɪˈspɒnd(ə)nt/ *n.* (*leg.*) соотве́тчик (в бракоразво́дном проце́ссе).

Corfu /kɔ:ˈfu:/ *n.* Ко́рфу (*m. indecl.*).

corgi /ˈkɔ:gɪ/ *n.* (*pl.* **~s**) ко́рги (*m. indecl.*) (*порода собак*).

coriander /ˌkɒrɪˈændə(r)/ *n.* (*bot., also* **~ seed**) кориа́ндр; (*cul.*) *fresh* (*leaves*) кинза́.

Corinthian /kəˈrɪnθɪən/ *n.* кори́нфян|ин (*fem.* -ка); (*pl., bibl.*) Посла́ние к кори́нфянам.

● *adj.* кори́нфский.

cork /kɔ:k/ *n.* (*material, stopper*) про́бка; (*attr.*) про́бковый; (*float*) поплаво́к.

● *v.t.* (*stop up*) зат|ыка́ть, -кну́ть про́бкой; **~ up one's feelings** сде́рживать (*impf.*) свои́ чу́вства; **the wine is ~ed** вино́ отдаёт про́бкой.

● *cpd.* **~screw** *n.* што́пор; *v.i.* дви́гаться (*impf.*) по спира́ли.

corker /ˈkɔ:kə(r)/ *n.* (*sl., excellent or astonishing thing or person*) (не́что) шика́рное/потряса́ющее; блеск.

cormorant /ˈkɔ:mərənt/ *n.* большо́й бакла́н.

corn[1] /kɔ:n/ *n.* **1** (*Br., grain, seed*) зерно́. **2** (*Br., cereals in general*) зерновы́е (*pl.*), хлеб; **~ exchange** хле́бная би́ржа. **3** (*Br., wheat*) пшени́ца; **a field of ~** пшени́чное по́ле. **4** (*US, maize*) кукуру́за.

● *cpds.* **~-cob** *n.* сте́ржень (*m.*) кукуру́зного поча́тка; **~crake** *n.* коросте́ль (*m.*); **~flakes** *n. pl.* корнфле́кс; **~flour** *n.* (*Br.*) кукуру́зная/ри́совая мука́; **~flower** *n.* василёк; **~ on the cob** *n.* кукуру́за в поча́тках; **~starch** *n.* (*US*) = **cornflour**

corn[2] /kɔ:n/ *n.* (*on foot*) мозо́ль; **tread on s.o.'s ~s** (*fig.*) наступи́ть (*pf.*) кому́-н. на люби́мую мозо́ль.

● *cpd.* **~-plaster** *n.* мозо́льный пла́стырь.

corn[3] /kɔ:n/ *v.t.*: **~ed beef** консерви́рованная говя́дина, консе́рв|ы (*pl., g.* -ов) из говя́дины.

cornea /ˈkɔ:nɪə/ *n.* рогови́ца; рогова́я оболо́чка.

cornel /ˈkɔ:n(ə)l/ *n.* кизи́л.

cornelian /kɔ:ˈni:lɪən/ = **carnelian**

corner /ˈkɔ:nə(r)/ *n.* **1** (*place where lines etc. meet*) у́гол; **at, on the ~** на углу́; **round the ~** (*lit.*) за угло́м; (*fig., near*) ря́дом, побли́зости; **cut a ~** (*of car*) сре́зать (*pf.*) поворо́т; **he was driven into a ~** (*fig.*) он был за́гнан в у́гол (*or* припёрт к стене́); **in a tight ~** в затрудне́нии; **turn the ~** (*of illness*) благополу́чно перенести́ (*pf.*) кри́зис (боле́зни); **~ of one's eye** кра́ешек гла́за; **he looked out of the ~ of his eye** он следи́л кра́ешком гла́за; он наблюда́л укра́дкой.
2 (*hidden place etc.*) уголо́к, закоу́лок; **money hidden in odd ~s** де́ньги, припря́танные по уголка́м и закоу́лкам.
3 (*region*) край; **all the ~s of the earth** все уголки́ земли́.
4 (*football*) углово́й уда́р, ко́рнер.

● *v.t.* заг|оня́ть, -на́ть в у́гол; **the fugitive was ~ed** беглеца́ загна́ли в у́гол; **he ~ed the market** он завладе́л ры́нком, скупи́в весь това́р.

● *v.i.* (*of car*) брать, взять углы́.

● *cpd.* **~-stone** *n.* углово́й ка́мень; (*fig.*) краеуго́льный ка́мень.

cornet /ˈkɔ:nɪt/ *n.* **1** (*mus. instrument*) корне́т; корне́т-а-пистóн. **2** (*Br., for ice-cream*) ва́фельный рожо́к.

cornettist /kɔ:ˈnetɪst/, /ˈkɔ:nɪtɪst/ *n.* корнети́ст.

cornice /ˈkɔ:nɪs/ *n.* **1** (*archit.*) карни́з. **2** (*of snow*) нави́сшая глы́ба.

cornucopia /ˌkɔ:njʊˈkəʊpɪə/ *n.* рог изоби́лия.

corny /ˈkɔ:nɪ/ *adj.* (**cornier, corniest**) (*coll., hackneyed*) пло́ский, изби́тый.

corolla /kəˈrɒlə/ *n.* ве́нчик.

corollary /kəˈrɒlərɪ/ *n.* сле́дствие, вы́вод.

coro|na /kəˈrəʊnə/ *n.* (*pl.* **~nae** /-ni:/) (*astron.*) коро́на; (*bot.*) коро́на, вене́ц.

coronary /ˈkɒrənərɪ/ *n.* коронаротромбо́з.

● *adj.* (*anat.*) корона́рный, вене́чный; **~ artery** вене́чная арте́рия; **~ (thrombosis)** тромбо́з вене́чных арте́рий, коронаротромбо́з, инфа́ркт.

coronation /ˌkɒrəˈneɪʃ(ə)n/ *n.* корона́ция.

coroner /ˈkɒrənə(r)/ *n.* сле́дователь (*m.*), веду́щий дела́ о наси́льственной или скоропости́жной сме́рти.

coronet /ˈkɒrənɪt/, /-ˌnet/ *n.* (*small crown*) коро́на, диаде́ма; (*garland*) вено́к, вене́ц.

Corp. /ˌkɔ:pəˈreɪʃ(ə)n/ *n.* (*abbr. of* ***Corporation***) корпора́ция.

corpora /ˈkɔ:pərə/ *pl. of* ⇒**corpus**

corporal[1] /ˈkɔ:pr(ə)l/ *n.* (*officer*) капра́л.

corporal[2] /ˈkɔ:pr(ə)l/ *adj.* теле́сный; **~ punishment** теле́сное наказа́ние.

corporate /ˈkɔ:pərət/ *adj.* **1** (*collective*) о́бщий, коллекти́вный; **~ responsibility** коллекти́вная отве́тственность, кругова́я пору́ка. **2** (*of, forming a corporation*) корпорати́вный; **~ hospitality** корпорати́вное гостеприи́мство; **body ~** корпора́ция, юриди́ческое лицо́. **3**: **~ state** корпорати́вное госуда́рство.

corporation /ˌkɔ:pəˈreɪʃ(ə)n/ *n.* (*public body*) корпора́ция; (*US, company*) акционе́рное о́бщество; (*coll., paunch*) пу́зо, брю́хо.

corporeal /kɔ:ˈpɔ:rɪəl/ *adj.* теле́сный, материа́льный.

corps /kɔ:(r)/ *n.* (*pl.* **~** /kɔ:z/) (*mil., dipl.*) ко́рпус; **~ de ballet** кордебале́т.

corpse /kɔ:ps/ *n.* труп.

corpulence /ˈkɔ:pjʊləns/ *n.* полнота́, ту́чность, доро́дность.

corpulent /ˈkɔ:pjʊlənt/ *adj.* по́лный, ту́чный, доро́дный.

corpus /ˈkɔ:pəs/ *n.* (*pl.* **corpora** *or* **corpuses**) (*body of writings etc.*) свод, ко́декс; **~ delicti** соста́в преступле́ния.

corpuscle /ˈkɔ:pʌs(ə)l/ *n.* корпу́скула, те́льце, части́ца.

corral /kɒˈrɑ:l/ *n.* (*enclosure*) заго́н.

● *v.t.* (**corralled, corralling**) (*drive together*) заг|оня́ть, -на́ть в заго́н.

correct /kəˈrekt/ *adj.* **1** (*right, true*)

пра́вильный, ве́рный, то́чный; **an answer ~ to three decimal places** отве́т с то́чностью до тре́тьего десяти́чного зна́ка. **2** (*of behaviour*) корре́ктный.

● *v.t.* **1** (*make right*) испр|авля́ть, -а́вить; попр|авля́ть, -а́вить; **I ~ed my watch by the time signal** я вы́верил свои́ часы́ по сигна́лу вре́мени; **~ proofs** пра́вить/держа́ть (*impf.*) корректу́ру/гра́нки. **2** (*admonish, punish*) нака́з|ывать, -а́ть; де́лать, с- замеча́ние +*d.*

correction /kəˈrekʃ(ə)n/ *n.* **1** (*act of correcting*) исправле́ние, поправле́ние, пра́вка; **these figures are subject to ~** э́ти ци́фры подлежа́т исправле́нию. **2** (*thing substituted for what is wrong*) попра́вка, исправле́ние. **3** (*punishment*) наказа́ние; **house of ~** исправи́тельный дом.

● *cpd.* **~ fluid** *n.* корректи́рующая жи́дкость.

correctional /kəˈrekʃ(ə)nəl/ *adj.* исправи́тельный.

correctitude /kəˈrektɪˌtjuːd/ *n.* корре́ктность.

corrective /kəˈrektɪv/ *n.* корректи́в, попра́вка.

● *adj.* исправи́тельный.

correctness /kəˈrektnɪs/ *n.* пра́вильность, ве́рность, то́чность; (*of behaviour*) корре́ктность.

corrector /kəˈrektə(r)/ *n.* корре́ктор.

correlate /ˈkɒrəˌleɪt/, /ˈkɒrɪ-/ *v.t.* прив|оди́ть, -ести́ в соотноше́ние.

correlation /ˌkɒrəˈleɪʃ(ə)n/, /ˌkɒrɪ-/ *n.* соотноше́ние, корреля́ция.

correlative /kɒˈrelətɪv/, /kə-/ *n.* корреля́т.

● *adj.* соотноси́тельный, корреляти́вный.

correspond /ˌkɒrɪˈspɒnd/ *v.i.* **1** (*match, harmonize*) соотве́тствовать (*impf.*) (+*d.*). **2** (*exchange letters*) перепи́сываться (*impf.*) (c+*i.*).

correspondence /ˌkɒrɪˈspɒnd(ə)ns/ *n.* **1** (*analogy, agreement*) соотве́тствие. **2** (*letter-writing*) корреспонде́нция, перепи́ска; **I am in ~ with him** я с ним перепи́сываюсь; **he dealt with his ~** он разобра́л свою́ корреспонде́нцию; **~ column** (*Br.*) ру́брика пи́сем (в газе́те); **~ course** курс зао́чного обуче́ния.

correspondent /ˌkɒrɪˈspɒnd(ə)nt/ *n.* (*writer of letters; reporter*) корреспонде́нт; **he is a good ~** он добросо́вестный корреспонде́нт.

corresponding /ˌkɒrɪˈspɒndɪŋ/ *adj.* **1** (*matching*) соотве́тственный, соотве́тствующий. **2**: **~ member** (*of a society*) член-корреспонде́нт.

corridor /ˈkɒrɪˌdɔː(r)/ *n.* коридо́р.

corrigend|um /ˌkɒrɪˈgendəm/, /-ˈdʒendəm/ *n.* (*pl.* **~a**) опеча́тка; (*pl., list of* **~a**) спи́сок опеча́ток.

corroborate /kəˈrɒbəˌreɪt/ *v.t.* подтвер|жда́ть, -ди́ть.

corroboration /kəˌrɒbəˈreɪʃ(ə)n/ *n.* подтвержде́ние; **in ~** в подтвержде́ние (*чего*).

corroborative /kəˈrɒbərətɪv/ *adj.* подтвержда́ющий.

corrode /kəˈrəʊd/ *v.t.* разъ|еда́ть, -е́сть.

● *v.i.* ржа́ве́ть, за-.

corrosion /kəˈrəʊʒ(ə)n/ *n.* корро́зия, ржа́вчина.

corrosive /kəˈrəʊsɪv/ *adj.* коррози́йный, разъеда́ющий, е́дкий; (*fig.*) разъеда́ющий.

corrosiveness /kəˈrəʊsɪvnɪs/ *n.* коррози́йное сво́йство.

corrugate /ˈkɒrʊˌgeɪt/ *v.t.* гофрирова́ть (*impf., pf.*); **~d iron** волни́стое/рифлёное желе́зо.

corrupt /kəˈrʌpt/ *adj.* **1** (*depraved*) развращённый. **2** (*venal*) прода́жный, коррумпи́рованный, (*coll.*) подкупно́й; **~ practices** корру́пция, подку́пность и прода́жность. **3** (*unreliable, erroneous; also comput.*) испо́рченный; **~ Latin** испо́рченная латы́нь.

● *v.t.* **1** (*deprave*) развра|ща́ть, -ти́ть; разл|ага́ть, -ожи́ть. **2** (*bribe*) подкуп|а́ть, -и́ть. **3** (*distort; also comput.*) иска|жа́ть, -зи́ть.

corruptibility /kəˌrʌptəˈbɪlɪtɪ/ *n.* (*moral*) развраща́емость; (*accessibility to bribes*) подку́пность, прода́жность.

corruptible /kəˈrʌptəbəl/ *adj.* (*morally*) легко́ развраща́емый; (*bribable*) подкупно́й, прода́жный.

corruption /kəˈrʌpʃ(ə)n/ *n.* **1** (*depravity*) разложе́ние; развраще́ние. **2** (*bribery*) корру́пция, взя́точничество. **3** (*deformation*) по́рча, искаже́ние; **this word is a ~ of that** э́то сло́во — испо́рченный вариа́нт того́ сло́ва.

corruptness /kəˈrʌptnɪs/ *n.* прода́жность, коррумпи́рованность.

corsage /kɔːˈsɑːʒ/ *n.* (*bodice*) корса́ж; (*US, flower adornment*) цвето́к, прико́лотый к корса́жу.

corset /ˈkɔːsɪt/ *n.* корсе́т.

Corsica /ˈkɔːsɪkə/ *n.* Ко́рсика.

cortège /kɔːˈteɪʒ/ *n.* корте́ж.

cortex /ˈkɔːteks/ *n.* (*pl.* **cortices**) (*bark*) кора́; (*anat.*) кора́ больши́х полуша́рий головно́го мо́зга.

cortices /ˈkɔːtɪˌsiːz/ *pl. of* ⇒**cortex**

cortisone /ˈkɔːtɪˌzəʊn/ *n.* (*med.*) кортизо́н.

corundum /kəˈrʌndəm/ *n.* (*min.*) кору́нд.

coruscat|e /ˈkɒrəˌskeɪt/ *v.i.* (*lit., fig.*) сверк|а́ть, -ну́ть; блиста́ть (*impf.*); **~ing wit** сверка́ющее остроу́мие.

cos /kɒs/ *n.* (*also* **~ lettuce**) сала́т ромэ́н.

cosecant /kəʊˈsiːkənt/ *n.* (*math.*) косе́канс.

cosh /kɒʃ/ *n.* (*Br.*) дуби́нка.

● *v.t.* тра́хнуть (*pf.*) по голове́.

co-signatory /kəʊˈsɪgnətərɪ/ *n.* лицо́/госуда́рство, подпи́сывающее (*что*) совме́стно с други́ми ли́цами/госуда́рствами.

cosine /ˈkəʊsaɪn/ *n.* ко́синус.

cosiness /ˈkəʊzɪnɪs/ *n.* ую́т.

cosmetic /kɒzˈmetɪk/ *n.* косме́тика.

● *adj.* космети́ческий.

cosmetician /ˌkɒzmeˈtɪʃ(ə)n/ *n.* космети́чка.

cosmic /ˈkɒzmɪk/ *adj.* косми́ческий.

cosmogony /kɒzˈmɒgənɪ/ *n.* космого́ния.

cosmologist /kɒzˈmɒlədʒɪst/ *n.* космо́лог.

cosmology /kɒzˈmɒlədʒɪ/ *n.* космоло́гия.

cosmonaut /ˈkɒzməˌnɔːt/ *n.* космона́вт.

cosmopolitan /ˌkɒzməˈpɒlɪt(ə)n/ *n.* космополи́т.

● *adj.* космополити́ческий.

cosmopolitanism /kɒzməˈpɒlɪtənˌɪz(ə)m/ *n.* космополити́зм.

cosmos /ˈkɒzmɒs/ *n.* (*universe*) ко́смос, вселе́нная.

Cossack /ˈkɒsæk/ *n.* каза́|к (*fem.* -чка); (*attr.*) каза́цкий, каза́чий; **~ hat** папа́ха.

cosset /ˈkɒsɪt/ *v.t.* (**cosseted, cosseting**) балова́ть (*impf.*); не́жить (*impf.*).

cost /kɒst/ *n.* **1** (*monetary*) цена́, сто́имость; **~ price** себесто́имость; **he sold it at ~** он про́дал э́то по себесто́имости; **~ accounting** хозрасчёт; **~, insurance and freight** (*abbr.* **c.i.f.**) сто́имость това́ра, страхова́ние и фрахт (*abbr.* сиф); **~ of living** прожи́точный ми́нимум; **~ of production** изде́ржки (*f. pl.*) произво́дства. **2** (*expense, loss*) цена́; **at all ~s** любо́й цено́й; **at the ~ of his life** цено́й жи́зни; **count the ~** (*fig.*) взве́сить (*pf.*) возмо́жные после́дствия. **3** (*pl., leg.*) суде́бные изде́ржки (*f. pl.*); **he was awarded ~s** ему́ присуди́ли суде́бные изде́ржки.

● *v.t. & i.* **1** (*past and p.p.* **~**) (*involve expense*) сто́ить (*impf.*); об|ходи́ться, -ойти́сь (*кому во что*); **this ~ me £5** э́то сто́ило мне 5 фу́нтов; э́то обошло́сь мне в 5 фу́нтов; **it ~ me much trouble** э́то сто́ило мне значи́тельных хлопо́т; **it will ~ you dear** э́то вам до́рого обойдётся. **2** (*past and p.p.* **~ed**) (*assess* **~** *of*) оце́н|ивать, -и́ть изде́ржки (*предприятия и т.п.*).

● *cpds.* **~-effective** *adj.* рента́бельный; **~-effectiveness** *n.* рента́бельность.

costal /ˈkɒst(ə)l/ *adj.* рёберный.

co-star /ˈkəʊstɑː(r)/ *n.* партнёр (*fem.* -ша) (в друго́й гла́вной ро́ли).

● *v.t.*: **a film ~ring X and Y** фильм с уча́стием двух звёзд — X и У.

● *v.i.*: **they ~red in that picture** они́ снима́лись в э́том фи́льме в гла́вных роля́х.

Costa Rica /ˈkɒstə ˈriːkə/ *n.* Ко́ста-Ри́ка.

Costa Rican /ˈkɒstə ˈriːkən/ *n.* костарика́нец (*fem.* -ка).

● *adj.* костарика́нский.

coster(monger) /ˈkɒstəˌmʌŋgə(r)/ *n.*

у́личный торго́вец фру́ктами и овоща́ми.

costing /ˈkɒstɪŋ/ *n.* калькуля́ция издéржек произво́дства (*чего*).

costive /ˈkɒstɪv/ *adj.* страда́ющий запо́ром.

costliness /ˈkɒstlɪnɪs/ *n.* дороговизна; высо́кая цена́.

costly /ˈkɒstlɪ/ *adj.* (**costlier, costliest**) дорого́й, дорогосто́ящий.

costume /ˈkɒstju:m/ *n.* костю́м; (*attr.*): ~ **jewellery** (*Br.*), **jewelry** (*US*) бижутéрия; ~ **play** истори́ческая пьéса.

costum(i)er /kɒˈstju:mɪə(r)/ *n.* (*theatr.*) костюмéр; (*maker or seller of costumes*) торго́вец театра́льными и маскара́дными костю́мами.

cosy /ˈkəʊzɪ/ (*US* **cozy**) *adj.* (**cosier, cosiest**) ую́тный.

cot /kɒt/ *n.* (*Br., child's bed*) дéтская крова́тка; (*US, camp bed*) раскладу́шка; ~ **death** (*Br.*) внеза́пная смéрть (ребёнка грудно́го во́зраста).

cotangent /kəʊˈtændʒ(ə)nt/ *n.* кота́нгенс.

co-tenancy /kəʊˈtenənsɪ/ *n.* соарéнда.

co-tenant /kəʊˈtenənt/ *n.* соарендáтор.

coterie /ˈkəʊtərɪ/ *n.* кружо́к; (*pej.*) кли́ка.

coterminous /kəʊˈtɜ:mɪnəs/ *adj.* смéжный, грани́чащий; (*in meaning*) синоними́чный.

cotill(i)on /kəˈtɪljən/ *n.* котильо́н.

cottage /ˈkɒtɪdʒ/ *n.* коттéдж; за́городный дом, до́мик, да́ча; ~ **cheese** (прессо́ванный) творо́г; ~ **industry** надо́мное произво́дство; куста́рная промы́шленность; ~ **pie** (*Br.*) картóфельная запека́нка с мя́сом.

cotton¹ /ˈkɒt(ə)n/ *n.* **1** (*plant*) хло́пок, хлопча́тник. **2** (*fabric*) хло́пок; (хлопча́то)бума́жная ткань; ~ **print** си́тец. **3** (*thread*) ни́тки (*f. pl.*); (*piece of thread*) ни́тка; **a needle and** ~ иго́лка с ни́ткой. **4** (*attr.*) хло́пковый, хлопча́тый, хлопча́тобума́жный. **5** (*US*) = ~**-wool**

● *cpds.* ~ **candy** (*US*) = **candyfloss;** ~**-gin** *n.* хлопкоочисти́тельная маши́на; ~**-grass** *n.* пуши́ца; ~**-mill** *n.* хлопкопряди́льная/хлопкотка́цкая фа́брика; ~**-picker** *n.* (*person*) хлопкоро́б; (*machine*) хлопкоубо́рочная маши́на; ~**-seed** *n.* хло́пковое сéмя; семена́ (*nt. pl.*) хлопча́тника; ~**tail** *n.* америка́нский кро́лик; ~**-waste** *n.* хло́пковые отбро́сы (*m. pl.*); уга́р; ~**-wool** *n.* (*Br.*) ва́та; **wrap in** ~**-wool** (*fig.*) оберега́ть (*impf.*); трясти́сь (*impf.*) над + *i.*

cotton² /ˈkɒt(ə)n/ *v.i.* (*coll.*): ~ **on to** поня́ть (*pf.*), (*coll.*) усéчь (*pf.*).

cotyledon /ˌkɒtɪˈli:d(ə)n/ *n.* семядо́ля.

couch¹ /kaʊtʃ/ *n.* (*sofa*) кушéтка, дива́н; (*bed*) крова́ть.

● *v.t.* (*express*): **he** ~**ed his reply in friendly terms** он облёк свой отвéт в дру́жескую фо́рму.

● *v.i.* (*of animal: crouch*) притаи́ться (*pf.*).

couch² /ku:tʃ/, /kaʊtʃ/ *n.* (*also* ~**-grass**) пырéй ползу́чий.

couchette /ku:ˈʃet/ *n.* спа́льное мéсто.

cougar /ˈku:gə(r)/ *n.* пу́ма, кугуа́р.

cough /kɒf/ *n.* ка́шель (*m.*); **he has a bad** ~ у негó си́льный ка́шель; **he gave a warning** ~ он предупрежда́юще кашляну́л.

● *v.t. & i.* ка́шлять (*impf.*); ~ **up** (*lit.*) отка́шл|ивать, -яну́ть; (*fig., coll.*) выкла́дывать, вы́ложить.

● *cpds.* ~**-drop,** ~**-lozenge** *nn.* пасти́лка/таблéтка от ка́шля; ~**-medicine,** ~**-mixture** (*Br.*) *nn.* миксту́ра от ка́шля.

could /kʊd/ *v. aux., see* ⇨**can**²

coulomb /ˈku:lɒm/ *n.* кул́он.

council /ˈkaʊns(ə)l/ *n.* совéт; **town** ~ городско́й совéт; муниципалитéт; ~ **of war** воéнный совéт; **Church** ~ церко́вный собо́р.

● *cpds.* ~**-chamber** *n.* зал заседа́ний совéта; ~**-house** *n.* (*Br., dwelling*) муниципа́льный дом; жило́й дом, принадлежа́щий муниципа́льному совéту; ~**man** *n.* (*US*) член совéта; ~ **tax** *n.* (*Br.*) муниципа́льный нало́г.

councillor /ˈkaʊnsələ(r)/ (*US also* **councilor**) *n.* член совéта; совéтник.

counsel /ˈkaʊns(ə)l/ *n.* **1** (*advice, consultation*) совéт, совеща́ние; **take** ~ **with s.o.** совеща́ться (*impf.*) с кем-н.; **keep one's (own)** ~ пома́лкивать (*impf.*). **2** (*barrister(s)*) адвока́т; ~ **for the defence** (*Br.*), **defense** (*US*) защи́тник; ~ **for the plaintiff** адвока́т истца́.

● *v.t.* (**counselled, counselling;** *US* **counseled, counseling**) совéтовать, по- (+*d.*).

counsellor /ˈkaʊnsələ(r)/ (*US* **counselor**) *n.* совéтник.

count¹ /kaʊnt/ *n.* (*nobleman*) граф.

count² /kaʊnt/ *n.* **1** (*reckoning*) счёт, подсчёт; **keep** ~ счита́ть (*impf.*); вести́ (*det.*) счёт; **lose** ~ потеря́ть (*pf.*) счёт. **2** (*total*) ито́г; **the** ~ **was 200** ито́г равня́лся 200 (двумста́м). **3** (*leg.*) пункт обвини́тельного заключéния; **he was found guilty on all** ~**s** егó призна́ли вино́вным по всем пу́нктам обвини́тельного заключéния. **4** (*boxing*): **he took** (*or* **went down for**) **the** ~ он был нокаути́рован.

● *v.t.* (*number, reckon*) счита́ть, со-; подсчи́т|ывать, -а́ть; пересчи́т|ывать, -а́ть; **he** ~**ed (up) the men** он пересчита́л солда́т; ~ **your change!** провéрьте сда́чу!; ~ **ten!** сосчита́йте до десяти́!; **50 people, not** ~**ing the children** 50 человéк, не счита́я детéй; **I** ~ **him among my friends** я счита́ю егó мои́м дру́гом; ~ **me in/out!** включи́те/исключи́те меня́; **I shall** ~ **it an honour** (*Br.*), **honor** (*US*) **to serve you** я почту́ за чéсть служи́ть вам; **do not** ~ **that against him** не ста́вьте емý э́того в винý; **the boxer was** ~**ed out** боксёр был объя́влен нокаути́рованным.

● *v.i.* **1** (*reckon, number*) счита́ть (*impf.*); ~ **up to 10!** счита́йте до десяти́!; ~ **down from 10 to 0!** счита́йте в обра́тном поря́дке от десяти́ до нуля́!; ~**ing-house** бухгалтéрия. **2** (*be reckoned*) счита́ться (*impf.*); **that doesn't** ~ э́то не в счёт (*or* не счита́ется); ~ **for much** имéть большо́е значéние; ~ **for little** не имéть (*impf.*) большо́го значéния; немно́го сто́ить (*impf.*); ~ **for nothing** не имéть никако́го значéния; не идти́ в счёт; ничего́ не сто́ить; **he** ~**s among our friends** он счита́ется на́шим дру́гом. **3** (*rely*) рассчи́тывать (*impf.*) (на + *a.*); **I** ~ **(up)on you to help** я рассчи́тываю на ва́шу по́мощь.

● *cpd.* ~**-down** *n.* отсчёт врéмени.

countable /ˈkaʊntəb(ə)l/ *adj.* (*gram.*) исчисля́емый.

countenance /ˈkaʊntɪnəns/ *n.* **1** (*face*) лицо́, о́блик; выражéние лица́. **2** (*composure*) споко́йствие; **keep one's** ~ сохраня́ть (*impf.*) невозмути́мое выражéние лица́. **3** (*sanction*) поддéржка.

● *v.t.* поддéрж|ивать, -а́ть.

counter¹ /ˈkaʊntə(r)/ *n.* **1** (*at games*) фи́шка, ма́рка; **bargaining** ~ (*fig.*) ко́зырь (*m.*) (в запа́се). **2** (*in shop*) прила́вок; **under the** ~ (*fig.*) из-под полы́/прила́вка. **3** (*device for counting*) счётчик; **Geiger** ~ счётчик Гéйгера.

counter² /ˈkaʊntə(r)/ *adj. & adv.* (*contrary*) противополо́жный; напро́тив; **this runs** ~ **to my wishes** э́то идёт вразрéз с мои́ми жела́ниями.

● *v.t. & i.* (*oppose, parry*) противодéйствовать (*impf.*) + *d.*; отра|жа́ть, -зи́ть.

counteract /ˌkaʊntəˈrækt/ *v.t.* противодéйствовать (*impf.*) + *d.*

counteraction /ˌkaʊntərˈækʃ(ə)n/ *n.* противодéйствие.

counter-attack /ˈkaʊntərəˌtæk/ *n.* контрата́ка.

● *v.t. & i.* контратакова́ть (*impf., pf.*).

counter-attraction /ˈkaʊntərəˌtrækʃ(ə)n/ *n.* зама́нчивая альтернати́ва.

counterbalance /ˈkaʊntəˌbæləns/ *n.* противовéс.

● *v.t.* уравновé|шивать, -сить.

counterblast /ˈkaʊntəˌblɑ:st/ *n.* отвéтный уда́р/вы́пад.

counterblow /ˈkaʊntərˌbləʊ/ *n.* контруда́р; встрéчный уда́р.

countercharge /ˈkaʊntəˌtʃɑ:dʒ/ *n.* встрéчное обвинéние.

● *v.t.* предъявл|я́ть, -и́ть встрéчное обвинéние + *p.*

counter-claim /ˈkaʊntəˌkleɪm/ *n.* встрéчный иск; контробвинéние.

● *v.t. & i.* предъяв|ля́ть, -и́ть встрéчный иск (*кому*) (на + *a.*).

counter-clockwise /ˌkaʊntəˈklɒkwaɪz/ *adj. & adv.* (*US*) (дви́жущийся) про́тив часово́й стрéлки.

counter-demonstration /ˈkaʊntərˌdemənˈstreɪʃən/ *n.* ко́нтрдемонстра́ция; встрéчная демонстра́ция.

counter-espionage /ˌkaʊntərˈespɪəˌnɑːʒ/, /-ɪdʒ/ *n.* контрразве́дка.

counterfeit /ˈkaʊntəfɪt/, /-ˌfiːt/ *n.* подде́лка, подло́г.
● *adj.* подде́льный, подло́жный.
● *v.t. & i.* подде́л|ывать, -ать; (*fig., simulate*) подража́ть (*impf.*) + *d.*; притвор|я́ться, -и́ться.

counterfeiter /ˈkaʊntəfɪtə(r)/, /-ˌfiːtə(r)/ *n.* фальшивомоне́тчик.

counterfoil /ˈkaʊntəˌfɔɪl/ *n.* (*Br.*) корешо́к (че́ка, квита́нции *и т.п.*).

counter-intelligence /ˌkaʊntərɪnˈtelɪdʒ(ə)ns/ *n.* контрразве́дка.

countermand /ˌkaʊntəˈmɑːnd/ *v.t.* отмен|я́ть, -и́ть.

counter-measure /ˈkaʊntəˌmeʒə(r)/ *n.* контрме́ра.

counter-move /ˈkaʊntəˌmuːv/ *n.* контруда́р.

counter-offensive /ˈkaʊntərəˌfensɪv/ *n.* контрнаступле́ние.

counterpane /ˈkaʊntəˌpeɪn/ *n.* покрыва́ло.

counterpart /ˈkaʊntəˌpɑːt/ *n.* па́ра (*к чему*), дополне́ние; (*person*) колле́га (*c.g.*).

counterpoint /ˈkaʊntəˌpɔɪnt/ *n.* контрапу́нкт.

counterpoise /ˈkaʊntəˌpɔɪz/ *n.* противове́с, равнове́сие.
● *v.t.* уравнове́|шивать, -сить.

counter-productive /ˌkaʊntəprəˈdʌktɪv/ *adj.* приводя́щий к обра́тным результа́там; нецелесообра́зный.

counter-proposal /ˈkaʊntəprəˌpəʊz(ə)l/ *n.* встре́чное предложе́ние; контрпредложе́ние.

counter-revolution /ˌkaʊntəˌrevəˈluːʃ(ə)n/ *n.* контрреволю́ция.

counter-revolutionary /ˌkaʊntəˌrevəˈluːʃənərɪ/ *n.* контрреволюционе́р.
● *adj.* контрреволюцио́нный.

countersign /ˈkaʊntəˌsaɪn/ *n.* (*watchword*) паро́ль (*m.*), о́тзыв.
● *v.t.* (*add signature to*) ста́вить, по-втору́ю по́дпись на + *p.*; скреп|ля́ть, -и́ть по́дписью.

countersignature /ˈkaʊntəˌsɪɡnətʃə(r)/ *n.* втора́я по́дпись.

countersink /ˈkaʊntəsɪŋk/ *v.t.* (*past and p.p.* **countersunk**) зенкова́ть (*impf.*).

counterstroke /ˈkaʊntəˌstrəʊk/ *n.* контруда́р.

countertenor /ˈkaʊntəˌtenə(r)/ *n.* те́нор-альт.

counterweight /ˈkaʊntəˌweɪt/ *n.* противове́с, контргру́з.

countess /ˈkaʊntɪs/ *n.* графи́ня.

countless /ˈkaʊntlɪs/ *adj.* бесчи́сленный, несчётный, неисчисли́мый.

countrified /ˈkʌntrɪˌfaɪd/ *adj.* име́ющий дереве́нский вид.

country /ˈkʌntrɪ/ *n.* **1** (*geog., pol.*) страна́; **~ of birth** ро́дина.
2 (*motherland*) ро́дина, оте́чество.
3 (*opp. town*) дере́вня; **in the ~** за́ городом, на да́че; (**~***side*) приро́да, се́льская ме́стность; **~ life** се́льская/ дереве́нская жизнь; **~ cousin** провинциа́л (*fem.* -ка), (*coll.*) дереве́нщина (*c.g.*); **~ gentleman** землевладе́лец, поме́щик; **~ house, seat** поме́стье; **~ club** за́городный клуб.
4 (*terrain*) ме́стность; **difficult ~** труднопроходи́мая ме́стность; **wooded ~** леси́стая ме́стность.
5 (*fig., domain*) о́бласть, сфе́ра; **the subject is unknown ~ to me** э́то неизве́стная для меня́ о́бласть.
6: **go to the ~** (*Br., pol.*) распусти́ть (*pf.*) парла́мент и назна́чить (*pf.*) но́вые вы́боры.
● *cpds.* **~folk** *n.* се́льские жи́тели (*m. pl.*); **~man** *n.* дереве́нский/се́льский жи́тель (*m.*); (*fellow-***~***man*) соотéчественник, земля́к; **~side** *n.* се́льская ме́стность; ландша́фт; **~-wide** *adj.* распространя́ющийся на всю страну́; *adv.* по всей стране́; **~woman** *n.* дереве́нская/се́льская жи́тельница; (*fellow-***~***woman*) соотéчественница, земля́чка.

county /ˈkaʊntɪ/ *n.* (*in Britain*) гра́фство; (*in the US*) о́круг; **~ seat** (*US*) = **~ town; ~ town** (*Br.*) гла́вный го́род гра́фства; **~ families** (*Br.*) се́мьи (*f. pl.*) дже́нтри.

coup /kuː/ *n.* (*pl.* **coups** /kuːz/) уда́чный ход; *see also* ⇒**~ d'état**
● *cpds.* **~ de grâce** *n.* заверша́ющий уда́р; **~ d'état** *n.* госуда́рственный переворо́т.

coupé /ˈkuːpeɪ/ *n.* закры́тый автомоби́ль с двумя́ дверя́ми.

couple /ˈkʌp(ə)l/ *n.* (*objects or people*) па́ра; **married ~** супру́жеская па́ра; **engaged ~** жени́х и неве́ста.
● *v.t.* **1** (*rail*) сцеп|ля́ть, -и́ть.
2 (*associate, assemble*) соедин|я́ть, -и́ть; свя́з|ывать, -а́ть; **the name of Oxford is ~d with the idea of learning** О́ксфорд ассоции́руется с нау́чными заня́тиями.

coupler /ˈkʌplə(r)/ *n.* (*tech.*) сце́пщик.

couplet /ˈkʌplɪt/ *n.* рифмо́ванное двусти́шие.

coupling /ˈkʌplɪŋ/ *n.* (*rail.*) сцепле́ние, сце́пка; (*tech.*) связь, му́фта.

coupon /ˈkuːpɒn/ *n.* купо́н, тало́н.

courage /ˈkʌrɪdʒ/ *n.* хра́брость, сме́лость, му́жество; **take, pluck up ~** мужа́ться (*impf.*); соб|ира́ться, -ра́ться с ду́хом; **lose ~** пасть (*pf.*) ду́хом; **take one's ~ in both hands** мобилизова́ть (*impf., pf.*) всё своё му́жество; **Dutch ~** хра́брость во хмелю́; **he has the ~ of his convictions** он де́йствует согла́сно свои́м убежде́ниям; **I had not the ~ to refuse** у меня́ не хвати́ло ду́ху отказа́ться; **~!** (*as int.*) мужа́йтесь!

courageous /kəˈreɪdʒəs/ *adj.* хра́брый, сме́лый, му́жественный.

courgette /kʊəˈʒet/ *n.* (*Br.*) кабачо́к.

courier /ˈkʊrɪə(r)/ *n.* (*messenger*) курье́р, на́рочный; (*travel guide*) экскурсово́д.

course /kɔːs/ *n.* **1** (*movement, process*) ход, тече́ние; **~ of events** ход собы́тий; **in ~ of time** с тече́нием вре́мени; **in the ordinary ~** (*of events*) при норма́льном разви́тии собы́тий; **in due ~** в до́лжное/своё вре́мя; до́лжным о́бразом; **of ~** коне́чно; **as a matter of ~** обы́чным поря́дком; **he takes my help as a matter of ~** он принима́ет мою́ по́мощь как не́что само́ собо́й разуме́ющееся; **the disease must run its ~** боле́знь должна́ пройти́ все ста́дии; **I let matters take their ~** я пусти́л дела́ на самотёк; **the law took its ~** де́ло пошло́ зако́нным хо́дом.
2 (*direction*) курс, направле́ние; (*of a river*) тече́ние; (*naut.*) курс; **our ~ is, lies due north** мы де́ржим курс (*or* направле́ние) на се́вер; **we are on ~** мы идём по ку́рсу; **we are off ~** мы сби́лись с ку́рса.
3 (*line of conduct*): **this is the only ~ open to us** э́то — еди́нственно возмо́жный путь для нас.
4 (*race-***~**) скаково́й круг, доро́жка; **stay the ~** (*fig.*) держа́ться (*impf.*) до конца́.
5 (*series*) курс; **a ~ of lectures** курс ле́кций; **a ~ of treatment** курс лече́ния.
6 (*cul.*) блю́до; **main ~** второ́е блю́до; **sweet ~** сла́дкое, десе́рт.
7 (*masonry*) горизонта́льный ряд кла́дки.
● *v.i.* (*run about*) бе́гать (*indet.*); (*of water*) бежа́ть (*det.*); (*of blood*) течь (*impf.*).

court /kɔːt/ *n.* **1** (*yard*) двор.
2 (*space for playing games*) площа́дка для игр; (*tennis*) корт; **hard ~** бетони́рованный корт; **grass ~** землян́ой корт.
3 (*sovereign's etc.*) двор; **hold ~** (*maintain a* **~**) содержа́ть (*impf.*) двор; **she was presented at ~** её предста́вили ко двору́.
4 (*leg.*) суд; **~ of law, justice** суд; **~ of inquiry** сле́дственная коми́ссия; **High C.** (*Br.*), **Supreme C.** (*US*) Верхо́вный суд; **higher ~** суд вы́сшей инста́нции; **they settled (the case) out of ~** они́ пришли́ к (полюбо́вному) соглаше́нию; **he was brought to ~** (*for trial*) он предста́л пе́ред судо́м; **the judge had the ~ cleared** судья́ очи́стил зал от пу́блики.
5: **pay ~ to s.o.** уха́живать (*impf.*) за кем-н.
● *v.t.* **1** (*a woman*) уха́живать (*impf.*) за + *i.*
2 (*seek*): **she ~ed his approval** она́ добива́лась его́ одобре́ния.
3 (*risk*): **he is ~ing disaster** он игра́ет с огнём.
● *cpds.* **~-card** *n.* (*Br.*) фигу́рная ка́рта; **~-house** *n.* зда́ние суда́; **~-martial** *n.* вое́нный суд; *v.t.* (**-martialled, -martialling;** (*US*) **-martialed, -martialing**) суди́ть (*impf.*) вое́нным судо́м; **~-room** *n.* зал суда́; **~yard** *n.* двор.

courteous /ˈkɜːtɪəs/ *adj.* ве́жливый, учти́вый.

courtesan /ˌkɔːtɪˈzæn/, /ˈkɔːt-/ *n.* куртиза́нка.

courtesy /ˈkɜːtɪsɪ/ *n.* (*politeness*) ве́жливость, учти́вость; (*polite act*) любе́зность; **by ~ of Mr X** с любе́зного разреше́ния г-на X.

● *cpds.* **~ car, ~ bus** *nn.* беспла́тный тра́нспорт.

courtier /ˈkɔːtɪə(r)/ *n.* придво́рный.

courtliness /ˈkɔːtlɪnɪs/ *n.* обходи́тельность.

courtly /ˈkɔːtlɪ/ *adj.* (**courtlier, courtliest**) обходи́тельный; **~ love** ры́царская любо́вь.

courtship /ˈkɔːtʃɪp/ *n.* уха́живание.

cousin /ˈkʌz(ə)n/ *n.* (*also* **first ~**) (*male*) кузе́н; двою́родный брат; (*fem.*) кузи́на; двою́родная сестра́; **second ~** троюро́дный брат (*fem.* троюро́дная сестра́); **first ~ once removed** (*son or daughter of first ~*) двою́родный племя́нник (*fem.* двою́родная племя́нница); (*first ~ of parent*) двою́родный дя́дя (*fem.* двою́родная тётя); **our American ~s** на́ши америка́нские ро́дственники.

couturier /kuːˈtjʊərɪˌeɪ/ *n.* моделье́р.

cove[1] /kəʊv/ *n.* (*bay*) бу́хточка.

cove[2] /kəʊv/ *n.* (*Br. sl., fellow*) па́рень (*m.*), ма́лый.

coven /ˈkʌv(ə)n/ *n.* ша́баш ведьм.

covenant /ˈkʌvənənt/ *n.* соглаше́ние, догово́р; **C~ of the League of Nations** уста́в Ли́ги На́ций; (*relig.*) заве́т.

● *v.t. & i.* заключ|а́ть, -и́ть соглаше́ние; догов|а́риваться, -ори́ться (*с кем о чём*).

Coventry /ˈkɒvəntrɪ/ *n.*: **send to ~** (*Br.*) подв|ерга́ть, -е́ргнуть остраки́зму/бойко́ту.

cover /ˈkʌvə(r)/ *n.* **1** (*lid*) кры́шка, покры́шка.
2 (*loose ~ing of chair etc.*) чехо́л; (*pl., bedclothes*) посте́ль.
3 (*of book etc.*) переплёт, обло́жка; **I read the book from ~ to ~** я прочёл кни́гу от ко́рки до ко́рки; (*dust-~*) суперобло́жка.
4 (*wrapper, envelope*) обёртка, конве́рт; **under separate ~** в отде́льном конве́рте.
5 (*shelter, protection*) укры́тие, прикры́тие; **take ~** укр|ыва́ться, -ы́ться; **the ground provided no ~** укры́тия на ме́стности не́ было; **under ~ of darkness** под покро́вом темноты́.
6 (*concealment*): **the fox broke ~** лиса́ вы́шла из укры́тия.
7 (*pretence, pretext*) личина, ма́ска, ши́рма; **under ~ of friendship** под личи́ной дру́жбы; (*ostensible business, e.g. spy's*) кры́ша, вы́веска; **~ address** подставно́й а́дрес.
8 (*mil., protective force*) прикры́тие; **fighter ~** прикры́тие истреби́телями.
9 (*at table*) прибо́р; **~ charge** пла́та «за куве́рт».
10 (*Br., insurance*) страхова́ние.

● *v.t.* **1** (*overspread etc.; also* **~ up, ~ over**) покр|ыва́ть, -ы́ть; закр|ыва́ть, -ы́ть; прикр|ыва́ть, -ы́ть; накр|ыва́ть, -ы́ть; **~ a chair** об|ива́ть, -и́ть стул; **cats are ~ed with hair** ко́шки покры́ты ше́рстью; **she ~ed her face in/with her hands** она́ закры́ла лицо́ рука́ми; **her face is ~ed with freckles** у неё всё лицо́ в весну́шках (*or* усе́яно весну́шками); **the hills are ~ed with pine-trees** холмы́ поросли́ со́снами; **the roads are ~ed with snow** доро́ги занесены́ сне́гом; **trees ~ed with blossom** дере́вья в цвету́; **well ~ed** (*with clothes*) тепло́ оде́тый; (*with flesh*) в те́ле; **the taxi ~ed us with mud** такси́ окати́ло нас гря́зью; **the city ~ed ten square miles** го́род раски́нулся на 10 квадра́тных миль; **~ed** (*indoor*) **court** (*for tennis*) закры́тый корт; **~ed way** кры́тая галере́я.
2 (*fig.*) покр|ыва́ть, -ы́ть; скр|ыва́ть, -ы́ть; **he laughed to ~ (up) his nervousness** он засмея́лся, что́бы скрыть своё волне́ние; **he ~ed himself with glory** он покры́л себя́ сла́вой.
3 (*protect*) закр|ыва́ть, -ы́ть; прикр|ыва́ть, -ы́ть; **warships ~ed the landing** вое́нные корабли́ прикрыва́ли вы́садку войск; **are you ~ed against theft?** вы застрахо́ваны от кра́жи?; **these words ~ you against a libel charge** э́ти слова́ огради́т вас от обвине́ния в клевете́.
4 (*aim weapon at*) це́литься (*impf.*) в + *a.*; **he ~ed him** (*with his revolver*) он це́лился в него́ (из револьве́ра); он держа́л его́ под прице́лом; **our guns ~ed the road** на́ши ору́дия прикрыва́ли доро́гу (от неприя́теля).
5 (*travel*) покр|ыва́ть, -ы́ть; **we ~ed 5 miles by nightfall** мы прошли́ расстоя́ние в 5 миль до наступле́ния темноты́.
6 (*meet, satisfy*) покр|ыва́ть, -ы́ть; **£10 will ~ my needs** 10 фу́нтов хва́тит на мои́ ну́жды; **we only just ~ed expenses** мы едва́ покры́ли свои́ расхо́ды.
7 (*embrace, deal with*): **the lectures ~ a wide field** ле́кции охва́тывают широ́кий круг вопро́сов; **the rules ~ every possible case** э́ти пра́вила предусма́тривают все возмо́жные слу́чаи; **the reporter ~ed the conference** корреспонде́нт дава́л репорта́жи о хо́де конфере́нции; **this salesman ~s Essex** э́тот торго́вый аге́нт обслу́живает Эссекс.
8 (*of correspondence*): **~ing letter** сопроводи́тельное письмо́.
9 (*of male animal*) покр|ыва́ть, -ы́ть.

● *cpd.* **~-up** *n.* сокры́тие.

coverage /ˈkʌvərɪdʒ/ *n.* **1** (*extent or amount dealt with*) охва́т; **news ~** освеще́ние в печа́ти (*or* по ра́дио). **2** (*fin.*) покры́тие; гаранти́йный фонд. **3** (*insurance*) страхова́ние.

coveralls /ˈkʌvəˌɔːlz/ *n. pl.* комбинезо́н.

coverlet /ˈkʌvəlɪt/ *n.* покрыва́ло.

covert[1] /ˈkʌvət/ *n.* (*thicket*) ча́ща.

covert[2] /ˈkʌvət/, /ˈkəʊvɜːt/ *adj.* скры́тый, завуали́рованный.

covet /ˈkʌvɪt/ *v.t.* (**coveted, coveting**) вожделе́ть (*impf.*) к + *d.*; жа́ждать (*impf.*) + *g.*; (*coll.*) за́риться (*impf.*) на + *a.*

covetous /ˈkʌvɪtəs/ *adj.* а́лчный, жа́дный.

covetousness /ˈkʌvɪtəsnɪs/ *n.* а́лчность, жа́дность.

cow[1] /kaʊ/ *n.* **1** (*bovine*) коро́ва; **till the ~s come home** (*coll.*) до второ́го прише́ствия; (*of other mammals*) са́мка, коро́ва; *expr. by Ru. suff., e.g.* **~ elephant** слони́ха; **sacred ~** (*fig.*) неприкоснове́нное; «и́стина в после́дней инста́нции». **2** (*pej., woman*) коро́ва; **silly ~** дурёха.

● *cpds.* **~bell** *n.* колоко́льчик на ше́е коро́вы; **~boy** *n.* ковбо́й; **~herd** *n.* пасту́х; **~hide** *n.* (*leather*) воло́вья ко́жа; **~-house** *n.* (*Br.*) хлев, коро́вник; **~-pat** *n.* коровя́к; **~pox** *n.* коро́вья о́спа; **~shed** *n.* = **~-house**

cow[2] /kaʊ/ *v.t.* запу́г|ивать, -а́ть.

coward /ˈkaʊəd/ *n.* трус (*fem.* -и́ха).

cowardice /ˈkaʊədɪs/ *n.* тру́сость.

cowardly /ˈkaʊədlɪ/ *adj.* трусли́вый.

cower /ˈkaʊə(r)/ *v.i.* съёжи|ваться, -ться.

cowl /kaʊl/ *n.* (*hood*) капюшо́н; (*hooded garment*) ря́са, сута́на с капюшо́ном; (*chimney-~*) зонт над домово́й трубо́й.

cowling /ˈkaʊlɪŋ/ *n.* (*tech.*) капо́т дви́гателя.

cowr|ie, -y /ˈkaʊrɪ/ *nn.* (*zool.*) ка́ури (*nt. indecl.*).

cowslip /ˈkaʊslɪp/ *n.* первоцве́т.

cox /kɒks/ *n.* рулево́й.

● *v.t.*: **~ a boat** управля́ть (*impf.*) рулём ло́дки; сиде́ть (*impf.*) на руле́.

coxswain /ˈkɒkswеɪn/, /-s(ə)n/ *n.* старшина́ шлю́пки; (*helmsman*) рулево́й.

coy /kɔɪ/ *adj.* (**coyer, coyest**) (*bashful*) стыдли́вый; (*affectedly*) жема́нный; (*secretive*) скры́тный.

coyness /ˈkɔɪnɪs/ *n.* стыдли́вость; жема́нство; скры́тность.

coyote /kɔɪˈəʊtɪ/, /ˈkɔɪəʊt/ *n.* (*pl.* **~** *or* **~s**) койо́т.

coypu /ˈkɔɪpuː/ *n.* (*pl.* **~s**) (*zool.*) ну́трия, койпу (*m. indecl.*).

cozy /ˈkəʊzɪ/ (*US*) = **cosy**

Cpl. /ˈkɔːpər(ə)l/ *n.* (*abbr. of* ***Corporal***) капра́л.

CPSU (*abbr. of* ***Communist Party of the Soviet Union***) КПСС (Коммунисти́ческая па́ртия Сове́тского Сою́за).

CPU (*abbr. of* ***central processing unit***) (*comput.*) ЦП (центра́льный проце́ссор).

crab[1] /kræb/ *n.* краб; (*astron.*): **the C~** Рак.

● *v.i.* (**crabbed, crabbing**) (*fish for* **~s**) лови́ть (*impf.*) кра́бов.

● *cpd.* **~-like** *adj.* (*sidelong*) дви́жущийся бо́ком.

crab[2] /kræb/ *n.* (*also* **~-apple**) ди́кое я́блоко.

crabbed /ˈkræbɪd/ *adj.* (*irritable*) брюзжа́щий; (*illegible, obscure*) неразбо́рчивый.

crabby /ˈkræbɪ/ *adj.* (**crabbier, crabbiest**) брюзгли́вый.

crack /kræk/ *n.* **1** (*in a cup, ice etc.*) тре́щина; (*in the ground*) рассе́лина; (*in wall, floor etc.*) щель.
2 (*sudden noise*) треск, щёлканье; (*of thunder*) треск, уда́р.
3: **at ~ of dawn** с (пе́рвой) зарёй.
4 (*blow*) затре́щина; **he got a ~ on the head** он получи́л затре́щину.
5 (*coll., facetious remark*) остро́та.
6 (*coll., attempt*) попы́тка; **have a ~ at something** попыта́ть (*pf.*) свои́ си́лы в чём-н.
7: **a ~ regiment** отбо́рный полк; **a ~ shot** первокла́ссный стрело́к.
8 (*drug*) крэк.
● *v.t.* **1** (*make a ~ in, break open*) проб|ива́ть, -и́ть щель в (чём); взл|а́мывать, -ома́ть; **he fell and ~ed his skull** он упа́л и пролом́ил себе́ го́лову; **~ a nut** расколо́ть (*pf.*) оре́х; **~** (*broach*) **a bottle** раздави́ть (*pf.*) буты́лочку; **~ a code** разгада́ть (*pf.*) шифр; **~ a safe** взлома́ть (*pf.*) сейф.
2: **~ a whip** щёлк|ать, -нуть бичо́м; **~ a joke** отпусти́ть (*pf.*) шу́тку.
3: **~ed** (*crazy*) чо́кнутый.
● *v.i.* **1** (*get broken or fissured*) да|ва́ть, -ть тре́щину; тре́снуть (*pf.*); **the glass ~ed** стекло́ тре́снуло; (*fig., give way*): **he did not ~ under torture** пы́тки его́ не сломи́ли.
2 (*of sound*) щёлк|ать, -нуть; **a rifle ~ed (out)** разда́лся винто́вочный вы́стрел.
3: **the boy's voice ~ed** у ма́льчика слома́лся го́лос.
4 *see* ⇒**cracking**
● *with advs.*: **~ down** *v.i.* **~ down on** прин|има́ть, -я́ть круты́е ме́ры про́тив + *g.*; **~ up** *v.t.* (*praise*) захва́л|ивать, -и́ть; **the book is not all it's ~ed up to be** э́та кни́га не та́к хороша́, как её расписы́вают; *v.i.* (*of person: suffer collapse*) надломи́ться (*pf.*); разв|а́ливаться, -и́ться.
● *cpds.* **~-brained, ~-pot** *adjs.* поме́шанный; **~-down** *n.* распра́ва; **~-up** *n.* (*breakdown*) упа́док сил.

cracker /ˈkrækə(r)/ *n.* **1** (*firework*) хлопу́шка, шути́ха. **2** (*biscuit*) кре́кер. **3** (*pl., nut-~s*) щипц|ы́ (*pl., g.* -о́в) для оре́хов.

crackerjack /ˈkrækəˌdʒæk/ *adj.* (*US coll.*) первокла́ссный; вы́сшего кла́сса.

crackers /ˈkrækəz/ *adj.* (*Br. sl., mad*) рехну́вшийся.

cracking /ˈkrækɪŋ/ *adj. & adv.*: **at a ~ pace** (*Br.*) стреми́тельно; бо́дрым ша́гом; **we had a ~ good time** (*Br.*) мы здо́рово провели́ вре́мя; **get ~!** пошеве́ливайся!; за рабо́ту!

crackle /ˈkræk(ə)l/ *n.* (*sound*) треск, потре́скивание.
● *v.i.* (*of sound*) потре́скивать (*impf.*).

crackling /ˈkræklɪŋ/ *n.* **1** (*sound*) треск, хруст. **2** (*cul.*) шква́рки (*f. pl.*).

Cracow /ˈkrækaʊ/ *n.* Кра́ков.

cradle /ˈkreɪd(ə)l/ *n.* **1** (*lit., fig.*) колыбе́ль; лю́лька; **from ~ to grave** всю жизнь; **Greece is the ~ of Western civilization** Гре́ция — колыбе́ль за́падной цивилиза́ции.
2 (*shipbuilding*) спусковы́е сала́з|ки (*pl., g.* -ок); (*teleph.*) рыча́г.
● *v.t.*: **~ a child in one's arms** держа́ть (*impf.*) ребёнка на рука́х; **~** (*put down*) **the receiver** класть, положи́ть тру́бку на рыча́г.
● *cpd.* **~-song** *n.* колыбе́льная (пе́сня).

craft /krɑːft/ *n.* **1** (*guile*) хи́трость, хитроу́мие. **2** (*skill*) ло́вкость, уме́ние. **3** (*occupation*) ремесло́; **arts and ~s** иску́сства и ремёсла (*nt. pl.*). **4** (*pl.* **~**) (*boat*) су́дно.
● *cpds.* **~sman** *n.* реме́сленник, ма́стер; **~smanship** *n.* мастерство́.

craftiness /ˈkrɑːftɪnɪs/ *n.* хи́трость.

crafty /ˈkrɑːftɪ/ *adj.* (**craftier, craftiest**) хи́трый.

crag /kræg/ *n.* скала́, утёс.

cragginess /ˈkrægɪnɪs/ *n.* скали́стость.

craggy /ˈkrægɪ/ *adj.* (**craggier, craggiest**) скали́стый.

cram /kræm/ *v.t.* (**crammed, cramming**) **1** (*insert forcefully*) запи́х|ивать, -а́ть/-ну́ть; впи́х|ивать, -ну́ть; (*fill*): **the shelves are ~med with books** по́лки ло́мятся от книг. **2** (*v.t. & i.*) (*teach, study intensively*) репети́ровать (*impf.*); (*coll.*) ната́ск|ивать, -а́ть; зубри́ть (*impf.*); **~ pupils** репети́ровать/ната́скивать (*impf.*) ученико́в.
● *cpd.* **~-full** *adj.* по́лный до отка́за; битко́м наби́тый.

crammer /ˈkræmə(r)/ *n.* (*Br., tutor*) репети́тор.

cramp /kræmp/ *n.* **1** (*of muscles*) су́дорога; **writer's ~** су́дорога в па́льцах; **the swimmer was seized with ~** пловца́ схвати́ла су́дорога. **2** (*also* **~-iron**) (*pl.*) клёщ|и (*pl., g.* -е́й).
● *v.t.* (*hamper*) стесн|я́ть, -и́ть; **we are ~ed for room** у нас здесь поверну́ться не́где; **~ s.o.'s style** (*fig.*) не дава́ть (*impf.*) кому́-н. разверну́ться; **a ~ed handwriting** ме́лкий (и) неразбо́рчивый по́черк.

crampon /ˈkræmpən/ *n.* (*on boot*) подо́шва с шипа́ми; (*pl.*) ко́шки (*f. pl.*).

cranberry /ˈkrænbərɪ/ *n.* клю́ква (*collect.*); (*single berry*) я́года клю́квы, клю́квина (*coll.*).

crane /kreɪn/ *n.* (*bird*) жура́вль (*m.*); (*machine*) (грузо)подъёмный кран.
● *v.t.*: **~ one's neck** вытя́гивать, вы́тянуть ше́ю.
● *cpd.* **~-fly** *n.* долгоно́жка.

crania /ˈkreɪnɪə/ *pl. of* ⇒**cranium**

cranial /ˈkreɪnɪəl/ *adj.* черепно́й.

crani|um /ˈkreɪnɪəm/ *n.* (*pl.* **~ums** *or* **~a**) че́реп.

crank[1] /kræŋk/ *n.* (*handle*) кривоши́п; коле́нчатый рыча́г; рукоя́тка; заводна́я ру́чка.
● *v.t.*: **~ a car** зав|оди́ть, -ести́ мото́р вручну́ю.
● *cpds.* **~case** *n.* (*tech.*) ка́ртер (дви́гателя); **~shaft** *n.* (*tech.*) коле́нчатый вал.

crank[2] /kræŋk/ *n.* (*person*) чуда́|к (*fem.* -чка); челове́к с причу́дами.

crankiness /ˈkræŋkɪnɪs/ *n.* скло́нность к причу́дам, чуда́чество; (*US*) раздражи́тельность.

cranky /ˈkræŋkɪ/ *adj.* (**crankier, crankiest**) (*eccentric*) с причу́дами/приве́том; (*US, peevish*) раздражи́тельный.

cranny /ˈkrænɪ/ *n.* тре́щина.

crap[1] /kræp/ (*vulg.*) *n.* (*shit*) говно́; (*nonsense*) вздо́р, чепуха́.
● *v.i.* (**crapped, crapping**) (*shit*) срать (*impf.*).

crap[2] /kræp/ *n.* (*pl., game; also* **~-shooting**) игра́ в ко́сти; **shoot ~s** броса́ть (*impf.*) ко́сти.
● *cpd.* **~shooter** *n.* игро́к в ко́сти.

crape /kreɪp/ *n.* креп.

crappy /ˈkræpɪ/ *adj.* (**crappier, crappiest**) (*vulg.*) лажо́вый, дрянно́й, дерьмо́вый.

crash /kræʃ/ *n.* **1** (*noise*) гро́хот, гром. **2** (*fall, smash*) ава́рия, круше́ние; **he was killed in a car/plane ~** он поги́б в автомоби́льной/авиацио́нной катастро́фе; (*comput.*) фата́льный сбой; (*fig., disaster*) катастро́фа, крах. **3**: **a ~** (*intensive*) **course** ускоренный курс.
● *v.t.* разб|ива́ть, -и́ть; гро́хнуть (*pf.*); **he ~ed his fist down on the table** он гро́хнул кулако́м по́ столу; **he ~ed the aircraft** он разби́л самолёт; **~** (*gate-~*) **a party** ворва́ться (*pf*) на ве́чер без приглаше́ния.
● *v.i.*: **the music ~ed out** загреме́ла му́зыка; **the plane ~ed** самолёт потерпе́л ава́рию (*or* разби́лся); **the cars ~ed together** автомоби́ли столкну́лись; **he ~ed into the room** он ворва́лся/вломи́лся в ко́мнату; **he is a ~ing bore** (*coll.*) он невыноси́мый зану́да.
● *cpds.* **~-helmet** *n.* шлем автого́нщика/мотоцикли́ста; мотошле́м; **~-land** *v.t. & i.* соверш|а́ть, -и́ть авари́йную поса́дку; **~-landing** *n.* авари́йная поса́дка.

crass /kræs/ *adj.* гру́бый; тупо́й; **~ stupidity** непроходи́мая ту́пость.

crassness /ˈkræsnɪs/ *n.* гру́бость; ту́пость.

crate /kreɪt/ *n.* я́щик.
● *v.t.* пакова́ть, у- в я́щик(и).

crater /ˈkreɪtə(r)/ *n.* кра́тер; (*bomb-~*) воро́нка.

cravat /krəˈvæt/ *n.* широ́кий га́лстук; ше́йный плато́к.

crave /kreɪv/ *v.t. & i.* (*desire*) жа́ждать (*impf.*) + *g.*; **he ~d for a drink** ему́ до́ сме́рти хоте́лось вы́пить.

craven /ˈkreɪv(ə)n/ *adj.* трусли́вый, малоду́шный.

craving /ˈkreɪvɪŋ/ *n.* стра́стное жела́ние.

craw /krɔː/ *n.* зоб

crawfish /ˈkrɔːfɪʃ/ = **crayfish**

crawl /krɔːl/ *n.* **1** (**~ing motion**) по́лзание; **traffic was reduced to a ~**

тра́нспорт тащи́лся е́ле-е́ле. **2** (*swimming stroke*) кроль (*m.*).

● *v.i.* **1** (*e.g. of reptile*) по́лзать (*indet.*), ползти́ (*det.*); **he ~ed on his hands and knees** он полз на четвере́ньках. **2** (*go very slowly*) ползти́ (*det.*); **the train ~ed over the damaged bridge** по́езд ме́дленно тащи́лся по повреждённому мосту́. **3** (*kowtow*) по́лзать (*indet.*) (*перед кем*); пресмыка́ться (*impf.*) (*перед кем*); **he ~s to the boss** он пресмыка́ется перед нача́льником. **4**: **the ground is ~ing with ants** земля́ кишмя́ киши́т муравья́ми. **5** (*tickle*): **my skin is ~ing** у меня́ мура́шки по те́лу бе́гают.

crawler /ˈkrɔ:lə(r)/ *n.* **1** (*Br., obsequious person*) низкопокло́нник, подхали́м. **2** (*pl., baby's garment*) ползунк|и́ (*pl., g.* -о́в).

cray|fish /ˈkreɪfɪʃ/, **craw-** /ˈkrɔ:fɪʃ/ *nn.* (*freshwater*) речно́й рак; (*marine*) лангу́ст(а).

crayon /ˈkreɪən/, /-ɒn/ *n.* цветно́й каранда́ш; цветно́й мело́к; пасте́ль.

● *v.t. & i.* рисова́ть (*impf.*) цветны́м карандашо́м (*or* пасте́лью).

craze /kreɪz/ *n.* ма́ния, помеша́тельство; пова́льная мо́да.

● *v.t.* св|оди́ть, -ести́ с ума́.

craziness /ˈkreɪzɪnɪs/ *n.* (*madness*) безу́мие, сумасше́ствие, помеша́тельство.

crazy /ˈkreɪzɪ/ *adj.* (**crazier, craziest**) **1** (*mad*) безу́мный, сумасше́дший; **~ about something** поме́шанный на чём-н.; **a ~ scheme** безу́мный план; **he is ~ about her** он без ума́ от неё. **2**: **~ paving** (*Br.*) моще́ние из камне́й разли́чной фо́рмы.

creak /kri:k/ *n.* скрип.

● *v.i.* скрипе́ть (*impf.*).

cream /kri:m/ *n.* **1** (*top part of milk*) сли́в|ки (*pl., g.* -ок); **whipped ~** взби́тые сли́вки; **~ cheese** сли́вочный сыро́к. **2** (*dish or sweet*) крем; **~ cake** торт с кре́мом; кре́мовое пиро́жное; **~ puff** сло́йка с кре́мом; **chocolate ~s** шокола́дные конфе́ты (*f. pl.*); **salad ~** (*Br.*) майоне́з; **~ of celery (soup)** суп-пюре́ из сельдере́я. **3** (*polish, cosmetic etc.*) крем, мазь; **shoe ~** крем для о́буви; **face ~** крем для лица́; **cold ~** кольдкре́м. **4** (*of other liquid*) пе́на; **~ of tartar** ви́нный ка́мень. **5** (*best part*): **the ~ of society** сли́вки о́бщества. **6** (*attr.*, **~-coloured**) кре́мового цве́та.

● *v.t.* (*apply ~ to*) на|кла́дывать, -ложи́ть крем на + *a*; нама́з|ывать, -ать кре́мом; **she ~ed her face** она́ наложи́ла на лицо́ крем; (*work together to form a paste*): **she ~ed the butter and sugar** она́ стира́ла ма́сло с са́харом; **~ off** от|бира́ть, -обра́ть.

● *cpds.* **~-coloured** (*US* **-colored**) *adj.* кре́мового цве́та; кре́мовый; **~-jug** *n.* сли́вочник.

creamer /ˈkri:mə(r)/ *n.* (*milk, cream substitute*) осветли́тель (*m.*); (*US*) = **cream-jug**

creamery /ˈkri:mərɪ/ *n.* (*place of sale*) моло́чная; (*factory*) маслобо́йный заво́д, маслобо́йня.

creaminess /ˈkri:mɪnɪs/ *n.* жи́рность (молока́).

creamy /ˈkri:mɪ/ *adj.* (**creamier, creamiest**) жи́рный; (*colour*) кре́мовый.

crease /kri:s/ *n.* скла́дка, морщи́на; (*in trousers*) скла́дка.

● *v.t.* (*wrinkle*) мять (*or* смина́ть), с-.

● *v.i.* (*form ~s*) мя́ться (*or* смина́ться), с-.

● *cpd.* **~-resistant** *adj.* немну́щийся.

create /kri:ˈeɪt/ *v.t.* созд|ава́ть, -а́ть; твори́ть, со-; произв|оди́ть, -ести́; **God ~d the world** Бог сотвори́л мир; **Dickens ~d many characters** Ди́ккенс со́здал мно́го о́бразов; **it ~d a bad impression** э́то произвело́ дурно́е впечатле́ние.

creation /kri:ˈeɪʃ(ə)n/ *n.* **1** (*act, process*) созда́ние, созида́ние; **~ of the world** сотворе́ние ми́ра. **2** (*the universe*) мирозда́ние. **3** (*product of imagination*) творе́ние, произведе́ние.

creative /kri:ˈeɪtɪv/ *adj.* тво́рческий.

creativeness /kri:ˈeɪtɪvnɪs/ *n.* тво́рческий дар.

creator /kri:ˈeɪtə(r)/ *n.* созда́тель (*m.*), творе́ц.

creature /ˈkri:tʃə(r)/ *n.* **1** (*living being*) созда́ние, тварь, существо́; **she is a lovely ~** она́ — очарова́тельное созда́ние/существо́; **poor ~** несча́стное созда́ние; бедня́жка (*c.g.*); **a good ~** хоро́ший/добросерде́чный челове́к. **2**: **~ comforts** земны́е бла́га.

crèche /kreʃ/, /kreɪʃ/ *n.* (*Br.*) (де́тские) я́сл|и (*pl., g.* -е́й).

credence /ˈkri:d(ə)ns/ *n.* ве́ра, дове́рие; **give ~ to** пове́рить (*pf.*) + *d.*

credential /krɪˈdenʃ(ə)l/ *n.* (*usu. pl.*) **1** (*pl., qualifications*) квалифика́ции; (*testimonial*) удостовере́ние; манда́т. **2** (*ambassador's*) вери́тельная гра́мота.

credibility /ˌkredɪˈbɪlɪtɪ/ *n.* (*of person*) спосо́бность вы́звать дове́рие; (*of thing*) правдоподо́бие, достове́рность; (*plausibility*) убеди́тельность.

credible /ˈkredɪb(ə)l/ *adj.* (*of person*) заслу́живающий дове́рия; (*of thing*) правдоподо́бный, вероя́тный, достове́рный.

credit /ˈkredɪt/ *n.* **1** (*belief, trust, confidence*) ве́ра, дове́рие; **give ~ to, place ~ in** (*a report etc.*) пове́рить (*pf.*) + *d.*; доверя́ть (*impf.*) + *d.*; **this lends ~ to the story** э́то де́лает расска́з правдоподо́бным. **2** (*honour, reputation*): **a man of the highest ~** челове́к с прекра́сной репута́цией; **the work does you ~** э́та рабо́та де́лает вам честь; **he is cleverer than I gave him ~ for** он умне́е, чем я счита́л; **this is to his ~** э́то говори́т в его́ по́льзу; **he took ~ for the success** он приписа́л успе́х себе́; **give ~ where ~ is due** возда́ть (*pf.*) до́лжное кому́ сле́дует; **~ titles** (*cin., also* **~s**) вступи́тельные ти́тры (*m. pl.*). **3** (*book-keeping*) кре́дит; (*fin.*) креди́т; **buy on ~** покупа́ть (*pf.*) в креди́т; **~ balance** кре́дитовый бала́нс, са́льдо (*indecl.*); **~ card** креди́тная ка́рточка; **letter of ~** аккредити́в; **this shop gives no ~** э́тот магази́н не отпуска́ет/продаёт това́ры в креди́т; **his ~ is good for £50** он име́ет креди́т на 50 фу́нтов; **place the sum to my ~** внеси́те э́ту су́мму на мой счёт.

● *v.t.* (**credited, crediting**) **1** (*believe something*) ве́рить, по- + *d.*; доверя́ть (*impf.*) + *d.* **2**: **I ~ed him with more sense** я счита́л его́ бо́лее благоразу́мным. **3** (*fin.*): **I ~ed him with £10** (*or* **£10 to him**) я внёс 10 фу́нтов на его́ счёт.

● *cpds.* **~-worthiness** *n.* кредитоспосо́бность; **~-worthy** *adj.* заслу́живающий креди́та, кредитоспосо́бный.

creditable /ˈkredɪtəb(ə)l/ *adj.* (*praiseworthy*) де́лающий честь (+ *d.*); (*believable*) правдоподо́бный, вероя́тный.

creditor /ˈkredɪtə(r)/ *n.* кредито́р.

credo /ˈkreɪdəʊ/, /ˈkri:-/ *n.* (*pl.* **~s**) кре́до (*indecl.*).

credulity /krɪˈdju:lɪtɪ/ *n.* легкове́рие, дове́рчивость.

credulous /ˈkredjʊləs/ *adj.* легкове́рный, дове́рчивый.

creed /kri:d/ *n.* вероуче́ние; (*fig.*) убежде́ния (*nt. pl.*), кре́до (*indecl.*).

creek /kri:k/ *n.* (*inlet*) зали́в, бу́хта; (*small river*) ре́чка; **up the ~** (*coll.*) в беде́.

creel /kri:l/ *n.* корзи́на для ры́бы.

creep /kri:p/ *n.* **1** (*act of ~ing*) по́лзание. **2** (*of metal*) пласти́ческая деформа́ция, крип. **3**: **it gives me the ~s** (*coll.*) от э́того у меня́ моро́з по ко́же. **4** (*sl., obnoxious person*) несно́сный/отврати́тельный тип.

● *v.i.* (*past and p.p.* **crept**) **1** (*crawl, move stealthily*) по́лзать (*indet.*), ползти́ (*det.*); кра́сться (*impf.*). **2** (*fig.*): **old age ~s up on one unnoticed** ста́рость подкра́дывается незаме́тно. **3** (*of plants*) стла́ться (*impf.*); ви́ться (*impf.*).

creeper /ˈkri:pə(r)/ *n.* (*plant*) ползу́чее/выю́щееся расте́ние.

creepiness /ˈkri:pɪnɪs/ *n.* жуть.

creepy /ˈkri:pɪ/ *adj.* (**creepier, creepiest**) **1** жу́ткий. **2** (*of flesh*) в мура́шках.

● *cpd.* **~-crawly** *n.* бука́шка.

cremate /krɪˈmeɪt/ *v.t.* креми́ровать (*impf., pf.*).

cremation /krɪˈmeɪʃ(ə)n/ *n.* крема́ция.

cremator /krɪˈmeɪtə(r)/ *n.* (*furnace*) кремацио́нная печь.

cremator|ium /ˌkreməˈtɔ:rɪəm/ *n.* (*pl.* **~ia** *or* **~iums**) кремато́рий.

crematory /ˈkremətərɪ/ *n.* (*US*) = **crematorium**

crème de la crème /ˌkrem də lɑ: ˈkrem/ *n.* сли́в|ки (*pl., g.* -ок) о́бщества, эли́та.

crème de menthe /ˌkrem də ˈmɑ̃t/, /ˈmɒnt/ *n.* мя́тный ликёр.

crenellate /ˈkrenə,leɪt/ *v.t.*: **~d walls** зу́бчатые сте́ны.

Creole /ˈkriːəʊl/ *n.* (*of European descent*) крео́л (*fem.* -ка); (*of part-Negro descent, also*) мула́т (*fem.* -ка).

● *adj.* крео́льский.

creosote /ˈkriːə,səʊt/ *n.* креозо́т.

crêpe /kreɪp/ *n.* креп; **~ paper** гофриро́ванная бума́га; **~ soles** каучу́ковые подо́швы; **~ de Chine** крепдеши́н.

crepitate /ˈkrepɪ,teɪt/ *v.i.* (*crackle*) хрусте́ть (*impf.*).

crept /krept/ *past and p.p. of* ⇒**creep**

crescen|do /krɪˈʃendəʊ/ *n.* (*pl.* **~dos** *or* **~di** /-dɪ/) креще́ндо (*indecl.*).

● *adj.* креще́ндо.

crescent /ˈkrez(ə)nt/, /ˈkres-/ *n.* **1** (*moon*) лу́нный серп. **2** (*symbol of Islam*) полуме́сяц. **3** (*Br., street, row of houses*) ряд домо́в, располо́женных полукру́гом.

● *cpd.* **~-shaped** *adj.* серпови́дный, серпообра́зный.

cress /kres/ *n.* кресс(-сала́т).

crest /krest/ *n.* **1** (*tuft of feathers*) гре́бень (*m.*), хохоло́к. **2** (*helmet*) шлем; (*top of helmet*) гре́бень (*m.*) шле́ма. **3** (*her. device*) герб. **4** (*of wave*) гре́бень (*m.*); **he is on the ~ of a wave** (*fig.*) он на верши́не сла́вы.

● *v.t.*: **~ed notepaper** пи́счая бума́га с гербо́м; **a golden ~ed bird** пти́ца с золоты́м хохолко́м.

● *cpd.* **~fallen** *adj.* упа́вший ду́хом; удручённый.

cretaceous /krɪˈteɪʃəs/ *adj.* мелово́й.

Cretan /ˈkriːt(ə)n/ *n.* жи́тель (*fem.* -ница) Кри́та.

● *adj.* кри́тский.

Crete /kriːt/ *n.* Крит.

cretin /ˈkretɪn/ *n.* (*lit., fig.*) крети́н.

cretinism /ˈkretɪ,nɪzəm/ *n.* кретини́зм.

cretinous /ˈkretɪnəs/ *adj.* слабоу́мный (*also fig.*).

cretonne /kreˈtɒn/, /ˈkre-/ *n.* (*text.*) крето́н.

crevasse /krəˈvæs/ *n.* рассе́лина в леднике́.

crevice /ˈkrevɪs/ *n.* щель, расще́лина.

crew[1] /kruː/ *n.* **1** (*of vessel*) кома́нда, экипа́ж; (*of aircraft*) экипа́ж; (*of train*) брига́да; (*aeron.*): **ground ~** назе́мный обслу́живающий персона́л. **2** (*team*) брига́да, арте́ль; (*lot, gang*) ба́нда. **3**: **~ cut** стри́жка ёжиком.

● *v.t.* обслу́живать (*impf.*) (*корабль*).

crew[2] /kruː/ *past of* ⇒**crow**[2]

crib /krɪb/ *n.* **1** (*US, cot*) де́тская крова́тка; **~ death** = **cot death** (*see* **cot**). **2** (*manger*) я́с|ли (*pl., g.* -ей), корму́шка. **3** (*plagiarism*) плагиа́т. **4** (*literal translation*) подстро́чник; (*for cheating*) шпарга́лка (*coll.*).

● *v.t.* (**cribbed, cribbing**) (*plagiarize*) спи́с|ывать, -а́ть (*что у кого*).

● *v.i.* (**cribbed, cribbing**) (*of schoolboy*) сду|ва́ть, -ть (*sl.*).

● *cpd.* **crib death** (*US*) = **cot death**

cribbage /ˈkrɪbɪdʒ/ *n.* кри́ббидж.

crick /krɪk/ *n.* растяже́ние мышц.

● *v.t.* растяну́ть (*pf.*) мы́шцу.

cricket[1] /ˈkrɪkɪt/ *n.* (*insect*) сверчо́к.

cricket[2] /ˈkrɪkɪt/ *n.* (*game*) кри́кет; **it isn't ~** (*fig., Br.*) э́то нече́стно; э́то не по пра́вилам.

cricketer /ˈkrɪkɪtə(r)/ *n.* игро́к в кри́кет.

cri de coeur /,kriː də ˈkɜː(r)/ *n.* (*pl.* ***cris de coeur*** *pronunc. same*) крик души́.

crier /ˈkraɪə(r)/ *n.* (*official*) глаша́тай.

crikey /ˈkraɪkɪ/ *int.* (*Br. sl.*) мать честна́я!; ну и ну!

crime /kraɪm/ *n.* **1** (*act*) преступле́ние; **~ of violence** преступле́ние с примене́нием наси́лия. **2** (**~*s in general***) престу́пность; **~ fiction** детекти́вный рома́н.

Crimea /kraɪˈmɪə/ *n.* Крым; **in the ~** в Крыму́; **native of ~** крымча́|к (*fem.* -чка).

Crimean /kraɪˈmɪən/ *adj.* кры́мский.

criminal /ˈkrɪmɪn(ə)l/ *n.* престу́пни|к (*fem.* -ца); **war ~** вое́нный престу́пник.

● *adj.* **1** (*guilty*) престу́пный; **he has a ~ history** у него́ престу́пное про́шлое. **2** (*pert. to crime*) уголо́вный, кримина́льный; **~ action** (*prosecution*) уголо́вное де́ло; **~ code** уголо́вный ко́декс; **~ court** суд по уголо́вным дела́м; **~ law** уголо́вное пра́во.

criminality /,krɪmɪˈnælɪtɪ/ *n.* престу́пность, кримина́льность.

criminologist /,krɪmɪˈnɒlədʒɪst/ *n.* криминоло́г.

criminology /,krɪmɪˈnɒlədʒɪ/ *n.* криминоло́гия.

crimp /krɪmp/ *n.* (*fold, curl*) гофриро́вка, го́фр|ы (*pl., g.* —).

● *v.t.* гофрирова́ть (*impf., pf.*); **~ing-iron** щипцы́ для зави́вки воло́с.

crimplene /ˈkrɪmpliːn/ *n.* (*propr.*) кримпле́н.

● *adj.* кримпле́новый.

crimson /ˈkrɪmz(ə)n/ *n.* мали́новый цвет; тёмно-кра́сный цвет.

● *adj.* мали́новый; тёмно-кра́сный.

cringe /krɪndʒ/ *v.i.* (**cringing**) (*shrink*) съёжи|ваться, -ться (*от чего*); (*behave servilely*) раболе́пствовать (*impf.*).

crinkle /ˈkrɪŋk(ə)l/ *n.* морщи́на.

● *v.t. & i.* мо́рщить(ся), на-/с-.

crinkly /ˈkrɪŋklɪ/ *adj.* (**crinklier, crinkliest**) смо́рщенный.

crinoline /ˈkrɪnəlɪn/ *n.* кринoли́н.

crippl|e /ˈkrɪp(ə)l/ *n.* кале́ка (*c.g.*).

● *v.t.* кале́чить, ис-; уро́довать, из-; (*fig.*): **the ship was ~ed by the storm** бу́ря покале́чила кора́бль; **strikes are ~ing industry** забасто́вки расша́тывают промы́шленность; **~ing expenses** разори́тельные расхо́ды.

crisis /ˈkraɪsɪs/ *n.* (*pl.* **crises** /-siːz/) кри́зис.

crisp /krɪsp/ *n.* (*Br.*) (*potato* **~**) жа́реная карто́фельная стру́жка; (*pl.*) хрустя́щий карто́фель, чи́пс|ы (*pl., g.* -ов) (*coll.*).

● *adj.* (*of substance*) хрустя́щий; **a ~ biscuit** рассы́пчатое пече́нье; **a ~ lettuce** све́жий сала́т; (*of style, orders etc.*) чека́нный, отчётливый; (*of air*) бодря́щий, све́жий.

● *cpd.* **~bread** *n.* сухари́ (*m. pl.*); хрустя́щие хле́бцы (*m. pl.*).

crispness /ˈkrɪspnɪs/ *n.* све́жесть; отчётливость, чека́нность.

crispy /ˈkrɪspɪ/ *adj.* (**crispier, crispiest**) хрустя́щий.

criss-cross /ˈkrɪskrɒs/ *n.* перекре́щивание.

● *adj.* перекре́щивающийся, перекрёстный.

● *adv.* крест-на́крест; (*fig.*) вкривь и вкось.

● *v.t.* расчёр|чивать, -ти́ть крест-на́крест.

criteri|on /kraɪˈtɪərɪən/ *n.* (*pl.* **~a**) крите́рий.

critic /ˈkrɪtɪk/ *n.* (*also* **adverse ~**) кри́тик.

critical /ˈkrɪtɪk(ə)l/ *adj.* **1** (*decisive; judicious*) крити́ческий; **the patient's condition is ~** больно́й в крити́ческом состоя́нии. **2** (*fault-finding*) крити́ческий, крити́чный.

criticism /ˈkrɪtɪ,sɪz(ə)m/ *n.* кри́тика; **textual ~** крити́ческий разбо́р те́кста; **I have only one ~ to make** у меня́ то́лько одно́ замеча́ние.

criticize /ˈkrɪtɪ,saɪz/ *v.t.* подв|ерга́ть, -е́ргнуть крити́ческому разбо́ру; (*adversely*) критикова́ть (*impf.*).

critique /krɪˈtiːk/ *n.* кри́тика; (*review*) реце́нзия, крити́ческая статья́.

croak /krəʊk/ *n.* ка́рканье, ква́канье.

● *v.t. & i.* ква́кать (*impf.*); (*coll., die*) загну́ться (*pf.*) (*sl.*).

Croat /ˈkrəʊæt/ *n.* хорва́т (*fem.* -ка).

Croatia /krəʊˈeɪʃə/ *n.* Хорва́тия.

Croatian /krəʊˈeɪʃ(ə)n/ *adj.* хорва́тский.

crochet /ˈkrəʊʃeɪ/, /-ʃɪ/ *n.* вя́зка крючко́м.

● *v.t. & i.* (**crocheted** /-ʃeɪd/, **crocheting** /-ʃeɪɪŋ/) вяза́ть (*impf.*) крючко́м.

● *cpd.* **~-hook** *n.* вяза́льный крючо́к.

croci /ˈkrəʊkaɪ/, /-kiː/ *pl. of* ⇒**crocus**

crock[1] /krɒk/ *n.* (*pot*) гли́няный кувши́н/горшо́к; (*pl., broken bits of pottery*) черепки́ (*m. pl.*); бой.

crock[2] /krɒk/ *n.* (*coll.*) (*worn-out person*) кля́ча; (*Br., car*) рыдва́н.

crockery /ˈkrɒkərɪ/ *n.* гли́няная/фая́нсовая посу́да.

crocodile /ˈkrɒkə,daɪl/ *n.* крокоди́л; **~ tears** крокоди́ловы слёзы; (*Br., of schoolchildren etc.*) строй па́рами.

crocus /ˈkrəʊkəs/ *n.* (*pl.* **crocuses** *or* **croci**) кро́кус, шафра́н; **autumn ~** осе́нний кро́кус.

croft /krɒft/ *n.* (*Br.*) ху́тор.

crofter /ˈkrɒftə(r)/ *n.* (*Br.*) хуторя́нин.

croissant /ˈkrwʌsɑ̃/ *n.* францу́зский рога́лик.

crone /krəʊn/ *n.* сго́рбленная стару́ха.

crony /ˈkrəʊnɪ/ *n.* дружо́к, закады́чный друг.

cronyism /ˈkrəʊnɪˌɪz(ə)m/ *n.* панибра́тство.

crook /krʊk/ *n.* **1** (*shepherd's*) по́сох. **2** (*bend*) поворо́т, изги́б. **3** (*coll., criminal*) моше́нник, жу́лик.

● *v.t.* сгиба́ть, согну́ть; из|гиба́ть, -огну́ть; **~ one's finger** согну́ть (*pf.*) па́лец.

crooked /ˈkrʊkɪd/ *adj.* (**crookeder, crookedest**) **1** (*bent*) со́гнутый, изо́гнутый; (*with age*) сго́рбленный. **2**: **you have got your hat on ~** у вас шля́па сиди́т/наде́та ко́со/набекре́нь. **3** (*coll., dishonest*) бесче́стный, моше́ннический.

crookedness /ˈkrʊkɪdnɪs/ *n.* со́гнутость, изо́гнутость; (*dishonesty*) бесче́стность, моше́нничество.

croon /kruːn/ *v.t. & i.* напева́ть (*impf.*) вполго́лоса.

crop /krɒp/ *n.* **1** (*craw*) зоб. **2** (*of whip*) кнутови́ще; (*hunting-~*) охо́тничий хлыст. **3** (*produce*) урожа́й, жа́тва; **potato ~** урожа́й карто́феля; (*pl.*) посе́вы (*m. pl.*); (*grain*) хлеба́ (*m. pl.*). **4** (*fig.*): **a ~ of questions** ку́ча вопро́сов.

● *v.t.* (**cropped, cropping**) **1** (*bite off*) щипа́ть (*impf.*); объ|еда́ть, -е́сть; **the sheep ~ped the grass short** о́вцы ощипа́ли траву́. **2** (*hair, hedge*) подстр|ига́ть, -и́чь. **3** (*sow, plant*) зас|ева́ть, -е́ять.

● *v.i.* (**cropped, cropping**) **1** (*yield a ~*) да|ва́ть, -ть урожа́й; **the beans ~ped well** бобы́ да́ли хоро́ший урожа́й. **2**: **~ out** (*of rock etc.*) обнаж|а́ться, -и́ться. **3** (*fig.*): **difficulties ~ped up** появи́лись/возни́кли тру́дности.

● *cpd.* **~-dusting** *n.* опы́ливание посе́вов.

cropper /ˈkrɒpə(r)/ *n.* **1**: **heavy ~** расте́ние, даю́щее хоро́ший урожа́й. **2**: **he came a ~** (*coll.*) (*lit.*) он шлёпнулся; (*fig.*) он провали́лся.

croquet /ˈkrəʊkeɪ/, /-kɪ/ *n.* кроке́т.

● *v.t.* (**croqueted** /-keɪd/, **croqueting** /-keɪɪŋ/) крокирова́ть (*impf., pf.*).

croquette /krəˈket/ *n.* кроке́т.

cro|sier, -zier /ˈkrəʊzɪə(r)/, /-ʒə(r)/ *n.* епи́скопский по́сох.

cross /krɒs/ *n.* **1** крест; **he made a ~ on the document** он поста́вил кре́стик на докуме́нте; **Red C~** Кра́сный Крест. **2** (*of crucifixion*) крест; **he made the sign of the ~** он перекрести́лся; он осени́л себя́ кресто́м (*or* кре́стным зна́мением). **3** (*fig.*): **take up one's ~** нести́ (*pf.*) свой крест; **he is a ~ I have to bear** он крест, кото́рый мне суждено́ нести́. **4**: **cut on the ~** (*diagonally*) разре́занный на́искось (*or* по диагона́ли). **5** (*mixing of breeds*) по́месь, гибри́д; **a mule is a ~ between a horse and an ass** мул — по́месь ло́шади с осло́м; **this is a ~ between a sermon and a fable** э́то смесь про́поведи с ба́сней.

● *adj.* (*see also cpds.*) **1** (*transverse*) попере́чный, перекрёстный; **~ ventilation** попере́чная/сквозня́я вентиля́ция; **~ wind** (*sidewind*) боково́й/косо́й ве́тер. **2** (*angry*) серди́тый; злой (на + *a.*); раздражённый.

● *v.t.* **1** (*go across, traverse; also* **~ over**): **~ a road/bridge** пере|ходи́ть, -йти́ че́рез доро́гу/мост; **~ the Channel** перепл|ыва́ть, -ы́ть Ла-Манш; **~ s.o.'s path** перебежа́ть (*pf.*) кому́-н. доро́гу; (*fig.*) повстреча́ться (*impf.*) с кем-н.; **the idea never ~ed my mind** э́та мысль никогда́ не приходи́ла мне в го́лову; **the ship ~ed our bows** кора́бль пересёк наш путь. **2** (*draw lines across*): **~ a cheque** (*Br.*) перечёрк|ивать, -ну́ть чек. **3** (*place across*) скре́|щивать, -сти́ть; **~ one's legs** скрести́ть (*pf.*) но́ги; **~ one's arms** скрести́ть (*pf.*) ру́ки; **~ swords with s.o.** (*fig.*) скрести́ть (*pf.*) мечи́/шпа́ги с кем-н.; **keep one's fingers ~ed** (*fig., expr. hope*) ≈ как бы не сгла́зить; **~ s.o.'s palm with silver** позолоти́ть (*pf.*) ру́чку кому́-н.; **the wires are ~ed** (*lit.*) провода́ запу́тались; **~ wires** (*fig.*) запу́т|ывать, -ать де́ло; мути́ть (*impf.*) во́ду. **4**: **~ o.s.** перекрести́ться (*pf.*); **~ my heart!** вот те крест! **5** (*travel in opposite direction to*): **we ~ed each other on the way** мы размину́лись в пути́; **my letter ~ed your telegram** моё письмо́ размину́лось с ва́шей телегра́ммой. **6** (*thwart*): **he was ~ed in love** он потерпе́л неуда́чу в любви́; **do not ~ me** не станови́тесь на моём пути́; не перебега́йте мне доро́гу. **7** (*breed*) скре́|щивать, -сти́ть.

● *v.i.* **1** (*go across*): **he ~ed to where I was sitting** он перешёл к тому́ ме́сту, где я сиде́л; **he ~ed from Dover to Calais** он перепра́вился из Ду́вра в Кале́. **2**: **our letters ~ed** на́ши пи́сьма размину́лись.

● *with advs.*: **~ off, out** *vv.t.* вычёркивать, вы́черкнуть.

● *cpds.* **~bar** *n.* попере́чина, тра́верса, ри́гель (*m.*); **~-bench** *n.* (*parl.*) скамья́ для незави́симых депута́тов; **~-bencher** *n.* (*parl.*) незави́симый депута́т; **~bow** *n.* самостре́л, арбале́т; **~-bred** *adj.* скрещённый, гибри́дный; **~-breed** *n.* по́месь, гибри́д; *v.t. & i.* скре́|щивать(ся), -сти́ть(ся); **~-channel** *adj.*: **~-channel steamer** парохо́д, пересека́ющий Ла-Ма́нш; **~-check** *n.* све́рка; *v.t. & i.* св|еря́ть(ся), -е́рить(ся); **~-country** *adj.*: **a ~-country race** бег по пересечённой ме́стности, кросс; **~-country runner** кроссме́н; **~-country vehicle** вездехо́д; **~-current** *n.* пересека́ющий пото́к; **~-cut** *adj.*: **~-cut saw** попере́чная пила́; **~-examination** *n.* перекрёстный допро́с; **~-examine** *v.t.* подв|ерга́ть, -е́ргнуть перекрёстному допро́су; (*fig.*) допр|а́шивать, -оси́ть; **~-eyed** *adj.* косогла́зый, косо́й; **~-fertilization** *n.* перекрёстное опыле́ние; скре́щивание (*lit., fig.*); **~-fertilize** *v.t.* перекрёстно опыл|я́ть, -и́ть; **~-fire** *n.* (*mil.*) перекрёстный ого́нь; **~-legged** *adj.* (сидя́щий) положи́в но́гу на́ ногу (*or* скрести́в но́ги по-туре́цки); **~-patch** *n.* (*coll.*) брюзга́ (*c.g.*), злю́ка (*c.g.*); **~piece** *n.* попере́чина, крестови́на; **~-pollinate** *v.t.* перекрёстно опыл|я́ть, -и́ть; **~-pollination** *n.* перекрёстное опыле́ние; **~-purposes** *n. pl.* недоразуме́ние; **~-question** *v.t.* допр|а́шивать, -оси́ть; **~-reference** *n.* перекрёстная ссы́лка; **~road** *n.* перекрёсток; пересека́ющая доро́га; **at the ~ roads** (*fig.*) на распу́тье; **~-section** *n.* попере́чное сече́ние; попере́чный разре́з; **~-section of the population** про́фильный срез/про́филь (*m.*) населе́ния; **~-stitch** *n.* вы́шивка кре́стиком; **~-talk** *n.* пререка́ния (*nt. pl.*); **~-tie** *n.* (*US*) шпа́ла; **~walk** *n.* (*US*) перехо́д; **~ways** *adj.* = **crosswise; ~word** *n.* кроссво́рд.

crosse /krɒs/ *n.* (*sport*) клю́шка (для игры́ в лакро́сс).

crossing /ˈkrɒsɪŋ/ *n.* **1** (*going across*) перехо́д; перее́зд. **2** (*of sea*) перепра́ва, перехо́д; **we had a rough ~** нас си́льно кача́ло (во вре́мя перепра́вы). **3** (*of road and/or rail*) перекрёсток; перехо́д; перее́зд; **grade ~** (*US*), **level ~** (*Br.*) пересече́ние желе́зной доро́ги с шоссе́ (на одно́м у́ровне), (железнодоро́жный) перее́зд; **pedestrian ~** пешехо́дный перехо́д. **4** (*cross-breeding*) скре́щивание.

crossness /ˈkrɒsnɪs/ *n.* (*ill-temper*) раздражи́тельность, сварли́вость.

cross|wise /ˈkrɒswaɪz/, **-ways** /ˈkrɒsweɪz/ *adjs.* крестообра́зный.

● *adv.* крест-на́крест.

crotch /krɒtʃ/ *n.* (*anat.; also* **crutch**) промéжность; **the trousers are tight in the ~** брю́ки жмут в шагу́.

crotchet /ˈkrɒtʃɪt/ *n.* (*Br., mus.*) четвертна́я но́та.

crotchety /ˈkrɒtʃɪtɪ/ *adj.* (*peevish*) раздражи́тельный, брюзгли́вый.

crouch /kraʊtʃ/ *v.i.* сгиба́ться, согну́ться.

croup[1] /kruːp/ *n.* (*rump*) круп.

croup[2] /kruːp/ *n.* (*med.*) круп.

croupier /ˈkruːpɪə(r)/, /-ɪˌeɪ/ *n.* (*at gambling*) крупье́ (*m. indecl.*).

crouton /ˈkruːtɒn/ *n.* (*cul.*) грено́к.

crow[1] /krəʊ/ *n.* воро́на; **carrion ~** чёрная воро́на; **they are a mile away as the ~ flies** они́ в ми́ле отсю́да, е́сли счита́ть по прямо́й; **eat ~** (*US, eat humble pie*) прийти́ (*pf.*) с пови́нной (голово́й); **~'s nest** (*naut.*) наблюда́тельный пост на ма́чте, «воро́нье гнездо́»; **~'s feet** (*wrinkles*) морщи́нки в уголка́х глаз; гуси́ные ла́пки.

● *cpd.* **~bar** *n.* лом, ва́га, а́ншпуг.

crow[2] /krəʊ/ *n.* (*of cock*) кукаре́канье.

C

● *v.i.* (*past* **~ed** *or* **crew;** *p.p.* **~ed**) (*of cock*) кукаре́кать (*impf.*); **~ over s.o.** восторжествова́ть (*pf.*) над кем-н.

crowd /kraʊd/ *n.* **1** (*throng*) толпа́; **follow** (*or* **go with**) **the ~** (*fig.*) плыть (*impf.*) по тече́нию. **2** (*clique, social set*) компа́ния, о́бщество.

● *v.t.* **1** (*overfill*) зап|олня́ть, -о́лнить; переп|олня́ть, -о́лнить; **spectators ~ed the stadium** зри́тели запо́лнили стадио́н; **the buses are ~ed** авто́бусы перепо́лнены; **~ed street** у́лица, запру́женная наро́дом; **the room was ~ed with furniture** ко́мната была́ загромождена́ ме́белью; **a life ~ed with incident** жизнь, бога́тая происше́ствиями. **2** (*press, hustle*) оса|жда́ть, -ди́ть. **3**: **patients are ~ed out of the hospitals** больни́цы перегру́жены; больны́м бо́льше нет ме́ста; **his article was ~ed out of the magazine** его́ статья́ была́ вы́теснена из журна́ла други́м материа́лом.

● *v.i.* (*assemble in a ~*) толпи́ться, с-; наб|ива́ться, -и́ться битко́м; **they ~ed round the teacher** они́ столпи́лись вокру́г учи́теля; **they ~ed into the room** они́ наби́лись в ко́мнату; **memories ~ed in upon me** на меня́ нахлы́нули воспомина́ния.

crown /kraʊn/ *n.* **1** коро́на, вене́ц. **2** (*fig., sovereignty or sovereign*) коро́на, престо́л; **he succeeded to the ~** он унасле́довал коро́ну; **this land belongs to the C~** э́та земля́ принадлежи́т короле́вской семье́; **witness for the C~** свиде́тель обвине́ния. **3** (*wreath*) вене́ц, вено́к; **martyr's ~** му́ченический вене́ц. **4** (*coin*) кро́на. **5** (*of head*) маку́шка, те́мя (*nt.*), голова́; (*of hat*) тулья́; (*of road*) вы́пуклость доро́ги; (*of tree*) кро́на, верху́шка. **6** (*dental work*) коро́нка. **7** (*fig., culmination or reward*) вене́ц, заверше́ние, верши́на; **the ~ of one's achievements** верши́на достиже́ний; **the ~ of one's labours** (*Br.*), **labors** (*US*) заверше́ние трудо́в. **8** (*attr.*): **~ jewels** короле́вские/ца́рские рега́лии (*f. pl.*); **~ lands** зе́мли, принадлежа́щие короле́вской семье́; **~ prince** кронпри́нц, насле́дный принц; **~ princess** кронпринце́сса, насле́дная принце́сса.

● *v.t.* **1**: **he was ~ed king** его́ корона́ли (на ца́рство); **~ed heads** коро́нованные осо́бы. **2**: **the hill is ~ed with a wood** верши́на холма́ покры́та ле́сом. **3** (*fig., reward*): **his efforts were ~ed with success** его́ уси́лия увенча́лись успе́хом. **4** (*put finishing touch to*) заверш|а́ть, -и́ть; **to ~ it all, a storm broke out** в доверше́ние всего́ разрази́лась бу́ря; **~ing mercy** вы́сшее (*or* всё превосходя́щее) милосе́рдие. **5** (*hit on the head*) тре́снуть (*pf.*) по башке́ (*coll.*). **6** (*at draughts*) пров|оди́ть, -ести́ в да́мки. **7**: **~ a tooth** ста́вить, по- коро́нку на зуб.

crozier /ˈkrəʊzɪə(r)/, /-ʒə(r)/ = **crosier**

CRT (*abbr. of* **cathode-ray tube**) ЭЛТ (электро́нно-лучева́я тру́бка).

cruces /ˈkru:si:z/ *pl. of* ⇨**crux**

crucial /ˈkru:ʃ(ə)l/ *adj.* (*decisive*) реша́ющий.

crucian /ˈkru:ʃ(ə)n/ *n.* (*also* **~ carp**) кара́сь (*m.*).

crucible /ˈkru:sɪb(ə)l/ *n.* ти́гель (*m.*); (*fig.*) горни́ло.

crucifix /ˈkru:sɪfɪks/ *n.* распя́тие; (*cross*) крест.

crucifixion /ˌkru:sɪˈfɪkʃ(ə)n/ *n.* распя́тие (на кресте́).

cruciform /ˈkru:sɪˌfɔ:m/ *adj.* крестообра́зный.

crucify /ˈkru:sɪˌfaɪ/ *v.t.* расп|ина́ть, -я́ть.

crude /kru:d/ *adj.* **1** (*of materials*): **~ oil** сыра́я нефть; **~ sugar** неочи́щенный са́хар. **2** (*graceless*) гру́бый, неотёсанный. **3** (*awkward, ill-made*): **~ paintings** аляпова́тые карти́ны; **a ~ log cabin** гру́бо сколо́ченная деревя́нная хи́жина. **4** (*unripe, undigested*): **~ schemes** неразрабо́танные/незре́лые пла́ны; **~ facts** го́лые фа́кты.

crud|eness /ˈkru:dnɪs/, **-ity** /ˈkru:dɪtɪ/ *nn.* гру́бость, неотёсанность.

cruel /ˈkru:əl/ *adj.* (**crueller, cruellest** *or* **crueler, cruelest**) жесто́кий.

cruelty /ˈkru:əltɪ/ *n.* жесто́кость; **~ to animals** жесто́кое обраще́ние с живо́тными.

cruet /ˈkru:ɪt/ *n.* (*Br.*) графи́нчик, сосу́д.

● *cpd.* **~-stand** *n.* судо́к.

cruis|e /kru:z/ *n.* (*of ship*) пла́вание, кре́йсерство; (*of aircraft*) полёт; (*pleasure voyage*) морско́е путеше́ствие, круи́з; **~ missile** крыла́тая раке́та; **~ ship** круи́зный кора́бль.

● *v.i.* крейси́ровать (*impf.*); соверша́ть (*impf.*) ре́йсы; **~ing speed** (*of aircraft*) кре́йсерская ско́рость; (*of car*) эксплуатацио́нная ско́рость.

cruiser /ˈkru:zə(r)/ *n.* (*warship*) кре́йсер; **cabin ~** прогу́лочный ка́тер с каю́той.

● *cpd.* **~-weight** *n.* (*Br., boxing*) полутяжёлый вес.

crumb /krʌm/ *n.* **1** (*small piece*) кро́шка; (*fig.*): **~s of information** кро́хи (*f. pl.*) обры́вки (*m. pl.*) све́дений; **~ of comfort** сла́бое утеше́ние. **2** (*inner part of bread*) мя́киш. **3**: **~s!** (*Br. coll.*) ну и ну!

crumble /ˈkrʌmb(ə)l/ *n.* (*Br., cul.*) фрукто́вый пу́динг.

● *v.t.* (*bread etc.*) кроши́ть, рас-.

● *v.i.* кроши́ться (*impf.*); (*of a wall*) обва́л|иваться, -и́ться; обру́ши|ваться, -ться; (*fig., of empires, hopes etc.*) ру́шиться (*impf., pf.*); ру́хнуть (*pf.*).

crumbly /ˈkrʌmblɪ/ *adj.* (**crumblier, crumbliest**) кроша́щийся; (*of bread*) рассы́пчатый.

crummy /ˈkrʌmɪ/ *adj.* (**crummier, crummiest**) (*inferior*) дрянно́й, жа́лкий.

crumpet /ˈkrʌmpɪt/ *n.* ≈ сдо́бная лепёшка.

crumple /ˈkrʌmp(ə)l/ *v.t.* мять (*or* смина́ть) с-; **~ one's clothes** смять (*pf.*) свою́ оде́жду; **~ up a sheet of paper** ско́мкать (*pf.*) лист бума́ги.

● *v.i.* мя́ться (*or* смина́ться), с-; **these sheets ~** э́ти про́стыни мну́тся; **the wings of the aircraft ~d up** кры́лья самолёта помя́лись.

crunch /krʌntʃ/ *n* (*noise*) хруст; (*crucial moment*) реша́ющий моме́нт.

● *v.t. & i.* грызть (*impf.*) с хру́стом; хрусте́ть (*impf.*); скрипе́ть (*impf.*); **our feet ~ed the gravel** гра́вий хрусте́л у нас под нога́ми.

crusade /kru:ˈseɪd/ *n.* (*lit., fig.*) кресто́вый похо́д.

● *v.i.* (*fig.*) идти́ (*det.*) в похо́д (*против чего or за что*).

crusader /kru:ˈseɪdə(r)/ *n.* крестоно́сец (*fig.*); боре́ц.

crush /krʌʃ/ *n.* **1** (*crowd*) толчея́, толкотня́, да́вка. **2** (*infatuation*): **she has a ~ on him** она́ от него́ без ума́. **3** (*fruit drink*) вы́жатый фрукто́вый сок.

● *v.t.* **1** (*press, squash*) разда́в|ливать, -и́ть; **some people were ~ed to death** кое-кого́ задави́ло. **2** (*crumple*) мять, из-/с-; **her dresses were badly ~ed** её пла́тья си́льно помя́лись. **3** (*defeat, overcome*) сокруш|а́ть, -и́ть; **he ~ed his enemies** он разгроми́л свои́х враго́в; **our hopes were ~ed** на́ши наде́жды ру́хнули; **she ~ed him with a look** она́ уничто́жила/испепели́ла его́ одни́м взгля́дом; **a ~ing defeat** по́лное пораже́ние, разгро́м.

● *v.i.* мя́ться, из-/с-; **this material does not ~** э́та мате́рия не мнётся; **they ~ed into the front seats** они́ проти́снулись/протолка́лись на места́ пе́рвого ря́да.

● *with advs.*: **~ out** *v.t.* (*extinguish*): **~ out a cigarette** погаси́ть (*pf.*) сигаре́ту; **~ up** *v.t.* (*make into powder*) толо́чь, рас-/ис-.

crust /krʌst/ *n.* (*of bread*) ко́рка; (*of pastry*) ко́рочка; **the earth's ~** земна́я кора́.

● *v.i.*: **the snow ~ed over** на снегу́ образова́лась твёрдая ко́рка.

crustacean /krʌˈsteɪʃ(ə)n/ *n.* ракообра́зное.

crusty /ˈkrʌstɪ/ *adj.* (**crustier, crustiest**) (*lit.*) покры́тый ко́ркой; с ко́рочкой; (*fig.*) ре́зкий, жёлчный.

crutch /krʌtʃ/ *n.* **1** (*support*) косты́ль (*m.*); (*fig.*) опо́ра. **2** = **crotch**

crux /krʌks/ *n.* (*pl.* **~es** *or* **cruces**) (*essential point*) суть; коренно́й вопро́с.

cry /kraɪ/ *n.* **1** (*weeping*) плач; **she had a good ~** она́ вспла́сть попла́кала. **2** (*shout*) крик; (*fig.*): **it is a far ~ to the**

days of the horse-carriage мы далеко́ ушли́ от времён лошади́ного тра́нспорта.
3 (*of animal*) крик; **in full ~** (*of hounds*) в бе́шеной пого́не.
4 (*watch-word*) клич, ло́зунг.
5 (*entreaty, demand*) мольба́; **there was a ~ for reform** подняли́сь голоса́, тре́бующие рефо́рмы; со всех сторо́н раздава́лись тре́бования рефо́рм.
6 (*outcry, clamour*) крик, вопль (*m.*); **they raised the ~ of discrimination** они́ по́дняли крик/во́пли о дискримина́ции.
● *v.t.* **1** (*weep*) пла́кать (*impf.*); **~ bitter tears** пла́кать (*impf.*) го́рькими слеза́ми; **~ one's eyes out** вы́плакать (*pf.*) (все) глаза́; **she cried herself to sleep** она́ усну́ла в слеза́х.
2 (*shout, exclaim*) крича́ть (*impf.*); вскри́к|ивать, -нуть; **'Enough!' he cried** «Дово́льно!» — закрича́л он.
● *v.i.* **1** (*weep*) пла́кать (*impf.*); **~ over something** опла́кивать (*impf.*) что-н.; **it's no good ~ing over spilt milk** (*fig.*) сде́ланного не воро́тишь; что с во́зу упа́ло, то пропа́ло.
2 (*shout, exclaim, plead*) крича́ть (*impf.*); вскри́к|ивать, -нуть; **he cried with pain** он вскри́кнул от бо́ли; **they cried for mercy** они́ умоля́ли о милосе́рдии.
● *with advs.*: **~ off** *v.t. & i.* (*an engagement*) отмен|я́ть, -и́ть (свида́ние); **~ out** *v.i.* (*in pain or distress*) вскри́к|ивать, -нуть.
● *cpd.* **~-baby** *n.* пла́кса (*c.g.*), рёва (*c.g.*).

crying /ˈkraɪɪŋ/ *n.* (*weeping*) плач; (*calling of wares*) крик, выклика́ние.
● *adj.*: **a ~ shame** вопию́щее безобра́зие; **~ need** о́страя нужда́.

crypt /krɪpt/ *n.* кри́пта, склеп.

cryptic /ˈkrɪptɪk/ *adj.* таи́нственный, зага́дочный.

crypto-Communist /ˌkrɪptəʊˈkɒmjʊnɪst/ *n.* та́йный коммуни́ст.

cryptogram /ˈkrɪptəˌgræm/ *n.* криптогра́мма, та́йнопись.

cryptographer /krɪpˈtɒgrəfə(r)/ *n.* шифрова́льщик

cryptographic /ˌkrɪptəˈgræfɪk/ *adj.* криптографи́ческий, шифрова́льный.

cryptography /krɪpˈtɒgrəfɪ/ *n.* криптогра́фия.

crystal /ˈkrɪst(ə)l/ *n.* **1** (*substance*) го́рный хруста́ль; **~ ornaments** хруста́льные украше́ния; **~ set** (*radio*) приёмник на криста́ллах.
2 (*glassware*) хруста́ль (*m.*); **~ ball** маги́ческий криста́лл. **3** (*aggregation of molecules*) криста́лл. **4** (*fig.*): **the ~ waters of the lake** прозра́чные во́ды о́зера. **5** (*US, watch-glass*) стекло́ ручны́х/карма́нных часо́в.
● *cpd.* **~-clear** *adj.* (*fig.*) я́сный как бо́жий день.

crystalline /ˈkrɪstəˌlaɪn/ *adj.* хруста́льный; (*fig., also*) криста́льный.

crystallization /ˌkrɪstəlaɪˈzeɪʃ(ə)n/ *n.* (*lit.*) кристаллиза́ция.

crystallize /ˈkrɪstəˌlaɪz/ *v.t.* **1** (*form into crystals*) кристаллизова́ть (*impf., pf.*); за- (*pf.*). **2** (*clarify*) вопло|ща́ть, -ти́ть в определённую фо́рму. **3**: **~d fruit** заса́харенные фру́кты.
● *v.i.* **1** (*form into crystals*) кристаллизова́ться (*impf., pf.*); вы- (*pf.*). **2**: **his plans ~d** его́ пла́ны определи́лись.

crystallographer /ˌkrɪstəˈlɒgrəfə(r)/ *n.* кристалло́граф.

crystallography /ˌkrɪstəˈlɒgrəfɪ/ *n.* кристаллогра́фия.

CSCE (*abbr. of* ***Conference on Security and Co-operation in Europe***) СБСЕ (Совеща́ние по безопа́сности и сотру́дничеству в Евро́пе).

CSE (*abbr. of* ***Certificate of Secondary Education***) (*hist.*) ≈ аттеста́т о сре́днем образова́нии.

cub /kʌb/ *n.* детёныш; (*bear*) медвежо́нок; (*fox*) лисёнок; (*lion*) львёнок; (*tiger*) тигрёнок; (*wolf*) волчо́нок.
● *v.i.* (**cubbed, cubbing**) **1** (*bring forth* **~s**) щени́ться, о-. **2** (*hunt fox-***~s**) охо́титься (*impf.*) на лися́т.

Cuba /ˈkjuːbə/ *n.* Ку́ба; **in ~** на Ку́бе.

Cuban /ˈkjuːbən/ *n.* куби́н|ец (*fem.* -ка).
● *adj.* куби́нский.

cubby-hole /ˈkʌbɪ-/ *n.* (*small room*) ко́мнатка, камо́рка.

cube /kjuːb/ *n.* **1** (*math.: of a number*) куб; **~ root** куби́ческий ко́рень.
2 (*solid*) ку́бик; **~ sugar** пилёный са́хар; **sugar ~** ку́бик/кусо́к са́хара.
● *v.t.* **1** (*calculate* **~** *of*) возв|оди́ть, -ести́ (*число*) в куб; **4 ~d** 4 в ку́бе; 4 в тре́тьей сте́пени. **2** (*cut into* **~s**) нар|еза́ть, -е́зать ку́биками.

cubic /ˈkjuːbɪk/ *adj.* куби́ческий.

cubicle /ˈkjuːbɪk(ə)l/ *n.* (*for changing in at a swimming pool; in a toilet*) каби́нка; (*for trying on clothes in a shop*) приме́рочная; (*in a hospital*) бокс.

cubism /ˈkjuːbɪz(ə)m/ *n.* куби́зм.

cubist /ˈkjuːbɪst/ *n.* куби́ст (*fem.* -ка).

cubit /ˈkjuːbɪt/ *n.* ло́коть (*m.*) (*мера длины*).

cuckold /ˈkʌkəʊld/ *n.* рогоно́сец.
● *v.t.* наст|авля́ть, -а́вить рога́ + *d.*

cuckoo /ˈkʊkuː/ *n.* куку́шка; **~ clock** часы́ (*m. pl.*) с куку́шкой; **~ flower** серде́чник лугово́й.
● *adj.* (*coll., crazy*) чо́кнутый, тро́нутый.
● *v.i.* (*utter* **~***'s cry*) кукова́ть (*impf.*).

cucumber /ˈkjuːkʌmbə(r)/ *n.* огуре́ц; **~ salad** сала́т из огурцо́в; **cool as a ~** хладнокро́вный, невозмути́мый.

cud /kʌd/ *n.* жва́чка; **chew the ~** (*lit., fig.*) жева́ть (*impf.*) жва́чку.

cuddle /ˈkʌd(ə)l/ *v.t. & i.* обн|има́ть(ся).
● *v.i.*: **~ up (to s.o.)** приж|има́ться, -а́ться (к кому́-н.).

cuddl|esome /ˈkʌd(ə)lsəm/, **-y** /ˈkʌdlɪ/ (*Br.*) *adjs.* располага́ющий к ла́ске; ми́лый, прия́тный; **~ toy** мя́гкая игру́шка.

cudgel /ˈkʌdʒ(ə)l/ *n.* дуби́нка, па́лка; **take up the ~s for s.o.** (*fig.*) вы́ступить (*pf.*) в защи́ту кого́-н.
● *v.t.* (**cudgelled, cudgelling;** *US* **cudgeled, cudgeling**) бить (*impf.*) дуби́нкой/па́лкой; **~ one's brains** лома́ть (*impf.*) го́лову (*над чем*).

cue[1] /kjuː/ *n.* (*theatr.*) ре́плика; (*fig., hint*) намёк; **take one's ~ from** взять (*pf.*) приме́р с (*кого*).

cue[2] /kjuː/ *n.* (*billiards*) кий.

cuff[1] /kʌf/ *n.* **1** (*part of sleeve; linen band*) манже́та; **off the ~** (*fig.*) экспро́мтом.
2 (*US, trouser turnup*) отворо́т.
● *cpd.* **~-links** *n. pl.* за́понки (*f. pl.*).

cuff[2] /kʌf/ *n.* (*blow*) шлепо́к.
● *v.t.* шлёп|ать, -нуть.

cuirass /kwɪˈræs/ *n.* (*armour*) кира́са.

cuirassier /ˌkwɪrəˈsɪə(r)/ *n.* кираси́р.

cuisine /kwɪˈziːn/ *n.* (*национальная*) ку́хня.

cul-de-sac /ˈkʌldəˌsæk/, /ˈkʊl-/ *n.* (*pl.* **culs-de-sac** *pronunc. same, or* **cul-de-sacs**) (*also fig.*) тупи́к.

culinary /ˈkʌlɪnərɪ/ *adj.* кулина́рный.

cull /kʌl/ *n.* (*of seals*) отбо́р, брако́вка.
● *v.t.* **1** (*select*) от|бира́ть, -обра́ть; под|бира́ть, -обра́ть; (*flowers etc.*) соб|ира́ть, -ра́ть. **2** (*slaughter*) бить (*impf.*).

culminate /ˈkʌlmɪˌneɪt/ *v.i.* дост|ига́ть, -и́гнуть вы́сшей то́чки (*or* апоге́я); **~ in** заверш|а́ться, -и́ться + *i.*

culmination /ˌkʌlmɪˈneɪʃ(ə)n/ *n.* кульмина́ция; кульминацио́нный пункт.

culottes /kjuːˈlɒts/ *n. pl.* ю́бка-брю́ки.

culpability /ˌkʌlpəˈbɪlɪtɪ/ *n.* вино́вность.

culpable /ˈkʌlpəb(ə)l/ *adj.* вино́вный.

culprit /ˈkʌlprɪt/ *n.* (*offender*) престу́пник; (*fig.*) вино́вник.

cult /kʌlt/ *n.* культ.

cultivable /ˈkultivəb(ə)l/ *adj.* (*of land*) приго́дный для возде́лывания.

cultivate /ˈkʌltɪˌveɪt/ *v.t.* **1** (*land*) возде́л|ывать, -ать; (*crops*) культиви́ровать (*impf.*); **~d area** посевна́я пло́щадь. **2**: **~ one's mind** развива́ть (*impf.*) ум; **~ one's style** соверше́нствовать (*impf.*) свой стиль; **a ~d person** культу́рный/интеллиге́нтный челове́к. **3**: **~ s.o.('s acquaintance)** подде́рживать (*impf.*) знако́мство с кем-н.

cultivation /ˌkʌltɪˈveɪʃ(ə)n/ *n.* **1** (*agric.*) (*of soil*) обрабо́тка, культива́ция, возде́лывание; (*of plants*) культиви́рование, разведе́ние. **2** (*culture*) культу́ра. **3** (*of acquaintance*) подде́рживание (знако́мства).

cultivator /ˈkʌltɪˌveɪtə(r)/ *n.* (*person*) земледе́лец; (*implement*) культива́тор.

cultural /ˈkʌltʃər(ə)l/ *adj.* культу́рный; **~ centre** (*Br.*), **center** (*US*) дом/дворе́ц культу́ры.

culture /ˈkʌltʃə(r)/ *n.* **1** (*tillage*) возде́лывание, культива́ция.
2 (*rearing, production*) разведе́ние, возде́лывание. **3** (*colony of bacteria*) культу́ра, шта́мм. **4** (*civilization, way of life*) культу́ра, быт; **a man of ~**

интеллиге́нтный челове́к; **Greek ~** гре́ческая культу́ра.

● *v.t.*: **~d pearls** культиви́рованный же́мчуг; **~d viruses** вы́ращенные ви́русы.

cultured /ˈkʌltʃəd/ *adj.* (*of person*) интеллиге́нтный, культу́рный.

culvert /ˈkʌlvət/ *n.* кульве́рт; дрена́жная труба́.

cumb|ersome /ˈkʌmbəsəm/, **-rous** /ˈkʌmbrəs/ *adjs.* громо́здкий, обремени́тельный.

cummerbund /ˈkʌməˌbʌnd/ *n.* широ́кий по́яс (под смо́кинг).

cum(m)in /ˈkʌmɪn/ *n.* тмин.

cumquat /ˈkʌmkwɒt/ *n.* (*bot.*) кумква́т.

cumulate /ˈkjuːmjʊˌleɪt/ *v.t.* соб|ира́ть, -ра́ть.

● *v.i.* аккумули́роваться (*impf.*); нак|а́пливаться, -опи́ться.

cumulation /ˌkjuːmjʊˈleɪʃ(ə)n/ *n.* аккумуля́ция, накопле́ние.

cumulative /ˈkjuːmjʊlətɪv/ *adj.* кумуляти́вный, нако́пленный; **~ evidence** (*leg.*) совоку́пность ули́к.

cumulo-nim|bus /ˈkjuːmjʊləʊ-/ *n.* (*pl.* **~buses** *or* **~bi** /-baɪ/) ку́чево-дождевы́е облака́.

cumu|lus /ˈkjuːmjʊləs/ *n.* (*pl.* **~li** /-laɪ/, /-liː/) (*cloud*) кучевы́е облака́.

cuneiform /ˈkjuːnɪˌfɔːm/ *n.* (**~** *writing*) кли́нопись.

cunning /ˈkʌnɪŋ/ *n.* (*craftiness*) хи́трость; (*skill*) ло́вкость.

● *adj.* (**cunninger, cunningest**) (*crafty*) хи́трый.

cunt /kʌnt/ *n.* (*vulg.*) пизда́ (*vulg.*).

cup /kʌp/ *n.* **1** (*for tea etc.*) ча́шка, (*liter.*) ча́ша; **that is my ~ of tea** (*fig.*) э́то по мне́; э́то в моём вку́се. **2** (*fig.*): **his ~ was full** (*sc. with happiness*) он был на верху́ блаже́нства. **3** (*as prize*) ку́бок; **~ final** фина́л ро́зыгрыша ку́бка.

● *v.t.* (**cupped, cupping**): **~ one's hand** держа́ть (*impf.*) ру́ку го́рстью; **~ one's hands round a glass** обхвати́ть (*pf.*) стака́н обе́ими рука́ми; **~ one's chin in one's hands** подп|ира́ть, -ере́ть подборо́док ладо́нями.

● *cpds.* **~-cake** *n.* кру́глый кекс; **~-tie** *n.* (*Br.*) футбо́льный матч на ку́бок.

cupboard /ˈkʌbəd/ *n.* шкаф, буфе́т.

cupful /ˈkʌpfʊl/ *n.* по́лная ча́шка (*чего*).

Cupid /ˈkjuːpɪd/ *n.* **1** (*myth.*) Купидо́н; **~'s bow** (*of lip*) гу́бы (*f. pl.*) ба́нтиком. **2** (*putto*) аму́р.

cupidity /kjuːˈpɪdɪtɪ/ *n.* а́лчность, жа́дность.

cupola /ˈkjuːpələ/ *n.* ку́пол.

cupro-nickel /ˌkjuːprəʊˈnɪk(ə)l/ *n.* мельхио́р.

cur /kɜː(r)/ *n.* дворня́жка.

curable /ˈkjʊərəb(ə)l/ *adj.* излечи́мый.

curacy /ˈkjʊərəsɪ/ *n.* прихо́д.

curate /ˈkjʊərət/ *n.* вика́рий.

curative /ˈkjʊərətɪv/ *adj.* целе́бный, цели́тельный.

curator /kjʊəˈreɪtə(r)/ *n.* (*of museum etc.*) храни́тель (*m.*).

curatorship /kjʊəˈreɪtə(r)ʃɪp/ *n.* до́лжность храни́теля.

curb /kɜːb/ *n.* **1** узда́. **2** = **kerb**

● *v.t.* **1** (*of horse*) над|ева́ть, -е́ть узду́ на + *a.* **2** (*fig.*) обу́зд|ывать, -а́ть.

curd /kɜːd/ *n.* тво́ро́г; **~ cheese** (*Br.*) тво́ро́г.

curdle /ˈkɜːd(ə)l/ *v.t.* створ|а́живать, -ожи́ть; **~ the blood** (*fig.*) леде́ни́ть (*impf.*) кровь.

● *v.i.* свёр|тываться, -ну́ться; створ|а́живаться, -о́житься; (*fig.*): **one's blood ~s** кровь леденеет; кровь сты́нет в жи́лах.

cure /ˈkjʊə(r)/ *n.* **1** (*remedy*) лека́рство, сре́дство; **this is a ~ for idleness** э́то лека́рство от безде́лья; **past ~** неизлечи́мый. **2** (*treatment*) лече́ние; **he went to Vichy for the ~** он пое́хал на лече́ние в Виши́.

● *v.t.* **1** (*make healthy*) выле́чивать, вы́лечить; **he was ~d of asthma** он вы́лечился от а́стмы; **he was ~d of gambling** он излечи́лся от стра́сти к аза́ртной игре́. **2** (*remedy*) (*disease*) выле́чивать, вы́лечить; излеч|ивать, -и́ть; (*poverty*) уничт|ожа́ть, -о́жить; (*drunkenness*) изж|ива́ть, -и́ть. **3** (*meat*) соли́ть, по-; вя́лить, про-; (*hides*) обраб|а́тывать, -о́тать; (*tobacco*) ферменти́ровать; (*impf.*, *pf.*).

● *cpd.* **~-all** *n.* панаце́я.

curettage /kjʊəˈretɪdʒ/, /-rɪˈtɑːdʒ/ *n.* выска́бливание.

curfew /ˈkɜːfjuː/ *n.* коменда́нтский час; **impose a ~** устан|а́вливать, -ови́ть коменда́нтский час; **lift a ~** отмен|я́ть, -и́ть коменда́нтский час.

curie /ˈkjʊərɪ/ *n.* (*unit*) кюри́ (*nt. indecl.*).

curio /ˈkjʊərɪəʊ/ *n.* (*pl.* **~s**) антиква́рная вещь, ре́дкость.

curiosity /ˌkjʊərɪˈɒsɪtɪ/ *n.* **1** (*inquisitiveness*) любопы́тство, любозна́тельность; **~ killed the cat** (*prov.*) любопы́тство до добра́ не доведёт. **2** (*unusual object*) дико́вин(к)а; ре́дкость.

curious /ˈkjʊərɪəs/ *adj.* **1** (*interested*): **I am ~ to know what he said** я хочу́ знать, что он сказа́л. **2** (*inquisitive*) любопы́тный, любозна́тельный. **3** (*odd*) стра́нный, дико́винный; **~ to relate, ~ly enough** как ни стра́нно.

curl /kɜːl/ *n.* (*of hair*) ло́кон, завито́к; (*pl.*, **~y hair**) кудря́вые во́лосы (*m. pl.*); (*of string*) завито́к, спира́ль; (*of smoke*) кольцо́; (*of wave*) изги́б; (*of lip*) презри́тельная усме́шка/улы́бка.

● *v.t.*: **~ a string around one's finger** закрути́ть (*pf.*) шнуро́к вокру́г па́льца; **~ one's hair** зав|ива́ть, -и́ть во́лосы; **~ing-irons/-tongs** щипцы́ (*m. pl.*) для зави́вки; **~ one's lip** презри́тельно скриви́ть (*pf.*) гу́бы.

● *v.i.*: **her hair ~s naturally** у неё вью́щиеся/кудря́вые от приро́ды во́лосы; **the smoke ~ed upwards** клу́бы ды́ма поднима́лись вверх; **the dog ~ed up by the fire** соба́ка сверну́лась клубко́м у ками́на; **he ~ed up (with shame)** он весь съёжился от стыда́.

curlers /ˈkɜːləz/ *n.* бигуди́ (*nt. pl.*, *indecl.*).

curlew /ˈkɜːljuː/ *n.* (*pl.* **~** *or* **~s**) кроншне́п.

curlicue /ˈkɜːlɪˌkjuː/ *n.* завиту́шка.

curliness /ˈkɜːlɪnɪs/ *n.* кудря́вость, курча́вость.

curly /ˈkɜːlɪ/ *adj.* (**curlier, curliest**) кудря́вый, курча́вый, вью́щийся.

● *cpd.* **~-headed** *adj.* кудря́вый.

curmudgeon /kəˈmʌdʒ(ə)n/ *n.* скваль́ига (*c.g.*); скря́га (*c.g.*).

curmudgeonly /kəˈmʌdʒ(ə)nlɪ/ *adj.* скваль́жный, ска́редный.

currant /ˈkʌrənt/ *n.* **1** (*fruit, bush*) сморо́дина. **2** (*in cake etc.*) изю́м, кори́нка; **~ bun** бу́лочка с изю́мом.

currency /ˈkʌrənsɪ/ *n.* **1** (*acceptance, validity*): **the rumour** (*Br.*), **rumor** (*US*) **gained ~** э́тот слух прони́к всю́ду; **give ~ to a rumour** (*Br.*), **rumor** (*US*) распространи́ть (*pf.*) слух (*о чём*); **during the ~ of the contract** в тече́ние сро́ка де́йствия догово́ра. **2** (*money*) валю́та; де́н|ьги (*pl.*, *g.* -ег); **paper ~** бума́жные де́ньги; **gold ~** золота́я валю́та; **hard ~** конверти́руемая валю́та; **soft ~** неконверти́руемая валю́та; **the dollar is American ~** до́ллар — де́нежная едини́ца Аме́рики; **~ reform** де́нежная рефо́рма.

current /ˈkʌrənt/ *n.* **1** (*of air, water*) струя́, пото́к. **2** (*elec.*) ток; **alternating ~** переме́нный ток; **direct ~** постоя́нный ток. **3** (*course, tendency*) тече́ние, ход.

● *adj.* **1** (*in general use, e.g. words, opinions*) ходя́чий, распространённый. **2** (*of present time*) теку́щий; **~ affairs, events** теку́щие собы́тия; **the ~ issue of a magazine** теку́щий/очередно́й но́мер журна́ла; **at ~ prices** по существу́ющим це́нам. **3**: **~ account** (*Br.*, *comm.*) теку́щий счёт.

currently /ˈkʌrəntlɪ/ *adv.* **1** (*generally, commonly*) обы́чно. **2** (*at present*) тепе́рь, ны́не, в настоя́щее вре́мя.

curricul|um /kəˈrɪkjʊləm/ *n.* (*pl.* **~a**) курс обуче́ния; програ́мма; уче́бный план; **~ vitae** (кра́ткая) биогра́фия.

curry[1] /ˈkʌrɪ/ *n.* (*cul.*) ке́рри (*nt. indecl.*).

● *v.t.*: **curried lamb** бара́нина, припра́вленная ке́рри.

● *cpd.* **~-powder** *n.* ке́рри; порошо́к из курку́мы.

curry[2] /ˈkʌrɪ/ *v.t.* **1** (*a horse etc.*) чи́стить, вы- скребни́цей. **2**: **~ favour** (*Br.*), **favor** (*US*) **with s.o.** подли́з|ываться, -а́ться к кому́-н.

● *cpd.* **~-comb** *n.* скребни́ца.

curse /kɜːs/ *n.* **1** (*execration*) прокля́тие; **he is under a ~, there is a ~ upon him** над ним тяготе́ет прокля́тие. **2** (*bane*) прокля́тие, бич; **the ~ of drink** бич пья́нства; **the ~** (*coll.*, *menses*) го́сти (*m. pl.*). **3** (*oath*) богоху́льство, руга́тельство.

● *v.t.* **1** (*pronounce ~ on*) прокл|ина́ть, -я́сть. **2** (*abuse, scold*) руга́ть (*impf.*); проклина́ть (*impf.*). **3**: **he is ~d with a**

violent temper Госпо́дь его́ награди́л необу́зданным нра́вом.

● *v.i.* (*swear, utter* ~*s*) руга́ться (*impf.*); ~ **at s.o.** осыпа́ть (*pf.*) кого́-н. прокля́тиями.

cursed /ˈkɜːsɪd/, /kɜːst/ *adj.* прокля́тый.

cursive /ˈkɜːsɪv/ *n.* (*script*) ско́ропись.

● *adj.* скоропи́сный.

cursor /ˈkɜːsə(r)/ *n.* (*comput.*) курсо́р.

cursoriness /ˈkɜːsərɪnɪs/ *n.* пове́рхностность.

cursory /ˈkɜːsərɪ/ *adj.* бе́глый, пове́рхностный.

curt /kɜːt/ *adj.* отры́вистый, ре́зкий.

curtail /kɜːˈteɪl/ *v.t.* (*shorten*) сокра|ща́ть, -ти́ть; ~ **an allowance** уре́зать (*impf.*) посо́бие.

curtailment /kɜːˈteɪlmənt/ *n.* сокраще́ние, уре́зывание.

curtain /ˈkɜːt(ə)n/ *n.* **1** (*of window, door*) занаве́ска, што́ра; **draw the** ~**s** (*close*) задёрнуть (*pf.*) занаве́ски; (*open*) отдёрнуть (*pf.*) занаве́ски. **2** (*fig.*) заве́са; **draw a** ~ **over something** покры́ть (*pf.*) что-н. заве́сой та́йны; **lift the** ~ **of secrecy** приподня́ть (*pf.*) заве́су та́йны; **Iron C**~ желе́зный за́навес. **3** (*theatr.*) за́навес; **ring up the** ~ подня́ть (*pf.*) за́навес; **ring down the** ~ опусти́ть (*pf.*) за́навес; **safety** ~ пожа́рный за́навес; ~ **call** вы́зов; **he took six** ~**s** его́ вызыва́ли шесть раз.

● *v.t.* занаве́|шивать, -сить; ~ **off** отгор|а́живать, -оди́ть занаве́ской.

● *cpd.* ~**-raiser** *n.* небольшо́е представле́ние, исполня́емое пе́ред нача́лом спекта́кля; (*fig.*) прелю́дия.

curtness /ˈkɜːtnɪs/ *n.* отры́вистость, ре́зкость.

curts(e)y /ˈkɜːtsɪ/ *n.*ревера́нс, приседа́ние.

● *v.i.* (*also* **make, drop a** ~) прис|еда́ть, -е́сть; де́лать, с- ревера́нс.

curvaceous /kɜːˈveɪʃəs/ *adj.* (*coll.*) пы́шный, соблазни́тельный.

curvature /ˈkɜːvətʃə(r)/ *n.* кривизна́, изги́б, крива́я; ~ **of the earth** кривизна́ земли́; ~ **of the spine** искривле́ние позвоно́чника.

curve /kɜːv/ *n.* (*line*) крива́я; (*pl., of female body*) изги́бы (*m. pl.*); (*bend in road*) изги́б.

● *v.t.* сгиба́ть, согну́ть; из|гиба́ть, -огну́ть.

● *v.i.* из|гиба́ться, -огну́ться; **the road** ~**s** доро́га извива́ется; **the river** ~**s round the town** река́ огиба́ет го́род.

curvet /kɜːˈvet/ *n.* (*sport*) курбе́т.

curvilinear /ˌkɜːvɪˈlɪnɪə(r)/ *adj.* криволине́йный.

cushion /ˈkʊʃ(ə)n/ *n.* (дива́нная) поду́шка; (*billiards*) борт.

● *v.t.*: ~**ed** (*padded*) **seats** мя́гкие сиде́нья; ~ **a blow** смягч|а́ть, -и́ть уда́р.

cushy /ˈkʊʃɪ/ *adj.* (**cushier, cushiest**) (*coll.*): ~ **job** непы́льная рабо́та.

cusp /kʌsp/ *n.* (*of moon*) рог; (*of leaf*) о́стрый коне́ц; (*of tooth*) ко́нчик.

cuspidor /ˈkʌspɪˌdɔː(r)/ *n.* (*US*) плева́тельница.

cussed /ˈkʌsɪd/ *adj.* стропти́вый.

cussedness /ˈkʌsɪdnɪs/ *n.* стропти́вость.

custard /ˈkʌstəd/ *n.* сла́дкий крем/со́ус из яи́ц и молока́; ~ **powder** заварно́й крем-концентра́т.

custodian /kʌˈstəʊdɪən/ *n.* (*guardian*) опеку́н; (*of property etc.*) администра́тор; (*of museum etc.*) храни́тель (*m.*); (*caretaker*) сто́рож.

custody /ˈkʌstədɪ/ *n.* **1** (*guardianship*) опе́ка, попече́ние. **2** (*keeping*): **in safe** ~ на (со)хране́нии. **3** (*arrest*): **take, give into** ~ брать, взять под стра́жу; аресто́в|ывать, -а́ть.

custom /ˈkʌstəm/ *n.* **1** (*habit, accepted behaviour*) обы́чай. **2** (*Br., business patronage, clientele*) клиенту́ра, покупа́тели (*m. pl.*). **3** (*pl., import duties*) тамо́женные по́шлины (*f. pl.*); ~**s officer** тамо́женник; **we got through the** ~**s** мы прошли́ тамо́женный досмо́тр.

● *cpds.* ~**-house** *n.* тамо́жня; ~**-built,** ~**-made** *adjs.* сде́ланный/изгото́вленный на зака́з.

customary /ˈkʌstəmərɪ/ *adj.* обы́чный, привы́чный; **it is** ~ **to tip** при́нято дава́ть на чай.

customer /ˈkʌstəmə(r)/ *n.* (*purchaser*) покупа́тель (*m.*); (*giving order*) зака́зчик; **regular** ~ постоя́нный покупа́тель; (*of bank etc.*) клие́нт; (*of restaurant*) посети́тель (*m.*); (*coll., fellow*) субъе́кт, тип; **ugly** ~ жу́ткий субъе́кт.

cut /kʌt/ *n.* **1** (*act of* ~*ting*) ре́зка, ре́зание; ~ **and thrust** схва́тка; (*result of stroke*) поре́з, разре́з; **he has** ~**s on his face from shaving** у него́ на лице́ поре́зы от бритья́; **he got a nasty** ~ он си́льно поре́зался.
2 (*reduction*) сниже́ние, пониже́ние; ~ **in salary** сниже́ние жа́лованья; **power** ~ прекраще́ние пода́чи электроэне́ргии.
3 (*omission*): **there were** ~**s in the film** в фи́льме бы́ли сде́ланы купю́ры (*f. pl.*).
4 (*piece or quantity* ~): **a nice** ~ **of beef** хоро́ший кусо́к вы́резки/филе́я; **a** ~ **off the joint** ломо́ть (*m.*)/кусо́к жа́реного мя́са; **cold** ~**s** мясно́й ассортиме́нт.
5 (*of clothes*) покро́й.
6: **short** ~ кратча́йший путь; **take a short** ~ пойти́ (*pf.*) напрями́к.
7: **he is a** ~ **above you** он на́ голову вы́ше вас.
8 (*coll., rake-off*) до́ля, часть; **his** ~ **was 20%** его́ до́ля составля́ла 20%.

● *v.t.* (**cutting;** *past and p.p.* ~)
1 (*divide, separate, wound, extract by* ~*ting*) ре́зать (*impf.*); разр|еза́ть, -е́зать; отр|еза́ть, -е́зать; **the knife** ~ **his finger** нож поре́зал ему́ па́лец; **he** ~ **himself on the tin** он поре́зался/пора́нился о консе́рвную ба́нку; **the wheat has been** ~ пшени́ца сжа́та; ~ **wood** руби́ть (*impf.*) лес; коло́ть (*impf.*) дрова́; ~ (*p.p.*) **flowers** сре́занные цветы́; ~ **coal** (*in a mine*) выруба́ть, вы́рубить у́голь; ~ **something in two** разр|еза́ть, -е́зать что-н. попола́м; ~ **to pieces** (*lit.*) разре́зать (*pf.*) на куски́; (*fig., defeat utterly*) изничто́жить (*pf.*); ~ **short** (*an article*) сокра|ща́ть, -ти́ть; (*s.o.'s life*) оборва́ть (*pf.*); ~ **open** (*e.g. an orange*) разр|еза́ть, -е́зать; (*cin.*): ~! (*stop shooting*) стоп!
2 (*make by* ~*ting*): ~ **me a piece of cake** отре́жьте мне кусо́к то́рта; ~ **steps in the ice** проруб|а́ть, -и́ть ступе́ньки во льду; ~ **an inscription** высека́ть, вы́сечь на́дпись (на ка́мне); ~ **a key** выта́чивать, вы́точить ключ; ~ **a jewel** грани́ть (*impf.*) драгоце́нный ка́мень; ~ **glass** гранёное стекло́; хруста́ль (*m.*).
3 (*trim*) подстр|ига́ть, -и́чь; ~ **one's nails** подстр|ига́ть, -и́чь но́гти; **have one's hair** ~ стри́чься, по-; ~ **s.o.'s hair** стричь, о- кого́-н.; **he** ~ **my hair too short** он сли́шком ко́ротко подстри́г мне во́лосы.
4 (*ignore, neglect*): **she** ~ **me (dead)** она́ не пожела́ла меня́ узна́ть; ~ **a lecture** (*US*) пропус|ка́ть, -ти́ть ле́кцию.
5 (*intersect*) пересека́ть (*impf.*); **the line** ~**s the vertical axis** ли́ния пересека́ет вертика́льную ось.
6 (*reduce*) сн|ижа́ть, -и́зить; сокра|ща́ть, -ти́ть; **fares were** ~ пла́та за прое́зд была́ сни́жена; **the play was** ~ пье́су сократи́ли.
7 (*of clothes*) кро́ить, с-.
8: **the baby** ~ **a tooth** у ребёнка прорезался зуб.
9 (*at cards*): ~ **the pack** сн|има́ть, -ять коло́ду.
10 (*fig.*): **he was** ~ **to the heart** э́то его́ заде́ло за живо́е; ~ (*break*) **one's connection with s.o.** пор|ыва́ть, -ва́ть отноше́ния с кем-н.; ~ **it fine** (*leave bare margin*) рассчита́ть (*pf.*) что-н. в обре́з; **that** ~**s no ice with me** (*coll.*) э́то на меня́ не де́йствует; ~ **the ground from under s.o.'s feet** вы́бить (*pf.*) у кого́-н. по́чву из-под ног.
11 (*excise, eschew*): **the third act was** ~ **(out)** тре́тье де́йствие бы́ло вы́резано/опу́щено.
12 (*hit sharply*): **he** ~ **him across the face with his whip** он хлестну́л его́ плётью по лицу́.

● *v.i.* (**cutting;** *past and p.p.* ~) **1** (*make incision*) ре́зать (*impf.*); **this knife doesn't** ~ э́тот нож не ре́жет.
2 (*in pass. sense*) ре́заться (*impf.*); **sandstone** ~**s easily** песча́ник легко́ ре́жется.
3 (*fig.*): **the argument** ~**s both ways** э́тот до́вод мо́жно испо́льзовать и так, и э́так; ~ **loose** (*sever connection*) прерва́ть (*pf.*) отноше́ния; (*behave wildly*) с цепи́ сорва́ться (*pf.*); **he** ~ **into the conversation** он вмеша́лся в разгово́р; **it** ~ **into** (*took up*) **his time** э́то отня́ло у него́ вре́мя.
4 (*aim a blow; thrust*): **he** ~ **at me with a stick** он замахну́лся на меня́ па́лкой; **it** ~**s across our plans** э́то срыва́ет на́ши пла́ны.
5 (*cards*): **we** ~ **for partners** сня́тием карт мы определи́ли партнёров.
6 (*run, take short* ~): **the boy** ~ **away** ма́льчик удра́л/умча́лся; **he** ~ **and ran**

он драпану́л (*or* дал стрекача́) (*coll.*); **we ~ across the fields** мы прошли́ кратча́йшим путём, напряму́ю че́рез поля́.

● *with advs.*: **~ away** *v.t.* (*e.g. dead wood from a tree*) ср|еза́ть, -е́зать; **~ back** *v.t.* (*prune*) подр|еза́ть, -е́зать; (*fig, reduce, limit*) сокра|ща́ть, -ти́ть; **~ down** *v.t.* (*e.g. a tree*) руби́ть, с-; (*an opponent*) сра|жа́ть, -зи́ть; **~ down expenses** сокра|ща́ть, -ти́ть расхо́ды; **~ down trousers** (*for s.o. shorter*) подкор|а́чивать, -оти́ть брю́ки; **~ down** (*abridge*) **an article** сокра|ща́ть, -ти́ть статью́; **~ s.o. down to size** (*coll.*) сбить (*pf.*) спесь с кого́-н.; **~ in** *v.t.*: **~ s.o. in** (*give them a share*) выделя́ть, вы́делить кому́-н. до́лю; *v.i.* (*interrupt a speaker*) вмеш|иваться, -а́ться; (*of a driver*) перере́зать (*pf.*) доро́гу кому́-н.; **~ off** *v.t.*: **he ~ the chicken's head off** он отруби́л цыплёнку го́лову; **he ~ off a yard from the roll (of cloth)** он отре́зал ярд мате́рии от куска́; **I was ~ off while talking** меня́ разъедини́ли/прерва́ли во вре́мя разгово́ра; **they ~ off our electricity** у нас отключи́ли/вы́ключили электри́чество; **the army was ~ off from its base** а́рмия была́ отре́зана от ба́зы; **we were ~ off by the tide** прили́в отре́зал нас от су́ши; **~ off supplies** прекра|ща́ть, -ти́ть подво́з припа́сов; **he ~ himself off from the world** он отгороди́лся от ми́ра; **he ~ his son off** он лиши́л своего́ сы́на насле́дства; **he was ~ off in his prime** он поги́б в расцве́те лет; **~ (off) a corner** ср|еза́ть, -е́зать у́гол; **~ out** *v.t.*: **he ~ out a picture from the paper** он вы́резал карти́нку из газе́ты; **the doctors cut out half his lung** врачи́ вы́резали ему́ полови́ну лёгкого; **she ~ out a dress** она́ скрои́ла пла́тье; **he is not ~ out for the work** он не со́здан для э́той рабо́ты; **he has his work ~ out** ему́ предстои́т нелёгкая зада́ча; (*eliminate*): **~ out the details** (*in talking*) отбр|а́сывать, -о́сить подро́бности; **~ out smoking** бро́сить (*pf.*) кури́ть; **the engine ~ out** (*failed*) мото́р сдал (*or* вы́шел из стро́я); **~ up** *v.t.*: **he ~ up his meat** он наре́зал мя́со; **he was ~ up by the news** (*coll.*) его́ срази́ло/подкоси́ло э́то изве́стие; **his book was ~ up by the reviewers** (*US*) рецензе́нты разнесли́ его́ кни́гу; *v.i.*: **the turkey ~s up well** в индю́шке мно́го мя́са; **he ~ up rough** (*Br. coll.*) он рассвирепе́л.

● *cpds.* **~-and-dried** *adj.*: **~-and-dried opinions** гото́вые/загото́вленные мне́ния; **~ and paste** *v.t.* (*comput.*) вы́резать и вста́вить; **~away** *adj.*: **~away view of an engine** разре́з маши́ны; **~back** *n.* (*reduction*) сокраще́ние; **~-off** *n.* (*device shutting off steam or liquid*) отсе́чка па́ра/жи́дкости; **~-off date** (*terminal date of a narrative etc.*) после́дний срок; **~-out** *n.* (*figure*) вы́резанная фигу́ра; (*elec.*) предохрани́тель (*m.*); автомати́ческий выключа́тель; **~-price** *adj.* продава́емый по сни́женной цене́; **~-rate** (*US*) = **cut-price; ~throat** *n.* головоре́з; **~throat razor** (*Br.*) опа́сная бри́тва; **~throat competition** ожесточённая/беспоща́дная конкуре́нция; **~water** *n.* (*of ship's prow*) волноре́з; водоре́з; (*of pier*) волноло́м.

cutaneous /kjuːˈteɪnɪəs/ *adj.* ко́жный.

cute /kjuːt/ *adj.* (*appealing*) симпати́чный, ми́лый.

cutesy /ˈkjuːtsɪ/ *adj.* (*coll.*) вы́чурный, претенцио́зный.

cuticle /ˈkjuːtɪk(ə)l/ *n.* кожи́ца (*у основания ногтей*).

cutlass /ˈkʌtləs/ *n.* аборда́жная са́бля.

cutler /ˈkʌtlə(r)/ *n.* ножо́вщик.

cutlery /ˈkʌtlərɪ/ *n.* ножевы́е изде́лия.

cutlet /ˈkʌtlɪt/ *n.* отбивна́я котле́та.

cutter /ˈkʌtə(r)/ *n.* (*tailor*) закро́йщик; (*boat*) ка́тер.

cutting /ˈkʌtɪŋ/ *n.* **1** (*road, rail etc.*) вы́емка. **2** (*Br., press ~*) вы́резка. **3** (*of plant*) отро́сток. **4** (*cin.*) монта́ж.

● *adj.*: **a ~ wind** ре́зкий/прони́зывающий ве́тер; **a ~ retort** язви́тельный/ре́зкий отве́т; **the ~ edge of technology** са́мая совреме́нная те́хника.

cuttle-fish /ˈkʌt(ə)lfɪʃ/ *n.* карака́тица, се́пия.

c.v. (*abbr. of* ***curriculum vitae***) (кра́ткая) автобиогра́фия.

cwt /ˈhʌndrəd,weɪt/ *n.* (*abbr. of* ***hundredweight***) (*Imperial — approx. 50.8 kilograms*) англи́йский це́нтнер; (*US — approx. 45.4 kilograms*) америка́нский це́нтнер.

cyanide /ˈsaɪə,naɪd/ *n.* циани́д.

cyanogen /saɪˈænədʒ(ə)n/ *n.* циа́н.

cyanosis /,saɪəˈnəʊsɪs/ *n.* циано́з, синю́ха.

cybercafé /ˈsaɪbə,kæfeɪ/ *n.* Интерне́т-кафе́.

cybernetic /,saɪbəˈnetɪk/ *adj.* кибернети́ческий.

cybernetics /,saɪbəˈnetɪks/ *n.* кибирне́тика.

cyberspace /ˈsaɪbə,speɪs/ *n.* киберпростра́нство.

cyclamen /ˈsɪkləmən/ *n.* (*pl.* **~** *or* **~s**) циклame´н.

cycle /ˈsaɪk(ə)l/ *n.* **1** (*series, rotation*) цикл, круг; **the ~ of the seasons** времена́ (*nt. pl.*) го́да; **song ~** цикл пе́сен; **menstrual ~** менструа́льный цикл. **2** (*bicycle*) велосипе́д. **3** (*elec.*) пери́од переме́нного то́ка.

● *v.i.* **1** (*revolve*) де́лать (*impf.*) оборо́ты. **2** (*ride ~*) е́здить (*indet.*) на велосипе́де.

● *cpds.* **~ race** *n.* велого́нка; **~-track** *n.* (*Br.*) велосипе́дная доро́жка; (*for race*) велотре́к.

cyclic(al) /ˈsaɪklɪk(ə)l/, /ˈsɪk-/ *adj.* цикли́ческий.

cycling /ˈsaɪklɪŋ/ *n.* езда́ на велосипе́де; велоспо́рт.

cyclist /ˈsaɪklɪst/ *n.* велосипеди́ст.

cyclone /ˈsaɪkləʊn/ *n.* цикло́н.

cyclonic /,saɪˈklɒnɪk/ *adj.* циклони́ческий.

cyclopedia /,saɪkləˈpiːdɪə/ *n.* энциклопе́дия.

cyclotron /ˈsaɪklə,trɒn/ *n.* циклотро́н.

cygnet /ˈsɪɡnɪt/ *n.* молодо́й ле́бедь.

cylinder /ˈsɪlɪndə(r)/ *n.* **1** (*geom. & eng.*) цили́ндр; **~ head** кры́шка цили́ндра; **fire on all ~s** (*lit., fig.*) рабо́тать (*impf.*) в по́лную мо́щность. **2** (*typ.*) цили́ндр, ва́лик.

cylindrical /,sɪˈlɪndrɪk(ə)l/ *adj.* цилиндри́ческий.

cymbal /ˈsɪmb(ə)l/ *n.* таре́лка.

cynic /ˈsɪnɪk/ *n.* ци́ник.

● *adj.* (*phil.*) цини́ческий.

cynical /ˈsɪnɪk(ə)l/ *adj.* цини́чный.

cynicism /ˈsɪnɪ,sɪz(ə)m/ *n.* цини́зм.

cynosure /ˈsaɪnə,zjʊə(r)/, /ˈsɪn-/ *n.* (*fig.*) центр внима́ния.

cypher /ˈsaɪfə(r)/ = **cipher**

cypress /ˈsaɪprəs/ *n.* кипари́с; (*attr.*) кипари́совый.

Cypriot /ˈsɪprɪət/ *n.* киприо́т (*fem.* -ка).

● *adj.* ки́прский.

Cyprus /ˈsaɪprəs/ *n.* Кипр; **in ~** на Ки́пре.

Cyrillic /sɪˈrɪlɪk/ *adj.* кирилли́ческий; **~ alphabet** кири́ллица.

cyst /sɪst/ *n.* киста́.

cystic fibrosis /,sɪstɪk faɪˈbrəʊsɪs/ *n.* кисто́зный фибро́з.

cystitis /sɪˈstaɪtɪs/ *n.* цисти́т.

cytology /saɪˈtɒlədʒɪ/ *n.* цитоло́гия.

czar /zɑː(r)/ *etc. see* ⇒**tsar** *etc.*

Czech /tʃek/ *n.* чех (*fem.* че́шка); (*language*) че́шский язы́к.

● *adj.* че́шский; **~ Republic** Че́хия.

Czechoslovak /,tʃekəˈsləʊvæk/ (*hist.*) *n.* жи́тель (*fem.* -ница) Чехослова́кии.

● *adj.* чехослова́цкий.

Czechoslovakia /,tʃekəsləˈvækɪə/ *n.* (*hist.*) Чехослова́кия.

Dd

D /diː/ *n.* **1** (*mus.*) ре (*indecl.*). **2** (*acad. mark*) «неудовлетвори́тельно», 2, дво́йка; **he got a ∼ in English** он получи́л дво́йку по англи́йскому языку́.

● *cpd.* **∼-day** *n.* день (*m.*) нача́ла вое́нной опера́ции, день «Д».

DA (*abbr. of* ***district attorney***) окружно́й прокуро́р.

dab[1] /dæb/ *n.* (*small quantity*) мазо́к.

● *v.t. & i.* (**dabbed, dabbing**) при|кла́дывать, -ложи́ть; **she ∼bed (at) her eyes with a handkerchief** она́ прикла́дывала к глаза́м плато́к; **he ∼bed paint on the picture** он нанёс кра́ски на холст.

dab[2] /dæb/ *n.* (*fish*) ершова́тка.

dab[3] /dæb/ *n.*: **∼ hand** (*Br.*) спец, до́ка (*c.g.*) (*coll.*).

dabble /ˈdæb(ə)l/ *v.i.*: **∼ at** (*fig.*) игра́ть (*impf.*) в + *a.*; балова́ться (*impf.*) + *i.*; **he ∼s in politics** он игра́ет в поли́тику.

dabbler /ˈdæblə(r)/ *n.* дилета́нт.

dabchick /ˈdæbtʃɪk/ *n.* пога́нка ма́лая.

DAC (*abbr. of* ***digital to analogue converter***) ЦАП (ци́фро-анало́говый преобразова́тель).

da capo /dɑː ˈkɑːpəʊ/ *adv.* (*mus.*) да-ка́по (*с начала*).

dace /deɪs/ *n.* (*pl.* ∼) (*zool.*) еле́ц.

dacha /ˈdætʃə/ *n.* да́ча.

dachshund /ˈdækshʊnd/ *n.* та́кса (*порода собак*).

dacron /ˈdeɪkrɒn/, /ˈdæk-/ *n.* (*propr.*) дакро́н (*ткань*).

dactyl /ˈdæktɪl/ *n.* да́ктиль (*m.*).

dactylic /dækˈtɪlɪk/ *adj.* дактили́ческий.

dad /dæd/, **-dy** /ˈdædɪ/ *nn.* (*coll.*) па́па (*m.*), па́почка (*m.*).

daddy /ˈdædɪ/ = **dad**

● *cpd.* **∼-long-legs** *n.* долгоно́жка.

dado /ˈdeɪdəʊ/ *n.* (*pl.* **∼s**) (*of pedestal*) цо́коль (*m.*); (*of wall*) пане́ль.

daffodil /ˈdæfədɪl/ *n.* нарци́сс жёлтый.

daft /dɑːft/ *adj.* (*Br.*) (*person*) тро́нутый (*coll.*); (*action*) бестолко́вый, глу́пый.

Dagestan /ˌdægɪˈstɑːn/ *n.* Дагеста́н.

Dagestani /ˌdægɪˈstɑːnɪ/ *n.* (*pl.* **∼s**) дагеста́н|ец (*fem.* -ка).

● *adj.* дагеста́нский.

dagger /ˈdægə(r)/ *n.* **1** (*weapon*) кинжа́л; **they are at ∼s drawn** они́ на ножа́х; **she looked ∼s at him** она́ пронзи́ла его́ взгля́дом. **2** (*typ.*) ≈ кре́стик.

daguerreotype /dəˈgerəʊˌtaɪp/ *n.* (*portrait*) дагеррoти́п.

dahlia /ˈdeɪlɪə/ *n.* георги́н.

daily /ˈdeɪlɪ/ *n.* **1** (*newspaper*) ежедне́вная газе́та. **2** (*Br., charwoman*) приходя́щая домрабо́тница.

● *adj.* ежедне́вный; **one's ∼ bread** хлеб насу́щный.

● *adv.* ежедне́вно, ка́ждый день; постоя́нно.

daintiness /ˈdeɪntɪnɪs/ *n.* изя́щество, изы́сканность.

dainty /ˈdeɪntɪ/ *n.* ла́комство, деликате́с.

● *adj.* (**daintier, daintiest**) (*refined, delicate*) изя́щный, изы́сканный; **∼ morsel** ла́комый кусо́чек.

dairy /ˈdeərɪ/ *n.* **1** (*room or building*) маслоде́льня. **2** (*shop*) моло́чный магази́н; (*attr.*) моло́чный.

● *cpds.* **∼maid** *n.* моло́чница; **∼man** *n.* моло́чник.

dais /ˈdeɪɪs/ *n.* помо́ст.

daisy /ˈdeɪzɪ/ *n.* (*flower*) маргари́тка; **fresh as a ∼** цвету́щий; пы́шущий здоро́вьем.

Dalai Lama /ˌdælaɪ ˈlɑːmə/ *n.* дала́й-ла́ма (*m.*).

dale /deɪl/ *n.* дол, доли́на.

dalliance /ˈdælɪəns/ *n.* (*trifling*) баловство́; (*flirtation*) флирт.

dally /ˈdælɪ/ *v.i.* **1** (*play, toy*) балова́ться (*impf.*) (*чем*). **2** (*flirt*) флиртова́ть (*impf.*). **3** (*waste time*) тра́тить (*impf.*) вре́мя по́пусту.

Dalmatian /dælˈmeɪʃ(ə)n/ *n.* (*dog*) далма́тский дог, далмати́н.

dam[1] /dæm/ *n.* **1** (*barrier*) да́мба, плоти́на, запру́да. **2** (*reservoir*) водохрани́лище.

● *v.t.* (**dammed, damming**) запру́|живать, -ди́ть; **∼ up a valley** перекр|ыва́ть, -ы́ть доли́ну.

dam[2] /dæm/ *n.* (*zool.*) ма́тка.

damag|e /ˈdæmɪdʒ/ *n.* **1** (*harm, injury*) вред, поврежде́ние; уще́рб; **do ∼e to something** нан|оси́ть, -ести́ уще́рб/вред чему́-н. **2** (*coll., cost*): **what's the ∼e?** ско́лько с нас (причита́ется)? **3** (*pl., leg.*) убы́тк|и (*pl., g.* -ов); **sue s.o. for ∼es** предъяв|ля́ть, -и́ть иск кому́-н. за убы́тки.

● *v.t.* (*physically*) повре|жда́ть, -ди́ть + *d.*; (*morally*) вреди́ть, на-, причин|я́ть, -и́ть вред + *d.*; **a ∼ing admission** призна́ние себе́ в уще́рб.

Damascus /dəˈmæskəs/ *n.* Дама́ск.

damask /ˈdæməsk/ *n.* **1** (*material*) камча́тная ткань; **∼ silk** дама́ст, камка́; **∼ table-cloth** камча́тная ска́терть. **2**: **∼ rose** дама́сская ро́за.

● *adj.* (*poet., rosy*) а́лый.

dame /deɪm/ *n.* **1** (*fem. equiv. of knight*) дейм, кавале́рственная да́ма. **2** (*US coll., woman*) бабёнка (*coll.*).

damn /dæm/ *n.* (*negligible amount*): **I don't care a ∼** мне наплева́ть.

● *v.t.* **1** (*doom to hell*) прокл|ина́ть, -я́сть; осу|жда́ть, -ди́ть на ве́чные му́ки. **2** (*condemn*): **the critics ∼ed the play** кри́тики забракова́ли пье́су; **∼ with faint praise** хвали́ть, по- так, что не поздоро́вится. **3** (*as expletive*): **∼ (it all)!** чёрт возьми́!; **I'm ∼ed if I know** разрази́ меня́ гром, е́сли я зна́ю; **well, I'm ∼ed!** чёрт бы меня́ побра́л!; **∼ your impudence!** чёрт бы побра́л твоё наха́льство!; **∼ all** (*Br. coll., nothing*) ни черта́; **I'm ∼ed if I'll go** провали́ться мне на э́том ме́сте, е́сли я пойду́; *see also* ⇨**damned**

damnable /ˈdæmnəb(ə)l/ *adj.* прокля́тый.

damnation /dæmˈneɪʃ(ə)n/ *n.* **1** (*condemnation to hell*) прокля́тие; осужде́ние на ве́чные му́ки. **2** (*adverse *judgment*) осуждéние. **3**: **~!** проклятие!

damned /dæmd/ *n., adj. & adv.* **1**: **the ~** осуждённые на вéчные мýки; прóклятые. **2**: **a ~ fool** набитый дурáк; **it's a ~ nuisance** это чертóвски досáдно; **he did his ~est** (*coll.*) он лез из кóжи вон.

damning /ˈdæmɪŋ/ *adj.* губительный; **~ evidence** изобличáющие ули́ки.

Damocles /ˈdæməˌkliːs/ *n.*: **sword of ~** дамóклов меч.

damp /dæmp/ *n.* **1** (*moisture*) влáжность, сы́рость. **2** (*~ atmosphere*) сы́рость, влáжность. **3** (*fig., depression*) уны́ние; **this cast a ~ over the outing** это испóртило прогýлку.

● *adj.* влáжный, сырóй; **~ course** гидроизоля́ция.

● *v.t.* (*also* **dampen**) **1** (*lit.*) см|áчивать, -очи́ть; увлажн|я́ть, -и́ть; **~ down a fire** туши́ть, по- огóнь. **2** (*fig.*): **~ s.o.'s ardour** (*Br.*), **ardor** (*US*) осту|жáть, -ди́ть чей-н. пыл. **3** (*mus.*): **~ a string** заглуш|áть, -и́ть струнý.

● *cpd.* **~-proof** *adj.* влагонепроницáемый; *v.t.* предохран|я́ть, -и́ть от влáги.

damper /ˈdæmpə(r)/ *n.* **1** (*plate in stove etc.*) заслóнка; (*shock absorber*) амортизáтор; (*silencer*) глуши́тель (*m.*). **2** (*fig.*): **the news put a ~ on the stock market** нóвости привели́ к понижéнию конъюнктýры на би́рже. **3** (*in piano*) дéмпфер.

dampish /ˈdæmpɪʃ/ *adj.* сыровáтый.

dampness /ˈdæmpnɪs/ *n.* сы́рость.

damsel /ˈdæmz(ə)l/ *n.* (*arch.*) дéва.

damson /ˈdæmz(ə)n/ *n.* (*fruit*) тернослúв; (*tree*) тёрн.

● *adj.* (*colour*) тёмно-крáсный.

dance /dɑːns/ *n.* **1** тáнец; **we joined the ~** мы присоедини́лись к танцýющим. **2** (*party*) танцевáльный вéчер; тáнцы (*m. pl.*); **give a ~** устр|áивать, -óить тáнцы. **3** (*fig.*): **lead s.o. a (fine/pretty) ~** (*Br.*) води́ть (*indet.*) когó-н. зá нос; **~ of death** пля́ска смéрти.

● *v.t.* **1** танцевáть, с-; исп|олня́ть, -óлнить (*танец*). **2**: **~ a baby on one's knee** качáть (*impf.*) ребёнка на колéнях. **3** (*fig.*): **~ attendance on s.o.** ходи́ть (*indet.*) пéред кем-н. на зáдних лáпках.

● *v.i.* танцевáть, с-; пляcáть, с-; **he ~d for joy** он плясáл от рáдости; **the leaves ~d in the wind** ли́стья кружи́лись на ветрý; **the boat ~d on the waves** лóдка качáлась на вóлнáх.

● *cpds.* **~-band** *n.* оркéстр (на тáнцах); **~-floor** *n.* танцевáльная площáдка; **~-hall** *n.* танцевáльный зал.

dancer /ˈdɑːnsə(r)/ *n.* танцóр (*fem.* -ка); (*professional*) танцóвщи|к (*fem.* -ца).

dancing /ˈdɑːnsɪŋ/ *n.* тáнцы (*m. pl.*).

● *cpds.* **~-girl** *n.* танцóвщица; **~-master** *n.* учи́тель (*m.*) тáнцев; **~-partner** *n.* партнёр; **~-shoes** *n. pl.* танцевáльные тýфли (*f. pl.*).

dandelion /ˈdændɪˌlaɪən/ *n.* одувáнчик.

dander /ˈdændə(r)/ *n.* (*coll.*): **get s.o.'s ~ up** выводи́ть, вы́вести когó-н. из себя́.

dandified /ˈdændɪˌfaɪd/ *adj.* щегольскóй.

dandle /ˈdænd(ə)l/ *v.t.* качáть (*impf.*).

dandruff /ˈdændrʌf/ *n.* пéрхоть.

dandy /ˈdændɪ/ *n.* дéнди (*m. indecl.*), щёголь (*m.*), франт.

● *adj.* (**dandier, dandiest**) (*US coll.*) превосхóдный; пéрвый класс (*pred.*).

dandyism /ˈdændɪˌɪz(ə)m/ *n.* денди́зм, франтовствó, щегольствó.

Dane /deɪn/ *n.* датчáн|ин (*fem.* -ка); **Great ~** дог.

danger /ˈdeɪndʒə(r)/ *n.* **1** (*risk of injury*) опáсность; **~!** осторóжно!; береги́сь!; **in ~** в опáсности; **out of ~** вне опáсности; **he is in ~ of falling** он рискýет упáсть; **~ money** плáта за опáсную рабóту; **~ zone** опáсная зóна. **2** (*person or thing presenting risk*) опáсность, угрóза; **the wreck is a ~ to shipping** облóмки представля́ют (собóй) опáсность/угрóзу для кораблéй; **~ point** опáсная тóчка; опáсный предéл.

dangerous /ˈdeɪndʒərəs/ *adj.* опáсный, рискóванный; **the dog looks ~** собáка имéет грóзный вид.

dangerousness /ˈdeɪndʒərəsnɪs/ *n.* опáсность, риск.

dangle /ˈdæŋg(ə)l/ *v.t.* болтáть (*impf.*) (+*i.*).

● *v.i.* болтáться (*impf.*).

Daniel /ˈdænj(ə)l/ *n.* (*bibl.*) Даниил; (*fig.*) неподкýпный/прáведный судья́.

Danish /ˈdeɪnɪʃ/ *n.* (*language*) дáтский язы́к.

● *adj.* дáтский.

dank /dæŋk/ *adj.* влáжный, сырóй.

dankness /ˈdæŋknɪs/ *n.* влáжность, сы́рость.

danse macabre /ˌdɑ̃s məˈkɑːbr/ *n.* пля́ска смéрти.

danseuse /dɑˈsɜːz/ *n.* танцóвщица.

Danube /ˈdænjuːb/ *n.* Дунáй.

daphne /ˈdæfnɪ/ *n.* (*bot.*) волчея́годник.

dapper /ˈdæpə(r)/ *adj.* щеголевáтый.

dapple /ˈdæp(ə)l/ *n.* (*dappled effect*) пестротá.

● *adj.* (*also* **~d**) пёстрый, пятни́стый.

● *cpd.* **~-grey** *n. & adj.* (*horse*) сéрый в я́блоках (конь).

Dardanelles /ˌdɑːdəˈnelz/ *n.* Дарданéлл|ы (*pl., g.* —).

dare /deə(r)/ *n.* (*challenge*) вы́зов; **take a ~** прин|имáть, -я́ть вы́зов.

● *v.t.* (*challenge*) бр|осáть, -óсить вы́зов +*d.*; (*egg on*) подзадóри|вать, -ть; **I ~ you to jump over the wall!** а ну, перепры́гни чéрез э́ту стéну!

● *v.i.* (*3rd pers. sing. pres. usu.* **~** *before an expressed or implied infinitive without 'to'*) **1** (*have courage*) осмéли|ваться, -ться; сметь, по-; отвáжи|ваться, -ться. **2** (*have impudence*) сметь, по-; **how ~ he say that!** как он смéет говори́ть такóе! **3**: **I ~ say (that)** . . . нáдо дýмать (*or* полагáю), что. . . .

● *cpd.* **~-devil** *adj.* отчáянный, бесшабáшный.

daring /ˈdeərɪŋ/ *n.* отвáга.

● *adj.* отвáжный, дéрзкий.

dark /dɑːk/ *n.* темнотá, тьма; **before/after ~** до/пóсле наступлéния темноты́; (*ignorance*) невéжество, невéдение; **I am in the ~ as to his plans** я в невéдении относи́тельно егó плáнов; егó плáны мне невéдомы; (*dark colour*) тень.

● *adj.* **1** (*lacking light*) тёмный; **pitch ~** кромéшная тьма, темны́м-темнó (*coll.*); **~ glasses** (*spectacles*) тёмные/сóлнечные очки́; **~ room** (*phot.*) тёмная кóмната. **2** (*of colour*) тёмный. **3** (*of complexion*) смýглый. **4** (*fig.*) тёмный; **a ~ horse** тёмная лошáдка; **the D~ Continent** чёрный континéнт; **keep the news ~** держáть (*impf.*) нóвость в секрéте; **the future is ~** бýдущее неизвéстно; **the D~ Ages** рáннее средневекóвье.

dark- /dɑːk/ *comb. form* **1** (*before colours*) тёмно-; **~blue** тёмно-си́ний. **2** (*before haired etc.*) темно (*no hyphen*); **~haired** темноволóсый; **~skinned** темнокóжий.

darken /ˈdɑːkən/ *v.t.* затемн|я́ть, -и́ть; **never ~ my door again!** не переступáйте бóльше моегó порóга!

● *v.i.* темнéть, по-; ста|нови́ться, -ть тёмным.

darkness /ˈdɑːknɪs/ *n.* темнотá; **the Prince of D~** принц тьмы.

darling /ˈdɑːlɪŋ/ *n.* дорогóй, ми́лый, роднóй, люби́мый; **she's a ~** онá прéлесть; (*favourite*) люби́мец; **mother's ~** (*boy*) мáменькин сынóк; (*girl*) мáменькина дóчка.

● *adj.* (*beloved*) люби́мый, дорогóй; (*delightful*) очаровáтельный.

darn[1] /dɑːn/ *n.* штóпка; заштóпанное мéсто; **his socks have a ~ in them** у негó носки́ заштóпаны.

● *v.t. & i.* (*mend*) штóпать, за-; *see also* ⇨**darning**

darn[2] /dɑːn/ *n.* (*coll.*): **I don't give a ~** мне наплевáть.

● *v.t.* (*as expletive*): **~ (it)!** чёрт возьми́!; чёрт подери́!

darnel /ˈdɑːn(ə)l/ *n.* плéвел.

darning /ˈdɑːnɪŋ/ *n.* **1** (*action*) штóпанье, штóпка. **2** (*things to be darned*) вéщи (*f. pl.*) для штóпки.

● *cpds.* **~-needle** *n.* штóпальная иглá; **~-wool** *n.* штóпка.

dart[1] /dɑːt/ *n.* **1** (*light javelin*) стрелá, дрóтик. **2** (*for indoor game*) стрелá, дрóтик.

● *cpd.* **~board** *n.* мишéнь для стрел.

dart[2] /dɑːt/ *n.* (*run*) бросóк, рывóк; **he made a ~ for the door** он рвану́лся/брóсился к двéри.

● *v.t.* мет|áть, -нýть; **she ~ed an angry look at him** онá метнýла на негó злóбный взгляд.

● *v.i.* устрем|ля́ться, -и́ться; мчáться, по-; бросáться, брóситься; **she ~ed into the shop** онá стрелóй влетéла в магази́н; **swallows were ~ing through the air** лáсточки носи́лись в вóздухе.

dart³ /dɑːt/ *n.* (*dressmaking*) вы́тачка, шов.

Darwinian /dɑːˈwɪnɪən/ *adj.* дарвини́стский.

Darwinism /ˈdɑːwɪn,ɪz(ə)m/ *n.* дарвини́зм.

Darwinist /ˈdɑːwɪnɪst/ *n.* дарвини́ст.

dash /dæʃ/ *n.* **1** (*sudden rush, race*) рыво́к, бросо́к; **let's make a ~ for it** дава́й побежи́м туда́; **the 100 yards ~** забе́г на 100 я́рдов.
2 (*impact*) уда́р, взмах; **the ~ of waves on a rock** уда́ры волн о скалу́; **the ~ of cold water revived him** струя́ холо́дной воды́ привела́ его́ в чу́вство.
3 (*admixture*): **a ~ of pepper in the soup** щепо́тка пе́рца в су́пе.
4 (*written stroke; also in Morse*) тире́ (*indecl.*).
5 (*vigour*) реши́тельность.
6 (*show*): **cut a ~** (*coll.*) (хорошо́) смотре́ться (*impf.*).
● *v.t.* **1** (*throw violently*) швыр|я́ть, -ну́ть; **the ship was ~ ed against the cliff** су́дно швырну́ло о скалу́; **he ~ed the book down** он швырну́л кни́гу.
2 (*perform rapidly*): **he ~ed off a sketch** он наброса́л эски́з.
3 (*fig., disappoint*) разр|уша́ть, -у́шить; разб|ива́ть, -и́ть; **his hopes were ~ed** его́ наде́жды ру́хнули.
4 (*Br., as expletive*): **~ it (all)!** к чёрту!; чёрт побери́!; *see also* ⇨**dashed**
● *v.i.* **1** (*move violently*) броса́ться, бро́ситься; ри́нуться (*pf.*); **the waves ~ed over the rocks** во́лны разбива́лись о ска́лы.
2 (*run*) мча́ться (*impf.*); нести́сь (*det.*); **she ~ed into the shop** она́ ворвала́сь в магази́н; **he ~ed off to town** он умча́лся в го́род.

dashboard /ˈdæʃbɔːd/ *n.* прибо́рная пане́ль/доска́.

dashed /dæʃt/ *adj.* (*Br.*) чёртов, прокля́тый.

dashing /ˈdæʃɪŋ/ *adj.* сти́льный.

dastard /ˈdæstəd/ *n.* трус, подле́ц.

dastardly /ˈdæstədlɪ/ *adj.* трусли́вый, по́длый.

data /ˈdeɪtə/ = **datum**

databank /ˈdeɪtə,bæŋk/ *n.* банк да́нных.

database /ˈdeɪtə,beɪs/ *n.* ба́за да́нных.

datable /ˈdeɪtəb(ə)l/ *adj.* поддаю́щийся датиро́вке.

date¹ /deɪt/ *n.* (**~-palm**) фи́никовая па́льма; (*fruit*) фи́ник.

date² /deɪt/ *n.* **1** (*indication of time*) да́та, число́; **what's the ~ today?** како́е сего́дня число́?; **the ~ of the letter is 6 October** письмо́ дати́ровано шесты́м октября́; **what were the ~s of your last employment?** укажи́те да́ты ва́шего после́днего ме́ста рабо́ты.
2 (*period*) пери́од; **at an early ~** (*soon*) в ближа́йшем бу́дущем; **by the earliest possible ~** в наикратча́йший срок; **out of ~** устаре́лый; **go out of ~** устар|ева́ть, -е́ть; выходи́ть, вы́йти из мо́ды; **up to ~** нове́йший, совреме́нный; **bring s.o. up to ~** вв|оди́ть, -ести́ кого́-н. в курс де́ла; **bring a catalogue up to ~** обнов|ля́ть, -и́ть катало́г; **our receipts to ~ are £5** на́ши поступле́ния на сего́дняшний день равны́ пяти́ фу́нтам.
3 (*coll., appointment*) свида́ние.
● *v.t.* **1** (*indicate ~ on*) дати́ровать (*impf., pf.*); **he ~d the letter 24 May** он дати́ровал письмо́ 24-ым ма́я; *see also* ⇨**dated.**
2 (*estimate ~ of*) дати́ровать (*impf., pf.*); **can you ~ these coins?** вы мо́жете дати́ровать э́ти моне́ты?
3 (*US coll., go out with*) встреча́ться (*impf.*) с + *i.*; **dating agency** аге́нтство знако́мств.
● *v.i.* **1** (*originate*): **this church ~s from the 14th century** э́та це́рковь отно́сится к 14-му ве́ку.
2 (*become obsolete, show signs of age*) старе́ть (*impf.*); устар|ева́ть, -е́ть; **the play ~s terribly** э́та пье́са ужа́сно устаре́ла.
● *cpds.* **~-line** *n.* (*meridian*) демаркацио́нная ли́ния (су́точного) вре́мени; (*journ.*) указа́ние ме́ста и да́ты репорта́жа; **~-stamp** *n.* ште́мпель-календа́рь (*m.*); календа́рный ште́мпель.

dated /ˈdeɪtɪd/ *adj.* (*out of date*) устаре́вший, устаре́лый.

dative /ˈdeɪtɪv/ *n.* да́тельный паде́ж. ● *adj.* да́тельный.

datum /ˈdeɪtəm/, /ˈdɑːtəm/ *n.* **1** (*thing known or granted*) исхо́дный факт.
2 (*assumption, premise*) исхо́дная то́чка. **3** (*pl.*, **data**) да́нные (*nt. pl.*); материа́л; **personal ~** биографи́ческие да́нные; **~ bank** банк да́нных; **~ input** ввод да́нных; **~ processing** обрабо́тка информа́ции.

daub /dɔːb/ *n.* **1** (*material*) штукату́рка. **2** (*bad painting*) мазня́, пачкотня́.
● *v.t. & i.* **1** (*smear*) обма́з|ывать, -ать; ма́зать, на-; **~ paint on a wall; ~ a wall with paint** ма́зать сте́ну кра́ской.
2 (*paint badly*) па́чкать; ма́зать (*both impf.*).

daughter /ˈdɔːtə(r)/ *n.* (*child*) дочь.
● *cpd.* **~-in-law** *n.* неве́стка, сноха́.

daughterly /ˈdɔːtərlɪ/ *adj.* доче́рний.

daunt /dɔːnt/ *v.t.* устраш|а́ть, -и́ть; обескура́жи|вать, -ть; **nothing ~ ed, he asked for more** нима́ло не смуща́ясь, он попроси́л доба́вки.

dauntless /ˈdɔːntlɪs/ *adj.* неустраши́мый, бесстра́шный.

dauphin /ˈdɔːfɪn/, /ˈdəʊfæ̃/ *n.* дофи́н.

davenport /ˈdævən,pɔːt/ *n.* (*Br., writing-desk*) пи́сьменный сто́лик; (*US, sofa*) дива́н.

davit /ˈdævɪt/, /ˈdeɪvɪt/ *n.* шлюпба́лка.

Davy Jones's locker /,deɪvɪ ˈdʒəʊnz/ (*fig.*) морска́я пучи́на; **he's gone to ~** он утону́л.

Davy lamp /ˈdeɪvɪ/ *n.* шахтёрская ла́мпа.

daw /dɔː/ *n.* га́лка.

dawdle /ˈdɔːd(ə)l/ *v.t.*: **~ away one's time** зря тра́тить (*impf.*) вре́мя.
● *v.i.* ме́шкать (*impf.*); **she dawdled along the road** она́ брела́ по доро́ге.

dawdler /ˈdɔːd(ə)lə(r)/ *n.* копу́ша (*coll., c.g.*).

dawn /dɔːn/ *n.* **1** (*daybreak*) рассве́т, заря́; **at ~** на рассве́те; на заре́; **~ chorus** у́тренний щебе́т. **2** (*fig.*): **the ~ of civilization** заря́ цивилиза́ции.
● *v.i.* **1** (*of daybreak*) света́ть (*impf.*); рассве|та́ть, -сти́; **the day is ~ing** света́ет. **2** (*fig.*): **it ~ ed on me that ...** меня́ осени́ло, что...; **the truth ~ed upon him** ему́ всё ста́ло я́сно.

day /deɪ/ *n.* **1** (*time of daylight*) день (*m.*); (*attr.*) дневно́й; **by ~** днём; **twice a ~** два ра́за в день; **time of ~** вре́мя дня; **pass the time of ~ with s.o.** обме́ниваться, обменя́ться приве́тствиями с кем-н.; **break of ~** рассве́т; **late in the ~** (*fig.*) сли́шком по́здно.
2 (*24 hours*) день (*m.*), су́т|ки (*pl., g.* -ок); **a ~ and a half** полтора́ дня.
3 (*as point of time*): **what ~ (of the week) is it?** како́й сего́дня день (неде́ли)?; **one ~** (*past*) одна́жды; (*future*) когда́-нибудь; **the other ~** на днях; **every other ~** че́рез день; **one of these (fine) ~s** в оди́н прекра́сный день; на днях; **some ~** когда́-нибу́дь; **some ~ soon** как-нибу́дь на днях; вско́ре; **this isn't my ~** (*coll.*) я сего́дня не в уда́ре; мне сего́дня что́-то не везёт; **the Last D~, the D~ of Judgement** су́дный день, день стра́шного суда́; **she's thirty if she's a ~** ей ника́к не ме́ньше тридцати́ лет; **live from ~ to ~** жить (*impf.*) со дня на́ день; **this ~ week** ро́вно че́рез неде́лю; **~ in, ~ out; ~ after ~** изо дня в день; **three years ago to a ~** ро́вно три го́да наза́д; **(on) the ~ I met you** в день на́шей встре́чи; **(on) the ~ before** накану́не (*чего*); **to this ~** по сей день; поны́не; **she named the ~** она́ назна́чила день сва́дьбы; **I took a ~ off** я взял выходно́й; **we had a ~ out** (*Br.*) мы провели́ день вне до́ма.
4 (*as work period*): **he works a 5-hour ~** у него́ пятичасово́й рабо́чий день; **he is paid by the ~** ему́ пла́тят подённо; **let's call it a ~** (*coll.*) на сего́дня хва́тит; **it's all in a/the ~'s work** э́то в поря́дке веще́й.
5 (*in names of festivals*): **May D~** день Пе́рвого ма́я; **Victory D~** День Побе́ды.
6 (*period*) пора́, вре́мя (*nt.*); **the present ~** сего́дня; теку́щий моме́нт; **these ~s** (*nowadays*) тепе́рь, в на́ши дни; **in those ~s** в те дни; в то вре́мя; **in ~s of old** в былы́е дни; **in ~s to come** в бу́дущем; **in this ~ and age** в на́ше вре́мя; **he has known better ~s** он знава́л лу́чшие времена́; **his ~s are numbered** его́ дни́ сочтены́; **end one's ~s** сконча́ться (*pf.*); **the great men of the ~** ви́дные лю́ди эпо́хи; **he has had his ~** он отслужи́л своё; **she was a beauty in her ~** в своё вре́мя она́ была́ краса́вицей; **save for a rainy ~** от|кла́дывать, -ложи́ть на чёрный день; **in all my born ~s** за всю мою́ жизнь; **salad ~s** пора́ ю́ношеской нео́пытности.
7 (*denoting contest*): **win/carry the ~**

одерж|ивать, -áть побéду; **the ~ is ours** мы одержáли побéду, нáша взялá (*coll.*); **his arrival saved the ~** его́ приéзд спас положéние.

● *cpds.* **~-bed** *n.* кушéтка; **~-boarder** *n.* полупансионéр; **~-book** *n.* журнáл; **~-boy** *n.* (*Br.*) учени́к, не живу́щий при шкóле; **~-break** *n.* рассвéт; **~-care** *adj.*: **~-care facilities** (*for children*) детсáд; (*for babies, toddlers*) я́сл|и (*pl., g.* -ей); дéтск|ие учреждéн|ия (*pl., g.* -их -ий); **~ (-care) centre** (*for elderly etc.*) центр пóмощи престарéлым, инвали́дам, и т.п.; **~-dream** *n.* грёза, мечтá; *v.i.* мечтáть (*impf.*); грéзить (*impf.*); **~dreamer** *n.* мечтáтель (*m.*) (*fem.* -ница); **~-girl** *n.* (*Br.*) учени́ца, не живу́щая при шкóле; **~-labourer** (*Br.*), **-laborer** (*US*) *n.* подёнщи|к (*fem.* -ца); **~light** *n.* (*period*): **in broad ~light** средь бéла дня; **~light robbery** *see* ⇒**robbery; ~light-saving time** лéтнее врéмя; (*dawn*) дневнóй свет; рассвéт; (*fig.*): **I begin to see ~light** мне ужé ви́ден просвéт; (*fig.*): **beat the ~lights out of s.o.** отколоти́ть (*pf.*) когó-н. до полусмéрти; **~-long** *n.* для́щийся цéлый день; **~-nursery** *n.* (*crèche*) дéтские я́сл|и (*pl., g.* -ей); **~-school** *n.* шкóла без пансиóна; **~-ticket** *n.* билéт, действи́тельный в течéние одногó дня; **~time** *n.* день (*m.*); **in the ~time** днём; *adj.* дневнóй; **~-to-~** *adj.* повседнéвный.

daze /deɪz/ *n.*: **he was in a ~** он был как в дурмáне.

● *v.t.* пора|жáть, -зи́ть; ошарáши|вать, -ть (*coll.*).

dazzle /'dæz(ə)l/ *n.* ослеплéние; ослепи́тельный блеск.

● *v.t.* **1** (*lit.*) ослеп|ля́ть, -и́ть. **2** (*fig.*) пора|жáть, -зи́ть; ослеп|ля́ть, -и́ть; **she was ~d by his wealth** онá былá ослепленá егó богáтством.

dB /'desɪˌbel/ *n.* (*abbr. of* **decibel(s)**) дБ. (децибéл).

DC (*abbr. of* ***direct current***) постоя́нный ток.

DDT (*abbr. of* ***dichlorodiphenyl-trichloroethane***) ДДТ (дихлордифенилтрихлорэтáн).

deacon /'di:kən/ *n.* дья́кон.

deaconess /ˌdi:kə'nes/, /'di:kənɪs/ *n.* дьяконéсса.

dead /ded/ *n.*: **at ~ of night** глубóкой нóчью.

● *adj.* **1** (*no longer living*) мёртвый, умéрший; (*in accident etc.*) поги́бший, уби́тый; (*of animal*) дóхлый; **~ body** труп, мёртвое тéло; **~ flowers/leaves** увя́дшие цветы́/ли́стья; **he is ~** он у́мер; (*killed*) уби́т; **~ and gone** (*fig.*) давнó прошéдший; **more ~ than alive** полумёртвый; **~ man's handle** автомати́ческий тóрмоз в электропоездáх; **~ wood** (*lit.*) сухостóй; (*fig.*) баллáст; **I wouldn't be seen ~ there** меня́ тудá аркáном не затáщишь; (*as n.*: **the ~**) умéршие, покóйные; **rise from the ~** воскрéснуть (*pf.*); восстáть (*pf.*) из мёртвых.
2 (*numb, insensitive*) онемéлый, омертвéлый; **my foot has gone ~** у меня́ ногá онемéла/затеклá; **~ with hunger** умирáющий с гóлоду; **~ with fatigue** смертéльно устáлый; **he is ~ to the world** (*drunk*) он мертвéцки пьян; (*asleep*) он спит мёртвым сном.
3 (*inert, motionless*) спокóйный, неподви́жный; **in the ~ hours of the night** глухóй нóчью; **~ end** (*lit., fig.*) тупи́к; **a ~ end job** бесперспекти́вная рабóта; **~ season** мёртвый сезóн.
4 (*used, spent, uncharged*): **~ match** испóльзованная спи́чка; **the telephone went ~** телефóн умóлк; **the furnace is ~** тóпка погáсла; **the law is a ~ letter** э́тот закóн утрáтил си́лу; **~ volcano** потýхший вулкáн.
5 (*dull, of sound or colour*) глухóй, ту́склый.
6 (*obsolete, no longer valid*): **~ language** мёртвый язы́к.
7 (*abrupt, exact, complete*) внезáпный; пóлный; совершéнный; **in ~ earnest** совершéнно серьёзно; **come to a ~ stop** остан|áвливаться, -ови́ться как вкóпанный; **~ calm** мёртвый штиль; **~ loss** (*irrecoverable amount*) чи́стый убы́ток; (*fig., failure*) пóлный провáл; **he's a ~ loss** он неудáчник, от негó тóлку не бу́дет; **a ~ faint** глубóкий óбморок; **a ~ certainty** пóлная увéренность; **he's a ~ shot** он мéткий стрелóк; он стреля́ет без прóмаха; **he made a ~ set at her** (*Br.*) он реши́л покори́ть её во что бы то ни стáло; **~ centre** (*mech.*) мёртвая тóчка.

● *adv.*: **he stopped ~** он останови́лся как вкóпанный; **~ on time** минýта в минýту; **~ drunk** мертвéцки пья́ный; **~ straight** совершéнно пря́мо; **~ tired** смертéльно устáлый; **~ against** реши́тельно прóтив; **he is ~ set on going to London** он реши́л поéхать в Лóндон во что бы то ни стáло; **~ slow** óчень мéдленно; **~ certain** совершéнно увéренный.

● *cpds.* **~-beat** *n.* (*coll., loafer*) бездéльник; парази́т; *adj.* (*coll., worn out*) смертéльно устáлый, изнурённый; **~-eye** *n.* (*naut.*) ю́ферс; **~head** *v.t.* (*Br.*) обр|езáть, -éзать сухи́е голóвки + *g.*; *n.* (*US, passenger*) человéк, имéющий прáво на бесплáтный проéзд; **~line** *n.* предéльный/крáйний срок; **~lock** *n.* мёртвая тóчка; тупи́к; **break a ~lock** выходи́ть, вы́йти из тупикá; *v.t.*: **the negotiations are ~locked** переговóры зашли́ в тупи́к; **~pan** *adj.* (*coll.*) невырази́тельный; **~-reckoning** *n.* навигациóнное счислéние.

deaden /'ded(ə)n/ *v.t.* осл|абля́ть, -áбить; заглуш|áть, -и́ть; **the drug ~s pain** лекáрство притупля́ет боль; **the walls ~ sound** стéны заглушáют шум; **gloves ~ the force of a blow** перчáтки ослабля́ют си́лу удáра.

deadliness /'dedlɪnɪs/ *n.* смертéльность.

deadly /'dedlɪ/ *adj.* (**deadlier, deadliest**) смертéльный; смертонóсный; **~ poison** смертéльный яд; **~ enemy** смертéльный враг; **~ sin** смéртный грех; (*intense*) ужáсный; **~ dullness** смертéльная скýка; **~ weapon** смертонóсное орýжие.

deadness /'dednɪs/ *n.* омертвéлость, омертвéние.

deaf /def/ *adj.* **1** глухóй; **~ in one ear** глухóй на однó ýхо; **~ as a post** глухáя тетéря; **~ and dumb** глухонемóй; **~ and dumb language** язы́к глухонемы́х; **~ mute** глухонемóй; (*as n.*: **the ~**) глухи́е.
2 (*fig.*): **turn a ~ ear to** не слýшать (*impf.*); не обращáть (*impf.*) внимáния на + *a.*; **he is ~ to all entreaty** он глух ко всем мольбáм.

● *cpd.* **~-aid** *n.* (*Br.*) слуховóй аппарáт.

deafen /'def(ə)n/ *v.t.* оглуш|áть, -и́ть.

deafening /'defənɪŋ/ *adj.* оглуши́тельный.

deafness /'defnɪs/ *n.* глухотá.

deal¹ /di:l/ *n.* (*wood*) хвóйная древеси́на; (*board*) елóвая/соснóвая доскá; дильс; **~ furniture** мéбель из сосны́.

deal² /di:l/ *n.* **1** (*amount*) коли́чество; **a great, good ~ (of)** мнóго + *g.*; **she's a good ~ better today** ей сегóдня гораздо лýчше.
2 (*business agreement*) сдéлка; **it's a ~!** договори́лись!; по рукáм!; **give s.o. a raw/square ~** (*coll.*) несправедли́во/чéстно обходи́ться, обойти́сь с кем-н.
3 (*at cards*) сдáча; **it's my ~** моя́ óчередь сдавáть.

● *v.t.* (*past and p.p.* **dealt**) **1** (*cards*) сда|вáть, -ть.
2 (*apportion*) разд|авáть, -áть; распредел|я́ть, -и́ть; **the money was ~t out fairly** дéньги бы́ли разделены́ чéстно.
3 (*inflict*): **~ s.o. a blow** нан|оси́ть, -ести́ комý-н. удáр.

● *v.i.* (*past and p.p.* **dealt**) **1** (*do business*) торговáть (*impf.*); **he is a difficult man to ~ with** с ним трýдно имéть дéло; **he ~s in furs** он торгýет мехáми.
2: **~ with** (*treat*) обращáться (с + *i.*); поступáть (с + *i.*) (*both impf*); **what is the best way of ~ing with young criminals?** как лýчше всегó поступáть с малолéтними престýпниками?; (*cope with, manage*) справ|ля́ться, ~иться (с + *i.*); **I'll ~ with him!** я с ним спрáвлюсь; **he ~t with the problem skilfully** он умéло подошёл к э́тому вопрóсу.
3: **~ with** (*discuss, treat*) (*of person*) зан|имáться, -я́ться (*impf.*) + *i.*; (*of book*) рассм|áтривать, -отрéть; **the book ~s with African affairs** э́та кни́га посвященá африкáнским проблéмам (*or* рассмáтривает африкáнские проблéмы).
4 (*behave, conduct o.s.*) обходи́ться (*impf.*) (с + *i.*); поступáть (*impf.*) (с + *i.*); **he ~s justly with all** он поступáет со всéми справедли́во.

dealer /'di:lə(r)/ *n.* **1** (*at cards*) сдаю́щий кáрты. **2** (*trader*) торгóвец, ди́лер.

dealing /'di:lɪŋ/ *n.* **1** (*action*) распределéние; **plain ~** прямотá.
2 (*trade*): **~ in real estate** торгóвля недви́жимостью. **3** (*pl., association*) торгóвые делá; сдéлки (*f. pl.*); **have**

~s with s.o. име́ть (*impf.*) дела́ с кем-н.

dealt /delt/ *past and p.p of* ⇒**deal²**

dean /di:n/ *n.* (*eccl.*) дека́н, настоя́тель (*m.*); (*acad.*) дека́н.

deanery /ˈdi:nərɪ/ *n.* (*function*) дека́нство; (*acad.*) декана́т; (*house*) дом дека́на.

dear /dɪə(r)/ *n.* ми́лый, дорого́й; **he's a (perfect) ~** он о́чень мил; **be a ~ and do this for me** бу́дь так добр, сде́лай э́то для меня́.

● *adj.* **1** (*beloved*) люби́мый, дорого́й. **2** (*lovable*) сла́вный, ми́лый. **3** (*as polite address*): **my ~ fellow** дорого́й (мой); (*in informal letters*) дорого́й; (*in formal letters*) уважа́емый. **4** (*precious*) дорого́й; **for ~ life** (*fig.*) отча́янно, изо всех сил. **5** (*heartfelt*): **his ~est wish** его́ сокрове́нное жела́ние. **6** (*costly*) дорого́й.

● *int.*: **oh ~!; ~ me!** о, Го́споди!; Бо́же ты мой!

dearly /ˈdɪəlɪ/ *adv.* (*fondly*) не́жно; (*at a high price*) до́рого.

dearness /ˈdɪənɪs/ *n.* (*high cost*) дороговизна.

dearth /dɜ:θ/ *n.* нехва́тка, недоста́ток.

death /deθ/ *n.* **1** (*act or fact of dying*) смерть; **die the ~** (*liter.*) пог|иба́ть, -и́бнуть; **meet one's ~** на|ходи́ть, -йти́ свою́ ги́бель; **natural ~** есте́ственная смерть; **violent ~** наси́льственная смерть; **~ certificate** свиде́тельство о сме́рти; **~ duties** нало́г на насле́дство; **~ penalty** сме́ртная казнь; **be burnt to ~** сгор|а́ть, -е́ть за́живо; **drink o.s. to ~** ум|ира́ть, -ере́ть от пья́нства; **work o.s. to ~** рабо́тать (*impf.*) на изно́с; **bleed to ~** ист|ека́ть, -е́чь кро́вью; **at ~'s door** на поро́ге сме́рти; **catch one's ~ (of cold)** простуди́ться (*pf.*) на́смерть; **put to ~** казни́ть (*impf., pf.*); убива́ть, уби́ть; **sentence to ~** пригов|а́ривать, -ори́ть к сме́рти; **stone to ~** заб|ива́ть, -и́ть камня́ми; **fight to the ~** би́ться (*impf.*) не на жизнь, а на смерть; **he held on like grim ~** он держа́лся изо всех сил; **he looks like ~** (*coll.*) ≈ кра́ше в гроб кладу́т; **~ in life; living ~** не жизнь, а ка́торга.
2 (*instance of dying*) ги́бель; **there were many ~s in the accident** в ава́рии поги́бло мно́го люде́й.
3 (*destruction*): **the ~ of his hopes** круше́ние его́ наде́жд.
4 (*utmost limit*): **he was bored to ~** ему́ бы́ло до́ смерти ску́чно; **tired to ~** смерте́льно уста́лый; **I'm sick to ~ of it** мне э́то до́ смерти надое́ло.
5 (*cause of death*): **this work will be the ~ of me** э́та рабо́та сведёт меня́ в моги́лу.

● *cpds.* **~-bed** *n.* сме́ртное ло́же; **~-blow** *n.* смерте́льный уда́р; **~like** *adj.*: **a ~like silence** гробово́е молча́ние; **~-mask** *n.* посме́ртная ма́ска; **~-rate** *n.* сме́ртность; **~-rattle** *n.* предсме́ртный хрип; **~-toll** *n.* число́ поги́бших; **~-trap** *n.*: **this theatre is a ~-trap in case of fire** в слу́чае пожа́ра э́тот теа́тр су́щая западня́; **~-warrant** *n.* распоряже́ние о приведе́нии сме́ртного пригово́ра в исполне́ние; **~-watch** *adj.*: **~-watch beetle** жук-моги́льщик; **~-wish** *n.* (*psych.*) стремле́ние к сме́рти.

deathly /ˈdeθlɪ/ *adj. & adv.* (**deathlier, deathliest**) смерте́льный; **~ pale** смерте́льно бле́дный; **~ silence** мёртвая тишина́.

deb /deb/ (*coll.*) = **debutante**

debacle /deɪˈbɑ:k(ə)l/ *n.* катастро́фа.

debar /dɪˈbɑ:(r)/ *v.t.* (**debarred, debarring**) препя́тствовать, вос- + *d.*; не допус|ка́ть, -ти́ть + *g.*; **~ s.o. from office** лиш|а́ть, -и́ть кого́-н. возмо́жности заня́ть каку́ю-н. до́лжность; **~ s.o. from voting** лиш|а́ть, -и́ть кого́-н. пра́ва го́лоса.

debark /di:ˈbɑ:k/, /dɪ-/ *v.t. & i.* = **disembark**

debarkation /ˌdi:bɑ:ˈkeɪʃ(ə)n/ *n.* = **disembarkation**

debase /dɪˈbeɪs/ *v.t.* **1** (*lower morally*) ун|ижа́ть, -и́зить. **2** (*depreciate, e.g. coinage*) сн|ижа́ть, -и́зить це́нность + *g.*

debasement /dɪˈbeɪsmənt/ *n.* униже́ние; сниже́ние це́нности (*чего*).

debatable /dɪˈbeɪtəb(ə)l/ *adj.* спо́рный.

debat|e /dɪˈbeɪt/ *n.* диску́ссия; (*after s.o.'s speech*) пре́ния (*nt. pl.*); (*in parliament*) деба́т|ы (*pl., g.* -ов); **the question under ~e** обсужда́емый вопро́с; **beyond ~e** бесспо́рный.

● *v.t. & i.* **1** (*discuss*) обсу|жда́ть, -ди́ть; дебати́ровать (*impf.*); дискути́ровать (*impf., pf.*); спо́рить (*impf.*) о + *p.*; **~ing society** дискуссио́нный клуб. **2** (*ponder*) обду́м|ывать, -ать; взве́|шивать, -сить; **I was ~ing whether to go out or not** я размышля́л, выходи́ть мне и́ли нет.

debater /dɪˈbeɪtə(r)/ *n.* уча́стник деба́тов; спо́рщик; **he's a good ~** он уме́ет спо́рить.

debauch /dɪˈbɔ:tʃ/ *v.t.* **1** (*pervert morally*) развра|ща́ть, -ти́ть. **2** (*seduce*) совра|ща́ть, -ти́ть; оболь|ща́ть, -сти́ть.

debauchee /ˌdɪbɔ:ˈtʃi:/, /ˌdeb-/ *n.* развра́тник.

debauchery /dɪˈbɔ:tʃərɪ/ *n.* развра́т, распу́щенность.

debenture /dɪˈbentʃə(r)/ *n.* долгово́е обяза́тельство; облига́ция акционе́рного о́бщества.

debilitate /dɪˈbɪlɪˌteɪt/ *v.t.* осл|абля́ть, -а́бить; рассл|абля́ть, -а́бить.

debility /dɪˈbɪlɪtɪ/ *n.* сла́бость, бесси́лие.

debit /ˈdebɪt/ *n.* де́бет; **~ side of an account** де́бетовая сторона́ счёта.

● *v.t.* (**debited, debiting**) дебетова́ть (*impf., pf.*); вн|оси́ть, -ести́ в де́бет.

debonair /ˌdebəˈneə(r)/ *adj.* обходи́тельный, учти́вый.

debouch /dɪˈbaʊtʃ/, /-ˈbu:ʃ/ *v.i.* **1** (*of stream etc.*) выходи́ть, вы́йти на откры́тую ме́стность; впа|да́ть, -сть (*or* вл|ива́ться, -и́ться) (*в море и т.п.*). **2** (*mil.*) дебуши́ровать (*impf., pf.*).

debrief /di:ˈbri:f/ *v.t.* расспр|а́шивать, -оси́ть; **~ s.o.** заслу́ш|ивать, -ать чей-н. отчёт.

debriefing /di:ˈbri:fɪŋ/ *n.* расспро́с, опро́с.

debris /ˈdebri:/, /ˈdeɪ-/ *n.* оско́лки (*m. pl.*); обло́мки (*m. pl.*).

debt /det/ *n.* **1** (*of money*) долг; **get/run into ~** входи́ть, войти́ в долги́; влез|а́ть, -ть в долги́ (*coll.*); **bad ~** безнадёжный долг; **~ of honour** (*Br.*), **honor** (*US*) долг че́сти; **National D~** госуда́рственный долг; **funded ~** консолиди́рованный долг; **floating ~** теку́щая задо́лженность.
2 (*obligation*): **I owe him a ~ of gratitude** я пе́ред ним в долгу́; **I am greatly in your ~** я вам чрезвыча́йно обя́зан.

debtor /ˈdetə(r)/ *n.* должни́к; **~'s prison** долгова́я тюрьма́.

debunk /di:ˈbʌŋk/ *v.t.* (*coll.*) разве́нч|ивать, -а́ть.

debunker /di:ˈbʌŋkə(r)/ *n.* (*coll.*) разоблачи́тель (*m.*).

debut /ˈdeɪbju:/, /-bu:/ *n.* дебю́т.

debutante /ˈdebju:ˌtɑ:nt/, /ˈdeɪb-/ *n.* (*making first appearance in fashionable society*) де́вушка, впервы́е выезжа́ющая в свет; (*theatr., sport*) дебюта́нтка.

decade /ˈdekeɪd/, *disp.* /dɪˈkeɪd/ *n.* (*10 years*) десятиле́тие; (*of one's age*) деся́ток.

decadence /ˈdekəd(ə)ns/ *n.* упа́док, декаде́нтство.

decadent /ˈdekəd(ə)nt/ *n.* декаде́нт.

● *adj.* упа́дочный, декаде́нтский.

decaffeinated /di:ˈkæfɪˌneɪtɪd/ *adj.* без кофеина; **~ coffee** бескофеи́новый ко́фе.

decagon /ˈdekəgən/ *n.* десятиуго́льник.

decamp /dɪˈkæmp/ *v.i.* (*leave camp*) сн|има́ться, -я́ться с ла́геря; (*abscond*) сбе|га́ть, -жа́ть; уд|ира́ть, -ра́ть (*coll.*).

decant /dɪˈkænt/ *v.t.* (*pour wine*) сце́|живать, -ди́ть; перел|ива́ть, -и́ть (из буты́лки в графи́н).

decanter /dɪˈkæntə(r)/ *n.* (*vessel*) графи́н.

decapitate /dɪˈkæpɪˌteɪt/ *v.t.* обезгла́в|ливать, -ить.

decapitation /dɪˌkæpɪˈteɪʃ(ə)n/ *n.* обезгла́вливание.

decarbonize /di:ˈkɑ:bəˌnaɪz/ *v.t.* **1** (*chem.*) обезуглеро́|живать, -дить. **2** (*of car engine*) оч|ища́ть, -и́стить от нага́ра.

decathlete /dɪˈkæθli:t/ *n.* десятибо́рец.

decathlon /dɪˈkæθlən/ *n.* десятибо́рье.

decay /dɪˈkeɪ/ *n.* **1** (*physical*) гние́ние, разложе́ние; **tooth ~** разруше́ние зубо́в; **the house is in ~** дом разруша́ется. **2** (*decayed part*) гниль. **3** (*moral*) упа́док, разложе́ние; **civilizations fall into ~** цивилиза́ции прихо́дят в упа́док.

● *v.i.* гнить, с-; разл|ага́ться, -ожи́ться; **~ing vegetables** гнию́щие о́вощи.

decease /dɪˈsiːs/ *n.* кончи́на.

deceased /dɪˈsiːst/ *adj.* поко́йный, сконча́вшийся, уме́рший; (*as n.*: **the ~**) поко́йник.

deceit /dɪˈsiːt/ *n.* обма́н, ложь.

deceitful /dɪˈsiːtfʊl/ *adj.* обма́нчивый, лжи́вый.

deceitfulness /dɪˈsiːtfʊlnɪs/ *n.* обма́нчивость, лжи́вость.

deceive /dɪˈsiːv/ *v.t. & i.* обма́н|ывать, -у́ть; **~ o.s.** обма́н|ываться, -у́ться; **I have been ~d in him** я в нём обману́лся; **we were ~d into believing that** ... нас обма́ном заста́вили пове́рить, что....

decelerate /diːˈseləˌreɪt/ *v.i.* зам|едля́ть, -е́длить ход.
● *v.t.* зам|едля́ть, -е́длить.

deceleration /diːˌseləˈreɪʃ(ə)n/ *n.* замедле́ние; торможе́ние.

December /dɪˈsembə(r)/ *n.* дека́брь (*m.*); (*attr.*) дека́брьский.

Decembrist /dɪˈsembrɪst/ *n.* декабри́ст.
● *adj.* декабри́стский.

decenc|y /ˈdiːsənsɪ/ *n.* (*seemliness*) прили́чие, благопристо́йность; **offence against ~y** наруше́ние прили́чий; **observe the ~ies** соблюда́ть (*impf.*) прили́чия.

decent /ˈdiːs(ə)nt/ *adj.* **1** (*not obscene*) прили́чный, присто́йный; благопристо́йный. **2** (*proper, adequate*) прили́чный, подходя́щий; **~ living conditions** прили́чные жили́щные усло́вия; **a ~ dinner** прили́чный у́жин. **3** (*Br. coll., kind, well-conducted*) поря́дочный; **he was very ~ to me** он вёл себя́ поря́дочно по отноше́нию ко мне.

decentralization /diːˌsentrəlaɪˈzeɪʃ(ə)n/ *n.* децентрализа́ция.

decentralize /diːˈsentrəˌlaɪz/ *v.t.* децентрализова́ть (*impf., pf.*).

deception /dɪˈsepʃ(ə)n/ *n.* обма́н; **practise a ~ on** обма́н|ывать, -у́ть.

deceptive /dɪˈseptɪv/ *adj.* обма́нчивый.

deceptiveness /dɪˈseptɪvnɪs/ *n.* обма́нчивость.

decibel /ˈdesɪˌbel/ *n.* децибе́л.

decide /dɪˈsaɪd/ *v.t.* реш|а́ть, -и́ть; прин|има́ть, -я́ть реше́ние о + *p.*; **~ a question** реш|а́ть, -и́ть вопро́с; **~ a dispute** разреш|а́ть, -и́ть спор; **that ~s me** тепе́рь мне всё я́сно; я бо́льше не сомнева́юсь; **what ~d you to give up your job?** почему́ вы реши́ли (*or* что вас заста́вило) бро́сить рабо́ту?
● *v.i.* реш|а́ться, -и́ться; прин|има́ть, -я́ть реше́ние; **~ between adversaries** рассуди́ть (*pf.*) проти́вников; **~ between alternatives** де́лать, с- вы́бор; **~ on going** реши́ть (*pf.*) пое́хать; **~ against going** реши́ть (*pf.*) не е́хать; **she ~d on the green hat** она́ вы́брала зелёную шля́пу; **they ~d on the youngest candidate** они́ останови́ли свой вы́бор на са́мом молодо́м кандида́те.

decided /dɪˈsaɪdɪd/ *adj.* (*clear-cut*) определённый; **a ~ difference** бесспо́рное разли́чие.

decidedly /dɪˈsaɪdɪdlɪ/ *adv.* реши́тельно, я́вно.

deciduous /dɪˈsɪdjʊəs/ *adj.* ли́ственный, листопа́дный.

decilitre /ˈdesɪˌliːtə(r)/ (*US* **deciliter**) *n.* децили́тр.

decimal /ˈdesɪm(ə)l/ *n.* десяти́чная дробь.
● *adj.* десяти́чный; **~ place: correct to six ~ places** с то́чностью до шесто́го зна́ка по́сле запято́й; **~ point** запята́я, отделя́ющая це́лое от дро́би; **~ coinage** десяти́чная моне́тная систе́ма.

decimalization /ˌdesɪməlaɪˈzeɪʃ(ə)n/ *n.* перехо́д/перево́д на десяти́чную систе́му.

decimalize /ˈdesɪməˌlaɪz/ *v.t.* перев|оди́ть, -ести́ на десяти́чную систе́му.

decimate /ˈdesɪˌmeɪt/ *v.t.* уничт|ожа́ть, -о́жить.

decimation /ˌdesɪˈmeɪʃ(ə)n/ *n.* уничтоже́ние.

decimetre /ˈdesɪˌmiːtə(r)/ (*US* **decimeter**) *n.* дециме́тр.

decipher /dɪˈsaɪfə(r)/ *v.t.* **1** (*lit.*) расшифро́в|ывать, -а́ть. **2** (*fig., make out*) раз|бира́ть, -обра́ть; разга́д|ывать, -а́ть.

decipherment /dɪˈsaɪfəmənt/ *n.* расшифро́вка, дешифро́вка.

decision /dɪˈsɪʒ(ə)n/ *n.* **1** (*deciding*) реше́ние; **make, take, come to a ~** прин|има́ть, -я́ть реше́ние. **2** (*decisiveness*) реши́мость, реши́тельность; **a man of ~** реши́тельный челове́к.

decisive /dɪˈsaɪsɪv/ *adj.* (*conclusive*) реша́ющий; **~ answer** оконча́тельный отве́т; (*resolute*) реши́тельный.

decisiveness /dɪˈsaɪsɪvnɪs/ *n.* реши́тельность.

deck[1] /dek/ *n.* **1** (*of ship*) па́луба; **~ house** ру́бка; **~ landing** (*aeron.*) поса́дка на па́лубу; **go up on ~** подн|има́ться, -я́ться на па́лубу; **below ~(s)** под па́лубой; **clear the ~s** (*for action*) (*nav.*) пригото́виться (*pf.*) к бо́ю; (*fig.*) пригото́виться (*pf.*) к де́йствиям; **all hands on ~!** свиста́ть все наве́рх!; авра́л! **2** (*of bus*): **top ~** ве́рхний эта́ж. **3** (*US, of cards*) коло́да.
● *cpds.* **~-chair** *n.* шезло́нг; **~-hand** *n.* матро́с.

deck[2] /dek/ *v.t.* (*adorn; also* **~ out**) укр|аша́ть, -а́сить.

declaim /dɪˈkleɪm/ *v.t. & i.* деклами́ровать (*impf.*).

declamation /ˌdekləˈmeɪʃ(ə)n/ *n.* (*act*) деклами́рование; (*art*) деклама́ция.

declamatory /dɪˈklæmətərɪ/ *n.* декламацио́нный; ора́торский.

declaration /ˌdekləˈreɪʃ(ə)n/ *n.* **1** (*proclamation*) заявле́ние, деклара́ция; **~ of independence** деклара́ция незави́симости; **~ of war** объявле́ние войны́. **2** (*affirmation*): **~ of love** призна́ние, объясне́ние в любви́. **3** (*statement*) деклара́ция; **customs ~** тамо́женная деклара́ция.

declarat|ive /ˌdeˈklærətɪv/, **-ory** /ˌdeˈklærətərɪ/ *adjs.* декларати́вный.

declare /dɪˈkleə(r)/ *v.t. & i.* **1** (*proclaim, make known*) объяв|ля́ть, -и́ть; **~ one's love** объясн|я́ться, -и́ться в любви́. **2** (*say solemnly*) заяв|ля́ть, -и́ть; провозгла|ша́ть, -си́ть; **he ~d that he was innocent** он заяви́л о свое́й невино́вности. **3** (*pronounce*) объяв|ля́ть, -и́ть; **I ~ the meeting open** объявля́ю собра́ние откры́тым; **~ o.s.** (*avow intentions*) де́лать, с- призна́ние; **~ for/against s.o.** выска́зываться, вы́сказаться за/про́тив кого́-н. **4** (*at customs*) деклари́ровать (*impf., pf.*); **have you anything to ~?** предъяви́те ве́щи, подлежа́щие обложе́нию по́шлиной.

declassification /ˌdiːklæsɪfɪˈkeɪʃ(ə)n/ *n.* рассекре́чивание (*докуме́нтов*).

declassify /diːˈklæsɪˌfaɪ/ *v.t.* рассекре́|чивать, -тить (*докуме́нты*).

declension /dɪˈklenʃ(ə)n/ *n.* (*gram.*) склоне́ние.

declinable /dɪˈklaɪnəb(ə)l/ *adj.* (*gram.*) склоня́емый.

declination /ˌdeklɪˈneɪʃ(ə)n/ *n.* (*astron.*) магни́тное склоне́ние; отклоне́ние.

decline /dɪˈklaɪn/ *n.* **1** (*fall*) паде́ние; **~ in prices** сниже́ние/паде́ние цен. **2** (*decay*) упа́док, зака́т; **~ of the Roman Empire** упа́док Ри́мской импе́рии. **3** (*in health*) ухудше́ние; **fall into a ~** слабе́ть, о-, ча́хнуть, за-.
● *v.t.* **1** (*refuse*) отклон|я́ть, -и́ть; **he ~d the invitation** он отклони́л приглаше́ние; **he ~d to answer** он отказа́лся отвеча́ть. **2** (*gram.*) склоня́ть, про-.
● *v.i.* **1** (*sink, draw to a close*) па́дать, упа́сть, при|ходи́ть, -йти́ в упа́док; **his strength is declining** его́ си́лы па́дают; **prices ~** це́ны па́дают; **in his declining years** в свои́ прекло́нные го́ды. **2** (*refuse*) отка́з|ываться, -а́ться.

declivity /dɪˈklɪvɪtɪ/ *n.* пока́тость, отко́с, склон.

declutch /diːˈklʌtʃ/ *v.i.* расцеп|ля́ть, -и́ть сцепле́ние/му́фту.

decoction /dɪˈkɒkʃ(ə)n/ *n.* (*boiling down*) вывари́вание; (*liquor*) отва́р, деко́кт.

decode /diːˈkəʊd/ *v.t.* расшифро́в|ывать, -а́ть; декоди́ровать (*impf., pf.*).

décolletage /ˌdeɪkɒlˈtɑːʒ/ *n.* декольте́ (*indecl.*), вы́рез.

décolleté /deɪˈkɒlteɪ/ *adj.* декольтиро́ванный.

decolonization /ˌdiːkɒlənaɪˈzeɪʃ(ə)n/ *n.* деколониза́ция.

decompose /ˌdiːkəmˈpəʊz/ *v.t.* разл|ага́ть, -ожи́ть.
● *v.i.* (*decay*) разл|ага́ться, -ожи́ться.

decomposition /ˌdiːkɒmpəˈzɪʃ(ə)n/ *n.* разложе́ние.

decompression /ˌdiːkəmˈpreʃ(ə)n/ *n.* сброс давле́ния, декомпре́ссия; (*comput.*) декомпре́ссия.

decompressor /ˌdiːkəmˈpresə(r)/ *n.* (*Br.*) декомпре́ссор.

decontaminate /ˌdiːkənˈtæmɪˌneɪt/ *v.t.* обеззара́|живать, -зить; (*remove harmful gases from*) дегази́ровать (*impf., pf.*); (*remove radioactivity from*) дезактиви́ровать (*impf., pf.*).

decontamination /ˌdiːkəntæmɪˈneɪʃ(ə)n/ *n.* обеззара́живание, дегаза́ция, дезактива́ция.

decontrol /ˌdiːkənˈtrəʊl/ *v.t.* (**decontrolled, decontrolling**) освобо|жда́ть, -ди́ть от контро́ля.

decor /ˈdeɪkɔː(r)/, /ˈde-/ *n.* (*of room*) убра́нство; (*of stage*) декора́ции (*f. pl.*).

decorate /ˈdekəˌreɪt/ *v.t.* **1** (*adorn*) укр|аша́ть, -а́сить; декори́ровать (*impf., pf.*); **~d style** (*archit.*) английская го́тика XIV ве́ка. **2** (*paint, furnish etc.*) отде́л|ывать, -ать. **3** (*confer medal upon*) награ|жда́ть, -ди́ть.

decoration /ˌdekəˈreɪʃ(ə)n/ *n.* **1** (*adornment*) украше́ние, убра́нство. **2** (*furnishing etc. of house*) обстано́вка, убра́нство. **3** (*order, medal*) награ́да.

decorative /ˈdekərətɪv/ *adj.* декорати́вный.

decorator /ˈdekəˌreɪtə(r)/ *n.* **1** (*Br., manual worker*) (*painter*) маля́р, (*paperer*) обо́йщик. **2**: **interior ~** худо́жник по интерье́ру.

decorous /ˈdekərəs/ *adj.* прили́чный, присто́йный.

decorum /dɪˈkɔːrəm/ *n.* вне́шнее прили́чие; этике́т, деко́рум.

decoy /ˈdiːkɔɪ/, /dɪˈkɔɪ/ *n.* прима́нка; **~ duck** подсадна́я у́тка.

● *v.t.* зама́н|ивать, -и́ть; прима́н|ивать, -и́ть.

decrease *n.* /ˈdiːkriːs/ уменьше́ние, убыва́ние; **crime is on the ~** престу́пность идёт на у́быль.

● *v.t.* /dɪˈkriːs/ ум|еньша́ть, -е́ньшить.

● *v.i.* /dɪˈkriːs/ ум|еньша́ться, -е́ньшиться; уб|ыва́ть, -ы́ть.

decreasingly /ˌdiːˈkriːsɪŋlɪ/ *adv.* всё ме́нее и ме́нее.

decree /dɪˈkriː/ *n.* **1** (*pol.*) ука́з, декре́т, постановле́ние. **2** (*leg.*) реше́ние.

● *v.t. & i.* изд|ава́ть, -а́ть декре́т; **fate ~d otherwise** судьба́ реши́ла ина́че.

decrepit /dɪˈkrepɪt/ *adj.* дря́хлый, ве́тхий.

decrepitude /dɪˈkrepɪtjuːd/ *n.* дря́хлость, ве́тхость.

decrescendo /ˌdiːkreˈʃendəʊ/, /ˌdeɪkrɪ-/ *n.* (*pl.* **~s**), *adj. & adv.* (*mus.*) диминуэ́ндо (*indecl.*).

decry /dɪˈkraɪ/ *v.t.* хули́ть (*impf.*).

dedicate /ˈdedɪˌkeɪt/ *v.t.* (*devote; also book etc.*) посвя|ща́ть, -ти́ть (*что-н. кому-н.*); (*assign, set apart*) предназн|ача́ть, -а́чить (*что-н. кому-н.*).

dedicated /ˈdedɪˌkeɪtɪd/ *adj.* пре́данный, беззаве́тный.

dedication /ˌdedɪˈkeɪʃ(ə)n/ *n.* (*devotion*) пре́данность, самоотве́рженность; (*inscription*) посвяще́ние.

dedicatory /ˈdedɪˌkeɪtərɪ/ *adj.* посвяти́тельный.

deduce /dɪˈdjuːs/ *v.t.* (*infer*) выводи́ть, вы́вести; заключ|а́ть, -и́ть.

deduct /dɪˈdʌkt/ *v.t.* вычита́ть, вы́честь; удерж|ивать, -а́ть.

deduction /dɪˈdʌkʃ(ə)n/ *n.* (*subtraction*) вы́чет, удержа́ние; (*amount deducted*) вы́чет; (*inference*) вы́вод, заключе́ние.

deductive /dɪˈdʌktɪv/ *adj.* дедукти́вный.

deed /diːd/ *n.* **1** (*something done*) де́йствие, посту́пок. **2** (*feat*) по́двиг. **3** (*actual fact*) де́ло, дея́ние; **in word and ~** сло́вом и де́лом. **4** (*leg.*) акт, докуме́нт.

● *cpd.* **~-poll** *n.* односторо́ннее обяза́тельство.

deem /diːm/ *v.t.* (*hold, consider*) полага́ть (*impf.*), счита́ть, счесть, призн|ава́ть, -а́ть.

deep /diːp/ *n.*: **the ~** (*poet.*) пучи́на.

● *adj.* **1** глубо́кий; **a ~ shelf** широ́кая по́лка; **in ~ water** (*trouble*) в беде́. **2** (*with measurement*): **a hole 6 feet ~** я́ма глубино́й в 6 фу́тов; **ankle ~ in mud** по щи́колотку в грязи́; **the soldiers were drawn up six ~** солда́ты стоя́ли в шесть шере́нг. **3** (*submerged, lit., fig.*): **a village ~ in the valley** дере́вня, располо́женная в глубине́ доли́ны; **~ in thought** заду́мавшийся; погружённый в разду́мья; **~ in a book** уше́дший с голово́й в кни́гу; **~ in debt** увя́зший в долга́х; **~ in love** без па́мяти влюблённый; по́ уши влюблённый (*coll.*). **4** (*extreme, profound*) глубо́кий; **~ sorrow** глубо́кая печа́ль; **in ~ mourning** в глубо́ком тра́уре; **take a ~ breath** де́лать, с- глубо́кий вдох; **heave a ~ sigh** глубоко́ взд|ыха́ть, -охну́ть; **that is too ~ for me** (*fig.*) э́то сли́шком умно́ для меня́. **5** (*of colour*) тёмный, насы́щенный; **~ red** тёмно-кра́сный. **6** (*low-pitched*) ни́зкий.

● *adv.* глубоко́; **dig ~** рыть (*impf.*) глубоко́; **~ into the night** до глубо́кой но́чи; **still waters run ~** в ти́хом о́муте че́рти во́дятся.

● *cpds.* **~-freeze** *n.* морози́льник; *v.t.* глубоко́ замор|а́живать, -о́зить; **~-frozen** *adj.* заморо́женный; **~-fry** *v.t.* зажа́ри|вать, -ть; жа́рить, за- во фритю́ре; **~-rooted** *adj.*: **~-rooted belief** глубоко́ укорени́вшееся мне́ние; **~-sea** *adj.*: **~-sea fishing** глубоково́дный лов; **~-seated** *adj.*: **~-seated emotion** затаённое чу́вство.

deepen /ˈdiːpən/ *v.t. & i.* **1** (*make, become deeper*) углуб|ля́ть(ся), -и́ть(ся). **2** (*intensify*) уси́ли|вать(ся), -ть(ся). **3** (*make, become lower in pitch*) пон|ижа́ть(ся), -и́зить(ся).

deeply /ˈdiːplɪ/ *adv.* глубо́ко; **he is ~ in debt** он влез в долги́; он по́ уши в долга́х (*coll.*); **he feels ~ about it** его́ э́то глубоко́ волну́ет.

deepness /ˈdiːpnɪs/ *n.* (*of water etc.*) глубина́; (*of colour*) со́чность, насы́щенность; (*of voice*) глубина́.

deer /dɪə(r)/ *n.* (*pl.* **~**) оле́нь (*m.*); **red ~** благоро́дный оле́нь; **roe ~** косу́ля; **fallow ~** лань.

● *cpds.* **~-forest, ~-park** *nn.* оле́ний запове́дник; **~-hound** *n.* шотла́ндская борза́я; **~skin** *n.* лоси́на, за́мша; (*attr.*) лоси́ный, за́мшевый; **~stalker** *n.* (*sportsman*) охо́тник на оле́ней; (*cap*) охо́тничий шлем.

de-escalate /diːˈeskəˌleɪt/ *v.t.* прекра|ща́ть, -ти́ть эскала́цию.

de-escalation /diːeskəˈleɪʃ(ə)n/ *n.* деэскала́ция.

deface /dɪˈfeɪs/ *v.t.* (*spoil appearance of*) иска|жа́ть, -зи́ть; уро́довать, из-; (*make illegible*) де́лать, с- неразбо́рчивым.

defacement /dɪˈfeɪsmənt/ *n.* искаже́ние; уро́дование.

de facto /diː ˈfæktəʊ/, /deɪ/ *adj.* факти́ческий.

● *adv.* де-фа́кто; на де́ле, факти́чески.

defamation /ˌdefəˈmeɪʃ(ə)n/, /ˌdiːf-/ *n.* клевета́, диффама́ция; **~ of character** диффама́ция ли́чности.

defamatory /dɪˈfæmətərɪ/ *adj.* клеветни́ческий.

defame /dɪˈfeɪm/ *v.t.* клевета́ть, на- (на + *a.*); поро́чить, о-.

default /dɪˈfɔːlt/, /-ˈfɒlt/ *n.* **1** (*want, absence*) отсу́тствие, недоста́ток; **in ~ of** за отсу́тствием + *g.* **2** (*neglect, failure to act or appear*): **he won the match by ~** он вы́играл матч из-за нея́вки проти́вника. **3** (*failure to pay*) неупла́та. **4** (*comput.*) значе́ние по умолча́нию; **~ font** шрифт по умолча́нию.

● *v.i.* **1** (*fail to perform a duty*) не выполня́ть, вы́полнить обяза́тельства. **2** (*fail to appear in court*) не яв|ля́ться, -и́ться в суд. **3** (*fail to meet debts*) прекра|ща́ть, -ти́ть платежи́; **~ on a debt** не выпла́чивать (*impf.*) долг.

defaulter /dɪˈfɔːltə(r)/, /-ˈfɒltə(r)/ *n.* **1** (*one who fails to perform duty*) не выполня́ющий свои́х обяза́тельств; (*one who fails to pay a debt*) неплате́льщик. **2** (*Br., mil.*) провини́вшийся солда́т.

defeat /dɪˈfiːt/ *n.* пораже́ние.

● *v.t.* нан|оси́ть, -ести́ пораже́ние + *d.*; разб|ива́ть, -и́ть; одерж|ивать, -а́ть побе́ду над + *i.*; **our hopes were ~ed** на́ши наде́жды ру́хнули; **they were ~ed** они́ потерпе́ли пораже́ние.

defeatism /dɪˈfiːtɪz(ə)m/ *n.* пораже́нчество.

defeatist /dɪˈfiːtɪst/ *n.* пораже́нец; (*fig.*) пессими́ст.

● *adj.* пораже́нческий, пессимисти́ческий.

defecate /ˈdefɪˌkeɪt/ *v.i.* испражн|я́ться, -и́ться.

defecation /ˌdefɪˈkeɪʃ(ə)n/ *n.* испражне́ние.

defect[1] /dɪˈfekt/, /ˈdiːfekt/ *n.*

недостáток, изъя́н; дефéкт; порóк (*also leg.*).

defect² /diːˈfekt/ *v.i.* перебе|гáть, -жáть; **he ~ed to the West** он перебежáл на Зáпад.

defection /dɪˈfekʃ(ə)n/ *n.* дезерти́рство; **there were several ~s from the party** нéсколько человéк вы́шло из пáртии.

defective /dɪˈfektɪv/ *adj.* несовершéнный; дефéктный; **~ memory** плохáя пáмять; **~ translation** нетóчный перевóд; **~ verb** (*gram.*) недостáточный глагóл.

defectiveness /dɪˈfektɪvnɪs/ *n.* неисправность, несовершéнство.

defector /dɪˈfektə(r)/ *n.* перебéжчи|к (*fem.* -ца).

defence /dɪˈfens/ (*US* **defense**) *n.* **1** оборóна, защи́та; **in ~ of** в защи́ту +*g.*; **he died in ~ of his country** он поги́б, защищáя рóдину; **~ industry** оборóнная промы́шленность. **2** (*means or system of defending*) укреплéния (*nt. pl.*); оборони́тельные сооружéния; **his ~s are down** он беззащи́тен. **3** (*leg.*) защи́та; **counsel for the ~** защи́тник (ответчика).

defenceless /dɪˈfenslɪs/ (*US* **defenseless**) *adj.* беззащи́тный.

defencelessness /dɪˈfenslɪsnɪs/ (*US* **defenselessness**) *n.* беззащи́тность.

defend /dɪˈfend/ *v.t.* **1** обороня́ть (*impf.*); защи|щáть, -ти́ть; **~ o.s.** защи|щáться, -ти́ться; **~ one's ideas** защи|щáть, -ти́ть (*or* отст|áивать, -оя́ть) свои́ идéи. **2** (*leg.*) защищáть (*impf.*); выступáть (*impf.*) защи́тником +*g.*

defendant /dɪˈfend(ə)nt/ *n.* ответчик, подсуди́мый, обвиня́емый.

defender /dɪˈfendə(r)/ *n.* (*person who defends something*; *also leg., sport*) защи́тник; (*defending champion*) чемпиóн, защищáющий своё звáние.

defense /dɪˈfens/ *etc.* (*US*) = **defence** *etc.*

defensibility /dɪˌfensɪˈbɪlɪtɪ/ *n.* **1** обороноспосóбность. **2** правомéрность.

defensible /dɪˈfensɪb(ə)l/ *adj.* **1** (*e.g. mil.*) хорошó обороня́емый. **2** (*e.g. of an argument*) правомéрный, опрáвданный.

defensive /dɪˈfensɪv/ *n.* оборóна; **on the ~** в оборóне.

● *adj.* оборони́тельный; **he has a ~ manner** он как бýдто опрáвдывается.

defer¹ /dɪˈfɜː(r)/ *v.t.* (**deferred, deferring**) (*postpone*) отсрóчи|вать, -ть; **~ one's departure** от|клáдывать, -ложи́ть отъéзд; **~red payment** отсрóчка платежá.

defer² /dɪˈfɜː(r)/ *v.i.* (**deferred, deferring**): **~ to** считáться (*impf.*) с+*i.*

deference /ˈdefərəns/ *n.* уважéние, почти́тельность; **show ~ to s.o.** относи́ться (*impf.*) почти́тельно к комý-н.; **with all (due) ~ to** при всём уважéнии к+*d.*; **he acted thus in (or out of) ~ to** ... он дéйствовал так из уважéния к....

deferential /ˌdefəˈrenʃ(ə)l/ *adj.* почти́тельный.

deferment /dɪˈfɜːmənt/ *n.* отклáдывание, отсрóчка.

defiance /dɪˈfaɪəns/ *n.* вы́зов; **in ~ of orders** вопреки́ распоряжéниям.

defiant /dɪˈfaɪənt/ *adj.* вызывáющий.

deficiency /dɪˈfɪʃənsɪ/ *n.* **1** (*lack*) нехвáтка, отсýтствие; **~ disease** авитаминóз. **2** (*pl., shortcomings*) недостáтки (*m. pl.*).

deficient /dɪˈfɪʃ(ə)nt/ *adj.* недостáточный, непóлный; **~ in courage** недостáточно смéлый; **mentally ~** слабоýмный.

deficit /ˈdefɪsɪt/ *n.* дефици́т, недочёт; **meet a ~** покр|ывáть, -ы́ть дефици́т.

defile /dɪˈfaɪl/ *v.t.* осквер|ня́ть, -ни́ть.

defilement /dɪˈfaɪlmənt/ *n.* осквернéние.

definable /dɪˈfaɪnəb(ə)l/ *adj.* определи́мый.

define /dɪˈfaɪn/ *v.t.* **1** (*state meaning of*) определ|я́ть, -и́ть; толковáть (*impf.*); да|вáть, -ть определéние +*d.* **2** (*state clearly*): **I ~d his duties** я определи́л круг егó обя́занностей; **he ~d his position** он определи́л своё отношéние. **3** (*delimit*): **his powers are ~d by law** егó полномóчия определя́ются закóном; **the frontier is not clearly ~d** нет определённой/чёткой грани́цы. **4** (*show clearly*): **a well ~d image** чётко очéрченный óбраз; **the tree was ~d against the sky** дéрево вырисóвывалось на фóне нéба.

definite /ˈdefɪnɪt/ *adj.* **1** (*specific*) определённый; **~ article** (*gram.*) определённый арти́кль. **2** (*clear, exact*) тóчный, чёткий.

definitely /ˈdefɪnɪtlɪ/ *adv.* определённо, тóчно; **he is ~ coming** он непремéнно, тóчно придёт.

definition /ˌdefɪˈnɪʃ(ə)n/ *n.* (*clearness of outline*) я́сность, чёткость; (*statement of meaning*) определéние.

definitive /dɪˈfɪnɪtɪv/ *adj.* окончáтельный.

deflate /dɪˈfleɪt/ *v.t.* **1** выкáчивать, вы́качать вóздух/газ из+*g.*; **~ a balloon/tyre** выпускáть, вы́пустить вóздух из шáра/ши́ны. **2** (*fig.*): **~ a rumour** (*Br.*), **rumor** (*US*) опроверг|áть, **~нуть** слух; **~ s.o.'s conceit** сбить (*pf.*) с когó-н. спесь. **3** (*currency*) пров|оди́ть, -ести́ дефля́цию+*g.*

deflation /dɪˈfleɪʃ(ə)n/ *n.* (*fin.*) дефля́ция.

deflationary /dɪˈfleɪʃ(ə)nərɪ/ *adj.* (*fin.*) дефляциóнный.

deflect /dɪˈflekt/ *v.t. & i.* отклон|я́ть(ся), -и́ть(ся).

deflection /dɪˈflekʃ(ə)n/ *n.* отклонéние.

deflower /diːˈflaʊə(r)/ *v.t.* лиш|áть, -и́ть дéвственности.

defogger /diːˈfɒgə(r)/ *US* = **demister**

defoliant /diːˈfəʊlɪənt/ *n.* дефолиáнт.

defoliate /diːˈfəʊlɪˌeɪt/ *v.t.* лиш|áть, -и́ть листвы́.

defoliation /diːˌfəʊlɪˈeɪʃ(ə)n/ *n.* лишéние листвы́.

deforest /diːˈfɒrɪst/ *v.t.* обезлéси|вать, -ть.

deforestation /diːˌfɒrɪˈsteɪʃ(ə)n/ *n.* обезлéсение.

deform /dɪˈfɔːm/ *v.t.* урóдовать, из-; иска|жáть, -зи́ть; деформи́ровать (*impf, pf.*); **he has a ~ed foot** у негó деформи́рована стопá.

deformation /ˌdiːfɔːˈmeɪʃ(ə)n/ *n.* урóдование, искажéние, деформáция.

deformity /dɪˈfɔːmɪtɪ/ *n.* урóдливость, урóдство.

defraud /dɪˈfrɔːd/ *v.t.* обмáн|ывать, -ýть; обмáном лиш|áть, -и́ть (*когó чегó*).

defray /dɪˈfreɪ/ *v.t.* оплá|чивать, -ти́ть; **~ expenses** возме|щáть, -сти́ть расхóды.

defray|al /dɪˈfreɪəl/, **-ment** /dɪˈfreɪmənt/ *nn.* оплáта; возмещéние расхóдов.

defreeze /diːˈfriːz/ *v.t.* размор|áживать, -óзить.

defrost /diːˈfrɒst/ *v.t.* (*food, refrigerator*) размор|áживать, -óзить; **~ the windscreen** (*US*) оч|ищáть, -и́стить ото льдá ветровóе стеклó.

defroster /diːˈfrɒstə(r)/ *n.* (*US, in car*) антиобледени́тель (*m.*); (*in refrigerator*) дефрóстер.

deft /deft/ *adj.* лóвкий, искýсный.

deftness /ˈdeftnɪs/ *n.* лóвкость, искýсность.

defunct /dɪˈfʌŋkt/ *adj.* несуществýющий, исчéзнувший; (*ineffective*) бесполéзный; **a ~ newspaper** газéта, прекрати́вшая существовáние.

defuse /diːˈfjuːz/ *v.t.* сн|имáть, -ять взрывáтель +*g.*; (*fig.*) разря|жáть, -ди́ть.

defy /dɪˈfaɪ/ *v.t.* **1** (*challenge*) вызывáть, вы́звать; бр|осáть, -óсить вы́зов +*d.*; **I ~ you to prove it** попрóбуйте, докажи́те э́то!; ручáюсь, что вы э́того не докáжете. **2** (*disobey*) пренебр|егáть, -éчь +*i.*; **~ the law** игнори́ровать (*impf., pf.*) закóн. **3** (*fig.*): **the problem defies solution** проблéму невозмóжно реши́ть.

degauss /diːˈgaʊs/ *v.t.* размагни́|чивать, -тить.

degeneracy /dɪˈdʒenərəsɪ/ *n.* дегенерати́вность, вырождéние.

degenerate *n.* /dɪˈdʒenərət/ дегенерáт, вы́родок.

● *adj.* /dɪˈdʒenərət/ вы́родившийся, дегенерати́вный.

● *v.i.* /dɪˈdʒenəˌreɪt/ вырождáться, вы́родиться; дегенери́ровать (*impf., pf.*).

degeneration /dɪˌdʒenəˈreɪʃ(ə)n/ *n.* вырождéние, дегенерáция.

degradation /ˌdegrəˈdeɪʃ(ə)n/ *n.* **1** (*in rank*) понижéние. **2** (*moral*) упáдок, деградáция.

degrade /dɪˈgreɪd/ *v.t.* **1** (*reduce in rank*)

пон|ижáть, -и́зить. **2** (*lower morally*) прин|ижáть, -и́зить; ун|ижáть, -и́зить.

● *v.i.* деградúровать (*impf., pf.*).

degrading /dɪˈgreɪdɪŋ/ *adj.* унизи́тельный.

degree /dɪˈgriː/ *n.* **1** (*unit of measurement*) грáдус; **30 ~s below zero** 30 грáдусов ни́же нуля́; **15 ~s centigrade** 15 грáдусов по Цéльсию. **2** (*step, stage*) стéпень; у́ровень (*m.*); **their work shows varying ~s of skill** их рабóта покáзывает разли́чную стéпень мастерствá; **by ~s** постепéнно; **in the highest ~** в наивы́сшей стéпени; **to the last ~** до послéдней стéпени; **to a ~** до извéстной стéпени; **not in the slightest ~** нискóлько, ни в какóй стéпени; **in some ~** в нéкоторой стéпени; **to what ~ is he interested?** в какóй стéпени э́то егó интересу́ет?; **third ~** допрóс с применéнием пы́ток; **prohibited ~s** стéпени родствá, при котóрых запрещáется брак; **murder in the first ~** тя́жкое уби́йство пéрвой стéпени. **3** (*social position*) положéние; **of high ~** высокопостáвленный. **4** (*acad.*) диплóм; (*higher ~*) стéпень; **take one's ~** получ|áть, -и́ть стéпень. **5** (*gram.*) стéпень; **~s of comparison** стéпени сравнéния.

dehumanization /diːˌhjuːmənaɪˈzeɪʃ(ə)n/ *n.* дегуманизáция.

dehumanize /diːˈhjuːməˌnaɪz/ *v.t.* дегуманизи́ровать (*impf., pf.*).

dehumidify /ˌdiːhjuːˈmɪdɪˌfaɪ/ *v.t.* осуш|áть, -и́ть.

dehydrate /diːˈhaɪdreɪt/, /ˌdiːhaɪˈdreɪt/ *v.t.* обезвó|живать, -дить; **~d eggs** яи́чный порошóк.

dehydration /ˌdiːhaɪˈdreɪʃ(ə)n/ *n.* обезвóживание, дегидратáция.

de-ice /diːˈaɪs/ *v.t.* устран|я́ть, -и́ть обледенéние +*g.*

de-icer /diːˈaɪsə(r)/ *n.* антиобледени́тель (*m.*).

deification /ˌdiːɪfɪˈkeɪʃ(ə)n/, /ˌdeɪɪfɪˈkeɪʃ(ə)n/ *n.* обожествлéние, обоготворéние.

deify /ˈdiːɪˌfaɪ/, /ˈdeɪɪ-/ *v.t.* обожеств|ля́ть, -и́ть; боготвори́ть, о-.

deign /deɪn/ *v.t.* сни|сходи́ть, -зойти́; соизвол|я́ть, -и́ть; **he did not ~ to answer us** он не соизвóлил отвéтить нам.

deism /ˈdiːɪz(ə)m/, /ˈdeɪ-/ *n.* деи́зм.

deist /ˈdiːɪst/, /ˈdeɪɪst/ *n.* деи́ст.

deity /ˈdiːɪtɪ/, /ˈdeɪɪ-/ *n.* (*divine nature*) божéственность; (*god*) божествó.

déjà vu /ˌdeɪʒɑː ˈvuː/ *n.* ощущéние, что нéчто ужé когдá-то случи́лось.

dejected /dɪˈdʒektɪd/ *adj.* удручённый, подáвленный.

dejection /dɪˈdʒekʃ(ə)n/ *n.* уны́ние, подáвленность.

de jure /diː ˈdʒʊərɪ/, /deɪ ˈjʊəreɪ/ *adj.* юриди́ческий.

● *adv.* де-ю́ре; юриди́чески.

delay /dɪˈleɪ/ *n.* задéржка, отсрóчка, промедлéние; **without ~** немéдленно, без промедлéния; **after several ~s** пóсле нéскольких отсрóчек.

● *v.t.* от|клáдывать, -ложи́ть; задéрж|ивать, -áть; мéдлить (*impf.*); **I was ~ed by traffic** я задержáлся из-за прóбок; **~ed action mine** ми́на замéдленного дéйствия.

● *v.i.* задéрж|иваться, -áться.

delectable /dɪˈlektəb(ə)l/ *adj.* услади́тельный, прелéстный.

delectation /ˌdiːlekˈteɪʃ(ə)n/ *n.* наслаждéние, удовóльствие.

delegate /ˈdelɪgət/: *v.* /ˈdelɪˌgeɪt/ *n.* делегáт, представи́тель (*m.*).

● *v.t.*: **~ s.o.** делеги́ровать (*impf., pf.*) когó-н.; пос|ылáть, -лáть когó-н. делегáтом; обл|екáть, -éчь когó-н. влáстью; **~ authority** перед|авáть, -áть полномóчие (*кому*): **~ a task** поруч|áть, -и́ть рабóту (*кому*).

delegation /ˌdelɪˈgeɪʃ(ə)n/ *n.* **1** (*of task*) поручéние; (*of authority*) передáча. **2** (*body of delegates*) делегáция, депутáция.

delete /dɪˈliːt/ *v.t.* вычёркивать, вы́черкнуть; (*comput.*) ст|ирáть, -ерéть.

deleterious /ˌdelɪˈtɪərɪəs/ *adj.* врéдный.

deletion /dɪˈliːʃ(ə)n/ *n.* вычёркивание.

Delhi /ˈdelɪ/ *n.* Дéли (*m. indecl.*).

deliberate[1] /dɪˈlɪbərət/ *adj.* (*intentional*) преднамéренный, умы́шленный; (*slow, prudent*) осмотри́тельный, основáтельный.

deliberate[2] /dɪˈlɪbəˌreɪt/ *v.i.* совещáться (*impf.*); **~ on/upon/over/about a matter** обсу|ждáть, -ди́ть вопрóс.

deliberation /ˌdɪlɪbəˈreɪʃ(ə)n/ *n.* (*pondering*) обду́мывание; (*pl.*) диску́ссия; (*slowness*) медли́тельность, неторопли́вость.

deliberative /dɪˈlɪbərətɪv/ *adj.* совещáтельный.

delicacy /ˈdelɪkəsɪ/ *n.* (*exquisiteness, subtlety*) утончённость, тóнкость; (*proneness to injury*) хру́пкость; (*critical nature*) щекотли́вость, деликáтность; (*sensitivity*) чувстви́тельность; (*tact*) деликáтность, щепети́льность; (*choice food*) деликатéс, лáкомство.

delicate /ˈdelɪkət/ *adj.* **1** (*fine, exquisite*) изя́щный, тóнкий; **~ complexion** нéжная кóжа; **~ workmanship** тóнкое мастерствó. **2** (*subtle, dainty*) тóнкий, утончённый; **a ~ shade of pink** блéдно-рóзовый оттéнок; **~ flavour** (*Br.*), **flavor** (*US*) тóнкий аромáт. **3** (*easily injured*) хру́пкий, слáбый; **~ health** слáбое здорóвье; **a ~ person** хру́пкий человéк; **a ~ child** болéзненный ребёнок. **4** (*critical, ticklish*) щекотли́вый, затрудни́тельный; **a ~ operation** тóнкая/слóжная операция. **5** (*sensitive*) тóнкий, óстрый; **a ~ sense of smell** тóнкое обоня́ние; **~ instruments** чувстви́тельные прибóры; **the pianist has a ~ touch** у пиани́ста мя́гкое тушé. **6** (*tactful, considerate*) деликáтный, такти́чный; **~ behaviour** (*Br.*), **behavior** (*US*) такти́чное поведéние. **7** (*careful of propriety*) щепети́льный, осторóжный.

delicatessen /ˌdelɪkəˈtes(ə)n/ *n.* (*food*) деликатéсы (*m. pl.*); (*shop*) гастрономи́ческий магази́н, гастронóм.

delicious /dɪˈlɪʃəs/ *adj.* óчень вку́сный; (*delightful*) восхити́тельный.

delict /dɪˈlɪkt/, /ˈdiː-/ *n.* (*leg.*) правонарушéние.

delight /dɪˈlaɪt/ *n.* **1** (*pleasure*) удовóльствие, наслаждéние; **take ~ in something** на|ходи́ть, -йти́ удовóльствие в чём-н. **2** (*source of pleasure*): **music is her ~** му́зыка для неё — istóчник наслаждéния.

● *v.t.* дост|авля́ть, -áвить наслаждéние +*d.*; **I am ~ed to accept the invitation** я с рáдостью принимáю приглашéние.

● *v.i.* насла|ждáться, -ди́ться; **he ~s in reading** он нахóдит большóе удовóльствие в чтéнии.

delightful /dɪˈlaɪtfʊl/ *adj.* восхити́тельный, очаровáтельный.

delimit /dɪˈlɪmɪt/ *v.t.* (**delimited, delimiting**) определ|я́ть, -и́ть грани́цы +*g.*; размежёв|ывать, -áть.

delimitation /dɪˌlɪmɪˈteɪʃ(ə)n/ *n.* размежевáние; определéние.

delineate /dɪˈlɪnɪˌeɪt/ *v.t.* (*e.g. a frontier*) очéр|чивать, -ти́ть; (*e.g. character*) изобра|жáть, -зи́ть.

delineation /dɪˌlɪnɪˈeɪʃ(ə)n/ *n.* очéрчивание, изображéние.

delinquency /dɪˈlɪŋkwənsɪ/ *n.* престу́пность; **juvenile ~** престу́пность несовершеннолéтних.

delinquent /dɪˈlɪŋkwənt/ *adj.* правонаруши́тель (*fem.* -ница), престу́пни|к (*fem.* -ца); **juvenile ~** малолéтний престу́пник.

● *adj.* винóвный.

delirious /dɪˈlɪrɪəs/ *adj.* (*raving*) в бреду́ (*pred.*); (*wildly excited*) вне себя́ (*pred.*).

delirium /dɪˈlɪrɪəm/ *n.* бред; **~ tremens** бéлая горя́чка.

deliver /dɪˈlɪvə(r)/ *v.t.* **1** (*rescue, set free*) освобо|ждáть, -ди́ть; изб|авля́ть, -áвить; **God ~ us!** упаси́, избáви Бог!; Гóсподи, поми́луй!
2 (*of birth*): **she was ~ed (of a child)** онá разреши́лась от брéмени; **she delivered a child** (*gave birth*) онá роди́ла ребёнка; (*assisted at birth*) онá принялá ребёнка; **he ~ed her** (*assisted her in giving birth*) он при́нял рóды у неё; **the child was ~ed by forceps** родоразрешéние произвели́ при пóмощи щипцóв.
3: **~ o.s. of an opinion** вы́сказывать, вы́сказать своё мнéние.
4 (*give, present*): **~ judgment** выноси́ть, вы́нести решéние; **~ a speech** произн|оси́ть, -ести́ речь; **a well ~ed sermon** хорошó прочи́танная прóповедь.
5 (*hand over*) сда|вáть, -ть; перед|авáть, -áть; **~ up stolen goods** сда|вáть, -ть укрáденные товáры.
6 (*aim, launch*) нан|оси́ть, -ести́; **~ a blow** нан|оси́ть, -ести́ удáр; **~ battle**

давáть, дать бой.
7 (*send out, convey*) дост|авля́ть, -áвить; **the shop ~s daily** магази́н доставля́ет товáры нá дом ежеднéвно; **the postman ~s letters** почтальóн доставля́ет пи́сьма; **~ the goods** (*fig., coll.*) выполня́ть, вы́полнить обéщанное.

deliverance /dɪˈlɪvərəns/ *n.* избавлéние.

deliverer /dɪˈlɪvərə(r)/ *n.* (*conveyor*) разнóсчик, достáвщик; (*saviour, rescuer*) избави́тель (*m.*), спаси́тель (*m.*).

delivery /dɪˈlɪvərɪ/ *n.* **1** (*childbirth*) рóды (*pl., g.* -ов); **~ room** роди́льная палáта. **2** (*distribution of goods or letters*) достáвка; **charges payable on ~** оплáта при достáвке; **the letter came by the first ~** письмó пришлó с пéрвой пóчтой; **~ note** накладнáя; **~ man** достáвщик; **~ van** фургóн для достáвки товáров. **3** (*of speech etc.*) произнесéние (рéчи); ди́кция; **his ~ was poor** он говори́л óчень невня́тно.

dell /del/ *n.* леси́стая доли́на; лощи́на.

delouse /diːˈlaʊs/ *v.t.* дезинсекти́ровать (*impf., pf.*); подв|ергáть, -éргнуть санобрабóтке/дезинсéкции.

delphinium /delˈfɪnɪəm/ *n.* (*pl.* **~s**) дельфи́ниум.

delta /ˈdeltə/ *n.* дéльта.

deltoid /ˈdeltɔɪd/ *adj.* дельтови́дный, треугóльный.

delude /dɪˈluːd/, /-ˈljuːd/ *v.t.* вв|оди́ть, -ести́ в заблуждéние; **he ~d himself into believing that . . .** он увéрил себя́ в тóм, что. . .

deluge /ˈdeljuːdʒ/ *n.* **1** (*lit.*) потóп; **the D~** (*bibl.*) всеми́рный потóп. **2** (*fig.*) потóк, град, лави́на; **a ~ of protest** потóк протéстов.
● *v.t.* затоп|ля́ть, -и́ть; **he was ~d with questions** егó засы́пали вопрóсами.

delusion /dɪˈluːʒ(ə)n/, /-ˈljuːʒ(ə)n/ *n.* заблуждéние; **be under a ~** заблуждáться (*impf.*); **~s of grandeur** мáния вели́чия.

de luxe /də ˈlʌks/, /ˈlʊks/ *adj.* роскóшный; **a ~ cabin** каю́та-люкс.

delve /delv/ *v.i.*: **~ in archives** ры́ться (*impf.*) в архи́вах; **~ in(to) one's pockets** ры́ться (*impf.*) в кармáнах.

demagnetize /diːˈmægnɪˌtaɪz/ *v.t.* размагни́|чивать, -тить.

demagogic /ˌdeməˈgɒgɪk/ *adj.* демагоги́ческий.

demagogue /ˈdeməˌgɒg/ *n.* демагóг.

demagogy /ˈdeməˌgɒgɪ/ *n.* демагóгия.

demand /dɪˈmɑːnd/ *n.* **1** (*claim*) трéбование; **payable on ~** подлежáщий оплáте по предъявлéнии; **there are many ~s on my time** у меня́ мнóго дел; **there were ~s for the minister to resign** раздавáлись трéбования об отстáвке мини́стра. **2** (*desire to obtain*) потрéбность, спрóс; **there is no ~ for this article** на э́тот товáр нет спрóса; **he is in great ~ for parties** все старáются зазвáть егó к себé в гóсти.
● *v.t.* трéбовать, по- +*g.*; **piety ~s it of us** э́того трéбует от нас благочéстие.

demarcate /ˈdiːmɑːˌkeɪt/ *v.t.* разграни́чи|вать, -ть.

demarcation /ˌdiːmɑːˈkeɪʃ(ə)n/ *n.* разграничéние, демаркáция; **~ line** демаркациóнная ли́ния.

démarche /deɪˈmɑːʃ/ *n.* демáрш.

demean /dɪˈmiːn/ *v.t.* (*abase*) ун|ижáть, -и́зить; **~ o.s.** роня́ть, урони́ть своё достóинство.

demeanour /dɪˈmiːnə(r)/ (*US* **demeanor**) *n.* поведéние; манéра вести́ себя́.

demented /dɪˈmentɪd/ *adj.* сумасшéдший.

dementia /dɪˈmenʃə/ *n.* слабоýмие.

demerit /diːˈmerɪt/ *n.* недостáток; изъя́н.

demesne /dɪˈmiːn/, /-ˈmeɪn/ *n.* (*estate*) владéние, помéстье.

demigod /ˈdemɪˌgɒd/ *n.* полубóг.

demijohn /ˈdemɪˌdʒɒn/ *n.* большáя оплетённая буты́ль.

demilitarization /diːˌmɪlɪtəraɪˈzeɪʃ(ə)n/ *n.* демилитаризáция.

demilitarize /diːˈmɪlɪtəˌraɪz/ *v.t.* демилитаризи́ровать (*impf., pf.*).

demi-mondaine /ˈdemɪmɒnˌdeɪn/, /-mɔ̃ˌdem/ *n.* дáма полусвéта.

demi-monde /ˈdemɪˌmɒnd/, /-ˈmɔ̃d/ *n.* полусвéт.

demise /dɪˈmaɪz/ *n.* кончи́на.

demisemiquaver /ˌdemɪˈsemɪˌkweɪvə(r)/, /ˈdemɪ-/ *n.* (*Br.*) три́дцать вторáя (нóта).

demist /diːˈmɪst/ *v.t.* (*Br.*) предохран|я́ть, -и́ть от запотевáния; обогр|евáть, -éть (*стекло*).

demister /diːˈmɪstə(r)/ *n.* (*Br.*) деми́стер; обогревáтель (*m.*) стеклá.

demiurge /ˈdemɪˌɜːdʒ/ *n.* (*creator*) творéц, демиýрг.

demo /ˈdeməʊ/ *n.* (*pl.* **~s**) (*coll.*) = **demonstration**

demob /diːˈmɒb/ *v.t.* (**demobbed, demobbing**) (*Br. coll.*) = **demobilize**

demobilization /diːˌməʊbɪlaɪˈzeɪʃ(ə)n/ *n.* демобилизáция.

demobilize /diːˈməʊbɪˌlaɪz/ *v.t.* демобилизовáть (*impf., pf.*).

democracy /dɪˈmɒkrəsɪ/ *n.* демокрáтия; **Britain is a ~** Великобритáния — демократи́ческое госудáрство.

democrat /ˈdeməˌkræt/ *n.* демокрáт.

democratic /ˌdeməˈkrætɪk/ *adj.* (*state, system*) демократи́ческий; (*manner, person*) демократи́чный; **she is very ~** онá óчень демократи́чна.

democratize /dɪˈmɒkrəˌtaɪz/ *v.t.* демократизи́ровать (*impf., pf.*).

demographer /dɪˈmɒgrəfə(r)/ *n.* демóграф.

demographic /ˌdeməˈgræfɪk/ *adj.* демографи́ческий.

demography /dɪˈmɒgrəfɪ/ *n.* демогрáфия.

demolish /dɪˈmɒlɪʃ/ *v.t.* (*e.g. house*) сн|оси́ть, -ести́; разр|ушáть, -ýшить; (*e.g. theory*) опров|ергáть, -éргнуть; разб|ивáть, -и́ть.

demolition /ˌdeməˈlɪʃ(ə)n/ *n.* **1** (*lit.*) разрушéние, снос; **~ gang** бригáда подры́вников. **2** (*of argument etc.*) опровержéние.

demon /ˈdiːmən/ *n.* **1** (*devil*) дéмон, дья́вол, бес; **the child is a little ~** э́тот ребёнок — сýщий бесёнок; **the ~ drink** дья́вольское зéлье. **2** (*fierce or energetic person*): **he's a ~ for work** он дья́вольски работоспосóбен.

demoniac(al) /ˌdiːməˈnaɪək(ə)l/ *adj.* демони́ческий.

demonology /ˌdiːməˈnɒlədʒɪ/ *n.* демонолóгия.

demonstrable /ˈdemɒnstrəb(ə)l/, /dɪˈmɒnstrəb(ə)l/ *adj.* доказýемый.

demonstrate /ˈdemənˌstreɪt/ *v.t.* **1** (*prove*) докáз|ывать, -áть; **~ one's sympathies** проя́в|ля́ть, -и́ть свои́ симпáтии. **2** (*show in operation*) демонстри́ровать, про-.
● *v.i.* (*organize demonstration*) устр|áивать, -óить демонстрáцию; (*take part in demonstration*) учáствовать (*impf.*) в демонстрáции.

demonstration /ˌdemənˈstreɪʃ(ə)n/ *n.* (*proof*) доказáтельство; (*exhibition*): **~ of affection** проявлéние чýвства; **~ of a machine** демонстрáция маши́ны; (*public manifestation*) демонстрáция.

demonstrative /dɪˈmɒnstrətɪv/ *adj.* **1** (*of proof*) нагля́дный, убеди́тельный. **2** (*showing feelings*) экспанси́вный, несдéржанный. **3** (*gram.*) указáтельный.

demonstrativeness /dɪˈmɒnstrətɪvnɪs/ *n.* экспанси́вность, несдéржанность.

demonstrator /ˈdemənˌstreɪtə(r)/ *n.* **1** (*art exhibition etc.*) демонстрáтор; (*in lab*) лаборáнт. **2** (*pol.*) демонстрáнт.

demoralization /dɪˌmɒrəlaɪˈzeɪʃ(ə)n/ *n.* деморализáция; (*corruption*) разложéние.

demoralize /dɪˈmɒrəˌlaɪz/ *v.t.* деморализовáть (*impf., pf.*); (*corrupt*) разл|агáть, -ожи́ть.

demote /dɪˈməʊt/, /diː-/ *v.t.* пон|ижáть, -и́зить (в дóлжности).

demotic /dɪˈmɒtɪk/ *adj.* (*ling.*) демоти́ческий.

demotion /dɪˈməʊʃ(ə)n/ *n.* понижéние (в дóлжности).

demur /dɪˈmɜː(r)/ *n.* возражéние; **without ~** без возражéний.
● *v.i.* (**demurred, demurring**) возра|жáть, -зи́ть (**at, to:** прóтив + *g.*).

demure /dɪˈmjʊə(r)/ *adj.* (**demurer, demurest**) скрóмный.

demureness /dɪˈmjʊənɪs/ *n.* скрóмность.

demythologize /ˌdiːmɪˈθɒləˌdʒaɪz/ *v.t.* развéнчивать, -ять миф о + *p.*

den /den/ *n.* **1** (*animal's lair*) берлóга, лóговище, лóгово. **2** (*of thieves*) притóн; **~ of vice** вертéп. **3** (*private room*) берлóга, убéжище.

D

denationalization /diːˌnæʃənəlaɪˈzeɪʃ(ə)n/ *n.* денационализа́ция.

denationalize /diːˈnæʃənəˌlaɪz/ *v.t.* денационализи́ровать (*impf., pf.*).

denature /diːˈneɪtʃə(r)/ *v.t.* измен|я́ть, -и́ть есте́ственные сво́йства +*g.*; денатури́ровать (*impf., pf.*); **~d alcohol** денатура́т.

denial /dɪˈnaɪəl/ *n.* **1** (*denying*) отрица́ние, опроверже́ние; **a flat ~** категори́ческое опроверже́ние/отрица́ние. **2** (*refusal*) отка́з; **I'll take no ~** я не приму́ отка́за; **~ of justice** отка́з в правосу́дии. **3** (*disavowal*) отрече́ние (от + *g.*).

denier /ˈdenjə(r)/ *n.* (*unit of fineness*) денье́ (*indecl.*).

denigrate /ˈdenɪˌgreɪt/ *v.t.* (*defame*) черни́ть, о-; клевета́ть, о-; поро́чить, о-.

denigration /ˌdenɪˈgreɪʃ(ə)n/ *n.* клевета́, опоро́чение.

denigrator /ˈdenɪˌgreɪtə(r)/ *n.* клеветни́к.

denim /ˈdenɪm/ *n.* джи́нсовая ткань.

● *adj.* джи́нсовый.

denizen /ˈdenɪz(ə)n/ *n.* (*inhabitant*) жи́тель (*m.*), обита́тель (*m.*); **~s of the deep** обита́тели глуби́н.

Denmark /ˈdenmɑːk/ *n.* Да́ния.

denomination /dɪˌnɒmɪˈneɪʃ(ə)n/ *n.* **1** (*name, nomenclature*) наименова́ние. **2** (*relig.*) вероисповéдание, конфе́ссия. **3**: **money of small ~s** де́нежные зна́ки (*m. pl.*) ма́лого досто́инства.

denominational /dɪˌnɒmɪˈneɪʃənəl/ *adj.* (*relig.*) конфессиона́льный, вероисповéдный.

denominator /dɪˈnɒmɪˌneɪtə(r)/ *n.* (*math.*) знамена́тель (*m.*); **reduce to a common ~** прив|оди́ть, -ести́ к о́бщему знамена́телю.

denotation /ˌdiːnəˈteɪʃ(ə)n/ *n.* обозначе́ние.

denote /dɪˈnəʊt/ *v.t.* обозн|ача́ть, -а́чить.

dénouement /deɪˈnuːmɑ̃/ *n.* развя́зка.

denounce /dɪˈnaʊns/ *v.t.* **1** (*inveigh against*) осу|жда́ть, -ди́ть. **2** (*inform against*) дон|оси́ть, -ести́ на + *a.*

dense /dens/ *adj.* **1** (*of liquids, vapour, population*) пло́тный, густо́й. **2** (*undergrowth, bush, forest*) густо́й; (*cloth*) пло́тный. **3** (*coll., stupid*) тупо́й. **4** (*fig., prose text*) пло́тный.

denseness /ˈdensnɪs/ *n.* пло́тность; густота́; (*stupidity*) ту́пость, тупоу́мие.

density /ˈdensɪtɪ/ *n.* пло́тность; густота́; **~ of population** пло́тность населе́ния; населённость.

dent /dent/ *n.* (*mark*) вмя́тина, (*hollow*) вы́боина.

● *v.t.* ост|авля́ть, -а́вить вмя́тину в/на + *p.*; вда́в|ливать, -и́ть; **the car got ~ed in the collision** при столкнове́нии маши́на получи́ла вмя́тину.

● *v.i.* гну́ться, про-; **this metal ~s easily** э́тот мета́лл легко́ гнётся.

dental /ˈdent(ə)l/ *n.* (*phon.*) зубно́й звук.

● *adj.* (*of teeth*) зубно́й; **~ floss** ни́тка для чи́стки зубо́в; **~ plaque** зубно́й налёт; **~ surgeon** = **dentist**; (*of dentistry*) зубовраче́бный, стоматологи́ческий.

dentifrice /ˈdentɪfrɪs/ *n.* (*powder*) зубно́й порошо́к; (*paste*) зубна́я па́ста.

dentist /ˈdentɪst/ *n.* зубно́й врач, данти́ст, стомато́лог.

dentistry /ˈdentɪstrɪ/ *n.* стоматоло́гия; лече́ние зубо́в.

denture /ˈdentʃə(r)/ *n.* зубно́й проте́з.

denuclearize /diːˈnjuːklɪəˌraɪz/ *v.t.* превра|ща́ть, -ти́ть в безъя́дерную зо́ну.

denudation /ˌdiːnjuːˈdeɪʃ(ə)n/ *n.* оголе́ние, обнаже́ние.

denude /dɪˈnjuːd/ *v.t.* огол|я́ть, -и́ть; обнаж|а́ть, -и́ть.

denunciation /dɪˌnʌnsɪˈeɪʃ(ə)n/ *n.* (*criticism*) осужде́ние; (*informing*) доно́с.

denunciatory /dɪˈnʌnsɪətərɪ/, /-ˈnʌnʃɪətərɪ/ *adj.* осуди́тельный.

den|y /dɪˈnaɪ/ *v.t.* **1** (*contest truth of*) отрица́ть (*impf.*). **2** (*repudiate*) отр|ека́ться, -е́чься от + *g.* **3** (*refuse*) отка́з|ывать, -а́ть (*кому в чём*); **he was ~ied admittance** его́ не впусти́ли; **~y o.s. something** отка́з|ывать, -а́ть себе́ в чём-н.

deodorant /diːˈəʊdərənt/ *n.* дезодора́нт.

deodorize /diːˈəʊdəˌraɪz/ *v.t.* дезодори́ровать (*impf., pf.*).

depart /dɪˈpɑːt/ *v.t.*: **~ this life** уйти́ (*pf.*) из жи́зни *or* в ино́й мир.

● *v.i.* **1** (*go away*) отпр|авля́ться, -а́виться; отб|ыва́ть, -ы́ть. **2**: **~ from** (*custom, plan etc.*) отступ|а́ть, -и́ть от + *g.*

departed /dɪˈpɑːtɪd/ *n.*: **the (dear) ~** поко́йный, почи́вший.

● *adj.* (*bygone*) было́й, мину́вший.

department /dɪˈpɑːtmənt/ *n.* **1** отде́л; **~ store** универма́г. **2** (*of government*) департа́мент, ве́домство. **3** (*of univ.*) ка́федра.

departmental /ˌdiːpɑːtˈment(ə)l/ *adj.* ве́домственный; (*in university*) кафедра́льный.

departure /dɪˈpɑːtʃə(r)/ *n.* **1** (*going away*) отъе́зд; (*from job*) ухо́д; (*of train*) отправле́ние; **~ lounge** зал ожида́ния. **2** (*deviation, change*) отклоне́ние; **new ~** нововведе́ние.

depend /dɪˈpend/ *v.i.* **1** (*be conditional*) зави́сеть (*impf.*) (**on**: от + *g.*); **that ~s; it all ~s** как сказа́ть; посмо́трим; смотря́ (*где, когда, что и т.п.*); как полу́чится. **2** (*rely*) пол|ага́ться, -ожи́ться (**on**: на + *a.*); рассчи́тывать (*impf.*) (**on**: на + *a.*).

dependable /dɪˈpendəb(ə)l/ *adj.* надёжный.

dependant /dɪˈpend(ə)nt/ (*US* **dependent**) *n.* иждиве́н|ец (*fem.* -ка).

dependence /dɪˈpend(ə)ns/ *n.* зави́симость (от + *g.*); (*reliance*) дове́рие (к + *d.*).

dependency /dɪˈpendənsɪ/ *n.* (*pol.*) коло́ния.

dependent /dɪˈpend(ə)nt/ *adj.* **1** (*conditional*) зави́симый, зави́сящий. **2** (*financial*) зави́симый, находя́щийся на иждиве́нии. **3** (*gram.*) подчинённый.

● *n.* = **dependant**

depersonalize /diːˈpɜːsənəˌlaɪz/ *v.t.* обезли́чи|вать, -ть.

depict /dɪˈpɪkt/ *v.t.* изобра|жа́ть, -зи́ть.

depiction /dɪˈpɪkʃ(ə)n/ *n.* описа́ние, изображе́ние.

depilatory /dɪˈpɪlətərɪ/ *n.* сре́дство для удале́ния воло́с.

● *adj.* удаля́ющий во́лосы.

deplane /diːˈpleɪn/ *v.t. & i.* (*US*) выса́живать(ся), вы́садить(ся) из самолёта.

deplete /dɪˈpliːt/ *v.t.* истощ|а́ть, -и́ть; исче́рп|ывать, -а́ть; **~d strength** (*physical*) уга́сшие си́лы.

depletion /dɪˈpliːʃ(ə)n/ *n.* истоще́ние, исче́рпывание.

deplorable /dɪˈplɔːrəb(ə)l/ *adj.* плаче́вный, приско́рбный; **~ handwriting** ужа́сный/невозмо́жный по́черк.

deplore /dɪˈplɔː(r)/ *v.t.* сожале́ть (*impf.*) о + *p.*; счита́ть (*impf.*) предосуди́тельным/возмути́тельным.

deploy /dɪˈplɔɪ/ *v.t.* развёр|тывать, -ну́ть.

deployment /dɪˈplɔɪmənt/ *n.* развёртывание; размеще́ние.

deponent /dɪˈpəʊnənt/ *n.* (*leg.*) свиде́тель (*m.*), даю́щий показа́ния под прися́гой; (*gram.*) отложи́тельный (глаго́л).

● *adj.* (*gram*) отложи́тельный.

depopulate /diːˈpɒpjʊˌleɪt/ *v.t.* лиш|а́ть, -и́ть населе́ния.

depopulation /diːˌpɒpjʊˈleɪʃ(ə)n/ *n.* сокраще́ние населе́ния.

deport /dɪˈpɔːt/ *v.t.* **1**: **~ o.s.** вести́ (*det.*) себя́. **2** (*remove, banish*) депорти́ровать (*impf., pf.*); высыла́ть, вы́слать.

deportation /ˌdiːpɔːˈteɪʃ(ə)n/ *n.* депорта́ция, вы́сылка.

deportee /ˌdiːpɔːˈtiː/ *n.* депорти́рованный, высыла́емый, со́сланный.

deportment /dɪˈpɔːtmənt/ *n.* (*Br.*) оса́нка; (*US*) мане́ры (*f. pl.*).

depose /dɪˈpəʊz/ *v.t.* (*monarch etc.*) св|ерга́ть, -е́ргнуть (с престо́ла); низл|ага́ть, -ожи́ть.

● *v.i.* (*testify*) свиде́тельствовать (*impf.*).

deposit /dɪˈpɒzɪt/ *n.* **1** (*sum in bank*) вклад. **2** (*act of placing*) депози́т; **~ account** (*Br.*) депози́тный счёт. **3** (*advance payment*) зада́ток; (*layer*) отложе́ние. **4** (*of ore etc.*) за́лежь; (*of precious metals and stones*) ро́ссыпь.

● *v.t.* (**deposited, depositing**) класть, положи́ть; (*place in bank*) депони́ровать (*impf., pf.*).

depositary /dɪ'pɒzɪtərɪ/ *n.* храни́тель (*m.*), дове́ренное лицо́.

deposition /ˌdiːpə'zɪʃ(ə)n/, /ˌdep-/ *n.* (*dethronement*) сверже́ние, низверже́ние; (*evidence*) показа́ние под прися́гой.

depositor /dɪ'pɒzɪtə(r)/ *n.* (*fin.*) депози́тор, депоне́нт, вкла́дчик.

depository /dɪ'pɒzɪtərɪ/ *n.* **1** (*storehouse*) храни́лище. **2** = **depositary**

depot /'depəʊ/ *n.* (*place of storage*) склад; (*for trams, buses, taxis*) парк; (*for trucks*) автоба́за; (*for trains*) депо́; (*US, train or bus station*) ста́нция.

deprave /dɪ'preɪv/ *v.t.* развра|ща́ть, -ти́ть.

depravity /dɪ'prævɪtɪ/ *n.* развра́т, развращённость.

deprecate /'deprɪˌkeɪt/ *v.t.* осу|жда́ть, -ди́ть; выска́зываться, вы́сказаться про́тив + *g.*

deprecation /ˌdeprɪ'keɪʃ(ə)n/ *n.* осужде́ние (*чего*).

depreciate /dɪ'priːʃɪˌeɪt/, /-sɪˌeɪt/ *v.t.* обесце́ни|ва́ть, -ть; (*disparage*) умал|я́ть, -и́ть.
● *v.i.* обесце́ни|ваться, -ться.

depreciation /dɪˌpriːʃɪ'eɪʃ(ə)n/, /-sɪ'eɪʃ(ə)n/ *n.* обесце́нивание, амортиза́ция; (*disparagement*) умале́ние.

depredation /ˌdeprɪ'deɪʃ(ə)n/ *n.* грабёж.

depredator /'deprɪˌdeɪtə(r)/ *n.* граби́тель (*m.*).

depress /dɪ'pres/ *v.t.* **1** (*push down*) наж|има́ть, -а́ть на + *a.* **2** (*fig.*) угнета́ть (*impf.*); **~ed classes** угнетённые кла́ссы; **~ed area** райо́н, пострада́вший от экономи́ческой депре́ссии. **3** (*make sad*) удруч|а́ть, -и́ть; угнета́ть (*impf.*); подав|ля́ть, -и́ть.

depressant /dɪ'pres(ə)nt/ *n.* (*med.*) успокои́тельное сре́дство.

depressing /dɪ'presɪŋ/ *adj.* удруча́ющий; тру́дный.

depression /dɪ'preʃ(ə)n/ *n.* **1** (*pressing down*) давле́ние. **2** (*hollow, sunken place*) впа́дина, углубле́ние. **3** (*slump*) депре́ссия, упа́док. **4** (*low spirits*) депре́ссия, тоска́. **5** (*meteor.*) депре́ссия.

deprivation /ˌdeprɪ'veɪʃ(ə)n/, /ˌdiːpraɪ-/ *n.* (*being deprived*) лише́ние; (*loss*) утра́та.

deprive /dɪ'praɪv/ *v.t.* лиш|а́ть, -и́ть (*кого чего*); **~d** (*underprivileged*) обездо́ленный.

depth /depθ/ *n.* **1** (*deepness*) глубина́; **what is the ~ of the well?** какова́ глубина́ коло́дца?; **6 feet in ~** глубино́й в шесть фу́тов; **at a ~ of 6 feet** на глубине́ шести́ фу́тов; **be out of one's ~** не достава́ть (*impf.*) нога́ми до дна; (*fig.*): **I am out of my ~ in this job** э́та рабо́та мне не по плечу́; **I am out of my ~ in this subject** э́тот предме́т вы́ше моего́ понима́ния; **in ~** (*fig., thoroughly*) глубоко́. **2** (*profundity*) глубина́. **3** (*extremity*): **~ of despair** глубо́кое отча́яние; **~ of winter** глубо́кая зима́; **in the ~(s) of the country** в глуши́, в захолу́стьи.
● *cpd.* **~-charge** *n.* глуби́нная бо́мба.

deputation /ˌdepjʊ'teɪʃ(ə)n/ *n.* депута́ция.

depute /dɪ'pjuːt/ *v.t.* (*a task*) поруч|а́ть, -и́ть; (*a person*) делеги́ровать (*impf., pf.*).

deputize /'depjʊˌtaɪz/ *v.i.*: **~ for s.o.** заме|ща́ть (*impf.*) кого́-н.

deputy /'depjʊtɪ/ *n.* **1** (*substitute*) замести́тель (*m.*); **~ chairman** замести́тель (*m.*) председа́теля. **2** (*member of parliament*) депута́т.

derail /dɪ'reɪl/, /diː-/ *v.t.* св|оди́ть, -ести́ с ре́льсов; **the train was ~ed** по́езд сошёл с ре́льсов; **the partisans ~ed the train** партиза́ны пусти́ли по́езд под отко́с.

derailment /dɪ'reɪlmənt/, /diː-/ *n.* сход с ре́льсов.

derange /dɪ'reɪndʒ/ *v.t.* св|оди́ть, -ести́ с ума́; лиш|а́ть, -и́ть рассу́дка.

derangement /dɪ'reɪndʒmənt/ *n.* у́мственное расстро́йство.

derby /'dɜːbɪ/ *n.* (*US, hat*) котело́к.

deregulate /diː'regjʊleɪt/ *v.t.* отменя́ть, отмени́ть (госуда́рственное) регули́рование (*чего*).

deregulation /ˌdiːregjʊ'leɪʃ(ə)n/ *n.* отме́на (госуда́рственного) регули́рования.

derelict /'derəlɪkt/, /'derɪ-/ *adj.* (*house, land*) забро́шенный; (*garden*) запу́щенный, забро́шенный.

dereliction /ˌderɪ'lɪkʃ(ə)n/ *n.* забро́шенность, запу́щенность; **~ of duty** наруше́ние до́лга.

derestriction /ˌdiːrɪ'strɪkʃ(ə)n/ *n.* сня́тие ограниче́ния.

deride /dɪ'raɪd/ *v.t.* высме́ивать, вы́смеять; осме́|ивать, -я́ть.

de rigueur /də rɪ'gɜː(r)/ *adj.* тре́буемый этике́том; **to be ~** тре́боваться этике́том.

derision /dɪ'rɪʒ(ə)n/ *n.* осмея́ние, высме́ивание.

derisive /dɪ'raɪsɪv/ *adj.* (*scornful*) насме́шливый.

derisory /dɪ'raɪsərɪ/ *adj.* (*ludicrous*) смешно́й, ничто́жный.

derivation /ˌderɪ'veɪʃ(ə)n/ *n.* происхожде́ние; (*action*) дерива́ция.

derivative /də'rɪvətɪv/, /dɪ-/ *adj.* (*gram.*) произво́дный; (*fig.*) неоригина́льный.

derive /dɪ'raɪv/ *v.t.* **1** (*obtain*) извл|ека́ть, -е́чь; **~ pleasure from** получ|а́ть, -и́ть удово́льствие от + *g.* **2** (*trace*) выводи́ть, вы́вести; возв|оди́ть, -ести́; **he ~d his origin from Caesar** он вёл свой род от Це́заря. **3** (*originate*) происходи́ть (*impf.*); **words ~d from Latin** слова́ лати́нского происхожде́ния.
● *v.i.*: **~ from** происходи́ть (*impf.*) от + *g.*

dermatitis /ˌdɜːmə'taɪtɪs/ *n.* дермати́т.

dermatologist /ˌdɜːmə'tɒlədʒɪst/ *n.* дермато́лог.

dermatology /ˌdɜːmə'tɒlədʒɪ/ *n.* дерматоло́гия.

derogate /'derəˌgeɪt/ *v.i.*: **~ from** (*detract from*) умал|я́ть, -и́ть.

derogation /ˌderə'geɪʃ(ə)n/ *n.* (*impairment*) умале́ние (*чего*).

derogatory /dɪ'rɒgətərɪ/ *adj.* пренебрежи́тельный.

derrick /'derɪk/ *n.* **1** (*crane*) де́ррик(-кран). **2** (*over oil-well*) бурова́я вы́шка.

derring-do /ˌderɪŋ'duː/ *n.* хра́брость, удальство́.

dervish /'dɜːvɪʃ/ *n.* де́рвиш.

desalinate /diː'sælɪˌneɪt/ *v.t.* опресн|я́ть, -и́ть.

desalination /diːˌsælɪ'neɪʃ(ə)n/ *n.* опресне́ние (воды́).

descant /'deskænt/ *n.* (*mus.*) ди́скант.

descend /dɪ'send/ *v.t.* сходи́ть, сойти́ с + *g.*; спус|ка́ться, -ти́ться с + *g.*; **~ a hill** спус|ка́ться, -ти́ться с холма́; **he ~ed the stairs** он спусти́лся с ле́стницы.
● *v.i.* **1** (*go down*) спус|ка́ться, -ти́ться; сходи́ть, сойти́; **in ~ing order (of importance)** в нисходя́щем поря́дке; от бо́лее ва́жного к ме́нее ва́жному. **2** (*originate*) происходи́ть (*impf.*); **he is ~ed from a ducal family** он происхо́дит из ге́рцогской семьи́. **3** (*pass by inheritance*) перед|ава́ться, -а́ться (по насле́дству). **4** (*make an attack*) набр|а́сываться, -о́ситься; **the bandits ~ed upon the village** банди́ты нагря́нули в дере́вню. **5** (*lower o.s. morally*) опус|ка́ться, -ти́ться; пасть (*pf.*); **~ to cheating** не гнуша́ться (*impf.*) жу́льничества.

descendant /dɪ'send(ə)nt/ *n.* пото́мок.

descent /dɪ'sent/ *n.* **1** (*downward slope*) склон, скат. **2** (*act of descending*) спуск; (*of plane*) сниже́ние. **3** (*ancestry*) происхожде́ние. **4** (*transmission by inheritance*) переда́ча по насле́дству. **5** (*attack*) нападе́ние.

describe /dɪ'skraɪb/ *v.t.* опи́с|ывать, -а́ть (*also geom.*); характеризова́ть, о-; **~ s.o. as a scoundrel** наз|ыва́ть, -ва́ть кого́-н. подлецо́м; **he ~s himself as a doctor** он называ́ет себя́ врачо́м.

description /dɪ'skrɪpʃ(ə)n/ *n.* **1** (*act of describing*) описа́ние; **answer a ~** соотве́тствовать (*impf.*) описа́нию; **by ~** по описа́нию; **beyond ~** неопису́емый; **it beggars ~** э́то не поддаётся описа́нию. **2** (*kind*) род, тип, сорт.

descriptive /dɪ'skrɪptɪv/ *adj.* описа́тельный.

descry /dɪ'skraɪ/ *v.t.* зам|еча́ть, -е́тить; различ|а́ть, -и́ть.

desecrate /'desɪˌkreɪt/ *v.t.* оскверн|я́ть, -и́ть.

desecration /ˌdesɪ'kreɪʃ(ə)n/ *n.* оскверне́ние.

desegregate /diː'segrɪˌgeɪt/ *v.t. & i.* десегреги́ровать (*impf., pf.*).

desegregation /ˌdiːsegrɪ'geɪʃ(ə)n/ *n.* десегрега́ция.

desensitize /diː'sensɪˌtaɪz/ *v.t.*

сн|ижа́ть, -и́зить чувстви́тельность +*g*.

desert[1] /dɪˈzɜːt/ *n.* (*merit*) заслу́га; **get one's ~s** получ|а́ть, -и́ть по заслу́гам.

desert[2] /ˈdezət/ *n.* (*waste land*) пусты́ня.

● *adj.* пусты́нный; **~ island** необита́емый о́стров.

desert[3] /dɪˈzɜːt/ *v.t.* **1** (*go away from*) ост|авля́ть, -а́вить; пок|ида́ть, -и́нуть; **the streets were ~ed** у́лицы бы́ли пусты́нны. **2** (*abandon*) пок|ида́ть, -и́нуть; **his courage ~ed him** му́жество измени́ло ему́; **he ~ed his wife** он бро́сил свою́ жену́; **he ~ed his post** он поки́нул свой пост.

● *v.i.* дезерти́ровать (*impf., pf.*); **the regiment ~ed to the enemy** полк перешёл на сто́рону проти́вника.

deserter /dɪˈzɜːtə(r)/ *n.* дезерти́р.

desertification /dɪˌsɜːtɪfɪˈkeɪʃ(ə)n/ *n.* опусты́нивание.

desertion /dɪˈzɜːʃ(ə)n/ *n.* дезерти́рство.

deserve /dɪˈzɜːv/ *v.t. & i.* заслу́ж|ивать, -и́ть; **he ~s to be well treated** он заслу́живает хоро́шего отноше́ния.

deserved /dɪˈzɜːvd/ *adj.* заслу́женный.

deserving /dɪˈzɜːvɪŋ/ *adj.* похва́льный, досто́йный.

desiccate /ˈdesɪˌkeɪt/ *v.t.* высу́шивать, вы́сушить; **~d coconut** сушёный коко́с.

desiderata *pl. of* ⇒**desideratum**

desiderat|um /dɪˌzɪdəˈrɑːtəm/, /dɪˌsɪd-/ *n.* жела́емое; **~a** (*pl.*) пожела́ния (*nt. pl.*).

design /dɪˈzaɪn/ *n.* **1** (*drawing, plan*) план, прое́кт; **~ for a dress** моде́ль пла́тья; **~ for a garden** план са́да. **2** (*art of drawing*) рисова́ние; **school of ~** худо́жественное учи́лище. **3** (*tech.: layout, system*) констру́кция, прое́кт; **~ of a car** констру́кция автомоби́ля; **~ of a building** прое́кт зда́ния. **4** (*pattern*) узо́р, рису́нок; **a vase with a ~ of flowers on it** ва́за с цвето́чным рису́нком. **5** (*purpose*) у́мысел; **by ~** с у́мыслом; **he has ~s on my job** он име́ет ви́ды на мою́ рабо́ту. **6** (*industrial*) диза́йн. **7** (*version of product*) моде́ль; **our latest ~** на́ша после́дняя моде́ль.

● *v.t.* **1** (*make designs for*) сост|авля́ть, -а́вить план +*g*.; проекти́ровать, с-; (*e.g. a book*) оф|ормля́ть, -о́рмить; **~ a garden** плани́ровать, рас- сад. **2** (*intend*) зам|ышля́ть, -ы́слить; предназн|ача́ть, -а́чить.

● *v.i.*: **he ~s for a dressmaker** он де́лает моде́ли для портни́хи.

designate[1] /ˈdezɪgnət/ *adj.* назна́ченный.

designate[2] /ˈdezɪgˌneɪt/ *v.t.* (*specify (a time) etc.*) обозн|ача́ть, -а́чить; (*appoint to a post*) назн|ача́ть, -а́чить.

designation /ˌdezɪgˈneɪʃ(ə)n/ *n.* (*appointment*) назначе́ние; (*title*) зва́ние.

designedly /dɪˈzaɪnɪdlɪ/ *adv.* умы́шленно.

designer /dɪˈzaɪnə(r)/ *n.* (*of dresses, decorations*) моделье́р; (*tech.*) констру́ктор; (*industrial*) диза́йнер.

designing /dɪˈzaɪnɪŋ/ *adj.* (*scheming*): **he is a ~ person** он — интрига́н.

desirability /dɪˌzaɪərəˈbɪlɪtɪ/ *n.* жела́тельность.

desirable /dɪˈzaɪərəb(ə)l/ *adj.* жела́тельный; **it is ~** жела́тельно; (*attractive*) привлека́тельный.

desire /dɪˈzaɪə(r)/ *n.* **1** (*wish, longing*) жела́ние, стремле́ние. **2** (*lust*) вожделе́ние. **3** (*request*) про́сьба, пожела́ние. **4** (*thing desired*) жела́ние, предме́т жела́ния; **he got all his ~s** все его́ жела́ния сбыли́сь/испо́лнились.

● *v.t.* **1** (*wish*) жела́ть, по-; **it leaves much to he ~ed** э́то оставля́ет жела́ть лу́чшего *or* мно́гого. **2** (*request*) проси́ть, по-.

desirous /dɪˈzaɪərəs/ *adj.* жела́ющий; **I am ~ of seeing him** я жела́ю его́ ви́деть.

desist /dɪˈzɪst/ *v.i.* возде́рж|иваться, -а́ться (от +*g*.).

desk /desk/ *n.* пи́сьменный стол; (*with sloping top*) конто́рка; (*school ~*) па́рта; (*information centre*) спра́вочный стол; (*Br., cash ~*) ка́сса; (*mus.*) пюпи́тр; (*attr.*) насто́льный; **~ set** пи́сьменный прибо́р; **~ work** канцеля́рская рабо́та.

desktop /ˈdesktɒp/ *adj.* насто́льный; **~ publishing** насто́льная полигра́фия.

● *n.* (*also comput.*) рабо́чий стол.

desolate[1] /ˈdesələt/ *adj.* (*ruined, neglected*) забро́шенный, запу́щенный; (*wretched, lonely*) забро́шенный, поки́нутый.

desolate[2] /ˈdesəˌleɪt/ *v.t.* (*lay waste*) разор|я́ть, -и́ть; опустош|а́ть, -и́ть; (*make sad*) прив|оди́ть, -ести́ в отчая́ние.

desolation /ˌdesəˈleɪʃ(ə)n/ *n.* (*waste*) забро́шенность, опустоше́ние; (*sorrow*) забро́шенность, скорбь.

despair /dɪˈspeə(r)/ *n.* отчая́ние; **he is the ~ of his teachers** он приво́дит свои́х учителе́й в отчая́ние.

● *v.i.* отча́|иваться, -яться; **I ~ of him** я утра́тил ве́ру в него́; **I ~ of convincing him** я отча́ялся убеди́ть его́.

despatch /dɪˈspætʃ/ = **dispatch**

desperado /ˌdespəˈrɑːdəʊ/ *n.* (*pl.* **~es** *or* **~s**) сорвиголова́ (*m.*); головоре́з.

desperate /ˈdespərət/ *adj.* **1** (*wretched, hopeless*) отча́янный, беспросве́тный. **2** (*in extreme need*): **he is ~ for money** он отча́янно нужда́ется в деньга́х; **a ~ remedy** кра́йнее сре́дство.

desperation /ˌdespəˈreɪʃ(ə)n/ *n.* отча́яние; **he drives me to ~** он приво́дит меня́ в отча́яние.

despicable /ˈdespɪkəb(ə)l/, /dɪˈspɪk-/ *adj.* презре́нный.

despise /dɪˈspaɪz/ *v.t.* презира́ть (*impf.*); **the salary is not to be ~d** э́то жа́лованье внуши́тельное.

despite /dɪˈspaɪt/ *prep.* несмотря́ на +*a*.

despoil /dɪˈspɔɪl/ *v.t.* гра́бить, о-; разор|я́ть, -и́ть; **~ of** лиш|а́ть, -и́ть +*g*.

despondency /dɪˈspɒndənsɪ/ *n.* уны́ние.

despondent /dɪˈspɒnd(ə)nt/ *adj.* уны́лый; пода́вленный.

despot /ˈdespɒt/ *n.* де́спот.

despotic /ˌdeˈspɒtɪk/ *adj.* (*system, rule*) деспоти́ческий, (*person, style*) деспоти́чный.

despotism /ˈdespəˌtɪz(ə)m/ *n.* деспоти́зм.

dessert /dɪˈzɜːt/ *n.* (*sweet course*) десе́рт, сла́дкое, тре́тье.

● *cpd.* **~-spoon** *n.* десе́ртная ло́жка.

destabilize /diːˈsteɪbɪˌlaɪz/ *v.t.* дестабилизи́ровать (*impf., pf.*).

destination /ˌdestɪˈneɪʃ(ə)n/ *n.* ме́сто назначе́ния.

destine /ˈdestɪn/ *v.t.* предназн|ача́ть, -а́чить; предопредел|я́ть, -и́ть; **his parents ~d him for the army** роди́тели наме́тили определи́ть его́ в а́рмию; **he was ~ed to become Prime Minister** ему́ суждено́ бы́ло стать премье́р-мини́стром; **the plan was ~ed to fail** э́тот план был обречён на прова́л.

destiny /ˈdestɪnɪ/ *n.* (*fate*) судьба́.

destitute /ˈdestɪˌtjuːt/ *adj.* (*in penury*) нужда́ющийся, обездо́ленный; (*devoid*) лишённый (*чего*).

destitution /ˌdestɪˈtjuːʃ(ə)n/ *n.* (*poverty*) обездо́ленность, нищета́.

destroy /dɪˈstrɔɪ/ *v.t.* (*building*) разр|уша́ть, -у́шить; (*friendship, hope*) разб|ива́ть, -и́ть; (*kill*) истреб|ля́ть, -и́ть; (*wreck*) уничт|ожа́ть, -о́жить; **his hopes were ~ed** его́ наде́жды ру́хнули; **the horse had to be ~ed** ло́шадь пришло́сь пристрели́ть.

destroyer /dɪˈstrɔɪə(r)/ *n.* **1** (*one who destroys*) разруши́тель (*m.*). **2** (*nav.*) эсми́нец; эска́дренный миноно́сец.

destructible /dɪˈstrʌktɪb(ə)l/ *adj.* разруши́мый.

destruction /dɪˈstrʌkʃ(ə)n/ *n.* (*act of destroying*) уничтоже́ние, разруше́ние; (*cause of ruin*) ги́бель; **gambling was his ~** аза́ртные и́гры погуби́ли его́.

destructive /dɪˈstrʌktɪv/ *adj.* разруши́тельный; (*of behaviour, influence, agent*) деструкти́вный; **~ criticism** уничтожа́ющая кри́тика; **he is a ~ child** э́тот ребёнок всё лома́ет.

destructiveness /dɪˈstrʌktɪvnɪs/ *n.* разруши́тельность.

desuetude /dɪˈsjuːɪˌtjuːd/, /ˈdeswɪ-/ *n.* неупотреби́тельность.

desultory /ˈdezəltərɪ/ *adj.* отры́вочный; **~ reading** бессисте́мное чте́ние.

detach /dɪˈtætʃ/ *v.t.* **1** (*separate*) отдел|я́ть, -и́ть; разъедин|я́ть, -и́ть. **2** (*send on separate mission*) отря|жа́ть, -ди́ть; высыла́ть, вы́слать.

detachable /dɪˈtætʃəb(ə)l/ *adj.* съёмный, отделя́емый.

detached /dɪˈtætʃd/ *adj.* (*impartial*) беспристра́стный; (*unemotional*) равноду́шный, отчуждённый; **a ~**

attitude равнодушный подход; **a ~ house** отдельный дом.

detachment /dɪˈtætʃmənt/ *n.* (*separation*) отделение, разъединение; (*indifference*) отчуждённость, равнодушие; (*body of troops etc.*) отряд.

detail¹ /ˈdi:teɪl/ *n.* **1** подробность, деталь; **go into ~(s)** входить, вдаваться (*both impf.*) в подробности; **in ~** подробно, детально. **2** (*of a picture*) деталь. **3** (*mil., detachment*) наряд.

detail² /ˈdi:teɪl/ *v.t.* **1** (*give particulars of*) входить, вдаваться (*both impf.*) в подробности + *g.* **2** (*appoint*) наря|жать, -дить.

detain /dɪˈteɪn/ *v.t.* **1** (*delay, cause to remain*) задерж|ивать, -ать; **he was ~ed at the office** его задержали на работе; **the question need not ~ us long** этот вопрос не потребует много времени; **he was ~ed by the police** он был задержан полицией. **2** (*withhold*) удерж|ивать, -ать.

detainee /ˌdi:teɪˈni:/ *n.* задержанный.

detect /dɪˈtekt/ *v.t.* (*track down*) выслеживать, выследить; на|ходить, -йти; (*discover*) обнаружи|вать, -ть; (*discern*) ул|авливать, -овить.

detectable /dɪˈtektəb(ə)l/ *adj.* заметный, различимый.

detection /dɪˈtekʃ(ə)n/ *n.* (*of crime*) расследование, раскрытие; **he escaped ~** он избежал разоблачения; (*discovery*) обнаружение.

detective /dɪˈtektɪv/ *n.* сыщик, детектив; **private ~** частный детектив, сыщик; **~ novel** детектив, детективный роман.

detector /dɪˈtektə(r)/ *n.* (*radio*) детектор.

détente /deɪˈtɑ̃t/ *n.* (*pol.*) разрядка.

detention /dɪˈtenʃ(ə)n/ *n.* (*at school*) оставление после уроков; (*arrest*) задержание; (*confinement*) заключение (под стражу).

deter /dɪˈtɜ:(r)/ *v.t.* (**deterred, deterring**) удерж|ивать, -ать.

detergent /dɪˈtɜ:dʒ(ə)nt/ *n.* моющее средство; (*washing powder*) стиральный порошок.

deteriorate /dɪˈtɪərɪəˌreɪt/ *v.t. & i.* ух|удшать(ся), -удшить(ся).

deterioration /dɪˌtɪərɪəˈreɪʃ(ə)n/ *n.* ухудшение.

determinable /dɪˈtɜ:mɪnəb(ə)l/ *adj.* (*ascertainable*) определимый; (*leg., terminable*) могущий быть решённым; **this case is ~** это дело можно решить.

determinant /dɪˈtɜ:mɪnənt/ *n.* решающий фактор.

● *adj.* решающий.

determinate /dɪˈtɜ:mɪnət/ *adj.* определённый.

determination /dɪˌtɜ:mɪˈneɪʃ(ə)n/ *n.* **1** (*deciding upon*) решение. **2** (*calculating*) установление, вычисление. **3** (*resoluteness*) решимость, решительность.

determine /dɪˈtɜ:mɪn/ *v.t.* **1** (*be deciding factor*) определ|ять, -ить; **this ~d him to accept** это убедило его согласиться. **2** (*take decision*) реш|ать, -ить; **he is ~d to go (*or* on going)** он твёрдо решил ехать; **~ the date of a meeting** устан|авливать, -овить дату собрания. **3** (*ascertain*) устан|авливать, -овить.

determined /dɪˈtɜ:mɪnd/ *adj.* (*resolute*) решительный.

determinism /dɪˈtɜ:mɪˌnɪz(ə)m/ *n.* детерминизм.

determinist /dɪˈtɜ:mɪnɪst/ *n.* детерминист.

deterministic /dɪˌtɜ:mɪˈnɪstɪk/ *adj.* детерминистический.

deterrence /dɪˈterəns/ *n.* устрашение, отпугивание.

deterrent /dɪˈterənt/ *n.* средство устрашения/сдерживания; сдерживающее средство; **nuclear ~** ядерный арсенал сдерживания.

detest /dɪˈtest/ *v.t.* ненавидеть (*impf.*); испытывать (*impf.*) отвращение к + *d.*

detestable /dɪˈtestəb(ə)l/ *adj.* отвратительный.

detestation /ˌdi:teˈsteɪʃ(ə)n/ *n.* ненависть, отвращение.

dethrone /di:ˈθrəʊn/ *v.t.* св|ергать, -ергнуть с престола.

dethronement /di:ˈθrəʊnmənt/ *n.* свержение с престола.

detonate /ˈdetəˌneɪt/ *v.t.* детонировать (*impf., pf.*).

● *v.i.* вз|рываться, -орваться.

detonation /ˌdetəˈneɪʃ(ə)n/ *n.* детонация.

detonator /ˈdetəˌneɪtə(r)/ *n.* (*part of bomb or shell*) детонатор; (*fog-signal*) петарда.

detour /ˈdi:tʊə(r)/ *n.* (*on foot*) обход; (*by transport*) объезд; окружной, окольный путь; **make a ~** делать, с-крюк.

detoxification /ˈdi:tɒksɪfɪˈkeɪʃ(ə)n/ *n.*: **~ centre** вытрезвитель (*m.*).

detract /dɪˈtrækt/ *v.i.*: **~ from** умал|ять, -ить.

detraction /dɪˈtrækʃ(ə)n/ *n.* (*disparagement*) умаление; (*slander*) клевета.

detractor /dɪˈtræktə(r)/ *n.* клеветник.

detrain /di:ˈtreɪn/ *v.t. & i.* высаживать(ся), высадить(ся) из поезда.

detriment /ˈdetrɪmənt/ *n.* ущерб; **he works long hours to the ~ of his health** он работает в ущерб своему здоровью.

detrimental /ˌdetrɪˈment(ə)l/ *adj.* вредный.

detritus /dɪˈtraɪtəs/ *n.* (*geol.*) детрит; (*debris*) осколки (*m. pl.*); обломки (*m. pl.*).

de trop /də ˈtrəʊ/ *adj.* излишний.

deuce¹ /dju:s/ *n.* (*US, cards or dice*) двойка; (*tennis*) равный счёт.

deuce² /dju:s/ *n.* (*euph., devil*) чёрт, дьявол; **~ take it!** чёрт подери!; **where the ~ did I put it?** куда к чёрту я это задевал?

deuterium /dju:ˈtɪərɪəm/ *n.* (*chem.*) дейтерий, тяжёлый водород.

Deuteronomy /ˌdju:təˈrɒnəmɪ/ *n.* Второзаконие.

devaluation /di:ˌvæljuːˈeɪʃ(ə)n/ *n.* обесценение; (*fin.*) девальвация.

devalue /di:ˈvælju:/ *v.t.* (**devalues, devalued, devaluing**) обесцени|вать, -ть; (*fin.*) девальвировать (*impf., pf.*).

● *v.i.* (**devalues, devalued, devaluing**) пров|одить, -ести девальвацию.

devastate /ˈdevəˌsteɪt/ *v.t.* опустош|ать, -ить; разор|ять, -ить; (*person, fig.*) убивать, убить; **a ~ing remark** уничтожающее замечание.

devastation /ˌdevəˈsteɪʃ(ə)n/ *n.* опустошение, разорение.

develop /dɪˈveləp/ *v.t.* (**developed, developing**) **1** (*cause to unfold*) разв|ивать, -ить; (*work up, polish*) обраб|атывать, -отать. **2** (*phot.*) прояв|лять, -ить. **3** (*contract*): **he ~ed a cough** у него появился кашель. **4** (*open up for residence etc.*) разв|ивать, -ить; (*resources*) осв|аивать, -оить; разраб|атывать, -отать.

● *v.i.* (**developed, developing**) **1** (*unfold*) разв|иваться, -иться; разв|ёртываться, -ернуться; **~ into** превра|щаться, -титься в + *a.*; **London ~ed into a huge city** Лондон превратился в огромный город. **2** (*come to light*) выясняться, выясниться.

developer /dɪˈveləpə(r)/ *n.* **1**: **he was a late ~** он поздно проявил свои способности. **2** (*phot., substance*) проявитель (*m.*). **3** (*builder*) застройщик.

development /dɪˈveləpmənt/ *n.* **1** (*unfolding*) развитие, рост. **2** (*event*) событие, обстоятельство. **3** (*of land etc.*) развитие (района); (*building*) застройка.

developmental /dɪˌveləpˈment(ə)l/ *adj.* **1** (*incidental to growth*) связанный с ростом; **~ disease** болезнь роста. **2** (*evolutionary*) эволюционный.

deviant /ˈdi:vɪənt/ *n.* (*e.g. sexual*) извращенец.

● *adj.* отклоняющийся от нормы.

deviate /ˈdi:vɪˌeɪt/ *v.i.* отклон|яться, -иться (от + *g.*).

deviation /ˌdi:vɪˈeɪʃ(ə)n/ *n.* отклонение, отход; (*of compass*) девиация.

deviationism /ˌdi:vɪˈeɪʃənˌɪz(ə)m/ *n.* уклонизм.

deviationist /ˌdi:vɪˈeɪʃənɪst/ *n.* уклонист.

device /dɪˈvaɪs/ *n.* **1** (*plan, scheme, trick*) план, схема, затея; (*method*) приём; **he was left to his own ~s** он был предоставлен самому себе. **2** (*instrument, contrivance*) приспособление, прибор. **3** (*sign, symbol*) эмблема.

devil /ˈdev(ə)l/ *n.* **1** чёрт, дьявол; **between the ~ and the deep (blue) sea** между двух огней; **go to the ~!** иди к чёрту!; **~ take it!** чёрт побери!; **~ take**

the hindmost к чертя́м неуда́чников; **talk of the ~!** лёгок на поми́не; **he has the ~'s own luck** ему черто́вски везёт. **2** (*wretched person*): **poor ~!** бедола́га!, бедня́га!
3 (*as expletive*): **what the ~ do you mean?** что вы э́тим хоти́те сказа́ть, чёрт возьми́?; **he ran like the ~** он побежа́л с дья́вольской быстрото́й; **I had the ~ of a time** я черто́вски хорошо́/пло́хо провёл вре́мя; **a ~ of a fellow** отча́янный па́рень; **there'll be the devil to pay** рассчи́таться за э́то бу́дет дья́вольски тру́дно.
● *v.t.* (**devilled, devilling;** *US* **deviled, deviling**) (*cul.*) гото́вить (*impf.*) с пря́ностями.
● *cpd.* **~-may-care** *adj.* бесшаба́шный, разуда́лый.
devilish /'devəlɪʃ/ *adj.* дья́вольский.
● *adv.* (*coll.*) черто́вски, дья́вольски.
devilment /'devəlmənt/ *n.* дья́вольщина, чертовщи́на.
devilry /'devɪlrɪ/ *n.* (*wickedness*) жесто́кость, зве́рства (*nt. pl.*); (*mischief*) прока́зы (*f. pl.*), проде́лки (*f. pl.*).
devious /'di:vɪəs/ *adj.* (*road*) изви́листый, око́льный; (*fig.*) лука́вый, нейскренний.
deviousness /'di:vɪəsnɪs/ *n.* (*of road*) изви́листость; (*fig.*) лука́вство, хи́трость.
devise /dɪ'vaɪz/ *v.t.* (*think out*) приду́м|ывать, -ать; изобре|та́ть, -сти́.
devitalize /di:'vaɪtə,laɪz/ *v.t.* лиш|а́ть, -и́ть жи́зненных сил.
devoid /dɪ'vɔɪd/ *adj.* лишённый; **~ of shame** бессты́дный; **~ of fear** бесстра́шный.
devolution /,di:və'lu:ʃ(ə)n/, /-'lju:ʃ(ə)n/ *n.* переда́ча/делеги́рование вла́сти.
devolve /dɪ'vɒlv/ *v.t.* (*delegate*) перед|ава́ть, -а́ть.
● *v.i.* пере|ходи́ть, -йти́; **the work ~d on/to me** рабо́ту переда́ли мне; **the estate ~d on/to a distant cousin** име́ние перешло́ к да́льнему ро́дственнику.
Devonian /dɪ'vəʊnɪən/ *n.*: (*geol.*) **~ period** дево́н, дево́нский пери́од.
● *adj.* (*geol.*) дево́нский.
devote /dɪ'vəʊt/ *v.t.* посвя|ща́ть, -ти́ть; **he ~s his time to study** он посвяща́ет всё своё вре́мя учёбе; **she is ~d to her children** она́ пре́дана свои́м де́тям; она́ всю себя́ отдаёт де́тям; **a ~d friend** пре́данный друг.
devotee /,devə'ti:/ *n.* приве́рженец.
devotion /dɪ'vəʊʃ(ə)n/ *n.* **1** (*being devoted*) пре́данность; **~ to tennis** увлече́ние те́ннисом. **2** (*love*) пре́данность, привя́занность. **3** (*pl., prayers*) моли́твы (*f. pl.*); **he was at his ~s** он моли́лся.
devotional /dɪ'vəʊʃənəl/ *adj.* моли́твенный, религио́зный.
devour /dɪ'vaʊə(r)/ *v.t.* **1** (*eat greedily*) пож|ира́ть, -ра́ть. **2** (*fig.*) погло|ща́ть, -ти́ть; пожира́ть (*impf.*); **she ~ed his story** она́ жа́дно слу́шала его́ расска́з; **he ~ed the book** он проглоти́л кни́гу; **~ed by anxiety** снеда́емый трево́гой; **the fire ~ed the forest** пожа́р уничто́жил лес.
devout /dɪ'vaʊt/ *adj.* (*religious*) благочести́вый; (*devoted*) пре́данный.
devoutness /dɪ'vaʊtnɪs/ *n.* благоче́стие, на́божность.
dew /dju:/ *n.* роса́.
● *cpds.* **~berry** *n.* ежеви́ка (*collect.*); я́года ежеви́ки; **~drop** *n.* роси́нка.
dewlap /'dju:læp/ *n.* подгру́док.
dewy /'dju:ɪ/ *adj.* (**dewier, dewiest**) роси́стый.
● *cpd.* **~-eyed** *adj.* (*fig.*) дове́рчивый; простоду́шный.
dexterity /dek'sterɪtɪ/ *n.* ло́вкость, прово́рство.
dext(e)rous /'dekstrəs/ *adj.* ло́вкий, прово́рный.
diabetes /,daɪə'bi:ti:z/ *n.* диабе́т; са́харная боле́знь.
diabetic /,daɪə'betɪk/ *n.* диабе́тик.
● *adj.* диабети́ческий.
diabolic(al) /,daɪə'bɒlɪk(l)/ *adj.* дья́вольский.
diachronic /,daɪə'krɒnɪk/ *adj.* диахрони́ческий.
diaconate /daɪ'ækə,neɪt/, /-nət/ *n.* дья́конство.
diacritic /,daɪə'krɪtɪk/ *n.* диакрити́ческий знак.
● *adj.* диакрити́ческий.
diadem /'daɪə,dem/ *n.* (*crown*) диаде́ма; (*wreath*) вено́к, вене́ц.
diaeresis /daɪ'ɪərəsɪs/ (*US* **dieresis**) *n.* (*pl.* **diaereses** /-,si:z/) (*ling.*) диере́за, трема́.
diagnose /'daɪəg,nəʊz/ *v.t.* диагности́ровать (*impf., pf.*); **he ~d (the illness as) cancer** он установи́л, что у больно́го рак; (*med.*) он диагности́ровал рак.
diagnosis /,daɪəg'nəʊsɪs/ *n.* (*pl.* **diagnoses** /-si:z/) диа́гноз; **make a ~** ста́вить, по- диа́гноз.
diagnostic /,daɪəg'nɒstɪk/ *adj.* диагности́ческий.
diagnostician /,daɪəgnɒ'stɪʃ(ə)n/ *n.* диагно́ст.
diagnostics /,daɪəg'nɒstɪks/ *n.* диагно́стика.
diagonal /daɪ'ægən(ə)l/ *n.* диагона́ль.
● *adj.* диагона́льный; **~ly** по диагона́ли.
diagram /'daɪə,græm/ *n.* диагра́мма, схе́ма.
diagrammatic(al) /,daɪəgrə'mætɪk(ə)l/ *adj.* схемати́ческий.
dial /'daɪ(ə)l/ *n.* **1** (*of clock*) цифербла́т. **2** (*of radio etc.*) шкала́. **3** (*of telephone*) диск.
● *v.t. & i.* (**dialled, dialling;** *US* **dialed, dialing**): **~ a number** наб|ира́ть, -ра́ть но́мер; **~ the police-station** звони́ть, по- в поли́цию; **~ling tone** дли́нный гудо́к; сигна́л «ли́ния свобо́дна».
dialect /'daɪə,lekt/ *n.* диале́кт, го́вор.
dialectal /,daɪə'lekt(ə)l/ *adj.* диалекта́льный, диале́ктный.
dialectic(s) /,daɪə'lektɪks/ *n.* диале́ктика.
● *adj.* (*also* **-al**) диалекти́ческий.
dialectician /,daɪəlek'tɪʃ(ə)n/ *n.* диале́ктик.
dialectology /,daɪəlek'tɒlədʒɪ/ *n.* диалектоло́гия.
dialogue /'daɪə,lɒg/ (*US also* **dialog**) *n.* диало́г, разгово́р; **written in ~** напи́санный в фо́рме диало́га.
dialysis /daɪ'ælɪsɪs/ *n.* диа́лиз.
diameter /daɪ'æmɪtə(r)/ *n.* диа́метр; **two feet in ~** два фу́та диа́метром.
diametric(al) /,daɪə'metrɪk(ə)l/ *adj.* диаметра́льный.
diamond /'daɪəmənd/ *n.* **1** (*precious stone*) алма́з; (*cut and set*) бриллиа́нт; **rough ~** (*fig.*) самоpо́док. **2** (*geom.*) ромб. **3** (*at cards*) бу́б|ны (*pl., g.* -ён); **the queen of ~s** да́ма бубён, бубно́вая да́ма. **4** (*baseball*) площа́дка для игры́ в бейсбо́л. **5** (*attr.*) алма́зный; бриллиа́нтовый; **~ mine** алма́зный рудни́к; **~ ring** бриллиа́нтовое кольцо́; **~ wedding** бриллиа́нтовая сва́дьба.
diapason /,daɪə'peɪz(ə)n/, /-'peɪs(ə)n/ *n.* диапазо́н.
diaper /'daɪəpə(r)/ *n.* (*US*) подгу́зник.
diaphanous /daɪ'æfənəs/ *adj.* прозра́чный, просве́чивающий.
diaphragm /'daɪə,fræm/ *n.* **1** (*anat.*) диафра́гма. **2** (*of camera lens*) перегоро́дка. **3** (*of telephone receiver*) мембра́на. **4** (*contraceptive device*) колпачо́к.
diarist /'daɪərɪst/ *n.* а́втор дневника́.
diarrhoea /,daɪə'rɪə/ (*US* **diarrhea**) *n.* поно́с; расстро́йство желу́дка.
diary /'daɪərɪ/ *n.* (*journal*) дневни́к; (*engagement book*) календа́рь (*m.*).
diaspora /daɪ'æspərə/ *n.* (*people*) диа́спора, (*dispersion*) рассе́яние.
diatonic /,daɪə'tɒnɪk/ *adj.* диатони́ческий.
diatribe /'daɪə,traɪb/ *n.* диатри́ба, вражде́бная кри́тика.
dibble /'dɪb(ə)l/ *n.* лункокопа́тель (*m.*) поса́дочный меч.
dice /daɪs/ *n.* (*see also* ⇒**die**) (*cube*) игра́льные ко́сти (*f. pl.*); (*game of ~*) игра́ в ко́сти; **no ~!** (*sl.*) так де́ло не пойдёт!; **the ~ are loaded against him** судьба́ — про́тив него́.
● *v.t. & i.* **1** (*play at ~*) игра́ть (*impf.*) в ко́сти; **~ away one's fortune** про|игрывать, -игра́ть состоя́ние. **2** (*cul.*) нар|еза́ть, -е́зать ку́биками.
dicey /'daɪsɪ/ *adj.* (**dicier, diciest**) (*sl.*) риско́ванный.
dichotomy /daɪ'kɒtəmɪ/ *n.* дихотоми́я; (*contrast*) противопоставле́ние.
dick /dɪk/ *n.* **1** (*US sl., detective*) сы́щик, хвост. **2** (*coll., fellow*): **a clever D~** (*Br.*) у́мник, всезна́йка (*c.g.*). **3** (*vulg.*) член.
dickens /'dɪkɪnz/ *n.* (*coll.*) чёрт; **what the ~ are you up to?** что вы там замышля́ете, чёрт возьми́?
dickhead /'dɪkhed/ *n.* (*vulg.*) муда́к, мудозво́н.

dicky[1] /ˈdɪkɪ/ *n.* (*shirt-front*) мани́шка.
dicky[2] /ˈdɪkɪ/ *adj.* (**dickier, dickiest**) (*Br. coll.*) хли́пкий; (*unstable*) ша́ткий, ва́лкий.
dicky-bird /ˈdɪkɪbɜ:d/ *n.* пти́чка; пта́шка.
dicta *pl. of* ⇒**dictum**
Dictaphone /ˈdɪktəˌfəʊn/ *n.* (*propr.*) диктофо́н.
dictate[1] /ˈdɪkteɪt/ *n.* веле́ние.
dictate[2] /dɪkˈteɪt/ *v.t. & i.* (*recite, specify, command*) диктова́ть, про-; **I won't be ~d to** я не позво́лю ста́вить мне усло́вия; я не позво́лю, что́бы мне диктова́ли.
dictation /dɪkˈteɪʃ(ə)n/ *n.* **1** (*to class*) дикта́нт; (*to secretary*) дикто́вка; **take ~** писа́ть (*impf.*) под дикто́вку. **2** (*orders*) приказа́ние, предписа́ние; **I did it at his ~** я сде́лал э́то по его́ приказа́нию.
dictator /dɪkˈteɪtə(r)/ *n.* (*ruler*) дикта́тор.
dictatorial /ˌdɪktəˈtɔ:rɪəl/ *adj.* дикта́торский.
dictatorship /dɪkˈteɪtəʃɪp/ *n.* диктату́ра.
diction /ˈdɪkʃ(ə)n/ *n.* ди́кция.
dictionary /ˈdɪkʃənrɪ/, /-nərɪ/ *n.* слова́рь (*m.*); **a walking ~** ≈ ходя́чая энциклопе́дия.
dictum /ˈdɪktəm/ *n.* (*pl.* **dicta** *or* **dictums**) изрече́ние, афори́зм.
did /dɪd/ *past of* ⇒**do**[1]
didactic /daɪˈdæktɪk/, /dɪ-/ *adj.* поучи́тельный, дидакти́ческий.
didacticism /daɪˈdæktɪˌsɪz(ə)m/, /dɪ-/ *n.* дидакти́зм.
diddle /ˈdɪd(ə)l/ *v.t.* (*coll.*) над|ува́ть, -у́ть.
die[1] /daɪ/ *n.* (*cf.* ⇒**dice**) игра́льная кость; **the ~ is cast** жре́бий бро́шен; **straight as a ~** (*fig.*) прямо́й, че́стный.
die[2] /daɪ/ *n.* (*engraving stamp*) штамп.
die[3] /daɪ/ *v.i.* (**dies, died, dying**) **1** (*of person*) ум|ира́ть, -ере́ть; сконча́ться (*pf.*); (*in accident, in war*) ги́бнуть, по-; (*of animals*) сд|ыха́ть, -о́хнуть; под|ыха́ть, -о́хнуть; (*of plants*) ув|яда́ть, -я́нуть; погиб|а́ть, ~нуть; **he ~d a beggar** он у́мер ни́щим; **never say ~!** никогда́ не отча́ивайся!; **old habits ~ hard** ста́рые привы́чки живу́чи; **he ~d by violence** он у́мер наси́льственной сме́ртью; **he ~d like a dog** он подо́х, как соба́ка; **he ~d by his own hand** он наложи́л на себя́ ру́ки; **he ~d in his bed** он у́мер свое́й сме́ртью.
2 (*fig.*): **I'm dying to see him** я до́ смерти хочу́ его́ ви́деть; **we ~d of laughing** мы умира́ли со́ смеху.
3 (*of things*): **his anger ~d** его́ гнев утих́; **the wind ~d** ве́тер зати́х; **his secret ~d with him** его́ та́йна умерла́ вме́сте с ним; **the engine ~d** мото́р загло́х.
● *with advs.*: **~ away** (*of sound*) зам|ира́ть, -ере́ть; (*of feeling etc.*) ум|ира́ть, -ере́ть; **~ down** (*of fire*) уг|аса́ть, -а́снуть; (*of noise*) ут|иха́ть, -и́хнуть; зам|ира́ть, -ере́ть; (*of feeling*) ум|ира́ть, -ере́ть; **~ off** умира́ть (*impf.*) оди́н за други́м; **~ out** вымира́ть, вы́мереть; **the family ~d out** э́та семья́ вы́мерла; **the dinosaur ~d out** диноза́вры вы́мерли; **the belief ~d out** э́то пове́рье о́тмерло.
● *cpd.* **~hard** *n.* консерва́тор, ретрогра́д; *adj.* твердоло́бый.
dieresis /daɪˈɪərəsɪs/ *US* = **diaeresis**
diesel /ˈdi:z(ə)l/ *n.* (**~ engine, motor**) ди́зель (*m.*); **~ locomotive** теплово́з; **~ oil** ди́зельное то́пливо.
diet /ˈdaɪət/ *n.* **1** (*customary food*) пи́ща, пита́ние. **2** (*medical régime*) дие́та; **he is on a ~** он (сиди́т) на дие́те; **go on a ~** сади́ться, сесть на дие́ту; **put s.o. on a ~** сажа́ть, посади́ть кого́-н. на дие́ту; **crash ~** ускоренная дие́та; **milk-free ~** безмоло́чная дие́та.
● *v.i.* (**dieted, dieting**) соблюда́ть (*impf.*) дие́ту; быть (*impf.*) на дие́те.
diet|ary /ˈdaɪətrɪ/, **-etic** /ˌdaɪəˈtetɪk/ *adjs.* диети́ческий.
dietetics /ˌdaɪəˈtetɪks/ *n.* диетоло́гия.
dietitian /ˌdaɪəˈtɪʃ(ə)n/ *n.* (врач-)дието́лог.
differ /ˈdɪfə(r)/ *v.i.* **1** (*be different*) отлича́ться (*impf.*); различа́ться (*impf.*); **we ~ in our tastes** на́ши вку́сы разли́чны; **tastes ~** (*prov.*) о вку́сах не спо́рят; **they ~ in size** они́ различа́ются разме́ром, по разме́ру. **2** (*disagree*) ра|сходи́ться, -зойти́сь во мне́ниях; **I ~ed with him** я с ним не согласи́лся; **I beg to ~** я позво́лю себе́ не согласи́ться; **we agreed to ~** мы реши́ли прекрати́ть бесполе́зный спор.
difference /ˈdɪfrəns/ *n.* **1** (*state of being unlike*) отли́чие, разли́чие, ра́зница; **that makes all the ~** в э́том вся ра́зница; **it makes no ~ whether you go or not** соверше́нно безразли́чно, идёте вы и́ли нет. **2** (*extent of inequality*) ра́зница; (*math.*) ра́зность; **let's split the ~** дава́йте поде́лим ра́зницу; **I will pay the ~** я доплачу́ ра́зницу. **3** (*dispute*) разногла́сие, спор.
different /ˈdɪfrənt/ *adj.* **1** (*unlike*) друго́й, ра́зный, разли́чный; **that is quite ~** э́то совсе́м друго́е де́ло; **they live in ~ houses** они́ живу́т в ра́зных дома́х; **she wears a ~ hat each day** на ней ка́ждый день друга́я шля́па; **of ~ kinds** ра́зного ро́да; **he became a ~ person** он стал други́м челове́ком; **~ from** непохо́жий на + *a.*; отли́чный от + *g.*; **everyone gave him a ~ answer** все отвеча́ли ему́ по-ра́зному.
2 (*unusual*) необы́чный; **this drink has a really ~ flavour** (*Br.*), **flavor** (*US*) э́тот напи́ток име́ет о́чень необы́чный вкус.
3 (*various*) разли́чный, ра́зный; **we talked of ~ things** мы говори́ли о ра́зных веща́х; **at ~ times** в ра́зное вре́мя.
differential /ˌdɪfəˈrenʃ(ə)l/ *n.* **1** (*Br., difference in wage-rates*) дифференци́рованная опла́та труда́. **2** (*of a car etc.; also* **~ gear**) дифференциа́л.
● *adj.* **1** (*differing according to circumstances*) дифференци́рованный. **2** (*math.*) дифференциа́льный.
differentiate /ˌdɪfəˈrenʃɪˌeɪt/ *v.t.* **1** (*constitute difference*) отлич|а́ть, -и́ть (от + *g.*). **2** (*perceive difference*) различ|а́ть, -и́ть. **3** (*make, point out difference*) пров|оди́ть, -ести́ разли́чие; различ|а́ть, -и́ть; **we do not ~ on grounds of sex** мы не прово́дим разли́чие по по́лу.
differentiation /ˌdɪfərenʃɪˈeɪʃ(ə)n/ *n.* **1** (*change*) видоизмене́ние. **2** (*act of distinguishing*) различе́ние. **3** (*discrimination*) дифференциа́ция.
differently /ˈdɪfrəntlɪ/ *adv.* по-ино́му; по-друго́му; (*looking, made*) ина́че; **I understand this ~ from you** я понима́ю э́то ина́че, чем вы.
difficult /ˈdɪfɪkəlt/ *adj.* тру́дный (*also of person*); **a ~ child** трудновоспиту́емый ребёнок; **he is ~ to please** ему́ тру́дно угоди́ть; **~ of access** труднодосту́пный.
difficult|y /ˈdɪfɪkəltɪ/ *n.* тру́дность, затрудне́ние; **I have ~y in understanding him** я с трудо́м его́ понима́ю; **don't make ~ies** не создава́йте тру́дностей; **we ran into ~ies** мы столкну́лись с тру́дностями; **he is in financial ~ies** он испы́тывает материа́льные затрудне́ния; **he is in ~ with his work** у него́ тру́дности в рабо́те.
diffidence /ˈdɪfɪdəns/ *n.* неуве́ренность в себе́; засте́нчивость; стесни́тельность.
diffident /ˈdɪfɪd(ə)nt/ *adj.* неуве́ренный в себе́; засте́нчивый, стесни́тельный.
diffuse[1] /dɪˈfju:s/ *adj.* (*of light etc.*) рассе́янный; (*of style*) расплы́вчатый.
diffuse[2] /dɪˈfju:z/ *v.t.* (*light, heat etc.*) рассе́|ивать, -ять; **~d lighting** рассе́янный свет; (*learning etc.*) распростран|я́ть, -и́ть.
● *v.i.* рассе́|иваться, -яться; распростран|я́ться, -и́ться.
diffuseness /dɪˈfju:snɪs/ *n.* расплы́вчатость.
diffusion /dɪˈfju:ʒ(ə)n/ *n.* (*phys.*) диффу́зия, рассе́ивание; распростране́ние.
dig /dɪg/ *n.* **1** (*thrust, poke*) толчо́к; **~ in the ribs** толчо́к в бок.
2 (*fig.*) шпи́лька, подковы́рка; **that remark was a ~ at me** э́то замеча́ние — шпи́лька мне.
3 (*archaeol.*) (*site*) раско́п; (*expedition*) раско́пки (*f. pl.*); **we went on a ~** мы вы́ехали на раско́пки.
4 (*pl., Br. coll., lodgings*) кварти́ра, берло́га, нора́.
● *v.t. & i.* (**digging;** *past and p.p.* **dug**) **1** (*excavate ground*) копа́ть, вы́-; рыть, вы́-; (*of animals*) рыть, вы́-; **the ground is hard to ~** э́ту зе́млю тру́дно копа́ть; **they are ~ging potatoes** они́ копа́ют карто́шку; **he dug a hole** он вы́рыл я́му; **they are ~ging for gold** они́ и́щут зо́лото; **he dug his way through the rubble** он с трудо́м пробира́лся че́рез обло́мки; **they dug through the mountain** они́ проры́ли тонне́ль в горе́.
2 (*fig.*) отк|а́пывать, -опа́ть; **you will**

have to ~ for the information вам нужно будет порыться, чтобы найти нужную информацию; **he dug into the archives** он зарылся в архивы.
3 (*thrust*) толк|ать, -нуть; ткнуть (*pf.*); **he dug me in the ribs** он толкнул/ткнул меня в бок; **he dug his fork into the pie** он вонзил вилку в пирог.

● *with advs.*: **~ in** *v.t.* зак|апывать, -опать; **the soldiers dug (themselves) in** солдаты окопались; **he dug his heels/toes in** (*fig.*) он упёрся на своём; **~ out** *v.t.* выкапывать, выкопать; раск|апывать, -опать; извл|екать, -ечь; **victims of the accident were dug out** жертвы катастрофы были отрыты; **~ up** *v.t.* отк|апывать, -опать; **they dug up the land** они вскопали землю; **the tree was dug up by the roots** дерево было выкопано/вырыто из земли с корнями; **they dug up an ancient statue** они откопали древнюю статую; **where did you ~ him up?** (*fig.*) где вы его откопали?

digest[1] /ˈdaɪdʒest/ *n.* сводка, резюме (*indecl.*), дайджест.

digest[2] /daɪˈdʒest/, /dɪ-/ *v.t.* (*food*) перевар|ивать, -ить; (*information etc.*) усв|аивать, -оить.

● *v.i.* перевар|иваться, -иться.

digestible /daɪˈdʒestɪb(ə)l/, /dɪ-/ *adj.* удобоваримый.

digestion /daɪˈdʒestʃ(ə)n/ *n.* (*of food*) переваривание; (*capacity to digest*) пищеварение; (*of knowledge*) усвоение.

digestive /dɪˈdʒestɪv/, /daɪ-/ *adj.* пищеварительный; (*aiding digestion*) способствующий пищеварениию.

digger /ˈdɪgə(r)/ *n.* (*one who digs*) копатель (*m.*); землекоп; (*searcher for gold*) золотоискатель (*m.*).

digging /ˈdɪgɪŋ/ *n.* (*action*) рытьё, копание, выемка.

digit /ˈdɪdʒɪt/ *n.* (*finger or toe*) палец; (*numeral*) цифра.

digital /ˈdɪdʒɪt(ə)l/ *adj.* цифровой; **~ clock** цифровые/электронные часы (*pl., g.* -ов).

digitalis /ˌdɪdʒɪˈteɪlɪs/ *n.* дигиталис, наперстянка.

digitize /ˈdɪdʒɪˌtaɪz/ *v.t.* оцифр|овывать, -овать; преобраз|овывать, -овать в цифровую форму.

dignified /ˈdɪgnɪˌfaɪd/ *adj.* полный достоинства; величавый.

dignify /ˈdɪgnɪˌfaɪ/ *v.t.* облагор|аживать, -одить; (*give name to*) величать (*impf.*).

dignitary /ˈdɪgnɪtərɪ/ *n.* сановник; высокопоставленное лицо.

dignity /ˈdɪgnɪtɪ/ *n.* **1** (*worth*) достоинство; **stand on one's ~** требовать (*impf.*) уважения к себе; **it is beneath my ~ to reply** отвечать на это — ниже моего достоинства.
2 (*dignified behaviour*): **keep one's ~** сохран|ять, -ить своё достоинство.
3 (*title*) сан, титул; **confer the ~ of a peerage** присв|аивать, -оить (*pf.*) титул пэра.

digress /daɪˈgres/ *v.i.* отвл|екаться, -ечься; отклон|яться, -иться; делать, с- отступление.

digression /daɪˈgreʃ(ə)n/ *n.* отклонение, отступление.

dike /daɪk/ *n.* (*ditch*) ров, канава; (*embankment*) дамба, плотина.

diktat /ˈdɪktæt/ *n.* диктат.

dilapidated /dɪˈlæpɪˌdeɪtɪd/ *adj.* ветхий, полуразрушенный.

dilapidation /dɪˌlæpɪˈdeɪʃ(ə)n/ *n.* (об)ветшание, износ.

dilatation /ˌdaɪləˈteɪʃ(ə)n/ = **dilation**

dilate /daɪˈleɪt/ *v.t.* расш|ирять, -ирить; **the horse ~d its nostrils** лошадь раздула ноздри.

● *v.i.* расш|иряться, -ириться; распростран|яться, -иться; **his eyes ~d** его глаза расширились.

dilation /daɪˈleɪʃ(ə)n/ *n.* расширение.

dilatoriness /ˈdɪlətərɪnɪs/ *n.* замедление, медлительность.

dilatory /ˈdɪlətərɪ/ *adj.* (*slow*) замедленный; (*person*) медлительный; (*intended to cause delay*) обструкционистский.

dilemma /daɪˈlemə/, /dɪ-/ *n.* дилемма; **he is on the horns of a ~** он стоит перед дилеммой.

dilettan|te /ˌdɪlɪˈtæntɪ/ *n.* (*pl.* **~ti** /-tɪ/ *or* **~tes**) дилетант.

● *adj.* дилетантский.

dilettantism /ˌdɪlɪˈtæntɪz(ə)m/ *n.* дилетантство.

diligence /ˈdɪlɪdʒ(ə)ns/ *n.* (*zeal*) прилежание, усердие, старательность.

diligent /ˈdɪlɪdʒ(ə)nt/ *adj.* прилежный, усердный, старательный.

dill /dɪl/ *n.* укроп; **~ pickle** маринованный огурец.

dilly-dally /ˌdɪlɪˈdælɪ/ *v.i.* (*coll.*) мешкать (*impf.*); колебаться (*impf.*).

dilute /ˈdaɪljuːt/ *adj.* разбавленный; разведённый.

● *v.t.* разв|одить, -ести; разб|авлять, -авить.

dilution /daɪˈljuːʃ(ə)n/ *n.* разведение, разбавление.

dim /dɪm/ *adj.* (**dimmer, dimmest**) (*of light etc.*) тусклый; (*of memory etc.*) смутный; (*of eyes*) затуманенный; (*of prospects, future*) мрачный; (*coll., stupid*) тупой; **I take a ~ view of it** (*coll.*) я смотрю на это неодобрительно.

● *v.t.* (**dimmed, dimming**) затумани|вать, -ть; (*shade*) затенять, -ить; **~ one's headlights** пере|ходить, -йти на ближний свет.

● *v.i.* (**dimmed, dimming**) (*of eyes*) затумани|ваться, -ться; (*of memory*) тускнеть, по-.

● *cpds.* (*coll.*): **~wit** *n.* тупица (*c.g.*); **~-witted** *adj.* тупоумный.

dime /daɪm/ *n.* десятицентовик.

dimension /daɪˈmenʃ(ə)n/, /dɪ-/ *n.* **1** (*extent*) размер; **a room of vast ~s** комната огромного размера; (*capacity*) объём. **2** (*direction of measurement*) измерение; **the fourth ~** четвёртое измерение.

diminish /dɪˈmɪnɪʃ/ *v.t.* ум|еньшать, -еньшить; уб|авлять, -авить; **~ed responsibility** (*leg.*) ограниченная уголовная ответственность; **law of ~ing returns** закон сокращающихся доходов; **~ed fifth** (*mus.*) уменьшенная квинта.

● *v.i.* ум|еньшаться, -еньшиться; уб|авляться, -авиться.

diminuen|do /dɪˌmɪnjʊˈendəʊ/ *n.* (*pl.* **~dos** *or* **~di** /-dɪ/), *adj. & adv.* (*mus.*) диминуэндо (*indecl.*).

diminution /ˌdɪmɪˈnjuːʃ(ə)n/ *n.* уменьшение.

diminutive /dɪˈmɪnjʊtɪv/ *n.* (*gram.*) уменьшительное слово.

● *adj.* (*small*) миниатюрный.

dimness /ˈdɪmnɪs/ *n.* (*of light*) тусклость; (*of wit*) тупость.

dimple /ˈdɪmp(ə)l/ *n.* ямочка; (*ripple*) рябь.

din /dɪn/ *n.* гам, грохот, галдёж.

● *v.t.* (**dinned, dinning**) вд|албливать, -олбить; **he ~ned it into me that I must obey** он вдолбил мне в голову, что я должен подчиниться.

dinar /ˈdiːnɑː(r)/ *n.* динар.

din|e /daɪn/ *v.t.*: **he was wined and ~ed** его кормили-поили; его потчевали на славу.

● *v.i.* (*at midday*) обедать, по- (**on, off**: *чем*); (*in the evening*) ужинать, по-; **~ing-car** вагон-ресторан; **~ing-hall** обеденный зал, столовая; **~ing-room** столовая (комната); **~ing-table** обеденный стол.

diner /ˈdaɪnə(r)/ *n.* (*person*) обедающий, ужинающий; (*dining-car*) вагон-ресторан.

● *cpd.* **~-out** *n.* любитель (*m.*) ужинать вне дома.

ding-dong /ˈdɪŋdɒŋ/ *n.* динь-дон.

● *adj.*: **a ~ battle** (*Br.*) битва с переменным успехом.

dinghy /ˈdɪŋɪ/, /ˈdɪŋgɪ/ *n.* маленькая шлюпка, ялик; (*inflatable*) надувная лодка.

dinginess /ˈdɪndʒɪnɪs/ *n.* темнота; мрачность.

dingle /ˈdɪŋg(ə)l/ *n.* лощина.

dingo /ˈdɪŋgəʊ/ *n.* (*pl.* **~es** *or* **~s**) динго (*m. or f., indecl.*).

dingy /ˈdɪndʒɪ/ *adj.* (**dingier, dingiest**) тёмный, мрачный.

dinkum /ˈdɪŋkəm/ *adj.* (*Austral. sl.*) настоящий, заправдашний.

dinky /ˈdɪŋkɪ/ *adj.* (**dinkier, dinkiest**) (*coll.*) (*Br.*) изящный, миленький; (*US*) дрянной.

dinner /ˈdɪnə(r)/ *n.* (*midday meal*) обед; (*evening meal*) ужин; **at ~** за обедом/ужином; **ask s.o. to ~** пригла|шать, -сить кого-н. на обед/ужин; **have ~** обедать, по-/ужинать, по-; **what's for ~?** что на обед/ужин?

● *cpds.* **~-hour** *n.* час обеда/ужина; **~-jacket** *n.* смокинг; **~-party** *n.* званый обед; **~-plate** *n.* мелкая тарелка; **~-service, ~-set** *nn.* обеденный сервиз; **~-time** *n.* обеденное время; время ужина.

dinosaur /ˈdaɪnəˌsɔː(r)/ *n.* динозавр.

D

dint /dɪnt/ *n.* **1** (*dent*) вмя́тина. **2**: **by ~ of** посре́дством + *g.*; при по́мощи + *g.*
● *v.t.* ост|авля́ть, -а́вить след/вмя́тину в/на + *p.*

diocesan /daɪˈɒsɪs(ə)n/ *n.* (*bishop*) епи́скоп.
● *adj.* епархиа́льный.

diocese /ˈdaɪəsɪs/ *n.* епа́рхия.

diode /ˈdaɪəʊd/ *n.* дио́д.

dioptre /daɪˈɒptə(r)/ (*US* **diopter**) *n.* (*unit*) диоптри́я.

diorama /ˌdaɪəˈrɑːmə/ *n.* диора́ма.

dioxide /daɪˈɒksaɪd/ *n.* двуо́кись.

dip /dɪp/ *n.* **1** (*immersion*) погруже́ние; **lucky ~** лотере́йный бараба́н.
2 (*bathe*) ныря́ние; купа́ние; **have/take a ~** вы́купаться (*pf.*), попла́вать (*pf.*).
3 (*sheep ~*) дезинфици́рующий раство́р.
4 (*slope*) спуск, укло́н; **a ~ among the hills** низи́на между холмо́в.
5 (*cul.*) со́ус.
● *v.t.* (**dipped, dipping**) **1** (*immerse*) окун|а́ть, -у́ть; мак|а́ть, -ну́ть; погру|жа́ть, -зи́ть; **~ one's pen into ink** обма́к|ивать, -ну́ть перо́ в черни́ла; **~ sheep** купа́ть, вы- ове́ц в дезинфици́рующем раство́ре; **~ one's hand into a bag** запус|ка́ть, -ти́ть ру́ку в су́мку.
2 (*lower briefly*) приспус|ка́ть, -ти́ть; **~ headlights** (*Br.*) переключ|а́ть, -и́ть фа́ры на (*or* включ|а́ть, -и́ть) бли́жний свет.
● *v.i.* (**dipped, dipping**) **1** (*go below surface*) окун|а́ться, -у́ться; погру|жа́ться, -зи́ться; **the sun ~ped below the horizon** со́лнце скры́лось за горизо́нтом (*or* нырну́ло за горизо́нт).
2 (*fig.*): **~ into one's purse** раскоше́ли|ваться, -ться.
3 (*slope away*): **the (plot of) land ~s to the south** уча́сток име́ет накло́н к ю́гу.
4 (*scan, peer*) загля́|дывать, -ну́ть; **~ into the future** загля́|дывать, -ну́ть в бу́дущее; **I ~ped into the book** я загляну́л в э́ту кни́гу.
5 (*fall slightly or temporarily*) пон|ижа́ться, -и́зиться; **the road ~s here** здесь доро́га идёт под укло́н.
● *cpd.* **~-stick** *n.* уровнеме́р, щуп.

diphtheria /dɪfˈθɪərɪə/, *disp.* /dɪp-/ *n.* дифтери́я, дифтери́т.

diphthong /ˈdɪfθɒŋ/ *n.* дифто́нг.

diploma /dɪˈpləʊmə/ *n.* дипло́м (**in**: по + *d.*).

diplomacy /dɪpˈləʊməsɪ/ *n.* диплома́тия; (*tact*) диплома́ти́чность.

diplomat /ˈdɪpləˌmæt/ *n.* (*lit., fig.*) диплома́т.

diplomatic /ˌdɪpləˈmætɪk/ *adj.* (*lit., fig.*) дипломати́ческий; **~ corps** дипломати́ческий ко́рпус; **~ service** дипломати́ческая слу́жба.

dipper /ˈdɪpə(r)/ *n.* **1** (*ladle*) ковш, черпа́к; **the Big/Little D~** (*astron.*) Больша́я/Ма́лая Медве́дица. **2** (*bird*) оля́пка. **3** (*switchback*) америка́нские го́ры (*f. pl.*).

dippy /ˈdɪpɪ/ *adj.* (**dippier, dippiest**) (*sl.*) поме́шанный, чо́кнутый.

dipso /ˈdɪpsəʊ/ *n.* (*pl.* **~s**) алка́ш (*sl.*).

dipsomania /ˌdɪpsəˈmeɪnɪə/ *n.* алкоголи́зм.

dipsomaniac /ˌdɪpsəˈmeɪnɪˌæk/ *n.* алкого́лик.
● *adj.* алкоголи́ческий.

dire /ˈdaɪə(r)/ *adj.* ужа́сный; **he is in ~ need of help** он кра́йне нужда́ется в по́мощи.

direct /daɪˈrekt/, /dɪ-/ *adj.* (*straight; without intermediary*) прямо́й; (*straightforward*) прямо́й, непосре́дственный; **he has a ~ way of speaking** он говори́т всё пря́мо в лицо́; **the ~ opposite** по́лная противополо́жность; **~ current** постоя́нный ток; **~ flight** прямо́й/беспереса́дочный полёт/рейс.
● *adv.* пря́мо.
● *v.t.* **1** (*indicate the way*): **can you ~ me to the station?** вы не ска́жете, как пройти́ на вокза́л?
2 (*address*) адресова́ть (*impf., pf.*); напр|авля́ть, -а́вить; **I ~ed the letter to his bank** я адресова́л письмо́ в его́ банк; **my remarks were ~ed to him** мои́ замеча́ния бы́ли адресо́ваны ему́.
3 (*manage, control*) руководи́ть (*impf.*) + *i.*; **he ~ed the orchestra** он дирижи́ровал орке́стром; **he ~ed the play** он поста́вил пье́су; **the policeman ~s traffic** полице́йский регули́рует движе́ние.
4 (*command*) предпи́с|ывать, -а́ть; да|ва́ть, -ть указа́ние; **I ~ed him to take no notice** я веле́л ему́ не обраща́ть внима́ния.

direction /daɪˈrekʃ(ə)n/, /dɪ-/ *n.* **1** (*course, point of compass*) направле́ние; **in the ~ of London** по направле́нию (*or* в направле́нии) к Ло́ндону; **they dispersed in all ~s** они́ разошли́сь в ра́зные сто́роны; **he has a good sense of ~** он хорошо́ ориенти́руется. **2** (*pl., instructions*) указа́ния (*nt. pl.*); **I followed the ~s on the label** я сле́довал указа́ниям на ярлыке́. **3** (*command, control*) руково́дство. **4** (*theatr.*): **~ of a play** постано́вка/режиссу́ра пье́сы; **stage ~** а́вторская рема́рка. **5** (*to a jury*) напу́тствие прися́жным.
● *cpds.* **~-finder** *n.* радиопеленга́тор; **~-finding** *adj.*: **~-finding equipment** радиопеленга́торное обору́дование.

directional /daɪˈrekʃən(ə)l/, /dɪ-/ *adj.* напра́вленный.

directive /daɪˈrektɪv/, /dɪ-/ *n.* директи́ва, указа́ние.

directly /daɪˈrektlɪ/, /dɪ-/ *adv.* **1** (*in var. senses of direct*) пря́мо. **2** (*soon*): **I'll be there ~** я вско́ре/сейча́с же там бу́ду. **3** (*at once*) неме́дленно, то́тчас.
● *conj.* (*Br.*) как то́лько.

directness /daɪˈrektnɪs/, /dɪ-/ *n.* прямота́, открове́нность.

director /daɪˈrektə(r)/, /dɪ-/ *n.* **1** (*one who directs*) руководи́тель (*m.*). **2** (*of company etc.*) дире́ктор; **managing ~** управля́ющий; **~-general** (*Br.*) гла́вный дире́ктор, генера́льный дире́ктор. **3** (*theatr.*) режиссёр.

directorate /daɪˈrektərət/, /dɪ-/ *n.* (*group of directors*) директора́т; (*admin. body*) управле́ние.

directorial /ˌdaɪrekˈtɔːrɪəl/, /ˌdɪ-/ *adj.* дире́кторский.

directorship /daɪˈrektəʃɪp/, /dɪ-/ *n.* дире́кторство.

directory /daɪˈrektərɪ/, /dɪ-/ *n.* (*reference work*) спра́вочник, указа́тель (*m.*); **~ assistance** (*US*), **~ enquiries** (*Br.*) спра́вочная; **telephone ~** телефо́нная кни́га.

direness /ˈdaɪənɪs/ *n.* у́жас.

dirge /dɜːdʒ/ *n.* погреба́льное пе́ние.

dirigible /ˈdɪrɪdʒɪb(ə)l/, /dɪˈrɪdʒ-/ *n.* дирижа́бль (*m.*).

dirk /dɜːk/ *n.* кинжа́л.

dirt /dɜːt/ *n.* **1** (*unclean matter*) грязь; **this dress shows the ~** э́то пла́тье ма́ркое; **treat s.o. like ~** трети́ровать (*impf.*) кого́-н.; не счита́ться (*impf.*) с кем-н. **2** (*loose earth or soil*) грунт, земля́; **a ~ road** грунтова́я доро́га; **~ track** мотоцикле́тный трек.
3 (*obscenity*) непристо́йность, га́дость.
● *cpd.* **~-cheap** *adv.* по дешёвке, деше́вле па́реной ре́пы; *adj.* копе́ечный; **I bought the radio ~-cheap** я купи́л ра́дио по дешёвке.

dirtiness /ˈdɜːtɪnɪs/ *n.* грязь, га́дость.

dirty /dɜːtɪ/ *adj.* (**dirtier, dirtiest**) **1** (*not clean*) гря́зный. **2** (*rough, stormy*) бу́рный. **3** (*obscene*) поха́бный, па́костный; **~ story** поха́бный анекдо́т. **4** (*nasty*) гря́зный, га́дкий; **he played a ~ trick on me** он подложи́л мне свинью́; **he gave me a ~ look** (*coll.*) он посмотре́л на меня́ серди́то; **do your own ~ work!** я не бу́ду де́лать за вас ва́шу гря́зную рабо́ту.
● *v.t. & i.* грязни́ть(ся), за-; па́чкать(ся), за-.

disability /ˌdɪsəˈbɪlɪtɪ/ *n.* (*inability to work*) нетрудоспосо́бность; (*physical defect*) инвали́дность.

disable /dɪsˈeɪb(ə)l/ *v.t.* (*physically*) кале́чить, ис-; **~d soldier** инвали́д войны́; **the ship was ~d** кора́бль был вы́веден из стро́я.

disablement /dɪsˈeɪbəlmənt/ *n.* нетрудоспосо́бность; инвали́дность.

disabuse /ˌdɪsəˈbjuːz/ *v.t.* выводи́ть, вы́вести из заблужде́ния; **~ s.o. of something** разув|еря́ть, -е́рить кого́-н. в + *p.*

disadvantage /ˌdɪsədˈvɑːntɪdʒ/ *n.* невы́годное положе́ние; невы́годность; **be at a ~** ока́з|ываться, -а́ться в невы́годном положе́нии; **put s.o. at a ~** ста́вить, по- кого́-н. в невы́годное положе́ние.
● *v.t.* де́йствовать (*impf.*) в уще́рб + *d.*; **~d** (*underprivileged*) обездо́ленный.

disadvantageous /dɪsˌædvənˈteɪdʒəs/ *adj.* невы́годный.

disaffected /ˌdɪsəˈfektɪd/ *adj.* недово́льный.

disaffection /ˌdɪsəˈfekʃ(ə)n/ *n.* недово́льство.

disagree /ˌdɪsəˈgriː/ *v.i.* (**disagrees, disagreed, disagreeing**) **1** (*differ, not correspond*) расходи́ться (*impf.*) (с + *i.*); не соотве́тствовать (*impf.*) (**with**: + *d.*). **2** (*in opinion*) не согла|ша́ться, -си́ться; **I ~ with you** я с ва́ми не согла́сен; **the witnesses ~** свиде́тели расхо́дятся в показа́ниях. **3** (*have adverse effect*): **oysters ~ with me** я пло́хо переношу́ у́стриц.

disagreeable /ˌdɪsəˈgriːəb(ə)l/ *adj.* (*unpleasant*) неприя́тный, непривлека́тельный; (*of person*) неприве́тливый, неприя́зненный.

disagreeableness /ˌdɪsəˈgriːəbəlnɪs/ *n.* непривлека́тельность, неприве́тливость.

disagreement /ˌdɪsəˈgriːmənt/ *n.* разногла́сие, разла́д, несогла́сие.

disallow /ˌdɪsəˈlaʊ/ *v.t.* (*reject*) отклон|я́ть, -и́ть; (*goal*) не засч|и́тывать, -ита́ть.

disappear /ˌdɪsəˈpɪə(r)/ *v.i.* исч|еза́ть, -е́знуть; проп|ада́ть, -а́сть.

disappearance /ˌdɪsəˈpɪərəns/ *n.* исчезнове́ние.

disappoint /ˌdɪsəˈpɔɪnt/ *v.t.* разочаро́в|ывать, -а́ть; **he was ~ed at this** он был разочаро́ван э́тим; **I am ~ed in you** я в вас разочарова́лся.

disappointing /ˌdɪsəˈpɔɪntɪŋ/ *adj.* разочаро́вывающий; **the weather has been ~** пого́да была́ нева́жная.

disappointment /ˌdɪsəˈpɔɪntmənt/ *n.* **1** (*state of being disappointed*) разочарова́ние; **to my ~** к моему́ огорче́нию; **he met with ~** его́ пости́гло разочарова́ние. **2** (*person or thing that disappoints*): **he turned out a ~** он обману́л возлага́емые на него́ наде́жды.

disappro|bation /dɪsˌæprəˈbeɪʃ(ə)n/, **-val** /ˌdɪsəˈpruːv(ə)l/ *nn.* неодобре́ние.

disapprove /ˌdɪsəˈpruːv/ *v.i.* **~ of**: не одобря́ть; осужда́ть (*both impf.*).

● *v.t.* (*refuse to agree to*) отклон|я́ть, -и́ть.

disapproving /ˌdɪsəˈpruːvɪŋ/ *adj.* неодобри́тельный.

disarm /dɪsˈɑːm/ *v.t.* разоруж|а́ть, -и́ть; (*fig.*) обезору́жи|вать, -ть; **he ~s criticism** он обезору́живает свои́х кри́тиков.

● *v.i.* разоруж|а́ться, -и́ться.

disarmament /dɪsˈɑːməmənt/ *n.* разоруже́ние.

disarrange /ˌdɪsəˈreɪndʒ/ *v.t.* прив|оди́ть, -ести́ в беспоря́док.

disarray /ˌdɪsəˈreɪ/ *n.* смяте́ние, расстро́йство.

disassemble /ˌdɪsəˈsemb(ə)l/ *v.t.* раз|бира́ть, -обра́ть; демонти́ровать (*impf., pf.*).

disassembly /ˌdɪsəˈsemblɪ/ *n.* разбо́рка; демонта́ж.

disassociate /ˌdɪsəˈsəʊʃɪˌeɪt/, /-sɪˌeɪt/ = **dissociate**

disaster /dɪˈzɑːstə(r)/ *n.* бе́дствие; **he is courting ~** он наклика́ет беду́.

disastrous /dɪˈzɑːstrəs/ *adj.* ги́бельный, бе́дственный.

disastrousness /dɪˈzɑːstrəsnɪs/ *n.* ги́бельность.

disavow /ˌdɪsəˈvaʊ/ *v.t.* отрица́ть (*impf.*); отр|ека́ться, -е́чься от + *g.*

disavowal /ˌdɪsəˈvaʊəl/ *n.* отрица́ние; отрече́ние.

disband /dɪsˈbænd/ *v.t.* распус|ка́ть, -ти́ть; расформиро́в|ывать, -а́ть.

● *v.i.* расп|ада́ться, -а́сться; **the (theatre) company ~ed** тру́ппа распа́лась.

disbandment /dɪsˈbændmənt/ *n.* расформирова́ние, ро́спуск.

disbar /dɪsˈbɑː(r)/ *v.t.* (**disbarred, disbarring**) лиш|а́ть, -и́ть зва́ния адвока́та.

disbarment /dɪsˈbɑːmənt/ *n.* лише́ние зва́ния адвока́та.

disbelief /ˌdɪsbɪˈliːf/ *n.* неве́рие.

disbelieve /ˌdɪsbɪˈliːv/ *v.t.* (*person*) не ве́рить (*impf.*) + *d.*; (*account, evidence*) не ве́рить (*impf.*) + *d.* (*or* в + *a.*).

disburse /dɪsˈbɜːs/ *v.t.* выпла́чивать, вы́платить.

disbursement /dɪsˈbɜːsmənt/ *n.* (*act of paying*) опла́та; (*sum paid*) вы́плаченная су́мма.

disc /dɪsk/ (*US and comput.* **disk**) *n.* **1** (*round object*) диск; **the sun's ~** со́лнечный диск; **identity ~** (*mil.*) ли́чный знак. **2** (*gramophone record*) пласти́нка, диск. **3** (*med.*): **slipped ~** смеще́ние межпозвоно́чного ди́ска. **4** (*comput.*): **floppy ~** ги́бкий диск; **~ drive** дисково́д.

● *cpd.* **~-jockey** *n.* диск-жоке́й.

discard /dɪˈskɑːd/ *v.t.* выбра́сывать, вы́бросить; **~ winter clothing** сбр|а́сывать, -о́сить зи́мнюю оде́жду; **~ old beliefs** отбр|а́сывать, -о́сить ста́рые убежде́ния.

discern /dɪˈsɜːn/ *v.t.* разгля́д|ывать, -е́ть; рассм|а́тривать, -отре́ть; различ|а́ть, -и́ть.

discernible /dɪˌsɜːnˈɪb(ə)l/ *adj.* различи́мый.

discerning /dɪˈsɜːnɪŋ/ *adj.* проница́тельный.

discernment /dɪˈsɜːnmənt/ *n.* проница́тельность.

discharge *n.* /ˈdɪstʃɑːdʒ/ **1** (*unloading*) разгру́зка. **2** (*of fluid*) слив, (*of gas*) вы́брос; (*elec.*) разря́д. **3** (*med.*) выделе́ние; (*matter discharged*) выделе́ния (*pl.*). **4** (*performance, e.g. of duty*) исполне́ние; (*of a debt*) упла́та. **5** (*release, dismissal*) увольне́ние, освобожде́ние; (*from the army*) демобилиза́ция, увольне́ние в запа́с. **6** (*firing of a gun*) вы́стрел, залп.

● *v.t.* /dɪsˈtʃɑːdʒ/ **1** (*unload*) разгру|жа́ть, -зи́ть. **2** (*emit liquid*) слива́ть, слить; спус|ка́ть, -ти́ть; (*emit current*) разря|жа́ть, -ди́ть; **the clouds ~ electricity** облака́ разряжа́ются электри́чеством. **3** (*med.*) выделя́ть, вы́делить. **4** (*missiles*) выпуска́ть, вы́пустить; **~ a rifle** разря|жа́ть, -ди́ть. **5** (*release, dismiss*) (*from the army*) демобилизова́ть (*impf., pf.*); (*from hospital*) выпи́сывать, вы́писать; (*from service*) ув|ольня́ть, -о́лить.

disciple /dɪˈsaɪp(ə)l/ *n.* учени́|к (*fem.* -ца); после́дователь (*fem.* -ница); (*relig.*) апо́стол.

discipleship /dɪˈsaɪpəlʃɪp/ *n.* учени́чество.

disciplinarian /ˌdɪsɪplɪˈneərɪən/ *n.* сторо́нник дисципли́ны; **he is a good ~** он уме́ет подде́рживать дисципли́ну.

disciplinary /ˈdɪsɪplɪnərɪ/, /-ˈplɪnərɪ/ *adj.* дисциплина́рный; **take ~ action** прин|има́ть, -я́ть дисциплина́рные ме́ры.

discipline /ˈdɪsɪplɪn/ *n.* (*good order; branch of studies*) дисципли́на.

● *v.t.* дисциплини́ровать (*impf., pf.*).

disclaim /dɪsˈkleɪm/ *v.t.* отр|ека́ться, -е́чься от + *g.*; отка́з|ываться, -а́ться от + *g.*

disclaimer /dɪsˈkleɪmə(r)/ *n.* отрече́ние, отка́з.

disclose /dɪsˈkləʊz/ *v.t.* (*make known*) раскр|ыва́ть, -ы́ть; (*uncover*) откр|ыва́ть, -ы́ть; (*reveal*) разоблач|а́ть, -и́ть.

disclosure /dɪsˈkləʊʒə(r)/ *n.* раскры́тие, откры́тие, разоблаче́ние.

disco /ˈdɪskəʊ/ *n.* (*pl.* **~s**) (*coll.*) = **discotheque**

discolor (*US*) = **discolour**

discoloration /dɪsˌkʌləˈreɪʃ(ə)n/ *n.* (*change of colour*) измене́ние цве́та; (*loss of colour*) обесцве́чивание; (*stains*) разво́д|ы (*pl., g.* -ов).

discolour /dɪsˈkʌlə(r)/ (*US* **discolor**) *v.i.* (*lose colour*) обесцве́|чиваться, -титься.

● *v.t.* (*make change colour*) меня́ть, по- цвет + *g.*; **rain discoloured the water** дождь поменя́л цвет воды́; **smoking had discoloured his teeth** его́ зу́бы пожелте́ли от куре́ния; (*make lose colour*) обесцве́|чивать, -тить.

discomfit /dɪsˈkʌmfɪt/ *v.t.* (**discomfited, discomfiting**) (*disconcert*) сму|ща́ть, -ти́ть; прив|оди́ть, -ести́ в замеша́тельство.

discomfiture /dɪsˈkʌmfɪtjə(r)/ *n.* смуще́ние, замеша́тельство.

discomfort /dɪsˈkʌmfət/ *n.* неудо́бство, диском́форт.

● *v.t.* причин|я́ть, -и́ть неудо́бство + *d.*; стесн|я́ть, -и́ть.

discommode /ˌdɪskəˈməʊd/ *v.t.* причин|я́ть, -и́ть неудо́бство + *d.*

discompose /ˌdɪskəmˈpəʊz/ *v.t.* волнова́ть, вз-; трево́жить, вс-.

discomposure /ˌdɪskəmˈpəʊʒə(r)/ *n.* волне́ние, трево́га.

disconcert /ˌdɪskənˈsɜːt/ *v.t.* волнова́ть, вз-.

disconnect /ˌdɪskəˈnekt/ *v.t.* (*two roughly equal things*) разъедин|я́ть, -и́ть; (*small part from larger part*) отсоедин|я́ть, -и́ть; (*gas etc.*) отключ|а́ть, -и́ть; **we were ~ed** (*telephone*) нас разъедини́ли/ прерва́ли.

disconnected /ˌdɪskəˈnektɪd/ *adj.* **1** (*tech.*) разъединённый, вы́ключенный. **2** (*ideas etc.*) обры́вочный, бессвя́зный.

disconnection /ˌdɪskəˈnekʃ(ə)n/ *n.* разъедине́ние, отключе́ние.

disconsolate /dɪsˈkɒnsələt/ *adj.* неуте́шный.

discontent /ˌdɪskənˈtent/ *n.* недово́льство.

discontented /ˌdɪskənˈtentɪd/ *adj.* недово́льный.

discontinuance /ˌdɪskənˈtɪnjuːəns/ *n.* прекраще́ние.

discontinue /ˌdɪskənˈtɪnjuː/ *v.t.* (**discontinues, discontinued, discontinuing**) прекра|ща́ть, -ти́ть.

discontinuity /dɪsˌkɒntɪˈnjuːɪtɪ/ *n.* отсу́тствие непреры́вности.

discontinuous /ˌdɪskənˈtɪnjʊəs/ *adj.* прерыва́ющийся, преры́вистый.

discord /ˈdɪskɔːd/ *n.* (*disagreement*) разногла́сие; (*disharmony*) разла́д, раздо́р; (*mus.*) диссона́нс.

discordance /dɪˈskɔːdəns/ *n.* разногла́сие, разла́д.

discordant /dɪˈskɔːd(ə)nt/ *adj.* несогла́сный; (*inharmonious*) диссони́рующий; нестро́йный.

discotheque /ˈdɪskəˌtek/ *n.* дискоте́ка.

discount *n.* /ˈdɪskaʊnt/ **1** ски́дка. **2** (*on bill of exchange etc.*) диско́нт.

● *v.t.* /dɪsˈkaʊnt/ (*reduce price of*) снижа́ть, сни́зить це́ну на + *a.*; (*bill of exchange etc.*) дисконти́ровать (*impf., pf.*); (*fig., treat sceptically*) отн|оси́ться, -ести́сь с недове́рием к + *d.*; **I ~ed his story** я отнёсся к его́ расска́зу с недове́рием.

discourage /dɪˈskʌrɪdʒ/ *v.t.* (*deprive of confidence*) обескура́жи|вать, -ть; (*dissuade*) отгов|а́ривать, -ори́ть.

discouragement /dɪˈskʌrɪdʒmənt/ *n.* обескура́живание; (*dissuasion*) отгова́ривание.

discourse[1] /ˈdɪskɔːs/, /-ˈskɔːs/ *n.* речь, рассужде́ние.

discourse[2] /dɪˈskɔːs/ *v.i.* рассужда́ть (*impf.*).

discourteous /dɪsˈkɜːtɪəs/ *adj.* неве́жливый.

discourtesy /dɪsˈkɜːtəsɪ/ *n.* неве́жливость.

discover /dɪˈskʌvə(r)/ *v.t.* (*find*) обнару́жи|вать, -ть; (*place, substance, fact*) откр|ыва́ть, -ы́ть; раскр|ыва́ть, -ы́ть; (*find out*) узн|ава́ть, -а́ть; выясня́ть, вы́яснить.

discoverer /dɪˈskʌvərə(r)/ *n.* иссле́дователь (*m.*) (но́вых земе́ль); (перво)открыва́тель (*m.*); **she was the ~ of radium** она́ откры́ла ра́дий.

discovery /dɪˈskʌvərɪ/ *n.* откры́тие; обнаруже́ние.

discredit /dɪsˈkredɪt/ *n.* (*loss of repute*) дискредита́ция; **bring s.o. into ~** (*or* **bring ~ upon s.o.**) компромети́ровать, с- кого́-н.; дискредити́ровать (*impf., pf.*) кого́-н.; **he is a ~ to the school** он дискредити́рует шко́лу.

● *v.t.* (**discredited, discrediting**) дискредити́ровать (*impf., pf.*).

discreditable /dɪsˈkredɪtəb(ə)l/ *adj.* дискредити́рующий; (*shameful*) позо́рный.

discreet /dɪˈskriːt/ *adj.* (**discreeter, discreetest**) осмотри́тельный; (*tactful*) такти́чный; **a ~ silence** благоразу́мное молча́ние.

discrepancy /dɪsˈkrepənsɪ/ *n.* расхожде́ние, разногла́сие, противоре́чие.

discrepant /dɪˈskrepənt/ *adj.* противоречи́вый.

discrete /dɪˈskriːt/ *adj.* обосо́бленный.

discreteness /dɪˈskriːtnɪs/ *n.* обосо́бленность.

discretion /dɪˈskreʃ(ə)n/ *n.* **1** (*prudence, good judgment*) осмотри́тельность, осторо́жность, благоразу́мие; **~ is the better part of valour** благоразу́мие — гла́вное досто́инство хра́брости; **years/age of ~** во́зраст, с кото́рого челове́к счита́ется отве́тственным за свои́ посту́пки. **2** (*freedom to judge*) усмотре́ние; **I leave this to your ~** я оставля́ю э́то на ва́ше усмотре́ние; **at ~** по усмотре́нию; **I gave him wide ~** я дал ему́ широ́кие полномо́чия.

discretionary /dɪˈskreʃənərɪ/ *adj.* дискрецио́нный.

discriminate /dɪˈskrɪmɪˌneɪt/ *v.t.* (*distinguish*) отлич|а́ть, -и́ть; различ|а́ть, -и́ть.

● *v.i.*: **~ against** дискримини́ровать (*impf., pf.*).

discriminating /dɪˈskrɪmɪˌneɪtɪŋ/ *adj.* разбо́рчивый; **~ taste** то́нкий/разбо́рчивый вкус.

discrimination /dɪˌskrɪmɪˈneɪʃ(ə)n/ *n.* (*judgment, taste*) разбо́рчивость; (*bias*) дискримина́ция; **~ against women** дискримина́ция же́нщин.

discriminatory /dɪˈskrɪmɪnətərɪ/ *adj.* пристра́стный.

discursive /dɪˈskɜːsɪv/ *adj.* (*digressive*) разбро́санный.

discursiveness /dɪˈskɜːsɪvnɪs/ *n.* разбро́санность.

discus /ˈdɪskəs/ *n.* (*pl.* **~es**) (*sport*) диск.

discuss /dɪˈskʌs/ *v.t.* дискути́ровать (*impf.*); обсу|жда́ть, -ди́ть.

discussion /dɪˈskʌʃ(ə)n/ *n.* обсужде́ние, диску́ссия; **the question is under ~** вопро́с обсужда́ется/рассма́тривается.

disdain /dɪsˈdeɪn/ *n.* презре́ние.

● *v.t.* през|ира́ть, -ре́ть; пренебр|ега́ть, -е́чь + *i.*; **he ~ed to reply** он не соизво́лил отве́тить.

disdainful /dɪsˈdeɪnfʊl/ *adj.* презри́тельный.

disease /dɪˈziːz/ *n.* боле́знь.

diseased /dɪˈziːzd/ *adj.* (*lit., fig.*) больно́й.

disembark /ˌdɪsɪmˈbɑːk/ (*also* **debark**) *v.t. & i.* выса́живать(ся), высадить(ся).

disembarkation /ˌdɪsɪmbɑːˈkeɪʃ(ə)n/ (*also* **debarkation**) *nn.* высадка, вы́грузка.

disembod|y /ˌdɪsɪmˈbɒdɪ/ *v.t.* (*set free from the body*) освобо|жда́ть, -ди́ть от теле́сной оболо́чки; **a ~ied spirit** освобождённая душа́.

disembowel /ˌdɪsɪmˈbaʊəl/ *v.t.* (**disembowelled, disembowelling;** *US* **disemboweled, disemboweling**) потроши́ть, вы-.

disembowelment /ˌdɪsɪmˈbaʊəlmənt/ *n.* потроше́ние.

disenchant /ˌdɪsɪnˈtʃɑːnt/ *v.t.* разочаро́в|ывать, -а́ть.

disenchantment /ˌdɪsɪnˈtʃɑːntmənt/ *n.* разочарова́ние.

disendow /ˌdɪsɪnˈdaʊ/ *v.t.* лиш|а́ть, -и́ть поже́ртвований.

disenfranchise /ˌdɪsɪnˈfræntʃaɪz/ *v.t.* = **disfranchise**

disengage /ˌdɪsɪnˈgeɪdʒ/ *v.t.* высвобожда́ть, вы́свободить; освобо|жда́ть, -ди́ть; (*clutch*) расцеп|ля́ть, -и́ть; (*mil.*) выводи́ть, вы́вести из бо́я.

● *v.i.* высвобожда́ться, вы́свободиться; освобо|жда́ться, -ди́ться; (*mil.*) выходи́ть, вы́йти из бо́я.

disengagement /ˌdɪsɪnˈgeɪdʒmənt/ *n.* (*disentangling*) освобожде́ние, высвобожде́ние; (*mil.*) вы́ход из бо́я; взаи́мный вы́вод вооружённых сил.

disentangle /ˌdɪsɪnˈtæŋg(ə)l/ *v.t. & i.* распу́т|ывать(ся), -ать(ся); выпу́тывать(ся), вы́путать(ся).

disentanglement /ˌdɪsɪnˈtæŋgəlmənt/ *n.* распу́тывание, выпу́тывание.

disestablish /ˌdɪsɪˈstæblɪʃ/ *v.t.* (*eccl.*) отдел|я́ть, -и́ть от госуда́рства (*церковь*).

disestablishment /ˌdɪsɪˈstæblɪʃmənt/ *n.* отделе́ние от госуда́рства (*церкви*).

disfavour /dɪsˈfeɪvə(r)/ (*US* **disfavor**) *n.* неми́лость, опа́ла.

disfigure /dɪsˈfɪgə(r)/ *v.t.* уро́довать, из-; обезобра́|живать, -зить; **she was ~d in the accident** она́ была́ изуро́дована в катастро́фе.

disfigurement /dɪsˈfɪgərmənt/ *n.* (*act*) обезобра́живание; (*result*) уро́дство.

disfranchise /dɪsˈfræntʃaɪz/ *v.t.* лиш|а́ть, -и́ть избира́тельного пра́ва.

disfranchisement /dɪsˈfræntʃaɪzmənt/ *n.* лише́ние избира́тельного пра́ва.

disgorge /dɪsˈgɔːdʒ/ *v.t.* изв|ерга́ть, -е́ргнуть.

● *v.i.* (*of river etc.*) впада́ть (*impf.*).

disgrace /dɪsˈgreɪs/ *n.* **1** (*loss of respect*) бесче́стье, позо́р; **bring ~ upon, bring into ~** навл|ека́ть, -е́чь позо́р на + *a.* **2** (*disfavour*) неми́лость, опа́ла; **he is in ~** он в неми́лости. **3** (*cause of shame*) позо́р; **he is a ~ to the school** он позо́р для всей шко́лы.

● *v.t.* позо́рить, о-; (*dismiss with ignominy*) разжа́ловать (*pf.*); (*bring shame upon*): **he ~d the family name** он покры́л позо́ром (*or* он опозо́рил) свою́ семью́.

disgraceful /dɪsˈgreɪsfʊl/ *adj.* позо́рный, недосто́йный.

disgruntled /dɪsˈgrʌnt(ə)ld/ *adj.* недово́льный; раздражённый.

disguise /dɪsˈgaɪz/ *n.* **1** (*clothing*) маскиро́вка; **in the ~ of a beggar** переоде́тый ни́щим. **2** (*concealment*) маскиро́вка, личи́на; **it is a blessing in ~** не́ было бы сча́стья, да несча́стье помогло́.

● *v.t.* (*weapons, objects, intentions*) маскирова́ть, за-; (*with clothing*) переод|ева́ть, -е́ть; (*emotions*) скрыва́ть, скрыть; **he ~d his voice/handwriting** он измени́л го́лос/по́черк; **a door ~d as a bookcase** потайна́я дверь в ви́де кни́жного шка́фа; (*fig.*): **he ~d his feelings** он скрыл свои́ чу́вства; **there is no disguising the fact that . . .** для вся́кого очеви́дно, что. . .

disgust /dɪsˈgʌst/ *n.* отвраще́ние; **he resigned in ~** он поки́нул пост в возмуще́нии.

● *v.t.* внуш|а́ть, -и́ть отвраще́ние +*d.*; **I am ~ed by his behaviour** (*Br.*), **behavior** (*US*) я возмущён его́ поведе́нием.

disgusting /dɪsˈgʌstɪŋ/ *adj.* отврати́тельный.

dish /dɪʃ/ *n.* **1** (*vessel*) (*for cooking*) (ку́хонная) посу́да; (*flat, for serving*) блю́до; **wash, do the ~es** мыть, вы́- посу́ду. **2** (*contents*) блю́до; (*type of food*) блю́до, ку́шанье. **3** (*coll., TV satellite ~*) таре́лка.

● *v.t.* (*serve; also ~* **up**) под|ава́ть, -а́ть к столу́; (*fig.*) под|ава́ть, -а́ть; преподн|оси́ть, -ести́; **~ out** (*food*) ра|скла́дывать, -зложи́ть по таре́лкам (*edy*); выкла́дывать, вы́ложить на блю́до (*edy*).

● *cpds.* **~-cloth** *n.* ку́хонная/посу́дная тря́пка; **~-towel** (*US*) *n.* ку́хонное/посу́дное полоте́нце; **~-washer** *n.* (*woman*) судомо́йка; (*machine*) посудомо́ечная маши́на; **~-water** *n.* помо́|и (*pl., g.* -ев).

disharmony /dɪsˈhɑːmənɪ/ *n.* дисгармо́ния, разла́д, разногла́сие.

dishearten /dɪsˈhɑːt(ə)n/ *v.t.* прив|оди́ть, -ести́ в уны́ние; **I was ~ed** я упа́л ду́хом.

dishevelled /dɪˈʃev(ə)ld/ (*US* **disheveled**) *adj.* взъеро́шенный, всклоко́ченный, растрёпанный.

dishevelment /dɪˈʃev(ə)lmənt/ *n.* взъеро́шенность, всклоко́ченность, растрёпанность.

dishonest /dɪsˈɒnɪst/ *adj.* нече́стный, бесче́стный.

dishonesty /dɪsˈɒnɪstɪ/ *n.* нече́стность, бесче́стность.

dishonour /dɪsˈɒnə(r)/ (*US* **dishonor**) *n.* бесче́стье, позо́р; **he brought ~ on his family** он навлёк на свою́ семью́ позо́р.

● *v.t.* бесче́стить, о-; позо́рить, о-; **~ one's promise** не сде́рживать, сдержа́ть обеща́ния; (*comm.*): **~ a bill** отка́з|ывать, -а́ть в акце́пте ве́кселя.

dishonourable /dɪsˈɒnərəb(ə)l/ (*US* **dishonorable**) *adj.* бесче́стный.

dishy /ˈdɪʃɪ/ *adj.* (**dishier, dishiest**) (*Br. coll.*) аппети́тный, привлека́тельный.

disillusion /ˌdɪsɪˈluːʒ(ə)n/, /-ˈljuːʒ(ə)n/ *v.t.* разочаро́в|ывать, -а́ть; разр|уша́ть, -у́шить иллю́зии +*g.*

disillusionment /ˌdɪsɪˈluːʒənmənt/, /-ˈljuːʒənmənt/ *n.* разочарова́ние; утра́та иллю́зий.

disincentive /ˌdɪsɪnˈsentɪv/ *n.* сде́рживающее обстоя́тельство.

disinclination /ˌdɪsɪnklɪˈneɪʃ(ə)n/ *n.* нежела́ние, неохо́та.

disincline /ˌdɪsɪnˈklaɪn/ *v.t.* отб|ива́ть, -и́ть чью-н. охо́ту к+*d.*; **he was ~d to help me** ему́ не хоте́лось мне помо́чь.

disinfect /ˌdɪsɪnˈfekt/ *v.t.* дезинфици́ровать (*impf., pf.*); обеззара́|живать, -зить.

disinfectant /ˌdɪsɪnˈfekt(ə)nt/ *n.* дезинфици́рующее сре́дство.

disinfection /ˌdɪsɪnˈfekʃ(ə)n/ *n.* дезинфе́кция.

disinformation /ˌdɪsɪnfəˈmeɪʃ(ə)n/ *n.* дезинформа́ция.

disingenuous /ˌdɪsɪnˈdʒenjʊəs/ *adj.* неи́скренний.

disingenuousness /ˌdɪsɪnˈdʒenjʊəsnɪs/ *n.* неи́скренность.

disinherit /ˌdɪsɪnˈherɪt/ *v.t.* (**disinherited, disinheriting**) лиш|а́ть, -и́ть насле́дства.

disinheritance /ˌdɪsɪnˈherɪtəns/ *n.* лише́ние насле́дства.

disintegrate /dɪsˈɪntɪˌgreɪt/ *v.t.* прив|оди́ть, -ести́ к распа́ду дезинтегра́ции.

● *v.i.* расп|ада́ться, -а́сться.

disintegration /dɪsˌɪntɪˈgreɪʃ(ə)n/ *n.* дезинтегра́ция, распа́д.

disinter /ˌdɪsɪnˈtɜː(r)/ *v.t.* (**disinterred, disinterring**) эксгуми́ровать (*impf., pf.*).

disinterest /dɪsˈɪntrɪst/ *n.* **1** (*lack of bias*) беспристра́стие. **2** (*lack of self-interest*) бескоры́стие. **3** (*lack of concern*) незаинтересо́ванность; безуча́стность.

disinterested /dɪsˈɪntrɪstɪd/ *adj.* **1** (*unprejudiced*) беспристра́стный. **2** (*not self-seeking*) бескоры́стный. **3** (*coll.*): **he is ~ in ballet** он не интересу́ется бале́том.

disinterestedness /dɪsˈɪntrɪstɪdnɪs/ *n.* беспристра́стие; бескоры́стие; отсу́тствие интере́са.

disinterment /ˌdɪsɪnˈtɜːmənt/ *n.* эксгума́ция.

disinvestment /ˌdɪsɪnˈvestmənt/ *n.* (*econ.*) сокраще́ние капиталовложе́ний.

disjoin /dɪsˈdʒɔɪn/ *v.t.* разъедин|я́ть, -и́ть.

disjointed /dɪsˈdʒɔɪntɪd/ *adj.* (*fig.*) бессвя́зный, несвя́зный.

disjunction /dɪsˈdʒʌŋkʃ(ə)n/ *n.* разделе́ние, разъедине́ние.

disjunctive /dɪsˈdʒʌŋktɪv/ *adj.* (*separating*) разъединя́ющий; (*gram.*) раздели́тельный.

disk /dɪsk/ (*US, comput.*) = **disc**

diskette /dɪˈsket/ *n.* (*comput.*) диске́та.

dislikable /dɪsˈlaɪkəb(ə)l/ *adj.* неприя́тный, антипати́чный, несимпати́чный.

dislike /dɪsˈlaɪk/ *n.* неприя́знь, нелюбо́вь, нерасположе́ние, антипа́тия; **I took a ~ to him** я невзлюби́л его́.

● *v.t.* не люби́ть (*impf.*) +*g.*; недолю́бливать (*impf.*) +*a. or g.*; **I ~ having to go** мне не хо́чется *or* я не располо́жен идти́; **he made himself ~d** он вы́звал к себе́ неприя́знь.

dislocate /ˈdɪsləˌkeɪt/ *v.t.* вы́вихнуть (*pf.*); (*fig.*): **traffic was ~d** движе́ние бы́ло нару́шено.

dislocation /ˌdɪsləˈkeɪʃ(ə)n/ *n.* вы́вих; наруше́ние.

dislodge /dɪsˈlɒdʒ/ *v.t.* сме|ща́ть, -сти́ть; (*fig.*) вытесня́ть, вы́теснить.

dislodgement /dɪsˈlɒdʒmənt/ *n.* смеще́ние, вытесне́ние.

disloyal /dɪsˈlɔɪəl/ *adj.* нелоя́льный, неве́рный.

disloyalty /dɪsˈlɔɪəltɪ/ *n.* нелоя́льность, неве́рность.

dismal /ˈdɪzm(ə)l/ *adj.* мра́чный, уны́лый, гнету́щий.

dismalness /ˈdɪzməlnɪs/ *n.* мра́чность, уны́лость.

dismantle /dɪsˈmænt(ə)l/ *v.t.* (*strip of defences etc.*) демонти́ровать (*impf., pf.*); (*take to pieces*) раз|бира́ть, -обра́ть.

dismay /dɪsˈmeɪ/ *n.* смяте́ние, (*extreme*) потрясе́ние.

● *v.t.* прив|оди́ть, -ести́ в смяте́ние; потряс|а́ть, -ти́.

dismember /dɪsˈmembə(r)/ *v.t.* расчлен|я́ть, -и́ть; (*fig.*) раздел|я́ть, -и́ть.

dismemberment /dɪsˈmembəmənt/ *n.* расчлене́ние, разделе́ние.

dismiss /dɪsˈmɪs/ *v.t.* **1** (*send away*) (*a group*) распус|ка́ть, -ти́ть; (*let go*) отпус|ка́ть, -ти́ть; **he ~ed her with a nod** он отпусти́л её кивко́м головы́. **2** (*discharge from service*) ув|ольня́ть, -о́лить; удал|я́ть, -и́ть. **3** (*put out of consideration, reject*): **he ~ed it from his mind** он вы́бросил э́то из головы́; **the argument is not to be ~ed lightly** нельзя́ от э́того до́вода про́сто отмахну́ться; **I ~ed the idea** я оста́вил э́ту мысль. **4** (*leg.*): (*a case*) прекра|ща́ть, -ти́ть; (*an appeal*) отклон|я́ть, -и́ть.

dismissal /dɪsˈmɪsəl/ *n.* (*of a goup of people*) ро́спуск; (*from service*) увольне́ние.

dismissive /dɪsˈmɪsɪv/ *adj.* (*contemptuous*) презри́тельный.

dismount /dɪsˈmaʊnt/ *v.i.* (*from horse*) спе́ши|ваться, -ться; (*from bicycle*) слез|а́ть, -ть.

disobedience /ˌdɪsəˈbiːdɪəns/ *n.* неповинове́ние, непослуша́ние.

disobedient /ˌdɪsəˈbiːdɪənt/ *adj.* непослу́шный.

disobey /ˌdɪsəˈbeɪ/ *v.t.* не слу́шаться, по- +*g.*; не повинова́ться (*impf., pf.*) +*d.*; **my orders were ~ed** мои́ приказа́ния не́ были вы́полнены.

disoblige /ˌdɪsəˈblaɪdʒ/ *v.t.* не счита́ться, по- с жела́ниями +*g.*; поступ|а́ть, -и́ть нелюбе́зно с+*i.*

D

disobliging /ˌdɪsəˈblaɪdʒɪŋ/ *adj.* нелюбе́зный.

disorder /dɪsˈɔːdə(r)/ *n.* (*untidiness*) беспоря́док; (*confusion*) ха́ос, неразбери́ха; (*riot*) беспоря́дки (*m. pl.*); (*med.*) расстро́йство; **mental ~** психи́ческое наруше́ние/расстро́йство.

● *v.t.* расстр|а́ивать, -о́ить; прив|оди́ть, -ести́ в беспоря́док.

disorderliness /dɪsˈɔːdəlɪnɪs/ *n.* беспоря́док; (*unruliness*) бу́йство.

disorderly /dɪsˈɔːdəlɪ/ *adj.* (*untidy*) беспоря́дочный; (*unruly*) бу́йный; **~ conduct** хулига́нство.

disorganization /dɪsˌɔːgənaɪˈzeɪʃ(ə)n/ *n.* дезорганиза́ция.

disorganize /dɪsˈɔːgəˌnaɪz/ *v.t.* дезорганизова́ть (*impf., pf.*).

disorient(ate) /dɪsˈɔːrɪənˌteɪt/ *v.t.* дезориенти́ровать (*impf., pf.*).

disorientation /dɪsˌɔːrɪənˈteɪʃ(ə)n/ *n.* дезориента́ция.

disown /dɪsˈəʊn/ *v.t.* отка́з|ываться, -а́ться от + *g.*; отр|ека́ться, -е́чься от + *g.*

disownment /dɪsˈəʊnmənt/ *n.* отка́з, отрече́ние (от + *g.*).

disparage /dɪˈspærɪdʒ/ *v.t.* (*belittle*) преум|еньша́ть, -е́ньшить; говори́ть (*impf.*) с пренебреже́нием о + *p.*

disparagement /dɪˈspærɪdʒmənt/ *n.* преуменьше́ние.

disparaging /dɪˈspærɪdʒɪŋ/ *adj.* пренебрежи́тельный.

disparate /ˈdɪspərət/ *adj.* несхо́жий.

disparity /dɪˈspærɪtɪ/ *n.* расхожде́ние; (*incongruity*) несоотве́тствие.

dispassionate /dɪˈspæʃənət/ *adj.* бесстра́стный.

dispassionateness /dɪˈspæʃənətnɪs/ *n.* бесстра́стность.

dispatch, despatch /dɪˈspætʃ/ *n.* **1** (*sending off*) отпра́вка. **2** (*message*) депе́ша, донесе́ние; (*for a newspaper*) сообще́ние; **he was mentioned in ~es** он был отме́чен в депе́шах. **3** (*promptitude*) быстрота́.

● *v.t.* **1** (*send off*) отпр|авля́ть, -а́вить. **2** (*deal with, e.g. business*) спр|авля́ться, -а́виться с + *i.* **3** (*kill*) поко́нчить (*pf.*) с + *i.*; отпр|авля́ть, -а́вить на тот свет (*coll.*).

● *cpds.* **~-box** *n.* вали́за (для официа́льных бума́г); **~-rider** *n.* курье́р.

dispatcher /dɪˈspætʃə(r)/ *n.* (*sender*) отправи́тель (*m.*); (*regulator*) диспе́тчер.

dispel /dɪˈspel/ *v.t.* (**dispelled, dispelling**) рассе́|ивать, -ять.

dispensable /dɪˈspensəb(ə)l/ *adj.* необяза́тельный.

dispensary /dɪˈspensərɪ/ *n.* апте́ка; (*clinic*) амбулато́рия.

dispensation /ˌdɪspenˈseɪʃ(ə)n/ *n.* **1** (*dealing out*) разда́ча. **2** (*order*) зако́н; **under the Mosaic ~** по моисе́еву зако́ну. **3** (*exemption*) освобожде́ние, исключе́ние; (*permission*) разреше́ние.

dispens|e /dɪˈspens/ *v.t.* **1** (*deal out*) разд|ава́ть, -а́ть. **2** (*of prescription*) пригот|овля́ть, -о́вить; **~ing chemist** (*Br.*) апте́карь (*m.*), фармаце́вт. **3** (*release*) освобо|жда́ть, -ди́ть (*от чего*).

● *v.i.*: **~ with** (*do without*) об|ходи́ться, -ойти́сь без + *g.*

dispenser /dɪˈspensə(r)/ *n.* **1** (*one who deals out*) раздаю́щий, распределя́ющий; **~ of justice** отправля́ющий правосу́дие. **2** (*of medicines*) фармаце́вт. **3** (*machine*) торго́вый автома́т; (*container*) доза́тор; **cash ~** банкома́т; **drinks ~** автома́т по прода́же напи́тков; **toilet-paper ~** доза́тор туале́тной бума́ги.

dispers|al /dɪˈspɜːsəl/, **-ion** /dɪˈspɜːʃ(ə)n/ *nn.* рассредото́чение, рассе́ивание; разго́н.

disperse /dɪˈspɜːs/ *v.t.* рассе́|ивать, -ять; раз|гоня́ть, -огна́ть; **the policeman ~d the crowd** полице́йский разогна́л толпу́; **the troops were ~d over a wide front** войска́ бы́ли рассредото́чены по широ́кому фро́нту.

● *v.i.* рассе́|иваться, -яться; ра|сходи́ться, -зойти́сь.

dispersion /dɪˈspɜːʃ(ə)n/ *n.* = **dispersal**

dispirit /dɪˈspɪrɪt/ *v.t.* удруч|а́ть, -и́ть; прив|оди́ть, -ести́ в уны́ние.

displace /dɪsˈpleɪs/ *v.t.* **1** (*put in wrong place*) сме|ща́ть, -сти́ть; **~d persons** перемещённые ли́ца. **2** (*replace*) заме|ща́ть, -сти́ть; (*remove from office*) сме|ща́ть, -сти́ть; (*oust*) вытесня́ть, вы́теснить; **he ~d his rival in her affections** он вы́теснил своего́ сопе́рника из её се́рдца.

displacement /dɪsˈpleɪsmənt/ *n.* (*ousting*) смеще́ние, вытесне́ние; (*replacement*) замеще́ние; (*of ship*) водоизмеще́ние; (*geol.*) сдвиг.

display /dɪˈspleɪ/ *n.* **1** (*manifestation*) пока́з, проявле́ние. **2** (*ostentation*) хвастовство́; **he made a ~ of his wealth** он кичи́лся свои́м бога́тством. **3** (*of goods etc.*) вы́ставка; **there was a fine ~ of flowers at the show** на вы́ставке демонстри́ровалось мно́го изуми́тельных цвето́в. **4** (*of computer*) диспле́й.

● *v.t.* (*quality, emotion*) проявл|я́ть, -и́ть; обнару́жи|вать, -ть; (*on screen, in a picture*) демонстри́ровать, про-; пок|а́зывать, -аза́ть; (*goods etc.*) выставля́ть, вы́ставить; **he ~s his ignorance** он проявля́ет *or* выка́зывает своё неве́жество.

displease /dɪsˈpliːz/ *v.t.* не нра́виться (*impf.*) + *d.*; серди́ть, рас-; вызыва́ть, вы́звать недово́льство у + *g.*; **he was ~d at this** он был недово́лен э́тим; э́то вы́звало у него́ недово́льство; **I am ~d with you** я недово́лен ва́ми.

displeasing /dɪsˈpliːzɪŋ/ *adj.* неприя́тный; доса́дный.

displeasure /dɪsˈpleʒə(r)/ *n.* недово́льство, неудово́льствие; **incur s.o.'s ~** навл|ека́ть, -е́чь на себя́ (*or* вызыва́ть, вы́звать) чьё-н. недово́льство.

disport /dɪˈspɔːt/ *v.t.*: **~ o.s.** резви́ться (*impf.*).

disposable /dɪˈspəʊzəb(ə)l/ *adj.* ра́зовый, одноразо́вый; одноразо́вого по́льзования (*pred.*).

disposal /dɪˈspəʊz(ə)l/ *n.* **1** (*getting rid of*) удале́ние, устране́ние; (*of sewage*) сброс, удале́ние; **the ~ of rubbish** убо́рка му́сора; **bomb ~** обезвре́живание бомб. **2** (*arrangement*) размеще́ние. **3** (*management, control*) распоряже́ние; **the money is at your ~** де́ньги в ва́шем распоряже́нии.

dispose /dɪˈspəʊz/ *v.t.* **1** (*arrange*) распол|ага́ть, -ожи́ть. **2** (*determine*) распол|ага́ть, -ожи́ть; **man proposes, God ~s** челове́к предполага́ет, а Госпо́дь располага́ет. **3** (*incline*) склон|я́ть, -и́ть; **this ~s me to believe that** ... э́то склоня́ет меня́ к мы́сли, что...; **I am not ~d to help him** я не скло́нен ему́ помога́ть; **he is well ~d towards me** он ко мне хорошо́ располо́жен.

● *v.i.* (*with prep.* **of**) **1** (*get rid of*) изб|авля́ться, -а́виться от + *g.* **2** (*deal with*): **he ~d of his work/dinner** он упра́вился с рабо́той/обе́дом. **3** (*account for, overcome*) разд|е́лываться, -ела́ться с + *i.*; **that argument is soon ~d of** э́тот аргуме́нт легко́ опрове́ргнуть.

disposition /ˌdɪspəˈzɪʃ(ə)n/ *n.* **1** (*arrangement*) расположе́ние. **2** (*character*) нрав, хара́ктер; **he has a cheerful ~** у него́ весёлый нрав. **3** (*inclination*) скло́нность; **there was a general ~ to leave early** большинство́ бы́ло скло́нно уйти́ ра́но.

dispossess /ˌdɪspəˈzes/ *v.t.* лиш|а́ть, -и́ть (*кого чего*); от|бира́ть, -обра́ть (*что у кого*).

dispossession /ˌdɪspəˈzeʃ(ə)n/ *n.* лише́ние (*собственности*).

disproportion /ˌdɪsprəˈpɔːʃ(ə)n/ *n.* диспропо́рция.

disproportionate /ˌdɪsprəˈpɔːʃənət/ *adj.* (*lacking proportion*) непропорциона́льный; (*too large*) чрезме́рный; (*too small*) незначи́тельный.

disprove /dɪsˈpruːv/ *v.t.* опров|ерга́ть, -е́ргнуть.

disputable /dɪˈspjuːtəb(ə)l/, /ˈdɪspjʊ-/ *adj.* спо́рный, недока́занный.

disputant /dɪˈspjuːt(ə)nt/ *n.* уча́стник диску́ссии, спо́рщик.

disputation /ˌdɪspjuːˈteɪʃ(ə)n/ *n.* ди́спут, спор.

disputatious /ˌdɪspjuːˈteɪʃ(ə)s/ *adj.*: **he is ~** он большо́й спо́рщик.

dispute /dɪˈspjuːt/, /ˈdɪspjuːt/ *n.* **1** (*debate, argument*) ди́спут; (*disagreement*) спор; **the ownership of the house is in ~** пра́во со́бственности на э́тот дом оспа́ривается; **beyond/past ~** бесспо́рно, вне вся́ких сомне́ний. **2** (*quarrel*) ссо́ра, разногла́сие.

● *v.t.* (*call in question, oppose*) осп|а́ривать, -о́рить; **I ~ that point** я оспа́риваю э́тот пункт; **the will was ~d** завеща́ние бы́ло опротесто́вано.

● *v.i.* (*argue*) спо́рить, по-; **they ~d whether to wait or not** они́ спо́рили, жда́ть им и́ли нет.

disqualification /dɪsˌkwɒlɪfɪˈkeɪʃ(ə)n/ *n.* дисквалифика́ция; **age is no ~** во́зраст — не поме́ха/препя́тствие.

disqualify /dɪsˈkwɒlɪˌfaɪ/ *v.t.* дисквалифици́ровать (*impf., pf.*).

disquiet /dɪsˈkwaɪət/ *n.* беспоко́йство, трево́га.

● *v.t.* беспоко́ить, о-, трево́жить, вс-.

disquieting /dɪsˈkwaɪətɪŋ/ *adj.* трево́жный; **a ~ly high number of mistakes** трево́жное коли́чество оши́бок.

disquietude /dɪsˈkwaɪəˌtju:d/ *n.* беспоко́йство, трево́га.

disquisition /ˌdɪskwɪˈzɪʃ(ə)n/ *n.* тракта́т.

disregard /ˌdɪsrɪˈgɑ:d/ *n.* пренебреже́ние + *i.*; **he showed ~ for his teachers** он проявля́л неуваже́ние к учителя́м.

● *v.t.* пренебр|ега́ть, -е́чь + *i.*; (*ignore*) игнори́ровать (*impf., pf.*).

disrepair /ˌdɪsrɪˈpeə(r)/ *n.* неиспра́вность; **the house is in ~** дом в запу́щенном состоя́нии; **fall into ~** при|ходи́ть, -йти́ в упа́док/запусте́ние; (*mechanism*) при|ходи́ть -йти́ в неиспра́вность.

disreputable /dɪsˈrepjʊtəb(ə)l/ *adj.* (*behaviour*) позо́рный; (*company, person*) по́льзующийся дурно́й сла́вой; **a ~ old hat** убо́гая ста́рая шля́па.

disrepute /ˌdɪsrɪˈpju:t/ *n.* дурна́я сла́ва; **fall into ~** приобре|та́ть, -сти́ дурну́ю сла́ву.

disrespect /ˌdɪsrɪˈspekt/ *n.* неуваже́ние (к + *d.*); непочте́ние (к + *d.*); непочти́тельность.

disrespectful /ˌdɪsrɪˈspektfʊl/ *adj.* непочти́тельный, неуважи́тельный.

disrobe /dɪsˈrəʊb/ *v.t. & i.* (*undress*) разд|ева́ть(ся), -е́ть(ся); (*take off robes*) разоблач|а́ть(ся), -и́ть(ся).

disrupt /dɪsˈrʌpt/ *v.t.* (*event*) срыва́ть, сорва́ть; (*process, system*) прер|ыва́ть, -ва́ть; нар|уша́ть, -у́шить.

disruption /dɪsˈrʌpʃ(ə)n/ *n.* срыв; наруше́ние.

disruptive /dɪsˈrʌptɪv/ *adj.* разруши́тельный, подрывно́й.

dissatisfaction /ˌdɪsætɪsˈfækʃ(ə)n/ *n.* неудовлетворённость, недово́льство, неудово́льствие.

dissatisf|y /dɪˈsætɪsˌfaɪ/ *v.t.* не удовлетвор|я́ть, -и́ть; **he is ~ied with his job** он недово́лен *or* неудовлетворён свое́й рабо́той.

dissect /dɪˈsekt/ *v.t.* вскр|ыва́ть, -ы́ть; (*fig.*) раз|бира́ть, -обра́ть.

dissection /dɪˈsekʃ(ə)n/ *n.* вскры́тие; разбо́р.

dissemble /dɪˈsemb(ə)l/ *v.t.* таи́ть (*impf.*); скры|ва́ть, -ть; **he ~s his emotions** он скрыва́ет свои́ чу́вства.

● *v.i.* притвор|я́ться, -и́ться; таи́ться (*impf.*) лицеме́рить (*impf.*).

dissembler /dɪˈsemblə(r)/ *n.* притво́рщик, лицеме́р.

dissembling /dɪˈsemblɪŋ/ *n.* притво́рство.

● *adj.* (*smile, behaviour*) притво́рный; (*person*) притворя́ющийся.

disseminate /dɪˈsemɪˌneɪt/ *v.t.* распростран|я́ть, -и́ть.

dissemination /dɪˌsemɪˈneɪʃ(ə)n/ *n.* распростране́ние.

disseminator /dɪˈsemɪˌneɪtə(r)/ *n.* распространи́тель (*m.*).

dissension /dɪˈsenʃ(ə)n/ *n.* разла́д, раздо́р.

dissent /dɪˈsent/ *n.* несогла́сие; (*eccl.*) раско́л.

dissenter /dɪˈsentə(r)/ *n.* диссиде́нт; (*rebel*) бунта́рь (*m.*); (*eccl.*) раско́льник.

dissentient /dɪˈsenʃ(ə)nt/ *n. & adj.* несогла́сный.

dissertation /ˌdɪsəˈteɪʃ(ə)n/ *n.* (*thesis*) диссерта́ция; (*as part of diploma*) дипло́мная рабо́та.

disservice /dɪsˈsɜ:vɪs/ *n.* плоха́я услу́га, уще́рб; **he did me a ~** он нанёс мне уще́рб; он навреди́л мне; **his words did great ~ to the cause** его́ слова́ нанесли́ большо́й уще́рб де́лу.

dissidence /ˈdɪsɪd(ə)ns/ *n.* несогла́сие, инакомы́слие.

dissident /ˈdɪsɪd(ə)nt/ *n.* (*pol.*) диссиде́нт; (*differently-minded person*) инакомы́слящий.

● *adj.* несогла́сный, диссиде́нтский, инакомы́слящий.

dissimilar /dɪˈsɪmɪlə(r)/ *adj.* несхо́дный.

dissimilarity /ˌdɪsɪmɪˈlærɪtɪ/ *n.* несхо́дство.

dissimulate /dɪˈsɪmjʊˌleɪt/ *v.t.* скры|ва́ть, -ть, таи́ть (*impf.*).

● *v.i.* лицеме́рить (*impf.*); притворя́ться (*impf.*).

dissimulation /dɪˌsɪmjʊˈleɪʃ(ə)n/ *n.* лицеме́рие, притво́рство.

dissimulator /dɪˈsɪmjʊˌleɪtə(r)/ *n.* лицеме́р, притво́рщик.

dissipate /ˈdɪsɪˌpeɪt/ *v.t.* (*lit., fig.*) рассе́|ивать, -ять; (*squander*) растра́|чивать, -тить; пром|а́тывать, -ота́ть.

dissipated /ˈdɪsɪˌpeɪtɪd/ *adj.* беспу́тный; (*life style*) разгу́льный.

dissipation /ˌdɪsɪˈpeɪʃ(ə)n/ *n.* беспу́тство, разгу́л.

dis|sociate /dɪˈsəʊʃɪˌeɪt/, /-sɪˌeɪt/, **-associate** /ˌdɪsəˈsəʊʃɪˌeɪt/, /-sɪˌeɪt/ *v.t.* (*disunite*) разобщ|а́ть, -и́ть; разъедин|я́ть, -и́ть; **~ o.s.** отмеж|ёвываться, -ева́ться (от + *g.*); **I ~ myself from what has been said** я отмежёвываюсь от того́, что бы́ло ска́зано; (*think of as separate*) отдел|я́ть, -и́ть

dissociation /dɪˌsəʊsɪˈeɪʃ(ə)n/, /-ʃɪˈeɪʃ(ə)n/ *n.* разобще́ние, разъедине́ние.

dissolubility /dɪˌsɒljʊˈbɪlɪtɪ/ *n.* (*phys.*) раствори́мость; (*of contract*) расторжи́мость.

dissoluble /dɪˈsɒljʊb(ə)l/ *adj.* (*phys.*) раствори́мый; (*of contract*) расторжи́мый.

dissolute /ˈdɪsəˌlu:t/, /-ˌlju:t/ *adj.* распу́щенный, беспу́тный, распу́тный.

dissoluteness /ˈdɪsəˌlu:tnɪs/, /-ˌlju:tnɪs/ *n.* распу́щенность, беспу́тство, распу́тство.

dissolution /ˌdɪsəˈlu:ʃ(ə)n/, /-ˈlju:ʃ(ə)n/ *n.* (*phys.*) растворе́ние; (*death*) конча́на; (*of marriage etc.*) расторже́ние; (*of parliament*) ро́спуск.

dissolvable /dɪˈzɒlvəb(ə)l/ *adj.* разложи́мый; (*contract*) расторжи́мый.

dissolve /dɪˈzɒlv/ *v.t.* **1** (*phys.*) раствор|я́ть, -и́ть. **2**: **the queen ~d parliament** короле́ва распусти́ла парла́мент. **3** (*marriage*) раст|орга́ть, -о́ргнуть; **the marriage was ~d** брак был расто́ргнут.

● *v.i.* (*phys.*) раствор|я́ться, -и́ться; **she ~d into tears** она́ залила́сь слеза́ми.

dissonance /ˈdɪsənəns/ *n.* диссона́нс.

dissonant /ˈdɪsənənt/ *adj.* диссони́рующий, нестро́йный.

dissuade /dɪˈsweɪd/ *v.t.* отгов|а́ривать, -ори́ть (*кого от чего*); отсове́товать (*pf.*) (*что кому*).

dissuasion /dɪˈsweɪʒ(ə)n/ *n.* отгова́ривание.

distaff /ˈdɪstɑ:f/ *n.* пря́лка; **on the ~ side** по же́нской ли́нии.

distance /ˈdɪst(ə)ns/ *n.* **1** (*measure of space*) диста́нция, расстоя́ние; **it can be seen from a ~ of two miles** э́то ви́дно с расстоя́ния двух миль; **it is some ~ to the school** до шко́лы дово́льно далеко́; **no ~ at all** совсе́м недалеко́; **he lives within walking ~ of the office** от его́ до́ма до рабо́ты мо́жно дойти́ пешко́м; **at what ~?** на како́м расстоя́нии?; **in the ~** вдалеке́; **from a ~** и́здали, издалека́; **middle ~** сре́дний план. **2** (*fig.*): **keep one's ~** держа́ться (*impf.*) в стороне́ (от + *g.*); **keep s.o. at a ~** держа́ть (*impf.*) кого́-н. на расстоя́нии.

● *v.t.*: **~ o.s.** отмеж|ёвываться, -ева́ться (от + *g.*).

distant /ˈdɪst(ə)nt/ *adj.* **1** (*in space*) далёкий, да́льний, отдалённый; **the school is three miles ~** шко́ла нахо́дится на расстоя́нии трёх миль; **we had a ~ view of the mountains** вдали́ мы ви́дели го́ры. **2** (*in time*) далёкий. **3** (*fig., remote*): **a ~ cousin** да́льний ро́дственник; **a ~ likeness** отдалённое схо́дство. **4** (*reserved*) сде́ржанный, холо́дный.

● *cpd.* **~ learning** *n.* зао́чное обуче́ние.

distaste /dɪsˈteɪst/ *n.* отвраще́ние (к + *d.*).

distasteful /dɪsˈteɪstfʊl/ *adj.* отврати́тельный, неприя́тный.

distemper[1] /dɪˈstempə(r)/ *n.* (*disease of dogs*) соба́чья чума́.

distemper[2] /dɪˈstempə(r)/ *n.* (*method of painting*) те́мпера; (*type of paint*) клеева́я кра́ска.

● *v.t.* кра́сить, по- клеево́й кра́ской.

distend /dɪ'stend/ *v.t. & i.* над|ува́ть(ся), -у́ть(ся); вз|дува́ть(ся), -у́ть(ся).

distension /dɪ'stenʃ(ə)n/ *n.* расшире́ние, взду́тие.

distil /dɪ'stɪl/ (*US* **distill**) *v.t.* (**distilled, distilling**) дистилли́ровать (*impf., pf.*); (*e.g. salt water*) опресн|я́ть, -и́ть; **~ whisky** перег|оня́ть, -на́ть ви́ски.

distillate /'dɪstɪ,leɪt/ *n.* дистилля́т.

distillation /,dɪstɪ'leɪʃ(ə)n/ *n.* (*process*) дистилля́ция, перего́нка; винокуре́ние.

distiller /dɪ'stɪlə(r)/ *n.* (*equipment*) дистилля́тор; (*person*) виноку́р; (*company*) ликёрово́дочная компа́ния.

distillery /dɪ'stɪlərɪ/ *n.* ликёрово́дочный заво́д.

distinct /dɪ'stɪŋkt/ *adj.* **1** (*sound*) вня́тный; (*picture*) отчётливый; (*idea, thought*) я́сный; (*improvement, change*) заме́тный; (*advantage, possibility*) очеви́дный. **2** (*different*) отли́чный (от + *g.*).

distinction /dɪ'stɪŋkʃ(ə)n/ *n.* **1** (*difference*) отли́чие. **2** (*discrimination*) разли́чие; **without ~ of rank** не взира́я на ра́нги. **3** (*special or superior quality*) отличи́тельная осо́бенность, своеобра́зие; **a writer of ~** выдаю́щийся писа́тель; **his style lacks ~** его́ стиль не отлича́ется своеобра́зием. **4** (*mark of honour*) отли́чие; **he received several ~s** он получи́л не́сколько зна́ков отли́чия.

distinctive /dɪ'stɪŋktɪv/ *adj.* своеобра́зный, осо́бый; (*feature*) отличи́тельный.

distinctly /dɪ'stɪŋktlɪ/ *adv.* отчётливо; (*perceptibly*) заме́тно; **~ better** значи́тельно лу́чше; **he spoke ~** он говори́л вня́тно/чётко; **I ~ heard** я я́сно слы́шал.

distinctness /dɪ'stɪŋktnɪs/ *n.* отчётливость, определённость.

distinguish /dɪ'stɪŋgwɪʃ/ *v.t.* **1** (*perceive*) разли́ч|а́ть, -и́ть; разгля́д|ывать, -е́ть. **2** (*discern or point out difference*) различ|а́ть, -и́ть. **3** (*characterize*) отлич|а́ть, -и́ть. **4**: **~ o.s.** отлич|а́ться, -и́ться.

distinguishable /dɪ'stɪŋgwɪʃəb(ə)l/ *adj.* (*visible*) различи́мый, заме́тный; (*different*) отличи́мый.

distinguished /dɪ'stɪŋgwɪʃt/ *adj.* выдаю́щийся, ви́дный.

distort /dɪ'stɔ:t/ *v.t.* иска|жа́ть, -зи́ть; (*twist, contort*) искрив|ля́ть, -и́ть; **~ facts** извра|ща́ть, -ти́ть фа́кты.

distortion /dɪ'stɔ:ʃ(ə)n/ *n.* искаже́ние, извраще́ние.

distract /dɪ'strækt/ *v.t.* **1** (*draw away; make inattentive*) отвл|ека́ть, -е́чь; **it ~s me from my work** э́то отвлека́ет меня́ от рабо́ты. **2** (*derange mentally*) св|оди́ть, -ести́ с ума́; дов|оди́ть, -ести́ до безу́мия; **he drove her ~ed** он довёл её до безу́мия.

distraction /dɪ'strækʃ(ə)n/ *n.* (*act of diverting*) отвлече́ние; (*cause of inattention*) поме́ха; (*amusement*) развлече́ние; (*frenzy, derangement*) безу́мие; **he loves her to ~** он безу́мно (*or* без па́мяти) её лю́бит; **drive s.o. to ~** дов|оди́ть, -ести́ кого́-н. до безу́мия.

distrain /dɪ'streɪn/ *v.i.* (*leg.*) опи́с|ывать, -а́ть иму́щество за долги́; **~ upon s.o.'s goods** на|кла́дывать, -ложи́ть аре́ст на чьи-н. това́ры для обеспече́ния до́лга.

distraint /dɪ'streɪnt/ *n.* (*leg.*) наложе́ние аре́ста на иму́щество в обеспече́ние до́лга.

distraught /dɪ'strɔ:t/ *adj.* обезу́мевший.

distress /dɪ'stres/ *n.* **1** (*physical suffering*) изнуре́ние, изнеможе́ние; **the runner showed signs of ~** бегу́н был изнурён. **2** (*mental suffering*) трево́га, депре́ссия. **3** (*indigence*) нужда́. **4** (*danger*) бе́дствие; **a ship in ~** су́дно, те́рпящее бе́дствие.

● *v.t.* **1** (*grieve*) огорч|а́ть, -и́ть. **2** (*impoverish*) истощ|а́ть, -и́ть; **~ed area** райо́н бе́дствия.

distressing /dɪ'stresɪŋ/ *adj.* огорчи́тельный, доса́дный.

distribute /dɪ'strɪbju:t/, /'dɪ-/ *v.t.* **1** (*deal out*) распредел|я́ть, -и́ть; разд|ава́ть, -а́ть; (*goods*) распростран|я́ть, -и́ть. **2** (*spread*) распредел|я́ть, -и́ть; **wealth is unfairly ~d** бога́тство распределя́ется несправедли́во; **~ a load evenly** равноме́рно распредел|я́ть, -и́ть груз.

distribution /,dɪstrɪ'bju:ʃ(ə)n/ *n.* **1** (*dealing out, spreading*) распределе́ние, разда́ча; (*of goods*) распростране́ние; **the ~ of population is uneven** распределе́ние населе́ния неравноме́рно; **~ of prizes** разда́ча награ́д. **2** (*marketing*) распределе́ние, распростране́ние.

distributive /dɪ'strɪbjʊtɪv/ *adj.* распредели́тельный; **the ~ trades** ро́зничная торго́вля; (*gram.*) раздели́тельный.

distributor /dɪ'strɪbjʊtə(r)/ *n.* (*person*) распредели́тель (*m.*); (*in car*) распредели́тель (*m.*) зажига́ния; (*comm.*) дистрибью́тор.

district /'dɪstrɪkt/ *n.* райо́н, о́круг; (*attr.*) райо́нный, окружно́й; **consular ~** ко́нсульский о́круг; **postal ~** почто́вый райо́н; (*US, constituency*) избира́тельный уча́сток; **D~ of Columbia** о́круг Колу́мбия; **~ attorney** (*US*) окружно́й прокуро́р; **~ nurse** (*Br.*) участко́вая (мед)сестра́.

distrust /dɪs'trʌst/ *n.* недове́рие.

● *v.t.* не доверя́ть (*impf.*) + *d.*

distrustful /dɪs'trʌstfʊl/ *adj.* недове́рчивый.

disturb /dɪ'stɜ:b/ *v.t.* беспоко́ить, о-; меша́ть, по- + *d.*; трево́жить, вс-; (*peace*) нар|уша́ть, -у́шить; **~ s.o.'s sleep** нар|уша́ть, -у́шить чей-н. сон; **~ the surface of the water** трево́жить, по- во́дную гладь; **he was ~ed by the news** он был обеспоко́ен но́востью; **his mind was ~ed** у него́ помути́лся рассу́док; **~ the peace** вызыва́ть, вы́звать обще́ственные беспоря́дки; **do not ~ these papers** не тро́гайте э́ти бума́ги.

disturbance /dɪ'stɜ:bəns/ *n.* (*act of troubling*) наруше́ние; (*cause of trouble*) трево́га; (*riot*) волне́ния (*nt. pl.*); беспоря́дки (*m. pl.*).

disturbing /dɪ'stɜ:bɪŋ/ *adj.* трево́жный.

disunite /'dɪsju:'naɪt/ *v.t.* (*separate, estrange*) разобщ|а́ть, -и́ть; разъедин|я́ть, -и́ть.

disuse /dɪs'ju:s/ *n.* забро́шенность, неупотребле́ние; **fall into ~** выходи́ть, вы́йти из употребле́ния.

disused /dɪs'ju:sd/ *adj.*: **a ~ well** забро́шенный коло́дец.

disyllabic /,dɪsɪ'læbɪk/, /,daɪ-/ *adj.* двусло́жный.

disyllable /dɪ'sɪləb(ə)l/, /'daɪ-/ *n.* двусло́жное сло́во.

ditch /dɪtʃ/ *n.* кана́ва; ров.

● *v.t.*: **~ one's plane** сажа́ть, посади́ть самолёт на́ воду; **~ one's plans** (*coll.*) забр|а́сывать, -о́сить свои́ пла́ны; **~ one's old clothes** (*coll.*) выбра́сывать, вы́бросить ста́рую оде́жду; **~ s.o.** (*sl.*) бр|оса́ть, -о́сить кого́-н.

● *v.i.* (*make ~es*) копа́ть, вы́- кана́вы; (*repair ~es*) чи́стить, вы́- кана́вы.

● *cpd.* **~-water** *n.* стоя́чая вода́; **dull as ~-water** смерте́льно ску́чный.

dither /'dɪðə(r)/ *n.* (*coll.*) смяте́ние; **she was in a ~** она́ не́рвничала *or* была́ в смяте́нии.

● *v.i.* (*coll.*) колеба́ться, по-.

dithery /'dɪðərɪ/ *adj.* (*coll.*) нереши́тельный, нерво́зный.

ditto /'dɪtəʊ/ *n.* (*pl.* **~s**) то же; сто́лько же.

ditty /'dɪtɪ/ *n.* пе́сенка.

diuretic /,daɪjʊ'retɪk/ *n.* мочего́нное сре́дство.

● *adj.* мочего́нный.

diurnal /daɪ'ɜ:n(ə)l/ *adj.* дневно́й, ежедне́вный.

diva /'di:və/ *n.* (*pl.* **~s**) примадо́нна, ди́ва.

divan /dɪ'væn/, /daɪ-/, /'daɪ-/ *n.* тахта́, дива́н; **~ bed** дива́н-крова́ть.

dive /daɪv/ *n.* **1** (*act of diving*) ныро́к, ныря́ние; **high ~** прыжо́к в во́ду с вы́шки; (*of submarine*) погруже́ние; (*of aircraft*) пики́рование; **the plane went into a ~** самолёт спики́ровал. **2** (*underground bar etc.*) погребо́к. **3** (*drinking or gambling den*) прито́н.

● *v.i.* (*past and p.p.* **dived** *or US also* **dove**) **1** (*plunge into water*) ныр|я́ть, -ну́ть; (*in diving suit; also of submarine*) погру|жа́ться, -зи́ться. **2** (*move sharply downwards*): **the animal ~d into its hole** зверёк юркну́л в но́ру; **he ~d into his pocket** он су́нул ру́ку в карма́н. **3** (*fig., immerse o.s.*) углуб|ля́ться, -и́ться; *see also* ⇒**diving**

● *cpds.* **~-bomb** *v.t.* бомби́ть (*impf.*) с пики́рования; **~-bomber** *n.* пики́рующий бомбардиро́вщик.

diver /'daɪvə(r)/ *n.* ныря́льщик; водола́з; (*for pearls*) иска́тель (*m.*) же́мчуга; (*bird*) гага́ра.

diverge /daɪ'vɜ:dʒ/ *v.i.* ра|сходи́ться,

-зойти́сь; (*from truth, standard*) отклон|я́ться, -и́ться.

divergence /daɪˈvɜ:dʒəns/ *n.* расхожде́ние, отклоне́ние.

divergent /daɪˈvɜ:dʒ(ə)nt/ *adj.* расходя́щийся, отклоня́ющийся.

diverse /daɪˈvɜ:s/, /ˈdaɪ-/, /dɪ-/ *adj.* разнообра́зный.

diversification /daɪ,vɜ:sɪfɪˈkeɪʃ(ə)n/ *n.* расшире́ние ассортиме́нта.

diversify /daɪˈvɜ:sɪ,faɪ/ *v.t.* разнообра́зить (*impf.*), варьи́ровать (*impf.*).

diversion /daɪˈvɜ:ʃ(ə)n/, /dɪ-/ *n.* **1** (*turning aside*) отклоне́ние; **~ of a stream** отво́д ручья́; **traffic ~** (*Br.*) объе́зд. **2** (*mil.*) дивéрсия. **3** (*amusement*) развлече́ние, заба́ва. **4**: **create a ~** отвл|ека́ть, -е́чь внима́ние.

diversionary /daɪˈvɜ:ʃənərɪ/, /dɪ-/ *adj.* диверсио́нный.

diversity /daɪˈvɜ:sɪtɪ/, /dɪ-/ *n.* (*variety*) разнообра́зие.

divert /daɪˈvɜ:t/, /dɪ-/ *v.t.* (*deflect*) отклон|я́ть, -и́ть; отвл|ека́ть, -е́чь; (*entertain*) развл|ека́ть, -е́чь.

divertimen|to /dɪ,vɜ:tɪˈmentəʊ/, /dɪ,veə-/ *n.* (*pl.* **~ti** /-tɪ/ *or* **~tos**) дивертисме́нт.

diverting /daɪˈvɜ:tɪŋ/, /dɪ-/ *adj.* развлека́ющий, развлека́тельный, заба́вный.

divertissement /,di:veəˈti:smɑ̃/ *n.* (*ballet*) дивертисме́нт.

divest /daɪˈvest/ *v.t.* (*fig.*) лиш|а́ть, -и́ть; **~ o.s. of functions** сложи́ть (*pf.*) с себя́ обя́занности.

divide /dɪˈvaɪd/ *n.* (*divergence*) расхожде́ние; (*geog.*) водоразде́л.

● *v.t.* **1** (*share*) дели́ть, по-, раз-; **they ~d the money equally** они́ раздели́ли де́ньги по́ровну; **he ~s his time between work and play** он де́лит своё вре́мя ме́жду рабо́той и развлече́ниями. **2** (*math.*) дели́ть, раз-; **~ 27 by 3** 27 дели́ть, раз- на́ 3. **3** (*separate*) раздел|я́ть, -и́ть; **dividing-line** разграничи́тельная ли́ния; **the river ~s the two estates** река́ разделя́ет э́ти два име́ния; **~d highway** (*US*) = **dual carriageway.** **4** (*cause disagreement*) разъедин|я́ть, -и́ть; раздел|я́ть, -и́ть; **such a small matter should not ~ us** не сто́ит нам спо́рить из-за тако́го пустяка́; **we are ~d on this question** мы расхо́димся в э́том вопро́се; **a ~-and-rule policy** поли́тика «разделя́й и вла́ствуй».

● *v.i.* дели́ться, раз-; **the road ~s** доро́га разветвля́ется; **the House ~d** пала́та проголосова́ла; (*math.*): **18 ~s by 3** 18 де́лится на́ 3.

dividend /ˈdɪvɪ,dend/ *n.* (*math.*) дели́мое; (*fin.*) дивиде́нд.

dividers /dɪˈvaɪdəz/ *n.* (*compasses*) ци́ркуль (*m.*).

divination /,dɪvɪˈneɪʃ(ə)n/ *n.* (*foretelling the future*) гада́ние, прорица́ние.

divin|e /dɪˈvaɪn/ *adj.* (**diviner, divinest**) боже́ственный; (*coll.*, *superb*) ди́вный, боже́ственный; **~e right of kings** пра́во пома́занника бо́жьего; **~e service** богослуже́ние.

● *v.t.* (*guess, intuit*) уга́д|ывать, -а́ть; **~ing-rod** прут для отыска́ния воды́.

diviner /dɪˈvaɪnə(r)/ *n.* (*seer*) гада́тель (*m.*), прорица́тель (*m.*); (*water-~*) лозоиска́тель (*m.*).

diving /ˈdaɪvɪŋ/ *n.* ныря́ние.

● *cpds.* **~-bell** *n.* водола́зный ко́локол; **~-board** *n.* трампли́н, вы́шка (для прыжко́в в во́ду); **~-suit** *n.* скафа́ндр.

divinity /dɪˈvɪnɪtɪ/ *n.* (*quality*) боже́ственность; (*divine being*) божество́; (*theology*) богосло́вие.

divinize /ˈdɪvɪnaɪz/ *v.t.* обожеств|ля́ть, -и́ть.

divisibility /dɪ,vɪzɪˈbɪlɪtɪ/ *n.* дели́мость.

divisible /dɪˈvɪzɪb(ə)l/ *adj.* (раз)дели́мый.

division /dɪˈvɪʒ(ə)n/ *n.* **1** (*math.*) деле́ние. **2** (*dividing*) разделе́ние, разде́л; **~ of labour** (*Br.*), **labor** (*US*) разделе́ние труда́; **a fair ~ of the money** справедли́вое распределе́ние де́нег. **3** (*separation*) разделе́ние; **class ~s** кла́ссовые разли́чия. **4** (*interval on a scale*) деле́ние. **5** (*discord*) расхожде́ние. **6** (*mil.*) диви́зия. **7** (*department*) отде́л. **8** (*Br.*, *electoral district*) избира́тельный о́круг. **9** (*parl. vote*) голосова́ние. **10** (*typ.*, *of words at end of line*) перено́с.

divisional /dɪˈvɪʒənəl/ *adj.* (*mil.*) дивизио́нный; **~ headquarters** штаб диви́зии.

divisive /dɪˈvaɪsɪv/ *adj.* вызыва́ющий разногла́сия.

divisor /dɪˈvaɪzə(r)/ *n.* (*math.*) дели́тель (*m.*).

divorce /dɪˈvɔ:s/ *n.* (*leg.*) разво́д; **~ court** суд по бракоразво́дным дела́м; **~ rate** проце́нт разво́дов.

● *v.t.* **1** (*separate*) отдел|я́ть, -и́ть; **~ a word from its context** вырыва́ть, вы́рвать сло́во из конте́кста. **2** (*leg.*) разв|оди́ть, -ести́; **he ~d his wife** он развёлся с жено́й; **she is ~d** она́ разведена́.

● *v.i.* разв|оди́ться, -ести́сь.

divorcee /,dɪvɔ:ˈsi:/ (*US* **divorcé** (*m.*), **divorcée** (*f.*)) *n.* разведённый (муж), разведённая (жена́).

divulge /daɪˈvʌldʒ/, /dɪ-/ *v.t.* разгла|ша́ть, -си́ть.

Dixieland /ˈdɪksɪ,lænd/ *n.* (*jazz*) диксиле́нд.

DIY (*abbr. of* ***do it yourself***) (*Br.*): **~ store** магази́н «Уме́лые ру́ки».

DIYer /di:aɪˈwaɪə(r)/ *n.* (*Br. coll.*) дома́шний уме́лец.

dizziness /ˈdɪzɪnɪs/ *n.* головокруже́ние.

dizzy /ˈdɪzɪ/ *adj.* (**dizzier, dizziest**) (*feeling giddy*) испы́тывающий головокруже́ние; (*causing giddiness*) головокружи́тельный; **I feel ~** у меня́ кру́жится голова́.

DJ (*abbr. of* ***disc jockey***) диск-жоке́й, ди-дже́й.

D. Litt. (*abbr. of* ***Doctor of Letters***) до́ктор филоло́гии.

DNA (*abbr. of* ***deoxyribonucleic acid***) ДНК (дезоксирибонуклеи́новая кислота́).

do[1] /du:/, /də/ *n.* (*pl.* **~s** *or* **~'s**) (*coll.*) **1** (*Br.*, *entertainment*) вечери́нка, гуля́нка. **2** (*Br.*, *share*): **fair do's!** всем по́ровну! **3** (*advice*): **~'s and don'ts** сове́ты (*m. pl.*).

● *v.t.* & *aux.* (*3rd pers. sing. pres.* **does;** *past* **did;** *p.p.* **done**) **1** (*as aux. or substitute for v. already used*: *not translated unless emph.*): **I ~ not smoke** я не курю́; **did you not see me?** ра́зве вы меня́ не ви́дели?; **I ~ want to go** я о́чень хочу́ пойти́; **~ tell me** пожа́луйста, расскажи́те мне; **they promised to help, and they did** они́ обеща́ли помо́чь и помогли́; **so ~ I** я то́же; **he went, but I did not** он пошёл, а я нет; **she plays better than she did** она́ игра́ет лу́чше, чем пре́жде; **he ~es not work, nor ~ I** ни он, ни я не рабо́таем. **2** (*perform, carry out*): **what can I ~ for you?** чем могу́ служи́ть?; **what ~es he ~ (for a living)?** чем он занима́ется?; кем/где он рабо́тает?; **what ~es your father ~?** кто ваш оте́ц?; **the team did well** кома́нда вы́ступила успе́шно; **what's ~ne cannot be undone** сде́ланного не воро́тишь/попра́вишь; **~ one's duty** выполня́ть, вы́полнить свой долг; **easier said than ~ne** легко́ сказа́ть; **well ~ne!** молоде́ц!; **it isn't ~ne!** (*Br.*) э́то не при́нято!, так не де́лают! **3** (*bestow, render*): **it ~es him credit** э́то де́лает ему́ честь; **he did me a service** он оказа́л мне услу́гу; **it won't ~ any good** э́то бесполе́зно, э́то ничего́ не даст. **4** (*effect, produce*): **that's ~ne it! now you've ~ne it!** (*iron.*) поздравля́ю! **5** (*finish*): **I have ~ne** я ко́нчил; **I have ~ne with algebra** я поко́нчил с а́лгеброй; **I have ~ne with him** я с ним поко́нчил. **6** (*work at*): **he's ~ing algebra** он изуча́ет а́лгебру. **7** (*solve*): **~ a sum** реш|а́ть, -и́ть арифмети́ческую зада́чу. **8** (*attend to*): **the barber did me first** парикма́хер обслужи́л меня́ пе́рвым; **he ~es book reviews** он рецензи́рует кни́ги; **we did geography today** сего́дня мы занима́лись геогра́фией. **9** (*arrange, clean, tidy*): **~ one's hair** прич|ёсываться, -еса́ться; **~ a room** уб|ира́ть, -ра́ть ко́мнату; **~ the dishes** мыть, по- посу́ду; **~ one's face** прив|оди́ть, -ести́ лицо́ в поря́док. **10** (*cook*): **~ne to a turn** зажа́рено как раз в ме́ру; **well ~ne** хорошо́ прожа́ренный; **the potatoes are ~ne** карто́шка свари́лась/гото́ва. **11** (*enact*): **he did Hamlet** он игра́л Га́млета. **12** (*undergo*): **he did 6 years for forgery** он отсиде́л 6 лет за подло́г. **13** (*cater for*): **they ~ you well at the Savoy** в «Саво́е» хоро́шее обслу́живание. **14** (*coll.*, *swindle*) над|ува́ть, -у́ть.

15 (*achieve speed etc.*): **we did 70 miles in two hours** мы проде́лали 70 миль за два часа́; **he was ~ing 60 (miles an hour)** он е́хал со ско́ростью 60 миль в час.
16: **~ne!** (*agreed*) по рука́м!
17: **I can ~** (*sell*) **you this coat at £50** я уступлю́ вам э́то пальто́ за 50 фу́нтов.

● *v.i.* (*3rd pers. sing. pres.* **does;** *past* **did;** *p.p.* **done**) **1** (*act, behave*): **~ as I tell you** де́лай, что тебе́ говоря́т; **~ as you would be ~ne by** поступа́йте так, как бы вы хоте́ли, что́бы поступа́ли с ва́ми; **you would ~ well to go there** вы хорошо́ сде́лаете, е́сли пойдёте туда́; **we must ~ or die** мы должны́ сде́лать э́то во что бы то ни ста́ло.
2 (*be satisfactory, fitting or advisable*): **the scraps will ~ for the dog** объе́дки пойду́т соба́ке; **this will never ~** э́то никуда́ не годи́тся; так не пойдёт; **that will ~!** (*is enough*) хва́тит!; дово́льно!; **it doesn't ~ to be rude** гру́бость тут не помо́жет; **tomorrow will ~** мо́жно и за́втра.
3 (*fare, succeed*): **how ~ you ~?** здра́вствуйте!; как пожива́ете?; **how did he ~ in his exams?** как он сдал экза́мены?; **she is ~ing well** у неё всё хорошо́; **my roses are ~ing well** мои́ ро́зы хорошо́ растут; **the patient is ~ing well** больно́й поправля́ется.
4 (*happen*): **is anything ~ing at the club?** что происхо́дит в клу́бе?; **nothing ~ing!** (*refusal*) не вы́йдет!
● *with preps.*: **what shall we ~ about lunch?** как насчёт обе́да?; **nothing can be ~ne about it** с э́тим ничего́ не поде́лаешь; **~ well by s.o.** хорошо́ обраща́ться (*impf.*) с кем-н.; **~ for** (*Br., clean house etc. for*) вести́ (*det.*) чьё-н. хозя́йство; (*defeat, destroy, damage*): **these shoes are ~ne for** э́тим ту́флям коне́ц; **if he finds out, I am ~ne for** е́сли он об э́том узна́ет, я пропа́л *or* мне коне́ц; **we're ~ne for** нам кры́шка (*coll.*) *or* нам коне́ц; **what will you ~ for food?** что вы бу́дете де́лать насчёт пита́ния?; **~ s.o. out of something** (*cheat, deprive of*) выма́нивать, вы́манить что-н. у кого́-н.; **what have you ~ne to my watch?** что вы сде́лали с мо́ими часа́ми?; **what have you ~ne with the keys?** куда́ вы де́ли ключи́?; **what is he ~ing with a car?** заче́м ему́ маши́на?; **I could ~ with a drink** я охо́тно (*or* с удово́льствием) вы́пил бы; **that coat could ~ with a clean** не помеша́ло бы вы́чистить э́то пальто́; **I can't be ~ing with her** (*Br.*) я её не выношу́; **we shall have to make ~ with margarine** нам придётся обойти́сь маргари́ном; **he ~esn't know what to ~ with himself** он не зна́ет, чем заня́ться; **it is nothing to ~ with you** э́то вас не каса́ется; **the letter is/has to ~ with the bazaar** э́то письмо́ каса́ется благотвори́тельного база́ра; **hard work had a lot to ~ with his success** упо́рный труд сыгра́л большу́ю роль в его́ успе́хе; **these books are ~ne with** э́ти кни́ги бо́льше не нужны́; **we must ~ without luxuries** мы должны́ обойти́сь без ро́скоши; **I can ~ without his silly jokes** мне надое́ли его́ дура́цкие шу́тки.

● *with advs.*: **~ away** *v.i.*: **~ away with** конча́ть, ко́нчить с + *i.*; поко́нчить (*pf.*) с + *i.*; **~ away with o.s.** поко́нчить (*pf.*) с собо́й; **~ down** *v.t.* (*Br. coll., cheat*) над|ува́ть, -у́ть; **~ in** *v.t.* (*sl., kill*) уб|ира́ть, -ра́ть; (*coll., exhaust*): **I am ~ne in** я измо́тан; **~ out** *v.t.* (*Br., clean, e.g. a room*) уб|ира́ть, -ра́ть; (*Br., clear, e.g. a cupboard*) вычища́ть, вы́чистить; **~ over (again)** *v.t.* (*US*) переде́л|ывать, -ать; **~ up** *v.t.* (*repair, refurnish*): **~ up a room** отде́л|ывать, -ать ко́мнату; (*fasten*): **~ up a parcel** завя́з|ывать, -а́ть паке́т; **~ up a dress** застёг|ивать, -ну́ть пла́тье.
● *cpds.* **~-it-yourself** *adj.* самоде́льный; **~-nothing** *n.* ло́дырь (*m.*); *adj.* лени́вый; **~-or-die** *adj.* отча́янный.

do² /dəʊ/ *n.* = **doh**

doable /ˈduːəb(ə)l/ *adj.* (*feasible*) выполни́мый.

Dobermann (pinscher) /ˈdəʊbəmən ˈpɪnʃə(r)/ (*US* **Doberman**) *n.* Доберма́н (-пи́нчер).

docile /ˈdəʊsaɪl/ *adj.* послу́шный, поко́рный.

docility /dəʊˈsɪlɪtɪ/ *n.* послуша́ние, поко́рность.

dock¹ /dɒk/ *n.* (*bot.*) ко́нский щаве́ль.

dock² /dɒk/ *n.* (*in court*) скамья́ подсуди́мых.

dock³ /dɒk/ *n.* **1** (*naut.*) док; **dry ~** сухо́й док; **floating ~** плаву́чий док; **wet ~** мо́крый док. **2** (*pl., port facilities*) верфь. **3** (*wharf*) при́стань.
● *v.t.* (*bring into ~*) ста́вить, по- в док (*су́дно*).
● *v.i.* (*go into ~*) входи́ть, войти́ в док; (*of space vehicles*) стыкова́ться, со-.
● *cpd.* **~yard** *n.* верфь.

dock⁴ /dɒk/ *v.t.* **1** (*shorten*) подр|еза́ть, -е́зать; (*shorten tail of*) обруб|а́ть, -и́ть хвост + *g. or* + *d.* **2** (*fig., reduce*) уре́з|ывать, -ать; **the soldiers were ~ed of their ration** солда́там уре́зали рацио́н.
● *cpd.* **~-tailed** *adj.* ку́цый.

docker /ˈdɒkə(r)/ *n.* до́кер; порто́вый рабо́чий.

docket /ˈdɒkɪt/ *n.* **1** (*summary*) аннота́ция; (*Br., list*) пе́речень (*m.*). **2** (*US, leg.*) рее́стр суде́бных дел.
● *v.t.* (**docketed, docketing**) аннoти́ровать (*impf., pf.*).

docking /ˈdɒkɪŋ/ *n.* (*of space vehicles*) стыко́вка.

doctor /ˈdɒktə(r)/ *n.* **1** (*acad.*) до́ктор. **2** (*of medicine*) врач, до́ктор; **woman ~** же́нщина-врач.
● *v.t.* (*Br. coll., castrate*) кастри́ровать (*impf., pf.*); (*falsify*) подде́л|ывать, -ать; (*food*) фальсифици́ровать (*impf., pf.*).

doctor|al /ˈdɒktər(ə)l/, **-ial** /ˌdɒkˈtɔːrɪəl/ *adjs.* до́кторский.

doctorate /ˈdɒktərət/ *n.* сте́пень до́ктора.

doctrinaire /ˌdɒktrɪˈneə(r)/ *n.* доктринёр.
● *adj.* доктринёрский.

doctrinal /dɒkˈtraɪn(ə)l/, /ˈdɒktrɪn(ə)l/ *adj.* (*relig.*) теологи́ческий; (*pol., phil.*) относя́щийся к доктри́не.

doctrine /ˈdɒktrɪn/ *n.* доктри́на, уче́ние.

docudrama /ˈdɒkjʊˌdrɑːmə/ *n.* полудокумента́льный фильм.

document /ˈdɒkjʊmənt/ *n.* (*also comput.*) докуме́нт.
● *v.t.* документи́ровать (*impf., pf.*).

documentary /ˌdɒkjʊˈmentərɪ/ *n.* документа́льный фильм.
● *adj.* документа́льный.

documentation /ˌdɒkjʊmenˈteɪʃ(ə)n/ *n.* документа́ция.

dodder /ˈdɒdə(r)/ *v.i.* трясти́сь (*impf.*); **a ~ing old man** дря́хлый стари́к.

doddery /ˈdɒdərɪ/ *adj.* трясу́щийся от ста́рости; дря́хлый.

doddle /ˈdɒd(ə)l/ *n.* (*Br. coll.*) плёвое де́ло, па́ра пустяко́в.

dodge /dɒdʒ/ *n.* (*evading movement*) увёртка; (*trick*) увёртка, уло́вка.
● *v.t.* увил|ивать, -ьну́ть от + *g.*; **~ a blow** увёртываться, уверну́ться от уда́ра; **~ a question** увил|ивать, -ьну́ть от отве́та; **~ military service** уклон|я́ться, -и́ться от вое́нной пови́нности.
● *v.i.* уклон|я́ться, -и́ться (от + *g.*); **he ~d behind a tree** он (бы́стро) укры́лся за де́ревом.

dodger /ˈdɒdʒə(r)/ *n.* изворо́тливый челове́к; хитре́ц.

dodgy /ˈdɒdʒɪ/ *adj.* (**dodgier, dodgiest**) (*Br. coll.*) (*suspicious*) подозри́тельный; (*dishonest*) нече́стный; (*tricky, difficult*) ка́верзный; (*risky*) риско́ванный; (*unsafe*) ненадёжный.

dodo /ˈdəʊdəʊ/ *n.* (*pl.* **~s** *or* **~es**) дронт; (*fig.*) ко́сный челове́к.

doe /dəʊ/ *n.* са́мка (*оленя, зайца и т.п.*).
● *cpd.* **~skin** *n.* оле́нья ко́жа; (*natural*) за́мша; (*text.*) шерстяна́я ткань, имити́рующая за́мшу.

doer /ˈduːə(r)/ *n.* (*performer; man of action*) де́ятель (*m.*), челове́к де́ла.

does /dʌz/ *3rd pers. sing. pres. of* ⇒**do¹**

doff /dɒf/ *v.t.* сн|има́ть, -ять (*шляпу*).

dog /dɒg/ *n.* **1** соба́ка, пёс (*also fig., pej.*); (*attr.*) соба́чий; **~ family** (*zool.*) семе́йство псо́вых *or* соба́чьих.
2 (*male*) кобе́ль (*m.*); **~ fox** саме́ц лисы́, кобе́ль (*m.*); **~ wolf** саме́ц во́лка, кобе́ль (*m.*).
3 (*astron.*): **~ star** Си́риус; **~ days** пе́кло; са́мые жа́ркие ле́тние дни.
4 (*fire-iron*) подста́вка для ками́нных щипцо́в.
5 (*coll., fellow*): **lucky ~** счастли́вчик; **lazy ~** лентя́й; **sly ~** хитре́ц; **dirty ~** су́кин сын; **top ~** хозя́ин положе́ния.
6 (*other fig. uses*): **go to the ~s** разори́ться (*pf.*), пойти́ (*pf.*) пра́хом; **die like a ~** подо́хнуть (*pf.*) как соба́ка; **a ~'s life** соба́чья жизнь; **give a ~ a bad name and hang him** клевета́ сме́рти подо́бна; от худо́й сла́вы вдруг не отде́лаешься; **let sleeping ~s lie** не тронь ли́ха, пока спит ти́хо; **not a ~'s chance** нет ни мале́йшего ша́нса; **~ in the manger** соба́ка на

се́не; **take a hair of the ~** опохме́л|яться, -и́ться; **there's life in the old ~ yet** есть ещё по́рох в пороховни́цах; **you can't teach an old ~ new tricks** ≈ нельзя́ переучи́ть кого́-н. на ста́рости лет; **~'s dinner** (*Br. sl., mess, hotchpotch*) мешани́на; неразбери́ха; **the ~s of war** у́жасы (*m. pl.*) войны́; **hot ~** (*coll.*) бу́лка с горя́чей соси́ской, хот-дог.

● *v.t.* (**dogged, dogging**) ходи́ть (*indet.*) по пята́м за + *i.*; (*fig.*) пресле́довать (*impf.*).

● *cpds.* **~-biscuit** *n.* соба́чья гале́та; **~cart** *n.* двуко́лка; **~-collar** *n.* оше́йник; (*coll., clergyman's*) кру́глый стоя́чий воротни́к; **~-ear** (*fig.*) *n.* за́гнутый уголо́к страни́цы; *v.t.* заг|иба́ть, -ну́ть уголки́ страни́ц в + *p.*; **~-eared** *adj.* потрёпанный; **~-eat-~** *adj.*: **~-eat-~ competition** жесто́кая/беспоща́дная конкуре́нция, конкуре́нция не на жизнь, а на смерть; **~fight** *n.* (*lit.*) соба́чья сва́лка; (*fig.*) дра́ка, потасо́вка; (*aeron.*) возду́шный бой; **~fish** *n.* аку́ла; **~-food** *n.* корм для соба́к; **~house** *n.* (*US*) конура́; **in the ~house** (*coll.*) в неми́лости; **~-Latin** *n.* ку́хонная латы́нь; **~-leg** *n.* зигза́г; **~like** *adj.*: **~like devotion** соба́чья пре́данность; **~-lover** *n.* (*coll.*) соба́чни|к (*fem.* -ца); **~-paddle** *v.i.* пла́вать (*indet.*) по-соба́чьи; **~-racing** *n.* соба́чьи бега́; **~rose** *n.* шипо́вник; **~sbody** *n.* (*Br.*) иша́к, работя́га (*c.g.*); **~-show** *n.* соба́чья вы́ставка; **~-sled** *n.* на́рт|ы (*pl., g.* —); **~-tired** *adj.*: **I am ~-tired** я уста́л как соба́ка; **~-watch** *n.* полува́хта; **~wood** *n.* кизи́л; свиди́на крова́во-кра́сная.

doge /dəʊdʒ/ *n.* дож.

dogged /ˈdɒgɪd/ *adj.* упо́рный, насты́рный (*coll.*).

doggedness /ˈdɒgɪdnɪs/ *n.* упо́рство, насты́рность (*coll.*).

doggerel /ˈdɒgər(ə)l/ *n.* ви́рш|и (*pl., g.* -ей).

doggo /ˈdɒgəʊ/ *adv.* (*Br.*) притая́сь; **lie ~** прит|а́иваться, -аи́ться.

doggone /ˈdɒgɒn/ *adj.* (*US sl.*) чёртов.

doggy /ˈdɒgɪ/ *n.* соба́чка, пёсик.

dogma /ˈdɒgmə/ *n.* до́гма; (*specific*) догма́т.

dogmatic /dɒgˈmætɪk/ *adj.* (*views*) догмати́ческий; (*person*) догмати́чный.

dogmatism /ˈdɒgmə,tɪz(ə)m/ *n.* догмати́зм.

dogmatist /ˈdɒgmətɪst/ *n.* догма́тик.

dogmatize /ˈdɒgmə,taɪz/ *v.i.* догматизи́ровать (*impf.*).

doh, do /dəʊ/ *n.* (*mus.*) пе́рвая но́та мажо́рной га́ммы; (*the note C*) до (*indecl.*).

doily /ˈdɔɪlɪ/ *n.* кружевна́я салфе́тка.

doing /ˈduːɪŋ/ *n.* **1** (*achievement*): **this was his ~** э́то его́ рук де́ло; **it will take some ~** э́то потре́бует труда́; э́то не та́к про́сто. **2** (*pl., activities*) дела́ (*nt. pl.*); посту́пки (*m. pl.*). **3** (*pl., coll., accessories*) принадле́жности (*f. pl.*).

doldrums /ˈdɒldrəmz/ *n.* (*geog.*) экваториа́льная штилева́я полоса́; (*fig.*) уны́ние, хандра́; **be in the ~** быть в уны́нии, хандри́ть (*impf.*).

dole /dəʊl/ *n.* (*Br.*) (*benefit*) посо́бие по безрабо́тице; **he is on the ~** он получа́ет посо́бие по безрабо́тице.

● *v.t.*: **~ out** разд|ава́ть, -а́ть.

doleful /ˈdəʊlfʊl/ *adj.* ско́рбный.

dolefulness /ˈdəʊlfʊlnɪs/ *n.* скорбь.

doll /ˈdɒl/ *n.* **1** (*toy*) ку́кла; **~'s house** ку́кольный до́мик. **2** (*coll., sweet creature*) ку́колка.

● *v.t. & i.*: **~ (o.s) up** разоде́ться (*pf.*).

dollar /ˈdɒlə(r)/ *n.* до́ллар; **~ diplomacy** диплома́тия до́ллара; **(one's) bottom ~** после́дний грош.

dollop /ˈdɒləp/ *n.* соли́дная по́рция.

dolly /ˈdɒlɪ/ *n.* **1** = **doll.** **2** (*platform for camera*) опера́торская теле́жка.

dolorous /ˈdɒlərəs/ *adj.* го́рестный, печа́льный.

dolphin /ˈdɒlfɪn/ *n.* дельфи́н.

dolphinarium /,dɒlfɪˈneərɪəm/ *n.* (*pl.* **~s**) дельфина́рий.

dolt /dəʊlt/ *n.* болва́н, тупи́ца.

doltish /ˈdəʊltɪʃ/ *adj.* тупо́й.

doltishness /ˈdəʊltɪʃnɪs/ *n.* ту́пость.

domain /dəˈmeɪn/ *n.* **1** (*estate*) владе́ние, име́ние. **2** (*realm*) сфе́ра. **3** (*fig.*) о́бласть; **these matters are in his ~** э́ти дела́ вхо́дят в его́ компете́нцию.

dome /dəʊm/ *n.* ку́пол.

domed /dəʊmd/ *adj.*: **~ forehead** вы́пуклый лоб.

domestic /dəˈmestɪk/ *n.* прислу́га, домрабо́тница.

● *adj.* **1** (*of the home or family*) дома́шний; **~ science** домово́дство; **~ troubles** семе́йные неприя́тности. **2** (*home-loving*) дома́шний. **3** (*of animals*) дома́шний. **4** (*not foreign*) оте́чественный, вну́тренний; **~ product** (*econ.*) вну́тренний проду́кт.

domesticate /dəˈmestɪ,keɪt/ *v.t.* (*tame*) приуч|а́ть, -и́ть; (*interest in household*) приуч|а́ть, -и́ть к веде́нию хозя́йства; **she is not ~d** она́ не домосе́дка.

domestication /də,mestɪˈkeɪʃ(ə)n/ *n.* одома́шнивание, приуче́ние; приуче́ние к веде́нию хозя́йства.

domesticity /,dɒməˈstɪsɪtɪ/, /,dəʊ-/ *n.* семе́йная/дома́шняя жизнь.

domicile /ˈdɒmɪ,saɪl/, /-sɪl/ *n.* (*dwelling*) ме́сто жи́тельства.

● *v.t.*: **~d in England** име́ющий постоя́нное местожи́тельство в А́нглии.

domiciliary /,dɒmɪˈsɪlɪərɪ/ *adj.* дома́шний; **~ visit** визи́т на дом.

dominance /ˈdɒmɪnəns/ *n.* преоблада́ние, госпо́дство.

dominant /ˈdɒmɪnənt/ *n.* (*mus., biol.*) домина́нта.

● *adj.* **1** (*prevailing*) домини́рующий, преоблада́ющий. **2** (*of heights etc.*) госпо́дствующий, домини́рующий. **3** (*mus.*) домина́нтовый. **4** (*biol.*) домина́нтный.

dominate /ˈdɒmɪ,neɪt/ *v.t. & i.* **1** (*prevail*) домини́ровать (*impf.*) (над + *i.*); преоблада́ть (*impf.*) (над + *i.*). **2** (*influence*) подавля́ть, командова́ть (*both impf.*); **she ~s her daughter** она́ подавля́ет дочь. **3** (*of heights, buildings etc.*) домини́ровать (*impf.*) над + *i.*; возвыша́ться (*impf.*) над + *i.*

domination /,dɒmɪˈneɪʃ(ə)n/ *n.* госпо́дство.

domineer /,dɒmɪˈnɪə(r)/ *v.i.*: **~ over** помыка́ть (*impf.*) (*кем*); кома́ндовать (*impf.*) (*кем*).

domineering /,dɒmɪˈnɪərɪŋ/ *adj.* вла́стный.

Dominican /dəˈmɪnɪkən/ *n.* (*relig., pol.*) доминика́н|ец (*fem.* -ка).

● *adj.* доминика́нский; **the ~ Republic** Доминика́нская Респу́блика.

dominion /dəˈmɪnɪən/ *n.* (*lordship*) влады́чество; (*realm*) владе́ние; (*pol. hist.*) доминио́н.

domino /ˈdɒmɪ,nəʊ/ *n.* (*pl.* **~es**) пласти́нка домино́; (*pl., also name of game*) домино́ (*indecl.*).

don[1] /dɒn/ *n.* **1** (*Spanish title*) дон; **D~ Juan** (*fig.*) донжуа́н. **2** (*univ.*) преподава́тель (*m.*).

don[2] /dɒn/ *v.t.* (**donned, donning**) над|ева́ть, -е́ть.

donate /dəʊˈneɪt/ *v.t.* дари́ть, по-; же́ртвовать, по-.

donation /dəʊˈneɪʃ(ə)n/ *n.* дар; поже́ртвование.

done /dʌn/ *p.p. of* ⇒**do[1]**

donkey /ˈdɒŋkɪ/ *n.* осёл (*also fig.*); **for ~'s years** (*coll.*) с незапа́мятных времён.

● *cpd.* **~-work** *n.* (*coll.*) чёрная рабо́та.

donnish /ˈdɒnɪʃ/ *adj.* педанти́чный.

donor /ˈdəʊnə(r)/ *n.* дари́тель (*fem.* -ница), же́ртвователь (*fem.* -ница); (*of blood, transplant*) до́нор.

donut (*US*) = **doughnut**

doodle /ˈduːd(ə)l/ *n.* кара́кули (*f. pl.*).

● *v.t. & i.* чи́ркать (*impf.*).

● *cpd.* **~-bug** *n.* (*Br. coll.*) самолёт-снаря́д.

doom /duːm/ *n.* (*ruin*) ги́бель.

● *v.t.* обр|ека́ть, -е́чь на + *a.*

● *cpd.* **~sday** *n.* стра́шный суд; день стра́шного суда́; **till ~sday** (*fig.*) до второ́го прише́ствия.

door /dɔː(r)/ *n.* **1** (*of room etc.*) дверь; (*of cupboard etc.*) две́рца; **sliding ~** раздвижна́я дверь; **revolving ~** враща́ющаяся дверь; **front ~** пара́дная дверь; **back ~** за́дняя дверь; чёрный ход; **side ~** бокова́я дверь; **answer the ~** откр|ыва́ть, -ы́ть дверь; **he lives next ~** он живёт в сосе́днем до́ме; **he lives two ~s off** он живёт че́рез два до́ма отсю́да; **the boy next ~** сосе́дский ма́льчик; **the taxi took us from ~ to ~** такси́ довезло́ нас от до́ма до до́ма; **out of ~s** на све́жем/откры́том во́здухе; на дворе́/у́лице; **within ~s** до́ма, в помеще́нии; **show s.o. the ~** (*expel*) выставля́ть, вы́ставить кого́-н. за дверь; пока́з|ывать, -а́ть кому́-н. на дверь;

behind closed ~s (*in secret*) за закры́тыми дверя́ми.
2 (*fig., expr. proximity*): **that is next ~ to slander** от э́того оди́н шаг до клеветы́; **lay a crime at s.o.'s ~** вали́ть, с- вину́ на кого́-н.; **he shall never darken my ~ again** ноги́ его́ бо́льше не бу́дет в моём до́ме.
3 (*fig.*): **a ~ to success** путь к успе́ху; **close the ~ against, to, upon** отр|еза́ть, -е́зать путь к+*d.*; **force an open ~** ломи́ться (*impf.*) в откры́тую дверь.
● *cpds.* **~-bell** *n.* дверно́й звоно́к; **~-curtain** *n.* портье́ра; **~-to-~** *adj.*: **~ salesman** коммивояжёр; **~-frame** *n.* дверна́я коро́бка/ра́ма; **~-handle** *n.* дверна́я ру́чка; **~-keeper, ~man** *nn.* приврáтник; швейца́р; **~knob** *n.* кру́глая дверна́я ру́чка; **~man** *n.* = **~keeper; ~mat** *n.* полови́к; **~post** *n.* дверно́й кося́к; **deaf as a ~post** глухо́й как пень; **~step** *n.* поро́г; **~stop** *n.* упо́р две́ри; **~way** *n.* дверно́й проём.

dope /dəʊp/ *n.* **1** (*drug*) дурма́н, нарко́тик; (*taken by athlete, horse*) до́пинг; **~ fiend** (*sl.*) наркома́н. **2** (*sl., fool*) ду́рень (*m.*). **3** (*sl., information*) све́дения (*nt. pl.*).
● *v.t.* **1** (*make unconscious*) дурма́нить, о-. **2** (*put narcotic in*) наркотизи́ровать (*impf., pf.*).
3 (*stimulate with drug*) стимули́ровать (*impf., pf.*) нарко́тиками.

dopey /ˈdəʊpɪ/ *adj.* (**dopier, dopiest**) (*bemused by drug or sleep*) одурма́ненный; (*sl., foolish*) чо́кнутый.

dopiness /ˈdəʊpɪnɪs/ *n.* (*stupor*) одуре́ние; (*stupidity*) ду́рость.

doppelgänger /ˈdɒp(ə)l,geŋə(r)/ *n.* виде́ние (*живого человека*); (*double*) двойни́к.

Doric /ˈdɒrɪk/ *adj.* дори́ческий.

dormant /ˈdɔːmənt/ *adj.* (*of animals*) в спя́чке; **~ volcano** спя́щий вулка́н; **lie ~** безде́йствовать (*impf.*).

dormer(-window) /ˈdɔːmə(r)/ *n.* слухово́е окно́.

dormice /ˈdɔːmaɪs/ *pl. of* ⇒**dormouse**

dormitory /ˈdɔːmɪtərɪ/ *n.* дортуа́р; **~ suburb** ≈ при́городный посёлок.

dormouse /ˈdɔːmaʊs/ *n.* (*pl.* **dormice**) со́ня.

dorsal /ˈdɔːs(ə)l/ *adj.* спинно́й; **~ fin** спинно́й плавни́к.

dory /ˈdɔːrɪ/ *n.* (*fish*) со́лнечник.

DOS /dɒs/ (*abbr. of* ***disk operating system***) ДОС (ди́сковая операцио́нная систе́ма).

dosage /ˈdəʊsɪdʒ/ *n.* (*dosing*) дозиро́вка; (*dose*) до́за.

dose /dəʊs/ *n.* до́за; (*fig.*) по́рция.
● *v.t.* лечи́ть (*impf.*) до́зами лека́рства.

dosh /dɒʃ/ *n.* (*Br. sl.*) деньжа́т|а (*pl. g.* —).

doss /dɒs/ *v.i.* (*Br. coll.; also* **~ down**) ночева́ть, пере-; (*also* **~ around**) безде́льничать (*impf.*).
● *cpd.* **~-house** *n.* ночле́жка.

dosser /ˈdɒsə(r)/ *n.* (*Br. coll.*) бомж.

dossier /ˈdɒsɪə(r)/, /-ɪ,eɪ/ *n.* досье́ (*indecl.*), де́ло.

dot /dɒt/ *n.* (*small mark or object*) то́чка; **on the ~** то́чно; **~s and dashes** а́збука Мо́рзе; **in the year ~** (*Br. coll.*) о́чень давно́; **~ matrix printer** (*comput.*) ма́тричный при́нтер.
● *v.t.* (**dotted, dotting**) **1** (*place ~ on*): **~ one's i's** (*lit., fig.*) ста́вить, по- то́чки над «i». **2** (*mark, indicate with ~s*) отм|еча́ть, -е́тить то́чками/пункти́ром; пункти́ровать (*impf., pf.*); **~ted line** пункти́р; пункти́рная ли́ния; **sign on the ~ted line** (*fig.*) безогово́рочно согла|ша́ться, -си́ться; **~ted note** (*mus.*) удлинённая на полови́ну но́та. **3** (*scatter*) усе́|ивать, -ять; **villages ~ted about** дере́вни, разбро́санные вокру́г; **sea ~ted with ships** мо́ре, усе́янное корабля́ми.

dotage /ˈdəʊtɪdʒ/ *n.* ста́рческое слабоу́мие, мара́зм; **he is in his ~** он впал в де́тство/мара́зм.

dote /dəʊt/ *v.i.*: **~ on** (*child, friend*) обожа́ть (*impf.*); (*film star*) сходи́ть (*impf.*) с ума́ по+*d.*

doting /ˈdəʊtɪŋ/ *adj.* обожа́ющий.

dotty /ˈdɒtɪ/ *adj.* (**dottier, dottiest**) (*Br. coll., silly*) чо́кнутый.

double /ˈdʌb(ə)l/ *n.* **1** (*twofold quantity*): **ten is the ~ of five** де́сять вдво́е бо́льше пяти́; **~ or nothing** (*or Br.* **quits**) вдвойне́ и́ли ничего́; (*two shots of vodka etc.*) двойна́я ме́ра.
2 (*person or thing resembling another*) двойни́к, (*thing*) дублика́т.
3 (*running pace*) бе́глый шаг; **at the ~** бе́глым ша́гом.
4 (*tennis*) па́рная игра́; **mixed ~s** сме́шанные па́ры (*f. pl.*).
● *adj.* **1** (*in two parts; twice as much*) двойно́й; (*happening twice*) двукра́тный; **~ bed** дву(х)спа́льная крова́ть; **~ bend** (*on road*) зигза́г; **~ doors** двойны́е две́ри; **~ eagle** двугла́вый орёл; **~ room** (*in house*) больша́я ко́мната; (*in hotel*) двухме́стный но́мер; **~ saucepan** (*Br.*) кастрю́ля с двойны́м дном; **'Anna' is spelt with a ~ 'n'** «А́нна» пи́шется с двумя́ «н»; **serve a ~ purpose** выполня́ть, вы́полнить двойну́ю роль.
2 (*ambiguous, deceitful*): **~ dealer** двуру́шник; **~ dealing** двуру́шничество; **~ meaning** двоя́кий смысл, двусмы́сленность; **~ standard** двули́чие.
3 (*mus.*): **~ bass** контраба́с.
● *adv.* вдво́е; **bend ~** сгиба́ть(ся), согну́ть(ся) вдво́е; **pay ~** плати́ть, за- вдвойне́; **he sees ~** у него́ двои́тся в глаза́х; **it costs ~ what it used to** э́то сто́ит вдво́е доро́же, чем ра́ньше; **I am ~ his age** я вдво́е ста́рше его́.
● *v.t.* **1** (*make twice as great*) удв|а́ивать, -о́ить.
2 (*fold, clench*): **~ a shawl** скла́дывать, сложи́ть шаль вдво́е; **~ one's fists** сж|има́ть, -ать кулаки́; **~ up one's legs** под|гиба́ть, -огну́ть под себя́ но́ги.
3 (*cause to bend in pain*) скрю́чи|вать, -ть; **the blow ~d him up** он сложи́лся попола́м от уда́ра.
4 (*round*) огиба́ть, обогну́ть; **the ship ~d Cape Horn** кора́бль обогну́л мыс Горн.
● *v.i.* **1** (*become twice as great*) удв|а́иваться, -о́иться.
2 (*turn sharply*): **he ~d back on his tracks** он пошёл обра́тно по своему́ следу́.
3 (*bend*) скрю́чи|ваться, -ться; **he ~d up with the pain** он скрю́чился от бо́ли.
4 (*share room etc.*): **you will have to ~ up** вам придётся подели́ть ко́мнату на двои́х.
5 (*combine roles*): **I ~d for him** я дубли́ровал его́; **the porter ~s as waiter** носи́льщик рабо́тает официа́нтом по совмести́тельству.
● *cpds.* **~-barrelled** (*US* **barreled**) *adj.* (*gun*) двуство́льный; **~-barrelled name** (*Br.*) двойна́я фами́лия; **~-breasted** *adj.* двубо́ртный; **~-check** *v.t.* перепров|еря́ть, -е́рить; **~-click** *v.i.* (*comput.*) два́жды щёлк|ать, -нуть; **~-cross** *n.* вероло́мство; *v.t.* обма́н|ывать, -у́ть; **~-crosser** *n.* вероло́мный челове́к; **~-decker** *n.* (*bus*) двухэта́жный авто́бус; **~ Dutch** *n.* (*Br.*) тараба́рщина, кита́йская гра́мота; **~-dyed** *adj.* закорене́лый; махро́вый (*coll.*); **~-edged** *adj.* (*lit., fig.*) обоюдоо́стрый; **~-faced** *adj.* двули́чный; **~-jointed** *adj.* ги́бкий; **~-lock** *v.t.* зап|ира́ть, -ере́ть на два поворо́та ключа́; **~-park** *v.t. & i.* ста́вить, по- (маши́ну) во второ́й ряд; **~-quick** *adv.* о́чень бы́стро; **~-take** *n.* (*fig.*) заме́дленная реа́кция; **~-talk** *n.* неопределённые ре́чи (*f. pl.*).

double entendre /,duːb(ə)l ɑːnˈtɑːndrə/ *n.* двусмы́сленность.

doublet /ˈdʌblɪt/ *n.* (*garment*) камзо́л.

doubly /ˈdʌb(ə)lɪ/ *adv.* вдвойне́.

doubt /daʊt/ *n.* сомне́ние; **I have my ~s** у меня́ есть сомне́ние; **there is no (room for) ~ that** … нет сомне́ния в том, что…; **the question is in ~** э́тот вопро́с ещё не я́сен; **he is in ~ what to do** он не зна́ет, что ему́ де́лать; **without ~** вне сомне́ния; несомне́нно; **no ~** несомне́нно, безусло́вно; **cast ~ upon** подв|ерга́ть, -е́ргнуть сомне́нию; **when in ~, don't!** не уве́рен — не бери́сь!
● *v.t. & i.* сомнева́ться (*impf.*) (в+*p.*); **I ~ that/whether he will come** я сомнева́юсь, что он придёт; **~ing Thomas** Фома́ неве́рный/неве́рующий.

doubter /ˈdaʊtə(r)/ *n.* ске́птик.

doubtful /ˈdaʊtfʊl/ *adj.* **1** (*feeling doubt*) сомнева́ющийся; **I am ~ about going** я сомнева́юсь, идти́ и́ли нет. **2** (*causing doubt*) сомни́тельный; **he is a ~ character** он сомни́тельная ли́чность; **~ weather** неопределённая пого́да.

doubtfulness /ˈdaʊtfʊlnɪs/ *n.* сомни́тельность.

doubtless /ˈdaʊtlɪs/ *adv.* несомне́нно.

douche /duːʃ/ *n.* **1** (*shower*) душ.
2 (*internal*) промыва́ние.

dough /dəʊ/ *n.* те́сто; (*sl., money*) деньга́.

D

● *cpd.* **~nut** *n.* пóнчик.

doughty /ˈdaʊtɪ/ *adj.* (**doughtier, doughtiest**) дóблестный, отвáжный.

doughy /ˈdəʊɪ/ *adj.* (**doughier, doughiest**) (*of or like dough*) тестообрáзный; (*soft, flabby*) рыхлый.

dour /dʊə(r)/ *adj.* сурóвый.

dourness /ˈdʊənɪs/ *n.* сурóвость.

douse /daʊs/ *v.t.* (*drench*) зал|ивáть, -и́ть; (*extinguish*) гаси́ть, по-.

dove¹ /dʌv/ *n.* гóлубь (*m.*).

● *cpds.* **~-colour** (*US* **-color**) *n.* си́зый цвет; **~-coloured** (*US* **-colored**) *adj.* си́зый; **~cote** *n.* голубя́тня; **~tail** *n.* (*tech.*) лáсточкин хвост; *v.t.* соедин|я́ть, -и́ть лáсточкиным хвостóм; (*fig.*) соглас|óвывать, -овáть; *v.i.* (*fig.*) совп|адáть, -áсть

dove² /dəʊv/ *US past and p.p. of* ⇒**dive**

Dover /ˈdəʊvə(r)/ *n.* Дувр.

dowager /ˈdaʊədʒə(r)/ *n.* вдовá; **~ empress** вдóвствующая императри́ца; (*elderly lady*) матрóна.

dowdy /ˈdaʊdɪ/ *adj.* (**dowdier, dowdiest**) неэлегáнтный.

dowel /ˈdaʊəl/ *n.* (*tech.*) штифт, штырь.

down¹ /daʊn/ *n.* (*open high land*) безлéсная возвы́шенность.

down² /daʊn/ *n.* (*hair, fluff*) пух, пушóк.

down³ /daʊn/ *n.* **1** (*reverse, of fortune etc.*) невзгóда; **ups and ~s** взлёты (*m. pl.*) и падéния (*nt. pl.*); преврáтности (*f. pl.*) судьбы́. **2** (*coll., dislike*): **have a ~ on** (*or* **be ~ on**) **s.o.** имéть (*impf.*) зуб на когó-н.

● *adj.* напрáвленный вниз/кни́зу; **~ draught** (*Br.*), **draft** (*US*) (*tech.*) ни́жняя тя́га; **~ payment** авáнс.

● *adv.* **1** (*expr. motion/place*) вниз/внизу́; (*in crosswords*) по вертикáли; **he is not ~ yet** (*from bedroom*) он ещё не сошёл вниз; **the sun is ~** сóлнце сéло; **the blinds are ~** штóры спу́щены; **~ south** на ю́ге; **prices are ~** цéны упáли; (*fig.*): **he is ~ with fever** он слёг с высóкой температу́рой; **he is ~ and out** он разби́т; **~ under** (*coll.*) в Австрáлии; **he is £15 ~** он в убы́тке на 15 фу́нтов; **be ~ on s.o.** *see* ⇒**~** *n.* 2.
2 (*expr. movement to lower level*): **climb ~** слез|áть, -ть; **come ~** спус|кáться, -ти́ться; **~!** (*to a dog*) лежáть!; **we have read ~ to here** мы дочитáли до э́того мéста.
3 (*expr. change of position*): **sit ~** сади́ться, сесть; **lie ~** ложи́ться, лечь; **fall ~** пáдать, упáсть; **knock s.o. ~** сби|вáть, -ть; **he bent ~** он нагну́лся.
4 (*movement to less important place*): **we went ~ to Brighton for the day** мы съéздили нá день в Брáйтон.
5 (*reduction*): **the soles have worn ~** подмётки износи́лись; **the wind died ~** вéтер ути́х; **boil the fat ~** раст|áпливать, -опи́ть жир; **the quality of these goods has gone ~** кáчество э́тих товáров уху́дшилось; **the house burnt ~** дом сгорéл дотлá.
6 (*of writing*): **write something ~** запи́с|ывать, -áть что-н.; **take ~ a letter** писáть, на- письмó под диктóвку; **he is ~ to speak** он в спи́ске выступáющих.
7 (*to end of scale*): **everyone from the manager ~ to the office-boy** все — от дирéктора вплоть до посы́льного.
8 (*at once*): **pay cash ~** плати́ть, за- нали́чными.
9 (*var.*): **shout s.o. ~** кри́ком заст|авля́ть, -áвить когó-н. замолчáть; **~ with tyranny!** долóй тирани́ю!; **get ~ to business** брáться, взя́ться за дéло; **up and ~** (*to and fro*) взад и вперёд; *for other phrasal vv. see relevant v. entry.*

● *v.t.* (*coll., overcome*) одол|евáть, -éть; оси́ли|вать, -ть; (*coll., swallow*) прогл|áтывать, -оти́ть; **~ a glass of beer** осуш|áть, -и́ть стакáн пи́ва; **~ tools** (*Br., leave off work*) прекра|щáть, -ти́ть рабóту; (*strike*) забастовáть (*pf.*).

● *prep.* **1** (*expr. downward direction*): **we walked ~ the hill** мы шли́ с горы́ (*or* пóд гору); **tears ran ~ her face** слёзы текли́/кати́лись у неё по лицу́; **he glanced ~ the list** он мéльком взгляну́л на спи́сок.
2 (*at, to a lower or further part of*): **further ~ the river** дáльше вниз по рекé; **we sailed ~ the Volga** мы плы́ли вниз по Вóлге; **he lives ~ the street** он живёт дáльше по э́той у́лице.
3 (*along*): **he walked ~ the street** он шёл по у́лице.
4 (*var.*): **~ (the) wind** (*expr. place*) под вéтром; (*expr. motion*) по вéтру; **~ the ages** (*since earliest times*) с дáвних пор/ времён; **~ stage** (*theatr.*) на авансцéне.

down-and-out /daʊnəˈnaʊt/ *n.* бродя́га (*m.*); бездóмный.

downcast /ˈdaʊnkɑːst/ *adj.* (*dejected*) удручённый; подáвленный.

downfall /ˈdaʊnfɔːl/ *n.* (*of rain*) ли́вень (*m.*); (*ruin*) падéние, ги́бель.

downgrade /ˈdaʊngreɪd/ *v.t.* пон|ижáть, -и́зить в чи́не.

● *n.* (*US*) (*on road*) спуск, уклóн; (*fig., decline*) упáдок.

downhearted /daʊnˈhɑːtɪd/ *adj.* подáвленный, угнетённый.

downhill /ˈdaʊnhɪl/ *adj.* наклóнный.

● *adv.* пóд гору; вниз; **go ~** (*fig.*) кати́ться (*det.*) по наклóнной плóскости.

download /daʊnˈləʊd/ *v.t.* (*comput.*) загру|жáть, -зи́ть.

down-market /ˈdaʊnˈmɑːkɪt/ *adj.* (*Br.*) дешёвый.

downpour /ˈdaʊnpɔː(r)/ *n.* ли́вень (*m.*).

downright /ˈdaʊnraɪt/ *adj.* (*straightforward, blunt*) прямóй; (*absolute*) совершéнный; я́вный.

● *adv.* совершéнно, я́вно.

downshift /ˈdaʊnʃɪft/ *v.i.* **1** (*US, change to lower gear*) переключ|áть, -и́ть на ни́жнюю скóрость. **2** (*change job*) меня́ть, по- рабóту на мéнее напряжённую.

Down's syndrome /daʊnz/ *n.* болéзнь *or* синдрóм Дáуна; **~ sufferer** человéк, страдáющий болéзнью *or* синдрóмом Дáуна; дáун.

downstairs /ˈdaʊnsteəz/ *adj.*: **~ rooms** кóмнаты пéрвого этажá.

● *adv.* (*expr. place*) внизу́; (*expr. motion*) вниз.

downstream /ˈdaʊnstriːm/ *adv.* вниз по течéнию.

down-to-earth /ˈdaʊntəˌɜːθ/ *adj.* практи́чный, реалисти́ческий.

downtown /ˈdaʊntaʊn/ *adj.* (*US*) располóженный в деловóй чáсти гóрода.

downtrodden /ˈdaʊnˌtrɒd(ə)n/ *adj.* угнетённый.

downturn /ˈdaʊntɜːn/ *n.* (*fall, reduction*) падéние, спад.

downward /ˈdaʊnwəd/ *adj.* спускáющийся, опускáющийся.

downwards /ˈdaʊnwədz/ *adv.* вниз.

downy /ˈdaʊnɪ/ *adj.* (**downier, downiest**) (*fluffy*) пуши́стый.

dowry /ˈdaʊərɪ/ *n.* придáное.

dowser /ˈdaʊzə(r)/ *n.* лозоискáтель (*m.*).

doyen /ˈdɔɪən/, /ˈdwɑːjæ̃/ *n.* дуайéн, старшинá (*m.*).

doze /dəʊz/ *n.* дремóта.

● *v.i.* дремáть (*impf.*); **~ off** задремáть (*pf.*).

dozen /ˈdʌz(ə)n/ *n.* **1** (*pl.* **~**) дю́жина; **by the ~** дю́жинами; **a round ~** кру́глая дю́жина; **baker's ~** чёртова дю́жина; **talk nineteen to the ~** (*Br.*) говори́ть (*impf.*) без у́молку; **six of one and half a ~ of the other** что в лоб, что пó лбу. **2**: **~s of** мнóжество, мáсса +*g.*; **~s of times** ты́сячу раз.

doziness /ˈdəʊzɪnɪs/ *n.* дремóта, сонли́вость; рассéянность.

dozy /ˈdəʊzɪ/ *adj.* (**dozier, doziest**) сонли́вый; (*Br., not alert*) рассéянный.

DPP (*abbr. of* ***Director of Public Prosecutions***) (*Br.*) Глáвный прокурóр.

Dr. /ˈdɒktə(r)/ *n.* (*abbr. of* ***Doctor***) д-р (дóктор).

drab /dræb/ *adj.* (**drabber, drabbest**) (*dull*) сéрый.

drabness /ˈdræbnɪs/ *n.* сéрость.

drach|ma /ˈdrækmə/ *n.* (*pl.* **~mas** *or* **~mae** /-miː/) дрáхма.

Draconian /drəˈkəʊnɪən/ *adj.* дракóновский.

draft /drɑːft/ *n. see also* ⇒**draught.** **1** (*outline, rough copy*) набрóсок, чернови́к. **2** (*order for payment*) чек, трáтта. **3** (*detachment of men for duty*) наря́д. **4** (*US, conscription*) призы́в; **~ dodger** лицó, уклоня́ющееся от воéнной слу́жбы; **~ evasion** уклонéние от воéнной слу́жбы.

● *v.t.* **1** (*detach for duty*) наря|жáть, -ди́ть; командировáть, от- **2** (*conscript*) приз|ывáть, -вáть. **3** (*prepare* **~** *of*) набр|áсывать, -осáть черновик +*g.*

draftsman /ˈdrɑːftsmən/ *n.* (*of contracts etc.*) состави́тель (*m.*) (*законопроекта и т.п.*); (*US, one who draws*) чертёжник.

drafty /ˈdrɑːftɪ/ (*US*) = **draughty**

drag /dræg/ *n.* **1** (*also* **~-net**) бре́день (*m.*), не́вод.
2 (*hindrance*) то́рмоз, препя́тствие; **she was a ~ on his progress** она́ препя́тствовала его́ успе́ху.
3 (*pull on cigarette etc.*) затя́жка.
4 (*coll.*) же́нское пла́тье (трансвести́та).
5 (*coll.*) (*person*) зану́да; (*thing*) тоска́ зелёная.
● *v.t.* (**dragged, dragging**) **1** (*pull*) тяну́ть, волочи́ть, тащи́ть (*all impf.*); **they ~ged him out of hiding** они́ вы́волокли его́ из укры́тия; **I had to ~ him to the party** мне пришло́сь потащи́ть его́ на вечери́нку; **he could hardly ~ his feet along** он е́ле волочи́л но́ги; **~ one's feet** (*fig.*) тяну́ть (*impf.*); ме́длить (*impf.*).
2 (*search, dredge*) драги́ровать (*impf., pf.*); чи́стить, вы́- дно +*g*.
● *v.i.* (**dragged, dragging**) **1** (*trail*) волочи́ться (*impf.*); тащи́ться (*impf.*).
2 (*be slow or tedious*) тяну́ться (*impf.*); затя́|гиваться, -ну́ться; **the soloist ~ged behind the orchestra** соли́ст отстава́л от орке́стра.
● *with advs.*: **~ down** *v.t.*: **he ~ged the luggage down** он стащи́л чемода́ны вниз; (*fig.*): **he ~ged her down with him** он увлёк её за собо́й к ги́бели; **~ in** *v.t.* прит|я́гивать, -яну́ть; **why ~ in Cicero?** при чём тут Цицеро́н?; **~ on** *v.i.*: **the performance ~ged on till 11** представле́ние затяну́лось до оди́ннадцати часо́в; **~ out** *v.t.* (*protract*) растя́|гивать, -ну́ть; **~ up** *v.t.* (*Br. coll., a child*) запус|ка́ть, -ти́ть.

dragon /ˈdrægən/ *n.* (*fabulous beast*) драко́н; (*formidable woman*) ме́гера, фу́рия.
● *cpd.* **~-fly** *n.* стрекоза́.

dragoon /drəˈguːn/ *n.* драгу́н.
● *v.t.* прину|жда́ть, -ди́ть; **he was ~ed into obeying** его́ заста́вили подчини́ться.

drain /dreɪn/ *n.* **1** (*channel carrying off sewage etc.*) водосто́к; (*pl., system of ~s*) канализа́ция; **throw money down the ~** (*fig.*) бр|оса́ть, -о́сить де́ньги на ве́тер; тра́тить, по- (*impf.*) де́ньги впусту́ю; **go down the ~** (*fig.*) кати́ться, по- по накло́нной пло́скости.
2 (*cause of exhaustion*) истоще́ние; **it is a ~ on my energy** э́то истоща́ет мою́ эне́ргию.
● *v.t.* **1** (*water etc.*) отв|оди́ть, -ести́.
2 (*land etc.*) осуш|а́ть, -и́ть; дрени́ровать (*impf., pf.*); **~ing-board** (*Br.*), **drain-board** (*US*) суши́лка.
3 (*deplete*) истощ|а́ть, -и́ть.
4 (*drink contents of*) осуш|а́ть, -и́ть.
● *v.i.* **1** (*flow away*) ут|ека́ть, -е́чь.
2 (*lose moisture, become dry*) высыха́ть, вы́сохнуть; **the field ~s into the river** вода́ с по́ля стека́ет в ре́ку.
3 (*fig.*): **his life was ~ing away** жизнь по ка́плям уходи́ла из него́.
● *cpd.* **~pipe** *n.* дрена́жная труба́; **~pipe trousers** брю́ки ду́дочкой.

drainage /ˈdreɪnɪdʒ/ *n.* **1** (*draining or being drained*) дрена́ж, осуше́ние.
2 (*system of drains*) канализа́ция.

drainer /ˈdreɪnə(r)/ *n.* (*surface*) суши́лка; (*colander*) дуршла́г.

drake /dreɪk/ *n.* се́лезень (*m.*).

dram /dræm/ *n.* (*tot of spirits*) глото́к спиртно́го; **he is fond of a ~** он не дура́к вы́пить.

drama /ˈdrɑːmə/ *n.* **1** (*play; exciting episode*) дра́ма. **2** (*dramatic art*) дра́ма, драматурги́я. **3** (*dramatic quality*) драмати́зм.

dramatic /drəˈmætɪk/ *adj.* (*pert. to drama*) драмати́ческий, театра́льный; (*exciting*) драмати́чный, порази́тельный.

dramatics /drəˈmætɪks/ *n.* **1** (*staging of plays*) драмати́ческое иску́сство; теа́тр; **amateur ~** люби́тельский/самоде́ятельный теа́тр. **2** (*theatrical behaviour*) драмати́зм.

dramatis personae /ˌdræmətɪs pɜːˈsəʊnaɪ/, /-niː/ *n.* (*characters*) де́йствующие ли́ца; (*list*) спи́сок де́йствующих лиц.

dramatist /ˈdræmətɪst/ *n.* драмату́рг.

dramatization /ˌdræmətaɪˈzeɪʃ(ə)n/ *n.* инсцениро́вка, драматиза́ция.

dramatize /ˈdræməˌtaɪz/ *v.t.* (*turn into a play*) инсцени́ровать (*impf., pf.*); драматизи́ровать (*impf., pf.*); (*exaggerate*) драматизи́ровать (*impf., pf.*).

drank /dræŋk/ *past of* ⇒**drink**

drape /dreɪp/ *n.* (*usu. pl.*) за́навес, портье́ра.
● *v.t.* драпирова́ть, за-; **~ a cloak over one's shoulders** оку́т|ывать, -ать пле́чи плащо́м; **~ walls with flags** драпирова́ть, за- сте́ны фла́гами.

drapery /ˈdreɪpərɪ/ *n.* (*goods*) тексти́льные изде́лия; тексти́ль (*m.*), тка́ни (*f. pl.*); (*cloth arranged in folds*) драпиро́вка.

drastic /ˈdræstɪk/, /ˈdrɑː-/ *adj.* реши́тельный, круто́й.

drat /dræt/ *v.t.* (*coll.*): **~ him** чтоб его́!; **~ted** проклятый.
● *int.* чёрт возьми́!, прокля́тие!

draught /drɑːft/ (*US* **draft**) *n. see also* ⇒**draft. 1** (*current of air*) тя́га; сквозня́к; (*in chimney, air-conditioning*) тя́га; **there is a ~ in this room** в э́той ко́мнате сквози́т; **sit in a ~** сиде́ть (*impf.*) на сквозняке́. **2** (*catch of fish*) уло́в. **3** (*of ships*) оса́дка. **4** (*supply of liquor*): **~ beer, beer on ~** пи́во из бо́чки. **5** (*amount drunk*) глото́к; **he drank the glassful in one ~** он за́лпом вы́пил це́лый стака́н. **6** (*traction by animals*) тя́га. **7** (*pl., Br., game*) ша́шки (*f. pl.*).
● *cpds.* **~-board** *n.* (*Br.*) ша́шечная доска́; **~-horse** *n.* ломова́я ло́шадь.

draughtsman /ˈdrɑːftsmən/ *n.* (*see also* ⇒**draftsman**) **1** (*one who makes drawings etc.*) чертёжник. **2** (*in game of draughts*) ша́шка.

draughtsmanship /ˈdrɑːftsmənʃɪp/ *n.* уме́ние черти́ть/рисова́ть; чертёжное иску́сство.

draughtswoman /ˈdrɑːftswʊmən/ *n.* чертёжница.

draughty /ˈdrɑːftɪ/ (*US* **drafty**) *adj.* (**draughtier, draughtiest**): **this is a ~ room** в э́той ко́мнате постоя́нный сквозня́к.

draw /drɔː/ *n.* (*in lottery*) ро́зыгрыш; (*attraction*) привлека́тельность, прима́нка; (*~n game*) ничья́.
● *v.t.* (*past* **drew;** *p.p.* **drawn**) **1** (*pull, move*) тяну́ть (*impf.*); таска́ть (*indet.*), тащи́ть, по-; **~ one's hand across one's forehead** пров|оди́ть, -ести́ руко́й по́ лбу; **~ s.o. aside** отв|оди́ть, -ести́ кого́-н. в сто́рону; **~ the curtains** (*close*) задёр|гивать, -нуть (*or* задв|ига́ть, -и́нуть) занаве́ски; (*open*) отдёр|гивать, -нуть (*or* раздв|ига́ть, -и́нуть) занаве́ски; **the train was ~n by two engines** по́езд тяну́ли два локомоти́ва.
2 (*extract*) выта́скивать, вы́тащить; **he drew a handkerchief out of his pocket** он вы́тащил плато́к из карма́на; **~ a knife** выхва́тывать, вы́хватить нож; **~ blood** ра́нить (*impf., pf.*) кого́-н. до кро́ви; **~ the sword** обнаж|а́ть, -и́ть меч; **have a tooth ~n, ~ a tooth** вырыва́ть, вы́рвать зуб; **~ s.o.'s teeth** (*fig.*) обезвре́|живать, -дить кого́-н.; **~ lots** тяну́ть, вы́- жре́бий; **~ a blank** (*fig.*) терпе́ть, по- неуда́чу; **~ a card from the pack** брать, взять ка́рту из коло́ды.
3 (*obtain from a source*): **~ (off) water from a well** брать (*impf.*) во́ду из коло́дца; **~ one's salary** получ|а́ть, -и́ть зарпла́ту; **~ money out of the bank** снима́ть, снять де́ньги в ба́нке; **~ a moral from a story** извл|ека́ть, -е́чь мора́ль из расска́за; **~ inspiration from nature** че́рпать (*impf.*) вдохнове́ние в приро́де; **~ on one's savings** тра́тить, по- свои́ сбереже́ния; **~ on s.o.'s help** приб|ега́ть, -е́гнуть к чье́й-н. по́мощи.
4 (*attract*) привл|ека́ть, -е́чь; **the film drew large audiences** фильм привлёк мно́го зри́телей; **I drew him into the conversation** я втяну́л *or* вовлёк его́ в разгово́р; **she felt ~n towards him** её тяну́ло *or* влекло́ к нему́.
5 (*stretch*): **he drew the metal into a long wire** он вы́тянул *or* протяну́л мета́лл в дли́нную про́волоку; **his face was ~n with pain** его́ лицо́ осу́нулось от бо́ли.
6 (*trace, depict*) рисова́ть, на-; черти́ть, на-; **~ a line** пров|оди́ть, -ести́ ли́нию.
7 (*of mental operations*): **~ a distinction/comparison** пров|оди́ть, -ести́ разли́чие/сравне́ние; **~ conclusions** при|ходи́ть, -йти́ к вы́водам.
8 (*of documents*): **~ a cheque** (*Br.*), **check** (*US*) выпи́сывать, вы́писать чек; **~ (up) a contract** сост|авля́ть, -а́вить догово́р.
9 (*of ship*): **the ship ~s 20 feet of water** су́дно име́ет оса́дку в 20 фу́тов.
10 (*of contest*): **the match was ~n** матч был сы́гран (*or* око́нчился) вничью́.
11 (*disembowel*): **hanged, ~n and quartered** пове́шен и четверто́ван; **~ a chicken** потроши́ть, вы́- ку́рицу.
● *v.i.* (*past* **drew;** *p.p.* **drawn**) **1** (*admit air*) тяну́ть (*impf.*); втя́|гивать, -ну́ть;

this pipe ~s well эта трубка хорошо тянет.
2 (*move, come*) придв|игаться, -инуться; **he drew near** он придвинулся поближе; **they drew round the table** они собрались вокруг стола; **the day drew to a close** день близился к концу; **the ships drew level** корабли поравнялись.
3 (*infuse*) наст|аиваться, -ояться; **he let the tea ~** он дал чаю настояться.
4 (*pull*): **~ at a cigarette** затя|гиваться, -нуться папиросой; *see also* ⇒**drawing.**

● *with advs.*: **~ back** *v.t.*: **he drew back the curtain** он отдёрнул занавеску; *v.i.*: **he drew back in alarm** он в страхе отпрянул; **~ down** *v.t.* (*e.g. blinds*) спус|кать, -тить; **he drew down reproaches on his head** он навлёк на себя упрёки; **~ in** *v.t.*: **he drew in the details** он изобразил детали; **the cat drew in its claws** кошка втянула когти; *v.i.*: **the train drew in** поезд подошёл к перрону; **the car drew in to the roadside** автомобиль подъехал к обочине; (*shorten*): **the days are ~ing in** дни становятся короче; **~ off** *v.t.* (*e.g. water*) черпать (*impf.*); **~ on** *v.t.*: **~ on one's gloves** натя|гивать, -нуть перчатки; *v.i.* (*advance*): **autumn ~s on** осень приближается; **~ out** *v.t.* (*extract*) вытаскивать, вытащить; вытягивать, вытянуть; (*prolong*) затя|гивать, -нуть; **the battle was long ~n-out** битва оказалась затяжной; (*encourage to speak*): **~ s.o. out** вызывать, вызвать кого-н. на разговор; *v.i.*: **the train drew out** поезд отошёл; **the car drew out into the road** автомобиль выехал на дорогу; **~ up** *v.t.*: **~ o.s. up** (*to one's full height*) выпрямляться, выпрямиться; **~ one's chair up to the table** пододв|игать, -инуть стул к столу; **~ up troops** выстраивать, выстроить войска; (*plan, contract etc.*) сост|авлять, -авить; оф|ормлять, -ормить; *v.i.*: **the taxi drew up at the door** такси подъехало к двери.

● *cpds.* **~back** *n.* (*disadvantage*) недостаток; (*refund of duty*) возвратная пошлина; **~bridge** *n.* подъёмный мост.

drawee /drɔ:ˈi:/ *n.* (*fin.*) трассат.

drawer /ˈdrɔ:ə(r)/, *senses* 3 *and* 4 /drɔ:(r)/ *n.* **1** (*author of drawing*) рисовальщик. **2** (*fin.*) трассант; (*of cheque*) чекодатель (*m.*). **3** (*in table etc.*) (выдвижной) ящик; **chest of ~s** комод; **bottom ~** (*fig., trousseau*) приданое; **she is out of the top ~** (*fig., well-bred*) она прекрасно воспитана. **4** (*pl., underpants*) кальсон|ы (*pl., g.* —).

drawing /ˈdrɔ:ɪŋ/ *n.* **1** (*technique*) рисование. **2** (*piece of ~*) рисунок.

● *cpds.* **~-board** *n.* чертёжная доска; **~-pin** *n.* (*Br.*) кнопка; **~-room** *n.* гостиная.

drawl /drɔ:l/ *n.* протяжное произношение.

● *v.t. & i.* тянуть (*impf.*) (слова).

drawn /drɔ:n/ *p.p. of* ⇒**draw**

dray /dreɪ/ *n.* ломовая телега.

● *cpds.* **~-horse** *n.* ломовая лошадь; **~man** *n.* ломовой извозчик.

dread /dred/ *n.* ужас, страх; **stand in ~ of s.o.** бояться (*impf.*) кого-н.; **in ~ of one's life** в страхе за свою жизнь.

● *adj.* ужасный, грозный.

● *v.t.* бояться (*impf.*) + *g.*; **I ~ to think what may happen** мне страшно подумать, что может случиться.

● *cpd.* **~nought** *n.* дредноут.

dreadful /ˈdredfʊl/ *adj.* ужасный.

dreadfulness /ˈdredfʊlnɪs/ *n.* ужас.

dream /dri:m/ *n.* **1** (*appearance in sleep*) сон, сновидение.
2 (*fantasy*) мечта, мечтание; (*poet.*) грёза; **land of ~s** царство грёз.
3 (*bemused state*): **he goes about in a ~** он ходит как во сне.
4 (*delightful object*) мечта, сказка; **she looked a perfect ~** она была сказочно хороша; **~ house** дом-сказка.

● *v.t. & i.* (*past and p.p.* **dreamed** /dremt/, /dri:md/ *or* **dreamt**) **1** (*in sleep*) видеть (*impf.*) сон; **I ~t that I was in the forest** мне снилось, что я в лесу; **I ~t of you** вы мне снились; я видел вас во сне.
2 (*imagine*) пом|ышлять, -ыслить о + *p.*; фантазировать (*impf.*); **I never ~t of doing so** я и не помышлял сделать это; **you must have ~t it** это вам померещилось/приснилось; **he ~t up a plan** (*coll.*) он сочинил план.
3 (*spend time in reverie*) грезить (*impf.*); мечтать (*impf.*); **he ~t away his life** он провёл жизнь в мечтах; он жил в мире грёз.

● *cpds.* **~-land, ~-world** *nn.* царство грёз; **~-like** *adj.* сказочный.

dreamer /ˈdri:mə(r)/ *n.* (*in sleep*) видящий сны; (*dreamy person*) мечтатель (*m.*); (*visionary*) фантазёр.

dreaminess /ˈdri:mɪnɪs/ *n.* мечтательность.

dreamless /ˈdri:mlɪs/ *adj.* без сновидений; **he fell into a ~ sleep** он погрузился в глубокий сон.

dreamt /dremt/ *past and p.p. of* ⇒**dream**

dreamy /ˈdri:mɪ/ *adj.* (**dreamier, dreamiest**) мечтательный; (*coll., lovely*) восхитительный.

dreariness /ˈdrɪərɪnɪs/ *n.* серость.

dreary /ˈdrɪərɪ/ *adj.* (**drearier, dreariest**) (*gloomy*) тоскливый; (*dull*) серый.

dredge /dredʒ/ *n.* (*net*) драга; (*machine*) драга, землечерпалка.

● *v.i. & i.* драгировать (*impf., pf.*); вычищать, вычистить; **~ up** вылавливать, выловить.

dredger /ˈdredʒə(r)/ *n.* землечерпалка, землесос.

dreg /dreg/ *n.* (*usu. pl.*) **1** (*of liquor*) отстой, осадок; **drain to the ~s** пить, вы- до дна. **2** (*pl., fig.*) подонки (*m. pl.*).

drench /drentʃ/ *v.t.* пром|ачивать, -очить; **we got a ~ing** мы промокли насквозь; **he was ~ed to the skin** он вымок до нитки; он промок до костей.

Dresden /ˈdrezd(ə)n/ *n.* Дрезден; (*attr.*) дрезденский.

dress /dres/ *n.* **1** (*clothing, costume*) одежда, наряд, туалет; **full ~** парадная форма; **morning ~** (*formal*) визитка; **national ~** национальный костюм; **evening ~** фрак; (*woman's*) вечернее платье; **~ circle** бельэтаж; **~ coat** фрак; **~ rehearsal** генеральная репетиция; **day ~** повседневная одежда; **~ suit** фрак; фрачная пара; **~ shirt** фрачная сорочка.
2 (*woman's garment*) платье.

● *v.t.* **1** (*clothe*) од|евать, -еть; **the boy can ~ himself** мальчик умеет сам одеваться; **she was ~ed in white** она была одета в белое; **~ed up to the nines, ~ed to kill** расфранчённый; разодетый в пух и прах.
2 (*prepare*) припр|авлять, -авить; **~ leather** выделывать, выделать кожу; **~ a salad** запр|авлять, -авить салат; **~** (*clean*) **a chicken** обраб|атывать, -отать курицу.
3 (*of a wound*) перевяз|ывать, -ать.
4 (*adorn*) наря|жать, -дить; **~ a shop window** оф|ормлять, -ормить витрину.
5 (*mil., align*) выравнивать, выровнять.

● *v.i.* **1** (*put on one's clothes*) од|еваться, -еться; **she takes an hour to ~** она одевается час; **~ up** (**~** *elaborately*) наря|жаться, -диться; разря|жаться, -диться; **they ~ed up as pirates** они нарядились пиратами.
2 (*put on evening ~*) переод|еваться, -еться в вечернее платье; **no-one ~es for dinner** никто не переодевается к обеду.
3 (*choose clothes*) од|еваться, -еться; **he ~es well** он хорошо одевается.
4 (*of troops*) выравниваться, выровняться; **right ~!** равнение направо!

● *cpds.* **~maker** *n.* портниха; **~maker's** *n.* ателье (*indecl.*) мод; **~making** *n.* пошив дамской одежды.

dressage /ˈdresɑ:ʒ/, /-sɑ:dʒ/ *n.* объездка лошадей.

dresser¹ /ˈdresə(r)/ *n.* **1** (*chooser of clothes etc.*): **she is a good ~** она хорошо одевается. **2** (*theatr.*) костюмер (*fem.* -ша). **3** (*Br., in hospital*) хирургическая сестра. **4** (*of leather*) кожевник.

dresser² /ˈdresə(r)/ *n.* (*sideboard*) буфет; (*US, chest of drawers*) комод.

dressiness /ˈdresɪnɪs/ *n.* шик, нарядность.

dressing /ˈdresɪŋ/ *n.* **1** (*med.*) повязка. **2** (*US, stuffing*) начинка. **3** (*of salad etc.*) заправка, приправа. **4** (*manure*) удобрение.

● *cpds.* **~down** *n.* (*coll.*) головомойка, трёпка; **~-gown** *n.* халат; **~-room** *n.* (*theatr.*) артистическая уборная; (*sport*) раздевалка; **~-station** *n.* (*mil.*) перевязочный пункт; **~-table** *n.* туалетный столик.

dressy /ˈdresɪ/ *adj.* (**dressier, dressiest**) шикарный, нарядный.

drew /druː/ *past of* ⇒**draw**

dribble /ˈdrɪb(ə)l/ *n.* (*trickle*) стру́йка.
● *v.t.*: **~ a ball** вести́ (*det.*) мяч.
● *v.i.* (*of baby*) пуска́ть, пусти́ть слю́ни.

dribbler /ˈdrɪblə(r)/ *n.* веду́щий мяч.

driblet /ˈdrɪblɪt/ *n.* ка́пелька; **in ~s** понемно́жку; по ка́пле.

drier /ˈdraɪə(r)/ *n.* (*drying agent*) сиккати́в; (**hair-~**) фен; (**clothes-~**) суши́льный автома́т.

drift /drɪft/ *n.* **1** (*continuous slow movement*) ме́дленное тече́ние; (*of tide etc.*) тече́ние, самотёк. **2** (*heap of snow, leaves etc.*) нано́с, ку́ча. **3** (*meaning*) смысл; **I get his ~** я понима́ю, куда́ он кло́нит. **4** (*tendency*) направле́ние. **5** (*inactivity*) пасси́вность.
● *v.t.*: **the wind ~ed the snow into high banks** ве́тер намёл высо́кие сугро́бы.
● *v.i.* дрейфова́ть (*impf.*); **the boat ~ed out to sea** ло́дку отнесло́ в мо́ре; **we ~ed downstream** нас отнесло́ вниз по тече́нию; **we are ~ing towards disaster** мы дви́жемся к катастро́фе; **they were friends but ~ed apart** они́ бы́ли друзья́ми, но их пути́ постепе́нно разошли́сь.
● *cpds.* **~-net** *n.* дри́фтерная сеть; **~wood** *n.* сплавно́й лес.

drifter /ˈdrɪftə(r)/ *n.* (*aimless person*) лету́н; перекати́-по́ле.

drill[1] /drɪl/ *n.* (*instrument*) (*small*) дрель; (*large*) бур, бура́в; (*dentist's*) бормаши́на.
● *v.t.* сверли́ть, про-; бури́ть, про-; **~ a hole** сверли́ть, про- отве́рстие; **~ a tooth** сверли́ть (*impf.*) зуб.
● *v.i.* бури́ть (*impf.*); **~ for oil** бури́ть (*impf.*) нефтяну́ю сква́жину.

drill[2] /drɪl/ *n.* **1** (*military exercise*) строева́я подгото́вка, (*coll.*) муштра́. **2** (*thorough practice*) трениро́вка. **3** (*coll., procedure*) процеду́ра; **what's the ~ for getting tickets?** какова́ процеду́ра получе́ния биле́тов?
● *v.t.* **1** (*troops*) обуч|а́ть, -и́ть стро́ю; муштрова́ть, вы́-. **2**: **~ s.o. in grammar** ната́ск|ивать, -а́ть кого́-н. по грамма́тике; **I have ~ed him in what he is to say** я вдолби́л ему́, что он до́лжен говори́ть.
● *v.i.* упражня́ться (*impf.*); про|ходи́ть, -йти́ строево́е обуче́ние; **the troops were ~ing all morning** войска́ занима́лись строево́й подгото́вкой всё у́тро.
● *cpd.* **~-sergeant** *n.* сержа́нт-инстру́ктор по строево́й подгото́вке.

drill[3] /drɪl/ *n.* (*text.*) тик.

drily, dryly /ˈdraɪlɪ/ *adv.* су́хо; (*humorously*) ирони́чно.

drink /drɪŋk/ *n.* **1** (*liquid*) напи́ток, питьё. **2** (*quantity*) глото́к; **give me a ~ of water** да́йте мне воды́/водíчки. **3** (*alcoholic*) вы́пивка, спиртно́й напи́ток; **take to ~** пристрасти́ться (*pf.*) к спиртно́му/вы́пивке; **drive s.o. to ~** дов|оди́ть, -ести́ кого́-н. до пья́нства; **in ~** в пья́ном ви́де; **he smells of ~** от него́ несёт спиртны́м. **4**: **the ~** (*coll., sea*) мо́ре.
● *v.t.* (*past* **drank;** *p.p.* **drunk**) **1** (*consume liquid*) пить, вы́-; **~ down** пить, вы́- за́лпом; **~ up** доп|ива́ть, -и́ть; **~ing-fountain** питьево́й фонта́нчик; **~ing-water** питьева́я вода́. **2** (*of plants, soil etc.*) впит|ывать, -а́ть; **the flowers have drunk all that water** цветы́ впита́ли всю во́ду. **3** (*absorb with the mind*) впи́т|ывать, -а́ть. **4** (*of alcoholic liquor*) пить (*or* выпива́ть), вы́-; **he drank himself to death** пья́нство свело́ его́ в моги́лу; **he ~s half his earnings** он пропива́ет полови́ну своего́ за́работка; **~ s.o. under the table** переп|ива́ть, -и́ть кого́-н.; **~ing-bout** попо́йка; **~ing-song** засто́льная пе́сня. **5**: **~ a toast** провозгла|ша́ть, -си́ть тост; подн|има́ть, -я́ть бока́л (за + *a.*); **~ s.o.'s health** пить, вы́- за чьё-н. здоро́вье; **I ~ to your success** я пью за ваш успе́х.
● *v.i.* (*past* **drank;** *p.p.* **drunk**) (*consume liquid*) пить (*impf.*); **~ deep** мно́го пить; (*be a drunkard*) пить (*impf.*) запо́ем, пья́нствовать (*impf.*); **do you ~?** вы пьёте?; **he ~s like a fish** он пьёт как сапо́жник.
● *cpd.* **~-driving** *n.* (*Br.*) вожде́ние в нетре́звом состоя́нии.

drinkable /ˈdrɪŋkəb(ə)l/ *adj.* (*capable of being drunk*) питьево́й, го́дный для питья́; (*palatable*) вку́сный.

drinker /ˈdrɪŋkə(r)/ *n.* (*one who drinks, esp. alcohol*) пью́щий; **he is an occasional ~** он иногда́ выпива́ет; (*drunkard*) пья́ница.

drip /drɪp/ *n.* (*action*) ка́панье; (*drop*) ка́пля; (*sl., dull person*) зану́да (*c.g.*); (*weak person*) слюнтя́й.
● *v.t.* (**dripped, dripping**): **he was ~ping sweat** кати́лся с него́ гра́дом.
● *v.i.* (**dripped, dripping**) ка́пать (*impf.*); стека́ть (*impf.*) по ка́плям; **his shirt ~ped with blood** его́ руба́шка промо́кла от кро́ви; **~ping wet** насквозь промо́кший; **the wall ~s** стена́ протека́ет.
● *cpds.* **~-dry** *adj.* не тре́бующий гла́жки; *v.t.* суши́ть (*impf.*) на ве́шалке, не выжима́я; **~-feed** *n.* ка́пельное внутриве́нное влива́ние; ка́пельная кли́зма.

dripping /ˈdrɪpɪŋ/ *n.* (*pl., US, liquid*) ка́пли (*f. pl.*); (*Br., cul.*) топлёный жир.

drive /draɪv/ *n.* **1** (*ride in vehicle*) езда́; **go for a ~** прокати́ться, поката́ться (*both pf.*) (на маши́не); **take s.o. for a ~** прокати́ть/поката́ть (*pf.*) кого́-н. (на маши́не); **the station is an hour's ~ away** до ста́нции час езды́. **2** (*private road*) подъездна́я доро́га. **3** (*hit, stroke, at tennis etc.*) драйв, си́льный уда́р. **4** (*energy*) напо́ристость, напо́р. **5** (*organized effort*) кампа́ния; **a ~ for new members** кампа́ния по привлече́нию но́вых чле́нов. **6** (*strong need*) стремле́ние. **7** (*Br., tournament*) состяза́ние. **8** (*driving gear*) переда́ча, приво́д; **front-wheel ~** пере́дний приво́д; **left-hand ~** ле́вое рулево́е управле́ние; **~ belt** приводно́й реме́нь; **~ shaft** веду́щий вал. **9** (*comput.*) дисково́д.
● *v.t.* (*past* **drove;** *p.p.* **driven**) **1** (*force to move*) гоня́ть (*indet.*), гнать (*det.*); выбива́ть, вы́бить; **~ away** прог|оня́ть, -на́ть; **~ in** заг|оня́ть, -на́ть; **~ out** выгоня́ть, вы́гнать; **~ cattle to market** гнать (*det.*) скот на ры́нок; **~ s.o. into a corner** (*fig.*) заг|оня́ть, -на́ть кого́-н. в у́гол. **2** (*operate*) управля́ть (*impf.*) + *i.*; пра́вить (*impf.*) + *i.*; **~ a car** води́ть (*indet.*) маши́ну; **the machinery is ~n by steam** маши́на приво́дится в де́йствие па́ром; маши́на рабо́тает на пару́. **3** (*convey*) отв|ози́ть, -езти́; **I was ~n to the station** меня́ отвезли́ на ста́нцию. **4** (*impel, of objects*): **the gale drove the ship on to the rocks** шторм гнал кора́бль к ска́лам; **the wind drove the rain against the windows** дождь и ве́тер стуча́ли в о́кна, **he drove a nail into the plank** он вбил гвоздь в до́ску; **he drove the ball into our court** (*tennis*) он посла́л мяч на на́шу полови́ну ко́рта; **~n snow** сугро́б; **~ home** (*nail etc.*) загоня́ть, загна́ть; вкол|а́чивать, -оти́ть; вби|ва́ть, -ть; **~ something home to s.o.** убе|жда́ть, -ди́ть кого́-н. в чём-н.; дов|оди́ть, -ести́ кого́-н. до осозна́ния чего́-н.; **this drove the matter out of my head** э́то заста́вило меня́ всё забы́ть. **5** (*impel, fig.*): **failure drove him to despair** неуда́ча довела́ его́ до отча́яния; **~ s.o. mad** св|оди́ть, -ести́ кого́-н. с ума́; **hunger drove him to steal** го́лод заста́вил его́ ворова́ть. **6** (*force to work hard*) гоня́ть, гна́ть; **he has been driving his staff too much** он соверше́нно загна́л свои́х подчинённых. **7** (*engineering*) про|кла́дывать, -ложи́ть; пров|оди́ть, -ести́; **~ a tunnel through a hill** про|кла́дывать, -ложи́ть тунне́ль че́рез го́ру. **8** (*effect, conclude*): **~ a bargain** заключ|а́ть, -и́ть сде́лку.
● *v.i.* (*past* **drove;** *p.p.* **driven**) **1** (*operate vehicle*) води́ть (*indet.*), вести́ (*det.*) маши́ну; **we drove up to the door** мы подъе́хали/подкати́ли пря́мо к две́ри. **2** (*be impelled*): **rain drove against the panes** дождь бил в око́нные стёкла; **driving rain** проливно́й дождь. **3**: **what is he driving at?** к чему́ он кло́нит?; куда́ он гнёт? (*coll.*). **4** (*of vehicle*): **the car ~s easily** э́ту маши́ну легко́ вести́.

drivel /ˈdrɪv(ə)l/ *n.* (*nonsense*) чушь, чепуха́.
● *v.i.* (**drivelled, drivelling;** *US* **driveled, driveling**) поро́ть (*impf.*) чушь; нести́ (*impf.*) вздор/чепуху́.

driven /ˈdrɪv(ə)n/ *p.p. of* ⇒**drive**

driver /ˈdraɪvə(r)/ *n.* (*of vehicle*) води́тель (*m.*), шофёр; (*of animals*) пого́нщик, гуртовщи́к; **~'s license**

D

(*US*) води́тельские права́; (*comput.*) дра́йвер.

driving /ˈdraɪvɪŋ/ *n.* езда́; вожде́ние автомоби́ля; **~ instructor** преподава́тель (*m.*) автошко́лы.

● *cpds.* **~-licence** (*Br.*) *n.* води́тельские права́; **~-mirror** *n.* зе́ркало за́днего обзо́ра; **~-school** *n.* автошко́ла; **~-test** *n.* экза́мен на вожде́ние; **~-wheel** *n.* веду́щее колесо́.

drizzle /ˈdrɪz(ə)l/ *n.* и́зморось.

● *v.i.* мороси́ть (*impf.*).

drizzly /ˈdrɪzlɪ/ *adj.* морося́щий.

droll /drəʊl/ *adj.* чудно́й, заба́вный.

drollness /ˈdrəʊlnɪs/ *n.* заба́вность.

dromedary /ˈdrɒmɪdərɪ/, /ˈdrʌm-/ *n.* дромаде́р.

drone /drəʊn/ *n.* **1** (*bee; also fig., idler*) тру́тень (*m.*). **2** (*of engine*) гуде́ние; (*of voice*) жужжа́ние.

● *v.t. & i.* (*hum*) жужжа́ть (*impf.*); гуде́ть (*impf.*); (*speak monotonously*) бубни́ть (*impf.*).

drool /dru:l/ *v.i.* пус|ка́ть, -ти́ть слю́ни.

droop /dru:p/ *v.t.* (*e.g. head*) опус|ка́ть, -ти́ть.

● *v.i.* (*of flowers, head*) ни́кнуть, по-; (*of branches*) склон|я́ться, -и́ться; (*fig.*): **his spirits ~ed** он пал ду́хом.

droopy /ˈdru:pɪ/ *adj.* (**droopier, droopiest**) (*lit.*) склонённый; (*fig.*) уны́лый.

drop /drɒp/ *n.* **1** (*small quantity of liquid*) ка́пля; **~ by ~** ка́пля по ка́пле; (*fig.*): **a ~ in the bucket, ocean** ка́пля в мо́ре; **he had a ~ too much** он хвати́л ли́шнего.

2 (*small round object*): **acid ~** монпансье́ (*indecl.*), ледене́ц; **ear ~** серьга́, подве́ска.

3 (*fall*) паде́ние; **~ in prices/temperature** паде́ние цен; пониже́ние температу́ры; **at the ~ of a hat** (*fig.*) сра́зу/то́тчас же; **there is a ~ of 30 feet behind this wall** за э́той стено́й обры́в в 30 фу́тов высоты́.

● *v.t.* (**dropped, dropping**) **1** (*allow, cause to fall*) роня́ть, урони́ть; **~ anchor** бр|оса́ть, -о́сить я́корь; **~ a stitch** спус|ка́ть, -ти́ть петлю́; **~ a letter into the box** опус|ка́ть, -ти́ть письмо́ в я́щик; **~ supplies by parachute** сбр|а́сывать, -о́сить припа́сы на парашю́те; **~ a parcel at s.o.'s house** ост|авля́ть, -а́вить паке́т у чьего́-н. до́ма.

2 (*impel, force down*) сра|жа́ть, -зи́ть; **~ shells into a town** обстре́л|ивать, -ять го́род; **he ~ped the ball to the back of the court** он посла́л мяч в коне́ц ко́рта.

3 (*give birth to young*) (*lamb or kid*) ягни́ться, о-; (*calf etc.*) тели́ться, о-.

4 (*lower*): **~ one's voice** пон|ижа́ть, -и́зить го́лос; **~ one's eyes** пот|упля́ть, -у́пить глаза́.

5 (*send, utter casually*): **~ s.o. a line** черкну́ть (*pf.*) кому́-н. па́ру строк; **~ a hint** oброни́ть (*pf.*) намёк.

6 (*omit, cease*) опус|ка́ть, -ти́ть; пропус|ка́ть, -ти́ть; **this word can safely be ~ped** э́то сло́во мо́жно сме́ло опусти́ть; **~ it!** переста́ньте!; бро́сьте!

7 (*allow to descend, disembark*) выса́живать, вы́садить; спус|ка́ть, -ти́ть с бо́рта; **please ~ me at the station** пожа́луйста, вы́садите меня́ у ста́нции.

8 (*abandon*) бр|оса́ть, -о́сить; **let us ~ the subject** дава́йте оста́вим э́ту те́му; **he ~ped all his friends** он порва́л со все́ми свои́ми друзья́ми.

9 (*coll., lose*) теря́ть, по-; **he ~ped £100** он потра́тил сто фу́нтов.

10: **~ a goal** заб|ива́ть, -и́ть гол.

● *v.i.* (**dropped, dropping**) **1** (*fall, descend*) па́дать, упа́сть; опус|ка́ться, -ти́ться; **you could hear a pin ~** (*fig.*) бы́ло слы́шно, как му́ха пролети́т; **~ into a habit** входи́ть, войти́ в привы́чку; приобре|та́ть, -сти́ привы́чку; **~ into one's club** загля́|дывать, -ну́ть в клу́б.

2 (*become weaker or lower*) па́дать, упа́сть; пон|ижа́ться, -и́зиться; **the wind ~ped** ве́тер стих/ути́х; **prices ~ped** це́ны упа́ли; **his voice ~ped** он пони́зил го́лос.

3 (*expr. separation etc.*): **~ behind the others** отст|ава́ть, -а́ть от остальны́х; **he ~ped from sight** он исче́з из по́ля зре́ния.

4 (*sink, collapse*) па́дать, упа́сть; опус|ка́ться, -ти́ться; **he ~ped into a chair** он опусти́лся на стул; **he ~ped (on) to his knees** он упа́л/опусти́лся на коле́ни; **I felt ready to ~** я вали́лся с ног; **his jaw ~ped** у него́ отви́сла че́люсть; **he ~ped dead** он внеза́пно у́мер; **~ dead!** (*coll.*) подо́хни!; чтоб ты сдох!

5 (*cease, be abandoned*): **we let the matter ~** мы бро́сили э́то де́ло.

● *with advs.*: **~ in** *v.i.* (*coll.*): **he ~ped in on me** он загляну́л ко мне; **~ off** *v.i.* (*become fewer or less*) ум|еньша́ться, -е́ньшиться; **attendance ~ped off** посеща́емость упа́ла; (*coll., doze off*) засну́ть (*pf.*); **~ out** *v.i.*: **five runners ~ped out** пять бегуно́в вы́были из состяза́ния; **he ~ped out of school** он бро́сил шко́лу.

● *cpds.* **~-curtain** *n.* (*theatr.*) опускно́й/па́дающий за́навес; **~-forging** *n.* горя́чая штампо́вка; **~-hammer** *n.* копёр; **~-head** *n.* (*Br.*) автомоби́ль с откидны́м ве́рхом; **~-kick** *n.* уда́р с полулёта; *v.t.* уд|аря́ть, -а́рить с полулёта; **~-leaf** *n.* откидна́я доска́; **~-leaf table** откидно́й сто́лик; **~-out** *n.* челове́к, поста́вивший себя́ вне о́бщества; (*from school*) недоу́чка (*c.g.*); **~-scene** *n.* (*curtain*) опускно́й за́навес; (*final scene*) заключи́тельная сце́на.

droplet /ˈdrɒplət/ *n.* ка́пелька.

dropper /ˈdrɒpə(r)/ *n.* (*instrument*) пипе́тка, ка́пельница.

dropping /ˈdrɒpɪŋ/ *n.* (*pl., of animals and birds*) помёт.

● *cpd.* **~-zone** *n.* (*for troops*) зо́на вы́садки деса́нта; (*for supplies*) зо́на сбра́сывания гру́за.

dropsy /ˈdrɒpsɪ/ *n.* водя́нка.

droshky /ˈdrɒʃkɪ/ *n.* дро́ж|ки (*pl., g.* -ек).

dross /drɒs/ *n.* шлак, дросс; (*fig.*) отбро́сы (*m. pl.*).

drought /draʊt/ *n.* за́суха.

drove¹ /drəʊv/ *n.* (*herd*) ста́до, гурт; (*crowd*) толпа́.

drove² /drəʊv/ *past of* ⇒**drive**

drover /ˈdrəʊvə(r)/ *n.* гуртовщи́к.

drown /draʊn/ *v.t.* **1** (*kill by immersion*) топи́ть, у-; **~ one's sorrows in drink** топи́ть, у- го́ре в вине́; **~ o.s.** топи́ться, у-; **be ~ed** тону́ть, у-. **2** (*of sound*) приглуш|а́ть, -и́ть. **3**: **like a ~ed rat** (*fig.*) мо́крый как мышь.

● *v.i.* тону́ть, у-; утопа́ть (*impf.*); **a ~ing man will catch at a straw** утопа́ющий за соло́минку хвата́ется; **death by ~ing** смерть че́рез утопле́ние.

drowse /draʊz/ *n.* полусо́н, сонли́вость; **in a ~** в дремо́те.

● *v.i.* дрема́ть (*impf.*); быть в полусне́.

drowsiness /ˈdraʊzɪnɪs/ *n.* дремо́та, сонли́вость.

drowsy /ˈdraʊzɪ/ *adj.* (**drowsier, drowsiest**) (*feeling sleepy*) со́нный; (*soporific*) усыпля́ющий, снотво́рный.

drub /drʌb/ *v.t.* (**drubbed, drubbing**) колоти́ть, по-; **~ an idea into s.o.'s head** вбива́ть, вбить/вда́лбливать, вдолби́ть мысль кому́-н. в го́лову.

drubbing /ˈdrʌbɪŋ/ *n.* битьё, трёпка, взбу́чка; **give s.o. a ~** зад|ава́ть, -а́ть взбу́чку/трёпку кому́-н.

drudge /drʌdʒ/ *n.* работя́га (*c.g.*), иша́к.

drudgery /ˈdrʌdʒərɪ/ *n.* изнури́тельная рабо́та.

drug /drʌg/ *n.* **1** (*medicinal substance*) медикаме́нт, лека́рство. **2** (*narcotic or stimulant*) нарко́тик; **~ addict** наркома́н; **~ addiction** наркома́ния; **~ ring** наркосиндика́т; **~ trafficker** *or* **pusher** наркоделе́ц; **~ trafficking** торго́вля нарко́тиками, наркоби́знес.

● *v.t.* (**drugged, drugging**) (*food etc.*) подме́ш|ивать, -а́ть нарко́тики в + *a.*; (*person*) да|ва́ть, -ть нарко́тики + *d.*; одурма́ни|вать, -ть.

● *cpds.* **~-abuse** *adj.* употребле́ние нарко́тиков; **~-abuse clinic** наркологи́ческий диспансе́р; **~store** *n.* (*US*) ≈ апте́ка.

drugget /ˈdrʌgɪt/ *n.* (*text.*) ковро́вая ткань.

druggist /ˈdrʌgɪst/ *n.* (*US*) фармаце́вт, апте́карь (*m.*).

Druid /ˈdru:ɪd/ *n.* друи́д.

Druidic(al) /dru:ˈɪdɪk(ə)l/ *adj.* друиди́ческий.

drum /drʌm/ *n.* **1** (*instrument*) бараба́н; **bass ~** большо́й бараба́н.

2 (*container for oil etc.*) металли́ческая бо́чка.

3 (*cylinder for winding cable etc.*) ка́бельный бараба́н.

4 (**ear~**) бараба́нная перепо́нка.

● *v.t.* (**drummed, drumming**) бараба́нить (*impf.*); бить (*impf.*) в бараба́н; **~ s.o. out of the army** с позо́ром выгоня́ть, вы́гнать кого́-н. из а́рмии; **~ up support** соз|ыва́ть, -ва́ть на подмо́гу; **~ something into**

s.o.'s head вд|а́лбливать, -олби́ть что-н. кому́-н. в го́лову.

● *v.i.* (**drummed, drumming**) бараба́нить (*impf.*); бить (*impf.*) в бараба́н; ~ **with one's fingers on the table** бараба́нить (*impf.*) па́льцами по́ столу.

● *cpds.* **~-beat** *n.* бараба́нный бой; **~fire** *n.* урага́нный ого́нь; **~head** *n.* ко́жа на бараба́не; **~head court martial** вое́нно-полево́й суд; **~-major** *n.* тамбурмажо́р; **~-majorette** *n.* тамбурмажоре́тка; **~ roll** *n.* бараба́нная дробь; **~stick** *n.* бараба́нная па́лочка; (*of fowl*) но́жка.

drummer /ˈdrʌmə(r)/ *n.* бараба́нщ|ик (*fem.* -ица); (*US, commercial traveller*) коммивояжёр.

drunk /drʌŋk/ *n.* пья́ный.

● *adj.* пья́ный; ~ **driver** пья́ный води́тель; **~-driving** = **drink-driving; half** ~ подвы́пивший; **dead** ~ мертве́цки пья́ный; ~ **as a lord** пья́ный в сте́льку; ~ **with success** опьянённый успе́хом; **get** ~ **on brandy** нап|ива́ться, -и́ться коньяка́; пьяне́ть, о- от коньяка́.

drunk /drʌŋk/ *p.p. of* ⇒**drink**

drunkard /ˈdrʌŋkəd/ *n.* пья́ница (*c.g.*), алкого́лик.

drunken /ˈdrʌŋkən/ *adj.* пья́ный; ~ **brawl** пья́ная дра́ка.

drunkenness /ˈdrʌŋkənnɪs/ *n.* пья́нство.

dry /draɪ/ *adj.* (**drier** /ˈdraɪə/; **driest** /ˈdraɪɪst/) **1** (*free from moisture or rain*) сухо́й; ~ **as a bone** сухо́й-пресухо́й; **wipe** ~ вытира́ть, вы́тереть на́сухо. **2** (*not supplying water etc.*) вы́сохший, сухо́й; **a** ~ **well** вы́сохший коло́дец; ~ **cow** недо́йная коро́ва; **the cows are** ~ коро́вы не до́ятся.
3: ~ **measure** ме́ра сыпу́чих тел; ~ **goods** (*sugar, grain, etc*) сухи́е проду́кты; (*US, fabrics*) тексти́ль (*m.*), тексти́льные това́ры.
4: ~ **run** (*trial*) про́бный забе́г.
5 (*of wine*) сухо́й.
6 (*dull, plain*) сухо́й; ~ **as dust** (*fig., of person*) суха́рь (*m.*).
7 (*of humour*) сухо́й; (*of remark etc.*) ирони́ческий; *see also* ⇒**drily.**
8: ~ **ice** сухо́й лёд; ~ **ski slope** лы́жный склон с иску́сственным покры́тием; ~ **battery** суха́я батаре́я.
9: ~ **state** штат, в кото́ром де́йствует сухо́й зако́н; **the country went dry** в стране́ ввели́ сухо́й зако́н.

● *v.t.* суши́ть (*or* высу́шивать), вы́-; ~ **o.s.** вытира́ться, вы́тереться; ~ **one's tears** ут|ира́ть, -ере́ть слёзы; ~ **the dishes** вытира́ть, вы́тереть посу́ду; ~ **one's hands** вытира́ть, вы́тереть ру́ки; **dried fruit(s)** сушёные фру́кты; **dried egg** яи́чный порошо́к; **dried milk** сухо́е молоко́; **the drought dried up the wells** за́суха вы́сушила коло́дцы; **the wind dries up one's skin** ве́тер су́шит ко́жу.

● *v.i.* со́хнуть, вы- суши́ться (*or* высу́шиваться), вы-; **our clothes have dried** на́ша оде́жда вы́сохла; **the well dried up** коло́дец вы́сох; **his imagination dried up** его́ фанта́зия исся́кла; ~ **up!** заткни́сь! (*coll.*); **he dried up** (*coll., theatr.*) он забы́л роль; **hang something up to** ~ ве́шать, пове́сить что-н. для просу́шки.

● *cpds.* **~-clean** *v.t.* подв|ерга́ть, -е́ргнуть хими́ческой чи́стке; **~-cleaning** *n.* хими́ческая чи́стка, химчи́стка; **~-eyed** *adj.* без слёз; с сухи́ми глаза́ми; **~-rot** *n.* суха́я гниль.

dryad /ˈdraɪæd/, /ˈdraɪəd/ *n.* дриа́да.

dryish /ˈdraɪɪʃ/ *adj.* сухова́тый.

dryly /ˈdraɪlɪ/ = **drily**

dryness /ˈdraɪnɪs/ *n.* су́хость, сушь.

DSS (*abbr. of* ***Department of Social Security***) Министе́рство социа́льного обеспе́чения.

DTI (*abbr. of* ***Department of Trade and Industry***) Министе́рство торго́вли и промы́шленности.

DTP (*abbr. of* ***desktop publishing***) насто́льная полигра́фия.

DT's /diːˈtiːz/ *n.* (*coll.*) бе́лая горя́чка.

dual /ˈdjuːəl/ *adj.* дво́йственный, двойно́й; ~ **ownership** совме́стное владе́ние; ~ **carriageway** (*Br.*) доро́га с двусторо́нним движе́нием и раздели́тельным барье́ром; ~ **personality** раздвое́ние ли́чности; ~ **control** двойно́е управле́ние; ~ **nationality** двойно́е по́дданство.

● *cpd.* **~-purpose** *adj.* двойно́го назначе́ния.

dualism /ˈdjuːəˌlɪz(ə)m/ *n.* дуали́зм.

duality /ˌdjuːˈælɪtɪ/ *n.* дво́йственность, раздво́енность.

dub /dʌb/ *v.t.* (**dubbed, dubbing**) **1** (*a knight*) посвя|ща́ть, -ти́ть в ры́цари; (*fig., call*) проз|ыва́ть, -ва́ть; крести́ть, о-. **2** (*coll., film*) дубли́ровать (*impf.*).

dubbing /ˈdʌbɪŋ/ *n.* (*of film*) дубли́рование.

dubiety /djuːˈbaɪətɪ/ *n.* сомне́ние.

dubious /ˈdjuːbɪəs/ *adj.* (*feeling doubt*) сомнева́ющийся; (*inspiring mistrust; ambiguous*) сомни́тельный.

dubiousness /ˈdjuːbɪəsnɪs/ *n.* сомни́тельность.

Dublin /ˈdʌblɪn/ *n.* Ду́блин.

ducal /ˈdjuːk(ə)l/ *adj.* ге́рцогский.

ducat /ˈdʌkət/ *n.* дука́т.

duchess /ˈdʌtʃɪs/ *n.* герцоги́ня; **grand** ~ (*wife*) вели́кая княги́ня; (*daughter*) вели́кая княжна́.

duchy /ˈdʌtʃɪ/ *n.* ге́рцогство, кня́жество.

duck[1] /dʌk/ *n.* (*pl.* ~ *or* **~s**) **1** (*water-bird*) у́тка; (*as food*) утя́чье мя́со, утя́тина (*coll.*); **wild** ~ ди́кая у́тка; **take to something like a** ~ **to water** чу́вствовать, по- себя́ в чём-н. как ры́ба в воде́; **sitting** ~ (*fig.*) лёгкая же́ртва/добы́ча; **like water off a ~'s back** как с гу́ся вода́; **like a dying** ~ как мо́края ку́рица; **dead** ~ (*fig.*) (*person*) ко́нченый челове́к; (*thing*) ги́блое де́ло; **lame** ~ неуда́чник. **2** (*Br., dear creature*) ду́шка, ду́шенька. **3** (*also* **~'s egg**: *zero score*) нулево́й счёт; **make a** ~ сыгра́ть (*pf.*) с нулевы́м счётом.

● *cpds.* **~-bill (platypus)** *n.* утконо́с; **~-boards** *n. pl.* доща́тый насти́л; **~-pond** *n.* пруд для у́ток; **~('s)-egg blue** *adj.* & *n.* зеленова́то-голубо́й (цвет); **~-shooting** *n.* охо́та на ди́ких у́ток; **~weed** *n.* ря́ска.

duck[2] /dʌk/ *n.* (**~ing** *motion, dip*) погруже́ние, ныря́ние, окуна́ние.

● *v.t.* погру|жа́ть, -зи́ть; окун|а́ть, -у́ть; ~ **one's head** бы́стро наг|иба́ть, -ну́ть го́лову; ~ **s.o.** окун|а́ть, -у́ть кого́-н.; тол|ка́ть, -ну́ть кого́-н. в во́ду; (*evade*): ~ **a question** увёр|тываться, -ну́ться от отве́та.

● *v.i.* окун|а́ться, -у́ться; ~ **to avoid a blow** наклон|я́ться, -и́ться, что́бы избежа́ть уда́ра.

ducking /ˈdʌkɪŋ/ *n.* погруже́ние в во́ду; **give s.o. a** ~ опус|ка́ть, -ти́ть чью-н. го́лову (в во́ду).

duckling /ˈdʌklɪŋ/ *n.* утёнок; **ugly** ~ га́дкий утёнок.

ducky /ˈdʌkɪ/ *n.* (*Br. coll.*) ду́шечка, голу́бушка.

duct /ˈdʌkt/ *n.* (*anat.*) кана́л, прото́к.

ductile /ˈdʌktaɪl/ *adj.* (*of metal*) тягу́чий, ко́вкий; (*of substance*) пласти́чный; (*of person*) пода́тливый.

ductility /ˌdʌkˈtɪlɪtɪ/ *n.* (*tech.*) тягу́честь, ко́вкость.

ductless /ˈdʌktlɪs/ *adj.*: ~ **gland** железа́ вну́тренней секре́ции.

dud /dʌd/ *n.* (*coll.*) (*bomb*) неразорва́вшаяся бо́мба; (*shell*) неразорва́вшийся снаря́д; (*counterfeit object*) подде́лка; (*person*) пусто́е ме́сто.

● *adj.* (*useless*) неприго́дный; (*counterfeit*) подде́льный.

dude /djuːd/, /duːd/ *n.* пижо́н (*coll.*).

dudgeon /ˈdʌdʒ(ə)n/ *n.* (*resentment*) возмуще́ние; (*feeling of offence*) оби́да; **in (high)** ~ с глубо́ким возмуще́нием; негоду́я.

due /djuː/ *n.* **1** (~ *credit*) до́лжное; **to give him his ~, he tried hard** на́до отда́ть ему́ до́лжное — он о́чень стара́лся.
2 (*pl., Br., charges*) сбо́ры (*m. pl.*); взно́сы (*m. pl.*); **membership ~s** чле́нские взно́сы; **harbour** (*Br.*), **harbor** (*US*) **~s** порто́вые сбо́ры.

● *adj.* **1** (*owing, payable*) причита́ющийся; **debts** ~ **to us** причита́ющиеся нам долги́; **when is the rent ~?** когда́ на́до плати́ть за кварти́ру?; **the bill falls** ~ **on October 1** срок платежа́ по ве́кселю наступа́ет пе́рвого октября́.
2 (*proper*) до́лжный, надлежа́щий; **with** ~ **attention** с до́лжным внима́нием; **in** ~ **time** в своё вре́мя; **after** ~ **consideration** по́сле надлежа́щего рассмотре́ния; **in** ~ **course** в свою́ о́чередь, свои́м чередо́м; **I am** ~ **for a haircut** мне пора́ постри́чься.
3 (*expected*): **he is** ~ **to speak twice** он до́лжен вы́ступить два́жды; **the mail is** ~ **tomorrow** по́чта должна́ быть за́втра.
4: ~ **to** (*coll., owing to*) благодаря́ + *d.*; (*because of*) из-за + *g.*

D

● *adv.* то́чно, пря́мо; **the village lies ~ south** дере́вня лежи́т пря́мо на юг отсю́да.

duel /'dju:əl/ *n.* дуэ́ль, поеди́нок; **~ of wits** состяза́ние в остроу́мии.

● *v.i.* (**duelled, duelling;** *US* **dueled, dueling**) дра́ться (*impf.*) на дуэ́ли.

duellist /'dju:əlɪst/ (*US* **duelist**) *n.* дуэля́нт.

duet /dju:'et/ *n.* дуэ́т.

duff|el, -le /'dʌf(ə)l/ *n.* **1** (*text.*): **~ coat** пальто́ из шерстяно́й ба́йки с капюшо́ном. **2**: **~ bag** вещево́й мешо́к.

duffer /'dʌfə(r)/ *n.* простофи́ля (*c.g.*) болва́н; **he is a ~ at games** в и́грах от него́ нет никако́го то́лку.

dug /dʌg/ *past and p.p. of* ⇨**dig**

dug-out /'dʌgaʊt/ *n.* (*shelter*) блинда́ж; (*canoe*) челно́к.

duke /dju:k/ *n.* ге́рцог; **grand ~** вели́кий князь, эрцге́рцог.

dukedom /'dju:kdəm/ *n.* (*territory*) ге́рцогство; кня́жество; (*title*) ти́тул ге́рцога.

dulcet /'dʌlsɪt/ *adj.* сла́дкий, не́жный.

dulcimer /'dʌlsɪmə(r)/ *n.* цимба́л|ы (*pl., g.* —).

dull /dʌl/ *adj.* **1** (*not clear or bright*) ту́склый; **a ~ sound** глухо́й звук; **a ~ mirror** ту́склое зе́ркало; **~ weather** па́смурная пого́да. **2** (*slow in understanding*) тупо́й. **3** (*uninteresting*) ску́чный. **4** (*not sharp*) тупо́й; **a ~ knife** тупо́й нож; **a ~ pain** тупа́я боль.

● *v.t.* притуп|ля́ть, -и́ть.

● *cpd.* **~-witted** *adj.* тупоу́мный.

dullard /'dʌləd/ *n.* тупи́ца.

dullish /'dʌlɪʃ/ *adj.* тупова́тый; скучнова́тый.

dullness /'dʌlnɪs/ *n.* ту́пость; ску́ка.

duly /'dju:lɪ/ *adv.* (*in due manner*) до́лжным о́бразом; (*at the right time*) в до́лжное вре́мя, своевре́менно; **I ~ went there** как и сле́довало, я пошёл туда́.

dumb /dʌm/ *adj.* **1** (*unable to speak*) немо́й; **~ animals** бесслове́сные живо́тные. **2** (*temporarily silent*) онеме́вший, немо́й; **he was struck ~** он онеме́л; **~ show** нема́я сце́на. **3** (*US coll., stupid*) глу́пый.

● *v.t.*: **~ down** (*coll.*) популяризи́ровать (*impf., pf.*).

● *cpds.* **~-bell** *n.* ганте́ль; **~-waiter** *n.* (*Br., table*) враща́ющийся сто́лик для заку́сок; (*lift*) лифт для пода́чи ку́шаний из ку́хни в столо́вую.

dum(b)found /dʌm'faʊnd/ *v.t.* ошара́ш|ивать, -ить; ошелом|ля́ть, -и́ть.

dumbness /'dʌmnɪs/ *n.* немота́.

dummy /'dʌmɪ/ *n.* **1** ку́кла; **tailor's ~** манеке́н; **baby's ~** (*Br.*) со́ска; **he stands there like a (stuffed) ~** он стои́т там истука́ном. **2** (*at cards*) «болва́н». **3** (*stand-in*) подставно́е лицо́. **4** (*US coll., fool*) болва́н.

● *adj.* (*imitation*) подставно́й; **~ run** про́бный забе́г.

dump /dʌmp/ *n.* **1** (*heap of refuse*) му́сорная ку́ча. **2** (*place for tipping refuse*) (му́сорная) сва́лка. **3** (*ammunition store*) вре́менный полево́й скла́д. **4** (*seedy place*) дыра́ (*coll.*).

● *v.t.* **1** (*throw away*) выбра́сывать, вы́бросить. **2** (*deposit carelessly*) сва́л|ивать, -и́ть. **3** (*coll., abandon*) броса́ть, бро́сить. **4** (*comput.*) (*copy data*) разгру|жа́ть, -зи́ть; (*print out data*) распеча́т|ывать, -ать.

dumping /'dʌmpɪŋ/ *n.* сва́лка; (*comm.*) де́мпинг.

dumpling /'dʌmplɪŋ/ *n.* клёцка.

dumps /dʌmps/ *n.* (*coll.*): **the ~** уны́ние.

dumpster /'dʌmpstə(r)/ *n.* (*US*) ёмкость для перево́зки му́сора.

dumpy /'dʌmpɪ/ *adj.* (**dumpier, dumpiest**) призе́мистый.

dun[1] /dʌn/ *v.t.* (**dunned, dunning**) нап|омина́ть, -о́мнить (кому́-н.) об упла́те до́лга.

dun[2] /dʌn/ *adj.* серова́то-кори́чневый; (*of animal*) мыша́стый.

dunce /dʌns/ *n.* тупи́ца (*m.*).

dunderhead /'dʌndə,hed/ *n.* болва́н.

dune /dju:n/ *n.* дю́на.

dung /dʌŋ/ *n.* (*manure*) наво́з; (*excrement*) помёт.

● *cpds.* **~-beetle** *n.* наво́зный жук; наво́зник; **~ heap, ~hill** *nn.* наво́зная ку́ча.

dungarees /,dʌŋgə'ri:z/ *n.* комбинезо́н.

dungeon /'dʌndʒ(ə)n/ *n.* темни́ца.

dunk /dʌŋk/ *v.t.* мак|а́ть, -ну́ть.

dunlin /'dʌnlɪn/ *n.* (*pl.* **~** *or* **~s**) чернозо́бик.

duo /'dju:əʊ/ *n.* (*pl.* **~s**) дуэ́т; (*of comedians*) коми́ческая па́ра.

duodenal /,dju:əʊ'di:nəl/ *adj.* дуодена́льный.

duodenary /,dju:əʊ'di:nərɪ/ *adj.* двена́дцатери́чный.

duodenum /,dju:əʊ'di:nəm/ *n.* двенадцатипе́рстная кишка́.

dupe /dju:p/ *n.* простофи́ля (*c.g.*).

● *v.t.* ост|авля́ть, -а́вить в дурака́х; над|ува́ть, -у́ть.

duplex /'dju:pleks/ *adj.* двойно́й; **~ house** (*US*) двухкварти́рный дом; **~ apartment** кварти́ра, располо́женная на двух этажа́х.

duplicate[1] /'dju:plɪkət/ *n.* дублика́т; (то́чная) ко́пия; **in ~** в двух экземпля́рах.

● *adj.* (*spare, extra*) запасно́й; (*twice as large or many*) двойно́й; (*identical*) одина́ковый; **~ document** ко́пия докуме́нта.

duplicate[2] /'dju:plɪ,keɪt/ *v.t.* (*double*) удв|а́ивать, -о́ить; сдв|а́ивать, -о́ить; (*activity*) дубли́ровать, про-; (*document*) сн|има́ть, -ять ко́пию с + *g.*; (*repeat*) повтор|я́ть, -и́ть.

duplication /,dju:plɪ'keɪʃ(ə)n/ *n.* удвое́ние; сня́тие ко́пии; **~ of effort** нену́жное повторе́ние уси́лий.

duplicator /'dju:plɪ,keɪtə(r)/ *n.* (*machine*) копирова́льный аппара́т.

duplicity /dju:'plɪsɪtɪ/ *n.* двули́чность.

durability /,djʊərə'bɪlɪtɪ/ *n.* про́чность, долгове́чность.

durable /'djʊərəb(ə)l/ *n.*: **consumer ~s** това́ры (*m. pl.*) дли́тельного по́льзования.

● *adj.* про́чный; долгове́чный.

Duralumin /djʊə'ræljʊmɪn/ *n.* (*propr.*) дюралюми́ний.

duration /djʊə'reɪʃ(ə)n/ *n.* продолжи́тельность; **for the ~ of the war** на (всё) вре́мя войны́; **of short ~** непродолжи́тельный.

duress /djʊə'res/, /'djʊə-/ *n.* принужде́ние, нажи́м, давле́ние; **under ~** под нажи́мом/давле́нием.

during /'djʊərɪŋ/ *prep.* (*throughout*) в тече́ние + *g.*; (*at some point in*) во вре́мя + *g.*

dusk /dʌsk/ *n.* су́мер|ки (*pl., g.* -ек); (*gloom*) су́мрак.

dusky /'dʌskɪ/ *adj.* (**duskier, duskiest**) су́меречный; (*of complexion*) сму́глый.

dust /dʌst/ *n.* **1** (*powdered earth etc.*) пыль; **gold ~** золотоно́сный песо́к; **bite the ~** (*coll.*) сконча́ться (*pf.*); **shake the ~ off one's feet** отрясти́ (*pf.*) прах с ног свои́х; **throw ~ in s.o.'s eyes** пус|ка́ть, -ти́ть пыль в глаза́ кому́-н.; втира́ть (*impf.*) кому́-н. очки́.
2 (*human remains*) прах; **~ and ashes** прах и тлен.
3 (*cloud of ~*) пыль; **make, raise a ~** (*lit.*) подн|има́ть, -я́ть пыль; (*fig.*) подн|има́ть, -я́ть шум/переполо́х.

● *v.t.* **1** (*remove ~ from*) ст|ира́ть, -ере́ть; (*or* стря́х|ивать, -ну́ть) пыль с + *g.*; **~ furniture** сма́х|ивать, -ну́ть (*or* ст|ира́ть, -ере́ть) пыль с ме́бели; **~ a room** уб|ира́ть, -ра́ть ко́мнату.
2 (*sprinkle*) пос|ыпа́ть, -ы́пать; **~ sugar on to a cake** пос|ыпа́ть, -ы́пать торт са́харной пу́дрой.

● *cpds.* **~bin** *n.* (*Br.*) му́сорный я́щик; **~-bowl** *n.* засу́шливый райо́н; **~-cart** *n.* (*Br.*) фурго́н для сбо́ра му́сора, мусорово́з; **~-cover** *n.* (*for chair etc.*) чехо́л; (*of book*) суперобло́жка; **~-jacket, ~-wrapper** *nn.* (*of book*) суперобло́жка; **~man** *n.* (*Br.*) му́сорщик; **~pan** *n.* сово́к для му́сора; **~-sheet** *n.* (*Br.*) защи́тное покрыва́ло; **~-storm** *n.* пы́льная бу́ря; **~-up** *n.* (*coll.*) ссо́ра, свара́; **~-wrapper** *n.* = **~-jacket**

duster /'dʌstə(r)/ *n.* (*Br., cloth*) тря́пка для пы́ли.

dustiness /'dʌstɪnɪs/ *n.* запылённость.

dusty /'dʌstɪ/ *adj.* (**dustier, dustiest**) пы́льный.

Dutch /dʌtʃ/ *n.* **1** (*language*) голла́ндский/нидерла́ндский язы́к; **double ~** кита́йская гра́мота, тараба́рщина. **2** (*pl., people*) голла́ндцы (*m. pl.*).

● *adj.*: **~ auction** «голла́ндский аукцио́н»; **~ cap** (*Br.*) колпачо́к; **~ tile** ка́фель (*m.*); изразе́ц; (*fig.*): **~ courage** хра́брость во хмелю́; **~ treat** угоще́ние в скла́дчину.

● *cpds.* **~man** *n.* голла́ндец; **that's Smith, or I'm a ~man** (*Br.*) я не я бу́ду, е́сли э́то не Смит; **the Flying ~man** лету́чий голла́ндец; **~woman** *n.* голла́ндка.

dutiable /ˈdju:tɪəb(ə)l/ *adj.* подлежа́щий обложе́нию по́шлиной.

dutiful /ˈdju:tɪ,fʊl/ *adj.* пре́данный; (*obedient*) послу́шный.

dutifulness /ˈdju:tɪfʊlnɪs/ *n.* послуша́ние, пре́данность.

duty /ˈdju:tɪ/ *n.* **1** (*moral obligation*) долг, обя́занность; **he has a strong sense of ~** у него́ си́льно ра́звито чу́вство до́лга; **a ~ call** официа́льный визи́т; **bounden ~** свяще́нная обя́занность; **we are in ~ bound** долг повелева́ет нам.
2 (*official employment*) служе́бные обя́занности; дежу́рство; **on ~** на дежу́рстве; **come on ~** при|ходи́ть, -йти́ на дежу́рство; **off ~** свобо́дный; вне слу́жбы; в свобо́дное/неслужéбное вре́мя; **I am off ~ today** я сего́дня не рабо́таю; **go off ~** уходи́ть, уйти́ с дежу́рства; **take up one's duties** присту́п|а́ть, -и́ть к исполне́нию свои́х обя́занностей; **~ officer** дежу́рный офице́р.
3 (*fig., of things*): **a box did ~ for a table** я́щик служи́л столо́м; **a heavy ~ engine** сверхмо́щный мото́р.
4 (*fin.*) по́шлина, сбор; **customs ~** тамо́женная по́шлина; **stamp ~** ге́рбовый сбор.
● *cpds.* **~-free, ~-paid** *adjs.* беспо́шлинный.

duvet /ˈdu:veɪ/ *n.* (*Br.*) стёганое одея́ло.

dwarf /dwɔ:f/ *n.* (*pl.* **dwarfs** *or* **dwarves**) ка́рлик; **~ plant** ка́рликовое расте́ние.
● *v.t.* (*stunt growth of*) меша́ть, по- ро́сту +*g.*; (*fig.*): **the skyscrapers dwarfed the church** ря́дом с небоскрёбами це́рковь каза́лась совсе́м кро́шечной; **our efforts are ~ed by his** его́ уси́лия затмева́ют на́ши.

dwarfish /ˈdwɔ:fɪʃ/ *adj.* ка́рликовый.

dwarves /dwɔ:vz/ *pl. of* ⇒**dwarf**

dwell /dwel/ *v.i.* (*past and p.p.* **dwelt** *or* **dwelled**) **1** (*live*) жить (*impf.*); обита́ть (*impf.*). **2**: **~ (up)on** (*expatiate on*) распространя́ться (*impf.*) о+*p.*; остан|а́вливаться, -ови́ться на+*p.*; **it is unnecessary to ~ on the difficulties** не ну́жно остана́вливаться на тру́дностях.

dweller /ˈdwelə(r)/ *n.* жи́тель, обита́тель (*fem.* -ница).

dwelling /ˈdwelɪŋ/ *n.* жильё, жили́ще.
● *cpds.* **~-house** *n.* жило́й дом; **~-place** *n.* местожи́тельство.

dwelt /dwelt/ *past and p.p. of* ⇒**dwell**

dwindle /ˈdwɪnd(ə)l/ *v.i.* сокра|ща́ться, -ти́ться; ум|еньша́ться, -е́ньшиться.

dye /daɪ/ *n.* кра́ска.
● *v.t.* (**dyeing**) (*colour artificially*) кра́сить, по-; окра́|шивать, -сить; **~ a dress black** кра́сить, по- пла́тье в чёрный цвет; **~d-in-the-wool** (*fig.*) закорене́лый.
● *v.i.* (**dyeing**) кра́ситься, по-; **this material ~s well** э́тот материа́л хорошо́ кра́сится.
● *cpds.* **~stuff** *n.* краси́тель (*m.*); **~-works** *n.* краси́льня.

dyer /ˈdaɪə(r)/ *n.* краси́льщик.

dying /ˈdaɪɪŋ/ *adj.* умира́ющий, предсме́ртный; **till one's ~ day** до конца́ свои́х дней.

D

dyke /daɪk/ = **dike**

dynamic /daɪˈnæmɪk/ *n.* (*force*) дви́жущая си́ла; (*pl., science*) дина́мика.
● *adj.* (*pertaining to force*) динами́ческий; (*energetic*), динами́чный.

dynamism /ˈdaɪnə,mɪz(ə)m/ *n.* динами́зм.

dynamite /ˈdaɪnə,maɪt/ *n.* динами́т (*also fig.*).
● *v.t.* вз|рыва́ть, -орва́ть динами́том.

dynamo /ˈdaɪnə,məʊ/ *n.* (*pl.* **~s**) дина́мо (*indecl.*); дина́мо-маши́на; **a human ~** энерги́чный/неутоми́мый челове́к.

dynastic /dɪˈnæstɪk/ *adj.* династи́ческий.

dynasty /ˈdɪnəstɪ/ *n.* дина́стия.

dysentery /ˈdɪsəntərɪ/, /-trɪ/ *n.* дизентери́я.

dysfunction /dɪsˈfʌŋkʃ(ə)n/ *n.* дисфу́нкция.

dyslexia /dɪsˈleksɪə/ *n.* дисле́ксия.

dyslexic /dɪsˈleksɪk/ *adj.*: **he is ~** он дисле́ктик.

dyspepsia /dɪsˈpepsɪə/ *n.* диспепси́я.

dyspeptic /dɪsˈpeptɪk/ *n. & adj.* страда́ющий диспепси́ей.

dystrophy /ˈdɪstrəfɪ/ *n.* дистрофи́я.

Ee

E /iː/ *n.* **1** (*mus.*) ми (*nt. indecl.*). **2** (*acad. mark*) 1, едини́ца, «кол»; **he got an ∼ in physics** он получи́л едини́цу по фи́зике.

each /iːtʃ/ *pron. & adj.* ка́ждый; **he gave ∼ (one) of us a book** он ка́ждому из нас дал по кни́ге; **he sat with a child on ∼ side of him** он сиде́л ме́жду двумя́ детьми́; **we took a tray ∼ from the table** мы взя́ли со сто́лика по подно́су; **the apples cost 20 pence ∼** я́блоки сто́ят два́дцать пе́нсов шту́ка (*or* за шту́ку); **∼ other** друг дру́га; **∼ and every one** все без исключе́ния; **2 ∼** по два/двое́; **5 ∼** по пяти́, (*coll.*) по пять; **100 ∼** по́ сто; **200 ∼** по две́сти; **500 ∼** по пятисо́т.

eager /ˈiːɡə(r)/ *adj.* стремя́щийся (к + *d.*); жа́ждущий (+ *g.*); **he is ∼ to go** он рвётся идти́.

eagerness /ˈiːɡənɪs/ *n.* рве́ние, стремле́ние.

eagle /ˈiːɡ(ə)l/ *n.* орёл; **∼ eye** зо́ркий взгляд; **∼ owl** фи́лин.

● *cpd.* **∼-eyed** *adj.* зо́ркий, проница́тельный.

eaglet /ˈiːɡlɪt/ *n.* орлёнок.

ear¹ /ɪə(r)/ *n.* **1** (*anat.*) у́хо; (*dim. e.g. baby's*) у́шко; **give s.o. a thick ∼** дать (*pf.*) в у́хо кому́-н.
2: **∼ for music** музыка́льный слух; **she plays by ∼** она́ игра́ет по слу́ху; **play it by ∼** (*fig.*) пол|ага́ться, -ожи́ться на чутьё.
3 (*var. idioms*): **I am all ∼s** я весь обрати́лся в слух; **it went in (at) one ∼ and out (at) the other** в одно́ у́хо вошло́, в друго́е вы́шло; **up to one's ∼s in work/debt** по́ уши в рабо́те/долга́х; **gain s.o.'s ∼** доби́ться (*pf.*) чьего́-н. благоскло́нного внима́ния; **(may I have) a word in your ∼** мне ну́жно кое-что́ вам сказа́ть на у́шко; **prick up one's ∼s** навостри́ть (*pf.*) у́ши; **were your ∼s burning last night?** у вас у́ши не горе́ли вчера́?; **I could not believe my ∼s** я свои́м уша́м не пове́рил; **lend an ∼, give ∼ to** прислу́ш|иваться, -аться к + *d.*; **his words fell on deaf ∼s** его́ слова́ бы́ли гла́сом вопию́щего в пусты́не; **turn a deaf ∼ to** пропусти́ть (*pf.*) ми́мо уше́й; **it came to my ∼s that** . . . до меня́ дошли́ слу́хи, что. . .; **he has his ∼ to the ground** (*fig.*) он де́ржит у́хо востро́.

● *cpds.* **∼ache** *n.* боль в у́хе; **∼drop** *n.* (*pendant*) (серьга́-)подве́ска; (*pl., medicinal*) ушны́е ка́пли (*f. pl.*); **∼drum** *n.* бараба́нная перепо́нка; **∼-flap** *n.* нау́шник ша́пки; **∼mark** *v.t.* на|кла́дывать, -ложи́ть тавро́ на + *a.*; (*fig.*) предназн|ача́ть, -а́чить; ассигнова́ть (*impf., pf.*); **∼phone, ∼piece** *nn.* нау́шник; ра́ковина телефо́нной тру́бки; **∼-piercing** *adj.* пронзи́тельный; **∼-plug** *n.* заты́чка для уше́й; **∼ring** *n.* серьга́; **∼shot** *n.*: **within ∼shot** в преде́лах слы́шимости; **out of ∼shot** вне преде́лов слы́шимости; **∼-splitting** *adj.* оглуши́тельный; **∼-trumpet** *n.* слухово́й рожо́к; **∼-wax** *n.* ушна́я се́ра.

ear² /ɪə(r)/ *n.* (*bot.*) ко́лос.

earl /ɜːl/ *n.* граф.

earldom /ˈɜːldəm/ *n.* гра́фство.

earl|y /ˈɜːlɪ/ *adj.* (**earlier, earliest**) ра́нний; **he is an ∼y riser** он ра́но встаёт; **in one's ∼y days/life** в ю́ности/мо́лодости; **in the ∼y part of this century** в нача́ле э́того столе́тия; **we are ∼y** мы пришли́ ра́но; **an ∼y reply** незамедли́тельный отве́т; **on Tuesday at (the) ∼iest** не ра́ньше вто́рника; **∼y man** первобы́тный челове́к; **∼y music** стари́нная му́зыка; **∼y peaches** ра́нние/скоропе́лые пе́рсики; **∼y warning** (*radar*) да́льнее обнаруже́ние.

● *adv.* ра́но; **come as ∼y as possible** приходи́те как мо́жно ра́ньше; **∼y on** в нача́ле; **∼ier on** ра́ньше, ра́нее; **two hours ∼ier** на два часа́ ра́ньше; **as ∼y as March** уже́/ещё в ма́рте.

earn /ɜːn/ *v.t. & i.* зараб|а́тывать, -о́тать; (*deserve*) заслу́ж|ивать, -и́ть; **∼ one's living** зараба́тывать (*impf.*) на жизнь; **∼ed income** трудово́й дохо́д.

earnest /ˈɜːnɪst/ *n.*: **in ∼** серьёзно, всерьёз; **I am in ∼** (*not joking*) я не шучу́; я говорю́ серьёзно; **it is raining in real ∼** дождь разошёлся не на шу́тку.

● *adj.* серьёзный.

earnestness /ˈɜːnɪstnɪs/ *n.* серьёзность.

earnings /ˈɜːnɪŋz/ *n.* за́работок.

earth /ɜːθ/ *n.* **1** (*planet, world*) земля́; **on the face of the ∼** на пове́рхности земли́; **to the ends of the ∼** на край све́та; **come back to ∼** (*fig.*) спусти́ться (*pf.*) с облако́в на зе́млю; **why on ∼?** с како́й ста́ти?; заче́м то́лько?; **who on ∼?** кто то́лько?; кто же?; **like nothing on ∼** ни на что не похо́жий; **move heaven and ∼** пусти́ть (*pf.*) в ход все сре́дства; **down to ∼** (*fig.*) практи́чный, тре́звый.
2 (*dry land*) земля́; **scorched ∼** вы́жженная земля́.
3 (*soil*) земля́, по́чва.
4 (*animal's hole*) нора́; **go to ∼** скр|ыва́ться, -ы́ться в но́ру; прита́иться (*pf.*); **run s.o. to ∼** (*fig.*) высле́живать, вы́следить кого́-н.
5 (*chem.*) по́чва, грунт.
6 (*Br., elec.*) земля́, заземле́ние.

● *v.t.* **1**: **∼ up the roots of a shrub** оку́чи|вать, -ть куст.
2: **∼ an aerial** (*Br.*) заземл|я́ть, -и́ть анте́нну.

● *cpds.* **∼-bound** *adj.* земно́й; **∼quake** *n.* землетрясе́ние; **∼-shaking** *adj.* всеми́рного значе́ния; **∼works** *n. pl.* земляны́е рабо́ты (*f. pl.*); **∼worm** *n.* земляно́й червь.

earthen /ˈɜːθ(ə)n/ *adj.* земляно́й.

● *cpd.* **∼ware** *n.* гонча́рные изде́лия; гли́няная посу́да.

earthiness /ˈɜːθɪnɪs/ *n.* приземлённость, грубова́тость.

earthly /ˈɜːθlɪ/ *adj.* земно́й; **there is no ∼ reason why** . . . нет ни мале́йшей причи́ны, что́бы. . .; **he hasn't an ∼** (*Br. coll.*) у него́ нет ни мале́йшего ша́нса.

earthy /ˈɜːθɪ/ *adj.* (**earthier, earthiest**) (*smell etc.*) земляно́й; (*fig.*) приземлённый, грубова́тый.

earwig /ˈɪəwɪɡ/ *n.* уховёртка.

ease /iːz/ *n.* **1** (*facility*) лёгкость.

2 (*comfort*) покóй, óтдых, досýг; **take one's ~** отд|ыхáть, -охнýть; **a life of ~** лёгкая жизнь; **he was ill at ~** емý бы́ло не по себé; **stand at ~** (*mil.*) стоя́ть (*impf.*) вóльно; **be, feel at ~** чýвствовать (*impf.*) себя́ непринуждённо; **put s.o. at his ~** приободри́ть (*pf.*) когó-н.

● *v.t.* **1** (*loosen*) отпус|кáть, -ти́ть. **2** (*make less severe, reduce*): **~ tension** ослабля́ть, ослáбить напряжённость; **~ congestion** разгру|жáть, -зи́ть движéние; **~ s.o.'s anxiety** успок|áивать, -óить когó-н.

● *v.i.* (*relax*) облегч|áться, -и́ться; слабéть, о-, ослáбнуть; **tension ~d (off)** напряжéние ослáбло; **~ off on drinking** (*coll.*) пить (*impf.*) мéньше; **the pressure of work ~d (up)** напряжённость рабóты спáла.

easel /'i:z(ə)l/ *n.* мольбéрт.

easement /'i:zmənt/ *n.* (*leg.*) сервитýт.

easily /'i:zɪlɪ/ *adv.* (*freely*) свобóдно; (*without difficulty*) легкó, без трудá; **he is ~ the best** он безуслóвно сáмый лýчший; **he may ~ be late** он вполнé мóжет опоздáть.

easiness /'i:zɪnɪs/ *n.* (*facility*) лёгкость; (*comfort*) удóбство; (*informality*) непринуждённость.

east /i:st/ *n.* & *adv.* востóк; на востóк; к востóку; **Far E~** Дáльний Востóк; **Near E~** Бли́жний Востóк; **Middle E~** Срéдний/Бли́жний Востóк; **the wind is in the ~** вéтер дýет с востóка; **~ by north** ост-тень-норд; **~ northeast** ост-норд-ост; **(to the) ~ of London** к востóку от Лóндона; **travel ~** дви́гаться (*impf.*) на востóк; **sail due ~** плыть (*impf.*) по направлéнию к востóку; **face ~** быть обращённым на востóк; **E~ German** (*hist.*) *adj.* восточногермáнский; *n.* жи́тель (*fem.* -ница) Востóчной Гермáнии; **E~ Germany** (*hist.*) Востóчная Гермáния; **~ wind** востóчный вéтер.

● *adj.* востóчный.

● *cpd.* **~bound** *adj.* идýщий/ дви́жущийся на востóк.

Easter /'i:stə(r)/ *n.* Пáсха; (*attr.*) пасхáльный; **at ~** на Пáсху; **~ Day, Sunday** Свéтлое/Христóво Воскресéнье; Пáсха; **~ egg** пасхáльное яйцó; **~ week** пасхáльная недéля; святáя/свéтлая сéдмица **~ Monday (Tuesday** *etc.***)** Свéтлый Понедéльник (Втóрник *и т.п.*).

easterly /'i:stəlɪ/ *n.* (*wind*) востóчный вéтер.

● *adj.* востóчный.

eastern /'i:st(ə)n/ *adj.* востóчный; **E~ bloc** (*hist.*) соцблóк.

easternmost /'i:st(ə)n,məust/ *adj.* сáмый востóчный.

eastward /'i:stwəd/ *adj.* дви́жущийся на востóк.

● *adv.* (*also* **~s**) на востóк; в востóчном направлéнии.

easy /'i:zɪ/ *adj.* **(easier, easiest)** **1** (*not difficult*) лёгкий; **~ of access** достýпный; **the book is ~ to read** кни́га легкó читáется; **~ money** легкó нáжитые дéньги; **~ come, ~ go** как нáжито, так и прóжито; **he is ~ to get on with** у негó лёгкий харáктер; **woman of ~ virtue** жéнщина лёгкого поведéния; **easier said than done** легкó сказáть; **as ~ as ABC (*or* falling off a log)** лéгче лёгкого; прóще простóго.

2 (*comfortable, unconstrained*) спокóйный, лёгкий; **he leads an ~ life** у негó лёгкая жизнь; **~ in one's mind** спокóйный; **~ chair** крéсло; **in E~ Street** в довóльстве/достáтке; **on ~ terms** на лёгких услóвиях; **I am ~** (*coll., have no preference*) мне всё равнó.

● *adv.*: **~ does it!** ти́ше éдешь — дáльше бýдешь; **~!** спокóйно!; **take it ~!** (*don't exert yourself*) не усéрдствуйте!; (*don't worry*) не волнýйтесь!; (*don't hurry*) не спеши́те!

● *cpds.* **~-going** *adj.* (*of person*) благодýшный; **~-goingness** *n.* благодýшие.

eat /i:t/ *v.t.* & *i.* (*past* **ate;** *p.p.* **eaten**) **1** (*of person*) есть, съ-; (*politely, of others*) кýшать, по-/с-; **~ one's dinner** пообéдать/поýжинать (*pf.*); **he ~s well** он хорóший едóк; у негó хорóший аппети́т; (**~*s good food***) он хорошó питáется; **~, drink and be merry** есть, пить и весели́ться (*all impf.*); **good to ~** (*edible*) съедóбный; (*palatable*) вкýсный.

2 (*of animal etc.*) есть, съ-; жрать, со-; **the moths ate holes in my coat** моё пальтó изъéдено мóлью; **what's ~ing you?** (*coll.*) какáя мýха вас укуси́ла?; что вас беспокóит?

3 (*of physical substances*) раз|ъедáть, -éсть; **acids ~ (into) metals** кислóты разъедáют метáллы.

4 (*idioms*): **~ one s words** брать, взять свои́ словá назáд; **~ one's heart out** исстрадáться (*pf.*); жестóко тосковáть (*impf.*); **~ humble pie** прийти́ (*pf.*) с пови́нной головóй; **~ s.o. out of house and home** объ|едáть, -éсть когó-н.; **~ out of s.o.'s hand** (*fig.*) ста|нови́ться, -ть ручны́м; **he can't ~ you** он вас не съест; **I'll ~ my hat if . . .** даю гóлову на отсечéние, éсли. . . .

● *with advs.*: **~ away** *v.t.* разъ|едáть, -éсть; **the wood was ~en away by worms** чéрви изгры́зли дéрево; **~ in** *v.i.* (*at home*) питáться (*impf.*) дóма; **~ out** *v.i.* есть (*impf.*) вне дóма; **~ up** *v.t.* до|едáть, -éсть; (*fig.*): **he is ~en up with pride/curiosity** егó съедáет гóрдость/ любопы́тство.

eatable /'i:təb(ə)l/ *adj.* съедóбный.

eaten /'i:t(ə)n/ *p.p. of* ⇨**eat**

eater /'i:tə(r)/ *n.* едóк; **he is a big ~** он мнóго ест; едóк он óчень хорóший.

eating /'i:tɪŋ/ *n.* едá.

● *adj.*: **are these ~ apples?** мóжно э́ти я́блоки есть сыры́ми?

● *cpd.* **~-house** *n.* рестorán.

eats /i:ts/ *n.* харчи́ (*m. pl.*) (*coll.*).

eau-de-cologne /,əudəkə'ləun/ *n.* одеколóн.

eaves /i:vz/ *n.* карни́з.

● *cpds.* **~drop** *v.i.* подслýш|ивать, -ать; **~dropper** *n.* подслýшивающий; **~dropping** *n.* подслýшивание.

ebb /eb/ *n.* (*of tide*) отли́в; **the tide is on the ~** наступи́л отли́в; **~ and flow** отли́в и прили́в; (*fig.*) упáдок; **his strength is at a low ~** егó си́лы иссякáют.

● *v.i.* (*of tide*) уб|ывáть, -ы́ть; (*fig.*) ослаб|евáть, -éть; **daylight is ~ing away** день угасáет; **his strength is ~ing** егó си́лы слабéют.

● *cpd.* **~-tide** *n.* отли́в.

ebonite /'ebə,naɪt/ *n.* эбони́т.

ebony /'ebənɪ/ *n.* эбéновое/чёрное дéрево; (*fig., black*) чёрный как смоль.

ebullience /ɪ'bʌlɪəns/ *n.* кипýчесть.

ebullient /ɪ'bʌlɪənt/ *adj.* кипýчий, пóлный энтузиáзма.

EC **1** (*abbr. of* ***European Commission***) ЕК (Европéйская коми́ссия). **2** (*abbr. of* ***European Community***) ЕС (Европéйское сóобщество).

eccentric /ɪk'sentrɪk/, /ek-/ *n.* **1** (*person*) чудáк; оригинáл; эксцентри́чный человéк. **2** (*tech.*) эксцéнтрик.

● *adj.* **1** (*of person*) эксцентри́чный. **2** (*math., astron.*) эксцентри́ческий.

eccentricity /,ɪksen'trɪsɪtɪ/, /,ek-/ *n.* (*quality*) чудáчество, эксцентри́чность; (*eccentric habit*) стрáнность.

Ecclesiastes /ɪ,kli:zɪ'æsti:z/ *n.* (*bibl.*) Кни́га Екклезиáста/Проповéдника.

ecclesiastic /ɪ,kli:zɪ'æstɪk/ *n.* духóвное лицó.

ecclesiastical /ɪ,kli:zɪ'æstɪk(ə)l/ *adj.* духóвный, церкóвный.

Ecclesiasticus /ɪ,kli:zɪ'æstɪkəs/ *n.* (*bibl.*) Кни́га Премýдрости Иисýса, сы́на Сирáхова.

ECG (*abbr. of* ***electrocardiogram***) ЭКГ (электрокардиогрáмма).

echelon /'eʃə,lɒn/, /'eɪʃə,lɔ̃/ *n.* **1** (*mil. formation*) эшелóн; **in ~** эшелóнами. **2** (*grade*) чин, ранг.

● *v.t.* (*mil.*) эшелони́ровать (*impf., pf.*).

echidna /ɪ'kɪdnə/ n. ехи́дна.

echo /'ekəu/ *n.* (*pl.* **echoes**) э́хо.

● *v.t.* **(echoes, echoed)** втóрить (*impf.*) + *d.*; **~ s.o.'s words** втóрить чьим-н. словáм.

● *v.i.* **(echoes, echoed)** отд|авáться, -áться э́хом; **the thunder ~ed amongst the hills** гром отдавáлся э́хом в горáх; **the house ~ed to the children's laughter** дом звенéл от дéтского смéха.

● *cpd.* **~-sounding** *n.* измерéние эхолóтом.

éclair /eɪ'kleə(r)/, /ɪ'kleə(r)/ *n.* эклéр.

eclectic /ɪ'klektɪk/ *adj.* эклекти́ческий; эклекти́чный.

eclecticism /ɪ'klektɪ,sɪz(ə)m/ *n.* эклекти́зм.

eclipse /ɪ'klɪps/ *n.* (*astron.*) затмéние; **partial/total ~** части́чное/пóлное затмéние.

● *v.t.* (*lit., fig.*) затм|евáть, -и́ть.

ecliptic /ɪ'klɪptɪk/ *n.* экли́птика.

eclogue /'eklɒg/ *n.* эклóга.

ecocide /ˈiːkəʊˌsaɪd/ *n.* экоци́д, разруше́ние приро́дной среды́.

eco-friendly /ˈiːkəʊˌfrendlɪ/ *adj.* экологи́чески безвре́дный.

ecological /ˌiːkəˈlɒdʒɪk(ə)l/ *adj.* экологи́ческий.

ecologist /ɪˈkɒlədʒɪst/ *n.* эко́лог.

ecology /ɪˈkɒlədʒɪ/ *n.* эколо́гия.

econometric /ɪˌkɒnəˈmetrɪk/ *adj.* эконометри́ческий.

econometrics /ɪˌkɒnəˈmetrɪks/ *n.* экономе́трия, экономе́трика.

economic /ˌiːkəˈnɒmɪk/, /ˌek-/ *adj.* **1** экономи́ческий, хозя́йственный; **~ warfare** экономи́ческая война́. **2** (*paying*) рента́бельный.

economical /ˌiːkəˈnɒmɪk(ə)l/, /ˌek-/ *adj.* эконо́мный, бережли́вый, хозя́йственный; **he is ~ with words** он скуп на слова́.

economics /ˌiːkəˈnɒmɪks/, /ˌek-/ *n.* эконо́мика; **the ~ of poultry-farming** эконо́мика птицево́дства.

economist /ɪˈkɒnəmɪst/ *n.* экономи́ст.

economize /ɪˈkɒnəˌmaɪz/ *v.i.* эконо́мить, с-; **~ on fuel** эконо́мить, с- то́пливо; **he ~d by drinking less** он эконо́мил на вы́пивке.

econom|y /ɪˈkɒnəmɪ/ *n.* **1** (*thrift*) эконо́мия, хозя́йственность, бережли́вость; **false ~y** бессмы́сленная эконо́мия; **little ~ies** эконо́мия на мелоча́х; **~y class** туристи́ческий класс; **~y of truth** (*iron.*) зама́лчивание пра́вды; лжи́вость. **2** (*~ic system*) эконо́мика, хозя́йство; **rural ~y** се́льское хозя́йство; **political ~y** полити́ческая эконо́мия.

ECOSOC /ˈiːkəʊˌsɒk/ *n.* (*abbr. of* ***Economic and Social Council***) ЭКОСОС (Экономи́ческий и Социа́льный Сове́т ООН).

ecosystem /ˈiːkəʊˌsɪstəm/ *n.* экосисте́ма.

ecstas|y /ˈekstəsɪ/ *n.* **1** (*strong emotion*) экста́з; **she went into ~ies over it** э́то привело́ её в экста́з. **2** (*the drug*) э́кстази (*indecl.*).

ecstatic /ɪkˈstætɪk/ *adj.* (*joyful*) экстати́ческий, в экста́зе.

ectopic /ekˈtɒpɪk/ *adj.* эктопи́ческий; **~ pregnancy** внема́точная бере́менность.

ectoplasm /ˈektəʊˌplæz(ə)m/ *n.* (*biol.*) эктопла́зма.

ecu /ˈekjuː/ *n.* (*pl.* **~** *or* **ecus**) экю́ (*m. and nt. indecl.*).

Ecuador /ˈekwəˌdɔː(r)/ *n.* Эквадо́р.

Ecuadorean /ˌekwəˈdɔːrɪən/ *n.* эквадо́р|ец (*fem.* -ка).

● *adj.* эквадо́рский.

ecumenical /ˌiːkjuːˈmenɪk(ə)l/, /ˈek-/ *adj.* (*eccl.*) экумени́ческий, вселе́нский; **~ council** вселе́нский собо́р.

ecumenism /iːˈkjuːməˌnɪz(ə)m/ *n.* (*eccles.*) экумени́зм, экумени́ческое движе́ние.

eczema /ˈeksɪmə/ *n.* экзе́ма.

eddy /ˈedɪ/ *n.* водоворо́т; вихрь (*m.*).

● *v.i.* клуби́ться (*impf.*); крути́ться (*impf.*).

edelweiss /ˈeɪd(ə)lˌvaɪs/ *n.* эдельве́йс.

edema /ɪˈdiːmə/ (*US*) = **oedema**

Eden /ˈiːd(ə)n/ *n.* Эде́м; **Garden of ~** эде́мский сад; (*paradise*) рай.

edge /edʒ/ *n.* **1** (*sharpened side*) остриё, ле́звие; **the knife has no ~** нож затупи́лся; **take the ~ off** (*lit.*) притуп|ля́ть, -и́ть; затуп|ля́ть, -и́ть; (*fig., e.g. appetite*) испо́ртить (*pf.*). **2** (*fig.*): **be on ~** быть в не́рвном состоя́нии; **set one's teeth on ~** вызыва́ть, вы́звать ощуще́ние оско́мины. **3** (*border*) грань; край. **4** (*of book*) обре́з; **gilt ~s** золото́й обре́з. **5** (*skating*): **inside ~** дуга́ внутрь; **outside ~** дуга́ нару́жу. **6**: **have the ~ on s.o.** (*coll.*) име́ть (*impf.*) преиму́щество над кем-н.

● *v.t. & i.* **1** (*border*) окайм|ля́ть, -и́ть; **~ a handkerchief with lace** окайм|ля́ть, -и́ть носово́й плато́к кру́жевом; **~ a path with plants** обса́|живать, -ди́ть доро́жку цвета́ми. **2** (*move obliquely*): **~ one's way through a crowd** проб|ира́ться, -ра́ться че́рез толпу́; **~ a piano through a door** с трудо́м прота́|скивать, -щи́ть пиани́но в дверь; **~ one's chair towards the fire** пододви́нуть (*pf.*) стул кками́ну; **he ~d closer to me** он пододви́нулся ко мне.

edgeways /ˈedʒweɪz/, **edgewise** /ˈedʒwaɪz/ *adv.* бо́ком; **I could not get a word in ~** я не мог сло́ва вста́вить.

edging /ˈedʒɪŋ/ *n.* (*border*) кайма́.

edgy /ˈedʒɪ/ *adj.* (**edgier, edgiest**) (*irritable*) раздражи́тельный.

edibility /ˌedɪˈbɪlɪtɪ/ *n.* съедо́бность.

edible /ˈedɪb(ə)l/ *adj.* съедо́бный.

edict /ˈiːdɪkt/ *n.* ука́з.

edification /ˌedɪfɪˈkeɪʃ(ə)n/ *n.* назида́ние, поуче́ние.

edifice /ˈedɪfɪs/ *n.* зда́ние; (*fig.*) структу́ра, систе́ма.

edify /ˈedɪˌfaɪ/ *v.t.* наст|авля́ть, -а́вить; поуча́ть (*impf.*).

edifying /ˈedɪˌfaɪɪŋ/ *adj.* назида́тельный, поучи́тельный.

edit /ˈedɪt/ *v.t.* (**edited, editing**) (*a text, newspaper*) редакти́ровать, от-; **the passage was ~ed out** э́тот отры́вок вы́черкнули; (*film etc.*) монти́ровать, с-.

editing /ˈedɪtɪŋ/ *n.* (*of text*) редакти́рование, реда́кция; (*of film*) монта́ж.

edition /ɪˈdɪʃ(ə)n/ *n.* изда́ние; (*e.g. of newspaper*) вы́пуск; **revised ~** испра́вленное изда́ние; **limited ~** изда́ние, вы́пущенное ограни́ченным тиражо́м; **an ~ of 50,000 copies** изда́ние в 50 000 экземпля́ров; **the book ran into 20 ~s** кни́га вы́держала 20 изда́ний.

editor /ˈedɪtə(r)/ *n.* реда́ктор; **sports ~** реда́ктор спорти́вного отде́ла.

editorial /ˌedɪˈtɔːrɪəl/ *n.* передови́ца, передова́я статья́.

● *adj.* редакцио́нный; реда́кторский; **~ office** реда́кция; **~ staff** редакцио́нная колле́гия, редколле́гия; **~ changes** (*in a text*) реда́кторская пра́вка.

editorship /ˈedɪtəʃɪp/ *n.* реда́кторство.

educa(ta)ble /ˈedjʊk(eɪt)əb(ə)l/ *adj.* обуча́емый, поддаю́щийся обуче́нию.

educate /ˈedjʊˌkeɪt/ *v.t.* да|ва́ть, -ть образова́ние + *d.*; воспи́т|ывать, -а́ть; **where were you ~d?** где вы получи́ли образова́ние?; **a well ~d man** образо́ванный челове́к; **~d speech** культу́рная речь; **~ s.o.'s taste** разв|ива́ть, -и́ть чей-н. вкус.

education /ˌedjʊˈkeɪʃ(ə)n/ *n.* образова́ние, культу́ра; (*upbringing*) воспита́ние; **universal compulsory ~** всео́бщее обяза́тельное обуче́ние; **higher ~** вы́сшее образова́ние; **college of ~** педагоги́ческий институ́т; **Ministry of E~** Министе́рство просвеще́ния; **lack of ~** необразо́ванность; **it was an ~ to work with him** рабо́та с ним мно́го мне дала́; **physical ~** физи́ческое воспита́ние, физкульту́ра.

educational /ˌedjʊˈkeɪʃənəl/ *adj.* (*pert. to education*) образова́тельный; (*instructive*) воспита́тельный, уче́бный; **~ film** уче́бный фильм.

education(al)ist /ˌedjʊˈkeɪʃən(əl)ɪst/ *n.* педаго́г(-методи́ст).

educative /ˈedjʊˌkətɪv/ *adj.* поучи́тельный.

educator /ˈedjʊˌkeɪtə(r)/ *n.* воспита́тель (*m.*), педаго́г.

EEC (*abbr. of* ***European Economic Community***) ЕЭС (Европе́йское экономи́ческое соо́бщество).

eel /iːl/ *n.* у́горь (*m.*); **he is as slippery as an ~** (*fig.*) он ско́льзкий как у́горь.

e'en /iːn/ (*poet.*) = **even¹, even²** *adv.*

e'er /eə(r)/ (*poet.*) = **ever**

eer|ie (*US* **-y**) /ˈɪərɪ/ *adj.* (**eerier, eeriest**) жу́ткий.

efface /ɪˈfeɪs/ *v.t.* ст|ира́ть, -ере́ть; (*fig.*) изгла́|живать, -дить; **~ o.s.** стушёв|ываться, -а́ться; держа́ться (*impf.*) в тени́.

effacement /ɪˈfeɪsmənt/ *n.* стира́ние.

effect /ɪˈfekt/ *n.* **1** (*result*) результа́т; **punishment had no ~ on him** наказа́ние на него́ не поде́йствовало; **of no ~** безрезульта́тный; **to no ~** безрезульта́тно; **take ~** (*e.g. medicine*) де́йствовать, по-; **in ~** в су́щности, факти́чески. **2** (*validity*) де́йствие; **come into ~** вступ|а́ть, -и́ть в си́лу; **put, bring into ~** вводи́ть (*impf.*) в де́йствие; **with ~ from today** начина́я с сего́дняшнего дня; **in ~** (*operative*) де́йствующий, в си́ле. **3** (*sensual etc. impression*) впечатле́ние, эффе́кт; **sound ~s** (*e.g. on radio*) шумовы́е эффе́кты; **special ~s** спецэффе́кты; **he does it all for ~** он де́лает всё напока́з. **4** (*meaning*) содержа́ние, смысл; **he spoke to this ~** смысл его́ слов был сле́дующий; **or words to that ~** и́ли что́-то в э́том ро́де.

5 (*pl., property*) пожи́тк|и (*pl., g.* -ов); иму́щество.

● *v.t.* осуществ|ля́ть, -и́ть; выполня́ть, вы́полнить; **~ one's purpose** осуществл|я́ть, -и́ть цель; **~ a cure** излечи́ть (*pf.*) больно́го; **~ payment** произв|оди́ть, -ести́ платёж; **~ a compromise** пойти́ (*pf.*) на компроми́сс; прив|оди́ть, -ести́ к компроми́ссу.

effective /ɪ'fektɪv/ *adj.* **1** (*efficacious*) эффекти́вный. **2** (*striking*) эффе́ктный. **3** (*operative*) име́ющий си́лу; де́йствующий; **become ~** входи́ть, войти́ в си́лу; **~ range** (*mil.*) да́льность действи́тельного огня́; **~ strength** (*of an army*) нали́чный соста́в. **4** (*virtual*) действи́тельный.

effectiveness /ɪ'fektɪvnɪs/ *n.* (*efficacy*) эффекти́вность, де́йственность; (*of decor etc.*) эффе́ктность.

effectual /ɪ'fektʃʊəl/, /-tjʊəl/ *adj.* де́йственный; действи́тельный.

effeminacy /ɪ'femɪnəsɪ/ *n.* изне́женность.

effeminate /ɪ'femɪnət/ *adj.* женоподо́бный.

effervesce /,efə'ves/ *v.i.* пузыри́ться (*impf.*); (*fig.*) искри́ться (*impf.*).

effervescence /,efə'vesəns/ *n.* шипе́ние; (*fig.*) весёлое оживле́ние, кипе́ние.

effervescent /,efə'vesənt/ *adj.* пузыря́щийся, шипу́чий; (*fig.*) искря́щийся, кипу́чий.

effete /ɪ'fi:t/ *adj.* сла́бый, упа́дочный; (*degenerate*) вы́родившийся.

efficacious /,efɪ'keɪʃəs/ *adj.* эффекти́вный, де́йственный.

efficacy /'efɪkəsɪ/ *n.* эффекти́вность, де́йственность.

efficiency /ɪ'fɪʃənsɪ/ *n.* делови́тость; эффекти́вность, производи́тельность.

efficient /ɪ'fɪʃ(ə)nt/ *adj.* делови́тый, исполни́тельный; эффекти́вный, производи́тельный.

effigy /'efɪdʒɪ/ *n.* изображе́ние; **burn s.o. in ~** сжечь (*pf.*) чьё-н. изображе́ние/чу́чело.

efflorescence /,eflɔ:'resəns/ *n.* расцве́т.

effluent /'eflʊənt/ *n.* пото́к, вытека́ющий из о́зера/реки́; (*of sewage etc.*) сток.

effluvi|um /ɪ'flu:vɪəm/ *n.* (*pl.* **~a**) испаре́ние; миа́змы (*f. pl.*).

effort /'efət/ *n.* уси́лие, попы́тка; (*pl.*) рабо́та; **make an ~** приложи́ть (*pf.*) уси́лие; **spare no ~** не щади́ть (*impf.*) уси́лий; **his ~s at persuading her failed** его́ уси́лия убеди́ть её оказа́лись тще́тными; (*coll., performance*): **a good ~** уда́чная попы́тка.

effortless /'efətlɪs/ *adj.* непринуждённый; не тре́бующий уси́лий; **with ~ skill** с непринуждённой ло́вкостью.

effrontery /ɪ'frʌntərɪ/ *n.* на́глость, наха́льство.

effulgence /ɪ'fʌldʒəns/ *n.* лучеза́рность, сия́ние.

effulgent /ɪ'fʌldʒ(ə)nt/ *adj.* лучеза́рный, сия́ющий.

effusion /ɪ'fju:ʒ(ə)n/ *n.* излия́ние (*also fig.*).

effusive /ɪ'fju:sɪv/ *adj.* экспанси́вный; **he was ~ in his gratitude** он рассыпа́лся в благода́рностях.

effusiveness /ɪ'fju:sɪvnɪs/ *n.* экспанси́вность.

EFTA /'eftə/ *n.* (*abbr. of* ***European Free Trade Association***) ЕАСТ (Европе́йская ассоциа́ция свобо́дной торго́вли).

e.g. (*abbr. of* ***exempli gratia***) напр. (наприме́р).

egalitarian /ɪ,gælɪ'teərɪən/ *adj.* эгалита́рный.

egalitarianism /ɪ,gælɪ'teərɪən,ɪz(ə)m/ *n.* эгалитари́зм.

egality /ɪ'gælɪtɪ/ *n.* ра́венство.

egg[1] /eg/ *n.* **1** (*lit.*) яйцо́; **lay ~s** нести́сь (*impf.*); нести́, с- яйца́; **new-laid ~** свежеснесённое яйцо́; **boiled ~** яйцо́ в мешо́чек; **soft-boiled ~** яйцо́ всмя́тку; **hard-boiled ~** крутое яйцо́; **fried ~** я́ичница-глазу́нья; **scrambled ~s** я́ичница-болту́нья; **poached ~** яйцо́-пашо́т; **rotten ~** ту́хлое яйцо́; **you have got ~ on your chin** у вас оста́тки яйца́ на подборо́дке; **~ and spoon race** шу́точный бег с ло́жкой, в кото́рой лежи́т сыро́е яйцо́; **put all one's ~s in one basket** класть, положи́ть все я́йца в одну́ корзи́ну; **as sure as ~s is ~s** (*coll.*) ≈ я́сно как два́жды два четы́ре; **don't teach your grandmother to suck ~s** ≈ яйца ку́рицу не у́чат.
2 (*coll., chap*) па́рень (*m.*).

● *cpds.* **~-beater, ~-whisk** *nn.* весёлка, муто́вка; **~-cosy** *n.* чехо́льчик для сохране́ния яйца́ горя́чим; **~-cup** *n.* рю́мка для яйца́; **~head** *n.* (*sl.*) интеллиге́нтик; **~-plant** *n.* (*US*) баклажа́н; **~-shaped** *adj.* яйцеви́дный; **~-shell** *n.* скорлупа́; **~-timer** *n* (песо́чные) часы́ для ва́рки яи́ц; **~-whisk** *n.* = **~-beater**

egg[2] /eg/ *v.t.*: **~ on** подстрек|а́ть, -ну́ть.

eggy /'egɪ/ *adj.* (**eggier, eggiest**) (*covered with egg*) вы́мазанный яйцо́м.

ego /'i:gəʊ/ *n.* (*pl.* **egos**) (*phil.*) э́го (*indecl.*); я (*nt. indecl.*); субъе́кт; (*amour-propre*) самолю́бие; (*selfishness*) эгои́зм.

egocentric /,i:gəʊ'sentrɪk/ *adj.* эгоцентри́ческий, эгоцентри́чный.

egocentrism /i:gəʊ'sentrɪz(ə)m/ *n.* эгоцентри́зм.

egoism /'i:gəʊ,ɪz(ə)m/ *n.* эгои́зм, эгоисти́чность.

egoist /'i:gəʊɪst/, /'eg-/ *n.* эгои́ст (*fem.* -ка).

egoistic(al) /,i:gəʊ'ɪstɪk(ə)l/, /'eg-/ *adj.* эгоисти́ческий, эгоисти́чный.

egomania /,i:gəʊ'meɪnɪə/ *n.* эгоцентри́зм.

egomaniac /,i:gəʊ'meɪnɪ,æk/, /,eg-/ *n.* эгоцентри́ст.

● *adj.* эгоцентри́ческий.

egotism /'i:gə,tɪz(ə)m/ *n.* эготи́зм.

egotist /'i:gə,tɪst/, /'eg-/ *n.* эготи́ст (*fem.* -ка), эгоце́нтрик.

egotistic(al) /,i:gə'tɪstɪk(ə)l/, /,eg-/ *adj.* эгоцентри́ческий.

egregious /ɪ'gri:dʒəs/ *adj.* вопию́щий, отъя́вленный.

egress /'i:gres/ *n.* (*exit*) вы́ход.

egret /'i:grɪt/ *n.* бе́лая ца́пля.

Egypt /'i:dʒɪpt/ *n.* Еги́пет.

Egyptian /ɪ'dʒɪpʃ(ə)n/ *n.* египтя́н|ин (*fem.* -ка).

● *adj.* еги́петский.

Egyptologist /,i:dʒɪp'tɒlədʒɪst/ *n.* египто́лог.

Egyptology /,i:dʒɪp'tɒlədʒɪ/ *n.* египтоло́гия.

eh /eɪ/ *int.* а?; да неуже́ли?; как?

eider /'aɪdə(r)/ *n.* (*also* **~ duck**) га́га.

● *cpd.* **~down** *n.* (*Br., quilt*) пухо́вое одея́ло.

eight /eɪt/ *n.* (число́/но́мер) во́семь; (**~** *people*) во́сьмеро, во́семь челове́к; **we ~, the ~ of us** мы ввосьмеро́м; мы, во́семь челове́к; **~ each** по восьми́; **in ~s, ~ at a time** по восьми́, восьмёрками; (*figure; thing numbered 8; group or crew of* **~**) восьмёрка; **he cut a figure of ~** он сде́лал восьмёрку; (*with var. nn. expressed or understood: cf. examples under* ⇒**five**): **he had one over the ~** (*Br. coll.*) он хвати́л ли́шнего.

● *adj.* во́семь +*g. pl.*; (*for people and pluralia tantum, also*) во́сьмеро +*g. pl.*; **~ twos are sixteen** во́семью (*or* во́семь на) два — шестна́дцать.

● *cpd.* **~fold** *adj.* восьмикра́тный; *adv.* в во́семь раз (бо́льше).

eighteen /eɪ'ti:n/ *n.* восемна́дцать; **in the 1820s** в двадца́тые го́ды (*or* в двадца́тых года́х) XIX (девятна́дцатого) ве́ка.

● *adj.* восемна́дцать +*g. pl.*

eighteenth /eɪ'ti:nθ/ *n.* (*date*) восемна́дцатое число́; (*fraction*) одна́ восемна́дцатая; восемна́дцатая часть.

● *adj.* восемна́дцатый.

eighth /eɪtθ/ *n.* (*date*) восьмо́е (число́); (*fraction*) одна́ восьма́я; восьма́я часть.

● *adj.* восьмо́й; **~ note** (*US, mus.*) восьма́я но́та.

eightieth /'eɪtɪɪθ/ *n.* одна́ восьмидеся́тая; восьмидеся́тая часть.

● *adj.* восьмидеся́тый.

eight|y /'eɪtɪ/ *n.* во́семьдесят; **in the ~ies** (*decade*) в восьмидеся́тых года́х, в восьмидеся́тые го́ды; (*temperature*) за во́семьдесят гра́дусов (по Фаренге́йту); **he is in his ~ies** ему́ за во́семьдесят.

Eire /'eərə/ *n.* Э́йре (*indecl.*).

either /'aɪðə(r)/, /'i:ðə(r)/ *pron. & adj.* (*one or other*) любо́й, ка́ждый; тот и́ли друго́й; **do ~ of these roads lead to town?** кака́я-нибудь из э́тих доро́г ведёт к го́роду?; **~ book will do** люба́я из э́тих книг годи́тся; **I do not like ~ (one)** мне не нра́вится ни тот, ни друго́й; **~ way you will lose** и так и э́так вы проигра́ете; **on ~ side of the window** по обе́им сторона́м окна́; **~ of you may come** любо́й из вас мо́жет прийти́; **has ~ of you seen him?** кто-нибу́дь из вас ви́дел его́?

● *adv. & conj.*: **I do not like Smith, or Jones ~** я не люблю́ ни Сми́та, ни Джо́нса; **he did not go, and I did not ~** ни он, ни я не пошли́; (*intensive*): **it was not long ago ~** э́то бы́ло не так уж давно́; **~ . . . or** и́ли. . . и́ли; ли́бо. . . ли́бо; то ли. . . то ли; не то. . . не то; **~ I or he will go** оди́н из нас пойдёт; и́ли он и́ли я пойдём.

ejaculate /ɪˈdʒækjʊˌleɪt/ *v.t.* (*utter suddenly*) воскл|ица́ть, -и́кнуть.

● *v.i.* (*physiol.*) изв|ерга́ть, -е́ргнуть се́мя.

ejaculation /ɪˌdʒækjʊˈleɪʃ(ə)n/ *n.* (*exclamation*) восклица́ние; (*physiol.*) эякуля́ция.

eject /ɪˈdʒekt/ *v.t.* (*lit., fig.*) выбра́сывать, вы́бросить; выселя́ть, вы́селить; (*emit*) изв|ерга́ть, -е́ргнуть.

● *v.i.* (*aeron.*): **the pilot ~ed** лётчик катапульти́ровался.

ejection /ɪˈdʒekʃ(ə)n/ *n.* (*expulsion*) исключе́ние; (*from house*) выселе́ние; (*emission*) изверже́ние.

ejector /ɪˈdʒektə(r)/ *n.*: **~ seat** (*aeron.*) катапульти́руемое сиде́нье.

eke /iːk/ *v.t.*: **~ out** (*supplement*) восп|олня́ть, -о́лнить; **~ out a livelihood** ко́е-как перебива́ться (*impf.*); скрипе́ть (*impf.*).

elaborate¹ /ɪˈlæbərət/ *adj.* иску́сно сде́ланный; сло́жный; **an ~ pattern** замыслова́тый рису́нок; **an ~ dinner** изы́сканный обе́д.

elaborate² /ɪˈlæbəˌreɪt/ *v.t.* разраб|а́тывать, -о́тать; **~ on** (*develop*) разв|ива́ть, -и́ть; (*make more precise*) уточн|я́ть, -и́ть.

elaboration /ɪˌlæbəˈreɪʃ(ə)n/ *n.* (*working out*) разрабо́тка; (*development*) разви́тие; уточне́ние.

elan /eɪˈlɑ̃/ *n.* поры́в, подъём.

elapse /ɪˈlæps/ *v.i.* про|ходи́ть, -йти́; прот|ека́ть, -е́чь.

elastic /ɪˈlæstɪk/, /ɪˈlɑːstɪk/ *n.* рези́нка.

● *adj.* (*lit.*) эласти́чный; упру́гий; **~ band** (*Br.*) рези́нка; (*fig.*) ги́бкий; **~ rules** нестро́гие пра́вила.

elasticity /ɪlæsˈtɪsɪtɪ/ *n.* эласти́чность, упру́гость; (*fig.*) ги́бкость.

elate /ɪˈleɪt/ *v.t.* прив|одить, -ести́ в восто́рг; **he was ~d at the news** но́вость окрыли́ла его́.

elation /ɪˈleɪʃ(ə)n/ *n.* ликова́ние, восто́рг.

Elba /ˈelbə/ *n.* Э́льба.

Elbe /elb/ *n.* Э́льба.

elbow /ˈelbəʊ/ *n.* ло́коть (*m.*); (*tech.*) коле́но; **at one's ~** (*fig.*) под руко́й; **more power to his ~!** (*coll.*) дай Бог ему́ уда́чи!; **rub ~s with** (*US*) якша́ться (*impf.*) с + *i.* (*coll.*).

● *v.t.* пих|а́ть, -ну́ть; толка́ть (*impf.*) локтя́ми; **~ one's way** прот|а́лкиваться, -олкну́ться; **~ s.o. aside** отпи́хивать, отпихну́ть кого́-н. в сто́рону.

● *cpds.* **~-grease** *n.* (*joc.*) уси́ленная полиро́вка; **it needs ~-grease** придётся попоте́ть; **~-room** *n.* просто́р.

elder¹ /ˈeldə(r)/ *n.* **1** (*older person*) ста́рец, ста́рший; **we should respect our ~s** мы должны́ уважа́ть ста́рших; **he is my ~ by seven years** он ста́рше меня́ на семь лет. **2** (*official, senior member of tribe*) старе́йшина (*m.*).

● *adj.* ста́рший; **Pitt the ~** Питт ста́рший; **which is the ~ of the two?** кто из них двух ста́рше?

elder² /ˈeldə(r)/ *n.* (*bot.*) бузина́.

● *cpd.* **~berry** *n.* я́года бузины́.

elderly /ˈeldəlɪ/ *adj.* пожило́й.

eldest /ˈeldɪst/ *adj.* са́мый ста́рший.

elect /ɪˈlekt/ *adj.* и́збранный; **president ~** и́збранный президе́нт.

● *v.t.* изб|ира́ть, -ра́ть; выбира́ть, вы́брать; **they ~ed him king** они́ избра́ли его́ королём; **the president is ~ed** президе́нт избира́ется; **he ~ed to go** он предпочёл пойти́.

election /ɪˈlekʃ(ə)n/ *n.* **1** (*pol.*) вы́боры (*m. pl.*); **general ~** всео́бщие вы́боры; **hold an ~** пров|оди́ть, -ести́ вы́боры; **~ campaign** предвы́борная/избира́тельная кампа́ния. **2** (*choice*) избра́ние.

electioneer /ɪˌlekʃəˈnɪə(r)/ *v.i.* агити́ровать (*impf.*); **~ing** (*campaign*) предвы́борная кампа́ния.

elective /ɪˈlektɪv/ *adj.* **1** (*filled by election*) избира́тельный; вы́борный; **an ~ office** вы́борная до́лжность. **2** (*empowered to elect*): **an ~ assembly** избира́тельное собра́ние. **3** (*optional*) факультати́вный.

elector /ɪˈlektə(r)/ *n.* (*voter*) избира́тель (*m.*).

electoral /ɪˈlektər(ə)l/ *adj.* избира́тельный; **~ college** колле́гия вы́борщиков; **~ register** спи́сок избира́телей.

electorate /ɪˈlektərət/ *n.* (*body of voters*) избира́тели (*m. pl.*).

electric /ɪˈlektrɪk/ *adj.* электри́ческий; **~ blanket** одея́ло-гре́лка; **~ blue** (*n. & adj.*) (цвет) электри́к (*indecl.*); **~ car** электромоби́ль (*m.*); **~ chair** электри́ческий стул; **~ field** электри́ческое по́ле; **~ guitar** электрогита́ра; **~ light** электри́ческий свет; **~ locomotive** электрово́з; **~ shock** уда́р электри́ческим то́ком; (*fig.*): **this had an ~ effect on him** э́то наэлектризова́ло его́.

electrical /ɪˈlektrɪk(ə)l/ *adj.* электри́ческий; **~ engineer** инжене́р-эле́ктрик; **~ engineering** электроте́хника.

electrician /ˌɪlekˈtrɪʃ(ə)n/ *n.* (электро)монтёр.

electricity /ˌɪlekˈtrɪsɪtɪ/, /ˌel-/ *n.* электри́чество.

electrification /ɪˌlektrɪfɪˈkeɪʃ(ə)n/ *n.* (*phys.*) электриза́ция; (*tech.*) электрифика́ция.

electrify /ɪˈlektrɪˌfaɪ/ *v.t.* **1** (*charge with electricity; also fig.*) электризова́ть, на-. **2** (*e.g. a railway*) электрифици́ровать (*impf., pf.*).

electro- /ɪˈlektrəʊ/ *pref.* эле́ктро. . .

electrocardiogram /ɪˌlektrəʊˈkɑːdɪəˌgræm/ *n.* электрокардиогра́мма.

electrocute /ɪˈlektrəˌkjuːt/ *v.t.* (*execute*) казни́ть (*impf., pf.*) на электри́ческом сту́ле; **he was ~d** (*by accident*) его́ уби́ло то́ком.

electrocution /ɪˌlektrəˈkjuːʃ(ə)n/ *n.* казнь на электри́ческом сту́ле.

electrode /ɪˈlektrəʊd/ *n.* электро́д.

electrodynamics /ɪˌlektrəʊdaɪˈnæmɪks/ *n.* электродина́мика.

electro-encephalogram /ɪˌlektrəʊɪnˈsefələˌgræm/ *n.* электроэнцефалогра́мма.

electrolysis /ˌɪlekˈtrɒlɪsɪs/, /ˌel-/ *n.* электро́лиз.

electrolyte /ɪˈlektrəˌlaɪt/ *n.* электроли́т.

electromagnet /ɪˌlektrəʊˈmægnɪt/ *n.* электромагни́т.

electromagnetic /ɪˌlektrəʊmægˈnetɪk/ *adj.* электромагни́тный.

electromotive /ɪˌlektrəʊˈməʊtɪv/ *adj.* электродви́жущий.

electron /ɪˈlektrɒn/ *n.* электро́н; **~ microscope** электро́нный микроско́п.

electronic /ˌɪlekˈtrɒnɪk/, /ˌel-/ *adj.* электро́нный; **~ mail** электро́нная по́чта; **~ tagging** электро́нная сле́жка.

electronics /ˌɪlekˈtrɒnɪks/, /ˌel-/ *n.* электро́ника.

electroplate /ɪˈlektrəˌpleɪt/ *v.t.* гальванизи́ровать (*impf., pf.*); покр|ыва́ть, -ы́ть мета́ллом с по́мощью электро́лиза.

elegance /ˈelɪgəns/ *n.* элега́нтность, изя́щество.

elegant /ˈelɪgənt/ *adj.* элега́нтный, изя́щный.

elegiac /ˌelɪˈdʒaɪək/ *adj.* элеги́ческий, элеги́чный.

elegiacs /ˌelɪˈdʒaɪəks/ *n.* элеги́ческие стихи́ (*m. pl.*).

elegy /ˈelɪdʒɪ/ *n.* эле́гия.

element /ˈelɪmənt/ *n.* **1** (*earth, air etc.*) стихи́я; **exposed to the ~s** бро́шенный на произво́л стихи́й; (*fig.*): **in one's ~** в свое́й стихи́и. **2** (*chem.*) элеме́нт. **3** (*pl., rudiments*) нача́ла (*nt. pl.*); азы́ (*m. pl.*). **4** (*feature, constituent*) элеме́нт; составна́я часть. **5** (*trace*) след, до́ля. **6** (*elec.*) элеме́нт.

elemental /ˌelɪˈment(ə)l/ *adj.* стихи́йный.

elementary /ˌelɪˈmentərɪ/ *adj.* элемента́рный; **~ school** нача́льная шко́ла.

elephant /ˈelɪfənt/ *n.* (*pl.* **~** *or* **~s**) слон; **~ calf** слонёнок; **~ cow** слони́ха; **white ~** (*fig.*) обремени́тельное иму́щество.

elephantiasis /ˌelɪfənˈtaɪəsɪs/ *n.* слоно́вая боле́знь.

elephantine /ˌelɪˈfæntaɪn/ *adj.*

слоно́вый; an ~ task непоси́льная зада́ча.

elevate /ˈelɪ,veɪt/ *v.t.* (*lit.*) подн|има́ть, -я́ть; **~d railway** надзе́мная желе́зная доро́га; (*fig.*) пов|ыша́ть, -ы́сить; (*ennoble*) облагор|а́живать, -о́дить; **he was ~d to the peerage** его́ возвели́ в зва́ние пэ́ра.

elevated /ˈelɪ,veɪtɪd/ *adj.* (*lofty*) высо́кий, возвы́шенный.

elevating /ˈelɪ,veɪtɪŋ/ *adj.* облагора́живающий; подъёмный.

elevation /,elɪˈveɪʃ(ə)n/ *n.* **1** (*act of raising*) подня́тие, возвыше́ние. **2** (*e.g. of a gun*) вертика́льная наво́дка. **3** (*height*) возвыше́ние, возвы́шенность. **4** (*drawing*) вертика́льный разре́з; **front ~** фаса́д; **side ~** боково́й фаса́д. **5** (*fig., of style etc.*) возвы́шенность. **6**: **~ to the peerage** возведе́ние в зва́ние пэ́ра.

elevator /ˈelɪ,veɪtə(r)/ *n.* **1** (*machine*) грузоподъёмник, элева́тор. **2** (*US, storehouse*) элева́тор. **3** (*US, lift*) лифт; **~ operator** лифтёр. **4** (*aeron.*) руль (*m.*) высоты́.

eleven /ɪˈlev(ə)n/ *n.* оди́ннадцать; **chapter ~** оди́ннадцатая глава́; (*team of ~ men*) кома́нда (из оди́ннадцати челове́к); **at ~ (o'clock)** в оди́ннадцать (часо́в); **half past ~** полови́на двена́дцатого.

elevenses /ɪˈlevənzɪz/ *n.* (*Br. coll.*) лёгкий за́втрак о́коло оди́ннадцати часо́в утра́.

eleventh /ɪˈlevənθ/ *n.* (*date*) оди́ннадцатое (число́); (*fraction*) одна́ оди́ннадцатая; оди́ннадцатая часть.
● *adj.* оди́ннадцатый; **at the ~ hour** (*fig.*) в после́днюю мину́ту.

elf /elf/ *n.* (*pl.* **elves**) эльф.

el|fin /ˈelfɪn/, **-fish** /ˈelfɪʃ/, **-vish** /ˈelvɪʃ/ *adjs.* подо́бный фе́е; волше́бный.

elicit /ɪˈlɪsɪt/, /eˈlɪsɪt/ *v.t.* (**elicited, eliciting**) извл|ека́ть, -е́чь; допы́т|ываться, -а́ться; **~ a fact** выявля́ть, вы́явить факт; **~ a reply** доби́ться (*pf.*) отве́та.

elide /ɪˈlaɪd/ *v.t.* выпуска́ть, вы́пустить; опус|ка́ть, -ти́ть.

eligibility /,elɪdʒɪˈbɪlɪtɪ/ *n.* пра́во на избра́ние.

eligible /ˈelɪdʒɪb(ə)l/ *adj.* могу́щий быть и́збранным; **be ~ for** име́ть пра́во на + *a.*; **an ~ young man** подходя́щий жени́х.

eliminate /ɪˈlɪmɪ,neɪt/ *v.t.* **1** (*do away with*) устран|я́ть, -и́ть. **2** (*rule out*) исключ|а́ть, -и́ть. **3** (*physiol., chem.*) оч|ища́ть, -и́стить. **4** (*sport*): **he was ~d on the first round** он вы́был в пе́рвом ту́ре.

elimination /ɪ,lɪmɪˈneɪʃ(ə)n/ *n.* устране́ние, исключе́ние, очище́ние; (*sport*) отбо́рочное соревнова́ние.

elision /ɪˈlɪʒ(ə)n/ *n.* (*phon.*) эли́зия.

élite /eɪˈli:t/, /ɪ-/ *n.* эли́та; **an ~ regiment** отбо́рный полк.

élitist /eɪˈli:tɪst/, /ɪ-/ *adj.* элита́рный.

elixir /ɪˈlɪksə(r)/ *n.* эликси́р.

Elizabethan /ɪ,lɪzəˈbi:θ(ə)n/ *n.* елизаве́тинец.
● *adj.* елизаве́тинский.

elk /elk/ *n.* (*pl.* **~** *or* **~s**) лось (*m.*).

ellipse /ɪˈlɪps/ *n.* э́ллипс, ова́л.

ellipsis /ɪˈlɪpsɪs/ *n.* (*pl.* **ellipses** /-si:z/) э́ллипсис.

ellipsoid /ɪˈlɪpsɔɪd/ *n.* эллипсо́ид.
● *adj.* (*also* **~al**) эллипсоида́льный, эллипсо́идный.

elliptical /ɪˈlɪptɪkəl/ *adj.* (*math., gram.*) эллипти́ческий.

elm /elm/ *n.* (*tree; wood*) вяз.

elocution /,eləˈkju:ʃ(ə)n/ *n.* ора́торское иску́сство; те́хника ре́чи.

elongate /ˈi:lɒŋ,geɪt/ *adj.* (*also* **~d**) удлинённый.
● *v.t.* удлин|я́ть, -и́ть.

elongation /,i:lɒŋˈgeɪʃ(ə)n/ *n.* удлине́ние.

elope /ɪˈləʊp/ *v.i.* (та́йно) бежа́ть (*det.*) (с возлю́бленным).

elopement /ɪˈləʊpmənt/ *n.* та́йное бе́гство (с возлю́бленным).

eloquence /ˈeləkwəns/ *n.* красноре́чие.

eloquent /ˈeləkwənt/ *adj.* красноречи́вый.

El Salvador /el ˈsælvə,dɔ:(r)/ *n.* Сальвадо́р.

else /els/ *adj. & adv.* друго́й; **no-one ~** никто́ друго́й; бо́льше никто́; **everyone ~** все остальны́е; **nowhere ~** ни в како́м друго́м ме́сте; **nowhere ~ but . . .** нигде́, кро́ме. . .; **everywhere ~** везде́, то́лько не зде́сь/там; **someone ~'s** не свой, чужо́й; **what ~ could I say?** что ещё я мог сказа́ть?; **do you want anything ~** (*more*)? вы хоти́те ещё что-нибу́дь?; **how ~ can I manage?** как (же) ещё я могу́ спра́виться с э́тим?; **or ~** и́ли же; ина́че; а (не) то; **run, or ~ you'll be late** беги́те, а то опозда́ете.
● *cpd.* **~where** *adv.* где́-нибудь ещё (в друго́м ме́сте); куда́-нибудь ещё (в друго́е ме́сто).

elucidate /ɪˈlu:sɪ,deɪt/, /ɪˈlju:s-/ *v.t.* разъясн|я́ть, -и́ть; прол|ива́ть, -и́ть свет на + *a.*

elucidation /ɪ,lu:sɪˈdeɪʃ(ə)n/, /ɪ,lju:s-/ *n.* разъясне́ние.

elucidatory /ɪˈlu:sɪ,deɪtərɪ/, /ɪˈlju:s-/ *adj.* поясни́тельный.

elude /ɪˈlu:d/, /ɪˈlju:d/ *v.t.* изб|ега́ть, -е́гнуть *g.*; ускольз|а́ть, -ну́ть от + *g.*

elusive /ɪˈlu:sɪv/, /ɪˈlju:sɪv/ *adj.* неулови́мый.

elusiveness /ɪˈlu:sɪvnɪs/, /ɪˈlju:sɪvnɪs/ *n.* неулови́мость.

elver /ˈelvə(r)/ *n.* молодо́й у́горь.

elves /elvz/ *pl. of* ⇒**elf**

elvish /ˈelvɪʃ/ = **elfin**

Elysian /ɪˈlɪzɪən/ *adj.* елисе́йский; (*fig.*) ра́йский.

emaciate /ɪˈmeɪsɪ,eɪt/, /ɪˈmeɪʃɪ,eɪt/ *v.t.* изнур|я́ть, -и́ть, истощ|а́ть, -и́ть.

emaciation /ɪ,meɪsɪˈeɪʃ(ə)n/, /ɪ,meɪʃɪˈeɪʃ(ə)n/ *n.* изнуре́ние, истоще́ние.

email /ˈi:meɪl/ *n.* (*also* **e-mail**) электро́нная по́чта; **~ address** электро́нный а́дрес; **I received/sent three ~s** я получи́л/посла́л три письма́ по электро́нной по́чте.
● *v.t.*: **I'll ~ you the file** я перешлю́ вам файл по электро́нной по́чте.

emanate /ˈemə,neɪt/ *v.i.* излуча́ться (*impf.*); истека́ть (*impf.*).

emanation /,eməˈneɪʃ(ə)n/ *n.* истече́ние, излуче́ние.

emancipate /ɪˈmænsɪ,peɪt/ *v.t.* эмансипи́ровать (*impf., pf.*); свобо|жда́ть, -ди́ть.

emancipation /ɪ,mænsɪˈpeɪʃ(ə)n/ *n.* эмансипа́ция, освобожде́ние.

emancipator /ɪˈmænsɪ,peɪtə(r)/ *n.* эмансипа́тор, освободи́тель (*m.*).

emasculate /ɪˈmæskjʊ,leɪt/ *v.t.* (*castrate*) кастри́ровать (*impf., pf.*); (*fig.*) выхола́щивать, вы́холостить.

emasculation /ɪ,mæskjʊˈleɪʃ(ə)n/ *n.* кастра́ция; выхола́щивание.

embalm /ɪmˈbɑ:m/ *v.t.* бальзами́ровать (*impf., pf.*) (*pf. also* за-, на-).

embalmer /ɪmˈbɑ:mə(r)/ *n.* бальзамиро́вщик.

embalmment /ɪmˈbɑ:mmənt/ *n.* бальзами́рование.

embankment /ɪmˈbæŋkmənt/ *n.* (*wall etc.*) на́сыпь, гать; (*roadway*) на́бережная.

embargo /emˈbɑ:gəʊ/, /ɪm-/ *n.* (*pl.* **~es**) эмба́рго (*indecl.*); **oil is under ~** торго́вля не́фтью запрещена́; **lay an ~ on** нал|ага́ть, -ожи́ть эмба́рго на + *a.*; **lift, raise an ~** сни|ма́ть, -ять эмба́рго (с + *g.*).
● *v.t.* (**~es, ~ed**) (*forbid trade in*) нал|ага́ть, -ожи́ть эмба́рго на + *a.*

embark /ɪmˈbɑ:k/ *v.t.* (*goods*) грузи́ть, на-; (*people*) грузи́ть, по-.
● *v.i.* (*go on board*) грузи́ться, по-; сади́ться, сесть на кора́бль; (*fig.*) пус|ка́ться -ти́ться (в + *a.*); прин|има́ться, -я́ться (за + *a.*); **~ on an undertaking** предприн|има́ть, -я́ть де́ло; **~ on a discussion** пус|ка́ться -ти́ться в диску́ссию.

embarkation /,embɑ:ˈkeɪʃ(ə)n/ *n.* (*of goods*) погру́зка; (*of people*) поса́дка.

embarrass /ɪmˈbærəs/ *v.t.* сму|ща́ть, -ти́ть; прив|оди́ть, -ести́ в замеша́тельство.

embarrassing /ɪmˈbærəsɪŋ/ *adj.* щекотли́вый, вызыва́ющий смуще́ние; затрудни́тельный.

embarrassment /ɪmˈbærəsmənt/ *n.* смуще́ние, замеша́тельство; **he was an ~ to his parents** он был уко́ром для роди́телей; **financial ~** фина́нсовые затрудне́ния.

embassy /ˈembəsɪ/ *n.* посо́льство.

embattled /ɪmˈbæt(ə)ld/ *adj.* (*ready for war*) приведённый в боеву́ю гото́вность; (*in difficulties*) в тру́дном положе́нии.

embed /ɪmˈbed/ *v.t.* (**embedded, embedding**): **stones ~ded in rock** ка́мни, вмуро́ванные в скалу́; **facts ~ded in one's memory** фа́кты, вре́завшиеся в па́мять.

embellish /ɪmˈbelɪʃ/ *v.t.* укр|аша́ть,

E

-а́сить; (*a tale etc.*) приукра́|шивать, -сить.

embellishment /ɪm'belɪʃmənt/ *n.* приукра́шивание.

embers /'embəz/ *n. pl.* (*coals etc.*) тле́ющие уголькú (*m. pl.*).

embezzle /ɪm'bez(ə)l/ *v.t.* растра́|чивать, -тить; присв|а́ивать, -о́ить.

embezzlement /ɪm'bezəlmənt/ *n.* растра́та, присвое́ние.

embezzler /ɪm'bezələ(r)/ *n.* растра́тчик.

embitter /ɪm'bɪtə(r)/ *v.t.* озл|обля́ть, -о́бить; ожесточ|а́ть, -и́ть.

emblazon /ɪm'bleɪz(ə)n/ *v.t.* (*to decorate, inscribe*) распи́с|ывать, -а́ть; украша́ть, укра́сить (**with** + *i.*).

emblem /'embləm/ *n.* (*symbol*) эмбле́ма; (*heraldic device*) герб.

emblematic /,emblə'mætɪk/ *adj.* эмблемати́ческий.

embodiment /ɪm'bɒdɪmənt/ *n.* воплоще́ние, олицетворе́ние.

embod|y /ɪm'bɒdɪ/ *v.t.* вопло|ща́ть, -ти́ть; олицетвор|я́ть, -и́ть; (*contain*) содержа́ть (*impf.*); **this model ~ies new features** э́та моде́ль включа́ет в себя́ но́вые элеме́нты.

embolden /ɪm'bəʊld(ə)n/ *v.t.* подбодр|я́ть, -и́ть; ободр|я́ть, -и́ть; да|ва́ть, -ть сме́лость + *d.*

embolism /'embə,lɪz(ə)m/ *n.* эмболи́я.

emboss /ɪm'bɒs/ *v.t.* выбива́ть, вы́бить; чека́нить, от-/вы-; **~ed notepaper** тиснёная бума́га.

embrace /ɪm'breɪs/ *n.* объя́тие.
● *v.t.* **1** (*clasp in one's arms*) обн|има́ть, -я́ть. **2** (*an offer, theory etc.*) прин|има́ть, -я́ть. **3** (*include, comprise*) включ|а́ть, -и́ть. **4** (*take in with eye or mind*) охва́т|ывать, -и́ть.
● *v.i.* обн|има́ться, -я́ться.

embrasure /ɪm'breɪʒə(r)/ *n.* (*for gun*) амбразу́ра, бойни́ца; (*of door, window*) проём.

embrocation /,embrəʊ'keɪʃ(ə)n/ *n.* примо́чка.

embroider /ɪm'brɔɪdə(r)/ *v.t.* вышива́ть, вы́шить; (*a story etc.*) приукра́|шивать, -сить.

embroidery /ɪm'brɔɪdərɪ/ *n.* вышива́ние, вы́шивка; **~ frame** пя́л|ьцы (*pl., g.* -ец).

embroil /ɪm'brɔɪl/ *v.t.* впу́т|ывать, -ать; вовл|ека́ть, -е́чь.

embroilment /ɪm'brɔɪlmənt/ *n.* впу́тывание; вовлече́ние.

embryo /'embrɪəʊ/ *n.* (*pl.* **~s**) (*biol.*) эмбрио́н; (*fig.*) заро́дыш; **in ~** в заро́дыше.

embryologist /,embrɪ'ɒlədʒɪst/ *n.* эмбрио́лог.

embryology /,embrɪ'ɒlədʒɪ/ *n.* эмбриоло́гия.

embryonic /,embrɪ'ɒnɪk/ *adj.* эмбриона́льный; (*fig.*) недора́звитый; в заро́дыше.

emend /ɪ'mend/ *v.t.* испр|авля́ть, -а́вить.

emendation /,i:men'deɪʃ(ə)n/ *n.* исправле́ние (те́кста).

emerald /'emər(ə)ld/ *n.* изумру́д; (*attr.*) изумру́дный; **~ green** изумру́дно-зелёный.

emerge /ɪ'mɜ:dʒ/ *v.i.* всплы|ва́ть, -ть; появ|ля́ться, -и́ться; **the moon ~d from behind clouds** луна́ вы́шла из-за облако́в; (*fig.*) возн|ика́ть, -и́кнуть; **no new facts ~d** никаки́х но́вых фа́ктов не всплы́ло.

emergence /ɪ'mɜ:dʒəns/ *n.* появле́ние, возникнове́ние.

emergency /ɪ'mɜ:dʒənsɪ/ *n.* кра́йняя необходи́мость; ава́рия; (*also* **state of ~**) чрезвыча́йное положе́ние; (*attr.*) чрезвыча́йный, э́кстренный; (*for use in ~*) запасно́й, запа́сный, вре́менный; **~ exit** запа́сный вы́ход; **~ landing** вы́нужденная поса́дка; **~ powers** чрезвыча́йные полномо́чия; **~ ration** неприкоснове́нный запа́с.

emergent /ɪ'mɜ:dʒ(ə)nt/ *adj.* всплыва́ющий на пове́рхность; (*fig.*) нараста́ющий, развива́ющийся.

emeritus /ɪ'merɪtəs/ *adj.*: **professor ~** заслу́женный профе́ссор в отста́вке.

emery /'emərɪ/ *n.* нажда́к; **~ board** нажда́чная па́лочка для ногте́й; **~ cloth** нажда́чное полотно́; шку́рка; **~ paper** нажда́чная бума́га.

emetic /ɪ'metɪk/ *n.* рво́тное сре́дство.
● *adj.* рво́тный; (*fig.*) тошнотво́рный.

emigrant /'emɪgrənt/ *n.* эмигра́нт (*fem.* -ка).
● *adj.* эмигра́нтский.

emigrate /'emɪ,greɪt/ *v.i.* эмигри́ровать (*impf., pf.*).

emigration /,emɪ'greɪʃ(ə)n/ *n.* эмигра́ция.

émigré /'emɪ,greɪ/ *n.* эмигра́нт (*fem.* -ка).

eminence /'emɪnəns/ *n.* **1** (*high ground*) высота́; возвыше́ние. **2** (*celebrity*) знамени́тость; **reach, win, attain ~** доби́ться (*pf.*) сла́вы/изве́стности. **3** (*title*): **His E~** Его́ Высокопреосвяще́нство.

eminent /'emɪnənt/ *adj.* (*of person*) выдаю́щийся, знамени́тый; (*of qualities*) замеча́тельный, выдаю́щийся; **~ly suitable** ве́сьма, чрезвыча́йно подходя́щий.

emir /e'mɪə(r)/ *n.* (*ruler*) эми́р.

emirate /'emɪərət/ *n.* эмира́т.

emissary /'emɪsərɪ/ *n.* эмисса́р.

emission /ɪ'mɪʃ(ə)n/ *n.* (*of gas, heat*) выделе́ние; (*of light*) излуче́ние; (*pl.*) вы́бросы.

emit /ɪ'mɪt/ *v.t.* (**emitted, emitting**) (*smoke, smell*) испус|ка́ть, -ти́ть; (*light*) излуч|а́ть, -и́ть; (*gas, heat*) выделя́ть, вы́делить; (*sound*) изд|ава́ть, -а́ть.

emollient /ɪ'mɒlɪənt/ *n.* мягчи́тельное сре́дство.
● *adj.* смягча́ющий; мягчи́тельный.

emolument /ɪ'mɒljʊmənt/ *n.* (*usu. pl.*) жа́лованье, дохо́д.

emotion /ɪ'məʊʃ(ə)n/ *n.* (*feeling*) эмо́ция; (*agitation*) волне́ние.

emotional /ɪ'məʊʃən(ə)l/ *adj.* эмоциона́льный; **an ~ appeal** волну́ющий призы́в.

emotionalism /ɪ'məʊʃənəl,ɪz(ə)m/ *n.* эмоциона́льность.

emotive /ɪ'məʊtɪv/ *adj.* эмоциона́льно волну́ющий.

empathetic /,empə'θetɪk/ *adj.* эмпати́ческий, сопережива́ющий.

empathy /'empəθɪ/ *n.* эмпа́тия, сопережива́ние.

emperor /'empərə(r)/ *n.* импера́тор; **~ penguin** импера́торский пингви́н; **purple ~** (*butterfly*) ба́бочка-нимфахи́на.

emphasis /'emfəsɪs/ *n.* (*pl.* **emphases** /-si:z/) **1** (*stress, prominence*) ударе́ние, вырази́тельность; **lay ~ on** подчёрк|ивать, -ну́ть. **2** (*phon.*) ударе́ние, акце́нт.

emphasize /'emfə,saɪz/ *v.t.* подчёрк|ивать, -ну́ть; де́лать, с- упо́р на + *a.*

emphatic /ɪm'fætɪk/ *adj.* эмфати́ческий, вырази́тельный; **he was ~ on this point** он придава́л осо́бое значе́ние э́тому; **that is my ~ opinion** э́то моё твёрдое убежде́ние.

emphysema /,emfɪ'si:mə/ *n.* (*med.*) эмфизе́ма.

empire /'empaɪə(r)/ *n.* (*state*) импе́рия; **Russian E~** Росси́йская импе́рия; **E~ style** стиль ампи́р.

empiric(al) /ɪm'pɪrɪk(ə)l/ *adj.* эмпири́ческий.

empiricism /ɪm'pɪrɪ,sɪz(ə)m/ *n.* эмпири́зм.

empiricist /ɪm'pɪrɪsɪst/ *n.* эмпи́рик.

emplacement /ɪm'pleɪsmənt/ *n.* **1** (*location*) местоположе́ние. **2** (*mil.*) ору́дийный око́п.

employ /ɪm'plɔɪ/ *n.* заня́тие, слу́жба; **he is in my ~** он рабо́тает у меня́.
● *v.t.* **1** (*engage*) нан|има́ть, -я́ть; держа́ть (*impf.*) на слу́жбе; предост|авля́ть, -а́вить рабо́ту + *d.*; **they ~ five servants** они́ де́ржат пять слуг (*or* пять челове́к прислу́ги); **~ o.s.** занима́ться (*impf.*) (*чем*); **be ~ed** (*for hire*) рабо́тать (*impf.*), служи́ть (*impf.*). **2** (*use*) примен|я́ть, -и́ть; употреб|ля́ть, -и́ть.

employable /ɪm'plɔɪəb(ə)l/ *adj.* трудоспосо́бный.

employee /,emplɔɪ'i:/, /-'plɔɪi:/ *n.* слу́жащий; **he is an ~ of this firm** он рабо́тает в э́той фи́рме; он слу́жащий э́той фи́рмы.

employer /ɪm'plɔɪə(r)/ *n.* работода́тель (*m.*); предпринима́тель (*m.*).

employment /ɪm'plɔɪmənt/ *n.* **1** (*service for pay*) рабо́та, слу́жба; **in ~** на слу́жбе/рабо́те; **out of ~** без рабо́ты; **full ~** по́лная за́нятость; **~ agency** ка́дровое аге́нтство; бюро́ (*indecl.*) по трудоустро́йству. **2** (*occupation*) заня́тие. **3** (*use*) примене́ние, испо́льзование.

empori|um /em'pɔ:rɪəm/ *n.* (*pl.* **~a** *or* **~ums**) (*shop*) большо́й магази́н, универма́г.

empower /ɪm'paʊə(r)/ *v.t.* уполномо́чи|вать, -ть.

empress /'emprɪs/ *n.* императри́ца; (*fig.*) цари́ца.

emptiness /'emptɪnɪs/ *n.* (*lit., fig.*) пустота́.

empt|y /'emptɪ/ *adj.* (**emptier, emptiest**) **1** пусто́й; поро́жний; (*fig.*): **~y words** пусты́е слова́; **on an ~y stomach** на пусто́й желу́док; натоща́к; **~y hours** бесце́льно проведённые часы́; **I feel ~y** я го́лоден.
2 (*pl.*, **~y** *bottles etc.*) поро́жняя та́ра; буты́лки из-под вина́ и т.п.

● *v.t.* опор|а́жнивать (*or* опорожня́ть), -о́жни́ть; **he ~ied his pockets** он опоро́жни́л карма́ны; **~y one drawer into another** пере|кла́дывать, -ложи́ть ве́щи из одного́ я́щика в друго́й; **~y water out of a jug** вы́лить (*pf.*) во́ду из кувши́на.

● *v.i.* опор|а́жниваться (*or* опорожня́ться), -о́жни́ться; **the water ~ies slowly** вода́ ме́дленно вытека́ет; **the Rhine ~ies into the North Sea** Рейн впада́ет в Се́верное мо́ре; **the streets ~ied** у́лицы опусте́ли.

● *cpds.* **~y-handed** *adj.* с пусты́ми рука́ми; **~y-headed** *adj.* пустоголо́вый.

EMS (*abbr. of* ***European Monetary System***) ЕВС (Европе́йская валю́тная систе́ма).

emu /'i:mju:/ *n.* э́му (*m. indecl.*).

emulate /'emjʊˌleɪt/ *v.t.* (*compete with*) соревнова́ться (*impf.*) с + *i.*; сопе́рничать (*impf.*) с + *i.*; (*imitate*) подража́ть (*impf.*) + *d.*

emulation /ˌemjʊ'leɪʃ(ə)n/ *n.* соревнова́ние, сопе́рничество; подража́ние.

emulator /'emjʊˌleɪtə(r)/ *n.* соревну́ющийся, сопе́рник; подража́тель (*m.*).

emulsion /ɪ'mʌlʃ(ə)n/ *n.* эму́льсия.

enable /ɪ'neɪb(ə)l/ *v.t.* (*make able*) да|ва́ть, -ть возмо́жность + *d.*; (*authorize*) уполномо́чи|вать, -ть; (*make possible*) де́лать, с- возмо́жным.

enact /ɪ'nækt/ *v.t.* (*make law*) вв|оди́ть, -ести́ в де́йствие; утвер|жда́ть, -ди́ть; (*act*) игра́ть, сыгра́ть (*роль*); разы́гр|ывать, -а́ть; (*carry out*) соверш|а́ть, -и́ть.

enactment /ɪ'næktmənt/ *n.* введе́ние зако́на в си́лу; утвержде́ние; игра́.

enamel /ɪ'næm(ə)l/ *n.* (*also of teeth*) эма́ль; **~ paint** эма́левые кра́ски; **~ware** эмалиро́ванная посу́да.

● *v.t.* (**enamelled, enamelling;** *US* **enameled, enameling**) эмалирова́ть (*impf.*).

enamour /ɪ'næmə(r)/ (*US* **enamor**) *v.t.*: **he was ~ed of her** он был е́ю очаро́ван.

en bloc /ɑ̃ 'blɒk/ *adv.* целико́м; **the government resigned ~** прави́тельство ушло́ в отста́вку в по́лном соста́ве.

encamp /ɪn'kæmp/ *v.t. & i.* распол|ага́ть(ся), -ожи́ть(ся) ла́герем.

encampment /ɪn'kæmpmənt/ *n.* расположе́ние ла́герем; (*camp*) ла́герь (*m.*).

encapsulate /ɪn'kæpsjʊˌleɪt/ *v.t.* (*fig.*) заключ|а́ть, -и́ть в себе́; **an ~d dream** сон во сне.

encase /ɪn'keɪs/ *v.t.*: **~d in armour** (*Br.*), **armor** (*US*) зако́ванный в ла́ты.

encash /ɪn'kæʃ/ *v.t.* (*Br.*) реализова́ть (*impf., pf.*); получ|а́ть, -и́ть нали́чными/деньга́ми.

encashment /ɪn'kæʃmənt/ *n.* (*Br.*) реализа́ция.

encephalitis /enˌkefə'laɪtɪs/, /enˌsef-/ *n.* энцефали́т.

enchant /ɪn'tʃɑ:nt/ *v.t.* (*bewitch*) зачаро́в|ывать, -а́ть; заколдо́в|ывать, -а́ть; (*delight*) обвор|а́живать, -ожи́ть; очаро́в|ывать, -а́ть; восхи|ща́ть, -ти́ть.

enchanter /ɪn'tʃɑ:ntə(r)/ *n.* (*wizard*) волше́бник, чароде́й; (*charmer*) чарovни́к.

enchanting /ɪn'tʃɑ:ntɪŋ/ *adj.* чару́ющий, обворожи́тельный.

enchantment /ɪn'tʃɑ:ntmənt/ *n.* (*spell*) волшебство́; (*charm*) очарова́ние, обая́ние; (*delight*) восхище́ние.

enchantress /ɪn'tʃɑ:ntrɪs/ *n.* (*witch, charmer*) волше́бница, чаро́де́йка; (*charmer*) чаровни́ца.

enchase /ɪn'tʃeɪs/ *v.t.* (*adorn with engravings*) укр|аша́ть, -а́сить гравиро́вкой; (*set*) обр|амля́ть, -а́мить; (*inlay*) инкрусти́ровать (*impf., pf.*).

encipher /ɪn'saɪfə(r)/ *v.t.* зашифро́в|ывать, -а́ть.

encipherment /ɪn'saɪfəmənt/ *n.* шифро́вка.

encircl|e /ɪn'sɜ:k(ə)l/ *v.t.* окруж|а́ть, -и́ть; **~ing manoeuvre** (*Br.*), **maneuver** (*US*) обхо́дный мане́вр; манёвр на окруже́ние.

encirclement /ɪn'sɜ:kəlmənt/ *n.* окруже́ние.

enclave /'enkleɪv/ *n.* ankла́в.

enclitic /en'klɪtɪk/ *n.* энкли́тика.

● *adj.* энклити́ческий.

enclos|e, inclose /ɪn'kləʊz/ *v.t.* **1** (*surround, fence*) окруж|а́ть, -и́ть; **~e a garden with a wall** обн|оси́ть, -ести́ сад стено́й; **~e in parentheses** заключ|а́ть, -и́ть в ско́бки. **2** (*in letter etc.*) при|кла́дывать, -ложи́ть; **I ~e herewith...** при сём прилага́ю...; **a letter ~ing an invoice** письмо́ с приложе́нием счёта.

enclosure /ɪn'kləʊʒə(r)/ *n.* (*act of enclosing*) огора́живание; (*fence*) огражде́ние, огра́да; (*in letter*) приложе́ние.

encode /ɪn'kəʊd/ *v.t.* коди́ровать (*impf., pf.*) (*pf. also* за-); шифрова́ть, за-.

encoder /ɪn'kəʊdə(r)/ *n.* (*comput.*) коди́рующее устро́йство.

encompass /ɪn'kʌmpəs/ *v.t.* (*surround*) окруж|а́ть, -и́ть; (*contain, comprise*) заключ|а́ть, -и́ть; (*cope with, accomplish*) осуществ|ля́ть, -и́ть; охва́т|ывать, -и́ть.

encore /'ɒŋkɔ:(r)/ *n. & int.* бис; **he gave six ~s** он биси́ровал шесть раз.

encounter /ɪn'kaʊntə(r)/ *n.* (*meeting*) встре́ча; (*contest, competition*) состяза́ние.

● *v.t.* встр|еча́ться, -е́титься с + *i.*; ст|а́лкиваться, -олкну́ться с + *i.*

encourage /ɪn'kʌrɪdʒ/ *v.t.* ободр|я́ть, -и́ть; поощр|я́ть, -и́ть; подде́рж|ивать, -а́ть; спосо́бствовать (*impf.*) + *d.*; **I ~d him to go** я угова́ривал его́ идти́; **do not ~ him in his idle ways** не поощря́йте его́ безде́лья; **I was ~d by the result** результа́т меня́ обнадёжил.

encouragement /ɪn'kʌrɪdʒmənt/ *n.* ободре́ние, поощре́ние, подде́ржка; **this acted as an ~ to him** э́то ободри́ло его́; **I gave him no ~** я не поощря́л его́.

encouraging /ɪn'kʌrɪdʒɪŋ/ *adj.* ободря́ющий, ободри́тельный, обнадёживающий.

encroach /ɪn'krəʊtʃ/ *v.i.* поку|ша́ться, -си́ться (на + *a.*); вт|орга́ться, -о́ргнуться (в + *a.*); **~ on s.o.'s rights** посяг|а́ть, -ну́ть на чьи-н. права́; **the sea is ~ing on the land** мо́ре наступа́ет на су́шу.

encroachment /ɪn'krəʊtʃmənt/ *n.* посяга́тельство; вторже́ние.

encrust /ɪn'krʌst/ *v.t. & i.* (*of ice, rust etc.*) покр|ыва́ть(ся), -ы́ть(ся); **salt ~ed on the bottom of the kettle** дно ча́йника покры́лось сло́ем со́ли.

encrypt /en'krɪpt/ *v.t.* шифрова́ть, за-.

encryption /en'krɪpʃ(ə)n/ *n.* шифро́вка.

encumber /ɪn'kʌmbə(r)/ *v.t.* (*burden*) обремен|я́ть, -и́ть; **~ o.s. with luggage** взва́л|ивать, -и́ть на себя́ бага́ж.

encumbrance /ɪn'kʌmbrəns/ *n.* обу́за, препя́тствие; (*leg.*) обремене́ние.

encyclical /en'sɪklɪk(ə)l/ *n.* энци́клика.

encyclopedia /enˌsaɪklə'pi:dɪə/, /ɪn-/ *n* энциклопе́дия; **walking ~** ходя́чая энциклопе́дия.

encyclopedic /enˌsaɪklə'pi:dɪk/, /ɪn-/ *adj.* энциклопеди́ческий.

end /end/ *n.* **1** (*extremity; lit., fig.*) коне́ц; **the ~ house** кра́йний дом; **I read the book from ~ to ~** я прочита́л кни́гу от ко́рки до ко́рки; **two hours on ~** (*in succession*) два часа́ подря́д; **he began at the wrong ~** он на́чал не с того́ конца́; **third from the ~** тре́тий с кра́ю; **is everything all right at your ~?** всё ли благополу́чно у вас?; **to the ~s of the earth** ≈ к чёрту на кули́чки; на край све́та; **at the ~ of the passage** в конце́ коридо́ра; **at the ~ of the world** на краю́ све́та; **at the ~ of August** в конце́ (*or* в после́дних чи́слах) а́вгуста.
2 (*of elongated object*) коне́ц, край; **he stood the box on (its) ~** он поста́вил я́щик стоймя́ (*or* на попа́); **the ships collided ~ on** корабли́ столкну́лись нос к но́су; **he placed the tables ~ to ~** он соста́вил столы́ в длину́ оди́н к друго́му; **her hair stood on ~** у неё во́лосы вста́ли ды́бом.

3 (*var. idioms*): **keep one's ~ up** ≈ не уда́рить (*pf.*) лицо́м в грязь; **I am at the ~ of my tether** (*Br.*), **rope** (*US*) я дошёл до то́чки/ру́чки; **this is the ~!** (*coll., last straw, limit*) да́льше е́хать не́куда!; **he got hold of the wrong ~ of the stick** он по́нял всё наоборо́т; **loose ~s** (*unfinished business*) запу́щенные дела́; **I am at a loose ~** я шата́юсь без де́ла; **he went off the deep ~** (*coll.*) он взорва́лся; **make (both) ~s meet** св|оди́ть, -ести́ концы́ с конца́ми.
4 (*remnant, small part*): **candle ~** ога́рок; **cigarette ~** оку́рок.
5 (*conclusion, termination*) оконча́ние; **in the ~** в конце́ концо́в; в коне́чном счёте; **the war is at an ~** войне́ коне́ц; **our stores are at an ~** на́ши запа́сы на исхо́де; **come to an ~** ок|а́нчиваться, -о́нчиться; конча́ться, ко́нчиться; **put an ~ to, make an ~ of** класть, положи́ть коне́ц +*d.*; **there s an ~ (of it)!** вот и всё!; **what will the ~ be?** чем э́то ко́нчится?; **till the ~ of time** наве́чно; до сконча́ния ве́ка; **dead ~** тупи́к; **he came to a bad ~** он пло́хо ко́нчил; **world without ~** на ве́ки ве́чные; **the ~ of the matter was that** . . . де́ло ко́нчилось те́м, что. . .; **we shall never hear the ~ of it** э́тому конца́-кра́ю не бу́дет; **they fought to the bitter ~** они́ сража́лись до после́дней ка́пли кро́ви; **he stayed till the bitter ~** он остава́лся на ме́сте до са́мого конца́; **~ product** коне́чный проду́кт; **I had no ~ of trouble finding him** мне сто́ило неверо́ятного труда́ найти́ его́.
6 (*death*) коне́ц; **he is nearing his ~** он при́ смерти; **she came to an untimely ~** она́ безвре́менно сконча́лась.
7 (*purpose*) цель; **an ~ in itself** самоце́ль; **gain, win, achieve one's ~** дост|ига́ть, -и́чь свое́й це́ли; **to this ~, with this ~ in view** с э́той це́лью; **to the ~ that** . . . для того́, что́бы; **to no ~** (*in vain*) бесце́льно; **any means to an ~** все сре́дства хороши́.
● *v.t.* конча́ть, ко́нчить; **~ a quarrel** прекра|ща́ть, -ти́ть ссо́ру; **~ one's days** рассчита́ться (*pf.*) с жи́знью.
● *v.i.* конча́ться, ко́нчиться; **the road ~s here** доро́га конча́ется здесь; **the story ~s happily** э́то расска́з со счастли́вым концо́м; **the meeting ~ed with a vote of thanks** собра́ние око́нчилось выраже́нием благода́рности; **he will ~ by marrying her** он в конце́ концо́в на ней же́нится; **all's well that ~s well** всё хорошо́, что хорошо́ конча́ется.
● *with advs.*: **~ off** *v.t.*: **he ~ed off his speech with a quotation** он зако́нчил свою́ речь цита́той; **~ up** *v.i.*: **he ~ed up in jail** он ко́нчил за решёткой; **he ~ed up at the opera** в конце́ концо́в он попа́л-таки в о́перу.
● *cpds.* **~-game** *n.* (*at chess*) э́ндшпиль (*m.*); **~paper** *n.* (*of a book*) форза́ц; **~ways, ~wise** *advs.* (*with end towards spectator*) за́дом наперёд; (*end to end*) в длину́ (оди́н к друго́му); (*upright*) стоймя́.

endanger /ɪnˈdeɪndʒə(r)/ *v.t.* подв|ерга́ть, -е́ргнуть опа́сности; ста́вить (*impf.*) под угро́зу; угрожа́ть (*impf.*) +*d.*; **~ed species** вымира́ющий вид.

endear /ɪnˈdɪə(r)/ *v.t.*: **~ o.s. to s.o.** внуш|а́ть, -и́ть кому́-н. любо́вь к себе́; **this speech ~ed him to me** э́та речь расположи́ла меня́ к нему́; **an ~ing smile** покоря́ющая/подкупа́ющая улы́бка.

endearment /ɪnˈdɪəmənt/ *n.* ла́ска; **term of ~** ла́сковое обраще́ние.

endeavour /ɪnˈdevə(r)/ (*US* **endeavor**) *n.* стара́ние, стремле́ние.
● *v.i.* стара́ться, по-.

endemic /enˈdemɪk/ *adj.* эндеми́ческий.

ending /ˈendɪŋ/ *n.* (*action*) оконча́ние (*also gram.*); (*of book, play*) коне́ц; **happy ~** счастли́вый коне́ц.

endive /ˈendaɪv/, /-dɪv/ *n.* сала́т энди́вий (зи́мний); (*US, chicory crown*) цико́рий-энди́вий.

endless /ˈendlɪs/ *adj.* бесконе́чный, несконча́емый; **~ patience** беспреде́льное терпе́ние; **~ attempts** бесконе́чные попы́тки.

endocrine /ˈendəʊˌkraɪn/, /-ˌkrɪn/ *adj.* эндокри́нный; **~ glands** же́лезы вну́тренней секре́ции.

endocrinologist /ˌendəʊkrɪˈnɒlədʒɪst/ *n.* эндокрино́лог.

endocrinology /ˌendəʊkrɪˈnɒlədʒɪ/ *n.* эндокриноло́гия.

endogamous /enˈdɒgəməs/ *adj.* (*anthrop.*) эндога́мный.

endogamy /enˈdɒgəmɪ/ *n.* (*anthrop.*) эндога́мия.

endorse /ɪnˈdɔːs/ *v.t.* **1** (*sign*) индосси́ровать (*impf., pf.*); распи́с|ываться, -а́ться; **~ a cheque** (*Br.*), **check** (*US*) распи́с|ываться, -а́ться на че́ке. **2** (*support*) подтвер|жда́ть, -ди́ть; подде́рж|ивать, -а́ть; **I ~ your opinion** я подде́рживаю ва́ше мне́ние.

endorsement /ɪnˈdɔːsmənt/ *n.* **1** переда́точная на́дпись; индоссаме́нт; резолю́ция (нача́льника на докуме́нте). **2** (*support, approval*) подтвержде́ние; одобре́ние.

endow /ɪnˈdaʊ/ *v.t.* одар|я́ть, -и́ть; надел|я́ть, -и́ть; **~ a school** поже́ртвовать (*pf.*) капита́л на содержа́ние шко́лы; **~ a professorial chair** осно́в|ывать, -а́ть ка́федру; **he is ~ed with patience** он наделён терпе́нием.

endowment /ɪnˈdaʊmənt/ *n.* **1** (*act of endowing*) поже́ртвование. **2** (*funds*) вклад, дар, поже́ртвование, фонд. **3** (*talent*) одарённость. **4**: **~ insurance** страхова́ние-вклад.

endurable /ɪnˈdjʊərəb(ə)l/ *adj.* прие́млемый, сно́сный.

endurance /ɪnˈdjʊərəns/ *n.* (*physical*) про́чность; **~ test** испыта́ние на про́чность; (*mental*) выно́сливость; **past, beyond ~** невыноси́мый.

endure /ɪnˈdjʊə(r)/ *v.t.* выноси́ть, вы́нести; терпе́ть, вы-; вы́де́рживать, вы́держать; перен|оси́ть, -ести́; **~ toothache** терпе́ть зубну́ю боль; **I cannot ~ him** я его́ терпе́ть не могу́;
● *v.i.* (*suffer*) терпе́ть (*impf.*); (*last*) прод|олжа́ться, -о́лжиться; дли́ться, про-.

enduring /ɪnˈdjʊərɪŋ/ *adj.* (*lasting*) дли́тельный, продолжи́тельный.

enema /ˈenɪmə/ *n.* (*pl.* **~s** *or* **~ta** /ɪˈnemətə/) (*injection; syringe*) кли́зма.

enemy /ˈenəmɪ/ *n.* **1** враг, не́друг; **make an ~ of s.o.** наж|ива́ть, -и́ть себе́ врага́ в ком-н.; **he is his own worst ~** он сам себе́ зле́йший враг. **2** (*mil., in collect. sense*) враг, проти́вник, непри́ятель (*m.*); **20 of the ~ were killed** проти́вник потеря́л 20 челове́к уби́тыми. **3** (*attr.*) вра́жеский; непри́ятельский.

energetic /ˌenəˈdʒetɪk/ *adj.* энерги́чный.

energize /ˈenəˌdʒaɪz/ *v.t.* побужда́ть (*impf.*) к де́йствию; (*tech.*) пита́ть (*impf.*) эне́ргией.

energ|y /ˈenədʒɪ/ *n.* (*phys. or mental*) эне́ргия; **devote all one's ~ies to a task** приложи́ть (*pf.*) все си́лы к выполне́нию зада́чи; **~y crisis** энергети́ческий кри́зис.

enervat|e /ˈenəˌveɪt/ *v.t.* обесси́ли|вать, -ть; рассл|абля́ть, -а́бить; **~ing** обесси́ливающий.

en famille /ɑ̃ fæˈmiːj/ *adv.* в семе́йном кругу́.

enfeeble /ɪnˈfiːb(ə)l/ *v.t.* осл|абля́ть, -а́бить; рассл|абля́ть, -а́бить.

enfeeblement /ɪnˈfiːbəlmənt/ *n.* ослабле́ние, расслабле́ние.

enfilade /ˌenfɪˈleɪd/ *n.* (*mil.*) продо́льный ого́нь.
● *v.t.* обстре́л|ивать, -я́ть продо́льным огнём.

enfold /ɪnˈfəʊld/ *v.t.* (*contain, envelop*) завёр|тывать, -ну́ть; заку́т|ывать, -ать; (*embrace*) обн|има́ть, -я́ть.

enforce /ɪnˈfɔːs/ *v.t.* **1** (*strengthen*) уси́ли|вать, -ть; **~ an argument** подкреп|ля́ть, -и́ть аргуме́нт. **2**: **~ obedience on s.o.** заст|авля́ть, -а́вить кого́-н. подчини́ться. **3**: **~ a judgment** (*leg.*) прив|оди́ть, -ести́ в исполне́ние суде́бное реше́ние; **~ a law** следи́ть (*impf.*) за соблюде́нием зако́на; **~ payment** взыска́ть (*pf.*) платёж.

enforceable /ɪnˈfɔːsəb(ə)l/ *adj.* осуществи́мый, обеспе́ченный правово́й са́нкцией.

enforcement /ɪnˈfɔːsmənt/ *n.* осуществле́ние; **law ~** наблюде́ние за соблюде́нием зако́нов.

enfranchise /ɪnˈfræntʃaɪz/ *v.t.* предост|авля́ть, -а́вить избира́тельные права́ +*d.*

enfranchisement /ɪnˈfræntʃaɪzmənt/ *n.* предоставле́ние избира́тельных прав (*кому*).

engage /ɪnˈgeɪdʒ/ *v.t.* **1** (*hire*) нан|има́ть, -я́ть; **~ a servant** нан|има́ть, -я́ть прислу́гу; **~ s.o. as a guide** нан|има́ть, -я́ть кого́-н. ги́дом. **2** (*occupy*) зан|има́ть, -я́ть; **he is ~d in reading** он за́нят чте́нием; **he ~d me in conversation** он вовлёк меня́ в

разговóр; **the line is ~d** (*teleph.*) нóмер зáнят; **~d signal, tone** (*Br.*) корóткие гудки́; сигнáл «зáнято»; **the lavatory is ~d** убóрная занятá.
3 (*attract*) привл|екáть, -éчь; **the sight ~d my attention** зрéлище привлеклó моё внимáние.
4 (*pledge to marry*): **Tom and Mary are ~d** Том и Мэ́ри помóлвлены; **to whom is he ~d?** с кем он помóлвлен?; **they got ~d** они́ обручи́лись.
5 (*attack*) вступ|áть, -и́ть в бой с + *i.*; **we ~d the enemy** мы откры́ли огóнь по врагý.
6 (*tech.*) зацеп|ля́ть, -и́ть; включ|áть, -и́ть.
● *v.i.* **1** (*undertake, promise*) брáться, взя́ться; обещáть (*impf.*, *pf.*).
2 (*embark, busy o.s.*) зан|имáться, -я́ться чем-н.; **he ~d in this venture** он взя́лся за э́то предприя́тие.
3 (*lock together*) зацеп|ля́ть, -и́ть; **the cogs ~d** зубцы́ шестерён вошли́ в зацеплéние.

engagé /ˌɑ̃gæ'ʒeɪ/ *adj.* идéйный.

engagement /ɪn'geɪdʒmənt/ *n.* **1** (*hiring*) наём. **2** (*to marry*) помóлвка; **she broke off the ~** онá растóргла помóлвку; **~ ring** обручáльное кольцó. **3** (*appointment to meet etc.*) свидáние, встрéча; **I have numerous ~s (for) next week** у меня́ óчень мнóго встреч на слéдующей недéле; **~ book** календáрь (*m.*). **4** (*theatr.*) контрáкт, приглашéние на рабóту. **5** (*mil.*) бой; **the enemy broke off the ~** прóтивник вы́шел из бóя. **6** (*of wheels etc.*) зацеплéние.

engaging /ɪn'geɪdʒɪŋ/ *adj.* располагáющий; привлекáтельный; **an ~ smile** располагáющая улы́бка; **with ~ frankness** с подкупáющей и́скренностью.

engender /ɪn'dʒendə(r)/ *v.t.* (*fig.*) порo|ждáть, -ди́ть.

engine /'endʒɪn/ *n.* двигатель (*m.*); мотóр; **we had ~ trouble** (*motoring*) у нас бы́ли неполáдки с мотóром.
● *cpds.* **~-driver** *n.* (*Br.*) машини́ст; **~-room** *n.* маши́нное отделéние.

engineer /ˌendʒɪ'nɪə(r)/ *n.* **1** (*technician*) инженéр, механик; **civil ~** инженéр-строи́тель; **mining ~** гóрный инженéр; **mechanical ~** инженéр-мехáник. **2** (*man in charge of engines*) мехáник; **chief ~** (*of a ship*) глáвный мехáник; (*US, engine-driver*) машини́ст. **3** (*mil.*) сапёр.
● *v.t.* (*tech.*) проекти́ровать, с-; конструи́ровать, с-; (*fig.*) зат|евáть, -éять; осуществ|ля́ть, -и́ть.

engineering /ˌendʒɪ'nɪərɪŋ/ *n.* машинострoéние; **civil ~** граждáнское строи́тельство; **chemical ~** хими́ческая технолóгия; **genetic ~** гéнная инженéрия.

England /'ɪŋglənd/ *n.* Áнглия.

English /'ɪŋglɪʃ/ *n.* **1** (*language*) англи́йский язы́к; **he speaks ~** он говори́т по-англи́йски; **in plain ~** (*fig.*) без обиняко́в; **Old ~** древнеангли́йский язы́к; **Middle ~** среднеангли́йский язы́к; **British/American ~** британский/американский вариáнт англи́йского языкá; **the King's, Queen's, standard ~** нормати́вный/литерату́рный англи́йский язы́к; **what is the ~ for 'стол'?** как по-англи́йски «стол»? **2**: **he studied, read ~ at university** он изучáл в университéте англи́йскую филолóгию. **3**: **the ~** (*people*) англичáне.
● *adj.* англи́йский; **~ teacher** учи́тель (*fem.* -ница) англи́йского языкá.
● *cpds.* **~man** *n.* англичáнин; **~woman** *n.* англичáнка.

engrave /ɪn'greɪv/ *v.t.* гравировáть, вы́-; **~d with an inscription** с вы́гравированной нáдписью; (*fig.*): **~ something on s.o.'s memory** запечатл|евáть, -éть что-н. в чьей-н. пáмяти.

engraver /ɪn'greɪvə(r)/ *n.* гравёр.

engraving /ɪn'greɪvɪŋ/ *n.* (*craft*) гравирóвка, гравировáние; (*product*) гравю́ра.

engross /ɪn'grəʊs/ *v.t.* (*absorb*) погло|щáть, -ти́ть; **an ~ing conversation** захвáтывающий разговóр; **he was ~ed in his work** он был поглощён рабóтой.

engulf /ɪn'gʌlf/ *v.t.* погло|щáть, -ти́ть.

enhance /ɪn'hɑːns/ *v.t.* уси́ли|вать, -ть; (*of price*) пов|ышáть, -ы́сить.

enhancement /ɪn'hɑːnsmənt/ *n.* усилéние, повышéние.

enharmonic /ˌenhɑː'mɒnɪk/ *adj.* (*mus.*) энгармони́ческий.

enigma /ɪ'nɪgmə/ *n.* загáдка.

enigmatic /ˌenɪg'mætɪk/ *adj.* загáдочный.

enjoin /ɪn'dʒɔɪn/ *v.t.* **1** (*order*) предпи́с|ывать, -áть; велéть (*impf.*, *pf.*); **~ silence upon s.o.** велéть (*impf.*, *pf.*) комý-н. молчáть. **2** (*leg., prohibit*) запре|щáть, -ти́ть.

enjoy /ɪn'dʒɔɪ/ *v.t.* **1** (*get pleasure from*) наслa|ждáться, -ди́ться + *i.*; **~ one's food** есть (*impf.*) с удовóльствием; люби́ть (*impf.*) поéсть; **I ~ed talking to him** мне доставля́ло удовóльствие говори́ть с ним; **he ~s a good laugh** он лю́бит хорóшую шýтку; **how did you ~ the play?** как вам понрáвилась пьéса?; **we ~ed our holiday** мы хорошó провели́ óтпуск; **~ o.s.** весели́ться (*impf.*); наслаждáться (*impf.*); хорошó пров|оди́ть, -ести́ врéмя; **we ~ed ourselves** нам бы́ло вéсело/прия́тно. **2** (*possess*) располагáть (*impf.*) + *i.*; обладáть (*impf.*) + *i.*; **~ good/bad health** обладáть хорóшим/плохи́м здорóвьем; **~ a good income** имéть хорóший дохóд.

enjoyable /ɪn'dʒɔɪəb(ə)l/ *adj.* прия́тный.

enjoyment /ɪn'dʒɔɪmənt/ *n.* **1** (*pleasure*) наслаждéние, удовóльствие; **~ of music** любóвь к мýзыке. **2** (*possession*) обладáние + *i.*, пóльзование + *i.*

enlarge /ɪn'lɑːdʒ/ *v.t.* увеличи|вать, -ть; расш|иря́ть, -и́рить; **~ one's house** дéлать, с- пристрóйку к дóму.
● *v.i.* расш|иря́ться, -и́риться; **the photograph will ~ well** фотогрáфия бýдет чёткой и при увеличéнии; **he ~d on the point** он подрóбнее останови́лся на э́том.

enlargement /ɪn'lɑːdʒmənt/ *n.* увеличéние; расширéние.

enlarger /ɪn'lɑːdʒə(r)/ *n.* (*phot.*) увеличи́тель (*m.*).

enlighten /ɪn'laɪt(ə)n/ *v.t.* просве|щáть, -ти́ть.

enlightening /ɪn'laɪt(ə)nɪŋ/ *adj.* поучи́тельный.

enlightenment /ɪn'laɪtənmənt/ *n.* просвещённость; **the E~** (*hist.*) Просвещéние.

enlist /ɪn'lɪst/ *v.t.* вербовáть, за-; **~ a recruit** вербовáть, за- новобрáнца; **~ed man** (*US*) рядовóй; **~ s.o.'s support** заруч|áться, -и́ться чьей-н. поддéржкой; **~ s.o. in a cause** привлекáть (*impf.*) когó-н. к дéлу.
● *v.i.* поступ|áть, -и́ть на воéнную слýжбу.

enlistment /ɪn'lɪstmənt/ *n.* вербóвка; поступлéние на воéнную слýжбу.

enliven /ɪn'laɪv(ə)n/ *v.t.* ожив|ля́ть, -и́ть.

en masse /ɑ̃ 'mæs/ *adv.* в мáссе.

enmesh /ɪn'meʃ/ *v.t.* опýт|ывать, -ать; запýт|ывать, -ать.

enmity /'enmɪtɪ/ *n.* враждá; **be at ~ with** враждовáть (*impf.*) с + *i.*

ennoble /ɪ'nəʊb(ə)l/ *v.t.* (*raise to peerage*) возв|оди́ть, -ести́ в дворя́нство; (*make nobler*) облагор|áживать, -óдить.

ennoblement /ɪ'nəʊbəlmənt/ *n.* пожáлование дворя́нством; облагорáживание.

enormity /ɪ'nɔːmɪtɪ/ *n.* (*grossness*) чудóвищность; (*crime*) чудóвищное преступлéние.

enormous /ɪ'nɔːməs/ *adj.* громáдный, огрóмный; **~ly** чрезвычáйно; **he enjoyed himself ~ly** он получи́л огрóмное удовóльствие.

enough /ɪ'nʌf/ *n.* достáточное коли́чество; довóльно, достáточно; **£5 is ~** пяти́ фýнтов достáточно; **he has ~ and to spare** у негó бóлее чем достáточно; **~ is as good as a feast** от добрá добрá не и́щут; **I had ~ to do to catch the train** я и так едвá успевáл на пóезд; **it is ~ to make one weep** э́того достáточно, чтóбы расплáкаться; **(that's) ~!** достáточно!; довóльно!; **~ said!** всё поня́тно; **there is ~ to go round** хвáтит на всех; **I have had ~ of your lies** надоéла мне вáша ложь; **it is not ~ to buy a book, one must also read it** мáло купи́ть кни́гу, нáдо ещё читáть её.
● *adj.* достáточный; **is there ~ wine for all of us?** хвáтит ли винá на всех?; **I have just ~ money** дéнег у меня́ в обрéз (на + *a.*).
● *adv.* достáточно; **are you warm ~?** вы не замёрзли?; вам теплó?; **you know well ~** вы прекрáсно знáете; **be kind/good ~ to do this** бýдьте добры́/любéзны сдéлать э́то; **I was foolish ~ to believe her** я был настóлько глуп, что повéрил ей; (*fairly, rather*) довóльно; **she sings well ~** онá

неплóхо поёт; **curiously ~** как ни стрáнно; **sure ~, he came** он действи́тельно пришёл.

en passant /ˌɑ̃ pæ'sɑ̃/ *adv.* (*by the way*) попу́тно, мимохóдом; (*chess*) на прохóде.

enquire (*see also* ⇒**inquire**) /ɪn'kwaɪə(r)/, /ɪŋ-/ *v.t.* спр|áшивать, -оси́ть; запр|áшивать, -оси́ть; **I ~d his name** я спроси́л, как егó зову́т.

● *v.i.* осв|едомля́ться, -éдомиться; **~ into a matter** расслéдовать (*pf.*) дéло; **~ after s.o.** спр|áшивать, -оси́ть о ком-н.; **I ~d after his wife** я спроси́л, как поживáет егó женá; **~ for s.o.** спр|áшивать, -оси́ть когó-н.

enquirer /ɪn'kwaɪərə(r)/, /ɪŋ-/ *n.* спрáшивающий, вопрошáющий.

enquiring /ɪn'kwaɪərɪŋ/, /ɪŋ-/ *adj.*: **an ~ look** вопроси́тельный взгляд; **an ~ mind** пытли́вый ум.

enquir|y /ɪn'kwaɪərɪ/, /ɪŋ-/ *n.* (*see also* ⇒**inquiry**) расспрóсы (*m. pl.*); расслéдование; **make ~ies** нав|оди́ть, -ести́ спрáвки.

enrage /ɪn'reɪdʒ/ *v.t.* беси́ть, вз-.

enrapture /ɪn'ræptʃə(r)/ *v.t.* восхи|щáть, -ти́ть.

enrich /ɪn'rɪtʃ/ *v.t.* обога|щáть, -ти́ть; (*soil*) уд|обря́ть, -óбрить.

enrichment /ɪn'rɪtʃmənt/ *n.* обогащéние; (*of soil*) удобрéние.

enrol /ɪn'rəʊl/ (*US* **enroll**) *v.t. & i.* (**enrolled, enrolling**) зач|исля́ть(ся), -и́слить(ся); запи́с|ывать(ся), -áться; **17,000 students are ~led at the university** в университéте 17 000 студéнтов.

enrolment /ɪn'rəʊlmənt/ *n.* зачислéние, приём.

en route /ɑ̃ 'ru:t/ *adv.* по/в пути́.

ensconce /ɪn'skɒns/ *v.t.*: **~ o.s.** устр|áиваться, -óиться; укр|ывáться, -ы́ться.

ensemble /ɒn'sɒmb(ə)l/ *n.* ансáмбль (*m.*).

enshrine /ɪn'ʃraɪn/ *v.t.* поме|щáть, -сти́ть в рáку; (*fig.*) храни́ть (*impf.*).

enshroud /ɪn'ʃraʊd/ *v.t.* заку́т|ывать, -ать; оку́т|ывать, -ать.

ensign /'ensaɪn/, /-s(ə)n/ *n.* **1** (*flag*) (кормовóй) флаг. **2** (*hist., standard-bearer*) прáпорщик. **3** (*US nav.*) млáдший лейтенáнт.

ensilage /'ensɪlɪdʒ/ *n.* (*storage*) силосовáние; (*fodder*) си́лос.

● *v.t.* (*also* **ensile** /ɪn'saɪl/) силосовáть (*impf., pf.*).

enslave /ɪn'sleɪv/ *v.t.* порабо|щáть, -ти́ть; **he is ~d to this habit** он раб э́той привы́чки; **she ~d him by her charms** онá покори́ла егó свои́м обая́нием.

enslavement /ɪn'sleɪvmənt/ *n.* порабощéние.

ensnare /ɪn'sneə(r)/ *v.t.* (*lit.*) лови́ть, поймáть в лову́шку; (*fig.*) замáн|ивать, -и́ть в западню́.

ensu|e /ɪn'sju:/ *v.i.* (**ensues, ensued, ensuing**) (*result*) слéдовать (*impf.*) из + *g.*; (*follow*) слéдовать (*impf.*) за + *i.*; **silence ~ed** послéдовало молчáние; **in ~ing years** в послéдующие гóды.

en suite /ɑ̃ 'swi:t/ *adj.* (*with bathroom*) с вáнной.

ensure (*see also* ⇒**insure**) /ɪn'ʃʊə(r)/ *v.t.* (*make certain; secure*) обеспéчи|вать, -ть.

entablature /ɪn'tæblətʃə(r)/ *n.* (*archit.*) антаблемéнт.

entail /ɪn'teɪl/, /en-/ *v.t.* (*necessitate*) влечь (*impf.*) за собóй; **the work ~s expense** э́та рабóта свя́зана с расхóдами.

entangle /ɪn'tæŋg(ə)l/ *v.t.* (*lit.*) запу́т|ывать, -ать; (*fig.*) впу́т|ывать, -ать; **he ~d himself with women** он запу́тался в отношéниях с жéнщинами.

entanglement /ɪn'tæŋg(ə)lmənt/ *n.* запу́танность.

enter /'entə(r)/ *v.t. & i.* **1** (*go into*) входи́ть, войти́ в + *a.*; **~ hospital** ложи́ться, лечь в больни́цу; **~ school** поступ|áть, -и́ть в шкóлу; **~ the army** вступ|áть, -и́ть в áрмию; **~ the Church** (*be ordained*) прин|имáть, -я́ть сан свящéнника; **~ s.o.'s service** поступ|áть, -и́ть на слу́жбу к комý-н.; **France ~ed the war** Фрáнция вступи́ла в войну́; **the idea never ~ed my head** э́та мысль никогдá не приходи́ла мне в гóлову; **~ Macbeth** (*stage direction*) вхóдит Мáкбет. **2** (*include in record*) запи́с|ывать, -áть; (*comput.*) вводи́ть, ввести́; **~ one's name in a list** вноси́ть, внести́ своё и́мя в спи́сок; **~ (up) an item in an account-book** дéлать, с- зáпись в расчётной кни́ге; **~ a horse for a race** заяв|ля́ть, -и́ть лóшадь для скáчек; **~ (o.s.) for an examination** под|авáть, -áть на учáстие в экзáмене; **~** (*make*) **an appearance** появ|ля́ться, -и́ться; **~ a protest** заяв|ля́ть, -и́ть протéст.

● *with preps.*: **~ into conversation** вступ|áть, -и́ть в разговóр; **~ into details** входи́ть (*impf.*) в подрóбности; **~ into s.o.'s feelings** пон|имáть, -я́ть чьи-н. чу́вства; **the fact ~ed into our calculations** э́тот факт входи́л в нáши расчёты; **he ~ed into the spirit of the game** он прони́кся ду́хом игры́; **~ (up)on a career** нач|инáть, -áть профессионáльную дéятельность.

enteric /en'terɪk/ *adj.* кишéчный, брюшнóй.

enteritis /ˌentə'raɪtɪs/ *n.* энтери́т.

enterprise /'entəˌpraɪz/ *n.* **1** (*undertaking, adventure*) предприя́тие. **2** (*initiative*) предприи́мчивость; **a man of ~** предприи́мчивый человéк. **3** (*econ.*): **free ~** свобóдное предпринимáтельство; **private ~** чáстное предпринимáтельство.

enterprising /'entəˌpraɪzɪŋ/ *adj.* предприи́мчивый.

entertain /ˌentə'teɪn/ *v.t.* развл|екáть, -éчь; прин|имáть, -я́ть; **~ friends** уго|щáть, -сти́ть друзéй; **he ~s a great deal** у негó чáсто бывáют гóсти; (*amuse*) развл|екáть, -éчь; **~ a proposal** разду́мывать (*impf.*) над предложéнием; **~ ideas** носи́ться (*impf.*) с идéями; **~ doubts** питáть (*impf.*) сомнéния.

entertainer /ˌentə'teɪnə(r)/ *n.* арти́ст эстрáды.

entertaining /ˌentə'teɪnɪŋ/ *adj.* интерéсный, занимáтельный.

entertainment /ˌentə'teɪnmənt/ *n.* **1** (*social*) приём гостéй; **~ allowance** срéдства на представи́тельские расхóды. **2** (*amusement*) развлечéние. **3** (*spectacle*) представлéние.

enthral /ɪn'θrɔ:l/ (*US* **enthrall**) *v.t.* (**enthralled, enthralling**) (*fascinate*) увл|екáть, -éчь; **an ~ling play** захвáтывающая пьéса.

enthralment /ɪn'θrɔ:lmənt/ (*US* **enthrallment**) *n.* увлечéние.

enthrone /ɪn'θrəʊn/ *v.t.* (*a king, bishop*) возв|оди́ть, -ести́ на престóл.

enthronement /ɪn'θrəʊnmənt/ *n.* возведéние на престóл.

enthuse /ɪn'θju:z/, /-'θu:z/ *v.i.* (*coll.*) восторгáться (*impf.*) (*чем*).

enthusiasm /ɪn'θju:zɪˌæz(ə)m/, /-'θu:zɪˌæz(ə)m/ *n.* востóрг, энтузиáзм.

enthusiast /ɪn'θju:zɪˌæst/, /-'θu:zɪˌæst/ *n.* энтузиáст (*fem.* -ка).

enthusiastic /ɪnˌθju:zɪ'æstɪk/, /-ˌθu:zɪ'æstɪk/ *adj.* востóрженный; пóлный энтузиáзма; **he was ~ about the play** он был в востóрге от пьéсы.

entice /ɪn'taɪs/ *v.t.* соблазн|я́ть, -и́ть; замáн|ивать, -и́ть; перемáн|ивать, -и́ть; **~ a man from his duty** заст|авля́ть, -áвить человéка забы́ть о дóлге.

enticement /ɪn'taɪsmənt/ *n.* (*action*) замáнивание; (*lure*) примáнка, соблáзн.

entire /ɪn'taɪə(r)/ *adj.* цéлый, пóлный, цéльный; **that is the ~ cost** э́то— пóлная стóимость; **~ly** целикóм, совершéнно; **he is ~ly wrong** он совершéнно неплрáв.

entirety /ɪn'taɪərətɪ/ *n.* полнотá, цéльность; **in its ~** пóлностью; во всей полнотé.

entitle /ɪn'taɪt(ə)l/ *v.t.* **1** (*a book etc.*) озаглáв|ливать, -ить; **a book ~d 'Progress'** кни́га под заглáвием «Прогрéсс». **2** (*bestow title on*) жáловать, по- ти́тул + *d.* **3** (*authorize*) да|вáть, -ть прáво на + *a.*; **you are ~d to two books a month** вам полагáется две кни́ги в мéсяц.

entitlement /ɪn'taɪt(ə)lmənt/ *n.* (*right*) прáво; (*regular due*) полóженная нóрма.

entity /'entɪtɪ/ *n.* (*object, body*) существó, органи́зм, организáция; **Germany as a single ~** Гермáния как еди́ное цéлое.

entomb /ɪn'tu:m/ *v.t.* (*bury*) погре|бáть, -сти́.

entombment /ɪn'tu:mmənt/ *n.* погребéние.

entomological /ˌentəmə'lɒdʒɪk(ə)l/ *adj.* энтомологи́ческий.

entomologist /ˌentə'mɒlədʒɪst/ *n.* энтомóлог.

entomology /ˌentə'mɒlədʒɪ/ *n.* энтомолóгия.

entourage /ˌɒntʊəˈrɑːʒ/ *n.* антура́ж, окруже́ние.

entrails /ˈentreɪlz/ *n.* вну́тренности (*f. pl.*); (*fig.*) не́дра|а (*pl., g.* —).

entrance¹ /ˈentrəns/ *n.* **1** (*door, passage etc.*) вход; **front ~** пара́дный ход; **back ~** чёрный ход. **2** (*entering*) вход, вступле́ние; **upon his ~** когда́ он вошёл; **~s and exits** (*theatr.*) вхо́ды и вы́ходы (*m. pl.*); **~ upon one's duties** вступле́ние в до́лжность; **~ examination** вступи́тельный экза́мен; **~ fee, money** вступи́тельный взно́с; **~ hall** прихо́жая, вестибю́ль (*m.*).

entranc|e² /ɪnˈtrɑːns/ *v.t.* восторга́ть (*impf.*); **an ~ing sight** восхити́тельный вид

entrant /ˈentrənt/ *n.* (*person entering school, profession etc.*) поступа́ющий, приступа́ющий; (*competitor*) уча́стник.

entrap /ɪnˈtræp/ *v.t.* (**entrapped, entrapping**) лови́ть, пойма́ть в лову́шку; **he was ~ped into confessing** обма́нным путём его́ заста́вили призна́ться.

entreat /ɪnˈtriːt/ *v.t.* умол|я́ть, -и́ть; упр|а́шивать, -оси́ть; **~ a favour** (*Br.*), **favor** (*US*) умоля́ть (*impf.*) (*кого*) об одолже́нии.

entreaty /ɪnˈtriːtɪ/ *n.* мольба́; **with a look of ~** умоля́ющим взгля́дом.

entrechat /ˌɒntrəˈʃɑː/ *n.* антраша́ (*m. indecl.*).

entrecôte /ˈɒntrəˌkəʊt/ *n.* антреко́т.

entrée /ˈɒntreɪ/, /ˈɑ̃treɪ/ *n.* **1** (*admittance*) до́ступ; **he has the ~ to the Minister** у него́ есть до́ступ к мини́стру. **2** (*cul.*) (*Br., dish between fish and meat courses*) блю́до, подава́емое пе́ред жарки́м; (*US, main dish*) гла́вное блю́до.

entrench /ɪnˈtrentʃ/ *v.t.* окруж|а́ть, -и́ть око́пами; **the enemy were ~ed nearby** враг окопа́лся вблизи́; **~ o.s.** ок|а́пываться, -опа́ться; (*fig.*): **customs ~ed by tradition** обы́чаи, закреплённые тради́цией.

entrenchment /ɪnˈtrentʃmənt/ *n.* (*mil.*) око́п.

entrepôt /ˈɒntrəˌpəʊ/ *n.* (*storehouse*) пакга́уз; (*trade centre*) склад; **~ trade** транзи́тная торго́вля.

entrepreneur /ˌɒntrəprəˈnɜː(r)/ *n.* предпринима́тель (*m.*).

entrepreneurial /ˌɒntrəprəˈnɜːrɪəl/, /-ˈnjʊərɪəl/ *adj.* предпринима́тельский.

entresol /ˈɒntrəˌsɒl/ *n.* антресо́ли (*f. pl.*); полуэта́ж.

entropy /ˈentrəpɪ/ *n.* (*phys.*) энтропи́я.

entrust /ɪnˈtrʌst/ *v.t.* вв|еря́ть, -е́рить; возл|ага́ть, -ожи́ть; **I ~ed the task to him** (*or* **~ed him with the task**) я дал ему́ (*or* возложи́л на него́) поруче́ние.

entry /ˈentrɪ/ *n.* **1** (*going in*) вход; **the ~ of the US into the war** вступле́ние США в войну́; **the Romans' ~ into Britain** вторже́ние ри́млян в Брита́нию; **the ~ of the Nile into the Mediterranean** впаде́ние Ни́ла в Средизе́мное мо́ре; **the actress made an impressive ~** актри́са сде́лала эффе́ктный вы́ход. **2** (*access*) до́ступ; **he gained ~ to the house** он пробра́лся в дом. **3** (*place of ~; ~ way*) вход; **the south ~ of a church** ю́жный вход це́ркви. **4** (*item*) за́пись; **dictionary ~** слова́рная статья́; **~ in a diary** за́пись в дневнике́; **bookkeeping by double ~** двойна́я бухгалте́рия. **5** (*inscription; competitor*): **~ form** вступи́тельная анке́та; **there was a large ~ for the race** на ска́чк записа́лось мно́го уча́стников. **6** (*immigration*) въезд; **~ permit** разреше́ние на въезд.

entryphone /ˈentrɪˌfəʊn/ *n.* (*Br., propr.*) домофо́н.

entwine /ɪnˈtwaɪn/ *v.t.* (*interweave*) впле|та́ть, -сти́; (*wreathe*) обв|ива́ть, -и́ть.

enumerate /ɪˈnjuːməˌreɪt/ *v.t.* переч|исля́ть, -и́слить.

enumeration /ɪˌnjuːməˈreɪʃ(ə)n/ *n.* перечисле́ние; (*list*) пе́речень (*m.*).

enunciate /ɪˈnʌnsɪˌeɪt/ *v.t.* (*set forth*) формули́ровать, с-; (*pronounce*) произн|оси́ть, -ести́.

enunciation /ɪˌnʌnsɪˈeɪʃ(ə)n/ *n.* формулиро́вка, произноше́ние.

enuresis /ˌenjʊəˈriːsɪs/ *n.* недержа́ние мочи́, энуре́з.

envelop /ɪnˈveləp/ *v.t.* (**enveloped, enveloping**) обёр|тывать, -ну́ть; оку́т|ывать, -ать; **hills ~ed in mist** холмы́, оку́танные тума́ном; **a baby ~ed in a shawl** младе́нец, завёрнутый в шаль; **~ed in mystery** покры́тый та́йной; (*mil.*) окруж|а́ть, -и́ть; охва́т|ывать, -и́ть.

envelope /ˈenvəˌləʊp/, /ˈɒn-/ *n.* (*of letter*) конве́рт.

envelopment /ɪnˈveləpmənt/ *n.* обёртывание; (*mil.*) окруже́ние, охва́т.

enviable /ˈenvɪəb(ə)l/ *adj.* зави́дный.

envious /ˈenvɪəs/ *adj.* зави́стливый.

environment /ɪnˈvaɪərənmənt/ *n.* окруже́ние, среда́; **the ~** окружа́ющая среда́.

● *cpd.* **~-friendly** *adj.* природобезвре́дный, природосберега́ющий.

environmental /ɪnˌvaɪərənˈment(ə)l/ *adj.* окружа́ющий; **~ studies** изуче́ние окружа́ющей среды́.

environmentalism /ɪnˌvaɪərənˈmentəlɪz(ə)m/ *n.* экологи́зм.

environmentalist /ɪnˌvaɪərənˈmentəlɪst/ *n.* сторо́нник защи́ты окружа́ющей среды́.

environs /ɪnˈvaɪərənz/, /ˈenvɪrənz/ *n.* окре́стности (*f. pl.*).

envisage /ɪnˈvɪzɪdʒ/ *v.t.* (*consider*) рассм|а́тривать, -отре́ть; (*visualize*) предви́деть (*impf.*); **I had not ~d seeing him so soon** я не предполага́л, что уви́жу его́ так ско́ро; **we ~ holding a meeting** мы наме́рены устро́ить собра́ние.

envision /ɪnˈvɪʒ(ə)n/ *v.t.* предст|авля́ть, -а́вить себе́.

envoy /ˈenvɔɪ/ *n.* (*messenger*) посла́нец; (*diplomat*) диплома́т; **~ extraordinary** чрезвыча́йный посла́нник.

envy /ˈenvɪ/ *n.* за́висть; **she was green with ~** она́ позелене́ла (*or* чуть не ло́пнула) от за́висти; **his skill was the ~ of his friends** его́ ло́вкость была́ предме́том за́вити его́ друзе́й.

● *v.t.* зави́довать, по- + *d.*; **I ~ him** я ему́ зави́дую; **I ~ his patience** я зави́дую его́ терпе́нию.

enzyme /ˈenzaɪm/ *n.* энзи́м.

eon /ˈiːɒn/ = **aeon**

epaulette /ˈepəlet/, /ˈepɔːˌlet/, /ˈepəʊˌlet/, /ˌepəˈlet/ *n.* эполе́т.

epée /ˈepeɪ/ *n.* шпа́га; **~ fencer** шпажи́ст.

ephemera /ɪˈfemərə/, /ɪˈfiːm-/ *n. pl.* (*ephemeral things, esp. writings*) эфемери́ды (*f. pl.*).

ephemeral /ɪˈfemər(ə)l/, /ɪˈfiːm-/ *adj.* эфеме́рный.

epic /ˈepɪk/ *n.* эпи́ческая поэ́ма, эпопе́я.

● *adj.* эпи́ческий; (*on a grand scale*) грандио́зный; **an ~ biography** биогра́фия эпи́ческого масшта́ба.

epicentre /ˈepɪˌsentə(r)/ (*US* **epicenter**) *n.* эпице́нтр.

epicure /ˈepɪˌkjʊə(r)/ *n.* эпикуре́ец.

epicurean /ˌepɪkjʊəˈriːən/ *n.* эпикуре́ец (*also phil.*).

● *adj.* эпикуре́йский.

epicur(ean)ism /ˌepɪkjʊə(ˈriːən)ˈɪz(ə)m/ *n.* эпикуре́йство.

epicycle /ˈepɪˌsaɪk(ə)l/ *n.* эпици́кл.

epidemic /ˌepɪˈdemɪk/ *n.* эпиде́мия.

● *adj.* эпидеми́ческий.

epidemiology /ˌepɪdiːmɪˈɒlədʒɪ/ *n.* эпидемиоло́гия.

epiderm|al /ˌepɪˈdɜːməl/, **-ic** /ˌepɪˈdɜːmɪk/ *adjs.* эпидерми́ческий.

epidermis /ˌepɪˈdɜːmɪs/ *n.* эпиде́рмис.

epidural /ˌepɪˈdjʊər(ə)l/ *n.* эпидура́льная инъе́кция.

epiglottis /ˌepɪˈglɒtɪs/ *n.* надгорта́нник.

epigone /ˈepɪˌgəʊn/ *n.* (*pl.* **epigones** *or* **epigoni** /ɪˈpɪgəˌnaɪ e-/) эпиго́н.

epigram /ˈepɪˌgræm/ *n.* эпигра́мма.

epigrammatic /ˌepɪgrəˈmætɪk/ *adj.* эпиграммати́ческий.

epigraph /ˈepɪˌgrɑːf/ *n.* эпи́граф.

epilepsy /ˈepɪˌlepsɪ/ *n.* эпиле́псия.

epileptic /ˌepɪˈleptɪk/ *n.* эпиле́птик.

● *adj.* эпилепти́ческий; **he had an ~ fit** у него́ был эпилепти́ческий припа́док.

epilogue /ˈepɪˌlɒg/ *n.* эпило́г.

Epiphany /eˈpɪfənɪ/, /ɪˈpɪf-/ *n.* Богоявле́ние, Креще́ние.

episcopal /ɪˈpɪskəp(ə)l/ *adj.* (*of bishop*) епи́скопский; (*of system*) епископа́льный.

Episcopalian /ɪˌpɪskəˈpeɪlɪən/ *n.* (*Anglican*) член англика́нской це́ркви; (*pl.*) англика́нцы.

episcopate /ɪˈpɪskəpət/ *n.* (*office of bishop*) епа́рхия; (*collect., bishops*) епископа́т; епи́скопы (*m. pl.*).

episode /ˈepɪˌsəʊd/ *n.* (*occurrence*) эпизо́д; (*instalment*) часть.

E

episodic /ˌepɪˈsɒdɪk/ *adj.* (*composed of episodes*) состоя́щий из отде́льных эпизо́дов; (*incidental, occasional*) эпизоди́ческий.

epistemological /ɪˌpɪstɪməˈlɒdʒɪk(ə)l/ *adj.* гносеологи́ческий, эпистемологи́ческий.

epistemology /ɪˌpɪstɪˈmɒlədʒɪ/ *n.* гносеоло́гия, эпистемоло́гия.

epistle /ɪˈpɪs(ə)l/ *n.* посла́ние.

epistolary /ɪˈpɪstələrɪ/ *adj.* эпистоля́рный.

epitaph /ˈepɪˌtɑːf/ *n.* эпита́фия, надгро́бная на́дпись.

epitheli|um /ˌepɪˈθiːlɪəm/ *n.* (*pl.* **~ums** *or* **~a**) эпите́лий.

epithet /ˈepɪˌθet/ *n.* эпи́тет.

epitome /ɪˈpɪtəmɪ/ *n.* (*summary*) конспе́кт; (*personification*) воплоще́ние, олицетворе́ние.

epitomize /ɪˈpɪtəˌmaɪz/ *v.t.* (*summarize*) резюми́ровать (*impf.*, *pf.*); (*personify*) вопло|ща́ть, -ти́ть.

epoch /ˈiːpɒk/ *n.* эпо́ха; **this discovery marks a new ~** э́то откры́тие знамену́ет собо́й но́вую эпо́ху.

● *cpd.* **~-making** *adj.* эпоха́льный.

eponym /ˈepənɪm/ *n.* эпони́м.

eponymous /ɪˈpɒnɪməs/ *adj.* эпони́мный.

Epsom salts /ˈepsəm/ *n.* англи́йская соль.

equable /ˈekwəb(ə)l/ *adj.* (*of climate, temper*) ро́вный, уравнове́шенный.

equal /ˈiːkw(ə)l/ *n.* (*person or thing*) ро́вня; **he has no ~** ему́ нет ра́вного; **he was her ~ at tennis** он игра́л в те́ннис не ху́же её; **he only mixes with his ~s** он обща́ется то́лько с ра́вными себе́.

● *adj.* **1** (*same, equivalent*) ра́вный, одина́ковый; **~ in** (*or* **of ~**) **ability** одина́ковых спосо́бностей; **the totals are ~** ито́ги равны́; **other things being ~** при про́чих ра́вных усло́виях; **~ shares** ра́вные до́ли; **two boys of ~ height** два ма́льчика одного́ ро́ста; **he speaks French and German with ~ ease** он одина́ково свобо́дно говори́т по-францу́зски и по-неме́цки. **2** (*capable, adequate*) спосо́бный; **he is ~ to the task** он вполне́ мо́жет спра́виться с э́той зада́чей. **3** (*unbiased, evenly balanced, stable*) ра́вный, равнопра́вный, уравнове́шенный; **~ laws** ра́вные права́; **an ~ fight** ра́вный бой.

● *v.t. & i.* (**equalled, equalling;** *US* **equaled, equaling**) **1** (*math.*) равня́ться (*impf.*) (*чему*); **twice 2 ~s 4** два́жды два равня́ется четырём; **x = y** x ра́вен y; **the ~s sign** знак ра́венства. **2**: **he ~s me in strength** он ра́вен мне по си́ле; **I know nothing to ~ it** я не зна́ю ничего́ подо́бного; **it will be hard to ~ his record** бу́дет тру́дно повтори́ть его́ реко́рд.

equality /ɪˈkwɒlɪtɪ/ *n.* ра́венство, равнопра́вие.

equalization /ˌiːkwəlaɪˈzeɪʃ(ə)n/ *n.* уравне́ние, ура́внивание.

equalize /ˈiːkwəˌlaɪz/ *v.t. & i.* ура́вн|ивать, -я́ть; **~ (the score)** равня́ть (*or* сра́внивать), с- счёт.

equalizer /ˈiːkwəˌlaɪzə(r)/ *n.* **1** (*sport*) сра́внивающий гол. **2** (*electronics*) выра́вниватель (*m.*).

equally /ˈiːkwəlɪ/ *adv.* **1** (*to an equal extent*) одина́ково; **he is ~ to blame** он винова́т в той же сте́пени. **2** (*also, likewise*) ра́вным о́бразом; наравне́; **~ it can be said that** ... с таки́м же успе́хом мо́жно сказа́ть, что.... **3** (*evenly*): **he divided the money ~** он раздели́л де́ньги по́ровну.

equanimity /ˌekwəˈnɪmɪtɪ/, /ˌiːk-/ *n.* душе́вное равнове́сие; споко́йствие; **with ~** споко́йно.

equate /ɪˈkweɪt/ *v.t.* (*make equal*) ура́вн|ивать, -я́ть; **they ~d his salary to mine** они́ уравня́ли его́ окла́д с мои́м; (*consider or treat as equal*) отождеств|ля́ть, -и́ть; прира́вн|ивать, -я́ть; **he ~s wealth with happiness** он отождествля́ет бога́тство со сча́стьем.

● *v.i.*: **~ with** (*be equal, correspond to*) быть ра́вным + *d.*

equation /ɪˈkweɪʒ(ə)n/ *n.* **1** (*making equal, balancing*) выра́внивание; **~ of demand and supply** соотве́тствие спро́са и предложе́ния. **2** (*math., chem.*) уравне́ние; **quadratic ~** квадра́тное уравне́ние.

equator /ɪˈkweɪtə(r)/ *n.* эква́тор.

equatorial /ˌekwəˈtɔːrɪəl/, /ˌiːk-/ *adj.* экваториа́льный.

equerry /ˈekwərɪ/, /ɪˈkwerɪ/ *n.* коню́ший, шталме́йстер.

equestrian /ɪˈkwestrɪən/ *n.* нае́здник, вса́дник.

● *adj.* ко́нный.

equestrianism /ɪˈkwestrɪəˌnɪz(ə)m/ *n.* ко́нный спорт.

equestrienne /ɪˌkwestrɪˈen/ *n.* вса́дница; (*in circus*) нае́здница.

equidistance /ˌiːkwɪˈdɪstəns/ *n.* равноудалённость.

equidistant /ˌiːkwɪˈdɪst(ə)nt/ *adj.* равноотстоя́щий; **these towns are ~ from London** э́ти города́ располо́жены на одина́ковом расстоя́нии от Ло́ндона.

equilateral /ˌiːkwɪˈlætər(ə)l/ *adj.* равносторо́нний.

equilibrate /ɪˈkwɪlɪˌbreɪt/, /ˌiːkwɪˈlaɪbreɪt/ *v.t.* уравнове́|шивать, -сить.

equilibration /ɪˌkwɪlɪˈbreɪʃ(ə)n/, /ˌiːkwɪlaɪˈbreɪʃ(ə)n/ *n.* уравнове́шивание.

equilibria /ˌiːkwɪˈlɪbrɪə/ *pl. of* ⇒**equilibrium**

equilibrist /ɪˈkwɪlɪbrɪst/ *n.* эквилибри́ст (*fem.* -ка).

equilibri|um /ˌiːkwɪˈlɪbrɪəm/ *n.* (*pl.* **~a**) (*lit., fig.*) равнове́сие; **in stable ~um** в усто́йчивом равнове́сии.

equine /ˈiːkwaɪn/, /ˈek-/ *adj.* лошади́ный, ко́нский.

equinoctial /ˌiːkwɪˈnɒkʃ(ə)l/, /ˌek-/ *adj.* равноде́нственный; **~ gales** што́рмы равноде́нствия.

equinox /ˈiːkwɪˌnɒks/, /ˈek-/ *n.* равноде́нствие; **autumnal ~** осе́ннее равноде́нствие; **vernal, spring ~** весе́ннее равноде́нствие.

equip /ɪˈkwɪp/ *v.t.* (**equipped, equipping**) снаря|жа́ть, -ди́ть; (*a ship*) осна|ща́ть, -сти́ть; (*soldiers*) снаря|жа́ть, -ди́ть; экипирова́ть (*impf.*, *pf.*); **~ o.s. with something** вооруж|а́ться, -и́ться чем-н.; **he is ~ped with sound sense** он наделён здра́вым рассу́дком.

equipage /ˈekwɪpɪdʒ/ *n.* (*carriage*) экипа́ж; (*attendants*) сви́та.

equipment /ɪˈkwɪpmənt/ *n.* снаряже́ние, экипиро́вка.

equipoise /ˈekwɪˌpɔɪz/, /ˈiː-/ *n.* (*balance*) равнове́сие.

equitable /ˈekwɪtəb(ə)l/ *adj.* справедли́вый.

equitation /ˌekwɪˈteɪʃ(ə)n/ *n.* верхова́я езда́.

equity /ˈekwɪtɪ/ *n.* **1** (*fairness*) справедли́вость. **2** (*pl., fin.*) обыкнове́нные а́кции (*f. pl.*).

equivalenc|e /ɪˈkwɪvələns/ *n.* эквивале́нтность.

equivalent /ɪˈkwɪvələnt/ *n.* эквивале́нт; **a university degree or the ~** университе́тский дипло́м и́ли ра́вное ему́ удостовере́ние.

● *adj.* эквивале́нтный; **his words were ~ to an insult** его́ слова́ бы́ли равноси́льны оскорбле́нию.

equivocal /ɪˈkwɪvək(ə)l/ *adj.* двусмы́сленный, сомни́тельный.

equivocate /ɪˈkwɪvəˌkeɪt/ *v.i.* говори́ть (*impf.*) двусмы́сленно; увил|ивать, -ну́ть от прямо́го отве́та.

equivocation /ɪˌkwɪvəˈkeɪʃ(ə)n/ *n.* укло́нчивость, увёртка.

equivocator /ɪˈkwɪvəˌkeɪtə(r)/ *n.* говоря́щий двусмы́сленно; нейскренний челове́к.

er /ɜː(r)/ *int.* (*expr. hesitation*) а; э-э.

era /ˈɪərə/ *n.* э́ра.

eradicable /ɪˈrædɪkəb(ə)l/ *adj.* искорени́мый.

eradicate /ɪˈrædɪˌkeɪt/ *v.t.* искорен|я́ть, -и́ть.

eradication /ɪˌrædɪˈkeɪʃ(ə)n/ *n.* искорене́ние.

erasable /ɪˈreɪzəb(ə)l/ *adj.* стира́емый.

erase /ɪˈreɪz/ *v.t.* ст|ира́ть, -ере́ть; **~ something from one's memory** вычёркивать, вы́черкнуть что-н. из па́мяти.

eraser /ɪˈreɪzə(r)/ *n.* рези́нка.

erasure /ɪˈreɪʒə(r)/ *n.* стира́ние, подчи́стка.

ere /eə(r)/ (*arch., poet.*) = **before**

erect /ɪˈrekt/ *adj.* прямо́й; **with head ~** с по́днятой голово́й; **stand ~** держа́ться (*impf.*) пря́мо.

● *v.t.* (*build, set up*) воздв|ига́ть, -и́гнуть; соору|жа́ть, -ди́ть; **~ a monument** воздв|ига́ть, -и́гнуть па́мятник; **~ a tent** ста́вить, по- пала́тку.

erection /ɪˈrekʃ(ə)n/ *n.* (*setting up*) сооруже́ние; (*building*) зда́ние; (*physiol.*) эре́кция.

erectness /ɪˈrektnɪs/ *n.* прямота́.

erector /ɪˈrektə(r)/ *n.* (*builder*) строи́тель (*m.*); **~ muscle** выпрямля́ющая мы́шца.

eremitic(al) /ˌerɪˈmɪtɪk(ə)l/ *adj.* отше́льнический.

erg /ɜ:g/ *n.* (*phys.*) эрг.

ergo /ˈɜ:gəʊ/ *adv.* сле́довательно.

ergonomic /ˌɜ:gəˈnɒmɪk/ *adj.* эргономи́ческий.

ergonomics /ˌɜ:gəˈnɒmɪks/ *n.* эргоно́мика, эргоно́мия.

ergonomist /ɜ:ˈgɒnəmɪst/ *n.* эргономи́ст.

Eritrea /ˌerɪˈtreɪə/ *n.* Эритре́я.

ERM (*abbr. of* ***exchange-rate mechanism***) МВК (механи́зм валю́тных ку́рсов).

ermine /ˈɜ:mɪn/ *n.* (*pl.* **~** *or* **~s**) (*animal, fur*) горноста́й.

erode /ɪˈrəʊd/ *v.t.* разъ|еда́ть, -е́сть; (*fig.*) подт|а́чивать, -очи́ть.

erogenous /ɪˈrɒdʒɪnəs/ *adj.* эроге́нный.

erosion /ɪˈrəʊʒ(ə)n/ *n.* разъеда́ние, эро́зия (*fig.*); **the ~ of his hopes** постепе́нное разруше́ние его́ наде́жд.

erosive /ɪˈrəʊsɪv/ *adj.* разъеда́ющий; эрози́вный.

erotic /ɪˈrɒtɪk/ *adj.* эроти́ческий.

erotica /ɪˈrɒtɪkə/ *n.* (*pl.*) эро́тика.

eroticism /ɪˈrɒtɪˌsɪz(ə)m/ *n.* эроти́зм.

erotomania /ɪˌrəʊtəˈmeɪnɪə/ *n.* эротома́ния.

err /ɜ:(r)/ *v.i.* ошиб|а́ться, -и́ться; заблужда́ться (*impf.*); **to ~ is human** челове́ку сво́йственно ошиба́ться.

errand /ˈerənd/ *n.* поруче́ние; предприя́тие; **go on ~s for s.o.** исполня́ть (*impf.*) чьи-н. поруче́ния.

● *cpd.* **~-boy** *n.* (*Br.*) посы́льный, рассы́льный.

errant /ˈerənt/ *adj.* **1** (*mistaken*) заблужда́ющийся. **2** (*stray, wandering*) стра́нствующий; **knight ~** стра́нствующий ры́царь. **3** (*misbehaving*) заблу́дший.

errata /ɪˈrɑ:tə/ *pl. of* **⇒erratum**

erratic /ɪˈrætɪk/ *adj.* неусто́йчивый; (*of person*) беспоря́дочный, сумасбро́дный; **~ally** нерегуля́рно; **the engine fires ~ally** мото́р рабо́тает с перебо́ями.

errat|um /ɪˈrɑ:təm/ *n.* (*pl.* **~a**) опеча́тка; **~a** (*pl., list*) спи́сок опеча́ток.

erring /ˈɜ:rɪŋ/ *adj.* заблу́дший, гре́шный.

erroneous /ɪˈrəʊnɪəs/ *adj.* оши́бочный.

error /ˈerə(r)/ *n.* **1** (*mistake*) оши́бка, заблужде́ние; **make, commit an ~** соверш|а́ть, -и́ть (*or* допус|ка́ть, -ти́ть) оши́бку; **he is in ~** он заблужда́ется; **fall into (an) ~** впа|да́ть, -сть в заблужде́ние; **the letter was sent in ~** письмо́ бы́ло по́слано по оши́бке; **clerical ~** опи́ска; **printer's ~** опеча́тка; **~ of fact** факти́ческая оши́бка; **~ of judgment** неве́рное сужде́ние; оши́бка в расчётах; **he saw the ~ of his ways** он осозна́л свои́ оши́бки; **~s and omissions excepted** не счита́я оши́бки и про́пуски. **2** (*transgression*) просту́пок; **the ~s of his youth** грехи́ (*m. pl.*) его́ мо́лодости.

ersatz /ˈɜ:zæts/, /ˈeə-/ *n.* эрза́ц, суррога́т; **~ coffee** эрза́ц-ко́фе (*m. indecl.*).

erstwhile /ˈɜ:stwaɪl/ *adj.* да́вний, давни́шний; **an ~ friend** да́вний/стари́нный друг.

eructation /ˌi:rʌkˈteɪʃ(ə)n/ *n.* (*of person*) отры́жка; (*of volcano etc.*) изверже́ние.

erudite /ˈeru:ˌdaɪt/ *adj.* эруди́рованный, учёный.

erudition /ˌeru:ˈdɪʃ(ə)n/ *n.* эруди́ция.

erupt /ɪˈrʌpt/ *v.i.* (*of volcano etc.*) изв|ерга́ться, -е́ргнуться; (*of teeth*) прор|еза́ться, -е́заться.

eruption /ɪˈrʌpʃ(ə)n/ *n.* **1** (*of volcano etc.*) изверже́ние. **2** (*of teeth*) проре́зывание. **3** (*on face etc.*) сыпь. **4** (*fig.*) взрыв.

erysipelas /ˌerɪˈsɪpɪləs/ *n.* ро́жа, ро́жистое воспале́ние.

escalate /ˈeskəˌleɪt/ *v.t.* эскали́ровать (*impf., pf.*); обостр|я́ть, -и́ть.

● *v.i.* разраста́ться (*impf.*).

escalation /ˌeskəˈleɪʃ(ə)n/ *n.* эскала́ция.

escalator /ˈeskəˌleɪtə(r)/ *n.* эскала́тор.

escalope /ˈeskəˌlɒp/ *n.* эскало́п.

escapade /ˈeskəˌpeɪd/, /ˌeskəˈpeɪd/ *n.* эскапа́да; вы́ходка.

escape /ɪˈskeɪp/ *n.* **1** (*becoming free*) побе́г, бе́гство; **make one's ~** убежа́ть (*pf.*); **there have been few ~s from this prison** побе́ги из э́той тюрьмы́ весьма́ ре́дки; **~ clause** пункт догово́ра, избавля́ющий сто́рону от отве́тственности; **~ hatch** авари́йный люк; **~ velocity** (*of rocket*) втора́я косми́ческая ско́рость. **2** (*avoidance*) спасе́ние, избавле́ние; **he had a narrow ~ from shipwreck** он едва́ спа́сся при кораблекруше́нии; **that was a lucky ~** э́то бы́ло счастли́вым избавле́нием. **3** (*of gas etc.*) уте́чка. **4** (*fig., mental relief*) ухо́д/бе́гство от действи́тельности.

● *v.t.* избе|га́ть, -жа́ть + *g.*; **he ~d death** он оста́лся в живы́х; **he ~d with a scratch** он отде́лался цара́пиной; **the words ~d his lips** слова́ сорвали́сь у него́ с языка́; **I cannot ~ the feeling that** ... я не могу́ отде́латься от чу́вства, что...; **nothing ~s you!** вы всё замеча́ете!; **his name ~s me** не могу́ припо́мнить его́ фами́лии.

● *v.i.* бежа́ть (*det.*); уходи́ть, уйти́; соверши́ть (*pf.*) побе́г; **the prisoner ~d** заключённый (с)бежа́л; **an ~d prisoner** бе́глый ареста́нт; **the canary ~d from its cage** канаре́йка вы́порхнула из кле́тки; **the lion ~d** лев вы́рвался на во́лю; **gas is escaping** происхо́дит уте́чка га́за.

escapee /ɪskeɪˈpi:/ *n.* бегле́ц.

escapism /ɪˈskeɪpɪz(ə)m/ *n.* бе́гство от действи́тельности; эскапи́зм.

escapist /ɪˈskeɪpɪst/ *n.* челове́к, уходя́щий от действи́тельности; эскапи́ст.

● *adj.* уходя́щий от действи́тельности; эскапи́стский.

escapologist /ˌeskəˈpɒlədʒɪst/ *n.* фо́кусник, выполня́ющий трюк самоосвобожде́ния от цепе́й.

escarp(ment) /ɪˈskɑ:pmənt/ *n.* (*geol.*) вертика́льное обнаже́ние поро́ды.

eschatological /ˌeskətəˈlɒdʒɪk(ə)l/ *adj.* (*theol.*) эсхатологи́ческий.

eschatology /ˌeskəˈtɒlədʒɪ/ *n.* (*theol.*) эсхатоло́гия.

escheat /ɪsˈtʃi:t/ *v.i.*: **the property ~ed to the Crown** (вы́морочное) иму́щество перешло́ в казну́.

eschew /ɪsˈtʃu:/ *v.t.* возде́рж|иваться, -а́ться от + *g.*; сторони́ться (*impf.*) + *g.*

eschscholtzia /ɪsˈkɒlʃə/, /eˈʃɒltsɪə/ *n.* (*bot.*) эшо́льция.

escort[1] /ˈeskɔ:t/ *n.* (*mil., nav.*) конво́й, эско́рт; **~ ship, vessel** сторожево́й/эско́ртный кора́бль; **police ~** (*of criminal*) конво́й; **her ~ to the ball** её кавале́р на балу́.

escort[2] /ɪˈskɔ:t/ *v.t.* сопрово|жда́ть, -ди́ть; (*mil., nav.*) эскорти́ровать (*impf., pf.*); конвои́ровать (*impf.*); **he ~ed her to the ball** он сопровожда́л её на бал; **I ~ed him to his seat** я провёл его́ на ме́сто; **he was ~ed from the hall** его́ вы́вели из за́ла.

escritoire /ˌeskrɪˈtwɑ:(r)/ *n.* секрете́р.

escutcheon /ɪˈskʌtʃ(ə)n/ *n.* щит герба́; **a blot on s.o.'s ~** (*fig.*) пятно́ на чьей-н. репута́ции.

Eskimo /ˈeskɪˌməʊ/ *n.* (*pl.* **~** *or* **~s**) эскимо́с (*fem.* -ка).

● *adj.* эскимо́сский; **~ dog** ла́йка.

esophagus /i:ˈsɒfəgəs/ (*US*) = **oesophagus**

esoteric /ˌi:səʊˈterɪk/, /ˌe-/ *adj.* эзотери́ческий.

ESP (*abbr. of* ***extra-sensory perception***) сверхчу́вственное восприя́тие, экстрасенсо́рика.

espagnolette /espanjəˈlet/ *n.* шпингале́т.

espalier /ɪˈspælɪə(r)/ *n.* (*lattice*) шпале́ра; (*plant*) шпале́рник.

esparto /eˈspɑ:təʊ/ *n.* (*pl.* **~s**) (*also* **~ grass**) эспа́рто (*indecl.*), трава́ а́льфа.

especial /ɪˈspeʃ(ə)l/ *adj.* специа́льный; осо́бенный.

Esperantist /ˌespəˈræntɪst/ *n.* эсперанти́ст (*fem.* -ка).

Esperanto /ˌespəˈræntəʊ/ *n.* эспера́нто (*m. & nt. indecl.*); **in ~** на языке́ эспера́нто.

espionage /ˈespɪəˌnɑ:ʒ/ *n.* шпиона́ж.

esplanade /ˌespləˈneɪd/ *n.* (*promenade*) эспланада.

espousal /ɪˈspaʊz(ə)l/ *n.* (*of a cause*) подде́ржка.

espouse /ɪˈspaʊz/ *v.t.*: **~ a cause** (целико́м) отд|ава́ться, -а́ться де́лу.

espresso /eˈspresəʊ/ *n.* (*pl.* **~s**) (*coffee*) ко́фе «экспре́ссо».

esprit de corps /eˈspri: də ˈkɔ:(r)/, /ˈespri:/ *n.* ≈ чу́вство солида́рности.

espy /ɪ'spaɪ/ *v.t.* зам|еча́ть, -е́тить.

esquire /ɪ'skwaɪə(r)/ *n.*: **W. Jones, E~** (*Br., on envelope*) г-ну В. Джо́нсу.

essay[1] /'eseɪ/ *n.* (*attempt*) попы́тка, про́ба; (*literary composition*) о́черк, эссе́ (*indecl.*); (*in school*) сочине́ние.

essay[2] /e'seɪ/ *v.t.* про́бовать, по-.

● *v.i.* пыта́ться, по-.

essayist /'eseɪɪst/ *n.* очерки́ст, эссеи́ст.

essence /'es(ə)ns/ *n.* **1** (*philos.*) су́щность, существо́; (*gist*) суть; **speed is of the ~** всё де́ло в ско́рости. **2** (*extract*) эссе́нция.

essential /ɪ'senʃ(ə)l/ *n.* (*~ feature, element*) су́щность; **~s of mathematics** осно́вы (*f. pl.*) матема́тики.

● *adj.* **1** (*necessary*) необходи́мый; **is wealth ~ to happiness?** необходи́мо ли бога́тство для сча́стья?; **it is ~ that I should know** о́чень ва́жно, что́бы я знал. **2** (*fundamental*) суще́ственный; **~ly** суще́ственно; по существу́; в су́щности; **he is ~ly an amateur** он в су́щности дилета́нт. **3**: **~ oils** эфи́рные масла́.

establish /ɪ'stæblɪʃ/ *v.t.* **1** (*found, set up*) учре|жда́ть, -ди́ть; устан|а́вливать, -ови́ть; **~ a republic** провозгл|аша́ть, -си́ть респу́блику; **~ contact** устан|а́вливать, -ови́ть конта́кт; **~ o.s. in business** осно́в|ывать, -а́ть де́ло; **~ one's son in business** помо́чь (*pf.*) сы́ну нача́ть делову́ю карье́ру. **2** (*settle*) устр|а́ивать, -о́ить; **we are ~ed in our new home** мы обжили́сь в но́вом до́ме. **3** (*prove, gain acceptance for*) утвер|жда́ть, -ди́ть; **~ a claim** обосно́в|ывать, -а́ть прете́нзию; **~ one's reputation** созд|ава́ть, -а́ть себе́ репута́цию; **it is ~ed that he saw her** устано́влено, что он её ви́дел; **an ~ed custom** укорени́вшийся обы́чай; **~ed church** госуда́рственная це́рковь.

establishment /ɪ'stæblɪʃmənt/ *n.* **1** (*setting up*) учрежде́ние, установле́ние. **2** (*of a claim, fact etc.*) установле́ние, обоснова́ние. **3** (*business concern*) заведе́ние, де́ло. **4** (*household*) дом; **he keeps a large ~** он живёт на широ́кую но́гу; **they maintain two ~s** они́ живу́т на́ два до́ма. **5** (*institution*) учрежде́ние, заведе́ние; **educational ~** уче́бное заведе́ние. **6** (*set of institutions or key persons*): **the E~** «истéблишмент».

estate /ɪ'steɪt/ *n.* **1** (*landed property*) поме́стье, име́ние; **~ agent** (*Br.*) аге́нт по прода́же недви́жимости; **~ car** (*Br.*) автомоби́ль (*m.*) с ку́зовом «универса́л»; универса́л (*coll.*); **housing ~** (*Br.*) жило́й масси́в; **industrial ~** (*Br.*) промы́шленный ко́мплекс. **2** (*property*) иму́щество; **real ~** недви́жимость; **personal ~** дви́жимость; **the deceased's ~ amounted to £150,000** состоя́ние поко́йного составля́ло 150 000 фу́нтов.

esteem /ɪ'sti:m/ *n.* уваже́ние; **we have great ~ for you** мы пита́ем к вам большо́е уваже́ние; **he fell in my ~** он упа́л в мои́х глаза́х.

● *v.t.* уважа́ть (*impf.*); **I ~ him highly** я его́ высоко́ ценю́.

Esther /'estə(r)/ *n.* (*bibl.*) Эсфи́рь.

esthete /'i:sθi:t/ *etc.* (*US*) = **aesthete** *etc.*

estimable /'estɪməb(ə)l/ *adj.* досто́йный уваже́ния.

estimate[1] /'estɪmət/ *n.* **1** (*assessment*) оце́нка. **2** (*comm.*) сме́та; **the builder exceeded his ~** строи́тель превы́сил сме́ту.

estimate[2] /'estɪ,meɪt/ *v.t.* оце́н|ивать, -и́ть; **I ~ his income at £20,000** по моим подсчётам его́ дохо́д ра́вен двадцати́ ты́сячам фу́нтов.

estimation /,estɪ'meɪʃ(ə)n/ *n.* (*judgment*) оце́нка, сужде́ние.

Estonia /ɪ'stəʊnɪə/ *n.* Эсто́ния.

Estonian /ɪ'stəʊnɪən/ *n.* эсто́н|ец (*fem.* -ка).

● *adj.* эсто́нский.

estrange /ɪ'streɪndʒ/ *v.t.* отдал|я́ть, -и́ть; **his ~d wife** жена́, с кото́рой он живёт разде́льно; **Mr X is ~d from his wife** г-н и г-жа X живу́т вро́зь; **the children were ~d from their mother** ме́жду детьми́ и их ма́терью возни́кло отчужде́ние.

estrangement /ɪ'streɪndʒmənt/ *n.* отчужде́ние, разры́в.

estrogen /'i:strədʒ(ə)n/ (*US*) = **oestrogen**

estrus /'i:strəs/ (*US*) = **oestrus**

estuary /'estjʊərɪ/ *n.* эстуа́рий, у́стье.

ETA (*abbr. of* ***estimated time of arrival***) предполага́емое вре́мя прибы́тия.

et al /et 'æl/ (*abbr. of* ***et alii***) и други́е.

etc. /et 'setərə/, /'setrə/ *adv.* (*abbr. of* ***et cetera***) и т.д., и т.п. (и так да́лее; и тому́ подо́бное).

et cetera /et 'setərə/, /'setrə/ *adv. & n.* и так да́лее; и тому́ подо́бное.

etch /etʃ/ *v.t. & i.* трави́ть, вы́-; гравирова́ть, вы́-; (*fig.*): **it is ~ed on my memory** э́то запечатле́лось у меня́ в па́мяти.

etcher /'etʃə(r)/ *n.* гравёр.

etching /'etʃɪŋ/ *n.* (*craft*) гравиро́вка; (*product*) офо́рт, гравю́ра.

eternal /ɪ'tɜ:n(ə)l/ *adj.* ве́чный (*also fig.*); **~ triangle** любо́вный треуго́льник.

eternity /ɪ'tɜ:nɪtɪ/ *n.* ве́чность; **for all ~** на ве́ки ве́чные; **it seemed an ~ till he came** каза́лось, прошла́ ве́чность, пока́ он (не) пришёл.

ethane /'eθeɪn/, /'i:θ-/ *n.* эта́н.

ether /'i:θə(r)/ *n.* (*phys., chem.*) эфи́р.

ether|eal, -ial /ɪ'θɪərɪəl/ *adj.* эфи́рный, неземно́й; **~ beauty** неземна́я красота́.

ethic /'eθɪk/ *n.* (*moral code; also* **~s**) э́тика; мора́ль.

● *adj.* эти́ческий; эти́чный.

ethical /'eθɪk(ə)l/ *adj.* (*pert. to ethics*) эти́ческий; (*conforming to a code*) эти́чный; **it is not ~ for doctors to advertise** врача́м неэти́чно создава́ть себе́ рекла́му.

Ethiopia /,i:θɪ'əʊpɪə/ *n.* Эфио́пия.

Ethiopian /,i:θɪ'əʊpɪən/ *n.* эфио́п (*fem.* -ка).

● *adj.* эфио́пский.

ethnic /'eθnɪk/ *adj.* этни́ческий; **~ group** (*within a state*) национа́льность; **~ cleansing** этни́ческая чи́стка.

ethnographer /eθ'nɒgrəfə(r)/ *n.* этно́граф.

ethnographic(al) /,eθnə'græfɪk(ə)l/ *adj.* этнографи́ческий.

ethnography /eθ'nɒgrəfɪ/ *n.* этногра́фия.

ethnological /,eθnə'lɒdʒɪk(ə)l/ *adj.* этнологи́ческий.

ethnologist /eθ'nɒlədʒɪst/ *n.* этно́лог.

ethnology /eθ'nɒlədʒɪ/ *n.* этноло́гия.

ethological /,i:θə'lɒdʒɪk(ə)l/ *adj.* этологи́ческий.

ethologist /i:'θɒlədʒɪst/ *n.* это́лог.

ethology /i:'θɒlədʒɪ/ *n.* этоло́гия.

ethos /'i:θɒs/ *n.* дух, хара́ктер.

ethyl /'i:θaɪl/, /'eθɪl/ *n.* эти́л.

etiolated /'i:tɪəʊ,leɪtɪd/ *adj.* (*fig.*) обескро́вленный, безжи́зненный.

etiology /,i:tɪ'ɒlədʒɪ/ (*US*) = **aetiology**

etiquette /'etɪ,ket/, /-'ket/ *n.* этике́т.

Etruscan /ɪ'trʌskən/ *n.* этру́ск; (*language*) этру́сский язы́к.

● *adj.* этру́сский.

étude /'eɪtju:d/, /-'tju:d/ *n.* (*mus.*) этю́д.

etymological /,etɪmə'lɒdʒɪk(ə)l/ *adj.* этимологи́ческий.

etymologist /,etɪ'mɒlədʒɪst/ *n.* этимо́лог.

etymology /,etɪ'mɒlədʒɪ/ *n.* этимоло́гия.

EU (*abbr. of* ***European Union***) ЕС (Европе́йское сообщество).

eucalyp|tus /ju:kə'lɪptəs/ *n.* (*pl.* **~tuses** *or* **~ti** /-taɪ/) эвкали́пт.

Eucharist /'ju:kərɪst/ *n.* евхари́стия, свято́е прича́стие.

Euclidean /ju:'klɪdɪən/ *adj.* эвкли́дов.

eugenic /ju:'dʒenɪk/ *adj.* евгени́ческий.

eugeni(ci)st /ju:'dʒenɪ(sɪ)st/ *n.* евгени́ст.

eugenics /ju:'dʒenɪks/ *n.* евге́ника.

eulogist /'ju:lədʒɪst/ *n.* панегири́ст.

eulogistic /,ju:lə'dʒɪstɪk/ *adj.* панегири́ческий.

eulogize /'ju:lə,dʒaɪz/ *v.t.* восхвал|я́ть, -и́ть.

eulogy /'ju:lədʒɪ/ *n.* панеги́рик; похвала́.

eunuch /'ju:nək/ *n.* е́внух, кастра́т.

euphemism /'ju:fɪ,mɪz(ə)m/ *n.* эвфеми́зм.

euphemistic /,ju:fɪ'mɪstɪk/ *adj.* эвфемисти́ческий.

euphonious /ju:'fəʊnɪəs/ *adj.* благозву́чный.

euphonium /ju:'fəʊnɪəm/ *n.* тенор́овая ту́ба.

euphony /'ju:fənɪ/ *n.* благозву́чность, благозву́чие.

euphorbia /juːˈfɔːbɪə/ *n.* (*bot.*) молоча́й.

euphoria /juːˈfɔːrɪə/ *adj.* эйфори́я.

euphoric /juːˈfɒrɪk/ *adj.* в припо́днятом настрое́нии.

Euphrates /juːˈfreɪtiːz/ *n.* Евфра́т.

Eurasia /jʊəˈreɪʒɪə/ *n.* Евра́зия.

Eurasian /jʊəˈreɪʒ(ə)n/ *adj.* еврази́йский.

Euratom /jʊəˈrætəm/ *n.* (*abbr. of* ***European Atomic Energy Community***) Евра́том (Европе́йское соо́бщество по а́томной эне́ргии).

eureka /jʊəˈriːkə/ *int.* э́врика.

euro /ˈjʊərəʊ/ *n.* (*pl.* **~s**) е́вро (*indecl.*).

Euro- /ˈjʊərəʊ/ *comb. form* евро. . .; **~-MP** депута́т Европарла́мента; **~sceptic** евроске́птик.

Europe /ˈjʊərəp/ *n.* Евро́па; **go into ~** (*pol.*) войти́ (*pf.*) в Евро́пу.

European /ˌjʊərəˈpɪən/ *n.* европе́|ец (*fem.* -йка); **a staunch ~** (*pol.*) рья́ный сторо́нник еди́ной Евро́пы.

● *adj.* европе́йский.

Europeanism /jʊərəˈpɪənɪz(ə)m/ *n.* иде́я еди́ной Евро́пы.

Europeanist /jʊərəˈpɪənɪst/ *n.* сторо́нник еди́ной Евро́пы.

Eustachian tube /juːˈsteɪʃ(ə)n/ *n.* евста́хиева труба́.

euthanasia /ˌjuːθəˈneɪzɪə/ *n.* умерщвле́ние из милосе́рдия; эйтана́зия.

evacuate /ɪˈvækjʊˌeɪt/ *v.t.* **1** (*person or place*) эвакуи́ровать (*impf., pf.*). **2** (*physiol.*) очи|ща́ть, -и́стить.

evacuation /ɪˌvækjʊˈeɪʃ(ə)n/ *n.* (*removal*) эвакуа́ция; (*physiol.*) очище́ние кише́чника, испражне́ние.

evacuee /ɪˌvækjuːˈiː/ *n.* эвакуи́рованный.

evade /ɪˈveɪd/ *v.t.* избе|га́ть, -жа́ть +*g.*; избе́гнуть (*pf.*) +*g.*; уклон|я́ться, -и́ться от+*g.*; **~ a blow/question** уклон|я́ться, -и́ться от уда́ра/отве́та; **~ paying one's debts** уклон|я́ться, -и́ться от упла́ты долго́в.

evaluate /ɪˈvæljʊˌeɪt/ *v.t.* оце́н|ивать, -и́ть; **he ~d the damage at £50** он оцени́л уще́рб в 50 фу́нтов.

evaluation /ɪˌvæljʊˈeɪʃ(ə)n/ *n.* оце́нка.

evanesce /ˌiːvəˈnes/, /ˌe-/ *v.i.* исч|еза́ть, -е́знуть.

evanescence /ˌiːvəˈnesəns/, /ˌe-/ *n.* исчезнове́ние.

evanescent /ˌiːvəˈnes(ə)nt/, /ˌe-/ *adj.* исчеза́ющий, мимолётный.

evangelical /ˌiːvænˈdʒelɪk(ə)l/ *n.* протеста́нт.

● *adj.* ева́нгельский; (*Protestant*) евангели́ческий.

evangelism /ɪˈvændʒəˌlɪz(ə)m/ *n.* про́поведь Ева́нгелия; (*fig.*) пропове́дничество.

evangelist /ɪˈvændʒəlɪst/ *n.* (*author of gospel*) евангели́ст; (*preacher*) пропове́дник Ева́нгелия.

evangelize /ɪˈvændʒəˌlaɪz/ *v.t.* обра|ща́ть, -ти́ть в христиа́нство.

● *v.i.* пропове́довать (*impf.*) Ева́нгелие.

evaporate /ɪˈvæpəˌreɪt/ *v.t. & i.* испар|я́ть(ся), -и́ть(ся) (*also fig.*); **his anger ~d** его́ гнев рассе́ялся; **~d milk** сгущённое молоко́ (*без сахара*).

evaporation /ɪˌvæpəˈreɪʃ(ə)n/ *n.* испаре́ние.

evasion /ɪˈveɪʒ(ə)n/ *n.* (*avoidance*) уклоне́ние; (*prevarication*) увёртка.

evasive /ɪˈveɪsɪv/ *adj.* (*of answer*) укло́нчивый; (*of person*) увёртливый; **the ship took ~ action** кора́бль маневри́ровал переме́нным ку́рсом.

eve /iːv/ *n.* (*day or evening before*) кану́н (*also fig.*); **on the ~ of** накану́не +*g.*; **Christmas E~** кану́н Рождества́; **New Year's E~** новогодняя ночь, кану́н Но́вого го́да.

even[1] /ˈiːv(ə)n/ *n.* (*poet.*) = **evening**

● *cpds.* **~song** *n.* вече́рняя моли́тва; **~tide** *n.* вече́рняя пора́.

even[2] /ˈiːv(ə)n/ *adj.* (**evener, evenest**) **1** (*level, smooth*) ро́вный; **fill** (*glass, etc.*) **~ with the brim** напо́лнить (*pf.*) до краёв; **~ with the ground** вро́вень с землёй.
2 (*uniform*) равноме́рный; **his work is not very ~** он рабо́тает дово́льно неро́вно; **at an ~ speed** с постоя́нной ско́ростью.
3 (*equal*) ра́вный; **the score is ~** счёт ра́вный; **an ~ chance** ра́вные ша́нсы; **get ~ with s.o.** расквита́ться (*pf.*) с кем-н.; **now we are ~** тепе́рь мы кви́ты; **break ~** ост|ава́ться, -а́ться при свои́х.
4 (*divisible by 2*) чётный; **on ~ dates** по чётным чи́слам.
5 (*calm*) ро́вный, споко́йный; **~ temper** ро́вный хара́ктер.
6 (*exact*) ро́вный; **an ~ dozen** ро́вно дю́жина.

● *adv.* да́же; и; хотя́ бы; **he disputes ~ the facts** он оспа́ривает да́же фа́кты; **he won't ~ notice** он и не заме́тит; **~ if** е́сли да́же; **~ so** всё равно́; да́же в тако́м слу́чае; **not ~** да́же не; **~ though I don't like him** хотя́ он мне не нра́вится; **does he ~ suspect the danger?** подозрева́ет ли он вообще́ об опа́сности?; **I have only one suit, and ~ it is shabby** у меня́ всего́ оди́н костю́м, да и тот потрёпанный; **this applies ~ more to French** э́то ещё в бо́льшей сте́пени отно́сится к францу́зскому языку́; **~ as I spoke, I realised** . . . уже́ когда́ я говори́л э́то, я по́нял. . .; **~ as a child he was** . . . ещё/уже́ ребёнком он был. . . .

● *v.t.* (*make even or equal*) выра́внивать, вы́ровнять; **that ~s (up) the score** э́то ура́внивает счёт.

● *v.i.* выра́вниваться, вы́ровняться.

● *cpds.* **~-handed** *adj.* беспристра́стный; **~-handedness** *n.* беспристра́стность; **~-tempered** *adj.* уравнове́шенный.

evening /ˈiːvnɪŋ/ *n.* ве́чер; **in the ~** ве́чером; **(on) that ~** в тот ве́чер; **one ~** одна́жды ве́чером; **this ~** сего́дня ве́чером; **tomorrow ~** за́втра ве́чером; **last, yesterday ~** вчера́ ве́чером; **on the ~ of the 8th** восьмо́го ве́чером; **musical ~** музыка́льный ве́чер; (*attr.*) вече́рний; **~ service** (*relig.*) вече́рня; вече́рняя моли́тва; **~ dress, clothes** (*men's or women's*) вече́рний туале́т; **~ dress, gown** (*woman's*) вече́рнее пла́тье.

evenly /ˈiːvənlɪ/ *adv.* ро́вно, равноме́рно; **spread the butter ~** нама́з|ывать, -ать ма́сло ро́вным сло́ем; **the odds are ~ balanced** ша́нсы — ра́вные.

evenness /ˈiːvənnɪs/ *n.* (*physical smoothness*) гла́дкость; (*uniformity*) равноме́рность; (*of temper, tone etc.*) ро́вность, уравнове́шенность; (*of odds, contest etc.*) ра́венство.

event /ɪˈvent/ *n.* **1** (*occurrence*) собы́тие; **current ~s** теку́щие собы́тия; **in the natural course of ~s** при норма́льном разви́тии собы́тий; **it was quite an ~** э́то бы́ло це́лое собы́тие. **2** (*outcome*) исхо́д; **in the ~ he was unsuccessful** в коне́чном счёте он потерпе́л неуда́чу; **wise after the ~** за́дним умо́м кре́пок.
3 (*hypothesis*) слу́чай; **in the ~ of his coming** в слу́чае его́ прихо́да; **in any ~** в любо́м слу́чае; **in either ~** так и́ли ина́че; **at all ~s** во вся́ком слу́чае.
4 (*sports item*) забе́г, зае́зд; вид спо́рта.

eventful /ɪˈventfʊl/ *adj.* насы́щенный собы́тиями.

eventing /ɪˈventɪŋ/ *n.* конноспорти́вное состяза́ние.

eventual /ɪˈventjʊəl/ *adj.* (*final*) коне́чный, оконча́тельный; **~ success** успе́шный коне́ц.

eventuality /ɪˌventjʊˈælɪtɪ/ *n.* возмо́жность, слу́чай; **prepared for any ~** гото́вый ко вся́ким случа́йностям.

eventually /ɪˈventjʊəlɪ/ *adv.* со вре́менем; в конце́ концо́в; в коне́чном счёте; ра́но и́ли по́здно.

eventuate /ɪˈventjʊˌeɪt/ *v.i.* (*happen*) случ|а́ться, -и́ться; возн|ика́ть, -и́кнуть; **~ in** конча́ться, ко́нчиться (*чем*).

ever /ˈevə(r)/ *adv.* **1** (*always*) всегда́; **for ~ (and a day** *or* **and ~)** навсегда́, наве́чно; **~ after, since** с тех (са́мых) пор; **~ since** (*conj.*) с тех пор, как. . .; **yours ~, ~ yours, as ~** (*in letters*) Ваш/Твой. . .; пре́данный Вам; **with ~-increasing pleasure** со всё возраста́ющим удово́льствием.
2 (*at any time*): **do you ~ see him?** вы его́ когда́-нибудь ви́дите?; **nothing ~ happens** ничего́ не происхо́дит; **scarcely, hardly ~** почти́ никогда́; о́чень ре́дко; **not then or ~** ни тогда́, ни когда́-либо ещё; **as good as ~** не ху́же, чем ра́ньше; **better than ~** лу́чше, чем когда́-либо; **this is the best ~** тако́го ещё не быва́ло.
3 (*intensive*): **as soon as ~ I can** при пе́рвой возмо́жности; **why ~ did you do it?** заче́м же вы э́то сде́лали?; **how ~ did you manage it?** как то́лько вам э́то удало́сь?; **~ so rich** (*Br.*) ужа́сно бога́тый; страсть как бога́тый (*coll.*); **thank you ~ so much** (*Br.*) я вам чрезвыча́йно благода́рен.

● *cpds.* **~green** *n.* (*bot.*) вечнозелёное расте́ние; *adj.* вечнозелёный;

~lasting *adj.* ве́чный; **~lasting flower** иммортéль (*m.*); бессмéртник; **~-loving** *adj.* всегдá лю́бящий; **~more** *adv.*: **for ~more** навсегдá, навéчно; **~-present** *adj.* постоя́нный.

every /'evrɪ/ *adj.* кáждый, вся́кий; **not ~ animal can swim** не все живóтные плáвают; **you have ~ reason to be satisfied** у вас есть все основáния быть довóльным; **I have ~ confidence in him** я в нём совершéнно увéрен; **I wish you ~ success** желáю вам вся́ческого/пóлного успéха; **~ ten minutes** кáждые дéсять минýт; **~ other car** кáждый вторóй автомоби́ль; **(on) ~ other day** чéрез день; **~ one of them** все до однóго; **~ now and again; ~ so often; ~ once in a while** врéмя от врéмени; по временáм; иногдá; **this is ~ bit as good** э́то ничýть не уступáет; **~ bit as much** тóчно стóлько же; **~ time (that) he comes** вся́кий раз, когдá он прихóдит; **in ~ way** во всех отношéниях.

● *cpds.* **~body, ~one** *prons.* кáждый; вся́кий; все (*pl.*); **~body knows that!** э́то кáждый знáет; **~body else** все остальны́е; **~body knows ~body else** все со всéми знакóмы; **~day** *adj.* повседнéвный; обыкновéнный, бытовóй; **E~man** *n.* (*the common man*) рядовóй/обыкновéнный человéк; **~one** *pron.* = **~body; ~thing** *pron.* всё; **speed is ~thing to him** для негó скóрость — э́то всё; **money is not ~thing** дéньги — э́то ещё не всё; **~thing is not clear** не всё я́сно **~where** *adv.* вездé, повсю́ду; **~where else** во всех други́х местáх.

evict /ɪ'vɪkt/ *v.t.* выселя́ть, вы́селить.

eviction /ɪ'vɪkʃ(ə)n/ *n.* выселéние.

evidence /'evɪd(ə)ns/ *n.* **1** (*clarity, visibility*) очеви́дность; **he was much in ~ at the party** он óчень выделя́лся на вечери́нке; **flowers were much in ~** цветы́ бы́ли повсю́ду. **2** (*indication, confirmation*) доказáтельство, свидéтельство; **there was ample ~ of foul play** всё свидéтельствовало о совершённом преступлéнии; **there is no ~ for this belief** нет основáний для э́того убеждéния. **3** (*leg.*) свидéтельское показáние; ули́ка; дáнные (*nt. pl.*); **the ~ of the charred letter** ули́ка в ви́де полусожжённого письмá; **give ~** да|вáть, -ть свидéтельское показáние; **circumstantial ~** кóсвенные ули́ки (*f. pl.*); **cumulative ~** совокýпность ули́к.

● *v.t.* служи́ть, по- доказáтельством, ули́кой (*чего*).

evident /'evɪd(ə)nt/ *adj.* очеви́дный, я́сный; **it was ~ from his behaviour** (*Br.*), **behavior** (*US*) **that . . .** бы́ло ви́дно по егó поведéнию, что. . .; **he is ~ly a fool** он я́вно дурáк; **~ly not** (*as reply*) разумéется, нет; окáзывается, что нет.

evidential /,evɪ'denʃ(ə)l/ *adj.* доказáтельный.

evil /'i:v(ə)l/, /-ɪl/ *n.* зло; **social ~s** я́звы óбщества.

● *adj.* злой, дурнóй; **she has an ~ tongue** у неё злой язы́к.

● *cpds.* **~-doer** *n.* злодéй; **~-doing** *n.* злодея́ние; **~-minded** *adj.* злонамéренный.

evilness /'i:vəlnɪs/, /-ɪlnɪs/ *n.* злóбность.

evince /ɪ'vɪns/ *v.t.* прояв|ля́ть, -и́ть.

eviscerate /ɪ'vɪsə,reɪt/ *v.t.* потроши́ть, вы́-.

evisceration /ɪ,vɪsə'reɪʃ(ə)n/ *n.* потрошéние.

evocation /,evə'keɪʃ(ə)n/ *n.* вызывáние; воскрешéние в пáмяти.

evocative /ɪ'vɒkətɪv/ *adj.* навевáющий воспоминáния.

evoke /ɪ'vəʊk/ *v.t.* вызывáть, вы́звать; пробу|ждáть, -ди́ть; нап|оминáть, -óмнить.

evolution /,i:və'lu:ʃ(ə)n/, /-'lju:ʃ(ə)n/ *n.* эволю́ция; **theory of ~** эволюциóнная теóрия.

evolutionary /,i:və'lu:ʃənərɪ/, /-'lju:ʃənərɪ/ *adj.* эволюциóнный.

evolutionism /,i:və'lu:ʃənɪz(ə)m/, /-'lju:ʃənɪz(ə)m/ *n.* эволюциони́зм; эволюциóнная теóрия.

evolutionist /,i:və'lu:ʃənɪst/, /-'lju:ʃənɪst/ *n.* эволюциони́ст.

evolve /ɪ'vɒlv/ *v.t.* разв|ивáть, -и́ть; **he ~d a plan** он разрабóтал план.

● *v.i.* разв|ивáться, -и́ться; эволюциони́ровать (*impf., pf.*).

ewe /ju:/ *n.* овцá.

ewer /'ju:ə(r)/ *n.* кувши́н.

ex /eks/ *prep.* (*comm.*): **~ warehouse** (*from warehouse*) со склáда; **shares ~ dividend** áкции без дивидéнда.

ex- /eks/ *pref.* (*former*) экс-. . ., бы́вший; **~ husband/president** бы́вший муж/ президéнт.

exacerbate /ek'sæsə,beɪt/, /ɪg-/ *v.t.* (*pain etc.*) обостр|я́ть, -и́ть.

exacerbation /ek,sæsə'beɪʃ(ə)n/, /ɪg-/ *n.* обострéние.

exact /ɪg'zækt/ *adj.* тóчный.

● *v.t.* (*e.g. payment*) взыск|ивáть, -áть; (*e.g. obedience*) трéбовать, по- + *g.*

exacting /ɪg'zæktɪŋ/ *adj.* взыскáтельный, трéбовательный.

exaction /ɪg'zækʃ(ə)n/ *n.* (*demand, extortion*) трéбование, вымогáтельство.

exact|itude /ɪg'zæktɪ,tju:d/ = **-ness**

exactly /ɪg'zæktlɪ/ *adv.* тóчно; (*of numbers, quantities*) рóвно; **he measured it ~** он э́то тóчно изме́рил; **~ a kilogram** рóвно килогрáмм; **(in) ~ (the same way) as** так тóчно как; **~ the same** то же сáмое; **~!** (*as reply*) и́менно!; **~ how much do you need?** скóлько и́менно вам нýжно?; **not ~ ugly** не такóй уж урóдливый; **he did not ~ complain, but he was discontented** он не то что(бы) жáловался, но был недовóлен.

exactness /ɪg'zæktnɪs/ *n.* тóчность.

exaggerate /ɪg'zædʒə,reɪt/ *v.t.* преувели́чи|вать, -ть.

exaggeration /ɪg,zædʒə'reɪʃ(ə)n/ *n.* преувеличéние.

exalt /ɪg'zɔ:lt/ *v.t.* (*make higher in rank etc.*) пов|ышáть, -ы́сить; (*praise*) превозн|оси́ть, -ести́.

exaltation /,egzɔ:l'teɪʃ(ə)n/ *n.* **1** (*raising in rank etc.*) повышéние. **2** (*worship*) возвели́чение. **3** (*mental or emotional transport*) экзальтáция.

exam /ɪg'zæm/ (*coll.*) = **examination** 3

examination /ɪg,zæmɪ'neɪʃ(ə)n/ *n.* **1** (*inspection*) осмóтр; **customs ~** тамóженный досмóтр; **~ of passports** провéрка паспортóв. **2** (*interrogation*) допрóс; **the prisoner is under ~** заключённого допрáшивают. **3** (*acad. etc.; also* **exam**) экзáмен; **~ paper** (*written by examinee*) экзаменациóнная рабóта; (*questions set*) вопрóсы (*m. pl.*) (для экзаменациóнной рабóты); **entrance ~** вступи́тельный экзáмен; **go in for** (*or* **take) an ~** сда|вáть, -ть экзáмен; **sit an ~** экзаменовáться, про-; **pass an ~** сдать/вы́держать (*both pf.*) экзáмен; **fail (in) an ~** провáл|иваться, -и́ться на экзáмене.

examine /ɪg'zæmɪn/ *v.t.* **1** (*inspect*) осм|áтривать, -отрéть; **~ passports** пров|еря́ть, -éрить паспортá; **~ records** изуч|áть, -и́ть докумéнты; **~ a signature** пров|еря́ть, -éрить пóдлинность пóдписи; **~ a patient** осм|áтривать, -отрéть больнóго; **~ one's conscience** спр|áшивать, -оси́ть свою́ сóвесть; **~ claims** рассм|áтривать, -отрéть жáлобы; **he had his eyes ~d (by s.o.)** он провéрил глазá (у когó-н.). **2** (*interrogate*) допр|áшивать, -оси́ть. **3** (*acad.*) экзаменовáть, про-.

examinee /ɪg,zæmɪ'ni:/ *n.* экзаменýющийся.

examiner /ɪg'zæmɪnə(r)/ *n.* (*acad.*) экзаменáтор; (*of a prisoner, witness etc.*) слéдователь (*m.*).

example /ɪg'zɑ:mp(ə)l/ *n.* **1** (*illustration, model*) примéр; **for (***or* **by way of) ~** напримéр; **follow s.o.'s ~** брать (*impf.*) с когó-н. примéр; **set an ~ to s.o.** подавáть (*impf.*) комý-н. примéр. **2** (*warning*) урóк; **let this be an ~ to you** пусть э́то послýжит вам урóком; **make an ~ of s.o.** накáз|ывать, -áть когó-н. в назидáние други́м. **3** (*specimen*) образéц.

exasperate /ɪg'zɑ:spə,reɪt/ *v.t.* изв|оди́ть, -ести́; раздраж|áть, -и́ть.

exasperating /ɪg'zɑ:spə,reɪtɪŋ/ *adj.* раздражáющий.

exasperation /ɪg,zɑ:spə'reɪʃ(ə)n/ *n.* раздражéние.

excavate /'ekskə,veɪt/ *v.t.* копáть (*impf.*); выкáпывать, вы́копать; раск|áпывать, -опáть; **~ a trench** копáть (*impf.*) окóп; **~ a buried city** раскопáть (*pf.*) погребённый гóрод.

excavation /,ekskə'veɪʃ(ə)n/ *n.* (*site*) раскóпки (*f. pl.*); (*action*) выкáпывание.

excavator /'ekskə,veɪtə(r)/ *n.* (*person*) землекóп; (*machine*) экскавáтор.

exceed /ɪk'si:d/ *v.t.* прев|ышáть, -ы́сить; **~ s.o. in height** быть вы́ше кого́-н. ро́стом; ~ **expectations** превзойти́ (*pf.*) ожида́ния.

exceedingly /ɪk'si:dɪŋlɪ/ *adv.* чрезвыча́йно.

excel /ɪk'sel/ *v.t.* (**excelled, excelling**) прев|осходи́ть, -зойти́.

● *v.i.* (**excelled, excelling**) выдава́ться (*impf.*); выделя́ться (*impf.*); **he ~s as an orator** он выдаю́щийся ора́тор; **he ~s in sport** он превосхо́дный спортсме́н.

excellence /'eksələns/ *n.* превосхо́дство; превосхо́дное ка́чество; ~ **in French** соверше́нство во францу́зском языке́.

excellency /'eksələnsɪ/ *n.*: **His E~** его́ превосходи́тельство.

excellent /'eksələnt/ *adj.* отли́чный.

except /ɪk'sept/ *v.t.* исключ|а́ть, -и́ть; **present company ~ed** о прису́тствующих не говоря́т.

● *prep.* (*also* **~ing**) исключа́я + *a.*; кро́ме + *g.*; за исключе́нием + *g.*; ра́зве лишь/то́лько; **the essay is good ~ for the spelling mistakes** сочине́ние хоро́шее, е́сли не счита́ть орфографи́ческих оши́бок; **I knew nothing ~ that he was away** я не знал ничего́, кроме того́, что его́ не́ было; **I would go ~ that it is too far** я бы пошёл, да то́лько э́то сли́шком далеко́.

exception /ɪk'sepʃ(ə)n/ *n.* **1** исключе́ние; **with the ~ of** за исключе́нием + *g.*; **an ~ to a rule** исключе́ние из пра́вила; **the ~ proves the rule** исключе́ние подтвержда́ет пра́вило. **2**: **take ~ to** об|ижа́ться, -и́деться на + *a.*

exceptionable /ɪk'sepʃənəb(ə)l/ *adj.* вызыва́ющий возраже́ния; небезупре́чный.

exceptional /ɪk'sepʃən(ə)l/ *adj.* исключи́тельный.

excerpt /'eksɜ:pt/ *n.* вы́держка, цита́та.

● *v.t.*: ~ **a passage from a book** процити́ровать (*pf.*) отры́вок из кни́ги; прив|оди́ть, -ести́ вы́держку из кни́ги.

excess /ɪk'ses/, /'ekses/ *n.* **1** (*amount that is more than necessary or exceeds another amount*) изли́шек, избы́ток; ~ **of imports over exports** превыше́ние и́мпорта над э́кспортом; **in ~ of £20** свы́ше двадцати́ фу́нтов; **expenditure in ~ of income** расхо́ды, превыша́ющие дохо́д. **2** (*in insurance claim*) превыше́ние, изли́шек. **3** (*lack of moderation*) эксце́сс, кра́йность; **the ~es of the military** бесчи́нства вое́нщины; **drink to ~** злоупотребля́ть (*impf.*) алкого́лем; ~ **fare** (*Br.*) допла́та; ~ **postage** (*Br.*) почто́вая допла́та; ~ **luggage** изли́шек багажа́; **we had to pay ~** мы должны́ бы́ли доплати́ть.

excessive /ɪk'sesɪv/ *adj.* изли́шний; (*extreme*) чрезме́рный.

excessiveness /ɪk'sesɪvnɪs/ *n.* изли́шество, чрезме́рность.

exchange /ɪks'tʃeɪndʒ/ *n.* **1** (*act of exchanging*) обме́н + *g.*/*i.*; **in ~ for** в обме́н на + *a.*; ~ **of prisoners** обме́н пле́нными; ~ **of shots** перестре́лка; ~ **professor** профе́ссор, преподаю́щий в друго́й стране́ в поря́дке обме́на; ~ **student** (иностра́нный) студе́нт (*fem.* -ка), прие́хавший по обме́ну; стажёр; ~ **is no robbery** ме́на — не грабёж. **2** (*fin.*) разме́н, обме́н; ~ **rate/control** валю́тный курс/контро́ль; **lose on the ~** потеря́ть (*pf.*) на обме́не де́нег. **3** (*place of business*) би́ржа; **stock ~** фо́ндовая би́ржа. **4** (*teleph.*) (центра́льная) телефо́нная ста́нция; (*in building*) коммута́тор.

● *v.t.* меня́ть, об-/по- (*что на что*); (*reciprocally*) меня́ться, об-/по- + *i.*; обме́ниваться (*impf.*) + *i.*; **we ~d places** мы поменя́лись места́ми; **we ~d opinions** мы обменя́лись мне́ниями; **he ~d one job for another** он перешёл с одно́й рабо́ты на другу́ю.

● *v.i.*: **he ~d with me on the roster** мы с ним поменя́лись дежу́рствами; **a mark ~s for one Swiss franc** ма́рка обме́нивается на оди́н швейца́рский франк.

exchangeable /ɪks'tʃeɪndʒəb(ə)l/ *adj.* подлежа́щий обме́ну, го́дный для обме́на; **this coupon is ~ for lunch** э́тот тало́н даёт пра́во на обе́д.

exchequer /ɪks'tʃekə(r)/ *n.* казначе́йство, казна́; **Chancellor of the E~** ка́нцлер казначе́йства.

excise[1] /'eksaɪz/ *n.* акци́з; ~ **officer** акци́зный чино́вник.

excise[2] /'eksaɪz/ *v.t.* выреза́ть, вы́резать; отр|еза́ть, -е́зать.

excision /ɪk'sɪʒ(ə)n/ *n.* выреза́ние, отреза́ние.

excitability /ɪk,saɪtə'bɪlɪtɪ/ *n.* повы́шенная возбуди́мость.

excitable /ɪk'saɪtəb(ə)l/ *adj.* легко́ возбуди́мый.

excite /ɪk'saɪt/ *v.t.* **1** (*cause, arouse, stimulate*) возбу|жда́ть, -ди́ть; вызыва́ть, вы́звать; ~ **a riot** подн|има́ть, -я́ть бунт. **2** (*thrill, agitate*) волнова́ть, вз-; **don't ~ yourself** (*or* **get ~d**) не волну́йтесь.

excitement /ɪk'saɪtmənt/ *n.* возбужде́ние, волне́ние; **what is all the ~ about?** что за шум?; в чём де́ло?

exciting /ɪk'saɪtɪŋ/ *adj.* захва́тывающий, увлека́тельный; **how ~!** как интере́сно!

exclaim /ɪk'skleɪm/ *v.t.* & *i.* воскл|ица́ть, -и́кнуть; ~ **at** удив|ля́ться, -и́ться + *d.*

exclamation /,ekslə'meɪʃ(ə)n/ *n.* восклица́ние; ~ **mark** восклица́тельный знак.

exclamatory /ɪk'sklæmətərɪ/ *adj.* восклица́тельный.

exclude /ɪk'sklu:d/ *v.t.* исключ|а́ть, -и́ть; ~ **from membership** лиш|а́ть, -и́ть чле́нства; ~ **immigrants** не впус|ка́ть, -ти́ть иммигра́нтов.

exclusion /ɪk'sklu:ʒ(ə)n/ *n.* исключе́ние.

exclusive /ɪk'sklu:sɪv/ *adj.* **1** (*sole*) исключи́тельный, еди́нственный; **he is the ~ agent for this product** он еди́нственный аге́нт по сбы́ту э́того това́ра. **2**: ~ **of** (*not counting*) без + *g.*, не счита́я + *g.* **3** (*reserved, restricted*) специа́льный, исключи́тельный; (*high-class*) эксклюзи́вный; **an ~ interview** интервью́, да́нное то́лько одно́й газе́те; **an ~ club** клуб для и́збранных; **we have ~ rights to his invention** мы владе́ем исключи́тельными права́ми на его́ изобрете́ние.

exclusiveness /ɪk'sklu:sɪvnɪs/ *n.* исключи́тельность.

excommunicate /,ekskə'mju:nɪ,keɪt/ *v.t.* отлуч|а́ть, -и́ть от це́ркви.

excommunication /ekskə,mju:nɪ'keɪʃ(ə)n/ *n.* отлуче́ние от це́ркви.

excoriate /eks'kɔ:rɪ,eɪt/ *v.t.* сдира́ть, содра́ть ко́жу с + *g.*; (*fig.*) разн|оси́ть, -ести́.

excoriation /eks,kɔ:rɪ'eɪʃ(ə)n/ *n.* сдира́ние ко́жи; (*fig.*) разно́с.

excrement /'ekskrɪmənt/ *n.* экскреме́нты (*m. pl.*).

excrescence /ɪk'skres(ə)ns/ *n.* наро́ст.

excreta /ek'skri:tə/, /ɪk-/ *n.* (*pl.*, *physiol.*) экскреме́нты (*m. pl.*), выделе́ния (*nt. pl.*).

excrete /ɪk'skri:t/ *v.t.* выделя́ть, вы́делить.

excretion /ɪk'skri:ʃ(ə)n/ *n.* экскре́ция, выделе́ние.

excretory /ɪk'skri:tərɪ/ *adj.* экскрето́рный, выдели́тельный.

excruciating /ɪk'skru:ʃɪ,eɪtɪŋ/ *adj.* мучи́тельный.

exculpate /'ekskʌl,peɪt/ *v.t.* опра́вд|ывать, -а́ть.

exculpation /,ekskʌl'peɪʃ(ə)n/ *n.* оправда́ние.

excursion /ɪk'skɜ:ʃ(ə)n/ *n.* (*trip*) экску́рсия; **make (*or* go on) an ~** идти́/пое́хать (*det.*) на экску́рсию; (*digression, interlude*) э́кскурс.

excursus /ek'skɜ:səs/, /ɪk-/ *n.* (*pl.* **~es** *or* **~**) э́кскурс.

excusable /ɪk'skju:zəb(ə)l/ *adj.* прости́тельный, извини́тельный.

excuse[1] /ɪk'skju:s/, /ek-/ *n.* извине́ние, оправда́ние, отгово́рка; **ignorance is no ~** незна́ние — не оправда́ние; **a lame, poor ~** сла́бая отгово́рка; **please make my ~s to the hostess** пожа́луйста, переда́йте мои́ извине́ния хозя́йке.

excuse[2] /ɪk'skju:z/ *v.t.* **1** (*justify, palliate*) опра́вд|ывать, -а́ть; ~ **o.s.** прин|оси́ть, -ести́ извине́ния. **2** (*forgive*) извин|я́ть, -и́ть; про|ща́ть, -сти́ть; **please ~ my coming late (*or* me for coming late)** извини́те, что я пришёл по́здно; ~ **me, what time is it?** прости́те, кото́рый час?; ~ **me, but you are wrong** прости́те, но вы непра́вы. **3** (*dispense, release*): **I ~d him from attending** я позво́лил ему́ не прису́тствовать; **may I be ~d from coming?** могу́ я не приходи́ть?

ex-directory /,eksdaɪ'rektərɪ/ *adj.* (*Br.*) не внесённый в телефо́нную кни́гу;

he's ~ его́ но́мера в телефо́нной кни́ге нет.

execrable /ˈeksɪkrəb(ə)l/ *adj.* отврати́тельный.

execrate /ˈeksɪˌkreɪt/ *v.t.* испы́т|ывать, -а́ть отвраще́ние к + *d.*

execration /ˌeksɪˈkreɪʃ(ə)n/ *n.* омерзе́ние; **hold s.o. up to ~** выставля́ть, вы́ставить кого́-н. на всео́бщее порица́ние.

executable /ˈeksɪˌkjuːtəb(ə)l/ *adj.* (*feasible*) исполни́мый, выполни́мый.

executant /ɪɡˈzekjʊt(ə)nt/ *n.* исполни́тель (*m.*).

execute /ˈeksɪˌkjuːt/ *v.t.* **1** (*carry out*) выполня́ть, вы́полнить; исп|олня́ть, -о́лнить; **~ a will** исп|олня́ть, -о́лнить завеща́ние. **2** (*put to death*) казни́ть (*impf., pf.*).

execution /ˌeksɪˈkjuːʃ(ə)n/ *n.* **1** (*carrying out*) исполне́ние, выполне́ние; **carry, put into ~** прив|оди́ть, -ести́ в исполне́ние. **2** (*capital punishment*) казнь; **there were five ~s last year** в про́шлом году́ казни́ли пятеры́х.

executioner /ˌeksɪˈkjuːʃənə(r)/ *n.* пала́ч.

executive /ɪɡˈzekjʊtɪv/ *n.* руководи́тель (*m.*); **chief ~** гла́вный исполни́тельный дире́ктор; (*US president*) президе́нт (США).
● *adj.* **1** (*executing laws etc.*) исполни́тельный. **2** (*managing*) руководя́щий; **~ ability** администрати́вные спосо́бности; **~ director** исполни́тельный дире́ктор.

executor[1] /ɪɡˈzekjʊtə(r)/ *n.* (*one who carries out*) исполни́тель (*m.*).

executor[2] /ɪɡˈzekjʊtə(r)/ *n.* (*of a will*) душеприка́зчик.

exegesis /ˌeksɪˈdʒiːsɪs/ *n.* (*pl.* **exegeses** /-siːz/) толкова́ние.

exemplar /ɪɡˈzemplə(r)/, /-plɑː(r)/ *n.* образе́ц, экземпля́р.

exemplary /ɪɡˈzemplərɪ/ *adj.* приме́рный, образцо́вый.

exemplification /ɪɡˌzemplɪfɪˈkeɪʃ(ə)n/ *n.* приведе́ние приме́ров; приме́р.

exemplify /ɪɡˈzemplɪˌfaɪ/ *v.t.* (*illustrate by example*) прив|оди́ть, -ести́ приме́р + *g.*; (*be an example of*) служи́ть, по- приме́ром + *g.*

exempt /ɪɡˈzempt/ *adj.* освобождённый, свобо́дный (*от чего*).
● *v.t.* освобо|жда́ть, -ди́ть.

exemption /ɪɡˈzempʃ(ə)n/ *n.* освобожде́ние (*от чего*).

exercise /ˈeksəˌsaɪz/ *n.* **1** (*use, exertion*) проявле́ние (*чего*); выка́зывание (*чего*); **the ~ of patience is essential** ва́жно прояви́ть терпе́ние. **2** (*physical activity*) заря́дка, упражне́ние, моцио́н; **you should take more ~** вам ну́жно де́лать бо́льше физи́ческих упражне́ний. **3** (*mental or physical training*) упражне́ние, трениро́вка; **~ bicycle** велотренажёр; **slimming ~s** упражне́ния для сниже́ния ве́са. **4** (*trial operation*) уче́ние; **military ~s** строево́е уче́ние, вое́нные уче́ния; (*fig.*): **the object of the ~** цель э́того предприя́тия.
● *v.t.* **1** (*exert, use*) выка́зывать, вы́казать; прояв|ля́ть, -и́ть; **~ authority** примен|я́ть, -и́ть власть; **~ one's rights** осуществ|ля́ть, -и́ть свои́ права́. **2** (*physically*) упражня́ть (*impf.*); **~ a dog** прогу́ливать (*impf.*) соба́ку. **3** (*worry, perplex*) беспоко́ить (*impf.*), трево́жить (*impf.*); **the problem ~d our minds** пробле́ма заста́вила нас заду́маться.
● *v.i.* упражня́ться (*impf.*).
● *cpd.* **~-book** *n.* (*Br.*) (учени́ческая) тетра́дь.

exert /ɪɡˈzɜːt/ *v.t.* осуществ|ля́ть, -и́ть; ока́з|ывать, -а́ть; **~ influence** ока́з|ывать, -а́ть влия́ние; **~ o.s.** постара́ться (*pf.*).

exertion /ɪɡˈzɜːʃ(ə)n/ *n.* напряже́ние, уси́лие; **the ~s of travelling** (*Br.*), **traveling** (*US*) тя́готы (*f. pl.*) пути́.

exeunt /ˈeksɪˌʌnt / *v.i.* (*stage direction*) ухо́дят.

ex gratia /eks ˈɡreɪʃə/ *adj.* доброво́льный; **an ~ payment** доброво́льная упла́та.

exhalation /ˌekshəˈleɪʃ(ə)n/ *n.* (*mist, vapour*) пар; испаре́ние; (*act of exhaling*) выдыха́ние.

exhale /eksˈheɪl/, /ɪɡz-/ *v.t.* (*give off*) испус|ка́ть, -ти́ть.
● *v.i.* (*breathe out*) выдыха́ть, вы́дохнуть.

exhaust /ɪɡˈzɔːst/ *n.* (*apparatus*) вы́хлоп, вы́пуск; (*expelled gas*) отрабо́танный газ; **~ pipe** выхлопна́я труба́; **I could smell the ~** я почу́вствовал за́пах выхлопны́х га́зов.
● *v.t.* **1** (*consume, tire out*) истощ|а́ть, -и́ть; изнур|я́ть, -и́ть; **my patience is ~ed** моё терпе́ние исся́кло; **the climb ~ed us** восхожде́ние изнури́ло нас; **be ~ed** изнем|oга́ть, -о́чь; **I feel ~ed** я соверше́нно без сил. **2** (*empty*) исче́рп|ывать, -ать; **~ land** истощ|а́ть, -и́ть зе́млю. **3** (*explore thoroughly*) исче́рп|ывать, -ать.

exhausting /ɪɡˈzɔːstɪŋ/ *adj.* изнури́тельный, утоми́тельный.

exhaustion /ɪɡˈzɔːstʃ(ə)n/ *n.* изнуре́ние, истоще́ние; (*fatigue*) переутомле́ние, изнеможе́ние.

exhaustive /ɪɡˈzɔːstɪv/ *adj.* исче́рпывающий, всесторо́нний.

exhaustiveness /ɪɡˈzɔːstɪvnɪs/ *n.* всесторо́нность, полнота́.

exhibit /ɪɡˈzɪbɪt/ *n.* (*in museum etc.*) экспона́т; (*leg.*) веще́ственное доказа́тельство.
● *v.t.* (**exhibited, exhibiting**) **1** (*e.g. painting*) экспони́ровать (*impf., pf.*); выставля́ть, вы́ставить. **2** (*fig., display*) прояв|ля́ть, -и́ть.

exhibition /ˌeksɪˈbɪʃ(ə)n/ *n.* (*public show*) вы́ставка; (*showing*) пока́з; **be on ~** быть вы́ставленным; **he made an ~ of himself** он сде́лал себя́ посме́шищем; (*Br., scholarship*) стипе́ндия.

exhibitioner /ˌeksɪˈbɪʃənə(r)/ *n.* (*Br.*) стипендиа́т.

exhibitionism /ˌeksɪˈbɪʃəˌnɪz(ə)m/ *n.* хвастовство́; эксгибициони́зм.

exhibitionist /eksɪˈbɪʃənɪst/ *n.* хвасту́н (*coll.*); эксгибициони́ст.

exhibitor /ɪɡˈzɪbɪtə(r)/ *n.* экспоне́нт.

exhilarat|e /ɪɡˈzɪləˌreɪt/ *v.t.* весели́ть, раз-; ра́довать, об-; **he felt ~ed** он был в припо́днятом настрое́нии; **~ing news** ра́достное изве́стие.

exhilaration /ɪɡˌzɪləˈreɪʃ(ə)n/ *n.* весе́лье; прия́тное возбужде́ние.

exhort /ɪɡˈzɔːt/ *v.t.* приз|ыва́ть, -ва́ть (*кого к чему*); увещева́ть (*impf.*).

exhortation /ˌeɡzɔːˈteɪʃ(ə)n/, /ˌeks-/ *n.* призы́в, увещева́ние.

exhumation /eksˌhjuːˈmeɪʃ(ə)n/, /ɪɡˌzjuːˈmeɪʃ(ə)n/ *n.* эксгума́ция, извлече́ние тру́па из земли́; (*fig.*) раска́пывание, выка́пывание.

exhume /eksˈhjuːm/, /ɪɡˈzjuːm/ *v.t.* эксгуми́ровать (*impf., pf.*); (*fig.*) раск|а́пывать, -опа́ть; выка́пывать, вы́копать.

exigency /ˈeksɪdʒənsɪ/, /ɪɡˈzɪdʒ-/ *n.* неотло́жность, кра́йность; кра́йняя необходи́мость; **the ~ies of the time** веле́ние вре́мени.

exigent /ˈeksɪdʒ(ə)nt/ *adj.* (*urgent*) неотло́жный, сро́чный; (*demanding*) тре́бовательный.

exiguity /eɡˌzɪˈɡjuːɪtɪ/, /ɪɡ-/ *n.* ску́дость, незначи́тельность.

exiguous /eɡˈzɪɡjʊəs/, /ɪɡ-/ *adj.* ску́дный, незначи́тельный, ма́лый.

exile /ˈeksaɪl/, /ˈeɡz-/ *n.* **1** (*banishment*) изгна́ние; ссы́лка; **send into ~** ссыла́ть, сосла́ть. **2** (*person*) изгна́нник; ссы́льный.
● *v.t.* изг|оня́ть, -на́ть; ссыла́ть, сосла́ть.

exist /ɪɡˈzɪst/ *v.i.* **1** (*be, live*) существова́ть (*impf.*), жить (*impf.*); **he ~s on £50 per week** он существу́ет на 50 фу́нтов в неде́лю. **2** (*be found*) име́ться, встреча́ться, находи́ться (*all impf.*).

existence /ɪɡˈzɪst(ə)ns/ *n.* существова́ние; (*presence*) нали́чие; (*life*) жизнь; **in ~** существу́ющий, нали́чный, име́ющийся; **the largest ship in ~** са́мый большо́й кора́бль из всех существу́ющих.

existent /ɪɡˈzɪst(ə)nt/ *adj.* существу́ющий.

existential /ˌeɡzɪˈstenʃ(ə)l/ *adj.* экзистенциа́льный.

existentialism /ˌeɡzɪˈstenʃəˌlɪz(ə)m/ *n.* экзистенциали́зм.

existentialist /ˌeɡzɪˈstenʃəlɪst/ *n.* экзистенциали́ст.

exit /ˈeksɪt/, /ˈeɡzɪt/ *n.* (*also comput.*) вы́ход; **make one's ~** у|ходи́ть, -йти́.
● *v.i.* (**exited, exiting**) у|ходи́ть, -йти́; **~ Macbeth** (*stage direction*) Макбе́т ухо́дит; (*comput.*) выходи́ть, вы́йти.

ex-libris /eksˈliːbrɪs/ *n.* (*pl.* **~**) экслибрис.

exodus /ˈeksədəs/ *n.* ма́ссовый отъе́зд/ухо́д; **E~** (*bibl.*) Исхо́д, Втора́я кни́га Моисе́ева.

ex officio /ˌeks əˈfɪʃɪəʊ/ *adv. & adj.* по до́лжности.

exogamous /ekˈsɒgəməs/ *adj.* экзога́мный.

exogamy /ekˈsɒgəmɪ/ *n.* экзога́мия.

exonerate /ɪgˈzɒnəˌreɪt/ *v.t.* опра́вд|ывать, -а́ть; сн|има́ть, -ять обвине́ние с + *g.* (*в чем*).

exoneration /ɪgˌzɒnəˈreɪʃ(ə)n/ *n.* оправда́ние.

exophthalmic /ˌeksɒfˈθælmɪk/ *adj.*: **~ goitre** (*Br.*), **goiter** (*US*) базе́дова боле́знь.

exorbitant /ɪgˈzɔ:bɪt(ə)nt/ *adj.* непоме́рный, чрезме́рный.

exorcism /ˈeksɔ:ˌsɪz(ə)m/ *n.* изгна́ние злых ду́хов.

exorcist /ˈeksɔ:sɪst/ *n.* заклина́тель (*m.*).

exorcize /ˈeksɔ:ˌsaɪz/ *v.t.* изг|оня́ть, -на́ть злых ду́хов из + *g.*

exotic /ɪgˈzɒtɪk/ *adj.* экзоти́ческий.

expand /ɪkˈspænd/ *v.t.* (*lit., fig.*) расш|иря́ть, -и́рить; **heat ~s metals** при нагрева́нии мета́ллы расширя́ются; **the essay was ~ed into a book** о́черк был развёрнут в кни́гу.

● *v.i.* расш|иря́ться, -и́риться; увели́чи|ваться, -ться в объёме; **trade ~ed** торго́вля расши́рилась.

expanse /ɪkˈspæns/ *n.* протяже́ние; широ́кое простра́нство; (*of sea, sky etc.*) просто́р; ширь.

expansion /ɪkˈspænʃ(ə)n/ *n.* расшире́ние; (*pol.*) экспа́нсия; (*increase*) подъём; **chest ~** расшире́ние грудно́й кле́тки; **territorial ~** территориа́льный захва́т.

expansionism /ɪkˈspænʃ(ə)ˌnɪz(ə)m/ *n.* (*pol.*) экспансиони́зм.

expansionist(ic) /ɪkˌspænʃ(ə)ˈnɪstɪk/ *adj.* (*pol.*) экспансиони́стский.

expansive /ɪkˈspænsɪv/ *adj.* (*extensive*) обши́рный; (*of person*) экспанси́вный.

expansiveness /ɪkˈspænsɪvnɪs/ *n.* (*of person*) экспанси́вность.

expatiate /ɪkˈspeɪʃɪˌeɪt/ *v.i.* распространя́ться (*impf.*) (*на какую-н. тему*).

expatiation /ɪkˌspeɪʃɪˈeɪʃ(ə)n/ *n.* простра́нное рассужде́ние.

expatriate¹ /eksˈpætrɪət/, /-ˈpeɪtrɪət/ *n. & adj.* экспатриа́нт (*fem.* -ка); **an ~ American** америка́нец-экспатриа́нт.

expatriate² /eksˈpætrɪˌeɪt/, /-ˈpeɪtrɪˌeɪt/ *v.t.* (*banish*) экспатрии́ровать (*impf., pf.*).

● *v.i.* (*emigrate*) эмигри́ровать (*impf., pf.*).

expatriation /eksˌpætrɪˈeɪʃ(ə)n/, /-ˌpeɪtrɪˈeɪʃ(ə)n/ *n.* (*banishing*) экспатриа́ция; (*emigration*) эмигра́ция.

expect /ɪkˈspekt/ *v.t.* **1** (*of future or probable event*) ждать (*impf.*), ожида́ть (*impf.*) + *g.*; **I ~ to see him** я рассчи́тываю встре́титься с ним; **I'm ~ing him to dinner** я жду его́ к обе́ду; **you would ~ them to have thought of that** каза́лось бы, они́ должны́ бы́ли об э́том поду́мать; **just as I ~ed** так я и ду́мал. **2** (*require*) ожида́ть (*impf.*) + *g.*; рассчи́тывать (*impf.*) на + *a.*; тре́бовать (*impf.*) + *g.*; **I ~ you to be punctual** я наде́юсь/рассчи́тываю, что вы бу́дете пунктуа́льны. **3** (*suppose*) полага́ть (*impf.*); предполага́ть (*impf.*); **I ~ you are hungry** я полага́ю, что вы голодны́. **4**: **she is ~ing** (*coll., pregnant*) она́ ожида́ет ребёнка.

expectancy /ɪkˈspektənsɪ/ *n.* ожида́ние; предвкуше́ние.

expectant /ɪkˈspekt(ə)nt/ *adj.* выжида́ющий; **an ~ mother** бу́дущая мать.

expectation /ˌekspekˈteɪʃ(ə)n/ *n.* **1** (*anticipation*) ожида́ние; **in ~ of** в ожида́нии + *g.*; **contrary to ~** вопреки́ ожида́ниям; **come up to ~s** оправда́ть (*pf.*) ожида́ния; **fall short of ~s** не оправда́ть (*pf.*) ожида́ний. **2** (*prospect*) наде́жда; **~ of life** вероя́тная продолжи́тельность жи́зни.

expectorant /ekˈspektərənt/ *n.* (*med.*) отха́ркивающее сре́дство.

expectorate /ekˈspektəˌreɪt/ *v.t. & i.* (*spit*) отха́рк|ивать(ся), -ать(ся), -нуть(ся).

expectoration /ekˌspektəˈreɪʃ(ə)n/ *n.* отха́ркивание.

expedienc|e /ɪkˈspi:dɪəns/, **-y** /ɪkˈspi:dɪənsɪ/ *nn.* (*suitability*) целесообра́зность; (*self interest*) вы́годность; (*pej.*) оппортуни́зм.

expedient /ɪkˈspi:dɪənt/ *n.* приём, спо́соб.

● *adj.* целесообра́зный; (*advantageous*) вы́годный.

expedite /ˈekspɪˌdaɪt/ *v.t.* уск|оря́ть, -о́рить.

expedition /ˌekspɪˈdɪʃ(ə)n/ *n.* экспеди́ция.

expeditionary /ˌekspɪˈdɪʃənərɪ/ *adj.* экспедицио́нный; **~ force** экспедицио́нные войска́.

expeditious /ˌekspɪˈdɪʃəs/ *adj.* бы́стрый, ско́рый.

expeditiousness /ˌekspɪˈdɪʃəsnɪs/ *n.* быстрота́, ско́рость.

expel /ɪkˈspel/ *v.t.* (**expelled, expelling**) (*emit*) пос|ыла́ть, -ла́ть; (*compel to leave*) исключ|а́ть, -и́ть; выгоня́ть, вы́гнать; (*dislodge, e.g. troops*) изг|оня́ть, -на́ть.

expend /ɪkˈspend/ *v.t.* (*capital*) расхо́довать, из-; тра́тить, ис-; (*ammunition*) расхо́довать, из-; (*time, efforts*) тра́тить, ис-/по-.

expendable /ɪkˈspendəb(ə)l/ *adj.* (*of acceptable sacrifice*) ≈ расхо́дуемый.

expenditure /ɪkˈspendɪtʃə(r)/ *n.* расхо́д, тра́та; **~ of energy** затра́та эне́ргии.

expense /ɪkˈspens/ *n.* **1** (*monetary cost*) расхо́д; **at my ~** (*lit.*) за мой счёт; **at public ~** за казённый счёт; **go to ~** нести́ (*det.*) расхо́ды; **put s.o. to ~** ввести́ (*pf.*) кого́-н. в расхо́д; **spare no ~** не жале́ть (*impf.*) расхо́дов; **~ account** ава́нсовый отчёт; **travelling** (*Br.*), **traveling** (*US*) **~s** доро́жные расхо́ды. **2** (*detriment*): **a joke at my ~** шу́тка на мой счёт; **idealism at others' ~** идеали́зм за чужо́й счёт.

expensive /ɪkˈspensɪv/ *adj.* дорого́й, дорогосто́ящий; **he has ~ tastes** у него́ вкус к дороги́м веща́м; **an ~ education** образова́ние, сто́ившее больши́х де́нег.

expensiveness /ɪkˈspensɪvnɪs/ *n.* дорогови́зна.

experience /ɪkˈspɪərɪəns/ *n.* **1** (*process of gaining knowledge etc.*) о́пыт; **we learn by ~** мы у́чимся на со́бственном о́пыте; **I know that from ~** я зна́ю э́то по о́пыту. **2** (*event*) слу́чай; **an unpleasant ~** неприя́тный слу́чай.

● *v.t.* испы́т|ывать, -а́ть, переж|ива́ть, -и́ть.

experienced /ɪkˈspɪərɪənst/ *adj.* о́пытный.

experiment /ɪkˈsperɪmənt/, /-ˌment/ *n.* экспериме́нт, о́пыт.

● *v.i.* эксперименти́ровать (*impf.*).

experimental /ɪkˌsperɪˈment(ə)l/ *adj.* эксперимента́льный, про́бный; **at the ~ stage** на ста́дии экспериме́нта.

experimentation /ɪkˌsperɪmenˈteɪʃ(ə)n/ *n.* эксперименти́рование.

experimenter /ɪkˈsperɪˌmentə(r)/ *n.* эксперимента́тор.

expert /ˈekspɜ:t/ *n.* экспе́рт, знато́к, специали́ст (*по чему*).

● *adj.* квалифици́рованный; **an ~ driver** о́пытный шофёр; **~ advice** сове́т специали́ста; **he is ~ at persuading people** он ма́стер угова́ривать.

expertise /ˌekspɜ:ˈti:z/ *n.* (*skill, knowledge*) компете́нтность.

expiate /ˈekspɪˌeɪt/ *v.t.* искуп|а́ть, -и́ть.

expiation /ˌekspɪˈeɪʃ(ə)n/ *n.* искупле́ние.

expiatory /ˈekspɪətərɪ/, /ˈekspɪˌeɪtərɪ/ *adj.* искупи́тельный.

expiration /ˌekspɪˈreɪʃ(ə)n/ *n.* (*breathing out*) вы́дох; (*expiry*) истече́ние (*срока*).

expire /ɪkˈspaɪə(r)/ *v.i.* **1** (*breathe out*) выдыха́ть, вы́дохнуть. **2** (*of period, truce, licence etc.*) ист|ека́ть, -е́чь. **3** (*die*) уг|аса́ть, -а́снуть.

expiry /ɪkˈspaɪərɪ/ *n.* истече́ние (сро́ка).

explain /ɪkˈspleɪn/ *v.t.* объясн|я́ть, -и́ть; изъясн|я́ть, -и́ть; **~ o.s.** (*make o.s. clear*) разъясни́ть (*pf.*) свою́ то́чку зре́ния; (*account for one's conduct*) опра́вд|ываться, -а́ться; **~ something away** на|ходи́ть, -йти́ объясне́ние (*неудобному факту*); отгов|а́риваться, -ори́ться от чего́-н.

explainable /ɪkˈspleɪnəb(ə)l/ *adj.* объясни́мый.

explanation /ˌekspləˈneɪʃ(ə)n/ *n.* объясне́ние; **in (by way of) ~** в ка́честве объясне́ния.

explanatory /ɪkˈsplænətərɪ/ *adj.* объясни́тельный.

expletive /ɪkˈspli:tɪv/ *n.* (*oath*) бра́нное выраже́ние; (*gram.*) вставно́е сло́во.

explicable /ɪkˈsplɪkəb(ə)l/, /ˈek-/ *adj.* объясни́мый.

E

explicit /ɪk'splɪsɪt/ *adj.* я́сный, чёткий, то́чный; (*of person*) прямо́й.

explicitness /ɪk'splɪsɪtnɪs/ *n.* я́сность, чёткость, то́чность; (*of person*) прямота́.

explode /ɪk'spləʊd/ *v.t.* вз|рыва́ть, -орва́ть; (*fig.*): **~ a theory** опров|ерга́ть, -е́ргнуть тео́рию.

● *v.i.* вз|рыва́ться, -орва́ться; (*fig.*): **he ~d with rage/laughter** он разрази́лся гне́вом/сме́хом.

exploit[1] /'eksplɔɪt/ *n.* по́двиг.

exploit[2] /ɪk'splɔɪt/ *v.t.* **1** (*use or develop economically*) разраб|а́тывать, -о́тать; эксплуати́ровать (*impf.*). **2** (*an advantage etc.*) по́льзоваться, вос- + *i.*; испо́льзовать (*impf., pf.*). **3** (*a person*) эксплуати́ровать (*impf.*).

exploitable /ɪk'splɔɪtəb(ə)l/ *adj.* го́дный для разрабо́тки.

exploitation /,eksplɔɪ'teɪʃ(ə)n/ *n.* разрабо́тка; эксплуата́ция (*also of person*).

exploitative /ɪk'splɔɪtətɪv/ *adj.* эксплуата́торский, эксплуатацио́нный.

exploiter /ɪk'splɔɪtə(r)/ *n.* эксплуата́тор.

exploration /,eksplə'reɪʃ(ə)n/ *n.* (*geog.*) иссле́дование; (*of possibilities etc.*) изуче́ние.

exploratory /ɪk'splɒrətərɪ/ *adj.* иссле́довательский; **~ talks** предвари́тельные перегово́ры.

explore /ɪk'splɔː(r)/ *v.t.* **1** (*geog.*) иссле́довать (*impf., pf.*); разве́д|ывать, -ать. **2** (*possibilities etc.*) изуч|а́ть, -и́ть. **3** (*by touch*) ощу́п|ывать, -ать.

explorer /ɪk'splɔːrə(r)/ *n.* иссле́дователь (*m.*) (*fem.* -ница).

explosion /ɪk'spləʊʒ(ə)n/ *n.* (*of bomb etc.*) взрыв; (*of rage etc.*) вспы́шка; (*fig.*): **population ~** демографи́ческий взрыв.

explosive /ɪk'spləʊsɪv/ *n.* взры́вчатое вещество́; **high ~** дробя́щее взры́вчатое вещество́.

● *adj.* взры́вчатый, взрывно́й; (*situation*) взрывоопа́сный; **~ bomb** фуга́сная бо́мба; **~ bullet** разрывна́я пу́ля; (*fig.*) вспы́льчивый.

explosiveness /ɪk'spləʊsɪvnɪs/ *n.* взрыва́емость, взры́вчатость.

exponent /ɪk'spəʊnənt/ *n.* **1** (*advocate*) сторо́нник; представи́тель (*m.*). **2** (*math.*) экспоне́нта, показа́тель (*m.*) сте́пени.

exponential /,ekspə'nenʃ(ə)l/ *adj.* (*math.*) экспоненциа́льный, показа́тельный.

export[1] /'ekspɔːt/ *n.* э́кспорт, вы́воз; **~ duty** э́кспортная по́шлина; **~s increased in value** це́нность/сто́имость э́кспорта возросла́; **~s amounted to . . .** э́кспорт соста́вил. . .; **sugar is an important ~** са́хар — ва́жная статья́ э́кспорта.

export[2] /ek'spɔːt/, /'ek-/ *v.t.* экспорти́ровать (*impf., pf.*); вывози́ть, вы́везти.

exportable /ek'spɔːtəb(ə)l/ *adj.* экспорти́руемый; го́дный на э́кспорт.

exportation /,ekspɔː'teɪʃ(ə)n/ *n.* экспорти́рование.

exporter /ek'spɔːtə(r)/ *n.* экспортёр.

expose /ɪk'spəʊz/ *v.t.* **1** (*physically*) выставля́ть, вы́ставить; **~ one's body to sunlight** подст|авля́ть, -а́вить те́ло со́лнцу; **~ o.s.** (*indecently*) обнаж|а́ться, -и́ться; **~d to the weather** незащищённый от непого́ды; **an ~d position** (*mil.*) незащищённая пози́ция. **2** (*fig., subject*) подв|ерга́ть, -е́ргнуть; **he was ~d to insult** его сде́лали мише́нью для оскорбле́ний. **3** (*display*) выставля́ть, вы́ставить. **4** (*fig., unfold*) раскр|ыва́ть, -ы́ть. **5** (*unmask*) разоблач|а́ть, -и́ть. **6** (*phot.*) экспони́ровать (*impf.*).

exposé /ek'spəʊzeɪ/ *n.* разоблаче́ние.

exposition /,ekspə'zɪʃ(ə)n/ *n.* (*setting forth facts etc.*) изложе́ние; (*exhibition*) экспози́ция, вы́ставка.

expository /ɪk'spɒzɪtərɪ/ *adj.* объясни́тельный.

ex post facto /,eks pəʊst 'fæktəʊ/ *adj. & adv.* пост фа́ктум.

expostulate /ɪk'spɒstjʊ,leɪt/ *v.i.*: **~ with s.o.** увещева́ть (*impf.*) кого́-н.; усо́вещивать (*impf.*) кого́-н.

expostulation /ɪk,spɒstjʊ'leɪʃ(ə)n/ *n.* увещева́ние.

expostulatory /ɪk'spɒstjʊlətərɪ/ *adj.* увещева́тельный.

exposure /ɪk'spəʊʒə(r)/ *n.* **1** (*physical*): **~ to light** выставле́ние на свет; **indecent ~** обнаже́ние; **he died of ~** он поги́б от хо́лода; **house with a southern ~** дом о́кнами на юг. **2** (*subjection*): **~ to ridicule** выставле́ние на посме́шище. **3** (*unmasking*) разоблаче́ние. **4** (*phot.*) экспози́ция; **~ meter** экспоно́метр.

expound /ɪk'spaʊnd/ *v.t.* (*a theory*) изл|ага́ть, -ожи́ть; (*a text*) толкова́ть (*impf.*).

express[1] /ɪk'spres/ *n.* (**~** *train*) экспре́сс; курье́рский по́езд.

● *adj.* (*urgent, high-speed*) сро́чный; **~ letter** сро́чное письмо́; **~ mail** э́кстренная по́чта.

● *adv.* сро́чно, спе́шно; с на́рочным; **the goods were sent ~** (*urgently*) това́р был отпра́влен большо́й ско́ростью.

express[2] /ɪk'spres/ *adj.* **1** (*clear*) чёткий; **~ orders** чёткие приказа́ния. **2** (*exact, specific*) то́чный, осо́бенный; **for the ~ purpose of** со специа́льной це́лью + *g.*

● *v.t.* **1** (*press out*) выжима́ть, вы́жать. **2** (*show in words etc.*) выража́ть, вы́разить; **~ o.s.** выража́ться, вы́разиться; выска́зывать, вы́сказать.

expressible /ɪk'spresɪb(ə)l/ *adj.* вырази́мый.

expression /ɪk'spreʃ(ə)n/ *n.* **1** (*act of expressing*) выраже́ние; **beyond ~** невырази́мый; **give ~ to** выража́ть, вы́разить; **find ~** выража́ться, вы́разиться. **2** (*mus.*): **he plays with ~** он игра́ет вырази́тельно. **3** (*word, term*) выраже́ние (*also math.*).

expressionism /ɪk'spreʃə,nɪz(ə)m/ *n.* экспрессиони́зм.

expressionist /ɪk'spreʃə,nɪst/ *n.* экспрессиони́ст.

expressionistic /ɪk,spreʃə'nɪstɪk/ *adj.* экспрессиони́стский.

expressive /ɪk'spresɪv/ *adj.* вырази́тельный.

expressiveness /ɪk'spresɪvnɪs/ *n.* вырази́тельность.

expressway /ɪk'spresweɪ/ *n.* (*US*) городска́я автомагистра́ль.

expropriate /eks'prəʊprɪ,eɪt/ *v.t.* (*person*) лиш|а́ть, -и́ть со́бственности; (*property*) экспроприи́ровать (*impf., pf.*).

expropriation /eks,prəʊprɪ'eɪʃ(ə)n/ *n.* экспроприа́ция; лише́ние со́бственности.

expulsion /ɪk'spʌlʃ(ə)n/ *n.* изгна́ние; исключе́ние.

expunge /ɪk'spʌndʒ/ *v.t.* вычёркивать, вы́черкнуть.

expurgate /'ekspə,geɪt/ *v.t.*: **~ a book** исключ|а́ть, -и́ть (*or* изыма́ть, изъя́ть) нежела́тельные места́ из кни́ги.

expurgation /,ekspə'geɪʃ(ə)n/ *n.* исключе́ние/изъя́тие нежела́тельных мест из кни́ги.

exquisite /'ekskwɪzɪt/, /ek'skwɪzɪt/ *adj.* (*perfected*) утончённый; (*delicate*) то́нкий; **~ sensibility** обострённая чувстви́тельность; **~ pain** о́страя боль.

exquisiteness /eks'kwɪzɪtnɪs/ *n.* утончённость; (*of pain*) острота́.

ex-service /eks'sɜːvɪs/ *adj.* (*Br.*) демобилизо́ванный, отставно́й.

ex-serviceman /eks'sɜːvɪsmən/ *n.* (*Br.*) демобилизо́ванный; отставно́й вое́нный.

extant /ek'stænt/, /ɪk'st-/, /'ekst(ə)nt/ *adj.* сохрани́вшийся.

extemporaneous /ɪk,stempə'reɪnɪəs/ *adj.* импровизи́рованный.

extempore /ɪk'stempərɪ/ *adj.* импровизи́рованный.

● *adv.* экспро́мтом.

extemporization /ɪks,tempəraɪ'zeɪʃ(ə)n/ *n.* импровиза́ция.

extemporize /ɪk'stempə,raɪz/ *v.t. & i.* и|мпровизи́ровать, сы-; **he ~d a speech** он произнёс импровизи́рованную речь.

extend /ɪk'stend/ *v.t.* **1** (*stretch out*) протя́|гивать, -ну́ть; **~ a rope between two posts** натя́|гивать, -ну́ть верёвку ме́жду двумя́ столба́ми; **an ~ed battle-line** растя́нутая ли́ния фро́нта. **2** (*offer, accord*) ока́з|ывать, -а́ть; **~ a welcome** выка́зывать, вы́казать раду́шие; раду́шно встр|еча́ть, -е́тить (*кого*). **3** (*make longer, wider or larger*) удлин|я́ть, -и́ть; расш|иря́ть, -и́рить; **~ a railway** продли́ть (*pf.*) железнодоро́жную ли́нию; **~ a table** (*by means of a leaf*) раздв|ига́ть, -и́нуть стол; **~ one's premises** расш|иря́ть, -и́рить помеще́ние. **4** (*prolong*) продл|ева́ть, -и́ть; **~ one's leave/passport** продл|ева́ть,

-и́ть о́тпуск/па́спорт; **an ~ed** (*lengthy*) **visit** дли́тельный визи́т.
5 (*fig., enlarge, widen*) увели́чи|вать, -ть; расш|иря́ть, -и́рить; **~ one's influence** распростран|я́ть, -и́ть своё влия́ние.
6 (*exert*): **~ o.s.** напр|яга́ться, -я́чься; стара́ться (*impf.*) изо всех сил; **we are fully ~ed** мы на преде́ле (на́ших) сил.
● *v.i.* простира́ться (*impf.*); **the garden ~s to the river** сад простира́ется до реки́; **my leave ~s till Tuesday** мой о́тпуск продолжа́ется до вто́рника; **this rule ~s to first-year students** э́то пра́вило распространя́ется и на первоку́рсников.

exten|dible /ɪk'stendɪb(ə)l/, **-sible** /ɪk'stensɪb(ə)l/ *adjs.* (*e.g. table, ladder*) раздвижно́й.

extension /ɪk'stenʃ(ə)n/ *n.* **1** (*extent*) протяже́ние. **2** (*stretching out*) вытя́гивание, удлине́ние. **3** (*enlarging in space or time*) расшире́ние, увеличе́ние; **~ of a railway** удлине́ние железнодоро́жной ли́нии; **~ of leave** продле́ние о́тпуска; **~ of time (to pay debt)** дополни́тельный срок (для упла́ты до́лга); **an ~ course in physics** дополни́тельный курс фи́зики; **~ lead** (*elec.*) удлини́тель (*m.*). **4** (*additional part of building etc.*) пристро́йка (к + *d.*). **5** (*teleph.*) (*telephone*) паралле́льный телефо́н; (*number*) доба́вочный (но́мер); **my number is 5652, ~ 10** мой но́мер 5652, доба́вочный 10.

extensive /ɪk'stensɪv/ *adj.* (*wide, far-reaching*) простра́нный; **an ~ park** обши́рный парк; **~ knowledge** обши́рные зна́ния; **~ plans** далеко́ иду́щие пла́ны; (*opp. intensive*) экстенси́вный.

extensiveness /ɪk'stensɪvnɪs/ *n.* простра́нность; обши́рность.

extensor /ɪk'stensə(r)/ *n.* (*also* **~ muscle**) разгиба́ющая мы́шца.

extent /ɪk'stent/ *n.* **1** (*phys. size, length etc.*) протяже́ние; **a vast ~ of marsh** обши́рное заболо́ченное простра́нство. **2** (*fig., range*) разме́р; круг; диапазо́н; **~ of s.o.'s knowledge** круг чьих-н. зна́ний; **~ of damage** разме́р поврежде́ний. **3** (*degree*) сте́пень; **to some (*or* a certain) ~** до не́которой/изве́стной сте́пени; **to a large ~** в значи́тельной ме́ре; **I have never played golf to any ~** я со́бственно почти́ никогда́ не игра́л в гольф; **he went to the ~ of borrowing money** он пошёл да́же на то, что́бы заня́ть де́ньги.

extenuat|e /ɪk'stenjʊ,eɪt/ *v.t.* преум|еньша́ть, -е́ньшить; **~ing circumstances** смягча́ющие обстоя́тельства.

extenuation /ɪkstenjʊ'eɪʃ(ə)n/ *n.* приуменьше́ние; оправда́ние.

exterior /ɪk'stɪərɪə(r)/ *n.* (*of object*) вне́шняя сторона́; (*archit.*) экстерье́р; (*of person*) вне́шность; нару́жность.
● *adj.* вне́шний.

exterminate /ɪk'stɜ:mɪ,neɪt/ *v.t.* (*disease; ideas*) искорен|я́ть, -и́ть; (*people*) уничт|ожа́ть, -о́жить; (*people, vermin*) истреб|ля́ть, -и́ть.

extermination /ɪk,stɜ:mɪ'neɪʃ(ə)n/ *n.* искорене́ние; уничтоже́ние; истребле́ние.

exterminator /ɪk'stɜ:mɪ,neɪtə(r)/ *n.* (*person, substance*) истреби́тель (*m.*).

external /ɪk'stɜ:n(ə)l/ *n.* вне́шность; **judge by ~s** суди́ть (*impf.*) по вне́шнему ви́ду.
● *adj.* вне́шний; **the ~ world** вне́шний мир; **~ affairs** иностра́нные дела́; **an ~ student** экстéрн, зао́чни|к (*fem.* -ца); **for ~ use only** то́лько для нару́жного употребле́ния.

externalize /ɪk'stɜ:nə,laɪz/ *v.t.* (*manifest*) прояв|ля́ть, -и́ть.

extinct /ɪk'stɪŋkt/ *adj.* (*of volcano*) поту́хший; (*of species, custom*) вы́мерший; (*of feelings etc.*) уга́сший.

extinction /ɪk'stɪŋkʃ(ə)n/ *n.* угаса́ние; (*of species etc.*) вымира́ние; (*of a disease*) ликвида́ция, искорене́ние.

extinguish /ɪk'stɪŋgwɪʃ/ *v.t.* (*light, fire*) гаси́ть, по-; (*hopes etc.*) уб|ива́ть, -и́ть; (*a debt*) пога|ша́ть, -си́ть.

extinguisher /ɪk'stɪŋgwɪʃə(r)/ *n.* (*for candle*) гаси́льник; (*fire ~*) огнетуши́тель (*m.*).

extirpate /'ekstə,peɪt/ *v.t.* вырыва́ть, вы́рвать с ко́рнем; искорен|я́ть, -и́ть.

extirpation /,ekstə'peɪʃ(ə)n/ *n.* искорене́ние.

extol /ɪk'stəʊl/, /ɪk'stɒl/ *v.t.* (**extolled, extolling**) превозн|оси́ть, -ести́.

extort /ɪk'stɔ:t/ *v.t.* вымога́ть (*impf.*).

extortion /ɪk'stɔ:ʃ(ə)n/ *n.* вымога́тельство.

extortionate /ɪk'stɔ:ʃənət/ *adj.* вымога́тельский.

extortioner /ɪk'stɔ:ʃənə(r)/ *n.* вымога́тель (*m.*).

extra /'ekstrə/ *n.* **1** (*additional item*) что-н. дополни́тельное; **music is an ~** му́зыка препода́ётся факультати́вно; **no ~s** без вся́ких припла́т; (*edition*) э́кстренный вы́пуск. **2** (*minor performer*) стати́ст (*fem.* -ка), актёр (*fem.* актри́са) массо́вки.
● *adj.* **1** (*additional*) доба́вочный, дополни́тельный; **~ time** (*sport*) дополни́тельное вре́мя; **it costs £1, postage ~** э́то сто́ит 1 фунт без пересы́лки; **I paid an ~ £5** я заплати́л ли́шних 5 фу́нтов; **£5 ~** 5 фу́нтов дополни́тельно. **2** (*special*) осо́бый.
● *adv.* сверх-, осо́бо; **~ strong** (*e.g. drink*) осо́бой кре́пости.

extra-cellular /,ekstrə'seljʊlə(r)/ *adj.* внекле́точный.

extract[1] /'ekstrækt/ *n.* **1** (*concentrated substance*) экстра́кт; **beef ~** мясно́й экстра́кт. **2** (*from book etc.*) вы́держка.

extract[2] /ɪk'strækt/ *v.t.* (*cork*) вытя́скивать, вы́тащить; (*tooth*) удал|я́ть, -и́ть; (*bullet from wound*) извл|ека́ть, -е́чь; (*information, admission*) вырыва́ть, вы́рвать; (*money*) вымога́ть (*impf.*); (*math.*) извл|ека́ть, -е́чь (*корень*); (*pleasure from a situation*) извл|ека́ть, -е́чь; **~ passages** (*from a book*) де́лать, с- вы́держки; (*juices etc.*) выжима́ть, вы́жать.

extractable /ɪk'stræktəb(ə)l/ *adj.* извлека́емый.

extraction /ɪk'strækʃ(ə)n/ *n.* (*extracting*) извлече́ние; (*of tooth*) удале́ние, экстра́кция; (*descent, origin*) происхожде́ние.

extractive /ɪk'stræktɪv/ *adj.*: **~ industries** добыва́ющие о́трасли промы́шленности.

extractor /ɪk'stræktə(r)/ *n.* экстра́ктор; **~ fan** вентиля́тор, воздухоочисти́тель (*m.*).

extra-curricular /,ekstrəkə'rɪkjʊlə(r)/ *adj.* проводи́мый сверх уче́бного пла́на; вне програ́ммы.

extraditable /'ekstrə,daɪtəb(ə)l/ *adj.* (*person*) подлежа́щий вы́даче; (*crime*) обусло́вливающий вы́дачу.

extradite /'ekstrə,daɪt/ *v.t.* (*hand over*) выдава́ть, вы́дать (*обвиняемого преступника*).

extradition /,ekstrə'dɪʃ(ə)n/ *n.* вы́дача (престу́пника); экстради́ция.

extragalactic /,ekstrəgə'læktɪk/ *adj.* внегалакти́ческий.

extra-judicial /,ekstrədʒu:'dɪʃ(ə)l/ *adj.*: **~ confession** внесуде́бное призна́ние; **~ execution** казнь без суда́.

extra-legal /'ekstrə-/ *adj.* не предусмо́тренный зако́ном.

extra-marital /,ekstrə'mærɪt(ə)l/ *adj.*: **~ affair** внебра́чная связь.

extramural /,ekstrə'mjʊər(ə)l/ *adj.* (*outside city*) за́городный; (*Br., acad.*) зао́чный; **~ studies** зао́чное обуче́ние; **~ student** ≈ зао́чни|к, вече́рни|к (*fem.* -ца).

extraneous /ɪk'streɪnɪəs/ *adj.* посторо́нний, чужо́й.

extraordinariness /ɪkstrə'ɔ:dɪnərɪnɪs/ *n.* стра́нность, необыча́йность.

extraordinary /ɪk'strɔ:dɪnərɪ/, /,ekstrə'ɔ:dɪnərɪ/ *adj.* чрезвыча́йный, необыча́йный, выдаю́щийся.

extrapolate /ɪk'stræpə,leɪt/ *v.t. & i.* (*math., fig.*) экстраполи́ровать (*impf., pf.*).

extrapolation /ɪk,stræpə'leɪʃ(ə)n/ *n.* (*math.*) экстраполя́ция.

extrasensory /,ekstrə'sensərɪ/ *adj.*: **~ perception** внечу́вственное восприя́тие.

extraterrestrial /,ekstrətɪ'restrɪəl/ *adj.* внеземно́й.
● *n.* инопланетя́н|ин (*fem.* -ка).

extraterritorial /,ekstrə,terɪ'tɔ:rɪəl/ *adj.* экстерриториа́льный.

extraterritoriality /,ekstrə,terɪ,tɔ:rɪ'ælɪtɪ/ *n.* экстерриториа́льность.

extravagance /ɪk'strævəgəns/ *n.* изли́шество; экстравага́нтность; расточи́тельность.

extravagant /ɪk'strævəgənt/ *adj.* **1** (*excessive*) изли́шний. **2** (*fantastic*) экстравага́нтный, сумасбро́дный. **3** (*over-spending*) расточи́тельный; **he was ~ with the hot water** он расхо́довал сли́шком мно́го горя́чей воды́.

E

extravaganza /ɪkˌstrævəˈgænzə/ *n.* феерия.

extravasate /ɪkˈstrævəˌseɪt/ *v.i.* вытека́ть, вы́течь из сосу́дов в ткань.

extravasation /ɪkˌstrævəˈseɪʃ(ə)n/ *n.* кровоподтёк, излия́ние кро́ви.

extravert /ˈekstrəˌvɜːt/ = **extrovert**

extreme /ɪkˈstriːm/ *n.* **1** (*high degree*) кра́йность; **wearisome in the ~** в вы́сшей сте́пени ску́чный. **2** (*of conduct etc.*) кра́йность; **he went to the opposite ~** он впал в другу́ю кра́йность; **he went to ~s to satisfy them** он пошёл на кра́йние ме́ры, что́бы угоди́ть им; **carry things to ~s** впада́ть (*impf.*) в кра́йность. **3** (*pl., opposing qualities etc.*): **~s of behaviour** (*Br.*), **behavior** (*US*) кра́йности поведе́ния; **~s of heat and cold** экстрема́льно/кра́йне высо́кие и ни́зкие температу́ры.

● *adj.* **1** (*furthest, utmost, last*) кра́йний, преде́льный; **the ~ edge of the city** са́мая окра́ина го́рода; **(the one) on the ~ right** кра́йний спра́ва; (*in politics*) кра́йне пра́вый; **~ old age** глубо́кая ста́рость; **the ~ penalty of the law** вы́сшая ме́ра наказа́ния; **~ unction** (*relig.*) собо́рование. **2** (*very great*) чрезвыча́йный. **3** (*taking something to its highest pitch*) кра́йний, преде́льный; **an ~ fashion** (*in clothes*) экстравага́нтная мо́да.

extremely /ɪkˈstriːmlɪ/ *adv.* кра́йне.

extremeness /ɪkˈstriːmnɪs/ *n.* (*of measures etc.*) кра́йность.

extremism /ɪkˈstriːmɪz(ə)m/ *n.* экстреми́зм.

extremist /ɪkˈstriːmɪst/ *n.* экстреми́ст.
● *adj.* экстреми́стский.

extremity /ɪkˈstremɪtɪ/ *n.* **1** (*end, extreme point*) край. **2** (*pl., hands and feet*) коне́чности (*f. pl.*). **3** (*extreme quality*) кра́йность; **the ~ of his grief** безме́рность его́ го́ря. **4** (*hardship*) кра́йность; **reduced to ~** доведённый до кра́йности. **5** (*pl., extreme measures*) кра́йние ме́ры (*f. pl.*).

extricate /ˈekstrɪˌkeɪt/ *v.t.* высвобожда́ть, вы́свободить; **~ o.s. from a difficulty** вы́путаться (*pf.*) из затрудне́ния.

extrication /ˌekstrɪˈkeɪʃ(ə)n/ *n.* высвобожде́ние, выпу́тывание.

extrinsic /ekˈstrɪnsɪk/ *adj.* посторо́нний; несуще́ственный.

extrovert /ˈekstrəˌvɜːt/ *n.* челове́к с откры́той нату́рой, экстрове́рт.

extrude /ɪkˈstruːd/ *v.t.* выта́лкивать, вы́толкнуть; вытесня́ть, вы́теснить.

extrusion /ɪkˈstruːʒ(ə)n/ *n.* вытесне́ние, выта́лкивание.

exuberance /ɪgˈzjuːbərəns/ *n.* (*profusion*) изоби́лие; (*of character*) экспанси́вность.

exuberant /ɪgˈzjuːbərənt/ *adj.* (*of foliage etc.*) бу́йный; (*of imagination etc.*) бога́тый, бу́йный; (*of spirits etc.*) экспанси́вный.

exudation /ˌeksjʊˈdeɪʃ(ə)n/ *n.* выделе́ние.

exude /ɪgˈzjuːd/ *v.i.* проступ|а́ть, -и́ть; выделя́ть, вы́делить; **he ~d cheerfulness** он излуча́л весе́лье.

exult /ɪgˈzʌlt/ *v.i.* торжествова́ть (*impf.*); ликова́ть (*impf.*).

exultant /ɪgˈzʌltənt/ *adj.* торжеству́ющий, лику́ющий.

exultation /ˌɪgzʌlˈteɪʃ(ə)n/ *n.* торжество́, ликова́ние.

eye /aɪ/ *n.* **1** (*organ of vision*) глаз; (*dim.*) глазо́к (*pl.* гла́зки); (*arch., poet.*) о́ко; **glass ~** стекля́нный глаз; **have a cast in one's ~** быть косогла́зым; **I can see well out of this ~** я хорошо́ ви́жу э́тим гла́зом; **I have something in my ~** мне что́-то попа́ло в глаз; **blind in one ~** криво́й; **evil ~** дурно́й глаз; **put the evil ~ on** сгла́зить (*pf.*). **2** (*var. idioms*): **give s.o. a black ~** подби́ть (*pf.*) глаз кому́-н.; **~s right!/left!** (*mil.*) равне́ние напра́во/нале́во!; **have a straight ~** име́ть ве́рный глаз; **with the naked ~** невооружённым гла́зом; **with half an ~** одни́м глазко́м; **in the twinkling of an ~** в мгнове́ние о́ка; **make ~s at s.o.; give s.o. the glad ~** (*coll.*) стро́ить (*impf.*) гла́зки кому́-н.; **be all ~s** гляде́ть (*impf.*) во все глаза́; **set, lay ~s on** зам|еча́ть, -е́тить; **fix one's ~s on** не спуска́ть (*impf.*) глаз с + *g.*; уста́виться (*pf.*) на + *a.*; **keep an ~ on** (*e.g. a saucepan*) следи́ть (*impf.*) за + *i.*; (*e.g. children*) следи́ть (*impf.*) за + *i.*; присм|а́тривать, -отре́ть за + *i.*; (*the time*) следи́ть (*impf.*) за + *i.*; **keep one's ~s open, skinned** (*Br.*), **peeled** (*coll.*) смотре́ть (*impf.*) в о́ба; **take one's ~s off s.o./sth.** отв|оди́ть, -ести́ глаза́ от кого́/чего́-н.; **an ~ for an ~** о́ко за о́ко; **pull the wool over s.o.'s ~s** вт|ира́ть, -ере́ть очки́ кому́-н.; **under, before s.o.'s very ~s** на глаза́х у кого́-н.; **he has an ~ for colour** (*Br.*), **color** (*US*) он чу́вствует цвет; **he has an ~ for the ladies** он зна́ет толк в же́нщинах; **cry one's ~s out** вы́плакать (*pf.*) все глаза́; **dry one's ~** осуши́ть (*pf.*) слёзы; **his ~s are bigger than his stomach** глаза́ у него́ завиду́щие; **in the mind's ~** мы́сленным взо́ром; **I could not believe my ~s** я не мог пове́рить свои́м глаза́м; **he ran his ~** (*or* **cast an ~**) **over the paper** он пробежа́л глаза́ми газе́ту; **feast one's ~s on** (*a sight*) наслажда́ться (*impf.*) (зре́лищем); **I caught her ~** я пойма́л её взгляд; **it offends the ~** э́то ре́жет глаз; **easy on the ~** (*coll.*) прия́тной нару́жности; **have ~s at the back of one's head** всё ви́деть/подмеча́ть (*impf.*); **see ~ to ~ with** сходи́ться (*impf.*) во взгля́дах с + *i.*; **up to the ~s in work** по́ уши в рабо́те; **I opened his ~s to the situation** я откры́л ему́ глаза́ на положе́ние веще́й; **he closed his ~s to the danger** он закрыва́л глаза́ на опа́сность; **turn a blind ~ to** смотре́ть (*impf.*) сквозь па́льцы на + *a.*; **in my ~s** (*judgment*) в мои́х глаза́х, на мой взгляд; **in the public ~** в це́нтре внима́ния; **with an ~ to pleasing her** что́бы понра́виться ей; **there is more in this than meets the ~** э́то не так про́сто, как ка́жется на пе́рвый взгляд. **3** (*special senses*): **~ of a needle** иго́льное ушко́; **in the ~ of the storm** в эпице́нтре бу́ри; **hooks and ~s** крючки́ (*m. pl.*) и пе́тли (*f. pl.*); (*of a potato*) глазо́к (*pl.* глазки́); **~s of a peacock's tail** глазки́ павли́ньего хвоста́; **private ~** (*sl., detective*) ча́стный сы́щик.

● *v.t.* (**eyes, eyed, eyeing** *or* **eying**) разгля́д|ывать, -е́ть; наблюда́ть (*impf.*); **he ~d me with suspicion** он разгля́дывал меня́ с подозре́нием.

● *cpds.* **~ball** *n.* глазно́е я́блоко; **~-bath** (*Br.*), **~-cup** (*US*) *nn.* глазна́я ва́нночка; **~bright** *n.* оча́нка; **~brow** *n.* бровь; **~brow pencil** каранда́ш для брове́й; **up to the ~brows** (*fig.*) по́ уши; **raise one's ~brows** (*fig.*) подня́ть (*pf.*) бро́ви от удивле́ния, неодобре́ния и т.п.; **~-catching** *adj.* эффе́ктный; **~-cup** *n.* = **~-bath; ~ doctor** *n.* глазни́к, глазно́й врач, окули́ст; **~-dropper** *n.* пипе́тка; **~ drops** *n.pl.* глазны́е ка́пли; **~glass** *n.* (*monocle*) моно́кль (*m.*); (*pl., spectacles*) очк|и́ (*pl., g.* -о́в); **~hole** *n.* (*spyhole*) глаз|о́к (*pl.* -ки́); **~ hospital** *n.* глазна́я больни́ца; **~lash** *n.* ресни́ца; **~-level** *n.*: **at ~-level** на у́ровне глаз; **~lid** *n.* ве́ко; **without batting an ~lid** (*coll.*) гла́зом не моргну́в; **~liner** *n.* каранда́ш для подкра́шивания глаз; **~-opener** *n.* (*coll., revelation*) открове́ние; **~-shadow** *n.* те́ни (*f. pl.*) для век; **~sight** *n.* зре́ние; **he has good ~sight** у него́ хоро́шее зре́ние; **his ~sight failed** его́ зре́ние уху́дшилось; **~-socket** *n.* глазни́ца, глазна́я впа́дина; **~sore** *n.* уро́дство; **~strain** *n.* напряже́ние зре́ния; **~-tooth** *n.* глазно́й зуб; **~wash** *n.* (*lotion*) примо́чка для глаз; (*fig., coll.*) очковтира́тельство; **~witness** *n.* очеви́дец.

-eyed /aɪd/ *suff.*: **blue-~** голубогла́зый.

eyeful /ˈaɪfʊl/ *n.* (*coll.*) зре́лище.

eyeless /ˈaɪlɪs/ *adj.* безгла́зый.

eyelet /ˈaɪlɪt/ *n.* ушко́; пе́телька.

eyrie /ˈaɪərɪ/, /ˈɪərɪ/, /ˈɜːrɪ/ *n.* орли́ное гнездо́.

Ezekiel /ɪˈziːkɪəl/ *n.* (*bibl.*) Иезеки́иль (*m.*).

Ezra /ˈezrə/ *n.* (*bibl.*) Е́з(д)ра.

Ff

F[1] /ef/ *n.* (*mus., also* **fa, fah**) фа (*nt. indecl.*).

F[2] /ˈfærən,haɪt/ (*abbr. of* ***Fahrenheit***) °Ф (шкала́ термо́метра Фаренге́йта); **30°F** 30°Ф (гра́дусов по Фаренге́йту).

FA (*abbr. of* ***Football Association***) (*Br.*) Футбо́льная ассоциа́ция; **~ Cup** кубо́к Футбо́льной ассоциа́ции.

fa /fɑ:/ *n.* = **fah**

Fabian /ˈfeɪbɪən/ *n.* (*socialist*) фабиа́нец.
● *adj.* (*of socialism*) фабиа́нский; (*of tactics generally*) выжида́тельный, медли́тельный.

Fabianism /ˈfeɪbɪə,nɪz(ə)m/ *n.* фабиа́нство.

fable /ˈfeɪb(ə)l/ *n.* ба́сня.

fabled /ˈfeɪbəld/ *adj.* (*celebrated*) легенда́рный; (*fictitious*) легенда́рный, ска́зочный.

fabric /ˈfæbrɪk/ *n.* (*text.*) ткань, мате́рия; (*of a building etc.*) констру́кция, структу́ра; (*fig.*) структу́ра.

fabricate /ˈfæbrɪ,keɪt/ *v.t.* (*invent*) сочин|я́ть, -и́ть; (*falsify, forge*) фабрикова́ть, с-; подде́л|ывать, -ать; **a ~d charge** сфабрико́ванное обвине́ние.

fabrication /,fæbrɪˈkeɪʃ(ə)n/ *n.* (*story etc.*) вы́думка; **complete ~** сплошна́я вы́думка; (*falsification*) фабрика́ция, подде́лка.

fabulist /ˈfæbjʊlɪst/ *n.* баснопи́сец.

fabulous /ˈfæbjʊləs/ *adj.* (*legendary*) легенда́рный; мифи́ческий; (*coll., marvellous*) роско́шный, басносло́вный.

façade /fəˈsɑ:d/ *n.* (*archit.*) фаса́д; (*fig.*): **his politeness is a ~** его́ ве́жливость чи́сто показна́я.

face /feɪs/ *n.* **1** (*front part of head*) лицо́; (*dim.*) ли́чико; **he fell on his ~** он упа́л ничко́м; **he hit him in the ~** он уда́рил его́ по лицу́; **look s.o. in the ~** (*lit.*) посмотре́ть (*pf.*) кому́-н. в глаза́; **I came ~ to ~ with him** я столкну́лся с ним лицо́м к лицу́; **I brought them ~ to ~** я свёл их друг с дру́гом; **I told him so to his ~** я сказа́л ему́ э́то в лицо́; **I dare not show my ~ there** я не сме́ю глаз показа́ть там; **the sun was shining in our ~s** со́лнце свети́ло нам пря́мо в лицо́; **she laughed in my ~** она́ рассмея́лась мне в лицо́; **he shut the door in my ~** он захло́пнул дверь пе́ред мои́м но́сом; **red in the ~** (*from anger/effort/embarrassment*) кра́сный/багро́вый (от гне́ва/уси́лия/смуще́ния); **it's written all over his ~** э́то у него на лице́/лбу/физионо́мии напи́сано; **you may talk till you are blue in the ~** мо́жете говори́ть, пока́ не охри́пнете; **she had her ~ lifted** ей подтяну́ли ко́жу на лице́; **in the ~ of danger** пе́ред лицо́м опа́сности; **in the ~ of difficulties** несмотря́ на тру́дности; **ruin stares us in the ~** нам грози́т разоре́ние.
2 (*facial expression*) лицо́; выраже́ние лица́; **he made a ~** он ско́рчил/состро́ил ро́жу; **he pulled a long ~** у него́ вы́тянулось лицо́; **he kept a straight ~** он храни́л невозмути́мый вид; **he put a bold ~ on the matter** он сде́лал хоро́шую ми́ну при плохо́й игре́; **his ~ fell** он измени́лся в лице́; у него́ вы́тянулось лицо́.
3 (*composure, effrontery*): **he saved his ~** он спас свою́ репута́цию; **he had the ~ to tell me …** у него́ хвати́ло на́глости сказа́ть мне…
4 (*outward show, aspect*) вне́шний вид; **on the ~ of it** (*apparently*) на вид, на пе́рвый взгляд; **this puts a new ~ on things** э́то представля́ет де́ло в но́вом све́те.
5 (*physical surface, facade*) лицо́; лицева́я сторона́; (*of clock*) цифербла́т; (*of banknote*) лицева́я сторона́; **they disappeared from the ~ of the earth** они́ исче́зли с лица́ земли́; **he laid the card ~ down** он положи́л ка́рту лицо́м вниз (*or* руба́шкой вверх); **the miner worked at the coal ~** шахтёр рабо́тал в у́гольном забо́е; **~ value** (*of currency*) номина́льная сто́имость; **I took his words at ~ value** я при́нял его́ слова́ за чи́стую моне́ту.
● *v.t.* **1** (*physically*) стоя́ть (*impf.*) лицо́м к + *d.*; смотре́ть (*impf.*) на + *a.*; **turn round and ~ me!** поверни́тесь ко мне лицо́м; **the man facing us** челове́к, сидя́щий *и т.п.* про́тив нас; **a seat facing the engine** сиде́нье по хо́ду по́езда.
2 (*confront*) смотре́ть (*impf.*) в лицо́ (*чему*); **we must ~ facts** на́до смотре́ть фа́ктам в лицо́; на́до счита́ться с фа́ктами; **let's ~ it!** (*coll.*) на́до гляде́ть пра́вде в глаза́!; **~ s.o. down** оса|жда́ть, -ди́ть кого́-н.; **the problem that ~s us** зада́ча, стоя́щая пе́ред на́ми; **we are ~d with bankruptcy** мы стои́м пе́ред банкро́тством.
3 (*mil., cause to turn*) пов|ора́чивать, -ерну́ть; **he ~d his men about** он поверну́л солда́т круго́м.
4 (*cover*) облицо́вывать, облицева́ть; **a wall ~d with stone** стена́, облицо́ванная ка́мнем; **a coat ~d with silk** пальто́, отде́ланное шёлком.
● *v.i.*: **the house ~s south** дом обращён фаса́дом на юг; **the house ~s on to a park** о́кна до́ма выхо́дят на парк; дом обращён фаса́дом к па́рку; **their house ~s ours** их дом — напро́тив на́шего; **he ~d up to the difficulties** он не испуга́лся тру́дностей; (*mil.*): **about ~!** круго́м!; **please ~ (towards) the camera** пожа́луйста, смотри́те в объекти́в.
● *cpds.* **~-card** *n.* (*US*) фигу́ра; **~-cloth** *n.* махро́вая рукави́чка для лица́; **~-cream** *n.* крем для лица́; **~-lift** *n.* опера́ция подня́тия ко́жи на лице́; (*fig.*) вне́шнее обновле́ние, космети́ческий ремо́нт; **~-pack** *n.* (*Br.*) космети́ческая ма́ска; **~-powder** *n.* пу́дра; **~-saving** *adj.* (*fig.*) для спасе́ния репута́ции/прести́жа; **~-worker** *n.* (*miner*) забо́йщик.

faceless /ˈfeɪslɪs/ *adj.* (*anonymous*) безли́чный, безли́кий.

facer /ˈfeɪsə(r)/ *n.* (*Br. coll., difficulty*) загво́здка.

facet /ˈfæsɪt/ *n.* грань, фасе́т; (*fig.*) аспе́кт.

faceted /ˈfæsɪtɪd/ *adj.* гранёный.

facetious /fəˈsi:ʃəs/ *adj.* шутли́вый, шу́точный; (*pej.*) неуме́стно-шутли́вый; **talk ~ly** остри́ть (*impf.*) (некста́ти).

facetiousness /fəˈsiːʃəsnɪs/ *n.* (неуме́стная) шутли́вость.

facia /ˈfeɪʃɪə/ *n.* (*Br.*) = **fascia**

facial /ˈfeɪʃ(ə)l/ *n.* масса́ж лица́.
● *adj.* лицево́й; **~ expression** выраже́ние лица́.

facile /ˈfæsaɪl/ *adj.* (*easy, fluent*) лёгкий, свобо́дный; (*superficial*) пове́рхностный.

facilitate /fəˈsɪlɪˌteɪt/ *v.t.* облегч|а́ть, -и́ть; спосо́бствовать (*impf.*) + *d.*; соде́йствовать (*impf.*) + *d.*

facilitation /fəˌsɪlɪˈteɪʃ(ə)n/ *n.* облегче́ние (*чего*); соде́йствие (*чему*).

facilit|y /fəˈsɪlɪtɪ/ *n.* (*ease*) лёгкость; (*skill*) спосо́бность (*к чему*); (*aid, appliance, installation*) сооруже́ние; **~ies for study** усло́вия (*nt. pl.*) для учёбы; **sports ~ies** спорти́вное обору́дование, помеще́ния (*nt. pl.*) для заня́тия спо́ртом.

facing /ˈfeɪsɪŋ/ *n.* (*of wall etc.*) облицо́вка; (*of coat etc.*) отде́лка.

facsimile /fækˈsɪmɪlɪ/ *n.* факси́миле (*indecl.*); (*fax*) факс.

fact /fækt/ *n.* факт; **the ~ that he was there shows that** ... тот факт, что он был там, говори́т о том, что...; **as a matter of ~** факти́чески; на са́мом де́ле; **the ~ is that** ... де́ло в том, что...; **in (point of) ~** (*actually*) факти́чески; в/на са́мом де́ле; (*intensifying*): **very much, in ~** о́чень да́же; **I think so, in ~ I'm quite sure** я так ду́маю, бо́лее того́, я уве́рен в э́том; (*summing up*): **in ~ the whole thing is most unsatisfactory** в су́щности, всё э́то весьма́ неудовлетвори́тельно; **a story founded on ~** расска́з, осно́ванный на действи́тельном происше́ствии.
● *cpd.* **~-finding** *adj.* занима́ющийся собира́нием фа́ктов; **~-finding tour** ознакоми́тельная пое́здка.

faction /ˈfækʃ(ə)n/ *n.* фра́кция, кли́ка.

factionalism /ˈfækʃənəlˌɪz(ə)m/ *n.* фракцио́нность.

factious /ˈfækʃəs/ *adj.* фракцио́нный.

factitious /fækˈtɪʃəs/ *adj.* иску́сственный.

factor /ˈfæktə(r)/ *n.* **1** (*math.*) мно́житель (*m.*), фа́ктор. **2** (*contributing cause*) фа́ктор; **this was a ~ in his success** э́то соде́йствовало его́ успе́ху.

factorial /fækˈtɔːrɪəl/ *adj.*: **~ 4** факториа́л 4.

factorize /ˈfæktəˌraɪz/ *v.t.* разложи́ть (*pf.*) на мно́жители.

factory /ˈfæktərɪ/ *n.* **1** (*place of manufacture*) фа́брика, заво́д; (*attr.*) фабри́чный, заводско́й. **2**: **~ ship** (*whaling*) плаву́чая китобо́йная ба́за.

factotum /fækˈtəʊtəm/ *n.* (*pl.* **~s**) факто́тум, дове́ренный слуга́.

factual /ˈfæktjʊəl/ *adj.* факти́ческий.

facult|y /ˈfækəltɪ/ *n.* **1** (*power, aptitude*) спосо́бность; **in possession of one's ~ies** в здра́вом уме́. **2** (*Br., part of university*) факульте́т. **3** (*US, body of teachers*) профе́ссорско-преподава́тельский соста́в.

fad /fæd/ *n.* (*craze*) увлече́ние, пове́трие; (*whim*) при́хоть, причу́да.

faddiness /ˈfædɪnɪs/ *n.* капри́зность.

faddish /ˈfædɪʃ/ *adj.* прихотли́вый.

faddist /ˈfædɪst/ *n.* приве́редник, чуда́к.

faddy /ˈfædɪ/ *adj.* (**faddier, faddiest**) (*Br.*) капри́зный.

fade /feɪd/ *v.t.* **1** (*cause to lose colour*) обесцве́|чивать, -тить; **the sunlight ~d the curtains** занаве́ски вы́горели на со́лнце. **2** (*cin., radio*): **~ one scene into another** пла́вно перев|оди́ть, -ести́ одну́ сце́ну в другу́ю; **~ out** постепе́нно ум|еньша́ть, -е́ньшить си́лу зву́ка; ув|оди́ть, -ести́ звук; **~ in** постепе́нно увели́чи|вать, -ть си́лу зву́ка.
● *v.i.* **1** (*lose colour*) обесцве́|чиваться, -титься; **the flowers ~d** цветы́ завя́ли/поблёкли; (*of sound*) зам|ира́ть, -ере́ть; (*of strength*) уг|аса́ть, -а́снуть. **2** (*fig.*): **his hopes ~d** его́ наде́жды испари́лись; **she is fading away** (*dying*) она́ та́ет на глаза́х.
● *cpds.* **~-in** *n.* (*cin., radio*) постепе́нное появле́ние зву́ка/изображе́ния; **~-out** *n.* (*cin., radio*) постепе́нное исчезнове́ние зву́ка/изображе́ния.

faecal /ˈfiːk(ə)l/ (*US* **fecal**) *adj.* фека́льный.

faeces /ˈfiːsiːz/ (*US* **feces**) *n.* фека́лии (*f. pl.*); испражне́ния (*nt. pl.*).

Faeroes /ˈfeərəʊz/ *n.*: **the ~** (*also* **Faeroe Islands**) Фаре́рские острова́ (*m. pl.*).

Faeroese /ˌfeərəʊˈiːz/ *n.* (*pl.* **~**) (*person*) фаре́р|ец (*fem.* -ка); (*language*) фаре́рский язы́к.
● *adj.* фаре́рский.

fag¹ /fæg/ *n.* (*Br.*) **1** (*coll., tiring task*) изнури́тельная рабо́та. **2** (*schoolboy*) мла́дший учени́к, прислу́живающий ста́ршему.
● *v.t.* (**fagged, fagging**) (*tire*) утом|ля́ть, -и́ть; выма́тывать, вы́мотать; **I am ~ged out** я вконе́ц вы́мотался.
● *v.i.* (**fagged, fagging**) (*toil*) корпе́ть (*impf.*) (*над чем*).

fag² /fæg/ *n.* (*Br. coll., cigarette*) сигаре́та, папиро́ска.
● *cpd.* **~-end** *n.* (*Br., butt*) оку́рок, (*sl.*) чина́рик; (*fig.*) коне́ц (*чего*); оста́ток (*чего*).

fag³ /fæg/ (*US*) = **faggot** *n.* 2

faggot /ˈfægət/ *n.* **1** (*US* **fagot**) (*bundle of sticks*) вяза́нка, фаши́на. **2** (*US sl. offens., homosexual*) гомосексуали́ст, пе́дик.

fa(h) /fɑː/ *n.* (*mus.*) четвёртая но́та мажо́рной га́ммы; (*the note F*) фа (*indecl.*).

Fahrenheit /ˈfærənˌhaɪt/ *n.* (*abbr.* **F**) Фаренге́йт; **at 30° ~** при тридцати́ гра́дусах по Фаренге́йту.

faience /ˈfaɪɑ̃s/ *n.* фая́нс.

fail /feɪl/ *n.*: **without ~** обяза́тельно, непреме́нно.
● *v.t.* **1** (*reject in exam*) прова́л|ивать, -и́ть. **2** (*disappoint, desert*) подв|оди́ть, -ести́; **words ~ me** я не нахожу́ слов; **his heart ~ed him** у него́ не хвати́ло ду́ху.
● *v.i.* **1** (*fall short, decline*) ух|удша́ться, -у́дшиться; недостава́ть (*impf.*); **the crops ~ed** хлеб не уроди́лся; **the water supply ~ed** водоснабже́ние прекрати́лось; **his eyesight is ~ing** его́ зре́ние слабе́ет; **he is in ~ing health** его́ здоро́вье ухудша́ется. **2** (*not succeed*): **he ~ed in the exam** он провали́лся на экза́мене; **his scheme ~ed** его́ план провали́лся; **he ~ed to convince her** ему́ не удало́сь (*or* он не суме́л) убеди́ть её; **I ~ to see why** ... я не понима́ю, почему́.... **3** (*omit*) упус|ка́ть, -ти́ть; **he never ~s to write** он никогда́ не забыва́ет писа́ть; **he ~ed to let us know** он не дал нам знать. **4** (*go bankrupt*): **the bank ~ed** банк ло́пнул.
● *cpd.* **~-safe** *adj.* самоотключа́ющийся (при ава́рии).

failing /ˈfeɪlɪŋ/ *n.* (*defect*) недоста́ток, сла́бость.
● *prep.* за неиме́нием + *g.*; **~ this** за неиме́нием э́того; е́сли э́того не слу́чится; **~ an answer** не получи́в отве́та.

failure /ˈfeɪljə(r)/ *n.* **1** (*unsuccess*) неуда́ча, неуспе́х, прова́л; **the venture was a ~** зате́я провали́лась. **2** (*person*) неуда́чник; **he was a ~ as a teacher** как педаго́г он никуда́ не годи́лся. **3** (*of crops etc.*) неурожа́й. **4** (*bankruptcy*) банкро́тство. **5** (*non-functioning*) ава́рия; **heart ~** парали́ч се́рдца; **engine ~** отка́з дви́гателя. **6** (*omission, neglect*): **his ~ to answer is a nuisance** о́чень доса́дно, что он не отвеча́ет.

fain /feɪn/ *adv.* (*poet.*) охо́тно, с ра́достью.

faint /feɪnt/ *n.* (*loss of consciousness*) о́бморок; **in a dead ~** в глубо́ком о́бмороке.
● *adj.* **1** (*weak, indistinct*) сла́бый, неотчётливый; **his strength grew ~** его́ си́лы угаса́ли; **he was ~ with hunger** он осла́б от го́лода; **I haven't the ~est idea** я не име́ю ни мале́йшего поня́тия. **2** (*timid*) ро́бкий; **~ heart never won fair lady** сме́лость города́ берёт. **3** (*giddy, likely to swoon*) бли́зкий к о́бмороку; **I feel ~** мне ду́рно.
● *v.i.* (*lose consciousness*) па́дать, упа́сть в о́бморок; (*grow weak*) слабе́ть (*impf.*); **he was ~ing with hunger** он е́ле стоя́л на нога́х от го́лода; **~ing fit** о́бморок.
● *cpds.* **~-hearted** *adj.* трусли́вый, малоду́шный; **~-heartedness** *n.* тру́сость, малоду́шие.

faintly /ˈfeɪntlɪ/ *adv.* (*feebly*) сла́бо; (*slightly*) сла́бо, слегка́.

faintness /ˈfeɪntnɪs/ *n.* сла́бость; (*giddiness*) дурнота́.

fair¹ /feə(r)/ *n.* (*open-air market etc.*) я́рмарка; (*exhibition*) вы́ставка; **book ~** кни́жная я́рмарка.

● *cpd.* **~-ground** *n.* я́рмарочная пло́щадь.

fair² /feə(r)/ *adj.* **1** (*beautiful*) прекра́сный, краси́вый; **the ~ sex** прекра́сный пол.
2 (*specious*) показно́й; **~ words** краси́вые слова́.
3 (*of weather*) я́сный.
4 (*abundant, favourable*): **a ~ wind** попу́тный ве́тер; **a ~ amount** (*a lot*) значи́тельное/изря́дное коли́чество.
5 (*average*) сно́сный, посре́дственный; **he has a ~ chance of success** у него́ неплохи́е ша́нсы на успе́х; **she has a ~ amount of sense** у неё доста́точно здра́вого смы́сла; **his performance was only ~** его́ выступле́ние бы́ло так себе́; **'~'** (*as school mark*) посре́дственно; **~ to middling** так себе́; нева́жный.
6 (*equitable*): **~ share** зако́нная до́ля; **~ price** подходя́щая цена́; **~ play** че́стная игра́; справедли́вость; **by ~ means or foul** любы́ми сре́дствами; **it is ~ to say that** ... со всей справедли́востью мо́жно сказа́ть, что...; **~ and square** откры́тый, че́стный; **~ game** зако́нная добы́ча; **~ comment** справедли́вая кри́тика.
7 (*clean, unblemished*): **~ copy** чистови́к.
8 (*of hair*) све́тлый, (*blond*) белоку́рый; **a ~ complexion** све́тлый цвет лица́; **a ~ man** блонди́н.

● *adv.*: **he fought ~** он боро́лся че́стно (*or* по пра́вилам); **I hit him ~ (and square) in the midriff** я уда́рил его́ пря́мо в со́лнечное сплете́ние; **I tell you ~ and square that** ... я скажу́ вам напрями́к, что...

● *cpds.* **~-complexioned** *adj.* све́тлой ма́сти; **~-dealing** *n.* че́стность, прямота́; *adj.* че́стный, прямо́й; **~-haired** *adj.* белоку́рый; **~-minded** *adj.* справедли́вый; **~-mindedness** *n.* справедли́вость; **~way** *n.* (*naut.*) фарва́тер; **~-weather** *adj.*: **~-weather friends** ненадёжные друзья́, друзья́ до пе́рвой беды́.

fairish /ˈfeərɪʃ/ *adj.* (*tolerably good*) сно́сный; (*hair*) светлова́тый.

fairly /ˈfeəlɪ/ *adv.* **1** (*completely, positively*) факти́чески, буква́льно; **he ~ shook with indignation** он буква́льно дрожа́л от негодова́ния. **2** (*moderately*) дово́льно, сно́сно, терпи́мо; **he writes ~ well** он дово́льно хорошо́ пи́шет. **3** (*justly*) че́стно, справедли́во.

fairness /ˈfeərnɪs/ *n.* (*equity*) справедли́вость, че́стность; **in all ~** со всей справедли́востью.

fairy /ˈfeərɪ/ *n.* **1** фе́я; **bad ~** зла́я фе́я; злой дух; (*attr.*) волше́бный, ска́зочный; **~ voices** волше́бные голоса́; **~ lights** (*Br.*) цветны́е фона́рики. **2** (*sl. offens., homosexual*) пе́дик.

● *cpds.* **~land** *n.* волше́бное ца́рство; волше́бная/ска́зочная страна́; **~-like** *adj.* подо́бный фе́е; **~-story, ~-tale** *nn.* ска́зка; (*fig.*) ска́зка, небыли́ца.

fait accompli /ˌfeɪt əˈkɒmpliː/, /əˈkɔ̃pliː/ *n.* (*pl.* ***faits accomplis*** *pronunc. same*) сверши́вшийся факт.

faith /feɪθ/ *n.* **1** (*trust*) ве́ра, дове́рие; **put one's ~ in s.o.** дов|еря́ться, -е́риться кому́-н.; **I have no ~ in doctors** я не ве́рю доктора́м. **2** (*relig. conviction*) ве́ра. **3** (*relig. system*) вероиспове́дание, ве́ра. **4** (*promise, warranty*) обеща́ние, руча́тельство; **keep/break ~ with s.o.** сдержа́ть/нару́шить (*pf.*) обеща́ние, да́нное кому́-н.; **breach of ~** наруше́ние обеща́ния. **5** (*sincerity*) че́стность; **good ~** добросо́вестность; **in bad ~** с нече́стными наме́рениями; **in good ~** че́стно, добросо́вестно; с чи́стой со́вестью.

● *cpds.* **~-healer** *n.* зна́хар|ь (*fem.* -ка); **~-healing** *n.* зна́харство, лече́ние внуше́нием.

faithful /ˈfeɪθfʊl/ *adj.* то́чный, достове́рный; **a ~ translation** то́чный перево́д; (*as n.*): **the ~** (*believers*) правове́рные.

faithfully /ˈfeɪθfʊlɪ/ *adv.* то́чно, ве́рно; **I promise you ~** я вам то́чно обеща́ю; **yours ~** (*Br., letter-ending*) с соверше́нным почте́нием; **deal ~ with** (*treat candidly*) добросо́вестно относи́ться (*impf.*) к + *d*.

faithfulness /ˈfeɪθfʊlnɪs/ *n.* ве́рность.

faithless /ˈfeɪθlɪs/ *adj.* вероло́мный.

faithlessness /ˈfeɪθlɪsnɪs/ *n.* вероло́мство.

fake /feɪk/ *n.* (*sham*) подде́лка, фальши́вка; (*attr.*) подде́льный, фальши́вый; **a ~ antique** подде́лка под антиквариа́т.

● *v.t.* подде́л|ывать, -ать; **a ~d illness** притво́рная боле́знь.

faker /ˈfeɪkə(r)/ *n.* (*fabricator*) подде́лыватель (*m.*); (*fraudulent person*) обма́нщик.

fakery /ˈfeɪkərɪ/ *n.* подде́лка; притво́рство.

fakir /ˈfeɪkɪə(r)/, /fəˈkɪə(r)/ *n.* faки́р.

falcon /ˈfɔːlkən/, /ˈfɒlkən/ *n.* со́кол.

falconer /ˈfɔːlkənə(r)/, /ˈfɒl-/ *n.* соко́льничий; соколи́ный охо́тник.

falconry /ˈfɔːlkənrɪ/, /ˈfɒl-/ *n.* соколи́ная охо́та.

Falkland /ˈfɔːlklənd/ *n.*: **the ~s (*also* the ~ Islands)** Фолкле́ндские острова́ (*m. pl.*).

fall /fɔːl/ *n.* **1** (*physical drop, act of ~ing*) паде́ние; **he had a bad ~** он упа́л и си́льно ушибся; **a heavy ~ of rain** ли́вень (*m.*), проливно́й дождь; **~ of snow** снегопа́д.
2 (*moral*) паде́ние; **~ from grace** нра́вственное паде́ние; паде́ние в чьих-то глаза́х; **the ~ of man** (*relig.*) грехопаде́ние.
3: **the ~ of the Roman Empire** паде́ние Ри́мской импе́рии.
4 (*diminution*) пониже́ние; **~ in prices** паде́ние цен.
5 (*pl., waterfall*) водопа́д; **Niagara F~s** Ниага́рский водопа́д.
6 (*US, autumn*) о́сень.

● *v.i.* (*past* **fell;** *p.p.* **fallen**) **1** па́дать, упа́сть; **he fell over a chair** он упа́л, споткну́вшись о стул; **he fell full length** он растяну́лся во весь рост; **rain fell at last** наконе́ц вы́пал дождь; **many trees fell in the storm** бу́рей повали́ло мно́го дере́вьев; **leaves ~** ли́стья летя́т/опада́ют; **the river ~s into the lake** река́ впада́ет в о́зеро; **the arrow fell short** стрела́ не долете́ла до це́ли; **he fell off his horse** он упа́л с ло́шади; **he fell on his feet** (*fig.*) он счастли́во отде́лался; **the joke fell flat** шу́тка не име́ла успе́ха; **his work fell short of expectations** его́ рабо́та не оправда́ла ожида́ний/наде́жд; **he fell into the trap** он попа́л(ся) в лову́шку; **~ over o.s.** (*coll.*) (*from eagerness*) перестара́ться (*pf.*); лезть (*impf.*) из ко́жи вон.
2 (*drop, sink*) па́дать, пасть (*or* упа́сть); **the river has ~en** вода́ в реке́ спа́ла; **prices fell** це́ны сни́зились/упа́ли; **the temperature fell** температу́ра упа́ла; **my spirits fell** я упа́л ду́хом; **the wind fell** ве́тер стих; **his voice fell to a whisper** он перешёл на шёпот.
3 (*of defeat etc.*) па́|дать, -сть; **the city fell** го́род пал; **he fell in battle** он пал в бою́; **the ~en** (*in war*) па́вшие (*m. pl.*) в боя́х; **the government fell** прави́тельство па́ло.
4 (*morally*): **~en women** па́дшие же́нщины.
5 (*hang down*) па́дать (*impf.*); **his beard fell to his chest** борода́ па́дала ему́ на грудь; **her hair fell over her shoulders** во́лосы па́дали ей на пле́чи.
6 (*pass into a state*): **he fell silent** он замолча́л; **he fell ill** он заболе́л; **the rent fell due** подошёл срок плати́ть за кварти́ру; **he fell into disgrace** он впал в неми́лость; **the garden fell into neglect** сад пришёл в запусте́ние; **he fell in love with her** он влюби́лся в неё; **they fell into conversation** они́ разговори́лись.
7 (*come, alight*): **darkness fell** наступи́ла темнота́; **fear fell upon them** на них нашёл/напа́л страх; **I fell to wondering** я заду́мался; **his eye fell on a strange object** его́ взгляд упа́л на стра́нный предме́т; **suspicion fell on her** подозре́ние па́ло на неё; **stress falls on the first syllable** ударе́ние па́дает на пе́рвый слог; **the subject ~s into four parts** э́тот предме́т де́лится на четы́ре ча́сти; **it fell to his lot** ему́ вы́пало на до́лю; **it fell to me to welcome the speaker** мне на́до бы́ло приве́тствовать ора́тора; **Christmas Day ~s on a Tuesday** Рождество́ прихо́дится на вто́рник; **Easter ~s early this year** в э́том году́ ра́нняя Па́сха.
8 (*be uttered*): **these words fell from his lips** э́то слете́ло у него́ с языка́; **she let ~ a few words** она́ оброни́ла не́сколько слов.

● *with preps.* (*further examples*): **~ for** (**~** *in love with*) увл|ека́ться, -е́чься + *i.*; влюб|ля́ться, -и́ться в + *a.*; (*be taken in by*): **he fell for her story** он пове́рил её слова́м; он попа́лся ей на у́дочку; **~ over: he fell over a cliff** он сорва́лся со скалы́; **he fell over a bucket** он споткну́лся о ведро́ и упа́л; **~ to** (*begin*): **he fell to work** он приня́лся за рабо́ту; **~ upon** (*attack*) нап|ада́ть,

F

-áсть; набр|áсываться, -óситься; **they fell upon the enemy** они́ напáли на врагá; **he fell upon his dinner** он набрóсился на едý.

● *with advs.*: **~ about (with laughter)** (*Br. coll.*) лежáть (*impf.*) (от смéха); **the audience fell about** (*Br.*) пýблика лежáла; **~ apart** расп|адáться, -áсться; **~ away: his supporters fell away** сторóнники поки́нули егó (*or* отступи́лись от негó); **prejudices fell away** предрассýдки исчéзли; **~ back** (*retreat*) приб|егáть, -éгнуть к чемý-н.; **~ back on something** приб|егáть, -éгнуть к чемý-н.; **~ behind** (*e.g. in walking*) отст|авáть, -áть; (*with letters*) задéрж|иваться, -áться с отвéтом; (*with rent*) зап|áздывать, -оздáть с уплáтой за квартиру; **~ down** (*lit.*) пáдать, упáсть; **he fell down on the task** (*coll.*) он не спрáвился с задáнием; **~ in** впасть (*во что*); **the roof fell in** кры́ша рýхнула/обвали́лась; **the soldiers fell in** солдáты стáли в строй (*or* пострóились); **~ in!** (*mil.*) станови́сь!; **he fell in with my views** он согласи́лся со мной; **~ off** пáдать, упáсть (*с чего*); **attendance is ~ing off** посещáемость пáдает; **the quality fell off** кáчество сни́зилось; **~ing-off** (*deterioration*) падéние, упáдок; **~ out** выпадáть, вы́пасть; **his hair fell out** у негó вы́пали вóлосы; (*quarrel*) поссóриться (*pf.*); **~ing-out** (*quarrel*) размóлвка, ссóра; (*mil.*) выходи́ть, вы́йти из стрóя; разойти́сь (*pf.*); **~ out!** разойди́сь!; (*withdraw*): **six competitors fell out** шéстеро вы́пали из соревновáний; **~ over** пáдать, упáсть; **he fell over backwards to please** он лез из кóжи вон, чтóбы угоди́ть +*d.*; **~ through** провáл|иваться, -и́ться; **~ to** (*start eating or fighting*) набр|áсываться, -óситься (друг на дрýга) (на едý).

● *cpd.* **~-out** *n.* (*nuclear*) радиоакти́вные осáдки (*m. pl.*); выпадéние радиоакти́вных осáдков.

fallacious /fəˈleɪʃəs/ *adj.* оши́бочный, лóжный.

fallaciousness /fəˈleɪʃəsnɪs/ *n.* оши́бочность, лóжность.

fallacy /ˈfæləsɪ/ *n.* (*false belief*) заблуждéние; **popular ~** распространённое заблуждéние; (*false reasoning*) оши́бочный вы́вод.

fallen /ˈfɔːl(ə)n/ *p.p. of* ⇒**fall**

fallibility /ˌfælɪˈbɪlɪtɪ/ *n.* погреши́мость; подвéрженность оши́бкам.

fallible /ˈfælɪb(ə)l/ *adj.* подвéрженный оши́бкам, могýщий ошибáться.

Fallopian tube /fəˈləʊpɪən/ *n.* Фаллóпиева трубá.

fallow /ˈfæləʊ/ *adj.* вспáханный под пар; **~ land** пар; **lie ~** ост|авáться, -áться под пáром.

fallow-deer /ˈfæləʊ/ *n.* лань.

false /fɒls/, /fɔːls/ *adj.* **1** (*wrong, incorrect*) лóжный, оши́бочный, фальши́вый; **a ~ note** фальши́вая нóта; **a ~ step** лóжный шаг; **he was in a ~ position** он оказáлся в лóжном положéнии; **is this statement true or ~?** вéрно э́то утверждéние и́ли нет?; **~ pride** лóжная гóрдость; **~ start** фальстáрт (*races*); срыв в сáмом начáле; **~ alarm** лóжная тревóга. **2** (*deceitful, treacherous*) лжи́вый, верелóмный; **bear ~ witness** лжесвидéтельствовать (*impf.*); **he was ~ to her** он был ей невéрен; **sail under ~ colours** (*Br.*), **colors** (*US*) плыть (*impf.*) под чужи́м флáгом; (*fig.*) выступáть (*impf.*) под мáской/личи́ной; **~ pretences** (*Br.*), **pretenses** (*US*) обмáн, притвóрство; (*adv.*): **he played me ~** он прéдал меня́. **3** (*sham, apparent*) фальши́вый; **~ hair** накладны́е вóлосы; **~ teeth** искýсственные зýбы; **~ bottom** двойнóе дно; **~ acacia** лóжная акáция, лжеакáция.

falsehood /ˈfɒlshʊd/, /ˈfɔːls-/ *n.* ложь, неправда; **he told a ~** он сказáл непрáвду.

falseness /ˈfɒlsnɪs/, /ˈfɔːlsnɪs/ *n.* (*wrongness*) лóжность, оши́бочность; (*insincerity*) нейскренность; (*treachery*) лжи́вость.

falsetto /fɒlˈsetəʊ/, /fɔːl-/ *n.* (*pl.* **~s**) фальцéт.

falsification /ˌfɒlsɪfɪˈkeɪʃ(ə)n/, /ˌfɔːls-/ *n.* фальсификáция.

falsifier /ˈfɒlsɪˌfaɪə(r)/, /ˈfɔːls-/ *n.* фальсификáтор.

falsif|y /ˈfɒlsɪˌfaɪ/, /ˈfɔːls-/ *v.t.* (*e.g. accounts*) поддéл|ывать, -ать; фальсифици́ровать (*impf.*, *pf.*); **my hopes were ~ied** мои́ надéжды бы́ли напрáсны.

falsity /ˈfɒlsɪtɪ/, /ˈfɔːlsɪtɪ/ *n.* (*falsehood, inaccuracy*) лóжность, оши́бочность.

falter /ˈfɒltə(r)/, /ˈfɔːl-/ *v.i.* (*move or act hesitatingly*) спотыкáться (*impf.*); (*in speaking*) зап|инáться, -нýться.

faltering /ˈfɒltərɪŋ/, /ˈfɔːl-/ *adj.* запинáющийся, прерывáющийся; **~ gait** невéрная похóдка; **a ~ voice** дрожáщий гóлос; **he spoke ~ly** он говори́л с запи́нкой.

fame /feɪm/ *n.* слáва; репутáция; **house of ill ~** публи́чный дом.

● *v.t.*: **he was ~d for valour** (*Br.*), **valor** (*US*) он прослáвился своéй дóблестью.

familial /fəˈmɪlɪəl/ *adj.* семéйный, фами́льный.

familiar /fəˈmɪlɪə(r)/ *n.* (*intimate*) бли́зкий друг.

● *adj.* **1** (*common, usual*) обы́чный, привы́чный. **2** (*of acquaintance*) знакóмый; **I am ~ with the subject** я знакóм с э́тим предмéтом; **your face is ~** вáше лицó мне знакóмо. **3** (*friendly*) дрýжеский. **4** (*casual, impudent*) бесцеремóнный, фамилья́рный.

familiarity /fəˌmɪlɪˈærɪtɪ/ *n.* **1** (*close acquaintance with person or thing*) бли́зкое знакóмство (с + *i.*); **~ breeds contempt** чем бли́же знáешь человéка, тем мéньше егó уважáешь. **2** (*of manner*) фамилья́рность.

familiarization /fəˌmɪlɪəraɪˈzeɪʃ(ə)n/ *n.* ознакомлéние (*с чем*).

familiarize /fəˈmɪlɪəˌraɪz/ *v.t.* ознак|омля́ть, -óмить (*кого с чем*); **~ o.s. with something** ознакóмиться (*pf.*) с чем-н.

family /ˈfæmɪlɪ/, /ˈfæmlɪ/ *n.* **1** (*parents and children*) семья́; **extended ~** расши́ренная семья́; **nuclear ~** нуклеáрная семья́; **the Holy F~** Святóе семéйство. **2** (*children*) дéт|и (*pl.*, *g.* -éй); **they have a large ~** у них мнóго детéй. **3** (*descendants of common ancestor*) семья́, род; **a man of good ~** человéк из хорóшей семьи́. **4** (*of animals etc.*) семéйство. **5** (*attr.*) семéйный; **a ~ man** семьяни́н, семéйный человéк; **~ likeness** семéйное/фами́льное схóдство; **~ friend** друг семьи́; **~ name** (*surname*) фами́лия; **~ tree** родослóвное дéрево; **~ planning** контрóль (*m.*) над рождáемостью; **in the ~ way** (*coll.*) в интерéсном положéнии.

famine /ˈfæmɪn/ *n.* гóлод.

famish /ˈfæmɪʃ/ *v.t.* мори́ть (*impf.*) гóлодом; **I'm ~ed** я си́льно проголодáлся; я умирáю с гóлоду; **the child looks half ~ed** у ребёнка голóдный вид.

famous /ˈfeɪməs/ *adj.* знамени́тый, прослáвленный; **the road is ~ for its views** э́та дорóга извéстна тем, что óчень живопи́сна.

fan[1] /fæn/ *n.* вéер; (*ventilator*) вентиля́тор.

● *v.t.* (**fanned, fanning**): **~ o.s.** обмáхиваться (*impf.*) вéером; **he ~ned the spark into a blaze** он разжёг из и́скры плáмя; **the breeze ~ned our faces** ветерóк обвевáл нам лицó.

● *v.i.* (**fanned, fanning**): **~ out** (*e.g. roads*) расходи́ться (*impf.*) вéером; (*e.g. soldiers*) развёр|тываться, -нýться вéером.

● *cpds.* **~-belt** *n.* ремéнь (*m.*) вентиля́тора; **~-light** *n.* веерообрáзное окнó; **~-vaulting** *n.* ребри́стый свод.

fan[2] /fæn/ *n.* (*coll., devotee*) болéльщи|к (*fem.* -ца), люби́тель (*m.*) (*fem.* -ница).

● *cpd.* **~-mail** *n.* пи́сьма (*nt. pl.*) от поклóнников.

fanatic /fəˈnætɪk/ *n.* фанáтик.

● *adj.* (*also* **~al**) фанати́чный, фанати́ческий.

fanaticism /fəˈnætɪˌsɪz(ə)m/ *n.* фанати́зм.

fancier /ˈfænsɪə(r)/ *n.* люби́тель (*m.*), знатóк (*чего*).

fanciful /ˈfænsɪˌfʊl/ *adj.* капри́зный; причýдливый.

fancifulness /ˈfænsɪˌfʊlnɪs/ *n.* прихотли́вость, причýдливость.

fancy /ˈfænsɪ/ *n.* **1** (*imagination*) фантáзия, воображéние. **2** (*thing imagined, supposition*) фантáзия. **3** (*liking*) склóнность; **he took a ~ to her** он éю увлёкся; **it caught my ~** э́то мне понрáвилось (*or* пришлóсь по вкýсу); **a passing ~** мимолётное увлечéние. **4** (*as adj.*) (**fancier, fanciest**): **~ cakes** фигýрные пирóжные; **~ dress**

маскара́дный костю́м; **~-dress ball** костюми́рованный бал; **a ~ price** непоме́рная цена́; **~ goods** безделу́шки (*f. pl.*); **this dress is too ~ to wear to work** для рабо́ты ну́жно пла́тье поскромне́е.

● *v.t.* **1** (*imagine*) вообра|жа́ть, -зи́ть; **~ (that)!** вообрази́те!; поду́мать то́лько!; **~ his being here!** кто б мог поду́мать, что он здесь!
2 (*suppose, feel*) полага́ть (*impf.*); счита́ть (*impf.*); **I ~ he will come** мне сдаётся, что он придёт.
3 (*Br., like, wish*) хоте́ть (*impf.*) +*g.*; жела́ть (*impf.*); **I don't ~ this place** мне не по душе́ (*or* не нра́вится) э́то ме́сто; **she fancies him** (*coll.*) он ей нра́вится; **he fancies himself as a speaker** он вообража́ет себя́ ора́тором; **what do you ~ for dinner?** чего́ бы вам хоте́лось на у́жин?

● *cpd.* **~-free** *adj.* свобо́дный от привя́занностей; невлюблённый.

fanfare /ˈfænfeə(r)/ *n.* фанфа́ра.

fang /fæŋ/ *n.* (*of wolf etc.*) клык; (*of snake*) ядови́тый зуб.

fanny /ˈfænɪ/ *n.* (*Br. vulg., female genitals*) пизда́; (*US sl., buttocks*) за́дница, по́пка.

● *cpd.* **~ pack** *n.* (*US sl.*) поясно́й кошелёк.

fantasia /fænˈteɪzɪə/, /ˌfæntəˈzɪə/ *n.* фанта́зия.

fantasize /ˈfæntəˌsaɪz/ *v.i.* фантази́ровать (*impf.*).

fantastic /fænˈtæstɪk/ *adj.* (*wild, strange, absurd*) фантасти́ческий, фантасти́чный; (*coll., marvellous*) потряса́ющий, изуми́тельный.

fantasy /ˈfæntəsɪ/, /-zɪ/ *n.* фанта́зия; (*genre*) фанта́стика.

FAO (*abbr. of* ***Food and Agriculture Organization of the United Nations***) ФА́О (Продово́льственная и сельскохозя́йственная организа́ция Объединённых На́ций).

f.a.o. (*abbr. of* ***for the attention of***) вним. (+*g.*), (внима́нию (+*g.*)).

FAQ (*abbr. of* ***frequently asked questions***) (*comput.*) ча́сто задава́емые вопро́сы.

far /fɑː(r)/ *n.* (*of distance or amount*): **have you come from ~?** вы издалека́ прие́хали?; **this is better by ~** э́то намно́го лу́чше.

● *adj.* (**further, furthest** *or* **farther, farthest**) да́льний, далёкий, отдалённый; **a ~ country** далёкая страна́; **a ~ journey** да́льнее путеше́ствие; **the F~ East** Да́льний Восто́к; **at the ~ end of the street** на друго́м конце́ у́лицы.

● *adv.* (**further, furthest** *or* **farther, farthest**) далеко́; **~ away, off** о́чень далеко́; **~ and near, wide** повсю́ду; **they came from ~ and wide** они́ съе́хались отовсю́ду (*or* со всех концо́в); **~ into the air** высоко́ в во́здух; **~ into the night** далеко́ за́ полночь; **~ better** (на)мно́го/гора́здо лу́чше; **~ different** соверше́нно друго́й; **~ (and away) the best** несравне́нно/намно́го лу́чше други́х; **it is ~ from true** э́то совсе́м не так; **~ from satisfactory** весьма́ неудовлетвори́тельный; **not ~ wrong** не так уж далеко́ от и́стины; **~ from it!** ничу́ть!; отню́дь нет!; **~ be it from me to condemn him** я далёк от того́, что́бы осужда́ть его́; **~ from helping, he made things worse** он не то́лько не помо́г де́лу, но про́сто всё испо́ртил; **as ~ back as January** ещё/уже́ в январе́; **so ~** (*until now*) до сих пор; пока́ (что); **so ~, so good** пока́ всё хорошо́; **as/so ~ as** (*of distance*) до (*чего*); (*of extent*) наско́лько; поско́льку; **as ~ as I know** наско́лько мне изве́стно; **as ~ as I am concerned** что каса́ется меня́; **he went so ~ as to say ...** он да́же сказа́л..., **in so ~ as** (*to the extent that*) поско́льку, насто́лько; **how ~** (*of distance*) как далеко́; (*of extent*) наско́лько; **he will go ~** (*succeed*) он далеко́ пойдёт; **£5 will not go ~** на пять фу́нтов далеко́ не уе́дешь; **this will go ~ to pay our expenses** э́то почти́ покро́ет на́ши расхо́ды; **he has gone too ~ this time** на э́то раз он зашёл сли́шком далеко́; **he is ~ gone** (*of illness*) он совсе́м плох; **few and ~ between** ре́дкие (*pl.*).

● *cpds.* **~-away** *adj.* (*distant*) далёкий, отдалённый; (*absent*): **a ~-away look** отсу́тствующий взгляд; **F~ Eastern** *adj.* дальневосто́чный; **~-fetched** *adj.* с натя́жкой; притя́нутый за́ волосы/уши; **~-flung** *adj.* обши́рный; широко́ раски́нувшийся; **~-off** *adj.* отдалённый; **~-reaching** *adj.* далеко́ иду́щий; **~-seeing** *adj.* дальнови́дный, прозорли́вый; **~-sighted** *adj.* (*prudent etc.*) дальнови́дный, предусмотри́тельный; (*long-sighted*) дальнозо́ркий.

farad /ˈfærəd/ *n.* (*electr.*) фара́да.

farce /fɑːs/ *n.* (*theatr., fig.*) фарс.

farcical /ˈfɑːsɪk(ə)l/ *adj.* смехотво́рный, неле́пый.

fare[1] /feə(r)/ *n.* **1** (*cost of journey*) пла́та за прое́зд; **what is the ~?** ско́лько сто́ит прое́зд/биле́т? **2** (*passenger*) пассажи́р.

● *v.i.* (*progress, prosper*): **how did you ~ on the journey?** как вы съе́здили?; **how's he faring?** как у него́ дела́?; **she ~d well in the exam** она́ хорошо́ сдала́ экза́мен.

● *cpd.* **~-paying** *adj.* платя́щий за прое́зд.

fare[2] /feə(r)/ *n.* (*food*) стол; съестны́е припа́с|ы (*pl., g.* -ов); **bill of ~** меню́ (*nt. indecl.*).

farewell /feəˈwel/ *n.* проща́ние; **~ dinner** проща́льный у́жин; **make one's ~s, bid ~ (to)** про|ща́ться, -сти́ться (с+*i.*).

● *int.* проща́й(те).

farinaceous /ˌfærɪˈneɪʃəs/ *adj.* мучни́стый, мучно́й.

farm /fɑːm/ *n.* фе́рма; (*in former USSR, collective ~*) колхо́з; **state ~** совхо́з; **dairy ~** моло́чная фе́рма; **~ worker** рабо́тни|к (*fem.* -ца) на фе́рме; сельскохозя́йственный рабо́чий.

● *v.t. & i.* **1** (*agric.*) занима́ться (*impf.*) се́льским хозя́йством; быть фе́рмером; **he ~s 200 hectares** он обраба́тывает 200 гекта́ров земли́.
2: **~ out** (*taxes*) отд|ава́ть, -а́ть на о́ткуп; **~ out work** отд|ава́ть, -а́ть часть рабо́ты.

● *cpds.* **~-hand, ~-labourer** (*US* **-laborer**) *nn.* рабо́тник на фе́рме; сельскохозя́йственный рабо́чий; **~house** *n.* фе́рмерский дом; **~stead** *n.* фе́рма со слу́жбами; хозя́йство; **~yard** *n.* двор фе́рмы.

farmer /ˈfɑːmə(r)/ *n.* фе́рмер.

faro /ˈfeərəʊ/ *n.* фарао́н.

farouche /fəˈruːʃ/ *adj.* ди́кий, нелюди́мый.

farrago /fəˈrɑːgəʊ/ *n.* (*pl.* **~s** *or US* **~es**) мешани́на; вся́кая вся́чина; (*nonsense*) чепуха́.

farrier /ˈfærɪə(r)/ *n.* ко́вочный кузне́ц; (*mil.*) конов́од.

farrow /ˈfærəʊ/ *n.* опоро́с; **in ~** супоро́с(н)ая.

● *v.i.* пороси́ться, о-.

fart /fɑːt/ (*vulg.*) *n.* пук.

● *v.i.* перде́ть, пёрнуть; пу́к|ать, -нуть.

farther /ˈfɑːðə(r)/ (*see also* ⇒**further**) *adj.* бо́лее отдалённый; дальне́йший.

● *adv.* да́льше, да́лее.

farthermost /ˈfɑːðəˌməʊst/ *adj.* (*see also* ⇒**furthermost**) са́мый да́льний/отдалённый.

farthest /ˈfɑːðɪst/ (*see also* ⇒**furthest**) *adj.* са́мый да́льний.

● *adv.* да́льше всего́.

farthing /ˈfɑːðɪŋ/ *n.* (*hist.*) фа́ртинг.

farthingale /ˈfɑːðɪŋˌgeɪl/ *n.* (*hist.*) ю́бка с фи́жмами.

fascia /ˈfeɪʃə/ *n.* (*pl.* **fasciae** /-ʃɪiː/ *or* **fascias**) (*Br., over shop-front*) вы́веска; (*Br., dashboard*) прибо́рная доска́; (*archit., flat piece of material*) полоса́; по́яс.

fascicle /ˈfæsɪk(ə)l/ *n.* (*bot.*) пучо́к, гро́здь; (*of book*) (отде́льный) вы́пуск.

fascinate /ˈfæsɪˌneɪt/ *v.t.* очаро́в|ывать, -а́ть; плен|я́ть, -и́ть.

fascinating /ˈfæsɪˌneɪtɪŋ/ *adj.* очарова́тельный, плени́тельный; (*story*) захва́тывающий.

fascination /ˌfæsɪˈneɪʃ(ə)n/ *n.* очарова́ние, обая́ние, пре́лесть.

Fascism /ˈfæʃɪz(ə)m/ *n.* фаши́зм.

Fascist /ˈfæʃɪst/ *n.* фаши́ст (*fem.* -ка).

● *adj.* фаши́стский.

fashion /ˈfæʃ(ə)n/ *n.* **1** (*way*) о́браз, мане́ра; **after a ~** (*indifferently*) до не́которой сте́пени; **after the ~ of** по образцу́ +*g.* **2** (*prevailing style*) мо́да; **in ~** в мо́де; **out of ~** вы́шедший из мо́ды; **in the height of ~** по после́дней мо́де; после́дний крик мо́ды; **~ designer** моделье́р; **~ house** дом моде́лей; **~ magazine, paper** журна́л мод; **~ parade/show** демонстра́ция мод.

● *v.t.* (*e.g. an object*) прид|ава́ть, -а́ть фо́рму +*d.*; (*e.g. s.o.'s taste*) формирова́ть, с-.

● *cpd.* **~-plate** *n.* мо́дная карти́нка.

fashionable /ˈfæʃnəb(ə)l/ *adj.* мóдный.

fashionableness /ˈfæʃ(ə)nəbəlnɪs/ *n.* соответствие мóде.

fast[1] /fɑːst/ *n.* пост; **break one's ~** разгов|ля́ться, -éться.

● *v.i.* пости́ться (*impf.*).

● *cpd.* **~-day** *n.* пóстный день.

fast[2] /fɑːst/ *adj.* (*firm, secure*) прóчный, крéпкий; **the post is ~ in the ground** столб прóчно вбит в зéмлю; **he made the boat ~** он привязáл лóдку; **the door is ~** дверь плóтно закры́та; **~ friends** вéрные друзья́; **~ colours** (*Br.*), **colors** (*US*) стóйкие цветá.

● *adv.* прóчно, крéпко; **she was ~ asleep** онá крéпко спалá; **he stood ~** он стоя́л твёрдо; (*fig.*) он твёрдо стоя́л на своём; **the car stuck ~** маши́на застря́ла/завя́зла;

fast[3] /fɑːst/ *adj.* **1** (*rapid*) скóрый, бы́стрый; **~ lane** (*on road*) скоростнóй ряд; **~ food restaurant** ресторáн бы́строго обслу́живания; **he is a ~ worker** он бы́стро рабóтает; **my watch is ~** мои́ часы́ спешáт; **pull a ~ one on s.o.** над|увáть, -у́ть когó-н. **2** (*dissipated*) беспу́тный; **a ~ woman** жéнщина лёгкого поведéния.

fasten /ˈfɑːs(ə)n/ *v.t.* **1** (*doors, windows*) зап|ирáть, -ерéть; (*dress, coat*) застёг|ивать, -ну́ть; (*shoelaces*) завя́з|ывать, -áть; (*seat-belt*) пристёг|ивать, -ну́ть; (*with rope etc.*) привя́з|ывать, -áть; (*make firmer*) прикреп|ля́ть, -и́ть; **he ~ed the sheets of paper together** он скрепи́л вмéсте листы́ бумáги. **2** (*fig.*): **he ~ed his eyes on me** он устáвился на меня́; **they ~ed the crime on him** емý приписáли э́то преступлéние.

● *v.i.* **1** зап|ирáться, -ерéться; **the door won't ~** дверь не закрывáется/запирáется; **the dress ~s down the back** плáтье застёгивается на спинé. **2**: **he ~ed upon the idea** он ухвати́лся за э́ту мысль.

fasten|er /ˈfɑːs(ə)nə(r)/, **-ing** /ˈfɑːsnɪŋ/ *nn.* запóр, задви́жка; (*on dress*) застёжка.

fastidious /fæˈstɪdɪəs/ *adj.* приверéдливый, щепети́льный; разбóрчивый.

fastidiousness /fæˈstɪdɪəsnɪs/ *n.* приверéдливость, щепети́льность; разбóрчивость.

fastness /ˈfɑːstnɪs/ *n.* (*of dyes etc.*) прóчность, стóйкость; (*stronghold*) оплóт, цитадéль.

fat /fæt/ *n.* **1** жир. **2** (*fig., richness*): **they live on the ~ of the land** они́ купáются в рóскоши.

● *adj.* (**fatter, fattest**) **1** (*of person etc.*) тóлстый, жи́рный, ту́чный; **get ~** толстéть, по-; **~ cheeks** пу́хлые щёки; **~ fingers** тóлстые пáльцы; (*of food*) жи́рный. **2** (*rich, fertile*): **a ~ profit** большáя при́быль; (*pej.*) жи́рный кусóк. **3** (*coll., iron.*): **a ~ lot you care!** а тебé наплевáть!; óчень тебя́ э́то беспокóит!; **that's a ~ lot of use** мнóго с э́того тóлку.

● *cpds.* **~head** *n.* (*coll.*) болвáн, тупи́ца (*c.g.*); **~-headed** *adj.* тупоголóвый.

fatal /ˈfeɪt(ə)l/ *adj.* **1** (*causing death*) смертéльный, ги́бельный, пáгубный; **a ~ accident** несчáстный слу́чай со смертéльным исхóдом. **2** (*disastrous*) роковóй, фатáльный; **he made a ~ error** он сдéлал роковýю оши́бку.

fatalism /ˈfeɪtəˌlɪz(ə)m/ *n.* фатали́зм.

fatalist /ˈfeɪtəlɪst/ *n.* фатали́ст.

fatalistic /ˌfeɪtəˈlɪstɪk/ *adj.* фаталисти́ческий, фаталисти́чный.

fatality /fəˈtælətɪ/ *n.* (*natural calamity*) стихи́йное бéдствие; (*fatal accident*) смерть от несчáстного слу́чая; (*destiny*) рок, фатáльность.

fate /feɪt/ *n.* **1** (*personified destiny*) судьбá, рок; **as sure as ~** несомнéнно. **2** (*what is in store for one*) судьбá, у́часть, удéл, дóля; **they met their various ~s** кáждому из них достáлся свой удéл. **3** (*death*) ги́бель, смерть; **he sent him to his ~** он послáл егó на ги́бель.

● *v.t.* предопредел|я́ть, -и́ть; **he was ~d to die** емý сужденó бы́ло поги́бнуть.

fateful /ˈfeɪtfʊl/ *adj.* роковóй.

father /ˈfɑːðə(r)/ *n.* **1** (*male parent, also fig.*) отéц, роди́тель (*m.*); **the wish was ~ to the thought** он при́нял желáемое за действи́тельное; **God the F~** Бог-Отéц; **our Heavenly F~** Отéц Небéсный; **Our F~** (*prayer*) Óтче наш. **2** (*pl., ancestors*) отцы́, дéды (*m. pl.*). **3** (*founder, leader*) отéц, родоначáльник; **city ~s** отцы́ гóрода; **the Pilgrim F~s** отцы́-пилигри́мы. **4** (*oldest member*) старéйшина (*m.*). **5** (*in personifications*): **F~ Christmas** дед-морóз; **F~ Thames** мáтушка Тéмза; **F~ Time** врéмя. **6** (*priest*) отéц, бáтюшка; **the Holy F~** егó святéйшество; (*as title*): **F~ Sergius** отéц Сéргий.

● *v.t.* **1** (*beget*) поро|ждáть, -ди́ть; быть (*impf.*)/стать (*pf.*) отцóм + *g.* **2** (*fig., originate*) поро|ждáть, -ди́ть. **3** (*fix responsibility*): **do not ~ this scheme on me** не припи́сывайте э́тот плáн мне.

● *cpds.* **~-figure** *n.* ктó-н., заменя́ющий отцá; **~-in-law** *n.* (*husband's ~*) свёкор; (*wife's ~*) тесть (*m.*); **~land** *n.* отéчество, отчи́зна, рóдина.

fatherhood /ˈfɑːðəˌhʊd/ *n.* отцóвство.

fatherless /ˈfɑːðəlɪs/ *adj.* без отцá.

fatherliness /ˈfɑːðəlɪnɪs/ *n.* отéческое отношéние.

fatherly /ˈfɑːðəlɪ/ *adj.* отéческий.

fathom /ˈfæð(ə)m/ *n.* морскáя сажéнь.

● *v.t.* (*lit.*) изм|еря́ть, -éрить глубинý + *g.*; (*fig.*) пост|игáть, -и́гнуть; вн|икáть, -и́кнуть в + *a.*

fathomless /ˈfæðəmlɪs/ *adj.* (*very deep*) бездóнный; (*incomprehensible*) непостижи́мый.

fatigue /fəˈtiːg/ *n.* устáлость (**also metal ~**); (*mil.*) (*pl., menial tasks*) хозя́йственная рабóта; (*pl., dress*) рабóчая одéжда, спецодéжда, комбинезóн (*в армии*).

● *v.t.* (**fatigues, fatigued, fatiguing**) утом|ля́ть, -и́ть.

● *cpds.* **~-dress** *n.* рабóчая одéжда; спецодéжда; **~-duty** *n.* хозя́йственные рабóты (*f. pl.*); **~-party** *n.* рабóчая комáнда.

fatness /ˈfætnɪs/ *n.* полнотá.

fatted /ˈfætɪd/ *adj.* откóрмленный; **kill the ~ calf** *see* ⇒**calf**[1]

fatten /ˈfæt(ə)n/ *v.t.* (*animal*) отк|áрмливать, -орми́ть на убóй.

● *v.i.* жирéть (*impf.*); толстéть (*impf.*).

fattening /ˈfæt(ə)nɪŋ/ *adj.* калори́йный.

fattiness /ˈfætɪnɪs/ *n.* (*of meat etc.*) жи́рность.

fattish /ˈfætɪʃ/ *adj.* толстовáтый, полновáтый.

fatty /ˈfætɪ/ *n.* (*coll.*) толстя́к.

● *adj.* (**fattier, fattiest**) жи́рный, жировóй; **~ bacon** жи́рный бекóн; **~ tissue** жировáя ткань.

fatuity /fəˈtjuːɪtɪ/ *n.* самодовóльная глу́пость.

fatuous /ˈfætjʊəs/ *adj.* самодовóльно-глу́пый; бессмы́сленный.

faucet /ˈfɔːsɪt/ *n.* (*US, tap*) кран.

fault /fɒlt/, /fɔːlt/ *n.* **1** (*imperfection*) недостáток, дефéкт; **generous to a ~** чересчу́р щéдрый; **find ~ with s.o.** на|ходи́ть, -йти́ недостáтки у когó-н.; прид|ирáться, -рáться к комý-н.; **my memory was at ~** пáмять мне измени́ла. **2** (*physical defect*) дефéкт; **there was a ~ in the electric connection** в электри́ческой сети́ былá неисправность. **3** (*error*) оши́бка. **4** (*blame*) винá; **it's (all) your ~** э́то вáша винá; э́то всё из-за вас; **the ~ lies with him** он виновáт. **5** (*at tennis etc.*) непрáвильная подáча; **double ~** двойнáя оши́бка. **6** (*geol.*) разлóм, сдвиг.

● *v.t.* на|ходи́ть, -йти́ недостáтки в + *p.*; прид|ирáться, -рáться к + *d.*; **I could not ~ his argument** я не мог придрáться к егó аргументáции.

● *cpds.* **~-finder** *n.* приди́ра (*c.g.*); **~-finding** *n.* приди́рчивость; *adj.* приди́рчивый.

faultiness /ˈfɒltɪnɪs/, /ˈfɔːltɪnɪs/ *n.* оши́бочность.

faultless /ˈfɒltlɪs/, /ˈfɔːlt-/ *adj.* (*without blame*) непогреши́мый; безоши́бочный; (*without blemish*): **~ precision** безупрéчная тóчность.

faulty /ˈfɒltɪ/, /ˈfɔːltɪ/ *adv.* (**faultier, faultiest**) оши́бочный; с изъя́ном; **a ~ memory** слáбая пáмять; **a ~ connection** (*tech.*) повреждённое соединéние.

faun /fɔːn/ *n.* фавн.

fauna /ˈfɔːnə/ *n.* (*pl.* **~s**) фáуна.

faute de mieux /ˌfəʊt də ˈmjɜː/ за неимéнием лу́чшего.

faux pas /fəʊ ˈpɑː/ *n.* (*pl.* **~**) бестáктность.

favour /ˈfeɪvə(r)/ (*US* **favor**) *n.* **1** (*goodwill*) благосклóнность; расположéние (к + *d.*); **win s.o.'s ~**; **find ~ in s.o.'s eyes** снискáть (*pf.*)

чьё-н. расположе́ние (*or* чью-н. благоскло́нность); **look with ~ on** благоскло́нно/доброжела́тельно относи́ться (*impf.*) к + *d.*; **curry ~ with s.o.** заискивать (*impf.*) пе́ред кем-н.; **he is out of ~ with his superiors** он не в че́сти́ у нача́льства; **I am in ~ of the plan** я — за э́тот план.
2 (*kindly act*) одолже́ние, любе́зность, услу́га; **he did me a ~** он оказа́л мне любе́зность; он сде́лал мне одолже́ние.
3 (*advantage, credit*) по́льза; **this is in his ~** э́то говори́т в его́ по́льзу; **the exchange rate is in our ~** курс обме́на валю́ты вы́годен для нас.
4 (*privilege*): **I don't ask for any ~s** я не прошу́ одолже́ний/привиле́гий.
5 (*prejudice*): **without fear or ~** беспристра́стно.
● *v.t.* **1** (*approve, support*) благоприя́тствовать (*impf.*) + *d.*; подде́рж|ивать, -а́ть; **fortune ~s the brave** сме́лость города́ берёт; **this ~s my theory** э́то подтвержда́ет мою́ тео́рию.
2 (*choose*) предпоч|ита́ть, -е́сть; **I ~ the grey horse (to win)** по-мо́ему, у се́рой ло́шади бо́льше ша́нсов вы́играть; **she ~ed a pink dress** она́ вы́брала ро́зовое пла́тье.
3 (*treat with partiality*) ока́з|ывать, -а́ть предпочте́ние + *d.*; быть приστра́стным к + *d.*; **he ~s certain pupils** он ока́зывает предпочте́ние не́которым ученика́м.
4 (*oblige, treat favourably*): **she ~ed us with a song** она́ оказа́ла нам любе́зность, испо́лнив пе́сню; **most ~ed nation** наибо́лее благоприя́тствуемая на́ция; **the ~ed few** немно́гие избра́нные.
5 (*resemble*) походи́ть (*impf.*) на + *a.*; **the child ~s its father** ребёнок похо́ж на своего́ отца́.

favourable /ˈfeɪvərəb(ə)l/ (*US* **favorable**) *adj.* благоприя́тный, благоскло́нный; **~ weather** благоприя́тная пого́да; **a ~ report** положи́тельный отчёт.

favourableness /ˈfeɪvərəbəlnɪs/ (*US* **favorableness**) *n.* благоприя́тность; благоприя́тное/благоскло́нное отноше́ние (к + *d.*).

favourite /ˈfeɪvərɪt/ (*US* **favorite**) *n.* (*preferred person*) люби́мец, фаворит; (*preferred thing*) люби́мая вещь; (*horse*) фаворит.
● *adj.* люби́мый, излю́бленный; **my ~ food** моя́ люби́мая еда́.

favouritism /ˈfeɪvərɪˌtɪz(ə)m/ (*US* **favoritism**) *n.* фаворити́зм.

fawn¹ /fɔːn/ *n.* (*deer*) молодо́й оле́нь; (*colour*) желтова́то-кори́чневый цвет.
● *adj.* (*also* **~-coloured** (*Br.*), **-colored** (*US*)) желтова́то-кори́чневый.

fawn² /fɔːn/ *v.i.* (*of dog*) ласка́ться (*impf.*); (*of person*): **~ on s.o.** подли́з|ываться, -а́ться к кому́-н.; выслу́живаться (*impf.*) пе́ред кем-н.

fax /fæks/ *n.* факс; **~ machine** факс, факси́мильный аппара́т.
● *v.t.* пос|ыла́ть, -ла́ть фа́ксом.

faze /feɪz/ *v.t.* сму|ща́ть, -ти́ть; прив|оди́ть, -ести́ в недоуме́ние.

FBI (*abbr. of* ***Federal Bureau of Investigation***) ФБР (Федера́льное бюро́ рассле́дований).

FCO (*abbr. of* ***Foreign and Commonwealth Office***) (*Br.*) МИД (*Министе́рство иностра́нных дел*).

fealty /ˈfiːəltɪ/ *n.* ве́рность васса́ла феода́лу; **swear, do ~ to s.o.** присяг|а́ть, -ну́ть на ве́рность кому́-н.

fear /fɪə(r)/ *n.* **1** (*terror, anxiety*) страх, боя́знь, опасе́ние; **in ~ and trembling** дрожа́ от стра́ха; **the ~ of God** страх бо́жий; **I put the ~ of God into him** (*coll.*) я нагна́л на него́ стра́ху; **he was in ~ of his life** он боя́лся за свою́ жизнь; **I could not speak for ~** от стра́ха я не мог говори́ть; **your ~s are groundless** ва́ши опасе́ния напра́сны.
2 (*of precaution, likelihood*): **I was silent for ~ of offending him** я молча́л, боя́сь оби́деть его́; **we tethered the horse for ~ it should escape** мы привяза́ли ло́шадь, что́бы она́ не убежа́ла; **there is no ~ of my losing the money** не бо́йтесь, я не потеря́ю де́ньги; **no ~!** (*Br. coll.*) ни-ни́!; ни за что!
● *v.t. & i.* боя́ться (*impf.*) + *g.*; опаса́ться (*impf.*) + *g.*; **he ~s death** он бои́тся сме́рти; **I ~ the worst** я опаса́юсь ху́дшего; **I ~ for his life** я опаса́юсь за его́ жизнь; **he will come, never ~!** не бо́йтесь, он придёт; (*expr. regret*): **I ~ you must stay** бою́сь, вам придётся оста́ться.

fearful /ˈfɪəfʊl/ *adj.* (*terrible*) стра́шный, ужа́сный; (*coll., frightful*) ужа́сный, стра́шный; (*timorous*) ро́бкий, боязли́вый; **I was ~ of waking him** я боя́лся разбуди́ть его́.

fearfulness /ˈfɪəfʊlnɪs/ *n.* страх, у́жас; (*timidity*) ро́бость, боязли́вость.

fearless /ˈfɪəlɪs/ *adj.* бесстра́шный, неустраши́мый; **he was ~ of the consequences** он не боя́лся после́дствий.

fearlessness /ˈfɪəlɪsnɪs/ *n.* бесстра́шие, неустраши́мость.

fearsome /ˈfɪəsəm/ *adj.* устраша́ющий, гро́зный.

feasibility /ˌfiːzɪˈbɪlɪtɪ/ *n.* осуществи́мость, выполни́мость; **~ study** изуче́ние техни́ческих возмо́жностей.

feasible /ˈfiːzɪb(ə)l/ *adj.* осуществи́мый, выполни́мый.

feast /fiːst/ *n.* **1** (*relig.*) (церко́вный) пра́здник; **movable ~** подвижно́й пра́здник. **2** (*meal*) пир; **enough is as good as a ~** от добра́ добра́ не и́щут.
● *v.t. & i.* пирова́ть (*impf.*); пра́здновать (*impf.*); **they ~ed away the night** они́ (про)пирова́ли всю ночь; **he ~ed his friends** он ще́дро угоща́л свои́х друзе́й; **he ~ed his eyes on the scene** он любова́лся э́тим зре́лищем.
● *cpd.* **~-day** *n.* пра́здник, пра́здничный день; **today is my ~-day** сего́дня мои́ имени́н|ы (*pl., g.* —).

feaster /ˈfiːstə(r)/ *n.* пиру́ющий, уча́стник пи́ра.

feat /fiːt/ *n.* по́двиг; **~ of engineering** выдаю́щееся достиже́ние инжене́рного иску́сства; **it was a ~ to get him to come** бы́ло нелёгким де́лом затащи́ть его́ сюда́.

feather /ˈfeðə(r)/ *n.* перо́; **that is a ~ in his cap** он мо́жет э́тим горди́ться; **you could have knocked me down with a ~** ни за что бы не пове́рил (э́тому).
● *v.t.* опер|я́ть, -и́ть; укр|аша́ть, -а́сить пе́рьями; **our ~ed friends** на́ши перна́тые друзья́; **~ one's nest** (*fig.*) наб|ива́ть, -и́ть себе́ карма́н; **~ an oar** выноси́ть, вы́нести весло́ плашмя́.
● *cpds.* **~-bed** *n.* пери́на, пухови́к; *v.t.* (*fig.*) балова́ть, из-; изне́жи|вать, -ть; **~-bedding** *n.* (*fig.*) баловство́; (*econ.*) иску́сственное раздува́ние шта́тов; **~-brain, ~-head** *nn.* пуста́я башка́; **~-brained, ~-headed** *adjs.* пустоголо́вый; **~weight** *n.* вес пера́; *adj.* в ве́се пера́; о́чень лёгкий.

feathery /ˈfeðərɪ/ *adj.* пухово́й; лёгкий.

feature /ˈfiːtʃə(r)/ *n.* **1** (*part of face*) черта́; **he has strong ~s** у него́ волево́е лицо́.
2 (*geog.*) черта́/подро́бность релье́фа; **a ~ of the landscape** осо́бенность ландша́фта.
3 (*aspect*) черта́, осо́бенность; **the main ~s of his programme** (*Br.*), **program** (*US*) основны́е пу́нкты (*m. pl.*) его́ програ́ммы.
4 (*object of special attention, main item*): **this journal makes a ~ of sport** э́тот журна́л широко́ освеща́ет спорти́вные собы́тия; **~ (article)** темати́ческая статья́; **~ (film)** худо́жественный фильм.
● *v.t.* (*give prominence to*) поме|ща́ть, -сти́ть на ви́дном ме́сте; **the newspaper ~d the murder story** газе́та помести́ла на ви́дном ме́сте сообще́ние об уби́йстве; **the film ~s a new actress** в фи́льме гла́вную роль поручи́ли но́вой актри́се.
● *v.i.* (*figure prominently*) быть характе́рной черто́й.
● *cpds.* **~-length** *adj.* (*film*) полнометра́жный; **~-writer** *n.* очерки́ст.

featureless /ˈfiːtʃəlɪs/ *n.* невырази́тельный; (*of landscape*) соверше́нно ро́вный; **a ~ existence** бесцве́тное существова́ние.

febrifuge /ˈfebrɪˌfjuːdʒ/ *n.* жаропонижа́ющее сре́дство.

febrile /ˈfiːbraɪl/ *adj.* (*lit., fig.*) лихора́дочный.

February /ˈfebrʊərɪ/ *n.* февра́ль (*m.*); (*attr.*) февра́льский.

fec|al /ˈfiːk(ə)l/, **-es** /ˈfiːsiːz/ (*US*) = **faec|al, -es**

feckless /ˈfeklɪs/ *adj.* безала́берный.

fecklessness /ˈfeklɪsnɪs/ *n.* безала́берность.

fecund /ˈfiːkənd/, /ˈfek-/ *adj.* плодоро́дный, плодови́тый.

fecundity /fɪˈkʌndɪtɪ/ *n.* плодоро́дие, плодови́тость.

fed /fed/ *past and p.p. of* ⇒**feed**

federal /ˈfedər(ə)l/ *adj.* федера́льный; (*in titles of states*) федерати́вный; **F~**

Republic of Germany Федерати́вная Респу́блика Герма́нии.

federalism /ˈfedərə,lɪz(ə)m/ *n.* федерали́зм.

federalist /ˈfedərəlɪst/ *n.* федерали́ст.

federate¹ /ˈfedərət/ *adj.* федерати́вный.

federate² /ˈfedə,reɪt/ *v.t. & i.* объедин|я́ть(ся), -и́ть(ся) на федерати́вных нача́лах.

federation /,fedəˈreɪʃ(ə)n/ *n.* федера́ция; (*of societies etc.*) объедине́ние.

federative /ˈfedərətɪv/ *adj.* федерати́вный.

fedora /fɪˈdɔːrə/ *n.* мя́гкая мужска́я шля́па с продо́льной вмя́тиной.

fee /fiː/ *n.* (*professional charge*) гонора́р; **school ~s** пла́та за обуче́ние; **club ~s** чле́нские взно́сы (*m. pl.*) в клуб; **(TV, radio) licence** (*Br.*), **license** (*US*) **~** абонеме́нтная пла́та.

● *v.t.* (*past and p.p.* **fee'd** *or* **feed**) плати́ть, за-/у- гонора́р + *d.*

feeble /ˈfiːb(ə)l/ *adj.* (**feebler, feeblest**) хи́лый, сла́бый.

● *cpds.* **~-minded** *adj.* слабоу́мный; **~-mindedness** *n.* слабоу́мие.

feebleness /ˈfiːbəlnɪs/ *n.* хи́лость, сла́бость.

feed /fiːd/ *n.* **1** (*animal's*) корм; (*baby's*) еда́, кормле́ние; (*coll.*): **we had a good ~** мы хорошо́ перекуси́ли. **2** (*of machine etc.*) пита́ние, пода́ча материа́ла.

● *v.t.* (*past and p.p.* **fed**) **1** (*give food to*) корми́ть, на-; пита́ть, на-; да|ва́ть, -ть корм + *d.*; **what do you ~ your dog on?** чем вы ко́рмите свою́ соба́ку?; **the hotel ~s you well** в гости́нице хорошо́ ко́рмят; **the child cannot ~ itself** ребёнок ещё не мо́жет есть сам; **the child needs ~ing up** ребёнка на́до подкорми́ть; **~ing-bottle** (*Br.*) (де́тский) рожо́к; (*fig.*): **I am fed up** (*coll.*) я сыт по го́рло; мне надое́ло. **2** (*give as food*) ск|а́рмливать, -орми́ть; **we ~ oats to horses** мы ко́рмим лошаде́й овсо́м. **3** (*fig.*): **the lake is fed by two rivers** э́то о́зеро пита́ют две реки́; **he fed information into the computer** он ввёл да́нные в компью́тер.

● *v.i.* (*past and p.p.* **fed**) (*of animals*) корми́ться (*impf.*); (*graze*) пасти́сь (*impf.*); (*coll., of person*) пита́ться (*impf.*).

● *cpds.* **~-back** *n.* (*elec.*) обра́тная связь; (*fig.*) о́тклик, реа́кция; **~-back from readers** о́тклики чита́телей; **~-bag** *n.* (*horse's*) то́рба; **~-pipe** *n.* (*tech.*) пита́тельная/подаю́щая труба́.

feeder /ˈfiːdə(r)/ *n.* **1** едо́к; **he is a big ~** он обжо́ра; он лю́бит пое́сть. **2** (*Br., feeding-bottle*) (де́тский) рожо́к. **3** (*Br., bib*) нагру́дник. **4** (*tributary*) прито́к; **~ line** (*railway*) ве́тка; (*tech.*) пита́тель (*m.*).

feel /fiːl/ *n.* (*sensation*) ощуще́ние; (*contact*) осяза́ние; **cold to the ~** холо́дный на о́щупь; **have a ~ of this cloth** пощу́пайте э́ту мате́рию; **it has a soapy ~** на о́щупь э́то похо́же на мы́ло; **there will be frost tonight by the ~ of it** чу́вствуется, что но́чью бу́дет моро́з; **there is money in that envelope by the ~ of it** похо́же, что в э́том конве́рте — де́ньги; **if you practise** (*Br.*), **practice** (*US*) **you'll soon get the ~ of it** е́сли вы бу́дете упражня́ться, то ско́ро осво́ите э́тот приём (*or* набьёте ру́ку); **he has a ~ for language** у него́ есть чу́вство языка́.

● *v.t.* (*past and p.p.* **felt**) **1** (*explore by touch*) щу́пать, по-; ощу́п|ывать, -ать; про́бовать, по-; **~ the edge of a knife** тро́гать, по- ле́звие ножа́; **~ s.o.'s pulse** щу́пать, по- кому́-н. пу́льс; (*fig.*) прощу́п|ывать, -ать кого́-н.; **he felt my muscles** он потро́гал мои́ мы́шцы; **~ the weight of this box!** чу́вствуете, ско́лько ве́сит э́тот я́щик!; **~ whether there are any bones broken** пощу́пайте, не сло́маны ли ко́сти. **2** (*grope*) пробира́ться (*impf.*) о́щупью; **he felt his way in the dark** он пробира́лся о́щупью в темноте́; **they are ~ing their way towards an agreement** они́ нащу́пывают по́чву для соглаше́ния. **3** (*be aware of*) чу́вствовать, по-; ощу|ща́ть, -ти́ть; испы́т|ывать, -а́ть; **I can ~ a nail in my shoe** я чу́вствую, у меня́ в боти́нке гвоздь; **did you ~ the earthquake?** вы почу́вствовали землетрясе́ние? **4** (*be affected by*) чу́вствовать, по-; ощу|ща́ть, -ти́ть; пережива́ть (*impf.*); **he felt the insult** он почу́вствовал оскорбле́ние; **he ~s** (*or* **is ~ing**) **the heat** жара́ на него́ пло́хо де́йствует; он пло́хо перено́сит жару́; **he felt the loss of his mother keenly** он о́стро пережива́л сме́рть ма́тери. **5** (*be of opinion*): **I ~ you should go** по-мо́ему, вам сле́дует пойти́; **I ~ the plan to be unwise** я счита́ю, что э́тот план неблагоразу́мен.

● *v.i.* (*past and p.p.* **felt**) **1** (*experience sensation*): **I ~ cold** мне хо́лодно; **I ~ hungry** я го́лоден; **I ~ sure** я уве́рен; **I don't ~ quite myself** мне не по себе́; **I ~ bound to say** … я до́лжен сказа́ть…; **I ~ bad about not inviting him** мне со́вестно, что я не пригласи́л его́; **I ~ as if my head were splitting** у меня́ тако́е чу́вство, сло́вно голова́ раска́лывается; **I ~ strongly about this** у меня́ твёрдое мне́ние на э́то счёт; **I ~ like (going for) a walk** мне хо́чется прогуля́ться; **do you ~ like dancing?** хоти́те потанцева́ть?; **I don't ~ up to going** я не в состоя́нии идти́; **how do you ~ about going there?** как вы отно́ситесь к тому́, что́бы пойти́ туда́?; **it ~s like rain** похо́же, что быть дождю́; **I ~ for you** я вам сочу́вствую. **2** (*produce sensation*) да|ва́ть, -ть ощуще́ние (*чего*); **your hands ~ cold** у вас холо́дные ру́ки; **the air ~s chilly** здесь прохла́дно; **how does it ~ to be home?** каково́ оказа́ться до́ма? **3** (*grope*): **he felt in his pocket for a coin** он поша́рил в карма́не, ища́ моне́ту; **he felt along the wall for the door** он пыта́лся нащу́пать дверь в стене́.

feeler /ˈfiːlə(r)/ *n.* (*zool.*) щу́пальце, у́сик; (*fig.*): **he put out ~s** он заки́нул у́дочку; он пусти́л про́бный шар.

feeling /ˈfiːlɪŋ/ *n.* **1** (*power of sensation*) ощуще́ние, чу́вство; **sense of ~** ощуще́ние; **he lost all ~ in his legs** у него́ онеме́ли но́ги. **2** (*sense, sensation*) созна́ние, чу́вство; **I had a ~ of safety** я чу́вствовал себя́ в безопа́сности. **3** (*opinion*): **I have a ~ he won't come** у меня́ предчу́вствие, что он не придёт; **the general ~ is that** … о́бщее мне́ние таково́, что… **4** (*emotion*) чу́вство, страсть; **he spoke with ~** он говори́л с чу́вством; **I have mixed ~s** у меня́ э́то вызыва́ет сме́шанные чу́вства; **good ~** доброжела́тельность; **no hard ~s, I hope** наде́юсь, никако́й оби́ды; **~ ran high** стра́сти разгоре́лись; **the speech aroused strong ~s** э́та речь разожгла́ стра́сти. **5** (*sensitivity*) чувстви́тельность; **you hurt his ~s** вы его́ оби́дели. **6** (*sympathy*) сочу́вствие; **have you no ~ for his troubles?** неуже́ли его́ бе́ды не вызыва́ют у вас сочу́вствия? **7** (*aptitude*) понима́ние, чутьё; **he has a ~ for the work** у него́ есть да́нные для э́той рабо́ты.

● *adj.* (*sensitive*) чувстви́тельный.

feet /fiːt/ *pl. of* ⇨**foot**

feign /feɪn/ *v.t.* (*simulate*) притвор|я́ться, -и́ться + *i.*; симули́ровать (*impf., pf.*); **~ madness** симули́ровать безу́мие.

feint¹ /feɪnt/ *n.* (*pretence*) притво́рство; (*sham attack*) ло́жная ата́ка, финт.

● *v.i.* нан|оси́ть, -ести́ отвлека́ющий уда́р.

feint² /feɪnt/ *adj.* бле́дный.

fel(d)spar /ˈfeldspɑː(r)/ *n.* полево́й шпат.

felicitate /fəˈlɪsɪ,teɪt/ *v.t.* поздр|авля́ть, -а́вить.

felicitation /fə,lɪsɪˈteɪʃ(ə)n/ *n.* (*usu. pl.*) поздравле́ние.

felicitous /fəˈlɪsɪtəs/ *adj.* ме́ткий, уме́стный, уда́чный.

felicity /fəˈlɪsɪtɪ/ *n.* (*bliss*) блаже́нство; (*aptness*) уме́стность.

feline /ˈfiːlaɪn/ *n.* живо́тное из семе́йства коша́чьих.

● *adj.* коша́чий.

fell¹ /fel/ *n.* (*hill*) гора́; (*moorland*) ве́ресковая пу́стошь.

fell² /fel/ *v.t.* (*person*) сби|ва́ть, -ть с ног; (*tree*) руби́ть, с-; вали́ть, с-/по-.

fell³ /fel/ *past of* ⇨**fall**

fellatio /fɪˈleɪʃɪəʊ/, /feˈlɑːtɪəʊ/ *n.* мине́т.

feller /ˈfelə(r)/ *n.* (*of trees*) дровосе́к.

fell|oe /ˈfeləʊ/, **-y** /ˈfelɪ/ *n.* (*pl.* **~oes** *or* **~ies**) обо́д колеса́, кося́к.

fellow /ˈfeləʊ/ *n.* **1** (*chap; also coll.* **fella, feller**) (*man, boy*) па́рень (*m.*); **a good ~** сла́вный ма́лый; **my dear ~** дорого́й мой!; **old ~!** старина́ (*m.*), дружи́ще (*m.*); **a little ~** малы́ш, мальчуга́н; **poor ~** бедня́га (*m.*); **what does the ~ want?** что э́тому челове́ку ну́жно? **2** (*comrade, companion*) това́рищ, собра́т; **~s in misfortune** това́рищи по несча́стью. **3** (*equal, contemporary etc.*) ра́вный;

све́рстник; това́рищ. **4** (*acad. & professional*) колле́га; сотру́дник; (*Br., of a college*) член сове́та колле́джа.

● *cpds.* **~-being** *n.* бли́жний; **~-citizen** *n.* сограждја|ни́н (*fem.* -а́нка); **~-countryman** *n.* соотечественник; **~-countrywoman** *n.* соотечественница; **~-creature** *n.* бли́жний; **~-feeling** *n.* симпа́тия, сочу́вствие; **~-man** *n.* бли́жний; **~-student** *n.* това́рищ по университе́ту; соку́рсник; **~-traveller** (*US* **-traveler**) *n.* (*lit., fig.*) попу́тчик.

fellowship /ˈfeləʊʃɪp/ *n.* (*companionship*) това́рищество, бра́тство; **good ~** това́рищеские взаимоотноше́ния; (*association*) корпора́ция; колле́гия (*адвокатов и т.п.*); (*of a college*) зва́ние чле́на сове́та колле́джа.

felly /ˈfelɪ/ = **felloe**

felon /ˈfelən/ *n.* уголо́вный престу́пник.

felonious /fɪˈləʊnɪəs/ *adj.* престу́пный.

felony /ˈfelənɪ/ *n.* уголо́вное преступле́ние.

felspar /ˈfelspɑː(r)/ = **fel(d)spar**

felt[1] /felt/ *n.* (*material*) во́йлок, фетр; **~ boots** ва́лен|ки (*pl., g.* -ок); **~ hat** фе́тровая шля́па.

● *v.t.* (*cover with ~*) покр|ыва́ть, -ы́ть во́йлоком.

● *cpd.* **~-tip (pen)** *n.* флома́стер.

felt[2] /felt/ *past and p.p. of* ⇒**feel**

felucca /fɪˈlʌkə/ *n.* (*naut.*) фелю́га.

female /ˈfiːmeɪl/ *n.* (*woman or girl*) же́нщина; (*pej.*) ба́ба; (*animal*) са́мка, ма́тка; (*plant*) же́нская о́собь.

● *adj.* же́нский; **~ child** де́вочка; **~ insect** насеко́мое-са́мка; **~ plant** же́нская о́собь; **~ worker** рабо́тница; **~ screw** га́йка.

feminine /ˈfemɪnɪn/ *adj.* же́нский; (*gram.*) же́нский; же́нского ро́да.

femininity /ˌfemɪˈnɪnɪtɪ/ *n.* же́нственность.

feminism /ˈfemɪˌnɪz(ə)m/ *n.* фемини́зм.

feminist /ˈfemɪnɪst/ *n.* фемини́ст (*fem.* -ка).

feministic /ˌfemɪˈnɪstɪk/ *adj.* фемини́стский.

femme fatale /ˌfæm fæˈtɑːl/ *n.* (*pl.* ***femmes fatales*** *pronunc. same*) рокова́я же́нщина.

femora /ˈfemərə/ *pl. of* ⇒**femur**

femoral /ˈfemər(ə)l/ *adj.* бе́дренный.

femur /ˈfiːmə(r)/ *n.* (*pl.* **femurs** *or* **femora**) бедро́.

fen /fen/ *n.* топь, боло́то.

fence[1] /fens/ *n.* **1** (*barrier*) забо́р, и́згородь, огра́да; **sit on the ~** держа́ться (*impf.*) нейтра́льной/выжида́тельной пози́ции; **mend one's ~** укреп|ля́ть, -и́ть свои́ пози́ции. **2** (*receiver of stolen goods*) бары́га (*m.*).

● *v.t.* (*also* **~ in, off, about, round**) огор|а́живать, -оди́ть.

fence[2] /fens/ *v.i.* фехтова́ть (*impf.*).

fenceless /ˈfenslɪs/ *adj.* (*unenclosed*) неогоро́женный.

fencer /ˈfensə(r)/ *n.* фехтова́льщик.

fencing /ˈfensɪŋ/ *n.* **1** (*fences*) и́згородь, забо́р, огра́да; (*material*) до́ски (*f. pl.*) для забо́ра; материа́л для и́згороди. **2** (*swordplay*) фехтова́ние.

● *cpd.* **~-master** *n.* учи́тель (*m.*) фехтова́ния.

fend /fend/ *v.t.* отра|жа́ть, -зи́ть; пари́ровать (*impf., pf.*); **~ off a blow** отра|жа́ть, -зи́ть уда́р.

● *v.i.*: **~ for o.s.** полага́ться (*impf.*) на себя́.

fender /ˈfendə(r)/ *n.* **1** (*in front of fire*) ≈ ками́нная решётка. **2** (*of train*) предохрани́тельная решётка. **3** (*US, of car*) крыло́.

fenestration /ˌfenɪˈstreɪʃ(ə)n/ *n.* (*archit.*) распределе́ние о́кон в зда́нии.

fennel /ˈfen(ə)l/ *n.* фе́нхель (*m.*), сла́дкий укро́п.

fenugreek /ˈfenjuːˌgriːk/ *n.* па́житник, шамбала́.

feral /ˈfɪər(ə)l/, /ˈfer(ə)l/ *adj.* ди́кий, одича́вший.

ferment[1] /ˈfɜːment/ *n.* заква́ска; ферме́нт; (*fig.*): **in a ~** в броже́нии.

ferment[2] /fəˈment/ *v.t.* (*e.g. beer*) выха́живать, вы́ходить.

● *v.i.* броди́ть (*impf.*).

fermentation /ˌfɜːmenˈteɪʃ(ə)n/ *n.* броже́ние (*also fig.*).

fern /fɜːn/ *n.* (*pl.* **~** *or* **~s**) па́поротник.

ferocious /fəˈrəʊʃəs/ *adj.* свире́пый, лю́тый.

ferocity /fəˈrɒsɪtɪ/ *n.* свире́пость, лю́тость.

ferret /ˈferɪt/ *n.* (*zool.*) хорёк.

● *v.t.* (**ferreted, ferreting**): **~ out** (*fig.*) выи́скивать, вы́искать; разню́х|ивать, -ать (*e.g. a secret*).

● *v.i.* (**ferreted, ferreting**) (*hunt with ~s*) охо́титься (*impf.*) с хорько́м; **~ about** (*fig.*) ры́скать (*impf.*); ша́рить (*impf.*).

ferrety /ˈferɪtɪ/ *adj.* хорько́вый; **~ eyes** ры́сьи глаза́.

Ferris wheel /ˈferɪs/ *n.* чёртово колесо́; колесо́ обозре́ния.

ferro-alloy /ˈferəʊ ˈælɔɪ/ *n.* ферроспла́в.

ferroconcrete /ˌferəʊˈkɒŋkriːt/ *n.* железобето́н.

ferromagnetic /ˌferəʊmægˈnetɪk/ *adj.* ферромагни́тный.

ferrous /ˈferəs/ *adj.* желе́зистый; **~ metals** чёрные мета́ллы.

ferruginous /fəˈruːdʒɪnəs/ *adj.* желе́зистый, железосодержа́щий; (*in colour*) цве́та ржа́вчины.

ferrule /ˈferuːl/ *n.* (*tip*) металли́ческий наконе́чник; (*strengthening band*) обод; му́фта.

ferry /ˈferɪ/ *n.* (*boat*) паро́м.

● *v.t.* (*convey to and fro*) перев|ози́ть, -езти́ (*or* перепр|авля́ть, -а́вить) на паро́ме; отв|ози́ть, -езти́.

● *cpds.* **~-boat** *n.* паро́м; **~man** *n.* паро́мщик, перево́зчик.

fertile /ˈfɜːtaɪl/ *adj.* **1** (*of soil*) плодоро́дный; (*of eggs*) оплодотворённый; (*of humans, animals*) плодови́тый. **2** (*fig.*): **a ~ imagination** бога́тое воображе́ние.

fertility /ˌfɜːˈtɪlɪtɪ/ *n.* плодоро́дие; плодови́тость; **~ drug** препара́т про́тив беспло́дия.

fertilization /ˌfɜːtɪlaɪˈzeɪʃ(ə)n/ *n.* (*biol.*) оплодотворе́ние; (*of soil*) удобре́ние.

fertilize /ˈfɜːtɪˌlaɪz/ *v.t.* (*biol.*) оплодотвор|я́ть, -и́ть; (*of soil*) уд|обря́ть, -о́брить.

fertilizer /ˈfɜːtɪˌlaɪzə(r)/ *n.* (*of soil*) удобре́ние.

fervent /ˈfɜːv(ə)nt/ *adj.* (*fig.*) горя́чий, пы́лкий.

fervid /ˈfɜːvɪd/ *adj.* пы́лкий, пла́менный.

fervour /ˈfɜːvə(r)/ (*US* **fervor**) *n.* жар, пыл, страсть.

fester /ˈfestə(r)/ *v.i.* гнои́ться, за-/на-; нагн|а́иваться, -ои́ться; **the cut ~ed** поре́з загнои́лся; **the insult ~ed** оскорбле́ние жгло́ (*его и т.п.*).

festival /ˈfestɪv(ə)l/ *n.* фестива́ль (*m.*); пра́зднество; **Church ~** церко́вный пра́здник; **~ of music** фестива́ль (*m.*) му́зыки.

festive /ˈfestɪv/ *adj.* пра́здничный.

festivit|y /feˈstɪvɪtɪ/ *n.* пра́зднество, торжество́; **wedding ~ies** сва́дебные торжества́.

festoon /feˈstuːn/ *n.* гирля́нда; (*archit.*) фесто́н.

● *v.t.* укр|аша́ть, -а́сить гирля́ндами/фесто́нами.

Festschrift /ˈfestʃrɪft/ *n.* (*pl.* **~en** *or* **~s**) юбиле́йный сбо́рник.

fet|al /ˈfiːt(ə)l/ = **foet|al**

fetch /fetʃ/ *v.t.* **1** (*go and get*) прин|оси́ть, -ести́; прив|оди́ть, -ести́; пойти́ (*pf.*) за + *i.*; **~ me my hat** принеси́те мою́ шля́пу; **they ~ed the doctor** они́ вы́звали врача́. **2**: **I ~ed him a blow** я нанёс ему́ уда́р. **3** (*of price*): **his house ~ed £150,000** он вы́ручил 150 000 фу́нтов за свой дом; **it won't ~ more than £20** кра́сная цена́ э́тому — 20 фу́нтов (*coll.*).

● *v.i.*: **~ up** (*coll., come to rest*) остан|а́вливаться, -ови́ться; **we ~ed up at the bar** в конце́ концо́в мы очути́лись в ба́ре.

fetching /ˈfetʃɪŋ/ *adj.* привлека́тельный, соблазни́тельный.

fête /feɪt/ *n.* пра́зднество, пра́здник; **village ~** се́льский пра́здник.

● *v.t.* пра́здновать, от-.

fetid /ˈfetɪd/, /ˈfiːtɪd/ *adj.* воню́чий, зловО́нный.

fetish /ˈfetɪʃ/ *n.* (*lit., fig.*) фети́ш.

fetishism /ˈfetɪʃˌɪz(ə)m/ *n.* фетиши́зм (*also psych.*).

fetishist /ˈfetɪʃɪst/ *n.* фетиши́ст.

fetishistic /ˌfetɪˈʃɪstɪk/ *adj.* фетиши́стский.

fetlock /ˈfetlɒk/ *n.* щётка.

fetor /ˈfiːtə(r)/ *n.* вонь, злово́ние.

fetter /ˈfetə(r)/ *n.* (*pl.*) ножные

F

кандал|ы́ (*pl.*, *g.* -ов); (*fig.*) окóв|ы (*pl.*, *g.* —).

● *v.t.* закóв|ывать, -áть в кандалы́; (*of horse*) спу́т|ывать, -ать; (*fig.*) скóв|ывать, -áть.

fettle /ˈfet(ə)l/ *n.*: **in fine ~** в хорóшем состоя́нии (*condition*)/настроéнии (*mood*).

fetus /ˈfiːtəs/ = **foetus**

feud /fjuːd/ *n.* враждá; **blood ~** крóвная месть; **be at ~ with** враждовáть (*impf.*) с + *i.*

● *v.i.* (*carry on a ~*) вести́ (*det.*) вражду́ (*с кем*).

feudal /ˈfjuːd(ə)l/ *adj.* феодáльный; **~ lord** феодáл; **~ system** феодáльный строй.

feudalism /ˈfjuːdəlˌɪz(ə)m/ *n.* феодали́зм.

fever /ˈfiːvə(r)/ *n.* **1** (*body temperature*) жар; высóкая температу́ра; **he has a high ~** у негó жар. **2** (*disease*) лихорáдка; **yellow ~** жёлтая лихорáдка; **rheumatic ~** ревмати́зм; **scarlet ~** скарлати́на. **3** (*fig.*): **in a ~ of impatience** сгорáя от нетерпéния; **at ~ heat** в си́льном возбуждéнии; в сáмом разгáре.

fevered /ˈfiːvəd/ *adj.* лихорáдочный, горя́чечный; **a ~ brow** пылáющий лоб; **~ imagination** бу́йное воображéние.

feverfew /ˈfiːvəˌfjuː/ *n.* (*bot.*) пирéтрум.

feverish /ˈfiːvərɪʃ/ *adj.* лихорáдочный; **the child is ~** у ребёнка повы́шенная температу́ра.

few /fjuː/ *n.* & *adj.* немнóгие (*pl.*); немнóго (+*g.*); мáло +*g.*; **the discriminating ~** немнóгие знатоки́; **a faithful ~ stayed with him** с ним остáлась ку́чка вéрных; **~ (people) know the truth** немнóгие знáют прáвду; **a ~ (people)** немнóгие (лю́ди); нéсколько человéк; **a, some ~** немнóго, нéсколько (+*g.*); **a good ~** (*Br.*), **quite a ~** довóльно мнóго +*g.*; **not a ~** немáло +*g.*; **his friends are ~** у негó мáло друзéй; **the ~ books (that) I have** те нéсколько книг, что у меня́ есть; те немнóгие кни́ги, каки́е у меня́ есть; **~ and far between** рéдкие; **every ~ minutes** кáждые нéсколько мину́т; **a man of ~ words** немногослóвный человéк.

fewer /ˈfjuːə(r)/ *n.* & *adj.* мéнее, мéньше; **few know and even ~ will tell** мáло кто знáет, и ещё мéньше тех, кто вы́скажутся; **he wrote no ~ than 60 books** он написáл ни мнóго ни мáло 60 книг.

fey /feɪ/ *adj.* (*clairvoyant*) ясновидящий; (*whimsical*) шальнóй, с чуди́нкой.

fez /fez/ *n.* (*pl.* **fezzes**) фéска.

Fez /fez/ *n.* Фес.

fezzes *pl. of* ⇒**fez**

fiancé /fɪˈɒnseɪ/, /fɪˈɑ̃seɪ/ *n.* жени́х.

fiancée /fɪˈɒnseɪ/, /fɪˈɑ̃seɪ/ *n.* невéста.

fiasco /fɪˈæskəʊ/ *n.* (*pl.* **~s**) фиáско (*indecl.*), провáл.

fiat /ˈfaɪæt/, /ˈfaɪət/ *n.* декрéт, укáз.

fib /fɪb/ *n.* вы́думка, непрáвда.

● *v.i.* (**fibbed, fibbing**) выду́мывать, вы́думать; подвирáть (*impf.*).

fibber /ˈfɪbə(r)/ *n.* врун (*fem.* -ья); враль (*m.*).

fibre /ˈfaɪbə(r)/ (*US* **fiber**) *n.* **1** (*filament*) волокнó. **2** (*substance made of ~s*) фи́бра (*also fig.*); **moral ~** морáльные устóи (*m. pl.*).

● *cpds.* **~-board** *n.* фи́бровый картóн; листовáя фи́бра; **~-glass** *n.* стекловолокнó, фибергля́с; стеклоплáстик; **~ optics** *n.* волокóнная óптика.

fibrositis /ˌfaɪbrəˈsaɪtɪs/ *n.* фибрóзное воспалéние.

fibrous /ˈfaɪbrəs/ *adj.* волокни́стый, фибрóзный.

fibula /ˈfɪbjʊlə/ *n.* (*pl.* **fibulae** /-ˌliː/ *or* **fibulas**) (*brooch*) фи́була.

fickle /ˈfɪk(ə)l/ *adj.* перемéнчивый, непостоя́нный.

fickleness /ˈfɪkəlnɪs/ *n.* перемéнчивость, непостоя́нство.

fiction /ˈfɪkʃ(ə)n/ *n.* **1** (*invention, pretence*) вы́мысел, вы́думка, фи́кция; **truth is stranger than ~** прáвда порóй чуднéе вы́мысла. **2** (*novels etc.*) беллетри́стика; **work of ~** худóжественное произведéние; **~ writer** беллетри́ст, романи́ст.

fictional /ˈfɪkʃənəl/ *adj.* вы́мышленный; беллетристи́ческий.

fictionalized /ˈfɪkʃənəlaɪzd/ *adj.* беллетризóванный.

fictitious /fɪkˈtɪʃəs/ *adj.* подлóжный, фикти́вный; **a ~ name** вы́мышленное и́мя.

fiddle /ˈfɪd(ə)l/ *n.* **1** (*violin*) скри́пка; (*fig.*): **fit as a ~** в дóбром здрáвии; **play second ~ to s.o.** игрáть (*impf.*) вторýю скри́пку у когó-н. (*or* при ком-н.). **2** (*Br. sl., piece of cheating*) жу́льничество.

● *v.t.* (*Br., falsify*) поддéл|ывать, -ать; подтасóв|ывать, -áть.

● *v.i.* **1** (*play ~*) игрáть (*impf.*) на скри́пке. **2** (*fidget, meddle, tamper*) вертéться (*impf.*); крути́ться (*impf.*); вози́ться (*impf.*); **he ~d with his tie** он тереби́л свой гáлстук; **don't ~ with my papers!** не трóгайте мои́ бумáги!

● *cpds.* **~-faddle** *n.* пустяки́ (*m. pl.*); чепухá, вздор; **~-sticks!** *int.* чепухá!, ерундá!

fiddler /ˈfɪdlə(r)/ *n.* (*musician*) скрипáч (*fem.* -ка); (*Br. coll., cheat*) мошéнник, жу́лик.

fiddling /ˈfɪdlɪŋ/ *adj.* (*trifling*) пустя́чный, пустякóвый.

fidelity /fɪˈdelɪtɪ/ *n.* (*loyalty*) вéрность; (*accuracy*) тóчность.

fidget /ˈfɪdʒɪt/ *n.* **1** (*~y person*) непосéда (*c.g.*), егозá (*c.g.*). **2**: **he's got the ~s** (*coll.*) емý на мéсте не сиди́тся.

● *v.i.* (**fidgeted, fidgeting**) (*make aimless movements*) ёрзать (*impf.*); сует́иться (*impf.*); (*show impatience*) нéрвничать (*impf.*).

fidgety /ˈfɪdʒɪtɪ/ *adj.* суетли́вый, непосéдливый.

fiduciary /fɪˈdjuːʃərɪ/ *n.* попечи́тель (*m.*); опеку́н.

● *adj.* довéренный, порýченный; **~ issue** (*fin.*) вы́пуск банкнóт, не покры́тых зóлотом.

fief /fiːf/ *n.* феóд.

field /fiːld/ *n.* **1** (*piece of ground*) пóле; **a fine ~ of wheat** прекрáсное пшени́чное пóле; **~ sports** спорти́вные заня́тия на откры́том вóздухе; **~ events** лёгкая атлéтика. **2** (*physical range, area*) пóле; **~ of vision** пóле зрéния; **gravitational ~** гравитациóнное пóле; пóле (зéмного) тяготéния. **3** (*mil.*): **~ of battle** пóле би́твы/сражéния; **~ artillery** полевáя артиллéрия; **~ officer** стáрший офицéр; **F~ Marshal** фельдмáршал; **~ hospital** полевóй гóспиталь. **4**: **in the ~** (*away from headquarters*) на местáх/мéстности. **5** (*area of activity or study*) óбласть; пóле/сфéра дéятельности; **an expert in his ~** специали́ст в своéй óбласти; **that is outside my ~** э́то не моя́ óбласть; **in the international ~** на междунарóдной арéне. **6** (*participants in race etc.*) учáстники (*m. pl.*) состязáния.

● *v.t.*: **~ a ball** прин|имáть, -я́ть мяч; (*fig.*): **~ a difficult question** спр|авля́ться, -áвиться с трýдным вопрóсом; **~** (*muster*) **a team** выставля́ть, вы́ставить komáнду.

● *v.i.* (*at cricket etc.*) находи́ться (*impf.*) в пóле.

● *cpds.* **~-day** *n.* (*fig., day of successful exploits*) знаменáтельный/пáмятный день; **~-glasses** *n. pl.* (*binoculars*) полевóй бинóкль; **~mouse** *n.* полевáя мышь; **~sman** *n.* принимáющий/полевóй игрóк (*крикет*); **~-work** *n.* (*research*) исслéдование на мéсте; **~-worker** *n.* (*researcher*) исслéдователь (*m.*) на мéстности.

fieldfare /ˈfiːldfeə(r)/ *n.* дрозд-ряби́нник.

fiend /fiːnd/ *n.* (*devil*) дья́вол; (*evil person*) злодéй, и́зверг; (*fig.*): **a bridge ~** заядлый игрóк в бридж.

fiendish /ˈfiːndɪʃ/ *adj.* дья́вольский, злодéйский.

fiendishness /ˈfiːndɪʃnɪs/ *n.* злодéйство.

fierce /fɪəs/ *adj.* (**fiercer, fiercest**) свирéпый, лю́тый; **~ heat** нестерпи́мая жарá; **~ competition** жестóкая конкурéнция.

fierceness /ˈfɪəsnɪs/ *n.* свирéпость, лю́тость.

fieriness /ˈfaɪərɪnɪs/ *n.* вспы́льчивость.

fiery /ˈfaɪərɪ/ *adj.* (**fierier, fieriest**) óгненный, плáменный; **a ~ temper** вспы́льчивый/горя́чий харáктер; **a ~ horse** горя́чая лóшадь.

fiesta /fɪˈestə/ *n.* прáздник, фиéста.

FIFA /ˈfiːfə/ *n.* (*abbr. of* ***Fédération Internationale de Football Association***) ФИФА (Междунарóдная федерáция футбóла).

fife /faɪf/ *n.* дýдка; мáленькая флéйта.

fifteen /fɪfˈtiːn/, /ˈfɪf-/ *n.* пятнáдцать;

she is ~ ей пятна́дцать лет; **a girl of ~** пятнадцатиле́тняя де́вушка.

● *adj.* пятна́дцать +*g. pl.*; **~ hundred** ты́сяча пятьсо́т, полторы́ ты́сячи.

fifteenth /fɪf'ti:nθ/, /'fɪf-/ *n.* (*date*) пятна́дцатое (число́); (*fraction*) одна́ пятна́дцатая; пятна́дцатая часть.

● *adj.* пятна́дцатый.

fifth /fɪfθ/ *n.* (*date*) пя́тое (число́); (*fraction*) одна́ пя́тая; пя́тая часть; (*mus.*) кви́нта.

● *adj.* пя́тый; **~ column** пя́тая коло́нна.

fifthly /'fɪfθlɪ/ *adv.* в-пя́тых.

fiftieth /'fɪftɪɪθ/ *n.* (*fraction*) одна́ пятидеся́тая; пятидеся́тая часть.

● *adj.* пятидеся́тый.

fift|y /'fɪftɪ/ *n.* пятьдеся́т, полсо́тни; **the ~ies** (*decade*) пятидеся́тые го́ды; (*latitude*) пятидеся́тые широ́ты; **he is in his ~ies** ему́ за пятьдеся́т (лет); ему́ пошёл шесто́й деся́ток; **we shared expenses ~-~** мы раздели́ли расхо́ды попола́м.

● *adj.* пятьдеся́т +*g. pl.*

fig¹ /fɪg/ *n.* (*fruit*) фи́га, инжи́р, ви́нная я́года; **I don't care a ~** мне наплева́ть.

● *cpds.* **~-leaf** *n.* фи́говый листо́к; **~-tree** *n.* фи́говое де́рево.

fig² /fɪg/ *n.* (*dress, get-up*): **in full ~** в по́лном облаче́нии.

fig. /fɪg/ *n.* (*abbr. of* ***figure*** 4) рис. (рису́нок); **in ~ 6** на рис. 6.

fight /faɪt/ *n.* **1** бой, схва́тка, дра́ка; **stand-up ~** кула́чный бой; **free ~** всео́бщая потасо́вка; сва́лка; **he is spoiling for a ~** он и́щет ссо́ры; **~ to the finish** борьба́ до побе́дного конца́; **he put up a (good) ~** он (упо́рно) сопротивля́лся.
2 (*boxing-match*) боксёрский поеди́нок/бой.
3 (*~ing spirit*) задо́р; **he has ~ in him yet** в нём ещё оста́лся боево́й задо́р; **the news took all the ~ out of him** от э́той но́вости он совсе́м приуны́л.

● *v.t. & i.* (*past and p.p.* **fought**) дра́ться, по-; сра|жа́ться, -зи́ться; (*wage war*) воева́ть (*impf.*); **the boys/dogs are ~ing** ма́льчики/соба́ки деру́тся; **Britain fought Germany** Великобрита́ния воева́ла с Герма́нией (*or* выступа́ла про́тив Герма́нии); **~ a battle** вести́ (*det.*) бой; **~ a duel** дра́ться (*impf.*) на дуэ́ли; **~ an election** вести́ (*det.*) предвы́борную борьбу́; **~ a lawsuit** суди́ться (*impf.*); **~ a case** (*leg.*) защища́ть (*impf.*) де́ло в суде́; **the patient is ~ing for breath** больно́й задыха́ется; **he fought shy of the problem** он уклоня́лся от реше́ния э́той зада́чи; **he fought his way forward** он пробива́лся/прота́лкивался вперёд; **he fought like a lion** он сража́лся как лев; **he fought off a cold** он (бы́стро) спра́вился с просту́дой; **I fought off my desire to sleep** я переборо́л сон; **they fought off the enemy** они́ отби́ли врага́; **they fought it out (*or* to a finish)** они́ сража́лись/боро́лись до конца́; **~ back** *v.i.* отб|ива́ться, -и́ться; **~ down** *v.t.* (*repress, e.g. a feeling*) побе|жда́ть, -ди́ть; **you should ~ down that tendency** вам на́до боро́ться с э́той накло́нностью.

fighter /'faɪtə(r)/ *n.* **1** (*one who fights*) бое́ц; (*fig.*) боре́ц. **2** (**~** *aircraft*) истреби́тель (*m.*); **~ cover** прикры́тие истреби́телями.

● *cpds.* **~-bomber** *n.* истреби́тель-бомбардиро́вщик; **~-pilot** *n.* лётчик-истреби́тель (*m.*).

fighting /'faɪtɪŋ/ *n.* бой, сраже́ние; **hand-to-hand ~** рукопа́шный бой.

● *adj.* боево́й; **we have a ~ chance** сто́ит попыта́ться.

figment /'fɪgmənt/ *n.* вы́мысел; фи́кция; **a ~ of the imagination** плод воображе́ния.

figurative /'fɪgjʊrətɪv/, /'fɪgər-/ *adj.* фигура́льный; перено́сный, метафори́ческий; (*pictorial*) изобрази́тельный.

figure /'fɪgə(r)/ *n.* **1** (*numerical sign*) ци́фра; **double ~s** двузна́чные чи́сла; **a six-~ number** шестизна́чное число́; **I bought it at a low ~** я э́то дёшево купи́л.
2 (*geom.*) фигу́ра, те́ло.
3 (*pl., arithmetic*): **he is good at ~s** он силён в арифме́тике.
4 (*diagram, illustration*) рису́нок.
5 (*image, effigy*) о́браз, изображе́ние, ста́туя, фигу́ра; **lay ~** манеке́н.
6 (*human form*) фигу́ра; **I saw a ~ approaching** я уви́дел приближа́вшуюся ко мне фигу́ру; **she has a good ~** у неё хоро́шая фигу́ра; **a fine ~ of a man** хорошо́ сложённый мужчи́на; **he is a ~ of fun** он про́сто смешо́н; **landscape with ~s** пейза́ж с фигу́рами люде́й.
7 (*person of importance*) фигу́ра, выдаю́щаяся ли́чность; **he is a great ~ in this town** он изве́стная фигу́ра в э́том го́роде; **he was the greatest ~ of his age** он был са́мой выдаю́щейся ли́чностью своего́ вре́мени.
8 (*show, appearance*) вид; **he cut a brilliant ~** он блиста́л; **he cut a poor ~** он име́л жа́лкий вид.
9 (**~** *of speech*) ритори́ческая фигу́ра; о́бразное выраже́ние.
10 (*in dancing*) фигу́ра.

● *v.t.* **1** (*make patterns etc. in*): **~d silk** узо́рчатый шёлк.
2: **~ out** (*calculate*) вычисля́ть, вы́числить; (*understand*) пон|има́ть, -я́ть; пост|ига́ть, -и́гнуть; **I can't ~ him out** я не могу́ его́ поня́ть (*or* раскуси́ть (*coll.*)); **~ out how much we owe you** подсчита́йте, ско́лько мы вам должны́.

● *v.i.* **1** (*appear*) фигури́ровать (*impf.*); **he ~s in history** он вошёл в исто́рию; **this did not ~ in my plans** э́то не входи́ло в мои́ пла́ны; **~ in a play** (*as actor*) игра́ть (*impf.*) в пье́се; (*as character*) фигури́ровать (*impf.*).
2 (*US coll.*): **it ~s** (*makes sense, is plausible*) э́то похо́же на пра́вду; **I ~d on seeing him** я рассчи́тывал уви́деться с ним; **I ~ they'll be late** я ду́маю, что они́ опозда́ют.

● *cpds.* **~-head** *n.* носово́е украше́ние, фигу́ра на носу́ корабля́; (*fig.*) номина́льный руководи́тель; **~-of-eight** *n.* восьмёрка; **~-skater** *n.* конькобе́жец-фигури́ст; **~skating** *n.* фигу́рное ката́ние.

figurine /ˌfɪgjʊ'ri:n/, /'fɪg-/ *n.* фигу́рка, стату́этка.

Fiji /'fi:dʒi:/ *n.* Фи́джи (*nt. indecl.*).

Fijian /fi:'dʒi:ən/ *n.* фиджи́|ец (*fem.* -йка).

● *adj.* фиджи́йский.

filament /'fɪləmənt/ *n.* (*animal fibre*) волокно́; (*bot.*) нить; (*elec.*) нить нака́ла; **~ lamp** ла́мпа нака́ливания.

filbert /'fɪlbət/ *n.* (*tree*) лещи́на; (*nut*) фунду́к.

filch /fɪltʃ/ *v.t.* стяну́ть (*pf.*) (*coll.*).

file¹ /faɪl/ *n.* (*tool*) напи́льник; (*nail-~*) пи́лочка для ногте́й.

● *v.t.* подпи́л|ивать, -и́ть; опи́л|ивать, -и́ть; **~ one's nails** подпи́л|ивать, -и́ть но́гти; **he ~d away the roughness** он отшлифова́л гру́бую пове́рхность.

file² /faɪl/ *n.* **1** (*for papers*) па́пка, регистра́тор для бума́г, скоросшива́тель (*m.*). **2** (*set of papers etc.*) де́ло, досье́ (*indecl.*); **a newspaper ~** подши́вка газе́ты; **the correspondence is on our ~s** э́та перепи́ска храни́тся у нас в де́ле.
3 (*comput.*) файл; **~ server** файл-се́рвер.

● *v.t.* **1** (*place on ~*) подш|ива́ть, -и́ть; регистри́ровать, за-; **the letters were ~d away** пи́сьма бы́ли подши́ты к де́лу. **2**: **~** (*lodge*) **a complaint** под|ава́ть, -а́ть жа́лобу; **~ suit against s.o.** возбу|жда́ть, -ди́ть суде́бное де́ло про́тив кого́-н.

file³ /faɪl/ *n.* **1** (*rank, row*) ряд, шере́нга; коло́нна; **in single, Indian ~** гусько́м; по одному́; **rank and ~** (*mil.*) рядовы́е (*m. pl.*); (*fig., as adj.*) рядово́й (*рабо́тник и т.п.*). **2** (*chess*) вертика́ль.

● *v.i.* идти́ (*det.*) гусько́м/коло́нной; **the prisoners ~d out** заключённые выходи́ли гусько́м друг за дру́гом.

filial /'fɪlɪəl/ *adj.* (*pert. to son or daughter*) сыно́вний, доче́рний; (*dutiful*) почти́тельный.

filibuster /'fɪlɪˌbʌstə(r)/ *n.* (*obstruction*) обстру́кция.

● *v.i.* (*fig.*) тормози́ть (*impf.*) приня́тие зако́на путём обстру́кции.

filigree /'fɪlɪˌgri:/ *n.* филигра́нь; (*fig.*) филигра́нная рабо́та; **a ~ brooch** филигра́нная брошь.

filing /'faɪlɪŋ/ *n.* (*of papers*) регистра́ция бума́г.

● *cpds.* **~-cabinet** *n.* шкаф, сейф; **~-clerk** *n.* делопроизводи́тель (*m.*), регистра́тор.

filings /'faɪlɪŋz/ *n. pl.* металли́ческие опи́л|ки (*pl., g.* -ок).

Filipino /ˌfɪlɪ'pi:nəʊ/ *n.* (*pl.* **~s**) филиппи́н|ец (*fem.* -ка).

● *adj.* филиппи́нский.

fill /fɪl/ *n.*: **he ate his ~** он нае́лся до́сыта.

● *v.t.* **1** (*make full*) нап|олня́ть, -о́лнить; зап|олня́ть, -о́лнить; **he ~ed the tank with petrol** он напо́лнил бак бензи́ном; **he ~ed the hole with sand** он запо́лнил я́му песко́м; **smoke ~ed**

F

the room ко́мната напо́лнилась ды́мом; **I was ~ed with admiration** я был по́лон восхище́ния; **tears ~ed her eyes** её глаза́ напо́лнились слеза́ми.
2: **~ a tooth** пломбирова́ть, за-.
3 (*fig., of office etc.*) зан|има́ть, -я́ть; **~ a vacancy** зап|олня́ть, -о́лнить вака́нтную до́лжность; ста́вить, по- кого́-н. на вака́нтное ме́сто; **~ s.o.'s place** зан|има́ть, -я́ть чьё-н. ме́сто.
4: **~ a need** удовлетвор|я́ть, -и́ть потре́бность.
● *v.i.* (*become full*) нап|олня́ться, -о́лниться; **the sails ~ed** (*with wind*) паруса́ наду́лись; **his cheeks ~ed (out)** у него́ округли́лись щёки.
● *with advs.*: **~ in** *v.t.* (*Br., complete*) зап|олня́ть, -о́лнить; **he ~ed in the form** (*Br.*) он запо́лнил бланк/анке́ту; **he ~ed in his name** он вписа́л своё и́мя; (*coll., inform*): **I ~ed him in** я ввёл его́ в курс де́ла; *v.i.*: **I am ~ing in while X is away** я замеща́ю X в его́ отсу́тствие; **~ out** *v.t.* (*US, a form*) зап|олня́ть, -о́лнить; *v.i.* расш|иря́ться, -и́риться; попр|авля́ться, -а́виться; нап|олня́ться, -о́лниться; **~ up** *v.t.* (*make full*) нап|олня́ть, -о́лнить; **we ~ed up** (*the car*) **with petrol** мы запра́вились (бензи́ном); (*a form*) зап|олня́ть, -о́лнить; *v.i.* (*become full*) нап|олня́ться, -о́лниться.
● *cpd.* **~-in** *n.* (*person or thing*) заме́на.

fillet /ˈfɪlɪt/ *n.* **1** (*head-band*) ле́нта, повя́зка. **2** (*of meat, fish*) филе́ (*indecl.*).
● *v.t.* (**filleted, filleting**) (*of fish, take off bone*) отдел|я́ть, -и́ть мя́со от косте́й.

filling /ˈfɪlɪŋ/ *n.* (*in tooth*) пло́мба; (*in pie*) начи́нка.
● *adj.* наполня́ющий, заполня́ющий; (*of food*) сы́тный.
● *cpd.* **~-station** *n.* автозапра́вочная *or* бензозапра́вочная ста́нция; (бензо)запра́вка.

fillip /ˈfɪlɪp/ *n.* щелчо́к, толчо́к; (*fig.*): **give a ~ to** да|ва́ть, -ть толчо́к +*d.*; стимули́ровать (*pf.*).

filly /ˈfɪlɪ/ *n.* молода́я кобы́ла.

film /fɪlm/ *n.* **1** (*thin coating*) плёнка; **a ~ of dust** налёт пы́ли; **a ~ of mist** ды́мка. **2** (*photographic material*) фотоплёнка; (*cin.*) киноплёнка; **a roll of ~** кату́шка фотоплёнки. **3** (*motion picture*) фильм; **~ actor** киноактёр; **~ actress** киноактри́са; **~ clip** отры́вок из фи́льма; **~ crew** съёмочная гру́ппа; **~ critic** кинообозрева́тель (*m.*); **~ distributor** кинопрока́тчик; **~ star** кинозвезда́; **~ studies** киноведе́ние; **~ studio** киносту́дия; **~ test** кинопро́ба актёра; **~ projector** киноустано́вка; **~ rights** права́ на экраниза́цию; **~ set** съёмочная площа́дка.
● *v.t. & i.* сн|има́ть, -ять.

filter /ˈfɪltə(r)/ *n.* (*for liquid*) фильтр, цеди́лка; (*for light*) светофи́льтр; **~ light** (*Br., traffic sign*) светофо́р со стре́лкой; **~ tip** (*cigarette*) сигаре́та с фи́льтром.
● *v.t.* (*purify*) фильтрова́ть (*impf.*); проце́|живать, -ди́ть.
● *v.i.* (*fig.*): **the news ~ed out** но́вости просочи́лись.

filth /fɪlθ/ *n.* грязь.

filthy /ˈfɪlθɪ/ *adj.* (**filthier, filthiest**) гря́зный.

fin /fɪn/ *n.* плавни́к.

finagle /fɪˈneɪɡ(ə)l/ *v.i.* (*coll.*) моше́нничать (*impf.*).

final /ˈfaɪn(ə)l/ *n.* **1** (*Br., pl., exam at end of degree course*) выпускно́й экза́мен; (*US, exam at end of term, year, class*) ито́говый экза́мен; **he took his ~s in June** он сдава́л выпускны́е/госуда́рственные экза́мены в ию́не.
2 (*match*) фина́л; **tennis ~s** фина́л по те́ннису. **3** (*newspaper edition*) после́дний вы́пуск.
● *adj.* **1** (*last in order*) после́дний; заверша́ющий, заключи́тельный.
2 (*decisive*) оконча́тельный, реша́ющий; **I won't come, and that's ~** я не приду́, и э́то моё после́днее сло́во.

finale /fɪˈnɑːlɪ/, /-leɪ/ *n.* (*mus., fig.*) фина́л; **grand ~** торже́ственный фина́л.

finalist /ˈfaɪnəlɪst/ *n.* финали́ст (*fem.* -ка).

finality /faɪˈnælɪtɪ/ *n.*: **he spoke with (an air of) ~** он говори́л об э́том, как о де́ле решённом.

finalization /ˌfaɪnəlaɪˈzeɪʃ(ə)n/ *n.* заверше́ние.

finalize /ˈfaɪnəˌlaɪz/ *v.t.* (*give final form to*) заверш|а́ть, -и́ть; прид|ава́ть, -а́ть оконча́тельную фо́рму +*d.*; (*settle, e.g. arrangements*) (оконча́тельно) ула́|живать, -дить.

finance /ˈfaɪnæns/, /fɪˈnæns/, /faɪˈnæns/ *n.* фина́нсы (*m. pl.*); дохо́ды (*m. pl.*); **Minister of F~** мини́стр фина́нсов; **my ~s are low** у меня́ с фина́нсами ту́го (*coll.*).
● *v.t.* финанси́ровать (*impf., pf.*).

financial /faɪˈnænʃ(ə)l/, /fɪ-/ *adj.* фина́нсовый; **he is in ~ difficulties** у него́ де́нежные затрудне́ния.

financier /faɪˈnænsɪə(r)/, /fɪ-/ *n.* финанси́ст.

finch /fɪntʃ/ *n.* зя́блик.

find /faɪnd/ *n.* (*discovery, esp. valuable*) нахо́дка; **the new cook is a ~** но́вый по́вар — настоя́щая нахо́дка.
● *v.t.* (*past and p.p.* **found**) **1** (*discover, encounter*) на|ходи́ть, -йти́; (*by search*) разыска́ть, отыска́ть (*both pf.*); **I could ~ nothing to say** я не нашёлся, что сказа́ть; **he found his tongue** он обрёл дар ре́чи; **a letter was found on him** на нём нашли́ письмо́; **pine-trees are found in several countries** сосна́ растёт/встреча́ется во мно́гих стра́нах; **I found him waiting for me** он уже́ ждал меня́; **the bullet found its mark** пу́ля попа́ла в цель; **water ~s its own level** вода́ устана́вливает свой у́ровень; **we found the beds comfortable** крова́ти оказа́лись удо́бными; **you must take us as you ~ us** вам приде́тся приня́ть нас таки́ми, каки́е мы есть; **I found I had forgotten the key** я обнару́жил, что забы́л ключ; **I ~ it hard to understand him** мне тру́дно поня́ть его́; **he found himself in hospital** он оказа́лся/очути́лся в больни́це; **I called, but found her out** я зашёл, но не заста́л её.
2 (*compute, ascertain, judge*): **I ~ the total to be £20** по мои́м подсчётам, о́бщая су́мма составля́ет 20 фу́нтов; **the jury found him guilty** прися́жные призна́ли его́ вино́вным; **the judge found for the plaintiff** судья́ реши́л де́ло в по́льзу истца́.
3 (*provide*) предост|авля́ть, -а́вить; **I will ~ the money for the excursion** я раздобу́ду де́ньги на экску́рсию.
4 (*obtain, achieve*) получ|а́ть, -и́ть; **I ~ pleasure in reading** я получа́ю удово́льствие от чте́ния; **he found time to read** он находи́л вре́мя для чте́ния; **he found courage to ask her to marry him** он набра́лся хра́брости и сде́лал ей предложе́ние.
5: **~ out** (*detect*) узн|ава́ть, -а́ть; (*ascertain*) выясня́ть, вы́яснить; **I found out the answer** я нашёл отве́т; **have you found out (about) the trains?** вы узна́ли расписа́ние поездо́в?

findable /ˈfaɪndəb(ə)l/ *adj.* находи́мый.

finder /ˈfaɪndə(r)/ *n.* (*person who finds*): **the ~ will be rewarded** наше́дший полу́чит вознагражде́ние; **'~s keepers'** кому́ на́ руку попа́ло...; нашёл — зна́чит моё; (*lens*) (видо)иска́тель (*m.*).

finding /ˈfaɪndɪŋ/ *n.* (*discovery*) откры́тие, нахо́дка, нахожде́ние; (*conclusion; also pl.*) вы́вод(ы); (*leg.*) постановле́ние, реше́ние.

fine[1] /faɪn/ *n.* (*punishment*) штраф, пе́ня.
● *v.t.* штрафова́ть, о-; **he was ~d £5** его́ оштрафова́ли на 5 фу́нтов.

fine[2] /faɪn/ *adj.* **1** (*of weather*) я́сный, хоро́ший; **it has turned ~** проясни́лось; **one ~ day, one of these ~ days** в оди́н прекра́сный день.
2 (*pleasant, handsome, excellent*) прекра́сный, замеча́тельный; **a ~ view** прекра́сный вид; **a ~ girl** (*looks or character*) преле́стная/чуде́сная де́вушка; **we had a ~ time** мы прекра́сно/замеча́тельно провели́ вре́мя; **that is all very ~, but ...** всё э́то о́чень хорошо́, но....
3 (*noble, virtuous*) благоро́дный, возвы́шенный; **a ~ gentleman/lady** ба́рин/ба́рышня.
4 (*delicate, exquisite*) то́нкий; **~ workmanship** то́нкая рабо́та; **~ silk** то́нкий шёлк.
5 (*of small particles*) ме́лкий; **~ dust** ме́лкая пыль; **~ rain** ме́лкий дождь.
6 (*slender, thin, sharp*) то́нкий, о́стрый; **~ thread** то́нкая нить/ни́тка; **a pencil with a ~ point** о́стро отто́ченный каранда́ш.
7 (*refined, subtle*) утончённый, то́нкий; **a ~ distinction** то́нкое разли́чие; **the ~ arts** изобрази́тельные/изя́щные иску́сства.
8 (*elegant, distinguished*) изя́щный.
● *adv.*: **he cut it ~** (*of time*) он оста́вил себе́ вре́мени в обре́з; **that suits me ~** (*coll.*) э́то меня́ вполне́ устра́ивает.
● *cpds.* **~-grained** *adj.*

мелкозерни́стый; **~-spun** *adj.* то́нкий; **~-tooth(ed) comb** *n. see* ⇒**tooth**.

fineness /ˈfaɪnnɪs/ *n.* (*delicacy*) то́нкость, утончённость, изя́щество.

finery /ˈfaɪnərɪ/ *n.* пы́шный наря́д.

finesse /fɪˈnes/ *n.* (*delicacy*) делика́тность, то́нкость.

finger /ˈfɪŋɡə(r)/ *n.* па́лец (*also of glove*); (*of clock*) стре́лка; **index ~** указа́тельный па́лец; **middle ~** сре́дний па́лец; **ring ~** безымя́нный па́лец; **little ~** мизи́нец; **eat something with one's ~s** есть что-н. рука́ми; **I can twist him round my little ~** он всё сде́лает, что я ни захочу́; **lay a ~ on** (*touch, molest*) тро́|гать, -нуть па́льцем; **he put his ~ on it** он попа́л в са́мую то́чку; **I will not lift a ~ to help him** я и па́льцем не пошевельну́, что́бы помо́чь ему́; **he's all ~s and thumbs** (*Br.*) у него́ ру́ки — крю́ки; **he has a ~ in the pie** он заме́шан в э́том; он приложи́л ру́ку к э́тому; **she worked her ~s to the bone** она́ рабо́тала не покладая рук; **snap one's ~s** (*lit.*) щёлк|ать, -нуть па́льцами; **the criminal slipped through our ~s** престу́пник ускользну́л у нас из-под но́са; **he burnt his ~s in that business** он обжёгся на э́том де́ле; **they can be counted on the ~s of one hand** их по па́льцам мо́жно сосчита́ть.

● *v.t.* тро́гать, по-; **~ a piece of cloth** щу́пать, по- мате́рию.

● *cpds.* **~-alphabet** *n.* (*for deaf and dumb*) а́збука глухонемы́х; **~-bowl** *n.* ча́шка для спола́скивания па́льцев; **~-hole** *n.* (*mus.*) кла́пан; **~-mark** *n.* пятно́ от па́льца; **~-plate** *n.* (*on door*) нали́чник дверно́го замка́; **~-post** *n.* указа́тельный столб; **~-nail** *n.* но́готь (*m.*); **~-print** *n.* отпеча́ток па́льца; дактилоскопи́ческий отпеча́ток; *v.t.* (*take s.o.'s ~-prints*) сн|има́ть, -ять отпеча́тки па́льцев у + *g.*; **~-stall** *n.* напа́льчник; **~-tip** *n.* ко́нчик па́льца; **he has the subject at his ~-tips** он зна́ет э́тот предме́т как свои́ пять па́льцев; **he is a musician to his ~-tips** он музыка́нт до мо́зга косте́й.

fingering /ˈfɪŋɡərɪŋ/ *n.* (*mus.*) апликату́ра, пальцо́вка.

finial /ˈfɪnɪəl/ *n.* (*archit.*) фиа́л; флеро́н.

finic|al /ˈfɪnɪk(ə)l/, **-king** /ˈfɪnɪkɪŋ/, **-ky** /ˈfɪnɪkɪ/ *adjs.* разбо́рчивый, приди́рчивый, привере́дливый.

finis /ˈfɪnɪs/, /ˈfiːnɪs/, /ˈfaɪnɪs/ *n.* коне́ц.

finish /ˈfɪnɪʃ/ *n.* **1** (*conclusion*) оконча́ние, коне́ц; **it was a close ~** они́ зако́нчили почти́ одновреме́нно; **he was in at the ~** он прису́тствовал при развя́зке.
2 (*polish*) отде́лка; **mahogany ~** отде́лка из кра́сного де́рева; **his manners lack ~** у него́ грубова́тые мане́ры.

● *v.t.* **1** (*smooth, polish*) отде́л|ывать, -ать; **the work is beautifully ~ed** рабо́та отлича́ется соверше́нством.
2 (*perfect*) соверше́нствовать (*impf.*); **a ~ed performance** отто́ченное исполне́ние; **~ing touch** после́дний штрих; **~ing-school** пансио́н для де́вушек (*готовящий их к светской жизни*).
3 (*end*) зак|а́нчивать, -о́нчить; конча́ть, ко́нчить; **I ~ed** (*sc. writing, reading*) **the book** я (за)ко́нчил кни́гу; **he ~ed (off, up) the pie** он дое́л весь пиро́г; **we will ~ the job** мы зако́нчим рабо́ту.
4 (*of manufacture*): **~ed goods** гото́вые изде́лия.
5 (*coll., exhaust, kill*) изнур|я́ть, -и́ть; прик|а́нчивать, -о́нчить; **the climb ~ed me** (*coll.*) э́тот подъём докона́л меня́; **the fever ~ed him off** лихора́дка докона́ла/прико́нчила его́.

● *v.i.* конча́ться, ко́нчиться; зак|а́нчиваться, -о́нчиться; **they ~ed (off, up) by singing a song** в заключе́ние они́ спе́ли пе́сню; **have you ~ed with that book?** вам бо́льше не нужна́ э́та кни́га?; **I am ~ed with him** ме́жду на́ми всё ко́нчено; (*in race*) финиши́ровать (*impf., pf.*); **he ~ed fourth** он за́нял четвёртое ме́сто; **~ing-post** фи́ниш.

finite /ˈfaɪnaɪt/ *adj.* коне́чный; име́ющий преде́л; (*gram.*): **~ verb** ли́чный глаго́л.

Finland /ˈfɪnlənd/ *n.* Финля́ндия.

Finn /fɪn/ *n.* фин|н (*fem.* -ка).

Finnish /ˈfɪnɪʃ/ *n.* (*language*) фи́нский язы́к.

● *adj.* фи́нский.

Finno-Ugric /ˌfɪnəʊˈuːɡrɪk/, /-ˈjuːɡrɪk/ *adj.* фи́нно-уго́рский.

fiord, fjord /fjɔːd/ *n.* фьорд, фио́рд.

fir /fɜː(r)/ *n.* (*also* **~-tree**) ель; **Scotch ~** сосна́.

● *cpd.* **~-cone** *n.* (*Br.*) ело́вая ши́шка.

fire /ˈfaɪə(r)/ *n.* **1** (*phenomenon of combustion*) ого́нь (*m.*); **the house is on ~** дом загоре́лся/гори́т; **set on ~, set ~ to** подж|ига́ть, -е́чь; **he will never set the world** (*or* **Thames** (*Br.*)) **on ~** он по́роха не вы́думает; **catch ~** загор|а́ться, -е́ться; **there is no smoke without ~** нет ды́ма без огня́; **play with ~** (*fig.*) игра́ть (*impf.*) с огнём.
2 (*burning fuel*) ого́нь (*m.*); **camp ~** костёр; **he lit a ~** он разжёг ого́нь/ками́н; **lay a ~** раскла́дывать, разложи́ть ого́нь; **make a ~** (*indoors*) зат|а́пливать, -опи́ть ками́н; **light a ~** разж|ига́ть, -е́чь ками́н; топи́ть, за-; печь; **there is a ~ in the next room** в сосе́дней ко́мнате то́пится (*or* гори́т ками́н).
3 (*conflagration*) пожа́р; **~!** пожа́р!; (*excl. by someone in burning building*) гори́м!; **where's the ~?** где гори́т?
4 (*of ~arms*) ого́нь (*m.*), стрельба́; **open ~** откр|ыва́ть, -ы́ть ого́нь; **cease ~** прекра|ща́ть, -ти́ть ого́нь; **under ~** (*lit., also fig., of criticism etc.*) под огнём; **draw s.o.'s ~** (*fig.*) стать (*pf.*) мише́нью для чьих-н. напа́док; **hold one's ~** (*fig.*) сдерж|иваться, -а́ться.
5 (*ardour*) пыл, ого́нь (*m.*); **a speech full of ~** пла́менная речь.

● *v.t.* **1** (*set fire to*) подж|ига́ть, -е́чь; заж|ига́ть, -е́чь; (*fig.*): **it ~d her imagination** э́то воспламени́ло её воображе́ние.
2 (*bake, e.g. bricks or pottery*) обж|ига́ть, -е́чь.
3 (*fuel*): **an oil-~d furnace** то́пка, рабо́тающая на жи́дком то́пливе.
4 (*of ~arms*) стреля́ть (*impf.*) из + *g.*; **~ a rifle** стреля́ть (*impf.*) из ружья́; **~ a shot** вы́стрелить (*pf.*); **~ a salute** (*of many guns*) произвести́ (*pf.*) артиллери́йский салю́т; **he ~d off his ammunition** он израсхо́довал все патро́ны.

● *v.i.* (*of ~arms*) стреля́ть (*impf.*); вы́стрелить (*pf.*); **the troops ~d at the enemy** войска́ стреля́ли по врагу́; **they ~d at the target** они́ стреля́ли в цель; **the guns ~d** ору́дия стреля́ли; **~ away!** (*fig., coll.*) валя́й!; выкла́дывай!

● *cpds.* **~-alarm** *n.* (*alert*) пожа́рная трево́га; (*device*) автомати́ческий пожа́рный сигна́л; **~arm** *n.* огнестре́льное ору́жие; **~ball** *n.* (*meteor*) боли́д; (*nuclear*) о́гненный шар; **~-bird** *n.* (*myth.*) жар-пти́ца; **~-bomb** *n.* зажига́тельная бо́мба; **~-box** *n.* то́пка, огнева́я коро́бка; **~brand** *n.* зачи́нщик, подстрека́тель (*m.*); **~-break** *n.* загради́тельная противопожа́рная полоса́; **~-brick** *n.* огнеупо́рный кирпи́ч; **~-brigade** *n.* (*Br.*) пожа́рная кома́нда; **~clay** *n.* огнеупо́рная гли́на; **~-cracker** *n.* фейерве́рк; **~damp** *n.* ру́дничный/грему́чий газ; **~ department** (*US*) = **~-brigade; ~dog** *n.* подста́вка для ками́нного прибо́ра; **~-drill** *n.* пожа́рное уче́ние, обуче́ние приёмам противопожа́рной защи́ты; **~eater** *n.* (*at circus*) пожира́тель (*m.*) огня́; **~-engine** *n.* пожа́рная маши́на; **~-escape** *n.* пожа́рная ле́стница; **~-extinguisher** *n.* огнетуши́тель (*m.*); **~-fighter** *n.* пожа́рник, пожа́рный; **~fly** *n.* светля́к; **~-guard** *n.* (*screen*) ками́нная решётка; (*US*) — **~-break; ~-hose** *n.* пожа́рный шланг; **~-insurance** *n.* страхова́ние от огня́; **~-irons** *n.* ками́нный прибо́р; **~light** *n.* свет от ками́на; **~-lighter** *n.* (*Br.*) расто́пка; **~man** *n.* (*stoker*) кочега́р; (*member of* **~-brigade**) пожа́рник, пожа́рный; **~-place** *n.* ками́н, оча́г; **~-plug** *n.* (*US*) пожа́рный кран, гидра́нт; **~-power** *n.* огнева́я мощь; **~proof** *adj.* огнеупо́рный; **a ~proof door** несгора́емая дверь; *v.t.* прид|ава́ть, -а́ть огнесто́йкость + *d.*; **~-raiser** *n.* (*Br.*) поджига́тель (*m.*); **~-screen** *n.* (*ornamental*) ками́нный экра́н; = **~-guard; ~-ship** *n.* бра́ндер; **~side** *n.* ме́сто о́коло ками́на; (*fig.*) дома́шний оча́г; **~-station** *n.* пожа́рное депо́ (*indecl.*); **~-tongs** *n. pl.* ками́нные щипц|ы́ (*pl., g.* -о́в); **~-trap** *n.* «лову́шка» (*в случае пожара*); **~-truck** (*US*) = **~-engine; ~-watcher** *n.* доброво́лец пожа́рной охра́ны; дежу́рный, следя́щий за зажига́тельными бо́мбами; **~-watching** *n.* охра́на от зажига́тельных бомб; **~-water** *n.* горячи́тельные напи́тки (*m. pl.*);

F

~wood *n.* дров|á (*pl., g.* —); **~work(s)** *n.* фейервéрк (*also fig.*); **~work display** фейервéрк; **~-worshipper** *n.* огнепоклóнник.

firing /ˈfaɪərɪŋ/ *n.* (*shooting*) стрельбá.
● *cpds.* **~-line** *n.* лúния огня́; **~-party, -squad** *nn.* (*at funeral etc.*) салю́тная комáнда; (*for execution*) комáнда, наряжённая для расстрéла.

firm¹ /fɜːm/ *n.* фи́рма.

firm² /fɜːm/ *adj.* **1** (*physical*) крéпкий, твёрдый; **~ ground** сýша; **we are on ~ ground in asserting this** мы с увéренностью утверждáем э́то.
2 (*fig.*) устóйчивый, стóйкий, непоколеби́мый; **he is ~ in his beliefs** он непоколеби́м в своéй вéре; **you must be ~ with him** вы должны́ быть с ним пострóже; **a ~ offer** твёрдое предложéние.
● *adv.* твёрдо, устóйчиво; **stand ~** стоя́ть (*impf.*) твёрдо.
● *v.t.* (*make ~; also ~ up*) (*e.g. a mixture*) уплотн|я́ть, -и́ть; (*e.g. a project*) укреп|ля́ть, -и́ть.
● *v.i.* (*also ~ up*) (*become ~*) уплотн|я́ться, -и́ться; укреп|ля́ться, -и́ться.

firmament /ˈfɜːməmənt/ *n.* небéсный свод.

firmness /ˈfɜːmnɪs/ *n.* (*physical*) твёрдость; (*moral*) стóйкость, непоколеби́мость.

firmware /ˈfɜːmweə(r)/ *n.* (*comput.*) встрóенные прогрáммы.
● *adj.* (*comput.*) аппарáтно-прогрáммный.

first /fɜːst/ *n.* **1** (*beginning*): **at ~** сначáла, сперва́; **from ~ to last** с начáла до концá; **from the ~** с сáмого начáла.
2 (*date*) пéрвое (числó); **on the ~ of May** пéрвого мáя.
3 (*Br., acad.*) вы́сшая оцéнка/отмéтка; **he got a ~ in physics** он получи́л вы́сшую оцéнку по фи́зике.
4 (*edition*) пéрвое издáние.
● *adj.* **1** (*in time or place*) пéрвый; **on the ~ floor** (*Br.*) на вторóм этажé; (*US*) на пéрвом этажé; **at ~ glance** на пéрвый взгляд; **hear something at ~ hand** узн|авáть, -áть что-н. из пéрвых рук; **at ~ light** как тóлько начáло/начнёт светáть; **~ name** и́мя; **~ night** (*theatr.*) премьéра; **I asked the ~ person I saw** я спроси́л пéрвого встрéчного; **~ person singular** пéрвое лицó еди́нственного числá; **in the ~ place** во-пéрвых, в пéрвую óчередь; **I will go there ~ thing tomorrow** зáвтра я пéрвым дéлом зайдý тудá; **he said the ~ thing that came to mind** он сказáл пéрвое, что пришлó емý в гóлову; **the ~ time I saw him** когдá я в пéрвый раз уви́дел егó; **he got it right ~ time (off)** у негó получи́лось э́то с пéрвого рáза; **he would be the ~ to admit that . . .** он пéрвый признáет, что. . . .
2 (*in rank or importance*) пéрвый; **he travels ~ class** он éздит пéрвым клáссом; **put ~ things ~** дéлать (*impf.*) в пéрвую óчередь сáмое глáвное; **~ team** (*sport*) основнóй состáв; **~ cousin** двою́родный брат, двою́родная сестрá; **~ violin** пéрвая скри́пка.
3 (*basic*) основнóй; **~ principles** основны́е при́нципы; **he doesn't know the ~ thing about dogs** он ничегó не понимáет в собáках.
● *adv.* **1** (*before all; also ~ and foremost, ~ of all*) прéжде всегó; в пéрвую óчередь; **~ come, ~ served** кто пéрвым пришёл, тогó пéрвым и обслýжат.
2 (*initially*) сперва́, сначáла; (*in the ~ place*) во-пéрвых; (*for the ~ time*) впервы́е; **I ~ met him last year** я познакóмился с ним в прóшлом годý; **when they were ~ married** в начáле их супрýжеской жи́зни; когдá они́ тóлько пожени́лись.
● *cpds.* **~-aid** *adj.* пéрвая пóмощь; **~-aid kit** санитáрная сýмка; аптéчка; **~-aid post** пункт пéрвой пóмощи; **~-aid room, station** медпýнкт; **~-born** *n.* пéрвенец; *adj.* стáрший; **~-class** *adj.* (*excellent*) первоклáссный; *adv.* (*of travel*) пéрвым клáссом; **~-floor** *adj.* (*Br.*) вторóго этажá, на вторóм этажé; (*US*) пéрвого этажá, на пéрвом этажé; **~ form** *n.* (*Br.*) пéрвый класс; **~-former** *n.* (*Br.*) первоклáссни|к (*fem.* -ца); **~-grader** (*US*) = **~-former; ~-hand** *adj.* из пéрвых рук; **~-night** *adj.*: **~-night nerves** волнéние пéред премьéрой; **~-nighter** *n.* завсегдáтай премьéр; **~-rate** *adj.* первоклáссный; *int.* прекрáсно!; **~-strike** *adj.*: **~-strike weapons** орýжие для пéрвого удáра.

firstly /ˈfɜːstlɪ/ *adv.* во-пéрвых.

firth /fɜːθ/ *n.* зали́в; лимáн; **the F~ of Forth** зали́в Форт.

fiscal /ˈfɪsk(ə)l/ *adj.* фискáльный, финáнсовый.

fish /fɪʃ/ *n.* (*pl.* **~** *or* **~es**) ры́ба; **catch ~** лови́ть, поймáть ры́бу; **drink like a ~** пить (*impf.*) запóем; **a ~ out of water** человéк, попáвший не в свою́ срéду; **neither ~, flesh, nor fowl** ни ры́ба, ни мя́со; **I have other ~ to fry** у меня́ есть делá поважнéе; (*fig., creature*): **a cold ~** холóдный человéк.
● *v.t. & i.* лови́ть/уди́ть (*impf.*) ры́бу; **~ a river** лови́ть (*impf.*) ры́бу в рекé; (*fig.*): **~ for compliments** напрáшиваться (*impf.*) на комплимéнты; **~ for information** вы́уживать, вы́удить свéдения; **he ~ed through his pockets** он поры́лся у себя́ в кармáнах.
● *with advs.*: **~ out** *v.t.* вы́уживать, вы́удить; **~ up** *v.t.* вытáскивать, вы́тащить.
● *cpds.* **~bone** *n.* ры́бья кость; **~-cake** *n.* ≈ ры́бная котлéта; **~-farm** *n.* рыборазвóдный садóк; **~-eye** *adj.*: **~-eye lens** фотообъекти́в «ры́бий глаз»; **~-finger** *n.* (*Br.*) ры́бная пáлочка; **~-hook** *n.* рыболóвный крючóк; **~-knife** *n.* нож для ры́бы; **~monger** *n.* торгóвец ры́бой; **~net** *n.* рыболóвная сеть; **~net stockings** ажýрные чулки́; **~-oil** *n.* ры́бий жир; **~-pond** *n.* пруд для разведéния ры́бы; ры́бный садóк; **~-slice** *n.* (*Br.*) нож для перевора́чивания ры́бы на сковородé; **~-tank** *n.* аквáриум; **~wife** *n.* торгóвка ры́бой.

fisher(man) /ˈfɪʃəmən/ *n.* ры́бак; (*angler for pleasure*) рыболóв.

fishery /ˈfɪʃərɪ/ *n.* рыболóвство; ры́бный прóмысел.

fishing /ˈfɪʃɪŋ/ *n.* ры́бная лóвля; **~ rights** прáво ры́бной лóвли; **the boys have gone ~** мáльчики ушли́ на рыбáлку.
● *cpds.* **~-line** *n.* лесá, лéска; **~-net** *n.* рыболóвная сеть; **~-rod** *n.* уди́лище; **~-tackle** *n.* рыболóвные снáсти (*f. pl.*).

fishy /ˈfɪʃɪ/ *adj.* (**fishier, fishiest**) ры́бий, ры́бный; **a ~ taste** ры́бный при́вкус; (*coll., suspect*) нечи́стый, подозри́тельный.

fissile /ˈfɪsaɪl/ *adj.* (*phys.*) расщепля́ющийся; (*geol.*) сланцевáтый.

fission /ˈfɪʃ(ə)n/ *n.* (*biol.*) размножéние путём делéния клéток; (*phys.*) расщеплéние/делéние (ядрá); **nuclear ~** áтомный распáд.

fissionable /ˈfɪʃənəb(ə)l/ *adj.* спосóбный к я́дерному распáду; расщепля́емый.

fissure /ˈfɪʃə(r)/ *n.* трéщина, расщéлина.
● *v.i.* трéскаться, по-; трéснуть (*pf.*).

fist /fɪst/ *n.* кулáк; (*dim., e.g. baby's*) кулачóк; **shake one's ~ at s.o.** грози́ть, по- комý-н. кулакóм; **with clenched ~s** сжав кулаки́.

fistful /ˈfɪstfʊl/ *n.* горсть, при́горшня.

fisticuffs /ˈfɪstɪˌkʌfs/ *n.* кулáчный бой.

fistula /ˈfɪstjʊlə/ *n.* (*pl.* **fistulas** *or* **fistulae** /-ˌliː/) (*med.*) фи́стула, свищ.

fit¹ /fɪt/ *n.* **1** (*attack of illness*) при́ступ, припáдок; **apoplectic ~** апоплекси́ческий удáр; **he was subject to ~s as a child** ребёнком он был подвéржен припáдкам; (*fig.*): **she would have, throw a ~ if she knew** онá закати́ла бы сцéну/истéрику, éсли бы узнáла. **2** (*outburst*): **~ of coughing** при́ступ кáшля; **the book sent me into ~s of laughter** э́та кни́га рассмеши́ла меня́ до слёз; **his jokes had us in ~s** от егó шýток мы покáтывались сó смеху; **in a ~ of passion** в пореы́ве стрáсти. **3**: **by/in ~s and starts** уры́вками.

fit² /fɪt/ *n.* (*of a garment etc.*): **this jacket is a tight ~** э́тот пиджáк узковáт; **six people in the car is a tight ~** шесть человéк едвá умещáются в маши́не.
● *adj.* (**fitter, fittest**) **1** (*suitable*) гóдный, пригóдный, подходя́щий; **this food is not ~ to eat** э́та пи́ща несъедóбна; **he was passed ~ for military service** егó при́знали гóдным к воéнной слýжбе; **survival of the ~test** естéственный отбóр; **see, think ~** считáть, счéсть нýжным; **he'll come when he thinks ~** он придёт когдá емý заблагорассýдится; **a meal ~ for a king** цáрская трáпеза; **you are not ~ to be seen** вам нельзя́ покáзываться в такóм ви́де.
2 (*ready*) готóвый, спосóбный; **he was ~ to drop** он едвá держáлся на

ногáх; **dressed ~ to kill** разодéтый в пух и прах.
3 (*in good health*) здорóвый; в хорóшей фóрме; **fighting ~** здорóвый как бык; **keep (o.s.) ~** поддéрживать (*impf.*) хорóшую (спорти́вную) фóрму.
● *v.t.* (**fitted, fitting**) **1** (*equip*: *also* **~ out; ~ up**) снаря|жáть, -ди́ть; снаб|жáть, -ди́ть; экипировáть (*impf., pf.*); обору́довать (*impf., pf.*); **the house is ~ted for electricity** в дóме есть провóдка; **he was ~ted out with a new suit** ему́ вы́дали нóвый костю́м; **he went to the tailors to be ~ted** он пошёл к портнóму на примéрку; **~ a ship out** снаря|жáть, -ди́ть корáбль.
2 (*install, fix in place*): **~ted carpet** (*Br.*) ковёр во всю кóмнату; **~ted kitchen** (*Br.*) встрóенная ку́хня; **~ted wardrobe** (*Br.*) встрóенный платянóй шкаф; **he ~ted a new lock on the door** он встáвил нóвый замóк в дверь; (*fig., accommodate*): **I can ~ you in next week** я могу́ назнáчить вам встрéчу на слéдующей недéле.
3 (*make suitable, adapt*) приспос|áбливать, -óбить; **he is not ~ted for heavy work** он не годи́тся для тяжёлых рабóт; **they are well ~ted for each other** они́ подхóдят друг дру́гу; **I had a suit ~ted** я примéрил костю́м; **I ~ted in my holiday with his** я подогнáл врéмя своегó óтпуска к егó; (*correspond to in dimensions*: *also v.i.*) под|ходи́ть, -ойти́ + *d.*; **the dress ~s you** э́то плáтье хорошó на вас сиди́т; **will the letter ~ (into) this envelope?** войдёт письмó в э́тот конвéрт?; **a key to ~ this lock** ключ к э́тому замку́; **that ~s in with my plans** э́то вполнé совпадáет с моúми плáнами; **his story ~s in with hers** егó расскáз подтверждáет её словá.
4 (*insert*: *also v.i.*): **he ~ted the cigarette into the holder** он встáвил сигарéту в мундшту́к; **tubes that ~ into one another** тру́бки, вставля́ющиеся однá в другу́ю.
5 (*suit*) соотвéтствовать (*impf.*) + *d.*; **he made the punishment ~ the crime** он определи́л наказáние, соотвéтствующее преступлéнию.

fitful /ˈfɪtfʊl/ *adj.* нерóвный, преры́вистый.

fitment /ˈfɪtmənt/ *n.* (*Br.*) предмéт обстанóвки; часть обору́дования.

fitness /ˈfɪtnɪs/ *n.* (*suitability*) соотвéтствие, пригóдность; (*health*) хорóшее здорóвье.

fitter /ˈfɪtə(r)/ *n.* (*tailor's assistant*) портнóй, занимáющийся примéркой; (*mechanic*) монтёр, сбóрщик.

fitting /ˈfɪtɪŋ/ *n.* **1** (*of clothes*) примéрка. **2** (*fixture in building*) обору́дование; **light ~s** освети́тельные прибóры (*m. pl.*). **3** (*installation*) обору́дование, установка.
● *adj.* подходя́щий, гóдный.
● *cpd.* **~-room** *n.* примéрочная.

five /faɪv/ *n.* (числó/нóмер) пять; (**~** *people*) пя́теро; пять человéк; **we ~** нас пя́теро; **(the) ~ of us went** мы пошли́ впятерóм; нас пошлó пять человéк; **~ each** по пяти́; **in ~s, ~ at a time** по пяти́, пятёрками; (*figure, thing numbered 5, group of* **~**) пятёрка; (*of things purchased in* **~s**, *e.g. eggs*) пятóк; (*with var. nn. expr. or understood; cf. also examples under* ⇨**two**): **~ (o'clock)** пять (часóв); **chapter ~ (5)** пя́тая (5) главá; **he is ~** ему́ пять лет; **at ~ (years old)** в пять лет; **~ of spades** пятёрка пик; **~ to 4 (o'clock)** без пяти́ четы́ре; **~ past 6** пять мину́т шестóго; **have you got this dress in a ~?** есть у вас пя́тый размéр э́того плáтья?; **she takes ~s in shoes** у неё пя́тый размéр óбуви; **let's take five** (*coll.*) пойдём на перéку́р.
● *adj.* пять + *g. pl.*; (*for people and pluralia tantum, also*) пя́теро + *g. pl.*; **~ sixes are thirty** пя́тью шесть — три́дцать; **~ times as good** впя́теро лу́чше.
● *cpds.* **~-day** *adj.*: **~-day week** пятиднéвная недéля, пятиднéвка; **~-finger** *adj.*: **~-finger exercise** упражнéние для пяти́ пáльцев; **~fold** *adj.* пятикрáтный; *adv.* впя́теро; **the crop has increased ~fold** урожáй увели́чился в пять раз; **~-pound** *adj.*: **~-pound note** (*Br.*) пятифунтóвая бумáжка; **~-sided** *adj.* пятисторóнний; **~-sided figure** пятиугóльник; **~-storey** (*US* **-story**) *adj.* пятиэтáжный; **~-year** *adj.* пятилéтний; **~-year plan** пятилéтний план, пятилéтка; **~-year-old** *n.* пятилéтний ребёнок.

fiver /ˈfaɪvə(r)/ *n.* (*Br.*) пятёрка (*coll.*).

fix /fɪks/ *n.* (*coll., dilemma*) затрудни́тельное положéние; затруднéние; (*determination of position*) определéние мéста; (*coll., injection of drug*) укóл.
● *v.t.* **1** (*fasten, make firm*) укреп|ля́ть, -и́ть; (*fig.*): **I ~ed him with a glance** я при́стально посмотрéл на негó; **the event was ~ed in his mind** э́то собы́тие запечатлéлось у негó в мозгу́; **~ the blame on s.o.** взвáл|ивать, -и́ть вину́ на когó-н.
2 (*direct steadily*) напр|авля́ть, -áвить; **~ one's eyes (up)on** останавл|ивать, -ови́ть взгляд на + *p.*; **~ one's attention on** сосредотóчи|вать, -ть внимáние на + *p.*; **~ed gaze** при́стальный/засты́вший взгляд.
3 (*determine, settle*: *also v.i.*): **let us ~ (on) a date** давáйте договори́мся о дáте.
4 (*chem.*) сгу|щáть, -сти́ть; свя́з|ывать, -áть.
5 (*phot.*) фикси́ровать (*impf., pf.*).
6 (*provide*: *also* **~ up**): **can you ~ (up) a room for me?** *or* **~ me up with a room?** мóжете ли вы найти́ для меня́ кóмнату?
7 (*coll., repair*): **he ~ed the radio in no time** он в два счёта почини́л радиоприёмник; (*US, prepare*): **I will ~ the drinks** я приготóвлю напи́тки.

fixation /fɪkˈseɪʃ(ə)n/ *n.* (*psych.*) фиксáция.

fixative /ˈfɪksətɪv/ *n.* фиксати́в, фиксáтор.

fixed /ˈfɪksd/ *adj.* неподви́жный, закреплённый, постоя́нный; **~ idea** навя́зчивая идéя, идéя фикс; **~ point** (*geom.*) постоя́нная тóчка; **~ rate** устанóвленная/постоя́нная стáвка; **~ star** неподви́жная звездá.

fixedly /ˈfɪksɪdlɪ/ *adv.* при́стально; в упóр.

fixer /ˈfɪksə(r)/ *n.* (*phot.*) фиксáж; (*sl., arranger*) посрéдник.

fixture /ˈfɪkstʃə(r)/ *n.* **1** (*fitting in building*) приспособлéние. **2** (*tech.*) неподви́жная/закреплённая детáль. **3** (*Br., sporting event*) предстоя́щее спорти́вное состязáние/мероприя́тие. **4** (*coll., permanent feature*) обы́чное явлéние.

fizz /fɪz/ *n.* (*sound*) шипéние; (*champagne*) игри́стое (*coll.*).
● *v.i.* шипéть (*impf.*); и́скри́ться (*impf.*).

fizzle /ˈfɪz(ə)l/ *v.i.* шипéть (*impf.*); **~ out** выдыхáться, вы́дохнуться; (*fig.*) окóнчиться (*pf.*) ничéм.

fizzy /ˈfɪzɪ/ *adj.* (**fizzier, fizziest**) шипу́чий.

fjord /fjɔ:d/ = **fiord**

flabbergast /ˈflæbəˌgɑ:st/ *v.t.* (*coll.*) ошелом|ля́ть, -и́ть; ошарáши|вать, -ть.

flabbiness /ˈflæbɪnɪs/ *n.* вя́лость, дря́блость; (*fig.*) слáбость, слабохарáктерность.

flabby /ˈflæbɪ/ *adj.* (**flabbier, flabbiest**) вя́лый, дря́блый; (*fig.*) слáбый, слабохарáктерный.

flaccid /ˈflæksɪd/, /ˈflæsɪd/ *adj.* отви́слый, вя́лый.

flag[1] /flæg/ *n.* (*emblem*) флаг, знáмя (*nt.*); **show the white ~** вывéшивать, вы́весить бéлый флаг; **hoist, raise, run up the ~** подн|имáть, -я́ть (*or* водру|жáть, -зи́ть) флаг; **lower, strike the ~** (*naut.*) опус|кáть, -ти́ть флаг; (*surrender*) сд|авáться, -áться; **show the ~** подн|имáть, -я́ть флаг; (*fig.*) нап|оминáть, -óмнить о своём существовáнии; **~ of convenience** удóбный флаг; **keep the ~ flying** (*fig.*) высокó держáть (*impf.*) знáмя (*чего*); **put the ~s out** (*fig.*) прáздновать (*impf.*) побéду; **F~ Day** (*US*) День установлéния госудáрственного флáга США; **~ officer** адмирáл, коммодóр; комáндующий.
● *v.t.* (**flagged, flagging**) **1** (*mark*) мéтить, по-.
2 (*signal*: *also v.i.*) сигнализи́ровать (*impf., pf.*) флáгом; (*fig.*): **~ (down) a passing car** остан|áвливать, -ови́ть проезжáющую маши́ну.
● *cpds.* **~-captain** *n.* команди́р флагмáнского корабля́; **~-day** *n.* (*Br.*) день сбóра дéнег на благотвори́тельные цéли; **~-lieutenant** *n.* флаг-адъютáнт; **~man** *n.* сигнáльщик; **~pole** *n.* флагштóк; **~ship** *n.* флагмáнский корáбль, флáгман; **~staff** *n.* флагштóк; **~-waving** *n.* (*coll., demonstrative patriotism*) урá-патриоти́зм.

flag[2] /flæg/ *n.* (*bot.*) касáтик, и́рис.

flag[3] /flæg/ *n.* (**~** *stone*) кáменная плитá, плитня́к.
● *v.t.* (**flagged, flagging**) выстилáть, вы́стлать пли́тами.

flag[4] /flæg/ *v.i.* (**flagged, flagging**) (*grow weary*) ослаб|ева́ть, -е́ть; (*fig.*): **the conversation was ~ging** разгово́р не кле́ился.

flagellant /ˈflædʒələnt/, /fləˈdʒelənt/ *n.* (*eccl.*) флагелла́нт.

flagellate /ˈflædʒəˌleɪt/ *v.t.* бичева́ть (*impf.*).

flagellation /ˌflædʒəˈleɪʃ(ə)n/ *n.* бичева́ние; (*self-~*) самобичева́ние.

flageolet /ˌflædʒəˈlet/, /ˈflædʒ-/ *n.* (*mus.*) флажоле́т.

flagon /ˈflægən/ *n.* графи́н/кувши́н для вина́.

flagrancy /ˈfleɪgrənsɪ/ *n.* чудо́вищность, возмути́тельность.

flagrant /ˈfleɪgrənt/ *adj.* вопию́щий, возмути́тельный.

flagrante delicto /fləˈgræntɪ dɪˈlɪktəʊ/ *adv.*: **in ~** на ме́сте преступле́ния.

flail /fleɪl/ *n.* цеп.

● *v.t. & i.* молоти́ть, с-; (*fig.*) маха́ть (*impf.*); **he charged with his hands ~ing** он наступа́л, разма́хивая рука́ми.

flair /ˈfleə(r)/ *n.* нюх, чутьё; **a ~ for languages** спосо́бности (*f. pl.*) к языка́м.

flak /flæk/ *n.* зени́тный ого́нь; **~ jacket** защи́тная ку́ртка; (*fig.*): **he took a lot of ~ from the critics** ему́ доста́лось от кри́тиков.

flake /fleɪk/ *n.* (*pl.*) хло́пь|я (*pl., g.* -ев); **~s of snow** снежи́нки (*f. pl.*); **corn ~s** корнфле́кс; **soap ~s** мы́льная стру́жка.

● *v.i.* (*peel*) шелуши́ться (*impf.*); слои́ться (*impf.*); **the rust ~d off** ржа́вчина отслои́лась; **~ out** (*coll.*) зас|ыпа́ть, -ну́ть; **~d out** (*coll.*) измо́танный.

flaky /ˈfleɪkɪ/ *adj.* (**flakier, flakiest**) слои́стый; **~ pastry** слоёное те́сто.

flamboyanc|e /flæmˈbɔɪəns/, **-y** /flæmˈbɔɪənsɪ/ *nn.* цвети́стость; я́ркость.

flamboyant /flæmˈbɔɪənt/ *adj.* (*person, behaviour*) колори́тный; (*clothing*) бро́ский, я́ркий; (*style*) цвети́стый.

flame /fleɪm/ *n.* **1** (*burning gas; pl., fire*) ого́нь (*m.*), пла́мя (*nt.*); **burst into ~(s)** вспы́х|ивать, -нуть; **the house was in ~s** дом был охва́чен пла́менем; **commit to the ~s** пред|ава́ть, -а́ть огню́; **add fuel to the ~s** (*fig.*) подл|ива́ть, -и́ть ма́сла в ого́нь.
2 (*blaze of light or colour*) пла́мя (*nt.*), вспы́шка. **3** (*specific colour: also adj.*) о́гненный (цвет). **4** (*coll., sweetheart*) предме́т стра́сти; **she is an old ~ of mine** она́ моя́ ста́рая па́ссия.

● *v.i.* горе́ть, пыла́ть, пламене́ть (*all impf.*).

● *cpds.* **~-proof** *adj.* огнесто́йкий; **~-thrower** *n.* огнемёт.

flamenco /fləˈmeŋkəʊ/ *n.* (*pl.* **~s**) фламе́нко (*indecl.*).

flaming /ˈfleɪmɪŋ/ *adj.* **1** (*ablaze; very hot*) пыла́ющий, горя́щий. **2** (*brightly coloured*) я́ркий, пламене́ющий.
3 (*fig., violent*): **they had a ~ row** у них произошёл стра́шный сканда́л; **he was in a ~ temper** он был в бе́шенстве. **4** (*sl.*): **it's a ~ nuisance** э́то чертовски доса́дно.

flamingo /fləˈmɪŋgəʊ/ *n.* (*pl.* **~s** *or* **~es**) флами́нго (*m. indecl.*).

flammable /ˈflæməb(ə)l/ *adj.* горю́чий; легко́ воспламеня́ющийся.

flan /flæn/ *n.* откры́тый пиро́г.

Flanders /ˈflɑːndəz/ *n.* Фла́ндрия.

flâneur /flæˈnɜːr/ *n.* фланёр.

flange /flændʒ/ *n.* фла́нец, кро́мка.

flank /flæŋk/ *n.* **1** (*of the body*) бок. **2** (*of a building*) торцо́вая сторона́. **3** (*of a hill*) склон. **4** (*of an army*) фланг; **~ attack** фла́нговая ата́ка.

● *v.t.* **1** (*be or go alongside*) находи́ться (*impf.*) (*or* идти́) сбо́ку. **2** (*menace or cut off by ~ing movement*) угрожа́ть (*impf.*) с фла́нга + *g.*; отр|еза́ть, -е́зать фланг; **he was ~ed by guards** по о́бе его́ стороны́ шла/стоя́ла стра́жа.

flannel /ˈflæn(ə)l/ *n.* **1** (*kind of cloth*) флане́ль. **2**: **face ~** (*Br.*) махро́вая рукави́чка для лица́. **3** (*pl., trousers*) флане́левые брю́к|и (*pl., g.* —). **4** (*Br. coll.*) очковтира́тельство.

● *adj.* флане́левый.

flannelette /ˌflænəˈlet/ *n.* фланеле́т, ба́йка.

flap[1] /flæp/ *n.* **1** (*hinged piece etc.*): **the table has two ~s** у стола́ две откидны́е доски́; **a jacket with a ~ at the back** пиджа́к с двумя́ разре́зами сза́ди; **a hat with ~s** ша́пка с уша́ми; (*of pocket, envelope*) кла́пан; (*aeron.*) закры́лок; **with ~s down** с опу́щенными закры́лками. **2** (*waving motion*) взмах. **3** (*sound*) хлопо́к.

● *v.t. & i.* (**flapped, flapping**) взма́х|ивать, -ну́ть + *i.*; мах|а́ть, -ну́ть + *i.*; хло́п|ать, -нуть; шлёп|ать, -нуть; развева́ть(ся) (*impf.*); **the bird ~ped its wings** пти́ца взмахну́ла кры́льями; **the flags ~ped in the wind** фла́ги развева́лись на ветру́; **he ~ped away the flies** он отгоня́л мух (хлопу́шкой).

flap[2] /flæp/ *n.* (*coll., state of alarm*) переполо́х; **don't get into a ~!** не паникуйте!

● *v.i.* (**flapped, flapping**) переполоши́ться (*pf.*).

flapdoodle /flæpˈduːd(ə)l/, /ˈflæp-/ *n.* (*US sl.*) чепуха́, белиберда́.

flapjack /ˈflæpdʒæk/ *n.* **1** (*Br., biscuit*) овся́ное пече́нье. **2** (*US, pancake*) блин.

flare[1] /fleə(r)/ *n.* (*effect of flame*) сверка́ние; вспы́шка; (*illuminating device*) сигна́льная ракета́; освети́тельный патро́н; **the ship sent up ~s** кора́бль вы́ступил сигна́льные раке́ты.

● *v.i.* сверк|а́ть, -ну́ть; горе́ть (*impf.*) неро́вным пла́менем; (*fig.*) вспы́х|ивать, -нуть; вспыли́ть (*pf.*); **she ~s up at the least thing** она́ взрыва́ется от ка́ждого пустяка́.

● *cpds.* **~-path** *n.* освещённая взлётно-поса́дочная полоса́; **~-up** *n.* (*lit., fig.*) вспы́шка.

flare[2] /fleə(r)/ *n.* (*widening-out*) расшире́ние; **~s** (*trousers*) брю́ки-клёш.

● *v.t. & i.* расш|иря́ться, -и́риться; **~d skirt** ю́бка-клёш.

flash /flæʃ/ *n.* **1** (*burst of light*) вспы́шка, про́блеск; **a ~ of lightning** вспы́шка мо́лнии; **~ in the pan** (*fig.*) осе́чка; **he had a ~ of inspiration** на него́ нашло́ вдохнове́ние.
2 (*instant*) мгнове́ние, миг; **he answered in a ~** он мгнове́нно отве́тил.
3 (*Br., on uniform*) нарука́вная наши́вка; эмбле́ма ча́сти/соедине́ния.
4: **news ~** э́кстренное сообще́ние.

● *adj.* (*gaudy*) шика́рный, крича́щий.

● *v.t.*: **he ~ed the light in my face** он напра́вил свет мне в лицо́; **they were ~ing signals to the enemy** они́ посыла́ли светови́е сигна́лы врагу́; (*fig.*): **he ~ed a glance at her** он метну́л на неё взгля́д.

● *v.i.* сверк|а́ть, -ну́ть; вспы́х|ивать, -нуть; мельк|а́ть, -ну́ть; **the light ~ed on and off** свет то вспы́хивал, то гас; **the lightning ~ed** сверкну́ла/блесну́ла мо́лния; **~ing eyes** сверка́ющие глаза́; **the thought ~ed across my mind** э́та мысль промелькну́ла у меня́ в голове́; **cars ~ed by** маши́ны мча́лись ми́мо.

● *cpds.* **~back** *n.* (*cin.*) ретроспе́кция, обра́тный кадр; **~-bulb** *n.* (*phot.*) ла́мпа-вспы́шка; **~-gun** *n.* ла́мпа для ма́гниевой вспы́шки, «блиц»; **~light** *n.* (*for signalling*) сигна́льный ого́нь; прожéктор; (*phot.*) вспы́шка (ма́гния); (*US, torch*) карма́нный/электри́ческий фона́рь; **~-point** *n.* температу́ра вспы́шки; то́чка воспламене́ния.

flashiness /ˈflæʃɪnɪs/ *n.* показу́ха.

flashy /ˈflæʃɪ/ *adj.* (**flashier, flashiest**) крича́щий, показно́й, эффе́ктный.

flask /flɑːsk/ *n.* фля́га, фля́жка; (*chem.*) ко́лба.

flat /flæt/ *n.* **1** (*level object or area*) пло́скость; пло́ская пове́рхность; **the ~ of the hand** ладо́нь; **on the ~** на пло́скости.
2 (*mus.*) бемо́ль (*m.*); **the key of A ~** тона́льность ля бемо́ль.
3 (*Br., apartment*) кварти́ра; **block of ~s** многокварти́рный дом; **~mate** (*Br.*) сосе́д (*fem.* -ка) по кварти́ре.
4 (*coll., punctured tyre*) спу́щенная ши́на.

● *adj. & adv.* (**flatter, flattest**) **1** (*level*) пло́ский, ро́вный; **~ car** (*US*) ваго́н-платфо́рма; **he has ~ feet** у него́ плоскосто́пие; **~ race, racing** ска́чка без препя́тствий; **~ spin** (*aeron.*) пло́ский што́пор; **get into a ~ spin** (*Br. sl.*) впада́ть, впасть в па́нику; **~ trajectory fire** насти́льный ого́нь; **~ tyre** (*Br.*), **tire** (*US*) спу́щенная ши́на; **the battery is ~** (*Br.*) батаре́я се́ла; **he fell ~ on his back** он упа́л на́взничь; **my hair won't lie ~** у меня́ во́лосы не лежа́т.
2 (*uniform, undifferentiated*) однообра́зный; **~ rate** еди́ная ста́вка.
3 (*unqualified*) прямо́й, категори́ческий; **~ broke** вконе́ц

разори́вшийся; ~ **out** (*sl., exhausted*) вы́дохшийся; **drive ~ out** (*coll., at top speed*) гнать (*impf.*) во весь опо́р (*or* во всю мочь); **in ten seconds ~** ро́вно за де́сять секу́нд; **I tell you ~!** я скажу́ вам пря́мо (*or* без обиняко́в)!; **I've said no, and that's ~** я сказа́л нет — и то́чка.
4 (*dull, insipid*) ску́чный, вя́лый, бесцве́тный; **the wine has gone ~** вино́ вы́дохлось; **the story fell ~** расска́з не вы́звал интере́са.
5 (*expressionless*) безжи́зненный, уны́лый.
6 (*mus.*): **she sings ~ on the high notes** она́ фальши́вит (*or* не дотя́гивает) на высо́ких но́тах.
● *cpds.* **~bed** *adj.* (*comput.*) планше́тный; **~bed scanner** планше́тный ска́нер; **~-fish** *n.* пло́ская ры́ба; **~-foot** *n.* (*policeman*) мильто́н (*sl.*); **~-footed** *adj.* страда́ющий плоскосто́пием; (*fig., clumsy*) неуклю́жий; **~-iron** *n.* утю́г.

flatlet /ˈflætlət/ *n.* (*Br.*) однокомнатная/малогабари́тная кварти́ра.

flatly /ˈflætlɪ/ *adv.* (*expressionlessly*) безжи́зненно, уны́ло; (*bluntly*) категори́чески, наотре́з, пря́мо.

flatness /ˈflætnɪs/ *n.* пло́скость; (*fig.*) бана́льность.

flatten /ˈflæt(ə)n/ *v.t.* **1** (*make smooth*) выра́внивать, вы́ровнять; разгла́|живать, -дить. **2** (*reduce thickness of*) расплю́щи|вать, -ть; **he ~ed himself against the wall** он прижа́лся к стене́. **3** (*lay low*) повали́ть, примя́ть (*both pf.*); **the gale ~ed the corn** бу́рей примя́ло хлеба́; (*fig.*): **he was ~ed by her look of scorn** он был изничто́жен её презри́тельным взгля́дом.
● *v.i.* выра́вниваться, вы́ровняться; **the pilot ~ed out at fifty metres** (*Br.*), **meters** (*US*) пило́т вы́ровнял самолёт на высоте́ 50 ме́тров; **the rise in prices will soon ~ out** це́ны ско́ро вы́ровняются.

flatter /ˈflætə(r)/ *v.t.* **1** (*praise insincerely or unduly*) льсти́ть, по- +*d.* **2** (*represent too favourably*) приукра́|шивать, -сить; **the picture ~s her** худо́жник ей польсти́л. **3** (*gratify vanity of*): **~ o.s.** те́шить (*impf.*) себя́; льсти́ть (*impf.*) себя́ наде́ждой; **it ~s his self-esteem** э́то льсти́т его́ самолю́бию; **I ~ myself I'm a good judge of horses** я сме́ю ду́мать, что разбира́юсь в лошадя́х.

flatterer /ˈflætərə(r)/ *n.* льсте́ц.

flattering /ˈflætərɪŋ/ *adj.* ле́стный, льсти́вый; (*of person*) льсти́вый; **that's a ~ hairstyle** э́та причёска вам о́чень к лицу́.

flattery /ˈflætərɪ/ *n.* лесть.

flatulence /ˈflætjʊləns/ *n.* скопле́ние га́зов; (*fig.*) напы́щенность, высокопа́рность.

flatulent /ˈflætjʊlənt/ *adj.* вызыва́ющий га́зы; взду́вшийся от га́зов; (*fig.*) напы́щенный, высокопа́рный.

flaunt /flɔːnt/ *v.t.* афиши́ровать (*impf.*); щеголь|я́ть, -ну́ть +*i.*; выставля́ть, вы́ставить напока́з.

flautist /ˈflɔːtɪst/ *n.* флейти́ст (*fem.* -ка).

flavour /ˈfleɪvə(r)/ (*US* **flavor**) *n.* арома́т, вкус; (*fig.*) при́вкус.
● *v.t.* припр|авля́ть, -а́вить; (*fig.*) прид|ава́ть, -а́ть при́вкус +*d.*; сд|а́бривать, -о́брить.

flavourful /ˈfleɪvəfʊl/ (*US* **flavorful**) *adj.* аппети́тный, арома́тный.

flavouring /ˈfleɪvərɪŋ/ (*US* **flavoring**) *n.* припра́ва; спе́ции (*f. pl.*); эссе́нция.

flavourless /ˈfleɪvəlɪs/ (*US* **flavorless**) *adj.* безвку́сный.

flavoursome /ˈfleɪvəsəm/ (*US* **flavorsome**) *adj.* аппети́тный, арома́тный.

flaw /flɔː/ *n.* (*crack*) тре́щина; (*defect*) изъя́н, недоста́ток; **I detect a ~ in your argument** я ви́жу сла́бое ме́сто в ва́ших доказа́тельствах.
● *v.t.* по́ртить, ис-; **all ~ed articles are reduced** брако́ванные това́ры продаю́тся по сни́женным це́нам.

flawless /ˈflɔːlɪs/ *adj.* безупре́чный.

flax /flæks/ *n.* (*plant*) лён; (*fibre*) куде́ль.

flaxen /ˈflæks(ə)n/ *adj.* **1** (*of flax*) льняно́й. **2** (*colour*) светло-жёлтый, соло́менный.
● *cpd.* **~-haired** *adj.* с льняны́ми волоса́ми.

flay /fleɪ/ *v.t.* свежева́ть, о-; сдира́ть, содра́ть ко́жу с +*g.*; **he will ~ me alive if he finds out** он с меня́ живьём шку́ру сдерёт, е́сли узна́ет; (*fig.*): **~ one's opponents** разн|оси́ть, -ести́ в пух и пра́х.

flea /fliː/ *n.* блоха́; **I sent him off with a ~ in his ear** он получи́л от меня́ хоро́ший разно́с; **~ market** барахо́лка, толку́чка.
● *cpds.* **~ bite** *n.* блоши́ный уку́с; (*coll.*) ме́лочь, була́вочный уко́л; **~-bitten** *adj.* поно́шенный, заса́ленный; **~-pit** *n.* (*Br. sl., cinema*) кино́шка.

fleck /flek/ *n.* кра́пинка, пятно́; (*of dust*) пыли́нка.
● *v.t.* покр|ыва́ть, -ы́ть пя́тнами/кра́пинками.

fled /fled/ *past and p.p. of* ⇒**flee**

fledge /fledʒ/ *v.t.* (*bird, arrow*) опер|я́ть, -и́ть; **fully ~d** (*lit., fig.*) опери́вшийся.

fledg(e)ling /ˈfledʒlɪŋ/ *n.* то́лько что опери́вшийся птене́ц; (*fig.*) желторо́тый юне́ц.

flee /fliː/ *v.t.* (*past and p.p.* **fled**) избе|га́ть, -жа́ть; **~ the country** бежа́ть (*impf.*) из страны́.
● *v.i.* (*past and p.p.* **fled**) бежа́ть, с-; исч|еза́ть, -е́знуть.

fleece /fliːs/ *n.* руно́, ове́чья шерсть.
● *v.t.* (*fig.*) об|ира́ть, -обра́ть.

fleecy /ˈfliːsɪ/ *adj.* (**fleecier, fleeciest**) шерсти́стый; **~ clouds** кудря́вые облака́; **~ lining** пуши́стая подкла́дка.

fleet[1] /fliːt/ *n.* **1** (*collection of vessels*) флоти́лия, флот. **2** (*naval force*) вое́нно-морско́й флот; **Admiral of the F~** адмира́л фло́та. **3** (*of vehicles*) парк.

fleet[2] /fliːt/ *adj.* (*liter.*) бы́стрый, прово́рный; **~ of foot** быстроно́гий.

fleeting /ˈfliːtɪŋ/ *adj.* бе́глый, мимолётный; **a ~ glimpse** бе́глый взгляд.

Fleet Street /fliːt/ *n.* (*fig.*) ло́ндонская пре́сса.

Fleming /ˈflemɪŋ/ *n.* флама́нд|ец (*fem.* -ка).

Flemish /ˈflemɪʃ/ *n.* (*language*) флама́ндский язы́к; **the ~** (*people*) флама́ндцы (*m. pl.*).
● *adj.* флама́ндский.

F

flesh /fleʃ/ *n.* **1** (*bodily tissue*) плоть, те́ло; **insist on one's pound of ~** (*fig.*) ≈ безжа́лостно тре́бовать (*impf.*) упла́ты до́лга (*u m.n.*); (*meat*) мя́со; **pig's ~** свини́на; (*surface of body*): **~ tint** теле́сный цвет; **~ wound** пове́рхностное ране́ние; **make s.o.'s ~ creep** (*fig.*) прив|оди́ть, -ести́ кого́-н. в содрога́ние.
2 (*fig.*): **he went the way of all ~** он раздели́л у́часть всех сме́ртных; **sins of the ~** пло́тские грехи́; **see s.o. in the ~** ви́деть, у- кого́-н. во плоти́; **appear in ~ and blood** появ|ля́ться, -и́ться со́бственной персо́ной; **more than ~ and blood can stand** свы́ше сил челове́ческих; **my own ~ and blood** (*children*) моя́ плоть и кровь; (*relatives*) моя́ родня́.
3 (*of plant or fruit*) мя́со, мя́коть.
● *v.t.* **1**: **~ a hound** приуч|а́ть, -и́ть соба́ку к охо́те вку́сом кро́ви.
2 (*fig.*): **his characters are well ~ed out** его́ геро́и о́чень жи́зненны.
● *cpd.* **~-coloured** (*US* **-colored**) *adj.* теле́сного цве́та.

fleshly /ˈfleʃlɪ/ *adj.* (**fleshlier, fleshliest**) (*carnal*) пло́тский, чу́вственный.

fleshy /ˈfleʃɪ/ *adj.* (**fleshier, fleshiest**) (*of persons*) то́лстый, ту́чный; (*of meat, plant, fruit*) мяси́стый.

fleur-de-lis /ˌflɜːdəˈliː/ *n.* (*pl.* **fleurs-de-lis** *pronunc. same*) (*her.*) геральди́ческая ли́лия.

flew /fluː/ *past of* ⇒**fly**[3]

flex[1] /fleks/ *n.* (*Br.*) (ги́бкий) шнур.

flex[2] /fleks/ *v.t.* сгиба́ть, согну́ть; **~ one's muscles** напр|яга́ть, -я́чь му́скулы.

flexibility /ˌfleksɪˈbɪlɪtɪ/ *n.* эласти́чность; (*fig.*) ги́бкость.

flexible /ˈfleksɪb(ə)l/ *adj.* эласти́чный, ги́бкий; (*fig.*) ги́бкий.

flexion /ˈflekʃ(ə)n/ *n.* изги́б, изо́гнутость.

flexitime /ˈfleksɪˌtaɪm/ *n.* ненорми́рованный рабо́чий день.

flexor /ˈfleksə(r)/ *n.* (~ *muscle*) сгиба́ющая мы́шца.

flibbertigibbet /ˌflɪbətɪˈdʒɪbɪt/, /ˈflɪb-/ *n.* болту́шка (*c.g.*).

flick /flɪk/ *n.* **1** (*jerk*) толчо́к; **with a ~ of the wrist** взмахну́в ки́стью руки́; (*light touch*): **a ~ of the whip** лёгкий уда́р хлысто́м. **2** (*coll., film*) кинофи́льм; (*pl., cinema*) кино́ (*indecl.*).
● *v.t.* (*shake with a jerk*) встр|я́хивать, -яхну́ть; (*propel with finger end*)

щёлк|ать, -нуть; (*touch e.g. with whip*) стегну́ть (*pf.*); хлестну́ть (*pf.*).

● *v.i.*: ~ **through** просм|а́тривать, -отре́ть.

● *cpd.* **~-knife** *n.* (*Br.*) пружи́нный нож.

flicker /ˈflɪkə(r)/ *n.* (*of light*) мерца́ние; (*movement*) трепета́ние; (*fig.*): **a ~ of hope** про́блеск наде́жды.

● *v.i.* (*flutter*) трепета́ть (*impf.*); колыха́ться (*impf.*); (*burn or shine fitfully*) мерца́ть (*impf.*); (*fig.*) мельк|а́ть, -ну́ть.

flier /ˈflaɪə(r)/ = **flyer**

flight[1] /flaɪt/ *n.* **1** полёт; **shoot birds in ~** стреля́ть (*impf.*) птиц на лету́; (*fig.*): **the ~ of time** бег вре́мени; (*journey by air*): **a non-stop ~** беспоса́дочный полёт; **a round-the-world ~** полёт вокру́г све́та; (*a particular ~*) рейс; **the next ~ from London to Paris** сле́дующий рейс по маршру́ту Ло́ндон-Пари́ж; **~ number** но́мер ре́йса; **~ path** курс полёта; **~ recorder** бортово́й самопи́сец; **~ simulator** лётный тренажёр.
2 (*fig.*): **~ of fancy** полёт фанта́зии.
3: **~ of steps** ле́стничный марш; (*in front of house*) крыльцо́.
4: **a ~ of birds** ста́я птиц.

● *cpds.* **~ attendant** *n.* стю́ард; (*fem.* -е́сса); **~ case** *n.* жёсткий футля́р; **~-deck** *n.* (*of carrier*) полётная па́луба; (*of aircraft*) каби́на экипа́жа; **~ engineer** *n.* бортмеха́ник; **~-lieutenant** *n.* капита́н авиа́ции; **~-sergeant** *n.* ста́рший сержа́нт авиа́ции.

flight[2] /flaɪt/ *n.* бе́гство, побе́г; **put to ~** обра|ща́ть, -ти́ть в бе́гство; **take (to) ~** обра|ща́ться, -ти́ться в бе́гство; **the soldiers took to ~** солда́ты бежа́ли; **the army was in full ~** а́рмия стреми́тельно отступа́ла.

flightiness /ˈflaɪtɪnɪs/ *n.* ве́треность.

flighty /ˈflaɪtɪ/ *adj.* (**flightier, flightiest**) ве́треный, капри́зный.

flimsiness /ˈflɪmzɪnɪs/ *n.* то́нкость, непро́чность.

flimsy /ˈflɪmzɪ/ *adj.* (**flimsier, flimsiest**) то́нкий, непро́чный; **a ~ dress** о́чень лёгкое пла́тье; **a ~ structure** непро́чная постро́йка; **a ~ excuse** сла́бое оправда́ние.

flinch /flɪntʃ/ *v.i.* (*wince*) вздр|а́гивать, -о́гнуть; (*give way*) уклон|я́ться, -и́ться (*от чего*).

fling /flɪŋ/ *n.* **1** (*sexual*) коро́ткий рома́н, интри́жка.
2: **Highland ~** шотла́ндский та́нец.
3: **he had his ~** он повесели́лся/ нагуля́лся вво́лю.

● *v.t.* (*past and p.p.* **flung**): **~ o.s. into a chair** бр|оса́ться, -о́ситься в кре́сло; **~ o.s. into the saddle** вск|а́кивать, -очи́ть в седло́; **he flung himself into the project** он с голово́й окуну́лся в осуществле́ние прое́кта; **he was flung into prison** его́ бро́сили в тюрьму́; **I ~ myself (up)on your mercy** я взыва́ю к ва́шему милосе́рдию; **she flung her arms around me** она́ обняла́ меня́.

● *v.i.* (*past and p.p.* **flung**): **~ out of the room** вы́скочить/вы́лететь (*both pf.*) из ко́мнаты.

● *with advs.*: **~ o.s. about** разбра́сываться (*impf.*); **~ one's money around** транжи́рить (*impf.*) де́ньги; сори́ть (*impf.*) деньга́ми; **he flung her aside** он оттолкну́л её в сто́рону; **~ away an advantage** отка́з|ываться, -а́ться от преиму́щества; **~ o.s. down on the ground** бр|оса́ться, -о́ситься на зе́млю; **she flung her clothes off** она́ сбро́сила с себя́ оде́жду; **~ open the window** распа́х|ивать, -ну́ть окно́; **he was flung out** его́ вы́швырнули вон; **he flung a few things together** он на́скоро собра́л свои́ ве́щи; **she flung up her arms in horror** она́ в у́жасе всплесну́ла рука́ми.

flint /flɪnt/ *n.* креме́нь (*m.*); (*attr.*) кремнёвый, ка́менный.

flinty /ˈflɪntɪ/ *adj.* (**flintier, flintiest**) кремнёвый, кремни́стый; (*fig.*) ка́менный, суро́вый.

flip /flɪp/ *n.* **1** (*flick*) щелчо́к. **2** (*coll.*): **the ~ side of a record** обра́тная сторона́ пласти́нки.

● *adj.* (*flippant*) де́рзкий.

● *v.t.* (**flipped, flipping**) (*flick*) щёлк|ать, -нуть; (*a coin*) подбр|а́сывать, -о́сить; **~ one's lid** (*or US* **wig**) (*coll., go crazy*) с ума́ с|ходи́ть, -ойти́.

● *v.i.* (*coll., go crazy*) с ума́ с|ходи́ть, -ойти́; **~ through** просм|а́тривать, -отре́ть.

flip-flop /ˈflɪpflɒp/ *n.* **1** (*US, backward somersault*) са́льто-морта́ле (*indecl.*). **2** (*footwear*) вьетна́мка. **3** (*elec.*) три́ггер.

flippancy /ˈflɪpənsɪ/ *n.* легкомы́слие, ве́треность.

flippant /ˈflɪpənt/ *adj.* легкомы́сленный, ве́треный.

flipper /ˈflɪpə(r)/ *n.* плавни́к, ласт; (*diver's appendage*) ласт; (*direction indicator of car*) стре́лка.

flirt /flɜːt/ *n.* коке́тка; люби́тель (*m.*) поуха́живать.

● *v.i.* флиртова́ть (*impf.*) (с + *i.*); коке́тничать (*impf.*) (с + *i.*); (*fig.*): **~ with danger** игра́ть (*impf.*) с огнём; **~ with** (*an idea etc.*) поду́мывать (*impf.*) о + *p.*

flirtation /flɜːˈteɪʃ(ə)n/ *n.* флирт; коке́тство (*fig.*) игра́.

flirtatious /flɜːˈteɪʃəs/ *adj.* коке́тливый.

flit /flɪt/ *n.* (*Br.*): **the tenants did a moonlight ~** жильцы́ потихо́ньку смы́лись (*coll.*).

● *v.i.* (**flitted, flitting**) (*fly lightly*) порх|а́ть, -ну́ть; (*fig.*): **the thought ~ted across my mind** э́та мысль пронесла́сь у меня́ в голове́.

float /fləʊt/ *n.* **1** (*for supporting line or net*) поплаво́к, буй; (*of a seaplane*) поплаво́к; (*for learning to swim*) пла́вательный пло́тик.
2 (*Br., cart*) платфо́рма на колёсах; **milk ~** электрока́р для разво́зки молока́.
3 (*small change*) разме́нные де́ньги, ме́лочь; (*Br., petty cash*) де́ньги на ме́лкие расхо́ды.

● *v.t.* спус|ка́ть, -ти́ть на́ воду; (*stranded boat*) сн|има́ть, -я́ть с мели́; (*comm.*): **~ a company** учре|жда́ть, -ди́ть акционе́рное о́бщество; **~ a loan** разме|ща́ть, -сти́ть заём; (*fin.*): **~ the pound** перев|оди́ть, -ести́ фунт сте́рлингов на пла́вающий курс.

● *v.i.* **1** пла́вать (*indet.*), плыть (*det.*); **oil ~s on water** ма́сло не то́нет в воде́; **the boat ~ed down-river** ло́дку несло́ тече́нием вниз по реке́.
2 (*in air*) (*aeroplane*) плани́ровать (*impf.*); (*clouds etc.*) плыть (*det.*).
3 (*fig.*): **his past ~ed before him** его́ про́шлое пронесло́сь пе́ред ним.

floater /ˈfləʊtə(r)/ *n.* (*Br., undecided voter*) колеблю́щийся избира́тель.

floating /ˈfləʊtɪŋ/ *adj.* пла́вающий, плаву́чий; **~ bridge** понто́нный/ наплавно́й мост; **~ capital** оборо́тный капита́л; **~ debt** краткосро́чный долг; теку́щая задо́лженность; **~ dock** плаву́чий док; **~ kidney** блужда́ющая по́чка; **~ light** плаву́чий мая́к; **~ population** теку́чее народонаселе́ние; **~ vote** избира́тели, на кото́рых нельзя́ твёрдо рассчи́тывать; **~ voter** колеблю́щийся избира́тель.

flock /flɒk/ *n.* (*of birds*) ста́я; (*of sheep or goats*) ста́до; (*of people*) толпа́; (*relig.*) па́ства.

● *v.i.* стека́ться (*impf.*); дви́гаться (*impf.*) толпо́й; **they ~ed for miles to hear him** они́ стека́лись отовсю́ду, что́бы послу́шать его́.

floe /fləʊ/ *n.* плаву́чая льди́на.

flog /flɒg/ *v.t.* (**flogged, flogging**)
1 (*beat*) стега́ть, от-; поро́ть, вы́-; сечь, вы́-; **he is ~ging a dead horse** (*fig.*) он пыта́ется возроди́ть то, что безнадёжно устаре́ло. **2** (*Br. coll., sell*) заг|оня́ть, -на́ть; толк|а́ть, -ну́ть (*both coll.*).

flogging /ˈflɒgɪŋ/ *n.* по́рка.

flood /flʌd/ *n.* **1** (*tide*) прили́в.
2 (*inundation*) наводне́ние, полово́дье, разли́в; **the F~** (*bibl.*) пото́п; **the river is in ~** река́ разлила́сь.
3 (*torrent of water*) пото́к.
4 (*fig.*): **she burst into ~s of tears** она́ разрыда́лась; **a ~ of abuse** пото́к оскорбле́ний.

● *v.t.* затоп|ля́ть, -и́ть; наводн|я́ть, -и́ть; **the basement was ~ed** подва́л затопи́ло; **he was ~ed with replies** о́тклики так и посы́пались на него́.

● *v.i.* разл|ива́ться, -и́ться; выходи́ть, вы́йти из берего́в; **the river ~s every spring** река́ разлива́ется ка́ждую весну́.

● *cpds.* **~-gate** *n.* шлюз; **open the ~-gates** (*fig.*) да|ва́ть, -ть во́лю (*чему*); **~light** *n.* проже́ктор; (*theatr.*) юпи́тер; *v.t.* осве|ща́ть, -ти́ть проже́кторами; **~lighting** *n.* проже́кторное освеще́ние; **~-plain** *n.* заливно́й луг; **~-tide** *n.* прили́в.

flooding /ˈflʌdɪŋ/ *n.* затопле́ние.

floor /flɔː(r)/ *n.* **1** пол; **the ring fell to the ~** кольцо́ упа́ло на́ пол; **the child**

was playing on the ~ ребёнок игра́л на полу́; **he could wipe the ~ with you** он мог бы смеша́ть вас с гря́зью; **~ lamp** (*US*) торше́р.
2: **take the ~** (*in public assembly*) брать, взять сло́во; (*in dance hall*) вы́ступить (*pf.*) в та́нце.
3 (*storey*) эта́ж; **ground ~** пе́рвый эта́ж.
4: **shop ~** цех; **threshing ~** гумно́, ток.
5 (*of ocean, cave*) дно.
6 (*minimum level of prices etc.*) минима́льный у́ровень.
● *v.t.* **1** (*provide floor for*) наст|ила́ть, -ла́ть пол в + *p.*
2 (*coll., knock down*) сби|ва́ть, -ть с ног; (*fig., nonplus*) сра|жа́ть, -зи́ть; ошелом|ля́ть, -и́ть; ста́вить, по- в тупи́к; **the question ~ed him** вопро́с срази́л его́.
● *cpds.* **~board** *n.* полови́ца; **~-cloth** *n.* (*Br.*) полова́я тря́пка; **~-polish** *n.* масти́ка (для нати́рки поло́в); **~-polisher** *n.* полотёр; **~-show** *n.* представле́ние в кабаре́; **~-space** *n.* пло́щадь по́ла; **~-walker** *n.* (*US*) дежу́рный администра́тор в универма́ге.
flooring /'flɔ:rɪŋ/ *n.* (*material*) насти́л, пол; (*action*) насти́лка поло́в.
floo|sie, -zie /'flu:zɪ/ *n.* (*sl.*) шлю́ха.
flop /flɒp/ *n.* (*motion, sound*) шлепо́к, хлопо́к; (*coll., failure*) прова́л.
● *v.i.* (**flopped, flopping**) **1** (*move limply*): **~ down in a chair** плю́х|аться, -нуться в кре́сло; **~ around in slippers** шлёпать (*impf.*) в дома́шних ту́флях.
2 (*coll., fail*) прова́л|иваться, -и́ться.
● *cpd.* **~-house** *n.* (*US sl.*) ночле́жка.
floppy /'flɒpɪ/ *adj.* (**floppier, floppiest**) болта́ющийся, свиса́ющий; мя́гкий, обви́слый; **~ disk** (*comput.*) ги́бкий диск.
flora /'flɔ:rə/ *n.* (*pl.* **floras** *or* **florae** /-ri:/) фло́ра.
floral /'flɔ:r(ə)l/, /'flɒ-/ *adj.* цвето́чный; **~ tribute** подноше́ние цвето́в.
Florence /'flɒrəns/ *n.* Флоре́нция.
Florentine /'flɒrən,taın/ *adj.* флоренти́йский.
florescence /flɔ:'res(ə)ns/, /flɒ-/ *n.* цвете́ние; (*fig.*) расцве́т.
floriculture /'flɒrɪ,kʌltʃə(r)/, /'flɔ:-/ *n.* цветово́дство.
florid /'flɒrɪd/ *adj.* (*ornate*) цвети́стый, витиева́тый; (*ruddy*) кра́сный, багро́вый.
Florida /'flɒrɪdə/ *n.* Флори́да.
florin /'flɒrɪn/ *n.* (*hist.*) флори́н.
florist /'flɒrɪst/ *n.* продаве́ц цвето́в; (*fem.*) цвето́чница.
floruit /'flɒrʊɪt/, /'flɔ:-/ *n.* пери́од де́ятельности (*кого*).
floss /flɒs/ *n.* шёлк-сыре́ц; **dental ~** ни́тка для чи́стки ме́жду зуба́ми.
flossy /'flɒsɪ/ *adj.* (**flossier, flossiest**) шелкови́стый.
flotation /fləʊ'teɪʃ(ə)n/ *n.* распрода́жа а́кций компа́нии.
flotilla /flə'tɪlə/ *n.* флоти́лия (ме́лких судо́в).
flotsam /'flɒtsəm/ *n.* вы́брошенный и пла́вающий на пове́рхности груз, му́сор; (*fig.*) облó́мки (*m. pl.*).
flounce[1] /flaʊns/ *n.* (*abrupt movement*) рыво́к.
● *v.i.* бр|оса́ться, -о́ситься; **~ out (of a room)** вылета́ть, вы́лететь из ко́мнаты.
flounce[2] /flaʊns/ *n.* (*trimming*) обо́рка.
● *v.t.* отде́л|ывать, -ать обо́рками.
flounder[1] /'flaʊndə(r)/ *n.* (*zool.*) ме́лкая ка́мбала.
flounder[2] /'flaʊndə(r)/ *v.i.* бара́хтаться (*impf.*); (*fig.*) пу́таться (*impf.*) в слова́х.
flour /'flaʊə(r)/ *n.* мука́.
● *cpd.* **~-mill** *n.* мукомо́льная ме́льница; мукомо́льня.
flourish /'flʌrɪʃ/ *n.* **1** (*wave of hand etc.*) широ́кий жест; разма́хивание.
2 (*embellishment of literary style*) цвети́стость; цвети́стое выраже́ние; (*fanfare*) фанфа́ры (*f. pl.*); туш; (*of penmanship*) ро́счерк, завиту́шка.
● *v.t.* разма́хивать (*impf.*) + *i.*
● *v.i.* (*grow healthily*) пы́шно расти́ (*impf.*); (*prosper; be active*) процвета́ть (*impf.*).
flourishing /'flʌrɪʃɪŋ/ *adj.* процвета́ющий, преуспева́ющий; **a ~ business** процвета́ющее де́ло.
floury /'flaʊərɪ/ *adj.* (**flourier, flouriest**) (*of potato*) рассы́пчатый, мучни́стый.
flout /flaʊt/ *v.t.* поп|ира́ть, -ра́ть.
flow /fləʊ/ *n.* тече́ние, пото́к; **ebb and ~** прили́в и отли́в; (*fig.*) тече́ние; **interrupt the ~ of conversation** прер|ыва́ть, -ва́ть пла́вное тече́ние разгово́ра; **in full ~** в разга́ре.
● *v.i.* **1** течь, ли́ться (*both impf.*); **a land ~ing with milk and honey** ≈ моло́чные ре́ки и кисе́льные берега́; **the wine ~ed freely** вино́ лило́сь реко́й; **the Oka ~s into the Volga** Ока́ впада́ет в Во́лгу. **2** (*fig., proceed, move freely*) ли́ться, течь (*both impf.*).
● *cpd.* **~ chart/diagram** *n.* блок-схе́ма.
flower /'flaʊə(r)/ *n.* цвето́к; цветко́вое расте́ние; **in ~** в цвету́; **come into ~** расцве|та́ть, -сти́; **~ arrangement** расположе́ние цвето́в; **~ show** вы́ставка цвето́в; (*fig.*): **the ~ of the nation's youth** цвет молодёжи страны́.
● *v.i.* (*blossom; flourish*) цвести́ (*impf.*).
● *cpds.* **~-bed** *n.* клу́мба; **~-pot** *n.* цвето́чный горшо́к.
flowering /'flaʊərɪŋ/ *n.* цвете́ние.
● *adj.* цвету́щий.
flowery /'flaʊərɪ/ *adj.* покры́тый цвета́ми; (*fig.*) цвети́стый.
flowing /'fləʊɪŋ/ *adj.*: **~ hair** развева́ющиеся во́лосы; **~ lines** мя́гкие/пла́вные ли́нии; **~ style** гла́дкий стиль.
flown /fləʊn/ *p.p. of* ⇒**fly**[3]
flu /flu:/ *n.* (*coll.*) грипп; **go down with ~** слечь (*pf.*) с гри́ппом.
fluctuate /'flʌktjʊ,eɪt/ *v.i.* колеба́ться (*impf.*).
fluctuation /,flʌktjʊ'eɪʃ(ə)n/ *n.* колеба́ние.
flue /flu:/ *n.* дымохо́д.
● *cpd.* **~-pipe** *n.* (*tech.*) жарова́я труба́.
fluency /'flu:ənsɪ/ *n.* пла́вность, бе́глость.
fluent /'flu:ənt/ *adj.* пла́вный, бе́глый; **he speaks Russian ~ly** он свобо́дно говори́т по-ру́сски.
fluff /flʌf/ *n.* пух, пушо́к.
● *v.t.* **1** (*make fluffy*) взби|ва́ть, -ть; распуши́ть (*pf.*); **~ up a cushion** взби|ва́ть, -ть поду́шку; **the bird ~ed out its feathers** пти́ца распуши́ла пе́рья. **2** (*coll., bungle*) пу́тать, с-; **~ one's lines** произн|оси́ть, -ести́ свою́ роль с запи́нкой.
fluffy /'flʌfɪ/ *adj.* (**fluffier, fluffiest**) пуши́стый, взби́тый.
fluid /'flu:ɪd/ *n.* жи́дкость; **cleaning ~** жи́дкость для чи́стки; **correction ~** бели́л|а (*pl., g.* —).
● *adj.* жи́дкий, теку́чий; (*fig.*) неопределённый, переме́нчивый; **~ ounce** жи́дкая у́нция.
fluidity /,flu:'ɪdɪtɪ/ *n.* теку́честь; (*fig.*) переме́нчивость, неопределённость.
fluke[1] /flu:k/ *n.* (*lucky stroke*) (неожи́данная) уда́ча, случа́йность.
fluke[2] /flu:k/ *n.* (*worm*) глист.
flummox /'flʌməks/ *v.t.* (*coll.*) ошелом|ля́ть, -и́ть.
flung /flʌŋ/ *past and p.p. of* ⇒**fling**
flunk /flʌŋk/ *v.t. & i.* (*US coll.*): **he ~ed his exam** он провали́лся/засы́пался на экза́мене.
flunkey /'flʌŋkɪ/ *n.* лаке́й.
fluoresce /flʊə'res/ *v.i.* флюоресци́ровать (*impf.*).
fluorescence /flʊə'res(ə)ns/ *n.* флюоресце́нция.
fluorescent /flʊə'res(ə)nt/ *adj.* флюоресце́нтный.
fluoridate /'flʊərɪ,deɪt/ *v.t.* фтори́ровать (*impf., pf.*).
fluoridation /,flʊərɪ'deɪʃ(ə)n/ *n.* фтори́рование.
fluoride /'flʊəraɪd/ *n.* фтори́д.
fluorine /'flʊəri:n/ *n.* фтор.
fluor|ite /'flʊəraɪt/, **-spar** /'flʊəspɑ:(r)/ *nn.* флюори́т; пла́виковый шпат.
flurry /'flʌrɪ/ *n.* (*gust, squall*) шквал; (*agitation*) волне́ние, сумато́ха.
flush[1] /flʌʃ/ *n.* (*flow of water*) внеза́пный прили́в; пото́к; (*flow of blood; blush*) прили́в кро́ви; румя́нец; кра́ска на лице́; **hot ~** прили́в; (*fig.*): **in the ~ of youth** в расцве́те ю́ности.
● *v.t.* **1** (*swill clean*) пром|ыва́ть, -ы́ть; **~ the lavatory** спус|ка́ть, -ти́ть во́ду в убо́рной. **2** (*make red*) зал|ива́ть, -и́ть кра́ской. **3**: **he is ~ed with pride** его́ распира́ет го́рдость.
● *v.i.* красне́ть, по-; зал|ива́ться, -и́ться кра́ской.
flush[2] /flʌʃ/ *n.* (*cards*) ка́рты одно́й ма́сти; **royal ~** флешь-роя́ль, коро́нка.
flush[3] /flʌʃ/ *adj.* **1** (*coll., well supplied with money*): **he is ~** у него́ де́нег ку́ры

не клюю́т. **2** (*on the same level*) заподлицо́ (*adv.*); (находя́щийся) на одно́м у́ровне (*с чем*).

flush[4] /flʌʃ/ *v.t.* (*birds etc.*) вспу́г|ивать, -ну́ть.

flushed /flʌʃd/ *adj.* охва́ченный (*чем*); упоённый; ~ **with victory** упоённый побе́дой.

fluster /ˈflʌstə(r)/ *n.* суета́, волне́ние.

● *v.t.* волнова́ть, вз-; будора́жить, вз-.

flute[1] /flu:t/ *n.* (*instrument*) фле́йта.

flute[2] /flu:t/ *n.* (*groove*) желобо́к; каннелю́ра.

● *v.t.* желоби́ть (*impf.*).

fluted /ˈflu:tɪd/ *adj.* гофриро́ванный, рифлёный.

fluting /ˈflu:tɪŋ/ *n.* (*archit.*) канелю́ры (*f. pl.*); ри́фля.

flutist /ˈflu:tɪst/ (*US*) = **flautist**

flutter /ˈflʌtə(r)/ *n.* **1** (*of wings, leaves, flags etc.*) трепета́ние, дрожь. **2** (*agitation*) волне́ние, тре́пет; **to be in a ~ of expectation** с тре́петом ждать (*impf.*). **3** (*Br. coll., small bet*): **he had a ~ on the horses** он попыта́л сча́стья на ска́чках.

● *v.t.* мах|а́ть, -ну́ть + *i.*

● *v.i.* трепета́ть (*impf.*); (*of birds*) переп|а́рхивать, -орхну́ть.

fluvial /ˈflu:vɪəl/ *adj.* речно́й.

flux /flʌks/ *n.* **1** (*succession of changes*) постоя́нная сме́на; **everything was in a state of ~** всё бы́ло в состоя́нии непреры́вного измене́ния. **2** (*med.*) патологи́ческое оби́льное истече́ние. **3** (*metall.*) флюс, пла́вень (*m.*).

fly[1] /flaɪ/ *n.* му́ха; (*fig.*): **~ in the ointment** ло́жка дёгтя в бо́чке мёду; **there are no flies on him** к нему́ не подкопа́ешься (*coll.*).

● *cpds.* **~-blown** *adj.* заси́женный му́хами; **~-catcher** *n.* (*bird*) мухоло́вка; **~-fishing** *n.* уже́ние ры́бы на му́ху; **~-paper** *n.* ли́пкая бума́га (*or* ли́пкие ле́нты (*f. pl.*)) от мух; **~-spray** *n.* (*fluid*) жи́дкость от мух; (*instrument*) аэрозо́ль (*m.*) от мух; **~-weight** *n.* вес «му́хи»; наилегча́йший боксёрский вес.

fly[2] /flaɪ/ *n.* (*on trousers*) шири́нка; **his ~ is open, undone** у него́ шири́нка расстёгнута.

● *cpds.* **~-button** *n.* пу́говица шири́нки; **~-leaf** *n.* форза́ц; **~sheet** *n.* (*Br.*) наве́с; **~-wheel** *n.* махово́е колесо́, махови́к.

fly[3] /flaɪ/ *v.t.* (*past* **flew;** *p.p.* **flown**): **~ the Atlantic** перелет|а́ть, -е́ть че́рез Атланти́ческий океа́н; **~ an aircraft** управля́ть (*impf.*) самолётом; **~ home the wounded** дост|авля́ть, -а́вить ра́неных в тыл самолётом; **~ a kite** запус|ка́ть, -ти́ть змея́; (*fig., put out feeler or lure*) пус|ка́ть, -ти́ть про́бный шар; **~ a flag** выве́шивать, вы́весить флаг; (*naut.*) носи́ть, нести́ флаг; **~ the British flag** пла́вать (*indet.*) под брита́нским фла́гом.

● *v.i.* (*past* **flew;** *p.p.* **flown**) **1** (*move through the air*) лета́ть (*indet.*), лете́ть, по- (*det.*); **as the crow flies** напрями́к; по прямо́й; **he has never flown** он никогда́ не лета́л; **~ in the face of fortune** искуша́ть (*impf.*) судьбу́; **the pieces flew in all directions** куски́ разлете́лись во все сто́роны. **2** (*move or pass swiftly*) пролет|а́ть, -е́ть; **I must ~!** ну, я побежа́л!; **he flew downstairs** он ку́барем скати́лся с ле́стницы; **the dog flew at him** соба́ка бро́силась на него́; **~ into a passion** вспыли́ть (*pf.*); **~ to s.o.'s defence** (*Br.*), **defense** (*US*) бро́ситься (*pf.*) на защи́ту кого́-н.; **let ~ (at s.o.)** вы́ругать (*pf.*) кого́-н.; **~ off the handle** (*coll.*) сорва́ться (*pf.*); взорва́ться (*pf.*); при|ходи́ть, -йти́ в я́рость; **send ~ing** швыр|я́ть, -ну́ть; (*of person*) сби|ва́ть, -ть с ног; **time flies** вре́мя лети́т; **the flag is ~ing** флаг развева́ется. **3** (*flee*) бежа́ть (*det.*); **the bird has flown** (*fig.*) пти́чка улете́ла.

● *with advs.*: **leaves were ~ing about** повсю́ду кружи́лись ли́стья; **~ away** улет|а́ть, -е́ть; **the plane flew in to refuel and flew off again** самолёт прилете́л на запра́вку и вновь/сно́ва улете́л; **~ off at a tangent** сорва́ться (*pf.*); отклон|я́ться, -и́ться; **the door flew open** дверь распахну́лась на́стежь; **she flew out to join her husband** она́ улете́ла к му́жу.

● *cpds.* **~-by-night** *n.* ненадёжный челове́к; **~over** *n.* (*Br., bridge, overpass*) эстака́да; путепрово́д; **~-past** *n.* (*Br.*) возду́шный пара́д.

flyer, flier /ˈflaɪə(r)/ *n.* **1** (*aviator*) лётчик. **2** (*handbill*) рекла́мный листо́к.

flying /ˈflaɪɪŋ/ *n.* полёт; **he likes ~** он лю́бит лета́ть; **~ instructor** лётчик-инстру́ктор; **~ school** лётная шко́ла; **~ visit** блицвизи́т; кра́ткое посеще́ние.

● *adj.*: **~ bomb** самолёт-снаря́д; **~ buttress** а́рочный контрфо́рс, аркбута́н; **pass with ~ colours** (*Br.*), **colors** (*US*) пройти́, сдать (*both pf.*) с бле́ском; **~ leap** прыжо́к с разбе́га; **F~ Officer** ста́рший лейтена́нт авиа́ции; **~ saucer** лета́ющая таре́лка; **F~ Squad** (*Br.*) специа́льный отря́д полице́йских для бы́строго налёта; **get off to a ~ start** сра́зу пойти́ (*pf.*) хорошо́ (*or* в го́ру); **pay a ~ visit** нанести́ (*pf.*) мимолётный визи́т.

● *cpds.* **~-boat** *n.* лета́ющая ло́дка; **~-fish** *n.* летýчая ры́ба; **~-machine** *n.* лета́тельный аппара́т.

FM *abbr. of* **1** ***Field Marshal*** фельдма́ршал. **2** ***frequency modulation*** ЧМ (частóтная модуля́ция); **~ radio** частóтно-модули́рованное ра́дио.

FO (*abbr. of* ***Foreign Office***) (*Br.*) = **FCO**

foal /fəʊl/ *n.* жеребёнок; **the mare is in ~** кобы́ла жерёбая.

● *v.i.* жереби́ться, о-.

foam /fəʊm/ *n.* пе́на; **~ rubber** по́ристая рези́на; пенопла́ст.

● *v.i.* пе́ниться (*impf.*); **he was ~ing at the mouth** у него́ была́ пе́на на губа́х; (*fig.*) он был в я́рости.

fob[1] /fɒb/ *n.* (*watch pocket*) карма́шек для часо́в.

fob[2] /fɒb/ *v.t.* (**fobbed, fobbing**): **~ s.o. off with promises** корми́ть (*impf.*) кого́-н. обеща́ниями; **~ off a cheap article on s.o.** всу́чивать, всучи́ть кому́-н. каку́ю-н. дешёвку.

f.o.b. (*abbr. of* ***free on board***) фоб (фра́нко-борт).

focal /ˈfəʊk(ə)l/ *adj.* фо́кусный; **~ distance, length** фо́кусное расстоя́ние; **~ point** фока́льная то́чка; (*fig.*): **the ~ point in his argument** гла́вный пункт его́ доказа́тельств.

foci /ˈfəʊsaɪ/ *pl. of* ⇒**focus**

fo'c's'le /ˈfəʊks(ə)l/ *n.* (*naut.*) бак, полуба́к.

focus /ˈfəʊkəs/ *n.* (*pl.* **focuses** *or* **foci**) (*math., phys., phot.*) фо́кус; **bring into ~** поме|ща́ть, -сти́ть в фо́кусе; **out of ~** не в фо́кусе; (*fig.*) центр, средото́чие; **he became the ~ of interest** он оказа́лся в це́нтре внима́ния.

● *v.t.* (**focused, focusing** *or* **focussed, focussing**) (*binoculars, camera*) настр|а́ивать, -о́ить; (*rays*) фокуси́ровать, с-; (*attention*) сосредо|та́чивать, -то́чить; **he ~(s)ed his attention on the book** он сосредото́чил всё своё внима́ние на кни́ге.

fodder /ˈfɒdə(r)/ *n.* корм для скота́; фура́ж.

foe /fəʊ/ *n.* враг, не́друг.

foetal (*Br.*), **fetal** /ˈfi:t(ə)l/ *adj.* заро́дышевый, эмбриона́льный; **~ position** положе́ние эмбрио́на (в ма́тке).

foetus (*Br.*), **fetus** /ˈfi:təs/ *n.* (*pl.* **~es**) плод, заро́дыш.

fog /fɒg/ *n.* тума́н; (*phot.*) вуа́ль; (*fig.*): **in a ~** как в тума́не.

● *v.t.* (**fogged, fogging**) оку́т|ывать, -ать тума́ном; затума́ни|вать, -ть; (*fig.*): **the windows are ~ged up** о́кна запоте́ли.

● *cpds.* **~-bank** *n.* полоса́ тума́на над мо́рем; **~-bound** *adj.* (*US also* **~ed in**) (*enveloped in ~*) оку́танный тума́ном; (*delayed because of ~*) задержа́вшийся из-за тума́на; (*closed because of ~*) закры́тый из-за тума́на; **~-horn** *n.* тума́нный горн; **~-lamp/-light** *nn.* противотума́нная фа́ра.

fog(e)y /ˈfəʊgɪ/ *n.* (*pl.* **fogeys** *or* **fogies**) старомо́дный/отста́лый челове́к.

fogg|y /ˈfɒgɪ/ *adj.* (**foggier, foggiest**) тума́нный; (*fig.*): **I haven't the ~iest idea** (*Br.*) я не име́ю ни мале́йшего представле́ния.

foible /ˈfɔɪb(ə)l/ *n.* сла́бость; сла́бая стру́нка.

foil[1] /fɔɪl/ *n.* (*thin metal*) фольга́, стани́оль (*m.*); (*fig., contrast*) контра́ст, противопоставле́ние; **her plainness serves as a ~ to the others** её некраси́вая вне́шность оттеня́ет/подчёркивает красоту́ остальны́х.

foil[2] /fɔɪl/ *n.* (*fencing sword*) рапи́ра; **~ fencer** рапири́ст (*fem.* -ка).

foil³ /fɔɪl/ *v.t.* сби|ва́ть, -ть со сле́да; расстр|а́ивать, -о́ить (*or* срыва́ть, сорва́ть) пла́ны + *g*.

foist /fɔɪst/ *v.t.* навя́з|ывать, -а́ть (*что кому*).

fold¹ /fəʊld/ *n.* скла́дка; **the ~s of a dress** скла́дки пла́тья; **a ~ in the hills** (*Br.*) ложби́на.
● *v.t.* **1** (*double over*) скла́дывать, сложи́ть; св|ёртывать (*or* -ора́чивать), -ерну́ть; **~ one's arms** скре́|щивать, -сти́ть ру́ки на груди́; **~ back the bedclothes** отки́|дывать, -нуть одея́ло; **~ (up) the newspaper** скла́дывать, сложи́ть газе́ту.
2 (*embrace*) обн|има́ть, -я́ть; **she ~ed the child in her arms** она́ заключи́ла ребёнка в объя́тия; **the hills were ~ed in mist** холмы́ бы́ли оку́таны мгло́й.
● *v.i.* скла́дываться, сложи́ться; (*fig.*): **the play ~ed after a week** пье́са сошла́ (со сце́ны) че́рез неде́лю; **their business ~ed** они́ сверну́ли де́ло.

fold² /fəʊld/ *n.* (*for sheep*) заго́н; **return to the ~** (*fig.*) верну́ться (*pf.*) в ло́но (*церкви и т.п.*).

folder /ˈfəʊldə(r)/ *n.* (*container for papers*) скоросшива́тель (*m.*); (*also comput.*) па́пка.

folding /ˈfəʊldɪŋ/ *adj.* складно́й; **~ doors** складны́е две́ри.
● *cpds.* **~-bed** *n.* раскладу́шка; **~-chair** *n.* складно́й стул.

foliage /ˈfəʊlɪɪdʒ/ *n.* листва́; **~ plant** ли́ственное расте́ние.

folio /ˈfəʊlɪəʊ/ *n.* (*pl.* **folios**) (*book*) фолиа́нт; (*ledger sheet*) лист бухга́лтерской кни́ги.

folk /fəʊk/ *n.* (*pl.* **folk** *or* **folks**) **1** (*sing. or pl., coll., persons*) наро́д, лю́д|и (*pl., g.* -е́й); **some ~ have all the luck!** везёт же лю́дям!; **the old ~s** старики́; роди́тели (*both m. pl.*); **old ~s' home** дом для преста́релых. **2** (*pl., coll., relatives*) родня́, родны́е (*pl.*).
● *cpds.* **~lore** *n.* фолькло́р; **~-music** *n.* наро́дная му́зыка; **~-song** *n.* наро́дная пе́сня.

folklorist /ˈfəʊkˌlɔːrɪst/ *n.* фольклори́ст.

folksy /ˈfəʊksɪ/ *adj.* (**folksier, folksiest**) (*coll.*) (*characteristic of traditional culture*) (просто)наро́дный; (*informal*) просте́цкий, фамилья́рный, панибра́тский.

follicle /ˈfɒlɪk(ə)l/ *n.* (*anat.*) фолли́кул; (*bot.*) стручо́к.

follow /ˈfɒləʊ/ *v.t. & i.* **1** (*proceed or happen after*) сле́довать, по- за + *i.*; **the dog ~s him about** соба́ка хо́дит за ним по пята́м; **he ~ed his wife to the grave** (*died soon after*) он после́довал за жено́й в моги́лу; **he ~ed (in) his father's footsteps** он пошёл по стопа́м отца́; **~ the crowd** (*fig.*) плыть (*det.*) по тече́нию; **~ suit** (*at cards*) ходи́ть (*indet.*) в масть; (*fig.*) сле́довать, по- чьему́-н. приме́ру; **the frost was ~ed by a thaw** моро́з смени́лся о́ттепелью; **as ~s** сле́дующим о́бразом; как сле́дует ни́же; **his plan was as ~s** его́ план был тако́в.
2 (*as inference*) сле́довать (*impf.*) из + *g.*; **it does not ~ that** ... э́то во́все не зна́чит, что. . . .
3 (*pursue*) следи́ть (*impf.*) за + *i.*; **he ~ed the ball with his eye** он следи́л за мячо́м; **don't look now, we're being ~ed** не огля́дывайтесь, за на́ми следя́т; (*fig.*): **~ one's bent** сле́довать (*impf.*) свои́м накло́нностям.
4 (*keep to*) приде́рживаться (*impf.*) + *g.*; **~ this road** сле́дуйте/иди́те по э́той доро́ге; **~ the policy of one's predecessor** продолжа́ть (*impf.*) поли́тику своего́ предше́ственника; (*fig., engage in*): **~ a trade** име́ть (*impf.*) профе́ссию; (*fig., be guided by*): **~ s.o.'s advice/example** сле́довать, по- чьему́-н. сове́ту/приме́ру.
5 (*fig., keep track of*): **~ s.o.'s arguments** следи́ть (*impf.*) за хо́дом чьих-н. рассужде́ний; **I don't ~ you** я вас не понима́ю; **~ the news in the papers** следи́ть (*impf.*) за новостя́ми в газе́тах.
● *with advs.*: **~ on** *v.t. & i.* сле́довать, по- (за + *i.*); **~ through** *v.t. & i.* сле́довать (*impf.*) (за + *i.*) до конца́; **~ up** *v.t.* (*look into*) раз|бира́ть, -обра́ть; **~ up a clue** рассле́довать ули́ку; **~ up a suggestion** уч|и́тывать, -е́сть чьё-н. предложе́ние.
● *cpd.* **~-up** *n.* продолже́ние; (*med.*) контро́ль (*m.*).

follower /ˈfɒləʊwə(r)/ *n.* после́дователь (*m.*) (*fem.* -ница); сторо́нни|к (*fem.* -ца).

following /ˈfɒləʊwɪŋ/ *n.* после́дователи (*m. pl.*); приве́рженцы (*m. pl.*); **the preacher gained a large ~** пропове́дник собра́л мно́го приве́рженцев.
● *adj.* **1** (*ensuing*) сле́дующий; **(on) the ~ day** на сле́дующий день; (*about to be specified*): **we shall need the ~** нам потре́буется сле́дующее. **2** (*coming behind*) попу́тный; **a ~ wind** попу́тный ве́тер.

folly /ˈfɒlɪ/ *n.* (*foolishness*) глу́пость; (*building*) декорати́вное сооруже́ние.

foment /fəˈment/, /fəʊ-/ *v.t.* класть, положи́ть припа́рку к + *d.*; (*fig.*) подстрек|а́ть, -ну́ть.

fond /fɒnd/ *adj.* **1** (*pred., with* **of**): **he became ~ of her** он привяза́лся к ней; **are you ~ of music?** вы лю́бите му́зыку? **2** (*loving*) не́жный, лю́бящий; (*nice*): **~ memories** прия́тные/до́брые воспомина́ния.
3 (*credulous*) дове́рчивый; **I ~ly imagined** я тще́тно вообража́л.

fondant /ˈfɒnd(ə)nt/ *n.* ≈ пома́дка.

fondle /ˈfɒnd(ə)l/ *v.t.* ласка́ть (*impf.*); гла́дить, по-.

font¹ /fɒnt/ *n.* (*eccl.*) купе́ль.

font² /fɒnt/ *n.* (*typ.*) шрифт.

food /fuːd/ *n.* пи́ща, пита́ние; еда́; **~ supplies** продово́льственные припа́сы (*m. pl.*); провиа́нт; **~ and drink** еда́ и питьё; **go without ~** голода́ть (*impf.*); **baby ~** де́тское пита́ние; (*fig.*): **~ for thought** пи́ща для размышле́ний.
● *cpds.* **~ poisoning** *n.* пищево́е отравле́ние; **~-processor** *n.* ку́хонный комба́йн; **~-store** *n.* продово́льственный магази́н; **~stuff** *n.* пищево́й проду́кт.

fool¹ /fuːl/ *n.* (*simpleton*) дура́к, глупе́ц; **any ~ could do that** э́то ка́ждый дура́к мо́жет; **he is nobody's ~** он совсе́м не дура́к; **I was a ~ to accept** дура́к я был, что согласи́лся; **like a ~, I told him** я был так глуп, что сказа́л ему́; **he lived in a ~'s paradise** он жил в вы́думанном ми́ре; **~'s mate** (*at chess*) «де́тский» мат; (*jester*) шут; **~'s cap** шутовско́й колпа́к; **play the ~** дура́читься (*impf.*); валя́ть (*impf.*) дурака́; **April ~** апре́льский дура́к; **All F~s' Day** пе́рвое апре́ля; **make a ~ (out) of s.o.** дура́чить, о- кого́-н.; **make a ~ of o.s.** ста́вить, по- себя́ в дура́цкое положе́ние; позо́риться, о-.
● *adj.* (*US coll.*) глу́пый, безрассу́дный.
● *v.t.* (*delude, deceive*) одура́чи|вать, -ть; **he was ~ed into going there** обма́ном его́ убеди́ли пойти́ туда́.
● *v.i.* дура́читься (*impf.*); **~ about, around** валя́ть (*impf.*) дурака́; **don't ~ about with the watch, you may break it!** поосторо́жней с часа́ми, а то слома́ете их!
● *cpd.* **~proof** *adj.* (*reliable*) безотка́зный, ве́рный; (*simple*) несло́жный.

fool² /fuːl/ *n.* (*Br., fruit dish*) ≈ десе́рт со взби́тыми сли́вками.

foolery /ˈfuːlərɪ/ *n.* дура́чество, глу́пость; глу́пое поведе́ние.

foolhardiness /ˈfuːlˌhɑːdɪnɪs/ *n.* безрассу́дная хра́брость.

foolhardy /ˈfuːlˌhɑːdɪ/ *adj.* (**foolhardier, foolhardiest**) безрассу́дно хра́брый.

foolish /ˈfuːlɪʃ/ *adj.* глу́пый; дура́цкий.

foolishness /ˈfuːlɪʃnɪs/ *n.* глу́пость.

foolscap /ˈfuːlskæp/ *n.* (*Br., stationery*) пи́счая бума́га форма́том 330 x 200 мм.

foot /fʊt/ *n.* (*pl.* **feet**) **1** (*extremity of leg*) ступня́, нога́; стопа́ ноги́; (*dim.*) но́жка; (*of an animal*) ла́па; (*lowest part, bottom*) ни́жняя часть, ни́жний край; **at the ~ of the hill** у подно́жия холма́; **at the ~ of the page** в конце́ страни́цы; **at the ~ of the stairs** внизу́ ле́стницы; **at the ~ of the bed** в нога́х крова́ти.
2 (*unit of length*) фут; **six ~ (or feet) tall** шести́ фу́тов ро́стом; **40-foot container** сорока́-футо́вый конте́йнер.
3 (*pros.*) стопа́.
4 (*Br., infantry*) пехо́та; **~ guards** гварде́йская пехо́та.
● *phrr.*: **we came here on ~** мы пришли́ сюда́ пешко́м; **she is on her feet all day** она́ це́лый день на нога́х; **he was on his feet in an instant** он то́тчас вскочи́л на́ ноги; **the business got off on the wrong ~** де́ло с са́мого нача́ла пошло́ не так; **she was swept off her feet** (*fig.*) она́ потеря́ла го́лову; **he fell on his feet** (*fig.*) он сча́стливо отде́лался; ему́ повезло́; **find one's feet** нащу́п|ывать, -ать по́чву под нога́ми; **get, rise to one's feet** подн|има́ться, -я́ться; встава́ть,

вста́ть; **have one ~ in the grave** стоя́ть (*impf.*) одно́й ного́й в моги́ле; **have both feet on the ground** (*fig.*) кре́пко стоя́ть (*impf.*) на нога́х; **have feet of clay** (*fig.*) стоя́ть (*impf.*) на гли́няных нога́х; **keep one's feet** уде́рживаться (*pf.*) на нога́х; **kneel at s.o.'s feet** па́дать, пасть на коле́ни пе́ред кем-н.; **put one's ~ down** (*fig.*) зан|има́ть, -я́ть твёрдую/реши́тельную пози́цию; (*Br.*, *accelerate*) дава́ть, дать га́зу; **put one's ~ in it** (*fig.*) дать (*pf.*) ма́ху; **put one's best ~ forward, foremost** приба́вить (*pf.*) ша́гу; **put one's feet up** сиде́ть (*impf.*) задра́в но́ги; (*fig.*) отдыха́ть (*impf.*); **set ~ in** ступ|а́ть, -и́ть в + *a.*; **set s.o. on his feet again** подн|има́ть, -я́ть кого́-н. на́ ноги; **stand on one's own (two) feet** стоя́ть (*impf.*) на нога́х; быть самостоя́тельным; **trample under ~** поп|ира́ть, -ра́ть; **it's wet under ~** на земле́ мо́кро; **wipe one's feet** вытира́ть, вы́тереть но́ги.

● *v.t.*: **~ the bill** опла́|чивать, -ти́ть счёт.

● *cpds.* **~-and-mouth** *n.* (*disease*) я́щур; **~ball** *n.* (*Br.*) футбо́л; (*US*) америка́нский футбо́л; **~ball match** (*Br.*) футбо́льный матч; **~ball player** футболи́ст; **~baller** *n.* (*Br.*) футболи́ст; **~-bath** *n.* ножна́я ва́нна; **~-brake** *n.* ножно́й то́рмоз; **~bridge** *n.* пешехо́дный мо́стик; **~-dragging** *n.* проволо́чка, затя́гивание; **~hills** *n. pl.* предго́рье; **~hold** *n.* то́чка опо́ры; (*mil.*) опо́рный пункт; **~lights** *n. pl.* ра́мпа (*sg.*); **~man** *n.* лаке́й; **~mark** *n.* след ноги́; **~note** *n.* сно́ска; **~path** *n.* тропа́, тропи́нка; **~plate** *n.* (*Br.*) площа́дка машини́ста; **~-pound** *n.* (*tech.*) футофу́нт; **~print** *n.* след ноги́; **~-rot** *n.* копы́тная гниль; **~-slog** *v.i.* тащи́ться (*impf.*) пешко́м; **~-slogger** *n.* пехоти́нец, пехтура́ (*m.*); **~-soldier** *n.* пехоти́нец; **~sore** *adj.* со стёртыми нога́ми; **~step** *n.* шаг, по́ступь; **~stool** *n.* скаме́ечка для ног; **~sure** *adj.* не спотыка́ющийся; уве́ренно ступа́ющий; (*fig.*) уве́ренно иду́щий к це́ли; **~way** *n.* (*Br.*) пешехо́дная доро́жка, тротуа́р; **~wear** *n.* о́бувь; **~work** *n.* рабо́та ног.

footage /ˈfʊtɪdʒ/ *n.* (*length*) метра́ж; (*cin.*) киноматериа́л.

footer /ˈfʊtə(r)/ *n.* (*line of text*) ни́жний колонти́тул.

footing /ˈfʊtɪŋ/ *n.* (*foothold*) опо́ра для ног(и́); **lose one's ~** оступи́ться (*pf.*); (*fig.*) потеря́ть (*pf.*) по́чву под нога́ми; **on an equal ~** на ра́вной ноге́; **on a friendly ~** на дру́жеской ноге́; **the army was placed on a war ~** а́рмия была́ поста́влена в боеву́ю гото́вность.

footle /ˈfuːt(ə)l/ *v.i.* (*Br. coll.*) дури́ть (*impf.*); дура́читься (*impf.*).

footling /ˈfuːtlɪŋ/ *adj.* (*coll.*) пустя́чный, ерундо́вый.

fop /fɒp/ *n.* фат, хлыщ, щёголь (*m.*).

foppish /ˈfɒpɪʃ/ *adj.* фатова́тый, щеголева́тый, щегольско́й.

for /fə(r)/, /fɔː(r)/ *prep.* **1** (*with the object or purpose of*) для + *g.*; ра́ди + *g.*; **~ example** наприме́р; **I did it ~ fun** я сде́лал э́то для сме́ху; **~ a laugh** шу́тки ра́ди; **~ the sake of peace** ра́ди ми́ра; **they have gone ~ a walk** они́ отпра́вились гуля́ть; **who's coming ~ dinner?** кто придёт к у́жину?; **what ~?** заче́м?; **there is no need ~ this** в э́том нет никако́й на́добности; **a house ~ sale** дом на прода́жу; **save up ~ a house** копи́ть (*impf.*) (де́ньги) на поку́пку до́ма; **he sent ~ the doctor** он посла́л за врачо́м; **I've come ~ the rent** я пришёл получи́ть за кварти́ру; **run ~ a train** бежа́ть (*det.*), по- к по́езду; **run ~ it!** беги́те изо всех сил!; (*destination*) на + *a.*; к + *d.*; **the train ~ Moscow** по́езд на Москву́; **he left ~ home** он отпра́вился домо́й; **you're in ~ a shock** вас ждёт больша́я неприя́тность; (*aspiration*): **who could ask ~ more?** чего́ же ещё жела́ть?; **he begged ~ money** он проси́л де́нег; **a cry ~ help** крик о по́мощи; зов на по́мощь; **oh ~ a drink!** эх, вы́пить бы!; **greed ~ money** жа́дность к деньга́м; **longing ~ home** тоска́ по ро́дине; **demand ~ coal** спрос на у́голь; **prospecting ~ oil** разве́дка на нефть.
2 (*denoting reason*; *on account of*) ра́ди + *g.*; для + *g.*; **cry ~ joy** пла́кать (*impf.*) от ра́дости; **~ fear of being found out** из боя́зни разоблаче́ния; **grateful ~ help** благода́рный за по́мощь; **you can't move here ~ books** из-за книг здесь не́где поверну́ться; **he can't see the wood ~ trees** он за дере́вьями не ви́дит ле́са; **~ the love of God** ра́ди Бо́га; **~ shame!** как не сты́дно; **~ pity's sake!** пощади́те!; ра́ди Бо́га!; **my shoes are the worse ~ wear** мои́ боти́нки поизноси́лись; **but (or if it had not been) ~ me he would have died** ка́бы не я, он бы у́мер; **he is known ~ his generosity** он изве́стен свое́й ще́дростью; **they married ~ love** они́ жени́лись по любви́; **selected ~ their physique** ото́бранные по физи́ческим да́нным; (*accorded to*): **the penalty ~ treason is death** наказа́ние за изме́ну — сме́ртная казнь; **a prize ~ a novel** пре́мия за рома́н; **a decoration ~ bravery** о́рден за отва́гу; (*on the occasion of*): **I gave him a book ~ his birthday** я подари́л ему́ кни́гу на день рожде́ния; **he went abroad ~ his holidays** он пое́хал за грани́цу в о́тпуск; **she wore black ~ the funeral** она́ наде́ла всё чёрное на по́хороны; **the church was decorated ~ Easter** це́рковь была́ укра́шена к Па́схе; **what are we having ~ dinner?** что у нас на у́жин?
3 (*representative of*): **A ~ Anna** А как в сло́ве «А́нна»; **the member (of parliament) ~ Oxford** член парла́мента от О́ксфорда; **red is ~ danger** кра́сный цвет означа́ет опа́сность; **he signed ~ the government** он поста́вил по́дпись от и́мени прави́тельства; (*in support*; *in favour of*): **a vote ~ freedom** го́лос за свобо́ду; **I'm all ~ it** я по́лностью за (э́то); **stand up ~ one's rights** отст|а́ивать, -оя́ть свои́ права́; (*denoting purpose*): **they need premises ~ a school** им ну́жно помеще́ние под шко́лу; **a report ~ the director** докладна́я на и́мя дире́ктора; **a candidate ~ the presidium** кандида́т в прези́диум; **the order ~ retreat** прика́з об отступле́нии; **this barrel is meant ~ wine** э́та бо́чка предназна́чена под вино́; **ready ~ departure** гото́в к отъе́зду; (*on behalf of*) за + *a.*, от + *g.*; **speak ~ yourself!** говори́те за себя́!; **see ~ yourself!** смотри́те са́ми!; **pray ~ the sick** моли́ться (*impf.*) за больны́х.
4 (*denoting intended recipient*): **a dinner ~ 10 people** обе́д на де́сять челове́к; **there is a letter ~ you** вам письмо́; **votes ~ women** пра́во го́лоса для же́нщин.
5 (*denoting duration or extent*): **~ a time** на вре́мя; **~ a long time** на до́лгое вре́мя; в тече́ние до́лгого вре́мени; **he stayed ~ the night** он оста́лся на́ ночь; **he was away ~ ages** он о́чень до́лго был в отъе́зде; **I haven't seen him ~ (some) days** я не ви́дел его́ не́сколько дней; **the forest stretches ~ miles** лес простира́ется на мно́гие киломе́тры; **there is no house ~ miles** круго́м на мно́го вёрст ни еди́ного до́ма; **a weather report ~ the past week** сво́дка пого́ды за про́шлую неде́лю; (*intended duration*): **~ ever and ever** навсегда́, на ве́ки ве́чные; **I've lost it ~ good** я навсегда́/оконча́тельно потеря́л его́/её; **I shan't stay ~ long** я до́лго не задержу́сь; **~ the future we must be more careful** в бу́дущем мы должны́ быть бо́лее осторо́жными; **they are going away ~ a few days** они́ уезжа́ют на не́сколько дней.
6 (*denoting relationship*; *in respect of*): **I ~ my part** ... со свое́й стороны́, я ...; **~ the rest** что каса́ется остально́го; **as ~ me, myself** что каса́ется меня́; **he is hard up ~ money** у него́ пло́хо/ту́го с деньга́ми; **luckily ~ her** на её сча́стье, к сча́стью для неё; **~ one thing it's too short, and ~ another I don't like it** во-пе́рвых, э́то о́чень ко́ротко, во-вторы́х, мне э́то не нра́вится; (*responsive to*): **an eye ~ a bargain** намётанный глаз на вы́годную поку́пку; **an ear ~ music** музыка́льный слух; **a weakness ~ sweets** сла́бость к сла́дкому; (*in relation to what is normal or suitable*): **warm ~ the time of year** тепло́ для э́того вре́мени го́да; **cold ~ summer** не по ле́тнему холо́дный (*or* хо́лодно); **it's cold enough ~ snow** хо́лодно — того́ и гляди́ пойдёт снег; **he is too thoughtful ~ his age** он заду́мчив не по лета́м; **not bad ~ a beginner** для новичка́ непло́хо; **that's no job ~ a woman** э́то не же́нская рабо́та; **how's that ~ a stroke of luck?** вот э́то уда́ча!
7 (*in return ~, instead of*): **an eye ~ an eye** о́ко за о́ко; **new lamps ~ old** но́вые ла́мпы вме́сто ста́рых; **get something ~ nothing** получ|а́ть, -и́ть что-н. да́ром; **so much ~ your promises!** вот чего́ сто́ят ва́ши обеща́ния; **not ~ the world** ни за что (на све́те); **once (and) ~ all** раз и навсегда́; **thank you ~ nothing!** ну́ уж, удружи́л — не́чего сказа́ть!; **seven ~ a pound** семь штук за фунт; **how many**

books can I buy ~ that money? сколько книг я смогу купить на эти деньги?; **you'll pay ~ this!** вы мне за это заплатите!; **~ every good apple there were 10 bad ones** на каждое хорошее яблоко было 10 плохих.
8 (*as being; in the capacity of*): **what do you take me ~?** за кого вы меня принимаете?; **take something ~ granted** прин|имать, -ять что-н. как само собой разумеющееся.
9 (*up to; incumbent upon*): **it's ~ you to decide** вам решать; **it's not ~ me to say** не мне судить.
10 (*despite*): **~ all that, I still love him** несмотря на всё это, я его люблю.
11 (*ethic dative*): **there's gratitude ~ you!** вот вам и благодарность!; **there's a marvellous** (*Br.*), **marvelous** (*US*) **shot ~ you!** вот замечательный выстрел!
12 (*with certain expressions of time*): **~ the first time** в первый раз; **~ the last time, will you shut up!** говорю тебе в последний раз — замолчи!; **~ once I agree with you** на этот раз я с вами согласен; **the wedding is arranged ~ June the 1st** свадьба назначена на первое июня; **I ordered meat ~ Thursday** я заказал мясо к четвергу.
13 (*with following inf.*): **it will be better ~ us all to leave** будет лучше нам всем уйти; **~ the experiment to succeed, certain conditions must be fulfilled** чтобы опыт удался, должны быть выполнены определённые условия; **it was absurd ~ him to do that** это было нелепо с его стороны.
14: **~ all I know, he may he there already** почём я знаю, может быть он уже там; **~ all his boasting** при всём его хвастовстве; как бы он ни хвастался; **you can go away ~ all I care** а по мне — хоть сейчас уходите.
● *conj.* так как, ибо.

forage /ˈfɒrɪdʒ/ *n.* фураж, корм.
● *v.i.* (*search*) разыскивать (*impf.*).
● *cpd.* **~-cap** *n.* пилотка.

foray /ˈfɒreɪ/ *n.* набег.
● *v.i.* соверш|ать, -ить набег.

forbade /fəˈbæd/, /fəˈbeɪd/, **forbad** /fəˈbæd/ *past of* ⇒**forbid**

forbear[1] /ˈfɔːbeə(r)/ *n.* = **forebear**

forbear[2] /fɔːˈbeə(r)/ *v.t. & i.* (*past* **forbore;** *p.p.* **forborne**) воздерж|иваться, -аться (*от чего*); быть терпеливым.

forbearance /fɔːˈbeərəns/ *n.* воздержанность, терпеливость, терпение.

forbid /fəˈbɪd/ *v.t.* (**forbidding;** *past* **forbade** *or* **forbad;** *p.p.* **forbidden**) запре|щать, -тить (*кому что*); **God ~!** Боже упаси!/сохрани!

forbidden /fəˈbɪd(ə)n/ *adj.* запрещённый, запретный.

forbidding /fəˈbɪdɪŋ/ *adj.* (*repellent*) отталкивающий; (*unfriendly*) неприязненный; (*threatening*) грозный; **a ~ air** неприступный вид.

forbore /fɔːˈbɔː(r)/ *past of* ⇒**forbear**[2]

forborne /fɔːˈbɔːn/ *p.p. of* ⇒**forbear**[2]

force /fɔːs/ *n.* **1** (*strength: lit., fig.*) сила; **use ~** приб|егать, -егнуть к силе; **in full ~** в полном составе; **by ~** силой, насильно; **from ~ of habit** в силу привычки; **by ~ of circumstance(s)** в силу обстоятельств; **the ~s of darkness** силы тьмы.
2 (*body of men, usu. armed*) вооружённый отряд; **he attacked with a small ~** он атаковал с небольшим отрядом; **Air F~** военно-воздушные силы; **(Police) F~** полиция; (*pl.*): **the (Armed) F~s** армия, вооружённые силы.
3 (*binding power, validity*) действенность; **the agreement has the ~ of law** это соглашение имеет силу закона; **in ~** (*of law etc.*) в силе; **come into ~** вступ|ать, -ить в силу; (*significance, cogency*) смысл, значение; **he explained the ~ of the word** он объяснил точное значение этого слова.
4 (*phys.*) сила; **the ~ of gravity** сила притяжения.
● *v.t.* **1** (*compel, constrain*) заст|авлять, -авить; прин|уждать, -удить; **he was ~ed to sell the house** он был вынужден продать дом; **you are not ~d to answer** вы не обязаны отвечать; **~ s.o.'s hand** прин|уждать, -удить кого-н. к действию; **~d** (*laugh etc.*) принуждённый; **~d labour** (*Br.*), **labor** (*US*) принудительный труд; **~d landing** вынужденная посадка.
2 (*effect by ~*): **~ an entry** вл|амываться, -омиться; врываться, ворваться; (*apply ~ to*): **~ (open) the door** выламывать, выломать дверь; **~ a lock** взл|амывать, -омать замок.
3 (*increase under stress*): **~ the pace** уск|орять, -орить шаг; (*produce under stress*): **~ a laugh** смеяться (*impf.*) через силу; выдавливать, выдавить из себя смешок.
4 (*plants*) выгонять, выгнать.
● *cpds.* **~-feed** *v.t.* кормить (*impf.*) насильно; **~-feeding** *n.* насильственное кормление.

forceful /ˈfɔːsfʊl/ *adj.* сильный, убедительный.

force majeure /ˌfɔːs mæˈʒɜː(r)/ *n.* форс-мажор.

forcemeat /ˈfɔːsmiːt/ *n.* фарш.

forceps /ˈfɔːseps/ *n.* хирургические щипц|ы (*pl., g.* -ов).

forcible /ˈfɔːsɪb(ə)l/ *adj.* насильственный; (*forceful*) веский; убедительный; **~ entry** насильственное вторжение.

ford /fɔːd/ *n.* брод.
● *v.t.* пере|ходить, -йти вброд.

fore /fɔː(r)/ *n.* **1**: **he finished the race well to the ~** он закончил бег, намного опередив других; **this subject has recently come to the ~** в последнее время этот вопрос оказался в центре внимания.
2 (*naut.*) нос; носовая часть.
● *adj.* передний; (*naut.*) носовой; (*as pref.*) пред. . . .
● *adv.* впереди; **~ and aft** на носу и на корме; вдоль всего судна.

forearm[1] /ˈfɔːrɑːm/ *n.* предплечье.

forearm[2] /fɔːrˈɑːm/ *v.t.* заранее вооруж|ать, -ить; **forewarned is ~ed** кто предостережён, тот вооружён.

forebear /ˈfɔːbeə(r)/ *n.* предок.

forebode /fɔːˈbəʊd/ *v.t.* (*portend*) предвещать (*impf.*) (дурное).

foreboding /fɔːˈbəʊdɪŋ/ *n.* дурное предчувствие.

forecast /ˈfɔːkɑːst/ *n.* предсказание; (*also* **weather ~**) прогноз погоды.
● *v.t.* (*past and p.p* **forecast** *or* **forecasted**) предсказ|ывать, -ать; **weather ~ing** синоптика.

forecaster /ˈfɔːkɑːstə(r)/ *n.*: **weather ~** синоптик.

forecastle /ˈfəʊks(ə)l/ *n.* (*naut.*) бак.

foreclose /fɔːˈkləʊz/ *v.t. & i.* (*preclude*) исключ|ать, -ить; (*mortgage*) лишать (*impf.*) права выкупа заложенного имущества.

foreclosure /fɔːˈkləʊzjə(r)/ *n.* (*leg.*) лишение права выкупа заложенного имущества.

forecourt /ˈfɔːkɔːt/ *n.* передний двор.

foredoom /fɔːˈduːm/ *v.t.* (заранее) обр|екать, -ечь.

forefather /ˈfɔːˌfɑːðə(r)/ *n.* предок, праотец.

forefinger /ˈfɔːˌfɪŋgə(r)/ *n.* указательный палец.

forefoot /ˈfɔːfʊt/ *n.* передняя лапа/нога.

forefront /ˈfɔːfrʌnt/ *n.* авангард; **in the ~ of the battle** на передовой (линии); **at the ~ of his mind** первым делом на уме.

foregather /fɔːˈgæðə(r)/ = **forgather**

forego[1] /fɔːˈgəʊ/ *v.i.* (*precede*) предшествовать (*impf.*) + *d.*; **the ~ing** вышеупомянутое; **a ~ne conclusion** предрешённый исход.

forego[2] /fɔːˈgəʊ/ = **forgo**

foreground /ˈfɔːgraʊnd/ *n.* (*lit., fig.*) передний план.

forehand /ˈfɔːhænd/ *adj.* (*tennis*): **~ stroke** удар справа.

forehead /ˈfɒrɪd/, /ˈfɔːhed/ *n.* лоб.

foreign /ˈfɒrɪn/, /ˈfɒrən/ *adj.* **1** (*of or pertaining to another country or countries*) иностранный, заграничный; **~ affairs** международные дела; **Ministry of F~ Affairs** Министерство иностранных дел; **F~ (and Commonwealth) Office** (*Br.*) Министерство иностранных дел; **~ passport** заграничный паспорт; **~ policy** внешняя политика; **F~ Secretary** (*Br.*) министр иностранных дел; **F~ Service** (*institution or career*) дипломатическая служба; **~ trade** внешняя торговля; **in ~ parts** в чужих краях. **2** (*alien*) чужой, чуждый; **~ soil** чужая земля, чужбина. **3** (*med.*) инородный; **~ body** (*lit., fig.*) инородное тело.

foreigner /ˈfɒrɪnə(r)/, /ˈfɒrənə(r)/ *n.* иностран|ец (*fem.* -ка).

foreignness /ˈfɒrɪnnɪs/, /ˈfɒrənnɪs/ *n.* иностранное происхождение; чуждость.

foreknow /fɔːˈnəʊ/ *v.t.* (*liter.*) знать (*impf.*) заранее.

F

foreknowledge /fɔːˈnɒlɪdʒ/ *n.* предви́дение.

foreland /ˈfɔːlænd/ *n.* мыс.

foreleg /ˈfɔːleg/ *n.* пере́дняя ла́па/нога́.

forelock /ˈfɔːlɒk/ *n.* прядь воло́с на лбу; чуб; вихо́р.

foreman /ˈfɔːmən/ *n.* ма́стер, деся́тник; прора́б (производи́тель рабо́т); **~ of the jury** старшина́ (*m.*) прися́жных.

foremast /ˈfɔːmɑːst/, /-məst/ *n.* фок-ма́чта.

foremost /ˈfɔːməʊst/ *adj.* са́мый пере́дний.

● *adv.*: **first and ~** пре́жде всего́; в пе́рвую о́чередь.

forename /ˈfɔːneɪm/ *n.* и́мя (*nt.*) (*в отличие от фамилии*).

forenoon /ˈfɔːnuːn/ *n.* вре́мя до полу́дня; у́тро.

forensic /fəˈrensɪk/ *adj.* суде́бный; **~ expert, scientist** суде́бно-медици́нский экспе́рт.

foreordain /ˌfɔːrɔːˈdeɪn/ *v.t.* предопредел|я́ть, -и́ть.

foreplay /ˈfɔːpleɪ/ *n.* эроти́ческое стимули́рование.

forerunner /ˈfɔːˌrʌnə(r)/ *n.* предше́ственни|к (*fem.* -ца).

foresail /ˈfɔːseɪl/, /-s(ə)l/ *n.* (*naut.*) фок.

foresee /fɔːˈsiː/ *v.t.* предви́деть (*impf.*).

foreseeable /fɔːˈsiːəb(ə)l/ *adj.*: **in the ~ future** в обозри́мом бу́дущем.

foreshadow /fɔːˈʃædəʊ/ *v.t.* предвеща́ть (*impf.*).

foreshore /ˈfɔːʃɔː(r)/ *n.* берегова́я полоса́, затопля́емая прили́вом.

foreshorten /fɔːˈʃɔːt(ə)n/ *v.t.* черти́ть, на- в ра́курсе.

foresight /ˈfɔːsaɪt/ *n.* **1** (*knowledge of future*) предви́дение. **2** (*care for future*) предусмотри́тельность. **3** (*of gun*) му́шка.

foreskin /ˈfɔːskɪn/ *n.* кра́йняя плоть.

forest /ˈfɒrɪst/ *n.* лес; **~ fire** лесно́й пожа́р; **a ~ of masts** лес ма́чт.

● *v.t.* заса́|живать, -ди́ть ле́сом; **heavily ~ed country** леси́стая/лесна́я ме́стность.

● *cpd.* **~ ranger** (*US*), **warden** (*Br.*) *nn.* лесни́к.

forestall /fɔːˈstɔːl/ *v.t.* предвос|хища́ть, -хи́тить; опере|жа́ть, -ди́ть; предупре|жда́ть, -ди́ть.

forester /ˈfɒrɪstə(r)/ *n.* (*official*) лесни́к; (*specialist*) лесни́чий.

forestry /ˈfɒrɪstrɪ/ *n.* лесово́дство; **F~ Commission** коми́ссия по охра́не лесо́в.

foretaste /ˈfɔːteɪst/ *n.* предвкуше́ние.

foretell /fɔːˈtel/ *v.t.* (*past and p.p.* **foretold**) предска́з|ывать, -а́ть.

forethought /ˈfɔːθɔːt/ *n.* предусмотри́тельность.

forever /fəˈrevə(r)/ *adv.* навсегда́, наве́чно; (*continually*) постоя́нно, ве́чно.

forewarn /fɔːˈwɔːn/ *v.t.* предупре|жда́ть, -ди́ть; предостер|ега́ть, -е́чь; **~ed is forearmed** кто предостережён, тот вооружён.

forewoman /ˈfɔːˌwʊmən/ *n.* (же́нщина-)деся́тник/ма́стер; (*of a jury*) (же́нщина-)старшина́ прися́жных.

foreword /ˈfɔːwɜːd/ *n.* предисло́вие.

forfeit /ˈfɔːfɪt/ *n.* (*penalty*) штраф, конфиска́ция; (*trivial fine, e.g. at games*) фант; **play at ~s** игра́ть, сыгра́ть в фа́нты.

● *v.t.* (**forfeited, forfeiting**) теря́ть, по- (пра́во на) + *a.*; **he ~ed his self-respect** он потеря́л уваже́ние к себе́.

forfeiture /ˈfɔːfɪtʃə(r)/ *n.* конфиска́ция; лише́ние пра́ва (на + *a.*).

forgather, foregather /fɔːˈgæðə(r)/ *v.i.* соб|ира́ться, -ра́ться.

forgave /fəˈgeɪv/ *past of* ⇨**forgive**

forge /fɔːdʒ/ *n.* (*workshop*) ку́зница; (*hearth or furnace*) кузне́чный горн.

● *v.t. & i.* **1** (*shape metal*) кова́ть (*impf.*). **2** (*fabricate*) изобре|та́ть, -сти́; выду́мывать, вы́думать; (*counterfeit*) подде́л|ывать, -ать. **3**: **~ ahead** вырыва́ться, вы́рваться вперёд.

forger /ˈfɔːdʒə(r)/ *n.* подде́лыватель (*m.*); фальсифика́тор.

forgery /ˈfɔːdʒərɪ/ *n.* (*act*) подде́лка, подло́г; (*object*) подде́лка; подло́жный докуме́нт.

forget /fəˈget/ *v.t. & i.* (**forgetting;** *past* **forgot;** *p.p.* **forgotten** *or esp. US* **forgot**) заб|ыва́ть, -ы́ть; **I forgot all about the lecture** я соверше́нно забы́л о ле́кции; **'What is his name?' — 'I ~'** «Как его́ зову́т?» — «Я забы́л»; **his deeds will never be forgotten** его́ дея́ния бу́дут по́мнить ве́чно; **it is easy to ~** э́то легко́ забыва́ется; **he drinks to ~** он пьёт, что́бы забы́ться; **~ it!** (*coll.*) ла́дно!; бро́сьте!; **~ o.s.** (*act unselfishly*) забыва́ть (*impf.*) себя́ ра́ди други́х; (*act without decorum*) заб|ыва́ться, -ы́ться.

● *cpd.* **~-me-not** *n.* (*bot.*) незабу́дка.

forgetful /fəˈgetfʊl/ *adj.* забы́вчивый.

forgetfulness /fəˈgetfʊlnɪs/ *n.* забы́вчивость.

forgivable /fəˈgɪvəb(ə)l/ *adj.* прости́тельный.

forgive /fəˈgɪv/ *v.t. & i.* (*past* **forgave;** *p.p.* **forgiven**) про|ща́ть, -сти́ть; **I ~ you for everything** я вам всё проща́ю; **~ me, I didn't hear what you said** прости́те, я не расслы́шал, что вы сказа́ли.

forgiveness /fəˈgɪvnɪs/ *n.* проще́ние.

forgiving /fɔːˈgɪvɪŋ/ *adj.* (все)проща́ющий.

for|go, fore|go /fɔːˈgəʊ/ *v.t.* (**~goes** /-ˈgəʊz/; *past* **~went;** *p.p.* **~gone** /-ˈgɒn/) отка́з|ываться, -а́ться от + *g.*; возде́рж|иваться, -а́ться от + *g.*

forgot /fəˈgɒt/ *past and esp. US p.p. of* ⇨**forget**

forgotten /fəˈgɒt(ə)n/ *p.p. of* ⇨**forget**

fork /fɔːk/ *n.* **1** (*for cul. or table use*) ви́лка. **2** (*agric.*) ви́лы (*f. pl.*). **3** (*bifurcation*) разви́лка, разветвле́ние.

● *v.t.* (*dig or turn with ~*): **~ over a rose-bed** взрыхл|я́ть, -и́ть ви́лами гря́дку с ро́зами; **~ out, up** (*lit., dig roots etc.*) выка́пывать, вы́копать.

● *v.i.* (*bifurcate*) раздв|а́иваться, -ои́ться; развет|вля́ться, -и́ться; (*of road-direction*): **you must ~ right at the church** у це́ркви (где доро́га разветвля́ется,) поверни́те напра́во; **~ out** (*sl., provide money*) отва́л|ивать, -и́ть; раскоше́ли|ваться, -ться (**for**: на + *a.*).

● *cpd.* **~-lift** *n.* (*in full* **~-lift truck**) автопогру́зчик.

forked /fɔːkt/ *adj.* раздво́енный, разветвлённый, вилообра́зный; **~ lightning** зигзагообра́зная мо́лния; **~ tongue** раздво́енный язы́к.

forlorn /fəˈlɔːn/ *adj.* забро́шенный, поки́нутый, жа́лкий, несча́стный; **~ hope** о́чень сла́бая наде́жда; **he looked ~** у него́ был жа́лкий вид.

form /fɔːm/ *n.* **1** (*shape, aspect*) фо́рма, вид; (*figure, body*) фигу́ра.
2 (*species, kind, variant*) вид, фо́рма; **~ of government** госуда́рственный строй; фо́рма правле́ния; (*gram.*) фо́рма.
3 (*accepted or expected behaviour*) но́рмы (*f. pl.*) прили́чия/поведе́ния; **that is not good ~** так вести́ себя́ не при́нято.
4 (*ritual, formality*) тип, вид; **~s of worship** обря́ды (*m. pl.*).
5 (*of health*) состоя́ние; **in good ~** в хоро́шей фо́рме; (*of spirits*): **he appeared in great ~** он был в отли́чной фо́рме.
6 (*document*) бланк, анке́та.
7 (*Br., class*) класс.
8 (*Br., bench*) скамья́.
9 (*mould*) фо́рма.

● *v.t.* **1** (*fashion, shape*) формирова́ть, с-; прид|ава́ть, -а́ть фо́рму + *d.*; **he ~ed the clay into a vase** гли́на под его́ рука́ми преврати́лась в ва́зу; **the rocks are ~ed by wave action** ска́лы формиру́ются под возде́йствием волн; **she ~s her letters well** она́ хорошо́ выво́дит бу́квы; **he can ~ simple sentences** он уме́ет составля́ть просты́е предложе́ния; (*by discipline, training etc.*) тренирова́ть, на-; дисциплини́ровать (*impf., pf.*); разв|ива́ть, -и́ть; **his character was ~ed at school** его́ хара́ктер сформирова́лся в шко́ле (*or* был сформиро́ван шко́лой).
2 (*organize, create*) организ|о́вывать, -ова́ть; образ|о́вывать, -ова́ть; созд|ава́ть, -а́ть; формирова́ть, с-; **they ~ed an alliance** они́ со́здали/образова́ли сою́з; **he was unable to ~ a government** он не смог сформирова́ть прави́тельство.
3 (*conceive*): **they ~ed a plan** они́ вы́работали план; **~ an opinion** соста́вить (*pf.*) мне́ние; **I ~ed the conclusion that ...** я пришёл к заключе́нию, что. . . .
4 (*develop, acquire*): **habits ~ed in childhood** привы́чки, сложи́вшиеся с де́тства.
5 (*constitute*) сост|авля́ть, -а́вить; представля́ть собо́й, явля́ться (*both*

impf.); **this ~s the basis of our discussion** э́то составля́ет осно́ву на́шей диску́ссии; **the room ~s part of the museum** э́та ко́мната составля́ет часть (*or* явля́ется ча́стью) музе́я.
6 (*gram.*) образ|о́вывать, -ова́ть; **the plural is ~ed by adding 's'** мно́жественное число́ образо́вывается при по́мощи добавле́ния бу́квы **'s'**.
7 (*mil. etc.*) стро́ить, по-; **the troops were ~ed (up) into line** солда́т вы́строили в ряд; **~ a queue** (*Br.*), **line** (*US*) образ|о́вывать, -ова́ть о́чередь.
● *v.i.* (*take shape, appear, come into being*): **mist was ~ing in the valley** в доли́не собира́лся тума́н; **ice ~ed on the window** на окне́ образова́лся/возни́к моро́зный узо́р; **an idea ~ed in his mind** в его́ мозгу́ возни́кла иде́я (*or* возни́кло представле́ние); (*mil. etc.; also* **~ up**) стро́иться, по-; **the children ~ed up in groups** де́ти стро́ились отде́льными гру́ппами/отря́дами.
● *cpds.* **~-filling** *n.* заполне́ние бла́нков; **~-master** *n.* (*Br.*) кла́ссный руководи́тель; **~-mistress** *n.* (*Br.*) кла́ссная руководи́тельница; **~-room** *n.* (*Br.*) кла́ссная ко́мната.

formal /ˈfɔːm(ə)l/ *adj.* **1** (*in outward form*) вне́шний; форма́льный. **2** (*conventional*) общепри́нятый; надлежа́щий; **~ garden** англи́йский сад/парк. **3** (*official*) официа́льный. **4** (*done for the sake of form*) для профо́рмы. **5** (*ceremonious*) церемо́нный.

formaldehyde /fɔːˈmældɪˌhaɪd/ *n.* формальдеги́д.

formalism /ˈfɔːməˌlɪz(ə)m/ *n.* формали́зм.

formalist /ˈfɔːməlɪst/ *n.* формали́ст.

formalistic /ˌfɔːməˈlɪstɪk/ *adj.* формалисти́ческий.

formality /fɔːˈmælɪtɪ/ *n.* форма́льность.

formalization /ˌfɔːməlaɪˈzeɪʃ(ə)n/ *n.* оформле́ние.

formalize /ˈfɔːməˌlaɪz/ *v.t.* оф|ормля́ть, -о́рмить.

format /ˈfɔːmæt/ *n.* (*also comput.*) форма́т.
● *v.t.* (*comput.*) формати́ровать (*impf., pf.*).

formation /fɔːˈmeɪʃ(ə)n/ *n.* **1** (*creation*) образова́ние, формирова́ние. **2** (*mil.*) строй, расположе́ние, поря́док; (*aeron.*) боево́й поря́док; строй самолётов в во́здухе; **~ flying** полёт в боево́м поря́дке. **3** (*geol.*) форма́ция.

formative /ˈfɔːmətɪv/ *adj.* формиру́ющий, образу́ющий; **he spent his ~ years in France** го́ды, когда́ скла́дывался его́ хара́ктер, он провёл во Фра́нции.

former /ˈfɔːmə(r)/ *adj.* **1** (*earlier*) предше́ствующий; **in ~ times** в пре́жние времена́; **my ~ husband** мой бы́вший муж. **2** (*first mentioned of two*) пе́рвый.

formerly /ˈfɔːməlɪ/ *adv.* пре́жде, ра́ньше.

formic /ˈfɔːmɪk/ *adj.* муравьи́ный; **~ acid** муравьи́ная кислота́.

formidable /ˈfɔːmɪdəb(ə)l/, *disp.* /fɔːˈmɪd-/ *adj.* (*frightening*) устраша́ющий, гро́зный; (*huge*) огро́мный; (*task*) невероя́тно тру́дный.

formless /ˈfɔːmlɪs/ *adj.* бесфо́рменный.

formula /ˈfɔːmjʊlə/ *n.* (*pl.* **formulas** *or* **formulae** /-ˌliː/) (*set form of words*) выраже́ние, формулиро́вка; (*recipe*) реце́пт; (*math., chem.*) фо́рмула.

formulary /ˈfɔːmjʊlərɪ/ *n.* спра́вочник; свод пра́вил; (*eccl.*) тре́бник.

formulate /ˈfɔːmjʊˌleɪt/ *v.t.* формули́ровать, с-.

formulation /ˌfɔːmjʊˈleɪʃ(ə)n/ *n.* формулиро́вка.

fornicate /ˈfɔːnɪˌkeɪt/ *v.i.* развра́тничать (*impf.*); вести́ (*det.*) распу́тную жизнь.

fornication /ˌfɔːnɪˈkeɪʃ(ə)n/ *n.* развра́т.

fornicator /ˈfɔːnɪˌkeɪtə(r)/ *n.* развра́тни|к (*fem.* -ца).

forsake /fəˈseɪk/, /fɔː-/ *v.t.* (*past* **forsook** /-ˈsʊk/; *p.p.* **forsaken** /-ˈseɪk(ə)n/) пок|ида́ть, -и́нуть; ост|авля́ть, -а́вить; бр|оса́ть, -о́сить.

forsooth /fəˈsuːθ/, /fɔː-/ *adv.* (*arch.*) воистину, поистине.

forswear /fɔːˈsweə(r)/ *v.t.* (*past* **forswore** /-ˈswɔː/; *p.p.* **forsworn** /-ˈswɔːn/) отр|ека́ться, -е́чься от + *g.*

fort /fɔːt/ *n.* форт; **hold the ~** (*fig.*) держа́ть/уде́рживать (*impf.*) пози́цию.

forte[1] /ˈfɔːteɪ/ *n.* (*strong point*) си́льная сторона́.

forte[2] /ˈfɔːteɪ/ *n.* & *adv.* (*mus.*) фо́рте (*indecl.*).

forth /fɔːθ/ *adv.* вперёд, да́льше; **back and ~** взад и вперёд; **and so ~** и так да́лее; **from this day ~** с э́того дня; впредь; **let ~ a yell** изд|ава́ть, -а́ть вопль.

forthcoming /fɔːθˈkʌmɪŋ/, *attrib.* /ˈfɔːθ-/ *adj.* предстоя́щий; (*helpful*) услу́жливый; **the money was not ~** де́ньги не поступа́ли; **the clerk was not very ~ with information** чино́вник не о́чень охо́тно дава́л сведе́ния.

forthright /ˈfɔːθraɪt/ *adj.* прямо́й, прямолине́йный.

forthwith /fɔːθˈwɪθ/, /-ˈwɪð/ *adv.* неме́дленно, то́тчас.

fortieth /ˈfɔːtɪɪθ/ *n.* (*fraction*) одна́ сорокова́я; сорокова́я часть.
● *adj.* сороково́й.

fortification /ˌfɔːtɪfɪˈkeɪʃ(ə)n/ *n.* укрепле́ние, фортифика́ция.

fortif|y /ˈfɔːtɪˌfaɪ/ *v.t.* укреп|ля́ть, -и́ть; **~ied wines** креплёные ви́на; (*food*) витаминизи́ровать (*impf. and pf.*).

fortissi|mo /fɔːˈtɪsɪˌməʊ/ *n.* & *adv.* (*pl.* **-mos** *or* **-mi** /-ˌmiː/) форти́ссимо (*indecl.*); **a ~ passage** отры́вок/часть форти́ссимо.

fortitude /ˈfɔːtɪˌtjuːd/ *n.* сто́йкость; си́ла ду́ха.

fortnight /ˈfɔːtnaɪt/ (*Br.*) *n.* две неде́ли; **next Tuesday ~** че́рез две неде́ли, счита́я со сле́дующего вто́рника; **last Tuesday ~** за две неде́ли до про́шлого вто́рника.

fortnightly /ˈfɔːtˌnaɪtlɪ/ *n.* (*Br.*) (*publication*) двухнеде́льное изда́ние.
● *adj.* двухнеде́льный.
● *adv.* раз в две неде́ли.

fortress /ˈfɔːtrɪs/ *n.* кре́пость.

fortuitous /fɔːˈtjuːɪtəs/ *adj.* случа́йный.

fortuit|ousness /fɔːˈtjuːɪtəsnɪs/, **-y** /fɔːˈtjuːɪtɪ/ *nn.* случа́йность, слу́чай.

fortunate /ˈfɔːtjʊnət/, /-tʃənət/ *adj.* счастли́вый, уда́чный; **he was ~ to escape** ему́ посчастли́вилось убежа́ть; **~ly** к сча́стью.

fortune /ˈfɔːtjuːn/, /-tʃuːn/ *n.* **1** (*chance*) уда́ча, сча́стье, форту́на; **by good ~** по сча́стью; **he had ~ on his side** сча́стье бы́ло на его́ стороне́; **the ~s of war** вое́нная форту́на, превра́тности (*f. pl.*) войны́; **try one's ~** попыта́ть (*pf.*) сча́стья. **2** (*fate*) судьба́; **the Gypsy (woman) told my ~** цыга́нка (по/на)гада́ла мне. **3** (*prosperity, large sum*) состоя́ние, бога́тство; **come into a ~** насле́довать, у- состоя́ние; получ|а́ть, -и́ть насле́дство; **make a ~** разбогате́ть (*pf.*); наж|ива́ть, -и́ть состоя́ние; **I spent a small ~ today** я истра́тил у́йму де́нег сего́дня.
● *cpd.* **~-teller** *n.* гада́лка, ворожея́.

fort|y /ˈfɔːtɪ/ *n.* со́рок; **the ~ies** (*decade*) сороковы́е го́ды (*m. pl.*); **they are both in their ~ies** (*age*) им обо́им за со́рок; **the roaring ~ies** (*stormy ocean tracts*) реву́щие сороковы́е.
● *adj.* со́рок + *g. pl.*; **a man of ~y** сорокале́тний челове́к; **have ~y winks** вздремну́ть (*pf.*).

forum /ˈfɔːrəm/ *n.* (*hist.*) фо́рум; (*fig., court*) суд; **the ~ of conscience** суд со́вести; (*fig., discussion*) обсужде́ние; (*meeting*) фо́рум, съезд; **the magazine provides a ~ for discussion** журна́л предоставля́ет чита́телям возмо́жность вести́ диску́ссии.

forward /ˈfɔːwəd/ *n.* (*sport*) напада́ющий.
● *adj.* (*situated to the fore*) пере́дний; (*progressive*) прогресси́вный; (*precocious*) скоропе́лый, преждевре́менный; (*prompt, ready*) гото́вый (*на что*); (*pert*) наглова́тый, развя́зный.
● *adv.* (*onward; towards one*) вперёд; **~, march!** ша́гом марш!; **please come ~** пожа́луйста, вы́йдите вперёд; **carry ~** (*on a ledger*) перен|оси́ть, -ести́ на другу́ю страни́цу; **the meeting has been brought ~ a day** собра́ние перенесли́ на́ день ра́ньше; **walk back(wards) and ~(s)** ходи́ть (*indet.*) взад и вперёд; (*towards the future*): **I look ~ to meeting her** я с нетерпе́нием жду встре́чи с ней; **from this time ~** начина́я с э́того вре́мени; (*naut.*) в носово́й ча́сти; в носову́ю часть.
● *v.t.* (*promote, encourage*) продв|ига́ть, -и́нуть; (*send*) пос|ыла́ть, -ла́ть; отпр|авля́ть, -а́вить; (*send on*) перес|ыла́ть, -ла́ть.
● *cpd.* **~-looking** *adj.*

F

предусмотри́тельный, дальнови́дный.

forwardness /ˈfɔːwədnɪs/ *n.* ра́ннее разви́тие; (*impudence*) наха́льство.

forwent /fɔːˈwent/ *past of* ⇒**forgo**

fossil /ˈfɒs(ə)l/ *n.* окамене́лость; (*also fig.*) ископа́емое.

● *adj.* окамене́лый, ископа́емый.

fossilization /ˌfɒsɪlaɪˈzeɪʃ(ə)n/ *n.* окамене́ние.

fossilize /ˈfɒsɪlaɪz/ *v.t. & i.* превра|ща́ть(ся), -ти́ть(ся) в окамене́лость; (*fig.*) закосне́ть (*pf.*).

foster /ˈfɒstə(r)/ *v.t.* (*rear*) воспи́т|ывать, а́ть; (*Br., assign to someone else to rear*) отд|ава́ть, -а́ть на воспита́ние; (*fig.*) (*hope*) пита́ть (*impf.*); (*hatred*) се́ять, по-; ~ **evil thoughts** выена́шивать (*impf.*) недо́брые мы́сли.

● *cpds.* **~-brother** *n.* моло́чный брат; **~-child** *n.* приёмыш, воспи́танник; **~-father** *n.* приёмный оте́ц; **~-mother** *n.* приёмная мать.

fought /fɔːt/ *past and p.p. of* ⇒**fight**

foul /faʊl/ *n.* (*sport*) наруше́ние (пра́вил игры́).

● *adj.* гря́зный, отврати́тельный; **a ~ smell** злово́ние; **~ air** загрязнённый во́здух; **~ language** руга́тельства (*nt. pl.*); сквернosло́вие; **~ weather** отврати́тельная пого́да; непого́да; **~ play** (*sport*) гру́бая игра́; (*violence*) нечи́стое де́ло; **by fair means or ~** любы́ми сре́дствами; **fall ~ of** поссо́риться (*pf.*) с + *i.*

● *v.t.* (*defile*) загрязн|я́ть, -и́ть; па́чкать, за-; засор|я́ть, -и́ть; **~ one's own nest** (*fig.*) га́дить, на- в своём гнезде́; (*obstruct*) образо́в|ывать, -а́ть зато́р в + *p.*

● *v.i.* (*become entangled*) запу́т|ываться, -аться.

● *cpds.* **~-mouthed** *adj.* сквернosло́вящий; **~-mouthed person** сквернosло́в; **~-up** *n.* неразбери́ха, завару́ха.

foulard /fuːˈlɑːd/ *n.* (*text.*) фуля́р.

found[1] /faʊnd/ *v.t.* осно́в|ывать, -а́ть; за|кла́дывать, -ложи́ть; **~ a city** за|кла́дывать, -ложи́ть го́род; (*endow*) осно́в|ывать, -а́ть; учре|жда́ть, -ди́ть; (*base*) осно́в|ывать, -а́ть; **the story is ~ed on fact** в осно́ву расска́за поло́жено действи́тельное происше́ствие.

found[2] /faʊnd/ *v.t.* (*melt metal etc.*) пла́вить (*impf.*); лить (*impf.*).

found[3] /faʊnd/ *past and p.p. of* ⇒**find**

foundation /faʊnˈdeɪʃ(ə)n/ *n.* **1** (*establishing*) основа́ние, учрежде́ние; (*endowment*) учрежде́ние; (*founded institution*) учрежде́ние, существу́ющее на поже́ртвованный фонд; (*fund*) фонд. **2** (*base of building etc.*) фунда́мент; **lay the ~** за|кла́дывать, -ложи́ть фунда́мент/осно́ву; (*fig.*) осно́ва; **lay the ~s of one's career** класть, положи́ть нача́ло свое́й карье́ре; **the story has no ~ in fact** расска́з не име́ет ни мале́йшего основа́ния. **3**: **~ cream** крем под пу́дру; **~ garment** корсе́т, гра́ция.

● *cpd.* **~-stone** *n.* фунда́ментный ка́мень; (*fig.*) краеуго́льный ка́мень, осно́ва.

founder[1] /ˈfaʊndə(r)/ *n.* основа́тель (*m.*) (*fem.* -ница); учреди́тель (*m.*) (*fem.* -ница).

● *cpd.* **~-member** *n.* член-основа́тель (*m.*).

founder[2] /ˈfaʊndə(r)/ *n.* (*metall.*) лите́йщик, плави́льщик.

founder[3] /ˈfaʊndə(r)/ *v.i.* (*collapse*) ос|еда́ть, -е́сть; (*of a horse, go lame*) хроме́ть, о-; (*from fatigue*) вали́ться, с-; (*of a ship*) идти́, пойти́ ко дну.

foundling /ˈfaʊndlɪŋ/ *n.* подки́дыш, найдёныш.

foundry /ˈfaʊndrɪ/ *n.* лите́йная; **~ hand** лите́йщик.

fount[1] /faʊnt/ *n.* (*source*) исто́чник, ключ.

fount[2] /faʊnt/ (*Br.*) = **font**[2]

fountain /ˈfaʊntɪn/ *n.* фонта́н; (*fig.*) исто́чник; **drinking ~** фонта́нчик для питья́.

● *cpds.* **~-head** *n.*: **go to the ~-head** обрати́ться (*pf.*) к первоисто́чнику; **~-pen** *n.* авторучка.

four /fɔː(r)/ *n.* (числó/нóмер) четы́ре; (~ *people*) че́тверо; **we ~** нас че́тверо; **(the, all) ~ of us went** мы пошли́ вчетверо́м; нас пошло́ четы́ре челове́ка; **~ each** по четы́ре; **in ~s, ~ at a time** по четы́ре; четвёрками; (*figure; thing numbered 4; set, team, crew of ~*) четвёрка; (*cut, divide*): **in ~** на четы́ре ча́сти; **fold in ~** сложи́ть (*pf.*) вче́тверо; (*with var. nn. expr. or understood: cf. also examples under* ⇒**two**): **carriage and ~** каре́та, запряжённая четвёркой лошаде́й; **make up a ~ at bridge** сост|авля́ть, -а́вить па́ртию в бридж; **he got down on all ~s** он опусти́лся на четвере́ньки.

● *adj.* четы́ре + *g. sg.*; (*for people and pluralia tantum, also*) че́тверо + *g. pl.* (*cf. examples under* ⇒**two**); **he and ~ others** он и ещё че́тверо други́х; **~ fives are twenty** четы́режды (*or* четы́ре на) пять — два́дцать; **~ times as good** вче́тверо (*or* в четы́ре ра́за) лу́чше; **~ times as big** в четы́ре ра́за бо́льше; **from the ~ corners of the earth** со всех концо́в земли́; **~ figures** (*sum*) четырёхзна́чная су́мма.

● *cpds.* **~-course** *adj.*: **~-course meal** обе́д из четырёх блюд; **~fold** *adj.* четырёхкра́тный; *adv.* в четы́ре ра́за (бо́льше); **~-footed** *adj.* четвероно́гий; **~-hundredth** *adj.* четырёхсо́тый; **~-lane** *adj.*: **~-lane highway** шоссе́ (*indecl.*) с движе́нием в четы́ре ря́да; **~-legged** *adj.* = **~-footed; ~-letter** *adj.*: **~-letter word** (*fig.*) руга́тельство; непристо́йное сло́во; **~-poster (bed)** *n.* крова́ть с по́логом на четырёх сто́лбиках; **~-square** *adj.* квадра́тный; (*fig.*) твёрдый, прямо́й; **~-stroke** *adj.*: **~-stroke engine** четырёхта́ктный дви́гатель (вну́треннего сгора́ния); **~-wheel** *adj.*: **~-wheel drive** (*attr.*) с приво́дом на четы́ре колеса́.

foursome /ˈfɔːsəm/ *n.* четвёрка; две па́ры; **we made a ~** мы игра́ли дво́е на́ двое (*or* вчетверо́м).

fourteen /fɔːˈtiːn/ *n. & adj.* четы́рнадцать (+ *g. pl.*).

fourteenth /fɔːˈtiːnθ/ *n.* (*date*) четы́рнадцатое (числó); (*fraction*) одна́ четы́рнадцатая; четы́рнадцатая часть.

● *adj.* четы́рнадцатый.

fourth /fɔːθ/ *n.* **1** (*date*) четвёртое (числó). **2** (*fraction*) одна́ четвёртая; четвёртая часть; че́тверть. **3** (*mus.*) ква́рта.

● *adj.* четвёртый; **the ~ dimension** четвёртое измере́ние.

fowl /faʊl/ *n.* (*pl.* ~ *or* ~**s**) (*domestic*) дома́шняя пти́ца; (*chicken*) ку́рица.

fowler /ˈfaʊlə(r)/ *n.* птицело́в.

fox /fɒks/ *n.* лиса́, лиси́ца; (*fur*) ли́сий мех; (*wily man*) хитре́ц; лиса́ (*c.g.*).

● *v.t.* (*deceive*) обма́н|ывать, -у́ть; (*puzzle*) ста́вить, по- в тупи́к; озада́чи|вать, -ть.

● *cpds.* **~glove** *n.* наперстя́нка; **~hole** *n.* ли́сья нора́; (*mil.*) стрелко́вая яче́йка; одино́чный око́п; **~hound** *n.* го́нчая; **~-hunting** *n.* (верхова́я) охо́та на лис; **~-terrier** *n.* фокстерье́р; **~trot** *n.* фокстро́т.

foxy /ˈfɒksɪ/ *adj.* (**foxier, foxiest**) (*crafty*) хи́трый; (*coll., sexually attractive*) привлека́тельный.

foyer /ˈfɔɪeɪ/ *n.* фойе́ (*indecl.*).

Fr. /ˈfɑːðə(r)/ *n.* (*abbr. of* ***Father***) оте́ц.

fr. /ˈfræŋk(z)/ *n.* (*abbr. of* **franc(s)**) фр. (франк).

fracas /ˈfrækɑː/ (*pl.* ~ /-kɑːz/) *n.* сканда́л, шу́мная ссо́ра.

fraction /ˈfrækʃ(ə)n/ *n.* **1** (*arith.*) дробь; **decimal ~** десяти́чная дробь; **common, vulgar ~** простая дробь; **improper ~** непра́вильная дробь; **~ of a second** до́ля секу́нды. **2** (*small piece or amount*) части́ца, крупи́ца; **£5 and not a ~ less** пять фу́нтов — и ни гроша́ ме́ньше. **3** (*chem.*) фра́кция. **4** (*small sect or party*) фра́кция.

fractional /ˈfrækʃən(ə)l/ *adj.* дро́бный, части́чный; **the difference is ~** ра́зница незначи́тельна.

fractious /ˈfrækʃəs/ *adj.* капри́зный.

fracture /ˈfræktʃə(r)/ *n.* тре́щина, разры́в; (*of a bone*) перело́м; **simple/compound ~** закры́тый/откры́тый перело́м.

● *v.t. & i.* лома́ть(ся), с-; раск|а́лывать(ся), -оло́ть(ся).

fragile /ˈfrædʒaɪl/, /-dʒɪl/ *adj.* (*brittle*) ло́мкий, хру́пкий; (*frail*) хру́пкий.

fragility /frəˈdʒɪlɪtɪ/ *n.* ло́мкость, хру́пкость.

fragment /ˈfrægmənt/ *n.* обло́мок, оско́лок; (*of writing or music*) фрагме́нт; **~s of conversation** обры́вки (*m. pl.*) разгово́ра.

fragmentary /ˈfrægməntərɪ/ *adj.* отры́вочный, фрагмента́рный.

fragmentation /ˌfrægmənˈteɪʃ(ə)n/ *n.* разры́в на ме́лкие ча́сти; **~ bomb** оско́лочная бо́мба.

fragrance /ˈfreɪgrəns/ *n.* арома́т.

fragrant /ˈfreɪgrənt/ *adj.* арома́тный.

frail /freɪl/ *adj.* хру́пкий, непро́чный; (*in health*) хи́лый, хру́пкий,боле́зненный; (*in moral sense*) сла́бый, неусто́йчивый.

frailty /ˈfreɪltɪ/ *n.* хру́пкость, непро́чность; (*of health*) хру́пкость, боле́зненность; (*of morals*) сла́бость, неусто́йчивость.

frame /freɪm/ *n.* **1** (*structural skeleton*) скеле́т, костя́к; (*of a ship or aircraft*) ко́рпус, о́стов; (*textiles*) тка́цкий стано́к.
2 (*wood or metal surround*) ра́ма, ра́мка; **picture ~** ра́ма (для) карти́ны; **window ~** око́нная ра́ма.
3 (*hort.*) парнико́вая ра́ма.
4 (*body*): **more than the human ~ can bear** свы́ше сил челове́ческих; **sobs shook her ~** рыда́ния сотряса́ли её (те́ло).
5: **~ of mind** настрое́ние; расположе́ние ду́ха.
6 (*order, system*) структу́ра, систе́ма.
7 (*cin.*) кадр.
● *v.t.* **1** (*compose, devise*) сост|авля́ть, -а́вить; созд|ава́ть, -а́ть; **~ a constitution/sentence** сост|авля́ть, -а́вить конститу́цию/предложе́ние; **he ~d his question carefully** он то́чно сформули́ровал свой вопро́с.
2 (*surround*): **~ a picture** вст|авля́ть, -а́вить карти́ну в ра́м(к)у; обр|амля́ть, -а́мить карти́ну; **he was ~d in the doorway** он стоя́л в проёме две́ри.
3 (*sl., concoct case against*) приши́ть (*pf.*) де́ло + *d.*; сфабрикова́ть (*pf.*) ули́ку про́тив + *g.*
● *cpds.* **~-house** *n.* (*US*) карка́сный дом; **~-saw** *n.* ра́мная пила́; **~-up** *n.* (*sl.*) сфабрико́ванное обвине́ние; **~work** *n.* карка́с, о́стов; (*fig.*): **within the ~work of the constitution** в ра́мках конститу́ции.

franc /fræŋk/ *n.* франк.

France /frɑːns/ *n.* Фра́нция.

franchise /ˈfræntʃaɪz/ *n.* (*right of voting*) пра́во го́лоса; (*comm.*) привиле́гия, франши́з.

Franciscan /frænˈsɪskən/ *n.* франциска́нец.
● *adj.* франциска́нский.

Francophile /ˈfræŋkəˌfaɪl/ *n.* франкофи́л.
● *adj.* франкофи́льский.

francophone /ˈfræŋkəˌfəʊn/ *n. & adj.* франкоязы́чный; говоря́щий на францу́зском языке́.

frank[1] /fræŋk/ *adj.* открове́нный, и́скренний.

frank[2] /fræŋk/ *v.t.* франки́ровать (*impf., pf.*); **~ing machine** франкирова́льная маши́на.

frankfurter /ˈfræŋkˌfɜːtə(r)/ *n.* соси́ска.

frankincense /ˈfræŋkɪnˌsens/ *n.* ла́дан.

frankness /ˈfræŋknɪs/ *n.* открове́нность, и́скренность.

frantic /ˈfræntɪk/ *adj.* неи́стовый, безу́мный; **she became ~ with grief** она́ обезу́мела от го́ря; **the noise is driving me ~** шум выво́дит меня́ из себя́; **he was in a ~ hurry** он ужа́сно спеши́л.

fraternal /frəˈtɜːn(ə)l/ *adj.* бра́тский.

fraternity /frəˈtɜːnɪtɪ/ *n.* бра́тство; (*student association*) студе́нческая общи́на.

fraternization /ˌfrætənaɪˈzeɪʃ(ə)n/ *n.* брата́ние.

fraternize /ˈfrætəˌnaɪz/ *v.i.* брата́ться (*impf.*).

fratricidal /ˌfrætrɪˈsaɪd(ə)l/ *adj.* братоуби́йственный.

fratricide /ˈfrætrɪˌsaɪd/ *n.* (*crime*) братоуби́йство; (*criminal*) братоуби́йца (*c.g.*).

fraud /frɔːd/ *n.* (*fraudulent act*) обма́н, моше́нничество; (*impostor*) обма́нщик, моше́нник; (*thing that deceives or disappoints*) фальши́вка, подде́лка.

fraudulence /ˈfrɔːdjʊləns/ *n.* обма́нчивость, фальши́вость.

fraudulent /ˈfrɔːdjʊlənt/ *adj.* обма́нный, фальши́вый, моше́ннический.

fraught /frɔːt/ *adj.* по́лный, преиспо́лненный, чрева́тый; **the expedition is ~ with danger** экспеди́ция чрева́та опа́сностями; (*tense*) напряжённый.

fray[1] /freɪ/ *n.* дра́ка; побо́ище.

fray[2] /freɪ/ *v.t. & i.* прот|ира́ть(ся), -ере́ть(ся); (*fig.*): **her nerves are ~ed** у неё соверше́нно истрёпаны не́рвы.

frazzle /ˈfræz(ə)l/ *n.*: **worn to a ~** доведённый до изнеможе́ния.

freak /friːk/ *n.* (*unusual occurrence*): **a ~ storm** необы́чная бу́ря; (*abnormal person or thing*) уро́д, вы́родок; уро́дство; (*absurd or fanciful idea*) причу́да, заско́к; **~ of nature** оши́бка приро́ды; (*enthusiast*) фана́т; **health ~** поме́шанный на здоро́вье; **film ~** киномáн.
● *v.i.*: **~ (out)** (*coll.*) при|ходи́ть, -йти́ в возбужде́ние.

freakish /ˈfriːkɪʃ/ *adj.* причу́дливый, чудно́й.

freckle /ˈfrek(ə)l/ *n.* весну́шка.
● *v.t.* покр|ыва́ть, -ы́ть весну́шками; **a ~d face** весну́шчатое лицо́.

free /friː/ *adj.* (**freer** /ˈfriːə(r)/, **freest** /ˈfriːɪst/) **1** свобо́дный, во́льный; **you are ~ to leave** вы мо́жете уйти́; **they gave us a ~ hand** они́ да́ли нам по́лную свобо́ду де́йствий; **he let the thief go ~** он упусти́л во́ра; (*after capture*) он отпусти́л во́ра (на во́лю); **break ~** вырыва́ться, вы́рваться на во́лю; **set ~** освобо|жда́ть, -ди́ть; **~ of disease** здоро́вый; **~ from blame** неви́нный; **~ composition** сочине́ние на свобо́дную те́му; **~ enterprise** свобо́дное предпринима́тельство; **~ fall** свобо́дное паде́ние; **~ on board** фра́нко-борт; **~ speech** свобо́да сло́ва; **~ translation** во́льный перево́д; **~ verse** во́льный стих; **~ will** свобо́да во́ли; **he left of his own ~ will** он ушёл доброво́льно/сам (*or* по свое́й во́ле).
2 (*without constraint*) непринуждённый, раско́ванный; **~ and easy** непринуждённый; **make ~ with** свобо́дно распоряжа́ться (*impf.*) + *i.*; **he made ~ with my cigars** он распоряжа́лся мои́ми сига́рами, как свои́ми.
3 (*without payment*) беспла́тный; **the price is £5 post ~** цена́ 5 фу́нтов с беспла́тной доста́вкой по по́чте; **~ of charge** беспла́тный; **~ gift** полу́ченное да́ром; **~ pass** (*on railway etc.*) беспла́тный прое́зд; (*admission*) про́пуск.
4 (*unoccupied*) свобо́дный, неза́нятый; **my hands are ~** (*fig.*) у меня́ развя́заны ру́ки.
5 (*liberal*) ще́дрый; **~ with one's money** ще́дрый, расточи́тельный; **~ with advice** всегда́ гото́вый дава́ть сове́ты.
6 (*chem.*) несвя́занный.
● *v.t.* (*release, e.g. a rope*) высвобожда́ть, вы́свободить; (*liberate*) освобо|жда́ть, -ди́ть.
● *cpds.* **~board** *n.* надво́дный борт; **~booter** *n.* граби́тель (*m.*); пира́т; **~-for-all** *n.* (*competition*) откры́тый для всех ко́нкурс; (*fight*) всео́бщая дра́ка/сва́лка; ку́ча мала́ (*indecl.*); **~hand** *adj.*: **~hand drawing** рису́нок, сде́ланный от руки́; **~hold** *n.* неограни́ченное пра́во со́бственности на недви́жимость; **~holder** *n.* свобо́дный со́бственник; **~lance(r)** *n.* лицо́ свобо́дной профе́ссии, рабо́тающий по догово́рам; внешта́тник (*coll.*); **F~mason** *n.* масо́н; **F~masonry** *n.* (*lit.*) масо́нство; **F~phone** *n.* (*Br.*) беспла́тный телефо́н; **~-range** *adj.*: **~-range eggs** я́йца от кур, не сидя́щих в клéтках; **~-range hens** ку́ры на свобо́дном вы́гуле; **~-thinker** *n.* вольноду́м|ец (*fem.* -ка); **~-thinking** *adj.* вольноду́мный; **~way** *n.* (*US*) скоростна́я автостра́да; **~-wheel** *v.i.* (*lit.*) дви́гаться (*impf.*) свобо́дным хо́дом; **~-wheeling** *adj.* (*fig.*) во́льный, неско́ванный.

freedom /ˈfriːdəm/ *n.* свобо́да; **~ of speech** свобо́да сло́ва.

freesia /ˈfriːzjə/, /-ʒə/ *n.* фре́зия.

freez|e /friːz/ *n.* (*period of frost*) замора́живание; хо́лод, моро́з; **wage ~e** замора́живание за́работной пла́ты.
● *v.t.* (*past* **froze**; *p.p.* **frozen**) замор|а́живать, -о́зить; **frozen food** моро́женые проду́кты; **the news froze his blood** от э́того изве́стия его́ охвати́л у́жас; **~e assets/prices** замор|а́живать, -о́зить фо́нды/це́ны; **~e out** (*exclude*) вы́курить (*pf.*) (*sl.*).
● *v.i.* (*past* **froze**; *p.p.* **frozen**)
1 (*impers.*) моро́зить (*impf.*); **it's ~ing outside** на дворе́ стра́шный моро́з; **will it ~e tonight?** бу́дет сего́дня но́чью моро́з?
2 (*congeal with cold*): **the lake is frozen up, over, across** о́зеро покры́лось льдом; **the roads are frozen** доро́ги покры́лись льдом; **the pipes are frozen (up)** тру́бы промёрзли; **~ing point** то́чка замерза́ния.
3 (*fig., become rigid*) заст|ыва́ть, -ы́ть;

F

he froze where he stood он засты́л на ме́сте; **his features froze** его́ лицо́ как бу́дто засты́ло; **'~e!'** (*coll., remain motionless*) замри́!
4 (*become chilled*) зам|ерза́ть, -ёрзнуть; **he froze to death** он промёрз до косте́й; **I'm ~ing** я замёрз.

freezer /'fri:zə(r)/ *n.* (*domestic appliance*) морози́льник; **~ compartment** морози́лка.

freight /freɪt/ *n.* **1** (*carriage of goods*) фрахт, груз; **~ charge** сто́имость прово́за. **2** (*goods carried*) груз.
● *v.t.* (*transport*) перев|ози́ть, -езти́.
● *cpd.* **~-train** *n.* (*US*) това́рный по́езд.

freighter /'freɪtə(r)/ *n.* (*vessel*) грузово́е су́дно; (*aircraft*) грузово́й самолёт.

French /frentʃ/ *n.* (*language*) францу́зский язы́к; **the ~** (*people*) францу́зы (*m. pl.*).
● *adj.* францу́зский; **~ bean** (*Br.*) фасо́ль; **French Canadian** кана́д|ец-францу́з (*fem.* -ка-францу́женка); **~ chalk** мы́льный ка́мень; портня́жный мел; **~ fried potatoes** (*Br.*), **~ fries** (*US*) жа́реная карто́шка, карто́фель-соло́мка, карто́фель-фри; **~ horn** валто́рна; **~ horn player** валторни́ст; **~ leave** (*coll.*) прогу́л; (*mil.*) самово́льная отлу́чка; **~ letter** (*Br. coll., contraceptive*) презервати́в; **~ loaf** (дли́нный) бато́н; **~ polish** политу́ра; **~ window** двуство́рчатое окно́ до по́ла; (*pl.*) две́ри в сад.
● *cpds.* **~man** *n.* францу́з; **~woman** *n.* францу́женка.

Frenchified /'frentʃɪ,faɪd/ *adj.* офранцу́женный.

frenetic /frə'netɪk/ *adj.* неи́стовый; лихора́дочный.

frenzied /'frenzɪd/ *adj.* неи́стовый, взбешённый; **~ applause** неи́стовая ова́ция.

frenzy /'frenzɪ/ *n.* неи́стовство, бе́шенство.

frequency /'fri:kwənsɪ/ *n.* частота́; (*rate*) ча́стность; **~ modulation** часто́тная модуля́ция.

frequent¹ /'fri:kwənt/ *adj.* ча́стый.

frequent² /frɪ'kwent/ *v.t.* ча́сто посеща́ть (*impf.*).

frequentative /frɪ'kwentətɪv/ *adj.* (*gram.*) многокра́тный.

frequently /'fri:kwəntlɪ/ *adv.* ча́сто.

fresco /'freskəʊ/ *n.* (*pl.* **~s** *or* **~es**) фре́ска.

fresh /freʃ/ *adj.* **1** (*new*) све́жий, но́вый; (*more*): **make some ~ tea** завари́ть (*pf.*) све́жего ча́ю. **2** (*recent in origin*): **~ bread** све́жий хлеб; **~ paint** све́жая кра́ска; **~ from university** пря́мо с университе́тской скамьи́; **it is still ~ in my memory** э́то ещё свежо́ в мое́й па́мяти. **3** (*as opposed to salt*) пре́сный. **4** (*cool, refreshing*) све́жий, прохла́дный; **a ~ breeze** све́жий ветеро́к. **5** (*unspoilt, unsullied*) све́жий, незапя́тнанный; **~ air** све́жий во́здух; **a ~ complexion** све́жий цвет лица́. **6** (*lively*) бо́дрый, живо́й. **7** (*impudent*) развя́зный, де́рзкий.
● *cpds.* **~man** *n.* новичо́к (в университе́те); первоку́рсник; **~-water** *adj.* пресново́дный.

freshen /'freʃ(ə)n/ *v.t.* освеж|а́ть, -и́ть.
● *v.i.* свеже́ть, по-; **the wind is ~ing** ве́тер свеже́ет; **she's gone to ~ up** она́ пошла́ привести́ себя́ в поря́док.

fresher /'freʃə(r)/ *n.* (*Br. coll.*) = **freshman**

freshly /'freʃlɪ/ *adv.* свежо́, бо́дро; (*recently*) неда́вно; то́лько что.

freshness /'freʃnɪs/ *n.* (*novelty*) све́жесть, оригина́льность; (*coolness*) све́жесть; (*brightness*) све́жесть, я́ркость; (*impudence*) развя́зность, де́рзость.

fret¹ /fret/ *n.* (*of a guitar etc.*) лад.

fret² /fret/ *n.* (*Br.*) волне́ние.
● *v.t.* (**fretted, fretting**) (*wear by rubbing etc.*) изн|а́шивать, -оси́ть; разъ|еда́ть, -е́сть; (*worry*) раздража́ть (*impf.*); волнова́ть, вз-.
● *v.i.* (**fretted, fretting**) волнова́ться; му́читься (*both impf.*); **babies ~ in hot weather** ма́ленькие де́ти пло́хо перено́сят жа́ркую пого́ду.

fret³ /fret/ *v.t.* (**fretted, fretting**) (*decorate by cutting*) укр|аша́ть, -а́сить резьбо́й.
● *cpds.* **~saw** *n.* ло́бзик; пи́лка для мета́лла; **~work** *n.* резно́е украше́ние, резьба́.

fretful /'fretfʊl/ *adj.* раздражи́тельный, капри́зный.

fretfulness /'fretfʊlnɪs/ *n.* раздражи́тельность.

Freudian /'frɔɪdɪən/ *n.* фрейди́ст.
● *adj.* фрейди́стский; **~ slip** огово́рка по Фре́йду.

FRG (*abbr. of* ***Federal Republic of Germany***) (*hist.*) ФРГ (Федерати́вная Респу́блика Герма́нии).

friable /'fraɪəb(ə)l/ *adj.* кроша́щийся, ры́хлый.

friar /'fraɪə(r)/ *n.* мона́х (ни́щенствующего о́рдена).

friary /'fraɪərɪ/ *n.* мужско́й монасты́рь.

fricassee /'frɪkə,si:/, /-'si:/ *n.* фрикасе́ (*indecl.*).
● *v.t.* (**fricassees, fricasseed**) гото́вить (*impf.*) фрикасе́ из + *g.*

fricative /'frɪkətɪv/ *n.* & *adj.* фрикати́вный (звук).

friction /'frɪkʃ(ə)n/ *n.* тре́ние; (*fig.*) тре́ния (*nt. pl.*).

Friday /'fraɪdeɪ/, /-dɪ/ *n.* пя́тница; **Good ~** Страстна́я/Вели́кая пя́тница.

fridge /frɪdʒ/ *n.* (*coll.*) холоди́льник.
● *cpd.* **~-freezer** *n.* (*Br.*) двухка́мерный холоди́льник, «дву́шка».

friend /frend/ *n.* **1** (*close ~*) друг, прия́тель (*fem.* -ница); (*acquaintance*) знако́м|ый (*fem.* -ая); (*woman's fem.* ~) подру́га; **be ~s** дружи́ть (*impf.*) (*с кем*); **make ~s** подружи́ться (*pf.*) (*с кем*); **he makes ~s easily** он легко́ схо́дится с людьми́. **2** (*in addressing or referring to persons in public*) колле́га (*c.g.*); **my honourable ~** (*Br.*) мой достопочте́нный колле́га/собра́т. **3** (*benefactor, sympathizer*) доброжела́тель (*m.*), сторо́нник; **I am no ~ to such measures** я не сочу́вствую таки́м ме́рам. **4** (*Quaker*) ква́кер; **Society of F~s** се́кта ква́керов.

friendless /'frendlɪs/ *adj.* не име́ющий друзе́й.

friendliness /'frendlɪnɪs/ *n.* дружелю́бие.

friendly /'frendlɪ/ *adj.* (**friendlier, friendliest**) дру́жеский, това́рищеский; **F~ Society** о́бщество взаимопо́мощи.

friendship /'frendʃɪp/ *n.* дру́жба.

frieze /fri:z/ *n.* (*decorative band*) бордю́р, фриз.

frigate /'frɪgɪt/ *n.* (*hist.*) фрега́т; (*small destroyer*) эска́дренный миноно́сец; сторожево́й кора́бль.
● *cpd.* **~-bird** *n.* фрега́т.

frigging /'frɪgɪŋ/ *adj.* (*vulg.*) прокля́тый.

fright /fraɪt/ *n.* **1** (*fear; frightening experience*) страх, испу́г; **I almost died of ~** я чуть не у́мер от стра́ха; **give s.o. a ~** испуга́ть (*pf.*) кого́-н.; напуга́ть (*pf.*) кого́-н.; **I got the ~ of my life** я жу́тко испуга́лся.
2 (*absurd-looking person*) пу́гало, страши́лище; **she looks a (perfect) ~** она́ вы́глядит страшне́е пу́гала.

frighten /'fraɪt(ə)n/ *v.t.* пуга́ть, на-/ис-; устраш|а́ть, -и́ть; **she is ~ed of the dark** она́ бои́тся темноты́; **don't ~ the birds away** не спугни́те птиц; **he was ~ed into signing** его́ угро́зами заста́вили подписа́ться.

frightening /'fraɪtnɪŋ/ *adj.* стра́шный.

frightful /'fraɪtfʊl/ *adj.* (*terrible*) ужа́сный, стра́шный; (*coll., hideous*) безобра́зный; (*coll., very great*) колосса́льный.

frigid /'frɪdʒɪd/ *adj.* **1** (*cold*) холо́дный; **~ zone** аркти́ческий по́яс.
2 (*unfeeling*) холо́дный, безразли́чный; (*sexually*) холо́дный, фриги́дный.

frigidity /,frɪ'dʒɪdɪtɪ/ *n.* хо́лодность, фриги́дность.

frill /frɪl/ *n.* обо́рочка; обо́рки (*f. pl.*); **~s** (*fig.*) выкрута́с|ы (*pl., g.* -ов).
● *v.t.*: **a ~ed skirt** ю́бка с обо́рками.

frilly /'frɪlɪ/ *adj.* (**frillier, frilliest**) с обо́рками.

fringe /frɪndʒ/ *n.* **1** (*ornamental border*) бахрома́. **2** (*Br., of hair*) чёлка. **3** (*fig., edge, margin*) край, каймá; **~ benefits** дополни́тельные льго́ты (*f. pl.*).
● *v.t.* окайм|ля́ть, -и́ть.

frippery /'frɪpərɪ/ *n.* мишура́, дешёвые украше́ния; безделу́шки (*f. pl.*).

frisk¹ /frɪsk/ *v.t.* (*search*) обыск|ивать, -а́ть.

frisk² /frɪsk/ *v.i.* резви́ться (*impf.*); пры́гать (*impf.*).

frisky /'frɪskɪ/ *adj.* (**friskier, friskiest**) ре́звый, игри́вый.

fritter¹ /'frɪtə(r)/ *n.* (*cul.*) ≈ ола́дья.

fritter² /'frɪtə(r)/ *v.t.*: **~ away**

транжи́рить, рас-; **~ one's time away** по́пусту тра́тить (*impf.*) вре́мя.

frivolity /frɪ'vɒlɪtɪ/ *n.* легкомы́слие.

frivolous /'frɪvələs/ *adj.* (*of object*) пустя́чный; (*of person*) легкомы́сленный, пусто́й.

frivolousness /'frɪvələsnɪs/ *n.* легкомы́сленность.

frizz /frɪz/ *n.* (*of hair*) ку́дри (*f. pl.*).
● *v.t.* зав|ива́ть, -и́ть.

frizzle /'frɪz(ə)l/ *v.t. & i.* (*fry etc.*) жа́рить(ся) (*impf.*) с шипе́нием; **the bacon is all ~d up** бeко́н пережа́рен.

frizzy /'frɪzɪ/ *adj.* (**frizzier, frizziest**) вью́щийся, курча́вый.

fro /frəʊ/ *adv.*: **to and ~** взад и вперёд.

frock /frɒk/ *n.* пла́тье; **party ~** вече́рнее пла́тье.
● *cpd.* **~-coat** *n.* сюрту́к.

frog /frɒg/ *n.* **1** (*zool.*) лягу́шка; **I've got a ~ in my throat** (*fig.*) я охри́п. **2** (**F~**: *sl. pej., Frenchman*) францу́зик.
● *cpds.* **~man** *n.* легководола́з, **~-march** *v.t.* вести́ (*impf.*) сило́й/силко́м; **~-spawn** *n.* лягуша́чья икра́.

froing /'frəʊɪŋ/ *see* ⇒**toing and froing**

frolic /'frɒlɪk/ *n.* ша́лость; весе́лье, ре́звость.
● *v.i.* (**frolicked, frolicking**) шали́ть (*impf.*); резви́ться (*impf.*).

frolicsome /'frɒlɪksəm/ *adj.* шаловли́вый, ре́звый.

from /frəm/, /frɒm/ *prep.* **1** (*denoting origin of movement, measurement or distance*): **the train ~ London to Paris** по́езд из Ло́ндона в Пари́ж; **guests ~ Ukraine** го́сти с Украи́ны; **where is he ~?** отку́да он? (*родом и т.п.*); **10 miles ~ here** в десяти́ ми́лях отсю́да; **we are 2 hours' journey ~ there** мы в двух часа́х пути́ отту́да; **~ the beginning of the book** с нача́ла кни́ги; **~ cradle to grave** от колыбе́ли до моги́лы; **the lamp hung ~ the ceiling** ла́мпа свиса́ла с потолка́; **she rose ~ the piano** она́ вста́ла из-за роя́ля; **extracts ~ a novel** отры́вки из рома́на; **bark ~ a tree** кора́ с де́рева; **~ end to end** от одного́ конца́ до друго́го; **~ the bottom** со дна; **~ the top** све́рху; **~ my point of view** с мое́й то́чки зре́ния; **far ~ it!** отню́дь!; во́все нет!
2 (*expr. separation*): **I took the key ~ him** я взял у него́ ключ; **part ~ s.o.** расст|ава́ться, -а́ться с кем-н.; **hide ~** пря́таться, с- от + *g.*; **saved ~ death** спасённый от сме́рти; **released ~ prison** вы́пущенный из тюрьмы́.
3 (*denoting personal origin*): **a letter ~ my son** письмо́ от моего́ сы́на; **tell him ~ me** переда́йте ему́ от меня́; **she is ~ a good family** она́ из хоро́шей семьи́.
4 (*expr. material origin*): **wine is made ~ grapes** вино́ де́лается из виногра́да.
5 (*expr. origin in time*): **~ the very beginning** с са́мого нача́ла; **~ beginning to end** с нача́ла до конца́; **blind ~ birth** слепо́й от приро́ды; **~ childhood** с де́тства; **~ the age of seven** с семиле́тнего во́зраста; **~ now on** с э́того моме́нта; **~ dusk to dawn** от зари́ до зари́; **~ day to day** изо дня в день; со дня на́ день; **~ February to October** с февраля́ по октя́брь; **~ spring to autumn** с весны́ до о́сени; **~ time to time** вре́мя от вре́мени.
6 (*expr. source or model*): **I see ~ the papers that . . .** я зна́ю из газе́т, что. . .; **he quoted ~ memory** он цити́ровал по па́мяти; **judging ~ appearances** су́дя по вне́шности (*or* вне́шнему ви́ду); **he spoke ~ the heart** он говори́л от души́; **~ mouth to mouth** из уст в уста́; **paint ~ nature** писа́ть (*impf.*) с нату́ры; **change ~ a rouble** сда́ча с рубля́.
7 (*expr. cause*) от/с + *g.*; **~ grief** с го́ря; **suffer ~ arthritis** страда́ть (*impf.*) артри́том; **die ~ poisoning** ум|ира́ть, -ере́ть от отравле́ния; **~ jealousy** из ре́вности; **~ the best of motives** из лу́чших побужде́ний; **he drinks ~ boredom** он пьёт от/со ску́ки.
8 (*expr. difference*): **I can't tell him ~ his brother** я не могу́ отличи́ть его́ от его́ бра́та; **they live differently ~ us** они́ живу́т не так как мы.
9 (*expr. change*): **things went ~ bad to worse** дела́ шли всё ху́же и ху́же; **~ being a nonentity, he became famous** из ничто́жества он преврати́лся в знамени́тость.
10 (*with numbers*): **~ 1 to 10** от одного́ до десяти́; **it will last ~ 10 to 15 days** э́то продли́тся 10-15 дней; **~ 15 August to 10 September** с пятна́дцатого а́вгуста по деся́тое сентября́; **they cost ~ £5 (upwards)** они́ сто́ят 5 фу́нтов и вы́ше.
11 (*with advs.*): **~ above** све́рху; **~ below** сни́зу; **~ inside** изнутри́; **~ outside** снару́жи; **~ afar** издалека́; **~ over the sea** из-за мо́ря; **~ under the table** из-под стола́.

frond /frɒnd/ *n.* ветвь с ли́стьями; лист (па́поротника).

front /frʌnt/ *n.* **1** (*foremost side or part*) перёд; пере́дняя сторона́; **he walked in ~ of the procession** он шёл впереди́ проце́ссии; **in ~ of the house** пе́ред до́мом; **at the ~ of the house** в пере́дней ча́сти до́ма; **in ~ of the children** при де́тях; **she sat at the ~ of the class** она́ сиде́ла на пере́дней па́рте; **back to ~** за́дом наперёд; **in the ~ of the book** в нача́ле кни́ги.
2 (*archit.*) фаса́д.
3 (*fighting line*) фронт; **he was sent to the ~** его́ посла́ли на фронт; **on all ~s** на всех фронта́х; **in the ~ line** на передово́й ли́нии; **popular ~** (*pol.*) наро́дный фронт; **present a united ~** выступа́ть, вы́ступить еди́ным фро́нтом.
4 (*Br., road bordering sea*) на́бережная.
5 (*meteor.*) фронт.
6 (*face, in fig. senses*): **put on a bold ~** напус|ка́ть, -ти́ть на себя́ хра́брый вид; **have the ~ to** име́ть (*impf.*) на́глость (*сделать что-н.*).
7 (*cover*): **~ (organization)** организа́ция, слу́жащая вы́веской (для чего́-н.).
8 (*attr.*): **~ benches** (*pol.*) скамьи́ для мини́стров и ли́деров оппози́ции в парла́менте; **~ door** пара́дная дверь; **~ garden** сад пе́ред до́мом; палиса́дник; **~ page** пе́рвая страни́ца/полоса́; **~ page news** основны́е но́вости в газе́те; **in the ~ rank** (*fig.*) в пе́рвых ряда́х; **we had ~ seats** мы сиде́ли в пе́рвых ряда́х.
● *v.t.* **1** (*face on to*) выходи́ть (*impf.*) на + *a.*; быть обращённым к + *d.*
2: **~ed with stone** облицо́ванный ка́мнем.
3: **double-~ed house** дом с двумя́ вхо́дами.

frontage /'frʌntɪdʒ/ *n.* (*of building*) пере́дний фаса́д.

frontal /'frʌnt(ə)l/ *adj.* лобово́й; (*mil.*) фронта́льный.

frontier /'frʌntɪə(r)/, /-'tɪə(r)/ *n.* грани́ца; (*fig.*) грани́ца, преде́л; **~s of knowledge** преде́лы зна́ний.
● *adj.* пограни́чный.

frontiersman /'frʌntɪəzmən/, /-'tɪəzmən/ *n.* жи́тель (*m.*) пограни́чной полосы́.

frontispiece /'frʌntɪs,pi:s/ *n.* фронтиспи́с.

frost /frɒst/ *n.* моро́з; **ten degrees of ~** (*Br.*) де́сять гра́дусов моро́за; **black ~** моро́з без и́нея; **hard, sharp ~** си́льный моро́з; **hoar, white ~** ине́й; **Jack F~** ≈ Моро́з Кра́сный Нос; **the ~ has got my beans** мои́ бобы́ прихва́чены моро́зом.
● *v.t.*: **the windows were ~ed over** о́кна замёрзли; (*fig.*): **~ a cake** (*US*) покр|ыва́ть, -ы́ть торт глазу́рью; **~ed glass** ма́товое стекло́.
● *cpds.* **~-bite** *n.* отмороже́ние, обмороже́ние; **~-bitten** *adj.* обморо́женный; **~-bound** *adj.* ско́ванный моро́зом.

frosting /'frɒstɪŋ/ *n.* (*US, cul.*) глазу́рь.

frosty /'frɒstɪ/ *adj.* (**frostier, frostiest**) моро́зный; (*fig., unfriendly*) холо́дный, ледяно́й.

froth /frɒθ/ *n.* пе́на; (*fig.*) чепуха́, болтовня́.
● *v.t.* сби|ва́ть, -ть в пе́ну.
● *v.i.* пе́ниться (*impf.*); **~ at the mouth** бры́згать (*impf.*) слюно́й; **the milk ~ed up** молоко́ подняло́сь.

frothy /'frɒθɪ/ *adj.* (**frothier, frothiest**) пе́нистый; (*fig.*) пусто́й.

frown /fraʊn/ *n.* хму́рый взгляд.
● *v.i.* хму́риться, на-; **the authorities ~ on gambling** вла́сти неодобри́тельно отно́сятся к аза́ртным и́грам.

frowsty /'fraʊstɪ/ *adj.* (**frowstier, frowstiest**) (*Br.*) спёртый, за́тхлый.

froze /frəʊz/ *past of* ⇒**freeze**

frozen /'frəʊz(ə)n/ *adj.* замёрзший, засты́вший; (*icebound*) ско́ванный льдом; (*fig.*): **~ smile** засты́вшая улы́бка.

FRS (*abbr. of* ***Fellow of the Royal Society***) член Короле́вского о́бщества.

frugal /'fru:g(ə)l/ *adj.* (*of person*) бережли́вый; **a ~ meal** ску́дная еда́.

frugality /fru:'gælɪtɪ/ *n.* бережли́вость.

F

frugivorous /fruːˈdʒɪvərəs/ *adj.* плодоя́дный.

fruit /fruːt/ *n.* **1** (*class of food*) фрукт; **dried ~** сухофру́кты; **soft ~** плоды́ (*m. pl.*) фрукто́вых дере́вьев; **forbidden ~** (*fig.*) запре́тный плод. **2** (*bot.*) плод. **3** (*vegetable products*) плоды́, фру́кты; **the ~s of the earth** плоды́ земли́. **4** (*offspring*): **the ~ of his loins** (*of her womb*) плод его́ чресл (её чре́ва). **5** (*fig., result, reward*) плод; **enjoy the ~s of one's labours** (*Br.*), **labors** (*US*) наслажда́ться (*impf.*) плода́ми свои́х трудо́в. **6** (*US, offens.*) гомосексуали́ст.

● *cpds.* **~-cake** *n.* фрукто́вый кекс; (*coll., crazy person*) чуда́к; **~-fly** *n.* плодо́вая му́шка; **~-grower** *n.* плодово́д; **~-growing** *n.* плодово́дство; **~-juice** *n.* фрукто́вый сок; **~ machine** *n.* (*Br.*) игрово́й автома́т; **~-salad** *n.* сала́т из сыры́х фру́ктов; **~-tree** *n.* фрукто́вое де́рево.

fruitarian /fruːˈteərɪən/ *n.* челове́к, пита́ющийся исключи́тельно фру́ктами; фруктое́д.

fruiterer /ˈfruːtərə(r)/ *n.* (*Br.*) торго́вец фру́ктами.

fruitful /ˈfruːtfʊl/ *adj.* (*of soil*) плодоро́дный; (*fig.*) плодотво́рный, тво́рческий.

fruitfulness /ˈfruːtfʊlnɪs/ *n.* плодоро́дие, плодотво́рность.

fruition /fruːˈɪʃ(ə)n/ *n.* (*realization*) осуществле́ние; **come to ~** осуществ|ля́ться, -и́ться.

fruitless /ˈfruːtlɪs/ *adj.* (*lit., fig.*) беспло́дный.

fruity /ˈfruːtɪ/ *adj.* (**fruitier, fruitiest**) фрукто́вый; напомина́ющий фру́кты; (*Br., sexually suggestive*) пика́нтный, сканда́льный; (*of voice*) со́чный, зву́чный.

frump /frʌmp/ *n.* старомо́дно и пло́хо оде́тая же́нщина.

frumpish /ˈfrʌmpɪʃ/ *adj.* = **frumpy**

frumpy /ˈfrʌmpɪ/ *adj.* (**frumpier, frumpiest**) старомо́дно оде́тый.

frustrate /frʌˈstreɪt/, /ˈfrʌs-/ *v.t.* разочаро́в|ывать, -а́ть; расстр|а́ивать, -о́ить (*планы*); **I feel ~d** я обескура́жен.

frustration /frʌˈstreɪʃ(ə)n/ *n.* **1** (*thwarting*) круше́ние (*планов/надежд*). **2** (*disappointment*) разочарова́ние; **sense of ~** чу́вство безысхо́дности. **3** (*psych.*) фрустра́ция.

frust|um /ˈfrʌstəm/ *n.* (*pl.* **~a** *or* **~ums**) усечённая пирами́да; усечённый ко́нус.

fry[1] /fraɪ/ *n.* (*fish*) мальк|и́ (*pl., g.* -о́в); **small ~** (*fig.*) мелюзга́; ме́лкая со́шка.

fry[2] /fraɪ/ *v.t.* жа́рить, за-/из-; **I have other fish to ~** у меня́ други́е забо́ты; **~ing-pan** сковорода́; **out of the ~ing-pan into the fire** из огня́ да в по́лымя.

● *v.i.* жа́риться (*impf.*).

fuchsia /ˈfjuːʃə/ *n.* фу́ксия.

fuck /fʌk/ (*vulg.*) *n.*: **he doesn't give a ~** ему́ насра́ть.

● *v.t.* еба́ть, вы́-; **~ it!** чёрт возьми́!

● *v.i.* еба́ться, по-.

● *with advs.*: **~ about/around** занима́ться (*impf.*) пустяка́ми; **~ off!** отъеби́сь (от меня́)!; пошёл на́ хуй!; **~ up** по́ртить, ис-; изга́|живать, -дить.

fucking /ˈfʌkɪŋ/ *adj.* (*vulg. expletive*) ёбаный.

fuddy-duddy /ˈfʌdɪˌdʌdɪ/ *n. & adj.* устаре́лый, с устаре́вшими взгля́дами.

fudge[1] /fʌdʒ/ *n. & int.* (*nonsense*) чепуха́, вздор.

fudge[2] /fʌdʒ/ *n.* (*sweetmeat*) сли́вочная пома́дка.

fudge[3] /fʌdʒ/ *v.t. & i.*: **~ accounts** подде́л|ывать, -ать счета́; **~ up an excuse** вы́думать (*pf.*) предло́г.

fuel /ˈfjuːəl/ *n.* то́пливо, горю́чее; **~ gauge** бензиноме́р; то́пливный расходоме́р; **~ oil** мазу́т; **~ pump** бензопо́мпа; **add ~ to the flames** подл|ива́ть, -и́ть ма́сла в ого́нь; **smokeless ~s** безды́мное то́пливо; **lighter ~** бензи́н/газ для зажига́лок.

● *v.t.* (**fuelled, fuelling;** *US* **fueled, fueling**) снаб|жа́ть, -ди́ть то́пливом; запр|авля́ть, -а́вить горю́чим.

● *v.i.* (**fuelled, fuelling;** *US* **fueled, fueling**) запр|авля́ться, -а́виться горю́чим.

fug /fʌg/ *n.* (*Br. coll.*) духота́.

fugal /ˈfjuːg(ə)l/ *adj.* фу́говый.

fugitive /ˈfjuːdʒɪtɪv/ *n.* бегле́ц.

● *adj.* (*runaway*) бе́глый; (*fleeting*) бе́глый, мимолётный.

fugue /fjuːg/ *n.* фу́га.

fulcr|um /ˈfʊlkrəm/, /ˈfʌl-/ *n.* (*pl.* **~a** *or* **~ums**) то́чка опо́ры; то́чка приложе́ния си́лы.

fulfil /fʊlˈfɪl/ (*US* **fulfill**) *v.t.* (**fulfilled, fulfilling**) выполня́ть, вы́полнить; исп|олня́ть, -о́лнить; **~ a task** выполня́ть, вы́полнить зада́чу; **~ all expectations** опра́вд|ывать, -а́ть все ожида́ния.

fulfilment /fʊlˈfɪl mənt/ (*US* **fulfillment**) *n.* (*accomplishment*) выполне́ние, исполне́ние; осуществле́ние; (*satisfaction*) удовлетворе́ние.

full /fʊl/ *n.* (*limit*): **enjoy something to the ~** в по́лной ме́ре наслажда́ться (*impf.*) чем-н.

● *adj.* **1** (*filled to capacity*) по́лный; **~ to to the brim** (*or* **to overflowing**) по́лный до краёв; **the hotel is ~ (up)** все ко́мнаты в гости́нице за́няты; **he ate till he was ~ (up)** он нае́лся до отва́ла; **my heart is too ~ for words** нет слов, что́бы вы́разить переполня́ющие меня́ чу́вства; **~ house** (*theatr.*) все биле́ты про́даны; аншла́г; (*having plenty*): **~ of ideas** по́лон иде́й/за́мыслов; **~ of life** жизнера́достный; по́лон жи́зни; (*thinking or talking only*): **~ of o.s.** за́нят одни́м собо́й; **she's very ~ of herself** она́ уж о́чень мно́го о себе́ мнит/вообража́ет.
2 (*copious*) подро́бный; **he gave ~ details** он сообщи́л все подро́бности.
3 (*complete; whole; reaching the limit*): **the radio was going ~ blast** ра́дио бы́ло включено́ на по́лную мо́щность; **in ~ bloom** в по́лном цвету́; **~ brother** родно́й брат; **~ dress** костю́м для торже́ственных слу́чаев; пара́дная фо́рма; **the ~ effect of the medicine** по́лное де́йствие лека́рства; **at ~ gallop** на по́лном скаку́; **we waited a ~ hour** мы жда́ли це́лый час; **he lay at ~ length** он растяну́лся во весь рост; **~ moon** полнолу́ние; **on ~ pay** на по́лной ста́вке; **at ~ speed** на по́лной ско́рости; **~ steam ahead!** по́лный вперёд!; **~ stop** то́чка; **he came to a ~ stop** он останови́лся; **in ~ swing** в по́лном разга́ре; **he ran ~ tilt into me** он так и налете́л на меня́.
4 (*plump*) по́лный; **~ in the face** круглоли́цый.
5 (*amply fitting*) широ́кий; **a ~ skirt** пы́шная ю́бка.

● *adv.* **1** (*very*): **you know ~ well** вы са́ми прекра́сно зна́ете; вам прекра́сно изве́стно.
2 (*completely*): **she turned the radio on ~** она́ включи́ла ра́дио на по́лную мо́щность; **~ out** по́лностью.
3 (*squarely*) пря́мо; **he took the blow ~ in the face** уда́р пришёлся ему́ пря́мо в лицо́.

● *cpds.* **~-back** *n.* защи́тник; **~-blooded** *adj.* полнокро́вный; **~-blown** *adj.* распусти́вшийся; (*fig.*) зре́лый; самостоя́тельный; **~-bodied** *adj.* кре́пкий; **~-face** *adv.* анфа́с; **~-fledged** *adj.* вполне́ опери́вшийся; (*fig.*) зако́нченный; полнопра́вный; **~-grown** *adj.* взро́слый; **~-length** *adj.* во всю длину́; **~-length dress** пла́тье до́ полу; **~-scale** *adj.* в по́лном объёме; **~-term** *adj.* (*baby*) доно́шенный; **~-time** *adj.* (*of job*) занима́ющий всё (рабо́чее) вре́мя; **~-timer** *n.* рабо́чий, за́нятый по́лную рабо́чую неде́лю.

fuller /ˈfʊlə(r)/ *n.* (*craftsman*) валя́льщик, сукнова́л; **~'s earth** сукнова́льная/валя́льная гли́на.

ful(l)ness /ˈfʊlnɪs/ *n.* **1** (*full state*) полнота́. **2** (*sense of repletion*) сы́тость. **3**: **in the ~ of time** в надлежа́щее вре́мя.

fully /ˈfʊlɪ/ *adv.* вполне́, по́лностью, соверше́нно, до конца́; **~ satisfied** по́лностью удовлетворённый; **it will take ~ five hours** э́то займёт це́лых пять часо́в.

● *cpds.* **~-clothed** *adj.* по́лностью оде́тый; **~-fashioned** *adj.*: **~-fashioned stockings** чулки́ со швом.

fulmar /ˈfʊlmə(r)/ *n.* глупы́ш (*птица*).

fulminate /ˈfʌlmɪˌneɪt/, /ˈfʊl-/ *v.i.* (*flash*) сверк|а́ть, -ну́ть; (*fig., protest vehemently*) греме́ть (*impf.*); мета́ть (*impf.*) гро́мы и мо́лнии.

fulmination /ˌfʌlmɪˈneɪʃ(ə)n/, /ˌfʊl-/ *n.* (*fig.*) я́ростный проте́ст, инвекти́ва.

fulness /ˈfʊlnɪs/ = **ful(l)ness**

fulsome /ˈfʊlsəm/ *adj.* чрезме́рный, тошнотво́рный.

fumble /ˈfʌmb(ə)l/ *v.t.* теребить (*impf.*) в рука́х; **~ a ball** упусти́ть (*pf.*) мяч.

● *v.i.* ры́ться (*impf.*); копа́ться (*impf.*);

неуме́ло обраща́ться (*impf.*) (*с чем-н.*); **he ~d in his pockets for a key** он ры́лся в карма́нах, ища́ ключ.

fume /fju:m/ *n.* дым, ко́поть; **~s of wine** ви́нные пары́ (*m. pl.*); **he was overcome by ~s** он потеря́л созна́ние от уду́шливых га́зов.

● *v.i.* (*fig.*): **fuming with rage** кипя́щий гне́вом.

fumigate /ˈfju:mɪˌgeɪt/ *v.t.* оку́р|ивать, -и́ть.

fumigation /ˌfju:mɪˈgeɪʃ(ə)n/ *n.* оку́ривание.

fumitory /ˈfju:mɪtərɪ/ *n.* дымя́нка.

fun /fʌn/ *n.* шу́тка, весе́лье, заба́ва, хо́хма (*coll.*); **it was only meant in ~** э́то была́ шу́тка; **just for the ~ of it** про́сто ра́ди удово́льствия; **he never has any ~** он никогда́ не весели́тся/развлека́ется; **make ~ of, poke ~ at** насмеха́ться (*impf.*) над + *i.*; **he is ~ to be with** с ним не соску́чишься; **it's no ~ walking in the rain** что за удово́льствие броди́ть под дождём!; **what ~!** вот здо́рово!; как ве́село!; **when my father finds out there will be ~ and games** (*iron.*) когда́ оте́ц узна́ет об э́том, вот бу́дет поте́ха; **figure of ~** предме́т насме́шек; **we had ~ at the party** в гостя́х бы́ло ве́село.

● *cpds.* **~-fair** *n.* (*Br.*) увесели́тельный парк; **~-run** *n.* джо́ггинг; **~-runner** *n.* бегу́н-люби́тель.

funambulist /fju:ˈnæmbjʊlɪst/ *n.* канатохо́дец.

function /ˈfʌŋkʃ(ə)n/ *n.* **1** (*proper activity, purpose*) фу́нкция, назначе́ние. **2** (*social gathering*) ве́чер; приём. **3** (*math.*) фу́нкция. **4**: **~ key** (*comput.*) функциона́льная кла́виша.

● *v.i.* функциони́ровать, де́йствовать (*both impf.*).

functional /ˈfʌŋkʃən(ə)l/ *adj.* функциона́льный.

functionary /ˈfʌŋkʃənərɪ/ *n.* функционе́р, должностно́е лицо́.

fund /fʌnd/ *n.* фонд, запа́с, резе́рв; **a ~ of common sense** запа́с здра́вого смы́сла; (*sum of money*) фонд, капита́л; **relief ~** фонд по́мощи; **sinking ~** амортизацио́нный фонд; (*pl., resources*) фо́нды (*m. pl.*); де́нежные сре́дства; **public ~s** госуда́рственные сре́дства; **he is in ~s** (*Br.*) он при деньга́х.

● *v.t.* финанси́ровать (*impf., pf.*); (*fin.*) консолиди́ровать (*impf., pf.*).

● *cpd.* **~-raising** *n.* сбор средств; **a ~-raising dinner** (*for charity*) благотвори́тельный банке́т.

fundamental /ˌfʌndəˈment(ə)l/ *n.* **1** (*usu. pl., principle*) осно́ва, при́нцип; **the ~s of mathematics** осно́вы матема́тики. **2** (*mus.*) основно́й тон.

● *adj.* **1** (*basic*) основно́й, суще́ственный; **~ly** в основно́м; по существу́. **2** (*mus.*) основно́й.

fundamentalism /ˌfʌndəˈmentəˌlɪz(ə)m/ *n.* фундаментали́зм.

fundamentalist /ˌfʌndəˈmentəlɪst/ *n.* фундаментали́ст.

funeral /ˈfju:nər(ə)l/ *n.* по́хор|оны (*pl., g.* -о́н); **that's your ~!** э́то ва́ша забо́та!; **~ march** похоро́нный марш; **~ parlour** (*Br.*), **parlor** (*US*), **home** бюро́ (*indecl.*) похоро́нных проце́ссий; **~ pyre** погреба́льный костёр; **~ rites** похоро́нный обря́д.

funereal /fju:ˈnɪərɪəl/ *adj.* мра́чный; тра́урный.

fungi /ˈfʌŋgaɪ/, /ˈfʌndʒaɪ/ *pl. of* **⇒fungus**

fungicide /ˈfʌndʒɪˌsaɪd/ *n.* фунгици́д.

fungoid /ˈfʌŋgɔɪd/ *adj.* грибови́дный, грибообра́зный.

fungus /ˈfʌŋgəs/ *n.* (*pl.* **fungi** *or* **funguses**) грибо́к; ни́зший гриб.

funicular /fju:ˈnɪkjʊlə(r)/ *n.* фуникулёр; кана́тная (желе́зная) доро́га.

● *adj.* кана́тный.

funk /fʌŋk/ (*Br. coll.*) *n.* (*fear*) страх; **in a (blue) ~** в у́жасе.

● *v.t.*: **he ~ed the contest** он увильну́л от уча́стия в соревнова́ниях.

funnel /ˈfʌn(ə)l/ *n.* воро́нка; (*of ship*) дымова́я труба́.

● *v.t.* (**funnelled, funnelling;** *US* **funneled, funneling**) лить (*impf.*) че́рез воро́нку; (*fig.*): **applications are ~ed through this office** заявле́ния направля́ются че́рез э́ту конто́ру.

funny /ˈfʌnɪ/ *adj.* (**funnier, funniest**) **1** (*amusing*) смешно́й, заба́вный; **no ~ business!** без фо́кусов! **2** (*strange*) стра́нный; **I have a ~ feeling you're right!** я подозрева́ю, что вы пра́вы; **it's a ~ thing, but** ... как э́то ни стра́нно, но...; **funnily enough I never met him** как э́то ни стра́нно, я никогда́ не встреча́лся с ним.

● *cpd.* **~-bone** *n.* локтево́й суста́в.

fur /fɜ:(r)/ *n.* **1** (*animal hair*) шерсть. **2** (*as worn*) мех (*pl.* -а́); **a fox ~** ли́сий мех; **~ coat** мехово́е пальто́; мехова́я шу́ба. **3** (*coating of tongue*) налёт. **4** (*Br., deposit on kettle*) на́кипь.

● *v.t.* (**furred, furring**): **~red tongue** обло́женный язы́к; **~red kettle** (*Br.*) ча́йник, покры́тый на́кипью.

● *cpd.* **~-bearing** *adj.* пушно́й; **~-seal** *n.* ко́тик.

furbelow /ˈfɜ:bɪˌləʊ/ *n.* обо́рка, фалбала́.

furious /ˈfjʊərɪəs/ *adj.* **1** (*violent*) бу́йный, нейсто́вый; **a ~ struggle** я́ростная схва́тка; **drive at a ~ pace** е́хать (*det.*) на бе́шеной ско́рости. **2** (*enraged*) взбешённый; **it makes me ~ to hear him abused** меня́ бе́сит, когда́ я слы́шу, как его́ поно́сят; **she was ~ with him** она́ разозли́лась на него́ не на шу́тку.

furl /fɜ:l/ *v.t.* (*sails*) свёр|тывать, -ну́ть; (*umbrella*) скла́дывать, сложи́ть.

furlong /ˈfɜ:lɒŋ/ *n.* восьма́я часть ми́ли.

furlough /ˈfɜ:ləʊ/ *n.* о́тпуск; **on ~** в отпуску́, в о́тпуске.

furnace /ˈfɜ:nɪs/ *n.* горн, оча́г, печь, то́пка; **blast ~** до́менная печь; до́мна.

furnish /ˈfɜ:nɪʃ/ *v.t.* **1** (*provide*) снаб|жа́ть, -ди́ть (*кого чем*); предост|авля́ть, -а́вить (*что кому*). **2** (*equip with furniture*) обст|авля́ть, -а́вить; **fully ~ed house** по́лностью обста́вленный дом; **~ed apartment** мебли́рованная кварти́ра.

furnishings /ˈfɜ:nɪʃɪŋz/ *n.* принадле́жности (*f. pl.*); (*furniture*) обстано́вка.

furniture /ˈfɜ:nɪtʃə(r)/ *n.* ме́бель; **~ polish** политу́ра/лак для ме́бели; **~ removers** аге́нтство по перево́зке ме́бели; **~ van** (*Br.*) автофурго́н для перево́зки ме́бели.

furore /fjʊəˈrɔ:rɪ/ *n.* фуро́р.

furrier /ˈfʌrɪə(r)/ *n.* мехови́щк, скорня́к.

furrow /ˈfʌrəʊ/ *n.* **1** (*in the earth etc.*) борозда́, жёлоб; **plough** (*Br.*), **plow** (*US*) **a lonely ~** (*fig.*) де́йствовать (*impf.*) в одино́чку. **2** (*wrinkle*) глубо́кая морщи́на.

● *v.t.* борозди́ть, вз-; (*fig.*): **~ed brow** намо́рщенный лоб.

furry /ˈfɜ:rɪ/ *adj.* (**furrier, furriest**) покры́тый ме́хом; пушно́й.

further /ˈfɜ:ðə(r)/ *adj.* (*see also* **⇒farther**) **1** дальне́йший; (*additional*) доба́вочный, дополни́тельный; **~ education** (*Br.*) дальне́йшее образова́ние; **until ~ notice** до дальне́йшего уведомле́ния; **without ~ ado** без ли́шних хлопо́т, слов; **we need ~ proof** нам необходи́мы дополни́тельные доказа́тельства; **we need a ~ five pounds** нам ну́жно ещё пять фу́нтов. **2** (*more distant*) да́льний; **on the ~ side** на друго́й стороне́; по ту сто́рону.

● *adv.* **1** (*additionally*) в дополне́ние; **~ to my last letter** в дополне́ние к моему́ после́днему письму́. **2** (*to or at a more distant point*) да́лее, да́льше; **I can go no ~** я не могу́ да́льше идти́; **I'll go ~ than that, he's a liar** бо́лее того́, он лгун; **we need look no ~** смотре́ть да́льше не́чего. **3** (*moreover*) бо́лее того́.

● *v.t.* продв|ига́ть, -и́нуть; соде́йствовать (*impf.*) + *d.*; спосо́бствовать (*impf.*) + *d.*

furtherance /ˈfɜ:ðərəns/ *n.* продвиже́ние; **in ~ of this plan** для осуществле́ния э́того пла́на.

furthermore /ˌfɜ:ðəˈmɔ:(r)/ *adv.* к тому́ же; кро́ме того́.

furthermost /ˈfɜ:ðəˌməʊst/ *adj.* са́мый да́льний/отдалённый.

furthest /ˈfɜ:ðɪst/ *adj.* са́мый да́льний.

● *adv.* да́льше всего́; **the ~ I can go is to say that** ... са́мое бо́льшее, что я могу́ сказа́ть, э́то то, что....

furtive /ˈfɜ:tɪv/ *adj.* (*of movements*) краду́щийся; та́йный; скры́тый; (*of a person*) скры́тный.

furtiveness /ˈfɜ:tɪvnɪs/ *n.* скры́тность.

fury /ˈfjʊərɪ/ *n.* **1** (*violence*) не́истовство, я́рость, бе́шенство; **the ~ of the elements** я́рость стихи́й. **2** (*fit of anger*) я́рость; **she flew into a ~** она́ пришла́ в я́рость. **3** (**F~**: *myth.*) фу́рия. **4** (*fig., termagant*) фу́рия.

furze /fɜ:z/ *n.* утёсник.

fuse[1] /fju:z/ *n.* (*elec.*) предохрани́тель (*m.*), про́бка.

● *v.t. & i.* **1** (*make or become liquid*) пла́вить(ся) (*impf.*). **2** (*join by fusion*) спл|авля́ть(ся), -а́вить(ся); (*fig.*) сли|ва́ть(ся), -ть(ся); (*Br., elec.*): **he ~d the lights** он пережёг про́бки; **the lights ~d** про́бки перегоре́ли.

● *cpds.* **~-box** *n.* коро́бка с про́бками; **~-wire** *n.* про́волока для предохрани́теля.

fuse², fuze /fju:z/ *n.* (*igniting device*) запа́л, затра́вка, фити́ль (*m.*); (*detonating device*) заря́дная тру́бка; взрыва́тель (*m.*).

● *v.t.* вст|авля́ть, -а́вить взрыва́тель в + *a.*

fuselage /ˈfju:zə,lɑ:ʒ/, /-lɪdʒ/ *n.* фюзеля́ж.

fusible /ˈfju:zɪb(ə)l/ *adj.* пла́вкий.

fusilier /,fju:zɪˈlɪə(r)/, /-zəˈlɪə(r)/ *n.* фузилёр, стрело́к.

fusillade /,fju:zɪˈleɪd/ *n.* стрельба́.

fusion /ˈfju:ʒ(ə)n/ *n.* **1** (*melting together*) сплавле́ние, пла́вка; **~ bomb** термоя́дерная бо́мба. **2** (*blending, coalition*) сплав, слия́ние.

fuss /fʌs/ *n.* суета́, шум (из-за пустяко́в); **cause a lot of ~ and bother** причин|я́ть, -и́ть ма́ссу хлопо́т и забо́т; **get into a ~** разволнова́ться (*pf.*); **make a ~ about, over something** суети́ться (*impf.*) вокру́г чего́-н.; **make a ~ of s.o.** (*Br.*) суетли́во опека́ть (*impf.*) кого́-н.

● *v.i.* суети́ться (*impf.*); **she ~es over her children** она́ ве́чно во́зится со свои́ми детьми́.

● *cpd.* **~-pot** *n.* (*coll.*) хлопоту́н (*fem.* -ья); суетли́вый челове́к.

fusser /ˈfʌsə(r)/ *n.* суетли́вый челове́к.

fussiness /ˈfʌsɪnɪs/ *n.* суетли́вость.

fussy /ˈfʌsɪ/ *adj.* (**fussier, fussiest**) **1** (*worrying over trifles*) суетли́вый, беспоко́йный. **2** (*coll., fastidious*) разбо́рчивый; **I'm not ~ (about) what I eat** я не привере́длив в еде́. **3** (*of dress, style etc.*) вы́чурный.

fustian /ˈfʌstɪən/ *n.* (*cloth*) бумазе́я, флане́ль; (*bombast*) напы́щенные высокопа́рные ре́чи (*f. pl.*).

fusty /ˈfʌstɪ/ *adj.* (**fustier, fustiest**) (*stale-smelling*) за́тхлый, спёртый; (*fig., old-fashioned*) старомо́дный.

futile /ˈfju:taɪl/ *adj.* напра́сный, тще́тный.

futility /,fju:ˈtɪlɪtɪ/ *n.* тще́тность, бесполе́зность.

futon /ˈfu:tɒn/ *n.* япо́нский матра́с; фу́тон.

future /ˈfju:tʃə(r)/ *n.* **1** бу́дущее; **in (the) ~** в бу́дущем; **for the ~** на бу́дущее; **he has a great ~ before him** у него́ большо́е бу́дущее; ему́ предстои́т блестя́щая бу́дущность; **there's not much ~ in teaching** преподава́ние не сули́т блестя́щей карье́ры. **2** (*gram.*) бу́дущее вре́мя. **3** (*pl., comm.*) фьючерс|ы (*pl., g.* -ов).

● *adj.* бу́дущий; **belief in a ~ life** ве́ра в загро́бную жизнь; (*gram.*): **~ tense** бу́дущее вре́мя; **~ perfect tense** бу́дущее соверше́нное вре́мя.

futurism /ˈfju:tʃə,rɪz(ə)m/ *n.* футури́зм.

futurist /ˈfju:tʃərɪst/ *n.* футури́ст.

futuristic /,fju:tʃəˈrɪstɪk/ *adj.* футуристи́ческий.

futurity /fju:ˈtjʊərɪtɪ/ *n.* бу́дущее, бу́дущность.

futurological /,fju:tʃərəˈlɒdʒɪk(ə)l/ *adj.* футурологи́ческий.

futurologist /,fju:tʃəˈrɒlədʒɪst/ *n.* футуро́лог.

futurology /,fju:tʃəˈrɒlədʒɪ/ *n.* футуроло́гия.

fuze /fju:z/ = **fuse²**

fuzz¹ /fʌz/ *n.* (*fluffy mass*) пух; (*blur*) мгла.

● *v.t.* (*blur*) затемн|я́ть, -и́ть.

fuzz² /fʌz/ *n.* (*sl., police*): **the ~** мусор|а́ (*pl. g.* -о́в), менту́ра.

fuzzy /ˈfʌzɪ/ *adj.* (**fuzzier, fuzziest**) (*fluffy*) пуши́стый; (*blurred*) расплы́вчатый.

Gg

G /dʒi:/ *n.* (*mus.*) соль (*nt. indecl.*).

● *cpds.* **~-string** *n.* (*cloth etc.*) набе́дренная повя́зка; **~-suit** *n.* противоперегру́зочный костю́м.

g. /græm/ *n.* (*abbr. of* ***gram(me)(s)***) гм (грамм).

gab /gæb/ (*coll.*) *n.*: **he has the gift of the ~** у него́ язы́к хорошо́ подве́шен.

● *v.i.* (**gabbed, gabbing**) трепа́ться (*impf.*); точи́ть (*impf.*) ля́сы (*coll.*).

gabardine, gaberdine /ˈgæbəˌdi:n/, /-ˈdi:n/ *n.* (*material*) габарди́н; (*attr.*) габарди́новый.

gabble /ˈgæb(ə)l/ *n.* бормота́ние; (*sl.*) трёп, трепотня́.

● *v.t. & i.* бормота́ть, про-.

gabbler /ˈgæblə(r)/ *n.* болту́н.

gabby /ˈgæbɪ/ *adj.* (**gabbier, gabbiest**) (*coll.*) болтли́вый, трепли́вый.

gaberdine /ˈgæbəˌdi:n/, /-ˈdi:n/ = **gabardine**

gable /ˈgeɪb(ə)l/ *n.* щипе́ц; (*pediment*) фронто́н; **~(d) roof** двуска́тная/щипцо́вая кры́ша.

Gabon /gəˈbɒn/ *n.* Габо́н.

gad /gæd/ *v.i.* (**gadded, gadding**) (*also* **~ about**) шля́ться (*impf.*); шата́ться (*impf.*).

● *cpd.* **~about** *n. & adj.* праздношата́ющийся.

gadfly /ˈgædflaɪ/ *n.* о́вод, слепе́нь (*m.*).

gadget /ˈgædʒɪt/ *n.* (*coll.*) шту́чка.

gadgetry /ˈgædʒɪtrɪ/ *n.* (*coll.*) техни́ческие нови́нки (*f. pl.*).

Gaelic /ˈgeɪlɪk/, /ˈgæ-/ *n.* (*language*) гэ́льский язы́к.

● *adj.* гэ́льский.

gaff[1] /gæf/ *n.* (*spear, stick*) баго́р, острога́; (*naut.*) га́фель (*m.*).

● *v.t.* багри́ть (*impf.*).

gaff[2] /gæf/ *n.*: **blow the ~** (*Br. coll.*) проболта́ться (*pf.*).

gaffe /gæf/ *n.* ло́жный шаг, опло́шность.

gaffer /ˈgæfə(r)/ *n.* стари́к, дед; (*Br., foreman*) ма́стер (це́ха); (*cin.*) бригади́р осветите́лей.

gag /gæg/ *n.* **1** (*to prevent speech etc.*) кляп; (*parl.*) прекраще́ние пре́ний; (*fig.*): **a ~ on free speech** подавле́ние свобо́ды сло́ва. **2** (*joke*) шу́тка, хо́хма.

● *v.t.* (**gagged, gagging**) вст|авля́ть, -а́вить кляп +*d.*; (*fig.*) зат|ыка́ть, -кну́ть рот +*d.*; **the press was ~ged** пре́ссу заста́вили замолча́ть.

● *v.i.* (**gagged, gagging**) (*theatr.*) шути́ть, хохми́ть (*both impf.*); (*retch, choke*) дави́ться (*impf.*).

● *cpds.* **~-man, ~-writer** *nn.* (*theatr.*) ко́мик; сочини́тель (*m.*) остро́т и шу́ток (*для эстрады и т.п.*).

gaga /ˈgɑ:gɑ:/ *adj.* (*sl.*) чо́кнутый, слабоу́мный; **go ~** впа|да́ть, -сть в мара́зм; выжива́ть, вы́жить из ума́.

gage /geɪdʒ/ (*US*) = **gauge**

gaggle /ˈgæg(ə)l/ *n.* (*of geese*) ста́я, ста́до; (*fig., joc.*) ста́йка, толпа́.

gaiety /ˈgeɪətɪ/ (*US* **gayety**) *n.* весёлость, весе́лье.

gain /geɪn/ *n.* **1** (*profit*) при́быль; вы́года; вы́игрыш.
2 (*pl., things ~ed*) дохо́ды (*m. pl.*); нажи́ва; (*achievements*) завоева́ния; **ill-gotten ~s** нече́стно на́житое.
3 (*increase*) увеличе́ние; **a ~ in weight** приба́вка в ве́се.

● *v.t.* **1** (*reach*) доб|ира́ться, -ра́ться до +*g.*; дост|ига́ть, -и́гнуть +*g.*; **the swimmer ~ed the shore** плове́ц дости́г бе́рега.
2 (*win, acquire*) овлад|ева́ть, -е́ть; доб|ива́ться, -и́ться +*g.*; доб|ыва́ть, -ы́ть; приобре|та́ть, -сти́; **~ one's living** зараба́тывать (*impf.*) на жизнь; **~ a victory** одержа́ть (*pf.*) побе́ду; **~ the upper hand** взять (*pf.*) верх (над +*i.*); **~ time** вы́игр|ывать, вы́играть вре́мя; **what ~ed him such a reputation?** что созда́ло ему́ таку́ю репута́цию?; **he ~ed 5 pounds in weight** он попра́вился на 5 фу́нтов; **the patient is ~ing strength** пацие́нт набира́ется сил.

● *v.i.* **1** (*reap profit, benefit, advantage*) извл|ека́ть, -е́чь по́льзу/вы́году; **how do I stand to ~ from it?** кака́я мне от э́того по́льза/вы́года?; **he has ~ed in experience** он приобрёл о́пыт.
2 (*move ahead*): **my watch ~s (three minutes a day)** мои́ часы́ спеша́т (на три мину́ты в день); **he ~ed on his rival** он нагоня́л сопе́рника.

gainer /ˈgeɪnə(r)/ *n.*: **he was a ~ by the transaction** он вы́играл на э́той сде́лке.

gainful /ˈgeɪnfʊl/ *adj.* при́быльный; дохо́дный; **~ employment** хорошо́ опла́чиваемая рабо́та.

gainsa|y /geɪnˈseɪ/ *v.t.* (*past and p.p.* **gainsaid**) (*liter.*) противоре́чить (*impf.*) +*d.*; **the facts cannot be ~id** фа́кты неопровержи́мы.

gait /geɪt/ *n.* похо́дка.

gaiter /ˈgeɪtə(r)/ *n.* гама́ша; (*pl.*) ге́тр|ы (*pl., g.* —).

gaitered /ˈgeɪtəd/ *adj.* в гама́шах.

gal /gæl/ *n.* (*joc.*) = **girl**

gala /ˈgɑ:lə/ *n.* пра́зднество; **~ day** пра́здничный день; **~ night** (*theatr.*) гала́-представле́ние.

galactic /gəˈlæktɪk/ *adj.* галакти́ческий.

galantine /ˈgælənˌti:n/ *n.* заливно́е.

Galatians /gəˈleɪʃ(ə)nz/, /-ʃɪənz/ *n.* (*bibl.*) гала́ты (*m. pl.*).

galaxy /ˈgæləksɪ/ *n.* гала́ктика; (*fig.*) плея́да.

gale /geɪl/ *n.* бу́ря; што́рм; **it is blowing a ~** ду́ет штормово́й ве́тер; (*fig.*): **~s of laughter** взры́вы (*m. pl.*) хо́хота.

Galicia /gəˈlɪʃɪə/, /-ˈlɪʃə/ *n.* (*in Spain*) Гали́сия; (*in Eastern Europe*) Гали́ция.

Galilee /ˈgælɪˌli:/ *n.* Галиле́я; **Sea of ~** Галиле́йское мо́ре.

gall[1] /gɔ:l/ *n.* **1** жёлчь; (*fig., bitterness*) жёлчность. **2** (*coll., impudence*) на́глость.

● *cpds.* **~-bladder** *n.* жёлчный пузы́рь; **~stone** *n.* жёлчный ка́мень.

gall[2] /gɔ:l/ *n.* (*swelling; sore*) потёртость; ссади́на.

● *v.t.* (*lit.*) ссади́ть (*pf.*); нат|ира́ть, -ере́ть; (*fig.*) злить, разо-.

gall[3] /gɔ:l/ *n.* (*bot.*) галл, черни́льный/дуби́льный оре́шек.

gallant /ˈgælənt/ *adj.* **1** (*attentive to*

ladies) гала́нтный. **2** (*brave*) до́блестный.

gallantry /ˈgæləntrɪ/ *n.* (*bravery*) до́блесть; (*courtliness to women*) гала́нтность.

galleon /ˈgælɪən/ *n.* (*naut., hist.*) галео́н.

gallery /ˈgælərɪ/ *n.* **1** (*walk, passage*) галере́я; **shooting ~** тир. **2** (*picture ~*) карти́нная галере́я. **3** (*raised floor or platform*) хо́р|ы (*pl., g.* -ов); **minstrels' ~** хо́ры (*pl.*); **press ~** места́ для представи́телей печа́ти. **4** (*theatr.*) галёрка; **play to the ~** (*fig.*) иска́ть (*impf.*) дешёвой популя́рности. **5** (*mining*) што́льня.

galley /ˈgælɪ/ *n.* (*pl.* **~s**) **1** (*ship*) гале́ра. **2** (*ship's kitchen*) ка́мбуз; (*in aircraft*) ку́хня на борту́ самолёта. **3** (*typ.*) (*~-proof*) гра́нка.

● *cpd.* **~-slave** *n.* раб на гале́рах.

Gallic /ˈgælɪk/ *adj.* (*Gaulish*) га́лльский; (*French*) францу́зский.

Gallicism /ˈgælɪˌsɪzəm/ *n.* галлици́зм.

Gallicize /ˈgælɪˌsaɪz/ *v.t.* офранцу́зить (*pf.*).

galling /ˈgɔːlɪŋ/ *adj.* (*fig.*) раздража́ющий.

gallium /ˈgælɪəm/ *n.* га́ллий.

gallivant /ˈgælɪˌvænt/ *v.i.* (*coll.*) шля́ться (*impf.*); слоня́ться (*impf.*).

Gallomania /ˌgæləʊˈmeɪnɪə/ *n.* галлома́ния.

gallon /ˈgælən/ *n.* галло́н.

galloon /gəˈluːn/ *n.* галу́н.

gallop /ˈgæləp/ *n.* гало́п; **at a ~** гало́пом; **he rode off at a/full ~** он поскака́л во весь опо́р; **we went for a ~** мы отпра́вились на верхову́ю прогу́лку.

● *v.t.*: **~ a horse** пус|ка́ть, -ти́ть ло́шадь гало́пом (*or* в гало́п); (*fig.*): **we ~ed through our work** мы бы́стро прoверну́ли всю рабо́ту.

gallows /ˈgæləʊz/ *n.* (*also* **~-tree**) ви́селица; **send s.o. to the ~** отпра́вить (*pf.*) кого́-н. на ви́селицу.

● *cpd.* **~ humour** (*US* **humor**) *n.* ю́мор ви́сельника.

galore /gəˈlɔː(r)/ *adv.* (*coll.*) в изоби́лии, ско́лько уго́дно.

galosh /gəˈlɒʃ/ *n.* гало́ша.

galvanic /gælˈvænɪk/ *adj.* (*elec.*) гальвани́ческий.

galvanism /ˈgælvəˌnɪz(ə)m/ *n.* гальвани́зм.

galvanization /ˌgælvənaɪˈzeɪʃ(ə)n/ *n.* гальваниза́ция.

galvanize /ˈgælvəˌnaɪz/ *v.t.* гальванизи́ровать (*impf., pf.*); **~d iron** оцинко́ванное желе́зо; (*fig.*) побу|жда́ть, -ди́ть; возбу|жда́ть, -ди́ть; гальванизи́ровать (*impf., pf.*).

galvanometer /ˌgælvəˈnɒmɪtə(r)/ *n.* гальвано́метр.

Gambia /ˈgæmbɪə/ *n.* Га́мбия.

gambit /ˈgæmbɪt/ *n.* (*chess*) гамби́т; (*trick*) ухва́тка.

gamble /ˈgæmb(ə)l/ *n.* аза́ртная игра́; (*risky undertaking*) риско́ванное предприя́тие; **take a ~** пойти́ (*pf.*) на риск.

● *v.t. & i.* игра́ть (*impf.*) в аза́ртные и́гры; **~ away a fortune** проигра́ть (*pf.*) состоя́ние.

gambler /ˈgæmblə(r)/ *n.* игро́к; картёжник.

gambling /ˈgæmblɪŋ/ *n.* аза́ртные и́гры (*f. pl.*).

● *cpds.* **~-den** *n.* иго́рный прито́н; **~-game** *n.* аза́ртная игра́.

gambol /ˈgæmb(ə)l/ *n.* прыжо́к, скачо́к.

● *v.i.* (**gambolled, gambolling;** *US* **gamboled, gamboling**) пры́г|ать, -нуть.

game¹ /geɪm/ *n.* **1** игра́; **we had a ~ of golf** мы сыгра́ли па́ртию в гольф; **he plays a good ~ of bridge** он хорошо́ игра́ет в бридж; **play the ~** (*fig.*) игра́ть (*impf.*) по пра́вилам; **I am off my ~** я не в фо́рме; **~s** (*Br., at school*) физкульту́ра; **Olympic G~s** Олимпи́йские и́гры; **what is the state of the ~?** (*score*) како́й счёт?; **he won two ~s in the first set** (*tennis*) в пе́рвом се́те он вы́играл две игры́ (*or* два ге́йма); **we bought the child a ~** мы купи́ли ребёнку насто́льную игру́; **beat s.o. at his own ~** поби́ть (*pf.*) кого́-н. его́ же ору́жием. **2** (*scheme, plan, trick*) игра́; **what's the ~?** что за э́тим кро́ется?; **he is playing a deep ~** он ведёт сло́жную игру́; **you are playing his ~** вы игра́ете ему́ на́ руку; **two can play at that ~** (*fig.*) я могу́ отплати́ть вам (*и т.п.*) той же моне́той; **he gave the ~ away** он раскры́л свои́ ка́рты; **the ~ is up** ста́вка би́та; ко́нчен бал! **3** (*hunted animal, quarry*) дичь; зверь (*m.*); **big ~** кру́пный зверь; **fair ~** (*fig.*) объе́кт тра́вли.

● *adj.* боево́й; задо́рный; **are you ~ for a ten-mile walk?** у вас есть настрое́ние соверши́ть прогу́лку миль на де́сять?

● *v.t. & i.* игра́ть, сыгра́ть; **gaming-house** иго́рный дом; **gaming-table** иго́рный стол.

● *cpds.* **~-bird** *n.* перна́тая дичь; **~-cock** *n.* бойцо́вый пету́х; **~keeper** *n.* лесни́к, охраня́ющий дичь; **~ plan** *n.* страте́гия; **~-reserve** *n.* охо́тничий запове́дник; **~ show** *n.* телеигра́, гейм-шо́у (*indecl.*); **~s-master/mistress** *nn.* (*Br.*) преподава́тель(ница) физкульту́ры; **~ theory** *n.* (*math.*) тео́рия игр; **~-warden** *n.* е́герь/лесни́к, охраня́ющий дичь.

game² /geɪm/ *adj.* (*lame*) хромо́й.

gamesmanship /ˈgeɪmzmənʃɪp/ *n.* (*joc.*) ≈ иску́сство вы́игрывать (*чаще сомнительными, хотя незапрещёнными приёмами*).

gamester /ˈgeɪmstə(r)/ *n.* игро́к; картёжник.

gamete /ˈgæmiːt/, /gəˈmiːt/ *n.* (*biol.*) гаме́та.

gamma /ˈgæmə/ *n.*: **~ rays** га́мма-лучи́ (*m. pl.*).

gammon /ˈgæmən/ *n.* (*ham, bacon*) о́корок.

gammy /ˈgæmɪ/ *adj.* (**gammier, gammiest**) (*Br. coll.*) хромо́й.

gamut /ˈgæmət/ *n.* (*mus.*) га́мма; (*fig.*) диапазо́н, га́мма; **she ran the ~ of the emotions** она́ переда́ла всю га́мму чувств.

gamy /ˈgeɪmɪ/ *adj.* (**gamier, gamiest**) (*of scent, flavour*) с душко́м.

gander /ˈgændə(r)/ *n.* (*male goose*) гуса́к; (*sl., look*): **take a ~ at** взгля|дывать, -ну́ть на + *a.*

gang /gæŋ/ *n.* (*of workmen*) брига́да; (*of prisoners*) па́ртия (заключённых); (*of criminals*) ша́йка, ба́нда; (*coll. or pej., company*) ша́йка, вата́га.

● *v.i.*: **they ~ together** они́ собира́ются в ба́нду (*or* ба́ндой); **they ~ed up on me** они́ ополчи́лись про́тив/на меня́.

● *cpds.* **~-bang** *n. & v.t.* (*sl.*) группово́е изнаси́лование; наси́ловать, из- гру́ппой; **~land** *n.* престу́пный мир; **~-board, ~-plank** *nn.* схо́дни (*f. pl.*); **~way** *n.* (*from ship to shore*) схо́дни (*f. pl.*); (*from aircraft to ground*) трап; (*Br., in theatre etc.*) прохо́д; (*coll. int., clear the way!*) прочь с доро́ги!; сторони́сь!

ganger /ˈgæŋə(r)/ *n.* (*Br.*) деся́тник, бригади́р.

Ganges /ˈgændʒiːz/ *n.* Га́нг.

ganglia /ˈgæŋglɪə/ *pl. of* ⇒**ganglion**

gangling /ˈgæŋglɪŋ/ *adj.* долговя́зый.

gangli|on /ˈgæŋglɪən/ *n.* (*pl.* **~a** *or* **~ons**) (*anat.*) га́нглий, не́рвный у́зел.

gangrene /ˈgæŋgriːn/ *n.* гангре́на.

gangrenous /ˈgæŋgrɪnəs/ *adj.* гангрено́зный.

gangster /ˈgæŋstə(r)/ *n.* га́нгстер.

gannet /ˈgænɪt/ *n.* (*bird*) о́луша; (*Br., fig., glutton*) обжо́ра.

gantry /ˈgæntrɪ/ *n.* помо́ст; **~ crane** эстака́дный кран.

gaol /dʒeɪl/ (*Br.*) = **jail**

gaoler /ˈdʒeɪlə(r)/ (*Br.*) = **jailer**

gap /gæp/ *n.* **1** (*in a wall etc.*) брешь, проло́м; (*in defences*) проры́в; (*in ranks*) брешь; **fill a ~** (*supply deficiency*) устрани́ть (*pf.*) недоста́тки; **he filled up the ~s in his education** он воспо́лнил пробе́лы в своём образова́нии; **there is a wide ~ between their views** они́ ре́зко расхо́дятся во взгля́дах; **export ~** э́кспортный дефици́т. **2** (*gorge, pass*) прохо́д; уще́лье.

● *cpd.* **~-toothed** *adj.* с ре́дкими зуба́ми.

gap|e /geɪp/ *v.i.* (*stare*) зева́ть (*impf.*) (по сторона́м); глазе́ть (*impf.*) (на + *a.*); **a ~ing wound** зия́ющая ра́на; **the chasm ~ed before him** пе́ред ним зия́ла про́пасть.

garage /ˈgærɑːdʒ/, /-rɪdʒ/ *n.* (*for keeping a car*) гара́ж; (*where petrol is sold*) бензозапра́вочная ста́нция; (*for repairing cars*) автомастерска́я.

● *v.t.* ста́вить, по- в гара́ж.

garb /gɑːb/ *n.* наря́д.

garbage /ˈgɑːbɪdʒ/ *n.* (*US, rubbish*) отбро́сы (*m. pl.*); му́сор; (*fig.*) му́сор; макулату́ра.

● *cpds.* **~-can** *n.* (*US*) (*outside*)

мýсорный бак; (*in kitchen*) мýсорное ведрó; (*in office*) мýсорная корзи́на; **~-collector** *n.* (*US*) мýсорщик; **~ truck** *n.* (*US*) мусороубóрочная маши́на.

garble /ˈgɑ:b(ə)l/ *v.t.* (*distort*) искa|жáть, -зи́ть; ковéркать, ис-.

garden /ˈgɑ:d(ə)n/ *n.* **1** (*plot of ground*) сад; **vegetable ~** огорóд; **we haven't much ~** у нас сад небольшóй; **lead up the ~ path** (*coll.*) води́ть (*indet.*) зá нос. **2** (*attr.*) садóвый; огорóдный; **common or ~** обы́денный; заурядный; **~ flowers/plants** садóвые цветы́/растéния; **~ centre** (*US* **center**) садóвый центр; **~ city** гóрод-сад; **~ gate** садóвая кали́тка; **~ party** приём на откры́том вóздухе; **~ seat** садóвая скамья́; **~ suburb** (*Br.*) дáчный посёлок. **3** (*pl., park*) сад; парк; **Zoological G~s** зоологи́ческий сад; зоопáрк.

● *v.i.* занимáться (*impf.*) садовóдством; **he is fond of ~ing** он лю́бит рабóтать в садý; **~ing tools** садóвые инструмéнты.

gardener /ˈgɑ:dnə(r)/ *n.* (*professional*) садóвник; (*amateur*) садовóд.

gardenia /gɑ:ˈdi:nɪə/ *n.* гардéния.

gargantuan /gɑ:ˈgæntjʊən/ *adj.* гигáнтский, колоссáльный.

gargle /ˈgɑ:g(ə)l/ *n.* полоскáние.

● *v.i.* полоскáть, про- гóрло.

gargoyle /ˈgɑ:gɔɪl/ *n.* (*archit.*) горгу́лья.

garish /ˈgeərɪʃ/ *adj.* пёстрый, брóский, крича́щий.

garishness /ˈgeərɪʃnɪs/ *n.* пестротá, брóскость.

garland /ˈgɑ:lənd/ *n.* гирля́нда; венóк.

● *v.t.* укр|ашáть, -áсить гирля́ндами.

garlic /ˈgɑ:lɪk/ *n.* чеснóк; **clove of ~** зубóк чеснокá.

garment /ˈgɑ:mənt/ *n.* предмéт одéжды; (*pl., clothes*) одéжда; **the ~ industry** (*dressmaking, tailoring*) швéйная промы́шленность.

garner /ˈgɑ:nə(r)/ *v.t.* (*liter.*) сс|ыпáть, -ы́пать в амбáр; (*fig.*): **~ experience** нак|áпливать, -опи́ть óпыт.

garnet /ˈgɑ:nɪt/ *n.* (*min.*) гранáт.

garnish /ˈgɑ:nɪʃ/ *n.* отдéлка, украшéние; (*cul.*) гарни́р.

● *v.t.* (*decorate*) укр|ашáть, -áсить; отдéл|ывать, -ать; (*cul.*) гарни́ровать (*impf., pf.*).

garret /ˈgærɪt/ *n.* мансáрда; чердáк.

garrison /ˈgærɪs(ə)n/ *n.* гарнизóн; (*attr.*) гарнизóнный.

● *v.t.*: **~ a town** стáвить, по- гарнизóн в гóроде.

garrotte /gəˈrɒt/ (*US* **garrote**) *n.* гарróта (*орудие казни*).

● *v.t.* (**garrotted, garrotting;** *US* **garroted, garroting**) души́ть, у-; дави́ть, у-.

garrulity /gəˈru:lɪtɪ/ *n.* болтли́вость, говорли́вость.

garrulous /ˈgærʊləs/ *adj.* болтли́вый, говорли́вый.

garter /ˈgɑ:tə(r)/ *n.* подвя́зка; **the G~** óрден Подвя́зки; **~ belt** (*US*) пóяс с подвя́зками.

● *cpd.* **~-snake** *n.* подвя́зковая змея́.

gas /gæs/ *n.* (*pl.* **~es**) **1** (*aeriform fluid*) газ; **natural ~** прирóдный газ; **put the kettle on the ~** стáвить, по- чáйник на газ; **turn the ~ on/off** включи́ть/вы́ключить газ; (*dentist's*) эфи́р; (*poison ~*) ядови́тый газ; отравля́ющее веществó; (*mining*) гремýчий газ; (*flatulence*) гáзы (*m. pl.*). **2** (*attr.*) гáзовый; **~ alarm, alert** хими́ческая тревóга; **~ bomb** хими́ческая бóмба; **~ bracket** гáзовый рожóк; **~ burner** гáзовая горéлка; **~ chamber** (*for lethal purposes*) гáзовая кáмера; **~ cooker** (*Br.*) гáзовая плитá; **~ fire** (*Br.*) гáзовыйками́н; **~ fitter** газовщи́к; **~ lighting** гáзовое освещéние; **~ main** газопровóд; **~ mantle** кали́льная сéтка; **~ mask** противогáз; **~ meter** гáзовый счётчик; **~ oven** (*domestic*) гáзовая духóвка; **~ pipe** гáзовая трубá; **~ ring** гáзовое кольцó; **~ stove** гáзовая плитá; *see also cpds.* **3** (*US, petrol*) бензи́н, горю́чее; **step on the ~** (*coll.*) да|вáть, -ть гáзу; **~ station** (*US*) бензозапрáвочная стáнция; **~ tank** (*US*) бензобáк. **4** (*coll., empty talk*) болтовня́, трепотня́.

● *v.t.* (**gases, gassed, gassing**) **1** (*poison with ~*) отрав|ля́ть, -и́ть гáзом; (*kill with ~*) умер|щвля́ть, -тви́ть гáзом.
2: **~ up a car** (*US coll.*) = *v.i.* 2

● *v.i.* (**gases, gassed, gassing**) **1** (*coll., talk long and emptily*) болтáть (*impf.*); молóть (*impf.*).
2: **~ up** (*US coll., take in petrol*) запр|авля́ться, -áвиться горю́чим.

● *cpds.* **~bag** *n.* оболóчка аэростáта; (*coll., chatterer*) пустомéля (*c.g.*); **~holder** *n.* газохрани́лище; **~light** *n.* гáзовое освещéние; **~-lit** *adj.* освещённый гáзом; **~man** *n.* (*fitter*) (слéсарь-)газовщи́к; (*inspector*) инспéктор-газовщи́к; **~-permeable** *adj.* воздухопроницáемый; **~works** *n.* гáзовый завóд.

gaseous /ˈgæsɪəs/ *adj.* гáзовый; газообрáзный.

gash /gæʃ/ *n.* разрéз; глубóкая рáна.

● *v.t.* разр|езáть, -éзать; полоснýть (*pf.*).

gasification /ˌgæsɪfɪˈkeɪʃ(ə)n/ *n.* газификáция.

gasify /ˈgæsɪˌfaɪ/ *v.t. & i.* газифици́ровать (*impf., pf.*).

gasket /ˈgæskɪt/ *n.* проклáдка; тесьмá.

gasohol /ˈgæsəˌhɒl/ *n.* бензоспи́рт.

gasol|ine, -ene /ˈgæsəˌli:n/ *n.* газоли́н; (*US, petrol*) бензи́н.

gasometer /gæˈsɒmɪtə(r)/ *n.* (*container*) газгóльдер.

gasp /gɑ:sp/ *n.* глотóк вóздуха; перехвáт дыхáния; **at one's last ~** при послéднем издыхáнии.

● *v.t. & i.* зад|ыхáться, -охнýться; áхнуть (*pf.*); **he ~ed out a few words** задыхáясь, он произнёс нéсколько слов; **he was ~ing for breath** он задыхáлся; **he ~ed with astonishment** он откры́л рот (*or* задохнýлся) от удивлéния.

gassy /ˈgæsɪ/ *adj.* (**gassier, gassiest**) (*of beer etc.*) газирóванный.

gasteropod /ˈgæstərəˌpɒd/ *n.* ули́тка из клáсса брюхонóгих.

gastric /ˈgæstrɪk/ *adj.* желýдочный; **~ fever** брюшнóй тиф; **~ juice** желýдочный сок; **~ ulcer** я́зва желýдка.

gastritis /gæˈstraɪtɪs/ *n.* гастри́т.

gastro-enteritis /ˌgæstrəʊˌentəˈraɪtɪs/ *n.* гастроэнтери́т.

gastronome /ˈgæstrəˌnəʊm/ *n.* гастронóм, гурмáн.

gastronomic /ˌgæstrəˈnɒmɪk/ *adj.* гастрономи́ческий.

gastronomy /gæˈstrɒnəmɪ/ *n.* гастронóмия.

gate /geɪt/ *n.* **1** вор|óта (*pl., g.* -óт); кали́тка; (*city ~*) городски́е ворóта; (*garden ~*) садóвая кали́тка; (*at airport*) вы́ход; (*water-~*) шлю́зные ворóта; **give s.o. the ~** (*US coll.*) выгоня́ть, вы́гнать когó-н. **2** (*fig.*) (*size of audience*) коли́чество зри́телей; (*takings*) сбор, вы́ручка.

● *cpds.* **~-crash** *v.t. & i.* при|ходи́ть, -йти́ незвáным; про|ходи́ть, -йти́ без билéта; **~-crasher** *n.* незвáный гость; (*spectator*) безбилéтный зри́тель (*m.*), «зáяц»; **~-house** *n.* сторóжка; **~-keeper** *n.* приврáтник; **~-leg(ged)** *adj.*: **~-legged table** стол с откиднóй кры́шкой; **~-money** *n.* входнáя плáта; **~post** *n.* ворóтный столб; **between you and me and the ~post** мéжду нáми (говоря́); **~way** *n.* подворóтня; (*fig.*) подхóд.

gateau /ˈgætəʊ/ *n.* (*pl.* **~s** *or* **~x** /-əʊz/) (*Br.*) торт.

gather /ˈgæðə(r)/ *n.* (*in cloth*) сбóрки (*f. pl.*).

● *v.t.* **1** (*pick, cull: e.g. flowers, nuts, harvest; also* **~ in**) соб|ирáть, -рáть.
2 (*collect, also* **~ up**) соб|ирáть, -рáть; **things ~ dust** вéщи собирáют пыль; **he ~ed his papers together** он собрáл свои́ бумáги; **~ experience** накáпливать (*impf.*) óпыт.
3 (*receive addition of*) наб|ирáть, -рáть + *a. or g.*; **the ship ~ed way** корáбль набрáл ход.
4 (*understand, conclude*) заключ|áть, -и́ть; дéлать, с- вы́вод (*pf.*) (*на основании чего-н.*); **I ~ he's abroad** он как бýдто за грани́цей; **I ~ you don't like him** мне сдаётся, что он вам не нрáвится; **as far as I can ~** наскóлько я могý суди́ть.
5 (*draw, pull together*): **he ~ed his cloak about him** он завернýлся в плащ; **he ~ed her in his arms** он заключи́л её в объя́тия; **~ one's thoughts, wits (together)** соб|ирáться, -рáться с мы́слями.
6 (*sewing*) соб|ирáть, -рáть в склáдки.

● *v.i.* **1** (*collect*) соб|ирáться, -рáться; **a crowd ~ed** собралáсь толпá.
2 (*increase*) нараст|áть, -и́; **the tale ~ed like a snowball** истóрия разрастáлась как снéжный ком.

gatherer /ˈgæðərə(r)/ *n.* (*picker-up, collector*) сбóрщи|к (*fem.* -ца).

G

gathering /ˈgæðərɪŋ/ *n.* (*assembly*) собра́ние; встре́ча.

GATT /gæt/ *n.* (*abbr. of* ***General Agreement on Tariffs and Trade***) ГАТТ (Генера́льное соглаше́ние по тари́фам и торго́вле).

gauche /gəʊʃ/ *adj.* нело́вкий; неуклю́жий.

gauche|ness /ˈgəʊʃnɪs/, **-rie** /ˈgəʊʃəˌriː/ *nn.* нело́вкость, неуклю́жесть.

gaudiness /ˈgɔːdɪnɪs/ *n.* безвку́сица; крикли́вость.

gaudy /ˈgɔːdɪ/ *n.* (*Br., feast*) пра́зднество.

● *adj.* (**gaudier, gaudiest**) (*of colour*) крича́щий; безвку́сный.

gauge /geɪdʒ/ (*US* **gage**) *n.* **1** (*thickness, diameter etc.*) разме́р; (*rail.*): **standard ~** станда́ртная колея́; **broad ~** широ́кая колея́; **narrow ~** у́зкая колея́. **2** (*instrument*) шабло́н; лека́ло; этало́н.

● *v.t.* **1** (*measure*) изм|еря́ть, -е́рить. **2** (*fig., estimate*) оце́н|ивать, -и́ть; взве́сить (*pf.*); **~ the strength of the wind** определ|я́ть, -и́ть си́лу ве́тра.

Gaul /gɔːl/ *n.* (*hist., country*) Га́ллия; (*inhabitant*) галл.

gaunt /gɔːnt/ *adj.* (*person*) исхуда́лый; измождённый; (*landscape*) пусты́нный; мра́чный.

gauntlet¹ /ˈgɔːntlɪt/ *n.* рукави́ца; (*armoured glove*) ла́тная рукави́ца; **throw down the ~** (*fig.*) бро́сить (*pf.*) перча́тку/вы́зов; **pick up the ~** приня́ть (*pf.*) вы́зов.

gauntlet² /ˈgɔːntlɪt/ *n.*: **run the ~** про|ходи́ть, -йти́ сквозь строй; (*fig., of criticism etc.*) подв|ерга́ться, -е́ргнуться суро́вой кри́тике.

gauntness /ˈgɔːntnɪs/ *n.* худоба́.

gauze /gɔːz/ *n.* ма́рля, газ.

gave /geɪv/ *past of* ⇨**give**

gavel /ˈgæv(ə)l/ *n.* молото́к.

gavotte /gəˈvɒt/ *n.* гаво́т (*стари́нный та́нец*).

gawk /gɔːk/ *v.i.* (*also* **gawp** (*Br.*)) глазе́ть (*impf.*); пя́лить (*impf.*) глаза́ (на + *a.*).

gawky /ˈgɔːkɪ/ *adj.* (**gawkier, gawkiest**) нело́вкий, неуклю́жий.

gawp /gɔːp/ = **gawk**

gay /geɪ/ *adj.* (**gayer, gayest**) весёлый; **~ colours** я́ркие цвета́; **the street was ~ with flags** у́лица пестре́ла фла́гами; (*coll., homosexual*) гомосексуа́льный, голубо́й; (*as n.*) го́мик, гомосексуали́ст, гей.

gayety /ˈgeɪətɪ/ (*US*) = **gaiety**

gaz|e /geɪz/ *n.* приста́льный взгляд; **a strange sight met his ~e** его́ взо́ру откры́лось стра́нное зре́лище.

● *v.i.* при́стально гляде́ть; **stop ~ing around!** переста́ньте глазе́ть по сторона́м!

gazebo /gəˈziːbəʊ/ *n.* (*pl.* **~s** *or* **~es**) бельведе́р.

gazelle /gəˈzel/ *n.* газе́ль.

gazette /gəˈzet/ *n.* (*official journal*) официа́льные ве́домости (*f. pl.*); (*newspaper*) газе́та.

● *v.t.* (*Br.*): **he was ~d colonel** он получи́л зва́ние полко́вника.

gazetteer /ˌgæzɪˈtɪə(r)/ *n.* географи́ческий рее́стр; слова́рь географи́ческих назва́ний.

gazumping /gəˈzʌmpɪŋ/ *n.* (*Br.*) наруше́ние догово́ра при поку́пке до́ма, когда́ продаю́щая сторона́ соблазня́ется бо́лее высо́кой цено́й.

GB (*abbr. of* ***Great Britain***) Великобрита́ния.

GBH (*abbr. of* ***grievous bodily harm***) (*Br., leg.*) тяжёлые теле́сные поврежде́ния.

GCSE (*abbr. of* ***General Certificate of Secondary Education***) (*Br.*) ≈ аттеста́т зре́лости.

GDP (*abbr. of* ***gross domestic product***) ВВП (валово́й вну́тренний проду́кт).

GDR (*abbr. of* ***German Democratic Republic***) (*hist.*) ГДР (Герма́нская Демократи́ческая Респу́блика).

gear /gɪə(r)/ *n.* **1** (*apparatus, mechanism*) механи́зм. **2** (*equipment, utensils, clothing*) принадле́жности (*f. pl.*), аксессуа́ры (*m. pl.*); оде́жда; (*sl., stylish clothing*) прики́д; **hunting ~** охо́тничье снаряже́ние; **household ~** хозя́йственные принадле́жности. **3** (*of car etc.*) зубча́тая переда́ча; **high ~** высо́кая переда́ча; **top ~** вы́сшая переда́ча; **bottom ~** пе́рвая переда́ча; **low ~** ни́зкая переда́ча; **reverse ~** за́дний ход; **change ~** переключ|а́ть, -и́ть переда́чу; **the car is in ~** маши́на на переда́че; у маши́ны включена́ переда́ча.

● *v.t.*: **~ up** гото́вить (*impf.*); пригот|а́вливать, -о́вить; (*fig., adjust, correlate*) приспос|обля́ть, -о́бить; **production is ~ed to demand** произво́дство приспосо́блено к спро́су.

● *cpds.* **~-box** *n.* коро́бка переда́ч; **~-lever** *n.* (*Br.*) рыча́г переключе́ния переда́ч/скоросте́й; **~-ratio** *n.* переда́точное число́; **~-shift** *n.* (*US*) = **~-lever; ~-wheel** *n.* зубча́тое колесо́.

gecko /ˈgekəʊ/ *n.* (*pl.* **~s** *or* **~es**) (*zool.*) гекко́н.

gee¹ /dʒiː/ *int.*: **~ up!** но!

● *cpd.* **~-gee** *n.* (*Br.*) лоша́дка.

gee² /dʒiː/ *int.* (*also* **~ whiz!**) вот здо́рово!; вот так шту́ка!; ух ты!

geese /giːs/ *pl. of* ⇨**goose**

geezer /ˈgiːzə(r)/ *n.* (*sl.*) (*fellow*) тип, мужи́к; (*old fellow*) старика́шка (*m.*).

Geiger /ˈgaɪgə(r)/ *n.*: **~-counter** счётчик Ге́йгера.

geisha /ˈgeɪʃə/ *n.* (*pl.* **~** *or* **~s**) ге́йша.

gel /dʒel/ *n.* гель (*m.*).

gelatine /ˈdʒeləˌtiːn/ *n.* желати́н.

gelatinous /dʒɪˈlætɪnəs/ *adj.* желати́новый.

geld /geld/ *v.t.* кастри́ровать (*impf., pf.*).

gelding /ˈgeldɪŋ/ *n.* ме́рин.

gelid /ˈdʒelɪd/ *adj.* ледяно́й; студёный; леденя́щий.

gelignite /ˈdʒelɪgˌnaɪt/ *n.* гелигни́т.

gem /dʒem/ *n.* (*jewel*) драгоце́нный ка́мень; (*fig., outstanding specimen*) жемчу́жина, сокро́вище.

● *cpd.* **~stone** *n.* драгоце́нный ка́мень.

Gemini /ˈdʒemɪˌnaɪ/, /-ˌniː/ *n.* Близнецы́ (*m. pl.*).

gen /dʒen/ *n.* (*Br. coll.*) да́нные (*nt. pl.*); информа́ция.

gendarme /ˈʒɒndɑːm/ *n.* жанда́рм.

gendarmerie /ʒɒnˈdɑːmərɪ/ *n.* жандарме́рия.

gender /ˈdʒendə(r)/ *n.* род; (*coll., sex*) пол.

gene /dʒiːn/ *n.* ген; **~ therapy** геноте́рапи́я.

genealogical /ˌdʒiːnɪəˈlɒdʒɪk(ə)l/ *adj.* родосло́вный; генеалоги́ческий; **~ tree** генеалоги́ческое де́рево.

genealogist /ˌdʒiːnɪˈælədʒɪst/ *n.* специали́ст по генеало́гии.

genealogy /ˌdʒiːnɪˈælədʒɪ/ *n.* генеало́гия.

genera /ˈdʒenərə/ *pl. of* ⇨**genus**

general /ˈdʒenər(ə)l/ *n.* генера́л.

● *adj.* **1** (*universal or nearly so*) о́бщий; генера́льный; **~ rule** о́бщее пра́вило; **~ election** всео́бщие вы́боры; **~ strike** всео́бщая забасто́вка; **~ knowledge** о́бщие зна́ния; **~ practitioner** участко́вый врач; терапе́вт; **~ hospital** больни́ца о́бщего ти́па; **~ reader** ма́ссовый чита́тель; **G~ Assembly** (*of UN*) Генера́льная Ассамбле́я; **~ store** небольшо́й универса́льный магази́н; **a book of ~ interest** неспециализи́рованная кни́га. **2** (*usual, prevalent*) обы́чный; повсеме́стный; **~ opinion** о́бщее мне́ние; **in ~, in a ~ way** вообще́; **as a ~ rule** как пра́вило, обыкнове́нно. **3** (*approximate; not specific*) о́бщий; **~ resemblance** о́бщее схо́дство; **~ idea** о́бщее представле́ние; **he spoke in ~ terms** он говори́л в о́бщих выраже́ниях. **4** (*chief*) гла́вный; **~ staff** генера́льный штаб; **~ headquarters** гла́вное кома́ндование, ста́вка; **G~ Post Office** главпочта́мт.

● *cpd.* **~-purpose** *adj.* многоцелево́й; универса́льный.

generalissimo /ˌdʒenərəˈlɪsɪˌməʊ/ *n.* (*pl.* **~s**) генерали́ссимус.

generalit|y /ˌdʒenəˈrælɪtɪ/ *n.* **1** (*majority*) большинство́. **2** (*general statement*) о́бщее ме́сто, о́бщая фра́за; **he spoke in ~ies** он говори́л/отде́лался о́бщими фра́зами.

generalization /ˌdʒenərəlaɪˈzeɪʃ(ə)n/ *n.* обобще́ние.

generalize /ˈdʒenərəˌlaɪz/ *v.t. & i.* обобщ|а́ть, -и́ть; (*make general*) распростран|я́ть, -и́ть.

generally /ˈdʒenərəlɪ/ *adv.* **1** (*usually*) обы́чно. **2** (*widely*) широко́; бо́льшей ча́стью; **the plan was ~ welcomed** план получи́л всео́бщее одобре́ние; **~ received ideas** общепри́нятые поня́тия. **3** (*approximately, summarily*) вообще́; ~ **speaking** вообще́ говоря́. **4** (*as a class*): **this is true of Frenchmen** ~ э́то отно́сится к францу́зам в це́лом.

generalship /ˈdʒenər(ə)lʃɪp/ *n.* (*military skill*) вое́нное иску́сство.

generat|e /ˈdʒenəˌreɪt/ *v.t.* поро|жда́ть, -ди́ть; вызыва́ть, вы́звать; генери́ровать (*impf.*); **~e heat** выделя́ть (*impf.*) тепло́; **~e hatred** вызыва́ть (*impf.*) не́нависть; **~ing station** электроста́нция.

generation /ˌdʒenəˈreɪʃ(ə)n/ *n.* **1** (*of heat etc.*) генера́ция, генери́рование, произво́дство, образова́ние. **2** (*geneal.*) поколе́ние; **from ~ to ~** из поколе́ния в поколе́ние; **the rising ~** подраста́ющее поколе́ние; **a ~ ago** в про́шлом поколе́нии; **I have known the family for three ~s** я знал (це́лых) три поколе́ния э́той семьи́; **the ~ gap** пробле́ма отцо́в и дете́й. **3** (*fig., of weapons etc.*) эта́п разви́тия.

generative /ˈdʒenərətɪv/ *adj.* (*productive*) производи́тельный, производя́щий; (*biol.*) генерати́вный.

generator /ˈdʒenəˌreɪtə(r)/ *n.* производи́тель (*m.*); (*tech.*) генера́тор.

generic /dʒɪˈnerɪk/ *adj.* (*of a class*) родово́й; (*general*) о́бщий; (*of drug*) непатенто́ванный, о́бщего ти́па.

generosity /ˌdʒenəˈrɒsɪtɪ/ *n.* великоду́шие; ще́дрость.

generous /ˈdʒenərəs/ *adj.* **1** (*magnanimous*) великоду́шный. **2** (*liberal*) ще́дрый; **he is ~ with his time** он ще́дро/расточи́тельно тра́тит своё вре́мя. **3** (*plentiful*) оби́льный; **a ~ helping of meat** ще́драя/соли́дная по́рция мя́са.

genesis /ˈdʒenɪsɪs/ *n.* гене́зис; возникнове́ние; **(Book of) G ~** кни́га Бытия́.

genetic /dʒɪˈnetɪk/ *adj.* генети́ческий; **~ engineering** ге́нная инжене́рия; **~ fingerprinting** ге́нная дактилоскопи́я; **~ally modified** генети́чески модифици́рованный.

geneticist /dʒɪˈnetɪsɪst/ *n.* гене́тик.

genetics /dʒɪˈnetɪks/ *n.* гене́тика.

Geneva /dʒɪˈniːvə/ *n.* Жене́ва; **Lake ~** Жене́вское о́зеро; **~ Convention** Жене́вская конве́нция.

genial /ˈdʒiːnɪəl/ *adj.* **1** (*jovial, kindly*) серде́чный, доброду́шный. **2** мя́гкий; **a ~ climate** мя́гкий/благотво́рный кли́мат.

geniality /ˌdʒiːnɪˈælɪtɪ/ *n.* раду́шие; доброду́шие.

genie /ˈdʒiːnɪ/ *n.* (*pl.* **genii** *or* **genies**) джинн, дух.

genii /ˈdʒiːnɪaɪ/ *pl. of* ⇒**genie, genius**

genital /ˈdʒenɪt(ə)l/ *adj.* полово́й; (*pl.*) половы́е о́рганы (*m. pl.*), гените́лии (*f. pl.*).

genitive /ˈdʒenɪtɪv/ *n. & adj.* роди́тельный (паде́ж).

genito-urinary /ˌdʒenɪtəʊˈjʊərɪnərɪ/ *adj.* мочеполово́й.

genius /ˈdʒiːnɪəs/ *n.* (*pl.* **geniuses** *or* **genii**) ге́ний; **a person of ~** гениа́льный челове́к.

Genoa /ˈdʒenəʊə/ *n.* Ге́нуя.

genocidal /ˌdʒenəˈsaɪd(ə)l/ *adj.* геноци́дный.

genocide /ˈdʒenəˌsaɪd/ *n.* геноци́д.

genome /ˈdʒiːnəʊm/ *n.* гено́м.

genre /ˈʒɑ̃rə/ *n.* жанр; (*attr.*) жа́нровый, бытово́й.

gent /dʒent/ *n.* (*coll.*) джентльме́н; **~s** (*Br., lavatory*) мужска́я убо́рная.

genteel /dʒenˈtiːl/ *adj.* благовоспи́танный; «благоро́дный»; с аристократи́ческими зама́шками; **they live in ~ poverty** они́ живу́т в го́рдой нищете́.

gentian /ˈdʒenʃ(ə)n/, /-ʃɪən/ *n.* (*bot.*) гореча́вка.

gentile /ˈdʒentaɪl/ *n.* неевре́й; (*bibl.*) язы́чник.

● *adj.* неевре́йский; язы́ческий.

gentility /dʒenˈtɪlɪtɪ/ *n.* благовоспи́танность.

gentle /ˈdʒent(ə)l/ *adj.* (**gentler, gentlest**) **1**: **a person of ~ birth** челове́к благоро́дного происхожде́ния. **2** (*mild, tender, kind*) мя́гкий, ти́хий, делика́тный; **~ heat** уме́ренная жара́; **a ~ slope** отло́гий скло́н; **a ~ breeze** лёгкий ветеро́к; **a ~ hint** то́нкий намёк.

● *cpds.* **~folk** *n.* дворя́нство; знать; **~woman** *n.* да́ма; ле́ди (*f. indecl.*).

gentleman /ˈdʒent(ə)lmən/ *n.* джентльме́н; **~'s agreement** джентльме́нское соглаше́ние; **a ~ has called to see you** како́й-то господи́н жела́ет вас ви́деть; **gentlemen!** господа́!

● *cpd.* **~-at-arms** *n.* лейб-гварде́ец.

gentleman|like /ˈdʒent(ə)lmənˌlaɪk/, **-ly** /ˈdʒent(ə)lmənlɪ/ *adjs.* джентльме́нский; по-джентльме́нски.

gentleness /ˈdʒent(ə)lnɪs/ *n.* мя́гкость, не́жность; делика́тность.

gently /ˈdʒentlɪ/ *adv.* мя́гко; делика́тно; **hold it ~!** держи́те осторо́жно!; **the road slopes ~** доро́га идёт слегка́ под укло́н; **~!** (*not so fast*) поле́гче!; осторо́жно!

gentry /ˈdʒentrɪ/ *n.* нетитуло́ванное дворя́нство.

genuflect /ˈdʒenjʊˌflekt/ *v.i.* преклон|я́ть, -и́ть коле́но.

genuflection /ˌdʒenjʊˈflekʃ(ə)n/ *n.* коленопреклоне́ние.

genuine /ˈdʒenjʊɪn/ *adj.* настоя́щий; по́длинный; **a ~ Rubens** по́длинный Ру́бенс; **~ sorrow** и́скренняя печа́ль; **a ~ person** прямо́й/и́скренний челове́к.

genus /ˈdʒiːnəs/, /ˈdʒenəs/ *n.* (*pl.* **genera**) род.

geocentric /ˌdʒiːəʊˈsentrɪk/ *adj.* геоцентри́ческий.

geodesy /dʒiːˈɒdɪsɪ/ *n.* геоде́зия.

geodetic /ˌdʒiːəʊˈdetɪk/ *adj.* геодези́ческий.

geographer /dʒɪˈɒgrəfə(r)/ *n.* гео́граф.

geographic(al) /ˌdʒiːəˈgræfɪk((ə)l)/ *adj.* географи́ческий.

geography /dʒɪˈɒgrəfɪ/ *n.* геогра́фия.

geological /ˌdʒiːəˈlɒdʒɪk(ə)l/ *adj.* геологи́ческий.

geologist /dʒɪˈɒlədʒɪst/ *n.* гео́лог.

geology /dʒɪˈɒlədʒɪ/ *n.* геоло́гия.

geometric(al) /ˌdʒɪəˈmetrɪk((ə)l)/ *adj.* геометри́ческий.

geometry /dʒɪˈɒmɪtrɪ/ *n.* геоме́трия; **plane ~** планиме́трия; **solid ~** стереоме́трия.

geophysical /ˌdʒiːəʊˈfɪzɪk(ə)l/ *adj.* геофизи́ческий.

geophysicist /ˌdʒiːəʊˈfɪzɪsɪst/ *n.* геофи́зик.

geophysics /ˌdʒiːəʊˈfɪzɪks/ *n.* геофи́зика.

geopolitical /ˌdʒiːəʊpəˈlɪtɪk(ə)l/ *adj.* геополити́ческий.

geopolitics /ˌdʒiːəʊˈpɒlɪtɪks/ *n.* геополи́тика.

geoprobe /ˈdʒiːəʊˌprəʊb/ *n.* геофизи́ческая раке́та.

Georgia /ˈdʒɔːdʒɪə/ *n.* (*in Caucasus*) Гру́зия.

Georgian[1] /ˈdʒɔːdʒ(ə)n/ *n.* грузи́н (*fem.* -ка).

● *adj.* грузи́нский.

Georgian[2] /ˈdʒɔːdʒ(ə)n/ *adj.* (*Br.*): **~ architecture** георгиа́нский стиль в архитекту́ре.

geoscience /ˌdʒiːəʊˈsaɪəns/ *n.* (*also* **geosciences**) нау́ки о Земле́.

geostationary /ˌdʒiːəʊˈsteɪʃənərɪ/ *adj.* геостациона́рный.

geranium /dʒəˈreɪnɪəm/ *n.* гера́нь.

gerfalcon /ˈdʒɜːˌfɔːlkən/, /ˌfɔːkən/ *n.* кре́чет.

geriatric /ˌdʒerɪˈætrɪk/ *adj.* гериатри́ческий, ста́рческий; **~ ward** гериатри́ческое отделе́ние.

geriatrician /ˌdʒerɪəˈtrɪʃ(ə)n/ *n.* гериатро́лог.

geriatrics /ˌdʒerɪˈætrɪks/ *n.* гериатри́я.

germ /dʒɜːm/ *n.* микро́б, бакте́рия; **~ warfare** бактериологи́ческая война́; (*fig.*) зача́ток; **the ~ of an idea** зарожде́ние иде́и.

● *cpd.* **~-cell** *n.* заро́дышевая кле́тка.

german /ˈdʒɜːmən/ *adj.*: **cousin ~** двою́родный брат; двою́родная сестра́.

German /ˈdʒɜːmən/ *n.* **1** (*person*) не́м|ец (*fem.* -ка); **Swiss ~ (or ~ Swiss)** швейца́рский не́мец. **2** (*language*) неме́цкий язы́к.

● *adj.* неме́цкий; (*esp. pol.*) герма́нский; **Old High ~** древневерхненеме́цкий; **High ~** ве́рхненеме́цкий; **Low ~** ни́жненеме́цкий; **~ measles** красну́ха; **~ shepherd (dog)** неме́цкая овча́рка; **~ silver** нейзи́льбер; мельхио́р.

germane /dʒɜːˈmeɪn/ *adj.* уме́стный; подходя́щий.

Germanic /dʒɜːˈmænɪk/ *adj.* герма́нский; **~ studies** германи́стика.

Germanism /ˈdʒɜːmənɪz(ə)m/ *n.* (*in language*) германи́зм.

Germanist /ˈdʒɜːmənɪst/ *n.* германи́ст.

G

germanium /dʒɜːˈmeɪnɪəm/ *n.* германий.

Germany /ˈdʒɜːmənɪ/ *n.* Германия; **Federal Republic of ~ (FRG)** (*hist.*) Федеративная Республика Германия (*abbr.* ФРГ).

germicidal /ˌdʒɜːmɪˈsaɪd(ə)l/ *adj.* бактерицидный.

germicide /ˈdʒɜːmɪˌsaɪd/ *n.* гермицид, бактерицидный препарат.

germinal /ˈdʒɜːmɪn(ə)l/ *adj.* зародышевый.

germinate /ˈdʒɜːmɪˌneɪt/ *v.i.* прораст|ать, -и́; (*fig.*) давать (*impf.*) всходы.

germination /ˌdʒɜːmɪˈneɪʃ(ə)n/ *n.* прорастание; (*fig.*) зарождение; развитие.

gerontocracy /ˌdʒerɒnˈtɒkrəsɪ/ *n.* правление старейших.

gerontologist /ˌdʒerɒnˈtɒlədʒɪst/ *n.* геронтолог.

gerontology /ˌdʒerɒnˈtɒlədʒɪ/ *n.* геронтология.

gerrymander(ing) /ˌdʒerɪˈmændər(ɪŋ)/ *n.* предвыборные махинации (*f. pl.*) (*связанные с неправильной разбивкой на округа*).

gerund /ˈdʒerənd/ *n.* герундий.

gerundive /dʒeˈrʌndɪv/ *n.* герундив.

gesso /ˈdʒesəʊ/ *n.* (*pl.* **~es**) гипс.

Gestapo /geˈstɑːpəʊ/ *n.* (*hist.*) гестапо (*indecl.*); (*attr.*) гестаповский; **~ man** гестаповец.

gestate /dʒeˈsteɪt/ *v.t.* вынашивать, выносить.

gestation /dʒeˈsteɪʃ(ə)n/ *n.* беременность; (*fig.*) созревание.

gesticulate /dʒeˈstɪkjʊˌleɪt/ *v.i.* жестикулировать (*impf.*).

gesticulation /dʒeˌstɪkjʊˈleɪʃ(ə)n/ *n.* жестикуляция.

gesture /ˈdʒestʃə(r)/ *n.* жест.

● *v.i.* жестикулировать (*impf.*).

get /get/ *v.t.* (**getting;** *past* **got;** *p.p.* **got** *or US* **gotten**) **1** (*obtain, receive*) получ|ать, -ить; **I got your telegram** я получил вашу телеграмму; **we got dinner at the hotel** мы поужинали в гостинице; **I got Paris on the radio** я поймал по приёмнику Париж; **I've got it!** (*answer to problem etc.*) эврика!; дошло!; **I ~ you** (*sl., understand*) понял!; **have you got that (down)?** (*e.g. to secretary*) (вы это) записали?; готово?; **I never ~ time to see him** никак не могу выбрать время повидаться с ним; **this room ~s a lot of sun** эта комната очень солнечная; **he got his own way** он добился своего; **I ~ 9.5** (*as answer to calculation*) у меня получилось 9,5; **I got** (*bought*) **a new suit** я приобрёл/купил новый костюм; **I got a glimpse of him** я его увидел мельком.
2 (*of suffering etc.*): **he got 2 years** (*sentence*) он получил 2 года (тюрьмы); **he got the measles** он заболел корью; **he got a blow on the head** он получил удар по голове; **she got her feet wet** она промочила ноги.
3 (*procure, fetch, reach, lay hands on*) дост|авать, -ать; доб|ывать, -ыть; **I got him a chair** я принёс ему стул; **the book is not in stock, but we can ~ it for you** этой книги нет на складе, но мы можем её вам достать; **we cannot ~ a plumber** мы не можем найти/добиться водопроводчика; **~ me the manager!** позовите мне заведующего!; **I got him by telephone** я с ним связался по телефону.
4 (*bring into a position or state*): **we got him home** мы доставили его домой; **he got the sum right** он правильно решил пример/задачу; **we got the room tidy** мы прибрали комнату; мы убрались в комнате; **we got the piano through the door** мы пронесли пианино через дверь; **I got the clock going** я починил часы; **I've got him where I want him** теперь он у меня в руках.
5 (*p.p., expr. possession*): **he has got a book** у него есть книга.
6 (*p.p., expr. obligation*): **I have got to go** я должен идти; (*coll., expr. inference*) **you've got to be joking** вы, конечно (*or* должно быть), шутите.
7 (*induce, persuade*) заст|авлять, -авить; **I got him to talk** я заставил его заговорить/разговориться; **I could not ~ the tree to grow** я не сумел вырастить это дерево; **I got the fire to burn** мне удалось разжечь огонь.
8 (*factitive*): **I got my hair cut** я подстригся; **I got the table made by the carpenter** я заказал стол у столяра.
9 (*conquer, captivate*) завоёв|ывать, -ать; **there you have got me** вот тут-то вы меня и поймали.
10 (*denoting progress or achievement*): **I got to know him** я его узнал ближе; **I could not ~ to see him** мне не удалось с ним увидеться; **I got to like travelling** (*Br.*), **traveling** (*US*) я полюбил путешествия; **they got to be friends** они стали друзьями; они подружились; **he got to be manager** он стал директором.
11 (*see, experience*): **you never ~ working men standing for parliament** вы не встретите рабочего, который бы выставлял свою кандидатуру в парламент; **you won't ~ me inviting him again** будьте покойны: я его никогда больше не позову!
12 (*sl., kill, 'do for'*) покончить (*pf.*) c + *i.*

● *v.i.* (**getting;** *past* **got;** *p.p.* **got** *or US* **gotten**) **1** (*become, be*) ста|новиться, -ть; **he got red in the face** он покраснел; **he got angry** он разозлился; **he got drunk** он напился; **he got married** он женился; **he got going** он разошёлся; **he got ready** он приготовился; **he got left behind** он отстал; **he got killed** его убили; он погиб; **we got talking** мы разговорились.
2 (*arrive*) приб|ывать, -ыть; **when did you ~ here?** когда вы сюда прибыли?; **I got to bed at 11** я лёг спать в 11 часов; **how far have you got in your work?** какую часть работы (*or* сколько) вы сделали?; **he did not ~ beyond chapter 5** он не пошёл дальше пятой главы; **where has my book got to?** куда делась/девалась моя книга?; **we cannot ~ home tonight** мы сегодня не попадём домой.

● *with preps.*: **he got above himself** он много о себе возомнил; **the officer got his troops across the river** офицер переправил свои войска через реку; **he got ahead of his competitors** он обогнал своих соперников; **I cannot ~ at the books** я не могу добраться до этих книг; **we must ~ at the truth** мы должны добраться до правды; **what is he ~ting at?** (*trying to say*) что он хочет сказать?; куда он гнёт?; **she is always ~ting at me** (*Br., criticizing, nagging*) она всегда ко мне придирается; **the witness was got at** на свидетеля было оказано давление со стороны; **he got in(to) the taxi** он сел в такси; **I cannot ~ into these shoes** я не могу влезть в эти туфли; **he got into a rage** он пришёл в ярость; **what got into him?** что на него нашло?; **he got into bad habits** у него завелись дурные привычки; **he got into bad company** он завёл (*or* попал в) плохую компанию; **he got into the club** его приняли в клуб; **he got into trouble** он попал в беду; **he got it into his head** (*imagined wrongly*) **that ...** он почему-то решил (*or* вбил себе в голову), что...; **I could not ~ it into his head that ...** я не мог вбить ему в голову, что...; **he got off his horse** он соскочил с коня; **~ off the grass!** сойдите с газона!; **she got the ring off her finger** она (с трудом) сняла кольцо с пальца; **he got on his bicycle** он сел на велосипед; **he got on his feet** он встал/вскочил на ноги; **I got on to** (*contacted*) **him by telephone** я связался с ним по телефону; **the lion got out of its cage** лев выскочил из клетки; **I got out of going to the party** я отвертелся/уклонился от вечеринки; **he got out of the habit of seeing her** он перестал с ней видеться/встречаться; **they got a confession out of him** они вырвали у него признание; **I got £6 out of him** я выжал из него 6 фунтов; **what did you ~ out of his lecture?** что вы вынесли/почерпнули из его лекции?; **we got over the wall** мы перелезли через стену; **I cannot ~ over his rudeness** я не могу опомниться (*or* прийти в себя) от его грубости; **he could not ~ over the loss** он не мог пережить этой утраты; **she got over her shyness** она преодолела свою застенчивость; **we got round the difficulty** нам удалось преодолеть эту трудность; **she got round him** ей удалось его уговорить/провести; **I got through the work** я проделал/провернул всю работу; **he got through all his money** (*Br.*) он истратил все свои деньги; **he got through his exam** он выдержал экзамен; **he got her through the exam** он помог ей сдать экзамен; **he got the bill through parliament** он провёл законопроект через парламент; **the rescuers got to the drowning man** спасатели добрались до утопающего; **let us ~ to business** давайте приступим к делу; **I cannot ~ to the meeting** я не могу явиться на собрание; **we got to Paris by noon** мы добрали́сь до Пари́жа в по́лдень; **when it ~s to 10 o'clock I begin to feel tired** к десяти́ часа́м я начина́ю чу́вствовать уста́лость; *see also v.t.* 10; **the children got up to mischief** (*Br.*) де́ти расшали́лись; **we got up to 10,000 feet** мы подняли́сь на высоту́ 10 000 (десяти́ ты́сяч) фу́тов; **we got up to chapter 5** мы дошли́ до 5-й (пя́той) главы́.

● *with advs.*: **~ about, ~ around** *v.i.*: **he ~s about a great deal** он мно́го разъезжа́ет; **a car makes it easier to ~ about** с маши́ной ле́гче поспева́ть всю́ду; **the news got about** но́вость распространи́лась; **~ across** *v.t.*: **the speaker got his point across** выступа́ющий чётко изложи́л свою́ то́чку зре́ния; **~ along** *v.i.*: **we can ~ along without him** мы мо́жем обойти́сь без него́; **they ~ along** (*agree*) **very well** они́ отли́чно ла́дят; **~ along/away with you!** (*Br.*) брось!; иди́ ты!; да ну тебя́!; **I must be ~ting along** я до́лжен идти́; **~ around** *v.i.* = **~ about** *or* **~ round; ~ away** *v.t.*: **we got him away to the seaside** мы увезли́ его́ к мо́рю; *v.i.*: **the prisoner got away** заключённый бежа́л; **you cannot ~ away from this fact** от э́того фа́кта не уйдёшь; **the thieves got away with the money** во́ры удра́ли с деньга́ми; **he got away with cheating** ему́ удало́сь сжу́льничать; **~ back** *v.t.*: **he got his books back** он получи́л обра́тно/наза́д свои́ кни́ги; **he got his own back** (*Br., revenge*) он отомсти́л за себя́; **I got him back to London** я привёз его́ обра́тно в Ло́ндон; *v.i.*: **he got back from the country** он верну́лся из дере́вни; **he got back into bed** он сно́ва лёг в крова́ть; **~ by** *v.i.*: **please let me ~ by** (*pass*) разреши́те мне пройти́, пожа́луйста; **can I ~ by** (*coll., pass muster*) **in a dark suit?** тёмный костю́м сойдёт?; **~ down** *v.t.*: **he got a book down from the shelf** он снял кни́гу с по́лки; **he got his weight down** он сбро́сил (ли́шний) вес; **the secretary got the conversation down** секрета́рша записа́ла разгово́р; **I could not ~ the medicine down** я не мог проглоти́ть лека́рство; **this weather ~s me down** э́та пого́да де́йствует на меня́ удруча́юще; **things got him down** его заёл быт; *v.i.*: **he got down from his horse** он соскочи́л/слез с коня́; **the child got down (from table)** ребёнок встал из-за стола́; **he got down to his work** он засе́л за рабо́ту; **let us ~ down to the facts** дава́йте займёмся фа́ктами; **~ in** *v.t.*: **they got the crops in** они́ убра́ли урожа́й; **we got a plumber in** мы позва́ли водопрово́дчика; **he got his blow in first** он пе́рвым нанёс уда́р; **I could not ~ a word in** я не мог вста́вить ни сло́ва; **I got my work in** (*done*) **before dinner** я зако́нчил рабо́ту до у́жина; *v.i.*: **the burglar got in through the window** взло́мщик прони́к в дом че́рез окно́; **the train got in early** по́езд пришёл ра́но; **we didn't ~ in to the concert** мы не попа́ли на конце́рт; **he got in** (*was elected*) **for Chester** он прошёл на вы́борах в Че́стере; **he got in with a bad crowd** он связа́лся с плохо́й компа́нией; **~ off** *v.t.* (*remove*) сн|има́ть, -ять; (*dispatch*): **we got the letters off** мы отпра́вили пи́сьма; **we got the children off to school** мы отпра́вили дете́й в шко́лу; **we got the baby off to sleep** мы (е́ле-е́ле) уложи́ли ребёнка спать; **his lawyer got him off** (*acquitted*) адвока́т доби́лся его́ оправда́ния; **I got him off** (*had him excused from*) **school** я попроси́л, что́бы ему́ разреши́ли пропусти́ть шко́лу; *v.i.*: **he got off at the next station** он сошёл (с по́езда) на сле́дующей ста́нции; **I got off (to sleep) early** я ра́но засну́л; **we got off** (*started*) **at 9 a.m.** мы вы́шли/вы́ехали/отпра́вились в 9 часо́в; **he got off with a fine** он отде́лался штра́фом; **I told him where to get/he got off** (*coll.*) я поста́вил его́ на ме́сто; **~ off on** *v.t.* (*sl., get high on*) при|ходи́ть, -йти́ в возбуждённое состоя́ние от + *g.*; **~ on** *v.t.*: **I cannot ~ the lid on** я не могу́ прила́дить/закры́ть кры́шку; **~ your clothes on!** оде́ньтесь!; *v.i.*: **how are you ~ting on?** как дела́?; **she is ~ting on** (*Br., making progress*) она́ де́лает успе́хи; (*growing old*) она́ старе́ет; **~ting on (in years)** в лета́х; **he is ~ting on for 70** (*Br.*) ему́ уже́ к семи́десяти идёт; **~ting on for** (*nearly*) почти́; **it is ~ting on for 4 o'clock** уже́ почти́ 4 часа́; вре́мя идёт к четырём часа́м; **~ on with your work!** займи́тесь свое́й рабо́той!; **they ~ on (well) together** (*Br.*) они́ ла́дят ме́жду собо́й; **he is easy to ~ on with** с ним легко́ ла́дить; **~ out** *v.t.*: **the chauffeur got the car out** шофёр вы́вел маши́ну; **he got out his spectacles** он вы́нул очки́; **they got the book out** (*published*) они́ изда́ли/вы́пустили кни́гу; **he managed to ~ out** (*utter*) **a few words** ему́ удало́сь вы́молвить не́сколько слов; *v.i.*: **~ out!** (*begone!*) убира́йтесь!; (*sl, expr. incredulity*) да ну́!; иди́ ты!; **the secret got out** секре́т стал изве́стен; **~ over** *v.t.*: **I got the main point over to him** я внуши́л/растолкова́л ему́ гла́вное/суть; **I shall be glad to ~ the meeting over (with)** скоре́е бы уж состоя́лось э́то собра́ние!; **~ (a)round** *v.i.*: **I haven't got round to writing to him** я ещё не собра́лся написа́ть ему́; **~ through** *v.t.* (*an exam*) выде́рживать, вы́держать экза́мен; *v.i.* (*of a bill*) про|ходи́ть, -йти́ в парла́менте; **the message got through to him** поруче́ние/запи́ску ему́ переда́ли; (*fig., coll.*) он по́нял, в чём де́ло; **~ together** *v.t.*: **he got an army together** он собра́л а́рмию; *v.i.*: **we must ~ together and have a talk** мы должны́ встре́титься и поговори́ть; **~ up** *v.t.*: **they got me up at 7** они́ по́дняли меня́ в 7 часо́в; **they got up a subscription** они́ организова́ли подпи́ску; **the engine-driver got up steam** машини́ст развёл пары́; **she got herself up beautifully** она́ была́ прекра́сно оде́та; **he got himself up as a pirate** он наряди́лся пира́том; **I must ~ up my German** я до́лжен нажа́ть/нале́чь на неме́цкий; *v.i.* (*from bed, chair etc.*) вста|ва́ть, -ть; **she got up behind him** (*on horse*) она́ усе́лась на ло́шадь сза́ди него́; **the wind/sea is ~ting up** поднима́ется ве́тер; мо́ре начина́ет волнова́ться.

● *cpds.* **~-at-able** *adj.* (*coll.*) досту́пный; **~away** *n.* бе́гство; **make one's ~away** бежа́ть (*det.; impf., pf.*); **~-out** *n.* (*Br., escape, subterfuge*) вы́ход; увёртка; **as all ~-out** (*US coll., extremely*) чрезвыча́йно, дья́вольски; **~-together** *n.* (*meeting, gathering*) встре́ча, сбо́рище; (*entertainment*) вечери́нка; **~-up** *n.* (*dress*) наря́д; **~-up-and-go** *n.* (*coll., energy*) эне́ргия; предприи́мчивость.

gewgaw /ˈgjuːgɔː/ *n.* безделу́шка; мишура́.

geyser /ˈgaɪzə(r)/, /ˈgiː-/ *n.* (*hot spring*) ге́йзер; (*Br., apparatus*) коло́нка для нагре́ва воды́.

Ghana /ˈgɑːnə/ *n.* Га́на.

Ghanaian /gɑːˈneɪən/ *n.* га́нец.

● *adj.* га́нский.

ghastliness /ˈgɑːstlɪnɪs/ *n.* у́жас; отврати́тельность.

ghastly /ˈgɑːstlɪ/ *adj.* (**ghastlier, ghastliest**) ужа́сный, отврати́тельный, кошма́рный; **a ~ crime** ужа́сное преступле́ние; **a ~ accident** ужа́сная катастро́фа; **you look ~** у вас жу́ткий вид; **a ~ dinner** отврати́тельный у́жин.

● *adv.* ужа́сно.

Ghent /gent/ *n.* Гент.

gherkin /ˈgɜːkɪn/ *n.* корнишо́н.

ghetto /ˈgetəʊ/ *n.* (*pl.* **~s** *or* **~es**) ге́тто (*indecl.*); **~ blaster** (*coll.*) перено́сный радиомагнитофо́н, магнито́ла.

ghost /gəʊst/ *n.* **1** (*life, spirit*): **give up the ~** испусти́ть (*pf.*) дух; **Holy G~** Свято́й Дух. **2** (*of dead person*) привиде́ние; дух; **do you believe in ~s?** вы ве́рите в привиде́ния?; **he looked as if he had seen a ~** у него́ был тако́й вид, сло́вно ему́ яви́лось привиде́ние. **3** (*vestige*): **he hasn't the ~ of a chance** у него́ нет ни мале́йшего ша́нса; **the ~ of a smile** чуть заме́тная улы́бка. **4** (**~-***writer*) литобрабо́тчик, «невиди́мка».

● *v.t.* (*also* **~-write**): **the autobiography was ~ed** автобиогра́фию за него́ написа́л друго́й.

● *cpds.* **~buster** *n.* охо́тник за привиде́ниями; **~-like** *adj.* = **ghostly; ~-story** *n.* расска́з с привиде́ниями; **~ town** *n.* го́род-при́зрак.

ghostly /ˈgəʊstlɪ/ *adj.* (**ghostlier, ghostliest**) похо́жий на привиде́ние.

ghoul /guːl/ *n.* **1** (*myth.*) вампи́р. **2** (*person delighting in horror*) люби́тель (*m.*) у́жасов.

ghoulish /ˈguːlɪʃ/ *adj.* жу́ткий, отврати́тельный.

GHQ (*abbr. of* ***General Headquarters***) ста́вка, гла́вное кома́ндование.

GI (*abbr. of* ***government issue;*** = *American soldier*) (*pl.* **GIs**) «джи-а́й» (*indecl.*); солда́т.

giant /ˈdʒaɪənt/ *n.* **1** (*fabulous being*) гигáнт. **2** (*very tall person etc.*) великáн, исполи́н. **3** (*fig.*): **an intellectual ~** гигáнт мы́сли. **4** (*attr.*) гигáнтский; исполи́нский; **~ cactus** исполи́нский кáктус; **G~ Panda** бамбу́ковый медвéдь; **he made ~ strides in his work** он сдéлал гигáнтские успéхи в рабóте.

giantess /ˈdʒaɪəntɪs/ *n.* великáнша.

gibber /ˈdʒɪbə(r)/ *v.i.* таратóрить (*impf.*); говори́ть (*impf.*) невня́тно; лопотáть (*impf.*) (*coll.*).

gibberish /ˈdʒɪbərɪʃ/ *n.* тарабáрщина, лопотáние.

gibbet /ˈdʒɪbɪt/ *n.* ви́селица.

● *v.t.* (**gibbeted, gibbeting**) вéшать, повéсить.

gibbon /ˈɡɪbən/ *n.* гиббóн.

gibe /dʒaɪb/ = **jibe¹**

giblets /ˈdʒɪblɪts/ *n.* потрох|á (*pl.*, *g.* -óв).

Gibraltar /ɡɪˈbrɔːltə(r)/ *n.* Гибралтáр; **Strait of ~** Гибралтáрский проли́в.

giddap /ɡɪˈdæp/ *int.* (*US*) но!

giddiness /ˈɡɪdɪnɪs/ *n.* головокружéние; вéтреность.

giddy /ˈɡɪdɪ/ *adj.* (**giddier, giddiest**) **1** головокружи́тельный; **I feel ~** у меня́ кру́жится головá; **a ~ height** головокружи́тельная высотá. **2** (*capricious*): **a ~ girl** вéтреная девчóнка.

giddy-up /ˌɡɪdɪˈʌp/ *int.* но!

gift /ɡɪft/ *n.* **1** (*thing given*) подáрок; дар; **~ shop** магази́н подáрков; **~ voucher** (*Br.*)/**token** (*Br.*)/**certificate** (*US*) подáрочный талóн. **2** (*talent*) даровáние; дар; **he has a ~ for languages** у негó спосóбности (*f. pl.*)/ талáнт к языкáм; **a man of many ~s** разносторóнне одарённый человéк. **3** (*coll.*, *easy*): **the exam was a ~** экзáмен был пустякóвый.

● *v.t.* **1** (*bestow*) дари́ть, по-. **2** (*endow with ~*) надел|я́ть, -и́ть; **he was ~ed with rare talents** он был наделён рéдкими талáнтами.

● *cpds.* **~-horse** *n.*: **you must not look a ~-horse in the mouth** дарёному конó в зу́бы не смóтрят; **~-wrap** *v.t.* завёр|тывать, -ну́ть в подáрочную упакóвку.

gifted /ˈɡɪftɪd/ *adj.* одарённый.

gig¹ /ɡɪɡ/ *n.* **1** (*carriage*) двукóлка. **2** (*boat*) ги́чка.

gig² /ɡɪɡ/ *n.* (*coll.*) (*performance*) выступлéние, концéрт (*осóбенно джáза или поп-му́зыки*).

giga- /ˈɡɪɡə/, /ˈɡaɪɡə/ *comb. form* гига…; **~byte** гигабáйт; **~watt** гигавáтт.

gigantic /dʒaɪˈɡæntɪk/ *adj.* гигáнтский.

giggle /ˈɡɪɡ(ə)l/ *n.* хихи́канье; **for a ~** смéха/шу́тки рáди; **he had a fit of the ~s** на негó смех(у́нчик) напáл.

● *v.i.* хихи́к|ать, -нуть.

gigolo /ˈʒɪɡəˌləʊ/, /ˈdʒɪɡ-/ *n.* (*pl.* **~s**) жи́голо (*m. indecl.*).

gild /ɡɪld/ *v.t.* **1** (*cover or tinge with gold*) золоти́ть, по-. **2** (*fig.*) укр|ашáть, -áсить; **~ the lily** перебáр|щивать, -орщи́ть; ≈ мáсло мáсляное; **~ed youth** золотáя молодёжь.

gilding /ˈɡɪldɪŋ/ *n.* позолóта.

gill¹ /ɡɪl/ *n.* (*of fish*) жáбра; **he looks green about the ~s** (*fig.*) он вы́глядит больны́м.

gill² /dʒɪl/ *n.* (*measure*) чéтверть пи́нты.

gillyflower /ˈdʒɪlɪˌflaʊə(r)/ *n.* левкóй.

gilt /ɡɪlt/ *n.* позолóта; **take the ~ off the gingerbread** лиш|áть, -и́ть (*что*) привлекáтельности.

● *cpd.* **~-edged** *adj.* (*book etc.*) с золочёным обрéзом; **~-edged securities** первоклáссные (*or* осóбо надёжные) цéнные бумáги.

gimbals /ˈdʒɪmb(ə)lz/ *n.* кардáнов подвéс, кардáн.

gimcrack /ˈdʒɪmkræk/ *adj.* мишу́рный.

gimlet /ˈɡɪmlɪt/ *n.* бурáв; бурáвчик.

● *cpd.* **~-eyed** *adj.* остроглáзый; проницáтельный.

gimmick /ˈɡɪmɪk/ *n.* (*coll.*) трюк; финт, ухищрéние.

gimmickry /ˈɡɪmɪkrɪ/ *n.* (*coll.*) трю́ки (*m. pl.*); трюкáчество.

gimmicky /ˈɡɪmɪkɪ/ *adj.* (*coll.*) трюкáческий; с выкрутáсами.

gin¹ /dʒɪn/ *n.* (*tech.*) (*cotton-~*) джин, волокноотдели́тель (*m.*).

● *v.t.* (**ginned, ginning**) оч|ищáть, -и́стить.

gin² /dʒɪn/ *n.* (*drink*) джин; **~ and tonic** джин с тóником.

ginger /ˈdʒɪndʒə(r)/ *n.* **1** (*bot.*, *cul.*) имби́рь (*m.*); (*attr.*) имби́рный. **2** (*mettle, dash*) задóр; **~ group** (*Br.*) активи́сты, инициати́вная грýппа; (*zest*) «изю́минка».

● *adj.* (*colour*) ры́жий.

● *v.t.*: **~ up** подзадóри|вать, -ть.

● *cpds.* **~ale, ~-beer, ~-pop** *nn.* имби́рное пи́во; **~bread** *n.* имби́рная коври́жка; **~-nut, ~-snap** *nn.* имби́рный пря́ник, имби́рное печéнье.

gingerly /ˈdʒɪndʒəlɪ/ *adj.* (крáйне) осторóжный.

● *adv.* осторóжно.

gingery /ˈdʒɪndʒərɪ/ *adj.* **1** (*like ginger in taste etc.*) имби́рный. **2** (*colour*) рыжевáтый.

gingham /ˈɡɪŋəm/ *n.* пестротќаная клéтчатая матéрия.

gingivitis /ˌdʒɪndʒɪˈvaɪtɪs/ *n.* воспалéние дёсен, гингиви́т.

gink /ɡɪŋk/ *n.* (*US sl.*) пáрень (*m.*), мáлый.

ginkgo /ˈɡɪŋkɡəʊ/, **gingko** /ˈɡɪŋkəʊ/ *n.* (*pl.* **~s** *or* **~es**) (*bot.*) ги́нкго (*indecl.*).

ginormous /dʒaɪˈnɔːməs/ *adj.* (*Br. coll.*) огромáдный.

ginseng /ˈdʒɪnseŋ/ *n.* женьшéнь (*m.*).

Gipsy, Gypsy /ˈdʒɪpsɪ/ *n.* цыгáн (*fem.* -ка); **~ caravan** киби́тка; **g~ moth** непáрный шелкопря́д.

● *adj.* цыгáнский.

giraffe /dʒɪˈrɑːf/, /-ˈræf/ *n.* (*pl.* **~** *or* **~s**) жирáф(а).

girandole /ˈdʒɪrənˌdəʊl/ *n.* канделя́бр.

gird /ɡɜːd/ *v.t.* (*past and p.p.* **~ed** *or* **girt**) **1** (*with belt etc.*) опоя́с|ывать, -áть; **~ (up) one's loins** (*fig.*) ≈ засучи́ть (*pf.*) рукавá; собрáться (*pf.*) с си́лами; **~ on one's sword** прикрепи́ть (*pf.*) сáблю к пóясу. **2** (*encircle, e.g. fortress or island*) окруж|áть, -и́ть.

girder /ˈɡɜːdə(r)/ *n.* (*beam*) бáлка; брус; (*span of bridge etc.*) переклáдина; фéрма.

girdle /ˈɡɜːd(ə)l/ *n.* **1** (*belt etc.*) пóяс; кушáк. **2** (*corset*) корсéт.

● *v.t.* (*encircle*) окруж|áть, -и́ть.

girl /ɡɜːl/ *n.* (*child*) дéвочка; (*young woman*) дéвушка; (*pej.*) девчóнка; **G~ Guide, Scout** дéвочка-скáут, гёрл-скáут, гёрл-гáйд; (*maid-servant*) служáнка; (*sweetheart*) возлю́бленная; **old ~** (*coll.*, *old woman; also as affectionate term of address*) стару́шка; (*ex-pupil of school*) выпускни́ца (*дáнной шкóлы*).

● *cpd.* **~-friend** *n.* (*female friend*) подру́га; (*mistress*) ≈ дéвушка/ приятельница.

girlhood /ˈɡɜːlhʊd/ *n.* деви́чество, óтрочество; **in her ~** в деви́честве.

girlie /ˈɡɜːlɪ/ *n.* (*coll.*) дéвочка, девчу́шка; **~ magazine** журнáл с фотогрáфиями (полу)обнажённых жéнщин.

girlish /ˈɡɜːlɪʃ/ *adj.* деви́ческий; (*of a boy*) изнéженный, как девчóнка (*coll.*).

girlishness /ˈɡɜːlɪʃnɪs/ *n.* поведéние, свóйственное дéвочке.

girt /ɡɜːt/ *past and p.p. of* ^**gird**

girth /ɡɜːθ/ *n.* (*of horse*) подпру́га; (*of tree, person etc.*) обхвáт; размéр.

gist /dʒɪst/ *n.* суть.

give /ɡɪv/ *n.* **1** (*elasticity*) подáтливость, эласти́чность; **there's no ~ in a stone floor** кáменный пол не прогибáется; **there is no ~ in this rope** э́та верёвка не растя́гивается; **there is no ~ in his attitude** он зáнял непреклóнную пози́цию. **2**: **~ and take** взаи́мные усту́пки (*f. pl.*).

● *v.t.* (*past* **gave**; *p.p.* **given** /ˈɡɪv(ə)n/) **1** да|вáть, -ть; **~ lessons** давáть (*impf.*) урóки; **I ~ you my word** даю́ вам слóво; **I gave the porter my luggage** я óтдал свой багáж носи́льщику; **you must ~ and take in this life** в жи́зни ну́жно не тóлько брать, но и давáть что-то взамéн; **two years, ~ or take a month or so** óколо двух лет, мéсяцем бóльше и́ли мéньше. **2** (*imper.*, *expr. preference*): **~ me the good old days!** где нáше дóброе стáрое врéмя?!; **~ me Bach every time** я всем и всегдá предпочитáю Бáха. **3** (*present, bestow, surrender*) дари́ть, по-; **he was ~n a book** ему́ подари́ли кни́гу; **he gave him his daughter in marriage** он отдáл ему́ свою́ дочь в жёны; **she gave herself to him** онá ему́ отдалáсь. **4** (*propose*): **I ~ you** (*the toast of*) **the Queen** я предлагáю тост за королéву. **5** (**~** *in exchange*): **I gave a good price for it** я за э́то хорошó заплати́л; **what**

will you ~ me for this coat? сколько вы мне дадите за это пальто?; **I would ~ anything to know where she is** я бы всё отдал, чтобы узнать, где она; **he gave as good as he got** он заплатил той же монетой; **I don't ~ a damn!** а мне наплевать!
6 (*provide, furnish, impart, inflict*): **the sun ~s light** солнце — источник света; **he ~s me a lot of trouble** он мне доставляет много хлопот; **he has ~n me his cold** я заразился от него насморком; **the place gave its name to the battle** битва берёт своё название от местности; **he gave** (*cited*) **an example** он привёл пример; **he gave me to understand that ...** он дал мне понять, что...; **~ him my regards** передайте ему от меня привет; **a literal translation is ~n** приводится буквальный перевод; **~ evidence** (*in court*) да|вать, -ть показания; **~ pleasure** дост|авлять, -авить удовольствие; **the court gave him 6 months** суд приговорил его к шести месяцам (тюрьмы); ему дали 6 месяцев; **I gave him a look** я (*сердито и т.п.*) взглянул на него; **the noise ~s me a headache** у меня голова болит от шума; **he gave the signal to start** он дал сигнал начинать; **he gave no sign of life** он не подавал признаков жизни.
7 (*indicate*): **this book ~s you the answers** ответы вы найдёте в этой книге; **he gave no reason for his absence** он не объяснил своего отсутствия.
8 (*decide*): **the case was ~n against him** дело решили не в его пользу.
9 (*devote, sacrifice*) удел|ять, -ить; посвя|щать, -тить; **he gave a lot of time to the work** он уделил этой работе много времени; **he gave his life for her** он отдал за неё жизнь; **he gave thought to the question** он много думал над этим вопросом; **he gave me his attention** он внимательно меня слушал.
10 (*allow, estimate*): **I ~ you an hour to get ready** я даю вам час (чтобы) приготовиться; **I ~ him three months to fail** вот увидите — через три месяца он провалится; **to ~ him his due, he tried hard** надо отдать ему должное — он очень старался; **I would ~ him** (*estimate his age at*) **50** я бы дал ему лет 50.
11 (*organize*) устр|аивать, -оить; **they gave a dance** они устроили танцевальный вечер.
12 (*perform action*): **the horse gave a kick** лошадь (вз)брыкнула; **he gave a loud laugh** он громко рассмеялся; **the dog gave a bark** собака залаяла.
13 (*with pronominal object*): **~ it to him!** (*beating etc.*) дай ему!; **I gave him what for** (*Br. coll.*) я задал ему трёпку; **I gave him one** (*a blow*) **over the head** я стукнул его по башке.
14 (*special uses of* **~n**): **under the ~n** (*existing*) **conditions** в данных обстоятельствах/условиях; **~n time, it can be done** при наличии времени это можно сделать; **at a ~n** (*specified, agreed, particular*) **time** в определённое время; **~n name** (*forename*) имя (*nt.*); **he is ~n to boasting** он склонен к хвастовству; **~ that ...** при том, что...

● *v.i.* (*past* **gave;** *p.p.* **given** /ˈgɪv(ə)n/) **1**: **he ~s generously** он очень щедр; **~ of one's best** вложить (*pf.*) душу. **2** (*yield*) подд|аваться, -аться; под|аваться, -аться; **the branch gave but did not break** ветка согнулась, но не сломалась; **his knees gave** его колени подкосились; **the ground gave under our feet** земля подалась под нашими ногами; **the rope gave** (*broke*) верёвка оборвалась.
3 (*Br., face*): **the window ~s on to the yard** окно выходит во двор.

● *with advs.*: **~ away** *v.t.* дарить, по ; (*distribute, e.g. prizes*) разд|авать, -ать; **he gave away the secret** он выдал секрет; **don't ~ me away!** не выдавайте меня!; **he gave the game away** (*revealed a secret*) он проболтался; он выдал секрет; **~ back** *v.t.* (*restore*) возвра|щать, -тить; отд|авать, -ать; **~ forth** *v.t.* (*emit*) изд|авать, -ать; испус|кать, -тить; **~ in** *v.t.*: **he gave in his** (*exam*) **paper** (*Br.*) он сдал свою экзаменационную работу; *v.i.* (*yield*) подд|аваться, -аться; уступ|ать, -ить; **he gave in to my persuasion** он поддался моим уговорам; **~ off** *v.t.* (*emit, e.g. smell or smoke*) испус|кать, -тить; изд|авать, -ать; **~ out** *v.t.* (*distribute*) распредел|ять, -ить; (*announce*) объяв|лять, -ить; *v.i.* кончаться, кончиться; **the rations gave out** продовольствие кончилось; **his strength gave out** его силы иссякли; **~ over** *v.t.* (*hand over*) перед|авать, -ать; **he was ~n over to vice** он предался пороку; **~ over!** (*Br. coll., desist!*) бросьте!; **~ over pushing!** перестаньте толкаться!; (*devote*): **the time was ~n over to discussion** время было отдано/посвящено дискуссии; **~ up** *v.t.* ост|авлять, -авить; (*resign, surrender*) отказ|ываться, -аться +*g.*; **he gave up his seat to her** он уступил ей место; **the murderer gave himself up** убийца сдался; (*desist from*) бр|осать, -осить; **he gave up smoking** он бросил курить; (*abandon hope of*): **they gave him up for lost** они решили, что он пропал; **you were so late that we gave you up** вы пришли так поздно, что мы вас и ждать перестали; **we gave it up as a bad job** (*desisted from hopeless attempt*) мы махнули рукой на это дело; **after the quarrel she gave him up** после ссоры она с ним порвала; *v.i.*: **the swimmer gave up** пловец сошёл с дистанции; **I ~ up!** сдаюсь!

● *cpd.* **~-away** *n.* (*coll.*) (*betrayal of secret etc.*): **her tears were a ~-away** слёзы выдавали её; (*free gift*) подарок.

giver /ˈgɪvə(r)/ *n.* дающий; **he is a generous ~** он очень щедр.

gizmo /ˈgɪzməʊ/ *n.* (*pl.* **~s**) штуковина.

gizzard /ˈgɪzəd/ *n.* второй желудок (*у птиц*); (*fig., coll.*) желудок; **it sticks in my ~** (*coll.*) мне это поперёк горла стало.

glacé /ˈglæseɪ/ *adj.*: **~ fruits** засахаренные фрукты.

glacial /ˈgleɪʃ(ə)l/, /-sɪəl/ *adj.* ледовый; ледяной; **the ~ era** ледниковый период.

glaciation /ˌgleɪsɪˈeɪʃ(ə)n/ *n.* оледенение; замерзание.

glacier /ˈglæsɪə(r)/ *n.* ледник; глетчер.

glacis /ˈglæsɪs/, /-siː/ *n.* (*pl.* **~** /-sɪz/, /-siːz/) (*mil.*) гласис, передний скат бруствера.

glad /glæd/ *adj.* (**gladder, gladdest**) **1** (*pleased*) довольный; **I am ~ to meet you** рад с вами познакомиться; **I should be ~ of a few pounds** я был бы рад (и) нескольким фунтам. **2** (*happy*) радостный; **this is the ~dest day of my life** это самый счастливый день в моей жизни. **3** (*coll.*): **~ rags** праздничное платье.

gladden /ˈglæd(ə)n/ *v.t.* радовать, об-; **flowers ~ the scene** цветы оживляют вид; **wine ~s the heart** вино веселит душу.

glade /gleɪd/ *n.* поляна, прогалина.

gladiator /ˈglædɪˌeɪtə(r)/ *n.* гладиатор.

gladiatorial /ˈglædɪəˈtɔːrɪəl/ *adj.* гладиаторский.

gladio|lus /ˌglædɪˈəʊləs/ *n.* (*pl.* **~li** /-laɪ/ *or* **~luses**) гладиолус.

gladly /ˈglædlɪ/ *adv.* (*joyfully*) радостно; (*willingly, with pleasure*) охотно.

gladness /ˈglædnɪs/ *n.* радость.

Glagolitic /ˌglægəˈlɪtɪk/ *adj.* глаголический; **the ~ alphabet, script** глаголица.

glamor /ˈglæmə(r)/ (*US*) = **glamour**

glamorous /ˈglæmərəs/ *adj.* обольстительный; пленительный; (*of job etc.*) заманчивый, роскошный.

glamour /ˈglæmə(r)/ (*US* **glamor**) *n.* волшебство, очарование; шик.

glamo(u)rize /ˈglæməˌraɪz/ *v.t.* приукра|шивать, -сить.

glanc|e /glɑːns/ *n.* **1** (*quick look*) взгляд; **I took a ~e at the newspaper** я заглянул в газету; **I recognised him at a ~e** я узнал его с первого взгляда. **2** (*flash*) блеск, блик.

● *v.t. & i.* **1** (*look*) взглянуть (*pf.*); бросить (*pf.*) взгляд; **he ~ed at the clock** он взглянул на часы; **he ~ed round the room** он оглядел комнату; **he ~ed over the figures** он скользнул взглядом по цифрам; **he ~ed down the page** он пробежал страницу глазами. **2** (*bounce*) отск|акивать -очить; (*be reflected*) отра|жаться, -зиться; **a ~ ing blow** скользящий удар.

gland /glænd/ *n.* железа.

glandular /ˈglændjʊlə(r)/ *adj.* железистый; **~ fever** инфекционный мононуклеоз.

glare /gleə(r)/ *n.* (*fierce light*) ослепительный свет/блеск; (*fig.*): **~ of publicity** рекламная шумиха; (*angry look*) свирепый взгляд.

● *v.t. & i.* ослепительно сверкать; **the sun ~d down** солнце палило; **~ at s.o.** испепел|ять, -ить кого-н. взглядом.

glaring /ˈgleərɪŋ/ *adj.* (*e.g. headlights*)

слепя́щий, ослепи́тельный; (*of colour*) крича́щий, я́ркий; (*fierce, angry*) свире́пый; (*of mistake etc.*) гру́бый.

glasnost /ˈglæznɒst/, /ˈglɑ:s-/ *n.* гла́сность.

glass /glɑ:s/ *n.* **1** (*substance*) стекло́; **~ eye** стекля́нный глаз; **~ case** стекля́нный колпа́к; **people who live in ~ houses should not throw stones** тот, кто сам не безупре́чен, не до́лжен осужда́ть други́х. **2** (*for drinking*) (*tumbler*) стака́н; (*wine-~*) рю́мка, бока́л; **they clinked ~es** они́ чо́кнулись. **3** (*~ware*) стекля́нная посу́да. **4**: **tomatoes under ~** (*in ~houses*) помидо́ры в тепли́це. **5** (*Br., mirror*) зе́ркало. **6** (*pl., spectacles*) очк|и́ (*pl., g.* -о́в).

● *v.t.*: **a ~ed-in veranda** застеклённая/остеклённая вера́нда.

● *cpds.* **~-blower** *n.* стеклоду́в; **~-blowing** *n.* стеклоду́вное де́ло; **~house** *n.* (*Br.*) тепли́ца; **~-making** *n.* стеко́льное де́ло; **~ware** *n.* стекля́нная посу́да.

glassful /ˈglɑ:sfʊl/ *n.* стака́н (*чего*).

glassiness /ˈglɑ:sɪnɪs/ *n.* (*e.g. of eyes*) ту́склость, безжи́зненность; (*e.g. of river, lake*) зерка́льность.

glassy /ˈglɑ:sɪ/ *adj.* (**glassier, glassiest**): **a ~ stare** ту́склый/засты́вший взгляд; **a ~ lake** зерка́льная гладь о́зера.

glaucoma /glɔ:ˈkəʊmə/ *n.* глауко́ма.

glaucous /ˈglɔ:kəs/ *adj.* ту́склый, серова́то-зелёный; (*bot.*) покры́тый налётом.

glaze /gleɪz/ *n.* глазу́рь.

● *v.t.* (*window*) застекл|я́ть, -и́ть; (*pottery, paint etc.*) глазурова́ть (*impf., pf.*).

● *v.i.*: **his eyes ~d over** его́ взгляд потускне́л.

glazier /ˈgleɪzjə(r)/ *n.* стеко́льщик.

glazing /ˈgleɪzɪŋ/ *n.* (*material*) глазу́рь; (*glasswork*) остекле́ние; **double ~** (*Br.*) двойны́е ра́мы (*f. pl.*).

gleam /gli:m/ *n.* про́блеск; **a ~ of hope** про́блеск наде́жды; **a dangerous ~ in the eye** опа́сный блеск в глаза́х; **without a ~ of humour** (*Br.*), **humor** (*US*) без те́ни ю́мора.

● *v.i.* поблёскивать (*impf.*); блесте́ть (*impf.*).

glean /gli:n/ *v.t.* (*lit., also v.i.*) подбира́ть (*impf.*) (колоски́); (*fig.*) соб|ира́ть, -ра́ть (по крупи́цам).

gleanings /ˈgli:nɪŋz/ *n.* (*fig.*) крупи́цы (*f. pl.*).

glee /gli:/ *n.* (*delight*) весе́лье; ликова́ние; (*song*) пе́ние «а капе́лла»; **~ club** клуб певцо́в-люби́телей.

gleeful /ˈgli:fʊl/ *adj.* лику́ющий.

glen /glen/ *n.* лощи́на.

glib /glɪb/ *adj.* (**glibber, glibbest**) бо́йкий на язы́к; **a ~ excuse** благови́дный предло́г.

glibness /ˈglɪbnɪs/ *n.* словоохо́тливость; краснобáйство.

glide /glaɪd/ *n.* скольже́ние.

● *v.i.* скольз|и́ть, -ну́ть; (*in aircraft*) плани́ровать, с-.

glider /ˈglaɪdə(r)/ *n.* планёр; **~ pilot** планери́ст.

gliding /ˈglaɪdɪŋ/ *n.* (*sport*) планери́зм.

glimmer /ˈglɪmə(r)/ *n.* ту́склый свет; мерца́ние; **a ~ of hope/intelligence** про́блеск наде́жды/ума́.

● *v.i.* мерца́ть (*impf.*).

glimpse /glɪmps/ *n.* про́блеск; **I caught a ~ of him** он промелькну́л у меня́ пе́ред глаза́ми.

● *v.t.* уви́деть (*pf.*) ме́льком.

glint /glɪnt/ *n.* блеск; (*reflection*) о́тблеск.

● *v.i.* блесте́ть (*impf.*); (*flash*) вспы́х|ивать, -нуть.

glissade /glɪˈsɑ:d/, /-ˈseɪd/ *n.* **1** (*mountaineering*) соска́льзывание. **2** (*ballet*) глиссе́ (*indecl.*).

● *v.i.* **1** сколь|зи́ть, -ну́ть. **2** де́лать, с- глиссе́.

glissan|do /glɪˈsændəʊ/ *n.* (*pl.* **~di** /-dɪ/ *or* **~dos**) (*mus.*) глисса́ндо (*indecl.*).

glisten /ˈglɪs(ə)n/ *v.i.* сверк|а́ть, -ну́ть.

glitch /glɪtʃ/ *n.* небольшо́е затрудне́ние.

glitter /ˈglɪtə(r)/ *n.* блеск, сверка́ние.

● *v.i.* блесте́ть (*impf.*); сверка́ть (*impf.*).

glitz /glɪts/ *n.* (показно́й) блеск, шик.

glitzy /ˈglɪtsɪ/ *adj.* (**glitzier, glitziest**) мишу́рный, показу́шный.

gloaming /ˈgləʊmɪŋ/ *n.* (*liter.*) су́мер|ки (*pl., g.* -ек).

gloat /gləʊt/ *v.i.* смотре́ть (*impf.*) с вожделе́нием (на + *a.*); (*maliciously*) злора́дствовать (*impf.*).

global /ˈgləʊb(ə)l/ *adj.* (*total*) всео́бщий; (*world-wide*) глоба́льный; **~ warming** глоба́льное потепле́ние.

globalization /ˌgləʊbəlaɪˈzeɪʃ(ə)n/ *n.* глобализа́ция.

globe /gləʊb/ *n.* **1** (*spherical body*) шар; гло́бус; **~ artichoke** артишо́к. **2**: **terrestrial ~** земно́й шар.

● *cpd.* **~-trotter** *n.* зая́длый тури́ст.

globular /ˈglɒbjʊlə(r)/ *adj.* шарови́дный.

globule /ˈglɒbju:l/ *n.* ша́рик; ка́пелька.

glockenspiel /ˈglɒkənˌspi:l/, /-ˌʃpi:l/ *n.* металлофо́н.

gloom /glu:m/ *n.* (*dark*) тьма; мрак; (*despondency*) мра́чность; уны́ние; **the news cast a ~ over us** но́вость омрачи́ла/испо́ртила нам настрое́ние.

gloominess /ˈglu:mɪnɪs/ *n.* мра́чность.

gloomy /ˈglu:mɪ/ *adj.* (**gloomier, gloomiest**) (*dark*) мра́чный; (*depressing*) гнету́щий; (*depressed*) хму́рый; уны́лый.

glorification /ˌglɔ:rɪfɪˈkeɪʃ(ə)n/ *n.* прославле́ние, восхвале́ние.

glorif|y /ˈglɔ:rɪˌfaɪ/ *v.t.* **1** (*worship*) восхваля́ть (*impf.*). **2** (*honour, extol*) просл|авля́ть, -а́вить. **3**: **the house is a ~ied barn** никако́й э́то не дом, а про́сто сара́й.

glorious /ˈglɔ:rɪəs/ *adj.* сла́вный, великоле́пный; **a ~ day** (*weather*) изуми́тельный день; (*iron.*): **he made a ~ mess of it** он запу́тал дела́ как нельзя́ лу́чше.

glor|y /ˈglɔ:rɪ/ *n.* **1** (*renown, honour*) сла́ва. **2** (*splendour*) великоле́пие. **3** (*source of honour*): **the ~ies of Rome** сла́ва/вели́чие Ри́ма.

● *v.i.* упива́ться (*impf.*) + *i.*; горди́ться (*impf.*) + *i.*; **~y in one's strength** упива́ться свое́й си́лой.

● *cpd.* **~-hole** *n.* (*coll.*) сва́лка.

gloss[1] /glɒs/ *n.* (*comment, explanation*) гло́сса, поясне́ние; (*interpretation*) толкова́ние.

● *v.t.* комменти́ровать, про-; толкова́ть (*impf.*).

gloss[2] /glɒs/ *n.* (*lit., fig.*) лоск; **~ paint** ма́сленная кра́ска.

● *v.t.*: **~ over faults** обойти́ (*pf.*) оши́бки молча́нием; зама́з|ывать, -ать недоста́тки.

glossary /ˈglɒsərɪ/ *n.* глосса́рий.

glossiness /ˈglɒsɪnɪs/ *n.* лоск.

glossy /ˈglɒsɪ/ *adj.* (**glossier, glossiest**) глянцеви́тый; лощёный; **a ~ photograph** гля́нцевая фотогра́фия; **~ magazines** ≈ дороги́е иллюстри́рованные журна́лы.

glottal /ˈglɒt(ə)l/ *adj.* относя́щийся к голосово́й ще́ли; **~ stop** горта́нный взрыв, твёрдый при́ступ.

glottis /ˈglɒtɪs/ *n.* голосова́я щель.

glove /glʌv/ *n.* перча́тка; (*fig.*): **fit like a ~** быть впо́ру; **handle s.o. with kid ~s** церемо́ниться (*impf.*) с кем-н.; **with the ~s off** всерьёз; **~ compartment** (*in car*) я́щик для мелоче́й; бардачо́к.

● *v.t.*: **a ~d hand** рука́ в перча́тке.

glow /gləʊ/ *n.* (*of bodily warmth*) жар; (*of fire, sunset etc.*) за́рево; (*of feelings*) пыл.

● *v.i.* (*incandesce*) нака́л|иваться, -и́ться; (*shine*) свети́ться (*impf.*), сверка́ть (*impf.*); **~ing metal** раскалённый мета́лл; **a forest ~ing with autumn tints** лес, пыла́ющий осе́нними кра́сками; **he ~ed with pride** его́ распира́ла го́рдость; **he described the trip in ~ing colours** он расписа́л путеше́ствие в ра́дужных тона́х.

● *cpd.* **~-worm** *n.* светля́к.

glower /ˈglaʊə(r)/ *v.i.* серди́то смотре́ть (*impf.*).

gloxinia /glɒkˈsɪnɪə/ *n.* глокси́ния.

glucose /ˈglu:kəʊs/, /-kəʊz/ *n.* глюко́за.

glue /glu:/ *n.* клей.

● *v.t.* (**glues, glued, gluing** *or* **glueing**) прикле́|ивать, -ть; (*fig.*): **he ~d his eyes to the floor** он уста́вился в пол; **he ~d his ear to the keyhole** он прини́к у́хом к замо́чной сква́жине.

● *cpds.* **~-sniffer** *n.* токсикома́н; **~-sniffing** *n.* токсикома́ния.

gluey /ˈglu:ɪ/ *adj.* (**gluier, gluiest**) кле́йкий, ли́пкий.

glum /glʌm/ *adj.* (**glummer, glummest**) угрю́мый.

glumness /ˈglʌmnɪs/ *n.* угрю́мость.

glut /glʌt/ *n.* избы́ток.

● *v.t.* (**glutted, glutting**) нас|ыща́ть, -ы́тить; **~ o.s.** нас|ыща́ться, -ы́титься; **~ the market** зава́л|ивать, -и́ть ры́нок; **the animals were ~ted** живо́тные нае́лись до отва́ла.

gluten /ˈgluːt(ə)n/ *n.* клейкови́на.

glutinous /ˈgluːtɪnəs/ *adj.* кле́йкий, ли́пкий, вя́зкий.

glutton /ˈglʌt(ə)n/ *n.* **1** обжо́ра (*c.g.*); **a ~ for work** жа́дный к рабо́те. **2** (*zool.*) росома́ха.

gluttonous /ˈglʌtənəs/ *adj.* прожо́рливый.

gluttony /ˈglʌtənɪ/ *n.* обжо́рство.

glycerine /ˈglɪsəˌriːn/ (*US* **glycerin**) *n.* глицери́н.

GM (*abbr. of* ***genetically modified***): **~ foods** генети́чески модифици́рованные проду́кты.

GMT = **Greenwich (mean) time**

gnarl|ed /nɑːld/, **-y** /ˈnɑːlɪ/ *adjs.* шишкова́тый; сучкова́тый.

gnash /næʃ/ *v.t.*: **~ one's teeth** скрежета́ть (*impf.*) зуба́ми.

gnat /næt/ *n.* кома́р, мо́шка.

gnaw /nɔː/ *v.t. & i.* (*p.p.* **gnawed** *or* **gnawn**) грызть (*impf.*); **the dog ~ed (at) a bone** соба́ка глода́ла кость; **rats ~ed away the woodwork** кры́сы изгры́зли де́рево; **~ing pangs of hunger** мучи́тельные при́ступы го́лода; **~ing anxiety** грызу́щее беспоко́йство.

gneiss /naɪs/ *n.* (*geol.*) гнейс.

gnome /nəʊm/ *n.* (*goblin etc.*) гном.

Gnostic /ˈnɒstɪk/ *n.* гно́стик.

● *adj.* гности́ческий.

Gnosticism /ˈnɒstɪˌsɪz(ə)m/ *n.* гностици́зм.

GNP (*abbr. of* ***Gross National Product***) ВНП (валово́й национа́льный проду́кт).

gnu /nuː/, /njuː/ *n.* гну (*m. indecl.*).

go /gəʊ/ *n.* (*pl.* **~es**) **1** (*movement, animation*) движе́ние; ход; **she's on the ~ from morning to night** она́ с утра́ до ве́чера на нога́х; **she has no ~ in her** нет в ней изю́минки/огонька́ (*coll.*). **2** (*turn, attempt, shot*) попы́тка; **now it's my ~** тепе́рь моя́ о́чередь; **why don't you have a ~?** почему́ бы вам не попро́бовать?; **he scored 50 in one ~** он набра́л 50 очко́в в одно́м захо́де. **3** (*coll., success*) успе́х; **he tried to make a ~ of it** он стара́лся доби́ться успе́ха (в э́том де́ле); **it's no ~** э́то де́ло безнадёжное. **4**: **let ~ of** отпус|ка́ть, -ти́ть.

● *v.i.* (*3rd pers. sing. pres.* **goes;** *past* **went;** *p.p.* **gone**) (*see also* Agone) **1** (*on foot*) (*det.*) идти́; (*indet.*) ходи́ть; (*ride etc.*) (*det.*) е́хать; (*indet.*) е́здить; (*by train*) е́хать по́ездом; (*by plane*) лете́ть (*det.*) (самолётом); **the clock is ~ing** часы́ иду́т/хо́дят; **this train ~es to London** э́тот по́езд идёт в Ло́ндон; **he went cycling** он пое́хал ката́ться на велосипе́де; **who ~es there?** кто идёт?; **mind how you ~!** осторо́жно! **2** (*fig., with general idea of motion or direction*): **~!** (*at games*) марш; **from the word ~** (*fig.*) с са́мого нача́ла; **where do we ~ from here?** (*what is next step or development?*) что же да́льше?; **this road ~es to York** э́та доро́га ведёт в Йорк; **he ~es to school** (*is a schoolboy*) он хо́дит в шко́лу; **he went to** (*was educated at*) **Eton** он око́нчил Йтон; **he went sick** (*mil.*) он получи́л освобожде́ние по боле́зни; **let me ~!** отпусти́те меня́!; **there you ~ again!** ну вот, опя́ть!; **there is still an hour to ~** ещё час в запа́се; **where do these forks ~?** куда́ положи́ть э́ти ви́лки?; **if you follow me, you can't ~ wrong** де́лайте как я, и вы не ошибётесь; **his plans went wrong** с его́ за́мыслами не получи́лось; **his arguments went unheeded** к его́ до́водам не прислу́шались; **the criminal decided to ~ straight** престу́пник реши́л испра́виться. **3** (*with cognate etc. object*): **he went a long way** он пошёл/ушёл далеко́; **they went halves** они́ раздели́ли всё попола́м; **can Britain ~ it alone?** спра́вится ли Великобрита́ния в одино́чку?; **he went one better than me** он превзошёл меня́; **the balloon went 'pop'** шар ло́пнул; **the sheep went 'baa'** овца́ заблея́ла. **4** (*idea of progress or outcome*): **how's it ~ing?** (*health, affairs*) как дела́?; как пожива́ете?; **everything is ~ing well** всё (идёт) хорошо́; **here ~es!** приступа́ю!; **~ easy!** (*slowly, gently*) осторо́жно!; **~ easy with the sugar!** не клади́те сто́лько са́хару!; **he is ~ing strong** он по́лон сил; он молоде́ц; **he is ~ing all out to win** он изо всех сил стара́ется вы́играть; **the party/play went well** вечери́нка/пье́са прошла́ хорошо́; **how did the election ~?** (*who won it?*) как прошли́ вы́боры?; **she is 6 months ~ne** она́ на седьмо́м ме́сяце (бере́менности). **5** (*idea of extension or distance*): **the differences ~ deep** разногла́сия захо́дят глубоко́/далеко́; **I will ~** (*offer*) **as high as £100** я гото́в вы́ложить и сто фу́нтов; **his land ~es as far as the river** его́ зе́мли простира́ются до реки́; **£5 will not ~ far** пяти́ фу́нтов надо́лго не хва́тит; **he will ~ far** (*attain distinction*) он далеко́ пойдёт; **you ~ too far** (*impudence, presumption*) вы захо́дите сли́шком далеко́; **he is far ~ne** (*sick in mind or body*) он совсе́м плох; пло́хо его́ де́ло; **I will ~ so far as to say** я бы да́же сказа́л, что...; **this is all right as far as it ~es** пока́ что всё в поря́дке. **6** (*expr. tenor or tendency*): **how does the poem ~?** как звучи́т э́то стихотворе́ние?; **the story ~es that ...** расска́зывают, что...; **it ~es against the grain** э́то не по нутру́/душе́/вку́су (*кому*); **this ~es to show that he is wrong** э́то пока́зывает, что он не прав; **qualities that ~ to make a hero** ка́чества, необходи́мые геро́ю. **7** (*set out, depart*): **the post ~es at 5 p.m.** по́чта ухо́дит в 5 часо́в дня. **8** (*pass, come to an end, disappear*): **our holiday went in a flash** на́ши кани́кулы пролете́ли мгнове́нно; **as soon as we buy cheese it ~es** не успе́ем мы купи́ть сыр, как его́ уже́ нет; **it's ~ne 4** (*o'clock*) уже́ бо́льше четырёх; пошёл пя́тый час; **the Minister must ~** (*be got rid of*) мини́стр до́лжен уйти́ в отста́вку; **be ~ne!** (*liter.*) убира́йтесь!; **my sight is ~ing** я теря́ю зре́ние; **I wish this pain would ~** хоть бы прошла́ э́та боль!; **all my money is ~ne** все мои́ де́ньги уплы́ли; **his interest in literature has ~ne** у него́ пропа́л интере́с к литерату́ре; **~ing, ~ne!** (*at auction*) кто бо́льше? про́дано!; **the committee is not the same now that George has ~ne** по́сле ухо́да Джо́рджа комите́т уже́ не тот. **9** (*be in a certain state*): **the children ~ barefoot** де́ти хо́дят боси́ком; **I went hungry last night** я не ел вчера́ ве́чером. **10** (*become*): **the milk went sour** молоко́ прокисло́; **she went red in the face** она́ покрасне́ла. **11** (*function, succeed*): **I can't get my watch to ~** у меня́ не заво́дятся часы́; **he made the party ~** он был душо́й о́бщества. **12** (*cease to function, die*): **if the bulb ~es, change it** е́сли ла́мпочка перегори́т, поменя́йте её; **poor old Smith has ~ne** бе́дного Сми́та не ста́ло. **13** (*sound*): **come in when the bell ~es** входи́те, когда́ зазвони́т звоно́к. **14** (*make specified motion*): **~ like this with your left foot** сде́лайте так ле́вой ного́й. **15** (*be known, accepted, usual*): **what he says ~es** его́ сло́во — зако́н; **anything ~es** всё сойдёт; **I let it ~ at that** я реши́л э́то так оста́вить; **it ~es without saying** э́то само́ собо́й разуме́ется **he ~es by the name of Smith** он изве́стен под и́менем Смит; **it is cheap as yachts ~** для я́хты э́то недо́рого. **16** (*be sold, offered for sale*): **the picture went for a song** карти́ну про́дали за бесце́нок; **these cakes are ~ing cheap** э́ти пиро́жные сто́ят дёшево (*or* иду́т по дешёвке). **17** (*expr. impending or predicted action*): **I'm ~ing to sneeze** я сейча́с чихну́; **it's ~ing to rain** собира́ется дождь; **you are ~ing to do as I tell you** вы сде́лаете то, что я вам скажу́; **he's not ~ing to** (*shan't*) **cheat me** меня́ он не проведёт; **he's not ~ing to argue over 25 pence** он не ста́нет спо́рить из-за двадцати́ пяти́ пе́нсов. **18** (*expr. intention*): **I am ~ing to ask him** я реши́л спроси́ть его́. **19** (*emph. v.*): **don't ~ telling him the whole story** не взду́майте рассказа́ть ему́ всё; **he went and told his mother** он взял и рассказа́л ма́тери; **what have you ~ne and done?** ну, что вы там натвори́ли?

● *with preps.*: **how shall I ~ about this?** как мне за э́то взя́ться; **he went about his business** он заня́лся свои́ми дела́ми; **if the price ~es above £50** е́сли цена́ превы́сит 50 фу́нтов; **he went after** (*sought to win*) **the prize** он боро́лся за приз; **the dog went after the hare** соба́ка погнала́сь за за́йцем; **the decision went against them** реше́ние бы́ло не в их по́льзу; **it ~es against my principles** э́то противоре́чит мои́м при́нципам; **he went at it like a bull at a gate** он бро́сился очертя́ го́лову; **he went before the magistrates** он предста́л пе́ред судо́м; **he went** (*passed*) **by the window** он прошёл ми́мо окна́; **his interests went by the board** с его́ интере́сами соверше́нно не посчита́лись; **I ~ by what I hear** я исхожу́ из того́, что слы́шу; **this book is nothing to ~ by** по э́той кни́ге нельзя́ ни о чём суди́ть; **they went down the river** они́ поплы́ли вниз по реке́; **I went for a drink** я отпра́вился вы́пить; **the dog went for his legs** соба́ка хвата́ла его́ за́ ноги; **I went for** (*fetched*) **him** я пошёл за ним; (*attacked, verbally or physically*) я обру́шился на него́; **my efforts went for nothing** мои́ уси́лия ни к чему́ не привели́; **he will always ~ for the best** он всегда́ бу́дет стреми́ться к лу́чшему; **I ~ for that** (*like it: US coll.*) э́то мне по душе́/вку́су; **that ~es for** (*applies to*) **you too** (*e.g. an order*) э́то вас то́же каса́ется; **he went into the house** он вошёл в дом; **the car went into a wall** маши́на вре́залась в сте́ну; **he had to ~ into hospital** ему́ пришло́сь лечь в больни́цу; **I shall not ~ into details** я не бу́ду вдава́ться в подро́бности; **it won't ~ into the box** (*is too big*) э́то не войдёт в коро́бку; **6 into 30 ~es 5 times** шесть соде́ржится в тридцати́ пять раз; **I will ~ into the matter** я э́то де́ло рассмотрю́; **the law ~es into effect** зако́н вхо́дит в си́лу; **they went into mourning** они́ наде́ли тра́ур; **they went into raptures** они́ пришли́ в восто́рг; **he went off his food** он переста́л есть; **he went off his head** он сошёл с ума́; **I've ~ne off prawns** (*Br. coll.*) я разлюби́л креве́тки; **the children wanted to ~ on the swings** де́ти хоте́ли покача́ться на каче́лях; **I am ~ing on a course** я поступа́ю на ку́рсы; **all his money went on food** все его́ де́ньги пошли́/уходи́ли на еду́; **he is ~ne on** (*obsessed by*) **her** он по́ уши влюблён в неё; он помеша́лся на ней; **he went on his way** он пошёл свои́м путём; **we have no evidence to ~ on** для э́того у нас нет никаки́х да́нных; **~ out of sight** исч|еза́ть, -е́знуть и́з виду; **he went out of his mind** он сошёл с ума́; **she went out of her way to help** она́ вся́чески стара́лась помо́чь; **we went over the house** мы осмотре́ли дом; **she went over the floor with a mop** она́ прошла́сь шва́брой по́ полу; **the shell went over his head** снаря́д пролете́л у него́ над голово́й; **his words went right over my head** я пропусти́л его́ слова́ ми́мо уше́й; **I went over his work with him** вме́сте с ним я прошёлся по его́ рабо́те; **we have ~ne over** (*discussed*) **that** мы э́то обсужда́ли; **we went round the gallery** мы обошли́ галере́ю; **we went round the block** мы обошли́ кварта́л; **we have to ~ round the one-way system** здесь прихо́дится де́лать объе́зд из-за односторо́ннего движе́ния; **my trousers won't ~ round me any longer** на мне уже́ не схо́дятся брю́ки; **~ through the main gate!** проходи́те че́рез гла́вные воро́та!; **the ball went through** (*i.e. broke*) **the window** мяч разби́л окно́; **she went through his pockets** она́ обша́рила у него́ все карма́ны; **he has ~ne through a lot** ему́ довело́сь мно́го испыта́ть; **I went through his papers** я просмотре́л его́ бума́ги; **he went through the money in a week** он растра́тил де́ньги за неде́лю; **large sums went through his hands** че́рез его́ ру́ки прошли́ больши́е су́ммы де́нег; **they went through the ceremony** они́ прошли́ че́рез (*or* вы́держали) э́ту церемо́нию; **I'll ~ through the main points again** я хочу́ повтори́ть гла́вные пу́нкты; **the estate went to her nephew** иму́щество перешло́ её племя́ннику; **the prize went to him** он вы́играл приз; **our best thanks ~ to Mr X** мы горячо́ благодари́м г-на X; **he went to great expense** он пошёл на больши́е расхо́ды; **~ to it!** (*Br.*) за де́ло!; **the money will ~ towards a new car** де́ньги пойду́т на поку́пку но́вой маши́ны; **this will ~ a long way towards satisfying him** э́то почти́ по́лностью его́ устро́ит; **he went under an assumed name** он жил под вы́мышленным/чужи́м и́менем; **~ up the hill** поднима́ться (*impf.*)/идти́/е́хать (*both det.*) в го́ру; **he went up the stairs** он стал поднима́ться (*or* пошёл вверх) по ле́стнице; **this tie ~es with your suit** э́тот га́лстук подхо́дит к ва́шему костю́му; **five acres ~ with the house** пять а́кров земли́ отхо́дят с до́мом; **crime ~es with poverty** престу́пность идёт рука́ о́б руку с бе́дностью; **he has been ~ing with her for months** он встреча́ется с ней уже́ не́сколько ме́сяцев; **we went without a holiday** мы обошли́сь без о́тпуска.

● *with advs.*: **~ about** *v.i.*: **he ~es about looking for trouble** он то́лько и де́лает, что ле́зет на рожо́н; **the story is ~ing about that ...** хо́дят слу́хи, что. . .; **they ~ about together** они́ повсю́ду хо́дят вме́сте; **~ ahead!** вперёд!; **~ along** *v.i.*: **I went along to see** я пошёл посмотре́ть; **they sang as they went along** они́ шли с пе́снями; **the play got better as it went along** к концу́ пье́са смотре́лась лу́чше; **will you ~ along to the station with him?** вы пойдёте с ним до ста́нции?; вы доведёте его́ до ста́нции?; **I cannot ~ along with that** я не могу́ с э́тим согласи́ться; **~ around** *v.i.*: **he went around with a long face** он ходи́л/разгу́ливал с ки́слым ви́дом; **he is ~ing around with my sister** он встреча́ется с мое́й сестро́й; (*US*) = **~ round** *v.i.*; **~ away** *v.i.* уходи́ть, уйти́; **~ away!** уходи́те!; **~ back** *v.i.* идти́ (*det.*) наза́д; возвра|ща́ться, -ти́ться; **to ~ back to what I was saying** возвраща́ясь к тому́, что я сказа́л; **he went back on his word** он не сдержа́л своего́ сло́ва; **this custom ~es back to the 15th century** э́тот обы́чай восхо́дит к пятна́дцатому ве́ку; **~ before** *v.i.* (*die*): **those who have ~ne before** отоше́дшие в мир ино́й; **~ below** (*deck*) *v.i.*: **when the storm broke they went below** когда́ разрази́лся шторм, они́ спусти́лись в каю́ту; **~ by** *v.i.*: **he let the opportunity ~ by** он упусти́л слу́чай; **as the years ~ by** с года́ми; с тече́нием лет; **in days ~ne by** в мину́вшие дни; **he has just ~ne by** он то́лько что прошёл ми́мо; **~ down** *v.i.*: спус|ка́ться, -ти́ться; **he went down on his knees** он опусти́лся на коле́ни; **the sun went down** со́лнце се́ло; **the ship went down** кора́бль затону́л; **she went down with flu** (*Br.*) она́ слегла́ с гри́ппом; **the undergraduates ~ down in July** (*Br.*) студе́нты зака́нчивают заня́тия в ию́ле; **he has ~ne down in the world** он опусти́лся; **prices are ~ing down** це́ны па́дают; **~ing down!** (*of lift*) вниз!; **the pill won't ~ down** табле́тка не прогла́тывается; **his story went down well** его́ расска́з был хорошо́ при́нят; **the wind has ~ne down** ве́тер ути́х; **~ forth** *v.i.*: **the order went forth** прика́з был опублико́ван; **~ forward** *v.i.*: **the plan went forward** план вступи́л в де́йствие; **~ in** *v.i.* (*enter*) входи́ть, войти́; **the sun went in** со́лнце зашло́; **he ~es in for sport** он занима́ется спо́ртом; **he went in for the competition** он при́нял уча́стие в ко́нкурсе; **~ off** *v.i.*: **he went off without a word** он ушёл без еди́ного сло́ва; **Hamlet ~es off** (*exits*) Га́млет ухо́дит; **the servant went off with** (*stole*) **the spoons** слуга́ укра́л ло́жки и скры́лся; **the goods went off** (*were sent*) **today** това́р отпра́вили сего́дня; **the gun went off** ружьё вы́стрелило; **has the baby ~ne off** (*to sleep*) **?** ребёнок засну́л?; **the alarm clock went off** буди́льник зазвене́л; **the light has ~ne off** свет пога́с; **the fruit has ~ne off** (*Br.*) фру́кты погни́ли; **his work has ~ne off lately** в после́днее вре́мя он стал рабо́тать ху́же; **the party went off well** вечери́нка прошла́ хорошо́; **it went off according to plan** всё прошло́ согла́сно пла́ну; **~ on** *v.i.*: **the shoe will not ~ on** э́тот боти́нок не ле́зет; **the lights went on** загоре́лся свет; **I can't ~ on any longer** я так бо́льше не могу́; **~ on from where you left off** продолжа́йте с того́ ме́ста, где останови́лись; **shall we ~ on to the next item?** дава́йте перейдём к сле́дующему пу́нкту?; **~ on playing!** продолжа́йте игра́ть; **~ on!** (*coll., expr. incredulity*) да ну́!; (*urging action*) дава́йте!; валя́йте!; **that is enough to ~** (*or* **be ~ing**) **on with** (*Br.*) э́того пока́ хва́тит; **he went on to say that ...** зате́м он сказа́л, что. . .; **it is ~ing on for a year since we met** (*Br.*) уже́ почти́ год, как мы познако́мились; **what is ~ing on here?** что тут происхо́дит?; **~ on at** (*nag*) пили́ть (*impf.*); набра́сываться (*impf.*) на + *a.*; **he does ~ on so** (*coll.*) он ве́чно нуди́т; **he went on ahead of the others** он опереди́л/обогна́л остальны́х; **he went on** (*stage*) **after the interval** он вы́шел на сце́ну по́сле антра́кта; **the show must ~ on** что бы ни случи́лось, спекта́кль продолжа́ется; **as time ~es on** со вре́менем; **~ out** *v.i.* (*exit*) выходи́ть, вы́йти; **the light went out** свет пога́с; **he went out to Australia** он вы́ехал в Австра́лию; **the tide was ~ing out** шёл отли́в; **our hearts ~ out to them** мы всей душо́й с ни́ми; **he went all out for success** он рва́лся к успе́ху; **~ over** *v.i.*: **he went over to the shop** он пошёл в магази́н; **~ over to the enemy** перейти́ (*pf.*) в стан врага́; **he went**

over to France он переправился во Францию; **the country went over to decimal coinage** страна перешла на десятичную монетную систему; **~ round** *v.i.*: **I went round to see him** (*Br.*) я пошёл его навестить; **we had to ~ round by the park** (*Br.*) нам пришлось идти в обход через парк; **he ~es round collecting money** (*Br.*) он обходит всех и собирает деньги; **is there enough food to ~ round?** (*Br.*) хватит ли еды на всех?; **everything's ~ing round** (*describing dizziness*) всё идёт кругом; **~ through** *v.i.*: **I cannot ~ through with the plan** я не могу осуществить этот план; **the deal went through** сделка состоялась; **has their divorce ~ne through?** они уже развелись?; **the bill went through** (*parl.*) проект был принят; **~ together** *v.i.*: **they were ~ing together** (*keeping company*) **for years** они встречались многие годы; **these colours** (*Br.*), **colors** (*US*) **~ together** эти цвета гармонируют; **poverty and disease ~ together** где бедность, там и болезни; **~ under** *v.i.*: **it is the poor who ~ under** бедному хуже всех; **his business went under** его дело лопнуло; **~ up** *v.i.* подн|иматься, -яться; **he went up to bed** он пошёл спать; **I went up to town** я поехал в город; **prices have ~ne up** цены повысились; **the lights went up** загорелся свет; **houses are ~ing up** (*being built*) дома поднимаются/строятся/растут; **the house went up in flames** дом сгорел; **his plans went up in smoke** его планы развеялись как дым; **he ~es up to Oxford next year** (*Br.*) он поступит в Оксфордский университет на будущий год; **he is ~ing up in the world** он выбивается в люди.

● *cpds.* **~-ahead** *n.* разрешение, «добро», «зелёная улица»; *adj.* предприимчивый; настырный; **~-between** *n.* посредник; **~-cart** *n.* (*handcart*) ручная тележка; (*pushchair*) (детская) коляска; (*for racing, also* **~-kart**) карт; **~-getter** *n.* (*coll.*) проныра (*c.g.*); **~-getting** *adj.* (*coll.*) пронырливый, пробивной; **~-slow** *n.* (*Br.*) частичная забастовка, «медленная работа».

goad /gəʊd/ *n.* кол; (*fig.*) стимул.

● *v.t.* погонять (*impf.*); (*prod*) пришпори|вать, -ть; (*tease, torment*) раздражать (*impf.*).

goal /gəʊl/ *n.* **1** (*destination, objective*) цель; **he set himself a difficult ~** он поставил себе трудную задачу/цель. **2** (*sport*) ворот|а (*pl., g.* —); **Jackson was in ~** в воротах стоял Джексон; **keep ~** защи|щать, -тить ворота; (*point scored*) гол; **our team won by three ~s to one** наша команда выиграла со счётом три — один.

● *cpds.* **~-keeper** *n.* вратарь (*m.*); **~-kick** *n.* удар от ворот; **~-post** *n.* штанга.

goalie /'gəʊlɪ/ *n.* (*coll.*) вратарь (*m.*).

goat /gəʊt/ *n.* **1** коза; (*male*) козёл; **he gets my ~** (*sl.*) он меня раздражает; **separate the sheep from the ~s** (*fig.*) отделить (*pf.*) агнцев от козлищ. **2** (*fig., lecherous man*) кобель (*m.*), (старый) козёл.

● *cpds.* **~-herd** *n.* козопас; **~skin** *n.* козья шуба; (*for wine*) бурдюк.

goatee /gəʊ'ti:/ *n.* козлиная бородка.

gob[1] /gɒb/ *n.* (*Br. vulg.*) (*of spittle*) плевок.

gob[2] /gɒb/ *n.* (*Br. vulg.*) (*mouth*) глотка; **shut your ~!** заткни глотку!

gobbet /'gɒbɪt/ *n.* (*lit., fig.*) кусок.

gobble[1] /'gɒb(ə)l/ *v.t.* жрать, по-/со-.

● *v.i.* лопать, с-; быстро и шумно есть (*impf.*).

gobble[2] /'gɒb(ə)l/ *v.i.* (*of a turkey*) кулдыкать (*impf.*).

gobbledygook /'gɒb(ə)ldɪ,gu:k/, /-,gʊk/ *n.* (*sl.*) напыщенность речи; бюрократический жаргон.

Gobelin /'gəʊbəlɪn/, /gɔ'blæ̃/ *n.* (*tapestry*) гобелен.

goblet /'gɒblɪt/ *n.* кубок, бокал.

goblin /'gɒblɪn/ *n.* домовой.

goby /'gəʊbɪ/ *n.* (*zool.*) бычок.

god /gɒd/ *n.* **1** (*deity*) бог; **in the lap of the ~s** у Христа за пазухой; **ye ~s!** (*joc.*) Боже мой!; силы небесные!; (*fig., revered object or person*) идол, кумир; (**G~**: *supreme being*) Бог; божество; **act of G~** стихийное бедствие; **Almighty G~** всемогущий Бог; **G~ bless** (*you*)**!** благослови вас Бог; (*after sneeze*) будьте здоровы!; **my G~!** Боже мой!; Господи!; **G~ damn you!** чёрт вас возьми!; **G~ help you!** да поможет вам Бог!; **on G~'s earth** на божьем/белом свете; **G~ forbid!** Боже сохрани!; избави Бог!; **so help me G~** Господь свидетель; **G~ knows where he is** Бог знает, где он; **I've suffered enough, G~ knows** видит Бог — я страдал достаточно; **for G~'s sake!** ради Бога!; **thank G~ (for that)!** слава Богу!; **G~'s truth** святая правда; **G~ willing** даст Бог; с божьей помощью; если будем живы; **he is with G~** его Бог прибрал. **2** (*pl., theatr.*) галёрка; **a seat in the ~s** место на галёрке.

● *cpds.* **~-awful** *adj.* (*coll.*) жуткий, богомерзкий; **~child** *n.* крестни|к (*fem.* -ца); **~dam** *adj.* (*US sl.*) чёртов; **~daughter** *n.* крестница; **~father** *n.* крёстный (отец); **~-fearing** *adj.* богобоязненный; **~-forsaken** *adj.* заброшенный; **~-forsaken place** медвежий угол; **~mother** *n.* крёстная (мать); **~parent** *n.* крёстный (отец); крёстная (мать); **~send** *n.* находка; ≈ сам Бог послал; **~son** *n.* крестник; **~-speed!** *int.* с Богом!

goddess /'gɒdɪs/ *n.* богиня.

godhead /'gɒdhed/ *n.* божественность; божество.

godless /'gɒdlɪs/ *adj.* безбожный.

godlike /'gɒdlaɪk/ *adj.* богоподобный.

godliness /'gɒdlɪnɪs/ *n.* набожность.

godly /'gɒdlɪ/ *adj.* (**godlier, godliest**) набожный.

goer /'gəʊə(r)/ *n.* **1** (*performer*): **this watch is a good ~** эти часы отлично идут. **2** (*coll., energetic person*) упорный человек. **3**: **comers and ~s** приезжающие и отъезжающие.

goes /gəʊz/ *3rd pers. sing. pres. of* ⇒**go**

gofer /'gəʊfə(r)/ *n.* (*US, coll.*) ишак (*coll.*); мальчик/девушка на побегушках.

goffer /'gəʊfə(r)/, /'gɒf-/ *v.t.* гофрировать (*impf., pf.*).

goggle /'gɒg(ə)l/ *v.i.* таращить (*impf.*) глаза; **she ~ed at the news** от этой новости у неё глаза на лоб полезли.

● *cpds.* **~-box** *n.* (*Br. sl.*) телик, «ящик»; **~-eyed** *adj.* пучеглазый.

goggles /'gɒg(ə)lz/ *n.* тёмные/защитные очк|и (*pl., g.* -ов).

going /'gəʊɪŋ/ *n.* **1** (*departure*) отъезд, уход; **there will be no tears at his ~** по нём плакать не будут. **2** (*state of track*) состояние беговой дорожки; **the next mile is rough ~** следующая миля будет трудной. **3** (*progress, speed*) скорость; **fifty miles an hour is good ~** 50 миль в час — это хорошая скорость; **let's get out while the ~ is good** смоемся, пока не поздно; **this book is heavy ~** эта книга трудно читается; **he is heavy ~** он нудный человек; **the conversation was heavy ~** разговор не клеился.

● *adj.* **1** (*working, flourishing*): **a ~ concern** действующее предприятие. **2** (*Br., to be had*): **one of the best newspapers ~** одна из лучших нынешних газет; **there are plenty of sandwiches ~** бутербродов сколько угодно.

● *cpd.* **~-away** *adj.*: **~-away dress** дорожное платье; **~-over** *n.* (*coll., scrutiny*) осмотр; (*coll., cleaning*) прочистка; (*sl., beating*) трёпка; **~s-on** *n. pl.* (*coll.*) поведение; поступки (*m. pl.*); дела (*nt. pl.*); «делишки» (*nt. pl.*); **there have been strange ~s-on lately** в последнее время творятся странные вещи.

goitre /'gɔɪtə(r)/ (*US* **goiter**) *n.* зоб; базедова болезнь.

gold /gəʊld/ *n. & adj.* (*metal*) золото; **~ braid** сусальное золото; **~ medal** золотая медаль; **~ plate** (*tableware*) золотая посуда; (*gilding*) позолота; **(made of) solid ~** из чистого золота; **the ~ standard** золотой стандарт; **a currency backed by ~** валюта, обеспеченная золотом; **£50 in ~** 50 фунтов золотом; **he's as good as ~** (*of child*) он золото, а не ребёнок; **she has a heart of ~** у неё золотое сердце.

● *cpds.* **~-bearing** *adj.* золотоносный; **~-digger** *n.* золотоискатель (*m.*); (*coll., of woman*) вымогательница; **~-dust** *n.* золотой песок; **~field** *n.* золотой прииск; **~finch** *n.* щегол; **~fish** *n.* золотая рыбка; **~-leaf** *n.* сусальное золото; **~-mine** *n.* золотой рудник; (*fig.*): **the shop is a ~-mine** этот магазин — золотое дно; **~-rush** *n.* золотая лихорадка; **~smith** *n.* золотых дел мастер.

golden /'gəʊld(ə)n/ *adj.* (*lit., fig.*) золотой; (*of colour*) золотистый; **the ~ age** золотой век; **~ rod** (*bot.*) золотарник; **~ syrup** (*Br.*) светлая

G

па́тока; **receive a ~ handshake on retirement** получи́ть (*pf.*) вознагражде́ние при ухо́де на пе́нсию; **~ hours** золота́я пора́; **the ~ mean** золота́я середи́на; **miss a ~ opportunity** упусти́ть (*pf.*) редча́йшую возмо́жность; **celebrate one's ~ wedding** пра́зсновать, от- золоту́ю сва́дьбу.

● *cpd.* **~-haired** *adj.* золотоволо́сый.

golf /gɒlf/ *n.* гольф.

● *v.i.* игра́ть (*impf.*) в гольф.

● *cpds.* **~-ball** *n.* мяч для игры́ в гольф; **~-club** *n.* (*association*) клуб люби́телей игры́ в гольф; (*implement*) клю́шка; **~-course, ~-links** *nn.* площа́дка/по́ле для игры́ в гольф.

golfer /ˈgɒlfə(r)/ *n.* игро́к в гольф.

golfing /ˈgɒlfɪŋ/ *n.* игра́ в гольф.

golliwog /ˈgɒlɪˌwɒg/ *n.* чёрная ку́кла.

golly /ˈgɒlɪ/ *int.* (*coll.*) Бо́же мой!; **by ~!** ей-Бо́гу!

gonad /ˈgəʊnæd/ *n.* гона́да; полова́я железа́.

gondola /ˈgɒndələ/ *n.* (*boat; airship car*) гондо́ла.

gondolier /ˌgɒndəˈlɪə(r)/ *n.* гондолье́р.

gone /gɒn/ *adj.* (*see also* ⇒**go**).
1 (*departed, past*) уе́хавший; уше́дший.
2 (*US, doomed, hopeless*) пропа́щий.
3 (*dead*) уме́рший, усо́пший. **4** (*coll., in a stupor, drunk*) отъе́хавший (*sl.*).

goner /ˈgɒnə(r)/ *n.* (*sl.*) ко́нченый челове́к, доходя́га (*sl.*).

gong /gɒŋ/ *n.* (*instrument*) гонг.

gonorrhoea /ˌgɒnəˈrɪə/ (*US* **gonorrhea**) *n.* гоноре́я.

goo /guː/ *n.* (*coll.*) что-н. кле́йкое, ли́пкое.

good /gʊd/ *n.* **1** (**~ness, ~ action**) добро́, бла́го; **there is some ~ in everyone** в ка́ждом челове́ке есть что́-то хоро́шее; **he spends his life doing ~** всю жизнь он де́лает/твори́т добро́; **he is up to no ~** он заду́мал что́-то недо́брое.
2 (*benefit*) по́льза; **drink it! it will do you ~** вы́пейте э́то — вам поле́зно; **it's no ~ complaining** что про́ку жа́ловаться?; **that will do no ~** э́то не принесёт по́льзы; **what's the ~ of making a fuss?** како́й смысл поднима́ть шум?; **it's all to the ~** всё к лу́чшему; **for the ~ of the cause** для по́льзы де́ла; **much ~ may it do you!** (*iron.*) ну и на здоро́вье.
3: **for ~** (*permanently*) навсегда́.
4 (*pl., property*) добро́; **~s and chattels** пожи́тк|и (*pl., g.* -ов).
5 (*pl., merchandise*) това́р(ы); **are you sure he can deliver the ~s?** (*coll.,fig.*) а вы уве́рены, что он не подведёт?; **~s train** това́рный по́езд; **~s vehicle** грузово́й автомоби́ль/фурго́н.

● *adj.* (**better, best**) **1** (*in most senses*) хоро́ший; до́брый; (*of food*) вку́сный; **~ old Dad!** ай да папа́ша!; **that shows ~ sense** в э́том ви́ден здра́вый смысл; **~ idea!** прекра́сная мысль!; **very ~** (*expr. acquiescence*) ла́дно; хорошо́; (*servant's reply*) (*arch.*) слу́шаюсь; **~ works** до́брые дела́; **a ~ player** си́льный игро́к; **lead a ~ life** вести́ (*det.*) досто́йную жизнь; **the G~ Book** би́блия; **G~ Friday** Страстна́я Пя́тница; **~ heavens!** Бо́же мой!
2 (*of health, condition etc.*) хоро́ший; здоро́вый; **I don't feel so ~ today** (*coll.*) я себя́ нева́жно чу́вствую сего́дня; **these eggs are not very ~** э́ти я́йца не о́чень све́жие; **apples are ~ for you** я́блоки поле́зны для здоро́вья.
3 (*favourable, fortunate*): **~ luck!** жела́ю успе́ха; **a ~ sign** до́брый знак; **it's a ~ thing we stayed at home** хорошо́, что мы оста́лись до́ма; **he's gone, and a ~ thing too!** он ушёл, и сла́ва Бо́гу!; **~ for you!** (*coll.*) молодчи́на (*c.g.*).
4 (*kind*) любе́зный, до́брый; **be a ~ fellow** бу́дьте (так) добры́; **be so ~ as to let me in** бу́дьте добры́, впусти́те меня́; **that's very ~ of you** э́то о́чень ми́ло с ва́шей стороны́.
5 (*of skill*): **~ at** спосо́бный к + *d.*; си́льный в + *p.*; **she's ~ at maths** она́ спосо́бна к матема́тике; **he is ~ at French** он силён во францу́зском; **he is no ~ at his job** он взя́лся не за своё де́ло.
6 (*suitable*) подходя́щий.
7 (*well-behaved*) воспи́танный; послу́шный; **be ~!** веди́ себя́ прили́чно!; **be a ~ boy!** веди́ себя́ хорошо́!; будь у́мницей!; **as ~ as gold** (*of child*) зо́лотко; **~ dog!** молоде́ц, соба́ка.
8 (*var.*): **~ morning!** до́брое у́тро!; **I bade him ~ night** я пожела́л ему́ споко́йной но́чи; **it's ~ to see you** прия́тно вас ви́деть; **a ~ joke** хоро́шая/заба́вная шу́тка; **~ looks** краси́вая вне́шность; **he's had a ~ few, many drinks already** он уже́ успе́л изря́дно вы́пить; **a ~ deal of noise** мно́го шу́ма; **a ~ way off** дово́льно далеко́; **a ~ while ago** давны́м-давно́; **the jug holds a ~ pint** кувши́н вмеща́ет до́брую пи́нту; **he was as ~ as his word** он сдержа́л своё сло́во; **he as ~ as refused to go** он факти́чески отказа́лся идти́; **the car is ~ for another 5 years** э́тот автомоби́ль прослу́жит ещё лет 5; **his credit is ~ for £5,000** он мо́жет по́льзоваться креди́том в 5000 фу́нтов.
9: **make ~** *v.t.* (*fulfil*) исп|олня́ть, -о́лнить; (*substantiate*) обосно́в|ывать, -а́ть; (*recompense for*) возме|ща́ть, -сти́ть; (*repair*) прив|оди́ть, -ести́ в поря́док; *v.i.* (*coll., succeed*) преусп|ева́ть, -е́ть.

● *cpds.* **~-for-nothing** *n.* негодя́й, безде́льник; *adj.* никуды́шный; никчёмный; **~-humoured** (*US* **-humored**) *adj.* доброду́шный; **~-looking** *adj.* краси́вый; хоро́ш/хороша́ собо́й; **~-natured** *adj.* доброду́шный; **~-neighbourliness** (*US* **-neighborliness**) *n.* добрососе́дство; **~-night** *n.* проща́ние пе́ред сном; *int.* споко́йной но́чи!; **~-tempered** *adj.* доброду́шный; **~-timer** *n.* гуля́ка (*m.*); весельча́к; **~will** *n.* (*friendship*) доброжела́тельность; (*willingness*) до́брая во́ля; (*of business*) репута́ция.

goodbye /gʊdˈbaɪ/ *n.* проща́ние; **a ~ kiss** проща́льный поцелу́й; **wave ~** помаха́ть (*pf.*) руко́й на проща́нье.

● *int.* до свида́ния!; проща́йте.

goodish /ˈgʊdɪʃ/ *adj.* (*fairly good*) дово́льно хоро́ший, неплохо́й; (*fairly large*) поря́дочный.

goodly /ˈgʊdlɪ/ *adj.* (**goodlier, goodliest**) (*large*) кру́пный, значи́тельный.

goodness /ˈgʊdnɪs/ *n.* **1** (*virtue*) доброта́. **2** (*kindness*) любе́зность; **please have the ~ to move** бу́дьте любе́зны, подви́ньтесь. **3** (*quality, nourishment*): **these apples are full of ~** э́ти я́блоки о́чень поле́зны, пита́тельны. **4** (*euph., God*): **G~ me!** вот те на́!; **G~ (only) knows** кто его́ зна́ет!; **I wish to ~ (that)** ... как бы мне хоте́лось, что́бы...; **thank ~!** сла́ва Бо́гу!

goody /ˈgʊdɪ/ *n.* (*coll.*) **1** (*sweetmeat*) конфе́та. **2** (*Br., character in film etc.*) положи́тельный геро́й. **3** (*int., coll.*) прекра́сно!; замеча́тельно!; отли́чно! **4**: **~-~** па́инька (*c.g.*).

gooey /ˈguːɪ/ (*coll.*) *adj.* (**gooier, gooiest**) кле́йкий; ли́пкий.

goof /guːf/ *n.* балбе́с, пе́нтюх (*coll.*).

● *v.i.* (*US sl.*) зава́л|ивать, -и́ть де́ло.

goon /guːn/ *n.* (*sl.*) (*stupid person*) болва́н; (*US, thug*) громи́ла (*m.*).

goosander /guːˈsændə(r)/ *n.* большо́й крoха́ль.

goose /guːs/ *n.* (*pl.* **geese**) **1** гусь (*m.*); (*fem., also*) гуся́ня; **his ~ is cooked** (*fig.*) его́ пе́сенка спе́та; **he killed the ~ that laid the golden eggs** (*prov.*) он уби́л ку́рицу, несу́щую золоты́е я́йца; **he couldn't say bo(o) to a ~** (*fig.*) он боязли́в как лань; **wild-~-chase** (*fig.*) сумасбро́дная зате́я; пого́ня за химе́рами.
2 (*simpleton*) простофи́ля (*c.g.*).

● *cpds.* **~berry** *n.* крыжо́вник (*collect.*); я́года крыжо́вника; **play ~berry** (*Br. coll.*) ока́з|ываться, -а́ться тре́тьим ли́шним; **~-flesh** *n.* гуся́тина; гуси́ная ко́жа; **it gives me ~-flesh** у меня́ от э́того мура́шки по те́лу бе́гают; **~-step** *n.* (*coll.*) строево́й/гуси́ный шаг.

gopher /ˈgəʊfə(r)/ *n.* го́фер; колумби́йский су́слик.

gore[1] /gɔː(r)/ *n.* (*blood*) проли́тая/запёкшаяся кровь.

gore[2] /gɔː(r)/ *n.* (*gusset*) клин, ла́стовица.

gore[3] /gɔː(r)/ *v.t.* бода́ть, за-.

gorge /gɔːdʒ/ *n.* **1** (*ravine*) уще́лье.
2: **the sight made my ~ rise** меня́ затошни́ло от э́того зре́лища.

● *v.t. & i.* объ|еда́ться, -е́сться; **the lion ~ed (itself) on its prey** лев жа́дно поглоща́л свою́ добы́чу.

gorgeous /ˈgɔːdʒəs/ *adj.* (*magnificent*) великоле́пный; (*richly coloured*) кра́сочный; (*coll., enjoyable*) изуми́тельный; **we had a ~ time** мы великоле́пно провели́ вре́мя.

Gorgon /ˈgɔːgən/ *n.* (*lit.*) Горго́на; Меду́за; (*fig.*) мегера, ве́дьма.

gorilla /gəˈrɪlə/ *n.* гори́лла.

G

gormless /'gɔ:mlɪs/ *adj.* (*Br. dial. and coll.*) безду́мный; дура́шливый.

gorse /gɔ:s/ *n.* (*bot.*) утёсник обыкнове́нный.

gory /'gɔ:rɪ/ *adj.* (**gorier, goriest**) (*covered in blood*) окрова́вленный; (*involving bloodshed*) кровопроли́тный; **~ details** крова́вые подро́бности.

gosh /gɒʃ/ *int.* (*coll.*) Бо́же мой!

goshawk /'gɒshɔ:k/ *n.* тетеревя́тник.

gosling /'gɒzlɪŋ/ *n.* гусёнок.

gospel /'gɒsp(ə)l/ *n.* ева́нгелие; **preach the ~** пропове́довать (*impf.*) Ева́нгелие; **the G~ according to St. John** Ева́нгелие от Иоа́нна; от Иоа́нна свято́е благове́ствование; (*fig.*): **~ truth** и́стинная пра́вда; **she takes everything for ~** она́ всё принима́ет на ве́ру.

gossamer /'gɒsəmə(r)/ *n.* **1** (*spider web*) осе́нняя паути́нка. **2** (*gauzy material*) газ.

gossip /'gɒsɪp/ *n.* **1** (*talk*) спле́тня; **they met to have a good ~** они́ встре́тились, что́бы хороше́нько посплéтничать. **2** (*person addicted to ~ing*) спле́тни|к (*fem.* -ца). **3** (*attr.*): **~ column/writer** коло́нка/репортёр све́тской хро́ники.

● *v.i.* (**gossiped, gossiping**) спле́тничать, на-.

gossipy /'gɒsɪpɪ/ *adj.* болтли́вый, лю́бящий посплéтничать.

got /gɒt/ *past and p.p. of* ⇒**get**

Goth /gɒθ/ *n.* гот.

Gothic /'gɒθɪk/ *n.* **1** (*language*) го́тский язы́к. **2** (*archit.*) готи́ческий стиль. **3** (*script*) готи́ческий шрифт.

● *adj.* (*of style or script*) готи́ческий.

gotten /'gɒt(ə)n/ *US p.p. of* ⇒**get**

gouache /gʊ'ɑ:ʃ/, /gwɑ:ʃ/ *n.* гуа́шь.

gouge /gaʊdʒ/ *n.* полукру́глое долото́.

● *v.t.* выда́лбливать, вы́долбить; **~ s.o.'s eyes out** выка́лывать, вы́колоть кому́-н. глаза́.

goulash /'gu:læʃ/ *n.* гуля́ш.

gourd /gʊəd/ *n.* (*bot.*) горля́нка, ты́ква буты́лочная; (*vessel*) сосу́д из ты́квы.

gourmandize /'gɔ:mən,daɪz/ *v.i.* объеда́ться (*impf.*).

gourmet /'gʊəmeɪ/ *n.* гурма́н; гастроно́м.

gout /gaʊt/ *n.* пода́гра.

govern /'gʌv(ə)n/ *v.t.* **1** (*rule; also v.i.*) пра́вить (*impf.*) + *i.*; **~ing body** (*of hospital, school etc.*) дире́кция, правле́ние; (*control, influence*) руководи́ть (*impf.*) + *i.*; управля́ть (*impf.*) + *i.*; **he finds it hard to ~ his tongue** он несде́ржан на язы́к; **be ~ed by my advice!** сле́дуйте моему́ сове́ту. **2** (*apply to*): **the same principle ~s both cases** оди́н и тот же при́нцип примени́м в обо́их слу́чаях. **3** (*gram.*) управля́ть (*impf.*) + *i.*

governance /'gʌvənəns/ *n.* управле́ние (*чем*); руково́дство (*чем*).

governess /'gʌvənɪs/ *n.* гуверна́нтка.

government /'gʌvənmənt/ *n.* (*rule*) правле́ние; (*system*) фо́рма правле́ния; **local ~** ме́стное самоуправле́ние; (*pol.*) прави́тельство; **central ~** центра́льное прави́тельство; **the Prime Minister formed a ~** премье́р-мини́стр сформирова́л прави́тельство; **G~ House** (*Br.*) резиде́нция губерна́тора; **~ securities** госуда́рственные це́нные бума́ги.

governmental /,gʌvən'ment(ə)l/ *adj.* прави́тельственный.

governor /'gʌvənə(r)/ *n.* **1** (*ruling official*) губерна́тор. **2** (*member of governing body*) член правле́ния. **3** (*Br. coll., boss*) хозя́ин; шеф. **4** (*regulating mechanism*) регуля́тор.

● *cpd.* **~-general** *n.* генера́л-губерна́тор.

governorship /'gʌvənəʃɪp/ *n.* губерна́торство.

gown /gaʊn/ *n.* (*woman's*) пла́тье; (*academic or official*) ма́нтия.

GP (*abbr. of* ***general practitioner***) врач о́бщей пра́ктики; **who's your ~?** кто ваш участко́вый врач?

grab /græb/ *n.* **1** (*snatch*): **he made a ~ for the money** он попыта́лся схвати́ть де́ньги. **2** (*mechanical device*) экскава́тор; черпа́к.

● *v.t. & i.* (**grabbed, grabbing**) хва́т|ывать, -и́ть; **he ~bed me by the lapels** он схвати́л меня́ за ла́цканы; **how does that ~ you?** (*coll.*) что вы на э́то ска́жете?

grace /greɪs/ *n.* **1** (*elegance*) гра́ция, изя́щество; **airs and ~s** (*iron.*) жема́нство; (*quality*): **his speech had the saving ~ of brevity** его́ речь отлича́лась спаси́тельной кра́ткостью. **2** (*favour*) благосклóнность; **act of ~** поми́лование; **by the ~ of God** бо́жьей ми́лостью; **there, but for the ~ of God, go I** то́лько ми́лость госпо́дня уберегла́ меня́ от тако́й же судьбы́; **I am not in his good ~s** я у него́ в неми́лости; (*dispensation*) отсро́чка; **the law allows 3 days' ~** зако́н даёт 3 дня отсро́чки (*or* льго́тных дня); **he fell from ~** он сошёл с пути́ и́стинного; (*fell into disgrace*) он впал в неми́лость; (*sense of the seemly*): **he had the ~ to apologize** он был насто́лько такти́чен, что извини́лся; (*easy or pleasant manner*): **he could lose the game with a good ~** он уме́л прои́грывать с досто́инством; **with an ill** (*or* **a bad**) **~** нелюбе́зно; (*prayer before meal*) моли́тва; **say ~** моли́ться (*impf.*) пе́ред едо́й. **3** (*myth.*): **the three G~s** три гра́ции. **4** (*courtesy title*): **his G~** све́тлость/сия́тельство; (*eccl.*) его́ преосвящéнство.

● *v.t.* удост|а́ивать, -о́ить; награ|жда́ть, -ди́ть; **he ~d the meeting with his presence** он удосто́ил собра́ние свои́м прису́тствием; **she is ~d with good looks** она́ наделена́ прия́тной вне́шностью.

● *cpd.* **~-note** *n.* (*mus.*) мели́зм; (*vocal*) фиориту́ра.

graceful /'greɪsfʊl/ *adj.* грацио́зный; изя́щный.

gracefulness /'greɪsfʊlnɪs/ *n.* грацио́зность; изя́щество.

graceless /'greɪslɪs/ *adj.* (*rude*) нетакти́чный; бессты́дный; (*inelegant*) неуклю́жий.

gracious /'greɪʃəs/ *adj.* ми́лостивый; любе́зный; **~ living** краси́вая жизнь.

● *int.*: **good(ness) ~ (me)!** ба́тюшки!; Бо́же мой!

graciousness /'greɪʃəsnɪs/ *n.* ми́лость; любе́зность.

gradation /grə'deɪʃ(ə)n/ *n.* града́ция.

grade /greɪd/ *n.* **1** (*assessed category*) сте́пень; (*of quality*) сорт; **low-~ oil** нефть ни́зкого ка́чества; (*of rank*) сте́пень; класс; (*US, class in school*) класс; **~ school** (*US*) нача́льная шко́ла. **2** (*school rating*) отме́тка; оце́нка; (*fig., coll.*): **he will scarcely make the ~** он едва́ ли с э́тим спра́вится. **3** (*US*): **~ crossing** (железнодоро́жный) перее́зд. **4** (*fig., coll.*): **on the down ~** на спа́де.

● *v.t.* **1** (*classify*) сортирова́ть, рас-. **2** (*reduce slope of*) профили́ровать (*impf.*).

grader /'greɪdə(r)/ *n.* (*road-building*) гре́йдер.

gradient /'greɪdɪənt/ *n.* **1** (*ratio of slope*) градие́нт; (*up/down*) градие́нт подъёма/укло́на; **a ~ of 1 in 5** укло́н оди́н к пяти́. **2** (*slope*) подъём; склон.

gradual /'grædjʊəl/ *adj.* постепе́нный.

gradualism /'grædjʊə,lɪz(ə)m/ *n.* уче́ние о постепе́нной рефо́рме.

gradualist /'grædjʊə,lɪst/ *n.* постепе́новец.

graduate[1] /'grædjʊət/ *n.* (*of university, school etc.*) выпускни́|к (*fem.* -ца); **he is an Oxford ~** он выпускни́к О́ксфордского университе́та; **~ student** аспира́нт (*fem.* -ка); **~ study** аспиранту́ра.

graduate[2] /'grædjʊ,eɪt/ *v.t.* **1** (*mark with degrees*) градуи́ровать, про-. **2** (*arrange by grade*) распол|ага́ть, -ожи́ть на шкале́.

● *v.i.* (*from university*) ок|а́нчивать, -о́нчить университе́т/вуз/(*US, from school*) шко́лу; (*coll.*) получи́ть (*pf.*) дипло́м.

graduation /,grædjʊ'eɪʃ(ə)n/ *n.* **1** (*marking with degrees*) градуиро́вка. **2** (*pl., degrees so marked*) деле́ния (*nt. pl.*). **3** (*arrangement in grades*) расположе́ние на шкале́. **4** (*receiving degree*) получе́ние дипло́ма/сте́пени; (*US*) оконча́ние шко́лы.

graffiti /grə'fi:ti:/ *n.* (*sing.* **graffito** /-təʊ/) на́дписи (*f. pl.*) (на сте́нах/забо́рах).

graft[1] /grɑ:ft/ *n.* **1** (*scion*) черено́к; (*tissue*) переса́женная ткань; (*process applied to trees*) приви́вка. **2** (*surgery*) опера́ция переса́дки. **3** (*Br. coll.*) (*hard work*) вка́лывание.

● *v.t.* (*surg.*) переса́|живать, -ди́ть; (*hort., also fig.*) прив|ива́ть, -и́ть.

● *v.i.* (*Br. coll.*) вка́лывать (*impf.*) (*sl.*).

graft[2] /grɑ:ft/ *n.* (*coll., bribery etc.*) взя́точничество; блат.

grafter[1] /ˈɡrɑːftə(r)/ *n.* (*coll.*) (*hard worker*) трудя́га (*c.g.*).

grafter[2] /ˈɡrɑːftə(r)/ *n.* (*coll.*) (*swindler*) жу́лик.

grail /ɡreɪl/ *n.*: **the Holy G~** свято́й гра́аль.

grain /ɡreɪn/ *n.* **1** (*collect., seed of cereal plants*) зерно́; хле́бные зла́ки (*m. pl.*); (*single seed*) зерно́, зёрнышко, крупи́нка. **2** (*small particle*) зёрнышко; крупи́нка; **~ of sand** песчи́нка; **you must take his words with a ~ of salt** его́ слова́ сле́дует принима́ть с огово́ркой; **this affords me some ~s of comfort** э́то даёт мне хоть како́е-то утеше́ние; **there is not a ~ of truth in it** в э́том нет ни крупи́цы/гра́на/ка́пли пра́вды. **3** (*weight*) гран. **4** (*of wood*) волокно́; **to saw along the ~** пили́ть (*impf.*) вдоль волокна́. **5**: **it goes against the ~ with me** (*fig.*) э́то мне не по душе́/нутру́.

gram /ɡræm/ = **gram(me)**

grammar /ˈɡræmə(r)/ *n.* грамма́тика; **this sentence is bad ~** э́то негра́мотная фра́за.

● *cpds.* **~-book** *n.* уче́бник грамма́тики; **~-school** *n.* (*Br.*) сре́дняя шко́ла с гуманита́рным укло́ном.

grammarian /ɡrəˈmeərɪən/ *n.* граммати́ст.

grammatical /ɡrəˈmætɪk(ə)l/ *adj.* граммати́ческий; **a ~ sentence** гра́мотное (*or* пра́вильно соста́вленное) предложе́ние.

gram(me) /ɡræm/ *n.* грамм.

gramophone /ˈɡræməˌfəʊn/ *n.* граммофо́н; **~ record** грампласти́нка.

gran /ɡræn/ (*Br.*) = **granny**

granary /ˈɡrænərɪ/ *n.* амба́р; зернохрани́лище.

grand /ɡrænd/ *n.* (*piano*) роя́ль (*m.*); (*pl.* **~**) (*sl., 1,000 dollars, pounds, etc.*) шту́ка, то́нна.

● *adj.* **1** (*title*) вели́кий; **~ duke** вели́кий князь (*m.*); **~ master** (*chess*) гроссме́йстер. **2** (*great, important*) вели́кий; грандио́зный; **~ opera** больша́я о́пера; **~ piano** роя́ль (*m.*). **3** (*elevated, imposing*) вели́чественный; **the ~ style** высо́кий стиль; **a ~ air** ва́жный вид. **4** (*all embracing*): **~ finale** торже́ственный фина́л; **~ total** о́бщая су́мма. **5** (*coll., very fine*) восхити́тельный; великоле́пный; **we had a ~ time** мы потряса́юще провели́ вре́мя.

● *cpds.* **~child** *n.* внук (*fem.* вну́чка); **~dad** *n.* (*coll.*) де́душка (*m.*); **~daughter** *n.* вну́чка; **~father** *n.* де́душка (*m.*); **~father clock** высо́кие напо́льные часы́; **~(mam)ma** *n.* (*coll.*) ба́бушка; **~mother** *n.* ба́бушка; **teach one's ~mother to suck eggs** ≈ я́йца ку́рицу не у́чат; **~(pa)pa** *n.* (*coll.*) де́душка (*m.*); **~parent** *n.* де́душка (*fem.* ба́бушка); **~son** *n.* внук; **~stand** *n.* трибу́на. *For kinship terms see also cpds. of* ⇒**great**

grandee /ɡrænˈdiː/ *n.* гранд.

grandeur /ˈɡrændjə(r)/, /-ndʒə(r)/ *n.* вели́чие; великоле́пие.

grandiloquence /ˌɡrænˈdɪləkwəns/ *n.* высокопа́рность.

grandiloquent /ˌɡrænˈdɪləkwənt/ *adj.* высокопа́рный.

grandiose /ˈɡrændɪˌəʊs/ *adj.* грандио́зный.

grange /ɡreɪndʒ/ *n.* (*Br., farmstead*) мы́за, фе́рма.

granite /ˈɡrænɪt/ *n.* грани́т.

● *adj.* грани́тный.

granny /ˈɡrænɪ/ *n.* (*coll.*) ба́бушка; **~ knot** «ба́бий» у́зел.

grant /ɡrɑːnt/ *n.* (*sum etc. conferred*) дота́ция; субси́дия; грант; (*to student*) стипе́ндия.

● *v.t.* **1** (*bestow*) дарова́ть (*impf., pf.*); жа́ловать, по-; **I ~ my consent** я даю́ согла́сие; **~ me this favour** (*Br.*), **favor** (*US*)! сде́лайте мне э́то одолже́ние! **2** (*concede*) призн|ава́ть; -а́ть; **I ~ you that** в э́том вы пра́вы; **~ed, he has done all he could** согла́сен, он сде́лал всё, что мог. **3**: **he takes my help for ~ed** он принима́ет мою́ по́мощь как до́лжное.

granular /ˈɡrænjʊlə(r)/ *adj.* гранули́рованный.

granulate /ˈɡrænjʊˌleɪt/ *v.t. & i.* дроби́ть, раз-; **~d sugar** са́харный песо́к.

granule /ˈɡrænjuːl/ *n.* зерно́, гра́нула.

grape /ɡreɪp/ *n.*: **a ~** виногра́дина; **the ~, ~s** виногра́д (*collect.*); **bunch of ~s** гроздь виногра́да; **sour ~s** (*fig.*) зе́лен виногра́д.

● *cpds.* **~fruit** *n.* гре́йпфру́т; **~-shot** *n.* кру́пная карте́чь; **~-vine** *n.* виногра́дная лоза́; (*fig.*): **I heard on the ~-vine that ...** молва́ донесла́ до меня́, что. . .

graph /ɡrɑːf/, /ɡræf/ *n.* гра́фик.

● *cpd.* **~-paper** *n.* бума́га в клётку, миллиметро́вка (*coll.*).

graphic /ˈɡræfɪk/ *adj.* **1** (*pertaining to drawing etc.*) изобрази́тельный; **the ~ arts** изобрази́тельные иску́сства; гра́фика. **2** (*vivid*) кра́сочный; нагля́дный; **the papers give a ~ account of the events** газе́ты даю́т я́ркое описа́ние собы́тий. **3** (*using diagrams*) графи́ческий.

graphics /ˈɡræfɪks/ *n.* гра́фика; **~ package** (*comput.*) графи́ческий паке́т.

graphite /ˈɡræfaɪt/ *n.* графи́т.

● *adj.* графи́товый.

graphologist /ɡrəˈfɒlədʒɪst/ *n.* графо́лог.

graphology /ɡrəˈfɒlədʒɪ/ *n.* графоло́гия.

grapnel /ˈɡræpn(ə)l/ *n.* (*anchor*) шлю́почный я́корь; (*for boarding*) аборда́жный крюк.

grappl|e /ˈɡræp(ə)l/ *v.t.* схва́т|ывать, -и́ть.

● *v.i.* схва́т|ываться, -и́ться; **~e with the enemy** схвати́ться с враго́м; **~e with a problem** бра́ться, взя́ться за пробле́му; **~ing-iron** крюк.

grasp /ɡrɑːsp/ *n.* **1** (*grip*) хва́тка; (*fig.*): **victory is within our ~** побе́да уже́ близка́. **2** (*comprehension*) понима́ние; **he has a good ~ of the subject** он хорошо́ в э́том разбира́ется; **it is beyond my ~** э́то вы́ше моего́ понима́ния.

● *v.t.* (*seize*) схва́т|ывать, -и́ть; **~ the nettle** (*Br., fig.*) взять (*pf.*) быка́ за рога́; (*embrace*) обхва́т|ывать, -и́ть; (*comprehend*) схва́т|ывать, -и́ть смысл + *g.*

● *v.i.*: **~ at, for** (*lit., fig.*) ухвати́ться (*pf.*) за + *a.*; **a ~ing person** стяжа́тель (*fem.* -ница).

grass /ɡrɑːs/ *n.* **1** трава́; **blade of ~** трави́нка; **he lets the ~ grow under his feet** он сиди́т сложа́ ру́ки; **the land was laid to ~** земля́ была́ отведена́/пу́щена под луг; (*gramineous species*) злак; (*pasture*) па́стбище; **the horse was put (out) to ~** ло́шадь вы́гнали на подно́жный корм; **~ widow** соло́менная вдова́. **2** (*lawn*) газо́н; **keep off the ~** (*notice*) по траве́ не ходи́ть. **3** (*sl., marijuana*) марихуа́на, «тра́вка». **4** (*Br. sl., police informer*) стука́ч.

● *v.t.* зас|ева́ть, -е́ять траво́й; об|кла́дывать, -ложи́ть дёрном; **the ground has been ~ed over** уча́сток засе́ян траво́й.

● *v.i.* (*Br. sl., inform*) стуча́ть, на-.

● *cpds.* **~hopper** *n.* кузне́чик; **~land** *n.* луг; **~-roots** *adj.* (*coll.*) низово́й, из низо́в; **~-roots opinion is against the plan** рядовы́е гра́ждане настро́ены про́тив э́того пла́на; **~-seed** *n.* семена́ (*nt. pl.*) трав; **~-snake** *n.* уж.

grassy /ˈɡrɑːsɪ/ *adj.* (**grassier, grassiest**) травяно́й; травяни́стый.

grate[1] /ɡreɪt/ *n.* (*fireplace*) ками́нная решётка; ками́н.

grate[2] /ɡreɪt/ *v.t.* тере́ть (*impf.*); **~d cheese** тёртый сыр; **~ one's teeth** скрежета́ть (*impf.*) зуба́ми.

● *v.i.* **1** (*rub*) тере́ться (*impf.*); **~ on** (*fig.*) раздража́ть (*impf.*); нерви́ровать (*impf.*); **it ~s on my ear** э́то мне ре́жет слух. **2** (*make harsh sound*) скр|ипе́ть, -и́пнуть.

grateful /ˈɡreɪtfʊl/ *adj.* благода́рный; призна́тельный.

gratefulness /ˈɡreɪtfʊlnɪs/ *n.* благода́рность.

grater /ˈɡreɪtə(r)/ *n.* тёрка.

gratification /ˌɡrætɪfɪˈkeɪʃ(ə)n/ *n.* удовлетворе́ние.

gratify /ˈɡrætɪˌfaɪ/ *v.t.* **1** (*give pleasure to*) дост|авля́ть, -а́вить удово́льствие + *d.*; ублаж|а́ть, -и́ть; **the results were most ~ing** результа́ты бы́ли са́мыми обнадёживающими. **2** (*indulge*) удовлетвор|я́ть, -и́ть.

grating /ˈɡreɪtɪŋ/ *n.* решётка.

gratis /ˈɡrɑːtɪs/, /ˈɡreɪ-/ *adj.* беспла́тный.

● *adv.* беспла́тно.

gratitude /ˈɡrætɪˌtjuːd/ *n.* благода́рность.

gratuitous /ɡrəˈtjuːɪtəs/ *adj.* **1** (*unwarranted*) беспричи́нный; **a ~**

insult незаслу́женное оскорбле́ние. **2** (*free*) даровой; безвозме́здный; ~ **advice** беспла́тный сове́т.

gratuity /grə'tju:ɪtɪ/ *n.* (*Br., bounty on retirement etc.*) посо́бие; пре́мия; (*tip*) чаевы́|е (*pl., g.* -х).

grava|men /grə'veɪmen/ *n.* (*pl.* **~mens** *or* **~mina** /-mɪnə/) (*leg.*) (*grievance*) жа́лоба; (*of accusation*) суть, основно́й пункт.

grave¹ /greɪv/ *n.* моги́ла; **an old man with one foot in the ~** стари́к, стоя́щий одно́й ного́й в моги́ле; **he would turn in his ~ if he heard you** е́сли бы он вас услы́шал, он переверну́лся бы в гробу́; **someone is walking over my ~** меня́ ни с того́ ни с сего́ дрожь пробира́ет; (*death*) смерть; **he went to his ~** он сошёл в моги́лу; **life beyond the ~** загро́бная жизнь.

● *cpds.* **~-digger** *n.* моги́льщик; **~side** *n.*: **at the ~** на краю́ моги́лы; **~stone** *n.* надгро́бная плита́; **~yard** *n.* кла́дбище.

grave² /greɪv/ *adj.* (*of person*) серьёзный; (*of events*) серьёзный, тяжёлый; **~ news** трево́жные ве́сти.

grave³ /grɑ:v/ *adj.* (*gram.*): **~ accent** тупо́е ударе́ние.

grave⁴ /greɪv/ *v.t.* (*p.p.* **graven** *or* **graved**) высека́ть, вы́сечь; гравирова́ть (*impf.*); **her face is ~d on my memory** её лицо́ запечатле́лось в мое́й па́мяти; **~n image** и́дол, куми́р.

gravel /'græv(ə)l/ *n.* гра́вий; **a ~ path** грави́йная тро́пка; доро́жка, посы́панная гра́вием.

● *v.t.* (**gravelled, gravelling;** *US* **graveled, graveling**) (*strew with ~*) пос|ыпа́ть, -ы́пать гра́вием.

gravelly /'grævəlɪ/ *adj.* грави́йный; (*fig., of the voice*) скрипу́чий.

graven /'greɪv(ə)n/ *p.p. of* ⇒**grave⁴**

graver /'greɪvə(r)/ *n.* (*person*) ре́зчик, гравёр; (*tool*) резе́ц.

Graves /greɪvz/ *n.*: **~' disease** базе́дова боле́знь.

gravitate /'grævɪˌteɪt/ *v.i.* прит|я́гиваться, -яну́ться; (*fig.*) тяготе́ть (*impf.*) (*к чему*).

gravitation /ˌgrævɪ'teɪʃ(ə)n/ *n.* (*sinking*) опуска́ние; (*phys. force*) гравита́ция, притяже́ние, тяготе́ние; (*fig.*) тяготе́ние.

gravitational /ˌgrævɪ'teɪʃən(ə)l/ *adj.* гравитацио́нный.

gravity /'grævɪtɪ/ *n.* **1** (*force*) си́ла притяже́ния. **2** (*weight*) тя́жесть; **centre** (*Br.*), **center** (*US*) **of ~** центр тя́жести; **law of ~** зако́н всеми́рного тяготе́ния; **specific ~** уде́льный вес. **3** (*seriousness*) серьёзность; тя́жесть. **4** (*solemnity*) торже́ственность.

gravy /'greɪvɪ/ *n.* подли́вка.

● *cpd.* **~-boat** *n.* со́усник.

gray /greɪ/ (*US*) = **grey**

grayish /'greɪɪʃ/ (*US*) = **greyish**

grayness /'greɪnɪs/ (*US*) = **greyness**

graze¹ /greɪz/ *n.* (*abrasion*) цара́пина; ссади́на.

● *v.t.* зад|ева́ть, -е́ть; сса́|живать, -ди́ть; **the bullet ~d his cheek** пу́ля оцара́пала ему́ щёку; **he fell and ~d his knee** он упа́л и ссади́л коле́но.

● *v.i.*: **the bullet ~d past him** пу́ля пролете́ла ми́мо, почти́ не заде́в его́.

graze² /greɪz/ *v.t.* пасти́; **~ sheep** пасти́ ове́ц; **~** (*feed in*) **a field** пасти́сь на по́ле/лугу́.

● *v.i.*: **he has 40 sheep out to ~** у него́ (в ста́де/ота́ре) пасётся 40 ове́ц.

grazier /'greɪzɪə(r)/ *n.* скотово́д.

grazing /'greɪzɪŋ/ *n.* па́стбище; **~ land** вы́пас.

grease /gri:s/ *n.* (*fat*) жир; (*lubricant*) сма́зка.

● *v.t.* сма́з|ывать, -ать; (*fig.*): **~ s.o.'s palm** (*with a bribe*) «подма́зать» кого́-н.; **he ran off like ~d lightning** он помча́лся пу́лей.

● *cpds.* **~-gun** *n.* шприц для сма́зки; **~-monkey** *n.* (*coll.*) меха́ник; **~-paint** *n.* грим; **~proof** *adj.* жиронепроница́емый.

greasy /'gri:sɪ/, /-zɪ/ *adj.* (**greasier, greasiest**) жи́рный; (*of a road*) ско́льзкий; (*fig., unctuous*) еле́йный.

great /greɪt/ *adj.* **1** большо́й, вели́кий; (*famous*) знамени́тый; **a ~ nuisance** большо́е неудо́бство; **they are ~ friends** они́ больши́е друзья́; **a ~ (big) boy** ро́слый ма́льчик; **a ~ many people** ма́сса наро́ду; **a ~ deal of courage** незауря́дная хра́брость; **I've a ~ mind to ...** мне бы о́чень хоте́лось. . .; **a ~ while ago** давны́м-давно́; **he lived to a ~ age** он до́жил до глубо́кой ста́рости; **the ~ majority** подавля́ющее большинство́; **take ~ care!** бу́дьте о́чень осторо́жны; **he shows ~ ignorance** он проявля́ет по́лное неве́жество (*в чём*). **2** (*enthusiastic, assiduous*): **a ~ reader** стра́стный чита́тель; **a ~ walker** завзя́тый ходо́к. **3** (*coll., splendid, marvellous*) замеча́тельный; **we had a ~ time** мы замеча́тельно провели́ вре́мя; **he thinks he's the ~est** (*sl.*) он мно́го о себе́ вообража́ет; **he is ~ at repairing a car** он великоле́пно ремонти́рует маши́ну. **4** (*eminent, distinguished*) вели́кий; **~ minds think alike** вели́кие умы́ схо́дятся; **the G~ Powers** вели́кие держа́вы; **Peter the G~** Пётр Вели́кий; **a ~ occasion** торже́ственное собы́тие. **5** (*var.*): **the G~ Bear** Больша́я Медве́дица; **G~ Britain** Великобрита́ния; **~ circle** большо́й круг; **~ circle sailing** пла́вание по ортодро́мии.

● *cpds.* **~-aunt** *n.* двою́родная ба́бушка; **~coat** *n.* пальто́ (*indecl.*); **~-granddaughter** *n.* пра́внучка; **~-grandfather** *n.* пра́дед; **~-grandmother** *n.* праба́бушка; **~-grandson** *n.* пра́внук; **~-hearted** *adj.* великоду́шный; **~-nephew** *n.* внуча́тый племя́нник; **~-niece** *n.* внуча́тая племя́нница; **~-uncle** *n.* двою́родный дед.

greatly /'greɪtlɪ/ *adv.* о́чень, си́льно, значи́тельно; **I was ~ amused** э́то меня́ си́льно позаба́вило.

greatness /'greɪtnɪs/ *n.* вели́чие.

grebe /gri:b/ *n.* пога́нка (*птица*).

Grecian /'gri:ʃ(ə)n/ *adj.* гре́ческий.

Greece /gri:s/ *n.* Гре́ция.

greed /gri:d/, **-iness** /'gri:dɪnɪs/ *nn.* жа́дность; а́лчность; (*for food*) прожо́рливость.

greedy /'gri:dɪ/ *adj.* (**greedier, greediest**) (*for money etc.*) жа́дный; а́лчный (*liter.*); (*for honour etc.*) жа́ждущий +*g.*; а́лчущий +*g.* (*liter.*); (*for food*) прожо́рливый.

● *cpd.* **~-guts** *n.* (*sl.*) жа́дина (*c.g.*).

Greek /gri:k/ *n.* **1** (*person*) гре|к (*fem.* -ча́нка). **2** (*language*) гре́ческий язы́к; **Ancient ~** древнегре́ческий язы́к; **Modern ~** новогре́ческий язы́к; **it's ~ to me** э́то для меня́ кита́йская гра́мота.

● *adj.* гре́ческий.

green /gri:n/ *n.* **1** (*colour*) зелёный цвет; зелёное; **dressed in ~** оде́тый в зелёное. **2** (*pl., vegetables*) зе́лень; **spring ~s** ра́нние о́вощи (*m. pl.*); (*cut foliage*) ли́стья (*pl.*). **3** (*grassy area*) лужа́йка; (*on golf course*) площа́дка вокру́г лу́нки.

● *adj.* зелёный; **a ~ belt round the city** зелёный поя́с (вокру́г) го́рода; **he got the ~ light and went ahead** (*fig.*) получи́в «зелёную у́лицу», он на́чал де́йствовать; **she has ~ fingers** (*Br.*), **a ~ thumb** (*US*) она́ уме́лый садово́д; **~ with envy** зелёный от за́висти; (*unripe*) незре́лый; **~ wood** невы́держанная/«зелёная» древеси́на; (*fig., inexperienced, gullible*) «зелёный».

● *cpds.* **~back** *n.* (*US*) банкно́та; **~-eyed** *adj.* зеленогла́зый; (*fig.*) ревни́вый; **the ~-eyed monster** ре́вность; **~finch** *n.* зелену́шка; **~fly** *n.* (*Br.*) тля; **~gage** *n.* ренкло́д; **~grocer** *n.* (*Br.*) зеленщи́к; **~grocery** *n.* (*Br.*) зеленная ла́вка; **~horn** *n.* новичо́к; **~house** *n.* тепли́ца; **~house effect** парнико́вый *or* тепли́чный эффе́кт; **~-room** *n.* артисти́ческая; **~stuff** *n.* о́вощ|и (*pl. g.* -е́й); **~sward** *n.* (*arch.*) газо́н.

greenery /'gri:nərɪ/ *n.* зе́лень.

greenish /'gri:nɪʃ/ *adj.* зеленова́тый.

Greenland /'gri:nlənd/ *n.* Гренла́ндия.

● *adj.* гренла́ндский.

greenness /'gri:nnɪs/ *n.* зе́лень; (*fig.*) нео́пытность.

Greenwich (mean) time /'grenɪtʃ/, /'grɪnɪdʒ/ *n.* вре́мя по Гри́нвичу.

greet /gri:t/ *v.t.* (*socially*) здоро́ваться, по- с+*i.*; (*welcome*) приве́тствовать (*impf.*); (*e.g. the dawn*) встр|еча́ть, -е́тить; **the soldiers were ~ed by abuse** солда́т встре́тили оскорбле́ниями; **a fine view ~ed us at the summit** с верши́ны нам откры́лся прекра́сный вид.

greeting /'gri:tɪŋ/ *n.* (*on meeting*) приве́тствие; **~s** (*in a letter*) приве́т; **~s!** приве́т!; приве́тствую!; (*on a special occasion*): **birthday ~s** поздравле́ние с днём рожде́ния; **~ card** поздрави́тельная откры́тка.

gregarious /grɪˈgeərɪəs/ *adj.* ста́дный; (*fig., also*) общи́тельный.

gregariousness /grɪˈgeərɪəsnɪs/ *n.* ста́дность; общи́тельность.

Gregorian /grɪˈgɔːrɪən/ *adj.* григориа́нский.

gremlin /ˈgremlɪn/ *n.* (*coll.*) злой дух.

grenade /grɪˈneɪd/ *n.* грана́та.

grenadier /ˌgrenəˈdɪə(r)/ *n.* гренаде́р.

grew /gruː/ *past of* ⇒**grow**

grey /greɪ/ (*US* **gray**) *n.* се́рый цвет; се́рое; **dressed in ~** оде́тый в се́рое.

● *adj.* се́рый; **~ area** (*fig.*) о́бласть неопределённости; **~ matter** (*fig.*) «се́рое вещество́»; ум; «мозги́» (*m. pl.*); **he has gone quite ~** он си́льно поседе́л; **his face turned ~** он побледне́л.

● *cpds.* **~beard** *n.* стари́к; **~-haired, ~-headed** *adjs.* седо́й, седовла́сый; **~hound** *n.* англи́йская борза́я.

greyish /ˈgreɪɪʃ/ (*US* **grayish**) *adj.* серова́тый.

greyness /ˈgreɪnɪs/ (*US* **grayness**) *n.* се́рость; (*of hair*) седина́.

grid /grɪd/ *n.* **1** (*grating*) решётка. **2** (*gridiron*) ра́шпер. **3** (*map reference squares*) координа́тная се́тка; **~ reference** координа́ты (*f. pl.*). **4** (*elec.*) сеть электропереда́ч. **5** (*power supply system*) энергосисте́ма.

● *cpd.* **~iron** *n.* ра́шпер; (*US*) футбо́льное по́ле.

griddle /ˈgrɪd(ə)l/ *n.* сковоро́дка.

● *cpd.* **~cake** *n.* лепёшка; блин.

gridlock /ˈgrɪdlɒk/ *n.* зато́р, про́бка; **~ed streets** заблоки́рованные у́лицы.

grief /griːf/ *n.* (*sorrow*) го́ре, печа́ль; (*cause of sorrow*) огорче́ние; (*disaster*): **he will come to ~** он пло́хо ко́нчит.

grievance /ˈgriːv(ə)ns/ *n.* прете́нзия; недово́льство; **he likes airing his ~s** он лю́бит излива́ть своё недово́льство.

grieve /griːv/ *v.t.* огорч|а́ть, -и́ть; печа́лить, о-; **I am ~d to hear of it** мне бо́льно э́то слы́шать.

● *v.i.* печа́литься, о-; горева́ть (*impf.*); **she ~d for her husband** она́ горева́ла о му́же.

grievous /ˈgriːvəs/ *adj.* го́рестный; печа́льный; **~bodily** (*leg.*) **harm** тяжёлые теле́сные поврежде́ния (*nt. pl.*); **~ pain** мучи́тельная боль.

griffin /ˈgrɪfɪn/, **griffon** /ˈgrɪf(ə)n/, **gryphon** /ˈgrɪf(ə)n/ *n.* грифо́н.

grill /grɪl/ *n.* (*Br., on cooker*) гриль (*m.*); (*gridiron*) ра́шпер; (*dish*) жа́реное мя́со; **mixed ~** ассорти́ (*nt. indecl.*) из жа́реного мя́са.

● *v.t.* (*Br., cook*) жа́рить, за-, из- на гри́ле; (*coll., interrogate*) учин|я́ть, -и́ть допро́с +*d.*

● *v.i.* (*Br., of food*) жа́риться, за-, из- на гри́ле.

● *cpd.* **~room** *n.* гриль-ба́р.

grille /grɪl/ *n.* решётка.

grim /grɪm/ *adj.* (**grimmer, grimmest**) суро́вый, мра́чный, гро́зный; **he held on like ~ death** он вцепи́лся мёртвой хва́ткой; **the prospect is ~** перспекти́вы мра́чные/безра́достные.

grimace /ˈgrɪməs/, /grɪˈmeɪs/ *n.* грима́са.

● *v.i.* грима́сничать (*impf.*).

grime /graɪm/ *n.* са́жа; грязь.

grimy /ˈgraɪmɪ/ *adj.* (**grimier, grimiest**) чума́зый; гря́зный.

grin /grɪn/ *n.* усме́шка; ухмы́лка.

● *v.i.* (**grinned, grinning**) усмех|а́ться, -ну́ться; ухмыл|я́ться, -ьну́ться; ска́лить (*impf.*) зу́бы; **you must ~ and bear it** вы должны́ му́жественно перенести́ э́то.

grind /graɪnd/ *n.* (*coll.*) изнури́тельный труд; рабо́та на изно́с; **this work is a fearful ~** э́та рабо́та до у́жаса изнуря́ет.

● *v.t.* (*past and p.p.* **ground**) **1** (*crush*) моло́ть, с-; **~ corn** моло́ть, пере- зерно́; **ground almonds** мо́лотый минда́ль. **2** (*wear down*) изн|а́шивать, -оси́ть; **ground glass** ма́товое стекло́; (*sharpen*) точи́ть, на-; **I have no axe to ~** (*fig.*) у меня́ нет своекоры́стных це́лей; (*make smooth*) шлифова́ть, от-. **3**: **~ one's teeth** скрежета́ть/скрипе́ть (*both impf.*) зуба́ми. **4**: **~ one's heel into the earth** вда́в|ливать, -и́ть каблу́к в зе́млю.

● *v.i.* (*past and p.p.* **ground**) **1** (*rub, grate*) раст|ира́ть, -ере́ть. **2** (*coll., work hard*) изм|а́тываться, -ота́ться; **~ away at one's studies** грызть (*impf.*) грани́т нау́ки. **3**: **~ to a halt** остан|а́вливаться, -ови́ться (с ля́згом); засто́пориться (*pf.*).

● *cpd.* **~stone** *n.* точи́ло; **he kept his nose to the ~stone** он труди́лся без о́тдыха.

grinder /ˈgraɪndə(r)/ *n.* **1** (*for crushing*) дроби́лка; (*coffee-~*) кофемо́лка, кофе́йная ме́льница. **2** (*for abrasive work*) точи́льный ка́мень; шлифова́льный стано́к.

grip /grɪp/ *n.* **1** (*grasp*) схва́тывание; (*fig.*) понима́ние; **he has a powerful ~** у него́ кре́пкая хва́тка; **he was in the ~ of an illness** боле́знь кре́пко держа́ла его́; **come to ~s with a problem** вплотну́ю заня́ться (*pf.*) пробле́мой; **take a ~ of yourself!** возьми́те себя́ в ру́ки!; **he got a ~ of the facts** он разобра́лся в фа́ктах; **he is losing his ~** хва́тка у него́ уже́ не та. **2** (*handle; part held*) рукоя́тка; ру́чка. **3** (*travelling-bag*) саквоя́ж.

● *v.t.* (**gripped, gripping**) (*hold tightly*) схва́т|ывать, -и́ть; (*of a disease*) не отпуска́ть, кре́пко держа́ть (*both impf.*); (*hold the attention of*) захва́т|ывать, -и́ть; **a ~ping story** захва́тывающий расска́з.

● *v.i.* (**gripped, gripping**) схва́т|ываться, -и́ться; **the brakes failed to ~** тормоза́ отказа́ли.

gripe /graɪp/ (*coll.*) *n.* **1** (*pl., colic pains*) ко́лик|и (*pl., g.* —). **2** (*grumble, complaint*) ворча́ние.

● *v.i.* (*complain*) ворча́ть (*impf.*).

● *cpd.* **~-water** *n.* (*Br.*) укро́пная вода́.

grisly /ˈgrɪzlɪ/ *adj.* (**grislier, grisliest**) ужаса́ющий.

grist /grɪst/ *n.* помо́л; зерно́ для помо́ла; (*fig.*): **it will bring ~ to the mill** э́то принесёт дохо́д; **all is ~ to his mill** он из всего́ извлека́ет вы́году.

gristle /ˈgrɪs(ə)l/ *n.* хрящ.

gristly /ˈgrɪslɪ/ *adj.* хрящево́й; с хрящáми.

grit /grɪt/ *n.* **1** (*small bits of stone*) гра́вий; песо́к; **I've a piece of ~ in my eye** мне в глаз попа́ла сори́нка. **2** (*coll., courage and endurance*) вы́держка; му́жество. **3** (*pl., coarse meal*) овся́нка.

● *v.t.* (**gritted, gritting**) **1** (*spread ~ on*): **the streets were ~ted at the first sign of frost** при пе́рвых при́знаках моро́за у́лицы посы́пали песко́м. **2**: **~ one's teeth** скрипе́ть (*impf.*) зуба́ми; (*fig.*) сти́снуть (*pf.*) зу́бы.

gritty /ˈgrɪtɪ/ *adj.* (**grittier, grittiest**) песча́ный; (*fig., of style*) шерохова́тый.

grizzle /ˈgrɪz(ə)l/ *v.i.* (*Br. coll., fret*) капри́зничать (*impf.*); хны́кать (*impf.*).

grizzled /ˈgrɪz(ə)ld/ *adj.* седо́й.

grizzly /ˈgrɪzlɪ/ *n.* (**~-bear**) гри́зли (*m. indecl.*).

groan /grəʊn/ *n.* стон.

● *v.i.* стона́ть, за-; **he was ~ing for help** он взыва́л о по́мощи.

groats /grəʊts/ *n.* крупа́.

grocer /ˈgrəʊsə(r)/ *n.* бакале́йщик.

grocery /ˈgrəʊsərɪ/ *n.* (*trade*) бакале́йное де́ло; (*shop*) бакале́йная ла́вка; магази́н бакале́йных това́ров; (*pl., goods*) бакале́я.

grog /grɒg/ *n.* грог; пунш.

groggy /ˈgrɒgɪ/ *adj.* (**groggier, groggiest**) нетвёрдый на нога́х.

groin /grɔɪn/ *n.* (*anat.*) пах; (*archit.*) кресто́вый свод.

groom /gruːm/ *n.* (*for horses*) ко́нюх; (*bride~*) жени́х.

● *v.t.* **1**: **~ a horse** ходи́ть (*impf.*) за ло́шадью. **2**: **well-~ed** (*of person*) хорошо́ причёсанный и оде́тый; (*coll.*) ухо́женный. **3** (*prepare, coach*) гото́вить, при-; **he is being ~ed for President** его́ про́чат в президе́нты.

groove /gruːv/ *n.* желобо́к; (*fig.*) рути́на.

● *v.t.* прор|еза́ть, -е́зать кана́вки +*p.*

groovy /ˈgruːvɪ/ *adj.* (**groovier, grooviest**) (*sl., smart in the fashion*) шика́рный; клёвый.

grope /grəʊp/ *v.t. & i.* идти́ (*det.*) о́щупью; ощу́п|ывать, -ать; **he ~d his way toward the door** он о́щупью добра́лся до две́ри; (*fig.*): **~ after truth** дои́скиваться (*impf.*) пра́вды.

grosgrain /ˈgrəʊgreɪn/ *n.* ткань в уто́чный ру́бчик.

gross /grəʊs/ *n.* (*pl.* **~**) (*number*) гросс.

● *adj.* **1** (*coarse; flagrant*) гру́бый; вульга́рный. **2** (*obese*) ту́чный. **3** (*opp. net*) валово́й; **~ domestic product** валово́й вну́тренний проду́кт; **~ national product** валово́й национа́льный проду́кт; **~ weight** вес брýтто; **in the ~** (*wholesale*) óптом, гуртóм.

● *v.t.* (*coll., make a ~ profit*): **we ~ed £1,000** мы получи́ли óбщую при́быль в 1 000 фýнтов.

grossness /ˈgrəʊsnɪs/ *n.* грýбость; вульгáрность; (*obesity*) тýчность.

grotesque /grəʊˈtesk/ *n.* (*person, figure etc.*) гротéск.

● *adj.* гротéскный; (*cinema, role*) гротéсковый.

grotto /ˈgrɒtəʊ/ *n.* (*pl.* **~es** *or* **~s**) грот.

grouch /graʊtʃ/ *n.* (*coll.*) (*complaint*) жáлоба; **he has a ~ against me** он на меня́ в оби́де; (*grumbler*) ворчýн; брюзгá (*c.g.*).

grouchy /ˈgraʊtʃɪ/ *adj.* (**grouchier, grouchiest**) (*coll.*) ворчли́вый; брюзгли́вый.

ground[1] /graʊnd/ *n.* **1** (*surface of earth*) земля́; грунт; **the tree fell to the ~** дéрево упáло на зéмлю; **he cut the ~ from under my feet** он вы́бил у меня́ пóчву из-под ног; **his plan fell to the ~** егó план рýхнул; **the plane was a long while getting off the ~** самолёт дéлал большóй разбéг пéред взлётом; **the plan will never get off the ~** прoéкт так и остáнется на бумáге; **he has both feet on the ~** (*fig.*) он прóчно стои́т на ногáх; **thin on the ~** (*coll., sparse*) ≈ раз, два и обчёлся; **it suits me down to the ~** э́то меня́ вполнé устрáивает; **from the ~ up** сни́зу дóверху; **~ crew** назéмная комáнда; **~ control** назéмное управлéние; **~ floor** пéрвый этáж; **~ forces** сухопýтные войскá; **~ speed** (*aeron.*) путевáя скóрость; **~ staff** нелётный состáв; **~ swell** мёртвая зыбь, дóнные вóлны (*f. pl.*); (*fig.*) волнá.
2 (*soil, also fig.*) пóчва; **~ frost** (*Br.*) зáморозк|и (*pl., g.* -ов); подмёрзшая земля́; **his words fell on stony ~** егó словá бы́ли глáсом вопиющего в пусты́не; **this theory breaks fresh ~** э́та теóрия проклáдывает нóвые пути́; **you are** (*treading*) **on dangerous ~** вы вступи́ли на скóльзкую пóчву.
3 (*position*) положéние; **our forces gained ~** нáши чáсти продвигáлись вперёд; **this opinion is gaining ~** э́та тóчка зрéния набирáет си́лу; **he had to give ~** он дóлжен был уступи́ть; **he stood his ~ like a man** он держáлся как мужчи́на; **they held their ~ well** они́ стóйко держáлись; **he has shifted his ~ so many times** он стóлько раз менял свою пози́цию; **I prefer to meet him on my own ~** я предпочитáю встречáться с ним на своéй террито́рии; **there is much common ~ between us** у нас мнóго óбщего.
4 (*area, distance*) расстоя́ние; **we covered a lot of ~** (*distance*) мы покры́ли большóе расстоя́ние; (*fig., work*) мы замéтно продви́нулись вперёд.
5 (*defined area of activity*) площáдка; **fishing ~s** местá, отведённые для ры́бной лóвли; **football ~** футбóльная площáдка; **parade ~** плац; **sports ~** спорти́вная площáдка; **home ~** своё пóле.
6 (*pl., estate*) сад, парк, зéмли (*f. pl.*); **house and ~s** дом и земéльный учáсток.
7 (*pl., dregs*) гýща; **coffee ~s** кофéйная гýща.
8 (*reason*) основáние; **I have no ~s for complaint** у меня́ нет основáний жáловаться; **he has good ~(s) for saying so** у негó есть все основáния так говори́ть.
9 (*surface for painting, printing etc.*) фон; **a design on a white ~** рисýнок на бéлом фóне.
10 (*US, elec.*) земля́, заземлéние.

● *v.t.* **1** (*run aground*) сажáть, посади́ть на мель.
2 (*prevent from flying*) запре|щáть, -ти́ть полёты + *g.*
3 (*base*) обоснóв|ывать, -áть; **his fears were well ~ed** егó опасéния бы́ли пóлностью обоснóваны.
4 (*give basic instruction to*) подгот|áвливать, -óвить.
5 (*US, elec., connect to earth*) заземл|я́ть, -и́ть.

● *v.i.* (*of a vessel*) сади́ться, сесть на мель.

● *cpds.* **~-bait** *n.* (*Br.*) дóнная блеснá; **~-floor** *adj.* на пéрвом этажé; **~-hog** *n.* сурóк леснóй (америкáнский); **~nut** *n.* земляной орéх; **~-plan** *n.* план пéрвого этажá здáния; (*fig.*) óбщие намéтки (*f. pl.*); **~-rent** *n.* (*Br.*) земéльная рéнта; **~-to-air** *adj.*: **~-to-air missile** ракéта клáсса «земля́ — вóздух»; **~-work** *n.* фундáмент, оснóвы (*f. pl.*).

ground[2] /graʊnd/ *past and p.p. of* ⇒**grind**

grounding /ˈgraʊndɪŋ/ *n.* (*basic instruction*) подготóвка.

groundless /ˈgraʊndlɪs/ *adj.* беспричи́нный, беспóчвенный, необоснóванный.

groundsel /ˈgraʊns(ə)l/ *n.* (*bot.*) крестóвник.

groundskeeper /ˈgraʊndzˌkiːpə(r)/ (*US*) = **groundsman**

groundsman /ˈgraʊndzmən/ *n.* (*Br.*) тот, кто содéржит спортплощáдку в поря́дке.

group /gruːp/ *n.* **1** (*assemblage*) грýппа; коллекти́в; (*for artistic purposes*) грýппа; ансáмбль (*m.*); (*interest ~, e.g. at school*) кружóк; (*political etc. unit*) группирóвка; фрáкция. **2** (*attr.*) группово́й; **~ practice** (*med.*) грýппа врачéй, ведýщих приём в однóм мéсте; **~ therapy** группова́я психотерапи́я.

● *v.t. & i.* группировáть(ся), с-.

● *cpd.* **~-captain** *n.* полкóвник авиáции.

grouping /ˈgruːpɪŋ/ *n.* (*action*) группировáние, классифици́рование; (*group*) группирóвка.

grouse[1] /graʊs/ *n.* (*pl.* **~**) (*bird*) шотлáндская куропáтка.

grouse[2] /graʊs/ *n.* (*coll.*) (*complaint*) жáлоба; претéнзия.

● *v.i.* ворчáть (*impf.*).

grout /graʊt/ *n.* (*mortar*) цемéнтный раствóр.

● *v.t.* зал|ивáть, -и́ть цемéнтом.

grove /grəʊv/ *n.* рóща.

grovel /ˈgrɒv(ə)l/ *v.i.* (**grovelled, grovelling;** *US* **groveled, groveling**) лежáть (*impf.*) ниц/ распростёршись; (*fig.*) пресмыкáться (*impf.*) (*перед кем*); пá|дать, -сть в нóги.

grow /grəʊ/ *v.t.* (*past* **grew;** *p.p.* **grown**) расти́ть, вы́-; выра́щивать (*impf.*); разводи́ть (*impf.*); **cotton is ~n in the South** хлóпок выра́щивают на ю́ге; **he is ~ing a beard** он отрáщивает бóроду.

● *v.i.* (*past* **grew;** *p.p.* **grown**) **1** (*of vegetable habitat*) расти́, вы́расти; **ivy ~s on walls** плющ растёт на стéнах; **money doesn't ~ on trees** дéньги не растýт на дерéвьях.
2 (*of vegetable or animal development*): **he has ~n tall** он óчень вы́рос/ вы́тянулся; **he grew (by) 5 inches** он вы́рос на 5 дю́ймов; **she has ~n into a young lady** онá преврати́лась в молодýю жéнщину; **she is letting her hair ~** онá отрáщивает вóлосы; **he looks quite ~n up** он вы́глядит совсéм взрóслым; **~n-ups** взрóслые (*pl.*); **I grew to like him** со врéменем он мне стал нрáвиться; **it grew out of nothing** всё началóсь с пустякá; **it's a habit I've never ~n out of** э́то привы́чка, от котóрой я никогдá не мог избáвиться; **he grew out of his clothes** он вы́рос из одéжды; **full(y)-~n** зрéлый; **a ~n man** взрóслый человéк; **~ing pains** невралги́ческие/ ревмати́ческие бóли в дéтском вóзрастс; (*fig.*) болéзнь рóста; (*increase*) увели́чи|ваться, -ться; уси́ли|ваться, -ться; **he grew daily in wisdom** он с кáждым днём набирáлся умá; **his influence is ~ing** егó влия́ние растёт; **he listened with ~ing impatience** он слýшал с растýщим нетерпéнием; **the tune ~s on one** э́тот моти́в начинáет нрáвиться со врéменем.
3 (*become*) станови́ться, стать; *also expr. by inchoative pref.*: **it grew suddenly dark** вдруг стáло темнó (*or* стемнéло); **as he grew older, he ...** с вóзрастом он...; **she grew pale** онá побледнéла; **he grew rich** он разбогатéл.

grower /ˈgrəʊə(r)/ *n.* (*cultivator*) садовóд; **a fast ~** (*plant*) быстрорастýщее растéние.

growl /graʊl/ *n.* рычáние; (*of thunder*) грóхот.

● *v.i.* рычáть (*impf.*); гремéть (*impf.*).

grown /grəʊn/ *p.p. of* ⇒**grow**

growth /grəʊθ/ *n.* (*development*) рост; (*increase*) прирóст; **three days' ~ of beard** трёхднéвная щети́на; (*path.*) нарóст.

grub[1] /grʌb/ *n.* (*larva*) личи́нка; червь (*m.*); (*food*) жратвá (*coll.*).

grub[2] /grʌb/ *v.t.* (**grubbed, grubbing**) выкáпывать, вы́копать; **a hoe for ~bing out weeds** моты́га для прополки сорнякóв.

● *v.i.* (**grubbed, grubbing**) ры́ться (*impf.*); **pigs ~ about for food** свиньи

G

ро́ются вокру́г/повсю́ду в по́исках пи́щи.

grubby /ˈgrʌbɪ/ *adj.* (**grubbier, grubbiest**) (*dirty*) гря́зный, запа́чканный.

grudg|e /grʌdʒ/ *n.* прете́нзия, недоброжела́тельность; **I bear him no ~e** я на него́ не в оби́де.

● *v.t.* зави́довать, по- + *d.*; жале́ть, по- (*чего*); **I do not ~e him his success** я не зави́дую его́ успе́ху; **I ~e paying so much** мне жаль плати́ть так мно́го; **~ing praise** скупа́я похвала́; **he obeyed ~ingly** он неохо́тно вы́полнил приказа́ние.

gruel /ˈgru:əl/ *n.* (жи́дкая) каши́ца.

gruelling /ˈgru:əlɪŋ/ (*US* **grueling**) *adj.* изма́тывающий; изнури́тельный.

gruesome /ˈgru:səm/ *adj.* жу́ткий.

gruff /grʌf/ *adj.* (*of demeanour*) ре́зкий, грубова́тый; (*of voice*) хри́плый.

gruffness /ˈgrʌfnɪs/ *n.* ре́зкость, гру́бость; хри́плость.

grumble /ˈgrʌmb(ə)l/ *n.* (*complaint*) ворча́ние; (*rumbling noise*) гро́хот.

● *v.i.* (*complain*) ворча́ть (*impf.*); жа́ловаться, по-; (*rumble*) грохота́ть (*impf.*).

grumbler /ˈgrʌmblə(r)/ *n.* ворчу́н.

grumpy /ˈgrʌmpɪ/ *adj.* (**grumpier, grumpiest**) сварли́вый.

grunt /grʌnt/ *n.* (*animal*) хрю́канье; (*human*) ворча́ние.

● *v.i.* (*of animals*) хрю́к|ать, -нуть; (*of humans; also v.t.*) ворча́ть, про-.

gryphon /ˈgrɪf(ə)n/ = **griffin**

guano /ˈgwɑ:nəʊ/ *n.* (*agric.*) гуа́но (*indecl.*).

guarantee /ˌgærənˈti:/ *n.* **1** (*undertaking*) гара́нтия; поручи́тельство; **this watch carries a ~** э́ти часы́ с гара́нтией. **2** (*guarantor*) гара́нт; поручи́тель (*m.*); **will you stand ~ for me?** вы за меня́ пору́читесь? **3** (*security*) гара́нтия (*чего*). **4** (*determinant*) зало́г; **money is no ~ of success** де́ньги ещё не гаранти́руют успе́х.

● *v.t.* (**guarantees, guaranteed**) **1** (*stand surety; undertake, promise*) гаранти́ровать (*impf., pf.*). **2** (*ensure*) обеспе́чи|вать, -ть. **3** (*coll., feel sure, wager*) руча́ться, поручи́ться. **4** (*insure*) страхова́ть, за-; **it is ~d to last 10 years** срок го́дности/гара́нтии — 10 лет; **~d against rust** гаранти́рованный от ржа́вчины.

guarantor /ˌgærənˈtɔ:(r)/, /ˈgærəntə(r)/ *n.* поручи́тель (*m.*); гара́нт.

guaranty /ˈgærəntɪ/ *n.* гара́нтия (по до́лгу), зало́г, поручи́тельство.

guard /gɑ:d/ *n.* **1** (*state of alertness*) насторожённость; **be on your ~ against pickpockets** остерега́йтесь карма́нников; **he was caught off his ~** его́ заста́ли врасплох́; (*defence*): **his ~ was down** (*fig.*) его́ бди́тельность осла́бла; он осла́бил бди́тельность; (*mil.*): **mount ~** вступ|а́ть, -и́ть в карау́л; **on ~ duty** на часа́х; в карау́ле; **they kept ~ by day and night** они́ стоя́ли на стра́же днём и но́чью; **the soldiers stood ~ over the prisoner** солда́ты охраня́ли заключённого. **2** (*man appointed to keep ~*) охра́нник, карау́льный; (*collect.*) охра́на, стра́жа; **advance ~** аванга́рд; **a ~ was set on the gates** у воро́т вы́ставили охра́ну; **changing of the ~** сме́на карау́ла; **prison ~** тюре́мный надзира́тель; охра́нник в тюрьме́; **~ of honour** (*Br.*), **honor** (*US*) почётный карау́л. **3** (*pl., collect.*) гва́рдия; **Brigade of G~s** гварде́йская брига́да. **4** (*Br., of a train*) проводни́к; **~'s van** (*Br.*) бага́жный ваго́н. **5** (*protective device*) защи́тное устро́йство, предохрани́тель (*m.*); (*of a sword*) эфе́с.

● *v.t.* охраня́ть (*impf.*); бере́чь (*impf.*); **the prisoners were closely ~ed** заключённые находи́лись под уси́ленной охра́ной; **he will ~ your interests** он бу́дет охраня́ть ва́ши интере́сы; **you must ~ your tongue** вам ну́жно быть бо́лее сде́ржанным на язы́к.

● *v.i.* бере́чься (*impf.*), остерега́ться (*impf.*) (**against** + *g.*); **everything was done to ~ against infection** бы́ли при́няты все ме́ры про́тив инфе́кции.

● *cpds.* **~ dog** *n.* сторожева́я соба́ка; **~-house** *n.* карау́льное помеще́ние; карау́льня; **~-rail** *n.* пери́л|а (*pl., g.* —); **~-room** *n.* гауптва́хта; **~sman** *n.* гварде́ец.

guarded /ˈgɑ:dɪd/ *adj.* сде́ржанный; осторо́жный.

guardian /ˈgɑ:dɪən/ *n.* **1** (*protector*) опеку́н; попечи́тель (*m.*); **~ angel** а́нгел-храни́тель (*m.*); **~ of the public interest** защи́тник obще́ственных интере́сов. **2** (*leg.*) опеку́н.

guardianship /ˈgɑ:dɪənˌʃɪp/ *n.* опе́ка; опеку́нство.

Guatemala /ˌgwɑ:təˈmɑ:lə/ *n.* Гватема́ла.

Guatemalan /ˌgwɑ:təˈmɑ:lən/ *n.* гватема́л|ец (*fem.* -ка).

● *adj.* гватема́льский.

guava /ˈgwɑ:və/ *n.* гуа́ва.

gudgeon /ˈgʌdʒ(ə)n/ *n.* (*zool.*) песка́рь (*m.*).

guelder-rose /ˈgeldə(r)/ *n.* кали́на.

Guernsey /ˈgɜ:nzɪ/ *n.* (о́стров) Ге́рнси (*m. indecl.*); (*attr.*) гернсе́йский.

guer(r)illa /gəˈrɪlə/ *n.* партиза́н; **~ warfare** партиза́нская война́.

guess /ges/ *n.* дога́дка; предположе́ние; **at a rough ~** гру́бо/ориентиро́вочно; **my ~ is that ...** мне сдаётся, что...; **it's anybody's ~** никому́ не изве́стно; кто зна́ет?

● *v.t.* **1** (*estimate*) прики́|дывать, -нуть; **I would ~ his age at 40** я дал бы ему́ лет 40. **2**: **~ a riddle** отга́д|ывать, -а́ть зага́дку. **3** (*conjecture*) дога́д|ываться, -а́ться (*о чём*); уга́д|ывать, -а́ть; **I can't ~ how it happened** ума́ не приложу́, как э́то случи́лось. **4** (*coll., expect, suppose*) полага́ть (*impf.*); **I ~ you are right** веро́ятно, вы пра́вы.

● *v.i.* гада́ть (*impf.*); **she likes to keep him ~ing** ей нра́вится держа́ть его́ в неве́дении; **~ing game** виктори́на; «угада́йка».

● *cpd.* **~work** *n.* дога́дки (*f. pl.*).

guest /gest/ *n.* **1** (*one privately entertained*) гость (*m.*); **paying ~** ≈ жиле́ц; **~ of honour** (*Br.*), **honor** (*US*) почётный гость; **~ artist, star** гастроли́рующий арти́ст; звезда́ на гастро́лях. **2** (*at a hotel etc.*) постоя́лец.

● *cpds.* **~-house** *n.* пансио́н; **~-night** *n.* ≈ зва́ный ве́чер; **~-room** *n.* ко́мната для госте́й.

guff /gʌf/ *n.* (*sl.*) трёп; трепотня́.

guffaw /gʌˈfɔ:/ *n.* го́гот.

● *v.i.* гогота́ть (*impf.*).

guidance /ˈgaɪd(ə)ns/ *n.* руково́дство.

guide /gaɪd/ *n.* **1** (*leader*) руководи́тель (*m.*); (*for travellers, tourists etc.*) гид, экскурсово́д; (*mil.*) разве́дчик. **2** (*directing principle*) руково́дство. **3** (*also* **~-book**): **~ to Germany** путеводи́тель (*m.*) по Герма́нии; (*manual*) уче́бник; **~ to fishing** руково́дство по ры́бной ло́вле. **4**: **(Girl) G~** де́вочка-ска́ут.

● *v.t.* **1** (*lead, take around*) води́ть (*indet.*), вести́, по- (*det.*); руководи́ть (*impf.*) + *i.*; **he ~d them around the city** он поводи́л их по го́роду; **be ~d by principles** руково́дствоваться (*impf.*) при́нципами; **be ~d by circumstances** де́йствовать (*impf.*) по обстоя́тельствам. **2** (*direct*) напр|авля́ть, -а́вить; **~d missile** управля́емая раке́та.

● *cpds.* **~-book** *n.* путеводи́тель (*m.*); **~-dog** *n.* соба́ка-поводы́рь; **~line** *n.* директи́ва; **~-post** *n.* указа́тель (*m.*).

guild /gɪld/ *n.* **1** (*hist.*) ги́льдия. **2** ассоциа́ция, сою́з.

● *cpd.* **~hall** *n.* ра́туша.

guilder /ˈgɪldə(r)/ *n.* гу́льден.

guile /gaɪl/ *n.* кова́рство, хи́трость.

guileful /ˈgaɪlfʊl/ *adj.* кова́рный, хи́трый.

guileless /ˈgaɪllɪs/ *adj.* простоду́шный; бесхи́тростный.

guillemot /ˈgɪlɪˌmɒt/ *n.* (*zool.*) ка́йра.

guillotine /ˈgɪləˌti:n/ *n.* **1** гильоти́на. **2** (*for paper, metal etc.*) ре́зальная маши́на. **3** (*Br., parl.*) гильотини́рование пре́ний.

● *v.t.* (*execute*) гильотини́ровать (*impf., pf.*); (*pages etc.*) обр|еза́ть, -е́зать.

guilt /gɪlt/ *n.* вина́; **~ complex** ко́мплекс вины́.

guiltiness /ˈgɪltɪnɪs/ *n.* вино́вность.

guiltless /ˈgɪltlɪs/ *adj.* невино́вный (*в чём*).

guilty /ˈgɪltɪ/ *adj.* (**guiltier, guiltiest**) вино́вный; **he pleaded ~ to the crime** он призна́л себя́ вино́вным в преступле́нии; **he was found ~** он был при́знан вино́вным; **a verdict of not ~** верди́кт невино́вности; **~ conscience** нечи́стая со́весть; **a ~ look** винова́тый вид.

guinea /ˈgɪnɪ/ *n.* (*Br.*) гине́я.

Guinea /ˈgɪnɪ/ *n.* Гвине́я.

● *cpds.* **g~-fowl, hen** *nn.* цеса́рка;

g~-pig *n.* (*lit.*) морска́я сви́нка; (*fig.*) «подо́пытный кро́лик».

Guinean /gɪn'eɪən/ *n.* гвине́|ец (*fem.* -йка).

● *adj.* гвине́йский.

guise /gaɪz/ *n.* (*dress*) наря́д; (*pretence*) предло́г; **under the ~ of friendship** под ви́дом дру́жбы.

guitar /gɪ'tɑ:(r)/ *n.* гита́ра.

guitarist /gɪ'tɑ:rɪst/ *n.* гитари́ст (*fem.* -ка).

gulch /gʌltʃ/ *n.* (*US*) у́зкое уще́лье.

gulf /gʌlf/ *n.* **1** (*deep bay*) зали́в; бу́хта; **the G~ Stream** Гольфстри́м. **2** (*abyss*) бе́здна. **3** (*fig.*) про́пасть.

gull /gʌl/ *n.* (*bird*) ча́йка.

gullet /'gʌlɪt/ *n.* пищево́д; **it sticks in my ~** (*fig.*) э́то мне поперёк го́рла.

gullibility /,gʌlɪ'bɪlɪtɪ/ *n.* легкове́рие.

gullible /'gʌlɪb(ə)l/ *adj.* легкове́рный.

gully /'gʌlɪ/ *n.* лощи́на; водосто́к.

gulp /gʌlp/ *n.* большо́й глото́к; **at one ~** за́лпом; **he took a ~ of tea** он глотну́л ча́ю.

● *v.t.* глот|а́ть, -ну́ть; **don't ~ down your food!** не глота́й еду́/пи́щу!; **she ~ed back her tears** она́ глота́ла слёзы.

● *v.i.*: **he ~ed with astonishment** он поперхну́лся от удивле́ния.

gum[1] /gʌm/ *n.* (*anat.*) десна́.

● *cpds.* **~boil** *n.* флюс; **~shield** *n.* (*sport*) назу́бник.

gum[2] /gʌm/ *n.* (*adhesive*) клей; (*resin*) каме́дь; (*chewing-~*) жева́тельная рези́нка.

● *v.t.* (**gummed, gumming**) скле́и|вать, -ть; **~ up the works** (*sl.*) испо́ртить (*pf.*) всё де́ло.

● *cpds.* **~-boots** *n. pl.* (*Br. coll.*) рези́новые сапоги́ (*m. pl.*); **~-tree** *n.*: **he was up a ~-tree** (*Br. sl.*) он попа́л в переде́лку.

gummy /'gʌmɪ/ *adj.* (**gummier, gummiest**) кле́йкий.

gumption /'gʌmpʃ(ə)n/ *n.* (*coll.*) смышлёность; нахо́дчивость.

gun /gʌn/ *n.* **1** (*cannon*) пу́шка, ору́дие; (*pistol*) пистоле́т; (*rifle*) ружьё; **~ crew** ору́дийный расчёт; **heavy ~s** тяжёлая артилле́рия; **starting ~** ста́ртовый пистоле́т; **the ~s fired a salute** был произведён ору́дийный залп; **he stuck to his ~s** (*fig.*) он не сдал пози́ций; **jump the ~** (*fig.*) сова́ться, су́нуться ра́ньше вре́мени; **son of a ~** (*sl.*) па́рень (*m.*), ма́лый; **spike s.o.'s ~s** (*fig.*) сорва́ть (*pf.*) чьи-н. пла́ны. **2** (*device resembling ~*) пистоле́т. **3** (*Br., member of shooting-party*) стрело́к; охо́тник.

● *v.t.* (**gunned, gunning**) стреля́ть (*impf.*); **the refugees were ~ned down** бе́женцев расстреля́ли.

● *v.i.* (**gunned, gunning**) охо́титься (*impf.*); **he is ~ning for me** (*sl.*) он то́чит на меня́ нож.

● *cpds.* **~-barrel** *n.* ду́ло; **~-battle, ~-fight** *nn.* перестре́лка; **~boat** *n.* каноне́рская ло́дка, каноне́рка; **~-carriage** *n.* лафе́т; **~-dog** *n.* охо́тничья соба́ка; **~-fight** *n.* = **~-battle; ~fire** *n.* ору́ди́йный ого́нь; **~man** *n.* банди́т; террори́ст; **~-metal** *n.* пу́шечный мета́лл; **~-point** *n.*: **at ~-point** угрожа́я ору́жием; под ду́лом пистоле́та; **~powder** *n.* по́рох; **~-room** *n.* (*Br., nav.*) каю́т-компа́ния; **~-runner** *n.* контрабанди́ст, торгу́ющий ору́жием; **~-running** *n.* незако́нный ввоз ору́жия; контраба́нда ору́жием; **~-ship** *n.* вооружённый вертолёт; **~shot** *n.* руже́йный вы́стрел; **~smith** *n.* оруже́йный ма́стер.

gung-ho /gʌŋ'həʊ/ *adj.* разуха́бистый, у́харский.

gunner /'gʌnə(r)/ *n.* канони́р; артиллери́ст.

gunnery /'gʌnərɪ/ *n.* артиллери́йское де́ло.

gunwale /'gʌn(ə)l/ *n.* (*naut.*) планши́р.

gurgle /'gɜ:g(ə)l/ *n.* бу́льканье.

● *v.i.* бу́лькать (*impf.*).

Gurkha /'gɜ:kə/ *n.* (*mil.*) гу́рк(х)а (*m. indecl.*).

● *adj.* гу́рк(х)ский.

guru /'gʊru:/, /'gu:ru:/ *n.* гу́ру (*m. indecl.*).

gush /gʌʃ/ *n.* пото́к.

● *v.i.* хлы́нуть (*pf.*); **the water ~ed from the tap** вода́ хлы́нула из кра́на; (*fig., speak effusively*) излива́ться (*impf.*).

gushing /'gʌʃɪŋ/ *adj.* (*person*) экспанси́вный, несде́ржанный; (*compliments etc.*) преувели́ченный, чрезме́рный.

gusset /'gʌsɪt/ *n.* (*in a garment*) клин.

gust /gʌst/ *n.* (*of wind etc.*) поры́в ве́тра; (*fig.*) взрыв.

gustatory /'gʌstətərɪ/ *adj.* вкусово́й.

gusto /'gʌstəʊ/ *n.* (*relish*) смак; (*zeal*) жар, рве́ние.

gusty /'gʌstɪ/ *adj.* (**gustier, gustiest**) бу́рный; поры́вистый; **a ~ day** ве́треный день.

gut /gʌt/ *n.* **1** (*intestine*) кишка́; (*for strings of instrument*) струна́. **2** (*pl.*) (*intestines, stomach*) кишки́ (*f. pl.*); потрох|а́ (*pl., g.* -о́в); (*fig., gist, essential contents*) су́щность; (*fig., courage and determination*) вы́держка; **he is a man with no ~s** он бесхара́ктерный челове́к; **he hadn't the ~s to tackle the burglar** у него́ не хвати́ло му́жества задержа́ть взло́мщика; **~ reaction** инстинкти́вная реа́кция; **I hate his ~s** (*coll.*) я его́ на́ дух не принима́ю.

● *v.t.* (**gutted, gutting**) **1** (*eviscerate*) потроши́ть, вы́-. **2** (*destroy contents of*) опустош|а́ть, -и́ть; **the house was ~ted by fire** дом сгоре́л дотла́.

gutless /'gʌtlɪs/ *adj.* бесхребе́тный, бесхара́ктерный.

gutsy /'gʌtsɪ/ *adj.* (**gutsier, gutsiest**) упо́рный, де́рзкий.

gutta-percha /,gʌtə'pɜ:tʃə/ *n.* гуттапе́рча.

gutted /'gʌtɪd/ *adj.* (*Br. coll.*) кра́йне разочаро́ванный.

gutter[1] /'gʌtə(r)/ *n.* (*under eaves*) водосто́чный жёлоб; (*at roadside*) сто́чная кана́ва; (*fig.*): **his name was dragged into, through the ~** его́ и́мя бы́ло вто́птано в грязь; **the ~ press** (*Br.*) бульва́рная пре́сса.

● *cpd.* **~-snipe** *n.* у́личный мальчи́шка.

gutter[2] /'gʌtə(r)/ *v.i.* (*of a candle*) опл|ыва́ть, -ы́ть.

guttural /'gʌtər(ə)l/ *n.* веля́рный звук.

● *adj.* горта́нный; горлово́й; (*phon.*) веля́рный, задненёбный.

guy[1] /gaɪ/ *n.* (**~-rope**) оття́жка.

guy[2] /gaɪ/ *n.* (*Br., effigy*) пу́гало; (*coll., fellow*) ма́лый; **tough ~** желе́зный/круто́й ма́лый; **wise ~** у́мник

● *v.t.* (*hold up to ridicule*) осме́|ивать, -я́ть.

Guyana /gaɪ'ænə/ *n.* Гайа́на.

Guyanese /,gaɪə'ni:z/ *n.* гайа́н|ец (*fem.* -ка).

● *adj.* гайа́нский.

guzzle /'gʌz(ə)l/ *v.t.* (*eat*) есть, съ- с жа́дностью; (*drink*) пить, вы́- с жа́дностью; (*fig., consume*) про|еда́ть, -е́сть.

guzzler /'gʌzlə(r)/ *n.* обжо́ра (*c.g.*).

gym /dʒɪm/ *n.* (*coll.*) (*gymnasium*) гимнасти́ческий зал; (*gymnastics*) гимна́стика.

● *cpds.* **~-shoe** *n.* спорти́вная та́почка; **~-slip** *n.* (*Br.*) пла́тье-сарафа́н в скла́дку (*одежда школьниц*).

gymkhana /dʒɪm'kɑ:nə/ *n.* конноспорти́вные состяза́ния (*nt. pl.*).

gymnasi|um /dʒɪm'neɪzɪəm/ *n.* (*pl.* **~ums** *or* **~a**) гимнасти́ческий зал; (*school*) гимна́зия.

gymnast /'dʒɪmnæst/ *n.* гимна́ст.

gymnastic /dʒɪm'næstɪk/ *adj.* гимнасти́ческий.

gymnastics /dʒɪm'næstɪks/ *n.* гимна́стика.

gynaecological /,gaɪnɪkə'lɒdʒɪk(ə)l/ (*US* **gynecological**) *adj.* гинекологи́ческий.

gynaecologist /,gaɪnɪ'kɒlədʒɪst/ (*US* **gynecologist**) *n.* гинеко́лог.

gynaecology /,gaɪnɪ'kɒlədʒɪ/ (*US* **gynecology**) *n.* гинеколо́гия.

gyp /dʒɪp/ *n.* (*Br. sl.*): **give s.o. ~** зад|ава́ть, -а́ть кому́-н. трёпку.

gypsum /'dʒɪpsəm/ *n.* гипс.

Gypsy /'dʒɪpsɪ/ = **Gipsy**

gyrate /,dʒaɪə'reɪt/ *v.i.* враща́ться (*impf.*).

gyration /,dʒaɪ'reɪʃ(ə)n/ *n.* враще́ние.

gyratory /'dʒaɪrətərɪ/, /-'reɪtərɪ/ *adj.* враща́тельный.

gyro /'dʒaɪrəʊ/ *n.* (*pl.* **~s**) = **gyroscope**

● *cpds.* **~-compass** *n.* гироко́мпас; **~plane** *n.* автожи́р.

gyroscope /'dʒaɪərə,skəʊp/ *n.* (*pl.* **~s**) гироско́п.

gyroscopic /,dʒaɪrə'skɒpɪk/ *adj.* гироскопи́ческий.

Hh

ha /hɑː/ *int.* ага́!; **~, ~** (*expr. laughter*) ха-ха-ха́!

ha. /ˈhekteə(r)/, /-tɑː(r)/ *n.* (*abbr. of* ***hectare(s)***) га (гекта́р).

habeas corpus /ˌheɪbɪəs ˈkɔːpəs/ *n.* (*leg.*) суде́бный прика́з о переда́че арестова́нного в суд; Ха́беас Ко́рпус (*indecl.*).

haberdasher /ˈhæbəˌdæʃə(r)/ *n.* (*Br.*) галантере́йщик.

haberdashery /ˈhæbəˌdæʃərɪ/ *n.* (*Br.*) (*shop*) галантере́йный магази́н; (*wares*) галантере́я.

habit /ˈhæbɪt/ *n.* **1** (*settled practice*) привы́чка; обыкнове́ние; **get into a ~** прив|ыка́ть, -ы́кнуть (+*inf.*); **get out of a ~** отв|ыка́ть, -ы́кнуть (+*inf. or* от+*g.*); **break (o.s.) of a bad ~** отуч|а́ть(ся), -и́ть(ся) от дурно́й привы́чки; **I am in the ~ (*or* make a ~) of rising early** я обыкнове́нно встаю́ ра́но; **he got into bad ~s** он усво́ил дурны́е привы́чки; **from force of ~** в си́лу привы́чки; по привы́чке. **2** (*monk's dress*) ря́са. **3** (*riding-~*) амазо́нка (*пла́тье*).

● *cpd.* **~-forming** *adj.* создаю́щий привы́чку.

habitable /ˈhæbɪtəb(ə)l/ *adj.* приго́дный для жилья́.

habitat /ˈhæbɪˌtæt/ *n.* есте́ственная среда́ (*расте́ния, живо́тного*).

habitation /ˌhæbɪˈteɪʃ(ə)n/ *n.*: **unfit for ~** неприго́дный для жилья́; (*dwelling-place*) жили́ще; (*process of inhabiting*) обита́ние.

habitual /həˈbɪtjʊəl/ *adj.* привы́чный; обы́чный; **a ~ drunkard** беспробу́дный пья́ница; **a ~ liar** завзя́тый лгун.

habituate /həˈbɪtjʊˌeɪt/ *v.t.* приуч|а́ть, -и́ть (*кого к чему*).

habitué /həˈbɪtjʊˌeɪ/ *n.* завсегда́тай.

hachures /hæˈʃjʊəz/ *n. pl.* гашю́ры; штрихи (для обозначе́ния про́филей ме́стности).

hack¹ /hæk/ *n.* (*chopping blow*) рубя́щий уда́р.

● *v.t.* разруб|а́ть, -и́ть; руби́ть (*impf.*).

● *v.i.* **1**: **a ~ing cough** си́льный сухо́й ка́шель. **2**: **~ into** (*comput.*) прон|ика́ть, -и́кнуть в+*a.*; взл|а́мывать, -ома́ть.

● *cpd.* **~-saw** *n.* ножо́вка.

hack² /hæk/ *n.* (*horse*) наёмная ло́шадь; (*writer*) халту́рщик.

● *v.i.* ≈ ката́ться (*impf.*) на ло́шади.

● *cpd.* **~-work** *n.* халту́ра.

hacker /ˈhækə(r)/ *n.* (*comput.*) ха́кер.

hackles /ˈhæk(ə)lz/ *n. pl.* пе́рья (*nt. pl.*) на ше́е петуха́; (*fig.*): **it makes my ~ rise** э́то приво́дит меня́ в бе́шенство.

hackney /ˈhæknɪ/ *v.t.*: **a ~ed expression** затёртое/иста́сканное выраже́ние.

● *cpd.* **~-carriage** *n.* (*Br.*) наёмный экипа́ж; (*car*) такси́ (*nt. indecl.*).

had /hæd/ *past and p.p. of* ⇒**have**

haddock /ˈhædək/ *n.* (*pl.* **~**) пи́кша.

Hades /ˈheɪdiːz/ *n.* Га́дес, Аи́д, преиспо́дняя.

haematite /ˈhiːməˌtaɪt/ (*US* **hematite**) *n.* кра́сный железня́к.

haematological /ˌhiːmətəˈlɒdʒɪk(ə)l/ (*US* **hematological**) *adj.* гематологи́ческий.

haematologist /ˌhiːməˈtɒlədʒɪst/ (*US* **hematologist**) *n.* гемато́лог.

haematology /ˌhiːməˈtɒlədʒɪ/ (*US* **hematology**) *n.* гематоло́гия.

haemoglobin /ˌhiːməˈgləʊbɪn/ (*US* **hemoglobin**) *n.* гемоглоби́н.

haemophilia /ˌhiːməˈfɪlɪə/ (*US* **hemophilia**) *n.* гемофили́я.

haemorrhage /ˈhemərɪdʒ/ (*US* **hemorrhage**) *n.* кровотече́ние; (*internal*) кровоизлия́ние; **brain ~** кровоизлия́ние в мозг.

haemorrhoids /ˈheməˌrɔɪdz/ (*US* **hemorrhoids**) *n. pl.* геморро́й.

haft /hɑːft/ *n.* рукоя́тка.

hag /hæg/ *n.* карга́.

haggard /ˈhægəd/ *adj.* измождённый; осу́нувшийся.

haggle /ˈhæg(ə)l/ *v.i.* торгова́ться (*impf.*).

hagiography /ˌhægɪˈɒgrəfɪ/ *n.* житие́ святы́х, агиогра́фия.

Hague /heɪg/ *n.*: **The ~** Гаа́га.

hail¹ /heɪl/ *n.* (*frozen rain*) град; (*fig.*): **a ~ of blows** град уда́ров.

● *v.i.*: **it is ~ing** идёт град; (*fig.*) сы́паться гра́дом.

● *cpds.* **~stone** *n.* гра́дина; **~storm** *n.* гроза́ с гра́дом.

hail² /heɪl/ *n.* (*salutation*) приве́тствие; **within ~** на расстоя́нии слы́шимости.

● *v.t.* **1** (*acclaim*) провозгла|ша́ть, -си́ть; (*praise*) превозноси́ть (*impf.*); **he was ~ed by the critics** кри́тики превозноси́ли его́. **2** (*greet*) приве́тствовать (*impf.*); окл|ика́ть, -и́кнуть; **he ~ed me in the street** он окли́кнул меня́ на у́лице. **3** (*summon*) под|зыва́ть, -озва́ть; **he ~ed a taxi** он подозва́л такси́.

● *v.i.* быть ро́дом из+*g.*, быть уроже́нцем+*g.*; **he ~s from Scotland** он ро́дом из Шотла́ндии.

● *cpd.* **~-fellow-well-met** *adj.* запаниб ра́тский.

hair /heə(r)/ *n.* **1** (*single strand*) во́лос, волосо́к; **he came within a ~'s breadth of death** он был на волосо́к от сме́рти; **he came within a ~'s breadth of success** он был бли́зок к успе́ху; **he never turned a ~** он и бро́вью не повёл; **that is splitting ~s** э́то спор по пустяка́м; **you should take a ~ of the dog that bit you** вам сле́дует опохмели́ться. **2** (*dim., e.g. baby's*) воло́сик(и). **3** (*head of ~*) во́лосы (*m. pl.*); **~ conditioner** бальза́м (для воло́с); **have, get one's ~ cut** стри́чься, по-; **lose one's ~** лысе́ть, об-/по-; **keep your ~ on!** (*Br. sl.*) споко́йно!; не горячи́тесь!; **let one's ~ down** (*lit.*) распус|ка́ть, -ти́ть во́лосы; (*fig.*) рассл|абля́ться, -а́биться; **this will make your ~ stand on end** от э́того у вас во́лосы вста́нут ды́бом; **she put her ~ up** она́ подобрала́ во́лосы. **4** (*of animals*) шерсть, щети́на.

● *cpds.* **~band** *n.* ободо́к; **~('s)-breadth** *n.*: **within a ~'s breadth of death** на волосо́к от сме́рти; **~-brush** *n.* щётка для воло́с; **~-clip** *n.* зако́лка; **~cut** *n.* стри́жка;

have a ~cut стри́чься, по-; **~-do** *n.* (*coll.*) причёска; **~dresser** *n.* парикма́хер; **~dresser's** *n.* (*shop, salon*) парикма́херская; **~dressing** *n.* парикма́херское иску́сство; **~-dryer** *n.* фен; **~-grip** *n.* (*Br.*) зако́лка; **~-line** *n.* (*edge of ~*) ли́ния воло́с; **~-line crack** волосна́я тре́щина; **~-net** *n.* се́тка для воло́с; **~-oil** *n.* ма́сло для воло́с; **~-piece** *n.* накладны́е во́лосы, накла́дка; **~pin** *n.* шпи́лька; **~pin bend** (*Br.*), **turn** (*US*) круто́й поворо́т; **~-raising** *adj.* жу́ткий; **~-restorer** *n.* сре́дство от облысе́ния; **~-shirt** *n.* власяни́ца; **~-splitting** *n.* привере́дливость; *adj.* привере́дливый, ме́лочный; **~spray** *n.* лак для воло́с; **~-spring** *n.* волоско́вая пружи́на; **~-style** *n.* причёска; **~stylist** *n.* парикма́хер; **~-trigger** *n.* шне́ллер; *adj.* (*fig.*) вспы́льчивый.

hairiness /ˈheərɪnɪs/ *n.* волоса́тость.

hairless /ˈheəlɪs/ *adj.* безволо́сый.

hairy /ˈheərɪ/ *adj.* (**hairier, hairiest**) **1** волоса́тый. **2** (*sl.*) (*frightening*) стра́шный.

Haiti /ˈheɪtɪ/, /hɑːˈiːtɪ/ *n.* Гаи́ти (*m. indecl.*).

Haitian /ˈheɪʃɪən/, /hɑːˈiːʃən/ *n.* гаитя́н|ин (*fem.* -ка).

● *adj.* гаитя́нский.

hake /heɪk/ *n.* хек.

halberd /ˈhælbəd/ *n.* алеба́рда.

halberdier /ˌhælbəˈdɪə(r)/ *n.* во́ин, вооружённый алеба́рдой.

halcyon /ˈhælsɪən/ *adj.* (*fig.*) ти́хий, безмяте́жный.

hale /heɪl/ *adj.* кре́пкий; **~ and hearty** кре́пкий и бо́дрый.

half /hɑːf/ *n.* (*pl.* **halves**) **1** (*one of two equal parts*) полови́на; пол- (*pref: see examples and cpds.*); **one and a ~** полтора́; **he cut the loaf in ~** он разре́зал хлеб попола́м; **getting there is ~ the battle** добра́ться туда́ — полови́на де́ла; **~ an hour** полчаса́; **~ an hour later** получа́сом по́зже; **~ and ~** попола́м, по́ровну; **I have ~ a mind to go** я не про́чь пойти́; **~ a minute!** (одну́) мину́точку!; **~ past two** полови́на тре́тьего; (*coll.*) полтре́тьего; **he is too clever by ~** он чересчу́р уж у́мный; **they agreed to go halves** они́ согласи́лись подели́ть попола́м; **that's not the ~ of it!** э́то ещё далеко́ не всё.
2 (*one of two parts*) полови́на, часть; **my better ~** моя́ дража́йшая/лу́чшая полови́на; **let's see how the other ~ lives** посмо́трим, как живу́т други́е.
3 (*of a game*) пери́од, тайм; (*of academic year*) семе́стр; (*~-back*) полузащи́тник.

● *adj.* (*see also cpds.*): **he's not one for ~ measures** он не сторо́нник полуме́р.

● *adv.*: **~ asleep** со́нный; **~ dead** полуживо́й; **I feel ~ dead** я едва́ жив; **the meat is only ~ done** мя́со недова́рено/недожа́рено; **~ as much** вдво́е ме́ньше; **~ as much again** в полтора́ ра́за бо́льше; **I ~ expected it** я почти́ ждал э́того; **that's not ~ bad!** (*coll.*) э́то совсе́м непло́хо!; **not ~!** (*Br. coll.*) ещё бы!; а как же!; **he wasn't ~ annoyed!** (*coll.*) он был поря́дком раздоса́дован!; **it was ~ raining, ~ snowing** шёл не то дождь, не то снег.

● *cpds.* **~-and-~** *adv.* полови́на на полови́ну; (*fig.*) ни то ни сё; **~-back** *n.* полузащи́тник; **~-baked** *adj.* недопечённый; (*fig.*) недорабо́танный, непроду́манный; (*person*) незре́лый; **~-breed** *n.* (*offens.*) = **~-caste; ~-brother** *n.* (*having same father*) единокро́вный брат; (*having same mother*) единоутро́бный брат; **~-caste** *n.* (*offens.*) мети́с; **~-cock** *n.* предохрани́тельный взвод; **the scheme went off at ~-cock** в ход был пу́щен совсе́м ещё сыро́й план; **~-dozen** *n.* (*also* **~ a dozen**) полдю́жины; **~-hearted** *adj.* нереши́тельный; без энтузиа́зма; **~-holiday** *n.* коро́ткий рабо́чий/уче́бный день; **~-hour** *n.* (*also* **~ an hour**) полчаса́; **every ~-hour** ка́ждые полчаса́; **the last ~-hour** после́дние полча́са; **after the first ~-hour** по́сле пе́рвого получа́са; *adj.* получасово́й; **~-hourly** *adj.* получасово́й; *adv.* ка́ждые полчаса́; **~-length** *n.* (*portrait*) поясно́й портре́т; **~-life** *n.* (*phys.*) пери́од полураспа́да; **~-light** *n.* полутьма́; **~-mast** *n.*: **at ~-mast** приспу́щенный; **~-mile** *n.* (*also* **~ a mile**) полми́ли; **~-moon** *n.* полуме́сяц; **~-nelson** *n.* (*sport*) полуне́льсон; **~ note** *n.* (*US, mus.*) полови́нная но́та; **~-pay** *n.* полови́нный/непо́лный окла́д; **~-pound** *n.* (*also* **~ a pound**) полфу́нта; *adj.* полуфунто́вый; **~-price** *adj.* полцены́; **at ~-price** за полцены́; **children under 5 ~-price** за дете́й до пяти́ лет пла́тят полцены́; **~-sister** *n.* (*having same father*) единокро́вная сестра́; (*having same mother*) единоутро́бная сестра́; **~-term** *n.*: **~-term (holiday)** (*Br.*) кани́кул|ы (*pl., g.* —) в середи́не триме́стра; **~-timbered** *adj.* фахве́рковый; **~-time** *n.* коне́ц та́йма; переры́в ме́жду та́ймами; **the teams changed ends at ~-time** кома́нды поменя́лись места́ми по́сле пе́рвого та́йма; (*reduced working hours*): **the men were put on ~-time** рабо́чих перевели́ на непо́лную рабо́чую неде́лю; **~-title** *n.* шмуцти́тул; **~-tone** *n.* (*mus.*) полуто́н; **~-track** *n.* полугу́сеничная автомаши́на; **~-truth** *n.* полупра́вда; **~-turn** *n.* пол-оборо́та; **~-volley** *n.* уда́р с полулёта; **~-way** *adj.* лежа́щий на полпути́; **~-way house** (*fig.*) компроми́сс; полуме́ра; *adv.* на полпути́; **we met ~-way from the station** мы встре́тились на полпути́ от вокза́ла; **we turned back ~-way** мы верну́лись с полпути́; **I'll meet you ~-way** (*fig.*) я гото́в пойти́ вам навстре́чу; **~-wit** *n.* дура́к; **~-witted** *adj.* слабоу́мный, полоу́мный; **~-yearly** *adj.* шестиме́сячный; *adv.* раз в полгода.

halibut /ˈhælɪbət/ *n.* (*pl.* **~**) па́лтус.

halitosis /ˌhælɪˈtəʊsɪs/ *n.* дурно́й за́пах изо рта́.

hall /hɔːl/ *n.* **1** (*place of assembly*) зал; **town ~** ра́туша; (*college dining-~*) столо́вая. **2** (*Br., country mansion*) поме́щичья уса́дьба. **3** (*lobby; also* **~way**) пере́дняя, прихо́жая, холл; **~ of mirrors** ко́мната сме́ха; **~ of residence** (*Br.*) общежи́тие.

● *cpds.* **~mark** *n.* проби́рное клеймо́; про́ба; (*fig.*) отличи́тельный при́знак; печа́ть; *v.t.* ста́вить, по- про́бу на + *p.*; **~-stand** *n.* ве́шалка в прихо́жей.

hallelujah /ˌhælɪˈluːjə/ *n.* & *int.* аллилу́йя.

hallo /həˈləʊ/ *n.* & *int.* (*greeting*) здра́вствуй(те)!; приве́т! (*coll.*); (*on telephone*) алло́!; (*expr. surprise*) вот те(бе́) на́!

halloo /həˈluː/ *int.* (*in hunting*) ату́!; (*calling attention*) эй!

● *v.i.* (**halloos, hallooed**) улюлю́кать (*impf.*).

hallow /ˈhæləʊ/ *v.t.* освя|ща́ть, -ти́ть; **~ed be thy name** да святи́тся и́мя твоё; **in ~ed memory of** све́тлой па́мяти + *g.*

Hallowe'en /ˌhæləʊˈiːn/ *n.* кану́н Дня всех святы́х (*31 октября*).

hallucination /həˌluːsɪˈneɪʃ(ə)n/ *n.* галлюцина́ция; **have ~s** галлюцини́ровать (*impf.*); (*recurrently*) страда́ть (*impf.*) галлюцина́циями.

hallucin|atory /həˈluːsɪnətərɪ/, **-ogenic** /həˌluːsɪnəˈdʒenɪk/ *adjs.* вызыва́ющий галлюцина́ции, галлюциноге́нный.

hallucinogen /həˈluːsɪnədʒen/ *n.* галлюциноге́н.

halo /ˈheɪləʊ/ *n.* (*pl.* **~es** *or* **~s**) (*astron.*) гало́ (*indecl.*); сия́ние; (*round saint's head*) нимб; (*fig.*) орео́л.

halt[1] /hɒlt/, /hɔːlt/ *n.* (*in march or journey*) остано́вка; **come to a ~** остан|а́вливаться, -ови́ться; прекра|ща́ться, -ти́ться; **the train came to a ~** по́езд останови́лся; **bring to a ~** остан|а́вливать, -ови́ть; прекра|ща́ть, -ти́ть; **his work was brought to a ~** он был вы́нужден приостанови́ть рабо́ту; **call a ~** де́лать, с- прива́л; (*fig.*) да|ва́ть, -ть отбо́й; (*Br., stopping-place on railway*) полуста́нок.

● *v.t.* остан|а́вливать, -ови́ть; **he ~ed his men** он останови́л солда́т; **progress was ~ed** прогре́сс был приостано́влен.

● *v.i.* (*stop*) остан|а́вливаться, -ови́ться; **~! who goes there?** стой! кто идёт?

halt[2] /hɒlt/, /hɔːlt/ *v.i.* (*esp. pres. part.: limp, falter*) хрома́ть (*impf.*); зап|ина́ться, -ну́ться; **a ~ing gait** неве́рная похо́дка; **a ~ing voice** запина́ющийся го́лос.

halter /ˈhɒltə(r)/, /ˈhɔːl-/ *n.* (*for a horse*) по́вод; недоу́здок.

halva /ˈhælvɑː/ *n.* халва́.

halve /hɑːv/ *v.t.* (*divide in two*) дели́ть, раз- попола́м; (*reduce by half*) ум|еньша́ть, -е́ньшить (*or* сокра|ща́ть, -ти́ть) наполови́ну.

halves /hɑːvz/ *pl. of* ⇒**half**

halyard /ˈhæljəd/ *n.* (*naut.*) фал.

ham /hæm/ *n.* **1** (*thigh of pig*) óкорок; (*meat from this*) ветчинá; **~ sandwich** бутербрóд с ветчинóй. **2** (*human thigh*) ля́жка; **he squatted on his ~s** он присéл на кóрточки. **3** (*sl., poor actor*) бездáрный актёр. **4** (*sl., amateur radio operator*) радиолюби́тель (*m.*).

● *v.t. & i.* (**hammed, hamming**) (*sl.*) сквéрно игрáть (*impf.*); **~ it up** переигр|ывать, -áть; превра|щáть, -ти́ть всё в мелодрáму.

● *cpds.* **~-fisted, ~-handed** *adjs.* тяжёлый нá руку; неуклю́жий; (*fig.*) топóрный; **~string** *v.t.* подр|езáть, -éзать поджи́лки + *d.*; (*fig.*) подрезáть, подрéзать кры́лья + *d.*

hamburger /ˈhæm,bɜːɡə(r)/ *n.* гáмбургер.

Hamitic /həˈmɪtɪk/ *adj.* хами́тский.

hamlet /ˈhæmlɪt/ *n.* деревýшка.

hammer /ˈhæmə(r)/ *n.* молотóк; (*large one*) мóлот; **~ and sickle** серп и мóлот; **throwing the ~** метáние мóлота; **he went at it ~ and tongs** он брóсил на э́то все си́лы; (*auctioneer's*) молотóк; **the estate came (*or* was brought) under the ~** имéние пошлó с молоткá.

● *v.t.* (*beat*) уд|aря́ть, -áрить; (*defeat*) бить, по-; **~ in** вби|вáть, -ть; вкол|áчивать, -оти́ть; приб|ивáть, -и́ть; **he ~ed in the nails** он вбил гвóзди; **the smith ~s the metal into shape** кузнéц куёт метáлл; **the mechanic ~ed out the dents** механик вы́ровнял зазýбрины молоткóм; **he was ~ing a box together** он сколáчивал я́щик; **the enemy got a good ~ing** неприя́телю крéпко достáлось; **the idea was ~ed into his head** э́ту мысль вби́ли емý в гóлову; **we ~ed out a plan** мы разрабóтали план.

● *v.i.* стучáть (*impf.*); колоти́ть (*impf.*); **someone was ~ing on the door** ктó-то колоти́л в дверь; **he ~ed away on the piano** он барабáнил по роя́лю; **he ~ed away at the problem** он упóрно би́лся над э́той задáчей.

● *cpds.* **~-blow** *n.* (*fig.*) сокруши́тельный/тяжёлый удáр; **~-head** *n.* гóловка молоткá; (*shark*) мóлот-ры́ба; **~-toe** *n.* молоткообрáзное искривлéние большóго пáльца ноги́.

hammock /ˈhæmək/ *n.* гамáк.

hammy /ˈhæmɪ/ *adj.* (**hammier, hammiest**) переигрывающий; **he is a ~ actor** он переигрывает.

hamper¹ /ˈhæmpə(r)/ *n.* корзи́на с кры́шкой.

hamper² /ˈhæmpə(r)/ *v.t.* мешáть, по- + *d.*; стесня́ть (*impf.*).

hamster /ˈhæmstə(r)/ *n.* хомя́к.

hand /hænd/ *n.* **1** (*lit., fig.*) рукá, кисть; **the ~ of God** перст Бóжий; (*dim., e.g. baby's*) рýчка; (*attr.*) ручнóй; **~ luggage** ручнóй багáж; (*of animal*) лáпа, лáпка; **she waits on him ~ and foot** онá у негó в пóлном подчинéнии; **he was bound ~ and foot** егó связáли по рукáм и ногáм; **they won ~s down** побéда достáлась им легкó; **I shall have my ~s full next week** на слéдующей недéле я бýду óчень зáнят; **he was ~ in glove with the enemy** он был в сгóворе с врагóм; **~ in ~** (*lit., fig.*) рукá óб руку; **~s up!** рýки вверх!; **~s off!** рýки прочь (от + *g.*)!; **he is making money ~ over fist** он загребáет дéньги лопáтой; **they fought ~ to ~** они́ би́лись врукопáшную; **it's too much for one pair of ~s** однóй пáры рук для э́того недостáточно.

2 (*vbl. phrr.*): **he asked for her ~** (*in marriage*) он попроси́л её руки́; **the money changed ~s** дéньги перешли́ в други́е рýки; **force s.o.'s ~** заст|авля́ть, -áвить когó-н. раскры́ть кáрты; **he gained, got the upper ~** он взял/одержáл верх; **get one's ~ in** наб|ивáть, -и́ть рýку (*на чём*); осв|áиваться, -óиться с рабóтой; **let me give, lend you a ~!** давáйте я вам помогý!; **they gave the singer a big ~** (*coll.*) певцý бýрно аплоди́ровали; **he was given a free ~** емý предостáвили пóлную свобóду дéйствий; **she had a ~ in his downfall** в егó падéнии онá сыгрáла не послéднюю роль; **I'll have no ~ in it!** я не хочý имéть к э́тому никакóго отношéния; **they were holding ~s** они́ держáлись зá руки; **hold one's ~** (*restrain o.s.*) сдéрж|иваться, -áться; **keep one's ~ in** поддéрживать (*impf.*) фóрму; **if only I could lay my ~s on a dictionary** éсли бы я тóлько мог раздобы́ть/достáть словáрь; **don't dare to lay a ~ on her** не смей прикасáться к ней; **he rules with an iron ~** он прáвит желéзной рукóй; **he set his ~ to** (*set about*) **the work** он взя́лся за рабóту; **let me shake your ~** позвóльте пожáть вáшу/вам рýку; **(let's) shake ~s on it!** по рукáм!; **try one's ~ at something** прóбовать, по- себя́ в чём-н.; **my ~s are tied** (*fig.*) у меня́ свя́заны рýки; **he can turn his ~ to anything** он умéет дéлать что угóдно; **I wash my ~s of it** я умывáю рýки.

3 (*prepositional phrr.*): **the hour is at ~** приближáется час/врéмя; **he lives close at ~** он живёт совсéм ря́дом; **she suffered at his ~s** онá натерпéлась от негó *or* с ним; **he started the car by ~** он завёл маши́ну вручнýю; **the letter was delivered by ~** письмó бы́ло достáвлено с нарóчным; **he died by his own ~** он наложи́л на себя́ рýки; **the watch passed from ~ to ~** часы́ переходи́ли из рук в рýки; **he lives from ~ to mouth** он кóе-как свóдит концы́ с концáми; **I have enough money in ~** у меня́ при себé достáточно дéнег; **he took the matter in ~** он взял дéло в свои́ рýки; **please attend to the matter in ~** пожáлуйста, займи́тесь э́тим вопрóсом; **you should take that child in ~** вы должны́ взять э́того ребёнка нá руки; **we have the situation well in ~** мы пóлностью контроли́руем ситуáцию; **the matter is no longer in my ~s** я бóльше э́тим не занимáюсь; **he fell into the ~s of money lenders** он попáл в лáпы к ростовщикáм; **don't let this book fall into the wrong ~s** смотри́те, чтóбы э́та кни́га не попáла в плохи́е рýки; **you are playing into his ~s** вы дéйствуете емý нá руку; **my eldest daughter is off my ~s** моя́ стáршая дочь ужé пристрóена; **on ~** в нали́чии; в распоряжéнии; **he has a sick father on his ~s** у негó на рукáх больнóй отéц; **he refused out of ~** он тут же отказáлся; **things are getting out of ~** собы́тия выхóдят из-под контрóля; **the letters passed through his ~s** пи́сьма проходи́ли чéрез егó рýки; **news has come to ~** дошли́ свéдения; есть свéдения, что...; **his gun was ready to ~** ружьё бы́ло у негó под рукóй.

4 (*member of crew or team*): **all ~s on deck!** все навéрх!; **the ship went down with all ~s** корáбль затонýл со всем экипáжем; **factory ~** фабри́чный рабóчий; **farm ~** рабóтник на фéрме.

5 (*practitioner*): **he is an old ~ (at the game)** он человéк бывáлый; (*coll.*) он тёртый калáч; **a picture by the same ~** карти́на тогó же худóжника.

6 (*source*): **I heard it at first/second ~** я узнáл э́то из пéрвых/вторы́х рук.

7 (*side*): **on the right ~** по прáвую рýку; **at his right ~** по егó прáвую рýку; **on the one ~ ..., on the other ~** (*fig.*) с однóй стороны́..., с другóй стороны́.

8 (*handwriting*): **a large/small ~** крýпный/мéлкий пóчерк.

9 (*signature*): **I cannot set my ~ to this document** я не могý подписáться под э́тим доку́мéнтом.

10 (*of a clock*) стрéлка.

11 (*measure*) ладóнь (*10 сантимéтров*).

12 (*player at cards*) игрóк; (*set of cards*) кáрты (*f. pl.*); **show one's ~** (*fig.*) раскр|ывáть, -ы́ть кáрты; (*round in a card game*) кон, пáртия.

● *v.t.* перед|авáть, -áть; под|авáть, -áть; **~ me the paper, please** передáйте мне газéту, пожáлуйста; **I ~ it to you** (*coll., acknowledge your skill etc.*) я дóлжен отдáть вам дóлжное.

● *with advs.*: **he ~ed back the money** он вернýл дéньги; **~ me down that book from the shelf** сними́те мне э́ту кни́гу с пóлки; **the custom was ~ed down** э́тот обы́чай передавáлся из поколéния в поколéние; **will you ~ in your resignation?** вы подади́те заявлéние об ухóде?; **the estate was ~ed on to the heirs** имéние перешлó к наслéдникам; **the teacher ~ed out books** учи́тель раздáл кни́ги; **the king ~ed over his authority to parliament** корóль передáл власть парлáменту.

● *cpds.* **~bag** *n.* (*Br.*) сýмочка, дáмская сýмка; **~ball** *n.* (*game*) ручнóй мяч, гандбóл; (*ball*) гандбóльный мяч; **~bell** *n.* колокóльчик; **~bill** *n.* реклáмный листóк; **~book** *n.* посóбие; руковóдство; **~-brake** *n.* ручнóй тóрмоз; **~cart** *n.* ручная тeлéжка; **~-clap** *n.* хлопóк (рукáми); **slow ~-clap** мéдленные аплодисмéнты в унисóн; **~cuff** *n.* нарýчник; *v.t.* над|евáть, -éть нарýчники + *d.*; **~-drier** *n.* (электро)суши́лка; **~-grenade** *n.* (*shell*) ручнáя гранáта; **~grip** *n.* (*grasp*) пожáтие/сжáтие руки́; (*handle*) рукоя́тка; **~hold** *n.* опóра; зацéпка (*coll.*); **~-made** *adj.* сде́ланный вручну́ю; ручно́й рабо́ты; **~maid** *n.* служа́нка; **~-out** *n.* (*gift*) подая́ние; ми́лостыня; (*for publicity*) рекла́мный листо́к; (*for students*) разда́точный материа́л; **~over** *n.* (*Br., e.g. of responsibility*) переда́ча; **~-picked** *adj.* тща́тельно отобранный; **~rail** *n.* пери́л|а (*pl., g.* —); **~saw** *n.* ножо́вка; **~set** *n.* (*telephone*) тру́бка; **~shake** *n.* рукопожа́тие; **golden ~shake** (*coll.*) отста́вка с хоро́шими награднЫми; **~s-off** *adj.*: **~s-off policy** поли́тика невмеша́тельства; **~s-on** *adj.*: **~s-on experience** практи́ческий о́пыт; **~spring** *n.* «колесо́», са́льто (*indecl.*); **~stand** *n.* сто́йка на рука́х; **~-to-~** *adj.* рукопа́шный; **~-to-~ fighting** рукопа́шный бой; **~-to-mouth** *adj.*: **a ~-to-mouth existence** жизнь впро́голодь; **~work** *n.* ручна́я рабо́та; **~writing** *n.* по́черк; **~writing expert** графо́лог; **~written** *adj.* напи́санный от руки́.

handful /ˈhændfʊl/ *n.* горсть; при́горшня; (*fig., a small number*) го́рстка, горсть; (*coll.*): **this child is a ~** с э́тим ребёнком хлопо́т не оберёшься.

handicap /ˈhændɪˌkæp/ *n.*
1 (*hindrance*) поме́ха, препя́тствие.
2 (*sport*) гандика́п.
● *v.t.* (**handicapped, handicapping**)
1 (*put at disadvantage*) чини́ть (*impf.*) препя́тствия (*кому*); ста́вить, по- в невы́годное положе́ние; **~ped person** (*physically*) инвали́д; (*mentally*) у́мственно отста́лый челове́к.
2 (*sport*) да|ва́ть, -ть гандика́п (*or*) фо́ру + *d.*

handicraft /ˈhændɪˌkrɑːft/ *n.* ремесло́, ручна́я рабо́та; (*attr.*) реме́сленный; куста́рный.

handiwork /ˈhændɪˌwɜːk/ *n.* ручна́я рабо́та; **this is his ~** э́то сде́лано его́ рука́ми; (*fig.*) э́то его́ рук де́ло.

handkerchie|f /ˈhæŋkətʃɪf/, /-ˌtʃiːf/ *n.* (*pl.* **~fs** *or* **~ves**) носово́й плато́к.

handle /ˈhænd(ə)l/ *n.* (*of door, cup*) ру́чка; (*of sword, tool*) рукоя́ть, рукоя́тка; (*fig.*): **don't fly off the ~!** (*coll.*) не кипяти́сь!; не лезь в буты́лку!
● *v.t.* **1** (*take or hold in the hands*) тро́гать (*impf.*); брать, взять в ру́ки.
2 (*manage, deal with, treat*) обраща́ться (*impf.*) с + *i.*; обходи́ться (*impf.*) с + *i.*; спр|авля́ться, -а́виться с + *i.*; **he can ~ a horse with skill** он уме́ет обраща́ться с лошадьми́; **he ~d the affair very well** он прекра́сно спра́вился с э́тим де́лом; **he ~d himself well** он хорошо́ держа́лся; **the officer ~d his men well** офице́р уме́ло кома́ндовал свои́ми солда́тами.
3 (*comm., deal in*) торгова́ть (*impf.*) + *i.*
● *v.i.*: **this car ~s well** э́та маши́на удо́бна в управле́нии.
● *cpd.* **~-bars** *n. pl.* (*of a bicycle*) руль (*m.*); **~-bar moustache** (*Br.*), **mustache** (*US*) (*joc.*) закру́ченные вверх усы́ (*m. pl.*).

handler /ˈhændlə(r)/ *n.* тре́нер, дрессиро́вщик.

handsome /ˈhænsəm/ *adj.* (**handsomer, handsomest**) (*of appearance*) краси́вый; (*generous*): **a ~ present** ще́дрый пода́рок; **~ is as ~ does** су́дят не по слова́м, а по дела́м.

handy /ˈhændɪ/ *adj.* (**handier, handiest**) **1** (*clever with hands*) уме́лый, мастерови́тый, рука́стый (*coll.*); **he is ~** у него́ золоты́е ру́ки.
2 (*easy to handle*) удо́бный для по́льзования. **3** (*to hand, available*) (име́ющийся) под руко́й.
4 (*convenient*) удо́бный, сподру́чный (*coll.*); **it may come in ~** э́то мо́жет пригоди́ться.
● *cpd.* **~-man** *n.* разнорабо́чий.

hang /hæŋ/ *n.* **1** (*way in which a thing hangs*) вид (*вися́щей ве́щи*).
2 (*knack, sense*) смысл; «что к чему́»; **I can't get the ~ of this machine** (*or* **of his argument**) я не могу́ разобра́ться в э́той маши́не (*or* в его́ до́водах).
3 (*coll.*) **I don't give, care a ~** а мне како́е де́ло?; мне (на)плева́ть.
● *v.t.* (*past and p.p.* **hung,** *except in senses 4, 5: past and p.p.* **hanged**) **1** (*suspend*) ве́шать, пове́сить; **game must be hung for several days** дичь должна́ висе́ть не́сколько дней; **this gate has been hung badly** воро́та пло́хо пове́сили; **~ the blame on s.o.** взва́л|ивать, -и́ть вину́ на кого́-н.
2 (*let droop*) опус|ка́ть, -ти́ть; **she hung her head in shame** она́ опусти́ла го́лову от стыда́.
3 (*decorate, furnish*) разве́|шивать, -сить; **the hall was hung with flags** зал был уве́шан фла́гами.
4 (*execute by ~ing*) ве́шать, пове́сить; **Judas ~ed himself** Иу́да пове́сился.
5 (*as imprecation*): **~ it all!** чёрт возьми́!; пропади́ всё про́падом!; **I'll be ~ed if I'll go!** (хоть) убе́йте — не пойду́ туда!
● *v.i.* (*past and p.p.* **hung,** *except in sense 4: past and p.p.* **hanged**) **1** (*be suspended*) висе́ть (*impf.*); (*fig.*): **his life ~s by a thread** его́ жизнь (виси́т) на волоске́; **the outcome ~s in the balance** ещё не я́сно, чем всё э́то ко́нчится (*or* како́й оборо́т при́мет де́ло); **the threat of dismissal hung over him** над ним нави́сла угро́за увольне́ния; **everything ~s on his decision** всё упира́ется в его́ реше́ние.
2 (*lean*) све́|шиваться, -ситься; **don't ~ out of the window** не высо́вывайтесь из окна́.
3 (*droop*) висе́ть (*impf.*); свиса́ть (*impf.*).
4 (*be executed*): **he will ~ for it** он попадёт за э́то на ви́селицу.
5 (*loiter, stay close*): **he hung round the door** он задержа́лся у две́ри; **the children hung about their mother** де́ти льну́ли к ма́тери.
● *with advs.*: **~ about** (*Br.*), **~ around** *v.i.* болта́ться (*impf.*); шата́ться (*impf.*); **~ back** *v.i.* отст|ава́ть, -а́ть; **~ on** *v.i.* (*cling*) держа́ться (*impf.*) (*за что*); цепля́ться (*impf.*); (*persist*) упо́рствовать (*impf.*); не сдава́ться (*impf.*); **~on!** (*coll.*) погоди́те!; постои́те!; **~ out** *v.t.* выве́шивать, вы́весить; **she hung out the washing** она́ вы́весила бельё; *v.i.* (*protrude*): **his shirt was ~ing out** руба́шка вы́лезла у него́ из брюк; (*coll., relax*) тусова́ться (*impf.*); **~ together** *v.i.* (*stand by one another*) держа́ться (*impf.*) вме́сте; (*make sense*): **the story doesn't ~ together** ≈ концы́ с конца́ми не схо́дятся; **~ up** *v.t.* (*fasten on peg, nail etc.*) веша́ть, пове́сить; *v.i.* (*end telephone conversation*) веша́ть, пове́сить тру́бку.
● *cpds.* **~dog** *adj.*: **a ~dog expression** затра́вленный вид; **~-glider** *n.* (*craft*) дельтапла́н; (*person*) дельтаплане́ри́ст; **~-gliding** *n.* дельтаплане́ри́зм; **~man** *n.* пала́ч; **~-nail** *n.* заусе́ница; **~out** *n.* (*sl.*) местожи́тельство, местопребыва́ние; **~over** *n.* (*survival*) пережи́ток, насле́дие; (*from drink*) похме́лье, перепо́й; **I had a ~over** у меня́ разболе́лась голова́ от похме́лья; **~-up** *n.* (*obsession, inhibition*) пу́нктик, бзик (*coll.*); (*complex*) ко́мплекс; **he has a ~-up about it** он закли́нился на э́том.

hangar /ˈhæŋə(r)/ *n.* анга́р.

hanger /ˈhæŋə(r)/ *n.* (*for clothes*) ве́шалка.
● *cpd.* **~-on** *n.* (*dependant*) прихлеба́тель (*m.*); (*follower*) приспе́шник.

hanging /ˈhæŋɪŋ/ *n.* **1** висе́ние; (*execution*) пове́шение; **it is not a ~ matter** (*fig.*) э́то не тако́е уж стра́шное преступле́ние. **2** (*pl., tapestry etc.*) портье́ры (*f. pl.*); драпиро́вка (*collect.*).
● *adj.* вися́чий.

hank /hæŋk/ *n.* мото́к.

hanker /ˈhæŋkə(r)/ *v.i.*: **~ after** жа́ждать + *g.*

hanky /ˈhæŋkɪ/ (*coll.*) = **handkerchief**

hanky-panky /ˌhæŋkɪˈpæŋkɪ/ *n.* (*coll.*) (*trickery*) проде́л|ки (*pl., g.* -ок); моше́нничество; (*sexual*) шу́ры-му́ры (*pl. indecl.*).

Hanoi /hæˈnɔɪ/ *n.* Хано́й; (*attr.*) хано́йский.

Hanover /ˈhænəʊvə(r)/ *n.* Ганно́вер.

Hanoverian /ˌhænəˈvɪərɪən/ *adj.* ганно́верский.

Hanseatic /ˌhænsɪˈætɪk/ *adj.* ганзе́йский.

Hansen's disease /ˈhæns(ə)nz/ *n.* прока́за.

hansom /ˈhænsəm/ *n.* (*also* **~ cab**) двухколёсный экипа́ж.

ha'penny /ˈheɪpnɪ/ *n.* полпе́нни (*indecl.*).

haphazard /hæpˈhæzəd/ *adj.* случа́йный.
● *adv.* случа́йно; науда́чу.

hapless /ˈhæplɪs/ *adj.* несча́стный; злополу́чный.

happen /ˈhæpən/ *v.i.* **1** (*occur*) случ|а́ться, -и́ться; прои|сходи́ть, -зойти́; получ|а́ться, -и́ться; **accidents will ~** ≈ вся́кое быва́ет; **I hope nothing has ~ed to him** наде́юсь, с ним ничего́ не случи́лось.
2 (*chance*): **it (so) ~ed that I was there** случи́лось так, что я был там; **as it ~s I can help you ~** я в да́нном слу́чае

могу́ вам помо́чь; **do you ~ to know her?** вы случа́йно не зна́ете её?; **I ~ed to be out** меня́ не оказа́лось до́ма; **we ~ed to meet** мы неожи́данно/случа́йно встре́тились; **this ~s to be my birthday** сего́дня как раз мой день рожде́ния; **he ~ed to mention it** он ка́к-то упомяну́л об э́том.
3: **~ on** случа́йно нат|ыка́ться, -кну́ться на + *g.*

happening /ˈhæpənɪŋ/, /-pnɪŋ/ *n.* слу́чай; собы́тие.

happily /ˈhæpɪlɪ/ *adv.* **1** (*contentedly*) сча́стливо; **and they lived ~ ever after** ≈ и ста́ли они́ жить-пожива́ть, да добра́ нажива́ть. **2** (*fortunately*) к сча́стью. **3** (*gladly*) с удово́льствием.

happiness /ˈhæpɪnɪs/ *n.* сча́стье.

happy /ˈhæpɪ/ *adj.* (**happier, happiest**) **1** (*contented*) счастли́вый. **2** (*fortunate, felicitous*) счастли́вый, уда́чливый; уда́чный; **by a ~ coincidence** по счастли́вой случа́йности; **a ~ thought** счастли́вая/уда́чная мысль; **~ medium** золота́я середи́на; **her death was a ~ release** смерть была́ её счастли́вым избавле́нием; **~ birthday!** с днём рожде́ния!; **~ Christmas!** с Рождество́м (Христо́вым)!
3 (*pleased*) дово́льный (*чем*); **we shall be ~ to come** мы с удово́льствием придём; **I'm not ~ about, with that suggestion** мне э́то предложе́ние не нра́вится; меня́ э́то предложе́ние не устра́ивает.
● *cpd.* **~-go-lucky** *adj.* беззабо́тный; беспе́чный.

hara-kiri /ˌhærəˈkɪrɪ/ *n.* хараки́ри (*nt. indecl.*).

harangue /həˈræŋ/ *n.* разглаго́льствование; увещева́ние.
● *v.t.* увещева́ть (*impf.*).
● *v.i.* разглаго́льствовать (*impf.*).

harass /ˈhærəs/, *disp.* /həˈræs/ *v.t.* изв|оди́ть, -ести́; трави́ть, за-; **~ the enemy** изм|а́тывать, -ота́ть врага́.

harassment /ˈhærəsmənt/, /həˈræs-/ *n.* тра́вля; изма́тывание; **sexual ~** сексуа́льное домога́тельство.

harbinger /ˈhɑːbɪndʒə(r)/ *n.* предве́стник.

harbour /ˈhɑːbə(r)/ (*US* **harbor**) *n.* га́вань, порт; **~ dues** порто́вые сбо́ры (*m. pl.*); (*fig.*) убе́жище.
● *v.t.* да|ва́ть, -ть убе́жище + *d.*; укр|ыва́ть, -ы́ть; **~ing a criminal** укрыва́тельство/сокры́тие престу́пника; **dirt ~s disease** грязь — расса́дник боле́зней; (*fig.*): **I ~ no grudge against him** я не держу́ на него́ зла.
● *cpd.* **~-master** *n.* нача́льник по́рта.

hard /hɑːd/ *adj.* **1** (*firm, resistant, solid*) твёрдый; про́чный; **~ core** (*fig., nucleus of resistance etc.*) ядро́; **~ and fast rules** жёсткие пра́вила; **~ bread** чёрствый хлеб; **~ copy** (*comput.*) распеча́тка; **~ disk** (*comput.*) жёсткий диск; **~ hat** защи́тный шлем; **~ tack** гале́та, суха́рь (*m.*).
2 (*of money*): **~ cash** нали́чность; нали́чные (де́ньги); **~ currency** твёрдая валю́та.
3 (*difficult*) тру́дный; **do something the ~ way** идти́, пойти́ тру́дным путём; **you're ~ to please** вам тру́дно угоди́ть; **she played ~ to get** она́ разыгрывала из себя́ недотро́гу; она́ набива́ла себе́ це́ну; **it's ~ to say yet** пока́ тру́дно сказа́ть; **bargains are ~ to come by** доста́ть ве́щи по дешёвой цене́ нелегко́.
4: **~ of hearing** глухова́тый; туго́й на́ ухо.
5 (*unsentimental, relentless*): **he drives a ~ bargain** с ним не сторгу́ешься; **a ~ drinker** го́рький пья́ница; **don't be too ~ on her!** не бу́дьте к ней сли́шком стро́ги; **~ sell** навя́зывание това́ра; **~ words** ре́зкие/жёстие слова́.
6 (*vigorous, harsh*): **~ times** тяжёлые времена́; **a ~ climate** суро́вый кли́мат; **it's a ~ life** жизнь трудна́; тру́дно живётся; **take a ~ line** зан|има́ть, -я́ть жёсткую пози́цию; **a ~ master** стро́гий хозя́ин; **as ~ as nails** (*fig.*) (*physically*) закалённый; (*~-hearted*) чёрствый, жестокосе́рдный; **a ~ light** ре́зкий свет; **~ liquor** кре́пкие напи́тки; **~ drugs** сильноде́йствующие нарко́тики; **~ carriage** (*rail.*) жёсткий ваго́н; **~ water** жёсткая вода́; **a ~ consonant** твёрдый согла́сный.
7 (*intensive*): **~ work** тяжёлая/тру́дная рабо́та; **a ~ blow** си́льный/жесто́кий уда́р; **~ labour** (*Br.*), **labor** (*US*) исправи́тельно-трудовы́е рабо́ты; (*fig.*) ка́торга; **a ~ worker** усе́рдный/приле́жный рабо́тник.
8 (*coll., unfortunate*): **~ luck/cheese** (*Br.*)/**lines** (*Br.*)! не везёт!; **he told a ~-luck story** он пыта́лся разжа́лобить слу́шателей свои́ми го́рестями; **his parents are ~ up** его́ роди́тели — лю́ди небога́тые.
● *adv.* **1** (*solid*): **the ground froze ~** земля́ промёрзла.
2 (*with force*): **it is raining ~** идёт си́льный дождь; **he had to brake ~** ему́ пришло́сь ре́зко затормози́ть; **~ hit** (*fig.*) си́льно пострада́вший.
3 (*unremittingly*) усе́рдно; **he rode ~ all day** он проскака́л на ло́шади весь день, нигде́ не остана́вливаясь; **he was ~ pressed for money** он о́чень нужда́лся (в де́ньгах); **I was ~ put to it to answer** мне нелегко́ бы́ло найти́ отве́т.
4 (*adversely*): **it will go ~ with him** ему́ придётся ту́го; **~ done by** (*Br.*) пострада́вший, оби́женный.
5 (*persistently*): **he looked ~ in my direction** он при́стально посмотре́л в мою́ сто́рону; **I looked ~ for the book** я до́лго иска́л кни́гу; **look ~!** хороше́нько поищи́те!; **did you look ~?** вы как сле́дует иска́ли?; **work** (*study*) **~** усе́рдно занима́ться (*impf.*); **we worked ~** мы мно́го рабо́тали; **work ~er** рабо́тать (*impf.*) (ещё) бо́льше/лу́чше; **I tried ~ to make him understand** я изо всех сил стара́лся разъясни́ть ему́ (*что*).
● *cpds.* **~back** *n.* (*book*) кни́га в жёстком переплёте *or* в твёрдой обло́жке; **~ball** *n.* (*US*) бейсбо́л; **~-bitten** *adj.* сто́йкий, несгиба́емый; **~board** *n.* древесно-волокни́стая плита́, ДВП; **~-boiled** *adj.* (*lit.*) сва́ренный вкруту́ю; **a ~-boiled egg** круто́е яйцо́; яйцо́ вкруту́ю; (*fig.*) прожжённый; вида́вший ви́ды; **~-core** *adj.* (*criminal*) закорене́лый; (*pornography*) открове́нный; *n.* (*Br., rubble*) ще́бень (*m.*); **~-cover** *adj.* в жёстком переплёте, в твёрдой обло́жке; **~-earned** *adj.* зарабо́танный тя́жким трудо́м; **~-faced** *adj.* с суро́вым ви́дом; **~-fisted** *adj.* прижи́мистый; **~-headed** *adj.* тре́звый; практи́чный; **~-hearted** *adj.* жестокосе́рдный; неумоли́мый; **~-hitting** *adj.* (*e.g. speech*) жёсткий; бескомпроми́ссный; **~-line** *adj.* неусту́пчивый, бескомпроми́ссный; **~-liner** *n.* (*coll., one who takes a ~ line*) сторо́нник жёсткой ли́нии; **~-nosed** *adj.* тре́звый; **~ware** *n.* скобяны́е изде́лия/това́ры; (*mil., coll.*) те́хника; (*comput.*) аппарату́ра; аппара́тные сре́дства (*nt. pl.*); **~-wearing** *adj.* но́ский; **~wood** *n.* твёрдая древеси́на; **~-working** *adj.* работя́щий; (*at studies*) усидчи́вый.

harden /ˈhɑːd(ə)n/ *v.t.* (*make hard*) де́лать, с- твёрдым; **~ed steel** закалённая сталь; (*fig.*) ожесточ|а́ть, -и́ть; **he ~ed his heart** он ожесточи́лся се́рдцем; **a ~ed criminal** закорене́лый престу́пник; рецидиви́ст.
● *v.i.* тверде́ть, за-; (*fig.*) ожесточа|ться, -и́ться; **opinion ~ed** мне́ние укрепи́лось; **suspicions ~ed** подозре́ния уси́ливались.

hardiness /ˈhɑːdɪnɪs/ *n.* выно́сливость.

hardly /ˈhɑːdlɪ/ *adv.* **1** (*with difficulty*) с трудо́м. **2** (*only just*) едва́; **I had ~ sat down when the phone rang** едва́ я сел, как зазвони́л телефо́н. **3** (*not reasonably*) вряд ли; **he can ~ have arrived yet** вряд ли он уже́ прие́хал; **you can ~ expect her to agree** вы едва́ (*or* вряд) ли мо́жете рассчи́тывать на её согла́сие. **4** (*almost not*): **~ ever** почти́ никогда́; **I ~ know him** я его́ почти́ не зна́ю; **there's ~ any money left** де́нег почти́ не оста́лось; **I need ~ say** само́ собо́й разуме́ется; са́ми понима́ете.

hardness /ˈhɑːdnɪs/ *n.* (*of material*) твёрдость; (*of person, attitude*) жёсткость; (*of water*) жёсткость; (*of task*) тру́дность.

hardship /ˈhɑːdʃɪp/ *n.* невзго́ды (*f. pl.*); испыта́ния (*nt. pl.*).

hardy /ˈhɑːdɪ/ *adj.* (**hardier, hardiest**) **1** (*bold*) отва́жный; дёрзкий. **2** (*robust*) закалённый; выно́сливый; (*of plants*) морозосто́йкий, морозоусто́йчивый; **~ annual** морозосто́йкое однолéтнее расте́ние.

hare /heə(r)/ *n.* за́яц; **run with the ~ and hunt with the hounds** (*Br., fig.*) служи́ть (*impf.*) и на́шим и ва́шим; **mad as a March ~** одуре́вший, ошале́вший.
● *v.i.* (*sl.*) уд|ира́ть, -ра́ть.
● *cpds.* **~bell** *n.* колоко́льчик (круглоли́стый); **~-brained** *adj.*

опроме́тчивый; шально́й; **~lip** *n.* за́ячья губа́.

Hare Krishna /ˌhɑːrɪ ˈkrɪʃnə/ *n.* (*pl.* **Hare Krishnas**) (*cult member*) кришнаи́т.

● *adj.* кришнаи́тский.

harem /ˈhɑːriːm/, /hɑːˈriːm/ *n.* гаре́м.

haricot /ˈhærɪˌkəʊ/ *n.* (*also* **~ bean**) фасо́ль (обыкнове́нная) (*collect.*).

hark /hɑːk/ *v.i.* **1** (*listen*) вн|има́ть, -ять +*d.*; **just ~ at him!** вы то́лько его́ послу́шайте! **2**: **~ back to** (*recall*) упом|ина́ть, -яну́ть; верну́ться (*pf.*) к (*теме и т.п.*).

harlequin /ˈhɑːlɪkwɪn/ *n.* арлеки́н.

harlot /ˈhɑːlət/ *n.* (*arch.*) блудни́ца.

harm /hɑːm/ *n.* вред, уще́рб; **it can do no ~** от э́того вреда́ не бу́дет; **there's no ~ (in) trying** попы́тка не пы́тка; **he will come to no ~** с ним ничего́ не случи́тся; **I meant no ~** я не хоте́л (вас *и т.п.*) оби́деть; **out of ~'s way** от греха́ пода́льше; **there is no ~ done** никто́ не пострада́л.

● *v.t.* вреди́ть, по- +*d.*; причин|я́ть, -и́ть (*or* нан|оси́ть, -ести́) вред +*d.*; об|ижа́ть, -и́деть; **be ~ed** страда́ть, по-.

harmful /ˈhɑːmfʊl/ *adj.* вре́дный.

harmless /ˈhɑːmlɪs/ *adj.* (*not injurious*) безвре́дный; безопа́сный; (*innocent*) безоби́дный.

harmonic /hɑːˈmɒnɪk/ *adj.* гармони́ческий.

● *n.* **1** (*mus.*) (*overtone*) оберто́н; (*note on stringed instrument*) флажоле́т. **2** (*phys.*) гармо́ника.

harmonica /hɑːˈmɒnɪkə/ *n.* гармо́ника.

harmonious /hɑːˈməʊnɪəs/ *adj.* (*lit., fig.*) гармони́чный; (*amicable*) дру́жный; сла́женный; согла́сный.

harmonium /hɑːˈməʊnɪəm/ *n.* фисгармо́ния.

harmonization /ˌhɑːmənaɪˈzeɪʃ(ə)n/ *n.* (*lit., fig.*) гармониза́ция.

harmonize /ˈhɑːməˌnaɪz/ *v.t.* **1** (*mus., put chords to melody*) гармонизи́ровать (*impf., pf.*). **2** (*bring into agreement*) согласо́в|ывать, -а́ть; увя́з|ывать, -а́ть.

● *v.i.*: **these colours** (*Br.*), **colors** (*US*) **~ well** э́ти цвета́ гармони́руют (ме́жду собо́й).

harmony /ˈhɑːmənɪ/ *n.* **1** (*mus., theory*) гармо́ния. **2** (*of sounds, colours*) гармони́чность. **3** (*agreement*) гармо́ния; сла́женность; **their thoughts are in ~** их иде́и созву́чны.

harness /ˈhɑːnɪs/ *n.* у́пряжь; (*fig.*): **he died in ~** он у́мер на (трудово́м) посту́.

● *v.t.* запр|яга́ть, -я́чь; (*fig.*) (*of natural forces*) обузд|ывать, -а́ть; покор|я́ть, -и́ть; (*of energies etc.*) мобилизова́ть (*impf., pf.*).

harp /hɑːp/ *n.* а́рфа.

● *v.i.* (*fig.*): **~ on something** тверди́ть (*impf.*) о чём-н.

harp|er /ˈhɑːpə(r)/, **-ist** /ˈhɑːpɪst/ *nn.* арфи́ст (*fem.* -ка).

harpoon /hɑːˈpuːn/ *n.* гарпу́н.

● *v.t.* бить (*impf.*) гарпуно́м; гарпу́нить, за-.

harpsichord /ˈhɑːpsɪˌkɔːd/ *n.* клавеси́н.

harpy /ˈhɑːpɪ/ *n.* (*myth.*) га́рпия; (*fig., unscrupulous woman*) меге́ра, га́рпия.

harridan /ˈhærɪd(ə)n/ *n.* ста́рая карга́.

harrier /ˈhærɪə(r)/ *n.* (*dog*) го́нчая.

harrow /ˈhærəʊ/ *n.* борона́.

● *v.t.* **1** (*agric.; also v.i.*) борони́ть, вз-. **2** (*fig., lacerate*) терза́ть, ис-; ра́нить (*impf., pf.*) (*чувства*); **a ~ing tale** душераздира́ющая исто́рия.

harry /ˈhærɪ/ *v.t.* (*ravage*) разор|я́ть, -и́ть; опустош|а́ть, -и́ть, (*harass*) изв|оди́ть, -ести́; му́чить, из-.

harsh /hɑːʃ/ *adj.* **1** (*rough*) гру́бый, ре́зкий; **a ~ taste** ре́зкий вкус; **~ colours** (*Br.*), **colors** (*US*) ре́зкие цвета́. **2** (*severe*) суро́вый.

harshness /ˈhɑːʃnɪs/ *n.* (*roughness*) ре́зкость; (*severity*) суро́вость.

hart /hɑːt/ *n.* саме́ц оле́ня.

hartebeest /ˈhɑːtɪˌbiːst/ *n.* коро́вья антило́па, буба́л.

harum-scarum /ˌheərəmˈskeərəm/ *adj.* беззабо́тный, бесшаба́шный.

Harvard /ˈhɑːvəd/ *n.* Га́рвард.

harvest /ˈhɑːvɪst/ *n.* (*yield*) урожа́й; (**~ing**) жа́тва, сбор урожа́я; (*garnering*) убо́рка; **the ~ is ripe** урожа́й созре́л; **~ festival** пра́здник урожа́я; **~ home** коне́ц жа́твы; (*fig.*) плоды́ (*m. pl.*) труда́.

● *v.t.* соб|ира́ть, -ра́ть; жать, с-.

● *v.i.* соб|ира́ть, -ра́ть урожа́й.

harvester /ˈhɑːvɪstə(r)/ *n.* (*reaper*) жн|ец (*fem.* -и́ца); (*machine*) убо́рочная маши́на.

has /hæz/, /hæs/ *3rd pers. sing. pres. of* ⇒**have**

has-been /ˈhæzbiːn/ *n.* (*coll.*) челове́к, пережи́вший свою́ сла́ву; **he is a ~** его́ вре́мя прошло́.

hash[1] /hæʃ/ *n.* блю́до из ме́лко наре́занного мя́са и овоще́й; (*fig.*): **he made a ~ of it** он загуби́л всё де́ло; **I'll settle his ~** я сде́лаю из него́ котле́ту (*coll.*); я его́ проучу́.

● *v.t.* (*also* **~ up**) ме́лко ре́зать, на- (*мясо*).

hash[2] /hæʃ/ *n.* (*coll., drug*) анаша́, гаши́ш.

hash[3] /hæʃ/ *n.* (*also* **~ sign**) си́мвол но́мера (#).

hashish /ˈhæʃiːʃ/ *n.* гаши́ш.

Hasidic /hæˈsɪdɪk/ *adj.* (*relig.*) хаси́дский.

hasp /hɑːsp/ *n.* засо́в.

hassle /ˈhæs(ə)l/ *n.* (*coll.*) кани́тель.

hassock /ˈhæsək/ *n.* **1** (*Br.*) поду́шечка для коленопреклоне́ния. **2** (*US*) пуф.

haste /heɪst/ *n.* спе́шка, торопли́вость; **he went off in great ~** он поспе́шно ушёл; **make ~!** пото́рапливайтесь!; **more ~, less speed** ти́ше е́дешь — да́льше бу́дешь.

hasten /ˈheɪs(ə)n/ *v.t.* (*hurry*) торопи́ть, по-; (*accelerate*) уск|оря́ть, -о́рить; убыстр|я́ть, -и́ть.

● *v.i.* торопи́ться, по-, спеши́ть (*impf.*); **I ~ to add that …** спешу́ доба́вить, что….

hasty /ˈheɪstɪ/ *adj.* (**hastier, hastiest**) (*hurried*) поспе́шный, торопли́вый; (*rash, ill-considered*) поспе́шный, скоропали́тельный; (*quick-tempered*) вспы́льчивый, горя́чий.

hat /hæt/ *n.* шля́па; (*fur, knitted*) ша́пка; (*cap*) ке́пка; **top ~** цили́ндр; **if he wins I'll eat my ~** (*coll.*) разрази́ меня́ гром, е́сли он вы́играет; **keep it under your ~** (*coll.*) никому́ об э́том ни сло́ва; **they passed, sent the ~ round** они́ пусти́ли ша́пку по кру́гу; **I take off my ~ to him** я склоня́ю го́лову/преклоня́юсь пе́ред ним; **he's talking through his ~** он несёт ахине́ю (*coll.*); **at the drop of a ~** (*coll.*) (*immediately*) неме́дленно, то́тчас же; (*on the slightest pretext*) по мале́йшему по́воду; **old ~** (*coll.*) зата́сканный; **it's old ~!** (*coll.*) старо́!

● *cpds.* **~-band** *n.* шля́пная ле́нта; **~-pin** *n.* зако́лка для шля́пы; **~rack** *n.* ве́шалка для шляп; **~-stand** *n.* ве́шалка для шляп; **~-trick** *n.*: **he scored a ~-trick** (*fig., of footballer etc.*) он заби́л три го́ла подря́д.

hatch[1] /hætʃ/ *n.* (*opening*) люк; (*cover*) кры́шка; две́рцы (*f. pl.*); **down the ~!** (*coll.*) пей до дна!

● *cpds.* **~-back** *n.* хэтчбе́к; **~way** *n.* люк.

hatch[2] /hætʃ/ *v.t.* (*chick*) выси́живать, вы́сидеть; (*egg*) нас|и́живать, -иде́ть; (*in incubator*) выводи́ть, вы́вести; (*fig., plot*) выና́шивать, вы́носить; зам|ышля́ть, -ы́слить; **what are you ~ing?** что вы там замышля́ете?

● *v.i.* (*also* **~ out**) (*bird*) вылу́пливаться, вы́лупиться; (*fish*) выклёвываться, вы́клюнуться; (*insect*) выводи́ться, вы́вестись.

hatchery /ˈhætʃərɪ/ *n.* инкуба́тор.

hatchet /ˈhætʃɪt/ *n.* топо́р, топо́рик; **let's bury the ~!** дава́йте поми́римся!

● *cpds.* **~-faced** *adj.* остроли́цый; **~man** *n.* наёмник; (*killer*) ки́ллер.

hatching /ˈhætʃɪŋ/ *n.* штрих, штрихо́вка.

hatchment /ˈhætʃmənt/ *n.* мемориа́льная табли́чка с изображе́нием фами́льного ге́рба.

hate /heɪt/ *n.* не́нависть.

● *v.t.* ненави́деть (*impf.*); (*dislike strongly*) ненави́деть (*impf.*), не выноси́ть (*impf.*); **I ~ getting up early** я ненави́жу ра́но встава́ть; **I ~ to trouble you, but …** мне о́чень не хо́чется вас беспоко́ить, но….

hateful /ˈheɪtfʊl/ *adj.* ненави́стный.

hatred /ˈheɪtrɪd/ *n.* не́нависть; **have a ~ of something** ненави́деть (*impf.*) что-н., не выноси́ть чего́-н.; **feel ~ for** пита́ть, испы́тывать (*both impf.*) не́нависть к +*d.*

hatter /ˈhætə(r)/ *n.* шля́пник; **mad as a ~** сумасше́дший; полоу́мный; **he is as mad as a ~** у него́ не все до́ма.

haughtiness /ˈhɔːtɪnɪs/ *n.* высокоме́рие, зано́счивость.

haughty /ˈhɔːtɪ/ *adj.* (**haughtier, haughtiest**) высокоме́рный, зано́счивый.

haul /hɔːl/ *n.* **1** (*distance pulled*) рейс, пробе́г; **a long ~** (*fig.*) до́лгое де́ло. **2**: **a ~ of fish** уло́в, то́ня; (*fig., booty*) добы́ча, уло́в.

● *v.t. & i.* тяну́ть (*impf.*); тащи́ть (*impf.*); (*fig.*): **they were ~ed before the magistrate** их привлекли́ к суду́.

● *with advs.*: **~ down** *v.t.*: **the flag was ~ed down** флаг был спу́щен; **~ in** *v.t.* вт|я́гивать, -яну́ть; **~ out** *v.t.* вытя́гивать, вы́тянуть; **~ up** *v.t.* подн|има́ть, -я́ть; (*coll., summon*) притащи́ть (*pf.*).

haulage /ˈhɔːlɪdʒ/ *n.* транспортиро́вка, перево́зка; **~ contractor** (*Br.*) подря́дчик на грузовы́е перево́зки.

hauler /ˈhɔːlə(r)/ (*US*) = **haulier**

haulier /ˈhɔːlɪə(r)/ *n.* (*Br.*) перево́зчик.

haunch /hɔːntʃ/ *n.* бедро́, ля́жка; **he got down on his ~es** он присе́л на ко́рточки.

haunt /hɔːnt/ *n.* излю́бленное ме́сто; **our childhood ~s** места́, где мы люби́ли быва́ть в де́тстве.

● *v.t. & i.* неотсту́пно пресле́довать (*impf.*); **a ~ed house** дом с привиде́ниями; **a ~ing melody** неотсту́пная мело́дия; **she ~s my memory** она́ пресле́дует меня́ в мои́х воспомина́ниях.

Havana /həˈvænə/ *n.* Гава́на; (*also* **~ cigar**) гава́нская сига́ра.

have /hæv/, /həv/ *n.*: **the ~s and the ~-nots** иму́щие и неиму́щие.

● *v.t.* (*3rd pers. sing. pres.* **has;** *past and p.p.* **had**) **1** име́ть; (*possess*) облада́ть + *i.*; *often expr. by* у + *g.*; **she has blue eyes** у неё голубы́е глаза́; **I ~ no doubt** у меня́ нет сомне́ний; **he has no equal** он не име́ет себе́ (*or* ему́ нет) ра́вных; **~ the goodness to ...** бу́дьте добры́ +*imper.*; **he had the courage to refuse** он име́л му́жество отказа́ться; **I ~ no idea** поня́тия не име́ю; **he has no languages** он не зна́ет иностра́нных языко́в; **they cannot ~ children** они́ не мо́гут име́ть дете́й; **they ~ large reserves of oil** они́ владе́ют больши́ми запа́сами не́фти. **2** (*contain*): **June has 30 days** в ию́не 30 дней. **3** (*experience*): **~ a good time!** жела́ю вам хорошо́ провести́ вре́мя; (*suffer from*): **he has a cold** у него́ на́сморк; **do you often ~ toothache?** у вас ча́сто боля́т зу́бы? **4** (*bear*) роди́ть (*impf., pf.*); рожа́ть (*impf.*); **she is having a baby in May** в ма́е у неё роди́тся ребёнок. **5** (*receive, obtain*): **we had news of him yesterday** вчера́ мы получи́ли о нём изве́стие; **you always ~ your own way** ты всегда́ поступа́ешь по-сво́ему; **there was nothing to be had** там ничего́ не́ было; **the play had a great success** пье́са име́ла большо́й успе́х; (*tolerate*): **I won't ~ it!** э́того я не потерплю́! **6** (*show, exercise*): **~ pity on** сжа́литься (*pf.*) над + *i.*; **~ pity on me** сжа́льтесь надо мно́й; **he had no mercy** он был безжа́лостен. **7** (*undertake, perform*): **~ a game of tennis** сыгра́ть (*pf.*) в те́ннис; **~ a go** (*coll.*) пыта́ться, по-; про́бовать, по-. **8** (*partake of, enjoy*): **~ dinner** у́жинать (*impf.*). **9** (*puzzle, put at a loss*): **you ~ me there** вы меня́ озада́чили. **10** (*coll., swindle*): **you've been had** вас провели́/околпа́чили. **11** (*cause, order*): **~ him come here!** заста́вьте его́ прийти́ сюда́; **I must ~ my shoes mended** мне на́до отда́ть ту́фли в почи́нку; я до́лжен почини́ть ту́фли; **I would ~ you know** да бу́дет вам изве́стно; **what would you ~ me do?** так что, по-ва́шему, я до́лжен де́лать? **12** (*with inf., be obliged to*) (*need to*): **I ~ to finish by tomorrow** я до́лжен зако́нчить к за́втрашнему дню; **I ~ to sit down** мне на́до сесть; **it has to be done** э́то на́до/необходи́мо сде́лать; (*be obliged*) быть обя́занным; **I ~ to report to my boss every day** я обя́зан отчи́тываться пе́ред нача́льником ка́ждый день; **you don't ~ to go** вы не обя́заны идти́; (*having no choice*) быть вы́нужденным; **I ~ to accept the invitation** я был вы́нужден приня́ть приглаше́ние; **I didn't want to, but I had to** я не хоте́л, но был вы́нужден. **13** (*phrr. with it*): **I ~ it!** (*the answer, solution*) нашёл!; **let him ~ it!** (*sl., attack him*) дай ему́ хороше́нько!; покажи́ ему́!; **he's had it!** (*sl.*) (*is too old or old-fashioned*) ему́ коне́ц; его́ пе́сенка спе́та; (*has missed an offer or opportunity*) пиши́ пропа́ло; **rumour** (*Br.*), **rumor** (*US*) has it that ... хо́дят слу́хи, что...; **as he would ~ it** как он утвержда́ет; **you can't ~ it both ways** (*coll.*) и́ли то, и́ли друго́е; ≈ вы хоти́те, что́бы во́лки бы́ли сы́ты и о́вцы це́лы; **he had it coming (to him)** (*coll.*) он сам на э́то нарва́лся; **he has it in for me** (*coll.*) у него́ зуб на меня́; **~ it off** (*Br.*, **~** *sexual intercourse*) переспа́ть (*pf.*); **~ it out with s.o.** объясн|я́ться, -и́ться с кем-н.; **I had it in mind to go there** у меня́ была́ мысль пойти́ туда́; **~ it your own way!** будь по ва́шему!; **he has never had it so good** ему́ ещё никогда́ так хорошо́ не жило́сь.

● *with advs.*: **can I ~ my watch back?** могу́ я получи́ть свои́ часы́ обра́тно?; **may we ~ the blinds down?** мо́жно опусти́ть што́ры?; **we had her parents down** (*to stay*) у нас гости́ли её роди́тели; **we are having the painters in next week** на сле́дующей неде́ле к нам приду́т маляры́; **~ we enough food in for the weekend?** у нас доста́точно проду́ктов на суббо́ту и воскресе́нье?; **he had his coat off** он был без пальто́; **she had his coat off** (*took it off him*) **in a moment** она́ сра́зу же сняла́ с него́ пальто́; **she had a red dress on** на ней бы́ло кра́сное пла́тье; **~ you anything on tonight?** (*Br.*) у вас есть пла́ны на сего́дняшний ве́чер?; **we ~ a lot of work on at present** (*Br.*) у нас сейча́с мно́го/ма́сса рабо́ты; **~ s.o. on** (*Br.*) разы́гр|ывать, -а́ть кого́-н.; **I must ~ this tooth out** мне ну́жно удали́ть э́тот зуб; **they had the road up last week** на про́шлой неде́ле э́ту доро́гу ремонти́ровали; **we'll ~ the tent up in no time** мы ми́гом устано́вим пала́тку; **he was had up for speeding** (*Br. coll.*) его́ задержа́ли за превыше́ние ско́рости.

● *misc. phrr.*: **I ~ nothing against it** я ничего́ про́тив э́того не име́ю; **you had better, best give the book back** вам на́до бы верну́ть кни́гу; **~ done with something** поко́нчить (*pf.*) с чем-н.; **you might as well pay and ~ done with it** заплати́те — и де́лу коне́ц; **it has to do with his work** э́то свя́зано с его́ рабо́той; **it has nothing to do with you** к вам э́то ника́к не отно́сится, вас э́то не каса́ется; **I'll ~ nothing to do with it** я не жела́ю име́ть никако́го отноше́ния к э́тому.

haven /ˈheɪv(ə)n/ *n.* га́вань; (*fig.*) прию́т, приста́нище; **tax ~** нало́говое убе́жище; **safe ~** убе́жище.

haver /ˈheɪvə(r)/ *v.i.* (*Br., dither*) ме́шкать, колеба́ться (*both impf.*); (*Sc., talk nonsense*) нести́ (*det.*) чушь.

haversack /ˈhævəˌsæk/ *n.* рюкза́к.

havoc /ˈhævək/ *n.* (*destruction*) разгро́м; (*chaos*) беспоря́док, сумя́тица; (*fig.*): **play ~ with** вн|оси́ть, -ести́ беспоря́док/хао́с в + *a.*

haw[1] /hɔː/ *n.* я́года боя́рышника.

● *cpd.* **~thorn** *n.* боя́рышник.

haw[2] /hɔː/ *v.i. see* ⇒**hum** *v.t. & i.* 3

Hawaii /həˈwaɪɪ/ *n.* (*island*) Гава́йи (*m. indecl.*); (*group of islands*) Гава́йские острова́ (*m. pl.*).

Hawaiian /həˈwaɪən/ *n.* гава́|ец (*fem.* -йка).

● *adj.* гава́йский.

hawk[1] /hɔːk/ *n.* я́стреб (*also fig., pol.*).

● *v.i.* охо́титься (*impf.*) с я́стребом.

● *cpds.* **~-eyed** *adj.* зо́ркий, с орли́ным взгля́дом; **~-moth** *n.* бра́жник; су́меречная ба́бочка.

hawk[2] /hɔːk/ *v.i.* (*clear throat*) отка́шл|иваться, -яться.

hawk[3] /hɔːk/ *v.t.* (*peddle*) торгова́ть (*impf.*) вразно́с + *i.*; (*fig.*) быть разно́счиком + *g.*

hawker /ˈhɔːkə(r)/ *n.* торго́вец вразно́с.

hawser /ˈhɔːzə(r)/ *n.* (стально́й) трос.

hay /heɪ/ *n.* се́но; **~ fever** сенна́я лихора́дка; **hit the ~** (*sl., go to bed*) отпр|авля́ться, -а́виться на боково́ю; **make ~** (*lit.*) загот|а́вливать, -о́вить се́но; **make ~ while the sun shines** ≈ куй желе́зо, пока горячо́.

● *cpds.* **~cock** *n.* копна́; **~-fork** *n.* ви́л|ы (*pl., g.* —); **~making** *n.* сеноко́с, загото́вка се́на; **~rick** *n.* стог се́на; **~stack** *n.* стог се́на; **~wire** *n.* (*sl.*): **everything went ~wire** всё пошло́ наперекося́к.

hazard /ˈhæzəd/ *n.* **1** (*risk*) риск. **2** (*danger*) опа́сность; **road ~s** опа́сности на доро́гах.

● *v.t.* **1** (*endanger*) риск|ова́ть, -ну́ть + *i.*; **he ~ed his life for her** ра́ди неё он рискова́л жи́знью. **2** (*venture to say*) отва́ж|иваться, -иться + *inf. or* на + *a.*;

he ~ed a remark он отва́жился вы́сказать замеча́ние.

● *cpd.* **~ lights** *n. pl.* авари́йные фа́ры (*f. pl.*).

hazardous /ˈhæzədəs/ *adj.* риско́ванный; опа́сный.

haze /heɪz/ *n.* ды́мка; (*fig.*) тума́н.

hazel /ˈheɪz(ə)l/ *n.* (*tree*) лесно́й оре́х; (*colour*) оре́ховый цвет; **~ eyes** ка́рие глаза́.

● *cpd.* **~-nut** *n.* лесно́й оре́х.

haziness /ˈheɪzɪnɪs/ *n.* (*atmospheric*) тума́нность; ды́мка; (*mental*) расплы́вчатость; тума́нность, сму́тность.

hazy /ˈheɪzɪ/ *adj.* (**hazier, haziest**) подёрнутый ды́мкой; затума́ненный; (*fig.*) сму́тный, тума́нный.

H-bomb /ˈeɪtʃbɒm/ *n.* водоро́дная бо́мба.

HDTV (*abbr. of* ***high-definition television***) ТВЧ (телеви́дение высо́кой чёткости).

he[1] /hi:/, /hɪ/ *pron.* (*obj.* **him**) он; (*in children's game*) водя́щий (*etc., acc. to game*); **who is '~'?** кто во́дит?; кому́ води́ть?; **~ who believes** тот, кто ве́рит; **~'s a clever man, our teacher** он у́мный челове́к, наш учи́тель.

● *cpds.* **~-bear** *n.* медве́дь-саме́ц; **~goat** *n.* козёл; **~-man** *n.* настоя́щий мужчи́на.

he[2] /hi:/, /hɪ/ *int.* **~, ~** (*expr. laughter*) хи-хи!

head /hed/ *n.* **1** голова́; (*dim., e.g. baby's*) голо́вка; **he was hit on the ~** его́ уда́рили по голове́; **~ first, foremost** голово́й вперёд; **he was ~ over heels in love** он был по́ уши влюблён; **covered in dust from ~ to foot, toe** покры́тый пы́лью с головы́ до ног; **a good ~ of hair** густы́е во́лосы; **I could do it standing on my ~** я могу́ э́то сде́лать одно́й ле́вой; **he goes about with his ~ in the air** он задира́ет но́с; он задаётся; **his ~ is in the clouds** он вита́ет в облака́х; **he is keeping his ~ above water** (*fig.*) он де́ржится на пове́рхности; **he will never hold up his ~ again** он бо́льше не смо́жет смотре́ть лю́дям в глаза́; **he hung his ~ for shame** он пону́рил го́лову от стыда́; **shake one's ~** кача́ть, по- голово́й; **he turned his ~** он поверну́л го́лову; **I cannot make ~ or tail of it** я не могу́ в э́том разобра́ться; **he was promoted over my ~** ему́ да́ли повыше́ние че́рез мою́ го́лову; **this is all completely over my ~** э́то всё вы́ше моего́ понима́ния; **keep your ~ down** (*lit.*) пригни́тесь; опусти́те го́лову; (*fig.*) не высо́вывайтесь; не ле́зьте на рожо́н; **it's time to get your ~ down** (*Br. coll., go to bed*) пора́ на бокову́ю; **he can talk your ~ off** он вас заговори́т; **bury one's ~ in the sand** (*fig.*) отка́зываться (*impf.*) смотре́ть фа́ктам в лицо́; (*attr.*) головно́й; **a ~ cold** на́сморк; **a ~ voice** головно́й реги́стр; **a ~ wind** встре́чный ве́тер.
2 (*as measure*): **he gave me a ~ start** он дал мне фо́ру; **he is taller by a ~** он на́ го́лову вы́ше; **he stands ~ and shoulders above the rest** (*fig.*) он на́ го́лову вы́ше всех остальны́х.
3 (*mind, brain*): **two ~s are better than one** ум хорошо́, а два лу́чше; **he has a good ~ for figures** он хорошо́ счита́ет; **he's a bit weak in the ~** у него́ ви́нтика не хвата́ет (*coll.*); **he's off his ~** он спя́тил (*coll.*); **you can do the sum in your ~** вы мо́жете вы́числить э́то в уме́; **it came into my ~ that …** мне пришло́ в го́лову, что. . .; **I can't keep it in my ~** э́то не де́ржится у меня́ в голове́; **they put their ~s together** они́ ста́ли ду́мать вме́сте; **I made it up out of my ~** я э́то вы́думал; **put it out of your ~!** вы́бросьте э́то из головы́!; **what put that into your ~?** отку́да вы э́то взя́ли?; **he took it into his ~ to invite them** ему́ взбрело́ в го́лову их пригласи́ть; **the date went clean out of my ~** да́та соверше́нно вы́скочила у меня́ из головы́; **it never entered my ~** мне э́то никогда́ не приходи́ло в го́лову; (*faculties*): **the wine went to his ~** вино́ уда́рило ему́ в го́лову; **success went to his ~** успе́х вскружи́л ему́ го́лову; (*balance, composure*): **he kept his ~** он сохраня́л прису́тствие ду́ха; он не теря́л го́лову; **he has no ~ for heights** у него́ кру́жится голова́ от высоты́; он бои́тся высоты́; (*freedom, scope*): **he gave the horse its ~** он дал ло́шади по́лную во́лю.
4 (*on a coin*): **~s or tails?** орёл и́ли ре́шка?; **~s I win** е́сли орёл, я вы́играл.
5 (*personage*): **crowned ~s** корони́ванные осо́бы.
6 (*unit*): **£5 a ~** пять фу́нтов с ка́ждого; **forty ~ of cattle** со́рок голо́в скота́.
7 (*life*): **it cost him his ~** он поплати́лся за э́то голово́й; **he had a price on his ~** за его́ го́лову бы́ло назна́чено вознагражде́ние; **on your own ~ be it!** на ваш страх и риск!
8 (*upper or principal end*): **at the ~ of the table** во главе́ стола́; **at the ~ of the stairs** на ве́рхней площа́дке ле́стницы; **at the ~ of the page** в нача́ле страни́цы; **at the ~ of the procession** во главе́ проце́ссии.
9 (*principal member*) глава́ (*c.g.*), ста́рший; **~ of state** глава́ госуда́рства; **~ of the family** глава́ семьи́; (*attr., principal*): **~ boy** ста́рший учени́к; ста́роста шко́лы; **~ waiter** метрдоте́ль (*m.*); **~ office** гла́вная householdконто́ра, центр.
10 (*category*): **these all come under one ~** всё э́то отно́сится к одному́ разря́ду.
11 (*culmination*): **come to a ~** назр|ева́ть, -е́ть; **things came to a ~** наступи́л перело́мный моме́нт; **the revolt came to a ~** бунт назре́л; **he brought the issue to a ~** он поста́вил вопро́с ребро́м.
12 (*of tool, plant, vegetable, flower*) голо́вка; **~ of cabbage** коча́н капу́сты; (*of river*) верхо́вье; (*of water, steam*) напо́р, давле́ние; (*froth*) пе́на; (*promontory*) мыс.

● *v.t.* **1** (*steer, direct*): **he is ~ed for home** он направля́ется домо́й; **I managed to ~ him off** (*fig.*) мне удало́сь переключи́ть его на другу́ю те́му.
2 (*strike with head*): **he ~ed the ball into the net** он заби́л мяч в се́тку голово́й.
3 (*be first in*) возгл|авля́ть, -а́вить; **he ~ed the team** он возглавля́л кома́нду.

● *v.i.* (*move, steer*) напр|авля́ться, -а́виться; (*fig.*): **he is ~ing for disaster** он пло́хо ко́нчит.

● *cpds.* **~ache** *n.* головна́я боль; **I have a ~ache** у меня́ боли́т голова́; **~-band** *n.* головна́я повя́зка; **~board** *n.* спи́нка в изголо́вьи крова́ти; **~dress** *n.* (замыслова́тый/экзоти́ческий) головно́й убо́р; **~gear** *n.* головно́й убо́р; **~-hunter** *n.* челове́к, собира́ющий го́ловы уби́тых как трофе́и; (*fig.*) челове́к, перема́нивающий специали́стов из други́х организа́ций; **~lamp, ~light** *nn.* фа́ра; **~land** *n.* (*promontory*) мыс; **~light** *n.* = **~lamp; ~line** *n.* заголо́вок; (*pl.*) (гла́вные) но́вости дня; **he hit the ~lines** о нём крича́ли все газе́ты; **~long** *adj.* (*fig.*): **~long flight** стреми́тельное бе́гство; *adv.* голово́й вперёд; (*in a rush*) стремгла́в; очертя́ го́лову; **~man** *n.* глава́; **~master, ~mistress** *nn.* (*Br.*) дире́ктор шко́лы; **~-on** *adj.* лобово́й, встре́чный; **a ~-on collision** лобово́е столкнове́ние; *adv.*: **the wind blew ~-on** дул встре́чный ве́тер; **~phone** *n.* нау́шник; **~quarters** *n.* штаб-кварти́ра; (*mil.*) штаб, ста́вка; **~-rest** *n.* подголо́вник; **~-room** *n.* габари́тная высота́; **~-scarf** *n.* косы́нка; **~set** *n.* (*pair of ~-phones*) нау́шники (*m. pl.*); **~-shrinker** *n.* (*coll., joc.*) психиа́тр; **~stone** *n.* (*tombstone*) надгро́бный ка́мень; **~strong** *adj.* своево́льный, упря́мый; **~ teacher** *n.* дире́ктор шко́лы; **~waters** *n.* исто́ки (*m. pl.*); **~way** *n.* продвиже́ние вперёд; (*fig.*): **we are not making much ~way** мы продвига́емся сли́шком ме́дленно; **~-word** *n.* загла́вное сло́во.

headed /ˈhedɪd/ *adj.*: **~ notepaper** (*of organization*) ге́рбовая бума́га; (*of person*) имення́я бума́га.

header /ˈhedə(r)/ *n.* **1** (*fall*) паде́ние вниз голово́й; **he took a ~** он упа́л голово́й вниз; (*dive*) ныро́к. **2** (*in soccer*) уда́р голово́й. **3** (*line of text*) колонти́тул, ша́пка.

heading /ˈhedɪŋ/ *n.* (*title*) заголо́вок, загла́вие; (*section*) ру́брика.

headless /ˈhedlɪs/ *adj.* обезгла́вленный.

headship /ˈhedʃɪp/ *n.* руково́дство.

heady /ˈhedɪ/ *adj.* (**headier, headiest**) хмельно́й; (*also fig.*) пьяня́щий.

heal /hi:l/ *v.t.* (*person*) исцел|я́ть, -и́ть; (*wound*) зале́ч|ивать, -и́ть; (*fig.*): **time ~s all wounds** вре́мя всё ле́чит.

● *v.i.* заж|ива́ть, -и́ть; **his wounds ~ed up, over** его́ ра́ны зажи́ли.

healer /ˈhi:lə(r)/ *n.* ле́карь (*m.*); (ис)цели́тель (*m.*); (*fig.*): **time is the great ~** вре́мя — лу́чший ле́карь.

healing /ˈhiːlɪŋ/ *n.* (*curing*) лече́ние; (*of wound*) заживле́ние.

health /helθ/ *n.* **1** (*state of body or mind*) здоро́вье; **in good ~** здоро́вый; **he suffers from poor ~** у него́ сла́бое здоро́вье; **Ministry of H~** Министе́рство здравоохране́ния; **mental ~** душе́вное здоро́вье; **~ centre** (*Br.*), **center** (*US*) поликли́ника; **~ food** натура́льная пи́ща; **~ insurance** медици́нская страхо́вка; **~ resort** куро́рт, санато́рий; **~ service** слу́жба здравоохране́ния, здравоохране́ние. **2** (*toast*): **we drank (to) his ~** мы вы́пили за его́ здоро́вье; **here's a ~ to her Majesty!** за здоро́вье Её вели́чества!

healthful /ˈhelθfʊl/ *adj.* здоро́вый, целе́бный.

healthy /ˈhelθɪ/ *adj.* (**healthier, healthiest**) здоро́вый; **a ~ economy** стаби́льная эконо́мика.

heap /hiːp/ *n.* **1** (*pile*) ку́ча, гру́да. **2** (*esp. pl., coll., large quantity*) ма́сса, ку́ча, у́йма; **he has ~s of money** у него́ у́йма/ку́ча де́нег; **I have ~s to tell you** у меня́ у́йма/ку́ча новосте́й для вас.

● *v.t.*: **a ~ed** (*Br.*), **heaping** (*US*) **spoonful** ло́жка с ве́рхом; **they ~ed honours** (*Br.*), **honors** (*US*) **on him** его́ осы́пали по́честями; **the table was ~ed with food** стол ломи́лся от яств.

hear /hɪə(r)/ *v.t. & i.* (*past and p.p.* **heard** /hɜːd/) **1** (*perceive with ear*) слы́шать, у-; **I can't ~ a word** я не слы́шу ни сло́ва; **he can't ~ as well as he used to** он стал ху́же слы́шать; **I ~ someone coming** я слы́шу, что кто-то идёт *or* (чьи-то) шаги́; **I ~d him shout** я услы́шал, как он закрича́л; **he was ~d to say** слы́шали, что/как он говори́л; **I have ~d it said that ...** я слы́шал, бу́дто...; **the shot was ~d a mile away** вы́стрел бы́ло слы́шно за ми́лю. **2** (*listen to*): **~ evidence** слу́шать, за- показа́ния свиде́телей; **his prayer was ~d** его́ моли́твы бы́ли услы́шаны; **~ s.o. out** выслу́шивать, вы́слушать кого́-н.; **I won't ~ of it!** я и слы́шать об э́том не хочу́! **3** (*be told; learn*) слы́шать, у-; **have you ~d the news?** вы слы́шали но́вости?; **have you ~d from your brother?** что слы́шно от ва́шего бра́та?; **I ~ he has been ill** я слы́шал, что он был бо́лен; **I ~d about it from a friend** я узна́л об э́том от моего́ дру́га; **I've never ~d of him** я о нём никогда́ не слы́шал; **I never ~d of such a thing** э́то неслы́ханно; **you will ~ more of this** вам э́то так не пройдёт. **4**: **~!, ~!** пра́вильно!; ве́рно ска́зано!

● *cpd.* **~say** *n.* слу́хи (*m. pl.*); то́лки (*m. pl.*); **by ~say** понаслы́шке; **~say evidence** показа́ние с чужи́х слов.

hearer /ˈhɪərə(r)/ *n.* слу́шатель (*fem.* -ница).

hearing /ˈhɪərɪŋ/ *n.* **1** (*perception*) слух; **~ aid** слухово́й аппара́т; **he is hard of ~** он туг на́ ухо. **2** (*earshot*): **wait till he gets out of ~** да́йте ему́ сперва́ отойти́(, а то он мо́жет услы́шать); **don't say that in my ~** не говори́те э́того при мне. **3** (*attention*): **give him a fair ~** вы́слушайте его́; да́йте ему вы́сказаться. **4** (*leg.*) слу́шание.

hearken /ˈhɑːkən/ *v.i.* вн|има́ть, -ять + *d.*; слу́шать (*impf.*).

hearse /hɜːs/ *n.* катафа́лк, похоро́нные дро́г|и (*pl., g.* —).

heart /hɑːt/ *n.* **1** (*organ*) се́рдце; **~ attack** серде́чный при́ступ; инфа́ркт; **~ disease** боле́знь се́рдца; **~ failure** разры́в се́рдца; **~ surgery** кардиохирурги́я; **~ transplant** переса́дка се́рдца; **his ~ stopped beating** у него́ останови́лось се́рдце; **my ~ was in my mouth** у меня́ душа́ в пя́тки ушла́; **it will break his ~** он бу́дет в отча́янии; **his ~ sank** у него́ се́рдце упа́ло. **2** (*soul; seat of emotions*) се́рдце, душа́; **she has a ~ of gold** у неё золото́е се́рдце; **at ~** в глубине́ души́; **I am sick at ~** у меня́ тяжело́ на душе́; **he's a man after my own ~** он мне по душе́/по́ сердцу; **his ~ is in the right place** он серде́чный челове́к; **in one's ~ of ~s** в глубине́ души́; **to one's ~'s content** ско́лько душе́ уго́дно; **she achieved her ~'s desire** её заве́тное жела́ние осуществи́лось; **I agree with you ~ and soul** я всей душо́й с ва́ми согла́сен; **bless my ~!** Бо́же мой!; вот те(бе́) на́!; **bless his ~** дай Бог ему́ здоро́вья; **from the bottom of one's ~** от всего́ се́рдца; **he had a change of ~** он переду́мал/разду́мал; **she cried her ~ out** она́ вы́плакала все глаза́; **it did his ~ good to see her so happy** у него́ душа́ ра́довалась, глядя́ на её сча́стье; **I cannot find it in my ~ to be angry** я не в си́лах серди́ться; **he has your interests at ~** ему́ до́роги ва́ши интере́сы; **have a ~!** (*coll.*) сжа́льтесь!; поми́луйте!; **I didn't have the ~ to tell him about it** у меня́ не хвати́ло ду́ху сказа́ть ему́ об э́том; **he lost his ~ to her** он полюби́л её всем се́рдцем; **my ~ goes out to you** я вам о́чень сочу́вствую; **with all my ~** всем се́рдцем; **he had set his ~ on winning** он стра́стно жела́л вы́играть; **he speaks from his ~** он говори́т от чи́стого се́рдца; **don't take it to ~** не принима́йте э́то бли́зко к се́рдцу; **he wears his ~ on his sleeve** у него́ душа́ нараспа́шку; **he won their ~s** он завоева́л их сердца́; (*enthusiasm*): **his ~ is not in his work** у него́ душа́ не лежи́т к рабо́те; (*courage*): **he lost ~** он пал ду́хом; **take ~!** не па́дайте ду́хом!; (*memory*): **I learnt it by ~** я вы́учил э́то наизу́сть. **3** (*centre*) середи́на, сердцеви́на; **in the ~ of the forest** в глуши́ ле́са; **this book gets to the ~ of the matter** э́та кни́га затра́гивает са́мую суть де́ла. **4** (*pl., cards*) че́рв|и (*pl., g.* -е́й); **ace of ~s** черво́нный туз, туз черве́й.

● *cpds.* **~ache** *n.* серде́чная боль; **~beat** *n.* сердцебие́ние; **~break** *n.* большо́е го́ре; **~-breaking** *adj.* душераздира́ющий; **~-broken** *adj.* с разби́тым се́рдцем; **~burn** *n.* изжо́га; **~felt** *adj.* душе́вный, глубоко́ прочу́вствованный; **~land** *n.* се́рдце, центр; **~-rending** *adj.* душераздира́ющий; **~-searching** *n.* душе́вные терза́ния; **~'s-ease** *n.* аню́тины гла́зки (*m. pl.*); **~-strings** *n. pl.* душе́вные стру́ны (*f. pl.*); **he played on her ~-strings** он игра́л её чу́вствами; **~-throb** *n.* (*coll.*) люби́мец; **~-to-~** *adj.*: **a ~-to-~ talk** разгово́р по душа́м; **~-warming** *adj.* ра́достный; тёплый; тро́гательный; **~wood** *n.* ядро́вая древеси́на.

hearten /ˈhɑːt(ə)n/ *v.t.* ободр|я́ть, -и́ть; **a ~ing experience** поднима́ющее настрое́ние собы́тие.

hearth /hɑːθ/ *n.* оча́г; (*fig., home*) дома́шний оча́г.

● *cpd.* **~-rug** *n.* ко́врик пе́редками́ном.

heartily /ˈhɑːtɪlɪ/ *adv.* **1** (*from the heart*) серде́чно, и́скренне; **I am ~ sick of it** мне э́то до́ смерти надое́ло. **2** (*with relish, enthusiasm*) охо́тно, усе́рдно; **he agreed with me ~** он всеце́ло со мной согласи́лся; **the boys ate ~** ма́льчики е́ли с аппети́том.

heartiness /ˈhɑːtɪnɪs/ *n.* серде́чность, доброду́шие.

heartless /ˈhɑːtlɪs/ *adj.* бессерде́чный.

heartlessness /ˈhɑːtlɪsnɪs/ *n.* бессерде́чие.

hearty /ˈhɑːtɪ/ *adj.* (**heartier, heartiest**) **1** (*cordial, sincere*) серде́чный. **2** (*healthy, vigorous*): **he is still hale and ~** он всё ещё здоро́в и бодр; **a ~ appetite** прекра́сный аппети́т. **3** (*abundant*): **he ate a ~ breakfast** он пло́тно поза́втракал. **4** (*cheerful*) весёлый.

heat /hiːt/ *n.* **1** (*hotness*) жара́; (*warmth*) тепло́, теплота́; **white ~** бе́лое кале́ние; **latent ~** уде́льная/скры́тая теплота́; (*hot weather*) жара́; **the ~ of the day** (*lit.*) полу́денный зной; **he feels the ~** (*badly*) он пло́хо перено́сит жару́; **prickly ~** потни́ца; (*heating*) отопле́ние; **the ~ was turned on** (*lit.*) отопле́ние бы́ло включено́; (*fig., pressure was applied*) бы́ло ока́зано давле́ние; **~ engine** теплово́й дви́гатель; **~ treatment** (*med.*) теплолече́ние; (*metall.*) теплообрабо́тка. **2** (*warmth of feeling*) теплота́; (*passion*) горя́чность; **in the ~ of the moment** сгоряча́; **this took the ~ out of the situation** э́то разряди́ло обстано́вку. **3** (*in running*) забе́г; (*in horse-racing*) зае́зд; (*in swimming*) заплы́в; **dead ~** одновре́ме́нный фи́ниш. **4** (*of animals*) те́чка; **our dog is on ~** у на́шей соба́ки те́чка.

● *v.t.* **1** (*raise temperature of*) нагр|ева́ть, -е́ть; **the potatoes were ~ed up** карто́шку разогре́ли; **~ed swimming pool** бассе́йн с подогре́вом. **2** (*inflame*) накал|я́ть, -и́ть; горячи́ть, раз-; **a ~ed argument** жа́ркий спор; **he replied ~edly** он отве́тил запа́льчиво.

● *cpds.* **~-proof, ~-resistant** *adjs.* жаросто́йкий, жаропро́чный; **~stroke** *n.* теплово́й уда́р; **~-wave** *n.* полоса́/пери́од си́льной жары́.

heater /ˈhiːtə(r)/ *n.* (*electric, gas, oil ~*) обогрева́тель (*m.*); (*tech.*) нагрева́тель; (*radiator*) батаре́я; (*large, connected to wall*) печь, пе́чка.

heath /hi:θ/ *n.* **1** (*Br., waste land*) пу́стошь. **2** (*shrub*) ве́реск.

heathen /ˈhi:ð(ə)n/ *n.* язы́чник.
● *adj.* язы́ческий

heathenism /ˈhi:ðən,ɪz(ə)m/ *n.* язы́чество.

heather /ˈheðə(r)/ *n.* ве́реск.

heating /ˈhi:tɪŋ/ *n.* обогрева́ние, отопле́ние; **central ~** центра́льное отопле́ние.

heave /hi:v/ *n.* (*lifting effort*) подъём; (*throw*) бросо́к.
● *v.t.* (*past and p.p.* **heaved** *or esp. naut.* **hove**) (*lift*) подн|има́ть, -я́ть; (*throw*) бр|оса́ть, -о́сить; **~ a sigh** (тяжело́) вздыха́ть, -охну́ть.
● *v.i.* (*past and p.p.* **heaved** *or esp. naut.* **hove**) **1** (*pull*): **they ~d on the rope** они́ вы́брали кана́т; **~ ho!** раз-два взя́ли!; эй, у́хнем! **2** (*retch*) ту́житься (*impf.*) (при рво́те). **3** (*rise and fall*) вздыма́ться (*impf.*); **her bosom was heaving** её грудь вздыма́лась; **heaving billows** вздыма́ющиеся во́лны. **4**: **~ to** (*naut.*) ложи́ться, лечь в дрейф. **5**: **~ in sight** пока́з|ываться, -а́ться; яв|ля́ться, -и́ться глаза́м.

heaven /ˈhev(ə)n/ *n.* **1** (*sky, firmament*) не́бо, небе́сный свод; **the ~s opened** (*of heavy rain*) небеса́ разве́рзлись; **move ~ and earth** прил|ага́ть, -ожи́ть все уси́лия. **2** (*state of bliss*) блаже́нство; **in the seventh ~** на седьмо́м не́бе. **3** (*paradise*) рай, ца́рство небе́сное. **4** (*God, Providence*) Бог, провиде́ние; **~ knows where he is** Бог зна́ет, где он; **~ forbid!** Бо́же упаси́!; **thank ~ for that** сла́ва Бо́гу; **for ~'s sake** ра́ди Бо́га; **(good) ~s (above)!** Го́споди!; Бо́же мой!
● *cpd.* **~sent** *adj.* благода́тный.

heavenly /ˈhevənlɪ/ *adj.* **1** (*in or of heaven*) небе́сный; **~ bodies** небе́сные тела́/свети́ла (*nt. pl.*). **2** (*coll., excellent, wonderful*) изуми́тельный; ди́вный; **we had a ~ time** мы ди́вно/чуде́сно провели́ вре́мя.

heavily /ˈhevɪ/ *adv.* (*very, seriously*) значи́тельно, си́льно; **the rain is falling ~** идёт си́льный дождь; **he fell ~** он тяжело́ ру́хнул; **they were ~ defeated** они́ потерпе́ли тяжёлое пораже́ние.

heaviness /ˈhevɪnɪs/ *n.* **1** (*weight*) тя́жесть. **2** (*drowsiness, lethargy*) вя́лость, апа́тия. **3**: **~ of heart** тя́жесть на се́рдце.

heavy /ˈhevɪ/ *adj.* (**heavier, heaviest**) тяжёлый; **~ artillery** тяжёлая артилле́рия; **a ~ blow** (*lit., fig.*) тяжёлый уда́р; **~ breathing** тяжёлое дыха́ние; **a ~ cold** си́льный на́сморк; **there will be a ~ crop this year** в э́том году́ бу́дет оби́льный урожа́й; **he had a ~ day** у него́ был тяжёлый день; **he is a ~ drinker** он си́льно пьёт; **he had a ~ fall** он си́льно уда́рился при паде́нии; **under ~ fire** под си́льным огнём; **~ food** тяжёлая пи́ща; **his book is ~ going** его́ кни́га тру́дно чита́ется; **with a ~ heart** с тяжёлым се́рдцем; **~ industry** тяжёлая промы́шленность; **~ losses** тяжёлые/больши́е поте́ри; **~ metal** (*coll., mus.*) металли́ческий рок; **~ metallist** (*coll., mus.*) металли́ст; **a ~ programme** (*Br.*), **program** (*US*) насы́щенная/напряжённая програ́мма; **~ rain** си́льный/проливно́й дождь; **a ~ sea** бу́рное мо́ре; **a ~ silence** тя́гостное молча́ние; **a ~ sleep** глубо́кий/тяжёлый сон; **he is a ~ sleeper** он кре́пко спит; **a ~ sky** хму́рое не́бо; **~ taxes** больши́е нало́ги; **~ traffic** интенси́вное движе́ние.
● *cpds.* **~-duty** *adj.* сверхпро́чный, но́ский; **~ goods vehicle** *n.* (*Br.*) грузови́к-тяжелово́з; **~-handed** *adj.* неуклю́жий; **~-hearted** *adj.* с тяжёлым се́рдцем; **~-laden** *adj.* тяжело́ нагру́женный (*чем*); **~weight** *n. & adj.* (*sport*) (боксёр/боре́ц) тяжёлого ве́са.

Hebraic /hi:ˈbreɪɪk/ *adj.* древнееврéйский.

Hebraist /ˈhi:breɪɪst/ *n.* гебраи́ст.

Hebrew /ˈhi:bru:/ *n.* **1** (*Jew*) евре́й. **2** (*language*) древнеевре́йский язы́к; (*modern*) иври́т.
● *adj.* древнеевре́йский; (*modern*) иври́тский.

Hebridean /,hebrɪˈdi:ən/ *adj.* гебри́дский.

Hebrides /ˈhebrɪ,di:z/ *n.*: **the ~** Гебри́дские острова́ (*m. pl.*).

heckle /ˈhek(ə)l/ *v.t.* (*fig.*) переб|ива́ть, -и́ть.
● *v.i.* переб|ива́ть, -и́ть ора́тора.

heckler /ˈheklə(r)/ *n.* челове́к, кото́рый пыта́ется переби́ть ора́тора; крику́н.

hectare /ˈhekteə(r)/, /-tɑ:(r)/ *n.* гекта́р.

hectic /ˈhektɪk/ *adj.* (*busy*) лихора́дочный, бу́рный.

hectolitre /ˈhektə,li:tə(r)/ (*US* **hectoliter**) *n.* гектоли́тр.

hector /ˈhektə(r)/ *v.t.* набр|а́сываться, -о́ситься на + *a.*

hedge /hedʒ/ *n.* жива́я и́згородь.
● *v.t.* **1** (*enclose*) обса́|живать, -ди́ть куста́рником; огор|а́живать, -оди́ть; (*fig.*): **~d in, round with regulations** в тиска́х пра́вил и предписа́ний. **2**: **~ one's bets** (*fig.*) перестрах|о́вываться, -ова́ться.
● *v.i.* (*prevaricate*) увил|ивать, -ьну́ть.
● *cpds.* **~hog** *n.* ёж, ёжик; **~row** *n.* шпале́ра, жива́я и́згородь; **~-sparrow** *n.* завиру́шка лесна́я.

hedonism /ˈhi:də,nɪz(ə)m/, /ˈhe-/ *n.* гедони́зм.

hedonist /ˈhi:dənɪst/, /ˈhe-/ *n.* гедони́ст.

hedonistic /,hi:dəˈnɪstɪk/, /ˈhe-/ *adj.* гедонисти́ческий.

heed /hi:d/ *n.* внима́ние; **she paid no ~ to his advice** она́ не вняла́ его́ сове́ту; **take ~** (*arch.*)! внемли́те!
● *v.t.* уч|и́тывать, -е́сть; внима́ть, вня́ть + *d.*

heedful /ˈhi:dfʊl/ *adj.* внима́тельный (*к чему*); (*careful*) предусмотри́тельный, осмотри́тельный.

heedfulness /ˈhi:dfʊlnɪs/ *n.* внима́тельность; предусмотри́тельность, осмотри́тельность.

heedless /ˈhi:dlɪs/ *adj.* беззабо́тный, беспе́чный; **she continued, ~ of danger** она́ продолжа́ла, не взира́я на опа́сность.

hee-haw /ˈhi:hɔ:/ *n.* и-а (*крик осла*); (*laugh*) ржа́ние.

heel[1] /hi:l/ *n.* **1** (*part of foot*) пя́тка; **he arrived on John's ~s** он пришёл вслед за Джо́ном; **the dog followed at, on his ~s** соба́ка сле́довала за ним по пята́м; **he called the dog to ~** он позва́л соба́ку «к ноге́»; **he fell head over ~s** он полете́л вверх торма́шками; **he took to his ~s** он бро́сился наутёк; **he showed a clean pair of ~s** то́лько его́ и ви́дели; он показа́л пя́тки; **he turned on his ~** он кру́то поверну́лся; **they suffered under the ~ of a tyrant** они́ страда́ли под пято́й тира́на.
2 (*of a shoe*) (*whole unit*) каблу́к; (*lower replaceable part*) набо́йка; **my shoes are down at ~** у мои́х ту́фель сби́лись каблуки́.
3 (*of a sock*) пя́тка.
4 (*US sl., cad*) хам, подо́нок.
● *v.t.*: **~ shoes** ста́вить, по- набо́йки на ту́фли.

heel[2] /hi:l/ *v.i.*: **the ship ~ed over** су́дно накрени́лось.

hefty /ˈheftɪ/ *adj.* (**heftier, heftiest**) (*person*) здорове́нный, ро́слый; (*sum*) кру́пный; (*blow*) здоро́вый.

hegemony /hɪˈdʒemənɪ/, /-ˈgemənɪ/ *n.* гегемо́ния.

heifer /ˈhefə(r)/ *n.* тёлка, не́тель.

height /haɪt/ *n.* **1** высота́; (*of person*) рост; **he was six feet in ~** он был ро́стом в 6 фу́тов; **a wall six feet in ~** стена́ высото́й в 6 фу́тов; **he drew himself up to his full ~** он встал во весь рост; **the house stands at a ~ of 500 feet** дом нахо́дится на высоте́ 500 фу́тов; **he fell from a great ~** он упа́л с большо́й высоты́; **the plane is losing ~** самолёт теря́ет высоту́.
2 (*high ground*) верши́на, верху́шка.
3 (*utmost degree*) вы́сшая сте́пень; **the ~ of folly** верх глу́пости; **the ~ of fashion** после́дний крик мо́ды; **the gale was at its ~** шторм был в разга́ре.

heighten /ˈhaɪt(ə)n/ *v.t.* (*make higher*) пов|ыша́ть, -ы́сить; (*increase*) уси́ли|вать, -ть; **~ed colour** (*Br.*), **color** (*US*) (*of face*) румя́нец.
● *v.i.* (*fig.*) уси́ли|ваться, -ться.

heinous /ˈheɪnəs/, /ˈhi:nəs/ *adj.* гну́сный, омерзи́тельный.

heir /eə(r)/ *n.* насле́дник; **~ apparent** прямо́й/непосре́дственный насле́дник; **~ presumptive** предполага́емый насле́дник.

heiress /ˈeərɪs/ *n.* насле́дница.

heirloom /ˈeəlu:m/ *n.* фами́льная рели́квия.

held /held/ *past and p.p. of* ⇒**hold**

helical /ˈhelɪk(ə)l/ *adj.* спира́льный, вито́й.

helices /ˈhi:lɪ,si:z/, /ˈhel-/ *pl. of* ⇒**helix**

helicopter /ˈhelɪˌkɒptə(r)/ *n.* вертолёт.
● *v.t.* перебр|áсывать, -óсить на вертолёте.

heliograph /ˈhiːlɪəˌgrɑːf/ *n.* гелиóграф.

heliotrope /ˈhiːlɪəˌtrəʊp/, /ˈhel-/ *n.* гелиотрóп.
● *adj.* (*colour*) лилóвый.

heliport /ˈhelɪˌpɔːt/ *n.* вертодрóм, вертолётная стáнция.

helium /ˈhiːlɪəm/ *n.* гéлий.

helix /ˈhiːlɪks/ *n.* (*pl.* **helices**) (*math.*) спирáль; (*archit.*) завитóк.

hell /hel/ *n.* **1** (*place or state*) ад; **he went through ~** он перенёс мýки áда; **he made her life ~** он преврати́л её жизнь в ад; **I gave him ~** (*coll.*) я зáдал емý жáру; **he hasn't a hope in ~** (*coll.*) ни чертá у негó не вы́йдет; **he will raise ~** (*coll.*) он подни́мет стрáшный шум.
2 (*coll. or sl., expr. vexation or emphasis*) **oh ~!** чёрт возьми́!; **go to ~!** иди́ к чёрту!; **what the ~ do you want?** что вам нýжно, чёрт возьми́/побери́?; **what the ~!** (*sc. does it matter*) какóго чёрта!; **I wish to ~ I'd never done it!** чёрт меня́ попýтал!; **'Do you agree?' — 'Like ~ I do!'** (*sc. not at all*) «Вы соглáсны?» — «Чёрта с два!»; **it hurts like ~** чертóвски бóльно; **to ~ with it!** чёрт с ним!; **they made the ~ of a noise** они́ ужáсно шумéли; **we had a ~ of a time** мы чертóвски хорошó повесели́лись; **all ~ broke loose** началáсь свистопля́ска; **he rode ~ for leather** он мчáлся сломя́ гóлову; **just for the ~ of it** за здóрово живёшь; **come ~ or high water** будь что бýдет; былá не былá.
● *cpds.* **~-bent** *adj.* с дья́вольским упóрством (добивáющийся чегó-н.); **~-fire** *n.* áдский огóнь; **~-raiser** *n.* скандали́ст.

hellebore /ˈhelɪˌbɔː(r)/ *n.* морóзник.

Hellene /ˈheliːn/ *n.* э́ллин.

Hellenic /heˈlenɪk/, /-ˈliːnɪk/ *adj.* э́ллинский.

Hellenist /ˈhelɪnɪst/ *n.* эллини́ст.

Hellenistic /ˌhelɪˈnɪstɪk/ *adj.* эллинисти́ческий.

Hellenize /ˈhelɪˌnaɪz/ *v.t.* подв|ергáть, -éргнуть грéческому влия́нию.

hellish /ˈhelɪʃ/ *adj.* áдский.

hello /həˈləʊ/ *int.* (*greeting*) здрáвствуй(те)!; привéт (*coll.*); (*on telephone*) аллó!; (*Br., expr. surprise*) вот те(бé) нá!

helm /helm/ *n.* (*tiller*) руль, рýмпель (*both m.*); **take the ~** (*lit., fig.*) вста|вáть, -ть у штурвáла/руля́.
● *cpd.* **~sman** *n.* рулевóй.

helmet /ˈhelmɪt/ *n.* шлем; (*modern soldier's or fireman's*) кáска.

help /help/ *n.* **1** (*assistance*) пóмощь; **he walks with the ~ of a stick** он хóдит с пáлкой; **she manages without** (*domestic*) **~** онá обхóдится без прислýги; **can I be of (any) ~?** я могý вам чéм-нибудь помóчь?; **your advice was a great ~ to us** ваш совéт нам óчень помóг; **they were not (of) much ~ to me** они́ мне не осóбенно помогли́.
2 (*remedy*): **there's no ~ for it** ничегó не подéлаешь.
3 (*domestic servant*) прислýга.
● *v.t.* **1** (*assist*) пом|огáть, -óчь; **please ~ me up** помоги́те мне, пожáлуйста, подня́ться; **he ~ed her out of the car** он помóг ей вы́йти из маши́ны; **he ~ed her off with her coat** он помóг ей снять пальтó.
2 (*alleviate*) облегч|áть, -и́ть.
3 (*serve with food etc.*) уго|щáть, -сти́ть; класть, положи́ть; да|вáть, -ть; (*что кому*); **may I ~ you to salad?** могý я положи́ть вам немнóго салáта?; **~ yourself!** угощáйтесь!; бери́те, пожáлуйста!; **he ~ed himself to the spoons** он стащи́л лóжки (*coll.*).
4 (*avoid, prevent; also v.i.*): **I can't ~ it** я не могý ничегó подéлать; от меня́ э́то не зави́сит; **I can't ~ laughing** я не могý удержáться от смéха; я не могý не смея́ться; **I won't go a step farther than I can ~** я не сдéлаю ни одногó ли́шнего шáга; **don't stay longer than you can ~** не оставáйтесь дóльше, чем нáдо; **it can't be ~ed** ничегó не подéлаешь.
5: **so ~ me (God)!** да помóжет мне Бог!
● *v.i.* (*avail, be of use*) быть полéзным; **crying won't ~** слезáми гóрю не помóжешь.
● *cpds.* **~-mate, ~-meet** *nn.* (*of woman*) подрýга жи́зни, спýтница жи́зни; (*of man*) спýтник жи́зни.

helper /ˈhelpə(r)/ *n.* помóщник; (*of a craftsman*) подрýчный.

helpful /ˈhelpfʊl/ *adj.* полéзный; (*obliging*) услýжливый.

helpfulness /ˈhelpfʊlnɪs/ *n.* полéзность; услýжливость.

helping /ˈhelpɪŋ/ *n.* пóрция.
● *adj.*: **she lent a ~ hand** онá протянýла рýку пóмощи.

helpless /ˈhelplɪs/ *adj.* беспóмощный, бесси́льный.

helplessly /ˈhelplɪslɪ/ *adv.* беспóмощно; **~ drunk** пья́ный вдрéбезги; **he was laughing ~** он смея́лся до упáду.

helplessness /ˈhelplɪsnɪs/ *n.* беспóмощность, бесси́лие.

Helsinki /ˈhelsɪŋkɪ/, /helˈsɪŋkɪ/ *n.* Хéльсинки (*m. indecl.*); (*attr.*) хéльсинкский.

helter-skelter /ˌheltəˈskeltə(r)/ *n.* спирáльная дéтская гóрка.
● *adv.* беспоря́дочно, как попáло; врассыпнýю.
● *adj.* беспоря́дочный, сумбýрный.

hem /hem/ *n.* край, подóл.
● *v.t.* (**hemmed, hemming**) **1** (*sew the edge of*) подш|ивáть, -и́ть. **2**: **~ in, ~ about, ~ round** окруж|áть, -и́ть.
● *cpds.* **~-line** *n.* ≈ подóл ю́бки; **~-stitch** *n.* подрýбочный шов; *v.t.* подш|ивáть, -и́ть.

hema- /ˈhiːmə/ (*US*) = **haema-**

hemisphere /ˈhemɪˌsfɪə(r)/ *n.* полушáрие.

hemispherical /ˌhemɪˈsferɪk(ə)l/ *adj.* полусфери́ческий.

hemlock /ˈhemlɒk/ *n.* (*plant*) болиголóв; (*tree*) тсýга, гемлóк.

hemo- /ˈhiːmə/ (*US*) = **haemo-**

hemp /hemp/ *n.* (*plant*) конопля́; (*fibre*) пенькá; **Indian ~** (*plant*) конопля́ инди́йская; (*drug*) гаши́ш, марихуáна.

hempen /ˈhempən/ *adj.* конопля́ный; пенькóвый.

hen /hen/ *n.* (*domestic fowl*) кýрица; (*female of bird species*) сáмка пти́цы.
● *cpds.* **~-bane** *n.* беленá; **~-coop, ~-house** *nn.* куря́тник; **~-party** *n.* (*coll.*) деви́чник; **~pecked** *adj.*: **he is ~pecked** жéна дéржит егó под каблукóм; **~pecked husband** подкаблýчник (*coll.*).

hence /hens/ *adv.* (*from here*) отсю́да; (*liter.*) отсéль; (*from now*): **3 years ~** чéрез три гóда; (*consequently*) отсю́да, слéдовательно.
● *cpds.* **~forth, ~forward** *advs.* впредь, с э́того врéмени.

henchman /ˈhentʃmən/ *n.* приспéшник.

henna /ˈhenə/ *n.* хна.
● *v.t.* (**hennaed, hennaing**): **~ed hair** вóлосы, крáшенные хнóй.

hepatitis /ˌhepəˈtaɪtɪs/ *n.* гепати́т.

heptagon /ˈheptəgən/ *n.* семиугóльник.

her /hɜː(r)/, /hə(r)/ *obj. of* **she; he loves ~** он лю́бит её; **he looks at ~** он смóтрит на неё; (*poss. adj.*) её; **~ husband** её муж; (*referring to subj. of sentence*) свой; **she loves ~ husband** онá лю́бит своегó мýжа.

herald /ˈher(ə)ld/ *n.* (*official*) член геральди́ческой палáты; (*messenger, forerunner*) вéстник.
● *v.t.* возве|щáть, -сти́ть; предвещáть (*impf.*).

heraldic /heˈrældɪk/ *adj.* геральди́ческий.

heraldry /ˈherəldrɪ/ *n.* герáльдика.

herb /hɜːb/ *n.* травá; (*as medicine*) лекáрственное растéние, лечéбная травá; (*pl., cul.*) трáвы; **~ tea** (*camomile etc.*) цветóчный чай; (*blackcurrant etc.*) фруктóвый чай.

herbaceous /hɜːˈbeɪʃəs/ *adj.* травянóй; **~ border** цветóчный бордю́р

herbal /ˈhɜːb(ə)l/ *n.* травни́к; **~ medicine** траволечéние.
● *adj.* травянóй; **~ tea** = **herb tea**

herbalist /ˈhɜːbəlɪst/ *n.* специали́ст по лекáрственным растéниям.

herbari|um /hɜːˈbeərɪəm/ *n.* (*pl.* **~a**) гербáрий.

herbicide /ˈhɜːbɪˌsaɪd/ *n.* гербици́д.

herbivore /ˈhɜːbɪˌvɔː(r)/ *n.* травоя́дное живóтное.

herbivorous /ˌhɜːˈbɪvərəs/ *adj.* травоя́дный.

Herculean /ˌhɜːkjʊˈliːən/, /-ˈkjuːlɪən/ *adj.* геркулéсов; (*fig.*): **~ efforts** титани́ческие уси́лия.

Hercules /ˈhɜːkjʊˌliːz/ *n.* Геркулéс,

Гера́кл; **the labours** (*Br.*), **labors** (*US*) **of ~** по́двиги Гера́кла.

herd /hɜ:d/ *n.* (*animals*) ста́до; (*people*) толпа́; **~ instinct** ста́дное чу́вство.

● *v.t.* сгоня́ть, согна́ть (вме́сте).

● *v.i.* (*fig.*) (*of animals*) ходи́ть (*indet.*) ста́дом; (*of people*) ходи́ть (*indet.*) ско́пом.

● *cpd.* **~-sman** *n.* пасту́х.

here /hɪə(r)/ *n.*: **from ~ to there** отсю́да — туда́; **my house is near ~** мой дом ря́дом.

● *adv.* **1** (*in this place*) здесь, тут; **the book doesn't belong ~** э́той кни́ге здесь не ме́сто.
2 (*to this place, in this direction*) сюда́; **come ~!** иди́те сюда́!; **look ~!** (*lit.*) посмотри́те сюда!; (*expr. emph., impatience etc.*) послу́шайте!
3 (*demonstrative*) вот; **~ I am!** вот и я!; я тут!; **~ he comes!** вот и он!; **~ we are at last!** наконе́ц-то (мы) пришли́/ прие́хали/при́были; **~ we go (again)!** (*coll., fig.*) ну вот опя́ть!; ≈ опя́ть два́дцать пять!; **~ goes!** (*coll.*) будь что бу́дет!; **~'s how it happened** вот как э́то случи́лось; **~'s to our victory!** за на́шу побе́ду!; **Mr Smith ~ is a surgeon** вот ми́стер Смит, он хиру́рг.
4 (*with offers*): **~ you are!** пожа́луйста!; **~ is my hand!** вот вам моя́ рука́!
5 (*at this point*): **~ she began to cry** тут она́ запла́кала.
6 (*for emph.*): **~, take this** вот, возьми́те э́то.
7: **same ~!** и я то́же!
8 (*misc. phrr.*): **he looked ~ and there** он поиска́л там и сям (*coll.*); **I've been ~, there and everywhere** я был повсю́ду; **it's neither ~ nor there** э́то здесь ни при чём; э́то ни к селу́ ни к го́роду.

hereabouts /ˌhɪərəˈbaʊts/ *adv.* побли́зости.

hereafter /hɪərˈɑ:ftə(r)/ *n.*: **the ~** загро́бная жизнь.

● *adv.* впосле́дствии.

hereby /hɪəˈbaɪ/ *adv.* сим (*arch.*); э́тим; настоя́щим.

hereditary /hɪˈredɪtərɪ/ *adj.* насле́дственный.

heredity /hɪˈredɪtɪ/ *n.* насле́дственность.

herein /hɪəˈrɪn/ *adv.*: **I enclose ~ ...** при сём прилага́ю. . . .

hereinafter /ˌhɪərɪnˈɑ:ftə(r)/ *adv.* ни́же, в дальне́йшем.

heresy /ˈherəsɪ/ *n.* е́ресь.

heretic /ˈherətɪk/ *n.* ерети́|к (*fem.* -чка).

heretical /hɪˈretɪk(ə)l/ *adj.* ерети́ческий.

hereto /hɪəˈtu:/ *adv.* к сему́, к э́тому.

heretofore /ˌhɪətʊˈfɔ:(r)/ *adv.* досе́ле, пре́жде, до сих пор.

hereupon /ˌhɪərəˈpɒn/ *adv.* вслед за э́тим.

herewith /hɪəˈwɪð/, /-ˈwɪθ/ *adv.* при сём.

heritable /ˈherɪtəb(ə)l/ *adj.* насле́дуемый.

heritage /ˈherɪtɪdʒ/ *n.* насле́дство; (*fig.*) насле́дие.

hermaphrodite /hɜ:ˈmæfrəˌdaɪt/ *n.* гермафроди́т.

hermetic /hɜ:ˈmetɪk/ *adj.* гермети́ческий; **~ally sealed** гермети́чески закры́тый.

hermit /ˈhɜ:mɪt/ *n.* отше́льник.

● *cpd.* **~-crab** *n.* рак-отше́льник.

hermitage /ˈhɜ:mɪtɪdʒ/ *n.* прию́т отше́льника; **H~** (*museum*) Эрмита́ж.

her|nia /ˈhɜ:nɪə/ *n.* (*pl.* **~nias** *or* **~niae** /-nɪˌi:/) гры́жа.

hero /ˈhɪərəʊ/ *n.* (*pl.* **~es**) геро́й.

● *cpd.* **~-worship** *n.* преклоне́ние пе́ред геро́ями; (*pej.*) культ ли́чности.

heroic /hɪˈrəʊɪk/ *adj.* (*person, attempt*) герои́ческий; (*action*) геро́йский.

heroics /hɪˈrəʊɪks/ *n.* напы́щенность, ходу́льность.

heroin /ˈherəʊɪn/ *n.* герои́н.

heroine /ˈherəʊɪn/ *n.* герои́ня.

heroism /ˈherəʊˌɪz(ə)m/ *n.* герои́зм.

heron /ˈherən/ *n.* ца́пля.

herpes /ˈhɜ:pi:z/ *n.* лиша́й.

herring /ˈherɪŋ/ *n.* сельдь; (*as food*) селёдка; **red ~** (*fig.*) отвлека́ющий манёвр.

● *cpds.* **~-bone** *n.* & *adj.*: **~bone stitch** переплете́ние «ло́маная са́ржа»; (*archit. pattern*) кла́дка «в ёлку»; **~-fishery** *n.* лов се́льди.

hers /hɜ:z/ *pron.* её; **is this handkerchief ~?** э́то её плато́к?; **your dress is prettier than ~** у вас пла́тье краси́вее, чем у неё; **I don't like that husband of ~** мне не нра́вится её муж!; **friends of ~** её друзья́.

herself /həˈself/ *pron.* **1** (*refl.*) себя́, -ся (*suff.*); **she looked at ~ in the mirror** она́ посмотре́ла на себя́ в зе́ркало; **she fell down and hurt ~** она́ упа́ла и ушибла́сь.
2 (*emph.*) сама́; **she said so ~** она́ сама́ э́то сказа́ла; **I saw the Queen ~** я ви́дел саму́ короле́ву.
3 (*after preps.*) одна́; сама́; **she lives by ~** она́ живёт одна́; **can she do it by ~?** она́ мо́жет сама́ э́то сде́лать?; **she kept it to ~** она́ ни с кем э́тим не дели́лась.
4 (*her normal state*): **she is not ~ today** сего́дня она́ сама́ не своя́; **she will soon come to ~** она́ ско́ро придёт в себя́.

hertz /hɜ:ts/ *n.* (*pl.* **~**) герц.

hesitanc|e /ˈhezɪtəns/, **-y** /ˈhezɪtənsɪ/ *nn.* колеба́ние; (*irresolution*) нереши́тельность.

hesitant /ˈhezɪt(ə)nt/ *adj.* колеблю́щийся; (*irresolute*) нереши́тельный; **to be ~** колеба́ться (*impf.*), сомнева́ться (*impf.*).

hesitate /ˈhezɪˌteɪt/ *v.i.* колеба́ться (*impf.*), сомнева́ться (*impf.*); (*in speech*) зап|ина́ться, -ну́ться; **don't ~ to ask** непреме́нно спроси́те; **I ~ to say this** не зна́ю, сле́дует ли мне э́то сказа́ть; **he who ~s is lost** ≈ промедле́ние сме́рти подо́бно.

hesitation /ˌhezɪˈteɪʃ(ə)n/ *n.* колеба́ние, сомне́ние; (*in speech*) запи́нка.

hessian /ˈhesɪən/ *n.* (*cloth*) мешкови́на.

het /het/ *adj.*: **he got ~ up** он распсихова́лся (*sl.*).

heterodox /ˈhetərəʊˌdɒks/ *adj.* неортодокса́льный.

heterodoxy /ˈhetərəʊˌdɒksɪ/ *n.* неортодокса́льность.

heterogeneity /ˌhetərəʊdʒɪˈni:ɪtɪ/ *n.* неодноро́дность, разнохара́ктерность.

heterogeneous /ˌhetərəʊˈdʒi:nɪəs/ *adj.* неодноро́дный, разнохара́ктерный.

heterosexual /ˌhetərəʊˈseksjʊəl/ *n.* гетеросексуа́льный челове́к.

● *adj.* гетеросексуа́льный.

heterosexuality /ˌhetərəʊseksjʊˈælɪtɪ/ *n.* гетеросексуа́льность.

hetman /ˈhetmən/ *n.* (*pl.* **hetmen**) ге́тман.

heuristic /hjʊəˈrɪstɪk/ *adj.* эвристи́ческий.

hew /hju:/ *v.t.* (*p.p.* **hewn** *or* **hewed**) (*chop, cut*) руби́ть (*impf.*); (*cut into shape*) теса́ть (*impf.*); **they ~ed down a tree** они́ сруби́ли де́рево; **a branch had been ~n off** ве́тка была́ сру́блена; **she ~ed a statue out of stone** она́ вы́тесала из ка́мня ста́тую.

hewer /ˈhju:ə(r)/ *n.*: **~s of wood and drawers of water** (*fig.*) тру́женики (*m. pl.*).

hewn /hju:n/ *p.p. of* ⇨**hew**

hex /heks/ *n.* (*US*) (*spell, curse*) дурно́й глаз; (*witch*) ве́дьма.

● *v.t.* сгла́зить (*pf.*).

hexagon /ˈheksəgən/ *n.* шестиуго́льник.

hexagonal /ˌhekˈsægən(ə)l/ *adj.* шестиуго́льный.

hexameter /hekˈsæmɪtə(r)/ *n.* гекза́метр.

hey /heɪ/ *int.* эй!; **~ presto!** (*Br.*) але́-гоп!

heyday /ˈheɪdeɪ/ *n.* расцве́т, зени́т.

HGV (*abbr. of* ***heavy goods vehicle***) (*Br.*) грузови́к-тяжелово́з.

hi /haɪ/ *int.* **1** (*to call attention*) эй! **2** (*in greeting, also* **~ there!**) приве́т!

hiatus /haɪˈeɪtəs/ *n.* (*pl.* **~es**) **1** (*gap*) про́пуск, пробе́л. **2** (*between vowels*) зия́ние.

hibernate /ˈhaɪbəˌneɪt/ *v.i.* впада́ть (*impf.*) в зи́мнюю спя́чку; **these animals ~** э́ти живо́тные впада́ют в зи́мнюю спя́чку; **to be hibernating** находи́ться (*impf.*) в зи́мней спя́чке.

hibernation /ˌhaɪbəˈneɪʃ(ə)n/ *n.* зи́мняя спя́чка.

hibiscus /hɪˈbɪskəs/ *n.* (*pl.* **~es**) гиби́скус.

hicc|up, -ough /ˈhɪkʌp/ *n.* ико́та; (*slight delay*) зами́нка.

● *v.i.* (**hiccuped, hiccuping**) ик|а́ть, -ну́ть.

hick /hɪk/ *n.* (*US coll.*) дереве́нщина (*c.g.*); **a ~ town** захолу́стный го́род.

hickory /ˈhɪkərɪ/ *n.* пека́н.

hid /hɪd/ *past of* ⇨**hide²**

hide¹ /haɪd/ *n.* (*skin*) шку́ра; (*leather*)

ко́жа; **I'll tan his ~ for him** я задам ему́ взбу́чку; **he lied to save his ~** он солга́л, что́бы спасти́ свою́ шку́ру.

● *cpd.* **~-bound** *adj.* ограни́ченный, с у́зким кругозо́ром.

hide² /haɪd/ *v.t.* (*past* **hid;** *p.p.* **hidden** /ˈhɪd(ə)n/) пря́тать, с-; скры|ва́ть, -ть; **~ one's face** закр|ыва́ть, -ы́ть лицо́ рука́ми; **~ one's feelings** скры|ва́ть, -ть свои́ чу́вства; **the house was hidden from the road** дом не́ был ви́ден с доро́ги; **clouds hid the sun** ту́чи закры́ли со́лнце; **a hidden meaning** скры́тый смысл.

● *v.i.* (*past* **hid;** *p.p.* **hidden** /ˈhɪd(ə)n/) пря́таться, с-; скр|ыва́ться, -ы́ться.

● *cpds.* **~-and-seek** *n.* пря́т|ки (*pl., g.* -ок); **~away, ~out** *nn.* укры́тие.

hideous /ˈhɪdɪəs/ *adj.* (*ugly*) уро́дливый, безобра́зный; (*unpleasant*) ме́рзкий.

hideousness /ˈhɪdɪəsnɪs/ *n.* уро́дливость, безобра́зие; ме́рзость.

hidey-hole /ˈhaɪdɪ,həʊl/ *n.* (*coll.*) укры́тие.

hiding¹ /ˈhaɪdɪŋ/ *n.* (*coll., thrashing*): **she gave him a good ~** она́ его́ вы́порола как сле́дует.

hiding² /ˈhaɪdɪŋ/ *n.* (*concealment*) укры́тие; **he went into ~** он скры́лся; (*revolutionary*) он ушёл в подпо́лье; **he is in ~** он скрыва́ется.

● *cpd.* **~-place** *n.* укры́тие.

hierarch /ˈhaɪə,rɑːk/ *n.* иера́рх

hierarchical /,haɪəˈrɑːkɪk(ə)l/ *adj.* иерархи́ческий, иерархи́чный.

hierarchy /ˈhaɪə,rɑːkɪ/ *n.* иера́рхия.

hieroglyph /ˈhaɪərəglɪf/ *n.* иеро́глиф.

hieroglyphic /,haɪərəˈglɪfɪk/ *adj.* иероглифи́ческий.

hieroglyphics /,haɪərəˈglɪfɪks/ *n.* иероглифи́ческое письмо́.

hi-fi /ˈhaɪfaɪ/ *n.* (*pl.* **~s**) (*coll.*) проигрыватель (*m.*) с высо́кой то́чностью воспроизведе́ния зву́ка.

higgledy-piggledy /,hɪgəldɪˈpɪgəldɪ/ *adj.* беспоря́дочный; сумбу́рный.

● *adv.* впереме́шку; беспоря́дочно.

high /haɪ/ *n.* **1** (*peak*) вы́сшая то́чка; **prices reached a new ~** це́ны дости́гли небыва́ло высо́кого у́ровня. **2** (*anticyclone*) антицикло́н. **3**: **on ~** на небеса́х; **from on ~** свы́ше.

● *adj.* **1** (*tall, elevated*) высо́кий (*also mus.*); **a ~ building** высо́кое/высо́тное зда́ние; **a ~ chair** высо́кий де́тский стул; **ten feet ~** высото́й в 10 фу́тов; **~ jump** прыжо́к в высоту́; **he's for the ~ jump** (*Br. sl.*) ему́ попадёт/влети́т; **~ tide, water** больша́я вода́, прили́в; **~ and dry** вы́брошенный на бе́рег; (*fig.*) на мели́; **don't get on your ~ horse** (*coll.*) не ва́жничайте; (*geog.*): **~ latitudes** высо́кие широ́ты. **2** (*chief, important*): **~ altar** гла́вный престо́л; **~ command** вы́сшее кома́ндование; **~ days and holidays** (*Br.*) выходны́е дни и пра́здники; **~ life** све́тская жизнь; **H~ Mass** торже́ственная ме́сса; **~ and mighty** (*coll., arrogant*) надме́нный, вла́стный; **the Most H~** Всевы́шний; **in ~ places** (*fig.*) в верха́х, в вы́сших сфе́рах; **~ priest** первосвяще́нник; **~ school** сре́дняя шко́ла; **~ society** вы́сшее о́бщество; **the ~ spot of the evening** гвоздь програ́ммы; **~ street** (*Br.*) гла́вная у́лица; **~ table** (*Br.*) почётный стол; **~ tea** (*Br.*) ≈ по́лдник; **~ treason** госуда́рственная изме́на. **3** (*greater than average; extreme*): **~ blood-pressure** высо́кое (кровяно́е) давле́ние; **a ~ colour** (*Br.*), **color** (*US*) (*complexion*) я́ркий румя́нец; **in the ~est degree** в вы́сшей сте́пени; **held in ~ esteem** по́льзующийся больши́м уваже́нием; **~ explosive** дробя́щее (briза́нтное) взры́вчатое вещество́; **in ~ gear** на большо́й ско́рости; **~ jinks** (*coll.*) шу́мное весе́лье; **they are having a ~ old time** они́ веселя́тся вовсю́; **it is a ~ price to pay** цена́ сли́шком велика́; **on the ~ seas** в откры́том мо́ре; **in ~ spirits** в отли́чном/припо́днятом настрое́нии; **~ tension** си́льное напряже́ние; **H~ Tory** кра́йний консерва́тор; **a ~ wind** си́льный ве́тер. **4** (*at its peak*): **~ noon** по́лдень; **~ summer** середи́на/разга́р ле́та; **it is ~ time** давно́ пора́; **it is ~ time I was gone** мне уже́ давно́ пора́ идти́. **5** (*noble, lofty*): **a ~ calling** высо́кое призва́ние. **6** (*of food, tainted*) с душко́м. **7** (*intoxicated*) навеселе́; (*on drugs*) в дурма́не.

● *adv.* **1** (*aloft; at or to a height*): **~ up** высоко́; (*of direction*) ввысь; **the ball rose ~ into the air** мяч взлете́л высоко́ в во́здух; **you must aim ~** (*fig.*) вы должны́ ме́тить вы́ше; **he held his head ~** (*fig.*) он ходи́л с высоко́ по́днятой голово́й; **I searched ~ and low** я иска́л повсю́ду. **2** (*at a ~ level*): **the seas were running ~** мо́ре бы́ло неспоко́йно; **feelings ran ~** стра́сти разгора́лись.

● *cpds.* **~ball** *n.* (*US*) хайбо́л; **~-born** *adj.* зна́тный, зна́тного происхожде́ния; **~boy** *n.* (*US*) высо́кий комо́д; **~brow** *n.* интеллектуа́л; *adj.* интеллектуа́льный, серьёзный; **~-calorie** *adj.* калори́йный; **~-class** *adj.* первокла́ссный, высо́кого кла́сса; **~-falutin(g)** *adj.* (*coll.*) высокопа́рный, велеречи́вый; **~-fidelity** *adj.* с высокой то́чностью воспроизведе́ния; **~-flown** *adj.* высокопа́рный; витиева́тый; **~-flyer, ~-flier** *nn.* (*person likely to succeed*) подаю́щий больши́е наде́жды (*or* многообеща́ющий) челове́к; **~-frequency** *adj.* высокочасто́тный; **~-grade** *adj.* высокока́чественный; **~-handed** *adj.* вла́стный, своево́льный; **~-hat** *adj.* (*US coll.*) спеси́вый, надту́тый (*coll.*); *v.t.* (*US coll.*) относи́ться (*impf.*) высокоме́рно к + *d.*; **~-heeled** *adj.* на высо́ком каблуке́; **~ heels** *n. pl.* ту́фли на высо́ком каблуке́; **~land** *adj.* го́рский; **H~lander** *n.* го́р|ец (*fem.* -янка); **the H~lands** *n. pl.* се́вер и се́веро-за́пад Шотла́ндии; **~-level** *adj.* на высо́ком у́ровне; **~light** *n.* (*in painting*) блик; (*pl., in hair*) цветны́е пря́ди (*f. pl.*); (*phot.*) светово́й эффе́кт; (*fig.*) кульминацио́нный моме́нт; *v.t.* (*fig., emphasize*) выделя́ть, вы́делить (*also comput.*); заостр|я́ть, -и́ть внима́ние на + *p.*; **~lighter** *n.* флома́стер; **~-minded** *adj.* благоро́дный, великоду́шный; **~-pitched** *adj.* высо́кий; **~-powered** *adj.* (*of an engine*) мо́щный, большо́й мо́щности; (*of a person*) динами́чный, операти́вный; (*of a job*) отве́тственный; **~-priced** *adj.* дорогосто́ящий; **~-ranking** *adj.* высокопоста́вленный; **~-rise** *adj.*: **~-rise apartment blocks** высо́тные многокварти́рные дома́; **~road** *n.* шоссе́ (*indecl.*); **~-sounding** *adj.* напы́щенный; **~-sounding words** гро́мкие слова́; **~-speed** *adj.* скоростно́й; **~-spirited** *adj.* оживлённый, весёлый; **~-strung** *adj.* (*US*) = **highly strung; -tech** *adj.* высокотехнологи́чный; **~-tech company** (*using latest technology*) компа́ния, испо́льзующая передову́ю те́хнику; (*producing ~-tech goods*) компа́ния, производя́щая изде́лия высо́кой сло́жности; **~ technology** *n.* техноло́гия высо́кой сло́жности; **~-up** *n.*: **the ~-ups** верхи́ (*m. pl.*); *adj.* высокопоста́вленный; **~-water line** *n.* ли́ния наибо́льшего прили́ва; **~-water mark** *n.* у́ровень по́лной воды́; (*fig.*) верши́на; **~way** *n.* шоссе́ (*indecl.*); **H~way Code** пра́вила доро́жного движе́ния; **~way robbery** (*lit.*) грабёж на большо́й доро́ге; (*fig.*) грабёж; **~wayman** *n.* разбо́йник (с большо́й доро́ги).

higher /ˈhaɪə(r)/ *adj.* (*senior, advanced*) вы́сший.

● *adv.*: **~ up the hill** вы́ше на холме́; **~ up the road** да́льше по э́той доро́ге/у́лице.

highly /ˈhaɪlɪ/ *adv.* весьма́, о́чень; **~ paid** высокоопла́чиваемый; **~ polished** (*lit.*) хорошо́ отполиро́ванный; **he speaks ~ of you** он о вас о́чень хорошо́ отзыва́ется; **~ strung** (*Br.*) взви́нченный, нерво́зный; **she is ~ thought of** её о́чень це́нят.

highness /ˈhaɪnɪs/ *n.* **1** (*loftiness*) высота́, возвы́шенность. **2** (*title*) высо́чество; **His Royal H~** Его́ короле́вское высо́чество.

hijack /ˈhaɪdʒæk/ *n.* уго́н, похище́ние.

● *v.t.* уг|оня́ть, -на́ть; пох|ища́ть, -и́тить.

hijacker /ˈhaɪ,dʒækə(r)/ *n.* уго́нщик, похити́тель (*m.*).

hike¹ /haɪk/ *n.* (*coll., walk*) турпохо́д.

● *v.i.* броди́ть (*impf.*).

hike² /haɪk/ (*coll.*) *n.* (*rise*) подъём.

● *v.t.* (*raise*) подн|има́ть, -я́ть.

hiker /ˈhaɪkə(r)/ *n.* пе́ший тури́ст.

hiking /ˈhaɪkɪŋ/ *n.* пе́ший тури́зм.

hilarious /hɪˈleərɪəs/ *adj.* весёлый, умори́тельный.

hilarity /hɪˈlærɪtɪ/ *n.* весе́лье, потёха.

hill /hɪl/ *n.* холм; **down the ~** с горы́, по́д гору; **as old as the ~s** старо́ как мир; **the village lies just over the ~**

деревня лежит прямо за холмом; **this car takes the ~s well** эта машина хорошо идёт в гору; **up the ~** в гору; **up ~ and down dale** повсюду.

● *cpds.* **~man** *n.* житель (*m.*) холмистых мест; **~side** *n.* склон холма; **~top** *n.* вершина холма.

hilliness /ˈhɪlmɪs/ *n.* холмистость.

hillock /ˈhɪlək/ *n.* холмик, бугор.

hilly /ˈhɪlɪ/ *adj.* (**hilier, hilliest**) холмистый.

hilt /hɪlt/ *n.* рукоятка, эфес.

him /hɪm/ *obj. of* ⇒**he**[1]

Himalayan /ˌhɪməˈleɪən/ *adj.* гималайский.

Himalayas /ˌhɪməˈleɪəz/ *n.* Гимала|и (*pl., g.* -ев).

himself /hɪmˈself/ *pron.* **1** (*refl.*) себя, -ся; **I hope he behaves ~** надеюсь, что он будет вести себя прилично; **he fell and hurt ~** он упал и ушибся.
2 (*emph.*) сам; **he did the job ~** он сам сделал эту работу; **I saw the king ~** я видел самого короля.
3 (*after preps.*) один; сам; **he lives by ~** он живёт один; **he did it by ~** он сделал это сам; **he was talking to ~** он разговаривал сам с собой.
4 (*in his normal state*): **he will see you when he is ~ again** он повидается с вами, когда придёт в себя; **he is not ~ today** он сегодня сам не свой.

hind[1] /haɪnd/ *n.* (*deer*) самка оленя.

hind[2] /haɪnd/ *adj.* задний; **the dog stood on its ~ legs** собака встала на задние лапы.

● *cpds.* **~-quarters** *n.* зад; **~sight** *n.* (*of gun*) задний прицел; (*coll., wisdom after the event*): **he spoke with ~sight** он говорил, зная, чем кончилось дело.

hinder /ˈhɪndə(r)/ *v.t.* мешать, по- (+*d.*); препятствовать, вос- (+*d.*); **he ~ed me from working** он мешал мне работать.

Hindi /ˈhɪndɪ/ *n.* (*language*) хинди (*m. indecl.*).

hindrance /ˈhɪndrəns/ *n.* помеха, препятствие.

Hindu /ˈhɪnduː/, /-ˈduː/ *n.* (*pl.* **~s**) индус (*fem.* -ка).

● *adj.* индусский.

Hinduism /ˈhɪnduːˌɪz(ə)m/ *n.* индуизм.

Hindustani /ˌhɪndʊˈstɑːnɪ/ *n.* (*language*) хиндустани (*m. indecl.*).

hinge /hɪndʒ/ *n.* шарнир; (*on door*) петля; (*fig.*) стержень (*m.*).

● *v.t.* (**hingeing** *or* **hinging**) наве|шивать, -сить на петли.

● *v.i.* (**hingeing** *or* **hinging**) висеть (*impf.*); вращаться (*impf.*); (*fig.*): **it all ~d on this event** всё было связано с этим событием.

hinny /ˈhɪnɪ/ *n.* лошак.

hint /hɪnt/ *n.* (*suggestion*) намёк; **can't you take a ~?** ты что, намёка не понимаешь?; **he is always dropping ~s** он всегда говорит намёками; **a broad/gentle ~** ясный/тонкий намёк; **there was a ~ of frost** начинало подмораживать; **~ of garlic** чуточка чеснока; (*written advice*) совет; **~s for housewives** советы домохозяйкам.

● *v.t. & i.* намек|ать, -нуть на + *a.*; **I ~ed that I needed a holiday** я намекнул, что мне нужен отпуск; **what are you ~ing (at)?** на что вы намекаете?

hinterland /ˈhɪntəˌlænd/ *n.* (*inland area*) районы (*m. pl.*), удалённые от побережья; (*remote area*) глушь.

hip[1] /hɪp/ *n.* бедро; **he stood with his hands on his ~s** он стоял подбоченясь; **what do you measure round the ~s?** какой у вас объём бёдер?

● *cpds.* **~-bath** *n.* сидячая ванна; **~-flask** *n.* карманная фляжка; **~-joint** *n.* тазобедренный сустав; **~-pocket** *n.* задний карман.

hip[2] /hɪp/ *n.* (*fruit*) ягода шиповника.

hip[3] /hɪp/ *int.*: **~, ~, hooray!** гип-гип, ура.

hip[4] /hɪp/ *adj.* (**hipper, hippest**) (*coll.*) модный, крутой (*sl.*).

hipp|ie, -y /ˈhɪpɪ/ *n.* (*coll.*) хиппи (*c.g., indecl.*).

hippo /ˈhɪpəʊ/ *n.* (*pl.* **~s**) (*coll.*) гиппопотам, бегемот.

Hippocratic /ˌhɪpəˈkrætɪk/ *adj.*: **~ oath** клятва Гиппократа.

hippodrome /ˈhɪpəˌdrəʊm/ *n.* (*hist.*) ипподром.

hippopota|mus /ˌhɪpəˈpɒtəməs/ *n.* (*pl.* **~muses** *or* **~mi** /-ˌmaɪ/) гиппопотам, бегемот.

hippy /ˈhɪpɪ/ = **hippie**

hire /ˈhaɪə(r)/ *n.* (*engagement of person*) наём; (*of thing*) наём, прокат; **cars for ~** машины напрокат; **he let his boat out on ~** он сдавал свою лодку напрокат.

● *v.t.* (*Br., a place*) сн|имать, -ять; (*Br., equipment, a car*) брать, взять напрокат; (*a worker*) нан|имать, -ять; **they ~d the hall for a night** они сняли зал на вечер; **~d help** (*domestic servant*) прислуга, домработница; **~ out** (*Br.*) (*a place*) сда|вать, -ть; (*equipment, a car*) сда|вать, -ть напрокат.

● *cpd.* **~-purchase** *n.* (*Br.*) покупка в рассрочку.

hireling /ˈhaɪəlɪŋ/ *n.* наёмник, наймит.

hirer /ˈhaɪərə(r)/ *n.* берущий напрокат; (*employer*) работодатель (*m.*).

Hiroshima /ˌhɪrɒˈʃiːmə/, /hɪˈrɒʃɪmə/ *n.* Хиросима.

hirsute /ˈhɜːsjuːt/ *adj.* волосатый, косматый.

his /hɪz/ *pron.* его; **is this book ~?** это его книга?; **what is ~ by right** то, что принадлежит ему по праву; **my bicycle is newer than ~** у меня велосипед новее, чем у него; **friends of ~** его друзья; **I don't like that wife of ~** мне не нравится его жена.

● *poss. adj.* его; **this is ~ book** это его книга; (*referring to subj. of sentence*) свой; **he loves ~ children** он любит своих детей.

Hispanic /hɪˈspænɪk/ *adj.* испанский; латиноамериканский; **~ studies** испанистика.

Hispanist /ˈhɪspənɪst/ *n.* испанист.

hiss /hɪs/ *n.* шипение, свист.

● *v.t.* шипеть, про-; **'be quiet' he ~ed** «помолчите», — прошипел он; (*an actor*) освист|ывать, -ать; **he was ~ed off the stage** его освистали.

● *v.i.* (*of snake*) шипеть, за-; (*of audience*) свистеть (*impf.*).

histogram /ˈhɪstəˌgræm/ *n.* гистограмма.

historian /hɪˈstɔːrɪən/ *n.* историк.

historic /hɪˈstɒrɪk/ *adj.* исторический; (*significant*) исторический, знаменательный; (*gram.*): **the ~ present** историческое/повествовательное настоящее.

historical /hɪˈstɒrɪk(ə)l/ *adj.* исторический.

historicity /ˌhɪstəˈrɪsɪtɪ/ *n.* историчность.

history /ˈhɪstərɪ/ *n.* история; **make (** *or* **go down in) ~** входить, войти в историю; **~ is silent on that point** история об этом умалчивает; **that is ancient ~!** (*fig.*) это старо!

● *cpd.* **~-book** *n.* учебник истории.

histrionic /ˌhɪstrɪˈɒnɪk/ *adj.* (*stagy*) театральный, мелодраматический.

histrionics /ˌhɪstrɪˈɒnɪks/ *n.* (*behaviour*) театральность.

hit /hɪt/ *n.* (*blow*) удар, толчок; **~ man** наёмный/профессиональный убийца; киллер; (*strike or shot which reaches target*) попадание; (*coll., success*) успех; (*popular song*) хит; шлягер.

● *v.t.* (**hitting;** *past and p.p.* **~**) **1** (*strike*) уд|арять, -арить; бить (*impf.*); стук|ать, -нуть; **he fell and ~ his head on a stone** он упал и ударился головой о камень; **he was ~ on the head** его ударили по голове; **don't ~ a man when he's down** лежачего не бьют; **the car ~ a tree** машина врезалась в дерево; **he was ~ by a car** его сбила машина; **to ~ the target/mark** поп|адать, -асть в цель; **he ~ the nail on the head** (*fig.*) он попал прямо в точку; **the bullet ~ him in the shoulder** пуля попала ему в плечо; **he was ~ by a falling stone** его задело падающим камнем.
2 (*fig. uses*): **you've ~ it!** вы попали в точку!; **the idea suddenly ~ me** меня вдруг осенило; **the town was ~ by an earthquake** город пострадал от землетрясения; **~ the trail, road** (*coll.*) отпр|авляться, -авиться в путь; **he ~s the bottle now and again** (*coll.*) он время от времени прикладывается к бутылке.
3 (*encounter*): **he ~ a bad patch** (*coll.*) у него началась полоса неудач.

● *v.i.* (**hitting;** *past and p.p.* **~**): **he ~ on an idea** ему пришла в голову мысль.

● *with advs.*: **~ back** *v.t.*: **he ~ the ball back** он отбил мяч; **if he ~s you, ~ him back** если он вас ударит, ударьте его тоже; (*fig., at critics etc.*) да|вать, -ть отпор (+*d.*); **~ off** *v.t.*: **~ it off** ладить (*impf.*); **~ out** *v.i.*: **he ~ out at his opponents** он дал резкий отпор своим противникам; **~ up** *v.t.*: **he ~ up a good score** он сыграл с хорошим счётом.

● *cpd.* **~-or-miss** *adj.* бестолковый, безалаберный.

H

hitch /hɪtʃ/ *n.* (*jerk*) рывóк; (*knot*) ýзел; (*temporary stoppage; snag*) задéржка, загвóздка; **without a ~** глáдко.
● *v.t.* **1** (*fasten*) привя́з|ывать, -áть; прицеп|ля́ть, -и́ть. **2** (*lift*): **~ up one's trousers** подтя́|гивать, -нýть брю́ки. **3** (*coll.*): **~ a lift** подъ|езжáть, -éхать на попýтной маши́не. **4** (*coll.*): **get ~ed** (*of man*) жени́ться (*impf., pf.*); (*of woman*) выходи́ть, вы́йти зáмуж; (*of couple*) пожени́ться (*pf.*).
● *v.i.* (*coll., travel by getting free rides; also* **~-hike**) éздить автостóпом.
● *cpds.* **~-hiker** *n.* (*coll.*) путешéствующий автостóпом; **~-hiking** *n.* «голосовáние», ездá автостóпом (*or* на попýтных маши́нах).

hi-tech /haɪ'tek/ *adj.* = **high-tech**

hither /'hɪðə(r)/ *adv.* сюдá.
● *cpd.* **~to** *adv.* до сих пор.

Hittite /'hɪtaɪt/ *n.* хетт; (*language*) хéттский язы́к.
● *adj.* хéттский.

HIV (*med., abbr. of* ***human immunodeficiency virus***) ВИЧ (ви́рус иммунодефици́та человéка); **~ positive** ВИЧ-инфици́рованный.

hive /haɪv/ *n.* ýлей; (*fig.*): **the office is a ~ of industry** рабóта в óфисе кипи́т.
● *v.t.* (*fig.*): **they ~d off and formed a new party** они́ отколóлись и сóздали нóвую пáртию; **certain jobs were ~d off to other departments** (*Br.*) нéкоторые ви́ды рабóт бы́ли порýчены други́м отдéлам.

hives /haɪvz/ *n.* (*med.*) крапи́вница.

hm /hm/ *int.* гм!

HND (*abbr. of* ***Higher National Diploma***) (*Br.*) диплóм о вы́сшем техни́ческом образовáнии.

ho /həʊ/ *int.*: **~, ~** (*laughter*) ха-ха; **westward ~!** на зáпад!

hoar /hɔ:(r)/ *adj.* седóй.
● *cpd.* **~-frost** *n.* и́ней, и́зморозь.

hoard /hɔ:d/ *n.* (тáйный) запáс, склад.
● *v.t.* припря́т|ывать, -ать; ск|áпливать, -опи́ть бóльшие запáсы; **~ing food is illegal** закóн запрещáет припря́тывать продовóльствие.

hoarding /'hɔ:dɪŋ/ *n.* **1** (*Br., for poster display*) реклáмный щит. **2** (*Br., fence round building site*) огрáда вокрýг стройплощáдки. **3** (*stocking up*) накоплéние.

hoarse /hɔ:s/ *adj.* хри́плый, си́плый; **he talked himself ~** он договори́лся до хрипоты́.

hoarseness /'hɔ:snɪs/ *n.* хрипотá, си́плость.

hoary /'hɔ:rɪ/ *adj.* (**hoarier, hoariest**) (*grey or white with age*) седóй; (*old and trite*) изби́тый; **a ~ joke** анекдóт с бородóй.

hoax /həʊks/ *n.* мистификáция; (*involving deceit*) надувáтельство; **~ call** обмáнный звонóк по телефóну.
● *v.t.* мистифици́ровать (*impf., pf.*); над|увáть, -ýть.

hoaxer /'həʊksə(r)/ *n.* мистификáтор.

hob /hɒb/ *n.* (*Br.*) повéрхность кýхонной плиты́.

hobble /'hɒb(ə)l/ *v.t.*: **~ a horse** тренóжить, с- лóшадь.
● *v.i.* ковыля́ть (*impf.*); прихрáмывать (*impf.*).
● *cpd.* **~-skirt** *n.* дли́нная заýженная кни́зу ю́бка.

hobby /'hɒbɪ/ *n.* (*leisure pursuit*) хóбби (*nt. indecl.*).
● *cpd.* **~-horse** *n.* игрýшечная лошáдка; (*fig.*) конёк.

hobgoblin /'hɒb,gɒblɪn/ *n.* чертёнок, бесёнок.

hobnail /'hɒbneɪl/ *n.*: **~ed boots** боти́нки с шипáми на подóшвах.

hobnob /'hɒbnɒb/ *v.i.* (**hobnobbed, hobnobbing**) води́ться (*impf.*), знáться (*impf.*) (*с кем*).

hobo /'həʊbəʊ/ *n.* (*pl.* **~es** *or* **~s**) (*US sl.*) бродя́га (*m.*).

Hobson's choice /'hɒbs(ə)nz/ *n.* безальтернати́вная ситуáция.

Ho Chi Minh City /həʊ tʃɪ 'mɪn/ *n.* Хошими́н (*город*).

hock[1] /hɒk/ *n.* (*leg joint*) колéнное сухожи́лие; (*joint of meat*) óкорок.

hock[2] /hɒk/ *n.* (*Br., wine*) рейнвéйн.

hock[3] /hɒk/ *n.* (*sl., pawn*): **in ~** в ломбáрде; в заклáде.
● *v.t.* за|клáдывать, -ложи́ть.

hockey /'hɒkɪ/ *n.* (*on field*) хоккéй на травé; **ice ~** хоккéй (с шáйбой/на льдý).
● *cpds.* **~-player** *n.* хоккеи́ст (*fem.* -ка); **~-stick** *n.* клю́шка.

hocus-pocus /,həʊkəs'pəʊkəs/ *n.* фóкус, трюк.

hod /hɒd/ *n.* (строи́тельный) лотóк.

hodge-podge /'hɒdʒpɒdʒ/ *n.* (*coll.*) мешани́на.

hoe /həʊ/ *n.* моты́га, тя́пка.
● *v.t. & i.* (**hoes, hoed, hoeing**) моты́жить (*impf.*); выпáлывать, вы́полоть; **he ~d up the weeds** он вы́полол сорняки́.

hog /hɒg/ *n.* бóров; (*US, also fig.*) свинья́; **go the whole ~** дов|оди́ть, -ести́ дéло до концá; идти́, пойти́ на всё.
● *v.t.* (**hogged, hogging**) (*coll.*) (*eat greedily*) жрать, со-; (*monopolize*): **he ~ged the conversation** он не давáл никомý слóва встáвить.
● *cpds.* **~'s-back** *n.* (*ridge*) грéбень (*m.*); хребéт; **~shead** *n.* (*barrel*) бóчка; (*measure*) мéра ёмкости, ≈ 240 ли́тров; **~wash** *n.* (*pig-swill*) пóйло; (*coll., rubbish*) чушь, вздор.

Hogmanay /'hɒgmə,neɪ/, /-'neɪ/ *n.* (*Sc.*) канýн Нóвого гóда.

hoi(c)k /hɔɪk/ *v.t.* (*Br., jerk, yank*) рванýть (*pf.*).

hoi polloi /,hɔɪ pə'lɔɪ/ *n.* простонарóдье.

hoist /hɔɪst/ *n.* подъёмник.
● *v.t.* подн|имáть, -я́ть; **he was ~ by his own petard** он попáл в сóбственную ловýшку.

hoity-toity /,hɔɪtɪ'tɔɪtɪ/ *adj.* кичли́вый, высокомéрный.

hokum /'həʊkəm/ *n.* (*sl.*) вздор, чепухá.

hold /həʊld/ *n.* **1** (*grasp, grip*) удéрживание, захвáт; **he caught ~ of the rope** он ухвати́лся за канáт; **he kept ~ of the reins** он не выпускáл повóдья из рук; **he laid, seized, took ~ of my arm** он схвати́л/взял меня́ зá руку; **don't lose ~; don't let go your ~** держи́те, не отпускáйте; (*fig.*) на|ходи́ть, -йти; от|ы́скивать, -ыскáть; **I got ~ of a plumber** я нашёл/отыскáл водопровóдчика; **where did you get ~ of that idea?** откýда вы э́то взя́ли?; **where did you get ~ of those tickets?** где вы достáли э́ти билéты; **it's difficult to get ~ of her** её трýдно застáть.
2 (*in boxing or wrestling*) захвáт; **they fought with no ~s barred** они́ борóлись с применéнием любы́х захвáтов; (*fig.*) они́ прибегáли к всевозмóжным улóвкам.
3 (*means of pressure*): **he has a ~ on, over him** он имéет над ним власть.
4 (*support*) опóра.
5 (*ship's*) трюм.
● *v.t.* (*past and p.p.* **held**) **1** (*clasp, grip*) держáть (*impf.*); **they sat ~ing hands** они́ сидéли, держáсь зá руки.
2 (*maintain, keep in a certain position*): **~ yourself straight!** держи́сь пря́мо!; **~ it!** (*coll.*) (*don't move*) не дви́гайтесь!; не шевели́тесь!; (*fig., keep*): **he held himself in readiness** он был наготóве; **they were held to a draw** их вы́нудили к ничьéй; **they held the enemy at bay** они́ не подпускáли неприя́теля; **I won't ~ you to your promise** я не трéбую, чтóбы вы сдержáли своё слóво; **~ the line!** (*teleph.*) не клади́те трýбку!; ждите у телефóна!
3 (*detain*) зад|éрживать, -ержáть; **he was held prisoner** егó держáли в пленý; **they held him for questioning** егó задержáли для допрóса.
4 (*contain*) вме|щáть, -сти́ть; **the hall ~s a thousand** зал вмещáет ты́сячу человéк; **~ one's liquor** переноси́ть (*impf.*) спиртнóе; **his theory will not ~ water** (*fig.*) егó теóрия несостоя́тельна (*or* не вы́держивает кри́тики).
5 (*consider, believe*) полагáть (*impf.*), считáть (*impf.*); **the court held that ...** суд признáл, что...; **~ dear** высокó цени́ть (*impf.*); **he is held in great esteem** он пóльзуется больши́м уважéнием; **he was held responsible** емý пришлóсь держáть отвéт; **I don't ~ it against him** я не стáвлю емý э́то в винý.
6 (*restrain*): **she held her breath** онá затаи́ла дыхáние; **~ everything!** (*coll.*) останови́тесь!; **~ your tongue!** помолчи́!, придержи́ язы́к!; **~ your horses!** (*coll.*) полéгче на поворóтах!; **there's no ~ing him** емý нет ýдержу.
7 (*have, own*) владéть (*impf.*) (+*i.*); **he ~s the ace** у негó туз; **all this land is held by one man** всей э́той землёй владéет оди́н человéк; **~ the record** быть рекордсмéном; **~ shares** держáть (*impf.*) áкции; **this opinion is widely held** э́то мнéние широкó распространенó; **it is widely held that** ... широкó распространенó мнéние, что...; **we ~ the same views** мы

придéрживаемся одинáковых взглядов.
8 (*occupy, remain in possession of*): **how long has he held office?** как давнó он занимáет эту дóлжность; **he held his ground** он не уступáл; он не сдавáлся; **I can ~ my own against anyone** я могý потягáться с кем угóдно; **he ~s the rank of sergeant** он имéет звáние сержáнта; **the sight held his attention** это зрéлище приковáло егó внимáние (*or* завладéло егó внимáнием).
9 (*carry on, conduct, convene*) пров|одить, -ести; **they were ~ing a conversation** онú бесéдовали; **the meeting was held at noon** собрáние состоялось (*or* провели) в пóлдень.

● *v.i.* (*past and p.p.* **held**) **1** (*grasp*): **~ tight!** держитесь крéпче/крéпко!
2 (*adhere*): **he ~s firmly to his beliefs** он твёрдо дéржится своих убеждéний.
3 (*agree, approve*): **I don't ~ with that** я этого не одобряю.
4 (*remain*): **he held aloof** он держáлся особнякóм; **~ still!** не двигайтесь!; **the argument ~s good** дóвод сохраняет силу.
5 (*remain unbroken, unchanged, intact*): **will the rope ~?** выдержит ли верёвка?; **how long will the weather ~?** дóлго ли продéржится (простоит) такáя погóда?

● *with advs.*: **~ back** *v.t.* (*restrain*) удéрживать, удержáть; **I couldn't ~ him back** я не мог егó удержáть; (*withhold*) удéрживать, удержáть; **he held back part of their wages** он удержáл часть их зарплáты; (*repress*) сдéрживать, сдержáть; **I had to ~ back a smile** мне пришлóсь сдержáть улыбку; *v.i.* (*hesitate*) мéшкать, по-; (*refrain*) воздéрж|иваться, -áться (*от чего*); **~ down** *v.t.* (*lit.*): **~ your head down!** не поднимáйте головы!; (*fig.*): **do you think you can ~ the job down?** сумéете ли вы удержáться на этой дóлжности?; **we will try to ~ prices down** мы постарáемся сдержáть рост цен; **~ forth** *v.i.* (*coll., orate*) разглагóльствовать (*impf.*); вещáть (*impf.*); **~ in** *v.t.* (*lit.*): **her waist was held in by a belt** её тáлия былá стянута пóясом; (*fig.*): **I could hardly ~ myself in** я едвá сдержáлся; **~ off** *v.t.* (*keep away, repel*): **he held his dog off** он придержáл собáку; **they held off the attack** онú отбили атáку; **he held off going to the doctor** он откладывал визит к врачý; *v.i.* (*stay away*): **the rain held off all morning** дождя так и не было всё утро; **~ on** *v.t.* (*keep in position*) прикреп|лять, -ить; **the handle was held on with glue** рýчка держáлась на клею; *v.i.* (*cling*) держáться (*impf.*) (*за что*); **she held on to the banisters** онá держáлась за перила; (*fig.*): **you should ~ on to those shares** вам нáдо держáться за эти áкции; (*coll., wait*): **~ on a minute till I'm ready** подождите — я бýду готóв чéрез минýту; (*on the telephone*): **~ on, please!** не вéшайте трýбку!; **~ out** *v.t.* (*extend*) прот|ягивать, -янýть; **he greeted me and held out his hand** он поздорóвался и протянýл мне рýку; (*fig., offer*): **I can't ~ out any hope** я не могý вас ничéм обнадёжить; *v.i.* (*endure, refuse to yield*) держáться, про-; **the fortress held out for 6 weeks** крéпость продержáлась 6 недéль; **the men are ~ing out for more money** рабóчие настáивают на повышéнии зарплáты; (*last*): **supplies cannot ~ out much longer** запáсов хвáтит не надóлго; **~ over** *v.t.* (*defer*) от|клáдывать, -ложить; **~ together** *v.t.* (*a box etc.*) обхв|áтывать, -атить; (*fig., party etc.*) сплáчивать, сплотить; *v.i.* (*fig., of arguments*) быть непоследóвательным; **~ under** *v.t.* (*fig.*) угнетáть (*impf.*); держáть (*impf.*) в повиновéнии; **~ up** *v.t.* (*lift, hold erect*) подн|имáть, -ять; **the boy held up his hand** мáльчик пóднял рýку; (*fig., display, expose*): **he was held up as an example** егó постáвили в примéр; **he was held up to ridicule** егó выставили на посмéшище; (*delay*) задéрж|ивать, -áть; **we were held up on the way** по дорóге нас задержáли; **traffic was held up by fog** движéние остановилось из-за тумáна; **work is** (*or* **has been) held up** рабóта остановилась/стáла; (*waylay*): **the robbers held them up at pistol point** бандиты огрáбили их, угрожáя пистолéтом; *v.i.*: **do you think the table will ~ up under the weight?** вы дýмаете, стол выдержит такóй вес?; (*fig.*): **if the weather ~s up, we can go out** éсли такáя погóда продéржится, мы мóжем пойти кудá-нибудь.

● *cpds.* **~-all** *n.* (*Br.*) вещевóй мешóк; **~-up** *n.* (*stoppage, delay*) задéржка; **what's the ~-up?** за чем дéло стáло?; (*robbery*) вооружённый грабёж.

holder /ˈhəʊldə(r)/ *n.* **1** (*possessor, e.g. of a passport*) владéлец; обладáтель (*m.*); (*of securities, insurance policy*) держáтель (*m.*); **~ of an office** занимáющий пост. **2** (*device for holding*) держáтель (*m.*).

holding /ˈhəʊldɪŋ/ *n.* **1** (*of land*) учáсток (землú). **2** (*property*) вклáды (*m. pl.*), авуáры (*m. pl.*). **3** (*pl.*) (*stock*) запáс; (*of library*) фонд.

● *adj.*: **~ company** хóлдинг-компáния, компáния-держáтель; **~ operation** оперáция для сохранéния стáтуса кво (*or* для удержáния позиций).

hole /həʊl/ *n.* **1** (*cavity*) дырá. **2** (*opening*) отвéрстие. **3** (*rent*) щель, прóрезь. **4** (*burrow*) норá. **5** (*pej. of a place*) дырá. **6** (*predicament*) бедá. **7** (*in golf*) лýнка. **8** (*phrr.*): **the purchase made a ~ in his savings** покýпка сдéлала брешь в егó сбережéниях; **he is always picking ~s** он ко всемý придирáется; **a square peg in a round ~** человéк не на своём мéсте; **~ in the wall** (*Br. coll.*) банкомáт.

● *v.t.* **1** (*make ~ in*) дéлать, с- отвéрстие в+*p.* **2** (*make ~ through*) дырявить, про-. **3** (*golf*) заг|онять, -нáть в лýнку.

● *cpd.* **~-puncher** *n.* дырокóл.

holiday /ˈhɒlɪ,deɪ/, /-dɪ/ *n.* (*Br.*) **1** (*day off*) выходнóй (день); **bank ~** нерабóчий день(, когдá закрыты бáнки); **church ~** церкóвный прáздник. **2** (*annual leave*) óтпуск, óтдых; (*school, university vacation*) канúкул|ы (*pl., g.* —); (*leisure time*) óтдых; **he is on ~** он в отпускý; у негó канúкулы; **I take my ~s in June** я берý óтпуск в июне; **where are you spending your ~?** где вы бýдете отдыхáть?; **~ camp** (лéтний) лáгерь; **~ home** дом óтдыха.

● *cpd.* **~-maker** *n.* отдыхáющий; турист (*fem.* -ка).

holiness /ˈhəʊlɪnɪs/ *n.* святость, свящéнность; **His H~ (the Pope)** Егó Святéйшество.

holistic /hɒˈlɪstɪk/, /həʊ-/ *adj.* цéлостный.

Holland /ˈhɒlənd/ *n.* (*country or province*) Голлáндия.

holland /ˈhɒlənd/ *n.* (*fabric*) холст.

holler /ˈhɒlə(r)/ *v.t. & i.* (*US coll.*) орáть (*impf.*); вопить (*impf.*).

hollow /ˈhɒləʊ/ *n.* **1** (*small depression*) выемка, впáдина; (*hole within something*) пóлость. **2** (*dell*) лощина, низина.

● *adj.* **1** (*not solid*) пустóй, пóлый. **2** (*of sounds*) глухóй. **3** (*fig., false, insincere*) фальшивый, лживый; **~ laughter** неестéственный смех; (*of no value*) бессмысленный; **a ~ victory** бесплóдная побéда. **4** (*sunken*) ввалившийся, впáлый; **~ cheeks** ввалившиеся щёки.

● *adv.*: **we beat them ~** (*coll.*) мы разбили их в пух и прах.

● *v.t.* (*usu.* **~ out**) выдáлбливать, выдолбить.

hollowness /ˈhɒləʊnɪs/ *n.* (*insincerity*) лживость, фальшь.

holly /ˈhɒlɪ/ *n.* остролист.

hollyhock /ˈhɒlɪ,hɒk/ *n.* алтéй рóзовый.

Hollywood /ˈhɒlɪ,wʊd/ *n.* Голливýд; (*attr.*) голливýдский.

holm-oak /həʊm/ *n.* дуб кáменный.

holocaust /ˈhɒlə,kɔːst/ *n.* мáссовое уничтожéние; бóйня; **the H~** холокóст; **nuclear ~** ядерная катастрóфа.

hologram /ˈhɒlə,græm/ *n.* гологрáмма.

holograph /ˈhɒlə,grɑːf/ *n.* собственнорýчно написанный докумéнт.

● *adj.* собственнорýчный.

holster /ˈhəʊlstə(r)/ n. кобурá.

holy /ˈhəʊlɪ/ *n.*: **the H~ of Holies** (*lit., fig.*) Святáя Святых.

● *adj.* (**holier, holiest**) свящéнный, святóй; **H~ Communion** Святóе Причáстие; **the H~ Father** Егó Святéйшество; **~ fool** юрóдивый; **the H~ Ghost, Spirit** Святóй Дух; **the H~ Land** Святáя земля; **~ orders** духóвный сан; **~ place** святилище; **H~ Russia** Святáя Русь; **the H~ See** Святéйший Престóл; **a ~ terror** (*coll.*) наказáние Госпóдне; **a ~ war** свящéнная войнá; **~ water** святáя водá; **H~ Week** Страстнáя недéля.

homage /ˈhɒmɪdʒ/ *n.* почтéние,

преклоне́ние; **we pay ~ to his genius** мы преклоня́емся пе́ред его ге́нием.

home /həʊm/ *n.* **1** (*place where one resides or belongs*) дом; (*attr.*) дома́шний; **~ economics** домово́дство; **~ help** (*Br.*) приходя́щая домрабо́тница; **it was a ~ from ~** там бы́ло как до́ма; **a ~ of one's own** со́бственный дом; **his ~ is in London** он жи́тель Ло́ндона; **he made his ~ in Bristol** он посели́лся в Бри́столе; **she left ~** она́ поки́нула (роди́тельский) дом; **at ~** (*in one's house*) до́ма; (*on one's ~ ground*) у себя́; (*e.g. football*) на своём по́ле; **she is not at ~ to anyone** она́ никого́ не принима́ет; **make yourself at ~** бу́дьте как до́ма; **I feel at ~ here** я чу́вствую себя́ здесь как до́ма; **he is away from ~** он в отъе́зде. **2** (*institution*): **a ~ for the disabled** дом инвали́дов; **he put his parents into a ~** он помести́л свои́х роди́телей в дом для престаре́лых. **3** (*habitat*) ме́сто распростране́ния, ареа́л. **4** (*in games*): **the ~ stretch** фи́нишная пряма́я. **5** (*attr., opp. foreign; native, local*): **~ affairs** вну́тренние дела́; **H~ Counties** гра́фства, окружа́ющие Ло́ндон; **H~ Guard** ме́стное ополче́ние; **the ~ market** вну́тренний ры́нок; **H~ Office** (*Br.*) Министе́рство вну́тренних дел; **~ Secretary** (*Br.*) мини́стр вну́тренних дел; **~ team** кома́нда хозя́ев по́ля; **~ rule** самоуправле́ние; **~ town** родно́й го́род.

● *adv.* **1** (*at or to one's own house*): **is he ~ yet?** он (уже́) до́ма?; **he was on his way ~** он шёл/е́хал домо́й; **nothing to write ~ about** (*fig.*) ничего́ осо́бенного; **he is ~ and dry** (*Br., fig.*) он цел и невреди́м. **2** (*in or to one's own country*): **things are different back ~** (*coll.*) у нас э́то не так (*or* ина́че); **he came ~ from abroad** он верну́лся из-за грани́цы. **3** (*to the point aimed at*): **the nails were driven ~** гво́зди бы́ли заби́ты; **he drove his argument ~** он растолкова́л свой до́воды; **bring something ~ to s.o.** дов|оди́ть, -ести́ что-н. до чьего́-н. созна́ния; **it was brought ~ to him how lucky he was** ему́ ста́ло я́сно/до него́ дошло́ (*coll.*), как ему́ повезло́; **his remarks struck ~** его́ замеча́ния попа́ли в цель; (*attr.*): **~ truths** го́рькая пра́вда; нелицеприя́тные и́стины (*f. pl.*).

● *v.i.*: **homing instinct** тя́га домо́й; **homing pigeon** почто́вый го́лубь.

● *cpds.* **~-bird** *n.* (*Br., fig.*) домосе́д (*fem.* -ка); **~-brewed** *adj.* дома́шний, дома́шнего изготовле́ния; **~coming** *n.* возвраще́ние домо́й; **~-grown** *adj.* (*vegetables*) дома́шний, с огоро́да; (*not foreign*) оте́чественный; **~land** *n.* ро́дина, родна́я страна́; **~-lover** *n.* домосе́д (*fem.* -ка); **~-made** *adj.* (*food, drink*) дома́шний; (*object*) самоде́льный; **~ page** *n.* (*comput.*) страни́ца в Интерне́те; дома́шняя страни́ца; **~sick** *adj.* скуча́ющий/тоску́ющий по до́му/ро́дине; **~sickness** *n.* ностальги́я, тоска́ по до́му/ро́дине; **~spun** *n. & adj.* домотка́ный; (*fig.*) сермя́жный, грубова́тый; **~stead** *n.* уса́дьба; фе́рма; **~work** *n.* дома́шнее зада́ние; **what was the ~work?** что бы́ло за́дано на́ дом?

homeless /ˈhəʊmlɪs/ *adj.* бездо́мный.

homeliness /ˈhəʊmlɪnɪs/ *n.* **1** (*cosiness*) дома́шний ую́т. **2** (*unpretentiousness*) непритяза́тельность, неприхотли́вость. **3** (*unattractiveness*) непригля́дность.

homely /ˈhəʊmlɪ/ *adj.* (**homelier, homeliest**) **1** (*Br., cosy*) дома́шний, ую́тный; **a ~ atmosphere** дома́шняя обстано́вка. **2** (*Br., unpretentious*): **a ~ old lady** ми́лая стару́шка; **a ~ meal** неприхотли́вая еда́. **3** (*US, unattractive*) некраси́вый.

homeopath /ˈhəʊmɪəʊ,pæθ/, /ˈhɒmɪ-/ *n.* гомеопа́т.

homeopathic /,həʊmɪəʊˈpæθɪk/, /ˈhɒmɪ-/ *adj.* гомеопати́ческий.

homeopathy /,həʊmɪˈɒpəθɪ/, /,hɒmɪ-/ *n.* гомеопа́тия.

homer /ˈhəʊmə(r)/ *n.* (*pigeon*) почто́вый го́лубь.

Homeric /həʊˈmerɪk/, /həˈm-/ *adj.* гоме́ровский; **the ~ poems** поэ́мы Гоме́ра; **~ laughter** гомери́ческий смех.

homeward /ˈhəʊmwəd/ *adj.* иду́щий/веду́щий к до́му; **~ voyage** обра́тный рейс/путь.

● *adv.* (*also* **~s**) домо́й.

hom(e)y /ˈhəʊmɪ/ *adj.* (**homier, homiest**) (*US coll.*) дома́шний, ую́тный.

homicidal /,hɒmɪˈsaɪd(ə)l/ *adj.* замышля́ющий уби́йство.

homicide /ˈhɒmɪ,saɪd/ *n.* (*crime*) уби́йство.

homily /ˈhɒmɪlɪ/ *n.* про́поведь; (*reprimand*) нота́ция.

hominy /ˈhɒmɪnɪ/ *n.* марёная кукуру́за, мамалы́га.

homo /ˈhəʊməʊ/ *n.* (*pl.* **~s**) (*offens.*) го́мо (*m. indecl.*), го́мик (*coll.*).

homoeopath /ˈhəʊmɪəʊ,pæθ/, /ˈhɒmɪ-/, **-ic** /,həʊmɪəʊˈpæθɪk/, /ˈhɒmɪ-/, **-y** /,həʊmɪˈɒpəθɪ/, /,hɒmɪ-/ = **homeopath** *etc.*

homogeneity /,həʊməʊdʒɪˈniːɪtɪ/ *n.* одноро́дность.

homogeneous /,həʊməʊˈdʒiːnɪəs/, /,hɒməʊ-/ *adj.* одноро́дный.

homogenization /həmɒdʒɪ,naɪˈzeɪʃ(ə)n/ *n.* гомогениза́ция.

homogenize /həˈmɒdʒɪ,naɪz/ *v.t.* гомогенизи́ровать (*impf.*).

homograph /ˈhɒmə,grɑːf/ *n.* омо́граф.

homonym /ˈhɒmənɪm/ *n.* омо́ним.

homonymous /həˈmɒnɪməs/ *adj.* омоними́ческий.

homophobe /ˈhəʊmə,fəʊb/ *n.* гомофо́б.

homophobia /,həʊməˈfəʊbɪə/ *n.* не́нависть к гомосексуали́стам, гомофо́бия.

homophone /ˈhɒmə,fəʊn/ *n.* омофо́н.

homo sapiens /,həʊməʊ ˈsæpɪenz/ *n.* хо́мо са́пиенс (*m. indecl.*), челове́к разу́мный.

homosexual /,həʊməʊˈseksjʊəl/, /,hɒm-/ *n.* гомосексуали́ст; **~ lobby** гомосексуали́стское ло́бби.

● *adj.* гомосексуа́льный.

homosexuality /,həʊməʊ,seksjʊˈælɪtɪ/, /,hɒm-/ *n.* гомосексуали́зм.

homy /ˈhəʊmɪ/ = **homey**

Honduran /hɒnˈdjʊərən/ *n.* гондура́с|ец (*fem.* -ка).

● *adj.* гондура́сский.

Honduras /hɒnˈdjʊərəs/ *n.* Гондура́с.

hone /həʊn/ *v.t.* точи́ть, за-; (*tech.*) хонингова́ть (*impf.*); (*fig.*) отт|а́чивать, -очи́ть.

honest /ˈɒnɪst/ *adj.* (*fair, straightforward*) че́стный; (*sincere*): **an ~ attempt** че́стная попы́тка; (*expressive of honesty*) че́стный, откры́тый; **an ~ face** че́стное/откры́тое лицо́; (*candid*): **if you want the ~ truth** е́сли вы хоти́те знать всю/чи́стую пра́вду; **to be ~ (with you)** че́стно говоря́; (*legitimate*): **he turns an ~ penny** он зараба́тывает (на жизнь) че́стным путём.

● *cpds.* **~-to-god, ~-to-goodness** *adjs.* настоя́щий, взапра́вдашний (*coll.*); *adv.* че́стно!; ей-Бо́гу!

honestly /ˈɒnɪstlɪ/ *adv.* **1** (*straightforwardly*) че́стно. **2** (*candidly*) пря́мо, чистосерде́чно; **~!** че́стное сло́во!; **~, that's all the money I have** э́то все мои де́ньги — че́стное сло́во. **3** (*remonstrance*) поми́луйте!; ну, зна́ете!

honesty /ˈɒnɪstɪ/ *n.* **1** (*integrity*) че́стность. **2** (*candour*) чистосерде́чие, прямота́. **3** (*bot.*) лу́нник.

honey /ˈhʌnɪ/ *n.* мёд; (*US coll., darling*) дорого́й, ми́лый.

● *cpds.* **~-bee** *n.* пчела́ медоно́сная; **~comb** *n.* со́т|ы (*pl., g.* -ов); *adj.* (*structure*) яче́истый; **~-dew** *n.* медвя́ная роса́; (*melon*) муска́тная ды́ня; **~moon** *n.* медо́вый ме́сяц; *v.i.* пров|оди́ть, -ести́ медо́вый ме́сяц; **~suckle** *n.* жи́молость.

hon|eyed, -ied /ˈhʌnɪd/ *adj.*: **~ words** сла́дкие ре́чи.

Hong Kong /hɒŋˈkɒŋ/ *n.* Гонко́нг.

honk /hɒŋk/ *n.* **1** (*of goose*) крик (ди́ких гусе́й). **2** (*of motor horn*) гудо́к.

● *v.i.* **1** крича́ть (*impf.*). **2** гуде́ть (*impf.*).

Honolulu /,hɒnəˈluːluː/ *n.* Гонолу́лу (*m. indecl.*).

honor /ˈɒnə(r)/ (*US*) = **honour**

honorable /ˈɒnərəb(ə)l/ (*US*) = **honourable**

honorari|um /,ɒnəˈreərɪəm/ *n.* (*pl.* **~ums** *or* **~a**) гонора́р.

honorary /ˈɒnərərɪ/ *adj.* (*conferred as honour*) почётный; (*Br., unpaid*): **~ treasurer** казначе́й на обще́ственных нача́лах.

honorific /,ɒnəˈrɪfɪk/ *n.* почти́тельное

обраще́ние; (*in oriental languages*) фо́рма ве́жливости.

● *adj.* почти́тельный, ве́жливый; **an ~ post** почётный пост.

honour /ˈɒnə(r)/ (*US* **honor**) *n.* **1** (*good character, reputation*) честь; **a man of ~** благоро́дный/че́стный челове́к; **code of ~** ко́декс че́сти; **debt of ~** долг че́сти; **he considered himself in ~ bound to obey** он счёл свои́м до́лгом подчини́ться; **his ~ is at stake** на ка́рту поста́влена его́ честь; **(on my) word of ~!** кляну́сь че́стью!; че́стное сло́во!; (*chastity*) честь, целому́дрие. **2** (*dignity, credit*) честь; **it's an ~ to work with him** рабо́тать с ним — больша́я честь; **guard of ~** почётный карау́л; **maid of ~** фре́йлина; **the reception was held in his ~** приём был устро́ен в его́ честь; **he won ~ in war** он был уве́нчан боево́й сла́вой; (*in polite formulae*): **will you do me the ~ of accepting this gift?** окажи́те мне честь, приня́в э́тот дар; **I have the ~ to inform you** име́ю честь сообщи́ть вам. **3** (*usu. pl., mark of respect, distinction*): **~s list** спи́сок пожа́лованных мона́рхом почётных зва́ний и ти́тулов; **he was buried with military ~s** он был похоро́нен с во́инскими по́честями; **let me do the ~s** я бу́ду за хозя́ина; (*as title*): **your H~** ва́ша честь. **4** (*pl., academic distinction*): **~s course** курс, даю́щий пра́во на выпускно́й дипло́м; **pass with ~s** сдать (*pf.*) экза́мен с отли́чием.

● *v.t.* **1** (*respect, do ~ to*) ока́з|ывать, -а́ть честь + *d.* **2** (*confer dignity on*) удост|а́ивать, -о́ить; **he ~ed me with a visit** он удосто́ил меня́ визи́том. **3** (*fulfil obligation*) выполня́ть, вы́полнить; **he failed to ~ the agreement** он не вы́полнил соглаше́ния; **will the cheque** (*Br.*), **check** (*US*) **be ~ed?** бу́дет ли упла́чено по э́тому че́ку?

honourable /ˈɒnərəb(ə)l/ (*US* **honorable**) *adj.* **1** (*upright*) че́стный, досто́йный. **2** (*consistent with honour*): **an ~ peace** почётный мир; **are his intentions ~?** честны́ ли его́ наме́рения? **3** (*title: also* **right ~**) достопочте́нный.

hooch /hu:tʃ/ *n.* (*sl.*) спиртно́е, дурма́н.

hood /hʊd/ *n.* **1** (*headgear*) капюшо́н, ка́пор. **2** (*Br., of car or carriage*) складно́й верх; откидна́я кры́ша. **3** (*US, of car engine*) капо́т. **4** (*US sl.*) = **hoodlum**

● *v.t.* (*cover with ~*) покр|ыва́ть, -ы́ть капюшо́ном.

hoodlum /ˈhu:dləm/ *n.* (*US sl.*) хулига́н, банди́т.

hoodoo /ˈhu:du:/ *n.* по́рча, сглаз.

● *v.t.* (**hoodoos, hoodooed**) (*also* **put the ~ on**) нав|оди́ть, -ести́ по́рчу на + *a.*; сгла́зить (*pf.*).

hoodwink /ˈhʊdwɪŋk/ *v.t.* одура́чи|вать, -ть; (*coll.*) пров|оди́ть, -ести́.

hooey /ˈhu:ɪ/ *n.* (*sl.*) бред, чушь.

hoof /hu:f/ *n.* (*pl.* **hoofs** *or* **hooves**) копы́то; **on the ~** (*of cattle*) живо́й.

● *v.t.* (*sl.*): **~ it** идти́ пёхом (*sl.*).

hoo-ha /ˈhu:hɑ:/ *n.* (*sl.*) суета́, шуми́ха.

hook /hʊk/ *n.* **1** (*curved, usu. metal, device*) крючо́к (*also for fishing*), крюк; **the receiver was off the ~** тру́бка была́ снята́; **~, line and sinker** (*fig.*) (целико́м и) по́лностью; со все́ми потроха́ми (*coll.*); **he swallowed the tale ~, line and sinker** он попа́лся на у́дочку; **get off the ~** (*coll.*) вызволя́ть, вы́зволить; **let off the ~** (*coll.*) выруча́ть, вы́ручить; (*dress fastening*): **~ and eye** крючо́к; (*agric. tool*) сека́ч; **by ~ or by crook** все́ми пра́вдами и непра́вдами. **2** (*boxing blow*) хук, боково́й уда́р.

● *v.t.* **1** (*catch*) лови́ть, пойма́ть; **she ~ed a rich husband** (*coll.*) она́ подцепи́ла бога́того му́жа; **he is ~ed on drugs** (*sl.*) он пристрасти́лся к нарко́тикам. **2** (*usu. with advs., fasten*): **she ~ed up her dress** она́ застегну́ла пла́тье (на крючки́).

● *v.i.* (*fasten*): **the dress ~s (up) at the back** пла́тье застёгивается сза́ди.

● *cpds.* **~-nosed** *adj.* с крючкова́тым но́сом; **~-up** *n.* подключе́ние; (*radio*) одновреме́нная трансля́ция; **~worm** *n.* немато́да, анклисто́ма.

hookah /ˈhʊkə/ *n.* кальа́н.

hooker /ˈhʊkə(r)/ *n.* (*sl., prostitute*) проститу́тка, пане́льная деви́ца.

hookey /ˈhʊkɪ/ *n.*: **play ~** (*US, sl.*) прог|у́ливать, -уля́ть (уро́ки).

hooligan /ˈhu:lɪgən/ *n.* хулига́н.

hooliganism /ˈhu:lɪgənɪz(ə)m/ *n.* хулига́нство.

hoop /hu:p/ *n.* **1** (*of barrel etc.; plaything; in circus*) о́бруч; **they put him through the ~s** (*fig.*) они́ подве́ргли его́ тру́дным испыта́ниям. **2** (*Br., croquet*) воро́т|а (*pl., g.* —).

● *v.t.* (*bind with ~s*) скреп|ля́ть, -и́ть о́бручем.

● *cpds.* **~-la** *n.* (*Br., game*) ко́льца (*nt. pl.*); **~-skirt** *n.* кринoли́н.

hoopoe /ˈhu:pu:/ *n.* удо́д.

hooray! /hʊˈreɪ/ *int.* ура́.

hoot /hu:t/ *n.* (*derisive noise*) ши́канье, улюлю́кивание; **he doesn't give two ~s (or a ~)** ему́ на э́то начха́ть (*coll.*); (*owl's cry*) у́ханье; (*warning note of vessel, car, siren etc.*) гудо́к, сигна́л.

● *v.t.* оши́к|ивать, -ать; **he was ~ed down; they ~ed him off (the stage)** его́ оши́кали.

● *v.i.* (*in derision or amusement*) улюлю́кать (*impf.*); ши́кать (*impf.*); **we ~ed with laughter** мы пока́тывались со́ смеху; (*of an owl*) у́х|ать, -нуть; (*of a vessel, car etc.*) гуде́ть, про-; сигна́лить, про-; да|ва́ть, -ть гудо́к.

hooter /ˈhu:tə(r)/ *n.* **1** (*Br., of car, factory*) гудо́к. **2** (*sl.*) (*nose*) руби́льник.

Hoover /ˈhu:və(r)/ (*Br.*) *n.* (*propr.*) пылесо́с.

● *v.t.* (**h~**) пылесо́сить, про-.

hooves /hu:vz/ *pl. of* ⇒**hoof**

hop¹ /hɒp/ *n.* **1** подско́к, скачо́к (на одно́й ноге́); **~, skip and jump** тройно́й прыжо́к; **I was caught on the ~** (*Br. coll.*) меня́ заста́ли враспло́х. **2** (*dance*) танцу́лька (*coll.*). **3** (*stage of flight*) перелёт.

● *v.t.* (**hopped, hopping**): **~ it!** (*Br. sl.*) кати́сь!

● *v.i.* (**hopped, hopping**) пры́гать, скака́ть (*both impf.*); **he ~ped over the ditch** он перепры́гнул че́рез кана́ву; **where has he ~ped off to?** (*coll.*) куда́ э́то он ускака́л?; **he was ~ping mad** (*coll.*) он рассвирепе́л/остервене́л.

● *cpd.* **~scotch** *n.* кла́ссы (*m. pl.*), кла́ссики (*m. pl.*) (*игра*).

hop² /hɒp/ *n.* (*bot.*) хмель (*m.*).

hop|e /həʊp/ *n.* наде́жда; **I have high ~es of him** я возлага́ю на него́ больши́е наде́жды; **we live in ~e** мы живём наде́ждой (*or* в наде́жде); **don't raise my ~es in vain** не обнадёживайте меня́ напра́сну; **~e chest** (*US*) сунду́к для прида́ного; **his ~es were dashed** его́ наде́жды ру́хнули; **I can hold out little ~e** я не могу́ вас обнадёжить; **I went in the ~e of finding him** я пошёл в наде́жде найти́ его́; **there's not much ~e of that** на э́то ма́ло наде́жды; **things are past all ~e** положе́ние безнадёжно.

● *v.t. & i.* наде́яться (*impf.*); **I ~e to see you soon** наде́юсь, ско́ро вас уви́деть; **let's ~e so!** бу́дем наде́яться!; **I ~e not** наде́юсь, что нет; **I am ~ing against ~e** я наде́юсь, несмотря́ ни на что; **~e for** наде́яться на + *a.*

hopeful /ˈhəʊpfʊl/ *n.*: **young ~** (*joc.*) подаю́щий наде́жды ребёнок.

● *adj.* **1** (*having hope*): **I am ~ of success** я наде́юсь/рассчи́тываю на успе́х. **2** (*inspiring hope*) обнадёживающий; **a ~ prospect** обнадёживающая перспекти́ва; **a ~ sign** обнадёживающий знак.

hopefully /ˈhəʊpfʊlɪ/ *adv.* (*in sense 'it is hoped'*): **~ he will arrive soon** на́до наде́яться, он ско́ро прие́дет.

hopefulness /ˈhəʊpfʊlnɪs/ *n.* наде́жда, оптими́зм.

hopeless /ˈhəʊplɪs/ *adj.* **1** (*feeling no hope*) отчая́вшийся. **2** (*affording no hope*) безнадёжный; **a ~ situation** безнадёжное положе́ние. **3** (*coll., incapable*): **he's quite ~ at science** то́чные нау́ки ему́ соверше́нно не даю́тся; **he is a ~ ass** он безнадёжно глуп. **4**: **~ly inadequate** соверше́нно недоста́точный; **he fell ~ly in love** он влюби́лся по́ уши.

hopelessness /ˈhəʊplɪsnɪs/ *n.* безнадёжность.

hopper /ˈhɒpə(r)/ *n.* (*for grain*) загру́зочная воро́нка.

horde /hɔ:d/ *n.* (*of nomads*) орда́; (*fig.*) по́лчище.

horizon /həˈraɪz(ə)n/ *n.* (*lit., fig.*) горизо́нт; **over the ~** (*motion*) за горизо́нт; (*place*) за горизо́нтом.

horizontal /ˌhɒrɪˈzɒnt(ə)l/ *n.* горизонта́ль.

● *adj.* горизонта́льный.

hormone /ˈhɔ:məʊn/ *n.* гормо́н; (*attr.*)

гормо́нный, гормона́льный; ~ **replacement therapy** гормона́льная терапи́я.

horn /hɔ:n/ *n.* **1** (*of cattle*) рог; **I took the bull by the ~s** (*fig.*) я взял быка́ за рога́; **he drew in his ~s** (*fig.*) он присмире́л/прити́х. **2** (*hist.*, *drinking-vessel*) рог; **~ of plenty** рог изоби́лия. **3** (*mus.*): **French ~** валто́рна; (*hunting-~*) рог. **4** (*warning device*) гудо́к, свисто́к; (*of a car*) клаксо́н, гудо́к; **he sounded his ~** он дал сигна́л. **5** (*substance*) рог. **6**: **on, between the ~s of a dilemma** в тиска́х диле́ммы. **7** (*geog.*): **the H~** мыс Горн.

● *v.i.*: **he ~ed in on our conversation** (*coll.*) он влез в наш разгово́р.

● *cpds.* **~beam** *n.* граб; **~bill** *n.* пти́ца-носоро́г; **~blende** *n.* амфибо́л; **~pipe** *n.* хо́рнпайп; **~-rimmed** *adj.* рогово́й; в рогово́й опра́ве.

horned /hɔ:nd/ *adj.* рога́тый, с рога́ми.

hornet /ˈhɔ:nɪt/ *n.* ше́ршень (*m.*); **his words stirred up a ~'s nest** его́ слова́ потрево́жили оси́ное гнездо́.

horny /ˈhɔ:nɪ/ *adj.* (**hornier, horniest**) **1** рогово́й; **~ hands** мозо́листые ру́ки. **2** (*coll.*, *lustful*) похотли́вый.

● *cpd.* **~-handed** *adj.* с мозо́листыми рука́ми.

horology /həˈrɒlədʒɪ/ *n.* (*measuring time*) измере́ние вре́мени; (*making clocks*) часово́е де́ло.

horoscope /ˈhɒrəˌskəʊp/ *n.* гороско́п.

horrendous /həˈrendəs/ *adj.* ужа́сный, жу́ткий.

horri|ble /ˈhɒrɪb(ə)l/, **-d** /ˈhɒrɪd/ *adjs.* ужа́сный, ужаса́ющий; (*coll.*, *unpleasant*) ужа́сный, проти́вный; **you're being ~!** ты проти́вный!

horrific /həˈrɪfɪk/ *adj.* ужаса́ющий.

horrif|y /ˈhɒrɪˌfaɪ/ *v.t.* (*fill with horror*) ужас|а́ть, -ну́ть; (*shock*) потряс|а́ть, -ти́; **I was ~ied at his behaviour** (*Br.*), **behavior** (*US*) его́ поведе́ние меня́ ужасну́ло.

horror /ˈhɒrə(r)/ *n.* у́жас; **~s!** како́й у́жас!; жуть!; **the ~s of war** у́жасы войны́; **~ film** фильм у́жасов; (*extreme dislike*): **I have a ~ of cats** я терпе́ть не могу́ ко́шек; (*joc.*, *shocking person*) жу́ткий тип.

● *cpd.* **~-struck** *adj.* объя́тый у́жасом.

hors de combat /ˌɒr də ˈkɔ̃bɑ:/ *adj.* вы́шедший из стро́я.

hors d'oeuvre /ɔ:ˈdɜ:vr/, /-ˈdɜ:v/ *n.* (*pl.* **~** *or* **~s** *pronunc. same or* /ˈdɜ:vz/) заку́ска.

horse /hɔ:s/ *n.* **1** (*animal*) ло́шадь, конь (*m.*); **he backs ~s** он игра́ет на ска́чках; **he lost (money) on the ~s** он проигра́лся на ска́чках; **he backed the wrong ~** (*fig.*) он просчита́лся; он поста́вил не на ту ло́шадь; **he drove a ~ and cart** он е́хал на теле́ге; **he eats like a ~** он ест за семеры́х; **you are flogging a dead ~** зря стара́етесь!; ги́блое де́ло!; **hold your ~s!** (*coll.*) поле́гче на поворо́тах!; **put the cart before the ~** (*fig.*) ста́вить, по- всё с ног на́ голову; **he learnt to ride a ~** он научи́лся е́здить верхо́м; **a dark ~** тёмная лоша́дка; **I had it straight from the ~'s mouth** я зна́ю э́то из пе́рвых рук; **he got on his high ~** он стал в по́зу.
2 (*cavalry*) ко́нница, кавале́рия; **H~ Guards** конногварде́йский полк.
3 (*in gymnasium*) конь (*m.*).

● *cpds.* **~back** *n.*: **on ~back** верхо́м; **~back riding** (*US*) = **~-riding;** **~-blanket** *n.* попо́на; **~-box** *n.* прице́п для перево́зки лошаде́й; фурго́н для перево́зки лошаде́й; **~-chestnut** *n.* кашта́н ко́нский; **~-cloth** *n.* попо́на; **~-drawn** *adj.* ко́нный; **~flesh** *n.* кони́на; **~-fly** *n.* слепе́нь (*m.*); **~hair** *n.* ко́нский во́лос; *adj.* из ко́нского во́лоса; **~man** *n.* нае́здник, вса́дник; **~manship** *n.* иску́сство верхово́й езды́; **~play** *n.* шу́мная игра́/возня́; **~-power** *n.* лошади́ная си́ла; **20 ~-power** 20 лошади́ных сил; **~-race, ~-racing** *nn.* ска́чки (*f. pl.*), бега́ (*m. pl.*); **~-radish** *n.* хрен; **~-riding** *n.* верхова́я езда́; **~shoe** *n.* подко́ва; **~-trading** *n.* (*fig.*) полити́ческие сде́лки (*f. pl.*); **~whip** *n.* хлыст; *v.t.* хлеста́ть (*impf.*); **~-woman** *n.* нае́здница, вса́дница.

horsy /ˈhɔ:sɪ/ *adj.* (**horsier, horsiest**) (*fond of horses*) лю́бящий лошаде́й.

hortatory /ˈhɔ:tətərɪ/ *adj.* увещева́тельный, наста́вительный.

horticultural /ˌhɔ:tɪˈkʌltʃər(ə)l/ *adj.* садово́дческий.

horticultur(al)ist /ˌhɔ:tɪˈkʌltʃər(əl)ɪst/ *n.* садово́д.

horticulture /ˈhɔ:tɪˌkʌltʃə(r)/ *n.* садово́дство.

hosanna /həʊˈzænə/ *n.* & *int.* оса́нна.

hose /həʊz/ *n.* **1** (*stockings*) чуло́чные изде́лия; (*US*) чулки́ (*m. pl.*). **2** (*tube, also* **~-pipe**) шланг; **fire ~** брандспо́йт, пожа́рный рука́в.

● *v.t.*: **he was hosing down the car** он помы́л маши́ну водо́й из шла́нга.

hosier /ˈhəʊzɪə(r)/, /ˈhəʊʒə(r)/ *n.* торго́вец чуло́чно-носо́чными изде́лиями.

hosiery /ˈhəʊzɪərɪ/, /ˈhəʊʒərɪ/ *n.* (*shop*) магази́н чуло́чно-носо́чных изде́лий; (*wares*) чуло́чно-носо́чные изде́лия (*nt. pl.*).

hospice /ˈhɒspɪs/ *n.* (*for terminal patients*) больни́ца для неизлечи́мо больны́х.

hospitable /ˈhɒspɪtəb(ə)l/, /hɒˈspɪt-/ *adj.* гостеприи́мный.

hospital /ˈhɒspɪt(ə)l/ *n.* больни́ца; **~ bed** больни́чная ко́йка; (*esp. military*) го́спиталь (*m.*); **he went into ~** он лёг в больни́цу; **he is in ~** он (лежи́т) в больни́це; **~ ship** плаву́чий го́спиталь.

hospitality /ˌhɒspɪˈtælɪtɪ/ *n.* гостеприи́мство.

hospitalization /ˌhɒspɪtəlaɪˈzeɪʃ(ə)n/ *n.* госпитализа́ция.

hospitalize /ˈhɒspɪtəˌlaɪz/ *v.t.* госпитализи́ровать (*impf.*, *pf.*); класть, положи́ть в больни́цу.

host[1] /həʊst/ *n.* хозя́ин (*also zool.*); **he is a good ~** он гостеприи́мный/раду́шный хозя́ин.

● *v.t.* организова́ть (*impf.*, *pf.*); **the conference was ~ed by the British** конфере́нция была́ организо́вана брита́нцами.

host[2] /həʊst/ *n.* (*army, multitude*) мно́жество, сонм, ма́сса; **the Heavenly H~** си́лы небе́сные (*f. pl.*); **the Lord of ~s** Госпо́дь сил; **a ~ of difficulties** ма́сса тру́дностей.

host[3] /həʊst/ *n.* (*sacrament*) го́стия.

hostage /ˈhɒstɪdʒ/ *n.* зало́жник.

hostel /ˈhɒst(ə)l/ *n.* общежи́тие; **youth ~** молодёжная тури́стская ба́за/турба́за.

hostelling /ˈhɒstəlɪŋ/ (*US* **hosteling**) *n.*: **they like to go ~** они́ лю́бят путеше́ствовать, остана́вливаясь на молодёжных турба́зах.

hostelry /ˈhɒstəlrɪ/ *n.* (*arch., joc.*) посто́ялый двор.

hostess /ˈhəʊstɪs/ *n.* хозя́йка; (*on aircraft*) стюарде́сса; (*in night-club*) пла́тная партнёрша.

hostile /ˈhɒstaɪl/ *adj.* вражде́бный; (*person, attitude*) неприя́зненный; (*weather*) неблагоприя́тный; **to be ~ to something/s.o.** относи́ться (*impf.*) вражде́бно к + *d.*

hostility /hɒˈstɪlɪtɪ/ *n.* (*enmity, ill-will*) вражде́бность; (*pl.*, *warlike activity*) вое́нные де́йствия.

hostler /ˈɒslə(r)/ (*US*) = **ostler**

hot /hɒt/ *adj.* (**hotter, hottest**)
1 (*water, object*) горя́чий; (*weather*) жа́ркий; **I am ~** мне жа́рко; **he got ~ playing** ему́ ста́ло жа́рко от игры́; **~ air** (*coll.*) бахва́льство; **these goods are selling like ~cakes** э́тот това́р идёт нарасхва́т; **a ~ day** жа́ркий день; **~ dog** хо́т-до́г; **a ~ flush** прили́в кро́ви; **~ rod** (*sl.*) маши́на с мо́щным мото́ром; **in the ~ seat** (*coll.*) (*in responsible job*) на отве́тственной до́лжности; (*in responsible situation*) в отве́тственной ситуа́ции; **the issue is too ~ to handle** (*fig.*) э́то сли́шком щекотли́вый вопро́с; **they made things ~ for him** они́ его́ прижа́ли; **you'll get into ~ water** вы попадёте в беду́; вам не поздоро́вится.
2 (*spicy*) о́стрый.
3 (*ardent*) горя́чий, пла́менный; **~ on the scent, trail** по горя́чему следу́.
4 (*angry*) раздражённый.
5 (*excited*) взволно́ванный, возбуждённый; **~ under the collar** (*coll.*) распалённый, взбешённый.
6 (*exciting*) отли́чный, шика́рный; **not so ~** (*coll.*) ничего́ осо́бенного; **~ stuff** (*coll.*) (*outstanding person*) молодчи́на; (*something new and exciting*) блеск!; шик!
7 (*fresh*): **~ news** све́жие но́вости; **~ from the press** то́лько что из типогра́фии.
8 (*racing etc.*): **~ favourite** (*Br.*), **favorite** (*US*) всео́бщий фаври́т; **a ~ tip** де́льный сове́т.

● *adv.* (*fig.*): **he blows ~ and cold** ≈ у него́ семь пя́тниц на неде́ле.

● *v.t.* (**hotted, hotting**): **~ up** (*Br. coll.*, *reinforce*) уси́л|ивать, -ить.

● *v.i.* (**hotted, hotting**): **~ up** (*Br. coll., become more lively*): **the game ~ted up** игра́ оживи́лась.

● *cpds.* **~bed** *n.* парни́к; (*fig.*) расса́дник, оча́г; **a ~bed of vice** расса́дник поро́ка; **~-blooded** *adj.* пы́лкий, стра́стный; **~foot** *adv.* стремгла́в, поспе́шно; **~head** *n.* бу́йная/бедо́вая голова́; **~-headed** *adj.* вспы́льчивый, горя́чий; **~house** *n.* оранжере́я, тепли́ца; **~-line** *n.* (*for help, enquiries*) горя́чая ли́ния; (*between governments*) пряма́я телефо́нная связь; **~-plate** *n.* пли́тка; **~pot** *n.* (*Br.*) тушёное мя́со с овоща́ми; **~-tempered** *adj.* вспы́льчивый; **~-water-bottle** *n.* гре́лка.

hotch-potch /ˈhɒtʃpɒtʃ/ *n.* мешани́на.

hotel /həʊˈtel/ *n.* гости́ница, оте́ль (*m.*).

hotelier /həʊˈtelɪə(r)/ *n.* хозя́ин гости́ницы.

hotly /ˈhɒtlɪ/ *adv.* (*angrily*) ре́зко; (*passionately*) горя́чо, жа́рко; **her cheeks flushed ~** её щёки зарде́лись.

hound /haʊnd/ *n.* (*for hunting*) охо́тничья соба́ка; **he rides to ~s** он охо́тится на лиси́ц (с соба́ками); (*coll., any dog*) пёс, соба́ка.

● *v.t.* (*also fig.*) трави́ть, за~; (*with adv.*): **~ out** выжива́ть, вы́жить.

hour /aʊə(r)/ *n.* **1** (*period*) час; **it will take me an ~** мне потре́буется час; **boats for hire by the ~** прока́т ло́док с почасово́й опла́той; **he works an 8-~ day** у него́ восьмичасово́й рабо́чий день; **~ after ~** час за ча́сом.
2 (*of clock-time*): **the clock strikes the ~s and half-~s** часы́ отбива́ют час и полчаса́; **every ~ on the ~** в нача́ле ка́ждого ча́са; **every ~ on the half-~** ка́ждый час в середи́не ча́са; **at the eleventh ~** (*fig.*) в после́дний моме́нт.
3 (*time of day or night*): **we are open at all ~s** мы откры́ты круглосу́точно; **at an early ~** ра́но; **they keep late ~s** они́ по́здно ложа́тся (и встаю́т); **in the small ~s** в предрассве́тные часы́; **regardless of the ~** в любо́е вре́мя (дня и но́чи).
4 (*specific period of time*): **our working ~s are long** у нас до́лгий рабо́чий день; **I had to work after ~s** мне пришло́сь рабо́тать сверхуро́чно; **in office ~s** в рабо́чее вре́мя; **out of ~s** в нерабо́чее вре́мя; **after ~s** по́сле оконча́ния рабо́чего дня.
5 (*fig., moment*) час; **the ~ has come** про́бил час; **in the ~ of danger** в мину́ту опа́сности.

● *cpds.* **~-glass** *n.* песо́чные час|ы́ (*pl., g.* -о́в); **~-hand** *n.* часова́я стре́лка; **~-long** *adj.* часово́й; продолжа́ющийся час.

hourly /ˈaʊəlɪ/ *adj.* **1** (*occurring once an hour*) ежеча́сный. **2** (*constant*) постоя́нный, непреста́нный. **3**: **an ~ wage** почасова́я опла́та.

● *adv.* (*once every hour*) ежеча́сно; (*at any time*) с ча́су на час; в любо́е вре́мя; (*constantly*) непреста́нно.

house[1] /haʊs/ *n.* **1** (*habitation*) дом, зда́ние; **~ arrest** дома́шний аре́ст; **~ guest** гость (живу́щий в до́ме); **~ of cards** (*lit., fig.*) ка́рточный до́мик; **~ of God** дом Бо́жий, це́рковь; **they get on like a ~ on fire** они́ прекра́сно ла́дят; **keep ~** вести́ (*det.*) хозя́йство; **they kept open ~** у них был откры́тый дом; **put, set one's ~ in order** (*fig.*) прив|оди́ть, -ести́ свои́ дела́ в поря́док; **as safe as ~s** (*Br.*) в по́лной безопа́сности; **set up ~ together** зажи́ть (*pf.*) вдвоём; **turn s.o. out of ~ and home** выгоня́ть, вы́гнать кого́-н. из дому; (*inn*): **public ~** паб, пивно́й бар; **have a drink on the ~** пить, вы́- за счёт хозя́ина; (*parl.*): **H~ of Commons** пала́та о́бщин; **H~ of Lords** пала́та ло́рдов; **H~ of Representatives** пала́та представи́телей; **the H~** (*Parliament*) парла́мент; (*Br., Stock Exchange*) би́ржа; (*US, House of Representatives*) пала́та представи́телей.
2 (*audience*) зал, аудито́рия; **they played to a full ~** на их выступле́нии зал был по́лон; **she brought down the ~** её выступле́ние произвело́ фуро́р; (*Br., performance*) (*theatr.*) представле́ние; (*cin.*) сеа́нс.
3 (*dynasty*) дом, дина́стия.
4 (*business concern*) учрежде́ние, фи́рма.
5 (*Br., at boarding school*) ученики́, живу́щие в одно́м общежи́тии.

● *cpds.* **~-agent** *n.* (*Br.*) аге́нт по прода́же недви́жимости, риэ́лтер; **~boat** *n.* плаву́чий дом; **~bound** *adj.*: **he is ~bound** он не выхо́дит из до́ма; **~-boy** *n.* (*boy*) ма́льчик-слуга́ (*m.*); (*man*) слуга́ (*m.*); **~breaker** *n.* граби́тель-взло́мщик, дому́шник (*coll.*); **~breaking** *n.* (*Br.*) грабёж со взло́мом; **~-broken** *adj.* (*US*) = **~-trained; ~coat** *n.* (дома́шний) хала́т; **~-father, ~-mother** *nn.* (*of boarding school/children's home*) заве́дующ|ий, -ая интерна́том/прию́том; **~-fly** *n.* му́ха ко́мнатная; **~hold** *n.* дом; дома́шний круг; (*attr.*): **~hold appliances** бытовы́е прибо́ры; **~hold goods** хозя́йственные това́ры; **~hold troops** гва́рдия; **a ~hold word** обихо́дное выраже́ние; **her name is a ~hold word; she is a ~hold name** её всё зна́ют; **~holder** *n.* домовладе́лец; **~-hunting** *n.* по́иски (*m. pl.*) до́ма; **~-husband** *n.* муж, веду́щий дома́шнее хозя́йство; **~keeper** *n.* эконо́мка; **~keeping** *n.* дома́шнее хозя́йство; **~keeping expenses** расхо́ды на хозя́йство; **~-maid** *n.* го́рничная; **~master** *n.* ≈ коменда́нт (общежи́тия интерна́та); **~painter** *n.* маля́р; **~-proud** *adj.* лю́бящий занима́ться благоустро́йством и украше́нием до́ма; **~-room** *n.*: **I wouldn't give it ~-room** (*Br.*) я не бу́ду захламля́ть э́тим дом; **~-to-~** *adj.*: **a ~-to-~ search** о́быск всех домо́в подря́д; пова́льный о́быск; **~top** *n.* кры́ша, кро́вля; **~-trained** *adj.* (*Br.*) приу́ченный жить (*or* не па́чкать) в до́ме (*о собаке, кошке*); **~-warming** *n.* новосе́лье; **~wife** *n.* домохозя́йка; **~work** *n.* дома́шние дела́.

house[2] /haʊz/ *v.t.* **1** (*provide house(s) for*) предост|авля́ть, -а́вить жильё + *d.*; сели́ть, по-. **2** (*accommodate*) вме|ща́ть, -сти́ть; **this building ~s the city council** в э́том зда́нии размеща́ется муниципалите́т.
3 (*store*) храни́ть (*impf.*).

housing /ˈhaʊzɪŋ/ *n.* **1** (*provision of houses*) обеспе́чение жильём; **~ benefit** (*Br.*) посо́бие по вы́плате квартпла́ты; **the ~ problem** жили́щная пробле́ма. **2** (*houses built in quantity*) жильё; **~ development, ~ estate** (*Br.*), **~ project** (*US*) жило́й микрорайо́н. **3** (*casing*) ко́рпус, ко́жух.

hove /həʊv/ *esp. naut. past and p.p. of* ⇒**heave**

hovel /ˈhɒv(ə)l/ *n.* лачу́га.

hover /ˈhɒvə(r)/ *v.i.* пари́ть (*impf.*); (*fig.*): **~ around s.o.** ви́ться (*impf.*) вокру́г + *g.*; **he ~ed around her** он ви́лся вокру́г неё; **he ~ed between life and death** он был ме́жду жи́знью и сме́ртью.

● *cpd.* **~craft** *n.* ховеркра́фт; су́дно на возду́шной поду́шке.

how /haʊ/ *adv.* **1** (*in direct and indirect questions*) как; каки́м о́бразом?; **~ come?** (*coll.*) как э́то?; **~ the devil did you find out?** как вы э́то узна́ли, чёрт возьми́?; **~ on earth did it happen?** как же э́то случи́лось?; **~ come you are late?** почему́ э́то вы опа́здываете?; **~ are you?** как пожива́ете?; **~ do I know?** а я отку́да я зна́ю?; **~ do you know that?** отку́да вы э́то зна́ете?; **~ do you mean?** что вы хоти́те сказа́ть?; в како́м смы́сле?; **~'s that?** (*enquiring reason*) ка́к э́то?; (*inviting comment*): **~'s that for a jump!** ну, как прыжо́к!; **~ about a drink?** не хоти́те ли вы́пить?; не вы́пить ли нам?; **~ about that!** (*coll., expr. admiration etc.*) ну и ну!; (*praising one's own achievement*) как насчёт э́того!; **~ so?** почему́ э́то?, то́ есть?; **~ ever does he do it?** как то́лько он э́то де́лает?
2 (*with adjs. and advs.*): **~ far is it?** как далеко́ э́то нахо́дится?; како́е расстоя́ние (до + *g.*)?; **~ many, much?** ско́лько?; **~ old is she?** ско́лько ей лет?
3 (*in indirect statements or questions*): **I told him ~ I'd been abroad** я рассказа́л ему́, как я съе́здил за грани́цу.
4 (*in exclamations*): **~ he goes on!** како́й же он зану́да!; **~ I wish I were there!** как бы мне хоте́лось сейча́с быть там!; **and ~!** (*coll.*) ещё как!; **~ beautifully she plays!** как она́ прекра́сно игра́ет!

how|ever /haʊˈevə(r)/ *adv.* (*with adj.*) како́й бы ни; как ни; **~ strong he is** како́й бы он ни был си́льный; **~ strong our anger is we must be objective** как не вели́к наш гнев, мы должны́ быть объекти́вны; (*with adv.*) как бы ни; **~ strongly he denied it** как бы реши́тельно но ни отрица́л э́то; **~ hard he tried** как он ни стара́лся; (*in questions*) как же; **~ did you find that out?** как же вы узна́ли э́то?; (*nevertheless*) одна́ко, и всё же; **~, he forgot** одна́ко, он забы́л.

howitzer /ˈhaʊɪtsə(r)/ *n.* га́убица.

howl /haʊl/ *n.* (*cry of pain or grief*) вопль (*m.*), стон; (*cry of derision*) вой, гул; (*of*

H

an animal) вой; (*of the wind*) завыва́ние.

● *v.t. & i.* выть (*impf.*); **the baby was ~ing its head off** ребёнок надрыва́лся от пла́ча; **he was ~ed down** его́ перекрича́ли; **listen to the wolves ~ing!** послу́шайте, как во́ют во́лки!; **the wind ~s in the chimney** ве́тер во́ет в трубе́; **a ~ing gale** завыва́ющий ве́тер.

howler /ˈhaʊlə(r)/ *n.* (*coll., solecism*) грубе́йшая оши́бка, ля́псус.

HP (*abbr. of* **hire-purchase**) (*Br.*) поку́пка в рассро́чку.

h.p. (*abbr. of* **horse-power**) л.с. (лошади́ная си́ла).

HQ (*abbr. of* **headquarters**) штаб-кварти́ра; (*mil.*) штаб, ста́вка.

HRH (*abbr. of* **Her/His Royal Highness**) (*Br.*) Её/Его́ короле́вское высо́чество.

HRT (*abbr. of* **hormone replacement therapy**) гормона́льная терапи́я.

hub /hʌb/ *n.* ступи́ца; (*fig.*): **the ~ of the universe** центр вселе́ной.

● *cpd.* **~cap** *n.* колпа́к.

hubbub /ˈhʌbʌb/ *n.* шум, го́вор, го́мон, гвалт.

hubby /ˈhʌbɪ/ *n.* (*coll.*) муженёк (*coll.*).

hubris /ˈhju:brɪs/ *n.* горды́ня, надме́нность.

hubristic /ˌhju:ˈbrɪstɪk/ *adj.* высокоме́рный, надме́нный.

huckleberry /ˈhʌkəlbərɪ/ *n.* (*bush; fruit*) черни́ка (*collect.*); (*single berry*) я́года черни́ки.

huckster /ˈhʌkstə(r)/ *n.* торго́вец вразно́с

huddle /ˈhʌd(ə)l/ *n.* **1** (*disorderly mass*) ку́ча, гру́да, во́рох. **2**: **they went into a ~** (*coll.*) они́ ста́ли та́йно совеща́ться/шушу́каться.

● *v.i.* толпи́ться, с-; **he lay ~d up** он лежа́л, сверну́вшись кала́чиком; **they ~d together for warmth** они́ прижа́лись друг к дру́гу, что́бы согре́ться.

hue[1] /hju:/ *n.* (*colour*) отте́нок, тон (*pl.* -а́).

hue[2] /hju:/ *n.*: **~ and cry** крик; (*outcry*) возмуще́ние; **raise a ~ and cry** подн|има́ть, -я́ть крик.

huff /hʌf/ *n.* вспы́шка раздраже́ния/оби́ды; **he walked off in a ~** он ушёл вконе́ц разоби́женный.

● *v.t.* **1** (*in game of draughts*) брать, взять фук у + *g.*; фу́к|ать, -нуть. **2**: **you can ~ and puff but you won't stop me** мо́жете зли́ться, но меня́ э́то не остано́вит.

huffy /ˈhʌfɪ/ *adj.* (**huffier, huffiest**) оби́женный, рассе́рженный.

hug /hʌg/ *n.* объя́тие.

● *v.t.* (**hugged, hugging**) **1** (*embrace*) обн|има́ть, -я́ть. **2** (*fig., cling to, keep close to*): **the ship ~ged the shore** кора́бль шёл вдоль са́мого бе́рега.

huge /hju:dʒ/ *adj.* огро́мный, грома́дный; (*event*) грандио́зный; **he ate a ~ supper** он съел огро́мный у́жин; **a ~ joke** великоле́пный ро́зыгрыш.

hugely /ˈhju:dʒlɪ/ *adv.* весьма́, чрезвыча́йно.

hugeness /ˈhju:dʒnɪs/ *n.* грома́дность, грандио́зность.

Huguenot /ˈhju:gəˌnəʊ/, /-ˌnɒt/ *n.* гугено́т.

● *adj.* гугено́тский

huh /hə/ *int.* (*interrogation*) гм?, а?; (*expr. contempt*) хм!, гм!

hulk /hʌlk/ *n.* (*body of dismantled ship*) ко́рпус; (*unwieldy vessel*) неповоро́тливое су́дно, коры́то; (*large clumsy person*) медве́дь (*m.*); у́валень (*m.*).

hulking /ˈhʌlkɪŋ/ *adj.* неуклю́жий, неповоро́тливый.

hull[1] /hʌl/ *n.* (*of ship*) ко́рпус; (*of aircraft*) фюзеля́ж.

● *v.t.*: **~ a ship** (*strike in ~*) проб|ива́ть, -и́ть ко́рпус корабля́.

hull[2] /hʌl/ *n.* (*shell, pod*) кожура́; шелуха́.

● *v.t.* лущи́ть (*impf.*), шелуши́ть (*impf.*).

hullabaloo /ˌhʌləbəˈlu:/ *n.* шум, шуми́ха.

hullo /hʌˈləʊ/ *int.* (*greeting*) здра́вствуй(те)!; приве́т! (*coll.*); (*on telephone*) алло́!; (*expr. surprise*) вот те на́!

hum /hʌm/ *n.* (*of insects*) жужжа́ние; (*of machines*) гуде́ние, гул.

● *v.t. & i.* (**hummed, humming**) **1** (*make murmuring sound*) (*of insects*) жужжа́ть (*impf.*); (*of cars*) гуде́ть (*impf.*); **~ming bird** коли́бри (*m. indecl.*). **2** (*sing with closed lips*) напева́ть (*impf.*). **3**: **~ and ha(w)** (*Br.*) мя́млить (*impf.*). **4** (*coll., be active*) идти́ (*det.*) по́лным хо́дом; кипе́ть (*impf.*); **he made things ~** у него́ рабо́та кипе́ла.

human /ˈhju:mən/ *n.* челове́к.

● *adj.* челове́ческий; **~ being** челове́к; **~ error** оши́бка, сво́йственная челове́ку; **~ kind** челове́чество; **~ nature** челове́ческая приро́да; **the ~ race** род людско́й; **~ rights** права́ челове́ка; **~ shield** живо́й щит; **he did all that was ~ly possible** он сде́лал всё, что в челове́ческих си́лах.

humane /hju:ˈmeɪn/ *adj.* **1** (*compassionate*) гума́нный, челове́чный. **2**: **~ studies** гуманита́рные нау́ки (*f. pl.*).

humaneness /hju:ˈmeɪnnɪs/ *n.* гума́нность, челове́чность.

humanism /ˈhju:məˌnɪz(ə)m/ *n.* (*classical studies; non-religious ethics*) гумани́зм.

humanist /ˈhju:mənɪst/ *n.* гумани́ст.

humanistic /ˌhju:məˈnɪstɪk/ *adj.* гуманисти́ческий.

humanitarian /hju:ˌmænɪˈteərɪən/ *n.* гумани́ст.

● *adj.* гуманита́рный; гума́нный; **~ aid** гуманита́рная по́мощь.

humanitarianism /hju:ˌmænɪˈteərɪəˌnɪz(ə)m/ *n.* гуманита́рность, гума́нность.

humanity /hju:ˈmænɪtɪ/ *n.* **1** (*human nature*) челове́чность, челове́ческие ка́чества. **2** (*the human race*) челове́чество; род людско́й. **3** (*crowd*) толпа́, наро́д. **4** (*humaneness*) гума́нность. **5**: **the ~ies** гуманита́рные нау́ки (*f. pl.*).

humanize /ˈhju:məˌnaɪz/ *v.t.* (*make human*) очелове́чи|вать, -ть; (*make humane*) де́лать, с- бо́лее челове́чным.

humble /ˈhʌmb(ə)l/ *adj.* (**humbler, humblest**) **1** (*lacking self-importance*) скро́мный, поко́рный, смире́нный; **in my ~ opinion** по моему́ скро́мному мне́нию; **your ~ servant** ваш поко́рный слуга́; **he was made to eat ~ pie** ему́ пришло́сь извини́ться. **2** (*lowly*) просто́й, скро́мный; **of ~ birth** из простонаро́дья, из просты́х.

● *v.t.* смир|я́ть, -и́ть; ун|ижа́ть, -и́зить; **~ o.s.** уничижа́ться (*impf.*).

humbleness /ˈhʌmbəlnɪs/ *n.* смире́ние, скро́мность.

humbug /ˈhʌmbʌg/ *n.* (*deceit, hypocrisy*) надува́тельство; (*hypocrite, fraud*) обма́нщик, очковтира́тель (*m.*); (*nonsense*) чушь, вздо́р; (*Br., boiled sweet*) ледене́ц.

● *v.t.* (**humbugged, humbugging**) над|ува́ть, -у́ть; провести́ (*pf.*).

humdinger /ˈhʌmˌdɪŋə(r)/ *n.* (*sl.*) блеск, чу́до.

humdrum /ˈhʌmdrʌm/ *adj.* однообра́зный, ну́дный.

hume|rus /ˈhju:mərəs/ *n.* (*pl.* **~ri** /-ˌraɪ/) плечева́я кость.

humid /ˈhju:mɪd/ *adj.* вла́жный.

humidifier /hju:ˈmɪdɪˌfaɪ(ə)r/ *n.* увлажни́тель (*m.*) во́здуха.

humidity /hju:ˈmɪdɪtɪ/ *n.* вла́жность.

humiliate /hju:ˈmɪlɪˌeɪt/ *v.t.* ун|ижа́ть, -и́зить.

humiliation /hju:ˌmɪlɪˈeɪʃ(ə)n/ *n.* униже́ние.

humility /hju:ˈmɪlɪtɪ/ *n.* смире́ние; скро́мность.

hummock /ˈhʌmək/ *n.* бугор́, приго́рок.

humor /ˈhju:mə(r)/ (*US*) = **humour**

humoresque /ˌhju:məˈresk/ *n.* юморе́ска.

humorist /ˈhju:mərɪst/ *n.* (*facetious person*) остря́к, весельча́к; (*humorous writer etc.*) юмори́ст.

humorless /ˈhju:məlɪs/ (*US*) = **humourless**

humorous /ˈhju:mərəs/ *adj.* юмористи́ческий; **a ~ author** писа́тель-юмори́ст; **a ~ situation** коми́ческая ситуа́ция.

humour /ˈhju:mə(r)/ (*US* **humor**) *n.* **1** (*disposition*) нрав, душе́вный склад; **in an ill ~** не в ду́хе; в плохо́м настрое́нии; **this will put you in a good ~** э́то подни́мет вам настрое́ние; **he is out of ~** он не в ду́хе; **I am in no ~ for argument** я не настро́ен спо́рить; **he will work when the ~ takes him** он рабо́тает по настрое́нию. **2** (*amusement*) ю́мор; **his speech was full of ~** в его́ ре́чи бы́ло мно́го ю́мора; **he has little sense of ~** у него́ сла́бое чу́вство ю́мора.

● *v.t.* потака́ть (*impf.*) +*d.*; ублаж|а́ть, -и́ть.

humourless /ˈhju:məlɪs/ (*US* **humorless**) *adj.* лишённый чу́вства ю́мора; ску́чный.

hump /hʌmp/ *n.* **1** (*protuberance on back*) горб. **2** (*rounded hillock*) буго́р, бугоро́к; **we are over the ~ now** (*fig.*) са́мое тру́дное позади́. **3** (*Br., irritation*) раздраже́ние, ки́слое настрое́ние; **it gives me the ~** э́то наво́дит на меня́ тоску́.

● *v.t.* **1** (*make ~-shaped*) выгиба́ть, вы́гнуть; го́рбить, с-; **the cat ~ed up its back** ко́шка вы́гнула спи́ну. **2** (*carry, shoulder*) тащи́ть (*det.*) (на спине́); взва́ливать, взвали́ть на́ спину. **3** (*vulg., engage in sexual intercourse with*) тра́х|ать, -нуть.

● *v.i.* (*vulg., engage in sexual intercourse*) тра́х|аться, -нуться.

● *cpd.* **~-backed** *adj.* горба́тый.

humph /həmf/ *int.* хм!

humus /ˈhju:məs/ *n.* гу́мус, перегно́й.

hunch /hʌntʃ/ *n.* **1** (*hump*) горб. **2** (*US coll., intuitive feeling*) чутьё, интуи́ция; **I had a ~ he would come** я предчу́вствовал, что он придёт; **he acted on a ~** он де́йствовал интуити́вно.

● *v.t.*: **he ~ed (up) his shoulders** он ссуту́лился/сго́рбился.

● *cpd.* **~-back** *n.* горбу́н.

hundred /ˈhʌndrəd/ *n.* (*pl.* **~s** *or* (*with numeral or qualifying word*) **~**) (число́, но́мер) сто; (*collect.*) со́тня; **about 100** о́коло ста; **100 each** по́ сто; **up to 100** до ста; **page 100** со́тая страни́ца; **room 100** со́тая ко́мната, ко́мната но́мер сто; **a ~ and fifty** сто пятьдеся́т, полтора́ста; **~s of people** со́тни люде́й; **sell by the ~** прод|ава́ть, -а́ть по сто штук (*or* со́тнями); **~s of thousands** со́тни ты́сяч; **I have a ~ and one things to do** у меня́ ты́сяча дел; **~ per cent** (*as adj.*) стопроце́нтный; (*adv.*) стопроце́нтно, на (все) сто проце́нтов; **I'm one ~ per cent behind you** я стопроце́нтно (*or* я целико́м и по́лностью) на ва́шей стороне́; **a ~ to one** наверняка́; оди́н шанс из ста; **it's a ~ to one they will not meet again** руча́юсь, что они́ бо́льше не встре́тятся; **he lived to be a ~** он до́жил до ста лет; **at fourteen ~ hours** (*mil.*) в четы́рнадцать (часо́в) ноль-ноль (мину́т); в 14 часо́в ро́вно; **in the nineteen ~s** в девятисо́тые го́ды.

● *adj.* сто +*g. pl.*; **two** (*etc. to* **nine**) **~** две́сти, три́ста, четы́реста, пятьсо́т, шестьсо́т, семьсо́т, восемьсо́т, девятьсо́т (*all* +*g. pl.*); **a ~ miles away** (*fig.*) за ты́сячу вёрст; далеко́.

● *cpds.* **~fold** *adj.* стокра́тный; *adv.* во́ сто крат, в сто раз; **~-rouble note** *n.* сторублёвая бума́жка, сторублёвка; **~weight** *n.* (*Imperial — approx. 50.8 kilograms*) англи́йский це́нтнер; (*US — approx. 45.4 kilograms*) америка́нский це́нтнер.

hundredth /ˈhʌndrədθ/ *n.* (*fraction*) одна́ со́тая.

● *adj.* со́тый.

hung /hʌŋ/ *past and p.p. of* ⇒**hang**

Hungarian /hʌŋˈgeərɪən/ *n.* (*person*) венгр (*fem.* венге́рка); (*language*) венге́рский язы́к.

● *adj.* венге́рский.

Hungary /ˈhʌŋgərɪ/ *n.* Ве́нгрия.

hunger /ˈhʌŋgə(r)/ *n.* го́лод; (*fig., strong desire*) жа́жда.

● *v.i.* (*fig.*) жа́ждать (*impf.*) (+*g.*); **she ~ed for excitement** она́ жа́ждала развлече́ний.

● *cpds.* **~-march** *n.* голо́дный марш; **~-strike** *n.* голодо́вка.

hungover /hʌŋˈəʊvə(r)/ *adj.* (*coll.*) страда́ющий с похме́лья/перепо́я.

hungry /ˈhʌŋgrɪ/ *adj.* (**hungrier, hungriest**) голо́дный; (*fig., avid*) жа́ждущий.

hunk /hʌŋk/ *n.* большо́й кусо́к; (*of bread*) ломо́ть (*m.*) хле́ба.

hunkers /ˈhʌŋkəz/ *n.* (*Sc.*) я́годицы (*f. pl.*); **on one's ~** на ко́рточках.

hunky-dory /ˌhʌŋkɪˈdɔ:rɪ/ *adj.* (*coll.*): **everything's ~** всё в ажу́ре.

hunt /hʌnt/ *n.* **1** (**~ing expedition**) охо́та. **2** (*search*) охо́та (на+*a.*); по́иск|и (*pl., g.* -ов) (*чего*).

● *v.t. & i.* (*e.g. animals*) охо́титься (*impf.*) (на+*a.*); (*persons or things*) охо́титься (*impf.*) за+*i.*; вести́ (*det.*) по́иски +*g.*; **he had a ~ed look** у него́ был затра́вленный вид.

● *with advs.*: **the criminal was ~ed down** престу́пника пойма́ли; **she ~ed out some old clothes** она́ отыска́ла где́-то ста́рую оде́жду; **will you ~ up the address for me?** вы мо́жете разыска́ть для меня́ э́тот а́дрес?

hunter /ˈhʌntə(r)/ *n.* **1** (*one who hunts*) охо́тник. **2** (*horse*) гу́нтер; охо́тничья ло́шадь.

hunting /ˈhʌntɪŋ/ *n.* охо́та.

● *cpds.* **~-crop** *n.* охо́тничий хлыст; **~-ground** *n.* охо́тничье уго́дье; **happy ~-ground** (*fig., heaven*) рай, раздо́лье; **~-horn** *n.* охо́тничий рог.

huntress /ˈhʌntrɪs/ *n.* охо́тница.

huntsman /ˈhʌntsmən/ *n.* охо́тник; (*hunt official*) е́герь (*m.*).

hurdle /ˈhɜ:d(ə)l/ *n.* (*fence*) (переносна́я) огра́да; (*in athletics & fig.*) барье́р, препя́тствие.

● *v.t.* (*fence off*) огор|а́живать, -оди́ть.

● *v.i.* (*engage in ~-jumping*) уча́ствовать (*impf.*) в бе́ге с барье́рами.

hurdler /ˈhɜ:dlə(r)/ *n.* (*athlete*) барьери́ст (*fem.* -ка).

hurdy-gurdy /ˈhɜ:dɪˌgɜ:dɪ/ *n.* шарма́нка.

hurl /hɜ:l/ *v.t.* бр|оса́ть, -о́сить; швыр|я́ть, -ну́ть; **he ~ed abuse at me** он осы́пал меня́ оскорбле́ниями.

hurly-burly /ˈhɜ:lɪˌbɜ:lɪ/ *n.* переполо́х, сумя́тица.

hurr|ah /hʊˈrɑ:/, **-ay** /hʊˈreɪ/ *n. & int.* ура́!

● *v.i.* крича́ть (*impf.*) «ура́».

hurricane /ˈhʌrɪkən/, /-ˌkeɪn/ *n.* урага́н; **~ lamp** фона́рь «мо́лния».

hurried /ˈhʌrɪd/ *adj.* (*departure*) поспе́шный; (*glance*) бы́стрый; **he had a ~ meal** он на́скоро перекуси́л.

hurr|y /ˈhʌrɪ/ *n.* спе́шка, поспе́шность; **what's the ~y?** куда́/заче́м спеши́ть?; **there's no ~y!** спеши́ть не́куда; **she is always in a great ~y** она́ ве́чно торо́пится; **he was in no ~y to go** он не спеши́л уходи́ть; **in his ~y, he forgot his brief-case** в спе́шке он забы́л взять портфе́ль; **you won't need that again in a ~y** вам тепе́рь э́то не ско́ро пона́добится; **you won't beat that in a ~y** попро́буйте переплю́нуть э́то! (*coll.*).

● *v.t.* **1** (*cause to move hastily*) торопи́ть, по-; под|гоня́ть, -огна́ть; **if you ~y him, he'll make mistakes** е́сли вы бу́дете его́ торопи́ть/подгоня́ть, он наде́лает оши́бок. **2** (*perform hastily*): **don't ~y the job** рабо́тайте не спеша́.

● *v.i.* (*move hastily*) спеши́ть, по-; торопи́ться, по-; **he ~ied home** он спеши́л домо́й; **they ~ied to finish the work** они́ спеши́ли зако́нчить рабо́ту; **he ~ied over his breakfast** он поспе́шно съел свой за́втрак; **she ~ied down the road** она́ торопли́во (за)шага́ла вдоль у́лицы.

● *with advs.*: **~y along there, please!** потора́пливайтесь, пожа́луйста!; **you need not ~y back** не спеши́те возвраща́ться; **he ~ied away, off** он бы́стро удали́лся; **the boy was ~ied off to bed** ма́льчика бы́стро уложи́ли спать; **~y up!** потора́пливайтесь!; **can't you ~y him up?** ра́зве вы не мо́жете его́ потороп́ить?

hurt /hɜ:t/ *n.* (*offence*) оби́да, оскорбле́ние; (*damage*) вред, уще́рб; (*bodily injury*) уши́б.

● *v.t.* (*past and p.p.* **~**) (*inflict pain on*) ушиб|а́ть, -и́ть; причин|я́ть, -и́ть боль (+*d.*); **I won't ~ you** я вам не причиню́ бо́ли (*or* не сде́лаю бо́льно); **these shoes ~ (me)** э́ти ту́фли мне жмут; (*injure*) ушиб|а́ть, -и́ть; **he fell and ~ his back** он упа́л и уши́б спи́ну; **he was more frightened than ~** он не сто́лько уши́бся, ско́лько испуга́лся; **~ o.s.** ушиб|а́ться, -и́ться, ударя́ться, уда́риться; (*damage*) вреди́ть, по-; **it won't ~ this chair to get wet** от воды́ э́тому сту́лу ничего́ не бу́дет; (*offend, pain*) об|ижа́ть, -и́деть; зад|ева́ть, -е́ть; **she was deeply ~ by my remark** моё замеча́ние её о́чень оби́дело/заде́ло; **now you've ~ his feelings** ну вот, вы его́ и оби́дели; **a ~ expression** оби́женное/оскорблённое выраже́ние.

● *v.i.* (*past and p.p.* **~**) (*be sore*) боле́ть (*impf.*); **my arm ~s** у меня́ боли́т/но́ет рука́; **it didn't ~ a bit** ниско́лько не́бывало бо́льно; **where does it ~?** что/где у вас боли́т?; (*do damage*): **it wouldn't ~ to try it** (*coll.*) попы́тка не пы́тка; **it won't ~ to wait** не меша́ло бы подожда́ть.

hurtful /ˈhɜ:tfʊl/ *adj.* оби́дный.

hurtle /ˈhɜ:t(ə)l/ *v.t. & i.* нести́сь (*impf.*), мча́ться (*impf.*).

H

husband /ˈhʌzbənd/ *n.* муж (*pl.* -ья́).
● *v.t.* бере́чь (*impf.*); **we must ~ our resources** мы должны́ бере́чь/эконо́мить на́ши ресу́рсы.

husbandry /ˈhʌzbəndrɪ/ *n.* **1** се́льское хозя́йство; **animal ~** скотово́дство. **2** (*management of resources*) веде́ние хозя́йства.

hush /hʌʃ/ *n.* молча́ние, тишь.
● *v.t.*: **she ~ed the baby to sleep** она́ убаю́кала ребёнка; **the scandal was ~ed up** сканда́л замя́ли.
● *v.i.*: **~!** (*as int.*) ти́ше!; молчи́те!
● *cpds.* **~-~** *adj.* (*coll.*) та́йный, засекре́ченный; **~-money** *n.* взя́тка за молча́ние.

husk /hʌsk/ *n.* шелуха́, скорлупа́.
● *v.t.* очища́ть, очи́стить; лущи́ть, об-.

huskiness /ˈhʌskɪnɪs/ *n.* (*hoarseness*) хрипова́тость.

husky[1] /ˈhʌskɪ/ *n.* (*Eskimo dog*) эскимо́сская ла́йка.

husky[2] /ˈhʌskɪ/ *adj.* (**huskier, huskiest**) **1** (*hoarse*) сухо́й, хри́плый. **2** (*coll., brawny*) ро́слый, здоро́вый.

hussar /hʊˈzɑː(r)/ *n.* гуса́р.

hussy /ˈhʌsɪ/ *n.* (*pert girl*) де́рзкая девчо́нка; (*trollop*) шлю́ха, потаску́ха.

hustings /ˈhʌstɪŋz/ *n. pl.* предвы́борные ми́тинги (*m. pl.*).

hustle /ˈhʌs(ə)l/ *n.* су́толока, да́вка.
● *v.t.* **1** (*jostle*) толка́ть (*impf.*); пиха́ть (*impf.*); **he ~d his way through the crowd** он протолка́лся че́рез толпу́. **2** (*thrust, impel*) увол|а́кивать, -о́чь; **the police ~d him away** его́ уволокли́ полице́йские.
● *v.i.* (*jostle*) толка́ться (*impf.*); проти́скиваться (*impf.*); (*try to obtain something*): **he was hustling for work** он выпра́шивал рабо́ту.

hustler /ˈhʌslə(r)/ *n.* (*enterprising person*) пробивно́й челове́к; (*coll., prostitute*) проститу́тка.

hut /hʌt/ *n.* (*small building*) хи́жина; (*barrack*) бара́к.

hutch /hʌtʃ/ *n.* (*for pets*) кле́тка.

hyacinth /ˈhaɪəsɪnθ/ *n.* гиаци́нт.

hybrid /ˈhaɪbrɪd/ *n.* гибри́д.
● *adj.* гибри́дный; сме́шанный.

hybridization /ˌhaɪbrɪdaɪˈzeɪʃ(ə)n/ *n.* гибридиза́ция, скре́щивание.

hybridize /ˈhaɪbrɪˌdaɪz/ *v.t.* скре́|щивать, -сти́ть; гибридизи́ровать (*impf.*).

hydra /ˈhaɪdrə/ *n.* ги́дра.

hydrangea /haɪˈdreɪndʒə/ *n.* горте́нзия.

hydrant /ˈhaɪdrənt/ *n.* гидра́нт.

hydrate /ˈhaɪdreɪt/ *n.* гидра́т, гидро́окись.
● *v.t.* гидрати́ровать (*impf., pf.*).

hydraulic /haɪˈdrɔːlɪk/, /-ˈdrɒlɪk/ *adj.* гидравли́ческий.

hydraulics /haɪˈdrɔːlɪks/, /-ˈdrɒlɪks/ *n.* гидра́влика.

hydrocarbon /ˌhaɪdrəʊˈkɑːbən/ *n.* углеводоро́д.

hydrocephalus /ˌhaɪdrəˈsefələs/, **hydrocephaly** /ˌhaɪdrəˈsefəlɪ/ *nn.* водя́нка головно́го мо́зга, гидроцефа́лия.

hydrochloric /ˌhaɪdrəˈklɔːrɪk/, /-ˈklɒrɪk/ *adj.*: **~ acid** соля́ная кислота́.

hydrodynamic /ˌhaɪdrəʊdaɪˈnæmɪk/ *adj.* гидродинами́ческий.

hydroelectric /ˌhaɪdrəʊɪˈlektrɪk/ *adj.* гидроэлектри́ческий; **~ power station** гидроэлектроста́нция (*abbr.* ГЭС).

hydrofoil /ˈhaɪdrəˌfɔɪl/ *n.* су́дно на подво́дных кры́льях (*abbr.* СПК); раке́та.

hydrogen /ˈhaɪdrədʒ(ə)n/ *n.* водоро́д; **~ bomb** водоро́дная бо́мба.

hydrographer /haɪˈdrɒɡrəfə(r)/ *n.* гидро́граф.

hydrographic /ˌhaɪdrəˈɡræfɪk/ *adj.* гидрографи́ческий.

hydrography /haɪˈdrɒɡrəfɪ/ *n.* гидрогра́фия.

hydrolysis /haɪˈdrɒlɪsɪs/ *n.* гидро́лиз.

hydrometer /haɪˈdrɒmɪtə(r)/ *n.* гидро́метр, водоме́р.

hydrophobia /ˌhaɪdrəˈfəʊbɪə/ *n.* водобоя́знь.

hydrophone /ˈhaɪdrəˌfəʊn/ *n.* гидрофо́н.

hydroplane /ˈhaɪdrəˌpleɪn/ *n.* гидросамолёт.

hydroxide /haɪˈdrɒksaɪd/ *n.* гидро́окись, гидра́т о́киси.

hyena /haɪˈiːnə/ *n.* гие́на.

hygiene /ˈhaɪdʒiːn/ *n.* гигие́на.

hygienic /haɪˈdʒiːnɪk/ *adj.* гигиени́ческий.

hygrometer /haɪˈɡrɒmɪtə(r)/ *n.* гигро́метр

hymen /ˈhaɪmen/ *n.* (*anat.*) де́вственная плева́.

hymn /hɪm/ *n.* (церко́вный) гимн.
● *v.t.*: **he insists on ~ing my praises** он не перестаёт петь мне дифира́мбы.
● *cpd.* **~-book** *n.* (*also* **hymnal**) сбо́рник церко́вных ги́мнов.

hype /haɪp/ *n.* (*coll.*) крикли́вая рекла́ма.
● *adj.*: **~d-up** ду́тый, ли́повый.

hyperactive /ˌhaɪpəˈræktɪv/ *adj.* чрезме́рно акти́вный.

hyperactivity /ˌhaɪpəræk'tɪvɪtɪ/ *n.* повы́шенная акти́вность.

hyperbo|la /haɪˈpɜːbələ/ *n.* (*pl.* **~las** *or* **~lae** /-ˌliː/) (*geom.*) гипе́рбола.

hyperbole /haɪˈpɜːbəlɪ/ *n.* гипе́рбола, преувеличе́ние.

hyperbolical /ˌhaɪpəˈbɒlɪk(ə)l/ *adj.* гиперболи́ческий, преувели́ченный.

hypercritical /ˌhaɪpəˈkrɪtɪk(ə)l/ *adj.* въе́дливый, приди́рчивый.

hyperglycaemia /ˌhaɪpəɡlaɪˈsiːmɪə/ (*US* **hyperglycemia**) *n.* гипергликеми́я.

hyperinflation /ˌhaɪpərɪnˈfleɪʃ(ə)n/ *n.* гиперинфля́ция.

hypermarket /ˈhaɪpəˌmɑːkɪt/ *n.* (*Br.*) кру́пный универса́м (*в пригороде*).

hypersensitive /ˌhaɪpəˈsensɪtɪv/ *adj.* с повы́шенной чувстви́тельностью.

hyperspace /ˈhaɪpəˌspeɪs/ *n.* гиперпростра́нство.

hypertension /ˌhaɪpəˈtenʃ(ə)n/ *n.* (*med.*) высо́кое кровяно́е давле́ние.

hypertext /ˈhaɪpəˌtekst/ *n.* (*comput.*) гиперте́кст.

hypertrophy /haɪˈpɜːtrəfɪ/ *n.* гипертрофи́я.

hyphen /ˈhaɪf(ə)n/ *n.* дефи́с, чёрточка (*coll.*).
● *v.t.*: **a ~ed word** сло́во, пи́шущееся че́рез дефи́с/чёрточку.

hyphenate /ˈhaɪfəˌneɪt/ *v.t.* писа́ть, на- че́рез дефи́с/чёрточку.

hypnosis /hɪpˈnəʊsɪs/ *n.* гипно́з.

hypnotic /hɪpˈnɒtɪk/ *n.* (*subject*) загипнотизи́рованный; (*drug*) гипноти́ческое сре́дство.
● *adj.* гипноти́ческий.

hypnotism /ˈhɪpnəˌtɪz(ə)m/ *n.* гипноти́зм.

hypnotist /ˈhɪpnətɪst/ *n.* гипнотизёр.

hypnotize /ˈhɪpnəˌtaɪz/ *v.t.* гипнотизи́ровать, за-.

hypoallergenic /ˌhaɪpəʊˌæləˈdʒenɪk/ *adj.* с пони́женным содержа́нием аллерге́нов.

hypochondria /ˌhaɪpəˈkɒndrɪə/ *n.* ипохо́ндрия.

hypochondriac /ˌhaɪpəˈkɒndrɪˌæk/ *n.* ипохо́ндрик.
● *adj.* ипохондри́ческий.

hypocrisy /hɪˈpɒkrɪsɪ/ *n.* лицеме́рие.

hypocrite /ˈhɪpəkrɪt/ *n.* лицеме́р.

hypocritical /ˌhɪpəˈkrɪtɪk(ə)l/ *adj.* лицеме́рный, неи́скренний.

hypodermic /ˌhaɪpəˈdɜːmɪk/ *adj.*: **~ injection** подко́жное впры́скивание; подко́жная инъе́кция; **~ syringe/needle** шприц/игла́ для подко́жных инъе́кций.

hypotenuse /haɪˈpɒtəˌnjuːz/ *n.* гипотену́за.

hypothecate /haɪˈpɒθɪˌkeɪt/ *v.t.* за|кла́дывать, -ложи́ть.

hypothermia /ˌhaɪpəʊˈθɜːmɪə/ *n.* гипотерми́я.

hypothesis /haɪˈpɒθɪsɪs/ *n.* (*pl.* **hypotheses** /-ˌsiːz/) гипо́теза.

hypothesize /haɪˈpɒθɪˌsaɪz/ *v.i.* предпол|ага́ть, -ожи́ть; стро́ить (*impf.*) дога́дки.

hypothetical /ˌhaɪpəˈθetɪk(ə)l/ *adj.* гипотети́ческий.

hyssop /ˈhɪsəp/ *n.* иссо́п.

hysterectomy /ˌhɪstəˈrektəmɪ/ *n.* удале́ние ма́тки.

hysteria /hɪˈstɪərɪə/ *n.* истери́я.

hysterical /hɪˈsterɪk(ə)l/ *adj.* истери́чный; **she was ~** она́ была́ в исте́рике.

hysterics /hɪˈsterɪks/ *n.* исте́рика.

Hz (*abbr. of* **hertz**) Гц (герц).

Ii

I /aɪ/ *pron.* (*obj.* **me**) я; **it is ~** э́то я; **he and ~ were there** мы с ним бы́ли там; **~ too** и я то́же; **he is older than ~** он ста́рше меня́.

iambi /aɪ'æmbaɪ/ *pl. of* ⇒**iambus**

iambic /aɪ'æmbɪk/ *n.* ямби́ческий стих.
● *adj.* ямби́ческий.

iam|bus /aɪ'æmbəs/ *n.* (*pl.* **~buses** *or* **~bi**) ямб.

Iberia /aɪ'bɪərɪə/ *n.* (*peninsula*) Ибе́рия.

Iberian /aɪ'bɪərɪən/ *n.* ибе́р (*fem.* -ка).
● *adj.* ибери́йский.

ibex /'aɪbeks/ *n.* (*pl.* **~es**) ка́менный козёл, козеро́г.

ibid(em) /'ɪbɪ,dem/ *adj.* там же, в том же ме́сте.

ibis /'aɪbɪs/ *n.* (*pl.* **~es**) и́бис.

ICBM (*abbr. of* ***intercontinental ballistic missile***) МБР (межконтинента́льная баллисти́ческая раке́та).

ice /aɪs/ *n.* **1** лёд; **black ~** гололе́дица; **he broke the ~** (*lit., fig.*) он слома́л/разби́л лёд; **that cuts no ~ with me** э́то меня́ ниско́лько не впечатля́ет; **he is skating on thin ~** (*fig.*) он игра́ет с огнём; **the proposal was kept on ~** прое́кт заморо́зили; **~ age** ледниќовый пери́од.
2 (*Br.*, *~-cream*) моро́женое; **do they sell ~s?** продаётся ли моро́женое?
● *v.t.* **1** (*freeze; of wine, coffee etc., chill*) замор|а́живать, -о́зить.
2 (*cover with ~*): **the pond was soon ~d over** пруд вско́ре затяну́ло/скова́ло льдом.
3 (*cul.*) глазирова́ть (*impf., pf.*).
● *cpds.* **~-axe** *n.* ледору́б; **~-blink** *n.* ледяно́й о́тблеск; **~-boat** *n.* бу́ер; **~bound** *adj.* затёртый/ско́ванный льда́ми; **~-box** *n.* ле́дник, холоди́льник; **~breaker** *n.* ледоко́л; **~-bucket** *n.* ведёрко со льдом; (*for making ~-cream*) моро́женица; **~-cap** *n.* леднико́вый покро́в, ледни́к; **~-cold** *adj.* ледяно́й; **~-cream** *n.* моро́женое; **~-cream man** моро́женщик; **~-cream maker** (*appliance*) моро́женица; **~-cream parlour** кафе́-моро́женое; **~-cube** *n.* ку́бик льда; **~field** *n.* ледяно́е по́ле; **~-floe** *n.* плаву́чая льди́на; **~-hockey** *n.* хокке́й (на льду); **~-house** *n.* льдохрани́лище; **~-lolly** *n.* (*Br. coll.*) моро́женое на па́лочке; **~man** *n.* (*US*) разво́зчик/продаве́ц льда; **~-pack** *n.* (*pack~*) ледяно́й пак, торо́систый лёд; (*med.*) пузы́рь со льдом; **~-pick** *n.* кайла́; (*cul.*) пешня́ для льда; **~-rink** *n.* като́к; **~-run** *n.* ледяна́я го́рка; **~-show** *n.* бале́т на льду; **~-skate** *n.* конёк; *v.i.* ката́ться (*impf.*) на конька́х; **~-yacht** *n.* бу́ер.

iceberg /'aɪsbɜːg/ *n.* а́йсберг.

Iceland /'aɪslənd/ *n.* Исла́ндия.

Icelander /'aɪsləndə(r)/ *n.* исла́нд|ец (*fem.* -ка).

Icelandic /aɪs'lændɪk/ *n.* исла́ндский язы́к.
● *adj.* исла́ндский.

ichneumon /ɪk'njuːmən/ *n.* **1** (*animal*) ихневмо́н; фарао́нова мышь.
2 (*insect*) (*also* **~ fly** *or* **~ wasp**) нае́здник.

ichthyological /,ɪkθɪə'lɒdʒɪk(ə)l/ *adj.* ихтиологи́ческий.

ichthyologist /,ɪkθɪ'ɒlədʒɪst/ *n.* ихтио́лог.

ichthyology /,ɪkθɪ'ɒlədʒɪ/ *n.* ихтиоло́гия.

ichthyosaurus /,ɪkθɪə'sɔːrəs/ *n.* ихтиоза́вр.

icicle /'aɪsɪk(ə)l/ *n.* сосу́лька.

icing /'aɪsɪŋ/ *n.* (*on cake*) са́харная глазу́рь; (*action*) глазиро́вка; (**~-up**) обледене́ние.

icon, ikon /'aɪkɒn/ *n.* ико́на; о́браз (*pl.* -а́); (*comput.*) ико́нка, пиктогра́мма; **~ lamp** лампа́д(к)а.

iconoclasm /aɪ'kɒnə,klæz(ə)m/ *n.* иконобо́рство.

iconoclast /aɪ'kɒnə,klæst/ *n.* иконобо́рец; (*fig.*) бунта́рь (*m.*).

iconoclastic /aɪ,kɒnə'klæstɪk/ *adj.* (*fig.*) иконобо́рческий.

iconography /,aɪkə'nɒgrəfɪ/ *n.* иконогра́фия.

iconostasis /,aɪkə'nɒstəsɪs/, /aɪ,kɒnə'stæsɪs/ *n.* (*pl.* **iconostases** /-,siːz/) иконоста́с.

icy /'aɪsɪ/ *adj.* (**icier, iciest**) (*cold, lit., fig.*) ледяно́й; (*covered with ice*) покры́тый льдом.

ID (*abbr. of* ***identification***) удостовере́ние ли́чности; **have you got some ~?** у вас есть удостовере́ние ли́чности?

id /ɪd/ *n.* (*psych.*) ид.

idea /aɪ'dɪə/ *n.* **1** (*mental concept*) иде́я; **fixed ~** навя́зчивая иде́я; **he tried to force his ~s on me** он стара́лся навяза́ть мне свои́ иде́и; **where did you get that ~?** отку́да вы э́то взя́ли?
2 (*thought*) мысль; **I can't bear the ~ of it** (одна́) мысль об э́том мне проти́вна; **he is disturbed by the ~ of a possible accident** его́ беспоко́ит мысль о возмо́жной беде́; **don't put ~s into his head** не внуша́йте ему́ нену́жных иде́й; **the (very) ~ (of it)!** поду́мать то́лько!
3 (*notion; understanding*) поня́тие; **I've no ~** я поня́тия не име́ю; **he has little ~ of physics** у него́ сла́бое представле́ние о фи́зике; **I have a good ~ of his abilities** я прекра́сно представля́ю себе́, на что он спосо́бен; **he gave me a general ~ of the story** он в о́бщих черта́х пересказа́л мне расска́з.
4 (*scheme; plan*) иде́я, за́мысел, наме́рение; **a bright ~** блестя́щая иде́я; **a man (full) of ~s** челове́к, по́лный иде́й; **my ~ is to start afresh** я ду́маю нача́ть всё снача́ла; **what's the big ~?** (*coll.*) в чём смысл всего́ э́того?; э́то ещё заче́м?; **I studied Russian with the ~ of visiting Moscow** я изуча́л ру́сский язы́к с наме́рением съе́здить в Москву́; **that's the ~!** вот и́менно!; э́то то, что ну́жно!

ideal /aɪ'diːəl/ *n.* идеа́л.
● *adj.* идеа́льный; соверше́нный; превосхо́дный.

idealism /aɪ'dɪə,lɪz(ə)m/ *n.* идеали́зм.

idealist /aɪ'dɪəlɪst/ *n.* идеали́ст.

idealistic /aɪ,dɪə'lɪstɪk/ *adj.* идеалисти́ческий.

idealization /aɪˌdɪəlaɪˈzeɪʃ(ə)n/ *n.* идеализа́ция.

idealize /aɪˈdɪəˌlaɪz/ *v.t.* идеализи́ровать (*impf., pf.*).

idée fixe /ˌiːdeɪ ˈfiːks/ *n.* (*pl.* ***idées fixes*** *pronunc. same*) навя́зчивая иде́я, иде́я фикс.

idem /ˈɪdem/ *n.* тот же.

identical /aɪˈdentɪk(ə)l/ *adj.* **1** (*the same*): **the ~ room where he was born** та са́мая ко́мната, в кото́рой он роди́лся. **2** (*exactly similar*) тожде́ственный, иденти́чный; **the handwriting in the two manuscripts is ~** по́черк обе́их ру́кописей иденти́чен; **~ twins** однояйцо́вые близнецы́.

identification /aɪˌdentɪfɪˈkeɪʃ(ə)n/ *n.* **1** (*recognition; establishing identity*): **~ of a body** опозна́ние тру́па; **~ of a prisoner** установле́ние ли́чности арестóванного; (*attr.*) опознава́тельный; **~ marks** опознава́тельные зна́ки; **~ papers** докуме́нты, удостоверя́ющие ли́чность; **~ parade** (*Br.*) = **identity parade. 2** (*treating as identical*) отождествле́ние.

identif|y /aɪˈdentɪˌfaɪ/ *v.t.* **1** (*recognize; establish identity of*) опозн|ава́ть, -а́ть; выявля́ть, вы́явить; устан|а́вливать, -ови́ть ли́чность +*g.*; идентифици́ровать (*impf., pf.*). **2** (*treat as identical*) отождеств|ля́ть, -и́ть. **3** (*associate*), *also v.i.* (*coll.*): **he ~ied (himself) with the movement** он солидаризова́лся с э́тим движе́нием.

identikit /aɪˈdentɪkɪt/ *n.* (*propr.*): **an ~ (picture)** фоторо́бот (*подозреваемого преступника, сделанный по описаниям очевидцев*).

identity /aɪˈdentɪtɪ/ *n.* **1** (*sameness*) иденти́чность, тожде́ственность. **2** (*who one is*) ли́чность; **he proved his ~** он предста́вил удостовере́ние свое́й ли́чности; **a case of mistaken ~** (суде́бная/сле́дственная) оши́бка в установле́нии престу́пника *и т.п.*; **~ card** удостовере́ние ли́чности; **~ disc** (*Br.*) ли́чный знак; **~ parade** (*Br.*) процеду́ра опозна́ния подозрева́емого (свиде́телем и́ли пострада́вшим).

ideo|gram /ˈɪdɪəˌgræm/, **-graph** /ˈɪdɪəˌgrɑːf/ *nn.* идеогра́мма.

ideological /ˌaɪdɪəˈlɒdʒɪk(ə)l/ *adj.* идеологи́ческий, иде́йный.

ideologist /ˌaɪdɪˈɒlədʒɪst/ *n.* идео́лог.

ideology /ˌaɪdɪˈɒlədʒɪ/ *n.* идеоло́гия.

Ides /aɪdz/ *n.* и́д|ы (*pl., g.* —).

idiocy /ˈɪdɪəsɪ/ *n.* (*mental condition*) идиоти́зм; (*med.*) слабоу́мие; (*stupidity; stupid behaviour*) идио́тство.

idiom /ˈɪdɪəm/ *n.* (*expression*) идио́ма; (*language; way of speaking*) наре́чие, го́вор, язы́к; (*fig., style of writing etc.*) стиль (*m.*).

idiomatic /ˌɪdɪəˈmætɪk/ *adj.* идиомати́ческий; **he speaks ~ Russian** он свобо́дно владе́ет ру́сским языко́м; он говори́т по-ру́сски как ру́сский.

idiosyncrasy /ˌɪdɪəʊˈsɪŋkrəsɪ/ *n.* своеобра́зие.

idiosyncratic /ˌɪdɪəʊsɪŋˈkrætɪk/ *adj.* своеобра́зный.

idiot /ˈɪdɪət/ *n.* идио́т (*fem.* -ка), дура́к (*fem.* ду́ра); **a drivelling ~** зако́нченный идио́т, кру́глый дура́к; **don't be an ~** (*coll.*) не валя́йте дурака́; не дури́те.

idiotic /ˌɪdɪˈɒtɪk/ *adj.* идио́тский, дура́цкий.

idle /ˈaɪd(ə)l/ *adj.* (**idler, idlest**) **1** (*not working*) нерабо́тающий, безде́йствующий; (*unemployed*) безрабо́тный; **the strike made thousands ~** из-за забасто́вки ты́сячи люде́й оказа́лись без рабо́ты; (*unoccupied*) неза́нятый, свобо́дный; (*inactive*) безде́ятельный; **he stands ~ while others work** он безде́льничает, пока́ други́е рабо́тают; (*of factories etc.*) безде́йствующий; (*of machinery*) проста́ивающий; **the machines stood ~ all week** маши́ны простоя́ли це́лую неде́лю; (*of money*): **~ capital** мёртвый капита́л; (*of time*): **in an ~ moment** в свобо́дную мину́ту. **2** (*lazy; slothful*) пра́здный, лени́вый; **he leads an ~ existence** он ведёт пра́здную жизнь. **3** (*purposeless*): **out of ~ curiosity** из пра́здного/пусто́го любопы́тства; **~ talk** пуста́я болтовня́; **~ gossip** пусты́е спле́тни; (*fruitless; vain*): **an ~ attempt** тще́тная попы́тка; напра́сное уси́лие; **~ hopes** пусты́е/тще́тные наде́жды; **~ dreams** пусты́е мечты́.

● *v.t.*: **he ~d away his life** он растра́тил свою́ жизнь впусту́ю.

● *v.i.* **1** (*be ~*) безде́льничать (*impf.*); **stop idling about!** переста́ньте безде́льничать!; (*loiter*): **they ~d about the streets** они́ пра́здно слоня́лись по у́лицам. **2** (*of an engine*): **the motor ~s well** мото́р хорошо́ рабо́тает на холосто́м ходу́.

idleness /ˈaɪdəlnɪs/ *n.* пра́здность; безде́лье; **she lives in ~** она́ живёт в пра́здности; она́ ведёт пра́здную жизнь.

idler /ˈaɪdlə(r)/ *n.* безде́льник, лентя́й.

idly /ˈaɪdlɪ/ *adv.* лени́во; (*absently*) рассе́янно.

idol /ˈaɪd(ə)l/ *n.* и́дол, куми́р; **the ~ of the public** люби́мец пу́блики.

idolater /aɪˈdɒlətə(r)/ *n.* идолопокло́нни|к (*fem.* -ца).

idolatrous /aɪˈdɒlətrəs/ *adj.* идолопокло́ннический, обоготворя́ющий; (*fig.*) поклоня́ющийся (*кому-н.*).

idolatry /aɪˈdɒlətrɪ/ *n.* идолопокло́нство; (*fig.*) обожа́ние.

idolization /ˌaɪdəlaɪˈzeɪʃ(ə)n/ *n.* обоготворе́ние; (*fig.*) обожа́ние.

idolize /ˈaɪdəˌlaɪz/ *v.t.* обоготвор|я́ть, -и́ть; (*fig.*) боготвори́ть (*impf.*); обожа́ть (*impf.*).

idyll /ˈɪdɪl/ *n.* иди́ллия.

idyllic /ɪˈdɪlɪk/ *adj.* идилли́ческий.

i.e. (*abbr. of* **id est**) т.е. (то есть).

if /ɪf/ *n.*: **I want no ~s and buts** (я не хочу́ слы́шать) никаки́х отгово́рок; **there are no ~s about it** никаки́х «е́сли»!; **it is a very big ~** э́то ещё о́чень сомни́тельно.

● *conj.* **1** (*condition or supposition*) е́сли, е́сли бы; **~ he is reading** е́сли он чита́ет; **~ he were reading** е́сли бы он чита́л; **~ he comes** е́сли он придёт; **~ I were you** на ва́шем ме́сте; **~ necessary** е́сли необходи́мо; **~ so** е́сли/коль так; **~ anything she is more stupid than he** е́сли уж на то пошло́, она́ глупе́е его́; **~ only they arrive in time!** хоть бы они́ прие́хали во́время!; **~ only I had known!** е́сли бы я то́лько знал!; **~ only to please him** хотя́ бы для того́, что́бы доста́вить ему́ удово́льствие; **he talks as ~ he were the boss** он говори́т, как бу́дто он нача́льник; **he stood there as ~ dumb** он стоя́л, бу́дто немо́й; **as ~ by chance** бу́дто бы случа́йно; **as ~ you didn't know!** как бу́дто вы не зна́ли!; **it's not as ~ you had no money** друго́е де́ло, е́сли б у вас не́ было де́нег; **even ~** е́сли да́же. **2** (*though*) хотя́, пусть; **~ they are poor, they are nevertheless happy** хотя́ они́ и бедны́, они́ всё же сча́стливы; **a pleasant, ~ chilly, day** прия́тный, хотя́ и прохла́дный день. **3** (*whether*): **do you know ~ he is at home?** вы не зна́ете, он до́ма?; **see ~ the door is locked** посмотри́те, заперта́ ли дверь. **4** (*in excl.*): **~ I haven't lost my gloves again!** поду́мать то́лько, я опя́ть потеря́л перча́тки!

igloo /ˈɪgluː/ *n.* иглу́ (*nt. indecl.*).

igneous /ˈɪgnɪəs/ *adj.* (*of rock*) изве́рженный, пироге́нный; вулкани́ческого происхожде́ния.

ignite /ɪgˈnaɪt/ *v.t.* заж|ига́ть, -е́чь; воспламен|я́ть, -и́ть; (*fig.*) возбу|жда́ть, -ди́ть; разж|ига́ть, -е́чь.

● *v.i.* заж|ига́ться, -е́чься; воспламен|я́ться, -и́ться.

ignition /ɪgˈnɪʃ(ə)n/ *n.* (*igniting*) зажига́ние, воспламене́ние; (*~ system in engine*) зажига́ние; **~ key** ключ зажига́ния.

ignoble /ɪgˈnəʊb(ə)l/ *adj.* (**ignobler, ignoblest**) (*base*) по́длый, ни́зкий, посты́дный; (*of lowly birth*) ни́зкого происхожде́ния.

ignominious /ˌɪgnəˈmɪnɪəs/ *adj.* позо́рный, посты́дный; **an ~ death** бесла́вная смерть.

ignominy /ˈɪgnəmɪnɪ/ *n.* (*dishonour*) позо́р, бесче́стье.

ignoramus /ˌɪgnəˈreɪməs/ *n.* (*pl.* **~es**) неве́жда.

ignorance /ˈɪgnərəns/ *n.* (*in general*) неве́жество; **he displayed total ~** он обнару́жил по́лное неве́жество; (*of certain facts*) незна́ние, неве́дение; **he did it in ~ of the facts** он сде́лал э́то по незна́нию фа́ктов (*or* по неве́дению); **in a state of blissful ~** в состоя́нии блаже́нного неве́дения.

ignorant /ˈɪgnərənt/ *adj.* неве́жественный; **~ of music** несве́дущий в му́зыке; **I was ~ of his intentions** я не знал о его́ наме́рениях.

ignore /ɪg'nɔ:(r)/ *v.t.* игнори́ровать (*impf., pf.*); не обра|ща́ть, -ти́ть внима́ния на + *a.*

iguana /ɪg'wɑ:nə/ *n.* игуа́на.

ikon /'aɪkɒn/ = **icon**

ilk /ɪlk/ *n.*: **and others of his ~** (*coll.*) и други́е того́ же ро́да; и ему́ подо́бные.

ill /ɪl/ *n.* **1** (*evil, harm*) зло; **I meant him no ~** я не жела́л ему́ зла. **2** (*pl., misfortunes*) бе́ды (*f. pl.*), несча́стья (*nt. pl.*).

● *adj.* **1** (*unwell*) больно́й, нездоро́вый; **he looks ~** он вы́глядит больны́м; **he was taken (or fell) ~ with a fever** он заболе́л лихора́дкой; **I feel ~** мне нехорошо́; я пло́хо себя́ чу́вствую; **the mentally ~** психи́чески больны́е. **2** (*bad*): **~ effects** па́губные после́дствия; **~ fame, repute** дурна́я сла́ва; плоха́я репута́ция; **house of ~ fame** публи́чный дом; **~ feeling** неприя́знь, вражде́бность, оби́да; **I did it to show there was no ~ feeling** я сде́лал э́то, что́бы показа́ть, что я не пита́ю оби́ды; **~ fortune** несча́стье, неуда́ча; **~ health** нездоро́вье, недомога́ние; **~ humour** (*US* **humor**), **temper** (*disposition*) дурно́й нрав/хара́ктер; (*mood*) дурно́е настрое́ние; **in an ~ humour** (*US* **humor**) в раздраже́нии; **he had ~ luck** ему́ не повезло́; **as ~ luck would have it** как на зло; как на грех/беду́; по несча́стью; **a run of ~ luck** полоса́ невезе́ния; **~ omen** дурно́е предзнаменова́ние; **bird of ~ omen** (*fig.*) предве́стник беды́/несча́стья; **~ treatment** дурно́е обраще́ние; **~ will** зла́я во́ля, зло́ба; *see also* **~ feeling; I bear you no ~ will** я не жела́ю вам зла; **it's an ~ wind (that blows nobody any good)** нет ху́да без добра́.

● *adv.* пло́хо, ду́рно; **~ at ease** не по себе́; **to feel ~ at ease** чу́вствовать, по- себя́ нело́вко; **I can ~ afford it** я с трудо́м могу́ себе́ э́то позво́лить; **it ~ becomes you** э́то вам не идёт; **he behaved ~** (*liter.*) он (по)вёл себя́ пло́хо/ду́рно; **he took it ~ that ...** он оби́делся на то, что...; **it went ~ with him** ему́ не повезло́; **I have never spoken ~ of him** я никогда́ не отзыва́лся о нём пло́хо.

● *cpds.* **~-advised** *adj.* не(благо)разу́мный; **~-bred, ~-mannered** *adjs.* невоспи́танный, пло́хо воспи́танный; **~-considered, ~-judged** *adjs.* необду́манный; **~-defined** *adj.* неопределённый; **~-disposed** *adj.* (*malicious*) зло́бный, злонра́вный; (*unfavourable*) недоброжела́тельный (*к кому*); не располо́жен (*к кому*); **~-fated** *adj.* злосча́стный, рокова́й; **~-favoured** *adj.* (*US* **-favored**) (*in appearance*) непривлека́тельный, некраси́вый; **~-gotten** *adj.* нече́стно на́житый; **~-humoured** *adj.* (*US* **-humored**) дурно́го нра́ва, в дурно́м настрое́нии; **~-informed** *adj.* пло́хо осведомлённый; **~-intentioned** *adj.* злове́дный, злонаме́ренный; **~-judged** *adj.* = **~-considered; ~-mannered** *adj.* = **~-bred; ~-starred** *adj.* злосча́стный; **~-tempered** *adj.* вспы́льчивый, зло́бный; **~-timed** *adj.* несвоевре́менный; **~-treat, ~-use** *vv.t.* пло́хо об|ходи́ться, -ойти́сь с + *i.*; пло́хо обраща́ться (*impf.*) с + *i.*; **~-will** *n.* недоброжела́тельность, вражде́бность.

illegal /ɪ'li:g(ə)l/ *adj.* незако́нный, нелега́льный.

illegality /,ɪli:'gælɪtɪ/ *n.* незако́нность, нелега́льность.

illegibility /ɪ,ledʒɪ'bɪlɪtɪ/ *n.* неразбо́рчивость.

illegible /ɪ'ledʒɪb(ə)l/ *adj.* неразбо́рчивый.

illegitimacy /,ɪlɪ'dʒɪtɪməsɪ/ *n.* (*of action*) незако́нность; (*of birth*) незаконнорождённость.

illegitimate /,ɪlɪ'dʒɪtɪmət/ *adj.* (*of action*) незако́нный, нелегити́мный; (*of person*) незаконнорождённый.

illiberal /ɪ'lɪbər(ə)l/ *adj.* (*narrow-minded*) ограни́ченный; (*intolerant*) нетерпи́мый.

illiberality /ɪ,lɪbə'rælɪtɪ/ *n.* ограни́ченность; нетерпи́мость.

illicit /ɪ'lɪsɪt/ *adj.* незако́нный, недозво́ленный.

illiteracy /ɪ'lɪtərəsɪ/ *n.* негра́мотность, безгра́мотность.

illiterate /ɪ'lɪtərət/ *n.* негра́мотный; (*pej.*) не́уч.

● *adj.* (*esp. of person*) негра́мотный; (*esp. of writing*) безгра́мотный.

illness /'ɪlnɪs/ *n.* боле́знь; **he caught a serious ~** он зарази́лся тяжёлой боле́знью; **she had a long ~** она́ перенесла́ дли́тельную боле́знь; **he was absent through ~** он отсу́тствовал по боле́зни; (*ill-health*) нездоро́вье, сла́бое здоро́вье; (*incidence of ~*) заболева́емость; **has there been much ~ in your family?** страда́ли ли чле́ны ва́шей семьи́ серьёзными заболева́ниями?; (*onset of ~*) заболева́ние; **his ~ began with a chill** заболева́ние начало́сь с озно́ба.

illogical /ɪ'lɒdʒɪk(ə)l/ *adj.* нелоги́чный.

illogicality /ɪ,lɒdʒɪ'kælɪtɪ/ *n.* нелоги́чность.

illuminat|e /ɪ'lu:mɪ,neɪt/, /ɪ'lju:-/ *v.t.* **1** (*light*) осве|ща́ть, -ти́ть; **an ~ed sign** светя́щаяся рекла́ма. **2** (*decorate with lights*) иллюмини́ровать (*impf., pf.*); **the town was ~ed for the festival** к пра́зднику в го́роде устро́или иллюмина́цию. **3** (*of manuscripts etc.*) иллюмини́ровать (*impf., pf.*); **an ~ed manuscript** заста́вочная ру́копись. **4** (*shed light on; explain*) осве|ща́ть, -ти́ть; прол|ива́ть, -и́ть свет на + *a.*; **an ~ing talk** поучи́тельная бесе́да.

illumination /ɪ,lu:mɪ'neɪʃ(ə)n/, /ɪ,lju:-/ *n.* **1** (*lighting*) освеще́ние. **2** (*pl., decorative lights*) иллюмина́ция; **let's go and see the ~s** пойдёмте посмо́трим иллюмина́цию. **3** (*of manuscript*) заста́вка.

illumine /ɪ,lju:mɪn/, /ɪ'lu:-/ *v.t.* (*liter.*) **1** (*light up*) осве|ща́ть, -ти́ть; (*with sunshine, a smile etc.*) озар|я́ть, -и́ть. **2** (*enlighten*) просве|ща́ть, -ти́ть.

illusion /ɪ'lu:ʒ(ə)n/, /ɪ'lju:-/ *n.* иллю́зия, обма́н; **optical ~** опти́ческая иллю́зия, обма́н зре́ния; **I was under an ~** я был во вла́сти иллю́зии; **I have no ~s about him** относи́тельно его́ у меня́ нет никаки́х иллю́зий.

illusionist /ɪ'lu:ʒənɪst/, /ɪ'lju:-/ *n.* иллюзиони́ст, фо́кусник.

illus|ive /ɪ'lu:sɪv/,/ɪ'lju:-/, **-ory** /ɪ'lu:sərɪ/, /ɪ'lju:-/ *adjs.* иллюзо́рный, при́зрачный.

illustrate /'ɪlə,streɪt/ *v.t.* **1** (*decorate with pictures*) иллюстри́ровать (*impf., pf.*). **2** (*make clear by examples*) иллюстри́ровать (*impf., pf.*); поясн|я́ть, -и́ть; **this ~s the advantages of cooperation** э́то пока́зывает преиму́щества сотру́дничества.

illustration /,ɪlə'streɪʃ(ə)n/ *n.* (*act*) иллюстри́рование; (*picture, example*) иллюстра́ция; (*example*) поясне́ние.

illustrative /'ɪləstrətɪv/ *adj.* иллюстрати́вный, поясни́тельный; **a work ~ of his genius** произведе́ние, пока́зывающее его́ гениа́льность.

illustrator /'ɪlə,streɪtə(r)/ *n.* иллюстра́тор.

illustrious /ɪ'lʌstrɪəs/ *adj.* просла́вленный, знамени́тый.

image /'ɪmɪdʒ/ *n.* **1** (*representation*) изображе́ние. **2** (*statue*) ста́туя, скульпту́ра; **graven ~** и́дол, куми́р. **3** (*likeness; counterpart*) ко́пия, портре́т; **he was the ~ of his father** он был то́чной ко́пией (*or* живы́м портре́том) своего́ отца́. **4** (*idea; conception*) о́браз. **5** (*simile or metaphor*) о́браз; **he spoke in ~s** он говори́л о́бразно. **6** (*opt.*) изображе́ние; (*reflection*) отраже́ние. **7** (*impression made on others*) и́мидж, репута́ция.

imagery /'ɪmɪdʒərɪ/ *n.* (*in writing*) о́бразность.

imaginable /ɪ'mædʒɪnəb(ə)l/ *adj.* вообрази́мый; **we had the greatest trouble ~** у нас бы́ли невообрази́мые хло́поты.

imaginary /ɪ'mædʒɪnərɪ/ *adj.* вообража́емый, вы́мышленный; (*also math.*) мни́мый.

imagination /ɪ,mædʒɪ'neɪʃ(ə)n/ *n.* воображе́ние; **he let his ~ run riot** он дал во́лю своему́ воображе́нию; **use your ~!** напряги́те своё воображе́ние!

imaginative /ɪ'mædʒɪnətɪv/ *adj.* (*person*) одарённый/облада́ющий (больши́м/бога́тым) воображе́нием; (*literature*) худо́жественный; **~ writing** худо́жественная литерату́ра, беллетри́стика.

imagin|e /ɪ'mædʒɪn/ *v.t.* **1** (*form mental picture of*) вообра|жа́ть, -зи́ть; **she is always ~ing things** ей ве́чно что́-то мере́щится. **2** (*conceive*) предст|авля́ть, -а́вить себе́; **I cannot ~e how it happened** я не могу́ предста́вить себе́, как э́то случи́лось; **I ~e Peter to be tall** я представля́ю себе́ Петра́ высо́ким. **3** (*suppose*) предпол|ага́ть, -ожи́ть; полага́ть (*impf.*); **do you ~e I like it?** неуже́ли вы полага́ете, что мне э́то нра́вится?

4 (*think*) ду́мать, по-; **I ~ed I heard footsteps** мне показа́лось, что я слы́шал шаги́.
5 (*fancy*): **~e seeing you here!** кто бы мог поду́мать, что я уви́жу вас здесь?
6 (*guess*) дога́д|ываться, -а́ться; пон|има́ть, -я́ть; **I cannot ~e what you mean** ума́ не приложу́, что вы име́ете в виду́.

imam /ɪ'mɑ:m/ *n.* има́м.

imbalance /ɪm'bæləns/ *n.* отсу́тствие равнове́сия, неусто́йчивость; несоотве́тствие.

imbecile /'ɪmbɪ,si:l/ *n.* (*person of weak intellect*) крети́н; слабоу́мный; (*fool*) глупе́ц, дура́к (*fem.* ду́ра) (*coll.*).
● *adj.* слабоу́мный; (*stupid*) глу́пый.

imbecility /,ɪmbɪ'sɪlɪtɪ/ *n.* (*med.*) имбеци́льность, кретини́зм; слабоу́мие; (*stupidity*) глу́пость.

imbib|e /ɪm'baɪb/ *v.t.* (*drink*) погло|ща́ть, -ти́ть; пить, вы́-; (*fig., assimilate*) усв|а́ивать, -о́ить; впи́т|ывать, -а́ть; **he ~ed new ideas** он впита́л но́вые иде́и.

imbroglio /ɪm'brəʊlɪəʊ/ *n.* (*pl.* **~s**) пу́таница.

imbue /ɪm'bju:/ *v.t.* (**imbues, imbued, imbuing**) **1** (*lit., saturate*) пропи́т|ывать, -а́ть; (*dye*) окра́|шивать, -сить. **2** (*fig., inspire*) всел|я́ть, -и́ть (*что в кого*); (*fill*): **~d with hatred** прони́кнутый не́навистью.

IMF (*abbr. of* ***International Monetary Fund***) МВФ (Междунаро́дный валю́тный фонд).

imitate /'ɪmɪ,teɪt/ *v.t.* **1** (*follow example of*) подража́ть (*impf.*) + *d.*; **you should ~ his virtues** вы должны́ подража́ть его́ доброде́телям. **2** (*copy; mimic*) копи́ровать (*impf.*); имити́ровать (*impf.*); передра́зн|ивать, -и́ть.
3 (*make something similar to*) имити́ровать (*impf.*); подде́л|ывать, -ать; **fabric made to ~ silk** материа́л, имити́рующий шёлк.

imitation /,ɪmɪ'teɪʃ(ə)n/ *n.* **1** (*imitating; mimicry*) подража́ние; **in ~ of her teacher** в подража́ние своему́ учи́телю; **(built in) ~ Gothic** постро́енный в псевдоготи́ческом сти́ле; **he does bird ~s** он уме́ет подража́ть пти́цам. **2** (*copy*) имита́ция, подде́лка; **wood painted in ~ of marble** де́рево, окра́шенное под мра́мор; **beware of ~s!** остерега́йтесь подде́лок!; (*attr.*) иску́сственный, подде́льный; **~ leather** иску́сственная ко́жа; **~ antiques** подде́льные антиква́рные изде́лия.

imitative /'ɪmɪtətɪv/ *adj.*: **~ words** звукоподража́тельные слова́; **~ behaviour** (*Br.*), **behavior** (*US*) подража́тельное поведе́ние.

imitator /'ɪmɪ,teɪtə(r)/ *n.* подража́тель (*fem.* -ница).

immaculate /ɪ'mækjʊlət/ *adj.* **1** (*pure*) незапя́тнанный; **the I~ Conception** непоро́чное зача́тие. **2** (*faultless*) безупре́чный, безукори́зненный.

immanence /'ɪmənəns/ *n.* прису́щность; (*phil.*) имманéнтность.

immanent /'ɪmənənt/ *adj.* (*inherent*) прису́щий; (*pervading*) вездесу́щий; (*phil.*) имманéнтный.

immaterial /,ɪmə'tɪərɪəl/ *adj.* (*not corporeal*) невеще́ственный; (*unimportant*) несуще́ственный; **it is quite ~ to me** мне реши́тельно всё равно́.

immature /,ɪmə'tjʊə(r)/ *adj.* незре́лый.

immaturity /,ɪmə'tjʊərɪtɪ/ *n.* незре́лость.

immeasurable /ɪ'meʒərəb(ə)l/ *adj.* неизмери́мый.

immediacy /ɪ'mi:dɪəsɪ/ *n.* **1** (*directness*) непосре́дственность. **2** (*in time*) незамедли́тельность; (*urgency*) безотлага́тельность.

immediate /ɪ'mi:dɪət/ *adj.* **1** (*direct, closest possible*) непосре́дственный, прямо́й, ближа́йший; (*next in order*) очередно́й; **in the ~ neighbourhood** в непосре́дственной бли́зости; **my ~ neighbours** (*Br.*), **neighbors** (*US*) мой ближа́йшие сосе́ди; **on his ~ left** сра́зу нале́во от него́; **in the ~ future** в ближа́йшем бу́дущем. **2** (*without delay*) неме́дленный, мгнове́нный; **there was an ~ silence** наступи́ла мгнове́нная тишина́. **3** (*urgent*) безотлага́тельный.

immediately /ɪ'mi:dɪətlɪ/ *adv.* (*directly*) непосре́дственно; (*without delay, at once*) неме́дленно, то́тчас (же), сра́зу, мгнове́нно.
● *conj.* (*Br.*): **~ I heard the news** как то́лько я узна́л но́вости.

immemorial /,ɪmɪ'mɔ:rɪəl/ *adj.* незапа́мятный; **from time ~** с незапа́мятных времён.

immense /ɪ'mens/ *adj.* (*huge*) огро́мный, грома́дный; (*vast*) безме́рный, необозри́мый; (*coll., very great*): **it was an ~ disappointment** э́то бы́ло огро́мным разочарова́нием; **we enjoyed ourselves ~ly** мы получи́ли огро́мное удово́льствие; **she was ~ly proud of her son** она́ невероя́тно горди́лась свои́м сы́ном.

immensity /ɪ'mensɪtɪ/ *n.* безме́рность, необъя́тность.

immerse /ɪ'mɜ:s/ *v.t.* **1** погру|жа́ть, -зи́ть; окун|а́ть, -у́ть; **~d in thought** поглощённый мы́слями; **she ~d herself in a book** она́ погрузи́лась в чте́ние. **2** (*fig., entangle*) запу́т|ывать, -ать; **he was ~d in debt** он погря́з в долга́х.

immersion /ɪ'mɜ:ʃ(ə)n/ *n.* (*lit., fig.*) погруже́ние; **~ heater** погружа́емый нагрева́тель.

immigrant /'ɪmɪgrənt/ *n.* иммигра́нт (*fem.* -ка).

immigrate /'ɪmɪ,greɪt/ *v.i.* иммигри́ровать (*impf., pf.*).

immigration /,ɪmɪ'greɪʃ(ə)n/ *n.* иммигра́ция; **~ officer** сотру́дник иммиграцио́нного ве́домства (*or* иммиграцио́нной слу́жбы).

imminence /'ɪmɪnəns/ *n.* немину́емость.

imminent /'ɪmɪnənt/ *adj.* надвига́ющийся; **a storm was ~** надвига́лась гроза́; (*of danger*) непосре́дственный, нави́сший; (*departure*) бли́зкий, немину́емый.

immobile /ɪ'məʊbaɪl/ *adj.* неподви́жный.

immobility /,ɪməʊ'bɪlɪtɪ/ *n.* неподви́жность.

immobilization /ɪ,məʊbɪlaɪ'zeɪʃ(ə)n/ *n.* лише́ние подви́жности; остано́вка; (*med.*) иммобилиза́ция; (*of troops*) ско́вывание.

immobilize /ɪ'məʊbɪ,laɪz/ *v.t.* лиш|а́ть, -и́ть подви́жности; остан|а́вливать, -ови́ть; (*med.*) иммобилизова́ть (*pf.*); (*mil.*) ско́в|ывать, -а́ть; парализова́ть (*impf., pf.*); **our troops were ~d** на́ши войска́ бы́ли парализо́ваны; **I was ~d by a broken leg** я не мог дви́гаться из-за сло́манной ноги́.

immoderate /ɪ'mɒdərət/ *adj.* неуме́ренный.

immodest /ɪ'mɒdɪst/ *adj.* нескро́мный; (*indecent*) неприли́чный.

immodesty /ɪ'mɒdɪstɪ/ *n.* нескро́мность; (*indecency*) неприли́чие.

immolate /'ɪmə,leɪt/ *v.t.* (*lit., fig.*) прин|оси́ть, -ести́ в же́ртву.

immolation /,ɪmə'leɪʃ(ə)n/ *n.* жертвоприноше́ние.

immoral /ɪ'mɒr(ə)l/ *adj.* безнра́вственный, амора́льный; **~ earnings** сомни́тельные дохо́ды.

immorality /,ɪmə'rælɪtɪ/ *n.* безнра́вственность, амора́льность.

immortal /ɪ'mɔ:t(ə)l/ *n. & adj.* бессме́ртный; **~ fame** неувяда́емая сла́ва.

immortality /,ɪmɔ:'tælɪtɪ/ *n.* бессме́ртие.

immortalization /ɪ,mɔ:təlaɪ'zeɪʃ(ə)n/ *n.* увекове́чение.

immortalize /ɪ'mɔ:tə,laɪz/ *v.t.* увекове́чи|вать, -ть; обессме́ртить (*pf.*).

immovability /ɪ,mu:və'bɪlɪtɪ/ *n.* неподви́жность; (*steadfastness*) непоколеби́мость.

immovable /ɪ'mu:vəb(ə)l/ *n.* (*usu. pl.*) недви́жимость.
● *adj.* (*that cannot be moved; stationary; fixed, e.g. of property*) недви́жимый; (*motionless*) неподви́жный; недви́жимый; (*steadfast*) непоколеби́мый; (*emotionless*) невозмути́мый.

immune /ɪ'mju:n/ *adj.*: **~ system** имму́ная систе́ма; **~ to disease** невосприи́мчивый к боле́зни; **~ from criticism** неподвла́стный кри́тике; **~ from taxes** свобо́дный/освобождённый от нало́гов.

immunity /ɪ'mju:nɪtɪ/ *n.* **1** (*to disease etc.*) невосприи́мчивость, иммуните́т (*к чему*). **2** (*in law*) неприкоснове́нность, иммуните́т; **diplomatic ~** дипломати́ческий иммуните́т. **3** (*from tax*) освобожде́ние (от нало́га).

immunization /,ɪmju:naɪ'zeɪʃ(ə)n/ *n.* иммуниза́ция.

immunize /'ɪmju:,naɪz/ *v.t.*

иммунизи́ровать (*impf., pf.*) (*кого к чему*).

immunology /ˌɪmjuːˈnɒlədʒɪ/ *n.* иммуноло́гия.

immunotherapy /ˌɪmjuːnəʊˈθerəpɪ/ *n.* иммунотерапи́я.

immure /ɪˈmjʊə(r)/ *v.t.* заточ|а́ть, -и́ть; замуро́в|ывать, -а́ть; зап|ира́ть, -ере́ть; **he ~d himself in his study** он заперся́ в кабине́те.

immutability /ɪˌmjuːtəˈbɪlɪtɪ/ *n.* неизме́нность, непрело́жность.

immutable /ɪˈmjuːtəb(ə)l/ *adj.* неизме́нный, непрело́жный.

imp /ɪmp/ *n.* (*lit.; fig., mischievous child*) дьяволёнок, чертёнок, бесёнок; (*fig. only*) постре́л.

impact /ˈɪmpækt/ *n.* (*collision*) столкнове́ние; (*striking force*) уда́р, толчо́к; (*fig., effect, influence*) возде́йствие, влия́ние; **his words made an immediate ~** его́ слова́ возыме́ли неме́дленное де́йствие.

impacted /ɪmˈpæktɪd/ *adj.* (*med.*): **~ fracture** вколо́ченный перело́м; **~ tooth** ретини́рованный зуб.

impair /ɪmˈpeə(r)/ *v.t.* (*damage*) повре|жда́ть, -ди́ть; (*spoil*) по́ртить, ис-; (*undermine*) под|рыва́ть, -орва́ть; (*weaken*) осл|абля́ть, -а́бить; (*make worse*) ух|удша́ть, -у́дшить; **smoking will ~ your health** куре́ние подорвёт ва́ше здоро́вье; **his vision was ~ed** его́ зре́ние пострада́ло.

impairment /ɪmˈpeəmənt/ *n.* повреждéние; по́рча; подры́в; ослабле́ние; ухудше́ние.

impale /ɪmˈpeɪl/ *v.t.* прок|а́лывать, -оло́ть; пронз|а́ть, -и́ть; прот|ыка́ть, -кну́ть; (*hist.*) сажа́ть, посади́ть на́ кол; **he ~d himself on his sword** он пронзи́л себя́ мечо́м; **he fell and was ~d on the railings** он свали́лся на огра́ду и проткну́л себе́ живо́т.

impalpable /ɪmˈpælpəb(ə)l/ *adj.* (*not felt by touch*) неосяза́емый; (*by senses or mind*) неощути́мый; (*elusive*) неулови́мый.

impart /ɪmˈpɑːt/ *v.t.* **1** (*lend; give*) прид|ава́ть, -а́ть; **he ~ed a serious tone to the conversation** он прида́л разгово́ру серьёзный тон. **2** (*communicate, e.g. news*) перед|ава́ть, -а́ть; сообщ|а́ть, -и́ть. **3** (*pass on, e.g. knowledge*) дели́ться, по- + *i.*; **he ~ed his skill to us** он подели́лся с на́ми свои́м уме́нием.

impartial /ɪmˈpɑːʃ(ə)l/ *adj.* беспристра́стный.

impartiality /ɪmˌpɑːʃɪˈælɪtɪ/ *n.* беспристра́стность.

impassable /ɪmˈpɑːsəb(ə)l/ *adj.* (*on foot*) непроходи́мый; (*for vehicles*) непрое́зжий.

impasse /ˈæmpæs/, /ˈɪm-/ *n.* (*lit., fig.*) тупи́к; **things reached an ~** дела́ зашли́ в тупи́к.

impassioned /ɪmˈpæʃ(ə)nd/ *adj.* стра́стный, пы́лкий.

impassive /ɪmˈpæsɪv/ *adj.* (*unmoved*) бесстра́стный; (*serene*) безмяте́жный.

impassivity /ˌɪmpæˈsɪvɪtɪ/ *n.* бесстра́стие; безмяте́жность.

impasto /ɪmˈpæstəʊ/ *n.* (*art*) наложе́ние кра́сок густы́м сло́ем.

impatience /ɪmˈpeɪʃ(ə)ns/ *n.* нетерпе́ние, нетерпели́вость; (*irritation*) раздраже́ние.

impatient /ɪmˈpeɪʃ(ə)nt/ *adj.* нетерпели́вый; (*irritable*) раздражи́тельный, раздражённый; **he was growing, getting ~** он теря́л терпе́ние, он раздража́лся; **he is ~ of advice** он не те́рпит сове́тов; **she was ~ for a letter** она́ нетерпели́во ждала́ письма́; **he is ~ to begin** ему́ не те́рпится нача́ть.

impeach /ɪmˈpiːtʃ/ *v.t.* **1** (*accuse*) обвин|я́ть, -и́ть (*кого в чём*); подв|ерга́ть, -е́ргнуть импи́чменту; **he was ~ed (for treason)** ему́ предъяви́ли обвине́ние в госуда́рственной изме́не. **2** (*call in question*) осп|а́ривать, -о́рить; **are you ~ing my honour** (*Br.*), **honor** (*US*)? неуже́ли вы ста́вите под сомне́ние мою́ честь?

impeachment /ɪmˈpiːtʃmənt/ *n.* **1** (*accusation*) обвине́ние; (*on charge of treason etc.*) импи́чмент. **2** (*calling in question*) выраже́ние сомне́ния в + *p.* (*or* недове́рия + *d.*).

impeccability /ɪmˌpekəˈbɪlɪtɪ/ *n.* безупре́чность.

impeccable /ɪmˈpekəb(ə)l/ *adj.* безупре́чный.

impecuniosity /ˌɪmpɪˌkjuːnɪˈɒsɪtɪ/ *n.* безде́нежье.

impecunious /ˌɪmpɪˈkjuːnɪəs/ *adj.* безде́нежный, малообеспе́ченный.

impedance /ɪmˈpiːd(ə)ns/ *n.* (*elec.*) по́лное сопротивле́ние; импеда́нс.

impede /ɪmˈpiːd/ *v.t.* (*obstruct*) препя́тствовать (*impf.*) + *d.*; прегра|жда́ть, -ди́ть; (*delay*) задéрж|ивать, -а́ть; (*hinder*) меша́ть, по- (*кому/чему*); затрудн|я́ть, -и́ть; осложн|я́ть, -и́ть; **the traffic was ~d** у́личное движе́ние бы́ло заде́ржано; **negotiations were ~d** перегово́ры бы́ли затруднены́.

impediment /ɪmˈpedɪmənt/ *n.* **1** (*obstruction*) препя́тствие, прегра́да, поме́ха; (*hindrance, delay*) заде́ржка; **an ~ to progress** препя́тствие на пути́ прогре́сса. **2** (*speech defect*) заика́ние; **he has an ~ in his speech** он заика́ется; у него́ дефе́кт ре́чи.

impedimenta /ɪmˌpedɪˈmentə/ *n.* (*mil.*) обо́зы (*m. pl.*); (*baggage*) бага́ж.

impel /ɪmˈpel/ *v.t.* (**impelled, impelling**) **1** (*propel*) прив|оди́ть, -ести́ в движе́ние. **2** (*drive; force*) прин|ужда́ть, -у́дить; пон|ужда́ть, -у́дить; заст|авля́ть, -а́вить; побу|жда́ть, -ди́ть; **conscience ~led him to speak the truth** со́весть прину́дила его́ говори́ть пра́вду; **I feel ~led to say** я вы́нужден сказа́ть.

impend /ɪmˈpend/ *v.i.* **1** (*be imminent; approach*) надв|ига́ться, -и́нуться; прибл|ижа́ться, -и́зиться; **war was ~ing** война́ надвига́лась; **his ~ing arrival** его́ предстоя́щий прие́зд. **2** (*threaten*) угрожа́ть (*impf.*); нав|иса́ть, -и́снуть; **~ing danger** нави́сшая опа́сность/угро́за.

impenetrability /ɪmˌpenɪtrəˈbɪlɪtɪ/ *n.* (*lit., fig.*) непроница́емость.

impenetrable /ɪmˈpenɪtrəb(ə)l/ *adj.* непроница́емый; **an ~ forest** непроходи́мый лес; **an ~ mystery** непостижи́мая та́йна; **~ darkness** непрогля́дная тьма.

impenitent /ɪmˈpenɪt(ə)nt/ *adj.* нераска́янный, закосне́лый.

imperative /ɪmˈperətɪv/ *n.* (*gram.*) повели́тельное наклоне́ние, императи́в.

● *adj.* **1** (*urgent; essential*): **an ~ request** настоя́тельное тре́бование; **it is ~ that you come at once** вам необходи́мо то́тчас яви́ться. **2** (*imperious*) повели́тельный, вла́стный. **3** (*gram.*) повели́тельный.

imperceptible /ˌɪmpəˈseptɪb(ə)l/ *adj.* (*that cannot be perceived*) незаме́тный; (*very slight, gradual*) незначи́тельный.

imperfect /ɪmˈpɜːfɪkt/ *n.* (*gram.*) проше́дшее несоверше́нное вре́мя, импе́рфект.

● *adj.* (*faulty*) несоверше́нный, дефе́ктный; (*incomplete*) непо́лный; (*unfinished*) незако́нченный; (*gram.*) проше́дший несоверше́нный, имперфе́ктный.

imperfection /ˌɪmpəˈfekʃ(ə)n/ *n.* (*incompleteness, faultiness*) несоверше́нство, неполнота́; (*fault*) дефе́кт, изъя́н; недоста́ток.

imperfective /ˌɪmpəˈfektɪv/ *n. & adj.* (*gram.*) несоверше́нный (вид).

imperial /ɪmˈpɪərɪəl/ *adj.* **1** (*of an empire*) импе́рский; **~ Rome/Russia** Ри́мская/Росси́йская импе́рия. **2** (*of an emperor*) импера́торский; **the ~ crown** импера́торская коро́на; **His I~ Majesty** его́ импера́торское вели́чество. **3** (*majestic*) великоле́пный; **with ~ disdain** с ца́рственным презре́нием. **4** (*of Br. measures*) импе́рский, англи́йский.

imperialism /ɪmˈpɪərɪəˌlɪz(ə)m/ *n.* империали́зм.

imperialist /ɪmˈpɪərɪəlɪst/ *n.* империали́ст.

imperialist(ic) /ɪmˈpɪərɪəlɪst/, /ɪmˌpɪərɪəˈlɪstɪk/ *adj.* империалисти́ческий, империали́стский.

imperil /ɪmˈperɪl/ *v.t.* (**imperilled, imperilling;** *US* **imperiled, imperiling**) подв|ерга́ть, -е́ргнуть опа́сности; ста́вить, по- под угро́зу.

imperious /ɪmˈpɪərɪəs/ *adj.* (*domineering*) повели́тельный, вла́стный.

imperiousness /ɪmˈpɪərɪəsnɪs/ *n.* повели́тельность, вла́стность.

imperishable /ɪmˈperɪʃəb(ə)l/ *adj.* (*lit.*) непо́ртящийся; (*fig.*) нетле́нный.

impermanence /ɪmˈpɜːmənəns/ *n.* непостоя́нство.

impermanent /ɪmˈpɜːmənənt/ *adj.* непостоя́нный.

impermeability /ɪmˌpɜːmɪəˈbɪlɪtɪ/ *n.* непроница́емость.

impermeable /ɪmˈpɜːmɪəb(ə)l/ *adj.* непроница́емый.

impermissible /ˌɪmpəˈmɪsɪb(ə)l/ *adj.* непозволи́тельный, недозво́ленный.

impersonal /ɪmˈpɜːsən(ə)l/ *adj.* безли́чный.

impersonality /ɪmˌpɜːsəˈnælɪtɪ/ *n.* безли́чность.

impersonate /ɪmˈpɜːsəˌneɪt/ *v.t.* (*act the part of*) игра́ть (*impf.*) роль + *g.*; изобра|жа́ть, -зи́ть; (*pretend to be*) выдава́ть (*impf.*) себя́ за + *a.*

impersonation /ɪmˌpɜːsəˈneɪʃ(ə)n/ *n.* изображе́ние; **he gave an ~ of the professor** он изобрази́л профе́ссора.

impersonator /ɪmˈpɜːsəˌneɪtə(r)/ *n.* пароди́ст, имита́тор; **female ~** эстра́дный арти́ст, изобража́ющий же́нщину.

impertinence /ɪmˈpɜːtɪnəns/ *n.* де́рзость, на́глость, наха́льство.

impertinent /ɪmˈpɜːtɪnənt/ *adj.* де́рзкий, на́глый, наха́льный.

imperturbability /ˌɪmpəˌtɜːbəˈbɪlɪtɪ/ *n.* невозмути́мость.

imperturbable /ˌɪmpəˈtɜːbəb(ə)l/ *adj.* невозмути́мый.

impervious /ɪmˈpɜːvɪəs/ *adj.* непроница́емый; **~ to light** све́тонепроница́емый; (*fig.*): **~ to criticism** глух к кри́тике.

impetuosity /ɪmˌpetjʊˈɒsɪtɪ/ *n.* стреми́тельность, поры́вистость, необду́манность, горя́чность.

impetuous /ɪmˈpetjʊəs/ *adj.* (*moving violently*) стреми́тельный, поры́вистый; (*acting or done with rash energy*) стреми́тельный, поры́вистый; горя́чий; (*impulsive*) импульси́вный; (*unpremeditated*) необду́манный.

impetus /ˈɪmpɪtəs/ *n.* толчо́к; и́мпульс; **the car travelled** (*Br.*), **traveled** (*US*) **for several yards under its own ~** автомоби́ль прое́хал не́сколько ме́тров по ине́рции; (*fig.*) толчо́к, сти́мул; **this will give an ~ to trade** э́то даст торго́вле толчо́к.

impiety /ɪmˈpaɪətɪ/ *n.* не(благо)чести́вость.

impinge /ɪmˈpɪndʒ/ *v.i.* (**impinging**): **~ on** посяг|а́ть, -ну́ть на + *a.*; (*phys.*) ударя́ться (*impf.*) о + *a.*

impious /ˈɪmpɪəs/ *adj.* не(благо)чести́вый.

impish /ˈɪmpɪʃ/ *adj.* прока́зливый, озорно́й.

impishness /ˈɪmpɪʃnɪs/ *n.* прока́зливость, озорство́.

implacability /ɪmˌplækəˈbɪlɪtɪ/ *n.* неумоли́мость.

implacable /ɪmˈplækəb(ə)l/ *adj.* неумоли́мый, безжа́лостный.

implant *n.* /ˈɪmplɑːnt/ (*med.*) имплантáт.

● *v.t.* /ɪmˈplɑːnt/ (*med.*) вв|оди́ть, -ести́; вжив|ля́ть, -и́ть; импланти́ровать (*impf., pf.*); (*fig., instil*) внедр|я́ть, -и́ть; наса|жда́ть, -ди́ть, всел|я́ть, -и́ть; **he ~ed a doubt in her mind** он посе́ял в ней сомне́ние.

implausibility /ɪmˌplɔːzɪˈbɪlɪtɪ/ *n.* неправдоподо́бность, невероя́тность.

implausible /ɪmˈplɔːzɪb(ə)l/ *adj.* неправдоподо́бный, невероя́тный.

implement[1] /ˈɪmplɪmənt/ *n.* ору́дие, инструме́нт; **farm ~s** сельскохозя́йственные ору́дия.

implement[2] /ˈɪmplɪˌment/ *v.t.* выполня́ть, вы́полнить; осуществ|ля́ть, -и́ть; пров|оди́ть, -ести́ в жизнь; **when the scheme is ~ed** когда́ план бу́дет осуществлён.

implementation /ˌɪmplɪmenˈteɪʃ(ə)n/ *n.* выполне́ние, осуществле́ние.

implicate /ˈɪmplɪˌkeɪt/ *v.t.* вовл|ека́ть, -е́чь; вме́ш|ивать, -а́ть; заме́ш|ивать, -а́ть; впу́т|ывать, -ать; **the evidence ~d him** у́лики пока́зывали на его́ прича́стность; **I refuse to be ~d** я отка́зываюсь быть заме́шанным.

implication /ˌɪmplɪˈkeɪʃ(ə)n/ *n.* (*involvement*) вовлече́ние; (*implying; thing implied*) скры́тый смысл; намёк; **by ~** ко́свенно; **I do not like your ~** мне не нра́вится ваш намёк; (*significance*) значе́ние.

implicit /ɪmˈplɪsɪt/ *adj.* **1** (*implied*) подразумева́емый, недоска́занный; **~ threat** скры́тая угро́за; **~ consent** молчали́вое согла́сие; **~ in his statement was a denial** его́ заявле́ние подразумева́ло отка́з. **2** (*unquestioning*) безогово́рочный; **I have ~ belief in him** я безогово́рочно ве́рю в него́.

implore /ɪmˈplɔː(r)/ *v.t.* умол|я́ть, -и́ть; **he ~d my forgiveness** он моли́л меня́ о проще́нии.

imploringly /ɪmˈplɔːrɪŋlɪ/ *adv.* умоля́юще.

impl|y /ɪmˈplaɪ/ *v.t.* **1** (*of a person: suggest, hint at*) подразумева́ть (*impf.*); намека́ть (*impf.*) на + *a.*; **what are you ~ying by that?** что вы хоти́те э́тим сказа́ть?; **he ~ied that I was wrong** он намека́л на то (*or* дал поня́ть), что я не прав. **2** (*of a statement, action etc.*) подразумева́ть (*impf.*); (об)означа́ть (*impf.*); **what do his words ~y?** что означа́ют его́ слова́?; **I knew what was ~ied** я знал, что подразумева́лось; **silence ~ies consent** молча́ние — знак согла́сия.

impolite /ˌɪmpəˈlaɪt/ *adj.* неве́жливый.

impoliteness /ˌɪmpəˈlaɪtnɪs/ *n.* неве́жливость.

impolitic /ɪmˈpɒlɪtɪk/ *adj.* не(благо)разу́мный, неполити́чный.

imponderable /ɪmˈpɒndərəb(ə)l/ *adj.* (*fig.*) неулови́мый.

import[1] /ˈɪmpɔːt/ *n.* **1** (*bringing from abroad*) и́мпорт, ввоз; (*pl., goods introduced*) и́мпортные/ввози́мые/ввозны́е това́ры (*m. pl.*); (*attr.*) и́мпортный, привозно́й; **~ duty** ввозна́я по́шлина. **2** (*meaning*) значе́ние; (*importance*) ва́жность; **a matter of great ~** весьма́ ва́жное де́ло.

import[2] /ɪmˈpɔːt/, /ˈɪm-/ *v.t.* **1** (*bring in*) импорти́ровать (*impf., pf.*); вв|ози́ть, -езти́; **wheat is ~ed from abroad** пшени́ца вво́зится из-за грани́цы. **2** (*signify*) означа́ть (*impf.*).

importance /ɪmˈpɔːt(ə)ns/ *n.* значе́ние, значи́тельность, ва́жность; (*standing*) вес; **attach ~ to something** придава́ть (*impf.*) значе́ние чему́-н.; **it is of no ~** э́то не име́ет значе́ния; э́то незначи́тельно; **a person of some ~** ва́жное лицо́; ли́чность, име́ющая вес; **of little ~** малова́жный; **a matter of great ~** де́ло огро́мной ва́жности; **it is of the utmost ~ that ...** кра́йне ва́жно, что́бы. . .

important /ɪmˈpɔːt(ə)nt/ *adj.* значи́тельный, ва́жный; (*weighty*) ве́ский; **he went away on ~ business** он уе́хал по ва́жному де́лу; **~ people** ва́жные/влия́тельные лю́ди; **he likes to look ~** он лю́бит ва́жничать; **it is ~ for you to realize it** ва́жно, что́бы вы по́няли э́то; **more ~ly ...** что ещё бо́лее ва́жно. . .

importation /ˌɪmpɔːˈteɪʃ(ə)n/ *n.* и́мпорт, ввоз.

importer /ɪmˈpɔːtə(r)/ *n.* импортёр.

importunate /ɪmˈpɔːtjʊnət/ *adj.* назо́йливый, навя́зчивый, доку́чливый; **~ demands** настоя́тельные тре́бования.

importune /ɪmˈpɔːtjuːn/, /-ˈtjuːn/ *v.t.* докуча́ть (*impf.*) + *d.*; **he ~d me for a loan** он докуча́л мне про́сьбами о ссу́де.

importunity /ˌɪmpɔːˈtjuːnɪtɪ/ *n.* назо́йливость, навя́зчивость, доку́чливость, домога́тельство.

impose /ɪmˈpəʊz/ *v.t.* (*obligation*) возл|ага́ть, -ожи́ть (*что на кого*); (*tax, penalty etc.*) нал|ага́ть, -ожи́ть (*что на кого*); обл|ага́ть, -ожи́ть (*кого чем*); **the judge ~d a fine of 20 roubles** судья́ наложи́л штраф в 20 рубле́й; **the government ~d a tax on wealth** госуда́рство обложи́ло бога́тых нало́гом; **this will ~ a heavy burden on the people** э́то ля́жет тя́жким бре́менем на наро́д; **he ~d himself on our company** он навяза́лся/наби́лся к нам в компа́нию; **he ~s his views on everyone** он навя́зывает всем свои́ взгля́ды.

● *v.i.* **~ on** (*take advantage of*): **he ~s on his friends** он испо́льзует свои́х друзе́й.

imposing /ɪmˈpəʊzɪŋ/ *adj.* внуши́тельный, импоза́нтный, представи́тельный.

imposition /ˌɪmpəˈzɪʃ(ə)n/ *n.* **1** (*imposing of obligation, burden etc.*) возложе́ние, наложе́ние. **2** (*thing imposed; tax etc.*) обложе́ние, нало́г. **3** (*unreasonable demand*) чрезме́рное тре́бование.

impossibility /ɪmˌpɒsɪˈbɪlɪtɪ/ *n.* невозмо́жность.

impossible /ɪmˈpɒsɪb(ə)l/ *adj.* невозмо́жный; **don't ask me to do the ~** не тре́буйте от меня́ невозмо́жного; **an ~ person** невозмо́жный/несно́сный челове́к.

impost /ˈɪmpəʊst/ *n.* нало́г.

impostor /ɪmˈpɒstə(r)/ *n.* обма́нщи|к (*fem.* -ца); самозва́н|ец (*fem.* -ка).

imposture /ɪmˈpɒstʃə(r)/ *n.* обма́н; самозва́нство.

impotence /ˈɪmpət(ə)ns/ *n.* бесси́лие; (*sexual*) импоте́нция.

impotent /ˈɪmpət(ə)nt/ *adj.* бесси́льный; **he is ~** (*sexually*) он импоте́нт.

impound /ɪmˈpaʊnd/ *v.t.* (*cattle etc.*) заг|оня́ть, -на́ть; (*property*) конфискова́ть (*impf., pf.*).

impoverish /ɪmˈpɒvərɪʃ/ *v.t.* (*reduce to poverty*) обедн|я́ть, -и́ть; дов|оди́ть, -ести́ до бе́дности/обнища́ния; **become ~ed** бедне́ть, о-; ница́ть, об-; **~ed** (*adj.*) бе́дный, обедне́вший; обнища́вший, ни́щий; (*of soil; make barren*) истощ|а́ть, -и́ть; (*of health*) расстр|а́ивать, -о́ить; (*of ideas, style etc.*) обедн|я́ть, -и́ть; **an ~ed mind** убо́гий/ску́дный ум.

impoverishment /ɪmˈpɒvərɪʃmənt/ *n.* обедне́ние, обнища́ние; истоще́ние.

impracticability /ɪm,præktɪkəˈbɪlɪtɪ/ *n.* невыполни́мость, неисполни́мость, неосуществи́мость.

impracticable /ɪmˈpræktɪkəb(ə)l/ *adj.* нереа́льный, невыполни́мый, неосуществи́мый.

impractical /ɪmˈpræktɪk(ə)l/ *adj.* (*person*) непракти́чный; (*US*) = **impracticable**

imprecation /,ɪmprɪˈkeɪʃ(ə)n/ *n.* прокля́тие.

impregnability /ɪm,pregnəˈbɪlɪtɪ/ *n.* непристу́пность.

impregnable /ɪmˈpregnəb(ə)l/ *adj.* непристу́пный; (*fig.*): **an ~ argument** неопровержи́мый до́вод.

impregnate /ˈɪmpreg,neɪt/ *v.t.* (*fertilize*) оплодотвор|я́ть, -и́ть; (*saturate*) пропи́т|ывать, -а́ть; **~d wood** импрегни́рованная древеси́на.

impregnation /,ɪmpregˈneɪʃ(ə)n/ *n.* оплодотворе́ние; пропи́тывание.

impresario /,ɪmprɪˈsɑːrɪəʊ/ *n.* (*pl.* **~s**) импреса́рио (*m. indecl.*), антрепренёр.

impress[1] /ˈɪmpres/ *n.* (*lit., typ.*) о́ттиск; (*also fig.*) отпеча́ток, печа́ть; **his work bears the ~ of genius** его́ рабо́та несёт печа́ть ге́ния.

impress[2] /ɪmˈpres/ *v.t.* **1** (*make by imprinting*) отти́с|кивать, -нуть; вытисня́ть, вы́тиснить; (*fig., on the mind*) запечатл|ева́ть, -е́ть; внуш|а́ть, -и́ть (*кому*); **the words were ~ed on his memory** слова́ запечатле́лись в его́ па́мяти; **we ~ed on them the need for caution** мы внуши́ли им необходи́мость соблюда́ть осторо́жность. **2** (*make imprint on*) де́лать, с- отпеча́ток на + *p.*; (*fig., have a strong effect on*) произв|оди́ть, -ести́ впечатле́ние на + *a.*; **he did not ~ me at all** он не произвёл на меня́ никако́го впечатле́ния.

● *v.i.* произв|оди́ть, -ести́ впечатле́ние.

impression /ɪmˈpreʃ(ə)n/ *n.* **1** (*imprint*) отпеча́ток, о́ттиск; **his fingers left an ~** его́ па́льцы оста́вили отпеча́тки; **the dentist took an ~** зубно́й врач сде́лал сле́пок. **2** (*typ., copies printed*) тира́ж; (*Br., reprint*) печа́тание, перепеча́тка. **3** (*effect*) эффе́кт, результа́т; впечатле́ние; **make, create an ~** произв|оди́ть, -ести́ впечатле́ние. **4** (*notion*) впечатле́ние, представле́ние; **I have, get an ~ (*or* my ~ is) that he is not sincere** у меня́ сложи́лось впечатле́ние, что он неи́скренен; **I was under the ~ that ...** я полага́л, что...; **I have a strong ~ that ...** я почти́ уве́рен, что...; **one cannot rely on first ~s** нельзя́ доверя́ть пе́рвому впечатле́нию.

impressionable /ɪmˈpreʃənəb(ə)l/ *adj.* впечатли́тельный, восприи́мчивый; **she is at an ~ age** она́ о́чень впечатли́тельна — у неё тако́й во́зраст.

impressionism /ɪmˈpreʃə,nɪz(ə)m/ *n.* импрессиони́зм.

impressionist /ɪmˈpreʃənɪst/ *n.* **1** (*art*) импрессиони́ст. **2** (*mimic*) пароди́ст, имита́тор; (*attr.*) импрессиони́стский.

impressionistic /ɪm,preʃəˈnɪstɪk/ *adj.* импрессионисти́ческий, импрессиони́стский.

impressive /ɪmˈpresɪv/ *adj.* внуши́тельный, впечатля́ющий, си́льный; **an ~ speech** я́ркая речь; **an ~ scene** впечатля́ющая/волну́ющая карти́на.

imprest /ˈɪmprest/ *n.* ава́нс, подотчётная су́мма.

imprimatur /,ɪmprɪˈmeɪtə(r)/, /-ˈmuːtə(r)/, /-tʊə(r)/ *n.* (*eccl.*) разреше́ние (на печа́тание); (*fig., sanction*) са́нкция, одобре́ние.

imprint[1] /ˈɪmprɪnt/ *n.* (*lit., fig.*) отпеча́ток; (*fig.*) печа́ть; **publisher's ~** выходны́е да́нные (*nt. pl.*); **her face bore the ~ of sorrow** на её лице́ запечатле́лась грусть.

imprint[2] /ɪmˈprɪnt/ *v.t.* отпеча́т|ывать, -ать; вытисня́ть, вы́тиснить; (*fig.*) запечатл|ева́ть, -е́ть; **the words became ~ed on our minds** э́ти слова́ запа́ли нам в ду́шу; **he ~ed a kiss on her cheek** он запечатле́л поцелу́й на её щеке́.

imprison /ɪmˈprɪz(ə)n/ *v.t.* заключ|а́ть, -и́ть в тюрьму́; заточ|а́ть, -и́ть.

imprisonment /ɪmˈprɪzənmənt/ *n.* тюре́мное заключе́ние; заточе́ние; **he was sentenced to life ~** его́ приговори́ли к пожи́зненному заключе́нию.

improbability /ɪm,prɒbəˈbɪlɪtɪ/ *n.* неправдоподо́бие, невероя́тность.

improbable /ɪmˈprɒbəb(ə)l/ *adj.* неправдоподо́бный, невероя́тный.

improbity /ɪmˈprəʊbɪtɪ/ *n.* бесче́стность.

impromptu /ɪmˈprɒmptjuː/ *n.* (*pl.* **~s**) (*mus.*) экспро́мт.

● *adj.* импровизи́рованный.

● *adv.* экспро́мтом, без подгото́вки.

improper /ɪmˈprɒpə(r)/ *adj.* **1** (*unsuitable*) неподходя́щий, несоотве́тствующий; неуме́стный; **behaviour** (*Br.*), **behavior** (*US*) **~ to the occasion** поведе́ние, неподходя́щее к слу́чаю; **an ~ question** неуме́стный вопро́с. **2** (*incorrect*) непра́вильный; **~ fraction** непра́вильная дробь; **put something to ~ use** испо́льзовать что-н. не по назначе́нию. **3** (*unseemly, indecent*) неприли́чный, непристо́йный.

impropriety /,ɪmprəˈpraɪətɪ/ *n.* неуме́стность; непра́вильность; непристо́йность, неприли́чие.

improvable /ɪmˈpruːvəb(ə)l/ *adj.* поддаю́щийся улучше́нию.

improv|e /ɪmˈpruːv/ *v.t.* (*make better*) ул|учша́ть, -у́чшить; **~ing** (*edifying*) **literature** поучи́тельная литерату́ра; **he ~ed his French** он сде́лал успе́хи во францу́зском языке́.

● *v.i.* **1** (*become better*) ул|учша́ться, -у́чшиться; **wine ~es with age** вино́ улучша́ется с года́ми; **it will ~e with use** э́то бу́дет улучша́ться по ме́ре по́льзования; **things are ~ing** дела́ нала́живаются; **his health is ~ing** он (*or* его́ здоро́вье) поправля́ется. **2**: **~e on** (*produce something better than*): **I can ~e on that** я могу́ предложи́ть не́что лу́чшее; **he ~ed on my ideas** он разви́л да́льше мои́ мы́сли; **the design cannot be ~ed upon** моде́ль не поддаётся дальне́йшему улучше́нию.

improvement /ɪmˈpruːvmənt/ *n.* улучше́ние; **there has been an ~ in the weather** пого́да улу́чшилась; **your writing is in need of ~** вам сле́дует испра́вить ваш по́черк; **there is room for ~** могло́ бы быть лу́чше; **this is an ~ on your first attempt** ва́ша втора́я попы́тка значи́тельно лу́чше пе́рвой; (*rebuilding etc.*) перестро́йка; перестано́вка; **he is carrying out ~s on his house** он за́нят усоверше́нствованием своего́ до́ма.

improvidence /ɪmˈprɒvɪd(ə)ns/ *n.* непредусмотри́тельность; расточи́тельность, небережли́вость.

improvident /ɪmˈprɒvɪd(ə)nt/ *adj.* (*heedless of the future*) непредусмотри́тельный; (*wasteful*) расточи́тельный, небережли́вый.

improvisation /,ɪmprəvaɪˈzeɪʃ(ə)n/ *n.* импровиза́ция.

improvise /ˈɪmprə,vaɪz/ *v.t. & i.* (*music, speech etc.*) импровизи́ровать (*impf.*); (*arrange as makeshift*) мастери́ть, с-; **she ~d a bed on the floor** она́ соору́дила посте́ль на полу́; **an ~d dinner** импровизи́рованный у́жин.

imprudence /ɪmˈpruːd(ə)ns/ *n.* опроме́тчивость, неблагоразу́мие, неосторо́жность.

imprudent /ɪmˈpruːd(ə)nt/ *adj.* опроме́тчивый, неблагоразу́мный, неосторо́жный.

impudence /ˈɪmpjʊd(ə)ns/ *n.* де́рзость; бессты́дство; наха́льство; на́глость.

impudent /ˈɪmpjʊd(ə)nt/ *adj.* (*audacious*) де́рзкий; (*shameless*) бессты́дный; (*insolent*) наха́льный, на́глый; **an ~ fellow** наха́л, нагле́ц.

impugn /ɪmˈpjuːn/ *v.t.* осп|а́ривать, -о́рить; **he ~ed my honesty** он подве́рг мою́ че́стность сомне́нию.

impulse /ˈɪmpʌls/ *n.* (*lit., phys.*) толчо́к; (*elec.*) и́мпульс; (*fig., impetus, stimulus*): **the war gave an ~ to trade** война́ дала́ толчо́к торго́вле; **he lost all ~ to work** он потеря́л вся́кое влече́ние к рабо́те.

impulsion /ɪmˈpʌlʃ(ə)n/ *n.* толчо́к, побужде́ние, и́мпульс.

impulsive /ɪmˈpʌlsɪv/ *adj.* импульси́вный.

impunity /ɪmˈpjuːnɪtɪ/ *n.*: **with ~** безнака́занно.

I

impure /ɪmˈpjʊə(r)/ *adj.* нечи́стый, гря́зный; (*indecent*) непристо́йный.

impurity /ɪmˈpjʊərɪtɪ/ *n.* нечистота́, грязь; (*unchastity*) нечистопло́тность; (*pl., foreign substances*) при́меси (*f. pl.*).

imputable /ɪmˈpju:təb(ə)l/ *adj.* припи́сываемый.

imputation /ˌɪmpju:ˈteɪʃ(ə)n/ *n.* **1** (*imputing, ascription*) вмене́ние в вину́; обвине́ние, припи́сывание; **he could not avoid the ~ of dishonesty** он не мог избежа́ть подозре́ния в бесче́стности. **2** (*aspersion*) тень, пятно́; **~s were cast on his character** на его́ репута́цию была́ бро́шена тень.

impute /ɪmˈpju:t/ *v.t.* вмен|я́ть, -и́ть; припи́с|ывать, -а́ть; **the faults ~d to him** недоста́тки, припи́сываемые ему́.

in /ɪn/ *n.*: **he knew all the ~s and outs of the affair** он знал все то́нкости де́ла.

● *adj.* (*coll., fashionable*) популя́рный, мо́дный; **he knows all the '~' people** он зна́ет всех ну́жных люде́й.

● *adv.* **1** (*at home*) до́ма; **tell them I'm not ~** скажи́те, что меня́ нет до́ма; (*in one's office etc.*): **the boss is not ~ yet** нача́льника (в кабине́те) ещё нет; **he has been ~ and out all day** он весь день то приходи́л, то уходи́л. **2** (*arrived at station, port etc.*): **the train has been ~ (for) 10 minutes** по́езд пришёл 10 мину́т тому́ наза́д. **3** (*inside*) внутри́, внутрь; **he wore a coat with the fur side ~** он носи́л пальто́ ме́хом вовну́трь. **4** (*harvested*): **the crops were ~** урожа́й был со́бран. **5** (*available for purchase*): **strawberries are ~** начался́ сезо́н клубни́ки. **6** (*in fashion*): **short skirts are ~ again** коро́ткие ю́бки опя́ть в мо́де. **7** (*in power*): **which party was ~ then?** кака́я па́ртия была́ тогда́ у вла́сти? **8** (*burning*): **is the fire still ~?** ками́н ещё гори́т? **9** (*batting*): **England were ~ all day** кома́нда А́нглии отбива́ла мяч весь день. **10**: **day ~, day out** изо дня в день. **11** (*involved*): **count me ~!** включи́те и меня́!; **he was ~ at, from the start** он принима́л уча́стие с са́мого нача́ла. **12** (*with preps.*): **we are ~ for a storm** грозы́ не минова́ть; быть грозе́; **he is ~ for a surprise** его́ ожида́ет сюрпри́з; **~ for a penny, ~ for a pound** семь бед — оди́н отве́т; **he has got it ~ for me** (*coll.*) он про́тив меня́ что́-то име́ет; **you'll be ~ for it when she finds out** вам доста́нется за э́то, когда́ она́ узна́ет; **are you ~ on his plans?** (*coll.*) вы в ку́рсе его́ пла́нов?; **~ with** (*coll., on good terms with*) вхож в + *a.*, к + *d.*; **he is well ~ with the council** у него́ в сове́те свои́ лю́ди.

● *prep.* **1** (*position*) в/на + *p.*; (*inhabited places*): **~ Moscow** в Москве́; **he is the best worker ~ the village** он пе́рвый рабо́тник на селе́; (*countries and territories*): **~ France** во Фра́нции; **~ the Crimea** в Крыму́; **~ Ukraine** на Украи́не; **~ Western Ukraine** в За́падной Украи́не; (*islands and promontories*): **~ the British Isles** на Брита́нских острова́х; **~ Alaska** на Аля́ске; (*mountainous regions within Russia*): **~ the Caucasus** на Кавка́зе; (*mountainous regions elsewhere*): **~ the Alps** в А́льпах; (*open spaces and flat areas*): **~ the street** на у́лице; **~ the square** на пло́щади; **in the country(side)** в дере́вне; **~ the garden** в саду́; **~ the field** в/на по́ле; **~ the fields** в/на поля́х; (*buildings*): **~ the theatre** (*Br.*), **theater** (*US*) в теа́тре; (*places of learning*): **~ school** в шко́ле; **~ the university** в университе́те; (*places of work*): **~ the factory** на заво́де, фа́брике; (*activities*): **~ the lesson** на уро́ке; **~ the war** на войне́; во вре́мя войны́; **~ the Civil War** в гражда́нской войне́; (*groups*): **~ the crowd** в толпе́; (*points of compass*): **~ the (Far) East** на (Да́льнем) Восто́ке; (*vehicles*): **let's go ~ the car** пое́дем на маши́не; **they were travelling** (*Br.*), **traveling** (*US*) **~ his car** они́ е́хали в его́ маши́не; (*parts of body*): **hold this ~ your hand** держи́те э́то в руке́; **she had a child ~ her arms** у неё на рука́х был ребёнок; **he is lame ~ one leg** он хром на одну́ но́гу; (*natural phenomena*): **~ the sun** на со́лнце; **~ the fresh air** на све́жем во́здухе; **~ darkness** в темноте́; **~ the rain** под дождём; **he went out ~ the rain** он вы́шел в дождь; **~ the sky** в/на не́бе; **~ a strong wind** при си́льном ве́тре; на си́льном ветру́; (*books*): **~ the Bible** в Би́блии; (*authors*): **~ Shakespeare** у Шекспи́ра; (*close to*): **she was sitting ~ the window** она́ сиде́ла у окна́. **2** (*motion*) в (*rarely* на) + *a.*: **they arrived ~ the city** они́ при́были в го́род; **look ~ the mirror** посмотри́те в зе́ркало; **he threw the letter ~ the fire** он бро́сил письмо́ в ого́нь; **he whispered ~ my ear** он шепта́л мне на́ ухо. **3** (*time*) (*i*) (*specific centuries, years and decades*): **~ the 20th century** в двадца́том ве́ке; **~ 1975** в ты́сяча девятьсо́т се́мьдесят пя́том году́; **~ the sixties** в шестидеся́тые го́ды; **~ May** в ма́е; **~ (the) future** в бу́дущем; **~ childhood** в де́тстве; **~ old age** на ста́рости лет; **he is ~ his fifties** ему́ за пятьдеся́т; ему́ шесто́й деся́ток; (*ii*) (*ages of history, events, periods*): **~ the Middle Ages** в сре́дние века́; **~ the Stone Age** в ка́менном ве́ке; **~ that period** в тот пери́од; **~ these days** в э́ти дни; **~ the days of my youth** в дни мое́й мо́лодости; **~ our day** в на́ши дни; **~ my time** в моё вре́мя; **~ my lifetime** на моём веку́; **~ peacetime** в ми́рное вре́мя; **injured ~ the explosion** ра́ненный во вре́мя взры́ва; **~ the course of** в тече́ние + *g.* (*see also vii*); **3 times ~ one day** три ра́за в оди́н день; (*iii*): **~ the first minute of the game** на пе́рвой мину́те игры́; (*iv*) (*seasons*): **~ spring** весно́й; (*times of day*): **~ the morning** у́тром; **~ the mornings** по утра́м; **~ the afternoon** днём; по́сле полу́дня; (*v*) (*with gerund*): **~ crossing the river** при перехо́де реки́; переходя́ ре́ку; (*of reigns: during*): **~ Napoleon's time** при Наполео́не; (*vi*) (*at the end of*): **I shall finish this book ~ 3 days' time** я ко́нчу э́ту кни́гу че́рез три дня; **~ less than 3 weeks** ра́ньше чем че́рез три неде́ли; (*vii*) (*in the course of*): **how many will come ~ one day?** ско́лько придёт за день?; **I haven't been there ~ the last 3 years** за после́дние три го́да я не́ был там; **I shall write the story ~ (the space of) 3 weeks** я напишу́ э́тот расска́з в три (*or* за три) неде́ли; **he wrote twice ~ one week** он написа́л два́жды за одну́ неде́лю; **he completed it ~ 6 weeks** он зако́нчил э́то за шесть неде́ль. **4** (*condition, situation*): **~ his absence** в его́ отсу́тствие; **~ his presence** в его́ прису́тствии; **~ these circumstances** при/в э́тих усло́виях; **~ custody** под аре́стом; **cry out ~ fear** вскри́кнуть (*pf.*) от стра́ха; **~ place** на ме́сте; **I am not ~ a position to** я не име́ю возмо́жности (+ *inf.*); **~ power** у вла́сти; **~ the wake of** вслед за + *i.*; **~ the way** (*lit.*) попере́к доро́ги; (*fig.*): **these books are ~ my way** э́ти кни́ги мне меша́ют. **5** (*dress*): **she was ~ white** она́ была́ в бе́лом (пла́тье); **he was dressed ~ ...** на нём был...; **she dresses ~ bright colours** она́ одева́ется в я́ркие цвета́. **6** (*form; mode; arrangement; quantity*): **~ pairs** па́рами; **~ folds** скла́дками; **payment ~ silver** опла́та серебро́м; **they died ~ (their) thousands** они́ умира́ли ты́сячами; **~ writing** в пи́сьменном ви́де (*or* пи́сьменно); **~ a row** в ряду́; (*successively*) подря́д; **~ a circle** в кругу́; **~ short** вкра́тце; в не́скольких слова́х. **7** (*manner*): **~ a whisper** шёпотом; **~ a businesslike way** делови́м о́бразом; по-делово́му; **~ a loud voice** гро́мким го́лосом; **~ detail** подро́бно; **~ full** по́лностью; **~ part** ча́стью, части́чно; **~ secret** под секре́том, по секре́ту; **~ succession** подря́д, после́довательно; **~ turn** по о́череди; **~ haste** в спе́шке, второпя́х. **8** (*language*): **~ Russian** по-ру́сски; **~ several languages** на не́скольких языка́х. **9** (*material*): **a statue ~ marble** ста́туя из мра́мора. **10** (*medium*): **he paints ~ oils** он пи́шет ма́слом. **11** (*cul.*): **~ butter** на ма́сле. **12** (*solvent; diluent*): **take the medicine ~ water** лека́рство принима́ть с водо́й. **13** (*contained ~; inherent ~*): **there are 7 days ~ a week** в неде́ле семь дней; **there's no sense ~ complaining** жа́ловаться бессмы́сленно; **he hasn't got it ~ him to succeed** у него́ нет зада́тков к успе́ху; **there's nothing ~ it** (*coll., it is easy*) па́ра пустяко́в; (*coll., there is no difference*) нет никако́й ра́зницы; **there's nothing ~ it** (*coll., no benefit*) **for me** мне э́то ничего́ не даст. **14** (*consisting ~*): **we have lost a good friend ~ him** в нём (*or* в его́ лице́) мы потеря́ли хоро́шего дру́га. **15** (*ratio: out of*): **only 1 ~ every 10 survived** из ка́ждых десяти́ то́лько оди́н вы́жил; **he has 1 chance ~ 5 of success** его́ ша́нсы на успе́х — оди́н к четырём; **they had to pay 10p ~ the pound** им пришло́сь плати́ть де́сять пе́нсов с фу́нта.

16 (*division*): **he broke the plate ~ pieces** он разби́л таре́лку на куски́.
17 (~ *respect of*): **they differ ~ size but not ~ colour** (*Br.*), **color** (*US*) они́ различа́ются по разме́ру, а не по цве́ту; **he was senior ~ rank** он был ста́рший по чи́ну; **a lecture ~ anatomy** ле́кция по анато́мии; **an expert ~ economics** специали́ст по эконо́мике; **strong ~ mathematics** силён (*pred.*) в матема́тике; **weak ~ French** слаб (*pred.*) во францу́зском языке́; **broad ~ the shoulders** широ́к (*pred.*) в плеча́х; (*dimension*): **4 feet ~ length** четы́ре фу́та в длину́; (*of bodily defects*): **blind ~ one eye** слеп (*pred.*) на оди́н глаз; (*of physique or natural characteristics*): **slight ~ build** хру́пкого сложе́ния; **poor ~ quality** плохо́го ка́чества; **he is young ~ appearance** он молодо́й на вид; **a land rich ~ iron** страна́, бога́тая желе́зом; **he was unfortunate ~ his friends** ему́ не везло́ с друзья́ми; **he is advanced ~ years** ему́ уже́ не ма́ло лет; он уже́ не мо́лод; **they were 7 ~ number** их бы́ло се́меро.
18 (*according to*): **~ my opinion** по моему́ мне́нию; по-мо́ему.
19: **~ reply to** в отве́т на + *a.*; **~ honour** (*Br.*), **honor** (*US*) **of** в честь + *g.*; **~ memory of** в па́мять + *g.*; **~ protest** в знак проте́ста.
20 (*engaged* ~): **~ business** в де́ле; **~ battle** в бою́; **~ search of** в по́исках + *g.*; **~ self-defence** (*Br.*), **-defense** (*US*) для самооборо́ны; в поря́дке самозащи́ты.
21 (*with other parts of speech, forming phrasal conjs.*): **~ that** тем, что; так как; **~ between** ме́жду + *i.*; **something ~ between** не́что сре́днее.

inability /ˌɪnəˈbɪlɪtɪ/ *n.* неспосо́бность.

in absentia /ˌɪn æbˈsentɪə/ *adv.* зао́чно.

inaccessibility /ˌɪnækˌsesɪˈbɪlɪtɪ/ *n.* недосту́пность, непристу́пность.

inaccessible /ˌɪnækˈsesɪb(ə)l/ *adj.* недосту́пный, непристу́пный.

inaccuracy /ɪnˈækjʊrəsɪ/ *n.* нето́чность.

inaccurate /ɪnˈækjʊrət/ *adj.* нето́чный.

inaction /ɪnˈækʃ(ə)n/ *n.* безде́йствие.

inactive /ɪnˈæktɪv/ *adj.* **1** безде́йственный, безде́йствующий; **he leads an ~ life** он ведёт безде́ятельный/пасси́вный о́браз жи́зни; **the machines were ~** маши́ны проста́ивали. **2** (*of chemicals etc.*) ине́ртный, неде́ятельный.

inactivity /ˌɪnækˈtɪvɪtɪ/ *n.* безде́йствие.

inadequacy /ɪnˈædɪkwəsɪ/ *n.* недоста́точность, неполноце́нность; (*personal*) неспосо́бность, неполноце́нность.

inadequate /ɪnˈædɪkwət/ *adj.* (*insufficient*) недоста́точный; **words are ~ to express my joy** слов недостаёт (*or* не хвата́ет), что́бы вы́разить мою́ ра́дость; (*less than capable of*) неспосо́бный, неполноце́нный; **he was ~ to the task** он оказа́лся неспосо́бным к выполне́нию э́той зада́чи.

inadmissible /ˌɪnədˈmɪsɪb(ə)l/ *adj.* (*unacceptable*) неприе́млемый; (*impermissible*) недопусти́мый.

inadvertence /ˌɪnədˈvɜːt(ə)ns/ *n.* (*inattention*) невнима́тельность; (*oversight*) недосмо́тр; (*false step*) неосторо́жность.

inadvertent /ˌɪnədˈvɜːt(ə)nt/ *adj.* неумы́шленный, неча́янный, нево́льный.

inadvisability /ˌɪnədˌvaɪzəˈbɪlɪtɪ/ *n.* нецелесообра́зность, нежела́тельность.

inadvisable /ˌɪnədˈvaɪzəb(ə)l/ *adj.* нецелесообра́зный, нежела́тельный.

inalienability /ɪnˌeɪlɪənəˈbɪlɪtɪ/ *n.* неотъе́млемость.

inalienable /ɪnˈeɪlɪənəb(ə)l/ *adj.* неотъе́млемый.

inalterable /ɪnˈɒltərəb(ə)l/ *adj.* неизменя́емый, неизме́нный.

inane /ɪˈneɪn/ *adj.* глу́пый, пусто́й, неле́пый.

inanimate /ɪnˈænɪmət/ *adj.* неодушевлённый, неживо́й; **~ nature** нежива́я приро́да; **an ~ noun** неодушевлённое существи́тельное; (*lifeless; also fig., without animation*) безжи́зненный.

inanity /ɪnˈænɪtɪ/ *n.* глу́пость; неле́пость.

inapplicability /ɪnˌæplɪkəˈbɪlɪtɪ/, /ˌɪnəˌplɪk-/ *n.* непримени́мость.

inapplicable /ɪnˈæplɪkəb(ə)l/, /ˌɪnəˈplɪk-/ *adj.* непримени́мый; (*unsuitable*) неподходя́щий.

inapposite /ɪnˈæpəzɪt/ *adj.* неуме́стный.

inappropriate /ˌɪnəˈprəʊprɪət/ *adj.* неуме́стный, неподходя́щий.

inappropriateness /ˌɪnəˈprəʊprɪətnɪs/ *n.* неуме́стность.

inapt /ɪnˈæpt/ *adj.* неподходя́щий, неуме́стный.

inarticulate /ˌɪnɑːˈtɪkjʊlət/ *adj.* (*of speech*) невня́тный, нечленоразде́льный; (*of person*) косноязы́чный.

inarticulateness /ˌɪnɑːˈtɪkjʊlətnɪs/ *n.* нечленоразде́льность; косноязы́чие.

inartistic /ˌɪnɑːˈtɪstɪk/ *adj.* нехудо́жественный.

inasmuch as /ˌɪnəzˈmʌtʃ/ *adj.* так как; ввиду́ того́, что; поско́льку.

inattent|ion /ˌɪnəˈtenʃ(ə)n/, **-iveness** /ˌɪnəˈtentɪvnɪs/ *nn.* невнима́ние, невнима́тельность (к + *d.*).

inattentive /ˌɪnəˈtentɪv/ *adj.* невнима́тельный.

inaudibility /ɪnˌɔːdɪˈbɪlɪtɪ/ *n.* плоха́я слы́шимость; невня́тность.

inaudible /ɪnˈɔːdɪb(ə)l/ *adj.* неслы́шный; (*indistinct*) невня́тный.

inaugural /ɪˈnɔːgjʊr(ə)l/ *n.* торже́ственная речь при вступле́нии в до́лжность.
● *adj.* вступи́тельный, инаугурацио́нный.

inaugurate /ɪˈnɔːgjʊˌreɪt/ *v.t.* **1** (*install with ceremony*) (торже́ственно) вв|оди́ть, -ести́ в до́лжность; инаугури́ровать (*impf., pf.*); **the President was ~d** президе́нт вступи́л в до́лжность. **2** (*launch; officiate at opening of*) откр|ыва́ть, -ы́ть; (*fig.*): **they ~d many reforms** они́ ввели́ мно́го рефо́рм; **he ~d a new policy** он положи́л нача́ло но́вой поли́тике; **a new era was ~d** начала́сь но́вая э́ра.

inauguration /ɪˌnɔːgjʊˈreɪʃ(ə)n/ *n.* вступле́ние/введе́ние в до́лжность; инаугура́ция; откры́тие; нача́ло.

inauspicious /ˌɪnɔːˈspɪʃəs/ *adj.* (*of ill omen*) злове́щий; (*unlucky*) несчастли́вый.

in-basket /ˈɪnbɑːskɪt/ *n.* (*US*) корзи́нка для входя́щей корреспонде́нции.

in-between /ˌɪnbɪˈtwiːn/ *adj.* промежу́точный.

inboard /ˈɪnbɔːd/ *adj.* располо́женный внутри́ су́дна.

inborn /ˈɪnbɔːn/ *adj.* врождённый, прирождённый.

inbred /ɪnˈbred/, /ˈɪn-/ *adj.* (*innate*) = **inborn;** (*result of inbreeding*) рождённый от роди́телей, состоя́щих в кро́вном родстве́ ме́жду собо́й.

inbreeding /ˈɪnbriːdɪŋ/ *n.* (*of animals*) ро́дственное спа́ривание; инбри́динг; (*of people*) бра́чные отноше́ния ме́жду ро́дственниками.

inbuilt /ɪnˈbɪlt/ *adj.* врождённый.

Inca /ˈɪŋkə/ *n.* и́нка (*c.g.*).

incalculable /ɪnˈkælkjʊləb(ə)l/ *adj.* **1** (*too great for calculation*) неисчисли́мый, бессчётный, бесчи́сленный, несме́тный; **it has done ~ harm** э́то причини́ло неисчисли́мый/огро́мный вред. **2** (*unpredictable*) капри́зный, причу́дливый.

in camera /ɪn ˈkæmərə/ *adv.*: **the trial will be held ~** проце́сс бу́дет закры́тым (*or* бу́дет идти́ при закры́тых двеpя́х).

incandescence /ˌɪnkænˈdes(ə)ns/ *n.* нака́л, кале́ние.

incandescent /ˌɪnkænˈdes(ə)nt/ *adj.* накалённый, раскалённый; (*of light*) светя́щийся от нагре́ва; **~ lamp (*or* light bulb)** ла́мпа нака́ливания.

incantation /ˌɪnkænˈteɪʃ(ə)n/ *n.* заклина́ние, закля́тие.

incapability /ɪnˌkeɪpəˈbɪlɪtɪ/ *n.* неспосо́бность.

incapable /ɪnˈkeɪpəb(ə)l/ *adj.* **1** (*not having a particular capacity*) неспосо́бный; **he is ~ of understanding** он неспосо́бен поня́ть (*что*); он неспосо́бен к понима́нию; **~ of speech** невладе́ющий ре́чью; **~ of lying** неспосо́бный на ложь; **they are an ~ lot** э́то никчёмные лю́ди. **2** (*not susceptible*) не поддаю́щийся (*чему*); **~ of improvement** не поддаю́щийся улучше́нию.

incapacitate /ˌɪnkəˈpæsɪˌteɪt/ *v.t.*: **~ for, from** (*render incapable of or unfit for*) де́лать, с- неспосо́бным/неприго́дным к + *d.*; **his illness ~d him for work** из-за боле́зни он стал нетрудоспосо́бным; (*disable*): **he was ~d for 3 weeks** он вы́был из стро́я на три неде́ли; (*mil.*) выводи́ть, вы́вести из стро́я; **the enemy's tanks were ~d** та́нки проти́вника бы́ли вы́ведены из стро́я.

incapacity /ˌɪnkəˈpæsɪtɪ/ *n.* неспосо́бность.

incarcerate /ɪnˈkɑːsəˌreɪt/ *v.t.* заточ|а́ть, -и́ть (в тюрьму́).

incarceration /ɪnˌkɑːsəˈreɪʃ(ə)n/ *n.* заточе́ние (в тюрьму́).

incarnate¹ /ɪnˈkɑːnət/ *adj.* (*in bodily form*) воплощённый; **he is the Devil ~** он дья́вол во пло́ти; (*personified*) олицетворённый.

incarnate² /ˈɪnkɑːˌneɪt/, /-ˈkɑːneɪt/ *v.t.* вопло|ща́ть, -ти́ть; олицетвор|я́ть, -и́ть; **she ~d all the virtues** она́ воплоща́ла в себе́ (*or* олицетворя́ла собо́й) все доброде́тели.

incarnation /ˌɪnkɑːˈneɪʃ(ə)n/ *n.* **1** (*taking on bodily form*): **the I~** воплоще́ние (божества́ в Христе́); (*re-birth*) инкарна́ция; **in a future ~** в но́вом рожде́нии. **2** (*embodiment, personification*) воплоще́ние, олицетворе́ние.

incautious /ɪnˈkɔːʃəs/ *adj.* неосторо́жный, опроме́тчивый.

incendiarism /ɪnˈsendɪəˌrɪz(ə)m/ *n.* поджо́г.

incendiary /ɪnˈsendɪərɪ/ *n.* **1** (*arsonist*) поджига́тель (*m.*); (*fig., firebrand*) подстрека́тель (*m.*). **2** (**~ bomb**) зажига́тельная бо́мба.

● *adj.* зажига́тельный; (*fig.*) подстрека́ющий.

incense¹ /ˈɪnsens/ *n.* ла́дан, фимиа́м (*also fig.*); **they were burning ~** они́ кади́ли ла́даном.

● *cpd.* **~-burner** *n.* (*vessel*) кади́льница.

incense² /ɪnˈsens/ *v.t.* разгне́вать (*pf.*); прив|оди́ть, -ести́ в я́рость; **she was ~d at, by his behaviour** (*Br.*), **behavior** (*US*) его́ поведе́ние привело́ её в я́рость.

incentive /ɪnˈsentɪv/ *n.* побужде́ние, сти́мул; **he lacks all ~ to work** у него́ нет никако́го сти́мула для рабо́ты; **~ bonus** поощри́тельная пре́мия.

inception /ɪnˈsepʃ(ə)n/ *n.* нача́ло, начина́ние.

incertitude /ɪnˈsɜːtɪˌtjuːd/ *n.* неуве́ренность.

incessant /ɪnˈses(ə)nt/ *adj.* непреста́нный, непреры́вный.

incest /ˈɪnsest/ *n.* кровосмеше́ние.

incestuous /ɪnˈsestjʊəs/ *adj.* кровосмеси́тельный; (*person*) вино́вный в кровосмеше́нии.

inch /ɪntʃ/ *n.* дюйм; **he moved forward by ~es** ма́ло-пома́лу он дви́гался вперёд; **the car missed me by ~es** автомоби́ль едва́ меня́ не задави́л; **he was every ~ a sailor** он был моряко́м с головы́ до пят; **he did not yield an ~** он не уступи́л ни на йо́ту; **give him an ~ and he'll take a mile** дай ему́ па́лец, он всю ру́ку отхва́тит; **he was flogged within an ~ of his life** его́ изби́ли до полусме́рти.

● *v.i. with advs.*: **he was ~ing along** он ме́дленно тащи́лся; **the car began to ~ forward** маши́на ме́дленно тро́нулась с ме́ста.

inchoate /ɪnˈkəʊeɪt/, /ˈɪn-/ *adj.* зача́точный.

inchoative /ɪnˈkəʊətɪv/ *adj.* (*gram.*) начина́тельный.

incidence /ˈɪnsɪd(ə)ns/ *n.* **1** (*phys., falling; contact*) паде́ние, накло́н; **angle of ~** у́гол паде́ния. **2** (*range or scope of effect*) охва́т, сфе́ра де́йствия; **the ~ of taxation** охва́т налогообложе́нием; **the ~ of a disease** число́ заболе́вших.

incident /ˈɪnsɪd(ə)nt/ *n.* слу́чай, собы́тие; происше́ствие, инциде́нт; **frontier ~** пограни́чный инциде́нт; **without ~** без происше́ствий; (*in play, novel etc.*) эпизо́д.

● *adj.*: **~ to** (*connected with*) свя́занный с+*i.*; (*characteristic of*) прису́щий +*d.*, сво́йственный +*d.*

incidental /ˌɪnsɪˈdent(ə)l/ *adj.* **1** (*casual*) случа́йный; (*passing*) попу́тный; (*inessential*) несуще́ственный; (*secondary*) побо́чный; **~ expenses** побо́чные расхо́ды; **~ music** музыка́льное сопровожде́ние. **2**: **~ to** (*accompanying, contingent on*) сопряжённый с+*i.*; (*resulting from*) вытека́ющий из+*g.*

incidentally /ˌɪnsɪˈdentəlɪ/ *adv.* (*in passing*) попу́тно; (*parenthetically*) ме́жду про́чим; кста́ти; к сло́ву сказа́ть.

incinerate /ɪnˈsɪnəˌreɪt/ *v.t.* испепел|я́ть, -и́ть; сж|ига́ть, -ечь дотла́.

incineration /ɪnˌsɪnəˈreɪʃ(ə)n/ *n.* сжига́ние дотла́.

incinerator /ɪnˈsɪnəˌreɪtə(r)/ *n.* мусоросжига́тельная печь; кремацио́нная печь.

incipient /ɪnˈsɪpɪənt/ *adj.* зарожда́ющийся.

incise /ɪnˈsaɪz/ *v.t.* (*make cut in*) надр|еза́ть, -е́зать; (*engrave*) выреза́ть, вы́резать.

incision /ɪnˈsɪʒ(ə)n/ *n.* надре́з.

incisive /ɪnˈsaɪsɪv/ *adj.* ре́жущий; (*fig.*): **an ~ tone** ре́зкий тон; **an ~ mind** о́стрый/проница́тельный ум.

incisiveness /ɪnˈsaɪsɪvnɪs/ *n.* ре́зкость; острота́, пронзи́тельность.

incisor /ɪnˈsaɪzə(r)/ *n.* (*tooth*) резе́ц.

incite /ɪnˈsaɪt/ *v.t.* (*stir up*) возбу|жда́ть, -ди́ть; (*encourage, urge, impel*) побу|жда́ть, -ди́ть; подстрек|а́ть, -ну́ть; **he ~d them to revolt** он подстрека́л их к мятежу́.

incitement /ɪnˈsaɪtmənt/ *n.* (*inciting*) подстрека́тельство; (*spur, stimulus*) побужде́ние, сти́мул.

incivility /ˌɪnsɪˈvɪlɪtɪ/ *n.* неучти́вость, неве́жливость.

inclemency /ɪnˈklemənsɪ/ *n.* суро́вость.

inclement /ɪnˈklemənt/ *adj.* суро́вый.

inclination /ˌɪnklɪˈneɪʃ(ə)n/ *n.* **1** (*bending; slanting*) наклоне́ние, накло́н; **an ~ of the head** киво́к; накло́н головы́. **2** (*slope*) накло́н, скат, отко́с; **the ~ of a roof** скат кры́ши. **3** (*tendency*) накло́нность, скло́нность; **an ~ to stoutness** скло́нность/предрасполо́женность к полноте́. **4** (*desire*) охо́та, жела́ние; **he has lost all ~ to work** он потеря́л вся́кую охо́ту к рабо́те; **I have no ~ to go out** у меня́ нет никако́го жела́ния выходи́ть.

incline¹ /ˈɪnklaɪn/ *n.* накло́нная пло́скость, накло́н, скат.

incline² /ɪnˈklaɪn/ *v.t.* **1** (*cause to lean or slant*) наклон|я́ть, -и́ть; **~d plane** накло́нная пло́скость; (*bend forward or down*) склон|я́ть, -и́ть. **2** (*turn, direct*) напр|авля́ть, -а́вить; **he ~d his ear to their plea** он благоскло́нно вы́слушал их про́сьбу. **3** (*fig., dispose*) склон|я́ть, -и́ть; **his heart ~d him to pity** его́ до́брое се́рдце склоня́ло его́ к жа́лости; **I am ~d to agree with you** я скло́нен с ва́ми согласи́ться; **if you feel ~d (to do so)** е́сли вы располо́жены э́то сде́лать; **favourably** (*Br.*), **favorably** (*US*) **~d to** благоскло́нный к+*d.*

● *v.i.* **1** (*lean, slope*) наклон|я́ться, -и́ться; склон|я́ться, -и́ться. **2** (*tend*) склон|я́ться, -и́ться; **he ~s to(wards) leniency** он скло́нен к снисходи́тельности; **I ~ to think that ...** я скло́нен ду́мать, что...

inclose /ɪnˈkləʊz/ = **enclose**

includ|e /ɪnˈkluːd/ *v.t.* включ|а́ть, -и́ть; (*place on a list*) вн|оси́ть, -ести́; **I ~e you among my friends** я включа́ю вас в число́ свои́х друзе́й; **they were all there, wives ~ed** все бы́ли в сбо́ре, включа́я жён; **5 members, ~ing the President** пять чле́нов, включа́я президе́нта; **we saw several of them, ~ing your brother** мы ви́дели не́которых из них, в том числе́ (и) ва́шего бра́та; **service ~ed** включа́я услу́ги; **your work will ~e sweeping the floor** в ва́ши обя́занности бу́дет входи́ть подмета́ние поло́в; (*contain*) заключа́ть (*impf.*); содержа́ть (*impf.*) в себе́; **this book ~es all his poems** в э́той кни́ге со́браны все его́ стихи́.

inclusion /ɪnˈkluːʒ(ə)n/ *n.* включе́ние.

inclusive /ɪnˈkluːsɪv/ *adj. & adv.* **1**: **~ of** (*including*) включа́я; включа́ющий в себя́; содержа́щий в себе́. **2**: **from Feb. 2nd to 20th ~** со второ́го февраля́ по двадца́тое включи́тельно. **3**: **~ terms** (*at hotel*) цена́ ко́мнаты с по́лным содержа́нием.

incognito /ˌɪnkɒɡˈniːtəʊ/ *n., adj. & adv.* (*pl.* **~s**) инко́гнито (*m., nt., indecl.*).

incoherence /ˌɪnkəʊˈhɪərəns/ *n.* несвя́зность, непосле́довательность, бессвя́зность.

incoherent /ˌɪnkəʊˈhɪərənt/ *adj.* несвя́зный, непосле́довательный; (*of speech*) бессвя́зный.

incombustible /ˌɪnkəmˈbʌstɪb(ə)l/ *adj.* негорю́чий, невоспламеня́емый, огнесто́йкий.

income /ˈɪnkʌm/, /ˈɪŋkəm/ *n.* дохо́д, прихо́д; **earned ~** за́работок; **unearned ~** ре́нта, нетрудовы́е дохо́ды (*m. pl.*); **private ~** ча́стные дохо́ды; **~ support** де́нежное посо́бие малоопла́чиваемым; **live within one's**

~ жить по сре́дствам; **live beyond one's ~** жить не по сре́дствам.

● *cpd.* **~-tax** *n.* подохо́дный нало́г.

incoming /ˈɪnˌkʌmɪŋ/ *n.* (*pl., income*) дохо́ды (*m. pl.*).

● *adj.* входя́щий, поступа́ющий, прибыва́ющий; **~ passengers** прибыва́ющие пассажи́ры; **the ~ tide** прили́в; **the ~ president** новои́збранный президе́нт; **~ calls** поступа́ющие звонки́; **~ mail** входя́щая по́чта.

incommensurability /ˌɪnkəˌmenʃərəˈbɪlɪtɪ/, /-sjərəˈbɪlɪtɪ/ *n.* несоизмери́мость.

incommensurable /ˌɪnkəˈmenʃərəb(ə)l/, /-sjərəb(ə)l/ *adj.* несоизмери́мый.

incommensurate /ˌɪnkəˈmenʃərət/, /-sjərət/ *adj.* (*out of proportion*) несоразме́рный (c + *i.*); (*inadequate*) несоотве́тствующий (+ *d.*); (*incommensurable*) несоизмери́мый.

incommode /ˌɪnkəˈməʊd/ *v.t.* (*disturb, put out*) беспоко́ить, о-; (*make difficulties for*) стесн|я́ть, -и́ть; (*hinder*) меша́ть, по- + *d.*

incommunicable /ˌɪnkəˈmjuːnɪkəb(ə)l/ *adj.* невырази́мый.

incom(m)unicado /ˌɪnkəˌmjuːnɪˈkɑːdəʊ/ *adj. & adv.* лишённый пра́ва перепи́ски и сообще́ния; в изоля́ции.

incomparable /ɪnˈkɒmpərəb(ə)l/ *adj.* (*not comparable to or with*) несравни́мый (c + *i.*); (*matchless*) несравне́нный, бесподо́бный.

incompatibility /ˌɪnkəmˌpætɪˈbɪlɪtɪ/ *n.* несоотве́тствие; несовмести́мость; **a divorce on grounds of ~** разво́д по причи́не несхо́дства хара́ктеров.

incompatible /ˌɪnkəmˈpætɪb(ə)l/ *adj.* несовмести́мый; **they are ~** у них несовмести́мые хара́ктеры.

incompetence /ɪnˈkɒmpɪt(ə)ns/ *n.* неспосо́бность, некомпете́нтность; неуме́ние.

incompetent /ɪnˈkɒmpɪt(ə)nt/ *adj.* (*lacking ability*) неспосо́бный (*к чему or inf.*); (*lacking qualifications*) некомпете́нтный (*в чём*); (*inefficient, unskilful*) неуме́лый.

incomplete /ˌɪnkəmˈpliːt/ *adj.* (*not full*) непо́лный; **an ~ set** непо́лный компле́кт; (*defective, lacking*) несоверше́нный; (*unfinished*) незаве́ршённый, незако́нченный.

incompleteness /ˌɪnkəmˈpliːtnɪs/ *n.* неполнота́; несоверше́нство; незаверше́нность; незако́нченность.

incomprehensibility /ɪnˌkɒmprɪˌhensɪˈbɪlɪtɪ/ *n.* непоня́тность, непостижи́мость.

incomprehensible /ɪnˌkɒmprɪˈhensɪb(ə)l/ *adj.* непоня́тный, непостижи́мый.

incomprehension /ɪnˌkɒmprɪˈhenʃ(ə)n/ *n.* непонима́ние.

incompressible /ˌɪnkəmˈpresɪb(ə)l/ *adj.* несжима́емый.

incomunicado /ˌɪnkəˌmjuːnɪˈkɑːdəʊ/ = **incom(m)unicado**

inconceivable /ˌɪnkənˈsiːvəb(ə)l/ *adj.* (*incomprehensible*) непостижи́мый; (*unimaginable*) невообрази́мый; (*coll., unbelievable, most unlikely*) немы́слимый.

inconclusive /ˌɪnkənˈkluːsɪv/ *adj.* (*of argument etc.*) неубеди́тельный; (*of action*) нереши́тельный; **the vote was ~** голосова́ние не́ дало определённых результа́тов.

inconclusiveness /ˌɪnkənˈkluːsɪvnɪs/ *n.* неубеди́тельность; нереши́тельность, неопределённость.

incongruity /ˌɪnkɒŋˈɡruːɪtɪ/ *n.* несоотве́тствие; неуме́стность.

incongruous /ɪnˈkɒŋɡrʊəs/ *adj.* (*out of keeping*) несоотве́тствующий, неподходя́щий, несоотве́тственный; (*out of place, inappropriate*) неуме́стный.

inconsequence /ɪnˈkɒnsɪkwəns/ *n.* непосле́довательность.

inconsequent /ɪnˈkɒnsɪkwənt/ *adj.* (*not following logically*) непосле́довательный; (*irrelevant, immaterial*) несуще́ственный.

inconsequential /ɪnˌkɒnsɪˈkwenʃ(ə)l/ *adj.* (*insignificant*) незначи́тельный; (*irrelevant, immaterial*) несуще́ственный.

inconsiderable /ˌɪnkənˈsɪdərəb(ə)l/ *adj.* незначи́тельный; **his income was ~** его́ за́работок был ничто́жным.

inconsiderate /ˌɪnkənˈsɪdərət/ *adj.* невнима́тельный (к други́м), нечу́ткий; **he is ~ of, to everyone** он невнима́телен ко всем.

inconsiderateness /ˌɪnkənˈsɪdərətnɪs/ *n.* невнима́тельность, нечу́ткость.

inconsistenc|y /ˌɪnkənˈsɪst(ə)nsɪ/ *n.* непосле́довательность; противоречи́вость; **there are ~ies in his argument** его́ до́воды непосле́довательны (*or* полны́ противоре́чий).

inconsistent /ˌɪnkənˈsɪst(ə)nt/ *adj* (*incompatible, not in keeping*) несовмести́мый (*с чем*); (*of a person*) непосле́довательный; (*of an account*) противоречи́вый.

inconsolable /ˌɪnkənˈsəʊləb(ə)l/ *adj.* неуте́шный, безуте́шный.

inconspicuous /ˌɪnkənˈspɪkjʊəs/ *adj.* незаме́тный; **he made himself ~** он постара́лся оста́ться незаме́ченным.

inconstancy /ɪnˈkɒnst(ə)nsɪ/ *n.* непостоя́нство, изме́нчивость, переме́нчивость; неве́рность.

inconstant /ɪnˈkɒnst(ə)nt/ *adj.* непостоя́нный, изме́нчивый, переме́нчивый; (*in love or friendship*) неве́рный.

incontestable /ˌɪnkənˈtestəb(ə)l/ *adj.* неоспори́мый.

incontinence /ɪnˈkɒntɪnəns/ *n.* невозде́ржанность; несде́ржанность; (*of urine/faeces*) недержа́ние мочи́/ка́ла.

incontinent /ɪnˈkɒntɪnənt/ *adj.* невозде́ржанный (*esp. sexually*); несде́ржанный; (*of urine/faeces*): **he was ~** он страда́л недержа́нием (мочи́/ка́ла).

incontrovertible /ˌɪnkɒntrəˈvɜːtɪb(ə)l/ *adj.* неоспори́мый.

inconvenience /ˌɪnkənˈviːnɪəns/ *n.* неудо́бство, беспоко́йство; **he was put to great ~** ему́ причини́ли большо́е неудо́бство; **at great personal ~** цено́й большо́го неудо́бства для себя́.

● *v.t.* причин|я́ть, -и́ть неудо́бство + *d.*; беспоко́ить, о-; стесн|я́ть, -и́ть.

inconvenient /ˌɪnkənˈviːnɪənt/ *adj.* неудо́бный; **if it is not ~ to you** е́сли э́то вам удо́бно.

inconvertibility /ˌɪnkənˌvɜːtɪˈbɪlɪtɪ/ *n.* (*fin.*) необрати́мость.

inconvertible /ˌɪnkənˈvɜːtɪb(ə)l/ *adj.* (*fin.*) необрати́мый, неконверти́руемый; **~ currency** неконверти́руемая валю́та.

incorporate /ɪnˈkɔːpəˌreɪt/ *v.t.* **1** (*unite, combine*) объедин|я́ть, -и́ть; соедин|я́ть, -и́ть; **fertilizers should be ~d with the soil** удобре́ния должны́ быть переме́шаны с землёй. **2** (*include, introduce*) включ|а́ть, -и́ть; содержа́ть (*impf.*); **his suggestions were ~d in the plan** его́ предложе́ния бы́ли включены́ в план; **~ in, into** (*annex to*) присоедин|я́ть, -и́ть; **Austria was ~d into Germany** Австрия была́ включена́ в Герма́нию (*or* присоединена́ к Герма́нии). **3** (*form into corporation*) регистри́ровать, за- как корпора́цию.

incorporation /ɪnˌkɔːpəˈreɪʃ(ə)n/ *n.* объедине́ние, соедине́ние; включе́ние (в соста́в); инкорпора́ция, присоедине́ние.

incorporeal /ˌɪnkɔːˈpɔːrɪəl/ *adj.* (*not material*) невеще́ственный; (*without bodily form*) бестеле́сный.

incorrect /ˌɪnkəˈrekt/ *adj.* (*inaccurate; displaying errors, of style etc.*) непра́вильный; (*untrue; erroneous, of statements etc.*) неве́рный.

incorrectness /ˌɪnkəˈrektnɪs/ *n.* непра́вильность; неве́рность.

incorrigibility /ɪnˌkɒrɪdʒɪˈbɪlɪtɪ/ *n.* неисправи́мость.

incorrigible /ɪnˈkɒrɪdʒɪb(ə)l/ *adj.* неисправи́мый.

incorruptibility /ˌɪnkəˌrʌptɪˈbɪlɪtɪ/ *n.* (*honesty*) неподку́пность.

incorruptible /ˌɪnkəˈrʌptɪb(ə)l/ *adj.* (*honest*) неподку́пный.

increase[1] /ˈɪnkriːs/ *n.* (*measurable*) увеличе́ние; **~ of speed** увеличе́ние ско́рости; **~ in value** увеличе́ние сто́имости; (*growth*) рост, возраста́ние; увеличе́ние; **~ in population** рост населе́ния; **unemployment is on the ~** безрабо́тица растёт/увели́чивается; (*amount of ~*) приро́ст; **my shares show an ~ of 5%** мой а́кции подняли́сь на пять проце́нтов; **we had an ~ (of pay)** мы получи́ли приба́вку/надба́вку.

increase[2] /ɪnˈkriːs/ *v.t.* увели́чи|вать, -ть; **he ~d his wealth** он увели́чил своё состоя́ние; (*extend*): **~ one's influence** расш|иря́ть, -и́рить своё влия́ние; (*raise*): **~ prices** пов|ыша́ть, -ы́сить це́ны; (*quicken*): **~ one's pace**

уск|оря́ть, -о́рить шаг; (*multiply*): **~ one's efforts** умн|ожа́ть, -о́жить (*or* удв|а́ивать, -о́ить) уси́лия; (*strengthen*): **this merely ~d his determination** э́то то́лько уси́лило его́ реши́мость.

● *v.i.* увели́чи|ваться, -ться; (*grow*) расти́ (*impf.*); возраст|а́ть, -и́ (с + *g.*, до + *g.*); (*intensify*) уси́ли|ваться, -тьcя; (*expand*) расш|иря́ться, -и́риться; **the speed ~d** ско́рость увели́чилась; **the pace of life ~s** темп жи́зни ускоря́ется; (*multiply*): **his efforts ~d tenfold** его́ уси́лия возросли́/умно́жились в де́сять раз; (*rise*): **sugar ~d in price** са́хар повы́сился в цене́ (*or* подорожа́л).

increasingly /ɪnˈkriːsɪŋlɪ/ *adv.* всё бо́лее; всё бо́льше и бо́льше; **it becomes ~ difficult** стано́вится всё трудне́е.

incredibility /ɪnˌkredɪˈbɪlɪtɪ/ *n.* неправдоподо́бность, невероя́тность.

incredibl|e /ɪnˈkredɪb(ə)l/ *adj.* (*lit., unbelievable*) неправдоподо́бный, невероя́тный, неимове́рный; (*coll., extraordinary*) невероя́тный, неслы́ханный; **he was ~y stupid** он был невероя́тно глуп.

incredulity /ˌɪnkrɪˈdjuːlɪtɪ/ *n.* недове́рчивость.

incredulous /ɪnˈkredjʊləs/ *adj.* недове́рчивый.

increment /ˈɪnkrɪmənt/ *n.* (*increase*) рост, приро́ст; (*profit*) при́быль; (*amount of regular increase*) приба́вка.

incriminate /ɪnˈkrɪmɪˌneɪt/ *v.t.* (*expose; show to be guilty*) изоблич|а́ть, -и́ть; **his confession ~d his brother in the affair** его́ призна́ние ука́зывало на прича́стность бра́та к де́лу; **he refused to ~ himself** он отказа́лся дава́ть показа́ния про́тив себя́.

incriminating /ɪnˈkrɪmɪˌneɪtɪŋ/, **incriminatory** /ɪnˈkrɪmɪnətərɪ/ *adjs.* изоблича́ющий.

incrustation /ˌɪnkrʌˈsteɪʃ(ə)n/ *n.* (*encrusting*) инкруста́ция; (*crust, hard coating*) на́кипь, кора́.

incubate /ˈɪŋkjʊbeɪt/ *v.t.* (*of a bird*) сиде́ть (*impf.*) на (я́йцах); (*hatch by artificial heat*) инкуби́ровать (*impf., pf.*).

● *v.i.* (*of a disease*) находи́ться (*impf.*) в инкубацио́нном пери́оде.

incubation /ˌɪŋkjʊˈbeɪʃ(ə)n/ *n.* (*of eggs; stage of disease*) инкуба́ция; **~ period** инкубацио́нный пери́од.

incubator /ˈɪŋkjʊˌbeɪtə(r)/ *n.* инкуба́тор.

inculcate /ˈɪnkʌlˌkeɪt/ *v.t.* внедр|я́ть, -и́ть; внуш|а́ть, -и́ть.

inculcation /ˌɪnkʌlˈkeɪʃ(ə)n/ *n.* внедре́ние, внуше́ние.

incumbency /ɪnˈkʌmbənsɪ/ *n.* (*holding of office*) пребыва́ние в до́лжности; (*eccl.*) бенефи́ций.

incumbent /ɪnˈkʌmbənt/ *n.* **1** (*eccl.*) прихо́дский свяще́нник. **2** занима́ющий (*какую-н.*) до́лжность.

● *adj.* (*holding office*) занима́ющий пост, до́лжность; **the ~ president** ны́нешний президе́нт; (*necessary as a duty*): **~ upon** возлежа́щий на + *p.*; возло́женный на + *a.*; **it is ~ upon you to warn them** вы обя́заны предупреди́ть их.

incur /ɪnˈkɜː(r)/ *v.t.* (**incurred, incurring**) (*bring on o.s.*) навл|ека́ть, -е́чь на себя́; **she ~red the blame** она́ навлекла́ на себя́ обвине́ния; (*run into*) подв|ерга́ться, -е́ргнуться + *d.*; **I ~red his displeasure** я навлёк на себя́ его́ неудово́льствие; **he ~red heavy expenses** он понёс больши́е расхо́ды.

incurable /ɪnˈkjʊərəb(ə)l/ *adj.* (*of sick person*) безнадёжный; (*fig.*): **an ~ optimist** неисправи́мый оптими́ст; (*of disease*) неизлечи́мый; (*of habit etc.*) неискорени́мый.

incurious /ɪnˈkjʊərɪəs/ *adj.* нелюбопы́тный.

incursion /ɪnˈkɜːʃ(ə)n/ *n.* вторже́ние, налёт, набе́г.

indebted /ɪnˈdetɪd/ *adj.* (*owing money*) в долгу́, до́лжный; (*owing gratitude*) обя́занный; **to whom am I ~ for this?** кому́ я обя́зан за э́то?

indebtedness /ɪnˈdetɪdnɪs/ *n.* задо́лженность; обя́занность.

indecency /ɪnˈdiːs(ə)nsɪ/ *n.* неприли́чие, непристо́йность; **an act of gross ~** непристо́йное де́йствие.

indecent /ɪnˈdiːs(ə)nt/ *adj.* **1** (*unseemly*) неподоба́ющий, неблагови́дный; **she left with ~ haste** она́ ушла́ с неподоба́ющей поспе́шностью. **2** (*obscene*) неприли́чный, непристо́йный; **~ exposure** непристо́йное обнаже́ние те́ла.

indecipherable /ˌɪndɪˈsaɪfərəb(ə)l/ *adj.* не поддаю́щийся расшифро́вке; (*of handwriting etc.*) неразбо́рчивый.

indecision /ˌɪndɪˈsɪʒ(ə)n/ *n.* нереши́тельность, неуве́ренность.

indecisive /ˌɪndɪˈsaɪsɪv/ *adj.* (*irresolute, hesitant*) нереши́тельный; (*not producing a decision or result*) не реша́ющий; **an ~ battle** бой, не име́ющий реша́ющего значе́ния; **an ~ argument** недоста́точно убеди́тельный аргуме́нт.

indeclinable /ˌɪndɪˈklaɪnəb(ə)l/ *adj.* несклоня́емый.

indecorous /ɪnˈdekərəs/ *adj.* (*improper*) неприли́чный; (*unseemly*) неподоба́ющий.

indecorum /ˌɪndɪˈkɔːrəm/ *n.* наруше́ние прили́чий; неблагопристо́йность.

indeed /ɪnˈdiːd/ *adv.* **1** (*really, actually*) действи́тельно; в са́мом де́ле; вот и́менно; **and ~** да и; (*confirmatory, 'to be sure'*) и то́чно; **if ~** е́сли то́лько/вообще́.
2 (*expr. emphasis*): **yes, ~** ну коне́чно!; ну да!; (а) ка́к же!; **very glad ~** о́чень, о́чень рад; **thanks very much ~** премно́го вам благода́рен; **no, ~** ну уж нет!; как бы не так; куда́!; где там!; **this is generosity ~** вот э́то ще́дрость!; **why ~?** действи́тельно, заче́м?; заче́м со́бственно?; **'Will you come?' — 'I will ~'** «Вы придёте?» — «Непреме́нно/обяза́тельно»; **'Did you have any trouble?' — 'We did ~'** «У вас бы́ли неприя́тности?» — «Ещё каки́е!».
3 (*expr. intensification*) к тому́ же; ма́ло/бо́лее того́; да́же; **she was worried, ~ desperate** она́ была́ озабо́чена, да́же в отча́янии; **I saw him recently, ~ yesterday** я ви́дел его́ неда́вно, не да́лее как вчера́.
4 (*admittedly*) пра́вда; хотя́ (и); коне́чно; разуме́ется; **there are ~ exceptions** коне́чно, есть и исключе́ния; **I may ~ be wrong** допуска́ю, что я, мо́жет быть, непра́в; **he is ~ rich, but ...** он, разуме́ется, бога́т, но. . . .
5 (*acknowledging information*) пра́вда?; вот как!
6 (*iron.*): **charity ~!** ничего́ себе́ благотвори́тельность!; **is it ~!** в са́мом де́ле!; **progress ~!** то́же мне шаг вперёд!; шаг вперёд, не́чего сказа́ть!

indefatigable /ˌɪndɪˈfætɪgəb(ə)l/ *adj.* неутоми́мый.

indefeasible /ˌɪndɪˈfiːzɪb(ə)l/ *adj.* неотъе́млемый.

indefensible /ˌɪndɪˈfensɪb(ə)l/ *adj.* (*mil.*) непригóдный для оборо́ны; (*unjustified*) не име́ющий оправда́ния, непрости́тельный; **an ~ statement** неприе́млемое утвержде́ние.

indefinable /ˌɪndɪˈfaɪnəb(ə)l/ *adj.* неопредели́мый.

indefinite /ɪnˈdefɪnɪt/ *adj.* **1** (*not clearly defined*) неопределённый.
2 (*unlimited*) неограни́ченный, бессро́чный; **he was away for an ~ time** он уе́хал на неопределённый срок; **an ~ strike** бессро́чная забасто́вка. **3** (*gram.*): **~ article** неопределённый арти́кль.

indelible /ɪnˈdelɪb(ə)l/ *adj.* (*lit., fig.*) несмыва́емый; **~ ink** несмыва́емые черни́ла; (*fig., unforgettable*) неизглади́мый.

indelicacy /ɪnˈdelɪkəsɪ/ *n.* неделика́тность; беста́ктность.

indelicate /ɪnˈdelɪkət/ *adj.* (*unrefined, immodest*) неделика́тный; (*tactless*) нетакти́чный, беста́ктный.

indemnification /ɪnˌdemnɪfɪˈkeɪʃ(ə)n/ *n.* страхова́ние; предоставле́ние индемните́та; возмеще́ние, компенса́ция.

indemnif|y /ɪnˈdemnɪˌfaɪ/ *v.t.* **1** (*insure, protect*) страхова́ть, за-; **~y s.o. against loss** застрахова́ть кого́-н. на слу́чай убы́тков. **2** (*give legal security to*) предост|авля́ть, -а́вить индемните́т + *d.*; освобо|жда́ть, -ди́ть от отве́тственности. **3** (*compensate*) возме|ща́ть, -сти́ть (*что кому*); компенси́ровать (*impf., pf.*) (*что кому*); **he was ~ied for all his expenses** ему́ бы́ли возмещены́ все расхо́ды.

indemnity /ɪnˈdemnɪtɪ/ *n.* (*security against damage or loss*) гара́нтия возмеще́ния убы́тков; (*legal security*) индемните́т; (*compensation*) возмеще́ние; (*paid to war victor*) контрибу́ция.

indent *v.t.* /ɪnˈdent/ **1** (*make notches or recesses in*) зазу́бр|ивать, -ить;

нас|екáть, -éчь; **an ~ed coastline** извилистая береговáя линия. **2** (*make dent in*) выдáлбливать, выдолбить. **3** (*draw up in duplicate*) сост|авлять, -áвить (докумéнт) в двух экземплярах. **4** (*typ.*): **~ed** (написанный/напечáтанный) с óтступом; **the first line of each paragraph is ~ed** кáждый абзáц начинáется с крáсной строки.

● *n.* /ˈɪndent/ (*typ.*) абзáц, óтступ.

indentation /ˌɪndenˈteɪʃ(ə)n/ *n.* (*notch, cut*) зубéц, вырез, зазýбрина; (*in coastline etc.*) извилина.

indenture /ɪnˈdentʃə(r)/ *n.* контрáкт, договóр мéжду ученикóм и хозяином.

● *v.t.* связ|ывать, -áть контрáктом.

independence /ˌɪndɪˈpend(ə)ns/ *n.* независимость (от + *g.*), самостоятельность; **war of ~** войнá за независимость; **I~ Day** День независимости.

independent /ˌɪndɪˈpend(ə)nt/ *n.* (*pol.*) независимый.

● *adj.* независимый, самостоятельный; не завися́щий (от + *g.*); **~ proof** объективное доказáтельство; **an ~ witness** непредубеждённый свидéтель; **an ~ clause** (*gram.*) глáвное предложéние; (*in adv. sense*): **~ of** независимо от + *g.*; помимо + *g.*; **she is an ~ person** у неё независимый харáктер; **an ~ state** независимое госудáрство; **an ~ income** независимый/самостоятельный дохóд; **we are travelling** (*Br.*), **traveling** (*US*) **~ly** (*separately*) мы путешéствуем врозь/отдéльно.

in-depth /ɪnˈdepθ/ *adj.* обстоятельный, углублённый.

indescribable /ˌɪndɪˈskraɪbəb(ə)l/ *adj.* неописýемый.

indestructibility /ˌɪndɪˌstrʌktɪˈbɪlɪtɪ/ *n.* неразрушимость.

indestructible /ˌɪndɪˈstrʌktɪb(ə)l/ *adj.* неразрушимый.

indeterminable /ˌɪndɪˈtɜːmɪnəb(ə)l/ *adj.* (*unascertainable, indefinable*) неопределимый.

indeterminacy /ˌɪndɪˈtɜːmɪnəsɪ/ *n.* неопределённость.

indeterminate /ˌɪndɪˈtɜːmɪnət/ *adj.* (*not fixed; indefinite*) неопределённый; **an ~ sentence** неопределённый приговóр; (*not settled; undecided*) нерешённый; неокончáтельный; **an ~ result** неокончáтельный результáт; (*vague; indefinable*) неясный, смýтный.

indeterminateness /ˌɪndɪˈtɜːmɪnətnɪs/ = **indeterminacy**

index /ˈɪndeks/ *n.* (*pl.* **indexes** *or esp. tech.* **indices**) **1** (*indicator, pointer on instrument*) стрéлка. **2** (*indicative figure or value*) индекс; **retail price ~** индекс рóзничных цен; (*fig., indication*) показáтель (*m.*); **his behaviour** (*Br.*), **behavior** (*US*) **was an ~ of his true feelings** по егó поведéнию мóжно было сдéлать вывод о егó истинных чýвствах. **3** (*alphabetical*) указáтель (*m.*); **subject ~** предмéтный указáтель; **card ~** картотéка; **~ card** (картотéчная) кáрточка. **4** (*math.*) показáтель (*m.*) стéпени. **5**: **~ finger** указáтельный пáлец.

● *v.t.* **1** (*compile ~ to*) снаб|жáть, -дить указáтелем. **2** (*insert in ~*) зан|осить, -ести в указáтель. **3** (*econ., also* **~-link** (*Br.*)) индексировать (*impf., pf.*).

India /ˈɪndɪə/ *n.* Индия; **~ paper** китáйская бумáга, библьдрук.

● *cpd.* **i~rubber** *n.* резинка, лáстик.

Indian /ˈɪndɪən/ *n.* **1** (*native of India*) инди|ец (*fem.* -áнка). **2 (American ~)** инд|éец (*fem.* -иáнка). **3**: **West ~** вест-инд|ец (*fem.* -ка).

● *adj.* **1** (*of India*) индийский; **~ hemp** (*plant*) коноплá индийская; (*drug*) гаши́ш, марихуáна; **~ ink** тушь; **~ Ocean** Индийский океáн. **2** (*North American*) индéйский; **~ club** булавá; **~ corn** кукурýза, маис; **in ~ file** гуськóм; **~ summer** бáбье лéто. **3**: **West ~** вест-индский.

indicate /ˈɪndɪˌkeɪt/ *v.t.* (*point out*) покáз|ывать, -áть; укáз|ывать, -áть (*кого/что or на кого/что*); **he ~d the way** он укáзал/показáл путь; (*fig., point to*) укáз|ывать, -áть; **he ~d the need for secrecy** он укáзал на необходимость соблюдéния тáйны; (*show*) обозн|ачáть, -áчить; **the frontier is ~d in red** границá обозначена крáсным (цвéтом); (*state*) выражáть, выразить; **he ~d his intentions** он выразил свои намéрения; (*be a sign of*) свидéтельствовать (*impf.*) о + *p.*; означáть (*impf.*); быть признаком + *g.*; **his manner ~d willingness to assist** егó поведéние свидéтельствовало о желáнии помóчь; **rust ~s neglect** ржáвчина свидéтельствует о плохóм ухóде; (*call for*) трéбовать (*impf.*) + *g.*; **an operation is ~d** оперáция необходима/покáзана.

indication /ˌɪndɪˈkeɪʃ(ə)n/ *n.* (*pointing out*) указáние; (*sign*) знак, указáтель (*m.*); **~ of a right of way** указáтель прáва проéзда; **all the ~s are that he has left the country** всё свидéтельствует о том, что он уéхал из страны; (*suggestion; intimation*) признак, намёк; **he gave no ~ of his feelings** он ничéм не выдал своих чувств; (*portent*) признак; **~s of trouble** признаки неприя́тностей.

indicative /ɪnˈdɪkətɪv/ *n.* (*gram.*) изъявительное наклонéние.

● *adj.* **1**: **~ of** (*suggesting, showing*) укáзывающий (*на что*); свидéтельствующий (*о чём*); **a headache may be ~ of eyestrain** головнáя боль иногдá свидéтельствует о перенапряжéнии глаз; **this may be ~ of his intentions** это, возмóжно, укáзывает на егó намéрения. **2** (*gram.*) изъявительный.

indicator /ˈɪndɪˌkeɪtə(r)/ *n.* **1** (*pointer of instrument*) стрéлка; указáтель (*m.*). **2** (*other indicating device*) индикáтор; (*Br., on vehicle*) указáтель (*m.*) поворóта; указáтели направлéния; **~ board** (*Br., showing train arrivals and departures*) таблó (*indecl.*). **3** (*chem.*) индикáтор; **litmus paper is an ~ of acid** лáкмусовая бумáга является индикáтором кислоты. **4** (*fig., sign, symptom*) показáтель (*m.*), признак.

indices /ˈɪndɪˌsiːz/ *pl. of* ⇒**index**

indict /ɪnˈdaɪt/ *v.t.* предъяв|лять, -ить обвинéние + *d.*; **he was ~ed for theft** он был обвинён в крáже.

indictable /ɪnˈdaɪtəb(ə)l/ *adj.*: **an ~ offence** преступлéние, преслéдуемое по обвинительному áкту.

indictment /ɪnˈdaɪtmənt/ *n.* (*charge*) обвинительный акт; (*action*) предъявлéние обвинéния; **bring an ~ against s.o.** предъяв|лять, -ить обвинéние комý-н.; (*fig.*): **these figures are an ~ of government policy** эти цифры слýжат обвинительным докумéнтом прóтив политики правительства.

Indies /ˈɪndɪz/ *n. pl.*: **the East ~** Ост-Индия; **the West ~** Вест-Индия.

indifference /ɪnˈdɪfrəns/ *n.* **1** (*absence of interest*) безразличие; индифферéнтность; равнодýшие; **he regarded the matter with ~** он отнёсся к этому дéлу с равнодýшием. **2** (*absence of feeling*) безразличие; равнодýшие; **he showed complete ~ to their sufferings** он проявил пóлное равнодýшие к их страдáниям. **3** (*small importance*) маловáжность; **it is a matter of ~ to me** мне это безразлично; это для меня не имéет значéния.

indifferent /ɪnˈdɪfrənt/ *adj.* (*without interest*) безразличный; равнодýшный; индифферéнтный; (*mediocre*) посрéдственный.

indigence /ˈɪndɪdʒ(ə)ns/ *n.* нищетá, нуждá.

indigenous /ɪnˈdɪdʒɪnəs/ *adj.* тузéмный; мéстный; **kangaroos are ~ to Australia** кенгурý вóдятся в Австрáлии.

indigent /ˈɪndɪdʒ(ə)nt/ *adj.* малоимýщий, бéдный, нищий.

indigestible /ˌɪndɪˈdʒestɪb(ə)l/ *adj.* неудобовари́мый.

indigestion /ˌɪndɪˈdʒestʃ(ə)n/ *n.* несварéние, диспепсия; **the meal has given me ~** эта едá вызвала у меня расстрóйство желýдка; **he gets ~ after eating** пóсле еды у негó бывáет изжóга.

indignant /ɪnˈdɪgnənt/ *adj.* возмущённый; негодýющий; **I was ~ at his remark** егó замечáние меня возмутило; **he became ~ with me** он вознегодовáл на меня; **an ~ protest** гнéвный протéст.

indignation /ˌɪndɪgˈneɪʃ(ə)n/ *n.* возмущéние, негодовáние, гнев; **the sight aroused his ~** это зрéлище вызвало у негó возмущéние; **he was full of ~ against the police** он был возмущён поведéнием полиции.

indignit|y /ɪnˈdɪgnɪtɪ/ *n.* унижéние, оскорблéние; **we were subjected to various ~ies** мы подвéрглись всячéским унижéниям.

indigo /ˈɪndɪˌgəʊ/ *n.* (*pl.* **~s**) (*dye*) индиго (*indecl.*); **~ blue** цвет индиго; сине-фиолéтовый цвет.

I

indirect /ˌɪndaɪˈrekt/ *adj.* непрямо́й, ко́свенный; опосре́дствованный; **an ~ route** обходно́й/око́льный путь; **~ lighting** отражённый свет; **~ tax** ко́свенный нало́г; **an ~ reference** ко́свенная ссы́лка; (*secondary*) побо́чный, втори́чный; **~ effect** побо́чный/дополни́тельный эффе́кт; (*gram.*): **~ object** ко́свенное дополне́ние; **~ speech** ко́свенная речь.

indiscernible /ˌɪndɪˈsɜːnɪb(ə)l/ *adj.* неразличи́мый.

indiscipline /ɪnˈdɪsɪplɪn/ *n.* недисциплини́рованность.

indiscreet /ˌɪndɪˈskriːt/ *adj.* (*incautious*) неосторо́жный; неосмотри́тельный; (*tactless*) беста́ктный; **an ~ question** нескро́мный вопро́с.

indiscretion /ˌɪndɪˈskreʃ(ə)n/ *n.* (*indiscreetness*) нескро́мность; (*indiscreet act*) неосторо́жный посту́пок; (*revelation of secret*) неосторо́жность в выска́зываниях; **he committed an ~** он проговори́лся.

indiscriminate /ˌɪndɪˈskrɪmɪnət/ *adj.* **1** (*undiscriminating*) неразбо́рчивый; **an ~ reader** нетре́бовательный/неразбо́рчивый чита́тель; **to be ~ in one's friendships** води́ться (*impf.*) с любы́м и ка́ждым; быть неразбо́рчивым в друзья́х. **2** (*random*) де́йствующий без разбо́ра; **he gives ~ praise** он хва́лит без разбо́ра; **he hit out ~ly** он наноси́л уда́ры куда́ попа́ло (*or* напра́во и нале́во). **3** (*disorderly; unselected*) беспоря́дочный; **an ~ mass of data** ку́ча беспоря́дочной информа́ции.

indispensability /ˌɪndɪˌspensəˈbɪlɪtɪ/ *n.* необходи́мость; незамени́мость.

indispensable /ˌɪndɪˈspensəb(ə)l/ *adj.* (*of thing*) необходи́мый; **air is ~ to life** во́здух необходи́м для жи́зни; (*of person*) незамени́мый.

indisposed /ˌɪndɪˈspəʊzd/ *adj.* (*disinclined*): **I am ~ to believe you** я не скло́нен вам ве́рить; (*unwell*) (немно́го) нездоро́вый; **the Queen is ~** короле́ве нездоро́вится.

indisposition /ˌɪndɪspəˈzɪʃ(ə)n/ *n.* (*disinclination*) нерасположе́ние, нежела́ние; (*feeling unwell*) недомога́ние.

indisputability /ˌɪndɪsˌpjuːtəˈbɪlɪtɪ/ *n.* неоспори́мость.

indisputabl|e /ˌɪndɪˈspjuːtəb(ə)l/ *adj.* неоспори́мый; **his genius is ~e** он бесспо́рно гениа́льный челове́к; **you are ~y correct** вы бесспо́рно пра́вы.

indissolubility /ˌɪndɪˌsɒljʊˈbɪlɪtɪ/ *n.* нерушимость.

indissoluble /ˌɪndɪˈsɒljʊb(ə)l/ *adj.* неразры́вный; неруши́мый; **~ bonds of friendship** неразры́вные у́зы дру́жбы; (*chem.*) нераствори́мый.

indistinct /ˌɪndɪˈstɪŋkt/ *adj.* (*of things seen or heard*) нея́сный; невня́тный; **his speech was ~** он говори́л невня́тно; (*vague; obscure*) сму́тный, расплы́вчатый; **I have only an ~ memory of him** я по́мню его́ о́чень сму́тно.

indistinctness /ˌɪndɪˈstɪŋktnɪs/ *n.* (*of sense objects*) нея́сность, неотчётливость; (*of mental images*) расплы́вчатость, нея́сность.

indistinguishable /ˌɪndɪˈstɪŋgwɪʃəb(ə)l/ *adj.* (*not recognizably different*) неразличи́мый, неотличи́мый; **he is ~ from his brother** его́ невозмо́жно отличи́ть от бра́та; **the two are ~** э́ти дво́е неразличи́мы.

individual /ˌɪndɪˈvɪdjʊəl/ *n.* **1** (*single being*) ли́чность, индиви́дуум, едини́ца, о́собь; **the rights of the ~** права́ ли́чности. **2** (*type of person*) челове́к, тип, субъе́кт; **an unpleasant ~** неприя́тный тип.

● *adj.* **1** (*single, particular*) отде́льный. **2** (*of or for one person*) ли́чный, ча́стный; **the teacher gave each pupil ~ attention** учи́тель уделя́л внима́ние ка́ждому ученику́. **3** (*distinctive*) характе́рный, осо́бенный; **he has an ~ style of writing** у него́ оригина́льный/осо́бый/своеобра́зный стиль письма́.

individualism /ˌɪndɪˈvɪdjʊəˌlɪz(ə)m/ *n.* индивидуали́зм.

individualist /ˌɪndɪˈvɪdjʊəlɪst/ *n.* индивидуали́ст.

individualistic /ˌɪndɪˌvɪdjʊəˈlɪstɪk/ *adj.* индивидуалисти́ческий.

individuality /ˌɪndɪˌvɪdjʊˈælɪtɪ/ *n.* индивидуа́льность.

individualization /ˌɪndɪˌvɪdjʊəlaɪˈzeɪʃ(ə)n/ *n.* индивидуализа́ция.

individualize /ˌɪndɪˈvɪdjʊəˌlaɪz/ *v.t.* (*give distinct character to*) индивидуализи́ровать (*impf., pf.*).

indivisibility /ˌɪndɪˌvɪzɪˈbɪlɪtɪ/ *n.* недели́мость.

indivisible /ˌɪndɪˈvɪzɪb(ə)l/ *adj.* недели́мый.

Indo-China /ˈɪndəʊˈtʃaɪnə/ *n.* Индокита́й.

indoctrinate /ɪnˈdɒktrɪˌneɪt/ *v.t.* внуш|а́ть, -и́ть при́нципы + *d.*; подв|ерга́ть, -е́ргнуть идеологи́ческой обрабо́тке.

indoctrination /ɪnˌdɒktrɪˈneɪʃ(ə)n/ *n.* идеологи́ческая обрабо́тка.

Indo-European /ˌɪndəʊˌjʊərəˈpiːən/ *adj.* индоевропе́йский.

indolence /ˈɪndələns/ *n.* ле́ность, вя́лость.

indolent /ˈɪndələnt/ *adj.* лени́вый, вя́лый.

indomitability /ɪnˌdɒmɪtəˈbɪlɪtɪ/ *n.* неукроти́мость.

indomitable /ɪnˈdɒmɪtəb(ə)l/ *adj.* неукроти́мый.

Indonesia /ˌɪndəʊˈniːzɪə/ *n.* Индоне́зия.

Indonesian /ˌɪndəˈniːzjən/, /-ʒ(ə)n/, /-ʃ(ə)n/ *n.* (*person*) индонези́|ец (*fem.* -йка); (*language*) индонези́йский язы́к.

● *adj.* индонези́йский.

indoor /ˈɪndɔː(r)/ *adj.* ко́мнатный; **~ aerial** вну́тренняя/ко́мнатная анте́нна; **~ games** ко́мнатные и́гры; **~ swimming-pool** закры́тый бассе́йн.

indoors /ɪnˈdɔːz/ *adv.* (*expr. position*) в до́ме; взаперти́; в четырёх сте́нах; **we stayed ~ all morning** мы просиде́ли до́ма (*or* никуда́ не выходи́ли) всё у́тро; (*expr. motion*) в дом, внутрь.

indubitable /ɪnˈdjuːbɪtəb(ə)l/ *adj.* несомне́нный; бесспо́рный.

induc|e /ɪnˈdjuːs/ *v.t.* **1** (*persuade, prevail on*) убеж|да́ть, -ди́ть; возде́йствовать (*impf., pf.*) на + *a.*; **nothing will ~e him to change his mind** ничто́ не заста́вит его́ измени́ть реше́ние. **2** (*bring about*) вызыва́ть, вы́звать; **illness ~ed by fatigue** боле́знь, вы́званная переутомле́нием; **sleep-~ing drugs** снотво́рные сре́дства; **~e labour** (*Br.*), **labor** (*US*)/**a birth** стимули́ровать (*impf., pf.*) ро́ды. **3** (*elec.*) индукти́ровать (*impf., pf.*); **~ed current** индукти́рованный ток. **4** (*log.*) выводи́ть, вы́вести путём инду́кции.

inducement /ɪnˈdjuːsmənt/ *n.* (*motive, incentive*) сти́мул; **there is no ~ for me to stay here** ничто́ не уде́рживает меня́ здесь; (*lure*) прима́нка; **the ~s of the capital** притяга́тельная си́ла столи́чной жи́зни (*or* столи́цы).

induct /ɪnˈdʌkt/ *v.t.* (*install in post*) вв|оди́ть, -ести́; назн|ача́ть, -а́чить на до́лжность; (*initiate*) вв|оди́ть, -ести́; посвя|ща́ть, -ти́ть; (*US, into armed forces*) приз|ыва́ть, -ва́ть на вое́нную слу́жбу.

inductance /ɪnˈdʌkt(ə)ns/ *n.* индукти́вность.

induction /ɪnˈdʌkʃ(ə)n/ *n.* **1** (*installation in post*) введе́ние в до́лжность; (*introduction, initiation*) введе́ние, вступле́ние; (*US, into armed forces*) призы́в на вое́нную слу́жбу. **2** (*log.*) инду́кция. **3** (*elec.*) инду́кция. **4** (*med., of a birth*) стимуля́ция ро́дов.

inductive /ɪnˈdʌktɪv/ *adj.* (*log.*) индукти́вный; (*elec.*) индукти́вный; индукцио́нный.

indulge /ɪnˈdʌldʒ/ *v.t.* (*gratify, give way to*) потво́рствовать (*impf., pf.*) + *d.*; потака́ть (*impf.*) + *d.*; **she ~d all his wishes** она́ потака́ла всем его́ жела́ниям; (*spoil*) по́ртить (*impf.*); балова́ть, из-; **their children have been over-~d** они́ избалова́ли свои́х дете́й; (*entertain*) пита́ть (*impf.*); леле́ять (*impf.*); **I still ~ the hope that** … я всё ещё леле́ю наде́жду, что…

● *v.i.* (*allow o.s. pleasure*) увлека́ться (*impf.*) (*чем*); не отказа́ть (*pf.*) себе́ в удово́льствии; **he ~s in a cigar** он позволя́ет себе́ вы́курить сига́ру; **she rarely ~s in a new dress** она́ ре́дко позволя́ет себе́ поку́пку но́вого пла́тья; (*coll., partake of drink*) выпива́ть (*impf.*).

indulgence /ɪnˈdʌldʒ(ə)ns/ *n.* **1** (*gratification of others*) потво́рство, потака́ние, побла́жка; (*of o.s.*) потво́рство свои́м при́хотям. **2** (*tolerance*) снисходи́тельность, терпи́мость. **3** (*pleasure indulged in*) удово́льствие; **smoking is his only ~** куре́ние — его́ еди́нственная сла́бость. **4** (*eccl.*) индульге́нция.

indulgent /ɪnˈdʌldʒ(ə)nt/ *adj.*

(*compliant*) потво́рствующий; (*tolerant*) снисходи́тельный, терпи́мый; **~ criticism** снисходи́тельная кри́тика; **~ parents** не сли́шком стро́гие роди́тели.

Indus /ˈɪndəs/ *n.* Инд.

industrial /ɪnˈdʌstrɪəl/ *adj.* промы́шленный, индустриа́льный; **~ accident** несча́стный слу́чай на произво́дстве; **~ action** (*Br.*) забасто́вочные де́йствия; **~ area** индустриа́льный райо́н; **~ design** промы́шленный диза́йн; **~ disease** профессиона́льное заболева́ние; **~ dispute** трудово́й конфли́кт; **~ estate** (*Br.*) промы́шленная зо́на; **~ park** (*US*) = **~ estate; ~ relations** взаимоотноше́ния ме́жду предпринима́телями и рабо́чей си́лой; **the I~ Revolution** промы́шленный переворо́т; **~ training** произво́дственное обуче́ние.

industrialism /ɪnˈdʌstrɪəˌlɪz(ə)m/ *n.* индустриали́зм.

industrialist /ɪnˈdʌstrɪəlɪst/ *n.* промы́шленник; фабрика́нт.

industrialization /ɪnˌdʌstrɪəlaɪˈzeɪʃ(ə)n/ *n.* индустриализа́ция.

industrialize /ɪnˈdʌstrɪəˌlaɪz/ *v.t.* индустриализи́ровать (*impf., pf.*).

industrious /ɪnˈdʌstrɪəs/ *adj.* трудолюби́вый, усе́рдный.

industr|y /ˈɪndəstrɪ/ *n.* **1** (*branch of manufacture*) о́трасль; **home ~ies** о́трасли оте́чественной промы́шленности; **cottage ~y** надо́мный про́мысел; куста́рная промы́шленность; **a dying ~y** отмира́ющая о́трасль промы́шленности. **2** (*the world of manufacture*) индустри́я; промы́шленность; **he intends to go into ~y** он хо́чет заня́ться промы́шленной де́ятельностью. **3** (*diligence*) трудолю́бие; усе́рдие.

indwelling /ɪnˈdwelɪŋ/ *adj.* прису́щий.

inebriate[1] /ɪˈniːbrɪət/ *n.* пья́ница (*c.g.*). ● *adj.* пья́ный; опьянённый.

inebriate[2] /ɪˈniːbrɪˌeɪt/ *v.t.* (*usu. in p.p.*) вызыва́ть, вы́звать опьяне́ние у + *g.*; **~d** пья́ный; **he became ~d** он опьяне́л.

inedible /ɪnˈedɪb(ə)l/ *adj.* несъедо́бный.

ineducable /ɪnˈedjʊkəb(ə)l/ *adj.* необуча́емый.

ineffable /ɪnˈefəb(ə)l/ *adj.* неопису́емый, невырази́мый.

ineffective /ˌɪnɪˈfektɪv/ *adj.* неэффекти́вный; безрезульта́тный; (*of person, inefficient*) неуме́лый, неспосо́бный.

ineffectiveness /ˌɪnɪˈfektɪvnɪs/ *n.* неэффекти́вность; безрезульта́тность, неуме́ние, неспосо́бность.

ineffectual /ˌɪnɪˈfektjʊəl/, /-tʃʊəl/ *adj.* безрезульта́тный, неуда́чный; **an ~ person** неуда́чник.

inefficacy /ɪnˈefɪkəsɪ/ *n.* бесполе́зность, неэффекти́вность.

inefficiency /ˌɪnɪˈfɪʃ(ə)nsɪ/ *n.* неэффекти́вность, неспосо́бность.

inefficient /ˌɪnɪˈfɪʃ(ə)nt/ *adj.* (*of persons*) неуме́лый, неспосо́бный; (*of organizations, measures etc.*) неэффекти́вный; малопроизводи́тельный; (*of machines*) непроизводи́тельный.

inelegance /ɪnˈelɪgəns/ *n.* неэлега́нтность.

inelegant /ɪnˈelɪgənt/ *adj.* неэлега́нтный.

ineligibility /ɪnˌelɪdʒɪˈbɪlɪtɪ/ *n.* неприго́дность.

ineligible /ɪnˈelɪdʒɪb(ə)l/ *adj.* (*for office*) неподходя́щий; (*for military service*) него́дный (к + *d.*); (*for a benefit*) не име́ющий пра́ва (на + *a.*).

ineluctable /ˌɪnɪˈlʌktəb(ə)l/ *adj.* неотврати́мый, неизбе́жный.

inept /ɪˈnept/ *adj.* (*clumsy*) неуме́лый.

ineptitude /ɪˈneptɪˌtjuːd/ *n.* неуме́ние; (*act*) глу́пая вы́ходка.

inequalit|y /ˌɪnɪˈkwɒlɪtɪ/ *n.* (*lack of equality*) нера́венство; (*difference*) ра́зница; **~ies in wealth** иму́щественное нера́венство.

inequitable /ɪnˈekwɪtəb(ə)l/ *adj.* несправедли́вый.

inequity /ɪnˈekwɪtɪ/ *n.* несправедли́вость.

ineradicable /ˌɪnɪˈrædɪkəb(ə)l/ *adj.* неискорени́мый.

inert /ɪˈnɜːt/ *adj.* (*of substance*) ине́ртный; (*of the body, movements etc.*) тяжёлый, неповоро́тливый; (*fig., of person*) вя́лый, безде́ятельный.

inertia /ɪˈnɜːʃə/, /-ʃɪə/ *n.* (*phys.*) ине́рция; (*inertness, sloth*) ине́ртность.

inertness /ɪˈnɜːtnɪs/ = **inertia**

inescapable /ˌɪnɪˈskeɪpəb(ə)l/ *adj.* неизбе́жный.

inessential /ˌɪnɪˈsenʃ(ə)l/ *adj.* незначи́тельный; несуще́ственный.

inestimable /ɪnˈestɪməb(ə)l/ *adj.* неоцени́мый.

inevitability /ɪnˌevɪtəˈbɪlɪtɪ/ *n.* неизбе́жность.

inevitable /ɪnˈevɪtəb(ə)l/ *adj.* неизбе́жный, немину́емый; (*coll., customary*) неизме́нный.

inexact /ˌɪnɪgˈzækt/ *adj.* нето́чный.

inexactitude /ˌɪnɪgˈzæktɪtjuːd/ *n.* нето́чность.

inexcusable /ˌɪnɪkˈskjuːzəb(ə)l/ *adj.* непрости́тельный.

inexhaustible /ˌɪnɪgˈzɔːstɪb(ə)l/ *adj.* (*unfailing*) неистощи́мый, неисчерпа́емый; **~ energy** неистощи́мая эне́ргия; **~ patience** неистощи́мое терпе́ние; **an ~ supply** неисчерпа́емый запа́с; (*untiring*) неутоми́мый.

inexorability /ɪnˌeksərəˈbɪlɪtɪ/ *n.* неумоли́мость, непрекло́нность.

inexorable /ɪnˈeksərəb(ə)l/ *adj.* (*relentless, unyielding*) неумоли́мый, непрекло́нный; безжа́лостный; **~ demands** непрекло́нные/безжа́лостные тре́бования; **~ logic** неумоли́мая ло́гика.

inexpedient /ˌɪnɪkˈspiːdɪənt/ *adj.* нецелесообра́зный.

inexpensive /ˌɪnɪkˈspensɪv/ *adj.* недорого́й.

inexperience /ˌɪnɪkˈspɪərɪəns/ *n.* нео́пытность.

inexperienced /ˌɪnɪkˈspɪərɪənst/ *adj.* нео́пытный.

inexpert /ɪnˈekspɜːt/ *adj.* неуме́лый.

inexplicable /ˌɪnɪkˈsplɪkəb(ə)l/, /ɪnˈeks-/ *adj.* необъясни́мый.

inexplicit /ˌɪnɪkˈsplɪsɪt/ *adj.* непоня́тный; нея́сный.

inexpressible /ˌɪnɪkˈspresɪb(ə)l/ *adj.* невырази́мый, неизъясни́мый.

inexpressive /ˌɪnɪkˈspresɪv/ *adj.* невырази́тельный.

inextinguishable /ˌɪnɪkˈstɪŋgwɪʃəb(ə)l/ *adj.* (*lit., fig.*) неугаси́мый; (*fig.*) неистреби́мый; **~ hatred** неугаси́мая не́нависть.

inextricabl|e /ɪnˈekstrɪkəb(ə)l/, /ˌɪnɪkˈstrɪk-/ *adj.* неразры́вный; **~y linked** неразры́вно свя́занный.

infallibility /ɪnˌfælɪˈbɪlɪtɪ/ *n.* **1** (*incapability of error*) безоши́бочность, непогреши́мость; **Papal ~** непогреши́мость Па́пы. **2** (*dependability*) надёжность.

infallible /ɪnˈfælɪb(ə)l/ *adj.* (*action, plan, decision*) безоши́бочный; (*person*) непогреши́мый; (*unfailing*) надёжный; **an ~ method** надёжный/ве́рный спо́соб; **~ proof** неопроверж́имое доказа́тельство.

infamous /ˈɪnfəməs/ *adj.* (*person*) безсла́вный; (*behaviour*) позо́рный.

infamy /ˈɪnfəmɪ/ *n.* (*evil repute*) дурна́я сла́ва; (*moral depravity*) ни́зость; (*infamous conduct*) позо́рное поведе́ние; (*shame, disgrace*) позо́р.

infancy /ˈɪnfənsɪ/ *n.* младе́нчество; **the child died in ~** ребёнок у́мер в младе́нчестве; **from his earliest ~** с ра́ннего де́тства.

infant /ˈɪnf(ə)nt/ *n.* младе́нец; **~ mortality** де́тская сме́ртность; **~ prodigy** вундерки́нд; **~ school** (*Br.*) шко́ла для малыше́й, мла́дшие кла́ссы нача́льной шко́лы.

infanticide /ɪnˈfæntɪˌsaɪd/ *n.* (*person*) детоуби́йца (*c.g.*); (*crime*) детоуби́йство.

infantile /ˈɪnfənˌtaɪl/ *adj.* **1** де́тский, младе́нческий; **~ paralysis** де́тский парали́ч. **2** (*childish*) инфанти́льный.

infantilism /ɪnˈfæntɪˌlɪz(ə)m/ *n.* инфантили́зм.

infantry /ˈɪnfəntrɪ/ *n.* пехо́та; **~ regiment** пехо́тный полк. ● *cpd.* **~man** *n.* пехоти́нец.

infatuate /ɪnˈfætjʊˌeɪt/ *v.t.*: **he is ~d with her** она́ покори́ла/плени́ла его́; **he was ~d with the idea** иде́я покори́ла его́.

infatuation /ɪnˌfætjʊˈeɪʃ(ə)n/ *n.* (*for s.o.*) влюблённость, увлече́ние; (*with something*) увлече́ние.

infect /ɪnˈfekt/ *v.t.* (*lit., fig.*) зара|жа́ть, -зи́ть; **the wound became ~ed** ра́на загно́илась.

infection /ɪnˈfekʃ(ə)n/ *n.* (*infecting*) инфе́кция; (*infectious disease*) инфекцио́нное заболева́ние; **he**

caught the ~ from his brother (*lit., fig.*) он заразúлся от брáта.

infectious /ɪnˈfekʃəs/ *adj.* (*disease*) зарáзный, инфекциóнный; (*person*) зарáзный; (*fig.*) заразúтельный; **his enthusiasm was ~** егó энтузиáзм оказáлся заразúтельным.

infelicitous /ˌɪnfɪˈlɪsɪtəs/ *adj.* неудáчный, неумéстный.

infelicity /ˌɪnfɪˈlɪsɪtɪ/ *n.* неумéстность.

infer /ɪnˈfɜː(r)/ *v.t.* (**inferred, inferring**) **1** (*deduce*) заключ|áть, -úть; предпол|агáть, -ожúть; **am I to ~ that you disagree?** слéдует ли мне заключúть, что вы несоглáсны?; **he ~red the worst from her expression** по выражéнию её лицá он предположúл сáмое хýдшее. **2** (*disp., imply*) подразумевáть (*impf.*).

inferable /ɪnˈfɜːrəb(ə)l/ *adj.* выводúмый.

inference /ˈɪnfərəns/ *n.* (*inferring*) выведéние; **by ~** путём выведéния; (*conclusion*) вы́вод; заключéние; **I drew the obvious ~** я сдéлал естéственный вы́вод.

inferential /ˌɪnfəˈrenʃ(ə)l/ *adj.* (*inferred*) вы́веденный.

inferior /ɪnˈfɪərɪə(r)/ *n.* (*in rank, social status etc.*) подчинённый; (*in skill, mental attributes etc.*): **he is her ~ in horsemanship** он éздит на лóшади хýже, чем онá.

● *adj.* **1** (*lower in position, rank etc.*) нúзший; **he held an ~ position** он занимáл (бóлее) нúзкое положéние; **the rank of captain is ~ to that of major** капитáн нúже майóра по звáнию.
2 (*poorer in quality*) хýдший; **this batch is in no way ~ to the others** э́та пáртия товáра ничýть не хýже другúх.
3 (*of poor quality*) плохóй, сквéрный, низкосóртный, низкопрóбный; **an ~ specimen** плохóй образéц.
4 (*of less importance*) неполноцéнный; **he makes me feel ~** в егó присýтствии у меня́ появля́ется кóмплекс неполноцéнности.

inferiority /ɪnˌfɪərɪˈɒrɪtɪ/ *n.* (*of position*) бóлее нúзкое положéние; (*of rank*) бóлее нúзкое звáние; (*of quality*) низкосóртность; (*of ability*) неполноцéнность; **~ complex** кóмплекс неполноцéнности.

infernal /ɪnˈfɜːn(ə)l/ *adj.* **1** (*of hell*) áдский; **the ~ regions** ад, преиспóдняя. **2** (*devilish, abominable*) áдский, дья́вольский, инфернáльный; **an ~ machine** áдская машúна.
3 (*coll., confounded*) чертóвский; **an ~ nuisance** проклятие.

inferno /ɪnˈfɜːnəʊ/ *n.* (*pl.* **~s**) (*lit., fig.*) ад; **the building became a blazing ~** дом преврати́лся в пылáющий/óгненный ад.

infertile /ɪnˈfɜːtaɪl/ *adj.* (*soil*) неплодорóдный; (*woman, man*) бесплóдный; (*cell*) стерúльный.

infertility /ˌɪnfəˈtɪlɪtɪ/ *n.* неплодорóдность, бесплóдность, стерúльность.

infest /ɪnˈfest/ *v.t.* наводн|я́ть, -úть; **the house is ~ed with rats** дом наводнён кры́сами; **his clothes were ~ed with lice** егó одéжда кишéла вшáми; **pirates ~ed the coast** прибрéжные вóды кишéли пирáтами.

infestation /ˌɪnfeˈsteɪʃ(ə)n/ *n.* (*of rats etc.*) наводнéние; (*med.*) заражéние паразúтами.

infidel /ˈɪnfɪd(ə)l/ *n. & adj.* (*rel.*) невéрный.

infidelity /ˌɪnfɪˈdelɪtɪ/ *n.* невéрность, измéна.

in-fighting /ˈɪnˌfaɪtɪŋ/ *n.* (*boxing*) инфáйтинг, блúжний бой; (*fig.*) междоусóбица, внýтренняя борьбá; внýтренний конфлúкт.

infiltrate /ˈɪnfɪlˌtreɪt/ *v.t.* (*permeate*) пропúт|ывать, -áть; (*fig.*) прон|икáть, -úкнуть; **the enemy ~d our lines** враг пронúк в наш тыл.

infiltration /ˌɪnfɪlˈtreɪʃ(ə)n/ *n.* (*fig., mil. and pol.*) проникновéние, инфильтрáция.

infinite /ˈɪnfɪnɪt/ *n.*: **the ~** (**~** *space*) бесконéчность.

● *adj.* (*boundless*) бесконéчный, беспредéльный; **the ~ goodness of God** беспредéльная благодáть Бóжья; (*countless*) несмéтный; **there are ~ possibilities** возмóжности неисчерпáемы; (*very great*) огрóмный.

infinitesimal /ˌɪnfɪnɪˈtesɪm(ə)l/ *adj.* бесконéчно мáлый.

infinitive /ɪnˈfɪnɪtɪv/ *n.* инфинитúв, неопределённая фóрма глагóла.

infinitude /ɪnˈfɪnɪˌtjuːd/ *n.* (*boundlessness*) бесконéчность, беспредéльность; (*boundless number*) бесконéчно большóе числó.

infinity /ɪnˈfɪnɪtɪ/ *n.* бесконéчность.

infirm /ɪnˈfɜːm/ *adj.* (*physically*) нéмощный, дря́хлый.

infirmary /ɪnˈfɜːmərɪ/ *n.* (*hospital*) больнúца; (*sick quarters*) изоля́тор.

infirmity /ɪnˈfɜːmɪtɪ/ *n.* нéмощь; дря́хлость.

inflame /ɪnˈfleɪm/ *v.t.* **1**: **her eyes were ~d with weeping** от слёз у неё воспалúлись глазá; **the wound became ~d** рáна воспалúлась/загноúлась. **2** (*arouse*) возбу|ждáть, -дúть; **~d with passion** пылáющий стрáстью.

inflammable /ɪnˈflæməb(ə)l/ *adj.* легкó воспламеня́ющийся, горю́чий.

inflammation /ˌɪnfləˈmeɪʃ(ə)n/ *n.* воспалéние.

inflammatory /ɪnˈflæmətərɪ/ *adj.* (*lit.*) воспалúтельный; (*fig.*) зажигáтельный; подстрекáтельский.

inflatable /ɪnˈfleɪtəb(ə)l/ *n.* (*boat*) надувнáя лóдка; (*toy*) надувнáя игрýшка.

● *adj.* надувнóй.

inflate /ɪnˈfleɪt/ *v.t.* **1** (*fill with air, gas etc.*) над|увáть, -ýть; накáч|ивать, -áть; (*fig.*): **~d with pride** надýтый от вáжности; **~d language** напы́щенный язы́к; **~d importance** раздýтое значéние. **2** (*fin.*): **~d prices** взвúнченные цéны.

inflation /ɪnˈfleɪʃ(ə)n/ *n.* (*of balloon, tyre etc.*) надувáние; (*econ.*) инфля́ция, обесцéнивание.

inflationary /ɪnˈfleɪʃənərɪ/ *adj.* инфляциóнный.

inflect /ɪnˈflekt/ *v.t.* (*gram.*) склоня́ть, про-; (*modulate*) модулúровать (*impf.*).

inflection /ɪnˈflekʃ(ə)n/ *n.* (*gram.*) склонéние; (*ending*) флéксия; (*of voice*) интонáция.

inflexibility /ɪnˌfleksɪˈbɪlɪtɪ/ *n.* негúбкость, жёсткость; (*fig.*) непреклóнность, непоколебúмость.

inflexible /ɪnˈfleksɪb(ə)l/ *adj.* негúбкий, жёсткий; (*fig.*) непреклóнный, непоколебúмый.

inflict /ɪnˈflɪkt/ *v.t.* (*a blow*) нан|осúть, -ести́; (*pain*) причин|я́ть, -úть; **he ~ed a mortal blow on the enemy** он нанёс врагý смертéльный удáр; **a self-~ed wound** рáна, нанесённая самомý себé; **the judge ~ed a severe penalty** судья́ наложúл сурóвое наказáние; **I don't wish to ~ myself upon you** я не хочý навя́зываться вам.

infliction /ɪnˈflɪkʃ(ə)n/ *n.* (*of blow*) нанесéние; (*of pain*) причинéние; (*of penalty etc.*) наложéние.

in-flight /ˈɪnflaɪt/ *adj.* происходя́щий в полёте/на бортý самолёта.

inflow /ˈɪnfləʊ/ *n.* (*of liquid*) втекáние; (*of goods, money etc.*) наплы́в, прितóк.

influence /ˈɪnflʊəns/ *n.* (*power to affect or change*) влия́ние, воздéйствие; **she is a good ~ on him** онá на негó хорошó влия́ет; **he is an ~ for good** он хорошó воздéйствует/влия́ет на окружáющих; **fall under s.o.'s ~** поп|адáть, -áсть под чьё-н. влия́ние; **under the ~ (of drink)** под воздéйствием (алкогóля); **he has ~ with the government** он имéет влия́ние на прави́тельство; (*power due to position or wealth*) влия́ние; авторитéт; **he used his ~ on my behalf** он испóльзовал своё влия́ние, чтóбы помóчь мне; **a man of ~** влия́тельный человéк.

● *v.t.* влия́ть, по- на + *a.*; окáз|ывать, -áть влия́ние на + *a.*; дéйствовать, по- (*or* воздéйствовать *impf., pf.*) на + *a.*; **nothing will ~ me to change my mind** ничтó не застáвит меня́ измени́ть моё решéние; **he was ~d by what he saw** увúденное повлия́ло на негó.

influential /ˌɪnflʊˈenʃ(ə)l/ *adj.* влия́тельный.

influenza /ˌɪnflʊˈenzə/ *n.* грипп.

influx /ˈɪnflʌks/ *n.* (*fig.*) наплы́в.

inform /ɪnˈfɔːm/ *v.t.* **1** (*tell; make aware*) сообщ|áть, -úть + *d.*; информúровать (*impf., pf.*); осв|едомля́ть, -éдомить; стáвить, по- в извéстность; **I was not ~ed of the facts** мне не сообщúли о фáктах; **keep me ~ed** держúте меня́ в кýрсе дел; **according to ~ed opinion** соглáсно осведомлённым истóчникам; **he is a well ~ed man** он óчень осведомлённый человéк; **an ~ed guess** обоснóванная догáдка.
2 (*inspire*) воодушев|ля́ть, -úть.

● *v.i.* дон|осúть, -ести́; **he ~ed against, on his comrades** он доносúл на своúх товáрищей.

informal /ɪnˈfɔ:m(ə)l/ *adj.* неофициа́льный; непринуждённый; **it will be an ~ party** ве́чер бу́дет дру́жеский; **~ dress** повседне́вная оде́жда; **an ~ meeting** неофициа́льная встре́ча.

informality /ˌɪnfɔ:ˈmælɪtɪ/ *n.* непринуждённость.

informant /ɪnˈfɔ:mənt/ *n.* информа́тор; исто́чник информа́ции; (*police informer*) осведоми́тель (*fem.* -ница); (*ling.*) информа́нт.

information /ˌɪnfəˈmeɪʃ(ə)n/ *n.* информа́ция; све́дения (*nt. pl.*); спра́вка; да́нные (*nt. pl.*); **a useful piece of ~** поле́зная информа́ция; **according to my ~** согла́сно мои́м све́дениям; **can you give me any ~ about fares?** да́йте мне, пожа́луйста, спра́вку о сто́имости прое́зда!; **he is a mine of ~** он кла́дезь зна́ний; **for your ~** к ва́шему све́дению; **~ bureau** спра́вочное бюро́; **~ desk** спра́вочный стол; **~ science, technology** информа́тика.

informative /ɪnˈfɔ:mətɪv/ *adj.* информи́рующий; поучи́тельный; **I found him most ~** он снабди́л меня́ о́чень поле́зной информа́цией; **an ~ article** содержа́тельная/поучи́тельная статья́.

informer /ɪnˈfɔ:mə(r)/ *n.* (*police ~*) осведоми́тель (*fem.* -ница); (*against s.o.*) доно́счи|к (*fem.* -ца).

infraction /ɪnˈfrækʃ(ə)n/ *n.* наруше́ние.

infra dig /ˌɪnfrə ˈdɪg/ *pred. adj.* (*coll.*) унизи́тельно.

infra-red /ˌɪnfrəˈred/ *adj.* инфракра́сный.

infrastructure /ˈɪnfrəˌstrʌktʃə(r)/ *n.* инфраструкту́ра.

infrequency /ɪnˈfri:kwənsɪ/ *n.* ре́дкость.

infrequent /ɪnˈfri:kwənt/ *adj.* ре́дкий.

infringe /ɪnˈfrɪndʒ/ *v.t. & i.* нар|уша́ть, -у́шить; посяг|а́ть, -ну́ть на + *a.*; ущем|ля́ть, -и́ть; **this does not ~ on your rights** э́то не ущемля́ет ва́ших прав.

infringement /ɪnˈfrɪndʒmənt/ *n.* наруше́ние; посяга́тельство; ущемле́ние.

infuriat|e /ɪnˈfjʊərɪˌeɪt/ *v.t.* прив|оди́ть, -ести́ в я́рость/бе́шенство; разъяр|я́ть, -и́ть; **an ~ing delay** возмути́тельная заде́ржка; **he became ~ed with me** он разозли́лся на меня́.

infuse /ɪnˈfju:z/ *v.t.* (*pour in*) вли|ва́ть, -ть; (*steep in liquid*) зава́р|ивать, -и́ть; наст|а́ивать, -оя́ть; (*inspire*) всел|я́ть, -и́ть; внуш|а́ть, -и́ть.

● *v.i.* наст|а́иваться, -оя́ться; **let the tea ~ for 5 minutes** пусть чай наста́ивается пять мину́т.

infusion /ɪnˈfju:ʒ(ə)n/ *n.* влива́ние; (*fig.*) внуше́ние; (*of tea, herbs etc.*) наста́ивание; (*liquid made by ~*) насто́йка.

ingenious /ɪnˈdʒi:nɪəs/ *adj.* изобрета́тельный; остроу́мный; **an ~ solution** остроу́мное/оригина́льное реше́ние; (*of a device, machine etc.*) иску́сный; замыслова́тый.

ingenuity /ˌɪndʒɪˈnju:ɪtɪ/ *n.* изобрета́тельность; оригина́льность.

ingenuous /ɪnˈdʒenjʊəs/ *adj.* (*sincere; candid*) и́скренний; открове́нный; (*simple, unsophisticated*) просто́й, простоду́шный; (*naive*) простоду́шный.

ingenuousness /ɪnˈdʒenjʊəsnɪs/ *n.* и́скренность; простоду́шие.

ingest /ɪnˈdʒest/ *v.t.* глота́ть (*impf.*), прогл|а́тывать, -оти́ть.

ingestion /ɪnˈdʒestʃ(ə)n/ *n.* (*physiol.*) приём (пи́щи).

ingle-nook /ˈɪŋg(ə)lˌnʊk/ *n.* месте́чко у ками́на.

inglorious /ɪnˈglɔ:rɪəs/ *adj.* (*ignominious*) бесcла́вный; (*obscure*) незаме́тный.

ingot /ˈɪŋgɒt/, /-gət/ *n.* сли́ток.

ingrained /ɪnˈgreɪnd/, *attrib.* /ˈɪn-/ *adj.* **1** въе́вшийся; **~ dirt** въе́вшаяся грязь. **2** (*fig.*) закорене́лый, врождённый; **~ prejudice** закорене́лый предрассу́док.

ingrate /ˈɪngreɪt/, /-ˈgreɪt/ *n.* (*liter.*) неблагода́рный челове́к.

ingratiat|e /ɪnˈgreɪʃɪˌeɪt/ *v.t.*: **~ o.s. with s.o.** сни́ск|ивать, -а́ть расположе́ние (+ *g.*); **he ~ed himself with the new manager** он сниска́л расположе́ние но́вого нача́льника; **an ~ing smile** заи́скивающая улы́бка.

ingratitude /ɪnˈgrætɪˌtju:d/ *n.* неблагода́рность.

ingredient /ɪnˈgri:dɪənt/ *n.* составна́я часть; (*of solution, mixture*) компоне́нт; ингредие́нт; **the ~s of a cake** ингредие́нты пирога́; **hard work is an important ~ of success** упо́рный труд — одно́ из основны́х усло́вий успе́ха.

ingress /ˈɪngres/ *n.* (*entry*) до́ступ; вхожде́ние; (*right of entry*) пра́во вхо́да.

ingrowing /ˈɪnˌgrəʊɪŋ/ *adj.* враста́ющий; **~ toe-nail** враста́ющий но́готь ноги́.

Ingush /ˈɪŋgʊʃ/ *n.* (*pl.* **~** *or* **~es**) ингу́ш (*fem.* -ка).

● *adj.* ингу́шский.

Ingushetia /ˌɪŋgʊˈʃetɪə/ *n.* Ингуше́тия.

inhabit /ɪnˈhæbɪt/ *v.t.* (**inhabited, inhabiting**) жить (*impf.*) в + *p.*; обита́ть (*impf.*) в + *p.*; населя́ть (*impf.*); **his family ~ed a large estate** его́ семья́ жила́ в большо́м поме́стье; **is the island ~ed?** э́тот о́стров обита́ем?; **the house was ~ed by foreigners** дом был населён иностра́нцами; **many birds ~ the forest** в лесу́ во́дится мно́го птиц.

inhabitable /ɪnˈhæbɪtəb(ə)l/ *adj.* приго́дный для жилья́; жило́й.

inhabitant /ɪnˈhæbɪt(ə)nt/ *n.* жи́тель (*fem.* -ница); жиле́ц.

inhalation /ˌɪnhəˈleɪʃ(ə)n/ *n.* вдыха́ние; (*med.*) ингаля́ция.

inhale /ɪnˈheɪl/ *v.t.* вд|ыха́ть, -охну́ть.

● *v.i.* зат|я́гиваться, -яну́ться (*сигаретой и т.п.*); **it is dangerous to ~** затя́гиваться вре́дно.

inhaler /ɪnˈheɪlə(r)/ *n.* (*device*) ингаля́тор.

inharmonious /ˌɪnhɑ:ˈməʊnɪəs/ *adj.* (*of sounds*) негармони́чный; (*fig.*) негармони́рующий.

inhere /ɪnˈhɪə(r)/ *v.i.* быть прису́щим/сво́йственным; принадлежа́ть (*impf.*) (+ *d.*).

inherent /ɪnˈhɪərənt/, /ɪnˈherənt/ *adj.* сво́йственный, прису́щий; (*inalienable*) неотъе́млемый.

inherit /ɪnˈherɪt/ *v.t.* (**inherited, inheriting**) насле́довать (*impf., pf.*; *pf. also* у-); полу|ча́ть, -и́ть в насле́дство.

● *v.i.* (**inherited, inheriting**) полу|ча́ть, -и́ть насле́дство.

inheritable /ɪnˈherɪtəb(ə)l/ *adj.* насле́дуемый.

inheritance /ɪnˈherɪt(ə)ns/ *n.* (*inheriting*) насле́дование; (*something inherited*) насле́дство.

inheritor /ɪnˈherɪtə(r)/ *n.* насле́дни|к (*fem.* -ца).

inhibit /ɪnˈhɪbɪt/ *v.t.* (**inhibited, inhibiting**) (*hinder, restrain*) угнета́ть (*impf.*); подав|ля́ть, -и́ть; ско́в|ывать, -а́ть; **fear ~s his actions** страх ско́вывает его́ де́йствия; **an ~ed person** ско́ванный челове́к.

inhibition /ˌɪnhɪˈbɪʃ(ə)n/ *n.* (*restraint*) подавле́ние; (*psych.*) торможе́ние.

inhospitable /ˌɪnhɒˈspɪtəb(ə)l/, /ɪnˈhɒsp-/ *adj.* негостеприи́мный, неприве́тливый; **an ~ coast** суро́вый бе́рег.

inhospitality /ɪnˌhɒspɪˈtælɪtɪ/ *n.* негостеприи́мность, неприве́тливость.

inhuman /ɪnˈhju:mən/ *adj.* (*cruel*) бесчелове́чный; (*not human*) нечелове́ческий.

inhumane /ˌɪnhju:ˈmeɪn/ *adj.* негума́нный, бесчелове́чный.

inhumanity /ˌɪnhju:ˈmænɪtɪ/ *n.* бесчелове́чность, жесто́кость.

inhume /ɪnˈhju:m/ *v.t.* погре|ба́ть, -сти́; пред|ава́ть, -а́ть земле́.

inimical /ɪˈnɪmɪk(ə)l/ *adj.* (*hostile; conflicting*) вражде́бный; недружелю́бный; (*harmful*) вре́дный, неблагоприя́тный; **factors ~ to success** обстоя́тельства, препя́тствующие успе́ху.

inimitable /ɪˈnɪmɪtəb(ə)l/ *adj.* неподража́емый; несравне́нный.

iniquitous /ɪˈnɪkwɪtəs/ *adj.* (*unjust*) несправедли́вый; (*monstrous*) чудо́вищный.

iniquity /ɪˈnɪkwɪtɪ/ *n.* (*injustice*) несправедли́вость; (*evil*) зло.

initial /ɪˈnɪʃ(ə)l/ *n.* нача́льная/пе́рвая бу́ква; **what are your ~s?** ва́ши инициа́лы?; (*pl., as signature*) инициа́лы (*m. pl.*).

● *adj.* нача́льный, исхо́дный; **in the ~ stage** на первонача́льной ста́дии; **~ cost** первонача́льная сто́имость; **~ velocity** нача́льная ско́рость; **~ letter** нача́льная бу́ква.

● *v.t.* (**initialled, initialling;** *US* **initialed, initialing**): **~ a document** ста́вить, по- инициа́лы под документом; парафировать (*impf., pf.*) документ.

initiate[1] /ɪˈnɪʃɪət/ *n.* посвящённый.

initiate[2] /ɪˈnɪʃɪˌeɪt/ *v.t.* **1** (*set in motion*) нач|инать, -ать. **2** (*introduce*) приобщ|ать, -ить (к + *d.*); вв|одить, -ести (в + *a.*); посвя|щать, -тить (в + *a.*); **they ~d him into society** они ввели его в общество; **he was ~d into the mysteries of science** его посвятили в тайны науки.

initiation /ɪˌnɪʃɪˈeɪʃ(ə)n/ *n.* (*beginning*) основание, установление; (*admission; introduction*) посвящение (в + *a.*); введение (в + *a.*); **~ ceremonies** обряды посвящения.

initiative /ɪˈnɪʃətɪv/, /ɪˈnɪʃɪətɪv/ *n.* **1** (*lead*) инициатива, почин; **he took the ~** он взял на себя инициативу; **he acted on his own ~** он действовал по собственной инициативе. **2** (*enterprise*) инициатива, инициативность; **a man of ~** инициативный человек.

initiator /ɪˈnɪʃɪeɪtə(r)/ *n.* инициатор.

inject /ɪnˈdʒekt/ *v.t.* вв|одить, -ести; впрыс|кивать, -нуть; **the drug was ~ed into the blood-stream** лекарство ввели в вену; **the nurse ~ed his arm with morphia** сестра сделала ему укол морфия в руку; **he learned to ~ himself with insulin** он научился делать себе уколы инсулина; (*fig.*): **he will ~ new life into the government** он вдохнёт новую жизнь в деятельность правительства.

injection /ɪnˈdʒekʃ(ə)n/ *n.* впрыскивание; инъекция; **have you had an ~ for cholera?** вы прививались против холеры?

injudicious /ˌɪndʒuːˈdɪʃəs/ *adj.* неблагоразумный, неразумный.

injudiciousness /ˌɪndʒuːˈdɪʃəsnɪs/ *n.* неблагоразумие.

injunction /ɪnˈdʒʌŋkʃ(ə)n/ *n.* (*command*) приказ, предписание; (*leg.*) судебный запрет.

injure /ˈɪndʒə(r)/ *v.t.* (*physically*) ушиб|ать, -ить; повре|ждать, -дить; ранить (*impf., pf.*); **he was ~d in a fall** он ушибся при падении; **he fell and ~d himself** он упал и ушибся; (*fig.*): **he will ~ his own reputation** он сам испортит себе репутацию; (*offend*) ранить (*impf., pf.*); об|ижать, -идеть; оскорб|лять, -ить; **you have ~d his feelings** вы ранили/оскорбили его чувства.

injured /ˈɪndʒəd/ *adj.* (*suffering injury*) раненый; **an ~ soldier** раненый солдат; **the ~ party** пострадавшая сторона; (*as n.*): **the dead and ~** убитые и раненые; (*showing sense of wrong*) обиженный, оскорблённый; **in an ~ voice** обиженным тоном.

injurious /ɪnˈdʒʊərɪəs/ *adj.* вредный, губительный; **~ to health** вредный для здоровья; **remarks ~ to his reputation** замечания, подрывающие его репутацию.

injur|y /ˈɪndʒərɪ/ *n.* (*to the body*) рана, ранение, ушиб, травма; **a war ~y** боевое ранение; **his ~ies were superficial** его раны были лёгкие; **he sustained multiple ~ies** он получил множество ранений; **he threatened to do me an ~y** он грозился меня побить; (*to property etc.*) ущерб; (*wrongful treatment*) оскорбление; **that is adding insult to ~y** это равносильно новому оскорблению; (*fig., damage*) вред, ущерб; **this will do great ~y to our cause** это нанесёт большой вред нашему делу.

injustice /ɪnˈdʒʌstɪs/ *n.* несправедливость; **you do him an ~** вы к нему несправедливы; **you are doing yourself an ~** вы действуете себе во вред.

ink /ɪŋk/ *n.* черниl|а (*pl., g.* —); **the words were underlined in red ~** слова были подчёркнуты красными чернилами; **an ~ drawing** рисунок тушью.

● *v.t., with advs.*: **~ in a drawing** покр|ывать, -ыть рисунок тушью; **~ over pencil lines** обв|одить, -ести карандашные линии чернилами.

● *cpds.* **~-blot** *n.* чернильная клякса; **~-bottle** *n.* пузырёк для чернил; **~-jet** *adj.*: **~-jet printer** (*comput.*) струйный принтер; **~-pad** *n.* штемпельная подушечка; **~-stand** *n.* чернильный прибор; **~-well** *n.* чернильница.

inkling /ˈɪŋklɪŋ/ *n.* (*hint*) намёк; (*knowledge, suspicion*) подозрение; **I had not the least ~ of their intentions** я не имел ни малейшего представления об их намерениях.

inky /ˈɪŋkɪ/ *adj.* (**inkier, inkiest**) (*stained with ink*) запачканный чернилами; (*black*) чёрный как смоль.

inland /ˈɪnlənd/, /ˈɪnlænd/ *adj.* расположенный внутри страны; **an ~ sea** море внутри континента; **~ trade** (*Br.*) внутренняя торговля; **I~ Revenue** (*Br.*) Государственная налоговая служба.

● *adv.* (*motion*) внутрь/вглубь страны; (*place*) внутри страны; **they travelled** (*Br.*), **traveled** (*US*) **~** они ехали вглубь страны; **storms are more frequent ~** бури бывают чаще в районах, удалённых от моря.

in-law /ˈɪnlɔː/ *n.* свойственник, родственник со стороны мужа/жены; **~s** родственники (*m. pl.*) со стороны мужа/жены, свояки (*coll.*) (*m. pl.*).

inla|y *n.* /ˈɪnleɪ/ инкрустация; (*dentistry*) пломба.

● *v.t.* /ɪnˈleɪ/ (*past and p.p.* **inlaid**) инкрустировать (*impf., pf.*); **an ~id floor** паркетный пол с инкрустацией.

inlet /ˈɪnlet/, /-lɪt/ *n.* **1** (*small arm of water*) узкий залив. **2** (*insertion in garment*) вставка. **3**: **~ valve** впускной клапан.

inmate /ˈɪnmeɪt/ *n.* (*of house*) жилец, обитатель (*fem.* -ница); (*of hospital, mental home etc.*) больной, пациент; (*of prison*) заключённый.

in memoriam /ɪn mɪˈmɔːrɪˌæm/ *prep.* в память + *g.*/о + *p.*; памяти + *g.*

inmost /ˈɪnməʊst/, /-məst/, **innermost** /ˈɪnəˌməʊst/, /-məst/ *adjs.* глубочайший; (*fig.*) сокровеннейший.

inn /ɪn/ *n.* трактир; постоялый двор.

● *cpds.* **~keeper** *n.* хозяин трактира; трактирщи|к (*fem.* -ца); **~-sign** *n.* вывеска трактира.

innards /ˈɪnədz/ *n.* (*coll.*) внутренности (*f. pl.*).

innate /ɪˈneɪt/, /ˈɪ-/ *adj.* врождённый, природный.

inner /ˈɪnə(r)/ *adj.* (*nearer to centre*) внутренний; **an ~ room** внутренняя комната; **~ tube** камера шины; (*intimate*) интимный, сокровенный; **my ~ convictions** мои внутренние убеждения.

innermost /ˈɪnəməʊst/, /-məst/ = **inmost**

inning /ˈɪnɪŋ/ *n.* (*US, baseball*) часть матча, когда обе команды отбивают мяч.

innings /ˈɪnɪŋz/ *n.* (*pl.* **~** *or coll.* **~es**) (*cricket*) отбивание мяча; (*fig.*): **the Socialists had a long ~** социалисты долго продержались у власти; **he had a good ~** (*Br.*) он прожил долгую жизнь.

innocence /ˈɪnəs(ə)ns/ *n.* **1** (*guiltlessness*) невиновность; **his ~ was established** его невиновность была доказана. **2** (*freedom from sin*) невинность; (*chastity*) целомудрие. **3**: **I thought in my ~ that he would repay me** я по наивности надеялся, что он вернёт мне долг.

innocent /ˈɪnəs(ə)nt/ *n.* невинный младенец; **slaughter of the ~s** (*bibl.*) избиение младенцев.

● *adj.* **1** (*leg.*) невиновный. **2** (*harmless*) невинный, безобидный; **an ~ amusement** невинное развлечение. **3** (*without sin*) невинный, безгрешный; **~ as a babe** невинный как дитя. **4** (*naive, simple*) наивный, простодушный.

innocuous /ɪˈnɒkjʊəs/ *adj.* безвредный, безобидный.

innovate /ˈɪnəˌveɪt/ *v.i.* вв|одить, -ести нововведения/новшества.

innovation /ˌɪnəˈveɪʃ(ə)n/ *n.* нововведение, новшество, новаторство.

innovative /ˈɪnəˌveɪtɪv/ *adj.* новаторский.

innovator /ˈɪnəˌveɪtə(r)/ *n.* новатор.

innuendo /ˌɪnjʊˈendəʊ/ *n.* (*pl.* **~es** *or* **~s**) инсинуация; (*hint*) намёк, недомолвка; **he spoke in ~es** он говорил намёками.

innumerable /ɪˈnjuːmərəb(ə)l/ *adj.* бесчисленный, неисчислимый, бессчётный.

innumeracy /ɪˈnjuːmərəsɪ/ *n.* цифровая неграмотность.

innumerate /ɪˈnjuːmərət/ *adj.* не умеющий считать.

inoculate /ɪˈnɒkjʊˌleɪt/ *v.t.* делать, с- прививку; приви|вать, -ить; **he was ~d against smallpox** ему привили оспу/ему сделали прививку от оспы.

inoculation /ɪˌnɒkjʊˈleɪʃ(ə)n/ *n.* прививка; **I have to have an ~ for typhoid** мне нужно сделать прививку от тифа.

inoffensive /ˌɪnəˈfensɪv/ *adj.* (*giving no offence*) необи́дный, неоскорби́тельный; (*harmless*) безоби́дный.

inoperable /ɪnˈɒpərəb(ə)l/ *adj.* (*untreatable by surgery*) неопера́бельный; (*unworkable*) неприме́нимый; **the plan proved to be ~** план оказа́лся невыполни́мым.

inoperative /ɪnˈɒpərətɪv/ *adj.* неэффекти́вный, неде́йственный.

inopportune /ɪnˈɒpəˌtjuːn/ *adj.* неуме́стный, несвоевре́менный.

inordinate /ɪˈnɔːdɪnət/ *adj.* непоме́рный, чрезме́рный, неуме́ренный.

inorganic /ˌɪnɔːˈgænɪk/ *adj.* неоргани́ческий.

in-patient /ˈɪnˌpeɪʃ(ə)nt/ *n.* стациона́рный/ко́ечный больно́й; **~ treatment** стациона́рное лече́ние.

input /ˈɪnpʊt/ *n.* (*investment, resources*) вложе́ние; (*contribution*) вклад; (*comput., of data*) ввод; (*information fed in*) входны́е да́нные; (*electrical signal*) входно́й сигна́л; (*energy supplied*) подводи́мая мо́щность; (*device through which energy enters system*) вход.

● *v.t.* (*past and p.p.* **input** *or* **inputted**) (*comput.*) вв|оди́ть, -ести́ (в + *a.*).

inquest /ˈɪnkwest/, /ˈɪŋ-/ *n.* (*official enquiry*) (администрати́вное) рассле́дование, дозна́ние; (*in criminal case*) сле́дствие; (*Br., coroner's ~*) сле́дствие, проводи́мое ко́ронером и его́ жюри́; (*investigation*) рассле́дование, разбира́тельство.

inquir|e /ɪnˈkwaɪə(r)/, /ɪŋ-/ (*see also* ⇒**enquire**) *v.t.* спр|а́шивать, -оси́ть; узн|ава́ть, -а́ть; **may I ~e your name?** могу́ я узна́ть, как вас зову́т?; **I ~ed of a passer-by how to find your house** я спроси́л прохо́жего, как найти́ ваш дом.

● *v.i.* спр|авля́ться, -а́виться; нав|оди́ть, -ести́ спра́вку; **we ~ed about the train service** мы спра́вились относи́тельно расписа́ния поездо́в; **she ~ed after your health** она́ справля́лась о ва́шем здоро́вье; **has he ~ed for me?** он меня́ спра́шивал?; **we must ~e into the matter** мы должны́ рассле́довать э́то де́ло; **an ~ing mind** пытли́вый ум.

inquirer /ɪnˈkwaɪərə(r)/, /ɪŋ-/ *n.* де́лающий запро́с.

inquir|y /ɪnˈkwaɪərɪ/, /ɪŋ-/ (*see also* ⇒**enquiry**) *n.* **1** (*question*) наведе́ние спра́вок; **I made ~ies** я навёл спра́вки; **on ~y** в отве́т на вопро́с. **2** (*investigation*) рассле́дование; **public ~** обще́ственное рассле́дование; (*in criminal case*) сле́дствие; **court of ~y** сле́дственная коми́ссия; **the police are making ~ies** поли́ция рассле́дует де́ло; **there will be a full ~y** назна́чено по́лное рассле́дование э́того де́ла.

inquisition /ˌɪnkwɪˈzɪʃ(ə)n/, /ˌɪŋ-/ *n.* (*questioning*) допро́с; **he was subjected to an ~** он был под сле́дствием; (*hist.*) инквизи́ция.

inquisitive /ɪnˈkwɪzɪtɪv/, /ɪŋ-/ *adj.* любозна́тельный, любопы́тный, пытли́вый.

inquisitiveness /ɪnˈkwɪzɪtɪvnɪs/, /ɪŋ-/ *n.* любозна́тельность, любопы́тство, пытли́вость.

inquisitor /ɪnˈkwɪzɪtə(r)/, /ɪŋ-/ *n.* (*hist.*) инквизи́тор.

inquisitorial /ɪnˌkwɪzɪˈtɔːrɪəl/, /ɪŋ-/ *adj.* (*leg.*) сле́дственный; (*prying*) инквизи́торский.

inroad /ˈɪnrəʊd/ *n.* (*raid*) набе́г; (*encroachment*) посяга́тельство; **the holiday will make a large ~ on my savings** кани́кулы поглотя́т бо́льшую часть мои́х сбереже́ний.

inrush /ˈɪnrʌʃ/ *n.* (*of water etc.*) внеза́пный прито́к.

insalubrious /ˌɪnsəˈluːbrɪəs/, /-ˈljuːbrɪəs/ *adj.* нездоро́вый.

insane /ɪnˈseɪn/ *adj.* безу́мный, сумасше́дший; (*leg.*) невменя́емый; **he went ~** он лиши́лся рассу́дка; он сошёл с ума́; **he was certified ~** врачи́ призна́ли его́ сумасше́дшим/невменя́емым; (*as n.*): **the ~** сумасше́дшие; **home for the ~** сумасше́дший дом; психиатри́ческая больни́ца.

insanitary /ɪnˈsænɪtərɪ/ *adj.* антисанита́рный, негигиени́чный.

insanity /ɪnˈsænɪtɪ/ *n.* **1** (*madness*) сумасше́ствие; безу́мие; (*leg.*) невменя́емость; **the defendant pleaded ~** обвиня́емый сосла́лся на невменя́емость. **2** (*folly*) безу́мие; **it would be ~ to proceed** бы́ло бы безу́мием продолжа́ть.

insatiability /ɪnˌseɪʃəˈbɪlɪtɪ/ *n.* ненасы́тность.

insatiable /ɪnˈseɪʃəb(ə)l/ *adj.* ненасы́тный; **his appetite is ~** у него́ ненасы́тный аппети́т.

inscribe /ɪnˈskraɪb/ *v.t.* **1** (*engrave*) высека́ть, вы́сечь; выреза́ть, вы́резать; начерта́ть (*pf.*); **the stone was ~d with their names** их имена́ бы́ли вы́сечены на ка́мне; **a verse is ~d on his tomb** на его́ надгро́бном ка́мне вы́сечена стихотво́рная эпита́фия. **2** (*autograph*) надпи́с|ывать, -а́ть; **please ~ your name in the book** пожа́луйста, распиши́тесь в кни́ге. **3** (*geom.*) впи́с|ывать, -а́ть. **4** (*comm.*): **~d stock** (*Br.*) зарегистри́рованные це́нные бума́ги.

inscription /ɪnˈskrɪpʃ(ə)n/ *n.* на́дпись.

inscrutability /ɪnˌskruːtəˈbɪlɪtɪ/ *n.* зага́дочность, непроница́емость; непостижи́мость.

inscrutable /ɪnˈskruːtəb(ə)l/ *adj.* (*smile*) зага́дочный; (*face*) непроница́емый; (*incomprehensible*) непостижи́мый.

insect /ˈɪnsekt/ *n.* насеко́мое; **~ bite** уку́с насеко́мого; **~ powder** порошо́к от насеко́мых.

insecticide /ɪnˈsektɪˌsaɪd/ *n.* инсектици́д.

insectivorous /ˌɪnsekˈtɪvərəs/ *adj.* насекомоя́дный.

insecure /ˌɪnsɪˈkjʊə(r)/ *adj.* **1** (*unsafe; unreliable*) ненадёжный, небезопа́сный; **the ladder was ~** ле́стница была́ неусто́йчива; **the window was ~ly fastened** окно́ бы́ло закры́то непло́тно; **his position in the firm is ~** его́ положе́ние в фи́рме ша́ткое. **2** (*lacking confidence*) неуве́ренный (в себе́); **I feel ~ about the future** я не уве́рен в бу́дущем.

insecurity /ˌɪnsɪˈkjʊərɪtɪ/ *n.* ненадёжность, небезопа́сность; неуве́ренность.

inseminate /ɪnˈsemɪˌneɪt/ *v.t.* оплодотвор|я́ть, -и́ть.

insemination /ɪnˌsemɪˈneɪʃ(ə)n/ *n.* оплодотворе́ние; **artificial ~** иску́сственное оплодотворе́ние.

insensate /ɪnˈsenseɪt/ *adj.* (*without sensibility*) бесчу́вственный, безду́шный; (*senseless; mad*) безу́мный.

insensibility /ɪnˌsensɪˈbɪlɪtɪ/ *n.* нечувстви́тельность; (*unconsciousness*) бесчу́вствие; (*lack of appreciation; indifference*) бесчу́вственность, безразли́чие.

insensible /ɪnˈsensɪb(ə)l/ *adj.* (*without physical sensation*) нечувстви́тельный; **his hands were ~ with cold** от хо́лода его́ ру́ки потеря́ли чувстви́тельность; (*unconscious*) бесчу́вственный; (*unaware*) не сознаю́щий; **he was ~ of his danger** он не сознава́л опа́сности; (*without emotion; unsympathetic*) бесчу́вственный.

insensitive /ɪnˈsensɪtɪv/ *adj.* нечувстви́тельный; невосприи́мчивый, равноду́шный; **~ to light** нечувстви́тельный к све́ту; **~ to beauty** равноду́шный к красоте́.

insensitivity /ɪnˌsensɪˈtɪvɪtɪ/ *n.* нечувстви́тельность; (*indifference*) невосприи́мчивость, равноду́шие.

insentient /ɪnˈsenʃ(ə)nt/ *adj.* неодушевлённый, неживо́й.

inseparable /ɪnˈsepərəb(ə)l/ *adj.* неразде́льный, неразры́вный; **~ companions** неразлу́чные прия́тели; **he was ~ from his books** его́ невозмо́жно бы́ло оторва́ть от книг.

insert¹ /ˈɪnsɜːt/ *n.* вста́вка; (*in book, newspaper etc.*) вкла́дыш, вкла́дка.

insert² /ɪnˈsɜːt/ *v.t.* вст|авля́ть, -а́вить; поме|ща́ть, -сти́ть; **he ~ed the key in the lock** он вста́вил ключ в замо́к; **have you ~ed a coin?** вы опусти́ли моне́ту?; **I ~ed an advertisement in the paper** я помести́л объявле́ние в газе́те.

insertion /ɪnˈsɜːʃ(ə)n/ *n.* (*inserting*) вкла́дывание, помеще́ние, введе́ние; (*something inserted*) вста́вка.

inset¹ /ˈɪnset/ *n.* (*in book*) вкла́дка, вкле́йка; (*small map*) ка́рта-вре́зка; (*in dress*) вста́вка.

inset² /ɪnˈset/ *v.t.* (**insetting;** *past and p.p.* **inset** *or* **insetted**) (*insert*) вст|авля́ть, -а́вить; вкла́дывать, вложи́ть.

inshore /ɪnˈʃɔː(r)/, /ˈɪn-/ *adj.* прибре́жный.

● *adv.* (*position*) у бе́рега; (*motion*) к бе́регу, на взмо́рье; **the wind was blowing ~** ве́тер дул по направле́нию к бе́регу.

inside /ɪnˈsaɪd/ *n.* **1** (*interior*) вну́треннее простра́нство;

вну́тренняя часть; **have you seen the ~ of the house?** вы бы́ли внутри́ до́ма?; **the door was bolted on the ~** дверь была́ заперта́ изнутри́; **~ out** наизна́нку; **the thieves turned everything ~ out** во́ры переверну́ли всё вверх дном; **he knows the subject ~ out** он зна́ет предме́т вдоль и поперёк.
2 (*of a garment*) изна́нка.
3 (*of road*): **it is forbidden to pass on the ~** обго́н спра́ва запрещён.
4 (*of circular objects: part nearest centre*) вну́тренняя пове́рхность; **the ~ of the bearing was worn** вну́тренняя пове́рхность подши́пника сноси́лась.
5 (*stomach; intestines*) вну́тренности (*f. pl.*); **he complained of a pain in his ~** он жа́ловался на боль в желу́дке.

● *adj.* /'ınsaıd/ вну́тренний; **~ pocket** вну́тренний карма́н; **~ left/right** (*football*) ле́вый/пра́вый полусре́дний; **he received ~ information** он получи́л информа́цию из вну́тренних исто́чников; **it was an ~ job** (*coll.*) э́то сде́лал кто́-то из свои́х.

● *adv.* **1** (*in or on the inner surface*) внутрь; **she wore her coat with the fur ~** она́ носи́ла шу́бу ме́хом внутрь.
2 (*in the interior*) внутри́; **I opened the box and there was nothing ~** я откры́л коро́бку — внутри́ бы́ло пу́сто.
3 (*indoors*) внутри́, в помеще́нии, до́ма; **stay ~ till the rain stops** остава́йтесь до́ма, пока́ дождь не прекрати́тся; **come ~ out of the rain!** заходи́те внутрь, не сто́йте под дождём!
4 (*in prison*) за решёткой; **he did 6 weeks ~** (*coll.*) он просиде́л 6 неде́ль за решёткой.

● *prep.* **1** (*of place*) (*motion*) в + *a.*, внутрь + *g.*; **dogs are not allowed ~ the shop** с соба́ками вход в магази́н запрещён; (*position*) в + *p.*, внутри́ + *g.*; **she was just ~ the door** она́ стоя́ла пря́мо в дверя́х; **have you seen ~ the house?** вы ви́дели дом изнутри́?
2 (*of time*) в преде́лах + *g.*, за + *a.*; **the job can't be done ~ (of) a month** э́ту рабо́ту невозмо́жно сде́лать/зако́нчить в преде́лах ме́сяца; **I shall be back ~ (of) a week** я верну́сь не поздне́е, чем че́рез неде́лю.

insider /ın'saıdə(r)/ *n.* свой/непосторо́нний челове́к; (*comm.*) инса́йдер; **~ trading** уча́стие в биржевы́х сде́лках с испо́льзованием информа́ции из вну́тренних исто́чников.

insidious /ın'sıdıəs/ *adj.* кова́рный.

insidiousness /ın'sıdıəsnıs/ *n.* кова́рство.

insight /'ınsaıt/ *n.* проница́тельность; понима́ние; **he shows great ~ into human character** он демонстри́рует глубо́кое понима́ние челове́ческой души́; **gain an ~ into something** пости́|гнуть, -чь (*both pf.*) что-н.; **a man of ~** проница́тельный челове́к; **she had a sudden ~ into the consequences** она́ вдруг предста́вила себе́ все после́дствия.

insignia /ın'sıgnıə/ *n.* (*decorations*) зна́ки (*m. pl.*) отли́чия, награ́ды (*f. pl.*); (*badges of rank etc.*) зна́ки (*m. pl.*) разли́чия.

insignificance /ˌınsıg'nıfıkəns/ *n.* малова́жность, ничто́жность.

insignificant /ˌınsıg'nıfıkənt/ *adj.* малова́жный, ничто́жный.

insincere /ˌınsın'sıə(r)/ *adj.* нeiскренний.

insincerity /ˌınsın'serıtı/ *n.* нeiскренность.

insinuat|e /ın'sınjʊˌeıt/ *v.t.* **1** (*introduce*): **he ~ed himself into their company** он втёрся/прони́к в их о́бщество. **2** (*hint*) намек|а́ть, -ну́ть на + *a.*; внуш|а́ть, -и́ть; нашёпт|ывать, -а́ть (*coll.*); говори́ть (*impf.*) намёками; **what are you ~ing?** на что вы намека́ете?

insinuation /ınˌsınjʊ'eıʃ(ə)n/ *n.* (*hint*) намёк; инсинуа́ция; **there was an ~ of foul play** намека́ли на возмо́жность нече́стной игры́.

insipid /ın'sıpıd/ *adj.* безвку́сный, пре́сный; (*fig.*) ску́чный, вя́лый.

insipidity /ˌınsı'pıdıtı/ *n.* отсу́тствие вку́са, пре́сность; (*fig.*) ску́ка; вя́лость.

insist /ın'sıst/ *v.t. & i.* наст|а́ивать, -оя́ть на + *p.*; тре́бовать, по- + *g.*; **he ~ed on his rights** он наста́ивал на свои́х права́х; **he ~ed on his innocence** он наста́ивал на свое́й невино́вности; **he ~ed on my accompanying him** он настоя́л на том, что́бы я его́ сопровожда́л; **very well, if you ~!** ну ла́дно, е́сли/раз вы наста́иваете!

insistence /ın'sıst(ə)ns/ *n.* (*quality*) насто́йчивость; (*act*) настоя́ние, насто́йчивое тре́бование.

insistent /ın'sıst(ə)nt/ *adj.* (*repeatedly urged*) насто́йчивый; **~ demands** насто́йчивые/настоя́тельные тре́бования; **he was ~ that I should go** он наста́ивал на том, что́бы я пошёл.

in situ /ın 'sıtju:/ *adv.* на ме́сте.

insobriety /ˌınsə'braııtı/ *n.* нетре́звость, пья́нство.

insofar as /ˌınsəʊ'fɑ:(r)/ *conj.* (посто́льку,) поско́льку; в той ме́ре/сте́пени, в како́й. . .; наско́лько.

insole /'ınsəʊl/ *n.* сте́лька.

insolence /'ınsələns/ *n.* (*contempt*) де́рзость; (*insulting behaviour*) наха́льство.

insolent /'ınsələnt/ *adj.* (*contemptuous*) де́рзкий; (*insulting; disrespectful*) наха́льный.

insolubility /ınˌsɒljʊ'bılıtı/ *n.* нерастворимость; неразреши́мость.

insoluble /ın'sɒljʊb(ə)l/ *adj.* (*of substance*) нерастворимый; (*of problem*) неразреши́мый.

insolvency /ın'sɒlv(ə)nsı/ *n.* неплатёжеспосо́бность; несостоя́тельность; банкро́тство.

insolvent /ın'sɒlv(ə)nt/ *adj.* неплатёжеспосо́бный; несостоя́тельный.

insomnia /ın'sɒmnıə/ *n.* бессо́нница.

insomniac /ın'sɒmnıˌæk/ *n.* страда́ющий бессо́нницей.

insouciance /ın'su:sıəns/ *n.* небре́жность.

insouciant /ın'su:sıənt/, /æ̃'susjɑ̃/ *adj.* небре́жный.

inspect /ın'spekt/ *v.t.* (*by looking*) осм|а́тривать, -отре́ть; (*by examining*) обсле́довать (*impf., pf.*); инспекти́ровать (*impf., pf.*); **the Queen ~ed the troops** короле́ва произвела́ смотр войск.

inspection /ın'spekʃ(ə)n/ *n.* (*examination*) осмо́тр, обсле́дование, инспе́кция; **on closer ~** при бо́лее внима́тельном рассмотре́нии; **medical ~** медици́нский осмо́тр; **the house is open to ~** дом откры́т для всео́бщего обозре́ния; **these goods will not pass ~** э́ти това́ры не пройду́т прове́рку; (*review*) пара́д, смотр; **the general held an ~** генера́л произвёл смотр войск.

inspector /ın'spektə(r)/ *n.* (*inspecting official*) инспе́ктор; (*financial*) ревизо́р; (*police officer*) инспе́ктор (поли́ции).

inspectorate /ın'spektərət/ *n.* (*body*) инспе́кция.

inspiration /ˌınspı'reıʃ(ə)n/ *n.* **1** (*source of creative activity; idea*) вдохнове́ние; **he drew his ~ from nature** он че́рпал вдохнове́ние в приро́де; **I had an ~** меня́ осени́ла мысль. **2** (*thing that inspires; stimulus*) вдохнове́ние; (*person*) вдохнови́тель (*m.*).

inspire /ın'spaıə(r)/ *v.t.* **1** (*influence creatively*) вдохнов|ля́ть, -и́ть; **his friend's death ~d him to write an elegy** смерть дру́га вдохнови́ла его́ на написа́ние эле́гии; **he is an ~d musician** он вдохнове́нный музыка́нт; **in an ~d moment** в моме́нт вдохнове́ния. **2** (*instil; imbue*) всел|я́ть, -и́ть; **she ~d hope in me** она́ всели́ла наде́жду в меня́; **his work does not ~ me with confidence** его́ рабо́та не вызыва́ет у меня́ дове́рия; **~ s.o. with courage** внуш|а́ть, -и́ть му́жество кому́-н.

inspirer /ın'spaıərə(r)/ *n.* вдохнови́тель (*fem.* -ница).

inst. /ınst/ *n.* (*comm., abbr. of **instant** adj.* 3) с.м. (сего́ ме́сяца).

instability /ˌınstə'bılıtı/ *n.* нестаби́льность, неусто́йчивость; (*of character*) неуравнове́шенность.

install /ın'stɔ:l/ *v.t.* (**installed, installing**) **1** (*place in office; induct*) вв|оди́ть, -ести́ в до́лжность. **2** (*settle*) устр|а́ивать, -о́ить; поме|ща́ть, -сти́ть; **he ~ed his family in a hotel** он помести́л/устро́ил свою́ семью́ в гости́нице; **we are comfortably ~ed in our new home** мы удо́бно устро́ились в но́вом до́ме. **3** (*fix in position*) устан|а́вливать, -ови́ть; **the workmen came to ~ a new cooker** рабо́чие пришли́ установи́ть но́вую ку́хонную плиту́.

installation /ˌınstə'leıʃ(ə)n/ *n.* (*of person*) введе́ние в до́лжность; (*of thing*) устано́вка; (*equipment etc. installed*) устано́вка, устро́йство; (*buildings etc. for tech. purposes*).

сооруже́ния (*nt. pl.*); **a military ~** вое́нные сооруже́ния; вое́нные устано́вки (*f. pl.*); (*art*) инсталля́ция.

instalment /ɪn'stɔ:lmənt/ *n.* (*US also* **installment**) **1** (*partial payment*) взнос; **we are paying for our carpet by ~s (***or* **on the ~ plan)** мы пла́тим за ковёр в рассро́чку. **2** (*of published work*) отры́вок, вы́пуск; отде́льная часть.

instance /'ɪnst(ə)ns/ *n.* **1** (*example*) приме́р; **for ~** наприме́р; **let me give you an ~** я приведу́ вам приме́р. **2** (*particular case*) слу́чай; **in this ~** в э́том/да́нном слу́чае; **in the first ~** в пе́рвую о́чередь.

● *v.t.* прив|оди́ть, -ести́ в ка́честве приме́ра.

instant /'ɪnst(ə)nt/ *n.* **1** (*precise moment*) мгнове́ние; **come here this ~!** иди́ сюда́ сию́ же мину́ту!; **he left that very ~** он момента́льно (*or* в то́т же моме́нт) удали́лся; **I recognized him the ~ I saw him** я узна́л его́, как то́лько я его́ уви́дел. **2** (*momentary duration*) мгнове́ние, миг; **I shall be back in an ~** я верну́сь че́рез мину́ту/ми́гом (*coll.*).

● *adj.* **1** (*immediate*) мгнове́нный; неме́дленный; **I felt ~ relief** я то́тчас же почу́вствовал облегче́ние; **the book was an ~ success** кни́га име́ла мгнове́нный успе́х. **2** (*of food preparation*): **~ coffee** раствори́мый ко́фе. **3** (*abbr.* **inst.**) теку́щий, сей; **your letter of the 5th ~** ва́ше письмо́ от пя́того числа́ сего́ (*or* теку́щего) ме́сяца (*abbr.* с.м.).

instantaneous /,ɪnstən'teɪnɪəs/ *adj.* (*done in an instant*) мгнове́нный; **it was an ~ decision** э́то бы́ло решено́ мгнове́нно; (*immediate*) неме́дленный; **death was ~** смерть наступи́ла мгнове́нно.

instead /ɪn'sted/ *adv.* взаме́н (+*g.*); **~ of** вме́сто + *g.*; **let me go ~ (of you)** дава́йте я пойду́ вме́сто вас; **if the steak is off I'll have chicken ~** е́сли бифште́ксов нет, я возьму́ ку́рицу; **why don't you go out ~ of reading?** вме́сто того́, что́бы чита́ть, вы лу́чше бы пошли́ погуля́ть; **we are going by train ~ of by car** мы е́дем по́ездом, а не на маши́не.

instep /'ɪnstep/ *n.* подъём (ноги́).

instigate /'ɪnstɪ,geɪt/ *v.t.* подстрека́ть (*impf.*), провоци́ровать, с-; **they were ~d to rebel** их подстрека́ли к бу́нту; **he ~d the murder** он спровоци́ровал уби́йство; (*introduce*) вв|оди́ть, -ести́.

instigation /,ɪnstɪ'geɪʃ(ə)n/ *n.* подстрека́тельство, науще́ние; **the boy stole at his brother's ~** ма́льчик соверши́л кра́жу по науще́нию бра́та; (*initiative*) инициати́ва; **at her ~** по её инициати́ве.

instigator /'ɪnstɪ,geɪtə(r)/ *n.* подстрека́тель (*fem.* -ница).

instil /ɪn'stɪl/ *v.t.* (**instilled, instilling**) (*lit.*) вл|ива́ть, -и́ть; (*fig.*) внуш|а́ть, -и́ть; прив|ива́ть, -и́ть; **he tried to ~ some discipline into his pupils** он пыта́лся приви́ть свои́м ученика́м чу́вство дисципли́ны (*or* приучи́ть свои́х ученико́в к дисципли́не); **his love of science was ~led at an early age** с ма́лых лет ему́ внуша́ли/привива́ли любо́вь к нау́ке.

instinct /'ɪnstɪŋkt/ *n.* инсти́нкт; **herd ~** ста́дное чу́вство; **my ~ told me to turn back** инсти́нкт подсказа́л мне поверну́ть наза́д; **he acted by, on ~** он де́йствовал по интуи́ции (*or* инстинкти́вно); (*natural liking or propensity*) спосо́бность, чутьё; **he has an ~ for a bargain** у него́ приро́дное чутьё к вы́годным поку́пкам; **he has an uncanny ~ for making mistakes** он облада́ет необыкнове́нной спосо́бностью де́лать оши́бки.

instinctive /ɪn'stɪŋktɪv/ *adj.* инстинкти́вный, безотчётный; **I took an ~ dislike to him** у меня́ возни́кла безотчётная неприя́знь к нему́.

institute /'ɪnstɪ,tju:t/ *n.* институ́т.

● *v.t.* **1** (*found; establish*) устан|а́вливать, -ови́ть; учре|жда́ть, -ди́ть; **~ a law** вв|оди́ть, -ести́ зако́н. **2** (*set in motion*) нач|ина́ть, -а́ть; **the police ~d proceedings** поли́ция возбуди́ла де́ло; **they ~d a search** они́ произвели́ о́быск.

institution /,ɪnstɪ'tju:ʃ(ə)n/ *n.* **1** (*organization with social purpose*) учрежде́ние, организа́ция, заведе́ние, институ́т; **charitable ~** благотвори́тельное учрежде́ние; **mental ~** психиатри́ческая лече́бница. **2** (*setting up*) установле́ние, учрежде́ние. **3** (*established custom or practice*) институ́т.

institutional /,ɪnstɪ'tju:ʃən(ə)l/ *adj.* институцио́нный; **~ religion** организо́ванная рели́гия; **she is in need of ~ care** её сле́дует госпитализи́ровать; **~ investor** институцио́нный инве́стор; **~ reform** рефо́рма учрежде́ний.

instruct /ɪn'strʌkt/ *v.t.* **1** (*teach*) учи́ть, на- (*кого чему*); обуч|а́ть, -и́ть (*кого чему*). **2** (*order; direct*) инструкти́ровать (*impf., pf.*; *pf. also* про-); прика́з|ывать, -а́ть; **I was ~ed to call on you** мне бы́ло прика́зано зайти́ к вам; **I shall ~ my solicitor** (*Br.*) я поручу́ де́ло своему́ адвока́ту.

instruction /ɪn'strʌkʃ(ə)n/ *n.* **1** (*teaching*) обуче́ние; **he received ~ in mathematics** он получи́л математи́ческое образова́ние. **2** (*direction*) указа́ние; руково́дство; **follow the ~s on the packet** сле́дуйте указа́ниям на паке́те; (*order*) распоряже́ние, прика́з; **I have my ~s** мне был дан прика́з; **he had ~s to return** ему́ веле́ли/приказа́ли (*or* он получи́л распоряже́ние) верну́ться.

● *cpd.* **~-book** *n.* руково́дство.

instructive /ɪn'strʌktɪv/ *adj.* поучи́тельный.

instruct|or /ɪn'strʌktə(r)/, **-ress** /ɪn'strʌktrɪs/ *nn.* (*sport*) инстру́ктор; (*teacher*) учи́тель (*fem.* -ница); преподава́тель (*fem.* -ница).

instrument /'ɪnstrəmənt/ *n.* **1** (*implement*) инструме́нт; **he was knocked out with a blunt ~** его́ оглуши́ли тупы́м предме́том; (*apparatus*) аппара́т, прибо́р; **~ panel** пульт управле́ния; (*machine or device*) ору́дие; **~ of torture** ору́дие пы́тки. **2** (*musical ~*) (музыка́льный) инструме́нт. **3** (*fig., means*) ору́дие; **he was the ~ of another's vengeance** он был ору́дием чужо́й ме́сти. **4** (*formal document*) докуме́нт; акт.

● *v.t.* инструментова́ть (*impf., pf.*); оркестрова́ть (*impf., pf.*); **the piece was ~ed for full orchestra** произведе́ние бы́ло инструменто́вано для по́лного соста́ва орке́стра.

instrumental /,ɪnstrə'ment(ə)l/ *n.* (*gram.*) твори́тельный паде́ж.

● *adj.* **1** (*serving as means*): **~ to our purpose** поле́зный для на́шей це́ли; **he was ~ in obtaining the order** он спосо́бствовал получе́нию (*or* соде́йствовал в получе́нии) зака́за. **2** (*mus.*) инструмента́льный. **3** (*gram.*) твори́тельный.

instrumentalist /,ɪnstrə'mentəlɪst/ *n.* инструментали́ст.

instrumentality /,ɪnstrəmen'tælɪtɪ/ *n.* соде́йствие; **by the ~ of** при соде́йствии + *g.*

instrumentation /,ɪnstrəmen'teɪʃ(ə)n/ *n.* **1** (*mus.*) инструменто́вка, оркестро́вка; (*composition of ensemble*) соста́в орке́стра/анса́мбля. **2** (*provision of tools etc.*) оснаще́ние инструме́нтами; (*collect., measuring instruments*) контро́льно-измери́тельные прибо́ры.

insubordinate /,ɪnsə'bɔ:dɪnət/ *adj.* непоко́рный; неподчиня́ющийся.

insubordination /,ɪnsə,bɔ:dɪ'neɪʃ(ə)n/ *n.* неподчине́ние; непоко́рность.

insubstantial /,ɪnsəb'stænʃ(ə)l/, /-'stɑ:nʃ(ə)l/ *adj.* (*not real, imaginary*) нереа́льный, иллюзо́рный; (*building, structure*) непро́чный; (*evidence*) сла́бый, неубеди́тельный; (*meal*) несы́тный.

insufferable /ɪn'sʌfərəb(ə)l/ *adj.* несно́сный, невыноси́мый.

insufficiency /,ɪnsə'fɪʃənsɪ/ *n.* недоста́точность, недоста́ток, нехва́тка.

insufficient /,ɪnsə'fɪʃ(ə)nt/ *adj.* недоста́точный; **our food supply is ~ for a week** на́ших проду́ктов не хва́тит на неде́лю; **that in itself is ~ excuse** само́ по себе́ э́то недоста́точное оправда́ние.

insular /'ɪnsjʊlə(r)/ *adj.* островно́й; (*fig.*) ограни́ченный, у́зкий.

insularity /,ɪnsjʊ'lærɪtɪ/ *n.* ограни́ченность, у́зость.

insulat|e /'ɪnsjʊ,leɪt/ *v.t.* (*separate; detach*) отдел|я́ть, -и́ть; изоли́ровать (*impf., pf.*); (*protect from escape of electricity*) изоли́ровать (*impf., pf.*); **~ing tape** изоляцио́нная ле́нта; (*protect from escape of heat*) утепл|я́ть, -и́ть, теплоизоли́ровать (*impf., pf.*); **~e one's roof** утепл|я́ть, -и́ть/теплоизоли́ровать (*impf., pf.*) кры́шу.

insulation /,ɪnsjʊ'leɪʃ(ə)n/ *n.* (*against*

escape of electricity) изоля́ция; (*against escape of heat*) теплоизоля́ция; (*substance*) изоляцио́нный материа́л.

insulator /ˈɪnsjʊˌleɪtə(r)/ *n.* непроводни́к.

insulin /ˈɪnsjʊlɪn/ *n.* инсули́н.

insult¹ /ˈɪnsʌlt/ *n.* оскорбле́ние; оби́да; **this book is an ~ to the intelligence** э́та кни́га возмуща́ет ра́зум; **he took it as a personal ~** он э́то воспри́нял как ли́чное оскорбле́ние; *see also* ⇒**injury**

insult² /ɪnˈsʌlt/ *v.t.* оскорб|ля́ть, -и́ть; **I have never been so ~ed** меня́ в жи́зни никто́ так не оскорбля́л; **~ing language** оскорби́тельные выраже́ния.

insuperable /ɪnˈsuːpərəb(ə)l/, /ɪnˈsjuː-/ *adj.* непреодоли́мый.

insupportable /ˌɪnsəˈpɔːtəb(ə)l/ *adj.* нестерпи́мый, невыноси́мый, несно́сный.

insurable /ɪnˈʃʊərəb(ə)l/ *adj.* могу́щий быть застрахо́ванным.

insurance /ɪnˈʃʊərəns/ *n.* страхова́ние, страхо́вка; (*sum insured*) су́мма страхова́ния; **~ agent** страхово́й аге́нт; **~ company** страхова́я компа́ния, страхово́е о́бщество; **~ policy** страхово́й по́лис; **~ premium** страхова́я пре́мия; **life ~** страхова́ние жи́зни; **National I~** (*Br.*) госуда́рственное страхова́ние; **take out ~** страхова́ться, за-; **he is a bad ~ risk** его́ риско́ванно страхова́ть.

insure /ɪnˈʃʊə(r)/ *v.t.* **1** (*pay for guarantee of*) страхова́ть, за-; **he ~d his house for £200,000** он застрахова́л свой дом на 200 000 фу́нтов; **is your life ~d?** вы застрахова́ли свою́ жизнь?; **the ~d** (*person*) застрахо́ванный. **2** (*guarantee*) гаранти́ровать (*impf.*); страхова́ть (*impf.*); **Lloyd's ~s ships** Ллойд страху́ет корабли́. **3** = **ensure**
● *v.i.* страхова́ться, за-; **have you ~d against fire?** вы застрахова́лись от пожа́ра?

insurer /ɪnˈʃʊərə(r)/ *n.* страхова́тель (*m.*), страхо́вщик.

insurgent /ɪnˈsɜːdʒ(ə)nt/ *n.* повста́нец.
● *adj.* восста́вший; (*army, troops*) повста́нческий.

insurmountable /ˌɪnsəˈmaʊntəb(ə)l/ *adj.* непреодоли́мый.

insurrection /ˌɪnsəˈrekʃ(ə)n/ *n.* восста́ние.

intact /ɪnˈtækt/ *adj.* (*untouched*) нетро́нутый, це́лый; **I hope to keep my savings ~** наде́юсь, что мне уда́стся сохрани́ть свои́ сбереже́ния; (*unharmed*) (*person*) невреди́мый; (*thing*) нетро́нутый.

intake /ˈɪnteɪk/ *n.* (*act*) впуск, вход; (*mechanism*) впускно́е устро́йство; (*Br., of recruits, students, etc.*) набо́р; (*amount taken into body*) потребле́ние; **~ of breath** вздох.

intangible /ɪnˈtændʒɪb(ə)l/ *adj.* **1** (*non-material*) неосяза́емый, неуловимый; **~ assets** нематериа́льные/неосяза́емые акти́вы. **2** (*vague, obscure*): **~ ideas** сму́тные/нея́сные представле́ния.

integer /ˈɪntɪdʒə(r)/ *n.* це́лое число́.

integral /ˈɪntɪgr(ə)l/ *adj.* **1** (*essential*) неотъе́млемый, суще́ственный. **2** (*whole; complete*) це́лостный, це́льный. **3** (*math.*) интегра́льный; **~ calculus** интегра́льное исчисле́ние.

integrate /ˈɪntɪˌgreɪt/ *v.t.* **1** (*combine into whole*) объедин|я́ть, -и́ть в одно́ це́лое; интегри́ровать (*impf., pf.*); **an ~d personality** це́льная ли́чность. **2** (*complete by adding parts*) заверш|а́ть, -и́ть; прид|ава́ть, -а́ть зако́нченный вид (*чему*). **3** (*assimilate*) ассимили́ровать (*impf., pf.*), интегри́ровать (*impf., pf.*); **racially ~d schools** шко́лы совме́стного обуче́ния для дете́й разли́чных рас. **4** (*math.*) интегри́ровать (*impf., pf.*).
● *v.i.* (*join together*) объедин|я́ться, -и́ться.

integrated /ˈɪntɪˌgreɪtɪd/ *adj.*: **~ circuit** интегра́льная схе́ма.

integration /ˌɪntɪˈgreɪʃ(ə)n/ *n.* интегра́ция, объедине́ние, интегри́рование.

integrity /ɪnˈtegrɪtɪ/ *n.* **1** (*uprightness, honesty*) че́стность, це́льность; **a man of ~** че́стный/принципиа́льный челове́к. **2** (*complete state*) це́лостность; **territorial ~** территориа́льная це́лостность.

integument /ɪnˈtegjʊmənt/ *n.* нару́жный покро́в.

intellect /ˈɪntɪˌlekt/ *n.* интелле́кт, ум, рассу́док; **the great ~s of the age** вели́кие умы́ эпо́хи.

intellectual /ˌɪntɪˈlektjʊəl/ *n.* интеллиге́нт (*fem.* -ка), интеллектуа́л (*fem.* -ка); (*pl., collect.*) интеллиге́нция.
● *adj.* интеллектуа́льный, у́мственный; **~ process** мысли́тельный проце́сс; **~ pursuits** у́мственная рабо́та, заня́тие для ума́.

intellectualism /ˌɪntɪˈlektjʊəˌlɪz(ə)m/ *n.* интеллектуали́зм.

intellectuality /ˌɪntɪˌlektjʊˈælɪtɪ/ *n.* интеллектуа́льность; интеллиге́нтность.

intelligence /ɪnˈtelɪdʒ(ə)ns/ *n.* **1** (*mental power*) ум, интелле́кт; **~ quotient** коэффицие́нт у́мственного разви́тия; **~ test** испыта́ние у́мственных спосо́бностей; **high/low ~** высо́кий/ни́зкий интелле́кт. **2** (*quickness of understanding; sagacity*) ум, сообрази́тельность; **he has ~** он сообрази́тельный; **a person of ~** у́мный/неглу́пый челове́к; **I had the ~ to refuse his offer** у меня́ хвати́ло ума́ не приня́ть его́ предложе́ния. **3** (*news, information*) све́дения (*nt. pl.*); информа́ция. **4** (*mil.*) разве́дка.

intelligent /ɪnˈtelɪdʒ(ə)nt/ *adj.* у́мный, смышлёный, сообрази́тельный.

intelligentsia /ˌɪntelɪˈdʒentsɪə/ *n.* интеллиге́нция.

intelligibility /ɪnˌtelɪdʒɪˈbɪlɪtɪ/ *n.* поня́тность, вня́тность, вразуми́тельность.

intelligible /ɪnˈtelɪdʒɪb(ə)l/ *adj.* поня́тный, вня́тный, вразуми́тельный; **his words were barely ~** его́ слова́ едва́ мо́жно бы́ло поня́ть.

intemperance /ɪnˈtempərəns/ *n.* (*immoderation*) невозде́ржанность; (*lack of self-control*) несде́ржанность; (*immoderate drinking*) невозде́ржанность; приста́стие к спиртны́м напи́ткам.

intemperate /ɪnˈtempərət/ *adj.* (*immoderate*) невозде́ржанный; (*lacking self-control*) несде́ржанный; (*addicted to drink*) невозде́ржанный, пью́щий.

intend /ɪnˈtend/ *v.t.* **1** (*purpose; have in mind*) намерева́ться, хоте́ть, собира́ться (*all impf.*); **I ~ed him to do it** (*or* **that he should do it**) я хоте́л, что́бы он э́то сде́лал; **was this ~ed?** э́то бы́ло сде́лано преднаме́ренно? **2** (*design; mean*) предназн|ача́ть, -а́чить; **a book ~ed for advanced students** кни́га, рассчи́танная на продви́нутый эта́п обуче́ния студе́нтов; **a measure ~ed to secure peace** ме́ра, напра́вленная на укрепле́ние ми́ра.

intended /ɪnˈtendɪd/ *n.* (*betrothed*) наречённый, жени́х; (*fem.*) наречённая, неве́ста.

intense /ɪnˈtens/ *adj.* (**intenser, intensest**) **1** (*extreme*) си́льный, интенси́вный; **~ cold** си́льный хо́лод; **~ hatred** о́страя не́нависть; **~ly annoyed** кра́йне раздражённый. **2** (*ardent; emotionally charged*) напряжённый; **an ~ expression** напряжённое выраже́ние.

intenseness /ɪnˈtensnɪs/ *n.* си́ла, напряже́ние, напряжённость.

intensification /ɪnˌtensɪfɪˈkeɪʃ(ə)n/ *n.* интенсифика́ция, усиле́ние, увеличе́ние.

intensif|y /ɪnˈtensɪˌfaɪ/ *v.t.* уси́ли|вать, -ть; увели́чи|вать, -ть; **he ~ied his efforts** он приложи́л ещё бо́льше уси́лий; (*process, efforts*); интенсифици́ровать (*impf., pf.*).

intensity /ɪnˈtensɪtɪ/ *n.* си́ла, интенси́вность.

intensive /ɪnˈtensɪv/ *adj.* интенси́вный; **~ methods of farming** интенси́вное земледе́лие; **~ care unit** отделе́ние интенси́вной терапи́и.

intent¹ /ɪnˈtent/ *n.* наме́рение, цель; **I did it with good ~** я сде́лал э́то из до́брых побужде́ний; **to all ~s and purposes** факти́чески, на са́мом де́ле.

intent² /ɪnˈtent/ *adj.* **1** (*earnest, eager*) увлечённый, ре́вностный; (*expression, gaze, look*) сосредото́ченный; **there was an ~ expression on his face** у него́ бы́ло сосредото́ченное выраже́ние лица́. **2** (*sedulously occupied*) погружённый (*во что*); увлечённый (*чем*); **he was ~ on his work** он был увлечён свое́й рабо́той. **3** (*resolved*) по́лный реши́мости; **he was ~ on getting a first** он был по́лон реши́мости получи́ть дипло́м с отли́чием.

intention /ɪnˈtenʃ(ə)n/ *n.* наме́рение; у́мысел; **it was quite without ~** э́то бы́ло сде́лано/ска́зано без у́мысла; **I**

have no ~ of going to the party у меня́ нет наме́рения идти́ на вечери́нку; **his ~s are good** у него́ хоро́шие наме́рения.

intentional /ɪn'tenʃən(ə)l/ *adj.* умы́шленный, наме́ренный; наро́чный, созна́тельный; **my absence was not ~** моё отсу́тствие не́ было наме́ренным; **he ignored me ~ly** он умы́шленно меня́ не заме́тил.

inter /ɪn'tɜː(r)/ *v.t.* (**interred, interring**) хорони́ть, по-/за-; погре|ба́ть, -сти́.

inter- /'ɪntə(r)/ *comb. form* взаи́мо..., меж(ду)....

interact /ˌɪntər'ækt/ *v.i.* взаимоде́йствовать (*impf.*).

interaction /ˌɪntər'ækʃ(ə)n/ *n.* взаимоде́йствие.

interactive /ˌɪntər'æktɪv/ *adj.* взаимоде́йствующий; (*comput.*) интеракти́вный, диало́говый.

inter alia /ˌɪntər 'eɪlɪə/, /'ælɪə/ *adv.* среди́ про́чих.

interbreed /ˌɪntə'briːd/ *v.t. & i.* скр|е́щивать(ся), -ести́ть(ся).

intercede /ˌɪntə'siːd/ *v.i.* заступ|а́ться, -и́ться (*за кого перед кем*); хода́тайствовать, по- (*о ком/чём перед кем*).

intercept /ˌɪntə'sept/ *v.t.* перехва́т|ывать, -и́ть; (*listen in on*) подслу́ш|ивать, -ать.

interception /ˌɪntə'sepʃ(ə)n/ *n.* перехва́тывание, перехва́т, подслу́шивание.

intercession /ˌɪntə'seʃ(ə)n/ *n.* хода́тайство; засту́пничество.

intercessor /ˌɪntə'sesə(r)/ *n.* хода́тай; засту́пник.

interchange /'ɪntəˌtʃeɪndʒ/ *n.* **1** (*transposition*) перестано́вка. **2** (*exchange*) обме́н; **~ of views** обме́н мне́ниями. **3** (*alternation*) чередова́ние.

● *v.t.* **1** (*transpose*) перест|авля́ть, -а́вить. **2** (*exchange*) обме́н|ивать, -я́ть; обме́н|иваться, -я́ться + *i.* **3** (*alternate*) чередова́ть (*impf.*).

interchangeability /ˌɪntəˌtʃeɪndʒə'bɪlɪtɪ/ *n.* (взаимо)заменя́емость; равноце́нность.

interchangeable /ˌɪntə'tʃeɪndʒəb(ə)l/ *adj.* взаимозаменя́емый; (*equivalent*) равноце́нный.

inter-city /ˌɪntə'sɪtɪ/ *adj.* междугоро́дный.

intercollegiate /ˌɪntəkə'liːdʒət/ *adj.* межуниверсите́тский.

intercom /'ɪntəˌkɒm/ *n.* (*in an office, plane*) селе́ктор; (*to get into a house*) домофо́н.

intercommunicat|e /ˌɪntəkə'mjuːnɪˌkeɪt/ *v.i.* (*of people*) обща́ться (*impf.*) (**with**: с + *i.*); **~ing bedrooms** сме́жные спа́льни.

intercommunication /ˌɪntəkəˌmjuːnɪ'keɪʃ(ə)n/ *n.* обще́ние, связь.

interconnect /ˌɪntəkə'nekt/ *v.i.* соедин|я́ться, -и́ться.

interconnected /ˌɪntəkə'nektɪd/ *adj.* взаимосвя́занный.

interconnecting /ˌɪntəkə'nektɪŋ/ *adj.*: **~ rooms** сме́жные ко́мнаты.

interconnection /ˌɪntəkə'nekʃ(ə)n/ *n.* взаимосвя́зь.

intercontinental /ˌɪntəˌkɒntɪ'nent(ə)l/ *adj.* межконтинента́льный.

intercourse /'ɪntəˌkɔːs/ *n.* (*social*) обще́ние; (*diplomatic or commercial*) сноше́ния (*nt. pl.*), свя́зи (*f. pl.*); (*sexual*) (полово́е) сноше́ние; **have ~ with s.o.** вступи́ть (*pf.*) в полово́е сноше́ние с кем-н.

interdepartmental /ˌɪntəˌdiːpɑːt'ment(ə)l/ *adj.* меж(ду)ве́домственный; (*in university*) межфакульте́тский.

interdependence /ˌɪntədɪ'pendəns/ *n.* взаимозави́симость.

interdependent /ˌɪntədɪ'pendənt/ *adj.* взаимозави́симый.

interdict /'ɪntədɪkt/ *n.* (*eccl.*) интерди́кт.

● *v.t.* (*US*) запре|ща́ть, -ти́ть.

interdiction /ˌɪntə'dɪkʃ(ə)n/ *n.* запре́т.

interest /'ɪntrəst/, /-trɪst/ *n.* **1** (*attention, curiosity, concern*) интере́с; **feel, show, take a great, keen ~ in something** прояв|ля́ть, -и́ть большо́й интере́с к чему́-н.; **I have no ~ in sport** спорт меня́ не интересу́ет. **2** (*quality arousing ~*) занима́тельность; **his books lack ~ for me** меня́ его́ кни́ги не занима́ют; **it is of ~ to note that ...** интере́сно заме́тить, что...; **it is of no ~ to me whether we win or lose** меня́ соверше́нно не интересу́ет, вы́играем мы и́ли нет; **matters of ~ to everybody** вопро́сы, ва́жные для всех. **3** (*pursuit*) интере́с; **my chief ~s are art and history** я интересу́юсь гла́вным о́бразом иску́сством и исто́рией; **a man of wide ~s** челове́к с широ́ким кру́гом интере́сов. **4** (*oft. pl., advantage, benefit*) интере́сы (*m. pl.*), по́льза, вы́года; **it is in, to your ~ to listen to his advice** в ва́ших же интере́сах прислу́шаться к его́ сове́там; **I acted in your ~s** я де́йствовал в ва́ших интере́сах; **you must look after your own ~s** вы должны́ блюсти́ свои́ интере́сы; **in the ~s of truth** в интере́сах и́стины; **I know where my ~s lie** я зна́ю свою́ вы́году. **5** (*legal or financial right or share*) до́ля, часть; **he has an ~ in that firm** он име́ет до́лю в э́той фи́рме; **American ~s in Europe** америка́нские капиталовложе́ния в Евро́пе. **6** (*group having common concern*) заинтересо́ванные круги́ (*m. pl.*); **business ~s** торго́вые круги́ (*m. pl.*). **7** (*charge on loan*) (*paid*) ссу́дный проце́нт; проце́нты (*m. pl.*); (*received*) проце́нтный дохо́д; **pay ~ on a loan** плати́ть (*impf.*) проце́нты по за́йму; **lend money at 7% ~ p.a.** дава́ть, дать де́ньги (в рост) под семь проце́нтов годовы́х; **rate of ~** проце́нтная ста́вка; **at a high rate of ~** под больши́е проце́нты; **he lives on the ~ from his investments** он живёт на дохо́д со свои́х вложе́ний; (*fig.*): **my kindness was repaid with ~** меня́ ще́дро вознагради́ли за мою́ доброту́.

● *v.t.* интересова́ть (*impf.*); **I shall be ~ed to know what happens** мне бу́дет интере́сно знать, что происхо́дит; **this will ~ you** вам э́то бу́дет интере́сно; (*cause a person to take interest*) заинтересова́ть (*pf.*); **when he mentioned money I was ~ed at once** как то́лько он заговори́л о деньга́х, я то́тчас же заинтересова́лся; **can I ~ you in another drink?** могу́ я вам предложи́ть ещё рю́мочку?

● *cpds.* **~-bearing** *adj.* проце́нтный, принося́щий проце́нт; **~-free** *adj.* беспроце́нтный.

interested /'ɪntrəstɪd/, /'ɪntrɪstɪd/ *adj.* **1** (*having or showing interest*) интересу́ющийся; **are you ~ in football?** вы интересу́етесь футбо́лом? **2** (*not impartial*) коры́стный (*pej.*), заинтересо́ванный; **an ~ party** заинтересо́ванная сторона́.

interesting /'ɪntrəstɪŋ/, /-trɪstɪŋ/ *adj.* интере́сный; **it is ~** э́то интере́сно.

interethnic /ˌɪntər'eθnɪk/ *adj.* межнациона́льный.

interface /'ɪntəˌfeɪs/ *n.* стык; (*comput.*) интерфе́йс; (*fig.*) взаимосвя́зь, взаимоде́йствие.

interfer|e /ˌɪntə'fɪə(r)/ *v.i.* **1** (*meddle; obtrude o.s.*) вме́ш|иваться, -а́ться; **don't ~e in my affairs** не вме́шивайтесь в мои́ дела́; **she is an ~ing old lady** она́ назо́йливая стару́ха; **don't ~e with this machine** не тро́гайте э́ту маши́ну; **my papers have been ~ed with** кто́-то тро́гал мои́ бума́ги. **2** (*come in the way; present an obstacle*) меша́ть, по- + *d.*; **I am going to London tomorrow if nothing ~es** я за́втра пое́ду в Ло́ндон, е́сли ничто́ мне не помеша́ет.

interference /ˌɪntə'fɪərəns/ *n.* вмеша́тельство, поме́ха; (*radio, TV*) поме́хи (*f. pl.*); (*phys.*) интерфере́нция.

intergalactic /ˌɪntəgə'læktɪk/ *adj.* межгалакти́ческий.

intergovernmental /ˌɪntəˌgʌvən'ment(ə)l/ *adj.* межправи́тельственный.

interim /'ɪntərɪm/ *n.* промежу́ток вре́мени; **in the ~** тем вре́менем.

● *adj.* (*temporary*) вре́менный; (*provisional*) промежу́точный; **~ report** предвари́тельный докла́д.

interior /ɪn'tɪərɪə(r)/ *n.* **1** (*inside*) вну́тренность; **the earth's ~** не́дра (*pl., g.* —) земли́. **2** (*of building*) интерье́р; **~ decorator** худо́жник по интерье́ру; **~ decoration** вну́треннее оформле́ние; **~ design** диза́йн интерье́ра; **~ designer** диза́йнер интерье́ра. **3** (*painting*) интерье́р. **4** (*inland areas*) глуби́нные райо́ны (*m. pl.*); **he made a journey into the ~ of Brazil** он соверши́л путеше́ствие вглубь Брази́лии. **5** (*home affairs*): **Minister of the I~** мини́стр вну́тренних дел.

● *adj.* вну́тренний.

interject /ˌɪntə'dʒekt/ *v.t.* вст|авля́ть,

-а́вить; (*coll.*) вверну́ть (*pf.*); **'It's not true,' he ~ed** «Э́то непра́вда», — вста́вил он.

interjection /ˌɪntəˈdʒekʃ(ə)n/ *n.* восклица́ние; (*gram.*) междоме́тие.

interlace /ˌɪntəˈleɪs/ *v.t. & i.* перепле|та́ть(ся), -сти́(сь); сплe|та́ть(ся), -сти́(сь).

interlard /ˌɪntəˈlɑːd/ *v.t.*: **his prose is ~ed with foreign words** его́ про́за пересы́пана иностра́нными слова́ми.

interleave /ˌɪntəˈliːv/ *v.t.* (*insert blank pages in*) про|кла́дывать, -ложи́ть чи́стые листы́ ме́жду страни́цами (+*g.*); **an ~d text** текст с проло́женными чи́стыми листа́ми; (*place something between layers of*) просл|а́ивать, -ои́ть (**with**: +*i.*).

interlibrary /ˌɪntəˈlaɪbrərɪ/ *adj.*: **~ loan** межбиблиоте́чный абонеме́нт.

interline /ˌɪntəˈlaɪn/ *v.t.* (*insert extra lining*) ста́вить, по- дополни́тельную подкла́дку (на+*a.*).

interlinear /ˌɪntəˈlɪnɪə(r)/ *adj.* междустро́чный.

interlink /ˌɪntəˈlɪŋk/ *v.t. & i.* взаимосвя́з|ывать(ся), -а́ть(ся).

interlock *v.t. & i.* /ˌɪntəˈlɒk/ соедин|я́ть(ся), -и́ть(ся), сцеп|ля́ть(ся), -и́ть(ся); **they ~ed hands** они́ сцепи́ли ру́ки.

● *n.* /ˈɪntəˌlɒk/ (*mech., elec.*) сцепле́ние, блокиро́вка.

interlocutor /ˌɪntəˈlɒkjʊtə(r)/ *n.* собесе́дни|к (*fem.* -ца).

interloper /ˈɪntəˌləʊpə(r)/ *n.* незва́ный гость.

interlude /ˈɪntəˌluːd/, /-ˌljuːd/ *n.* (*interval of play*) антра́кт; (*mus. & fig.*) интерлю́дия.

intermarriage /ˌɪntəˈmærɪdʒ/ *n.* брак ме́жду людьми́ разли́чной ра́совой, национа́льной *и т.п.* принадле́жности.

intermarry /ˌɪntəˈmærɪ/ *v.i.* сме́ш|иваться, -а́ться; родни́ться, по- путём бра́ка.

intermediary /ˌɪntəˈmiːdɪərɪ/ *n.* посре́дни|к (*fem.* -ца).

● *adj.* (*acting as go-between*) посре́днический; (*intermediate*) промежу́точный, посре́дствующий.

intermediate /ˌɪntəˈmiːdɪət/ *adj.* промежу́точный; **at an ~ stage** на перехо́дной ста́дии.

interment /ɪnˈtɜːmənt/ *n.* погребе́ние.

intermezz|o /ˌɪntəˈmetsəʊ/ *n.* (*pl.* **~i** /-ɪ/ *or* **~os**) интерме́ццо (*indecl.*).

interminable /ɪnˈtɜːmɪnəb(ə)l/ *adj.* бесконе́чный, несконча́емый, ве́чный.

intermingle /ˌɪntəˈmɪŋg(ə)l/ *v.t. & i.* сме́ш|ивать(ся), -а́ть(ся).

intermission /ˌɪntəˈmɪʃ(ə)n/ *n.* переры́в, па́уза; (*theatr.*) антра́кт.

intermittent /ˌɪntəˈmɪt(ə)nt/ *adj.* преры́вистый.

intermix /ˌɪntəˈmɪks/ *v.t. & i.* переме́ш|ивать(ся), -а́ть(ся); сме́ш|ивать(ся), -а́ть(ся).

intermixture /ˌɪntəˈmɪkstʃə(r)/ *n.* смесь; смеше́ние.

intern¹ /ˈɪntɜːn/ *n.* (*US*) (*medical student*) молодо́й врач, инте́рн; (*trainee*) стажёр, практика́нт.

intern² /ɪnˈtɜːn/ *v.t.* интерни́ровать (*impf., pf.*).

internal /ɪnˈtɜːn(ə)l/ *adj.* вну́тренний; **~ strife** вну́тренние конфли́кты (*m. pl.*); **~ injuries** поврежде́ние вну́тренних о́рганов; **~ combustion engine** дви́гатель (*m.*) вну́треннего сгора́ния; **I~ Revenue Service** (*US*) Госуда́рственная нало́говая слу́жба.

internally /ɪnˈtɜːn(ə)lɪ/ *adv.* (*inside an object*) изнутри́, внутри́; (*inside an organization*) внутри́; (*in one's mind*) вну́тренне; **shudder ~** вну́тренне содрогну́ться (*pf.*).

international /ˌɪntəˈnæʃən(ə)l/ *n.* (*socialist organization*) Интернациона́л; (*Br., sporting event*) междунаро́дные состяза́ния (*nt. pl.*); (*participant*) уча́стни|к (*fem.* -ца) междунаро́дных состяза́ний.

● *adj.* междунаро́дный, интернациона́льный; **I~ Monetary Fund** Междунаро́дный валю́тный фонд.

Internationale /ˌɪntəˌnæʃjəˈnɑːl/ *n.* Интернациона́л.

internecine /ˌɪntəˈniːsaɪn/ *adj.* (*destructive to both sides*) взаимоуничтожа́ющий, взаиморазруши́тельный; (*of conflict between groups*) междоусо́бный.

internee /ˌɪntɜːˈniː/ *n.* интерни́рованный.

Internet /ˈɪntənet/ *n.* (**the ~**) Интерне́т; **on the ~** на Интерне́те.

internment /ɪnˈtɜːnmənt/ *n.* интерни́рование; **~ camp** ла́герь (*m.*) для интерни́рованных (лиц).

internship /ɪnˈtɜːnʃɪp/ *n.* (*US*) (*of medical student*) интерна́тура; (*traineeship*) стажиро́вка, пра́ктикум.

interpellation /ɪnˌtɜːpeˈleɪʃ(ə)n/ *n.* запро́с, интерпелля́ция.

interpersonal /ˌɪntəˈpɜːsən(ə)l/ *adj.* межли́чностный.

interplanetary /ˌɪntəˈplænɪtərɪ/ *adj.* межплане́тный.

interplay /ˈɪntəˌpleɪ/ *n.* взаимоде́йствие, взаимосвя́зь.

interpolate /ɪnˈtɜːpəˌleɪt/ *v.t.* интерполи́ровать (*impf., pf.*); вст|авля́ть, -а́вить.

interpolation /ɪnˌtɜːpəˈleɪʃ(ə)n/ *n.* интерполя́ция, вста́вка.

interpose /ˌɪntəˈpəʊz/ *v.t.* **1** (*remark, word*) вст|авля́ть, -а́вить; **~ an objection** выдвига́ть, вы́двинуть возраже́ние. **2** (*place, insert, between two things*) ста́вить, по-, поме|ща́ть, -сти́ть (*что-н.*) ме́жду (+*i.*).

● *v.i.* (*intervene*) вме́ш|иваться, -а́ться.

interposition /ˌɪntəpəˈzɪʃ(ə)n/ *n.* (*intervention*) вмеша́тельство.

interpret /ɪnˈtɜːprɪt/ *v.t.* (**interpreted, interpreting**) **1** (*expound meaning of*) толкова́ть (*impf.*); истолк|о́вывать, -ова́ть; интерпрети́ровать (*impf., pf.*); **how do you ~ this dream?** как вы объясня́ете э́тот сон?; **this passage has been ~ed in various ways** э́тот отры́вок толкова́ли/интерпрети́ровали по-ра́зному; (*of an actor*) интерпрети́ровать (*impf., pf.*), трактова́ть (*impf.*). **2** (*understand*) истолко́в|ывать, -а́ть; **I ~ed his silence as a refusal** я истолкова́л его́ молча́ние как отка́з.

● *v.i.* (**interpreted, interpreting**) перев|оди́ть, -ести́ (у́стно); **he ~ed for the President** он был перево́дчиком президе́нта.

interpretation /ɪnˌtɜːprɪˈteɪʃ(ə)n/ *n.* (*expounding; exposition*) интерпрета́ция, толкова́ние; (*by an actor*) тракто́вка, интерпрета́ция; (*understanding, construction*) толкова́ние; **he puts a different ~ on the facts** он ина́че истолко́вывает э́ти фа́кты; (*oral translation*) (у́стный) перево́д.

interpreter /ɪnˈtɜːprɪtə(r)/ *n.* (у́стный) перево́дчи|к (*fem.* -ца).

interracial /ˌɪntəˈreɪʃ(ə)l/ *adj.* межра́совый.

interregn|um /ˌɪntəˈregnəm/ *n.* (*pl.* **~ums** *or* **~a**) междуца́рствие.

interrelate /ˌɪntərɪˈleɪt/ *v.t.* взаимосвя́зывать (*impf.*).

interrelation(ship) /ˌɪntərɪˈleɪʃ(ə)nʃɪp/ *n.* взаимоотноше́ние.

interrogate /ɪnˈterəˌgeɪt/ *v.t.* допр|а́шивать, -оси́ть.

interrogation /ɪnˌterəˈgeɪʃ(ə)n/ *n.* допро́с.

interrogative /ˌɪntəˈrɒgətɪv/ *adj.* вопроси́тельный.

interrogator /ɪnˈterəˌgeɪtə(r)/ *n.* сле́дователь (*m.*).

interrogatory /ˌɪntəˈrɒgətərɪ/ *adj.* вопроси́тельный.

interrupt /ˌɪntəˈrʌpt/ *v.t.* **1** (*break in on; also v.i.*) прер|ыва́ть, -ва́ть; переб|ива́ть, -и́ть; **don't ~ when I am speaking** не перебива́йте, когда́ я говорю́; **he ~ed me as I was reading** он прерва́л моё чте́ние. **2** (*disturb*) нар|уша́ть, -у́шить; меша́ть, по- +*d.*; **my sleep was ~ed by the noise of trains** шум поездо́в нару́шил мой сон; **his performance was ~ed by coughing** его́ выступле́ние прерыва́лось ка́шлем в за́ле. **3** (*obstruct*) заслон|я́ть, -и́ть; препя́тствовать (*impf.*) +*d.*; **these trees ~ the view** э́ти дере́вья заслоня́ют вид.

interruption /ˌɪntəˈrʌpʃ(ə)n/ *n.* поме́ха; наруше́ние; вторже́ние; **he continued to speak despite ~s** он продолжа́л говори́ть, невзира́я на поме́хи; **~ of communications** наруше́ние свя́зи.

intersect /ˌɪntəˈsekt/ *v.t. & i.* перес|ека́ть(ся), -е́чь(ся); перекр|е́щивать(ся), -ести́ть(ся).

intersection /ˌɪntəˈsekʃ(ə)n/ *n.* (*intersecting*) пересече́ние; (*point of ~*) то́чка пересече́ния; (*crossroads*) перекрёсток.

intersperse /ˌɪntəˈspɜːs/ *v.t.* разбр|а́сывать, -оса́ть; расс|ыпа́ть, -ы́пать; **red flowers ~d with yellow**

ones кра́сные цветы́ вперемéжку с жёлтыми; **his talk was ~d with anecdotes** он пересыпа́л своё выступле́ние анекдо́тами.

interstate /ˈɪntəˌsteɪt/ *adj.* (*between regions of country*) межшта́тный; (*between countries*) межгосуда́рственный.

interstellar /ˌɪntəˈstelə(r)/ *adj.* межзвёздный.

interstice /ɪnˈtɜːstɪs/ *n.* (*intervening space*) промежу́ток; (*crevice*) расще́лина.

intertribal /ˌɪntəˈtraɪb(ə)l/ *adj.* межплеменно́й.

intertwine /ˌɪntəˈtwaɪn/ *v.t.* & *i.* спле|та́ть(ся), -сти́(сь); **their arms were ~d** их ру́ки бы́ли сплетены́; **the two subjects are ~d** э́ти два предме́та те́сно свя́заны ме́жду собо́й.

interval /ˈɪntəv(ə)l/ *n.* **1** (*of time*) промежу́ток, отре́зок вре́мени; интерва́л; **there was an ~ of a week between his two visits** ме́жду двумя́ его́ посеще́ниями прошла́ неде́ля; **we see each other at ~s** мы ви́димся вре́мя от вре́мени; **at ~s of an hour** с интерва́лами в час. **2** (*of place*) расстоя́ние; **the posts were set at ~s of 10 feet** столбы́ бы́ли расста́влены на расстоя́нии десяти́ фу́тов. **3** (*Br., theatr.*) антра́кт. **4** (*mus.*) интерва́л.

intervene /ˌɪntəˈviːn/ *v.i.* **1** (*of an event*): **we were to have met, but his death ~d** мы должны́ бы́ли встре́титься, но его́ смерть э́тому помеша́ла; **if nothing ~s** е́сли ничего́ не случи́тся; **some years ~d** с тех пор прошло́ не́сколько лет. **2** (*interpose one's influence*) вмéш|иваться, -а́ться; **the government ~d in the dispute** в конфли́кт вмеша́лось прави́тельство.

intervention /ˌɪntəˈvenʃ(ə)n/ *n.* вмеша́тельство; (*mil.*) интерве́нция.

interventionism /ˌɪntəˈvenʃəˌnɪz(ə)m/ *n.* поли́тика вмеша́тельства.

interventionist /ˌɪntəˈvenʃənɪst/ *n.* интерве́нт.

interview /ˈɪntəˌvjuː/ *n.* делова́я встре́ча; собесе́дование; (*with the media*) интервью́ (*nt. indecl.*); **I am having an ~ for the job** у меня́ бу́дет собесе́дование для но́вой рабо́ты; **he gave an ~ to the press** он дал интервью́ журнали́стам.

● *v.t.* & *i.* (*with the media*) интервьюи́ровать (*impf., pf.*); брать, взять интервью́ у + *g.*; **only certain candidates were ~ed** собесе́дование провели́ то́лько с не́сколькими кандида́тами; **he ~s well** (*acquits himself*) он хорошо́ де́ржится во вре́мя интервью́.

interviewee /ˌɪntəvjuːˈiː/ *n.* интервьюи́руемый, даю́щий интервью́.

interviewer /ˈɪntəˌvjuːə(r)/ *n.* (*for media*) интервьюе́р; (*for job*) проводя́щий собесе́дование.

inter-war /ˌɪntəˈwɔː(r)/ *adj.*: **~ period** пери́од ме́жду двумя́ мировы́ми во́йнами.

inter|weave /ˌɪntəˈwiːv/ *v.t.* (*past* **-wove** /-ˈwəʊv/; *p.p.* **-woven** /-ˈwəʊv(ə)n/) впле|та́ть, -сти́; (*insert*) вст|авля́ть, -а́вить; **truth ~woven with fiction** пра́вда, переплета́ющаяся с вы́мыслом.

intestacy /ɪnˈtestəsɪ/ *n.* отсу́тствие завеща́ния.

intestate /ɪnˈtesteɪt/ *adj.* уме́рший без завеща́ния.

intestinal /ˌɪnteˈstaɪn(ə)l/ *adj.* кише́чный.

intestine /ɪnˈtestɪn/ *n.* кише́чник.

intimacy /ˈɪntɪməsɪ/ *n.* инти́мность, бли́зость.

intimate¹ /ˈɪntɪmət/ *n.* бли́зкий друг.

● *adj.* **1** (*close, familiar*) бли́зкий, закады́чный (*coll.*); **they are on ~ terms** они́ в бли́зких отноше́ниях. **2** (*private, personal*) инти́мный, ли́чный; **the ~ details of his life** подро́бности его́ ли́чной жи́зни. **3** (*detailed*) основа́тельный, глубо́кий, доскона́льный; **he has an ~ knowledge of the subject** он доскона́льно зна́ет предме́т.

intimate² /ˈɪntɪˌmeɪt/ *v.t.* (*convey*) ув|едомля́ть, -е́домить; (*hint, imply*) намек|а́ть, -ну́ть на + *a.*

intimation /ˌɪntɪˈmeɪʃ(ə)n/ *n.* намёк, уведомле́ние.

intimidate /ɪnˈtɪmɪˌdeɪt/ *v.t.* запу́г|ивать, -а́ть; угрожа́ть (*impf.*) + *d.*

intimidation /ɪnˌtɪmɪˈdeɪʃ(ə)n/ *n.* запу́гивание, угро́зы (*f. pl.*).

into /ˈɪntʊ/, /ˈɪntə/ *prep.* **1** (*expr. motion to a point within*) в + *a.*; **I was going ~ the shop** я входи́л в магази́н. **2** (*expr. extent*) до; **far ~ the night** до по́здней но́чи. **3** (*expr. change or process*) *usu.* в + *a. or* на + *a.*; **the rain turned ~ snow** дождь перешёл в снег; **translate ~ French** перев|оди́ть, -ести́ на францу́зский. **4** (*coll., of a devotee*): **I'm not ~ Shakespeare** я не увлека́юсь Шекспи́ром; **he's ~ jazz** он увлека́ется джа́зом.

intolerable /ɪnˈtɒlərəb(ə)l/ *adj.* невыноси́мый.

intolerance /ɪnˈtɒlərəns/ *n.* нетерпи́мость; **his body developed an ~ to antibiotics** у него́ развила́сь неперенос́имость антибио́тиков.

intolerant /ɪnˈtɒlərənt/ *n.* нетерпи́мый; **~ of** (*unable to bear*) не вынося́щий + *g.*

intonation /ˌɪntəˈneɪʃ(ə)n/ *n.* интона́ция.

intone /ɪnˈtəʊn/ *v.t.* (*utter in particular tone*) интони́ровать (*impf.*); (*recite with prolonged sounds*) чита́ть (*impf.*) нараспе́в.

in toto /ɪn ˈtəʊtəʊ/ *adv.* целико́м, по́лностью, в це́лом.

intoxicat|e /ɪnˈtɒksɪˌkeɪt/ *v.t.* (*lit., fig.*) опьян|я́ть, -и́ть; **~ing liquor** опьяня́ющий напи́ток; **become ~ed** пьяне́ть, о-.

intoxication /ɪnˌtɒksɪˈkeɪʃ(ə)n/ *n.* опьяне́ние.

intra- /ˈɪntrə/ *pref.* внутри . . .

intractability /ɪnˌtræktəˈbɪlɪtɪ/ *n.* упря́мство, непоко́рность, несгово́рчивость.

intractable /ɪnˈtræktəb(ə)l/ *adj.* (*of person*) упря́мый, непоко́рный, несгово́рчивый; (*of problems, metal*) непода́тливый; **~ illness** трудноизлечи́мое заболева́ние; **~ pain** неустрани́мая боль.

intransigence /ɪnˈtrænsɪdʒ(ə)ns/, /-zɪdʒ(ə)ns/ *n.* непреклóнность.

intransigent /ɪnˈtrænsɪdʒ(ə)nt/, /-zɪdʒ(ə)nt/ *adj.* непрекло́нный.

intransitive /ɪnˈtrænsɪtɪv/, /ɪnˈtrɑːn-/, /-zɪtɪv/ *adj.* неперехо́дный.

intra-uterine /ˌɪntrəˈjuːtəˌraɪn/, /-rɪn/ *adj.*: **~ device** (*abbr.* **IUD**) внутрима́точный контрацепти́в.

intravenous /ˌɪntrəˈviːnəs/ *adj.* внутриве́нный.

in-tray /ˈɪntreɪ/ *n.* (*Br.*) корзи́нка для входя́щей корреспонде́нции.

intrepid /ɪnˈtrepɪd/ *adj.* неустраши́мый, бесстра́шный.

intrepidity /ˌɪntrɪˈpɪdɪtɪ/ *n.* неустраши́мость, бесстра́шие.

intricacy /ˈɪntrɪkəsɪ/ *n.* запу́танность, сло́жность.

intricate /ˈɪntrɪkət/ *adj.* запу́танный, сло́жный.

intrigu|e /ɪnˈtriːg/, /ˈɪn-/ *n.* (*secret plotting*) интри́га; про́иски (*m. pl.*); (*amour*) любо́вная связь, интри́га, интри́жка (*coll.*).

● *v.t.* (**intrigues, intrigued, intriguing**) интригова́ть, за-; интересова́ть, за-; **I was ~ed to learn** мне бы́ло интере́сно узна́ть; **an ~ing prospect** зама́нчивая перспекти́ва.

● *v.i.* (**intrigues, intrigued, intriguing**) интригова́ть (*impf.*); **they ~ed against the king** они́ интригова́ли про́тив короля́.

intrinsic /ɪnˈtrɪnzɪk/ *adj.* прису́щий, сво́йственный, по́длинный; **~ value** по́длинная це́нность/сто́имость.

intro /ˈɪntrəʊ/ *n.* (*pl.* **~s**) (*coll.*) введе́ние.

introduc|e /ˌɪntrəˈdjuːs/ *v.t.* **1** (*insert*) вст|авля́ть, -а́вить; **he ~ed the key into the lock** он вста́вил ключ в замо́к. **2** (*bring in*) вв|оди́ть, -ести́; (при)вн|оси́ть, -ести́; **the motor works are ~ing a new model** автозаво́д вво́дит в произво́дство но́вую моде́ль; **many improvements have been ~ed** ввели́ мно́го усоверше́нствований; **tobacco was ~ed from America** таба́к был завезён из Аме́рики; **~e a bill** вв|оди́ть, -ести́ законопрое́кт; **~e a custom** зав|оди́ть, -ести́ обы́чай. **3** (*present*) предст|авля́ть, -а́вить; знако́мить, по- (*кого с кем*); **may I ~e my fiancée?** разреши́те предста́вить вам мою́ неве́сту; **have we been ~ed (to each other)?** мы знако́мы?; **my father ~ed me to chess** мой оте́ц познако́мил меня́ с ша́хматами. **4** (*begin*): **he ~ed his speech with a quotation** он нача́л своё выступле́ние с цита́ты.

introduction /ˌɪntrəˈdʌkʃ(ə)n/ *n.* **1** (*inserting*) ввод, введе́ние, включéние. **2** (*bringing in, instituting*) введéние, установлéние. **3** (*something brought in*) нóвшество, нововведéние; **a recent ~ from abroad** нóвшество из-за рубежá. **4** (*presentation*) представлéние; **the hostess made ~s all round** хозяйка всех перезнакóмила; **this wine needs no ~ from me** э́то винó в моéй рекомендáции не нуждáется; **letter of ~** рекомендáтельное письмó. **5** (*title of book*): **An I~ to Nuclear Physics** «Введéние в я́дерную фи́зику». **6** (*preliminary matter in book, speech etc.*) введéние, вступлéние.

introductory /ˌɪntrəˈdʌktərɪ/ *adj.* вступи́тельный, ввóдный.

introspection /ˌɪntrəˈspekʃ(ə)n/ *n.* интроспéкция, самоанáлиз.

introspective /ˌɪntrəˈspektɪv/ *adj.* интроспекти́вный.

introvert /ˈɪntrəˌvɜːt/ *n.* зáмкнутый человéк, интровéрт.

● *v.t.*: **an ~ed nature** зáмкнутая натýра.

intrud|e /ɪnˈtruːd/ *v.t.* нав|я́зывать, -язáть; **he ~ed himself into our company** он навязáл нам своё óбщество; **I don't wish to ~e my opinions on you** я не хочý навя́зывать вам свои́ мнéния; **the thought ~ed itself into my mind** э́та мысль засéла у меня́ в головé.

● *v.i.* вт|оргáться, -óргнуться; **I hope I'm not ~ing** надéюсь, я вам не помешáю; **you are ~ing on my time** вы посягáете на моё врéмя.

intruder /ɪnˈtruːdə(r)/ *n.* (*intrusive person*) навя́зчивый человéк; (*burglar*) граби́тель (*m.*).

intrusion /ɪnˈtruːʒ(ə)n/ *n.* вторжéние; **an ~ on my privacy** нарушéние моегó покóя; вторжéние в мою́ ли́чную жизнь.

intrusive /ɪnˈtruːsɪv/ *adj.* назóйливый.

intuit /ɪnˈtjuːɪt/ *v.t.* пост|игáть, -и́гнуть интуити́вно.

intuition /ˌɪntjuːˈɪʃ(ə)n/ *n.* интуи́ция; чутьё.

intuitive /ɪnˈtjuːɪtɪv/ *adj.* интуити́вный; **women are more ~ than men** жéнщины обладáют бóлее рáзвитой интуи́цией, чем мужчи́ны.

inundate /ˈɪnənˌdeɪt/ *v.t.* затоп|ля́ть, -и́ть; наводн|я́ть, -и́ть; **floods ~d the valley** доли́на былá затóплена в результáте наводнéний; (*fig.*) нап|олня́ть, -óлнить; наводн|я́ть, -и́ть; **I was ~d with letters** меня́ засы́пали пи́сьмами; **the town was ~d with tourists** гóрод был наводнён тури́стами.

inundation /ˌɪnənˈdeɪʃ(ə)n/ *n.* наводнéние; (*fig.*) наплы́в.

inure /ɪˈnjʊə(r)/ *v.t.* приуч|áть, -и́ть; прив|ивáть, -и́ть нáвык (*к чему*); **working in the fields ~d his body to heat and cold** рабóта в пóле приучи́ла егó органи́зм к жáре и хóлоду.

invade /ɪnˈveɪd/ *v.t.* вторгáться, втóргнуться в + *a.*; **Germany ~d France** Гермáния втóрглась во Фрáнцию; (*fig.*) охвáт|ывать, -и́ть; наводн|я́ть, -и́ть; овлад|евáть, -éть + *i.*; **doubts ~d her mind** éю овладéли сомнéния; **crowds of tourists ~d the restaurants** тóлпы тури́стов наводни́ли ресторáны.

invader /ɪnˈveɪdə(r)/ *n.* захвáтчик.

invalid[1] /ˈɪnvəˌliːd/, /-lɪd/ *n.* (*sick person*) больнóй; (*disabled person*) инвали́д.

● *v.t.* (**invalided, invaliding**): **he was ~ed out (of the army)** егó демобилизовáли по состоя́нию здорóвья; егó комиссовáли.

invalid[2] /ɪnˈvalɪd/ *adj.* (*groundless*) несостоя́тельный, непригóдный; **~ argument** несостоя́тельный дóвод; (*having no legal force*) недействи́тельный, не имéющий (закóнной) си́лы.

invalidate /ɪnˈvælɪˌdeɪt/ *v.t.* (*argument*) дéлать, с- несостоя́тельным; (*treaty, contract*) лиш|áть, -и́ть закóнной си́лы; аннули́ровать (*impf., pf.*).

invalidation /ɪnˌvælɪˈdeɪʃ(ə)n/ *n.* лишéние (закóнной) си́лы; аннули́рование.

invalidity /ˌɪnvəˈlɪdɪtɪ/ *n.* **1** (*Br., being an invalid*) инвали́дность. **2** (*being invalid*) недействи́тельность.

invaluable /ɪnˈvæljʊəb(ə)l/ *adj.* неоцени́мый, бесцéнный.

invariable /ɪnˈveərɪəb(ə)l/ *adj.* неизмéнный, постоя́нный.

invasion /ɪnˈveɪʒ(ə)n/ *n.* вторжéние, нашéствие; **the ~ of Europe** вторжéние в Еврóпу; **~ of privacy** нарушéние покóя/уединéния; вторжéние в ли́чную жизнь.

invective /ɪnˈvektɪv/ *n.* инвекти́ва, брань.

inveigh /ɪnˈveɪ/ *v.i.*: **~ against** я́ростно нап|адáть, -áсть на + *a.*; поноси́ть (*impf.*).

inveigle /ɪnˈveɪg(ə)l/, /-ˈviːg(ə)l/ *v.t.* соблазн|я́ть, -и́ть; оболь|щáть, -сти́ть; **they ~d him into the conspiracy** они́ вовлекли́ егó в загóвор; **he was ~d into signing a cheque** (*Br.*), **check** (*US*) егó обмáном застáвили подписáть чек.

invent /ɪnˈvent/ *v.t.* (*devise, originate*) изобре|тáть, -сти́; **when was this machine ~ed?** когдá былá изобретенá э́та маши́на?; (*think up*) приду́м|ывать, -ать; вы́ду́мывать, вы́думать.

invention /ɪnˈvenʃ(ə)n/ *n.* (*designing; contrivance*) изобретéние; (*inventiveness*) изобретáтельность, нахóдчивость; (*fabrication*) вы́думка; **his story is pure ~** егó расскáз — пóлная вы́думка; **a writer of great ~** писáтель с богáтой фантáзией.

inventive /ɪnˈventɪv/ *adj.* изобретáтельный, нахóдчивый.

inventor /ɪnˈventə(r)/ *n.* изобретáтель (*m.*).

inventory /ˈɪnvəntərɪ/ *n.* инвентáрь (*m.*).

inverse /ˈɪnvɜːs/, /-ˈvɜːs/ *adj.* обрáтный, противополóжный; **in ~ proportion to (or ~ly proportional to)** обрáтно пропорционáльно + *d.*

inversion /ɪnˈvɜːʃ(ə)n/ *n.* (*turning upside down*) перевёртывание; (*reversing order or relation*) перестанóвка; (*gram.*) инвéрсия.

invert /ɪnˈvɜːt/ *v.t.* (*turn upside down*) перев|орáчивать, -ернýть; **~ed commas** (*Br.*) кавы́чки (*f. pl.*); (*reverse order or relation*) перест|авля́ть, -áвить.

invertebrate /ɪnˈvɜːtɪbrət/, /-ˌbreɪt/ *n.* беспозвонóчное (живóтное).

● *adj.* беспозвонóчный.

invest /ɪnˈvest/ *v.t.* **1** (*clothe, usu. fig.*) обл|екáть, -éчь; **he was ~ed with full authority** егó облекли́ всéми полномóчиями. **2** (*lay out as ~ment*) вклáдывать, вложи́ть; инвести́ровать (*impf., pf.*).

● *v.i.* вклáдывать, вложи́ть дéньги/капитáл; (*coll., spend money usefully*): **I must ~ in a new hat** мне придётся потрáтиться на (*or* приобрести́) нóвую шля́пу.

investigate /ɪnˈvestɪˌgeɪt/ *v.t.* (*crime, facts*) расслéдовать (*impf., pf.*); (*study, research*) исслéдовать (*impf., pf.*).

investigation /ɪnˌvestɪˈgeɪʃ(ə)n/ *n.* (*criminal*) расслéдование, слéдствие; (*study, research*) исслéдование.

investigative /ɪnˈvestɪgətɪv/ *adj.*: **~ journalism** журнали́стика расслéдований.

investigator /ɪnˈvestɪˌgeɪtə(r)/ *n.* (*in police*) слéдователь (*m.*); (*researcher*) исслéдователь (*m.*).

investiture /ɪnˈvestɪˌtjʊə(r)/ *n.* инвеститýра; формáльное введéние в дóлжность; пожáлование звáния.

investment /ɪnˈvestmənt/ *n.* (*investing*) инвести́рование, капиталовложéние, помещéние капитáла; **a wise ~** разýмное вложéние дéнег; (*sum invested*) инвести́ция; вклад; **~ bank** инвестициóнный банк; (*lucrative acquisition*) удáчное приобретéние.

investor /ɪnˈvestə(r)/ *n.* вклáдчик, инвéстор.

inveterate /ɪnˈvetərət/ *adj.* закоренéлый, зая́длый.

invidious /ɪnˈvɪdɪəs/ *adj.* оскорби́тельный; оби́дный; **an ~ comparison** оби́дное/оскорби́тельное сравнéние.

invidiousness /ɪnˈvɪdɪəsnɪs/ *n.* оскорби́тельность.

invigilate /ɪnˈvɪdʒɪˌleɪt/ *v.t. & i.* (*Br.*) надзирáть (*impf.*) за (*кем*); наблюдáть (*impf.*) за экзаменýющимися.

invigilation /ɪnˌvɪdʒɪˈleɪʃ(ə)n/ *n.* наблюдéние за экзаменýющимися.

invigilator /ɪnˈvɪdʒɪˌleɪtə(r)/ *n.* официáльный наблюдáтель (*на экзамене*).

invigorat|e /ɪnˈvɪgəˌreɪt/ *v.t.* укреп|ля́ть, -и́ть; прид|авáть, -áть си́лу + *d.*; (*fig.*) воодушев|ля́ть, -и́ть; вдохнов|ля́ть, -и́ть; **his ideas are ~ing** егó идéи вдохновля́ют.

invincibility /ɪnˌvɪnsɪˈbɪlɪtɪ/ *n.* непобеди́мость.

invincible /ɪnˌvɪnsɪb(ə)l/ *adj.* непобеди́мый; **~ will** несгибáемая вóля.

inviolability /ɪnˌvaɪələˈbɪlɪtɪ/ *n.* нерушимость; неприкосновéнность.

inviolable /ɪn'vaɪələb(ə)l/ *adj.* нерушимый; неприкосновенный.

inviolate /ɪn'vaɪələt/ *adj.* нетронутый.

invisibility /ɪn,vɪzɪ'bɪlɪtɪ/ *n.* невидимость.

invisible /ɪn'vɪzɪb(ə)l/ *adj.* невидимый, незримый; **~ to the naked eye** незаметный для невооружённого глаза; **~ exports** невидимый экспорт; **~ ink** симпатические чернила; **~ man** человек-невидимка.

invitation /,ɪnvɪ'teɪʃ(ə)n/ *n.* приглашение; **send out ~s** ра|ссылать, -зослать приглашения; **an ~ to lunch** приглашение на обед; **I came at your ~** я пришёл по вашему приглашению; **admission by ~ only** вход только по пригласительным билетам.

invite[1] /'ɪnvaɪt/ *n.* (*coll., invitation*) приглашение.

invit|e[2] /ɪn'vaɪt/ *v.t.* **1** (*request to come*) пригла|шать, -сить; **she ~ed him into her flat** она пригласила его к себе на квартиру; **I am seldom ~ed out** меня редко куда-либо приглашают; **I was not ~ed** меня не приглашали/звали; **~e o.s.** напр|ашиваться, -оситься в гости.
2 (*request*) предл|агать, -ожить; просить, по-; **I ~ed him to reconsider** я предложил ему пересмотреть своё решение; **we were ~ed to choose** нам был предоставлен выбор; **the speaker ~ed questions from the audience** лектор предложил публике задавать вопросы.
3 (*encourage*) вызывать, вызвать; **his manner ~es confidence** его стиль вызывает доверие; (*provoke*) провоцировать, с-, напр|ашиваться, -оситься на + *a.*; **are you trying to ~e trouble?** вы что, напрашиваетесь на неприятности?
4 (*attract*) привл|екать, -ечь; **her clothes ~ed attention** её одежда привлекала внимание; **the water looks ~ing** вода манит.

invocation /,ɪnvə'keɪʃ(ə)n/ *n.* взывание (к Богу); молитва.

invoice /'ɪnvɔɪs/ *n.* счёт, счёт-фактура.
● *v.t.* выписывать, выписать счёт кому-н. (на товары).

invoke /ɪn'vəʊk/ *v.t.* **1** (*call on*) взывать, воззвать; приз|ывать, -вать; **~ the law** взывать, воззвать к закону; **he ~d the dictionary in support of his statement** он сослался на словарь для подкрепления своего утверждения.
2 (*call for*) взывать, воззвать о + *p.*; молить (*impf.*) (о + *p.*); **~ God's blessing** молить Бога о благословении; **she ~d his aid** она взывала к нему о помощи.

involuntary /ɪn'vɒləntərɪ/ *adj.* (*forced*) вынужденный; (*accidental, unintentional*) нечаянный; (*uncontrollable*) невольный, непроизвольный.

involve /ɪn'vɒlv/ *v.t.* **1** (*entangle; implicate*) вовл|екать, -ечь; впут|ывать, -ать (*coll., pej.*); **I don't want to get ~d in this business** я не хочу впутываться в это дело; **he is ~d with stocktaking just now** он сейчас занят инвентаризацией; **he was ~d in debt** он запутался в долгах; **it will not ~ you in any expense** это не введёт вас в расходы. **2** (*have as consequence; entail*) влечь, по- за собой; вызывать, вызвать; **it would ~ my living in London** в таком случае мне бы пришлось жить в Лондоне; **I want to know what is ~d** я хочу знать, с чем это сопряжено.

involved /ɪn'vɒlvd/ *adj.* сложный, запутанный.

involvement /ɪn'vɒlvmənt/ *n.* (*participation*) причастность; (*complicated situation*) сложное положение; (*financial*) денежное затруднение; (*personal*) связь, вовлечённость.

invulnerability /ɪn,vʌlnərə'bɪlɪtɪ/ *n.* неуязвимость.

invulnerable /ɪn'vʌlnərəb(ə)l/ *adj.* неуязвимый.

inward /'ɪnwəd/ *adj.* (*lit., fig.*) внутренний; **I was ~ly relieved** внутренне/в душе я почувствовал облегчение.
● *adv.* = **inward(s)**

inward(s) /'ɪnwədz/ *adv.* (*expr. motion*) внутрь; **she turned her thoughts ~** она обратила мысли на себя.

iodine /'aɪə,di:n/, /-ɪn/ *n.* йод.

ion /'aɪən/ *n.* ион.

Ionic /aɪ'ɒnɪk/ *adj.* ионический.

ionization /,aɪənaɪ'zeɪʃ(ə)n/ *n.* ионизация.

ionize /'aɪə,naɪz/ *v.t.* ионизировать (*impf., pf.*).

ionosphere /aɪ'ɒnə,sfɪə(r)/ *n.* ионосфера.

iota /aɪ'əʊtə/ *n.* (*lit., fig.*) йота; **we will not yield one ~** мы не отступим ни на йоту; **I don't care one ~** мне решительно всё равно.

IOU /,aɪəʊ'ju:/ *n.* долговая расписка.

IPA (*abbr. of* ***International Phonetic Alphabet***) МФА (Международный фонетический алфавит).

ipso facto /,ɪpsəʊ 'fæktəʊ/ *adv.* тем самым; в силу самого факта.

IQ (*abbr. of* ***intelligence quotient***) коэффициент умственного развития.

IRA 1 (*abbr. of* ***Irish Republican Army***) ИРА (Ирландская республиканская армия). **2** (*abbr. of* ***individual retirement account***) (*US*) индивидуальные пенсионные вклады (*m. pl.*).

Iran /ɪ'rɑ:n/ *n.* Иран.

Iranian /ɪ'reɪnɪən/ *n.* иран|ец (*fem.* -ка).
● *adj.* иранский.

Iraq /ɪ'rɑ:k/ *n.* Ирак.

Iraqi /ɪ'rɑ:kɪ/ *n.* (*pl.* **~s**) иракец, житель (*fem.* -ница) Ирака.
● *adj.* иракский.

irascibility /ɪ,ræsɪ'bɪlɪtɪ/ *n.* раздражительность, вспыльчивость.

irascible /ɪ'ræsɪb(ə)l/ *adj.* раздражительный, вспыльчивый.

irate /aɪ'reɪt/ *adj.* сердитый, гневный.

irateness /aɪ'reɪtnɪs/ *n.* гнев, злоба.

ire /'aɪə(r)/ *n.* (*liter.*) гнев, злоба.

Ireland /'aɪələnd/ *n.* Ирландия.

iridescence /,ɪrɪ'des(ə)ns/ *n.* радужность; игра цветов.

iridescent /,ɪrɪ'des(ə)nt/ *adj.* радужный, переливчатый.

iridium /ɪ'rɪdɪəm/ *n.* иридий.

iridologist /,ɪrɪ'dɒlədʒɪst/ *n.* иридолог.

iridology /,ɪrɪ'dɒlədʒɪ/ *n.* иридодиагностика.

iris /'aɪərɪs/ *n.* **1** (*plant*) ирис. **2** (*of eye*) радужная оболочка.

Irish /'aɪərɪʃ/ *n.* **1** (*language*) ирландский язык. **2**: **the ~** ирландцы (*m. pl.*).
● *adj.* ирландский; **~ stew** ≈ тушёная баранина с картофелем.
● *cpds.* **~man** *n.* ирландец; **~woman** *n.* ирландка.

irk /ɜ:k/ *v.t.* надоедать (*impf.*) + *d.*; раздражать (*impf.*).

irksome /'ɜ:ksəm/ *adj.* надоедливый, докучливый.

irksomeness /'ɜ:ksəmnɪs/ *n.* надоедливость, докучливость.

iron /'aɪən/ *n.* **1** (*metal*) железо; **the I~ Age** железный век; **his muscles are of ~** у него стальные мускулы; **the ~ entered into his soul** «в железо вошла душа его»; он был подавлен горем; **strike while the ~ is hot** (*prov.*) куй железо, пока горячо.
2 (*flat- or smoothing ~*) утюг; **electric ~** электрический утюг; **run the ~ over my trousers, please** погладьте, пожалуйста, мои брюки.
3 (*pl., fire-~s*) каминный прибор; **he has too many ~s in the fire** он завален работой.
4 (*pl., fetters*) оков|ы (*pl., g.* —); (*handcuffs*) наручники (*m. pl.*).
5 (*support for leg*) ножной протез.
● *adj.* (*lit., fig.*) железный; **the I~ Curtain** железный занавес; **~ lung** боксовый респиратор, аппарат «железные лёгкие»; **~ rations** неприкосновенный запас; **he ruled with an ~ hand** он правил железной рукой; **the ~ hand in the velvet glove** железный кулак в бархатной перчатке; **an ~ will** железная воля.
● *v.t.* (*smooth with flat-~*) утюжить, вы-; гладить, по-/вы-; **~ out** (*fig.*) сгла|живать, -дить; **the difficulties have all been ~ed out** все трудности устранены.
● *v.i.* гладить (*impf.*); **she spent the whole evening ~ing** она гладила весь вечер.
● *cpds.* **~-age** *adj.* принадлежащий железному веку; **~clad** *n.* броненосец; *adj.* бронированный; (*fig.*) твёрдый, жёсткий; **~-foundry** *n.* чугунолитейный цех; **~-grey** (*US* **-gray**) *adj.* стального цвета; **~master** *n.* производитель (*m.*) железа; **~monger** *n.* (*Br.*) торговец скобяными изделиями; **~monger's (shop)** *n.* (*Br.*) магазин скобяных изделий/товаров; **~-ware** *n.* скобяные изделия (*nt. pl.*); **~work** *n.* чугунные/железные изделия; **~-works** *n.* чугунолитейный завод.

ironic(al) /aɪˈrɒnɪk(ə)l/ *adj.* ирони́ческий.

ironing /ˈaɪənɪŋ/ *n.* **1** (*action*) утю́жка, гла́женье, гла́жка (*coll.*); **~-board** глади́льная доска́. **2** (*linen*) бельё для гла́женья.

ironist /ˈaɪrənɪst/ *n.* насме́шник.

iron|y /ˈaɪrənɪ/ *n.* иро́ния; **the ~y of fate** иро́ния судьбы́; **one of life's ~ies** одна́ из превра́тностей судьбы́; **the ~y of it is that ...** иро́ния в том, что. . . .

irradiate /ɪˈreɪdɪˌeɪt/ *v.t.* (*illuminate*) осве|ща́ть, -ти́ть; озар|я́ть, -и́ть; (*phys.*) облуч|а́ть, -и́ть.

irradiation /ɪˌreɪdɪˈeɪʃ(ə)n/ *n.* (*illumination*) освеще́ние; (*phys.*) облуче́ние.

irrational /ɪˈræʃən(ə)l/ *adj.* (*not endowed with reason*) неразу́мный; (*illogical; absurd*) иррациона́льный, нелоги́чный, неразу́мный; (*math.*) иррациона́льный.

irrationality /ɪˌræʃəˈnælɪtɪ/ *n.* неразу́мность, иррациона́льность, нелоги́чность.

irreconcilability /ɪˌrekənˌsaɪləˈbɪlɪtɪ/ *n.* непримири́мость; несовмести́мость.

irreconcilable /ɪˈrekənˌsaɪləb(ə)l/ *adj.* (*of persons*) непримири́мый; (*of ideas etc.*) несовмести́мый, противоречи́вый; **this is ~ with his previous statement** э́то противоре́чит его́ предыду́щему заявле́нию.

irrecoverable /ˌɪrɪˈkʌvərəb(ə)l/ *adj.* невозмести́мый; (*irremediable*) непоправи́мый.

irredeemable /ˌɪrɪˈdi:məb(ə)l/ *adj.* непоправи́мый; (*of currency*) неразме́нный; (*of an annuity*) не подлежа́щий вы́купу.

irreducible /ˌɪrɪˈdju:sɪb(ə)l/ *adj.* (*that cannot be simplified*) не поддаю́щийся упроще́нию; (*that cannot be reduced*) преде́льный, минима́льный; **the ~ minimum** преде́льный ми́нимум; (*that cannot be controlled*): **~ to order** не поддаю́щийся упоря́дочению; (*math.*) несократи́мый.

irrefutability /ɪˌrefjʊtəˈbɪlɪtɪ/, /ˌɪrɪˌfju:-/ *n.* неопровержи́мость.

irrefutable /ɪˈrefjʊtəb(ə)l/, /ˌɪrɪˈfju:-/ *adj.* неопровержи́мый.

irregular /ɪˈregjʊlə(r)/ *n.* (*usu. pl., mil.*) нерегуля́рные войска́.

● *adj.* **1** (*contrary to rule*) непра́вильный; (*contrary to custom, norm*) непри́нятый; **~ proceeding** де́йствие, наруша́ющее заведённый поря́док; **he leads an ~ life** он ведёт беспоря́дочную жизнь. **2** (*variable in occurrence*) нерегуля́рный; **he keeps ~ hours** у него́ неупоря́доченный режи́м. **3** (*unsymmetrical*) непра́вильный, несимметри́чный; **an ~ polygon** несимметри́чный многоуго́льник. **4** (*uneven*) неро́вный; **~ teeth** неро́вные зу́бы; **an ~ surface** неро́вная пове́рхность. **5** (*unequal; heterogeneous*) неравноме́рный, неодина́ковый; **at ~ intervals** с неодина́ковыми интерва́лами. **6** (*not straight*) неро́вный; **an ~ coastline** изре́занная берегова́я ли́ния. **7** (*gram.*) непра́вильный.

irregularity /ɪˌregjʊˈlærɪtɪ/ *n.* (*of conduct*) беспоря́док; (*of procedure*) незако́нность; (*of occurrence*) непра́вильность, нерегуля́рность; (*of form*) несимметри́чность, непра́вильность, неро́вность.

irrelevanc|e /ɪˈrelɪv(ə)ns/, **-y** /ɪˈrelɪv(ə)nsɪ/ *nn.* неуме́стность; (*remark*) неуме́стное замеча́ние.

irrelevant /ɪˈrelɪv(ə)nt/ *adj.* неуме́стный, неподходя́щий; **~ to the matter in hand** не относя́щийся к де́лу.

irreligious /ˌɪrɪˈlɪdʒəs/ *adj.* неве́рующий.

irremediable /ˌɪrɪˈmi:dɪəb(ə)l/ *adj.* непоправи́мый.

irremovable /ˌɪrɪˈmu:vəb(ə)l/ *adj.* неустрани́мый; (*from office*) **he is ~** его́ невозмо́жно смести́ть (с поста́).

irreparable /ɪˈrepərəb(ə)l/ *adj.*: **an ~ mistake** непоправи́мая оши́бка; **an ~ loss** безвозвра́тная поте́ря/утра́та; **my watch suffered ~ harm** мои́ часы́ оконча́тельно слома́лись.

irreplaceable /ˌɪrɪˈpleɪsəb(ə)l/ *adj.* незамени́мый.

irrepressible /ˌɪrɪˈpresɪb(ə)l/ *adj.* неукроти́мый, неугомо́нный, неудержи́мый; **an ~ child** неугомо́нный ребёнок; **~ optimism** неистреби́мый оптими́зм.

irreproachable /ˌɪrɪˈprəʊtʃəb(ə)l/ *adj.* безукори́зненный, безупре́чный.

irresistible /ˌɪrɪˈzɪstɪb(ə)l/ *adj.* (*overwhelming*) непреодоли́мый; (*very attractive*) неотрази́мый; **an ~ impulse** безу́держный поры́в; **an ~ argument** неопровержи́мый до́вод; **her smile was ~** у неё была́ неотрази́мая улы́бка.

irresolute /ɪˈrezəˌlu:t/, /-ˌlju:t/ *adj.* нереши́тельный.

irresolut|ion /ɪˌrezəˈlu:ʃ(ə)n/, /-ˈlju:ʃ(ə)n/, **-eness** /ɪˈrezəˌlu:tnɪs/, /-ˌlju:tnɪs/ *nn.* нереши́тельность.

irrespective /ˌɪrɪˈspektɪv/ *adj.*: **~ of** невзира́я/несмотря́ на + *a*.

irresponsibility /ˌɪrˌɪspɒnsɪˈbɪlɪtɪ/ *n.* безотве́тственность.

irresponsible /ˌɪrɪˈspɒnsɪb(ə)l/ *adj.* безотве́тственный.

irretrievable /ˌɪrɪˈtri:vəb(ə)l/ *adj.* (*unrecoverable*) невозмести́мый; (*beyond rescue*) безнадёжный; (*irreparable*) непоправи́мый.

irreverence /ɪˈrevərəns/ *n.* непочти́тельность, неуваже́ние.

irreverent /ɪˈrevərənt/ *adj.* непочти́тельный, неуважи́тельный.

irreversibility /ˌɪrɪˌvɜ:sɪˈbɪlɪtɪ/ *n.* необрати́мость.

irreversible /ˌɪrɪˈvɜ:sɪb(ə)l/ *adj.* (*process*) необрати́мый; (*decision*) неотменя́емый.

irrevocability /ɪˌrevəkəˈbɪlɪtɪ/ *n.* бесповоро́тность.

irrevocable /ɪˈrevəkəb(ə)l/ *adj.* бесповоро́тный.

irrigate /ˈɪrɪˌgeɪt/ *v.t.* **1** (*supply water to*) оро|ша́ть, -си́ть. **2** (*med.*) пром|ыва́ть, -ы́ть; оро|ша́ть, -си́ть.

irrigation /ˌɪrɪˈgeɪʃ(ə)n/ *n.* **1** (*supply of water*) ороше́ние, ирригáция; **~ canal** ирригацио́нный/ороси́тельный кана́л. **2** (*med.*) промыва́ние, ороше́ние.

irritability /ˌɪrɪtəˈbɪlɪtɪ/ *n.* раздражи́тельность; чувстви́тельность.

irritable /ˈɪrɪtəb(ə)l/ *adj.* **1** (*easily annoyed*) раздражи́тельный. **2** (*of skin etc.*) чувстви́тельный.

irritant /ˈɪrɪt(ə)nt/ *n.* раздражи́тель (*m.*).

● *adj.* раздража́ющий.

irritat|e /ˈɪrɪˌteɪt/ *v.t.* **1** (*annoy*) раздража́ть (*impf.*); **he was in an ~ing mood** он был соверше́нно невозмо́жен. **2** (*cause discomfort to*) раздража́ть (*impf.*); **the smoke ~es one's eyes** дым ест глаза́.

irritation /ˌɪrɪˈteɪʃ(ə)n/ *n.* раздраже́ние.

irruption /ɪˈrʌpʃ(ə)n/ *n.* вторже́ние.

IRS (*abbr. of* ***Internal Revenue Service***) (*US*) ГНС (Госуда́рственная нало́говая слу́жба).

is /ɪz/ *3rd pers. sing. pres. of* ⇨**be**

ISA /ˈaɪsə/ *n.* (*abbr. of* ***individual savings account***) (*Br.*) сберега́тельный счёт, не облага́емый нало́гом.

Isaiah /aɪˈzaɪə/ *n.* (*bibl.*) Иса́йя (*m.*).

ISBN (*abbr. of* ***international standard book number***) междунаро́дный станда́ртный кни́жный но́мер.

isinglass /ˈaɪzɪŋˌglɑ:s/ *n.* ры́бий желати́н/клей.

Islam /ˈɪzlɑ:m/, /-læm/, /-ˈlɑ:m/ *n.* исла́м, мусульма́нство.

Islamic /ɪzˈlæmɪk/ *adj.* мусульма́нский, исла́мский.

island /ˈaɪlənd/ *n.* о́стров; **traffic ~** островóк безопа́сности.

islander /ˈaɪləndə(r)/ *n.* островитя́н|ин (*fem.* -ка).

isle /aɪl/ *n.* о́стров; **the British I~s** Брита́нские острова́.

islet /ˈaɪlɪt/ *n.* островóк.

isobar /ˈaɪsəʊˌbɑ:(r)/ *n.* изоба́ра.

isolate /ˈaɪsəˌleɪt/ *v.t.* **1** изоли́ровать (*impf., pf.*) (*also med.*); разобщ|а́ть, -и́ть; **an ~d village** отдалённая дере́вня; **an ~d occasion** ча́стный/отде́льный слу́чай; **you cannot ~ one aspect of the problem** нельзя́ выделя́ть оди́н аспе́кт пробле́мы. **2** (*chem.*) выделя́ть, вы́делить.

isolation /ˌaɪsəˈleɪʃ(ə)n/ *n.* (*separation*) изоля́ция, разобще́ние; **a policy of ~** поли́тика изоля́ции; (*detachment*) уедине́ние; **he lives in splendid ~** он живёт в благословенном уедине́нии; **a case considered in ~** отде́льно взя́тый слу́чай; (*med.*) изоля́ция; **~ hospital** инфекцио́нная больни́ца.

isolationism /ˌaɪsəˈleɪʃəˌnɪz(ə)m/ *n.* изоляциони́зм.

isolationist /ˌaɪsəˈleɪʃənɪst/ *n.* изоляциони́ст.

isometric /ˌaɪsəʊˈmetrɪk/ *adj.* изометри́ческий.

isosceles /aɪˈsɒsɪˌliːz/ *adj.* равнобе́дренный.

isotherm /ˈaɪsəʊˌθɜːm/ *n.* изоте́рма.

isotope /ˈaɪsəˌtəʊp/ *n.* изото́п.

Israel /ˈɪzreɪl/ *n.* (*bibl., pol.*) Изра́иль (*m.*); **children, sons of ~** сыны́ Изра́илевы.

Israeli /ɪzˈreɪlɪ/ *n.* (*pl.* **~s**), **Israelite** /ˈɪzrɪəˌlaɪt/, /-rəˌlaɪt/ *n.* израильтя́н|ин (*fem.* -ка).

● *adj.* изра́ильский.

issue /ˈɪʃuː/, /ˈɪsjuː/ *n.* **1** (*outflowing; emergence*) вытека́ние; (*place of emergence*) вы́ход.
2 (*putting out, publication, production*) вы́пуск, изда́ние; **an ~ of stamps** вы́пуск ма́рок; **on the day of ~** в день вы́хода/вы́пуска; (*something published or produced*) вы́пуск, изда́ние; **recent ~s of a magazine** после́дние номера́ журна́ла; **an ~ of winter clothing** компле́кт зи́мней оде́жды.
3 (*question, topic*) вопро́с; предме́т обсужде́ния; **the point at ~** предме́т обсужде́ния; **I don't want to make an ~ of it** я не хочу́ де́лать из э́того пробле́му; **join take ~ with s.o. on something** нач|ина́ть, -а́ть спо́рить с кем-н. о чём-н.
4 (*leg., offspring*) пото́мство.

● *v.t.* (**issues, issued, issuing**)
1 (*utter, publish*) выпуска́ть, вы́пустить; изд|ава́ть, -а́ть; **an order was ~d for everyone to remain at home** был и́здан прика́з не выходи́ть на у́лицу; **he ~d a solemn warning** он сде́лал серьёзное предупрежде́ние; **a book ~d last year** кни́га, и́зданная в про́шлом году́.
2 (*supply*) выдава́ть, вы́дать; снаб|жа́ть, -ди́ть; **everyone was ~d with ration cards** всем вы́дали продово́льственные ка́рточки.

● *v.i.* (**issues, issued, issuing**) **1** (*go, come out*) выходи́ть, вы́йти; вытека́ть, вы́течь; **smoke ~d from the chimney** дым шёл/вали́л из трубы́; **water ~d from the rock** вода́точи́лась из скалы́; **no sound ~d from his lips** он не изда́л ни зву́ка.
2 (*proceed, emanate*) прои|сходи́ть, -зойти́; **where do these rumours** (*Br.*), **rumors** (*US*) **~ from?** отку́да происхо́дят э́ти слу́хи?

Istanbul /ˌɪstænˈbuːl/, /-ˈbʊl/ *n.* Стамбу́л.

isthmus /ˈɪsməs/, /ˈɪsθ-/ *n.* (*pl.* **~es**) перешеек, перемы́чка.

IT (*abbr. of* ***information technology***) информа́тика.

it /ɪt/ *pron.* **1** он (она́, оно́); (*impersonal*) э́то; *often untranslated, see examples*: **he loved his country and died for ~** он люби́л свою́ страну́ и поги́б за неё; **who is ~?** кто э́то?; **~'s the postman** э́то почтальо́н; **I don't speak Russian but I understand ~** я не говорю́ по-ру́сски, но понима́ю; **the shed has no roof over ~** у сара́я нет кры́ши; **that's just ~** то́-то и оно́; в то́м-то и де́ло; **that's not ~** э́то не то; не в э́том де́ло.
2 (*impersonal or indefinite*): **~ is winter** (стои́т) зима́; **~ was in winter** де́ло/э́то бы́ло зимо́й; **~ is cold** хо́лодно; **~ is 6 o'clock** (сейча́с) шесть часо́в; **~ is raining** идёт дождь; **~ is 5 miles to Oxford** до О́ксфорда пять миль; **we had to walk ~** нам пришло́сь пойти́ пешко́м; **run for ~!** беги́те изо всех сил (*or* что есть мо́чи)!; **he had a bad time of ~** ему́ здо́рово доста́лось; **if ~ were not for him** е́сли бы не он; не будь его́; **how goes ~?** как дела́?; **~ is said** говоря́т; **~ is no use going there** не́зачем идти́ туда́.
3 (*anticipating logical subject*): **~ is hard to imagine** тру́дно себе́ предста́вить; **I thought ~ best to inform you** я почёл за лу́чшее сообщи́ть вам; **~ appears I was wrong** выхо́дит, что я был непра́в.
4 (*emph. another word*): **~ was John who laughed** э́то Джон смея́лся; **~ is to him you must write** э́то ему́ вы должны́ написа́ть; **~ is here that the trouble lies** вот в чём беда́; **~ was here that I met her** э́то здесь-то мы с ней и встре́тились.
5 (*other emph. uses*): **he thinks he's ~** (*coll.*) он (поря́дком) зазнаётся; **that's ~** (*the problem*) вот и́менно; (*right*) (вот) и́менно, ве́рно; (*coll., the end*) вот и всё; и то́чка; **this is ~** (*expected event*) наконе́ц-то.
6: **'~'** (*at children's games*) водя́щий (*etc., depending on game; see also* ⇒**he**): **who is ~?** кто во́дит?

Italian /ɪˈtæljən/ *n.* (*person*) италья́н|ец (*fem.* -ка); (*language*) италья́нский язы́к.

● *adj.* италья́нский.

italicize /ɪˈtælɪˌsaɪz/ *v.t.* выделя́ть, вы́делить курси́вом.

italics /ɪˈtælɪks/ *n.* курси́в; **in ~** курси́вом.

Italy /ˈɪtəlɪ/ *n.* Ита́лия.

itch /ɪtʃ/ *n.* **1** (*irritation of skin*) зуд. **2** (*disease*) чесо́тка. **3** (*hankering*) стремле́ние; зуд; **he has an ~ to travel** он жа́ждет путеше́ствовать.

● *v.i.* **1** (*irritate*) чеса́ться (*impf.*). **2** (*feel a longing*) испы́тывать (*impf.*) зуд; **I was ~ing to strike him** у меня́ рука́ так и зуде́ла/чеса́лась уда́рить его́.

itchy /ˈɪtʃɪ/ *adj.* (**itchier, itchiest**) (*skin*) зудя́щий; (*causing itchiness*) вызыва́ющий зуд.

item /ˈaɪtəm/ *n.* пункт, но́мер; **~s on the agenda** пу́нкты пове́стки дня; **the first ~ on the programme** (*Br.*), **program** (*US*) (*entertainment*) пе́рвый но́мер програ́ммы; **~ of expenditure** статья́ расхо́да; **the list comprises 11 ~s** спи́сок включа́ет 11 предме́тов; **news ~** (коро́ткое) сообще́ние.

itemization /ˌaɪtəmaɪˈzeɪʃ(ə)n/ *n.* (*list*) пе́речень (*m.*); спи́сок.

itemize /ˈaɪtəˌmaɪz/ *v.t.* переч|исля́ть, -и́слить; сост|авля́ть, -а́вить пе́речень +*g.*; **an ~d account** подро́бный счёт.

iterate /ˈɪtəˌreɪt/ *v.t.* повтор|я́ть, -и́ть; возобнов|ля́ть, -и́ть.

iteration /ˌɪtəˈreɪʃ(ə)n/ *n.* повторе́ние, возобновле́ние.

itinerant /aɪˈtɪnərənt/, /ɪ-/ *adj.* стра́нствующий, скита́ющийся; **~ musicians** стра́нствующие/бродя́чие музыка́нты; **~ worker** рабо́чий-мигра́нт.

itinerary /aɪˈtɪnərərɪ/, /ɪ-/ *n.* (*route*) маршру́т, путь (*m.*).

its /ɪts/ *poss. adj.* его́, её (*pert. to subject of sentence*) свой; **the horse broke ~ leg** ло́шадь слома́ла но́гу.

itself /ɪtˈself/ *n.* **1** (*refl.*) себя́; -ся (*suff.*); **the cat was washing ~** кот мы́лся; **the monkey saw ~ in the mirror** обезья́на уви́дела себя́ в зе́ркале. **2** (*emph.*) сам; **she is kindness ~** она́ сама́ доброта́; **the house ~ is not worth much** дом сам по себе́ мно́гого не сто́ит; **by ~** (*alone*) оди́н, одино́ко, в отдале́нии; (*automatically*) самостоя́тельно; **in ~** сам по себе́; **of ~** сам (по себе́); **the house looked ~ again** дом приобрёл пре́жний вид.

ITV (*abbr. of* ***Independent Television***) (*Br.*) Незави́симое (комме́рческое) телеви́дение (*телеканал в Великобритании*).

IUD (*abbr. of* ***intra-uterine device***) ВМК (внутрима́точный контрацепти́в).

ivory /ˈaɪvərɪ/ *n.* **1** (*substance*) слоно́вая кость; **the I~ Coast** Бе́рег Слоно́вой Ко́сти. **2** (*colour*) цвет слоно́вой ко́сти. **3** (*pl., coll., piano keys*) кла́виши (*m. pl.*).

● *adj.* (*made of ~*) из слоно́вой ко́сти; **~ brooch** брошь из слоно́вой ко́сти; (*of the colour of ~*) ма́товый, кре́мовый; **~ skin** ма́товая ко́жа.

ivy /ˈaɪvɪ/ *n.* плющ.

Jj

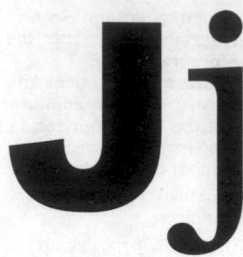

jab /dʒæb/ *n.* **1** (*sharp blow*) тычо́к; **he gave me a ~ in the ribs with his elbow** он ткнул меня́ ло́ктем в бок; (*with foot or knee*) пино́к.
2 (*Br. coll., injection*) уко́л; **they gave him (*or* he got) a ~** ему́ сде́лали уко́л; **have you had your smallpox ~?** вам уже́ сде́лали приви́вку от о́спы?
● *v.t.* (**jabbed, jabbing**) **1** (*poke*) ты́кать, ткнуть; **don't ~ me in the eye with your umbrella!** смотри́те, не проткни́те мне ва́шим зо́нтиком глаз!; (*pierce*) кол|о́ть, -ьну́ть; пырну́ть (*pf.*) (ножо́м) (*coll.*); **he was ~bed with a bayonet** его́ проткну́ли штыко́м.
2 (*thrust*) втыка́ть, воткну́ть; **he ~bed his knee into my stomach** он пнул меня́ в живо́т коле́ном; **they ~bed a needle into his arm** они́ воткну́ли ему́ в ру́ку иго́лку.
● *v.i.* (**jabbed, jabbing**): **he ~bed at my chin** он ткнул меня́ в подборо́док; **a ~bing pain** ко́лющая боль.

jabber /ˈdʒæbə(r)/ *n.* трескотня́.
● *v.t.* тарато́рить, про-.
● *v.i.* треща́ть (*impf.*), тарато́рить (*impf.*).

jabot /ˈʒæbəʊ/ *n.* жабо́ (*indecl.*).

jacaranda /ˌdʒækəˈrændə/ *n.* (*bot.*) джакара́нда.

jacinth /ˈdʒæsɪnθ/, /ˈdʒeɪ-/ *n.* гиаци́нт.

jack /dʒæk/ *n.* **1** (*name*): **J~ Frost** Моро́з Кра́сный Нос; **before you could say J~ Robinson** в мгнове́ние о́ка; ≈ и а́хнуть не успе́л; **J~ Tar** (*Br.*) матро́с; **every man ~** все до еди́ного; **~ of all trades** ма́стер на все ру́ки; **he is ~ of all trades and master of none** он за всё берётся и ничего́ то́лком не уме́ет; **~ rabbit** (*US*) кро́лик-саме́ц.
2 (*card*) вале́т; **~ of spades** вале́т пик, пи́ковый вале́т.
3 (*flag*) гюйс; **Union J~** госуда́рственный флаг Соединённого Короле́вства Великобрита́нии.
4 (*lifting device*) домкра́т.
5 (**~** *socket*) вход, гнездо́.
● *v.t.*: **~ in** (*Br. coll., give up*) бр|оса́ть, -о́сить; **~ up** (*of car etc.*) подн|има́ть, -я́ть домкра́том; (*fig., of prices etc.*) пов|ыша́ть, -ы́сить.
● *cpds.* **~ass** *n.* осёл; (*fool*) осёл, дура́к; **~boot** *n.* (*worn by Nazis*) сапо́г; (*hist.*) ботфо́рт; **~daw** *n.* га́лка; **~-in-the-box** *n.* чёртик в табаке́рке; **~knife** *n.* большо́й складно́й нож; (*fig., dive*) прыжо́к (в во́ду) согну́вшись; *v.i.* (*dive*) пры́гать (*impf.*) в во́ду согну́вшись; (*of lorry*): **the lorry ~knifed** грузови́к занесло́; **~-plane** *n.* шерхе́бель (*m.*), руба́нок; **~ plug** *n.* ште́ккер; **~pot** *n.* (*at cards*) банк при «пра́зднике»; (*in lottery*) джэ́кпот; **he hit the ~pot** (*fig.*) ему́ кру́пно повезло́.

jackal /ˈdʒæk(ə)l/ *n.* шака́л.

jacket /ˈdʒækɪt/ *n.* **1** ку́ртка; (*part of suit*) пиджа́к; (*woman's*) жаке́т.
2 (*tech., insulating cover*) кожу́х; обши́вка. **3** (*of book*) суперобло́жка.
4 (*skin of potato*) кожура́; **potatoes in their ~s** (*or* **~ potatoes** (*Br.*)) карто́фель в мунди́ре.

Jacobin /ˈdʒækəbɪn/ *n.* (*hist.*) якоби́нец.
● *adj.* якоби́нский.

Jacobinism /ˈdʒækəbɪnˌɪz(ə)m/ *n.* (*hist.*) якоби́нство.

Jacobite /ˈdʒækəˌbaɪt/ *n.* (*hist.*) якоби́т, приве́рженец Я́кова II.

jade¹ /dʒeɪd/ *n.* **1** (*min.*) нефри́т; (*attr.*) нефри́товый. **2** (**~ green**) цвет нефри́та.

jade² /dʒeɪd/ *v.t.* (*esp. p.p.*): **you look ~d** у вас утомлённый вид; **a ~d appetite** вя́лый аппети́т.

jag /dʒæg/ *n.* (*sharp projection*) о́стрый вы́ступ; зубе́ц; (*notch*) зазу́брина.

jagged /ˈdʒægɪd/ *adj.* (*notched*) зазу́бренный; **~ mountain tops** зубча́тые верши́ны; (*unevenly cut, torn*) неро́вно наре́занный/ото́рванный.

jaguar /ˈdʒægjʊə(r)/ *n.* ягуа́р.

jail /dʒeɪl/ *n.* тюрьма́; (*imprisonment*) тюре́мное заключе́ние; **break ~** бежа́ть (*impf., pf.*) из тюрьмы́.
● *v.t.* заключ|а́ть, -и́ть в тюрьму́.
● *cpds.* **~-bird** *n.* (*coll.*) закорене́лый престу́пник; **~-break** *n.* побе́г из тюрьмы́.

jailer /ˈdʒeɪlə(r)/ *n.* тюре́мщик.

jalopy /dʒəˈlɒpɪ/ *n.* (*sl., car*) драндуле́т.

jalousie /ˈʒælʊˌziː/ *n.* (*blind*) жалюзи́ (*nt. indecl.*); (*shutter*) ста́вень (*m.*).

jam¹ /dʒæm/ *n.* (*Br., preserve*) джем; (*of runnier consistency*) варе́нье; **~ tart** пиро́г с варе́ньем; **it was money for ~** э́то бы́ло одно́ удово́льствие.
● *cpds.* **~-jar, ~-pot** *nn.* ба́нка для дже́ма; (*empty*) ба́нка из-под дже́ма.

jam² /dʒæm/ *n.* **1** (*crush*) да́вка; **traffic ~** зато́р, про́бка.
2 (*stoppage*) остано́вка.
3 (*dilemma*) нело́вкое положе́ние; **get into a ~** влипа́ть, вли́пнуть (*coll.*).
● *v.t.* (**jammed, jamming**) **1** (*cram*) зап|и́хивать, -ихну́ть; вти́с|кивать, -нуть; **she ~med everything into the cupboard** она́ всё запихну́ла в шкаф; **he ~med his foot into the doorway** он просу́нул но́гу в дверь; **he ~med his hat on his head** он нахлобу́чил шля́пу; **they were ~med in like sardines** они́ наби́лись (туда́) как се́льди в бо́чке; (*force*): **a chair was ~med up against the door** дверь подпёрли кре́слом; **he ~med the brakes on** он ре́зко затормози́л.
2 (*trap*) прищем|ля́ть, -и́ть; **the child ~med its fingers in the door** ребёнок прищеми́л себе́ па́льцы две́рью.
3 (*cause to stick or stop*): **the machine got ~med** стано́к засто́порило/заклини́ло; (*wedge*): **~ the door open!** закрепи́те дверь, что́бы она́ не закрыва́лась.
4 (*obstruct; crowd*) заб|ива́ть, -и́ть; **the crowds ~med every exit** толпа́ заби́ла все вы́ходы; **the roads were ~med with cars** доро́ги бы́ли заби́ты/запру́жены маши́нами; **the room was ~med with people** ко́мната была́ битко́м наби́та людьми́; **the room was ~med with furniture** ко́мната была́ загромождена́ ме́белью; (*radio*) глуши́ть, за-.
● *v.i.* (**jammed, jamming**) (*get stuck*) застр|ева́ть, -я́ть; за|еда́ть, -е́сть; **the door ~med** дверь зае́ло/заклини́ло.
● *cpds.* **~-packed** *adj.* наби́тый до

отка́за; битко́м наби́тый; **~-session** *n.* джэм-се́йшен.

Jamaica /dʒəˈmeɪkə/ *n.* Яма́йка.

Jamaican /dʒəˈmeɪkən/ *n.* яма́ец; жи́тель (*fem.* -ница) Яма́йки.

● *adj.* яма́йский.

jamb /dʒæm/ *n.* (*of door, window*) кося́к.

jamboree /ˌdʒæmbəˈriː/ *n.* **1** (*of Scouts etc.*) слёт. **2** (*celebration*) пра́здество; (*spree*) весе́лье.

jangl|e /ˈdʒæŋg(ə)l/ *n.* ре́зкий звук.

● *v.i.* издава́ть (*impf.*) ре́зкий звук; бренча́ть (*impf.*); **a ~ing piano** разби́тый роя́ль.

● *v.t.* (*cause to make a sound*) звя́к|ать, -нуть +*i.*; бренча́ть (*impf.*) +*i.*; **their voices ~ed my nerves** их голоса́ де́йствовали мне на не́рвы.

jani|ssary /ˈdʒænɪsərɪ/, **-zary** /-zərɪ/ *nn.* яныче́р.

janitor /ˈdʒænɪtə(r)/ *n.* (*doorkeeper*) привра́тник, швейца́р; (*caretaker*) вахтёр.

January /ˈdʒænjʊərɪ/ *n.* янва́рь (*m.*); (*attr.*) янва́рский.

Japan /dʒəˈpæn/ *n.* Япо́ния.

japan /dʒəˈpæn/ *n.* (*varnish*) чёрный лак.

● *v.t.* (**japanned, japanning**) лакирова́ть, от-.

Japanese /ˌdʒæpəˈniːz/ *n.* (*pl.* ~) (*person*) япо́н|ец (*fem.* -ка); (*language*) япо́нский язы́к.

● *adj.* япо́нский.

jape /dʒeɪp/ *n.* ро́зыгрыш, шу́тка.

● *v.i.* шути́ть, по-.

japonica /dʒəˈpɒnɪkə/ *n.* айва́ япо́нская.

jar¹ /dʒɑː(r)/ *n.* (*vessel*) (стекля́нная) ба́нка.

jar² /dʒɑː(r)/ *n.* (*shock, vibration*) сотрясе́ние; (*on nerves or feelings*) шок; **the news gave him a ~** изве́стие потрясло́ его́.

● *v.t.* (**jarred, jarring**) (*shake*) сотряс|а́ть, -ти́; (*fig., shock*) потряс|а́ть, -ти́.

● *v.i.* (**jarred, jarring**) **1** (*emit harsh sound*) скрежета́ть (*impf.*); (*sound discordantly*) дисгармони́ровать (*impf.*). **2**: **~ on, against** (*strike with grating sound*) скрежета́ть (*impf.*) по+*d.*; **~ on** (*irritate, annoy*) раздраж|а́ть, -и́ть. **3** (*fig.*): **these colours** (*Br.*), **colors** (*US*) **~** э́ти цвета́ не сочета́ются.

jargon /ˈdʒɑːgən/ *n.* жарго́н.

jasmine /ˈdʒæsmɪn/, /ˈdʒæz-/, **jessamine** /ˈdʒesəmɪn/ *nn.* жасми́н.

jasper /ˈdʒæspə(r)/ *n.* я́шма.

jaundice /ˈdʒɔːndɪs/ *n.* желту́ха.

● *v.t.* (*usu. p.p.*): **a ~d complexion** жёлтый цвет лица́; **he took a ~d view of the affair** он мра́чно смотре́л на э́то де́ло.

jaunt /dʒɔːnt/ *n.* увесели́тельная пое́здка/прогу́лка.

jauntiness /ˈdʒɔːntɪnɪs/ *n.* бо́йкость, ли́хость; беспе́чность, небре́жность.

jaunty /ˈdʒɔːntɪ/ *adj.* (**jauntier, jauntiest**) (*sprightly*) бо́йкий, лихо́й; (*carefree*) беспе́чный, небре́жный.

Java /ˈdʒɑːvə/ *n.* Я́ва.

Javanese /ˌdʒɑːvəˈniːz/ *n.* (*pl.* ~) (*person*) ява́н|ец (*fem.* -ка); (*language*) ява́нский язы́к.

● *adj.* ява́нский.

javelin /ˈdʒævəlɪn/, /-vlɪn/ *n.* (мета́тельное) копьё; **(throwing) the ~** (*contest*) мета́ние копья́.

● *cpd.* **~-thrower** *n.* мета́тель (*fem.* -ница) копья́.

jaw /dʒɔː/ *n.* **1** че́люсть; (*pl., mouth*) рот; (*of animal*) пасть; **the dog held the bird in its ~s** соба́ка держа́ла пти́цу в зуба́х; **in the ~s of a vice** в тиска́х; **in the ~s of death** в когтя́х сме́рти. **2** (*coll., talk*): **they had a good ~** они́ вдоволь наговори́лись.

● *v.i.* (*coll., talk at length*) рассусо́ливать (*impf.*).

● *cpd.* **~bone** *n.* челюстна́я кость.

jay /dʒeɪ/ *n.* со́йка.

● *cpds.* **~-walk** *v.i.* пере|ходи́ть, -йти́ у́лицу неосторо́жно; **~-walker** *n.* неосторо́жный пешехо́д.

jazz /dʒæz/ *n.* джаз; **and all that ~** (*sl.*) и всё тако́е про́чее; (*attr.*) джа́зовый.

● *v.t.*: **~ up** (*fig., enliven*) ожив|ля́ть, -и́ть.

● *cpds.* **~-band** *n.* джаз-орке́стр, джаз-ба́нд; **~man, ~-player** *nn.* джази́ст; уча́стник джаз-орке́стра.

jazzy /ˈdʒæzɪ/ *adj.* (**jazzier, jazziest**) (*like jazz*) джа́зовый; (*showy*) бро́ский, я́ркий.

JCB /ˌdʒeɪsiːˈbiː/ *n.* (*Br. propr.*) экскава́тор.

JCR (*abbr. of* ***Junior Common Room***) (*Br.*) студе́нческая ко́мната о́тдыха.

jealous /ˈdʒeləs/ *adj.* **1** (*of affection etc.*) ревни́вый; **she was ~ of her husband's secretary** она́ ревнова́ла му́жа к секрета́рше; **a ~ god** бог ревни́тель. **2** (*vigilant in defence*): **he is ~ of his rights** он ревни́во оберега́ет свои́ права́. **3** (*envious*) зави́стливый; **I am ~ of his success!** я зави́дую его́ успе́ху.

jealousy /ˈdʒeləsɪ/ *n.* ре́вность, ревни́вость; (*envy*) за́висть.

jean /dʒiːn/ *n.* (*text.*) джи́нсо́вая ткань; (*pl., trousers*) джи́нс|ы (*pl., g.* -ов).

jeep /dʒiːp/ *n.* (*propr.*) джип, вездехо́д.

jeer /dʒɪə(r)/ *n.* (*scoff*) насме́шка; (*taunt*) глумле́ние.

● *v.t. & i.* (*taunt*) глуми́ться (*impf.*) (над+*i.*); (*deride*) насмеха́ться (*impf.*) (над+*i.*); **the crowd ~ed (at) him** толпа́ глуми́лась над ним; **he was ~ed off the stage** он ушёл со сце́ны под улюлю́канье.

Jehovah /dʒəˈhəʊvə/ *n.* Иего́ва (*m.*); **~'s witnesses** Свиде́тели Иегови́.

jejune /dʒɪˈdʒuːn/ *adj.* (*shallow*) пусто́й; бессодержа́тельный; (*dry, uninteresting*) сухо́й, неинтере́сный.

jejuneness /dʒɪˈdʒuːnnɪs/ *n.* ску́дность; бессодержа́тельность.

jell /dʒel/ *v.i.* (*coll., set into jelly*) заст|ыва́ть, -ы́ть; (*fig.*) формирова́ться, с-.

jellied /ˈdʒelɪd/ *adj.* засты́вший; преврати́вшийся в желе́; **~ eels** заливно́е из угре́й.

jelly /ˈdʒelɪ/ *n.* **1** (*Br.*) желе́ (*indecl.*); (*aspic*) сту́день (*m.*). **2** (*US, jam*) джем. **3**: **royal ~** ма́точное молочко́.

● *cpd.* **~fish** *n.* меду́за.

jemmy /ˈdʒemɪ/ (*US* **jimmy**) *n.* отмы́чка, «фо́мка» (*coll.*).

jeopardize /ˈdʒepəˌdaɪz/ *v.t.* (*endanger*) подв|ерга́ть, -е́ргнуть опа́сности; (*put at risk*) рискова́ть (*impf.*) +*i.*; **he ~d his chances of success** он рискова́л свои́ми ша́нсами на успе́х.

jeopardy /ˈdʒepədɪ/ *n.* (*danger*) опа́сность; (*risk*) риск; **his life was in ~** его́ жизнь была́ в опа́сности.

jerboa /dʒɜːˈbəʊə/ *n.* тушка́нчик.

Jeremiah /ˌdʒerɪˈmaɪə/ *n.* (*bibl.*) Иереми́я (*m.*).

jerk /dʒɜːk/ *n.* **1** (*pull*) рыво́к; (*jolt; shock*) уда́р; **the train stopped with a ~** по́езд ре́зко затормози́л; **he gave the handle a ~** он дёрнул за ру́чку. **2** (*twitch*) су́дорожное вздра́гивание; **with a ~ of his head** дёрнув голово́й. **3**: **physical ~s** (*coll.*) гимна́стика, заря́дка. **4** (*US sl., idiot*) ду́рень (*m.*), идио́т.

● *v.t.* (*push*) ре́зко толк|а́ть, -ну́ть; (*pull, twitch*) дёр|гать, -нуть; (*throw*) швыр|я́ть, -ну́ть; **he ~ed his head back** он вски́нул го́лову.

● *v.i.*: **the train ~ed to a halt** по́езд ре́зко останови́лся.

jerkin /ˈdʒɜːkɪn/ *n.* ку́ртка-безрука́вка.

jerk|y /ˈdʒɜːkɪ/ *adj.* (**jerkier, jerkiest**) (*moving in jerks*) дви́гающийся ре́зкими толчка́ми; **~y movements** су́дорожные движе́ния; **we had a ~y ride** в доро́ге нас си́льно трясло́; **he spoke ~ily** он говори́л отры́висто.

jerry /ˈdʒerɪ/ *n.* (*Br.*) **1** (*sl., chamber pot*) ночно́й горшо́к. **2** (**J~**: *German*) фриц (*coll.*).

● *cpds.* **~-builder** *n.* строи́тель (*m.*) недороги́х/непро́чных домо́в; го́ре-строи́тель (*m.*) (*coll.*); **~-building** *n.* недорога́я/непро́чная постро́йка; **~-built** *adj.* постро́енный недо́рого/ко́е-как (*coll.*); **~can** *n.* кани́стра.

jersey /ˈdʒɜːzɪ/ *n.* (*pl.* **~s**) (*fabric, garment*) дже́рси (*nt. indecl.*); **football ~** футбо́лка; **J~ cow** джерсе́йская коро́ва.

Jerusalem /dʒəˈruːsələm/ *n.* Иерусали́м; **~ artichoke** земляна́я гру́ша.

jessamine /ˈdʒesəmɪn/ = **jasmine**

jest /dʒest/ *n.* шу́тка; **in ~** в шу́тку; **many a true word is spoken in ~** в ка́ждой шу́тке есть до́ля пра́вды.

● *v.i.* шути́ть, по-; **~ at** шути́ть, по- над+*i.*

jester /ˈdʒestə(r)/ *n.* (*hist.*) шут; **court ~** придво́рный шут.

jesting /ˈdʒestɪŋ/ *adj.* шутли́вый.

Jesuit /ˈdʒezjʊɪt/ *n.* иезуи́т; (*attr.*) иезуи́тский.

J

Jesuitical /ˌdʒezjʊˈɪtɪk(ə)l/ *adj.* иезуи́тский.

Jesus /ˈdʒiːzəs/ *n.* Иису́с; **~ Christ** Иису́с Христо́с; (*as expletive*): **~ (Christ)!** Бо́же!

jet¹ /dʒet/ *n.* (*min.*) гага́т.

● *adj.* гага́товый; (**~**-*black*) чёрный как смоль.

jet² /dʒet/ *n.* **1** (*stream of water etc.*) струя́. **2** (*spout, nozzle*) со́пло. **3** (**~ engine**) реакти́вный дви́гатель; (**~ aircraft**) реакти́вный самолёт; **~ pilot** пило́т реакти́вного самолёта.

● *v.i.* (**jetted, jetting**) (*spurt, gush*) бить (*impf.*) струёй; (*coll., fly by* **~**) лета́ть (*indet.*) на реакти́вном самолёте.

● *cpds.* **~-fighter** *n.* реакти́вный истреби́тель; **~-lag** *n.* наруше́ние су́точного ри́тма; **~-propelled** *adj.* реакти́вный; **~-set** *n.* у́зкий круг бога́тых путеше́ственников; междунаро́дная эли́та.

jetsam /ˈdʒetsəm/ *n.* груз, вы́брошенный за́ борт при угро́зе затопле́ния.

jettison /ˈdʒetɪs(ə)n/, /-z(ə)n/ *v.t.* (*lit., fig.*) выбра́сывать, вы́бросить (за́ борт).

jetty /ˈdʒetɪ/ *n.* при́стань, мол.

Jew /dʒuː/ *n.* евре́й (*fem.* -ка).

● *cpd.* **j~'s-harp** *n.* варга́н.

jewel /ˈdʒuːəl/ *n.* (*precious stone*) драгоце́нный ка́мень; (*in watch*) ка́мень; (*ornament containing* **~**) ювели́рное изде́лие; драгоце́нность; (*fig., of person or thing*) сокро́вище.

● *v.t.* (**jewelled, jewelling;** *US* **jeweled, jeweling**) (*esp. p.p.*): **a ~led watch** час|ы́ (*pl., g.* -о́в) на камня́х; (*set in* **~s**) часы́, укра́шенные драгоце́нными камня́ми; **a ~led sword** меч, укра́шенный драгоце́нными камня́ми.

● *cpds.* **~-box, ~-case** *nn.* футля́р/шкату́лка для ювели́рных изде́лий.

jeweller /ˈdʒuːələ(r)/ (*US* **jeweler**) *n.* ювели́р; **~'s (shop)** ювели́рный магази́н.

jewellery /ˈdʒuːəlrɪ/ (*US also* **jewelry**) *n.* ювели́рные изде́лия; драгоце́нности (*f. pl.*).

Jewess /ˈdʒuːes/ *n.* (*often offens.*) евре́йка.

Jewish /ˈdʒuːɪʃ/ *adj.* евре́йский.

Jewry /ˈdʒʊərɪ/ *n.* (*collect., Jews*) евре́и (*m. pl.*), евре́йство.

Jezebel /ˈdʒezəˌbel/ *n.* (*bibl.*) Иезаве́ль; (*fig.*) (*immoral*) распу́тная же́нщина; (*shameless*) на́глая же́нщина.

jib¹ /dʒɪb/ *n.* **1** (*naut.*) кли́вер. **2** (*of crane*) стрела́.

● *cpd.* **~-boom** *n.* утле́гарь (*m.*).

jib² /dʒɪb/ *v.i.* (**jibbed, jibbing**) (*of horse or person*) уп|ира́ться, -ере́ться; **~ at someting** уклоня́ться (*impf.*) от чего́-н.

jibe¹ /dʒaɪb/ *n.* (*taunt*) насме́шка.

● *v.i.*: **~ at** насмеха́ться (*impf.*) над + *i.*

jibe² /dʒaɪb/ (*US, agree, accord*) соотве́тствовать (*impf.*) (+*d.*), соглас|о́вываться, -ова́ться (с + *i.*).

jiffy /ˈdʒɪfɪ/ *n.* (*coll.*) миг; **wait a ~!** подожди́те мину́тку; **in a ~** ми́гом; **I'll come in a ~** я ми́гом.

jig¹ /dʒɪg/ *n.* (*dance*) джи́га.

● *v.t.* (**jigged, jigging: she was ~ging the baby up and down** она́ подбра́сывала ребёнка.

● *v.i.* (**jigged, jigging**) (*dance*) танцева́ть (*impf.*) джи́гу; (*move jerkily; fidget*): **~ about** припля́сывать (*impf.*); **~ up and down** пры́гать (*impf.*).

jig² /dʒɪg/ *n.* (*tech.*) зажи́мное приспособле́ние.

● *cpd.* **~-saw** *n.* (*tool*) ажу́рная пила́; (*puzzle*) (составна́я) карти́нка-зага́дка.

jigger /ˈdʒɪgə(r)/ *v.t.* (*Br. coll.*): **I'll be ~ed!** (*expr. surprise*) ну и ну!; ну и дела́!; не мо́жет быть!

jiggery-pokery /ˌdʒɪgərɪˈpəʊkərɪ/ *n.* (*Br. coll.*) ко́зн|и (*pl., g.* -ей); плу́тни (*f. pl.*).

jiggle /ˈdʒɪg(ə)l/ *v.t.* пока́ч|ивать (*impf.*).

jilt /dʒɪlt/ *v.t.* бр|оса́ть, -о́сить.

jimmy /ˈdʒɪmɪ/ = **jemmy**

jingle /ˈdʒɪŋg(ə)l/ *n.* (*ringing sound*) звя́канье; (*advertising tune*) рекла́мная песе́нка.

● *v.t. & i.* звя́к|ать, -нуть (+*i.*); **he ~d the keys** он звя́кал ключа́ми; **the bell ~d** колоко́льчик звя́кнул.

jingo /ˈdʒɪŋgəʊ/ *n.*: **by ~!** ей-Бо́гу!

jingoism /ˈdʒɪŋgəʊˌɪz(ə)m/ *n.* шовини́зм, ура́-патриоти́зм.

jingoistic /ˌdʒɪŋgəʊˈɪstɪk/ *adj.* шовинисти́ческий.

jink /dʒɪŋk/ *n.* (*coll.*): **high ~s** (шу́мное/бу́рное) весе́лье.

jinx /dʒɪŋks/ *n.* (*coll.*) злы́е ча́ры (*f. pl.*); **put a ~ on** сгла́зить (*pf.*).

jitter /ˈdʒɪtə(r)/ *n.* (*coll.*): **have the ~s** не́рвничать (*impf.*); **it gave me the ~s** меня́ о́торопь взяла́.

● *v.i.* не́рвничать (*impf.*).

● *cpd.* **~bug** *n.* (*nervous person*) псих (*coll.*).

jittery /ˈdʒɪtərɪ/ *adj.* (*coll.*) не́рвный.

jive /dʒaɪv/ *n.* (*sl.*) джайв (*быстрая джазовая музыка*).

● *v.i.* танцева́ть (*impf.*) под джайв.

Jnr. /ˈdʒuːnɪə(r)/ *n.* (*abbr. of* **Junior**) мл. (мла́дший).

Job /dʒəʊb/ *n.* (*bibl.*) Ио́в; **it would try the patience of ~** э́то и свято́го вы́ведет из терпе́ния; **a ~'s comforter** го́ре-утеши́тель (*m.*).

job /dʒɒb/ *n.* **1** (*piece of work; task*) рабо́та; зада́ние; **he does a good ~ (of work)** он хорошо́ рабо́тает; **my ~ is to wash the dishes** моя́ обя́занность — мыть посу́ду; **odd ~s** случа́йная рабо́та; **payment by the ~** сде́льная опла́та; (*difficult task*): **we had a ~ finding them** мы с трудо́м их отыска́ли.
2 (*product of work*): **you've made a good ~ of that** вы сде́лали э́то хорошо́; **just the ~** (*Br. coll.*) то, что на́до.
3 (*employment; position*) рабо́та; ме́сто; **what is your ~?** кака́я у вас рабо́та?; кем/где вы рабо́таете?; **he has a good ~** у него́ хоро́шая рабо́та; **he is good at his ~** он хоро́ший рабо́тник; **look for a ~** иска́ть (*impf.*) рабо́ту; **get a ~** на|ходи́ть, -йти́ рабо́ту; **lose one's ~** теря́ть, по- рабо́ту/ме́сто; **out of a ~** без рабо́ты; **~s for the boys** (*Br.*) «рабо́та для ма́льчиков» (*coll.*).
4 (*coll., crime, esp. theft*) воровство́, «де́ло».
5 (*circumstance, fact*): **a put-up ~** махина́ция; **it's a good ~ you stayed at home** (*Br.*) хорошо́, что вы оста́лись до́ма; **it's a good ~ for you the inspector's not here** (*Br.*) ва́ше сча́стье, что инспе́ктора здесь нет; **he's gone, and a good ~ too!** (*Br.*) он ушёл — и сла́ва Бо́гу!; **make the best of a bad ~** (*Br.*) дово́льствоваться (*impf.*) ма́лым; не уныва́ть (*impf.*); **give up as a bad ~** махну́ть (*pf.*) руко́й на + *a.*

● *v.i.* (**jobbed, jobbing**) (*deal in stocks*) быть ма́клером; (*do* **~s**): **~bing gardener** наёмный садо́вник;

● *cpds.* **~ lot** *n.* па́ртия разро́зненных това́ров; **~-share** *v.i.* дели́ть (*impf.*) рабо́чее ме́сто и за́рплату.

jobber /ˈdʒɒbə(r)/ *n.* (*broker*) ма́клер.

jobbery /ˈdʒɒbərɪ/ *n.* испо́льзование служе́бного положе́ния в коры́стных це́лях.

jobcentre /ˈdʒɒbˌsentə(r)/ *n.* (*Br.*) бюро́ (*indecl.*) по трудоустро́йству.

jobless /ˈdʒɒblɪs/ *adj.* безрабо́тный.

jockey /ˈdʒɒkɪ/ *n.* (*pl.* **~s**) жоке́й.

● *v.t.* (**jockeys, jockeyed**) (*cheat*) обма́н|ывать, -у́ть; (*manoeuvre*): **~ s.o. into someting** обма́ном склон|я́ть, -и́ть кого́-н. к чему́-н.; **he was ~ed out of his job** его́ вы́толкали с рабо́ты.

● *v.i.* (**jockeys, jockeyed**): **~ for position** (*fig.*) оттесня́ть (*impf.*) друг дру́га (*в борьбе за выгодное положение и т.п.*).

jock-strap /ˈdʒɒkstræp/ *n.* суспензо́рий.

jocose /dʒəˈkəʊs/ *adj.* игри́вый.

jocos|eness /dʒəˈkəʊsnɪs/, **-ity** /dʒəˈkɒsɪtɪ/ *nn.* игри́вость.

jocular /ˈdʒɒkjʊlə(r)/ *adj.* (*merry*) весёлый; (*humorous*) шутли́вый, заба́вный.

jocularity /ˌdʒɒkjʊˈlærɪtɪ/ *n.* весёлость; шутли́вость.

jocund /ˈdʒɒkənd/ *adj.* (*cheerful*) весёлый; (*lively*) живо́й.

jodhpurs /ˈdʒɒdpəz/ *n.* брю́к|и (*pl., g.* —) для верхово́й езды́.

jog /dʒɒg/ *n.* **1** (*push; nudge*) толчо́к. **2** (*trot*) (*of animals*) рысь; (*of humans*) бег трусцо́й; оздорови́тельный бе́г.

● *v.t.* (**jogged, jogging: ~ up and down** подбра́сывать (*impf.*); **~ s.o.'s elbow** толк|а́ть, -ну́ть кого́-н. под ло́коть; **~ s.o.'s memory** освеж|а́ть, -и́ть чью-н. па́мять.

● *v.i.* (**jogged, jogging**) **1** (*run slowly*) бе́гать (*indet.*) трусцо́й; **he ~ged along (on horseback)** он труси́л (на ло́шади); **business is ~ging along** делá идýт своим чередóм. **2**: **~ up and down** подпрыгивать (*impf.*).

● *cpd.* **~-trot** *n.*: **at a ~-trot** рысью, рысцóй.

jogger /ˈdʒɒgə(r)/ *n.* любитель (*m.*) оздоровительного бéга, джóггер.

jogging /ˈdʒɒgɪŋ/ *n.* (*trot*) бег рысью/трусцóй; (*sport*) оздоровительный бéг; джóггинг.

joggle /ˈdʒɒg(ə)l/ *v.t.* & *i.* покáчиваться (*impf.*).

Johannesburg /dʒəʊˈhænɪsˌbɜːg/ *n.* Йохáннесбург.

john /dʒɒn/ *n.* (*US coll., lavatory*) сортир (*coll.*).

joie de vivre /ˌʒwɑː də ˈviːvrə/ *n.* жизнерáдостность.

join /dʒɔɪn/ *n.* связь, соединéние.

● *v.t.* **1** (*connect*) соедин|ять, -и́ть; **the towns are ~ed by a railway** эти городá соединяет желéзная дорóга; **~ hands** брáться, взя́ться зá руки; (*fasten*) свя́з|ывать, -áть (*что с чем*); (*unite*) объедин|ять, -и́ть; **they ~ed forces** они соединили (свои) си́лы; **~ in marriage** соедин|ять, -и́ть брáком. **2** (*enter*) вступ|áть, -и́ть в + *a.*; **he ~ed the party** (*pol.*) он вступил в пáртию; **~ battle** вступ|áть, -и́ть в бой; **~ a club** вступ|áть, -и́ть в клуб; **~ the army** вступ|áть, -и́ть (*or* идти́, пойти́) в áрмию; **~** (*sc. rejoin*) **one's regiment** (*or* **ship**) возвра|щáться, -ти́ться в полк (*or* на корáбль). **3** (*enter s.o.'s company*) присоедин|я́ться, -и́ться к + *d.*; (*side with*) прим|ыкáть, -кнýть к + *d.*; (*meet*) встр|ечáться, -éтиться с + *i.*; **may I ~ you?** разреши́те присоедини́ться к вам?; **will you ~ us in a walk?** не хоти́те ли прогуля́ться с нáми?; **he ~ed us in approving the decision** он поддержáл нас в одобрéнии э́того решéния. **4** (*flow or lead into*) соедин|я́ться, -и́ться с + *i.*; сл|ивáться, -и́ться с + *i.*; **where the Cherwell ~s the Thames** там, где рекá Чéрвелл впадáет в Тéмзу; **there is a restaurant where you ~ the motorway** у въéзда на автострáду есть ресторáн.

● *v.i.* **1** (*be connected, fastened*) соедин|я́ться, -и́ться; свя́з|ываться, -áться; (*be united*) объедин|я́ться, -и́ться; (*come together*) сходи́ться, сойти́сь; (*flow together*) сл|ивáться, -и́ться; (*border on each other*) грани́чить (*impf.*) друг с дрýгом. **2** (*take part*): **may I ~ in the game?** мóжно мне поигрáть с вáми?; **he ~ed in the applause** он присоедини́лся к аплоди́рующим; **they all ~ed in the chorus** припéв пéли все хóром. **3** (*become a member*) стать (*impf.*) члéном (*чего*).

● *with advs.*: **~ in** *v.i.* (*take part*) прин|имáть, -я́ть учáстие; (*in conversation, discussion etc.*) вступ|áть, -и́ть в + *a.*; **~ on** *v.t.* & *i.* присоедин|я́ть(ся), -и́ть(ся); **~ together** *v.t.* свя́з|ывать, -áть; соедин|я́ть, -и́ть; **~ up** *v.t.* & *i.* соедин|я́ть(ся), -и́ть(ся); *v.i.* (*coll., enlist*) идти́, пойти́ в áрмию.

joiner /ˈdʒɔɪnə(r)/ *n.* **1** (*woodworker*) столя́р; **~'s shop** столя́рная мастерскáя; **be a ~** столя́рничать (*impf.*). **2** (*coll., one who joins societies etc.*) член мнóгих организáций и клýбов.

joinery /ˈdʒɔɪnərɪ/ *n.* столя́рная рабóта; **do, practise** (*Br.*), **practice** (*US*) **~** столя́рничать (*impf.*).

joint /dʒɔɪnt/ *n.* **1** (*place of juncture; means of joining*) соединéние; стык; **the pipe is leaking at the ~s** трубá течёт на сты́ке; **ball and socket ~** шарни́р; шаровóе соединéние. **2** (*anat.*) сустáв, сочленéние; **out of ~** (*pred.*) вы́вихнут; (*fig.*) не в порядке; **my ~s ache** у меня́ лóмит в сустáвах. **3**: **a ~ of meat** (*Br.*) кусóк мя́са (к обéду). **4** (*coll.*) (*snack-bar*) закýсочная; (*dive*) притóн. **5** (*sl., marijuana cigarette*) кося́к, масты́рка.

● *adj.* **1** (*combined; shared*) совмéстный; **~ action** совмéстные дéйствия (*nt. pl.*); **take ~ action** дéйствовать (*impf.*) сообщá; (*common*) óбщий; **~ account** óбщий/совмéстный счёт; **~ efforts** óбщие/совмéстные уси́лия; **~ venture** совмéстное предприя́тие. **2** (*sharing*): **~ owner** совладéлец; **~ author** соáвтор.

● *v.t.* **1** (*connect by ~s*) соедин|я́ть, -и́ть; **a ~ed doll** кýкла на шарни́рах. **2** (*divide into ~s*) расчлен|я́ть, -и́ть.

● *cpd.* **~-stock** *n.* (*attr.*) акционéрный.

joist /dʒɔɪst/ *n.* бáлка.

jok|e /dʒəʊk/ *n.* шýтка; (*story*) анекдóт; (*witticism*) острóта; (*laughing-stock*) посмéшище; **it's no ~e** э́то не шýтка!; **crack, make a ~e** шути́ть, по-; **make a ~e of someting** оборáчивать, оберну́ть что-н. в шýтку; **play a ~e on s.o.** сыгрáть (*pf.*) шýтку с кем-н.; подшý|чивать, -ти́ть над кем-н.; **he couldn't see the ~e** он не пóнял шýтки; **can't you take a ~e?** вы что, шýток не понимáете?; **it was a standing ~e** э́то бы́ло объéктом постоя́нных шýток; **practical ~e** рóзыгрыш; **the ~e was on him** э́то он остáлся в дуракáх.

● *v.i.* шути́ть, по-; **I was only ~ing** я всегó лишь пошути́л; **~ing apart** шýтки в стóрону; крóме шýток.

joker /ˈdʒəʊkə(r)/ *n.* (*one who jokes*) шутни́к; (*coll., fellow*) пáрень (*m.*); (*cards*) джóкер.

jokey, joky /ˈdʒəʊkɪ/ *adj.* (**jokier, jokiest**) шутли́вый.

jollification /ˌdʒɒlɪfɪˈkeɪʃ(ə)n/ *n.* увеселéние.

jollity /ˈdʒɒlɪtɪ/ *n.* весéлье, увеселéние.

jolly /ˈdʒɒlɪ/ *adj.* (**jollier, jolliest**) (*cheerful*) весёлый; (*festive; entertaining*) рáдостный, прáздничный; (*coll., pleasant*) прия́тный.

● *adv.* (*Br. coll., very*) óчень; **~ well** (*Br. coll., definitely*) тóчно, óчень дáже; **you'll ~ well have to do it** тебé тóчно придётся э́то сдéлать.

● *v.t.*: **~ s.o. along** умáсл|ивать, -ить когó-н. (*coll.*).

jolt /dʒəʊlt/, /dʒɒlt/ *n.* толчóк; (*fig.*) удáр, потрясéние.

● *v.t.* & *i.* трясти́(сь) (*impf.*); **we were ~ed about** нас швыря́ло во все стóроны; **the cart ~ed along** телéгу трясло́; (*fig.*) потряс|áть, -ти́; порa|жáть, -зи́ть; **it ~ed him out of his routine** э́то вы́било егó из колéи.

Jonah /ˈdʒəʊnə/ *n.* (*bibl.*) Ио́на (*m.*).

jonquil /ˈdʒɒnkwɪl/ *n.* жонки́лия.

Jordan /ˈdʒɔːd(ə)n/ *n.* (*river*) Иордáн; (*country*) Иордáния.

Jordanian /dʒɔːˈdeɪnɪən/ *n.* иордáн|ец (*fem.* -ка).

● *adj.* иордáнский.

josh /dʒɒʃ/ (*US sl.*) *n.* дóбрая шýтка.

● *v.t.* подшý|чивать, -ти́ть над + *i.*

● *v.i.* шути́ть, по-.

joss-stick /dʒɒs/ *n.* пахýчая пáлочка.

jostle /ˈdʒɒs(ə)l/ *v.t.* толк|áть, -нýть; отт|ирáть, -ерéть; **I was ~d from every side** меня́ толкáли со всех сторóн.

● *v.i.* толкáться (*impf.*); **he ~d against me** он оттирáл меня́.

jot[1] /dʒɒt/ *n.* (*small amount*) йóта; **he was not one ~ the worse for it** э́то емý ничýть не повреди́ло.

jot[2] /dʒɒt/ *v.t.* (**jotted, jotting**): **~ down** набр|áсывать, -осáть.

jotter /ˈdʒɒtə(r)/ *n.* (*Br., pad*) блокнóт.

jottings /ˈdʒɒtɪŋz/ *n.* зáписи (*f. pl.*).

joule /dʒuːl/ *n.* джóуль (*m.*).

journal /ˈdʒɜːn(ə)l/ *n.* (*newspaper*) газéта; (*periodical*) журнáл; (*ship's log*) (судовóй) журнáл; (*bookkeeping*) журнáл.

journalese /ˌdʒɜːnəˈliːz/ *n.* газéтный штамп.

journalism /ˈdʒɜːnəˌlɪz(ə)m/ *n.* журнали́стика.

journalist /ˈdʒɜːnəlɪst/ *n.* журнали́ст (*fem.* -ка).

journalistic /ˌdʒɜːnəˈlɪstɪk/ *adj.* журнали́стский.

journey /ˈdʒɜːnɪ/ *n.* (*pl.* **~s**) (*expedition; trip*) (*long*) путешéствие; (*shorter*) поéздка; (*of train, bus etc.*) рейс; **(under)take a ~** предприн|имáть, -я́ть (*or* соверш|áть, -и́ть) путешéствие; **break one's ~** прер|ывáть, -вáть поéздку; **be, go on a ~** путешéствовать (*impf.*); **he did the ~ on foot** он соверши́л путешéствие пешкóм; **the bus makes 6 ~s a day** автóбус совершáет шесть рéйсов в день; (*travel; travelling time*) путь; **on the return ~** на обрáтном пути́; **will there be any refreshments on the ~?** бýдут ли в пути́ корми́ть/давáть лёгкие закýски?; **London is 6 hours' ~ from here** отсю́да до Лóндона шесть часóв езды́; **it was a wasted ~** путешéствие бы́ло напрáсным.

● *v.i.* (**journeys, journeyed**) путешéствовать (*impf.*).

● *cpd.* **~man** *n.* (*hired worker*) наёмный рабóтник.

joust /dʒaʊst/ *n.* (ры́царский) турни́р.

● *v.i.* состязáться (*impf.*) на турни́ре.

Jove /dʒəʊv/ *n.* Юпи́тер; **by ~!** вот те нá!; ну и делá!

J

jovial /'dʒəʊvɪəl/ *adj.* (*merry*) весёлый; (*convivial*) общи́тельный.

joviality /ˌdʒəʊvɪ'ælɪtɪ/ *n.* весёлость; общи́тельность.

jowl /dʒaʊl/ *n.* (*jaw*) че́люсть; (*dewlap*) подгру́док; (*chin*): **a heavy ~** тяжёлый подборо́док.

joy /dʒɔɪ/ *n.* **1** (*gladness*) ра́дость; (*pleasure*) удово́льствие; **jump for ~** скака́ть (*impf.*) от ра́дости; **one of the ~s of life** одна́ из ра́достей жи́зни; **life was no ~** жизнь была́ не в ра́дость. **2** (*Br. coll., success, response*): **I kept phoning but got no ~** я звони́л-звони́л, но никако́го то́лку.

● *cpds.* **~ride** *n.* пое́здка ра́ди заба́вы на укра́денной автомаши́не; **~rider** *n.* автово́р-лиха́ч, уго́нщик-лиха́ч; **~stick** *n.* (*aeron., sl.*) рыча́г/ру́чка управле́ния; (*comput.*) джо́йстик.

joyful /'dʒɔɪfʊl/ *adj.* ра́достный, счастли́вый.

joyfulness /'dʒɔɪfʊlnɪs/ *n.* ра́дость.

joyless /'dʒɔɪlɪs/ *adj.* безра́достный.

joylessness /'dʒɔɪlɪsnɪs/ *n.* безра́достность.

joyous /'dʒɔɪəs/ *adj.* ра́достный; (*happy*) весёлый.

JP (*abbr. of* ***Justice of the Peace***) мирово́й судья́.

jubilant /'dʒu:bɪlənt/ *adj.* лику́ющий; **be ~** ликова́ть (*impf.*).

jubilation /ˌdʒu:bɪ'leɪʃ(ə)n/ *n.* ликова́ние.

jubilee /'dʒu:bɪˌli:/ *n.* (*anniversary*) юбиле́й; **golden/silver ~** пятидесятиле́тний/двадцатипятиле́тний юбиле́й; (*attr.*) юбиле́йный.

Judaic /dʒu:'deɪɪk/ *adj.* иуде́йский.

Judaism /'dʒu:deɪˌɪz(ə)m/ *n.* иудаи́зм.

Judas /'dʒu:dəs/ *n.* (*bibl.*) Иу́да (*m.*); (*fig.*) преда́тель (*m.*).

● *cpd.* **~-tree** *n.* багря́нник; иу́дино де́рево.

judder /'dʒʌdə(r)/ *v.i.* (*Br.*) вибри́ровать (*impf.*) с гро́хотом.

judge /dʒʌdʒ/ *n.* **1** (*legal functionary*) судья́ (*m.*). **2** (*arbiter*) арби́тр, судья́; **let me be the ~ of that** мне суди́ть об э́том; **the ~s** (*of a contest*) су́дьи, жюри́ (*nt. indecl.*); **he is one of the ~s** он в соста́ве жюри́. **3** (*expert, connoisseur*) знато́к, цени́тель (*m.*); **a ~ of wines** знато́к вин.

● *v.t.* **1** (*pass ~ment on*) суди́ть (*impf.*) о + *i.*; **don't ~ him by appearances!** не суди́те о нём по вне́шности!; **who ~d the race?** кто суди́л на э́том состяза́нии?; (*assess*) оце́н|ивать, -и́ть. **2** (*consider*) счита́ть (*impf.*); **he was ~d to be innocent** его́ сочли́ невино́вным; (*suppose*) предпол|ага́ть, -ожи́ть; **I ~d him to be about 50** я предположи́л, что ему́ о́коло пяти́десяти. **3** (*hear and try*): **the case was ~d in secret** де́ло слу́шалось в закры́том суде́.

● *v.i.* **1** (*make an appraisal or decision*) суди́ть (*impf.*); **to ~ from what you say** су́дя по тому́, что вы сказа́ли. **2** (*act as ~; arbitrate*) суди́ть (*impf.*), быть арби́тром.

judg(e)ment /'dʒʌdʒmənt/ *n.* **1** (*sentence*) суде́бное реше́ние, пригово́р; **pass ~ (on)** (*in court*) выноси́ть, вы́нести пригово́р + *d.*; (*express opinion*) суди́ть (*impf.*) о + *p.*; **a reserved ~** отсро́ченное реше́ние; **the ~ was in his favour** (*Br.*), **favor** (*US*) реше́ние суда́ бы́ло в его́ по́льзу; (*act or process of judging*): **sit in ~** (*fig.*) суди́ть (*impf.*) други́х свысока́; **J~ Day** Су́дный день; **the Last J~** Стра́шный суд. **2** (*opinion; estimation*) мне́ние; сужде́ние; **in my ~** по моему́ мне́нию; **a hasty ~** опроме́тчивое сужде́ние; **against one's better ~** вопреки́ го́лосу ра́зума; **an error of ~** оши́бка в сужде́нии; **I reserve ~ about that** я (пока́) воздержу́сь от сужде́ния по э́тому по́воду. **3** (*criticism*) осужде́ние. **4** (*discernment*) рассуди́тельность; **he shows good ~** он здра́во су́дит.

judgeship /'dʒʌdʒʃɪp/ *n.* суде́йская до́лжность.

judicial /dʒu:'dɪʃ(ə)l/ *adj.* **1** (*of a law court*) суде́бный; **~ proceedings** суде́бный проце́сс; (*of a judge*) суде́йский. **2** (*critical; impartial*) рассуди́тельный; беспристра́стный.

judiciary /dʒu:'dɪʃɪərɪ/ *n.* су́дьи (*m. pl.*); суде́бная власть.

judicious /dʒu:'dɪʃəs/ *adj.* здравомы́слящий, рассуди́тельный.

judiciousness /dʒu:'dɪʃəsnɪs/ *n.* рассуди́тельность.

judo /'dʒu:dəʊ/ *n.* дзюдо́ (*indecl.*).

judoist /'dʒu:dəʊɪst/ *n.* дзюдои́ст (*fem.* -ка).

jug /dʒʌg/ *n.* (*vessel*) кувши́н; (*coll., prison*) тюря́га (*sl.*).

jugful /'dʒʌgfʊl/ *n.* по́лный кувши́н (*чего*).

juggernaut /'dʒʌgəˌnɔ:t/ *n.* (*fig.*) безжа́лостная/неумоли́мая си́ла; (*Br., lorry*) многото́нный грузови́к, автопо́езд.

juggle /'dʒʌg(ə)l/ *v.t.* (*lit., fig., manipulate*) жонгли́ровать (*impf.*) + *i.*

● *v.i.* (*lit., fig.*) жонгли́ровать (*impf.*).

juggler /'dʒʌglə(r)/ *n.* жонглёр.

Jugoslav /'ju:gəˌslɑ:v/, **-ia** /ˌju:gə'slɑ:vɪə/ = **Yugoslav, -ia**

jugular /'dʒʌgjʊlə(r)/ *n.* **(~ vein)** яре́мная ве́на.

juice /dʒu:s/ *n.* **1** (*bot., physiol.*) сок; (*fruit ~*) (фрукто́вый) сок; **stew in one's own ~** (*coll.*) вари́ться (*impf.*) в со́бственном соку́. **2** (*sl., petrol*) бензи́н. **3** (*sl., elec. current*) (электри́ческий) ток.

juicer /'dʒu:sə(r)/ *n.* соковыжима́лка.

juiciness /'dʒu:sɪnɪs/ *n.* со́чность.

juicy /'dʒu:sɪ/ *adj.* (**juicier, juiciest**) со́чный; (*coll., racy, scandalous*) сма́чный.

ju-jitsu /dʒu:'dʒɪtsu:/ *n.* джиу-джи́тсу (*nt. indecl.*).

jujube /'dʒu:dʒu:b/ *n.* (*bot*) ю́юба; (*US, lozenge*) лека́рственная лепёшка.

juke-box /'dʒu:kbɒks/ *n.* автома́т-прои́грыватель (*m.*).

julep /'dʒu:lep/ *n.*: **mint ~** (*US*) мя́тный напи́ток из ви́ски со льдом.

Julian /'dʒu:lɪən/ *adj.*: **~ calendar** юлиа́нский календа́рь.

July /dʒu:'laɪ/ *n.* (*pl.* **Julys**) ию́ль (*m.*); (*attr.*) ию́льский.

jumble /'dʒʌmb(ə)l/ *n.* (*untidy heap*) ку́ча; (*disorder, muddle*) беспоря́док, пу́таница; (*coll., unwanted articles*) хлам; **~ sale** (*Br.*) дешёвая распрода́жа (*в благотворительных целях*).

● *v.t.* (*also* **~ up**) переме́ш|ивать, -а́ть.

jumbo /'dʒʌmbəʊ/ *n.* (*pl.* **~s**) (*coll., elephant*) слон; (*attr., very large*) гига́нтский; большу́щий; **~ jet** реакти́вный ла́йнер.

jump /dʒʌmp/ *n.* прыжо́к, скачо́к; **long/high ~** прыжо́к в длину́/высоту́; **take a running ~** (*lit.*) пры́г|ать, -нуть с разбе́га; (*fig., coll.*): **I told him to take a running ~** я веле́л ему́ прова́ливать; (*obstacle in steeplechase*) препя́тствие; **water ~** ров с водо́й; (*fig., abrupt rise*) скачо́к; **there was a big ~ in the temperature** температу́ра си́льно подскочи́ла; (*fig., start, shock*) вздра́гивание.

● *v.t.* **1** (**~ over, across**) перепры́г|ивать, -нуть че́рез + *a.* **2** (*cause to ~*): **he ~ed his horse over the fence** он посла́л свою́ ло́шадь че́рез забо́р. **3** (*var. fig. uses*): **~ bail** наруша́ть, нару́шить усло́вия освобожде́ния под зало́г; **~ the gun** (*coll.*) нач|ина́ть, -а́ть ска́чки до сигна́ла; (*fig.*) нач|ина́ть, -а́ть что-н. ра́ньше вре́мени; **~ the queue** про|ходи́ть, -йти́ без о́череди; **the train ~ed the rails** по́езд сошёл с ре́льсов; **~ ship** дезерти́ровать (*impf., pf.*) с су́дна; **you've ~ed a few lines** вы пропусти́ли (*or* перескочи́ли че́рез) не́сколько строк.

● *v.i.* **1** пры́г|ать, -нуть; (*on horseback*) вск|а́кивать, -очи́ть; (*with parachute*) пры́г|ать, -нуть с парашю́том. **2** (*fig.*) переска́кивать (*impf.*); **he ~ed from one topic to another** он переска́кивал с одно́й те́мы на другу́ю. **3** (*start*) подск|а́кивать, -очи́ть; **the noise made me ~** звук заста́вил меня́ подскочи́ть. **4** (*make sudden movement*) подск|а́кивать, -очи́ть; **shares ~ed to a new level** а́кции подскочи́ли. **5** (*fig. uses*): **I would ~ at the chance** я бы ухвати́лся за э́ту возмо́жность; **he ~ed at my offer** он ухвати́лся за моё предложе́ние; **~ for joy** пры́гать/скака́ть (*impf.*) от ра́дости; **~ on s.o.** (*attack*) набр|а́сываться, -о́ситься на кого́-н.; (*rebuke*) ре́зко оса|жда́ть, -ди́ть кого́-н.; **~ to conclusions** де́лать (*impf.*) поспе́шные вы́воды; **~ to it!** поторапливайтесь!; **he ~ed to his feet** он вскочи́л на́ ноги.

● *with advs.*: **they ~ed about to keep warm** они́ пры́гали, что́бы согре́ться;

he ~ed back in surprise он отпря́нул в удивле́нии; **she ~ed down from the fence** она́ спры́гнула с забо́ра; **he took off his clothes and ~ed in** он разде́лся и пры́гнул в во́ду; **if you want a lift, ~ in!** е́сли хоти́те, что́бы я вас подбро́сил, залеза́йте в маши́ну!; **don't ~ off before the bus stops!** не спры́гивайте на ходу́ (*or* до по́лной остано́вки авто́буса); **~ing-off point** (*fig.*) отправна́я то́чка; **as the train began to move I ~ed on** я впры́гнул в по́езд, когда́ он уже́ тро́нулся; **~ up from one's chair** вск|а́кивать, -очи́ть со сту́ла; **~ up and down** пры́гать/подпры́гивать (*impf.*) вверх и вниз; **~ed-up** *adj.* (*coll.*): **a ~ed-up person** вы́скочка (*c.g.*).

● *cpds.* **~-jet** *n.* реакти́вный самолёт вертика́льного взлёта; **~ lead** *n.* (*Br.*) электри́ческий ка́бель для запуска автодви́гателя; **~-off** *n.* (*to decide tie*) дополни́тельный круг на бега́х с препя́тствиями (*при одинаковых результатах*); **~ rope** *n.* (*US*) скака́лка; **~-seat** *n.* откидно́е сиде́нье; **~-suit** *n.* комбинезо́н.

jumper /'dʒʌmpə(r)/ *n.* (*athlete*) прыгу́н; (*horse*) скаку́н; (*Br., sweater*) дже́мпер; (*US, pinafore dress*) сарафа́н.

● *cpd.* **~ cable** *n.* (*US*) = **jump lead**

jumpy /'dʒʌmpɪ/ *adj.* (**jumpier, jumpiest**) не́рвный, дёрганый.

junction /'dʒʌŋkʃ(ə)n/ *n.* **1** (*joining*) соедине́ние, стык. **2** (*meeting point*: *of railways*) у́зел; узлово́й пункт; (*of roads*) скреще́ние (доро́г), перекрёсток; (*of rivers*) слия́ние. **3** (*elec.*): **~ box** соедини́тельная му́фта.

juncture /'dʒʌŋktʃə(r)/ *n.* (*joining*) соедине́ние; **at a critical ~** в крити́ческий моме́нт; **at this ~** в да́нный моме́нт.

June /dʒu:n/ *n.* ию́нь (*m.*); (*attr.*) ию́ньский.

jungle /'dʒʌŋg(ə)l/ *n.* джу́нгл|и (*pl., g.* -ей); **concrete ~** ка́менные джу́нгли; **the law of the ~** зако́н джу́нглей; **~ warfare** боевы́е де́йствия в джу́нглях.

junior /'dʒu:nɪə(r)/ *n.* & *adj.* мла́дший; **John Jones ~** Джон Джонс мла́дший; **he is 6 years my ~** он моло́же меня́ на шесть лет; **~ partner** мла́дший партнёр; **~ school** (*Br.*) нача́льная шко́ла (*для детей 7-11 лет*); **~ high school** (*US*) непо́лная сре́дняя шко́ла (*7, 8, 9 классы*); **~ common room** (*Br.*) студе́нческая ко́мната о́тдыха; **in his ~ year** (*US*) на предпосле́днем ку́рсе.

juniper /'dʒu:nɪpə(r)/ *n.* можжеве́льник; (*attr.*) можжевёловый.

junk[1] /dʒʌŋk/ *n.* (*rubbish*) ру́хлядь, хлам; **~ food** неполноце́нная пи́ща.

● *v.t.* (*sl., discard*) выбра́сывать, вы́бросить.

● *cpds.* **~-heap** *n.*: **it is only fit for the ~-heap** э́то пора́ вы́бросить на сва́лку; **~ mail** *n.* макулату́рная по́чта; **~-shop** *n.* ла́вка старьёвщика.

junk[2] /dʒʌŋk/ *n.* (*sailing vessel*) джо́нка.

junket /'dʒʌŋkɪt/ *n.* **1** (*dish*) сла́дкий творо́г. **2** (*business trip at public expense*) увесели́тельная пое́здка за казённый счёт; (*celebration*) пра́зднество, пиру́шка.

junk|ie, -y /'dʒʌŋkɪ/ *n.* (*sl., drug addict*) наркома́н, торчо́к (*sl.*).

junta /'dʒʌntə/ *n.* ху́нта.

Jupiter /'dʒu:pɪtə(r)/ *n.* (*myth., astron.*) Юпи́тер.

Jurassic /dʒʊə'ræsɪk/ *n.* (**~ period**) ю́рский пери́од; ю́ра.

● *adj.* ю́рский.

juridical /dʒʊə'rɪdɪk(ə)l/ *adj.* юриди́ческий.

jurisdiction /ˌdʒʊərɪs'dɪkʃ(ə)n/ *n.* (*legal authority*) юрисди́кция; **have ~ over** име́ть (*impf.*) юрисди́кцию над + *i.*; **it does not lie within my ~** э́то не вхо́дит в мою́ компете́нцию.

jurisprudence /ˌdʒʊərɪs'pru:d(ə)ns/ *n.* юриспруде́нция.

jurist /'dʒʊərɪst/ *n.* юри́ст.

juristic /ˌdʒʊə'rɪstɪk/ *adj.* юриди́ческий.

juror /'dʒʊərə(r)/ *n.* (*in competition*) член жюри́; (*in court*) прися́жный (заседа́тель).

jury /'dʒʊərɪ/ *n.* (*in competition*) жюри́ (*nt. indecl.*); (*in court*) прися́жные (заседа́тели) (*m. pl.*); **grand ~** (*US*) большо́е жюри́.

● *cpds.* **~-box** *n.* скамья́ прися́жных; **~man** *n.* прися́жный; **~woman** *n.* же́нщина — прися́жный заседа́тель.

just /dʒʌst/ *adj.* (*equitable*) справедли́вый; **act ~ly to(wards) s.o.** быть справедли́вым (по отноше́нию) к кому́-н.; (*deserved*) справедли́вый, заслу́женный; **receive one's ~ deserts** получ|а́ть, -и́ть по заслу́гам; (*well-grounded*) обосно́ванный, справедли́вый.

● *adv.* **1** то́чно, как раз, и́менно; **it was ~ 3 o'clock** бы́ло ро́вно три часа́; **~ then** как раз/и́менно тогда́; в ту мину́ту; **that's ~ the trouble** в то́м-то и беда́; **~ how did you do it?** как и́менно вам удало́сь э́то сде́лать? **2**: **~ like, as** (*expr. comparison*) то́чно так же, как (и); то́чно, как; **that's ~ like him** (*typical*) э́то так похо́же на него́; **that's ~ like me** ну то́чно, как я; **that's ~ it** вот и́менно; **that's ~ the point** в то́м-то и де́ло; **~ the thing** и́менно то, что на́до; **the hat is ~ my size** шля́па мне в са́мую по́ру; **~ so** то́чно/и́менно так; (*exactly arranged*) то́чно; **~ so** (*you are quite right*) так то́чно; **he is ~ as lazy as ever** он всё тако́й же лени́вый; **~ as much** сто́лько же; **I'd ~ as soon stay at home** я предпочёл бы оста́ться до́ма; **it's ~ as well I warned you** хорошо́, что я вас предупреди́л; **thank you ~ the same** спаси́бо и на э́том. **3 ~ about** (*approximately*): **~ about right** почти́ так/пра́вильно; (*almost*): **I've ~ about finished** я почти́ ко́нчил. **4** (*expr. time*) то́лько что; (*very recently*): **I saw him ~ now** я то́лько что ви́дел его́; **as you were ~ saying** как вы то́лько что сказа́ли; **~ as** (*expr. time*) (как) то́лько; **~ as he entered the room** то́лько он вошёл в ко́мнату; (*at this moment*): **I'm ~ off** я ухожу́ пря́мо сейча́с/как раз сейча́с; **the show is ~ beginning** представле́ние как раз начина́ется. **5** (*barely, no more than*) едва́; **I ~ caught the train** я едва́ успе́л на по́езд; **he had ~ come in when the phone rang** едва́ он вошёл, как зазвони́л телефо́н; **I've got ~ enough for my fare** мои́х де́нег то́лько-то́лько хва́тит на биле́т; **(wait) ~ a minute!** (одну́) мину́т(к)у! **6** (*merely, simply*) то́лько; **~ listen to this!** вы то́лько послу́шайте!; **I went ~ to hear him** я пошёл то́лько, что́бы послу́шать его́; **it's ~ that I don't like him** де́ло про́сто в том, что он мне неприя́тен; **~ fancy!** поду́мать то́лько!; (то́лько) предста́вьте себе́!; **~ you wait!** ну, погоди́!; **~ for fun** шу́тки ра́ди; **~ in case** на вся́кий слу́чай. **7** (*positively, absolutely*) так и; про́сто(-на́просто); **the coffee ~ would not boil** ко́фе ника́к не закипа́л; **it's ~ splendid!** э́то про́сто великоле́пно!; **don't I ~!** ещё бы!; **not ~ yet** ещё не/нет.

justice /'dʒʌstɪs/ *n.* **1** (*fairness; equity*) справедли́вость; **do ~ to** отд|ава́ть, -а́ть до́лжное + *d.*; **you are not doing yourself ~** вы не проявля́ете себя́ в по́лную си́лу; **to do him ~** отдава́я ему́ до́лжное; **with ~** со всей справедли́востью. **2** (*system of institutions*) юсти́ция; (*judicial proceedings*) правосу́дие; **administer ~** отправля́ть (*impf.*) правосу́дие; **bring s.o. to ~** отд|ава́ть, -а́ть кого́-н. под суд; привл|ека́ть, -е́чь кого́-н. к суде́бной отве́тственности; **Court of J~** суд. **3** (*magistrate; judge*) судья́ (*m.*); **J~ of the Peace** (*Br.*) мирово́й судья́.

justifiable /'dʒʌstɪˌfaɪəb(ə)l/ *adj.* опра́вданный; **~ homicide** уби́йство в це́лях самозащи́ты *и т.п.*

justification /ˌdʒʌstɪfɪ'keɪʃ(ə)n/ *n.* **1** оправда́ние; **he objected, and with ~** он возрази́л и не без основа́ний. **2** (*typ.*) вы́ключка строки́.

justificatory /'dʒʌstɪfɪˌkeɪtərɪ/ *adj.* оправда́тельный.

justif|y /'dʒʌstɪˌfaɪ/ *v.t.* **1** (*establish rightness of*) опра́вд|ывать, -а́ть; **I was ~ied in suspecting ...** я име́л все основа́ния подозрева́ть...; **~y o.s.** опра́вд|ываться, -а́ться. **2** (*typ.*) выключа́ть, вы́ключить (*строку*).

jut /dʒʌt/ *v.i.* (**jutted, jutting**) (*usu.* **~ out**) выступа́ть (*impf.*); выдава́ться (*impf.*).

jute /dʒu:t/ *n.* (*bot.*) джут.

juvenile /'dʒu:vəˌnaɪl/ *n.* подро́сток.

● *adj.* ю́ный, ю́ношеский; **~ delinquent** малоле́тний престу́пник; **~ delinquency** де́тская престу́пность; **~ court** суд по дела́м несовершенноле́тних.

juvenilia /ˌdʒu:və'nɪlɪə/ *n.* ю́ношеские произведе́ния.

juxtapose /ˌdʒʌkstə'pəʊz/ *v.t.* поме|ща́ть, -сти́ть бок о́ бок; (*for comparison*) сопост|авля́ть, -а́вить (*кого с кем or что с чем*).

J

juxtaposition /ˌdʒʌkstəpəˈzɪʃ(ə)n/ *n.* сосе́дство, бли́зость; (*for comparison*) сопоставле́ние.

Kk

K *abbr. of* **1** ***Kelvin(s)*** °К (по Ке́львину). **2** ***kilobyte*** килоба́йт. **3** ***£1,000, $1,000*** ты́сяча фу́нтов, до́лларов, коса́я (*sl.*); **he earns 35K a year** он зараба́тывает 35 косы́х в год.

k (*abbr. of* ***kilometre(s)***) км (киломе́тр).

Kabul /kəˈbʊl/, /ˈkɑːbʊl/ *n.* Кабу́л.

kaftan /ˈkæftæn/ = **caftan**

Kaiser /ˈkaɪzə(r)/ *n.* ка́йзер.

kale /keɪl/ *n.* листова́я капу́ста.

kaleidoscope /kəˈlaɪdəˌskəʊp/ *n.* (*lit., fig.*) калейдоско́п.

kaleidoscopic /kəˌlaɪdəˈskɒpɪk/ *adj.* калейдоскопи́ческий.

kalends /ˈkælendz/ = **calends**

Kalmuck, Kalmyk /ˈkælmʌk/ *n.* (*pl.* **~** *or* **~s**) (*person*) калмы́|к (*fem.* -чка); (*language*) калмы́кский язы́к.

● *adj.* калмы́цкий.

kamikaze /ˌkæmɪˈkɑːzɪ/ *n.* (*pilot*) камика́дзе (*m. indecl.*), лётчик-сме́ртник.

Kampuchea /ˌkæmpʊˈtʃɪə/ *n.* Кампучи́я.

Kampuchean /ˌkæmpʊˈtʃɪən/ *n.* кампучи́|ец (*fem.* -йка).

● *adj.* кампучи́йский.

kangaroo /ˌkæŋɡəˈruː/ *n.* кенгуру́ (*m. indecl.*); **~ court** незако́нное суде́бное разбира́тельство.

kaolin /ˈkeɪəlɪn/ *n.* (*min.*) каоли́н.

kapok /ˈkeɪpɒk/ *n.* (*substance*) капо́к, ва́та из семя́н капка́; (*tree*) капо́к.

Karachi /kəˈrɑːtʃɪ/ *n.* Кара́чи (*m. indecl.*).

karakul /ˈkærəˌkʊl/ = **carakul**

karaoke /ˌkærɪˈəʊkɪ/ *n.* карао́ке (*nt. indecl.*) (*имитация профессионального певца под запись аккомпанемента*).

karat /ˈkærət/ (*US*) = **carat**

karate /kəˈrɑːtɪ/ *n.* карате́ (*nt. indecl.*).

karateka /kəˈrɑːtɪˌkæ/ *n.* карате́ка, карати́ст.

Karelia /kəˈriːlɪə/ *n.* Каре́лия.

Karelian /kəˈriːlɪən/ *n.* каре́л (*fem.* -ка).

● *adj.* каре́льский.

karma /ˈkɑːmə/ *n.* (*relig.*) ка́рма.

Kashmir /kæʃˈmɪə(r)/ *n.* Кашми́р.

Kashmiri /kæʃˈmɪərɪ/ *n.* (*person*) кашми́р|ец (*fem.* -ка); (*language*) кашми́рский язы́к.

kayak /ˈkaɪæk/ *n.* кая́к (*эскимосская лодка*).

Kazakh /kəˈzɑːk/, /kɑː-/ *n.* (*pl.* **~s**) (*person*) каза́|х (*fem.* -шка); (*language*) каза́хский язы́к.

Kazakhstan /ˌkɑːzɑːkˈstæn/, /-ˈstɑːn/ *n.* Казахста́н.

Kazan /kəˈzæn/, /-ˈzɑːn/ *n.* Каза́нь.

kebab /kɪˈbæb/ *n.* кеба́б, шашлы́к; **~ house** кеба́бная, шашлы́чная.

keel /kiːl/ *n.* (*of ship*) киль (*m.*); **false ~** фальшки́ль (*m.*); **on an even ~** не кача́ясь; (*fig.*) усто́йчивый, стаби́льный.

● *v.t.* (*impf.*) перев|ора́чивать, -ерну́ть ки́лем вверх; килева́ть (*impf., pf.*).

● *v.i.*: **~ over** опроки́|дываться, -нуться.

● *cpd.* **~-haul** *v.t.* прота́скивать (*impf.*) под ки́лем; (*fig., reprimand*) пропесо́чи|вать, -ть (*coll.*).

keen¹ /kiːn/ *n.* (*lament*) причита́ние/плач по поко́йнику.

● *v.i.* голоси́ть (*impf.*).

keen² /kiːn/ *adj.* (*lit., fig.: sharp, acute*) о́стрый; **~ eyesight** о́строе зре́ние; **a ~ intellect** о́стрый/проница́тельный ум; (*piercing*) пронзи́тельный; **a ~ glance** пронзи́тельный/о́стрый взгляд; **a ~ wind** ре́зкий/пронизы́вающий ве́тер; **~ frost** си́льный моро́з; (*strong, intense*) си́льный; **~ desire** си́льное/о́строе жела́ние; **~ interest** живо́й интере́с; (*eager; energetic*) ре́вностный; энерги́чный; **a ~ businessman** энерги́чный деле́ц; **a ~ pupil** усе́рдный/приле́жный учени́к; **~ competition** тру́дное соревнова́ние; **a ~ demand for something** большо́й спрос на что-н.; (*enthusiastic*) стра́стный; **a ~ sportsman** стра́стный спортсме́н; энтузиа́ст/люби́тель (*m.*) спо́рта; **be ~ on** си́льно/стра́стно увл|ека́ться, -е́чься + *i.*; **I am not ~ on chess** я не осо́бенно увлека́юсь ша́хматами; **he is ~ on your coming** ему́ о́чень хо́чется, что́бы вы пришли́.

keenness /ˈkiːnnɪs/ *n.* (*sharpness*) острота́; (*of cold etc.*) си́ла, интенси́вность; (*eagerness, enthusiasm*) усе́рдие; энтузиа́зм.

keep¹ /kiːp/ *n.* (*tower*) гла́вная ба́шня (за́мка).

keep² /kiːp/ *n.* **1** (*maintenance*) содержа́ние. **2** (*sustenance*) прокóрм, пропита́ние; **earn one's ~** зараб|а́тывать, -о́тать себе́ на пропита́ние; **he's not worth his ~** от него́ про́ку ма́ло. **3**: **for ~s** насовсе́м (*coll.*).

● *v.t.* (*past and p.p.* **kept**) **1** (*retain possession of*) держа́ть (*impf.*), не отдава́ть (*impf.*); ост|авля́ть, -а́вить (себе́ *or* при себе́); **~ the change!** сда́чи не на́до!; (*preserve*) храни́ть (*impf.*); сохран|я́ть, -и́ть; (*save, put by*): **I shall ~ this paper to show my mother** я сохраню́ э́ту газе́ту, что́бы показа́ть ма́тери; **I'm ~ing this for a rainy day** я берегу́ э́то на чёрный день; **you can't ~ milk for more than a day** молоко́ ки́снет в тече́ние су́ток; **he ~s all her letters** он храни́т все её пи́сьма; (*hold on to*): **she kept the book a long time** она́ до́лго держа́ла (*or* не возвраща́ла) кни́гу; (*appropriate*) присв|а́ивать, -о́ить себе́; **when I lent you my umbrella I didn't mean you to ~ it** одолжи́в вам зо́нтик, я не ду́мал, что вы его́ присво́ите. **2** (*cause to remain*): **the traffic kept me awake** у́личное движе́ние не дава́ло мне спать; **the garden ~s me busy** сад не даёт мне сиде́ть сложа́ ру́ки; **this will ~ him quiet for a bit** всё э́то отвлечёт его́ немно́жко; **~ something safe** храни́ть (*impf.*) что-н. в безопа́сности; **~ o.s. alive** подде́рживать (*impf.*) свою́ жизнь (*чем*); **~ hope alive** подде́рж|ивать, -а́ть наде́жду; **~ an issue alive** не да|ва́ть, -ть вопро́су заглóхнуть; **~ the house clean** содержа́ть (*impf.*) дом в чистоте́/поря́дке; **~ one's hands clean** держа́ть (*impf.*) ру́ки чи́стыми; (*fig.*) не мара́ть (*impf.*) рук; **~ your mouth shut!** держи́те язы́к за зуба́ми!;

I want the door kept open я хочу́, чтобы дверь остава́лась откры́той; **I'm ~ing my ears open** я держу́ у́шки на маку́шке; **~ s.o. supplied** снабжа́ть (*impf.*) кого́-н.; **~ the grass cut** регуля́рно стричь (*impf.*) траву́; **~ s.o. in the dark** держа́ть (*impf.*) кого́-н. в неве́дении; **~ s.o. in suspense** держа́ть (*impf.*) кого́-н. в напряжённом ожида́нии; **he kept his hands in his pockets** он держа́л ру́ки в карма́нах; **~ it to yourself** пома́лкивайте об э́том; **~ an eye on something** пригля́дывать (*impf.*) за чем-н.; **~ your mind on your work** не отвлека́йтесь от свое́й рабо́ты; **~ something in mind, view** име́ть (*impf.*) что-н. в виду́; **~ something in order** держа́ть (*impf.*) что-н. в поря́дке; **~ s.o. in order** держа́ть (*impf.*) кого́-н. в узде́; **where do you ~ the salt?** где вы храни́те соль?

3 (*cause to continue*): **he kept me standing for an hour** он продержа́л меня́ на нога́х це́лый час; **I don't like to be kept waiting** я не люблю́, когда́ меня́ заставля́ют ждать; **they kept him working late** они́ заде́рживали его́ на рабо́те допоздна́; **that will ~ you going till lunch-time** тепе́рь вы проде́ржитесь до обе́да.

4 (*remain in, on*): **~ one's seat** (*remain sitting*) не встава́ть (*impf.*); **~ the saddle** уде́рж|иваться, -а́ться в седле́; **~ one's feet** удержа́ться на нога́х, устоя́ть (*both pf.*); (*retain, preserve*): **~ one's balance** сохраня́ть/уде́рживать (*both impf.*) равнове́сие; **~ one's own counsel** молча́ть (*impf.*); **~ one's distance** соблю|да́ть, -сти́ расстоя́ние/диста́нцию; **she has kept her figure** она́ сохрани́ла стро́йность; (*for phrr. of the kind* **'~ company'; '~ guard'; '~ order'; '~ time'** *etc. see under nn.*).

5 (*have charge of; manage, own; rear, maintain*) име́ть, держа́ть, содержа́ть (*all impf.*); **who ~s the keys?** у кого́ храня́тся ключи́?; **the shop was kept by an Italian** владе́льцем ла́вки был италья́нец; **he wants to ~ pigs** он хо́чет держа́ть свине́й; **a kept woman** содержа́нка; **I have a wife and family to ~** у меня́ на иждиве́нии жена́ и де́ти; **that won't even ~ him in cigarettes** э́того ему́ не хва́тит да́же на сигаре́ты; **~ house** вести́ (*det.*) (дома́шнее) хозя́йство; **he ~s open house** у него́ дом откры́т для всех; **a well-kept garden** хорошо́ ухо́женный сад.

6 (*maintain, ~ entries in*) вести́ (*det.*); **~ books/accounts** вести́ счета́; **do you ~ a diary?** ведёте ли вы дневни́к?; **how long have records been kept?** как до́лго вели́сь за́писи?; **are you ~ing the score?** вы ведёте счёт?

7 (*detain*) заде́рж|ивать, -а́ть; **I won't ~ you** я вас не задержу́; **there was nothing to ~ me there** меня́ там ничто́ не держа́ло; **they kept him in prison** его́ держа́ли в тюрьме́.

8 (*stock; have for sale*): **we don't ~ cigarettes** мы не продаём сигаре́ты; **we do not ~ such goods** таки́х това́ров мы не де́ржим.

9 (*defend, protect*): **~ goal** стоя́ть (*impf.*) на воро́тах; защища́ть (*impf.*) воро́та; **God ~ you!** да храни́т вас Госпо́дь!

10 (*observe; be faithful to; fulfil*) сде́рж|ивать, -а́ть; соблю|да́ть, -сти́; **~ the law** соблюда́ть (*impf.*) зако́н; **~ one's word** держа́ть, с- сло́во; **~ faith** сохран|я́ть, -и́ть ве́рность; **I can't ~ the appointment** я не могу́ прийти́ на встре́чу.

11 (*celebrate*) пра́здновать, от-; отм|еча́ть, -е́тить.

12 (*guard, not divulge*) храни́ть (*impf.*); сохран|я́ть, -и́ть.

● *v.i.* (*past and p.p.* **kept**) **1** (*remain*) держа́ться (*impf.*); остава́ться (*impf.*); **the weather kept fine** стоя́ла хоро́шая пого́да; **if it ~s fine** е́сли проде́ржится хоро́шая пого́да; е́сли пого́да не испо́ртится; **I can't ~ warm here** я здесь не могу́ согре́ться; **~ cool** (*fig.*) не теря́ть (*impf.*) головы́; **the food will ~ warm in the oven** в духо́вке еда́ оста́нется тёплой; **please ~ quiet!** пожа́луйста, не шуми́те!; **how are you ~ing?** (*Br.*) как живёте-мо́жете? (*coll.*); **I'm ~ing quite well** (*Br.*) (я) на здоро́вье не жа́луюсь; **I exercise to ~ fit** я занима́юсь гимна́стикой/спо́ртом, что́бы быть в фо́рме; **we still ~ in touch** мы всё ещё подде́рживаем отноше́ния/связь; **~ in step** шага́ть (*impf.*) в но́гу.

2 (*continue*) продолжа́ть (*impf.*) + *inf.*; **she ~s giggling** она́ всё хихи́кает; **~ going!** продолжа́йте идти́!; **~ straight on!** иди́те/поезжа́йте пря́мо вперёд!

3 (*remain fresh*): **the food will ~ in the refrigerator** еда́ в холоди́льнике не испо́ртится; (*fig.*): **my news will ~ till tomorrow** с мои́ми новостя́ми мо́жно подожда́ть до за́втра.

● *with preps.*: (*for phrr. with* **in** *or* **on** + *n. see under v.t.* 2 *or v.i.* 1 *or under nn.*): **~ after** (*continue to pursue*) продолжа́ть (*impf.*) пого́ню за + *i.*; **we are ~ing ahead of schedule** мы продолжа́ем опережа́ть гра́фик; **he ~s his pupils at it** он заставля́ет ученико́в труди́ться; **you must ~ at it till it's finished** не отрыва́йтесь, пока́ не ко́нчите; **I kept at him to start the job** я наста́ивал, что́бы он на́чал рабо́ту; **he kept his hands behind his back** он держа́л ру́ки за спино́й; **he kept behind me all the way** он шёл позади́ меня́ всю доро́гу; **his brothers kept his share from him** его́ бра́тья удержа́ли его́ до́лю; **what are you trying to ~ from me?** что вы скрыва́ете от меня́?; **my umbrella ~s me from getting wet** зо́нтик спаса́ет меня́ от дождя́; **I kept him from hurting himself** я не дал ему́ ушиби́ться; **I could hardly ~ (myself) from laughing** я едва́ удержа́лся от сме́ха; **'~ off the grass!'** «по газо́нам не ходи́ть»; **I have to ~ off sugar** мне на́до избега́ть са́хара; **he can't ~ off (the subject of) politics** он никак не мо́жет съе́хать с разгово́ров о поли́тике; **I couldn't ~ my eyes off her** я не мог отвести́ от неё глаз; **they tried to ~ me out of the room** они́ пыта́лись не пуска́ть меня́ в ко́мнату; **he kept out of the room** он не входи́л в ко́мнату; **I kept the sweets out of his reach** я держа́л конфе́ты пода́льше от него́; **they kept him out of the talks** его́ не допуска́ли к перегово́рам; **~ out of s.o.'s way** (*avoid him*) избега́ть (*impf.*) кого́-н.; (*not hinder him*) не меша́ть (*impf.*) кому́-н.; **I kept out of their quarrel** я не вме́шивался в их ссо́ру; **he cannot ~ out of trouble for long** он ве́чно попада́ет в исто́рии; **I kept him to his promise** я заста́вил его́ вы́полнить обеща́ние; **he kept the news to himself** он ни с кем не дели́лся но́востью; **he ~s his feelings to himself** он скрыва́ет свои́ чу́вства; **he ~s himself to himself** он замыка́ется в себе́; **we must ~ costs to a minimum** мы должны́ свести́ расхо́ды до ми́нимума; **~ to the path** держа́ться (*impf.*) тропи́нки; **~ to the point** не отклоня́ться (*impf.*) от те́мы; **he ~s the boys under control** он де́ржит ма́льчиков в узде́; **~ s.o. under observation** следи́ть (*impf.*) за кем-н.

● *with advs.*: **~ away** *v.t.*: **the rain kept people away** дождь отпугну́л наро́д; **she kept her daughter away from school** она́ не пуска́ла дочь в шко́лу; **a spray to ~ flies away** аэрозо́ль (*m.*) для отпу́гивания мух; **we could not ~ him away from books** мы не могли́ удержа́ть его́ от чте́ния; *v.i.*: **he tried to ~ away from them** он стара́лся их избега́ть; **he kept away from spirits** он держа́лся пода́льше от спиртны́х напи́тков; **~ back** *v.t.* (*restrain*) сде́рж|ивать, -а́ть; **the police could not ~ the crowd back** поли́ция не могла́ сдержа́ть толпу́; (*retain*): **they ~ back £1 from my wages** из мое́й зарпла́ты уде́рживают оди́н фунт; (*repress*): **she could hardly ~ back her tears** она́ с трудо́м сде́рживала слёзы; (*conceal*): **he kept back the sad news from her** он скрыва́л от неё печа́льные изве́стия; *v.i.* держа́ться (*impf.*) в стороне́; **~ down** *v.t.*: **~ your head down!** не поднима́йте головы́!; (*fig., coll.*) не высо́вывайся!; **~ your voice down!** не повыша́йте го́лоса!; (*limit, control*): **they tried to ~ down expenses** они́ стара́лись расхо́довать как мо́жно ме́ньше; **a mistaken policy was ~ing production down** оши́бочная поли́тика затормáживала произво́дство; **unemployment was kept down** безрабо́тице не дава́ли разраста́ться; **how do you ~ the weeds down?** как вы бо́ретесь с сорняка́ми?; (*oppress*) держа́ть (*impf.*) в подчине́нии; (*suppress*) подав|ля́ть, -и́ть; (*digest*): **he can't ~ anything down** у него́ желу́док ничего́ не принима́ет; *v.i.* (*lie low*) притаи́ться (*pf.*); **~ in** *v.t.* (*confine*): **I ~ the children in when it rains** когда́ идёт дождь, я держу́ дете́й до́ма; **he was kept in after school** его́ оста́вили по́сле уро́ков; (*maintain*): **we ~ the fire in overnight** мы подде́рживаем ого́нь всю ночь; **I practise** (*Br.*), **practice** (*US*) **to ~ my eye, hand in** я трениру́юсь/практику́юсь, что́бы не отвы́кнуть; *v.i.*: **~ in with s.o.** подде́рживать (*impf.*) хоро́шие отноше́ния с кем-н.; **~ off** *v.t.* (*restrain*): **they kept the hounds off till the signal was given** го́нчих не подпуска́ли, пока́ не да́ли сигна́л; (*ward off, repel*): **I kept his blows off with my stick** я отрази́л его́ уда́ры па́лкой; **my hat will ~ the rain off** моя́ шля́па защити́т меня́ от дождя́; *v.i.* (*stay at a distance*): **I hope the rain ~s off** я наде́юсь, что дождь не начнётся; **the crowd kept off till the very end** толпа́ до са́мого конца́ держа́лась в отдале́нии; **~ on** *v.t.* (*continue to wear*): **women ~ their hats on in church** в це́ркви же́нщины не снима́ют шляп; **~ your hair** (*US* **shirt**) **on!** (*sl.*) споко́йно!; не не́рвничайте!; (*continue to employ, educate*): **they kept the workers on** они́ оста́вили рабо́чих; **they won't ~ you on after 60** они́ уво́лят вас, когда́ вам испо́лнится 60 лет; **I'm ~ing my boy on (at school) for another year** я оставля́ю сы́на в шко́ле ещё на́ год; (*leave in place*): **~ the lid on** не снима́йте кры́шку; *v.i.* (*with pres. part., continue*): **he kept on reading** он продолжа́л чита́ть; **she kept on glancing out of the window** она́ беспреста́нно выгля́дывала из окна́; **he kept on falling** он постоя́нно па́дал; (*continue, persist*): **the rain kept on all day** дождь шёл весь день; **she kept on till the job was finished** она́ рабо́тала, пока́ всё не зако́нчила; (*continue talking*): **he will ~ on about his dogs** он как зала́дит (*coll.*) о соба́ках; (*nag*): **if you ~ on at him, he'll take you to the theatre** (*Br.*), **theater** (*US*) е́сли вы бу́дете продолжа́ть наста́ивать, он в конце́ концо́в сво́дит вас в теа́тр; **~ out** *v.t.* (*exclude*): **this coat ~s out the cold very well** э́то пальто́ хорошо́ защища́ет от хо́лода; **we put up a fence to ~ out trespassers** мы постро́или/поста́вили забо́р, что́бы посторо́нние не заходи́ли на террито́рию; (*leave in view*): **I kept these papers out to show you** я оста́вил э́ти бума́ги, что́бы показа́ть их вам; *v.i.*: **'Private — ~ out!'** (*notice*) «посторо́нним вход воспрещён/запрещён!»; **~ together** *v.t.*: **this folder will ~ your papers together** в э́ту па́пку вы смо́жете сложи́ть все докуме́нты; **he has hardly enough to ~ body and soul together** он едва́ сво́дит концы́ с конца́ми; **the conductor kept the band together** дирижёр сплоти́л орке́стр; *v.i.*: **the mountaineers kept together for safety** для безопа́сности альпини́сты держа́лись вме́сте; **~ under** *v.t.* держа́ть (*impf.*) в подчине́нии; **~ up** *v.t.* (*prevent from falling or sinking*): **he could not ~ his trousers up** у него́ всё вре́мя сва́ливались брю́ки; **the wall was kept up by a buttress** стена́ держа́лась на подпо́рке; (*fig., sustain, maintain*): **~ up one's spirits** не па́дать (*impf.*) ду́хом; **~ one's strength up** подкрепля́ть (*impf.*) си́лы; **~ one's end up** держа́ть (*impf.*) хвост пистоле́том (*coll.*); не уда́рить (*pf.*) лицо́м в грязь; **~ up appearances** соблюда́ть (*impf.*) прили́чия/ви́димость прили́чий; **the house is expensive to ~ up** э́тот дом до́рого содержа́ть; **~ up the conversation** подде́рживать (*impf.*) разгово́р; (*continue*): **~ up the good work!** продолжа́йте в том же ду́хе!; **he can ~ it up for hours** он в э́том неутоми́м; **he could not ~ up the payments** он не мог регуля́рно плати́ть; **the custom has been kept up for centuries** э́тот обы́чай сохраня́лся столе́тия; **I wish I had kept up my Latin** жаль, что я забро́сил латы́нь; (*prevent from going to bed*): **the baby kept us up half the night** ребёнок не дава́л нам спать полно́чи; *v.i.* (*stay high, e.g. a kite; temperature*) держа́ться (*impf.*); (*continue*): **if the weather ~s up we will have a picnic** е́сли хоро́шая пого́да продержи́тся, мы устро́им пикни́к; (*stay level*): **we kept up with them the whole way** всю доро́гу мы не отстава́ли от них; **stop! I can't ~ up** подожди́те! я за ва́ми не поспева́ю; **the unions demand that wages should ~ up with prices** профсою́зы тре́буют, что́бы зарпла́та росла́ вме́сте с це́нами; **~ up with the times** не отстава́ть (*impf.*) от собы́тий; шага́ть (*impf.*) в но́гу со вре́менем; **~ up with the Joneses** быть не ху́же други́х/люде́й; (*remain in touch*): **I try to ~ up with the news** я стара́юсь следи́ть за собы́тиями; **I ~ up with several old friends** я подде́рживаю отноше́ния ко́е с кем из ста́рых друзе́й.

● *cpd.* **~-fit** *adj.* (*Br.*): **~-fit exercises** здоро́вительная гимна́стика.

keeper /ˈkiːpə(r)/ *n.* (*guardian*) храни́тель (*m.*), сто́рож; (*in zoo*) служи́тель (*m.*) (зоопа́рка); **I am not my brother's ~** я не сто́рож моему́ бра́ту; (*Br., museum-~*) смотри́тель (*m.*); (*of shop, restaurant etc.*) владе́лец; хозя́ин; (*goal-~*) врата́рь (*m.*).

keeping /ˈkiːpɪŋ/ *n.* **1**: **in safe ~** в надёжных рука́х; в по́лной сохра́нности. **2**: **be in ~ with** соотве́тствовать (*impf.*) + *d.*; **that remark is out of ~ with his character** э́то замеча́ние для него́ не типи́чно; **the furniture is not in ~ with the house** ме́бель не в сти́ле до́ма; обстано́вка не в сти́ле.

keepsake /ˈkiːpseɪk/ *n.* сувени́р; **as a ~** на па́мять.

keg /keg/ *n.* бочо́нок.

ken /ken/ *n.*: **beyond my ~** вне мое́й компете́нции; за преде́лами мои́х позна́ний.

kennel /ˈken(ə)l/ *n.* **1** конура́. **2** (*pl., for hounds*) пса́рня.

● *v.t.* (**kennelled, kennelling;** *US* **kenneled, kenneling**) (*keep in ~*) держа́ть (*impf.*) в конуре́; (*drive into ~*) заг|оня́ть, -на́ть в конуру́.

Kenya /ˈkenjə/, /ˈkiːnjə/ *n.* Ке́ния.

Kenyan /ˈkenjən/, /ˈkiːnjən/ *n.* кени́|ец (*fem.* -йка).

● *adj.* кени́йский.

kept /kept/ *past and p.p. of* ⇒**keep**

keratin /ˈkerətɪn/ *n.* (*biol.*) керати́н.

kerb /kɜːb/ (*US* **curb**) *n.* обо́чина.

● *cpds.* **~-crawler** *n.* (*Br.*) мотори́ст, кото́рый ме́дленно ведёт маши́ну в по́исках проститу́тки; **~stone** *n.* бордю́рный ка́мень.

kerchief /ˈkɜːtʃiːf/, /-tʃɪf/ *n.* плато́к, косы́нка.

kerfuffle /kəˈfʌf(ə)l/ *n.* (*Br.*) шум, завару́ха.

kernel /ˈkɜːn(ə)l/ *n.* (*of nut or fruit-stone*) ядро́; (*of seed, e.g. wheat grain*) зерно́; (*fig., essence*) суть, су́щность.

keros|ene, -ine /ˈkerəˌsiːn/ *n.* кероси́н; (*attr.*) кероси́новый.

kestrel /ˈkestr(ə)l/ *n.* (*zool*) пустельга́.

ketch /ketʃ/ *n.* (*naut.*) кеч (*двухмачтовое парусное судно*).

ketchup /ˈketʃʌp/ *n.* ке́тчуп.

kettle /ˈket(ə)l/ *n.* ча́йник; (*pot for boiling, e.g. fish*) котело́к; **here's a pretty ~ of fish!** вот так но́мер!; хоро́шенькое де́ло!; **that's quite another ~ of fish** э́то совсе́м из друго́й о́перы.

● *cpds.* **~-drum** *n.* лита́вра; **~-drummer** *n.* литаври́ст, лита́врщик.

key /kiː/ *n.* (*pl.* **keys**) **1** ключ; **~ to the door** ключ от две́ри. **2** (*fig., something providing access or solution*) ключ; **the ~ to understanding the political situation** ключ к понима́нию полити́ческой ситуа́ции; **the ~ to a mystery** разга́дка та́йны; **the ~ to success is hard work** зало́г успе́ха — упо́рная рабо́та; (*to map*) леге́нда. **3** (*attr., important, essential*) ва́жный, важне́йший; веду́щий; **~ position** ключева́я пози́ция; **~ question** стержнево́й вопро́с; **~ industries** веду́щие о́трасли промы́шленности. **4** (*of piano or computer*) кла́виш, кла́виша; (*pl.*) клавиату́ра; (*of wind instrument*) кла́пан. **5** (*mus.*) ключ, тона́льность; **in a low ~** (*fig.*) сде́ржанно.

● *v.t.* (**keys, keyed**): **~ up** взви́н|чивать, -ти́ть.

● *cpds.* **~board** *n.* (*mus., comput.*) клавиату́ра; **~board instrument** кла́вишный инструме́нт; **~boarder** *n.* опера́тор компью́тера; **~hole** *n.* замо́чная сква́жина; **~hole surgery** *n.* (*Br.*) полостна́я опера́ция с минима́льным вскры́тием; **~note** *n.* (*mus.*) основна́я но́та ключа́; (*fig.*) лейтмоти́в; основна́я мы́сль; **~note address** *n.* програ́ммная речь; **~pad** *n.* пане́ль управле́ния; **~-ring** *n.* кольцо́ для ключе́й; **~stone** *n.* замко́вый ка́мень; (*fig.*) краеуго́льный ка́мень; **~stroke** *n.* уда́р по кла́више; **~word** *n.* ключево́е сло́во.

kg. /ˈkɪləˌgræm/ *n.* (*abbr. of* ***kilogram(me)(s)***) кг (килогра́мм).

KGB (*abbr. of Russian*) КГБ (Комите́т госуда́рственной безопа́сности); **~ agent** кагебе́шник, гебист.

khaki /ˈkɑːkɪ/ *n.* (*pl.* **~s**) защи́тный цвет, ха́ки (*nt. indecl.*); **dressed in ~** оде́тый в ха́ки.

● *adj.*: **a ~ shirt** руба́шка цве́та ха́ки.

khan /kɑːn/, /kæn/ *n.* хан.

khanate /ˈkɑːneɪt/, /ˈkæneɪt/ *n.* ха́нство.

Kharkov /ˈhɑːkɒv/ *n.* Ха́рьков.

Khedive /kɪˈdiːv/ *n.* (*hist.*) хеди́в.

Khmer /kmeə(r)/ *n.* кхмер; **~ Rouge** кра́сные кхме́ры.

● *adj.* кхме́рский.

kibbu|tz /kɪ'bʊts/ *n.* (*pl.* **~tzim** /-'tsi:m/) кибб(б)у́ц.

kibosh /'kaɪbɒʃ/ *n.* (*sl.*): **put the ~ on** прихло́пнуть (*pf.*).

kick /kɪk/ *n.* **1** уда́р, пино́к; **give s.o. a ~** уд|ари́ть, -а́рить (*or* ляг|а́ть, -ну́ть) кого́-н. ного́й; **give a ~** (*of horse*) ляг|а́ться, -ну́ться; (*soccer*): **the referee gave a free ~** судья́ объяви́л штрафно́й уда́р.
2 (*recoil*) отда́ча.
3 (*fig., resilience*): **he has no ~ left in him** он вы́дохся.
4 (*coll., stimulus*): **get a ~ out of something** получ|а́ть, -и́ть удово́льствие от чего́-н.; **he does it for ~s** (*sl.*) он де́лает э́то из озорства́; **this vodka has real ~ in it** в э́той во́дке есть гра́дус.

● *v.t.* уд|аря́ть, -а́рить ного́й; **he ~ed me on the shin** он уда́рил меня́ по го́лени; **you mustn't ~ a man when he's down** нельзя́ бить лежа́чего; **I could have ~ed myself** я рвал на себе́ во́лосы; **he ~ed the ball** он уда́рил по мячу́; **he ~ed a goal** он заби́л гол; **~ the bucket** дать (*pf.*) ду́ба (*sl.*); **~ one's heels** ждать (*impf.*) с нетерпе́нием; **~ the habit** (*sl., give up addiction*) бро́сить (*pf.*) нарко́тики/кури́ть/пить *и т.д.*

● *v.i.* (*of animals*) ляга́ться (*impf.*); брыка́ться (*impf.*); (*fig.*): **~ at, against something** протестова́ть (*impf.*) про́тив чего́-н.; **~ over the traces** взбунтова́ться (*pf.*); **he is still alive and ~ing** он всё ещё жив-здоро́в.

● *with advs.*: **~ about, around** *v.t.*: **they were ~ing a ball about** они́ гоня́ли мяч; (*discuss informally*): **~ an idea around** обсужда́ть (*impf.*) пробле́му в ча́стном поря́дке; (*treat badly*): **he felt he had been ~ed around too long** он чу́вствовал, что его́ сли́шком уж шпыня́ли; *v.i.* (*coll.*): **is his father still ~ing around?** его́ оте́ц ещё жив?; **there are plenty of jobs ~ing around** круго́м вака́нсий рабо́ты ско́лько уго́дно; **~ back** *v.t.*: **the goalie ~ed the ball back into play** вратáрь ввёл мяч в игру́; *v.i.* (*retaliate*) соверши́ть (*pf.*) отве́тный уда́р; (*recoil*) отдава́ть (*impf.*); (*US coll., relax*) рассл|абля́ться, -а́биться; **~ in** *v.t.*: **~ the door in** взл|а́мывать, -ома́ть дверь; **~ s.o.'s teeth in** выбива́ть, вы́бить кому́-н. зу́бы; **~ off** *v.t.* (*e.g. shoes*) сбр|а́сывать, -о́сить; *v.i.* (*football*) нач|ина́ть, -а́ть игру́; (*coll., begin*) нач|ина́ть, -а́ть; **~ out** *v.t.* (*eject, expel*) выгоня́ть, вы́гнать; вы́швырнуть (*pf.*); *v.i.* выбра́сывать, вы́бросить но́ги; ляга́ться (*impf.*); **~ over** *v.t.* опроки́|дывать, -нуть; **~ up** *v.t.*: **the herd ~ed up a cloud of dust** ста́до по́дняло о́блако пы́ли; **the horse ~ed up its heels** ло́шадь взбрыкну́ла; **he ~ed up a stone** он подбро́сил ка́мень ного́й; (*coll., create*): **~ up a row** устр|а́ивать, -о́ить сканда́л; **~ up a din** подн|има́ть, -я́ть шум.

● *cpds.* **~-back** *n.* (*recoil*) отда́ча; (*payment*) магары́ч; **~-boxing** *n.* кикбо́ксинг; **~-off** *n.* нача́ло (игры́); **~-start** *v.t.* (*lit. and fig.*): **to ~-start the economy** дать толчо́к эконо́мике; **~-starter** *n.* ножно́й ста́ртер.

kicker /'kɪkə(r)/ *n.* **1** (*sport*) игро́к, бью́щий по мячу́. **2** (*horse*) брыкли́вая ло́шадь. **3** (*US coll., clause in contract*) невы́годная статья́ (*в контра́кте*).

kid[1] /kɪd/ *n.* **1** (*young goat*) козлёнок. **2** (*leather*) шевро́ (*indecl.*); (*attr.*) шевро́вый; (*for gloves*) ла́йка; **~ glove** ла́йковая перча́тка; **use, wear ~ gloves** (*fig.*) осторо́жно/мя́гко обраща́ться (*impf.*) (*с кем*). **3** (*coll., child*) малы́ш; **he's just a ~** он всего́ лишь ребёнок; **my ~ brother** мой мла́дший брат; **that's ~(s') stuff!** ≈ просто́е де́ло; раз плю́нуть.

● *cpd.* **~-glove** *adj.*: **~-glove methods** делика́тные/осторо́жные ме́тоды.

kid[2] /kɪd/ *v.t.* (**kidded, kidding**) **1** (*coll., deceive*) над|ува́ть, -у́ть; **who are you ~ding?** кого́ вы хоти́те обману́ть?; **don't ~ yourself!** не обма́нывайте себя́! **2** (*tease*) дразни́ть (*impf.*); **~ s.o. on, along** води́ть (*impf.*) кого́-н. за́ нос.

● *v.i.* (**kidded, kidding**) (*tease with untruths*): **you're ~ding!** врёшь!

kidnap /'kɪdnæp/ *v.t.* (**kidnapped, kidnapping;** *US* **kidnaped, kidnaping**) пох|ища́ть, -и́тить.

kidnapper /'kɪdnæpə(r)/ *n.* похити́тель (*m.*).

kidney /'kɪdnɪ/ *n.* (*pl.* **~s**) по́чка; **~ machine** аппара́т «иску́сственная по́чка»; **~ transplant** переса́дка по́чек.

● *cpds.* **~-bean** *n.* фасо́ль (*collect.*); **~-shaped** *adj.* почкови́дный; **~-stone** *n.* по́чечный ка́мень.

Kiev /'ki:ev/ *n.* Ки́ев.

Kievan /'ki:ev(ə)n/ *n.* киевля́н|ин (*fem.* -ка).

● *adj.* ки́евский.

kill /kɪl/ *n.* **1** (*of hunted animal*) отстре́л; (*of enemy aircraft etc.*) уничтоже́ние; **be in at the ~** (*fig.*) прибы́ть (*pf.*) к дележу́ добы́чи.
2 (*animal(s) ~ed*) добы́ча; **a good ~** бога́тая добы́ча.

● *v.t.* **1** уб|ива́ть, -и́ть; (*rats etc.*) мори́ть, вы́-; **he was ~ed in an accident** он поги́б при ава́рии; **~ed in action** уби́т в бою́ (*or* на по́ле сраже́ния); **~ o.s.** (*lit.*) ко́нчить самоуби́йством; (*fig., coll.*) перенапряга́ться (*impf.*); **the villain gets ~ed in the end** злоде́й в конце́ концо́в погиба́ет; **~ two birds with one stone** уби́ть (*pf.*) двух за́йцев (одни́м уда́ром); **the shock ~ed her** она́ умерла́ от потрясе́ния; **my feet are ~ing me** я без за́дних ног; **the frost ~ed my roses** мои́ ро́зы поги́бли от моро́за.
2 (*animals for food*) ре́зать, за-; (*esp. in quantity*) заб|ива́ть, -и́ть; **the wolf ~ed the calf** волк заре́зал телёнка.
3 (*destroy, put an end to*) уничт|ожа́ть, -о́жить; разб|ива́ть, -и́ть; **this drug ~s the pain** э́то лека́рство снима́ет боль; **~ a proposal** провали́ть (*pf.*) предложе́ние.
4 (*neutralize, e.g. colours*) нейтрализова́ть (*impf., pf.*); **cigarettes ~ the appetite** сигаре́ты по́ртят аппети́т; **~ time** уб|ива́ть, -и́ть вре́мя.
5 (*coll., switch off*) выключа́ть, вы́ключить.
6 (*coll., finish off*): **shall we ~ the bottle?** разда́вим/прико́нчим буты́лку?
7 (*sport*): **~ the ball** (*football*) останови́ть (*pf.*) мяч; (*tennis*) погаси́ть (*pf.*) мяч.
8 (*overwhelm*): **~ s.o. with kindness** губи́ть, по- кого́-н. чрезме́рной доброто́й; **your jokes are ~ing me!** ва́ши шу́тки меня́ умори́ли!; **dressed to ~** разоде́тый в пух и прах.

● *v.i.*: **thou shalt not ~!** не убий!; **~ or cure** (*Br.*) ≈ риско́ванное сре́дство.

● *with adv.*: **~ off** *v.t.* переб|ива́ть, -и́ть.

● *cpd.* **~joy** *n.* брюзга́ (*c.g.*).

killer /'kɪlə(r)/ *n.* (*murderer*) уби́йца (*c.g.*); (*coll., something formidable*) что-н. производя́щее си́льный эффе́кт; **that wind's a ~** э́тот ве́тер невыноси́мый; **~ whale** коса́тка; (*coll., something hilarious*) что-н. умори́тельное; (*fatal disease*): **typhus is a ~** тиф — смерте́льная боле́знь.

killing /'kɪlɪŋ/ *n.* (*murder*) уби́йство; (*slaughter of animals*) убо́й, забо́й; (*fig., coll.*): **he made a ~** он сорва́л большо́й куш.

● *adj.* (*exhausting*) уби́йственный; (*amusing*) умори́тельный.

kiln /kɪln/ *n.* печь.

● *cpd.* **~-dry** *v.t.* суши́ть, вы́- в печи́.

kilo /'ki:ləʊ/ *n.* (*pl.* **kilos**) кило́ (*indecl.*).

kilobyte /'kɪlə,baɪt/ *n.* килоба́йт.

kilogram(me) /'kɪlə,græm/ *n.* килогра́мм.

kilohertz /'kɪlə,hɜ:ts/ *n.* килоге́рц.

kilometre /'kɪlə,mi:tə(r)/, *disp.* /kɪ'lɒmɪtə(r)/ (*US* **kilometer**) *n.* киломе́тр.

kiloton /'kɪlə,tʌn/ *n.* килото́нна.

kilowatt /'kɪlə,wɒt/ *n.* килова́тт.

● *cpd.* **~-hour** *n.* килова́тт-час.

kilt /kɪlt/ *n.* (шотла́ндская) ю́бка.

kimono /kɪ'məʊnəʊ/ *n.* (*pl.* **~s**) кимоно́ (*indecl.*).

kin /kɪn/ *n.* (*family*) семья́; (*relations*) родня́ (*collect.*); ро́дственники (*m. pl.*); **kith and ~** родны́е и бли́зкие; (*fig.*) бра́тья по кро́ви; **next of ~** ближа́йший ро́дственник, ближа́йшая ро́дственница.

kind /kaɪnd/ *n.* **1** (*race*) род; **human ~** род челове́ческий.
2 (*class, sort, variety*) род, сорт, разнови́дность; **all ~s of goods** вся́кие това́ры; **something of the ~** что́-то (*or* что́-нибудь) в э́том ро́де; **of a different (*or* another) ~** друго́го ро́да; **nothing of the ~** ничего́ подо́бного; **an actor of a ~** в изве́стном смы́сле актёр; **a ~ of** своего́ ро́да; **he is a ~ of actor** он в своём ро́де актёр; **one of a ~** у́никум; уника́льный; **two of a ~** (*at cards*) па́ра; (*fig.*) два сапога́ па́ра; **what ~ of?** что за?; како́й?; **what ~ of a painter is he?** что он за худо́жник?; **what ~ of box do you want?** како́го ро́да коро́бка вам нужна́?; **that ~ of**

person is never satisfied тако́й челове́к всегда́ че́м-то недово́лен; **that ~ of thing** таки́е ве́щи/шту́ки; всё в тако́м ро́де; **these ~s of people annoy me** лю́ди тако́го ти́па меня́ раздража́ют.
3: **~ of** (*coll., to some extent*): **I ~ of expected it** я как бы ожида́л э́того; **I felt ~ of sorry for him** мне его́ бы́ло ка́к-то жаль.
4 (*natural character*) ка́чество; **differ in ~** отлича́ться по ка́честву; различа́ться по свое́й приро́де.
5: **in ~** нату́рой; **pay in ~** плати́ть, за- нату́рой; **repay in ~** (*fig.*) отпла́|чивать, -ти́ть то́й же моне́той.
● *adj.* до́брый, любе́зный; **be so ~ as to close the door** бу́дьте любе́зны, закро́йте дверь; **with ~ regards** с серде́чным приве́том.
● *cpds.* **~-hearted** *adj.* добросерде́чный; **~heartedness** *n.* доброта́.

kinda /ˈkaɪndə/ *contraction of* ***kind of*** (*see* ⇨**kind** 3).

kindergarten /ˈkɪndəˌgɑːt(ə)n/ *n.* де́тский сад.

kindle /ˈkɪnd(ə)l/ *v.t.* разж|ига́ть, -е́чь; (*fig., arouse*) возбу|жда́ть, -ди́ть; (*evoke*) вызыва́ть, вы́звать.
● *v.i.* загор|а́ться, -е́ться; (*fig.*) вспы́х|ивать, -нуть.

kindliness /ˈkaɪndlɪnɪs/ *n.* доброта́.

kindling /ˈkɪndlɪŋ/ *n.* (*firewood*) расто́пка; ще́пки (*f. pl.*).

kindly /ˈkaɪndlɪ/ *adj.* (**kindlier, kindliest**) до́брый, доброду́шный; (*fig., of climate etc.*) благоприя́тный, мя́гкий.
● *adv.* **1** (*in a kind manner*) любе́зно, ми́ло. **2** (*please*): **~ ring me tomorrow** бу́дьте добры́, позвони́те мне за́втра. **3**: **he took ~ to my suggestion** он хорошо́ отнёсся к моему́ предложе́нию; **he does not take ~ to criticism** он не лю́бит кри́тики.

kindness /ˈkaɪndnɪs/ *n.* **1** (*benevolence, kind nature*) доброта́; **he was ~ itself** он был сама́ доброта́; **he did it out of (the) ~ (of his heart)** он сде́лал э́то по доброте́ (серде́чной). **2** (*kind act; service*) любе́зность; одолже́ние; **do s.o. a ~** ока́з|ывать, -а́ть кому́-н. любе́зность; де́лать, с- кому́-н. одолже́ние.

kindred /ˈkɪndrɪd/ *adj.* (*lit., fig.*) ро́дственный; **~ ideas** ро́дственные иде́и; **a ~ spirit** родна́я душа́.

kinetic /kɪˈnetɪk/, /kaɪ-/ *adj.* кинети́ческий.

kinetics /kɪˈnetɪks/, /kaɪ-/ *n.* кине́тика.

king /kɪŋ/ *n.* **1** коро́ль (*m.*); (*anc. and bibl.*) царь (*m.*); **the K~'s English** пра́вильный англи́йский язы́к; **K~ of K~s** Царь Царе́й. **2** (*fig.*): **~ of beasts/birds** царь звере́й/птиц; (*chess*): **White K~** бе́лый коро́ль; **~'s pawn** короле́вская пе́шка; (*draughts, checkers*) да́мка; (*cards*): **~ of diamonds** бубно́вый коро́ль.
● *cpds.* **~fisher** *n.* (голубо́й) зиморо́док; **~pin** *n.* (*bolt*) шкво́рень (*m.*); (*fig.*) гла́вное лицо́; **~-size(d)** *adj.* кру́пный; бо́льшего разме́ра.

kingdom /ˈkɪŋdəm/ *n.* короле́вство; **the United K~** Соединённое Короле́вство; **the animal ~** живо́тное ца́рство; **the ~ of heaven** ца́рство небе́сное; **you'll wait from now to ~ come** (*coll.*) ну, тепе́рь бу́дете ждать до второ́го прише́ствия.

king|like /ˈkɪŋlaɪk/, **-ly** /ˈkɪŋlɪ/ *adjs.* короле́вский, ца́рский; (*fig.*) вели́чественный.

kink /kɪŋk/ *n.* (*in rope etc.*) переги́б; (*in metal*) изги́б; (*fig., in character*) причу́да.

kinky /ˈkɪŋkɪ/ *adj.* (**kinkier, kinkiest**) (*twisted*) кручёный; (*coll., perverted*) извращённый; со стра́нностями.

kinsfolk /ˈkɪnzfəʊk/ *n.* родня́ (*collect.*).

kinship /ˈkɪnʃɪp/ *n.* (*relationship*) родство́; (*similarity*) схо́дство.

kinsman /ˈkɪnzmən/ *n.* ро́дственник.

kinswoman /ˈkɪnzˌwʊmən/ *n.* ро́дственница.

kiosk /ˈkiːɒsk/ *n.* кио́ск; **telephone ~** (*Br.*) телефо́нная бу́дка, автома́т.

kip /kɪp/ (*Br.*) *n.* (*coll., sleep*) сон.
● *v.i.* (**kipped, kipping**) **1**: **~ down for the night** устро́иться (*pf.*) на ночь. **2** (*sleep*) кема́рить, по- (*coll.*).

kipper /ˈkɪpə(r)/ *n.* копчёная селёдка.
● *v.t.* копти́ть, за-.

Kirghiz /kɪəˈgɪz/, /ˈkɜːgɪz/ *n.* (*pl.* **~**) (*person*) кирги́з (*fem.* -ка); (*language*) кирги́зский язы́к.
● *adj.* кирги́зский.

Kirghizia /kɜːˈgiːzɪə/ *n.* Кирги́зия.

kirk /kɜːk/ *n.* шотла́ндская (пресвитериа́нская) це́рковь.

kirsch /kɪəʃ/ *n.* вишнёвая во́дка, киршва́ссер.

kiss /kɪs/ *n.* поцелу́й; **give s.o. a ~ on the cheek** поцелова́ть (*pf.*) кого́-н. в щёку; **blow s.o. a ~** посла́ть (*pf.*) кому́-н. возду́шный поцелу́й; **steal a ~** сорва́ть (*pf.*) поцелу́й; **~ of life** иску́сственное дыха́ние; **Judas ~** поцелу́й Иу́ды.
● *v.t.* целова́ть, по-; **he ~ed away her tears** поцелу́ями он осуши́л её слёзы; **they ~ed each other goodbye** они́ поцелова́лись на проща́ние; **you can ~ goodbye to the inheritance** вы мо́жете распроща́ться с насле́дством; пла́кало ва́ше насле́дство; **~ the rod** (*fig.*) поко́рно прин|има́ть, -я́ть наказа́ние.
● *v.i.* целова́ться, по-.
● *cpd.* **~-curl** *n.* ло́кон на лбу (*or* у виска́).

kisser /ˈkɪsə(r)/ *n.* (*sl., mouth*) ва́режка (*sl.*).

kit /kɪt/ *n.* (*Br., personal equipment, esp. clothing*) снаряже́ние; **a soldier's ~** солда́тское снаряже́ние; (*workman's tools*) набо́р инструме́нтов; (*for particular sport or activity*) набо́р/компле́кт (спорти́вных) принадле́жностей; **survival ~** набо́р са́мого необходи́мого; (*set of parts for assembly*) констру́ктор.
● *v.t. & i.* (**kitted, kitting**) (*Br.*) (*usu.* **~ out, up**) снаря|жа́ть(ся), -ди́ть(ся).
● *cpd.* **~bag** *n.* вещево́й мешо́к/ра́нец; вещмешо́к.

kitchen /ˈkɪtʃɪn/, /-tʃ(ə)n/ *n.* ку́хня; **~ garden** огоро́д; **~ sink** мо́йка; ра́ковина.
● *cpd.* **~-ware** *n.* ку́хонная у́тварь.

kitchenette /ˌkɪtʃɪˈnet/, /-tʃəˈnet/ *n.* ма́ленькая ку́хонька.

kite /kaɪt/ *n.* **1** (*bird*) (кра́сный) ко́ршун. **2** (*toy*) (возду́шный/бума́жный) змей; **fly a ~** (*lit.*) запус|ка́ть, -ти́ть змея́; (*fig., to test reaction*) пус|ка́ть, -ти́ть про́бный шар.

kith /kɪθ/ *see* ⇨**kin**

kitsch /kɪtʃ/ *n.* китч, дешёвка.

kitten /ˈkɪt(ə)n/ *n.* котёнок; **our cat has had ~s** на́ша ко́шка окоти́лась; у на́шей ко́шки котя́та; **she nearly had ~s** (*coll.*) она́ чуть на сте́нку не поле́зла.

kittenish /ˈkɪtənɪʃ/ *adj.* игри́вый.

kittiwake /ˈkɪtɪˌweɪk/ *n.* моёвка.

kitty /ˈkɪtɪ/ *n.* (*at cards etc.*) пу́лька, банк; (*cat*) ки́ска.

kiwi /ˈkiːwiː/ *n.* (*pl.* **kiwis**) ки́ви (*f. indecl.*); **K~** (*coll.*) новозела́нд|ец (*fem.* -ка).

KKK /ˌkuːklʌksˈklæn ˌkjuː-/ *n.* (*abbr. of* ***Ku Klux Klan***) ККК (ку-клукс-кла́н).

Klansman /ˈklænzmən/ *n.* куклуксклა́новец.

klaxon /ˈklæks(ə)n/ *n.* (*propr.*) кла́ксон.

kleptomania /ˌkleptəʊˈmeɪnɪə/ *n.* клептома́ния.

kleptomaniac /ˌkleptəʊˈmeɪnɪˌæk/ *n.* клептома́н (*fem.* -ка).

km. /ˈkɪləˌmiːtə(r)(z)/, *disp.* /kɪˈlɒmɪtə(r)(z)/ *n.* (*abbr. of* ***kilometre(s)***) км (киломе́тр).

knack /næk/ *n.* (*skill, faculty*) сноро́вка, уме́ние; **have the ~ of** име́ть (*impf.*) сноро́вку (*в чём*); **there's a ~ to it** де́ло тре́бует сноро́вки.

knacker /ˈnækə(r)/ *n.* (*Br.*) ску́пщик ста́рых лошаде́й; **~'s yard** живодёрня.

knackered /ˈnækəd/ *adj.* (*Br. coll.*) измо́танный.

knapsack /ˈnæpsæk/ *n.* ра́нец.

knave /neɪv/ *n.* **1** (*arch., rogue*) плут, моше́нник. **2** (*cards*) вале́т; **~ of hearts** вале́т черве́й.

knavery /ˈneɪvərɪ/ *n.* плутовство́.

knavish /ˈneɪvɪʃ/ *adj.* плутовско́й.

knead /niːd/ *v.t.* (*e.g. dough or clay*) меси́ть, за-/с-; (*massage*) масси́ровать (*impf., pf.*).

knee /niː/ *n.* коле́н|о (*pl.* -и); **he was on his ~s** он стоя́л на коле́нях; **go down on one's ~s** (*or* **on bended ~**) стать/упа́сть (*pf.*) на коле́ни (*fig.*); **go on one's ~s to s.o.** на коле́нях моли́ть (*impf.*) кого́-н.; **bring s.o. to his ~s** ста́вить, по- кого́-н. на коле́ни; **I went weak at the ~s** у меня́ задрожа́ли поджи́лки (*or* подкоси́лись но́ги); **I learnt it at my mother's ~** я впита́л э́то

K

с молоко́м ма́тери; **they were up to their ~s in mud** они́ бы́ли по коле́но в грязи́; **the ~s of his trousers were worn** его́ брю́ки протёрлись в коле́нках.

● *v.t.* (**knees, kneed, kneeing**) уд|аря́ть, -а́рить коле́ном.

● *cpds.* **~-bend** *n.* приседа́ние; **~-breeches** *n. pl.* бри́дж|и (*pl., g.* -ей); **~-cap** *n.* коле́нная ча́шка; (*protection*) наколе́нник; **~-capping** *n.* (*Br.*) вы́стрел в коле́нную ча́шку; **~-deep** *pred. adj. & adv.*: **he stood ~-deep in water** он стоя́л по коле́но в воде́; **~-high** *pred. adj. & adv.* (*reaching to the* ~): **the grass was ~-high** трава́ была́ по коле́но; **~-jerk** *adj.* автомати́ческий, непроизво́льный; **~ joint** *n.* (*anat.*) коле́нный суста́в; (*tech.*) коле́нчатое сочлене́ние; **~-length** *adj.* до коле́н; **~s-up** *n.* (*Br. coll.*) весёлая вечери́нка.

kneel /ni:l/ *v.i.* (*past and p.p.* **knelt** *or esp. US* **kneeled**) **1** (*also* **~ down**: *go down on one's knees*) ста|нови́ться, -ть на коле́ни; **~ to s.o.** преклон|я́ть, -и́ть коле́на пе́ред кем-н. **2** (*be in ~ing position*) стоя́ть (*impf.*) на коле́нях; **they knelt in prayer** они́ моли́лись на коле́нях.

knell /nel/ *n.* погреба́льный/похоро́нный звон; (*fig.*): **his death sounded the ~ of their hopes** его́ смерть означа́ла коне́ц их наде́ждам.

knelt /nelt/ *past and p.p. of* ⇒**kneel**

knew /nju:/ *past of* ⇒**know**

knickerbockers /ˈnɪkəˌbɒkəz/ *n.* бри́дж|и (*pl., g.* -ей).

knickers /ˈnɪkəz/ *n.* (*Br., undergarment*) тру́сик|и (*pl., g.* -ов).

(k)nick-(k)nack /ˈnɪknæk/ *n.* безделу́шка.

knife /naɪf/ *n.* (*pl.* **knives**) нóж; (*pocket* ~) но́жик; **hold a ~ to s.o.'s throat** прист|ава́ть, -а́ть с ножо́м к го́рлу к кому́-н.; **you could cut the atmosphere with a ~** во́здух был тако́й, что хоть топо́р ве́шай; атмосфе́ра была́ накалённая.

● *v.t.* зак|а́лывать, -оло́ть ножо́м.

● *cpds.* **~-edge** *n.* (*blade*) остриё ножа́; **on a ~-edge** (*fig.*) craft вися́щий на волоске́; **~-grinder** *n.* точи́льщик; **~-point** *n.*: **at ~-point** угрожа́я ножо́м.

knight /naɪt/ *n.* **1** (*hist.*) ры́царь (*m.*). **2** (*member of order*) кавале́р; **K~ of the Garter** кавале́р о́рдена Подвя́зки. **3** (*chess*) конь (*m.*).

● *v.t.* (*hist.*) возв|оди́ть, -ести́ в ры́царское досто́инство; (*mod.*) ≈ присв|а́ивать, -о́ить (*кому*) ненасле́дственное дворя́нское зва́ние.

● *cpds.* **~-errant** *n.* стра́нствующий ры́царь; **~-errantry** *n.* донкихо́тство.

knighthood /ˈnaɪthʊd/ *n.* ры́царство; ры́царское зва́ние; **he was recommended for a ~** его́ предста́вили к ры́царскому зва́нию.

knit /nɪt/ *v.t.* (**knitting;** *past and p.p.* **knitted** *or* **knit**) **1**: **~ wool into stockings** (*or* **stockings from wool**) вяза́ть, с- чулки́ из ше́рсти; **~ up** (*repair*) што́пать, за-; **hand-/machine-~ted garments** вя́заная/трикота́жная оде́жда; вя́занки (*f. pl.*). **2** (*fasten; also* **~ together**) скреп|ля́ть, -и́ть; (*unite*) соедин|я́ть, -и́ть. **3**: **~ one's brows** хму́рить, на-бро́ви; хму́риться, на-.

● *v.i.* (**knitting;** *past and p.p.* **knitted** *or* **knit**) **1** (*do ~ting*) вяза́ть (*impf.*). **2** (*of bones*) сраст|а́ться, -и́сь.

● *cpd.* **~wear** *n.* трикота́жные изде́лия.

knitting /ˈnɪtɪŋ/ *n.* (*action*) вяза́ние; (*fig.*) скрепле́ние, соедине́ние; (*material being knitted*) вяза́нье.

● *cpds.* **~-machine** *n.* вяза́льная маши́на; **~-needle** *n.* вяза́льная спи́ца; **~-yarn** *n.* трикота́жная пря́жа.

knives /naɪvz/ *pl. of* ⇒**knife**

knob /nɒb/ *n.* **1** (*protuberance*) вы́пуклость; (*on body*) ши́шка. **2** (*handle*) ру́чка; (*button*) кно́пка. **3** (*of butter etc.*) кусо́чек.

knobbly /ˈnɒblɪ/ *adj.* шишкова́тый.

knock /nɒk/ *n.* **1** (*rap, rapping sound*) стук; **double ~** двукра́тный стук; **give a ~ on the door** стуча́ть, по- в дверь; **there came a loud ~** разда́лся гро́мкий стук. **2** (*sound of ~ing in engine*) (детонацио́нный) стук; детона́ция; **anti-~** (*additive*) антидетона́тор. **3** (*blow*) уда́р; **he got a nasty ~ on the head** он си́льно уда́рился голово́й. **4** (*fig.*): **the pound has taken some ~s lately** в после́днее вре́мя курс фу́нта сте́рлингов си́льно пострада́л.

● *v.t.* **1** (*hit*) удар|я́ть, -а́рить; **the blow ~ed him flat** уда́р сбил его́ с ног; **he ~ed the ball into the net** он заби́л мяч в се́тку; **he ~ed the table with his hammer** он уда́рил по́ столу молотко́м; **she ~ed her arm against the chair** она́ сту́кнулась руко́й о стул; **he ~ed a nail into the wall** он вбил гвоздь в сте́ну; **he ~ed a hole in, through the wall** он проби́л ды́рку в стене́; **he ~ed the glass off the table** он смахну́л стака́н со стола́; **~ s.o. on, over the head** уда́рить/сту́кнуть (*both pf.*) кого́-н. по голове́; **I ~ed the gun out of his hand** я вы́бил из его́ руки́ пистоле́т. **2** (*fig. uses*): **the idea was ~ed on the head** (*Br.*) э́тому предложе́нию не да́ли хо́ду; **I tried to ~ some sense into his head** я пыта́лся впра́вить ему́ мозги́ (*or* образу́мить его́); **~ into shape** прив|оди́ть, -ести́ в поря́док; **he ~ed the ash off his cigarette** он стряхну́л пе́пел с папиро́сы; **I'll ~ a pound off the price** я сбро́шу/ски́ну/сба́влю фунт с цены́; **he ~ed five seconds off the record time** он поби́л реко́рд на пять секу́нд. **3** (*criticize*) ха́ять (*impf.*) (*sl.*).

● *v.i.* **1** (*rap*) стуча́ть; **~ at the door** стуча́ть(ся), по- в дверь; **'~ before entering'** «без сту́ка не входи́ть»; **~ on wood** (*US*) тьфу-тьфу́, не сгла́зить! **2**: **~ against** (*collide with*) нат|ыка́ться, -кну́ться на + *a.*; (*coll., meet*) столкну́ться (*pf.*) с + *i.* **3** (*of engine*) стуча́ть (*impf.*). **4** (*coll., travel*): **he spent a year ~ing round Europe** он год болта́лся по Евро́пе.

● *with advs.*: **~ about** *v.t.* (*treat roughly*) помя́ть/намя́ть (*pf.*) бока́ (*кому*); лома́ть, по-/с- (*что*); *v.i. also* **~ (a)round** (*travel, wander*): **he's ~ed about a bit in his time** он в своё вре́мя побродил/поёздил по све́ту; (*Br. coll., keep company*): **she's ~ing around with a married man** она́ связа́лась с жена́тым челове́ком; **~ back** *v.t.* (*lit.*): **the electric shock ~ed him back against the wall** уда́ром то́ка его́ отбро́сило к стене́; (*Br., disconcert*): **the news ~ed me back** изве́стие привело́ меня́ в замеша́тельство; (*coll., consume*): **he can ~ back 5 pints in as many minutes** он за пять мину́т мо́жет опроки́нуть/вы́лакать пять кру́жек (пи́ва); (*Br. coll., cost*): **that will ~ me back a bit** э́то ста́нет мне в копе́ечку; **~ down** *v.t.* (*strike to ground*) сби|ва́ть, -ть с ног; вали́ть, с-; **he was ~ed down by a car** его́ сбила маши́на; **you could have ~ed me down with a feather** я был поражён как мо́лнией; (*demolish*) сн|оси́ть, -ести́; (*dismantle*) раз|бира́ть, -обра́ть; (*reduce*) сн|ижа́ть, -и́зить; **~ in** *v.t.*: **~ a nail in** вби|ва́ть, -ть (*or* заб|ива́ть, -и́ть) гвоздь; **~ off** *v.t.* (*lit.*) сби|ва́ть, -ть; сшиб|а́ть, -и́ть; сма́х|ивать, -ну́ть; (*coll. uses*): (*deduct from price*) сб|авля́ть, -а́вить; (*compose or complete rapidly*): **he can ~ off an article in half an hour** он мо́жет состря́пать/сварга́нить (*sl.*) статью́ за полчаса́; (*Br., steal*) ти́брить, с- (*sl.*); (*kill*) прик|а́нчивать, -о́нчить (*coll.*); *v.i.* (*stop work*) шаба́шить, по- (*sl.*); **~ out** *v.t.* (*lit.*): **he ~ed a pane out** он вы́бил стекло́ из ра́мы; **he ~ed two of my teeth out** он вы́бил мне два зу́ба; (*empty by ~ing*): **he ~ed out his pipe** он вы́колотил/вы́бил тру́бку; (*make unconscious*) оглуш|а́ть, -и́ть; **the blow on his head ~ed him out** он был оглушён уда́ром по голове́; (*boxing*) нокаути́ровать (*impf., pf.*); (*overwhelm*) потряс|а́ть, -ти́; (*eliminate from contest*): **he was ~ed out in the first round** он вы́был в пе́рвом ту́ре; **~ over** *v.t.* опроки́|дывать, -нуть; **~ together** *v.t.*: **he ~ed together a cupboard** он на́спех сколоти́л шкаф; **~ up** *v.t.* (*Br., prepare*): **I can soon ~ up a meal** я на́скоро/бы́стренько пригото́влю еду́; (*Br., waken*) буди́ть, раз-; (*sl., exhaust*) выма́тывать, вы́мотать; (*US, make pregnant*) обрюха́тить (*pf.*) (*sl.*); *v.i.* (*Br., tennis*) разм|ина́ться, -я́ться (*coll.*).

● *cpds.* **~about** *adj.*: **~about humour** (*Br.*), **humor** (*US*) гру́бый фарс; **~down** *adj.*: **at a ~down price** по дешёвке (*coll.*); **~-kneed** *adj.* с вы́вернутыми внутрь коле́нями; **~out** *n.* (*boxing*) нока́ут; (*Br., competition*) соревнова́ния (*nt. pl.*) по олимпи́йской систе́ме; (*fig., something striking*) не́что сногсшиба́тельное; (*attr.*): **~out blow** сокруши́тельный уда́р; **~-up** *n.* (*Br., tennis*) разми́нка.

knocker /ˈnɒkə(r)/ *n.* (*on door*) (дверно́й) молото́к.

knocking /ˈnɒkɪŋ/ *n.* (*noise*) стук.

knocking-shop /ˈnɒkɪŋˌʃɒp/ *n.* (*Br. sl.*) публи́чный дом.

knoll /nəʊl/ *n.* хо́лмик, буго́р, бугоро́к.

knot /nɒt/ *n.* **1** (*in rope etc.*; *in wood*; *measure of speed*) у́зел; **tie a ~ in a rope** завя́з|ывать, -а́ть у́зел на верёвке; **tie something in a ~** завя́з|ывать, -а́ть что-н. узло́м; **tie o.s. (up) in(to) ~s** (*fig.*) запу́таться (*pf.*); **cut the Gordian ~** разруби́ть (*pf.*) го́рдиев у́зел; **a vessel of 20 ~s** су́дно со ско́ростью два́дцать узло́в; **we are flying at 500 ~s** мы лети́м со ско́ростью 500 узло́в. **2** (*group, cluster*) ку́чка.

● *v.t. & i.* (**knotted, knotting**) завя́з|ывать(ся), -а́ть(ся).

● *cpd.* **~-hole** *n.* дыра́ от сучка́.

knotted /ˈnɒtɪd/ *adj.* **1** (*also* **knotty**: *gnarled*) узлова́тый, сучкова́тый. **2**: **a ~ed rope** верёвка с узла́ми; верёвка, завя́занная узло́м.

knotty /ˈnɒtɪ/ *adj.* (**knottier, knottiest**) **1** = **knotted** 1. **2**: **a ~ problem** запу́танная/тру́дная пробле́ма.

knout /naʊt/, /nu:t/ *n.* кнут.

know /nəʊ/ *n.*: **be in the ~** быть в ку́рсе де́ла.

● *v.t.* (*past* **knew;** *p.p.* **known**) **1** (*be aware, have knowledge of*) знать (*impf.*); **I ~ nothing about it** я об э́том ничего́ не зна́ю; **I ~ for a fact that ...** я достове́рно зна́ю, что...; **as far as I ~** наско́лько мне изве́стно; **for all I ~** почём (*sl.*) мне знать; кто его́ зна́ет; **don't I ~!** мне да (*or* мне ли э́того) не знать!; **who ~s?** как знать?; **I wouldn't ~** пра́во, не зна́ю; отку́да мне знать?; **he let it be ~n that ...** он дал поня́ть, что...; **never let it be ~n** никогда́ в э́том не признава́йтесь; **you (should) ~ best** вам лу́чше знать; **father ~s best** оте́ц зна́ет лу́чше; **before I knew it we had arrived** я не успе́л огляну́ться, как мы при́были; **before you ~ where you are** не успе́ешь огляну́ться; в два счёта; **I knew it!** (я) так и знал!; **I don't ~ that I like this** я не уве́рен, что мне э́то нра́вится; мне э́то не сли́шком нра́вится; **he ~s what's what** он зна́ет, что к чему́; **he ~s his own mind** он зна́ет, чего́ (он) хо́чет; **he doesn't ~ his own mind** он сам не зна́ет, чего́ хо́чет; он не мо́жет ни на что реши́ться; **he ~s a thing or two** он ко́е в чём разбира́ется; он зна́ет, что к чему́; **he has been ~n to be wrong** у него́ быва́ли оши́бки; **he has been ~n to steal** ворова́ть ему́ не вно́ве; **he is ~n to have been married before** изве́стно, что он уже́ был жена́т; **I ~ what!** вот что!; зна́ете что?; **you ~ what? (***US* **you ~ something?)** зна́ете что?; **you ~ what he is** (ну, да) вы его́ зна́ете; вы зна́ете, како́й он; **he ~s what he is about** он своё де́ло зна́ет; **I meant to be early, but you ~ what it is** я собира́лся прийти́ пора́ньше, но зна́ете, как э́то быва́ет. **2** (*recognize, distinguish*) знать, у-; узн|ава́ть, -а́ть; отлич|а́ть, -и́ть; **I ~ him by sight** я зна́ю его́ в лицо́; **he knew her at once** он её сра́зу узна́л; **I shouldn't ~ him from his brother** я его́ не отличи́л бы от бра́та; **I don't ~ him from Adam** я его́ (в жи́зни) в глаза́ не вида́л; **I knew him for a liar** я знал, что он лжец; **I'd ~ him anywhere** я узна́ю его́ да́же во сне; **he is ~n as a gambler** за ним во́дится сла́ва игрока́; **he is ~n to his friends as Jumbo** друзья́ кли́чут его́ Слоно́м; **he ~s a good thing when he sees it** он понима́ет, что хорошо́ и что пло́хо; у него́ губа́ не ду́ра.
3 (*be acquainted, familiar with*) знать (*impf.*); быть знако́мым с + *i.*; **get to ~ s.o.** знако́миться, по- с кем-н.; **I have ~n him since childhood** я с ним знако́м с де́тства; **I ~ him slightly** у меня́ с ним ша́почное знако́мство; **I don't ~ him to speak to** я с ним недоста́точно знако́м, что́бы вступа́ть в разгово́р; **make o.s. ~n to s.o.** предст|авля́ться, -а́виться кому́-н.; **he is ~n to the police** он у поли́ции на заме́тке.
4 (*be versed in; understand; have experience in*) зна́ть (*impf.*), понима́ть (*impf.*), разбира́ться (*impf.*) в + *p.*; **he ~s Russian** он зна́ет ру́сский язы́к; он владе́ет ру́сским языко́м; **~ by heart** знать наизу́сть/назубо́к (*coll.*); **~ how to** уме́ть, с-.
5 (*experience*): **he ~s no peace** он не зна́ет поко́я; **he has ~n many privations** он пережи́л/испыта́л мно́го лише́ний; **I have ~n worse to happen** мне изве́стны слу́чаи и поху́же; **I have never ~n him tell a lie** я не по́мню, что́бы он когда́-нибудь солга́л.
6 (*be subject to*): **he ~s no shame** он не ве́дает стыда́; **her happiness knew no bounds** её сча́стье не зна́ло грани́ц; её сча́стью не́ было преде́ла; *see also* ⇒**known**

● *v.i.* (*past* **knew;** *p.p.* **known**): **let s.o. ~** сообщ|а́ть, -и́ть (*or* да|ва́ть, -ть знать) кому́-н.; **will you let me ~?** вы сообщи́те мне?; **(the) Lord only ~s!** Бог его́ зна́ет!; одному́ Бо́гу изве́стно!; **how should I ~?** почём я зна́ю?; **what do you ~ (about that)?** поду́майте (то́лько)!; ишь ты!; **you never ~** как знать?; **he doesn't want to ~** (*refuses to take notice, interest*) он (и) знать не хо́чет; **you never ~, he may come back** как знать, он мо́жет и верну́ться; **I ~ better than to ...** я не так прост, что́бы...; **I should have ~n better than to ask his advice** и дёрнуло же меня́ спроси́ть его́ сове́та!; **(do) you ~** (*in parenthesis*) зна́ете ли; понима́ете; **it's too hot to work, you ~** жа́рко рабо́тать-то; **do you ~ of a good restaurant?** вы зна́ете (*or* вы мо́жете порекомендова́ть) хоро́ший рестора́н?; **'Have you met him?' — 'Not that I ~ of'** «Вы встреча́лись с ним?» — «Наско́лько мне изве́стно, нет»; **I don't ~ him, but I ~ of him** ли́чно я с ним незнако́м, но наслы́шан о нём; **did you ~ about the accident?** вы зна́ли об э́том несча́стном слу́чае?; **he ~s about cars** он разбира́ется в маши́нах; **I don't ~ about that** (*expr. doubt*) я не зна́ю; сомнева́юсь.

● *cpds.* **~-all** *n.* (*US* **~-it-all**) всезна́йка (*c.g.*); **~-how** *n.* уме́ние; но́у-ха́у; о́пыт; у́ровень (*m.*) зна́ний; секре́ты (*m. pl.*) произво́дства; техноло́гия; **have the ~-how** облада́ть (*impf.*) уме́нием; (*body of experience*): **professional/technical ~-how** профессиона́льные/техни́ческие на́выки (*m. pl.*).

knowable /ˈnəʊəb(ə)l/ *adj.* познава́емый.

knowing /ˈnəʊɪŋ/ *n.*: **there's no ~ what may happen** невозмо́жно предви́деть, что мо́жет случи́ться/произойти́; **I did it without ~** я сде́лал э́то бессозна́тельно.

● *adj.* (*significant*): **a ~ look** понима́ющий/многозначи́тельный взгляд.

knowingly /ˈnəʊɪŋlɪ/ *adv.* (*significantly*) многозначи́тельно; (*intentionally, consciously*) наро́чно, созна́тельно.

K

knowledge /ˈnɒlɪdʒ/ *n.* зна́ние; **he has a thorough ~ of Russian** у него́ основа́тельные зна́ния по ру́сскому языку́; **field, branch of ~** о́бласть зна́ния; о́трасль нау́ки; (*understanding*): **our ~ of the subject is as yet limited** на́ши позна́ния в э́той о́бласти пока́ ограни́чены; (*experience*) о́пыт; (*information*) изве́стия (*nt. pl.*), све́дения (*nt. pl.*); **our earliest ~ of the Slavs** на́ши пе́рвые све́дения о славя́нах; **I have no ~ of that** я не име́ю об э́том све́дений; (*range of information or experience*): **to the best of my ~** наско́лько мне изве́стно; **it came to my ~ that ...** мне ста́ло изве́стно, что...; **to my certain ~** как мне достове́рно изве́стно; **not to my ~** мне э́то неизве́стно; наско́лько я зна́ю — нет; **without s.o.'s ~** без чьего́-н. ве́дома.

knowledgeable /ˈnɒlɪdʒəb(ə)l/ *adj.* хорошо́ осведомлённый.

known /nəʊn/ *adj.* изве́стный; **it is a ~ fact that ...** изве́стно, что...; **a scene ~ to him from childhood** карти́на, знако́мая ему́ с де́тства; *see also* ⇒**know** *v.t.*

knuckle /ˈnʌk(ə)l/ *n.* **1** (*anat.*) суста́в; **rap s.o. over the ~s** (*fig.*) дать (*pf.*) нагоня́й кому́-н.; **near the ~** (*Br. coll.*) на гра́ни неприли́чного; скабрёзный, риско́ванный. **2** (*joint of meat*) но́жка, голя́шка.

● *v.i.*: **~ down to one's work** прин|има́ться, -я́ться за де́ло; **~ under (to)** уступ|а́ть, -и́ть (+ *d.*); покор|я́ться, -и́ться (+ *d.*).

● *cpds.* **~-bone** *n.* ба́бка; **~-duster** *n.* касте́т.

KO (*abbr. of* ***knockout***) нока́ут.

● *v.t.* нокаути́ровать (*impf., pf.*).

koala /kəʊˈɑːlə/ *n.* **(~ bear)** коа́ла (*m.*), су́мчатый медве́дь.

kohlrabi /kəʊlˈrɑːbɪ/ *n.* (*pl.* **~es**) кольра́би (*f. indecl.*).

kolinsky /kəˈlɪnskɪ/ *n.* колоно́к; (*fur*) мех колонка́.

kolkhoz /ˈkɒlkɒz/, /kʌlkˈhɔːz/ *n.* колхо́з.

Komsomol /ˈkɒmsəˌmɒl/ *n.* (*association*) комсомо́л; (*member*) комсомо́л|ец (*fem.* -ка); (*attr.*) комсомо́льский.

kopeck /ˈkəʊpek/, /ˈkɒpek/ = **copeck**

Koran /kɔːˈrɑːn/, /kə-/ *n.* кора́н.

Korea /kəˈriːə/ *n.* Коре́я.

Korean /kəˈriːən/ *m.* (*person*) коре́|ец (*fem.* -я́нка); (*language*) коре́йский язы́к.

● *adj.* коре́йский.

kosher /ˈkəʊʃə(r)/, /ˈkɒʃ-/ *adj.* коше́рный.

Kosovan /ˈkɒsəv(ə)n/ *n.* жи́тель (*fem.* -ница) Ко́сово.

● *adj.* ко́совский.

Kosovar /ˈkɒsəˌvɑː(r)/ *n.* & *adj.* = **Kosovan**

Kosovo /ˈkɒsəvə/ *n.* Ко́сово (*indecl.*).

koumiss /ˈkuːmɪs/ *n.* кумы́с.

ko(w)tow /kaʊˈtaʊ/ *n.* ни́зкий покло́н.

● *v.i.* де́лать, с- ни́зкий покло́н; (*fig.*) раболе́пствовать (*impf.*), пресмыка́ться (*impf.*) (*перед кем*).

kremlin /ˈkremlɪn/ *n.* кремль (*m.*); **the K~** Кремль; (*attr.*) кремлёвский.

Kremlinologist /ˌkremlɪnˈɒlədʒɪst/ *n.* кремлеве́д, кремлино́лог.

Kremlinology /ˌkremlɪnˈɒlədʒɪ/ *n.* кремлеве́дение, кремлиноло́гия.

krypton /ˈkrɪptɒn/ *n.* (*chem.*) крипто́н.

kudos /ˈkjuːdɒs/ *n.* сла́ва.

Ku Klux Klan /ˌkuːklʌksˈklæn/, /ˌkjuː-/ *n.* ку-клукс-кла́н.

Ku Klux Klaner /ˌkuːklʌksˈklænə(r)/, /ˌkjuː-/ куклукскла́новец.

kulak /ˈkuːlæk/ *n.* (*hist.*) кула́к.

kumquat /ˈkʌmkwɒt/ *n.* (*bot.*) кумква́т.

kung fu /kʊŋ ˈfuː/, /kʌŋ/ *n.* кун-фу́ (*nt. indecl.*).

Kurd /kɜːd/ *n.* курд (*fem.* -ка).

Kurdish /ˈkɜːdɪʃ/ *n.* ку́рдский язы́к.

● *adj.* ку́рдский.

Kurdistan /ˌkɜːdɪˈstɑːn/ *n.* Курдиста́н.

Kuwait /kʊˈweɪt/ *n.* Куве́йт.

Kuwaiti /kʊˈweɪtɪ/ *n.* куве́йт|ец (*fem.* -ка).

● *adj.* куве́йтский.

kvass /kvɑːs/ *n.* квас.

kW /ˈkɪləˌwɒt/ *n.* (*abbr. of* ***kilowatt(s)***) кВт (килова́тт).

Ll

L (*abbr. of* **learner**) (*Br.*): **~-plate** ≈ щито́к с на́дписью «учёбная» (*на машине*).

l. /ˈliːtə(r)(z)/ *n.* (*abbr. of* **litre(s)**) л (литр).

la /lɑː/ *n.* = **lah**

lab /læb/ (*coll.*) = **laboratory**

label /ˈleɪb(ə)l/ *n.* ярлы́к, этике́тка; **(stick-on ~)** накле́йка; (*tag*) би́рка; **pin, stick a ~ on** (*lit., fig.*) прикле́и|вать, -ть ярлы́к/этике́тку + *d.*; (*gram. or stylistic ~, gloss*) поме́та.

● *v.t.* **(labelled, labelling;** *US* **labeled, labeling)** (*stick ~ on*) накле́и|вать, -ть ярлы́к на + *a.*; (*fasten ~ to*) привя́з|ывать, -а́ть ярлы́к/би́рку к + *d.*; (*fig.*): **he was ~led a fascist** ему́ прикле́или ярлы́к фаши́ста.

labial /ˈleɪbɪəl/ *n.* **(~ consonant)** губно́й/лабиа́льный согла́сный.

● *adj.* (*of the lips*) губно́й; (*phon.*) губно́й, лабиа́льный.

labile /ˈleɪbaɪl/, /-bɪl/ *adj.* (*phys., chem.*) неусто́йчивый, лаби́льный.

labiodental /ˌleɪbɪəʊˈdent(ə)l/ *adj.* гу́бно-зубно́й, ла́био-дента́льный.

labor /ˈleɪbə(r)/ *etc. see* ⇒**labour** *etc.*; **~ union** (*US*) профсою́з.

laboratory /ləˈbɒrətərɪ/ *n.* лаборато́рия; (*in school*) кабине́т; **in ~ conditions** в лаборато́рных усло́виях; **~ assistant** лабора́нт (*fem.* -ка).

laborious /ləˈbɔːrɪəs/ *adj.* **1** (*difficult*) тру́дный, тяжёлый, тя́жкий; (*toilsome*) трудоёмкий; (*wearying*) утоми́тельный. **2** (*of style, forced*) вы́мученный; (*involved*) громо́здкий, тяжёлый.

laboriousness /ləˈbɔːrɪəsnɪs/ *n.* трудоёмкость; (*of style*) громо́здкость.

labour /ˈleɪbə(r)/ (*US* **labor**) *n.* **1** (*toil, work*) труд, рабо́та; **manual ~** физи́ческий труд; **a ~ of love** бескоры́стный труд; **~ camp** исправи́тельно-трудово́й ла́герь.
2 (*pol., workers*) трудя́щиеся, рабо́чий класс; **Ministry of L~** (*Br., hist.*) министе́рство труда́; **International L~ Organization (ILO)** Междунаро́дная организа́ция труда́ (МОТ); **L~ Day** День (*m.*) труда́.
3 (*workforce*) рабо́чие (*pl.*), рабо́чая си́ла; **skilled ~** квалифици́рованные рабо́чие; **shortage of ~** нехва́тка рабо́чей си́лы; **~ dispute** трудово́й конфли́кт; **~ exchange** би́ржа труда́; **~ relations** трудовы́е отноше́ния.
4: **(L~ Party)** лейбори́стская па́ртия, лейбори́сты (*m. pl.*); **Vote L~!** голосу́йте за лейбори́стскую па́ртию!; **the L~ government** лейбори́стское прави́тельство; **a L~ MP** член парла́мента от лейбори́стской па́ртии.
5 (*childbirth*) ро́д|ы (*pl., g.* -ов); **~ pains** родовы́е схва́тки (*f. pl.*); **~ ward** роди́льная пала́та; **she went into ~** у неё начали́сь ро́ды; **be in ~** рожа́ть (*impf.*).

● *v.t.*: **~ a point** входи́ть (*impf.*) в изли́шние подро́бности; распространя́ться (*impf.*) о чём-н.

● *v.i.* **1** (*toil, work*) труди́ться (*impf.*), рабо́тать (*impf.*); **a ~ing man** рабо́чий.
2 (*strive, exert o.s.*): **he is ~ing to finish his book** он прилага́ет все уси́лия, что́бы ко́нчить кни́гу.
3 (*move, work etc. with difficulty*): **~ for breath** дыша́ть (*impf.*) с трудо́м; **the car ~ed up the hill** маши́на с трудо́м взбира́лась в го́ру.
4: **~ under** (*suffer from*): **you are ~ing under a delusion** вы нахо́дитесь в заблужде́нии.

● *cpds.* **~-intensive** *adj.* трудоёмкий; **~-saving** *adj.* рационализа́торский; трудосберега́ющий.

laboured /ˈleɪbəd/ (*US* **labored**) *adj.* **1** (*difficult*): **~ breathing** затруднённое дыха́ние. **2** (*forced*): **~ style/compliment** вы́мученный стиль/комплиме́нт.

labourer /ˈleɪbərə(r)/ (*US* **laborer**) *n.* рабо́чий.

Labourite /ˈleɪbəˌraɪt/ (*US* **Laborite**) *n.* лейбори́ст (*fem.* -ка).

● *adj.* лейбори́стский.

Labrador /ˈlæbrəˌdɔː(r)/ *n.* Лабрадо́р; (*dog*) лабрадо́р.

laburnum /ləˈbɜːnəm/ *n.* золото́й дождь.

labyrinth /ˈlæbərɪnθ/ *n.* (*lit., fig.*) лабири́нт.

labyrinthine /ˌlæbəˈrɪnθaɪn/ *adj.* (*lit.*) лабири́нтный; (*fig.*) запу́танный.

lac /læk/ *n.* (*resin, varnish*) лак; сыро́й шелла́к.

lace /leɪs/ *n.* **1** (*open-work fabric*) кру́жево, кружева́ (*nt. pl.*); **~ collar** кружевно́й воротни́к. **2** (*braid*) позуме́нт; (*mil.*) галу́н. **3** (*of shoe etc.*) шнуро́к.

● *v.t.* **1** (*fasten or tighten with ~*) шнурова́ть, за-; зашнуро́в|ывать, -а́ть; **he ~d up his shoes** он зашнурова́л боти́нки. **2** (*interlace*) спле|та́ть, -сти́. **3** (*fortify*): **~ coffee with rum** подли|ва́ть, -ть ром в ко́фе.

● *v.i.*: **~ into s.o.** намя́ть (*pf.*) бока́ кому́-н. (*coll.*).

● *cpds.* **~-maker** *n.* (*fem.*) кружевни́ца; **~-making** *n.* (*by hand*) плете́ние кру́жев; (*by machine*) произво́дство кру́жев; **~-ups** *n. pl.* (*Br.*) о́бувь на шнуро́вке.

lacerate /ˈlæsəˌreɪt/ *v.t.* (*lit., fig.*) терза́ть, рас-/ис-; растерз|ывать, -а́ть; (*wound*) ра́нить (*impf., pf.*).

laceration /ˌlæsəˈreɪʃ(ə)n/ *n.* (*tearing*) терза́ние, разрыва́ние; (*wound*) рва́ная ра́на.

lachrymal /ˈlækrɪm(ə)l/ *adj.* слёзный.

lachrymose /ˈlækrɪˌməʊs/ *adj.* слезли́вый, плакси́вый.

lack /læk/ *n.* недоста́ток; **for ~ of money** из-за недоста́тка (*or* за неиме́нием) де́нег; **for ~ of evidence** за отсу́тствием ули́к; **there was no ~ of water** воды́ бы́ло вполне́ доста́точно.

● *v.t. & i.*: **he ~s something** ему́ чего́-то недостаёт; **he ~s, is ~ing in courage** у него́ не хвата́ет хра́брости; **we ~ money** мы нужда́емся в деньга́х; **a subject on which information is ~ing** предме́т, о кото́ром ничего́ не изве́стно; **a week ~ing in incident** неде́ля, бе́дная собы́тиями; **he ~s for**

nothing у негó ни в чём нет недостáтка.

● *cpd.* **~-lustre** (*US* **-luster**) *adj.* тýсклый, без блéска.

lackadaisical /ˌlækəˈdeɪzɪk(ə)l/ *adj.* вя́лый, апати́чный; **in a ~ manner** спустя́ рукавá, без воодушевлéния.

lackey /ˈlækɪ/ *n.* (*pl.* **~s**) (*lit., fig.*) лакéй; (*fig.*) подхали́м.

laconic /ləˈkɒnɪk/ *adj.* (*of person*) неразговóрчивый, немногослóвный; (*of speech etc.*) лакони́чный, сжáтый.

lacon(ic)ism /ˈlækəˌnɪz(ə)m/, /ləˈkɒnɪˌsɪz(ə)m/ *n.* лакони́зм.

lacquer /ˈlækə(r)/ *n.* политýра (*no pl.*); лак.

● *v.t.* лакировáть (*impf.*).

● *cpd.* **~-ware** *n.* лакирóванные издéлия.

lacrosse /ləˈkrɒs/ *n.* лакрóсс.

lactate /lækˈteɪt/ *v.i.* выделя́ть (*impf.*) молокó.

lactation /lækˈteɪʃ(ə)n/ *n.* лактáция, выделéние молокá; (*breast-feeding*) кормлéние грýдью.

lactic /ˈlæktɪk/ *adj.* молóчный.

lacuna /ləˈkjuːnə/ *n.* (*pl.* **lacunae** /-niː/ *or* **lacunas**) прóбел, лакýна.

lad /læd/ *n.* (*boy*) мáльчик; (*fellow, youth*) пáрень (*m.*), мáлый; (*pl.*) ребя́т|а (*pl.*, *g.* —); **good ~!** молодéц!; **a bit of a ~** (*Br.*) гуля́ка (*m.*).

ladder /ˈlædə(r)/ *n.* **1** лéстница; **folding/extending ~** складнáя/выдвижнáя лéстница; (*fig.*): **~ of success** путь к успéху; **climb the social ~** продв|игáться, -и́нуться в óбществе; **he has one foot on the ~** он начáл дéлать карьéру. **2** (*on a ship*) трап. **3** (*Br., in stocking*) спусти́вшаяся пéтля.

● *v.t. & i.* (*Br.*): **I have ~ed my stocking; my stocking has ~ed** у меня́ спусти́лась петля́ на чулкé; **you have ~ed my stocking** вы мне порвáли чулóк.

laddie /ˈlædɪ/ = **lad**

lade /leɪd/ *v.t.* (*p.p.* **laden** /ˈleɪd(ə)n/) (*usu. p.p.*) грузи́ть, на-; нагру|жáть, -зи́ть; **he returned ~n with books** он вернýлся нагрýженный кни́гами; **the table was ~n with food** стол ломи́лся от еды́/яств; **she was ~n with cares** онá былá обремененá забóтами.

la-di-da /ˌlɑːdɪˈdɑː/ *adj.* (*coll.*) манéрный, жемáнный.

ladies /ˈleɪdɪz/ *n. see* ⇨**lady** *n.* 6

lading /ˈleɪdɪŋ/ *n.* (*process*) погрýзка; (*cargo*) груз; (*on hired ship*) фрахт; **bill of ~** коносáмент, трáнспортная накладнáя.

ladle /ˈleɪd(ə)l/ *n.* (*cul.*) поварёшка (*coll.*), полóвник (*coll.*); (*tech.*) ковш.

● *v.t.* чéрпать (*impf.*); отчéрп|ывать, -áть; **~ out soup** разл|ивáть, -и́ть суп.

lady /ˈleɪdɪ/ *n.* **1** (*woman of social status*) дáма, лéди (*indecl.*); **society ~** свéтская дáма; **first ~** (*US*) пéрвая дáма; супрýга президéнта; (*as title*) лéди (*f. indecl.*).
2 (*relig.*): **Our L~** Богорóдица; **L~ chapel** придéл Богомáтери; **L~ Day** Благовéщение.
3 (*courteous or formal for woman*) дáма, госпожá; **Ladies and Gentlemen** дáмы и господá; **ladies first!** дорóгу дáмам; **old ~** пожилáя жéнщина; **young ~** бáрышня; (*sweetheart*) возлю́бленная; (*fiancée*) невéста; **leading ~** (*theatr.*) ведýщая актри́са; **ladies' man** дáмский угóдник, волоки́та (*m.*).
4 (*attr.*): **~ doctor** жéнщина-врач.
5 (*wife*): **your good ~; your ~ wife** вáша супрýга.
6: **the ladies'** (*or* **ladies**) (*sg., Br.*), **ladies' room** (*US*) (*lavatory*) жéнская убóрная.

● *cpds.* **~bird,** (*US*) **~bug** *nn.* бóжья корóвка; **~-in-waiting** *n.* фрéйлина; **~-killer** *n.* сердцеéд; **~like** *adj.* (*refined, elegant*) изя́щный, деликáтный, благорóдный; **~-love** *n.* возлю́бленная; **~'s-maid** *n.* камери́стка.

ladyship /ˈleɪdɪʃɪp/ *n.*: **her/your ~** её/вáша ми́лость.

lag[1] /læg/ *n.* (*delay*) запáздывание.

● *v.i.* (**lagged, lagging**) отст|авáть, -áть; **the children were ~ging (behind)** дéти тащи́лись сзáди.

lag[2] /læg/ *n.* (*Br. coll., convict*) каторжáнин, кáторжник; **old ~** рецидиви́ст.

lag[3] /læg/ *v.t.* (**lagged, lagging**) (*wrap in felt etc.*) изоли́ровать/покрывáть (*impf.*) (вóйлоком).

lager /ˈlɑːgə(r)/ *n.* свéтлое пи́во.

● *cpd.* **~ lout** *n.* (*Br. coll.*) пья́ный хулигáн.

laggard /ˈlægəd/ *n.* лóдырь (*m.*); отстаю́щий.

lagging /ˈlægɪŋ/ *n.* (*for pipes etc.*) утепли́тельный материáл; (*tech.*) термоизоля́ция.

lagoon /ləˈguːn/ *n.* лагýна.

la(h) /lɑː/ *n.* (*mus.*) шестáя нóта мажóрной гáммы; (*the note A*) ля (*indecl.*).

laicization /ˌleɪɪsaɪˈzeɪʃ(ə)n/ *n.* секуляризáция.

laicize /ˈleɪɪˌsaɪz/ *v.t.* секуляризи́ровать (*impf., pf.*).

laid /leɪd/ *past and p.p. of* ⇨**lay**[2]

laid-back /leɪdˈbæk/ *adj.* непринуждённый, спокóйный.

lain /leɪn/ *p.p. of* ⇨**lie**[2]

lair /leə(r)/ *n.* лóговище; (*of bear*) берлóга; (*fig.*): **thieves' ~** воровскóй при́тон.

laird /ˈleəd/ *n.* помéщик (в Шотлáндии).

laissez-faire /ˌleseɪˈfeə(r)/ *n.* невмешáтельство; поли́тика невмешáтельства прави́тельства в эконóмику.

laity /ˈleɪɪtɪ/ *n.* (*relig.*) миря́не (*m. pl.*); (*non-professionals*) профáны (*m. pl.*); непрофессионáлы (*m. pl.*).

lake[1] /leɪk/ *n.* óзеро; (*attr.*): **L~ District** Озёрный край; **L~ Superior** Вéрхнее óзеро.

● *cpds.* **~-dwelling** *n.* свáйная пострóйка; **~side** *n.* бéрег óзера.

lake[2] /leɪk/ *n.* (*pigment*) крáсочный лак.

lam /læm/ *v.t.* (**lammed, lamming**) (*coll.*) колоти́ть, от-.

● *v.i.* (**lammed, lamming**): **~ into s.o.** (*coll., attack*) набр|áсываться, -óситься на когó-н.

lama /ˈlɑːmə/ *n.* лáма (*m.*).

Lamaism /ˈlɑːməˌɪz(ə)m/ *n.* ламаи́зм.

lamasery /ˈlɑːməsərɪ/, /ləˈmɑːsərɪ/ *n.* ламаи́стский монасты́рь.

lamb /læm/ *n.* ягнёнок, барáшек; **L~ of God** Áгнец Бóжий; **Persian ~** карáкуль (*m.*); **lead like a ~ to the slaughter** повести́ (*pf.*) как áгнца на заклáние; **as well be hanged for a sheep as a ~** семь бед — оди́н отвéт; (*fig., of child or mild person*) ягнёнок, овéчка; (*meat*) барáшек; **~ chop** барáнья котлéта; **leg of ~** барáнья ногá.

● *v.i.* (*of ewe*) ягни́ться, о(б)-; **the ~ing season** врéмя ягнéния.

● *cpds.* **~skin** *n.* овчи́на; барáшек; мерлýшка; **~'s-wool** *n.* поя́рок.

lambast(e) /læmˈbeɪst/ *v.t.* дубáсить, от- (*coll.*).

lambent /ˈlæmbənt/ *adj.* (*flickering*) игрáющий, мерцáющий; (*glowing*) светя́щийся, сия́ющий.

lame /leɪm/ *adj.* **1** хромóй; **be, walk ~** хромáть (*impf.*); **he is ~ in one leg** он хромáет на однý нóгу; **go ~** хромéть, о-. **2** (*fig., of argument, speech etc.*) слáбый; **a ~ excuse** слáбая отговóрка.

● *v.t.* калéчить, ис-; (*maim*) увéчить, из-.

● *cpd.* **~ duck** *n.* неудáчн|ик (*fem.* -ица).

lamé /ˈlɑːmeɪ/ *n.* ламé (*indecl.*).

lameness /ˈleɪmnɪs/ *n.* хромотá; (*fig., of excuse etc.*) неубеди́тельность.

lament /ləˈment/ *n.* (*expression of grief*) сéтование, причитáние; (*in music or verse*) плач; элéгия.

● *v.t.*: **~ one's fate** сéтовать, по- (*or* роптáть, воз-) на судьбý; **~ one's youth/the death of a friend** оплáк|ивать, -ать свою́ мóлодость/смерть дрýга; **late ~ed** покóйный, незабвéнный.

● *v.i.* сéтовать, по-; причитáть (*impf.*) (по + *d.*).

lamentable /ˈlæməntəb(ə)l/ *adj.* плачéвный; прискóрбный, жáлкий.

lamentation /ˌlæmənˈteɪʃ(ə)n/ *n.* (*lamenting*) сéтование, причитáние; (*lament*) плач, жáлобы (*f. pl.*); **L~s** (*bibl.*) Плач Иереми́и.

laminate[1] /ˈlæmɪnət/ *adj.* (*in plates*) пласти́нчатый; (*in layers*) расслоённый, слои́стый.

laminate[2] /ˈlæmɪˌneɪt/ *v.t.* (*roll into plates*) прокáт|ывать, -áть в листы́; (*split into layers*) рассл|áивать, -ои́ть.

lamination /ˌlæmɪˈneɪʃ(ə)n/ *n.* (*splitting*) расслоéние; (*rolling*) прокáтка; раскáтывание; (*geol.*) слои́стость.

lamp /læmp/ *n.* лáмпа; **standard ~** торшéр; **table ~** настóльная лáмпа; (*on vehicle*) фáра; (*lantern; street ~*)

фона́рь (*m.*); (*electric bulb*) ла́мп(очк)а; (*icon-*~) лампа́да.

● *cpds.* **~light** *n.* (*indoors*) свет ла́мпы; (*in street*) фона́рный свет; **~lighter** *n.* фона́рщик; **~-post, ~-standard** *nn.* у́личный фона́рь; **~shade** *n.* абажу́р.

lampoon /læmˈpuːn/ *n.* па́сквиль (*m.*).

● *v.t.* писа́ть, на- па́сквиль на + *a.*

lampoonist /læmˈpuːnɪst/ *n.* пасквиля́нт.

lamprey /ˈlæmprɪ/ *n.* (*pl.* **~s**) мино́га.

LAN (*abbr. of* ***local area network***) (*comput.*) лока́льная сеть.

lance /lɑːns/ *n.* (*for throwing*) копьё; (*cavalry weapon*) пи́ка; (*for fishing*) острога́.

● *v.t.* (*pierce with* ~) коло́ть, за- пи́кой; (*med.*) вскры|ва́ть, -ть ланце́том.

● *cpd.* **~-corporal** *n.* мла́дший капра́л.

lancer /ˈlɑːnsə(r)/ *n.* ула́н; (*pl., regiment*) ула́нский полк; (*pl., dance*) лансье́ (*indecl.*).

lancet /ˈlɑːnsɪt/ *n.* (*surg.*) ланце́т; (*archit.*): **~ arch** ланце́тная/стре́льчатая а́рка; **~ window** стре́льчатое окно́.

land /lænd/ *n.* **1** земля́; **~ mass** земе́льный масси́в; (*dry* ~) су́ша; **they sighted ~** они́ уви́дели су́шу/зе́млю; **travel by ~** е́хать (*det.*) су́шей (*or* по су́ше); **~ forces** (*mil.*) сухопу́тные войска́; **reach, make ~** дост|ига́ть, -и́гнуть бе́рега; **~ breeze** берегово́й ве́тер; **see how the ~ lies** (*fig.*) пров|еря́ть, -е́рить как обстоя́т дела́. **2** (*ground, soil*) грунт, по́чва; **he works on the ~** он рабо́тает на земле́; **work the ~** обраба́тывать (*impf.*) зе́млю; **good farming ~** плодоро́дная по́чва; **a house with some ~** дом с земе́льным уча́стком; **~ tax** поземе́льный нало́г. **3** (*country*) земля́, страна́; (*state*) госуда́рство; **~ of dreams** страна́ грёз; **native ~** ро́дина, отчи́зна; край родно́й; оте́чество; **in a foreign ~** за грани́цей; **in the ~ of the living** в живы́х; **no man's ~** ничья́ земля́; (*mil.*) ниче́йная полоса́. **4** (*property*) земля́, име́ние; **he owns ~** он владе́ет землёй; **his ~s extend for several miles** его́ владе́ния простира́ются на не́сколько миль.

● *v.t.* **1** (*bring to shore*): **~ a vessel** прив|оди́ть, -ести́ су́дно к бе́регу; **~ cargo** выгружа́ть, вы́грузить груз; **~ passengers** выса́живать, вы́садить пассажи́ров. **2**: **~ an aircraft** сажа́ть, посади́ть (*or* приземл|я́ть, -и́ть) самолёт. **3**: **~ a fish** вытаскивать, вы́тащить ры́бу на бе́рег; **a ~ed fish** по́йманная ры́ба. **4** (*win*) выи́грывать, вы́играть; (*secure*): **he ~ed himself a good job** он пристро́ился на хоро́шую рабо́ту. **5** (*get, involve*): **that will ~ you in jail** э́то доведёт вас до тюрьмы́; **he ~ed himself in trouble** он навлёк на себя́ беду́; **he ~ed himself with a lot of work** он загрузи́л себя́ рабо́той. **6** (*deal*): **I ~ed him one on the nose** я заéхал ему́ по́ носу (*coll.*).

● *v.i.* **1** (*of passengers*) выса́живаться, вы́садиться. **2** (*of aircraft*) приземл|я́ться, -и́ться; де́лать, с- поса́дку; (*on water*) приводн|я́ться, -и́ться; (*space-craft on moon*) прилун|я́ться, -и́ться; (*on Mars*) примарси́ться (*pf.*). **3** (*of athlete, after jump*) приземл|я́ться, -и́ться. **4** (*fall, lit. or fig.*): **she ~ed in trouble** она́ попа́ла в беду́; **we ~ed in a bog** мы угоди́ли в боло́то; **the ball ~ed on his head** мяч попа́л ему́ в го́лову. **5**: **~ up** (*coll., arrive*) приб|ыва́ть, -ы́ть; **I ~ed up in the wrong street** я очути́лся не на той у́лице.

● *cpds.* **~-agent** *n.* (*Br.*) (*steward*) управля́ющий име́нием; (*dealer in property*) аге́нт по прода́же земе́льных уча́стков; **~fall** *n.*: **make a ~fall** под|ходи́ть, -ойти́ к бе́регу; **~-girl** *n.* (*Br., hist.*) рабо́тница на фе́рме; **~holder** *n.* землевладе́л|ец (*fem.* -ица); **~lady** *n.* (*Br., of pub*) хозя́йка; (*of building*) домовладе́лица, хозя́йка; **~line** *n.* назе́мная ли́ния свя́зи; **~-locked** *adj.* окружённый су́шей, закры́тый; без вы́хода к мо́рю; **~lord** *n.* (*Br., of pub*) хозя́ин; (*owner of* ~) землевладе́лец; (*of building*) домовладе́лец, хозя́ин; **~lubber** *n.* сухопу́тная кры́са; **~mark** *n.* (*prominent feature*) заме́тный предме́т на ме́стности; (назе́мный) ориенти́р; (*fig.*) ве́ха; **~-mine** *n.* фуга́с; **~owner** *n.* землевладе́л|ец (*fem.* -ица); **~slide** *n.* о́ползень (*m.*); (*pol.*): **they won by a ~slide** они́ одержа́ли реши́тельную побе́ду; **~slip** *n.* (*Br.*) о́ползень (*m.*); **~sman** *n.* неморя́к; **~-surveying** *n.* (геодези́ческая) съёмка, межева́ние; **~-surveyor** *n.* землеме́р; **~-tax** *n.* земе́льный нало́г.

landau /ˈlændɔː/ *n.* ландо́ (*indecl.*).

landed /ˈlændɪd/ *adj.* **1** (*possessing land*) землевладе́льческий; **~ gentry** поме́щики (*m. pl.*). **2** (*consisting of land*): **~ property** земе́льные владе́ния.

lander /ˈlændə(r)/ *n.* (*aeron.*) спуска́емый аппара́т.

landing /ˈlændɪŋ/ *n.* **1** (*bringing or coming to earth*) поса́дка, приземле́ние; **~ approach** захо́д на поса́дку; **forced ~** вы́нужденная поса́дка. **2** (*on water*) приводне́ние; (*on the moon*) прилуне́ние. **3** (*putting ashore; depositing by air*) вы́садка; (*of goods*) вы́грузка. **4** (*mil.*) деса́нт, вы́садка деса́нта. **5** (*on stairs*) (ле́стничная) площа́дка.

● *cpds.* **~-craft** *n.* деса́нтное су́дно; **~-field** *n.* лётное по́ле; **~-gear** *n.* шасси́ (*nt. indecl.*); **~-ground** *n.* взлётно-поса́дочная площа́дка; **~-net** *n.* подсачо́к, сачо́к; **~-party** *n.* деса́нтная гру́ппа, деса́нт; **~-stage** *n.* дебарка́дер, при́стань; **~-strip** *n.* поса́дочная полоса́.

landless /ˈlændlɪs/ *adj.* безземе́льный.

landscape /ˈlændskeɪp/, /ˈlæns-/ *n.* (*picture*) пейза́ж; (*scenery*) ландша́фт.

● *cpds.* **~-gardening** *n.* садо́во-па́рковая архитекту́ра; **~-painter** *n.* пейзажи́ст; **~-painting** *n.* (*picture*) пейза́ж; (*art*) иску́сство пейза́жа.

landscapist /ˈlænd,skeɪpɪst/, /ˈlæn,s-/ *n.* пейзажи́ст.

landward /ˈlændwəd/ *n.*: **to ~** к бе́регу.

● *adj.*: **on the ~ side** со стороны́ су́ши.

● *adv.* (*also* **~s**) к бе́регу.

lane /leɪn/ *n.* **1** (*narrow street*) переу́лок, у́зкая у́лочка; (*country road*) доро́жка. **2** (*of traffic*) ряд; **get into ~** вста|ва́ть, -ть в ряд; **four-~ highway** автостра́да с четырьмя́ ряда́ми движе́ния. **3** (*air route*) тра́сса. **4** (*for shipping*) морско́й путь. **5** (*on race-track, swimming-pool*) доро́жка.

language /ˈlæŋgwɪdʒ/ *n.* язы́к; (*esp. spoken*) речь; **~ and literature** (*as subj. of study*) филоло́гия; **in a foreign ~** на иностра́нном языке́; **they don't speak the same ~** (*fig.*) они́ говоря́т на ра́зных языка́х; **a degree in ~s** дипло́м об оконча́нии филологи́ческого факульте́та; (*words, expressions*): **he has a great command of ~** он прекра́сно владе́ет языко́м; **bad ~** сквернасло́вие; **strong ~** си́льные выраже́ния; **science of ~** языкове́дение, языкозна́ние; **native ~** родно́й язы́к; **spoken ~** разгово́рный язы́к; **~ student** (*at university*) фило́лог; **~ laboratory** лингафо́нный кабине́т.

languid /ˈlæŋgwɪd/ *adj.* то́мный, вя́лый.

languish /ˈlæŋgwɪʃ/ *v.i.* томи́ться (*impf.*); изныва́ть (*impf.*); **a ~ing look** то́мный взгляд.

languor /ˈlæŋgə(r)/ *n.* то́мность, вя́лость; (*pleasant*) исто́ма.

languorous /ˈlæŋgərəs/ *adj.* то́мный; по́лный исто́мы.

lank /læŋk/ *adj.*: **~ hair** гла́дкие/прямы́е во́лосы.

lanky /ˈlæŋkɪ/ *adj.* (**lankier, lankiest**) долговя́зый; **~ person** верзи́ла (*c.g.*) (*coll.*).

lanolin /ˈlænəlɪn/ *n.* ланоли́н.

lantern /ˈlænt(ə)n/ *n.* **1** фона́рь (*m.*). **2** (*of lighthouse*) светова́я ка́мера.

● *cpd.* **~-jawed** *adj.* с впа́лыми щека́ми.

lanthanum /ˈlænθənəm/ *n.* ланта́н.

lanyard /ˈlænjəd/, /-jɑːd/ *n.* (*cord*) реме́нь (*m.*); (*for securing sail*) та́лреп; (*mil.*) вытяжно́й шнур.

Laos /laʊz/, /laʊs/ *n.* Лао́с.

Laotian /ˈlaʊʃɪən/, /lɑːˈəʊʃɪən/ *n.* **1** (*person*) лао́с|ец (*fem.* -ка). **2** (*language*) лао́сский язы́к.

● *adj.* лао́сский.

lap[1] /læp/ *n.* **1**: **the boy sat on his mother's ~** ма́льчик сиде́л у ма́тери на коле́нях; **the cat climbed on to my ~** ко́шка забрала́сь ко мне на коле́ни; (*fig.*): **in the ~ of the gods** в руце́ бо́жьей; **he lives in the ~ of luxury** ≈ он живёт как у Христа́ за па́зухой. **2** (*of garment*) пола́, фа́лда, подо́л.

● *cpds.* **~-dog** *n.* боло́нка; **~top** *adj.*: **~top computer** портати́вный компью́тер.

lap[2] /læp/ *n.* **1** (*coil or turn e.g. of rope*)

вито́к, оборо́т. **2** (*circuit of race-track*) круг; **he won by 3 ~s** он победи́л, обойдя́ проти́вника на 3 кру́га.

● *v.t.* (**lapped, lapping**) **1** (*wrap*): **~ cloth round something** обёр|тывать, -ну́ть что-н. мате́рией; **~ something in cloth** зав|ора́чивать, -ерну́ть что-н. в мате́рию; (*fig., surround, enfold*) окруж|а́ть, -и́ть. **2** (*sport*: *be a ~ ahead of*) об|ходи́ть, -ойти́ (*or* об|гоня́ть, -огна́ть) (*кого*) на круг.

lap³ /læp/ *n.* (*sound of waves*) плеск.

● *v.t.* (**lapped, lapping**) **1** (*drink with tongue*) лака́ть, вы́-; **the cat ~ped up the milk** ко́шка вы́лакала молоко́. **2** (*fig., accept eagerly*) жа́дно глота́ть (*impf.*); **he ~ped up their compliments** он жа́дно лови́л их комплиме́нты.

● *v.i.* (**lapped, lapping**) (*of waves*) плеска́ться (*impf.*); **waves ~ on the beach** во́лны плеще́тся о бе́рег.

lapel /lə'pel/ *n.* ла́цкан, отворо́т.

lapidary /'læpɪdərɪ/ *n.* (*gem cutter*) грани́льщик; (*polisher*) шлифова́льщик; (*engraver*) гравёр.

● *adj.* **1** грани́льный. **2** (*fig.*) лапида́рный.

lapis lazuli /ˌlæpɪs 'læzju:lɪ/, /-ˌlaɪ/ *n.* (*min.*) ля́пис-лазу́рь.

Lapland /'læplænd/ *n.* Лапла́ндия.

Laplander /'læpˌlændə(r)/ *n.* лапла́нд|ец (*fem.* -ка).

Lapp /læp/ *n.* **1** (*person*) саа́ми (*indecl.*); лопа́р|ь (*fem.* -ка). **2** (*also* **~ish**: *language*) саа́мский/лопа́рский язы́к; язы́к саа́ми.

● *adj.* **1** (*also* **~ish**) лопа́рский, саа́мский. **2** (*of Lapland*) лапла́ндский.

lapse /læps/ *n.* **1** (*slight mistake, slip*) упуще́ние, оплóшность; (*of memory*) прова́л па́мяти; (*of the pen*) опи́ска; (*of the tongue*) обмо́лвка, огово́рка. **2** (*moral deviation*) просту́пок; (*decline*) паде́ние. **3** (*leg., ending of right etc.*) прекраще́ние; недействи́тельность. **4** (*passage of time*) тече́ние; **after the ~ of a month** по истече́нии ме́сяца; (*interval*) промежу́ток.

● *v.i.* **1** (*decline morally; slip back*) пасть (*pf.*); **they ~d into heresy** они́ впа́ли в е́ресь; **he ~d into his old ways** он приня́лся́ за ста́рое; **~ into idleness** облени́ться (*pf.*); **~ into silence** зам|олка́ть, -о́лкнуть; **a ~d Catholic** бы́вший като́лик. **2** (*leg., become void*) теря́ть, по- си́лу; (*revert*): **the property ~d to the Crown** име́ние отошло́ к казне́. **3** (*of time*) про|ходи́ть, -йти́; минова́ть (*impf., pf.*).

lapwing /'læpwɪŋ/ *n.* чи́бис, пи́галица.

larcenous /'lɑ:sənəs/ *adj.* воровско́й; **with ~ intent** с наме́рением соверши́ть кра́жу.

larceny /'lɑ:sənɪ/ *n.* кра́жа; **grand/petty ~** кру́пная/ме́лкая кра́жа.

larch /lɑ:tʃ/ *n.* (*tree*) ли́ственница; (**~wood**) древеси́на ли́ственницы.

lard /lɑ:d/ *n.* лярд, топлёное свино́е са́ло.

● *v.t.* (*cul.*) шпигова́ть, на-; (*fig.*) усна|ща́ть, -сти́ть.

larder /'lɑ:də(r)/ *n.* кладова́я.

lares and penates /'lɑ:ri:z/ *n.* ла́ры и пена́ты (*pl.*); родны́е пена́ты.

large /lɑ:dʒ/ *n.*: **at ~** (*free*) на во́ле, на свобо́де; **set at ~** освобо|жда́ть, -ди́ть; (*in general*) целико́м; во всём объёме; **the public at ~** широ́кая пу́блика; **people at ~ were dissatisfied** наро́д в основно́м был недово́лен; **ambassador at ~** (*US*) посо́л по осо́бым поруче́ниям.

● *adj.* большо́й, кру́пный; **on a ~ scale** в большо́м/кру́пном масшта́бе; **~ handwriting** кру́пный по́черк; **in ~ type** кру́пным шри́фтом; **a ~ population** многочи́сленное/большо́е населе́ние; (*spacious*) просто́рный; (*considerable*) значи́тельный; (*copious*) оби́льный; (*extensive*) широ́кий; (*fat*) по́лный; **as ~ as life** (*fig.*) во всей красе́; **here he is, as ~ as life** он тут как тут; **he turned up as ~ as life** он яви́лся со́бственной персо́ной; **~r than life** бо́лее, чем в натура́льную величину́; (*fig., flamboyant*) колори́тный.

● *adv.*: **by and ~** вообще́ говоря́.

● *cpds.* **~-hearted** *adj.* великоду́шный; **~-minded** *adj.* широ́ких взгля́дов; **~-scale** *adj.* крупномасшта́бный; **a ~-scale map** крупномасшта́бная ка́рта.

largely /'lɑ:dʒlɪ/ *adv.* (*to a great extent*) по бо́льшей ча́сти; в значи́тельной сте́пени.

largess(e) /lɑ:'ʒes/ *n.* щедро́ты (*f. pl.*).

largish /'lɑ:dʒɪʃ/ *adj.* дово́льно большо́й; великова́тый.

largo /'lɑ:gəʊ/ *n., adj. & adv.* (*pl.* **largos**) ла́рго (*indecl.*).

lark¹ /lɑ:k/ *n.* (*bird*) жа́воронок; **rise with the ~** вста|ва́ть, -ть с петуха́ми.

● *cpd.* **~spur** *n.* (*bot.*) жи́вокость, шпо́рник.

lark² /lɑ:k/ *n.* (*coll.*), (*prank*) прока́за; (*amusement*) заба́ва; **for a ~** шу́тки ра́ди; **what a ~!** вот потéха!

● *v.i.*: **~ about** резви́ться (*impf.*).

larrikin /'lærɪkɪn/ *n.* хулига́н.

larrup /'lærəp/ *v.t.* (**larruped, larruping**) (*coll.*) поро́ть, вы́-; да|ва́ть, -ть (*кому*) трёпку/по́рку.

larva /'lɑ:və/ *n.* (*pl.* **larvae** /-vi:/) личи́нка.

laryngeal /lə'rɪndʒɪəl/ *adj.* горта́нный.

larynges /lə'rɪn(d)ʒi:z/ *pl. of* ⇒**larynx**

laryngitis /ˌlærɪn'dʒaɪtɪs/ *n.* ларинги́т.

laryngoscope /lə'rɪŋgəˌskəʊp/ *n.* ларингоско́п.

larynx /'lærɪŋks/ *n.* (*pl.* **larynges**) горта́нь.

lascivious /lə'sɪvɪəs/ *adj.* похотли́вый.

lasciviousness /lə'sɪvɪəsnɪs/ *n.* по́хоть, похотли́вость.

laser /'leɪzə(r)/ *n.* ла́зер; (*attr.*) ла́зерный; **~ printer** (*comput.*) ла́зерный при́нтер.

lash¹ /læʃ/ *n.* (**eye~**) ресни́ца.

lash² /læʃ/ *n.* **1** (*thong*) реме́нь (*m.*); **he got the ~** он был нака́зан плетью́. **2** (*stroke*) уда́р (плетью́); **he got fifty ~es** он получи́л пятьдеся́т уда́ров плетью́; (*fig.*): **the ~ of criticism** бич кри́тики; **he felt the ~ of her tongue** он по себе́ знал, како́й у неё о́стрый язы́к.

● *v.t.* **1** (*with whip; also of wind, rain*) хлест|а́ть, -ну́ть; (*fig., with satire, criticism, abuse*) бичева́ть (*impf.*). **2** (*wave about*): **the dog ~ed its tail** соба́ка би́ла хвосто́м. **3** (*fasten with rope etc.*) свя́з|ывать, -а́ть; привя́з|ывать, -а́ть.

● *v.i.*: **the rain ~ed against the window** ве́тер хлеста́л в окно́; **he ~ed into his opponent** он набро́сился на своего́ проти́вника.

● *with advs.*: **~ down** *v.t.* привя́з|ывать, -а́ть (*что к чему*); **~ out** *v.i.* (*with fists*) наки́|дываться, -нуться (*на кого*); (*kick*) ляг|а́ть, -ну́ть; (*verbally*) разра|жа́ться, -зи́ться бра́нью; (*Br. coll., spend lavishly*) сори́ть (*impf.*) деньга́ми; **~ together** *v.i.* свя́з|ывать, -а́ть.

lashing /'læʃɪŋ/ *n.* (*whipping*) по́рка; (*pl., Br. coll., plenty*): **~s of cream** ма́сса сли́вок.

lass /læs/, **-ie** /'læsɪ/ *nn.* (*child*) де́вочка; (*young woman*) де́вушка.

lassitude /'læsɪˌtju:d/ *n.* уста́лость, утомле́ние, вя́лость.

lasso /læ'su:/, /'læsəʊ/ *n.* (*pl.* **~s** *or* **~es**) арка́н, лассо́ (*indecl.*).

● *v.t.* (**lassoes, lassoed**) арка́нить, за-.

last¹ /lɑ:st/ *n.* (*shoemaker's*) коло́дка; **stick to your ~!** (*fig.*) занима́йся свои́м де́лом!; ≈ всяк сверчо́к знай свой шесто́к.

last² /lɑ:st/ *n.* (*final or most recent person or thing*): **he was the ~ of his line** он был после́дним в роду́; **he was the ~ to go** он ушёл после́дним; **our house is the ~ in the road** наш дом после́дний/кра́йний на у́лице; **the ~ of the wine** оста́тки (*m. pl.*) вина́; **the ~ shall be first** ≈ мно́гие после́дние бу́дут пе́рвыми; **on the ~ of the month** в после́дний день ме́сяца; **breathe one's ~** испусти́ть (*pf.*) после́дний вздох; **we have seen the ~ of him** мы его́ бо́льше не уви́дим; **he remained impenitent to the ~** он не раска́ялся до са́мого конца́; **at ~** наконе́ц; (*as excl.*) наконе́ц-то!; **at long ~** в конце́ концо́в, наконе́ц.

● *adj.* **1** (*latest; final; ~ of series*) после́дний; **in the ~ 7 years** в после́дние 7 лет; **at the very ~ moment** в са́мый после́дний моме́нт; **the L~ Judgement** Стра́шный суд; Су́дный день; светопреставле́ние; **~ rites, sacrament** причаще́ние пе́ред сме́ртью; **this chair is on its ~ legs** э́тот стул е́ле ды́шит; **~ name** фами́лия; **~ but not least of his talents** после́дний по счёту, но не по ва́жности из его́ тала́нтов; **~ but one** предпосле́дний; **~ but two** тре́тий от конца́; **the ~ thing I heard was that he was getting married** после́днее, что я о нём слы́шал, э́то то, что он

собира́ется жени́ться; ~ **thing at night** по́здно ве́чером; пре́жде, чем лечь спать; пе́ред сном.
2 (*preceding, of time*) про́шлый; **in the ~ century/year/month** в про́шлом столе́тии/году́/ме́сяце; **~ week** на про́шлой неде́ле; **~ night we got home late** вчера́ ве́чером мы по́здно верну́лись; **~ night I slept badly** про́шлой но́чью я пло́хо спал; **the week before ~** позапро́шлая неде́ля; **the night before ~** позавчера́ ве́чером.
3 (*least likely or suitable*): **he is the ~ person I expected to see** вот кого́ я ме́ньше всего́ ожида́л уви́деть; **she is the ~ person to help** от неё ме́ньше всего́ мо́жно ожида́ть по́мощи; **that's the ~ thing I would have expected** э́того я ника́к не ожида́л.
● *adv.* **1** (*in order*) по́сле всех; **he finished ~** он ко́нчил после́дним.
2 (*for the ~ time*) в после́дний раз; **when I ~ saw him** когда́ я в после́дний раз ви́дел его́.
3 (*~ly, in the ~ place*) на после́днем ме́сте; **~ but not least I wish you success** и, наконе́ц, — но отню́дь не в после́днюю о́чередь, — я жела́ю вам успе́ха.
● *v.i.* **1** (*go on, continue*) дли́ться, про-; продо|лжа́ться, -о́лжиться; **winter ~s six months** зима́ дли́тся шесть ме́сяцев; **the rain won't ~ long** дождь ско́ро пройдёт; **if the good weather ~s** е́сли продержи́тся (*or* простои́т) хоро́шая пого́да.
2 (*hold out*) выде́рживать, вы́держать; **as long as my health ~s (out)** пока́ у меня́ хва́тит здоро́вья; (*be preserved, survive*) сохран|я́ться, -и́ться; **the tradition has ~ed until today** э́та тради́ция сохрани́лась до настоя́щего вре́мени.
3 (*of clothes*): **this suit has ~ed well** э́тому костю́му сно́су нет.
4 (*of the dying*): **he won't ~ long** он до́лго не протя́нет (*coll.*).
5 (*be sufficient for*) хват|а́ть, -и́ть на + *a.*; **£30 ~s me a week** 30 фу́нтов мне хвата́ет на неде́лю; **the bread won't ~ us today** хле́ба нам на сего́дня не хва́тит.
● *cpds.* **~-ditch** *adj.* отча́янный; **a ~-ditch stand** упо́рная оборо́на; **~-minute** *adj.* (сде́ланный) в после́днюю мину́ту; **~ name** *n.* фами́лия; **~-named** *adj.* после́дний (из упомя́нутых).

lasting /'lɑ:stɪŋ/ *adj.* (*durable, enduring*) про́чный, продолжи́тельный; **~ peace** про́чный мир; **a ~ monument** ве́чный па́мятник; (*persistent, permanent*) постоя́нный; **~ regrets** постоя́нное чу́вство сожале́ния; **leave a ~ impression** произв|оди́ть, -ести́ неизглади́мое впечатле́ние.

lastly /'lɑ:stlɪ/ *adv.* в заключе́ние; наконе́ц.

latch /lætʃ/ *n.* (*bar*) щеко́лда; (*lock*) защёлка; **on the ~** на щеко́лде/защёлке.
● *v.t.* (*put on ~*) закр|ыва́ть, -ы́ть на щеко́лду.
● *v.i.*: **~ on to** смекну́ть (*pf.*) (*coll.*).
● *cpd.* **~-key** *n.* ключ (от америка́нского замка́); соба́чка; **~-key child** безнадзо́рный ребёнок.

late /leɪt/ *adj.* **1** (*far on in time*) по́здний; **it is ~** по́здно; **it's getting ~** де́ло идёт к но́чи; **in the ~ evening** по́здним ве́чером; **in ~ summer** к концу́ ле́та; **in ~ May** к концу́ ма́я; в после́дних чи́слах ма́я; **the ~ 19th century** коне́ц 19-го ве́ка; **he is in his ~ 40s** ему́ почти́ пятьдеся́т; **~ edition** вече́рний вы́пуск; **keep ~ hours** по́здно ложи́ться (*impf.*) спать; **it is ~ in the day for that** для э́того позднова́то; **~r events** после́дующие собы́тия; **at, by 2 o'clock at the ~st** са́мое по́зднее в 2 часа́.
2 (*behind time*): **be ~ for the train** оп|а́здывать, -озда́ть на по́езд (**for the theatre** (*Br.*), **theater** (*US*) в теа́тр; **for dinner** к у́жину); **he was an hour ~** он опозда́л на ча́с; **the train is running an hour ~** по́езд идёт с опозда́нием в (оди́н) час; по́езд опа́здывает на час; **the concert began an hour ~** конце́рт начался́ ча́сом (*or* на час) по́зже; **I was ~ in replying** я опозда́л отве́тить (*or* с отве́том); **plums are ~ this year** сли́вы в э́том году́ поспе́ли по́здно; **he is a ~ riser** он по́здно встаёт.
3 (*recent*) неда́вний, после́дний; **in ~ years** за после́дние го́ды; **his ~st book** его́ после́дняя кни́га; **~st news** после́дние изве́стия.
4 (*former*) пре́жний; (*immediately preceding*) бы́вший; **the ~ government** пре́жнее прави́тельство.
5 (*deceased*) поко́йный.
6 (*belated*) запозда́лый; **a few ~ swallows** не́сколько запозда́лых ла́сточек.
● *adv.* по́здно; **better ~ than never** лу́чше по́здно, чем никогда́; **sooner or ~r** ра́но и́ли по́здно; **stay up ~** по́здно ложи́ться (*impf.*); **~ in life** в пожило́м во́зрасте; на ста́рости лет; **a year ~r** спустя́ год; **see you ~r!** уви́димся!; пока́!; **~ into the night** до по́здней но́чи; **of ~** (в/за) после́днее вре́мя.
● *cpd.* **~-night** *adj.* ночно́й (*сеанс и т.п.*).

latecomer /'leɪt,kʌmə(r)/ *n.* опозда́вший.

lately /'leɪtlɪ/ *adv.* неда́вно; **have you seen him ~?** ви́дели ли вы его́ в после́днее вре́мя?; **I've been working hard ~** после́днее вре́мя я мно́го рабо́тал.

latency /'leɪt(ə)nsɪ/ *n.* скры́тое состоя́ние; (*tech.*) лате́нтность; **~ period** (*med.*) инкубацио́нный пери́од.

lateness /'leɪtnɪs/ *n.*: **the ~ of the train** опозда́ние по́езда; **despite the ~ of the hour** несмотря́ на по́здний час.

latent /'leɪt(ə)nt/ *adj.* скры́тый, лате́нтный; (*chem.*) свя́занный.

lateral /'lætər(ə)l/ *adj.* боково́й, горизонта́льный; **~ section** попере́чный разре́з.

latest /'leɪtɪst/ *adj.* после́дний; са́мый но́вый; **the ~ thing** после́днее сло́во, но́вость, нови́нка; *see also* ⇨**late**

latex /'leɪteks/ *n.* (*pl.* **latexes** *or* **latices**) мле́чный сок, ла́текс.

lath /lɑ:θ/ *n.* ре́йка, пла́нка; **~ and plaster** дра́нка и штукату́рка; (*on roof*) обрешётка; **~ fence** штаке́тник.

lathe /leɪð/ *n.* тока́рный стано́к.

lather /'lɑ:ðə(r)/, /'læðə(r)/ *n.* (мы́льная) пе́на; (*on horse*) мы́ло, пе́на; **in a ~** в мы́ле; (*fig., agitated*) в запа́рке.
● *v.t.* мы́лить (*impf.*); намы́ли|вать, -ть; (*coll., thrash*) взду́ть (*pf.*); да|ва́ть, -ть трёпку + *d.*
● *v.i.* (*of soap*) мы́литься.

lathering /'lɑ:ðərɪŋ/, /'læðərɪŋ/ *n.* (*coll.*) трёпка, взбу́чка.

latices /'leɪtɪ,si:z/ *pl. of* ⇨**latex**

Latin /'lætɪn/ *n.* **1** (*language*) латы́нь; лати́нский язы́к. **2** (*Frenchman, Italian etc.*) челове́к рома́нского происхожде́ния.
● *adj.* лати́нский; **~ America** Лати́нская Аме́рика; **~ languages/nations** рома́нские языки́/наро́ды; **~ scholar** латини́ст.
● *cpd.* **~-American** *adj.* латиноамерика́нский; *n.* латиноамерика́н|ец (*fem.* -ка).

Latinism /'lætɪ,nɪz(ə)m/ *n.* латини́зм.

Latinist /'lætɪnɪst/ *n.* латини́ст (*fem.* -ка).

Latino /lə'ti:nəʊ/ *n.* (*pl.* **~s**) & *adj.* = **Latin-American**

latish /'leɪtɪʃ/ *adj.* позднова́тый.

latitude /'lætɪ,tju:d/ *n.* **1** (*distance from equator; pl., regions*) широта́; **~ 25° N** 25° се́верной широты́. **2** (*freedom of action*) свобо́да (де́йствий); (*liberality*) широта́ (взгля́дов). **3** (*breadth, extent*) обши́рность.

latitudinal /,lætɪ'tju:dɪn(ə)l/ *adj.* широ́тный.

latitudinarian /lætɪ,tju:dɪ'neərɪən/ *adj.* веротерпи́мый.

latrine /lə'tri:n/ *n.* убо́рная, отхо́жее ме́сто.

latter /'lætə(r)/ *pron. & adj.* после́дний, второ́й; **in the ~ half of June** во второ́й полови́не ию́ня; **the former ... the ~** пе́рвый... второ́й/после́дний; **the ~** то, после́дний.
● *cpd.* **~-day** *adj.* совреме́нный, нове́йший; **L~-day Saints** мормо́ны (*m. pl.*).

latterly /'lætəlɪ/ *adv.* (*of late*) (в/за) после́днее вре́мя; (*towards the end*) к концу́, под коне́ц.

lattice /'lætɪs/ *n.* решётка; (*attr.; also* **~d**) решётчатый.

Latvia /'lætvɪə/ *n.* Ла́твия.

Latvian /'lætvɪən/ *n.* (*person*) латви́|ец (*fem.* -йка); латы́ш (*fem.* -ка); (*language*) латы́шский язы́к.
● *adj.* латви́йский, латы́шский.

laud /lɔ:d/ *v.t.* восхвал|я́ть, -и́ть; сла́вить (*impf.*).

laudability /,lɔ:də'bɪlɪtɪ/ *n.* похва́льность.

laudable /'lɔ:dəb(ə)l/ *adj.* похва́льный.

laudanum /'lɔ:dnəm/, /'lɒd-/ *n.* насто́йка о́пия.

L

laudatory /ˈlɔːdətərɪ/ *adj.* хвалéбный.

laugh /lɑːf/ *n.* смех; (*loud* **~**) хóхот; **it was a ~** смéху-то бы́ло; **we had a good ~ over it** мы от души́ посмея́лись над э́тим; **he had the last ~** в концé концóв посмея́лся он; **have the ~ on s.o.** ост|авля́ть, -áвить когó-н. в дуракáх; **the ~ was on him** он остáлся в дуракáх; **I could not raise a ~** меня́ э́то ничýть не рассмеши́ло; **he joined in the ~** он присоедини́лся к óбщему смéху; **he gave a loud ~** он грóмко рассмея́лся.

● *v.t.*: **~ to scorn** высмéивать, вы́смеять; **he was ~ed out of court** он был осмéян; **he was ~ing his head off** он хохотáл как безýмный.

● *v.i.* смея́ться (*impf.*); хохот|áть, -нýть; (*begin* **~ing**) засмея́ться (*pf.*); **burst out ~ing** рассмея́ться (*pf.*); расхохотáться (*pf.*); **I almost burst out ~ing** я чуть бы́ло не пры́снул; **he who ~s last, ~s longest** хорошó смеётся тот, кто смеётся послéдним; **he ~s at my jokes** он смеётся, когдá я шучý; **what/who are you ~ing at?** над чем/кем вы смеётесь?; **it's nothing to ~ at** ничегó смешнóго; **I should ~ if he came in** бы́ло бы смешнó, éсли бы он вошёл; **he ~ed in my face** он рассмея́лся мне в лицó; **he ~ed fit to burst** (*coll.*) он чуть не лóпнул сó смеху; **I ~ed till I cried** я смея́лся до слёз; **he was ~ing up his sleeve** он смея́лся в кулáк (*or* исподти́шка); **he'll soon be ~ing on the other side of his face** емý скóро бýдет не до смéху; **make s.o. ~** смеши́ть, рас- когó-н.; **don't make me ~!** (*iron.*) не смеши́те (меня́); **I couldn't help ~ing** я не мог удержáться от смéха; **I couldn't stop ~ing** я смея́лся так, что не мог останови́ться.

● *with adv.*: **~ off** *v.t.*: **~ it off** отшý|чиваться, -ти́ться; **~ something off** отдéл|ываться, -аться от чегó-н. шýткой; св|оди́ть, -ести́ что-н. на шýтку.

laughable /ˈlɑːfəb(ə)l/ *adj.* смешнóй, смехотвóрный.

laughing /ˈlɑːfɪŋ/ *n.* смех; **I was in no mood for ~** мне бы́ло не до смéху; **I couldn't speak for ~** от смéха я не мог произнести́ ни словá; **it is no ~ matter** э́то не шýточное дéло; **he burst out ~** он рассмея́лся/расхохотáлся.

● *cpds.* **~-gas** *n.* веселя́щий газ; **~-stock** *n.* посмéшище; **make a ~-stock of s.o.** выставля́ть, вы́ставить когó-н. на посмéшище.

laughter /ˈlɑːftə(r)/ *n.* смех; (*loud*) хóхот; **die of, with ~** ум|ирáть, -ерéть сó смеху; смея́ться (*impf.*) до упáду; **roar with ~** хохотáть (*impf.*) во всё гóрло.

launch¹ /lɔːntʃ/ *n.* (*motor-boat*) кáтер.

launch² /lɔːntʃ/ *n.* (*of ship*) спуск (нá воду); (*of rocket or spacecraft*) зáпуск; (*of torpedo, product*) вы́пуск.

● *v.t.* (*set afloat*): **~ a ship** спус|кáть, -ти́ть корáбль нá воду; (*send into air*): **~ a rocket** запус|кáть, -ти́ть ракéту; (*aircraft from flight deck*) катапульти́ровать (*impf., pf.*); (*hurl, discharge*): **~ a spear** мет|áть, -нýть (*or* бр|осáть, -óсить) копьё; **~ a torpedo** выпускáть, вы́пустить торпéду; (*initiate*): **~ an attack** нач|инáть, -áть атáку; **~ a campaign** нач|инáть, -áть (*or* откр|ывáть, -ы́ть) кампáнию; **~ an enterprise/product** пус|кáть, -ти́ть предприя́тие/продýкт в продáжу.

● *v.i.* пус|кáться, -ти́ться; **he ~ed into an argument** он пусти́лся в спор; **we are ~ing (out) on, into a new enterprise** мы начинáем нóвое дéло.

● *cpds.* **~(ing)-pad** *n.* стáртовая площáдка; **~(ing)-site** *n.* стáртовая пози́ция; **~(ing)-tower** *n.* пусковáя вы́шка; **~-vehicle** *n.* ракéта-носи́тель (*m.*).

launder /ˈlɔːndə(r)/ *v.t. & i.* **1** стирáть(ся), вы́-; **this cloth ~s well** э́та матéрия хорошó стирáется. **2** (*fig.*): **~ money** отм|ывáть, -ы́ть дéньги; **money ~ing** отмывáние дéнег.

laund(e)rette /lɔːnˈdret/ *n.* (*Br.*) прáчечная самообслýживания.

laundress /ˈlɔːndrɪs/ *n.* прáчка.

laundromat /ˈlɔːndrəˌmæt/ *n.* (*US propr.*) = **laund(e)rette**

laundry /ˈlɔːndrɪ/ *n.* **1** (*establishment*) прáчечная; **send to the ~** отд|авáть, -áть в сти́рку (*or* в прáчечную); **my shirt came back torn from the ~** в прáчечной мне порвáли рубáшку. **2** (*clothes*) бельё (для сти́рки *or* из сти́рки).

● *cpd.* **~man** *n.* рабóчий в прáчечной.

laureate /ˈlɒrɪət/, /ˈlɔː-/ *n.*: **Poet L~** поэ́т-лауреáт.

laurel /ˈlɒr(ə)l/ *n.* лавр; (*attr.*) лаврóвый; (*fig., pl.*): **reap, win ~s** пожинáть (*impf.*) лáвры; **rest on one's ~s** поч|ивáть, -и́ть на лáврах; **look to one's ~s** защи|щáть, -ти́ть своё пéрвенство.

lava /ˈlɑːvə/ *n.* лáва; **~ bed** пласт лáвы; **~ flow** потóк лáвы.

lavatory /ˈlævətərɪ/ *n.* (*WC*) убóрная, туалéт; (*washroom*) умывáльная (кóмната); **~ paper** (*Br.*) туалéтная бумáга.

lave /leɪv/ *v.t.* (*liter.*) омывáть (*impf.*).

lavender /ˈlævɪndə(r)/ *n.* лавáнда; **~ water** лавáндовая водá; **a ~ gown** плáтье блéдно-лилóвого цвéта.

lavish /ˈlævɪʃ/ *adj.* **1** (*generous*) щéдрый; (*prodigal*) расточи́тельный; **he is ~ in his praise** он щедр на похвалы́; **a ~ reception** богáтый приём. **2** (*abundant*) оби́льный.

● *v.t.*: **~ money on something** расточáть (*impf.*) дéньги на что-н.; **~ praise on s.o.** расточáть (*impf.*) похвалы́ комý-н.; **~ care on s.o.** окружáть (*impf.*) когó-н. чрезмéрными забóтами.

lavishness /ˈlævɪʃnɪs/ *n.* щéдрость; расточи́тельность.

law /lɔː/ *n.* **1** (*rule or body of rules for society*) закóн; **the ~ of the land** закóн страны́; **the bill became ~** законопроéкт был при́нят; **above the ~** вы́ше закóна; **by ~** по закóну; **within the ~** в рáмках (*or* без нарушéния) закóна; **break, violate the ~** нар|ушáть, -ýшить закóн; **keep, observe the ~** соблюдáть (*impf.*) закóн; **pass a ~** прин|имáть, -я́ть закóн; **his word is ~** егó слóво — закóн; **he is a ~ unto himself** он живёт по сóбственным закóнам; **natural ~** закóн прирóды; **the ~ of supply and demand** закóн спрóса и предложéния; **the ~s of the game** прáвила (*nt. pl.*) игры́.
2 (*as subject of study, profession, system*) прáво, юсти́ция; **civil ~** граждáнское прáво; **in international ~** по междунарóдному прáву; **declare martial ~** объяв|ля́ть, -и́ть воéнное положéние; **~ and order** правопоря́док; **rule of ~** правопоря́док; **~ school** юриди́ческая шкóла; **read, study ~** изуч|áть, -и́ть прáво; **go in for the ~** учи́ться, вы́- на юри́ста; **follow, practise** (*Br.*), **practice** (*US*) **~** быть юри́стом; **doctor of ~s** дóктор юриди́ческих наýк; **court of ~** суд.
3 (*process of* **~**; **~suit**) судéбный процéсс; **go to ~** возбу|ждáть, -ди́ть судéбное дéло; **have the ~ on s.o.** подáть (*pf.*) на когó-н. в суд; **take the ~ into one's own hands** поступ|áть, -и́ть самочи́нно; верши́ть (*impf.*) самосýд.
4 (*phys., math.*): **~ of gravity** закóн тяготéния; **~ of probability** теóрия вероя́тностей.

● *cpds.* **~-abiding** *adj.* законопослýшный; **~-breaker** *n.* правонаруши́тель (*m.*) (*fem.* -ни́ца); **~-court** *n.* суд; **~-enforcement** *n.* (*attr.*): **~-enforcement agencies** правоохрани́тельные óрганы; **~-giver, ~-maker** *nn.* законодáтель (*m.*) (*fem.* -ница); **~man** *n.* (*US*) полицéйский, шери́ф; **~suit** *n.* судéбный процéсс; **bring a ~suit against s.o.** возбу|ждáть, -ди́ть (судéбное) дéло прóтив когó-н.

lawful /ˈlɔːfʊl/ *adj.* закóнный.

lawfulness /ˈlɔːfʊlnɪs/ *n.* закóнность.

lawless /ˈlɔːlɪs/ *adj.* (*of country etc.*) ди́кий, анархи́чный; (*of person*) непокóрный, мятéжный.

lawlessness /ˈlɔːlɪsnɪs/ *n.* беззакóние; непокóрность, мятéжность.

lawn¹ /lɔːn/ *n.* (*area of grass*) газóн; **~ tennis** тéннис.

● *cpd.* **~-mower** *n.* газóнокоси́лка.

lawn² /lɔːn/ *n.* (*linen*) бати́ст.

lawyer /ˈlɔɪə(r)/, /ˈlɔːjə(r)/ *n.* юри́ст; (*advocate, barrister*) адвокáт.

lax /læks/ *adj.* (*negligent, inattentive*) небрéжный; (*not strict*) нестрóгий; **~ discipline** слáбая дисципли́на; **~ morals** распýщенные нрáвы.

laxative /ˈlæksətɪv/ *n.* слаби́тельное (срéдство).

● *adj.* слаби́тельный.

lax|ity /ˈlæksɪtɪ/, **-ness** /ˈlæksnɪs/ *nn.* небрéжность; (*of morals*) распýщенность.

lay¹ /leɪ/ *n.* (*liter.*) пéсня, баллáда.

lay² /leɪ/ *n.* **1** (*vulg.*): **she's an easy ~** онá давáлка (*sl.*). **2** *see* **⇒lie²** *n.*

● *v.t.* (*past and p.p.* **laid**) **1** (*put down, deposit*) класть, положи́ть; **he laid his hand on my shoulder** он положи́л ру́ку мне на плечо́; **~ a child to sleep** укла́дывать, уложи́ть ребёнка (спать); **~ to rest** (*bury*) хорони́ть, по-; (*fig.*): **his fears were laid to rest** его́ опасе́ния исче́зли; **~ an egg** нести́, с- яйцо́; (*US coll., fail*) пров|а́ливаться, -али́ться; (*set in position*): **~ bricks** класть (*impf.*) кирпичи́; **~ a foundation** (*lit., fig.*) за|кла́дывать, -ложи́ть фунда́мент; **~ a carpet** стлать, по- ковёр; **~ cable/pipes** про|кла́дывать, -ложи́ть ка́бель/тру́бы; **~ rails** укла́дывать, уложи́ть ре́льсы; **~ an ambush** устр|а́ивать, -о́ить заса́ду; **~ a trap** ста́вить, по- лову́шку.
2 (*fig., place*): **~ a bet** держа́ть (*impf.*) пари́; **~ £10 on a horse** ста́вить, по- 10 фу́нтов на ло́шадь; **~ the facts before s.o.** дов|оди́ть, -ести́ фа́кты до све́дения кого́-н.; **~ a charge** предъяв|ля́ть, -и́ть обвине́ние (*кому в чём*); **the scene is laid in London** де́йствие происхо́дит в Ло́ндоне.
3 (*prepare*): **~ a fire** пригото́вить (*pf.*) всё, что́бы развести́ ого́нь; **~ the table for dinner** накр|ыва́ть, -ы́ть стол к обе́ду; **~ plans** сост|авля́ть, -а́вить пла́ны.
4 (*cause to subside*): **~ a ghost** изг|оня́ть, -на́ть ду́ха.
5 (*cover*) укла́дывать, уложи́ть; покр|ыва́ть, -ы́ть; **a floor laid with linoleum** пол, покры́тый лино́леумом.
6 (*cause to be*): **~ bare** (*lit.*) обнаж|а́ть, -и́ть; (*fig., reveal*) раскр|ыва́ть, -ы́ть; **~ low** (*knock over*) вали́ть, с-; (*overthrow*) низл|ага́ть, -ожи́ть; **he was laid low with a fever** он слёг с лихора́дкой; **~ o.s. open to attack** подст|авля́ть, -а́вить себя́ под уда́р; **~ o.s. open to suspicion** навл|ека́ть, -е́чь на себя́ подозре́ние; **~ waste** опустош|а́ть, -и́ть.
7 (*vulg., copulate with*) тра́х|ать, -нуть.

● *v.i.* (*past and p.p.* **laid**) **1** (*sc. eggs*) нести́сь (*impf.*).
2 (*sc. the table*): **she laid for six** она́ накры́ла на шестеры́х.
3 (*strike*): **~ about s.o.** колоти́ть, по- кого́-н.; **~ about one** раздава́ть (*impf.*) уда́ры напра́во и нале́во; **~ into s.o.** набр|а́сываться, -о́ситься на кого́-н.; нап|ада́ть, -а́сть на кого́-н.

● *with advs.*: **~ aside** (*also* **~ by**) *v.t.* (*lit.*) от|кла́дывать, -ложи́ть; **he laid aside his work** он отложи́л рабо́ту; (*relinquish, abandon*) ост|авля́ть, -а́вить; **you must ~ aside your prejudices** вы должны́ оста́вить/(от)бро́сить свои́ предрассу́дки; (*save*) от|кла́дывать, -ложи́ть; **~ back** *v.t.*: **the dog laid back its ears** соба́ка прижа́ла у́ши; **~ by** *v.t.* = **~ aside; ~down** *v.t.* (*on ground, bed etc.*) укла́дывать, уложи́ть; **~ down one's arms** (*surrender*) скла́дывать, сложи́ть ору́жие; **~ down a field to grass** пус|ка́ть, -ти́ть по́ле под траву́; (*formulate, prescribe*): **~ down conditions/rules** устан|а́вливать, -ови́ть (*or* формули́ровать, с-; выраба́тывать, вы́работать) усло́вия/пра́вила; **he laid it down as a condition that ...** он поста́вил усло́вием, что́бы. . .; **this is laid down in the regulations** э́то предпи́сано пра́вилами; **he is fond of ~ing down the law** он лю́бит диктова́ть/распоряжа́ться; (*sacrifice*): **~ down one's life for one's friends** же́ртвовать, по- жи́знью (*or* класть, положи́ть жизнь) за друзе́й; (*begin to build*): **~ down a ship** за|кла́дывать, -ложи́ть кора́бль; **~ in** *v.t.* (*stock up with*) загот|а́вливать (*or* -овля́ть), -о́вить; запас|а́ть, -ти́; запас|а́ться, -ти́сь + *i.*; **~ off** *v.t.* (*suspend from work*) ув|ольня́ть, -о́лить (со слу́жбы); отстран|я́ть, -и́ть (от рабо́ты); (*coll., desist from*) перест|ава́ть, -а́ть; *v.i.*: **~ off!** (*coll.*) бро́сь(те)!; отста́нь(те)!; **~ on** *v.t.* (*Br., provide supply of*) пров|оди́ть, -ести́; **is water laid on here?** здесь есть водопрово́д?; (*coll.*): **he promised to ~ on some drinks** он обеща́л поста́вить вы́пивку; (*arrange*) устр|а́ивать, -о́ить; **it's all laid on** всё устро́ено; (*fig.*): **~ it on thick** (*coll., of exaggerated praise*) гру́бо льсти́ть (*impf.*); **~ out** *v.t.* (*arrange for display etc.*) выставля́ть, вы́ставить; **~ out clothes** выкла́дывать, вы́ложить оде́жду; (*design*) плани́ровать, рас-; (*garden etc.*) разб|ива́ть, -и́ть; (*for burial*): **~ out a corpse** уб|ира́ть, -ра́ть поко́йника; (*spend*) тра́тить, ис-; (*knock down*) сби|ва́ть, -ть (с ног); **~ to** *v.i.* (*of ship*) ложи́ться, лечь в дрейф (*or* на курс); **~ up** *v.t.* (*save, store*) копи́ть, на-; запас|а́ть, -ти́; **you are ~ing up trouble for yourself** вы лишь навлечёте неприя́тности себе́ на́ го́лову; (*make inactive*): **my car was laid up all winter** всю зи́му моя́ маши́на простоя́ла; **he was laid up with a broken leg** он был прико́ван к посте́ли из-за сло́манной ноги́.

● *cpds.* **~about** *n.* (*coll.*) безде́льни|к (*fem.* -ца); **~-by** *n.* (*Br.*) придоро́жная площа́дка для стоя́нки автомоби́лей; **~-off** *n.* (*of workers*) сокраще́ние ка́дров; **~out** *n.* (*arrangement*) расположе́ние; (*of town etc.*) планиро́вка; (*of garden etc.*) разби́вка; (*plan*) чертёж, план.

lay³ /leɪ/ *adj.* **1** (*opp. clerical*) мирско́й; **~ brother** беле́ц. **2** (*opp. professional*): **~ opinion** мне́ние неспециали́стов.

● *cpds.* **~man** *n.* (*relig.*) миря́нин; (*non-specialist*) непрофессиона́л, неспециали́ст; **~woman** *n.* миря́нка; непрофессиона́лка.

layer¹ /ˈleɪə(r)/ *n.* (*thickness, stratum*) слой, пласт; (*inserted* **~**) прокла́дка; **~ cake** слоёный пиро́г.

● *v.t.* (*lay or cut in* **~***s*) пластова́ть (*impf.*); насл|а́ивать, -о́ить.

layer² /ˈleɪə(r)/ *n.* (*person laying flooring, rails*) укла́дчик; (*laying hen*) несу́шка; **these hens are good ~s** э́ти ку́ры хорошо́ несу́тся.

layette /leɪˈet/ *n.* прида́ное новорождённого.

lay-figure /leɪ/ *n.* манеке́н.

laying /leɪɪŋ/ *n.* (*of eggs*) кла́дка; (*of cable*) прокла́дка; (*of bricks*) укла́дка; (*of carpet*) расстила́ние; (*of turf*) дерно́вка; (*of rails, pipes*) укла́дка.

● *cpd.* **~-on** *n.*: **~-on of hands** рукоположе́ние.

laze /leɪz/ *v.t. & i.*: **~ about** слоня́ться (*impf.*) без де́ла; **~ away the time** безде́льничать (*impf.*).

laziness /ˈleɪzɪnɪs/ *n.* лень, ле́ность.

lazy /ˈleɪzɪ/ *adj.* (**lazier, laziest**) лени́вый; **become ~** разле́н|иваться, -и́ться; **be ~** лени́ться (*impf.*); **I was too ~ to write to him** я лени́лся (*or* мне бы́ло лень) ему́ писа́ть.

● *cpds.* **~bones** *n.* лентя́й (*fem.* -ка), ло́дырь (*m.*); (*coll.*) лежебо́ка (*c.g.*); **~ Susan** *n.* враща́ющийся подно́с для ку́шаний; **~-tongs** *n.* пантогра́фный захва́т.

lb. /paʊnd(z)/ *n.* (*abbr. of* **libra**) фунт.

LCD (*abbr. of* ***liquid-crystal display***) ЖКИ (жидкокристалли́ческий индика́тор).

L/Cpl. /lɑːns ˈkɔːpər(ə)l/ *n.* (*abbr. of* ***Lance-Corporal***) мла́дший капра́л.

LEA (*abbr. of* ***local education authority***) (*Br.*) ме́стные о́рганы образова́ния.

leach /liːtʃ/ *v.t.* выщела́чивать, вы́щелочить.

lead¹ /led/ *n.* **1** (*metal*) свине́ц; (*attr.*) свинцо́вый; **red ~** свинцо́вый су́рик; **white ~** свинцо́вые бели́ла; **~ poisoning** отравле́ние свинцо́м. **2** (*in pencil*) графи́т; **~ pencil** (графи́товый) каранда́ш; **the ~ keeps breaking** гри́фель постоя́нно лома́ется. **3** (*on fishing line*) грузи́ло; (*as ammunition*) дробь; (*bullets*) пу́ли (*f. pl.*). **4** (*naut., for sounding*) лот. **5** (*typ.*) шпон. **6** (*pl., Br., on roof*) свинцо́вые листы́ (*m. pl.*) для покры́тия кры́ши. **7** (*pl., on window*) свинцо́вые ра́мки (*f. pl.*).

● *v.t.* (*cover with* **~**) освинц|о́вывать, -ева́ть.

● *cpd.* **~-free** *adj.* неэтили́рованный.

lead² /liːd/ *n.* **1** (*direction, guidance; initiative*) руково́дство; инициати́ва; **give a ~ to s.o.** под|ава́ть, -а́ть приме́р кому́-н.; **take the ~** брать, взять на (себя́) руково́дство/инициати́ву; **follow s.o.'s ~** (*lit., fig.*) сле́довать, по- за кем-н.
2 (*first place*): **be in the ~** стоя́ть (*impf.*) во главе́; (*sport*) быть впереди́; вести́ (*det.*); (*fig.*) стоя́ть (*impf.*) во главе́, пе́рвенствовать (*impf.*); **take the ~** (*sport*) выходи́ть, вы́йти вперёд; **he had a ~ of 10 metres** (*Br.*), **meters** (*US*) он опереди́л други́х на 10 ме́тров.
3 (*clue*): **give s.o. a ~ on something** нав|оди́ть, -ести́ кого́-н. на след чего́-н.; **the police are looking for a ~** поли́ция пыта́ется напа́сть на след.
4 (*Br., cord, strap*) поводо́к, при́вязь; **'dogs must be kept on a ~'** (*notice*) «соба́к держа́ть на поводке́».
5 (*elec.*) про́вод (*pl.* -а́).
6 (*theatr.*) гла́вная роль; актёр, игра́ющий гла́вную роль.
7 (*cards*) ход; **your ~!** ваш ход!

● *v.t.* (*past and p.p.* **led**) **1** (*conduct*) води́ть (*indet.*), вести́, по- (*det.*); **~ by the hand** вести́ за́ руку; **~ a horse by**

L

the bridle вести́ ло́шадь под уздцы́; ~ **s.o. by the nose** вести́ кого́-н. на поводу́; ~ **astray** сби|ва́ть, -ть с пути́ и́стинного; **he led his troops into battle** он повёл солда́т в бой; ~ **the way** идти́ (*det.*) во главе́; **he was led off the premises** его́ вы́вели из помеще́ния.
2 (*fig., bring, incline, induce*): **what led you to this idea?** что навело́ вас на э́ту мысль?; ~ **s.o. to believe** созда́ть (*pf.*) впечатле́ние у кого́-н., что. . .; **he led us to expect much** он пробуди́л у нас больши́е наде́жды.
3 (*cause to go, e.g. water*) пров|оди́ть, -ести́.
4 (*be in charge of*): ~ **an expedition/orchestra** руководи́ть (*impf.*) экспеди́цией/орке́стром; (*direct*) управля́ть (*impf.*) + *i.*; (*command*) кома́ндовать (*impf.*) + *i.*; (*act as chief or head of*) возгл|авля́ть, -а́вить; (*be in the forefront of*): **the choir** ~**s the procession** хор идёт во главе́ проце́ссии.
5 (*pass, spend*): ~ **an idle life** вести́ (*det.*) пра́здную жизнь; ~ **a wretched existence** влачи́ть (*impf.*) жа́лкое существова́ние.
6 (*cause to spend or undertake*): ~ **s.o. a (merry) dance** (*Br.*) заст|авля́ть, -а́вить кого́-н. попляса́ть/пому́читься.
7 (*cards*): ~ **trumps** ходи́ть, пойти́ с ко́зыря.
● *v.i.* (*past and p.p.* **led**) **1** (*of a road etc.*) вести́ (*det.*): **all roads** ~ **to Rome** все доро́ги веду́т в Рим; (*fig.*) вести́; прив|оди́ть, -ести́; **this method will** ~ **to difficulties** э́тот ме́тод вы́зовет сло́жности.
2 (*be first or ahead*) быть впереди́; вести́ (*det.*); лиди́ровать (*impf.*); **our team is** ~**ing by 5 points** на́ша кома́нда впереди́ на пять очко́в.
3 (*cards*) ходи́ть, пойти́.
4 (*journalism*): **the Times led with an article on the strike** «Таймс» посвяти́ла свою́ передову́ю статью́ забасто́вке.
● *with advs.*: ~ **away** *v.t.* отв|оди́ть, -ести́; ув|оди́ть, -ести́; ~ **in** *v.t.* вв|оди́ть, -ести́; ~ **off** *v.t.* (*take away*) ув|оди́ть, -ести́; (*start*): **they led off the dance** они́ откры́ли та́нец; *v.i.*: **he led off with an apology** он на́чал с извине́ния; ~ **on** *v.t.* (*lit.*): **he led his troops on to victory** он вёл свой во́йска к побе́де; (*encourage*) поощр|я́ть, -и́ть; (*deceive*) обма́н|ывать, -у́ть; (*flirt with*): **she is** ~**ing him on** она́ его́ завлека́ет; *v.i.*: ~ **on!** вперёд!; ~ **up** *v.i.*: ~ **up to** (*lit.*) подв|оди́ть, -ести́ к + *d.*; (*precede, form preparation for*) подгот|овля́ть, -о́вить; **the events that led up to the war** собы́тия, приве́дшие к войне́; (*direct conversation towards*) нав|оди́ть, -ести́ разгово́р на + *a.*; **what are you** ~**ing up to?** куда́ вы кло́ните?
● *cpd.* ~**-in** *n.* (*introduction*) введе́ние, ввод; (*elec.*) ввод.

leaded /ˈledɪd/ *adj.* (*petrol*) этили́рованный; (*window*) со свинцо́выми ра́мами.

leaden /ˈled(ə)n/ *adj.* (*lit., fig.*) свинцо́вый.

leader /ˈliːdə(r)/ *n.* **1** (*pol.*) руководи́тель (*m.*) (*fem.* -ница), ли́дер; (*comm.*) ли́дер; (*rhet.*) вождь (*m.*). **2** (*of group*) вожа́к; (*of gang*) глава́рь (*m.*). **3** (*mil.*) команди́р. **4** (*Br., of orchestra*) пе́рвая скри́пка; (*US, conductor*) дирижёр. **5** (*front horse in team*) пере́дняя ло́шадь. **6** (*Br., leading article*) передова́я (статья́), передови́ца.

leadership /ˈliːdəʃɪp/ *n.* (*role of leader; group of leaders*) руково́дство; (*pre-eminence*) пе́рвенство; (*qualities of a leader*) ли́дерство, инициати́вность.

leading /ˈliːdɪŋ/ *adj.* (*foremost*) веду́щий; (*outstanding*) выдаю́щийся; ~ **aircraftman** рядово́й авиа́ции пе́рвого кла́сса; ~ **article** (*Br.*) передова́я (статья́), передови́ца; ~ **company** (*comm.*) лиди́рующая компа́ния; ~ **lady** исполни́тельница гла́вной ро́ли; ~ **light** (*of art, science etc.*) свети́ло, корифе́й; (*of society*) знамени́тость, свети́ло; ~ **question** наводя́щий вопро́с; ~ **seaman** ста́рший матро́с; ~ **team** (*sport*) лиди́рующая кома́нда.
● *cpd.* ~**-rein** *n.* по́вод.

leaf /liːf/ *n.* (*pl.* **leaves**) **1** (*of tree or plant*) лист (*pl.* -ья); **in** ~ покры́тый листво́й; **come into** ~ распус|ка́ться, -ти́ться; **tobacco** ~ листово́й таба́к.
2 (*of book*) лист (*pl.* -ы́); (*fig.*): **take a** ~ **out of s.o.'s book** брать, взять приме́р с кого́-н.; **turn over a new** ~ нач|ина́ть, -а́ть но́вую жизнь, испра́виться (*pf.*). **3** (*of metal etc.*) лист (*pl.* -ы́); **gold** ~ листово́е зо́лото. **4** (*of table etc.*) откидна́я доска́; (*inserted section*) вставна́я доска́. **5** (*of shutter*) ство́рка.
● *v.t.*: ~ **over, through** перели́ст|ывать, -а́ть.
● *cpds.* ~**-green** *adj.* цве́та зелёной листвы́; ~**-mould** (*US* **-mold**) *n.* ли́ственный перегно́й.

leafless /ˈliːflɪs/ *adj.* безли́стный.

leaflet /ˈliːflɪt/ *n.* **1** (*bot.*) листо́к. **2** (*printed*) брошю́рка; (*fold-out*) букле́т; (*pol.*) листо́вка.

leafy /ˈliːfɪ/ *adj.* (**leafier, leafiest**) густоли́ственный.

league¹ /liːg/ *n.* (*measure*) лье (*indecl.*).

league² /liːg/ *n.* (*alliance*) ли́га; **L**~ **of Nations** Ли́га на́ций; **in** ~ **with** в сою́зе с + *i.*; в сго́воре с + *i.* (*pej.*); **be not in the same** ~ **as s.o.** быть не того́ кла́сса; **football** ~ футбо́льная ли́га; ~ **table** (*Br.*) (*sport*) табли́ца результа́тов; (*fig.*) сравни́тельный гра́фик.
● *v.i.* (**leagues, leagued, leaguing**): ~ **together** образо́в|ывать, -а́ть сою́з; (*pej.*) сгов|а́риваться, -ори́ться.

leak /liːk/ *n.* (*hole*) течь; **spring a** ~ да|ва́ть, -ть течь; **stop a** ~ остан|а́вливать, -ови́ть течь; (*escape of fluid*) уте́чка; (*fig., of information*) уте́чка/проса́чивание информа́ции.
● *v.t.* (*fig.*) выдава́ть, вы́дать.
● *v.i.* (*lit.*) течь (*impf.*); протека́ть (*impf.*); прос|а́чиваться, -очи́ться; (*fig.*): **the affair** ~**ed out** де́ло вы́плыло нару́жу; **take a** ~ (*coll., urinate*) отл|ива́ть, -и́ть.
● *cpd.* ~**-proof** *adj.* непроница́емый, гермети́чный.

leakage /ˈliːkɪdʒ/ *n.* (*lit., fig.*) уте́чка.

leaky /ˈliːkɪ/ *adj.* (**leakier, leakiest**) дыря́вый, име́ющий течь; **a** ~ **pipe** протека́ющая труба́; **these barrels are** ~ э́ти бо́чки теку́т.

lean¹ /liːn/ *n.* (*of meat*) по́стная часть.
● *adj.* **1** (*thin*) то́щий; (*fig.*): ~ **years** ску́дные го́ды; **a** ~ **harvest** ску́дный/плохо́й урожа́й. **2** (*of meat*) нежи́рный, по́стный.

lean² /liːn/ *n.* (*inclination*) укло́н, накло́н.
● *v.t.* (*past and p.p.* **leaned** /liːnd/, /lent/ *or esp. Br.* **leant**) прислон|я́ть, -и́ть (*что к чему*); оп|ира́ть, -ере́ть (*что обо что*); ~ **the ladder against the wall!** прислони́те ле́стницу к стене́!; **he was** ~**ing his arm on the table** он опира́лся руко́й о стол.
● *v.i.* (*past and p.p.* **leaned** /liːnd/, /lent/ *or esp. Br.* **leant**) (*incline from vertical*) наклон|я́ться, -и́ться; **the tower** ~**s slightly** ба́шня слегка́ наклони́лась; **the trees are** ~**ing in the wind** дере́вья клоня́тся от ве́тра; **the L**~**ing Tower of Pisa** Па́дающая ба́шня в Пи́зе; **sit** ~**ing backward/forward** сиде́ть (*impf.*), пода́вшись наза́д/вперёд; **he** ~**s over backwards to help** (*fig.*) он из ко́жи вон ле́зет, что́бы помо́чь; ~ **out of the window** высо́вываться, вы́сунуться из окна́; **he** ~**ed over to her** он наклони́лся к ней; **he was** ~**ing over my shoulder** он загля́дывал мне че́рез плечо́; **he** ~**t towards clemency** он был скло́нен к милосе́рдию; **I** ~ **towards the same opinion** я скло́нен ду́мать то же са́мое.
2 (*support o.s.*) прислон|я́ться, -и́ться; оп|ира́ться, -ере́ться; **he was** ~**ing against a tree** он стоя́л, прислони́вшись к де́реву; **he walked** ~**ing on a stick** он шёл, опира́ясь на трость; (*fig.*): **he** ~**s** (*depends*) **on his wife for support** он опира́ется на подде́ржку жены́; **I had to** ~ (*coll., put pressure*) **on him to get results** мне пришло́сь нажа́ть на него́, что́бы доби́ться результа́тов.
● *cpd.* ~**-to** *n.* односка́тная пристро́йка.

leaning /ˈliːnɪŋ/ *n.* (*inclination*) скло́нность; (*tendency*) пристра́стие.

leanness /ˈliːnnɪs/ *n.* худоба́, истоще́ние.

leant /lent/ *esp. Br. past and p.p. of* ⇒**lean²**

leap /liːp/ *n.* прыжо́к, скачо́к; **take a** ~ пры́гнуть (*pf.*); **his heart gave a** ~ се́рдце у него́ дро́гнуло/ёкнуло; (*fig.*): **a** ~ **in the dark** прыжо́к в неизве́стность; **by** ~**s and bounds** стреми́тельно.
● *v.t.* (*past and p.p.* **leaped** /liːpt/, /lept/ *or* **leapt** /lept/) (~ *over*) переск|а́кивать, -очи́ть (*or* перепры́г|ивать, -нуть) че́рез + *a.*
● *v.i.* (*past and p.p.* **leaped** /liːpt/, /lept/ *or* **leapt** /lept/) пры́г|ать, -нуть; **my heart** ~**t for joy** у меня́ се́рдце подскочи́ло от ра́дости; ~ **to one's feet** вск|а́кивать, -очи́ть; **he** ~**t** (*fig.*) **at**

my offer он так и ухвати́лся за моё предложе́ние.

● *cpds.* **~-frog** *n.* чехарда́; *v.t.* перепры́г|ивать, -нуть че́рез + *a.*; (*surpass, overtake*) обск|а́кивать, -aка́ть; (*avoid an obstacle*) об|ходи́ть, -ойти́; **~-year** *n.* високо́сный год.

learn /lɜ:n/ *v.t.* (*past and p.p.* **learned** /lɜ:nt/, /lɜ:nd/ *or esp. Br.* **learnt**) **1** (*get knowledge of*) учи́ться, на- + *d. or inf.*; изуч|а́ть, -и́ть; (*study*) занима́ться (*impf.*) + *i.*; **he ~ed (how) to ride** он научи́лся е́здить верхо́м; (**~** *a trade*) обуч|а́ться, -и́ться + *d. or inf.*; **he is ~ing to be an interpreter** он у́чится на перево́дчика; (**~** *off or by heart*) учи́ть, вы́-; вы́учиться (*pf.*) + *d.*; **he ~t French** он вы́учился францу́зскому языку́; **where did you ~ Russian?** где вы изуча́ли ру́сский язы́к?; **she is ~ing her part** она́ у́чит/разу́чивает свою́ роль; **he ~t the prayer by heart** он вы́учил моли́тву наизу́сть/назубо́к; **he ~t his lesson** (*fig.*) он получи́л хоро́ший уро́к.
2 (*be informed*) узн|ава́ть, -а́ть; **I have yet to ~ where we are going** я ещё не зна́ю, куда́ мы пойдём.

● *v.i.* (*past and p.p.* **learned** /lɜ:nt/, /ɜ:nd/ *or esp. Br.* **learnt**): **he ~s slowly** он у́чится с трудо́м; **you can ~ from his mistakes** учи́тесь на его́ оши́бках; **I was sorry to ~ of your illness** я с сожале́нием узна́л о ва́шей боле́зни.

learned /ˈlɜ:nɪd/ *adj.* учёный; **my ~ friend** (*Br., Counsel*) мой учёный колле́га; **a ~ society** нау́чное о́бщество.

learner /ˈlɜ:nə(r)/ *n.* начина́ющий; **he is a good ~** он хорошо́ у́чится; (**~***-driver*) начина́ющий води́тель (не име́ющий води́тельских прав); шофёр-учени́|к (*fem.* -ца).

learning /ˈlɜ:nɪŋ/ *n.* (*process*) уче́ние; изуче́ние; **~ did not come easily to him** уче́ние ему́ дава́лось нелегко́; (*possession of knowledge*) учёность, эруди́ция; (*body of knowledge*) нау́ка; **seat of ~** оча́г просвеще́ния.

learnt /lɜ:nt/ *esp. Br. past and p.p. of* ⇒**learn**

lease /li:s/ *n.* аре́нда; **long ~** долгосро́чная аре́нда; **the ~ is running out** срок аре́нды истека́ет; **we took the house on a 20-year ~** мы взя́ли дом в аре́нду на 20 лет; (*fig.*): **the doctors gave him a new ~ of life** врачи́ ему́ продли́ли жизнь; **he took on a new ~ of life** он сло́вно за́ново роди́лся.

● *v.t.* (*of lessee*) арендова́ть (*impf., pf.*); брать, взять в аре́нду/наём; (*of lessor*) сд|ава́ть, -ать в аре́нду.

● *cpds.* **~hold** *n.* аре́нда; владе́ние на права́х аре́нды; **~hold property** арендо́ванная со́бственность; **~holder** *n.* аренда́тор.

leash /li:ʃ/ *n.* при́вязь, поводо́к; **let off the ~** (*lit.*) спус|ка́ть, -ти́ть с поводка́; (*fig.*) развяза́ть (*pf.*) ру́ки + *d.*; **strain at the ~** (*fig.*) рва́ться (*impf.*) в бой.

● *v.t.* брать, взять на поводо́к.

least /li:st/ *n.*: **~ said, soonest mended** чем ме́ньше ска́зано, тем ле́гче испра́вить де́ло; **to say the ~** мя́гко говоря́; **the ~ he could do is to pay for the damage** он мог бы по кра́йней ме́ре возмести́ть уще́рб; **at ~** по кра́йней ме́ре; са́мое ме́ньшее; не ме́ньше + *g.*; **at the very ~** по ме́ньшей ме́ре; **give me ten at the (very) ~** да́йте мне ми́нимум де́сять; **at ~ once a year** не ре́же, чем раз в год; **he is at ~ as tall as you** он ва́шего ро́ста, а мо́жет быть и вы́ше; **you should at ~ have warned me** вы бы хоть предупреди́ли меня́; **you can at ~ try** попы́тка не пы́тка; **not in the ~** ни в мале́йшей сте́пени, ничу́ть, ниско́лько; **not in the ~ interested** совсе́м не заинтересо́ван (*pred.*).

● *adj.* (*smallest*) наиме́ньший; минима́льный; **that's the ~ of my worries** э́то меня́ ме́ньше всего́ волну́ет; (*slightest*) мале́йший; **he hasn't the ~ idea about it** он об э́том не име́ет ни мале́йшего поня́тия.

● *adv.* ме́ньше всего́; **I like this the ~ of all his plays** э́та его́ пье́са мне нра́вится ме́ньше всех други́х; **it is the ~ successful of his books** э́то наиме́нее уда́чная из его́ книг; **no-one can complain, you ~ of all** никто́ не мо́жет жа́ловаться, а вы и пода́вно; **with the ~ possible trouble** с наиме́ньшими хло́потами; с наиме́ньшей затра́той сил; **not ~** не в после́днюю о́чередь.

leather /ˈleðə(r)/ *n.* **1** ко́жа; **patent ~** лакиро́ванная ко́жа; **imitation ~** кожими́т; **as tough as ~** жёсткий как подо́шва. **2** (*wash-~*) за́мша; бархо́тка. **3** (**~** *thong*) реме́нь (*m.*).

● *adj.* **1** (*made of* **~**) ко́жаный; **~ jacket** ко́жаная ку́ртка; ко́жанка. **2** (*pert. to* **~**) коже́венный; **~ goods** коже́венный това́р.

● *v.t.* (*thrash*) лупи́ть, от- (*coll.*); поро́ть, вы́-.

leatherette /ˌleðəˈret/ *n.* кожими́т.

leathery /ˈleðərɪ/ *adj.* (*tough*) жёсткий; **~ skin** загрубе́вшая ко́жа.

leave /li:v/ *n.* **1** (*permission*) позволе́ние, разреше́ние; **who gave you ~ to go?** кто дал вам разреше́ние уйти́?; **I take ~ to remark** я позво́лю себе́ заме́тить; **by your ~** с ва́шего разреше́ния; **without (so much as) a 'by your ~'** без спро́са/спро́су.
2 (**~** *of absence*) о́тпуск; **he is on ~** он в о́тпуску́; **when are you going on ~?** когда́ вы ухо́дите в о́тпуск?; **~ pass** увольни́тельная запи́ска; отпускно́е свиде́тельство.
3 (*farewell*): **take (one's) ~ (of s.o.)** про|ща́ться, -сти́ться (с кем-н.); **take ~ of one's senses** с ума́ сойти́ (*pf.*); (*coll.*) рехну́ться (*pf.*).

● *v.t.* (*past and p.p.* **left**) **1** (*allow or cause to remain*) ост|авля́ть, -а́вить; **the wound left a scar** от ра́ны оста́лся шрам; **his words left a deep impression** его́ слова́ произвели́ большо́е впечатле́ние; **I was left with the feeling that ...** у меня́ оста́лось чу́вство, что...; **let us ~ it at that** пусть так; **you can take it or ~ it!** ва́ша во́ля!; **has anyone left a message?** никто́ ничего́ не передава́л?; **he left a wife and three children** по́сле его́ сме́рти жена́ оста́лась одна́ с тремя́ детьми́; **two from five ~s three** пять ми́нус два равня́ется трём; (*with indication of state or circumstances*): **~ me alone!** оста́вьте меня́ (в поко́е)!; **~ my books alone!** не тро́гайте мои́ кни́ги; **~ well alone!** от добра́ добра́ не и́щут; лу́чшее — враг хоро́шего; **it ~s me cold** (*fig.*) э́то меня́ не тро́гает; **I left him in no doubt as to my intention** я ему́ я́сно объясни́л своё наме́рение; **they left him in the lurch** они́ бро́сили его́ в беде́; **it ~s much to be desired** э́то оставля́ет жела́ть мно́го лу́чшего; **~ the door open!** оста́вьте дверь откры́той!; не закрыва́йте дверь!; **he ~s himself open to attack** он ста́вит себя́ под уда́р; **some things are better left unsaid** о не́которых веща́х лу́чше не говори́ть; **she was left a widow** она́ оста́лась вдово́й; **the illness left him weak** по́сле боле́зни он осла́б; (*p.p., remaining*): **I have no money left** у меня́ не оста́лось де́нег; **how much milk is there left?** ско́лько оста́лось молока́?
2 (**~** *behind by accident*) заб|ыва́ть, -ы́ть; **I left my umbrella at home** я забы́л зо́нтик до́ма.
3 (*bequeath*) завеща́ть (*impf., pf.*); ост|авля́ть, -а́вить в насле́дство; **she was left a large inheritance by her uncle** дя́дя оста́вил ей большо́е насле́дство.
4 (*abandon*) бр|оса́ть, -о́сить; пок|ида́ть, -и́нуть; **he left his wife for another woman** он бро́сил свою́ жену́ ра́ди друго́й же́нщины.
5 (*relinquish*): **~ hold, go of** выпуска́ть, вы́пустить из рук.
6 (*commit, entrust*) предост|авля́ть, -а́вить; **I ~ the decision to you** предоставля́ю реше́ние вам; **it was left to him to decide** реша́ть до́лжен был он; **~ it to him** пусть он э́то сде́лает; **~ it to me** я э́тим займу́сь; **he ~s nothing to chance** он чрезвыча́йно осторо́жен; **he was left to himself** он был предоста́влен самому́ себе́.
7 (*go away from*) выходи́ть, вы́йти из + *g.*; (*by vehicle*) выезжа́ть, вы́ехать из + *g.*; (*by air*) вылета́ть, вы́лететь из + *g.*; (*for vv. used when subj. is a mode of transport, see v.i.*); **I ~ the house at eight** я выхожу́ из дому в во́семь часо́в; **~ the room!** вы́йдите из ко́мнаты; **the train was an hour late leaving Oxford** по́езд о́тбыл из О́ксфорда с часовы́м опозда́нием; **I left him in good health** когда́ я его́ поки́нул, он был соверше́нно здоро́в; (*come off*): **the train left the rails** по́езд сошёл с ре́льсов; (*rise from*): **~ the table** вст|ава́ть, -ать из-за стола́; (**~** *for good, quit*) бр|оса́ть, -о́сить; пок|ида́ть, -и́нуть; **he left his job** он бро́сил свою́ рабо́ту; **our typist left us** на́ша машини́стка уво́лилась; **he left the Communist party** он вы́шел из коммунисти́ческой па́ртии; **has he left the country for good?** он навсегда́ поки́нул страну́?; **he left home at 16** в 16 лет он ушёл из дому; **he ~s school this year** он конча́ет шко́лу в э́том году́.

● *v.i.* (*past and p.p.* **left**) **1** (*of person on foot*) уходи́ть, уйти́; (*by transport*)

L

уезжáть, уéхать; (*by air*) улет|áть, -éть; **when do you ~ for the South?** когдá вы уезжáете на юг?; (**~** *for good*): **she left** (*her job*) **without giving notice** онá ушлá с рабóты, не увéдомив начáльства.
2 (*of train*) от|ходи́ть, -ойти́; (*of boat*) от|ходи́ть, -ойти́; отпл|ывáть, -ы́ть; (*of aircraft*) вылетáть, вы́лететь.

● *with advs.*: **~ about, ~ around** *v.t.*: **don't ~ your money around** не оставля́йте дéньги, где попáло; **~ aside** *v.t.* ост|авля́ть, -áвить в сторонé; **leaving expense aside, it's not a practical idea** э́то бесполéзная затéя, уж не говоря́ о расхóдах; **~ behind** *v.t.* ост|авля́ть, -áвить пóсле себя́; (*forget to take*): **he left his hat behind** он забы́л свою́ шля́пу; (*abandon*): **he was left behind on the island** егó поки́нули на óстрове; (*bequeath*): **he left behind a tidy sum** он остáвил изря́дную сýмму; (*outstrip*): **we left him far behind** мы егó остáвили далекó позади́; **~ down** *v.t.*: **~ the blinds down!** не поднимáйте штóры!; **~ in** *v.t.*: **we ~ the fire in overnight** у насками́н гори́т всю ночь; **he left in all the quotations** он сохрани́л все цитáты; **~ off** *v.t.* (*not put on*): **I posted the letter but left off the stamp** я отослáл письмó, но не приклéил мáрки; (*not wear*): **I ~ off my waistcoat in hot weather** в жарý я не ношý жилéта; (*stop*) перест|авáть, -áть + *inf.*; кончáть, кóнчить + *a.*; **~ off smoking** бр|осáть, -óсить кури́ть; *v.i.* (*halt*) остан|áвливаться, -ови́ться; **where did we ~ off?** на чём мы останови́лись?; **~ on** *v.t.*: **I left the light on** я остáвил свет включённым; **I left my jacket on** я не снял пиджакá; **~ out** *v.t.*: **she left the washing out in the rain** онá остáвила бельё под дождём; (*omit*) пропус|кáть, -ти́ть; **~ me out of this!** не втя́гивайте меня́ в э́то!; **I felt left out** я почýвствовал себя́ ли́шним; **~ over** *v.t.* (*defer*) от|клáдывать, -ложи́ть; (*pass., remain*): ост|авáться, -áться; **a lot was left over after dinner** пóсле обéда остáлось ещё мнóго еды́.

● *cpd.* **~-taking** *n.* прощáние, расставáние.

leaven /ˈlev(ə)n/ *n.* (*lit., fig.*) заквáска.
● *v.t.* (*lit.*) заквá|шивать, -сить; (*fig.*): **he ~ed his speech with a few jokes** он оживи́л свою́ речь двумя́-тремя́ анекдóтами.

leavening /ˈlevənɪŋ/ *n.* заквáска.

leaves /liːvz/ *pl. of* ⇨**leaf**

leavings /ˈliːvɪŋz/ *n.* остáтк|и (*pl., g.* -ов); (*of food*) объéдк|и (*pl., g.* -ов); (*of drink*) опи́в|ки (*pl., g.* -ок).

Lebanese /ˌlebəˈniːz/ *n.* (*pl.* **~**) ливáн|ец (*fem.* -ка).
● *adj.* ливáнский.

Lebanon /ˈlebəˌnən/ *n.* Ливáн.

lecher /ˈletʃə(r)/ *n.* развратник, распýтник.

lecherous /ˈletʃərəs/ *adj.* разврáтный, распýтный.

lecherousness /ˈletʃərəsnɪs/ *n.* разврáтность, распýтство.

lechery /ˈletʃərɪ/ *n.* разврáт.

lectern /ˈlektɜːn/, /-t(ə)n/ *n.* аналóй; (*in lecture-room*) пюпи́тр.

lector /ˈlektɔː(r)/ *n.* доцéнт, преподавáтель (*m.*).

lecture /ˈlektʃə(r)/ *n.* **1** (*dissertation*) лéкция; **attend a ~** слýшать, про- лéкцию; **give a ~** читáть, про- (*or* прочéсть) лéкцию. **2** (*reproof*) нотáция; **give, read s.o. a ~** читáть, про- нотáцию комý-н.
● *v.t.* читáть, про- лéкцию/нотáцию + *d.*
● *v.i.*: **he ~s in Russian** он читáет лéкции по рýсскому языкý; **he ~s in Roman law** он преподаёт ри́мское прáво.
● *cpd.* **~-hall, ~-room, ~ theatre** (*US* **theater**) *nn.* аудитóрия.

lecturer /ˈlektʃərə(r)/ *n.* (*speaker*) доклáдчи|к (*fem.* -ца); (*professional* **~**) лéктор; (*univ.*) преподавáтель (*m.*) (*fem.* -ница).

lectureship /ˈlektʃəʃɪp/ *n.* лéкторство; (*senior* **~**) доцентýра.

LED (*abbr. of* ***light-emitting diode***) СИД (светоизлучáющий диóд).

led /led/ *past and p.p. of* ⇨**lead²**

ledge /ledʒ/ *n.* (*shelf*) плáнка, пóлочка; (*projection*) вы́ступ; (*edge*) край; (*under water*) шельф, бар.

ledger /ˈledʒə(r)/ *n.* (*book*) гроссбýх; (глáвная) учётная кни́га.

lee /liː/ *n.* (*shelter*): **under the ~ of** под защи́той + *g.*; (**~** *side*) подвéтренная сторонá; **~ shore** подвéтренный бéрег.
● *cpd.* **~way** *n.* (*naut.*) дрейф; (*fig.*) свобóда дéйствий; **make up ~way** (*lit.*) компенси́ровать (*impf., pf.*) снос вéтром; (*Br., fig.*) навёрст|ывать, -áть упýщенное; **he has much ~way to make up** емý предстои́т мнóгое наверстáть.

leech /liːtʃ/ *n.* (*worm*) пия́вка.

leek /liːk/ *n.* лук-порéй.

leer /lɪə(r)/ *n.* ухмы́лка.
● *v.i.* ухмыл|я́ться, -ьнýться; **~ at** хи́тро/злóбно смотрéть, по- на + *a.*

leery /ˈlɪərɪ/ *adj.* (**leerier, leeriest**) (*sl.*) хи́трый; (*wary*) недовéрчивый.

lees /liːz/ *n.* (*lit., fig.*) подóнки (*m. pl.*); **drain to the ~** (*lit.*) вы́пить (*pf.*) до днá; (*fig.*) испи́ть (*pf.*) чáшу (*чего*).

leeward /ˈliːwəd/, *naut.* /ˈluːəd/ *n.* подвéтренная сторонá; **to ~ (of)** на подвéтренной сторонé (от + *g.*).
● *adj.* подвéтренный.
● *adv.* под вéтром.

left¹ /left/ *n.* **1** (*side, direction*): **from the ~** слéва; **from ~ to right** слéва напрáво; **on the ~ of the street** по лéвой сторонé ýлицы; **on, to my ~** (*location or motion*) налéво от меня́; **on, from my ~** слéва от меня́; **he turned to the ~** он повернýл налéво.
2 (*mil.*: **~** *flank*) лéвый фланг.
3 (*pol.*): **the L~** лéвые (*pl.*) (пáртии).
● *adj.* лéвый; **~ turn** лéвый поворóт; **~ wing** (*pol.*) лéвое крылó.
● *adv.* налéво; **turn ~** св|орáчивать, -ернýть налéво; **~ turn!** (*mil.*) налéво!
● *cpds.* **~-hand** *adj.* лéвый; **~-hand service** (*tennis*) подáча лéвой рукóй; **car with ~-hand drive** маши́на с левосторóнним управлéнием (*or* с рулём слéва); **~-hand screw** винт с лéвым хóдом; **~-handed** *adj.* дéлающий всё лéвой рукóй; **~-handed person** левшá (*c.g.*); **~-handed blow** удáр лéвой рукóй; **~-handed compliment** сомни́тельный комплимéнт; **~-wing** *adj.* лéвый, с лéвыми тендéнциями; **~-winger** *n.* представи́тель (*m.*) лéвого крылá (пáртии), лéвый.

left² /left/ *past and p.p. of* ⇨**leave**

leftism /ˈleftɪz(ə)m/ *n.* левизнá, лéвые взгля́ды (*m. pl.*).

leftist /ˈleftɪst/ *n.* левá|к (*fem.* -чка).
● *adj.* лéвый.

leftovers /ˈleftˌəʊvəz/ *n. pl.* остáтк|и (*pl., g.* -ов); (*food*) объéдк|и (*pl., g.* -ов).

leftwards /ˈleftwədz/ *adv.* налéво, влéво.

lefty /ˈleftɪ/ *n.* (*coll.*) (*left-handed person*) левшá (*c.g.*); (*pol.*) левá|к (*fem.* -чка).

leg /leg/ *n.* **1** ногá; (*dim.*) нóжка; (*of bird*) лáпа, лáпка; **with one's ~s in the air** вверх ногáми; **he is on his ~s again** (*after illness*) он встал нá ноги; **I've been on my ~s all day** я был на ногáх цéлый день; **he is on his last ~s** (*dying*) он ды́шит на лáдан; **the car is on its last ~s** маши́на вот-вóт развáлится; **get on one's hind ~s** (*of dog etc.*) вста|вáть, -ть на зáдние лáпы; **give s.o. a ~ up** (*lit.*) помóчь (*pf.*) комý-н. взобрáться; (*fig., assist*) окáз|ывать, -áть пóмощь комý-н.; **pull s.o.'s ~** разы́гр|ывать, -áть когó-н.; подшý|чивать, -ти́ть над кем-н.; **be run off one's ~s** сб|ивáться, -и́ться с ног; **shake a ~** (*coll., dance*) танцевáть (*impf.*); (*coll., get going*) дви́гаться (*impf.*); шевели́ть (*impf.*) ногáми; **show a ~!** (*Br. coll.*) подъём!; **he hasn't a ~ to stand on** емý нет оправдáния; егó дóводы не вы́держивают (ни малéйшей) кри́тики; **stretch one's ~s** размя́ть (*pf.*) нóги.
2 (*meat*): **~ of lamb** барáнья ногá; **~ of pork** óкорок.
3 (*of furniture etc.*) нóжка.
4 (*of garment*): **trouser ~** штани́на; (*of sock or stocking*) пáголенок.
5 (*stage of journey etc.*) этáп.
● *v.t.* (**legged, legging**): **~ it** (*coll.*) идти́ (*det.*) пешкóм; **we ~ged it for 20 miles** мы отмахáли 20 миль пешкóм.
● *cpds.* **~-pull** *n.* (*coll.*) мистификáция, рóзыгрыш; **~-room** *n.* мéсто для ног.

legacy /ˈlegəsɪ/ *n.* наслéдство, наслéдие.

legal /ˈliːg(ə)l/ *adj.* **1** (*pert. to or based on law*) юриди́ческий, правовóй; **~ department** юриди́ческий отдéл; **~ aid** (*Br.*) бесплáтная юриди́ческая пóмощь неимýщим; **~ obligation** правовóе обязáтельство; **~ practitioner** адвокáт; **~ adviser** юрискóнсульт; **the ~ profession** профéссия юри́ста; (*lawyers*) юри́сты, адвокáты (*both m. pl.*); **take ~ advice** консульти́роваться, про- с юри́стом.
2 (*permitted or ordained by law*)

зако́нный, лега́льный; **~ holiday** (*US*) официа́льный нерабо́чий день; **~ tender** зако́нное платёжное сре́дство; **~ offence** правонаруше́ние; **within one's ~ rights** в зако́нном пра́ве.
3 (*involving court proceedings*) суде́бный; **~ action** суде́бный иск; суде́бное де́ло; **take ~ action against** возбу|жда́ть, -ди́ть де́ло про́тив + *g*.; под|ава́ть, -а́ть в суд на + *a*.; **~ costs** суде́бные изде́ржки.

legalism /ˈli:gə,lɪz(ə)m/ *n*. буквое́дство, бюрократи́зм.

legalist /ˈli:gə,lɪst/ *n*. зако́нник.

legalistic /,li:gəˈlɪstɪk/ *adj*. бюрократи́ческий.

legality /lɪˈgælɪtɪ/, /li:ˈg-/ *n*. зако́нность, лега́льность.

legalization /ˈli:gə,laɪˈzeɪʃ(ə)n/ *n*. узаконе́ние, легализа́ция.

legalize /ˈli:gə,laɪz/ *v.t.* узако́ни|вать, -ть; легализи́ровать (*impf., pf.*).

legate /ˈlegɪt/ *n*. лега́т.

legatee /,legəˈti:/ *n*. насле́дни|к (*fem*. -ца), легата́рий.

legation /lɪˈgeɪʃ(ə)n/ *n*. представи́тельство, ми́ссия.

legato /lɪˈgɑ:təʊ/ *n. & adv.* (*pl.* **~s**) (*mus.*) лега́то (*indecl.*).

legend /ˈledʒ(ə)nd/ *n*. **1** леге́нда.
2 (*inscription, explanatory matter*) на́дпись, леге́нда.

legendary /ˈledʒəndərɪ/ *adj*. легенда́рный.

legerdemain /,ledʒədəˈmeɪn/ *n*. (*sleight of hand*) ло́вкость рук; (*trickery*) надува́тельство; (*trick*) уло́вка.

leger line /ˈledʒə(r)/ *n*. (*mus.*) доба́вочная лине́йка.

leggings /ˈlegɪŋz/ *n*. (*stretch trousers*) рейту́з|ы (*pl., g.* —); (*gaiters*) гама́ши (*f. pl.*); кра́ги (*f. pl.*).

leggy /ˈlegɪ/ *adj*. (**leggier, leggiest**) длинноно́гий.

legibility /,ledʒɪˈbɪlɪtɪ/ *n*. разбо́рчивость.

legible /ˈledʒɪb(ə)l/ *adj*. разбо́рчивый.

legion /ˈli:dʒ(ə)n/ *n*. **1** (*body of soldiers*) легио́н; **Foreign L~** иностра́нный легио́н; **L~ of Honour** (*Br.*), **Honor** (*US*) о́рден Почётного легио́на.
2 (*multitude*) легио́н, тьма; **her fans are ~** у неё тьма покло́нников; **their name is ~** и́мя им легио́н.

legion|ary /ˈli:dʒənərɪ/, **-naire** /,li:dʒəˈneə(r)/ *nn*. легионе́р.

legislate /ˈledʒɪs,leɪt/ *v.i.* изд|ава́ть, -а́ть зако́ны.

legislation /,ledʒɪsˈleɪʃ(ə)n/ *n*. законода́тельство.

legislative /ˈledʒɪslətɪv/ *adj*. законода́тельный.

legislator /ˈledʒɪs,leɪtə(r)/ *n*. законода́тель (*m.*) (*fem*. -ница).

legislature /ˈledʒɪs,leɪtʃə(r)/, /-lətʃə(r)/ *n*. (*assembly*) законода́тельный о́рган; (*institutions*) законода́тельные учрежде́ния.

legit /lɪˈdʒɪt/ *adj*. (*coll.*) (*lawful*) зако́нный; (*honest*) че́стный.

legitimacy /lɪˈdʒɪtɪməsɪ/ *n*. зако́нность.

legitimate[1] /lɪˈdʒɪtɪmət/ *adj*. **1** (*lawful*) зако́нный; **~ sovereign** зако́нный мона́рх; (*justifiable*): **~ demands** справедли́вые тре́бования; (*reasonable, admissible*) обосно́ванный.
2 (*by birth*) законнорождённый.

legitimate[2] /lɪˈdʒɪtɪ,meɪt/ *v.t.*, **legitimation** /lɪ,dʒɪtɪˈmeɪʃ(ə)n/ *n*. = **legitimiz|e, -ation**

legitim|ization /lɪ,dʒɪtɪmaɪˈzeɪʃ(ə)n/, **-ation** /lɪ,dʒɪtɪˈmeɪʃ(ə)n/ *nn*. узаконе́ние, узако́нивание, легитима́ция.

legitim|ize /lɪˈdʒɪtɪ,maɪz/, **-ate** /lɪˈdʒɪtɪ,meɪt/ *v.t.* узако́ни|вать, -ть.

legless /ˈleglɪs/ *adj*. безно́гий; (*Br. coll., drunk*) пья́ный в сте́льку.

legume /ˈlegju:m/ *n*. (*pod*) стручо́к; (*pl., crops*) бобо́вые (*pl.*).

leguminous /lɪˈgju:mɪnəs/ *adj*. бобо́вый, стручко́вый.

Le Havre /ləˈhɑ:vrə/ *n*. Гавр.

Leipzig /ˈlaɪpsɪg/ *n*. Ле́йпциг.

leisure /ˈleʒə(r)/ *n*. свобо́дное вре́мя; досу́г; **at ~** на досу́ге; **at one's ~** (*in free time*) в свобо́дное вре́мя; (*unhurriedly*) не спеша́; **I have ~ for reading** у меня́ есть вре́мя для чте́ния; **~ centre** (*Br.*), **center** (*US*) спорти́вно-развлека́тельный ко́мплекс; **~ clothes** дома́шняя оде́жда; **in one's ~ hours** в свобо́дное вре́мя; **~ time** вре́мя досу́га.

leisured /ˈleʒəd/ *adj*. досу́жий, пра́здный; **the ~ classes** нетрудовы́е кла́ссы.

leisureliness /ˈleʒəlɪnɪs/ *n*. нетороплі́вость.

leisurely /ˈleʒəlɪ/ *adj*. неспе́шный, нетороплі́вый; **at a ~ pace** споко́йным ша́гом.
● *adv*. не спеша́, ме́дленно.

leitmoti|f, -v /ˈlaɪtməʊ,ti:f/ *n*. лейтмоти́в.

lemming /ˈlemɪŋ/ *n*. (*zool.*) ле́мминг.

lemon /ˈlemən/ *n*. **1** (*fruit, tree*) лимо́н; (*attr.*) лимо́нный; **~ drop** лимо́нный леденéц; **~ squeezer** соковыжима́лка для лимо́на. **2** (*colour*) лимо́нный цвет.

lemonade /,leməˈneɪd/ *n*. **1** (*Br., carbonated drink*) лимона́д. **2** (*drink of lemon juice and water*) напи́ток из со́ка лимо́на с водо́й.

lemon sole /ˈlemən/ *n*. морско́й язы́к.

lemur /ˈli:mə(r)/ *n*. лему́р.

lend /lend/ *v.t.* (*past and p.p.* **lent**)
1 да|ва́ть, -ть взаймы́; од|а́лживать (*or* -олжа́ть), -олжи́ть; ссу|жа́ть, -ди́ть (*кого чем or что кому*); **~ me £5** одолжи́те мне (*or* да́йте мне взаймы́) пять фу́нтов; **~ me the book for a while** да́йте мне кни́гу на вре́мя; **he lent me the book to read** он дал мне почита́ть э́ту кни́гу.
2 (*impart*) прид|ава́ть, -а́ть; **their costumes lent a note of gaiety to the scene** их костю́мы придава́ли карти́не жизнера́достный тон.
3 (*proffer*): **~ an ear to** выслу́шивать, вы́слушать; **~ a hand** (*help*) ока́з|ывать, -а́ть по́мощь (*кому*); (*cooperate*) ока́з|ывать, -а́ть соде́йствие (*кому*); (*help out in difficulty*) выруча́ть, вы́ручить.
4: **~ o.s. to** (*agree to*) позво́лить (*pf.*) себе́ согласи́ться на + *a*.; (*accommodate o.s. to*) подд|ава́ться, -а́ться на + *a*.; **the novel ~s itself to filming** рома́н подхо́дит для экраниза́ции; (*allow of*) допус|ка́ть, -ти́ть; **the affair ~s itself to many interpretations** де́ло мо́жно толкова́ть по-ра́зному; (*be serviceable for*) годи́ться (*impf.*) на + *a*. (*or* для + *g*.).
● *with adv*.: **~ out** *v.t.* (*of library etc.*) выдава́ть, вы́дать на́ дом.

lender /ˈlendə(r)/ *n*. заимода́вец, кредито́р.

lending /ˈlendɪŋ/ *n*. ссу́да; (*of money*) да́ча взаймы́; **he does not approve of ~** он не одобря́ет долго́в; **~ library** библиоте́ка (с вы́дачей книг на́ дом).

length /leŋθ/, /leŋkθ/ *n*. **1** (*dimension, measurement*) длина́; **2 metres** (*Br.*), **meters** (*US*) **in ~** 2 ме́тра длино́й; **this material is sold by ~** э́та мате́рия продаётся на ме́тры/я́рды; **he lay at full ~** он лежа́л вы́тянувшись во всю длину́; **he travelled** (*Br.*), **traveled** (*US*) **the ~ and breadth of Europe** он изъе́здил Евро́пу вдоль и поперёк.
2 (*racing etc.*): **the horse won by a ~** ло́шадь опереди́ла други́х на ко́рпус; **they lost (the boat-race) by half a ~** (в состяза́ниях по гре́бле) они́ отста́ли на полко́рпуса.
3 (*of time*) продолжи́тельность, дли́тельность, срок; **the ~ of the visit was excessive** визи́т затяну́лся; **the chief fault of this film is its ~** гла́вный недоста́ток э́того фи́льма — его́ растя́нутость; **he objected to the ~ of the play** он счита́л, что пье́са сли́шком дли́нная; **seniority by ~ of service** старшинство́ по вы́слуге лет; **I shall be away for a certain ~ of time** меня́ не бу́дет не́которое вре́мя; **~ of the course** (*of study*) срок обуче́ния; **at ~** (*finally*) наконе́ц; (*in detail*) во всех подро́бностях; **he explained at some ~** он объясни́л дово́льно простра́нно; (*for a long time*) до́лго; **he spoke at great ~** он говори́л о́чень до́лго.
4 (*distance, extent*) расстоя́ние; **keep s.o. at arm's ~** (*fig.*) держа́ть (*impf.*) кого́-н. на почти́тельном расстоя́нии; **the ships passed at a cable's ~ apart** суда́ прошли́ друг от дру́га на расстоя́нии ка́бельтова.
5 (*extent, degree*): **go to any ~(s)** идти́ (*det.*) на всё; ни пе́ред чем не остана́вливаться (*impf.*); **he went to great ~s not to offend them** он сде́лал всё возмо́жное, что́бы их не оби́деть; **she went to all ~s to get her own way** она́ из ко́жи ле́зла, что́бы доби́ться своего́.
6 (*of vowel or syllable*) долгота́.
7 (*piece of material*) кусо́к; отре́з.

lengthen /ˈleŋθ(ə)n/, /ˈleŋkθ(ə)n/ *v.t. & i.* удлин|я́ть(ся), -и́ть(ся).

lengthening /ˈleŋθənɪŋ/, /ˈleŋkθənɪŋ/ *n*. удлине́ние.

L

lengthiness /'leŋθɪnɪs/, /'leŋkθɪnɪs/ *n.* растя́нутость; длинно́ты (*f. pl.*).

length|ways /'leŋθweɪz/, /'leŋkθ-/, **-wise** /'leŋθwaɪz/, /'leŋkθ-/ *adv.* (*along its length*): **fold the blanket ~** сложи́те одея́ло вдоль; (*in length*): **this piece measures not quite 3 feet ~** в длину́ в э́том куске́ без ма́лого три фу́та.

lengthy /'leŋθɪ/, /'leŋkθɪ/ *adj.* (**lengthier, lengthiest**) дли́нный, затя́нутый; (*in time*) дли́тельный; (*of speech etc.*) растя́нутый, простра́нный.

leniency /'li:nɪənsɪ/ *n.* снисхожде́ние; мя́гкость.

lenient /'li:nɪənt/ *adj.* (*of person*) снисходи́тельный; (*of punishment etc.*) мя́гкий.

Leningrad /'lenɪn,græd/ *n.* (*hist.*) Ленингра́д; (*attr.*) ленингра́дский.

Leninism /'lenɪ,nɪz(ə)m/ *n.* ленини́зм.

Leninist /'lenɪ,nɪst/ *n.* ле́нинец.
● *adj.* ле́нинский.

lenity /'lenɪtɪ/ *n.* милосе́рдие.

lens /lenz/ *n.* (*anat., opt.*) ли́нза; (*anat.*) хруста́лик гла́за; (*phot.*) объекти́в.

Lent /lent/ *n.* вели́кий пост; (*Br.*) **~ term** весе́нний триме́стр.

lent /lent/ *past and p.p. of* ⇒**lend**

Lenten /'lent(ə)n/ *adj.* (*of Lent*) великопо́стный; (*fasting*): **~ fare** по́стный стол.

lentil /'lentɪl/ *n.* чечеви́ца; **~ soup** чечеви́чная похлёбка.

lento /'lentəʊ/ *adv.* ле́нто (*indecl.*).

Leo /'li:əʊ/ *n.* (*pl.* **Leos**) (*astr.*) Лев.

leonine /'li:ə,naɪn/ *adj.* льви́ный.

leopard /'lepəd/ *n.* леопа́рд; **snow, mountain ~** сне́жный леопа́рд/барс, и́рбис; **a ~ cannot change his spots** ≈ горба́того моги́ла испра́вит.

leopardess /'lepədɪs/ *n.* са́мка леопа́рда.

leotard /'li:ə,tɑ:d/ *n.* трико́ (*indecl.*), леота́рд.

leper /'lepə(r)/ *n.* прокажённый.

lepidoptera /,lepɪ'dɒptərə/ *n. pl.* чешуекры́лые (*pl.*).

lepidopterous /,lepɪ'dɒptərəs/ *adj.* чешуекры́лый.

leprechaun /'leprə,kɔ:n/ *n.* гном.

leprosy /'leprəsɪ/ *n.* прока́за.

leprous /'leprəs/ *adj.* (*infected by leprosy*) прокажённый.

lesbian /'lezbɪən/ *n.* (*homosexual*) лесбия́нка.
● *adj.* лесби́йский.

lesbianism /'lezbɪən,ɪz(ə)m/ *n.* лесби́йская любо́вь.

lèse majesté /li:z 'mædʒɪstɪ/ *n.* оскорбле́ние мона́рха.

lesion /'li:ʒ(ə)n/ *n.* поврежде́ние, пораже́ние.

less /les/ *n.* ме́ньшее коли́чество; **you should eat ~** вам сле́дует ме́ньше есть; **I cannot accept ~ than £50** ме́ньше, чем на 50 фу́нтов я не соглашу́сь; **no ~ than £500** не ме́нее пятисо́т фу́нтов; **no more and no ~ than ...** не бо́лее и не ме́нее, как. . .; **all the ~ because ...** ещё ме́ньше из-за того́, что. . .; **it is nothing ~ than disgraceful** э́то позо́р и бо́льше ничего́; **he knew it would mean nothing ~ than the sack** он знал, что за э́то ему́ не минова́ть увольне́ния; **in ~ than no time** в одно́ мгнове́ние; **in ~ than an hour** ме́ньше чем за час; **you will see ~ of me in future** впосле́дствии вы не бу́дете ви́деть меня́ так ча́сто; **(I want) ~ of your cheek!** не хами́те!; **the ~ said, the better** чем ме́ньше слов, тем лу́чше; **I don't think any the ~ of him for that** э́то не умаля́ет моего́ мне́ния о нём; **he was a father to them, no ~** он был для них как родно́й оте́ц.
● *adj.* **1** (*smaller*) ме́ньший; **of ~ importance** ме́ньшей ва́жности; **of ~ magnitude** ме́ньшего разме́ра; **in a ~(er) degree** в ме́ньшей сте́пени; **grow ~** ум|еньша́ться, -е́ньшиться. **2** (*not so much*) ме́ньше; **eat ~ meat!** е́шьте ме́ньше мя́са!; **~ noise!** поти́ше! **3** (*of lower rank*): **no ~ a person than ...** никто́ ино́й, как. . ..
● *adv.* ме́ньше, ме́нее; не так, не сто́лько; **he is ~ intelligent than his sister** он не так умён, как его́ сестра́; **the ~ you think about it the better** чем ме́ньше об э́том ду́мать, тем лу́чше; **~ and ~** всё ме́ньше и ме́ньше; **none the ~** тем не ме́нее.
● *prep.* ми́нус; за вы́четом +*g.*; **I paid him his wages, ~ what he owed me** я вы́дал ему́ зарпла́ту за вы́четом су́ммы, кото́рую он мне задолжа́л.

lessee /le'si:/ *n.* (*of house etc.*) съёмщик; (*of land*) аренда́тор, нанима́тель (*m.*) (*fem.* -ница).

lessen /'les(ə)n/ *v.t. & i.* ум|еньша́ть(ся), -е́ньшить(ся).

lessening /'lesənɪŋ/ *n.* уменьше́ние.

lesser /'lesə(r)/ *adj.* ме́ньший; (*of plants, animals*) ма́лый; **the ~ evil** ме́ньшее из двух зол.

lesson /'les(ə)n/ *n.* **1** уро́к, заня́тие; **English ~s** уро́ки англи́йского языка́; **give ~s in physics** да|ва́ть, -ть уро́ки фи́зики; **~s begin on 1 September** (*Br.*) заня́тия начина́ются пе́рвого сентября́; **take ~s** брать (*impf.*) уро́ки; **teach s.o. a ~** (*rebuke, punish*) дать (*pf.*) уро́к кому́-н.; проучи́ть (*pf.*) кого́-н.; **let that be a ~ to you!** да бу́дет э́то вам нау́кой! **2** (*eccl.*) чте́ние.

lessor /le'sɔ:(r)/ *n.* арендода́тель (*m.*), сдаю́щий в аре́нду (*or* внаём).

lest /lest/ *conj.* что́бы не; **I fear ~ he should see her** я бою́сь, как бы он её не уви́дел.

let¹ /let/ *n.* **1**: **without ~ or hindrance** беспрепя́тственно. **2** (*tennis*): **~ ball!** се́тка!

let² /let/ *n.* (*Br., of property*) аре́нда; **take a house on a long ~** снять (*pf.*) дом на дли́тельный срок.
● *v.t.* (**letting;** *past and p.p.* **let**) (*also* **~ out**) сда|ва́ть, -ть в наём; **the flat is already ~** кварти́ра уже́ сдана́; **'house to ~ furnished'** (*notice*) «сдаётся дом с ме́белью».
● *v.i.* (**letting;** *past and p.p.* **let**): **this house would ~ easily** э́тот дом сни́мут бы́стро.

let³ /let/ *v.t.* (**letting;** *past and p.p.* **let**) **1** (*allow*) позв|оля́ть, -о́лить +*d.*; разреш|а́ть, -и́ть +*d.*; **~ me help you** позво́льте вам помо́чь; **why not ~ him try?** да́йте ему́ возмо́жность попро́бовать; **he won't ~ me work** он не даёт мне рабо́тать; **~ s.o. be** ост|авля́ть, -а́вить кого́-н. в поко́е; **~ something be** не тро́|гать, -нуть чего́-н.; **~ drop, fall** роня́ть, урони́ть; **~ fly at** (*go for*) **s.o.** напус|ка́ться, -ти́ться на кого́-н.; **~ fly at** (*shoot at*) **something** стреля́ть (*impf.*) во что-н.; **~ go** (*relax grip on*) выпуска́ть, вы́пустить из рук; отпус|ка́ть, -ти́ть; **~ go (of) my hand** отпусти́те мою́ ру́ку; **~ o.s. go** увл|ека́ться, -е́чься; (*set free*) выпуска́ть, вы́пустить; **~ things go** вести́ (*det.*) дела́ спустя́ рукава́; (*sell*): **he ~ the chair go for a song** он про́дал стул по дешёвке; (*ignore*): **this was untrue but I ~ it go, pass** э́то бы́ло непра́вдой, но я не стал возража́ть; **~ one's hair grow** отпус|ка́ть, -ти́ть во́лосы; **we ~ the storm pass and then went out** мы пережда́ли грозу́, пото́м вы́шли; **~ slide** пусти́ть (*pf.*) на самотёк (*see also* ⇒**~ go**); **~ slip** (*chance etc.*) упус|ка́ть, -ти́ть. **2** (*cause to*): **~ s.o. have it** (*coll., punish*) суро́во нак|а́зывать, -аза́ть кого́-н.; **~ s.o. know** да|ва́ть, -ть кому́-н. знать; **~ it not be said that we were afraid** да не обвиня́т нас в тру́сости. **3** (*in imper. or hortatory sense*): **~ me see** (*reflect*) погоди́те; да́йте поду́мать; **~ him do it** пусть он э́то сде́лает; **just ~ him try it!** пусть то́лько попро́бует!; **~ X equal the height of the building** пусть высота́ зда́ния равня́ется X; **~ us drink** вы́пьем(те); дава́й(те) вы́пьем/пить; **~ us pray** помо́лимся; **~ us not be greedy** не бу́дем жа́дничать; **~ them come in** пусть войду́т; **~ there be light** да бу́дет свет. **4** (**~** *come or go*): **he ~ me into the room** он впусти́л меня́ в ко́мнату; **shall I ~ you into a secret?** хоти́те я раскро́ю вам та́йну?; **he was ~ out of prison** его́ вы́пустили из тюрьмы́.
● *with advs.*: **~ alone** *v.t.* ост|авля́ть, -а́вить (*кого*) в поко́е; не тро́|гать, -нуть (*чего*); **~ him alone to finish it** не меша́йте ему́ зако́нчить э́то; **~ alone** (*not to mention*) не то́лько что, не говоря́ уже́ о +*p.*; **they haven't got a radio, ~ alone television** у них и ра́дио нет, не говоря́ уже́ о телеви́зоре; **he can't even walk, ~ alone run** он и ходи́ть-то не мо́жет, а бе́гать и пода́вно; **~ well alone** не вме́шиваться без нужды́; **~ down** *v.t.* (*lower*) опус|ка́ть, -ти́ть; **~ one's hair down** (*lit.*) распус|ка́ть, -ти́ть во́лосы; (*fig.*) держа́ть (*impf.*) себя́ раско́ванно; **~ s.o. down gently** (*fig.*) щади́ть, по-; чьё-н. самолю́бие; (*disappoint*) разочаро́в|ывать, -а́ть; **I feel ~ down** я разочаро́ван; (*fail to support*) подв|оди́ть, -ести́ (*coll.*); **I was badly ~ down** меня́ здо́рово подвели́; (*Br., deflate*): **~ down tyres** (*Br.*), **tires** (*US*)

спус|ка́ть, -ти́ть ши́ны; (*lengthen*): ~ **down a dress** отпуска́ть, отпусти́ть пла́тье; ~ **in** *v.t.* (*admit*) впус|ка́ть, -ти́ть; **the window doesn't ~ in much light** че́рез э́то окно́ проника́ет ма́ло све́та; **my shoes ~ in water** мои́ ту́фли протека́ют; **he ~ himself in** он сам откры́л дверь и вошёл; **he ~ me in for endless trouble** он впу́тал меня́ в бесконе́чные неприя́тности; **what have I ~ myself in for?** во что я ввяза́лся?; **we ~ him in on the secret** мы посвяти́ли его́ в та́йну; (*insert*) вст|авля́ть, -а́вить; (*into garment*) вши|ва́ть, -ть; (*engage*): ~ **the clutch in** включ|а́ть, -и́ть сцепле́ние; ~ **off** *v.t.* (*discharge*) разря|жа́ть, -ди́ть; ~ **off fireworks** запуска́ть (*impf.*) фейерве́рк; (*emit*): ~ **off steam** (*lit., fig.*) выпуска́ть, вы́пустить пары́; ~ **off a smell** испуска́ть (*impf.*) за́пах; (*allow to dismount*): ~ **me off at the next stop** ссади́те меня́ на сле́дующей остано́вке; (*acquit; not punish*) не нака́зывать (*impf.*); **he was ~ off lightly** он легко́ отде́лался; (*excuse*) про|ща́ть, -сти́ть + *d.*; **they ~ him off his debt** ему́ прости́ли долг; (*liberate*) освобо|жда́ть, -ди́ть; **he ~ them off work for the day** он их освободи́л от рабо́ты на день; *v.i.* (*fire*) вы́стрелить (*pf.*); ~ **on** *v.t. & i.* (*coll., divulge*) прогов|а́риваться, -ори́ться; **don't ~ on about it** ни сло́ва об э́том!; (*pretend*) прики́|дываться, -нуться; ~ **out** *v.t.* выпуска́ть, вы́пустить; ~ **the air out of a tyre** (*Br.*), **tire** (*US*) выпуска́ть, вы́пустить во́здух из ши́ны; спусти́ть (*pf.*) ши́ну; ~ **the water out of the bath** выпуска́ть, вы́пустить/спус|ка́ть, -ти́ть во́ду из ва́нны; ~ **out a scream** завизжа́ть (*pf.*); взви́згнуть (*pf.*); ~ **out a secret** прогов|а́риваться, -ори́ться; проболта́ться (*pf.*); **he ~ out the whole story** он вы́болтал всю исто́рию; **she ~ out the sleeves** она́ вы́пустила рукава́; ~ **the fire out** да|ва́ть, -ть поту́хнуть огню́; ~ **past** *v.t.* да|ва́ть, -ть пройти́; ~ **through** *v.t.* пропус|ка́ть, -ти́ть; ~ **up** *v.i.* (*weaken, diminish*) ослаб|ева́ть, -е́ть; (*stop for a while*) приостан|а́вливаться, -ови́ться; (*relax, take a rest*) перед|ыха́ть, -охну́ть; **he never ~s up in his work** он рабо́тает без переды́шки (*or* не поклада́я рук).

● *cpds.* **~-down** *n.* (*disappointment, anticlimax*) разочарова́ние; **~-off** *n.*: **that was a ~-off!** пронесло́!; **~-out** *n.* (*Br.*) возмо́жность отступле́ния; **a ~-out clause** усло́вие об освобожде́нии от отве́тственности; **~-up** *n.* (*respite*) переды́шка; остано́вка.

lethal /ˈli:θ(ə)l/ *adj.* (*fatal*) смерте́льный; **a ~ dose** смерте́льная до́за; (*designed to kill*) смертоно́сный.

lethargic /lɪˈθɑ:dʒɪk/ *adj.* вя́лый; (*med.*) летарги́ческий.

lethargy /ˈleθədʒɪ/ *n.* вя́лость; летарги́я.

Lett /let/ *n.* латы́ш (*fem.* -ка).

letter /ˈletə(r)/ *n.* **1** (*of alphabet*) бу́ква; **capital ~** прописна́я бу́ква; **the word is written with a capital ~** э́то сло́во пи́шется с прописно́й бу́квы; **small ~** строчна́я бу́ква; **it was written in small ~s** э́то бы́ло напи́сано строчны́ми бу́квами; (*fig., precise detail*): **to the ~** буква́льно; **the ~ of the law** бу́ква зако́на; **he follows the law to the ~** он соблюда́ет зако́н до после́дней запято́й; **in ~ and in spirit** по фо́рме и по существу́.
2 (*written communication*) письмо́; (*official*) паке́т; **registered ~** заказно́е письмо́; **~ of intent** протоко́л о наме́рениях; **~ of introduction** рекоменда́тельное письмо́.
3 (*pl., literature*) литерату́ра; **man of ~s** литера́тор.

● *v.t.* **1** (*impress title on*) отти́с|кивать, -нуть загла́вие на + *a.*; **the title was ~ed in gold** загла́вие бы́ло вытеснено золоты́ми бу́квами.
2 (*classify by means of ~s*) пом|еча́ть, -е́тить бу́квами.

● *cpds.* **~-bomb** *n.* письмо́, начинённое взрывча́ткой; бо́мба в конве́рте; **~-box** *n.* (*Br.*) почто́вый я́щик; **~-head(ing)** *n.* (*heading*) ша́пка на фи́рменном бла́нке; (*paper*) фи́рменный бланк; **~press** *n.* (*Br., text, captions*) печа́тный текст; (*printing from raised type*) высо́кая печа́ть.

lettering /ˈletərɪŋ/ *n.* (*inscription*) на́дпись; (*impressing of title*) тисне́ние (бу́квами); (*script*) шрифт.

Lettish /ˈletɪʃ/ *n.* латы́шский язы́к.

● *adj.* латы́шский.

lettuce /ˈletɪs/ *n.* (*plant, dish*) сала́т; (*plant*) лату́к.

leucocyte /ˈlu:kəˌsaɪt/ *n.* лейкоци́т.

leukaemia /lu:ˈki:mɪə/ (*US* **leukemia**) *n.* белокро́вие, лейкеми́я.

levee /ˈlevɪ/, /lɪˈvi:/ *n.* (*US, embankment*) на́бережная.

level /ˈlev(ə)l/ *n.* **1** (*instrument*) ватерпа́с; у́ровень (*m.*); **spirit ~** спиртово́й у́ровень.
2 (*horizontal plane or line*) у́ровень; **on a ~ with** на одно́м у́ровне с + *i.*; **at eye ~** на у́ровне глаз; (*fig., coll.*): **on the ~!** че́стно!; **is he on the ~?** мо́жно ли ему́ ве́рить?
3 (*social etc., standing*): **students at an advanced ~** бо́лее продви́нутые студе́нты; **a higher ~ of civilization** бо́лее высо́кий у́ровень цивилиза́ции; **subsistence ~** прожи́точный ми́нимум; **talks at Cabinet ~** перегово́ры на у́ровне прави́тельства.
4 (*geog., plain*) равни́на.

● *adj.* (*even*) ро́вный; (*flat*) пло́ский; (*horizontal*) горизонта́льный; **~ crossing** (*Br.*) (железнодоро́жный) перее́зд; **the room was ~ with the street** ко́мната была́ на одно́м у́ровне с у́лицей; **the water was ~ with the banks** вода́ была́ вро́вень с берега́ми; **draw ~ with** наг|оня́ть, -на́ть; **have, keep a ~ head** сохраня́ть (*impf.*) споко́йствие; **do one's ~ best** че́стно стара́ться (*impf.*).

● *v.t.* (**levelled, levelling;** *US* **leveled, leveling**) **1** (*make ~*) ур|а́внивать, -овня́ть; выра́внивать, вы́ровнять.
2 (*raze to ground*) ср|а́внивать, -овня́ть с землёй.
3 (*geol.*) нивели́ровать (*impf., pf.*).
4 (*direct, aim*) нав|оди́ть, -ести́; наце́ли|вать, -ть; **she ~led a gun at his head** она́ прице́лилась ему́ в го́лову; (*fig.*) напр|авля́ть, -а́вить (*что против кого*).

● *with advs.*: **~ down** *v.t.* выра́внивать, вы́ровнять; (*fig.*) нивели́ровать (*impf., pf.*); **~ off, ~ out** *vv.t.* (*smooth out*) сгла́|живать, -дить; (*make ~, even, identical*) ур|а́внивать, -овня́ть; *v.i.* (*of aircraft*) выра́вниваться, вы́ровняться; **~ up** *v.t.* ур|а́внивать, -овня́ть.

● *cpd.* **~-headed** *adj.* тре́звый, рассуди́тельный.

lever /ˈli:və(r)/ *n.* (*lit., fig.*) рыча́г.

● *v.t.*: **~ something out** высвобожда́ть, вы́свободить что-н. рычаго́м; **~ something up** подн|има́ть, -я́ть что-н. рычаго́м; **he ~ed the stone into position** он установи́л ка́мень с по́мощью рычага́.

leverage /ˈli:vərɪdʒ/ *n.* (*action*) де́йствие/уси́лие рычага́; **use ~ on s.o.** (*fig.*) повлия́ть (*pf.*) на кого́-н.

leveret /ˈlevərɪt/ *n.* зайчо́нок.

leviathan /lɪˈvaɪəθ(ə)n/ *n.* (*bibl., fig.*) левиафа́н.

levitate /ˈlevɪˌteɪt/ *v.t. & i.* подн|има́ть(ся), -я́ть(ся) в во́здух.

levitation /ˌlevɪˈteɪʃ(ə)n/ *n.* левита́ция.

Leviticus /lɪˈvɪtɪkəs/ *n.* (*bibl.*) Леви́т.

levity /ˈlevɪtɪ/ *n.* легкомы́слие.

levy /ˈlevɪ/ *n.* **1** (*collection of taxes etc.*) сбор; (*imposition*) обложе́ние; (*raising*) взима́ние; **capital ~** нало́г на капита́л. **2** (*of recruits*) набо́р.

● *v.t.* **1** (*raise*) взима́ть (*impf.*) (*что с кого*). **2** (*recruit*) наб|ира́ть, -ра́ть.

lewd /lju:d/ *adj.* (*of person*) развра́тный; (*of thing*) са́льный.

lewdness /ˈlju:dnɪs/ *n.* развра́тность; са́льность.

lexical /ˈleksɪk(ə)l/ *adj.* лекси́ческий.

lexicographer /ˌleksɪˈkɒgrəfə(r)/ *n.* лексико́граф.

lexicographical /ˌleksɪkəˈgræfɪk(ə)l/ *adj.* лексикографи́ческий.

lexicography /ˌleksɪˈkɒgrəfɪ/ *n.* лексикогра́фия.

lexicon /ˈleksɪkən/ *n.* (*dictionary*) слова́рь, лексико́н; (*vocabulary of writer etc.*) ле́ксика.

lexis /ˈleksɪs/ *n.* ле́ксика, слова́рь.

Lhasa /ˈlɑ:sə/ *n.* Лха́са.

liabilit|y /ˌlaɪəˈbɪlɪtɪ/ *n.* **1** (*responsibility*) отве́тственность; **limited ~y company** компа́ния с ограни́ченной отве́тственностью; **admit ~y for something** призн|ава́ть, -а́ть себя́ отве́тственным за что-н.
2 (*obligation*) обяза́тельство; **meet one's ~ies** выполня́ть, вы́полнить обяза́тельства; (*pl., debts*) долги́ (*m. pl.*). **3** (*burden, handicap*): **he's nothing but a ~y** он про́сто обу́за; **this is a terrible ~y** э́то нам стра́шно меша́ет; **I shall only be a ~y** я бу́ду то́лько поме́хой.

liable /ˈlaɪəb(ə)l/ *adj.* **1** (*answerable*) отве́тственный (за + *a.*). **2** (*subject*): **he is ~ to a heavy fine** его́ мо́гут подве́ргнуть большо́му штра́фу. **3** (*apt, likely*): **difficulties are ~ to arise** мо́гут возни́кнуть тру́дности; **she is ~ to forget it** она́ скло́нна забыва́ть об э́том.

liaise /lɪˈeɪz/ *v.i.* (*coll.*) устана́вливать/подде́рживать (*impf.*) связь (с + *i.*).

liaison /lɪˈeɪzɒn/ *n.* **1** (*mil. etc.*) связь; **~ officer** (*mil.*) офице́р свя́зи (*non-military*) челове́к, отве́тственный за поддержа́ние свя́зи ме́жду организа́циями. **2** (*love affair*) (любо́вная) связь.

liana /lɪˈɑːnə/ *n.* лиа́на.

liar /ˈlaɪə(r)/ *n.* лгун (*fem.* -ья); врун (*fem.* -ья).

Lib /lɪb/ *n.* (*coll.*): **Women's ~** фемини́стское движе́ние (*за равенство женщин и мужчин*).

libation /laɪˈbeɪʃ(ə)n/, /lɪ-/ *n.* возлия́ние.

libel /ˈlaɪb(ə)l/ *n.* клевета́; **~ action** де́ло по обвине́нию в клевете́; **law of ~** зако́н о диффама́ции.

● *v.t.* (**libelled, libelling;** *US* **libeled, libeling**) клевета́ть, о- (*кого*), на- (*на кого*).

libeller /ˈlaɪbələ(r)/ (*US* **libeler**) *n.* клеветни́|к (*fem.* -ца).

libellous /ˈlaɪbələs/ (*US* **libelous**) *adj.* клеветни́ческий.

liberal /ˈlɪbər(ə)l/ *n.* либера́л.

● *adj.* **1** (*generous, open-handed*) ще́дрый; (*abundant*) оби́льный. **2** (*open or broadminded*): **a man of ~ views** челове́к широ́ких взгля́дов; (*progressive*) передово́й; (*non-specialist*): **a ~ education** гуманита́рное образова́ние; **the ~ arts** гуманита́рные нау́ки. **3** (*pol.*) либера́льный; **the L~s** либера́льная па́ртия.

● *cpds.* **L~ Democrat** *n.* (*pol.*) либера́л-демокра́т; **~ democratic** *adj.* либера́льный-демократи́ческий.

liberalism /ˈlɪbərəl,ɪz(ə)m/ *n.* либерали́зм.

liberality /,lɪbəˈrælɪtɪ/ *n.* ще́дрость; широта́ взгля́дов.

liberalization /,lɪbərəlaɪˈzeɪʃ(ə)n/ *n.* демократиза́ция, либерализа́ция.

liberalize /ˈlɪbərə,laɪz/ *v.t.*: **~ trade** облегч|а́ть, -и́ть усло́вия торго́вли; (*ideas, regime*) либерализи́ровать (*impf., pf.*).

liberate /ˈlɪbə,reɪt/ *v.t.* освобо|жда́ть, -ди́ть.

liberation /,lɪbəˈreɪʃ(ə)n/ *n.* освобожде́ние.

liberator /ˈlɪbə,reɪtə(r)/ *n.* освободи́тель (*fem.* -ница).

Liberia /laɪˈbɪərɪə/ *n.* Либе́рия.

Liberian /laɪˈbɪərɪən/ *n.* либери́|ец (*fem.* -йка).

● *adj.* либери́йский.

libertarian /,lɪbəˈteərɪən/ *n.* (*advocate of freedom*) боре́ц за демократи́ческие свобо́ды.

libertine /ˈlɪbə,tiːn/, /-tɪn/, /-,taɪn/ *n.* распу́тник.

● *adj.* распу́щенный.

libertinism /ˈlɪbətiːn,ɪz(ə)m/, /-tɪn,ɪz(ə)m/, /-taɪn,ɪz(ə)m/ *n.* распу́щенность.

libert|y /ˈlɪbətɪ/ *n.* **1** (*freedom*) свобо́да; **~y of the subject** (*Br.*) свобо́да по́дданного; **~y of action** свобо́да де́йствий; **at ~y** находя́щийся на свобо́де; **you are at ~y to go** вы вольны́ уйти́; **set at ~y** выпуска́ть, вы́пустить на во́лю/свобо́ду; **regain one's ~y** (*escape*) верну́ть (*pf.*) себе́ свобо́ду; (*be released*) быть вы́пущенным на свобо́ду. **2** (*licence*) во́льность; **take ~ies** позв|оля́ть, -о́лить себе́ во́льности; **the author takes ~ies with facts** а́втор сли́шком во́льно обраща́ется с фа́ктами; **take the ~y** осме́ли|ваться, -ться + *inf.*; позв|оля́ть, -о́лить себе́ + *inf.*; **may I take the ~y of asking your name?** позво́льте спроси́ть, как вас зову́т?

libidinous /lɪˈbɪdɪnəs/ *adj.* похотли́вый.

libido /lɪˈbiː,dəʊ/, /lɪˈbaɪdəʊ/ *n.* (*pl.* **~s**) либи́до (*indecl.*).

Libra /ˈliːbrə/, /ˈlɪb-/, /ˈlaɪb-/ *n.* (*astron.*) Вес|ы́ (*pl., g.* -о́в).

librarian /laɪˈbreərɪən/ *n.* библиоте́карь (*m.*).

librarianship /laɪˈbreərɪənʃɪp/ *n.* библиоте́чное де́ло, библиотекове́дение.

library /ˈlaɪbrərɪ/ *n.* библиоте́ка; (*reading-room*) чита́льный зал; **reference ~** спра́вочная библиоте́ка; (*attr.*) библиоте́чный; **sound ~** фоноте́ка; **~ ticket** чита́тельский биле́т.

libretti /lɪˈbretɪ/ *pl. of* ⇒**libretto**

librettist /lɪˈbretɪst/ *n.* либретти́ст.

librett|o /lɪˈbretəʊ/ *n.* (*pl.* **~i** *or* **~os**) либре́тто (*indecl.*).

Libya /ˈlɪbɪə/, /ˈlɪbjə/ *n.* Ли́вия.

Libyan /ˈlɪbɪən/, /ˈlɪbjən/ *n.* ливи́|ец (*fem.* -йка).

● *adj.* ливи́йский.

licence /ˈlaɪs(ə)ns/ (*US also* **license**) *n.* **1** (*permission*) разреше́ние; (*for trade*) лице́нзия; **grant s.o. a ~** выдава́ть, вы́дать лице́нзию кому́-н. **2** (*permit, certificate*) свиде́тельство; **driving ~** води́тельские права́. **3** (*freedom*) во́льность, свобо́да; **poetic ~** поэти́ческая во́льность.

● *cpds.* **~-holder** *n.* = **licensee; ~-plate** *n.* (*US*) номерно́й знак.

license /ˈlaɪs(ə)ns/ (*US also* **licence**) *v.t.* **1** (*permit, authorize*) разреш|а́ть, -и́ть (*что*); да|ва́ть, -ть разреше́ние на (*что*); **the police would not ~ his gun** поли́ция отказа́ла ему́ в разреше́нии на огнестре́льное ору́жие. **2** (*grant permit, permission to*) разреш|а́ть, -и́ть + *d.*; **a shop ~d to sell tobacco** ла́вка, облада́ющая лице́нзией на прода́жу таба́чных изде́лий; **~d premises** (*inn*) заведе́ние, в кото́ром разреша́ется прода́жа спиртны́х напи́тков.

licensee /,laɪsənˈsiː/ *n.* облада́тель (*fem.* -ница) разреше́ния/лице́нзии; (*of public house*) хозя́|ин (*fem.* -йка) ба́ра.

licensing /ˈlaɪsənsɪŋ/ *n.* лицензи́рование; **~ hours** (*Br.*) часы́ прода́жи спиртны́х напи́тков; **~ system** лицензио́нная систе́ма.

licentiate /laɪˈsenʃɪət/, /-ʃət/ *n.* лиценциа́т; облада́тель (*fem.* -ница) дипло́ма.

licentious /laɪˈsenʃəs/ *adj.* распу́щенный.

licentiousness /laɪˈsenʃəsnɪs/ *n.* распу́щенность.

lichee /ˈlaɪtʃɪ/, /ˈlɪ-/ *n.* = **lychee**

lichen /ˈlaɪkən/, /ˈlɪtʃ(ə)n/ *n.* лиша́йник.

lich-gate /ˈlɪtʃgeɪt/ = **lych-gate**

licit /ˈlɪsɪt/ *adj.* зако́нный.

lick /lɪk/ *n.* **1**: **he gave the stamp a ~** он лизну́л ма́рку. **2** (*sl., speed*): **he went at a fair ~** он мча́лся очертя́ го́лову.

● *v.t.* **1** лиз|а́ть, -ну́ть; (**~** *all over*) обли́з|ывать, -а́ть; **~ one's lips**/(*coll.*) **chops** обли́з|ывать, -а́ть гу́бы; обли́з|ываться, -а́ться; (*fig.*): **~ s.o.'s boots** лиза́ть (*impf.*) сапоги́ кому́-н.; **~ one's wounds** зали́з|ывать, -а́ть ра́ны; **~ something into shape** прид|ава́ть, -а́ть вид чему́-н.; **~ s.o. into shape** обтёс|ывать, -а́ть кого́-н. **2** (*coll., thrash*) зад|ава́ть, -а́ть взбу́чку + *d.* **3** (*coll., defeat*) поб|ива́ть, -и́ть.

● *v.t.*: **~ off, ~ up** сли́з|ывать, -а́ть (*or* -ну́ть).

● *cpd.* **~spittle** *n.* подхали́м.

licking /ˈlɪkɪŋ/ *n.* (*coll.*): **he took a ~** (*thrashing*) ему́ доста́лась взбу́чка; (*was defeated*) он был разби́т в пух и прах.

licorice /ˈlɪkərɪs/, /-rɪʃ/ = **liquorice**

lid /lɪd/ *n.* кры́шка; (*fig.*): **flip one's ~** *see* ⇒**flip; keep the ~ on** (*keep secret*) держа́ть (*impf.*) в секре́те; **take the ~ off** (*disclose*) выта́скивать, вы́тащить на свет бо́жий.

lido /ˈliːdəʊ/, /ˈlaɪ-/ *n.* (*pl.* **lidos**) (обще́ственный) пляж.

lie[1] /laɪ/ *n.* (*falsehood*) ложь; **white ~** ложь во спасе́ние; **tell a ~** лгать, со-; **give the ~ to something** опров|ерга́ть, -е́ргнуть что-н.

● *v.t.* (**lies, lied, lying**): **he ~d his way out** он вы́путался с по́мощью лжи.

● *v.i.* (**lies, lied, lying**) лгать, со-; врать, со-/на-; **he ~d to me** он мне солга́л; **~ through one's teeth** на́гло/бессты́дно лгать, со-; **the camera cannot ~** фотогра́фия не (со)врёт.

● *cpd.* **~-detector** *n.* дете́ктор лжи, полигра́ф.

lie[2] /laɪ/ *n.* (*also* **lay**): **the ~ of the land** хара́ктер ме́стности; обстано́вка.

● *v.i.* (**lying;** *past* **lay;** *p.p.* **lain**) **1** (*repose*) лежа́ть, по-; **she lay on the grass all morning** она́ всё у́тро пролежа́ла на траве́; **here ~s ...** здесь поко́ится прах + *g.*; (*remain*): **~ in wait for s.o.** выжида́ть (*impf.*) кого́-н. в заса́де; **~ low** прита́иться (*pf.*); **~ idle** (*of machinery etc.*) прост|а́ивать, -оя́ть. **2** (*be; be situated*) находи́ться (*impf.*); быть располо́женным; **~ at anchor** стоя́ть (*impf.*) на я́коре; **London ~s on**

the Thames Ло́ндон стои́т на Те́мзе; **the town lay in ruins** го́род лежа́л в руи́нах; **see how the land ~s** (*fig.*) узн|ава́ть, -а́ть, как обстои́т де́ло; **the coast ~s open to attack** бе́рег не защищён от нападе́ния.
3 (*fig., reside, rest*): **the choice ~s with you** вы́бор зави́сит от вас; вам выбира́ть; **do you know what ~s behind it all?** вы зна́ете, что за э́тим кро́ется?; **do your interests ~ in that direction?** э́та о́бласть вас интересу́ет?; **she knows where her interests ~** она́ зна́ет свою́ вы́году; **the blame ~s at his door** вина́ на нём; **I will do all that ~s in my power** сде́лаю всё, что в мои́х си́лах.
4 (**~** *down*) ложи́ться, лечь; приле́чь (*pf.*); **he went and lay on the bed** он лёг на крова́ть.

● *with advs.*: **~ about, ~ around** валя́ться (*impf.*); быть разбро́санным; **~ ahead** предстоя́ть (*impf.*); **~ back** (*in chair etc.*) отки́|дываться, -нуться; (*take things easy*) сиде́ть (*impf.*) сложа́ ру́ки; **~ down** ложи́ться, лечь; **I shall ~ down for an hour** я приля́гу на час/часо́к; **take an insult lying down** безро́потно прин|има́ть, -я́ть оскорбле́ние; **~ down on the job** (*fig., slack*) лени́ться (*impf.*); **~ in** (*Br.*) остава́ться (*impf.*) в посте́ли; не встава́ть (*impf.*); **~ to** (*naut.*) лежа́ть (*impf.*) в дре́йфе; **~ up** (*naut.*) находи́ться (*impf.*) в до́ке.

● *cpds.* **~-down** *n.* (*Br.*): **she had a ~-down** она́ полежа́ла; **~-in** *n.* (*Br.*): **we had a ~-in** мы вста́ли по́здно.

liege /li:dʒ/ *n.* ле́нник.
● *adj.* ле́нный; **~ lord** сеньо́р.
● *cpd.* **~man** *n.* васса́л.

lien /ˈli:ən/ *n.* (*leg.*) пра́во удержа́ния.

lieu /lju:/ *n.*: **in ~ of** вме́сто + *g.*

lieutenancy /lefˈtenənsɪ/ *n.* зва́ние лейтена́нта.

lieutenant /lefˈtenənt/ *n.* **1** (*mil.*) лейтена́нт; **first, second ~:** *corresponding to these two Br. Army ranks are the three Russian Army ranks of* ста́рший лейтена́нт, лейтена́нт *and* мла́дший лейтена́нт. **2** (*civilian*) замести́тель (*m.*).
● *cpds.* **~-colonel** *n.* подполко́вник; **~-commander** *n.* (*nav.*) капита́н-лейтена́нт; **~-general** *n.* генера́л-лейтена́нт.

life /laɪf/ *n.* (*pl.* **lives**) **1** (*being alive*) жизнь, (*coll.*) житьё; **a matter of ~ and death** вопро́с жи́зни и сме́рти; **bring back to ~** (*from the dead*) воскре|ша́ть, -си́ть; возвра|ща́ть, -ти́ть к жи́зни; **escape with one's ~** вы́жить (*pf.*), уцеле́ть (*pf.*); **give** (*or* **lay down**) **one's ~ for s.o.** отда́ть/положи́ть (*both pf.*) жизнь за кого́-н.; **lose one's ~** ги́бнуть, по-; **many lives were lost** мно́гие поги́бли; мно́го наро́ду поги́бло; **great loss of ~** мно́го челове́ческих жертв; **run for one's ~** (*or* **for dear ~**) бежа́ть (*det.*) слом́я го́лову; **save one's ~** спас|а́ться, -ти́сь от сме́рти; **save s.o.'s ~** спасти́ (*pf.*) кого́-н. от сме́рти; спасти́ жизнь кому́-н.; **take one's (own) ~** конча́ть, (по)ко́нчить с собо́й; **take one's ~ in one's hands** рискова́ть (*impf.*) жи́знью; **take s.o.'s ~** лиши́ть (*pf.*) кого́-н. жи́зни; **upon my ~!** че́стное сло́во!; ей-Бо́гу!; **not on your ~!** ни за что!; **I couldn't for the ~ of me ...** хоть убе́й, я не мог (бы)...; **insure one's ~** страхова́ть, за- свою́ жизнь; **~ insurance**/(*Br.*) **assurance** страхова́ние жи́зни; (*existence*): **this (earthly) ~** земно́е бытие́; **the next ~, ~ beyond the grave** загро́бная/потусторо́нняя жизнь; **~ eternal, everlasting** ве́чная жизнь; **do you believe in a future ~?** вы ве́рите в загро́бную жизнь?; **that's ~!** такова́ жизнь!; **what a ~!** (*pej.*) ра́зве э́то жизнь?; **make ~ easy for s.o.** облегча́ть (*impf.*) кому́-н. жизнь; **with all the pleasure in ~** с превели́ким удово́льствием; (*way or style of ~*) быт; житьё-бытьё; **family ~** дома́шний быт; **country, village ~** дереве́нская жизнь; **a dog's ~** соба́чья жизнь; **high ~** све́тская жизнь; **low ~** жизнь низо́в; **the simple ~** просто́й о́браз жи́зни; **this is the ~!** вот э́то жизнь!; **anything for a quiet ~!** ли́шь бы поко́й!; (*department of ~*): **in private/public ~** в ча́стной/обще́ственной жи́зни; **sex ~** полова́я жизнь; **see ~** повида́ть (*pf.*) свет.
2 (*period, span of ~*): **at my time of ~** в моём во́зрасте; **get the fright of one's ~** перепуга́ться (*pf.*) на́смерть; **have the time of one's ~** прекра́сно проводи́ть (*impf.*) вре́мя; **he has had a good/quiet ~** он про́жил хоро́шую/споко́йную жизнь; **he got ~; he is in for ~** (*coll.*) он получи́л пожи́зненное заключе́ние; **~ peerage** ли́чное/пожи́зненное пэ́рство; **~ sentence** пригово́р к пожи́зненному заключе́нию; **it was his ~ work** э́то бы́ло трудо́м (всей) его́ жи́зни; (*of inanimate things, durability*) долгове́чность; срок слу́жбы; **these machines have an average ~ of 10 years** сре́дний срок слу́жбы э́тих маши́н 10 лет.
3 (*animation*) жи́вость, оживле́ние; **put some ~ into it!** живе́е!; пошеве́ливайтесь!; **the ~ and soul of the party** душа́ о́бщества; **the child is full of ~** ребёнок о́чень живо́й; **there's no ~ in her playing** её игра́ безжи́зненна; **bring (back) to ~** (*after fainting etc.*) прив|оди́ть, -ести́ в чу́вства; (*fig.*) вдохну́ть (*pf.*) жизнь в + *a.*; воскре|ша́ть, -си́ть; **come to ~** (*recover senses*) очну́ться (*pf.*); **the play came to ~ in the third act** к тре́тьему де́йствию пье́са оживи́лась.
4 (*living things*) жизнь; **is there ~ on Mars?** есть ли жизнь на Ма́рсе?; **animal ~** живо́тный мир; **marine ~** морска́я фа́уна; **still ~** натюрмо́рт; **wild~** жива́я приро́да; **draw from ~** рисова́ть, на- с нату́ры; **~ model** нату́рщи|к (*fem.* -ца); моде́ль.
5 (*actuality*): **true to ~** реалисти́чный; **as large as ~** в натура́льную величину́; как живо́й; со́бственной персо́ной; **larger than ~** преувели́ченный; **that's him to the ~!** э́то вы́литый он!
6 (*biography*) жизнь, биогра́фия; **lives of the saints ~** жития́ святы́х; **the ~ history of a plant** жи́зненный цикл расте́ния; **he told me his ~ story** он пове́дал мне исто́рию свое́й жи́зни.

● *cpds.* **~-and-death** *adj.* жи́зненно ва́жный, реша́ющий; **a ~-and-death struggle** борьба́ не на жизнь, а на́ смерть; **~belt** *n.* (*Br.*) спаса́тельный круг; **~-blood** *n.* кровь; (*fig.*) жи́зненная си́ла; **~boat** *n.* спаса́тельная ло́дка; **~buoy** *n.* (*Br.*) спаса́тельный круг; **~-cycle** *n.* жи́зненный цикл; цикл разви́тия; **~ expectancy** *n.* вероя́тная продолжи́тельность жи́зни; **~-force** *n.* жи́зненная си́ла; **~-giving** *adj.* живи́тельный; **~-guard, ~-saver** *nn.* спаса́тель (*fem.* -ница) (на пля́же); **~jacket** *n.* спаса́тельная жиле́т; **~like** *adj.* реалисти́чный; **~-line** *n.* (*naut.*) спаса́тельный коне́ц; (*diver's*) сигна́льный коне́ц; (*palmistry*) ли́ния жи́зни; (*fig.*) я́корь (*m.*) спасе́ния; **~long** *adj.* пожи́зненный; **they were ~long friends** они́ бы́ли друзья́ми всю жизнь; **~-preserver** *n.* (*Br., weapon*) дуби́нка, запо́лненная свинцо́м; (*US, lifebelt*) спаса́тельный по́яс; **~-saver** *n.* = **~-guard;** (*US*) = **~-belt, ~-jacket;** (*fig.*) спасе́ние; **~-saving** *n.* спасе́ние; *adj.* спаса́тельный; **~size(d)** *adj.* в натура́льную величину́; **~-span** *n.* продолжи́тельность/протяже́ние жи́зни; **~-style** *n.* о́браз жи́зни; **~-support** *adj.*: **~-support system** систе́ма жизнеобеспе́чения; **~time** *n.* жизнь; **in s.o.'s ~time** при жи́зни кого́-н.; **the chance of a ~time** ре́дкий/исключи́тельный слу́чай; **it's a ~time since I saw her** я её не ви́дел це́лую ве́чность.

lifeless /ˈlaɪflɪs/ *adj.* (*dead*) мёртвый; (*inanimate*) неживо́й; (*inert, without animation*) безжи́зненный.

lifelessness /ˈlaɪflɪsnɪs/ *n.* безжи́зненность.

lifer /ˈlaɪfə(r)/ *n.* (*coll.*) заключённый пожи́зненно; приговорённый к пожи́зненной ка́торге.

lift /lɪft/ *n.* **1** (*act of raising*) подня́тие, подъём; (*extent of rise*) высота́ подъёма; (*aeron., upward pressure*) подъёмная си́ла.
2 (*transport by air*) возду́шные перево́зки (*f. pl.*).
3 (*transport of passenger in car etc.*): **give s.o. a ~** подв|ози́ть, -езти́ кого́-н.; (*coll.*) подки́|дывать, -нуть кого́-н.; **he thumbed a ~ to London** он доéхал на попу́тных маши́нах до Ло́ндона.
4 (*fig., of spirits*): **the news gave her a ~** от э́той но́вости она́ воспря́ла ду́хом.
5 (*Br., apparatus*) лифт; (*tech.*) подъёмник; **~ attendant, operator** лифтёр (*fem.* -ша); **~ cage** кле́тка подъёмника; **take the ~** подн|има́ться, -я́ться ли́фтом (*or* на ли́фте).

● *v.t.* **1** (*raise*) подн|има́ть, -я́ть; **he barely ~ed his eyes to her** он едва́ взгляну́л на неё; **he did not ~ a finger** (*fig.*) он и па́льцем не пошевельну́л.
2 (*dig up*): **~ potatoes** выка́пывать,

вы́копать карто́фель.
3 (*transport by air*): **the troops were ~ed to Africa** войска́ бы́ли доста́влены в А́фрику по во́здуху.
4 (*steal*) спере́ть (*pf.*) (*coll.*); (*of a plagiarist*) спи́с|ывать, -а́ть, красть, у-.
5 (*remove*): **~ a ban** сн|има́ть, -ять запре́т.

● *v.i.* (*rise*) подн|има́ться, -я́ться; (*disperse*) рассе́|иваться, -яться; (*cease*) прекра|ща́ться, -ти́ться.

● *with advs.*: **~ down** *v.t.* снять (*pf.*) и поста́вить (*pf.*) на́ пол (*or* на зе́млю); **~ off** *v.t.* сн|има́ть, -ять; *v.i.* (*of rocket*) от|рыва́ться, -орва́ться от земли́; **~ out** *v.t.* вынима́ть, вы́нуть; **~ up** *v.t.* подн|има́ть, -я́ть; **~ up one's voice** (*sing*) запе́ть (*pf.*).

● *cpds.* **~-boy** *n.* (*Br.*) лифтёр; **~-off** *n.* отры́в от земли́.

ligament /ˈlɪgəmənt/ *n.* свя́зка.

ligature /ˈlɪgətʃə(r)/ *n.* (*med., typ.*) лигату́ра; (*mus.*) ли́га.

light[1] /laɪt/ *n.* **1** свет; **in the ~** на свету́; **in the ~ of day** при дневно́м све́те; **in artificial ~** при иску́сственном освеще́нии; **at first ~** на рассве́те; **stand against the ~** стоя́ть (*impf.*) про́тив све́та; **get in s.o.'s ~** заслон|я́ть, -и́ть свет кому́-н.; (*attr.*) светово́й; (*fig.*): **see the ~ (of day)** (*be born*) уви́деть (*pf.*) свет; (*be made public*) быть обнаро́дованным, уви́деть (*pf.*) свет; **see the ~** (*realize truth*) прозр|ева́ть, -е́ть; **in the ~ of experience** исходя́ из о́пыта; **bring to ~** выводи́ть, вы́вести на чи́стую во́ду; раскр|ыва́ть, -ы́ть; **come to ~** обнару́жи|ваться, -ться; выплыва́ть, вы́плыть; **shed, throw ~ on something** прол|ива́ть, -и́ть свет на что-н.; **hide one's ~ under a bushel** зарыва́ть (*impf.*) свой тала́нт в зе́млю; (*brightness*): **northern ~s** се́верное сия́ние; **there was a ~ in his eyes** у него́ блесте́ли глаза́; (*in a picture*): **effects of ~ and shade** эффе́кты све́та и те́ни; светоте́нь; (*lighting*) освеще́ние; **electric ~** электри́ческое освеще́ние; (*fig.*): **this book shows him in a bad ~** э́та кни́га пока́зывает его́ в невы́годном све́те; **there was a ~ in the window** в окне́ был свет; окно́ свети́лось; **put on the ~** заж|ига́ть, -е́чь свет; (*point of ~*): **the ~s of the town** огни́ го́рода.
2 (*lamp*) ла́мпа; **~ bulb** ла́мпочка; **'L~s out!'** «погаси́ть ого́нь/свет!»; (*of car*) фа́ра; **we saw the ~s of a car** мы уви́дели свет автомоби́льных фар; **dip the ~s** переключ|а́ть, -и́ть на бли́жний свет; **navigation ~s** (*of ship*) сигна́льно-отличи́тельные огни́; (*of aircraft*) аэронавигацио́нные огни́; **traffic ~s** светофо́р; **go against the ~s** е́хать (*impf.*) (*or* про|езжа́ть, -е́хать) на кра́сный свет; **give s.o. the green ~** (*fig.*) да|ва́ть, -ть зелёную у́лицу кому́-н.; **see the red ~** (*fig.*) зам|еча́ть, -е́тить опа́сность; (*fig.*): **a leading ~** (*in society*) свети́ло, знамени́тость.
3 (*flame*) ого́нь (*m.*); **strike a ~** (*with match*) заж|ига́ть, -е́чь спи́чку; **have you a ~?** нет ли у вас огонька́?; **give me a ~** да́йте прикури́ть.
4 (*fig., natural ability*): **according to one's ~s** по ме́ре свои́х спосо́бностей.
5 (*archit.*) окно́; просве́т.

● *adj.* **1** (*opp. dark*) све́тлый; **get ~** рассве|та́ть, -сти́; **we must leave while it's still ~** нам на́до уйти́ за́светло.
2 (*in colour*) све́тлый; све́тлого цве́та; **a ~ green** светло-зелёный цвет.

● *v.t.* (*past* **lit;** *p.p.* **lit** *or* (*attrib.*) **lighted**) (*also* **~ up**) **1** (*kindle*) заж|ига́ть, -е́чь; **~ a fire** разв|оди́ть, -ести́ ого́нь; **~ (up) a cigarette** заку́р|ивать, -и́ть папиро́су.
2 (*illuminate*) осве|ща́ть, -ти́ть; **the house is lit by electricity** в до́ме электри́ческое освеще́ние; **the town is lit up for the carnival** по слу́чаю карнава́ла в го́роде иллюмина́ция; **~ the way for s.o.** свети́ть, по- кому́-н.; (*fig.*): **a smile lit up his face** улы́бка озари́ла его́ лицо́.

● *v.i.* (*past* **lit;** *p.p.* **lit** *or* (*attrib.*) **lighted**): **~ up** (*switch on ~s*) включ|а́ть, -и́ть свет; **~ing-up time** (*Br.*) вре́мя для включе́ния фар; (*of the face*) свети́ться, за-; ожив|ля́ться, -и́ться; (*start smoking*) заку́р|ивать, -и́ть.

● *cpds.* **~-emitting** *adj.*: **~-emitting diode** светоизлуча́ющий дио́д, светодио́д; **~house** *n.* мая́к; **~house keeper** смотри́тель (*m.*) маяка́; **~-meter** *n.* экспоно́метр; **~ship** *n.* плаву́чий мая́к; **~-year** *n.* светово́й год.

light[2] /laɪt/ *adj.* (*opp. heavy*) лёгкий; **~ artillery** лёгкая артилле́рия; **a ~ blow** лёгкий уда́р; **our casualties were ~** на́ши поте́ри бы́ли незначи́тельны; **a ~ crop** ску́дный урожа́й; **a ~ diet** облегчённая дие́та; **with a ~ heart** с лёгким се́рдцем; **~ industry** лёгкая промы́шленность; **a ~ meal** неплóтная еда́; **we had a ~ meal** мы перекуси́ли; **~ music** лёгкая му́зыка; **~ rain** небольшо́й/ме́лкий дождь; **~ reading** лёгкое чте́ние; **a ~ sentence** мя́гкий пригово́р; **a ~ sleep** лёгкий/ чу́ткий/неглубо́кий сон; **I am a ~ sleeper** я чу́тко сплю; **~ soil** ры́хлая по́чва; **traffic is ~ today** сего́дня неинтенси́вное движе́ние; **the bridge is suitable for ~ traffic only** мост годи́тся то́лько для легковы́х маши́н; **in ~ type** све́тлым шри́фтом; **give s.o. ~ weight** обве́|шивать, -сить кого́-н.; **he made ~ work of it** он легко́ спра́вился с э́тим де́лом; **he made ~ of the difficulties** он преуменьша́л тру́дности.

● *adv.*: **travel ~** путеше́ствовать (*impf.*) налегке́.

● *cpds.* **~-armed** *adj.* (*with ~ weapons*) легковооружённый; **~-fingered** *adj.* нечи́стый на́ руку; **~-footed** *adj.* прово́рный, легконо́гий; **~-headed** *adj.*: **she felt ~-headed** у неё закружи́лась голова́; **~-hearted** *adj.* (*carefree*) беспе́чный; (*gay*) весёлый; (*thoughtless*) легкомы́сленный; (*of action*) необду́манный; (*joking*) игри́вый, шутли́вый; **~-heartedness** *n.* беспе́чность; **~-weight** *n.* (*sportsman*) легкове́с; боре́ц/боксёр лёгкого ве́са; (*fig.*) несерьёзный челове́к; *adj.* (*suit*) лёгкий; (*fig.*) несерьёзный, легкове́сный.

light[3] /laɪt/ *v.i.* (*past and p.p.* **lit** *or* **lighted**): **~ on** (*encounter*) набрести́ (*pf.*) на + *a.*; **his eyes ~ed on her face** его́ взгляд упа́л на её лицо́.

light- /laɪt/ *comb. form* **1** (*before colours*) све́тло-; **~-green** све́тло-зелёный.
2 (*before 'haired' etc.*) светло (*no hyphen*); **~haired** светловоло́сый; **~skinned** светлоко́жий.

lighten[1] /ˈlaɪt(ə)n/ *v.t.* (*make less heavy or easier*) облегч|а́ть, -и́ть; **it ~ed our task** э́то облегчи́ло на́шу зада́чу; (*mitigate*): **~ a sentence** смягч|а́ть, -и́ть пригово́р.

● *v.i.*: **his heart ~ed** у него́ ста́ло ле́гче на душе́; **~ up** (*become less serious*): **~ up!** бу́дьте повеселе́е!

lighten[2] /ˈlaɪt(ə)n/ *v.t.* (*illuminate, make brighter*) осве|ща́ть, -ти́ть; просветл|я́ть, -и́ть.

● *v.i.* **1** (*grow brighter*) светле́ть, про-; проясн|я́ться, -и́ться. **2** (*of lightning*) сверк|а́ть, -ну́ть; **it is ~ing** сверка́ет мо́лния.

lighter[1] /ˈlaɪtə(r)/ *n.* (*for cigarettes etc.*) зажига́лка.

lighter[2] /ˈlaɪtə(r)/ *n.* (*boat*) ли́хтер.

● *cpd.* **~man** *n.* матро́с на ли́хтере.

lighting /ˈlaɪtɪŋ/ *n.* освеще́ние.

lightish /ˈlaɪtɪʃ/ *adj.* (*of colour*) светлова́тый.

lightly /ˈlaɪtlɪ/ *adv.* легко́; **tread ~** легко́/осторо́жно ступа́ть (*impf.*); **he touched ~ on the past** он слегка́ косну́лся про́шлого; **he jumped ~ to the ground** он ло́вко спры́гнул на зе́млю; **it's not a thing to enter upon ~** за таки́е дела́ не сле́дует бра́ться необду́манно; **he takes everything ~** он ничего́ не принима́ет всерьёз; **you have got off ~** вы легко́ отде́лались; **the accused got off ~** обвиня́емый отде́лался лёгким наказа́нием.

lightness /ˈlaɪtnɪs/ *n.* (*of weight*) лёгкость; (*nimbleness*) ло́вкость; (*mildness*) мя́гкость; (*of colour*) све́тлость, светлота́.

lightning /ˈlaɪtnɪŋ/ *n.* мо́лния; **forked ~** зигзагообра́зная мо́лния; **sheet, summer ~** зарни́ца; **swift as ~** молниено́сный; **he was struck by ~** в него́ уда́рила мо́лния.

● *adj.*: **with ~ speed** молниено́сно; **a ~ attack** молниено́сная ата́ка.

● *cpds.* **~-conductor** (*Br.*), **~-rod** (*US*) *nn.* громоотво́д.

lights /laɪts/ *n.* (*animal's lungs*) лёгкие (*nt. pl.*).

lightsome /ˈlaɪtsəm/ *adj.* (*graceful*) лёгкий, грацио́зный; (*merry*) беспе́чный, весёлый.

lignite /ˈlɪgnaɪt/ *n.* (*min.*) лигни́т, бу́рый у́голь.

lignum vitae /ˌlɪgnəm ˈvaɪtɪ/, /ˈviːtaɪ/ *n.* гвая́ковое де́рево.

likable /ˈlaɪkəb(ə)l/ = **lik(e)able**

like[1] /laɪk/ *n.* (*something equal or similar*) подо́бное; **did you ever hear the ~ (of**

it)? слы́шали ли вы что́-нибудь подо́бное?; как вам э́то нра́вится?; **music, dancing and the ~** му́зыка, та́нцы и тому́ подо́бное; (*person*) подо́бный; **we shall not look upon his ~ again** тако́го (челове́ка) мы никогда́ бо́льше не встре́тим; **the ~s of me, us** наш брат; **the ~s of you** ваш брат.

● *adj.* (**more like, most like**) подо́бный, похо́жий; **in ~ manner** подо́бным о́бразом; **as ~ as two peas** похо́жи как две ка́пли воды́; **~ father, ~ son** я́блоко от я́блони недалеко́ па́дает; (*equal*) ра́вный; **~ poles repel each other** одноимённые по́люсы отта́лкиваются; *see also prep. uses.*

● *adv.* **1** (*probably*): **~ enough, very ~** весьма́ возмо́жно; **(as) ~ as not** верне́е всего́.
2 (*coll., as it were*) вро́де, похо́же, так сказа́ть, как бы сказа́ть.

● *prep.* **1** (*similar to, characteristic of*) похо́жий на + *a.*; **she is ~ her mother** она́ похо́жа на мать; **that's just ~ him!** э́то похо́же на него́!; узнаю́ его́!; **what's she ~?** что она́ за челове́к?; кака́я она́?; что она́ собо́й представля́ет?; **I don't care for films ~ that** я не люблю́ подо́бных фи́льмов; **a house ~ yours** дом вро́де ва́шего; **don't be ~ that!** (*coll., behave unhelpfully*) бро́сьте!; **there's nothing ~ walking to keep you fit** для здоро́вья нет ничего́ поле́знее, чем ходьба́; **his second book is nothing ~ as good as the first** его́ втора́я кни́га значи́тельно ху́же пе́рвой; **that is nothing ~ enough** э́того не мо́жет хвати́ть; **£500 would be more ~ it** скоре́е фу́нтов 500; **they sold something ~ 1,000 copies** они́ прода́ли (что́-то) о́коло 1 000 экземпля́ров; **look ~** *see* ⇒**look** *v.i.* 3; **it smells ~ something burning** па́хнет горе́лым; **it sounds ~ thunder** как бу́дто греми́т гром; **the crowd buzzed ~ a swarm of bees** толпа́ гуде́ла, то́чно рой пчёл; **it sounds ~ a good idea** э́то, пожа́луй, хоро́шая иде́я; **he drinks ~ a fish** он пьёт как бо́чка; **don't talk ~ that!** не на́до так говори́ть; **a person ~ that** тако́й челове́к; **he was working ~ anything** он труди́лся изо всех сил; **it's ~ nothing on earth** э́то ни на что не похо́же.
2 (*inclined towards*): **do you feel ~ going for a walk?** вам (не) хо́чется пройти́сь?; **I don't feel ~ it** мне (что́-то) не хо́чется; **I felt ~ crying** мне хоте́лось пла́кать; **I feel ~ an ice-cream** я бы не прочь съесть моро́женое; **I feel ~ nothing on earth** (*dreadful*) я себя́ отврати́тельно чу́вствую.

● *conj.* (*coll.*): **he talks ~ I do** он говори́т так же, как я.

● *cpd.* **~-minded** *adj.* приде́рживающийся тех же взгля́дов; **~-minded person** единомы́шленник.

like² /laɪk/ *n.*: **~s and dislikes** симпа́тии и антипа́тии (*both f. pl.*); **she has her ~s and dislikes** у неё о́чень определённый вкус.

● *v.t.* (*take pleasure in*) люби́ть (*impf.*), цени́ть (*impf.*); **he ~s living in Paris** ему́ нра́вится жить в Пари́же; **she ~d dancing** она́ люби́ла танцева́ть; **I ~ him** он мне нра́вится; **we ~d the play** пье́са нам понра́вилась; **how do you ~ that?** как вам э́то нра́вится?; **I ~ that!** (*iron.*) ничего́ себе́!; ну и ну!; **I ~ his impudence** вот э́то наха́льство!; **what don't you ~ about it?** что вас в э́том не устра́ивает?; **I don't ~** (*am reluctant*) **to disturb you** прости́те, что беспоко́ю вас; **(you can) ~ it or lump it!** (*coll.*) нра́вится — не нра́вится, а ничего́ не поде́лаешь; **whether you ~ it or not** во́лей-нево́лей; **would you ~ a drink?** хоти́те вы́пить (чего́-нибудь)?; **if you ~** е́сли хоти́те; **I should ~ to meet him** мне хоте́лось бы познако́миться с ним; **he would ~ to come** он хоте́л бы прийти́; **I would have ~d to (***or* **would like to have) come** я жале́ю, что не мог прийти́; **I ~ this picture better than that** мне э́та карти́на нра́вится бо́льше, чем та; **I wouldn't ~ there to be any misunderstanding** я хоте́л бы, что́бы меня́ по́няли пра́вильно; **I ~ to think he values my advice** мне хоте́лось бы ду́мать (*or* я наде́юсь), что он це́нит мой сове́т; **I ~ people to tell the truth** (я) люблю́, когда́ (лю́ди) говоря́т пра́вду; **I ~ to be sure** я предпочита́ю знать наверняка́; **how do you ~ your tea?** вы пьёте чай с са́харом/молоко́м (*и т.п.*)?; **as you ~** как уго́дно; **come whenever you ~** приходи́те в любо́е вре́мя; **he was outspoken if you ~, but not rude** он был, е́сли хоти́те, открове́нен, но ника́к не груб.

lik(e)able /ˈlaɪkəb(ə)l/ *adj.* симпати́чный.

likelihood /ˈlaɪklɪˌhʊd/ *n.* вероя́тность; **in all ~** по всей вероя́тности; **there is little ~ of his coming** ма́ло вероя́тно, что он прие́дет.

likely /ˈlaɪklɪ/ *adj.* (**likelier, likeliest**) **1** (*probable*) вероя́тный; (*plausible*) правдоподо́бный; **a ~ story!** (*iron.*) так я и пове́рил! **2** (*suitable*) подходя́щий; (*promising*) многообеща́ющий. **3** (*to be expected*): **he is ~ to come** он, вероя́тно, придёт; **that is never ~ to happen** э́то вряд ли когда́-нибудь случи́тся.

● *adv.* вероя́тно; **most, very ~** наве́рно; скоре́е всего́; **not ~!** (на)вря́д ли!; как бы не так!; **as ~ as not** вполне́ вероя́тно/возмо́жно; не исключено́.

liken /ˈlaɪkən/ *v.t.* упод|обля́ть, -о́бить (*кого/что кому/чему*); сра́вн|ивать, -и́ть (*кого/что с кем/чем*).

likeness /ˈlaɪknɪs/ *n.* **1** (*resemblance*) схо́дство, подо́бие; **a family ~** фами́льное схо́дство; **in his own image and ~** по своему́ о́бразу и подо́бию. **2** (*guise*) обли́чие; **in the ~ of** в ви́де + *g.*; под личи́ной + *g.*
3 (*representation, portrait*) изображе́ние, портре́т.

likewise /ˈlaɪkwaɪz/ *adv.* подо́бно.

● *conj.* таки́м же о́бразом.

liking /ˈlaɪkɪŋ/ *n.* симпа́тия (*к кому*); расположе́ние (*к чему*); **he has a ~ for quotations** он лю́бит цита́ты; **I took a ~ to him** я почу́вствовал к нему́ симпа́тию; **she has no ~ for this work** э́та рабо́та ей не по душе́; **is the meat done to your ~?** э́то мя́со пригото́влено, как вы лю́бите?

lilac /ˈlaɪlək/ *n.* сире́нь.

● *adj.* (*pert. to ~; ~-coloured*) сире́невый.

lilliputian /ˌlɪlɪˈpjuːʃ(ə)n/ *adj.* миниатю́рный, кро́шечный.

lilo /ˈlaɪləʊ/ *n.* (*propr.*) (*pl.* **~s**) надувно́й пля́жный матра́ц.

lilt /lɪlt/ *n.* (*tune*) напе́в; (*rhythm*) ритм.

● *v.i.*: **a ~ing melody** мелоди́чный напе́в.

lily /ˈlɪlɪ/ *n.* ли́лия; **~ of the valley** ла́ндыш.

● *cpds.* **~-livered** *adj.* трусли́вый; **~-pond** *n.* пруд с ли́лиями; **~-white** *adj.* лиле́йный.

limb /lɪm/ *n.* **1** (*of body; also fig.*). член; коне́чность; **escape with life and ~** вы́йти (*pf.*) це́лым и невреди́мым; **tear s.o. ~ from ~** раз|рыва́ть, -орва́ть кого́-н. на ча́сти. **2** (*branch of tree*) сук, ветвь; **out on a ~** (*fig.*) в невы́годном/опа́сном положе́нии.

limber¹ /ˈlɪmbə(r)/ *n.* (*mil.*) передо́к.

limber² /ˈlɪmbə(r)/ *adj.* (*flexible, pliable*) ги́бкий, пода́тливый; (*nimble*) прово́рный.

● *v.i.*: **~ up** разм|ина́ться, -я́ться.

limbless /ˈlɪmlɪs/ *adj.* (*armless*) безру́кий; (*legless*) безно́гий.

limbo /ˈlɪmbəʊ/ *n.* (*pl.* **~s**) **1** (*relig.*) лимб; преддве́рие а́да. **2** (*fig.*) неопределённость, перехо́дное состоя́ние; **our plans are in ~** на́ши пла́ны ви́снут в во́здухе.

lime¹ /laɪm/ *n.* (*fruit*) лайм; **~ juice** сок ла́йма.

lime² /laɪm/ *n.* (*tree*) ли́па; (*attr.*) ли́повый.

lime³ /laɪm/ *n.* (*calcium oxide*) и́звесть; **slaked/quick ~** гашёная/негашёная и́звесть; **~ water** известко́вая вода́.

● *v.t.* (*soil*) известкова́ть (*impf., pf.*); уд|обря́ть, -о́брить и́звестью.

● *cpds.* **~-kiln** *n.* печь для о́бжига и́звести; **~light** *n.* (*lit.*) свет ра́мпы; (*fig.*): **be in the ~light** быть знамени́тостью; быть в це́нтре внима́ния; быть на виду́; **come into the ~light** ста|нови́ться, -ть знамени́тостью; **~stone** *n.* известня́к; (*attr.*) известняко́вый.

limey /ˈlaɪmɪ/ *n.* (*pl.* **~s**) (*US sl.*) англича́нин.

limit /ˈlɪmɪt/ *n.* **1** (*terminal point*) преде́л; (*comm.*) лими́т; **the ~s of endurance** преде́лы выно́сливости; **he exceeded the speed ~** он превы́сил устано́вленную ско́рость; **set, fix a ~ to something** устан|а́вливать, -ови́ть преде́л чему́-н.; **lower/upper ~** ми́нимум/ма́ксимум; **that's the ~!** э́то перехо́дит все грани́цы; **he is the (very) ~!** он невозмо́жен!; **without ~** без конца́; (*endlessly*) бесконе́чно; **there is a ~ to what I can stand** моему́ терпе́нию есть преде́л; **his greed knows no ~s** его́ жа́дность не зна́ет преде́лов; **I am willing to help you,**

within ~s я гото́в помо́чь вам в преде́лах возмо́жного (*or* в изве́стных преде́лах).
2 (*border, boundary*) грани́ца; **he has gone beyond the ~s of decency** он перешёл грани́цы прили́чия; **city ~s** городска́я черта́; **'off ~s to military personnel'** (*US*) «вход военнослу́жащим запрещён».
3 (*time* ~) (преде́льный) срок; **age ~** преде́льный во́зраст.
● *v.t.* (**limited, limiting**) ограни́чи|вать, -ть (*кого/что чем*); **I shall ~ myself to a single chapter** я ограни́чусь одно́й главо́й; **~ed monarchy** ограни́ченная мона́рхия; **~ed edition** изда́ние, вы́пущенное ограни́ченным тиражо́м; **~ed (liability) company** (*Br.*) компа́ния с ограни́ченной отве́тственностью.

limitation /,lɪmɪ'teɪʃ(ə)n/ *n.* (*limiting, being limited*) ограниче́ние; (*condition*) огово́рка; (*drawback*) недоста́ток; **he has his ~s** он не лишён недоста́тков.

limitless /'lɪmɪtlɪs/ *adj.* безграни́чный, беспреде́льный; (*of time*) бесконе́чный.

limousine /'lɪmʊ,zi:n/, /,lɪmʊ'zi:n/, /'lɪmə,zi:n/ *n.* лимузи́н.

limp[1] /lɪmp/ *n.* хромота́; **he has (*or* walks with) a ~** он хрома́ет/прихра́мывает.
● *v.i.* хрома́ть (*impf.*); **he was ~ing along the street** он ковыля́л по у́лице; (*fig.*): **the plane ~ed back to base** самолёт с трудо́м добра́лся до ба́зы.

limp[2] /lɪmp/ *adj.* **1** (*flexible*) мя́гкий; **a book in ~ covers** кни́га в мя́гком переплёте. **2** (*without energy; flabby*) вя́лый; **I feel ~** я совсе́м без сил; **go ~** обм|яка́ть, -я́кнуть.

limpet /'lɪmpɪt/ *n.* блю́дечко (*моллюск*); **stick like a ~** приста́ть (*pf.*) как ба́нный лист; **~ mine** прилипа́ющая ми́на.

limpid /'lɪmpɪd/ *adj.* прозра́чный.

limpidity /lɪm'pɪdɪtɪ/ *n.* прозра́чность.

limy /'laɪmɪ/ *adj.* (**limier, limiest**) (*of soil*) известко́вый.

linchpin, lynchpin /'lɪntʃpɪn/ *n.* чека́; (*fig., of person or thing*) тот/то, на ком/чём всё де́ржится; незамени́мый челове́к; опо́ра.

linctus /'lɪŋktəs/ *n.* (*Br.*) миксту́ра.

linden /'lɪnd(ə)n/ *n.* ли́па.

line[1] /laɪn/ *n.* **1** (*cord*) верёвка; **hang washing on the ~** разве́сить (*pf.*) бельё на верёвке; (*fishing-*~) ле́ска; (*plumb-*~) отве́с.
2 (*wire, cable for communication*) ли́ния (свя́зи); ка́бель (*m.*); про́вод; **direct ~** пряма́я ли́ния; **party ~** паралле́льные телефо́ны; **hot ~** (*coll.*) прямо́й про́вод; **the ~ is bad** пло́хо слы́шно; **the ~ is engaged** (*Br.*), **busy** (*US*) ли́ния занята́; **he is on the ~** он говори́т по телефо́ну; он у телефо́на; **give me a ~ to the Ministry** соедини́те меня́ с министе́рством; **an outside ~, please** да́йте го́род, пожа́луйста; **hold the ~!** подожди́те у телефо́на!; не ве́шайте тру́бку!; **lay ~s** про|кла́дывать, -ложи́ть ка́бель.
3 (*rail.*) ли́ния; **~s of communication** (*mil.*) коммуника́ции (*f. pl.*); **main ~** гла́вный путь, магистра́ль; **branch ~** (железнодоро́жная) ве́тка; **he has reached the end of the ~** (*fig.*) он дошёл до ру́чки/то́чки/преде́ла; (*track*) полотно́; ре́льсы (*m. pl.*); (ре́льсовый) путь; **I crossed the ~ by the bridge** я перешёл ли́нию по мосту́.
4 (*transport system*) ли́ния; **air ~s** возду́шные ли́нии.
5 (*long narrow mark*) ли́ния, черта́; (*geom., geog. etc.*): **~s of force** силовы́е ли́нии; **date ~** ли́ния су́точного вре́мени; (*imagined straight* ~): **~ of fire** направле́ние стрельбы́.
6 (*on face etc.*) скла́дка, морщи́ны.
7 (*drawn, painted etc.*) штрих; **~ drawing** штрихово́й/каранда́шный рису́нок; **in broad ~s** в о́бщих черта́х; **drawn in bold ~s** нарисо́ванный сме́лыми штриха́ми; (*pl., contour, outline, shape*) ко́нтур, очерта́ние; **~s of a ship** обво́ды (*m. pl.*) корабля́.
8 (*boundary, limit*) грани́ца, преде́л, черта́; **dividing ~** раздели́тельная черта́; (*fig.*): **draw a ~ between** различ|а́ть, -и́ть; **draw the ~** пров|оди́ть, -ести́ грани́цу; **one must draw the ~ somewhere** всему́ есть преде́л; **I draw the ~ at that** на э́то я уж не согла́сен; (*sport*): **the ball went over the ~** мяч перешёл черту́; **at the starting ~** на ста́рте; **toe the ~** (*fig.*) беспрекосло́вно слу́шаться/подчиня́ться (*impf.*); ходи́ть (*indet.*) по ни́точке.
9 (*row*) ряд, ли́ния; **stand in ~** стоя́ть (*impf.*) в ряд; (*US, queue*) стоя́ть (*impf.*) в о́череди; (в)стать (*pf.*) в о́чередь; **in ~ with** в одну́ ли́нию (*or* в ряд) с + *i.*; (*fig.*) в согла́сии/соотве́тствии с + *i.*; **bring into ~** (*fig.*) привле́чь (*pf.*) (*кого*) на свою́ сто́рону; согласо́в|ывать, -а́ть (*что*); **come, fall into ~** согла|ша́ться, -си́ться; (*fig.*) согласова́ться (*impf., pf.*); **be out of ~** (*fig.*) не соотве́тствовать (*impf.*) но́рме; (*mil.*): **in ~** в развёрнутом строю́; **draw up in ~** стро́ить, по- в ряд.
10 (*mil., entrenched position*): **front ~** ли́ния фро́нта; **in the front ~** на передово́й; **~s of defence** оборони́тельный рубе́ж; **behind the enemy ~s** за расположе́нием (*or* в (бли́жнем) тылу́) проти́вника; **he was beaten all along the ~** (*fig.*) он потерпе́л пораже́ние на всех фронта́х.
11 (*mil., nav.: main, not auxiliary, formation*): **~ regiment** лине́йный полк; **ship of the ~** лине́йный кора́бль (*abbr.* линко́р).
12 (*of print or writing*) строка́; **on ~ 10** в строке́ деся́той; **begin a new ~!** начни́те с но́вой строки́!; **read between the ~s** (*fig.*) чита́ть (*impf.*) ме́жду строк; **marriage ~s** (*Br.*) свиде́тельство о бра́ке; **send (*coll.*, drop) s.o. a ~ (*or* a few ~s)** черкну́ть (*pf.*) кому́-н. не́сколько слов; (*pl., verse*) стихи́ (*m. pl.*); (*pl., actor's part*) роль.
13 (*lineage*) ли́ния; **in direct ~ of descent** по прямо́й (нисходя́щей) ли́нии; **the last of a long ~ of kings** после́дний в стари́нном короле́вском роду́; **in the male ~** по мужско́й ли́нии.
14 (*course, direction, track*) направле́ние, ли́ния; **~ of action** ли́ния поведе́ния/де́йствия; **take a firm, hard, strong ~** зан|има́ть, -я́ть твёрдую пози́цию; стро́го об|ходи́ться, -ойти́сь (*с кем*); **take the ~ of least resistance** пойти́ (*pf.*) по ли́нии наиме́ньшего сопротивле́ния; **follow the party ~** приде́рживаться (*impf.*) парти́йной ли́нии; **take a different ~** зан|има́ть, -я́ть ину́ю пози́цию; **get a ~ on something** навести́ (*pf.*) спра́вки о чём-нибудь; **on similar ~s** аналоги́чным о́бразом; на тех же основа́ниях; **you and I are thinking along the same ~s** мы с ва́ми ду́маем в одно́м направле́нии; **on different ~s** по-друго́му; (*principle*): **the business is run on co-operative ~s** предприя́тие де́йствует на кооперати́вных нача́лах.
15 (*province, sphere of activity*): **cards are not in my ~** ка́рточная игра́ — не по мое́й ча́сти; **in the ~ of duty** при исполне́нии служе́бных обя́занностей; **his ~ of business** род его́ заня́тий; **what's your ~?** чем вы занима́етесь?; кака́я у вас профе́ссия?
16 (*class of goods*) сорт, род, моде́ль (това́ра); **they are bringing in a new ~ in bicycles** они́ вво́дят/внедря́ют но́вую моде́ль велосипе́да; **consumer ~s** потреби́тельские това́ры (*m. pl.*).
17 (*pl., coll., fortune*): **it was hard ~s on him** (ужа́сно) не повезло́ ему́; **hard ~s!** бедня́га! (*c.g.*).
● *v.t.* **1** (*mark with ~s*) линова́ть, раз-; **~d paper** лино́ванная бума́га; **his face was deeply ~d** его́ лицо́ бы́ло изборождено́ морщи́нами.
2 (*form a ~ along*) стоя́ть (*impf.*) (*or* быть расста́вленными) вдоль + *g.*; **police ~d the street** полице́йские стоя́ли по обе́им сторона́м у́лицы; **the road was ~d with trees** доро́га была́ обса́жена дере́вьями.
● *with adv.*: **~ up** *v.t.* (*align*) выстра́ивать, вы́строить в ряд/ли́нию; **they were ~d up against a wall** их вы́строили вдоль стены́; (*coll., arrange*): **I have something ~d up for you** я для вас ко́е-что устро́ил; *v.i.* выстра́иваться, вы́строиться в ряд/ли́нию; (*queue up*) ста|нови́ться, -ть в о́чередь.
● *cpds.* **~man** *n.* (*rail.*) путево́й обхо́дчик; (*US, teleg.*) лине́йный надсмо́трщик; **~sman** *n.* (*sport*) боково́й судья́; (*Br., teleg.*) лине́йный надсмо́трщик; **~-up** *n.* (*sport*) соста́в кома́нды; (*mus.*) соста́в анса́мбля/поп-гру́ппы; (*telev.*) расписа́ние переда́ч; (*US, queue*) о́чередь; (*US, identification parade*) процеду́ра опозна́ния подозрева́емого.

line[2] /laɪn/ *v.t.* **1** (*put lining into*) ста́вить, по- на подкла́дку; подб|ива́ть, -и́ть; **~ a coat with silk** поста́вить (*pf.*) пальто́ на шёлковую подкла́дку; **her coat is ~d with silk** у неё пальто́ на шёлковой подкла́дке.
2 (*fig.*) заст|авля́ть, -а́вить; **the wall was ~d with books** стена́ была́ заста́влена кни́гами; (*fig., fill*): **~ one's pockets** наб|ива́ть, -и́ть себе́

карма́ны; ~ **one's stomach** подкреп|ля́ться, -и́ться. **3** (*tech., of walls etc.*) облиц|о́вывать, -ева́ть.

lineage /ˈlɪnɪɪdʒ/ *n.* (*ancestry*) происхожде́ние; (*genealogy*) родосло́вная.

lineal /ˈlɪnɪəl/ *adj.* происходя́щий по прямо́й ли́нии (*от кого*).

lineament /ˈlɪnɪəmənt/ *n.* черта́; (*pl.*) очерта́ния (*nt. pl.*), ко́нтуры (*m. pl.*).

linear /ˈlɪnɪə(r)/ *adj.* лине́йный.

linen /ˈlɪnɪn/ *n.* **1** (*material: smooth*) лён, (льняно́е) полотно́; (*coarse*) холст. **2** (~ *articles*) бельё; (*clothing*) (носи́льное) бельё; (*bed-*~) посте́льное бельё; **table** ~ столо́вое бельё; **wash one's dirty** ~ **in public** (*fig.*) выноси́ть (*impf.*) сор из избы́.

● *adj.* **1** (*pert. to flax*) льняно́й; ~ **industry** льняна́я промы́шленность; ~ **cloth** льняно́е полотно́. **2** (*made of* ~) полотня́ный.

liner /ˈlaɪnə(r)/ *n.* (*ship*) ла́йнер; **air** ~ возду́шный ла́йнер.

ling[1] /lɪŋ/ *n.* (*heather*) ве́реск.

ling[2] /lɪŋ/ *n.* (*fish*) морска́я щу́ка; морско́й нали́м.

linger /ˈlɪŋgə(r)/ *v.i.* (*take one's time*) ме́длить (*impf.*); ме́шкать (*impf.*); **without** ~**ing a minute** не ме́для ни мину́ты; **she** ~**ed over her dressing** она́ до́лго одева́лась; **a** ~**ing death** ме́дленная смерть; (*stay on*) задёрж|иваться, -а́ться; ~**ing disease** затяжна́я боле́знь; **I have** ~**ing doubts** мои́ сомне́ния не рассе́ялись; **the guests** ~**ed over their coffee** го́сти засиде́лись за ко́фе; **she gave him a** ~**ing glance** она́ посмотре́ла на него́ до́лгим взгля́дом; (*of time: drag*) затя́гиваться (*impf.*); (*continue to live*): **the old man** ~**ed for another week** стари́к протяну́л ещё одну́ неде́лю.

● *with advs.*: ~ **about**, ~ **around** *v.i.* болта́ться (*impf.*); ~ **on** *v.i.* (*of doubt etc.: remain*) ост|ава́ться, -а́ться; (*of customs; be preserved*) сохраня́ться (*impf.*); (*of invalid*) влачи́ть (*impf.*) существова́ние.

lingerie /ˈlæ̃ʒərɪ/ *n.* да́мское бельё.

lingo /ˈlɪŋgəʊ/ *n.* (*pl.* ~**s** *or* ~**es**) (*pej.*) (иностра́нный) язы́к; (*jargon*) жарго́н.

lingua franca /ˌlɪŋgwə ˈfræŋkə/ *n.* (*pl.* **lingua francas**) сме́шанный язы́к.

lingual /ˈlɪŋgw(ə)l/ *adj.* язы́чный.

linguist /ˈlɪŋgwɪst/ *n.* (*speaker of foreign languages*): **he is a good** ~ ему́ легко́ даю́тся языки́; он о́чень спосо́бен к языка́м; (*philologist*) лингви́ст, языкове́д.

linguistic /lɪŋˈgwɪstɪk/ *adj.* лингвисти́ческий, языкове́дческий; ~ **problems** пробле́мы языка́.

linguistics /lɪŋˈgwɪstɪks/ *n.* лингви́стика, языкозна́ние, языкове́дение.

liniment /ˈlɪnɪmənt/ *n.* мазь.

lining /ˈlaɪnɪŋ/ *n.* (*of garment*) подкла́дка; (*of walls etc.*) облицо́вка; (*of stomach*) сте́нки (*f. pl.*); **brake** ~ тормозна́я прокла́дка; **every cloud has a silver** ~ нет ху́да без добра́.

link /lɪŋk/ *n.* **1** (*of chain; also fig.*) звено́; **missing** ~ недостаю́щее звено́. **2** (*connection*) связь; (*comput.*) ссы́лка.

● *v.t.* (*unite*) соедин|я́ть, -и́ть; (*join*) свя́з|ывать, -а́ть; (*tech., couple*) сцеп|ля́ть, -и́ть; ~ **arms with s.o.** идти́ (*det.*) по́д руку с кем-н.; ~ **one's arm through another's** взять кого́-н. по́д руку.

● *v.i.*: ~ **on to something** прим|ыка́ть, -кну́ть к чему́-н.; ~ **with** (*fit in with*) **something** вяза́ться (*impf.*) с чем-н.

● *with advs.*: ~ **together** *v.t.* свя́з|ывать, -а́ть; ~ **up** *v.t. & i.* соедин|я́ться, -и́ться.

● *cpds.* ~**-man** *n.* (*Br., on TV*) веду́щий програ́мму; ~**-up** *n.* связь, соедине́ние.

linkage /ˈlɪŋkɪdʒ/ *n.* (*chem.*) связь; (*pol.*) **a** ~ **policy** поли́тика «увя́зок».

links /lɪŋks/ *n.* (*golf-*~) по́ле для игры́ в гольф.

linnet /ˈlɪnɪt/ *n.* коноплё́нка.

lino /ˈlaɪnəʊ/ (*pl.* **linos**) (*Br.*) = **linoleum**

linocut /ˈlaɪnəʊˌkʌt/ *n.* гравю́ра на лино́леуме, линогравю́ра.

linoleum /lɪˈnəʊlɪəm/ *n.* лино́леум.

linotype /ˈlaɪnəʊˌtaɪp/ *n.* линоти́п.

linseed /ˈlɪnsiːd/ *n.* льняно́е се́мя; ~ **cake** льняны́е жмыхи́ (*m. pl.*); ~ **oil** льняно́е ма́сло.

lint /lɪnt/ *n.* **1** (*Br., med.*) ко́рпия; (*gauze*) ма́рля. **2** (*fluff*) пух.

lintel /ˈlɪnt(ə)l/ *n.* при́толока.

lion /ˈlaɪən/ *n.* лев; ~**'s share** (*fig.*) льви́ная до́ля.

● *cpds.* ~**-cub** *n.* львёнок; ~**-hearted** *adj.* неустраши́мый.

lioness /ˈlaɪənɪs/ *n.* льви́ца.

lionize /ˈlaɪəˌnaɪz/ *v.t.*: ~ **s.o.** носи́ться (*impf.*) с ке́м-нибудь, как со знамени́тостью.

lip /lɪp/ *n.* **1** губа́ (*dim.* гу́бка); **lower/upper** ~ ни́жняя/ве́рхняя губа́; **bite one's** ~ (*in vexation*) куса́ть (*impf.*) гу́бы; (*in thought*) заку́с|ывать, -и́ть губу́; **curl one's** ~ (*in scorn*) презри́тельно криви́ть, с- гу́бы; **not a word escaped, passed his** ~**s** он не пророни́л ни сло́ва; **keep a stiff upper** ~ сохран|я́ть, -и́ть самооблада́ние; **lick one's** ~**s** обли́з|ываться, -ну́ться; **smack one's** ~**s** чмо́к|ать, -нуть; **I heard it from his own** ~**s** я слы́шал э́то от него́ самого́; **the news is on everyone's** ~**s** но́вость у всех на уста́х. **2** (*edge of cup, wound etc.*) край; (*of ladle*) но́сик. **3** (*coll., impudence*) де́рзость; **none of your** ~**!** не дерзи́!; **I won't take any** ~ **from him!** я ему́ покажу́ дерзи́ть!; пусть он не про́бует мне дерзи́ть.

● *cpds.* ~ **balm** *n.* = ~ **salve;** ~**-read** *v.t. & i.* чита́ть (*impf.*) с губ; ~**-reading** *n.* чте́ние с губ; ~ **salve** *n.* (*Br.*) мазь для смягче́ния губ; ~**-service** *n.* нейскренние призна́ния/завере́ния; **pay** ~**-service to something** призн|ава́ть, -а́ть что-н. то́лько на слова́х; ~**stick** *n.* (*substance*) губна́я пома́да; (*applicator*) тю́бик губно́й пома́ды.

lipped /lɪpt/ *adj.* (*of vessel*) с но́сиком; (*of edge*) за́гнутый.

● *comb. form*: **thick-**~ толстогу́бый.

liquefaction /ˌlɪkwɪˈfækʃ(ə)n/ *n.* расплавле́ние; сжиже́ние.

liquefy /ˈlɪkwɪˌfaɪ/ *v.t. & i.* (*of metals etc.*) распл|авля́ть(ся), -а́вить(ся); (*of gas*) сжи|жа́ть(ся), -ди́ть(ся).

liqueur /lɪˈkjʊə(r)/ *n.* ликёр.

● *cpd.* ~**-glass** *n.* ликёрная рю́м(оч)ка.

liquid /ˈlɪkwɪd/ *n.* **1** (*substance*) жи́дкость; ~ **measure** ме́ра жи́дкости. **2** (*phon.*) пла́вный.

● *adj.* **1** (*in* ~ *form*) жи́дкий; ~ **oxygen** жи́дкий кислоро́д. **2** (*translucent*): ~ **eyes** я́сные глаза́. **3** (*of sounds*) певу́чий, мелоди́чный, пла́вный. **4**: ~ **assets** ликви́дные акти́вы.

● *cpd.* ~**-crystal** *adj.*: ~**-crystal display** жидкокристалли́ческий индика́тор.

liquidate /ˈlɪkwɪˌdeɪt/ *v.t.* (*all senses*) ликвиди́ровать (*impf., pf.*).

liquidation /ˌlɪkwɪˈdeɪʃ(ə)n/ *n.* ликвида́ция; **go into** ~ ликвиди́роваться (*impf., pf.*); ~ **of debts** погаше́ние долго́в.

liquidator /ˈlɪkwɪˌdeɪtə(r)/ *n.* ликвида́тор.

liquidity /lɪˈkwɪdɪtɪ/ *n.* (*fin.*) ликви́дность.

liquidize /ˈlɪkwɪˌdaɪz/ *v.t.* (*Br., cul.*) пропус|ка́ть, -ти́ть че́рез смеси́тель/ми́ксер; (*by hand*) прот|ира́ть, -ере́ть сквозь си́то.

liquidizer /ˈlɪkwɪˌdaɪzə(r)/ *n.* (*Br., cul.*) смеси́тель (*m.*), ми́ксер.

liquor /ˈlɪkə(r)/ *n.* **1** (*alcoholic drink*) (спиртно́й) напи́ток; ~ **store** (*US*) ви́нный магази́н. **2** (*liquid*) жи́дкость.

liqu|orice, lic- /ˈlɪkərɪs/, /-rɪʃ/ *n.* (*plant*) соло́дка, лакри́чник; (*substance*) лакри́ца.

lira /ˈlɪərə/ *n.* (*pl.* **lire** /ˈlɪərə/, /ˈlɪəreɪ/, /ˈlɪərɪ/) ли́ра.

Lisbon /ˈlɪzbən/ *n.* Лиссабо́н.

lisle /laɪl/ *n.* (~ **thread**) фильдеко́с; ~ **stockings** фильдеко́совые чулки́.

lisp /lɪsp/ *n.* шепеля́вость; **he has** (*or* **speaks with**) **a** ~ он шепеля́вит.

● *v.i.* шепеля́вить (*impf.*); сюсю́кать (*impf.*).

lissom(e) /ˈlɪsəm/ *adj.* ги́бкий.

list[1] /lɪst/ *n.* (*roll, inventory, enumeration*) спи́сок, пе́речень (*m.*); **black** ~ чёрный спи́сок; **casualty** ~ спи́сок потéрь; **enter something on a** ~ вн|оси́ть, -ести́ что-н. в спи́сок; **make a** ~ сост|авля́ть, -а́вить спи́сок; ~ **price** цена́ по прейскура́нту.

● *v.t.* (*make a* ~ *of*) сост|авля́ть, -а́вить спи́сок +*g.*; (*enter on a* ~) вн|оси́ть, -ести́ в спи́сок; (*enumerate*) переч|исля́ть, -и́слить; ~**ed building** зда́ние, находя́щееся под охра́ной госуда́рства.

list[2] /lɪst/ *n.* (*leaning*) крен; накло́н; **have a** ~ крени́ться (*impf.*).

● *v.i.* (*of ship*) накреня́ться (*impf.*); крени́ться, на-.

L

listen /ˈlɪs(ə)n/ *v.i.* слу́шать, по-; ~ **to** слу́шать, по- +*a.*; **do you ~ (in) to the radio?** слу́шаете ли вы ра́дио?; (*pay attention, heed to*) прислу́ш|иваться, -аться к+*d.*; **don't ~ to him!** не обраща́йте на него́ внима́ния!; **I was ~ing for the bell** я (напряжённо) ждал звонка́; (*hear out*) выслу́шивать, вы́слушать; **~ to me and then decide** вы́слушайте меня́, а пото́м реша́йте!; (*for a certain time*) прослу́ш|ивать, -ать; **he ~s to the radio all evening** он це́лый ве́чер слу́шает ра́дио; **the doctor ~ed to his heart** врач прослу́шал его́ се́рдце; (*overhear, eavesdrop on*) подслу́ш|ивать, -ать; **he ~ed in on their conversation** он подслу́шал их разгово́р; **~ing-post** пост подслу́шивания.

listener /ˈlɪsənə(r)/ *n.* слу́шатель (*m.*); **he is a good ~** он уме́ет слу́шать; (*to radio*) радиослу́шатель (*m.*).

listing /ˈlɪstɪŋ/ *n.* (*list*) спи́сок; (*entry*) упомина́ние.

listless /ˈlɪstlɪs/ *adj.* апати́чный, вя́лый.

listlessness /ˈlɪstlɪsnɪs/ *n.* апа́тия, вя́лость.

lit /lɪt/ *past and p.p. of* ⇨**light**[1,3]

litany /ˈlɪtənɪ/ *n.* (*Orthodox*) ектенья́; (*Catholic*) лита́ния; (*fig., tedious enumeration*) ску́чное перечисле́ние.

liter /ˈli:tə(r)/ (*US*) = **litre**

literacy /ˈlɪtərəsɪ/ *n.* гра́мотность.

literal /ˈlɪtər(ə)l/ *adj.* **1** (*of, or expr. in, letters*) бу́квенный; **~ error** опеча́тка, бу́квенная оши́бка. **2** (*following the text exactly; taking words in primary sense*) буква́льный; **he has a ~ mind** у него́ педанти́чный/прозаи́ческий ум.

literalness /ˈlɪtərəlnɪs/ *n.* буква́льность.

literary /ˈlɪtərərɪ/ *adj.* **1** (*pert. to literature, books, writing*) литерату́рный; (*of ~ studies*) литературове́дческий; **~ history** исто́рия литерату́ры; **a ~ man** литера́тор. **2** (*of style or vocabulary*) кни́жный.

literate /ˈlɪtərət/ *adj.* гра́мотный.

literati /ˌlɪtəˈrɑ:ti:/ *n.* литера́торы (*m. pl.*)

literature /ˈlɪtərətʃə(r)/, /ˈlɪtrə-/ *n.* литерату́ра; **student of ~** литературове́д; **study of ~** литературове́дение; (*printed matter*) литерату́ра; кни́ги, брошю́ры и т.п.

lithe /laɪð/ *adj.* ги́бкий.

litheness /ˈlaɪðnɪs/ *n.* ги́бкость.

lithium /ˈlɪθɪəm/ *n.* ли́тий.

lithograph /ˈlɪθəˌgrɑ:f/, /ˈlaɪθə-/ *n.* литогра́фия; **~ print** литогра́фский о́ттиск.

● *v.t.* литографи́ровать (*impf., pf.*).

lithographer /lɪˈθɒgrəfə(r)/ *n.* лито́граф.

lithographic /ˌlɪθəˈgræfɪk/ *adj.* литогра́фский.

lithography /lɪˈθɒgrəfɪ/ *n.* литогра́фия.

Lithuania /ˌlɪθju:ˈeɪnɪə/, /ˌlɪθu:-/ *n.* Литва́.

Lithuanian /ˌlɪθju:ˈeɪnɪən/, /ˌlɪθu:-/ *n.* (*person*) лито́в|ец (*fem.* -ка); (*language*) лито́вский язы́к.

● *adj.* лито́вский.

litigant /ˈlɪtɪgənt/ *n.* тя́жущаяся сторона́.

litigate /ˈlɪtɪˌgeɪt/ *v.i.* суди́ться (*impf.*).

litigation /ˌlɪtɪˈgeɪʃ(ə)n/ *n.* тя́жба; суде́бный проце́сс.

litigious /lɪˈtɪdʒəs/ *adj.* **1** (*fond of going to law*) сутя́жнический; **a ~ person** сутя́га (*c.g.*); сутя́жни|к (*fem.* -ца). **2** (*pert. to litigation*): **~ procedure** процеду́ра суде́бного разбира́тельства.

litmus /ˈlɪtməs/ *n.* ла́кмус; **~ paper** ла́кмусовая бума́га.

litre /ˈli:tə(r)/ (*US* **liter**) *n.* литр.

litter /ˈlɪtə(r)/ *n.* **1** (*refuse*) сор, отбро́с|ы (*pl., g.* -ов). **2** (*straw etc. for animals*) подсти́лка; **cat ~** коша́чья подсти́лка. **3** (*newly-born animals*) помёт. **4** (*hist., means of transport*) паланки́н; (*stretcher*) носи́л|ки (*pl., g.* -ок).

● *v.t.* **1** (*make untidy*) сори́ть, на-; **he ~ed the room with paper** он разброса́л бума́гу по всей ко́мнате; **the table is ~ed with books** стол зава́лен кни́гами. **2** (*provide with straw for bedding*): **~ a horse** де́лать, с- подсти́лку для ло́шади.

● *v.i.* (*give birth: of dogs*) щени́ться, о-; (*of pigs*) пороси́ться, о-.

● *cpds.* **~-bin** *n.* (*Br.*) му́сорный я́щик; **~-bug** *n.* челове́к сора́щий в обще́ственных места́х.

littérateur /ˌlɪtərɑ:ˈtɜ:(r)/ *n.* литера́тор.

little /ˈlɪt(ə)l/ *n.* (*not much*) ма́ло, немно́го, немно́жко +*g.*; **there was ~ left** оста́лось ма́ло/немно́го; **it had ~ to do with me** э́то де́ло меня́ ма́ло каса́лось; **he makes ~ of physical pain** он не бои́тся физи́ческой бо́ли; **he thinks ~ of me** он обо мне́ ни́зкого/невысо́кого мне́ния; **it takes ~ to make him angry** его́ нетру́дно рассерди́ть; **I see ~ of him now** я тепе́рь ре́дко ви́жу его́; **~ or nothing** почти́ ничего́; ма́ло что; **he has done ~ or nothing for us** он нам почти́ ниче́м не помо́г; (*small amount*): **I did what ~ I could** я сде́лал то немно́гое, что мог; **I'd like a ~ of that salad** я бы хоте́л немно́го/чу́точку э́того сала́та; **he knows a ~ Japanese** он немно́го зна́ет япо́нский; **he knows a ~ of everything** он зна́ет обо всём понемно́гу; (*short time or distance*): **after a ~ he returned** вско́ре он верну́лся; **won't you stay (for) a ~?** побу́дьте/посиди́те ещё немно́го!; **~ by ~** ма́ло-пома́лу; постепе́нно.

● *adj.* (**littler, littlest; less** *or* **lesser; least**) **1** (*small*) ма́ленький, небольшо́й; **~ finger** мизи́нец; **~ toe** мизи́нец ноги́; **L~ Bear** (*astron.*) Ма́лая Медве́дица; (*expr. by dim., e.g.*): **~ house** до́мик; **~ man** челове́чек. **2** (*young*): **~ boy** (ма́ленький) ма́льчик; **~ girl** (ма́ленькая) де́вочка; **my ~ brother** мой брати́шка; **~ ones** (*children*) де́т|и (*pl., g.* -е́й); малыши́ (*m. pl.*); де́тки (*f. pl.*); (*animals*) детёныши (*m. pl.*). **3** (*trivial, unpretentious*) ме́лкий; незначи́тельный; **the ~ things of life** жите́йские ме́лочи (*f. pl.*). **4** (*not tall or long*) невысо́кий; недли́нный; **he was a ~ man** он был челове́к небольшо́го ро́ста; **I went a ~ way with him** я с ним прошёл не́сколько шаго́в; **wait here for a ~ while** подожди́те здесь немно́жко. **5** (*small, of quantity*) ма́ло, немно́го, немно́жко +*g.*; **there is ~ butter left** ма́сла оста́лось ма́ло; **he knows ~ Japanese** он пло́хо зна́ет япо́нский; **have a ~ something to eat!** перекуси́те чу́точку!; ску́шайте что́-нибудь!; **it gives me no ~ pleasure** э́то доста́вит мне и́стинное удово́льствие. **6** (*in var. emotive senses*): **that poor ~ girl!** бедня́жка!; **he's quite the ~ gentleman** э́тот ма́льчик — настоя́щий джентльме́н; **so that's your ~ game!** так вы вон что заду́мали!; **I know your ~ ways** я зна́ю ва́ши штý́чки; зна́ем мы вас!; **you ~ liar!** ах ты, лгуни́шка! (*c.g.*).

● *adv.* (**less, least**) **1** (*not much*) ма́ло; **I see him very ~** я ма́ло/ре́дко с ним ви́жусь; **~ more** ненамно́го/немно́гим бо́льше; **it is ~ more than speculation** э́то но́сит предположи́тельный хара́ктер; **he is ~ better than a thief** он про́сто-напро́сто вор; **~ short of madness** су́щее безу́мие; (*not at all*): **~ did he know I was following him** он и не подозрева́л, что я иду́ за ним; **we ~ thought he would go to those lengths** мы ника́к не ожида́ли, что он дойдёт до тако́й кра́йности. **2** (**a ~**: *slightly, somewhat*) немно́го, немно́жко; **this hat is a ~ too big for me** э́та шля́па мне немно́го велика́; **I was a ~ afraid you would not come** я немно́го боя́лся, что вы не придёте; **he was not a ~ annoyed** он был не на шу́тку раздражён; **I am a ~ happier now** я тепе́рь не́сколько успоко́ился; **she is a ~ over 40** ей немно́гим бо́льше сорока́.

littoral /ˈlɪtər(ə)l/ *n.* побере́жье.

● *adj.* прибре́жный.

liturgical /lɪˈtɜ:dʒɪk(ə)l/ *adj.* литурги́ческий.

liturgy /ˈlɪtədʒɪ/ *n.* (*eccl.*) литурги́я.

livable /ˈlɪvəb(ə)l/ = **liv(e)able**

live[1] /laɪv/ *adj.* **1** (*living*) живо́й; **~ bait** живе́ц; (*pert. to living person or thing*): **~ birth** рожде́ние живо́го ребёнка; **~ weight** живо́й вес; (*fig.*): **a ~ issue** актуа́льный вопро́с. **2** (*burning*): **~ coals** горя́щие у́гли. **3** (*not spent or exploded*): **~ ammunition** боевы́е патро́ны; **~ rail** токопроводя́щий ре́льс; **a ~ wire** (*lit.*) про́вод под то́ком/напряже́нием; (*fig.*) челове́к с изю́минкой, «жи́вчик». **4** (*not recorded*): **~ broadcast** пряма́я переда́ча; (*away from studio*) внестуди́йная переда́ча; **~ music** музыка́льное выступле́ние; **~ performance** публи́чное выступле́ние; **the game was broadcast ~** матч трансли́ровался непосре́дственно со стадио́на (*or* шёл в прямо́й трансля́ции).

● *cpd.* **~stock** *n.* дома́шний скот.

live² /lɪv/ *v.t.* (*spend, experience*) пров|оди́ть, -ести́; прож|ива́ть, -и́ть; **he ~d his whole life there** он там про́жил всю жизнь; **he is living a double life** он ведёт двойну́ю жизнь; **he ~s life to the full** он живёт по́лной жи́знью; **life is not worth living** жить не сто́ит; **~ a lie** жить (*impf.*) по лжи.

● *v.i.* **1** (*be alive*) жить (*impf.*); (*with reference to habitat*) води́ться, обита́ть (*both impf.*).

2 (*subsist*): **they ~ on vegetables** они́ пита́ются овоща́ми; **you can't ~ on air** нельзя́ пита́ться во́здухом; **they ~ off the land** они́ живу́т на подно́жном корму́; **they ~ from hand to mouth** они́ перебива́ются с хле́ба на во́ду; они́ е́ле сво́дят концы́ с конца́ми.

3 (*depend for one's living*) жить (*impf.*); **he ~s on his wife** он живёт на иждиве́нии жены́; **he ~s on his earnings** он живёт на свои́ за́работки; **they ~ quietly, within their income** они́ живу́т скро́мно, по сре́дствам; **he ~s on, off his friends** он живёт за счёт друзе́й; **he ~s on his reputation** он живёт на ста́рый капита́л, засчёт бы́лых заслу́г.

4 (*conduct o.s.*) жить (*impf.*); **he ~s up to his principles/reputation** он стро́го приде́рживается свои́х при́нципов; **he ~d up to my expectations** он не обману́л мои́х ожида́ний; (*arrange one's diet, habits etc.*): **he ~s well** он живёт хорошо́ (*or* на широ́кую но́гу); **two can ~ as cheaply as one** вдвоём жить не доро́же, чем одному́; **~ like a lord** ката́ться (*impf.*) как сыр в ма́сле.

5 (*enjoy life*): **now at last I'm really living** вот э́то я называ́ю жи́знью!; **if you've never been to Paris, you haven't ~d** кто в Пари́же не быва́л, тот жи́зни не вида́л.

6 (*continue alive*): **the doctors think he won't ~** врачи́ ду́мают, что он не вы́живет; **he ~d to a great (***or* **ripe old) age** он до́жил до глубо́кой ста́рости; **they ~d happily ever after** они́ ста́ли жить-пожива́ть да добра́ нажива́ть; **he ~d to regret it** впосле́дствии он об э́том жале́л; **he did not ~ to finish the work** он у́мер, не заверши́в рабо́ту; **long ~ the Queen!** да здра́вствует короле́ва!; **she has ~d through a great deal** она́ мно́го пережила́; **you, we ~ and learn** век живи́ — век учи́сь; **~ and let ~** сам живи́ и други́м не меша́й; **I have nothing to ~ for** мне не́зачем жить; **he ~s for his work** он живёт свое́й рабо́той; для него́ рабо́та — всё; (*fig., survive*): **his fame will ~ for ever** сла́ва его́ не умрёт.

7 (*reside*) жить, прожива́ть (*both impf.*); обита́ть (*impf.*); **where do you ~?** где вы живёте; **I ~ at No. 17** я живу́ в до́ме но́мер 17; **the house has a ~d-in appearance** у до́ма обжито́й вид; **he is living with his secretary** он живёт/сожи́тельствует с секрета́ршей; **they are living apart** (*of married couple*) они́ живу́т врозь; они́ разъе́хались; **~ with** (*fig. tolerate*) мири́ться, при- c + *i.*

● *with advs.*: **~ down** *v.t.* загла́|живать, -дить; **he will never ~ down the scandal** ему́ никогда́ не уда́стся загла́дить сканда́л; **~ in** *v.i.* (*of student*) жить (*impf.*) в общежи́тии; **the servants all ~ in/out** вся прислу́га — живу́щая/приходя́щая; **~ on** *v.i.*: **his memory ~s on** па́мять о нём жива́; **~ out** *v.i.* (*of student*) не жить (*impf.*) в общежи́тии; **most officers ~ out** бо́льшая часть офице́ров не живёт в каза́рмах; *see also* ⇒**~ in**; **~ together** *v.i.*: **are they married or only living together?** они́ жена́ты и́ли так живу́т (*or* сожи́тельствуют)?; **France and Germany have learnt to ~ together** Фра́нция и Герма́ния научи́лись жить в ми́ре; **~ up** *v.t.*: **~ it up** (*coll.*) жить (*impf.*) широко́, вести́ (*impf.*) бу́рную жизнь.

● *cpds.* **~-in** *adj.*: **~-in nanny** ня́ня, живу́щая в семье́; **~-in lover** сожи́тель (*fem.* -ница); **~long** *adj.* це́лый; **the ~long day** день-деньско́й.

liv(e)able /ˈlɪvəb(ə)l/ *adj.* **1** (*of house etc.*) го́дный для жилья́. **2** (*of life*) сно́сный. **3**: **~-with** (*of person*) тако́й, с кото́рым мо́жно ужи́ться.

livelihood /ˈlaɪvlɪˌhʊd/ *n.* сре́дства (*nt. pl.*) к существова́нию; **earn, gain one's ~** зараба́тывать (*impf.*) на жизнь; добыва́ть (*impf.*) сре́дства к существова́нию.

liveliness /ˈlaɪvlɪnɪs/ *n.* жи́вость, оживлённость.

lively /ˈlaɪvlɪ/ *adj.* (**livelier, liveliest**) (*lit., fig.*) живо́й; **take a ~ interest in something** проявля́ть (*impf.*) живо́й интере́с к чему́-н.; (*animated*) оживлённый; **trade was ~** торго́вля шла бо́йко; (*energetic*) живо́й, де́ятельный; (*bright*): **~ colours** (*Br.*), **colors** (*US*) я́ркие кра́ски; (*brisk*): **we walked at a ~ pace** мы шли бы́стрым ша́гом; **look ~!** быстре́е!; жи́во!; повора́чивайся!

liven /ˈlaɪv(ə)n/ *v.t. & i.* (*also* **~ up**) ожив|ля́ть(ся), -и́ть(ся).

liver¹ /ˈlɪvə(r)/ *n.* (*anat.*) пе́чень; **~ complaint** боле́знь пе́чени; (*food*) печёнка; **~ sausage** (*Br.*) ли́верная колбаса́.

● *cpd.* **~-fluke** *n.* печёночная двуу́стка.

liver² /ˈlɪvə(r)/ *n.*: **loose ~** распу́тник; **fast ~** прожига́тель (*m.*) жи́зни.

liveried /ˈlɪvərɪd/ *adj.* ливре́йный.

liver|ish /ˈlɪvərɪʃ/, **-y** /ˈlɪvərɪ/ *adjs.*: **he is feeling ~ish** у него́ поша́ливает пе́чень; (*fig., peevish*) жёлчный.

livery¹ /ˈlɪvərɪ/ *n.* (*of servants*) ливре́я; (*of a guild etc.*) фо́рма; (*for horses*) прoко́рм; **~ stable** пла́тная коню́шня.

livery² /ˈlɪvərɪ/ = **liverish**

lives¹ /laɪvz/ *pl. of* ⇒**life**

lives² /lɪvz/ *see* ⇒**live²**

livid /ˈlɪvɪd/ *adj.* (*grey-blue*) серова́то-си́ний; (*crimson*) багро́вый; (*coll., of temper*): **be ~** черне́ть, по-; **I was ~** я был взбешён.

living /ˈlɪvɪŋ/ *n.* **1** (*process, manner of ~*): **~ conditions** усло́вия жи́зни; **a ~ wage** прожи́точный ми́нимум; **the art of ~** уме́ние жить; **loose ~** распу́тство; **cost of ~** сто́имость жи́зни; **standard of ~** жи́зненный у́ровень.

2 (*livelihood*) сре́дства (*nt. pl.*) к жи́зни; **earn one's ~** зараб|а́тывать, -о́тать себе́ на жизнь; **he makes his ~ by teaching** он зараба́тывает преподава́нием; **the world owes us a ~** о́бщество обя́зано содержа́ть нас.

3 (*fare*): **good, high ~** бога́тый стол; **plain ~** просто́й стол.

4 (*Br., eccl.*) бенефи́ций.

● *adj.* **1** (*alive*) живо́й; **a ~ language** живо́й язы́к; **a ~ death** жа́лкое существова́ние; **within ~ memory** на па́мяти живу́щих; **not a ~ soul** (*as obj.*) ни (одно́й) живо́й души́; **no man ~ could do better** никто́ на све́те не мог бы сде́лать лу́чше; (*as n.*): **the ~** живы́е (*pl.*); **he is in the land of the ~** он ещё жив; он ещё не поки́нул э́тот свет.

2 (*true to life*): **he is the ~ image of his father** он вы́литый оте́ц.

3 (*contemporary*): **he is the greatest of ~ writers** он крупне́йший из совреме́нных писа́телей.

● *cpds.* **~-room** *n.* гости́ная; **~ space** *n.* жи́зненное простра́нство.

lizard /ˈlɪzəd/ *n.* я́щерица.

Ljubljana /luːˈbljɑːnə/ *n.* Люблья́на.

llama /ˈlɑːmə/ *n.* ла́ма.

lo /ləʊ/ *int.* (*arch.*): **~ and behold** и вдруг, о чу́до.

loach /ləʊtʃ/ *n.* (*zool.*) голе́ц.

load /ləʊd/ *n.* **1** (*what is carried; burden*) но́ша; груз, нагру́зка; тя́жесть; (*fig.*) бре́мя; **a ~ of worries** бре́мя забо́т; **that was a ~ off my mind** у меня́ как гора́ с плеч; **you have taken a ~ off my mind** от ва́ших слов мне ста́ло ле́гче.

2 (*amount carried by vehicle etc.*) груз; **a ~ of bricks** груз кирпиче́й; (*fig., coll.*): **it's a ~ of rubbish** э́то сплошна́я чепуха́.

3 (*phys., elec.*) нагру́зка; **test under ~** испы́т|ывать, -а́ть под нагру́зкой.

4 (*pl., coll., large amount*) у́йма, ма́сса.

● *v.t.* **1** (*cargo etc.*) грузи́ть, по-; **the goods were ~ed on to the ship** това́ры погрузи́ли на су́дно.

2 (*ship, vehicle etc.*) грузи́ть, на-; нагру|жа́ть, -зи́ть (*что чем*).

3 (*fig., with cares etc.*) обремен|я́ть, -и́ть (*кого чем*); **don't ~ yourself with extra work** не взва́ливайте на себя́ ли́шнюю рабо́ту.

4 (*with gifts, praises etc.*) ос|ыпа́ть, -ы́пать (*кого чем*).

5 (*firearm, camera etc.*) заря|жа́ть, -ди́ть; **he ~ed the camera with film** он заряди́л аппара́т (плёнкой).

6 (*weight with lead*) нал|ива́ть, -и́ть свинцо́м; **~ed dice** нали́тые свинцо́м ко́сти; **the dice were ~ed against him** (*fig.*) все ша́нсы бы́ли про́тив него́; (*fig.*): **a ~ed question** провокацио́нный вопро́с.

7 (*fill to capacity*): **the bus was ~ed with people** авто́бус был перепо́лнен.

8 (*sl.*): **he's ~ed** (*rich*) у него́ де́нег ку́ры не клюю́т; (*US, drunk*) он нагрузи́лся.

9 (*comput.*) загру|жа́ть, -зи́ть.

● *v.i.* грузи́ться, на-.

L

● *with advs.*: ~ **down** *v.t.* обремен|я́ть, -и́ть; ~ **up** *v.t.* нагру|жа́ть, -зи́ть; *v.i.* грузи́ться, на-.

● *cpds.* **~-bearing** *adj.*: **~-bearing capacity** грузоподъёмность; **~-line** *n.* грузова́я ватерли́ния; **~stone** *see* **⇒lode-**

loader /ˈləʊdə(r)/ *n.* (*person*) гру́зчик.

loading /ˈləʊdɪŋ/ *n.* **1** (*of cargo*) погру́зка. **2** (*of ship, vehicle etc.*) нагру́зка; ~ **bay** разгру́зочная площа́дка; ~ **berth** погру́зочный прича́л; ~ **hatch** грузово́й люк. **3** (*of gun, camera etc.*) заря́дка. **4** (*elec.*) нагру́зка. **5** (*comput.*) загру́зка.

loaf[1] /ləʊf/ *n.* (*pl.* **loaves**) **1** (*of bread*) буха́нка; **cottage** ~ карава́й; **small** ~ бу́лка; **half a ~ is better than no bread** ≈ на безры́бье и рак ры́ба; (**~**-*shaped food*): **meat** ~ мясно́й руле́т; **sugar** ~ са́харная голова́. **2** (*Br. sl., head*) башка́; **use one's** ~ шевели́ть (*impf.*) мозга́ми.

loaf[2] /ləʊf/ *v.i.* (*coll.; also* ~ **about**) ло́дырничать, гоня́ть ло́дыря (*both impf.*); шата́ться (*impf.*) без де́ла.

loafer /ˈləʊfə(r)/ *n.* ло́дырь (*m.*); пра́здношата́ющийся; (*propr., shoe*) ко́жаная ту́фля, ти́па мокаси́н.

loam /ləʊm/ *n.* сугли́нок.

loamy /ˈləʊmɪ/ *adj.* сугли́нистый.

loan /ləʊn/ *n.* **1** (*sum lent*) заём, ссу́да; **government ~s** госуда́рственные за́ймы (*m. pl.*); **student** ~ студе́нческий заём; **he asked for a ~ of £10** он попроси́л 10 фу́нтов взаймы́. **2** (*lending or being lent*): **take on ~; have the ~ of** (*of money*) брать, взять взаймы́; (*of objects*) брать, взять на вре́мя; **may I have the ~ of this book?** могу́ ли я взять на вре́мя э́ту кни́гу?; **this exhibit is on ~ from the museum** э́тот экспона́т вре́менно взят из музе́я.

● *v.t.* одолж|а́ть, -и́ть; да|ва́ть, -ть взаймы́.

● *cpds.* ~ **shark** *n.* (*coll.*) ростовщи́к; **~-translation** *n.* (*ling.*) ка́лька; **~-word** *n.* (*ling.*) заи́мствованное сло́во.

loaner /ˈləʊnə(r)/ *n.* (*US, car*) заёмная маши́на, дава́емая зака́зчику в заме́н во вре́мя ремо́нта со́бственного автомоби́ля.

lo(a)th /ləʊθ/ *pred. adj.*: **he was ~ to do anything** он ничего́ не хоте́л де́лать.

loathe /ləʊð/ *v.t.* (*detest*) ненави́деть (*impf.*); (*feel disgust for*) чу́вствовать/испы́тывать (*impf.*) отвраще́ние к + *d.*; (*be unable to bear*) быть не в состоя́нии терпе́ть; **I ~ asking him about it** мне ужа́сно неприя́тно его́ спра́шивать об э́том.

loathing /ˈləʊðɪŋ/ *n.* отвраще́ние; **feel ~ for** испы́тывать (*impf.*) отвраще́ние к + *d.*

loathsome /ˈləʊðsəm/ *adj.* отврати́тельный, омерзи́тельный.

loaves /ləʊvz/ *pl. of* **⇒loaf**[1]

lob /lɒb/ *n.* (*high-pitched ball*) свеча́.

● *v.t.* (**lobbed, lobbing**): ~ **a ball** под|ава́ть, -а́ть свечу́.

lobby /ˈlɒbɪ/ *n.* вестибю́ль (*m.*); (*theatr.*) фойе́ (*indecl.*); (*in Parliament*) кулуа́р|ы (*pl., g.* -ов); (*group*) ло́бби.

● *v.t.* агити́ровать (*impf.*) (в кулуа́рах).

lobbying /ˈlɒbɪɪŋ/ *n.* агита́ция (в кулуа́рах), лобби́рование.

lobbyist /ˈlɒbɪɪst/ *n.* лобби́ст.

lobe /ləʊb/ *n.* (*of liver, brain etc.*) до́ля; (*of ear*) мо́чка.

lobelia /ləˈbiːlɪə/ *n.* (*bot.*) лобе́лия.

lobotomy /ləˈbɒtəmɪ/ *n.* (*med.*) лоботоми́я.

lobster /ˈlɒbstə(r)/ *n.* ома́р; **red as a** ~ кра́сный как рак.

● *cpd.* **~-pot** *n.* ве́рша для ома́ров.

local /ˈləʊk(ə)l/ *n.* (*inhabitant*) ме́стный жи́тель; (*paper*) ме́стная газе́та; (*train*) ме́стный по́езд; (*Br., public house*) ме́стный паб, ме́стная пивна́я.

● *adj.* ме́стный; зде́шний; (*of that place*) (*coll.*) та́мошний; ~ **anaesthetic** (*Br.*), **anesthetic** (*US*) ме́стный нарко́з; ~ **authority** (*Br.*) ме́стные вла́сти; ~ **call** ме́стный телефо́нный разгово́р; ~ **colour** (*Br.*), **color** (*US*) ме́стный колори́т; ~ **government** ме́стное самоуправле́ние; ~ **pain** локализо́ванная боль; ~ **population** коренно́е населе́ние; ~ **showers** ≈ места́ми дожди́; **2 o'clock ~ time** два часа́ по ме́стному вре́мени; **he is a ~ man** он из зде́шних мест; он зде́шний.

locale /ləʊˈkɑːl/ *n.* ме́сто (де́йствия); ме́стность.

localism /ˈləʊkəˌlɪz(ə)m/ *n.* (*local custom or idiom*) ме́стный обы́чай; ме́стное/областно́е выраже́ние.

locality /ləʊˈkælɪtɪ/ *n.* ме́стность; (*neighbourhood*): **there is no cinema in the** ~ нигде́ побли́зости нет кино́.

localization /ˌləʊkəlaɪˈzeɪʃ(ə)n/ *n.* локализа́ция.

localize /ˈləʊkəˌlaɪz/ *v.t.* локализова́ть (*impf., pf.*).

locally /ˈləʊkəlɪ/ *adv.*: **he is well-known** ~ он изве́стен в э́тих края́х; **he works** ~ он рабо́тает побли́зости.

locate /ləʊˈkeɪt/ *v.t.* **1** (*establish in a place*) поме|ща́ть, -сти́ть; (*designate place of*) назн|ача́ть, -а́чить ме́сто (*чему or для чего*); **be ~d** (*situated*) находи́ться (*impf.*). **2** (*determine position of*) определ|я́ть, -и́ть ме́сто/местоположе́ние + *g.*; **has the fault been ~d?** нашли́ поврежде́ние?; определи́ли ли ме́сто поврежде́ния?; (*discover*) обнару́жи|вать, -ть; **he ~d the source of the Nile** он нашёл исто́ки Ни́ла.

location /ləʊˈkeɪʃ(ə)n/ *n.* **1** (*determining of place*) определе́ние (ме́ста). **2** (*position, situation*) местонахожде́ние, местоположе́ние, расположе́ние. **3**: **on** ~ (*cin.*) на нату́ре.

locative /ˈlɒkətɪv/ *n. & adj.* (*gram.*) ме́стный (паде́ж).

loch /lɒk/, /lɒx/ *n.* о́зеро (*в Шотландии*); **L~ Ness** о́зеро Лох-Не́сс.

loci /ˈləʊsaɪ/, /ˈləʊkaɪ/, /ˈləʊkiː/ *pl. of* **⇒locus**

loci classici /ˌləʊsaɪ ˈklæsɪˌsaɪ/, /ˌlɒkiː ˈklæsɪˌkiː/ *pl. of* ***locus classicus***

lock[1] /lɒk/ *n.* (*of hair*) ло́кон, прядь.

lock[2] /lɒk/ *n.* **1** (*on door or firearm*) замо́к; **under ~ and key** под замко́м; **~, stock and barrel** целико́м и по́лностью; (*on door or gate*) запо́р; (*on mechanism*) сто́пор. **2** (*of vehicle's wheels*) у́гол поворо́та; **full** ~ до упо́ра; **other** ~ поворо́т в другу́ю сто́рону. **3** (*wrestling hold*) захва́т. **4** (*on canal*) шлюз.

● *v.t.* **1** (*secure; restrict movement of*) зап|ира́ть, -ере́ть (на замо́к); **is the door ~ed?** дверь заперта́?; **she ~ed him into the bedroom** она́ заперла́ его́ в спа́льне; **I was ~ed out** дверь была́ заперта́, и я не мог войти́. **2** (*cause to stop moving or revolving*) тормози́ть, за-; **he ~ed the steering** он за́пер руль. **3** (*engage, interlace*) спле|та́ть, -сти́; **his fingers were ~ed together** он сцепи́л ру́ки; **they were ~ed in an embrace** они́ сжима́ли друг дру́га в объя́тиях.

● *v.i.* **1**: **does this chest ~?** э́тот сунду́к запира́ется? **2** (*become rigid or immovable*) застр|ева́ть, -я́ть. **3** (*interlace*) перепле|та́ться, -сти́сь; сцеп|ля́ться, -и́ться; **the parts ~ into each other** дета́ли взаи́мно блоки́руются.

● *with advs.*: ~ **away** *v.t.* спря́тать (*pf.*) под замо́к; ~ **in** *v.t.* зап|ира́ть, -ере́ть (*кого*) в ко́мнате/до́ме *и т.п.*; **he ~ed himself in** он заперся́ на ключ; ~ **out** *v.t.* зап|ира́ть, -ере́ть дверь и не впуска́ть; **the workers were ~ed out** рабо́чих подве́ргли локау́ту; ~ **up** *v.t.* зап|ира́ть, -ере́ть на замо́к; (*imprison*) сажа́ть, посади́ть; **his capital is ~ed up in land** весь его́ капита́л в земе́льных владе́ниях; *v.i.*: **when do you ~ up for the night?** в кото́ром часу́ вы ве́чером закрыва́етесь?

● *cpds.* **~-gate** *n.* шлю́зные воро́та; **~jaw** *n.* тризм че́люсти; **~-keeper** *n.* смотри́тель (*m.*) шлю́за; **~out** *n.* локау́т; **~smith** *n.* сле́сарь (*m.*); **~smith's trade** слеса́рное де́ло; **~-up** *n.* (*for prisoners*) катала́жка (*coll.*); (*Br., shed*) сара́й; (*Br., garage*) гара́ж.

locker /ˈlɒkə(r)/ *n.* (*cupboard*) шка́фчик; (*naut.*) рунду́к.

● *cpd.* **~-room** *n.* раздева́лка.

locket /ˈlɒkɪt/ *n.* медальо́н.

loco[1] /ˈləʊkəʊ/ (*pl.* **locos**) (*coll.*) = **locomotive**

loco[2] /ˈləʊkəʊ/ *adj.* (*coll., insane*) чо́кнутый (*sl.*).

locomotion /ˌləʊkəˈməʊʃ(ə)n/ *n.* передвиже́ние.

locomotive /ˌləʊkəˈməʊtɪv/ *n.* локомоти́в; (*steam*) парово́з; (*electric*) электрово́з; (*diesel*) ди́зель (*m.*), теплово́з; ~ **shed** депо́ (*indecl.*).

● *adj.* дви́жущий, дви́гательный; ~ **engine** = *n.*

locum /ˈləʊkəm/ (*pl.* **~s**) (*coll.*) = **locum tenens**

locum tenens /ˌləʊkəm ˈtiːnenz/,

/ˈtenenz/ *n.* (*pl.* **locum tenentes** /ˌləʊkəm trˈnentiːz/) (*doctor or clergyman*) вре́менный замести́тель (*m.*).

locus /ˈləʊkəs/, /ˈlɒkəs/ *n.* (*pl.* **loci**) (*math.*) траекто́рия; **~ of points** геометри́ческое ме́сто то́чек.

locus classicus /ˌləʊkəs ˈklæsɪkəs/, /ˌlɒkəs/ *n.* (*pl.* ***loci classici***) класси́ческая цита́та, наибо́лее подходя́щая в да́нном слу́чае.

locust /ˈləʊkəst/ *n.* (*insect*) саранча́ (*also collect.*).

locution /ləkˈjuːʃ(ə)n/ *n.* оборо́т (ре́чи), идио́ма.

lode /ləʊd/ *n.* ру́дная жи́ла.

● *cpds.* **~star** *n.* (*fig.*) путево́дная звезда́; **~stone** (*also* **loadstone**) *n.* магни́тный железня́к; (*fig.*) магни́т.

lodge /lɒdʒ/ *n.* **1** (*cottage e.g. at entrance to park*) дом привра́тника. **2** (*porter's apartment*) сторо́жка. **3** (*hunting ~*) охо́тничий до́мик. **4** (*freemason's ~*) масо́нская ло́жа. **5** (*trade union branch*) ме́стная профсою́зная организа́ция. **6** (*beaver's etc. lair*) нора́.

● *v.t.* **1** (*accommodate*) да|ва́ть, -ть помеще́ние +*d.*; поме|ща́ть, -сти́ть. **2** (*deposit*) сда|ва́ть, -ть на хране́ние. **3** (*fig., enter*): **~ a complaint/appeal** обра|ща́ться, -ти́ться с жа́лобой/апелля́цией; **~ a claim** предъяв|ля́ть, -и́ть прете́нзию; **~ an objection** заяв|ля́ть, -и́ть проте́ст.

● *v.i.* **1** (*reside*) жить (*impf.*); прожива́ть (*impf.*); **he ~s with us** он наш жиле́ц. **2** (*become embedded, stuck*) застр|ева́ть, -я́ть; **a bone ~d in his throat** кость застря́ла у него́ в го́рле.

lodger /ˈlɒdʒə(r)/ *n.* жил|е́ц (*fem.* -и́ца); (*occupant of flat*) квартира́нт (*fem.* -ка).

lodging /ˈlɒdʒɪŋ/ *n.* (*dwelling-place*) жильё; (*rented accommodation*) наёмная кварти́ра; (*pl.*) меблиро́ванные ко́мнаты (*f. pl.*); **he lives in ~s** он снима́ет ко́мнату.

loess /ˈləʊɪs/, /lɜːs/ *n.* (*geol.*) лёсс.

loft /lɒft/ *n.* (*room in roof*) черда́к; (*hay-~*) сенова́л; (*pigeon-~*) голубя́тня; (*organ-~*) хо́р|ы (*pl., g.* -ов).

● *v.t.*: **~ a ball** пос|ыла́ть, -ла́ть мяч высоко́/вверх.

loftiness /ˈlɒftɪnɪs/ *n.* (больша́я) высота́; возвы́шенность; (*fig., haughtiness*) высокоме́рие, надме́нность.

lofty /ˈlɒftɪ/ *adj.* (**loftier, loftiest**) (*high*) высо́кий; (*exalted*) возвы́шенный; (*haughty*) высокоме́рный, надме́нный.

log[1] /lɒg/ *n.* **1** (*of wood*) бревно́, чурба́н; **2** (*for fire*) поле́но; **he slept like a ~** он спал как уби́тый; **~ cabin** (бреве́нчатая) хи́жина.

● *cpds.* **~jam** *n.* зато́р; (*fig.*) засто́й, тупи́к; **~-rolling** *n.* (*US fig.*) поли́тика «ты мне — я тебе́».

log[2] /lɒg/ *n.* (**~-book**) ва́хтенный журна́л; (*of aircraft*) бортово́й журна́л; формуля́р; (*of lorry or car*) формуля́р.

● *v.t.* (**logged, logging**) (*record*) занос|и́ть, -ести́ в ва́хтенный журна́л; регистри́ровать (*impf., pf.*); (*attain*) разв|ива́ть, -и́ть (*ско́рость по ла́гу*); **~ in/on** (*comput.*) входи́ть, войти́ в систе́му; **~ out/off** (*comput.*) выходи́ть, вы́йти из систе́мы.

● *cpd.* **~-book** *n.* = *n.*

log[3] /lɒg/ = **logarithm**

loganberry /ˈləʊgənbərɪ/ *n.* лога́нова я́года (*гибрид малины с ежевикой*).

logarithm /ˈlɒgəˌrɪð(ə)m/ *n.* логари́фм.

logarithmic /ˌlɒgəˈrɪðmɪk/ *adj.* логарифми́ческий.

loggerhead /ˈlɒgəˌhed/ *n.*: **they are at ~s** они́ в ссо́ре (*or* не в лада́х) друг с дру́гом.

loggia /ˈləʊdʒə/, /ˈlɒ-/ *n.* ло́джия.

logging /ˈlɒgɪŋ/ *n.* (*tree-felling*) лесозагото́вки (*f. pl.*).

logic /ˈlɒdʒɪk/ *n.* ло́гика.

● *cpd.* **~-chopping** *n.* софи́стика.

logical /ˈlɒdʒɪk(ə)l/ *adj.* логи́ческий; (*consistent*) логи́чный, после́довательный.

logician /ləˈdʒɪʃ(ə)n/ *n.* ло́гик.

logistics /ləˈdʒɪstɪks/ *n.* (*mil.*) матриа́льно-техни́ческое обеспе́чение.

logo /ˈləʊgəʊ/, /ˈlɒgəʊ/ *n.* (*pl.* **logos**) эмбле́ма.

loin /lɔɪn/ *n.* **1** (*pl.*) поясни́ца; **gird up one's ~s** препоя́сать (*pf.*) свои́ чре́сла (*bibl.*). **2** (*joint of meat*) филе́ (*indecl.*).

● *cpd.* **~-cloth** *n.* набе́дренная повя́зка.

Loire /lwɑː(r)/ *n.* Луа́ра.

loiter /ˈlɔɪtə(r)/ *v.i.* (*dawdle*) ме́шкать (*impf.*); заме́шкаться (*pf.*); (*hang about*) слоня́ться (*impf.*) (без де́ла).

loiterer /ˈlɔɪtərə(r)/ *n.* праздношата́ющийся.

loll /lɒl/ *v.i.* **1** (*sit or stand in lazy attitude*) сиде́ть/стоя́ть (*impf.*) разваля́сь. **2** (*of tongue etc.: hang loose*) выва́ливаться (*impf.*).

lollipop /ˈlɒlɪˌpɒp/ *n.* леденец на па́лочке.

lollop /ˈlɒləp/ *v.i.* (**lolloped, lolloping**): **~ along** идти́ (*det.*) вразва́лку.

lolly /ˈlɒlɪ/ *n.* (*Br.*) **1** (*coll.*) = **lollipop. 2** (*sl., money*) гро́ш|и (*pl., g.* -ей).

London /ˈlʌnd(ə)n/ *n.* Ло́ндон; (*attr.*) ло́ндонский.

● *cpd.* **~ pride** *n.* (*bot.*) камнело́мка тени́стая.

Londoner /ˈlʌndənə(r)/ *n.* ло́ндон|ец (*fem.* -ка).

lone /ləʊn/ *adj.* одино́кий, уединённый; **~ wolf** (*lit., fig.*) бирю́к; **play a ~ hand** де́йствовать (*impf.*) в одино́чку.

loneliness /ˈləʊnlɪnɪs/ *n.* одино́чество.

lonely /ˈləʊnlɪ/ *adj.* (**lonelier, loneliest**) **1** (*solitary, alone*) одино́кий; **feel ~** чу́вствовать (*impf.*) себя́ одино́ким; **lead a ~ existence** вести́ (*det.*) одино́кий о́браз жи́зни; жить (*impf.*) уединённо. **2** (*isolated*) уединённый.

loner /ˈləʊnə(r)/ *n.* (*coll.*) бирю́к, одино́чка (*c.g.*).

lonesome /ˈləʊnsəm/ *adj.* одино́кий; **on one's ~** (*Br. coll.*) оди́н-одинёшенек; **feel ~** тоскова́ть (*impf.*); томи́ться (*impf.*) одино́чеством.

long[1] /lɒŋ/ *n.* **1** (*a ~ time*): **I shan't be away for ~** я уезжа́ю ненадо́лго; я ско́ро верну́сь; **it won't take ~** э́то не займёт мно́го вре́мени; **will you take ~ over it?** вы ско́ро ко́нчите?; **he did not take ~ to answer** он не заме́длил отве́тить; **it is ~ since he was here** он давно́ здесь не́ был; **at the ~est** са́мое бо́льшее.

2: **the ~ and the short of it is that ...** сло́вом, де́ло в том, что. . .

● *adj.* **1** (*of space, measurement*) дли́нный; **the table is 2 metres** (*Br.*), **meters** (*US*) **~** э́тот стол длино́й в 2 ме́тра (*or* име́ет 2 ме́тра длины́); **how ~ is this river?** какова́ длина́ э́той реки́?; **~ form** (*of Russian adj.*) по́лная фо́рма; **~ jump** прыжо́к в длину́; **~ measure** ме́ра длины́; **in the ~ run** в коне́чном ито́ге/счёте; с тече́нием вре́мени; **~ in the tooth** (*fig.*) не пе́рвой мо́лодости; **on ~ wave** на дли́нной волне́.

2 (*of distance*) да́льний; **a ~ journey** да́льний/до́лгий путь; **a ~ way off** далеко́; **from a ~ way off** издалека́.

3 (*of time*) до́лгий; **a ~ life** до́лгая жизнь; **a ~ memory** хоро́шая па́мять; **my holiday is 2 weeks ~** мой о́тпуск дли́тся две неде́ли; **a quarrel of ~ standing** да́вняя/многоле́тняя ссо́ра; **for a ~ time** до́лго, давно́; надо́лго; **a ~ time ago** мно́го вре́мени тому́ наза́д; давны́м-давно́; **a ~ time before the war** задо́лго до войны́; **it will be a ~ time before we meet again** мы встре́тимся сно́ва ещё не ско́ро.

4 (*prolonged*) дли́тельный; **a ~ illness** затяжна́я боле́знь.

● *adv.* **1** (*a ~ time*): **I shan't be ~** я ско́ро верну́сь; я не задержу́сь; **she is ~ since dead** она́ давно́ умерла́; **it was ~ past midnight** бы́ло далеко́ за́ полночь; **~ after** (*prep.*) до́лгое вре́мя по́сле+*g.*; **~ before** (*prep.*) задо́лго до+*g.*; **~ after(wards)** до́лгое вре́мя спустя́; гора́здо по́зже/поздне́е; **~ before** (*adv.*) давно́, гора́здо ра́ньше; **these events are ~ past** всё э́то случи́лось давно́; **~ ago** (давны́м-)давно́; **before ~** вско́ре, ско́ро.

2 (*for a ~ time*): **I have ~ thought so** я давно́ так ду́маю; **how ~ have you been here?** как давно́ вы здесь?; **~ live the Queen!** да здра́вствует короле́ва!

3 (*throughout*): **all day ~** це́лый день; **all night ~** всю ночь напролёт.

4: **as ~ as I live** пока́ я жив; **stay as ~ as you like** остава́йтесь, ско́лько хоти́те; **as ~ as you don't mind** е́сли вам всё равно́; е́сли вы не возража́ете.

5: **so ~!** пока́! (*coll.*).

6: **no ~er** бо́льше не; **I can't wait much ~er** мно́го до́льше ждать я не могу́.

● *cpds.* **~-awaited** *adj.* долгожда́нный; **~boat** *n.* барка́с; **~bow** *n.* большо́й лук; **~-distance** *adj.*: **~-distance call** междугоро́дный/междунаро́дный вы́зов; **~-distance train** по́езд да́льнего сле́дования; **~-distance runner** ста́йер, бегу́н на дли́нные

L

дистáнции; **~-drawn-out** *adj.* (*of conversation*) затянýвшийся; (*of story*) растя́нутый; (*of illness*) затяжнóй; **~-haired** *adj.* длинноволóсый; **~hand** *n.* обы́чное письмó (от руки́); **~ johns** *n. pl.* кальсóн|ы (*pl., g.* —); **~-legged** *adj.* длинноно́гий; **~-lived** *adj.* долговéчный; **~-lost** *adj.* давнó потéрянный/утрáченный; **~-playing** *adj.* долгоигрáющий; **~-range** *adj.* (*of gun*) дальнобóйный; (*of aircraft*) дáльнего дéйствия; (*of forecast, policy etc.*) долгосрóчный; **~shoreman** *n.* портóвый грýзчик; **~-sighted** *adj.* дальнозóркий; (*fig.*) дальнови́дный; **~-standing** *adj.* стари́нный, долголéтний; **a ~-standing promise** дáвнее обещáние; **~-suffering** *adj.* многострадáльный; **~-term** *adj.* долгосрóчный; (*of plans etc.*) перспекти́вный; **~-wave** *adj.* длинновóлновый; **~-winded** *adj.* многослóвный.

long² /lɒŋ/ *v.i.*: **~ for something** жáждать (*impf.*) чегó-н.; **we are ~ing for your return** мы ждём не дождёмся вáшего возвращéния; **I ~ed for a drink** я ужáсно хотéл пить; я томи́лся жáждой; **~ for s.o.** тосковáть (*impf.*) по комý-н.; скучáть (*impf.*) по комý-н.; **~ to do something** мечтáть (*impf.*) чтó-то дéлать; **he ~ed to get away from town** емý не терпéлось уéхать из гóрода.

longevity /lɒn'dʒevɪtɪ/ *n.* (*of person*) долголéтие; (*of thing*) долговéчность.

longing /'lɒŋɪŋ/ *n.* желáние, жáжда (*чего*); тоскá (*по чему*).

● *adj.* тоскýющий; **he looked at the books with ~ eyes** он смотрéл на кни́ги с вожделéнием.

longish /'lɒŋɪʃ/ *adj.* (*of size*) длиннováтый; (*of duration*) долговáтый.

longitude /'lɒŋgɪˌtju:d/, /'lɒndʒ-/ *n.* долготá; **at 20° ~ West** на двадцáтом грáдусе зáпадной долготы́.

longitudinal /ˌlɒŋgɪ'tju:dɪn(ə)l/, /ˌlɒndʒ-/ *adj.* (*of longitude*) долгóтный; (*lengthwise*) продóльный.

longw|ays /'lɒŋweɪz/, **-ise** /'lɒŋwaɪz/ *adv.* в длинý.

loo /lu:/ *n.* (*Br. coll., lavatory*) сорти́р (*coll.*); **I need (to use) the ~** мне нáдо кóе-кудá сбéгать; мне нáдо в «однó мéсто».

loofah /'lu:fə/ *n.* люфá.

look /lʊk/ *n.* **1** (*glance*) взгляд; **he gave me a ~** он брóсил взгляд (*or* взглянýл) на меня́; **there were angry ~s from the crowd** толпá глядéла с негодовáнием; **give s.o. a black ~** злóбно посмотрéть/взглянýть (*pf.*) на когó-н.; **may I have, take a ~ at your paper?** позвóльте просмотрéть вáшу газéту.

2: **have, take a ~ at** (*examine*) осм|áтривать, -отрéть; рассм|áтривать, -отрéть; **the doctor had a good ~ at his throat** дóктор внимáтельно посмотрéл егó гóрло; (*fig.*): **we must take a long ~ at these terms** мы должны́ разобрáться в постáвленных услóвиях тщáтельно (*or* как слéдует).

3: **have a ~ for** (*search for*) искáть, по-.

4 (*expression*) выражéние; **there was a ~ of horror on his face** егó лицó выражáло ýжас; **a ~ of pleasure came over her features** выражéние удовóльствия разлилóсь по её лицý.

5 (*appearance*) вид; **he had an odd ~ about him** у негó был стрáнный вид; **this house has a homely ~** у э́того дóма ую́тный вид; **I don't like the ~ of things** плóхо дéло!; **he has given the shop a new ~** он совсéм преобрази́л магази́н; **this is the new ~ in evening wear** вот нóвый силуэ́т вечéрних туалéтов; (*pl., personal appearance*) нарýжность, внéшность; **~s don't count** по внéшности не сýдят; **she has good ~s** онá хорошá собóй; **lose one's (good) ~s** дурнéть, по-.

● *v.t.* **1** (*inspect, scrutinize*): **~ s.o. in the face, eye** смотрéть, по- в глазá комý-н.; **don't ~ a gift horse in the mouth** дарёному коню́ в зýбы не смóтрят; **~ s.o. up and down** смéрить (*pf.*) когó-н. взгля́дом.

2 (*express with eyes*): **she ~ed daggers at him** онá злóбно посмотрéла на негó.

3 (*have the appearance of; see also v.i.* 3) вы́глядеть (*impf.*) + *i.*: **he ~s an old man** он вы́глядит старикóм; **he made me ~ a fool** он постáвил меня́ в дурáцкое положéние; **he ~s his age** емý впóлне дашь егó гóды; **she is thirty, but she does not ~ it** ей три́дцать, но ей стóлько не дашь; **he is not ~ing himself** на нём лицá нет; **you are ~ing yourself again** тепéрь вы снóва стáли похóжи на себя́; **she ~s her best in blue** ей си́нее бóльше всегó к лицý.

4 (*with ind. questions: observe*) смотрéть, по-; **~ who's here!** когó я ви́жу!; **now ~ what you've done!** смотри́те, что вы надéлали!; **~ where you're going!** смотри́те, кудá идёте!

● *v.i.* **1** (*use one's eyes; pay attention*) смотрéть, по-; **he ~ed out of the window to see if she was coming** он посмотрéл в окнó, не идёт ли онá; **~ over there!** посмотри́те/взгляни́те тудá!; **~ before you leap** ≈ семь раз отмéрь, оди́н отрéжь; не знáя брóду, не сýйся в вóду; **~ here!** послýшайте; **~ lively, sharp!** живéй!; поторáпливайтесь!; (*fig., consider*) вдýматься (*impf.*); **when one ~s more closely** при ближáйшем рассмотрéнии; (*search*) искáть, по-.

2 (*face*) выходи́ть (*impf.*); **the windows ~ on to the garden (street)** óкна выхóдят в сад (на ýлицу).

3 (*appear; see also v.i.* 3) вы́глядеть (*impf.*) + *i.*; **she is ~ing well** онá хорошó вы́глядит; **everybody ~ed tired** у всех был устáлый вид; **that ~s tasty** у э́того блю́да аппети́тный вид; **that hat ~s well on you** вам идёт (*or* к лицý) э́та шля́па; **he made me ~ small** он меня́ уни́зил; **things ~ black** плóхо дéло; **the situation ~s promising** ситуáция как бýдто благоприя́тная/обнадёживающая; **that ~s suspicious** э́то подозри́тельно; **it ~s as if ...** кáжется(, что)...; похóже на то, что...; **~ like** (*resemble*) вы́глядеть (*impf.*) + *i.*; походи́ть (*impf.*) на + *a.*; **the old man ~s like a tramp** у старикá вид бродя́ги; **he ~s like his father** он похóж на отцá; **she ~s like nothing on earth** онá Бог знáет на что похóжа; (*give expectation of*): **it ~s like rain** собирáется (*or* похóже, что бýдет) дождь; **it ~s like a fine day** день обещáет быть хорóшим; **'Shall we be late?' — 'It ~s like it'** «Мы опáздываем?» — «Похóже(, что так)»; **he ~s like winning** он, кáжется, вы́йдет победи́телем; похóже, что он вы́играет.

● *with preps.*: **~ about one** огля́д|ываться, -éться; **he ~ed about the room** он обвёл глазáми кóмнату; **~ after** (*follow with eye*) следи́ть (*impf.*) глазáми за + *i.*; (*care for*) смотрéть (*impf.*) за + *i.*; присмáтривать (*impf.*) за + *i.*; ухáживать (*impf.*) за + *i.*; **she has four children to ~ after** на её попечéнии чéтверо детéй; **he needs ~ing after** он нуждáется в ухóде; **he seems well ~ed after** у негó ухóженный вид; **he had to ~ after himself** емý приходи́лось всё дéлать самомý; **I can ~ after myself** я не нуждáюсь в посторóнней пóмощи; **~ after yourself!** (*in leave-taking*) береги́те себя́!; (*keep safe*) храни́ть (*impf.*); **I gave my valuables to the bank to ~ after** я сдал свои́ цéнности в банк на хранéние; (*be responsible for*) вéдать (*impf.*) + *i.*; занимáться (*impf.*) + *i.*; **a lawyer is ~ing after my affairs** мои́ми делáми вéдает юри́ст; **don't worry, I'll ~ after the bill** не беспокóйтесь, я займýсь счётом; **~ at** (*direct gaze on*) смотрéть, по- на + *a.*; **he was ~ing at a book** он смотрéл на кни́гу; **just ~ at the time!** подýмайте, как пóздно!; **he's not much to ~ at** внéшность у негó не сли́шком внуши́тельная; **to ~ at him, you would think ...** сýдя по егó ви́ду, мóжно подýмать, что...; **he won't even ~ at milk** он и смотрéть не хóчет на молокó; (*inspect, examine*) смотрéть, по- на + *a.*; осм|áтривать, -отрéть; **the doctor ~ed at the patient** врач осмотрéл больнóго; **I must get my car ~ed at** нáдо, чтóбы посмотрéли мою́ маши́ну; **the customs men ~ed at our luggage** тамóженники осмотрéли наш багáж; (*fig., consider*) вдýматься (*impf.*) в + *a.*; обра|щáть, -ти́ть внимáние на + *a.*; **we must ~ at the matter carefully** нáдо как слéдует подýмать об э́том дéле (*or* разобрáться в э́том вопрóсе); **I ~ed down the street** я оки́нул взгля́дом ýлицу; **he ~ed down the page** он пробежáл страни́цу глазáми; **~ for** (*seek*) искáть, по-; **he is ~ing for his wife** он и́щет свою́ женý; **he is ~ing for a wife** он и́щет себé женý; **he is ~ing for a job** он и́щет мéсто/рабóту; **he is ~ing for trouble** он напрáшивается на неприя́тности; (*hope for, expect*) надéяться (*impf.*) на + *a.*; ожидáть (*impf.*) + *g.*; **I ~ed for better things from him** я ожидáл от негó лýчшего; **we obtained the ~ed-for result** мы доби́лись желáемого результáта; **~ in the mirror** смотрéться, по- в зéркало; **~ into** (*lit.*) смотрéть, по- в + *a.*; (*investigate, examine*) исслéдовать (*impf.*); рассм|áтривать, -отрéть; **it is something that needs ~ing at** с э́тим нáдо разобрáться; **I shall ~ into the matter** я займу́сь э́тим вопрóсом; **~ on** (*regard*) считáть (*impf.*); **I ~ on him as my son** я считáю егó своúм сы́ном; **he ~ed on the remark as an insult** он восприня́л замечáние как оскорблéние; **he ~s on me with contempt** он меня́ презирáет; **~ on the bright side** смотрéть (*impf.*) оптимисти́чески; **~ on to** (*face*) *see v.i.* 2; **he ~ed out of the window** он посмотрéл в окнó; **he ~ed over the wall** он посмотрéл чéрез стéну; **~ over one's shoulder** огля́|дываться, -ну́ться; **~ over s.o.'s shoulder** смотрéть, по- комý-н. чéрез плечó; **the teacher was ~ing over our homework** учи́тель просмáтривал нáшу домáшнюю рабóту; **he left us to ~ over the house** он остáвил нас одни́х осмáтривать дом; **~ round** (*inspect*) осм|áтривать, -отрéть; **he ~ed through the window** он посмотрéл в окнó; **he ~ed right through** (*ignored*) **me** он смотрéл ми́мо меня́; **they ~ed through** (*examined*) **our papers** они́ просмотрéли нáши бумáги; **he quickly ~ed through the newspaper** он бы́стро пробежáл глазáми газéту; **~ to** (*turn to*) обра|щáться, -ти́ться к + *d.*; **we ~ed to him for help** мы рассчи́тывали на егó пóмощь; (*heed*): **he should ~ to his manners** емý слéдует обрати́ть внимáние на свои́ манéры; **~ upon** *see* ⇒**~ at, on**.

● *with advs.*: **~ about, ~ around** *v.i.* осм|áтриваться, -отрéться; **~ ahead** *v.i.* (*lit., fig.*) смотрéть (*impf.*) вперёд; **~ around** *see* ⇒**~ about, ~ round; ~ aside** *v.i.* смотрéть, по- в стóрону; **~ away** *v.i.* отв|орáчиваться, -ерну́ться; **~ back** *v.i.* (*lit., fig.*) огл|я́дываться, -яну́ться; **once started, there was no ~ing back** раз уж мы нáчали, отступáть бы́ло пóздно; **~ back on** вспоминáть (*impf.*); припоминáть (*impf.*); **~ behind** *v.i.* смотрéть, по- назáд; **~ down** *v.i.* (*lower one's gaze*) опус|кáть, -ти́ть глазá; **~ down on** смотрéть (*impf.*) свысокá на + *a.*; презирáть (*impf.*); **~ forward** смотрéть (*impf.*) вперёд; **~ forward to** предвкушáть (*impf.*); ждать (*impf.*) + *g.* с нетерпéнием; **I ~ forward to meeting you** жду с нетерпéнием, когдá уви́жусь с вáми; **I am so ~ing forward to it** я так жду э́того; **I ~ forward to his arrival** я жду не дожду́сь егó приéзда; **~ in** *v.i.*: **~ in** (*call*) **on s.o.** загля́|дывать, -ну́ть (*or* забе|гáть, -жáть) к комý-н.; **~ on** *v.i.* наблюдáть, смотрéть (*both impf.*); **~ out** *v.t.* (*Br., select*): **I must ~ out some old dresses** мне нáдо отобрáть каки́е-то стáрые плáтья; **he ~ed out some examples** он подыскáл нéсколько примéров; *v.i.* (*from a window*) смотрéть, по- в окнó; (*be careful*) быть насторожé; **~ out!** осторóжно!; **if you don't ~ out you'll lose your ticket** смотри́те, как бы не потеря́ть билéт!; (*keep one's eyes open*): **she stood at the door ~ing out for the postman** онá стоя́ла в дверя́х, высмáтривая почтальóна; **we are ~ing out for a house** мы присмáтриваем дом; **~ over** *v.t.* (*scrutinize*) просм|áтривать, -отрéть; **~ round, ~ around** *v.i.* (*turn one's head*) огля́|дываться, -ну́ться; озирáться (*impf.*); (*make an inspection*) осм|áтриваться, -отрéться; **~ round for** (*seek*) поды́скивать (*impf.*); **~ up** *v.t.* (*visit*) наве|щáть, -сти́ть; (**~** *for, seek information on*) оты́ск|ивать, -áть; и|скáть, разы-; **~ up trains** посмотрéть (*pf.*) расписáние; *v.i.* (*raise one's eyes*) подн|имáть, -ять глазá (**at s.o.**: на когó-н.); (*improve*) ул|учшáться, -у́чшиться; **things are ~ing up** делá идýт на поправку; **~ up to** (*respect*) уважáть (*impf.*); **he is ~ed up to by everybody** все егó уважáют.

● *cpds.* **~-alike** *n.* двойни́к; **a Prince Charles ~-alike** вы́литый принц Чарлз, двойни́к при́нца Чáрлза; **~-in** *n.*: **I didn't get a ~-in** меня́ не подпусти́ли к пирогý; **~-out** *n.* (*watchman*) наблюдáтель (*m.*); (*post*) наблюдáтельный пункт; (*watch*): **be on the ~-out** быть начекý (*or* насторожé *or* на стрáже); **be on the ~-out for** (*e.g. a house*) присмáтривать (*impf.*) себé; **be on the ~-out for the enemy** подстерегáть (*impf.*) неприя́теля; (*Br., prospect*): **it's a poor ~-out for us** у нас перспекти́ва невáжная; (*Br., concern*): **that's his ~-out** э́то егó дéло/забóта; **~-see** *n.* (*coll.*) бéглый просмóтр.

looker-on /ˈlʊkə(r)/ *n.* зри́тель (*m.*), наблюдáтель (*m.*).

looking-glass /ˈlʊkɪŋˌglɑːs/ *n.* зéркало.

loom¹ /luːm/ *n.* ткáцкий станóк.

loom² /luːm/ *v.i.* **1** (*appear indistinctly; also* **~ up**) неясно вырисóвываться (*impf.*); мая́чить (*impf.*); **a black shape ~ed in the distance** что-то чернéло вдали́. **2** (*impend*) нав|исáть, -и́снуть; **~ large** (*threateningly*) прин|имáть, -ять угрожáющие размéры; (*prominently*): **the risk ~ed large in his mind** мысль об опáсности егó преслéдовала неотсту́пно.

loon /luːn/ *n.* (*US, bird*) гагáра.

loony /ˈluːnɪ/ *n. & adj.* (**loonier, looniest**) (*coll.*) рехну́вшийся; чóкнутый (*coll.*), псих (*coll.*).

● *cpd.* **~-bin** *n.* (*coll. offens.*) психбольни́ца.

loop /luːp/ *n.* **1** пéтля. **2** (*rail.; also* **~-line**) вéтка. **3** (*aeron.*) мёртвая петля́. **4** (*comput.*) цикл.

● *v.t.* **1** (*form into* **~**) дéлать, с- пéтлю из + *g.* **2** (*fasten with* **~**) закреп|ля́ть, -и́ть петлёй. **3** **~ the ~** (*aeron.*) дéлать, с- мёртвую пéтлю.

loophole /ˈluːphəʊl/ *n.* (*fig.*) лазéйка.

loopy /ˈluːpɪ/ *adj.* (**loopier, loopiest**) (*coll.*) рехну́вшийся (*coll.*).

loose /luːs/ *n.*: **on the ~** в загу́ле; на свобóде; на вóле.

● *adj.* **1** (*free, unconfined, unrestrained*) свобóдный; **break ~** вы́рваться (*pf.*) на свобóду; (*of a dog*) сорвáться с цепи́; **let ~** (*e.g. a dog*) спус|кáть, -ти́ть с цепи́; (*e.g. lion, maniac*) выпускáть, вы́пустить; **~ box** (*Br.*) денни́к.
2 (*not fastened or held together*): **~ papers** отдéльные листы́; **~ cover** (*Br., on armchair etc.*) чехóл; **he carries his change ~ in his pocket** мéлочь у негó пря́мо в кармáне (без кошелькá); **she wears her hair ~** онá хóдит с распу́щенными волосáми; (*not packed*) без упакóвки.
3 (*not secure or firm*): **a ~ end** (*of rope*) свобóдный конéц; **at a ~ end** (*fig.*) без дéла; **he was at a ~ end** он не знал, за что приня́ться; **I have a ~ tooth** у меня́ зуб шатáется; **the nut is ~** гáйка разболтáлась; **the button is ~** пу́говица болтáется; **the screw came, worked ~** винт развинти́лся; **he has a screw ~** (*sl.*) у негó ви́нтика не хватáет; **the string is ~** верёвка слáбо завя́зана; **the string came ~** верёвка развязáлась; **hang ~** болтáться (*impf.*).
4 (*slack*) слáбо натя́нутый; **with a ~ rein** с отпу́щенными вожжáми; **~ bowels** понóс; **he has a ~ tongue** он сли́шком болтли́в; **~ clothes** ширóкая/простóрная одéжда; **a ~ collar** свобóдный вóрот.
5 (*not compact or dense*): **~ soil** ры́хлая пóчва; **~ weave** рéдкая ткань.
6 (*imprecise*): **a ~ translation** приблизи́тельный/вóльный перевóд; **~ thinking** нечёткость мы́сли.
7 (*morally lax*) распу́щенный; **~ living** распу́тство; распу́тный óбраз жи́зни; **a ~ woman** распу́тная жéнщина.

● *v.t.* (*release*) освобо|ждáть, -ди́ть; отпус|кáть, -ти́ть; (*undo*) развя́з|ывать, -áть; (*relax*) распус|кáть, -ти́ть.

● *cpds.* **~-fitting** *adj.* ширóкий, простóрный; **~-leaf** *adj.* со вкладны́ми листкáми; **~-leaf binder** скоросшивáтель (*m.*); **~-limbed** *adj.* ги́бкий; **~-tongued** *adj.* болтли́вый.

loosen /ˈluːs(ə)n/ *v.t.* (*tongue*) развя́з|ывать, -áть; (*screw*) отви́н|чивать, -ти́ть; (*by shaking or pulling*) расшáт|ывать, -áть; (*soil*) разрыхл|я́ть, -и́ть; (*tie, rope, belt etc.*) осл|абля́ть, -áбить; **the wine ~ed his tongue** винó развязáло емý язы́к; **~ one's grip** ослáбить (*pf.*) хвáтку; **~ one's hold on something** выпускáть, вы́пустить что-н. из рук.

looseness /ˈluːsnɪs/ *n.* (*slackness*) слáбость; (*of morals*) распу́щенность; (*of bowels*) понóс.

loosestrife /ˈluːsstraɪf/ *n.* (*bot.*) вербéйник.

loot /luːt/ *n.* добы́ча, наѓрабленное добрó.

● *v.t.* грáбить, раз-.

● *v.i.* ун|оси́ть, -ести́ добы́чу.

looter /ˈluːtə(r)/ *n.* марóдёр, граби́тель (*m.*).

looting /ˈluːtɪŋ/ *n.* марóдёрство, грабёж.

L

lop /lɒp/ *v.t.* (lopped, lopping) (*also* ~ off) руби́ть (*impf.*); отруб|а́ть, -и́ть.

lope /ləʊp/ *v.i.* бежа́ть (*det.*) вприпры́жку.

lop-eared /ˈlɒp,ɪəd/ *adj.* вислоу́хий.

lop-sided /lɒpˈsaɪdɪd/ *adj.* (*building*) кривобо́кий; (*grin*) криво́й; (*fig.*) неравноме́рный, односторо́нний.

loquacious /lɒˈkweɪʃəs/ *adj.* словоохо́тливый, болтли́вый.

loquaci|ousness /lɒˈkweɪʃəsnɪs/, **-ty** /lɒˈkwæsɪtɪ/ *n.* словоохо́тливость, болтли́вость.

lord /lɔːd/ *n.* **1** (*ruler*; *also fig.*) власти́тель (*m.*), властели́н; ~ of the manor владе́лец поме́стья; live like a ~ жить (*impf.*) припева́ючи, по-ба́рски; drunk as a ~ пьян в сте́льку/как сапо́жник.
2 (*Br., nobleman*) лорд; House of L~s пала́та ло́рдов; ~s temporal and spiritual «све́тские» и «духо́вные» ло́рды; My ~! мило́рд!
3 (*God*) Госпо́дь; Our L~ (*Christ*) Госпо́дь; L~ have mercy! Го́споди, поми́луй!; (the) L~ only knows Бог (его́) зна́ет; in the year of our L~ ... в ...ом году́ от рождества́ Христо́ва; L~'s day воскре́сный день; L~'s Prayer моли́тва госпо́дня, О́тче наш; L~'s Supper Евхари́стия.
● *v.t.*: ~ it over s.o. кома́ндовать (*impf.*) кем-н.
● *cpd.* L~ Mayor *n.* (*Br.*) лорд-мэ́р.

lordly /ˈlɔːdlɪ/ *adj.* (lordlier, lordliest) (*magnificent*) пы́шный; (*haughty*) надме́нный.

lordship /ˈlɔːdʃɪp/ *n.*: Your L~ ва́ша све́тлость/ми́лость.

lore /lɔː(r)/ *n.* (специа́льные) зна́ния (*nt. pl.*); bird ~ зна́ния о пти́цах; (*traditions*) преда́ния (*nt. pl.*).

lorgnette /lɔːˈnjet/ *n.* лорне́т.

lorry /ˈlɒrɪ/ *n.* (*Br.*) грузови́к.

Los Angeles /lɒs ˈændʒɪ,liːz/ *n.* Лос-А́нджелес.

los|e /luːz/ *v.t.* (*past and p.p.* lost)
1 теря́ть, по-; утра́|чивать, -тить; лиш|а́ться, -и́ться +*g.*; give something up for ~t счита́ть (*impf.*) что-н. (безвозвра́тно) пропа́вшим; the goods were ~t in transit това́ры пропа́ли в пути́; ~t property office (*Br.*), ~t and found department (*US*) бюро́ нахо́док; I ~t count of his mistakes я потеря́л счёт его́ оши́бкам; I am beginning to ~e faith in him я начина́ю теря́ть ве́ру в него́; he ~t his head (*fig.*) он потеря́л го́лову; Charles I ~t his head Карл I был обезгла́влен; ~e heart па́|дать, -сть ду́хом; the plane was ~ing height самолёт теря́л высоту́; he ~t a leg он потеря́л но́гу, он лиши́лся ноги́; ~e one's mind сходи́ть, сойти́ с ума́; ~e patience выходи́ть, вы́йти из терпе́ния; ~e one's place (*job*) быть уво́ленным; (*in queue*) теря́ть, по- о́чередь; (*while reading*) сби́ться (*pf.*), потеря́ть (*pf.*) ме́сто; ~e one's reason лиш|а́ться, -и́ться рассу́дка; сходи́ть, сойти́ с ума́; ~e (*forfeit*) one's rights утра́|чивать, -тить свои́ права́; ~e sight of (*lit.*) упус|ка́ть, -ти́ть и́з виду; (*fig.*) не уч|и́тывать, -е́сть; заб|ыва́ть, -ы́ть; ~e one's sight сле́пнуть, о-; теря́ть, по- зре́ние; ~e one's temper серди́ться, рас-; have you ~t your tongue? вы что — язы́к проглоти́ли?; I ~t touch with him я потеря́л связь с ним; we ~t track of the time мы утра́тили вся́кое представле́ние о вре́мени; he ~t the use of his legs у него́ отняли́сь но́ги; he ~t his voice он потеря́л/сорва́л го́лос; ~e one's way заблуди́ться (*pf.*); I am trying to ~e weight я стара́юсь похуде́ть; a ~t art утра́ченное иску́сство; a ~t cause безнадёжное де́ло; (*person*) неисправи́мый челове́к; a ~t soul (*fig.*) пропа́щий челове́к; I am ~t without her без неё я как без рук.
2 (~*e by death*): ~e an old friend лиши́ться (*pf.*) ста́рого дру́га; he ~t his wife у него́ умерла́ жена́; he ~t his son in the war у него́ на войне́ поги́б сын; she ~t the baby (*by miscarriage*) у неё был вы́кидыш; be ~t (*perish, die*) ги́бнуть (*impf.*); пог|иба́ть, -и́бнуть; the ship was ~t with all hands су́дно со всем экипа́жем поги́бло.
3: be, get ~t (~*e one's way*) заблуди́ться (*pf.*); get ~t! исче́зни!, кати́сь! (*coll.*); (*fig.*): ~t in thought заду́мавшись; ~e o.s. in something погру|жа́ться, -зи́ться во что́-н.
4 (*cease to see, understand etc.*): I've ~t you; you've ~t me (*coll., I can't follow you*) я потеря́л нить (ва́шей мы́сли); be ~t (*disappear*) исч|еза́ть, -е́знуть; проп|ада́ть, -а́сть; the church was ~t in the fog це́рковь скры́лась в тума́не; what he said was ~t in the noise его́ слова́ потону́ли в шу́ме.
5 (*fail to use; waste*): ~e an opportunity упус|ка́ть, -ти́ть возмо́жность; he ~t no opportunity он по́льзовался вся́кой возмо́жностью; ~e time теря́ть, по- вре́мя; he ~t no time in getting away он тут же убежа́л, не теря́я вре́мени; there is not a moment to be ~t нельзя́ теря́ть ни мину́ты (вре́мени); вре́мя не те́рпит; make up for ~t time навёрст|ывать, -а́ть упу́щенное вре́мя; the joke was ~t on him шу́тка не дошла́ до него́.
6 (*in contest, sport, gambling*) прои́гр|ывать, -а́ть; he ~t the argument его́ поби́ли в спо́ре; the motion was ~t предложе́ние не прошло́; they ~t the match они́ проигра́ли; I ~t my bet я проигра́л пари́.
7 (*of a clock*) отст|ава́ть, -а́ть на +*a.*; my watch ~es 5 minutes a day мои́ часы́ отстаю́т на 5 мину́т в день.
● *v.i.* (*past and p.p.* lost)
1 прои́гр|ывать, -а́ть; теря́ть, по-; fight a ~ing battle вести́ (*det.*) безнадёжную борьбу́; they ~t by 3 points они́ недобра́ли трёх очко́в; he ~t on the deal в э́той сде́лке он оста́лся в про́игрыше; ~e out (*coll.*) потерпе́ть (*pf.*) неуда́чу.
2 (*of a clock*): my watch is ~ing мои́ часы́ отстаю́т.

loser /ˈluːzə(r)/ *n.* (*at a game*) проигра́вший; (*person who habitually fails*) неуда́чник; he is a good (bad) ~ он (не) уме́ет досто́йно прои́грывать; come off (*or* be) a ~ оста́ться (*pf.*) в про́игрыше.

losings /ˈluːzɪŋz/ *n.* про́игрыш.

loss /lɒs/ *n.* **1** поте́ря; ~ of sight поте́ря зре́ния; ~ of heat теплопоте́ря; ~ of life поте́ри уби́тыми; челове́ческие же́ртвы (*f. pl.*); suffer heavy ~es понести́ (*pf.*) больши́е поте́ри.
2 (*detriment*) утра́та; his death was a great ~ его́ смерть была́ большо́й утра́той; his resignation is no great ~ его́ отста́вка — небольша́я поте́ря; it's your ~, not mine э́то ва́ша беда́, не моя́.
3 (*monetary*) убы́ток; cover a ~ покр|ыва́ть, -ы́ть убы́ток; incur ~es терпе́ть, по- убы́тки; meet a ~ нести́ (*det.*) убы́ток; sell at a ~ прод|ава́ть, -а́ть с убы́тком (*or* в убы́ток); dead ~ чи́стый убы́ток; (*coll., useless person etc.*) пусто́е ме́сто; gambling ~es про́игрыши (*m. pl.*) (в ка́ртах, на бега́х *и т.п.*).
4 (*destruction, wreck*) ги́бель.
5: I am at a ~ to answer я затрудня́юсь отве́тить; he was at a ~ what to say он не нашёлся, что сказа́ть; in my presence he was always at a ~ при мне он всегда́ теря́лся.

lost /lɒst/ *past and p.p. of* ⇒**lose**

lot /lɒt/ *n.* **1**: decide by ~ реш|а́ть, -и́ть жеребьёвкой; cast ~s бр|оса́ть, -о́сить жре́бий; draw ~s тяну́ть (*impf.*) жре́бий; (*fig., destiny*) судьба́, у́часть, до́ля; cast in one's ~ with s.o. свя́з|ывать, -а́ть свою́ судьбу́ с кем-н.; it fell to his ~ to go ему́ вы́пал жре́бий (*or* пришло́сь) идти́.
2 (*plot of land*) уча́сток; parking ~ (*US*) стоя́нка для маши́н/автомоби́лей.
3 (*Br. coll., of persons*) наро́д; our/your ~ наш/ваш брат.
4 (*in auction*) па́ртия, лот; (*Br. coll.*): he is a bad ~ он плохо́й челове́к.
5: the ~ (*Br. coll., everything*) всё; that's the ~! вот и всё!
6 (a ~, ~s: *a large number, amount*) мно́го; ма́ло ли что; a ~ of people мно́го наро́ду; мно́гие; ма́ло ли кто (+*sg. verb*); what a ~ of people there were! ско́лько бы́ло наро́ду!; I have seen a ~ in my time на своём веку́ я мно́гое повида́л; I don't see a ~ of him nowadays мы с ним ма́ло/ре́дко ви́димся ны́нче; he has ~s of friends у него́ мно́го друзе́й; there were ~s of apples left оста́лась у́йма я́блок; he plays a ~ of football он мно́го игра́ет в футбо́л.
● *adv.* (a ~) **1** (*often*) ча́сто; we went to the theatre (*Br.*), theater (*US*) a ~ мы ча́сто ходи́ли в теа́тр.
2 (*with comps.: much*) гора́здо, си́льно; a ~ worse гора́здо ху́же; a ~ better куда́ лу́чше; the patient became a ~ worse больно́му ста́ло намно́го ху́же.

loth /ləʊθ/ = lo(a)th

Lothario /ləˈθɑːrɪəʊ/, /-ˈθeərɪəʊ/ *n.* (*pl.* ~s) (*fig.*) волоки́та (*m.*), пове́са (*m.*), донжуа́н.

lotion /ˈləʊʃ(ə)n/ *n.* примо́чка; (*cosmetic*) лосьо́н.

lottery /ˈlɒtərɪ/ *n.* лотере́я; **~ ticket** лотере́йный биле́т.

lotto /ˈlɒtəʊ/ *n.* лото́ (*indecl.*).

lotus /ˈləʊtəs/ *n.* (*bot., myth.*) ло́тос.

● *cpd.* **~-eater** *n.* сибари́т.

loud /laʊd/ *adj.* гро́мкий; (*noisy*) шу́мный; (*fig.*): **~ colours** (*Br.*), **colors** (*US*) крича́щие/крикли́вые кра́ски/цвета́.

● *adv.* гро́мко; **we laughed long and ~** мы до́лго и гро́мко смея́лись; **out ~** вслух.

● *cpds.* **~-hailer** *n.* (*Br.*) ру́пор; **~-mouthed** *adj.* крикли́вый; **~speaker** *n.* громкоговори́тель (*m.*), дина́мик.

loudness /ˈlaʊdnɪs/ *n.* гро́мкость; (*of colour*) крикли́вость.

lounge /laʊndʒ/ *n.* (*Br., sitting-room*) гости́ная; (*public room*) сало́н; (*at airport*) зал ожида́ния; (*bar*) бар пе́рвого кла́сса; (*US, couch*) куше́тка.

● *v.i.* (*sit in relaxed position*) сиде́ть (*impf.*) разваля́сь (*or* вразва́лку); (*sit or stand, leaning against something*) сиде́ть/стоя́ть (*impf.*) прислоня́сь (*к чему*); **~ about** (*idly*) безде́льничать (*impf.*); слоня́ться (*impf.*).

● *cpds.* **~ lizard** *n.* (*sl.*) све́тский безде́льник; **~ suit** *n.* (*Br.*) костю́м, пиджа́чная па́ра.

lounger /ˈlaʊndʒə(r)/ *n.* шезло́нг.

lour /ˈlaʊə(r)/, **lower** /ˈləʊə(r)/ *v.i.* (*lit., fig.*) насу́п|ливаться, -иться; **he ~ed at me** он смотре́л на меня́ насу́пившись; **a ~ing sky** мра́чное не́бо; **a ~ing expression** угрю́мое выраже́ние.

louse /laʊs/ *n.* **1** (*pl.* **lice**) (*insect*) вошь. **2** (*pl.* **~s**) (*sl., person*) гни́да.

● *v.t.*: **~ up** (*sl.*) испо́ртить, испога́нить (*both pf.*).

lousiness /ˈlaʊzɪnɪs/ *n.* вши́вость; (*fig.*) гну́сность.

lousy /ˈlaʊzɪ/ *adj.* (**lousier, lousiest**) **1** (*infested with lice*) вши́вый. **2** (*sl., disgusting, rotten*) парши́вый, отврати́тельный; **he played a ~ trick on me** он мне сде́лал га́дость; он мне подложи́л свинью́; **I feel ~ today** я сего́дня чу́вствую себя́ отврати́тельно.

lout /laʊt/ *n.* хам.

loutish /ˈlaʊtɪʃ/ *adj.* ха́мский; неотёсанный.

loutishness /ˈlaʊtɪʃnɪs/ *n.* ха́мство; неотёсанность.

louvre /ˈlu:və(r)/ *n.* (*US also* **louver**) (*slatted opening; also* **~-boards**) жалюзи́ (*nt. pl. indecl.*); (*skylight*) слухово́е окно́.

lovable /ˈlʌvəb(ə)l/ *adj.* ми́лый, обая́тельный.

lovage /ˈlʌvɪdʒ/ *n.* (*bot.*) любисток лека́рственный.

love /lʌv/ *n.* **1** любо́вь; **he has a ~ of adventure** он большо́й люби́тель приключе́ний; **feel ~ for, towards s.o.** испы́тывать (*impf.*) любо́вь к кому́-н.; **show ~ to s.o.** проявл|я́ть, -и́ть любо́вь к кому́-н.; **for ~ of** из любви́ к + *d.*; ра́ди + *g.*; **for the ~ of God** ра́ди Бо́га; **labour** (*Br.*), **labor** (*US*) **of ~** бескоры́стный труд; люби́мое де́ло; **he sent you his ~** он проси́л переда́ть вам серде́чный приве́т; **there is no ~ lost between them** они́ друг дру́га недолю́бливают; **not for ~ or money** ни за что на све́те; **they were playing for ~** они́ игра́ли не на де́ньги; **they married for ~** они́ жени́лись по любви́; **be in ~ (with s.o.)** быть влюблённым в кого́-н.; **fall in ~ with s.o.** влюбл|я́ться, -и́ться в кого́-н.; **fall out of love with s.o.** разлюби́ть (*pf.*) кого́-н.; **make ~ to** (*court*) уха́живать (*impf.*) за + *i.*; **make ~** (*have sexual intercourse*) зан|има́ться, -я́тся любо́вью; **his ~ was not returned** он люби́л без взаи́мности; **unrequited ~** неразделённая любо́вь; любо́вь без взаи́мности; **~ affair** рома́н; (*pej.*) любо́вная связь; **~ story** рома́н про любо́вь; (*in address*): **(my) ~!** (мой) ми́лый!; (моя́) ми́лая!; ра́дость моя́! **2** (*delightful person, esp. child*) пре́лесть; (*sweetheart, mistress*) люби́мая, ми́лая, возлю́бленная; **he has had many ~s** он люби́л мно́го раз. **3** (*zero score*) ноль (*m.*); **~ all** счёт ноль-ноль; **~ game** «суха́я».

● *v.t.* люби́ть (*impf.*); **I ~ the way he smiles** мне ужа́сно нра́вится, как он улыба́ется; я люблю́ его́ улы́бку; **I ~ my work** я люблю́ мою́ рабо́ту; **I ~ walking in the rain** я обожа́ю гуля́ть под дождём; **he ~s finding fault** он ве́чно придира́ется; **I'd ~ to go to Italy** мне о́чень хоте́лось бы съе́здить в Ита́лию; **I'd ~ you to come** я был бы сча́стлив, е́сли бы вы пришли́; **'Will you come?' — 'Yes. I'd ~ to'** «Вы придёте?» — «Да, с удово́льствием/ра́достью».

● *cpds.* **~-bird** *n.* (попуга́йчик-)неразлу́чник; (*pl., fig.*) влюблённые; **~-child** *n.* дитя́ (*nt.*) любви́; **~-hate** *adj.*: **they have a ~-hate relationship** у них любо́вь-не́нависть; у них отноше́ние любви́-не́нависти; **~-in-a-mist** *n.* (*bot.*) черну́шка; **~-letter** *n.* любо́вная запи́ска; **~-lorn** *adj.* безнадёжно влюблённый; **~-making** *n.* (*intimacy*) физи́ческая бли́зость; **~-match** *n.* брак по любви́; **~-nest** *n.* гнёздышко; **~-seat** *n.* кре́сло-дива́н на двои́х; **~sick** *adj.* снеда́емый любо́вью; **~-song** *n.* любо́вная пе́сня.

loveless /ˈlʌvlɪs/ *adj.* нелю́бящий, без любви́; **~ marriage** брак без любви́.

loveliness /ˈlʌvlɪnɪs/ *n.* (*beauty*) красота́; (*attractiveness*) очарова́ние.

lovely /ˈlʌvlɪ/ *adj.* (**lovelier, loveliest**) (*beautiful*) краси́вый, прекра́сный; (*charming, attractive*) преле́стный, милови́дный; **we had a ~ time** мы прекра́сно провели́ вре́мя; **~!** (*excellent!*) замеча́тельно!; отли́чно!

lover /ˈlʌvə(r)/ *n.* **1** любо́вни|к (*fem.* -ца); (*pl.*) влюблённые; **they became ~s** (*had intercourse*) они́ сошли́сь/сбли́зились. **2** (*devotee*) люби́тель (*m.*) (*fem.* -ница); покло́нни|к (*fem.* -ца).

lovey /ˈlʌvɪ/ *n.* (*pl.* **loveys**) (*Br. coll.*) ми́лый, голу́бчик.

loving /ˈlʌvɪŋ/ *n.*: **the child needs a lot of ~** ребёнок нужда́ется в любви́ и ла́ске.

● *adj.* лю́бящий; **from your ~ father** от лю́бящего тебя́ отца́; (*tender*) не́жный.

● *cpds.* **~-cup** *n.* кругова́я ча́ша; **~-kindness** *n.* не́жная забо́тливость; милосе́рдие.

low[1] /ləʊ/ *n.* **1** (*meteor.*) цикло́н. **2** (**~ point or level**): **the pound fell to an all-time ~** фунт дости́г небыва́ло ни́зкого у́ровня.

● *adj.* **1** ни́зкий, невысо́кий; **the chair is too ~** стул сли́шком ни́зкий/ни́зок; **of ~ stature** невысо́кого ро́ста; **the switch was very ~ down** выключа́тель был располо́жен о́чень ни́зко; **~ gear** пе́рвая ско́рость; **the sun was ~ in the sky** со́лнце стоя́ло ни́зко (над горизо́нтом); **~ pressure/voltage** ни́зкое давле́ние/напряже́ние; **~ blood pressure** пони́женное кровяно́е давле́ние; **~ tide, water** ма́лая вода́, отли́в; **at ~ tide, water** во вре́мя отли́ва; **~ visibility** пони́женная/плоха́я/сла́бая ви́димость; (*geog.*, **~-lying**) ни́зкий, ни́зменный; **Low Countries** Нидерла́нды, Бе́льгия и Люксембу́рг; (*of pitch of sound*) ни́зкий; **in a ~ key** (*fig.*) приглушённо, сде́ржанно, без шу́ма; (*of volume of sound*) негро́мкий, ти́хий; **he spoke in a ~ voice** он говори́л, пони́зив го́лос (*or* ти́хим го́лосом); **keep a ~ profile** вести́ себя́ сде́ржанно; **I have a ~ opinion of him** я невысо́кого/нева́жного мне́ния о нём; **~ birth** ни́зкое происхожде́ние. **2** (*vulgar, common*): **~ life** жизнь низо́в; **~ Latin** вульга́рная латы́нь; **a ~ style** вульга́рный стиль; **~ comedy** ни́зкая коме́дия; фарс. **3** (*base*) ни́зкий, по́длый; **a ~ trick** по́длая уло́вка; **~ cunning** ни́зкое кова́рство. **4** (*nearly empty; scanty*): **the river is ~** река́ мелка́/обмеле́ла; **a ~ attendance** ма́лая/плоха́я посеща́емость; **we are getting ~ on sugar** у нас остаётся малова́то са́хару. **5** (*poor, depressed*): **in ~ spirits** в пода́вленном настрое́нии; **I was feeling ~** я чу́вствовал себя́ нева́жно.

● *adv.* ни́зко; **bow ~** отве́сить (*pf.*) ни́зкий покло́н; ни́зко кла́няться, поклони́ться; **lay ~** (*fig.*) низв|ерга́ть, -е́ргнуть; **lie ~** (*fig.*) зата́|иваться, -и́ться; **stocks are running ~** запа́сы конча́ются; **sink ~** опус|ка́ться, -ти́ться; **sink ~ in the water** глубоко́ погру|жа́ться, -зи́ться в во́ду; **he sank ~ in my esteem** он ни́зко пал в мои́х глаза́х; **I didn't think he would stoop so ~** я не ожида́л, что он падёт так ни́зко.

● *cpds.* **~-alcohol** *adj.* слабоалкого́льный; **~-born** *adj.* ни́зкого происхожде́ния; **~brow** *n.* челове́к, облада́ющий нера́звитым вку́сом; *adj.* нера́звитый, обыва́тельский; **~brow tastes** меща́нские вку́сы; **~-calorie** *adj.* малокалори́йный; **~-cut** *adj.* с

L

ни́зким/глубо́ким вы́резом; **~-down** *n.* (*information*) подного́тная (*coll.*); *adj.* по́длый, скве́рный; **~-fat** *adj.* маложи́рный; **~-frequency** *adj.* низкочасто́тный; **~-grade** *adj.* низкосо́ртный; (*of ore*) бе́дный; **~-key** *adj.* (*fig.*) сде́ржанный; **~land** *n.* (*usu. pl.*) ни́зменность, низи́на; *adj.* низи́нный; **~-lying** *adj.* ни́зменный; **~-lying areas** ни́зменности (*f. pl.*); **~-necked** *adj.* с ни́зким/глубо́ким вы́резом; **~-paid** *adj.* малоопла́чиваемый; **~-pitched** *adj.* (*of sound*) ни́зкий; ни́зкого то́на; (*of roof*) поло́гий; **~-powered** *adj.* маломо́щный; **~-profile** *adj.* сде́ржанный; ти́хий; **~-spirited** *adj.* уны́лый, пода́вленный; **~-water** *adj.*: **~-water mark** отме́тка у́ровня ни́зкой воды́.

low² /ləʊ/ *v.i.* (*of cattle*) мыча́ть, за-.

lower¹ /ˈləʊə(r)/ *adj.* ни́жний; **~ case** (*typ.*) строчны́е бу́квы (*f. pl.*); **the L~ Chamber, House** ни́жняя пала́та; пала́та о́бщин; **~ deck** ни́жняя па́луба; **on a ~ floor** (этажо́м) ни́же; **the ~ orders** ни́зшие сосло́вия; **~ reaches** (*of a river*) низо́вь|е, -я; **the ~ regions** (*hell*) преиспо́дняя; **~ school** (*Br.*) мла́дшие кла́ссы; пе́рвая ступе́нь.

● *v.t.* **1** (*e.g. boat, flag*) спус|ка́ть, -ти́ть; (*eyes*) опус|ка́ть, -ти́ть; пот|упля́ть, -у́пить; (*price*) сн|ижа́ть, -и́зить; (*voice*) пон|ижа́ть, -и́зить. **2** (*decrease*) ум|еньша́ть, -е́ньшить. **3** (*debase*) ун|ижа́ть, -и́зить.

● *cpd.* **~-class** *adj.* принадлежа́щий к ни́зшему сосло́вию.

lower² /ˈlaʊə(r)/ = **lour**

lowermost /ˈləʊəməʊst/ *adj.* нижа́йший; (са́мый) ни́жний.

lowlander /ˈləʊləndə(r)/ *n.* жи́тель (шотла́ндских) низи́н.

lowliness /ˈləʊlɪnɪs/ *n.* скро́мность, непритяза́тельность.

lowly /ˈləʊlɪ/ *adj.* (**lowlier, lowliest**) (*humble*) скро́мный; (*primitive*) ни́зший.

loyal /ˈlɔɪəl/ *adj.* (*faithful*) ве́рный; **he is ~ to his comrades** он ве́рен това́рищам; (*devoted*) пре́данный; **a ~ wife** пре́данная жена́; **~ supporters of the local team** постоя́нные боле́льщики ме́стной кома́нды; (*pol., supporting established authority*) верноподданный, лоя́льный.

loyalist /ˈlɔɪəlɪst/ *n.* лояли́ст (*fem.* -ка).

loyalty /ˈlɔɪəltɪ/ *n.* ве́рность, пре́данность, лоя́льность; **political ~** полити́ческая благонадёжность.

lozenge /ˈlɒzɪndʒ/ *n.* (*shape*) ромб; (*pastille*) табле́тка, лепёшка, пасти́лка.

● *cpd.* **~-shaped** *adj.* ромбови́дный.

LP (*abbr. of* ***long-playing record***) долгоигра́ющая пласти́нка.

LSD *abbr. of* **1** (*Br.*) ***pounds, shillings and pence*** де́н|ьги (*pl., g.* -ег). **2** (*pharm.*) ***lysergic acid diethylamide*** ЛСД (диэтилами́д лизерги́новой кислоты́).

Lt /lefˈtenənt/ *n.* (*abbr. of* ***Lieutenant***) л-т (лейтена́нт).

Ltd. /ˈlɪmɪtɪd/ *adj.* (*Br., comm., abbr. of* ***limited liability company***) ООО (о́бщество с ограни́ченной отве́тственностью).

lubricant /ˈlu:brɪkənt/ *n.* сма́зка, мазь.

lubricat|e /ˈlu:brɪˌkeɪt/ *v.t.* сма́з|ывать, -ать; **~ing oil** сма́зочное ма́сло.

lubrication /ˌlu:brɪˈkeɪʃ(ə)n/ *n.* сма́зывание.

lubricator /ˈlu:brɪˌkeɪtə(r)/ *n.* (*oil*) сма́зка; (*machine component*) лубрика́тор.

lubricious /lu:ˈbrɪʃəs/ *adj.* (*lewd*) похотли́вый.

lubricity /lu:ˈbrɪsɪtɪ/ *n.* похотли́вость.

lucerne /lu:ˈsɜ:n/ *n.* люце́рна.

lucid /ˈlu:sɪd/ *adj.* я́сный; **he has a ~ mind** у него́ я́сная голова́; **a ~ interval** све́тлый промежу́ток; про́блеск созна́ния.

lucidity /ˌlu:ˈsɪdɪtɪ/ *n.* я́сность.

luck /lʌk/ *n.*: **good/bad ~** сча́стье/несча́стье; везе́ние/невезе́ние; уда́ча/неуда́ча; **good ~!; the best of ~!** жела́ю сча́стья/уда́чи/успе́ха!; **... and good ~ to him** ...дай ему́ Бог; **bad, hard ~!** не повезло́!; **what rotten ~!** како́е невезе́ние!; **worse ~!** к несча́стью/сожале́нию; **no such ~!** увы́, нет; **as ~ would have it** по/к сча́стью; (*unfortunately*) по/к несча́стью; как назло́; (*in neutral sense*) получи́лось так, что...; **it was just a matter of ~** э́то был вопро́с везе́ния; **just my ~!** тако́е уж у меня́ везе́ние!; **I had the (good) ~ to be selected** мне посчастли́вилось попа́сть в число́ и́збранных; **he had the bad ~ to break his leg** как на грех, он слома́л себе́ но́гу; **we're in ~** нам везёт; **we're out of ~** (нам) не везёт; **he's down on his ~** ему́ не везёт; **it was a great piece of ~** э́то была́ больша́я/ре́дкая уда́ча; **I did it by sheer ~** мне про́сто повезло́; **a run of (bad) ~** полоса́ (не)везе́ния; **his ~ is in** ему́ везёт; **try one's ~** пыта́ть, по- сча́стья; **push one's ~** искуша́ть (*impf.*) судьбу́; **you never know your ~** как знать, вдруг да и посчастли́вится; **he wears a mascot for ~** он но́сит талисма́н на сча́стье.

luckily /ˈlʌkɪlɪ/ *adv.* к сча́стью.

luckless /ˈlʌklɪs/ *adj.* несчастли́вый, незада́чливый.

lucky /ˈlʌkɪ/ *adj.* (**luckier, luckiest**) **1** (*of person*) счастли́вый, уда́чливый; (*of things, actions, events*) уда́чный; **a ~ person** счастли́вец, уда́чник; **~ dog, beggar** счастли́вчик; **he's ~ in everything** ему́ во всём везёт; **he's ~ in business** он уда́члив в дела́х; **~ for you he's not here** ва́ше сча́стье, что его́ здесь нет; **you're ~ to be alive** скажи́ спаси́бо, что оста́лся в живы́х; **a ~ shot** уда́чный вы́стрел; (*fig., guess*) счастли́вая дога́дка; ≈ попа́л в то́чку. **2** (*bringing luck*): **a ~ charm** счастли́вый талисма́н.

lucrative /ˈlu:krətɪv/ *adj.* (*profitable*) при́быльный; (*remunerative*) дохо́дный.

lucre /ˈlu:kə(r)/ *n.* при́быль, нажи́ва; **filthy ~** презре́нный мета́лл.

ludicrous /ˈlu:dɪkrəs/ *adj.* (*absurd*) неле́пый; (*laughable*) смехотво́рный, смешно́й.

lug¹ /lʌg/ *n.* (*projection*) ушко́; (*sl., ear*) у́хо.

lug² /lʌg/ *v.t.* (**lugged, lugging**) (*coll.*) волочи́ть (*impf.*); тащи́ть (*impf.*).

luggage /ˈlʌgɪdʒ/ *n.* бага́ж; **piece of ~** вещь, ме́сто; **left ~ office** (*Br.*) ка́мера хране́ния.

● *cpds.* **~-carrier** *n.* (*e.g. on bicycle*) бага́жник; **~-label** *n.* бага́жный ярлы́к; **~-rack** *n.* (*in train*) се́тка/по́лка для багажа́; **~-trolley** *n.* бага́жная теле́жка; **~-van** *n.* (*Br.*) бага́жный ваго́н.

lugubrious /lu:ˈgu:brɪəs/, /lʊ-/ *adj.* (*mournful*) ско́рбный; (*dismal*) мра́чный.

lugubriousness /lu:ˈgu:brɪəsnɪs/, /lʊ-/ *n.* мра́чность.

lugworm /ˈlʌgwɜ:m/ *n.* (*zool.*) пескожи́л.

lukewarm /lu:kˈwɔ:m/, /ˈlu:k-/ *adj.* теплова́тый, чуть тёплый; (*fig., indifferent*) прохла́дный.

lull /lʌl/ *n.* (*in storm, fighting etc.*) зати́шье; (*in conversation*) па́уза, переры́в.

● *v.t.* (**~ to sleep**) убаю́к|ивать, -ать; (*allay*) усып|ля́ть, -и́ть; рассе́|ивать, -ять.

lullaby /ˈlʌləˌbaɪ/ *n.* колыбе́льная (пе́сня).

lumbago /lʌmˈbeɪgəʊ/ *n.* люмба́го (*indecl.*); простре́л.

lumbar /ˈlʌmbə(r)/ *adj.* поясни́чный.

lumber¹ /ˈlʌmbə(r)/ *n.* (*Br., disused furniture etc.*) ру́хлядь, хлам; (*US, timber*) пиломатериа́лы (*m. pl.*).

● *v.t.* (*fill, obstruct, make untidy with ~*) зава́л|ивать, -и́ть (*что чем*); (*Br., encumber*) обременя́ть (*impf.*); **I'm ~ed with my mother-in-law** тёща у меня́ на ше́е.

● *v.i.* (*work on tree-felling etc.*) руби́ть/вали́ть (*impf.*) дере́вья; распи́ливать/загота́вливать (*impf.*) лес.

● *cpds.* **~jack, ~man** *nn.* лесору́б; **~-jacket** *n.* (коро́ткая) рабо́чая ку́ртка; **~-mill** *n.* (*US*) лесопи́льный заво́д; **~-room** *n.* (*Br.*) чула́н; **~-yard** *n.* (*US*) склад пиломатериа́лов.

lumber² /ˈlʌmbə(r)/ *v.i.* (*also* **~ along**) дви́гаться (*impf.*) тяжело́; перева́ливаться (*impf.*).

lumbering¹ /ˈlʌmbərɪŋ/ *n.* (*US, tree-felling*) лесозаготовки (*f. pl.*).

lumbering² /ˈlʌmbərɪŋ/ *adj.* (*of person*) дви́гающийся тяжело́/неуклю́же; (*of cart etc.*) громыха́ющий.

luminary /ˈlu:mɪnərɪ/, /ˈlju:-/ *n.* (*lit., fig.*) свети́ло.

luminescence /ˌlu:mɪˈnes(ə)ns/, /ˌlju:-/ *n.* свече́ние, люминесце́нция.

luminescent /ˌlu:mɪˈnes(ə)nt/, /ˌlju:-/ *adj.* светя́щийся, люминесце́нтный.

luminosity /ˌlu:mɪ'nɒsɪtɪ/, /ˌlju:-/ *n.* освещённость, яркость.

luminous /'lu:mɪnəs/, /'lju:-/ *adj.* светя́щийся; (*bright*) све́тлый, я́ркий.

lumme /'lʌmɪ/ *int.* (*Br. coll.*) Бо́же мой!

lump /lʌmp/ *n.* **1** (*of earth, dough etc.*) ком; **~ of clay** ком гли́ны; (*large piece*) (кру́пный) кусо́к; **~ of sugar** кусо́к са́хара; **~ sugar** пилёный/кусково́й са́хар; **~ of ice/snow** глы́ба льда/ сне́га; **~ of wood** чурба́н; **~ in the throat** комо́к в го́рле.
2 (*swelling*) ши́шка, о́пухоль.
3 (*coll., person*) дуби́на (*c.g.*).
4: **~ sum** пауша́льная су́мма; единовре́менная пла́та; **they get paid a ~ sum** им пла́тят акко́рдно.
● *v.t.* **1**: **~ together** (*collect into heap*) вали́ть (*impf.*), сва́л|ивать, -и́ть в ку́чу; (*treat alike; place in single category*) ста́вить (*impf.*) на одну́ до́ску; **the passengers were ~ed in with the crew** пассажи́ров помести́ли вме́сте с экипа́жем.
2: **~ it** (*coll., put up with it*) примири́ться (*pf.*) (*с чем*); **you must ~ it** нра́вится — не нра́вится, а придётся проглоти́ть.
● *cpd.* **~-fish** *n.* морско́й воробе́й.

lumpish /'lʌmpɪʃ/ *adj.* неуклю́жий.

lumpy /'lʌmpɪ/ *adj.* (**lumpier, lumpiest**) комкова́тый.

lunacy /'lu:nəsɪ/ *n.* безу́мие.

lunar /'lu:nə(r)/, /'lju:-/ *adj.* лу́нный; **~ rover** лунохо́д.

lunatic /'lu:nətɪk/ *n.* сумасше́дший; душевнобольно́й.
● *adj.* (*mad*) сумасше́дший; **~ asylum** сумасше́дший дом; психиатри́ческая больни́ца; (*foolish, senseless*) безу́мный; (*eccentric*) чуда́ческий; **~ fringe** ку́чка фана́тиков.

lunch /lʌntʃ/ *n.* (*midday meal*) обе́д; (второ́й) за́втрак, ланч.
● *v.i.* обе́дать, по-; за́втракать, по-.
● *cpds.* **~-break, ~-hour, ~-time** *nn.* обе́денный переры́в; **~-party** *n.* зва́ный обе́д/за́втрак.

luncheon /'lʌntʃ(ə)n/ *n.* обе́д.
● *cpds.* **~-meat** *n.* мясно́й руле́т; **~-voucher** *n.* (*Br.*) тало́н на обе́д.

lung /lʌŋ/ *n.* лёгкое; **~ cancer** рак лёгк|ого, -их.

lunge¹ /lʌndʒ/ *n.* (*forward movement*) бросо́к; (*in fencing*) вы́пад.
● *v.i.* (**lungeing** *or* **lunging**): бро́ситься (*pf.*), ри́нуться (*pf.*) (**forward**: вперёд; **at**: на + *a.*); (*fencing, boxing etc.*) сде́лать (*pf.*) вы́пад (**at**: про́тив + *g.*).

lunge² /lʌndʒ/ *n.* (*rein*) ко́рда.
● *v.t.* (**lungeing**) гоня́ть (*impf.*) на ко́рде.

lupin /'lu:pɪn/ *n.* люпи́н.

lupine /'lu:paɪn/ *adj.* во́лчий.

lupus /'lu:pəs/ *n.* волча́нка; туберкулёз ко́жи.

lurch¹ /lɜ:tʃ/ *n.*: **leave s.o. in the ~** пок|ида́ть, -и́нуть кого́-н. в беде́; подв|оди́ть, -ести́ кого́-н.

lurch² /lɜ:tʃ/ *n.*: (*stagger*) **the ship gave a ~** кора́бль дал крен (*or* накрени́лся).
● *v.i.* шата́ться (*impf.*); поша́т|ываться, -ну́ться; **the drunken man ~ed across the street** пья́ный, поша́тываясь, перешёл у́лицу.

lure /ljʊə(r)/, /lʊə(r)/ *n.* (*decoy*) прима́нка; (*fig., enticement*) собла́зн; **the ~ of foreign travel** зама́нчивость загрáничных путеше́ствий.
● *v.t.* (*fish*) прима́н|ивать, -и́ть; (*persons*) зама́н|ивать, -и́ть; завл|ека́ть, -е́чь; **a rival firm ~d him away** конкури́рующая фи́рма перемани́ла его́ (к себе́); **I was ~d (on) by the promise of a reward** меня́ соблазни́ла перспекти́ва награ́ды; **they were ~d on to destruction** их замани́ли на (по)ги́бель.

lurid /'ljʊərɪd/, /'lʊə-/ *adj.* (*gaudy*) крича́щий, аляпова́тый; (*fiery, crimson*) о́гненный, багро́вый; (*sensational*) сенсацио́нный; **a ~ novel** бульва́рный рома́н; **~ details** жу́ткие подро́бности.

lurk /lɜ:k/ *v.i.* прита́|иваться, -и́ться; **~ about** ждать (*impf.*) притаи́вшись.

luscious /'lʌʃəs/ *adj.* (*succulent*) со́чный; (*ripe, also fig.*) наливно́й.

lusciousness /'lʌʃəsnɪs/ *n.* со́чность.

lush¹ /lʌʃ/ *n.* (*US, drunkard*) пьянчу́жка (*c.g.*), алка́ш (*sl.*).

lush² /lʌʃ/ *adj.* пы́шный, роско́шный.

lust /lʌst/ *n.* **1** (*sexual passion*) по́хоть, вожделе́ние. **2** (*craving*): **~ for power** жа́жда вла́сти.
● *v.i.*: **~ for, after s.o.** испы́т|ывать, -а́ть вожделе́ние к кому́-н.; жела́ть (*impf.*) кого́-н.

luster /'lʌstə(r)/ (*US*) = **lustre**

lustful /'lʌstfʊl/ *adj.* похотли́вый.

lustfulness /'lʌstfʊlnɪs/ *n.* похотли́вость.

lustiness /'lʌstɪnɪs/ *n.* (*health*) здоро́вье; (*vigour*) бо́дрость.

lustre /'lʌstə(r)/ (*US* **luster**) *n.* (*glaze*) глазу́рь; (*gloss, brilliance*) блеск, гля́нец; (*bright light*) сия́ние; (*splendour, glory*) сла́ва; **add ~ to something** прид|ава́ть, -а́ть блеск чему́-н.

lustreless /'lʌstəlɪs/ (*US* **lusterless**) *adj.* ту́склый.

lustrous /'lʌstrəs/ *adj.* (*brilliant*) блестя́щий; (*glossy*) глянцеви́тый.

lusty /'lʌstɪ/ *adj.* (**lustier, lustiest**) (*healthy*) здоро́вый; (*robust*) здорове́нный; (*vigorous*) бо́дрый.

lute /lu:t/, /lju:t/ *n.* (*mus.*) лю́тня.

lutenist /'lu:tənɪst/, /'lju:-/ *n.* игра́ющий на лю́тне.

Lutheran /'lu:θərən/, /'lju:-/ *n.* лютера́н|ин (*fem.* -ка).
● *adj.* лютера́нский.

Lutheranism /'lu:θərənˌɪz(ə)m/, /'lju:-/ *n.* лютера́нство.

Luxembourg /'lʌksəmˌbɜ:g/ *n.* Люксембу́рг.
● *adj.* люксембу́ргский.

Luxembourger /'lʌksəmˌbɜ:gə(r)/ *n.* люксембу́ржец; жи́тель (*fem.* -ница) Люксембу́рга.

luxuriance /lʌg'zjʊərɪəns/, /lʌk'sj-/, /lʌg'ʒʊə-/ *n.* изоби́лие; бога́тство; пы́шность.

luxuriant /lʌg'zjʊərɪənt/, /lʌk'sj-/, /lʌg'ʒʊə-/ *adj.* (*profuse*) оби́льный; (*of imagination etc.*) бога́тый; (*splendid*) пы́шный; (*of growth*) бу́йный.

luxuriate /lʌg'zjʊərɪˌeɪt/, /lʌk'sj-/, /lʌg'ʒʊə-/ *v.i.* (*enjoy o.s.*): **~ in something** наслажда́ться (*impf.*) чем-н.

luxurious /lʌg'zjʊərɪəs/, /lʌk'sj-/, /lʌg'ʒʊə-/ *adj.* (*sumptuous*) роско́шный; (*splendid*) пы́шный; (*self-indulgent*) расточи́тельный.

luxury /'lʌkʃərɪ/ *n.* **1** (*luxuriousness*) ро́скошь; **live in the lap of ~** жить (*impf.*) в ро́скоши; (*pleasure*) удово́льствие. **2** (*object of ~*) предме́т ро́скоши; **wine is my only ~** еди́нственная ро́скошь, кото́рую я себе́ позволя́ю — э́то вино́; **~ goods** предме́ты ро́скоши; **~ apartment** роско́шная кварти́ра; но́мер-люкс.

LV /'lʌntʃ(ə)n 'vaʊtʃə(r)/ *n.* (*Br.*) (*abbr. of* ***luncheon voucher***) тало́н на обе́д.

LW (*abbr. of* **long wave**) ДВ (дли́нные во́лны).

lycée /'li:seɪ/ *n.* лице́й.

lychee /'laɪtʃɪ/, /'lɪ-/ *n.* личжи́ (*indecl.*), кита́йский крыжо́вник (*collect.*).

lych- (*also* **lich-)gate** /'lɪtʃgeɪt/ кры́тый вход на кла́дбище (*для вноса гробов*).

lye /laɪ/ *n.* щёлок.

lying¹ /'laɪɪŋ/ *n.* (*telling lies*) ложь, враньё.
● *adj.* ло́жный, лжи́вый.

lying² /'laɪɪŋ/ *n.*: **~ in state** до́ступ к те́лу имени́того поко́йника.

lymph /lɪmf/ *n.* (*physiol.*) ли́мфа.

lymphatic /lɪm'fætɪk/ *adj.* лимфати́ческий.

lynch /lɪntʃ/ *n.*: **~ law** суд/зако́н Ли́нча; самосу́д.
● *v.t.* линчева́ть (*impf., pf.*).

lynchpin /'lɪntʃpɪn/ = **linchpin**

lynx /lɪŋks/ *n.* рысь.
● *cpd.* **~-eyed** *adj.* остроглáзый.

lyre /'laɪə(r)/ *n.* ли́ра.
● *cpd.* **~-bird** *n.* пти́ца-ли́ра, лирохво́ст.

lyric /'lɪrɪk/ *n.* **1** (**~** *poem*) лири́ческое стихотворе́ние; (*pl.*) лири́ческие стихи́ (*m. pl.*); (**~** *poetry*) ли́рика.
2 (*theatr., words of song*) слова́ (*nt. pl.*)/ текст пе́сни.
● *adj.* лири́ческий; **~ writer** ли́рик; поэ́т-пе́сенник.

lyrical /'lɪrɪk(ə)l/ *adj.* лири́ческий; **he waxed ~ about, over ...** он расчу́вствовался, говоря́ о...; **he was ~ in his praise of the play** он с воодушевле́нием расхва́ливал пье́су.

lyricism /'lɪrɪˌsɪz(ə)m/ *n.* лири́зм.

L

Mm

m. /ˈmiːtə(r)(z)/ *n.* (*abbr. of* ***metre(s)***) м (метр).

MA (*abbr. of* ***Master of Arts***) магистр гуманита́рных нау́к.

ma /mɑː/ *n.* (*coll.*) ма́ма.

ma'am /mæm/, /mɑːm/, /məm/ *n.* суда́рыня.

mac /mæk/ (*Br. coll.*) = **mac(k)intosh**

macabre /məˈkɑːbr/ *adj.* мра́чный, жу́ткий.

macadam /məˈkædəm/ *n.* макада́м, щебёночное покры́тие.

macadamize /məˈkædəmaɪz/ *v.t.*: **~d road** доро́га с щебёночным покры́тием.

macaroni /ˌmækəˈrəʊnɪ/ *n.* макаро́н|ы (*pl.*, *g.* —).

macaroon /ˌmækəˈruːn/ *n.* минда́льное пече́нье.

macaw /məˈkɔː/ *n.* а́ра (*m. indecl.*).

mace[1] /meɪs/ *n.* (*club; staff of office*) булава́; жезл.

● *cpd.* **~-bearer** *n.* булавоно́сец, жезлоно́сец.

mace[2] /meɪs/ *n.* (*spice*) муска́т.

Macedonia /ˌmæsəˈdəʊnɪə/ *n.* Македо́ния.

Macedonian /ˌmæsəˈdəʊnɪən/ *n.* македо́н|ец (*fem.* -ка).

● *adj.* македо́нский.

macerate /ˈmæsəˌreɪt/ *v.t.* выма́чивать, вы́мочить; мацери́ровать (*impf., pf.*).

● *v.i.* выма́чиваться, вы́мочиться.

maceration /ˌmæsəˈreɪʃ(ə)n/ *n.* выма́чивание, мацера́ция.

machete /məˈtʃetɪ/, /məˈʃetɪ/ *n.* маче́те (*indecl.*).

Machiavellian /ˌmækɪəˈvelɪən/ *adj.* макиаве́ллевский.

machination /ˌmækɪˈneɪʃ(ə)n/, /ˌmæʃ-/ *n.* (*usu. pl.*) махина́ции; ко́зни (*f. pl.*); интри́га.

machine /məˈʃiːn/ *n.* **1** (*mechanical device, apparatus*) маши́на, механи́зм; (*vending* ~) автома́т; **the ~ age** век маши́н/те́хники; **~ translation** маши́нный перево́д; **~ shop** механи́ческий цех; (**~**-*tool*) стано́к; **grinding ~** шлифова́льный стано́к.
2 (*means of transport*) маши́на.
3 (*controlling organization*) аппара́т; **party ~** парти́йный аппара́т.

● *v.t.* (*on lathe etc.*) обраба́|тывать, -о́тать (на станке́ *or* механи́ческим спо́собом); (*Br., on sewing*-~) шить, с- на маши́не.

● *cpds.* **~ code** *n.* маши́нный код; **~-gun** *n.* пулемёт; **~-gun fire** пулемётный ого́нь; *v.t.* (*fire at*) обстре́л|ивать, -я́ть; (*shoot down*) расстре́л|ивать, -я́ть; **~-gunner** *n.* пулемётчик; **~ language** *n.* маши́нный язы́к; **~-made** *adj.*: **~-made goods** това́р фабри́чного произво́дства; **~-minder** *n.* рабо́чий у станка́; **~operator** *n.* (*agric.*) механиза́тор; **~-readable** *adj.* (*comput.*) машиночита́емый.

machinery /məˈʃiːnərɪ/ *n.* (*collect., machines*) маши́ны (*f. pl.*), те́хника; (*mechanism*) механи́зм; (*fig.*): **the ~ of government** прави́тельственные структу́ры (*f. pl.*).

machinist /məˈʃiːnɪst/ *n.* машини́ст; (*Br., sewing-machine operator*) шве́йник, (*fem.*) швея́.

mack /mæk/ (*coll.*) = **mac(k)intosh**

mackerel /ˈmækr(ə)l/ *n.* (*pl.* ~ *or* **~s**) макре́ль, ску́мбрия; **~ sky** не́бо в бара́шках.

mac(k)intosh /ˈmækɪnˌtɒʃ/ *n.* (*Br.*) непромока́емый плащ, дождеви́к, макинто́ш.

macramé /məˈkrɑːmɪ/ *n.* макраме́ (*indecl.*).

macro /ˈmækrəʊ/ *n.* (*pl.* **~s**) (*comput.*) макрокома́нда.

macrocosm /ˈmækrəʊˌkɒz(ə)m/ *n.* макроко́см(ос).

macroeconomic /ˌmækrəʊˌiːkəˈnɒmɪk/, /-ˌekəˈnɒmɪk/ *adj.* макроэкономи́ческий.

macroeconomics /ˌmækrəʊˌiːkəˈnɒmɪks/, /-ˌekəˈnɒmɪks/ *n.* макроэконо́мика.

mad /mæd/ *adj.* (**madder, maddest**) **1** (*insane*) сумасше́дший; **he is as ~ as a hatter** он соверше́нно сумасше́дший; **go ~** сходи́ть, сойти́ с ума́; **drive s.o. ~** св|оди́ть, -ести́ кого́-н. с ума́; **this is bureaucracy gone ~** э́то бюрокра́тия, доведённая до безу́мия.
2 (*of animals*) бе́шеный; **~ cow disease** боле́знь «бе́шеной коро́вы».
3 (*wildly foolish*) шально́й; **a ~ escapade** безрассу́дная вы́ходка; **that was a ~ thing to do** поступи́ть так бы́ло про́сто безу́мием; **~ly in love** безу́мно влюблённый; **~ly expensive** безу́мно дорого́й.
4 (*coll., angry, annoyed*) серди́тый; **be, get ~** вы́йти (*pf.*) из себя́; **I was ~ at missing the train** я был вне себя́ из-за того́, что опозда́л на по́езд; **be, get ~ with s.o.** серди́ться, рас- на кого́-н.; **she was ~ with me for breaking the vase** она́ разозли́лась на меня́ за то, что я разби́л ва́зу.
5: **~ about** (*infatuated with, enthusiastic for*) в восто́рге (*or* без па́мяти) от + *g.*; **she was ~ about him** она́ была́ от него́ без ума́; **the boy is ~ about ice-cream** ма́льчик обожа́ет моро́женое; **his wife was ~ about cats** его́ жена́ была́ поме́шана на ко́шках.
6: **like ~** безу́держно; **I rushed like ~** я помча́лся как угоре́лый; **he is working like ~** он рабо́тает как одержи́мый; **he drove like ~** он е́хал с бе́шеной ско́ростью.

● *cpds.* **~cap** *n.* сорвиголова́ (*c.g.*); *adj.* сумасбро́дный; **~house** *n.* сумасше́дший дом; **~man** *n.* сумасше́дший; **~woman** *n.* сумасше́дшая.

Madagascar /ˌmædəˈgæskə(r)/ *n.* Мадагаска́р.

madam /ˈmædəm/ *n.* (*form of address*) мада́м, суда́рыня; (*coll., brothel-keeper*) мада́м.

madden /ˈmæd(ə)n/ *v.t.* (*persons*) раздраж|а́ть, -и́ть; (*animals*) беси́ть, вз-.

maddening /ˈmædənɪŋ/ *adj.* несно́сный.

madder /ˈmædə(r)/ *n.* (*plant*) маре́на; (*dye*) маре́новый краси́тель, крапп.

made /meɪd/ *past and p.p. of* ⇒**make**

Madeira /məˈdɪərə/ *n.* Мадéйра; (*wine*) мадéра.

made-to-measure /ˈmeɪdtəˈmeʒə(r)/ *adj.* (*Br.*) сдéланный (как) на закáз.

madness /ˈmædnɪs/ *n.* (*insanity*) сумасшéствие; (*of animals*) бéшенство; (*folly*) безýмие.

madonna /məˈdɒnə/ *n.* мадóнна; **~ lily** бéлая лúлия.

Madrid /məˈdrɪd/ *n.* Мадрúд.

madrigal /ˈmædrɪg(ə)l/ *n.* мадригáл.

maelstrom /ˈmeɪlstrəm/ *n.* водоворóт; (*fig.*) вихрь (*m.*).

maestro /ˈmaɪstrəʊ/ *n.* (*pl.* **maestri** /-strɪ/ *or* **~s**) маэ́стро (*m. indecl.*).

Mafia /ˈmæfɪə/, /ˈmɑ:-/ *n.* мáфия; (*fig.*) клúка.

Mafio|so /ˌmæfɪˈəʊsəʊ/, /-zəʊ/ *n.* (*pl.* **~si** /-sɪ/, /-zɪ/) мафиóзи, мафиóзо (*both indecl.*).

magazine¹ /ˌmægəˈzi:n/ *n.* **1** (*mil. store*) склад боеприпáсов. **2** (*cartridge chamber*) магазúн; (*attr.*) магазúнный.

magazine² /ˌmægəˈzi:n/ *n.* (*periodical*) журнáл; (*TV, radio*) тележурнáл, радиожурнáл; (*attr.*) журнáльный.

magenta /məˈdʒentə/ *n.* фуксúн.

● *adj.* красновáто-лилóвого цвéта.

maggot /ˈmægət/ *n.* личúнка.

maggoty /ˈmægətɪ/ *adj.* червúвый.

Magi /ˈmeɪdʒaɪ/ *n.*: **the ~** волхвы́ (*m. pl.*); **Adoration of the ~** поклонéние волхвóв.

magic /ˈmædʒɪk/ *n.* (*lit., fig.*) мáгия, волшебствó; **as if by ~** как по волшебствý.

● *adj.* волшéбный, магúческий; **~ lantern** волшéбный фонáрь; **~ wand** волшéбная пáлочка.

magical /ˈmædʒɪk(ə)l/ *adj.* феерúческий, волшéбный.

magician /məˈdʒɪʃ(ə)n/ *n.* (*sorcerer*) волшéбник; (*conjurer*) фóкусник.

magisterial /ˌmædʒɪˈstɪərɪəl/ *adj.* (*of a magistrate*) судéйский; (*authoritative*) авторитéтный.

magistracy /ˈmædʒɪstrəsɪ/, **magistrature** /ˈmædʒɪstrəˌtjʊə(r)/ *nn.* магистратýра, мировы́е сýдьи.

magistrate /ˈmædʒɪstrət/ *n.* судья́ (*m.*) (нúзшей инстáнции), мировóй судья́.

Magna Carta /ˌmægnə ˈkɑ:tə/ *n.* Велúкая хáртия вóльностей.

magnanimity /ˌmægnəˈnɪmɪtɪ/ *n.* великодýшие.

magnanimous /mægˈnænɪməs/ *adj.* великодýшный.

magnate /ˈmægneɪt/, /-nɪt/ *n.* магнáт.

magnesia /mægˈni:ʒə/, /-ʃə/, /-zjə/ *n.* магнéзия, óкись мáгния.

magnesium /mægˈni:zɪəm/ *n.* мáгний.

magnet /ˈmægnɪt/ *n.* (*lit., fig.*) магнúт.

magnetic /mægˈnetɪk/ *adj.* магнúтный; **~ tape** магнúтная лéнта, магнитолéнта; (*fig.*): **~ personality** притягáтельная/магнетúческая лúчность.

magnetism /ˈmægnɪˌtɪz(ə)m/ *n.* магнетúзм; (*fig.*) притягáтельность.

magnetization /ˌmægnɪtaɪˈzeɪʃ(ə)n/ *n.* (*process*) намагнúчивание; (*state*) намагнúченность.

magnetize /ˈmægnɪˌtaɪz/ *v.t.* намагнú|чивать, -тить; (*fig.*) гипнотизúровать, за-.

magneto /mægˈni:təʊ/ *n.* (*pl.* **~s**) магнéто (*indecl.*).

magnification /ˌmægnɪfɪˈkeɪʃ(ə)n/ *n.* увеличéние; (*of a radio signal*) усилéние; (*exaggeration*) преувеличéние.

magnificence /mægˈnɪfɪs(ə)ns/ *n.* великолéпие.

magnificent /mægˈnɪfɪs(ə)nt/ *adj.* великолéпный.

magnify /ˈmægnɪˌfaɪ/ *v.t.* (*cause to appear larger*) увелú|чивать, -ть; **~ing-glass** увеличúтельное стеклó, лýпа; (*exaggerate*) преувелú|чивать, -ть.

magniloquence /mægˈnɪləkwəns/ *n.* высокопáрность.

magniloquent /mægˈnɪləkwənt/ *n.* высокопáрный.

magnitude /ˈmægnɪˌtju:d/ *n.* (*size*) величинá; **a star of the first ~** звездá пéрвой величины́; (*importance*) вáжность; **a matter of the first ~** дéло первостепéнной вáжности.

magnolia /mægˈnəʊlɪə/ *n.* магнóлия.

magnum /ˈmægnəm/ *n.* (*pl.* **~s**) вúнная бутыль, вмещáющая полторá лúтра.

magpie /ˈmægpaɪ/ *n.* сорóка; (*fig., collector, hoarder*) барахóльщик.

Magyar /ˈmægjɑ:(r)/ *n.* **1** (*person*) мадья́р (*fem.* -ка); венг|р (*fem.* -éрка). **2** (*language*) венгéрский язы́к.

● *adj.* мадья́рский, венгéрский.

Maharaja(h) /ˌmɑ:həˈrɑ:dʒə/ *n.* магарáджа (*m.*).

mah-jong /mɑ:ˈdʒɒŋ/ *n.* маджóнг (*китайская игра*).

mahogany /məˈhɒgənɪ/ *n.* (*wood, tree*) крáсное дéрево; (*colour*) цвет крáсного дéрева.

maid /meɪd/ *n.* **1** (*girl, unmarried woman*) дéва, девúца; **old ~** стáрая дéва; **~ of honour** (*Br.*), **honor** (*US*) фрéйлина. **2** (*domestic servant*) прислýга, домрабóтница; (*in hotel*) гóрничная.

● *cpd.* **~servant** *n.* прислýга, служáнка.

maiden /ˈmeɪd(ə)n/ *n.* дéва.

● *adj.* **1** (*of a girl*) дéвичий; **~ name** дéвичья фамúлия. **2** (*unmarried*): **~ aunt** незамýжняя тётка. **3** (*first*): **~ speech** пéрвая речь (новоúзбранного члéна парлáмента); **~ voyage** пéрвый рейс.

● *cpds.* **~hair (fern)** *n.* адиáнтум; **~head** *n.* дéвственность; **~ly** *adj.* дéвичий.

mail¹ /meɪl/ *n.* **1** (*postal system*) пóчта; **~ order** почтóвый закáз/перевóд. **2** (**~-train**) почтóвый поéзд. **3** (*letters*) пóчта, пúсьма (*nt. pl.*); **has the ~ come?** пóчта былá?; **I had a lot of ~ today** я получúл сегóдня мнóго пúсем.

● *v.t.* отпр|авля́ть, -áвить (по пóчте); **where can I ~ this letter?** где тут почтóвый я́щик?; **the firm has me on its ~ing-list** я состою́ в спúске подпúсчиков фúрмы.

● *cpds.* **~bag** *n.* мешóк для почтóвой корреспондéнции; **~box** *n.* (*US; also comput.*) почтóвый я́щик; **~-coach** *n.* почтóвая карéта; **~man** *n.* (*US*) почтальóн; **~-order** *adj.* торгýющий по почтóвым закáзам; **~-order firm** торгóво-посы́лочная фúрма; **~shot** *n.* (*Br.*) реклáма, разóсланная по пóчте; **~-van** *n.* (*Br.*) (*road*) автомобúль, собирáющий и развозя́щий пóчту; (*rail*) почтóвый вагóн.

mail² /meɪl/ *n.* (*coat of* **~**) кольчýга.

mailed /meɪld/ *adj.*: **~ fist** (*fig.*) бронирóванный кулáк.

maim /meɪm/ *v.t.* калéчить, ис-; **he was ~ed for life** он остáлся калéкой на всю жизнь.

main /meɪn/ *n.* **1**: **in the ~** в основнóм. **2**: **with might and ~** изо всех сил. **3** (*arch., sea*) (откры́тое) мóре. **4** (*sg. and* (*Br.*) *pl., principal supply line*) магистрáль; (*sewerage*) канализáция; **our house is not on the mains** к нáшему дóму не подведенá канализáция; (*water*) водопровóд; водопровóдная магистрáль; **turn the water off at the ~(s)!** перекрóйте водопровóд; (*gas*) газопровóд; (*electricity*) кáбель (*m.*); **~s supply** электроснабжéние; **the ~s voltage is 250** напряжéние электросéти 250 вольт.

● *adj.* глáвный, основнóй; **~ course** (*of meal*) основнóе блю́до; **~ line** (*rail*) железнодорóжная магистрáль; **the ~ point** основнóй/глáвный пункт, суть; **~ road** магистрáль, глáвная дорóга; **~ street** глáвная ýлица.

● *cpds.* **~brace** *n.* (*naut.*) грóта-брас; **splice the ~brace** (*coll., serve rum ration*) вы́дать (*pf.*) дополнúтельную пóрцию рóма; (*take a drink*) напúться (*pf.*); **~-deck** *n.* глáвная пáлуба; **~land** *n.* (*continent*) материк; (*opp. island*): **they live on the ~land** онú живýт на большóй землé; **~mast** *n.* грот-мáчта; **~sail** *n.* грот; **~spring** *n.* (*of watch*) ходовáя пружúна; (*fig.*) глáвная двúжущая сúла; **~stay** *n.* (*naut.*) грóта-штаг; (*fig.*) опóра; **~stream** *n.* (*fig.*) госпóдствующая тендéнция.

mainframe /ˈmeɪnfreɪm/ *adj.*: **~ computer** большáя ЭВМ.

mainly /ˈmeɪnlɪ/ *adv.* глáвным óбразом.

maintain /meɪnˈteɪn/ *v.t.* **1** (*keep up*) поддéрживать (*impf.*); (*preserve*) сохран|я́ть, -úть; (*continue*) продолжáть (*impf.*); **the pilot ~ed a constant speed** пилóт поддéрживал постоя́нную скóрость; **if prices are ~ed** éсли цéны удéржатся на прéжнем ýровне; **law and order must be ~ed** законопоря́док дóлжен соблюдáться; **he ~ed his ground** он стоя́л на своём; **he ~ed silence** он хранúл молчáние. **2** (*support*) содержáть (*impf.*); **he has a wife and child to ~** емý прихóдится

M

содержа́ть жену́ и ребёнка.
3 (*keep in repair*): **he ~s his car himself** он ремонти́рует свою́ маши́ну сам.
4 (*defend*) отст|а́ивать, -оя́ть; **he ~ed his rights** он отста́ивал свои́ права́.
5 (*assert as true*) утвержда́ть (*impf.*); **he ~ed his innocence** он наста́ивал на свое́й невино́вности.

maintenance /ˈmeɪntənəns/ *n.* **1** (*maintaining*) поддержа́ние; сохране́ние; **price ~** поддержа́ние цен. **2** (*payment in support of dependants*) содержа́ние. **3** (*care or repair of machinery etc.*) техни́ческое обслу́живание; **~ crew** ремо́нтная брига́да/кома́нда; **~ manual** руково́дство по ухо́ду и обслу́живанию.

maison(n)ette /ˌmeɪzəˈnet/ *n.* двухэта́жная кварти́ра.

maître d'hôtel /ˌmetrə dəʊˈtel/, /ˌmeɪt-/ *n.* (*pl.* ***maîtres d'hôtel*** *pronunc. same*) метрдоте́ль (*m.*).

maize /meɪz/ *n.* кукуру́за, маи́с.

Maj. /ˈmeɪdʒə(r)/ *n.* (*abbr. of* **Major(-)**) м (майо́р).

majestic /məˈdʒestɪk/ *adj.* вели́чественный.

majesty /ˈmædʒɪstɪ/ *n.* (*stateliness*) вели́чественность; (*title*): **His/Her M~** его́/её вели́чество.

majolica /məˈjɒlɪkə/, /məˈdʒɒl-/ *n.* майо́лика.

major /ˈmeɪdʒə(r)/ *n.* **1** (*rank*) майо́р. **2** (*mus.*: **~ key**) мажо́р. **3** (*US, main subject of study*) основно́й предме́т (*в колледже*).
● *adj.* **1** (*greater*) бо́льший; **the ~ part** бо́льшая часть; (*principal, more important*) гла́вный; **~ road** гла́вная доро́га; **the ~ part in a play** гла́вная роль в пье́се. **2** (*significant*) кру́пный; **a ~ success** кру́пный успе́х; **~ advances in science** кру́пные/значи́тельные успе́хи в нау́ке; **a ~ operation** кру́пная опера́ция; **a ~ war** больша́я война́. **3** (*Br., elder*): **Smith M~** Смит ста́рший. **4** (*mus.*) мажо́рный; **~ key** мажо́рная тона́льность; **~ third** больша́я те́рция.
● *v.i.*: **he ~ed in physics** (*US*) он специализи́ровался в фи́зике.
● *cpds.* **~-domo** *n.* мажордо́м; **~-general** *n.* генера́л-майо́р.

Majorca /məˈjɔːkə/, /-ˈdʒɔː-/ *n.* Мальо́рка, Майо́рка.

majority /məˈdʒɒrɪtɪ/ *n.* **1** (*greater part or number*) бо́льшая часть; большинство́; (*in elections etc.*): **absolute ~** абсолю́тное большинство́; **they gained a ~ of 30** они́ получи́ли на 30 голосо́в бо́льше; **the government has a ~ of 60** у прави́тельства — большинство́ в (*or* на) 60 голосо́в бо́льше, чем у оппози́ции; **he won by a large ~** он победи́л значи́тельным большинство́м (голосо́в); **~ verdict** пригово́р, за кото́рый проголосова́ло бо́льше полови́ны прися́жных заседа́телей. **2** (*full age*) совершеннолéтие; **when will he attain his ~?** когда́ он дости́гнет совершенноле́тия?

make /meɪk/ *n.* (*product of particular firm or person*): **a good ~ of car** автомоби́ль хоро́шей ма́рки.
● *v.t.* (*past and p.p.* **made**) **1** (*fashion, create, construct*) де́лать, с-; (*build*) стро́ить, по-; **what is this made of?** из чего́ э́то сде́лано?; **you must think I'm made of money** вы, наве́рно, ду́маете, что я де́нежный мешо́к; **this chair is made to last** э́тот стул сде́лан про́чно/добро́тно; **they were made for each other** они́ бы́ли со́зданы друг для дру́га.
2 (*sew together*) шить, с-; **a suit made to order** костю́м, сши́тый на зака́з.
3 (*utter*) произн|оси́ть, -ести́; **he made a speech** он произнёс речь; он вы́ступил с ре́чью; **she made a remark** она́ сде́лала замеча́ние; **don't ~ a noise** не шуми́те; соблюда́йте тишину́.
4 (*compile, compose*) сост|авля́ть, -а́вить; **~ a list!** соста́вьте спи́сок!; **have you made your will?** вы соста́вили завеща́ние?
5 (*bodily movements, etc.: execute*) де́лать, с-; *see also under n. obj.*
6 (*manufacture, produce*) изгот|овля́ть, -о́вить; произв|оди́ть, -ести́; **the factory ~s shoes** заво́д изготовля́ет о́бувь; **paper is made here** здесь произво́дится бума́га; **he made a good impression** он произвёл хоро́шее впечатле́ние; **he made a sketch** он сде́лал рису́нок/набро́сок; **~ a film** сн|има́ть, -ять фильм.
7 (*prepare*) гото́вить, при-; вари́ть, с-; **she made breakfast** она́ пригото́вила за́втрак; **is the coffee made?** ко́фе гото́в?; **~ a fire** разв|оди́ть, -ести́ ого́нь; **~ a bed** (*prepare it for sleeping*) стлать, по- (*or* стели́ть, по-) посте́ль; (*tidy it after use*) уб|ира́ть, -ра́ть посте́ль.
8 (*establish, create*): **~ a rule** устан|а́вливать, -ови́ть пра́вило; **he ~s a rule of going to bed early** он взял (себе́) за пра́вило ложи́ться ра́но.
9 (*equal, result in*) равня́ться (*impf.*) + *d.*; **four plus two ~s six** четы́ре плюс два равня́ется шести́; **it ~s no difference** всё равно́; **this book ~s pleasant reading** э́ту кни́гу чита́ешь с удово́льствием; (*constitute*) **he ~s a good chairman** он хоро́ший председа́тель; **it ~s (good) sense** э́то разу́мно; (*become, turn out to be*): **she will ~ a good pianist** из неё вы́йдет хоро́шая пиани́стка.
10 (*construe, understand*) пон|има́ть, -я́ть; **can you ~ anything of it?** вы что́-нибудь тут понима́ете?; **what do you ~ of this sentence?** как вы понима́ете э́то предложе́ние?; (*estimate, consider to be*): **what do you ~ the time?** кото́рый час на ва́ших часа́х?
11: **~ much of**: **he has not made much of his opportunities** он ма́ло испо́льзовал свои́ возмо́жности; **the author ~s much of his childhood** а́втор придаёт большо́е значе́ние своему́ де́тству; **~ little of** не придава́ть (*impf.*) большо́го значе́ния + *d.*; (*minimize*) преум|еньша́ть, -е́ньшить; **~ the best of** испо́льзовать наилу́чшим о́бразом; **~ the best of a bad job** де́лать, с- хоро́шую ми́ну при плохо́й игре́; **~ the most of** испо́льзовать (*impf., pf.*) максима́льно; **you only have a week, so ~ the most of it** у вас всего́ неде́ля, так что проведи́те её с максима́льной по́льзой.
12 (*reach*) дост|ига́ть, -и́чь + *g.*; **we made the bridge by dusk** мы добра́лись до моста́, когда́ ста́ло смерка́ться; **we just made the train** мы е́ле поспе́ли на по́езд; **he made it** (*succeeded*) **after three years** он дости́г успе́ха че́рез три го́да; (*gain*) получ|а́ть, -и́ть; **he made a clear profit** он получи́л чи́стую при́быль; (*earn*) зараб|а́тывать, -о́тать; **he ~s a good living** он хорошо́ зараба́тывает; (*ensure*) обеспе́чи|вать, -ть; **this success made his career** э́тот успе́х обеспе́чил ему́ карье́ру; **he's got it made (for him)** (*coll.*) ему́ обеспе́чен успе́х.
13 (*cause to be*) де́лать, с- + *a. and i.*; **the rain ~s the road slippery** от дождя́ доро́га де́лается ско́льзкой; **she made his life miserable** она́ отрави́ла ему́ жизнь; **~ s.o. angry** серди́ть, рас- кого́-н.; (*appoint, elect*): **I made him my helper** я сде́лал его́ свои́м помо́щником; **they made him a general** его́ произвели́ в генера́лы; **they made him chairman** его́ вы́брали председа́телем.
14 (*compel, cause to*) заст|авля́ть, -а́вить; побу|жда́ть, -ди́ть; **he made them suffer for it** за э́то он им отплати́л; **he was made to kneel** его́ заста́вили стать на коле́ни; **I'll ~ you pay for this!** вы у меня́ за э́то запла́тите!; **don't ~ me laugh!** не смеши́те меня́!; **the book made me laugh, but it made her cry** меня́ кни́га рассмеши́ла, а её расстро́гала до слёз; **it ~s you think** э́то заставля́ет заду́маться; **look what you made me do!** ≈ всё из-за вас!; смотри́, до чего́ ты меня́ довёл!; **she made believe she was crying** она́ сде́лала вид, бу́дто пла́чет; **~ something do, ~ do with something** об|ходи́ться, -ойти́сь с чем-н.; **we must ~ do on our pension** мы должны́ обойти́сь одно́й пе́нсией; **can you ~ do without coal for another week?** мо́жете ли вы обойти́сь ещё одну́ неде́лю без угля́?
● *v.i.* (*past and p.p.* **made**) **1** (*with certain preps.: move, proceed*): **~ after** пус|ка́ться, -ти́ться в пого́ню (*or* вслед) за + *i.*; **~ for** (*head towards*) напр|авля́ться, -а́виться на + *a. or* к + *d.*; (*assail*) кида́ться, ки́нуться на + *a.*; (*conduce to*) спосо́бствовать (*impf.*) + *d.*; **~ with** (*US coll., hurry up, get on*): **~ with the drinks!** неси́те скоре́е напи́тки!
2 (*act, behave*): **he made as if to go** он сде́лал вид, что хо́чет уйти́; **may I ~ so bold as to come in?** позво́льте мне взять на себя́ сме́лость войти́.
3 (**~** *a profit*): **did you ~ on the deal?** ну как, получи́ли при́быль на э́той сде́лке? (*coll.*).

● *with advs.*: **~ away** *v.i.* = **~ off; ~ away with** (*get rid of*) изб|авля́ться, -а́виться от + *g.*; (*kill*) прик|а́нчивать, -о́нчить; **~ away with o.s.** (*or* **one's life**) поко́нчить (*pf.*) с собо́й; **~ off** *v.i.* (*hurry away*) сбе|га́ть, -жа́ть; **he made off with all speed** он пусти́лся бежа́ть со всех ног; (*escape, abscond*) скр|ыва́ться, -ы́ться; **the thieves made off with the jewellery** во́ры скры́лись, захвати́в с собо́й драгоце́нности; **~ out** *v.t.* (*write out*): **~ out a bill/cheque** (*Br.*), **check** (*US*) выпи́сывать, вы́писать счёт/чек; **~ out a report** сост|авля́ть, -а́вить отчёт; (*assert, maintain*) утвержда́ть (*impf.*); **they ~ out he was drunk** они́ утвержда́ют, что он был пьян; **you ~ me out to be a liar** по-ва́шему выхо́дит, что я лгу; (*conclude*): **how do you ~ that out?** как э́то у вас получа́ется?; (*argue*): **he made out a good case for it** он привёл ве́ские до́воды в по́льзу э́того; (*understand*) раз|бира́ться, -обра́ться в + *p.*; **I can't ~ him out** я не могу́ его́ поня́ть; (*discern, distinguish*) различ|а́ть, -и́ть; *v.i.* (*coll., get on*): **how did he ~ out?** как он спра́вился (с э́той зада́чей)?; **~ over** *v.t.* (*refashion*) переде́л|ывать, -ать; (*transfer*) перев|оди́ть, -ести́; **he made the money over to me** он перевёл де́ньги на моё и́мя; **~ up** *v.t.* (*complete*): **~ up the complement** сост|авля́ть, -а́вить кома́нду, гру́ппу *и т.п.*; (*pay; pay the residue of*) допла́|чивать, -ти́ть; **I shall ~ up the difference out of my own pocket** я доплачу́ ра́зницу из своего́ карма́на; (*repay*) возме|ща́ть, -сти́ть; **we must ~ it up to him somehow** мы должны́ ка́к-то возмести́ть ему́ э́то; (*recover*) навёрст|ывать, -а́ть; (*fig.*): **he quickly made up leeway in his studies** он бы́стро ликвиди́ровал отстава́ние в свои́х заня́тиях; **he made up his losses in a single night** он возмести́л свои́ убы́тки за одну́ ночь; (*prepare, ~ ready*) гото́вить, при-/из-; **ask the chemist to ~ up this prescription** попроси́те фармаце́вта пригото́вить лека́рство по э́тому реце́пту; **~ up a bed** заст|ила́ть, -ла́ть (*or* -ели́ть) посте́ль; **~ up a road** асфальти́ровать (*impf., pf.*) доро́гу; **we ~ up the fire before going to bed** пе́ред сном мы разжига́ем ками́н; (*arrange type*) верста́ть, с-; (*sew together*) шить, с-; (*fig.*): **~ up one's mind** реш|а́ть, -и́ть; **my mind is made up** я при́нял реше́ние; **~ up your mind!** реша́йтесь на что́-нибудь!; (*form, compose; compile*) сост|авля́ть, -а́вить; **life is made up of disappointments** жизнь полна́ разочарова́ний; (*concoct, invent*) выду́мывать, вы́думать; сочин|я́ть, -и́ть; **the whole story was made up** вся э́та исто́рия была́ вы́думана; **he ~s it up as he goes along** он сочиня́ет на ходу́; (*assemble*) соб|ира́ть, -ра́ть; (*settle*) ула́|живать, -дить; **~ (it) up** (*be reconciled*) мири́ться, по-; **let's ~ it up and be friends** дава́йте помири́мся; (*for a stage performance*) гримирова́ть, за-; **he was made up to look the part** его́ загримирова́ли как тре́бовалось для ро́ли; (*with cosmetics*) кра́сить, по-; ма́заться, на-; **she was heavily made up** она́ была́ си́льно накра́шена; *v.i.* (*be reconciled*) мири́ться, по-; (*for the stage*) гримирова́ться, за-; (*use cosmetics*) кра́ситься, на-; **~ up for** (*compensate for*) возме|ща́ть, -сти́ть; **this will ~ up for everything** э́тим всё бу́дет компенси́ровано; **he was lazy at school but he has made up for it since** в шко́ле он лени́лся, но пото́м наверста́л всё (с лихво́й); **~ up to** (*curry favour with*) подли́з|ываться, -а́ться к + *d.*

● *cpds.* **~-believe** *n.*: **he lives in a world of ~-believe** он живёт в ми́ре грёз; **it's all ~-believe** э́то — сплошна́я фанта́зия; **~shift** *n.* вре́менное приспособле́ние/сре́дство; (*attr.*): **a ~shift shelter** на́скоро сколо́ченное укры́тие; время́нка; **a ~shift dinner** на́скоро пригото́вленный обе́д; **~-up** *n.* (*composition*): **there is some cowardice in his ~-up** он не́сколько трусова́т; (*theatr., etc.*) грим; **~-up room** *n.* гримёрная; **put on ~-up** гримирова́ться, за-; (*cosmetics*) макия́ж, косме́тика; **she wears, uses a lot of ~-up** она́ си́льно кра́сится; **~weight** *n.* дове́сок; противове́с.

maker /ˈmeɪkə(r)/ *n.* (*manufacturer*) производи́тель (*m.*), изготови́тель (*m.*); (*relig., creator*): **the M~ of the universe** творе́ц вселе́нной.

making /ˈmeɪkɪŋ/ *n.* **1** (*that which makes s.o. successful etc.; decisive influence*): **this incident was the ~ of him** благодаря́ э́тому собы́тию, он вы́шел в лю́ди. **2** (*pl., profits*) за́работок. **3** (*pl., potential qualities*): **he has all the ~s of a general** у него́ есть все зада́тки, что́бы стать генера́лом. **4** (*construction*) стро́йка, построе́ние; (*creation*) созда́ние; **the difficulties were not of my ~** э́ти тру́дности возни́кли не из-за меня́; (*compilation*) составле́ние; (*manufacture, production*) изготовле́ние, произво́дство; (*preparation*) приготовле́ние.

malachite /ˈmæləˌkaɪt/ *n.* малахи́т; (*attr.*) малахи́товый.

maladjusted /ˌmæləˈdʒʌstɪd/ *adj.* (*fig., of person*) пло́хо приспосо́бленный; **~ children** трудновоспиту́емые де́ти.

maladjustment /ˌmæləˈdʒʌstmənt/ *n.* плоха́я приспособля́емость.

maladministration /ˌmælədˌmɪnɪˈstreɪʃ(ə)n/ *n.* плохо́е управле́ние.

maladroit /ˌmæləˈdrɔɪt/, /ˈmæl-/ *adj.* (*clumsy*) нело́вкий; (*tactless*) беста́ктный.

maladroitness /ˌmæləˈdrɔɪtnɪs/ *n.* нело́вкость; беста́ктность.

malady /ˈmælədɪ/ *n.* (*lit., fig.*) неду́г, боле́знь.

Malagasy /ˌmæləˈgæsɪ/ *n.* (*person*) малагаси́|ец (*fem.* -йка); (*language*) малагаси́йский язы́к.

● *adj.* малагаси́йский.

malaise /məˈleɪz/ *n.* (*bodily discomfort*) недомога́ние; (*disquiet*) беспоко́йство.

malapropism /ˈmæləprɒˌpɪz(ə)m/ *n.* непра́вильное употребле́ние слов.

malaria /məˈleərɪə/ *n.* маляри́я.

malarial /məˈleərɪəl/ *adj.* маляри́йный.

Malawi /məˈlɑːwɪ/ *n.* Мала́ви (*nt. indecl.*).

Malaya /məˈleɪə/ *n.* Мала́йя.

Malay(an) /məˈleɪ(ən)/ *n.* (*person*) мала́|ец (*fem.* -йка); (*language*) мала́йский язы́к.

● *adj.* мала́йский.

Malaysia /məˈleɪzɪə/, /-ʒə/ *n.* Мала́йзия.

Malaysian /məˈleɪzɪən/, /-ʒ(ə)n/ *adj.* малайзи́йский.

● *n.* малайзи́|ец (*fem.* -йка).

malcontent /ˈmælkənˌtent/ *n.* & *adj.* недово́льный.

male /meɪl/ *n.* (*person*) мужчи́на (*m.*); (*animal etc.*) саме́ц.

● *adj.* мужско́й; **~ animal** саме́ц; **~ model** манеке́нщик; **~ nurse** санита́р; **~(-voice) choir** мужско́й хор; (*tech.*): **~ screw** винт, болт, шуру́п.

malediction /ˌmælɪˈdɪkʃ(ə)n/ *n.* прокля́тие.

malefactor /ˈmælɪˌfæktə(r)/ *n.* злоде́й.

maleficent /məˈlefɪs(ə)nt/ *adj.* (*hurtful*) па́губный; (*criminal*) престу́пный.

malevolence /məˈlevələns/ *n.* недоброжела́тельность, злора́дство.

malevolent /məˈlevələnt/ *adj.* недоброжела́тельный, злора́дный.

malfeasance /mælˈfiːz(ə)ns/ *n.* должностно́е преступле́ние.

malformation /ˌmælfɔːˈmeɪʃ(ə)n/ *n.* непра́вильное образова́ние; уро́дство.

malformed /mælˈfɔːmd/ *adj.* непра́вильно/пло́хо сформиро́ванный; уро́дливый.

malfunction /mælˈfʌŋkʃ(ə)n/ *n.* неиспра́вная рабо́та, отка́з.

● *v.i.* неиспра́вно де́йствовать (*impf.*).

Mali /ˈmɑːlɪ/ *n.* Мали́ (*nt. indecl.*).

Malian /ˈmɑːlɪən/ *n.* мали́|ец (*fem.* -йка).

● *adj.* мали́йский.

malice /ˈmælɪs/ *n.* **1** (*ill-will*) зло́ба; **bear ~ to(wards), against s.o.** таи́ть, за- зло́бу на кого́-н. (*or* про́тив кого́-н.); **I bear you no ~** я не пита́ю к вам зло́бы. **2** (*leg., wrongful intent*): **with ~ aforethought** злоумы́шленно.

malicious /məˈlɪʃəs/ *adj.* (*of person*) злой; (*of thought, act etc.*) зло́бный; **~ tongues** злы́е языки́; **~ intent** престу́пное наме́рение.

malign /məˈlaɪn/ *adj.* па́губный.

● *v.t.* (*slander*) клевета́ть, на- на + *a.*; оклевета́ть (*pf.*); (*defame*) поро́чить, о-; **much-~ed** оклеве́танный.

malignancy /məˈlɪgnənsɪ/ *n.* зло́бность; (*med.*) злока́чественность.

malignant /məˈlɪgnənt/ *adj.* злой, зло́бный; (*med.*) злока́чественный.

malignity /məˈlɪgnɪtɪ/ *n.* зло́бность.

malinger /məˈlɪŋgə(r)/ *v.i.* симули́ровать (*impf., pf.*) боле́знь.

malingerer /məˈlɪŋgərə(r)/ *n.* симуля́нт (*fem.* -ка).

M

mall /mæl/, /mɔːl/ *n.* аллéя; (*shopping precinct*) торгóвый центр.
mallard /ˈmælɑːd/ *n.* (*pl.* ~ *or* ~**s**) кря́ква.
malleability /ˌmælɪəˈbɪlɪtɪ/ *n.* кóвкость; (*fig.*) подáтливость.
malleable /ˈmælɪəb(ə)l/ *adj.* (*of metal etc.*) кóвкий; (*of person*) подáтливый.
mallet /ˈmælɪt/ *n.* деревя́нный молотóк; колотýшка.
mallow /ˈmæləʊ/ *n.* мáльва, просвиря́к.
malnutrition /ˌmælnjuːˈtrɪʃ(ə)n/ *n.* недоедáние.
malodorous /mælˈəʊdərəs/ *adj.* зловóнный.
malpractice /mælˈpræktɪs/ *n.* (*wrongdoing*) противозакóнное дéйствие; (*leg., of physician*) престýпная небрéжность (врачá); (*leg., abuse of trust*) злоупотреблéние довéрием.
malt /mɔːlt/, /mɒlt/ *n.* сóлод; ~ **liquor** солодóвый напи́ток.
● *v.t.* (*make into* ~) солоди́ть. на-.
● *cpd.* ~**house** *n.* солодóвня.
Malta /ˈmɔːltə/, /ˈmɒltə/ *n.* Мáльта.
Maltese /mɔːlˈtiːz/, /mɒl-/ *n.* (*pl.* ~) (*person*) мальти́|ец (*fem.* -йка); (*language*) мальти́йский язы́к.
● *adj.* мальти́йский.
Malthusian /mælˈθjuːzɪən/ *n.* мальтузиáнец.
● *adj.* мальтузиáнский.
maltreat /mælˈtriːt/ *v.t.* дýрно обращáться (*impf.*) с + *i.*; **he was jailed for** ~**ing his children** он был заключён в тюрьмý за дурнóе обращéние с детьми́.
maltreatment /mælˈtriːtmənt/ *n.* дурнóе обращéние (*с кем*).
malversation /ˌmælvəˈseɪʃ(ə)n/ *n.* злоупотреблéние по слýжбе.
mama /ˈmæmə/, /məˈmɑː/, **mamma** /ˈmæmə/, **mammy** /ˈmæmɪ/ *n.* мáма, мáмочка; ~**'s boy** мáменькин сынóк.
mamba /ˈmæmbə/ *n.* мáмба.
mamma /ˈmæmə/ = **mama**
mammal /ˈmæm(ə)l/ *n.* млекопитáющее (живóтное).
mammalian /ˌmæˈmeɪlɪən/ *adj.* относя́щийся к млекопитáющим.
mammary /ˈmæmərɪ/ *adj.*: ~ **gland** молóчная железá.
mammogram /ˈmæməˌgræm/ *n.* маммогрáмма.
Mammon /ˈmæmən/ *n.* (*also* **m**~, *fig.*) мамóна, богáтство.
mammoth /ˈmæməθ/ *n.* мáмонт.
● *adj.* (*huge*) гигáнтский, громáдный.
mammy /ˈmæmɪ/ = **mama**
Man /mæn/ *n.*: **the Isle of** ~ óстров (*abbr.* ó-в) Мэн.
man /mæn/ *n.* (*pl.* **men**) **1** (*person, human being*) человéк (*pl.* лю́ди); **what can a** ~ **do?** что (тут) подéлаешь?; **as one** ~ все как оди́н; **to a** ~ все до одногó; **any** ~ = **anybody; no** ~ = **nobody;** ~ **about town** свéтский человéк; ~ **in the street** срéдний человéк; **a** ~ **in a thousand** рéдкостный человéк; ~ **of action** человéк дéйствия/дéла; ~ **of character** человéк с харáктером; ~ **of God** (*saint*) святóй угóдник; (*priest*) свящéнник; ~ **of honour** (*Br.*), **honor** (*US*) человéк чéсти; чéстный человéк; ~ **of ideas** изобретáтельный человéк; ~ **of letters** литерáтор; ~ **of means** состоя́тельный человéк; ~ **of the moment** человéк, пóсланный самóй судьбóй; ~ **of principle** принципиáльный человéк; ~ **of property** состоя́тельный человéк; ~ **of taste** человéк со вкýсом; ~ **of his word** человéк слóва; ~ **of few words** немногослóвный человéк; ~ **of the world** бывáлый человéк; **he is an Oxford** ~ он выпускни́к Óксфорда; **the inner** ~ душá; внýтреннее «я»; (*joc.*) желýдок; **I feel a new** ~ я чýвствую себя́ обновлённым; **he is his own** ~ он сам себé хозя́ин; **he's just the** ~ **for the job** он сóздан для э́того; **I'm your** ~ я и́менно тот, кто вам нýжен.
2 (*mankind*) человéк, человéчество; **the rights of** ~ правá человéка; (*typifying an era*): **Renaissance** ~ человéк эпóхи Возрождéния; **Neanderthal** ~ неандертáлец.
3 (*adult male*) мужчи́на (*m.*); **they talked** ~ **to** ~ они́ говори́ли как мужчи́на с мужчи́ной; **I have known him** ~ **and boy** я егó знáю с дéтства; **old** ~ стари́к; **young** ~ молодóй человéк; (*implying virility or fortitude*): **it will make a** ~ **of him** э́то сдéлает из негó настоя́щего мужчи́ну; **be a** ~**!** бýдьте мужчи́ной!
4 (*in address*): **speak up,** ~**!** говори́те же!; **tell me, my (good)** ~ **...** (*Br.*) скажи́те мне, дружóк...; **old** ~ старинá (*m.*).
5 (*husband*) муж; **they lived as** ~ **and wife** они́ жи́ли как муж и женá; **my old** ~**'s a dustman** мой стари́к рабóтает мýсорщиком.
6: **best** ~ (*at wedding*) шáфер.
7 (*servant, esp. valet*) слугá (*m.*).
8 (*pl., soldiers*) солдáты; (*sailors*) матрóсы; (*employees*) рабóчие.
9 (*piece in chess*) фигýра; (*in draughts, checkers*) шáшка; (*in other games*) фи́шка.
● *v.t.* (**manned, manning**) **1** (*mil., equip*) укомплектóв|ывать, -áть ли́чным состáвом.
2 (*occupy*) зан|имáть, -я́ть; ~ **the guns** обслýживать (*impf.*) орýдия; **a** ~**ned spacecraft** пилоти́руемый косми́ческий корáбль.
● *cpds.* ~**-at-arms** *n.* (*arch.*) вóин, солдáт; ~**-eater** *n.* людоéд; ~**-eating tiger** тигр-людоéд; ~**hole** *n.* люк; ~**-hour** *n.* человéко-час; ~**-hunt** *n.* рóзыск, полицéйская облáва; ~**-made** *adj.* искýсственный; (*text.*) синтети́ческий; ~**-of-war,** ~**-o'-war** *nn.* (*hist.*) воéнный корáбль; ~**power** *n.* рабóчая си́ла; ~**servant** *n.* слугá (*m.*); ~**-size(d)** *adj.* для взрóслого человéка; ~**-trap** *n.* западня́.
manacle /ˈmænək(ə)l/ *n.* нарýчник; (*pl., fetters, lit., fig.*) окóв|ы (*pl., g.* —).
● *v.t.* над|евáть, -éть нарýчники + *d.*
manag|e /ˈmænɪdʒ/ *v.t.* **1** (*control, conduct*) управля́ть, руководи́ть, завéдовать (*all impf.* + *i.*); **they** ~**ed the business between them** они́ вдвоём управля́ли предприя́тием; **the estate was** ~**ed by his brother** имéнием управля́л егó брат; ~**e a household** вести́ (*det.*) (домáшнее) хозя́йство; ~**ing director** дирéктор-распоряди́тель (*m.*).
2 (*handle*) владéть (*impf.*) + *i.*; **she can** ~**e a bicycle** онá умéет éздить на велосипéде; **can you** ~**e the car by yourself?** вы мóжете сáми спрáвиться с маши́ной?; **I can't** ~**e it** э́то мне не по си́лам.
3 (*be* ~**er** *of*): **he has** ~**ed the team for 10 years** он руководи́л комáндой в течéние десяти́ лет; **the singer was looking for someone to** ~**e him** певéц поды́скивал себé импресáрио; **who** ~**es this department?** кто завéдует э́тим отдéлом?
4 (*cope with*) спр|авля́ться, -áвиться с + *i.*; **I can't** ~**e this work** я не спрáвлюсь с э́той рабóтой; э́та рабóта мне не по плечý; **can't you** ~**e another sandwich?** неужéли вы не оси́лите ещё оди́н бутербрóд?
5 (*contrive*) суméть (*pf.*); умудр|я́ться, -и́ться; ухитр|я́ться, -и́ться; **he** ~**ed to answer** он суméл отвéтить; **I** ~**ed to convince him** мне удалóсь убеди́ть егó; **he** ~**ed to break his neck** он умудри́лся сломáть себé шéю; **can you** ~ **dinner?** вы смóжете пообéдать с нáми?
● *v.i.* (*cope*) спр|авля́ться, -áвиться; **you will never** ~**e on your pension** вы ни за что не проживёте на свою́ пéнсию; (*get by, make do*) об|ходи́ться, -ойти́сь; **we must** ~**e without bread today** сегóдня нам придётся обойти́сь без хлéба.
manageable /ˈmænɪdʒəb(ə)l/ *adj.* (*of task etc.*) выполни́мый; **of** ~ **dimensions** удóбных размéров; (*of person*) сговóрчивый.
management /ˈmænɪdʒmənt/ *n.* **1** (*control, controlling*) управлéние (*чем*), руковóдство, мéнеджмент, организáция; **estate** ~ управлéние имéнием; **it was all due to bad** ~ всё дéло бы́ло в плохóм управлéнии.
2 (*handling person or thing*) обращéние; умéние владéть + *i.*; **staff** ~ обращéние с ли́чным состáвом.
3 (*governing body*) правлéние; (*managerial staff*) администрáция; (*senior staff*) дирéкция.
manager /ˈmænɪdʒə(r)/ *n.* **1** (*controller of business etc.*) завéдующий (*чем*); начáльник, дирéктор, мéнеджер; (*sport*) стáрший трéнер; (*of s.o.'s career*) мéнеджер; **sales** ~ завéдующий отдéлом сбы́та. **2** (*person with administrative skill*) администрáтор.
3 (*comput.*): **program** ~ диспéтчер прогрáмм.
manageress /ˌmænɪdʒəˈres/ *n.* завéдующая; **canteen** ~ завéдующая столóвой.

managerial /ˌmænɪˈdʒɪərɪəl/ *adj.* административный; управленческий.

manatee /ˌmænəˈtiː/ *n.* (*zool.*) ламантин.

Manchuria /mænˈtʃʊərɪə/ *n.* Маньчжурия.

mandarin¹ /ˈmændərɪn/ *n.* **1** (*official*) мандарин; (*bureaucrat*) чиновник. **2** (**M~**, *language*) мандаринское наречие китайского языка.

mandarin² /ˈmændərɪn/ *n.* (*orange*) мандарин.

mandate /ˈmændeɪt/ *n.* (*official order*) мандат; (*authority*) полномочие; (*hist., to govern territory*) мандат; (*given by voters*) наказ; (*leg.*) постановление суда.

● *v.t.*: (*authorize*) уполномочи|вать, -ть; (*require*) требовать, по- +*g.*; **~d territory** подмандатная территория.

mandatory /ˈmændətərɪ/ *adj.* (*compulsory*) обязательный.

mandible /ˈmændɪb(ə)l/ *n.* (*of mammals*) нижняя челюсть; (*of birds*) створка клюва; (*of insects*) жвало.

mandolin /ˌmændəˈlɪn/ *n.* мандолина.

mandrake /ˈmændreɪk/ *n.* мандрагора.

mandrill /ˈmændrɪl/ *n.* (*zool.*) мандрил.

mane /meɪn/ *n.* грива.

manège /mæˈneɪʒ/ *n.* манеж.

maneuver /məˈnuːvə(r)/, **-ability** /məˌnuːvrəˈbɪlɪtɪ/, **-able** /məˈnuːvrəb(ə)l/ (*US*) = **manoeuvre** *etc.*

manful /ˈmænfʊl/ *adj.* мужественный.

manganese /ˈmæŋgəˌniːz/ *n.* марганец.

● *adj.* марганцевый.

mange /meɪndʒ/ *n.* парша.

mangel(-wurzel) /ˈmæŋg(ə)l/ *n.* кормовая свёкла.

manger /ˈmeɪndʒə(r)/ *n.* ясл|и (*pl., g.* -ей); **dog in the ~** собака на сене.

mangle¹ /ˈmæŋg(ə)l/ (*Br.*) *n.* (отжимный) каток.

● *v.t.* отж|имать, -ать.

mangle² /ˈmæŋg(ə)l/ *v.t.* (*mutilate*) уродовать, из-; (*cut to pieces*) кромсать, ис-; (*fig.*) иска|жать, -зить.

mango /ˈmæŋgəʊ/ *n.* (*pl.* **~es** *or* **~s**) манго (*indecl.*).

mangold /ˈmæŋg(ə)ld/ *n.* = **mangel(-wurzel)**

mangrove /ˈmæŋgrəʊv/ *n.* мангровое дерево.

mangy /ˈmeɪndʒɪ/ *adj.* (**mangier, mangiest**) паршивый, шелудивый (*coll.*).

manhandle /ˈmænˌhænd(ə)l/ *v.t.* (*move by manual effort*) та|скать (*indet.*), -щить (*det.*) (вручную); (*treat roughly*) изби|вать, -ить.

manhood /ˈmænhʊd/ *n.* **1** (*state of being a man; adult status*) возмужалость; взрослость, зрелость, совершеннолетие. **2** (*manly qualities*) мужественность.

mania /ˈmeɪnɪə/ *n.* мания; (*lit., fig.*) **a ~ for work** мания работы/работать.

maniac /ˈmeɪnɪˌæk/ *n.* маньяк; (*fig.*): **football ~** заядлый футболист; **homicidal ~** маньяк с навязчивой идеей убийства; **speed ~** любитель (*m.*) скорости.

● *adj.* (*also* **~al, manic**) маниакальный.

manic-depressive /ˈmænɪk/ *adj.* страдающий маниакально-депрессивным психозом.

manicur|e /ˈmænɪˌkjʊə(r)/ *n.* маникюр; (*attr.*) маникюрный.

● *v.t.* делать, с- маникюр +*d.*; **she was ~ing her nails** она делала себе маникюр.

manicurist /ˈmænɪˌkjʊərɪst/ *n.* (*fem.*) маникюрша.

manifest /ˈmænɪˌfest/ *adj.* явный, очевидный; **he was ~ly disturbed** он был явно взволнован.

● *v.t.* (*show clearly*) ясно показ|ывать, -ать; (*exhibit*) прояв|лять, -ить; **he ~ed a desire to leave** он проявил желание уйти; **this tendency ~s itself in...** эта тенденция проявляется в...; (*prove*) доказ|ывать, -ать.

manifestation /ˌmænɪfeˈsteɪʃ(ə)n/ *n.* проявление.

manifesto /ˌmænɪˈfestəʊ/ *n.* (*pl.* **~s**) манифест.

manifold /ˈmænɪˌfəʊld/ *adj.* (*numerous*) многочисленный; (*various*) разнообразный.

manikin /ˈmænɪkɪn/ *n.* (*undersized person*) человечек; (*dwarf*) карлик; (*artist's dummy*) манекен.

Manila /məˈnɪlə/ *n.* Манила.

● *adj.* манильский; **~ paper** манильская бумага.

manipulate /məˈnɪpjʊˌleɪt/ *v.t.* (*lit., fig.; also pej.*) манипулировать (*impf.*) +*i.*; (*influence*) влиять, по- на+*a.*; (*distort*) подтас|овывать, -овать; **he ~d the arguments in his own favour** (*Br.*), **favor** (*US*) он умело орудовал доводами в свою пользу.

manipulation /məˌnɪpjʊˈleɪʃ(ə)n/ *n.* манипуляция, махинация, подтасовка.

manipulator /məˈnɪpjʊˌleɪtə(r)/ *n.* манипулятор.

mankind /mænˈkaɪnd/ *n.* человечество, человеческий род.

manlike /ˈmænlaɪk/ *adj.* мужской; (*of a woman*) мужеподобная; (*of animal*) похожий на человека.

manliness /ˈmænlɪnɪs/ *n.* мужественность.

manly /ˈmænlɪ/ *adj.* (**manlier, manliest**) (*bold, resolute*) мужественный; (*of qualities etc.*) подобающий мужчине.

manna /ˈmænə/ *n.* манна; **like ~ from heaven** манна небесная.

mannequin /ˈmænɪkɪn/ *n.* (*person*) манекенщица; (*dummy*) манекен.

manner /ˈmænə(r)/ *n.* **1** (*way, fashion, mode*) образ; **in, after this ~** таким образом; **in a ~ of speaking** в некотором смысле; **~ of proceeding** принятый порядок (*чего*). **2** (*pl., ways of life; customs*) обычаи (*m. pl.*); нравы (*m. pl.*); **comedy of ~s** комедия нравов. **3** (*personal bearing, style of behaviour*) манера; **he has a strange ~ of speaking** у него странная манера говорить; **he has an awkward ~** он держится неловко; (*style in literature or art*): **after the ~ of Dickens** в стиле Диккенса. **4** (*pl., behaviour*) манеры (*f. pl.*); **good, bad ~s** хорошие/плохие манеры; **it is bad ~s to yawn** зевать неприлично; **the children have good table ~s** дети умеют себя вести за столом; (*polite behaviour*): **have you no ~s?** как ты себя ведёшь?; **have you forgotten your ~s?** вы забыли, как надо себя вести? **5** (*kind*): **what ~ of man is he?** что он за человек?; **all ~ of things** всякого рода вещи; **by no ~ of means** никоим образом.

mannered /ˈmænəd/ *adj.* (*showing mannerism*) манерный.

mannerism /ˈmænəˌrɪz(ə)m/ *n.* манера, манерность; (*style of art*) маньеризм.

mannerist /ˈmænəˌrɪst/ *n.* (*art*) маньерист.

mannerly /ˈmænəlɪ/ *adj.* вежливый.

mannish /ˈmænɪʃ/ *adj.* (*of a woman*) мужеподобная.

manoeuvrability /məˌnuːvrəˈbɪlɪtɪ/ (*US* **maneuverability**) *n.* манёвренность, подвижность.

manoeuvrable /məˈnuːvrəb(ə)l/ (*US* **maneuverable**) *adj.* манёвренный, подвижной.

manoeuvre /məˈnuːvə(r)/ (*US* **maneuver**) *n.* **1** (*mil.*) манёвр; **on ~s** на манёврах; **the Army is holding ~s** сухопутные войска проводят манёвры. **2** (*adroit management*) манёвр, махинация; **the conditions leave us no room for ~** обстановка такова, что маневрировать невозможно; (*intrigue*) интрига.

● *v.t.* маневрировать (*impf.*) +*i.*; **I ~d him to his chair** мне удалось подвести его к стулу; **he ~d his queen out of a difficult position** он вывел ферзя из трудного положения.

● *v.i.* (*lit., fig.*) маневрировать (*impf.*).

manometer /məˈnɒmɪtə(r)/ *n.* манометр.

manor /ˈmænə(r)/ *n.* (*estate*) поместье; **lord of the ~** помещик; (**~-house**) усадьба, помещичий дом.

manorial /məˈnɔːrɪəl/ *adj.* манориальный.

manqué /ˈmɒŋkeɪ/ *adj.*: **a poet ~** неудавшийся поэт.

mansard /ˈmænsɑːd/ *n.* (**~ roof**) мансардная крыша; (*garret*) мансарда.

manse /mæns/ *n.* дом пастора (*в Шотландии*).

mansion /ˈmænʃ(ə)n/ *n.* особняк; **country ~** загородный дом; (*pl., Br., house of flats*) многоквартирный дом.

manslaughter /ˈmænˌslɔːtə(r)/ *n.* непредумышленное убийство; убийство по неосторожности.

mantel(piece) /ˈmænt(ə)l,piːs/ *n.* каминная полка.

mantilla /mænˈtɪlə/ *n.* мантилья.

mantis /ˈmæntɪs/ *n.* (*pl.* ~ *or* ~**es**) (*zool.*): (**praying** ~) богомол.

mantissa /mænˈtɪsə/ *n.* (*math.*) мантисса.

mantle /ˈmænt(ə)l/ *n.* **1** (*cloak*) мантия; (*fig.*): **he assumed the prophet's** ~ он взял на себя роль пророка. **2** (*fig., covering*) покров. **3** (*for gas-jet*) калильная сетка.

● *v.t.* (*liter.*): **the fields were** ~**d with snow** поля были покрыты снегом.

manual /ˈmænjʊəl/ *n.* (*handbook*) руководство; пособие.

● *adj.* (*operated by hand*) ручной; ~**ly** ручным способом, вручную (*coll.*); (*performed by hand*): ~ **labour** (*Br.*), **labor** (*US*) физический труд.

manufactur|e /ˌmænjʊˈfæktʃə(r)/ *n.* изготовление; (*on large scale*) производство; **goods of foreign** ~**e** изделия иностранного производства.

● *v.t.* **1** (*produce*) изгот|овлять, -овить; произв|одить, -ести; ~**ed goods** промтовары (*m. pl.*); ~**ing industry** обрабатывающая промышленность; ~**ing town** промышленный город. **2** (*make up, invent*) фабриковать, с-.

manure /məˈnjʊə(r)/ *n.* навоз.

● *v.t.* унаво|живать, -зить.

manuscript /ˈmænjʊskrɪpt/ *n.* рукопись; **the book is still in** ~ книга ещё в рукописи; (*attr.*) рукописный.

● *cpd.* ~ **paper** (*mus.*) нотная бумага.

Manx /mæŋks/ *n.* (*language*) мэнский язык; **the** ~ (*people*) жители (*m. pl.*) острова Мэн.

● *adj.* мэнский; ~ **cat** (кошка-)манкс, бесхвостая кошка.

● *cpds.* ~**man**, ~**woman** *nn.* житель(ница) (*or* урожен|ец, -ка) острова Мэн.

many /ˈmenɪ/ *adj.* (**more, most**) многие; **a good, great** ~ большое количество +*g.*; ~ **people** много людей; многие (люди); ~ **years passed** прошло много лет; ~ **a one** многие; ~ **a time,** ~ **times** много раз; ~**'s the time** очень часто, частенько; **half as** ~ вдвое меньше; **twice as** ~ вдвое больше; **I haven't seen him for** ~ **a day** я его давно не видел; **as, so** ~ **(as)** столько(, сколько); **not as** ~ **as** не так много, как; **there were as** ~ **as forty people there** там было целых сорок человек; **not** ~ немного, не так уж много; ~ **more** гораздо больше +*g.*; **one too** ~ (*not wanted; in the way*) третий лишний; **he's had one too** ~ (*coll.*) он выпил лишнего.

● *cpds.* ~**-coloured** (*US* **-colored**) *adj.* пёстрый, многоцветный; ~**-sided** *adj.* (*lit., fig.*) многосторонний.

Maoism /ˈmaʊɪz(ə)m/ *n.* маоизм.

Maoist /ˈmaʊɪst/ *adj.* маоистский.

Maori /ˈmaʊrɪ/ *n.* (*pl.* ~ *or* ~**s**) (*person*) маори (*c.g., indecl.*); (*language*) маорийский язык.

● *adj.* маорийский.

map /mæp/ *n.* карта; (*e.g. of rail system*) схема; **town** ~ план города; **they wiped the village off the** ~ они стёрли деревню с лица земли; **this scandal put the village on the** ~ село получило известность из-за этого скандала.

● *v.t.* (**mapped, mapping**): (*make* ~ *of*): **this district was first** ~**ped a hundred years ago** карта этого района была впервые составлена сто лет назад; **he** ~**ped out his route before leaving** он составил маршрут перед отъездом; (*fig., plan*) планировать, за-; сост|авлять, -авить план +*g.*; **he** ~**ped out his plans** он прикинул, что ему нужно делать; ~**ping pen** рейсфедер.

● *cpds.* ~**-maker** *n.* картограф; ~**-reader** *n.*: **he is an excellent** ~**-reader** он прекрасно читает карту; ~**-reading** *n.* чтение карт.

maple /ˈmeɪp(ə)l/ *n.* клён; ~ **sugar/syrup** кленовый сахар/сироп.

● *cpds.* ~**-leaf** *n.* кленовый лист; ~**-wood** *n.* клён; (*attr.*) кленовый.

maquette /məˈket/ *n.* макет.

mar /mɑː(r)/ *v.t.* (**marred, marring**) портить, ис-.

marabou /ˈmærəˌbuː/ *n.* (*zool.*) марабу (*m. indecl.*).

maraschino /ˌmærəˈskiːnəʊ/ *n.* (*pl.* ~**s**) мараскин (*вишнёвый ликёр*).

marathon /ˈmærəθ(ə)n/ *n.* (~ **race**) марафон, марафонский бег; ~ **runner** марафонец; (*attr.*): **a** ~ **effort** гигантское усилие.

maraud /məˈrɔːd/ *v.i.* мародёрствовать (*impf., pf.*).

marauder /məˈrɔːdə(r)/ *n.* мародёр.

marble /ˈmɑːb(ə)l/ *n.* **1** (*substance*) мрамор; (*pl., collection of statuary*) коллекция скульптур из мрамора. **2** (*in child's game*) стеклянный шарик; **play** ~**s** играть (*impf.*) в шарики.

● *adj.* (*lit., fig.*) мраморный.

● *v.t.* раскра|шивать, -сить под мрамор; ~**d paper** мраморная бумага.

● *cpd.* ~**-topped** *adj.* с мраморным верхом.

March /mɑːtʃ/ *n.* март; (*attr.*) мартовский.

march /mɑːtʃ/ *n.* (*mil.*) марш; **on the** ~ в походе; ~ **past** (*Br.*) торжественный марш; **forced** ~ форсированный марш; **quick/slow** ~ быстрый/медленный марш; (*mus.*): **in** ~ **time** в темпе марша; (*pol.*) поход, демонстрация; **peace** ~ поход за мир; (*fig., distance*): **it was a long day's** ~ был длинный переход; **steal a** ~ **on one** опере|жать, -дить; (*fig., progress*): ~ **of events** ход событий; **the** ~ **of time** поступь времени.

● *v.t.* **1** (*cause to* ~) водить (*indet.*), вести, по- строем; **he** ~**ed them up to the top of the hill** он повёл их строем на вершину холма. **2** (*cover by* ~**ing**) про|ходить, -йти.

● *v.i.* **1** (*mil.*) маршировать (*impf., pf.*); **German troops** ~**ed into Austria** немецкие войска вступили в Австрию; **we watched them** ~ **past** мы смотрели, как они прошли строем; **quick** ~**!** шагом марш! **2** (*walk determinedly*): **he** ~**ed into the room** он смело вошёл в комнату; **with these words he** ~**ed out** с этими словами он демонстративно вышел.

● *with advs.*: ~ **along** *v.i.*: **they were** ~**ing along singing** они маршировали с песнями; ~ **back** *v.t.*: **I caught him running off and** ~**ed him back** я поймал его, когда он убегал, и препроводил обратно; *v.i.*: **they** ~**ed back to barracks** они строем вернулись в казармы; ~ **by** *v.i.* прошагать (*pf.*) мимо; ~ **in** *v.t.*: **he was** ~**ed in to see the boss** его ввели в кабинет начальника; *v.i.*: **when the soldiers** ~**ed in** когда солдаты вступили (в город *и т.п.*); ~ **off** *v.t.*: **he was** ~**ed off to prison** его препроводили в тюрьму; *v.i.*: **she** ~**ed off in disgust** ей стало противно, и она вышла; ~ **out** *v.t.* выводить, вывести *v.i.*: **the workers** ~**ed out on strike** рабочие вышли на забастовку; ~ **up** *v.i.*: **they** ~**ed up to the wall** они прошагали к стене; **he** ~**ed up and hit her** он решительно подошёл к ней и ударил её.

marcher /ˈmɑːtʃə(r)/ *n.* демонстрант (*fem.* -ка).

marching /ˈmɑːtʃɪŋ/ *n.* походное движение; ~ **drill** строевая подготовка; **in** ~ **order** в походном порядке; ~ **orders** (*mil.*) приказ о выступлении; (*fig.*): **get one's** ~ **orders** получ|ать, -ить расчёт; **they gave him his** ~ **orders** они уволили его.

marchioness /ˌmɑːʃəˈnes/, /ˈmɑː-/ *n.* маркиза.

Mardi Gras /ˌmɑːdɪ ˈgrɑː/ *n.* вторник на масленой неделе.

mare /meə(r)/ *n.* кобыла.

margarine /ˌmɑːdʒəˈriːn/, /ˌmɑːgə-/, /ˈmɑː-/ *n.* маргарин.

marge /mɑːdʒ/ (*Br. coll.*) = **margarine**

margin /ˈmɑːdʒɪn/ *n.* **1** (*edge, border*) край; (*of page*) поле (*usu. pl.*); **in the** ~ на полях. **2** (*extra amount*) запас; коэффициент; **safety** ~ запас прочности; **he won by a narrow** ~ он победил с небольшим преимуществом; ~ **of/for error** допустимая погрешность; **he was allowed a certain** ~ ему оставили кое-какую свободу действий; **profit** ~ прибыль, размер прибыли.

marginal /ˈmɑːdʒɪn(ə)l/ *adj.* **1** (*written in margin*) (написанный) на полях; ~ **notes** заметки (*f. pl.*) (на полях). **2** (*pert. to an edge or limit*) краевой; предельный; ~ **utility** предельная полезность; ~ **land** малоплодородная земля. **3** (*insignificant, minimal*) незначительный; минимальный; ~ **seat** (*Br.*) место в парламенте, завоёванное минимальным перевесом голосов.

marginalia /ˌmɑːdʒɪˈneɪlɪə/ *n.* заметки (*f. pl.*) на полях.

marguerite /ˌmɑːgəˈriːt/ *n.* нивяник.

marigold /ˈmærɪˌgəʊld/ *n.* (**common** *or* **pot** ~) ноготки (*m. pl.*); (**French** *or* **African** ~) бархатцы (*m. pl.*).

mari|juana, -huana /ˌmærɪˈhwɑːnə/ *n.* марихуа́на.

marina /məˈriːnə/ *n.* мари́на (*пристань для яхт*).

marinade /ˌmærɪˈneɪd/, /ˈmæ-/ *n.* марина́д.

● *v.t.* (*also* **marinate**) маринова́ть, за-.

marine /məˈriːn/ *n.* **1** (*fleet*): **mercantile, merchant ~** торго́вый флот. **2** (*naval infantryman*) солда́т морско́й пехо́ты, морско́й пехоти́нец; **the ~s** морска́я пехо́та; **tell that to the ~s!** расскажи́те э́то свое́й ба́бушке! (*coll.*).

● *adj.* морско́й; **~ engineer** судово́й меха́ник.

mariner /ˈmærɪnə(r)/ *n.* морепла́ватель (*m.*); **master ~** капита́н, шки́пер; **~'s compass** морско́й ко́мпас.

marionette /ˌmærɪəˈnet/ *n.* марионе́тка.

marital /ˈmærɪt(ə)l/ *adj.* (*of marriage*): **~ union** бра́чный сою́з; (*of husband or wife*): **~ rights** супру́жеские права́; **~ status** семе́йное положе́ние.

maritime /ˈmærɪˌtaɪm/ *adj.* (*of the sea*): **~ law** морско́е пра́во; (*situated by the sea*) примо́рский.

marjoram /ˈmɑːdʒərəm/ *n.* майора́н, души́ца.

mark¹ /mɑːk/ *n.* **1** (*surface imperfection; stain, spot etc.*) пятно́; **the horse has a white ~ on its nose** у ло́шади на носу́ бе́лое пятно́; (*scratch*) цара́пина; (*cut*) поре́з; (*scar*) рубе́ц, шрам; **there were ~s of smallpox on his face** его́ лицо́ бы́ло изры́то о́спой.
2 (*trace*) след; **tyre** (*Br.*), **tire** (*US*) **~s** следы́ шин; **you have left dirty ~s on the floor** вы наследи́ли на полу́.
3 (*sign, symbol*) знак; **punctuation ~s** зна́ки препина́ния; **question ~** вопроси́тельный знак; **as a ~ of goodwill** в знак расположе́ния; (*indication, feature, symptom*) при́знак; **politeness is the ~ of a gentleman** ве́жливость — отличи́тельная черта́ джентльме́на.
4 (*for purpose of distinction or identification*) ме́тка; (*fig.*): **make one's ~** выдвига́ться, вы́двинуться; (*as signature*): **he could not write his name but made his ~** он вме́сто по́дписи поста́вил крест; (*on an industrial product*) фабри́чная ма́рка; (*fig., stamp*): **it bears the ~ of hurried work** ви́дно, что э́то де́лалось в спе́шке.
5 (*reference point*) ме́тка; **the ~s show the depth of water in feet** отме́тки пока́зывают глубину́ воды́ в фу́тах; (*fig., standard*): **his work was not up to the ~** его́ рабо́та была́ не на высоте́; **I'm not quite up to the ~ today** я сего́дня не совсе́м в фо́рме; **come up to the ~** опра́вд|ывать, -а́ть ожида́ния; **overstep the ~** (*fig.*) выходи́ть, вы́йти за грани́цы дозво́ленного.
6 (*starting-line*) старт; **get off the ~** стартова́ть (*impf., pf.*); **quick/slow off the ~** (*fig.*) лёгкий/тяжёлый на подъём; **on your ~s; get set; go!** на старт; внима́ние; марш!
7 (*assessment of performance*) отме́тка; **he always gets good ~s** он всегда́ получа́ет хоро́шие отме́тки; **she got top ~s in the exam** она́ сдала́ (экза́мен) на «отли́чно»; (*unit of assessment*) балл; **they gave him 7 ~s out of 10** он набра́л 7 ба́ллов из 10; (*fig.*): **I give him full ~s for trying** я высоко́ ценю́ его́ стара́тельность; **this is a black ~ against him** э́то ему́ припо́мнят.
8 (*target*) цель; **hit the ~** (*lit., fig.*) поп|ада́ть, -а́сть в цель; **miss** (*or* **fall wide of**) **the ~** прома́х|иваться, -ну́ться; **you're way off the ~** вы попа́ли па́льцем в не́бо (*coll.*).

● *v.t.* **1** (*stain, scar, scratch etc.*): **a tablecloth ~ed with coffee stains** ска́терть, забры́зганная ко́фе; **the table was badly ~ed** стол был си́льно запа́чкан; **features ~ed by grief** черты́ лица́, отме́ченные го́рем.
2 (*for recognition purposes*) ме́тить, по-; **~ed cards** крапле́ные ка́рты; (*with price*): **all the goods are ~ed** на всех това́рах проста́влена цена́.
3 (*distinguish*): **his reign was ~ed by great victories** его́ ца́рствование бы́ло ознаменова́но вели́кими побе́дами; **he called for champagne to ~ the occasion** он заказа́л шампа́нское, что́бы отме́тить (э́то) собы́тие.
4 (*indicate*) отм|еча́ть, -е́тить; **is our village ~ed on this map?** на́ша дере́вня нанесена́ на э́ту ка́рту?; **the prices are clearly ~ed** це́ны чётко проста́влены; **to ~ his displeasure he remained silent** он храни́л молча́ние в знак недово́льства.
5 (*record*) запи́с|ывать, -а́ть; (*observe and remember*): **a ~ed man** челове́к, взя́тый на заме́тку; (*promising*) многообеща́ющий челове́к; (*Br., football etc.: follow closely*) закр|ыва́ть, -ы́ть; (*notice; pay heed to*) зам|еча́ть, -е́тить; **~ you, I don't agree with all he says** (*Br.*) заме́тьте, я согла́сен не со все́м, что он говори́т; **~ my words!** помяни́те моё сло́во!
6 (*assign ~s to; assess*): **~ an exercise** пров|еря́ть, -е́рить упражне́ние; **the judges ~ed his performance very high** су́дьи высоко́ оцени́ли его́ выступле́ние.
7: **~ time** (*mil.*) обознача́ть (*impf.*) шаг на ме́сте; **~ time!** на ме́сте ша́гом — марш!; (*fig.*) топта́ться (*impf.*) на ме́сте; тяну́ть (*impf.*) вре́мя.

● *with advs.*: **~ down** *v.t.* (*reduce price of*): **all the goods were ~ed down for the sale** для распрода́жи це́ны на все това́ры бы́ли сни́жены; (*give low ~ to*): **he was ~ed down for bad spelling** ему́ сни́зили оце́нку за орфографи́ческие оши́бки; **~ off** *v.t.* отм|еча́ть, -е́тить; **an area was ~ed off for the guests** часть мест *и т.п.* была́ отведена́ для госте́й; **~ out** *v.t.*: **a tennis court had been ~ed out** те́ннисный корт был расче́рчен/разме́чен; (*plan*): **their course was ~ed out several weeks in advance** их маршру́т был разрабо́тан не́сколькими неде́лями ра́нее; (*preselect, destine*): **he was ~ed out for promotion** его́ реши́ли повы́сить в до́лжности; **cattle ~ed out for slaughter** скот, ото́бранный на убо́й; **~ up** *v.t.* (*raise; raise price of*): **prices were ~ed up every month** це́ны повыша́ли ка́ждый ме́сяц; **goods were ~ed up after the budget** це́ны бы́ли повы́шены по́сле объявле́ния фина́нсовой сме́ты; (*record*): **who will ~ up the score?** кто бу́дет запи́сывать счёт?; (*raise ~s of*) зав|ыша́ть, -ы́сить оце́нку + *d.*

● *cpd.* **~-up** *n.* наце́нка.

mark² /mɑːk/ *n.* (*currency*) ма́рка.

marked /mɑːkt/ *adj.* (*distinct, noticeable*) заме́тный.

markedly /ˈmɑːkɪdlɪ/ *adv.*: **they were ~ different** они́ заме́тно отлича́лись друг от дру́га.

marker /ˈmɑːkə(r)/ *n.* (*recorder of score*) маркёр; (*indicator*) индика́тор; (*flag*) сигна́льный флажо́к; (*beacon*) ма́ркерный (ра́дио)мая́к; (*buoy*) буёк; (*bookmark*) закла́дка; (*tool*) отме́тчик; (*pen*) флома́стер; (*of exams*) челове́к, проверя́ющий экзаменацио́нные рабо́ты.

market /ˈmɑːkɪt/ *n.* **1** (*gathering; event; place of business*) ры́нок, база́р; **he sends his pigs to ~** он продаёт свои́х свине́й на база́ре; (*attr.*) ры́ночный, база́рный; **~ hall** ры́ночный павильо́н/зал; (*fig., area of sale*): **world ~** мирово́й ры́нок; **the Common M~** О́бщий ры́нок.
2 (*trade*) торго́вля; **the ~ in wool** торго́вля ше́рстью; (*opportunity for sale*) сбыт; **there is no ~ for these goods** на э́ти това́ры нет спро́са; **they will find a ready ~** они́ легко́ найду́т сбыт.
3 (*rates of purchase and sale; share prices*) це́ны (*f. pl.*); **the ~ is falling** це́ны па́дают; **the coffee ~ is steady** цена́ на ко́фе стаби́льна (*or* де́ржится твёрдо); **play the ~** спекули́ровать (*impf.*) на би́рже; **~ research** изуче́ние конъюнкту́ры/возмо́жностей ры́нка; **~ value** ры́ночная сто́имость.
4: **in the ~ for** (*ready to buy*) обду́мывающий поку́пку (*чего*).
5: **on the ~** (*available for purchase*): **he put his house on the ~** он вы́ставил свой дом на прода́жу; **his estate will soon come on to the ~** его́ име́ние ско́ро посту́пит в прода́жу.

● *v.t.* (**marketed, marketing**) (*sell in ~*) продава́ть (*impf.*); (*put up for sale*) пус|ка́ть, -ти́ть в прода́жу.

● *cpds.* **~-day** *n.* (*Br.*) база́рный день; **~ economy** *n.* ры́ночная эконо́мика; **~ forces** *n. pl.* ры́ночные си́лы (*f. pl.*); **~-garden** *n.* (*Br.*) огоро́д (для выра́щивания овоще́й на прода́жу); **~-gardener** *n.* (*Br.*) владе́лец огоро́да; **~-gardening** *n.* (*Br.*) выра́щивание овоще́й на прода́жу; **~-place** *n.* база́рная пло́щадь; **~ town** *n.* го́род, в кото́ром есть ры́нок.

marketable /ˈmɑːkɪtəb(ə)l/ *adj.* (*produced for sale*) това́рный; (*selling quickly*) хо́дкий.

marketing /ˈmɑːkɪtɪŋ/ *n.* ма́ркетинг; **~ department** отде́л ма́ркетинга; **~ manager** ме́неджер по ма́ркетингу.

M

marking /ˈmɑːkɪŋ/ *n.* **1** (*coloration of animals etc.*) окра́ска. **2** (*for identification*): **aircraft ~s** опознава́тельные зна́ки (*m. pl.*) самолёта. **3** (*assessment*) оце́нка.

marksman /ˈmɑːksmən/ *n.* стрело́к; **a good ~** ме́ткий стрело́к; (*sniper*) сна́йпер.

marksmanship /ˈmɑːksmən,ʃɪp/ *n.* ме́ткая стрельба́; стрелко́вое мастерство́.

marl /mɑːl/ *n.* (*geol.*) ме́ргель (*m.*).

marmalade /ˈmɑːmə,leɪd/ *n.*: **orange ~** апельси́новый/апельси́нный джем.

Marmara /ˈmɑːmərə/ *n.*: **Sea of ~** Мра́морное мо́ре.

marmoreal /mɑːˈmɔːrɪəl/ *adj.* (*fig.*) мра́морный.

marmoset /ˈmɑːmə,zet/ *n.* марты́шка.

marmot /ˈmɑːmət/ *n.* суро́к.

maroon¹ /məˈruːn/ *n. & adj.* (*colour*) тёмно-бордо́вый цвет.

maroon² /məˈruːn/ *v.t.* выса́живать, вы́садить на необита́емый о́стров *и т.п.*; (*fig., pass.*) застр|ева́ть, -я́ть; **we were ~ed in Paris** мы застря́ли в Пари́же; **we were ~ed by the tide** мы бы́ли отре́заны прили́вом.

marquee /mɑːˈkiː/ *n.* (*Br.*) (больша́я) пала́тка.

marquetry /ˈmɑːkɪtrɪ/ *n.* маркетри́ (*nt. indecl.*), инкруста́ция по де́реву.

marqu|is /ˈmɑːkwɪs/, **-ess** /ˈmɑːkwɪs/ *n.* марки́з.

marquise /mɑːˈkiːz/ *n.* марки́за.

marriage /ˈmærɪdʒ/ *n.* **1** (*ceremony*) сва́дьба; бракосочета́ние. **2** (*contraction of ~ by man*) жени́тьба; **his ~ to Liza** его́ жени́тьба на Ли́зе; **he made her an offer of ~** он сде́лал ей предложе́ние; **he took her in ~** он взял её в жёны; (*by woman*) вы́ход за́муж; **he gave his daughter in ~** он вы́дал дочь за́муж. **3** (*married state*) брак, супру́жество; (*of woman, also*) заму́жество; **~s are made in heaven** бра́ки заключа́ются на небеса́х; **~ of convenience** фикти́вный брак; брак по расчёту; **they were joined in ~** они́ сочета́лись бра́ком; **their ~ broke up** их брак распа́лся; **relative by ~** сво́йственни|к (*fem.* -ца); ро́дственни|к (*fem.* -ца) по му́жу/жене́. **4** (*attr.*) бра́чный; **~ bureau** бракопосре́днический аге́нтство; **~ certificate** свиде́тельство о бра́ке; **~ guidance** (*Br.*) семе́йная консульта́ция; **~ licence** (*Br.*), **license** (*US*) разреше́ние на брак; **~ portion** прида́ное; **~ settlement** (*Br.*) бра́чный догово́р. **5** (*fig., union*) сочета́ние.

● *cpds.* **~-bed** *n.* бра́чное/супру́жеское ло́же; **~-broker** *n.* сват; (*fem.*) сва́ха; **~-lines** *n. pl.* (*Br.*) свиде́тельство о бра́ке.

marriageable /ˈmærɪdʒəb(ə)l/ *adj.*: **of ~ age** бра́чного во́зраста; **a ~ girl** де́вушка на вы́данье (*coll.*); неве́ста.

married /ˈmærɪd/ *adj.* **1** (*of man*) жена́тый; (*of woman*) заму́жняя, (*pred.*) за́мужем (за + *i.*); **they are ~** (*to each other*) они́ жена́ты. **2** (*pert. to marriage*) супру́жеский; **a ~ couple** супру́жеская па́ра; **~ life** супру́жеская жизнь, супру́жество; (*n. pl.*): **young ~s** молодожёны.

marrow /ˈmærəʊ/ *n.* **1** (*anat.*) (ко́стный) мозг; **I was chilled to the ~** я продро́г до мо́зга косте́й. **2 (vegetable ~)** (*Br.*) кабачо́к.

● *cpd.* **~-bone** *n.* мозгова́я кость.

marr|y /ˈmærɪ/ *v.t.* **1** (*of man*) жени́ться (*impf., pf.*) на + *p.* **2** (*of woman*) выходи́ть, вы́йти за́муж за + *a.* **3** (*of parent; give daughter in marriage*) выдава́ть, вы́дать за́муж (*за кого*); (*give son in marriage*) жени́ть (*на ком*). **4** (*of priest*) венча́ть, об-. **5** (*fig., join*) сочета́ть (*impf., pf.*); (*devote*): **he was ~ied to his work** он был поглощён свое́й рабо́той.

● *v.i.* (*of man*) жени́ться (*impf., pf.*); (*of woman*) выходи́ть, вы́йти за́муж; (*of couple*) пожени́ться (*pf.*); вступ|а́ть, -и́ть в брак; (*relig.*) венча́ться, об-.

Mars /mɑːz/ *n.* (*myth., astron.*) Марс.

Marseillaise /,mɑːseɪˈjeɪz/, /,mɑːsəˈleɪz/ *n.* Марселье́за.

Marseilles /mɑːˈseɪ/ *n.* Марсе́ль (*m.*).

marsh /mɑːʃ/ *n.* боло́то; (*attr.*) боло́тный.

● *cpds.* **~land** *n.* боло́тистая ме́стность; топь; **~mallow** *n.* (*plant*) лека́рственный алте́й; (*confection*) пастила́; **~-marigold** *n.* боло́тная калу́жница.

marshal /ˈmɑːʃ(ə)l/ *n.* **1** (*mil.*) ма́ршал; **air ~** ма́ршал авиа́ции. **2** (*organizer of ceremonies*) обер-церемонийме́йстер. **3** (*US, head of police department*) нача́льник полице́йского уча́стка.

● *v.t.* (**marshalled, marshalling;** *US* **marshaled, marshaling**) **1** (*draw up in order*): **~ troops** выстра́ивать, вы́строить войска́; (*fig.*): **~ one's forces** соб|ира́ть, -ра́ть си́лы; **~ facts, arguments** прив|оди́ть, -ести́ фа́кты/до́воды в систе́му. **2** (*direct*): **~ a crowd** напр|авля́ть, -а́вить толпу́; **they were ~led into the dining-room** они́ бы́ли торже́ственно введены́ в столо́вую. **3** (*rail.*) сортирова́ть (*impf.*); **~ling-yard** сортиро́вочная (ста́нция).

marshy /ˈmɑːʃɪ/ *adj.* (**marshier, marshiest**) боло́тистый, то́пкий.

marsupial /mɑːˈsuːpɪəl/ *n.* су́мчатое живо́тное.

● *adj.* су́мчатый.

mart /mɑːt/ *n.* (*market-place*) ры́нок; (*centre of trade*) торго́вый центр; (*auction-room*) аукцио́нный зал.

marten /ˈmɑːtɪn/ *n.* куни́ца.

martial /ˈmɑːʃ(ə)l/ *adj.* (*military*) вое́нный; **~ arts** спорти́вная борьба́; **~ law** вое́нное положе́ние.

Martian /ˈmɑːʃ(ə)n/ *n.* марсиа́н|ин (*fem.* -ка).

● *adj.* марсиа́нский.

martin /ˈmɑːtɪn/ *n.*: **house-~** городска́я ла́сточка; **sand-~** берегова́я ла́сточка.

martinet /,mɑːtɪˈnet/ *n.* приди́рчивый нача́льник; сторо́нник стро́гой дисципли́ны.

martingale /ˈmɑːtɪŋ,geɪl/ *n.* мартинга́л (*часть упряжи*).

martlet /ˈmɑːtlɪt/ *n.* стриж (чёрный).

martyr /ˈmɑːtə(r)/ *n.* му́чени|к (*fem.* -ца); (*fig., sufferer*) страда́л|ец (*fem.* -ица); **be a ~ to, for a cause** страда́ть, по- за де́ло; **she makes a ~ of herself** она́ стро́ит из себя́ му́ченицу.

● *v.t.* му́чить, за-; (*fig.*): **she had a ~ed air** у неё был му́ченический вид.

martyrdom /ˈmɑːtədəm/ *n.* му́ченичество; (*ordeal*) муче́ние; **suffer ~** (*lit., fig.*) быть му́чеником.

marvel /ˈmɑːv(ə)l/ *n.* чу́до; **he's a ~** он чуде́сный челове́к; **she is a ~ of patience** она́ само́ терпе́ние; **it's a ~ that he escaped** э́то су́щее чу́до, что ему́ удало́сь спасти́сь; **the medicine worked ~s** лека́рство сотвори́ло чудеса́.

● *v.t. & i.* (**marvelled, marvelling;** *US* **marveled, marveling**) (*wonder*) диви́ться (*impf.*) + *d.*; удив|ля́ться, -и́ться + *d.*; **he ~led that ...** он порази́лся тому́, что...; **~ at** (*be surprised at*) изум|ля́ться, -и́ться + *d.*; (*admire*) восхи|ща́ться, -ти́ться + *i.*

marvellous /ˈmɑːvələs/ *adj.* (*US* **marvelous**) (*astonishing*) изуми́тельный; (*splendid*) чуде́сный.

Marxian /ˈmɑːksɪən/ *adj.* маркси́стский.

Marxism /ˈmɑːksɪz(ə)m/ *n.* маркси́зм.

Marxist /ˈmɑːksɪst/ *n.* маркси́ст (*fem.* -ка).

● *adj.* маркси́стский.

marzipan /ˈmɑːzɪ,pæn/, /-ˈpæn/ *n.* марципа́н.

mascara /mæˈskɑːrə/ *n.* тушь для ресни́ц.

mascot /ˈmæskɒt/ *n.* талисма́н.

masculine /ˈmæskjʊlɪn/, /ˈmɑːs-/ *n.* (**~ gender**) мужско́й род; (**~ noun**) существи́тельное мужско́го ро́да.

● *adj.* мужско́й; (*manly*) му́жественный; (*of a woman*) мужеподо́бная.

masculinity /,mæskjʊˈlɪnɪtɪ/ *n.* му́жественность.

mash /mæʃ/ *n.* (*for brewing*) су́сло; (*animal fodder*) ме́сиво, болту́шка из отрубе́й; (*Br., potato*) пюре́ (*indecl.*).

● *v.t.* (*brewing*): **~ malt** зава́р|ивать, -и́ть со́лод; (*cul.*): **~ turnips** де́лать, с- пюре́ из ре́пы; **~ed potatoes** карто́фельное пюре́.

mask /mɑːsk/ *n.* ма́ска; **under the ~ of friendship** под личи́ной дру́жбы; **he threw off the ~** (*fig.*) он сбро́сил ма́ску/личи́ну.

● *v.t.* над|ева́ть, -е́ть ма́ску на + *a.*; **~ed men** лю́ди в ма́сках; **~ed ball** маскара́д; (*fig.*): **she ~ed her feelings** она́ скрыва́ла свои́ чу́вства; **the drug ~ed the pain** лека́рство притупи́ло боль; (*cover*) закр|ыва́ть, -ы́ть.

masochism /ˈmæsə,kɪz(ə)m/ *n.* мазохи́зм.

masochist /ˈmæsəkɪst/ *n.* мазохи́ст.

masochistic /ˌmæsəˈkɪstɪk/ *adj.* мазохи́стский.

mason /ˈmeɪs(ə)n/ *n.* (*builder*) ка́менщик; (*stone-dresser*) каменотёс; **(M~, Free~)** масо́н.

Masonic /məˈsɒnɪk/ *adj.* масо́нский; **~ lodge** масо́нская ло́жа.

masonry /ˈmeɪsənrɪ/ *n.* (*stonework*) ка́менная кла́дка; **(M~, Free~)** масо́нство.

masquerad|e /ˌmɑːskəˈreɪd/, /ˌmæs-/ *n.* (*lit., fig.*) маскара́д.

● *v.i.*: **he ~ed as a general** он выдава́л себя́ за генера́ла; **he is ~ing under an assumed name** он скрыва́ется под вы́мышленной фами́лией.

Mass¹ /mæs/ *n.* (*relig.*) ме́сса, литурги́я; (*in Orthodox church*) обе́дня; **high ~** торже́ственная ме́сса; **low ~** ме́сса без пе́ния; **~es were said for his soul** за упоко́й его́ души́ служи́ли обе́дни.

mass² /mæs/ *n.* **1** (*phys. etc.*) ма́сса; **in the ~** в ма́ссе, в це́лом; **his body is a ~ of bruises** он весь в синяка́х; **his story was a ~ of lies** его́ расска́з был сплошно́й ло́жью; **a ~ of earth/rock** гру́да земли́/камне́й.
2 (*large number*) мно́жество; **~es of people** ма́сса наро́ду; **the ~es** (наро́дные/широ́кие) ма́ссы; (*pl., coll., a large amount*): **there's ~es of food** полно́ еды́.
3 (*greater part*) бо́льшая часть.
4 (*attr.*) ма́ссовый; **~ destruction** ма́ссовое уничтоже́ние; **~ education** всео́бщее обуче́ние/образова́ние; **the ~ media** сре́дства ма́ссовой информа́ции (СМИ); **~ market** ма́ссовый спрос; **~ meeting** ма́ссовый ми́тинг; **~ production** ма́ссовое произво́дство.

● *v.t.* соб|ира́ть, -ра́ть; **~ troops** масси́ровать (*impf., pf.*) войска́; **~ed bands** объединённые (вое́нные) орке́стры; **the flowers were ~ed for effect** для созда́ния эффе́кта цветы́ бы́ли со́браны вме́сте.

● *v.i.* соб|ира́ться, -ра́ться; **the clouds are ~ing** собира́ются облака́.

● *cpd.* **~-produce** *v.t.*: **these toys are ~-produced** э́ти игру́шки ма́ссового/сери́йного произво́дства.

massacre /ˈmæsəkə(r)/ *n.* бо́йня.

● *v.t.* переб|ива́ть, -и́ть; (*fig., in sport*) разгроми́ть (*pf.*).

massage /ˈmæsɑːʒ/, /-sɑːdʒ/ *n.* масса́ж.

● *v.t.* масси́ровать (*impf., pf.*).

masseur /mæˈsɜː(r)/ *n.* массажи́ст.

masseuse /mæˈsɜːz/ *n.* массажи́стка.

massif /ˈmæsiːf/, /mæˈsiːf/ *n.* (го́рный) масси́в.

massive /ˈmæsɪv/ *adj.* масси́вный; (*very considerable, substantial*): **he received ~ support** он получи́л огро́мную подде́ржку.

mast¹ /mɑːst/ *n.* (*ship's ~, flagpole, radio ~*) ма́чта.

● *cpd.* **~head** *n.* (*naut.*) топ ма́чты; (*US, of newspaper*) заголо́вок газе́ты.

mast² /mɑːst/ *n.* (*bot.*) плодоко́рм.

mastectomy /mæsˈtektəmɪ/ *n.* мастэктоми́я (*ампутация молочной железы*).

master /ˈmɑːstə(r)/ *n.* **1** (*one in control, boss*) хозя́ин; (*owner*) владе́лец; **~ of the house** хозя́ин до́ма; **is the ~ in?** до́ма хозя́ин?; **be one's own ~** быть самому́ по себе́; ни от кого́ не зави́сеть; **be ~ of o.s.** владе́ть (*impf.*) собо́й; **~ of ceremonies** распоряди́тель (*m.*), конферансье́ (*indecl.*); **~ of the situation** хозя́ин положе́ния; **like ~, like man** ≈ како́в поп, тако́в прихо́д; (*of a ship*) капита́н; **~ mariner** капита́н, шки́пер.
2 (*Br., teacher*) учи́тель (*m.*); **maths ~** учи́тель матема́тики; (*in university*): **M~ of Arts** маги́стр гуманита́рных нау́к.
3 (*skilled craftsman, expert*) ма́стер; **~ builder** строи́тель-подря́дчик; **he was a ~ of satire** он был ма́стером сати́ры; **old ~s** (*artists*) ста́рые мастера́; (*paintings*) карти́ны ста́рых мастеро́в; **grand ~** (*chess*) гроссме́йстер; **he made himself ~ of the language** он овладе́л языко́м.
4 (*original*) по́длинник, моде́ль, оригина́л.
5 (*pref. to boy's name*) ма́стер, господи́н.
6 (*attr.*): **~ bedroom** гла́вная спа́льня; **~ plan** генера́льный план; **~ race** ра́са госпо́д; **~ switch** гла́вный выключа́тель; **~ touch** рука́ ма́стера.

● *v.t.* **1** (*gain control of, deal with*) спр|авля́ться, -а́виться с+*i.*; **the problem was easily ~ed** с пробле́мой легко́ удало́сь спра́виться.
2 (*acquire knowledge of, skill in*) овлад|ева́ть, -е́ть +*i.*; **it is a language which can be ~ed in 6 months** э́тим языко́м мо́жно овладе́ть за шесть ме́сяцев.
3 (*overcome*) овлад|ева́ть, -е́ть +*i.*; **~ one's feelings** владе́ть, о- свои́ми чу́вствами.

● *cpds.* **~-at-arms** *n.* гла́вный старшина́ корабе́льной поли́ции; **~-hand** *n.* ма́стер, специали́ст; **~-key** *n.* отмы́чка; **~-mind** *n.* (*genius*) ге́ний; (*leader*) руководи́тель (*m.*); *v.t.*: **he ~-minded the plan** он разрабо́тал весь план; **~piece** *n.* шеде́вр; **~-stroke** *n.* гениа́льный ход.

masterful /ˈmɑːstəˌfʊl/ *adj.* (*imperious*) вла́стный; (*skilful*) мастерско́й.

masterfulness /ˈmɑːstəˌfʊlnɪs/ *n.* вла́стность, деспоти́чность; уве́ренность; мастерство́.

masterly /ˈmɑːstəlɪ/ *adj.* мастерско́й; **in (a) ~ fashion** мастерски́.

mastery /ˈmɑːstərɪ/ *n.* **1** (*authority*) власть; (*supremacy*) госпо́дство; **~ of the seas** госпо́дство на мо́ре; **gain the ~ of** доб|ива́ться, -и́ться госпо́дства над+*i.* **2** (*skill*) мастерство́.
3 (*knowledge*) владе́ние; **~ of a subject** основа́тельное зна́ние предме́та.

mastic /ˈmæstɪk/ *n.* (*resin*) масти́ка; (*tree*) масти́ковое де́рево.

masticate /ˈmæstɪˌkeɪt/ *v.t. & i.* жева́ть, раз-.

mastication /ˌmæstɪˈkeɪʃ(ə)n/ *n.* жева́ние.

mastiff /ˈmæstɪf/, /ˈmɑːs-/ *n.* масти́фф (*порода собак*).

mastitis /mæˈstaɪtɪs/ *n.* масти́т.

mastodon /ˈmæstəˌdɒn/ *n.* мастодо́нт.

mastoid /ˈmæstɔɪd/ *n.* (*also* **~ process**) сосцеви́дный отро́сток; (*pl., coll., mastoiditis*) мастоиди́т.

masturbate /ˈmæstəˌbeɪt/ *v.i.* онани́ровать (*impf.*), мастурби́ровать (*impf.*).

masturbation /ˌmæstəˈbeɪʃ(ə)n/ *n.* онани́зм, мастурба́ция.

mat¹ /mæt/ *n.* **1** (*floor covering*) ко́врик; **(door-~)** рого́жка, полови́к; **wipe your feet on the ~** вы́трите но́ги о полови́к; **the boss had him on the ~** (*fig., coll.*) хозя́ин дал ему́ нагоня́й.
2 (*placed under an object to protect surface*) подста́вка, подсти́лка.

mat² /mæt/ *n.* (*tangled mass of hair etc.*) колту́н, клубо́к.

● *v.t.* **(matted, matting): his hair was ~ted with blood** его́ во́лосы сли́плись от кро́ви.

mat³ /mæt/ *adj.* = **mat(t)**

matador /ˈmætəˌdɔː(r)/ *n.* матадо́р.

match¹ /mætʃ/ *n.* (*for producing flame*) спи́чка; **box of ~es** коро́бка спи́чек; **put a ~ to** заж|ига́ть, -е́чь; подж|ига́ть, -е́чь; **strike a ~** заж|ига́ть, -е́чь спи́чку; чи́ркнуть (*pf.*) спи́чкой; **safety ~es** безопа́сные/обыкнове́нные спи́чки.

● *cpds.* **~board** *n.* шпунтова́я доска́; **~box** *n.* спи́чечная коро́бка; **~stick** *n.*: **he's as thin as a ~stick** он худо́й как ще́пка; **he drew ~stick figures** он рисова́л па́лочных челове́чков; **~wood** *n.* (*splinters*) спи́чечная соло́мка; **make ~wood of** разб|ива́ть, -и́ть вдре́безги.

match² /mætʃ/ *n.* **1** (*equal in strength or ability*) па́ра, ро́вня; **he's no ~ for her** он ей не па́ра; куда́ ему́ с ней равня́ться; **he found, met his ~** он нашёл/встре́тил досто́йного проти́вника; **he was more than a ~ for me** он был сильне́е меня́.
2 (*thing resembling or suiting another*): **these curtains are a good ~ for the carpet** э́ти занаве́ски подхо́дят к ковру́; **a perfect ~ of colours** (*Br.*), **colors** (*US*) прекра́сное сочета́ние цвето́в; **I can't find a ~ for this glove** я не могу́ подобра́ть па́ру к э́той перча́тке; (*of man and woman*): **they are, make a good ~** они́ хоро́шая па́ра.
3 (*marriage; possible marriage partner*) па́ртия; **she wants to make a good ~ for her daughter** она́ и́щет хоро́шей па́ртии свое́й до́чери.
4 (*contest; game*) соревнова́ние, состяза́ние; матч, игра́; **wrestling ~** состяза́ние по борьбе́; **football ~** футбо́льный матч; **doubles ~** па́рная игра́; **the ~ was drawn** игра́ ко́нчилась вничью́; **we lost all our away ~es** мы проигра́ли все и́гры/ма́тчи на чужо́м по́ле.

● *v.t.* **1** (*suit; correspond to*) под|ходи́ть, -ойти́ к+*d.*; гармони́ровать с+*i.*; **her hat doesn't ~ her dress** у неё шля́па не подхо́дит к пла́тью; **a hat trimmed**

M

with velvet to ~ шля́па, отде́ланная ба́рхатом подходя́щего цве́та; **she bought 6 chairs and 6 cushions to ~** она́ купи́ла 6 сту́льев и к ним 6 поду́шек соотве́тствующего цве́та; (*find a ~ for*): **can you ~ this button?** мо́жете ли вы подобра́ть таку́ю же пу́говицу?; **we try to ~ the jobs with the applicants** мы стара́емся подобра́ть подходя́щую рабо́ту для кандида́тов; **the contestants were well ~ed** уча́стники состяза́ния бы́ли уда́чно подо́браны.
2 (*equal*) сравня́ться (*impf.*) с + *i.*
3 (*pit, oppose*) противопост|авля́ть, -а́вить (*кого/что кому/чему*); **she ~ed her wits against his strength** она́ противопоста́вила его́ си́ле свою́ хи́трость.

● *v.i.* (*correspond: be identical*): **the handbag and gloves don't ~** су́мочка и перча́тки не гармони́руют друг с дру́гом.

● *cpds.* **~-maker** *n.* сват; (*fem.*) сва́ха; **~ point** *n.* очко́, реша́ющее исхо́д ма́тча.

matchless /ˈmætʃlɪs/ *adj.* несравне́нный.

mate[1] /meɪt/ *n.* **1** (*Br., companion; (coll.) form of address*) брат, друг, ко́реш; (*fellow-worker*) напа́рник; (*schoolfellow*) соучени́к. **2** (*one of a pair of animals or birds*) саме́ц; (*fem.*) са́мка; (*marriage partner*) супру́г (*fem.* -а). **3** (*assistant*) помо́щник; **surgeon's ~** ассисте́нт хиру́рга. **4** (*ship's ~*) помо́щник капита́на; **second ~** второ́й помо́щник.

● *v.t. & i.* спа́ри|вать(ся), -ть(ся).

mate[2] /meɪt/ *n.* (*chess*) мат; **~!** шах и мат!

● *v.t.* де́лать, с- мат + *d.*

matelot /ˈmætləʊ/ *n.* (*Br. coll.*) моря́к.

material /məˈtɪərɪəl/ *n.* **1** (*substance*) материа́л; **raw ~(s)** сырьё; (*fig., of person*): **he is good officer ~** из него́ вы́йдет хоро́ший офице́р; (*subject matter*): **there is good ~ there for a novel** там есть хоро́ший материа́л для рома́на. **2** (*fabric, stuff*) мате́рия; **dress ~** платяна́я ткань; **made of waterproof ~** сде́ланный из непромока́емого материа́ла. **3** (*pl.*): **writing ~s** пи́сьменные принадле́жности.

● *adj.* **1** (*pert. to matter or material; physical; bodily*) материа́льный; **~ needs** физи́ческие потре́бности; **the ~ world** материа́льный мир; **~ pleasures** земны́е ра́дости.
2 (*important, essential*) суще́ственный; **a ~ witness** ва́жный свиде́тель; **~ evidence** веще́ственные доказа́тельства; **the position has not changed ~ly** положе́ние по существу́ не измени́лось.

materialism /məˈtɪərɪəˌlɪz(ə)m/ *n.* материали́зм.

materialist /məˈtɪərɪəˌlɪst/ *n.* материали́ст.

materialistic /məˌtɪərɪəˈlɪstɪk/ *adj.* материалисти́ческий.

materialization /məˌtɪərɪəlaɪˈzeɪʃ(ə)n/ *n.* (*taking bodily form*) материализа́ция; (*fulfilment*) осуществле́ние; материализа́ция.

materialize /məˈtɪərɪəˌlaɪz/ *v.t.* материализова́ть (*impf., pf.*).

● *v.i.* материализова́ться; (*come to pass, be fulfilled*) осуществ|ля́ться, -и́ться.

matériel /məˌtɪərɪˈel/ *n.* (*mil.*) материа́льная часть, те́хника.

maternal /məˈtɜːn(ə)l/ *adj.* (*motherly*) матери́нский; (*on mother's side*): **~ uncle** дя́дя с матери́нской стороны́ (*or* по ма́тери).

maternity /məˈtɜːnɪtɪ/ *n.* матери́нство; (*attr.*): **~ benefit** посо́бие роже́нице; **~ dress** пла́тье для бере́менных; **~ hospital** роди́льный дом; **~ leave** декре́тный о́тпуск.

mat(e)y /ˈmeɪtɪ/ *adj.* (**matier, matiest**) (*Br.*) общи́тельный, компане́йский.

math /mæθ/ *n.* (*US coll., abbr.*) = **mathematics**

mathematical /ˌmæθɪˈmætɪk(ə)l/ *adj.* математи́ческий.

mathematician /ˌmæθɪməˈtɪʃ(ə)n/ *n.* матема́тик.

mathematics /ˌmæθɪˈmætɪks/ *n.* матема́тика.

maths /mæθs/ *n.* (*Br. coll., abbr.*) = **mathematics**

matinée /ˈmætɪˌneɪ/ *n.* дневно́е представле́ние; у́тренник; **~ idol** актёр, по́льзующийся популя́рностью у зая́длых театра́лок.

mating /ˈmeɪtɪŋ/ *n.* спа́ривание; **~ season** сезо́н спа́ривания.

matins /ˈmætɪnz/ *n.* (за)у́треня.

matriarchy /ˈmeɪtrɪˌɑːkɪ/ *n.* матриарха́т.

matrices /ˈmeɪtrɪˌsiːz/ *pl. of* ⇒**matrix**

matricide /ˈmeɪtrɪˌsaɪd/ *n.* (*crime*) матереуби́йство; (*criminal*) матереуби́йца (*c.g.*).

matriculate /məˈtrɪkjʊˌleɪt/ *v.i.* быть при́нятым в вы́сшее уче́бное заведе́ние.

matriculation /məˌtrɪkjʊˈleɪʃ(ə)n/ *n.* зачисле́ние в вы́сшее уче́бное заведе́ние.

matrilineal /ˌmætrɪˈlɪnɪəl/ *adj.* по матери́нской ли́нии.

matrimonial /ˌmætrɪˈməʊnɪəl/ *adj.* супру́жеский; бра́чный.

matrimony /ˈmætrɪmənɪ/ *n.* брак.

matri|x /ˈmeɪtrɪks/ *n.* (*pl.* **~ces** /-ˌsiːz/ *or* **~xes**) ма́трица.

matron /ˈmeɪtrən/ *n.* **1** (*elderly married woman*) матро́на. **2** (*Br., in hospital*) ста́ршая сестра́; сестра́-хозя́йка. **3** (*in school*) эконо́мка.

matronly /ˈmeɪtrənlɪ/ *adj.* подоба́ющий почте́нной же́нщине.

mat(t) /mæt/ *adj.* ма́товый; **~ paint** ма́товая кра́ска.

matter /ˈmætə(r)/ *n.* **1** (*phys., phil.*) мате́рия; (*substance*) вещество́.
2 (*physiol.*): **grey ~** се́рое вещество́; (*pus*) гной.
3 (*content, opp. form or style*) содержа́ние.
4 (*material for reading*) материа́лы (*m. pl.*); **printed ~** печа́тный материа́л; (*as category for postal purposes*) ≈ бандеро́ль.
5 (*material for discussion*) те́ма, предме́т; **the article provided ~ for debate** статья́ дала́ пи́щу для диску́ссии; (*question; issue*) вопро́с; де́ло; **that's quite another ~** э́то совсе́м друго́е де́ло; **it is a ~ of course** само́ собо́й разуме́ется; **as a ~ of fact** (*to tell the truth*) по пра́вде сказа́ть; (*in reality*) на са́мом де́ле; (*incidentally*) со́бственно (говоря́); **a ~ of some importance** ва́жный вопро́с; **it is a ~ for the police** э́то де́ло поли́ции; **it's no laughing ~** э́то де́ло не шу́точное; **a ~ of life and death** вопро́с жи́зни и сме́рти; **it's a ~ of money** всё де́ло в деньга́х; **that's a ~ of opinion** э́то вопро́с мне́ния; **a ~ of principle** де́ло при́нципа; **a ~ of taste** де́ло вку́са; **it's only a ~ of time before he gives in** ра́но и́ли по́здно он сда́стся; **a ~ of urgency** сро́чное де́ло; (*pl., affairs*) дела́; **money ~s** де́нежные дела́; **as ~s stand** при тепе́решнем положе́нии дел; **to make ~s worse** в доверше́ние ко всем бе́дам.
6: **the ~** (*wrong, amiss*): **what's the ~?** в чём де́ло?; **is (there) anything the ~?** что́-нибудь не ла́дно?; **what's the ~ with him?** что с ним?; **there's nothing the ~ (with me)** (у меня́) всё в поря́дке.
7 (*importance*): **(it's) no ~** э́то нева́жно; **no ~ what I do, the result will be the same** что бы я ни сде́лал, результа́т бу́дет тот же; **he could not do it, no ~ how he tried** как он ни стара́лся, он не мог э́того сде́лать.
8: **a ~ of** (*a few*): **he was back again in a ~ of hours** он верну́лся че́рез не́сколько часо́в.
9: **for that ~; for the ~ of that** е́сли уж на то пошло́.
10: **in the ~ of** в отноше́нии + *g.*; относи́тельно + *g.*; что каса́ется + *g.*

● *v.i.* име́ть (*impf.*) значе́ние; **it doesn't ~ to me** э́то не име́ет для меня́ значе́ния; **does it ~ if I come late?** ничего́, е́сли я опозда́ю? **it doesn't ~ much if you come late** ничего́ стра́шного, е́сли вы опозда́ете; **what does it ~ what I say?** ра́зве мои́ слова́ име́ют хоть како́е-то значе́ние?; **what can it possibly ~ to him?** како́е значе́ние, в конце́ концо́в, э́то име́ет для него́?

● *cpd.* **~-of-fact** *adj.* приземлённый, лишённый фанта́зии; сухо́й, делово́й.

matting /ˈmætɪŋ/ *n.* рого́жка, цино́вка.

mattins /ˈmætɪnz/ = **matins**

mattock /ˈmætək/ *n.* моты́га.

mattress /ˈmætrɪs/ *n.* матра́ц; **air ~** надувно́й матра́ц.

maturation /ˌmætjʊˈreɪʃ(ə)n/ *n.* созрева́ние.

mature /məˈtjʊə(r)/ *adj.* (**maturer, maturest**) **1** (*of fruit etc., ripe*) спе́лый; (*lit., fig., ripe, developed*) зре́лый; **on ~ consideration** по зре́лом размышле́нии; **a person of ~ years** челове́к зре́лых лет; **~ student** (*Br.*) студе́нт (*fem.* -ка) зре́лого во́зраста.
2 (*ready, prepared*) гото́вый.

3 (*comm., ready for payment*) подлежа́щий опла́те; (*of debt*) подлежа́щий погаше́нию.

● *v.t.* (*crops, wine etc.*) выде́рживать, вы́держать.

● *v.i.* **1** (*lit., fig., ripen, develop*) созр|ева́ть, -е́ть; **the grapes ~d in the sun** виногра́д созре́л на со́лнце; **children ~ earlier nowadays** в на́ши дни де́ти развива́ются быстре́е; **his plans have not yet ~d** его́ пла́ны ещё не созре́ли/офо́рмились. **2** (*become due for payment*): **the policy ~s next year** в бу́дущем году́ наступа́ет срок вы́платы по страхово́му по́лису.

maturity /məˈtjʊərɪtɪ/ *n.* зре́лость.

matzo /ˈmɑːtsəʊ/ *n.* (*pl.* **matzos** *or* **matzoth** /-əʊt/) маца́.

maudlin /ˈmɔːdlɪn/ *adj.* слюня́во сентимента́льный; плакси́вый во хмелю́.

maul /mɔːl/ *v.t.* **1** (*of person*) изб|ива́ть, -и́ть; **stop ~ing me about!** переста́ньте меня́ терза́ть!; (*of animal*) терза́ть, рас-; **he was ~ed to death by a tiger** его́ растерза́л тигр. **2** (*fig., by criticism*) громи́ть, раз-; **his last book got a ~ing from the critics** кри́тики разгроми́ли его́ после́днюю кни́гу в пух и прах.

Maundy Thursday /ˈmɔːndɪ/ *n.* Страстно́й/Вели́кий четве́рг.

Mauritania /ˌmɒrɪˈteɪnɪə/ *n.* Маврита́ния.

Mauritanian /ˌmɒrɪˈteɪnɪən/ *n.* маврита́н|ец (*fem.* -ка).

● *adj.* маврита́нский.

Mauritius /məˈrɪʃəs/ *n.* Маври́кий.

mausole|um /ˌmɔːsəˈliːəm/ *n.* (*pl.* **~a** *or* **~ums**) мавзоле́й.

mauve /məʊv/ *n. & adj.* розова́то-лило́вый (цвет).

maverick /ˈmævərɪk/ *n.* (*US, calf*) неклеймёный телёнок; (*fig., dissenter*) диссиде́нт, «бе́лая воро́на»; (*attr.*) неприка́янный.

maw /mɔː/ *n.* утро́ба; (*fig.*) пасть.

mawkish /ˈmɔːkɪʃ/ *adj.* при́торный.

mawkishness /ˈmɔːkɪʃnɪs/ *n.* при́торность.

maxilla /mækˈsɪlə/ *n.* (*pl.* **maxillae** /-liː/) ве́рхняя че́люсть.

maxillary /mækˈsɪlərɪ/ *adj.* верхнечелюстно́й.

maxim /ˈmæksɪm/ *n.* (*aphorism*) афори́зм; (*principle*) при́нцип.

maxima /ˈmæksɪmə/ *pl. of* ⇒**maximum**

maximize /ˈmæksɪˌmaɪz/ *v.t.* максима́льно увели́чи|вать, -ть.

maxim|um /ˈmæksɪməm/ *n.* (*pl.* **~a** *or* **~ums**) ма́ксимум.

● *adj.* максима́льный.

May /meɪ/ *n.* **1** (*month*) май; **~ Day** Пе́рвое мая; пра́здник Пе́рвого ма́я; **~ Day parade** первома́йский пара́д. **2** (*attr.*) ма́йский. **3**: **(m~)** (*hawthorn*) боя́рышник.

● *cpds.* **~day** *n.* (*distress signal*) сигна́л бе́дствия; **~fly** *n.* подёнка; **~pole** *n.* ма́йское де́рево.

may /meɪ/ *v. aux.* (*3rd pers. sing. pres.* **may;** *past* **might**) **1** (*expr. possibility*) мо́жет быть; пожа́луй; **it ~ be true** возмо́жно, э́то пра́вда; **it ~ not be true** возмо́жно, э́то не так; **he ~, might lose his way** он мо́жет заблуди́ться; **he might have lost his way without my help** без мое́й по́мощи он мог бы заблуди́ться; **I was afraid he might have lost his way** я боя́лся, как бы он не заблуди́лся; **you ~ well be right** вполне́ возмо́жно, вы и пра́вы; **we ~, might as well stay** почему́ бы нам не оста́ться?; **and who ~, might you be?** а кто вы тако́й?; **that's as ~ be** э́то ещё вопро́с; **be that as it ~** как бы то ни́ было. **2** (*expr. permission*): **~ I come and see you?** мо́жно мне (*or* могу́ я) к вам зайти́?; **you ~ go if you wish** е́сли хоти́те, мо́жете идти́; **you ~ not smoke** нельзя́ кури́ть; **where have you been, ~ I ask?** могу́ я узна́ть, где вы пропада́ли? **3** (*expr. suggestion*): **you might call at the butcher's** вы бы зашли́ к мяснику́. **4** (*expr. reproach*): **you might offer to help!** вы могли́ бы предложи́ть свою́ по́мощь!; **you might have asked my permission** мо́жно бы́ло бы спроси́ть моего́ согла́сия. **5** (*in subord. clauses, expr. purpose, fear, wish, hope*): **I wrote (so) that you might know** я вам написа́л, что́бы вы зна́ли; **I fear he ~ be dead** я бою́сь, что он у́мер; **I hope he ~ come** наде́юсь, он придёт; **I hoped he might come** я наде́ялся, что он придёт. **6** (*in main clause, expr. wish or hope*): **~ you live long!** жела́ю вам до́лгой жи́зни!; **~ you live to repent it!** наде́юсь, вы об э́том ещё пожале́ете!; **~ the best man win!** да победи́т сильне́йший! **7** (*be able*): **try as I ~, I shall never learn to speak Russian well** как бы я ни стара́лся, я никогда́ не научу́сь хорошо́ говори́ть по-ру́сски.

● *cpd.* **~be** *adv.* мо́жет быть.

mayhem /ˈmeɪhem/ *n.* (*chaos*) разгро́м; **cause, create ~** учин|я́ть, -и́ть разгро́м.

mayonnaise /ˌmeɪəˈneɪz/ *n.* майоне́з.

mayor /meə(r)/ *n.* городско́й голова́; мэр.

mayoralty /ˈmeərəltɪ/ *n.* (*office*) до́лжность мэ́ра; (*period*): **during his ~** в бы́тность его́ мэ́ром.

mayoress /ˈmeərɪs/ *n.* (*mayor's wife*) жена́ мэ́ра; (*female mayor*) же́нщина-мэр.

maze /meɪz/ *n.* лабири́нт; (*fig.*) пу́таница.

mazurka /məˈzɜːkə/ *n.* мазу́рка.

Mb /ˈmegəˌbaɪt(s)/ *n.* (*comput., abbr. of* ***megabyte(s)***) мегаба́йт.

MBA (*abbr. of* ***Master of Business Administration***) маги́стр ме́неджмента.

MBE (*abbr. of* ***Member of the Order of the British Empire***) кавале́р о́рдена Брита́нской импе́рии 5-й сте́пени.

MC (*abbr. of* ***Master of Ceremonies***) конферансье́ (*indecl.*), распоряди́тель (*m.*).

MD *abbr. of* **1** ***Doctor of Medicine*** до́ктор медици́ны. **2** ***Managing Director*** (*Br.*) дире́ктор-распоряди́тель.

ME 1 (*abbr. of* ***myalgic encephalitis***) миалги́ческий энцефали́т. **2** (*abbr. of* ***medical examiner***) (*US*) суде́бно-медици́нский экспе́рт.

me¹ /miː/ *obj. of* ⇒**I**

me² /miː/ (*mus.*) тре́тья но́та мажо́рной га́ммы; (*the note E*) ми (*indecl.*).

mead /miːd/ *n.* (*drink*) мёд.

meadow /ˈmedəʊ/ *n.* луг.

● *cpds.* **~-grass** *n.* мя́тлик лугово́й; **~-lark** *n.* жа́воронок лугово́й; **~-saffron** *n.* безвреме́нник осе́нний, зимо́вник; **~-sweet** *n.* та́волга; лаба́зник.

meagre /ˈmiːgə(r)/ (*US* **meager**) *adj.* **1** (*of person, thin*) худо́й, то́щий. **2** (*poor, scanty*) ску́дный; **~ fare** по́стная еда́.

meal¹ /miːl/ *n.* (*ground grain*) мука́ (гру́бого помо́ла).

meal² /miːl/ *n.* еда́, тра́песа; **don't talk during ~s** не разгова́ривайте во вре́мя еды́; **have a good ~** пло́тно пое́сть (*pf.*); **have a light ~** заку́с|ывать, -и́ть; **it's a long time since I had a square ~** я давно́ не ел сы́тно; **don't make a ~ of it** (*Br. coll., fig.*) не раздува́йте из э́того це́лую исто́рию; **we have 3 ~s a day** мы еди́м три ра́за в день; **we have our ~s in the canteen** мы пита́емся в столо́вой; **let's have a ~ out this evening** дава́йте сего́дня поу́жинаем в рестора́не; **shall we ask them round for a ~?** не пригласи́ть ли их пообе́дать/поу́жинать с на́ми?; **evening ~** у́жин; **midday ~** обе́д.

● *cpds.* **~-ticket** *n.* тало́н на обе́д; **he is my ~-ticket** я живу́ за его́ счёт; **~time** *n.*: **at ~times** за едо́й.

mealy /ˈmiːlɪ/ *adj.* (**mealier, mealiest**) **1** (*consisting of meal*) мучни́стый; (*resembling meal, floury*): **~ potatoes** рассы́пчатый карто́фель. **2** (*fig., of complexion*) мучни́стый.

● *cpd.* **~-mouthed** *adj.* чрезме́рно делика́тный.

mean¹ /miːn/ *n.* (*intermediate or average point, condition etc.*) середи́на; **a happy (*or* the golden) ~** золота́я середи́на; (*math.*) сре́дняя величина́; (*pl., method, resources*) *see* ⇒**means**

● *adj.* сре́дний; **Greenwich ~ time** сре́днее вре́мя по Гри́нвичу.

● *cpds.* **~time** *n.*: **in the ~time** ме́жду тем; **~while** *adv.* ме́жду тем, тем вре́менем.

mean² /miːn/ *adj.* **1** (*lowly*) ни́зкий. **2** (*inferior*): **he is a man of no ~ abilities** он челове́к незауря́дных спосо́бностей. **3** (*shabby, squalid*): **~ streets** убо́гие у́лицы (*f. pl.*). **4** (*niggardly*) скупо́й. **5** (*ignoble; discreditable*) ни́зкий, по́длый. **6** (*ill-natured, spiteful*) зло́бный; **don't be ~ to him** не обижа́йте его́.

M

mean³ /miːn/ *v.t.* (*past and p.p.* **meant**) **1** (*intend*) имéть (*impf.*) в видý; намеревáться (*impf.*); **I ~ to solve this problem** я намéрен решúть э́тот вопрóс; **he ~s business** он берётся за дéло всерьёз; **he ~s mischief** у негó дурны́е намéрения; **he ~s well by you** он желáет вам добрá; **I ~t no harm** я не желáл зла; **I ~t it as a joke** я хотéл пошутúть; **I ~t to leave yesterday, but couldn't** я собирáлся вчерá уéхать, но не смог; **I didn't ~ to hurt you** я не хотéл вас обúдеть.
2 (*design, destine*) предназн|ачáть, -áчить; **his parents ~t him to be a doctor** родúтели прóчили егó в доктораá; **they were ~t for each other** онú бы́ли сóзданы друг для дрýга; **this letter is ~t for you** э́то письмó предназначáется вам.
3 (*of person, intend to convey*) хотéть (*impf.*) сказáть; **what do you ~?** что вы э́тим хотúте сказáть?; **he ~s what he says** он говорúт то, что дýмает; **do you ~ Charles I or Charles II?** вы говорúте о Кáрле I úли о Кáрле II?; **what do you ~ by it?** (*how dare you?*) как вы смéете?
4 (*of words etc., signify*) знáчить (*impf.*), означáть (*impf.*); **this sentence ~s nothing to me** э́то предложéние ничегó мне не говорúт; **what is ~t by this word?** как нáдо понимáть э́то слóво?; **modern music ~s nothing to me** совремéнная мýзыка мне совершéнно непоня́тна; **this ~s we can't go** знáчит, мы не смóжем пойтú; **her promises don't ~ a thing** её обещáния ничегó не стóят; **does my friendship ~ nothing to you?** неужéли моя́ дрýжба ничегó для вас не знáчит?; (*entail, involve*): **organizing a fête ~s a lot of hard work** подготóвка к прáзднику трéбует мнóго усúлий; (*portend*): **this ~s war** э́то приведёт к войнé; знáчит, бýдет войнá.

meander /mɪˈændə(r)/ *v.i.* (*of streams, roads etc.*) извивáться (*impf.*), вúться (*impf.*); **a ~ing river** извúлистая рекá; (*of person, wander along*) бродúть (*impf.*); (*in speech etc.*) сбивáться (*impf.*) с мы́слей (в рéчи *и т.п.*).

meaning /ˈmiːnɪŋ/ *n.* значéние; **what is the ~ of this word?** что э́то слóво означáет?; **get the ~ of** пон|имáть, -я́ть смысл + *g.*; **what is the ~ of this?** (*querying another's action*) что э́то знáчит?

meaningful /ˈmiːnɪŋfʊl/ *adj.* (*full of meaning*) многозначúтельный; (*making sense*) содержáтельный, толкóвый.

meaningless /ˈmiːnɪŋlɪs/ *adj.* бессмы́сленный.

meanness /ˈmiːnnɪs/ *n.* пóдлость, нúзость; скýпость.

means /miːnz/ *n.* **1** (*instrument, method*) спóсоб; **a ~ to an end** срéдство для достижéния цéли; **we shall find ways and ~ of persuading him** мы найдём спóсоб убедúть егó; **by ~ of** посрéдством + *g.*; с пóмощью + *g.*; **by all (manner of) ~** всéми срéдствами; **by all ~** (*US, without fail*) непремéнно; (*expr. permission*) конéчно; пожáлуйста; **by no ~** никóим óбразом; **it was by no ~ easy** э́то бы́ло отню́дь не легкó.
2 (*facilities*): **~ of communication** (*transport*) срéдства сообщéния; (*telecommunication*) срéдства свя́зи.
3 (*resources*) срéдства; **~ of existence** срéдства к существовáнию; **a man of ~** человéк со срéдствами; **he has private ~** у негó есть сóбственные срéдства; **~ test** провéрка нуждáемости; **live beyond one's ~** жить (*impf.*) не по срéдствам.

meant /ment/ *past and p.p. of* ⇒**mean³**

measles /ˈmiːz(ə)lz/ *n.* корь; **German ~** краснýха; **a child with ~** ребёнок, больнóй кóрью.

measly /ˈmiːzlɪ/ *adj.* (**measlier, measliest**) (*coll., miserably small*) жáлкий.

measurable /ˈmeʒərəb(ə)l/ *adj.* измерúмый.

measure /ˈmeʒə(r)/ *n.* **1** (*calculated quantity, size etc.*; *system of ~ment*) мéра; **dry ~** мéра сыпýчих тел; **linear ~** линéйная мéра; **liquid ~** мéра жúдкостей; **clothes made to ~** одéжда, сшúтая на закáз; **short ~** (*of weight*) недовéс; (*of length etc.*) недомéр; **full ~** пóлная мéра; (*portion, of whisky etc.*) пóрция; (*fig.*): **he repaid my kindness in full ~** он отплатúл мне за мою́ добротý сполнá; **it took him less than a day to get the ~ of his new assistant** не прошлó и дня, как он раскусúл своегó нóвого помóщника.
2 (*degree, extent*) стéпень; **his reply showed the ~ of his intelligence** по егó отвéту мóжно бы́ло судúть о стéпени егó умá; **in large ~** во мнóгом; **in some ~** до нéкоторой стéпени; (*prescribed limit, extent*) предéл; **she was irritated beyond ~** онá пришлá в невероя́тное раздражéние.
3 (*measuring device*): **metre** (*Br.*), **meter** (*US*) **~** метр; **litre** (*Br.*), **liter** (*US*) **~** литрóвый мéрный сосýд.
4 (*proceeding, step*) мéра, мероприя́тие; **take ~s against** прин|имáть, -я́ть мéры прóтив + *g.*; **adopt severe ~s** примен|я́ть, -úть стрóгие мéры.
5 (*law*) закóн; **pass a ~** приня́ть (*pf.*) закóн.
6 (*verse rhythm*) размéр; (*US, mus.*) такт.
7 (*mineral stratum*): **coal ~s** каменноугóльные пластьí (*m. pl.*).

● *v.t.* **1** (*find size etc. of*) мéрить, с-; изм|еря́ть, -éрить; **he was ~d for a suit** с негó сня́ли мéрку для костю́ма; (*fig.*): **I ~d him up and down** я смéрил егó взгля́дом.
2 (*amount to when ~d*): **the room ~s 12 ft. across** кóмната ширинóй в двенáдцать фýтов.

● *with advs.*: **~ off, ~ out** *vv.t.* отм|еря́ть, -éрить; **he ~d out a litre** (*Br.*), **liter** (*US*) **of milk** он отмéрил литр молокá; **the football pitch had been ~d out** футбóльное пóле бы́ло ужé размéчено; **~ up** *v.i.*: **the team has not ~d up to our expectations** комáнда не оправдáла нáших ожидáний.

measured /ˈmeʒəd/ *adj.* **1** (*rhythmical*) размéренный; **~ tread** мéрная пóступь. **2** (*of speech, moderate*) умéренный; (*carefully considered*) обдýманный, осторóжный.

measureless /ˈmeʒələs/ *adj.* безмéрный.

measurement /ˈmeʒəmənt/ *n.* (*measuring*) измерéние; (*dimension*) размéр; **take s.o.'s ~s** снять (*pf.*) мéрку с когó-н.; **waist ~** объём тáлии.

meat /miːt/ *n.* мя́со; **one man's ~ is another man's poison** что полéзно однomý, то другóму врéдно; ≈ что рýсскому здóрово, то нéмцу смерть; **argument is ~ and drink to him** (*Br.*) егó хлéбом не кормú, дай поспóрить.

● *cpds.* **~-ball** *n.* фрикадéлька; **~-eater** *n.* (*animal*) плотоя́дное живóтное; (*person*) человéк, не избегáющий мяснóй диéты; **~-eating** *adj.* плотоя́дный; **~-pie** *n.* пирóг с мя́сом; **~-safe** *n.* (*Br.*) холодúльник для хранéния мя́са.

meaty /ˈmiːtɪ/ *adj.* (**meatier, meatiest**) мясúстый; (*fig., pithy*) содержáтельный.

Mecca /ˈmekə/ *n.* (*lit., fig.*) Мéкка.

mechanic /mɪˈkænɪk/ *n.* мехáник.

mechanical /mɪˈkænɪk(ə)l/ *adj.* **1** (*pert. to machines*) механúческий; **~ engineer** инженéр-мехáник; **~ engineering** машинострoéние; **a ~ failure** механúческое повреждéние; **~ly operated** с механúческим управлéнием. **2** (*of person or movements: automatic*) машинáльный.

mechanics /mɪˈkænɪks/ *n.* (*lit., fig.*) мехáника.

mechanism /ˈmekəˌnɪz(ə)m/ *n.* механúзм.

mechanistic /ˌmekəˈnɪstɪk/ *adj.* (*phil.*) механистúческий.

mechanization /ˌmekənaɪˈzeɪʃ(ə)n/ *n.* механизáция.

mechanize /ˈmekəˌnaɪz/ *v.t. & i.* механизúровать(ся) (*impf., pf.*).

Med /med/ *n.* (*Br. coll., abbr.*): **the ~** Средизéмное мóре.

medal /ˈmed(ə)l/ *n.* медáль; (*mil. award*) óрден (*pl.* -á).

medallion /mɪˈdæljən/ *n.* медальóн.

medallist /ˈmedəlɪst/ (*US* **medalist**) *n.* (*recipient*) медалúст (*fem.* -ка); призёр; (*engraver*) медальéр.

meddle /ˈmed(ə)l/ *v.i.*: **~ in** (*interfere in*) вмéш|ивaться, -áться в + *a.*; **~ with** (*touch, tamper with*) трó|гать, -нуть.

meddlesome /ˈmedəlsəm/ *adj.* назóйливый; **he is a ~ person** он всё врéмя вмéшивается не в свой делá.

media /ˈmiːdɪə/ *see* ⇒**medium** *n.* 6

mediaeval /ˌmedɪˈiːv(ə)l/ = **medieval**

median /ˈmiːdɪən/ *n.* (*math., stat.*) медиáна.

● *adj.* срединный.

mediate /ˈmiːdɪˌeɪt/ *v.t.*: **the settlement was ~d by Britain** соглашéние бы́ло достúгнуто при посрéдничестве Великобритáнии.

● *v.i.* выступáть, вы́ступить посрéдником; посрéдничать (*impf.*).

mediation /ˌmi:dɪ'eɪʃ(ə)n/ *n.* посрéдничество.

mediator /'mi:dɪˌeɪtə(r)/ *n.* посрéдник.

mediatory /'mi:dɪətərɪ/ *adj.* посрéднический.

medic /'medɪk/ *n.* (*coll.*) (студéнт-)мéдик.

medical /'medɪk(ə)l/ *n.* (*coll.*, ~ *examination*): **have a ~** про|ходи́ть, -йти́ медици́нский осмóтр (*abbr.* медосмóтр).

● *adj.* медици́нский; врачéбный; (*opp. surgical*) терапевти́ческий; **~ certificate** спрáвка от врачá; **~ examiner** (*US, forensic scientist*) судéбно-медици́нский экспéрт; **~ history** истóрия болéзни; **~ man, practitioner** врач, терапéвт; **~ officer** (*Br.*) офицéр медици́нской слýжбы; **~ orderly** санитáр; **~ service** медици́нское обслýживание; **~ unit** санитáрная часть; санчáсть.

medicament /mɪ'dɪkəmənt/, /'medɪkəmənt/ *n.* лекáрство, медикамéнт.

medicate /'medɪˌkeɪt/ *v.t.* (*treat medically*) лечи́ть (*impf.*); (*impregnate*) нас|ыщáть, -ы́тить лекáрством.

medication /ˌmedɪ'keɪʃ(ə)n/ *n.* (*medicine*) лекáрство; (*treatment*) лечéние.

medicinal /mɪ'dɪsɪn(ə)l/ *adj.* (*of medicine*) лекáрственный; (*curative*) целéбный.

medicine /'medsɪn/, /-dɪsɪn/ *n.* **1** (*science, practice*) медици́на; **practise** (*Br.*), **practice** (*US*) **~** практиковáть/ рабóтать (*impf.*) врачóм. **2** (*substance*) лекáрство; медикамéнт, микстýра; **he is taking ~ for a cough** он принимáет лекáрство от кáшля; **I gave him a taste of his own ~** (*fig.*) я емý отплати́л той же монéтой.

● *cpds.* **~-ball** *n.* (*sport*) медицинбóл; **~-cabinet, ~-chest** *nn.* аптéчка; **~-man** *n.* знáхарь (*m.*).

medico /'medɪˌkəʊ/ *n.* (*pl.* **~s**) (*coll.*) мéдик.

medieval /ˌmedɪ'i:v(ə)l/ *adj.* средневекóвый.

medievalist /ˌmedɪ'i:v(ə)lɪst/ *n.* медиеви́ст.

mediocre /ˌmi:dɪ'əʊkə(r)/ *adj.* посрéдственный.

mediocrity /ˌmi:dɪ'ɒkrɪtɪ/ *n.* посрéдственность.

meditate /'medɪˌteɪt/ *v.t.* замышля́ть (*impf.*).

● *v.i.* размышля́ть (*impf.*) (**on:** о + *p.*).

meditation /ˌmedɪ'teɪʃ(ə)n/ *n.* размышлéние.

meditative /'medɪtətɪv/ *adj.* задýмчивый.

Mediterranean /ˌmedɪtə'reɪnɪən/ *n.* (**~ Sea**) Средизéмное мóре.

● *adj.* средиземномóрский.

medium /'mi:dɪəm/ *n.* (*pl.* **media** *or* **mediums**) **1** (*middle quality*) середи́на; **he strikes a happy ~** он придéрживается золотóй середи́ны. **2** (*phys., intervening substance*) средá. **3** (*means, agency*) срéдство; **through the ~ of** посрéдством + *g.* **4** (*solvent*) растворитель (*m.*). **5** (*spiritualist*) мéдиум. **6** (*means or channel of expression*) срéдство; **the media** (*sc. of communication*) срéдства мáссовой информáции; (*of sculptor*) материáл. **7** (*phys.*) средá.

● *adj.* (*intermediate*) промежýточный; (*average*) срéдний; **a man of ~ height** человéк срéднего рóста.

● *cpds.* **~-dry** *adj.* полусухóй; **~-sized** *adj.* срéднего размéра; **~-wave** *adj.* (*Br.*) средневóлновый.

medlar /'medlə(r)/ *n.* (*bot.*) мушмулá.

medley /'medlɪ/ *n.* (*pl.* **medleys**) смесь; (*mus.*) попурри́ (*nt. indecl.*).

medusa /mɪ'dju:zə/, /-sə/ *n.* (*pl.* **medusae** /-zi:/, /-si:/ *or* **medusas**) (*zool.*) медýза.

meek /mi:k/ *adj.* крóткий.

meekness /'mi:knɪs/ *n.* крóтость.

meerschaum /'mɪəʃəm/ *n.* (*clay*) морскáя пéнка; (*pipe*) пéнковая трýбка.

meet /mi:t/ *n.* (*of sportsmen, etc.*) сбор.

● *v.t.* (*past and p.p.* **met**) **1** (*encounter*) встр|ечáть, -éтить; **fancy ~ing you!** ну и встрéча!; **~ s.o. halfway** (*fig.*) идти́, пойти́ навстрéчу комý-н.; (*greet*): **she met her guests at the door** онá встрéтила гостéй в дверя́х; **a bus ~s all trains** к прихóду кáждого пóезда подаю́т автóбус; **they were met by a hail of bullets** они́ бы́ли встрéчены шквáльным огнём; (*make acquaintance of*) знакóмиться, по- с + *i.*; **I met your sister in Moscow** я познакóмился с вáшей сестрóй в Москвé; **(I want you to) ~ my fiancée** я хочý познакóмить вас с моéй невéстой.
2 (*reach point of contact with*): **where the river ~s the sea** там, где рекá впадáет в мóре; при впадéнии реки́ в мóре; **there is more in this than ~s the eye** здесь дéло не так прóсто.
3 (*face*): **they advanced to ~ the enemy** они́ продви́нулись навстрéчу проти́внику; **I am ready to ~ your challenge** я готóв приня́ть ваш вы́зов.
4 (*experience, suffer*): **~ one's death** поги́бнуть (*pf.*); **he met misfortune with a smile** он мýжественно переноси́л невзгóды.
5 (*satisfy, answer, fulfil*): **I cannot ~ your wishes** я не могý вы́полнить (*pf.*) вáши трéбования; **the request was met by a sharp refusal** прóсьба натолкнýлась на рéзкий откáз; **he met all their objections** он учёл все их возражéния.
6 (*pay, settle*): **~ a bill** уплá|чивать, -ти́ть по счёту; **this will barely ~ my expenses** э́то с трудóм покрóет мои́ расхóды.

● *v.i.* (*past and p.p.* **met**) **1** (*of persons, come together*) встр|ечáться, -éтиться; **we seldom ~** мы рéдко встречáемся; **haven't we met before?** мы с вáми не знакóмы?; **I hope to ~ you again soon** я надéюсь скóро с вáми встрéтиться; **our eyes met** нáши глазá встрéтились; (*become acquainted*) знакóмиться, по-; **we met at a dance** мы познакóмились на тáнцах.
2 (*assemble*) соб|ирáться, -рáться; **the council met to discuss the situation** совéт собрáлся, чтóбы обсуди́ть положéние.
3 (*of things, qualities etc.: come into contact, unite*) сходи́ться (*impf.*); **this belt won't ~ round his waist** э́тот пóяс на нём не схóдится; **there are traffic lights where the roads ~** на перекрёстке — светофóр; **the rivers Oka and Volga ~ at Nizhniy Novgorod** Ни́жний Нóвгород — мéсто слия́ния рек Оки́ и Вóлги; **make (both) ends ~** (*fig.*) св|оди́ть, -ести́ концы́ с концáми.
4 ~ with: ~ with difficulties испы́т|ывать, -áть затруднéния; **I met with much opposition** я натолкнýлся на си́льное сопротивлéние; **~ with approval/refusal** встрéтить (*pf.*) одобрéние/откáз; **he met with an accident** с ним произошёл несчáстный слýчай.

● *with advs.*: **~ together** *v.i.* соб|ирáться, -рáться; **~ up** *v.i.* (*coll.*): **we met up (***or* **I met up with him) in London** мы встрéтились в Лóндоне.

meeting /'mi:tɪŋ/ *n.* **1** (*encounter*) встрéча; **our ~ was purely accidental** мы встрéтились совершéнно случáйно; (*by arrangement*) свидáние. **2** (*gathering*) собрáние; **address a ~** выступáть, вы́ступить на собрáнии; (*political* **~**) ми́тинг; (*session*) заседáние. **3** (*sports* **~**) (спорти́вное) состязáние; (*race-***~**) скáчки (*f. pl.*).

● *cpds.* **~-house** *n.* моли́твенный дом; **~-place, -point** *nn.* мéсто встрéчи.

megabyte /'megəˌbaɪt/ *n.* (*comput.*) мегабáйт.

megacycle /'megəˌsaɪk(ə)l/ *n.* мегагéрц.

megalith /'megəlɪθ/ *n.* мегали́т.

megalithic /ˌmegə'lɪθɪk/ *n.* мегалити́ческий.

megalomania /ˌmegələ'meɪnɪə/ *n.* мегаломáния, мáния вели́чия.

megalomaniac /ˌmegələ'meɪnɪˌæk/ *n.* страдáющий мáнией вели́чия.

megaphone /'megəˌfəʊn/ *n.* мегафóн.

megaton /'megəˌtʌn/ *n.* мегатóнна.

megawatt /'megəˌwɒt/ *n.* мегавáтт.

meiosis /maɪ'əʊsɪs/ *n.* (*pl.* **meioses** /-si:z/) **1** (*biol.*) мейóз. **2** (*rhet.*) мейóзис.

melancholia /ˌmelən'kəʊlɪə/ *n.* меланхóлия.

melancholy /'melənkəlɪ/ *n.* уны́ние.

● *adj.* (*of person*) уны́лый; (*of things: saddening*) грýстный, печáльный.

Melanesia /ˌmelə'ni:zɪə/, /-ʃə/ *n.* Меланéзия.

Melanesian /ˌmelə'ni:zɪən/, /-ʃ(ə)n/ *n.* меланези́|ец (*fem.* -йка).

● *adj.* меланези́йский.

mélange /meɪ'lɑ̃ʒ/ *n.* смесь.

melee /'meleɪ/ *n.* (*also* **mêlée**) свáлка.

M

mellifluous /mɪˈlɪfluəs/ *adj.* медоточи́вый.

mellow /ˈmeləʊ/ *adj.* **1** (*of wine*) вы́держанный; (*of fruit*) мя́гкий; спе́лый и со́чный. **2** (*of voice, sound, colour, light*) со́чный. **3** (*of character: softened*) подобре́вший; (*genial*) доброду́шный. **4** (*coll., tipsy*) подвы́пивший.

● *v.t.*: **age has ~ed him** го́ды смягчи́ли его́ хара́ктер.

● *v.i.* (*of wine*) станови́ться (*impf.*) вы́держанным; (*of voice*) станови́ться (*impf.*) сочне́е; (*of person*) смягч|а́ться, -и́ться; добре́ть, по-.

mellowness /ˈmeləʊnɪs/ *n.* вы́держанность; со́чность; мя́гкость.

melodic /mɪˈlɒdɪk/ *adj.* мелоди́чный.

melodious /mɪˈləʊdɪəs/ *adj.* мелоди́чный; **~ voice** певу́чий го́лос.

melodiousness /mɪˈləʊdɪəsnɪs/ *n.* мелоди́чность, певу́честь.

melodrama /ˈmeləˌdrɑːmə/ *n.* (*lit., fig.*) мелодра́ма.

melodramatic /ˌmelədrəˈmætɪk/ *adj.* мелодрамати́ческий.

melody /ˈmelədɪ/ *n.* (*tune*) мело́дия; (*tunefulness*) мелоди́чность.

melon /ˈmelən/ *n.* ды́ня; **(water-~)** арбу́з.

melt /melt/ *v.t.* **1** (*reduce to liquid: of ice, snow, butter, wax*) раст|а́пливать, -опи́ть; (*of metal*) пла́вить, рас-. **2** (*dissolve*) раствор|я́ть, -и́ть. **3** (*fig., soften*) размягч|а́ть, -и́ть.

● *v.i.* **1** (*become liquid: of ice, snow, butter, wax*) та́ять, рас-; (*of metal*) пла́виться, рас-. **2** (*dissolve*) раствор|я́ться, -и́ться. **3** (*fig., soften*) смягч|а́ться, -и́ться; та́ять, от-; **her heart ~ed at the sight** её се́рдце смягчи́лось при ви́де э́того. **4** (*change slowly; merge*): **one colour** (*Br.*), **color** (*US*) **~ed into another** оди́н цвет переходи́л в друго́й. **5** (*coll., suffer from heat*): **I'm ~ing!** я весь распла́вился (от жары́).

● *with advs.*: **~ away** *v.i.* (*lit., fig., disappear*) та́ять, рас-; (*fig., disperse*) рассе́|иваться, -яться; **~ down** *v.t.* распл|авля́ть, -а́вить.

melting /ˈmeltɪŋ/ *n.* плавле́ние.

● *adj.* (*fig., of looks*) то́мный.

● *cpds.* **~-point** *n.* температу́ра плавле́ния; **~-pot** *n.* ти́гель (*m.*); (*fig.*): **throw into the ~-pot** подв|ерга́ть, -е́ргнуть коренно́му измене́нию.

member /ˈmembə(r)/ *n.* член, уча́стни|к (*fem.* -ца) (о́бщества *и т.п.*); **~s only** вход то́лько для чле́нов; **full ~** полнопра́вный член.

membership /ˈmembəʃɪp/ *n.* (*being a member*) чле́нство; (*collect., members*) чле́ны (*m. pl.*); (*number of members*) число́ чле́нов; (*composition*) соста́в; **admission to ~** приня́тие (*в клуб и т.п.*); **~ card** чле́нский биле́т.

membrane /ˈmembreɪn/ *n.* перепо́нка, мембра́на.

memento /mɪˈmentəʊ/ *n.* (*pl.* **~es** *or* **~s**) суве́нир; **as a ~** на па́мять.

memo /ˈmeməʊ/ *n.* (*pl.* **~s**) = **memorandum**

memoir /ˈmemwɑː(r)/ *n.* (*brief biography*) (биографи́ческая) заме́тка; (*pl., autobiography*) воспомина́ния (*nt. pl.*), мемуа́р|ы (*pl., g.* -ов); **author of ~s** мемуари́ст.

memorable /ˈmemərəb(ə)l/ *adj.* достопа́мятный.

memorand|um /ˌmeməˈrændəm/ *n.* (*pl.* **~a** *or* **~ums**) (*written reminder*) запи́ска; (*record of events, facts, transactions etc.*) докладна́я запи́ска; (*dipl.*) мемора́ндум; **memo(randum) book, pad** записна́я кни́жка; блокно́т.

memorial /mɪˈmɔːrɪəl/ *n.* (*commemorative object, custom etc.*) па́мятник; (*pl., chronicles*) хро́ника, ле́топись.

● *adj.*: **~ plaque** мемориа́льная доска́; **~ service** помина́льная слу́жба.

memorialize /mɪˈmɔːrɪəˌlaɪz/ *v.t.* (*commemorate*) увекове́чи|вать, -ть.

memorize /ˈmeməˌraɪz/ *v.t.* (*commit to memory*) зап|омина́ть, -о́мнить; (*learn by heart*) зау́ч|ивать, -и́ть (наизу́сть).

memory /ˈmemərɪ/ *n.* **1** (*faculty; its use*) па́мять; **I have a bad ~ for faces** у меня́ плоха́я па́мять на ли́ца; **a ~ like a sieve** дыря́вая па́мять; **search, rack one's ~** ры́ться, по- в па́мяти; **play from ~** игра́ть (*impf.*) на па́мять, по па́мяти; **lose one's ~** лиш|а́ться, -и́ться па́мяти; **loss of ~** поте́ря па́мяти; **it escapes my ~** я не по́мню э́того; **may I refresh, jog your ~?** позво́льте вам напо́мнить; **in ~ of** в па́мять *+g.*; **within living ~** на па́мяти живу́щих. **2** (*recollection*) воспомина́ние; **I have a clear ~ of what happened** я я́сно по́мню, что случи́лось. **3** (*comput.*) па́мять; запомина́ющее устро́йство.

men /men/ *pl. of* ⇒**man**

● *cpd.* **~'s room** *n.* (*US*) мужска́я убо́рная.

menace /ˈmenɪs/ *n.* (*threat*) угро́за; (*obnoxious person*) (*coll.*) зану́да (*c.g.*).

● *v.t.* угрожа́ть (*impf.*) *+d.*

ménage /meɪˈnɑːʒ/ *n.* хозя́йство; **~ à trois** брак втроём.

menagerie /mɪˈnædʒərɪ/ *n.* (*lit., fig.*) звери́нец.

mend /mend/ *n.* **1** (*patch*) запла́та; (*darn*) што́пка. **2**: **be on the ~** идти́ (*det.*) на попра́вку.

● *v.t.* **1** (*repair; make sound again*) чини́ть, по-; зашива́ть, -и́ть; **~ socks** што́пать, за- носки́; **the road was ~ed only last week** доро́гу почини́ли то́лько на про́шлой неде́ле. **2** (*improve, reform*) испр|авля́ть, -а́вить; **~ one's ways** испр|авля́ться, -а́виться.

● *v.i.* (*regain health*) выздора́вливать, вы́здороветь; **his leg is ~ing nicely** его́ нога́ заживае́т хорошо́.

mendacious /menˈdeɪʃəs/ *adj.* лжи́вый.

mendacity /menˈdæsɪtɪ/ *n.* лжи́вость.

mendicant /ˈmendɪkənt/ *n. & adj.* ни́щий.

mending /ˈmendɪŋ/ *n.* (*of clothes*) почи́нка, што́пка; **invisible ~** худо́жественная што́пка.

menfolk /ˈmenfəʊk/ *n.* мужчи́ны (*m. pl.*).

menial /ˈmiːnɪəl/ *n.* слуга́, лаке́й.

● *adj.* лаке́йский; **~ work** чёрная рабо́та.

meningitis /ˌmenɪnˈdʒaɪtɪs/ *n.* менинги́т.

menis|cus /mɪˈnɪskəs/ *n.* (*pl.* **~ci** /-saɪ/) (*phys.*) мени́ск.

menopause /ˈmenəˌpɔːz/ *n.* кли́макс.

menses /ˈmensiːz/ *n.* менструа́ции (*f. pl.*).

Menshevik /ˈmenʃəvɪk/ *n.* меньшеви́к; (*attr.*) меньшеви́стский.

menstrual /ˈmenstrʊəl/ *adj.* менструа́льный.

menstruate /ˈmenstrʊˌeɪt/ *v.i.* менструи́ровать (*impf.*).

menstruation /ˌmenstrʊˈeɪʃ(ə)n/ *n.* менструа́ция.

menswear /ˈmenzweə(r)/ *n.* мужска́я оде́жда.

mental /ˈment(ə)l/ *adj.* **1** (*of the mind*) у́мственный; **~ powers** у́мственные спосо́бности; **he has a ~ age of 7** у него́ у́ровень семиле́тнего ребёнка; **~ deficiency** слабоу́мие; **~ly handicapped** у́мственно отста́лый. **2** (*pert. to ~ illness*) психи́ческий; **~ disease** психи́ческая боле́знь; **~ home, hospital** психиатри́ческая больни́ца; **~ patient** душевнобольно́й. **3** (*carried out in the mind*) мы́сленный; **~ reservation** мы́сленная огово́рка; **he made a ~ note of the number** он отме́тил но́мер в уме́; **~ arithmetic** у́стный счёт.

mentality /menˈtælɪtɪ/ *n.* (*way of thinking*) мента́льность, менталите́т, склад ума́, умонастрое́ние; (*capacity*) у́мственные спосо́бности (*f. pl.*).

menthol /ˈmenθɒl/ *n.* (*chem.*) менто́л.

mentholated /ˈmenθəˌleɪtɪd/ *adj.* менто́ловый.

mention /ˈmenʃ(ə)n/ *n.* упомина́ние; **there was a ~ of him in the paper** в газе́те упомина́лось его́ и́мя; **receive a ~** быть упомя́нутым; **honourable** (*Br.*), **honorable** (*US*) **~** похва́льный о́тзыв; **he made no ~ whatever of your illness** он ни сло́вом не обмо́лвился о ва́шей боле́зни.

● *v.t.* упом|ина́ть, -яну́ть (*кого/что or о ком/чём*); **I shall ~ it to him** я скажу́ ему́ об э́том; **~ s.o.'s name** наз|ыва́ть, -ва́ть чьё-н. и́мя; **forgive me for ~ing it, but ...** прости́те, что я говорю́ об э́том, но...; **don't ~ it!** не́ за что!; ничего́; не сто́ит!; **not to ~ (or without ~ing)** не говоря́ уж о *+p.*; не то́лько что; **yes, now you ~ it** ах да, вы мне напо́мнили.

mentor /ˈmentɔː(r)/ *n.* наста́вник, ме́нтор.

menu /ˈmenjuː/ *n.* (*also comput.*) меню́ (*nt. indecl.*); **pop-up ~** (*comput.*) всплыва́ющее меню́; **pull-down ~** (*comput.*) выпада́ющее меню́.

MEP (*abbr. of* ***Member of the European Parliament***) депута́т европарла́мента.

mercantile /ˈmɜːkən,taɪl/ *adj.* торго́вый; **~ marine** торго́вый флот.

mercenary /ˈmɜːsɪnərɪ/ *n.* наёмник.

● *adj.* (*hired*) наёмный; (*motivated by money*) коры́стный.

merchandise /ˈmɜːtʃən,daɪz/ *n.* това́ры (*m. pl.*).

merchant /ˈmɜːtʃ(ə)nt/ *n.* **1** (*trader*) купе́ц; (*attr.*) купе́ческий; **the ~ class** купе́чество; (*with qualifying word*: *dealer, tradesman*) торго́вец; **wine ~** торго́вец ви́нами; (*attr.*) торго́вый; **~ ship** торго́вое су́дно; **~ marine** (*US*), **navy** (*Br.*) торго́вый флот; **~ bank** (*Br.*) комме́рческий банк. **2** (*coll., in cpds.: addict*): **speed-~** лиха́ч.

● *cpd.* **~man** *n.* торго́вое су́дно.

merciful /ˈmɜːsɪ,fʊl/ *adj.* милосе́рдный, сострада́тельный; **Lord, be ~ to us** Го́споди, сми́луйся над на́ми; **his death was a ~ release** смерть была́ для него́ бла́гом; **we were ~ly spared the details** к сча́стью, нас не посвяти́ли во все подро́бности.

mercifulness /ˈmɜːsɪfʊlnɪs/ *n.* милосе́рдие.

merciless /ˈmɜːsɪlɪs/ *adj.* беспоща́дный, безжа́лостный.

mercilessness /ˈmɜːsɪlɪsnɪs/ *n.* беспоща́дность, безжа́лостность.

mercurial /mɜːˈkjʊərɪəl/ *adj.* **1** (*of mercury*) рту́тный; **~ poisoning** отравле́ние рту́тью. **2** (*of person, lively*) живо́й; (*volatile*) непостоя́нный, изме́нчивый.

mercuric /mɜːˈkjʊərɪk/ *adj.*: **~ chloride** сулема́; **~ oxide** о́кись рту́ти.

Mercury /ˈmɜːkjʊrɪ/ *n.* (*myth., astron.*) Мерку́рий.

mercury /ˈmɜːkjʊrɪ/ *n.* (*metal*) ртуть; **~ column** (*of barometer*) рту́тный столб.

merc|y /ˈmɜːsɪ/ *n.* **1** (*compassion, forbearance, clemency*) милосе́рдие; поща́да; **beg for ~y** проси́ть (*impf.*) поща́ды; **show ~y to** (*or* **have ~y on**) щади́ть, по-; **they were given no ~y** им не́ было поща́ды; **throw o.s. on s.o.'s ~y** сда́ться (*pf.*) на ми́лость кого́-н.; (*leg., pardon*) помилова́ние; **act of ~y** акт милосе́рдия; **~y killing** эйтана́зия, умерщвле́ние неизлечи́мых больны́х; **God's ~y** ми́лость Бо́жья; **Lord, have ~y upon us!** Го́споди, поми́луй!
2 (*power*): **at the ~y of** во вла́сти + *g.*; **they left him to the ~y of fate** они́ оста́вили его́ на произво́л судьбы́; **he was left to Natasha's tender ~ies** (*iron.*) его́ оста́вили на ми́лость/попече́ние Ната́ши.
3 (*blessing*): **it's a ~y he wasn't drowned** сча́стье, что он не утону́л; **one must be thankful for small ~ies** на́до ра́доваться и ма́лому.

mere¹ /mɪə(r)/ *n.* (*lake*) о́зеро.

mere² /mɪə(r)/ *adj.* (**merest**) **1** (*simple; pure*) просто́й; чи́стый; (*absolute*) су́щий; (*no more than, nothing but*) не бо́лее чем; всего́ лишь; то́лько; **~ coincidence** просто́е совпаде́ние; **by the ~st chance** по чи́стой случа́йности; **it's a ~ trifle** э́то су́щая ме́лочь; **he is a ~ child** он всего́ лишь ребёнок; **they received a ~ pittance** они́ получа́ли су́щие гроши́. **2** (*single; ...alone*) оди́н (то́лько); **~ words are not enough** слова́ми де́лу не помо́жешь; **at the ~ thought** при одно́й мы́сли; **the ~ sight of him disgusts me** оди́н его́ вид вызыва́ет у меня́ отвраще́ние.

merely /ˈmɪəlɪ/ *adv.* (*simply*) про́сто; (*only*) то́лько.

meretricious /,merɪˈtrɪʃəs/ *adj.* мишу́рный.

merganser /mɜːˈgænsə(r)/ *n.* (*zool.*) кроха́ль (*m.*).

merge /mɜːdʒ/ *v.t. & i.* сл|ива́ть(ся), -и́ть(ся); **twilight ~d into darkness** су́мерки смени́лись темното́й.

merger /ˈmɜːdʒə(r)/ *n.* слия́ние; (*comm.*) объедине́ние.

meridian /məˈrɪdɪən/ *n.* (*geog.*) меридиа́н; **Greenwich/principal ~** гри́нвичский/нулево́й меридиа́н; (*astr. and fig.*) зени́т.

meringue /məˈræŋ/ *n.* безе́ (*indecl.*), мере́нга.

merino /məˈriːnəʊ/ *n.* (*pl.* **~s**) (*sheep*) мерино́с; (*wool*) мерино́совая шерсть.

merit /ˈmerɪt/ *n.* (*deserving quality, worth*) досто́инство; **a man of ~** челове́к с несомне́нными досто́инствами; **the suggestion has ~; there is some ~ in the suggestion** в э́том предложе́нии есть свои́ плю́сы; (*action etc. deserving recognition*) заслу́га; **he was rewarded according to his ~s** он был вознаграждён по заслу́гам; (*pl., rights and wrongs*): **one must decide each question on its ~s** на́до реша́ть ка́ждый вопро́с по существу́.

● *v.t.* (**merited, meriting**) заслу́ж|ивать, -и́ть.

meritocracy /,merɪˈtɒkrəsɪ/ *n.* о́бщество, управля́емое людьми́ с наибо́льшими спосо́бностями.

meritorious /,merɪˈtɔːrɪəs/ *adj.* похва́льный.

merlin /ˈmɜːlɪn/ *n.* (*zool.*) де́рбник.

mermaid /ˈmɜːmeɪd/ *n.* руса́лка.

merriment /ˈmerɪmənt/ *n.* весе́лье.

merry /ˈmerɪ/ *adj.* (**merrier, merriest**) (*happy, full of gaiety*) весёлый; **make ~** (*have fun*) весели́ться, по-; **M~ Christmas!** с Рождество́м (Христо́вым)!

● *cpds.* **~-go-round** *n.* карусе́ль; **~-making** *n.* весе́лье, поте́ха.

mésalliance /meɪˈzælɪ,ɑ̃s/ *n.* нера́вный брак, мезалья́нс.

mescalin(e) /ˈmeskə,liːn/ *n.* мескали́н.

Mesdames /meɪˈdɑːm/, /-ˈdæm/ *n.* (*pl.*) да́мы, госпожи́ (*f. pl.*).

mesh /meʃ/ *n.* **1** (*space in net etc.*) ячéйка; **~ bag** аво́ська. **2** (*pl., network*) сеть; (*fig., snares*) се́ти (*f. pl.*). **3**: **in ~** (*mech.*) сцéпленный.

● *v.t.* (*catch*) зацеп|ля́ть, -и́ть.

● *v.i.* (*interlock*) зацеп|ля́ться, -и́ться; (*fig., harmonize, of people*) найти́ (*pf.*) о́бщий язы́к.

mesmeric /mezˈmerɪk/ *adj.* гипноти́ческий.

mesmerism /ˈmezmə,rɪz(ə)m/ *n.* гипноти́зм.

mesmerist /ˈmezmərɪst/ *n.* гипнотизёр.

mesmerize /ˈmezmə,raɪz/ *v.t.* (*lit., fig.*) гипнотизи́ровать, за-.

mesolithic /,mezəʊˈlɪθɪk/ *adj.* мезолити́ческий; **~ age** сре́дний ка́менный век.

meson /ˈmezɒn/, /ˈmiːzɒn/ *n.* (*phys.*) мезо́н.

Mesozoic /,mesəʊˈzəʊɪk/ *adj.* мезозо́йский.

mess¹ /mes/ *n.* **1** (*disorder*) беспоря́док; **the room was in a complete ~** ко́мната была́ в соверше́нном беспоря́дке; **make a ~ of** (*spoil; bungle*) прова́л|ивать, -и́ть; **he made a ~ of his life** он загуби́л свою́ жизнь.
2 (*dirt*) грязь; **your shirt is in a ~** у вас руба́шка запа́чкалась; **make a ~ of** (*soil*) па́чкать, за-.
3 (*confusion*) пу́таница.
4 (*trouble*) неприя́тность, беда́, го́ре; **get o.s. into a ~** вли́пнуть (*pf.*) (*coll.*).

● *v.t.* (*make dirty, esp. with excrement*): **Johnny's ~ed his pants** Джо́нни замара́л штани́шки.

● *v.i.*: **~ with** (*interfere with*) вме́шиваться (*impf.*) в + *a.*

● *with advs.*: **~ about** *v.t.* (*Br., inconvenience*) причиня́ть (*impf.*) неудо́бство + *d.*; *v.i.* (*work half-heartedly or without plan*) ковыря́ться (*impf.*); (*potter, idle about*) каните́литься (*impf.*); **~ about with** (*fiddle with*) вози́ться (*impf.*) с + *i.*; **don't ~ about with matches** не игра́йте со спи́чками; **~ around** *v.t. & i.* = **~ about; ~ up** *v.t.* (*make dirty*) па́чкать, пере-; (*bungle*) прова́л|ивать, -и́ть; (*put into confusion*) перепу́т|ывать, -ать.

mess² /mes/ *n.* (*eating-place*) столо́вая; **officers' ~** офице́рский клуб; (*on ship*) каю́т-компа́ния.

● *cpds.* **~ hall** *n.* (*US*) столо́вая; **~-jacket** *n.* обе́денный ки́тель; **~-kit** *n.* (*utensils*) столо́вый набо́р; (*uniform*) пара́дная фо́рма оде́жды; **~-tin** *n.* (*Br.*) котело́к.

message /ˈmesɪdʒ/ *n.* **1** (*formal*) сообще́ние; (*informal*) запи́ска, за́пись; **I received a ~ by telephone** мне переда́ли по телефо́ну; **can I take a ~ for him?** что ему́ переда́ть?; **have you got the ~?** (*understood*) до вас дошло́?; поня́тно?; усекли́? **2** (*writer's theme*) иде́йное содержа́ние; (*prophet's teaching*) уче́ние.

messenger /ˈmesɪndʒə(r)/ *n.* курье́р, посы́льный.

● *cpd.* **~-boy** *n.* ма́льчик на посы́лках.

Messiah /mɪˈsaɪə/ *n.* Месси́я (*m.*).

Messianic /,mesɪˈænɪk/ *adj.* мессиа́нский.

Messrs /ˈmesəz/ *n. pl.* (*abbr. of* ***Messieurs***) господа́ (*pl., g.* госпо́д).

messy /ˈmesɪ/ *adj.* (**messier, messiest**) (*untidy*) неу́бранный; (*dirty*) гря́зный; (*slovenly*)

M

неря́шливый; (*difficult, unpleasant*) неприя́тный.

met /met/ *past and p.p. of* ⇒**meet**

metabolic /ˌmetəˈbɒlɪk/ *adj.*: ~ **disease** наруше́ние обме́на веще́ств.

metabolism /mɪˈtæbəˌlɪz(ə)m/ *n.* обме́н веще́ств.

metacarpal /ˌmetəˈkɑːp(ə)l/ *n.* (*also* ~ **bone**) пя́стная кость.

● *adj.* пя́стный.

metacar|pus /ˌmetəˈkɑːpəs/ *n.* (*pl.* ~**pi** /-paɪ/, /-piː/) (*anat.*) пясть.

metal /ˈmet(ə)l/ *n.* **1** мета́лл; **ferrous/non-ferrous** ~**s** чёрные/цветны́е мета́ллы. **2**: (**road-**~) ще́бень (*m.*). **3** (*pl., rails*) ре́льсы (*m. pl.*); **the train jumped the** ~**s** по́езд сошёл с ре́льсов.

● *adj.* металли́ческий.

● *v.t.* (**metalled, metalling;** *US* **metaled, metaling**) **1** (*cover with metal*) покр|ыва́ть, -ы́ть мета́ллом. **2** (*Br.*): ~**led road** шоссе́ (*indecl.*).

● *cpds.* ~**-detector** *n.* металлоиска́тель (*m.*); ~**work** *n.* металлообрабо́тка; ~**worker** *n.* металли́ст, сле́сарь (*m.*).

metallic /mɪˈtælɪk/ *adj.* металли́ческий.

metalliferous /ˌmetəˈlɪfərəs/ *adj.* рудоно́сный.

metallurgic(al) /ˌmetəˈlɜːdʒɪk(ə)l/ *adj.* металлурги́ческий.

metallurgist /meˈtælədʒɪst/ *n.* металлу́рг.

metallurgy /mɪˈtælədʒɪ/, /ˈmetəˌlɜːdʒɪ/ *n.* металлурги́я.

metamorphose /ˌmetəˈmɔːfəʊz/ *v.t.* превра|ща́ть, -ти́ть.

metamorphosis /ˌmetəˈmɔːfəsɪs/, /ˌmetəmɔːˈfəʊsɪs/ *n.* (*pl.* **metamorphoses** /-siːz/) метаморфо́за.

metaphor /ˈmetəˌfɔː(r)/ *n.* мета́фора; **mixed** ~ сме́шанная мета́фора.

metaphorical /ˌmetəˈfɒrɪk(ə)l/ *adj.* метафори́ческий; ~**ly speaking** о́бразно говоря́.

metaphysical /ˌmetəˈfɪzɪk(ə)l/ *adj.* метафизи́ческий; ~ **poet** поэ́т метафизи́ческой шко́лы.

metaphysics /ˌmetəˈfɪzɪks/ *n.* метафи́зика.

metatarsal /ˌmetəˈtɑːsəl/ *n.* (*also* ~ **bone**) плюснева́я кость.

● *adj.* плюснево́й.

metatar|sus /ˌmetəˈtɑːsəs/ *n.* (*pl.* ~**si** /-saɪ/, /-siː/) (*anat.*) плюсна́.

metathesis /mɪˈtæθɪsɪs/ *n.* (*pl.* **metatheses** /-ˌsiːz/) (*gram., phon.*) перестано́вка букв/зву́ков; метате́за.

mete /miːt/ *v.t.*: ~ **out** выделя́ть, вы́делить.

meteor /ˈmiːtɪə(r)/ *n.* метео́р; ~ **shower** пото́к метео́ров.

meteoric /ˌmiːtɪˈɒrɪk/ *adj.* **1** (*of meteors*) метео́рный, метеори́ческий; (*fig.*): **a** ~ **career** молниено́сная карье́ра; **a** ~ **rise to success** метео́рный взлёт к успе́ху. **2** (*of the atmosphere*) метеорологи́ческий.

meteorite /ˈmiːtɪəˌraɪt/ *n.* метеори́т.

meteorological /ˌmiːtɪərəˈlɒdʒɪk(ə)l/ *adj.* метеорологи́ческий; ~ **office** (*US* **center**) слу́жба пого́ды.

meteorologist /ˌmiːtɪəˈrɒlədʒɪst/ *n.* метеоро́лог.

meteorology /ˌmiːtɪəˈrɒlədʒɪ/ *n.* метеороло́гия.

meter[1] /ˈmiːtə(r)/ *n.* (*apparatus*) счётчик; **gas** ~ га́зовый счётчик; **a man came to read the** ~ слу́жащий пришёл снять показа́ния счётчика.

● *v.t.* изм|еря́ть, -е́рить; зам|еря́ть, -е́рить.

meter[2] /ˈmiːtə(r)/ (*US*) = **metre**

methane /ˈmiːθeɪn/, /ˈmeθeɪn/ *n.* мета́н.

method /ˈmeθəd/ *n.* (*mode, way*) ме́тод, спо́соб; (*system*) систе́ма, мето́дика; **there's** ~ **in his madness** в его́ безу́мии есть систе́ма.

methodical /mɪˈθɒdɪk(ə)l/ *adj.* (*systematic*) системати́ческий; (*of regular habits*) методи́чный.

Methodism /ˈmeθəˌdɪz(ə)m/ *n.* методи́зм.

Methodist /ˈmeθədɪst/ *n.* методи́ст (*fem.* -ка); (*attr.*) методи́стский.

methodological /ˌmeθədəˈlɒdʒɪk(ə)l/ *adj.* методологи́ческий.

meths /meθs/ (*Br. coll.*) = **methylated spirit**

Methuselah /mɪˈθjuːzələ/ *n.* Мафусаи́л.

methyl /ˈmiːθaɪl/, /ˈmeθɪl/ *n.* мети́л; (*attr.*): ~ **alcohol** мети́ловый спирт.

methylated /ˈmeθɪˌleɪtɪd/ *adj.*: ~ **spirit** денатура́т.

meticulous /məˈtɪkjʊləs/ *adj.* тща́тельный, аккура́тный.

meticulousness /məˈtɪkjʊləsnɪs/ *n.* тща́тельность, аккура́тность.

métier /ˈmetjeɪ/ *n.* (*profession*) профе́ссия; (*trade*) ремесло́.

metre /ˈmiːtə(r)/ (*US* **meter**) *n.* (*unit of length*) метр; (*verse rhythm*) разме́р.

metric /ˈmetrɪk/ *adj.* метри́ческий; ~ **system** метри́ческая систе́ма мер.

metrical /ˈmetrɪk(ə)l/ *adj.* (*of, or composed in, metre*) метри́ческий; (*pert. to measurement*) измери́тельный.

metrication /ˌmetrɪˈkeɪʃ(ə)n/ *n.* введе́ние метри́ческой систе́мы.

metrics /ˈmetrɪks/ *n.* ме́трика.

Metro /ˈmetrəʊ/ *n.* (*pl.* ~**s**) метро́ (*indecl.*).

metronome /ˈmetrəˌnəʊm/ *n.* метроно́м.

metropolis /mɪˈtrɒpəlɪs/ *n.* столи́ца.

metropolitan /ˌmetrəˈpɒlɪt(ə)n/ *n.* (*eccl.*) митрополи́т.

● *adj.* (*of capital*) столи́чный; (*of see*) митрополи́чий.

mettle /ˈmet(ə)l/ *n.* (*strength of character*) си́ла хара́ктера; **show one's** ~ прояв|ля́ть, -и́ть си́лу хара́ктера; (*spirit, combativeness*) боево́е настрое́ние.

mettlesome /ˈmetəlsəm/ *adj.* (*of person*) рья́ный; (*of horse*) рети́вый.

mew[1] /mjuː/ *n.* (*of cat*) мяу́канье.

● *v.i.* мяу́к|ать, -нуть.

mew[2] /mjuː/ *n.* (*gull*) ча́йка.

mewl /mjuːl/ *v.i.* попи́скивать (*impf.*).

mews /mjuːz/ *n.* (*Br.*) коню́шни (*f. pl.*) (переде́ланные в жило́е помеще́ние).

Mexican /ˈmeksɪkən/ *n.* мексика́н|ец (*fem.* -ка).

● *adj.* мексика́нский.

Mexico /ˈmeksɪˌkəʊ/ *n.* Ме́ксика; ~ **City** Ме́хико (*m. indecl.*).

mezzanine /ˈmetsəˌniːn/, /ˈmez-/ *n.* мезони́н, полуэта́ж.

mezzo /ˈmetsəʊ/ *adv.* полу-; ~ **forte** дово́льно гро́мко.

● *cpd.* ~**-soprano** *n.* ме́ццо-сопра́но (*indecl.*).

mezzotint /ˈmetsəʊtɪnt/ *n.* ме́ццо-ти́нто (*nt. & f. indecl.*).

mg. /ˈmɪlɪˌɡræm(z)/ *n.* (*abbr. of* ***milligram(me)(s)***) мг (миллигра́м).

Mgr. *abbr. of* **1** ***manager*** заве́дующий. **2** ***Monsignor*** монсеньёр.

mi /miː/ = **me**[2]

MIA (*abbr. of* ***missing in action***) пропа́вший бе́з вести.

M.I.5 (*abbr. of* ***Military Intelligence Section 5***) (*Br.*) эм ай 5.

M.I.6 (*abbr. of* ***Military Intelligence Section 6***) (*Br.*) эм ай 6.

miaou, miaow /mɪˈaʊ/ *n.* мяу́канье; (*onomat.*) мя́у!

● *v.i.* мяу́кать (*impf.*).

miasma /mɪˈæzmə/, /maɪ-/ *n.* (*pl.* ~**ta** *or* ~**s**) миа́зм|ы (*pl., g.* —).

mica /ˈmaɪkə/ *n.* слюда́; (*attr.*) слюдяно́й.

mice /maɪs/ *pl. of* ⇒**mouse**

Michaelmas /ˈmɪkəlməs/ *n.* Миха́йлов день; ~ **term** (*Br., acad.*) осе́нний триме́стр.

mickey /ˈmɪkɪ/ *n.* (*Br. sl.*): **take the** ~ **out of s.o.** издева́ться (*impf.*) над кем-н.

Mickey Finn /ˌmɪkɪ ˈfɪn/ *n.* (*drink*) ёрш (*sl.*).

Mickey Mouse /ˌmɪkɪ ˈmaʊs/ *adj.* (*pej.*) ребя́ческий.

microbe /ˈmaɪkrəʊb/ *n.* микро́б.

microbiological /ˌmaɪkrəʊbaɪəˈlɒdʒɪk(ə)l/ *adj.* микробиологи́ческий.

microbiologist /ˌmaɪkrəʊbaɪˈɒlədʒɪst/ *n.* микробио́лог.

microbiology /ˌmaɪkrəʊbaɪˈɒlədʒɪ/ *n.* микробиоло́гия.

microchip /ˈmaɪkrəʊtʃɪp/ *n.* микросхе́ма, чип.

microcircuit /ˈmaɪkrəʊˌsɜːkɪt/ *n.* микросхе́ма.

microcomputer /ˈmaɪkrəʊkəmˈpjuːtə(r)/ *n.* микрокомпью́тер.

microcosm /ˈmaɪkrəˌkɒz(ə)m/ *n.* микроко́см.

microeconomic /ˌmaɪkrəʊˌiːkəˈnɒmɪk/, /-ˌekəˈnɒmɪk/ *adj.* микроэкономи́ческий.

microeconomics /ˌmaɪkrəʊˌiːkəˈnɒmɪks/, /-ˌekəˈnɒmɪks/ *n.* микроэконо́мика.

micro-electronics /ˌmaɪkrəʊlekˈtrɒnɪks/ *n.* микроэлектро́ника.

microfibre /ˈmaɪkrəʊˌfaɪbə(r)/ *n.* (*US* **microfiber**) микроволокно́.

microfiche /ˈmaɪkrəʊˌfiːʃ/ *n.* микрофи́ша.

microfilm /ˈmaɪkrəʊfɪlm/ *n.* микрофи́льм.

● *v.t.* микрофильми́ровать (*impf.*); де́лать, с- микрофи́льм +*g.*

microlight /ˈmaɪkrəʊˌlaɪt/ *n.* (*Br.*) сверхлёгкий персона́льный самолёт.

micrometer /maɪˈkrɒmɪtə(r)/ *n.* микро́метр.

micron /ˈmaɪkrɒn/ *n.* микро́н.

micro-organism /ˌmaɪkrəʊˈɔːgənɪz(ə)m/ *n.* микроорганизм.

microphone /ˈmaɪkrəˌfəʊn/ *n.* микрофо́н.

microprocessor /ˌmaɪkrəʊˈprəʊsesə(r)/ *n.* микропроце́ссор.

microscope /ˈmaɪkrəˌskəʊp/ *n.* микроско́п.

microscopic /ˌmaɪkrəˈskɒpɪk/ *adj.* микроскопи́ческий.

microsurgery /ˈmaɪkrəʊˌsɜːdʒərɪ/ *n.* микрохирурги́я.

microwave /ˈmaɪkrəʊˌweɪv/ *n.* микроволна́; (*attr.*) микрово́лновый; **~ oven** микроволно́вая печь.

mid /mɪd/ *adj.* & *pref.*: **in ~ air** (высоко́) в во́здухе; **in ~ Channel** посреди́ Ла-Ма́нша; **in ~ course** посреди́не пути́; **from ~ June to ~ July** с середи́ны ию́ня до середи́ны ию́ля; **she interrupted him in ~ sentence** она́ прервала́ его́ на полусло́ве.

● *cpds.* **~day** *n.* по́лдень (*m.*); *adj.*: **the ~day sun** полу́денное со́лнце; **~land** *adj.* располо́женный внутри́ страны́; **the M~lands** центра́льные гра́фства А́нглии; **~night** *n.* по́лночь; **during the ~night hours** в по́лночь; **he was burning the ~night oil** он рабо́тал по ноча́м; он полуно́чничал; **~night sun** полу́но́чное со́лнце; **~summer** *n.* середи́на ле́та; **at ~summer** среди́ ле́та; *adj.*: **M~summer Day** Ива́нов день; **~way** *adv.* на полпути́; **the M~(dle)-west** *n.* Сре́дний За́пад США; **~winter** *n.* середи́на зимы́.

midden /ˈmɪd(ə)n/ *n.* наво́зная ку́ча.

middle /ˈmɪd(ə)l/ *n.* **1** середи́на; **in the ~ of** среди́ +*g.*; **there is a pain in the ~ of my back** у меня́ боль в поясни́це; **in the ~ of nowhere** Бог зна́ет где; (*of time*): **in the ~ of the night** посреди́ но́чи; **I was in the ~ of getting ready** в тот моме́нт я как раз собира́лся. **2** (*waist*) та́лия; **he caught her round the ~** он о́бнял/схвати́л её за та́лию.

● *adj.* сре́дний; **in ~ age** в сре́днем во́зрасте; **the M~ Ages** сре́дние века́; **the ~ classes** сре́дние сло́и о́бщества; буржуази́я; **upper/lower ~ class** кру́пная/ме́лкая буржуази́я; **he followed a ~ course** он держа́лся уме́ренного ку́рса; он вы́брал сре́дний путь; **~ distance** сре́дний план; **M~ America** сре́дняя Аме́рика; **M~ American** сре́дний америка́нец; **M~ East** Бли́жний Восто́к; **M~ English** среднеангли́йский язы́к; **~ finger** сре́дний па́лец; **in ~ life** в середи́не жи́зни; **his ~ name is George** его́ второ́е и́мя — Гео́ргий; **~ school** (*Br.*) сре́дняя шко́ла; **M~ West** = **Mid-west**

● *cpds.* **~-aged** *adj.* сре́дних лет; **~-class** *adj.* буржуа́зный; **~man** *n.* посре́дник; **~-of-the-road** *adj.* (*pol.*) уме́ренных (полити́ческих) взгля́дов; (*mus.*) лёгкий; **~weight** *n.* & *adj.* (боксёр) сре́днего ве́са.

middling /ˈmɪdlɪŋ/ *adj.* сре́дний, второсо́ртный; **fair to ~** так себе́.

midge /mɪdʒ/ *n.* кома́р, мо́шка.

midget /ˈmɪdʒɪt/ *n.* ка́рлик; (*attr.*) ка́рликовый.

midi /ˈmɪdɪ/ *n.* (*pl.* **midis**) ми́ди (*юбка и т.д.*).

midpoint /ˈmɪdˌpɔɪnt/ *n.* сре́дняя то́чка.

midriff /ˈmɪdrɪf/ *n.* ве́рхняя часть живота́.

midshipman /ˈmɪdʃɪpmən/ *n.* ми́чман, гардемари́н.

midst /mɪdst/ *n.* середи́на; **in the ~ of** среди́, в разга́р +*g.*, ме́жду +*i.*; **a stranger in our ~** чужо́й среди́ нас.

midwife /ˈmɪdwaɪf/ *n.* акуше́рка; повива́льная ба́бка.

midwifery /ˈmɪdˌwɪfərɪ/ *n.* акуше́рство.

mien /miːn/ *n.* (*liter.*) вид, нару́жность.

miff /mɪf/ *v.t.* (*coll.*): **he was ~ed by my remark** моё замеча́ние его́ оби́дело/заде́ло.

might[1] /maɪt/ *n.* **1** (*power to enforce will*) мощь; **~ is right** кто силён, тот и прав. **2** (*strength*) си́ла; **with (all his) ~ and main** изо всей мо́чи.

might[2] /maɪt/ *v. aux. see* ⇒**may**

mightiness /ˈmaɪtɪnɪs/ *n.* (*power*) мо́щность; (*size*) величи́е.

mighty /ˈmaɪtɪ/ *adj.* (**mightier, mightiest**) **1** (*powerful*) мо́щный; (*great*) вели́кий; **high and ~** (*pompous, arrogant*) зано́счивый. **2** (*massive*) грома́дный.

● *adv.* (*US coll.*) о́чень.

mignonette /ˌmɪnjəˈnet/ *n.* резеда́.

migraine /ˈmiːgreɪn/, /ˈmaɪ-/ *n.* мигре́нь.

migrant /ˈmaɪgrənt/ *n.* переселе́нец; (*bird*) перелётная пти́ца.

● *adj.* кочу́ющий; перелётный.

migrate /maɪˈgreɪt/ *v.i.* пересел|я́ться, -и́ться; мигри́ровать (*impf.*); (*of birds*) соверш|а́ть, -и́ть перелёт.

migration /maɪˈgreɪʃ(ə)n/ *n.* мигра́ция; перелёт.

migratory /maɪˈgreɪtərɪ/ *adj.* перелётный.

mike /maɪk/ (*coll.*) = **microphone**

milage /ˈmaɪlɪdʒ/ = **mil(e)age**

milch /mɪltʃ/ *adj.*: **~ cow** до́йная коро́ва.

mild /maɪld/ *adj.* мя́гкий; (*of person*) кро́ткий, ти́хий; **a ~ reproof** мя́гкий упрёк; **to put it ~ly** мя́гко говоря́; **a ~ day** тёплый день; **a ~ cheese** нео́стрый/мя́гкий сыр; **~ steel** мя́гкая сталь; **~ tobacco** сла́бый таба́к.

mildew /ˈmɪldjuː/ *n.* (*disease of plants*) ми́лдью (*nt. indecl.*), ложномучни́стая роса́; (*on paper, leather*) пле́сень.

mildness /ˈmaɪldnɪs/ *n.* мя́гкость; (*of food etc.*) пре́сность.

mile /maɪl/ *n.* ми́ля; **for ~s around** на мно́го миль вокру́г; **30 ~s an hour** 30 миль в час; **he ran the ~ in 4 minutes** он пробежа́л ми́лю за 4 мину́ты; (*fig.*): **I am feeling ~s better** мне намно́го лу́чше; **I was ~s away** я замечта́лся; **it sticks out a ~** э́то броса́ется в глаза́; э́то ви́дно за версту́.

● *cpd.* **~stone** *n.* ка́мень с указа́нием расстоя́ния; (*fig.*) ве́ха.

mil(e)age /ˈmaɪlɪdʒ/ *n.* **1** (*distance in miles*) расстоя́ние в ми́лях; (*of car*) пробе́г автомоби́ля в ми́лях; **~ indicator** счётчик про́йденного пути́. **2** (*travel expenses*) проездны́е (*pl.*). **3** (*coll., benefit*) по́льза, вы́года.

miler /ˈmaɪlə(r)/ *n.* (*athlete*) бегу́н на диста́нцию в одну́ ми́лю.

milieu /mɪˈljɜː/, /ˈmiːljɜː/ *n.* (*pl.* **~x** *or* **~s**) окруже́ние, среда́.

militancy /ˈmɪlɪt(ə)nsɪ/ *n.* вои́нственность.

militant /ˈmɪlɪt(ə)nt/ *n.* бое́ц, боре́ц; воя́ка (*m.*); активи́ст (*fem.* -ка).

● *adj.* вои́нствующий; **~ students** вои́нственно настро́енные студе́нты.

militarism /ˈmɪlɪtəˌrɪz(ə)m/ *n.* милитари́зм.

militarist /ˈmɪlɪtərɪst/ *n.* милитари́ст.

militaristic /ˌmɪlɪtəˈrɪstɪk/ *adj.* милитаристи́ческий.

militarize /ˈmɪlɪtəˌraɪz/ *v.t.* милитаризи́ровать (*impf., pf.*).

military /ˈmɪlɪtərɪ/ *n.*: **the ~** военнослу́жащие (*m. pl.*), войска́ (*nt. pl.*).

● *adj.* вое́нный; **of ~ age** призывно́го во́зраста; **~ band** вое́нный орке́стр; **~ engineering** вое́нно-инжене́рное де́ло; **a ~ man** военнослу́жащий, вое́нный; **~ service** вое́нная слу́жба; (*as liability*) во́инская пови́нность; **~ training** вое́нная подгото́вка.

militate /ˈmɪlɪˌteɪt/ *v.i.*: **~ against** препя́тствовать (*impf.*) +*d.*; говори́ть (*impf.*) про́тив +*g.*; **his age ~s against him** ему́ меша́ет во́зраст.

militia /mɪˈlɪʃə/ *n.* мили́ция.

● *cpd.* **~man** *n.* милиционе́р.

milk /mɪlk/ *n.* молоко́; **it's no good crying over spilt ~** слеза́ми го́рю не помо́жешь; (*attr.*) моло́чный; **~ pudding** (*Br.*) моло́чный пу́динг; **~ tooth** моло́чный зуб.

● *v.t.* дои́ть, по-; (*fig.*): **they ~ed him of all his cash** они́ вы́жали из него́ все де́ньги.

● *v.i.*: **the cows are ~ing well** коро́вы хорошо́ до́ятся.

● *cpds.* **~-bar** *n.* (*Br.*) кафе́-моло́чная; **~-churn** *n.* маслобо́йка; **~-float** *n.* (*Br.*) теле́жка для разво́зки молока́; **~maid** *n.* доя́рка; **~man** *n.* продаве́ц молока́, моло́чник; **~-powder** *n.* порошко́вое молоко́;

M

~-shake *n.* моло́чный коктейль; **~sop** *n.* тря́пка; мя́мля (*c.g.*); **~-white** *adj.* моло́чно-бе́лый.

milky /ˈmɪlkɪ/ *adj.* (**milkier, milkiest**) моло́чный; **the M~ Way** Мле́чный путь.

mill /mɪl/ *n.* (*for grinding corn*) ме́льница; **they put him through the ~** (*fig.*) они́ подве́ргли его́ тяжёлым испыта́ниям; (*factory*) фа́брика.

● *v.t.* **1** (*grind*) моло́ть, пере-. **2** (*cut with ~ing-machine*) фрезерова́ть (*impf.*); **a coin with a ~ed edge** моне́та с насе́чкой по краю́.

● *v.i.* (*coll.*): **a crowd was ~ing around the entrance** лю́ди толпи́лись у вхо́да.

● *cpds.* **~-pond** *n.* ме́льничный пруд; **the sea is like a ~-pond** мо́ре соверше́нно споко́йно; **~-race** *n.* (*trough*) ме́льничный лото́к; **~stone** *n.* жёрнов; (*fig.*) ка́мень (*m.*) на ше́е; **~-wheel** *n.* ме́льничное колесо́.

millennia /mɪˈlenɪə/ *pl. of* ⇒**millennium**

millennial /mɪˈlenɪəl/ *adj.* тысячеле́тний.

millenni|um /mɪˈlenɪəm/ *n.* (*pl.* **~ums** *or* **~a**) тысячеле́тие; (*fig.*) золото́й век; **~ bug** (*comput.*) компью́терная пробле́ма двухты́сячного го́да.

miller /ˈmɪlə(r)/ *n.* ме́льник.

millet /ˈmɪlɪt/ *n.* (*plant*) про́со; (*grain*) пшено́.

millibar /ˈmɪlɪˌbɑː(r)/ *n.* миллиба́р.

milligram(me) /ˈmɪlɪˌgræm/ *n.* миллигра́м.

millilitre /ˈmɪlɪˌliːtə(r)/ (*US* **-liter**) *n.* миллили́тр.

millimetre /ˈmɪlɪˌmiːtə(r)/ (*US* **-meter**) *n.* миллиме́тр.

milliner /ˈmɪlɪnə(r)/ *n.* (*fem.*) моди́стка.

millinery /ˈmɪlɪnərɪ/ *n.* (*trade*) произво́дство/прода́жа да́мских шляп; (*women's hats*) да́мские шля́пки (*f. pl.*).

million /ˈmɪljən/ *n.* & *adj.* (*pl.* **~s** *or* (*with numeral or qualifying word*) **~**) миллио́н (+*g.*); **thanks a ~** (*coll.*) огро́мное спаси́бо.

millionaire /ˌmɪljəˈneə(r)/ *n.* миллионе́р.

millionairess /ˌmɪljəˈneərɪs/ *n.* миллионе́рша.

millionth /ˈmɪljənθ/ *n.* миллио́нная часть.

● *adj.* миллио́нный.

millipede /ˈmɪlɪˌpiːd/ *n.* многоно́жка.

millivolt /ˈmɪlɪˌvɒlt/ *n.* милливо́льт.

milometer /maɪˈlɒmɪtə(r)/ *n.* (*Br.*) счётчик пробе́га.

milt /mɪlt/ *n.* семенники́ (*m. pl.*).

mime /maɪm/ *n.* (*drama; performer*) мим; (*dumb-show*) пантоми́ма.

● *v.t.* (*act by miming*) изобра|жа́ть, -зи́ть мими́чески.

● *v.i.* (*pretend to sing*) петь, с~/про~ под фоногра́мму.

mimeograph /ˈmɪmɪəˌgrɑːf/ *n.* мимео́граф.

● *v.t.* печа́тать на мимео́графе.

mimic /ˈmɪmɪk/ *n.* имита́тор; мими́ст (*fem.* -ка); **he is a good ~** он облада́ет да́ром подража́ния.

● *v.t.* (**mimicked, mimicking**) **1** (*ridicule by imitation*) передра́зн|ивать, -и́ть; пароди́ровать (*impf.*). **2** (*biol.*) принима́ть (*impf.*) защи́тную окра́ску +*g.*

mimicry /ˈmɪmɪkrɪ/ *n.* (*imitation*) имити́рование; подража́ние (+*d.*); (*biol.*) мимикри́я.

mimosa /mɪˈməʊzə/ *n.* мимо́за.

min. /ˈmɪnɪt(s)/ *n.* (*abbr. of* **minute(s)**) мин. (мину́та).

minaret /ˌmɪnəˈret/ *n.* минаре́т.

minatory /ˈmɪnətərɪ/ *adj.* угрожа́ющий.

mince /mɪns/ *n.* (*Br., chopped meat*) фарш.

● *v.t.* (*chop small*) руби́ть (*impf.*); пропус|ка́ть, -ти́ть че́рез мясору́бку; **~d beef** говя́жий фарш; **mincing-machine** мясору́бка; (*fig.*): **he does not ~ matters** он говори́т без обиняко́в.

● *v.i.* (*behave affectedly*) жема́ниться (*impf.*); (*of walk*) семени́ть (*impf.*); **he ~d up to me** он подошёл ко мне семеня́щей похо́дкой.

● *cpds.* **~meat** *n.* сла́дкая начи́нка из изю́ма для пирожко́в; **they made ~meat of our team** (*fig.*) они́ разгроми́ли на́шу кома́нду в пух и прах; **~-pie** *n.* (*Br.*) ≈ сла́дкий пирожо́к (с начи́нкой из изю́ма).

mincer /ˈmɪnsə(r)/ *n.* мясору́бка.

mind /maɪnd/ *n.* **1** (*intellect*) ум, ра́зум; **he has a very good ~** он о́чень спосо́бный; **you must be out of your ~** вы с ума́ сошли́; **a triumph of ~ over matter** торжество́ ду́ха над мате́рией; **his ~ has gone; he has lost his ~** он не в своём уме́; **great ~s** вели́кие умы́; **he is one of the best ~s of our time** он оди́н из велича́йших/лу́чших умо́в на́шего вре́мени.

2 (*remembrance*): **bear in ~** по́мнить (*impf.*); **bring to ~** нап|омина́ть, -о́мнить о+*p.*; **I called his words to ~** я вспо́мнил его́ слова́; **it puts me in ~ of something** э́то мне что́-то напомина́ет; **the tune went clean out of my ~** я на́чисто забы́л э́ту мело́дию; **out of sight, out of ~** с глаз доло́й — из се́рдца вон; **time out of ~** испоко́н веко́в.

3 (*opinion*) мне́ние; **he spoke his ~ on the subject** он открове́нно вы́сказался на э́ту те́му; **I gave him a piece of my ~** я ему́ вы́ложил всё, что ду́мал; **we are of one (*or* of the same) ~** мы одина́кового мне́ния; **is he still of the same ~?** он всё ещё того́ же мне́ния?; **he doesn't know his own ~** он сам не зна́ет, чего́ он хо́чет; **try to keep an open ~!** попыта́йтесь сохрани́ть объекти́вный подхо́д.

4 (*intention*) наме́рение; **I have a good (*or* half a) ~ not to go** я скло́нен не ходи́ть/идти́; **he changed his ~** он переду́мал; **I have made up my ~ to stay** я реши́л оста́ться; **my ~ is made up** я твёрдо реши́л; **I was in two ~s whether to accept the invitation** я колеба́лся, приня́ть мне приглаше́ние и́ли нет.

5 (*direction of thought or desire*): **she set her ~ on a holiday abroad** ей о́чень хоте́лось провести́ кани́кулы за грани́цей.

6 (*thought*) мы́сли (*f. pl.*); **my ~ was on other things** я ду́мал о друго́м; **I had something on my ~** меня́ что́-то трево́жило; **I set his ~ at rest** я его́ успоко́ил; **it took her ~ off her troubles** э́то отвлекло́ её от её забо́т/невзго́д; **I cannot read his ~** я не могу́ разгада́ть его́ мы́сли; **I can see him in my ~'s eye** он стои́т у меня́ пе́ред глаза́ми.

7 (*way of thinking*) настрое́ние; **in his present frame, state of ~** в его́ ны́нешнем состоя́нии; **to my ~** на мой взгляд; мне ка́жется (*or* я счита́ю), что.

8 (*attention*): **he turned his ~ to his work** он сосредото́чился на свое́й рабо́те; **if you set your ~ to your work** е́сли вы настро́итесь на рабо́ту; **keep your ~ on what you are doing** не отвлека́йтесь; **absence of ~** рассе́янность; **he showed great presence of ~** он проявля́л огро́мное прису́тствие ду́ха.

● *v.t.* **1** (*take care, charge of*) присм|а́тривать, -отре́ть за+*i.*; **~ your own business!** не вме́шивайтесь не в своё де́ло!

2 (*worry about*) забо́титься (*impf.*) о+*p.*; беспоко́иться (*impf.*) о+*p.*; **never ~ the expense** не ду́майте о расхо́дах; **~ your head!** осторо́жнее, не ушиби́те го́лову.

3 (*object to*) возра|жа́ть, -зи́ть на+*a.*; име́ть (*impf.*) что-н. про́тив+*g.*; **I don't ~ the cold** я не бою́сь хо́лода; **would you ~ opening the door?** откро́йте, пожа́луйста, дверь; **I wouldn't ~ going for a walk** я не про́чь прогуля́ться; **I don't ~ going alone** мне всё равно́, я могу́ пойти́ оди́н.

4 (*heed, note*) прислу́ш|иваться, -аться к+*d.*; слу́шаться (*impf.*) +*g.*; **if I had ~ed his advice** е́сли бы я прислу́шался к его́ сове́ту; **~ you lock the door!** не забу́дьте запере́ть/закры́ть дверь!

● *v.i.* **1** (*worry*) беспоко́иться (*impf.*); трево́житься (*impf.*); **we're rather late, but never ~** мы немно́го опа́здываем, ну, ничего́!; **but I do ~!** но мне не всё равно́!; **'Where have you been?' — 'Never you ~!'** «Где вы бы́ли?» — «Не ва́ше де́ло!».

2 (*object*) возра|жа́ть, -зи́ть; **do you ~ if I smoke?** вы не про́тив, е́сли я закурю́?; **if you don't ~** с ва́шего разреше́ния; **do you ~, you're treading on my foot!** прости́те, вы наступи́ли мне на́ ногу.

3 (*bear something in ~*) не заб|ыва́ть, -ы́ть; **~ you, I don't altogether approve** ме́жду про́чим, я э́то не совсе́м одобря́ю; **not a word, ~!** смотри́те, никому́ ни сло́ва!

● *cpds.* **~-bending** *adj.* умопомрачи́тельный (*coll.*); **~-boggling** *adj.* порази́тельный; **~-reader** *n.* телепа́т; **~-reading** *n.* телепа́тия.

minded /ˈmaɪndɪd/ *adj.* **1** (*disposed*): **I am ~ to go and see him** мне хо́чется его́ повида́ть. **2** (*as suff. expr. interest*) скло́нный к+*d.*; проявля́ющий интере́с к+*d.*; **mathematically-~** с математи́ческими накло́нностями.

minder /ˈmaɪndə(r)/ *n.* (*Br., child minder*) ня́ня; (*coll., bodyguard*) телохрани́тель (*m.*).

mindful /ˈmaɪndfʊl/ *adj.* забо́тливый; **we must be ~ of the children** мы должны́ ду́мать о де́тях; **I was ~ of his advice** я по́мнил его́ сове́т; **he was ~ of his duty** он сознава́л свой долг.

mindless /ˈmaɪndlɪs/ *adj.* **1** (*without care*) беззабо́тный; **~ of danger** не сознава́я опа́сности. **2** (*not requiring intelligence*): **~ drudgery** механи́ческий труд. **3** (*without intelligence*) глу́пый; **~ youths** безмо́зглые юнцы́.

mindlessness /ˈmaɪndlɪsnɪs/ *n.* (*unconcern*) беззабо́тность; легкомы́слие; (*stupidity*) глу́пость, безмо́зглость.

mine[1] /maɪn/ *n.* **1** (*excavation*) ша́хта; рудни́к; копь; **(gold-~)** (золото́й) при́иск; **the men went down the ~** рабо́чие спусти́лись в ша́хту; (*fig.*) сокро́вищница; кла́дезь (*m.*); **he is a ~ of information** он неиссяка́емый исто́чник информа́ции. **2** (*explosive device*) ми́на.

● *v.t.* **1** (*excavate*): **~ coal/ore** добыва́ть (*impf.*) у́голь/руду́. **2** (*mil.*) мини́ровать, за-; под|рыва́ть, -орва́ть; **they ~d the approaches to the harbour** (*Br.*), **harbor** (*US*) они́ замини́ровали подхо́ды к га́вани; **the vessel was ~d** су́дно подорва́ли.

● *v.i.* разраб|а́тывать, -о́тать рудни́к; **they were mining for gold** они́ добыва́ли зо́лото; **the mining industry** го́рная промы́шленность; **a mining town** шахтёрский го́род/посёлок; **mining engineer** го́рный инжене́р.

● *cpds.* **~-detector** *n.* миноиска́тель (*m.*); **~field** *n.* ми́нное по́ле; **~layer** *n.* ми́нный загради́тель; **~laying** *n.* мини́рование; **~sweeper** *n.* ми́нный тра́льщик.

mine[2] /maɪn/ *pron.*: **that book is ~** э́то моя́ кни́га; **a friend of ~** (оди́н) мой друг/знако́мый.

miner /ˈmaɪnə(r)/ *n.* (*coal-~*) шахтёр; (*gold-~*) золотоиска́тель (*m.*).

mineral /ˈmɪnər(ə)l/ *n.* минера́л, руда́.

● *adj.* минера́льный; **~ oil** нефть; **~ water** минера́льная вода́.

mineralogical /ˌmɪnərəˈlɒdʒɪk(ə)l/ *adj.* минералоги́ческий.

mineralogist /ˌmɪnəˈrælədʒɪst/ *n.* минерало́г.

mineralogy /ˌmɪnəˈrælədʒɪ/ *n.* минерало́гия.

minestrone /ˌmɪnɪˈstrəʊnɪ/ *n.* италья́нский овощно́й суп.

mingle /ˈmɪŋg(ə)l/ *v.t.* сме́ш|ивать, -а́ть.

● *v.i.* сме́шиваться (*impf.*); **~ with** (*frequent*) обща́ться (*impf.*) с+*i.*; враща́ться (*impf.*) среди́+*g.*

mingy /ˈmɪndʒɪ/ *adj.* (**mingier, mingiest**) (*coll.*) скупо́й, прижи́мистый.

mini /ˈmɪnɪ/ *n.* (*pl.* **minis**) (*garment*) ми́ни (*юбка и т.д.*).

miniature /ˈmɪnɪtʃə(r)/ *n.* (*portrait; branch of painting*) миниатю́ра; (*small-scale model*) маке́т; (*fig.*): **she is her mother in ~** она́ вы́литая мать, то́лько в миниатю́ре.

● *adj.* миниатю́рный.

miniaturist /ˈmɪnɪtʃərɪst/ *n.* миниатюри́ст.

miniaturization /ˌmɪnɪtʃəraɪˈzeɪʃ(ə)n/ *n.* миниатюриза́ция.

minibus /ˈmɪnɪˌbʌs/ *n.* микроавто́бус.

minicab /ˈmɪnɪˌkæb/ *n.* (*Br.*) микротакси́ (*nt. indecl.*).

minidisc /ˈmɪnɪˌdɪsk/ *n.* миниди́ск.

minim /ˈmɪnɪm/ *n.* (*Br., mus.*) полови́нная но́та.

minima /ˈmɪnɪmə/ *pl. of* ⇨**minimum**

minimal /ˈmɪnɪm(ə)l/ *adj.* (*least possible*) минима́льный; (*minute*) о́чень ма́ленький, наиме́ньший.

minimize /ˈmɪnɪˌmaɪz/ *v.t.* (*reduce to minimum*) дов|оди́ть, -ести́ до ми́нимума; (*make light of*) преум|еньша́ть, -е́ньшить.

minim|um /ˈmɪnɪməm/ *n.* (*pl.* **~a** *or* **~ums**) ми́нимум; (*attr.*) минима́льный; **~ wage** минима́льная за́работная пла́та.

mining /ˈmaɪnɪŋ/ *n.* го́рное де́ло, го́рная промы́шленность; *see also* ⇨**mine** *v.t.*

minion /ˈmɪnjən/ *n.* приспе́шник.

miniskirt /ˈmɪnɪˌskɜːt/ *n.* мини-ю́бка.

minister /ˈmɪnɪstə(r)/ *n.* **1** (*head of government dept.*) мини́стр; **Prime M~** премье́р-мини́стр. **2** (*in dipl. service*) посла́нник. **3** (*clergyman*) свяще́нник, па́стор.

● *v.i.*: **~ to** служи́ть (*impf.*) +*d.*; прислу́живать (*impf.*) +*d.*; **he ~ed to her wants** он ей прислу́живал; **a ~ing angel** а́нгел-храни́тель (*m.*).

ministerial /ˌmɪnɪˈstɪərɪəl/ *adj.* министе́рский.

ministration /ˌmɪnɪˈstreɪʃ(ə)n/ *n.* (*pl., services*) по́мощь; обслу́живание; (*of a priest*) отправле́ние свяще́нником свои́х обя́занностей.

ministry /ˈmɪnɪstrɪ/ *n.* **1** (*department of state*) министе́рство. **2** (*period of government*) срок пребыва́ния у вла́сти. **3** (*relig.*): **he entered the ~** он при́нял духо́вный сан.

mink /mɪŋk/ *n.* но́рка; (*attr.*) но́рковый; **~ coat** но́рковое пальто́/манто́.

minnow /ˈmɪnəʊ/ *n.* песка́рь (*m.*).

Minoan /mɪˈnəʊən/ *adj.* мино́йский.

minor /ˈmaɪnə(r)/ *n.* (*person under age*) несовершенноле́тний.

● *adj.* **1** (*of lesser importance*) второстепе́нный; малозначи́тельный, ме́лкий, небольшо́й; **~ repairs** ме́лкий ремо́нт. **2** (*Br., younger*) ме́ньший, мла́дший; **Smith M~** Смит мла́дший. **3** (*mus.*) мино́рный, ма́лый.

minority /maɪˈnɒrɪtɪ/ *n.* **1** (*being under age*) несовершенноле́тие. **2** (*smaller number of votes etc.*) меньшинство́, ме́ньшая часть; **you are in the ~** вы в меньшинстве́; (*attr.*): **~ group** меньшинство́. **3** (**~** *nationality*) национа́льное меньшинство́.

Minsk *n.* Минск.

minster /ˈmɪnstə(r)/ *n.* кафедра́льный собо́р.

minstrel /ˈmɪnstr(ə)l/ *n.* менестре́ль (*m.*).

mint[1] /mɪnt/ *n.* (*bot.*) мя́та; **~ sauce** со́ус из мя́ты; (*a sweet*) мя́тная конфе́та.

mint[2] /mɪnt/ *n.* (*fin.*) моне́тный двор; **he made a ~ of money** он сколоти́л (*coll.*) состоя́ние; (*attr., lit., fig.*) но́венький, но́вый.

● *v.t.* чека́нить (*impf.*).

minuet /ˌmɪnjʊˈet/ *n.* менуэ́т.

minus /ˈmaɪnəs/ *n.* ми́нус; **two ~es make a plus** (*in multiplication*) ми́нус на ми́нус даёт плюс.

● *adj.* отрица́тельный; **~ sign** (знак) ми́нус; **~ quantity** отрица́тельная величина́.

● *prep.* ми́нус; без+*g.*; **~ 1** ми́нус едини́ца; **he came back ~ an arm** он верну́лся без руки́.

minuscule /ˈmɪnəˌskjuːl/ *adj.* (*tiny*) кро́шечный, о́чень ма́ленький.

minute[1] /ˈmɪnɪt/ *n.* **1** (*fraction of hour or degree*) мину́та; **he left it to the last ~** он всё оста́вил до после́дней мину́ты; **the train left several ~s ago** по́езд отошёл не́сколько мину́т наза́д. **2** (*moment*) мгнове́ние, моме́нт, миг; **I'll come in a ~** я сейча́с/ми́гом приду́; **come here this ~!** сейча́с же иди́ сюда́!; **just a ~** одну́ мину́тку!; **I won't be a ~** я на мину́тку; сейча́с верну́сь!; **I'll tell him the ~ he arrives** как то́лько он придёт, я ему́ скажу́; **he came in and the next ~ he was gone** он пришёл и че́рез секу́нду его́ не́ было; **they left at 2 o'clock to the ~** они́ ушли́ в 2 часа́ ро́вно; **he is always up to the ~ with his news** он всегда́ в ку́рсе после́дних новосте́й. **3** (*usu. pl., record*) протоко́л; **the ~s of the last meeting** протоко́л после́днего совеща́ния; (*memorandum*) (делова́я) запи́ска.

● *v.t.* вести́ протоко́л +*g.*; запи́с|ывать, -а́ть.

● *cpd.* **~-hand** *n.* мину́тная стре́лка.

minute[2] /maɪˈnjuːt/ *adj.* (**minutest**) (*tiny*) ме́лкий, кро́хотный; **in ~ detail** подробне́йшим о́бразом; (*detailed*) подро́бный, дета́льный.

minutiae /maɪˈnjuːʃɪˌiː/, /mɪ-/ *n.* ме́лочи (*f. pl.*); дета́ли (*f. pl.*).

minx /mɪŋks/ *n.* озорни́ца; (*coquette*) коке́тка.

Miocene /ˈmaɪəˌsiːn/ *n.* миоце́н.

● *adj.* миоце́новый.

miracle /ˈmɪrək(ə)l/ *n.* чу́до; **~ play** мира́кль (*m.*); **he escaped by a ~** он чу́дом уцеле́л; **a ~ of ingenuity** чу́до изобрета́тельности.

miraculous /mɪˈrækjʊləs/ *adj.* (*surprising*) чуде́сный; (*miracle-working*) чудотво́рный.

mirage /ˈmɪrɑːʒ/ *n.* (*lit., fig.*) мира́ж.

M

mire /ˈmaɪə(r)/ *n.* трясина; болото; **his name was dragged through the ~** его смешали с грязью.

mirror /ˈmɪrə(r)/ *n.* зеркало; **~ image** (*lit.*, *fig.*) (зеркальное) отображение.

● *v.t.* отра|жать, -зить; (*fig.*) отобра|жать, -зить; изобра|жать, -зить.

mirth /mɜːθ/ *n.* (*gladness*) веселье, радость; (*laughter*) смех.

mirthful /ˈmɜːθfʊl/ *adj.* весёлый, радостный.

mirthless /ˈmɜːθlɪs/ *adj.* безрадостный.

miry /ˈmaɪərɪ/ *adj.* болотистый; грязный.

misadventure /ˌmɪsədˈventʃə(r)/ *n.* несчастье, несчастный случай; **death by ~** смерть от несчастного случая.

misalliance /ˌmɪsəˈlaɪəns/ *n.* мезальянс.

misandrist /mɪˈzændrɪst/ *n.* мужененавистница.

misanthrope /ˈmɪzənˌθrəʊp/, /ˈmɪs-/ *n.* мизантроп.

misanthropic /ˌmɪzənˈθrɒpɪk/, /ˈmɪs-/ *adj.* мизантропический, человеконенавистнический.

misanthropy /mɪˈzænθrəpɪ/ *n.* мизантропия.

misapplication /mɪsˌæplɪˈkeɪʃ(ə)n/ *n.* неправильное использование (+*g.*); злоупотребление (+*i.*).

misapply /ˌmɪsəˈplaɪ/ *v.t.* неправильно использовать (*impf.*, *pf.*); злоупотреб|лять, -ить +*i.*

misapprehend /ˌmɪsæprɪˈhend/ *v.t.* пон|имать, -ять превратно.

misapprehension /ˌmɪsæprɪˈhenʃ(ə)n/ *n.* превратное понимание; недоразумение; **I was under a ~** я заблуждался.

misappropriate /ˌmɪsəˈprəʊprɪˌeɪt/ *v.t.* (незаконно) присв|аивать, -оить; соверш|ать, -ить растрату +*g.*

misappropriation /ˌmɪsəˌprəʊprɪˈeɪʃ(ə)n/ *n.* незаконное присвоение; растрата.

misbehave /ˌmɪsbɪˈheɪv/ *v.i.* дурно себя вести (*det.*).

misbehaviour /ˌmɪsbɪˈheɪvɪə(r)/ (*US* **misbehavior**) *n.* дурное поведение.

miscalculate /ˌmɪsˈkælkjʊˌleɪt/ *v.t.* плохо рассчит|ывать, -ать.

● *v.i.* просчит|ываться, -аться.

miscalculation /ˌmɪskælkjʊˈleɪʃ(ə)n/ *n.* просчёт.

miscarriage /ˈmɪsˌkærɪdʒ/, /mɪsˈkærɪdʒ/ *n.* **1** (*biol.*) выкидыш; **she had a ~** у неё произошёл выкидыш. **2**: **~ of justice** ошибка правосудия.

miscarr|y /mɪsˈkærɪ/ *v.i.* **1** (*of a woman*) иметь (*impf.*) выкидыш. **2** (*fail*) терпеть (*impf.*) неудачу; **his plans ~ied** его планы провалились.

miscast /mɪsˈkɑːst/ *v.t.* да|вать, -ть неподходящую роль +*d.*; **he was ~ as Falstaff** ему не следовало поручать роль Фальстафа; **the play was ~** роли в пьесе были распределены неудачно.

miscellanea /ˌmɪsəˈleɪnɪə/ *n. pl.* разное.

miscellaneous /ˌmɪsəˈleɪnɪəs/ *adj.* смешанный; разнообразный, разношёрстный.

miscellany /mɪˈselənɪ/ *n.* смесь, всякая всячина; **literary ~** литературный альманах/сборник.

mischance /mɪsˈtʃɑːns/ *n.* неудача; невезение; **by ~** к несчастью.

mischief /ˈmɪstʃɪf/ *n.* **1** (*harm, damage*) вред; **put that knife away, or you'll do someone a ~** уберите нож, а то кого-нибудь пораните. **2** (*discord, ill-feeling*) раздор; **he is out to make ~ between us** он хочет нас поссорить. **3** (*naughtiness*) озорство; проказы (*f. pl.*); **he is always getting into ~** он всегда проказничает/шалит; **can't you keep him out of ~?** неужели вы не можете удержать его от проказ? **4** (*mockery*): **his eyes were full of ~** его глаза были полны лукавства. **5** (*coll., mischievous child*) озорник; проказник.

● *cpds.* **~-maker** *n.* интриган, смутьян; **~-making** *n.* интриги (*f. pl.*), интриганство.

mischievous /ˈmɪstʃɪvəs/ *adj.* (*harmful*) вредный; (*spiteful, malicious*) злой, злобный; (*given to pranks*) озорной, шаловливый.

misconceive /ˌmɪskənˈsiːv/ *v.t.* неправильно пон|имать, -ять.

misconception /ˌmɪskənˈsepʃ(ə)n/ *n.* неправильное представление/понимание.

misconduct¹ /mɪsˈkɒndʌkt/ *n.* **1** (*mismanagement*) плохое ведение (дел). **2** (*improper conduct*) дурное поведение; **professional ~** нарушение профессиональной этики; должностное преступление.

misconduct² /ˌmɪskənˈdʌkt/ *v.t.* (*mismanage*) плохо вести (*det.*) (дела); **~ o.s.** дурно себя вести (*det.*).

misconstruction /ˌmɪskənˈstrʌkʃ(ə)n/ *n.* неправильное/неверное толкование; **his words were open to ~** его слова могли быть истолкованы неверно/неправильно.

misconstrue /ˌmɪskənˈstruː/ *v.t.* неправильно истолков|ывать, -ать.

miscount *n.* /ˈmɪskaʊnt/ неправильный подсчёт.

● *v.t. & i.* /mɪsˈkaʊnt/ ошиб|аться, -иться в подсчёте; обсчит|ываться, -аться.

miscreant /ˈmɪskrɪənt/ *n.* подлец, негодяй.

miscue *n.* /ˈmɪskjuː/ неправильный/плохой удар (*в бильярде*).

● *v.i.* /mɪsˈkjuː/ делать, с- плохой удар.

misdate /mɪsˈdeɪt/ *v.t.* неправильно датировать (*impf.*, *pf.*).

misdeal *n.* /ˈmɪsˈdiːl/ неправильная сдача.

● *v.i.* /mɪsˈdiːl/ ошиб|аться, -иться при сдаче карт.

misdeed /mɪsˈdiːd/ *n.* преступление.

misdemeanour /ˌmɪsdɪˈmiːnə(r)/ (*US* **misdemeanor**) *n.* проступок.

misdirect /ˌmɪsdaɪˈrekt/, /-dɪˈrekt/ *v.t.* неверно напр|авлять, -авить; **the letter was ~ed** письмо было неправильно адресовано; **his efforts were ~ed** его усилия были направлены не по адресу; **the jury was ~ed** присяжным дали неправильное напутствие.

misdirection /ˌmɪsdaɪˈrekʃ(ə)n/, /-dɪˈrekʃ(ə)n/ *n.* неправильное указание направления/пути.

mise-en-scène /ˌmiːz ɑ̃ ˈsen/ *n.* мизансцена; (*fig., setting, environment*) окружающая обстановка.

miser /ˈmaɪzə(r)/ *n.* скряга (*c.g.*), скупец.

miserable /ˈmɪzərəb(ə)l/ *adj.* **1** (*wretched; unhappy*) жалкий, несчастный. **2** (*causing wretchedness*) плохой, скверный; **what ~ weather!** какая скверная погода!; **a ~ hovel** жалкая лачуга/хибарка. **3** (*mean; contemptible*): **a ~ sum (of money)** ничтожная/мизерная сумма.

miserliness /ˈmaɪzəlmɪs/ *n.* скупость, скаредность.

miserly /ˈmaɪzəlɪ/ *adj.* скупой, скаредный.

misery /ˈmɪzərɪ/ *n.* **1** (*suffering; wretchedness*) страдание; мучение; **he put the dog out of its ~** он положил конец страданиям собаки. **2** (*extreme poverty*) нищета, бедность. **3** (*Br. coll., person who complains*) зануда (*c.g.*), нытик.

misfire *n.* /ˈmɪsfaɪə(r)/ осечка.

● *v.i.* /mɪsˈfaɪə(r)/ да|вать, -ть осечку; (*tech., of ignition*) выпадать, выпасть; **the gun ~d** ружьё дало осечку; (*fig.*) не состояться (*impf.*); **his plans ~d** его план сорвался.

misfit /ˈmɪsfɪt/ *n.* (*person*) неприспособленный человек; (*failure*) неудачник.

misfortune /mɪsˈfɔːtʃuːn/, /-tjuːn/ *n.* (*bad luck*) беда, несчастье; **I had the ~ to lose my purse** я имел несчастье потерять кошелёк; **companions in ~** друзья по несчастью; (*stroke of bad luck*) несчастье, неудача.

misgiving /mɪsˈɡɪvɪŋ/ *n.* опасение; дурное предчувствие.

misgovern /mɪsˈɡʌv(ə)n/ *v.t.* плохо управлять (*impf.*) +*i.*; плохо руководить (*impf.*) +*i.*

misgovernment /mɪsˈɡʌvənmənt/ *n.* плохое управление/руководство (*чем*).

misguided /mɪsˈɡaɪdɪd/ *adj.*: **I was ~ enough to trust him** я имел неосторожность ему доверить; **~ enthusiasm** энтузиазм, достойный лучшего применения.

mishandle /mɪsˈhænd(ə)l/ *v.t.* (*ill-treat*) плохо/дурно обращаться (*impf.*) с+*i.*; (*manage inefficiently*) плохо вести (*det.*) (дело).

mishap /ˈmɪshæp/ *n.* неудача; неприятное происшествие.

mishear /mɪsˈhɪə(r)/ *v.t.* неточно расслышать (*pf.*).

mishit /ˈmɪshɪt/ *n.* промах.

mishmash /ˈmɪʃmæʃ/ *n.* (*coll.*) путаница, мешанина.

misinform /ˌmɪsɪnˈfɔːm/ *v.t.* непра́вильно информи́ровать (*impf., pf.*).

misinformation /ˌmɪsɪnfəˈmeɪʃ(ə)n/ *n.* неве́рная информа́ция; дезинформа́ция.

misinterpret /ˌmɪsɪnˈtɜːprɪt/ *v.t.* непра́вильно пон|има́ть, -я́ть; непра́вильно истолко́в|ывать, -а́ть.

misinterpretation /ˌmɪsɪnˌtɜːprɪˈteɪʃ(ə)n/ *n.* непра́вильное понима́ние/толкова́ние.

misjudge /mɪsˈdʒʌdʒ/ *v.t.* неве́рно оце́н|ивать, -и́ть; **he ~d the distance and fell** он не рассчита́л расстоя́ние и упа́л; **he has been ~d** о нём соста́вили непра́вильное мне́ние; его́ недооцени́ли.

misjudg(e)ment /mɪsˈdʒʌdʒmənt/ *n.* непра́вильное мне́ние/сужде́ние.

mislay /mɪsˈleɪ/ *v.t.* (*lose*) зате́ривать, затеря́ть; (*put in wrong place*) класть, положи́ть не на ме́сто.

mislead /mɪsˈliːd/ *v.t.* (*fig., cause to do wrong*) сби|ва́ть, -ть с пути́; (*fig., give wrong impression to*) вв|оди́ть, -ести́ в заблужде́ние; **a ~ing statement** заявле́ние, вводя́щее в заблужде́ние.

mismanage /mɪsˈmænɪdʒ/ *v.t.* пло́хо управля́ть (*impf.*) + *i.*; пло́хо руководи́ть (*impf.*) + *i.*

mismanagement /mɪsˈmænɪdʒmənt/ *n.* плохо́е управле́ние/руково́дство; (*inefficiency*) нераспоряди́тельность.

misname /mɪsˈneɪm/ *v.t.* неве́рно имнова́ть (*impf.*).

misnomer /mɪsˈnəʊmə(r)/ *n.* непра́вильное назва́ние/и́мя.

misogynist /mɪˈsɒdʒɪnɪst/ *n.* женоненави́стник.

misogyny /mɪˈsɒdʒɪnɪ/ *n.* женоненави́стничество.

misplace /mɪsˈpleɪs/ *v.t.* положи́ть (*pf.*) не на ме́сто.

misplaced /mɪsˈpleɪst/ *adj.* (*out of place*) неуме́стный; (*unfounded*) безоснова́тельный.

misprint /ˈmɪsprɪnt/ *n.* опеча́тка.

mispronounce /ˌmɪsprəˈnaʊns/ *v.t.* непра́вильно произн|оси́ть, -ести́.

mispronunciation /ˌmɪsprəˌnʌnsɪˈeɪʃ(ə)n/ *n.* непра́вильное произноше́ние.

misquotation /ˌmɪskwəʊˈteɪʃ(ə)n/ *n.* нето́чная цита́та.

misquote /mɪsˈkwəʊt/ *v.t.* нето́чно цити́ровать, про-; **I have been ~d** мои́ слова́ искази́ли.

misread /mɪsˈriːd/ *v.t.* (*read incorrectly*) чита́ть, про- непра́вильно; (*misinterpret*) непра́вильно истолко́в|ывать, -а́ть.

misremember /ˌmɪsrɪˈmembə(r)/ *v.t. & i.* пло́хо/нето́чно по́мнить (*impf.*).

misrepresent /ˌmɪsreprɪˈzent/ *v.t.* иска|жа́ть, -зи́ть; **he ~ed the facts** он искази́л фа́кты; **I was ~ed** меня́ предста́вили в ло́жном све́те.

misrepresentation /ˌmɪsreprɪzenˈteɪʃ(ə)n/ *n.* искаже́ние (фа́ктов).

misrule /mɪsˈruːl/ *n.* (*bad government*) плохо́е правле́ние; (*lawlessness*) беспоря́док, ана́рхия.

miss¹ /mɪs/ *n.* (*failure to hit etc.*) про́мах; **a ~ is as good as a mile** «чуть-чу́ть» не счита́ется; **near ~** (*lit.*) попада́ние/разры́в вблизи́ це́ли; (*fig.*) бли́зкая дога́дка *и т.п.*; **I gave the meeting a ~** (*Br.*) я не пошёл на собра́ние.

● *v.t.* **1** (*fail to hit or catch*): **he ~ed the ball** он пропусти́л мяч; **he ~ed the target** он не попа́л в цель; **the bullet ~ed him by inches** пу́ля чуть-чу́ть его́ не заде́ла; **he ~ed the bus** (*lit.*) он опозда́л на авто́бус; (*fig.*) он упусти́л слу́чай.
2 (*fig., fail to grasp*) не пон|има́ть, -я́ть; не улови́ть (*pf.*); **you have ~ed the point** вы не по́няли су́ти.
3 (*fail to secure*): **he ~ed his footing and fell** он оступи́лся и упа́л.
4 (*fail to hear or see*) не услы́шать (*pf.*); пропус|ка́ть, -ти́ть; **I ~ed your last remark** я прослу́шал ва́ше после́днее замеча́ние; **you must not ~ this film** не пропусти́те э́тот фильм; **you haven't ~ed much** вы немно́го потеря́ли; **it's the corner house; you can't ~ it** э́то углово́й дом — вы его́ не мо́жете не заме́тить.
5 (*fail to meet*): **you've just ~ed him!** вы с ним чуть-чу́ть размину́лись!
6 (*escape by chance*) избе|га́ть, -жа́ть; **we just ~ed having an accident** мы чуть не попа́ли в катастро́фу; ещё немно́го и мы попа́ли бы в катастро́фу.
7 (*discover or regret absence of*): **when did you ~ your purse?** когда́ вы обнару́жили, что у вас нет кошелька́?; **she ~es her husband** она́ скуча́ет по му́жу; **we ~ed you** нам вас недостава́ло; **he won't be ~ed** его́ отсу́тствия не заме́тят; (*sc. lamented*) никто́ не пожале́ет, что его́ нет; **I ~ his talks** я скуча́ю по его́ ле́кциям; **he wouldn't ~ a hundred pounds** что ему́ сто фу́нтов!

● *v.i.* **1** (*fail to hit target*) прома́х|иваться, -ну́ться; не поп|ада́ть, -а́сть в цель; **he shot at me but ~ed** он вы́стрелил в меня́, но промахну́лся.
2 (*of an engine*): **it is ~ing on one cylinder** оди́н цили́ндр барахли́т.

● *with adv.*: **~ out** *v.t.* упус|ка́ть, -ти́ть; пропус|ка́ть, -ти́ть; **you have ~ed out the most important thing** вы пропусти́ли/упусти́ли са́мое ва́жное; **I shall ~ out the first course** я не бу́ду есть пе́рвое; *v.i.* (*coll.*): **he ~ed out on all the fun** он пропусти́л са́мое весе́лье; **I felt I was ~ing out** я чу́вствовал, что мно́гое упуска́ю.

miss² /mɪs/ *n.* (*young girl; also voc.*) де́вушка; (**M~**: *as title, abbr. of* ***mistress***) мисс.

missal /ˈmɪs(ə)l/ *n.* служе́бник, моли́твенник.

missel-thrush /ˈmɪs(ə)l/ *n.* дрозд-деря́ба.

misshapen /mɪsˈʃeɪpən/ *adj.* уро́дливый, деформи́рованный.

missile /ˈmɪsaɪl/ *n.* **1** (*object thrown*) мета́тельный предме́т. **2** (*weapon thrown or fired*) снаря́д. **3** (*rocket weapon*) раке́та; **guided ~** управля́емая раке́та; **ballistic ~** баллисти́ческая раке́та; **~ site** ста́ртовая пози́ция; ста́ртовый ко́мплекс.

missing /ˈmɪsɪŋ/ *adj.* недостаю́щий; потеря́вшийся; **there is a page ~** не хвата́ет страни́цы; **he was ~ing for a whole day** он где́-то пропада́л це́лый день; **he went ~** он пропа́л (без вести); **the dead and ~** уби́тые и пропа́вшие бе́з вести; **the ~ link** недостаю́щее звено́.

● *quasi-prep.* (*coll., short of*): **I am ~ two shirt buttons** у меня́ на руба́шке оторва́лись две пу́говицы.

mission /ˈmɪʃ(ə)n/ *n.* **1** (*errand*) поруче́ние; командиро́вка. **2** (*vocation*) ми́ссия, призва́ние; **his ~ in life** цель его́ жи́зни. **3** (*mil., sortie or task*) зада́ние. **4** (*dipl.*) ми́ссия, (*to UN*) делега́ция. **5** (*relig.*) ми́ссия.

missionary /ˈmɪʃənərɪ/ *n.* миссионе́р (*fem.* -ка).

● *adj.* миссионе́рский.

missis /ˈmɪsɪz/ *n.* (*coll.*) жена́; хозя́йка.

missive /ˈmɪsɪv/ *n.* посла́ние.

misspell /mɪsˈspel/ *v.t. & i.* непра́вильно написа́ть (*pf.*); сде́лать (*pf.*) орфографи́ческую оши́бку.

misspelling /mɪsˈspelɪŋ/ *n.* непра́вильное написа́ние.

misspen|d /mɪsˈspend/ *v.t.* (*of funds*) тра́тить, рас-; **a ~t youth** (напра́сно) растра́ченная мо́лодость.

misstate /mɪsˈsteɪt/ *v.t.* де́лать, с- ло́жное заявле́ние о + *p.*; предст|авля́ть, -а́вить в ло́жном све́те.

misstatement /mɪsˈsteɪtmənt/ *n.* ло́жное заявле́ние.

missus /ˈmɪsəz/ = **missis**

mist /mɪst/ *n.* (*lit., fig.*) тума́н, ды́мка, мгла.

● *v.t. & i.* затума́ни|вать(ся), -ть(ся); **my glasses have ~ed over** у меня́ запоте́ли очки́.

mistakable /mɪˈsteɪkəb(ə)l/ *adj.*: **he is easily ~ for his brother** его́ легко́ приня́ть за бра́та.

mistak|e /mɪˈsteɪk/ *n.* оши́бка; заблужде́ние; **by ~e** по оши́бке; **make no ~e (about it)** бу́дьте уве́рены.

● *v.t.* (*misunderstand*) ошиб|а́ться, -и́ться в + *p.*; **there is no ~ing his meaning** смысл его́ слов преде́льно я́сен; (*misrecognize*): **he mistook me for my brother** он при́нял меня́ за моего́ бра́та.

mistaken /mɪˈsteɪkən/ *adj.* **1** (*in error*): **if I am not ~** е́сли я не ошиба́юсь. **2** (*ill-judged; erroneous*) неосмотри́тельный; оши́бочный, непра́вильный; **a ~ kindness** неуме́стная любе́зность.

mister /ˈmɪstə(r)/ *n.* (*coll., as voc.*) ми́стер, сэр; граждани́н.

mistime /mɪsˈtaɪm/ *v.t.* (*action*) сде́лать (*pf.*) не во́время; **he ~d his blow** он пло́хо/не рассчита́л уда́р; (*speech*) сказа́ть (*pf.*) не во́время; **a ~d remark** неуме́стное замеча́ние.

M

mistiness /ˈmɪstɪnɪs/ *n.* тума́нность.

mistletoe /ˈmɪs(ə)l,təʊ/ *n.* оме́ла.

mistral /ˈmɪstrɑːl/, /mɪˈstrɑːl/ *n.* мистра́ль (*m.*).

mistranslate /,mɪstrænzˈleɪt/, /,mɪstrɑː-/, /-sˈleɪt/ *v.t.* непра́вильно перев|оди́ть, -ести́.

mistranslation /,mɪstrænzˈleɪʃ(ə)n/, /,mɪstrɑː-/, /-sˈleɪʃ(ə)n/ *n.* непра́вильный перево́д.

mistress /ˈmɪstrɪs/ *n.* **1** (*of household etc.*) хозя́йка; **~ of the situation** хозя́йка положе́ния. **2** (*Br.*, *schoolteacher*) учи́тельница. **3** (*lover*) любо́вница.

mistrial /mɪsˈtraɪəl/ *n.* непра́вильное суде́бное разбира́тельство.

mistrust /mɪsˈtrʌst/ *n.* недове́рие.

● *v.t.* не доверя́ть (*impf.*) + *d.*

mistrustful /mɪsˈtrʌstfʊl/ *adj.* недове́рчивый.

misty /ˈmɪstɪ/ *adj.* (**mistier, mistiest**) тума́нный; (*fig.*) сму́тный.

misunder|stand /,mɪsʌndəˈstænd/ *v.t.* непра́вильно пон|има́ть, -я́ть; **she felt ~stood** она́ чу́вствовала, что её не понима́ют.

misunderstanding /,mɪsʌndəˈstændɪŋ/ *n.* недоразуме́ние.

misuse[1] /mɪsˈjuːs/ *n.* непра́вильное употребле́ние; злоупотребле́ние (*чем*); дурно́е обраще́ние (*с чем*).

misuse[2] /mɪsˈjuːz/ *v.t.* (*use improperly*) непра́вильно употреб|ля́ть, -и́ть; (*treat badly*) ду́рно обраща́ться (*impf.*) с + *i.*

mite[1] /maɪt/ *n.* (*small coin*) полу́шка; грош; (*fig.*, *small contribution*) ле́пта; (*bit*) чу́точка, ка́пелька; **he was not a ~ ashamed** ему́ не́ было ни ка́пельки сты́дно; (*small child*) малю́тка (*c.g.*), кро́шка.

mite[2] /maɪt/ *n.* (*insect*) клещ.

miter /ˈmaɪtə(r)/ (*US*) = **mitre**

mitigat|e /ˈmɪtɪ,geɪt/ *v.t.* смягч|а́ть, -и́ть; облегч|а́ть, -и́ть; **~ing circumstances** смягча́ющие обстоя́тельства.

mitigation /,mɪtɪˈgeɪʃ(ə)n/ *n.* смягче́ние, ослабле́ние; **a plea in ~** хода́тайство о смягче́нии пригово́ра.

mitre[1] /ˈmaɪtə(r)/ (*US* **miter**) *n.* (*headgear*) ми́тра.

mitre[2] /ˈmaɪtə(r)/ (*US* **miter**) *n.* (*joint*) соедине́ние в ус.

● *v.t.* соедин|я́ть, -и́ть в ус.

mitt /mɪt/ *n.* **1** = **mitten. 2** (*fingerless mitten*) мите́нка.

mitten /ˈmɪt(ə)n/ *n.* рукави́ца, ва́режка.

mix /mɪks/ *n.* смесь; соста́в; **cake ~** порошо́к для ке́кса *и т.п.*

● *v.t.* **1** (*mingle*) сме́ш|ивать, -а́ть; (*combine*) сочета́ть (*impf.*, *pf.*); **you can't ~ oil and water** ма́сло с водо́й не сме́шивается; **I like to ~ business with pleasure** я люблю́ сочета́ть прия́тное с поле́зным. **2** (*prepare by ~ing*) сме́ш|ивать, -а́ть; переме́ш|ивать, -а́ть; **~ me a cocktail** пригото́вьте мне кокте́йль. **3** (*in sound recording etc.*) мики́ровать (*impf.*, *pf.*), св|оди́ть, -ести́; **~ing desk** ми́кшерский пульт.

● *v.i.* (*mingle*) сме́шиваться (*impf.*); (*combine*) сочета́ться (*impf.*, *pf.*); (*of persons*) обща́ться (*impf.*); **she won't ~ with her neighbours** (*Br.*), **neighbors** (*US*) она́ не хо́чет обща́ться с сосе́дями.

● *with advs.*: **~ in** *v.t.* заме́|шивать, -си́ть; **beat the eggs and ~ in the flour** взбе́йте я́йца и смеша́йте с муко́й; **~ up** *v.t.* (**~** *thoroughly*) (хорошо́) переме́|шивать, -си́ть; (*confuse*) перепу́т|ывать, -ать; **I ~ed him up with his father** я перепу́тал его́ с отцо́м; **I ~ed up the dates** я перепу́тал чи́сла; **a ~ed-up child** (*coll.*) тру́дный ребёнок; (*involve*) впу́т|ывать, -ать; **I don't want to become ~ed up in the affair** я не хочу́ вввя́зываться в э́то де́ло.

● *cpd.* **~-up** *n.* недоразуме́ние.

mixed /mɪkst/ *adj.* сме́шанный, переме́шанный; **(place for) ~ bathing** о́бщий пляж; **a ~ bunch** (*of flowers*) сме́шанный буке́т; (*of people*) разношёрстная компа́ния; **~ doubles** сме́шанная па́рная игра́; **~ farming** сме́шанное хозя́йство; **I have ~ feelings about it** у меня́ на э́тот счёт разноречи́вые чу́вства; **~ grill** (*Br.*) ассорти́ (*nt. indecl.*) из жа́реного мя́са; **~ marriage** сме́шанный брак; **~ metaphor** сме́шанная мета́фора; **~ school** шко́ла совме́стного обуче́ния.

mixer /ˈmɪksə(r)/ *n.* **1** (*for cement*) меша́лка; (*for food*) ми́ксер; **~ tap** (*Br.*) смеси́тель (*m.*). **2** (*sociable person*): **he is a good ~** он общи́тельный челове́к. **3** (*cin. etc.*) ми́кшер.

mixture /ˈmɪkstʃə(r)/ *n.* (*mixing*) сме́шивание; (*something mixed*) смесь; **cough ~** миксту́ра от ка́шля.

miz(z)en /ˈmɪz(ə)n/ *n.* (**~-sail**) биза́нь.

● *cpd.* **~-mast** *n.* биза́нь-ма́чта.

ml. *n. abbr. of* **1** ***millilitre(s)*** /ˈmɪlɪ,liːtə(r)(z)/ мл (миллили́тр). **2** ***mile(s)*** /maɪl(z)/ ми́ля.

mm. /ˈmɪlɪ,miːtə(r)(z)/ *n.* (*abbr. of* ***millimetre(s)***) мм (миллиме́тр).

mnemonic /nɪˈmɒnɪk/ *n.* (*aid to memory*) мнемони́ческий приём.

● *adj.* мнемони́ческий.

mo /məʊ/ (*pl.* **mos**) (*Br. coll.*) = **moment**

moan /məʊn/ *n.* стон; (*coll.*, *complaint*) стон, нытьё.

● *v.t. & i.* стона́ть (*impf.*); (*coll.*, *complain*) ныть (*impf.*); (*fig.*) выть (*impf.*); завыва́ть (*impf.*); **the ~ing of the wind** завыва́ние ве́тра.

moaner /ˈməʊnə(r)/ *n.* ны́тик (*coll.*).

moat /məʊt/ *n.* ров с водо́й.

mob /mɒb/ *n.* **1** (*rabble, crowd*) толпа́. **2**: **the ~** (*common people*) толпа́; чернь; **~ rule** самосу́д; суд Ли́нча. **3**: **the Mob** (*mafia*) ма́фия.

● *v.t.* (**mobbed, mobbing**) нап|ада́ть, -а́сть на + *a.*; **the singer was ~bed by his fans** певца́ осажда́ли покло́нники.

mobile /ˈməʊbaɪl/ *n.* подвесна́я констру́кция, «моба́йл».

● *adj.* **1** (*easily moved*) передвижно́й, перено́сный; **~ home** жило́й автоприце́п; **~ phone** портати́вный/со́товый телефо́н; **~ troops** подвижны́е войска́. **2** (*lively, agile*) подви́жный; **~ features** живо́е лицо́.

mobility /məˈbɪlɪtɪ/ *n.* подви́жность, моби́льность.

mobilization /,məʊbɪlaɪˈzeɪʃ(ə)n/ *n.* мобилиза́ция.

mobilize /ˈməʊbɪ,laɪz/ *v.t.* мобилизова́ть (*impf.*, *pf.*); **he ~d all his resources to help us** он мобилизова́л все свои́ ресу́рсы, что́бы нам помо́чь.

● *v.i.* мобилизова́ться (*impf.*, *pf.*).

mobster /ˈmɒbstə(r)/ *n.* банди́т; (*Mafioso*) мафио́зи (*m. indecl.*).

moccasin /ˈmɒkəsɪn/ *n.* мокаси́н.

mocha /ˈmɒkə/ *n.* ко́фе (*m.*) мо́кко (*indecl.*).

mock /mɒk/ *n.*: **this makes a ~ of all my work** э́то сво́дит всю мою́ рабо́ту на нет.

● *adj.* подде́льный, фальши́вый; **~ battle** уче́бный бой; **~ examination** (*Br.*) предэкзаменацио́нная прове́рка; **~ trial** инсцени́рованный проце́сс.

● *v.t.* **1** (*ridicule*) насмеха́ться (*impf.*) над + *i.*; издева́ться (*impf.*) над + *i.*; высме́ивать, вы́смеять; **they ~ed the teacher** они́ издева́лись над учи́телем. **2** (*mimic*) передра́зн|ивать, -и́ть; **~ing-bird** пересме́шник.

● *v.i.*: **~ at** = **~** *v.t.* 1.

● *cpds.* **~-heroic** *adj.* ироикоми́ческий; **~-turtle soup** *n.* суп из теля́чьей головы́; **~-up** *n.* маке́т.

mocker /ˈmɒkə(r)/ *n.* насме́шни|к (*fem.* -ца).

mockery /ˈmɒkərɪ/ *n.* (*ridicule*) издева́тельство, осмея́ние; **he was held up to ~** над ним издева́лись; (*parody*) паро́дия; **the trial was a ~ of justice** суд был паро́дией на правосу́дие.

MOD (*abbr. of* ***Ministry of Defence***) Министе́рство оборо́ны.

mod /mɒd/ *n.* (*Br. sl.*) стиля́га (*c.g.*), мо́дник.

● *adj.*: **~ cons** (*Br.*) совреме́нные удо́бства.

modal /ˈməʊd(ə)l/ *adj.* (*logic, gram.*) мода́льный; (*mus.*) ла́довый.

modality /məˈdælɪtɪ/ *n.* (*in pl.*) ме́тоды (*m. pl.*), приёмы (*m. pl.*), мето́дика.

mode /məʊd/ *n.* **1** (*manner*) ме́тод, спо́соб; **~ of operation** спо́соб рабо́ты; **~ of life** о́браз жи́зни. **2** (*fashion*) мо́да; обы́чай. **3** (*mus.*) лад; тона́льность.

model /ˈmɒd(ə)l/ *n.* **1** (*representation*) моде́ль, маке́т, схе́ма; **working ~** де́йствующая моде́ль; **~ aircraft** моде́ль самолёта. **2** (*pattern*) образе́ц, станда́рт; **he made each box on the ~ of the first** он сде́лал все коро́бки по образцу́ пе́рвой; **he is a ~ of gallantry** он образе́ц гала́нтности; **a ~ husband** идеа́льный муж. **3** (*person posing for artist*) нату́рщи|к (*fem.* -ца); **life ~** жива́я моде́ль.

4 (*woman displaying clothes etc.*) манеке́нщица, моде́ль; **male ~** манеке́нщик.
5 (*dress*) моде́ль.
6 (*design*) моде́ль, тип; **sports ~** (*car*) спорти́вный автомоби́ль.

● *v.t.* (**modelled, modelling;** *US* **modeled, modeling**) де́лать, с- моде́ль +*g.*; **he ~led her face in wax** он вы́лепил из во́ска её лицо́; **she ~led the dress** (*wore it as a ~*) она́ демонстри́ровала пла́тье; **clay ~ling** ле́пка из гли́ны; (*fig.*): **he ~s himself upon his father** он сле́дует приме́ру своего́ отца́; **she ~s for a living** она́ рабо́тает манеке́нщицей.

modeller /ˈmɒdlə(r)/ *n.* ле́пщик, моде́льщик.

modem /ˈməʊdem/ *n.* мо́де́м.

moderate¹ /ˈmɒdərət/ *n.* уме́ренный челове́к; челове́к, приде́рживающийся уме́ренных взгля́дов.

● *adj.* уме́ренный; сре́дний; **~ appetite** уме́ренный аппети́т; **~ drinker** челове́к, пью́щий уме́ренно; **~ly well dressed** дово́льно хорошо́ оде́тый.

moderat|e² /ˈmɒdəˌreɪt/ *v.t.* ум|еря́ть, -е́рить; смягч|а́ть, -и́ть; **he ~ed his demands** он уме́рил свои́ тре́бования; **~e your language** выбира́йте выраже́ния.

● *v.i.* **1** (*become less violent*) смягч|а́ться, -и́ться. **2** (*preside*) председа́тельствовать (*impf.*).

moderation /ˌmɒdəˈreɪʃ(ə)n/ *n.* (*moderating*) сде́рживание; регули́рование; (*moderateness*) уме́ренность, сде́ржанность; **in ~** уме́ренно.

moderator /ˈmɒdəˌreɪtə(r)/ *n.* (*mediator*) арби́тр, посре́дник; (*chairman*) председа́тель (*m.*).

modern /ˈmɒd(ə)n/ *adj.* совреме́нный; **~ languages** но́вые языки́; **~ history** но́вая исто́рия.

modernism /ˈmɒdəˌnɪz(ə)m/ *n.* модерни́зм.

modernist /ˈmɒdəˌnɪst/ *n.* модерни́ст.

modernistic /ˌmɒdəˈnɪstɪk/ *adj.* модерни́стский.

modernity /mɒˈdɜːnɪtɪ/ *n.* совреме́нность.

modernization /ˌmɒdənaɪˈzeɪʃ(ə)n/ *n.* модерниза́ция.

modernize /ˈmɒdəˌnaɪz/ *v.t.* модернизи́ровать (*impf., pf.*).

modest /ˈmɒdɪst/ *adj.* скро́мный.

modesty /ˈmɒdɪstɪ/ *n.* скро́мность.

modicum /ˈmɒdɪkəm/ *n.* о́чень ма́лое коли́чество.

modification /ˌmɒdɪfɪˈkeɪʃ(ə)n/ *n.* модифика́ция; видоизмене́ние.

modif|y /ˈmɒdɪˌfaɪ/ *v.t.* **1** (*make changes in*) модифици́ровать (*impf.*); видоизмен|я́ть, -и́ть. **2** (*make less severe, violent etc.*) смягч|а́ть, -и́ть; ум|еря́ть, -е́рить. **3** (*gram.*) определ|я́ть, -и́ть; **the adverb ~ies the verb** наре́чие определя́ет глаго́л.

modi operandi /ˌməʊdɪ ˌɒpəˈrændɪ/ *pl. of* ***modus operandi***

modish /ˈməʊdɪʃ/ *adj.* мо́дный.

modi vivendi /ˌməʊdɪ vɪˈvendɪ/ *pl. of* ***modus vivendi***

modular /ˈmɒdjʊlə(r)/ *adj.* бло́чный.

modulate /ˈmɒdjʊˌleɪt/ *v.t.* (*vary pitch of; also radio*) модули́ровать (*impf.*).

modulation /ˌmɒdjʊˈleɪʃ(ə)n/ *n.* модуля́ция.

module /ˈmɒdjuːl/ *n.* (*independent unit*) блок, се́кция; (*unit of study*) курс; (*spacecraft*) отсе́к; **command ~** кома́ндный отсе́к; **lunar ~** лу́нная ка́псула.

modus operandi /ˌməʊdəs ˌɒpəˈrændɪ/ *n.* (*pl.* ***modi operandi***) спо́соб де́йствия.

modus vivendi /ˌməʊdəs vɪˈvendɪ/ *n.* (*pl.* ***modi vivendi***) мо́дус виве́нди (*indecl.*).

mogul /ˈməʊg(ə)l/ *n.* (*fig., tycoon*) магна́т.

mohair /ˈməʊheə(r)/ *n.* мохе́р; (*attr.*) мохе́ровый.

moire /mwɑː(r)/ *n.* муа́р.

moiré /ˈmwɑːreɪ/ *adj.* муа́ровый.

moist /mɔɪst/ *adj.* вла́жный, сыро́й.

moisten /ˈmɔɪs(ə)n/ *v.t.* увлажн|я́ть, -и́ть; см|а́чивать, -очи́ть; **she ~ed the cloth** она́ смочи́ла тря́пку; **he ~ed his lips** он облизну́л гу́бы.

moisture /ˈmɔɪstʃə(r)/ *n.* вла́жность, вла́га.

moisturize /ˈmɔɪstʃəˌraɪz/ *v.t.* увлажн|я́ть, -и́ть.

moisturizer /ˈmɔɪstʃəˌraɪzə(r)/ *n.* увлажня́ющий крем.

molar /ˈməʊlə(r)/ *n.* моля́р, коренно́й зуб.

● *adj.* коренно́й.

molasses /məˈlæsɪz/ *n.* мела́сса, чёрная па́тока.

mold /məʊld/, **-er** /ˈməʊldə(r)/, **-ing** /ˈməʊldɪŋ/, **-y** /ˈməʊldɪ/ (*US*) = **mould** *etc.*

Moldavia /mɒlˈdeɪvɪə/ *n.* Молда́вия.

Moldavian /mɒlˈdeɪvɪən/ *n.* (*person*) молдава́н|ин (*fem.* -ка); (*language*) молда́вский язы́к.

● *adj.* молда́вский.

Moldova /mɒlˈdəʊvə/ *n.* Молдо́ва.

Moldovan /mɒlˈdəʊv(ə)n/ *n.* молдава́н|ин (*fem.* -ка).

● *adj.* молда́вский.

mole¹ /məʊl/ *n.* (*blemish*) ро́динка, борода́вка.

mole² /məʊl/ *n.* (*zool.*) крот; (*secret agent*) аге́нт, внедри́вшийся в иностра́нную разве́дку.

● *cpds.* **~-hill** *n.* крото́вина; **~skin** *n.* крото́вый мех; *adj.* крото́вый.

mole³ /məʊl/ *n.* (*breakwater*) мол, да́мба.

molecular /məˈlekjʊlə(r)/ *adj.* молекуля́рный.

molecule /ˈmɒlɪˌkjuːl/ *n.* моле́кула.

molest /məˈlest/ *v.t.* прист|ава́ть, -а́ть к + *d.*

molestation /ˌmɒleˈsteɪʃ(ə)n/, /ˌməʊl-/ *n.* пристава́ние.

moll /mɒl/ *n.* (*gangster's mistress*) шалашо́вка, мару́ха (*sl.*).

mollify /ˈmɒlɪˌfaɪ/ *v.t.* смягч|а́ть, -и́ть; успок|а́ивать, -о́ить.

mollusc /ˈmɒləsk/ *n.* моллю́ск.

mollycoddle /ˈmɒlɪˌkɒd(ə)l/ *n.* не́женка.

● *v.t.* не́жить (*impf.*); балова́ть, из-.

Molotov cocktail /ˈmɒləˌtɒf/ *n.* буты́лка с зажига́тельной сме́сью.

molt /məʊlt/ (*US*) = **moult**

molten /ˈməʊlt(ə)n/ *adj.* распла́вленный, ли́тый; **~ metal** распла́вленный мета́лл.

molybdenum /məˈlɪbdɪnəm/ *n.* молибде́н.

mom /mɒm/ *n.* (*US coll.*) ма́ма.

moment /ˈməʊmənt/ *n.* **1** (*instant; short period of time*) моме́нт, миг; **this ~** (*at once*) сию́ мину́ту; **at the right ~** в подходя́щий моме́нт; **at the last ~** в после́днюю мину́ту; **he will be here (at) any ~ now** он здесь бу́дет с мину́ты на мину́ту; **half, just a ~!** оди́н моме́нт; мину́точку!; **it was all done in a ~** всё бы́ло сде́лано в миг; **I am busy at the ~** я сейча́с за́нят; **at this ~** в да́нную мину́ту; **only a ~ ago** мину́ту наза́д; **at odd ~s** ме́жду де́лом; **I would not agree to that for a ~** я ника́к не могу́ с э́тим согласи́ться; **the ~** (*as soon as*) **I saw him** как то́лько я его́ уви́дел.
2 (*mech.*) моме́нт.
3 (*importance*) ва́жность, значе́ние; **affairs of (great) ~** ва́жные дела́; дела́ первостепе́нной ва́жности.

momenta /məˈmentə/ *pl. of* ⇒**momentum**

momentarily /ˈməʊməntərɪlɪ/ *adv.* на мгнове́ние; (*US, very soon*) че́рез не́сколько мину́т.

momentary /ˈməʊməntərɪ/, /-trɪ/ *adj.* (*lasting a moment*) момента́льный.

momentous /məˈmentəs/ *adj.* ва́жный, знамена́тельный.

momentum /məˈmentəm/ *n.* (*pl.* **momenta**) (*phys.*) ине́рция; (*fig., impetus*) дви́жущая си́ла; и́мпульс; **the conspiracy gathered ~** за́говор разраста́лся.

mommy /ˈmɒmɪ/ *n.* (*US coll.*) ма́ма, ма́мочка.

Monaco /ˈmɒnəˌkəʊ/, /məˈnɑːkəʊ/ *n.* Мона́ко (*indecl.*).

monarch /ˈmɒnək/ *n.* мона́рх.

monarchic(al) /məˈnɑːkɪk(ə)l/ *adj.* монархи́ческий.

monarchism /ˈmɒnəˌkɪz(ə)m/ *n.* монархи́зм.

monarchist /ˈmɒnəkɪst/ *n.* монархи́ст (*fem.* -ка).

● *adj.* монархи́стский.

monarchy /ˈmɒnəkɪ/ *n.* мона́рхия.

monastery /ˈmɒnəstərɪ/, /-strɪ/ *n.* монасты́рь (*m.*).

monastic /məˈnæstɪk/ *adj.* (*of monasteries*) монасты́рский; **~ order** мона́шеский о́рден; **~ life** мона́шеская жизнь.

M

monasticism /məˈnæstɪˌsɪz(ə)m/ *n.* мона́шество.

Monday /ˈmʌndeɪ/, /-dɪ/ *n.* понеде́льник.

monetarism /ˈmʌnɪtəˌrɪz(ə)m/ *n.* монетари́зм.

monetarist /ˈmʌnɪtəˌrɪst/ *n.* монетари́ст.
● *adj.* монетари́стский.

monetary /ˈmʌnɪtərɪ/ *adj.* де́нежный; моне́тный; **~ unit** де́нежная едини́ца; **~ reform** де́нежная рефо́рма; **~ fund** валю́тный фонд.

money /ˈmʌnɪ/ *n.* (*pl.* **moneys** *or* **monies**) де́н|ьги (*pl.*, *g.* -ег); **ready ~** нали́чные (*pl.*); **he's after your ~** он охо́тится за ва́шими деньга́ми; **for ~** для/ра́ди/из-за де́нег; **they play** (*cards*) **for ~** они́ игра́ют на де́ньги; **for my ~** (*fig.*) на мой взгля́д; **I got my ~'s worth** я получи́л сполна́ за свои́ де́ньги; **make ~** (*earn money*) зараб|а́тывать, -о́тать; (*become rich*) разбогате́ть (*pf.*); **do you think I'm made of ~?** вы ду́маете, у меня́ де́нег полно́?; **he put his ~ into the business** он вложи́л свой капита́л в де́ло; **I put my ~ on the favourite** (*Br.*), **favorite** (*US*) я поста́вил на фавори́та; **throw good ~ after bad** упо́рствовать (*impf.*) в безнадёжном де́ле; **~ for jam** (*or* **for old rope**) (*Br. coll.*) де́ньги, полу́ченные ни за что́; **there's ~ in it for you** вы́годное для вас де́ло; **~ talks** с деньга́ми всего́ мо́жно доби́ться.
● *cpds.* **~-box** *n.* (*Br.*) копи́лка; **~-changer** *n.* меня́ла (*m.*); **~-grubber** *n.* стяжа́тель (*m.*); **~-grubbing** *adj.* стяжа́тельский; **~-laundering** *n.* отмыва́ние де́нег; **~lender** *n.* ростовщи́к; **~-market** *n.* де́нежный/валю́тный ры́нок; **~-order** *n.* почто́вый перево́д; **~-spinner** *n.* (*Br. coll.*) де́нежное де́ло.

moneyed /ˈmʌnɪd/ *adj.*: **a ~ man** де́нежный челове́к.

moneyless /ˈmʌnɪlɪs/ *adj.* безде́нежный.

Mongol /ˈmɒŋg(ə)l/ *n.* (*racial type*) монго́л (*fem.* -ка); (**m~**: *offens.*, *sufferer from Down's syndrome*) челове́к, страда́ющий боле́знью Да́уна.
● *adj.* монго́льский.

Mongolia /mɒŋˈgəʊlɪə/ *n.* Монго́лия.

Mongolian /mɒŋˈgəʊlɪən/ *n.* (*person*) монго́л (*fem.* -ка); (*language*) монго́льский язы́к.
● *adj.* монго́льский.

mongolism /ˈmɒŋgəˌlɪz(ə)m/ *n.* (*offens.*) боле́знь Да́уна.

mongoose /ˈmɒŋguːs/ *n.* (*pl.* **~s**) мангу́ста.

mongrel /ˈmʌŋgr(ə)l/, /ˈmɒŋ-/ *n.* дворня́жка, по́месь, ублю́док.
● *adj.* нечистокро́вный, беспоро́дный.

monies /ˈmʌnɪz/ *pl. of* ⇒**money**

monitor /ˈmɒnɪt(ə)r/ *n.* **1** (*in school*) ста́роста (*c.g.*). **2** (*of broadcasts*) слуха́ч; сотру́дник слу́жбы радиопрослу́шивания. **3** (*detector apparatus*) устано́вка для радиоперехва́та. **4** (*TV, comput.*) монито́р.
● *v.t.* проверя́ть, контроли́ровать, изуча́ть (*all impf.*); **~ a treaty** наблюда́ть (*impf.*) за исполне́нием догово́ра.

monitoring /ˈmɒnɪt(ə)ˌrɪŋ/ *n.* монито́ринг, слеже́ние; **environmental ~** монито́ринг за окружа́ющей средо́й.

monk /mʌŋk/ *n.* мона́х.

monkey /ˈmʌŋkɪ/ *n.* (*pl.* **~s**) обезья́на; **~ business, tricks** (*Br.*) ша́лости (*f. pl.*), проде́лки (*f. pl.*); **he made a ~ out of me** (*fig.*) он вы́ставил меня́ на посме́шище; **you young ~!** ах ты, прока́зник/озорни́к!
● *v.i.* (**monkeys, monkeyed**) дура́читься (*impf.*); забавля́ться (*impf.*); **stop ~ing about with the radio!** переста́ньте копа́ться в приёмнике!
● *cpds.* **~-jacket** *n.* матро́сская ку́ртка; **~-nut** *n.* (*Br.*) ара́хис; **~-puzzle** *n.* араука́рия; **~-wrench** *n.* разводно́й га́ечный ключ.

mono /ˈmɒnəʊ/ *n.* мо́но; **recorded in ~** запи́санный монофони́чески.
● *adj.* монофони́ческий.

monochrome /ˈmɒnəˌkrəʊm/ *n.* однокра́сочное изображе́ние.
● *adj.* монохро́мный.

monocle /ˈmɒnək(ə)l/ *n.* моно́кль (*m.*).

monogamous /məˈnɒgəməs/ *adj.* монога́мный, единобра́чный.

monogamy /məˈnɒgəmɪ/ *n.* монога́мия, единобра́чие.

monogram /ˈmɒnəˌgræm/ *n.* моногра́мма.

monograph /ˈmɒnəˌgrɑːf/ *n.* моногра́фия.

monohull /ˈmɒnəʊˌhʌl/ *n.* однoко́рпусное су́дно.

monolith /ˈmɒnəlɪθ/ *n.* моноли́т.

monolithic /ˌmɒnəˈlɪθɪk/ *adj.* (*lit., fig.*) моноли́тный.

monologue /ˈmɒnəˌlɒg/ *n.* моноло́г.

monomania /ˌmɒnəˈmeɪnɪə/ *n.* монома́ния.

monomaniac /ˌmɒnəˈmeɪnɪæk/ *n.* монома́н.

monophonic /ˌmɒnəˈfɒnɪk/ *adj.* монофони́ческий.

monoplane /ˈmɒnəˌpleɪn/ *n.* монопла́н.

monopolist /məˈnɒpəlɪst/ *n.* монополи́ст.

monopolistic /məˌnɒpəˈlɪstɪk/ *adj.* монополисти́ческий.

monopolize /məˈnɒpəˌlaɪz/ *v.t.* монополизи́ровать (*impf., pf.*); **he ~s the conversation** он не даёт никому́ вста́вить сло́ва.

monopoly /məˈnɒpəlɪ/ *n.* монопо́лия.

monorail /ˈmɒnəʊˌreɪl/ *n.* одноре́льсовая/моноре́льсовая подвесна́я желе́зная доро́га.

monosodium glutamate /ˌmɒnəˈsəʊdɪəm ˈgluːtəˌmeɪt/ *n.* глутамина́т на́трия.

monosyllabic /ˌmɒnəsɪˈlæbɪk/ *adj.* односло́жный.

monosyllable /ˈmɒnəˌsɪləb(ə)l/ *n.* односло́жное сло́во.

monotheism /ˈmɒnəˌθiːɪz(ə)m/ *n.* монотеи́зм, единобо́жие.

monotheistic /ˌmɒnəʊθiːˈɪstɪk/ *adj.* монотеисти́ческий.

monotone /ˈmɒnəˌtəʊn/ *n.*: **in a ~** без вся́кого выраже́ния, моното́нно.

monotonous /məˈnɒtənəs/ *adj.* моното́нный.

monotony /məˈnɒtənɪ/ *n.* моното́нность, однообра́зие.

monotype /ˈmɒnəˌtaɪp/ *n.* моноти́п.

monoxide /məˈnɒksaɪd/ *n.* одноо́кись; **carbon ~** о́кись углеро́да.

Monsignor /mɒnˈsiːnjə(r)/, /-ˈnjɔː(r)/ *n.* (*pl.* ***Monsignori*** /-ˈnjɔːrɪ/) монсеньёр.

monsoon /mɒnˈsuːn/ *n.* (*wind*) муссо́н; (*season*) сезо́н дожде́й.

monster /ˈmɒnstə(r)/ *n.* (*misshapen creature*) уро́д; (*imaginary animal*) чудо́вище; (*person of exceptional cruelty etc.*) чудо́вище, и́зверг; (*something abnormally large*) грома́дина; (*attr.*) чудо́вищный.

monstrosity /mɒnˈstrɒsɪtɪ/ *n.* (*quality*) уро́дство, чудо́вищность; (*object*) чудо́вище.

monstrous /ˈmɒnstrəs/ *adj.* (*monster-like*) ужа́сный, безобра́зный; (*huge*) грома́дный, исполи́нский; (*outrageous*) чудо́вищный, ужа́сный.

montage /mɒnˈtɑːʒ/ *n.* (*cinema*) монта́ж; (*composite picture*) фо́томонта́ж.

Mont Blanc /mɔ̃ ˈblɑ̃/ *n.* Монбла́н.

Monte Carlo /ˌmɒntɪ ˈkɑːləʊ/ *n.* Мо́нте-Ка́рло (*m. indecl.*).

Montenegrin /ˌmɒntɪˈniːgrɪn/ *n.* черного́р|ец (*fem.* -ка).
● *adj.* черного́рский.

Montenegro /ˌmɒntɪˈniːgrəʊ/ *n.* Черного́рия.

month /mʌnθ/ *n.* ме́сяц; **he will never do it in a ~ of Sundays** он никогда́ э́того не сде́лает; **the last six ~s** после́дние полго́да.

monthly /ˈmʌnθlɪ/ *n.* (*periodical*) ежеме́сячник; (*pl., coll., woman's period*) ме́сячные (*pl.*).
● *adj.* ме́сячный.
● *adv.* ежеме́сячно.

Montreal /ˌmɒntrɪˈɔːl/ *n.* Монреа́ль (*m.*).

monty /ˈmɒntɪ/ *n.*: **the full ~** (*Br. coll.*) (*the full amount*) до отка́за, до конца́, в по́лную ме́ру.

monument /ˈmɒnjʊmənt/ *n.* па́мятник, монуме́нт; **a ~ to Pushkin** па́мятник Пу́шкину; **ancient ~** дре́вний па́мятник; (*fig. model, example*) образе́ц, приме́р.

monumental /ˌmɒnjʊˈment(ə)l/ *adj.* увекове́чивающий, монумента́льный; **~ mason** (*Br.*) ма́стер, де́лающий надгро́бные пли́ты; (*fig.*) колосса́льный; **a ~ achievement** колосса́льное достиже́ние; **he showed**

~ ignorance он прояви́л порази́тельное неве́жество.

moo /muː/ *n.* (*pl.* **moos**) мыча́ние.

● *v.i.* (**moos, mooed**) мыча́ть, про-.

mooch /muːtʃ/ *v.i.* **1** (*usu.* **~ about/around**) (*Br. coll., loiter*) слоня́ться (*impf.*) (без де́ла). **2** (*US coll., cadge*) попроша́йничать (*impf.*).

mood¹ /muːd/ *n.* (*state of mind*) настрое́ние; **I am not in the ~ for conversation** я не располо́жен к разгово́ру; **he works as the ~ takes him** он рабо́тает по настрое́нию; **she is in one of her ~s** она́ опя́ть не в ду́хе.

mood² /muːd/ *n.* (*gram.*) наклоне́ние.

moodiness /ˈmuːdɪnɪs/ *n.* угрю́мость; капри́зность.

moody /ˈmuːdɪ/ *adj.* (**moodier, moodiest**) (*gloomy*) угрю́мый; (*subject to changes of mood*) капри́зный; переме́нчивого настрое́ния.

moon¹ /muːn/ *n.* луна́; (*astron.*) Луна́; (*esp. poet.*) ме́сяц; **is there a ~ tonight?** ночь сего́дня лу́нная?; **new ~** молодо́й ме́сяц, новолу́ние; **the ~ was full** бы́ло полнолу́ние; **the ~s of Jupiter** спу́тники Юпи́тера; (*month*): **many ~s ago** давны́м-давно́; **once in a blue ~** раз в год по обеща́нию.

● *cpds.* **~beam** *n.* луч луны́; **~-faced** *adj.* круглоли́цый; **~-landing** *n.* прилуне́ние; **~light** *n.* лу́нный свет; **by ~light** при луне́; **a ~light walk** прогу́лка при луне́; **do a ~light flit** (*sl.*) та́йно съе́хать с кварти́ры (*чтобы не платить за неё*); *v.i.* (*coll.*) подхалту́ри|вать, -ть; **~lighter** *n.* (*coll., one who does a second job*) халту́рщик; **~lighting** *n.* (*coll.*) халту́ра; **~lit** *adj.* зали́тый лу́нным све́том; **~scape** *n.* лу́нный ландша́фт; **~shine** *n.* (*visionary talk etc.*) фанта́зия; бред; (*US, smuggled spirits*) контраба́ндный спирт; **~-shot** *n.* за́пуск на Луну́; **~stone** *n.* лу́нный ка́мень; **~-struck** *adj.* поме́шанный.

moon² /muːn/ *v.i.*: **stop ~ing around the house!** переста́ньте слоня́ться/болта́ться по до́му!

moonless /ˈmuːnlɪs/ *adj.* безлу́нный.

moony /ˈmuːnɪ/ *adj.* (**moonier, mooniest**) (*listless*) вя́лый; (*dreamy*) мечта́тельный.

Moor /mʊə(r)/, /mɔː(r)/ *n.* мавр; (*fem.*) маврита́нка.

moor¹ /mʊə(r)/, /mɔː(r)/ *n.* ме́стность, поро́сшая ве́реском.

● *cpds.* **~hen** *n.* камы́шница; **~land** *n.* ве́ресковая пу́стошь.

moor² /mʊə(r)/, /mɔː(r)/ *v.t.* ста́вить, по- на прича́л; швартова́ть, при-; **the boat was ~ed to a stake** ло́дка была́ зача́лена за ко́лышек.

● *v.i.*: **they ~ed in the harbour** (*Br.*), **harbor** (*US*) они́ пришвартова́лись в га́вани.

mooring|s /ˈmʊərɪŋz/, /ˈmɔːrɪŋz/ *n.* (*gear*) мёртвые якоря́; (*place*) ме́сто стоя́нки; прича́л.

● *cpd.* **~-rope** *n.* швартóв.

Moorish /ˈmʊərɪʃ/, /ˈmɔːrɪʃ/ *adj.* маврита́нский.

moose /muːs/ *n.* (*pl.* **~**) америка́нский лось.

moot /muːt/ *adj.*: **a ~ point** спо́рный пункт.

● *v.t.*: **the question was ~ed** вопро́с поста́вили на обсужде́ние.

mop /mɒp/ *n.* шва́бра; **~ of hair** копна́ воло́с.

● *v.t.* (**mopped, mopping**) прот|ира́ть, -ере́ть; вытира́ть, вы́тереть; **she ~ped the floor** она́ протёрла пол; **he ~ped his brow** он вы́тер лоб.

● *with adv.*: **~ up** *v.t. & i.* (*fig.*): **~ping-up operations** (*mil.*) прочёсывание райо́на; очи́стка захва́ченной террито́рии от проти́вника.

mope /məʊp/ *v.i.* хандри́ть (*impf.*).

moped /ˈməʊped/ *n.* мопе́д.

moquette /mɒˈket/ *n.* ковёр «моке́т»; плюш «моке́т».

moraine /məˈreɪn/ *n.* море́на.

moral /ˈmɒr(ə)l/ *n.* **1** мора́ль; **the ~ of this story is ...** мора́ль сей ба́сни такова́. . .; **the book points a ~** в кни́ге соде́ржится нравоуче́ние.
2 (*pl.*) нра́в|ы (*pl., g.* -ов); **loose ~s** свобо́дные нра́вы, распу́щенность; **a man without ~s** безнра́вственный челове́к.

● *adj.* **1** (*ethical*) мора́льный; нра́вственный; **~ sense** уме́ние отлича́ть добро́ от зла; **~ standards** мора́льные крите́рии/усто́и; **~ philosophy** э́тика.
2 (*virtuous*) нра́вственный; **he leads a ~ life** он ведёт доброде́тельную жизнь.
3 (*capable of ~ action*): **man is a ~ agent** челове́к — носи́тель эти́ческого нача́ла.
4 (*conducive to ~ behaviour*) нравоучи́тельный; **a ~ tale** нравоучи́тельный расска́з.
5 (*non-physical*) мора́льный, духо́вный; **he won a ~ victory** он одержа́л мора́льную побе́ду; **I gave him ~ support** я оказа́л ему́ мора́льную подде́ржку; **he had the ~ courage to refuse** у него́ хвати́ло си́лы ду́ха отказа́ть.

morale /məˈrɑːl/ *n.* мора́льное состоя́ние.

moralist /ˈmɒrəlɪst/ *n.* морали́ст (*fem.* -ка).

morality /məˈrælɪtɪ/ *n.* **1** (*moral conduct*) мора́ль. **2** (*system of morals*) нра́вственность, э́тика.

moralize /ˈmɒrəˌlaɪz/ *v.i.* морализи́ровать (*impf.*).

morass /məˈræs/ *n.* бо́лото; тряси́на.

moratorium /ˌmɒrəˈtɔːrɪəm/ *n.* (*pl.* **moratoriums** *or* **moratoria** /-rɪə/) морато́рий; **impose a ~** объяв|ля́ть, -и́ть морато́рий.

morbid /ˈmɔːbɪd/ *adj.* **1** (*pert. to disease*): **~ anatomy** патологи́ческая анато́мия; **~ growth** (злока́чественное) новообразова́ние. **2** (*unwholesome*) боле́зненный, нездоро́вый.

morbid|ity /mɔːˈbɪdɪtɪ/, **-ness** /ˈmɔːbɪdnɪs/ *n.* боле́зненность.

mordant /ˈmɔːd(ə)nt/ *adj.* ко́лкий; язви́тельный.

mordent /ˈmɔːd(ə)nt/ *n.* (*mus.*) морде́нт.

Mordvin /ˈmɔːdvɪn/ *n.* мордви́н (*fem.* -ка).

Mordvinia /mɔːˈdvɪnɪə/ *n.* Мордо́вия.

more /mɔː(r)/ *n. & adj.* (*greater amount or number*) бо́льше, бо́лее; **a little ~** побо́льше; **he received ~ than I did** он получи́л бо́льше меня́; **~ than enough** предоста́точно; **you thanked her, which is ~ than I did** вы поблагодари́ли её, чего́ я не сде́лал; (*additional amount or number*) ещё; бо́льше; **~ tea** ещё ча́ю; **I hope to see ~ of you** я наде́юсь ви́деться с ва́ми поча́ще; **and what is ~** а кро́ме того́; и бо́льше того́; **have you any ~ matches?** у вас ещё оста́лись спи́чки?; **there is no ~ soup** бо́льше нет су́па; **twice ~** ещё два ра́за.

● *adv.* бо́льше, бо́лее; (*rather*) скоре́е; **~ or less** бо́лее и́ли ме́нее; **I like beef ~ than mutton** я предпочита́ю говя́дину бара́нине; **he is no ~ a professor than I am** он тако́й же профе́ссор как я; **~ ridiculous** бо́лее смехотво́рный; **she is ~ beautiful than her sister** она́ краси́вее свое́й сестры́; **~ and ~** всё бо́лее и бо́лее; **I became ~ and ~ tired** я всё бо́льше устава́л; **the ~ the better** чем бо́льше, тем лу́чше; **~ than once** не раз; **once ~** сно́ва, опя́ть, ещё раз; **I saw him no ~** я его́ бо́льше не ви́дел; **he is no ~** его́ уже́ нет с на́ми (*or* нет в живы́х); **all the ~ because ...** тем бо́лее, что. . .

morel /məˈrel/ *n.* (*mushroom*) сморчо́к.

morello /məˈreləʊ/ *n.* (*pl.* **~s**) ви́шня море́ль.

moreover /mɔːˈrəʊvə(r)/ *adv.* кро́ме того́; сверх того́.

mores /ˈmɔːreɪz/, /-riːz/ *n.* нра́вы (*m. pl.*).

morganatic /ˌmɔːgəˈnætɪk/ *adj.* морганати́ческий.

morgue /mɔːg/ *n.* морг, мертве́цкая.

moribund /ˈmɒrɪˌbʌnd/ *adj.* умира́ющий, отмира́ющий.

Mormon /ˈmɔːmən/ *n.* мормо́н (*fem.* -ка).

Mormonism /ˈmɔːmənˌɪz(ə)m/ *n.* мормони́зм.

morn /mɔːn/ *n.* (*poet.*) у́тро; денни́ца.

morning /ˈmɔːnɪŋ/ *n.* **1** у́тро; **in the ~** у́тром; **it began to rain in the ~** дождь пошёл с утра́; **on Monday ~** в понеде́льник у́тром; **next ~** на (сле́дующее) у́тро; **three o'clock in the ~** три часа́ но́чи/пополу́ночи; **this ~** сего́дня у́тром; **from ~ till night** с утра́ до ве́чера; **one ~** в одно́ у́тро; одна́жды у́тром; **when he awoke it was ~** когда́ он просну́лся, света́ло; **good ~!** до́брое у́тро! **2** (*attr.*) у́тренний; **~ coat** визи́тка; **~ glory** вьюно́к пурпу́рный; **~ sickness** тошнота́ и рво́та бере́менных по утра́м; **~ star** у́тренняя звезда́, Вене́ра.

Moroccan /məˈrɒkən/ *n.* марокка́н|ец (*fem.* -ка).

● *adj.* марокка́нский.

M

Morocco /mə'rɒkəʊ/ *n.* Маро́кко (*indecl.*); (**m~:** *leather*) сафья́н, (*attr.*) сафья́новый.

moron /'mɔːrɒn/ *n.* слабоу́мный.

moronic /mə'rɒnɪk/ *adj.* слабоу́мный, идио́тский.

morose /mə'rəʊs/ *adj.* (*gloomy*) мра́чный; (*unsociable*) необщи́тельный.

moroseness /mə'rəʊsnɪs/ *n.* мра́чность; необщи́тельность.

morpheme /'mɔːfiːm/ *n.* морфе́ма.

morph|ia /'mɔːfɪə/, **-ine** /'mɔːfiːn/ *n.* мо́рфий.

morphological /,mɔːfə'lɒdʒɪk(ə)l/ *adj.* морфологи́ческий.

morphology /mɔː'fɒlədʒɪ/ *n.* морфоло́гия.

morris dance /'mɒrɪs/ *n.* мо́ррис (*народный английский танец*).

morrow /'mɒrəʊ/ *n.* (*liter.*): **on the ~** на сле́дующий день.

Morse /mɔːs/ *n.* (**also ~ code**) а́збука Мо́рзе.

morsel /'mɔːs(ə)l/ *n.* кусо́чек; (*fig.*) ка́пелька.

mortal /'mɔːt(ə)l/ *n.* сме́ртный.

● *adj.* **1** (*subject to death*) сме́ртный; **in this ~ life** в э́той преходя́щей жи́зни. **2** (*leading to death*) смерте́льный, смертоно́сный; **a ~ accident** катастро́фа со смерте́льным исхо́дом; **a ~ wound** смерте́льная ра́на; **~ combat** сме́ртный бой; **they were ~ enemies** они́ бы́ли смерте́льные враги́; **~ sin** сме́ртный грех. **3** (*extreme*) смерте́льный, ужа́сный; **~ fear** смерте́льный страх; **he was in a ~ hurry** он был в стра́шной спе́шке.

mortality /mɔː'tælɪtɪ/ *n.* (*being mortal; number or rate of deaths*) сме́ртность; **the ~ rate was high** проце́нт сме́ртности был высо́кий.

mortar[1] /'mɔːtə(r)/ *n.* (*building material*) известко́вый раство́р.

● *v.t.* скреп|ля́ть, -и́ть известко́вым раство́ром.

● *cpd.* **~-board** (*used in building*) со́кол; (*cap*) академи́ческая ша́почка.

mortar[2] /'mɔːtə(r)/ *n.* (*bowl*) сту́п(к)а.

mortar[3] /'mɔːtə(r)/ *n.* (*mil.*) миномёт.

● *v.t.* обстре́л|ивать, -я́ть миномётным огнём.

● *cpd.* **~-fire** *n.* миномётный ого́нь.

mortgage /'mɔːgɪdʒ/ *n.* ссу́да на поку́пку до́ма; **pay off the ~** вы́купить (*pf.*) зало́женный дом; **raise a ~** получ|а́ть, -и́ть заём под закладну́ю.

● *v.t.* за|кла́дывать, -ложи́ть; **the house was ~d for £100,000** дом был зало́жен за 100 000 фу́нтов сте́рлингов.

mortgagee /,mɔːgɪ'dʒiː/ *n.* залогодержа́тель (*m.*).

mortgagor /,mɔːgɪ'dʒɔː(r)/ *n.* должни́к по закладно́й.

mortice /'mɔːtɪs/ = **mortise**

mortician /mɔː'tɪʃ(ə)n/ *n.* (*US*) похоро́нных дел ма́стер.

mortification /,mɔːtɪfɪ'keɪʃ(ə)n/ *n.* **1** (*hurt, humiliation, grief*) оби́да, униже́ние. **2** (*subduing*) подавле́ние, укроще́ние; **~ of the flesh** умерщвле́ние пло́ти. **3** (*med.*) омертве́ние, некро́з.

mortify /'mɔːtɪ,faɪ/ *v.t.* **1** (*cause shame or humiliation to*) об|ижа́ть, -и́деть; ун|ижа́ть, -и́зить; **a ~ing defeat** унизи́тельное пораже́ние. **2** (*subdue*) под|авля́ть, -ави́ть; укро|ща́ть, -ти́ть; умер|щвля́ть, -тви́ть.

● *v.i.* гангренизи́роваться (*impf., pf.*); мертве́ть, о-.

mort|ise, -ice /'mɔːtɪs/ *n.* гнездо́; **~ lock** врезно́й замо́к.

● *v.t.* запус|ка́ть, -ти́ть в паз.

mortuary /'mɔːtjʊərɪ/ *n.* морг, поко́йницкая.

● *adj.* похоро́нный, погреба́льный.

Mosaic /məʊ'zeɪɪk/ *adj.* Моисе́ев; **the ~ law** Моисе́евы зако́ны.

mosaic /məʊ'zeɪɪk/ *n.* моза́ика.

● *adj.* моза́ичный.

Moscow /'mɒskəʊ/ *n.* Москва́; (*attr.*) моско́вский; **in the ~ area** в райо́не Москвы́; под Москво́й.

Moselle /məʊ'zel/ *n.* Мо́зель (*m.*); (*wine*) мозельве́йн.

mosey /'məʊzɪ/ *v.i.* (*coll.*) (*walk in a leisurely manner*) идти́ лени́вой похо́дкой; **~ around** слоня́ться (*impf.*) по (+*d.*).

Moslem /'mɒzləm/ = **Muslim**

mosque /mɒsk/ *n.* мече́ть.

mosquito /mɒs'kiːtəʊ/ *n.* (*pl.* **~es**) кома́р.

● *cpd.* **~-net** *n.* противомоски́тная се́тка; накома́рник.

moss /mɒs/ *n.* мох.

● *cpd.* **~-green** *adj.* тёмно-зелёный.

mossy /'mɒsɪ/ *adj.* (**mossier, mossiest**) мши́стый.

most /məʊst/ *n.* (*greatest part*) бо́льшая часть; **I was in bed ~ of the time** бо́льшую часть вре́мени я провёл в посте́ли; (*greatest amount*) наибо́льшее коли́чество; **who scored the ~?** кто получи́л наибо́льшее коли́чество очко́в?; **at (the) ~** са́мое бо́льшее; ма́ксимум; максима́льно; не бо́льше (+*g., or* чем...); **£5 at the ~** ма́ксимум 5 фу́нтов; **that is the ~ I can do** э́то ма́ксимум того́, что я могу́ сде́лать; **you must make the ~ of your chances** вам ну́жно наилу́чшим о́бразом испо́льзовать свои́ возмо́жности.

● *adj.*: **the play was boring for the ~ part** в основно́м пье́са была́ ску́чная; **~ people** большинство́ люде́й; **~ of us** большинство́ из нас; **who has the ~ money?** у кого́ бо́льше всех де́нег?

● *adv.* **1** (*expr. comparison*): **what I ~ desire** чего́ я бо́льше всего́ хочу́; **the ~ beautiful** са́мый краси́вый. **2** (*very*) о́чень, весьма́, в вы́сшей сте́пени.

mostly /'məʊstlɪ/ *adv.* гла́вным о́бразом; **the weather was ~ dull** в основно́м пого́да стоя́ла па́смурная.

MOT (*abbr. of* ***Ministry of Transport***) (*Br.*) Министе́рство тра́нспорта; **~ (test)** ≈ техосмо́тр; **~ certificate** листо́к техосмо́тра.

mote /məʊt/ *n.* (*speck*) пыли́нка; **he sees the ~ in his brother's eye** (*fig.*) он ви́дит суčо́к в глазе бра́та своего́; он ви́дит лишь чужи́е недоста́тки.

motel /məʊ'tel/ *n.* моте́ль (*m.*).

motet /məʊ'tet/ *n.* (*mus.*) моте́т.

moth /mɒθ/ *n.* мотылёк, ночна́я ба́бочка; **(clothes) ~** (платяна́я) моль.

● *cpds.* **~ball** *n.* нафтали́новый ша́рик; **in ~balls** (*fig.*) на хране́нии; *v.t.* (*fig.*): **the ship was ~balled** кора́бль поста́вили на консерва́цию; **~-eaten** *adj.* (*lit.*) изъе́денный мо́лью; (*fig.*) устаре́вший.

mother /'mʌðə(r)/ *n.* **1** мать; (*dim.*) ма́ма, ма́тушка; **she was like a ~ to him** она́ была́ ему́ как родна́я мать; **unmarried ~** мать-одино́чка; (*fig. origin*) исто́чник, нача́ло; **necessity is the ~ of invention** (*prov.*) голь на вы́думки хитра́. **2** (*attr.*) матери́нский; **~ country** ро́дина; **M~ Earth** земля́-корми́лица; мать сыра́ земля́; **~ ship** плаву́чая ба́за; **~ tongue** родно́й язы́к; **~ wit** здра́вый смысл. **3** (*head of religious community*): **M~ Superior** мать-игу́менья.

● *v.t.* относи́ться (*impf.*) по-матери́нски к+*d.*; уха́живать (*за кем*) как за ребёнком; вск|а́рмливать, -орми́ть; **a child needs ~ing** ребёнку нужна́ матери́нская забо́та; **M~ing Sunday** (*Br.*) матери́нское воскресе́нье.

● *cpds.* **~board** *n.* (*comput.*) матери́нская пла́та; **~-in-law** *n.* (*wife's mother*) тёща; (*husband's mother*) свекро́вь; **~land** *n.* ро́дина, отчи́зна, оте́чество; **~-of-pearl** *n.* перламу́тр; *adj.* перламу́тровый; **~'s help** *n.* ня́ня.

motherhood /'mʌðə,hʊd/ *n.* матери́нство.

motherless /'mʌðəlɪs/ *adj.* лишённый ма́тери.

motherliness /'mʌðəlɪnɪs/ *n.* матери́нская не́жность/забо́тливость.

motherly /'mʌðəlɪ/ *adj.* не́жный, забо́тливый.

motif /məʊ'tiːf/ *n.* (*in music, literature*) лейтмоти́в; гла́вная мысль; (*in painting*) моти́в; (*ornament on dress*) вы́шитое украше́ние.

motion /'məʊʃ(ə)n/ *n.* **1** (*movement*) движе́ние; **perpetual ~** ве́чное движе́ние; **the car was in ~** маши́на дви́галась; **he put the machine in ~** он привёл маши́ну в де́йствие; **he set the plan in ~** он приступи́л к осуществле́нию пла́на; **~ picture** (*US*) кинофи́льм; (*fig.*): **he went through the ~s of asking my permission** он попроси́л моего́ разреше́ния лишь для профо́рмы. **2** (*gesture*) телодвиже́ние; жест; **I made a ~ to him to stop** я показа́л ему́ же́стом, что́бы он останови́лся. **3** (*proposal*) предложе́ние; **the ~ was carried** предложе́ние бы́ло при́нято; **we put the ~ to the vote** мы поста́вили предложе́ние на голосова́ние.

● *v.t. & i.*: **he ~ed to them to leave** он показа́л же́стом, что́бы они́ ушли́; **he**

~ed to the auctioneer он дал знак аукциони́сту.

motionless /ˈməʊʃənlɪs/ *adj.* неподви́жный.

motivate /ˈməʊtɪ,veɪt/ *v.t.* (*induce*) побу|жда́ть, -ди́ть; толк|а́ть, -ну́ть; **he is highly ~d** у него́ есть мо́щный сти́мул; **he is insufficiently ~d** ему́ не хвата́ет сти́мула.

motivation /,məʊtɪˈveɪʃ(ə)n/ *n.* побужде́ние, сти́мул; (*interest*) заинтересо́ванность.

motive /ˈməʊtɪv/ *n.* (*inducement, cause*) по́вод, моти́в, побужде́ние; (*motif*) моти́в.

● *adj.* дви́жущий; **~ power/force** дви́жущая си́ла.

motley /ˈmɒtlɪ/ *adj.* (**motlier, motliest**) (*multi-coloured*) разноцве́тный, пёстрый; (*varied*): **a ~ crowd** разношёрстная/пёстрая толпа́.

moto-cross /ˈməʊtəʊ,krɒs/ *n.* мотокро́сс; **~ racer** мотокроссме́н.

motor /ˈməʊtə(r)/ *n.* **1** (*engine*) дви́гатель (*m.*), мото́р; **electric ~** электродви́гатель (*m.*); **~ oil** авто́л; **~ vehicle** автомаши́на, автомоби́ль (*m.*). **2** (**~-car**) (легково́й) автомоби́ль (*m.*); **~ show** автосало́н; **the ~ trade** торго́вля автомоби́лями. **3** (*anat.*): **~ nerve** дви́гательный нерв; **~ neurone disease** боле́знь дви́гательных нейро́нов.

● *v.i.*: (*Br.*) **they ~ed down to the country** они́ пое́хали на автомоби́ле за́ город.

● *cpds.* **~-bicycle, ~-bike** (*coll.*) *nn.* мотоци́кл; **~-boat** *n.* мото́рная ло́дка; **~-car** *n.* автомоби́ль (*m.*); **~-coach** *n.* экскурсио́нный/междугоро́дный авто́бус; **~-cycle** *n.* мотоци́кл; **~-cycle racing** мотого́нки (*f. pl.*); **~-cyclist** *n.* мотоцикли́ст; **~-racing** *n.* (*Br.*) автомоби́льные го́нки (*abbr.* автого́нки) (*f. pl.*); **~scooter** *n.* моторо́ллер; **~-ship** *n.* теплохо́д; **~way** *n.* (*Br.*) автостра́да, автомагистра́ль.

motorcade /ˈməʊtə,keɪd/ *n.* автоколо́нна; корте́ж автомоби́лей.

motorist /ˈməʊtərɪst/ *n.* автомобили́ст (*fem.* -ка).

motorize /ˈməʊtə,raɪz/ *v.t.* моторизова́ть (*impf., pf.*).

mottled /ˈmɒtəld/ *adj.* пятни́стый, кра́пчатый.

motto /ˈmɒtəʊ/ *n.* (*pl.* **~es** *or* **~s**) **1** (*inscription*) эпи́граф; (*her.*) на́дпись на гербе́. **2** (*maxim*) деви́з; ло́зунг.

moue /muː/ *n.* грима́са.

moujik, muzhik /ˈmuːʒɪk/ *n.* мужи́к.

mould[1] /məʊld/ (*US* **mold**) *n.* (*hollow form for casting etc.*) лите́йная фо́рма; (*for making jellies etc.*) фо́рмочка, фо́рма; (*fig.*): **they are not cast in the same ~** они́ лю́ди ра́зные.

● *v.t.* отлива́ть (*impf.*); формова́ть (*impf.*): **she ~ed the dough into loaves** она́ формова́ла буха́нки из те́ста; **the head was ~ed in clay** голова́ была́ вы́леплена из гли́ны (*or* в гли́не); (*fig.*) формирова́ть (*impf.*); **his character was ~ed by experience** его́ хара́ктер сформирова́лся под влия́нием жи́зненного о́пыта.

mould[2] /məʊld/ (*US* **mold**) *n.* (*fungus*) пле́сень.

mould[3] /məʊld/ (*US* **mold**) *n.* (*loose earth*) взрыхлённая земля́.

moulder[1] /ˈməʊldə(r)/ (*US* **molder**) *n.* формо́вщик, лите́йщик.

moulder[2] /ˈməʊldə(r)/ (*US* **molder**) *v.i.* расс|ыпа́ться, -ы́паться; **~ing ruins** ве́тхие разва́лины.

moulding /ˈməʊldɪŋ/ (*US* **molding**) *n.* **1** (*shaping*) формо́вка; отли́вка. **2** (*archit.*) лепно́е украше́ние.

mould|y /ˈməʊldɪ/ (*US* **moldy**) *adj.* (**~ier, ~iest**) (*affected by mould*) запле́сневелый; (*stale*) чёрствый; (*coll., inferior*) скве́рный, парши́вый.

moult /məʊlt/ (*US* **molt**) *n.* ли́нька.

● *v.i.* линя́ть (*impf.*); меня́ть (*impf.*) опере́ние.

mound /maʊnd/ *n.* (*for burial or fortification*) на́сыпь; курга́н; (*heap*) ку́ча.

mount /maʊnt/ *n.* **1** (*mountain; hill*): **M~ Everest** гора́ Эвере́ст. **2** (*horse*) (верхова́я) ло́шадь. **3** (*of a picture*) паспарту́ (*nt. indecl.*). **4** (*glass slide for specimens*) предме́тное стекло́. **5** (*of a jewel*) опра́ва. **6** (*mil.*) стано́к, лафе́т.

● *v.t.* **1** (*ascend, get on to*) вз|бира́ться, -обра́ться на + *a.*; подн|има́ться, -я́ться на + *a.*; **he ~ed the hill** он подня́лся на холм; **he ~ed his horse** он сел на ло́шадь; **he ~ed the throne** он взошёл на престо́л; **the stallion ~ the mare** жеребе́ц покры́л кобы́лу. **2** (*provide with horse*): **~ed police** ко́нная поли́ция. **3** (*put, fix on a ~*) вст|авля́ть, -а́вить в опра́ву; опр|авля́ть, -а́вить; **do you want your photographs ~ed?** вы хоти́те накле́ить фотогра́фии на паспарту́?; **the guns were ~ed** ору́дия бы́ли устано́влены на лафе́ты. **4** (*set up*): **they ~ed guard over the jewels** они́ охраня́ли драгоце́нности; **the enemy ~ed an offensive** враг предприня́л наступле́ние. **5** (*present on stage or for display*) ста́вить, по-; **the play was lavishly ~ed** спекта́кль был пы́шно офо́рмлен.

● *v.i.* **1** (*increase*) расти́ (*impf.*); (*also* **~ up**) нак|а́пливаться, -опи́ться. **2**: **he ~ed and rode off** он вскочи́л в седло́ и ускака́л.

mountain /ˈmaʊntɪn/ *n.* **1** гора́; **he is making a ~ out of a molehill** он де́лает из му́хи слона́. **2** (*attr.*) го́рный; **~ chain, range** го́рная цепь; **~ sickness** го́рная боле́знь; **~ ash** ряби́на (ликёрная); **~ bike** тури́стский велосипе́д; **~ lion** пу́ма, кугуа́р. **3** (*fig.*) ма́сса, ку́ча; **a ~ of debts** ма́сса долго́в; **a butter ~** (*glut*) избы́ток ма́сла.

● *cpd.* **~side** *n.* го́рный скат.

mountaineer /,maʊntɪˈnɪə(r)/ *n.* альпини́ст (*fem.* -ка).

mountaineering /,maʊntɪˈnɪərɪŋ/ *n.* альпини́зм.

mountainous /ˈmaʊntɪnəs/ *adj.* гори́стый; (*huge*) грома́дный.

mountebank /ˈmaʊntɪ,bæŋk/ *n.* шарлата́н.

mourn /mɔːn/ *v.t.* опла́кивать (*impf.*); **he ~ed the loss of his wife** он скорбе́л по по́воду сме́рти свое́й жены́.

● *v.i.* скорбе́ть (*impf.*); печа́литься (*impf.*); **she ~ed for her child** она́ опла́кивала смерть своего́ ребёнка.

mourner /ˈmɔːnə(r)/ *n.* прису́тствующий на похорона́х; (*hired*) пла́кальщи|к (*fem.* -ца).

mournful /ˈmɔːnfʊl/ *adj.* скорбный, тра́урный.

mourning /ˈmɔːnɪŋ/ *n.* **1** (*grief; respect for the dead*) скорбь; тра́ур; **day of ~** тра́урный день. **2** (*black clothes*) тра́ур; **she was in deep ~** она́ была́ в глубо́ком тра́уре.

● *cpd.* **~-band** *n.* тра́урная повя́зка.

mouse /maʊs/ *n.* (*pl.* **mice**) мышь; (*fig.*) мы́шка, мышо́нок; (*comput.*) мышь, мы́шка.

● *v.i.* (*of cat*) лови́ть (*impf.*) мыше́й.

● *cpds.* **~-coloured** (*US* **-colored**) *adj.* мыши́ного цве́та; **~-trap** *n.* мышело́вка.

mouser /ˈmaʊsə(r)/ *n.* мышело́в.

mousse /muːs/ *n.* мусс.

moustache /məˈstɑːʃ/ (*US* **mustache**) *n.* ус|ы́ (*pl., g.* -о́в).

mousy /ˈmaʊsɪ/ *adj.* (**mousier, mousiest**) **1** (*timid*) ро́бкий, ти́хий. **2** (*colour*) мыши́ный.

mouth[1] /maʊθ/ *n.* рот; (*dim., e.g. baby's*) ро́тик; **I shouldn't have opened my ~** мне не сле́довало говори́ть; **keep your ~ shut!** молчи́!; пома́лкивай!; **he was down in the ~** он ходи́л, как в во́ду опу́щенный; **the word passed from ~ to ~** но́вость передава́лась из уст в уста́; **by word of ~** у́стно; **they live from hand to ~** они́ е́ле сво́дят концы́ с конца́ми; **don't put words into my ~** не припи́сывайте мне того́, что я не говори́л; **you have taken the words out of my ~** я и́менно э́то хоте́л сказа́ть; **the food made his ~ water** при ви́де еды́ у него́ потекли́ слю́нки; (*fig.*): **~ of a bottle** го́рлышко; **~ of a cave** вход в пеще́ру; **~ of a river** у́стье реки́.

● *cpds.* **~-organ** *n.* губна́я гармо́ника; **~piece** *n.* (*of instrument, pipe etc.*) мундшту́к; (*fig., spokesman*) ру́пор; глаша́тай; **~-to-~ resuscitation** *n.* иску́сственное дыха́ние; **~-wash** *n.* полоска́ние для рта; **~-watering** *adj.* вку́сный, аппети́тный.

mouth[2] /maʊð/ *v.t.*: **the actor ~ed his words** актёр напы́щенно деклами́ровал; **he ~ed the words 'Go away'** «Уйди́те», сказа́л он одни́ми губа́ми.

mouthful /ˈmaʊθfʊl/ *n.* кусо́к, глото́к; (*fig., long word*) тру́дно произноси́мое сло́во.

movable /ˈmuːvəb(ə)l/ *adj.* (*portable*) подвижно́й, портати́вный; (*varying in date*): **~ feast** переходя́щий пра́здник.

M

movables /ˈmuːvəb(ə)lz/ *n.* (*furniture etc.*) дви́жимое иму́щество.

move /muːv/ *n.* **1** (*in games*) ход; **it's your ~** ваш ход!; **make a ~** (*also fig.*) де́лать, с- ход; (*fig., action*) посту́пок; ход, шаг.
2 (*initiation of action or motion*) движе́ние; **it's time we made a ~** (*Br.*) нам пора́ дви́гаться; **they made a ~ to go** они́ ста́ли собира́ться уходи́ть; **what's the next ~?** что тепе́рь на́до де́лать?; **get a ~ on!** дви́гайтесь!, потора́пливайтесь!; **the enemy is on the ~** враг на ма́рше.
3 (*change of residence*) перее́зд; **when does your ~ take place?** когда́ вы переезжа́ете?

● *v.t.* **1** (*change position of; put in motion*) дви́гать (*impf.*); передв|ига́ть, -и́нуть; **he ~d his chair nearer the fire** он пододви́нул стул к ками́ну; **~ your books out of the way!** убери́те свои́ кни́ги!; **do you mind moving your car?** бу́дьте любе́зны, переста́вьте свою́ маши́ну; **he couldn't ~ his queen** (*at chess*) он не мог продви́нуть ферзя́; **he never ~d a muscle** он не шевельну́л ни одни́м му́скулом; (*fig.*) он и бро́вью не повёл; **I ~d heaven and earth to get him the job** я сде́лал всё возмо́жное, что́бы устро́ить его́ на э́ту рабо́ту.
2 (*affect, provoke*) тро́гать (*impf.*); волнова́ть (*impf.*); **the play ~d me deeply** пье́са меня́ глубоко́ взволнова́ла; **the sight ~d him to tears** зре́лище тро́нуло его́ до слёз; **a moving experience** волну́ющее пережива́ние; **he is easily ~d to anger** его́ легко́ рассерди́ть.
3 (*prompt, induce*) побу|жда́ть, -ди́ть; заст|авля́ть, -а́вить; **I was ~d to intervene** я не мог не вмеша́ться; **he works when the spirit ~s him** он рабо́тает, когда́ у него́ есть настрое́ние.
4 (*propose*) вн|оси́ть, -ести́ предложе́ние; **I ~ that the meeting be adjourned** я предлага́ю отложи́ть заседа́ние.

● *v.i.* **1** (*change position; be in motion*) дви́гаться (*impf.*); шевел|и́ться, -ьну́ться; **the lever won't ~** рыча́г не сдвига́ется; **don't ~!** не дви́гайтесь!; **a moving staircase** эскала́тор; **moving pictures** кинокарти́на; **we were certainly moving** (*going fast*) мы бы́стро мча́лись/дви́гались.
2 (*in games*) ходи́ть (*impf.*); **whose turn is it to ~?** чей ход?
3 (*change one's residence*) пере|езжа́ть, -е́хать; **moving-day** день перее́зда; **moving-van** фурго́н для перево́зки ме́бели.
4 (*make progress*) развива́ться (*impf.*); **things began to ~ fast** собы́тия нача́ли бы́стро развива́ться; **work ~s slowly** рабо́та идёт ме́дленно; **one must ~ with the times** на́до шага́ть в но́гу со вре́менем.
5 (*stir*) шевели́ться (*impf.*); **nobody ~d to help him** никто́ не пошевели́лся, что́бы ему́ помо́чь.
6 (*go about*) враща́ться (*impf.*); **he ~s in exalted circles** он враща́ется в вы́сших сфе́рах.
7 (*leg., make application*) хода́тайствовать (*impf.*); **I ~ for a new trial** я хода́тайствую о пересмо́тре де́ла.

● *with advs.*: **~ about, ~ around** *v.t.* перест|авля́ть, -а́вить; **they ~d the furniture about** они́ переста́вили ме́бель; **he was ~d about a lot** его́ ча́сто переводи́ли с одно́й до́лжности на другу́ю; *v.i.* пере|езжа́ть, -е́хать; разъезжа́ть (*impf.*); **he ~s about a lot** он мно́го разъезжа́ет; **~ along** *v.i.*: **~ along there, please!** проходи́те, пожа́луйста!; **~ around** *v.t.* = **~ about, ~ round; ~ aside** *v.t. & i.* отодв|ига́ть(ся), -и́нуть(ся); **~ away** *v.t. & i.* удал|я́ть(ся), -и́ть(ся); **~ your hand away!** убери́те ру́ку!; **they ~d away from here** они́ перее́хали отсю́да; **~ back** *v.t.*: **he ~d the books back** (*away from him*) он отодви́нул кни́ги; (*to where they had been*) он поста́вил кни́ги наза́д (на по́лку); *v.i.*: **he ~d** (*stepped*) **back** он отошёл; **they ~d back** (*to where they had lived*) они́ верну́лись (на ста́рую кварти́ру *и т.п.*); **~ forward** *v.t. & i.* дви́|гать(ся), -нуть(ся) вперёд; **~ in** *v.t.*: **troops were ~d in** бы́ли введены́ войска́; *v.i.* (*take up abode*): **they ~d in next door** они́ посели́лись в сосе́днем до́ме; **~ off** *v.i.*: **the train was moving off** по́езд на́чал отходи́ть (*or* тро́нулся); **~ on** *v.t.* продв|ига́ть, -и́нуть; **he ~d the hands** (*of the clock*) **on** он переста́вил стре́лки вперёд; **the police ~d the crowd on** поли́ция не дава́ла толпе́ собира́ться; *v.i.* продв|ига́ться, -и́нуться; идти́ (*det.*) да́льше; **she stopped and then ~d on** она́ останови́лась, а пото́м опя́ть продолжа́ла путь; **he ~d on to a better job** он перешёл на бо́лее подходя́щую рабо́ту; **~ out** *v.t.*: **the squatters were ~d out** скваттеров вы́селили; *v.i.*: **we have to ~ out tomorrow** мы должны́ съе́хать за́втра; **~ over** *v.t.* отодв|ига́ть, -и́нуть; *v.i.* (*to make room*) подв|ига́ться, -и́нуться; **~ round** *v.t.*: **she ~d the furniture round** она́ переста́вила ме́бель; *v.i.*: **the sails of the windmill ~d round** кры́лья ме́льницы враща́лись; **~ together** *v.t.* сдв|ига́ть, -и́нуть; *v.i.* сходи́ться, сойти́сь; съ|езжа́ться, -е́хаться; **~ up** *v.t.*: **~ up a chair!** пододви́ньте стул!; **he was ~d up into the next class** его́ перевели́ в сле́дующий класс; *v.i.* подв|ига́ться, -и́нуться; **~ up and let me sit down!** подви́ньтесь и да́йте мне сесть; **they ~d up in the world** они́ вы́шли в лю́ди.

movement /ˈmuːvmənt/ *n.* **1** (*state of moving, motion*) движе́ние, перемеще́ние; **his hands were in constant ~** ру́ки у него́ не зна́ли поко́я; **what are your ~s today?** како́е у вас сего́дня расписа́ние?
2 (*of the body or part of it*) жест, телодвиже́ние; **he made a ~ to go** он собра́лся уходи́ть; **with a ~ of his head** движе́нием головы́.
3 (*mil. evolution*) передвиже́ние.
4 (*from one place to another*) переселе́ние; **~ of populations** переселе́ние наро́дов.
5 (*of the bowels*) акт дефека́ции.
6 (*mus., section of composition*) часть; **slow ~** ме́дленная часть.
7 (*moving parts*) ход; механи́зм; **a clock's ~** ход часо́в.
8 (*group united by common purpose*) движе́ние; **the labour** (*Br.*), **labor** (*US*) **~** рабо́чее движе́ние; **peace ~** движе́ние за мир.
9 (*change*) измене́ние, сдвиг.

mover /ˈmuːvə(r)/ *n.* **1** (*initiator of idea etc.*) инициа́тор. **2** (*of proposal*) а́втор предложе́ния. **3**: **prime ~** перви́чный дви́гатель.

movie /ˈmuːvɪ/ *n.* (*coll.*) фильм, кинокарти́на; **he's gone to the ~s** он пошёл в кино́.
● *cpds.* **~-goer** *n.* люби́тель (*fem.* -ница) кино́; **~-maker** *n.* режиссёр.

moving /ˈmuːvɪŋ/ *adj.* волну́ющий, тро́гательный.

mow /məʊ/ *v.t. & i.* (*p.p.* **mowed** *or* **mown**) коси́ть, с-; **they were ~ing the hay** они́ коси́ли се́но; **he ~ed the lawn** он подстри́г траву́/газо́н.
● *with adv.*: **~ down** (*fig.*) ск|а́шивать, -оси́ть; **they were ~n down by a burst of machine-gun fire** их скоси́ла пулемётная о́чередь.

mower /ˈməʊə(r)/ *n.* коси́лка.

Mozambican /ˌməʊzæmˈbiːkən/ *n.* жи́тель (*fem.* -ница) Мозамби́ка.
● *adj.* мозамби́кский.

Mozambique /ˌməʊzæmˈbiːk/ *n.* Мозамби́к.

MP (*abbr. of* ***Member of Parliament***) чле́н парла́мента.

mpg (*abbr. of* ***miles per gallon***) (*сто́лько-то*) миль на галло́н бензи́на.

mph (*abbr. of* ***miles per hour***) (*сто́лько-то*) миль в час.

Mr /ˈmɪstə(r)/ *n.* (*abbr. of* ***mister***) (*pl.* **Messrs**) г-н (господ|и́н, *pl.* -а́); ми́стер.

Mrs /ˈmɪsɪz/ *n.* (*abbr. of* ***mistress***) (*pl.* **~**) г-жа (госпожа́); ми́ссис.

MS *abbr. of* **1** ***manuscript*** /ˈmænjʊskrɪpt/ ру́копись. **2** ***multiple sclerosis*** рассе́янный склеро́з.

Ms /mɪz/, /məz/ *n.* миз, г-жа (госпожа́).

M.Sc. (*abbr. of* ***Master of Science***) маги́стр (есте́ственных) нау́к.

Mt. /maʊnt/ *n.* (*abbr. of* ***Mount***) г (гора́).

much /mʌtʃ/ *n. & adj.* (**more, most**) мно́гое; мно́го *+g.*; **~ of what you say is true** мно́гое из того́, что вы говори́те, справедли́во; **I have ~ to tell you** мне есть что вам рассказа́ть; **I will say this ~** сто́лько (и не бо́льше) я гото́в сказа́ть; **his work is not up to ~** его́ рабо́та не отлича́ется высо́ким ка́чеством; **too ~** сли́шком (мно́го); мно́го; **it was too ~ for me** э́то бы́ло для меня́ (уж) сли́шком; **he thinks too ~ of himself** он сли́шком высо́кого мне́ния о себе́; **don't make too ~ of the incident** не придава́йте э́той исто́рии сли́шком большо́го значе́ния; **I couldn't make ~ of the lecture** ле́кция была́ мне не о́чень поня́тна; **I don't see ~ of him** я его́ ре́дко ви́жу; **he doesn't read ~** он ма́ло чита́ет; **he is**

not ~ of an actor он актёр нева́жный; **she is not ~ to look at** она́ далеко́ не краса́вица; **I don't think ~ of this cheese** мне не о́чень нра́вится э́тот сыр; **we are not devoting ~ attention** мы не уделя́ем большо́го внима́ния; мы уделя́ем ма́ло внима́ния; **how ~** ско́лько +*g.*; **very ~** о́чень (мно́го); о́чень си́льно; **as ~ again** ещё сто́лько же; **I thought as ~** я так и ду́мал; **I didn't get as ~ as he** я получи́л ме́ньше его́; **as ~ as to say** как бы говоря́; **it is as ~ my idea as yours** э́то сто́лько же моя́ иде́я, ско́лько ва́ша; **it was as ~ as I could do to stop laughing** я с трудо́м уде́рживался от сме́ха; **so ~** сто́лько +*g.*; **without so ~ as a 'by your leave'** не сказа́в да́же «с ва́шего позволе́ния»; **a bit ~** (*coll.*) немно́жко-мно́жко/уж сли́шком.

● *adv.* (**more, most**) **1** (*by far*) гора́здо; **~ better** гора́здо лу́чше; **~ the best** гора́здо лу́чше други́х/остальны́х. **2** (*greatly*) о́чень; нема́ло; **I am ~ obliged to you** премно́го вам обя́зан; **I was ~ amused** мне бы́ло о́чень заба́вно; **it doesn't ~ matter** э́то не име́ет большо́го значе́ния; **it does not differ ~** э́то немно́гим отлича́ется; **so ~ the better** тем лу́чше; **he was not ~ the worse** он не о́чень пострада́л; **I couldn't see him, ~ less speak to him** я не смог его́ уви́деть, не то что поговори́ть с ним; **how ~ do you love me?** как си́льно ты меня́ лю́бишь?; **~ to my surprise** к моему́ вели́кому удивле́нию; **~ as I should like to go** как бы я ни хоте́л пойти́; **not ~!** (*coll., very ~*) о́чень да́же!; а как же! **3** (*about*) приме́рно, почти́; **his condition is ~ the same** его́ состоя́ние приме́рно тако́е же; **they are ~ of a size** они́ почти́ одного́ разме́ра; **~ of a ~ness** (*coll.*) приме́рно одного́ ка́чества; почти́ одина́ково.

mucilage /ˈmju:sɪlɪdʒ/ *n.* (*viscous secretion*) расти́тельная слизь; (*US, glue*) клей.

muck /mʌk/ (*coll.*) *n.* **1** (*manure*) наво́з. **2** (*dirt*) грязь; (*fig., anything disgusting*) дрянь. **3** (*Br., mess*): **he tried to finish the job and made a ~ of it** он попыта́лся доде́лать рабо́ту и то́лько загуби́л её.

● *with advs.*: **~ about** (*Br.*) *v.t.* (*inconvenience*) причин|я́ть, -и́ть неудо́бство +*d.*; *v.i.*: **he was ~ing about with the radio** он вози́лся с ра́дио; **~ in** *v.i.* (*Br.*): **if we all ~ in we shall soon get it done** е́сли мы вме́сте за э́то возьмёмся, мы э́то бы́стро сде́лаем; **~ out** *v.t.*: **he ~ed out the stables** он почи́стил коню́шни; **~ up** *v.t.* (*make dirty*) загрязн|я́ть, -и́ть; па́чкать, ис-; (*spoil, bungle*) испо́ртить (*pf.*); напорта́чить (*pf.*); **I ~ed up my exam** я завали́л экза́мен.

● *cpds.* **~-heap** *n.* наво́зная ку́ча; **~-raker** *n.* (*fig.*) выгреба́тель (*m.*) му́сора; **~-raking** *n.* копа́ние в грязи́; **~-up** *n.* пу́таница.

mucky /ˈmʌkɪ/ *adj.* (**muckier, muckiest**) (*coll.*) гря́зный; пога́ный.

mucous /ˈmju:kəs/ *adj.* сли́зистый; **~ membrane** сли́зистая оболо́чка.

mucus /ˈmju:kəs/ *n.* слизь.

mud /mʌd/ *n.* грязь; сля́коть; **his name was ~** (*fig.*) он был опозо́рен; его́ и́мя бы́ло опоро́чено; (*attr.*): **~ flat** вя́зкое дно, обнажа́ющееся при отли́ве; **~ hut** земля́нка.

● *cpds.* **~-bath** *n.* грязева́я ва́нна; **~guard** *n.* крыло́; **~-pack** *n.* космети́ческая ма́ска; **~-slinging** *n.* (*fig.*) клевета́.

muddle /ˈmʌd(ə)l/ *n.* **1** (*mess; disorder*) беспоря́док; неразбери́ха; **you have made a ~ of it** вы всё перепу́тали; **things have got into a ~** всё перепу́талось/смеша́лось; **he left everything in a dreadful ~** он оста́вил по́сле себя́ ужа́сный беспоря́док. **2** (*confusion of mind*) пу́таница; **I was in a ~ over the dates** я запу́тался в да́тах.

● *v.t.* **1** (*bring into disorder*) перепу́т|ывать, -ать; вн|оси́ть, -ести́ беспоря́док в + *a.*; **you have ~d (up) my papers** вы смеша́ли мои́ бума́ги. **2** (*confuse*) пу́тать, на-; сби|ва́ть, -ть с то́лку; **don't ~ me (up)** не сбива́йте меня́ с то́лку.

● *v.i.*: **~ along, ~ through** вози́ться (*impf.*); копа́ться (*impf.*); **they ~ed along** они́ де́йствовали наобу́м; **we shall ~ through somehow** мы ко́е-как спра́вимся.

● *cpds.* **~-headed** *adj.* бестолко́вый; **~-headedness** *n.* бестолко́вость.

muddy /ˈmʌdɪ/ *adj.* (**muddier, muddiest**) **1** (*covered or soiled with mud*) гря́зный, запа́чканный; **a ~ road** гря́зная доро́га; **~ boots** забры́зганные гря́зью боти́нки. **2** (*of colours*) нечи́стый, гря́зный. **3** (*of liquids*) му́тный; **a ~ stream** му́тный руче́й.

● *v.t.* обры́зг|ивать, -ать (*or* забры́зг|ивать, -ать) гря́зью.

muesli /ˈm(j)u:zlɪ/ *n.* (*pl.* **~s**) смесь зла́ков, оре́хов и сухи́х фру́ктов.

muezzin /mu:ˈezɪn/ *n.* муэдзи́н.

muff[1] /mʌf/ *n.* (*for hands*) му́фта.

muff[2] /mʌf/ *v.t.* (*coll.*) ма́зать, про-; пропус|ка́ть, -ти́ть; **he ~ed the catch** он пропусти́л мяч; (*spoil*) по́ртить, ис-; **the actor ~ed his lines** актёр перепу́тал ре́плики.

muffin /ˈmʌfɪn/ *n.* (*Br.*) ≈ горя́чая бу́лочка; (*US*) сдо́бная бу́лочка.

muffle /ˈmʌf(ə)l/ *v.t.* **1** (*wrap up*) ку́тать, за-; **he was ~d up in an overcoat** он был заку́тан в пальто́. **2** (*of sound*) глуши́ть, за-; **a ~d peal of bells** приглушённый звон колоколо́в; **~ed voices** приглушённые голоса́.

muffler /ˈmʌflə(r)/ *n.* (*scarf*) кашне́ (*indecl.*), шарф; (*silencer*) глуши́тель (*m.*).

mufti[1] /ˈmʌftɪ/ *n.* (*in Islam*) му́фтий.

mufti[2] /ˈmʌftɪ/ *n.* (*civilian clothes*) шта́тское пла́тье; **in ~** в шта́тском.

mug[1] /mʌg/ *n.* (*vessel*) кру́жка; (*sl., face*) мо́рда.

● *cpd.* **~ shot** *n.* (*coll.*) официа́льное фо́то.

mug[2] /mʌg/ *n.* (*Br., simpleton*) балбе́с; **it's a ~'s game** э́то для дурако́в; безнадёжное де́ло.

mug[3] /mʌg/ *v.t.* (**mugged, mugging**): **~ up** (*Br. sl., study hard*) зубри́ть, вы-.

mug[4] /mʌg/ *v.t.* (**mugged, mugging**) (*Br. sl., attack*) напада́ть, -а́сть на + *a.*; (*rob*) гра́бить, о-; **~ging** у́личный грабёж.

mugger /ˈmʌgə(r)/ *n.* у́личный граби́тель.

muggins /ˈmʌgɪnz/ *n.* (*pl.* **~** *or* **~es**) (*Br. sl., fool, dupe*) простофи́ля (*c.g.*).

muggy /ˈmʌgɪ/ *adj.* (**muggier, muggiest**) (*damp and warm*) вла́жный и тёплый; (*close*) ду́шный, уду́шливый.

Muhammad /məˈhæməd/ *n.* Муха́ммед.

mulatto /mju:ˈlætəʊ/ *n.* (*pl.* **~s** *or* **~es**) мула́т (*fem.* -ка).

mulberry /ˈmʌlbərɪ/ *n.* (*tree*) ту́товое де́рево, шелкови́ца; (*fruit*) ту́товая я́года; (*attr., colour*) багро́вый.

mulch /mʌltʃ/, /mʌlʃ/ *n.* му́льча.

● *v.t.* мульчи́ровать (*impf., pf.*).

mulct /mʌlkt/ *v.t.* (*fine*) штрафова́ть, о-; (*swindle*): **he was ~ed of £5** у него́ вы́манили 5 фу́нтов; его́ нагре́ли (*coll.*) на 5 фу́нтов.

mule[1] /mju:l/ *n.* мул; (*fig., of person*) упря́мый осёл.

mule[2] /mju:l/ *n.* (*slipper*) шлёпанец.

muleteer /ˌmju:lɪˈtɪə(r)/ *n.* пого́нщик му́лов.

mulish /ˈmju:lɪʃ/ *adj.* упря́мый.

mull[1] /mʌl/ *v.t.*: **~ wine** вари́ть, с- глинтве́йн.

mull[2] /mʌl/ *v.t.*: **~ over** (*ponder*) размышля́ть (*impf.*) над + *i.*; обду́м|ывать, -ать.

mullah /ˈmʌlə/ *n.* мулла́ (*m.*).

mullet /ˈmʌlɪt/ *n.* кефа́ль.

mulligatawny /ˌmʌlɪgəˈtɔ:nɪ/ *n.* о́стрый инди́йский суп.

mullion /ˈmʌljən/ *n.* сре́дник; **~ed window** сво́дчатое окно́.

multi- /ˈmʌltɪ/ *comb. form* много. . ., мульти. . .

multicoloured /ˈmʌltɪˌkʌləd/ (*US* **multicolored**) *adj.* многоцве́тный, кра́сочный.

multifaceted /ˌmʌltɪˈfæsɪtɪd/ *adj.* многогра́нный.

multifarious /ˌmʌltɪˈfeərɪəs/ *adj.* разнообра́зный.

multiform /ˈmʌltɪˌfɔ:m/ *adj.* многообра́зный.

multilateral /ˌmʌltɪˈlætər(ə)l/ *adj.* многосторо́нний.

multilingual /ˌmʌltɪˈlɪŋgw(ə)l/ *adj.* многоязы́чный, разноязы́чный.

multimedia /ˌmʌltɪˈmi:dɪə/ *n.* мультиме́диа.

● *adj.* мультимеди́йный.

multimillionaire /ˌmʌltɪˌmɪljəˈneə(r)/ *n.* мультимиллионе́р.

multinational /ˌmʌltɪˈnæʃ(ə)n(ə)l/ *n.* междунаро́дная корпора́ция.

● *adj.* многонациона́льный.

M

multipartite /ˌmʌltɪˈpɑːtaɪt/ *adj.* многосторóнний.

multiparty /ˌmʌltɪˈpɑːtɪ/ *adj.* многопартúйный.

multiple /ˈmʌltɪp(ə)l/ *n.* крáтное числó; **lowest common ~** наимéньшее óбщее крáтное.

● *adj.* составнóй; многочúсленный; **~ injuries** многочúсленные ранéния/трáвмы; **~ sclerosis** рассéянный склерóз; **~ store** (*Br.*) фúрменный магазúн; **~ warhead** многозарядная боеголóвка.

● *cpd.* **~-choice** *adj.*: **~-choice test/exam** пúсьменный тест/экзáмен, в котóром учáщийся из нéскольких ответóв выбирáет прáвильный.

multiplex /ˈmʌltɪˌpleks/ *adj.* составнóй, слóжный.

multiplication /ˌmʌltɪplɪˈkeɪʃ(ə)n/ *n.* умножéние; **~ table** таблúца умножéния.

multiplicity /ˌmʌltɪˈplɪsɪtɪ/ *n.* многочúсленность, разнообрáзие.

multiplier /ˈmʌltɪˌplaɪə(r)/ *n.* мнóжитель (*m.*).

multipl|y /ˈmʌltɪˌplaɪ/ *v.t.* **1** (*math.*) умн|ожáть, -óжить; **seven ~ied by two** двáжды семь; **66 ~ied by 36** 66 помнóженное на 36. **2** (*increase*) увелúчи|вать, -ть; мнóжить, по-/у-.

● *v.i.* размн|ожáться, -óжиться; **rabbits ~ rapidly** крóлики быстро размножáются.

multi-purpose /ˌmʌltɪˈpɜːpəs/ *adj.* многоцелевóй.

multiracial /ˌmʌltɪˈreɪʃ(ə)l/ *adj.* многонационáльный, многорáсовый.

multi-storey /ˌmʌltɪˈstɔːrɪ/ (*US* **multi-story**) *adj.* многоэтáжный.

multitasking /ˌmʌltɪˈtɑːskɪŋ/ *n.* (*comput.*) многозадáчный режúм (рабóты).

multitude /ˈmʌltɪˌtjuːd/ *n.* (*great number*) мнóжество, мáсса; **the ~** (*mass of people*) толпá; чернь, мáсса.

multitudinous /ˌmʌltɪˈtjuːdɪnəs/ *adj.* многочúсленный, многообрáзный.

multivitamins /ˌmʌltɪˈvɪtəmɪnz/ *n. pl.* поливитамúн|ы (*pl.*, *g.* -ов).

mum¹ /mʌm/ *n.* (*Br. coll.*, *mother*) мамýля, мáма.

mum² /mʌm/ *adj.* (*coll.*, *quiet*): **I kept ~ about it** я об э́том помáлкивал; **~'s the word** молчóк!; ни слóва!

mumble /ˈmʌmb(ə)l/ *n.* бормотáние.

● *v.t.* & *i.* (*mutter*) бормотáть, про-.

mumbo-jumbo /ˌmʌmbəʊˈdʒʌmbəʊ/ *n.* тарабáрщина.

mummer /ˈmʌmə(r)/ *n.* ря́женый.

mummery /ˈmʌmərɪ/ *n.* (*dumb-show*) пантомúма; (*pej.*, *ceremonial*) нелéпый ритуáл; маскарáд.

mummify /ˈmʌmɪˌfaɪ/ *v.t.* мумифицúровать (*impf.*, *pf.*).

mummy¹ /ˈmʌmɪ/ *n.* (*embalmed corpse*) мýмия.

mummy² /ˈmʌmɪ/ *n.* (*Br. coll.*, *mother*) мáма, мáмочка; **~'s boy, darling** мáменькин сынóк.

mumps /mʌmps/ *n.* свúнка.

munch /mʌntʃ/ *v.t.* & *i.* жевáть (*impf.*); чáвкать (*impf.*).

mundane /mʌnˈdeɪn/ *adj.* земнóй, мирскóй, свéтский.

Munich /ˈmjuːnɪk/ *n.* Мю́нхен.

municipal /mjuːˈnɪsɪp(ə)l/ *adj.* муниципáльный, городскóй.

municipality /mjuːˌnɪsɪˈpælɪtɪ/ *n.* муниципалитéт.

munificence /mjuːˈnɪfɪs(ə)ns/ *n.* щéдрость.

munificent /mjuːˈnɪfɪs(ə)nt/ *adj.* щéдрый.

muniment /ˈmjuːnɪmənt/ *n.* грáмота; докумéнт.

munitions /mjuːˈnɪʃ(ə)nz/ *n.* снаряжéние, вооружéние; (*attr.*): **~ factory** воéнный завóд.

mural /ˈmjʊər(ə)l/ *n.* фрéска, стеннáя рóспись.

● *adj.* стеннóй.

murder /ˈmɜːdə(r)/ *n.* убúйство; **he was accused of ~** егó обвинúли в убúйстве; **~ weapon** орýдие убúйства; **~ will out** (*fig.*) ≈ шúла в мешкé не утаúшь; (*fig.*): **the traffic was (sheer) ~** (*coll.*) движéние бы́ло стрáшное/смертоубúйственное.

● *v.t.* уб|ивáть, -úть; **a man was ~ed** убúли человéка; человéк убúт; (*fig.*, *of a bad performance*) пóртить (*impf.*); губúть (*impf.*); **she ~ed the sonata** онá загубúла сонáту; **he ~s the language** он коверкает язы́к.

● *v.i.*: **he ~ed for gain** он совершúл преднамéренное убúйство с цéлью нажúвы.

murderer /ˈmɜːdərə(r)/ *n.* убúйца (*c.g.*).

murderess /ˈmɜːdərɪs/ *n.* (жéнщина-)убúйца.

murderous /ˈmɜːdərəs/ *adj.* смертонóсный, убúйственный.

murk /mɜːk/ *n.* мрак, темнотá.

murkiness /ˈmɜːkɪnɪs/ *n.* мрáчность.

murky /ˈmɜːkɪ/ *adj.* (**murkier, murkiest**) мрáчный, тёмный; **his ~ past** егó тёмное прóшлое.

murmur /ˈmɜːmə(r)/ *n.* **1** (*low sound*) бормотáние, шёпот; **his voice sank to a ~** он заговорúл шёпотом; егó гóлос понúзился до шёпота; **a ~ of conversation** тúхая бесéда; **the ~ of bees** жужжáние пчёл; **the ~ of the waves** рóпот волн; **a heart ~** (*med.*) шýмы (*m. pl.*) в сéрдце. **2** (*fig.*, *complaint*) рóпот, ворчáние; **~s of discontent** выражéния (*nt. pl.*) недовóльства; **he paid up without a ~** он заплатúл без звýка.

● *v.t.* & *i.* говорúть (*impf.*) тúхо; бормотáть, про-; шептáть, про-; **he ~ed a prayer** он прошептáл молúтву; (*complain*) роптáть (*impf.*); ворчáть (*impf.*).

muscatel /ˌmʌskəˈtel/ *n.* (*wine*) мускáт.

muscle /ˈmʌs(ə)l/ *n.* мы́шца, мýскул; **he didn't move a ~** (*remained motionless*) он не (по)шевельнýлся; он и ýхом не повёл.

● *v.i.* (*coll.*): **he ~d in on the conversation** он ввязáлся в разговóр.

● *cpd.* **~man** *n.* силáч, геркулéс; (*bouncer*) вышибáла (*m.*).

Muscovite /ˈmʌskəˌvaɪt/ *n.* (*native of Moscow*) москвúч (*fem.* -ка).

● *adj.* москóвский.

Muscovy /ˈmʌskəvɪ/ *n.* Москóвия.

muscular /ˈmʌskjʊlə(r)/ *adj.* (*pert. to muscle*) мы́шечный; **~ dystrophy** мýскульная дистрофúя; (*with strong muscles*; *robust*) мускулúстый; сúльный.

musculature /ˈmʌskjʊlətʃə(r)/ *n.* мускулатýра.

muse¹ /mjuːz/ *n.* (*myth.*) мýза.

muse² /mjuːz/ *v.i.* размышля́ть (*impf.*); задýмываться (*impf.*).

museum /mjuːˈzɪəm/ *n.* музéй; **~ piece** (*lit.*, *fig.*) музéйный экспонáт; музéйная рéдкость.

mush /mʌʃ/ *n.* (*pulpy mass*) кáша, кашúца; (*US*, *boiled meal*) кáша; (*coll.*, *sentimental writing or music*) сентиментáльщина.

mushroom /ˈmʌʃrʊm/, /-ruːm/ *n.* гриб; **~ cloud** грибовúдное óблако.

● *v.i.* (*pick ~s*) собирáть (*impf.*) грибы́; (*fig.*, *grow rapidly*) бы́стро распространя́ться (*impf.*); растú (*impf.*) как грибы́ под дождём.

mushy /ˈmʌʃɪ/ *adj.* (**mushier, mushiest**) мя́гкий; (*fig.*) слащáвый.

music /ˈmjuːzɪk/ *n.* **1** мýзыка; **the lines were set to ~ by Brahms** Брамс положúл стихú на мýзыку; **it was ~ to his ears** э́то ласкáло егó слух; **you will have to face the ~** (*criticism*, *outcry*) вам придётся за э́то расплáчиваться. **2** (*attr.*) **~ centre** (*Br.*) музыкáльный комбáйн; **~ lesson** урóк мýзыки; **~ teacher** учúтель (*m.*) мýзыки. **3** (*sheet ~*, **~al score**) нóты (*f. pl.*).

● *cpds.* **~-hall** *n.* (*place*, *entertainment*) мю́зик-хóлл; **~-hall artist** эстрáдный артúст (*fem.* -ка); **~-room** *n.* музыкáльная кóмната; **~-stand** *n.* пюпúтр.

musical /ˈmjuːzɪk(ə)l/ *n.* мю́зикл.

● *adj.* (*pert. to*, *fond of music*) музыкáльный; **~ box** (*Br.*) музыкáльная шкатýлка; **~ glasses** стекля́нная гармóника; **a ~ voice** мелодúчный гóлос; **~ talent** музыкáльность.

musicality /ˌmjuːzɪˈkælɪtɪ/ *n.* музыкáльность.

musician /mjuːˈzɪʃ(ə)n/ *n.* музыкáнт.

musicianship /mjuːˈzɪʃənʃɪp/ *n.* музыкáльность.

musicologist /ˌmjuːzɪˈkɒlədʒɪst/ *n.* музыковéд.

musicology /ˌmjuːzɪˈkɒlədʒɪ/ *n.* музыковéдение.

musk /mʌsk/ *n.* мýскус.

● *cpds.* **~-deer** *n.* мýскусный олéнь; **~-melon** *n.* ды́ня мýскусная; **~-ox** *n.* овцебы́к; **~-rat** *n.* ондáтра; **~-rose** *n.* мýскусная рóза.

musket /ˈmʌskɪt/ *n.* мушкéт.

musketeer /ˌmʌskɪˈtɪə(r)/ *n.* мушкетёр.

musketry /ˈmʌskɪtrɪ/ *n.* (*small arms firing*) стрельба́ из винто́вки.

musky /ˈmʌskɪ/ *adj.* (**muskier, muskiest**) му́скусный, па́хнущий му́скусом.

Muslim /ˈmʊzlɪm/, /ˈmʌ-/, **Moslem** /ˈmɒzləm/ *n.* мусульма́н|ин (*fem.* -ка).

● *adj.* мусульма́нский.

muslin /ˈmʌzlɪn/ *n.* мусли́н, кисея́.

● *adj.* мусли́новый, кисе́йный.

musquash /ˈmʌskwɒʃ/ *n.* (*Br., fur*) мех онда́тры.

muss /mʌs/ *v.t.* (*US coll.*): **~ up** (*e.g. hair*) взъеро́шить (*pf.*); растрепа́ть (*pf.*).

mussel /ˈmʌs(ə)l/ *n.* ми́дия.

must /mʌst/ *n.* (*coll., necessary item*): **the Tower of London is a ~ for visitors** тури́сты должны́ непреме́нно посмотре́ть Ло́ндонский Та́уэр.

● *v. aux.* (*3rd pers. sing. pres.* **must;** *past* **had to** *or in indirect speech* **must**) **1** (*expr. necessity*): **one ~ eat to live** что́бы жить, ну́жно есть; **~ you go so soon?** неуже́ли вам на́до уже́ уходи́ть?; **if you ~, you ~** в конце́ концо́в, ну́жно зна́чит ну́жно; **~ you behave like that?** неуже́ли вы ина́че не мо́жете?; (*expr. obligation*): **you ~ do as you're told** ты до́лжен слу́шаться; **we ~ not be late** нам нельзя́ опа́здывать; **you ~ not forget to write** непреме́нно напиши́те; **I ~ ask you to leave** я вы́нужден попроси́ть вас уйти́; **I ~ admit** я до́лжен призна́ть; **we ~ see what can be done** сле́дует поду́мать, что здесь мо́жно сде́лать. **2** (*with neg., expr. prohibition*): **cars ~ not be parked here** стоя́нка маши́н запрещена́. **3** (*expr. certainty or strong probability*): **you ~ be tired** вы, наве́рно, уста́ли; **this ~ be the bus coming now** э́то вероя́тно/наве́рно (*or* должно́ быть), авто́бус; **you ~ have known that** не мо́жет быть, что́бы вы э́того не зна́ли.

mustache /məˈstɑːʃ/ (*US*) = **moustache**

mustang /ˈmʌstæŋ/ *n.* муста́нг.

mustard /ˈmʌstəd/ *n.* (*plant; relish*) горчи́ца; **keen as ~** (*Br.*) по́лный энтузиа́зма; **~ gas** горчи́чный газ, ипри́т.

● *cpds.* **~-plaster** *n.* горчи́чник; **~-pot** *n.* горчи́чница.

muster /ˈmʌstə(r)/ *n.* **1** (*mil., assembly*) сбор, смотр. **2** (*numbers attending a function*) о́бщее число́. **3** (*inspection; roll-call*) пове́рка; перекли́чка; **will his work pass ~?** (*fig.*) его́ рабо́та годи́тся? **4** (*~-book, ~-roll*) спи́сок ли́чного соста́ва.

● *v.t.* (*summon together*) соз|ыва́ть, -ва́ть; соб|ира́ть, -ра́ть; (*fig.*): **he ~ed up all his courage** он собра́лся с ду́хом.

● *v.i.* (*assemble*) соб|ира́ться, -ра́ться.

mustiness /ˈmʌstɪnɪs/ *n.* за́тхлость; ко́сность, отста́лость.

musty /ˈmʌstɪ/ *adj.* (**mustier, mustiest**) (*smelling of mould or age*) за́тхлый; (*fig., ancient; out-of-date*) ко́сный, отста́лый, устаре́лый.

mutability /ˌmjuːtəˈbɪlɪtɪ/ *n.* изме́нчивость.

mutable /ˈmjuːtəb(ə)l/ *adj.* изме́нчивый.

mutant /ˈmjuːt(ə)nt/ *adj.* мута́нтный.

● *n.* мута́нт.

mutate /mjuːˈteɪt/ *v.i.* (*biol.*) видоизменя́ться (*impf.*).

mutation /mjuːˈteɪʃ(ə)n/ *n.* измене́ние; (*biol.*) мута́ция.

mutatis mutandis /muːˌtɑːtɪs muːˈtændɪs/, /mjuː-/, /-iːs/ *adv.* внося́ необходи́мые измене́ния.

mute /mjuːt/ *n.* **1** (*dumb person*) немо́й. **2** (*mus.*) сурди́н(к)а.

● *adj.* **1** (*silent*) безмо́лвный; **he made a ~ appeal** он бро́сил моля́щий взгля́д. **2** (*dumb*) немо́й. **3** (*phon., silent*) немо́й, непроизноси́мый.

● *v.t.* приглуш|а́ть, -и́ть; **they played with ~d strings** они́ игра́ли под сурди́нку.

mutilate /ˈmjuːtɪˌleɪt/ *v.t.* уве́чить, из-; кале́чить, ис-; (*fig.*) иска|жа́ть, -зи́ть; **the book was ~d in the film version** в фи́льме содержа́ние кни́ги бы́ло искажено́.

mutilation /ˌmjuːtɪˈleɪʃ(ə)n/ *n.* уве́чье; (*fig.*) искаже́ние.

mutineer /ˌmjuːtɪˈnɪə(r)/ *n.* мяте́жник.

mutinous /ˈmjuːtɪnəs/ *adj.* мяте́жный.

mutiny /ˈmjuːtɪnɪ/ *n.* мяте́ж.

● *v.i.* бунтова́ть, взбунтова́ться; под|ыма́ть, -ня́ть мяте́ж.

mutt /mʌt/ *n.* (*sl.*) (*stupid person*) остоло́п, о́лух; (*dog*) пёс.

mutter /ˈmʌtə(r)/ *n.* бормота́ние; **he spoke in a ~** он бормота́л.

● *v.t. & i.* бормота́ть (*impf.*); говори́ть (*impf.*) невня́тно; **he ~ed an apology** он пробормота́л извине́ние; **~ings of discontent** глухо́й ро́пот недово́льства.

mutton /ˈmʌt(ə)n/ *n.* бара́нина; **~ dressed as lamb** (*Br., fig.*) молодя́щаяся стару́шка; **~ chop** бара́нья отбивна́я; **~-chop whiskers** ба́ки.

mutual /ˈmjuːtʃʊəl/, /-tjʊəl/ *adj.* взаи́мный; **~ admiration society** (*iron.*) о́бщество взаи́много восхище́ния/восхвале́ния; **~ aid** взаимопо́мощь; **our ~ friend** наш о́бщий друг.

muzhik /ˈmuːʒɪk/ = **moujik**

muzzle /ˈmʌz(ə)l/ *n.* **1** (*animal's*) мо́рда, ры́ло. **2** (*guard for this*) намо́рдник. **3** (*of firearm*) ду́ло; **~ velocity** нача́льная ско́рость.

● *v.t.* над|ева́ть, -е́ть намо́рдник на + *a.*; (*fig.*) заст|авля́ть, -а́вить молча́ть; зат|ыка́ть, -кну́ть; **he tried to ~ the press** он пыта́лся заста́вить печа́ть молча́ть.

● *cpd.* **~-loading** *adj.* заряжа́ющийся с ду́ла.

muzzy /ˈmʌzɪ/ *adj.* (**muzzier, muzziest**) (*coll.*) нея́сный; тума́нный.

MW *abbr. of* **1** ***megawatt(s)*** МВт (мегава́тт). **2** ***medium wave*** СВ (сре́дние во́лны).

my /maɪ/ *poss. adj.* мой; (*belonging to speaker*) свой; **I lost ~ pen** я потеря́л свою́ ру́чку; **for ~ part** что каса́ется меня́; **I was all on ~ own** я был оди́н-одинёшенек/одинёхонек (*or* соверше́нно оди́н); **I did it all on ~ own** я сде́лал э́то самостоя́тельно (*or* без посторо́нней по́мощи); (*with words of address*): **~ dear** дорого́й; **~ dear fellow** дорого́й мой; **~ good man/woman** мой друг; (*in exclamations*): **~ goodness!; oh, ~!** Бо́же мой!; **~, ~!** ну и ну́! поду́мать то́лько!

Mycenae /maɪˈsiːniː/ *n.* Мике́н|ы (*pl., g.* —).

Mycenean /ˌmaɪsɪˈniːən/ *adj.* мике́нский.

mycology /maɪˈkɒlədʒɪ/ *n.* миколо́гия.

myna(h) /ˈmaɪnə/ *n.* ма́йна.

myopia /maɪˈəʊpɪə/ *n.* миопи́я, близору́кость.

myopic /maɪˈɒpɪk/ *adj.* миопи́ческий, близору́кий.

myriad /ˈmɪrɪəd/ *n.* мириа́д|ы (*pl., g.* —).

● *adj.* несчётный.

myrmidon /ˈmɜːmɪd(ə)n/ *n.* (*fig.*) прислу́жник; **~s of the law** блюсти́тели (*m. pl.*) зако́на/поря́дка.

myrrh /mɜː(r)/ *n.* (*resin*) ми́рра.

myrtle /ˈmɜːt(ə)l/ *n.* мирт.

myself /maɪˈself/ *pron.* **1** (*refl.*) себя́; **I said to ~** я сказа́л себе́; **I felt pleased with ~** я был дово́лен собо́й. **2** (*emph.*) сам; **I ~ did it** э́то я сде́лал; **I did it ~** я сам э́то сде́лал; **I did it by ~** (*without help*) я э́то сде́лал сам; **I am not ~ today** я сего́дня немно́го не в фо́рме. **3** (*after preps.*): **for ~, I prefer tea** что каса́ется меня́, я предпочита́ю чай; **dancing takes me out of ~** та́нцы развлека́ют меня́. **4** (*representing 'I' or 'me'*): **my wife and ~ were there** мы с жено́й бы́ли там.

mysterious /mɪˈstɪərɪəs/ *adj.* таи́нственный, зага́дочный.

mystery /ˈmɪstərɪ/ *n.* **1** (*secret, secrecy; obscurity*) та́йна, секре́т, зага́дка; **the murder remained a ~** э́то уби́йство оста́лось зага́дкой/та́йной; **their origins are wrapped in ~** их происхожде́ние покры́то мра́ком неизве́стности; **don't make a ~ of it** не де́лайте из э́того та́йну. **2** (*relig.*) та́инство, та́йные обря́ды (*m. pl.*); **~ play** мисте́рия. **3** (*novel etc.*) детекти́в.

mystic /ˈmɪstɪk/ *n.* ми́стик.

● *adj.* (*also* **~al**) мисти́ческий.

mysticism /ˈmɪstɪˌsɪz(ə)m/ *n.* мистици́зм, ми́стика.

mystification /ˌmɪstɪfɪˈkeɪʃ(ə)n/ *n.* мистифика́ция.

mystify /ˈmɪstɪˌfaɪ/ *v.t.* мистифици́ровать (*impf., pf.*); озада́чи|вать, -ть.

mystique /mɪˈstiːk/ *n.* таи́нственность, зага́дочность.

myth /mɪθ/ *n.* (*lit., fig.*) миф.

mythic(al) /ˈmɪθɪk(ə)l/ *adj.* мифи́ческий.

M

mythological /ˌmɪθəˈlɒdʒɪk(ə)l/ *adj.* мифологи́ческий.

mythology /mɪˈθɒlədʒɪ/ *n.* мифоло́гия.

myxomatosis /ˌmɪksəməˈtəʊsɪs/ *n.* миксомато́з (*заболевание кроликов*).

Nn

NAACP (*abbr. of* ***National Association for the Advancement of Colored People***) (*US*) Национа́льная ассоциа́ция соде́йствия прогре́ссу цветно́го населе́ния.

nab /næb/ *v.t.* (**nabbed, nabbing**) (*arrest*) накр|ыва́ть, -ы́ть (*coll.*); (*catch in wrong-doing*) заст|ига́ть, -и́чь/-и́гнуть, засту́к|ивать, -ать (*coll.*).

nadir /ˈneɪdɪə(r)/, /ˈnæd-/ *n.* (*astron.*) нади́р; (*fig.*) ни́зшая то́чка.

nag¹ /næg/ *n.* лоша́дка; (*pej.*) кля́ча.

nag² /næg/ *v.t.* (**nagged, nagging**) пили́ть (*impf.*); **she ~ged him into going to the theatre** (*Br.*), **theater** (*US*) она́ пили́ла его́, пока́ он не согласи́лся пойти́ с ней в теа́тр.

● *v.i.* (**nagged, nagging**) брюзжа́ть (*impf.*); **~ at s.o.** пили́ть (*impf.*) кого́-н.

nagger /ˈnægə(r)/ *n.* брюзга́ (*c.g.*).

nagging /ˈnægɪŋ/ *n.* (*harassing*) пиле́ние; (*grumbling*) брюзжа́ние; (*criticism*) приди́рки (*f. pl.*).

● *adj.* приди́рчивый; (*quarrelsome*) сварли́вый; **a ~ pain** но́ющая боль.

naiad /ˈnaɪæd/ *n.* (*pl.* **naiads** *or* **naiades** /ˈnaɪə,diːz/) ная́да.

nail /neɪl/ *n.* **1** (*on finger or toe*) но́готь (*m.*); **bite one's ~s with impatience** куса́ть (*impf.*) но́гти от нетерпе́ния. **2** (*metal spike*) гвоздь (*m.*); **he's as hard as ~s** (*unfeeling*) э́то жесто́кий, бесчу́вственный челове́к; (*physically*) у него́ желе́зное здоро́вье; **you've hit the ~ on the head** вы попа́ли в (са́мую) то́чку; **he pays on the ~** он расплачивается на ме́сте; **a ~ in s.o.'s coffin** (*fig.*) гвоздь (*m.*) в чей-н. гроб.

● *v.t.* **1** приб|ива́ть, -и́ть (*что к чему*); пригво|жда́ть, -зди́ть; **he ~ed the picture (on) to the wall** он приби́л карти́ну к стене́; **I am ~ing the lid down** я прибива́ю кры́шку; **the windows were ~ed up** о́кна бы́ли заколо́чены; (*fig.*): **he stood ~ed to the ground** он стоя́л как вко́панный; его́ сло́вно к земле́ пригвозди́ли; **he ~ed his colours** (*Br.*), **colors** (*US*) **to the mast** он стоя́л на своём. **2** (*catch, get hold of*): **he ~ed me as I was leaving** он перехвати́л меня́ на вы́ходе; (*pin down*): **he tried to evade the issue but I ~ed him down** он пыта́лся уйти́ от пробле́мы, но я прижа́л его́ к сте́нке; (*confute*): **that lie must be ~ed** э́ту ложь на́до разоблачи́ть.

● *cpds.* **~-brush** *n.* щёт(оч)ка для ногте́й; **~-file** *n.* пи́лка (для ногте́й); **~-polish** *n.* лак для ногте́й; **~-scissors** *n. pl.* но́жниц|ы (*pl., g.* —) для ногте́й; **~-varnish** *n.* (*Br.*) лак для ногте́й.

Nairobi /naɪˈrəʊbɪ/ *n.* Найро́би *m. indecl.*

naive /nɑːˈiːv/, /naɪˈiːv/ *adj.* наи́вный, простоду́шный; (*of art*) примити́вный.

naïveté /nɑːˈiːvteɪ/, **naivety** /nɑːˈiːvtɪ/, /naɪ-/ *nn.* наи́вность, простоду́шие.

naked /ˈneɪkɪd/ *adj.* го́лый; **strip ~** разд|ева́ть(ся), -е́ть(ся) (догола́); **~ wire** го́лый/оголённый про́вод; **~ flame, light** откры́тый ого́нь; (*of natural objects*: *bare*) го́лый, откры́тый; (*plain, undisguised, unadorned*) просто́й; **the ~ truth** го́лая и́стина; **with the ~ eye** невооружённым гла́зом.

nakedness /ˈneɪkɪdnɪs/ *n.* нагота́, обнажённость.

namby-pamby /ˌnæmbɪˈpæmbɪ/ *adj.* (*weak*) мягкоте́лый; (*sentimental*) слаща́вый, сентимента́льный.

name /neɪm/ *n.* **1** (*esp.* **fore~**) и́мя (*nt.*); (*surname*) и́мя, фами́лия; (*of pet*) кли́чка; **what is his ~?** как его́ зову́т/фами́лия?; **a man by, of the ~ of ...** челове́к по и́мени/фами́лии. . .; **your ~ was given me by Ivanov** Ивано́в сказа́л мне о вас; **a certain doctor, Crippen by ~** не́кий до́ктор по и́мени Кри́ппен; **they are known to me by ~** мне изве́стны их имена́; я зна́ю их понаслы́шке; **he goes by various ~s** он изве́стен под ра́зными имена́ми/фами́лиями; **he knows all the staff by ~** он зна́ет и́мя ка́ждого сотру́дника; **he goes by, under the ~ of Smith** он изве́стен под и́менем Смит; **in heaven's ~** ра́ди Бо́га; **in the ~** (*on behalf*) **of** от и́мени *+g.*; **in the ~ of common sense** во и́мя здра́вого смы́сла; **in the ~ of the law** и́менем зако́на; **he kept the money in his own ~** он держа́л де́ньги на своё и́мя; **he published the book in his own ~** он изда́л кни́гу под свои́м и́менем (*or* под свое́й фами́лией); **she was his wife in ~ only** она́ была́ его́ жено́й лишь форма́льно; **he lent his ~ to the petition** он поддержа́л пети́цию свои́м авторите́том; **I put my ~ down for a flat** я записа́лся в о́чередь на кварти́ру; **he has a house to his ~** у него́ со́бственный дом; **she hasn't a penny to her ~** у неё за душо́й нет ни гроша́; **he has £500 to his ~** он мо́жет похва́статься пятью́стами фу́нтами; **you may use my ~** мо́жете сосла́ться на меня́. **2** (*of a thing*) назва́ние; **what is the ~ of your school?** как называ́ется ва́ша шко́ла?; **this street has changed its ~** э́ту у́лицу переименова́ли. **3** (*personage*) и́мя, ли́чность; **the great ~s of history** вели́кие истори́ческие имена́/ли́чности. **4** (*reputation*) и́мя, репута́ция; **he made a ~ for himself** он со́здал/соста́вил себе́ и́мя; **he has a bad ~** у него́ дурна́я репута́ция; **this firm has a ~ for honesty** э́та фи́рма изве́стна свое́й че́стностью. **5**: **call s.o. ~s** руга́ть (*impf.*) кого́-н (нехоро́шими слова́ми).

● *v.t.* **1** (*give ~ to*) наз|ыва́ть, -ва́ть; да|ва́ть, -ть и́мя *+d.*; **they haven't yet ~d the baby** они́ ещё не да́ли ребёнку и́мя; **he was ~d Andrew after his grandfather** его́ назва́ли Андре́ем в честь де́да **the street is ~d after Napoleon** у́лица но́сит и́мя Наполео́на; **the Moscow underground railway was ~d after Lenin** моско́вскому метро́ бы́ло присво́ено и́мя Ле́нина; **Cape Kennedy was ~d in honour of the President** назва́ние «Мыс Ке́ннеди» бы́ло дано́ в честь президе́нта. **2** (*recite*) наз|ыва́ть, -ва́ть; **the pupil ~d the chief cities of Europe** учени́к назва́л/перечи́слил гла́вные города́ Евро́пы; (*state, mention*) наз|ыва́ть, -ва́ть; **~ your price!** назна́чьте це́ну!;

you ~ it, we've got it (*coll.*) чего́ то́лько у нас нет!; (*identify*): **how many stars can you ~** (*sc. identify*)? ско́лько звёзд вы мо́жете определи́ть?; (*appoint*) назн|ача́ть, -а́чить; **he asked her to ~ the day** он проси́л её назна́чить день (сва́дьбы); (*nominate*): **he was ~d for the professorship** (*proposed*) его́ кандидату́ра была́ вы́двинута на до́лжность профе́ссора; (*appointed*) он был назна́чен профе́ссором; (*as an example*) прив|оди́ть, -ести́.

● *cpds.* **~-day** *n.* имени́н|ы (*pl., g.* —); **~-dropping** *n.* (*coll.*) ≈ хвастовство́ свои́ми знако́мствами/свя́зями; **~-plate** *n.* доще́чка/табли́чка с и́менем; **~sake** *n.* (*with same first ~*) тёзка (*c.g.*); (*with same surname, but unrelated*) однофами́л|ец (*fem.* -ица); **~ tag** *n.* именно́й значо́к; **~-tape** *n.* тесьма́ с фами́лией (*для метки белья и т.п.*).

nameless /ˈneɪmlɪs/ *adj.* (*without a name*) безымя́нный; (*unnamed, unmentioned*) нена́званный, неупомя́нутый; **someone who shall be ~** не́кто, кого́ мы не ста́нем называ́ть по и́мени; (*unmentionable, unspeakable*): **~ horror** невырази́мый у́жас.

namely /ˈneɪmlɪ/ *adv.* (а) и́менно; то есть.

Namibia /nəˈmɪbɪə/ *n.* Нами́бия.

Namibian /nəˈmɪbɪən/ *adj.* намиби́йский.

nancy(-boy) /ˈnænsɪ/ *n.* ба́ба; (*homosexual*) пе́дик (*sl.*).

nankeen /næŋˈkiːn/, /næn-/ *n.* на́нка, кита́йка.

nanny /ˈnænɪ/ *n.* (*for child*) ня́ня, ня́нечка.

● *cpd.* **~-goat** *n.* коза́.

nanosecond /ˈnænəʊˌsekənd/ *n.* наносеку́нда.

nanotechnology /ˌnænəʊtekˈnɒlədʒɪ/ *n.* нанотехноло́гия.

nap¹ /næp/ *n.* (*short sleep*) коро́ткий сон; **have, take a ~** вздремну́ть (*pf.*); **catch s.o. ~ping** заста́ть/засти́гнуть (*pf.*) кого́-н. врасплóх.

nap² /næp/ *n.* ворс, начёс.

nap³ /næp/ *n.* (*game*) наполео́н; **go ~** ста́вить, по- всё на ка́рту.

napalm /ˈneɪpɑːm/ *n.* напа́лм; (*attr.*) напа́лмовый.

nape /neɪp/ *n.* загри́вок.

napery /ˈneɪpərɪ/ *n.* столо́вое бельё.

naphtha /ˈnæfθə/ *n.* (*chem.*) лигрои́н.

naphthalene /ˈnæfθəˌliːn/ *n.* нафтали́н.

napkin /ˈnæpkɪn/ *n.* **(table-~)** салфе́тка.

● *cpd.* **~-ring** *n.* кольцо́ для салфе́тки.

Napoleonic /nəˌpəʊlɪˈɒnɪk/ *adj.* наполео́новский.

nappy /ˈnæpɪ/ *n.* (*Br. coll.*) подгу́зник; **~ rash** потни́ца.

narcissi /nɑːˈsɪsaɪ/ *pl. of* ⇒**narcissus**

narcissism /ˈnɑːsɪˌsɪz(ə)m/, /nɑːˈsɪs-/ *n.* нарцисси́зм, самолюбова́ние.

narcissistic /ˌnɑːsɪˈsɪstɪk/ *adj.* самовлюблённый.

narciss|us /nɑːˈsɪsəs/ *n.* (*pl.* **~i** *or* **~uses**) нарци́сс.

narcosis /nɑːˈkəʊsɪs/ *n.* нарко́з.

narcotic /nɑːˈkɒtɪk/ *n.* нарко́тик.

● *adj.* наркоти́ческий.

nark¹ /nɑːk/ *n.* (*Br. coll., police decoy or spy*) лега́вый (*coll.*); (*informer*) стука́ч (*coll.*).

nark² /nɑːk/ *v.t.* (*Br. coll.*) раздраж|а́ть, -и́ть.

narrate /nəˈreɪt/ *v.t.* **1** (*story*) расска́з|ывать, -а́ть; (*events*) изл|ага́ть, -ожи́ть. **2** (*film, broadcast*) чита́ть (*impf.*) текст от а́втора.

narration /nəˈreɪʃ(ə)n/ *n.* **1** (*of story*) повествова́ние; (*of events*) изложе́ние; (*story*) по́весть. **2** (*of film, broadcast*) а́вторский коммента́рий.

narrative /ˈnærətɪv/ *n.* (*story*) расска́з.

● *adj.* повествова́тельный.

narrator /nəˈreɪtə(r)/ *n.* расска́зч|ик (*fem.* -ица); (*theatr., cin.*) а́вторский го́лос, ди́ктор.

narrow /ˈnærəʊ/ *n.* (*usu. pl., strait*) (у́зкий) проли́в.

● *adj.* **(narrower, narrowest)** (*lit., fig.*) **1** у́зкий; **within ~ limits** в у́зких преде́лах/ра́мках; **a ~ circle of acquaintances** у́зкий/те́сный круг знако́мых; **a ~ mind** у́зкий/ограни́ченный ум; **take a ~ view of something** у́зко под|ходи́ть, -ойти́ к чему́-н.
2 (*with little margin*): **a ~ majority** незначи́тельное большинство́; **a ~ victory** побе́да с небольши́м преиму́ществом; **he had a ~ escape from death** он чу́дом избежа́л сме́рти; **he ~ly escaped drowning** он чуть не утону́л.
3 (*close; precise*): **he was ~ly watched** за ним при́стально наблюда́ли.

● *v.t.* сужа́ть/су́|живать, -зить; **~ one's eyes, gaze** сощу́ри|ваться, -ться; (*limit*) ограни́чи|вать, -ть; **the choice was ~ed down to two candidates** вы́бор свёлся к двум кандидату́рам; **this ~s the field** (*of search*) э́то сужа́ет круг по́исков.

● *v.i.* (*of river etc.*) су́|живаться, -зиться; **his eyes ~ed** он прищу́рился; он сощу́рил глаза́.

● *cpds.* **~-gauge** *adj.* узкоколе́йный; **~-minded** *adj.* узколо́бый, ограни́ченный; **~-mindedness** *n.* у́зость взгля́дов, ограни́ченность.

narrowness /ˈnærəʊnɪs/ *n.* у́зость.

narwhal /ˈnɑːw(ə)l/ *n.* нарва́л.

NASA /ˈnæsə/ *n.* (*abbr. of* ***National Aeronautics and Space Administration***) НАСА (Национа́льное управле́ние по аэрона́втике и иссле́дованию косми́ческого простра́нства).

nasal /ˈneɪz(ə)l/ *n.* (*phon.*) носово́й (звук).

● *adj.* **1** (*of, for the nose*) носово́й; (*of the voice*) гнуса́вый; **speak in a ~ voice** говори́ть (*impf.*) в нос; гнуса́вить (*impf.*). **2** (*phon.*) носово́й, наза́льный.

nasalization /ˌneɪzəlaɪˈzeɪʃ(ə)n/ *n.* назализа́ция.

nasalize /ˈneɪzəlaɪz/ *v.t.* назализи́ровать (*impf., pf.*); произн|оси́ть, -ести́ в нос; **this sound has become ~d** э́тот звук назализи́ровался/преврати́лся в носово́й.

nascent /ˈnæs(ə)nt/, /ˈneɪs-/ *adj.* зарожда́ющийся.

nastiness /ˈnɑːstɪnɪs/ *n.* (*of actions*) гну́сность; (*of smell, disposition*) проти́вность.

nasturtium /nəˈstɜːʃəm/ *n.* насту́рция.

nasty /ˈnɑːstɪ/ *adj.* **(nastier, nastiest) 1** (*offensive, e.g. smell or taste*) неприя́тный, проти́вный; **the medicine tastes ~** у э́того лека́рства неприя́тный/проти́вный вкус; (*repellent, sickening*) отврати́тельный.
2 (*morally offensive*) ме́рзкий, га́дкий, гну́сный; **a ~ piece of work!** (*of man*) ну и мерза́вец!; (*of woman*) ну и мерза́вка!
3 (*unkind, spiteful, unpleasant*) злой; **a ~ remark** зло́е замеча́ние; **a ~ temper** тяжёлый хара́ктер; **he played a ~ trick on me** он сыгра́л со мной злу́ю шу́тку; **turn ~** обозли́ться (*pf.*); (*of the elements*): **~ weather** скве́рная пого́да; **a ~ wind** пронзи́тельный ве́тер; **there's a ~ storm brewing** надвига́ется си́льный шторм.
4 (*threatening*) опа́сный; **there was a ~ look in his eye** его́ вид не предвеща́л ничего́ до́брого.
5 (*troublesome*): **a ~ bout of bronchitis** тяжёлый при́ступ бронхи́та; **he had a ~ fall** он неуда́чно упа́л.
6 (*difficult*): **that's a ~ rock to climb** на э́ту скалу́ нелегко́ взобра́ться; **it's a ~ situation to be in** очути́ться в тако́м положе́нии неприя́тно; **that's a ~ one!** (*question*) тру́дный вопро́с!; (*insult*) э́то уж чересчу́р!

nation /ˈneɪʃ(ə)n/ *n.* на́ция; (*people*) наро́д; (*state*) госуда́рство; (*country*) страна́.

● *cpd.* **~-wide** *adj.* общенациона́льный, всенаро́дный; **a ~-wide search** ро́зыск/по́иски (*m. pl.*) по всей стране́; **~-wide poll** всенаро́дный опро́с.

national /ˈnæʃən(ə)l/ *n.* (*citizen*) гражд|ани́н (*fem.* -а́нка); (*subject*) по́дданн|ый (*fem.* -ая).

● *adj.* (*of the state*) госуда́рственный; (*of the country or population as a whole*) наро́дный, всенаро́дный; (*central; opp. provincial*) центра́льный; (*pert. to a particular nation or ethnic group*) национа́льный; **~ anthem** госуда́рственный гимн; **~ debt** госуда́рственный долг; **~ economy** национа́льная эконо́мика, наро́дное хозя́йство; **~ elections** всео́бщие вы́боры; **~ emergency** чрезвыча́йное положе́ние в стране́; **~ feeling** национали́зм, патриоти́зм; **~ flag** госуда́рственный флаг; **~ government** национа́льное/центра́льное прави́тельство; **a ~ (*all-party*) government** коалицио́нное правительство; ~ **holiday/income/language** государственный праздник/доход/язык; **N~ Health Service** Национальная служба здравоохранения; **N~ Insurance** Государственное страхование; ~ **newspapers** центральные газеты; ~ **park** заповедник, национальный парк; ~ **service** воинская повинность; ~ **theatre** (*Br.*), **theater** (*US*) национальный театр.

nationalism /ˈnæʃənəˌlɪz(ə)m/ *n.* национализм.

nationalist /ˈnæʃənəlɪst/ *n.* националист (*fem.* -ка).

● *adj.* (*also* **-ic**) националистический.

nationality /ˌnæʃəˈnælɪtɪ/ *n.* (*membership of a nation, country*) подданство; гражданство; **(of) what ~ are you?** какое у вас подданство/гражданство?; (*ethnic group, e.g. within Russia*) национальность; (*smaller one*) народность.

nationalization /ˌnæʃənəlaɪˈzeɪʃ(ə)n/ *n.* национализация.

nationalize /ˈnæʃənəˌlaɪz/ *v.t.* национализировать (*impf., pf.*); **steel was ~d** сталелитейная промышленность была национализирована.

native /ˈneɪtɪv/ *n.* **1** (*indigenous inhabitant*) тузем|ец (*fem.* -ка); коренной житель (*fem.* коренная жительница).
2: **a ~ of** (*born in*) урожен|ец (*fem.* -ка) +*g.*; (*living in*) житель (*fem.* -ница) +*g.*
3 (*of animal*): **the kangaroo is a ~ of Australia** кенгуру водятся в Австралии; (*of plant*): **the eucalyptus is a ~ of Australia** родина эвкалипта — Австралия.

● *adj.* **1** (*innate*) врождённый, природный.
2 (*of one's birth*) родной; ~ **language** родной язык; ~ **land** родина, родная земля.
3 (*indigenous, esp. of non-European countries*) туземный; **N~ American** американск|ий индеец (*fem.* -ая индианка); ~ **customs** туземные/местные обычаи (*m. pl.*); ~ **population** туземное/коренное/местное население; **go ~** отуземиться (*pf.*) (*coll.*); ~ **plants** местные растения.
4 (*natural, in natural state*) естественный; (*of minerals*): ~ **gold** самородное золото.

nativity /nəˈtɪvɪtɪ/ *n.* (*birth of Christ; picture of this*) Рождество Христово; (*N~ of the Virgin*) Рождество Богородицы.

NATO /ˈneɪtəʊ/ *n.* (*abbr. of* ***North Atlantic Treaty Organization***) НАТО (Организация Североатлантического договора); ~ **member** страна-участник НАТО, натовец (*coll.*).

● *adj.* натовский (*coll.*); ~ **troops** войска НАТО; ~ **generals** генералы НАТО.

natter /ˈnætə(r)/ (*Br. coll.*) *n.*: **I came in for a ~** я зашёл поболтать.

● *v.i.* болтать (*impf.*).

natt|y /ˈnætɪ/ *adj.* (**nattier, nattiest**) (*coll., spruce, trim*) элегантный; **he is ~ily dressed** он одет с иголочки.

natural /ˈnætʃər(ə)l/ *n.* **1** (*mus. sign*) бекар.
2: **he's a ~ for the part** он рождён/создан для этой роли.

● *adj.* **1** (*found in, established by, conforming or pertaining to nature*) естественный, природный; стихийный; ~ **death** естественная смерть; **she died a ~ death** она умерла естественной/своей смертью; ~ **forces** силы природы; ~ **gas** природный газ; ~ **history** естествознание; ~ **law** естественное право; ~ **life** земное существование; **for the rest of one's ~ life** до конца жизни; ~ **phenomena** явления природы; ~ **resources** природные ресурсы/богатства; ~ **sciences** естественные науки; ~ **selection** естественный отбор.
2 (*normal, ordinary, not surprising*) естественный, нормальный; **he spoke in his ~ voice** он говорил своим обычным голосом; **his presence seems quite ~** его присутствие кажется вполне естественным; **it is ~ for parents to love their children** для родителей естественно любить своих детей.
3 (*unforced, spontaneous*) естественный, непринуждённый; (*simple, unaffected*) простой; простодушный.
4 (*innate*) врождённый, природный; ~ **gifts** природные дарования.
5 (*destined by nature*): **he is a ~ linguist** он прирождённый лингвист.
6 (*illegitimate*) побочный, внебрачный.
7 (*mus.*): **B ~** си-бекар.

● *cpd.* **~-born** *adj.* прирождённый.

naturalism /ˈnætʃərəˌlɪz(ə)m/ *n.* натурализм.

naturalist /ˈnætʃərəlɪst/ *n.* **1** (*student of animals etc.*) натуралист, естествоиспытатель (*m.*). **2** (*in art*) натуралист.

naturalistic /ˌnætʃərəˈlɪstɪk/ *adj.* натуралистический.

naturalization /ˌnætʃərəlaɪˈzeɪʃ(ə)n/ *n.* натурализация; акклиматизация.

naturalize /ˈnætʃərəˌlaɪz/ *v.t.* (*admit to citizenship*) натурализовать (*impf., pf.*); (*of animals, plants: introduce to another country*) акклиматизировать (*impf., pf.*).

naturally /ˈnætʃərəlɪ/ *adv.* **1** (*not surprisingly*) естественно; (*of course*) естественно, конечно.
2 (*spontaneously, without affectation*) естественно. **3** (*by nature*) от рождения; по природе (своей); (*as by instinct*): **he took ~ to swimming** плавание далось ему легко; **oratory comes ~ to him** он прирождённый оратор.

naturalness /ˈnætʃərəlnɪs/ *n.* (*absence of affectation*) непринуждённость, естественность.

nature /ˈneɪtʃə(r)/ *n.* **1** (*force, natural phenomena*) природа; **N~'s laws** законы природы; **in the course of ~** естественным ходом/путём; **against (or contrary to) ~** противоестественный; ~ **reserve** заповедник; ~ **study** природоведение; **paint from ~** писать (*impf.*) с натуры; **one of N~'s gentlemen** джентльмен по природе (своей); **in a state of ~** (*e.g. primitive man*) в диком/первобытном состоянии; (*naked*) в чём мать родила.
2 (*of humans or animals: character, temperament*) натура, характер; **a generous ~** щедрый характер; **she was cautious by ~** она была от природы/по натуре (своей) осторожна; **human ~** человеческая природа; **second ~** вторая натура; **it was his ~ to be proud** он был гордым по натуре.
3 (*of things: essential quality*) природа, характер; **the ~ of the evidence** характер доказательств; **by, in the (very) ~ of things** по природе вещей; **the ~ of gases** свойства (*nt. pl.*) газов; (*sort, kind*) род; **things of this ~** такого рода вещи; **our talk was of a confidential ~** наша беседа носила конфиденциальный характер; **something in the ~ of a disappointment** нечто вроде разочарования.

naturism /ˈneɪtʃəˌrɪz(ə)m/ *n.* (*nudism*) нудизм.

naturist /ˈneɪtʃərɪst/ *n.* (*nudist*) нудист (*fem.* -ка).

naturopath /ˈneɪtʃərəˌpæθ/ *n.* натуропат.

naturopathy /ˈneɪtʃəˌrɒpəθɪ/ *n.* натуропатия.

naught /nɔːt/ *n.* (*arch. exc. in phrr.*): **come to ~** св|одиться, -естись к нулю; ни к чему не прив|одить, -ести; **set at ~** ни во что не ставить (*impf.*); *see also* ⇒**nought**

naughtiness /ˈnɔːtɪnɪs/ *n.* озорство.

naughty /ˈnɔːtɪ/ *adj.* (**naughtier, naughtiest**) **1** (*e.g. child's behaviour*) озорной; **be ~** озорничать (*impf.*); баловаться (*impf.*); **you were ~ today** ты сегодня плохо себя вёл; **that is ~ of you** (*to adult*) это нехорошо с вашей стороны; **don't be ~!** не шали!; (*to child*) не балуйся! **2** (*risqué*) рискованный.

nausea /ˈnɔːzɪə/, /-sɪə/ *n.* (*physical*) тошнота; **I was overcome by ~** меня затошнило/стошнило; (*mental disgust*) отвращение.

nauseat|e /ˈnɔːzɪˌeɪt/, /-sɪˌeɪt/ *v.t.* **1** (*physically*) вызывать, вызвать тошноту у +*g.*; **~ing** тошнотворный; **I find rich food ~ing** меня тошнит от жирной пищи. **2** (*fig., disgust*) вызывать, вызвать отвращение у +*g.*; претить (*impf.*) +*d.*; **I am ~ed by hypocrisy** мне противно лицемерие; **~ing** отвратительный.

nauseous /ˈnɔːzɪəs/, /-sɪəs/ *adj.* тошнотворный; (*fig.*) отвратительный.

nautical /ˈnɔːtɪk(ə)l/ *adj.* морской; ~ **mile** морская миля.

nauti|lus /ˈnɔːtɪləs/ *n.* (*pl.* **~luses** *or*

N

~li /-ˌlaɪ/, /-ˌliː/) наути́лус, кора́блик (*моллюск*).

naval /ˈneɪv(ə)l/ *adj.* **1** морско́й; (*of the navy*) вое́нно-морско́й; (*of a fleet*) фло́тский; **~ barracks** морска́я каза́рма; **~ base** вое́нно-морска́я ба́за; **~ officer** морско́й офице́р; **~ stores** шки́перское иму́щество. **2** (*pert. to ships*) корабе́льный, судово́й; **~ architect** инжене́р-судострои́тель (*m.*); **~ yard** вое́нная верфь; судострои́тельный заво́д.

nave /neɪv/ *n.* (*of church*) неф.

navel /ˈneɪv(ə)l/ *n.* пупо́к, пуп (*coll.*).

navigability /ˌnævɪgəˈbɪlɪtɪ/ *n.* судохо́дность.

navigable /ˈnævɪgəb(ə)l/ *adj.* (*of river, sea*) судохо́дный.

navigate /ˈnævɪˌgeɪt/ *v.t.* **1** (*of person*): **~ a ship/aircraft** управля́ть (*impf.*) кораблём/самолётом; вести́ (*det.*) кора́бль/самолёт; **~ a river/sea** пл|а́вать (*indet.*), -ыть (*det.*) по реке́/мо́рю; (*fig.*): **he ~d the difficulties with skill** он уме́ло обходи́л тру́дности. **2** (*of vessel*): **the yacht easily ~d the locks** я́хта легко́ прошла́ шлю́зы.

● *v.i.* (*in ship*) пла́вать (*indet.*), плыть (*det.*); (*in aircraft*) лета́ть (*indet.*), лете́ть (*det.*).

navigation /ˌnævɪˈgeɪʃ(ə)n/ *n.* **1** (*process*) управле́ние (кораблём, самолётом *и т.п.*). **2** (*skill*) навига́ция; **~ lights** навигацио́нные огни́. **3** (*passage of ships*) судохо́дство; **inland ~** речно́е судохо́дство.

navigator /ˈnævɪˌgeɪtə(r)/ *n.* (*naut., aeron.*) шту́рман, навига́тор; (*hist., explorer*) морепла́ватель (*m.*).

navvy /ˈnævɪ/ *n.* (*Br.*) землеко́п; чернорабо́чий.

navy /ˈneɪvɪ/ *n.* **1** (*naval forces*) вое́нно-морски́е си́лы (*f. pl.*); (*ships of war*) вое́нно-морско́й флот; **merchant ~** торго́вый флот; **~ yard** (*US*) вое́нная верфь. **2** (*department of naval affairs*) вое́нно-морско́е ве́домство. **3** (**~ blue**) тёмно-си́ний цвет.

● *cpd.* **~-blue** *adj.* тёмно-си́ний.

nay /neɪ/ *adv.* (*arch.*) нет; **he asked, ~ begged us to stay** он проси́л, нет, умоля́л нас оста́ться.

Nazareth /ˈnæzərəθ/ *n.* Назаре́т; **Jesus of ~** Иису́с из Назаре́та; Иису́с Назаря́нин/Назоре́й.

Nazi /ˈnɑːtsɪ/, /ˈnɑːzɪ/ *n.* (*pl.* **Nazis**) наци́ст (*fem.* -ка).

● *adj.* наци́стский.

Nazism /ˈnɑːtsɪz(ə)m/ *n.* наци́зм.

NB (*abbr. of* ***nota bene***) нотабе́не.

NCO *n.* = **non-commissioned officer**

Neanderthal /nɪˈændəˌtɑːl/ *n.* (**~ man**) неандерта́лец; неандерта́льский челове́к.

neap /niːp/ *n.* (**~ tide**) квадрату́рный прили́в.

Neapolitan /nɪəˈpɒlɪt(ə)n/ *adj.* неаполита́нский.

near /nɪə(r)/ *adj.* **1** (*close at hand, in space or time*) бли́зкий; **how ~ is the sea?** (как) бли́зко/далеко́ отсю́да мо́ре?; **the station is quite ~ (to) our house** ста́нция (нахо́дится) совсе́м бли́зко от на́шего до́ма; **which is the ~est way to the stadium?** како́й са́мый коро́ткий путь до стадио́на?; **in the ~ future** в ближа́йшем бу́дущем; **spring is ~** бли́зится весна́; **I spoke to the man ~est me** я заговори́л со свои́м ближа́йшим сосе́дом; **the N~ East** Бли́жний Восто́к; **~ sight** близору́кость. **2** (*closely connected*) бли́зкий; **a ~ relative** бли́зкий ро́дственник; **his ~est and dearest** его́ бли́зкие (*pl.*). **3**: **the ~ side** (*of road or vehicle or horse in Britain*) ле́вая сторона́. **4** (*narrowly achieved*): **he had a ~ escape** он едва́ избежа́л (*чего*); **a ~ miss** непрямо́е попада́ние; **we won, but it was a ~ thing** мы победи́ли, но с трудо́м.

● *adv.* **1** (*of place or time*) бли́зко; **he was standing ~ at hand** (*or* **~ by**) он стоя́л бли́зко/ря́дом; **they looked far and ~** они́ иска́ли повсю́ду; **people came from far and ~** лю́ди прибыва́ли отовсю́ду (*or* со всех концо́в страны́); **the procession drew ~** проце́ссия приближа́лась; **Christmas is drawing ~** бли́зится Рождество́; **it is ~ (up)on midnight** почти́ по́лночь; **come a little ~er** подойди́те побли́же. **2** (*fig.*): **I came ~ to believing him** я чуть бы́ло ему́ не пове́рил; **as ~ as I can guess** наско́лько я могу́ суди́ть; **the bus was nowhere ~ full** авто́бус был далеко́ не по́лный; **she is nowhere ~ as old as her husband** она́ далеко́ не так стара́, как её муж; она́ гора́здо моло́же му́жа.

● *v.t.* прибл|ижа́ться, -и́зиться к + *d.*; **he is ~ing his end** он при́ смерти.

● *prep.* о́коло, во́зле, близ, бли́зко от, у (*all* +*g.*); **she sat ~ the door** она́ сиде́ла о́коло/во́зле две́ри; **there are woods ~ the town** о́коло го́рода есть лес; **he lives ~ us** он живёт во́зле нас; **~ here** недалеко́ отсю́да; **is there a hotel ~ here?** есть здесь побли́зости гости́ница?; **come ~er the fire!** подвига́йтесь к ками́ну; **I'm getting ~ the end of the book** я зака́нчиваю кни́гу; **it must be ~ dinner-time** ско́ро до́лжен быть обе́д; **no-one can come ~ him for skill** никто́ не мо́жет сравни́ться с ним в мастерстве́; **we are no ~er a solution** мы ничу́ть не бли́же к реше́нию.

● *cpds.* **~by** *adj.* располо́женный побли́зости; близлежа́щий, сосе́дний; **~-side** *adj.* (*in Britain*) ле́вый; **~-sighted** *adj.* близору́кий.

nearly /ˈnɪəlɪ/ *adv.* (*almost*) почти́; **we are ~ there** мы почти́ прие́хали/пришли́; **I was ~ run over** меня́ чуть не сби́ла маши́на; **he ~ fell** он чуть не упа́л; **there is not ~ enough to eat** еды́ далеко́ не доста́точно.

nearness /ˈnɪənɪs/ *n.* бли́зость.

neat /niːt/ *adj.* **1** (*of appearance: tidy*) опря́тный, аккура́тный; **a ~ figure** изя́щная фигу́ра. **2** (*clear, precise, e.g. of handwriting, style*) чёткий, изя́щный. **3** (*of liquor etc., undiluted*) неразба́вленный; **drink one's whisky ~** пить (*impf.*) чи́стое ви́ски. **4** (*skilful*) иску́сный; **he made a ~ job of it** он вы́полнил рабо́ту иску́сно; он э́то здо́рово сде́лал (*coll.*). **5** (*US coll., excellent*) отли́чный, кла́ссный.

neatness /ˈniːtnɪs/ *n.* опря́тность; аккура́тность; изя́щность; чёткость; иску́сность.

Nebuchadnezzar /ˌnebjuːkədˈnezə(r)/ *n.* Навуходоно́сор.

nebula /ˈnebjʊlə/ *n.* (*pl.* **nebulae** /-ˌliː/ *or* **nebulas**) (*astron.*) тума́нность.

nebular /ˈnebjʊlə(r)/ *adj.* небуля́рный.

nebulizer /ˈnebjʊˌlaɪzə(r)/ *n.* пульверизáтор.

nebulosity /ˌnebjʊˈlɒsɪtɪ/ *n.* (*cloudiness*) о́блачность; (*fig., vagueness*) тума́нность.

nebulous /ˈnebjʊləs/ *adj.* (*cloudy*) о́блачный; (*fig.*) тума́нный, сму́тный.

necessarily /ˈnesəsərɪlɪ/, /-ˈserɪlɪ/ *adv.* обяза́тельно; **it is not ~ true** э́то не обяза́тельно так.

necessar|y /ˈnesəsərɪ/ *n.*: **I did the ~y** я сде́лал (всё), что необходи́мо.

● *adj.* (*inevitable, inescapable*) неизбе́жный; **a ~y evil** неизбе́жное зло; (*indispensable*) необходи́мый; **food is ~y to life** пи́ща необходи́ма для жи́зни; (*compulsory, obligatory*) необходи́мый, обяза́тельный; **it is ~y to eat in order to live** что́бы жить, необходи́мо пита́ться; **it is not ~y to dress for dinner** переодева́ться к обе́ду необяза́тельно; мо́жно не одева́ться к обе́ду.

necessitate /nɪˈsesɪˌteɪt/ *v.t.* (*a person*) вынужда́ть, вы́нудить; (*make necessary*) вызыва́ть, вы́звать, обусло́в|ливать, -ить; **his illness ~d his retirement** из-за боле́зни он вы́нужден был пода́ть в отста́вку; **the weather ~s a change of plan** пого́да обусло́вила измене́ние пла́нов.

necessitous /nɪˈsesɪtəs/ *adj.* (*needy*) нужда́ющийся, бе́дный.

necessity /nɪˈsesɪtɪ/ *n.* **1** (*inevitability*) неизбе́жность; **logical ~** логи́ческая неизбе́жность. **2** (*compulsion, need*) нужда́, необходи́мость; **physical ~** физи́ческая необходи́мость; **of ~** по необходи́мости; **in case of ~** в слу́чае необходи́мости; **~ is the mother of invention** ≈ голь на вы́думки хитра́. **3** (*necessary thing*): **the telephone is a ~** телефо́н не ро́скошь, а предме́т пе́рвой необходи́мости.

neck /nek/ *n.* **1** ше́я; (*dim.*) ше́йка; **I have a stiff ~** мне проду́ло ше́ю; **break s.o.'s ~** свёр|тывать, -ну́ть (*or* лома́ть, с-) ше́ю кому́-н.; **he got it in the ~** ему́ да́ли по ше́е; **he's a pain in the ~** он ужа́сная зану́да (*coll.*); **risk one's ~** рискова́ть (*impf.*) голово́й; **save one's ~** спас|а́ть, -ти́ свою́ го́лову/шку́ру; **stick one's ~ out** (*coll.*) ста́вить, по- себя́ под уда́р; **he was up to his ~ in water** он стоя́л по го́рло в воде́; **he is up to his ~ in debt** у него́ долго́в по го́рло; **he is up to his ~ in work** у него́ рабо́ты по го́рло; **the horse won by a ~** ло́шадь опереди́ла други́х на го́лову; **wring s.o.'s ~**

свёр|тывать, -ну́ть ше́ю кому́-н.; **I'll wring his ~** (*fig.*) я ему́ го́лову/ше́ю сверну́; **~ and ~** ноздря́ в ноздрю́; голова́ в го́лову.
2 (*geog., promontory*) мыс; (*isthmus*) перешеек.
3 (*of var. objects*): **~ of a bottle** го́рлышко буты́лки; **~ of a violin** гриф скри́пки; **~ of a shirt** во́рот руба́шки; **grab s.o. by the ~** хвата́ть, схвати́ть кого́-н. за ши́ворот.
4 (*sl., impudence*) наха́льство.
● *v.i.* (*coll.*) не́жничать (*impf.*).
● *cpds.* **~lace** *n.* ожере́лье; **~line** *n.* вы́рез (пла́тья); **low ~line** декольте́ (*indecl.*); **~tie** *n.* га́лстук.

necrology /neˈkrɒlədʒɪ/ *n.* (*obituary notice*) некроло́г; (*death-roll*) спи́сок уме́рших.

necromancer /ˈnekrəʊˌmænsə(r)/ *n.* некрома́нт; колду́н.

necromancy /ˈnekrəʊˌmænsɪ/ *n.* некрома́нтия; колдовство́; чёрная ма́гия.

necromantic /ˌnekrəʊˈmæntɪk/ *adj.* колдовско́й.

necrophilia /ˌnekrəˈfɪlɪə/ *n.* некрофили́я.

necropolis /neˈkrɒpəlɪs/ *n.* некро́поль (*m.*).

necrosis /neˈkrəʊsɪs/ *n.* омертве́ние, некро́з.

nectar /ˈnektə(r)/ *n.* некта́р.

nectarine /ˈnektərɪn/, /-ˌri:n/ *n.* гла́дкий пе́рсик, нектари́н.

née /neɪ/ *adj.* урождённая.

need /ni:d/ *n.* (*want, requirement*) нужда́; **be, stand in ~ of** нужда́ться (*impf.*) в + *p.*; **the house is in ~ of repair** дом нужда́ется в ремо́нте; **I have ~ of a rest** мне ну́жен о́тдых; **she feels a ~ for (***or* **the ~ of) company** у неё есть потре́бность в обще́нии; ей не хвата́ет обще́ния; **my ~s are few** у меня́ скро́мные потре́бности; (*emergency*) нужда́; **in one's (hour of) ~** в нужде́; **a friend in ~ is a friend indeed** друзья́ познаю́тся в беде́; (*necessity*) необходи́мость; **if ~ be** в слу́чае необходи́мости; **is there any ~ to hurry?** ра́зве ну́жно торопи́ться?; **there's no ~ to get upset** не́зачем расстра́иваться; **there is no ~ for him to read the whole book** ему́ необяза́тельно/не́зачем чита́ть всю кни́гу.
● *v.t.* **1** (*want, require*) нужда́ться (*impf.*) в + *p.*; **the grass ~s cutting** газо́н сле́дует подстри́чь; **the tap ~s a new washer** в кра́не ну́жно смени́ть прокла́дку; **he ~s a haircut** ему́ пора́ (под)стри́чься; **we shall ~ every penny** нам потре́буется/пона́добится ка́ждая копе́йка; **what he ~s is a good hiding** его́ сле́дует хороше́нько вы́пороть.
2 (*with inf., be obliged, under necessity*): **~ I come today?** мне ну́жно приходи́ть сего́дня?; **you ~n't do it all tomorrow** вам не обяза́тельно ко́нчить всю рабо́ту за́втра; **one ~s to be on one's guard with him** с ним сле́дует/ну́жно держа́ть у́хо востро́; **it ~s to be done** э́то ну́жно сде́лать; **don't be away longer than you ~** не заде́рживайтесь до́льше, чем ну́жно/необходи́мо; **~ she have come at all?** на́до ли бы́ло ей приходи́ть вообще́?; **you ~ not have bothered** напра́сно вы беспоко́ились; **I ~ not** (*have no reason to*) мне не́зачем; **he ~ not come** он мо́жет не (*or* он не до́лжен *or* ему́ не на́до) приходи́ть.
● *v.i.* (*be in want*) нужда́ться (*impf.*).

needful /ˈni:dfʊl/ *adj.* необходи́мый.

needle /ˈni:d(ə)l/ *n.* **1** (*for sewing etc.*) игла́, иго́лка; **thread a ~** вд|ева́ть, -еть ни́тку в иго́лку; **eye of a ~** (иго́льное) ушко́; **as sharp as a ~** (*fig.*) у́мный, как чёрт; черто́вски проница́тельный; **look for a ~ in a haystack** иска́ть (*impf.*) иго́лку в сто́ге се́на; **gramophone ~** патефо́нная игла́; (*for knitting*) спи́ца; (*instrument pointer*) стре́лка. **2** (*leaf of conifer*): **pine/fir ~** сосно́вая/ело́вая игла́; (*pl.*) хвоя́ (*collect.*).
● *v.t.* (*irritate, tease*) подд|ева́ть, -е́ть.
● *cpds.* **~-case** *n.* иго́льник; **~craft** *n.* рукоде́лие; **~point** *n.* (*embroidery*) ручна́я вы́шивка га́русом по канве́; (*lace*) иго́льное кру́жево; **~woman** *n.* швея́; (*non-professional*) рукоде́льница; **~work** *n.* (*sewing, embroidery*) рукоде́лие; (*sewing*) шитьё; (*embroidery*) вышива́ние.

needless /ˈni:dlɪs/ *adj.* (*unnecessary*) нену́жный; (*superfluous*) (из)ли́шний; (*inappropriate, uncalled for*) неуме́стный; **~ to say** (само́ собо́й) разуме́ется.

needlessness /ˈni:dlɪsnɪs/ *n.* нену́жность; неуме́стность.

needs /ni:dz/ *adv.* (*liter.*): **I ~ must go** я непреме́нно до́лжен идти́; **~ must when the devil drives** ≈ про́тив рожна́ не попрёшь.

needy /ˈni:dɪ/ *adj.* (**needier, neediest**) нужда́ющийся; (*as n.*): **the poor and ~** беднота́.

ne'er /neə(r)/ *adv.* (*arch.*) никогда́.
● *cpd.* **~-do-well** *n.* него́дник.

nefarious /nɪˈfeərɪəs/ *adj.* злоде́йский.

negate /nɪˈgeɪt/ *v.t.* (*deny the existence of*) отрица́ть (*impf.*) существова́ние + *g.*; (*nullify*) св|оди́ть, -ести́ на нет; (*be opposite of; contradict*) противоре́чить (*impf.*) (+ *dat.*).

negation /nɪˈgeɪʃ(ə)n/ *n.* (*denial*) отрица́ние; (*nullification*) опроверже́ние; (*contradiction*): **this is a ~ of common sense** э́то противоре́чит здра́вому смы́слу.

negative /ˈnegətɪv/ *n.* **1** (*statement, reply, word*) отрица́ние; **he answered in the ~** он дал отрица́тельный отве́т; **a sentence in the ~** отрица́тельное предложе́ние. **2** (*elec.*) отрица́тельный по́люс. **3** (*phot.*) негати́в.
● *adj.* **1** отрица́тельный; **take a ~ attitude** отрица́тельно/негати́вно отн|оси́ться, -ести́сь к (*чему*); **~ sign** (*math.*) знак ми́нус. **2** (*phot.*) негати́вный.
● *v.t.* (*reject, veto*) отв|ерга́ть, -е́ргнуть; (*disprove*) опров|ерга́ть, -е́ргнуть; (*contradict*) противоре́чить (*impf.*) + *d.*

negativism /ˈnegətɪˌvɪz(ə)m/ *n.* негативи́зм.

neglect /nɪˈglekt/ *n.* **1** (*failure to attend to*) пренебреже́ние + *i.*; **~ of one's duties** пренебреже́ние свои́ми обя́занностями, хала́тность; **~ of one's appearance** пренебреже́ние свое́й вне́шностью.
2 (*lack of care*) запу́щенность; **the wound festered through ~** ра́на загнои́лась, оттого́ что была́ запу́щена; **~ of one's children** отсу́тствие забо́ты о свои́х де́тях.
3 (*failure to notice; disregard*) невнима́ние (**of**: к + *d.*); **she scolded him for his ~ of her** она́ его́ руга́ла за невнима́ние к ней.
4 (*uncared-for state*) запу́щенность, забро́шенность; **the house was in a state of ~** дом был запу́щен/забро́шен.
● *v.t.* **1** (*leave undone, let slip*) запус|ка́ть, -ти́ть; забр|а́сывать, -о́сить; (*duty*) пренебр|ега́ть, -е́чь; **he ~ed his studies** он запусти́л заня́тия; **you ~ed your duty** вы пренебрегли́ свои́м до́лгом.
2 (*leave uncared for*) забр|а́сывать, -о́сить, ост|авля́ть, -а́вить без внима́ния; **he ~s his family** он забро́сил свою́ семью́; **~ed children** безнадзо́рные/забро́шенные де́ти; **a ~ed garden** запу́щенный/забро́шенный сад; **you have been ~ing me all these months** все э́ти ме́сяцы вы не обраща́ли на меня́ никако́го внима́ния; (*of books, writers etc.*): **he is a ~ed composer** он (несправедли́во) забы́тый компози́тор.
3 (*with inf., fail, forget*) заб|ыва́ть, -ы́ть; **he ~ed to wind up the clock** он забы́л завести́ часы́.

neglectful /nɪˈglektfʊl/ *adj.* небре́жный, невнима́тельный; **he is ~ of his interests** он не забо́тится о со́бственных интере́сах.

negligée /ˈneglɪˌʒeɪ/ *n.* пеньюа́р.

negligence /ˈneglɪdʒ(ə)ns/ *n.* небре́жность, хала́тность; **criminal ~** престу́пная небре́жность; невнима́тельность.

negligent /ˈneglɪdʒ(ə)nt/ *adj.* (*careless*) небре́жный; **he is ~ of his duties** он отно́сится небре́жно/хала́тно к свои́м обя́занностям; (*inattentive*) невнима́тельный; (*slovenly*) неря́шливый; **he is ~ in dress/appearance** он одева́ется неря́шливо.

negligible /ˈneglɪdʒɪb(ə)l/ *adj.* незначи́тельный.

negotiable /nɪˈgəʊʃəb(ə)l/ *adj.* **1**: **~ conditions, terms** усло́вия, кото́рые мо́гут служи́ть предме́том перегово́ров. **2** (*of cheques etc.*) с пра́вом переда́чи; (*of securities*) обраща́ющийся, оборо́тный.
3 (*navigable*) проходи́мый; (*of roads*) прое́зжий.

negotiate /nɪˈgəʊʃɪˌeɪt/ *v.t.* **1** (*arrange*) догов|а́риваться, -ори́ться о + *p.*; (*conduct negotiations over*) вести́ (*impf.*) перегово́ры о + *p.*; (*conclude agreement*

N

on) при|ходи́ть, -йти́ к соглаше́нию о + *p.* **2** (*get over or through*) проб|ира́ться, -ра́ться че́рез + *a.*; **~ a corner** брать, взять поворо́т; (*fig., surmount*): **~ an obstacle/difficulty** преодол|ева́ть, -е́ть препя́тствие/тру́дность.

● *v.i.* догов|а́риваться, -ори́ться.

negotiation /nɪˌgəʊʃɪˈeɪʃ(ə)n/, /nɪˌgəʊsɪˈeɪʃ(ə)n/ *n.* **1** (*process*) обсужде́ние; **~ of terms** обсужде́ние усло́вий; (*usu. pl., talks*) перегово́ры (*m. pl.*); **conduct ~s** вести́ перегово́ры. **2** (*fig.*): **~ of difficulties** преодоле́ние тру́дностей.

negotiator /nɪˈgəʊʃɪˌeɪtə(r)/ *n.* уча́стник перегово́ров; (*representative*) представи́тель (*m.*).

Negress /ˈniːgrɪs/ *n.* негритя́нка.

negritude /ˈniːgrɪˌtjuːd/ *n.* принадле́жность к негро́идной ра́се.

Negro /ˈniːgrəʊ/ *n.* (*pl.* **Negroes**) негр.

● *adj.* негритя́нский.

Negroid /ˈniːgrɔɪd/ *adj.* негро́идный.

neigh /neɪ/ *n.* ржа́ние.

● *v.i.* ржать (*impf.*).

neighbour /ˈneɪbə(r)/ (*US* **neighbor**) *n.* (*lit., and of countries, guests at dinner etc.*) сосе́д (*fem.* -ка); **my next-door ~** мой ближа́йший сосе́д (по у́лице); **this house and its ~s** э́тот и сосе́дние с ним дома́; **love of one's ~** любо́вь к бли́жнему; **love thy ~!** возлюби́ бли́жнего своего́!

● *v.i.*: **~ on** прилега́ть (*impf.*) к + *d.*; сосе́дствовать (*impf.*) с + *i.*; **~ing countries** сосе́дние стра́ны; пограни́чные госуда́рства.

neighbourhood /ˈneɪbəˌhʊd/ (*US* **neighborhood**) *n.* **1** (*locality*) ме́стность, окре́стность; (*district*) райо́н; (*vicinity*) сосе́дство; **in the ~ of the park** о́коло (*or* недалеко́ от) па́рка; **in the ~ of 20 tons** в райо́не двадцати́ тонн; приблизи́тельно два́дцать тонн. **2** (*neighbours; community*) сосе́ди (*m. pl.*); окружа́ющие (*pl.*).

neighbourliness /ˈneɪbəlmɪs/ (*US* **neighborliness**) *n.* добрососе́дское отноше́ние.

neighbourly /ˈneɪbəlɪ/ (*US* **neighborly**) *adj.* добрососе́дский; **in a ~ fashion** по-сосе́дски; **that's not a ~ thing to do** э́то не по-сосе́дски.

neither /ˈnaɪðə(r)/, /ˈniːð-/ *pron. & adj.* ни тот, ни друго́й; **~ of them knows** ни оди́н (*or* никто́) из них не зна́ет; они́ о́ба не зна́ют; **~ of them likes it** э́то не нра́вится ни тому́, ни друго́му; **he took ~ side in the argument** в спо́ре он не присоедини́лся ни к той, ни к друго́й стороне́ (*or* ни к одно́й из сторо́н).

● *adv.* **1**: **~ ... nor ...** ни... ни...; **~ one thing nor the other** ни то, ни друго́е; **~ fish nor fowl** ни ры́ба ни мя́со; **one must ~ smoke nor spit here** здесь нельзя́ ни кури́ть, ни плева́ть; **he ~ knows nor cares** он не зна́ет и не хо́чет знать; **it's of no interest to you, nor to me ~** (*sl.*) э́то никому́ не интере́сно — ни вам, ни мне; **that's ~ here nor there** ≈ э́то тут ни к селу́ ни к го́роду; э́то тут ни при чём; **~ he nor I went** ни он, ни я не пошли́. **2** (*after neg. clause*): **he didn't go and ~ did I** он не пошёл, и я то́же.

nelson /ˈnels(ə)n/ *n.* (*wrestling-hold*) не́льсон.

nem. con. /nem ˈkɒn/ *adv.* (*abbr. of* ***nemine contradicente***) без возраже́ний.

nemesis /ˈnemɪsɪs/ *n.* (*pl.* **nemeses** /-ˌsiːz/) (*retribution*) возме́здие, ка́ра.

neoclassical /ˌniːəʊˈklæsɪk(ə)l/ *adj.* неоклассический.

neoclassicism /ˌniːəʊˈklæsɪˌsɪz(ə)m/ *n.* неоклассици́зм.

neocolonial /ˌniːəʊkəˈləʊnɪəl/ *adj.* неоколониали́стский.

neocolonialism /ˌniːəʊkəˈləʊnɪəˌlɪz(ə)m/ *n.* неоколониали́зм.

neo-Fascist /ˌniːəʊˈfæʃɪst/ *n.* неофаши́ст.

● *adj.* неофаши́стский.

neolithic /ˌniːəˈlɪθɪk/ *n.* (*the ~ period*) неоли́т.

● *adj.* неолити́ческий.

neologism /niːˈɒləˌdʒɪz(ə)m/ *n.* неологи́зм.

neon /ˈniːɒn/ *n.* нео́н.

● *adj.* нео́новый; **~ light** нео́новый свет; **~ sign** нео́новая рекла́ма.

neonate /ˈniːəˌneɪt/ *n.* новорождённый.

neophyte /ˈniːəˌfaɪt/ *n.* неофи́т.

Neozoic /ˌniːəʊˈzəʊɪk/ *adj.* кайнозо́йский.

Nepal /nɪˈpɔːl/ *n.* Непа́л.

Nepal|ese /ˌnepəˈliːz/, **-i** /nɪˌpɔːlɪ/ *n.* (*pl.* **~ese, ~i** *or* **~is**) непа́л|ец (*fem.* -ка).

● *adj.* непа́льский.

nephew /ˈnevjuː/, /ˈnef-/ *n.* племя́нник.

nephrite /ˈnefraɪt/ *n.* нефри́т.

nephritic /nɪˈfrɪtɪk/ *adj.* по́чечный.

nephritis /nɪˈfraɪtɪs/ *n.* нефри́т.

ne plus ultra /ˌneɪ plʊs ˈʊltrɑː/ *n.* вы́сшая то́чка + *g.*

nepotism /ˈnepəˌtɪz(ə)m/ *n.* непоти́зм, кумовство́.

Neptune /ˈneptjuːn/ *n.* (*myth., astron.*) Непту́н.

nerd /nɜːd/ *n.* зану́да (*c.g.*).

nerve /nɜːv/ *n.* **1** нерв; **~ gas** не́рвный газ; **he has ~s of steel** у него́ желе́зные не́рвы; **he doesn't know what ~s are** он не зна́ет, что тако́е не́рвы; **he's just a bundle of ~s** он про́сто комо́к не́рвов; **he suffers from ~s** у него́ расстро́ены не́рвы; **he gets on my ~s** он де́йствует мне на не́рвы. **2** (*courage, assurance*) сме́лость; **lose one's ~** робе́ть, о-; (*coll., impudence*): **have the ~ to ...** име́ть на́глость + *inf.*; **he's got a ~!** ну и нагле́ц!; **he had the ~ to ask me ...** у него́ хвати́ло на́глости спроси́ть меня́.... **3** (*sinew*) жи́ла; **strain every ~ to ...** напр|яга́ть, -я́чь все си́лы, что́бы....

● *v.t.* (*impart vigour/courage to*): **he ~d himself to make a speech** он собра́лся с ду́хом и произнёс речь.

● *cpds.* **~-cell** *n.* не́рвная кле́тка; **~-centre** (*US* **-center**) *n.* не́рвный центр; **~-racking** *adj.* (*situation*) нерво́зный; (*time*) напряжённый.

nerveless /ˈnɜːvlɪs/ *adj.* (*inert*) ине́ртный; (*limp, flabby*) вя́лый; (*powerless*) бесси́льный; (*confident*) уве́ренный; **his arm fell ~ to his side** его́ рука́ бесси́льно упа́ла.

nervous /ˈnɜːvəs/ *adj.* **1** (*pert. to nerves*) не́рвный; **~ system** не́рвная систе́ма; **~ strain** не́рвное напряже́ние; **he had a ~ breakdown** у него́ бы́ло не́рвное расстро́йство; **he's a ~ wreck** э́то челове́к с подо́рванной не́рвной систе́мой. **2** (*highly strung*) не́рвный. **3** (*agitated*) не́рвный, взволно́ванный; **I'm ~** я не́рвничаю; **he was ~ before making his speech** он волнова́лся/не́рвничал пе́ред выступле́нием. **4** (*apprehensive*) не́рвный, не́рвничающий; **I am ~ of asking him** я не реша́юсь спроси́ть его́.

nervousness /ˈnɜːvəsnɪs/ *n.* не́рвность, нерво́зность.

nervy /ˈnɜːvɪ/ *adj.* (**nervier, nerviest**) **1** (*Br., nervous*) не́рвный, нерво́зный; **feel ~** не́рвничать (*impf.*). **2** (*US, impudent*) наха́льный, на́глый.

nest /nest/ *n.* гнездо́, (*dim.*) гнёздышко; (*fig.*): **feather one's ~** ≈ наб|ива́ть, -и́ть себе́ карма́н; наж|ива́ться, -и́ться; нагре́ть (*pf.*) ру́ки; **foul one's own ~** ≈ плева́ть (*impf.*) в со́бственный коло́дец; **~ of tables** компле́кт сто́ликов (*вставляющихся один в другой*).

● *v.i.* **1** (*of birds*) гнезди́ться (*impf.*). **2** (*hunt for birds' ~s*) охо́титься (*impf.*) за гнёздами.

● *cpd.* **~-egg** *n.* (*fig., savings*) сбереже́ния (*nt. pl.*).

nestle /ˈnes(ə)l/ *v.t. & i.*: **~ (one's head/face) against s.o./something** приж|има́ться, -а́ться (голово́й/лицо́м) к кому́/чему́-н.; **~ down** устр|а́иваться, -о́иться поудо́бнее; приюти́ться (*pf.*); **~ up to s.o.** ласка́ться, при- к кому́-н.; льну́ть, при- к кому́-н.; **a village (lay) ~d at the foot of the hill** у подно́жия горы́ приюти́лась дере́вня.

nestling /ˈneslɪŋ/, /ˈnest-/ *n.* птене́ц, пте́нчик (*dim.*).

net[1] /net/ *n.* **1** (*fruit-~, mosquito-~ etc.*) се́тка; (*snare for birds, fishing-~ and fig.*) сеть, се́ти (*f. pl.*); (*hair-~, tennis, cricket-~ etc.*) се́тка; (*butterfly-~*) сачо́к. **2** (*fabric*) тюль (*m.*); **~ curtains** тю́левые занаве́ски. **3** (*network, of communications etc.*) сеть. **4**: **the Net** (*comput.*) Сеть, Интерне́т.

● *v.t.* (**netted, netting**) **1** (*fish, birds etc.*) лови́ть, пойма́ть в сеть/се́ти. **2** (*fruit etc.*) накр|ыва́ть, -ы́ть се́ткой. **3**: **he ~ted the ball** он заки́нул мяч в се́тку; (*at football*) он заби́л гол.

● *cpds.* **~ball** *n.* нетбо́л (*род баскетбола*); **~work** *n.* сеть; *v.t.* (*Br., T.V., radio*) перед|ава́ть, -а́ть по (телевизио́нной/

радиотрансляцио́нной) се́ти; (*comput.*) свя́з|ывать, -а́ть в о́бщую сеть; *v.i.* (*fig.*) нала́живать, нала́дить конта́кты/свя́зи; **~worked** *adj.* (*comput.*) сетево́й.

net², nett /net/ *adj.* чи́стый; **~ income** чи́стый дохо́д; **~ weight** чи́стый вес; вес не́тто.

● *v.t.* (**netted, netting**) (*obtain as profit*) получ|а́ть, -и́ть чи́стыми; де́лать, с-; **he ~ted a handsome profit** он получи́л соли́дную при́быль.

nether /ˈneðə(r)/ *adj.* ни́жний; **~ regions** преиспо́дняя.

● *cpd.* **~most** *adj.* са́мый ни́жний.

Netherlander /ˈneðələndə(r)/ *n.* голла́нд|ец (*fem.* -ка).

Netherlandish /ˈneðələndɪʃ/ *adj.* нидерла́ндский.

Netherlands /ˈneðələndz/ *n.* Нидерла́нд|ы (*pl., g.* -ов).

nett /net/ (*Br.*) = **net²**

netting /ˈnetɪŋ/ *n.* се́тка.

nettle /ˈnet(ə)l/ *n.* крапи́ва.

● *v.t.* (*fig.*) зад|ева́ть, -е́ть; раздраж|а́ть, -и́ть.

● *cpd.* **~-rash** *n.* крапи́вница.

neural /ˈnjʊər(ə)l/ *adj.* не́рвный.

neuralgia /njʊəˈrældʒə/ *n.* невралги́я.

neuralgic /njʊəˈrældʒɪk/ *adj.* невралги́ческий.

neurasthenia /ˌnjʊərəsˈθiːnɪə/ *n.* неврастени́я.

neurasthenic /ˌnjʊərəsˈθenɪk/ *adj.* неврастени́ческий.

neuritis /njʊəˈraɪtɪs/ *n.* неври́т.

neurological /ˌnjʊərəˈlɒdʒɪk(ə)l/ *adj.* неврологи́ческий.

neurologist /njʊəˈrɒlədʒɪst/ *n.* невропато́лог, невро́лог.

neurology /njʊəˈrɒlədʒɪ/ *n.* невроло́гия.

neuron /ˈnjʊərɒn/ *n.* нейро́н.

neuropathologist /ˌnjʊərəʊpəˈθɒlədʒɪst/ *n.* невропато́лог.

neuropathology /ˌnjʊərəʊpəˈθɒlədʒɪ/ *n.* невропатоло́гия.

neurosis /njʊəˈrəʊsɪs/ *n.* (*pl.* **neuroses** /-siːz/) невро́з.

neurotic /njʊəˈrɒtɪk/ *n.* невро́тик.

● *adj.* невроти́ческий.

neuter /ˈnjuːtə(r)/ *n.* (*gram., gender*) сре́дний род.

● *adj.* (*gram.*) сре́дний; сре́днего ро́да; (*zool.*) кастри́рованный; (*bot.*) бespо́лый.

● *v.t.* кастри́ровать (*impf., pf.*).

neutral /ˈnjuːtr(ə)l/ *n.* (*of gears*) холосто́й ход; **in ~** в сре́днем положе́нии.

● *adj.* **1** (*of state or person*) нейтра́льный; **be ~** зан|има́ть, -я́ть нейтра́льную пози́цию. **2** (*of colour etc., indeterminate*) неопределённый, нейтра́льный. **3** (*chem.*) сре́дний. **4** (*elec.*) нулево́й, нейтра́льный. **5** (*of gears*) холосто́й.

neutrality /njuːˈtrælɪtɪ/ *n.* нейтралите́т.

neutralization /ˌnjuːtrəlaɪˈzeɪʃ(ə)n/ *n.* нейтрализа́ция.

neutralize /ˈnjuːtrəˌlaɪz/ *v.t.* нейтрализова́ть (*impf., pf.*); (*paralyse*) парализова́ть (*impf., pf.*).

neutron /ˈnjuːtrɒn/ *n.* нейтро́н; **~ bomb** нейтро́нная бо́мба.

Neva /ˈniːvə/ *n.* Нева́.

never /ˈnevə(r)/ *adv.* **1** никогда́ (... не); (*not once*) ни ра́зу (... не); **~ a dull moment!** не соску́чишься!; **you ~ know** как знать?; **~ before** никогда́ ра́ньше; **I have ~ before** (*or* **in my life**) **seen such tomatoes** я в жи́зни не ви́дел таки́х помидо́ров; **I believed him once, but ~ again** одна́жды я ему́ пове́рил, но бо́льше никогда́ не пове́рю; (*emphatic for not*) так и не; **that will ~ do** э́то никуда́ не годи́тся; **he ~ even tried** он да́же не попро́бовал; **I ~ slept a wink** я глаз не сомкну́л; (*Br., expr. incredulity*) **~!** не мо́жет быть!; (*with imper.*): **~ fear!** не бо́йтесь!; не беспоко́йтесь!; **~ say die!** не отча́ивайтесь!; **~ mind!** (*don't trouble yourself*) не беспоко́йтесь!; (*in answer to apology*) не ва́жно!; ничего́! (*coll.*).
2 (*expr. surprise*): **surely you ~ told him!** неуже́ли вы ему́ сказа́ли?; **well, I ~ (did)!** не мо́жет быть!; на́до же!

● *cpds.* **~-ceasing** *adj.* беспреста́нный, непреры́вный; **~-ending** *adj.* бесконе́чный; **it's a ~-ending job** э́той рабо́тє конца́ нет; **~-failing** *adj.* надёжный; **~more** *adv.* никогда́ бо́льше/вперёдь; **~-~** *n.*: **~-~ land** (*sc. of plenty*) ска́зочная страна́ изоби́лия; **he bought his car on the ~-~** (*Br. coll.*) он купи́л маши́ну в рассро́чку; **~theless** *adv.* одна́ко; *conj.* тем не ме́нее; **~-to-be-forgotten** *adj.* незабве́нный.

new /njuː/ *adj.* **1** но́вый; **the N~ World** Но́вый Свет; **the N~ Testament** Но́вый заве́т; **N~ Year** Но́вый год; *see also* ⇒**Year; as good as ~** совсе́м как но́вый; **what's ~?** что но́вого?; **he became a ~ man** он стал други́м челове́ком.
2 (*modern, advanced*) нове́йший, после́дний; **the ~est fashions** нове́йшие/после́дние мо́ды.
3 (*fresh*) молодо́й; **~ potatoes** молодо́й карто́фель; **~ moon** молодо́й ме́сяц, новолу́ние; **~ wine** молодо́е вино́.
4 (*unaccustomed*): **I am ~ to this work** я в э́том де́ле новичо́к; (*unfamiliar*): **this work is ~ to me** э́та рабо́та для меня́ непривы́чна.

● *cpds.* **N~ Age** *n.* филосо́фская систе́ма, бази́рующаяся на ве́ре в альтернати́вный о́браз жи́зни; **~-born** *adj.* новорождённый; **~comer** *n.* новичо́к; **he's a ~comer to the village** он посели́лся в э́той дере́вне неда́вно; **~-fangled, ~-fashioned** *adjs.* новомо́дный; **~-found** *adj.*: **a ~-found interest** но́вое увлече́ние (+*i.*); **N~foundland** *n.* Ньюфаундле́нд; (*dog*) ньюфа́ундленд, водола́з; **~-laid** *adj.* све́жий; **~-mown** *adj.* свежеско́шенный; **~-year** *adj.* нового́дний.

newel /ˈnjuːəl/ *n.* коло́нна винтово́й ле́стницы; баля́сина.

New Guinea /njuː ˈɡɪnɪ/ *n.* Но́вая Гвине́я.

newly /ˈnjuːlɪ/ *adv.* **1** (*recently*) неда́вно, но́во-; **~ arrived** неда́вно прибы́вший, новоприбы́вший.
2 (*anew*) вновь; **a ~ painted gate** свежевы́крашенная кали́тка. **3** (*in a new way*) за́ново; по-ино́му; по-но́вому.

● *cpds.* **~-built** *adj.* неда́вно вы́строенный; **~-wed** *n.*: **the ~-weds** молодожён|ы (*pl., g.* -ов); *adj.* новобра́чный.

newness /ˈnjuːnɪs/ *n.* новизна́.

news /njuːz/ *n.* **1** но́вости (*f. pl.*); (*piece of ~*) но́вость, весть; **have you heard the ~?** вы слы́шали но́вость?; **is there any** (*or* **what's the**) **~?** что но́вого?, каки́е но́вости?; **what ~ of him?** что слы́шно о нём?; **that's good ~!** рад слы́шать!; э́то прия́тная но́вость!; **I had bad ~ from home** я получи́л плохи́е но́вости/ве́сти из до́му; **he brought bad ~** он принёс дурну́ю весть; **that's no ~ to me!** для меня́ э́то не но́вость; я э́то и ра́ньше знал; **no ~ is good ~** отсу́тствие весте́й — хоро́шая весть; **we had ~ from him** мы получи́ли от него́ ве́сточку; **have you had ~ of the results?** вам уже́ изве́стны результа́ты?
2 (*in press or radio*) но́вости (*f. pl.*), после́дние изве́стия; **he is in the ~** про него́ сообща́ют в новостя́х; **~ agency** информацио́нное аге́нтство; **~ bulletin** (*Br.*) вы́пуск новосте́й; информацио́нный бюллете́нь; **~ conference** пресс-конфере́нция; **~ flash** э́кстренное сообще́ние.

● *cpds.* **~agent** *n.* (*shop*) газе́тный кио́ск; (*person*) = **~-vendor; ~boy** *n.* ма́льчик-газе́тчик; **~cast** *n.* после́дние изве́стия (*по радио/телевидению*); **~caster** *n.* ди́ктор; **~-dealer** *n.* = **~agent; ~-girl** *n.* де́вочка-газе́тчица; **~-letter** *n.* информацио́нный бюллете́нь; **~monger** *n.* сплетни́|к (*fem.* -ца); **~paper** *n.* газе́та; (*attr.*) газе́тный; **~print** *n.* газе́тная бума́га; **~-reader** *n.* (*Br.*) ди́ктор (*последних известий*); **~reel** *n.* кинохро́ника; **~room** *n.* отде́л новосте́й; **~sheet** *n.* информацио́нный листо́к; **~stand** *n.* газе́тный лото́к; **~-vendor** *n.* (*Br.*) продав|е́ц (*fem.* -щи́ца) газе́т; (газе́тный) киоскёр; **~worthy** *adj.* интере́сный; представля́ющий интере́с для пре́ссы.

newsy /ˈnjuːzɪ/ *adj.* (**newsier, newsiest**) (*coll.*) по́лный новосте́й.

newt /njuːt/ *n.* трито́н.

Newtonian /njuːˈtəʊnɪən/ *adj.* ньюто́нов.

New York /njuː ˈjɔːk/ *n.* Нью-Йо́рк; (*attr.*) нью-йо́ркский.

New Zealand /njuː ˈziːlənd/ *n.* Но́вая Зела́ндия; (*attr.*) новозела́ндский.

New Zealander /njuː ˈziːləndə(r)/ *n.* новозела́нд|ец (*fem.* -ка).

next /nekst/ *n.* (*in order*): **the week after ~** че́рез неде́лю; **~, please!**

N

следующий!; **~ of kin** ближайший родственник.

● *adj.* **1** (*of place: nearest*) ближайший; (*adjacent*) соседний, смежный; **in the ~ house** в соседнем доме; **the house ~ to ours** дом рядом с нашим; **he lives ~ door** он живёт рядом; **he lives ~ door but one to us** он живёт через дом от нас; **the chair was ~ to the fire** стул стоял возле камина.
2: **~ to** (*fig., almost*) почти; **it was ~ to impossible** это было почти невозможно; **I got it for ~ to nothing** я купил это за бесценок.
3 (*in a series*) очередной; (*future*) будущий, следующий; (*past or future*) следующий; **~ day** на другой/следующий день; **~ Friday** в следующую пятницу; **~ October** в следующем октябре; **the ~ day but one was a holiday** это было за два дня до праздника; **~ week** на будущей/следующей неделе; **~ year** в будущем году; **~ time we'll go to London** в следующий раз мы поедем в Лондон; **better luck ~ time!** может, в следующий раз больше повезёт!; **he is ~ in line** он первый на очереди; он следующий; **the ~ thing I knew, I was lying on the floor** в следующую минуту я уже лежал на полу; **the ~ world** другой/потусторонний мир.

● *adv.*: **he stood ~ to the fire** он стоял возле камина; **he placed his chair ~ to hers** он поставил свой стул рядом с её (стулом); **what ~?** этого ещё не хватало!; **what will he do ~?** а теперь что он надумает?; **when I ~ saw him** когда я увидел его в следующий раз; **~ we come to the library** дальше/а теперь — библиотека.

● *cpd.* **~-door** *adj.* соседний; **~-door neighbour** (*Br.*), **neighbor** (*US*) ближайший сосед.

nexus /ˈneksəs/ *n.* (*pl.* **nexuses**) (*connection*) связь.

NHS (*abbr. of* ***National Health Service***) Национальная служба здравоохранения.

nib /nɪb/ *n.* перо.

nibble /ˈnɪb(ə)l/ *n.*: **have, take a ~ at something** надкус|ывать, -ить что-н.

● *v.t.* покусывать (*impf.*); (*at bait*) дёрг|ать, -нуть; (*at grass*) щипать (*impf.*); пощипывать (*impf.*); (*of fish*) кл|евать, -юнуть.

● *v.i.*: **~ at something** грызть (*impf.*) что-н.

Nicaragua /ˌnɪkəˈrægjʊə/ *n.* Никарагуа (*indecl.*).

Nicaraguan /ˌnɪkəˈrægjʊən/ *n.* никарагуан|ец (*fem.* -ка).

● *adj.* никарагуанский.

nice /naɪs/ *adj.* **1** (*agreeable*) приятный, милый; (*good*) хороший; (*of person*) приятный, милый, симпатичный, любезный; **they have a ~** (*comfortable*) **home** у них милый/приятный дом; **that's very ~ of you** это очень мило с вашей стороны; **this soup tastes ~** этот суп вкусный; **the house was ~ and big** дом был просторный; **get the room ~ and tidy!** хорошенько уберите комнату!; **the soup was ~ and hot** суп был по-настоящему горячий; **the children were ~ and clean** дети были чистенькие; (*iron.*): **a ~ state of affairs!** хорошенькое дело!
2 (*subtle*) тонкий; **a ~ shade of meaning** тонкий смысловой оттенок; **~ distinctions** тонкие различия.

● *cpd.* **~-looking** *adj.* милый, симпатичный.

nicely /ˈnaɪslɪ/ *adv.* (*well, satisfactorily*) хорошо; **he is getting along ~** у него всё хорошо; (*of progress*) он делает успехи; (*of invalid*) он поправляется; (*agreeably*) приятно; (*kindly*) мило; **that will suit me ~** это мне вполне подойдёт; (*aptly*): **~ put** метко сказано.

niceness /ˈnaɪsnɪs/ *n.* (*amiability*) любезность; (*exactitude*) точность.

nicety /ˈnaɪsɪtɪ/ *n.* **1** (*exactness*) точность; (*accuracy*) аккуратность; **to a ~** точно. **2** (*subtle quality*) тонкость; **a point of great ~** очень тонкий вопрос. **3** (*minute distinction, detail*) мелочь, мелкая подробность.

niche /nɪtʃ/, /niːʃ/ *n.* ниша; (*fig.*) ниша, место в жизни.

Nick /nɪk/ *n.*: **Old ~** чёрт, сатана (*m.*).

nick /nɪk/ *n.* **1** (*notch*) зарубка. **2** (*Br., prison*) кутузка (*sl.*). **3**: **in good ~** (*Br. coll.*) в хорошем состоянии; **in the ~ of time** в (самый) последний момент; как раз вовремя.

● *v.t.* **1** (*cut notch in*) делать, с- зарубку на + *p.*; **he ~ed his chin shaving** он порезал себе подбородок во время бритья. **2** (*Br. sl., arrest*) брать, взять; заб|ирать, -рать. **3** (*Br., steal*) стибрить (*pf.*) (*sl.*).

nickel /ˈnɪk(ə)l/ *n.* (*metal*) никель (*m.*); (*US coin*) пятицентовик.

● *adj.* никелевый.

● *v.t.* (**nickelled, nickelling;** *US* **nickeled, nickeling**) никелировать (*impf., pf.*).

● *cpd.* **~-plated** *adj.* никелированный.

nick-nack /ˈnɪknæk/ = **knick-knack**

nickname /ˈnɪkneɪm/ *n.* прозвище, кличка.

● *v.t.* проз|ывать, -вать + *a.* & *i.*; **he was ~d Shorty** его прозвали Коротышкой.

nicotine /ˈnɪkəˌtiːn/ *n.* никотин; **~ poisoning** отравление никотином.

● *cpd.* **~-stained** *adj.* жёлтый от табака.

niece /niːs/ *n.* племянница.

niello /nɪˈeləʊ/ *n.* чернь (*на металле*).

nifty /ˈnɪftɪ/ *adj.* (**niftier, niftiest**) (*sl.*) (*adept*) ловкий; (*stylish*) стильный.

Niger /ˈnaɪdʒə(r)/ *n.* Нигер.

Nigeria /naɪˈdʒɪərɪə/ *n.* Нигерия.

Nigerian /naɪˈdʒɪərɪən/ *n.* нигери|ец (*fem.* -йка).

● *adj.* нигерийский.

niggard /ˈnɪgəd/ *n.* скряга (*c.g.*).

niggardliness /ˈnɪgədlɪnɪs/ *n.* скупость.

niggardly /ˈnɪgədlɪ/ *adj.* скупой.

nigger /ˈnɪgə(r)/ *n.* (*offens.*) черномазый (*offens.*).

niggle /ˈnɪg(ə)l/ *v.t.* (*irritate*) дёргать (*impf.*), придираться (*impf.*) к + *d.*

● *v.i.* (*fuss over detail*) мелочиться (*impf.*).

niggling /ˈnɪglɪŋ/ *adj.* (*nagging*) придирчивый; (*petty*) мелочный; **~ criticism** мелочная критика, придирки (*f. pl.*).

nigh /naɪ/ (*arch.*) = **near**

night /naɪt/ *n.* **1** ночь; (*waking hours of darkness*) вечер; **dark, black as ~** чёрный как смоль; **all ~ (long)** всю ночь (напролёт); **last ~** вчера вечером/ночью; **tomorrow ~** завтра вечером/ночью; **at, by ~** ночью; **at ~s** по ночам; **at dead of ~** в глухую ночь; **~ and day** днём и ночью; **we reached home before ~** мы пришли домой засветло; **on Saturday ~** в субботу вечером; **on the ~ of the 12th/13th** в ночь с двенадцатого на тринадцатое; **good ~!**; (*coll.*) **~-~!** спокойной ночи!; **have a good ~ (~'s sleep)** хорошо спать (*impf.*); **it's my ~ off today** сегодня у меня свободный вечер; **stay the ~** ночевать, пере-; **work ~s** работать (*impf.*) по ночам.
2 (*attr.*) ночной; **~ life** ночная жизнь (города); **~ shift** ночная смена.

● *cpds.* **~-bird** *n.* (*fig.*) полуночник, сова; **~-blindness** *n.* куриная слепота; **~cap** *n.* (*clothing*) ночной колпак; (*beverage*) стакан (*чего*) на ночь; **~-club** *n.* ночной клуб; **~-dress** *n.* ночная сорочка/рубашка; **~fall** *n.* сумер|ки (*pl., g.* -ек); **by ~fall** к вечеру; **~-gown** *n.* ночная рубашка/сорочка; **~jar** *n.* козодой; **~-light** *n.* ночник; **~-long** *adj.* продолжающийся всю ночь; **~mare** *n.* (*also fig.*) кошмар; **have a ~mare** видеть (*impf.*) кошмарный сон; **he had ~s all through the night** всю ночь ему снились кошмары; **~marish** *adj.* кошмарный; **~-owl** *n.* (*fig.*) = **~-bird; ~-porter** *n.* ночной швейцар/портье (*m. indecl.*); **~-school** *n.* вечерняя школа; **~shade** *n.* паслён; **deadly ~shade** красавка, белладонна; **~-shirt** *n.* ночная рубашка; **~-soil** *n.* нечистоты (*f. pl.*); **~-time** *n.* ночное время; **in the ~-time** ночью; **~-watchman** *n.* ночной сторож; **~-work** *n.* ночная работа.

nightie /ˈnaɪtɪ/ *n.* ночная рубашка/сорочка.

nightingale /ˈnaɪtɪŋˌgeɪl/ *n.* соловей.

nightly /ˈnaɪtlɪ/ *adj.* (*happening every night*) еженощный; ежевечерний; **~ performances** ежедневные вечерние представления.

● *adv.* еженощно; каждую ночь; каждый вечер.

nihilism /ˈnaɪɪˌlɪz(ə)m/, /ˈnaɪhɪˌlɪz(ə)m/ *n.* нигилизм.

nihilist /ˈnaɪɪlɪst/, /ˈnaɪhɪlɪst/ *n.* нигилист (*fem.* -ка).

nihilistic /ˌnaɪɪˈlɪstɪk/, /ˌnaɪhɪˈlɪstɪk/ *adj.* нигилистический, нигилистский.

nil /nɪl/ *n.* нуль (*m.*); **his influence is ~** его влияние равно нулю.

Nile /naɪl/ *n.* Нил; **Blue ~** Голубой Нил.

nimbi /ˈnɪmbaɪ/ *pl. of* ⇒**nimbus**

nimble /'nɪmb(ə)l/ *adj.* (**nimbler, nimblest**) (*agile*) прово́рный, шу́стрый (*coll.*); (*lively*) живо́й; (*swift*) бы́стрый; (*dextrous*) ло́вкий; **he is ~ on his feet** он о́чень прово́рен; (*mentally quick, sharp*) нахо́дчивый; **a ~ wit** живо́й ум.

● *cpds.* **~-footed** *adj.* быстроно́гий; **~-witted** *adj.* нахо́дчивый, остроу́мный.

nimbus /'nɪmbəs/ *n.* (*pl.* **nimbi** *or* **nimbuses**) (*halo*) нимб; (*meteor.*) дождево́е о́блако.

nincompoop /'nɪŋkəm,puːp/ *n.* дура́к, болва́н.

nine /naɪn/ *n.* (число́/но́мер) де́вять; (**~** *people*) де́вятеро, де́вять челове́к; **~ each** по девяти́ ка́ждый; **in ~s, ~ at a time** по девяти́, девя́тками; (*figure; thing numbered 9; group of* **~**) девя́тка; (*with var. nn. expr. or understood: cf. examples under* ⇒**five**); **dressed (up) to the ~s** разоде́тый в пух и прах.

● *adj.* де́вять + *g. pl.*; **~ twos are eighteen** два помно́жить на де́вять — восемна́дцать; **a ~ days' wonder** скоропреходя́щая сенса́ция; **~ times out of ten** в девяти́ слу́чаях из десяти́.

● *cpds.* **~fold** *adj.* девятикра́тный; *adv.* вде́вятеро, в де́вять раз; **~pins** *n.* ке́гл|и (*pl., g.* -ей).

nineteen /naɪn'tiːn/ *n.* девятна́дцать; **in the 1920s** в двадца́тые го́ды 20-го ве́ка; **talk ~ to the dozen** тарато́рить (*impf.*); треща́ть (*impf.*) без у́молку.

● *adj.* девятна́дцать + *g. pl.*

nineteenth /naɪn'tiːnθ/ *n.* (*date*) девятна́дцатое число́; (*fraction*) одна́ девятна́дцатая, девятна́дцатая часть.

● *adj.* девятна́дцатый.

ninetieth /'naɪntɪɪθ/ *n.* одна́ девяно́стая; девяно́стая часть.

● *adj.* девяно́стый.

ninet|y /'naɪntɪ/ *n.* девяно́сто; **he is in his ~ies** ему́ за девяно́сто; **in the ~ies** (*decade*) в девяно́стых года́х; (*temperature*) за девяно́сто гра́дусов (по Фаренге́йту).

● *adj.* девяно́сто + *g. pl.*; **~y-nine times out of a hundred** в девяно́ста девяти́ слу́чаях из ста.

ninny /'nɪnɪ/ *n.* дурачо́к.

ninth /naɪnθ/ *n.* (*date*) девя́тое число́; (*fraction*) одна́ девя́тая; девя́тая часть; (*mus. interval*) но́на.

● *adj.* девя́тый.

nip /nɪp/ *n.* **1** (*pinch*) щипо́к. **2** (*small bite*) уку́с; **the puppy gave his finger a ~** щено́к укуси́л его́ за па́лец. **3** (*of frost*): **there's a ~ in the air today** сего́дня (моро́з) пощи́пывает. **4** (*of liquor etc.*) рю́мочка.

● *v.t.* (**nipped, nipping**) **1** (*pinch*) щип|а́ть, -ну́ть; **his fingers were ~ped in the door** ему́ прищеми́ло па́льцы две́рью. **2** (*bite*) укуси́ть, кусну́ть (*both pf.*). **3** (*of frost etc.*) щип|а́ть, -ну́ть; **the blossom was ~ped by the frost** за́морозки поби́ли ра́нний цвет; **~ something in the bud** (*fig.*) подави́ть (*pf.*) что-н. в заро́дыше. **4**: **~ off** отку́с|ывать, -и́ть.

● *v.i.* (**nipped, nipping**) **1** (*pinch*) щипа́ться (*impf.*); **a crab can ~ quite severely** краб о́чень бо́льно щи́плется. **2** (*strike cold*) щипа́ть (*impf.*). **3** (*Br., usu. with advs., move smartly*): **I must ~ along to the shop** мне ну́жно сбе́гать в магази́н; **he ~ped in just ahead of me** он заскочи́л как раз пе́редо мной; **he ~ped off home** он удра́л домо́й; **I'll (just) ~ on ahead** я побегу́ вперёд; **he ~ped out to have a smoke** он вы́скочил покури́ть.

nipper /'nɪpə(r)/ *n.* (*claw*) клешня́; (*pl., pincers*) клещ|и́ (*pl., g.* -е́й); (*sl., child*) малы́ш, кро́шка.

nipple /'nɪp(ə)l/ *n.* (*of breast*) сосо́к; (*of feeding-bottle*) со́ска; (*tech.*) ни́ппель (*m.*).

nippy /'nɪpɪ/ *adj.* (**nippier, nippiest**) **1** (*nimble*) прово́рный. **2** (*chilly*): **a ~ wind** ре́зкий ве́тер; **the weather is ~** моро́зит.

nirvana /nɜː'vɑːnə/, /nɪə-/ *n.* нирва́на.

nisi /'naɪsaɪ/ *conj.*: **decree ~** усло́вный разво́д.

nit /nɪt/ *n.* гни́да; (*Br. sl., fool*) о́лух (*coll.*).

● *cpds.* **~-pick** *v.i.* (*sl.*) придира́ться (*impf.*) к мелоча́м; **~-picking** *adj.* приди́рчивый.

niter /'naɪtə(r)/ (*US*) = **nitre**

nitrate /'naɪtreɪt/ *n.* соль/эфи́р азо́тной кислоты́; (*fertilizer*) нитра́т; **copper ~** азотноки́слая медь.

nitre /'naɪtə(r)/ (*US* **niter**) *n.* сели́тра.

nitric /'naɪtrɪk/ *adj.* азо́тный; **~ acid** азо́тная кислота́; **~ oxide** о́кись азо́та.

nitrogen /'naɪtrədʒ(ə)n/ *n.* азо́т.

● *adj.* азо́тный.

nitrogenous /,naɪ'trɒdʒɪnəs/ *adj.* азо́тный.

nitroglycerine /,naɪtrəʊ'glɪsəriːn/ *n.* нитроглицери́н.

nitrous /'naɪtrəs/ *adj.* азо́тистый; **~ acid** азо́тистая кислота́; **~ oxide** за́кись азо́та.

nitty-gritty /,nɪtɪ'grɪtɪ/ *n.* (*sl.*) суть де́ла; дета́ли (*f. pl.*); ку́хня (*coll.*); **the ~ of politics** полити́ческая ку́хня.

nitwit /'nɪtwɪt/ *n.* о́лух (*coll.*).

no /nəʊ/ *n.* (*pl.* **noes**) (*refusal*) отка́з; (*vote against*) го́лос про́тив; **the ~es have it** большинство́ (голосо́в) про́тив.

● *adj.* **1** (*not any*) никако́й; **there's ~ food in the house** в до́ме нет (никако́й) еды́; **~ two people are alike** нет двух одина́ковых люде́й; **it's ~ use complaining** нет (никако́го) смы́сла жа́ловаться; **~ doubt** несомне́нно; **~ end of something** о́чень мно́го чего́-н., бесконе́чно мно́го чего́-н.; **in ~ way** (*not at all*) ничу́ть; нисколько; **it's ~ go** не вы́йдет/пойдёт (*coll.*); **~ way** (*coll., certainly not*) ни в ко́ем слу́чае; **~ words can describe ...** слова́ беси́льны описа́ть...; **there is ~ question of that** об э́том не мо́жет быть и ре́чи; **they are in ~ way alike** они́ ни в чём не похо́жи; **~ man, ~ one** никто́; **I spoke to ~ one** я ни с кем не говори́л; **~ one was there** там никого́ не́ было; **~ one man can do this** в одино́чку э́то никому́ не под си́лу; *see also* ⇒**nobody.** **2** (*not a; quite other than*) не; **he's ~ fool** он (во́все) не дура́к; он совсе́м не глуп; **he's ~ friend of mine** он мне отню́дь не друг; **it's ~ distance at all** э́то совсе́м недалеко́; **in ~ time** (*very quickly*) в коро́ткий срок, в два счёта (*coll.*). **3** (*expr. refusal or prohibition*): **~ children!** де́ти не допуска́ются!; **~ smoking** кури́ть воспреща́ется; **~ talking!** разгова́ривать воспреща́ется!; **~ entry** вход воспрещён; нет вхо́да.

● *adv.* (*with comps., not at all, in no way*) не; **~ better than before** ничу́ть не лу́чше, чем ра́ньше; **he is ~ less than a scoundrel** он про́сто-на́просто подле́ц; **he gave him ~ less than 10,000** он дал ему́ це́лых де́сять ты́сяч; **we met the president, ~ less** мы да́же ви́дели само́го президе́нта; **he ~ longer lives there** он бо́льше там не живёт; **I have ~ more to say** мне бо́льше не́чего сказа́ть; **there is ~ more bread** хле́ба бо́льше нет; **he is ~ more a professor than I am** он тако́й же профе́ссор, как я; **~ sooner said than done!** ска́зано — сде́лано!; **~ sooner had he said it than ...** не успе́л он сказа́ть, как...

● *particle* **1** (*in replies*) нет; **~ thank you** нет, спаси́бо; **he can never say ~ to an invitation** он никогда́ не отка́зывается от приглаше́ния; **he will not take ~ for an answer** он не при́мет отка́за; (*after negative statement or question, sometimes*) да; **'You don't like him, do you?' — 'No, I don't'** «Вам ведь он не нра́вится?» — «Да, не нра́вится»; **'He's not a nice man' — 'No, he isn't'** «Он челове́к нева́жный» — «Да, нева́жный». **2** (*expr. incredulity*): **~!** не мо́жет быть!

● *cpds.* **~-fly** *adj.*: **~-fly zone** запре́тная возду́шная зо́на; **~-go** *adj.*: **~-go area** (*Br.*) запре́тная о́бласть; **~-good** *adj.* никчёмный; **~-man's-land** *n.* ниче́йная земля́; нейтра́льная зо́на; **~-one** *pron.*: *see* ⇒**no** *adj.* 1, **nobody; ~-show** *n.* (*person*) нея́вившийся пассажи́р.

No. /'nʌmbə(r)/ *n.* (*abbr. of* **number**) №.

nob /nɒb/ *n.* (*Br. sl., bigwig*) (больша́я) ши́шка.

nobble /'nɒb(ə)l/ *v.t.* (*Br. sl.*) **1** (*horse*) по́ртить, ис-. **2** (*bribe*) подма́з|ывать, -ать; подкуп|а́ть, -и́ть.

Nobel prize /'nəʊbel/, /-'bel/ *n.* Нобе́левская пре́мия (**for**: в о́бласти +*g.*).

nobility /nəʊ'bɪlɪtɪ/ *n.* (*quality*) благоро́дство; (*titled class*) дворя́нство.

noble /'nəʊb(ə)l/ *n.* дворя|ни́н (*fem.* -я́нка).

● *adj.* (**nobler, noblest**) **1** (*of character or conduct*) благоро́дный. **2** (*belonging to the nobility*) дворя́нский; **of ~ birth** дворя́нского происхожде́ния. **3** (*imposing, impressive*)

N

внуши́тельный; (*majestic*) велича́вый; (*excellent*) превосхо́дный. **4**: ~ **metal** благоро́дный мета́лл.

● *cpds.* ~**man** *n.* дворяни́н; ~**-minded** *adj.* великоду́шный, благоро́дный; ~**-mindedness** *n.* (душе́вное) благоро́дство; ~**woman** *n.* дворя́нка.

noblesse /nəʊ'bles/ *n.*: ~ ***oblige*** положе́ние обя́зывает.

nobody /'nəʊbədɪ/ *n.* ничто́жный челове́к, ничто́жество.

● *pron.* (*also* **no(-)one**) никто́ (. . . не); ~ **knows** никто́ не зна́ет; **there was** ~ **present** никого́ не́ было; **it's** ~**'s business but his own** э́то никого́ не каса́ется, кро́ме его́ самого́; *see also* ⇒**no** *adj.* 1

nocturnal /nɒk'tɜ:n(ə)l/ *adj.* ночно́й.

nocturne /'nɒktɜ:n/ *n.* ноктю́рн.

nod /nɒd/ *n.* киво́к; **give a** ~ **of the head to s.o.** кив|а́ть, -ну́ть голово́й кому́-н.; **he was given the job on the** ~ (*Br.*) он получи́л рабо́ту с ходу́; **to pass a motion on the** ~ (*Br.*) приня́ть (*pf.*) предложе́ние без голосова́ния; **the land of** ~ (*joc.*) со́нное ца́рство.

● *v.t.* (**nodded, nodding**): ~ **one's head** кив|а́ть, -ну́ть; ~ **assent** кив|а́ть, -ну́ть в знак согла́сия.

● *v.i.* (**nodded, nodding**) **1** кив|а́ть, -ну́ть; **he** ~**ded to me in the street** он кивну́л мне на у́лице; **a** ~**ding acquaintance** ша́почное знако́мство. **2** (*become drowsy*) клева́ть (*impf.*) но́сом (*coll.*); **he** ~**ded off during the lecture** он задрема́л на ле́кции.

node /nəʊd/ *n.* (*bot., phys.*) у́зел; (*astron., math.*) то́чка пересече́ния.

nodule /'nɒdju:l/ *n.* (*bot., med.*) узело́к.

noggin /'nɒgɪn/ *n.* кру́жечка.

noise /nɔɪz/ *n.* **1** (*din*) шум; **make a** ~ шуме́ть, за-; **don't make so much** ~**!** не шуми́те так! **2** (*sound*) звук; **can you hear a funny** ~**?** вы слы́шите э́тот стра́нный звук?; **he made sympathetic** ~**s** (*coll.*) он подава́л сочу́вственные сигна́лы. **3**: **a big** ~ (*coll.*) ши́шка. **4** (*elec., TV, radio*) поме́хи (*f. pl.*).

● *v.t.*: ~ **abroad** распростран|я́ть, -и́ть.

noiseless /'nɔɪzlɪs/ *adj.* бесшу́мный.

noisiness /'nɔɪzɪnɪs/ *n.* (*of person*) шумли́вость; (*of sound, machine*) гро́мкость.

noisome /'nɔɪsəm/ *adj.* (*harmful*) вре́дный; (*fetid*) злово́нный; (*offensive*) отврати́тельный.

noisy /'nɔɪzɪ/ *adj.* (**noisier, noisiest**) (*of thing*) шу́мный; **a** ~ **party** шу́мная вечери́нка; **your engine sounds** ~ у вас шуми́т мото́р; (*of person*) шумли́вый; ~ **laughter** гро́мкий смех.

nomad /'nəʊmæd/ *n.* коче́вник; (*attr.*) кочево́й.

nomadic /nəʊ'mædɪk/ *adj.* кочево́й; **lead a** ~ **life** кочева́ть (*impf.*); вести́ (*impf.*) кочево́й о́браз жи́зни.

nom de plume /ˌnɒm də 'plu:m/ *n.* (*pl.* ***noms de plume*** *pronunc. same*) псевдони́м.

nomenclature /nəʊ'menklətʃə(r)/, /'nəʊmənˌkleɪtʃə(r)/ *n.* номенклату́ра.

nominal /'nɒmɪn(ə)l/ *adj.* номина́льный.

nominate /'nɒmɪˌneɪt/ *v.t.* (*appoint, e.g. date, place, person*) назн|ача́ть, -а́чить; (*propose, e.g. candidate*) выставля́ть, вы́ставить кандидату́ру +*g.*

nomination /ˌnɒmɪ'neɪʃ(ə)n/ *n.* назначе́ние; выставле́ние кандидату́ры; **how many** ~**s are there for chairman?** ско́лько вы́ставлено кандида́тов на пост председа́теля?; (*for an award*) номина́ция.

nominative /'nɒmɪnətɪv/ *n.* (~ **case**) имени́тельный паде́ж.

● *adj.* имени́тельный.

nominee /ˌnɒmɪ'ni:/ *n.* кандида́т; (*for a prize*) номина́нт.

non- /nɒn/ *pref.* не. . .

non-addictive /ˌnɒnə'dɪktɪv/ *adj.* не вызыва́ющий привыка́ния, не вырaба́тывающий зави́симости.

non-aggression /ˌnɒnə'greʃ(ə)n/ *n.*: ~ **pact** догово́р о ненападе́нии.

non-alcoholic /ˌnɒnælkə'hɒlɪk/ *adj.* безалкого́льный.

non-aligned /ˌnɒnə'laɪnd/ *adj.* (*pol.*) неприсоедини́вшийся (к бло́кам).

non-alignment /ˌnɒnə'laɪnmənt/ *n.* поли́тика неприсоедине́ния.

non-appearance /ˌnɒnə'pɪərəns/ *n.* нея́вка.

non-attendance /ˌnɒnə'tend(ə)ns/ *n.* непосеще́ние, нея́вка.

non-believer /ˌnɒnbɪ'li:və(r)/ *n.* неве́рующий.

non-belligerency /ˌnɒnbə'lɪdʒərənsɪ/ *n.* неуча́стие в войне́.

non-belligerent /ˌnɒnbə'lɪdʒərənt/ *n.* & *adj.* не уча́ствующий в войне́; нево́юющий.

non-biodegradable /ˌnɒnbaɪəʊdɪ'greɪdəb(ə)l/ *adj.* не разлага́емый микрооргани́змами.

nonce /nɒns/ *n.*: **for the** ~ для да́нного слу́чая; на э́то вре́мя.

● *cpd.* ~**-word** *n.* (*ling.*) окказиона́льное сло́во.

nonchalance /'nɒnʃələns/ *n.* беззабо́тность; безразли́чие.

nonchalant /'nɒnʃələnt/ *adj.* (*carefree*) беззабо́тный; (*indifferent*) безразли́чный.

non-combatant /nɒn'kɒmbət(ə)nt/ *n.* (*non-fighting soldier*) нестроево́й солда́т; (*pl., civilians*) гражда́нское населе́ние.

● *adj.* небоево́й; (*of units*) нестроево́й.

non-commissioned /ˌnɒnkə'mɪʃ(ə)nd/ *adj.*: ~ **officer** сержа́нт; военнослу́жащий сержа́нтского соста́ва.

non-committal /ˌnɒnkə'mɪt(ə)l/ *adj.* (*evasive*) укло́нчивый.

non-compliance /ˌnɒnkəm'plaɪəns/ *n.*: ~ **with regulations** несоблюде́ние пра́вил.

non compos mentis /ˌnɒn kɒmpɒs 'mentɪs/ *adj.* невменя́емый.

non-conducting /ˌnɒnkən'dʌktɪŋ/ *adj.* непроводя́щий.

non-conductor /ˌnɒnkən'dʌktə(r)/ *n.* непроводни́к.

nonconformist /ˌnɒnkən'fɔ:mɪst/ *n.* нонконформи́ст (*fem.* -ка), челове́к незави́симых взгля́дов; (*pol.*) инакомы́слящий; (*relig.*, **N.**) нонконформи́ст (*fem.* -ка), секта́нт, раско́льник.

● *adj.* неконфо́рмный; незави́симый; секта́нтский.

nonconformity /ˌnɒnkən'fɔ:mɪtɪ/ *n.* несоблюде́ние (пра́вил), неподчине́ние; (*relig.*) секта́нтство, раско́л.

non-contributory /ˌnɒnkən'trɪbjʊtərɪ/ *adj.* не тре́бующий взно́сов.

non-cooperation /ˌnɒnkəʊˌɒpə'reɪʃ(ə)n/ *n.* (*lack of cooperation*) нежела́ние сотру́дничать; (*failure to cooperate*) отка́з от сотру́дничества.

non-delivery /ˌnɒndɪ'lɪvərɪ/ *n.* (*of mail, goods*) недоста́вка.

nondescript /'nɒndɪskrɪpt/ *adj.* невзра́чный, безли́чный.

none /nʌn/ *pron.* (*person*) никто́; ~ **of us is perfect** никто́ из на́с не явля́ется соверше́нством; **I saw** ~ **of the people I wanted to** я не ви́дел никого́ из ну́жных мне люде́й; **it was** ~ **other than Smith himself** э́то был не кто ино́й, как Смит; ~ **of the people died** ни оди́н челове́к не у́мер; (*thing*) ничто́; **there is** ~ **of it left** из э́того ничего́ не оста́лось; ~ **of this is mine** ничто́ из э́того мне не принадлежи́т; ~ **of the books is red** среди́ э́тих книг нет ни одно́й кра́сной; ~ **of the houses collapsed** ни оди́н дом не ру́хнул; ~ **of the exhibition is worth seeing** на вы́ставке нет ничего́ сто́ящего; **it's better than** ~ **at all** э́то лу́чше, чем ничего́; **he would have** ~ **of it** он и слу́шать не хоте́л; ~ **of that!** так не пойдёт!; дово́льно!; ~ **of your impudence!** без де́рзостей, пожа́луйста!; **it's** ~ **of your business** э́то не ва́ше де́ло; **you have money and I have** ~ у вас есть де́ньги, а у меня́ нет.

● *adv.*: **I feel** ~ **the better for seeing the doctor** по́сле визи́та к врачу́ мне ниско́лько/ничу́ть не лу́чше; **he is** ~ **the worse for his accident** он ничу́ть не пострада́л по́сле ава́рии; **the pay is** ~ **too high** пла́та отню́дь не высо́кая; ~ **the less** тем не ме́нее.

nonentity /nɒ'nentɪtɪ/ *n.* (*person*) ничто́жество.

non-essential /ˌnɒnɪ'senʃ(ə)l/ *n.* несуще́ственная вещь.

● *adj.* несуще́ственный.

non-European /ˌnɒnjʊərə'pɪən/ *n.* неевропе́|ец (*fem.* -йка).

● *adj.* неевропе́йский.

non-event /ˌnɒnɪ'vent/ *n.* собы́тие сомни́тельной ва́жности.

non-existence /ˌnɒnɪg'zɪst(ə)ns/ *n.* небытие́.

non-existent /ˌnɒnɪg'zɪst(ə)nt/ *adj.* несуществу́ющий.

non-ferrous /nɒn'ferəs/ *adj.*: ~ **metals** цветны́е мета́ллы.

non-fiction /nɒnˈfɪkʃ(ə)n/ *n.* документа́льная про́за/литерату́ра.

non-flammable /nɒnˈflæməb(ə)l/ *adj.* невоспламеня́ющийся.

non-fulfilment /ˌnɒnfʊlˈfɪlmənt/ *n.* невыполне́ние.

non-interference /ˌnɒnɪntəˈfɪərəns/ *n.* невмеша́тельство.

non-intervention /ˌnɒnɪntəˈvenʃ(ə)n/ *n.* невмеша́тельство.

non-member /nɒnˈmembə(r)/ *n.* нечле́н.

non-metal /nɒnˈmet(ə)l/ *n.* немета́лл, металло́ид.

non-metallic /ˌnɒnmɪˈtælɪk/ *adj.* неметалли́ческий.

non-negotiable /ˌnɒnnɪˈgəʊʃəb(ə)l/ *adj.* (*comm.*) непередава́емый, необраща́ющийся; (*not for discussion*) не подлежа́щий обсужде́нию.

non-nuclear /nɒnˈnju:klɪə(r)/ *adj.* нея́дерный; (*State*) не облада́ющий я́дерным ору́жием; (*of zone, area*) безъя́дерный; (*of weapons*) обы́чный, нея́дерный.

non-observance /ˌnɒnəbˈzɜ:v(ə)ns/ *n.* несоблюде́ние, невыполне́ние, наруше́ние.

no-nonsense /ˌnəʊˈnɒns(ə)ns/ *adj.* (*serious*) серьёзный, нешу́точный (*coll.*); (*business-like*) делово́й; (*strict*) стро́гий.

nonpareil /ˈnɒnpər(ə)l/, /ˌnɒnpəˈreɪl/ *n.* (*perfect specimen*) верх соверше́нства; идеа́л.

non-party /nɒnˈpɑ:tɪ/ *adj.* беспарти́йный.

non-payment /nɒnˈpeɪmənt/ *n.* неупла́та, невы́плата.

nonplus /nɒnˈplʌs/ *v.t.* (**nonplussed, nonplussing**) прив|оди́ть, -ести́ в замеша́тельство; сму|ща́ть, -ти́ть.

non-political /ˌnɒnpəˈlɪtɪk(ə)l/ *adj.* неполити́ческий.

non-polluting /ˌnɒnpəˈlu:tɪŋ/ *adj.* экологи́чески чи́стый; не загрязня́ющий окружа́ющую среду́.

non-productive /ˌnɒnprəˈdʌktɪv/ *adj.* непроизводи́тельный.

non-profit(-making) /nɒnˈprɒfɪtˌmeɪkɪŋ/ *adj.* некомме́рческий.

non-proliferation /ˌnɒnprəˌlɪfəˈreɪʃ(ə)n/ *n.* нераспростране́ние (я́дерного ору́жия).

non-recognition /ˌnɒnrekəgˈnɪʃ(ə)n/ *n.* непризна́ние.

non-renewable /ˌnɒnrɪˈnju:əb(ə)l/ *adj.* невозобновля́емый.

non-residence /nɒnˈrezɪd(ə)ns/ *n.* непрожива́ние (где-н.).

non-resident /nɒnˈrezɪd(ə)nt/ *n.* & *adj.* непрожива́ющий (где-н.); прие́зжий.

non-resistance /ˌnɒnrɪˈzɪst(ə)ns/ *n.* непротивле́ние (*кому/чему*).

non-resistant /ˌnɒnrɪˈzɪst(ə)nt/ *adj.* (*person*) не ока́зывающий сопротивле́ния; (*material*) неусто́йчивый.

non-sectarian /ˌnɒnsekˈteərɪən/ *adj.* включа́ющий все рели́гии.

nonsense /ˈnɒns(ə)ns/ *n.* **1** (*something without meaning*) бессмы́слица; (*rubbish*) вздор; ерунда́ (*coll.*); чепуха́ (*coll.*); **talk ~** говори́ть (*impf.*) вздор/ерунду́. **2** (*foolish conduct*) глу́пость; **let's have no more ~!** хва́тит валя́ть дурака́!; **what ~ is this?** э́то что за глу́пости!

nonsensical /nɒnˈsensɪk(ə)l/ *adj.* бессмы́сленный; неле́пый, глу́пый.

non sequitur /nɒn ˈsekwɪtə(r)/ *n.* нелоги́чное заключе́ние.

non-skid /nɒnˈskɪd/ *adj.* небуксу́ющий.

non-slip /nɒnˈslɪp/ *adj.* нескользкий.

non-smoker /nɒnˈsməʊkə(r)/ *n.* (*person*) некуря́щий; (*Br., compartment*) *see* ⇒**non-smoking**

non-smoking /nɒnˈsməʊkɪŋ/ *adj.*: **~ compartment** купе́ (*indecl.*) для некуря́щих.

non-starter /nɒnˈstɑ:tə(r)/ *n.* (*coll.*) до́хлый но́мер, до́хлое де́ло.

non-stick /nɒnˈstɪk/ *adj.*: **a ~ saucepan** кастрю́ля с непригора́ющим покры́тием.

non-stop /nɒnˈstɒp/ *adj.* **1** (*of train or coach*) иду́щий/е́дущий без остано́вок; (*of aircraft or flight*) беспоса́дочный. **2** (*continuous*) непреры́вный.

● *adv.* **1** беспоса́дочно; без остано́вок. **2**: **he talks ~** он говори́т без у́молку.

nonsuit /nɒnˈsju:t/, /-ˈsu:t/ *v.t.*: **~ a plaintiff** прекра|ща́ть, -ти́ть иск.

non-swimmer /nɒnˈswɪmə(r)/ *n.* не уме́ющий пла́вать; **she's a ~** она́ не уме́ет пла́вать.

non-transferable /ˌnɒntrænsˈfɜ:rəb(ə)l/ *adj.* не подлежа́щий переда́че (друго́му).

non-U /nɒnˈju:/ *adj.* (*Br.*) просте́цкий; (*pej.*) плебе́йский.

non-union /nɒnˈju:nɪən/ *adj.*: **he employs ~ labour** (*Br.*), **labor** (*US*) он принима́ет на рабо́ту не чле́нов профсою́за.

non-violence /nɒnˈvaɪələns/ *n.* отка́з от примене́ния наси́лия/наси́льственных ме́тодов.

non-violent /nɒnˈvaɪələnt/ *adj.* ненаси́льственный.

non-white /nɒnˈwaɪt/ *n.* & *adj.* (*of race*) цветно́й.

noodles /ˈnu:d(ə)lz/ *n. pl.* (*cul.*) лапша́.

nook /nʊk/ *n.* уголо́к; **I searched every ~ and cranny** я обша́рил ка́ждый уголо́к.

noon /nu:n/ *n.* (*also* **~day, ~tide, ~time, high ~**) по́лдень (*m.*); **at ~** в по́лдень; **12 ~** двена́дцать часо́в дня; (*attr.*) полу́денный, полдне́вный.

noose /nu:s/ *n.* (*loop*) пе́тля; (*lasso*) арка́н; **put one's head in the ~** (*fig.*) лезть (*impf.*) в пе́тлю.

nor /nɔ:(r)/, /nə(r)/ *conj.*: **they had neither arms ~ provisions** у них не́ было ни ору́жия, ни провиа́нта; **he can't do it, ~ can I** он не мо́жет э́того сде́лать, да и я то́же; **you are not well, ~ am I** вам нездоро́вится, и мне то́же; **I said I had not seen him, ~ had I** я сказа́л, что не ви́дел его́, и э́то пра́вда; **he had neither the means ~, apparently, the inclination** у него́ не́ было средств, да, похо́же, и жела́ния; **~ will I deny that ...** не ста́ну та́кже отрица́ть, что...; **~ is this all** и э́то ещё не всё.

Nordic /ˈnɔ:dɪk/ *adj.* (*north-European*) норди́ческий; (*Scandinavian*) скандина́вский.

norm /nɔ:m/ *n.* но́рма, пра́вило.

normal /ˈnɔ:m(ə)l/ *adj.* (*regular, standard*) норма́льный; **it is ~ weather for the time of year** э́то обы́чная/норма́льная пого́да для э́того вре́мени го́да; (*usual*) обы́чный; **I ~ly use the bus** обы́чно я е́зду авто́бусом; (*sane, well-balanced*) норма́льный.

normal|cy /ˈnɔ:məlsɪ/, **-ity** /nɔ:ˈmælɪtɪ/ *nn.* норма́льность; обы́чное состоя́ние.

normalization /ˌnɔ:məlaɪˈzeɪʃ(ə)n/ *n.* нормализа́ция.

normalize /ˈnɔ:məˌlaɪz/ *v.t.* нормализова́ть (*impf., pf.*).

● *v.i.* нормализова́ться (*impf., pf.*).

Norman /ˈnɔ:mən/ *n.* норма́нд|ец (*fem.* -ка).

● *adj.* норма́ндский; **the ~ Conquest** Норма́ндское завоева́ние А́нглии; **~ architecture** рома́нский стиль в архитекту́ре.

Normandy /ˈnɔ:məndɪ/ *n.* Норма́ндия.

normative /ˈnɔ:mətɪv/ *adj.* нормати́вный.

Norse /nɔ:s/ *n.*: **Old ~** древнескандина́вский язы́к.

● *adj.* норма́ннский.

● *cpd.* **~man** *n.* норма́нн; (*Russian hist.*) варя́г.

north /nɔ:θ/ *n.* се́вер; (*naut.*) норд; **the far ~** Кра́йний Се́вер; **the ~ of England** се́вер А́нглии/се́верная часть А́нглии; **the ~ of Europe** Се́верная Евро́па; **in the ~** на се́вере; **from the ~** с се́вера; **to the ~** на се́вер; **to the ~ of** к се́веру от + *g.*; се́вернее + *g.*; **magnetic ~** се́верный магни́тный по́люс; **~ by east/west** норд-тень-ост/вест.

● *adj.* се́верный; **N~ America** Се́верная Аме́рика; **N~ American** (*n.*) североамерика́н|ец (*fem.* -ка); (*adj.*) североамерика́нский; **the ~ country** се́верная А́нглия; **N~ Pole** Се́верный по́люс; **N~ Sea** Се́верное мо́ре; **N~ star** Поля́рная звезда́.

● *adv.*: **we went ~** мы пое́хали на се́вер;

● *cpds.* **~bound** *adj.* направля́ющийся на се́вер; **~countryman** *n.* уроже́нец се́верной А́нглии; **~-east** *n.* се́веро-восто́к; (*naut.*) норд-о́ст; *adj.* (*also* **~-easterly, ~-eastern**) се́веро-восто́чный; **~-east wind** (*also* **~-easter** *n.*) норд-о́ст; *adv.* (*also* **~-easterly, ~-eastward**) к се́веро-восто́ку; на се́веро-восто́к; **~-west** *n.* се́веро-за́пад; (*naut.*) норд-ве́ст; *adj.* (*also* **~-westerly, ~-western**) се́веро-за́падный; **~-west wind** (*also* **~-wester(ly)** *nn.*) норд-ве́ст; *adv.* (*also* **~-westerly,**

~-westward) к се́веро-за́паду; на се́веро-за́пад.

northerly /ˈnɔːðəlɪ/ *n.* (*wind*) се́верный ве́тер.

● *adj.* се́верный.

northern /ˈnɔːð(ə)n/ *adj.* се́верный; **~ Ireland** Се́верная Ирла́ндия; **~ Irish** североирла́ндский; **~ lights** се́верное сия́ние.

northerner /ˈnɔːðənə(r)/ *n.* северя́н|ин (*fem.* -ка).

northernmost /ˈnɔːðən,məʊst/ *adj.* са́мый се́верный.

northward /ˈnɔːθwəd/ *n.*: **to ~** к се́веру.

● *adj.* се́верный.

● *adv.* на се́вер.

Norway /ˈnɔːweɪ/ *n.* Норве́гия.

Norwegian /nɔːˈwiːdʒ(ə)n/ *n.* (*person*) норве́ж|ец (*fem.* -ка); (*language*) норве́жский язы́к.

● *adj.* норве́жский.

nose /nəʊz/ *n.* **1** нос; (*dim.*) но́сик; **my ~ is bleeding** у меня́ идёт кровь и́з носу; **his ~ is running** у него́ на́сморк; **I have a stuffy ~** у меня́ заложи́ло нос; **with one's ~ in the air** (*fig.*) задра́в нос; **as plain as the ~ on your face** я́сно как два́жды два — четы́ре; **blow one's ~** сморка́ться, вы-; **bury one's ~ in a book** уткну́ться (*pf.*) но́сом в кни́гу; **cut off one's ~ to spite one's face** с доса́ды сде́лать (*pf.*) ху́же себе́; **follow one's ~** (*go straight ahead*) идти́ (*det.*) пря́мо (вперёд); (*be guided by instinct*) руково́дствоваться (*impf.*) интуи́цией/чутьём; **hold one's ~** заж|има́ть, -а́ть нос; **keep one's ~ clean** (*coll., avoid trouble*) держа́ться (*impf.*) пода́льше от греха́; **keep your ~ out of my business!** не су́йте нос в мои́ дела́; **keep one's ~ to the grindstone** не отрыва́ться (*impf.*) от де́ла; рабо́тать (*impf.*) не покладая́ рук; **keep s.o.'s ~ to the grindstone** не дава́ть (*impf.*) кому́-н. ни о́тдыху, ни сро́ку; **lead s.o. by the ~** вести́ (*det.*) кого́-н. на поводу́; **look down one's ~ at s.o.** смотре́ть, по- свысока́ на кого́-н.; **pay through the ~** плати́ть, за- втри́дорога; **poke one's ~ into something** сова́ть, су́нуть нос во что-н.; **punch s.o. on the ~** да|ва́ть, -ть кому́-н. по́ носу; **put s.o.'s ~ out of joint** ≈ утира́ть, утере́ть нос кому́-н.; **rub s.o.'s ~ in something** ты́кать, ткнуть кого́-н. но́сом во что-н.; **he can see no further than his ~** он да́льше своего́ но́са не ви́дит; **talk through one's ~** говори́ть (*impf.*) в нос; **turn up one's ~ at something** вороти́ть (*impf.*) нос от чего́-н.; **under one's ~** под са́мым но́сом; **he stole the purse from under my ~** он укра́л у меня́ кошелёк из-под но́са.
2 (*sense of smell; also fig., flair*) нюх, чутьё; **my dog has a good ~** у мое́й соба́ки хоро́ший нюх/хоро́шее чутьё; **he has a ~ for gossip** у него́ настоя́щий нюх на спле́тни.
3 (*of car, aircraft etc.*) нос; **they were driving ~ to tail** они́ е́хали вплотну́ю друг за дру́гом/ба́мпер в ба́мпер.
4 (*of wine*) буке́т.

● *v.t.* **1** (*of animals, smell*) чу́ять (*impf.*). **2** (*nuzzle*) ты́каться, ткну́ться но́сом в + *a.*
3: **~ one's way** проб|ира́ться, -ра́ться; **the ship ~d her way through the channel** кора́бль ме́дленно шёл по фарва́теру.
4: **~ into** (*pry, meddle*) сова́ться, су́нуться (*or* сова́ть, су́нуть нос) (*impf.*) в + *a.*

● *with advs.*: **~ about** *v.i.* (*sniff, smell*) ню́хать (*impf.*); **the dog ~d about the room** соба́ка обню́хивала ко́мнату; **~ out** *v.t.* (*of animals*) учу́ять (*pf.*); разню́х|ивать, -ать; оты́ск|ивать, -а́ть чутьём; (*fig.*) разню́х|ивать, -ать, разве́д|ывать, -ать.

● *cpds.* **~-bag** *n.* то́рба; **~-bleed** *n.*: **he has frequent ~-bleeds** у него́ ча́сто идёт кровь из но́са; **~-cone** *n.* (*of rocket etc.*) носово́й ко́нус; **~-dive** *n.* пики́рование, пике́ (*indecl.*); **prices took a ~-dive** це́ны ре́зко упа́ли; *v.i.* пики́ровать (*impf., pf.*); **~gay** *n.* буке́т души́стых цвето́в.

noseless /ˈnəʊzlɪs/ *adj.* безно́сый.

nosey /ˈnəʊzɪ/ = **nosy**

nosh /nɒʃ/ *n.* жратва́ (*sl.*).

nostalgia /nɒˈstældʒɪə/, /-dʒə/ *n.* ностальги́я.

nostalgic /nɒˈstældʒɪk/ *adj.* (*person*) тоску́ющий; (*thing*) ностальги́ческий, вызыва́ющий воспомина́ния.

nostril /ˈnɒstrɪl/ *n.* ноздря́.

no-strings /nəʊˈstrɪŋz/ *adj.* (*coll.*): **~ agreement** безусло́вный догово́р.

nostrum /ˈnɒstrəm/ *n.* (*lit., fig.*) панаце́я.

nos|y, -ey /ˈnəʊzɪ/ *adj.* (**nosier, nosiest**) (*coll.*) любопы́тный.

not /nɒt/ *adv.* **1** не; (*as pred.*) нет; **it is my book, ~ yours** э́то моя́ кни́га, а не ва́ша; **~ till after dinner** то́лько по́сле обе́да; **she is ~ here** её здесь нет.
2 (*elliptical phrr.*): **guilty or ~, he is my son** вино́вен он и́ли нет, а он мой сын; **if it's fine, we'll go, but if ~ we'll stay here** е́сли бу́дет хоро́шая пого́да, мы пое́дем, а е́сли нет — оста́немся здесь; **we must hurry, if ~ we may be late** на́до потора́пливаться, а (не) то опозда́ем; **whether or ~** так и́ли ина́че; **I hope ~** наде́юсь, что нет; **'Are you afraid?' — 'I should say ~!'** «Вы бои́тесь?» — «Да ничу́ть!».
3 (**~ *even***): **~ one of them moved** ни оди́н из них не подви́нулся; **there's ~ a drop left** не оста́лось ни (одно́й) ка́пли; **~ a day passed without ...** и дня не проходи́ло без (того́, что́бы)...; **'Have you heard any news?' — 'N~ a thing'** «Вы слы́шали каки́е-нибу́дь но́вости?» — «Никаки́х».
4 (*litotes*): **~ a few** мно́гие, дово́льно мно́го; **~ infrequently** дово́льно ча́сто; **~ unconnected with ...** име́ющий не́которую связь с + *i.*; **'Was he annoyed?' — 'N~ half!'** «Он рассерди́лся?» — «Ещё как!».
5 (**~ *at all***): **'Do you mind if I smoke?' — 'N~ at all!'** «Вы не возража́ете, е́сли я закурю́?» — «Ниско́лько/ничу́ть»; **'Many thanks!' — 'N~ at all!'** «Большо́е спаси́бо!» — «Не сто́ит! (*or* Пожа́луйста!)»; **it's ~ at all clear** совсе́м/во́все не я́сно.
6 (*introducing concession*): **it's ~ that I don't want to, I can't** я не то что́бы не хочу́, а не могу́; **(it is) ~ that I fear him, but ...** я не то что́бы его́ боя́лся, а....
7 (*var. phrr.*): **~ for the world** ни за что на све́те; **~ on your life** ни в ко́ем слу́чае; **~ really!** (*not very much*) (пожа́луй) не о́чень; (*when disbelieving*) да нет!; не мо́жет быть!; **~ in the least** ничу́ть; ниско́лько; **he's ~ much of an actor** он нева́жный (*or* так себе́) актёр.

notability /,nəʊtəˈbɪlɪtɪ/ *n.* знамени́тость.

notable /ˈnəʊtəb(ə)l/ *n.* знамени́тость.

● *adj.* (*perceptible*) заме́тный; (*worthy of note, remarkable*) замеча́тельный; (*eminent, outstanding*) ви́дный, выдаю́щийся; (*well-known*) изве́стный; (*celebrated*) знамени́тый; (*noteworthy*) достопримеча́тельный; (*famed, renowned*) сла́вящийся, изве́стный (*чем*); **a city ~ for its buildings** го́род, сла́вящийся свое́й архитекту́рой.

notably /ˈnəʊtəblɪ/ *adv.* осо́бенно; в осо́бенности; (*perceptibly*) заме́тно.

notary /ˈnəʊtərɪ/ *n.* (*also* **~ public**) нота́риус.

notation /nəʊˈteɪʃ(ə)n/ *n.* нота́ция; **musical ~** но́тное письмо́.

notch /nɒtʃ/ *n.* зару́бка.

● *v.t.* **1** (*mark with ~*) де́лать, с- зару́бку на + *p.* **2**: **~ up a point** (*in game*) выи́грывать, вы́играть очко́.

note /nəʊt/ *n.* **1** (*mus., as written, sounded or sung*) но́та; (*key of instrument*) кла́виша; **eighth/quarter ~** (*US*) восьма́я/четве́ртая но́та; **strike the ~s** брать, взять но́ты; ударя́ть, уда́рить по кла́вишам; (*fig.*): **he sounded a ~ of warning** он вы́разил опасе́ние; **there was a ~ of irony in his voice** в его́ го́лосе слы́шалась иро́ния; **the ~ of pessimism in his writings** пессимисти́ческая но́тка в его́ сочине́ниях; **strike the right ~** поп|ада́ть, -а́сть в тон; **strike a false ~** не поп|ада́ть, -а́сть в тон; брать, взять неве́рный тон.
2 (*distinction*): **a family of ~** изве́стная семья́; **a man of ~** ва́жное лицо́.
3 (*attention, notice*) внима́ние; **take ~ of** (*observe*) прин|има́ть, -я́ть во внима́ние; (*heed*) прин|има́ть, -я́ть к све́дению; **worthy of ~** заслу́живающий внима́ния.
4 (*written record*) за́пись; **make a ~ of something** запи́с|ывать, -а́ть что-н.; **he made, took ~s of the lecture** он законспекти́ровал ле́кцию; **he made a ~ in his diary** он сде́лал за́пись в дневнике́; **he spoke from ~s** он говори́л по конспе́кту; **compare ~s** (*fig.*) обме́н|иваться, -я́ться впечатле́ниями.
5 (*annotation*) примеча́ние.
6 (*communication*) запи́ска; **he left a ~ for you** он оста́вил вам запи́ску; **diplomatic ~** дипломати́ческая но́та.
7 (*Br., currency*) банкно́т; ба́нковский биле́т.

● *v.t.* **1** (*observe, notice*) зам|еча́ть, -е́тить; (*heed*) обра|ща́ть, -ти́ть

внима́ние на + *a*.
2: **~ down** (*in writing*) запи́с|ывать, -а́ть.

● *cpds.* **~book** *n.* записна́я кни́жка, (*pad*) блокно́т, (*exercise-book*) тетра́дь; **~book computer** *n.* компью́тер-блокно́т, но́утбу́к; **~pad** *n.* блокно́т; **~paper** *n.* пи́счая бума́га; **~worthy** *adj.* досто́йный внима́ния; (*of thing*) достопримеча́тельный.

noted /'nəʊtɪd/ *adj.* изве́стный, знамени́тый; **~ for his courage** изве́стный свои́м му́жеством.

nothing /'nʌθɪŋ/ *n.* (*trifle*) ме́лочь, пустя́к; **a mere ~** су́щий пустя́к; **sweet ~s** ми́лый вздор; (*nonentity*) ничто́, ничто́жество; (*zero*) нуль (*m.*).

● *pron.* ничто́, ничего́ (*coll.*); **~ came of it** из э́того ничего́ не вы́шло; **~ I did was right** что бы я ни де́лал, всё (бы́ло) не так; **~ whatever** ро́вно ничего́; **~ interests him** он ниче́м не интересу́ется; **~ worries him** ничто́ не забо́тит его́; **he's a politician and ~ more** он поли́тик и ничего́ бо́лее; **~ but peace can save mankind** то́лько мир мо́жет спасти́ челове́чество; **I heard ~ but reproaches** я не слы́шал ничего́, кро́ме упрёков; я слы́шал одни́ упрёки; **he is ~ but a liar** он про́сто-на́просто лгун; **in ~ but a shirt** в одно́й руба́шке; **he is ~ if not conscientious** чего́-чего́, а добросо́вестности у него́ хвата́ет; **she is ~ to me** она́ для меня́ ничто́, она́ мне безразли́чна; **it's ~ to what I felt** э́то ничто́ по сравне́нию с тем, что мне пришло́сь пережи́ть; **it's ~ to him to work all night** ему́ ничего́ не сто́ит прорабо́тать всю ночь; **it's ~ to him what I say** мои́ слова́ для него́ — ничто́; **there's ~ to do** (*or* **be done**) не́чего де́лать; **there's ~ to be ashamed of** в э́том нет ничего́ посты́дного; **there's ~ worse than getting wet through** нет ничего́ ху́же, чем промо́кнуть насквозь; **~ doing!** не вы́йдет!; (э́тот) но́мер не пройдёт!; **there was ~ for it but to tell the truth** (*Br.*) оста́лось то́лько сказа́ть пра́вду; **there's ~** (*no difficulty*) **to it** э́то пустяки́; **there's ~** (*no truth*) **in it** э́то (сплошна́я) вы́думка; **there's ~** (*no advantage*) **in it for me** мне э́то ничего́ не да́ст; **there's ~ like a hot bath** нет ничего́ лу́чше горя́чей ва́нны; **~ much** ма́ло; **what's wrong? ~ much!** что случи́лось? Ничего́ осо́бенного!; **there's ~ wrong with that** ничего́ в э́том плохо́го нет; **bring to ~** св|оди́ть, -ести́ на нет; **our efforts came to ~** на́ши уси́лия ниче́м не увенча́лись; **that music does ~ for me** э́та му́зыка меня́ не тро́гает; **he did ~ to help** он ниче́м не помо́г; **you knew, and did ~ about it** вы зна́ли и ничего́ не сде́лали; **he did ~ but look at her** он то́лько и де́лал, что смотре́л на неё; **you do ~ but complain** вы то́лько и зна́ете, что жа́ловаться; **I feel like ~ (on earth)** я чу́вствую себя́ (пре)отврати́тельно; **I have ~ to do** мне не́чего де́лать; **it has ~ to do with me** э́то меня́ не каса́ется; я здесь ни при чём; **they had ~ to eat** им не́чего бы́ло есть, у них не́ было никако́й еды́; **I have ~ against him** я ничего́ про́тив него́ не име́ю; **I have ~ but praise for him** я не могу́ им нахвали́ться; **I had ~ to do with him** я с ним ника́к не́ был свя́зан (*or* не име́л никаки́х дел); **he had ~ on** (*was naked*) он был соверше́нно го́лый; **the police have ~ on me** (*to my discredit*) у поли́ции не мо́жет быть ко мне никаки́х прете́нзий; **our investigations led to ~** на́ши рассле́дования ни к чему́ не привели́; **I like ~ better than ...** я бо́льше всего́ люблю́...; **he looks like ~ on earth** он вы́глядит соверше́нным пу́галом; **I could make ~ of his statement** я ничего́ не по́нял из его́ заявле́ния; **he made ~ of his illness** он не придава́л никако́го значе́ния свое́й боле́зни; **~ of the kind** ничего́ подо́бного; **does it mean ~ to you that I am unhappy?** а то, что я несча́стен — для вас ничто́?; **to say ~ of the expense** не говоря́ уже́ о расхо́дах; **he started from ~** он на́чал с нуля́; **he will stop at ~** он ни пе́ред чем не остано́вится; **he thinks ~ of walking 20 miles** ему́ ничего́ не сто́ит пройти́ два́дцать миль пешко́м; **when it first happened I thought ~ of it** в пе́рвый раз я не прида́л э́тому никако́го значе́ния; **think ~ of it!** (*replying to thanks etc.*) э́то пустяки́!; ничего́!; **for ~** (*without cause*) ни за́ что, ни про́ что; (*to no purpose*) зря, напра́сно, да́ром; (*free of charge*) беспла́тно; **he was not his father's son for ~** неда́ром он был сы́ном своего́ отца́; **she wants for ~** она́ ни в чём не нужда́ется.

● *adv.*: **she is ~ like her sister** она́ совсе́м не похо́жа на сестру́; **this exam is ~ like as hard as the last** э́тот экза́мен гора́здо/куда́ ле́гче предыду́щего; **it is ~ short of scandalous** э́то настоя́щее/су́щее безобра́зие.

nothingness /'nʌθɪŋnɪs/ *n.* (*non-existence*) небытие́; (*insignificance*) ничто́жество.

notice /'nəʊtɪs/ *n.* **1** (*intimation*) предупрежде́ние; **give ~ of something to s.o.** предупре|жда́ть, -ди́ть кого́-н. о чём-н.; **have ~ of something** быть предупреждённым о чём-н.; **~ is hereby given** настоя́щим сообща́ется. **2** (*time-limit*): **he gave me a week's ~** (*of dismissal*) он предупреди́л меня́ об увольне́нии за неде́лю; **I have to give my employer a month's ~** (*of resignation*) я до́лжен предупреди́ть хозя́ина за ме́сяц (об ухо́де с рабо́ты); **the employees were all given ~** всем слу́жащим объяви́ли об увольне́нии; **the landlord gave the tenant ~ to quit** домовладе́лец предупреди́л съёмщика о расторже́нии контра́кта; **he gave me due/ample ~** он предупреди́л меня́ своевре́менно/заблаговре́менно; **at short ~** в после́днюю мину́ту; в сро́чном поря́дке; **at a moment's ~** то́тчас, незамедли́тельно; **till further ~** впредь до дальне́йшего уведомле́ния. **3** (*written or printed announcement*) объявле́ние; **obituary ~** (*reporting death*) объявле́ние о сме́рти. **4** (*attention*) внима́ние; **it has come to my ~ that ...** мне ста́ло изве́стно, что...; до меня́ дошли́ све́дения о том, что...; **he took no ~ of me** он не обраща́л на меня́ внима́ния; **he sat up and took ~** он внеза́пно заинтересова́лся. **5** (*critique*) реце́нзия, о́тзыв; **the play got good ~s** пье́са получи́ла положи́тельные о́тзывы в пре́ссе.

● *v.t.* (*observe*) зам|еча́ть, -е́тить; **he didn't even ~ me** он меня́ да́же не заме́тил; **I couldn't help but ~ what she was wearing** я нево́льно обрати́л внима́ние на её оде́жду; **I ~d fear in his voice** я почу́вствовал страх в его́ го́лосе; **he ~s things** он наблюда́тельный челове́к; он всё замеча́ет.

● *cpd.* **~-board** *n.* (*Br.*) доска́ объявле́ний.

noticeable /'nəʊtɪsəb(ə)l/ *adj.* заме́тный.

notifiable /'nəʊtɪˌfaɪəb(ə)l/ *adj.* (*of disease etc.*) подлежа́щий регистра́ции.

notification /ˌnəʊtɪfɪ'keɪʃ(ə)n/ *n.* (*announcement*) объявле́ние, извеще́ние, предупрежде́ние; (*official registration*) регистра́ция.

notif|y /'nəʊtɪˌfaɪ/ *v.t.* **1** (*give notice of, announce*) объяв|ля́ть, -и́ть о + *p.*; **he ~ied the loss of his wallet to the police** он заяви́л в поли́цию о пропа́же своего́ бума́жника; (*register*) регистри́ровать (*impf., pf.*); **all births must be ~ied** все рожде́ния подлежа́т регистра́ции. **2** (*inform*) изве|ща́ть, -сти́ть; сообщ|а́ть, -и́ть + *d.*; **I was ~ied of your arrival** меня́ извести́ли/мне сообщи́ли о ва́шем (предстоя́щем) прие́зде; **he ~ied me of his address** он сообщи́л мне свой а́дрес.

notion /'nəʊʃ(ə)n/ *n.* **1** (*idea, conception*) поня́тие, представле́ние; (*opinion*) мне́ние, взгляд; (*impulse, idea*) мысль, иде́я; **I haven't the slightest ~** я не име́ю ни мале́йшего поня́тия; **I had no ~ of leaving my country** я и в мы́слях не держа́л покида́ть ро́дину; **the ~ of my resigning is absurd** предположе́ние, что я уйду́ в отста́вку, абсу́рдно; **he got the ~ of selling the house** ему́ пришло́ в го́лову прода́ть дом; **his head is full of stupid ~s** голова́ его́ наби́та дура́цкими иде́ями. **2** (*pl., US, small wares*) галантере́я.

notional /'nəʊʃən(ə)l/ *adj.* (*ostensible, imaginary*) вообража́емый, мни́мый.

notoriety /ˌnəʊtə'raɪətɪ/ *n.* дурна́я сла́ва, печа́льная изве́стность; **his arrest won him a brief ~** его́ аре́ст созда́л/принёс ему́ на вре́мя печа́льную изве́стность.

notorious /nəʊ'tɔːrɪəs/ *adj.* (*well-known*) (обще)изве́стный; **a ~ criminal** изве́стный престу́пник; (*pej.*) пресловýтый; печа́льно изве́стный.

notwithstanding /ˌnɒtwɪθ'stændɪŋ/, /-wɪð'stændɪŋ/ *adv.* всё-таки.

● *prep.* несмотря́ на + *a.*

● *conj.*: **~ that ...** несмотря́ на то что...

nougat /ˈnu:gɑ:/ *n.* нуга́.

nought /nɔ:t/ *n.* **1** (*nothing*) = **naught. 2** (*zero*) нуль (*m.*); **6 from 6 leaves ~** шесть ми́нус шесть равня́ется нулю́. **3** (*figure 0*) ноль (*m.*); **add a ~** приб|авля́ть, -а́вить ноль; **~ point one (0.1)** ноль це́лых и одна́ деся́тая.

noun /naʊn/ *n.* (и́мя) существи́тельное.

nourish /ˈnʌrɪʃ/ *v.t.* (*lit., fig.*) пита́ть (*impf.*); **~ing food** пита́тельная еда́; **he was ~ed on radical ideas** с де́тства ему́ привива́ли радика́льные иде́и; он вы́рос на радика́льных иде́ях.

nourishment /ˈnʌrɪʃmənt/ *n.* пита́ние; **he is able to take ~ again** он сно́ва мо́жет принима́ть пи́щу.

nous /naʊs/ *n.* (*Br., common sense*) здра́вый смысл; (*coll.*) смётка.

nouveau riche /ˌnu:vəʊ ˈri:ʃ/ *n.* (*pl.* **nouveaux riches** *pronunc. same*) нувори́ш.

nova /ˈnəʊvə/ *n.* (*pl.* **novae** /-vi:/ *or* **novas**) но́вая звезда́.

Nova Scotia /ˈnəʊvə ˈskəʊʃə/ *n.* Но́вая Шотла́ндия.

Novaya Zemlya /ˈnɒvəjə ˈzemljə/ *n.* Но́вая Земля́.

novel /ˈnɒv(ə)l/ *n.* рома́н.

● *adj.* (*new*) но́вый; (*unusual*) необы́чный.

novelist /ˈnɒvəlɪst/ *n.* писа́тель (*fem.* -ница); романи́ст (*fem.* -ка).

novella /nəˈvelə/ *n.* (*pl.* **~s**) по́весть, нове́лла.

novelt|y /ˈnɒvəltɪ/ *n.* (*newness*) новизна́; (*new thing*) нови́нка; но́вшество; **it was a ~y for him to travel by plane** бы́ло ему́ в нови́нку путеше́ствовать самолётом; **the shops were full of Christmas ~ies** магази́ны бы́ли полны́ рожде́ственскими нови́нками.

November /nəˈvembə(r)/ *n.* ноя́брь (*m.*); (*attr.*) ноя́брьский; **on ~ the fifth** пя́того ноября́.

novice /ˈnɒvɪs/ *n.* **1** (*relig.*) по́слушни|к (*fem.* -ца). **2** (*beginner*) новичо́к.

novi|ciate, -tiate /nəˈvɪʃɪət/ *n.* послу́шничество; (*fig., probation*) иску́с, испыта́ние.

now /naʊ/ *adv.* **1** (*at the present time*) тепе́рь, сейча́с, ны́не; в настоя́щее вре́мя; (*opp. previously*): **I'm married ~** я тепе́рь жена́т; **(it's) ~ or never** тепе́рь и́ли никогда́; **~ and again** вре́мя от вре́мени; **(every) ~ and then** вре́мя от вре́мени; поро́й; **~ he's cheerful, ~ he's sad** он то ве́сел, то гру́стен; **~ he says one thing, ~ another** он говори́т то одно́, то друго́е; (*with preps.*): **before ~** (*hitherto*) до сих пор; (*in the past*) в про́шлом; **by ~** к э́тому вре́мени; **he should be here by ~** он до́лжен уже́ быть здесь; **from ~ on** впредь; отны́не; **till (*or* up to) ~** до сих пор. **2** (*this time*): **~ you've broken the glass** ну, вот вы и слома́ли стака́н; **~ you're talking!** (*coll.*) э́то друго́е де́ло. **3** (*at once; at this moment*) сейча́с; **I must go ~** мне пора́ (уходи́ть); **he was here just ~** он то́лько что был здесь; **only ~** то́лько тепе́рь. **4** (*in historic narrative*) тепе́рь; (*then*) тогда́; (*by then*) к тому́ вре́мени; (*next*) по́сле э́того, тогда́. **5** (*introducing new factor or aspect; summing up*) так вот; и вот; **~ it turned out that** и вот оказа́лось, что; **~ there lived a blacksmith in the village** так вот, в селе́ жил кузне́ц. **6** (*emphatic*) ну, так, ита́к; **~ you just listen to me** нет, вы послу́шайте, что я вам скажу́; **~ don't get upset** вы то́лько не расстра́ивайтесь; **~ what do you mean by that?** что вы, со́бственно, хоти́те э́тим сказа́ть?; **~ what's the matter with you?** что э́то с ва́ми?; **~ then** ну́-ка; ну-ну́; послу́шайте!; **~ why didn't I think of that?** как же я об э́том не поду́мал?

● *conj.* (*also* **~ that**) по́сле того́ как; **~ you mention it, I do remember** тепе́рь, когда́ вы упомя́нули об э́том, я вспо́мнил; **~ that I know you better ...** тепе́рь, узна́в вас бли́же. . .; **~ (that) he has come** раз/поско́льку он пришёл.

nowadays /ˈnaʊəˌdeɪz/ *adv.* ны́не, ны́нче (*coll.*); в на́ши дни; в ны́нешние времена́.

nowhere /ˈnəʊweə(r)/ *adv.* нигде́; (*motion*) никуда́; **the house was ~ near the park** дом стоя́л о́чень далеко́ от па́рка; **he was ~ near 60** ему́ ещё бы́ло далеко́ до шести́десяти (лет); **£5 is ~ near enough** пяти́ фу́нтов далеко́ не доста́точно; **this conversation is getting us ~** э́тот разгово́р нас ни к чему́ не приведёт; **a bottle of vodka appeared from ~** отку́да ни возьми́сь, появи́лась буты́лка во́дки; **there's ~ to sit** не́где сесть; **he has ~ to go** ему́ не́куда идти́; **in the middle of ~** у чёрта на кули́чках.

noxious /ˈnɒkʃəs/ *adj.* вре́дный, па́губный.

nozzle /ˈnɒz(ə)l/ *n.* сопло́; **jet ~** форсу́нка; **fire ~** брандспо́йт.

NSPCC (*abbr. of* ***National Society for the Prevention of Cruelty to Children***) Национа́льное о́бщество защи́ты дете́й от жесто́кого обраще́ния.

nth /enθ/ *adj.* э́нный; **to the ~ degree** (*fig.*) в вы́сшей сте́пени.

nuance /ˈnju:ɑ̃s/ *n.* отте́нок, нюа́нс.

nub /nʌb/ *n.* (*fig., point, gist*) суть.

nubile /ˈnju:baɪl/ *adj.* (*mature*) зре́лый, созре́вший; (*alluring*) прельсти́тельный.

nuclear /ˈnju:klɪə(r)/ *adj.* **1** (*phys.*) я́дерный; **~ bomb** я́дерная бо́мба; **~ energy** я́дерная эне́ргия; **~ fallout** радиоакти́вные оса́дки (*m. pl.*); **~ physics** я́дерная фи́зика; **~ power station** а́томная электроста́нция; **~ reactor** а́томный/я́дерный реа́ктор; **~ test** испыта́ние я́дерного ору́жия; **~ warfare** я́дерная война́; **~ weapons** я́дерное ору́жие. **2**: **~ family** ма́лая/нуклеа́рная семья́.

nuclei /ˈnju:klɪˌaɪ/ *pl. of* ⇒**nucleus**

nucleus /ˈnju:klɪəs/ *n.* (*pl.* **nuclei**) (*phys., fig.*) ядро́; (*biol.*) заро́дыш.

nude /nju:d/ *n.* **1** (*art*) обнажённая (фигу́ра). **2**: **in the ~** в го́лом ви́де, нагишо́м (*coll.*).

● *adj.* го́лый, обнажённый, наго́й.

nudge /nʌdʒ/ *n.* толчо́к ло́ктем; **give s.o. a ~** (*lit., fig.*) подт|а́лкивать, -олкну́ть кого́-н.

● *v.t.* подт|а́лкивать, -олкну́ть.

nudism /ˈnju:dɪz(ə)m/ *n.* нуди́зм.

nudist /ˈnju:dɪst/ *n.* нуди́ст (*fem.* -ка).

nudity /ˈnju:dɪtɪ/ *n.* нагота́.

nugatory /ˈnju:gətərɪ/ *adj.* пусто́й, пустя́чный.

nugget /ˈnʌgɪt/ *n.* самоpо́док.

nuisance /ˈnju:s(ə)ns/ *n.* (*annoyance*) доса́да; (*inconvenience*) неудо́бство; **what a ~!** кака́я доса́да!; **that boy is a perfect ~** э́тот мальчи́шка — су́щее наказа́ние; **go away, you are a ~!** уходи́, ты мне меша́ешь!; **be a ~ to s.o.** (*of person*) доса|жда́ть, -ди́ть кому́-н.; (*of thing*) раздража́ть (*impf.*) кого́-н.; **make a ~ of o.s. to s.o.** надо|еда́ть, -е́сть кому́-н.; **he makes a ~ of himself** он тако́й надое́дливый.

nuke /nju:k/ (*coll.*) *n.* (*weapon*) я́дерное ору́жие; (*power station*) а́томная электроста́нция.

● *v.t.* атакова́ть (*impf., pf.*), испо́льзуя я́дерное ору́жие.

null /nʌl/ *adj.* недействи́тельный; **become ~ and void** утра́|чивать, -тить (зако́нную) си́лу.

nullification /ˌnʌlɪfɪˈkeɪʃ(ə)n/ *n.* аннули́рование.

nullify /ˈnʌlɪˌfaɪ/ *v.t.* (*annul*) аннули́ровать (*impf., pf.*); (*bring to nothing*) св|оди́ть, -ести́ к нулю́.

nullity /ˈnʌlɪtɪ/ *n.* (*invalidity*) недействи́тельность; **~ decree** суде́бное реше́ние о призна́нии бра́ка недействи́тельным.

numb /nʌm/ *adj.* **1** (*of body*) онеме́лый, онеме́вший; (*of extremities*: **~** *with cold*) окочене́лый; **go ~** неме́ть, о-. **2** (*of mind, senses*) онеме́вший, оцепене́вший; **go ~** неме́ть, о-, цепене́ть, о-.

● *v.t.*: **my hand was ~ed with cold** моя́ рука́ окочене́ла от хо́лода; **my senses were ~ed with terror** я оцепене́л/онеме́л от у́жаса.

number /ˈnʌmbə(r)/ *n.* **1** (*numeral*) число́, ци́фра; **odd and even ~s** чётные и нечётные чи́сла; **in round ~s** в кру́глых ци́фрах; приме́рно. **2** (*quantity, amount, total*) число́, коли́чество; **the average ~ in a class is 30** сре́дняя чи́сленность кла́сса — 30 челове́к/ученико́в; **we were 20 in ~** нас бы́ло два́дцать (челове́к); **there were a large ~ of people there** там бы́ло мно́го наро́ду/большо́е коли́чество люде́й; **a ~ of professors attended the lecture** ле́кцию слу́шали не́сколько профессоро́в; **a ~ of people thought otherwise** (*some*) не́которые/(*a lot*) мно́гие ду́мали ина́че; **a small ~ of children** небольша́я гру́ппа дете́й; **they won by force of ~s** они́ победи́ли благодаря́ чи́сленному превосхо́дству; (*company*): **among our ~ there were several students** среди́ нас бы́ло

несколько уча́щихся; **times without ~** несчётное число́ раз.
3 (*identifying*) но́мер; **he was ~ 3 on the list** он шёл тре́тьим но́мером в спи́ске; **look after ~ one** (*fig.*) забо́титься (*impf.*) о со́бственной персо́не; **he lives at ~ 5** он живёт в до́ме но́мер 5; **telephone ~** но́мер телефо́на; **what is your ~?** како́й у вас но́мер?; **you have the wrong ~** вы не туда́ звони́те/попа́ли; **a car's (registration) ~** но́мер автомоби́ля; **catalogue** (*Br.*), **catalog** (*US*) **~** шифр по катало́гу; **he's got your ~** (*fig., has sized you up*) он вас раскуси́л; **when your ~ comes up** (*fig.*) когда́ придёт ваш черёд (*or* ва́ша о́чередь); **his ~ is up** (*coll.*) его́ пе́сенка спе́та; (*issue of magazine*): **the current ~** после́дний/очередно́й но́мер; **back ~** ста́рый но́мер; (*song or item in stage performance*) но́мер; (*coll., garment*): **she wore a fetching little ~** на ней бы́ло преми́ленькое пла́тьице.
4 (*gram.*) число́.
● *v.t.* **1** (*count*) переч|исля́ть, -и́слить; **his days are ~ed** его́ дни сочтены́.
2 (*give ~ to*) нумерова́ть, про-/за-; **all the seats are ~ed** все места́ пронумеро́ваны.
3 (*amount to*) насчи́тываться (*impf.*); **they ~ed sixty all told** их в о́бщей сло́жности насчи́тывалось шестьдеся́т (челове́к).
4 (*include*) включ|а́ть, -и́ть; **I ~ him among my friends** я включа́ю его́ в число́ свои́х друзе́й.
● *cpd.* **~-plate** *n.* (*Br.*) номерно́й знак.

numberless /'nʌmbəlɪs/ *adj.* бесчи́сленный.

numbness /'nʌmnɪs/ *n.* оцепене́ние, онеме́ние.

numbskull /'nʌmskʌl/ = **numskull**

numeracy /'nju:mərəsɪ/ *n.* зна́ние арифме́тики.

numeral /'nju:mər(ə)l/ *n.* **1** ци́фра; **Arabic/Roman ~s** ара́бские/ри́мские ци́фры. **2** (*gram.*) (и́мя) числи́тельное.

numerate /'nju:mərət/ *adj.* облада́ющий зна́нием арифме́тики.

numeration /ˌnju:mə'reɪʃ(ə)n/ *n.* (*numbering*) нумера́ция; (*calculation*) вычисле́ние.

numerator /'nju:məˌreɪtə(r)/ *n.* числи́тель (*m.*).

numerical /nju:'merɪk(ə)l/ *adj.* чи́сленный, числово́й; **~ superiority** чи́сленное превосхо́дство; **~ly superior** превосходя́щий чи́сленностью; **~ value** числово́е значе́ние.

numerous /'nju:mərəs/ *adj.* многочи́сленный.

numismatics /ˌnju:mɪz'mætɪks/ *n.* нумизма́тика.

numismatist /ˌnju:'mɪzmətɪst/ *n.* нумизма́т.

numskull, numbskull /'nʌmskʌl/ *n.* тупи́ца (*c.g.*), о́лух.

nun /nʌn/ *n.* мона́хиня, мона́шенка.

nuncio /'nʌnʃɪəʊ/, /-sɪəʊ/ *n.* (*pl.* **~s**) ну́нций.

nunnery /'nʌnərɪ/ *n.* же́нский монасты́рь.

nuptial /'nʌpʃ(ə)l/ *adj.* сва́дебный.

nuptials /'nʌpʃəlz/ *n. pl.* сва́дьба.

Nuremberg /'njʊərəmˌbɜ:g/ *n.* Ню́рнберг.

nurse /nɜ:s/ *n.* **1** (**~** *maid*) ня́ня, ня́нька (*coll.*). **2** (*of the sick*) сиде́лка; (*orderly*) санита́рка; (*senior* **~**) медсестра́; **male ~** (*orderly*) санита́р; (*senior*) медбра́т.
● *v.t.* **1** (*suckle*) корми́ть (*impf.*) (гру́дью); **nursing mother** кормя́щая мать. **2** (*take charge of; attend to*) уха́живать (*impf.*) за + *i.* **3** (*hold in one's arms*) держа́ть (*impf.*) на рука́х.
4 (*fig.*): **~ hopes** леле́ять (*impf.*) наде́жду; **~ a grudge, grievance against s.o.** таи́ть (*impf.*) оби́ду про́тив кого́-н.; **~ a cold** (сиде́ть (*impf.*) до́ма и) лечи́ться (*impf.*) от на́сморка.
● *v.i.* (*US, feed at the breast*) соса́ть (*impf.*) грудь.

nursery /'nɜ:sərɪ/ *n.* **1** (*room*) де́тская. **2** (*institution etc. for care of young*): **day ~** (дневны́е) я́сл|и (*pl., g.* -ей). **3**: **~ nurse** (*Br.*) воспита́тельница я́слей/де́тского са́да; **~ school** де́тский сад, детса́д; **~ rhyme** де́тские стишки́ (*m. pl.*); де́тская пе́сенка; **~ slopes** (*Br., skiing*) спу́ски для начина́ющих лы́жников. **4** (*hort.*) расса́дник, пито́мник.
● *cpd.* **~man** *n.* (*proprietor*) владе́лец пито́мника; (*employee*) рабо́тник пито́мника.

nursing /'nɜ:sɪŋ/ *n.* (*career*) профе́ссия медсестры́; **take up ~** учи́ться (*impf.*) на медсестру́; (*of man*) учи́ться (*impf.*) на медбра́та; **~ sister** медици́нская сестра́, медсестра́; **~ home** (ча́стная) лече́бница, (ча́стный) санато́рий; (*old people's home*) дом для престаре́лых.

nursling /'nɜ:slɪŋ/ *n.* (*baby*) грудно́й младе́нец.

nurture /'nɜ:tʃə(r)/ *n.* (*nourishment*) пита́ние; (*training*) воспита́ние; (*care*) ухо́д.
● *v.t.* (*nourish*) пита́ть (*impf.*); (*rear*) воспи́т|ывать, -а́ть.

nut /nʌt/ *n.* **1** оре́х; **crack ~s** раск|а́лывать, -оло́ть (*or* щёлкать, *impf.*) оре́хи; **a hard ~ to crack** (*fig.*) кре́пкий оре́шек; **he can't sing for ~s** (*coll.*) он соверше́нно не уме́ет петь.
2 (*for securing bolt*) га́йка; **~s and bolts** (*fig., practical details*) практи́ческая сторона́ де́ла.
3 (*sl., head*) башка́; **he is off his ~** он спя́тил; **do one's ~** (*Br.*) беси́ться, вз-.
4 (*pl., coll., crazy*): **he is ~s** у него́ не все до́ма; **he is ~s about motor-cycles** он поме́шан на мотоци́клах.
5 (*pl., vulg., testicles*) я́йца (*nt. pl.*).
● *cpds.* **~-brown** *adj.* кашта́новый; **~-case** *n.* (*sl.*) псих; **~crackers** *n. pl.* щипц|ы́ (*pl., g.* -о́в) для оре́хов; **~hatch** *n.* по́ползень (*m.*); **~-house** *n.* (*sl.*) психу́шка, дурдо́м; **~shell** *n.* оре́ховая скорлупа́; **in a ~shell** (*fig.*) кра́тко; в двух слова́х; **he put the problem in a ~shell** он кра́тко и чётко сформули́ровал пробле́му; **~-tree** *n.* оре́х(овое де́рево); (*hazel tree*) оре́шник.

nutmeg /'nʌtmeg/ *n.* муска́тный оре́х.

nutria /'nju:trɪə/ *n.* ну́трия.

nutrient /'nju:trɪənt/ *n.* пита́тельное вещество́.

nutrition /nju:'trɪʃ(ə)n/ *n.* пита́ние; (*food*) пи́ща.

nutritional /nju:'trɪʃən(ə)l/ *adj.* (*deficiency, standards, value*) пита́тельный; (*advice, information, requirement*) диети́ческий; **~ status** состоя́ние пита́ния.

nutritionist /nju:'trɪʃənɪst/ *n.* дието́лог.

nutritious /nju:'trɪʃəs/ *adj.* пита́тельный.

nutritive /'nju:trɪtɪv/ *adj.* пита́тельный.

nutter /'nʌtə(r)/ *n.* (*Br. sl.*) псих.

nutty /'nʌtɪ/ *adj.* (**nuttier, nuttiest**) **1** (*of taste*) с при́вкусом оре́ха. **2** (*crazy*) чо́кнутый (*coll.*).

nuzzle /'nʌz(ə)l/ *v.t. & i.*: **~ (against, up to) s.o./sth.** (*prod, rub with nose*) ты́каться (*impf.*) но́сом в кого́-н./что-н.

NY /nju: 'jɔ:k/ *n.* (*abbr. of* ***New York***) Нью-Йо́рк.

nylon /'naɪlɒn/ *n.* нейло́н; (*pl.*, **~** *stockings*) нейло́новые чулки́ (*m. pl.*).
● *adj.* нейло́новый.

nymph /nɪmf/ *n.* **1** (*myth.*) ни́мфа; **water ~** ная́да; (*Russian*) руса́лка; **sea ~** нере́йда; **wood ~** дриа́да. **2** (*zool.*) ни́мфа.

nympho /'nɪmfəʊ/ *n.* (*pl.* **~s**) (*coll.*) = **nymphomaniac**

nymphomania /ˌnɪmfə'meɪnɪə/ *n.* нимфома́ния.

nymphomaniac /ˌnɪmfə'meɪnɪæk/ *n.* нимфома́нка.

NZ /nju: 'zi:lənd/ *n.* (*abbr. of* ***New Zealand***) Но́вая Зела́ндия; (*attr.*) новозела́ндский.

N

Oo

O /əʊ/ *n.* (*nought*) нуль (*m.*), ноль (*m.*).
● *int.* о!; **~ God!** о Бо́же!; *see also* ⇒**oh**

oaf /əʊf/ *n.* (*pl.* **~s**) (*awkward lout*) у́валень (*m.*); (*stupid person*) ду́рень (*m.*).

oafish /ˈəʊfɪʃ/ *adj.* (*clumsy*) неуклю́жий; (*stupid*) придуркова́тый.

oak /əʊk/ *n.* (*tree; wood*) дуб; (*attr.*) дубо́вый.
● *cpds.* **~ apple, gall** *nn.* черни́льный оре́шек; **~-wood** *n.* (*copse*) дубо́вая ро́ща, дубня́к, дубра́ва; (*timber*) дуб.

oaken /ˈəʊkən/ *adj.* дубо́вый.

oakum /ˈəʊkəm/ *n.* па́кля.

OAP (*abbr. of* ***old-age pensioner***) (*Br.*) пенсионе́р (*fem.* -ка) (по ста́рости).

oar /ɔ:(r)/ *n.* **1** весло́; **put, shove, stick one's ~ into something** вме́шиваться/влеза́ть (*both impf.*) в чужи́е дела́. **2** (*rower*) гребе́ц; **he is a good ~** он хоро́ший гребе́ц; он хорошо́ гребёт.
● *cpds.* **~lock** *n.* (*US*) уклю́чина; **~sman** *n.* гребе́ц; **~smanship** *n.* иску́сство гребли́; **~swoman** *n.* (же́нщина-)гребе́ц.

oared /ɔ:d/ *adj. & comb. form* (-)весе́льный.

oasis /əʊˈeɪsɪs/ *n.* (*pl.* **oases** /-si:z/) оа́зис.

oasthouse /ˈəʊsthaʊs/ *n.* хмелесуши́льня.

oat /əʊt/ *n.* (*in pl.*) овёс; **he is off his ~s** (*coll.*) у него́ пропа́л аппети́т; **sow one's wild ~s** (*fig.*) прож|ига́ть, -е́чь мо́лодость; перебеси́ться (*pf.*); **he has sown his wild ~s** он уже́ перебеси́лся/остепени́лся.
● *adj.* овся́ный.
● *cpds.* **~-cake** *n.* овся́ная лепёшка; **~meal** *n.* толокно́; овся́ная крупа́.

oath /əʊθ/ *n.* **1** прися́га; **on** (*Br.*), **under ~** под прися́гой; **~ of allegiance** прися́га на ве́рность; **take, swear an ~** да|ва́ть, -ть кля́тву; присяг|а́ть, -ну́ть. **2** (*profanity*) прокля́тие, руга́тельство.

OAU (*abbr. of* ***Organization of African Unity***) ОАЕ (Организа́ция африка́нского еди́нства).

Obadiah /ˌəʊbəˈdaɪə/ *n.* (*bibl.*) А́вдий.

obbligato /ˌɒblɪˈgɑ:təʊ/ *n.* (*mus.*) (*pl.* **~s**) облига́то (*indecl.*).

obduracy /ˈɒbdjʊrəsɪ/ *n.* упря́мство; ожесточе́ние.

obdurate /ˈɒbdjʊrət/ *adj.* (*stubborn*) упря́мый; (*hard-headed*) ожесточённый.

OBE (*abbr. of* ***Officer of the Order of the British Empire***) кавале́р о́рдена Брита́нской импе́рии 4-й сте́пени.

obedience /əʊˈbi:dɪəns/ *n.* послуша́ние, поко́рность, повинове́ние; **~ to rules** повинове́ние пра́вилам; **~ to one's parents** послуша́ние роди́телям; **in ~ to the law** согла́сно зако́ну; в соотве́тствии с зако́ном.

obedient /əʊˈbi:dɪənt/ *adj.* послу́шный, поко́рный.

obeisance /əʊˈbeɪs(ə)ns/ *n.* (*bow*) покло́н; (*curtsey*)ревера́нс; (*fig., homage*) почте́ние, уваже́ние; **do, pay ~ to** выража́ть, вы́разить почте́ние + *d.*

obelisk /ˈɒbəlɪsk/ *n.* обели́ск.

obelus /ˈɒbələs/ *n.* (*pl.* **obeli** /-ˌlaɪ/, /-ˌli:/) кре́стик, обели́ск (*в полиграфии*).

obese /əʊˈbi:s/ *adj.* ту́чный.

obesity /əʊˈbi:sɪtɪ/ *n.* ту́чность; (*med.*) ожире́ние.

obey /əʊˈbeɪ/ *v.t.* (*comply with*): **~ the laws** подчин|я́ться, -и́ться зако́нам; (*be obedient to*): **~ one's parents** слу́шаться, по- роди́телей; (*execute*): **~ an order** выполня́ть, вы́полнить кома́нду/прика́з/приказа́ние; (*act in response to*): **~ an impulse** подда|ва́ться, -́ться поры́ву.
● *v.i.* повинова́ться (*impf., pf.*).

obfuscate /ˈɒbfʌˌskeɪt/ *v.t.* (*darken, obscure*) затемн|я́ть, -и́ть; (*confuse*) сму|ща́ть, -ти́ть.

obfuscation /ˌɒbfʌsˈkeɪʃ(ə)n/ *n.* затемне́ние; смуще́ние.

obituary /əˈbɪtjʊərɪ/ *n.* некроло́г.
● *adj.* некрологи́ческий.

object[1] /ˈɒbdʒɪkt/ *n.* **1** (*material thing*) предме́т, вещь; **~ lesson** (*lit.*) нагля́дный уро́к; (*fig.*): **he is an ~ lesson in courtesy** он образе́ц ве́жливости. **2** (*focus of feeling, effort etc.*) предме́т, объе́кт; **an ~ of curiosity** предме́т любопы́тства; **a suitable ~ for study** объе́кт, подходя́щий для изуче́ния. **3** (*purpose, aim*) цель; **what was your ~ in writing that?** с како́й це́лью вы э́то писа́ли?; **I had no particular ~ in view** я никако́й определённой це́ли не пресле́довал; **I visited him with the ~ of settling my debts** я пошёл к нему́ с це́лью расплати́ться с долга́ми; **his one ~ in life** цель всей его́ жи́зни. **4** (*consideration*): **money/time is no ~** де́ньги/вре́мя не прегра́да. **5** (*philos.*) объе́кт. **6** (*gram.*) дополне́ние; **a transitive verb takes a direct ~** перехо́дный глаго́л тре́бует прямо́го дополне́ния.

object[2] /əbˈdʒekt/ *v.i.* возра|жа́ть, -зи́ть (про́тив + *g.*); протестова́ть (*impf.*) (про́тив + *g.*); выдвига́ть, вы́двинуть возраже́ния (про́тив + *g.*); **I ~ to being treated like this** я протесту́ю про́тив тако́го обраще́ния; я не жела́ю, что́бы со мно́й так обраща́лись; **do you ~ to my smoking?** вас не беспоко́ит, что я курю́?; **I'll open a window if you don't ~** я откро́ю окно́, е́сли вы не возража́ете.

objection /əbˈdʒekʃ(ə)n/ *n.* возраже́ние, проте́ст; **raise (an) ~ to, against something** возра|жа́ть, -зи́ть про́тив чего́-н.; **are there any ~s?** есть возраже́ния?; **~ overruled/sustained** возраже́ние отклоня́ется/принима́ется; **I have no ~ to your going abroad** я не возража́ю (*or* я ничего́ не име́ю) про́тив ва́шей пое́здки за грани́цу.

objectionable /əbˈdʒekʃənəb(ə)l/ *adj.* (*undesirable; unpleasant*) нежела́тельный; неприе́млемый.

objective /əbˈdʒektɪv/ *n.* **1** (*aim*) цель. **2** (*mil.*) объе́кт, цель. **3** (*gram.*) объе́ктный паде́ж. **4** (*lens*) объекти́в.

● *adj.* (*var. senses*) объекти́вный.

objectivity /ˌɒbdʒekˈtɪvɪtɪ/ *n.* объекти́вность.

objector /əbˈdʒektə(r)/ *n.* возража́ющий; **conscientious ~** челове́к, отка́зывающийся от вое́нной слу́жбы из принципиа́льных соображе́ний.

objet d'art /ˌɒbʒeɪ ˈdɑː/ *n.* (*pl.* ***objets d'art*** *pronunc. same*) предме́т иску́сства.

oblation /əʊˈbleɪʃ(ə)n/ *n.* жертвоприноше́ние; же́ртва.

obligate /ˈɒblɪˌgeɪt/ *v.t.* обя́з|ывать, -а́ть.

obligation /ˌɒblɪˈgeɪʃ(ə)n/ *n.* (*promise, engagement*) обяза́тельство; (*duty, responsibility*) обя́занность; **be under an ~ to s.o.** быть обя́занным кому́-н.; быть в долгу́ пе́ред кем-н.; **fulfil, repay an ~** выполня́ть, вы́полнить обяза́тельство; отблагодари́ть (*pf.*); **meet one's ~s** покр|ыва́ть, -ы́ть свои́ обяза́тельства; **you are under no ~ to reply** вы не обя́заны отвеча́ть.

obligatory /əˈblɪgətərɪ/ *adj.* обяза́тельный.

oblige /əˈblaɪdʒ/ *v.t.* **1** (*bind by promise etc.; require*) обя́з|ывать, -а́ть. **2** (*compel*) вынужда́ть, вы́нудить; **we are ~d to remind you** мы вы́нуждены напо́мнить вам; **I am ~d to say** я до́лжен (вам) сказа́ть; **if you do not leave I shall be ~d to call the police** е́сли вы не поки́нете помеще́ние, я бу́ду вы́нужден вы́звать поли́цию. **3** (*do favour to*) обя́з|ывать, -а́ть; **I would be ~d if you would close the door** сде́лайте одолже́ние, закро́йте, пожа́луйста, дверь; **I am much ~d to you** я вам о́чень обя́зан/благода́рен; **can you ~ me with a pen?** не мо́жете ли вы одолжи́ть мне ру́чку?

● *v.i.*: **he ~d with a song** он любе́зно спел пе́сню.

obliging /əˈblaɪdʒɪŋ/ *adj.* услу́жливый, любе́зный.

oblique /əˈbliːk/ *adj.* **1** (*slanting*) косо́й; **~ surface** накло́нная пло́скость. **2** (*gram. and fig.*) ко́свенный.

obliterate /əˈblɪtəˌreɪt/ *v.t.* (*lit., fig., erase, wipe out*) ст|ира́ть, -ере́ть (с лица́ земли́); (*destroy*) уничт|ожа́ть, -о́жить.

obliteration /əˌblɪtəˈreɪʃ(ə)n/ *n.* стира́ние; уничтоже́ние.

oblivion /əˈblɪvɪən/ *n.* забве́ние; **fall, sink into ~** быть забы́тым (*or* пре́данным забве́нию).

oblivious /əˈblɪvɪəs/ *adj.* (*forgetful*) забы́вчивый; (*not aware*): **be ~ of** не име́ть (*impf.*) никако́го поня́тия о + *p.*; **he was ~ of the time** он (соверше́нно) забы́л о вре́мени; **he was ~ to her objections** он был глух к её возраже́ниям.

obliviousness /əˈblɪvɪəsnɪs/ *n.* забы́вчивость.

oblong /ˈɒblɒŋ/ *n.* (*figure*) продолгова́тая фигу́ра; (*object*) продолгова́тый предме́т.

● *adj.* продолгова́тый.

obloquy /ˈɒbləkwɪ/ *n.* (*defamation*) клевета́; (*reproach*) поноше́ние.

obnoxious /əbˈnɒkʃəs/ *adj.* (*offensive*) проти́вный; (*intolerable*) несно́сный.

obnoxiousness /əbˈnɒkʃəsnɪs/ *n.* проти́вность; несно́сность.

oboe /ˈəʊbəʊ/ *n.* гобо́й.

oboist /ˈəʊbəʊɪst/ *n.* гобои́ст (*fem.* -ка).

obscene /əbˈsiːn/ *adj.* непристо́йный, неприли́чный.

obscenit|y /əbˈsenɪtɪ/ *n.* непристо́йность, нецензу́рное сло́во; **he was shouting ~ies** он гро́мко выкри́кивал непристо́йности/нецензу́рные слова́.

obscurantism /ˌɒbskjʊˈræntɪz(ə)m/ *n.* мракобе́сие, обскуранти́зм.

obscurantist /ˌɒbskjʊˈræntɪst/ *n.* мракобе́с, обскура́нт.

● *adj.* обскуранти́стский.

obscuration /ˌɒbskjʊˈreɪʃ(ə)n/ *n.* помраче́ние; (*astron.*) затме́ние.

obscure /əbˈskjʊə(r)/ *adj.* **1** (*not easily understood or clearly expressed*) непоня́тный, нея́сный; невня́тный; **his motives were ~** моти́вы его́ бы́ли нея́сны́. **2** (*remote; hidden*) уединённый; скры́тый; **an ~ village** глуха́я дереву́шка; (*inconspicuous; little-known*) незаме́тный, малоизве́стный, безве́стный; **an ~ poet** малоизве́стный поэ́т; **a man of ~ origins** челове́к скро́много происхожде́ния. **3** (*dark, sombre, dim, dull*) тёмный, сму́тный.

● *v.t.* (*darken; also fig., make less noticeable or clear*) затемн|я́ть, -и́ть; (*dim the glory of, eclipse*) затм|ева́ть, -и́ть; (*conceal from sight*) заслон|я́ть, -и́ть; загор|а́живать, -оди́ть.

obscurity /əbˈskjʊərɪtɪ/ *n.* (*darkness, gloom*) тьма, мрак; (*vagueness, lack of clarity*) нея́сность; (*unintelligibility*) непоня́тность; (*being unknown or unheard of*) неизве́стность, безве́стность.

obsequies /ˈɒbsɪkwɪz/ *n. pl.* погребе́ние, по́хор|оны (*pl., g.* -о́н).

obsequious /əbˈsiːkwɪəs/ *adj.* подобостра́стный, рабол́епный.

obsequiousness /əbˈsiːkwɪəsnɪs/ *n.* подобостра́стие, рабол́епие.

observable /əbˈzɜːvəb(ə)l/ *adj.* заме́тный, различи́мый.

observance /əbˈzɜːv(ə)ns/ *n.* **1** (*of rule, law, custom etc.*) соблюде́ние. **2** (*rite, ceremony*) обря́д; (*ritual*) ритуа́л.

observant /əbˈzɜːv(ə)nt/ *adj.* **1** (*attentive*) наблюда́тельный; внима́тельный. **2**: **~ of the rules** соблюда́ющий пра́вила.

observation /ˌɒbzəˈveɪʃ(ə)n/ *n.* **1** (*observing, surveillance*) наблюде́ние; **keep s.o. under ~** держа́ть (*impf.*) кого́-н. под наблюде́нием; **he was sent to hospital for ~** его́ положи́ли в больни́цу на обсле́дование; **~ post** наблюда́тельный пункт. **2** (*remark*) замеча́ние, выска́зывание.

observatory /əbˈzɜːvətərɪ/ *n.* обсервато́рия; (*meteorological*) наблюда́тельная ста́нция.

observe /əbˈzɜːv/ *v.t.* **1** (*notice*) зам|еча́ть, -е́тить; (*see*) ви́деть, у-. **2** (*watch*) наблюда́ть (*impf.*) за + *i.*; следи́ть (*impf.*) за + *i.*; (*examine, study*) изуч|а́ть, -и́ть. **3** (*keep, adhere to*) соблю|да́ть, -сти́; **~ silence** храни́ть (*impf.*) молча́ние. **4** (*remark, comment*) зам|еча́ть, -е́тить. **5** (*commemorate*) отм|еча́ть, -е́тить. **6** (*celebrate*) пра́здновать, от-.

observer /əbˈzɜːvə(r)/ *n.* **1** (*spectator, watcher*) наблюда́тель (*m.*). **2**: **he is an ~ of old customs** он соблюда́ет ста́рые обы́чаи; он приде́рживается ста́рых обы́чаев.

obsess /əbˈses/ *v.t.* завлад|ева́ть, -е́ть (*or* овлад|ева́ть, -е́ть) (*чьим-н.*) умо́м; (*haunt*) пресле́довать, му́чить (*both impf.*); **he was ~ed by the thought of failure** его́ пресле́довала мы́сль о неуда́че; **he is ~ed by money** он поме́шан на деньга́х.

obsession /əbˈseʃ(ə)n/ *n.* (*being obsessed*) одержи́мость; (*fixed idea*) навя́зчивая иде́я; **dieting became an ~ with him** он был одержи́м/поглощён мы́слью о дие́те.

obsess|ive /əbˈsesɪv/, **-ional** /əbˈseʃən(ə)l/ *adjs.* навя́зчивый, всепоглоща́ющий.

obsolescence /ˌɒbsəˈles(ə)ns/ *n.* устарева́ние; **planned, built-in ~** заплани́рованная устаре́лость.

obsolescent /ˌɒbsəˈles(ə)nt/ *adj.* устарева́ющий.

obsolete /ˈɒbsəˌliːt/ *adj.* устаре́лый; вы́шедший из употребле́ния; **become ~** выходи́ть, вы́йти из употребле́ния; отж|ива́ть, -и́ть.

obstacle /ˈɒbstək(ə)l/ *n.* (*physical obstruction*) препя́тствие; **~ course** (*sport*) полоса́ препя́тствий; **~ race** бег/ска́чки с препя́тствиями; **clear an ~** брать, взять препя́тствие; (*hindrance*) препя́тствие, поме́ха; **put, throw ~s in s.o.'s way** чини́ть (*impf.*) препя́тствия кому́-н.; **~s to world peace** препя́тствия на пути́ к всео́бщему ми́ру.

obstetric(al) /əbˈstetrɪk(əl)/ *adj.* акуше́рский, родовспомога́тельный.

obstetrician /ˌɒbstəˈtrɪʃ(ə)n/ *n.* акуше́р (*fem.* -ка).

obstetrics /əbˈstetrɪks/ *n.* акуше́рство.

obstinacy /ˈɒbstɪnəsɪ/ *n.* упря́мство; насто́йчивость.

obstinate /ˈɒbstɪnət/ *adj.* (*stubborn*) упря́мый; (*persistent*) насто́йчивый.

obstreperous /əbˈstrepərəs/ *adj.* (*unruly*) бу́йный; (*noisy*) шу́мный.

obstreperousness /əbˈstrepərəsnɪs/ *n.* бу́йность, шумли́вость.

obstruct /əbˈstrʌkt/ *v.t.* меша́ть (*impf.*) + *d.*, препя́тствовать, вос- + *d.*; **~ the road** загра|жда́ть, -ди́ть доро́гу; **~ s.o.'s movement** препя́тствовать, вос- кому́-н.; **~ progress** препя́тствовать, вос- прогре́ссу; **~ the view** заслон|я́ть, -и́ть вид; **~ the light** загор|а́живать, -оди́ть свет.

obstruction /əbˈstrʌkʃ(ə)n/ *n.* загражде́ние; (*hindrance*) препя́тствие, поме́ха; (*parl.*) обстру́кция.

obstructive /əbˈstrʌktɪv/ *adj.* (*policy*) препя́тствующий; (*object*) загора́живающий; (*parl.*) обструкцио́нный.

obstructiveness /əbˈstrʌktɪvnɪs/ *n.* обструкцио́нность.

obtain /əbˈteɪn/ *v.t.* **1** (*receive*) получ|а́ть, -и́ть; **he ~ed a prize** он получи́л приз; **have you ~ed permission?** вы получи́ли разреше́ние? **2** (*procure*) доб|ыва́ть, -ы́ть; **he ~ed the services of a secretary** он получи́л возмо́жность по́льзоваться услу́гами секретаря́; (*acquire*) приобре|та́ть, -сти́; **this book was ~ed for me by the library** библиоте́ка вы́писала э́ту кни́гу для меня́. **3** (*attain*) дост|ига́ть, -и́гнуть + *g.*; **they ~ed good results** они́ дости́гли/доби́лись хоро́ших результа́тов.

● *v.i.* (*be current, prevalent*) нали́чествовать, существова́ть (*both impf.*); **these views no longer ~** э́ти взгля́ды уже́ устаре́ли.

obtainable /əbˈteɪnəb(ə)l/ *adj.* достижи́мый, досту́пный; **is this model still ~?** э́ту моде́ль мо́жно ещё приобрести́?

obtrude /əbˈtruːd/ *v.t.* навя́з|ывать, -а́ть; **~ o.s. on s.o.** навя́з|ываться, -а́ться кому́-н.

● *v.i.* навя́з|ываться, -а́ться.

obtrusive /əbˈtruːsɪv/ *adj.* (*importunate*) навя́зчивый, назо́йливый; (*conspicuous*) броса́ющийся в глаза́.

obtrusiveness /əbˈtruːsɪvnɪs/ *n.* навя́зчивость, назо́йливость; (*prominence*) заме́тность.

obtuse /əbˈtjuːs/ *adj.* (*lit., fig.*) тупо́й.

obtuseness /əbˈtjuːsnɪs/ *n.* ту́пость.

obverse /ˈɒbvɜːs/ *n.* (*of a coin etc.*) лицева́я сторона́.

obviate /ˈɒbvɪˌeɪt/ *v.t.* (*evade, circumvent*) избе|га́ть, -жа́ть + *g.*; (*remove*) устран|я́ть, -и́ть.

obvious /ˈɒbvɪəs/ *adj.* очеви́дный, я́сный; **for an ~ reason** по вполне́ поня́тной причи́не.

obviousness /ˈɒbvɪəsnɪs/ *n.* очеви́дность, я́сность.

ocarina /ˌɒkəˈriːnə/ *n.* (*mus.*) окари́на.

occasion /əˈkeɪʒ(ə)n/ *n.* **1** слу́чай; **on many ~s** во мно́гих слу́чаях; ча́сто; **I was there on one ~** я там был оди́н раз; **on ~** (*when the ~ arises*) при слу́чае; (*now and then*) вре́мя от вре́мени, иногда́; **on the ~ of his marriage** по слу́чаю его́ бра́ка; **today is a special ~** сего́дня осо́бый день; **he was dressed for the ~** он был соотве́тственно оде́т; **profit by the ~** воспо́льзоваться (*pf.*) слу́чаем; **choose one's ~** выбира́ть, вы́брать подходя́щий моме́нт; **rise to the ~** ока́зываться, оказа́ться на высоте́ положе́ния.
2 (*reason, ground*) причи́на, основа́ние; **give ~ to** служи́ть, по- причи́ной/основа́нием для + *g.*; **I had no ~ to meet him** у меня́ не́ было по́вода встреча́ться с ним; **there is no ~ for laughter** здесь смея́ться не́чему.

● *v.t.* (*cause*) причин|я́ть, -и́ть; вызыва́ть, вы́звать; **his behaviour** (*Br.*), **behavior** (*US*) **~ed his parents much anxiety** его́ поведе́ние доставля́ло роди́телям мно́го волне́ний; (*be reason for*) служи́ть, по- по́водом к + *d.*

occasional /əˈkeɪʒən(ə)l/ *adj.* случа́йный; (*infrequent*) ре́дкий; **~ table** сто́лик.

occasionally /əˈkeɪʒən(ə)lɪ/ *adv.* вре́мя от вре́мени, поро́й, иногда́, и́зредка; **very ~** ре́дко.

Occident /ˈɒksɪd(ə)nt/ *n.* За́пад.

occidental /ˌɒksɪˈdent(ə)l/ *adj.* за́падный.

occipital /ɒkˈsɪpɪt(ə)l/ *adj.* заты́лочный.

occiput /ˈɒksɪˌpʌt/ *n.* затылок.

occlude /əˈkluːd/ *v.t.* (*obstruct, block*) прегра|жда́ть, -ди́ть; (*stop, close up*) закр|ыва́ть, -ы́ть; (*pores*) заку́пори|вать, -ть.

occlusion /əˈkluːʒ(ə)n/ *n.* преграждéние; закры́тие; заку́порка; (*dental*) прику́с (зубо́в).

occult[1] /ɒˈkʌlt/, /ˈɒkʌlt/ *n.*: **the ~** оккульти́зм.

● *adj.* (*secret*) окку́льтный; (*powers*) маги́ческий, та́йный.

occult[2] /ɒˈkʌlt/ *v.t.* (*astron.*) затм|ева́ть, -и́ть; заслон|я́ть, -и́ть.

occultation /ˌɒkʌlˈteɪʃ(ə)n/ *n.* (*astron.*) затме́ние.

occultism /ɒˈkʌltɪz(ə)m/ *n.* оккульти́зм.

occupancy /ˈɒkjʊpənsɪ/ *n.* заня́тие; (*taking, holding possession*) завладе́ние; (*holding on lease*) аре́нда, владе́ние.

occupant /ˈɒkjʊpənt/ *n.* **1** (*inhabitant*) жи́тель (*fem.* -ница). **2** (*tenant, lessee*) жиле́ц, аренда́тор, нанима́тель (*m.*). **3**: **the ~s of the car** е́хавшие в маши́не.

occupation /ˌɒkjʊˈpeɪʃ(ə)n/ *n.*
1 (*taking possession*) завладе́ние; **the house is ready for immediate ~** дом гото́в для неме́дленного вселе́ния; (*forcible ~ of building etc.*) захва́т.
2 (*mil.*) оккупа́ция; **army of ~** оккупацио́нная а́рмия. **3** (*holding, inhabiting as owner or tenant*) прожива́ние (в до́ме *и т.п.*). **4** (*way of spending time*) заня́тие, время(пре)провожде́ние.
5 (*employment*) заня́тие; профе́ссия; **what is his ~?** чем он занима́ется?; кто он по профе́ссии?

occupational /ˌɒkjʊˈpeɪʃən(ə)l/ *adj.* профессиона́льный; **~ disease** профессиона́льное заболева́ние; **~ hazard** риск, свя́занный с хара́ктером рабо́ты; профессиона́льный риск; **~ therapy** трудотерапи́я.

occupier /ˈɒkjʊˌpaɪə(r)/ *n.* (*Br., person living in a property*) прожива́ющий; (*Br., owner*) владе́л|ец (*fem.* -ица); (*Br., lessee*) съёмщи|к (*fem.* -ца); (*conqueror*) оккупа́нт.

occup|y /ˈɒkjʊˌpaɪ/ *v.t.* **1** (*take over or move into property, house, country etc.; take possession of*) занима́ть, заня́ть; завлад|ева́ть, -е́ть + *i.*; **the building was ~ied by squatters** зда́ние бы́ло за́нято сква́ттерами.
2 (*be in possession of; hold*) занима́ть (*impf.*); (*mil.*) оккупи́ровать (*impf., pf.*); **all the rooms are ~ied** все ко́мнаты за́няты; **he ~ied the position of treasurer** он занима́л до́лжность казначе́я.
3 (*take up*): **the bed ~ies most of the room** крова́ть занима́ет бо́льшую часть ко́мнаты; **the whole day was ~ied in shopping** весь день ушёл на хожде́ние по магази́нам; **the work ~ies my whole attention** рабо́та занима́ет всё моё внима́ние.
4 (*employ*): **he ~ies his time with crossword puzzles** он заполня́ет всё своё вре́мя реше́нием кроссво́рдов; **my day is fully ~ied** мой день по́лностью за́нят; я за́нят весь день; **~y o.s. with something** занима́ться, заня́ться чем-н.

occur /əˈkɜː(r)/ *v.i.* (**occurred, occurring**) **1** (*be met, found*) встр|еча́ться, -е́титься. **2** (*take place*) случа́ться, -и́ться; прои|сходи́ть, -зойти́; **~ again** повтор|я́ться, -и́ться.
3 (*of thought, ideas*) при|ходи́ть, -йти́ в го́лову, на ум; **it ~red to me that ...** мне пришло́ в го́лову, что....

occurrence /əˈkʌrəns/ *n.* (*incident, event*) происше́ствие, слу́чай; (*phenomenon*) явле́ние; **an everyday ~** обы́чное явле́ние; (*incidence*): **of frequent ~** ча́сто встреча́ющийся, распространённый.

ocean /ˈəʊʃ(ə)n/ *n.* океа́н; (*attr.*) океа́нский.

● *cpd.* **~-going** *adj.* океа́нский.

Oceania /ˌəʊsɪˈɑːnɪə/, /ˌəʊʃɪ-/ *n.* Океа́ния.

oceanic /ˌəʊʃɪˈænɪk/, /ˌəʊsɪ-/ *adj.* океани́ческий, океа́нский.

oceanographer /ˌəʊʃəˈnɒgrəfə(r)/ *n.* океано́граф.

oceanographic /ˌəʊʃənəˈgræfɪk/ *adj.* океанографи́ческий.

oceanography /ˌəʊʃəˈnɒgrəfɪ/ *n.* океаногра́фия.

ocelot /ˈɒsɪˌlɒt/ *n.* (*zool.*) оцело́т.

ochre /ˈəʊkə(r)/ *n.* (*US* **ocher**) о́хра.

o'clock /əˈklɒk/ *adv.*: **two ~** два часа́; **at 10 ~ at night** в де́сять часо́в ве́чера; **the 8 ~ train** восьмичасово́й по́езд; **the 9 ~ news** девятичасовы́е но́вости.

OCR (*comput.*) (*abbr. of* ***optical character recognition***) опти́ческое распознава́ние си́мволов.

octagon /ˈɒktəgən/ *n.* восьмиуго́льник.

octagonal /ɒkˈtægən(ə)l/ *adj.* восьмиуго́льный.

octahedra /ˌɒktəˈhiːdrə/, /-ˈhedrə/ *pl. of* ⇒**octahedron**

octahedral /ˌɒktəˈhiːdr(ə)l/ *adj.* восьмигра́нный.

octahedr|on /ˌɒktəˈhiːdrən/, /-ˈhedrən/ *n.* (*pl.* **~a** *or* **~ons**) восьмигра́нник, окта́эдр.

octane /ˈɒkteɪn/ *n.* окта́н; **high-~** высокоокта́новый.

octave /ˈɒktɪv/ *n.* окта́ва.

octet /ɒk'tet/ *n.* октéт.

October /ɒk'təʊbə(r)/ *n.* октя́брь (*m.*); (*attr.*) октя́брьский; **the ~ Revolution** Октя́брьская револю́ция.

octogenarian /ˌɒktəʊdʒɪ'neərɪən/ *n.* восьмидесятиле́тний стари́к; (*fem.*) восьмидесятиле́тняя стару́ха.

● *adj.* восьмидесятиле́тний.

octopus /'ɒktəpəs/ *n.* (*pl.* **octopuses**) осьмино́г, спрут.

octosyllabic /ˌɒktəʊsɪ'læbɪk/ *adj.* восьмисло́жный.

ocular /'ɒkjʊlə(r)/ *adj.* глазно́й.

oculist /'ɒkjʊlɪst/ *n.* окули́ст.

odd /ɒd/ *adj.* **1** (*not even*) нечётный; **~ numbers** нечётные чи́сла; **houses with ~ numbers** дома́ с нечётными номера́ми.
2 (*not matching*) непа́рный; **I was wearing ~ socks** я был в ра́зных носка́х.
3 (*not in a set*) разро́зненный.
4 (*with some remainder or excess*) с ли́шним; **40 ~** со́рок с ли́шним (*or* с чем-то); **£12 ~** двена́дцать с ли́шним фу́нтов; **~ change** сда́ча; (*small coins*) ме́лочь.
5 (*spare, extra*) доба́вочный; **~ player** запасно́й игро́к; **~ man out** (*person or thing outside group*) исключе́ние.
6 (*occasional, casual*) случа́йный; **~ jobs** случа́йная рабо́та; **at ~ times** (*now and then*) поро́й; **he made the ~ mistake** (*coll.*) ему́ случа́лось ошиба́ться; (*unoccupied*): **in an ~ moment** ме́жду де́лом.
7 (*strange*) стра́нный, эксцентри́чный, чудно́й; **his behaviour** (*Br.*), **behavior** (*US*) **was very ~** он о́чень стра́нно себя́ вёл.
● *cpds.* **~ball** *n.* (*sl.*) чуда́к, оригина́л; **~ job** *n.* (*attr.*): **~-job man** разнорабо́чий; **~-looking** *adj.* стра́нного ви́да; чудно́й.

oddity /'ɒdɪtɪ/ *n.* (*quality*) стра́нность, чудакова́тость; (*person*) чуда́|к (*fem.* -чка); (*thing*) причу́дливая вещь; (*event*) стра́нное/необы́чное явле́ние.

oddly /'ɒdlɪ/ *adv.*: **~ enough** как (э́то) ни стра́нно; предста́вьте себе́.

oddment /'ɒdmənt/ *n.* (*left-over piece*) оста́ток; (*odd item*) шту́ка.

oddness /'ɒdnɪs/ *n.* стра́нность.

odds /ɒdz/ *n. pl.* **1** (*difference*) ра́зница; **it makes no ~** (*Br.*) э́то не де́лает ра́зницы; без ра́зницы (*coll.*); **what's the ~?** кака́я ра́зница?
2 (*balance of advantage*): **the ~ are in our favour** (*Br.*), **favor** (*US*) переве́с на на́шей стороне́; **the ~ were against his winning** ша́нсы (*m. pl.*) на вы́игрыш бы́ли про́тив него́; **he won against heavy ~** он вы́играл про́тив значи́тельного превосхо́дства сил; **by long ~** намно́го, значи́тельно.
3 (*chances, likelihood*): **the ~ are that he will do so** вероя́тнее всего́, что он так и посту́пит.
4 (*equalizing allowance*): **give s.o. ~** да|ва́ть, -ть кому́-н. преиму́щество.
5 (*betting*): **lay, give ~ of 10 to 1** ста́вить, по- де́сять про́тив одного́; **long ~** нера́вные ша́нсы (*m. pl.*); **short ~** почти́ ра́вные ша́нсы; **it is ~ on that he will win** его́ ша́нсы на вы́игрыш вы́ше, чем у проти́вника; **over the ~** (*Br., fig., excessive*) чересчу́р.
6 (*variance*): **be at ~ with s.o.** не ла́дить (*impf.*) с кем-н.
7: **~ and ends** (*leftovers*) оста́тки (*m. pl.*); (*sundries*) вся́кая вся́чина; (*of material*) обре́зки (*m. pl.*).

ode /əʊd/ *n.* о́да.

odious /'əʊdɪəs/ *adj.* (*hateful*) ненави́стный, одио́зный; (*foul, vile*) гну́сный; (*repulsive*) отврати́тельный.

odiousness /'əʊdɪəsnɪs/ *n.* гну́сность, отврати́тельность.

odium /'əʊdɪəm/ *n.* (*hatred*) не́нависть; (*disgust*) отвраще́ние; (*reprobation*) осужде́ние, позо́р.

odometer /əʊ'dɒmɪtə(r)/ *n.* одо́метр.

odor /'əʊdə(r)/ (*US*) = **odour**

odor|iferous /ˌəʊdə'rɪfərəs/, **-ous** /'əʊdərəs/ *adjs.* благоуха́ющий, благово́нный.

odorless /'əʊdəlɪs/ (*US*) = **odourless**

odour /'əʊdə(r)/ (*US* **odor**) *n.* (*smell*) за́пах; (*aroma*) арома́т; (*fig., savour, trace*) при́вкус; (*fig., repute, reputation*): **be in good/bad ~ with s.o.** быть в ми́лости/неми́лости у кого́-н.

odourless /'əʊdəlɪs/ (*US* **odorless**) *adj.* без за́паха.

odyssey /'ɒdɪsɪ/ *n.* (*pl.* **~s**) одиссе́я, приключе́ния (*nt. pl.*).

oedema /ɪ'di:mə/ (*US* **edema**) *n.* отёк.

Oedipus /'i:dɪpəs/ *n.* Эди́п; **~ complex** эди́пов ко́мплекс.

o'er /'əʊə(r)/ = **over**

oersted /'ɜ:sted/ *n.* (*phys.*) э́рстед.

oesopha|gus /i:'sɒfəgəs/ (*US* **esophagus**) *n.* (*pl.* **~gi** /-ˌdʒaɪ/ *or* **~guses**) пищево́д.

oestrogen /'i:strədʒ(ə)n/ (*US* **estrogen**) *n.* эстроге́н.

oestrus /'i:strəs/ (*US* **estrus**) *n.* те́чка.

oeuvre /'ɜ:vrə/ *n.* труды́ (*m. pl.*); произведе́ния (*nt. pl.*).

of /ɒv/, /əv/ *prep., expr. by g. and/or var. preps.*: **1** (*origin*): **he is ~ noble descent** он благоро́дного происхожде́ния; **there was one child ~ that marriage** от э́того бра́ка роди́лся оди́н ребёнок; **Lawrence ~ Arabia** Ло́уренс Арави́йский; **that's what comes ~ being careless** вот к чему приво́дит неосторо́жность; **what will become ~ us?** что с на́ми бу́дет?
2 (*cause*): **he died ~ fright** он у́мер от испу́га; **he did it ~ necessity** он сде́лал э́то из необходи́мости; **~ one's own accord** доброво́льно; по со́бственному жела́нию; **it happened ~ itself** э́то произошло́ само́ по себе́.
3 (*authorship*): **the works ~ Shakespeare** произведе́ния Шекспи́ра.
4 (*material*) из + *g.*; **what is it made ~?** из чего́ э́то сде́лано?; **a house ~ cards** ка́рточный до́мик.
5 (*composition*): **a bunch ~ keys** свя́зка ключе́й; **a family ~ 8** семья́ из восьми́ челове́к; **a work ~ 250 pages** рабо́та в 250 страни́ц; **a loan ~ £20** заём в 20 фу́нтов.
6 (*contents*): **a bottle ~ milk** (*full*) буты́лка молока́.
7 (*qualities, characteristics*): **a man ~ strong character** челове́к си́льного хара́ктера (*or* с си́льным хара́ктером); **a man ~ ability** спосо́бный челове́к.
8 (*description*): **a case ~ smallpox** слу́чай (чёрной) о́спы; **an accusation ~ theft** обвине́ние в кра́же; **a vow ~ friendship** кля́тва в дру́жбе; **an act ~ violence** акт наси́лия; **the King ~ Denmark** коро́ль Да́нии, да́тский коро́ль; **a man ~ 80** челове́к восьми́десяти лет; восьмидесятиле́тний стари́к.
9 (*identity, definition*): **the name ~ George** и́мя Гео́ргий; **the city ~ Rome** (го́род) Рим; **the Port ~ London** Ло́ндонский порт; **that fool ~ a driver** э́тот глу́пый води́тель; **a letter ~ introduction** рекоменда́тельное письмо́; **a letter ~ complaint** письмо́ с жа́лобой; **your letter ~ the 14th** ва́ше письмо́ от 14-го числа́.
10 (*objective*): **a lover ~ music** люби́тель (*m.*) му́зыки; **love ~ study** любо́вь к заня́тиям; **the use ~ a car** по́льзование маши́ной; **a view ~ the river** вид на́ реку; **a copy ~ the letter** ко́пия (с) письма́.
11 (*subjective*): **the love ~ a mother** любо́вь ма́тери; матери́нская любо́вь.
12 (*possession, belonging*): **the property ~ the state** госуда́рственная со́бственность; **a thing ~ the past** де́ло про́шлого.
13 (*partitive*): **some ~ us** не́которые/ ко́е-кто из нас; **5 ~ us** пя́теро из нас; **a quarter ~ an hour** че́тверть часа́; **most ~ all** осо́бенно; бо́льше всего́/ всех; **~ all the cheek!** (*Br.*) ну и на́глость!; **here ~ all places you expect punctuality** где-где́, а здесь мо́жно рассчи́тывать на то́чность; **a friend ~ ours** оди́н из на́ших знако́мых; **a great friend ~ ours** большо́й наш друг; **he is ~ the same opinion** он того́ же мне́ния.
14 (*concerning*): **we talked ~ politics** мы говори́ли о поли́тике; **what ~ it?** что из того́?; ну и что?
15 (*during*): **~ an evening** ве́чером; по вечера́м; **~ late years** в после́дние го́ды.
16 (*separation, distance, direction*): **within 10 miles ~ London** в десяти́ ми́лях от Ло́ндона; **north ~** к се́веру от + *g.*; се́вернее + *g.*
17 (*on the part ~*): **it was good ~ you** бы́ло о́чень ми́ло с ва́шей стороны́.

off /ɒf/ *n.* (*Br., start of race*): **they were waiting for the ~** они́ жда́ли ста́рта.
● *adj.* **1** (*nearer to centre of road*): **on the ~ side** (*in Britain*) на пра́вой стороне́.
2 (*improbable*): **I went on the ~ chance of finding him in** я пошёл туда́ на аво́сь — вдруг заста́ну (его́).
3 (*substandard*): **it was one of my ~ days** в тот день я был не в са́мой лу́чшей фо́рме.
4 (*inactive*): **the ~ season** мёртвый сезо́н.
● *adv.* (*for phrasal vv. with* **off** *see relevant v. entries*) **1** (*away*): **two miles ~** в двух ми́лях отту́да/отсю́да; **the elections**

are still two years ~ до вы́боров ещё два го́да; **~ with you!** пойди́те прочь!; **he's ~ to France tomorrow** за́втра он уезжа́ет во Фра́нцию; **it's time I was ~; I must be ~** мне пора́ (уходи́ть); **~ we go!** пошли́!; **they're ~!** (*racing*) они́ старту́ют!; **~ with his head!** го́лову с плеч!
2 (*removed*): **hats ~!** (*fig.*) ша́пки доло́й!
3 (*disconnected*): **the light is ~** свет отключён; **the electricity was ~** электри́чество бы́ло отключено́; **are the brakes ~?** вы отпусти́ли тормоза́?; (*Br., not available*): **ice-cream is ~** моро́женое ко́нчилось.
4 (*ended, cancelled*): **their engagement is ~** их помо́лвка расто́ргнута; **the match is ~** матч отменён.
5 (*not working*): **day ~** выходно́й (день); **today is my day ~** я (*or* у меня́) сего́дня выходно́й; **night ~** свобо́дный ве́чер; **he was ~ sick** он не́ был на рабо́те по боле́зни; **he was always taking time ~** он постоя́нно брал отгу́лы; **I'm ~ now till Monday** меня́ не бу́дет до понеде́льника.
6 (*of food: not fresh; tainted*): **the fish is ~** ры́ба испо́ртилась (*or* с душко́м (*coll.*)).
7 (*theatr.*): **noises ~** шум за сце́ной.
8 (*Br. coll., ill-behaved*): **I thought it a bit ~ when he left me to pay the bill** по-мо́ему, бы́ло не о́чень краси́во с его́ стороны́ оста́вить меня́ распла́чиваться.
9 (*supplied*): **they are quite well ~** они́ вполне́ обеспе́чены; **he is badly ~** он бе́ден, он нужда́ется; **how are you ~ for money?** как у вас с деньга́ми?
10: **~ and on** (*intermittently*) с переры́вами; вре́мя от вре́мени.
● *prep.* (*from; away from; up or down from*): **the car went ~ the road** маши́на съе́хала с доро́ги; **~ the beaten track** по непротоpённой доро́ге; **just ~ the High Street** неподалёку от гла́вной у́лицы; **~ balance** несбаланси́рованный; **~ work** не на рабо́те; **he fell ~ the ladder** он упа́л с ле́стницы; **he took 50p ~ the price** он сни́зил це́ну на пятьдеся́т пе́нсов; он сба́вил с цены́ пятьдеся́т пе́нсов; **I picked it up ~ the floor** я по́днял э́то с по́ла; **they were eating ~ the same plate** они́ е́ли из одно́й таре́лки; **I won £5 ~ him** (*coll.*) я вы́играл у него́ пять фу́нтов; **the ship lay ~ the coast** су́дно стоя́ло недалеко́ от бе́рега; **I broke the spout ~ the teapot** я отби́л у ча́йника но́сик; **I was run ~ my feet** я сби́лся с ног; **~ form** не в фо́рме; **he was ~ his game** он был не в лу́чшей фо́рме; **he must be ~ his head** он, должно́ быть, спя́тил; **he got ~ the point** он сби́лся с те́мы; (*disinclined for*): **he is ~ his food** он потеря́л аппети́т; **I'm ~ smoking** мне надое́ло кури́ть; (*have given it up*) я бро́сил кури́ть.

offal /ˈɒf(ə)l/ *n.* (*of meat*) потроха́ (*m. pl.*); (*entrails*) требуха́.

off-beat /ˈɒfbiːt/ *n.* (*mus.*) неуда́рная но́та.
● *adj.* (*fig.*) необы́чный, оригина́льный.

off-centre /ɒfˈsentə(r)/ (*US* **-center**) *adj.* смещённый от це́нтра, нецентра́льный, периферийный.

off-colour /ɒfˈkʌlə(r)/ (*US* **-color**) *adj.* (*Br., out of sorts*) нездоро́вый; не в фо́рме; не в себе́; (*risqué*) риско́ванный.

offence /əˈfens/ (*US* **offense**) *n.*
1 (*wrong-doing*) просту́пок; (*crime*) правонаруше́ние, преступле́ние; **an ~ against the law** наруше́ние зако́на; **commit an ~** соверш|а́ть, -и́ть правонаруше́ние. **2** (*affront; wounded feeling; annoyance*) оби́да; **cause, give ~ to** оскорб|ля́ть, -и́ть; **take ~ at** об|ижа́ться, -и́деться на + *a.*; **quick to take ~** оби́дчивый; **no ~ (meant)!** не в оби́ду бу́дет ска́зано! **3** (*mil.*) наступле́ние.

offend /əˈfend/ *v.t.* **1** (*give offence to; wound*) об|ижа́ть, -и́деть; **I hope you won't be ~ed** наде́юсь, вы не оби́дитесь; **are you ~ed with me?** вы на меня́ (не) оби́делись? **2** (*outrage*) оскорб|ля́ть, -и́ть; **it ~s my sense of decency** э́то оскорбля́ет моё чу́вство прили́чия.
● *v.i.* греши́ть (*impf.*); **~ against the law** нар|уша́ть, -у́шить зако́н; **he deleted the ~ing words** он вы́черкнул слова́, вы́звавшие возраже́ния.

offender /əˈfendə(r)/ *n.* (*against law*) правонаруши́тель (*m.*) (*fem.* -ница); престу́пни|к (*fem.* -ца); **first ~** соверши́вший преступле́ние впервы́е.

offense /əˈfens/ (*US*) = **offence**

offensive /əˈfensɪv/ *n.* нападе́ние; (*mil.*) наступле́ние; **take (or go on) the ~** пере|ходи́ть, -йти́ в наступле́ние; (*fig.*) зан|има́ть, -я́ть наступа́тельную пози́цию.
● *adj.* **1** (*causing offence*) оскорби́тельный; (*of person*) отврати́тельный, проти́вный.
2 (*repulsive*) отврати́тельный. **3** (*mil.*) наступа́тельный; **~ weapon** наступа́тельное ору́жие.

offer /ˈɒfə(r)/ *n.* **1** предложе́ние; **make an ~** де́лать, с- предложе́ние; **decline an ~** отклон|я́ть, -и́ть предложе́ние.
2: **be on ~** (*Br., for sale at reduced price*) прод|ава́ться, -а́ться со ски́дкой.
● *v.t.* **1** (*present for acceptance or refusal*) предл|ага́ть, -ожи́ть; **~ one's hand** (*lit.*) протя́|гивать, -ну́ть ру́ку; (*in marriage*) де́лать, с- предложе́ние; предл|ага́ть, -ожи́ть ру́ку; **he ~ed me a drink** он предложи́л мне вы́пить; **I was ~ed a lift** меня́ предложи́ли подвезти́; **they are ~ing a reward** объя́влено вознагражде́ние; **may I ~ my congratulations?** позво́льте вас поздра́вить!; **~ something for sale** выставля́ть, вы́ставить что-н. на прода́жу; **~ an opinion** выража́ть, вы́разить своё мне́ние; **~ an apology** прин|оси́ть, -ести́ извине́ния; **~ one's services** предл|ага́ть, -ожи́ть свои́ услу́ги; **he did not ~ to help** он не предложи́л помо́чь; **~ prayers** возн|оси́ть, -ести́ моли́твы.
2 (*provide*) предост|авля́ть, -а́вить.
3 (*attempt*): **~ resistance** ока́з|ывать, -а́ть сопротивле́ние.
● *v.i.*: **as opportunity ~s** как/когда́ предста́вится слу́чай.

offering /ˈɒfərɪŋ/ *n.* **1** предложе́ние.
2 (*of a sacrifice*) жертвоприноше́ние; (*thing or creature offered*) подноше́ние, же́ртва. **3** (*contribution*) поже́ртвование.

offertory /ˈɒfətərɪ/, /-trɪ/ *n.* (*collection*) церко́вные поже́ртвования (*nt. pl.*).

off-hand /ɒfˈhænd/, /ˈɒfhænd/ *adj.* (*also* **off-handed**) развя́зный, бесцеремо́нный.
● *adv.* сра́зу, без подгото́вки.

office /ˈɒfɪs/ *n.* **1** (*position of responsibility; service*) до́лжность, слу́жба; **the party in ~** па́ртия, находя́щаяся у вла́сти; **he held ~ for 10 years** он занима́л до́лжность/пост де́сять лет; **take (or enter upon) ~** вступ|а́ть, -и́ть в до́лжность; **run for ~** (*US*) выставля́ть, вы́ставить свою́ кандидату́ру; **term of ~** срок полномо́чий.
2 (*premises*) о́фис, конто́ра, канцеля́рия; (*room, also doctor's or dentist's*) кабине́т; **~ block** администрати́вное зда́ние; **~ equipment** оргте́хника; **~ hours** часы́ рабо́ты; рабо́чее/служе́бное вре́мя; **she's at the ~** она́ на рабо́те.
3 (*for services*) бюро́ (*indecl.*); **booking ~** биле́тная ка́сса; **enquiry ~** спра́вочное бюро́; **lost property ~** бюро́/стол нахо́док; **recruitment ~** (*mil.*) призывно́й пункт; (*non-mil.*) бюро́ по на́йму; (*department, agency*) отде́л, департа́мент; управле́ние; **editorial ~** реда́кция; **branch ~** филиа́л, отделе́ние; (*of central government*) ве́домство; **Home/Foreign O~** Министе́рство вну́тренних/иностра́нных дел; **Record O~** Госуда́рственный архи́в.
4 (*usu. pl., service, assistance*) услу́га; **through his good ~s** благодаря́ его́ посре́дничеству.
5 (*rite*) обря́д; **the last ~s** погреба́льный обря́д.
● *cpds.* **~-boy** *n.* рассы́льный; посы́льный; **~-work** *n.* канцеля́рская рабо́та; **~-worker** *n.* (конто́рский) слу́жащий; рабо́тни|к (*fem.* -ца) о́фиса.

officer /ˈɒfɪsə(r)/ *n.* **1** (*in armed forces*) офице́р; (*pl., collect.*) офице́рский соста́в; **commanding ~** команди́р; **~s' mess** офице́рская столо́вая.
2 (*official*) должностно́е лицо́, чино́вник; **medical ~ of health** санита́рный инспе́ктор; **customs ~** тамо́женник; **research ~** нау́чный сотру́дник; **~s of a club** руково́дство (*or* чле́ны правле́ния) клу́ба.

official /əˈfɪʃ(ə)l/ *n.* должностно́е лицо́, чино́вник; **government ~s** прави́тельственные чино́вники.
● *adj.* (*relating to an office*) служе́бный, должностно́й; **~ duties** служе́бные обя́занности; **~ position** служе́бное положе́ние; (*formal*): **an ~ style** форма́льный стиль; (*authoritative*) официа́льный; **~ language** официа́льная терминоло́гия; (*of a country*) госуда́рственный язы́к; **~ly I**

am not here официа́льно меня́ здесь нет.

officialdom /əˈfɪʃəldəm/ *n.* чино́вничество, бюрократи́ческий аппара́т.

officialese /əˌfɪʃəˈliːz/ *n.* казённый язы́к, бюрократи́ческий жарго́н.

officiate /əˈfɪʃɪˌeɪt/ *v.i.*: **~ at a wedding** соверш|а́ть, -и́ть обря́д бракосочета́ния; **~ as host** быть за хозя́ина; **~ as chairman** председа́тельствовать (*impf.*).

officious /əˈfɪʃəs/ *adj.* навя́зчивый, назо́йливый.

officiousness /əˈfɪʃəsnɪs/ *n.* навя́зчивость, назо́йливость.

offing /ˈɒfɪŋ/ *n.*: **in the ~** (*fig.*) в перспекти́ве.

off-key /ɒfˈkiː/ *adj.* (*lit., fig.*) фальши́вый.

off-licence /ˈɒflaɪs(ə)ns/ *n.* (*Br.*) ви́нный магази́н.

off-line /ɒfˈlaɪn/ *adj.* (*comput.*) автоно́мный; (*disconnected*) отключённый.

off-load /ˈɒfləʊd/, /ɒfˈləʊd/ *v.t.* разгру|жа́ть, -зи́ть.

off-peak /ˈɒfpiːk/ *adj.* непи́ковый; **~ hours** часы́ зати́шья, непи́ковые часы.

offprint /ˈɒfprɪnt/ *n.* о́ттиск.

off-putting /ˈɒfpʊtɪŋ/ *adj.* (*coll.*) отта́лкивающий.

off-season /ˈɒfsiːz(ə)n/ *n.* межсезо́нье.

● *adj.* несезо́нный.

offset *n.* /ˈɒfset/ (*compensation*) возмеще́ние; (*typ.*) офсе́т.

● *v.t.* /ɒfˈset/ (*compensate for*) возме|ща́ть, -сти́ть; (*neutralize*) противостоя́ть (*impf.*) + *d.*

offshoot /ˈɒfʃuːt/ *n.* побе́г; (*fig.*) о́трасль.

offshore /ˈɒfʃɔː(r)/ *adj.* (*close to shore*) прибре́жный; (*at a distance*) морско́й; (*foreign*) загрнани́чный; (*fin.*) оф(ф)шо́рный; **~ wind** берегово́й ве́тер; **~ fishery** морско́й рыболо́вный про́мысел.

off-side /ɒfˈsaɪd/ *n.* (*football*) положе́ние вне игры́, офса́йд.

offspring /ˈɒfsprɪŋ/ *n.* (*pl.* **~**) пото́мок, о́тпрыск; (*pl.*) пото́мство; (*fig.*) плод.

off-stage /ɒfˈsteɪdʒ/ *adj.* (*life, behaviour*) реа́льный; **~ whisper** шёпот за кули́сами.

off-the-cuff /ˌɒfðəˈkʌf/ *adj.* импровизи́рованный.

off-the-peg /ˌɒfðəˈpeg/ *adj.* гото́вый (*об одежде*).

off-the-record /ˌɒfðəˈrekɔːd/ *adj.* неофициа́льный.

off-the-shelf /ˌɒfðəˈʃelf/ *adj.* станда́ртный, типово́й.

off-white /ˈɒfwaɪt/ *adj.* серова́то-бе́лый.

often /ˈɒf(ə)n/, /ˈɒft(ə)n/ *adv.* (**oftener, oftenest**) ча́сто; **every so ~** вре́мя от вре́мени; **as ~ as not** нере́дко; **more ~ than not** бо́льшей ча́стью, в большинстве́ слу́чаев.

ogee /ˈəʊdʒiː/, /-ˈdʒiː/ *n.* си́нус; (*archit.*) гусёк.

ogle /ˈəʊg(ə)l/ *v.t.* пожира́ть (*impf.*) глаза́ми.

ogre /ˈəʊgə(r)/ *n.* велика́н-людое́д.

ogress /ˈəʊgrɪs/ *n.* велика́нша-людое́дка.

oh /əʊ/ *int.* о!, ах!; (*expr. surprise, fright, pain*) ой!; **~ yes, ~ really?** пра́вда?; неуже́ли?; да?; **~ for a drink!** ах, как хо́чется пить!

ohm /əʊm/ *n.* ом.

oho /əʊˈhəʊ/ *int.* ого́.

OHP (*abbr. of* ***overhead projector***) графопрое́ктор.

oil /ɔɪl/ *n.* **1** ма́сло; **mineral/vegetable ~** минера́льное/расти́тельное ма́сло; **fixed/volatile ~s** жи́рные/эфи́рные масла́; **cod-liver ~** ры́бий жир; **engine ~** маши́нное ма́сло; **fuel ~** мазу́т; **burn the midnight ~** рабо́тать (*impf.*) по ноча́м; **pour ~ on troubled waters** снима́ть, снять напряже́ние.

2 (*petroleum*) нефть; **strike ~** обнару́жи|вать, -ть/на|ходи́ть, -йти́ месторожде́ние не́фти.

3 (*paint, usu. pl.*) ма́сляная кра́ска; (*painting*) ма́сло; **paint in ~s** писа́ть (*impf.*) ма́слом.

● *v.t.* (*lubricate*) сма́з|ывать, -ать; **~ the wheels** (*fig.*) ула́|живать, -дить де́ло; (*treat with* ~) пропи́т|ывать, -а́ть ма́слом; **well ~ed** (*drunk*) навеселе́ (*coll.*).

● *cpds.* **~-bearing** *adj.* нефтено́сный; **~-can** *n.* маслёнка; **~cloth** *n.* клеёнка; (*linoleum*) лино́леум; **~-colour** (*US* **-color**) *n.* ма́сляная кра́ска; **~field** *n.* месторожде́ние не́фти; **~ filter** *n.* ма́сляный фильтр; **~-fired** *adj.*: **~-fired central heating** (*Br.*), **~ heat** (*US*) нефтяно́е центра́льное отопле́ние; **~ gauge** *n.* индика́тор у́ровня ма́сла; **~-heater** *n.* парафи́новая пе́чка; **~-lamp** *n.* кероси́новая ла́мпа; **~-paint** *n.* ма́сляная кра́ска; **~-painting** *n.* (*activity*): **he does ~-painting** он пи́шет ма́слом; (*genre*) ма́сло; (*object*) ма́сло, холст, карти́на; **she's no ~-painting** (*Br.*) она́ далеко́ не краса́вица; **~-rig** *n.* нефтяна́я вы́шка; **~skin** *n.* (*material*) клеёнка; (*garment*) непромока́емый костю́м; **~-slick** *n.* плёнка не́фти на воде́; **~stone** *n.* точи́льный ка́мень; **~-tank** *n.* нефтяна́я цисте́рна; **~-tanker** *n.* (*ship*) та́нкер; (*vehicle*) нефтево́з; **~-well** *n.* нефтяна́я сква́жина.

oiliness /ˈɔɪlɪnɪs/ *n.* масляни́стость, вя́зкость; (*fig.*) еле́йность.

oily /ˈɔɪlɪ/ *adj.* (**oilier, oiliest**) **1** ма́сляный; **~ cheese** масляни́стый сыр. **2** (*fig., fawning, unctuous*) еле́йный.

ointment /ˈɔɪntmənt/ *n.* мазь.

OK, okay /əʊˈkeɪ/ *n.* (*pl.* **~s**) (*coll.*) одобре́ние, «добро́».

● *adj.* (*safe, well*): **she is ~** она́ в поря́дке; (*acceptable*): **are you sure it's ~?** э́то ничего́?; **I'll be back soon, ~?** я ско́ро верну́сь, ла́дно?; **it's ~** ничего́; годи́тся; **it's ~ by me** я согла́сен; **it looks ~ to me** по-мо́ему, ничего́/норма́льно; **an ~ expression** приe̋млемое выраже́ние.

● *adv.*: **the meeting went off ~** собра́ние прошло́ норма́льно; **he is doing ~** у него́ всё хорошо́/норма́льно.

● *v.t.* (**OK's, OK'd, OK'ing**) од|обря́ть, -обрить; **he ~'d the proposal** он одо́брил э́то предложе́ние.

● *int.* (*agreeing*) ла́дно!, хорошо́!; (*marking the end of topic etc.*) ла́дно, ну вот.

okra /ˈəʊkrə/, /ˈɒkrə/ *n.* (*bot.*) о́кра.

old /əʊld/ *n.* **1**: **the ~** (*people*) старики́ (*m. pl.*), пожилы́е/престаре́лые (лю́ди); **young and ~** (*everyone*) стар и млад.

2: **of ~** в пре́жнее вре́мя; в пре́жние времена́; **in days of ~** в старину́.

● *adj.* (**older, oldest**) **1** ста́рый; (*object, house*) стари́нный; **~ age** ста́рость; **~ age pension** (*Br.*) пе́нсия по ста́рости; **~ man** (*also coll., husband or father*) стари́к; **~ woman** (*also coll., wife*) стару́ха; **~ lady** ста́рая да́ма, стару́ха; **~ folk** старики́; **~ folk's home** дом для престаре́лых; **~ maid** ста́рая де́ва; **grow ~** ста́риться, со-.

2 (*expr. age in years etc.*): **how ~ is he?** ско́лько ему́ лет?; **my son is 4 years ~** моему́ сы́ну четы́ре го́да; **he is ~ enough to understand** в его́ во́зрасте пора́ понима́ть э́то; **he is ~ enough to be her father** он ей в отцы́ годи́тся; **he could read at 4 years ~** в четы́ре го́да он уже́ чита́л; **a four-year-~** четырёхле́тний; **this newspaper is two weeks ~** э́та газе́та двухнеде́льной да́вности.

3 (*practised, experienced*) о́пытный; (*inveterate*) закорене́лый; **he is an ~ hand at such things** он в таки́х дела́х ма́стер.

4 (*Br. coll., expr. familiarity*): **~ man, chap, fellow** старина́ (*m.*), стари́к; **~ boy, thing** дружо́к, дружи́ще (*m.*); **the ~ man** (*employer*) стари́к, хозя́ин, шеф; (*father, husband*) стари́к; **we had a good, fine, high ~ time** мы хорошо́/здо́рово провели́ вре́мя.

5 (*coll., whatever*): **any ~ time** когда́ уго́дно; **he dresses any ~ how** он одева́ется, как попа́ло.

6 (*dating from the past; ancient; longstanding*) стари́нный, давни́шний; **an ~ family** стари́нный род; **one of the ~ school** челове́к ста́рого зака́ла; **that story is as ~ as the hills** э́тот расска́з стар как мир; **they are ~ friends** они́ стари́нные/да́вние друзья́; **the ~ guard** ста́рая гва́рдия; **the O~ World** Ста́рый Свет; **the O~ Testament** Ве́тхий заве́т; **he was paying off ~ scores** он своди́л ста́рые счёты.

7 (*former*) бы́вший, пре́жний; **an ~ boy** (*of school*) бы́вший учени́к; пито́мец; **~-boy network** круг бы́вших однока́шников; **the good ~ days** до́брое ста́рое вре́мя; **the ~ country** ро́дина (отцо́в); **O~ English** (*language*) древнеангли́йский (язы́к); **O~ French** старофранцу́зский (язы́к); **~ ways** стари́нные обы́чаи; **~ master** (*artist*) ста́рый ма́стер; (*painting*) карти́на ста́рого ма́стера; **see the ~**

O

year out встр|еча́ть, -е́тить Но́вый год.
8 (*worn, shabby*) поно́шенный, потрёпанный; **I was wearing my ~est clothes** я был в са́мом поно́шенном из мои́х костю́мов.
● *cpds.* **~-established** *adj.* да́вний, стари́нный; **~-fashioned** *adj.* старомо́дный; (*obsolete*) устаре́лый; **~-maidish** *adj.* староде́вичий, чо́порный; **~-time** *adj.* стари́нный; **~-timer** *n.* старожи́л; **~-womanish** *adj.* стару́шечий; **~-world** *adj.* (*ancient*) стари́нный; (*belonging to former days*) старозаве́тный, старосве́тский.

olden /ˈəʊld(ə)n/ *adj.* (*arch.*) ста́рый, было́й; **in ~ days, times** в было́е времена́.

olde-worlde /ˌəʊldɪˈwɜːldɪ/ *adj.* (*coll.*) стилизо́ванный под старину́.

oldish /ˈəʊldɪʃ/ *adj.* старова́тый.

oleaginous /ˌəʊlɪˈædʒɪnəs/ *adj.* (*oily*) масляни́стый; (*yielding oil*) ма́сличный.

oleander /ˌəʊlɪˈændə(r)/ *n.* олеа́ндр.

O level /ˈəʊ lev(ə)l/ *n.* (*Br., hist.*) экза́мен (по програ́мме сре́дней шко́лы) на обы́чном у́ровне.

olfactory /ɒlˈfæktərɪ/ *adj.* обоня́тельный; **~ organ** о́рган обоня́ния.

oligarch /ˈɒlɪˌgɑːk/ *n.* олига́рх.

oligarchic(al) /ˌɒlɪˈgɑːkɪk((ə)l)/ *adj.* олигархи́ческий.

oligarchy /ˈɒlɪˌgɑːkɪ/ *n.* олига́рхия.

olive /ˈɒlɪv/ *n.* **1** (*tree*) масли́на; оли́вковое де́рево; (*fruit*) масли́на, оли́вка. **2** (*colour*) оли́вковый цвет.
● *adj.* оли́вковый; **hold out an ~ branch** (*fig.*) предл|ага́ть, -ожи́ть мири́ться; **~ oil** оли́вковое ма́сло.

Olympiad /əˈlɪmpɪˌæd/ *n.* олимпиа́да.

Olympian /əˈlɪmpɪən/ *n.* (*godlike person; participant in Olympic games*) олимпи́ец.
● *adj.* олимпи́йский.

Olympic /əˈlɪmpɪk/ *adj.* олимпи́йский; **~ games, ~s** Олимпи́йские и́гры.

Olympus /əˈlɪmpəs/ *n.* Оли́мп.

Oman /əʊˈmɑːn/ *n.* Ома́н.

ombudsman /ˈɒmbʊdzmən/ *n.* о́мбудсмен (*чиновник, рассматривающий претензии граждан к правительственным служащим*).

omega /ˈəʊmɪgə/ *n.* оме́га.

omelet(te) /ˈɒmlɪt/ *n.* омле́т; **you can't make an ~ without breaking eggs** ≈ лес ру́бят — ще́пки летя́т.

omen /ˈəʊmən/, /-men/ *n.* предзнаменова́ние; (*sign*) знак.

ominous /ˈɒmɪnəs/ *adj.* злове́щий.

omission /əˈmɪʃ(ə)n/ *n.* **1** (*thing excluded; act of excluding*) про́пуск. **2** (*failure to do something*) упуще́ние.

omit /əˈmɪt/ *v.t.* (**omitted, omitting**) **1** (*leave out*) пропус|ка́ть, -ти́ть. **2** (*neglect*) упус|ка́ть, -ти́ть; **I ~ted to lock the door** я забы́л запере́ть дверь.

omnibus /ˈɒmnɪbəs/ *n.* **1** (*obs.*) о́мнибус, авто́бус. **2** (**~** *volume*) сбо́рник, антоло́гия.

omnipotence /ɒmˈnɪpət(ə)ns/ *n.* всемогу́щество.

omnipotent /ɒmˈnɪpət(ə)nt/ *adj.* всемогу́щий.

omnipresence /ˌɒmnɪˈprez(ə)ns/ *n.* вездесу́щность.

omnipresent /ˌɒmnɪˈprez(ə)nt/ *adj.* вездесу́щий.

omniscience /ɒmˈnɪsɪəns/, /-ʃɪəns/ *n.* всеве́дение.

omniscient /ɒmˈnɪsɪənt/, /-ʃɪənt/ *adj.* всеве́дущий.

omnivorous /ɒmˈnɪvərəs/ *adj.* (*lit., fig.*) всея́дный.

on /ɒn/ *adv.* (*for phrasal vv. with* **on** *see relevant v. entries*). **1** (*expr. continuation*): **straight ~** пря́мо; **and so ~** и так да́лее; **from now ~** (начина́я) с э́того дня; **read ~!** продолжа́йте чита́ть!; чита́йте да́льше!; **he looked at me and then walked ~** он взгляну́л на меня́ и пошёл да́льше; **we walked ~ and ~** мы всё шли и шли; **he went ~ (and ~) about his dog** он без конца́ говори́л о свое́й соба́ке; **what is he ~ about?** (*Br. coll.*) о чём э́то он?; **he was ~ at me to lend him my bicycle** (*Br.*) он пристава́л ко мне, что́бы я одолжи́л ему́ мой велосипе́д; (*expr. extension*): **further ~** да́льше; **later ~** по́зже; **a garage has been built ~ (to the house)** (к до́му) пристро́или гара́ж.
2 (*placed, fixed, spread etc.* **~** *something*): **the kettle is ~** ча́йник стои́т/поста́влен; **the light-switch is ~** свет включён; **he had his glasses ~** он был в очка́х; он наде́л очки́; **your badge is ~ upside-down** у вас значо́к вверх нога́ми.
3 (*arranged, available*): **what's ~ this week?** (*at theatre*) что идёт/даю́т на э́той неде́ле?; **what's ~ tonight?** (*TV*) кака́я сего́дня програ́мма?; что сего́дня пока́зывают?; **he is ~** (*performing*) **tonight** он выступа́ет сего́дня ве́чером; **have you anything ~ next week?** у вас что́-нибудь наме́чено на бу́дущую неде́лю?; **is the match still ~?** матч не отмени́ли/отменён?
4 (*turned, switched* **~**): **the radio was ~ full blast** ра́дио бы́ло включено́ на всю мощь; **the tap was left ~** кран был не вы́ключен; **leave the light ~!** не гаси́те свет!; **is the brake ~?** то́рмоз включён?
5 (**~** *stage*): **you're ~ next!** сле́дующий вы́ход — ваш!
6 (*expr. contact*): **I've been ~ to him this morning** (*by telephone*) я связа́лся с ним (по телефо́ну) сего́дня у́тром; **he's ~ to a good thing** (*coll.*) ему́ повезло́; **the police are ~ to him** (*coll.*) поли́ция его́ раскуси́ла.
7: **you're ~!** (*coll., I accept your offer, bet etc.*) идёт!; **it's not ~** (*coll., feasible*) так не пойдёт/идёт.
● *prep.* (*for some senses see also* ⇒**upon**) **1** (*expr. position*) на + *p.*; **~ the table** на столе́; **Rostov-~-Don** Росто́в-на-Дону́; (*supported by*): **stand ~ one leg** стоя́ть (*impf.*) на одно́й ноге́; **he walks ~ crutches** он хо́дит на костыля́х; **the look ~ his face** выраже́ние его́ лица́; (*as means of transport*) на + *p.*; **ride ~ a donkey** е́хать (*det.*) верхо́м на осле́; **~ horseback** верхо́м; **~ foot** пешко́м; **I came ~ the bus** я прие́хал на авто́бусе; (**~** *one's person*): **I have no money ~ me** у меня́ нет при себе́ де́нег; **a gun was found ~ him** у него́ нашли́ ору́жие; (*over the surface of; along*) по + *d.*; **the fly was crawling ~ the ceiling** му́ха по́лзала по потолку́; **the boat floated ~ the current** ло́дка плыла́ по тече́нию; (*expr. relative position, with* **left, right, side, hand** *etc.*): **~ all sides** со всех сторо́н; повсю́ду; **~ my left** сле́ва от меня́; **~ my part** с мое́й стороны́; **~ the one hand ... ~ the other (hand)** с одно́й стороны́... с друго́й (стороны́); **~ either side of the street** по о́бе стороны́ у́лицы; **he walked ~ the other side of the street** он шёл по противополо́жной стороне́ у́лицы; **uncle ~ the father's side** дя́дя со стороны́ отца́.
2 (*expr. final position of movement or action*) на + *a.*; **she threw her gloves ~(to) the floor** она́ бро́сила перча́тки на́ пол; **he sat down ~ the sofa** он сел на дива́н; **they went ~ deck** они́ вы́шли на па́лубу; **the windows open ~(to) the garden** о́кна выхо́дят в сад.
3 (*expr. point of contact*): **he hit me ~ the head** он уда́рил меня́ по голове́; **I hit my head ~ a stone** я уда́рился голово́й о ка́мень; **I cut my finger ~ the glass** я поре́зал себе́ па́лец о стекло́; **he kissed her ~ the lips** он поцелова́л её в гу́бы; **he knocked ~ the door** он постуча́л в дверь; **I cut my finger ~ a knife** я поре́зал себе́ па́лец ножо́м; **she dried her hands ~ a towel** она́ вы́терла ру́ки полоте́нцем; **her dress caught ~ a nail** она́ зацепи́лась пла́тьем за гвоздь.
4 (*of musical instrument*) на + *p.*; **he played a tune ~ the fiddle** он сыгра́л мело́дию на скри́пке.
5 (*of a medium of communication*) по + *d.*; **~ the radio/telephone/television** по ра́дио/телефо́ну/телеви́зору.
6 (*expr. membership*) в + *p.*; **she is ~ the committee** она́ член комите́та; **~ our staff** у нас в шта́те.
7 (*expr. time*): **~ that same day** в тот же день; **~ Tuesday** во вто́рник; **~ time** во́время; своевре́менно; **~ the instant** то́тчас; **~ the next day** на сле́дующий день; **~ this occasion** на э́тот раз; **~ the 8th of May** восьмо́го ма́я; **~ the morning of the 8th of May** у́тром восьмо́го ма́я; **~ a winter morning** зи́мним у́тром; **~ Tuesdays** по вто́рникам; **~ our holidays we work on a farm** во вре́мя о́тпуска мы рабо́таем на фе́рме; **~ the occasion of his death** по слу́чаю его́ сме́рти.
8 (*at the time of; immediately after*): **~ his arrival** по его́ прие́зде; **~ my return** по возвраще́нии; когда́ я верну́лся/верну́сь; **cash ~ delivery** опла́та по доста́вке; **~ seeing him she ran off** уви́дев его́, она́ убежа́ла; **~ his father's death** по/по́сле сме́рти отца́; (*during*): **~ my way home** по доро́ге

домо́й; ~ **his rounds** во вре́мя (его́) обхо́да; ~ **examination** при осмо́тре.
9 (*concerning*): **an article ~ Pushkin** статья́ о Пу́шкине; **decisions ~ reparations** реше́ния по репара́циям; **a poem ~ X's death** стихотворе́ние на смерть X; ~ **that subject** на э́ту те́му, по э́той те́ме.
10 (*on the strength, basis of*) на + *p.*; **he was acquitted ~ my evidence** он был опра́вдан на осно́ве мои́х показа́ний; ~ **easy terms** на льго́тных усло́виях; ~ **half-pay** на полста́вке.
11 (*expr. direction of effort*): **work ~ a book** рабо́та над кни́гой; **work ~ building a house** рабо́та по постро́йке до́ма; **I spent two hours ~ that job** я потра́тил на э́ту рабо́ту два часа́; **he spent £500 ~ his daughter's wedding** он потра́тил пятьсо́т фу́нтов на сва́дьбу до́чери.
12 (*at the expense of*): **drinks are ~ me** я угоща́ю; **the joke was ~ me** шу́тка оберну́лась про́тив меня́; **he lives ~ his friends** он живёт за счёт друзе́й.
13 (*by means of*) на + *a. or p.*; **he lives ~ slender means** он живёт на ску́дные сре́дства; **he lives ~ fish** он пита́ется ры́бой; **the machine runs ~ oil** маши́на рабо́тает на ма́сле.
14 (*imposed ~*) на + *a.*; **a tax ~ tobacco** по́шлина на таба́чные изде́лия.
15 (*taking drugs etc.*): **he's ~ drugs** он по́льзуется нарко́тиками; **she's ~ medicine** она́ принима́ет лека́рство.

onanism /ˈəʊnəˌnɪz(ə)m/ *n.* онани́зм.

on-board /ˈɒnbɔːd/ *adj.* бортово́й.

once /wʌns/ *adv.* **1** (оди́н) раз; **he read the letter only ~** он прочита́л письмо́ то́лько оди́н раз; ~ **is enough** одного́ ра́за (вполне́) доста́точно; ~ **six is six** оди́ножды шесть — шесть; **it happened only that ~** э́то случи́лось в тот еди́нственный раз; **more than ~** не раз; ~ **a day** (оди́н) раз в день; ~ **every 6 weeks** ка́ждые шесть неде́ль; раз в шесть неде́ль; **just (for) this ~** то́лько на э́тот раз, в ви́де исключе́ния; хотя́ бы на э́тот раз; **for ~** хотя́ бы на сей раз; ~ **again, more** ещё раз; **(every) ~ in a while** (*occasionally*) и́зредка; вре́мя от вре́мени; ~ **(and) for all** (*finally*) раз и навсегда́; ~ **or twice** не́сколько раз, па́ру раз; **not ~** ни ра́зу, никогда́.
2 (*whenever, as soon as*): ~ **he understands this** как то́лько он поймёт э́то; ~ **you hesitate you are lost** сто́ит заколеба́ться и ты пропа́л.
3 (*at one time, formerly*) не́когда; одно́ вре́мя; одна́жды; когда́-то; (*at some point*) как-то; ~ **upon a time there was** (давны́м-давно́) жил-был; (*on one occasion in the past*) одна́жды.
4: **at ~** (*immediately*) сейча́с же; сра́зу же; то́тчас; неме́дленно; (*simultaneously*) в то же вре́мя; **don't all talk at ~!** не говори́те все сра́зу/вме́сте!; **all at ~** (*suddenly*) внеза́пно/вдруг.

● *conj. see adv.* ⇒2

● *cpd.* **~-over** *n.* (*coll.*): **give s.o./sth. the ~-over** бе́гло осм|а́тривать, -отре́ть кого́/что-н.

oncological /ˌɒŋkəˈlɒdʒɪk(ə)l/ *adj.* онкологи́ческий.

oncologist /ɒŋˈkɒlədʒɪst/ *n.* онко́лог.

oncology /ɒŋˈkɒlədʒɪ/ *n.* онколо́гия.

oncoming /ˈɒnˌkʌmɪŋ/ *adj.* приближа́ющийся, наступа́ющий.

OND (*abbr. of* ***Ordinary National Diploma***) (*Br., hist*) дипло́м о сре́днем техни́ческом образова́нии.

on-duty /ˈɒndjuːtɪ/ *adj.* дежу́рный.

one /wʌn/ *n.* **1** (*number*) оди́н; (*in counting*): **~, 2, 3** раз/оди́н, два, три; (*figure 1*) оди́н; едини́ца; **minus ~** ми́нус оди́н; **a row of ~s** ряд едини́ц; **they arrived in ~s and twos** они́ приходи́ли по одному́ и по́ двое; **5 ~s are 5** пя́тью оди́н — пять; ~ **or two** (*several*) не́сколько; (*a few*) немно́го; ~ **in 10** оди́н из десяти́; **ten to ~ he will forget** ста́влю де́сять про́тив одного́ — он забу́дет; **he's ~ in a thousand** таки́х, как он — оди́н на ты́сячу; **last but ~** предпосле́дний; ~ **and a half** полтора́ + *g.*; **you're ~ up on me** (одно́) очко́ в ва́шу по́льзу; вы меня́ опереди́ли.
2 (*in a series*): **Part O~** часть пе́рвая, I часть (*read as* пе́рвая часть); **Volume O~** том пе́рвый, I том (*read as* пе́рвый том); **Act I** де́йствие пе́рвое; **room ~** ко́мната (но́мер) оди́н; пе́рвая ко́мната; (*in hotel*) пе́рвый но́мер; **a no. 1** (*bus*) пе́рвый но́мер; **he looks after number ~** (*i.e. himself*) он забо́тится (лишь) о само́м себе́.
3 (*hour*) час; **I'll see you at ~** я вас уви́жу в час; **it was past ~** шёл второ́й час; **quarter/half past ~** че́тверть/полови́на второ́го; **at a quarter to ~** (в) без че́тверти час; ~ **o'clock** (*a.m.*) час но́чи; (*p.m.*) час дня.
4 (*age*): **he's only ~** ему́ всего́/то́лько год(ик).
5 (*expr. unity or identity*): **he is a scholar and a musician all in ~** он и учёный, и музыка́нт; **we are at ~ in thinking ...** мы согла́сны в том, что...; **it's all ~ to me** мне безразли́чно (*or* всё равно́).
6 (*being, person, creature*): **the Evil O~** чёрт, дья́вол, нечи́стый; **little ~s** де́ти; **our loved ~s** на́ши бли́зкие; **he fought like ~ possessed** он боро́лся, как одержи́мый; **he is not ~ to refuse** он не тако́в, что́бы отказа́ться; **what a ~ you are for making excuses!** вы ма́стер находи́ть предло́ги; **he is ~ who never complains** он не из тех, кто жа́луется.
7 (*member of a group*) оди́н; ~ **of my friends** оди́н из мои́х друзе́й; **he was ~ of the first to arrive** он пришёл одни́м из пе́рвых; **many a ~** мно́гие, не оди́н; ~ **of the women** одна́/кто́-то из же́нщин; **the ~ with the beard** тот(, кото́рый) с бородо́й; **which ~ of you did it?** кто из вас э́то сде́лал?; ~ **and all** все как оди́н; **I for ~ don't believe him** что каса́ется меня́, то я не ве́рю ему́; ~ **of these days** ка́к-нибудь на днях; **he is not ~ of our customers** э́то не наш клие́нт; он не из на́ших клие́нтов; **not ~ of them** ни оди́н из них; никто́ из них; ~ **another** друг дру́га; ~ **after the other;** ~ **by** ~ оди́н за други́м; **(the) ~ ... the other ...** оди́н/тот... друго́й...; ~ **each** по одному́ (ка́ждому); ~ **at a time** по одному́; по о́череди; ~ **of a kind** (*unique specimen*) еди́нственный в своём ро́де.
8 (*referring to category specified or understood*): **Do you play the piano? There's ~ in the study** Игра́ете ли вы на роя́ле? В кабине́те есть роя́ль; **which book do you want, the red or the green ~?** каку́ю кни́гу вы хоти́те, кра́сную и́ли зелёную?; **'Take my pen!' — 'Thanks, I have ~'** «Возьми́те мою́ ру́чку!» — «Спаси́бо, у меня́ есть»; **this pencil is better than that ~** э́тот каранда́ш лу́чше того́; **this book is more interesting than the ~ I read yesterday** э́та кни́га интере́снее чем та, кото́рую я чита́л вчера́; **I gave him ~** (*blow*) **on the chin** я дал ему́ по че́люсти (*or* в зу́бы); **that's ~ in the eye for you/him** (*fig.*) получи́л!; **we had ~** (*drink*) **for the road** мы вы́пили на доро́жку; **let's have a quick ~!** пропу́стим по одно́й! (*coll.*); **he had ~ too many** он вы́пил ли́шнего.

● *pron.*: ~ **never knows** никогда́ не зна́ешь; кто его́ зна́ет?; ~ **doesn't say that in Russian** по-ру́сски так не говоря́т; ~ **can say anything nowadays** в на́ше вре́мя мо́жно всё сказа́ть; **how can ~ do it?** как э́то сде́лать?; ~ **gets used to anything** челове́к ко всему́ привыка́ет; **~'s own** свой (со́бственный).

● *adj.* **1** оди́н; (*sometimes untranslated, e.g.*) **price ~ rouble** цена́ (оди́н) рубль; (*with pluralia tantum*) одни́; ~ **watch** одни́ часы́; ~ **hundred and ~** сто оди́н; **not ~ man in a hundred will understand you** вас не поймёт да́же оди́н из ста; **I have ~ or two things to do** у меня́ есть ко́е-каки́е дела́.
2 (*only*) еди́нственный; **the ~ way to do it** еди́нственный спо́соб э́то сде́лать; **the ~ thing I detest is ...** бо́льше всего́ я ненави́жу...; что я ненави́жу — так э́то...; (*single*): **no ~ man can lift it** одному́ э́то ника́к не подня́ть; **with ~ accord** как оди́н, единоду́шно; **they spoke with ~ voice** они́ говори́ли в оди́н го́лос.
3 (*the same*) тот же са́мый; **all in ~ direction** всё в том же (са́мом) направле́нии; **at ~ and the same time** в одно́ и то же вре́мя.
4 (*particular but unspecified*): **at ~ time** когда́-то; одно́ вре́мя; не́когда; ~ **evening** ка́к-то/одна́жды ве́чером; ~ **day** (*in past*) одна́жды; (*in future*) когда́-нибудь; ~ **fine day** в оди́н прекра́сный день.
5 (*a certain*) не́кий; **we bought the house from ~ Jones** мы купи́ли дом у не́коего Джо́нса.
6 (*opp. other*): **I'll go ~ way and you go the other** я пойду́ в одну́ сто́рону, а вы — в другу́ю; я пойду́ одно́й доро́гой, а вы — друго́й; **neither ~ thing nor the other** ни то ни друго́е, ни то́ ни сё (*coll.*); **(just) ~ thing after another** не одно́, так друго́е; **for ~ thing, I'm not ready** во-пе́рвых, я не гото́в.

● *cpds.* **~-act** *adj.* одноа́ктный; **~-armed** *adj.* одноannotated ру́кий; **~-armed bandit** (*sl.*) игрово́й автома́т; **~-eyed**

O

adj. одногла́зый; **~-horse** *adj.*: **~-horse town** заштáтный городи́шко; **~-legged** *adj.* одноно́гий; **~-man** *adj.* (*seating* **~** *man*) одномéстный; **~-man band** человéк-оркéстр; **~-man exhibition, show** персонáльная вы́ставка; **~-man show** (*theatr.*) теáтр одногó актёра; **~-man business** единоли́чное предприя́тие; **~-night** *adj.*: **~-night stand** (*theatr.*) еди́нственное представлéние; (*liaison*) ромáн на однý ночь; **~-off** *adj.* (*Br. coll.*) уникáльный, еди́нственный; **~-parent family** *n.* семья́ с одни́м роди́телем; **~-piece** *adj.* цéльный; **~-shot** *adj.* (*US coll.*) = **~-off; ~-sided** *adj.* (*prejudiced*) однобóкий, односторóнний; **~-time** *adj.* бы́вший; былóй; *see also* ⇒**~-off; ~-to-~** *adj.* непосрéдственный; **~-track** *adj.* (*rail*) одноколéйный; (*fig.*): **~-track mind** ýзкий кругозóр; **~-upmanship** *n.* умéние доби́ться чýвства превосхóдства; **~-way** *adj.*: **~-way traffic** односторóннее движéние; **~-way street** ýлица с односторóнним движéнием; **~-way ticket** билéт в однý стóрону (*or* в однóм направлéнии).

oneness /'wʌnnɪs/ *n.* (*unity*) еди́нство; (*uniqueness*) еди́нственность, едини́чность.

onerous /'ɒnərəs/, /'əʊn-/ *adj.* обремени́тельный, тя́гостный.

onerousness /'ɒnərəsnɪs/, /'əʊn-/ *n.* обремени́тельность, тя́гостность.

oneself /wʌn'self/ *pron.* (*refl.*) себя́, . . .ся; **talk to ~** говори́ть (*impf.*) с сами́м собóй; **sit by ~** сидéть (*impf.*) в сторонé/одинóчестве; **for ~** самостоя́тельно; **cooking for ~ is a bore** скýчно готóвить для самогó себя́ (*or* для себя́ одногó); **see for ~** убеди́ться (*pf.*) самомý.

ongoing /'ɒn,gəʊɪŋ/ *adj.* (*continuing*): **~ conflict** непрекращáющийся конфли́кт; **~ process** поступáтельный процéсс; (*in progress*) текýщий; **~ negotiations** текýщие перегово́ры, проходя́щие сейчáс перегово́ры.

onion /'ʌnjən/ *n.* лýковица; (*pl., collect.*) лук (рéпчатый); **spring ~s** зелёный лук; (*attr.*) лýковый; **~ dome** кýпол-лýковка.

● *cpd.* **~-skin** *n.* лýковичная шелухá.

on-line /ɒn'laɪn/ *adj.* (*comput.*) (*information, program*) онлáйновый, диалóговый, интеракти́вный; (*connected*) подключённый.

onlooker /'ɒn,lʊkə(r)/ *n.* зри́тель (*m.*), наблюдáтель (*m.*); (*witness*) свидéтель (*m.*).

only /'əʊnlɪ/ *adj.* еди́нственный; **one and ~** оди́н еди́нственный; **she was an ~ child** онá былá еди́нственным ребёнком; **this ring is the ~ one of its kind** э́то кольцó — еди́нственное в своём рóде; **she is not the ~ one** онá не исключéние; **I was the ~ one there** крóме меня́ там никогó нé было; **he was the ~ one to object** он оди́н возражáл; **~ women attended the meeting** на заседáнии бы́ли одни́/тóлько жéнщины; **~ a month ago** не дáлее как мéсяц томý назáд; **the ~ thing is, I can't afford it** дéло тóлько/лишь в том, что мне э́то не по срéдствам; **the ~ thing for 'flu is to go to bed** прóтив гри́ппа есть тóлько/лишь однó срéдство — отлежáться (в постéли).

● *adv.* тóлько; всегó; **~ just** (*recently*) тóлько что; (*barely*) едвá; **I have ~ just arrived** я тóлько что при́был; **he was ~ just in time** он чуть (бы́ло) не опоздáл; он едвá успéл; **if ~ you knew** éсли бы вы тóлько знáли; **I am ~ too pleased** я óчень рад; **the engine started, ~ to stop again** мотóр завёлся, но тут же заглóх; **the soup was ~ warm** суп был éле тёплый.

● *conj.* но; **I would go myself, ~ I'm tired** я пошёл бы сам, но я устáл; **he's a good speaker, ~ he shouts a lot** он хорóший орáтор, тóлько сли́шком кричи́т.

● *cpd.* **~-begotten** *adj.* единорóдный.

o.n.o. (*abbr. of* ***or near(est) offer***) (*Br.*) ≈ ценá в райóне дáнной сýммы.

on-off /'ɒn'ɒf/ *adj.*: **~-switch** выключáтель (*m.*).

onomastic /,ɒnə'mæstɪk/ *adj.* ономасти́ческий.

onomastics /,ɒnə'mæstɪks/ *n.* ономáстика.

onomatopoeia /,ɒnə,mætə'pi:ə/ *n.* звукоподражáние.

onomatopoeic /,ɒnə,mætə'pi:ɪk/ *adj.* звукоподражáтельный.

onrush /'ɒnrʌʃ/ *n.* нáтиск; (*attack*) атáка.

on-screen /ɒn'skri:n/ *adj.* (*comput.*) экрáнный; **~ graphics** экрáнная грáфика.

onset /'ɒnset/ *n.* начáло, наступлéние.

onshore /'ɒnʃɔ:(r)/ *adj.*: **~ wind** морскóй вéтер.

on-site /'ɒnsaɪt/ *adj.* на местáх/мéсте.

onslaught /'ɒnslɔ:t/ *n.* атáка, нападéние.

onto /'ɒntu:/ = **on** *prep.* 2

ontological /,ɒntə'lɒdʒɪk(ə)l/ *adj.* онтологи́ческий.

ontology /ɒn'tɒlədʒɪ/ *n.* онтолóгия.

onus /'əʊnəs/ *n.* (*pl.* **onuses**) брéмя, отвéтственность; **~ of proof** брéмя докáзывания.

onward /'ɒnwəd/ *adj.* продвигáющийся; **~ movement** движéние вперёд.

● *adv.* (*also* **~s**) вперёд, дáлее; **from now ~** впредь, отны́не; **from then ~** с тех пор; с той поры́; (*in future*) с тогó врéмени.

onyx /'ɒnɪks/ *n.* óникс.

oodles /'u:d(ə)lz/ *n.* (*coll.*) мáсса, ýйма, кýча; **~ of money** кýча дéнег.

oolite /'əʊə,laɪt/ *n.* (*geol.*) ооли́т.

oolitic /,əʊə'lɪtɪk/ *adj.* ооли́товый.

oomph /ʊmf/ *n.* энéргия.

oops! /u:ps/, /ʊps/ *int.* (*coll.*) ой!

ooze /u:z/ *n.* (*slime*) ил, ти́на; (*wet mud*) жи́жа; (*exudation*) просáчивание.

● *v.t.* (*emit*): **the wound ~d blood** из рáны сочи́лась кровь; (*fig.*): **he ~d self-confidence** он источáл самоувéренность.

● *v.i.* (*flow slowly*) мéдленно течь (*impf.*); (*in drops*) сочи́ться (*impf.*); (*fig.*): **~ away** уб|ывáть, -ы́ть; **his strength ~d away** си́лы покидáли егó.

opacity /ə'pæsɪtɪ/ *n.* **1** непрозрáчность. **2** (*obscurity*) нея́сность; смýтность.

opal /'əʊp(ə)l/ *n.* опáл.

● *adj.* опáловый; **~ glass** молóчное/мáтовое стеклó.

opal|escent /,əʊpə'les(ə)nt/, **-ine** /'əʊpə,laɪn/ *adjs.* опáловый.

opaque /əʊ'peɪk/ *adj.* (**opaquer, opaquest**) непрозрáчный; (*dark, obscure*) тёмный; (*obtuse, dull-witted*) тупóй, глýпый.

opaqueness /əʊ'peɪknɪs/ *n.* непрозрáчность; темнотá; тýпость, глýпость.

op-art /ɒp'ɑ:t/ *n.* оп-искýсство.

op. cit. /ɒp 'sɪt/ (*abbr. of* ***opere citato***) в цити́рованном трудé.

OPEC /'əʊpek/ *n.* (*abbr. of* ***Organization of Petroleum-Exporting Countries***) ОПЕ́К (Организáция стран-экспортёров нéфти).

open /'əʊpən/ *n.* **1** (**~** *space;* **~** *air*) откры́тое прострáнство; **in the ~** под откры́тым нéбом; на откры́том вóздухе. **2** (*fig.*): **bring something into the ~** выявля́ть, вы́явить; выводи́ть, вы́вести что-н. на чи́стую вóду (*coll.*); **come into the ~** выявля́ться, вы́явиться; (*be frank*) быть откровéнным.

● *adj.* **1** откры́тый; **in the ~ air** на откры́том вóздухе; **receive, welcome with ~ arms** (*fig.*) встр|ечáть, -éтить с распростёртыми объя́тиями (*or* тепл́о/радýшно); **~ boat** беспáлубное сýдно; **~ car/carriage** откры́тая маши́на/откры́тый экипáж; **~ competition** откры́тое состязáние; **~ contempt** я́вное/нескрывáемое презрéние; **in ~ country** в непересечённой мéстности; средú полéй и лугóв; **in ~ court** на откры́том судéбном заседáнии; **~ day** (*Br., at school*) день откры́тых дверéй; **keep one's ears ~** прислýшиваться (*impf.*); навостри́ть (*pf.*) ýши; **with ~ eyes (*or* one's eyes ~)** с откры́тыми глазáми; (*fig.*) вполнé сознáтельно; **~ flower** распусти́вшийся цветóк; **~ hostility** откры́тая враждá; **they keep ~ house** у них откры́тый/гостеприи́мный дом; **~ letter** откры́тое письмó; **~ market** откры́тый ры́нок; **have an ~ mind on something** не имéть (*impf.*) предвзя́того мнéния о + *p.*; **~ prison** (*Br.*) тюрьмá откры́того ти́па; **an ~ question** откры́тый/нерешённый вопрóс; **on the ~ road** на большóй дорóге; **on the ~ sea** в откры́том мóре; **~ season** охóтничий сезóн; **~ secret** секрéт полишинéля; **~ space** откры́тое прострáнство; **~ ticket** билéт с откры́той дáтой; **~ verdict** смерть при неустано́вленных обстоя́тельствах; **~ warfare** откры́тая война́; **~ winter** мя́гкая зима́; **~ wound** откры́тая/незажи́вшая ра́на; **break ~** (*v.t.*) вскры|ва́ть, -ть; (*letter*) распеча́т|ывать, -ать; взл|а́мывать, -ома́ть; **the door flew ~** дверь распахну́лась; **he threw the window ~** он распахну́л окно́; **we left the matter ~** мы оста́вили вопро́с откры́тым. **2** (*accessible, available*) досту́пный; **the road is ~ to traffic** доро́га откры́та для движе́ния; **the chairman threw the debate ~** председа́тель объяви́л пре́ния откры́тыми; **~ to attack** уязви́мый; **~ to question** спо́рный; **~ to misinterpretation** спосо́бный вы́звать непра́вильное толкова́ние; **~ to offer** гото́вый рассмотре́ть предложе́ние. **3** (*frank*) откры́тый, открове́нный.

● *v.t.* **1** откр|ыва́ть, -ы́ть; (*unseal*) распеча́т|ывать, -ать; (*unwrap*) разв|ора́чивать, -ерну́ть; (*book, newspaper*) откр|ыва́ть, -ы́ть; раскр|ыва́ть, -ы́ть; (*vein; parcel at customs etc.*) вскр|ыва́ть, -ыть; (*bottle*) отку́пори|вать, -ть; **~ wide** (*e.g. door*) распа́х|ивать, -ну́ть; **he ~ed his mouth wide** он широко́ откры́л рот; **don't ~ your umbrella indoors** не раскрыва́йте зо́нтик в ко́мнате. **2** (*fig.*): **she ~ed her heart to me** она́ откры́ла мне ду́шу; **I ~ed his eyes to the situation** я откры́л ему́ глаза́ на положе́ние дел; **he ~ed an account** он откры́л счёт; **the secretary ~ed the debate** секрета́рь откры́л пре́ния; **the enemy ~ed fire** неприя́тель откры́л ого́нь; **we ~ed negotiations** мы приступи́ли к перегово́рам; **a new business has been ~ed** откры́ли но́вый би́знес. **3**: **a road was ~ed through the forest** че́рез лес проложи́ли доро́гу; **they are planning to ~ a mine** они́ собира́ются заложи́ть ша́хту.

● *v.i.* **1** откр|ыва́ться, -ы́ться; (*unfold*, **~ wide**) раскр|ыва́ться, -ы́ться; **the heavens ~ed** (*fig.*) дождь поли́л как из ведра́. **2** (*fig., begin*) нач|ина́ться, -а́ться; **the play ~s with a long speech** пье́са начина́ется дли́нным моноло́гом; **the new play ~s on Saturday** но́вая пье́са идёт с суббо́ты; **I shall ~ by reading the minutes** я начну́ с чте́ния протоко́ла. **3** (*of door, room etc.*): **the study ~s into the drawing-room** кабине́т сообща́ется с гости́ной; **the windows ~ on to a courtyard** о́кна выхо́дят во двор.

● *with advs.*: **~ out** *v.i.*: **the roses ~ed out** ро́зы распусти́лись; **~ up** *v.t.*: **~ up!** (*command to open*) откро́йте дверь!; **he ~ed up the boot (of the car)** он откры́л бага́жник; (*territory*) осв|а́ивать, -о́ить; **his stories ~ up a new world** его́ расска́зы раскрыва́ют но́вый мир; *v.i.*: **he ~ed up about his visit** он открове́нно рассказа́л о свое́й пое́здке; **a machine-gun ~ed up** пулемёт на́чал стреля́ть.

● *cpds.* **~-air** *adj.*: **~-air life** жизнь на откры́том во́здухе; **~cast** *adj.* (*Br.*): **~cast mining** откры́тые го́рные рабо́ты; **~ended** *adj.* (*fig.*) (*with no preconditions*) не име́ющий зара́нее предусмо́тренных усло́вий; (*with no time limit*) бессро́чный; **~-handed** *adj.* ще́дрый; **~-heart** *adj.*: **~-heart operation** опера́ция, проводи́мая на отключённом се́рдце; **~-hearted** *adj.* (*sincere*) чистосерде́чный; (*generous*) великоду́шный; **~-hearth** *adj.*: **~-hearth furnace** марте́новская печь; **~-minded** *adj.* непредубеждённый; **~-mouthed** *adj.* рази́нувший (от удивле́ния) рот; **~-plan** *adj.* с откры́той плани́ровкой; **~-work** *n.* мере́жка; ажу́рная стро́чка; *adj.* ажу́рный.

opener /ˈəʊpənə(r)/, /ˈəʊpnə(r)/ *n.* (*for cans etc.*) консе́рвный нож; (*coll.*) открыва́лка (*also for bottles*).

opening /ˈəʊpənɪŋ/, /ˈəʊpnɪŋ/ *n.* **1** (*vbl. senses*) откры́тие, раскры́тие, вскры́тие. **2** (*aperture*) отве́рстие; прохо́д. **3** (*beginning*) нача́ло; (*of play, speech*) вступле́ние; (*initial part*) вступи́тельная часть. **4** (*job*) ме́сто, вака́нсия. **5** (*favourable opportunity*) удо́бный слу́чай; благоприя́тная возмо́жность. **6** (*chess*) дебю́т.

● *adj.* (*initial*) нача́льный, пе́рвый; (*introductory*) вступи́тельный; **~ remarks** вступи́тельные замеча́ния; **~ night** премье́ра; (*working*): **~ hours** рабо́чие часы́; часы́ рабо́ты.

openly /ˈəʊpənlɪ/ *adv.* откры́то; (*frankly*) открове́нно; (*publicly*) публи́чно, откры́то.

openness /ˈəʊpənnɪs/ *n.* (*frankness*) откры́тость, открове́нность; (*pol.*) гла́сность.

opera[1] /ˈɒpərə/ *n.* о́пера; **at the ~** на о́пере; **to the ~** на о́перу; (*branch of art*) о́перное иску́сство, о́пера.

● *cpds.* **~-glass(es)** *n.* театра́льный бино́кль; **~-house** *n.* о́перный теа́тр; **~-singer** *n.* о́перный певе́ц (*fem.* о́перная певи́ца).

opera[2] /ˈɒpərə/ *pl. of* ⇒**opus**

operable /ˈɒpərəb(ə)l/ *adj.* **1** (*med.*) опера́бельный. **2** (*workable*) де́йствующий, функциони́рующий.

operate /ˈɒpəˌreɪt/ *v.t.* **1** (*control work of*) управля́ть (*impf.*) + *i.*; эксплуати́ровать (*impf.*); **he ~s a lathe** он рабо́тает на тока́рном станке́; **the company ~s three factories** э́та компа́ния управля́ет тремя́ фа́бриками; **the machine is ~d by electricity** э́та маши́на рабо́тает на электри́честве. **2** (*bring into motion*) прив|оди́ть, -ести́ в движе́ние. **3** (*put into effect*): **we ~ a simple system** мы применя́ем просту́ю систе́му.

● *v.i.* **1** (*work, act*) рабо́тать (*impf.*); де́йствовать (*impf.*); **the brakes failed to ~** тормоза́ отказа́ли. **2** (*produce effect or influence*) ока́з|ывать, -а́ть влия́ние (на + *a.*); де́йствовать, по- (на + *a.*). **3**: **~ on** (*surg.*) опери́ровать (*impf., pf.*) (**for**: по по́воду + *g.*). **4** (*mil.*) де́йствовать (*impf.*); опери́ровать (*impf., pf.*).

operatic /ˌɒpəˈrætɪk/ *adj.* о́перный.

operating /ˈɒpəˌreɪtɪŋ/ *adj.* **1** (*surg.*): **~ room** (*US*), **theatre** (*Br.*) операцио́нная; **~ table** операцио́нный стол. **2**: **~ costs** эксплуатацио́нные расхо́ды. **3** (*comput.*): **~ system** операцио́нная систе́ма.

operation /ˌɒpəˈreɪʃ(ə)n/ *n.* **1** (*action, effect*) де́йствие; рабо́та; **bring into ~** прив|оди́ть, -ести́ в де́йствие; **come into ~** нач|ина́ть, -а́ть де́йствовать; **go out of ~** выходи́ть, вы́йти из стро́я. **2** (*force, validity*) си́ла, де́йствие. **3** (*process*) проце́сс, опера́ция. **4** (*control, making work*) эксплуата́ция, управле́ние. **5** (*business transaction*) опера́ция. **6** (*mil.*) опера́ция, де́йствия (*nt. pl.*); **combined ~s** совме́стные де́йствия; **~s room** кома́ндный пункт. **7** (*med.*) опера́ция; операти́вное вмеша́тельство; **an ~ for cancer** опера́ция по по́воду ра́ка; **perform an ~** де́лать, с- (*or* произв|оди́ть, -ести́) опера́цию. **8** (*math.*) де́йствие.

operational /ˌɒpəˈreɪʃən(ə)l/ *adj.* **1** (*mil.*) операти́вный; **~ unit** боево́е подразделе́ние. **2** де́йствующий; **the fleet is ~** флот нахо́дится в состоя́нии боево́й гото́вности; **the factory is fully ~** заво́д по́лностью гото́в к эксплуата́ции. **3** (*needed for operating*): **~ data** рабо́чие да́нные.

operative /ˈɒpərətɪv/ *n.* (*machine operator*) стано́чник; (*on production line*) квалифици́рованный рабо́чий.

● *adj.* **1** (*working, operating*) де́йствующий; (*having force*) действи́тельный; (*effective*) де́йственный; **become ~** (*of law etc.*) входи́ть, войти́ в си́лу. **2** (*practical*) операти́вный.

operator /ˈɒpəˌreɪtə(r)/ *n.* **1** (*one who works a machine*) опера́тор. **2** (*telephonist*) телефони́ст (*fem.* -ка); (*radio ~*) связи́ст, ради́ст (*fem.* -ка). **3** (*comm.*) деле́ц.

operetta /ˌɒpəˈretə/ *n.* опере́тта.

ophthalmic /ɒfˈθælmɪk/ *adj.* глазно́й; **~ optician** (*Br.*) окули́ст.

ophthalmological /ˌɒfθælməˈlɒdʒɪk(ə)l/ *adj.* офтальмологи́ческий.

ophthalmologist /ˌɒfθælˈmɒlədʒɪst/ *n.* офтальмо́лог.

ophthalmology /ˌɒfθælˈmɒlədʒɪ/ *n.* офтальмоло́гия.

ophthalmoscope /ɒfˈθælməˌskəʊp/ *n.* офтальмоско́п.

opiate /ˈəʊpɪət/ *n.* опиа́т; (*fig.*) о́пиум.

opine /əʊˈpaɪn/ *v.t.* (*express opinion*) выска́зывать, вы́сказать мне́ние, что...

opinion /əˈpɪnjən/ *n.* (*judgement, belief*) мне́ние; (*view*) взгляд; **in the ~ of** по мне́нию + *g.*; **in my ~** по моему мне́нию, по-мо́ему, на мой взгляд; **be of the ~ that ...** держа́ться (*impf.*) того́ мне́ния, что...; полага́ть (*impf.*) (*or* счита́ть (*impf.*)), что...; **change one's ~** меня́ть (*impf.*), перемени́ть (*pf.*) мне́ние; **form an ~** сост|авля́ть, -а́вить себе́ мне́ние; **that is a matter of ~** э́то зави́сит от то́чки зре́ния; **~ poll**

O

опро́с обще́ственного мне́ния; (*estimate*): **have a high/low ~ of** быть высо́кого/невысо́кого мне́ния о + *p.*; (*conviction*) убежде́ние; (*expert judgment*) заключе́ние; **I wish to get another ~** я хоте́л бы пригласи́ть ещё одного́ специали́ста.

opinionated /əˈpɪnjəˌneɪtɪd/ *adj.* догмати́чный.

opium /ˈəʊpɪəm/ *n.* о́пиум; **~ den** прито́н кури́льщиков о́пиума.

opossum /əˈpɒsəm/ *n.* опо́ссум.

opponent /əˈpəʊnənt/ *n.* оппоне́нт, проти́вник; (*sport*) проти́вник.

opportune /ˈɒpəˌtjuːn/ *adj.* (*timely*) своевре́менный, уме́стный; (*suitable*) подходя́щий.

opportunism /ˌɒpəˈtjuːnɪz(ə)m/, /ˈɒpə-/ *n.* оппортуни́зм.

opportunist /ˌɒpəˈtjuːnɪst/ *n.* оппортуни́ст.
● *adj.* оппортунисти́ческий.

opportunistic /ˌɒpətjuːˈnɪstɪk/ *adj.* оппортунисти́ческий.

opportunit|y /ˌɒpəˈtjuːnɪtɪ/ *n.* (*favourable circumstance*) удо́бный слу́чай; (*good chance*) возмо́жность; **as ~y offers** при слу́чае; **there were few ~ies of, for hearing music** почти́ не́ было возмо́жности слу́шать му́зыку; **I had no ~y to thank him** у меня́ не́ было возмо́жности поблагодари́ть его́; **ring me up if you get the ~y!** позвони́те, е́сли бу́дет возмо́жность (*or* предста́вится слу́чай); **he seized, took the ~y to ...** он воспо́льзовался слу́чаем, что́бы...; **he let slip a golden ~y** он упусти́л блестя́щую возмо́жность.

oppos|e /əˈpəʊz/ *v.t.* **1** (*set against or in contrast to*) противопост|авля́ть, -а́вить (*что чему*); **two ~ed ideas** две противополо́жные иде́и; **as ~ed to** в отли́чие от + *g.*; **I am firmly ~ed to the idea** я реши́тельно про́тив э́той иде́и. **2** (*set o.s. against*) возра|жа́ть, -зи́ть (*or* выступа́ть, вы́ступить) про́тив + *g.*; **the ~ing side** проти́вная сторона́; (*sport*) кома́нда проти́вника; (*show opposition to*) проти́виться (*impf.*) + *d.*; ока́з|ывать, -а́ть сопротивле́ние + *d.*; (*reject; propose rejection of*) отклон|я́ть, -и́ть; **he ~ed my request** он отклони́л мою́ про́сьбу.

opposite /ˈɒpəzɪt/ *n.* противополо́жность; **he was quite the ~ of what I expected** он оказа́лся по́лной противополо́жностью того́, что я ожида́л; **just the ~** как раз наоборо́т.
● *adj.* противополо́жный; **the ~ sex** противополо́жный пол; **in the ~ direction** в обра́тном направле́нии; **~ poles** (*elec.*) разноимённые по́люсы; **~ number** лицо́, занима́ющее таку́ю же до́лжность в друго́й организа́ции.
● *adv.* напро́тив.
● *prep.* (на)про́тив + *g.*; **his house is ~ ours** его́ дом (стои́т) напро́тив на́шего; **put a tick ~ your name** поста́вьте га́лочку про́тив ва́шей фами́лии.

opposition /ˌɒpəˈzɪʃ(ə)n/ *n.* **1** (*placing or being placed opposite*) противопоставле́ние; **they found themselves in ~ (to each other)** они́ оказа́лись в противополо́жных ла́герях. **2** (*contrast*) противополо́жность. **3** (*resistance, contrary action*) сопротивле́ние, противоде́йствие, оппози́ция; **the infantry encountered heavy ~** пехо́та встре́тила си́льное сопротивле́ние; **he offered no ~** он не оказа́л никако́го сопротивле́ния. **4** (*Br., pol.*) оппози́ция; **the Leader of the O~** ли́дер оппози́ции; **the party was in ~** па́ртия находи́лась в оппози́ции. **5** (*astron.*) противостоя́ние.

oppositionist /ˌɒpəˈzɪʃənɪst/ *n.* оппозиционе́р.

oppress /əˈpres/ *v.t.* **1** (*of a ruler or government*) угнета́ть (*impf.*); притесн|я́ть, -и́ть; подав|ля́ть, -и́ть. **2** (*weigh down; weary*) удруч|а́ть, -и́ть; томи́ть (*impf.*); **feel ~ed with the heat** томи́ться (*impf.*) от жары́.

oppression /əˈpreʃ(ə)n/ *n.* (*oppressing*) угнете́ние, гнёт, притесне́ние, тирани́я; (*being oppressed*) угнетённость.

oppressive /əˈpresɪv/ *adj.* угнета́ющий, давя́щий; (*tyrannical*) деспоти́ческий; (*burdensome*) тя́гостный; (*wearisome*) утоми́тельный; **~ weather** угнета́ющая/ду́шная пого́да.

oppressor /əˈpresə(r)/ *n.* угнета́тель (*m.*).

opprobrious /əˈprəʊbrɪəs/ *adj.* (*injurious*) оскорби́тельный; (*shameful*) позо́рный.

opprobrium /əˈprəʊbrɪəm/ *n.* (*reproach*) напа́дки (*m. pl.*); негодова́ние, возмуще́ние; (*shame, disgrace*) позо́р.

opt /ɒpt/ *v.i.*: **~ for** выбира́ть, вы́брать; **~ out of** отка́з|ываться, -а́ться от уча́стия в + *prep.*; (доброво́льно) выбыва́ть, вы́быть из + *g.*
● *cpd.* **~-out** *n.* отка́з от уча́стия в чём-н.

optative /ɒpˈteɪtɪv/, /ˈɒptətɪv/ *n.* **(~ mood)** оптати́в, жела́тельное наклоне́ние.
● *adj.* оптати́вный.

optic /ˈɒptɪk/ *n.* **1** (*lens*) ли́нза. **2** (*joc., eye*) глаз.
● *adj.* зри́тельный, глазно́й; **~ angle** у́гол зре́ния; **~ nerve** зри́тельный нерв.

optical /ˈɒptɪk(ə)l/ *adj.* опти́ческий; **~ fibre** (*Br.*), **fiber** (*US*) опти́ческое волокно́; **~ illusion** опти́ческий обма́н.

optician /ɒpˈtɪʃ(ə)n/ *n.* окули́ст.

optics /ˈɒptɪks/ *n.* о́птика.

optimism /ˈɒptɪˌmɪz(ə)m/ *n.* оптими́зм.

optimist /ˈɒptɪmɪst/ *n.* оптими́ст (*fem.* -ка).

optimistic /ˌɒptɪˈmɪstɪk/ *adj.* оптимисти́ческий, оптимисти́чный.

optimum /ˈɒptɪməm/ *adj.* оптима́льный.

option /ˈɒpʃ(ə)n/ *n.* **1** (*choice*) вы́бор; **soft ~** лёгкий вы́бор; **I have no ~ but to ...** у меня́ нет друго́го вы́бора, как...; **keep, leave one's ~s open** ост|авля́ть, -а́вить вы́бор за собо́й. **2** (*right of choice*) пра́во вы́бора; **I have an ~ on the house** я облада́ю преиму́щественным пра́вом на поку́пку э́того до́ма. **3** (*stock exchange etc.*) опцио́н; **~ price** курс пре́мий.

optional /ˈɒpʃən(ə)l/ *adj.* необяза́тельный, факультати́вный.

optometrist /ɒpˈtɒmɪtrɪst/ *n.* (*US*) окули́ст.

opulence /ˈɒpjʊləns/ *n.* бога́тство, оби́лие, изоби́лие.

opulent /ˈɒpjʊlənt/ *adj.* (*wealthy*) бога́тый; (*abundant*) оби́льный.

opus /ˈəʊpəs/, /ˈɒp-/ *n.* (*pl.* **opuses** *or* **opera**) **1** (*mus.*) о́пус. **2**: **magnum ~** труд всей жи́зни.

or /ɔː(r)/, /ə(r)/ *conj.* **1** и́ли; **will you be here ~ not?** вы здесь бу́дете и́ли нет?; **he came for a day ~ two** он прие́хал на день-друго́й; **two ~ three** два-три. **2** (**~ else**) и́ли, ина́че; и́ли же; а (не) то; **wear your coat ~ you'll catch cold** наде́ньте пальто́, ина́че (*or* а то) просту́дитесь; **we must hurry ~ we'll be late** ну́жно торопи́ться, а то опозда́ем; **do as I say ~ else!** де́лай что ска́зано и́ли пеня́й на себя́! **3**: **there were 20 ~ so people present** там бы́ло челове́к 20 (*or* о́коло двадцати́ челове́к). **4**: **storm ~ no storm, I shall go** гроза́ не гроза́, а я пойду́.

oracle /ˈɒrək(ə)l/ *n.* ора́кул; (*oracular statement*) прорица́ние, предсказа́ние.

oracular /əˈrækjʊlə(r)/ *adj.* (*prophetic*) проро́ческий; (*ambiguous*) двусмы́сленный; (*obscure*) зага́дочный.

oral /ˈɔːr(ə)l/ *n.* у́стный экза́мен.
● *adj.* (*by word of mouth*) у́стный; (*pert. to mouth*) стоматологи́ческий; **~ cavity** ротова́я по́лость; **~ contraceptive** противозача́точная табле́тка; **~ history** изу́стная исто́рия; **~ sex** ора́льный секс.

orange /ˈɒrɪndʒ/ *n.* **1** (*fruit*) апельси́н; (*attr.*) апельси́новый (*see also cpds.*); **Seville ~** помера́нец. **2** (*tree*) апельси́новое де́рево; **~ marmalade** апельси́новый джем. **3** (*colour*) ора́нжевый цвет.
● *adj.* (*colour*) ора́нжевый.
● *cpds.* **~-blossom** *n.* флёрдора́нж; помера́нцевые цветы́ (*m. pl.*); **~ juice** *n.* апельси́новый сок; **O~man** *n.* (*Br., pol.*) оранжи́ст; **~-peel** *n.* апельси́нная ко́рка; (*candied*) апельси́нный цука́т; **~-pip** (*Br.*), **-seed** (*US*) *nn.* зёрнышко апельси́на; **O~woman** *n.* (*Br., pol.*) оранжи́стка.

orangeade /ˌɒrɪndʒˈeɪd/ *n.* (*Br.*) оранжа́д (*напиток*).

orangery /ˈɒrɪndʒərɪ/ *n.* оранжере́я (для выра́щивания апельси́новых дере́вьев).

orang-utan /ɔːˌræŋuːˈtæn/ *n.* орангута́нг.

orate /ɔːˈreɪt/ *v.i.* ора́торствовать (*impf.*).

oration /ɔːˈreɪʃ(ə)n/, /ə-/ *n.* речь.

orator /ˈɒrətə(r)/ *n.* ора́тор.

oratorical /ˌɒrəˈtɒrɪk(ə)l/ *adj.* ора́торский.

oratorio /ˌɒrəˈtɔːrɪəʊ/ *n.* (*pl.* **~s**) орато́рия.

oratory /ˈɒrətərɪ/ *n.* (*rhetoric*) красноре́чие, рито́рика; (*chapel*) моле́льня.

orb /ɔːb/ *n.* (*globe, sphere*) шар, сфе́ра; (*heavenly body*) небе́сное свети́ло; (*part of regalia*) держа́ва.

orbit /ˈɔːbɪt/ *n.* **1** (*of planet etc.*) орби́та; (*circuit completed by space vehicle*) вито́к. **2** (*eye-socket*) глазна́я впа́дина, орби́та, глазни́ца. **3** (*fig., sphere of action*) сфе́ра де́ятельности, орби́та.

● *v.t.* (**orbited, orbiting**) (*move in ~ round*) враща́ться (*impf.*) вокру́г (+*g.*).

● *v.i.* (**orbited, orbiting**) (*move in ~*) враща́ться (*impf.*) по орби́те.

orbital /ˈɔːbɪt(ə)l/ *adj.* (*astron.*) орбита́льный; (*Br., of road*) кольцево́й; (*of eye*) глазно́й.

Orcadian /ɔːˈkeɪdɪən/ *n.* жи́тель (*fem.* -ница) Оркне́йских острово́в; оркне́|ец (*fem.* -йка).

● *adj.* оркне́йский.

orchard /ˈɔːtʃəd/ *n.* (фрукто́вый) сад; **cherry ~** ви́шнёвый сад.

orchestra /ˈɔːkɪstrə/ *n.* орке́стр; **full ~** симфони́ческий орке́стр; **~ pit** оркестро́вая я́ма; **~ stalls** (*Br.*) парте́р.

orchestral /ɔːˈkestr(ə)l/ *adj.* оркестро́вый.

orchestrate /ˈɔːkɪˌstreɪt/ *v.t.* оркестрова́ть (*impf., pf.*); (*fig.*) организова́ть, с-.

orchestration /ˌɔːkɪˈstreɪʃ(ə)n/ *n.* оркестро́вка.

orchid /ˈɔːkɪd/ *n.* орхиде́я.

ordain /ɔːˈdeɪn/ *v.t.* **1** (*eccl.*) посвя|ща́ть, -ти́ть в духо́вный сан; **he was ~ed priest** он был посвящён в свяще́нники. **2** (*destine, decree*) предпи́с|ывать, -а́ть.

ordeal /ɔːˈdiːl/ *n.* му́ка; (*unpleasant situation*) тяжёлое испыта́ние.

order /ˈɔːdə(r)/ *n.* **1** (*arrangement*) поря́док; (*sequence, succession*) после́довательность; **~ of the day** (*agenda*) пове́стка дня; **in alphabetical ~** в алфави́тном поря́дке; **in ~ of size** по разме́ру; **in ~ of importance** по сте́пени ва́жности; **out of ~, not in the right ~** не по поря́дку; не на (том) ме́сте; **put something in ~** прив|оди́ть, -ести́ что-н. в поря́док.
2 (*mil. formation*) строй; **battle ~** боево́й поря́док.
3 (*result of arrangement or control*) поря́док; **everything is in ~** всё в поря́дке; (*settled state*): **keep ~** подде́рживать/соблюда́ть (*both impf.*) поря́док; **restore ~** восстан|а́вливать, -ови́ть поря́док; **law and ~** правопоря́док; (*efficient state*) поря́док; (*of machinery*) испра́вность; **out of ~** неиспра́вный, в плохо́м состоя́нии; **the bell is out of ~** звоно́к не рабо́тает (*or* в неиспра́вности); **he got the typewriter into working ~** он почини́л (*or* привёл в поря́док) маши́нку.
4 (*procedure*) поря́док; (*procedural rules*) регла́мент; **call s.o. to ~** приз|ыва́ть, -ва́ть кого́-н. к поря́дку; **call a meeting to ~** откр|ыва́ть, -ы́ть заседа́ние; **maintain, keep ~ (in the hall)** обеспе́чи|вать, -ть соблюде́ние поря́дка (в за́ле); следи́ть (*impf.*) за поря́дком; **O~!** к поря́дку!; **he raised a point of ~** он вы́ступил по поря́дку веде́ния заседа́ния; **is it in ~ to ask questions?** позволя́ется ли задава́ть вопро́сы?; **out of ~** (*against procedure*) в наруше́ние процеду́ры.
5 (*command, instruction*) прика́з, распоряже́ние, поруче́ние; **by ~ of the president** по поруче́нию/прика́зу президе́нта; **give an, the ~** отд|ава́ть, -а́ть прика́з; **I won't take ~s from you** вы мной не распоряжа́йтесь/кома́ндуйте; **obey ~s** подчин|я́ться, -и́ться прика́зу; **till further ~s** до дальне́йшего распоряже́ния; **under s.o.'s ~s** под кома́ндой кого́-н.; **get one's marching ~s** (*dismissal*) (*fig.*) получ|а́ть, -и́ть отста́вку; (*warrant*) о́рдер (*pl.* -а́); **~ to view (a house)** (*Br.*) смотрово́й о́рдер.
6 (*direction to supply*) зака́з (на + *a.*); **on ~** по зака́зу; **is on ~** зака́зан; **put in an ~ for** зака́з|ывать, -а́ть; **I am having a suit made to ~** я шью себе́ костю́м на зака́з; **that's a tall ~** (*fig.*) э́то нелёгкая/тру́дная зада́ча.
7 (*direction to bank*): **standing ~** прика́з о регуля́рных платежа́х; (*pl., parl.*) пра́вила (*nt. pl.*) процеду́ры.
8 (*direction to Post Office*): **money/postal ~** де́нежный/почто́вый перево́д.
9 (*social group, stratum*) социа́льная гру́ппа; слой; **lower ~s** ни́зшие слои́;
10 (*pl., eccl.*): **holy ~s** духо́вный сан; **confer ~s on** рукопол|ага́ть, -ожи́ть; **take ~s** прин|има́ть, -я́ть духо́вный сан.
11 (*distinction; insignia*) о́рден (*pl.* -а́); **O~ of Lenin** (*hist.*) о́рден Ле́нина; **he was awarded the O~ of the Garter** его́ награди́ли о́рденом Подвя́зки.
12 (*kind, sort, category*) сорт, род; **talent of another ~** тала́нт ино́го поря́дка; (*math.*) поря́док; **a sum of the ~ of £10** су́мма поря́дка десяти́ фу́нтов; (*biol.*) отря́д; (*archit.*) о́рдер (*pl.* -ы), о́рден (*pl.* -ы).
13 (*of chivalry or relig.*) о́рден (*pl.* -ы).
14: **in ~ to** (для того́,) что́бы + *inf.*; **in ~ that** (для того́,) что́бы + *past tense*.

● *v.t.* **1** (*arrange, regulate*) прив|оди́ть, -ести́ в поря́док.
2 (*command*) прика́з|ывать, -а́ть; распоряж|а́ться, -ди́ться; **he ~ed an enquiry** он приказа́л (*or* дал распоряже́ние) провести́ рассле́дование; **he ~ed the soldiers to leave** он приказа́л солда́там разойти́сь; **he ~ed the gates to be closed** он приказа́л закры́ть воро́та; **he was ~ed home** ему́ приказа́ли верну́ться домо́й.
3 (*prescribe*) пропи́с|ывать, -а́ть.
4 (*reserve; request; arrange for supply of*) зака́з|ывать, -а́ть.
5: **~ s.o. about** кома́ндовать (*impf.*) + *i.*; **I don't like being ~ed about** я не люблю́, когда́ мно́ю кома́ндуют/распоряжа́ются.

● *cpds.* **~-book** *n.* (*Br.*) кни́га зака́зов; **~-form** *n.* бланк зака́за.

orderliness /ˈɔːdəlɪnɪs/ *n.* (*order*) поря́док; (*methodical nature*) аккура́тность; (*good behaviour*) хоро́шее поведе́ние, послуша́ние.

orderly /ˈɔːdəlɪ/ *n.* (*mil.*) ордина́рец; (*in hospital*) санита́р.

● *adj.* **1** (*methodical, neat, tidy*) аккура́тный, опря́тный. **2** (*quiet; well-behaved*) ти́хий, послу́шный. **3** (*organized*) организо́ванный. **4** (*mil.*): **~ officer** (*Br.*) дежу́рный офице́р.

ordinal /ˈɔːdɪn(ə)l/ *n.* (**~** *number*) поря́дковое числи́тельное.

ordinance /ˈɔːdɪnəns/ *n.* ука́з; (*decree*) декре́т.

ordinand /ˈɔːdɪˌnænd/ *n.* ожида́ющий рукоположе́ния.

ordinariness /ˈɔːdɪnərɪnɪs/ *n.* обы́чность, зауря́дность.

ordinary /ˈɔːdɪnərɪ/ *n.*: **out of the ~** необы́чный, незауря́дный.

● *adj.* (*usual*) обы́чный; (*average, common*) обыкнове́нный; (*simple*) просто́й; (*normal*) норма́льный; (*commonplace*) зауря́дный; **~ seaman** (*Br.*) мла́дший матро́с.

ordination /ˌɔːdɪˈneɪʃ(ə)n/ *n.* (*eccl.*) рукоположе́ние.

ordnance /ˈɔːdnəns/ *n.* (*artillery*) артилле́рия; **piece of ~** ору́дие; (*military stores and material*) артиллери́йско-техни́ческое и вещево́е снабже́ние; **O~ Survey** (*Br.*) госуда́рственное картографи́ческое управле́ние; **O~ Survey map** ка́рта картографи́ческого управле́ния.

ordure /ˈɔːdjʊə(r)/ *n.* (*dung*) наво́з; (*filth*) грязь.

ore /ɔː(r)/ *n.* руда́.

organ /ˈɔːgən/ *n.* **1** (*mus.*) орга́н; (*attr.*) орга́нный; **mouth ~** губна́я гармо́ника, гармо́шка (*coll.*); **street ~** шарма́нка. **2** (*biol., pol. etc.*) о́рган; **~ donor** до́нор; **~ transplant** переса́дка о́ргана.

● *cpds.* **~-grinder** *n.* шарма́нщик; **~-loft** *n.* хо́р|ы (*pl., g.* -ов); галере́я; **~-pipe** *n.* орга́нная труба́; **~-stop** *n.* реги́стр орга́на.

organdie /ˈɔːgəndɪ/, /-ˈgændɪ/ (*US also* **organdy**) *n.* органди́ (*f. indecl.*); кисе́я.

organic /ɔːˈgænɪk/ *adj.* органи́ческий; **~ food** натура́льные пищевы́е проду́кты; **~ whole** еди́ное це́лое.

organism /ˈɔːgəˌnɪz(ə)m/ *n.* органи́зм.

organist /ˈɔːgənɪst/ *n.* органи́ст (*fem.* -ка).

organization /ˌɔːgənaɪˈzeɪʃ(ə)n/ *n.* организа́ция.

organize /ˈɔːgəˌnaɪz/ *v.t.* организо́в|ывать, -а́ть; устр|а́ивать, -о́ить; (*play, performance*) ста́вить, по-; **it took him a long time to get ~d** он до́лго собира́лся; **she is an ~d person** она́ челове́к организо́ванный; **~d crime** организо́ванная престу́пность.

organizer /ˈɔːgəˌnaɪzə(r)/ *n.* организа́тор; **personal ~** органа́йзер.

organophosphate /ɔːˌgænəʊˈfɒsfeɪt/ *n.* органофосфа́т.

orgasm /ˈɔːgæz(ə)m/ *n.* орга́зм.

orgiastic /ˌɔːdʒɪˈæstɪk/ *adj.* (*fig.*) разну́зданный.

orgy /ˈɔːdʒɪ/ *n.* о́ргия; (*fig.*) разгу́л.

oriel /ˈɔːrɪəl/ *n.* э́ркер; **~ window** э́ркер.

Orient /ˈɔːrɪənt/ *n.* Восто́к.

● *v.t.* = **orient(ate)**

oriental /ˌɔːrɪˈent(ə)l/, /ˌɒr-/ *adj.* восто́чный; **~ studies** востокове́дение, ориентали́стика.

orientalism /ˌɔːrɪˈentəˌlɪz(ə)m/, /ˌɒr-/ *n.* ориентали́зм.

orientalist /ˌɔːrɪˈentəlɪst/, /ˌɒr-/ *n.* востокове́д, ориентали́ст.

orient(ate) /ˈɒrɪenˌteɪt/, /ˈɔːr-/ *v.t.* (*determine position of*) ориенти́ровать (*impf., pf.*); определ|я́ть, -и́ть местонахожде́ние +*g.*; **~ o.s.** ориенти́роваться (*impf., pf.*).

orientation /ˌɒrɪenˈteɪʃ(ə)n/, /ˌɔːr-/ *n.* (*lit., fig.*) ориентиро́вка, ориента́ция.

orienteering /ˌɔːrɪenˈtɪərɪŋ/, /ˌɒr-/ *n.* спорти́вное ориенти́рование, ориенти́рование на ме́стности.

orifice /ˈɒrɪfɪs/ *n.* (*aperture*) отве́рстие; (*mouth*) у́стье.

origin /ˈɒrɪdʒɪn/ *n.* (*beginning, source*) нача́ло, исто́чник; (*derivation, extraction*) происхожде́ние; **he is of peasant ~** он вы́ходец из крестья́н.

original /əˈrɪdʒɪn(ə)l/ *n.* **1** по́длинник, оригина́л; **a copy of the ~** ко́пия с по́длинника/оригина́ла; **I am reading Tolstoy in the ~** я чита́ю Толсто́го в по́длиннике, в оригина́ле. **2** (*eccentric*) оригина́л, чуда́к.

● *adj.* **1** (*first, earliest*) первонача́льный; **~ sin** первоpо́дный грех; **the ~ inhabitants** иско́нные жи́тели. **2** (*archetypal; genuine*) по́длинный; **~ manuscript** по́длинная ру́копись. **3** (*constructive, inventive*) оригина́льный, своеобы́тный; **an ~ mind** изобрета́тельный/самобы́тный ум. **4** (*novel, fresh*) но́вый, све́жий; своеобра́зный.

originality /əˌrɪdʒɪˈnælɪtɪ/ *n.* оригина́льность, самобы́тность.

originally /əˈrɪdʒɪnəlɪ/ *adv.* (*in the first place*) первонача́льно, исхо́дно; (*in origin*) по происхожде́нию.

originate /əˈrɪdʒɪˌneɪt/ *v.t.* **1** (*cause to begin, initiate*) поро|жда́ть, -ди́ть; дав|а́ть, -ть нача́ло +*d.* **2** (*create*) созд|ава́ть, -а́ть; поро|жда́ть, -ди́ть.

● *v.i.* брать, взять нача́ло; (*arise*) возн|ика́ть, -и́кнуть; (*of something bad*) зав|оди́ться, -ести́сь; **the quarrel ~d in a remark of mine** ссо́ра возни́кла из-за моего́ замеча́ния.

origination /əˌrɪdʒɪˈneɪʃ(ə)n/ *n.* (*source, origin*) нача́ло, происхожде́ние; (*creation*) созда́ние.

originator /əˈrɪdʒɪˌneɪtə(r)/ *n.* (*initiator*) инициа́тор; (*author*) а́втор; (*creator*) созда́тель (*m.*); (*inventor*) изобрета́тель (*m.*); (*sender of message*) отправи́тель (*m.*).

oriole /ˈɔːrɪəʊl/ *n.* и́волга.

Orkney /ˈɔːknɪ/ *n.*: **the ~s (also the ~ Islands)** Оркне́йские острова́ (*m. pl.*); (*attr.*) оркне́йский.

ormolu /ˈɔːməˌluː/ *n.* золочёная бро́нза.

ornament[1] /ˈɔːnəmənt/ *n.* **1** (*adornment, embellishment*) украше́ние. **2** (*decorative article or feature*) орна́мент.

ornament[2] /ˈɔːnəˌment/ *v.t.* укр|аша́ть, -а́сить.

ornamental /ˌɔːnəˈment(ə)l/ *adj.* орнамента́льный; (*decorative*) декорати́вный.

ornamentation /ˌɔːnəmenˈteɪʃ(ə)n/ *n.* украше́ние.

ornate /ɔːˈneɪt/ *adj.* бога́то укра́шенный; (*of style*) витиева́тый, цвети́стый.

ornithological /ˌɔːnɪθəˈlɒdʒɪk(ə)l/ *adj.* орнитологи́ческий.

ornithologist /ˌɔːnɪˈθɒlədʒɪst/ *n.* орнито́лог.

ornithology /ˌɔːnɪˈθɒlədʒɪ/ *n.* орнитоло́гия.

orotund /ˈɒrəˌtʌnd/, /ˈɔːr-/ *adj.* (*of voice*) зву́чный, полнозву́чный; (*of style*) высокопа́рный; (*pretentious*) напы́щенный.

orphan /ˈɔːf(ə)n/ *n.* сирота́ (*c.g.*).

● *adj.* сиро́тский.

● *v.t.* лиш|а́ть, -и́ть (*кого*) роди́телей; де́лать, с- сирото́й; **an ~ed child** осироте́вший ребёнок.

orphanage /ˈɔːfənɪdʒ/ *n.* прию́т для сиро́т.

orris /ˈɒrɪs/ *n.* (*bot.*) каса́тик флоренти́йский.

● *cpd.* **~-root** *n.* фиа́лковый ко́рень; (*powder*) порошо́к из фиа́лкового ко́рня.

orthodox /ˈɔːθəˌdɒks/ *adj.* (*relig.*) ортодокса́льный, правове́рный; **the O~ Church** правосла́вная це́рковь; (*fig.*) ортодокса́льный.

orthodoxy /ˈɔːθəˌdɒksɪ/ *n.* (*relig.*) ортодокса́льность, правове́рность; (*denomination*) правосла́вие; (*fig.*) ортодокса́льность.

orthographic(al) /ˌɔːθəˈgræfɪk((ə)l)/ *adj.* орфографи́ческий.

orthography /ɔːˈθɒgrəfɪ/ *n.* правописа́ние, орфогра́фия.

orthopaedic /ˌɔːθəˈpiːdɪk/ (*US* **orthopedic**) *adj.* ортопеди́ческий.

orthopaedics /ˌɔːθəˈpiːdɪks/ (*US* **orthopedics**) *n.* ортопе́ди́я.

orthopaedist /ˌɔːθəˈpiːdɪst/ (*US* **orthopedist**) *n.* ортопе́д.

ortolan /ˈɔːtələn/ *n.* садо́вая овся́нка (*птица*).

oryx /ˈɒrɪks/ *n.* сернобы́к.

Oscar /ˈɒskə(r)/ *n.* (*cin.*) пре́мия О́скара.

● *cpds.* **~-winner** *n.* лауреа́т пре́мии О́скара; **~-winning** *adj.*: **~-winning picture** фильм, получи́вший О́скара.

oscillate /ˈɒsɪˌleɪt/ *v.t.* кача́ть (*impf.*).

● *v.i.* (*swing*) кача́ться (*impf.*); (*elec., radio; also fig.*) колеба́ться (*impf.*).

oscillation /ˌɒsɪˈleɪʃ(ə)n/ *n.* колеба́ние; (*elec.*) осцилля́ция.

oscillator /ˈɒsɪˌleɪtə(r)/ *n.* осцилля́тор; (*radio*) генера́тор.

oscillatory /ɒˈsɪlətərɪ/, /ˈɒsɪˌleɪtərɪ/ *adj.* колеба́тельный.

oscillograph /əˈsɪləˌgrɑːf/ *n.* осцилло́граф.

oscilloscope /əˈsɪləˌskəʊp/ *n.* осциллоско́п.

osier /ˈəʊzɪə(r)/ *n.* (*plant*) и́ва; (*shoot*) лоза́.

● *adj.* и́вовый.

● *cpd.* **~-bed** *n.* ивня́к.

Oslo /ˈɒzləʊ/ *n.* О́сло (*m. indecl.*).

osmium /ˈɒzmɪəm/ *n.* (*chem.*) о́смий.

osmosis /ɒzˈməʊsɪs/ *n.* (*biol., chem.*) о́смос.

osmotic /ɒzˈmɒtɪk/ *adj.* (*biol., chem.*) осмоти́ческий.

osprey /ˈɒspreɪ/, /-prɪ/ *n.* (*pl.* **~s**) (*zool.*) скопа́.

osseous /ˈɒsɪəs/ *adj.* (*of bone*) костяно́й; (*bony*) кости́стый.

ossification /ˌɒsɪfɪˈkeɪʃ(ə)n/ *n.* окостене́ние (*also fig.*).

ossif|y /ˈɒsɪˌfaɪ/ *v.t. & i.* превра|ща́ть(ся), -ти́ть(ся) в кость; (*fig.*) заст|ыва́ть, -ы́ть; костене́ть, о-.

Ostend /ɒsˈtend/ *n.* Осте́нде (*m. indecl.*).

ostensibl|e /ɒˈstensɪb(ə)l/ *adj.* (*for show*) показно́й; (*professed*) мни́мый; **he called ~y to thank me** он пришёл я́кобы для того́, что́бы поблагодари́ть меня́.

ostentation /ˌɒstenˈteɪʃ(ə)n/ *n.* (*display*) выставле́ние напока́з; (*boasting*) хвастовство́, бахва́льство.

ostentatious /ˌɒstenˈteɪʃəs/ *adj.* показно́й, хвастли́вый.

osteoarthritis /ˌɒstɪəʊɑːˈθraɪtɪs/ *n.* остеоартри́т.

osteopath /ˈɒstɪəˌpæθ/ *n.* остеопа́т.

osteopathic /ˌɒstɪəˈpæθɪk/ *adj.* остеопати́ческий.

osteopathy /ˌɒstɪˈɒpəθɪ/ *n.* остеопа́тия.

osteoporosis /ˌɒstɪəʊpəˈrəʊsɪs/ *n.* остеопоро́з.

ostler /ˈɒslə(r)/ (*US* **hostler**) *n.* ко́нюх.

ostracism /ˈɒstrəˌsɪz(ə)m/ *n.* (*hist., fig.*) острaки́зм; (*fig.*) изгна́ние (из о́бщества).

ostracize /ˈɒstrəˌsaɪz/ *v.t.* подв|ерга́ть, -е́ргнуть острaки́зму; изг|оня́ть, -на́ть.

ostrich /ˈɒstrɪtʃ/ *n.* стра́ус; (*attr.*) стра́усовый.

other /ˈʌðə(r)/ *pron.* друго́й, ино́й; **the ~** (*liter., person referred to*) тот; **one (thing) or the ~** одно́ из двух; **~s may disagree with you** други́е/ины́е мо́гут с ва́ми не согласи́ться; **as an example to ~s** в приме́р други́м/про́чим; **'~s'** (*in classification*) про́чие; **one after the ~** оди́н за други́м; **we talked of this, that and the ~** мы говори́ли о том о сём (*coll.*); **someone or ~** кто́-нибудь; **some day or ~** когда́-нибудь, ка́к-нибудь; **somehow or ~** ка́к-нибудь; **I want this book and no ~** я хочу́ и́менно э́ту кни́гу; **it was none ~ than Mr Brown** э́то был не кто ино́й, как сам г-н Бра́ун; **no one ~ than he** никто́ кро́ме него́; **I could do no ~ than agree** мне не остава́лось ничего́ друго́го, как согласи́ться; (*expr. reciprocity*): **they were in love with each ~** они́ бы́ли влюблены́ друг в дру́га; **they got in each ~'s way** они́ друг дру́гу меша́ли; (*pl., additional ones; more*) ещё +*g.*; **let me see some ~s** покажи́те ещё каки́е-нибудь!; **there are no ~s** други́х нет; (*remaining ones*) остальны́е; **the ~s had already gone** остальны́е уже́ ушли́; **why this day of all ~s?** почему́ и́менно сего́дня?

● *adj.* **1** друго́й; **on the ~ hand** с друго́й стороны́; **on the ~ side of the road** на друго́й/той стороне́ доро́ги; **the ~ world** тот свет; **the ~ side of the moon** обра́тная сторона́ Луны́; **we must find some ~ way** мы должны́ найти́ друго́й спо́соб; **there was no ~ place to go** бо́льше идти́ бы́ло не́куда; **some ~ time** в друго́й раз.
2 (*additional*) ещё +*g.*; **how many ~ children have you?** ско́лько у вас ещё дете́й?
3 (*remaining*) остально́й; **we shall visit the ~ museums tomorrow** мы посети́м остальны́е музе́и за́втра; **~ things being equal** при про́чих ра́вных усло́виях.
4: **the ~ day** на днях; **every ~** ка́ждый второ́й; **every ~ day** че́рез день.
5: **~ ranks** (*Br., mil.*) сержа́нтско-рядово́й соста́в.

● *adv.*: *see* ⇒**otherwise** *adv.* **1**

● *cpd.* **~-worldly** *adj.* (*not of this world*) не от ми́ра сего́; (*relating to life after death*) потусторо́нний.

otherness /ˈʌðənɪs/ *n.* непохо́жесть, отли́чие.

otherwise /ˈʌðəˌwaɪz/ *adj.*: **the matter is quite ~** де́ло обстои́т совсе́м ина́че/не так.

● *adv.* **1** (*in a different way*) ина́че, по-друго́му, други́м спо́собом; **I was ~ engaged** я был за́нят други́м (де́лом); **~ known as ...** та́кже имену́емый +*i.*; (*of person*) он же; **I could do no ~ (or other)** я не мог поступи́ть ина́че.
2 (*in other respects or circumstances*) в други́х отноше́ниях; **the house is cold but ~ comfortable** дом холо́дный, но в остально́м удо́бный; **I will go if you do, but not ~** я пойду́ то́лько, е́сли вы то́же пойдёте.
3 (*if not; or else*) ина́че, а то; **I went, ~ I would have missed them** я пошёл, ина́че я бы их не заста́л; **shut the windows, ~ it will be noisy** закро́йте о́кна, а то бу́дет шу́мно.
4: **the merits or ~ of the plan** досто́инства и́ли недоста́тки э́того пла́на.

otiose /ˈəʊʃɪəʊs/, /ˈəʊt-/, /-əʊz/ *adj.* изли́шний.

otitis /əˈtaɪtɪs/ *n.* (*med.*) оти́т.

OTT (*abbr. of* ***over-the-top***) (*Br. coll.*) чрезме́рный; **it's/that's ~** э́то уже́ сли́шком.

Ottawa /ˈɒtəwə/ *n.* Отта́ва.

otter /ˈɒtə(r)/ *n.* вы́дра; **sea ~** морско́й бобр.

Ottoman /ˈɒtəmən/ *n.* (*pl.* **~s**) **1** (*hist.*) оттома́н. **2** (*sofa*) оттома́нка, тахта́.

● *adj.* оттома́нский.

ouch /aʊtʃ/ *int.* ой!, ай!

ought /ɔːt/ *v. aux.* **1** (*expr. duty*) до́лжен; **you ~ to go there** вы должны́ (*or* вам сле́дует) туда́ пойти́; **you ~ to have gone yesterday** вам сле́довало пойти́ туда́ вчера́; **he ~ never to have done it** он ни в ко́ем слу́чае не до́лжен был так поступа́ть.
2 (*expr. desirability*) до́лжен; на́до (+*d.*); **you ~ to see that film** вы (непреме́нно) должны́ посмотре́ть э́тот фильм; **you ~ to have seen his face** на́до бы́ло ви́деть его́ лицо́; **I told him the house ~ to be painted** я сказа́л ему́, что дом на́до покра́сить.
3 (*expr. probability*) должно́ быть, вероя́тно; **if he started early he ~ to be there by now** е́сли он отпра́вился ра́но, то он, вероя́тно (*or* должно́ быть), сейча́с уже́ там; **it ~ not to take you long** э́то не должно́ заня́ть у вас мно́го вре́мени.

ouija-board /ˈwiːdʒə/ *n.* планше́тка для спирити́ческих сеа́нсов.

ounce[1] /aʊns/ *n.* (*weight*) у́нция; (*fig.*): **he hasn't an ~ of sense** у него́ нет ни ка́пли/гра́мма здра́вого смы́сла.

ounce[2] /aʊns/ *n.* (*zool.*) и́рбис.

our /ˈaʊə(r)/ *poss. adj.* наш; **O~ Father** О́тче наш; **O~ Lady** Бо́жья ма́терь, Пресвята́я де́ва; **in ~ midst** среди́ нас, в на́шей среде́; **in ~ opinion** (*i.e. of the writer, editor*) по на́шему мне́нию.

ours /ˈaʊəz/ *pron. & pred. adj.* наш; **~ is a blue car** на́ша маши́на си́няя; **this tree is ~** э́то де́рево на́ше; **this government of ~** э́то на́ше прави́тельство; **if you are short of chairs, borrow ~** е́сли у вас не хвата́ет сту́льев, возьми́те на́ши (*or* у нас).

ourselves /aʊəˈselvz/ *pron.* **1** (*refl.*) себя́; **we washed ~** мы умы́лись; (*after preps.*): **we can only depend on ~** мы мо́жем полага́ться то́лько на себя́ (сами́х); **we were not satisfied with ~** мы бы́ли недово́льны собо́й.
2 (*emph.*) са́ми; **we ~ were not present** са́ми мы не прису́тствовали.
3: **by ~** (*alone*) са́ми (по себе́); (*without aid*) са́ми, одни́; **we can't do it by ~** мы не мо́жем сде́лать э́то са́ми/одни́.

oust /aʊst/ *v.t.* (*force out; also fig.*) вытесня́ть, вы́теснить; (*expel*) выгоня́ть, вы́гнать.

out /aʊt/ *pred. adj. & adv.* (*for phrasal vv. with* **out** *see relevant v. entries*) **1** (*away from home, office, room, usual place etc.*): **he is ~** его́ нет до́ма; **he is, was ~ for lunch** он ушёл обе́дать; **let's have dinner ~!** пойдёмте обе́дать в рестора́н!; **the jury was ~ for 2 hours** прися́жные совеща́лись два часа́; **the book was ~** (*of the library*) кни́га была́ вы́дана (*or* на рука́х); **the children are ~** (*of school*) **early today** сего́дня дете́й отпусти́ли ра́но; (*of expulsion*): **the crowd were shouting 'Stevens ~!'** толпа́ крича́ла: «доло́й Сти́венса!» (*or* «Сти́венса вон!»); **the workers are ~** (*on strike*) рабо́чие басту́ют; (*sport*) вне игры́; **~!** (*at tennis*) а́ут!
2 (**~** *of doors*) на дворе́; на у́лице; **it is quite warm ~ today** сего́дня на дворе́ тепло́; **he was ~ and about all day** он был на нога́х весь день; **we were ~ in the garden** мы бы́ли в саду́; (*fig., intent*): **they are ~ to get him** они́ (во что бы то ни ста́ло) наме́рены его́ пойма́ть; **he is ~ for my blood** он жа́ждет мое́й кро́ви; **he is ~ for what he can get** он блюдёт свои́ интере́сы.
3 (*extracted*): **you will feel better when the tooth is ~** вы почу́вствуете себя́ лу́чше, когда́ вам удаля́т зуб.
4 (*open*): **the blossom is ~** цветы́ распусти́лись; (*visible*): **the moon came ~** луна́ показа́лась/появи́лась; **the stars are ~** звёзды вы́сыпали; **the sun will be ~ this afternoon** по́сле полу́дня пока́жется/поя́вится со́лнце; (*revealed*): **the secret is, was ~** секре́т раскры́лся (*or* стал всем изве́стен); **murder will ~** ≈ ши́ла в мешке́ не утаи́шь; **~ with it!** выкла́дывайте!; говори́те же, что́ у вас на уме́!; (*published, issued*): **my book is ~ at last** моя́ кни́га, наконе́ц, вы́шла (из печа́ти); **when will the results be ~?** когда́ объя́вят результа́ты?; **there is a warrant ~ for his arrest** на его́ аре́ст вы́писан/вы́дан о́рдер.
5 (*with superl.*): **whisky is the best thing ~ for a cold** ви́ски — лу́чшее сре́дство от просту́ды.
6 (*at departure*): **will you see me ~?** вы меня́ прово́дите (до двере́й)?; **on the voyage ~** на пути́ туда́; **he stumbled on the way ~** выходя́, он споткну́лся; (*at a distance*): **he is ~ in the Far East** он на Да́льнем Восто́ке; **~ at sea** в откры́том мо́ре; **when they were four days ~** на четвёртый день пла́вания; **the tide is ~** сейча́с отли́в.
7 (*coll.,* **~** *of favour, fashion*): **short hair is ~** коро́ткая стри́жка не в мо́де; (*inadmissible*): **that idea is ~ for a start** э́та иде́я исключа́ется с са́мого нача́ла; (*astray, wrong*): **be ~ in one's calculations** ошиб|а́ться, -и́ться в расчётах; **I wasn't far ~** я не на мно́го оши́бся; **my watch is 10 minutes ~** мои́ часы́ отстаю́т/спеша́т/(*coll.*) врут на де́сять мину́т.
8 (*ended, over*): **before the week is ~** до оконча́ния неде́ли; (*extinguished*): **the fire is ~** ого́нь поту́х; (*conflagration*) пожа́р ко́нчился; **lights ~!** гаси́те свет!; (*unconscious*) без созна́ния; **he was ~ (for the count)** он был в нока́уте.
9: **~ and ~** соверше́нно, по́лностью; **~ and away** безусло́вно, несравне́нно.
10: **~ of** (*movement*) из+*g.*; **he fell ~ of the window** он вы́пал из окна́; **as they came ~ of the theatre** (*Br.*), **theater** (*US*) когда́ они́ вы́шли из теа́тра; **he leapt ~ of bed** он вскочи́л с посте́ли; (*material*): **made ~ of silk** (сши́тый) из шёлка, шёлковый; (*from among*): **2 students ~ of 40** два студе́нта из сорока́; **one week ~ of ten** одна́ неде́ля из десяти́; (*motive*): **~ of pity/love/respect** из жа́лости/любви́/уваже́ния (*к кому/чему*); **~ of grief/joy** с го́ря/ра́дости; **~ of boredom** от/со

O

скýки; (*outside*): **~ of danger** вне опáсности; **~ of doors** на ýлице, на дворé, на вóздухе; **~ of hours** вне рабóчего врéмени; не в приёмные часы́; **~ of (its) place** не на мéсте; **it's ~ of the question** об э́том не мóжет быть и рéчи; **~ of town** зá городом; **he is ~ of town** егó нет в гóроде; он уéхал; **feel ~ of it** чýвствовать (*impf.*) себя́ чужи́м (*or* ни при чём); (*not conforming or amenable to*): **~ of condition** не в фóрме; **~ of control** вне контрóля; **~ of fashion** не в мóде; **get ~ of hand** выходи́ть, вы́йти из-под контрóля; отби́ться (*pf.*) от рук; **~ of sorts** не в своéй тарéлке; не в дýхе/настроéнии; **~ of step** не в нóгу; **~ of tune** расстрóенный; не в тон; (*without*): **~ of breath** запыхáвшийся; **~ of work** безрабóтный; **we are ~ of sugar** у нас кóнчился сáхар; (*origin*): **a scene ~ of a play** сцéна из пьéсы.

● *v.t.* (*knock ~*) нокаути́ровать (*impf., pf.*); (*coll., expose as being homosexual*) изоблич|áть, -и́ть в гомосексуали́зме.

outage /ˈaʊtɪdʒ/ *n.* (*of machine*) бездéйствие, простóй; (*of power supply*) отключéние.

out-and-out /ˌaʊtəndˈaʊt/ *adj.* совершéнный, пóлный, отъя́вленный.

outback /ˈaʊtbæk/ *n.* глушь.

outbid /aʊtˈbɪd/ *v.t.* (*at auction*): **~ s.o.** предл|агáть, -ожи́ть бóлее высóкую цéну, чем ктo-н.

outboard /ˈaʊtbɔːd/ *adj.*: **~ motor** подвеснóй мотóр.

outbound /ˈaʊtbaʊnd/ *adj.* выходя́щий/уходя́щий в рейс.

outbreak /ˈaʊtbreɪk/ *n.* (*of disease, anger etc.*) вспы́шка; **~ of hostilities** начáло воéнных дéйствий.

outbuilding /ˈaʊtˌbɪldɪŋ/ *n.* надвóрное строéние, надвóрная пострóйка.

outburst /ˈaʊtbɜːst/ *n.* (*of rage etc.*) вспы́шка, взрыв; (*of applause or laughter*) взрыв.

outcast /ˈaʊtkɑːst/ *n.* изгнáнник, отвéрженный.

● *adj.* и́згнанный, отвéрженный.

outclass /aʊtˈklɑːs/ *v.t.* прев|осходи́ть, -зойти́.

outcome /ˈaʊtkʌm/ *n.* (*result*) исхóд, результáт; (*consequence*) (по)слéдствие.

outcrop /ˈaʊtkrɒp/ *n.* (*geol.*) обнажéние.

● *v.i.* обнаж|áться, -и́ться; выходи́ть, вы́йти на повéрхность.

outcry /ˈaʊtkraɪ/ *n.* (*noise*) крик, вы́крик; (*protest*) протéст; (общéственное) негодовáние.

outdated /aʊtˈdeɪtɪd/ *adj.* устарéлый, устарéвший.

outdistance /aʊtˈdɪst(ə)ns/ *v.t.* перег|онять, -нáть.

outdo /aʊtˈduː/ *v.t.* прев|осходи́ть, -зойти́.

outdoor /ˈaʊtdɔː(r)/ *adj.*: **~ games** и́гры на откры́том вóздухе, подвижны́е и́гры; **~ clothes** вéрхнее плáтье.

outdoors /aʊtˈdɔːz/ *n.*: **the great ~** мáтушка прирóда.

● *adv.* на откры́том вóздухе, на дворé; (*expr. motion*) на вóздух.

outer /ˈaʊtə(r)/ *adj.* (*external*) внéшний; **the ~ world** внéшний мир; (*turned to the outside*) нарýжный; (*further away*): **~ space** кóсмос; **the ~ suburbs** дáльний при́город.

outermost /ˈaʊtəˌməʊst/ *adj.* сáмый дáльний.

outface /aʊtˈfeɪs/ *v.t.* (*defy*) смy|щáть, -ти́ть; конфýзить, с-.

outfall /ˈaʊtfɔːl/ *n.* (*of river*) ýстье; (*of drain*) вы́ход.

outfield /ˈaʊtfiːld/ *n.* (*sport*) дáльняя часть пóля; (*outlying land*) отдалённое пóле.

outfit /ˈaʊtfɪt/ *n.* **1** (*set of equipment*) снаряжéние, комплéкт; (*of clothes*) комплéкт (одéжды). **2** (*coll., group of people*) компáния, грýппа, бáнда (*coll.*).

outfitter /ˈaʊtˌfɪtə(r)/ *n.*: **gentlemen's ~** (*Br.*) магази́н мужскóй одéжды.

outflank /aʊtˈflæŋk/ *v.t.* об|ходи́ть, -ойти́ (*or* охвáт|ывать, -и́ть) фланг + *g.*; (*fig., outwit*) перехитри́ть (*pf.*).

outflow /ˈaʊtfləʊ/ *n.* (*of liquid*) истечéние; (*e.g. of currency*) утéчка.

outfox /aʊtˈfɒks/ *v.t.* (*coll.*) перехитри́ть (*pf.*).

outgoing /ˈaʊtˌgəʊɪŋ/ *adj.* **1** (*departing*): **~ ship** уходя́щее сýдно; **~ mail** исходя́щая пóчта; **the ~ president** президéнт, уходя́щий с постá. **2** (*sociable*): **an ~ person** общи́тельный/ужи́вчивый человéк.

outgoings /ˈaʊtˌgəʊɪŋz/ *n.* (*Br.*) расхóды (*m. pl.*), издéржки (*f. pl.*).

outgrow /aʊtˈgrəʊ/ *v.t.* **1** (*grow taller than*) перераст|áть, -и́; (*grow too large for*) вырастáть, вы́расти из + *g.*; **my family has ~n our house** наш дом стал тéсен для моéй семьи́. **2** (*discard with time*) вырастáть, вы́расти из + *g.*

outgrowth /ˈaʊtgrəʊθ/ *n.* **1** (*of plants etc.*) нарóст. **2** (*result, development*) продýкт, результáт. **3** (*off-shoot*) óтпрыск, побéг.

outgun /aʊtˈgʌn/ *v.t.* (*be better armed than*) дост|игáть, -и́чь огневóго превосхóдства над + *i.*; (*shoot better than*) стреля́ть (*impf.*) лýчше чем.

outhouse /ˈaʊthaʊs/ *n.* надвóрное строéние; (*US, lavatory*) убóрная во дворé, отхóжее мéсто.

outing /ˈaʊtɪŋ/ *n.* прогýлка, экскýрсия; (*on foot*) похóд; (*picnic*) пикни́к.

outlandish /aʊtˈlændɪʃ/ *adj.* дикóвинный, чуднóй.

outlast /aʊtˈlɑːst/ *v.t.* (*outlive*) переж|ивáть, -и́ть.

outlaw /ˈaʊtlɔː/ *n.* лицó, объя́вленное вне закóна.

● *v.t.* объяв|ля́ть, -и́ть вне закóна.

outlay /ˈaʊtleɪ/ *n.* (*expenses*) издéржки (*f. pl.*), затрáты (*f. pl.*); **~ on clothes** расхóды (*m. pl.*) на одéжду.

outlet /ˈaʊtlet/, /-lɪt/ *n.* **1** (*lit.*) выходнóе/выпускнóе отвéрстие. **2** (*market*) сбыт; (*shop*) фи́рменный магази́н. **3** (*for energies etc.*) отдýшина, вы́ход. **4** (*elec.*) штéпсельная розéтка.

outline /ˈaʊtlaɪn/ *n.* **1** (*contour*) кóнтур, áбрис; (*of badly visible object*) очертáние; (*attr.*) кóнтурный. **2** (*summary*) план, схéма; (*of speech, article*) конспéкт; **in ~** в óбщих чертáх.

● *v.t.* **1** (*drawing*) рисовáть, на- кóнтур (*чего*). **2** (*give an ~ of*) нам|ечáть, -éтить в óбщих чертáх; набр|áсывать, -осáть.

outlive /aʊtˈlɪv/ *v.t.* переж|ивáть, -и́ть.

outlook /ˈaʊtlʊk/ *n.* **1** (*prospect, lit., fig.*) вид, перспекти́ва; **the ~ for trade is good** перспекти́вы для торгóвли хорóшие; (*weather etc.*) прогнóз. **2** (*point of view*) тóчка зрéния; (*mental horizon*) кругозóр.

outlying /ˈaʊtˌlaɪɪŋ/ *adj.* отдалённый, удалённый.

outmanoeuvre /ˌaʊtməˈnuːvə(r)/ (*US* **outmaneuver**) *v.t.* (*fig.*) перехитри́ть (*pf.*).

outmatch /aʊtˈmætʃ/ *v.t.* прев|осходи́ть, -зойти́.

outmoded /aʊtˈməʊdɪd/ *adj.* старомóдный, немóдный, устарéлый.

outnumber /aʊtˈnʌmbə(r)/ *v.t.* прев|осходи́ть, -зойти́ (*кого, что*) чи́сленно.

out-of-date /ˌaʊtəvˈdeɪt/ *adj.* устарéлый, старомóдный.

out-of-fashion /ˌaʊtəvˈfæʃ(ə)n/ *adj.* старомóдный, немóдный.

out-of-the-way /ˌaʊtəvðəˈweɪ/ *adj.* **1** (*remote*) отдалённый, удалённый. **2** (*obscure*) малоизвéстный.

out-of-work /ˌaʊtəvˈwɜːk/ *adj.* безрабóтный.

outpace /aʊtˈpeɪs/ *v.t.* об|гоня́ть, -огнáть.

out-patient /ˈaʊtˌpeɪʃ(ə)nt/ *n.* амбулатóрный больнóй; **~ department** амбулатóрия, поликли́ника.

outperform /ˌaʊtpəˈfɔːm/ *v.t.* прев|осходи́ть, -зойти́.

outplay /aʊtˈpleɪ/ *v.t.* обыгр|ывать, -áть.

outpost /ˈaʊtpəʊst/ *n.* (*mil.*) аванпóст; (*settlement*) отдалённое поселéние.

outpouring /ˈaʊtˌpɔːrɪŋ/ *n.* излия́ние.

output /ˈaʊtpʊt/ *n.* **1** (*production*) вы́пуск, продýкция, произвóдство; **literary ~** литератýрная продýкция; (*of mine*) добы́ча; (*of power station*) мóщность; (*of computer*) выходя́щая информáция. **2** (*productivity*) производи́тельность.

● *v.t.* (*past and p.p.* **output** *or* **outputted**) (*comput.*) выводи́ть, вы́вести.

outrage /ˈaʊtreɪdʒ/ *n.* (*outrageous situation*) безобрáзие; (*outrageous act*) безобрáзный постýпок; (*anger*) негодовáние.

● *v.t.* (*offend, insult*) оскорб|ля́ть, -и́ть; (*anger*) вызывáть, вы́звать негодовáние у + *g.*, возму|щáть, -ти́ть.

outrageous /aʊtˈreɪdʒəs/ *adj.*

безобра́зный, возмути́тельный, вопию́щий, сканда́льный; **an ~ remark** возмути́тельное замеча́ние.

outré /ˈuːtreɪ/ *adj.* (*eccentric*) экстравага́нтный; (*improper*) неприе́млемый.

outrider /ˈaʊt,raɪdə(r)/ *n.* (*usu. pl.*) эско́рт.

outrigger /ˈaʊt,rɪɡə(r)/ *n.* (*rowlock*) выносна́я уклю́чина; (*boat*) аутри́гер.

outright /ˈaʊtraɪt/ *adj.* (*open, direct*) прямо́й, откры́тый; (*absolute*) соверше́нный; **an ~ scoundrel** отъя́вленный моше́нник; **he gave an ~ denial** он категори́чески отрица́л (свою́ вину́ *и т.п.*).

● *adv.* (*openly, right out*) пря́мо, откры́то; (*at once*) сра́зу; (*once and for all*) раз (и) навсегда́; **own something ~** владе́ть (*impf.*) чем-н. по́лностью.

outrun /aʊtˈrʌn/ *v.t.* (*outstrip*) опере|жа́ть, -ди́ть; (*run farther than*) перег|оня́ть, -на́ть.

outsell /aʊtˈsel/ *v.t.*: **~ something** продава́ться (*impf.*) бо́льше, чем что-н.; **~ s.o.** прод|ава́ть, -а́ть бо́льше, чем кто-н.

outset /ˈaʊtset/ *n.* нача́ло; **at the ~** внача́ле; **from the ~** с са́мого нача́ла.

outshine /aʊtˈʃaɪn/ *v.t.* (*past and p.p.* **outshone**) (*lit., fig.*) затм|ева́ть, -и́ть.

outside /aʊtˈsaɪd/, /ˈaʊtsaɪd/ *n.* нару́жная сторона́; (*outer surface*) вне́шняя пове́рхность; (*of cloth*) лицева́я сторона́, лицо́; **from ~** извне́; **from, on the ~** снару́жи; **the door opens from the ~** дверь открыва́ется снару́жи; **the ~ of the house needs painting** нару́жные сте́ны до́ма нужда́ются в покра́ске; **at the (very) ~** са́мое бо́льшее.

● *adj.* **1** (*external, exterior*) нару́жный, вне́шний; **~ repairs** нару́жный ремо́нт; **~ broadcast** (*Br.*) внестуди́йная переда́ча.
2 (*extreme*) кра́йний; **he has an ~ chance of winning** у него́ есть небольшо́й шанс на вы́игрыш; **~ left/right** (*sport*) ле́вый/пра́вый кра́йний.
3 (*not belonging*) посторо́нний, вне́шний; **~ help** посторо́нняя по́мощь; **the ~ world** вне́шний мир.

● *adv.* снару́жи; извне́; (*to the ~*) нару́жу; (*out of doors*) на у́лице; на дворе́; (*in the open air*) на откры́том во́здухе.

● *prep.* **1** вне + *g.*, из + *g.*; (*beyond bounds of*) за преде́лами + *g.*; **~ the door/window** за две́рью/окно́м; **he went ~ the house** он вы́шел из дому во двор; **it is ~ my field** э́то не вхо́дит в мою́ компете́нцию.
2 (*apart from*) за исключе́нием + *g.*, кро́ме + *g.*; **he has no interests ~ his work** кро́ме/вне рабо́ты его ничего́ не интересу́ет.

outsider /aʊtˈsaɪdə(r)/ *n.* посторо́нний; (*in contest, lit., fig.*) аутса́йдер.

outsize /ˈaʊtsaɪz/ *n.* разме́р бо́льше станда́ртного.

● *adj.* нестанда́ртный; больши́х разме́ров.

outskirts /ˈaʊtskɜːts/ *n.* (*of town*) окра́ина.

outsmart /aʊtˈsmɑːt/ *v.t.* (*coll.*) перехитри́ть (*pf.*).

outspoken /aʊtˈspəʊkən/ *adj.* прямо́й, открове́нный.

outspread /aʊtˈspred/, /ˈaʊtspred/ *adj.* распростёртый.

outstanding /aʊtˈstændɪŋ/ *adj.* (*prominent, eminent*) выдаю́щийся; (*still to be done*) невы́полненный; (*unpaid*) неопла́ченный.

outstay /aʊtˈsteɪ/ *v.t.* (*other guests*) переси́|живать, -де́ть; **~ one's welcome** загости́ться (*pf.*); злоупотреб|ля́ть, -и́ть гостеприи́мством.

outstretched /ˈaʊtstretʃt/, /aʊtˈstretʃt/ *adj.* (*hand*) протя́нутый; (*body*) растяну́вшийся.

outstrip /aʊtˈstrɪp/ *v.t.* (*lit., fig.*) опере|жа́ть, -ди́ть; об|гоня́ть, -огна́ть.

out-tray /ˈaʊttreɪ/ *n.* корзи́нка/я́щик для исходя́щих бума́г.

outvote /aʊtˈvəʊt/ *v.t.*: **~ s.o.** наб|ира́ть, -ра́ть бо́льше голосо́в, чем кто-н.

outward /ˈaʊtwəd/ *adj.* (*external*) нару́жный, вне́шний; **~ calm** вне́шнее споко́йствие; **~ form** вне́шность; (*visible*) ви́димый; **to all ~ appearances** су́дя по вне́шности; (*superficial*) пове́рхностный.

● *adv.* = **outwards**; **~ bound** выходя́щий/уходя́щий в пла́вание/рейс.

outwardly /ˈaʊtwədlɪ/ *adv.* вне́шне, снару́жи; (*at sight*) на вид.

outwards /ˈaʊtwədz/ *adv.* нару́жу.

outweigh /aʊtˈweɪ/ *v.t.* переве́|шивать, -сить.

outwit /aʊtˈwɪt/ *v.t.* (**outwitted, outwitting**) перехитри́ть (*pf.*).

outworn /aʊtˈwɔːn/ *adj.* (*lit.*) изно́шенный; (*of ideas etc.*) устаре́лый, изби́тый.

ouzel /ˈuːz(ə)l/ *n.* чёрный дрозд.

ova /ˈəʊvə/ *pl. of* ⇒**ovum**

oval /ˈəʊv(ə)l/ *n.* ова́л.

● *adj.* ова́льный.

ovarian /əˈveərɪən/ *adj.* яи́чниковый; **~ cancer** рак яи́чников.

ovary /ˈəʊvərɪ/ *n.* яи́чник.

ovation /əʊˈveɪʃ(ə)n/ *n.* ова́ция.

oven /ˈʌv(ə)n/ *n.* духо́вка; (*baker's, industrial*) печь.

● *cpds.* **~glove** *n.* ку́хонная рукави́чка; **~proof** *adj.* жаропро́чный; **~ware** *n.* огнеупо́рная посу́да.

over[1] /ˈəʊvə(r)/ *n.* (*cricket*) се́рия бросков́.

over[2] /ˈəʊvə(r)/ *adv.* (*for phrasal vv. with* **over** *see relevant v. entries*) **1** (*across; to, on the other side*): **~ there** (вон) там; **~ against** (*opposite*) про́тив/напро́тив + *g.*; (*compared to*) по сравне́нию с + *i.*; **I asked him ~** я пригласи́л его́ к себе́; **he's ~!** (*has jumped clear*) он перепры́гнул!; он взял высоту́!; **~ (to you)!** (*said by radio operator*) перехожу́ на приём!; **see ~** (*instruction to reader*) смотри́ (см.) на оборо́те!; (*to the ground*): **one push and ~ I went!** толчо́к — и я растяну́лся на земле́!
2 (*covering surface*): **all ~** (*everywhere*) повсю́ду; **hills covered ~ with trees** холмы́, сплошь покры́тые дере́вьями; **there is mud all ~ your shoes** ва́ши ту́фли все в грязи́; **the whole world ~** по всему́ ми́ру; во всём ми́ре; **I felt hot and cold all ~** меня́ (всего́) броса́ло в жар и хо́лод; **that's John all ~** э́то типи́чный Джон.
3 (*at an end*): **the meeting is ~** собра́ние ко́нчилось; **the holidays are half ~** уже́ прошла́/минова́ла полови́на кани́кул; **I shall be glad to get it ~ (with)** я бу́ду рад, когда́ всё э́то зако́нчится; **it's all ~ with their marriage** их супру́жеской жи́зни пришёл коне́ц; **the doctor could see it was all ~ with him** врачу́ бы́ло я́сно, что он безнадёжен.
4 (*also* **~ again**: *for a second time; once more*) опя́ть, сно́ва, ещё раз; **~ and ~ again** ты́сячу раз, сно́ва и сно́ва; **he read it three times ~** он три́жды э́то перечита́л; **if I had my life ~ again** е́сли б мне довело́сь прожи́ть жизнь за́ново.
5 (*in excess*): **sums of £5 and ~** су́ммы в 5 фу́нтов и вы́ше; **the parcel weighs 2 pounds or ~** посы́лка ве́сит два фу́нта, е́сли не бо́льше (*or* а то и бо́льше); **I had £3 (left) ~** у меня́ ещё остава́лось три фу́нта.

● *prep.* **1** (*above*) над + *i.*; **a roof ~ one's head** кры́ша над голово́й; **the threat hanging ~ them** нави́сшая над ни́ми угро́за; **a seagull flew ~ us** над на́ми пролете́ла ча́йка; (*expr. division*): **five ~ two** (*math.*) пять дробь два; **1 ~ 2** одна́ втора́я; (*fig.*): **the lecture was ~ their heads** ле́кция была́ вы́ше их понима́ния; **his voice was heard ~ the crowd** его́ го́лос раздава́лся над толпо́й.
2 (*to the far side of*) че́рез + *a.*; **a bridge ~ the river** мост че́рез ре́ку; **he climbed ~ the fence** он переле́з че́рез забо́р; **~ the sea** за́ море; **~ the hills** за го́ры; **I threw the ball ~ the wall** я переки́нул мяч че́рез сте́ну; **he jumped ~ the puddles** он перепры́гнул (че́рез) лу́жи; **he swam ~ the river** он переплы́л ре́ку; **he looked ~ his shoulder** он огляну́лся; **he read the letter ~ my shoulder** он чита́л письмо́, загля́дывая че́рез моё плечо́; **he looked at her ~ his spectacles** он смотре́л на неё пове́рх очко́в; (*down from*): **he fell ~ the cliff** он упа́л со скалы́; (*against*): **he tripped ~ a stone** он споткну́лся о ка́мень.
3 (*on the far side of*): **he lives ~ the ocean** он живёт по ту сто́рону океа́на (*or* за океа́ном); **he lives ~ the way** он живёт че́рез у́лицу; **she is ~ the operation** опера́ция прошла́ у неё благополу́чно.
4 (*resting on; covering*): **he carried a raincoat ~ his arm** он шёл, переки́нув плащ че́рез ру́ку; **he pulled his cap ~ his eyes** он надви́нул ша́пку на глаза́; **crossing one leg ~ the other** переки́нув но́гу за́ ногу; **a change came ~ him** с ним произошла́

перемéна; **what has come ~ you?** что с вáми случи́лось?; что на вас нашлó?; (*across, ~ the surface of*) по + *d.*; **~ the whole country** по всей странé; **a flush spread ~ her face** крáска залилá её лицó (*or* разлилáсь по её лицý); **all ~ the world** во всём ми́ре; по всемý свéту; **the news was all ~ town** нóвость разошлáсь по всемý гóроду; **he was all ~ me** (*coll., of flattery, attention*) он засы́пал меня́ комплимéнтами.
5 (*more than*) бóльше/свы́ше + *g.*; **~ a year ago** бóльше/свы́ше гóда (томý) назáд; **he can't be ~ 60** емý (никáк) не бóльше шести́десяти (лет); **~ and above his wages** в добавлéние к егó зарплáте; **~ and above that** (*moreover*) к томý же; **children ~ 5** дéти стáрше пяти́ лет; **~ 600** свы́ше шестисóт.
6 (*in command, charge, control of*): **he was ruler ~ several tribes** он был вождём нéскольких племён; **I have two people ~ me** нáдо мной ещё два начáльника; **have you no control ~ your dog?** вы что, не мóжете спрáвиться со своéй собáкой?; **he has an advantage ~ me** у негó есть пéредо мной преимýщество; **a victory ~ the forces of reaction** побéда над си́лами реáкции.
7 (*as long as*): **can you stay ~ the whole week?** мóжете ли вы остáться на всю/цéлую недéлю?; **I can only stay ~ Saturday night** я могý остáться тóлько до воскресéнья; (*during*): **much has happened ~ the past two years** за послéдние два гóда мнóгое случи́лось.
8 (*near; leaning, bending ~*): **they were sitting ~ the fire** они́ сидéли уками́на; **I stood ~ him while he finished it** я не отходи́л от негó, покá он не кóнчил.
9 (*while engaged in*): **he takes too long ~ his work** он сли́шком дóлго вóзится со своéй рабóтой; **he fell asleep ~ the job** он заснýл за рабóтой; (*while consuming*): **we chatted ~ a bottle of wine** мы болтáли за буты́лкой винá.
10 (*on the subject of; because of*): **he laughed ~ our misfortune** он смея́лся над нáшей бедóй; **it's no good crying ~ spilt milk** потéрянного не ворóтишь; слезáми гóрю не помóжешь; **he gets angry ~ nothing** он зли́тся из-за пустякóв; **a quarrel ~ money** ссóра из-за дéнег.
11 (*through the medium of*): **I heard it ~ the radio** я слы́шал э́то по рáдио.

over-abundance /ˌəʊvərəˈbʌnd(ə)ns/ *n.* избы́ток.

over-abundant /ˌəʊvərəˈbʌnd(ə)nt/ *adj.* избы́точный.

overact /ˌəʊvərˈækt/ *v.t. & i.* переигр|ывать, -áть.

over-active /ˌəʊvərˈæktɪv/ *adj.* сверхакти́вный.

over-activity /ˌəʊvrækˈtɪvɪtɪ/ *n.* повы́шенная акти́вность.

overall /ˈəʊvərˌɔːl/ *n.* (*Br.*) рабóчий халáт; (*pl.*) комбинезóн.
● *adj.* (*total*) пóлный; (*general*) (все)óбщий; **~ dimensions** габари́тные/предéльные размéры.
● *adv.* /ˌəʊvərˈɔːl/(*taken as a whole*) в цéлом.

over-ambitious /ˌəʊvəræmˈbɪʃəs/ *adj.* чересчýр честолюби́вый.

over-anxious /ˌəʊvərˈæŋkʃəs/ *adj.* сли́шком обеспокóенный; **~ mother** изли́шне забóтливая мать.

overarching /ˌəʊvərˈɑːtʃɪŋ/ *adj.* (*all-embracing*) всеобъéмлющий, всеохвáтывающий.

overarm /ˈəʊvərˌɑːm/ *adj. & adv.* с рукóй, пóднятой над головóй; **~ throw** вéрхняя подáча.

overawe /ˌəʊvərˈɔː/ *v.t.* внуш|áть, -и́ть благоговéйный страх + *d.*

overbalance /ˌəʊvəˈbæləns/ (*Br.*) *v.t.* (*knock over*) опроки́|дывать, -нуть; (*capsize*) перев|орáчивать, -ернýть.
● *v.i.* терять, по- равновéсие.

overbear /ˌəʊvəˈbeə(r)/ *v.t.* подав|ля́ть, -и́ть; **an ~ing manner** влáстная манéра.

overblown /ˌəʊvəˈbləʊn/ *adj.* (*inflated, pretentious*) раздýтый; (*of flower etc.*) осыпáющийся; **an ~ beauty** перезрéлая красáвица.

overboard /ˈəʊvəˌbɔːd/ *adv.*: **man ~!** человéк за бóртом!; **go ~** (*fig.*) переб|áрщивать, -орщи́ть; **throw ~** (*also fig.*) выки́дывать, вы́кинуть зá борт.

overbook /ˌəʊvəˈbʊk/ *v.t.*: **the plane was ~ed** билéтов на самолёт бы́ло прóдано бóльше, чем мест.

overbuild /ˌəʊvəˈbɪld/ *v.t. & i.* (чрезмéрно) застр|áивать, -óить.

overburden /ˌəʊvəˈbɜːd(ə)n/ *v.t.* перегру|жáть, -зи́ть.

over-careful /ˌəʊvəˈkeəfʊl/ *adj.* чрезмéрно осторóжный.

overcast /ˈəʊvəˌkɑːst/ *adj.* (*of sky*) покры́тый облакáми; (*of weather*) хмýрый.

over-cautious /ˌəʊvəˈkɔːʃəs/ *adj.* чрезмéрно осторóжный/рóбкий; изли́шне предусмотри́тельный.

overcharge /ˌəʊvəˈtʃɑːdʒ/ *v.t.* запр|áшивать, -оси́ть чрезмéрную цéну у (*кого*); (*elec.*) перезаря|жáть, -ди́ть; (*fig.*) перегру|жáть, -зи́ть.

overcloud /ˌəʊvəˈklaʊd/ *v.t.* заст|илáть, -лáть облакáми/тýчами; (*fig.*) омрач|áть, -и́ть.

overcoat /ˈəʊvəˌkəʊt/ *n.* пальтó (*indecl.*); (*mil.*) шинéль.

overcome /ˌəʊvəˈkʌm/ *v.t.* (*prevail over, get the better of*) преодол|евáть, -éть; (*be victorious over*) побе|ждáть, -ди́ть; (*of emotion*) охвáт|ывать, -и́ть; **he was ~ by rage** он был охвáчен я́ростью; **~ by the sight** растрóганный зрéлищем; (*of heat*) изнур|я́ть, -и́ть; (*of hunger*) истощ|áть, -и́ть.

over-confidence /ˌəʊvəˈkɒnfɪd(ə)ns/ *n.* самонадéянность, самоувéренность.

over-confident /ˌəʊvəˈkɒnfɪd(ə)nt/ *adj.* самонадéянный, самоувéренный; **he was ~ of success** он был сли́шком увéрен в успéхе.

overcook /ˌəʊvəˈkʊk/ *v.t.* (*by roasting, frying*) пережáр|ивать, -ить; (*by boiling*) перевáр|ивать, -и́ть.

over-critical /ˌəʊvəˈkrɪtɪk(ə)l/ *adj.* чрезмéрно крити́чный/сурóвый.

overcrop /ˌəʊvəˈkrɒp/ *v.t.* истощ|áть, -и́ть (*почву*).

overcrowd /ˌəʊvəˈkraʊd/ *v.t.* переп|олня́ть, -óлнить.

overdevelop /ˌəʊvədɪˈveləp/ *v.t.* (*phot.*) передéрж|ивать, -áть (при проявлéнии); **~ed** чрезмéрно разви́тый.

overdo /ˌəʊvəˈduː/ *v.t.* (*by roasting, frying*) пережáри|вать, -ть; (*by boiling*) перевáр|ивать, -и́ть; **the comic scenes were ~ne** они́ перестарáлись в коми́ческих сцéнах; **~ it** перестарáться (*pf.*); переб|áрщивать, -орщи́ть (*coll.*); переусéрдствовать (*pf.*) (*в чём*); **don't ~ it** (*work too hard*) не перенапрягáйтесь/переутомля́йтесь.

overdose /ˈəʊvəˌdəʊs/ *n.* передозирóвка, чрезмéрная дóза; **she died of an ~** онá умерлá от чрезмéрной дóзы (*наркотика и т.п.*).

overdraft /ˈəʊvəˌdrɑːft/ *n.* (*deficit in bank account*) овердрáфт, перерасхóд; превышéние креди́та; (*agreement*) разрешéние на превышéние креди́та.

overdraw /ˌəʊvəˈdrɔː/ *v.t.* **1**: **~ one's account** прев|ышáть, -ы́сить креди́т; **I am £100 ~n** я превы́сил креди́т в бáнке на 100 фýнтов. **2** (*exaggerate*): **his characters are ~n** егó персонáжи карикатýрны.

overdress /ˌəʊvəˈdres/ *v.t. & i.*: **she ~es (***or* **is ~ed)** онá одевáется/одéта сли́шком наря́дно.

overdrive /ˈəʊvəˌdraɪv/ *n.* (*of vehicle*) ускоря́ющая передáча.

overdue /ˌəʊvəˈdjuː/ *adj.* запоздáлый; **the train is ~** пóезд опáздывает; **recognition of his services is long ~** давнó порá признáть егó заслýги; **the baby is 2 weeks ~** ребёнок дóлжен был роди́ться две недéли томý назáд; (*of payment*) просрóченный.

over-eager /ˌəʊvərˈiːgə(r)/ *adj.* сли́шком усéрдный/рéвностный.

overeat /ˌəʊvərˈiːt/ *v.i.* пере|едáть, -éсть; объ|едáться, -éстся.

over-emphasis /ˌəʊvərˈemfəsɪs/ *adj.* изли́шнее подчёркивание.

over-emphasize /ˌəʊvərˈemfəˌsaɪz/ *v.t.* изли́шне подчёрк|ивать, -нýть.

over-enthusiasm /ˌəʊvərɪnˈθjuːzɪˌæz(ə)m/, /-ˌθuːzɪˌæz(ə)m/ *n.* чрезмéрный энтузиáзм.

over-enthusiastic /ˌəʊvərɪnˌθjuːzɪˈæstɪk/, /-ˌθuːzɪˈæstɪk/ *adj.* с изли́шним энтузиáзмом; **he was not ~** он нé был в востóрге.

overestimate[1] /ˌəʊvərˈestɪmət/ *n.* переоцéнка.

overestimate[2] /ˌəʊvərˈestɪˌmeɪt/ *v.t.* переоцéн|ивать, -и́ть.

over-excite /ˌəʊvərɪkˈsaɪt/ *v.t.* крáйне возбу|ждáть, -ди́ть.

over-excitement /ˌəʊvərɪkˈsaɪtmənt/ *n.* перевозбуждéние.

over-exert /ˌəʊvərɪgˈzɜːt/ *v.t.* перенапр|ягáть, -я́чь.

over-exertion /ˌəʊvərɪɡˈzɜːʃ(ə)n/ *n.* перенапряже́ние.

over-expose /ˌəʊvərɪkˈspəʊz/ *v.t.* (*phot.*) передéрж|ивать, -áть; (*fig.*) сли́шком чáсто упом|инáть, -янýть в печáти *и т.д.*

over-exposure /ˌəʊvərɪkˈspəʊʒə(r)/ *n.* передéржка; (*fig.*) сли́шком чáстое упоминáние в печáти *и т.д.*

over-familiar /ˌəʊvəfəˈmɪlɪə(r)/ *adj.* сли́шком фамилья́рный.

over-familiarity /ˌəʊvəfəˌmɪlɪˈærɪtɪ/ *n.* чрезмéрная фамилья́рность.

overfeed /ˌəʊvəˈfiːd/ *v.t.* перек|áрмливать, -орми́ть.

overfeeding /ˌəʊvəˈfiːdɪŋ/ *n.* перекáрмливание.

overfish /ˌəʊvəˈfɪʃ/ *v.t.* истощ|áть, -и́ть запáсы ры́бы в + *p.*

overflight /ˈəʊvəˌflaɪt/ *n.* перелёт.

overflow /ˈəʊvəˌfləʊ/ *n.* (*flowing* ~) разли́в; (*superfluity*) избы́ток; (*outlet*) сливнóе отвéрстие.

● *v.t. & i.* перел|ивáться, -и́ться (*через что*); **the river ~s its banks** рекá наводня́ет берегá (*or* выхóдит из берегóв); **~ing with** переполненный + *i.*; (*fig.*) преиспóлненный + *g./i.*

overfly /ˌəʊvəˈflaɪ/ *v.t.* перелет|áть, -éть чéрез + *a.*

overfond /ˌəʊvəˈfɒnd/ *adj.*: **I am not ~ of skating** я не сли́шком-то люблю́ катáться на конькáх.

overfulfil /ˌəʊvəfʊlˈfɪl/ (*US* **overfulfill**) *v.t.* перев|ыполня́ть, -ы́полнить.

overfulfilment /ˌəʊvəfʊlˈfɪlmənt/ (*US* **overfulfillment**) *n.* перевыполнéние.

overfull /ˌəʊvəˈfʊl/ *adj.* перепóлненный (+ *i.*).

over-generous /ˌəʊvəˈdʒenərəs/ *adj.* сли́шком щéдрый.

overglaze /ˈəʊvəˌɡleɪz/ *n.* вéрхний слой глазýри.

overground /ˈəʊvəˌɡraʊnd/ *adj.* надзéмный.

overgrow /ˌəʊvəˈɡrəʊ/ *v.t.*: **be ~n (with)** зараст|áть, -и́ (+ *i.*); **the garden was ~n with nettles** сад зарóс крапи́вой.

overgrowth /ˈəʊvəˌɡrəʊθ/ *n.* (*excessive growth*) чрезмéрный рост; (*of weeds etc.*) зáросль.

overhand /ˈəʊvəˌhænd/ *adj.* (*delivery of ball*) производи́мый свéрху вниз.

● *adv.* свéрху вниз.

overhang /ˈəʊvəˌhæŋ/ *n.* вы́ступ.

● *v.t. & i.* (*past and p.p.* **overhung**) выступáть, выдавáться (*both impf.*) над + *i.*; (*fig.*) нав|исáть, -и́снуть над + *i.*

over-hasty /ˌəʊvəˈheɪstɪ/ *adj.* опромéтчивый.

overhaul /ˈəʊvəˌhɔːl/ *n.* (*of machine, equipment*) осмóтр; (*reconditioning*) восстановлéние; (*thorough repair*) капитáльный ремóнт; (*of plan, system*) пересмóтр.

● *v.t.* **1** осм|áтривать, -отрéть; восстан|áвливать, -ови́ть; ремонти́ровать, от-; пересм|áтривать, -отрéть. **2** (*Br., overtake*) дог|оня́ть, -нáть.

overhead /ˈəʊvəˌhed/ *n.* (*usu. pl.*) накладны́е расхóды (*m. pl.*).

● *adj.* **1** (*above ground level*): **~ projector** графопроéктор; **~ railway** надзéмная желéзная дорóга; **~ wires, lines** воздýшные проводá. **2** (*comm.*): **~ charges, costs** накладны́е расхóды.

● *adv.* /ˌəʊvəˈhed/ наверхý, вверхý; (*above one's head*) над головóй; (*in the sky*) на нéбе.

overhear /ˌəʊvəˈhɪə(r)/ *v.t.* (*intentionally*) подслýш|ивать, -ать; (*accidentally*) нечáянно услы́шать (*pf.*).

overheat /ˌəʊvəˈhiːt/ *v.t. & i.* перегр|евáть(ся), -éть(ся).

over-indulge /ˌəʊvərɪnˈdʌldʒ/ *v.t.* (*spoil*) сли́шком баловáть, из-.

● *v.i.*: **~ in something** злоупотреб|ля́ть, -и́ть чем-н.

over-indulgence /ˌəʊvərɪnˈdʌldʒ(ə)ns/ *n.* чрезмéрное баловствó; злоупотреблéние (+ *i.*).

over-indulgent /ˌəʊvərɪnˈdʌldʒ(ə)nt/ *adj.* потакáющий, сли́шком снисходи́тельный.

overjoyed /ˌəʊvəˈdʒɔɪd/ *adj.* вне себя́ от рáдости.

overkill /ˈəʊvəkɪl/ *n.* (*fig.*) вы́ход за предéлы необходи́мости; ≈ пýшками по воробья́м.

overladen /ˌəʊvəˈleɪd(ə)n/ *adj.* перегрýженный.

overland /ˈəʊvəˌlænd/ *adj.* сухопýтный.

● *adv.* по сýше.

overlap *n.* /ˈəʊvəˌlæp/ (*tech.*) перекры́тие; (*fig.*) части́чное совпадéние.

● *v.t.* /ˌəʊvəˈlæp/ покр|ывáть, -ы́ть части́чно.

● *v.i.* /ˌəʊvəˈlæp/ за|ходи́ть, -йти́ оди́н на другóй; (*coincide*) (части́чно) совп|адáть, -áсть; **my holidays ~ with yours** мой óтпуск части́чно совпадáет с вáшим.

overlay *n.* /ˈəʊvəˌleɪ/ покры́тие.

● *v.t.* /ˌəʊvəˈleɪ/ покр|ывáть, -ы́ть.

overleaf /ˌəʊvəˈliːf/ *adv.* на оборóте (страни́цы).

overlie /ˌəʊvəˈlaɪ/ *v.t.* лежáть (*impf.*) над + *i.*

overload *n.* /ˈəʊvəˌləʊd/ перегрýзка.

● *v.t.* /ˌəʊvəˈləʊd/ перегру|жáть, -зи́ть.

over-long /ˌəʊvəˈlɒŋ/ *adj.* сли́шком дли́нный/дóлгий.

● *adv.* сли́шком дóлго.

overlook /ˌəʊvəˈlʊk/ *v.t.* **1** (*look down on*) смотрéть, по- свéрху на + *a.*; (*tower above*) возвышáться (*impf.*) над (+ *i.*); **the mountains ~ the sea** гóры возвышáются над мóрем. **2** (*open on to*) выходи́ть (*impf.*) на + *a.*; **our house is not ~ed** наш дом защищён от посторóнних взгля́дов; **a view ~ing the lake** вид на óзеро. **3** (*fail to notice*) просмотрéть (*pf.*), проглядéть (*pf.*), пропус|кáть, -ти́ть; **the mistake was completely ~ed** оши́бку пóлностью просмотрéли/проглядéли; (*disregard*) упус|кáть, -ти́ть; **you've ~ed one important thing** вы упусти́ли из ви́ду однó вáжное обстоя́тельство; **he was ~ed** (*not promoted*) егó обошли́. **4** (*excuse*) про|щáть, -сти́ть; **I will ~ his mistakes** я прощý емý егó оши́бки.

overlord /ˈəʊvəˌlɔːd/ *n.* (*feudal*) сюзерéн; (*master*) повели́тель (*m.*).

overly /ˈəʊvəlɪ/ *adv.* сли́шком, чересчýр.

overman /ˌəʊvəˈmæn/ *v.t.*: **the department is ~ned** в отдéле раздýты штáты; отдéл перегрýжен людьми́.

overmanning /ˌəʊvəˈmænɪŋ/ *n.* раздувáние штáтов.

overmantel /ˈəʊvəˌmænt(ə)l/ *n.* украшéние надками́ном.

overmastering /ˌəʊvəˈmɑːstərɪŋ/ *adj.* непреодоли́мый.

over-modest /ˌəʊvəˈmɒdɪst/ *adj.* чересчýр скрóмный.

over-much /ˌəʊvəˈmʌtʃ/ *adv.* сли́шком мнóго; чрезмéрно.

overnight /ˌəʊvəˈnaɪt/ *adj.*: **~ preparations** подготóвка наканýне; **an ~ stay** ночёвка, ночлéг; **~ bag** дорóжная сýмка, саквоя́ж; **~ train** ночнóй пóезд.

● *adv.* (*on the previous evening*) наканýне вéчером; (*through the night*) всю ночь; (*during the night*) зá ночь; **stay ~** ночевáть, за-; (*fig.*): **he rose to fame ~** слáва пришлá к немý в одночáсье.

overpass /ˈəʊvəˌpɑːs/ *n.* эстакáда.

overpay /ˌəʊvəˈpeɪ/ *v.t.* перепла|чивать, -ти́ть.

overpayment /ˌəʊvəˈpeɪmənt/ *n.* переплáта.

overplay /ˌəʊvəˈpleɪ/ *v.t.* (*overact*) переигр|ывать, -áть; (*overemphasize*) прид|авáть, -áть чрезмéрное значéние + *d.*; **~ one's hand** (*fig.*) переоцéн|ивать, -и́ть свои́ возмóжности.

overpopulated /ˌəʊvəˈpɒpjʊˌleɪtɪd/ *adj.* перенаселённый.

overpopulation /ˌəʊvəˌpɒpjʊˈleɪʃ(ə)n/ *n.* перенаселéние.

overpower /ˌəʊvəˈpaʊə(r)/ *v.t.* одол|евáть, -éть; (*overwhelm*) сокрушáть, -и́ть; **~ing grief** сокрушáющее гóре; **~ing smell** óчень си́льный зáпах; **I found the heat ~ing** я изнемогáл от жары́.

overpraise /ˌəʊvəˈpreɪz/ *v.t.* перехвáл|ивать, -и́ть.

over-produce /ˌəʊvəprəˈdjuːs/ *v.t.* перепроизв|оди́ть, -ести́.

over-production /ˌəʊvəprəˈdʌkʃ(ə)n/ *n.* перепроизвóдство.

overrate /ˌəʊvəˈreɪt/ *v.t.* переоцéн|ивать, -и́ть.

overreach /ˌəʊvəˈriːtʃ/ *v.t.* (*outwit*) перехитри́ть (*pf.*); **~ o.s.** (*defeat one's object*) перестарáться (*pf.*).

over-react /ˌəʊvərɪˈækt/ *v.i.* реаги́ровать, от- *or* про- чрезмéрно рéзко.

over|ride /ˌəʊvəˈraɪd/ *v.t.* (*reject*) отв|ергáть, -éргнуть; **he ~rode my objections** он отвéрг/отмёл мои́ возражéния; **~riding** (*aim, importance*) основнóй, первостепéнный; (*factor, consideration*) глáвный, решáющий; **an**

~riding objection неопровержи́мое возраже́ние.

overrider /ˈəʊvə,raɪdə(r)/ *n.* (*Br.*) клык ба́мпера.

over-ripe /,əʊvəˈraɪp/ *adj.* перезре́лый.

overrule /,əʊvəˈru:l/ *v.t.* (*annul*) аннули́ровать (*impf., pf.*); отмен|я́ть, -и́ть; **~ a claim/objection** отв|ерга́ть, -е́ргнуть (*or* отклон|я́ть, -и́ть) прете́нзию/возраже́ние; **I was ~d** моё возраже́ние отве́ргли.

overrun /,əʊvəˈrʌn/ *v.t.* **1** (*of enemy*) соверш|а́ть, -и́ть набе́г на + *a.* **2** (*of vermin, weeds etc.: infest*): **the garden is ~ with weeds** сад заро́с сорняка́ми; **the house is ~ with rats** дом киши́т кры́сами. **3** (*go beyond*): **the speaker overran his time** выступа́ющий превы́сил регла́мент.

● *v.i.*: **the broadcast is ~ning by 20 minutes** переда́ча идёт на 20 мину́т до́льше поло́женного вре́мени.

overseas *adj.* /ˈəʊvə,si:z/ (*trip*) загранú́чный; (*visitor*) иностра́нный; **~ trade** вне́шняя торго́вля.

● *adv.* /,əʊvəˈsi:z/ за́ мо́рем; (*abroad*) за грани́цей; **go ~** е́хать (*det.*), по- за грани́цу.

oversee /,əʊvəˈsi:/ *v.t.* надзира́ть (*impf.*) за + *i.*

overseer /ˈəʊvə,si:ə(r)/ *n.* надсмо́трщик, надзира́тель (*m.*).

over-sensitive /,əʊvəˈsensɪtɪv/ *adj.* чересчу́р чувстви́тельный.

over-sensitiveness /,əʊvəˈsensɪtɪvnɪs/ *n.* чрезме́рная чувстви́тельность.

over-sexed /,əʊvəˈsekst/ *adj.* чрезме́рно чу́вственный.

overshadow /,əʊvəˈʃædəʊ/ *v.t.* (*lit., fig.*) заслон|я́ть, -и́ть; затм|ева́ть, -и́ть.

overshoe /ˈəʊvə,ʃu:/ *n.* гало́ша.

overshoot *n.* /ˈəʊvə,ʃu:t/ (*aeron.*) перелёт (*при посадке*).

● *v.t.* /,əʊvəˈʃu:t/ (*junction, traffic lights*) про|езжа́ть, -е́хать; проск|а́кивать, -очи́ть; **~ the mark** (*lit.*) брать, взять вы́ше це́ли; (*fig.*) за|ходи́ть, -йти́ сли́шком далеко́.

● *v.i.* /,əʊvəˈʃu:t/ : **the plane overshot on landing** самолёт перелете́л то́чки приземле́ния.

oversight /ˈəʊvə,saɪt/ *n.* (*failure to notice*) недосмо́тр, упуще́ние; (*supervision*) надзо́р.

over-simplification /,əʊvə,sɪmplɪfɪˈkeɪʃ(ə)n/ *n.* чрезме́рное упроще́ние; вульгариза́ция.

over-simplify /,əʊvəˈsɪmplɪ,faɪ/ *v.t.* сли́шком упро|ща́ть, -сти́ть.

oversize(d) /ˈəʊvə,saɪzd/ *adj.* о́чень/сли́шком большо́го разме́ра.

oversleep /,əʊvəˈsli:p/ *v.i.* прос|ыпа́ть, -па́ть.

overspend /,əʊvəˈspend/ *v.i.* тра́тить, по- сли́шком мно́го.

overspill /ˈəʊvəspɪl/ *n.* (*Br., of population*) избы́ток населе́ния.

overstate /,əʊvəˈsteɪt/ *v.t.* преувели́ч|ивать, -ить.

overstatement /ˈəʊvə,steɪtmənt/ *n.* преувеличе́ние.

overstay /,əʊvəˈsteɪ/ *v.t.*: **~ one's welcome** загости́ться (*pf.*); злоупотреб|ля́ть, -и́ть гостеприи́мством.

overstep /,əʊvəˈstep/ *v.t.* переступ|а́ть, -и́ть.

overstock /,əʊvəˈstɒk/ *v.t.* (*with goods*) переп|олня́ть, -о́лнить.

over-strain /,əʊvəˈstreɪn/ *n.* перенапряже́ние.

● *v.t.* перенапр|яга́ть, -я́чь; (*over-exert*) переутом|ля́ть, -и́ть.

over-stress /,əʊvəˈstres/ *v.t.* (*over-strain*) перенапр|яга́ть, -я́чь; (*over-emphasize*) изли́шне подчёрк|ивать, -ну́ть.

oversubscribe /,əʊvəsəbˈskraɪb/ *v.t.*: **the course is ~d** курс перепо́лнен; **the school is ~d** шко́ла перепо́лнена; **the share issue was ~d** бы́ло сли́шком мно́го жела́ющих на приобрете́ние а́кций.

overt /əʊˈvɜ:t/, /ˈəʊvɜ:t/ *adj.* (*open*) откры́тый; (*obvious, evident*) я́вный, очеви́дный.

overtak|e /,əʊvəˈteɪk/ *v.t.* (*outstrip*) об|гоня́ть, -огна́ть; перег|оня́ть, -на́ть; **no ~ing!** обго́н запрещён!; **misfortune overtook him** его́ пости́гло несча́стье.

overtax /,əʊvəˈtæks/ *v.t.* (*lit.*) обремен|я́ть, -и́ть чрезме́рными нало́гами; (*strength, patience etc.*) истощ|а́ть, -и́ть.

over-the-top /,əʊvəðəˈtɒp/ *adj.* чрезме́рный.

overthrow[1] /ˈəʊvə,θrəʊ/ *n.* ниспроверже́ние, сверже́ние.

overthrow[2] /,əʊvəˈθrəʊ/ *v.t.* ниспров|ерга́ть, -е́ргнуть; св|ерга́ть, -е́ргнуть.

overtime /ˈəʊvə,taɪm/ *n.* сверхуро́чное вре́мя; (*work*) сверхуро́чная рабо́та.

● *adv.* сверхуро́чно.

overtired /,əʊvəˈtaɪəd/ *adj.* переутомлённый.

overtone /ˈəʊvə,təʊn/ *n.* оберто́н; (*fig., also*) отте́нок.

overture /ˈəʊvə,tjʊə(r)/ *n.* **1** (*mus.*) уверт ю́ра. **2** (*pl.*): **peace ~s** ми́рные предложе́ния, ми́рная инициати́ва.

overturn /,əʊvəˈtɜ:n/ *v.t. & i.* опроки́|дывать(ся), -нуть(ся).

overvalue /,əʊvəˈvælju:/ *v.t.* переоц|е́нивать, -ени́ть.

overview /ˈəʊvə,vju:/ *n.* обзо́р.

overweening /,əʊvəˈwi:nɪŋ/ *adj.* (*arrogant*) высокоме́рный; (*pride, ambition*) чрезме́рный.

overweight /ˈəʊvə,weɪt/ *adj.* ве́сящий бо́льше но́рмы; **he is several pounds ~** он ве́сит на не́сколько фу́нтов бо́льше но́рмы.

overwhelm /,əʊvəˈwelm/ *v.t.* (*weigh down*) подав|ля́ть, -и́ть; (*submerge*) погру|жа́ть, -зи́ть; (*in battle*) сокруш|а́ть, -и́ть; (*fig.*): **his kindness ~ed me** я был ошеломлён/пода́влен его́ доброто́й; **I was ~ed with joy** моё се́рдце перепо́лнилось ра́достью; **he was ~ed with grief** он был охва́чен го́рем; **~ing majority** подавля́ющее большинство́.

overwind /,əʊvəˈwaɪnd/ *v.t.*: **~ a watch** перекр|у́чивать, -ути́ть пружи́ну у часо́в.

overwork /,əʊvəˈwɜ:k/ *n.* (*overstrain*) перенапряже́ние, переутомле́ние.

● *v.t. & i.* переутом|ля́ть(ся), -и́ть(ся); (*fig.*): **that phrase has been ~ed** э́то выраже́ние заtáскано.

overwrite /,əʊvəˈraɪt/ *v.t.* (*comput.*) (*a file*) перезапи́с|ывать, -а́ть; (*data*) запи́с|ывать, -а́ть пове́рх (+ *g.*).

overwrought /,əʊvəˈrɔ:t/ *adj.* сли́шком возбуждённый, не́рвный; **she is ~** у неё не́рвное истоще́ние.

oviduct /ˈəʊvɪ,dʌkt/ *n.* яйцево́д.

ovoid /ˈəʊvɔɪd/ *adj.* яйцеви́дный.

ovulate /ˈɒvjʊ,leɪt/ *v.i.* овули́ровать (*impf., pf.*).

ovulation /,ɒvjʊˈleɪʃ(ə)n/ *n.* овуля́ция.

ovum /ˈəʊvəm/ *n.* (*pl.* **ova**) яйцо́.

owe /əʊ/ *v.t. & i.* **1** (*be under obligation to pay*) быть до́лжным + *d.*; **you ~ us £50** вы должны́ нам 50 фу́нтов; **I ~d him a large sum** я до́лжен был ему́ большу́ю су́мму; **I ~ you for the ticket** я до́лжен вам за биле́т; **he ~s 4 roubles** он до́лжен четы́ре рубля́; **he still ~s for last year** он ещё до́лжен (*or* у него́ ещё задо́лженность) за про́шлый год; **you ~ it to yourself to take a holiday** вам необходи́мо взять о́тпуск. **2** (*be indebted for*) быть обя́занным (*кому чем*); **I ~ it to you that I am still alive** я обя́зан вам жи́знью; **he ~s his success to hard work** свои́м успе́хом он обя́зан неуста́нной рабо́те.

owing /ˈəʊɪŋ/ *adj.* **1** (*yet to be paid*) причита́ющийся; **there is 2 roubles ~ to you from me** вам причита́ется два рубля́ с меня́. **2**: **~ to** (*attributable to; caused by*) по причи́не + *g.*; вслéдствие + *g.*; (*thanks to*) благодаря́ + *d.*; (*on account of, because of*) из-за + *g.*; **~ to fog we were late** из-за тума́на мы опозда́ли.

owl /aʊl/ *n.* сова́; **barn ~** сипу́ха; **little ~** домо́вый сыч; **tawny ~** нея́сыть.

owlish /ˈaʊlɪʃ/ *adj.* (*fig.*) серьёзный.

own /əʊn/ *pron.*: **come into one's ~** доб|ива́ться, -и́ться призна́ния; **each to his ~** кому́ как; по вку́су; **get one's ~ back on s.o.** поквита́ться (*pf.*) с кем-н.; **hold one's ~** стоя́ть (*impf.*) на своём; **on one's ~** (*alone*) в одино́честве; (*unaided, independently*) самостоя́тельно, сам (по себе́).

● *adj.* со́бственный, свой; **my ~ house** мой со́бственный дом; **this house is not my ~** э́тот дом мне не принадлежи́т; **I want a dog of** (*or* **for**) **my very ~** я хочу́ соба́ку для себя́; **my time is my ~** я хозя́ин своего́ вре́мени; **can I have a room of my ~?** мо́жно получи́ть отде́льную ко́мнату?; **a flavour** (*Br.*), **flavor** (*US*) **all its ~** осо́бенный арома́т; **with one's ~ hand** собственнору́чно; **he died by his ~ hand** он поко́нчил с собо́й; он наложи́л на себя́ ру́ки; **he had reasons of his ~** у него́ бы́ли (на то) свои́ причи́ны; **he has nothing of his ~** он ничего́ не име́ет; **I love truth for its ~ sake** я люблю́ пра́вду ра́ди пра́вды; **of one's ~ accord** по со́бственному побужде́нию; доброво́льно; **he is his ~ master** он сам себе́ хозя́ин; **she makes all her ~ clothes** она́ сама́ себя́ обшива́ет; **my ~ father** мой родно́й оте́ц.

● *v.t.* **1** (*have as property*) владе́ть (*impf.*) + *i.*; **who ~s this bag?** чья э́то су́мка?; **be ~ed (by)** принадлежа́ть (*impf.*) (+ *d.*); **the land was ~ed by my father** (э́та) земля́ принадлежа́ла моему́ отцу́ (*or* э́той землёй владе́л мой оте́ц).
2 (*acknowledge, admit*) призн|ава́ть, -а́ть; **he would not ~ his faults** он не признава́л за собо́й недоста́тков.

● *v.i.*: **~ (up) to something; ~ up** призн|ава́ться, -а́ться в чём-н.; **I ~ to having told a lie** я признаю́сь, что солга́л.

owner /'əʊnə(r)/ *n.* владе́л|ец (*fem.* -ица); хозя́|ин (*fem.* -йка); **at ~'s risk** на отве́тственность владе́льца; **joint ~** совладе́л|ец (*fem.* -ица).

● *cpd.* **~-occupier** *n.* (*Br.*) домовладе́л|ец (*fem.* -ица), квартировладе́л|ец (*fem.* -ица).

ownerless /'əʊnəlɪs/ *adj.* бесхо́зный, без хозя́ина.

ownership /'əʊnəʃɪp/ *n.* владе́ние (**of**: + *i.*); со́бственность; **joint ~** о́бщее владе́ние; **private/state ~** ча́стная/госуда́рственная со́бственность.

ox /ɒks/ *n.* (*pl.* **oxen**) бык; (*castrated*) вол.

● *cpds.* **~-bow** *n.* (*geog.*) подковообра́зная излу́чина (*реки*); **~hide** *n.* воло́вья/бы́чья шку́ра; **~tail** *n.* воло́вий/бы́чий хвост; **~-tongue** *n.* воло́вий/бы́чий язы́к.

oxalic /ɒk'sælɪk/ *adj.* щаве́левый.

Oxbridge /'ɒksbrɪdʒ/ *n.* (*coll.*) О́ксфорд и Ке́мбридж (университе́ты).

oxen /'ɒks(ə)n/ *pl. of* ⇒**ox**

Oxford /'ɒksfəd/ *n.* О́ксфорд; (*attr.*) о́ксфордский.

oxidation /,ɒksɪ'deɪʃ(ə)n/ = **oxidization**

oxide /'ɒksaɪd/ *n.* о́кись.

oxidization /,ɒksɪ,daɪ'zeɪʃ(ə)n/ *n.* окисле́ние.

oxidize /'ɒksɪ,daɪz/ *v.t.* окисл|я́ть, -и́ть.

oxyacetylene /,ɒksɪə'setɪ,li:n/ *adj.* кислоро́дно-ацетиле́новый.

oxygen /'ɒksɪdʒ(ə)n/ *n.* кислоро́д; **~ mask** кислоро́дная ма́ска; **~ tent** кислоро́дная пала́тка.

oxygenate /'ɒksɪdʒə,neɪt/, /ɒk'sɪ-/ *v.t.* нас|ыща́ть, -ы́тить кислоро́дом.

oxygenation /,ɒksɪdʒə'neɪʃ(ə)n/ *n.* насыще́ние кислоро́дом.

oxymoron /,ɒksɪ'mɔ:rɒn/ *n.* оксю́морон.

oyster /'ɔɪstə(r)/ *n.* у́стрица; **the world is his ~** весь мир у его́ ног.

● *cpds.* **~-bed** *n.* у́стричный садо́к; **~-catcher** *n.* (*zool.*) кули́к-соро́ка.

Oz /ɒz/ *n.* (*Austral. coll.*) Австра́лия.

oz. /aʊns(ɪz)/ *n.* (*abbr. of* ***ounce(s)***) у́нция.

ozone /'əʊzəʊn/ *n.* озо́н; **~ layer** озо́нный слой.

● *cpd.* **~-friendly** *adj.* не разруша́ющий озо́нный слой.

Pp

P /piː/ *n.*: **we must mind our ~'s and Q's** на́до быть осторо́жным; на́до соблюда́ть прили́чия.

p. *n. abbr. of* **1** ***penny*** /'penɪ/ (*pl.* ***pence***) (*Br.*) пе́нни (*nt. indecl.*), пенс. **2** ***page*** /peɪdʒ/ стр (страни́ца).

PA *abbr. of* **1** (*Br.*) ***personal assistant*** ли́чный секрета́рь. **2** ***public address*** **(*system*)** звукоусили́тельная аппарату́ра.

pa /pɑː/ *n.* (*coll.*) па́па (*m.*).

p.a. /pər 'ænəm/ *adv.* (*abbr. of* ***per annum***) в год.

pace /peɪs/ *n.* **1** (*step*) шаг. **2** (*speed of progression*): **mend, quicken one's ~** уск|оря́ть, -о́рить шаг; **keep ~ with** посп|ева́ть, -е́ть за + *i.*; **at a snail's ~** с черепа́шьей ско́ростью; (*fig.*): **this pupil sets the ~ for the whole class** э́тот учени́к задаёт темп всему́ кла́ссу. **3** (*gait, esp. of horse*) аллю́р; (*of person*) по́ступь; **he put the horse through its ~s** он пуска́л ло́шадь ра́зными аллю́рами; (*fig.*): **she put me through my ~s** она́ меня́ как сле́дует погоня́ла (*coll.*).

● *v.t.* **1** (*measure out, traverse in ~s*) шага́ть (*impf.*) по + *d.*; расха́живать (*impf.*) по + *d.*; **he ~d the floor** он ме́рил ко́мнату шага́ми; **I ~d out the distance** я изме́рил расстоя́ние шага́ми. **2** (*set the ~ for*) за|дава́ть, -да́ть темп + *d.*

● *v.i.* ходи́ть (*indet.*); расха́живать (*impf.*); **he ~d up and down** он ходи́л взад и вперёд.

● *cpd.* **~-maker** *n.* ли́дер, задаю́щий темп; (*cardiac aid*) ритмиза́тор се́рдца, пейсме́йкер.

pace /'pɑːtʃeɪ/, /'peɪsɪ/ *prep.*: **~ the critics** с позволе́ния кри́тиков.

pachyderm /'pækɪˌdɜːm/ *n.* толстоко́жее (живо́тное).

pacific /pə'sɪfɪk/ *n.*: **the P~ (Ocean)** Ти́хий океа́н; (*attr.*) тихоокеа́нский; **the P~ Islands** Океа́ния.

● *adj.* (*peaceful, calm*) споко́йный; (*promoting peace*) миролюби́вый.

pacification /ˌpæsɪfɪ'keɪʃ(ə)n/ *n.* успокое́ние; умиротворе́ние.

pacifier /'pæsɪˌfaɪə(r)/ *n.* (*one who soothes*) успоко́итель (*m.*); (*bringer of peace*) миротво́рец; (*US, child's dummy*) со́ска, пусты́шка.

pacifism /'pæsɪˌfɪz(ə)m/ *n.* пацифи́зм.

pacifist /'pæsɪfɪst/ *n.* пацифи́ст (*fem.* -ка) (*attr.*) пацифи́стский.

pacify /'pæsɪˌfaɪ/ *v.t.* (*soothe; appease*) успок|а́ивать, -о́ить; умиротвор|я́ть, -и́ть; (*bring peace to, esp. by force*) усмир|я́ть, -и́ть.

pack /pæk/ *n.* **1** (*knapsack*) ра́нец; (*rucksack*) рюкза́к; (*carried by animal*) вьюк. **2** (*packet; packaged quantity of goods*) па́чка, паке́т. **3** (*collection*) набо́р; **it's all a ~ of lies** э́то сплошна́я ложь; **a ~ of thieves** ша́йка воро́в. **4** (*animals*): **~ of hounds** сво́ра го́нчих; **~ of wolves** ста́я волко́в. **5** (*Rugby forwards*) нападе́ние. **6** (*Br., cards*) коло́да.

● *v.t.* **1** (*put into container*) упако́в|ывать, -а́ть; укла́дывать, уложи́ть; **~ed lunch** бутербро́ды с собо́й, сухо́й паёк; (*for preservation*) консерви́ровать, за-. **2** (*put into small space*) наб|ива́ть, -и́ть; **they were ~ed in there like sardines** они́ наби́лись туда́ как се́льди в бо́чке. **3** (*cover for protection in transit etc.*) упак|о́вывать, -ова́ть; **the glass is ~ed in cotton wool** стекло́ упако́вано в ва́ту. **4** (*fill*) зап|олня́ть, -о́лнить; **he ~ed his bags and left** он уложи́л чемода́ны и уе́хал; **the hall was ~ed** зал был битко́м наби́т. **5**: **~ a jury/committee** под|бира́ть, -обра́ть соста́в жюри́/комите́та. **6**: **he ~s a punch** (*coll.*) у него́ си́льный уда́р.

● *v.i.* **1**: **(~ one's clothes)** укла́дываться, уложи́ться. **2** (*crowd together*): **they ~ed into the car** они́ вти́снулись в автомоби́ль. **3**: **send s.o. ~ing** прог|оня́ть, -на́ть кого́-н.

● *with advs.*: **~ away** *v.t.* от|кла́дывать, -ложи́ть; **I ~ed my overcoat away for the summer** я убра́л своё пальто́ на ле́то; **~ down** *v.t.* уплотн|я́ть, -и́ть; **the soil should be ~ed down firmly** грунт сле́дует хорошо́ утрамбова́ть; **~ in** *v.t.*: **she took her bag and ~ed everything in** она́ взяла́ су́мку и всё в неё уложи́ла; (*fig., accomplish in given time*): **I'm only going for a week, so I have a lot to ~ in** я е́ду то́лько на неде́лю, и поэ́тому у меня́ бу́дет о́чень пло́тная програ́мма; (*coll., stop, give up*) прекра|ща́ть, -ти́ть; **he's ~ing in his job** он броса́ет рабо́ту; **~ it in, will you!** бро́сьте (э́то), пожа́луйста; *v.i.*: **it was a small car but they all ~ed in somehow** автомоби́ль был ма́ленький, но все ко́е-как в него́ вти́снулись; **~ off** *v.t.* (*dispatch*) отгру|жа́ть, -зи́ть; отпр|авля́ть, -а́вить; **she ~ed the children off to school** она́ отпра́вила дете́й в шко́лу; **~ out** *v.t.* (*Br.*): **the hall was ~ed out** зал был запо́лнен до отка́за; **~ up** *v.t.*: **have the presents been ~ed up yet?** пода́рки уже́ упако́ваны?; (*coll., stop*): **I ~ed up smoking last year** я бро́сил кури́ть в про́шлом году́; *v.i.*: **we spent the day ~ing up** мы це́лый день укла́дывались; (*coll., stop working*): **the workmen ~ed up at 5** рабо́чие зако́нчили в 5 часо́в; **the engine ~ed up** (*Br.*) мото́р отказа́л.

● *cpds.* **~-drill** *n.* наказа́ние марширо́вкой с по́лной вы́кладкой; **~-horse** *n.* вью́чная ло́шадь; **~-ice** *n.* пак; па́ковый лёд; **~-saddle** *n.* вью́чное седло́.

package /'pækɪdʒ/ *n.* (*parcel*) посы́лка; (*bundle*) свёрток, паке́т; (*comput.*) паке́т; (*fig.*): **~ deal** ко́мплексная сде́лка.

● *v.t.* упак|о́вывать, -ова́ть; (*fig.*): **a ~ holiday, tour** (*Br.*) организо́ванная туристи́ческая пое́здка; пое́здка по путёвке.

packer /'pækə(r)/ *n.* (*person*) упако́вщик; (*firm*) упако́вочная фи́рма.

packet /'pækɪt/ *n.* **1** (*of cigarettes, biscuits*) па́чка; (*of crisps*) паке́т. **2** (*Br.*

coll., large sum of money): **that must have cost him a ~** это, наверное, ему стоило уйму денег.

packing /'pækɪŋ/ *n.* **1** (*action, process*) упаковка; **I have all my ~ to do to-night** я должен собраться сегодня вечером. **2** (*material*) упаковка, упаковочный материал; (*seal for pipes etc.*) уплотнительный материал.

● *cpd.* **~-case** *n.* упаковочный ящик.

pact /pækt/ *n.* пакт.

pad /pæd/ *n.* **1** (*small cushion*) подушечка; (*for protection*) прокладка; **he played with ~s on his shins** он играл в щитках. **2** (*block of paper*) блокнот. **3** (*of animal's foot*) подушечка. **4** (*launching platform*) пусковой/стартовый стол; (*for rockets*) стартовая площадка. **5** (*sl., home*) пристанище, свой угол.

● *v.t.* (**padded, padding**) **1** (*provide with padding*) (*cushion*) наб|ивать, -ить; (*coat*) подб|ивать, -ить; **~ded cell** палата, обитая войлоком; **~ded shoulders** плечевые накладки (*f. pl.*). **2** (*fig., also* **~ out**) перегру|жать, -зить; разб|авлять, -авить; **his essays are ~ded out with quotations** его очерки перегружены цитатами.

● *v.i.* (**padded, padding**) (*coll., move softly*) бесшумно двигаться (*impf.*).

padding /'pædɪŋ/ *n.* (*lit.*) (*for cushion*) набивка; (*for coat*) подбивка; (*fig.*) многословие; вода.

paddle¹ /'pæd(ə)l/ *n.* (*oar*) (*single-bladed*) гребок; (*two-bladed*) байдарочное весло.

● *v.t. & i.* грести (*impf.*); **I learned to ~ my own canoe** (*fig.*) я научился действовать самостоятельно.

● *cpds.* **~-steamer** *n.* колёсный пароход; **~-wheel** *n.* гребное колесо.

paddl|e² /'pæd(ə)l/ *n.*: **the children have gone for a ~e** дети пошли поплескаться в воде.

● *v.i.* (*walk in shallow water*) шлёпать (*impf.*) по воде; мочить (*impf.*) ноги; **~ing-pool** детский бассейн, лягушатник (*coll.*).

paddock /'pædək/ *n.* (*small field, esp. for horses*) выгул; (*at racecourse*) паддок.

Paddy /'pædɪ/ *n.* (*coll., often offens. Irishman*) Пэдди (*m. indecl.*), ирландец.

paddy¹ /'pædɪ/ *n.*: **~-field** *n.* (заливное) рисовое поле.

paddy² /'pædɪ/ *n.* (*Br. coll., fit of temper*) ярость.

padlock /'pædlɒk/ *n.* висячий замок.

● *v.t.* вешать, повесить замок на + *a.*

padre /'pɑːdrɪ/, /-dreɪ/ *n.* (*coll.*) падре (*m. indecl.*).

paean /'piːən/ *n.* пеан.

paederast /'pedəˌræst/, **-y** /'pedəˌræstɪ/ = **pederast, -y**

paediatric /ˌpiːdɪ'ætrɪk/ (*US* **pediatric**) *adj.* педиатрический.

paediatrician /ˌpiːdɪə'trɪʃ(ə)n/ (*US* **pediatrician**) *n.* педиатр.

paediatrics /ˌpiːdɪ'ætrɪks/ (*US* **pediatrics**) *n.* педиатрия.

paedophile /'piːdəˌfaɪl/ (*US* **pedophile**) *n.* педофил.

paedophilia /ˌpiːdə'fɪlɪə/ (*US* **pedophilia**) *n.* педофилия.

paella /paɪ'elə/ *n.* (*cul.*) паэлья.

pagan /'peɪgən/ *n.* язычни|к (*fem.* -ца).

● *adj.* языческий.

paganism /'peɪgənˌɪz(ə)m/ *n.* язычество.

page¹ /peɪdʒ/ *n.* (*of a book etc.; also comput. and fig.*) страница; **~ proof** корректура в листах; вёрстка (*collect.*).

● *v.t.* нумеровать, про- страницы + *g.*

page² /peɪdʒ/ *n.* (*boy servant*) мальчик-прислужник; (*attending person of rank*) паж; (*at wedding*) мальчик, несущий шлейф невесты.

● *v.t.*: **please have Mr Smith ~d** пожалуйста, вызовите господина Смита по пейджеру.

pageant /'pædʒ(ə)nt/ *n.* (*sumptuous spectacle*) церемония, процессия; (*open-air enactment of historical events*) представление, действо.

pageantry /'pædʒəntrɪ/ *n.* пышность, парадность.

pager /'peɪdʒə(r)/ *n.* пейджер.

paginate /'pædʒɪˌneɪt/ *v.t.* нумеровать, про- страницы + *g.*

pagination /ˌpædʒɪ'neɪʃ(ə)n/ *n.* пагинация.

pagoda /pə'gəʊdə/ *n.* пагода.

paid /peɪd/ *past and p.p. of* ⇒**pay; put ~ to** (*coll.*) класть, положить конец + *d.*

pail /peɪl/ *n.* ведро.

paillasse /'pælɪˌæs/ = **palliasse**

pain /peɪn/ *n.* **1** (*suffering*) боль; **he is in great ~** его мучают боли; **he cried out in ~** он вскрикнул от боли; **her words caused me ~** её слова причинили мне боль; (*particular or localized*): **he had severe stomach ~s** у него были острые боли в желудке; **she felt her (labour** (*Br.*), **labor** (*US*)) **~s coming on** она чувствовала приближение (родовых) схваток; **he is a ~ in the neck** (*coll.*) он действует всем на нервы.
2 (*pl., trouble, effort*) старания (*nt. pl.*), хлоп|оты (*pl., g.* -от); **she spared no ~s to make us comfortable** она приложила все усилия, чтобы устроить нас поудобнее; **he takes great ~s over every picture** он подолгу работал над каждой картиной; **he was at ~s to show us everything** он позаботился о том, чтобы показать нам всё; **you will get nothing for your ~s** вы ничего не получите за свои труды.
3 (*penalty*): **he goes there on ~ of death** он идёт туда под страхом смерти.

● *v.t.* причин|ять, -ить боль + *d.*; **it ~s me to have to say this** мне больно это говорить; **a ~ed expression** обиженное выражение лица.

● *cpd.* **~-killer** *n.* болеутоляющее (средство).

painful /'peɪnfʊl/ *adj.* (*of part of body*) больной; (*causing mental or physical pain*) болезненный, мучительный; **it is my ~ duty to tell you ...** мой тягостный долг сообщить вам, что ...

painfully /'peɪnfʊlɪ/ *adv.* болезненно, мучительно; **~ slow** мучительно медленный; **~ familiar** до боли знакомый; **he was ~ aware...** он мучительно сознавал....

painfulness /'peɪnfʊlnɪs/ *n.* болезненность, мучительность.

painless /'peɪnlɪs/ *adj.* безболезненный.

painlessness /'peɪnlɪsnɪs/ *n.* безболезненность.

painstaking /'peɪnzˌteɪkɪŋ/ *adj.* старательный, усердный; кропотливый.

paint /peɪnt/ *n.* краска; **wet ~!** осторожно, окрашено!; **that door could do with a touch of ~** эту дверь хорошо бы подкрасить.

● *v.t.* **1** (*portray in colours*) рисовать, на-; писать, на- красками; (*fig., in words*) распис|ывать, -ать; **he's not as black as he is ~ed** не так уж он плох, как его описывают.
2 (*cover or adorn with ~*) красить, по-/вы-; **the house is ~ed white** дом выкрашен в белый цвет; **she never ~s her face** она никогда не красится; **they ~ed the town red** (*fig.*) они загуляли (*or* устроили кутёж); **~ed lady** (*butterfly*) репейница.

● *v.i.* рисовать (*impf.*); писать (*impf.*) красками; **he ~s** он художник; он занимается живописью.

● *with advs.*: **~ in** *v.t.* впис|ывать, -ать; **~ out** *v.t.* закра|шивать, -сить.

● *cpds.* **~-box** *n.* набор красок; **~-brush** *n.* кисть; **~-remover, -stripper** *nn.* растворитель (*m.*); **~-roller** *n.* валик; **~work** *n.* (*Br.*) краска.

painter¹ /'peɪntə(r)/ *n.* (*artist*) художник; (*decorator*) маляр.

painter² /'peɪntə(r)/ *n.* (*rope*) фалинь (*m.*).

painterly /'peɪntəlɪ/ *adj.* художественный, живописный.

painting /'peɪntɪŋ/ *n.* **1** (*profession*) живопись; **he took up ~** он занялся живописью. **2** (*work of art*) картина.

pair /peə(r)/ *n.* пара; **I have only one ~ of hands** у меня всего две руки; **I have found one boot, but its ~ is missing** я нашёл один ботинок, а парного нет; **they walked along in ~s** они шли парами; **~ of scissors** ножниц|ы (*pl., g.* —); **one ~ of scissors** одни ножницы; **~ of spectacles** очк|и (*pl., g.* -ов); **two ~s of trousers** двое (*or* две пары) брюк.

● *v.t.* (*unite*) спари|вать, -ть; (*mate*) случ|ать, -ить.

● *with adv.*: **~ off** *v.t. & i.* разб|ивать(ся), -ить(ся) на пары; (*coll., marry*) жениться (*impf., pf.*), пожениться (*pf.*).

pajamas /pɪ'dʒɑːməz/, /pə-/ (*US*) = **pyjamas**

Paki /'pækɪ/ *n.* (*pl.* **~s**) (*Br. coll., offens.*) пакистан|ец (*fem.* -ка).

● *adj.* пакистанский.

P

Pakistan /,pɑːkɪ'stɑːn/, /,pækɪ-/ *n.* Пакиста́н.

Pakistani /,pɑːkɪ'stɑːnɪ/, /,pækɪ-/ *n.* (*pl.* **~s**) пакиста́н|ец (*fem.* -ка).

● *adj.* пакиста́нский.

pal /pæl/ (*coll.*) *n.* ко́реш, дружо́к; **he was a real ~ to me** он был мне настоя́щим дру́гом; **be a ~ and lend me a cigarette** будь дру́гом, дай закури́ть.

● *v.i.* (**palled, palling**): **~ up** подружи́ться (*pf.*).

palace /'pælɪs/ *n.* дворе́ц.

palaeographer /,pælɪ'ɒgrəfə(r)/ (*US* **paleographer**) *n.* палео́граф.

palaeographic /,pælɪə'græfɪk/ (*US* **paleographic**) *adj.* палеографи́ческий.

palaeography /,pælɪ'ɒgrəfɪ/ (*US* **paleography**) *n.* палеогра́фия.

palaeolithic /,pælɪəʊ'lɪθɪk/ (*US* **paleolithic**) *adj.* палеолити́ческий.

palaeontologist /,pælɪɒn'tɒlədʒɪst/, /,peɪlɪ-/ (*US* **paleontologist**) *n.* палеонто́лог.

palaeontology /,pælɪɒn'tɒlədʒɪ/, /,peɪlɪ-/ (*US* **paleontology**) *n.* палеонтоло́гия.

Palaeozoic /,pælɪəʊ'zəʊɪk/ (*US* **Paleozoic**) *n.* палеозо́й.

● *adj.* палеозо́йский.

palatable /'pælətəb(ə)l/ *adj.* вку́сный; (*fig.*) прие́млемый.

palatal /'pælət(ə)l/ *n.* (*phon.*) палата́льный звук.

● *adj.* палата́льный.

palatalization /,pælətəlaɪ'zeɪʃ(ə)n/ *n.* палатализа́ция, смягче́ние.

palatalize /'pælətə,laɪz/ *v.t.* палатализи́ровать (*impf.*); смягч|а́ть, -и́ть.

palate /'pælət/ *n.* (*roof of mouth*) нёбо; (*lit., fig. taste*) вкус.

palatial /pə'leɪʃ(ə)l/ *adj.* роско́шный, великоле́пный.

palaver /pə'lɑːvə(r)/ *n.* (*coll.*) сует́а.

pale¹ /peɪl/ *n.* (*stake*) кол; (*boundary*) черта́, грани́ца; **his conduct puts him beyond the ~** (*fig.*) его́ поведе́ние перехо́дит все грани́цы; **~ of settlement** (*hist.*) черта́ осе́длости.

pale² /peɪl/ *adj.* **1** (*of complexion*) бле́дный; **she turned ~** она́ побледне́ла; (*of colours*) све́тлый; **~ ale** све́тлое пи́во; **~ blue** све́тло-голубо́й. **2** (*dim*) бле́дный, ту́склый; **a ~ reflection of its former glory** бле́дная тень было́й сла́вы.

● *v.i.* бледне́ть, по-; (*fig.*) тускне́ть, по-; **the event ~d into insignificance** э́то собы́тие отошло́ на за́дний план.

● *cpd.* **~faced** *adj.* бледноли́цый.

paleness /'peɪlnɪs/ *n.* бле́дность.

paleo- (*US*) = **palaeo-**

Palestine /'pælɪ,staɪn/ *n.* Палести́на.

Palestinian /,pælɪ'stɪnɪən/ *n.* палести́н|ец (*fem.* -ка).

● *adj.* палести́нский.

palette /'pælɪt/ *n.* (*lit., fig.*) пали́тра.

● *cpd.* **~-knife** *n.* (*art*) шпа́тель (*m.*).

palimpsest /'pælɪmp,sest/ *n.* палимпсе́ст.

palindrome /'pælɪn,drəʊm/ *n.* палиндро́м.

paling /'peɪlɪŋ/ *n.* палиса́д, частоко́л.

palisade /,pælɪ'seɪd/ *n.* (*wooden*) частоко́л; (*iron*) огра́да.

palish /'peɪlɪʃ/ *adj.* бледнова́тый.

pall¹ /pɔːl/ *n.* покро́в; **a ~ of smoke hung over the city** пелена́ ды́ма висе́ла над го́родом.

● *cpd.* **~-bearer** *n.* несу́щий гроб.

pall² /pɔːl/ *v.i.* при|еда́ться, -е́стся/надо|еда́ть, -е́сть (**on**: +*d.*).

pallet¹ /'pælɪt/ *n.* (*straw bed*) соло́менный тюфя́к.

pallet² /'pælɪt/ *n.* (*for loads*) поддо́н.

palliasse /'pælɪ,æs/ *n.* тюфя́к.

palliate /'pælɪ,eɪt/ *v.t.* (*alleviate*) облегч|а́ть, -и́ть; (*extenuate*) смягч|а́ть, -и́ть.

palliative /'pælɪətɪv/ *n.* паллиати́в.

● *adj.* паллиати́вный; смягча́ющий.

pallid /'pælɪd/ *adj.* бле́дный.

pallor /'pælə(r)/ *n.* бле́дность.

pally /'pælɪ/ *adj.* (**pallier, palliest**) (*coll.*) (*friendly*) дружелю́бный; **be ~ with s.o.** быть с кем-н. на коро́ткой ноге́.

palm¹ /pɑːm/ *n.* (*tree*) па́льма; (*branch, symbol of victory*) па́льмовая ветвь; **P~ Sunday** Ве́рбное воскресе́нье.

● *cpd.* **~-oil** *n.* па́льмовое ма́сло.

palm² /pɑːm/ *n.* (*of hand*) ладо́нь; **he greased the doorman's ~** (*bribed him*) он подма́зал портье́ (*coll.*).

● *v.t.*: **~ something off on s.o.** (*or* **s.o. off with something**) подс|о́вывать, -у́нуть что-н. кому́-н.

palmist /'pɑːmɪst/ *n.* хирома́нт (*fem.* -ка).

palmistry /'pɑːmɪstrɪ/ *n.* хирома́нтия.

palpable /'pælpəb(ə)l/ *adj.* ощути́мый; **a ~ error** я́вная оши́бка.

palpate /pæl'peɪt/ *v.t.* пальпи́ровать (*impf.*).

palpitate /'pælpɪ,teɪt/ *v.i.* (*pulsate*) пульси́ровать (*impf.*); (*tremble*) трепета́ть (*impf.*).

palpitation /,pælpɪ'teɪʃ(ə)n/ *n.* сердцебие́ние; **just to watch him gave me ~s** оди́н его́ вид приводи́л меня́ в тре́пет.

palsy /'pɔːlzɪ/, /'pɒl-/ *n.* парали́ч.

paltriness /'pɔːltrɪnɪs/, /'pɒl-/ *n.* ничто́жность.

paltry /'pɔːltrɪ/, /'pɒl-/ *adj.* (**paltrier, paltriest**) (*worthless*) ничто́жный; (*petty, mean*) ме́лкий; (*contemptible*) презре́нный.

pampas /'pæmpəs/ *n.* пампа́с|ы (*pl., g.* -ов).

● *cpd.* **~-grass** *n.* трава́ пампа́сная.

pamper /'pæmpə(r)/ *v.t.* балова́ть, из-; **she ~ed herself and stayed in bed all morning** она́ не́жилась в посте́ли всё у́тро.

pamphlet /'pæmflɪt/ *n.* (*printed leaflet*) брошю́ра; (*satirical*) памфле́т.

pamphleteer /,pæmflɪ'tɪə(r)/ *n.* памфлети́ст.

pan¹ /pæn/ *n.* **1** (*kitchen utensil; sauce~*) кастрю́ля; (**frying-~**) сковорода́. **2** (*of scales*) ча́шка. **3** (*Br., of water-closet*) унита́з. **4** (*ore-washing screen*) лото́к, поддо́н.

● *v.t.* (**panned, panning**) **1** (*coll., criticize severely*) разн|оси́ть, -ести́. **2** (*also* **~ out**: *wash gravel etc.*) пром|ыва́ть, -ы́ть.

● *v.i.* (**panned, panning**) (*fig.*): **everything ~ned out well** де́ло вы́шло как нельзя́ лу́чше.

● *cpds.* **~handle** *n.* (*US*) у́зкий высту́п земли́; *v.t. & i.* (*US*) попроша́йничать (*impf.*); **~tile** *n.* желобча́тая черепи́ца.

pan² /pæn/ *n.* (*camera movement*) панорами́рование.

● *v.t.* (**panned, panning**) панорами́ровать (*impf.*).

● *v.i.* (**panned, panning**) (*of camera*) повора́чиваться (*impf.*).

pan³ /pæn/: **~-pipes** *n. pl.* фле́йта Па́на.

pan- /pæn/ *comb. form* пан. . . .

panacea /,pænə'siːə/ *n.* панаце́я.

panache /pə'næʃ/ *n.* (*flamboyance*) рисо́вка, щегольство́.

Panama /'pænə,mɑː/ *n.* Пана́ма; **~ Canal** Пана́мский кана́л; **~ hat** пана́ма.

Panamanian /,pænə'meɪnɪən/ *n.* пана́м|ец (*fem.* -ка); жи́тель (*fem.* -ница) Пана́мы.

● *adj.* пана́мский.

Pan-American /,pænə'merɪkən/ *adj.* панамерика́нский.

pancake /'pæŋkeɪk/ *n.* блин; ола́дья; **P~ Day** вто́рник на ма́сленой неде́ле, в кото́рый пеку́т блины́.

panchromatic /,pænkrəʊ'mætɪk/ *adj.* панхромати́ческий.

pancreas /'pæŋkrɪəs/ *n.* поджелу́дочная железа́.

pancreatic /,pæŋkrɪ'ætɪk/ *adj.* панкреати́ческий.

panda /'pændə/ *n.* па́нда, бамбу́ковый медве́дь; **~ car** (*Br. coll.*) полице́йская патру́льная автомаши́на.

pandemic /pæn'demɪk/ *n.* пандеми́я.

● *adj.* всео́бщий.

pandemonium /,pændɪ'məʊnɪəm/ *n.* (*uproar, confusion*) смяте́ние, столпотворе́ние.

pander /'pændə(r)/ *v.i.* (*minister*) потво́рствовать (*impf.*) (**to**: +*d.*); **this newspaper ~s to the lowest tastes** э́та газе́та потво́рствует са́мым ни́зменным вку́сам.

Pandora's box /pæn'dɔːrəz/ *n.* я́щик Пандо́ры.

pane /peɪn/ *n.* око́нное стекло́.

panegyric /,pænɪ'dʒɪrɪk/ *n.* панеги́рик.

panel /'pæn(ə)l/ *n.* **1** (*of door etc.*) пане́ль. **2** (*of cloth*) вста́вка. **3** (*register*) спи́сок. **4** (*group of speakers*) ≈ кру́глый стол; **~ of judges** жюри́ (*indecl.*), суде́йская гру́ппа; **~ of experts** гру́ппа экспе́ртов; **~ game** (*Br.*) виктори́на.

5 (*for instruments*) пульт; **control ~** пульт управле́ния.

● *v.t.* (**pannelled, pannelling;** *US* **paneled, paneling**) обш|ива́ть, -и́ть (пане́лями).

panelling /'pænəlɪŋ/ (*US* **paneling**) *n.* пане́льная обши́вка; (*in frame*) филёнка.

panellist /'pænəlɪst/ (*US* **panelist**) *n.* (*in discussion*) уча́стник диску́ссии/кру́глого стола́; (*judge*) член жюри́.

Pan-European /,pæn,jʊrə'pɪən/ *adj.* панъевропе́йский.

pang /pæŋ/ *n.* **1** (*physical*) боль; (*sharp pain*) ко́лики (*f. pl.*), резь; **~s of hunger** голо́дные бо́ли; **birth ~s** родовы́е схва́тки (*f. pl.*). **2** (*mental*) му́ки (*f. pl.*); **a ~ of conscience** угрызе́ния (*nt. pl.*) со́вести.

panic /'pænɪk/ *n.* па́ника; **~ measures** отча́янные ме́ры.

● *v.t.* (**panicked, panicking**) (*coll.*): **they were ~ked into surrender** они́ впа́ли в па́нику и сдали́сь.

● *v.i.* (**panicked, panicking**) впа|да́ть, -сть в па́нику; паникова́ть (*impf.*).

● *cpds.* **~-monger** *n.* паникёр; **~-stricken** *adj.* охва́ченный па́никой.

panicky /'pænɪkɪ/ *adj.* (*coll.*) (*action*) пани́ческий; (*person*): **he was ~** он паникова́л.

pannier /'pænɪə(r)/ *n.* корзи́на.

panoplied /'pænəplɪd/ *adj.* во всеору́жии (*pred.*).

panoply /'pænəplɪ/ *n.* доспе́х|и (*pl., g.* -ов).

panorama /,pænə'rɑːmə/ *n.* (*lit., fig.*) панора́ма.

panoramic /,pænə'ræmɪk/ *adj.* панора́мный.

pansy /'pænzɪ/ *n.* (*flower*) аню́тины гла́з|ки (*pl., g.* -ок); (*coll., homosexual*) пе́дик.

pant /pænt/ *v.i.* тяжело́ дыша́ть (*impf.*); пыхте́ть (*impf.*); задыха́ться (*impf.*).

pantaloon /,pæntə'luːn/ *n.* (*in pl.*) (*hist.*) пантало́н|ы (*pl., g.* —); (*coll., trousers*) штан|ы́ (*pl., g.* -о́в).

pantechnicon /pæn'teknɪkən/ *n.* (*Br., van*) фурго́н.

pantheism /'pænθɪ,ɪz(ə)m/ *n.* пантеи́зм.

pantheist /'pænθɪ,ɪst/ *n.* пантеи́ст.

pantheistic /,pænθɪ'ɪstɪk/ *adj.* пантеисти́ческий.

pantheon /'pænθɪən/ *n.* (*lit., fig.*) пантео́н.

panther /'pænθə(r)/ *n.* панте́ра; (*US*) пу́ма.

panties /'pæntɪz/ *n.* тру́сик|и (*pl., g.* -ов).

panto /'pæntəʊ/ (*pl.* **~s**) (*Br. coll.*) = **pantomime**

pantograph /'pæntə,grɑːf/ *n.* панто́граф.

pantomime /'pæntə,maɪm/ *n.* (*Br., entertainment*) рожде́ственское представле́ние; (*dumb show*) пантоми́ма; (*fig.*) фарс.

pantry /'pæntrɪ/ *n.* кладова́я.

pants /pænts/ *n.* (*Br., underwear*) трус|ы́ (*pl., g.* -о́в); (*long*) кальсо́н|ы (*pl., g.* —); (*coll. or US, trousers*) брю́к|и (*pl., g.* —); штан|ы́ (*pl., g.* -о́в); **~** (*or* **pant**) **suit** (*US*) (же́нский) брю́чный костю́м.

pantyhose /'pæntɪ,həʊz/ *n.* (*US*) колго́т|ки (*pl., g.* -ок).

panzer /'pæntsə(r)/, /'pænz-/ *adj.* бронета́нковый.

pap /pæp/ *n.* (*soft food*) каши́ца; (*trivial reading matter*) чти́во, макулату́ра.

papa /pə'pɑː/ *n.* па́па (*m.*).

papacy /'peɪpəsɪ/ *n.* па́пство.

papal /'peɪp(ə)l/ *adj.* па́пский.

papara|zzo /,pæpə'rætsəʊ/ *n.* (*pl.* **~zzi** /-tsɪ/) фотокорреспонде́нт, рабо́тающий на бульва́рную пре́ссу; (*pl.*) папара́цци (*indecl.*).

papaw, pawpaw /pə'pɔː/ *n.* **1** (*Carica papaya*) папа́йя. **2** (*Asimina triloba*) азими́на.

paper /'peɪpə(r)/ *n.* **1** бума́га; (*attr.*): **~ bag** бума́жный паке́т; **~ handkerchief, tissue** бума́жная салфе́тка; **~ napkin** бума́жная салфе́тка; **a ~ tiger** бума́жный тигр. **2**: (**news~**) газе́та; **what do the ~s say?** что пи́шут газе́ты?; (*attr.*): **~ round** доста́вка газе́т (на́ дом); **~ shop** газе́тный кио́ск. **3** (*currency*) банкно́ты (*f. pl.*), бума́жные де́н|ьги (*pl., g.* -ег). **4** (*pl., documents*) докуме́нты (*m. pl.*), бума́ги (*f. pl.*). **5**: (**examination ~**) (*Br.*) экзаменацио́нная рабо́та. **6** (*essay, lecture*) докла́д; (*school essay*) сочине́ние. **7**: (**wall~**) обо́|и (*pl., g.* -ев).

● *v.t.* (*put wall~ on*) окле́и|вать, -ть обо́ями.

● *with adv.*: **~ over** *v.t.* закле́и|вать, -ть бума́гой; (*fig.*): **his speech merely ~ed over the cracks in the party** его́ речь была́ попы́ткой зама́зать раско́л в па́ртии.

● *cpds.* **~back** *n.* кни́га в бума́жном/мя́гком переплёте; **~-boy** *n.* (ма́льчик-)разно́счик газе́т; **~-chase** *n.* (*Br.*) игра́ «за́яц и соба́ки» с бума́жным «сле́дом»; **~-clip** *n.* канцеля́рская скре́пка; **~-girl** *n.* (де́вушка-)разно́счица газе́т; **~-hanger** *n.* обо́йщик; **~-knife** *n.* листоре́з; **~-mill** *n.* бума́жная фа́брика; **~-weight** *n.* пресс-папье́ (*indecl.*); **~-work** *n.* канцеля́рская рабо́та.

papier mâché /,pæpjeɪ 'mæʃeɪ/ *n.* папье́-маше́ (*indecl.*).

papist /'peɪpɪst/ *n.* (*pej.*) папи́ст; като́лик.

papistry /'peɪpɪstrɪ/ *n.* (*pej.*) папи́зм, католици́зм.

papoose /pə'puːs/ *n.* инде́йский ребёнок.

paprika /'pæprɪkə/, /pə'priːkə/ *n.* (*spice*) па́прика.

Papua New Guinea /'pæpjʊə njuː'gɪnɪ/ *n.* Па́пуа-Но́вая Гвине́я.

Papua New Guinean /'pæpjʊə njuː'gɪnɪən/ *n.* папуа́с (*fem.* -ка).

● *adj.* папуа́сский.

papyrus /pə'paɪərəs/ *n.* (*pl.* **papyri** /-raɪ -riː/) папи́рус.

par /pɑː(r)/ *n.* **1** (*equality*) ра́венство; **this is on a ~ with his other work** э́то на у́ровне други́х его́ рабо́т. **2** (*face value*) цена́; **above ~** вы́ше номина́льной цены́; **at ~** по номина́льной цене́; **below ~** ни́же номина́льной цены́. **3** (*standard, normal condition*) норма́льное состоя́ние; **I feel below ~ today** я себя́ сего́дня нева́жно чу́вствую; **~ for the course** (*fig., coll.*) сре́дняя но́рма.

para /'pærə/ (*coll.*) *abbr. of* ***paratrooper*** деса́нтник, авиадеса́нтник.

parable /'pærəb(ə)l/ *n.* при́тча.

parabola /pə'ræbələ/ *n.* (*pl.* **parabolas** *or* **parabolae** /-,liː/) пара́бола.

parabolic /,pærə'bɒlɪk/ *adj.* (*math.*) параболи́ческий.

paracetamol /,pærə'siːtə,mɒl/ *n.* (*Br.*) парацетамо́л.

parachute /'pærə,ʃuːt/ *n.* парашю́т; (*attr.*): **~ jump/landing** прыжо́к/приземле́ние с парашю́том; **~ troops** возду́шно-деса́нтные войска́.

● *v.t.*: **the stores were ~d to the ground** припа́сы бы́ли сбро́шены с парашю́том.

● *v.i.*: **the pilot ~d out of the aircraft** пило́т вы́бросился из самолёта с парашю́том.

● *cpds.* **~-jumper** *n.* парашюти́ст (*fem.* -ка); **~-jumping** *n.* прыжки́ (*m. pl.*) с парашю́том.

parachutist /'pærə,ʃuːtɪst/ *n.* парашюти́ст (*fem.* -ка).

parade /pə'reɪd/ *n.* **1** (*public procession*) ше́ствие, пара́д; (*display*) пока́з; **fashion ~** пока́з мод. **2** (*muster of troops*) пара́д; **be on ~** уча́ствовать (*impf.*) в пара́де. **3** (*Br., public promenade*) промена́д.

● *v.t.* (*display*) выставля́ть, вы́ставить напока́з; (*flaunt*) щеголя́ть (*impf.*) + *i.* (*coll.*); (*march through*) ше́ствовать (*impf.*) по + *d.*; (*muster*) стро́ить, вы́-/по-.

● *v.i.* (*muster*) стро́иться, вы́-/по-; (*march in procession*) ше́ствовать (*impf.*); маршировать (*impf.*).

● *cpd.* **~-ground** *n.* плац.

paradigm /'pærə,daɪm/ *n.* паради́гма.

paradise /'pærə,daɪs/ *n.* рай; **bird of ~** ра́йская пти́ца; **a ~ on earth** рай на земле́, рай земно́й; **he is living in a fool's ~** он живёт в ми́ре иллю́зий.

paradis(i)al /'pærə,daɪs(ə)l/ *adj.* ра́йский.

paradox /'pærə,dɒks/ *n.* парадо́кс.

paradoxical /,pærə'dɒksɪk(ə)l/ *adj.* парадокса́льный.

paraffin /'pærəfɪn/ *n.* **1** (*Br.*, **~ oil**) кероси́н; **~ heater** кероси́новый обогрева́тель; **~ lamp** кероси́новая ла́мпа. **2** (**~** *wax*) парафи́н; **liquid ~** парафи́новое ма́сло.

paragon /'pærəgən/ *n.* образе́ц.

paragraph /'pærə,grɑːf/ *n.* абза́ц,

пара́граф; (*of legal document*) пара́граф.

Paraguay /ˈpærəˌgwaɪ/ *n.* Парагва́й.

Paraguayan /ˌpærəˈgwaɪən/ *n.* парагва́|ец (*fem.* -йка).

● *adj.* парагва́йский.

parakeet /ˈpærəˌkiːt/ *n.* длиннохво́стый попуга́й.

parallax /ˈpærəˌlæks/ *n.* (*astron.*) паралла́кс.

parallel /ˈpærəˌlel/ *n.* **1** (*line or direction*) паралле́льная ли́ния; **in ~** паралле́льно; (*of latitude*) паралле́ль. **2** (*fig., similar thing; comparison*) паралле́ль; **one cannot draw a ~ between the two wars** невозмо́жно провести́ паралле́ль ме́жду э́тими двумя́ во́йнами.

● *adj.* паралле́льный; **~ bars** (паралле́льные) бру́сь|я (*pl., g.* -ев); (*analogous, similar*) аналоги́чный.

● *v.t.* (**paralleled, paralleling**) (*correspond to*) соотве́тствовать (*impf.*) + *d.*

parallelepiped /ˌpærəlelˈepɪˌped/, /-ləˈpaɪpɪd/ *n.* параллелепи́пед.

parallelism /ˈpærəlelˌɪz(ə)m/ *n.* (*lit., fig.*) параллели́зм.

parallelogram /ˌpærəˈleləˌgræm/ *n.* параллелогра́мм.

paralyse /ˈpærəˌlaɪz/ (*US* **paralyze**) *v.t.* (*lit., fig.*) парализова́ть (*impf., pf.*).

paralysis /pəˈrælɪsɪs/ *n.* (*pl.* **paralyses** /-ˌsiːz/) (*lit., fig.*) парали́ч.

paralytic /ˌpærəˈlɪtɪk/ *n.* парали́тик.

● *adj.* (*lit.*) паралити́ческий, парализо́ванный; (*Br., incapably drunk*) мертве́цки пья́ный.

paralyze /ˈpærəˌlaɪz/ (*US*) = **paralyse**

paramedic /ˌpærəˈmedɪk/ *n.* медрабо́тник (*без высшего образования*).

parameter /pəˈræmɪtə(r)/ *n.* (*math., comput.; also fig.*) пара́метр.

paramilitary /ˌpærəˈmɪlɪtərɪ/ *adj.* военизи́рованный.

paramount /ˈpærəˌmaʊnt/ *adj.* первостепе́нный; **his influence was ~** он име́л огро́мное влия́ние.

paramour /ˈpærəˌmʊə(r)/ *n.* любо́вни|к (*fem.* -ца).

paranoia /ˌpærəˈnɔɪə/ *n.* парано́йя.

paranoi|d /ˈpærəˌnɔɪd/, **-ac, -c** /ˌpærəˈnəʊɪk/, /-ˈnɔɪk/ *nn.* парано́ик.

● *adjs.* парано́идный, параноп́ческий; **you think I'm ~d** ты ду́маешь, что я парано́ик.

paranormal /ˌpærəˈnɔːm(ə)l/ *adj.* паранорма́льный.

parapet /ˈpærəpɪt/ *n.* (*low wall*) парапе́т; (*trench defence*) бру́ствер.

paraphernalia /ˌpærəfəˈneɪlɪə/ *n.* (*belongings*) ли́чные ве́щи (*f. pl.*); (*trappings*) причинда́л|ы (*pl., g.* -ов) (*coll., joc.*).

paraphrase /ˈpærəˌfreɪz/ *n.* переска́з.

● *v.t.* переска́з|ывать, -а́ть.

paraplegia /ˌpærəˈpliːdʒə/ *n.* параплеги́я.

paraplegic /ˌpærəˈpliːdʒɪk/ *adj.* парализо́ванный.

parapsychology /ˌpærəsaɪˈkɒlədʒɪ/ *n.* парапсихоло́гия.

parasite /ˈpærəˌsaɪt/ *n.* парази́т; (*fig.*) парази́т; тунея́дец.

parasitic /ˌpærəˈsɪtɪk/ *adj.* (*lit., fig.*) паразити́ческий.

parasol /ˈpærəˌsɒl/ *n.* зо́нтик (от со́лнца).

paratrooper /ˈpærəˌtruːpə(r)/ *n.* (авиа)деса́нтник.

paratroops /ˈpærəˌtruːps/ *n.* парашю́тно-деса́нтные войска́ (*nt. pl.*).

paratyphoid /ˌpærəˈtaɪfɔɪd/ *n.* парати́ф.

parboil /ˈpɑːbɔɪl/ *v.t.* слегка́ отв|а́ривать, -ари́ть.

parcel /ˈpɑːs(ə)l/ *n.* **1** (*for posting*) паке́т, бандеро́ль, посы́лка; (*wrapped object*) свёрток. **2** (*arch., portion*) часть; **a ~ of land** уча́сток земли́; **part and ~** составна́я/неотъе́млемая часть (*чего*).

● *v.t.* (**parcelled, parcelling;** *US* **parceled, parceling**) (*pack up; also* **~ up**) пакова́ть, у-; (*divide; also* **~ out**) дроби́ть, раз-.

parch /pɑːtʃ/ *v.t.* иссуш|а́ть, -и́ть; **the ground was ~ed** земля́ высохла; **his throat was ~ed with thirst** от жа́жды у него́ пересо́хло в го́рле; **my lips are ~ed** у меня́ запекли́сь гу́бы.

parchment /ˈpɑːtʃmənt/ *n.* перга́мент.

pardon /ˈpɑːd(ə)n/ *n.* **1** извине́ние, проще́ние; **I beg your ~** (*apology*) прошу́ проще́ния; (*request for repetition*) повтори́те, пожа́луйста!; прости́те, не расслы́шал. **2** (*leg.*) поми́лование; **they were granted a free ~** их поми́ловали.

● *v.t.* (*forgive*) про|ща́ть, -сти́ть; (*excuse*) извин|я́ть, -и́ть; **if you'll ~ the expression** извини́те за выраже́ние; (*leg.*) ми́ловать, по-

pardonabl|e /ˈpɑːdənəb(ə)l/ *adj.* прости́тельный.

pare /peə(r)/ *v.t.* (*trim*) стричь, о(б)-; (*peel*) чи́стить, по-; (*reduce; also* **~ away, ~ down**) ур|е́зывать (*or* -еза́ть), -е́зать.

parent /ˈpeərənt/ *n.* (*father or mother*) роди́тель (*fem.* -ница); (*attr., original*) первонача́льный; **~ company** компа́ния-учреди́тель; **~ stock** (*bot.*) корнева́я по́росль.

parentage /ˈpeərəntɪdʒ/ *n.* происхожде́ние; **he is of mixed ~** он происхо́дит от сме́шанного бра́ка.

parental /pəˈrent(ə)l/ *adj.* роди́тельский.

parenthes|is /pəˈrenθəsɪs/ *n.* (*pl.* **parentheses** /-ˌsiːz/) (*word*) вво́дное сло́во; (*sentence*) вво́дное предложе́ние; (*pl., text mark*) кру́глые ско́бки (*f. pl.*); **in ~es** в ско́бках.

parenthetic(al) /ˌpærənˈθetɪkəl/ *adj.* вво́дный.

parenthetically /ˌpærənˈθetɪkəlɪ/ *adv.* ме́жду де́лом/про́чим.

parenthood /ˈpeərəntˌhʊd/ *n.* (*fatherhood*) отцо́вство; (*motherhood*) матери́нство; **planned ~** плани́рование семьи́.

parenting /ˈpeərəntɪŋ/ *n.* воспита́ние.

par excellence /ˌpɑːr eksəˈlɑ̃s/ *adv.*: **this is the fashionable quarter ~** э́то са́мый что ни на есть мо́дный райо́н.

pariah /pəˈraɪə/, /ˈpærɪə/ *n.* (*lit. fig.*) па́рия (*c.g.*).

paring /ˈpeərɪŋ/ *n.* (*peeling*) очище́ние; чи́стка; (*trimming: of nails etc.*) стри́жка; (*slicing: of cheese etc.*) нареза́ние; **nail ~s** обре́зки (*m. pl.*) ногте́й.

Paris /ˈpærɪs/ *n.* (*geog.*) Пари́ж.

parish /ˈpærɪʃ/ *n.* (*eccles.*) прихо́д; (*Br., civil*) о́круг; **~ council** (*Br.*) окружно́е управле́ние.

parishioner /pəˈrɪʃənə(r)/ *n.* прихожа́н|ин (*fem.* -ка).

Parisian /pəˈrɪzɪən/ *n.* парижа́н|ин (*fem.* -ка).

● *adj.* пари́жский.

parity /ˈpærɪtɪ/ *n.* (*equality*) ра́венство, парите́т.

park /pɑːk/ *n.* **1** (*public garden*) парк. **2** (*protected area of countryside*) запове́дник; парк. **3** (*grounds of country mansion*) уго́дь|я (*pl., g.* -ий). **4** (*Br., for vehicles etc.*) стоя́нка, парк.

● *v.t.* паркова́ть, за-; (*coll., stow, dispose*) скла́дывать, сложи́ть; **you can ~ your things in my room** вы мо́жете оста́вить свои́ ве́щи в моей ко́мнате; **he ~ed himself in the best chair** он усе́лся в лу́чшее кре́сло.

● *v.i.* паркова́ться, за-; ста́вить, по- маши́ну (на стоя́нку).

● *cpd.* **~-keeper** *n.* сто́рож (при па́рке).

parka /ˈpɑːkə/ *n.* па́рка.

parking /ˈpɑːkɪŋ/ *n.* (авто)стоя́нка; **'no ~!'** «стоя́нка запрещена́!»

● *cpds.* **~-light** *n.* подфа́рник; **~-lot** *n.* (*US*) стоя́нка; ме́сто стоя́нки; **~-meter** *n.* стоя́ночный счётчик; счётчик на стоя́нке; **~ place** *n.* ме́сто для парко́вки; **~ ticket** *n.* штраф за наруше́ние пра́вил стоя́нки.

Parkinson's disease /ˈpɑːkɪns(ə)nz/ *n.* боле́знь Паркинсо́на.

Parkinson's law /ˈpɑːkɪns(ə)nz/ *n.* зако́н Паркинсо́на.

parkland /ˈpɑːklənd/ *n.* парк, па́рковая террито́рия; **the house is set in ~** дом располо́жен на террито́рии па́рка.

parkway /ˈpɑːkweɪ/ *n.* (*US*) шоссе́ (*indecl.*), обса́женное дере́вьями.

parky /ˈpɑːkɪ/ *adj.* (**parkier, parkiest**) (*Br. coll.*) холоднова́тый.

parlance /ˈpɑːləns/ *n.* язы́к; мане́ра выраже́ния; **in common ~** в просторе́чии.

parley /ˈpɑːlɪ/ *n.* (*pl.* **~s**) перегово́р|ы (*pl., g.* -ов).

● *v.i.* (**parleys, parleyed**) вести́ (*impf.*) перегово́ры.

parliament /ˈpɑːləmənt/ *n.* парла́мент; **P~ is sitting** парла́мент заседа́ет; **P~ rose** парла́мент око́нчил заседа́ние; **the Queen opened P~** короле́ва откры́ла се́ссию парла́мента.

parliamentarian /ˌpɑːləmenˈteərɪən/ *n.* (*member of parliament*) парламента́рий.

parliamentary /ˌpɑːləˈmentərɪ/ *adj.* парла́ментский, парламента́рный.

parlour /ˈpɑːlə(r)/ (*US* **parlor**) *n.* (*in house*) гости́ная; **beauty ~** космети́ческий кабине́т/сало́н; **funeral ~** похоро́нное бюро́ (*indecl.*); **ice-cream ~** кафе́-моро́женое.

● *cpd.* **~-game** *n.* фа́нт|ы (*pl., g.* -ов).

parlous /ˈpɑːləs/ *adj.* (*arch., joc.*) стра́шный.

Parmesan /ˌpɑːmɪˈzæn/, /ˈpɑː-/ *n.* (**~ cheese**) сыр пармеза́н.

parochial /pəˈrəʊkɪəl/ *adj.* прихо́дский; (*fig.*) ограни́ченный, у́зкий.

parochialism /pəˈrəʊkɪəˌlɪz(ə)m/ *n.* ограни́ченность, у́зость.

parodist /ˈpærədɪst/ *n.* пароди́ст.

parody /ˈpærədɪ/ *n.* паро́дия.

● *v.t.* пароди́ровать (*impf., pf.*).

parole /pəˈrəʊl/ *n.* че́стное сло́во; **he was released on ~** его́ освободи́ли под че́стное сло́во.

● *v.t.* освобо|жда́ть, -ди́ть под че́стное сло́во (*or* на пору́ки).

paroxysm /ˈpærəkˌsɪz(ə)m/ *n.* пароксизм.

parquet /ˈpɑːkɪ/, /-keɪ/ *n.* парке́т; **~ floor** парке́тный пол.

parrot /ˈpærət/ *n.* (*lit., fig.*) попуга́й.

● *v.t.* (**parroted, parroting**) повтор|я́ть, -и́ть как попуга́й.

● *cpd.* **~-fashion** *adv.* как попуга́й.

parry /ˈpærɪ/ *v.t.* отра|жа́ть, -зи́ть; (*question*) пари́ровать (*impf., pf.*).

parse /pɑːz/ *v.t. & i.* де́лать, с- граммати́ческий разбо́р (*чего*).

parsimonious /ˌpɑːsɪˈməʊnɪəs/ *adj.* скупо́й.

parsimony /ˈpɑːsɪmənɪ/ *n.* ску́пость.

parsley /ˈpɑːslɪ/ *n.* петру́шка.

parsnip /ˈpɑːsnɪp/ *n.* пастерна́к.

parson /ˈpɑːs(ə)n/ *n.* па́стор; **~'s nose** (*of fowl*) «архиере́йский нос», кури́ная гу́зка.

parsonage /ˈpɑːsənɪdʒ/ *n.* пастора́т.

part /pɑːt/ *n.* **1** часть; (*portion*) до́ля; **the greater ~** (*majority*) бо́льшая часть; **for the most ~** бо́льшей ча́стью; по бо́льшей ча́сти; **in ~** части́чно, отча́сти; **this book is good in ~s** э́та кни́га хороша́ места́ми; **inquisitiveness is ~ of being young** мо́лодости сво́йственна любозна́тельность; **~ and parcel** *see* ⇒**parcel** *n.* 2; (*equal division*): **he received a fifth ~ of the estate** он получи́л пя́тую часть состоя́ния; (*instalment*): **the journal comes out in weekly ~s** журна́л выхо́дит еженеде́льными вы́пусками; (*component*): **spare ~s** запасны́е ча́сти; (*gram.*): **~s of speech** ча́сти ре́чи; **principal ~s of a verb** основны́е фо́рмы (*f. pl.*) глаго́ла.
2 (*share, contribution*) уча́стие; **take ~ in** прин|има́ть, -я́ть уча́стие в + *p.*; **I'll have no ~ in it** я не бу́ду принима́ть в э́том уча́стия; **I have done my ~** я сде́лал своё де́ло (*or* свою́ часть рабо́ты).
3 (*actor's role or lines*) роль; **he is only playing a ~** он про́сто игра́ет (роль); **luck played a large ~ in his success** уда́ча сыгра́ла большу́ю роль в его́ успе́хе.
4 (*side in dispute etc.*) сторона́; **take s.o.'s ~** вст|ава́ть, -ать на чью-н. сто́рону; **there will be no objection on his ~** с его́ стороны́ возраже́ний не бу́дет; **for my ~** с мое́й стороны́, что каса́ется меня́; **he took my criticism in good ~** он не оби́делся на мою́ кри́тику.
5 (*region*) места́ (*nt. pl.*), край; **in our ~ of the world** в на́ших края́х; **I'm a stranger in these ~s** я в э́тих места́х чужо́й; **do you know these ~s?** зна́ете вы э́ти места́/края́?
6 (*mus.*) па́ртия; **it is a difficult ~ to sing** э́ту па́ртию тру́дно петь; **a song for four ~s** пе́сня на четы́ре го́лоса.
7 (*US, in one's hair*) пробо́р.
8 (*pl., abilities*) спосо́бности (*f. pl.*); **a man of ~s** спосо́бный челове́к.

● *adv.* части́чно, ча́стью, отча́сти; **the wall is ~ brick and ~ stone** стена́ сло́жена части́чно из кирпича́, части́чно из ка́мня.

● *v.t.* раздел|я́ть, -и́ть; **he ~ed the fighters** он разня́л деру́щихся; **the policeman ~ed the crowd** полице́йский раздви́нул толпу́; **his hair was ~ed in the middle** его́ во́лосы бы́ли расчёсаны на прямо́й пробо́р; **he ~s it at the side** он де́лает пробо́р сбо́ку; **we ~ed company** (*went different ways*) мы разошли́сь/разъе́хались; (*ended our relationship*) мы расста́лись; (*differed*) мы разошли́сь во мне́ниях.

● *v.i.* расст|ава́ться, -а́ться; **they ~ed friends** они́ расста́лись друзья́ми; **she has ~ed from her husband** она́ разошла́сь с му́жем; **he hates to ~ with his money** он о́чень не лю́бит расстава́ться с деньга́ми.

● *cpds.* **~ exchange** *n.* (*Br.*) сде́лка, при кото́рой ста́рая вещь обме́нивается на но́вую с допла́той; **~-exchange** *v.t.*: **she ~-exchanged her car for a new one** она́ обменя́ла свою́ ста́рую маши́ну на но́вую с допла́той; **~-owner** *n.* совладе́лец; **~-time** *adj., adv.* на полста́вки; **I want a ~-time job** я хочу́ рабо́тать на полста́вки; **a ~-time teacher** учи́тель (*fem.* -ница) на полста́вки; **he works ~-time** он рабо́тает на полста́вки.

partake /pɑːˈteɪk/ *v.i.* (*past* **partook** -ˈtʊk; *p.p.* **partaken** /-ˈteɪk(ə)n/) (*take a share*) прин|има́ть, -я́ть уча́стие; **they partook of our meal** они́ пое́ли с на́ми.

parterre /pɑːˈteə(r)/ *n.* (*in garden*) цветни́к; (*US, theatr.*) парте́р.

parthenogenesis /ˌpɑːθɪnəʊˈdʒenɪsɪs/ *n.* партеногене́з.

Parthian /ˈpɑːθɪən/ *adj.*: **a ~ shot** парфя́нская стрела́.

partial /ˈpɑːʃ(ə)l/ *adj.* **1** (*opp. total*) части́чный; **~ eclipse** непо́лное затме́ние. **2** (*biased*) пристра́стный. **3**: **~ to** (*fond of*) неравноду́шный к + *d.*

partiality /ˌpɑːʃɪˈælɪtɪ/ *n.* (*bias*) пристра́стность; (*fondness*) неравноду́шие (*к кому/чему*).

participant /pɑːˈtɪsɪpənt/ *n.* уча́стник.

participate /pɑːˈtɪsɪˌpeɪt/ *v.i.* (*take part*) уча́ствовать (*impf.*).

participation /pɑːˌtɪsɪˈpeɪʃ(ə)n/ *n.* уча́стие.

participle /ˈpɑːtɪˌsɪp(ə)l/ *n.* прича́стие; **present and past ~s** прича́стия настоя́щего и проше́дшего вре́мени.

particle /ˈpɑːtɪk(ə)l/ *n.* **1** части́ца, крупи́ца; **a ~ of dust** пыли́нка. **2** (*gram.*) части́ца.

particoloured /ˈpɑːtɪˌkʌləd/ (*US* **particolored**) *adj.* разноцве́тный.

particular /pəˈtɪkjʊlə(r)/ *n.* ча́стность; **in ~** (*specifically*) в ча́стности; (*especially*) осо́бенно; (*pl.*) да́нные (*pl.*); **let me take down your ~s** разреши́те мне записа́ть ва́ши да́нные; **they sent me ~s of the house** они́ присла́ли мне (подро́бное) описа́ние до́ма.

● *adj.* **1** (*specific, special*) осо́бенный, осо́бый; **for no ~ reason** без осо́бой причи́ны. **2** (*detailed*) обстоя́тельный; **a ~ account** обстоя́тельный/дета́льный отчёт. **3** (*fastidious*) привере́дливый; **I am not ~ what I eat** я неразбо́рчив в еде́; **she is not ~ about her dress** ей всё равно́, что наде́ть.

particularity /pəˌtɪkjʊˈlærɪtɪ/ *n.* специ́фика.

particularize /pəˈtɪkjʊləˌraɪz/ *v.t.* переч|исля́ть, -и́слить.

particularly /pəˈtɪkjʊləlɪ/ *adv.* осо́бенно.

parting /ˈpɑːtɪŋ/ *n.* **1** (*leave-taking*) проща́ние; **a kiss at ~** поцелу́й на проща́ние; **a ~ gift** проща́льный пода́рок; **~ shot** = **Parthian shot.** **2** (*separation*) расстава́ние; проща́ние; **at the ~ of the ways** (*lit., fig.*) на распу́тье. **3** (*Br., of the hair*) пробо́р.

parti|san, -zan /ˈpɑːtɪˌzæn/ *n.* **1** (*zealous supporter*) приве́рженец; **you say that in a ~ spirit** вы говори́те пристра́стно. **2** (*resistance fighter*) партиза́н (*fem.* -ка).

● *adj.* пристра́стный.

partisanship /ˈpɑːtɪˌzænʃɪp/ *n.* приве́рженность.

partition /pɑːˈtɪʃ(ə)n/ *n.* (*division*) разде́л; **the ~ of Yugoslavia** разде́л Югосла́вии; (*dividing structure*) перегоро́дка.

● *v.t.* дели́ть, раз-/по-; **~ off** отгор|а́живать, -оди́ть.

partitive /ˈpɑːtɪtɪv/ *adj.* (*gram.*) раздели́тельный.

partizan /ˌpɑːtɪˈzæn/ = **partisan**

partly /ˈpɑːtlɪ/ *adv.* части́чно, отча́сти.

partner /ˈpɑːtnə(r)/ *n.* (*business, sexual, cards, dancing etc.*) партнёр (*fem.* -ша) (*coll.*); **~s in crime** соуча́стники (*m. pl.*) преступле́ния; (*in marriage*) супру́г (*fem.* -а).

● *v.t.* (*be ~ to*) быть партнёром + *g.*

partnership /ˈpɑːtnəʃɪp/ *n.*

P

товáрищество; партнёрство; **go into ~ (with)** входи́ть, войти́ в партнёрство (с + *i.*); образ|óвывать, -овáть товáрищество (с + *i.*).

partridge /ˈpɑːtrɪdʒ/ *n.* (*pl.* ~ *or* ~**s**) куропáтка.

parturition /ˌpɑːtjʊˈrɪʃ(ə)n/ *n.* разрешéние от брéмени; рóд|ы (*pl., g.* -ов).

party /ˈpɑːtɪ/ *n.* **1** (*political group*) пáртия; ~ **line** партийная ли́ния; ~ **politics** партийная поли́тика; **the** ~ **system** партийная систéма.
2 (*group with common interests or pursuits*) компáния, грýппа; **we travelled** (*Br.*), **traveled** (*US*) **abroad in a** ~ мы поéхали за грани́цу грýппой.
3 (*social gathering*) вечери́нка; (*official*) приём; ~ **dress** вечéрнее плáтье; **he lacks the** ~ **spirit** он не компанéйский человéк.
4 (*outing*) экскýрсия.
5 (*participant in contract etc.*) сторонá; **the wife was the injured** ~ женá былá пострадáвшей сторонóй; **I won't be** ~ **to such a scheme** я не приму́ учáстия в э́той затée.
6 (*attr., shared*): ~ **line** (*telephone*) óбщая телефóнная ли́ния (*see also sense* 1); ~ **wall** óбщая стенá.
● *cpd.* ~**-political** *adj.* партийный; ~**-political broadcast** (*Br.*) пропагандистское выступлéние пáртии по рáдио и́ли телеви́дению.

paschal /ˈpæsk(ə)l/ *adj.* пасхáльный.

pas de deux /pɑː də ˈdɜː/ *n.* (*pl.* ~) па-де-дé (*m., nt. indecl.*).

pass /pɑːs/ *n.* **1** (*qualifying standard in exam*) сдáча экзáмена; **he got a** ~ **in French** он сдал экзáмен по францу́зскому языку́.
2 (*situation*) положéние; **things reached a pretty** ~ делá при́няли сквéрный оборóт.
3 (*permit, document*) прóпуск (*pl.* -á); **free** ~ свобóдный вход.
4 (*transfer of ball in game*) пас, передáча.
5 (*lunge, thrust*) вы́пад; (*coll., amorous approach*): **he made a** ~ **at her** он к ней приставáл (*coll.*).
6 (*mountain defile*) ущéлье, перевáл.
7 (*at cards*) пас.
● *v.t.* **1** (*go by*) про|ходи́ть, -йти́ (ми́мо + *g.*); **he** ~**es the shop on his way to work** по дорóге на рабóту он прохóдит ми́мо магази́на; **I** ~**ed him in the street** я прошёл ми́мо негó на у́лице.
2 (*overtake*) об|гоня́ть, -огнáть.
3 (*go, get through*) про|ходи́ть, -йти́; **not a word** ~**ed his lips** он не произнёс ни слóва; **will your car** ~ **the test?** пройдёт ли вáша маши́на провéрку?; ~ **an exam** сдать/вы́держать (*pf.*) экзáмен.
4 (*spend*) пров|оди́ть, -ести́; **he** ~**ed a pleasant evening there** он провёл там прия́тный вéчер.
5 (*surpass, exceed*) прев|ышáть, -ы́сить; **it** ~**es all reason** э́то выхóдит за предéлы разу́много.
6 (*examine and accept*) пропус|кáть, -ти́ть; **only one candidate was** ~**ed by the board** коми́ссия утверди́ла тóлько однý кандидату́ру; (*approve, sanction*) од|обря́ть, -óбрить.
7 (*hand over*) перед|авáть, -áть; ~ **(me) the salt, please!** передáйте мне соль, пожáлуйста!
8 (*utter*) произн|оси́ть, -ести́; **he refrained from** ~**ing judgement** он воздержáлся выноси́ть суждéние; **the judge** ~**ed sentence** судья́ вы́нес пригово́р; **we met and** ~**ed the time of day** мы встрéтились и поздорóвались.
9 (*cause to go, move*): **he** ~**ed his eye over the goods** он просмотрéл товáры; **he** ~**ed a rope round his waist** он обвязáл свою́ тáлию верёвкой; ~ **a ball** перед|авáть, -áть (*or* бр|осáть, -óсить) мяч.
10 (*excrete*) испус|кáть, -ти́ть; **he could not** ~ **water** он не мог мочи́ться.
● *v.i.* **1** (*proceed, move*) про|ходи́ть, -йти́; перепр|авля́ться, -áвиться; **he** ~**ed by the window** он прошёл ми́мо окнá; **he** ~**ed through the door** он прошёл в/ чéрез дверь; **she** ~**ed out of sight** онá исчéзла и́з виду; (*get through*): **let me** ~**!** дáйте мне пройти́; (*circulate*) перед|авáться, -áться; **the magazine** ~**ed from hand to hand** журнáл передавáлся/переходи́л из рук в ру́ки; (*in opposite directions*) миновáть (*impf., pf.*); **they** ~**ed without speaking** они́ мóлча прошли́ ми́мо друг дрýга.
2 (*be transferred*): **the business** ~**ed into other hands** предприя́тие перешлó в други́е ру́ки; (*by inheritance*): **the estate** ~**ed to his son** имéние бы́ло унаслéдовано сы́ном.
3 (*overtake*) об|гоня́ть, -огнáть; ~**ing prohibited for 2 miles** обгóн запрещён на две ми́ли.
4 (*go by, elapse*) про|ходи́ть, -йти́; **the procession** ~**ed** процéссия прошлá ми́мо; **time** ~**es slowly** врéмя прохóдит мéдленно; **six years have** ~**ed since then** с тех пор прошлó шесть лет.
5 (*change*) превра|щáться, -ти́ться; **day** ~**es into night** день перехóдит в ночь; **his mood** ~**ed from fear to anger** страх смени́лся в нём я́ростью.
6 (*be said or done*) прои|сходи́ть, -зойти́; **did you hear what** ~**ed between them?** вы знáете, что произошлó мéжду ни́ми?
7 (*go without comment*): **his words** ~**ed unnoticed** егó словá остáлись незамéченными; на егó словá никтó не обрати́л внимáния; **let it** ~**!** не нáдо об э́том говори́ть!
8 (*come to an end*) про|ходи́ть, -йти́; прекра|щáться, -ти́ться; **the pain will** ~ боль пройдёт.
9 (*qualify in exam etc.; be valid, accepted, recognized*) про|ходи́ть, -йти́; **he** ~**es for an expert** он счи́тается специали́стом.
10 (*at cards*) пасовáть, с-.
● *with advs.*: ~ **along** *v.i.* про|ходи́ть, -йти́; ~ **away** *v.i.* (*die*) скончáться (*pf.*); ~ **by** *v.t. & i.* про|ходи́ть, -йти́ (ми́мо + *g.*); ~ **down** *v.t.* перед|авáть, -áть; **the custom was** ~**ed down from father to son** обы́чай передавáлся от отцá к сы́ну; ~ **off** *v.t.* (*dismiss*): **he** ~**ed off the whole affair as a joke** он обрати́л всё дéло в шу́тку; (*palm off, get rid of*) подс|óвывать, -у́нуть; сбы|вáть, -ть; (*falsely represent*): **he** ~**es himself off as a foreigner** он выдаёт себя́ за инострáнца; **he tried to** ~ **off the picture as genuine** он выдавáл карти́ну за пóдлинник; *v.i.* (*go away*) прекра|щáться, -ти́ться; **the pain was slow to** ~ **off** боль проходи́ла мéдленно; (*be carried through*) про|ходи́ть, -йти́; **the wedding** ~**ed off without a hitch** свáдьба прошлá без проблéм; ~ **on** *v.t.* перед|авáть, -áть; (*charge, tax etc.*) пере|клáдывать, -ложи́ть (*на кого*); *v.i.* про|ходи́ть, -йти́; **let us** ~ **on to other topics** давáйте перейдём/ переключи́мся на други́е тéмы; (*euph., die*) скончáться (*pf.*); ~ **out** *v.i.* (*Br., qualify, graduate*) про|ходи́ть, -йти́; ~**ing-out parade** парáд выпускникóв; (*coll., lose consciousness*) отключ|áться, -и́ться; ~ **over** *v.t.* (*hand over*) перед|авáть, -áть; (*omit; overlook, ignore*) пропус|кáть, -ти́ть; **we shall** ~ **over your previous offences** (*Br.*), **offenses** (*US*) мы не бу́дем инкримини́ровать вам предыду́щие нарушéния; **he was** ~**ed over for a younger man** они́ емý предпочли́ бóлее молодóго человéка; *v.i.* про|ходи́ть, -йти́; **the storm** ~**ed over** буря́ прошлá; (*euph., die*) скончáться (*pf.*); ~ **round** *v.t.* перед|авáть, -áть; ~ **the hat round** пус|кáть, -ти́ть шáпку по крýгу; ~ **through** *v.t.* прод|евáть, -éть; ~ **up** *v.t.* (*hand up*) под|авáть, -áть; (*coll., refuse*) откáз|ываться, -áться от + *g.*
● *cpds.* ~**-book** *n.* бáнковская кни́жка; ~**-key** *n.* отмы́чка; **P**~**over** *n.* еврéйская Пáсха; ~**word** *n.* (*also comput.*) парóль (*m.*).

passable /ˈpɑːsəb(ə)l/ *adj.* (*affording passage*) проходи́мый, проéзжий; (*tolerable*) снóсный.

passage /ˈpæsɪdʒ/ *n.* **1** (*going by*) прохóд; **the** ~ **of time** течéние врéмени; (*going across, over*) переéзд; перелёт; **a bird of** ~ перелётная пти́ца; (*transition, change*) перехóд; (*going through, way through*) прохóд; **the police forced a** ~ **through the crowd** поли́ция проложи́ла себé путь чéрез толпу́; (*right to go through*) прáво прохóда.
2 (*crossing by ship etc.*) рейс; **have you booked your** ~**?** вы заказáли билéт на парохóд?; **we had a rough** ~ нáше плáвание бы́ло бу́рным; (*fig.*): **the bill had a rough** ~ законопроéкт был при́нят пóсле бу́рного обсуждéния; **work one's** ~ отраб|áтывать, -óтать свой проéзд.
3 (*passing of law etc.*) проведéние.
4 (*corridor*) коридóр.
5 (*alley*) прохóд.
6 (*coll., duct in body*) прохóд, протóк; **back** ~ (*rectum*) зáдний прохóд; (*pl., breathing tubes*) дыхáтельные пут|и́ (*pl., g.* -éй).
7 (*literary excerpt*) отры́вок, текст; (*mus.*) пассáж.
● *cpd.* ~**-way** *n.* коридóр; прохóд.

passé /ˈpæseɪ/ *adj.* устарéлый, немóдный.

passenger /ˈpæsɪndʒə(r)/ *n.* пассажи́р; **~ train** пассажи́рский по́езд; **~ seat** ме́сто ря́дом с води́телем.

passer-by /ˌpɑːsəˈbaɪ/ *n.* прохо́жий.

passim /ˈpæsɪm/ *adv.* везде́, повсю́ду.

passing /ˈpɑːsɪŋ/ *n.* **1** (*going by*) прохожде́ние; **I just called in ~** я зашёл мимохо́дом; **I will mention in ~** я заме́чу попу́тно (*or* вскользь *or* ме́жду про́чим). **2** (*death*) смерть, конча́на.

● *adj.* (*transient*): **a ~ fancy** мимолётное увлече́ние; **the ~ fashion** преходя́щая мо́да.

● *cpd.* **~-note** *n.* (*mus.*) перехо́дная но́та.

passion /ˈpæʃ(ə)n/ *n.* **1** (*strong emotion; sexual feeling*) страсть; **his ~s were quickly aroused** его́ бы́ло нетру́дно разъяри́ть; (*burst of anger*) взрыв; **fly into a ~** при|ходи́ть, -йти́ в я́рость; (*enthusiasm*) страсть, пыл; **she has a ~ for Bach** она́ стра́стно увлечена́ му́зыкой Ба́ха. **2** (*relig.*): **the P~** стра́сти Госпо́дни (*f. pl.*); кре́стные му́ки (*f. pl.*); **P~ play** библе́йская мисте́рия.

passionate /ˈpæʃənət/ *adj.* (*having strong emotions*) стра́стный, пы́лкий; (*sexually ardent*) стра́стный; (*impassioned, of language etc.*) пы́лкий, стра́стный, пла́менный.

passionately /ˈpæʃənətlɪ/ *adv.* стра́стно, пы́лко; **he is ~ fond of golf** он стра́стно/до стра́сти увлечён го́льфом.

passive /ˈpæsɪv/ *n.* (*gram.*) (*form of verb*) пасси́вная фо́рма; (*voice*) страда́тельный зало́г.

● *adj.* пасси́вный; **~ smoking** пасси́вное куре́ние; (*gram.*) пасси́вный, страда́тельный.

passiv|eness /ˈpæsɪvnɪs/, **-ity** /pæˈsɪvɪtɪ/ *nn.* пасси́вность.

passport /ˈpɑːspɔːt/ *n.* (*lit.*) па́спорт; (*fig.*) зало́г (+*g.*), путёвка (к+*d.*); **hard work is the ~ to success** усе́рдие — зало́г успе́ха.

past /pɑːst/ *n.* **1** про́шлое; **courtesy is a thing of the ~** ве́жливость вы́шла из мо́ды; **in the ~** в про́шлом; **one cannot undo the ~** нельзя́ зачеркну́ть про́шлое.
2 (*gram.*) проше́дшее вре́мя.

● *adj.* **1** (*bygone*) мину́вший, про́шлый; **that is all ~ history** всё э́то уже́ исто́рия; (*pred., gone by*) ми́мо; **the time for that is ~** вре́мя для э́того давно́ минова́ло; **that is all ~ and done with** с э́тим поко́нчено; **what's ~ is ~** де́ло про́шлое.
2 (*preceding*) про́шлый, после́дний; **for the ~ few days** за после́дние не́сколько дней; **during the ~ week** за после́днюю/э́ту неде́лю.
3 (*gram.*) проше́дший; **~ participle** прича́стие проше́дшего вре́мени; **~ tense** проше́дшее вре́мя.
4: **a ~ master** (*Br.*) непревзойдённый ма́стер.

● *adv.* ми́мо; **the soldiers marched ~** солда́ты прошли́ ми́мо; **he pushed ~** он протолка́лся/проби́лся вперёд.

● *prep.* **1** (*after*) по́сле +*g.*; **it is ~ eight o'clock** сейча́с девя́тый час; **ten ~ one** де́сять мину́т второ́го; **he lived to be ~ eighty** ему́ бы́ло за во́семьдесят, когда́ он у́мер.
2 (*by*) ми́мо+*g.*; **he drove ~ the house** он прое́хал ми́мо до́ма; **he hurried ~ me** он пробежа́л ми́мо меня́.
3 (*to the far side of*) за+*a.*; (*on the far side of*) за+*i.*; **you've gone ~ the turning** вы прое́хали поворо́т; **his house is ~ the church** его́ дом за це́рковью.
4 (*beyond, exceeding*) свы́ше+*g.*, сверх+*g.*; **I am ~ caring** тепе́рь мне уже́ всё равно́; **he was a fine actor, but he's ~ it now** (*coll.*) когда́-то он был хоро́шим актёром, но э́то в про́шлом; **this is ~ a joke** э́то перехо́дит грани́цы шу́ток; **I wouldn't put it ~ him to steal the money** я ду́маю, что он спосо́бен укра́сть де́ньги.

pasta /ˈpæstə/ *n.* макаро́н|ы (*pl., g.* —); макаро́нные изде́лия.

paste /peɪst/ *n.* (*soft dough*) те́сто; (*malleable mixture; savoury preparation*) па́ста; (*adhesive*) клей; (*gem substitute*) страз.

● *v.t.* **1** (*stick*) накле́|ивать, -ить; прикле́|ивать, -ить; **the notice was ~d up on the wall** объявле́ние бы́ло прикле́ено к стене́; **she ~d the pictures into her album** она́ вкле́ила карти́нки в альбо́м. **2** (*sl., beat*) бить, по-; **their team got a good pasting** их кома́нда здо́рово поби́ли. **3** (*comput.*) встав|ля́ть, -ить.

● *cpd.* **~board** *n.* клеёный карто́н.

pastel /ˈpæst(ə)l/ *n.* (*crayon*) пасте́ль; **~ shades** пасте́льные кра́ски; (*drawing in ~*) рису́нок пасте́лью.

pasteurization /ˌpɑːstjəraɪˈzeɪʃ(ə)n/, /-tʃəraɪˈzeɪʃ(ə)n/, /ˌpæst-/ *n.* пастериза́ция.

pasteurize /ˈpɑːstjəˌraɪz/, /-tʃəˌraɪz/, /ˈpæst-/ *v.t.* пастеризова́ть (*impf., pf.*).

pastiche /pæˈstiːʃ/ *n.* (*literary imitation*) стилиза́ция (под+*a.*); подде́лка.

pastille /ˈpæstɪl/ *n.* пастила́.

pastime /ˈpɑːstaɪm/ *n.* время(пре)провожде́ние.

pastor /ˈpɑːstə(r)/ *n.* па́стор.

pastoral /ˈpɑːstər(ə)l/ *n.* (*literary or artistic work*) пастора́ль.

● *adj.* (*pert. to country life*) пастора́льный; (*pert. to clergy*) па́сторский.

pastry /ˈpeɪstrɪ/ *n.* (*dough*) те́сто; (*tart, cake*) пиро́жное.

● *cpd.* **~-cook** *n.* конди́тер.

pasturage /ˈpɑːstʃərɪdʒ/ *n.* (*grazing land*) па́стбище; (*grazing*) вы́пас.

pasture /ˈpɑːstjə(r)/ *n.* = **pasturage; the sheep were put out to ~** ове́ц вы́гнали на па́стбище.

● *v.t.* (*put to graze*) пасти́ (*impf.*).

pasty[1] /ˈpæstɪ/ *n.* (*Br.*) пирожо́к.

pasty[2] /ˈpeɪstɪ/ *adj.* (**pastier, pastiest**) (*like paste*) тестообра́зный; (*palefaced*) бле́дный.

pat[1] /pæt/ *n.* **1** (*light touch or sound*) хлопо́к; шлепо́к; **he deserves a ~ on the back** (*fig.*) он заслу́живает одобре́ния/похвалы́. **2** (*small mass*): **the butter was served in ~s** ма́сло пода́ли кро́хотными кусо́чками.

● *v.t.* (**patted, patting**) похло́п|ывать, -ать; (*a dog*) гла́дить, по-; **he ~ted my shoulder** он похло́пал меня́ по плечу́.

pat[2] /pæt/ *adj.* гото́вый; **he had his lesson off** (*US* **down**) **~** он знал уро́к назубо́к; **stand ~** (*US, stick to one's decision or bet*) стоя́ть (*impf.*) на своём; (*at cards etc.*) ост|ава́ться, -а́ться при свои́х; не брать, взять при́купа.

● *cpd.* **~-a-cake** *n.* (*child's game*) ла́душ|ки, (*pl., g.* -ек).

patch /pætʃ/ *n.* **1** (*covering over hole*) запла́та; **he wore ~es on his elbows** у него́ на локтя́х бы́ли запла́ты; (*over wound*) пла́стырь (*m.*); (*over eye*) повя́зка; (*fig., coll.*): **the film is not a ~ on the book** (*Br.*) фильм не идёт ни в како́е сравне́ние с кни́гой.
2 (*superficial mark or stain*) пятно́; (*distinctive area*) клочо́к; **~es of blue sky** клочки́ голубо́го не́ба; **we ran into a fog ~** мы попа́ли в полосу́ тума́на; **there were ~es of ice on the road** на доро́ге места́ми была́ гололе́дица; (*fig.*): **he has struck a bad ~** (*Br.*) ему́ не везёт; **in ~es** места́ми.
3 (*piece of ground*) уча́сток.
4 (*scrap, remnant*) лоску́т.

● *v.t.* (*mend*) лата́ть, за-.

● *with advs.*: **~ over** *v.t.* лата́ть, за-; **~ up** *v.t.* (*lit.*) чини́ть, по-; заде́л|ывать, -ать; (*fig.*) ула́|живать, -дить; **the quarrel was soon ~ed up** ссо́ра была́ вско́ре ула́жена.

● *cpds.* **~-pocket** *n.* накладно́й карма́н; **~work** *n.* (*needlework*) лоску́тное шитьё; **~work of fields** моза́ика поле́й; (*fig., muddle*) мешани́на; **~work quilt** лоску́тное одея́ло.

patchy /ˈpætʃɪ/ *adj.* (**patchier, patchiest**) (*marked with patches, blotchy*) пятни́стый; (*fig., of knowledge, information*) отры́вочный; (*fig., of uneven quality*) неро́вный.

pate /peɪt/ *n.* (*arch.*) башка́.

pâté /ˈpæteɪ/ *n.* паштéт; **~ *de foie gras*** гуси́ный паштéт.

patella /pəˈtelə/ *n.* (*pl.* **patellae** /-liː/) (*anat.*) пате́лла.

patent /ˈpeɪt(ə)nt/, /ˈpæt-/ *n.* пате́нт; **P~ Office** пате́нтное бюро́ (*indecl.*).

● *adj.* **1** (*protected by ~*) патенто́ванный; **~ leather** лакиро́ванная ко́жа; **~-leather shoes** лакиро́ванные ту́фли. **2** (*obvious*) очеви́дный.

● *v.t.* патентова́ть, за-.

patentee /ˌpeɪtənˈtiː/ *n.* патентодержа́тель (*m.*).

paterfamilias /ˌpeɪtəfəˈmɪlɪˌæs/ *n.* глава́ (*m.*) семьи́.

paternal /pəˈtɜːn(ə)l/ *adj.* **1** (*fatherly*) отцо́вский; (*of feelings*) оте́ческий; **~ instinct** отцо́вский инсти́нкт; (*fig.*): **~ government** прави́тельство, оте́чески относя́щееся к наро́ду. **2** (*related through father*) ро́дственный по отцу́,

P

по отцóвской лúнии; ~ **grandmother** бáбушка со стороны́ отцá.

paternalism /pəˈtɜːnəˌlɪz(ə)m/ *n.* покровúтельство, попечéние; (*pol.*) патерналúзм.

paternalistic /pəˌtɜːnəˈlɪstɪk/ *adj.* (*pol.*) патерналúстский; (*manner, tone*) покровúтельственный.

paternity /pəˈtɜːnɪtɪ/ *n.* отцóвство; ~ **leave** óтпуск по ухóду за ребёнком (для отцá); ~ **suit** иск по установлéнию отцóвства.

path /pɑːθ/ *n.* (*track for walking*) тропá, тропúнка; дорóжка; ~ **through the woods** леснáя тропá/тропúнка; **garden** ~ садóвая дорóжка; (*fig.*) путь (*m.*); **if ever he crosses my** ~ éсли он когдá-нибудь встрéтится мне на путú; **he swept aside all who stood in his** ~ он сметáл всех, кто стоя́л на егó путú; **he followed the** ~ **of duty** он вéрно слéдовал дóлгу; **our** ~**s diverged** нáши дорóги/путú разошлúсь; (*course, trajectory*) траектóрия; **the** ~ **of a bullet** траектóрия полёта пýли.

● *cpds.* ~**finder** *n.* (*explorer*) исслéдователь (*m.*), первопрохóдец; (*aircraft*) самолёт наведéния; ~**way** *n.* тропá, путь (*m.*).

pathetic /pəˈθetɪk/ *adj.* (*arousing pity*) печáльный, жáлкий; (*coll., wretchedly inadequate*) жáлкий.

pathless /ˈpɑːθlɪs/ *adj.* бездорóжный.

pathological /ˌpæθəˈlɒdʒɪk(ə)l/ *adj.* патологúческий.

pathologist /pəˈθɒlədʒɪst/ *n.* патóлог.

pathology /pəˈθɒlədʒɪ/ *n.* патолóгия.

pathos /ˈpeɪθɒs/ *n.* гóречь, печáль.

patience /ˈpeɪʃ(ə)ns/ *n.* **1** терпéние; **I have no** ~ **with him** он бы́стро вывóдит меня́ из терпéния; **she lost** ~ **with him** онá потеря́ла с ним вся́кое терпéние; **my** ~ **is exhausted** моё терпéние кóнчилось/лóпнуло (*coll.*). **2** (*Br., card game*) пасья́нс.

patient /ˈpeɪʃ(ə)nt/ *n.* пациéнт (*fem.* -ка), больн|óй (*fem.* -áя).

● *adj.* терпелúвый.

patina /ˈpætɪnə/ *n.* (*pl.* ~**s**) пáтина.

patio /ˈpætɪəʊ/ *n.* (*pl.* ~**s**) пáтио (*indecl.*), двóрик.

patois /ˈpætwɑː/ *n.* (*pl.* ~ /-wɑːz/) мéстный гóвор.

patriarch /ˈpeɪtrɪˌɑːk/ *n.* патриáрх.

patriarchal /ˌpeɪtrɪˈɑːk(ə)l/ *adj.* патриархáльный.

patriarchate /ˈpeɪtrɪˌɑːkət/ *n.* (*eccl.*) патриáршество.

patriarchy /ˈpeɪtrɪˌɑːkɪ/ *n.* патриархáт.

patrician /pəˈtrɪʃ(ə)n/ *n.* (*Roman noble*) патрúций; (*aristocrat*) аристокрáт.

● *adj.* патрициáнски; аристократúческий.

patricide /ˈpætrɪˌsaɪd/ *n.* (*crime*) отцеубúйство; (*criminal*) отцеубúйца (*c.g.*).

patrimony /ˈpætrɪmənɪ/ *n.* (*inheritance from father*) отцóвское наслéдие; (*fig.*) наслéдие.

patriot /ˈpeɪtrɪət/, /ˈpæt-/ *n.* патриóт (*fem.* -ка).

patriotic /ˌpeɪtrɪˈɒtɪk/, /ˌpæt-/ *adj.* патриотúческий.

patriotism /ˈpeɪtrɪətˌɪz(ə)m/, /ˈpæt-/ *n.* патриотúзм.

patrol /pəˈtrəʊl/ *n.* **1** (*action*) патрулúрование, дозóр; **on** ~ в дозóре; ~ **car** (полицéйская) патрýльная машúна; ~ **vessel** сторожевóе сýдно. **2** (~*ling body*) патрýль (*m.*); (~*ling official*) патрýльный.

● *v.t. & i.* (**patrolled, patrolling**) патрулúровать (*impf.*).

● *cpd.* ~**man** *n.* (*US, policeman*) полицéйский.

patron /ˈpeɪtrən/ *n.* **1** (*supporter, protector*) покровúтель (*m.*), патрóн; **a** ~ **of the arts** покровúтель искýсств, меценáт; ~ **saint** свят|óй застýпни|к (*fem.* -áя -ца). **2** (*customer*) (постоя́нный) клиéнт, покупáтель (*m.*).

patronage /ˈpætrənɪdʒ/ *n.* (*support, sponsorship*) покровúтельство, шéфство; (*right of appointment*) прáво назначéния на дóлжность; (*customer's support*) постоя́нная клиентýра.

patroness /ˈpeɪtrənɪs/ *n.* покровúтельница, патронéсса.

patroniz|e /ˈpætrəˌnaɪz/ *v.t.* (*support, encourage*) покровúтельствовать (*impf.*) + *d.*; (*visit as customer*) постоя́нно посещáть (*impf.*); (*treat condescendingly*) отн|осúться, -естúсь свысокá к + *d.*; ~**ing airs** покровúтельственные/снисходúтельные манéры (*f. pl.*).

patronymic /ˌpætrəˈnɪmɪk/ *n.* (*Russian*) óтчество.

patter[1] /ˈpætə(r)/ *n.* (*of salesman, conjurer etc.*) скороговóрка.

patter[2] /ˈpætə(r)/ *n.* (*tapping sound*) стук, постýкивание; (*of feet*) тóпот.

● *v.i.* барабáнить (*impf.*); (*of feet*) топотáть (*impf.*); **the rain** ~**ed on the windows** дождь барабáнил по óкнам; **her footsteps** ~**ed down the hall** её шагú простучáли по зáлу.

pattern /ˈpæt(ə)n/ *n.* **1** (*decorative design*) узóр. **2** (*laudable example*) образéц; **a** ~ **of virtue** образéц добродéтели; (*attr.*) образцóвый. **3** (*model for production*) вы́кройка; **dress** ~ вы́кройка плáтья. **4** (*model*) модéль. **5** (*arrangement, system*) óбраз, манéра; **new** ~**s of behaviour** (*Br.*), **behavior** (*US*) нóвые нóрмы (*f. pl.*) поведéния; **events are following the usual** ~ делá идýт своúм чередóм.

● *v.t.* **1** (*model*) копúровать, с-; **he** ~**ed himself on his father** он брал примéр со своегó отцá. **2** (*decorate with design*) укр|ашáть, -áсить; **a** ~**ed dress** плáтье с узóрами.

patty /ˈpætɪ/ *n.* (*pie*) пирожóк; (*of minced meat*) котлéта.

paucity /ˈpɔːsɪtɪ/ *n.* нехвáтка, скýдость.

paunch /pɔːntʃ/ *n.* брюшкó, пýзо.

paunchy /ˈpɔːntʃɪ/ *adj.* (**paunchier, paunchiest**) пузáтый.

pauper /ˈpɔːpə(r)/ *n.* бедня́к, пáупер.

pauperism /ˈpɔːpəˌrɪz(ə)m/ *n.* нищетá, пауперúзм.

pauperization /pɔːpəraɪˈzeɪʃ(ə)n/ *n.* обнищáние, пауперизáция.

pause /pɔːz/ *n.* (*intermission, temporary halt*) переры́в; переды́шка; (*in speaking, reading, mus.*) пáуза; **give s.o.** ~ **(for thought)** заст|авля́ть, -áвить когó-н. задýматься.

● *v.i.* остан|áвливаться, -овúться; **she scarcely** ~**d for breath** онá не переводúла дыхáния; **if you** ~ **to think** éсли задýматься.

pavan(e) /pəˈvɑːn/ *n.* (*mus.*) павáна.

pave /peɪv/ *v.t.* мостúть, вы́-; ~**d road** мощёная дорóга; **the road to hell is** ~**d with good intentions** благúми намéрениями вы́мощена дорóга в ад; (*fig.*): **his proposal** ~**d the way to a lasting peace** егó предложéние проложúло путь к прóчному мúру.

pavement /ˈpeɪvmənt/ *n.* **1** (*Br., footway*) тротуáр; ~ **artist** худóжник, рисýющий на тротуáре. **2** (*US, paved surface*) мостовáя.

pavilion /pəˈvɪljən/ *n.* (*Br., sport*) павильóн; (*large tent*) шатёр.

paving /ˈpeɪvɪŋ/ *n.* (*material*) дорóжное покры́тие; (*act*) мощéние.

● *cpd.* ~**-stone** *n.* брусчáтка.

paw /pɔː/ *n.* лáпа; (*coll.*): **take your** ~**s off me!** рýки прочь!

● *v.t.* (*touch with* ~) трóгать, по- лáпой; **the horse** ~**ed the ground** конь бил зéмлю копы́тами; (*handle, fondle clumsily*) лáпать (*impf.*).

pawn[1] /pɔːn/ *n.* (*chessman, also fig.*) пéшка.

pawn[2] /pɔːn/ *n.* (*pledge*) залóг, заклáд; **in** ~ залóженный в заклáде; **he took his watch out of** ~ он вы́купил часы́ из заклáда.

● *v.t.* за|клáдывать, -ложúть.

● *cpds.* ~**broker** *n.* заклáдчик; ~**shop** *n.* ломбáрд.

pawpaw /ˈpɔːpɔː/ = **papaw**

pay /peɪ/ *n.* (*for work, goods, services*) плáта, (*wages*) зарплáта; жáлованье; ~ **clerk** бухгáлтер-расчётчик; **a** ~ **cut** снижéние зарплáты; **a** ~ **increase** повышéние зарплáты; **on half** ~ на половúнной стáвке; **he is in the** ~ **of the enemy** он на слýжбе у врагá.

● *v.t.* (*past and p.p.* **paid**) **1** (*give in return for something*) платúть, за-, у-; **she always** ~**s cash** онá всегдá плáтит налúчными; **he has paid the penalty for his greed** он поплатúлся за свою́ жáдность; (*contribute*): **everyone must** ~ **his share** кáждый дóлжен внестú своío дóлю; **I'll** ~ **the difference** я доплачý рáзницу; ~ **one's fare** платúть, за- за проéзд; оплá|чивать, -тúть проéзд. **2** (*remunerate, recompense*) платúть, за-, оплá|чивать, -тúть (**s.o.**: + *d.*); **they are paid by the hour** онú получáют почасовýю оплáту; **we are paid on Fridays** нам плáтят по пя́тницам; мы получáем зарплáту по пя́тницам; **he who** ~**s the piper calls the tune** кто плáтит музыкáнту, тот и закáзывает мýзыку; **there will be the**

devil to ~ будет грандиозный скандал.
3 (*settle*, **~** *for*) упла|чивать, -тить; **the defendant must ~ costs** обвиняемый должен уплатить судебные издержки; **he paid his way through college** он сам зарабатывал себе на высшее образование.
4 (*bestow, render*): **~ attention to me!** послушайте меня!; **~ s.o. a compliment** делать, с- кому-н. комплимент; **~ heed to** обра|щать, -тить внимание на + *a.*; **~ one's respects to** свидетельствовать, за- своё почтение + *d.*; **~ s.o. a visit** наве|щать, -стить кого-н.
5 (*benefit, profit*): **it will ~ you to wait** вам стоит подождать.

● *v.i.* (*past and p.p.* **paid**) **1** (*give money*) распла|чиваться, -титься; **he ~s on the nail** он платит на месте; **I paid through the nose for it** я заплатил за это бешеные деньги.
2 (*suffer*) платить, за- (*or* платиться, по-) за + *a.*; **you'll ~ dearly for this** вы за это дорого заплатите; **he paid for his carelessness** он поплатился за своё легкомыслие.
3 (*yield a return*) окуп|аться, -иться; давать, дать прибыль; (*fig.*) иметь смысл; оправд|ывать, -ать себя; **it ~s to advertise** реклама окупается.

● *with advs.*: **~ back** *v.t.* (*return*) возвра|щать, -тить (*also* вернуть); **he paid back every penny** он вернул всё до последней копейки; (*reimburse*): **he paid me back in person** он самолично вернул мне деньги; (*have revenge on*) отплатить (*pf.*) + *d.*; **I'll ~ you back for this** я вам за это отплачу; **~ in** *v.t.* вн|осить, -ести; **~ off** *v.t.* рассчит|ываться, -аться с + *i.*; **the workers were paid off** с рабочими рассчитались; **I have paid off my debts** я расплатился со своими долгами; **he is ~ing off old scores** он сводит старые счёты; (**~** *wages and discharge*) рассчит|ывать, -ать; (*bribe*) подкуп|ать, -ить; *v.i.* (*bring profit*) окуп|аться, -иться; **~ out** *v.t.* (*expend, make payment of*) выплачивать, выплатить; (*rope etc.*) отпус|кать, -тить; травить, по-; **~ up** *v.t.* (*settle*) выплачивать, выплатить; **a paid-up account** закрытый счёт; *v.i.* (**~** *amount due*) рассчит|ываться, -аться сполна.

● *cpds.* **~-day** *n.* платёжный день; **~-desk** *n.* касса; **~ envelope** (*US*) = **~ packet; ~load** *n.* (*of vehicle*) полезный груз; (*of missile*) полезная нагрузка; **~master** *n.* кассир; **P~master-General** (*Br.*) главный казначей; **~-off** *n.* (*settlement*) выплата; (*profit, reward*) награда; (*bribe*) взятка; (*coll., climax, e.g. of a joke*) развязка; **~ packet** (*Br.*) *n.* заработок, получка (*coll.*); **~phone** *n.* телефон-автомат; **~roll, ~-sheet** *nn.* платёжная ведомость; **there are 500 men on the ~roll** в платёжной ведомости (*or* в штате) числится 500 человек; **~slip** *n.* (*Br.*) квитанция о выдаче зарплаты; **~ station** (*US*) = **~phone; ~ TV** *n.* абонентское телевидение.

payable /ˈpeɪəb(ə)l/ *adj.* оплачиваемый; подлежащий уплате.

PAYE (*abbr. of* **pay-as-you-earn**) (*Br.*) автоматическое отчисление подоходного налога из зарплаты.

payee /peɪˈiː/ *n.* получатель (*fem.* -ница) (денег).

payer /ˈpeɪə(r)/ *n.* плательщи|к (*fem.* -ца).

payment /ˈpeɪmənt/ *n.* (*paying*) оплата, платёж; (*sum paid*) плата; (*of debt etc.*) уплата; **prompt ~ is requested** просьба уплатить немедленно; **he made a cash ~ of £50** он заплатил 50 фунтов наличными; (*requital*): **this is in ~ of your services** это вознаграждение за ваши услуги.

PC *abbr. of* **1** (*Br.*) ***Police Constable*** полицейский, констебль (*m.*).
2 ***personal computer*** ПК, (персональный компьютер).
3 ***politically correct*** политически корректный; ***political correctness*** политическая корректность.

p.d.q. (*abbr. of* ***pretty damn quick***) (*coll.*) в темпе.

PE (*abbr. of* ***physical education***) физкультура.

pea /piː/ *n.* горошина; (*pl., collect.*) горох; **they are as like as two ~s** они похожи как две капли воды; **~ soup** гороховый суп; **split ~s** колотый горох.

● *cpds.* **~-green** *adj.* ярко-зелёный; **~nut** *n.* земляной орех, арахис; **~nut butter** паста из тёртого арахиса; **~nuts** *n. pl.* (*US sl., trifling amount*) гроши (*m. pl.*); **~-shooter** *n.* трубка для стрельбы горохом; **~-souper** *n.* (*coll., fog*) густой туман.

peace /piːs/ *n.* **1** (*freedom from war*) мир; **our countries are at ~ again** между нашими странами снова установлен мир; **~ talks** мирные переговоры; **~ treaty** мирный договор; (*fig.*): **make one's ~ with s.o.** мириться, по- с кем-н.
2 (*freedom from civil disorder*) спокойствие, порядок; **they were bound over to keep the ~** им предписали соблюдать порядок; **breach of the ~** нарушение общественного порядка; **Justice of the P~** мировой судья.
3 (*rest, quiet*) спокойствие, покой; **~ be with you!** мир вам!; **may he rest in ~** мир праху его; **she found ~** (*died*) **at last** она, наконец, упокоилась/нашла вечный покой; **can we have some ~ and quiet?** нельзя ли потише?; **~ of mind** спокойствие духа; **he never gives me a moment's ~** он не даёт мне ни минуты покоя.

● *cpds.* **~-keeping** *adj.*: **~-keeping force** миротворческие войска (*nt. pl.*)/силы (*f. pl.*); **~-loving** *adj.* миролюбивый; **~maker** *n.* миротворец; **~offering** *n.* (*relig.*) благодарственная жертва; (*fig.*) задабривание; **~-pipe** *n.* трубка мира; **~time** *n.* мирное время.

peaceable /ˈpiːsəb(ə)l/ *adj.* миролюбивый, мирный.

peaceful /ˈpiːsfʊl/ *adj.* мирный; **~ coexistence** мирное сосуществование.

peach[1] /piːtʃ/ *n.* **1** (*fruit*) персик. **2** (*tree*) персиковое дерево. **3** (*coll., superb specimen*) первый сорт. **4** (*coll., attractive girl*) красотка.

● *cpd.* **~-coloured** (*US* **-colored**) *adj.* персиковый, персикового цвета.

peach[2] /piːtʃ/ *v.i.* стучать, на- (*на кого*) (*sl.*).

peacock /ˈpiːkɒk/ *n.* павлин; **~ blue** переливчатый синий цвет.

peahen /ˈpiːhen/ *n.* пава, самка павлина.

peajacket /ˈpiːˌdʒækɪt/ *n.* бушлат, тужурка.

peak /piːk/ *n.* **1** (*mountain top*) пик, вершина. **2** (*of cap*) козырёк. **3** (*fig., highest point, maximum*) пик, вершина; **at the ~ of her career** на вершине своей карьеры; **~ load** (*elec.*) максимальная нагрузка; **his excitement reached its ~** его возбуждение достигло предела; **~ hours** часы пик; **~ viewing hours** наиболее популярные часы для показа телепередач.

● *v.i.*: **demand ~ed** спрос достиг высшей точки.

peaked /piːkd/ *adj.* **1** остроконечный; **~ cap** (форменная) фуражка.
2 (*haggard; also* **peaky**) осунувшийся, измождённый.

peaky /ˈpiːkɪ/ *adj.* (**peakier, peakiest**) = **peaked** 2

peal /piːl/ *n.* (*of bell*) звон; (*of bells*) трезвон; (*of thunder*) грохот, раскат; (*of laughter*) взрыв.

● *v.i.* (*of bells*) трезвонить (*impf.*); (*of thunder*) греметь, про-; (*of laughter*) разд|аваться, -аться.

pear /peə(r)/ *n.* **1** (*fruit*) груша. **2** (*tree*) грушевое дерево, груша. **3**: **prickly ~** (*bot.*) опунция.

pearl /pɜːl/ *n.* жемчужина; (*pl., collect.*) жемчуг; (*mother-of-~*) (*bot.*) перламутр; (*fig.*) перл; **cast ~s before swine** метать (*impf.*) бисер перед свиньями; **(mother-of-)~ buttons** перламутровые пуговицы.

● *cpds.* **~-barley** *n.* перловая крупа; **~-diver, ~-fisher** *nn.* ловец/искатель (*m.*) жемчуга.

pearly /ˈpɜːlɪ/ *adj.* (**pearlier, pearliest**) жемчужного цвета, жемчужный.

peasant /ˈpez(ə)nt/ *n.* крестьян|ин (*fem.* -ка).

peasantry /ˈpezəntrɪ/ *n.* крестьянство.

pease pudding /piːz/ *n.* (*Br.*) гороховая запеканка.

peat /piːt/ *n.* торф.

● *cpd.* **~-bog** *n.* торфяное болото.

pebble /ˈpeb(ə)l/ *n.* галька, голыш (*coll.*).

● *cpd.* **~-dash** (*Br.*) *n.* гравийная набро́ска; *adj.* гравийный.

pebbly /ˈpeblɪ/ *adj.* покрытый галькой.

pecan /ˈpiːkən/ *n.* орех-пекан.

peccadillo /ˌpekəˈdɪləʊ/ *n.* (*pl.* **~es** *or* **~s**) грешок.

peck /pek/ *n.* (*made by beak*) клево́к; (*fig., hasty kiss*): **he gave her a ~ on the cheek** он чмо́кнул её в щёку.

● *v.t.* клева́ть, клю́нуть; поклева́ть (*pf.*).

● *v.i.* (*fig.*): **she ~ed at her food** она́ едва́ дотро́нулась до еды́; она́ немно́жко поклева́ла и всё; **~ing order** ≈ неофициа́льная иера́рхия.

pecker /ˈpekə(r)/ *n.* **1** (*Br. sl.*): **keep your ~ up!** не ве́шай но́са! **2** (*US sl., penis*) член, со́лоп.

peckish /ˈpekɪʃ/ *adj.* (*Br. coll.*) голо́дный; **I'm feeling a bit ~** я не про́тив чего́-нибудь перекуси́ть.

pectoral /ˈpektər(ə)l/ *adj.* грудно́й.

peculiar /pɪˈkjuːlɪə(r)/ *adj.* **1** (*exclusive, distinctive*) осо́бенный, своеобра́зный; **this custom is ~ to the English** э́то чи́сто англи́йский обы́чай. **2** (*particular*) осо́бенный; **a building of ~ interest** зда́ние, представля́ющее осо́бый интере́с. **3** (*strange*) стра́нный; **his behaviour** (*Br.*), **behavior** (*US*) **was rather ~** он вёл себя́ дово́льно стра́нно.

peculiarity /pɪˌkjuːlɪˈærɪtɪ/ *n.* (*characteristic*) сво́йство; осо́бенность; (*oddity*) стра́нность.

pecuniary /pɪˈkjuːnɪərɪ/ *adj.* де́нежный.

pedagogic(al) /ˌpedəˈgɒgɪk((ə)l)/, /-ˈgɒdʒɪk((ə)l)/ *adj.* педагоги́ческий.

pedagogue /ˈpedəˌgɒg/ *n.* педаго́г.

pedagogy /ˈpedəˌgɒdʒɪ/, /-ˌgɒgɪ/ *n.* педаго́гика.

pedal /ˈped(ə)l/ *n.* педа́ль.

● *v.i.* (**pedalled, pedalling;** *US* **pedaled, pedaling**) (*cycle*) е́хать (*det.*) на велосипе́де; (*turn pedals*) крути́ть (*impf.*) педа́ли.

● *v.t.* (**pedalled, pedalling;** *US* **pedaled, pedaling): she ~led her bicycle into town** она́ е́хала в го́род на велосипе́де.

● *cpd.* **~-cycle** *n.* велосипе́д.

pedalo /ˈpedəˌləʊ/ *n.* (*pl.* **~s** *or* **~es**) (*Br.*) морско́й/во́дный велосипе́д.

pedant /ˈped(ə)nt/ *n.* педа́нт (*fem.* -ка).

pedantic /pɪˈdæntɪk/ *adj.* педанти́чный.

pedantry /ˈped(ə)ntrɪ/ *n.* педанти́чность.

peddle /ˈped(ə)l/ *v.t.* торгова́ть (*impf.*) вразно́с; **he ~s his wares in every town** он разво́зит свои́ това́ры по всем города́м; (*fig.*): **she likes to ~ gossip** она́ лю́бит разноси́ть спле́тни.

peddler /ˈpedlə(r)/ *n.* **1** (*of drugs*) торго́вец нарко́тиками. **2** (*US*) = **pedlar**

pe|derast, pae- /ˈpedəˌræst/ *n.* педофи́л.

pe|derasty, pae- /ˈpedəˌræstɪ/ *n.* педофи́лия.

pedestal /ˈpedɪst(ə)l/ *n.* (*of column or statue*) пьедеста́л; **he set her on a ~** (*fig.*) он вознёс её на пьедеста́л; (*of desk etc.*) основа́ние.

pedestrian /pɪˈdestrɪən/ *n.* пешехо́д.

● *adj.* **1** (*of or for walking*) пешехо́дный; **~ crossing** (*Br.*) перехо́д; **~ precinct** пешехо́дная зо́на. **2** (*fig., prosaic*) прозаи́ческий, ску́чный.

pedestrianization /pɪˌdestrɪənaɪˈzeɪʃ(ə)n/ *n.* созда́ние пешехо́дных зон.

pedestrianize /pɪˈdestrɪəˌnaɪz/ *v.t.* запре|ща́ть, -ти́ть автомоби́льное движе́ние в + *p.*

pediatric /ˌpiːdɪˈætrɪk/, **-ian** /ˌpiːdɪəˈtrɪʃ(ə)n/, **-s** /ˌpiːdɪˈætrɪks/ (*US*) = **paediatric** *etc.*

pedicure /ˈpedɪˌkjʊə(r)/ *n.* (*treatment*) педикю́р; (*person*) педикю́рша.

pedigree /ˈpedɪˌgriː/ *n.* (*genealogical table*) родосло́вная; (*line of descent*) происхожде́ние; (*ancient descent*): **a man of ~** челове́к с хоро́шей родосло́вной; (*attr.*): **~ cattle** племенно́й скот.

pediment /ˈpedɪmənt/ *n.* фронто́н.

pedlar /ˈpedlə(r)/ (*US* **peddler**) *n.* разно́счик, коробе́йник.

pedometer /pɪˈdɒmɪtə(r)/ *n.* шагоме́р.

pedophile /ˈpiːdəˌfaɪl/ (*US*) = **paedophile**

pedophilia /ˌpiːdəˈfɪlɪə/ (*US*) = **paedophilia**

pee /piː/ (*coll.*) *n.* (*urination*) пи-пи́ (*nt. indecl.*); (*urine*) моча́.

● *v.i.* (**pees, peed**) мочи́ться, по-.

peek /piːk/ (*coll.*) *n.* взгляд укра́дкой.

● *v.i.* взгля|дывать, -ну́ть; **~ in** загля́|дывать, -ну́ть; **~ out** выгля́дывать, вы́глянуть.

peel /piːl/ *n.* (*thin skin of fruit*) кожура́; (*of vegetables*) шелуха́; (*rind of orange etc.*) ко́рка.

● *v.t.* **1** (*remove skin from*) оч|ища́ть, -и́стить; (*fig.*): **he kept his eyes ~ed** (*coll.*) он смотре́л в о́ба. **2** (*remove from surface*) сн|има́ть, -ять; **he ~ed the stamp off the envelope** он откле́ил ма́рку от конве́рта.

● *v.i.* **1** (*lose skin, bark etc.*) шелуши́ться (*impf.*); **the sun makes my arms ~** у меня́ шелуша́тся пле́чи от со́лнца; **the walls were ~ing with the damp** сте́ны обле́зли от сы́рости. **2** (*come away from surface; also* **~ away, ~ off**) слез|а́ть, -ть; обл|еза́ть, -е́зть; **the paint has begun to ~ (off)** кра́ска начала́ облеза́ть.

● *with advs.*: **~ away** *v.t.* сн|има́ть, -ять; *v.i.* = **peel** *v.i.* 2; **~ off** *v.t.*: **he ~ed off his clothes and dived in** он сбро́сил с себя́ оде́жду и нырну́л; *v.i.* (*lit.*) = **peel** *v.i.* 2; (*fig., detach o.s. from group*) отрыва́ться, оторва́ться; выходи́ть, вы́йти из стро́я; **the aircraft ~ed off to attack** самолёт оторва́лся для ата́ки.

peeler /ˈpiːlə(r)/ *n.* (*device for peeling*) шелуши́тель (*m.*).

peeling /ˈpiːlɪŋ/ *n.* (*of fruit*) кожура́; (*of vegetables*) шелуха́; **potato ~s** карто́фельные очи́стки (*f. pl.*).

peep[1] /piːp/ *n.* **1** (*furtive or hasty look*) взгляд укра́дкой; **~ing Tom** ≈ любопы́тная Варва́ра; **take, have a ~ at** взгляну́ть (*pf.*) на + *a.* **2** (*first appearance*) про́блеск; **at ~ of day, dawn** на рассве́те.

● *v.i.* погля́д|ывать, -е́ть; **he ~ed in at the window** он загляну́л в окно́; **during the morning the sun ~ed out** у́тром вы́глянуло со́лнце.

● *cpds.* **~-hole** *n.* глазо́к; **~-show** *n.* кинетоско́п.

peep[2] /piːp/ *n.* (*chirp*) писк, чири́канье; (*fig.*): **I couldn't get a ~ out of him** я не смог вы́жать из него́ ни сло́ва.

● *v.i.* пища́ть, пи́скнуть; чири́к|ать, -нуть.

peer[1] /pɪə(r)/ *n.* **1** (*equal*) ро́вня́; **you will not find his ~** вы не найдёте ему́ ра́вного; **~ group** гру́ппа све́рстников, све́рстники (*m. pl.*); **~ group pressure** группово́й нажи́м; давле́ние гру́ппы (све́рстников). **2** (*noble*) лорд, пэр; **he was made a ~** его́ возвели́ в ло́рды.

peer[2] /pɪə(r)/ *v.i.* (*look closely*) всм|а́триваться, -отре́ться (в + *a.*).

peerage /ˈpɪərɪdʒ/ *n.* (*body of peers*) сосло́вие пэ́ров; (*rank*) пэ́рство, ти́тул пэ́ра.

peeress /ˈpɪərɪs/ *n.* супру́га пэ́ра; же́нщина, име́ющая ти́тул пэ́ра.

peerless /ˈpɪərlɪs/ *adj.* несравне́нный.

peeve /piːv/ (*coll.*) *n.* (*grievance*) прете́нзия.

● *v.t.*: **he looks ~d** у него́ недово́льный вид.

peevish /ˈpiːvɪʃ/ *adj.* брюзгли́вый; капри́зный.

peewit, pewit /ˈpiːwɪt/ *n.* (*Br.*) чи́бис.

peg /peg/ *n.* ко́лышек; **(clothes-~)** (*Br.*) крючо́к; **(hat-, coat-~)** ве́шалка; **he buys his clothes off the ~** (*Br.*) он покупа́ет гото́вую оде́жду; **(tent-~)** ко́лышек для натя́гивания пала́тки; (*fig.*): **he is a square ~ in a round hole** он не на своём ме́сте; **it provided a ~ to hang a discussion on** э́то послужи́ло по́водом для бесе́ды; **he should be taken down a ~** с него́ на́до сбить спесь; его́ на́до поста́вить на ме́сто.

● *v.t.* (**pegged, pegging**) (*fasten*) прикреп|ля́ть, -и́ть; (*comm., fix level of*): **~ prices** замор|а́живать, -о́зить це́ны.

● *with advs.*: **~ away** *v.i.* вка́лывать (*impf.*); корпе́ть (*impf.*) (*coll.*); **~ down** *v.t.* (*lit.*) укреп|ля́ть, -и́ть; (*fig., restrict*) свя́з|ывать, -а́ть; **~ out** *v.t.* (*mark with* **~s**): **he ~ged out his claim** (*lit.*) он отме́тил грани́цы своего́ уча́стка; (*fig.*) он закрепи́л своё пра́во; (*hang out with* **~s**): **~ out the clothes** разве́|шивать, -сить оде́жду; *v.i.* (*Br. sl., expire*) выдыха́ться, вы́дохнуться.

● *cpd.* **~-leg** *n.* (*leg*) деревя́нная нога́; (*person*) челове́к с деревя́нной ного́й.

peignoir /ˈpeɪnwɑː(r)/ *n.* пеньюа́р.

pejorative /pɪˈdʒɒrətɪv/, /ˈpiːdʒə-/ *adj.* уничижи́тельный, пренебрежи́тельный.

peke /piːk/ (*coll.*) = **pekin(g)ese** 2

Pekin(g)ese /ˌpiːkɪˈniːz/ *n.* (*pl.* **~**) (*dog*) кита́йский мопс, пекине́с.

pelargonium /ˌpeləˈgəʊnɪəm/ *n.* пеларго́ния.

pelican /ˈpelɪkən/ *n.* пелика́н; **~ crossing** (*Br.*) пешехо́дный перехо́д со светофо́ром, включа́емым пешехо́дом.

pellet /'pelɪt/ *n.* ша́рик; (*small shot*) пу́лька.

pell-mell /pel'mel/ *adv.* вперемéшку; беспоря́дочно.

pellucid /prɪ'lu:sɪd/, /-'lju:sɪd/ *adj.* прозра́чный.

pelmet /'pelmɪt/ *n.* ламбреке́н.

pelt¹ /pelt/ *n.* (*skin*) ко́жа, шку́ра.

pelt² /pelt/ *n.*: **at full ~** по́лным хо́дом.

● *v.t.* (*assail*) забр|а́сывать, -оса́ть; **they ~ed him with stones/insults** они́ заброса́ли его́ камня́ми/оскорбле́ниями.

● *v.i.* стуча́ть (*impf.*), бараба́нить (*impf.*); **the rain was ~ing down** дождь бараба́нил вовсю́.

pelvic /'pelvɪk/ *adj.* та́зовый; **~ girdle** та́зовый по́яс.

pelvis /'pelvɪs/ *n.* (*pl.* **pelvises**) таз.

pen¹ /pen/ *n.* (*writing instrument*) ру́чка; **he never puts ~ to paper** он никогда́ не берётся за перо́.

● *v.t.* (**penned, penning**) писа́ть, на-; сочин|я́ть, -и́ть.

● *cpds.* **~-and-ink** *adj.* нарисо́ванный перо́м; **a ~-and-ink drawing** рису́нок перо́м/ту́шью; **~-friend** *n.* (*Br.*) друг (*fem.* подру́га) по перепи́ске; **~knife** *n.* перочи́нный но́ж(ик); **~manship** *n.* каллигра́фия; **~-name** *n.* (литерату́рный) псевдони́м; **~-nib** *n.* перо́ (пи́счее); **~ pal** (*US*) = **~-friend; ~-pusher** *n.* (*coll.*) писа́ка (*c.g.*).

pen² /pen/ *n.* (*enclosure*) заго́н.

● *v.t.* (**penned, penning**) (*also* **~ in, ~ up**) зап|ира́ть, -ере́ть.

penal /'pi:n(ə)l/ *adj.*: **~ code** уголо́вный ко́декс; **~ colony** штрафна́я коло́ния; **~ laws** уголо́вное пра́во; **~ offence** (*Br.*), **offense** (*US*) уголо́вное преступле́ние; **~ servitude** ка́торжные/исправи́тельно-трудовы́е рабо́ты.

penalize /'pi:nə,laɪz/ *v.t.* нака́з|ывать, -а́ть; (*to fine*) штрафова́ть, о-; **he was ~d for a foul** он был нака́зан за гру́бую игру́.

penalty /'penəltɪ/ *n.* (*punishment*) наказа́ние; (*fine*) штраф; **on, under ~ of death** под стра́хом сме́ртной ка́зни; (*football, also* **~ kick**) пена́льти (*indecl.*); **they won on penalties** они́ вы́играли по пена́льти; **~ area** штрафна́я площа́дка; **~ clause** (*comm.*) пункт о штра́фах (за невыполне́ние усло́вий догово́ра).

penance /'penəns/ *n.* епитимья́; покая́ние; **he must do ~ for his sins** он до́лжен замоли́ть/искупи́ть свои́ грехи́.

pence /pens/ *n. see* ⇒**penny**

penchant /'pɑ̃ʃɑ̃/ *n.* скло́нность (*к чему*).

pencil /'pensɪl/ *n.* каранда́ш; **coloured** (*Br.*), **colored** (*US*) **~** цветно́й каранда́ш; **eyebrow ~** каранда́ш для брове́й; **a ~ drawing** рису́нок карандашо́м.

● *v.t.* (**pencilled, pencilling;** *US* **penciled, penciling**) рисова́ть, на-; **~led eyebrows** подрисо́ванные бро́ви; **the corrections were ~led in** попра́вки бы́ли внесены́ карандашо́м; **~ in** (*arrange provisionally*) де́лать, с- предвари́тельную заме́тку насчёт *+g.*

● *cpds.* **~ case** *n.* пена́л; **~ sharpener** *n.* точи́лка.

pendant /'pend(ə)nt/ *n.* (*attached to necklace*) куло́н, подве́ска.

pendent /'pend(ə)nt/ *adj.* (*lit., hanging*) свиса́ющий, вися́чий; (*fig., incomplete, in suspense*) нерешённый.

pending /'pendɪŋ/ *adj.* рассма́триваемый; нерешённый; **~ tray, file** я́щик, па́пка для бума́г, отло́женных для рассмотре́ния; па́пка «К рассмотре́нию».

● *prep.* **1** (*during*) во вре́мя *+g.*; в тече́ние *+g.* **2** (*until*) до *+g.*; в ожида́нии *+g.*

pendulous /'pendjʊləs/ *adj.* подвесно́й.

pendulum /'pendjʊləm/ *n.* ма́ятник.

penetrability /,penɪtrə'bɪlɪtɪ/ *n.* проница́емость.

penetrable /'penɪtrəb(ə)l/ *adj.* проница́емый.

penetrate /'penɪ,treɪt/ *v.t.* **1** (*pierce, find access to*) прон|ика́ть, -и́кнуть в *+a.*; **the bullet ~d his brain** пу́ля прони́кла ему́ в мозг; **they ~d the enemy's defences** (*Br.*), **defenses** (*US*) они́ прони́кли че́рез оборо́ну проти́вника; (*see through*): **our eyes could not ~ the darkness** мы не могли́ ничего́ разгляде́ть в темноте́; (*fig.*) прон|ика́ть, -и́кнуть в *+a.*; разга́д|ывать, -а́ть; **I soon ~d his designs** я вско́ре разгада́л его́ наме́рения.
2 (*pervade*) прон|ика́ть, -и́кнуть в *+a.*; прони́з|ывать, -а́ть; **the smell ~d the whole house** за́пах распространи́лся по всему́ до́му.

● *v.i.* **1** (*make one's way*) проб|ира́ться, -а́ться, прон|ика́ть, -и́кнуть (**into:** в *+a.*); **Livingstone ~d into the interior of Africa** Ливингсто́н прони́к вглубь Африки.
2 (*be heard clearly*): **his voice ~d into the next room** его́ го́лос доноси́лся в сосе́днюю ко́мнату.

penetrating /'penɪ,treɪtɪŋ/ *adj.* си́льный; о́стрый; **a ~ mind** проница́тельный/о́стрый ум; **a ~ voice** пронзи́тельный го́лос.

penetration /,penɪ'treɪʃ(ə)n/ *n.* (*penetrating*) проника́ние; проникнове́ние; (*mil., breach of defences*) проры́в; (*mental acumen*) проница́тельность; (*sexual*) проникнове́ние.

penetrative /'penɪtrətɪv/ *adj.* (*able to penetrate*) проника́ющий; (*perspicacious*) проница́тельный.

penguin /'peŋgwɪn/ *n.* пингви́н.

penicillin /,penɪ'sɪlɪn/ *n.* пеницилли́н.

peninsula /pɪ'nɪnsjʊlə/ *n.* полуо́стров.

peninsular /pɪ'nɪnsjʊlə(r)/ *adj.* полуостровно́й.

penis /'pi:nɪs/ *n.* (*pl.* **penises**) пе́нис, полово́й член.

penitence /'penɪt(ə)ns/ *n.* раска́яние.

penitent /'penɪt(ə)nt/ *n.* ка́ющийся гре́шник.

● *adj.* раска́ивающийся.

penitential /,penɪ'tenʃ(ə)l/ *adj.* покая́нный.

penitentiary /,penɪ'tenʃərɪ/ *n.* (*house of correction*) исправи́тельный дом; (*prison*) тюрьма́.

pennant /'penənt/ *n.* флажо́к, вы́мпел.

penniless /'penɪlɪs/ *adj.* безде́нежный, без гроша́ (*pred.*).

pennon /'penən/ *n.* флажо́к, вы́мпел.

penny /'penɪ/ *n.* (*pl. for separate coins* **pennies,** *for a sum of money* **pence**, *US* **cents**) пе́нни (*nt. indecl.*), пенс; (*US cent*) цент; **a ~ for your thoughts** о чём вы заду́мались?; **in for a ~, in for a pound** ≈ взя́лся за гуж, не говори́, что не дюж; **he turned up like a bad ~** ≈ то́лько его́ не хвата́ло; **that cost him a pretty ~** э́то влете́ло ему́ в копе́ечку; **at last the ~ has dropped!** (*Br. coll.*) наконе́ц-то дошло́; **I must (go and) spend a ~** (*coll.*) мне ну́жно кой-куда́.

● *cpds.* **~-farthing** *n.* (*bicycle*) велосипе́д-пау́к; **~-pinching** *adj.* скупо́й; *n.* ску́пость.

pension /'penʃ(ə)n/ *n.* пе́нсия; **old-age ~** пе́нсия по ста́рости; **war ~** пе́нсия ветера́на войны́; **widow's ~** вдо́вья пе́нсия.

● *with adv.*: **~ off** *v.t.* отпр|авля́ть, -а́вить на пе́нсию.

pension /pɑ̃'sjɔ̃/ *n.* (*boarding-house*) пансио́н.

pensionable /'penʃənəb(ə)l/ *adj.*: **he is a ~ employee** он име́ет пра́во на пе́нсию; **his job is ~** э́то рабо́та даёт ему́ пра́во на пе́нсию.

pensioner /'penʃənə(r)/ *n.* пенсионе́р (*fem.* -ка).

pensive /'pensɪv/ *adj.* заду́мчивый.

pensiveness /'pensɪvnɪs/ *n.* заду́мчивость.

pent /pent/ *adj.* за́пертый; **~-up feelings** сде́рживаемые/подавля́емые чу́вства.

pentagon /'pentəgən/ *n.* пятиуго́льник; **the P~** (*U.S. War Dept.*) Пентаго́н.

pentagram /'pentə,græm/ *n.* пентагра́мма, маги́ческий пятиуго́льник.

pentameter /pen'tæmɪtə(r)/ *n.* пента́метр.

Pentateuch /'pentə,tju:k/ *n.* (*bibl.*) Пятикни́жие.

pentathlete /pen'tæθli:t/ *n.* пятибо́рец.

pentathlon /pen'tæθlən/ *n.* пятибо́рье.

Pentecost /'pentɪ,kɒst/ *n.* Пятидеся́тница.

Pentecostal /,pentɪ'kɒst(ə)l/ *adj.* пятидеся́тнический.

Pentecostalist /,pentɪ'kɒstəlɪst/ *n.* пятидеся́тни|к (*fem.* -ца).

penthouse /'penthaʊs/ *n.* (*apartment*)

P

роско́шная кварти́ра на после́днем этаже́ небоскрёба; пе́нтхаус.

penultimate /pɪˈnʌltɪmət/ *adj.* предпосле́дний.

penumbra /pɪˈnʌmbrə/ *n.* (*pl.* **penumbrae** /-briː/ *or* **penumbras**) полуте́нь.

penurious /pɪˈnjʊərɪəs/ *adj.* (*poor*) бе́дный; (*mean*) скупо́й.

penury /ˈpenjʊrɪ/ *n.* бе́дность, нужда́.

peony /ˈpiːənɪ/ *n.* пио́н.

people /ˈpiːp(ə)l/ *n.* **1** (*race, nation*) наро́д; **the ~s of the former Soviet Union** наро́ды бы́вшего Сове́тского Сою́за; **~'s republic** наро́дная респу́блика.
2 (*proletariat*) наро́д; **the common ~** просто́й наро́д; **a man of the ~** челове́к из наро́да.
3 (*inhabitants*) жи́тели (*m. pl.*); (*citizens*) гра́ждане (*m. pl.*).
4 (*persons grouped by class, place etc.*): **poor ~** бедняки́ (*m. pl.*), бе́дные лю́ди; **country ~** се́льские жи́тели; **young ~** молодёжь, молоды́е лю́ди; **old ~** старики́ (*m. pl.*); **our ~** на́ши лю́ди.
5 (*relatives, parents*) родны́е (*pl.*).
6 (*persons in general*) лю́ди (*pl., g.* -е́й); **few ~** ма́ло люде́й; **four ~** четы́ре челове́ка; че́тверо; **there were 20 ~ present** прису́тствовало 20 челове́к; **most ~ will object** большинство́ (люде́й) бу́дет про́тив; **~ say he's mad** говоря́т, что он сумасше́дший; **he doesn't care what ~ say** ему́ всё равно́, что о нём говоря́т.
● *v.t.* засел|я́ть, -и́ть; **a thickly-~d district** густонаселённый райо́н.

pep /pep/ (*coll.*) *n.* бо́дрость ду́ха; эне́ргия; **put some ~ into it!** веселе́е!; живе́е!; **~ pill** стимули́рующая табле́тка (*наркотик*); **~ talk** нака́чка.
● *v.t.* (**pepped, pepping**) (*usu.* **~ up**) подбодр|я́ть, -и́ть.

pepper /ˈpepə(r)/ *n.* (*condiment*) пе́рец; (*vegetable*) (*sweet* **~**) (сла́дкий) пе́рец; (*chilli* **~**) стручко́вый пе́рец.
● *v.t.* **1** (*sprinkle or season with* **~**) пе́рчить, на-/по-. **2** (*fig., sprinkle*) усе́|ивать, -ять. **3** (*fig., pelt*) забр|а́сывать, -оса́ть; **he was ~ed with questions** его́ заброса́ли вопро́сами.
● *cpds.* **~corn** *n.* пе́речное зерно́, горо́шина пе́рца; (*Br., fig., rent*) номина́льная аре́ндная пла́та; **~-mill** *n.* ме́льница (для пе́рца); **~mint** *n.* (*plant; its essence*) мя́та пе́речная; (*flavoured sweet*) мя́тный ледене́ц; **~-pot** (*US* **~-shaker**) *nn.* пе́речница.

peppery /ˈpepərɪ/ *adj.* (*of food*) напе́рченный; (*fig., irascible*) вспы́льчивый.

Pepsi(-Cola) /ˈpepsɪ/, /ˌpepsɪˈkəʊlə/ *n.* (*propr.*) Пе́пси(-ко́ла).

pepsin /ˈpepsɪn/ *n.* пепси́н.

peptic /ˈpeptɪk/ *adj.* пепти́ческий, пищевари́тельный; **~ ulcer** я́зва желу́дка.

per /pɜː(r)/ *prep.* **1** (*for each*) в + *a.*; на + *a.*; с + *g.*; **60 miles ~ hour** 60 миль в час; **grams ~ square centimetre** (*Br.*), **centimeter** (*US*) гра́ммы на оди́н квадра́тный сантиме́тр; **they collected 20 pence ~ man** они́ собра́ли по 20 пе́нсов с челове́ка.
2: **as ~ usual** (*coll.*) по обыкнове́нию.

perambulate /pəˈræmbjʊˌleɪt/ *v.t.* расха́живать (*impf.*) по + *d.*

perambulation /pəˌræmbjʊˈleɪʃ(ə)n/ *n.* прогу́лка.

perambulator /pəˈræmbjʊˌleɪtə(r)/ *n.* (*Br.*) де́тская коля́ска.

per annum /pər ˈænəm/ *adv.* в год.

per capita /pə ˈkæpɪtə/ *adv.* на ду́шу (населе́ния).

perceivable /pəˈsiːvəb(ə)l/ *adj.* ощути́мый.

perceive /pəˈsiːv/ *v.t.* (*with mind*) пост|ига́ть, -и́гнуть/-и́чь; пон|има́ть, -я́ть; (*through senses*) восприн|има́ть, -я́ть; ощу|ща́ть, -ти́ть.

per cent /pə ˈsent/ (*US* **percent**) *n., adv.* проце́нт; **three ~** три проце́нта; **a discount of 20 ~** ски́дка в два́дцать проце́нтов; **in 20 ~ of cases** в двадцати́ проце́нтах таки́х слу́чаев.

percentage /pəˈsentɪdʒ/ *n.* (*rate per cent*) проце́нтное содержа́ние; (*proportion*) проце́нт; (*share in profits*) до́ля, часть.

perceptibility /pəˌseptɪˈbɪlɪtɪ/ *n.* ощути́мость.

perceptibl|e /pəˈseptɪb(ə)l/ *adj.* ощути́мый; **he was ~y moved** он был заме́тно растро́ган.

perception /pəˈsepʃ(ə)n/ *n.* (*process or faculty of perceiving*) восприя́тие, ощуще́ние; (*quality of discernment*) осозна́ние, понима́ние.

perceptive /pəˈseptɪv/ *adj.* восприи́мчивый; (*observant*) проница́тельный.

perceptiveness /pəˈseptɪvnɪs/ *n.* восприи́мчивость; проница́тельность.

perch[1] /pɜːtʃ/ *n.* (*pl.* **~** *or* **~es**) (*zool.*) о́кунь (*m.*).

perch[2] /pɜːtʃ/ *n.* (*of bird*) насе́ст, жёрдочка.
● *v.t. & i.* сади́ться, сесть; устр|а́иваться, -о́иться; **birds ~ on the boughs** пти́цы садя́тся на ве́тви; **he ~ed (himself) on a stool** он присе́л на табуре́т; **the town was ~ed on a hill** го́род расположи́лся на верши́не холма́.

perchance /pəˈtʃɑːns/ *adv.* (*arch. or joc.*) случа́йно.

percipience /pəˈsɪpɪəns/ *n.* спосо́бность восприя́тия.

percipient /pəˈsɪpɪənt/ *adj.* воспринима́ющий.

percolate /ˈpɜːkəˌleɪt/ *v.t.* про|ходи́ть, -йти́ че́рез + *a.*
● *v.i.* прос|а́чиваться, -очи́ться; **water ~s through sand** вода́ проса́чивается/прохо́дит сквозь песо́к; **I'm waiting for the coffee to ~** я жду, пока́ ко́фе профильтру́ется; (*fig.*): **the news ~d through at last** но́вости наконе́ц просочи́лись.

percolator /ˈpɜːkəˌleɪtə(r)/ *n.* (*cul.*) перколя́тор, кофева́рка.

percussion /pəˈkʌʃ(ə)n/ *n.* **1** (*striking*) уда́р; **~ cap** уда́рный писто́н. **2**: (**~ instruments**) уда́рные инструме́нты (*m. pl.*).

percussionist /pəˈkʌʃ(ə)nɪst/ *n.* уда́рник.

per diem /pə ˈdiːem/, /ˈdaɪem/ *adv.* в день.

perdition /pəˈdɪʃ(ə)n/ *n.* ги́бель.

peregrination /ˌperɪgrɪˈneɪʃ(ə)n/ *n.* стра́нствие, стра́нствование.

peregrine /ˈperɪgrɪn/ *n.* (**~ falcon**) со́кол; сапса́н.

peremptory /pəˈremptərɪ/, /ˈperɪm-/ *adj.* (*imperious*) повели́тельный; непререка́емый.

perennial /pəˈrenɪəl/ *n.* (*plant*) многоле́тнее расте́ние, многоле́тник; **hardy ~** (*lit.*) выно́сливый многоле́тник.
● *adj.* (*plant*) многоле́тний; (*enduring*) (веко)ве́чный; (*regularly repeated*) повторя́ющийся.

perestroika /ˌperɪˈstrɔɪkə/ *n.* перестро́йка.

perfect[1] /ˈpɜːfɪkt/ *n.* (*gram.*) перфе́кт; **the future ~** бу́дущее соверше́нное вре́мя.
● *adj.* **1** (*entire, complete; absolute*) соверше́нный; по́лный; **the child was a ~ nuisance** ребёнок всем до́ смерти надое́л; **that is ~ nonsense** э́то по́лный абсу́рд; э́то абсолю́тная чепуха́; **you have a ~ right to your opinion** вы име́ете по́лное пра́во приде́рживаться своего́ мне́ния; **a ~ stranger** соверше́нно чужо́й (челове́к); **I am ~ly sure of it** я соверше́нно уве́рен в э́том.
2 (*faultless*) соверше́нный, безупре́чный; **a ~ diamond** безупре́чный алма́з; **he speaks ~ English** он в соверше́нстве владе́ет англи́йским (языко́м); (*thoroughly accomplished*) соверше́нный; **the actors were word-~** актёры зна́ли роль назубо́к; (*corresponding to an ideal*) соверше́нный, идеа́льный; (*corresponding to definition; archetypal*): **a ~ circle** то́чный круг; **he committed the ~ murder** он соверши́л класси́ческое уби́йство.
3 (*exact, precise*) абсолю́тный; **~ pitch** (*mus.*) абсолю́тный слух; (*corresponding to requirements*) безупре́чный; **the dress is a ~ fit** пла́тье сиди́т безупре́чно.
4 (*gram.*) перфе́ктный, соверше́нный; **~ tense** перфе́кт.
5 (*mus.*): **~ fifth** чи́стая кви́нта.

perfect[2] /pəˈfekt/ *v.t.* (*complete; accomplish, achieve*) заверш|а́ть, -и́ть; выполня́ть, вы́полнить; (*bring to highest standard*) соверше́нствовать, у-.

perfection /pəˈfekʃ(ə)n/ *n.* **1** (*perfecting*) заверше́ние, соверше́нствование. **2** (*faultlessness, excellence*) соверше́нство; **she dances to ~** она́ безупре́чно танцу́ет. **3** (*ideal or its embodiment*) зако́нченность; **the ~ of beauty** верх красоты́.

perfectionism /pəˈfekʃəˌnɪz(ə)m/ *n.* стремле́ние к соверше́нству, перфекциони́зм.

perfectionist /pəˈfekʃənɪst/ *n.*

взыска́тельный челове́к, перфекциони́ст.

perfective /pəˈfektɪv/ *n.* (*gram.*) соверше́нный вид.

● *adj.* соверше́нный; соверше́нного ви́да.

perfidious /ˌpɜːˈfɪdɪəs/ *adj.* вероло́мный, кова́рный.

perfid|iousness /ˌpɜːˈfɪdɪəsnɪs/, **-y** /ˈpɜːfɪdɪ/ *nn.* вероло́мство, кова́рство.

perforate /ˈpɜːfəˌreɪt/ *v.t.* перфори́ровать (*impf.*); **a ~d appendix** прободно́й/перфорати́вный аппендици́т.

perforation /ˌpɜːfəˈreɪʃ(ə)n/ *n.* (*piercing*) перфора́ция; (*row of pierced holes*) перфори́рованный ряд.

perform /pəˈfɔːm/ *v.t.* **1** (*carry out*) выполня́ть, вы́полнить; исп|олня́ть, -о́лнить. **2** (*enact*) исп|олня́ть, -о́лнить; **Hamlet will be ~ed next week** «Га́млета» даю́т/игра́ют на сле́дующей неде́ле; **~ing rights** права́ на постано́вку/исполне́ние; **he ~ed conjuring tricks** он пока́зывал фо́кусы.

● *v.i.* **1** (*act, play instrument etc.*) игра́ть, сыгра́ть; выступа́ть, вы́ступить; (*execute tricks*): **~ing seal** дрессиро́ванный тюле́нь. **2** (*function*) рабо́тать (*impf.*), **my car ~s well on hills** моя́ маши́на хорошо́ идёт в го́ру.

performance /pəˈfɔːməns/ *n.* **1** (*execution*) исполне́ние, выполне́ние, проведе́ние; **in the ~ of his duty** при исполне́нии до́лга. **2** (*achievement, feat*) успе́х, сверше́ние. **3** (*of a machine, vehicle etc.*) ход, характери́стика. **4** (*public appearance*) выступле́ние. **5** (*of play etc.*) представле́ние; постано́вка; (*play*) спекта́кль (*m.*); (*of music*) исполне́ние; (*concert*) конце́рт. **6** (*coll., tedious process, fuss*): **he made a ~ of it** он устро́ил из э́того це́лую исто́рию.

performer /pəˈfɔːmə(r)/ *n.* исполни́тель (*m.*) (*fem.* -ница); **he is a fine ~ on the flute** он прекра́сно игра́ет на фле́йте.

perfume /ˈpɜːfjuːm/ *n.* (*odour*) благоуха́ние; (*fluid*) дух|и́ (*pl., g.* -о́в).

● *v.t.* (*impart odour to*) де́лать, с- благоуха́нным; (*apply scent to*) души́ть, на-.

perfumer /pəˈfjuːmə(r)/ *n.* парфюме́р.

perfumery /pəˈfjuːmərɪ/ *n.* (*business*) парфюме́рия; (*shop*) парфюме́рный магази́н; **~ department** парфюме́рия.

perfunctoriness /pəˈfʌŋktərɪnɪs/ *n.* пове́рхностность; небре́жность.

perfunctory /pəˈfʌŋktərɪ/ *adj.* (*glance, inspection*) пове́рхностный; (*kiss, smile*) небре́жный.

pergola /ˈpɜːgələ/ *n.* садо́вая а́рка.

perhaps /pəˈhæps/ *adv.* мо́жет быть; возмо́жно; пожа́луй; **~ not** мо́жет быть и нет; (*in requests*) пожа́луйста, бу́дьте добры́; **could you ~ read this?** бу́дьте добры́, прочти́те э́то.

pericardium /ˌperɪˈkɑːdɪəm/ *n.* (*pl.* **pericardia** /-dɪə/) (*anat.*) перика́рд.

perigee /ˈperɪˌdʒiː/ *n.* (*astron.*) периге́й.

perihelion /ˌperɪˈhiːlɪən/ *n.* (*pl.* **perihelia** /-lɪə/) (*astron.*) периге́лий.

peril /ˈperɪl/ *n.* опа́сность; риск; **at one's ~** на свой страх и риск; **he goes in ~ of his life** его́ жизнь в постоя́нной опа́сности.

perilous /ˈperɪləs/ *adj.* опа́сный; риско́ванный.

perimeter /pəˈrɪmɪtə(r)/ *n.* (*of a geom. figure*) пери́метр; (*of an airfield etc.*) вне́шняя грани́ца, пери́метр; **~ fence** окружна́я и́згородь.

period /ˈpɪərɪəd/ *n.* **1** пери́од; **she has ~s of depression** у неё быва́ют пери́оды депре́ссии; **he will be away for a long ~** его́ не бу́дет до́лгое вре́мя. **2** (*previous age*) эпо́ха; **she wore the dress of the ~** она́ была́ оде́та в сти́ле эпо́хи; **~ furniture** ме́бель в сти́ле определённой эпо́хи; стари́нная ме́бель; **a ~ play** пье́са, рису́ющая нра́вы определённой эпо́хи. **3** (*session of instruction*) уро́к. **4** (*menses*) ме́сячные (*pl.*); **~ pains** (*Br.*) ме́сячные бо́ли (*f. pl.*). **5** (*US, full stop*) то́чка.

periodic /ˌpɪərɪˈɒdɪk/ *adj.* периоди́ческий; **~ table** (*chem.*) периоди́ческая табли́ца.

periodical /ˌpɪərɪˈɒdɪk(ə)l/ *n.* периоди́ческое изда́ние; (*pl.*) перио́дика.

● *adj.* = **periodic**

periodicity /ˌpɪərɪəˈdɪsɪtɪ/ *n.* периоди́чность.

peripatetic /ˌperɪpəˈtetɪk/ *adj.* (*teacher*) приходя́щий; (*itinerant*) бродя́чий.

peripheral /pəˈrɪfər(ə)l/ *n.* (*comput.*) перифери́йное устро́йство.

● *adj.* (*lit.*) перифери́йный; (*fig., not central to a subject*) несуще́ственный; побо́чный.

periphery /pəˈrɪfərɪ/ *n.* (*boundary*) грани́ца, черта́; (*also fig.*) перифери́я.

periphrasis /pəˈrɪfrəsɪs/ *n.* (*pl.* **periphrases** /-ˌsiːz/) перифра́з.

periphrastic /ˌperɪˈfræstɪk/ *adj.* перифрасти́ческий.

periscope /ˈperɪˌskəʊp/ *n.* периско́п.

periscopic /ˌperɪˈskɒpɪk/ *adj.* перископи́ческий; **~ sight** периско́пный прице́л.

perish /ˈperɪʃ/ *v.t.*: **we were ~ed with cold** (*Br.*) мы погиба́ли от хо́лода; **strong sun will ~ rubber** си́льные со́лнечные лучи́ разруша́ют рези́ну.

● *v.i.* **1** пог|иба́ть, -и́бнуть; **they shall ~ by the sword** они́ поги́бнут от меча́; **~ the thought!** Бо́же упаси́! **2**: **the rubber has ~ed** рези́на пришла́ в него́дность.

perishable /ˈperɪʃəb(ə)l/ *adj.* непро́чный, скоропо́ртящийся; (*pl., as n.*) скоропо́ртящийся това́р.

perishing /ˈperɪʃɪŋ/ *adj.* (*Br. coll.*) (*cold*): **it's ~ here** здесь а́дский хо́лод; (*wretched*) ужа́сный, стра́шный.

peristyle /ˈperɪˌstaɪl/ *n.* (*archit.*) перисти́ль (*m.*).

peritone|um /ˌperɪtəˈniːəm/ *n.* (*pl.* **~ums** *or* **~a**) брюши́на.

peritonitis /ˌperɪtəˈnaɪtɪs/ *n.* перитони́т.

periwig /ˈperɪwɪg/ *n.* (пу́дреный) пари́к.

periwinkle /ˈperɪˌwɪŋk(ə)l/ *n.* (*mollusc*) litори́на; (*plant*) барви́нок.

perjure /ˈpɜːdʒə(r)/ *v.t.*: **~ o.s.** да|ва́ть, -ть ло́жное показа́ние под прися́гой, лжесвиде́тельствовать (*impf.*); **a ~d witness** лжесвиде́тель (*fem.* -ница).

perjurer /ˈpɜːdʒərə(r)/ *n.* лжесвиде́тель (*fem.* -ница).

perjury /ˈpɜːdʒərɪ/ *n.* лжесвиде́тельство; **commit ~** = **perjure o.s.**

perk[1] /pɜːk/ *n.* (*coll.*) = **perquisite**

perk[2] /pɜːk/ *v.t.* **1** (*move smartly*): **the dog ~ed up its tail** соба́ка задрала́ хвост. **2**: **~ up** (*enliven*) ожив|ля́ть, -и́ть.

● *v.i.*: **~ up** (*liven up*) ожив|ля́ться, -и́ться; **I hope the weather ~s up** (*coll.*) наде́юсь, что пого́да прояснится/улу́чшится.

perkiness /ˈpɜːkɪnɪs/ *n.* бо́йкость, весёлость, оживлённость.

perky /ˈpɜːkɪ/ *adj.* (**perkier, perkiest**) (*cheerful*) весёлый, оживлённый; (*cheeky*) бо́йкий.

perm /pɜːm/ *n.* (*coll., permanent wave*) пермане́нт.

● *v.t.*: **she had her hair ~ed** она́ сде́лала себе́ пермане́нтную зави́вку/перманéнт.

permafrost /ˈpɜːməˌfrɒst/ *n.* ве́чная мерзлота́.

permanence /ˈpɜːmənəns/ *n.* неизме́нность.

permanent /ˈpɜːmənənt/ *adj.* постоя́нный; **~ wave** перманéнт.

permanganate /pɜːˈmæŋgəˌneɪt/, /-nət/ *n.* перманганáт; **potassium ~** марганцовоки́слый ка́лий.

permeability /ˌpɜːmɪəˈbɪlɪtɪ/ *n.* проница́емость.

permeable /ˈpɜːmɪəb(ə)l/ *adj.* проница́емый.

permeate /ˈpɜːmɪˌeɪt/ *v.t.* пропи́т|ывать, -а́ть; прон|ика́ть, -и́кнуть в + *a.*

● *v.i.* прос|а́чиваться, -очи́ться.

permeation /ˌpɜːmɪˈeɪʃ(ə)n/ *n.* (*lit.*) проникнове́ние, проса́чивание; (*fig.*) проникнове́ние.

Permian /ˈpɜːmɪən/ *adj.* пе́рмский.

permissible /pəˈmɪsɪb(ə)l/ *adj.* допусти́мый, позволи́тельный.

permission /pəˈmɪʃ(ə)n/ *n.* позволе́ние, разреше́ние; **you must get ~ to go there** что́бы пойти́ туда́, необходи́мо получи́ть разреше́ние; **she has my ~ to stay** я разреша́ю ей оста́ться; **with your ~ I'll leave** с ва́шего позволе́ния я ухожу́.

permissive /pəˈmɪsɪv/ *adj.*: **~ society** о́бщество вседозво́ленности.

permissiveness /pəˈmɪsɪvnɪs/ *n.* вседозво́ленность.

permit[1] /ˈpɜːmɪt/ *n.* разреше́ние, про́пуск (*pl.* -а́); **work ~** разреше́ние

P

на рабо́ту; **residence ~** вид на жи́тельство.

permit² /pəˈmɪt/ *v.t.* (**permitted, permitting**) разреш|а́ть, -и́ть, позв|оля́ть, -о́лить; **smoking ~ted** кури́ть разреша́ется; **if I may be ~ted to speak** е́сли мне бу́дет позво́лено вы́сказаться.

● *v.i.* (**permitted, permitting**): **if circumstances ~** е́сли обстоя́тельства позво́лят; **weather ~ting** е́сли пого́да позво́лит; **the situation ~s of no delay** ситуа́ция не те́рпит отлага́тельства.

permutation /ˌpɜːmjʊˈteɪʃ(ə)n/ *n.* (*math.*) перестано́вка; (*fig.*) вариа́нт, модифика́ция.

pernicious /pəˈnɪʃəs/ *adj.* па́губный, вре́дный; **~ anaemia** (*Br.*), **anemia** (*US*) злока́чественное малокро́вие.

perniciousness /pəˈnɪʃəsnɪs/ *n.* па́губность.

pernickety /pəˈnɪkɪtɪ/ *adj.* (*coll.*) приверé́дливый.

peroxide /pəˈrɒksaɪd/ *n.* пе́рекись; **hydrogen ~** пе́рекись водоро́да; **a ~ blonde** кра́шеная блонди́нка.

● *v.t.* обесцве́|чивать, -тить.

perpendicular /ˌpɜːpənˈdɪkjʊlə(r)/ *n.* перпендикуля́р; **out of the ~** невертика́льный.

● *adj.* (*at right angles*) перпендикуля́рный; (*vertical*) вертика́льный.

perpetrate /ˈpɜːpɪˌtreɪt/ *v.t.* соверш|а́ть, -и́ть.

perpetration /ˌpɜːpɪˈtreɪʃ(ə)n/ *n.* соверше́ние.

perpetrator /ˈpɜːpɪˌtreɪtə(r)/ *n.* вино́вник (+*g.*), вино́вный (в+*p.*); **~ of crime** престу́пник.

perpetual /pəˈpetjʊəl/ *adj.* ве́чный; **~ motion** ве́чное движе́ние; (*for life*) бессро́чный, пожи́зненный.

perpetuate /pəˈpetjʊˌeɪt/ *v.t.* увекове́чи|вать, -ть.

perpetuation /pəˌpetjʊˈeɪʃ(ə)n/ *n.* увекове́чение.

perpetuity /ˌpɜːpɪˈtjuːɪtɪ/ *n.* ве́чность; **in ~** навсегда́, (на)ве́чно.

perplex /pəˈpleks/ *v.t.* (*puzzle*) озада́чи|вать, -ть; (*complicate*) усложн|я́ть, -и́ть; запу́т|ывать, -ать.

perplexity /pəˈpleksɪtɪ/ *n.* (*bewilderment*) озада́ченность, недоуме́ние.

perquisite /ˈpɜːkwɪzɪt/ *n.* льго́та.

per se /pɜː ˈseɪ/ *adv.* сам (*fem.* -а, *nt.* -о) по себе́.

persecute /ˈpɜːsɪˌkjuːt/ *v.t.* пресле́довать (*impf.*).

persecution /ˌpɜːsɪˈkjuːʃ(ə)n/ *n.* пресле́дование; **~ mania** ма́ния пресле́дования.

persecutor /ˈpɜːsɪˌkjuːtə(r)/ *n.* пресле́дователь (*m.*) (*fem.* -ница).

perseverance /ˌpɜːsɪˈvɪərəns/ *n.* упо́рство, насто́йчивость.

persever|e /ˌpɜːsɪˈvɪə(r)/ *v.i.* прояв|ля́ть, -и́ть упо́рство (в+*p.*); **you must ~e in (at, with) your work** вы должны́ прояви́ть упо́рство в свое́й рабо́те; **he is very ~ing** он о́чень упо́рный.

Persia /ˈpɜːʃə/ *n.* Пе́рсия.

Persian /ˈpɜːʃ(ə)n/ *n.* (*person*) перс (*fem.* -ия́нка); (*language*) перси́дский язы́к.

● *adj.* перси́дский; **~ Gulf** Перси́дский зали́в; **~ lamb** кара́куль (*m.*).

persiflage /ˈpɜːsɪˌflɑːʒ/ *n.* подшу́чивание.

persimmon /pɜːˈsɪmən/ *n.* хурма́.

persist /pəˈsɪst/ *v.i.* **1** (*resist dissuasion*) упо́рствовать (*impf.*); **he ~ed in his opinion** он упо́рствовал в своём мне́нии; он упо́рно отста́ивал своё мне́ние; **he ~ed in coming with me** он настоя́л на том, что́бы пойти́ со мной. **2** (*continue to exist, remain*) сохран|я́ться, -и́ться; **the custom ~s to this day** э́тот обы́чай сохрани́лся по сей день; **fog will ~ all day** тума́н продéржится весь день.

persistence /pəˈsɪst(ə)ns/ *n.* (*obstinacy*) упо́рство, насто́йчивость; (*continuation*) продолже́ние.

persistent /pəˈsɪst(ə)nt/ *adj.* **1** (*obstinate*) упо́рный. **2** (*slow to go or change*) усто́йчивый, постоя́нный.

person /ˈpɜːs(ə)n/ *n.* **1** (*individual*) челове́к; **a young ~** молодо́й челове́к; **not a single ~ was injured** ни оди́н челове́к не был ра́нен; (*of particular category*) лицо́; **a very important ~** о́чень ва́жное/значи́тельное лицо́; **displaced ~s** перемещённые ли́ца. **2** (*body*) лицо́; **an offence** (*Br.*), **offense** (*US*) **against the ~** преступле́ние про́тив ли́чности; **he appeared in ~** он яви́лся со́бственной персо́ной. **3** (*gram.*) лицо́; **first ~ singular** пе́рвое лицо́ еди́нственного числа́.

persona /pɜːˈsəʊnə/ *n.* (*pl.* **personas** *or* **personae** /-niː/) нару́жность, вне́шняя сторона́; **~ (non) grata** персо́на (нон) гра́та (*indecl.*).

personable /ˈpɜːsənəb(ə)l/ *adj.* привлека́тельный.

personage /ˈpɜːsənɪdʒ/ *n.* (*important person*) ли́чность, персо́на; (*in a play*) персона́ж.

personal /ˈpɜːsən(ə)l/ *adj.* ли́чный; **she is a ~ acquaintance of mine** я её ли́чно зна́ю; **she has great ~ charm** у неё большо́е ли́чное обая́ние; **~ assistant** ли́чный секрета́рь; **~ column** (*of newspaper*) коло́нка ча́стных объявле́ний; **~ computer** персона́льный компью́тер; **~ estate** (*leg.*) дви́жимое иму́щество; **~ organizer** органа́йзер; **~ pronoun** ли́чное местоиме́ние; **~ stereo** пле́йер; **don't make ~ remarks!** не переходи́те на ли́чности!

personality /ˌpɜːsəˈnælɪtɪ/ *n.* **1** (*character*) ли́чность; **a strong ~** си́льная ли́чность; **~ cult** культ ли́чности. **2** (*famous person*) знамени́тость. **3** (*pl., offensive remarks*) вы́пады (*m. pl.*).

personalize /ˈpɜːsənəˌlaɪz/ *v.t.* вн|оси́ть, -ести́ ли́чный элеме́нт в+*a.*; **~d stationery** именна́я пи́счая бума́га.

personally /ˈpɜːsənəlɪ/ *adv.* ли́чно; **he was ~ involved** он был ли́чно заме́шан; **don't take it ~!** не принима́йте э́то на свой счёт!; **~ I prefer this** ли́чно я предпочита́ю э́то.

personification /pəˌsɒnɪfɪˈkeɪʃ(ə)n/ *n.* олицетворе́ние, воплоще́ние; **he is the ~ of selfishness** он явля́ется воплоще́нием эгои́зма.

personif|y /pəˈsɒnɪˌfaɪ/ *v.t.* (*give personal attributes to*) олицетвор|я́ть, -и́ть; (*exemplify*) вопло|ща́ть, -ти́ть; **she was kindness ~ied** она́ была́ воплоще́нием доброты́.

personnel /ˌpɜːsəˈnel/ *n.* персона́л; штат; ка́дры (*m. pl.*); **~ officer** рабо́тник отде́ла ка́дров; **~ department** отде́л ка́дров.

perspective /pəˈspektɪv/ *n.* **1** (*system of representation*) перспекти́ва; **the roof is out of ~** (*in a drawing*) кры́ша изображена́ вне перспекти́вы. **2** (*fig.*): **you must see, get things in (their right) ~** на́до ви́деть ве́щи в их и́стинном све́те.

● *adj.* перспекти́вный; **~ drawing** чертёж в перспекти́ве.

perspex /ˈpɜːspeks/ *n.* (*Br. propr.*) плексигла́с, органи́ческое стекло́.

perspicacious /ˌpɜːspɪˈkeɪʃəs/ *adj.* проница́тельный.

perspicacity /ˌpɜːspɪˈkæsɪtɪ/ *n.* проница́тельность.

perspicuous /pəˈspɪkjʊəs/ *adj.* я́сный, поня́тный.

perspicu|ousness /pəˈspɪkjʊəsnɪs/, **-ity** /ˌpɜspɪˈkjuːɪtɪ/ *nn.* я́сность, поня́тность.

perspiration /ˌpɜːspɪˈreɪʃ(ə)n/ *n.* (*sweating*) поте́ние; (*sweat*) пот.

perspire /pəˈspaɪə(r)/ *v.i.* поте́ть, вс-.

persuadable /pəˈsweɪdəb(ə)l/ *adj.* внуша́емый; поддаю́щийся убежде́нию.

persuade /pəˈsweɪd/ *v.t.* **1** (*convince*) убе|жда́ть, -ди́ть; **I ~d him of my innocence** я убеди́л его́ в мое́й невино́вности. **2** (*induce*) угов|а́ривать, -ори́ть; **he was ~d to sing** его́ уговори́ли спеть.

persuasion /pəˈsweɪʒ(ə)n/ *n.* (*persuading*) убежде́ние; (*persuasiveness*) убеди́тельность; (*conviction*) убежде́ние; (*denomination*) вероисповéдание.

persuasive /pəˈsweɪsɪv/ *adj.* убеди́тельный; (*of person*) облада́ющий да́ром убежде́ния.

persuasiveness /pəˈsweɪsɪvnɪs/ *n.* убеди́тельность.

pert /pɜːt/ *adj.* де́рзкий, наха́льный.

pertain /pəˈteɪn/ *v.i.* (*relate*) относи́ться (*impf.*) (*к кому/чему*).

pertinacious /ˌpɜːtɪˈneɪʃəs/ *adj.* упря́мый, неусту́пчивый.

pertinac|iousness /ˌpɜːtɪˈneɪʃəsnɪs/, **-ity** /ˌpɜːtɪˈnæsɪtɪ/ *nn.* упря́мство, неусту́пчивость.

pertinence /ˈpɜːtɪnəns/ *n.* уме́стность.

pertinent /ˈpɜːtɪnənt/ *adj.* уме́стный; подходя́щий.

pertness /ˈpɜːtnɪs/ *n.* дéрзость, нахáльство.

perturb /pəˈtɜːb/ *v.t.* тревóжить, вс-; волновáть, вз-.

perturbation /ˌpɜːtəˈbeɪʃ(ə)n/ *n.* встревóженность, волнéние.

Peru /pəˈruː/ *n.* Перý (*indecl.*).

perusal /pəˈruːzəl/ *n.* (внимáтельное) чтéние.

peruse /pəˈruːz/ *v.t.* (*read*) внимáтельно читáть, про-, вчи́тываться (*impf.*) в + *a.*; (*examine*) рассм|áтривать, -отрéть.

Peruvian /pəˈruːvɪən/ *n.* перуáн|ец (*fem.* -ка).

● *adj.* перуáнский.

pervade /pəˈveɪd/ *v.t.* (*smell*) прон|икáть, -и́кнуть, распростран|я́ться, -и́ться по + *d.*; (*influence, quality*) прон|и́зывать, -изáть, прин|икáть, -и́кнуть.

pervasion /pəˈveɪʒ(ə)n/ *n.* распространéние; наполнéние.

pervasive /pəˈveɪsɪv/ *adj.* (*able to pervade*) всепроникáющий; (*pervading*) настóйчивый, неотстýпный.

pervasiveness /pəˈveɪsɪvnɪs/ *n.* проникновéние; неотстýпность.

perverse /pəˈvɜːs/ *adj.* (*unreasonable*) преврáтный; (*persistent in wrongdoing*) порóчный, извращённый.

pervers|eness /pəˈvɜːsnɪs/, **-ity** /pəˈvɜːsɪtɪ/ *nn.* преврáтность; извращённость.

perversion /pəˈvɜːʃ(ə)n/ *n.* (*distortion, misrepresentation*) искажéние; (*corruption, leading astray*) извращéние; (*sexual deviation*) извращéние, первéрсия.

pervert[1] /ˈpɜːvɜːt/ *n.* (*sexual deviant*) извращéнец.

pervert[2] /pəˈvɜːt/ *v.t.* (*distort*) извра|щáть, -ти́ть; (*corrupt*) развра|щáть, -ти́ть; **~ the course of justice** иска|жáть, -зи́ть ход правосýдия.

pervious /ˈpɜːvɪəs/ *adj.* (*allowing passage; permeable*) проходи́мый; достýпный; (*receptive*) восприи́мчивый.

peseta /pəˈseɪtə/ *n.* песéта.

pesky /ˈpeskɪ/ *adj.* (**peskier, peskiest**) (*US coll.*) докýчливый, занýдный.

pessary /ˈpesərɪ/ *n.* (*med.*) пессáрий.

pessimism /ˈpesɪˌmɪz(ə)m/ *n.* пессими́зм.

pessimist /ˈpesɪmɪst/ *n.* пессими́ст (*fem.* -ка).

pessimistic /ˌpesɪˈmɪstɪk/ *adj.* пессимисти́ческий; (*person*) пессимисти́чный.

pest /pest/ *n.* (*harmful creature*) вреди́тель (*m.*); (*of person*) занýда (*c.g.*).

pester /ˈpestə(r)/ *v.t.* докучáть (*impf.*); **he keeps ~ing me for money** он всё врéмя пристаёт ко мне насчёт дéнег; **she ~ed her father to take her with him** онá приставáла к отцý, чтóбы он взял её с собóй.

pesticide /ˈpestɪˌsaɪd/ *n.* пестици́д.

pestilence /ˈpestɪləns/ *n.* чумá.

pestilent /ˈpestɪlənt/ *adj.* смертонóсный; (*fig.*) губи́тельный.

pestilential /ˌpestɪˈlenʃ(ə)l/ *adj.* чумнóй; пáгубный.

pestle /ˈpes(ə)l/ *n.* пéстик.

pet /pet/ *n.* **1** (*animal, bird etc.*) питóмец, домáшнее живóтное; **~ food** корм для домáшних живóтных; **~ shop** зоомагази́н. **2** (*favourite*) люби́м|ец (*fem.* -ица), бáловень (*m.*); **teacher's ~** люби́мчик учи́теля; **his ~ subject** егó излюбленная тéма; **onions are my ~ aversion** я бóльше всегó не люблю лук; **~ name** ласкáтельное/уменьши́тельное и́мя.

● *v.t.* (**petted, petting**) (*treat with affection*) баловáть, из-; (*fondle*) ласкáть, при-.

● *v.i.* (**petted, petting**) (*coll., fondle each other*) обнимáться (*impf.*).

petal /ˈpet(ə)l/ *n.* лепестóк.

petard /pɪˈtɑːd/ *n.* петáрда; **he was hoist with his own ~** он попáл в сóбственную ловýшку.

Peter /ˈpiːtə/ *n.*: **he is robbing ~ to pay Paul** берёт у одногó, чтóбы отдáть другóму.

peter /ˈpiːtə(r)/ *v.i.*: **~ out** (*run dry, low*) исс|якáть, -я́кнуть; (*of a path, road*) постепéнно исч|езáть, -éзнуть; **the track ~ed out** след постепéнно пропáл.

petit bourgeois /ˌpətɪ ˈbʊəʒwɑː/ *adj.* (*pl.* **petits bourgeois** *pronunc. same*) мелкобуржуáзный.

petite /pəˈtiːt/ *adj.* мáленький, миниатю́рный.

petite bourgeoisie /pəˈtiːt ˌbʊəʒwɑːˈziː/ *n.* мéлкая буржуази́я.

petit four /ˌpetɪ ˈfɔː(r)/ *n.* (*pl.* **petits fours**) петифýр.

petition /pɪˈtɪʃ(ə)n/ *n.* (*signed by many people*) пети́ция; (*formal request*) ходáтайство, прошéние; (*application to court*) исковóе заявлéние.

● *v.t.* под|авáть, -áть прошéние + *d.*/в + *a.*; ходáтайствовать, по- в + *p.*/пéред + *i.*

● *v.i.*: **~ for** взывáть, воззвáть о + *p.*; **~ for divorce** под|авáть, -áть заявлéние о развóде.

petitioner /pɪˈtɪʃənə(r)/ *n.* (*with request*) проси́тель (*m.*); (*in a divorce suit*) ис|тéц (*fem.* -и́ца); (*pol.*) подáтель (*m.*) пети́ции.

petits bourgeois *pl. of* ⇨**petit bourgeois**

petits fours /ˌpetɪ ˈfɔːz/ *pl. of* ⇨**petit four**

petits pois /ˌpetɪ ˈpwɑː/ *n.* мéлкий зелёный горóшек.

petrel /ˈpetr(ə)l/ *n.* буревéстник; **stormy ~** (*zool.*) качýрка мáлая.

petrification /ˌpetrɪfɪˈkeɪʃ(ə)n/ *n.* (*lit.*) петрификáция, окаменéние; (*fig.*) оцепенéние.

petrif|y /ˈpetrɪˌfaɪ/ *v.t.* (*lit.*) превра|щáть, -ти́ть в кáмень; (*fig.*) прив|оди́ть, -ести́ в оцепенéние; **I was ~ied** я остолбенéл/оцепенéл.

petrochemicals /ˌpetrəʊˈkemɪk(ə)ls/ *n. pl.* нефтепродýкты (*m. pl.*), нефтехими́ческие продýкты (*m. pl.*).

petrodollar /ˈpetrəʊˌdɒlə(r)/ *n.* нефтедóллар.

petrol /ˈpetr(ə)l/ *n.* (*Br.*) бензи́н; **fill up with ~** запр|авля́ться, -áвиться бензи́ном; **~ bomb** буты́лка с зажигáтельной смéсью; **~ can** кани́стра для бензи́на; **~ engine** бензи́новый дви́гатель; **~ pump** (*at garage*) бензоколóнка; (*in engine*) бензонасóс; **~ pump attendant** слýжащий бензоколóнки; **~ station** бензозаправочная стáнция, бензоколóнка; **~ tank** бензобáк; **~ tanker** бензовóз.

petroleum /pɪˈtrəʊlɪəm/ *n.* нефть; **the ~ industry** нефтянáя проми́шленность; **~ jelly** вазели́н.

petticoat /ˈpetɪˌkəʊt/ *n.* ни́жняя ю́бка.

pettifogger /ˈpetɪˌfɒgə(r)/ *n.* крючкотвóр.

pettifogging /ˈpetɪˌfɒgɪŋ/ *n.* крючкотвóрство.

● *adj.* мéлочный.

pettiness /ˈpetɪnɪs/ *n.* мéлочность.

petty /ˈpetɪ/ *adj.* (**pettier, pettiest**) **1** (*trivial*) мéлкий, маловáжный. **2** (*small-minded*) мéлочный. **3** (*of small amounts*): **~ cash** дéньги на мéлкие расхóды; **~ theft** мéлкая крáжа. **4**: **~ officer** (*nav.*) старшинá (*m.*).

petulance /ˈpetjʊləns/ *n.* раздражи́тельность.

petulant /ˈpetjʊlənt/ *adj.* раздражи́тельный.

petunia /pɪˈtjuːnɪə/ *n.* петýния.

pew /pjuː/ *n.* (*enclosed compartment*) отгорóженное мéсто в цéркви; (*bench*) скамья́; **take a ~!** (*Br. coll.*) присáживайтесь!

pewit /ˈpiːwɪt/ = **peewit**

pewter /ˈpjuːtə(r)/ *n.* (*alloy*) сплав óлова с мéдью/со свинцóм; (*vessels made of ~*) оловя́нная посýда.

● *adj.* оловя́нный.

pfennig /ˈpfenɪg/, /ˈfenɪg/ *n.* пфéнниг.

phaeton /ˈfeɪt(ə)n/ *n.* фаэтóн.

phalan|x /ˈfælæŋks/ *n.* (*pl.* **~xes** *or* **~ges** /fəˈlændʒiːz/) (*hist.*) фалáнга; (*anat.*) фалáнга пáльца.

phalarope /ˈfæləˌrəʊp/ *n.* (*zool.*) плавýнчик.

phalli /ˈfælaɪ/, /ˈfæliː/ *pl. of* ⇨**phallus**

phallic /ˈfælɪk/ *adj.* фалли́ческий; **~ symbol** фалли́ческий си́мвол.

phallus /ˈfæləs/ *n.* (*pl.* **phalli** *or* **phalluses**) фáллос.

phantasm /ˈfænˌtæz(ə)m/ *n.* (*ghost*) фантóм, при́зрак.

phantasmagoria /ˌfæntæzməˈgɔːrɪə/ *n.* фантасмагóрия.

phantasy /ˈfæntəsɪ/, /-zɪ/ = **fantasy**

phantom /ˈfæntəm/ *n.* **1** (*ghost*) при́зрак, фантóм; (*attr.*) при́зрачный. **2** (*illusion*): **a ~ of the imagination** плод воображéния/фантáзии.

P

Pharaoh /ˈfeərəʊ/ *n.* фарао́н.

Pharisaical /ˌfærɪˈseɪɪk(ə)l/ *adj.* (*fig.*) фарисе́йский; (*fig.*) ха́нжеский.

Pharisaism /ˈfærɪseɪˌɪz(ə)m/ *n.* фарисе́йство; (*fig.*) ханжество́.

Pharisee /ˈfærɪˌsiː/ *n.* фарисе́й; (*fig.*) ханжа́ (*c.g.*).

pharmaceutical /ˌfɑːməˈsjuːtɪk(ə)l/ *adj.* фармацевти́ческий; **~ chemist** фармаце́вт, апте́карь (*m.*).

pharmaceuticals /ˌfɑːməˈsjuːtɪk(ə)lz/ *n.* медикаме́нты (*m. pl.*).

pharmaceutics /ˌfɑːməˈsjuːtɪks/ *n.* (*pharmaceutical industry*) фармаци́я; (*dispensing*) апте́чное де́ло.

pharmacist /ˈfɑːməsɪst/ *n.* фармаце́вт.

pharmacologist /ˌfɑːməˈkɒlədʒɪst/ *n.* фармако́лог.

pharmacology /ˌfɑːməˈkɒlədʒɪ/ *n.* фармаколо́гия.

pharmacopoeia /ˌfɑːməkəˈpiːə/ *n.* фармакопе́я.

pharmacy /ˈfɑːməsɪ/ *n.* (*dispensing*) апте́чное де́ло, о́тпуск лека́рственных средств; (*dispensary*) апте́ка.

pharyng(e)al /ˌfærɪŋˈdʒiːəl/ *adj.* гло́точный.

pharynges /fəˈrɪndʒiːz/ *pl. of* **⇒pharynx**

pharyngitis /ˌfærɪŋˈdʒaɪtɪs/ *n.* фаринги́т.

pharynx /ˈfærɪŋks/ *n.* (*pl.* **pharynges**) зев; гло́тка.

phase /feɪz/ *n.* фа́за; (*stage*) ста́дия; **be in (out of) ~ with** (не) совпада́ть с + *i.*

● *v.t.*: **a ~d withdrawal** поэта́пный вы́вод; **~ out** (*weapons*) поэта́пно сн|има́ть, -ять с вооруже́ния; (*bases*) поэта́пно св|ёртывать, -ерну́ть; ликвиди́ровать (*impf., pf.*).

Ph.D. (*abbr. of* ***Doctor of Philosophy***) ≈ сте́пень кандида́та нау́к.

pheasant /ˈfez(ə)nt/ *n.* фаза́н.

phenomena /fɪˈnɒmɪnə/ *pl. of* **⇒phenomenon**

phenomenal /fɪˈnɒmɪn(ə)l/ *adj.* (*perceptible*) ощуща́емый; (*extraordinary, prodigious*) феномена́льный.

phenomenon /fɪˈnɒmɪnən/ *n.* (*pl.* **phenomena**) (*object of perception*) фено́мен, явле́ние; (*remarkable person or thing*) фено́мен, чу́до.

phew /fjuː/ *int.* (*expr. astonishment*) ну и ну!; **~, what a crowd!** ну и толпа́!; (*discomfort*): **~, isn't it hot!** уф, ну и жара́!; (*weariness*): **~, what a day it's been!** уф, ну и денёк вы́дался!; (*disgust*): **~, that meat's bad!** фу, э́то мя́со проту́хло!; (*relief*): **~, that was a near one!** ф-фу/уф, пронесло́! (*coll.*).

phial /ˈfaɪəl/ *n.* пузырёк.

philander /fɪˈlændə(r)/ *v.i.* флиртова́ть (*impf.*).

philanderer /fɪˈlændərə(r)/ *n.* волоки́та (*c.g.*).

philanthropic /ˌfɪlənˈθrɒpɪk/ *adj.* филантропи́ческий.

philanthropist /fɪˈlænθrəpɪst/ *n.* филантро́п (*fem.* -ка).

philanthropy /fɪˈlænθrəpɪ/ *n.* филантро́пия.

philatelic /ˌfɪləˈtelɪk/ *adj.* филателисти́ческий.

philatelist /fɪˈlætəlɪst/ *n.* филатели́ст (*fem.* -ка).

philately /fɪˈlætəlɪ/ *n.* филатели́я.

philharmonic /ˌfɪlhɑːˈmɒnɪk/ *n.* (**~** *society*) филармо́ния.

● *adj.* филармони́ческий.

philippic /fɪˈlɪpɪk/ *n.* (*fig.*) обличи́тельная речь, фили́ппика.

Philippine /ˈfɪlɪˌpiːn/ *adj.* филиппи́нский; **the ~s** (*islands*) Филиппи́н|ы (*pl., g.* —).

Philistine /ˈfɪlɪˌstaɪn/ *n.* (*bibl.*) филисти́млянин; (*fig.*) фили́стер, обыва́тель (*m.*).

● *adj.* обыва́тельский.

Philistinism /ˈfɪlɪstɪˌnɪz(ə)m/ *n.* фили́стерство.

Phillips /ˈfɪlɪps/ *n.* (*propr.*): **~ screwdriver** крестова́я отвёртка.

philological /ˌfɪləˈlɒdʒɪk(ə)l/ *adj.* языкове́дческий; филологи́ческий.

philologist /fɪˈlɒlədʒɪst/ *n.* языкове́д; фило́лог.

philology /fɪˈlɒlədʒɪ/ *n.* (*language*) языкове́дение; (*language and literature*) филоло́гия.

philosopher /fɪˈlɒsəfə(r)/ *n.* фило́соф.

philosophic(al) /ˌfɪləˈsɒfɪk(ə)l/ *adj.* филосо́фский.

philosophize /fɪˈlɒsəˌfaɪz/ *v.i.* филосо́фствовать (*impf.*).

philosophy /fɪˈlɒsəfɪ/ *n.* филосо́фия.

philtre /ˈfɪltə(r)/ (*US* **philter**) *n.* любо́вный напи́ток.

phlegm /flem/ *n.* (*secretion*) мокро́та; (*fig.*) флегмати́чность.

phlegmatic /flegˈmætɪk/ *adj.* флегмати́чный.

phlox /flɒks/ *n.* флокс.

phobia /ˈfəʊbɪə/ *n.* фо́бия, страх.

Phoenician /fəˈnɪʃ(ə)n/, /fəˈniː-/ *adj.* финики́йский.

phoenix /ˈfiːnɪks/ *n.* фе́никс.

phone /fəʊn/ (*see also* **⇒telephone**) *n.* телефо́н; (*attr.*) телефо́нный.

● *v.t. & i.* звони́ть, по- (*кому*).

● *with advs.*: **~ back** *v.t. & i.* сде́лать (*pf.*) отве́тный телефо́нный звоно́к; перезвони́ть (*pf.*); **~ up** *v.t. & i.* звони́ть, по- (*кому*).

● *cpds.* **~card** *n.* телефо́нная ка́рточка; **~-in** *n.* програ́мма «Звони́те — отвеча́ем».

phoneme /ˈfəʊniːm/ *n.* фоне́ма.

phonetic /fəˈnetɪk/ *adj.* фонети́ческий.

phonetician /ˌfəʊnɪˈtɪʃ(ə)n/, **phoneticist** /fəˈnetɪsɪst/ *n.* фонети́ст.

phonetics /fəˈnetɪks/ *n.* фоне́тика.

phon(e)y /ˈfəʊnɪ/ (*sl.*) *n.* (*pl.* **phoneys** *or* **phonies**) (*person*) шарлата́н, обма́нщик; (*thing*) подде́лка, фальши́вка, ли́па (*coll.*).

● *adj.* (**phonier, phoniest**) подде́льный, фальши́вый, ли́повый.

phonograph /ˈfəʊnəˌgrɑːf/ *n.* (*US, gramophone*) граммофо́н, патефо́н.

phonological /ˌfəʊnəˈlɒdʒɪk(ə)l/, /ˌfɒn-/ *adj.* фонологи́ческий.

phonologist /fəˈnɒlədʒɪst/ *n.* фоно́лог.

phonology /fəˈnɒlədʒɪ/ *n.* фоноло́гия.

phony /ˈfəʊnɪ/ = **phon(e)y**

phosgene /ˈfɒzdʒiːn/ *n.* фосге́н.

phosphate /ˈfɒsfeɪt/ *n.* фосфа́т.

phosphorescence /ˌfɒsfəˈres(ə)ns/ *n.* фосфоресце́нция.

phosphorescent /ˌfɒsfəˈres(ə)nt/ *adj.* фосфоресци́рующий.

phosphoric /ˌfɒsˈfɒrɪk/ *adj.* фосфори́ческий.

phosphorous /ˈfɒsfərəs/ *adj.* фо́сфористый.

phosphorus /ˈfɒsfərəs/ *n.* фо́сфор.

photo /ˈfəʊtəʊ/ *n.* (*pl.* **photos**) (*coll.*) фо́то (*indecl.*), сни́мок; **~ call** (*Br.*), **~ opportunity** сеа́нс фотосъёмки (*для прессы*).

● *cpds.* **~copier** *n.* фотокопирова́льный аппара́т; **~-copy** *n.* фотоко́пия, ксероко́пия; *v.t.* сн|има́ть, -ять фотоко́пию (c) + *g.*; **~-finish** *n.* фотофи́ниш; **~fit** *n.* (*Br.*) фотокомпозицио́нный портре́т.

photoelectric /ˌfəʊtəʊɪˈlektrɪk/ *adj.* фотоэлектри́ческий.

photogenic /ˌfəʊtəʊˈdʒenɪk/, /-ˈdʒiːnɪk/ *adj.* (*photographing well*) фотогени́чный.

photograph /ˈfəʊtəˌgrɑːf/ *n.* фотогра́фия.

● *v.t.* фотографи́ровать, с-.

● *v.i.*: **she ~s well** она́ хорошо́ выхо́дит на фотогра́фиях.

photographer /fəˈtɒgrəfə(r)/ *n.* фото́граф.

photographic /ˌfəʊtəˈgræfɪk/ *adj.* фотографи́ческий.

photography /fəˈtɒgrəfɪ/ *n.* фотогра́фия, фотосъёмка.

photogravure /ˌfəʊtəʊgrəˈvjʊə(r)/ *n.* фотогравю́ра.

photojournalism /ˌfəʊtəʊˈdʒɜːnəˌlɪz(ə)m/ *n.* фотожурнали́зм.

photojournalist /ˌfəʊtəʊˈdʒɜːnəlɪst/ *n.* фотожурнали́ст (*fem.* -ка).

photostat /ˈfəʊtəʊˌstæt/ *n.* (*propr.*) фотоко́пия.

● *v.t.* (**photostatted, photostatting**) сн|има́ть, -ять фотоко́пию (c) + *g.*

photosynthesis /ˌfəʊtəʊˈsɪnθɪsɪs/ *n.* фотоси́нтез.

phototypesetter /ˌfəʊtəʊˈtaɪpˌsetə(r)/ *n.* (*phototypesetting machine*) фотонабо́рный аппара́т.

phrase /freɪz/ *n.* (*group of words or mus. notes*) фра́за; (*expression*) оборо́т, словосочета́ние; **empty ~s** пусты́е слова́.

● *v.t.* **1** (*express in words*) формули́ровать, с-. **2** (*mus.*) фрази́ровать (*impf.*).

● *cpd.* **~-book** *n.* разгово́рник.

phraseological /ˌfreɪzɪəˈlɒdʒɪk(ə)l/ *adj.* фразеологи́ческий.

phraseology /ˌfreɪzɪˈɒlədʒɪ/ *n.* фразеоло́гия.

phrenetic /frɪˈnetɪk/ *adj.* исступлённый.

phrenological /ˌfrɪnəˈlɒdʒɪk(ə)l/ *adj.* френологи́ческий.

phrenologist /frɪˈnɒlədʒɪst/ *n.* френо́лог.

phrenology /frɪˈnɒlədʒɪ/ *n.* френоло́гия.

phylum /ˈfaɪləm/ *n.* (*pl.* **phyla**) (*biol.*) фи́лум, тип.

physical /ˈfɪzɪk(ə)l/ *adj.* физи́ческий; **~ properties** физи́ческие сво́йства; **the ~ universe** материа́льный мир; **it is a ~ impossibility** э́то физи́чески невозмо́жно; (*relating to the body*): **~ education/training** физи́ческое воспита́ние/трениро́вка; физкульту́ра; **~ exercises** гимнасти́ческие упражне́ния; заря́дка; **~ly handicapped** физи́чески неполноце́нный; **have you had your ~ (examination)?** вы прошли́ медици́нский осмо́тр?

physician /fɪˈzɪʃ(ə)n/ *n.* врач.

physicist /ˈfɪzɪsɪst/ *n.* фи́зик.

physics /ˈfɪzɪks/ *n.* фи́зика.

physiognomy /ˌfɪzɪˈɒnəmɪ/ *n.* физионо́мия; (*of country etc.*) о́блик.

physiological /ˌfɪzɪəˈlɒdʒɪk(ə)l/ *adj.* физиологи́ческий.

physiologist /ˌfɪzɪˈɒlədʒɪst/ *n.* физио́лог.

physiology /ˌfɪzɪˈɒlədʒɪ/ *n.* физиоло́гия.

physiotherapist /ˌfɪzɪəʊˈθerəpɪst/ *n.* физиотерапе́вт.

physiotherapy /ˌfɪzɪəʊˈθerəpɪ/ *n.* физиотерапи́я.

physique /fɪˈziːk/ *n.* телосложе́ние.

pi /paɪ/ *n.* (*geom.*) число́ «пи».

pianissi|mo /ˌpɪəˈnɪsɪˌməʊ/ *n., adj. & adv.* (*pl.* **~mos** *or* **~mi** /-mɪ/) пиани́ссимо (*indecl.*).

pianist /ˈpɪənɪst/ *n.* пиани́ст (*fem.* -ка).

piano¹ /pɪˈænəʊ/ *n.* (*pl.* **pianos**) фортепья́но (*indecl.*), роя́ль (*m.*); (*upright*) пиани́но (*indecl.*); **~ accordion** аккордео́н; **~ lessons** уро́ки игры́ на фортепья́но.

● *cpds.* **~forte** *n.* фортепья́но (*indecl.*); **~-player** *n.* пиани́ст (*fem.* -ка); (*instrument*) пиано́ла; **~-stool** *n.* табуре́т для пиани́ста; **~-tuner** *n.* настро́йщик (пиани́но).

piano² /pɪˈænəʊ/ *adj. & adv.* (*mus.*) пиа́но; **a ~ passage** пасса́ж пиа́но.

pianola /pɪəˈnəʊlə/ *n.* пиано́ла.

piastre /pɪˈæstə(r)/ *n.* пиа́стр.

piazza /pɪˈætsə/ *n.* (*square*) пло́щадь; (*market place*) ры́ночная пло́щадь; (*in names*) пиа́цца; (*US, verandah*) вера́нда.

picador /ˈpɪkəˌdɔː(r)/ *n.* пикадо́р.

picaresque /ˌpɪkəˈresk/ *adj.* плутовско́й.

piccalilli /ˌpɪkəˈlɪlɪ/ *n.* марино́ванные о́вощ|и (*pl.*, *g.* -е́й).

piccolo /ˈpɪkəˌləʊ/ *n.* (*pl.* **~s**) пи́кколо (*indecl.*).

pick /pɪk/ *n.* **1** (**~***axe*) кирка́, кайло́. **2** (*probing instrument, e.g. dentist's*) про́бник. **3** (*selection*) отбо́р, вы́бор; **take your ~!** выбира́йте!; **I had first ~** мне пе́рвому доста́лось; **the ~ of the bunch** са́мый лу́чший; (*of many objects*) отбо́рный.

● *v.t.* **1** (*pluck*) рвать, со-; (*gather*) соб|ира́ть, -ра́ть; **they were ~ing apples** они́ собира́ли я́блоки; **don't ~ the flowers!** не рви́те цветы́!; **she ~ed the thread from her dress** она́ сняла́ ни́тку с пла́тья. **2** (*extract contents of*): **he is ~ing your brains** он испо́льзует ва́ши иде́и/позна́ния; **his pocket was ~ed in the crowd** в толпе́ ему́ зале́зли в карма́н. **3** (*remove flesh from*) обгл|а́дывать, -ода́ть; **the birds ~ed the bones clean** пти́цы склева́ли с косте́й всё мя́со; **I have a bone to ~ with you** (*fig.*) у меня́ к вам кру́пный разгово́р. **4** (*probe*) ковыря́ть (*impf.*); **it's not nice to ~ one's teeth** ковыря́ть (*impf.*) в зуба́х — некраси́во; **stop ~ing your nose!** не ковыря́й в носу́!; (*probe to open*) откр|ыва́ть, -ы́ть отмы́чкой; **the lock has been ~ed** замо́к взло́ман. **5** (*pull apart*) (*fig.*): **he ~ed my argument to pieces** он разнёс мою́ аргумента́цию в пух и прах. **6** (*make by ~ing*): **he ~ed a hole in the cloth** он продыря́вил ткань; **he ~s holes in everything I say** он придира́ется ко вся́кому моему́ сло́ву. **7** (*select*) выбира́ть, вы́брать; **he ~ed his words carefully** он тща́тельно подбира́л слова́; **she ~ed her way through the mud** она́ осторо́жно ступа́ла по гря́зи; **the captains ~ed sides** капита́ны подобра́ли соста́в кома́нд; **can you ~ the winner?** вы мо́жете зара́нее угада́ть победи́теля?; **he's trying to ~ a quarrel** он и́щет по́вода для ссо́ры.

● *v.i.* (*select*) выбира́ть, вы́брать; **~ and choose** быть разбо́рчивым.

● *with preps.*: **~ at** ковыря́ть, по-; **the child ~ed at** (*trifled with*) **his food** ребёнок поковыря́л еду́ ви́лкой; **~ on** (*find fault with*) прид|ира́ться, -ра́ться к + *d.*; (*single out*) выбира́ть, вы́брать.

● *with advs.*: **~ off** *v.t.* (*pluck*) срыва́ть, сорва́ть; (*shoot by deliberate aim*) подстр|е́ливать, -ели́ть; **~ out** *v.t.* (*select*): **he ~ed out the best for himself** са́мое лу́чшее он отобра́л для себя́; (*distinguish*): **I ~ed him out in the crowd** я узна́л его́ в толпе́; **the pattern was ~ed out in red** узо́р выделя́лся кра́сным цве́том; (*play note by note*): **she can ~ out tunes by ear** она́ подбира́ет мело́дии по слу́ху; **~ over** *v.t.* (*examine*) переб|ира́ть, -ра́ть; **~ up** *v.t.* (*lift*) подн|има́ть, -я́ть; **he ~ed himself up off the ground** он подня́лся с земли́; **he ~ed up his bag** он взял свою́ су́мку; (*acquire, gain*) приобре|та́ть, -сти́; **he has ~ed up an American accent** он приобрёл америка́нский акце́нт; **he went there to ~ up information** он пошёл туда́ раздобы́ть све́дения; **I ~ed up a bargain at the sale** я сде́лал вы́годную поку́пку на распрода́же; **he ~ed her up on the street corner** он подцепи́л (*coll.*) её на у́лице; **where can I have ~ed up this germ?** где я мог подцепи́ть э́ту инфе́кцию? (*coll.*); **the car began to ~ up speed** маши́на начала́ набира́ть ско́рость; **can you ~ up Moscow on your radio?** вы мо́жете пойма́ть Москву́ на своём приёмнике?; (*provide transport for*) заб|ира́ть, -ра́ть; под|бира́ть, -обра́ть; **the train stops to ~ up passengers** по́езд остана́вливается, что́бы забра́ть пассажи́ров; **I never ~ up hitch-hikers** я никогда́ не беру́ «голосу́ющих» на доро́гах; (*collect*): **I ~ her up from school** я забира́ю её из шко́лы; (*apprehend*) заде́рж|ивать, -а́ть; **the culprit was ~ed up by the police** престу́пник был заде́ржан поли́цией; (*regain*) приобре|та́ть, -сти́; **he soon ~ed up spirits** он вско́рс повесели́л; (*resume*) возобнов|ля́ть, -и́ть; **he ~ed up the thread where he had left off** он возобнови́л бесе́ду с того́ ме́ста, где останови́лся; *v.i.* (*recover health*) опр|авля́ться, -а́виться; попр|авля́ться, -а́виться; **he soon ~ed up after his illness** он бы́стро опра́вился по́сле боле́зни; (*improve*) ул|учша́ться, -у́чшиться; **trade is ~ing up** торго́вля оживля́ется; (*gain speed*): **after a slow start the engine ~ed up** по́сле ме́дленного ста́рта мото́р зарабо́тал как сле́дует.

● *cpds.* **~axe** (*US also* **~ax**) *n.* кирка́; **~-me-up** *n.* тонизи́рующее сре́дство; **~pocket** *n.* карма́нник, карма́нный вор; **~-up** *n.* (*microphone*) да́тчик; (*of record-player*) ада́птер; (*van*) пика́п; (*casual acquaintance*) случа́йное знако́мство; (*acceleration*) ускоре́ние.

pick-a-back /ˈpɪkəˌbæk/, **piggy-back** /ˈpɪgɪˌbæk/ *adv.* на спине́; на зако́рках.

picker /ˈpɪkə(r)/ *n.* (*of fruit etc.*) сбо́рщи|к (*fem.* -ца).

picket /ˈpɪkɪt/ *n.* **1** (*pointed stake*) кол; **~ fence** частоко́л. **2** (*also* **picquet**: *small body of troops*) заста́ва, карау́л. **3** (*of strikers*) пике́т; (*individual*) пике́тчик.

● *v.t.* (**picketed, picketing**) **1** (*secure with stakes*) обн|оси́ть, -ести́ частоко́лом; (*tether*): **the horse was ~ed nearby** ло́шадь была́ привя́зана неподалёку. **2** (*guard*) охраня́ть (*impf.*); **the camp was securely ~ed** ла́герь надёжно охраня́лся. **3** (*deploy as guards*) выставля́ть, вы́ставить; **he ~ed his men round the house** он вы́ставил свои́х люде́й охраня́ть дом. **4** (*mount guards on*): **the enemy has ~ed the bridge** враг вы́ставил карау́л у моста́. **5** (*deny entry to*) пикети́ровать (*impf.*); **the workers are ~ing the factory** рабо́чие пикети́руют фа́брику.

picking /ˈpɪkɪŋ/ *n.* **1** (*gathering*) сбор. **2** (*pl., remains*) оста́тки (*m. pl.*); объе́дки (*m. pl.*). **3** (*pl., profits*) нажи́ва.

pickle /ˈpɪk(ə)l/ *n.* **1** (*preservative*) (*in vinegar*) марина́д; (*in salt*) рассо́л. **2** (*usu. pl., preserved vegetables*) соле́нья

P

(*pl.*). **3** (*coll., predicament*) напа́сть; (*mess*) заваруха.

● *v.t.* **1** мариновать, за-; **~d herrings** маринованная селёдка. **2**: **he came home ~d** (*coll.*) он пришёл домой под градусом/газом (*coll.*).

picky /ˈpɪkɪ/ *adj.* (**pickier, pickiest**) (*US coll.*) разборчивый, придирчивый.

picnic /ˈpɪknɪk/ *n.* пикник; (*fig., coll., something easily done*) пара пустяков, детская игра; **it was no ~** это было нелёгкое дело.

● *v.i.* (**picnicked, picnicking**) устр|аивать, -оить пикник.

● *cpd.* **~-basket** *n.* корзинка для пикника.

picnicker /ˈpɪknɪkə(r)/ *n.* участни|к (*fem.* -ца) пикника.

picquet /ˈpɪkɪt/ = **picket** *n.* 2

Pict /pɪkt/ *n.* пикт.

pictogram /ˈpɪktə,græm/ *n.* пиктограмма.

pictograph /ˈpɪktə,grɑːf/ = **pictogram**

pictorial /pɪkˈtɔːrɪəl/ *n.* иллюстрированное издание.

● *adj.* изобразительный; (*illustrated*) иллюстрированный.

picture /ˈpɪktʃə(r)/ *n.* **1** (*depiction; pictorial composition*) картина; **~s** (*in general*) живопись; (*illustration*) изображение; (*portrait*) портрет; (*fig.*): **she is the very ~ of her mother** она вылитая мать/копия матери; (*drawing*) рисунок; (*image on TV screen*) картин(к)а.
2 (*beautiful object*) картинка.
3 (*embodiment*) олицетворение; **he looks the ~ of health** он пышет здоровьем.
4 (*coll., of information*): **he will soon put you in the ~** он вскоре введёт вас в курс (дела); **don't fail to keep me in the ~** не забудьте держать меня в курсе дела.
5 (*film*) (кино)фильм, картина; (*pl., cinema show, cinema*) кино (*indecl.*); **what's on at the ~s?** что идёт в кино?

● *v.t.* (*depict*) опис|ывать, -ать; изобра|жать, -зить; **~ to yourself** вообразите/представьте себе.

● *cpds.* **~-book** *n.* книжка с картинками; **~-card** *n.* (*court card*) фигурная карта; **~-gallery** *n.* картинная галерея; **~-house, ~-palace** (*Br.*), **~-theater** (*US*) *nn.* кинотеатр.

picturesque /,pɪktʃəˈresk/ *adj.* живописный.

piddle /ˈpɪd(ə)l/ *v.i.* (*coll.*) мочиться, по-.

piddling /ˈpɪdlɪŋ/ *adj.* (*coll., trifling*) пустячный.

pidgin /ˈpɪdʒɪn/, **pigeon** /ˈpɪdʒɪn/, /-dʒ(ə)n/ *n.*: **that's not my ~** это не моя забота; (*language*) пиджин; **~ English** английский пиджин.

pie /paɪ/ *n.* (*pastry with filling*) пирог; (*small one*) пирожок; (*fig.*): **~ in the sky** ≈ журавль в небе; (*misleading promise*) пустые посулы; **it's as easy as ~** это плёвое дело (*coll.*); **he has a finger in the ~** он замешан в этом деле.

● *cpds.* **~-crust** *n.* корочка (пирога); **~-eyed** *adj.* (*sl.*) косой, пьяный вдрызг.

piebald /ˈpaɪbɔːld/ *n.* пегая лошадь.

● *adj.* пегий.

piece /piːs/ *n.* **1** (*portion, fragment, bit*) кусок; **a ~ of bread** кусок хлеба; **a ~ of cake** (*lit.*) кусок торта; (*coll., something easily accomplished*) легче лёгкого, пара пустяков; **a ~ of paper** листок бумаги, бумажка; **(all) of a ~ with** в соответствии с + *i.*; **all in one ~** неразобранный; (*fig., unharmed*) целый и невредимый; **the record was smashed to ~s** пластинка разбилась вдребезги; **he took the watch to ~s** он разобрал часы; **pull, tear to ~s** раз|рывать, -орвать на части/куски; **he was left to pick up the ~s** (*fig.*) его оставили расхлёбывать кашу (*coll.*); **go to ~s** ломаться, с-; **he went to ~s under interrogation** он сломался на допросе; **he went to ~s after his wife's death** он совсем сломался после смерти жены.
2 (*small area*) участок; **a ~ (*plot*) of land** участок земли.
3 (*example, instance*) образец; **a ~ of news** новость; **here's a ~ of luck!** вот это удача!; **may I give you a ~ of advice?** можно дать вам один совет?; **I gave him a ~ of my mind** я его отчитал.
4 (*single composition*) произведение; **a ~ of music** пьеса.
5 (*object of art or craft*) произведение (искусства); вещь, вещица; **there were some nice ~s at the sale** на распродаже было несколько хороших вещей; **~ of furniture** предмет мебели; **three-~ suite** диван с двумя креслами; **museum ~** (*lit.*) музейная вещь; (*fig.*) музейная редкость; **a beautiful ~ of work** великолепная работа; **nasty ~ of work** (*coll.*) противный тип.
6 (*one of a set*): **he set out the ~s on the chessboard** он расставил фигуры на шахматной доске; **a 52-~ dinner service** обеденный сервиз из пятидесяти двух предметов.
7 (*coin*) монета; **a ten-cent ~** монета в десять центов.
8 (*instrument*) инструмент; **a six-~band** секстет.

● *with adv.*: **~ together** *v.t.* соедин|ять, -ить; (*fig.*) связ|ывать, -ать.

● *cpds.* **~meal** *adj.* частичный; *adv.* по частям; **~-rates** *n. pl.* сдельная оплата; **~-work** *n.* сдельная работа, сдельщина (*coll.*); **~-worker** *n.* сдельщи|к (*fem.* -ца).

pièce de résistance /,pjes də reɪˈziːstɑ̃s/ *n.* (*pl.* ***pièces de résistance*** *pronunc. same*) (*cul.*) главное блюдо; (*fig.*) достопримечательность.

pied /paɪd/ *adj.* пёстрый; **P~ Piper** дудочник в пёстром костюме, ≈ крысолов.

pied-à-terre /,pjeɪdɑːˈteə(r)/ *n.* (*pl.* ***pieds-à-terre*** *pronunc. same*) пристанище.

pier /pɪə(r)/ *n.* **1** (*structure projecting into sea*) пирс; (*breakwater*) волнолом; (*landing stage*) мол. **2** (*bridge support*) бык, (береговой) устой. **3** (*masonry between windows*) простенок.

● *cpd.* **~-glass** *n.* трюмо (*indecl.*).

pierc|e /pɪəs/ *v.t.* прок|алывать, -олоть; **she had her ears ~ed** ей прокололи уши; **~ing cold** пронизывающий холод; **a ~ing cry** пронзительный крик; **a ~ing gaze** проницательный взгляд.

● *v.i.* прон|икать, -икнуть; проб|иваться, -иться; **they ~ed through the enemy lines** они прорвались сквозь линии укреплений врага.

pietà /,pieˈtɑː/ *n.* пиета, плач Богоматери.

piety /ˈpaɪɪtɪ/ *n.* набожность.

piffle /ˈpɪf(ə)l/ *n.* (*coll.*) вздор, чепуха.

piffling /ˈpɪflɪŋ/ *adj.* (*coll., trifling*) ничтожный, пустячный.

pig /pɪg/ *n.* **1** (*animal*) свинья; **~s might fly** (*Br.*) ≈ бывает, что коровы летают; **he bought a ~ in a poke** он купил кота в мешке; (*greedy or disagreeable person*): **he made a ~ of himself** он нажрался, как свинья.
2 (*mass of iron*) брусок.

● *cpds.* **~-farm** *n.* свиноферма; **~-headed** *adj.* упрямый, крепкоголовый; **~-iron** *n.* чушковый чугун; **~skin** *n.* свиная кожа; **~sty** *n.* (*lit., fig.*) свинарник; **~swill** *n.* помо|и (*pl., g.* -ев); **~tail** *n.* косичка.

pigeon[1] /ˈpɪdʒɪn/, /-dʒ(ə)n/ *n.* голубь (*m.*); **carrier, homing ~** почтовый голубь; **clay ~** глиняная летающая мишень.

● *cpds.* **~-breasted, ~-chested** *adjs.* с «куриной» грудью; **~hole** *n.* (*compartment*) отделение для бумаг; ящик для корреспонденции; (*fig.*) категория; *v.t.* (*categorize*) классифицировать (*impf., pf.*), накле́и|вать, -ть ярлык на + *a.*; (*put aside*) от|кладывать, -ложить; **~-toed** *adj.* косолапый.

pigeon[2] /ˈpɪdʒɪn/, /-dʒ(ə)n/ = **pidgin**

piggery /ˈpɪgərɪ/ *n.* (*sty*) свинарник; (*farm*) свиноферма.

piggy /ˈpɪgɪ/ *n.* (*piglet; greedy child*) поросёнок.

● *adj.* (**piggier, piggiest**) свиной, поросячий.

● *cpds.* **~-back** *adv.* = **pick-a-back; ~-bank** *n.* копилка.

piglet /ˈpɪglɪt/ *n.* поросёнок.

pigment /ˈpɪgmənt/ *n.* пигмент.

pigmentation /,pɪgmənˈteɪʃ(ə)n/ *n.* пигментация.

pigmented /ˈpɪgməntɪd/ *adj.* пигментированный.

pigmy /ˈpɪgmɪ/ = **pygmy**

pike /paɪk/ *n.* **1** (*pl.* **~s**) (*weapon*) копьё. **2** (*pl.* **~**) (*fish*) щука.

● *cpd.* **~staff** *n.*: **plain as a ~staff** ясный как день.

pila|ff /pɪˈlæf/, **-u** /pɪˈlaʊ/ *n.* пилав, плов.

pilaster /pɪˈlæstə(r)/ *n.* пилястр(а).

pilau /pɪ'laʊ/ = **pilaff**

pilchard /'pɪltʃəd/ *n.* пи́льчард, европе́йская сарди́на.

pile¹ /paɪl/ *n.* (*stake, post*) сва́я.

● *cpd.* **~-driver** *n.* копёр.

pile² /paɪl/ *n.* **1** (*heap*) ку́ча, гру́да; **funeral ~** погреба́льный костёр; (*coll., of money*): **he made his ~** он на́жил состоя́ние; (*coll., any large quantity*) ку́ча, ма́сса.
2 (*massive building*) строе́ние; грома́да.
3 (*elec.*) батаре́я.
4: **atomic ~** а́томный реа́ктор.

● *v.t.* **1** (*heap up*) сва́ливать, свали́ть в ку́чу; **he ~d coal on to the fire** он подбро́сил у́гля в ками́н.
2 (*load*) нав|а́ливать, -али́ть; заст|авля́ть, -а́вить; **the table was ~d high with dishes** стол был заста́влен вся́кими я́ствами.

● *with advs.*: **~ in** *v.i.* (*coll., crowd into a vehicle etc.*) наб|ива́ться, -и́ться; **~ on** *v.t.* нава́л|ивать, -и́ть; (*fig.*) преувели́чи|вать, -ть; **~ up** *v.t.* (*heap up objects*) сва́ливать, свали́ть; (*debts*) наде́лать (*pf.*); (*store up*) копи́ть, на-/с-; *v.i.* (*accumulate*) (*of objects*) нагромо|жда́ться, -зди́ться; (*of work, debts*) нак|а́пливаться, -опи́ться.

● *cpd.* **~-up** *n.* (*crash*) столкнове́ние не́скольких маши́н.

pile³ /paɪl/ *n.* (*down, soft hair*) шерсть, во́лос; (*nap on cloth, carpet etc.*) ворс.

pile⁴ /paɪl/ *n.* (*usu. pl., haemorrhoid*) геморро́й.

pilfer /'pɪlfə(r)/ *v.t. & i.* ворова́ть (*impf.*), таска́ть (*impf.*).

pilfer|age /'pɪlfərɪdʒ/, **-ing** /'pɪlfərɪŋ/ *nn.* ме́лкая кра́жа.

pilferer /'pɪlfərə(r)/ *n.* вори́шка (*c.g.*); (*from work place*) несу́н.

pilgrim /'pɪlgrɪm/ *n.* пилигри́м, пало́мник.

pilgrimage /'pɪlgrɪmɪdʒ/ *n.* пало́мничество; **they went on a ~ to Lourdes** они́ соверши́ли пало́мничество в Лурд.

pill /pɪl/ *n.* пилю́ля, табле́тка; **take ~s** прин|има́ть, -я́ть пилю́ли; (*fig.*): **a bitter ~** го́рькая пилю́ля; **contraceptive ~** противозача́точная табле́тка; **she is on the ~** она́ принима́ет противозача́точные табле́тки.

● *cpd.* **~box** *n.* (*receptacle*) коро́бочка для табле́ток; (*mil.*) долговре́менная огнева́я то́чка (*abbr.* дот); (*hat*) шля́пка без поле́й.

pillage /'pɪlɪdʒ/ *n.* мародёрство, грабёж.

● *v.i.* мародёрствовать (*impf.*); гра́бить (*impf.*).

● *v.t.* гра́бить, о-.

pillager /'pɪlɪdʒə(r)/ *n.* мародёр.

pillar /'pɪlə(r)/ *n.* (*column*) столб, коло́нна; (*support*) опо́ра; **he was driven from ~ to post** он мета́лся с ме́ста на ме́сто; (*fig.*) столп; **~s of society** столпы́ о́бщества.

● *cpd.* **~-box** *n.* (*Br.*) (стоя́чий) почто́вый я́щик.

pillion /'pɪljən/ *n.* (*on motor-cycle*) за́днее сиде́нье; **she rode ~** она́ е́хала на за́днем сиде́нье мотоци́кла.

pillock /'pɪlək/ *n.* (*Br. coll.*) идио́т (*fem.* -ка).

pillory /'pɪlərɪ/ *n.* позо́рный столб.

● *v.t.* (*fig.*) пригво|жда́ть, -зди́ть к позо́рному столбу́.

pillow /'pɪləʊ/ *n.* поду́шка.

● *v.t.*: **~ one's head** класть, положи́ть го́лову (на + *a.*); **he ~ed his head in his hands** он подпёр го́лову рука́ми.

● *cpds.* **~-case, ~-slip** *nn.* на́волочка.

pilot /'paɪlət/ *n.* **1** (*of vessel*) ло́цман; (*of aircraft*) лётчи|к (*fem.* -ца), пило́т; **~ officer** лейтена́нт авиа́ции. **2** (*attr., fig.*) про́бный, о́пытный; **~ scheme** экспериме́нт.

● *v.t.* (**piloted, piloting**) (*lit.*) пилоти́ровать (*impf.*); (*fig.*) напр|авля́ть, -а́вить.

● *cpds.* **~-boat** *n.* ло́цманское су́дно; **~-fish** *n.* ры́ба-ло́цман; **~-light** *n.* (*burner*) га́зовая горе́лка; (*indicator light*) контро́льная/сигна́льная ла́мпа.

pilotage /'paɪlətɪdʒ/ *n.* пилота́ж.

pim(i)ento /ˌpɪmɪ'entəʊ/, /pɪm'jentəʊ/ *n.* (*pl.* **~s**) (*sweet pepper*) пе́рец души́стый, пиме́нт.

pimp /pɪmp/ *n.* сутенёр.

● *v.i.* быть сутенёром.

pimpernel /'pɪmpəˌnel/ *n.* (*bot.*) о́чный цвет.

pimple /'pɪmp(ə)l/ *n.* прыщ, пры́щик.

pimply /'pɪmplɪ/ *adj.* прыща́вый.

PIN /pɪn/ *n.* (*abbr. of* ***personal identification number***) персона́льный код.

pin /pɪn/ *n.* **1** була́вка; (*for hair, hat*) шпи́лька; **for two ~s I'd knock you down** ещё немно́го, и я вас сту́кну; **you could have heard a ~ drop** мо́жно бы́ло услы́шать, как му́ха пролети́т; **~s and needles** (*tingling sensation*) колотьё по́сле до́лгого сиде́нья; **I've got ~s and needles in my leg** у меня́ нога́ затекла́.
2 (*securing peg*) прище́пка.
3 (*pl., coll., legs*) но́ги (*f. pl.*).

● *v.t.* (**pinned, pinning**) **1** (*fasten*) прик|а́лывать, -оло́ть; **she ~ned a rose to her dress** она́ приколо́ла ро́зу к пла́тью; (*fig.*): **~ accusation, blame on s.o.** сва́л|ивать, -и́ть вину́ на кого́-н.; **I ~ my faith on the captain** я возлага́ю все наде́жды на капита́на.
2 (*immobilize*) приж|има́ть, -а́ть; **the bandits ~ned him against the wall** банди́ты прижа́ли его́ к стене́; **he was ~ned beneath the vehicle** его́ придави́ло маши́ной; **his arms were ~ned behind him** ему́ связа́ли ру́ки за спино́й.

● *with advs.*: **~ down** *v.t.* (*lit.*) прик|а́лывать, -оло́ть; (*fig., commit to an action or opinion*) прип|ира́ть, -ере́ть к сте́нке; **~ on** *v.t.* прик|а́лывать, -оло́ть; **~ together** *v.t.* ск|а́лывать, -оло́ть; скреп|ля́ть, -и́ть; **~ up** *v.t.* прик|а́лывать, -оло́ть; ве́шать, пове́сить; **she ~ned up her hair** она́ заколо́ла во́лосы.

● *cpds.* **~ball** *n.* (*game, machine*) пинбо́л, кита́йский билья́рд; **~ball machine** билья́рд-автома́т; **~cushion** *n.* иго́льник; **~-money** *n.* де́ньги на ме́лкие расхо́ды; **~point** *n.* (*lit.*) остриё була́вки; *v.t.* (*fig.*) то́чно определ|я́ть, -и́ть; **~-prick** *n.* (*lit.*) була́вочный уко́л; (*fig.*) шпи́лька, ме́лкая приди́рка; **~-stripe** (*suit*) *n.* костю́м в то́нкую све́тлую поло́ску; **~-up** *n.* фотогра́фия красо́тки (в журна́ле); **~-up girl** красо́тка.

pinafore /'pɪnəˌfɔ:(r)/ *n.* (*Br., apron*) фа́ртук, пере́дник; **~ dress** пла́тье-сарафа́н.

pince-nez /pæs'neɪ/ *n.* (*pl.* **~**) пенсне́ (*indecl.*).

pincer /'pɪnsə(r)/ *n.* **1** (*of crustacean*) клешня́. **2** (*pl.*) щипц|ы́ (*pl., g.* -о́в); клещ|и́ (*pl., g.* -е́й); **~ movement** (*mil.*) захва́т в кле́щи.

pinch /pɪntʃ/ *n.* **1** (*nip*) щипо́к; **he gave her a ~ on the cheek** он ущипну́л её за щёку; (*fig., constraint*) тру́дность; **at a ~; if it comes to the ~** в кра́йнем слу́чае; е́сли придётся ту́го/прижмёт.
2 (*small amount*) щепо́тка; **a ~ of snuff** поню́шка табаку́; **you must take that with a ~ of salt** (*fig.*) вы должны́ отнести́сь к э́тому крити́чески.

● *v.t.* **1** (*nip, squeeze*) (*objects*) прищем|ля́ть, -и́ть; (*person*) щипа́ть, ущипну́ть; **his fingers were ~ed in the door** он прищеми́л па́льцы две́рью; (*fig.*): **his face was ~ed with cold** моро́з щипа́л ему́ лицо́.
2 (*Br., steal*) стяну́ть (*pf.*), стащи́ть (*pf.*) (*coll.*).
3 (*arrest, charge*) заца́пать (*pf.*) (*sl.*).

● *v.i.* (*be niggardly*) скупи́ться, по-; **she had to ~ and scrape to make ends meet** ей приходи́лось эконо́мить на всём, что́бы своди́ть концы́ с конца́ми.

pine¹ /paɪn/ *n.* сосна́.

● *cpds.* **~apple** *n.* анана́с; **~apple juice** анана́совый сок; **~-cone** *n.* сосно́вая ши́шка; **~-needle** *n.* хвоя́.

pin|e² /paɪn/ *v.i.* **1** (*languish, waste*) ча́хнуть, за-; томи́ться (*impf.*); **she is ~ing away** она́ ча́хнет. **2** (*long*): **~e for** жа́ждать (*impf.*) + *g.*; **I ~e for sea air** так хо́чется подыша́ть морски́м во́здухом.

pineal /'pɪnɪəl/, /'paɪ-/ *adj.* шишкови́дный.

ping /pɪŋ/ *n.* звон.

● *v.i.* звони́ть (*impf.*).

ping-pong /'pɪŋpɒŋ/ *n.* пинг-по́нг.

pinion¹ /'pɪnjən/ *n.* (*end of wing*) оконе́чность пти́чьего крыла́; (*poet., wing*) крыло́.

● *v.t.* (*immobilize by cutting wing*) подр|еза́ть, -е́зать кры́лья + *g.*; (*bind arms of*) свя́з|ывать, -а́ть ру́ки + *d.*

pinion² /'pɪnjən/ *n.* (*cog-wheel*) шестерня́.

pink¹ /pɪŋk/ *n.* (*flower*) гвозди́ка; (*colour*) ро́зовый цвет; (*perfection*): **he is in the ~ (of health)** он пы́шет здоро́вьем.

● *adj.* (*of colour*) ро́зовый; (*pol.*) ле́вый.

pink² /pɪŋk/ *v.t.* (*prick with sword*)

прок|áлывать, -олóть; (*decorate by perforation*) укр|аш**á**ть, -áсить ды́рочками; **~ing shears** фестóнные нóжницы.

pink³ /pɪŋk/ *v.i.* (*Br., of engine*) стреля́ть (*impf.*).

pinnacle /ˈpɪnək(ə)l/ *n.* (*of building*) шпиц; (*fig.*) верши́на.

pinny /ˈpɪnɪ/ *n.* (*coll.*) пéредничек.

pint /paɪnt/ *n.* пи́нта; **~ jug** кувши́н ёмкостью в пи́нту.

● *cpd.* **~-sized** *adj.* (*fig.*) мáленький, крóхотный.

pioneer /ˌpaɪəˈnɪə(r)/ *n.* (*one who is first in the field*) пионéр, новáтор, первооткрывáтель (*m.*); (*mil.*) сапёр; **P~ Corps** сапёрно-строи́тельные чáсти.

● *v.t. & i.* быть пионéром (*в чём*); про|клáдывать, -ложи́ть путь (*в чём*); **~ing** *adj.* новáторский; первопрохóдческий.

pious /ˈpaɪəs/ *adj.* нáбожный.

pip /pɪp/ *n.* **1** (*Br., fruit seed*) сéмечко; зёрнышко. **2** (*Br., sound*) гудóк, сигнáл. **3** (*spot on playing-card etc.*) очкó. **4** (*Br. coll., star on officer's uniform*) звёздочка.

● *v.t.* (**pipped, pipping**) (*Br. sl., defeat*) бить, по-; **he was ~ped at the post** егó побили в послéднюю минýту.

● *cpd.* **~-squeak** *n.* (*coll.*) ничтóжество.

pipe /paɪp/ *n.* **1** (*conduit*) трубá; (*small, thin one*) трýбка.
2 (*mus. instrument*) свирéль; дýдка; (*bagpipe*) волы́нка.
3 (*shrill voice or sound*) вопль (*m.*); писк; (*note of bird*) свист; пéние.
4 (*for smoking*) трýбка; **your ~ has gone out** вáша трýбка потýхла; **put that in your ~ and smoke it!** (*coll.*) намотáйте э́то себé на ус!
5 (*cask of wine*) бóчка (вмести́мостью в 477 ли́тров).

● *v.t.* **1** (*also v.i.*) (*play on ~*) игрáть, сыгрáть на свирéли/дýдке/волы́нке.
2 (*lead, summon by piping*) свистéть (*impf.*), свистáть (*impf.*); **he ~d all hands on deck** он свистáл всех навéрх.
3 (*utter in shrill voice*) визжáть, про-.
4 (*decorate cake*) покр|ывáть, -ы́ть крéмом; (*ornament dress*) отдéл|ывать, -ать кáнтом.
5 (*convey by ~s*) пус|кáть, -ти́ть по трýбам; **a ~d water supply** водопровóд.
6: **~d music** музыкáльная трансля́ция (в общéственном мéсте).

● *with advs.*: **~ down** *v.i.* (*be quiet*) замолчáть (*pf.*); **~ up** (*coll.*) (*start to speak*) под|авáть, -áть гóлос; (*start to sing*) запéть (*pf.*); (*start to play*) заигрáть (*pf.*).

● *cpds.* **~-clay** *n.* бéлая гли́на; трýбочная гли́на; *v.t.* отб|éливать, -ели́ть трýбочной гли́ной; **~-cleaner** *n.* ёршик для чи́стки трýбки; **~-dream** *n.* несбы́точная мечтá; **~line** *n.* трубопровóд; (*for oil*) нефтепровóд; (*fig.*) комуникациóнная ли́ния; **in the ~line** (*fig.*) на подхóде (*coll.*); **~-rack** *n.* подстáвка для трýбок; **~-tobacco** *n.* трýбочный табáк.

piper /ˈpaɪpə(r)/ *n.* (*bag ~*) волы́нщи|к (*fem.* -ца); **he who pays the ~ calls the tune** кто плáтит, тот и распоряжáется.

pipette /pɪˈpet/ *n.* пипéтка.

piping /ˈpaɪpɪŋ/ *n.* (*system of pipes*) трубопровóд; (*ornamental cord*) кант; (*cake decoration*) отдéлка, узóр.

● *adj.* (*of voice etc.*) пронзи́тельный.

● *adv.*: **~ hot** с пы́лу, с жáру.

piquancy /ˈpiːkənsɪ/, /-kɑːnsɪ/ *n.* (*lit., fig.*) пикáнтность.

piquant /ˈpiːkənt/, /-kɑːnt/ *adj.* (*lit., fig.*) пикáнтный.

pique /piːk/ *n.* досáда; раздражéние; **in a fit of ~** в поры́ве раздражéния.

● *v.t.* (**piques, piqued, piquing**) (*hurt the pride of*) уязв|ля́ть, -и́ть; (*stimulate*) возбу|ждáть, -ди́ть.

piqué /ˈpiːkeɪ/ *n.* пикé (*indecl.*).

piquet /pɪˈket/ *n.* пикéт.

piracy /ˈpaɪrəsɪ/ *n.* пирáтство.

pirate /ˈpaɪərət/ *n.* пирáт; **~ ship** пирáтский корáбль; (*infringer of copyright*) наруши́тель (*m.*) áвторского прáва, пирáт; **~ radio station** пирáтская радиостáнция.

● *v.t.* (*literary work*) публиковáть, о- в нарушéние áвторских прав; **~d edition** пирáтское издáние; (*video etc.*) выпускáть, вы́пустить пирáтскую кóпию + *g.*

piratical /ˌpaɪəˈrætɪk(ə)l/ *adj.* пирáтский.

pirouette /ˌpɪrʊˈet/ *n.* пируэ́т.

● *v.i.* дéлать, с- пируэ́т.

Pisces /ˈpaɪsiːz/, /ˈpɪskiːz/ *n.* (*pl. ~*) Ры́бы (*f. pl.*).

pisciculture /ˈpɪsɪˌkʌltʃə(r)/ *n.* рыбовóдство.

piss /pɪs/ *n.* (*vulg.*) мочá; **~ artist** (*Br., drunkard*) забулды́га (*c.g.*); **take the ~ (out of)** (*Br.*) насмехáться (*impf.*) (над + *i.*).

● *v.t.*: **~ blood** мочи́ться, по- крóвью; **~ s.o. off** злить, обо- когó-н.

● *v.i.* мочи́ться, по-; **~ off!** (*Br.*) отцепи́сь!; провáливай!

● *cpds.* **~-taker** *n.* (*Br.*) насмéшник; **~-taking** *n.* (*Br.*) насмехáтельство; **~-up** *n.* (*Br.*) выпивóн.

pissed /pɪsd/ *adj.* (*vulg.*) **1** (*Br., drunk*) пья́ный в стéльку. **2** (*US, annoyed*) обозлённый; **~ off** обозлённый.

pistachio /pɪˈstɑːʃɪəʊ/ *n.* (*pl.* **~s**) фистáшка.

pistil /ˈpɪstɪl/ *n.* пéстик.

pistol /ˈpɪst(ə)l/ *n.* пистолéт.

● *cpds.* **~-shot** *n.* пистолéтный вы́стрел; **~-whip** *v.t.* бить, по- рукоя́ткой пистолéта.

piston /ˈpɪst(ə)n/ *n.* пóршень (*m.*); (*mus.*) пистóн.

● *cpds.* **~-engine** *n.* поршневóй дви́гатель; **~-ring** *n.* поршневóе кольцó; **~-rod** *n.* поршневóй шток.

pit¹ /pɪt/ *n.* **1** (*hole*) я́ма; (*a large hole*) котловáн; (*for gravel*) карьéр; **gravel from the ~** грáвий из карьéра.
2 (*coal-mine*) шáхта; **he works down the ~** он рабóтает в шáхте; **~ pony** (*Br.*) шáхтная лóшадь.
3 (*covered hole, trap*) западня́, ловýшка; **the ~** (*hell*) преиспóдняя, ад; **the ~s** (*sl.*) áдская ситуáция.
4 (*depression*) углублéние, я́мка; **~ of the stomach** подлóжечная я́мка.
5 (*scar*) ряби́на; (*after smallpox*) óспина.
6 (*theatr.*) оркестрóвая я́ма; **~ stalls** партéр.
7 (*in workshop*) ремóнтная я́ма, смотровáя канáва; (*on motor-racing circuit*) ремóнтная площáдка, пит.

● *v.t.* (**pitted, pitting**) **1** (*oppose*): **he ~ted his wits against the law** он пытáлся обойти́ закóн.
2 (*scar*): **his face was ~ted by smallpox** егó лицó бы́ло изры́то óспой.

● *cpds.* **~ bull terrier** *n.* пит-бýль (*m.*); **~fall** *n.* (*lit., fig.*) западня́, капкáн; **~head** *n.* надшáхтное здáние; **~-prop** *n.* рудни́чный пропс, рудни́чная подпóрка.

pit² /pɪt/ *n.* (*US, fruit-stone*) кóсточка.

● *v.t.* (**pitted, pitting**) (*remove stones from*) вынимáть, вы́нуть кóсточки из + *g.*

pit-a-pat /ˈpɪtəˌpæt/ *n.* биéние, трéпет.

● *adv.* топ-тóп; с биéнием/трéпетом; **her heart went ~** её сéрдце затрепетáло.

pitch¹ /pɪtʃ/ *n.* **1** (*plunging motion of ship*) (килевáя) кáчка; (*lurch forward*) бросóк.
2 (*throw*) бросóк; (*delivery of ball*) подáча.
3 (*Br., area for games*) пóле, площáдка.
4 (*Br., spot where trader or entertainer operates*) (постоя́нное/обы́чное) мéсто.
5 (*of voice or instrument*) высотá.
6 (*height, intensity, degree*) ýровень (*m.*), стéпень; **excitement reached fever ~** возбуждéние дости́гло истери́ческого накáла; **things came to such a ~ that ...** дéло дошлó до тогó, что. . .
7 (*slope of roof*) скат.

● *v.t.* **1** (*set up, erect*): **they ~ed camp for the night** они́ разби́ли нá ночь лáгерь; **a ~ed battle** заплани́рованное сражéние.
2 (*throw*) бр|осáть, -óсить; (*fig.*): **he was ~ed into the centre** (*Br.*), **center** (*US*) of events он очути́лся в сáмом цéнтре собы́тий.
3 (*mus.*): **the song is ~ed too high for me** э́та пéсня сли́шком высокá для моегó гóлоса.

● *v.i.* (*of ship*): **the ship was ~ing** корáбль испы́тывал килевýю кáчку; (*of person, fall forwards*) пáдать, упáсть нáвзничь; (*lurch forward*) качнýться (*pf.*); (*fig.*) набр|áсываться, -óситься; **he ~ed into the work** он окунýлся в рабóту; **he ~ed into me** он набрóсился на меня́.

● *with adv.*: **~ in** *v.i.* (*join in with vigour*) горячó/энерги́чно брáться, взя́ться (*за что*).

● *cpd.* **~fork** *n.* (сенные) вил|ы (*pl.*, *g.* —).

pitch[2] /pɪtʃ/ *n.* (*bituminous substance*) смола́; **~ darkness** тьма кроме́шная.

● *cpds.* **~-black** *adj.* чёрный как смоль; **~blende** *n.* уранини́т; **~-dark** *adj.*: **it is ~-dark here** здесь кроме́шная тьма; здесь темны́м-темно́ (*coll.*); **~-pine** *n.* сосна́ жёсткая.

pitcher /ˈpɪtʃə(r)/ *n.* (*jug*) кувши́н; (*at baseball*) подаю́щий.

piteous /ˈpɪtɪəs/ *adj.* жа́лкий; (*voice, song, words*) жа́лобный.

pith /pɪθ/ *n.* (*plant tissue*) паренхи́ма; сердцеви́на; (*essential part*) суть; (*vigour, force*) эне́ргия, си́ла.

pithy /ˈpɪθɪ/ *adj.* (**pithier, pithiest**) (*fig.*) сжа́тый; содержа́тельный.

pitiable /ˈpɪtɪəb(ə)l/ *adj.* несча́стный; (*contemptible*) жа́лкий.

pitiful /ˈpɪtɪˌfʊl/ *adj.* жа́лкий.

pitiless /ˈpɪtɪlɪs/ *adj.* безжа́лостный.

pittance /ˈpɪt(ə)ns/ *n.* жа́лкие гроши́ (*m. pl.*).

pitter-patter /ˈpɪtəˌpætə(r)/ *n.* & *adv.* топ-то́п.

● *v.i.* посту́кивать (*impf.*).

pituitary /pɪˈtjuːɪtərɪ/ *n.* (*also* **~ gland**) гипо́физ.

pit|y /ˈpɪtɪ/ *n.* **1** (*compassion*) жа́лость; **have, take ~y on** сжа́литься (*pf.*) над + *i.*; **I feel ~y for him** мне его́ жа́лко; **he married her out of ~y** он жени́лся на ней из жа́лости; **for ~y's sake!** (*expr. impatience*) Го́споди Бо́же мой! **2** (*cause for regret*) жаль; **what a ~y!** как жаль/жа́лко!; **more's the ~y** тем ху́же; **it's a great ~y** о́чень жаль.

● *v.t.* жале́ть, по-; **she is much to be ~ied** её о́чень жаль.

pivot /ˈpɪvət/ *n.* то́чка враще́ния; (*fig.*) то́чка опо́ры.

● *v.i.* (**pivoted, pivoting**) враща́ться (*impf.*); верте́ться (*impf.*); **everything ~s on his decision** всё упира́ется в его́ реше́ние.

pivotal /ˈpɪvətəl/ *adj.* осево́й; центра́льный; (*fig.*) центра́льный, основно́й.

pixel /ˈpɪks(ə)l/ *n.* (*comput.*) пи́ксел, элеме́нт изображе́ния.

pix|y, -ie /ˈpɪksɪ/ *n.* эльф.

pizazz /ˌpɪˈzæz/ *n.* огонёк, аза́рт.

pizza /ˈpiːtsə/ *n.* пи́цца; **~ parlour** (*Br.*), **parlor** (*US*) пиццери́я.

pizzeria /ˌpiːtsəˈriːə/ *n.* пиццери́я.

pizzica|to /ˌpɪtsɪˈkɑːtəʊ/ *n.*, *adj.* & *adv.* (*pl.* **~tos** *or* **~ti** /-tɪ/) (*mus.*) пиццика́то (*indecl.*).

pl. /ˈplʊər(ə)l/ *n.* (*abbr. of* ***plural***) мн. ч. (мно́жественное число́).

placard /ˈplækɑːd/ *n.* плака́т; (*advertising performance*) афи́ша.

placate /pləˈkeɪt/, /ˈplæ-/, /ˈpleɪ-/ *v.t.* умиротвор|я́ть, -и́ть; успок|а́ивать, -о́ить.

placatory /pləˈkeɪtərɪ/ *adj.* зада́бривающий; умиротворя́ющий.

place /pleɪs/ *n.* **1** ме́сто; **I have put my money in a safe ~** я положи́л де́ньги в надёжное ме́сто; **all over the ~** (*everywhere*) повсю́ду; (*in confusion*) повсю́ду, в беспоря́дке; (*correct, appropriate* **~**): **everything is in ~** всё на ме́сте; **there's a time and a ~ for everything** всему́ своё вре́мя и ме́сто; **her hair was out of ~** её причёска растрепа́лась; **your laughter is out of ~** ваш смех неуме́стен; **that put him in his ~** э́то поста́вило его́ на ме́сто; (*reserved, occupied* **~**): **he took his ~ in the queue** (*Br.*), **in (the) line** (*US*) он за́нял ме́сто в о́череди; (*seat*): **he gave up his ~ to a lady** он уступи́л своё ме́сто да́ме; **take your ~s!** займи́те свои́ места́!; (*fig.*, *position*): **put yourself in my ~** поста́вьте себя́ на моё ме́сто; **in your ~ I would go** на ва́шем ме́сте я бы пошёл; (*at table*): **six ~s were laid** стол был накры́т на шесть персо́н; (*fig.*): **take ~** (*occur*) состоя́ться (*pf.*); име́ть (*impf.*) ме́сто; **when will the race take ~?** когда́ состоя́тся го́нки?; **take the ~ of** (*replace*) замен|я́ть, -и́ть; **give ~ to** смен|я́ться, -и́ться + *i.*; **her tears gave ~ to smiles** её слёзы смени́лись улы́бкой; **in ~ of** вме́сто + *g.*
2 (*locality; specific area or point*) ме́сто; **in ~s** (*here and there*) места́ми; **we visited all the ~s of interest** мы осмотре́ли все интере́сные места́; **small ~s are not marked on the map** ме́лкие пу́нкты не обозна́чены на ка́рте; **there's no ~ like home** ≈ в гостя́х хорошо́, а до́ма лу́чше.
3 (*building; domicile*) дом; жили́ще; **~ of worship** моли́твенный дом; **~ of work** ме́сто рабо́ты; **he has a little ~ in the country** у него́ есть небольшо́й до́мик в дере́вне; **come round to my ~!** заходи́те ко мне!
4 (*employment*) ме́сто, слу́жба.
5 (*point or passage in book etc.*) ме́сто, страни́ца; **I put in a pencil to mark my ~** я заложи́л страни́цу карандашо́м.
6 (*position in race or contest*) ме́сто; **our team took first ~** на́ша кома́нда заняла́ пе́рвое ме́сто; (*stage, position in series*): **in the first ~** во-пе́рвых.
7 (*math.*): **correct to three decimal ~s** с то́чностью до тре́тьего десяти́чного зна́ка.

● *v.t.* **1** (*stand*) ста́вить, по-; (*lay*) класть, положи́ть; (*set*) сажа́ть, посади́ть; (*dispose*) разме|ща́ть, -сти́ть; расс|тавля́ть, -а́вить.
2 (*appoint*) поме|ща́ть, -сти́ть.
3 (*comm.*) поме|ща́ть, -сти́ть (*деньги и т.п.*); **I ~d an order with them** я помести́л у них зака́з.
4 (*repose*) возл|ага́ть, -ожи́ть (*надежды и т.п.*); **no-one ~s any confidence in his reports** его́ сообще́ния не вызыва́ют ни у кого́ дове́рия.
5 (*identify*) определ|я́ть, -и́ть; **I know those lines, but I cannot ~ them** мне знако́мы э́ти стро́чки, но я не могу́ вспо́мнить, отку́да они́.

● *cpds.* **~-kick** *n.* уда́р по неподви́жному мячу́; **~-mat** *n.* подста́вка/салфе́тка под столо́вый прибо́р; **~-name** *n.* географи́ческое назва́ние; **~-names** (*collect.*) топони́мика, топони́мия.

placebo /pləˈsiːbəʊ/ *n.* (*pl.* **~s**) (*med.*) плаце́бо (*indecl.*); имита́ция лека́рственного сре́дства.

placement /ˈpleɪsmənt/ *n.* (*action*) размеще́ние; (*for work*) назначе́ние.

placen|ta /pləˈsentə/ *n.* (*pl.* **~tae** /-tiː/ *or* **~tas**) плаце́нта.

placid /ˈplæsɪd/ *adj.* споко́йный, безмяте́жный.

placidity /pləˈsɪdɪtɪ/ *n.* споко́йствие, безмяте́жность.

plagiarism /ˈpleɪdʒəˌrɪz(ə)m/ *n.* плагиа́т.

plagiarist /ˈpleɪdʒərɪst/ *n.* плагиа́тор.

plagiarize /ˈpleɪdʒəˌraɪz/ *v.i.* занима́ться (*impf.*) плагиа́том.

● *v.t.*: **he ~d my book** его́ рабо́та целико́м спи́сана с мое́й кни́ги.

plague /pleɪg/ *n.* **1** (*pestilence*) чума́. **2** (*infestation*) бе́дствие; **a ~ of rats** наше́ствие крыс. **3** (*annoyance*) напа́сть, зара́за (*coll.*).

● *v.t.* (**plagues, plagued, plaguing**) (*afflict*) нас|ыла́ть, -ла́ть чуму́/бе́дствие на + *a.*; (*pester*) докуча́ть (*impf.*) + *d.*

plaice /pleɪs/ *n.* (*pl.* **~**) ка́мбала.

plaid /plæd/ *n.* (*garment*) плед; (*fabric*) шотла́ндка (*ткань*).

plain /pleɪn/ *n.* равни́на.

● *adj.* **1** (*clear, evident*) я́сный, я́вный; **it is as ~ as the nose on one's face** э́то я́сно как день; **her distress was ~ to see** она́ я́вно страда́ла; **it was ~ sailing from then on** с тех пор всё пошло́ как по ма́слу.
2 (*easy to understand*) я́сный, поня́тный; **why can't you speak ~ English?** почему́ вы не говори́те просты́м языко́м?
3 (*straightforward, candid*) прямо́й, открове́нный; **I am a ~ man** я челове́к просто́й; **I will be ~ with you** я бу́ду с ва́ми открове́нен; **~ dealing** че́стность, прямота́.
4 (*not patterned*): **~ wallpaper** одното́нные (*or* гла́дкие) обо́и; **~ blue shirt** одното́нная (*or* гла́дкая) голуба́я руба́шка; **~ paper** нелино́ванная бума́га; (*simple, ordinary, unembellished*) просто́й, скро́мный, неприхотли́вый; **~ clothes** (*opp. to uniform*) шта́тское (пла́тье); **~ food** проста́я пи́ща; **~ living** скро́мная жизнь; **~ words** просты́е слова́.
5 (*unattractive*) некраси́вый.
6: **~ chocolate** чёрный шокола́д; **~ flour** (*Br.*) мука́ без доба́вок.

● *adv.* я́сно, про́сто.

● *cpds.* **~-chant, ~-song** *nn.* одното́нный напе́в; **~-clothes** *adj.* оде́тый в шта́тское; **~-clothes man, officer** оде́тый в шта́тское полице́йский; **~-spoken** *adj.* открове́нный, прямо́й.

plainness /ˈpleɪnnɪs/ *n.* (*candour*) прямота́, открове́нность; (*simplicity*) простота́, скро́мность, неприхотли́вость; (*unattractiveness*) непривлека́тельность.

plaintiff /ˈpleɪntɪf/ *n.* ист|е́ц (*fem.* -и́ца).

plaintive /ˈpleɪntɪv/ *adj.* печа́льный, гру́стный.

P

plait /plæt/ *n.* (*Br.*) коcá; **she wears her hair in a ~** она́ но́сит ко́су/заплета́ет во́лосы в ко́су.

● *v.t.* запле|та́ть, -сти́.

plan /plæn/ *n.* план; (*drawing, diagram*) чертёж; **~s were drawn up** бы́ли соста́влены пла́ны; (*map*) ка́рта, план; **a ~ of the city** план го́рода; (*schedule*): **all went according to ~** всё прошло́ по пла́ну; (*project*) план, прое́кт; **five-year ~** пятиле́тний план; **master ~** генера́льный план; **they made ~s for the future** они́ стро́или пла́ны на бу́дущее; (*system*) за́мысел; **on the instalment ~** в рассро́чку; **an open-~ house** дом откры́той планиро́вки.

● *v.t.* (**planned, planning**) **1** (*make a ~ of*) плани́ровать, рас-. **2** (*arrange*) плани́ровать, за-; (*design*) проекти́ровать, с-; **~ned economy** пла́новая эконо́мика.

● *v.i.* (**planned, planning**) намерева́ться (*impf.*), плани́ровать (*impf.*); **where are you ~ning to go this year?** куда́ вы плани́руете пое́хать в э́том году́?; **we must ~ ahead** на́до ду́мать о бу́дущем.

planchette /plɑːnˈʃet/ *n.* планше́тка (для спирити́ческих сеа́нсов).

plane[1] /pleɪn/ *n.* (*tree*) плата́н.

plane[2] /pleɪn/ *n.* (*tool*) руба́нок, струг.

● *v.t.* строга́ть, вы́-.

● *v.i.* строга́ть (*impf.*).

● *with advs.*: **~ away, ~ down** *v.t.* сostrа́г|ивать, -а́ть.

plane[3] /pleɪn/ *n.* **1** (*flat surface*) пло́скость. **2** (*aeroplane*) самолёт. **3** (*fig., level*) у́ровень (*m.*); **her thoughts are on a higher ~** у неё бо́лее высо́кий строй мы́слей.

● *adj.* пло́ский, плоскостно́й.

planet /ˈplænɪt/ *n.* плане́та.

planetari|um /ˌplænɪˈteərɪəm/ *n.* (*pl.* **~ums** *or* **~a**) планета́рий.

planetary /ˈplænɪtərɪ/ *adj.* планета́рный, плане́тный.

plangent /ˈplændʒ(ə)nt/ *adj.* (*plaintive*) зауны́вный.

plank /plæŋk/ *n.* доска́; (*fig., item in election programme*) пункт предвы́борной програ́ммы.

● *v.t.* (*US coll., also* **plunk**): **he ~ed down his money on the table** он вы́ложил де́ньги на стол.

planking /ˈplæŋkɪŋ/ *n.* (*flooring*) насти́л; (*planks*) до́ски (*f. pl.*).

plankton /ˈplæŋkt(ə)n/ *n.* планкто́н.

planner /ˈplænə(r)/ *n.* планови́к; проектиро́вщик.

planning /ˈplænɪŋ/ *n.* плани́рование; **long-term ~** перспекти́вное плани́рование; **family ~** плани́рование семьи́; **town ~** градострои́тельство; **~ department** отде́л плани́рования и застро́йки; **~ permission** (*Br.*) разреше́ние на строи́тельство.

plant /plɑːnt/ *n.* **1** (*vegetable organism*) расте́ние; **house ~** ко́мнатное расте́ние. **2** (*industrial fixtures or machinery*) обору́дование. **3** (*factory*) заво́д. **4** (*coll., article placed to incriminate; incrimination*) сфабрико́ванная ули́ка.

● *v.t.* **1** (*put in ground*) сажа́ть, посади́ть; (*seeds*) се́ять; **I have ~ed out the cabbages** я вы́садил капу́сту в грунт. **2** (*furnish with ~s*) заса́|живать, -ди́ть; **the beds were ~ed with roses** гря́дки бы́ли заса́жены ро́зами. **3** (*fig.*): **he ~ed a doubt in my mind** он посе́ял во мне сомне́ние; **he ~ed himself in front of the fire** он расположи́лся пе́ред ками́ном; **~ a blow** нан|оси́ть, -ести́ то́чный уда́р; **~ a bomb** под|кла́дывать, -ложи́ть бо́мбу; **~ evidence** подстр|а́ивать, -о́ить (*or* подбр|а́сывать, -о́сить) ули́ки.

plantain /ˈplæntɪn/ *n.* (*herb*) подоро́жник; (*tropical tree*) ди́кий бана́н.

plantation /plænˈteɪʃ(ə)n/, /plɑːn-/ *n.* (*area of planted trees*) насажде́ния (*pl.*), зелёный масси́в; (*estate*) планта́ция.

planter /ˈplɑːntə(r)/ *n.* (*person who plants seeds*) сажа́льщик (*plantation owner*) планта́тор; (*agric. machine*) се́ялка; (*container for plants*) декорати́вный горшо́к (для расте́ний).

plaque /plæk/, /plɑːk/ *n.* (*tablet*) доще́чка; (*on teeth*) зубно́й ка́мень.

plash /plæʃ/ *n.* (*splashing sound*) плеск, всплеск.

● *v.i.* плес|ка́ть, -ну́ть; плеска́ться (*impf.*).

plasm(a) /ˈplæzmə/ *n.* пла́зма.

● *adj.* пла́зменный.

plaster /ˈplɑːstə(r)/ *n.* **1** (*for coating walls etc.*) штукату́рка; **~ cast** ги́псовый сле́пок; **~ of Paris** гипс. **2** (*Br., med.*) пла́стырь (*m.*).

● *v.t.* **1** (*coat with ~*) штукату́рить, о(т)-; (*coat*) покр|ыва́ть, -ы́ть; **his boots were ~ed with mud** его́ боти́нки бы́ли обле́плены гря́зью. **2** (*cover*) облеп|ля́ть, -и́ть; **the suitcase was ~ed with labels** чемода́н был весь обле́плен накле́йками. **3**: **get ~ed** (*sl., drunk*) нализа́ться (*pf.*); упи́ться (*pf.*).

● *cpd.* **~board** *n.* лист сухо́й штукату́рки.

plasterer /ˈplɑːstərə(r)/ *n.* штукату́р.

plastic /ˈplæstɪk/ *n.* пла́стик, пластма́сса; (*sl., credit card*) креди́тная ка́рточка, пла́стиковая ка́рточка.

● *adj.* **1** (*made of ~*) пластма́ссовый; пла́стиковый; **~ bag** полиэтиле́новый мешо́к; **~ bomb** пла́стиковая бо́мба. **2** (*pert. to moulding; sculptural*) лепно́й; скульпту́рный; **the ~ arts** пласти́ческие иску́сства; **~ surgery** (*medical practice*) пласти́ческая хирурги́я; (*operation*) пласти́ческая опера́ция. **3** (*malleable*) пласти́чный.

plasticine /ˈplæstɪˌsiːn/ *n.* (*propr.*) пластили́н.

plasticity /ˌplæsˈtɪsɪtɪ/ *n.* пласти́чность.

plate /pleɪt/ *n.* **1** (*shallow dish*) (ме́лкая) таре́лка; **side ~** таре́лка для хле́ба; (*fig.*): **he has a lot on his ~** (*Br.*) у него́ дел по го́рло (*coll.*); **the game was handed to him on a ~** ему́ преподнесли́ побе́ду на блю́дечке. **2** (*collect., metal tableware*) посу́да; **silver ~** сере́бряная посу́да. **3** (*sheet of metal, glass etc.*) лист, пласти́н(к)а; **a ~ on the door gave the doctor's name** на две́ри была́ табли́чка с фами́лией до́ктора; **the battery has zinc ~s** батаре́я име́ет ци́нковые пласти́ны; **armour** (*Br.*), **armor** (*US*) **~** бронев́ые пли́ты (*f. pl.*). **4** (*phot.*) фотопласти́нка; **half ~** полуто́новое клише́ (*indecl.*). **5** (*lithographic*) гальваноклише́ (*indecl.*); (*illustration*) вкладна́я иллюстра́ция. **6** (*typ.*) стереоти́п. **7**: (**dental ~**) вставна́я че́люсть, (зубно́й) проте́з. **8** (*cup as racing prize*) ку́бок. **9** (*rail.*) ре́льсовая накла́дка. **10** (*number-~*) номерно́й знак.

● *v.t.* **1** (*cover with metal ~s*) обш|ива́ть, -и́ть. **2** (*coat with layer of metal*) плакирова́ть (*impf.*); нан|оси́ть, -ести́ покры́тие на + *a.*; **silver-~d spoons** посеребрённые ло́жки.

● *cpds.* **~-glass** *adj.* из зерка́льного стекла́; **~layer** *n.* (*Br.*) путево́й рабо́чий; **~-rack** *n.* (*Br.*) суши́лка для посу́ды; **~ tectonics** *n.* плитотекто́ника.

plateau /ˈplætəʊ/ *n.* (*pl.* **~x** /-z/ *or* **~s**) плато́ (*indecl.*).

plateful /ˈpleɪtfʊl/ *n.* (по́лная) таре́лка (*чего*).

platen /ˈplæt(ə)n/ *n.* (*of typewriter*) ва́лик.

platform /ˈplætfɔːm/ *n.* **1** (*at station*) платфо́рма, перро́н; **at ~ No. 3** на платфо́рме № 3; **~ ticket** (*Br.*) перро́нный биле́т. **2** (*for speakers*) трибу́на; (*fig., pol.*) (полити́ческая) платфо́рма. **3** (*comput.*) платфо́рма.

plating /ˈpleɪtɪŋ/ *n.* покры́тие; обши́вка.

platinum /ˈplætɪnəm/ *n.* пла́тина; **~ blonde** о́чень све́тлая блонди́нка.

platitude /ˈplætɪˌtjuːd/ *n.* пло́скость, бана́льность.

platitudinous /ˌplætɪˈtjuːdɪnəs/ *adj.* пло́ский, бана́льный.

Platonic /pləˈtɒnɪk/ *adj.* платони́ческий.

platoon /pləˈtuːn/ *n.* взвод.

platter /ˈplætə(r)/ *n.* блю́до; **cold ~** холо́дное ассорти́ (*indecl.*).

platypus /ˈplætɪpəs/ *n.* (*pl.* **platypuses**) утконо́с.

plaudit /ˈplɔːdɪt/ *n.* (*usu. pl.*) (*applause*) аплодисме́нт|ы (*pl., g.* -ов); (*praise*) похвала́ (*sg.*).

plausibility /ˌplɔːzɪˈbɪlɪtɪ/ *n.* вероя́тность, правдоподо́бие.

plausible /ˈplɔːzɪb(ə)l/ *adj.* (*story, statement*) правдоподо́бный, вероя́тный; (*person*) убеди́тельный.

play /pleɪ/ *n.* **1** (*recreation, amusement*) игра́; **the children were at ~** де́ти игра́ли; **mathematics is child's ~ to him** матема́тика для него́ — де́тские

игру́шки; **~ on words** игра́ слов.
2 (*conduct of game etc.*) игра́; мане́ра игры́; **there was a lot of rough ~** бы́ло мно́го гру́бой игры́; **I am here to see fair ~** я слежу́ за тем, что́бы игра́ вела́сь по пра́вилам; **the police suspect foul ~** поли́ция подозрева́ет незако́нные де́йствия/, что де́ло нечи́сто (*coll.*).
3 (*state of being played with*): **the ball was out of ~** мяч был вне игры́.
4 (*fig., action*) де́йствие, де́ятельность; **all his strength was brought into ~** он мобилизова́л все свои́ си́лы; **the ~ of market forces** возде́йствие ры́ночных фа́кторов.
5 (*dramatic work*) пье́са; (*in theatre*) спекта́кль (*m.*).
6 (*visual effect*) игра́; перели́вы (*m. pl.*); **the ~ of light on the water** игра́ све́та на воде́.
7 (*free movement*) люфт, свобо́дный ход; **there is too much ~ in the brake pedal** тормо́зная педа́ль име́ет сли́шком большо́й свобо́дный ход.
8 (*fig., scope*) во́ля; просто́р; **she allowed her curiosity free ~** она́ дала́ во́лю своему́ любопы́тству.

● *v.t.* **1** (*perform, take part in*) игра́ть, сыгра́ть в + *a.*; **~ football** игра́ть (*impf.*) в футбо́л; **he wouldn't ~ ball** (*coll., cooperate*) он не хоте́л сотру́дничать; **~ it cool** (*coll.*) сохраня́ть (*impf.*) хладнокро́вие.
2 (*perform on*) игра́ть, сыгра́ть на + *p.*; **can you ~ the piano?** вы игра́ете на роя́ле?; **he ~s second fiddle** (*fig.*) он игра́ет втору́ю скри́пку.
3 (*perform piece of music*) исп|олня́ть, -о́лнить; (*record*) про|и́грывать, -игра́ть; **they ~ed records** они́ поста́вили/проигра́ли пласти́нки; **he ~ed it by ear** (*fig., of extempore action*) он де́йствовал в зави́симости от обстоя́тельств.
4 (*perpetrate*): **he is always ~ing tricks on me** он всегда́ надо мно́й подшу́чивает; **my memory ~s tricks** па́мять меня́ подво́дит.
5 (*enact role of*) игра́ть, сыгра́ть; **I ~ed Horatio** я игра́л Гора́цио; **stop ~ing the fool!** переста́ньте валя́ть дурака́; **~ truant** прогу́л|ивать, -я́ть заня́тия/уро́ки.
6 (*enact drama of*) дава́ть (*impf.*); дава́ть представле́ние + *g.*, игра́ть (*impf.*); **they are ~ing Othello** (в теа́тре) даю́т/игра́ют «Оте́лло».
7 (*contend against*): **will you ~ me at chess?** вы сыгра́ете со мной в ша́хматы?
8 (*cards*): **he ~ed the ace** он пошёл с туза́; **he ~ed his trump card** (*fig.*) он пусти́л в ход свой ко́зырь; **he ~ed his cards well** (*fig.*) он де́йствовал уме́ло.
9 (*use as ~er*): **they ~ed Jones at full back** Джо́нса поста́вили игра́ть защи́тником.
10 (*strike, propel*) уд|аря́ть, -а́рить; (*fig.*): **he ~ed the affair skilfully** он иску́сно провёл де́ло.

● *v.i.* **1** игра́ть, сыгра́ть; (*amuse o.s., have fun*) игра́ть (*impf.*), забавля́ться (*impf.*); **they were ~ing at soldiers** они́ игра́ли в войну́; **what are you ~ing at?** что за игру́ вы ведёте?; **she ~ed on his vanity** она́ игра́ла на его́ тщесла́вие; **he is fond of ~ing on words** он лю́бит каламбу́ры; **she is ~ing with his affections** она́ игра́ет его́ чу́вствами; **I am ~ing with the idea of resigning** я поду́мываю об отста́вке; **he ~ed with his glasses while he was talking** разгова́ривая, он верте́л в рука́х очки́; **don't ~ with fire!** (*fig.*) не игра́йте с огнём!; (*take part in game or sport*) игра́ть (*impf.*); **they ~ed to win** они́ игра́ли с аза́ртом; **two can ~ at that game!** (*fig.*) посмо́трим ещё, чья возьмёт!; **I have always ~ed fair with you** я всегда́ поступа́л с ва́ми че́стно; (*gamble*) игра́ть (*impf.*); **what shall we ~ for?** по ско́льку бу́дем игра́ть/ста́вить?; **he is ~ing for high stakes** (*fig.*) он игра́ет по-кру́пному; (*perform music*): **it's an old instrument but it ~s well** э́то ста́рый инструме́нт, но у него́ хоро́ший звук; (*on stage etc.*): **they ~ed to full houses** они́ игра́ли при по́лном за́ле; **~ to the gallery** (*fig.*) иска́ть (*impf.*) дешёвой популя́рности; игра́ть (*impf.*) на пу́блику; (*move, be active*): **a smile ~ed on her lips** улы́бка игра́ла на её губа́х; **a breeze ~ed in the trees** в дере́вьях шелесте́л ветеро́к; **the light ~ed on the water** на воде́ игра́ли светові́ые бли́ки; **the fountains were ~ing** би́ли фонта́ны.
2 (*be directed*): **searchlights ~ed on the aircraft** проже́кторы бы́ли напра́влены на самолёт.
3 (*strike ball*) де́лать, с- бросо́к; (*fig.*): **he ~ed into my hands** он сыгра́л мне на́ руку.

● *with advs.*: **~ about, ~ around** *v.i.* игра́ть (*impf.*); резви́ться (*impf.*); **the children were ~ing about in the garden** де́ти резви́лись в саду́; **~ back** *v.t.* воспроизв|оди́ть, -ести́; прослу́ш|ивать, -ать; **the tape was ~ed back** плёнку проигра́ли; **~ down** *v.t.* (*fig., minimize*) преум|еньша́ть, -е́ньшить; **I ~ed down his faults in my report** в своём отчёте я не заостря́лся на его́ недоста́тках; **~ o.s. in** *v.i.* (*Br.*) разы́гр|ываться, -а́ться; входи́ть, войти́ в игру́/рабо́ту; **~ off** *v.t.* (*replay*): **the drawn game must be ~ed off next week** ничья́ должна́ быть переи́грана на сле́дующей неде́ле; (*set in opposition*) натра́в|ливать, -ить (*кого на кого*); **he ~ed his rivals off against one another** он стра́вливал свои́х сопе́рников; **~ out** *v.t.* (**~** *to the end, to a result*) доигр|ывать, -а́ть; (*pass., be exhausted*) выдыха́ться, вы́дохнуться; **~ over** *v.t.* переигр|ывать, -а́ть; **may I ~ over my new composition?** мо́жно вам проигра́ть моё но́вое произведе́ние?; **~ through** *v.t.* игра́ть, сыгра́ть (целико́м); **the conductor made them ~ the movement through again** дирижёр заста́вил их сыгра́ть/проигра́ть э́ту часть за́ново; **~ up** *v.t.* (*give emphasis, importance to*) обы́гр|ывать, -а́ть; **he ~ed up the advantages of the scheme** он обыгра́л преиму́щества пла́на; (*Br. coll., give trouble to*) му́чить, за-; **Tommy has been ~ing me up all morning** То́мми досажда́л мне всё у́тро; **my car is ~ing me up again** моя́ маши́на опя́ть барахли́т; *v.i.* (*Br., misbehave*) распус|ка́ться, -ти́ться; **the boys ~ up when their father is away** ма́льчики распуска́ются, когда́ отца́ нет до́ма; **~ up to** (*humour*) подда́к|ивать, -нуть + *d.*; **she ~s up to her husband** она́ подда́кивает своему́ му́жу; (*give flattering attention to*) льстить (*impf.*) + *d.*; подли́зываться (*impf.*) к + *d.*

● *cpds.* **~-act** *v.i.* притворя́ться (*impf.*); **~-acting** *n.* (*fig.*) притво́рство, на́игрыш (*coll.*); **~back** *n.* воспроизведе́ние; **~bill** *n.* (*poster*) театра́льная афи́ша; **~-box** *n.* я́щик для игру́шек; **~boy** *n.* плейбо́й, пове́са (*m.*); **~fellow, ~mate** *nn.*: **the child needs a ~fellow** ребёнку на́до с ке́м-то игра́ть; **~goer** *n.* театра́л; **~ground** *n.* (*at school*) площа́дка для игр; (*fig.*) излю́бленное ме́сто развлече́ния; **~group** *n.* (*Br.*) дошко́льная гру́ппа; **~house** *n.* теа́тр; **~mate** *n.* = **~fellow; ~-off** *n.* реша́ющая встре́ча; повто́рная встре́ча по́сле ничье́й; **~-pen** *n.* де́тский мане́ж; **~school** *n.* ≈ де́тский сад; **~-suit** *n.* спорти́вный костю́м; **~thing** *n.* (*lit., fig.*) игру́шка; **~time** *n.* (шко́льная) переме́на; **~wright** *n.* драмату́рг.

player /ˈpleɪə(r)/ *n.* **1** (*of game*) игро́к; спортсме́н. **2** (*actor*) актёр. **3** (*musician*) исполни́тель; **a ~ on the clarinet** кларнети́ст. **4** (*record-~*) прои́грыватель (*m.*).
● *cpd.* **~-piano** *n.* пиано́ла.

playful /ˈpleɪfʊl/ *adj.* игри́вый, шаловли́вый.

playfulness /ˈpleɪfʊlnɪs/ *n.* игри́вость.

playing /ˈpleɪɪŋ/ *n.* игра́.
● *cpds.* **~-card** *n.* игра́льная ка́рта; **~-field** *n.* спорти́вное по́ле.

playlet /ˈpleɪlɪt/ *n.* пье́ска.

plaza /ˈplɑːzə/ *n.* пло́щадь.

PLC, plc (*abbr. of* ***public limited company***) (*Br.*) обще́ственная компа́ния с ограни́ченной отве́тственностью.

plea /pliː/ *n.* **1** (*leg.*) заявле́ние (отве́тчика); **he entered a ~ of guilty** он призна́л себя́ вино́вным. **2** (*excuse*) предло́г; **on the ~ of ill-health** под предло́гом боле́зни. **3** (*request, appeal*) про́сьба.
● *cpd.* **~-bargaining** *n.* (*leg.*) призна́ние подсуди́мым вино́вности в соверше́нии ме́нее тя́жкого преступле́ния в обме́н на бо́лее мя́гкий пригово́р.

plead /pliːd/ *v.t.* **1** (*case*) вести́ (*impf.*); **he had a lawyer to ~ his case** его́ де́ло вёл адвока́т; (*cause*) защища́ть (*impf.*); **he ~ed the cause of the pensioners** он защища́л интере́сы пенсионе́ров.
2 (*offer as excuse*) ссыла́ться, сосла́ться на + *a.*; **the defendant ~ed insanity** подсуди́мый сосла́лся на невменя́емость; **I must ~ ignorance of the facts** я до́лжен призна́ться, что мне неизве́стны э́ти фа́кты.
3 (*declare o.s.*): **my client ~s (not) guilty** мой клие́нт (не) признаёт себя́ вино́вным.
● *v.i.* **1** (*address court as advocate*)

выступа́ть, вы́ступить в суде́. **2** (*appeal, entreat*) приз|ыва́ть, -ва́ть; умоля́ть (*impf.*); **the prisoners ~ed for mercy** заключённые просили о поми́ловании; **he ~ed with me to stay** он умоля́л меня́ оста́ться.

pleading /ˈpli:dɪŋ/ *n.* выступле́ние защи́ты; хода́тайство; (*of cause of an action*) заявле́ние основа́ний и́ска; (*of defence*) защи́та про́тив и́ска; **special ~** тенденцио́зный подбо́р фа́ктов/аргуме́нтов.

pleasant /ˈplez(ə)nt/ *adj.* (**pleasanter, pleasantest**) прия́тный.

pleasantness /ˈplezəntnɪs/ *n.* прия́тность.

pleasantry /ˈplezəntrɪ/ *n.* (*amiable remark*) любе́зность.

please /pli:z/ *v.t.* нра́виться, по- +*d.*; ра́довать, по-; дост|авля́ть, -а́вить удово́льствие +*d.*; **it ~s the eye** э́то ра́дует глаз; **his attitude ~s me** меня́ ра́дует его́ отноше́ние; **I was not very ~d at, by, with the results** я был не о́чень дово́лен результа́тами; **I feel better, I'm ~d to say** рад сообщи́ть, что я чу́вствую себя́ лу́чше; **I was ~d to note** мне бы́ло прия́тно отме́тить; **I shall be ~d to attend** я бу́ду рад приня́ть уча́стие; **~ God** дай Бог; **~ yourself** как вам бу́дет уго́дно; **he ~s himself what he does** он поступа́ет, как ему́ заблагорассу́дится.

● *v.i.* **1** (*give pleasure*) уго|жда́ть, -ди́ть; **she is very anxious to ~** она́ о́чень стара́ется угоди́ть. **2** (*think fit*) изво́лить (*impf.*); **do as you ~** де́лайте, как хоти́те; **take as many as you ~** возьми́те ско́лько уго́дно/хоти́те. **3** (*polite request*): **~ shut the door** пожа́луйста, закро́йте дверь; **won't you ~ sit down?** пожа́луйста, сади́тесь; **~ do try the jam** пожа́луйста/прошу́ вас, попро́буйте варе́нья; **~ forgive our long silence** о́чень про́сим извини́ть нас за до́лгое молча́ние; **if you ~** е́сли вам уго́дно; о́чень вас прошу́; (*iron.*): **he's taken a day's leave, if you ~** предста́вьте себе́ (*or* поду́мать то́лько), он взял выходно́й.

pleasing /ˈpli:zɪŋ/ *adj.* прия́тный.

pleasurable /ˈpleʒərəb(ə)l/ *adj.* прия́тный, отра́дный.

pleasure /ˈpleʒə(r)/ *n.* **1** (*enjoyment*) удово́льствие; **it's a ~!** (*sc. to oblige*) не сто́ит!; **it gives me great ~ to see you** мне о́чень прия́тно вас ви́деть; **may I have the ~ of a dance?** разреши́те пригласи́ть вас на та́нец?; **he takes ~ in teasing her** ему́ доставля́ет удово́льствие подтру́нивать над ней. **2** (*will, desire*) жела́ние; **at your ~** по ва́шему жела́нию.

● *cpds.* **~-boat** *n.* прогу́лочный ка́тер; **~-ground** *n.* сад; парк; **~-seeking** *adj.* и́щущий удово́льствий.

pleat /pli:t/ *n.* скла́дка.

● *v.t.* плиссирова́ть (*impf.*); **~ed skirt** плиссиро́ванная ю́бка; ю́бка в скла́дку.

plebeian /plɪˈbi:ən/ *n.* плебе́й.

● *adj.* плебе́йский.

plebiscite /ˈplebɪsɪt/, /-ˌsaɪt/ *n.* плебисци́т.

plebs /plebz/ *n.* плебс.

plectr|um /ˈplektrəm/ *n.* (*pl.* **~ums** *or* **~a**) (*mus.*) (*for guitar etc.*) медиа́тор, плектр.

pledge /pledʒ/ *n.* **1** (*thing left as earnest of intent; token*) зало́г. **2** (*promise*) обе́т, обеща́ние; **he has signed the** (*temperance*) **~** он дал заро́к не пить.

● *v.t.* **1** (*give as security*) отд|ава́ть, -а́ть в зало́г; (*pawn*) за|кла́дывать, -ложи́ть; **~ o.s.** обя́з|ываться, -а́ться; руча́ться, поручи́ться; **I ~ my word** даю́ сло́во; руча́юсь. **2** (*enjoin*): **I ~d him to secrecy** я взял с него́ сло́во не разглаша́ть э́то.

Pleiades /ˈplaɪəˌdi:z/ *n.* Плея́д|ы (*pl., g.* —).

Pleistocene /ˈplaɪstəˌsi:n/ *n.* плейстоце́н.

plenary /ˈpli:nərɪ/ *adj.*: **~ powers** неограни́ченные полномо́чия; **~ session** плена́рное заседа́ние, пле́нум.

plenipotentiary /ˌplenɪpəˈtenʃərɪ/ *n.* полномо́чный представи́тель.

● *adj.* (*having power*) полномо́чный; (*absolute*) неограни́ченный;

plenitude /ˈplenɪˌtju:d/ *n.* (*fullness*) полнота́; (*abundance*) изоби́лие, оби́лие.

plenteous /ˈplentɪəs/ *adj.* оби́льный.

plentiful /ˈplentɪˌfʊl/ *adj.* изоби́льный, оби́льный.

plenty /ˈplentɪ/ *n.* **1** (*abundance*) изоби́лие; **there was food in ~** еда́ была́ в изоби́лии. **2** (*large quantity or number*) мно́го; мно́жество; **we have ~** у нас мно́го; **he has ~ of money** у него́ мно́го/по́лно (*coll.*) де́нег; **we have ~ of time to spare** у нас мно́го вре́мени в запа́се. **3** (*sufficient*) доста́ток; **that will be ~** э́того бу́дет (пре)доста́точно.

plenum /ˈpli:nəm/ *n.* пле́нум.

plesiosaurus /ˌpli:sɪəˈsɔ:rəs/ *n.* плезиоза́вр.

plethora /ˈpleθərə/ *n.* (*med.*) полнокро́вие; (*fig., over-abundance*) избы́ток.

pleurisy /ˈplʊərɪsɪ/ *n.* плеври́т.

plexus /ˈpleksəs/ *n.* (*pl.* **~** *or* **~es**) сплете́ние; **solar ~** со́лнечное сплете́ние.

pliability /ˌplaɪəˈbɪlɪtɪ/ *n.* ги́бкость; усту́пчивость, сгово́рчивость.

pliable /ˈplaɪəb(ə)l/ *adj.* (*material*) ги́бкий; (*person*) усту́пчивый, сгово́рчивый

pliant /ˈplaɪənt/ *adj.* = **pliable**

pliers /ˈplaɪəz/ *n.* (*for holding things*) щипц|ы́ (*pl., g.* -о́в); (*for pulling things out*) клещ|и́ (*pl., g.* -е́й); (*for bending, cutting*) плоскогу́бц|ы (*pl., g.* -ев).

plight /plaɪt/ *n.* (незави́дная) у́часть.

plimsoll /ˈplɪms(ə)l/ *n.* **1** (*Br., light shoe*): **~s** паруси́новые ту́фли (*f. pl.*); спорти́вные та́почки (*f. pl.*). **2**: **P~ line** грузова́я ма́рка (*судна*).

plinth /plɪnθ/ *n.* плинт.

Pliocene /ˈplaɪəˌsi:n/ *n.* (*geol.*) плиоце́н.

PLO (*abbr. of* ***Palestine Liberation Organization***) ООП (Организа́ция освобожде́ния Палести́ны).

plod /plɒd/ *n.* (*walk*) тяжёлая по́ступь.

● *v.t. & i.* (**plodded, plodding**) тащи́ться (*impf.*); **he ~ded home** он уста́ло тащи́лся домо́й; (*fig.*): **~ away at something** корпе́ть (*impf.*) над чем-н.

plodder /ˈplɒdə(r)/ *n.* (*fig.*) труд́яга (*c.g.*); работя́га (*c.g.*).

plonk /plɒŋk/ *n.* (*Br. sl., cheap wine*) дешёвое вино́, бормоту́ха (*coll.*).

● *v.t.* (*coll., put down heavily*) гро́х|ать, -нуть; ба́х|ать, -нуть; **he ~ed himself in an armchair** он плю́хнулся в кре́сло.

plonker /ˈplɒŋkə(r)/ *n.* (*Br. coll.*) пентю́х, фо́фан.

plop /plɒp/ *n.* бульты́х.

● *adv.*: **fall ~** бултыхну́ться (*pf.*).

● *v.i.* (**plopped, plopping**) шлёпаться, шлёпнуться, бултыхну́ться (*pf.*).

● *int.* бух!

plosive /ˈpləʊsɪv/ *n.* (*phon.*) взрывно́й звук.

● *adj.* взрывно́й.

plot /plɒt/ *n.* **1** (*piece of ground*) уча́сток (земли́). **2** (*outline of play etc.*) фа́була, сюже́т. **3** (*conspiracy*) за́говор.

● *v.t.* (**plotted, plotting**) **1** (*conspire to achieve*): **they ~ted his ruin** они́ гото́вили ему́ ги́бель. **2** (*mark on a chart or graph*) нан|оси́ть, -ести́ (*данные*) на ка́рту/гра́фик. **3** (*naut., aeron.*) про|кла́дывать, -ложи́ть (*курс*).

● *v.i.* (**plotted, plotting**) (*conspire*) вына́шивать, составля́ть (*both impf.*) за́говор.

plotter /ˈplɒtə(r)/ *n.* **1** (*person*) загово́рщи|к (*fem.* -ца). **2** (*instrument*) графопострои́тель (*m.*), пло́ттер.

plough /plaʊ/ (*US* **plow**) *n.* **1** плуг; **we have 100 acres under ~** у нас 100 а́кров па́шни (*or* па́хотной земли́); **(snow-~)** снегоочисти́тель (*m.*). **2**: **the P~** (*astron.*) Больша́я Медве́дица.

● *v.t.* паха́ть, вс-; **he ~s a lonely furrow** (*fig.*) он де́йствует в одино́чку; (*fig.*): **he ~ed his way through the mud** он шлёпал по гря́зи.

● *v.i.* (*fig.*) продв|ига́ться, -и́нуться; **the ship ~ed through the waves** кора́бль рассека́л во́лны; **I ~ed through the book** я с трудо́м осилил кни́гу.

● *with advs.*: **~ back** *v.t.*: **profits are ~ed back** при́быль вкла́дывается в де́ло/реинвести́руется; **~ in** *v.t.* запа́х|ивать, -а́ть.

● *cpds.* **~land** *n.* па́хотная земля́; **~man** *n.* па́харь (*m.*); **~man's lunch** проста́я еда́, состоя́щая из хле́ба с сы́ром и припра́вами; **~share** *n.* плу́жный ле́мех.

plover /ˈplʌvə(r)/ *n.* (*zool.*) ржа́нка.

plow /plaʊ/ = **plough**

ploy /plɔɪ/ *n.* (*manoeuvre*) уло́вка.

pluck /plʌk/ *n.* **1** (*pull*) дёрганье; (*twitch*) щипо́к. **2** (*coll., courage*) сме́лость, отва́га.

● *v.t.* **1** (*pull off, pick*) срыва́ть, сорва́ть; соб|ира́ть, -ра́ть. **2** (*strip of feathers*) ощи́п|ывать, -а́ть. **3** (*cause to vibrate by twitching*) щипа́ть (*impf.*); **~ed instrument** щипко́вый инструме́нт. **4** (*twitch, pull at; also v.i.*) дёр|гать, -нуть.

● *with advs.*: **~ off** *v.t.* выдёргивать, вы́дернуть; **~ out** *v.t.* выщи́пывать, вы́щипать; **~ up** *v.t.*: **~ up courage** соб|ира́ться, -ра́ться с ду́хом.

plucky /ˈplʌkɪ/ *adj.* (**pluckier, pluckiest**) (*coll.*) сме́лый, отва́жный.

plug /plʌg/ *n.* **1** (*stopper, e.g. of bath*) про́бка, заты́чка; **ear-~** заты́чка для уше́й. **2** (*elec. connector*) ви́лка; (*socket*) розе́тка. **3** (*spark-~*) свеча́ зажига́ния. **4** (*coll., advertisement*) рекла́ма.

● *v.t.* (**plugged, plugging**) (*stop up*) затыка́ть, заткну́ть; (*coll., boost*) реклами́ровать (*impf., pf.*), прота́лкивать (*impf.*); (*US sl., shoot*) уложи́ть, хло́пнуть (*both pf.*).

● *with advs.*: **~ away** *v.i.* (*coll., persevere*) корпе́ть (*impf.*); **~ in** *v.t.* включ|а́ть, -и́ть; **~ up** *v.t.* (*hole*) затыха́ть, заткну́ть.

● *cpds.* **~hole** *n.* (*Br.*) сто́чное отве́рстие; **~-in** *adj.* вставно́й; **~-ugly** *n.* (*US sl.*) (*thug*) хулига́н; (*ruffian*) банди́юга.

plum /plʌm/ *n.* **1** (*fruit, tree*) сли́ва. **2** (*raisins*) изю́м, (*currants*) кори́нка; **~ pudding** изю́мный пу́динг, плампу́динг. **3** (*fig., prized object or possession*) ла́комый кусо́чек; **a ~ job** тёплое месте́чко.

plumage /ˈpluːmɪdʒ/ *n.* опере́ние.

plumb /plʌm/ *n.* отве́с, грузи́ло; **out of ~** накло́нный, отве́сный.

● *adj.* (*vertical*) вертика́льный.

● *adv.* (*exactly*) то́чно; (*US sl., utterly*) соверше́нно, совсе́м.

● *v.t.* (*sound*) изм|еря́ть, -е́рить ло́том; (*fig.*) прон|ика́ть, -и́кнуть в + *a.*; **he ~ed the depths of absurdity** он дошёл до по́лного абсу́рда; **~ in** (*install*) подсоедин|я́ть, -и́ть.

● *cpd.* **~-line** *n.* отве́с.

plumber /ˈplʌmə(r)/ *n.* водопрово́дчик, санте́хник.

plumbing /ˈplʌmɪŋ/ *n.* (*occupation*) слеса́рно-водопрово́дное де́ло; (*installation*) канализа́ция, водопрово́дно-канализацио́нная сеть.

plume /pluːm/ *n.* **1** (*feather*) перо́; **a ~ of smoke** шлейф ды́ма. **2** (*in headdress*) султа́н, плюма́ж.

● *v.t.*: **the bird ~s its feathers** пти́ца охора́шивается (*or* чи́стит пёрышки); (*fig.*): **he ~s himself on his skill** он ки́чится свои́м мастерство́м.

plummet /ˈplʌmɪt/ *v.i.* (**plummeted, plummeting**) об|рыва́ться, -орва́ться; (*fig.*): **shares ~ed** а́кции ре́зко упа́ли.

plummy /ˈplʌmɪ/ *adj.* (**plummier, plummiest**) (*Br. coll., of voice*) со́чный.

plump¹ /plʌmp/ *adj.* (*rounded, chubby*) пу́хлый, окру́глый; (*fattish*) по́лный.

● *v.t.*: **~ up 1** (*fatten*) отк|а́рмливать, -орми́ть. **2** (*shake up*) взб|ива́ть, -и́ть; **she ~ed up the cushions** она́ взби́ла поду́шки.

plump² /plʌmp/ *v.t.* (*drop; usu.* **~ down**) бу́х|ать, -нуть; швыр|я́ть, -ну́ть.

● *v.i.* (*fall heavily; usu.* **~ down**) бу́х|аться, -нуться; шлёп|аться, -нуться; (*make one's choice*) реш|а́ть, -и́ть; **I ~ for the roast beef** я — за ро́стбиф.

plunder /ˈplʌndə(r)/ *n.* (*looting*) грабёж; (*loot*) добы́ча.

● *v.t.* (*a person*) гра́бить, о-; (*goods*) расх|ища́ть, -и́тить; (*place*) разгр|абля́ть, -а́бить.

plunge /plʌndʒ/ *n.* **1** (*dive*) ныря́ние; (*fig.*): **he took the ~** он реши́л: была́ не была́. **2** (*violent movement*) бросо́к.

● *v.t.* погру|жа́ть, -зи́ть; **the room was ~d into darkness** ко́мната погрузи́лась во мрак; **he ~d his hands into water** он погрузи́л ру́ки в во́ду; **they were ~d into despair** они́ бы́ли пове́ргнуты в отча́яние.

● *v.i.* **1** (*dive*) окун|а́ться, -у́ться; (*fig.*): **a plunging neckline** глубо́кий вы́рез. **2** (*lunge forward*) бр|оса́ться, -о́ситься (вперёд); **the horse ~d forward** ло́шадь рвану́лась вперёд; **the ship ~d through the waves** кора́бль шёл, рассека́я во́лны; (*fig.*) погру|жа́ться, -зи́ться.

plunger /ˈplʌndʒə(r)/ *n.* (*for clearing pipes*) прока́чка; (*in mechanism*) плу́нжер, по́ршень (*m.*).

plunk /plʌŋk/ = **plank** *v.t.*

pluperfect /pluːˈpɜːfɪkt/ *n.* плюсквамперфе́кт, давнопроше́дшее вре́мя.

● *adj.* плюсквамперфе́ктный, давнопроше́дший.

plural /ˈplʊər(ə)l/ *n.* мно́жественное число́.

● *adj.*: **~ noun/pronoun** существи́тельное/местоиме́ние во мно́жественном числе́.

pluralism /ˈplʊərəˌlɪz(ə)m/ *n.* плюрали́зм.

pluralistic /plʊərəˈlɪstɪk/ *adj.* плюралисти́ческий.

plurality /plʊəˈrælɪtɪ/ *n.* (*plural state*) мно́жественность; (*large number*) мно́жество; (*relative majority*) относи́тельное большинство́.

plus /plʌs/ *n.* **1** (*symbol*) плюс. **2** (*additional or positive quantity*) доба́вочное коли́чество.

● *adj.* (*additional, extra*) доба́вочный; (*math., elec.*) положи́тельный.

● *prep.* плюс; **3 ~ 4 is 7** три плюс четы́ре — семь; **~ or minus** плюс-ми́нус.

● *cpd.* **~-fours** *n. pl.* го́льфы (*pl., g.* -ов).

plush /plʌʃ/ *n.* плюш.

● *adj.* (*made of* **~**) плю́шевый; (*sl., sumptuous; also* **plushy**) шика́рный.

plutocracy /pluːˈtɒkrəsɪ/ *n.* плутокра́тия.

plutocrat /ˈpluːtəˌkræt/ *n.* плутокра́т.

plutocratic /ˌpluːtəˈkrætɪk/ *adj.* плутократи́ческий.

plutonium /pluːˈtəʊnɪəm/ *n.* плуто́ний.

ply¹ /plaɪ/ *n.* (*layer*) слой; (*strand*) отде́льная нить; **three-~ cable** трёхсло́йный/трёхжи́льный ка́бель.

● *cpd.* **~wood** *n.* фане́ра; *adj.* фане́рный.

ply² /plaɪ/ *v.t.* **1** (*manipulate*) ору́довать (*impf.*) + *i.*; **they plied the oars** они́ налега́ли на вёсла. **2** (*work at*): **he plies an honest trade** он зараба́тывает на хлеб че́стным трудо́м. **3** (*keep supplied*) по́тчевать, по-; корми́ть, на-; **I was plied with food** меня́ хорошо́ попо́тчевали/накорми́ли; **they plied him with questions** они́ засы́пали его́ вопро́сами.

● *v.i.* курси́ровать (*impf.*).

PM (*abbr. of* ***Prime Minister***) премье́р-мини́стр.

p.m. (*abbr. of* ***post meridiem***) пополу́дни; **at 5 ~** в 5 часо́в дня/пополу́дни.

PMS (*abbr. of* ***premenstrual syndrome***) предменструа́льный синдро́м.

PMT (*abbr. of* ***premenstrual tension***) (*Br.*) предменструа́льное напряже́ние.

pneumatic /njuːˈmætɪk/ *adj.* пневмати́ческий; возду́шный; **~ drill** пневмати́ческий бури́льный молото́к.

pneumonia /njuːˈməʊnɪə/ *n.* воспале́ние лёгких, пневмони́я.

PO *abbr. of* **1** ***Post Office*** по́чта. **2** ***postal order*** (де́нежный) почто́вый перево́д. **3** ***Petty Officer*** старшина́ (*во флоте*).

● *cpd.* **~ box** *n.* абонеме́нтный я́щик.

poach¹ /pəʊtʃ/ *v.t.* (*cul.*): **~ eggs** вари́ть, с- (яйцо́-)пашо́т.

poach² /pəʊtʃ/ *v.t.* & *i.*: **~ game** браконье́рствовать (*impf.*); незако́нно охо́титься (*or* лови́ть ры́бу) (*both impf.*); **you are ~ing on my preserves** вы вме́шиваетесь в мои́ дела́.

poacher /ˈpəʊtʃə(r)/ *n.* браконье́р.

pocket /ˈpɒkɪt/ *n.* **1** (*in clothing*) карма́н; **they live in each other's ~s** они́ неразлу́чны; **he has the chairman in his ~** председа́тель у него́ в карма́не. **2** (*money resources*): **your ~ will suffer** ваш карма́н пострада́ет; э́то уда́рит по ва́шему карма́ну; **he was in ~ at the end of the day** под коне́ц дня он сде́лал при́быль/был в вы́игрыше; **I shall be out of ~** у меня́ бу́дет убы́ток; я бу́ду в про́игрыше; **out-of-~ expenses** расхо́ды, опла́чиваемые нали́чными. **3** (*at billiards*) лу́за. **4** (*small area*): **~ of resistance** оча́г сопротивле́ния; **~s of unemployment** райо́ны безрабо́тицы. **5**: **air ~** возду́шная я́ма; возду́шный мешо́к. **6** (*geol.*) карма́н, гнездо́.

P

7 (*attr., miniature*) карма́нный; **~ edition** карма́нное изда́ние.

● *v.t.* (**pocketed, pocketing**)
1 класть, положи́ть в карма́н; (*fig., appropriate*) прикарма́ни|вать, -ть.
2: **he ~ed the ball** (*billiards*) он загна́л шар в лу́зу.

● *cpds.* **~-book** *n.* (*Br., notebook*) записна́я кни́жка; (*US, handbag*) су́мочка; (*US, wallet*) бума́жник; **~-handkerchief** *n.* носово́й плато́к; **~-knife** *n.* карма́нный но́ж(ик); **~-money** *n.* (*Br.*) карма́нные де́н|ьги (*pl., g.* -er); **~-size(d)** *adj.* карма́нного форма́та; миниатю́рный.

pocketful /'pɒkɪt,fʊl/ *n.* по́лный карма́н (*чего*).

pock-marked /'pɒkmɑ:kt/ *adj.* рябо́й.

pod /pɒd/ *n.* (*seed vessel*) стручо́к.
● *v.t.* (**podded, podding**) (*shell*) лущи́ть (*impf.*).

podgy /'pɒdʒɪ/ *adj.* (**podgier, podgiest**) (*Br.*) то́лстенький, призе́мистый; (*of face*) пу́хлый, толстощёкий.

podiatrist /pə'daɪətrɪst/ *n.* специали́ст (*fem.* -ка) по лече́нию заболева́ний стоп; мозо́льный опера́тор.

podiatry /pə'daɪətrɪ/ *n.* лече́ние заболева́ний стоп.

podi|um /'pəʊdɪəm/ *n.* (*pl.* **~ums** *or* **~a**) (*archit.*) по́диум, по́дий; (*rostrum*) трибу́на; (*raised platform*) возвыше́ние, по́диум.

poem /'pəʊɪm/ *n.* стихотворе́ние; (*long narrative*) поэ́ма.

poet /'pəʊɪt/ *n.* поэ́т.

poetess /'pəʊɪtɪs/ *n.* поэте́сса.

poetic /pəʊ'etɪk/ *adj.* поэти́ческий; **~ licence** (*Br.*), **license** (*US*) поэти́ческая во́льность; **~ justice** справедли́вое возме́здие.

poetical /pəʊ'etɪk(ə)l/ *adj.* поэти́ческий, поэти́чный; **~ works** поэти́ческие произведе́ния.

poetry /'pəʊɪtrɪ/ *n.* (*also fig.*) поэ́зия; (*poetical work*) стих|и́ (*pl., g.* -о́в); (*poetical quality*) поэти́чность.

po-faced /pəʊ'feɪst/ *adj.* (*Br.*) надме́нный, чва́нный.

pogrom /'pɒgrəm/, /-rɒm/ *n.* погро́м.

poignancy /'pɔɪnjənsɪ/ *n.* острота́; го́речь.

poignant /'pɔɪnjənt/ *adj.* (*of taste etc.*) о́стрый; (*painfully moving*) о́стрый, го́рький.

point /pɔɪnt/ *n.* **1** (*sharp end*) остриё; **not to put too fine a ~ on it** (*fig.*) без обиняко́в; не делика́тничая.
2 (*tip*) ко́нчик.
3 (*promontory*) мыс.
4 (*dot*) то́чка; **full ~** то́чка; **decimal ~** (*in Russian usage*) запята́я (*отделяющая десятичную дробь от целого числа*); **two ~ five (2.5)** две це́лых и пять деся́тых; **forty-five ~ nought (45.0)** со́рок пять це́лых и ноль деся́тых; **36.6** (*human temperature Centigrade*) три́дцать шесть и шесть.
5 (*mark, position*) ме́сто, пункт; **~ of contact** (*lit., fig.*) то́чка соприкоснове́ния; **~ of departure** отправна́я/исхо́дная то́чка; **~ of view** то́чка зре́ния; **they have reached the ~ of no return** возвра́та наза́д для них уже́ нет.
6 (*moment*) моме́нт; **at this ~ he turned round** в э́тот моме́нт/тут он поверну́лся; **I was on the ~ of leaving** я уже́ собра́лся уходи́ть; **at the ~ of death** при́ смерти; **when it came to the ~, he refused** в реша́ющий моме́нт он отказа́лся.
7 (*mark on scale*) отме́тка, деле́ние; (*unit*) едини́ца; **boiling-~** то́чка кипе́ния; **up to a ~** до изве́стной сте́пени.
8 (*of the compass*) страна́ све́та.
9 (*unit of evaluation, score*) пункт, очко́; **they won on ~s** они́ вы́играли по очка́м.
10 (*chief idea, meaning, purpose*) суть, вопро́с, смысл; **that is beside the ~** не в э́том суть/де́ло; **come to the ~** до|ходи́ть, -йти́ до гла́вного/су́ти (де́ла); **that's just the ~** вот и́менно; в то́м-то и де́ло; **I don't see the ~ of the joke** э́та шу́тка мне непоня́тна; **you have a ~ there** тут вы пра́вы; **a case in ~** нагля́дный приме́р; **in ~ of fact** в действи́тельности, факти́чески; **I made a ~ of seeing him** я счёл необходи́мым повида́ться с ним; **you missed the ~** вы не по́няли су́ти (де́ла); **there was no ~ in staying** не име́ло смы́сла остава́ться; **that's not the ~** не в э́том суть; **off the ~** некста́ти, не к ме́сту; **he is off the ~** он говори́т не по существу́; **I see your ~** я вас понима́ю; **what's the ~ of it?** како́й в э́том смысл?
11 (*item*) пункт; **we agree on certain ~s** по не́которым пу́нктам мы схо́димся; **I explained the theory ~ by ~** я разъясни́л тео́рию по пу́нктам; **I suppose we can stretch a ~** я полага́ю, мы мо́жем сде́лать ски́дку; **it is a ~ of honour** (*Br.*), **honor** (*US*) **with him** для него́ э́то вопро́с че́сти; **~ of order** вопро́с по регла́менту/к поря́дку веде́ния; **that is a ~ in his favour** (*Br.*), **favor** (*US*) э́то говори́т в его́ по́льзу.
12 (*quality, trait*) черта́; **the plan has its good ~s** э́тот план не лишён досто́инств; **singing is not my strong ~** я не силён в пе́нии.
13 (*pl., in internal combustion engine*) конта́ктные прерыва́тели (*m. pl.*); (*pl., rail.*) (*Br.*) стре́лочный перево́д; стре́лки (*f. pl.*).
14 (*typ.*) пункт.

● *v.t.* **1** (*aim*) ука́з|ывать, -а́ть; пока́з|ывать, -а́ть; **he ~ed a gun at her** он навёл на неё пистоле́т; **he ~ed a finger at her** он указа́л па́льцем на неё.
2 (*fill with mortar*): **~ brickwork** расш|ива́ть, -и́ть швы кла́дки.

● *v.i.* ука́з|ывать, -а́ть (**at, to**: на + *a.*); **she ~ed at/to the door** она́ указа́ла на дверь; **the sign ~ed to the station** доро́жный знак ука́зывал направле́ние к ста́нции; **everything ~s to his guilt** всё ука́зывает на его́ вину́.

● *with adv.*: **~ out** *v.t.* ука́з|ывать, -а́ть на + *a.*; подч|ёркивать, -еркну́ть; **he ~ed out my mistakes** он указа́л мне на мои́ оши́бки.

● *cpds.* **~-blank** *adj.* (*lit.*) прямо́й; (*fig.*) категори́ческий; *adv.* пря́мо, в упо́р; **~-duty** *n.* (*Br.*) обя́занности (*f. pl.*) регулиро́вщика движе́ния; **~sman** *n.* (*Br., rail*) стре́лочник; **~-to-~** *n.* (*race*) ска́ч|ки (*pl., g.* -ек) по пересечённой ме́стности.

pointed /'pɔɪntɪd/ *adj.* **1** (*e.g. a stick*) остроконе́чный. **2** (*significant, directed against s.o.*) о́стрый, ко́лкий; подчёркнутый; **she gave me a ~ look** она́ на меня́ многозначи́тельно посмотре́ла.

pointer /'pɔɪntə(r)/ *n.* **1** (*rod*) ука́зка. **2** (*of balance etc.*) стре́лка, указа́тель (*m.*). **3** (*indication, hint*) намёк. **4** (*dog*) по́йнтер.

pointillism /'pwæntɪ,lɪz(ə)m/ *n.* (*art*) пуантили́зм.

pointillist /'pwæntɪlɪst/ *n.* (*art*) пуантили́ст.

pointing /'pɔɪntɪŋ/ *n.* (*of wall etc.*) расши́вка швов.

pointless /'pɔɪntlɪs/ *adj.* бессмы́сленный.

poise /pɔɪz/ *n.* (*equilibrium*) равнове́сие; (*self-possession*) уравнове́шенность, самооблада́ние.
● *v.t.* удерж|ивать, -а́ть в равнове́сии; **he is ~d to attack** он гото́в к нападе́нию.

poison /'pɔɪz(ə)n/ *n.* яд, отра́ва.
● *v.t.* (*lit., fig.*) отрав|ля́ть, -и́ть; **food ~ing** пищево́е отравле́ние; **he has food ~ing** он отрави́лся.
● *cpds.* **~-gas** *n.* ядови́тый газ; **~-ivy** *n.* сума́х ядоно́сный; **~-pen** *adj.*: **~-pen letter** анони́мное письмо́, анони́мка (*coll.*).

poisoner /'pɔɪzənə(r)/ *n.* отрави́тель (*m.*) (*fem.* -ница).

poisonous /'pɔɪzənəs/ *adj.* ядови́тый; (*fig.*) вре́дный; (*vicious*) злой, ядови́тый.

poke /pəʊk/ *n.* (*prod*) толчо́к; **give the fire a ~!** помеша́йте у́гли в ками́не!; **he gave me a ~ in the ribs** он ткну́л меня́ в бок.
● *v.t.* **1** (*prod*) ты́кать, ткнуть; **~ the fire** меша́ть, по- у́гли в ками́не.
2 (*thrust*) пиха́ть, пихну́ть; сова́ть, су́нуть; **he ~d his stick through the fence** он просу́нул па́лку че́рез забо́р; **he ~d his tongue out** он вы́сунул язы́к; **he ~s his nose into other people's business** он суёт нос не в своё де́ло; **he ~d fun at me** он насмеха́лся надо мно́й.
3 (*cause by prodding*): **the boy ~d a hole in his drum** ма́льчик продыря́вил бараба́н.
● *v.i.*: **he ~d about among the rubbish** он ры́лся в му́соре.

poker /'pəʊkə(r)/ *n.* **1** (*for a fire*) кочерга́; **gas ~** га́зовая зажига́лка.
2 (*game*) по́кер.
● *cpds.* **~-face** *n.* бесстра́стное/ ка́менное лицо́; **~-faced** *adj.* с ка́менным лицо́м; **~-work** *n.* (*Br.*) выжига́ние по де́реву.

poky /ˈpəʊkɪ/ *adj.* (**pokier, pokiest**) (*coll.*) тéсный, убóгий.

Poland /ˈpəʊlənd/ *n.* Пóльша.

polar /ˈpəʊlə(r)/ *adj.* **1** (*of or near either Pole*) поля́рный; **~ bear** бéлый медвéдь; **~ exploration** поля́рные исслéдования (*nt. pl.*). **2** (*elec.*) поля́рный, пóлюсный. **3** (*geom.*) поля́рный.

polarity /pəˈlærɪtɪ/ *n.* (*lit., fig.*) поля́рность.

polarization /ˌpəʊləraɪˈzeɪʃ(ə)n/ *n.* (*lit., fig.*) поляриза́ция.

polarize /ˈpəʊləˌraɪz/ *v.t. & i.* (*lit., fig.*) поляризовáть(ся) (*impf., pf.*).

Pole /pəʊl/ *n.* (*person*) поля́к (*fem.* пóлька).

pole[1] /pəʊl/ *n.* (*of the earth; also elec. and fig.*) пóлюс; **an expedition to the P~** поля́рная экспеди́ция; **he and his sister are ~s apart** они́ с сестрóй — две противоположности.

● *cpd.* **~-star** *n.* Поля́рная звездá.

pole[2] /pəʊl/ *n.* (*post, rod etc.*) столб, шест.

● *cpds.* **~-jumping, ~-vaulting** *nn.* прыжки́ (*m. pl.*) с шестóм; **~-vault** *n.* прыжóк с шестóм; **~-vaulter** *n.* шестови́к.

pole-axe /ˈpəʊlæks/ (*US also* **-ax**) *n.* (*old weapon*) секи́ра; (*butcher's implement*) топóр.

● *v.t.* заб|ивáть, -и́ть (*скот*).

polecat /ˈpəʊlkæt/ *n.* леснóй хорёк.

polemic /pəˈlemɪk/ *n.* полéмика, спор.

● *adj.* (*also* **~al**) полеми́ческий, спóрный.

polemicist /pəˈlemɪsɪst/ *n.* полеми́ст; спóрщик.

police /pəˈliːs/ *n.* поли́ция; (*in Russia*) мили́ция; **~ constable** (*Br.*) полицéйский; **~ force** поли́ция; **~ inquiry** расслéдование дéла поли́цией; **a ~ state** полицéйское госудáрство.

● *v.t.* охраня́ть, поддéрживать (*both impf.*) поря́док в+*p.*; нести́ (*det.*) полицéйскую слу́жбу в+*p.*

● *cpds.* **~man** *n.* полисмéн, полицéйский; (*in Russia*) милиционéр; **~-officer** *n.* полицéйский; **~-station** *n.* (полицéйский) учáсток; (*in Russia*) отделéние мили́ции; **~woman** *n.* жéнщина-полицéйский/милиционéр.

policy /ˈpɒlɪsɪ/ *n.* (*planned course of action*) поли́тика; (*insurance*) (страховóй) пóлис.

● *cpd.* **~holder** *n.* держáтель (*m.*) страховóго пóлиса.

polio(myelitis) /ˌpəʊlɪəʊˌmaɪˈlaɪtɪs/ *n.* полиомиели́т.

Polish /ˈpəʊlɪʃ/ *n.* (*language*) пóльский язы́к.

● *adj.* пóльский.

polish /ˈpɒlɪʃ/ *n.* **1** (*smoothness, brightness*) полирóвка. **2** (*substance used for ~ing*) полировáльная пáста. **3** (*act of ~ing*) полирóвка; **I must give my shoes a ~** я дóлжен вы́чистить тýфли. **4** (*fig., refinement*) лоск, блеск.

● *v.t.* полировáть, от-; (*metal; also fig.*) шлифовáть, от-; **~ed** (*behaviour etc.*) свéтский, утончённый.

● *with advs.*: **~ off** *v.t.* (*coll., finish*) раздéл|ываться, -аться с+*i.*, покóнчить (*pf.*) с+*i.*; **I must ~ off this letter** я дóлжен покóнчить с э́тим письмóм; **he ~ed off the cake** он бы́стро расправился с пирогóм; **~ up** *v.t.* (*lit., give gloss to*) нат|ирáть, -ерéть; **she ~ed up the silver** онá до блéска начи́стила серебрó; (*fig., improve*) совершéнствовать, у-; **I must ~ up my French** мне нýжно освежи́ть (в пáмяти) францýзский язы́к.

polisher /ˈpɒlɪʃə(r)/ *n.* (*workman*) полирóвщик; (*machine*) полировáльная маши́на.

Politburo /ˈpɒlɪtˌbjʊərəʊ/ *n.* (*pl.* **~s**) политбюрó (*indecl.*).

polite /pəˈlaɪt/ *adj.* (**politer, politest**) вéжливый, учти́вый; **~ society** изы́сканное/благовоспи́танное óбщество.

politeness /pəˈlaɪtnɪs/ *n.* вéжливость, учти́вость.

politic /ˈpɒlɪtɪk/ *adj.* **1** (*prudent*) благоразýмный. **2**: **the body ~** госудáрство.

political /pəˈlɪtɪk(ə)l/ *adj.* полити́ческий; (*pert. to internal politics*) внутриполити́ческий; **~ correctness** полити́ческая коррéктность; **~ly correct** полити́чески коррéктный; **~ prisoner** полити́ческий заключённый; **~ science** политолóгия; **~ scientist** политóлог.

politician /ˌpɒlɪˈtɪʃ(ə)n/ *n.* поли́тик; (*pej.*) политикáн.

politicization /pəˌlɪtɪsaɪˈzeɪʃ(ə)n/ *n.* политизáция.

politicize /pəˈlɪtɪˌsaɪz/ *v.t.* политизи́ровать (*impf., pf.*).

politics /ˈpɒlɪtɪks/ *n.* поли́тика; **party ~** парти́йная поли́тика; **he went into ~ as a young man** он зáнялся поли́тикой/вступи́л на полити́ческое пóприще в мóлодости; (*political views*) полити́ческие взгля́ды (*m. pl.*)/убеждéния (*nt. pl.*); **what are his ~?** каковы́ егó полити́ческие взгля́ды/убеждéния?

polka /ˈpɒlkə/, /ˈpəʊlkə/ *n.* пóлька.

● *cpd.* **~-dot** *n.* (*pattern*) узóр в горóшек; (*attr.*): **~-dot dress** плáтье в горóшек.

poll /pəʊl/ *n.* (*voting process*) голосовáние; **the country will go to the ~s in May** в странé бýдут вы́боры в мáе; **he came head of the ~** он получи́л наибóльшее коли́чество/числó голосóв; (*number of votes*) коли́чество пóданных голосóв; (*opinion canvass*) опрóс.

● *v.t.* **1** (*receive*) получ|áть, -и́ть; наб|ирáть, -рáть; **he ~ed 60,000 votes** он получи́л/набрáл 60 000 голосóв. **2** (*take votes of*): **they ~ed the meeting** они́ постáвили вопрóс на голосовáние.

● *cpd.* **~-tax** *n.* (*hist.*) подýшный налóг.

pollard /ˈpɒləd/ *n.* подстри́женное дéрево; (*attr.*) подстри́женный.

● *v.t.* подстр|игáть, -и́чь (*дерево*).

pollen /ˈpɒlən/ *n.* цветóчная пыльцá.

pollinate /ˈpɒlɪˌneɪt/ *v.t.* опыл|я́ть, -и́ть.

pollination /ˌpɒlɪˈneɪʃ(ə)n/ *n.* опылéние.

polling /ˈpəʊlɪŋ/ *n.* голосовáние.

● *cpds.* **~-booth** *n.* (*Br.*) каби́на для голосовáния; **~-day** *n.* день вы́боров; **~-station** *n.* избирáтельный учáсток.

pollster /ˈpəʊlstə(r)/ *n.* лицó, производя́щее опрóс общéственного мнéния.

pollutant /pəˈluːtənt/ *n.* загрязни́тель (*m.*); поллютáнт.

pollute /pəˈluːt/ *v.t.* загрязн|я́ть, -и́ть.

pollution /pəˈluːʃ(ə)n/ *n.* загрязнéние; **environmental ~** загрязнéние окружáющей среды́.

polo /ˈpəʊləʊ/ *n.* пóло (*indecl.*).

● *cpd.* **~-neck** (*sweater*) *n.* (*Br.*) сви́тер с кру́глым высóким воротникóм; (*of thin material*) водолáзка.

polonaise /ˌpɒləˈneɪz/ *n.* полонéз.

polonium /pəlˈəʊnɪəm/ *n.* полóний.

poltergeist /ˈpɒltəˌgaɪst/ *n.* полтергéйст.

polyandry /ˈpɒlɪˌændrɪ/ *n.* полиáндрия, многомýжие.

polyanthus /ˌpɒlɪˈænθəs/ *n.* (*pl.* **polyanthuses**) при́мула высóкая.

polyclinic /ˈpɒlɪˌklɪnɪk/ *n.* поликли́ника.

polygamist /pəˈlɪgəmɪst/ *n.* полигами́ст.

polygamous /pəˈlɪgəməs/ *adj.* полигáмный.

polygamy /pəˈlɪgəmɪ/ *n.* полигáмия, многобрáчие.

polyglot /ˈpɒlɪˌglɒt/ *n.* полиглóт.

● *adj.* многоязы́чный.

polygon /ˈpɒlɪgən/, /-ˌgɒn/ *n.* многоугóльник.

polygonal /pəˈlɪgən(ə)l/ *adj.* многоугóльный.

polygraph /ˈpɒlɪˌgrɑːf/ *n.* (*lie-detector*) полигрáф.

polymath /ˈpɒlɪˌmæθ/ *n.* эруди́т; всесторóнне осведомлённый человéк.

polymer /ˈpɒlɪmə(r)/ *n.* полимéр.

Polynesia /ˌpɒlɪˈniːʒə/ *n.* Полинéзия.

Polynesian /ˌpɒlɪˈniːʒ(ə)n/ *n.* полинези́|ец (*fem.* -йка).

● *adj.* полинези́йский.

polyp /ˈpɒlɪp/ *n.* (*zool., med.*) поли́п.

polyphonic /ˌpɒlɪˈfɒnɪk/ *adj.* полифони́ческий.

polyphony /pəˈlɪfənɪ/ *n.* полифони́я.

polypropylene /ˌpɒlɪˈprəʊpɪˌliːn/ *n.* полипропилéн.

polystyrene /ˌpɒlɪˈstaɪəˌriːn/ *n.* полистирóл.

polysyllabic /ˌpɒlɪsɪˈlæbɪk/ *adj.* многослóжный.

polytechnic /ˌpɒlɪˈteknɪk/ *n.*

политехни́ческий институ́т, полите́х (*coll.*).

● *adj.* политехни́ческий.

polytheism /ˈpɒlɪθiːˌɪz(ə)m/ *n.* политеи́зм.

polytheist /ˈpɒlɪˌθiːɪst/ *n.* политеи́ст.

polytheistic /ˌpɒlɪθiːˈɪstɪk/ *adj.* политеисти́ческий.

polythene /ˈpɒlɪˌθiːn/ *n.* (*Br.*) полиэтиле́н; (*attr.*) полиэтиле́новый.

polyunsaturated /ˌpɒlɪʌnˈsætʃəˌreɪtɪd/ *adj.*: **~ fats** полиненасы́щенные жиры́.

polyurethane /ˌpɒlɪˈjʊərəˌθeɪn/ *n.* полиурета́н.

pomade /pəˈmɑːd/ *n.* пома́да.

● *v.t.* пома́дить, на-.

pomander /pəˈmændə(r)/ *n.* ша́рик с арома́тическими тра́вами.

pomegranate /ˈpɒmɪˌgrænɪt/, /ˈpɒmˌgrænɪt/ *n.* грана́т.

Pomeranian /ˌpɒməˈreɪnɪən/ *n.* (*dog*) шпиц.

pommel /ˈpʌm(ə)l/ *n.* (*of saddle*) лука́; (*of sword*) голо́вка.

● *v.t.* (**pommelled, pommelling;** *US* **pommeled, pommeling**) = **pummel**

pomp /pɒmp/ *n.* пы́шность, по́мпа.

pom-pom /ˈpɒmpɒm/ *n.* (*Br., mil.*) малокали́берная зени́тная устано́вка.

pompom /ˈpɒmpɒm/, **pompon** /ˈpɒmpɒn/ *nn.* (*tuft*) помпо́н.

pomposity /pɒmˈpɒsɪtɪ/ *n.* помпе́зность; (*of person*) напы́щенность.

pompous /ˈpɒmpəs/ *adj.* помпе́зный; (*of person*) напы́щенный.

ponce /pɒns/ (*Br.*) *n.* (*coll.*) сутенёр.

● *v.i.*: **~ about/around** шикова́ть (*impf.*), выпе́ндриваться (*impf.*) (*sl.*).

poncho /ˈpɒntʃəʊ/ *n.* (*pl.* **~s**) по́нчо (*indecl.*).

pond /pɒnd/ *n.* пруд.

● *cpds.* **~-life** *n.* прудова́я фа́уна; **~weed** *n.* (*bot.*) рдест.

ponder /ˈpɒndə(r)/ *v.t.* обду́м|ывать, -ать; взве́|шивать, -сить.

● *v.i.* размышля́ть (*impf.*).

ponderous /ˈpɒndərəs/ *adj.* (*heavy*) тяжёлый; (*bulky*) масси́вный; (*of style etc.*) тяжелове́сный.

pong /pɒŋ/ *n.* (*Br. coll.*) вонь, злово́ние.

pontiff /ˈpɒntɪf/ *n.*: **supreme ~** (*the Pope*) Па́па ри́мский.

pontifical /pɒnˈtɪfɪk(ə)l/ *adj.* па́пский; (*fig.*) догмати́ческий.

pontificate /pɒnˈtɪfɪkət/ *v.i.* (*fig., lay down the law*) веща́ть (*impf.*).

pontoon /pɒnˈtuːn/ *n.* **1** (*boat*) понто́н; **~ bridge** понто́нный мост. **2** (*Br., card game*) два́дцать одно́.

pony /ˈpəʊnɪ/ *n.* (*horse*) по́ни (*m. indecl.*).

● *cpd.* **~-tail** *n.* хво́стик.

poodle /ˈpuːd(ə)l/ *n.* пу́дель (*m.*).

poof(ter) /pʊf/, /ˈpʊftə(r)/ *n.* (*Br. pej. sl.*) го́мик.

pooh /puː/ *int.* фу!; уф!

pooh-pooh /puːˈpuː/ *v.t.* фы́ркать (*impf.*) на + *a.*; относи́ться (*impf.*) пренебрежи́тельно к + *d.*

pool¹ /puːl/ *n.* (*small body of water*) пруд; (*puddle*) лу́жа; (**swimming-~**) (пла́вательный) бассе́йн; (*still place in river*) за́водь.

pool² /puːl/ *n.* **1** (*total of staked money*) совоку́пность ста́вок; (*in cards*) банк; **football ~s** футбо́льный тотализа́тор. **2** (*cartel*) пул. **3** (*common reserve*) о́бщий фонд. **4** (*billiards game*) пул; **~ hall, ~ room** помеще́ние для игры́ в пул. **5**: **typing ~** машинопи́сное бюро́ (*indecl.*).

● *v.t.* объедин|я́ть, -и́ть (в о́бщий фонд); **we ~ed our resources** мы объедини́ли на́ши ресу́рсы.

poop /puːp/ *n.* (*of ship*) корма́.

poor /pʊə(r)/ *n.* (*collect.*: **the ~**) бедно́та, бедняки́ (*m. pl.*), бе́дные (*pl.*).

● *adj.* **1** (*indigent*) бе́дный. **2** (*unfortunate, deserving of sympathy*) бе́дный, несча́стный; **~ fellow** бедня́га (*m.*); **~ little chap!** бедня́жка! (*c.g.*). **3** (*small, scanty*) ску́дный; плохо́й; **a ~ supply** плохо́е снабже́ние; **a ~ harvest** ни́зкий урожа́й; **a ~ response** сла́бый о́тклик. **4** (*of low quality*) плохо́й; **~ soil** бе́дная, неплодоро́дная по́чва; **~ health** плохо́е/сла́бое здоро́вье. **5** (*miserable, spiritless*) несча́стный, жа́лкий.

poorly /ˈpʊəlɪ/ *adj.* (*Br.*) нездоро́вый; **are you feeling ~?** вам нездоро́вится?

● *adv.* бе́дно; пло́хо; **his parents are ~ off** его́ роди́тели живу́т бе́дно; **this book is ~ written** э́та кни́га пло́хо напи́сана.

poorness /ˈpʊənɪs/ *n.* (*poor quality*) бе́дность; недоста́точность; **the ~ of the soil** ску́дость/неплодоро́дность по́чвы.

pop¹ /pɒp/ *n.* (*explosive sound*) щёлк, хлопо́к; (*coll., gaseous drink*) газиро́вка.

● *adv.*: **the balloon went ~** ша́рик ло́пнул; **the cork went ~** про́бка хло́пнула/вы́стрелила.

● *v.t.* (**popped, popping**) **1** (*cause to explode*): **~ a balloon** прок|а́лывать, -оло́ть ша́рик. **2** (*put suddenly*) сова́ть, су́нуть; **he ~ped his head through the window** он вы́сунул го́лову из окна́; **~ the question** (*coll.*) де́лать, с- предложе́ние.

● *v.i.* (**popped, popping**) (*make explosive sound*) хло́п|ать, -нуть, щёлк|ать, -нуть; **the sound of a cork ~ping** звук вы́стрелившей про́бки; (*shoot*) стрел|я́ть, -ьну́ть; **they were ~ping away at the target** они́ пали́ли по мише́ни.

● *with advs.* (*coll.*): **they ~ped in for a drink** они́ заскочи́ли/забежа́ли вы́пить; **I am ~ping off home now** ну, я побежа́л домо́й; **he ~ped off** (*died*) **last week** на про́шлой неде́ле он отда́л концы́ (*sl.*); **she kept ~ping out all day** она́ весь день куда́-то выска́кивала; **his eyes ~ped out** он вы́лупил глаза́; **I'll ~ over to the shop** я сбе́гаю в магази́н; **he ~ped up unexpectedly** он появи́лся неожи́данно.

● *cpds.* **~corn** *n.* попко́рн, возду́шная кукуру́за; **~-gun** *n.* пуга́ч.

pop² /pɒp/ *n.* (*coll., abbr. of* **popular** 2) (*music*) поп-му́зыка.

● *adj.*: **~ art** поп-а́рт; **~ concert** поп-конце́рт; **~ group** поп-гру́ппа; **~ singer** поп-пев|е́ц (*fem.* -и́ца); поп-музыка́нт; **~ star** поп-звезда́.

pop³ /pɒp/ *n.* (*US coll., father*) па́пка, ба́тька (*both m.*).

pope /pəʊp/ *n.* (*bishop of Rome*) Па́па ри́мский (*m.*); (*Orthodox priest*) поп.

popery /ˈpəʊpərɪ/ *n.* (*pej.*) папи́зм.

popish /ˈpəʊpɪʃ/ *adj.* (*pej.*) католи́ческий.

poplar /ˈpɒplə(r)/ *n.* то́поль (*m.*).

poplin /ˈpɒplɪn/ *n.* попли́н.

poppa /ˈpɒpə/ *n.* (*US coll.*) па́пка, па́па (*both m.*).

popper /ˈpɒpə(r)/ *n.* (*Br. coll.*) кно́пка.

poppet /ˈpɒpɪt/ *n.* (*Br., as term of endearment*) кро́шка, малы́шка; **she is a ~** она́ пре́лесть.

poppy /ˈpɒpɪ/ *n.* мак; (*attr.*) ма́ковый.

● *cpd.* **~-seed** *n.* мак.

poppycock /ˈpɒpɪˌkɒk/ *n.* чепуха́ (*coll.*).

populace /ˈpɒpjʊləs/ *n.* (*the masses*) ма́ссы (*f. pl.*).

popular /ˈpɒpjʊlə(r)/ *adj.* **1** (*of the people*) наро́дный; **~ front** наро́дный фронт. **2** (*suited to the needs, tastes etc. of the people*): **the ~ press** ма́ссовая пре́сса/печа́ть; **~ prices** общедосту́пные це́ны; **~ science** нау́чно-популя́рная литерату́ра; **~ song** популя́рная пе́сня. **3** (*generally liked*) по́льзующийся о́бщей симпа́тией; **she is ~ at school** её лю́бят в шко́ле; **he is ~ with the ladies** он име́ет успе́х у же́нщин.

popularity /ˌpɒpjʊˈlærɪtɪ/ *n.* популя́рность; успе́х.

popularization /ˌpɒpjʊləraɪˈzeɪʃ(ə)n/ *n.* популяриза́ция.

popularize /ˈpɒpjʊləˌraɪz/ *v.t.* популяризи́ровать (*impf., pf.*).

popularly /ˈpɒpjʊləlɪ/ *adv.*: **he was ~ supposed to be a magician** в наро́де его́ счита́ли волше́бником.

populate /ˈpɒpjʊˌleɪt/ *v.t.* насел|я́ть, -и́ть; засел|я́ть, -и́ть.

population /ˌpɒpjʊˈleɪʃ(ə)n/ *n.* населе́ние; жи́тели (*m. pl.*).

populism /ˈpɒpjʊlɪz(ə)m/ *n.* попули́зм; (*Russian hist.*) наро́дничество.

populist /ˈpɒpjʊlɪst/ *n.* попули́ст; (*Russian hist.*) наро́дник.

● *adj.* попули́стский; наро́днический.

populous /ˈpɒpjʊləs/ *adj.* многолю́дный, густонаселённый.

porcelain /ˈpɔːsəlɪn/ *n.* фарфо́р; (*attr.*) фарфо́ровый.

porch /pɔːtʃ/ *n.* (*covered entrance*) крыльцо́; (*a grand one*) подъе́зд; (*of church*) па́перть; (*US, veranda*) вера́нда.

porcine /ˈpɔːsaɪn/ *adj.* свино́й.

porcupine /ˈpɔ:kjʊ,paɪn/ *n.* дикобра́з.

pore[1] /pɔ:(r)/ *n.* по́ра.

pore[2] /pɔ:(r)/ *v.i.*: **he likes to ~ over old books** он лю́бит сиде́ть над ста́рыми кни́гами.

pork /pɔ:k/ *n.* свини́на; **~ chop** свина́я отбивна́я котле́та; **~ pie** пиро́г со свини́ной.

● *cpd.* **~-butcher** *n.* свинобо́ец.

porker /ˈpɔ:kə(r)/ *n.* отко́рмленный на убо́й поросёнок.

pork|y /ˈpɔ:kɪ/ *n.* (*Br. sl.*): **tell ~ies** залива́ть (*impf.*), врать (*impf.*).

● *adj.* (**porkier, porkiest**) (*coll.*) то́лстый.

porn(o) /ˈpɔ:n(əʊ)/ *n.* (*coll.*) порногра́фия, порну́ха (*coll.*).

pornographer /pɔ:ˈnɒgrəfə(r)/ *n.* челове́к, распространя́ющий порногра́фию.

pornographic /,pɔ:nəˈgræfɪk/ *adj.* порнографи́ческий.

pornography /pɔ:ˈnɒgrəfɪ/ *n.* порногра́фия.

porosity /pɔ:ˈrɒsɪtɪ/ *n.* по́ристость.

porous /ˈpɔ:rəs/ *adj.* по́ристый.

porphyry /ˈpɔ:rfɪrɪ/ *n.* (*geol.*) порфи́р.

porpoise /ˈpɔ:pəs/ *n.* (*zool.*) морска́я свинья́.

porridge /ˈpɒrɪdʒ/ *n.* овся́ная ка́ша.

port[1] /pɔ:t/ *n.* (*harbour*) порт, га́вань; **P~ of London** Ло́ндонский порт; **~ of call** порт захо́да; **free ~** во́льная га́вань.

port[2] /pɔ:t/ *n.* (*left side*) ле́вый борт; **hard to ~!** ле́во руля́!; **on the ~ bow** сле́ва по́ носу.

port[3] /pɔ:t/ *n.* (*wine*) портве́йн.

port[4] /pɔ:t/ *n.* (*comput.*) порт.

portability /,pɔ:təˈbɪlɪtɪ/ *n.* портати́вность.

portable /ˈpɔ:təb(ə)l/ *adj.* портати́вный.

portage /ˈpɔ:tɪdʒ/ *n.* перепра́ва (*судна*) во́локом; (*place*) во́лок.

● *v.t.* перепр|авля́ть, -а́вить во́локом.

portal /ˈpɔ:t(ə)l/ *n.* порта́л.

portcullis /pɔ:tˈkʌlɪs/ *n.* опускна́я решётка.

portend /pɔ:ˈtend/ *v.t.* предвеща́ть (*impf.*).

portent /ˈpɔ:tent/, /-t(ə)nt/ *n.* (*omen*) предзнаменова́ние; (*marvel*) чу́до.

portentous /pɔ:ˈtentəs/ *adj.* (*prophetic*) ве́щий; (*significant*) многозначи́тельный; (*pompous*) напы́щенный.

porter /ˈpɔ:tə(r)/ *n.* **1** (*carrier of luggage etc.*) носи́льщик. **2** (*US, sleeping car attendant*) проводни́к. **3** (*Br., door-keeper*) швейца́р. **4** (*type of beer*) по́ртер.

porterage /ˈpɔ:tərɪdʒ/ *n.* перено́ска.

portfolio /pɔ:tˈfəʊlɪəʊ/ *n.* (*pl.* **~s**) **1** (*case*) портфе́ль (*m.*); (*folder*) па́пка. **2** (*of investments*) портфе́ль (*m.*). **3** (*ministerial office*) портфе́ль (*m.*); **minister without ~** мини́стр без портфе́ля.

porthole /ˈpɔ:thəʊl/ *n.* иллюмина́тор.

portico /ˈpɔ:tɪ,kəʊ/ *n.* (*pl.* **~es** *or* **~s**) по́ртик.

portière /,pɔ:trˈeə(r)/ *n.* портье́ра.

portion /ˈpɔ:ʃ(ə)n/ *n.* (*part, share*) часть; до́ля; (*of food*) по́рция.

● *v.t.* (*divide*) дели́ть, раз-; **~ out** (*distribute*) распредел|я́ть, -и́ть.

portliness /ˈpɔ:tlɪnɪs/ *n.* доро́дство, полнота́, ту́чность.

portly /ˈpɔ:tlɪ/ *adj.* (**portlier, portliest**) доро́дный, по́лный, ту́чный.

portmanteau /pɔ:tˈmæntəʊ/ *n.* (*pl.* **~s** *or* **~x** /-z/) (складно́й) саквоя́ж.

portrait /ˈpɔ:trɪt/ *n.* портре́т.

portraitist /ˈpɔ:trɪtɪst/ *n.* портрети́ст.

portralture /ˈpɔ:trɪtʃə(r)/ *n.* портре́тная жи́вопись.

portray /pɔ:ˈtreɪ/ *v.t.* (*depict, describe*) рисова́ть, на- портре́т +*g.*; изобра|жа́ть, -зи́ть; (*act part of*) игра́ть, сыгра́ть; созд|ава́ть, -а́ть о́браз +*g.*

portrayal /pɔ:ˈtreɪəl/ *n.* (*process*) изображе́ние; (*image*) о́браз.

Portugal /ˈpɔ:tjʊg(ə)l/ *n.* Португа́лия.

Portuguese /,pɔ:tjʊˈgi:z/, /,pɔ:tʃ-/ *n.* (*pl.* **~**) **1** (*person*) португа́л|ец (*fem.* -ка); **the P~** (*pl.*) португа́льцы (*m. pl.*). **2** (*language*) португа́льский язы́к.

● *adj.* португа́льский.

● *cpd.* **~ man-of-war** *n.* (*zool.*) португа́льский кора́блик.

pose /pəʊz/ *n.* (*of body or mind*) по́за.

● *v.t.* (*put forward, propound*) предл|ага́ть, -ожи́ть; изл|ага́ть, -ожи́ть; **this ~s an awkward problem** э́то создаёт серьёзную пробле́му.

● *v.i.* **1** (*take up a position or attitude*) пози́ровать (*impf.*); **they ~d for the photograph** они́ пози́ровали для фотогра́фии; **he ~s as an expert** он выдаёт себя́ за знатока́/специали́ста. **2** (*behave in an affected way*) рисова́ться (*impf.*).

poser /ˈpəʊzə(r)/ *n.* (*problem*) загво́здка, закавы́ка; (*person*) позёр.

poseur /pəʊˈzɜ:(r)/ *n.* позёр.

posh /pɒʃ/ *adj.* (*coll.*) шика́рный, фешене́бельный; (*people*) све́тский.

posit /ˈpɒzɪt/ *v.t.* (**posited, positing**) (*postulate*) постули́ровать (*impf., pf.*).

position /pəˈzɪʃ(ə)n/ *n.* **1** (*place occupied by s.o. or something*) ме́сто, положе́ние; **he took up his ~ by the door** он заня́л своё ме́сто у две́ри; (*mil.*) пози́ция; **the enemy's ~s were stormed** пози́ции врага́ бы́ли взя́ты шту́рмом. **2** (*situation, circumstances*) положе́ние; **the ~ is desperate** положе́ние отча́янное; **that puts me in an awkward ~** э́то ста́вит меня́ в неудо́бное положе́ние; **I am not in a ~ to say** я не в состоя́нии сказа́ть. **3** (*posture*) по́за, положе́ние; **he assumed a sitting ~** он при́нял сидя́чую по́зу. **4** (*mental attitude, line of argument*) пози́ция; **allow me to state my ~** разреши́те мне вы́сказать свою́ то́чку зре́ния. **5** (*place in society, status*) положе́ние; **he is a man of wealth and ~** у него́ есть и бога́тство, и положе́ние. **6** (*post, employment*) до́лжность, ме́сто; **I am looking for a ~ as tutor** я ищу́ ме́сто репети́тора.

● *v.t.* (*place in ~*) поме|ща́ть, -сти́ть; ста́вить, по-.

positive /ˈpɒzɪtɪv/ *n.* (*gram.*) положи́тельная сте́пень; (*math.*) положи́тельное число́, положи́тельная величина́; (*phot.*) позити́в.

● *adj.* **1** (*definite, explicit*) несомне́нный, определённый; **~ proof** несомне́нное доказа́тельство. **2** (*convinced, certain*) уве́ренный, убеждённый; **are you ~ you saw him?** вы уве́рены, что ви́дели его́?; **I am quite ~ on that point** я в э́том абсолю́тно убеждён. **3** (*assertive*) самоуве́ренный. **4** (*practical, helpful*) позити́вный, конструкти́вный; **a ~ suggestion** де́льное предложе́ние; **~ discrimination** дискримина́ция в по́льзу определённой гру́ппы. **5** (*downright*) положи́тельный, зако́нченный; **he is a ~ fool** он зако́нченный дура́к. **6** (*gram., math., elec.*) положи́тельный; **a ~ charge** положи́тельный заря́д; **the ~ sign** знак плюс. **7** (*phot.*) позити́вный.

positively /ˈpɒzɪtɪvlɪ/ *adv.* несомне́нно, я́сно, абсолю́тно; положи́тельно; **she was ~ rude to me** она́ была́ со мной про́сто груба́.

positivism /ˈpɒzɪtɪ,vɪz(ə)m/ *n.* позитиви́зм.

positivist /ˈpɒzɪt,vɪst/ *n.* позитиви́ст.

positron /ˈpɒzɪ,trɒn/ *n.* позитро́н.

posse /ˈpɒsɪ/ *n.* отря́д полице́йских.

possess /pəˈzes/ *v.t.* **1** (*own, have*) владе́ть (*impf.*) +*i.*; облада́ть (*impf.*) +*i.*; име́ть (*impf.*); **all I ~ is yours** всё, что я име́ю, — ва́ше. **2** (*dominate, influence*) овлад|ева́ть, -е́ть; захва́т|ывать, -и́ть; **he is ~ed by one idea** он одержи́м одно́й иде́ей; **whatever ~ed him to do that?** что его́ заста́вило/дёрнуло (*coll.*) поступи́ть таки́м о́бразом?

possession /pəˈzeʃ(ə)n/ *n.* **1** (*ownership, occupation*) владе́ние; **they took ~ of the house** они́ ста́ли владе́льцами до́ма; **the documents are in my ~** докуме́нты в мои́х рука́х/в моём владе́нии; **he is in full ~ of his senses** он в здра́вом уме́; **~ is nine points of the law** владе́ние иму́ществом почти́ равно́ пра́ву на него́. **2** (*property*) иму́щество, со́бственность. **3** (*territory*) владе́ния (*nt. pl.*). **4** (*diabolic etc.*) одержи́мость.

possessive /pəˈzesɪv/ *n.* (*gram.*) притяжа́тельный паде́ж.

● *adj.* **1** (*gram.*) притяжа́тельный. **2** (*of person*) со́бственнический; (*jealous*) ревни́вый; **she is a ~ mother** она́ вла́стная мать.

possessiveness /pəˈzesɪvnɪs/ *n.* ревни́вость, собственни́ческий инсти́нкт.

possessor /pəˈzesə(r)/ *n.* (*owner*) владе́лец, облада́тель (*m.*).

possibility /,pɒsɪˈbɪlɪtɪ/ *n.*

P

возмóжность; (*likelihood*) веростность; **there is no ~ of his coming** возмóжность егó прихóда исключенá; **it is within the bounds of ~** э́то в предéлах возмóжного; (*pl., potentiality*) возмóжности (*f. pl.*); перспектúвы (*f. pl.*).

possible /ˈpɒsɪb(ə)l/ *n.* (**~** *choice*) возмóжное.

● *adj.* возмóжный; (*achievable*) осуществúмый; **as soon as ~** как мóжно скорéе; **I have done everything ~ to help** я сдéлал всё возмóжное, чтóбы помóчь.

possibly /ˈpɒsɪblɪ/ *adv.* **1** (*in accordance with what is possible*) возмóжно; верóятно; **how can I ~ do that?** как же я могý э́то сдéлать? **2** (*perhaps*) возмóжно; мóжет быть.

post¹ /pəʊst/ *n.* (*of wood, metal etc.*) столб; **starting ~** стáртовый столб; **winning ~** фи́нишный столб.

● *v.t.* (*display publicly*) вывéшивать, вы́весить; объяв|ля́ть, -и́ть; **'~ no bills'** «вывéшивать объявлéния воспрещáется»; **the results will be ~ed (up) on the board** результáты бýдут вы́вешены на доскé; **the ship was ~ed as missing** сýдно бы́ло объя́влено пропáвшим без вéсти.

post² /pəʊst/ *n.* (*Br., mail*) пóчта; **by ~** пóчтой, по пóчте; **by return of ~** с обрáтной пóчтой; **parcel ~** почтóво-посы́лочная слýжба; **I must take these letters to the ~** я дóлжен отнести́ э́ти пи́сьма на пóчту; **if you hurry you will catch the ~** éсли вы поспеши́те, то успéете до отпрáвки пóчты; **has the ~ come yet?** пóчта ужé былá?; **the letter came by the first ~** письмó пришлó с ýтренней пóчтой.

● *v.t.* **1** (*Br., dispatch by mail*) отпр|авля́ть, -áвить по пóчте. **2** (*book-keeping*) перен|оси́ть, -ести́ в гроссбýх; зан|оси́ть, -ести́ в бухгáлтерские кни́ги; (*fig.*) изве|щáть, -сти́ть; **keep me ~ed (of events)** держи́те меня́ в кýрсе (дел)!

● *cpds.* **~-bag** *n.* (*Br.*) сýмка почтальóна; (*mail received*) пóчта; **~-box** *n.* почтóвый я́щик; **~card** *n.* откры́тка; **picture ~card** худóжественная откры́тка; **~code** *n.* (*Br.*) почтóвый и́ндекс; **~-free** *adj.* (*Br.*) оплáченный отправи́телем; *adv.* бесплáтно; **~-haste** *adv.* óчень бы́стро; **~man** *n.* (*Br.*) почтальóн; **~mark** *n.* почтóвый штéмпель; *v.t.* стáвить, по- почтóвый штéмпель на + *a.*/*p.*; **~master** *n.* начáльник почтóвого отделéния; **~mistress** *n.* начáльница почтóвого отделéния; **~-office** *n.* пóчта; (*branch office*) отделéние свя́зи; (*main office*) почтáмт; **~-paid** *adj.* с оплáченными почтóвыми расхóдами; *adv.* бесплáтно.

post³ /pəʊst/ *n.* **1** (*place of duty*) пост; **at one's ~** на постý. **2** (*fort*) форт. **3** (*trading station*) торгóвый пост; фактóрия. **4** (*appointment, job*) дóлжность, пост. **5** (*bugle-call*): **last ~** повéстка/сигнáл к зóре.

● *v.t.* **1** (*assign to place of duty*) назн|ачáть, -áчить на дóлжность. **2** (*mil., guard, sentry*) выставля́ть, вы́ставить.

post- /pəʊst/ *pref.* по..., пóсле..., пост....

postage /ˈpəʊstɪdʒ/ *n.* почтóвый сбор; почтóвые расхóды (*m. pl.*).

● *cpd.* **~-stamp** *n.* почтóвая мáрка.

postal /ˈpəʊst(ə)l/ *adj.* почтóвый; **~ order** (*Br.*) (дéнежный) почтóвый перевóд.

post-Communist /pəʊst ˈkɒmjʊnɪst/ *adj.* посткоммунисти́ческий.

post-date /pəʊstˈdeɪt/ *v.t.* **1** (*give a date later than the actual one*) дати́ровать (*impf.*) бóлее пóздним числóм. **2** (*occur later than*) слéдовать, по- за + *i.*

poster /ˈpəʊstə(r)/ *n.* (*placard*) афи́ша, плакáт; (*advertising*) пóстер; **(bill-~)** расклéйщик афи́ш.

● *cpd.* **~-paint** *n.* плакáтная тушь.

poste restante /ˌpəʊst reˈstɑ̃t/ *n.* (*Br.*) до востребования.

posterior /pɒˈstɪərɪə(r)/ *n.* зад.

● *adj.* (*subsequent*) послéдующий; (*behind*) зáдний.

posterity /pɒˈsterɪtɪ/ *n.* (*descendants*) потóмство; (*future generations*) потóмк|и (*pl., g.* -ов); послéдующие поколéния (*nt. pl.*); **go down to ~** жить (*impf.*) в векáх, войти́ (*pf.*) в векá.

postern /ˈpɒst(ə)n/, /ˈpəʊ-/ *n.* (*back door*) зáдняя дверь; (*side entrance*) боковóй вход.

post-graduate /pəʊstˈgrædjʊət/ *n.*: **~ student** аспирáнт (*fem.* -ка); **~ studies** аспирантýра.

● *adj.* аспирáнтский.

posthumous /ˈpɒstjʊməs/ *adj.* посмéртный.

postil(l)ion /pɒˈstɪljən/ *n.* форéйтор.

post-Impressionism /ˌpəʊstɪmˈpreʃəˌnɪz(ə)m/ *n.* постимпрессиони́зм.

post-Impressionist /ˌpəʊstɪmˈpreʃənɪst/ *n.* постимпрессиони́ст.

post-industrial /ˌpəʊstɪnˈdʌstrɪəl/ *adj.* постиндустриáльный.

postmodern /pəʊstˈmɒd(ə)n/ *adj.* постмодерни́стский.

postmodernism /pəʊstˈmɒdəˌnɪz(ə)m/ *n.* постмодерни́зм.

post-mortem /pəʊstˈmɔːtəm/ *n.* (*on dead body*) вскры́тие (трýпа), аутопси́я; (*coll., on game etc.*) разбóр.

post-natal /pəʊstˈneɪt(ə)l/ *adj.* послеродовóй.

postpone /pəʊstˈpəʊn/, /pəˈspəʊn/ *v.t.* отсрóчи|вать, -ть; от|клáдывать, -ложи́ть.

postponement /pəʊstˈpəʊnmənt/, /pəˈspəʊnmənt/ *n.* отсрóчка, отклáдывание.

post-prandial /pəʊstˈprændɪəl/ *adj.* послеобéденный.

postscript /ˈpəʊstskrɪpt/, /ˈpəʊskrɪpt/ *n.* постскри́птум.

postulate¹ /ˈpɒstjʊlət/ *n.* постулáт.

postulate² /ˈpɒstjʊˌleɪt/ *v.t.* постули́ровать (*impf., pf.*).

posture /ˈpɒstʃə(r)/ *n.* (*physical attitude*) пóза; (*carriage of body*) осáнка; (*situation, condition*) положéние.

● *v.i.* пози́ровать (*impf.*).

posturer /ˈpɒstʃərə(r)/ *n.* позёр.

post-war /pəʊstˈwɔː(r)/, /ˈpəʊst-/ *adj.* послевоéнный.

posy /ˈpəʊzɪ/ *n.* букéт цветóв.

pot¹ /pɒt/ *n.* **1** (*vessel*) горшóк; (*of glass*) бáнка; (*of metal*) котелóк; **a ~ of jam** бáнка варéнья; **~s and pans** кýхонная посýда/ýтварь; **a ~ of tea** чáйник с завáренным чáем; **~ plant** (*Br.*) горшéчное растéние; **his work is going to ~** (*coll.*) егó рабóта идёт насмáрку; **a watched ~ never boils** кто над чáйником стои́т, у тогó он не кипи́т. **2** (*coll., usu. pl., large sum*): **~s of money** кýча дéнег. **3** (*coll., prize cup*) кýбок. **4** (*coll., paunch*) пýзо.

● *v.t.* (**potted, potting**) **1** (*e.g. preserves*) консерви́ровать, за-; **~ted meat** консерви́рованное мя́со. **2** (*e.g. plants*) сажáть, посади́ть в горшóк; **~ting shed** помещéние для пересáдки растéний. **3** (*fig., abridge*) сокра|щáть, -ти́ть; урéз|ывать, -ать; **~ted history** крáткая истóрия. **4** (*billiards*) заг|оня́ть, -нáть в лýзу. **5** (*coll., kill with a ~-shot*) подстрéл|ивать, -и́ть.

● *cpds.* **~-bellied** *adj.* пузáтый; **~-belly** *n.* пýзо; брю́хо (*pej.*); **~-boiler** *n.* (*book etc.*) халтýра; **~-holder** *n.* кýхонная рукави́ца, прихвáтка; **~hole** *n.* (*in road surface*) вы́боина, ры́твина; (*in the ground*) котлови́на; (*underground*) провáл; **~-holer** *n.* (спортсмéн-)спелеóлог; **~-holing** *n.* (*Br.*) спелеолóгия; **~-roast** *n.* тушёное мя́со; *v.t.* туши́ть, по-; **~-shot** *n.* неприцéльный вы́стрел.

pot² /pɒt/ *n.* (*coll., marijuana*) трáвка, анашá; **~ smoker** анаши́ст.

● *cpd.* **~head** *n.* (*sl.*) анаши́ст.

potash /ˈpɒtæʃ/ *n.* (*chem.*) потáш; (*hydroxide*) гидрокси́д кáлия, éдкое кáли; (*carbonate*) карбонáт кáлия.

potassium /pəˈtæsɪəm/ *n.* кáлий; (*attr.*) кáлиевый.

potato /pəˈteɪtəʊ/ *n.* (*pl.* **~es**) (*collect., and pl.*) картóфель (*m.*), картóшка (*coll.*); (*single* **~**) картóфелина; **mashed ~es** картóфельное пюрé (*indecl.*); **~ chips** (*US*) хрустя́щий картóфель; чи́пс|ы (*pl., g.* -ов); **~ crop** урожáй картóфеля; **~ crisps** (*Br.*) хрустя́щий картóфель; чи́пс|ы (*pl., g.* -ов).

potency /ˈpəʊt(ə)nsɪ/ *n.* си́ла; могýщество; эффекти́вность; (*of alcoholic drink*) крéпость; (*sexual*) потéнция.

potent /ˈpəʊt(ə)nt/ *adj.* (*powerful*) си́льный, могýщественный; (*efficacious*) эффекти́вный; (*of alcoholic drink*) крéпкий.

potentate /'pəʊtən,teɪt/ *n.* повели́тель (*m.*), властели́н.

potential /pə'tenʃ(ə)l/ *n.* потенциа́л.
● *adj.* потенциа́льный.

potentialit|y /pə,tenʃɪ'ælɪtɪ/ *n.* потенциа́льность; **he has great ~ies** у него́ бо́льшие зада́т|ки (*pl., g.* -ов)/ возмо́жности.

potion /'pəʊʃ(ə)n/ *n.* насто́йка, сна́добье; **love ~** любо́вный напи́ток.

potpourri /pəʊ'pʊərɪ/, /-'ri:/ *n.* (*pl.* **~s**) (*lit., fig.*) попурри́ (*nt. indecl.*).

potsherd /'pɒtʃɜ:d/ *n.* черепо́к.

pottage /'pɒtɪdʒ/ *n.* (*arch.*) похлёбка.

potter[1] /'pɒtə(r)/ *n.* гонча́р; **~'s wheel** гонча́рный круг.

potter[2] /'pɒtə(r)/ *v.i.* (*e.g. in garden*) копа́ться (*impf.*), ковыря́ться (*impf.*); **he ~ed along the road** он плёлся по доро́ге.

pottery /'pɒtərɪ/ *n.* (*ware*) кера́мика; (*craft*) гонча́рное де́ло; (*workshop*) гонча́рня.

potty[1] /'pɒtɪ/ *n.* (*coll., chamber-pot*) горшо́к.

potty[2] /'pɒtɪ/ *adj.* (**pottier, pottiest**) (*Br.*) (*trifling*) ме́лкий, пустяко́вый; (*crazy*) чо́кнутый (*coll.*).

pouch /paʊtʃ/ *n.* су́мочка, мешо́чек; **tobacco ~** кисе́т; (*container for documents etc.*) па́пка; **diplomatic ~** (*US*) дипломати́ческая по́чта; (*kangaroo's*) су́мка; (*fig., loose skin*) мешо́к.

pouf(fe) /pu:f/ *n.* (*seat*) пуф.

poulterer /'pəʊltərə(r)/ *n.* (*Br.*) торго́вец пти́цей и ди́чью.

poultice /'pəʊltɪs/ *n.* припа́рка.
● *v.t.* ста́вить, по- припа́рки на + *a.*

poultry /'pəʊltrɪ/ *n.* дома́шняя пти́ца (*collect.*).
● *cpds.* **~-farm** *n.* птицефе́рма; **~-farmer** *n.* птицево́д; **~farming** *n.* птицево́дство; **~-house** *n.* пти́чник; **~man** *n.* птицево́д; торго́вец дома́шней пти́цей; **~-run** *n.* пти́чий волье́р; **~-yard** *n.* пти́чий двор.

pounce /paʊns/ *n.* (*swoop*) налёт, прыжо́к.
● *v.i.* набр|а́сываться, -о́ситься; **the cat ~d on the mouse** ко́шка бро́силась на мышь; (*fig.*) кида́ться, ки́нуться (*or* наки́дываться, наки́нуться) (*на кого/что*).

pound[1] /paʊnd/ *n.* **1** (*weight*) фунт; **butter is 60p a ~** ма́сло сто́ит 60 пе́нсов за фунт. **2** (*money*) фунт (сте́рлингов); **a five-~ note** банкно́т в 5 фу́нтов сте́рлингов.

pound[2] /paʊnd/ *n.* (*enclosure*) заго́н.

pound[3] /paʊnd/ *v.t.* **1** (*crush*) разб|ива́ть, -и́ть; **the ship was ~ed on the rocks** кора́бль уда́рило о ска́лы. **2** (*thump*) колоти́ть (*impf.*).
● *v.i.* **1** (*thump*): **the guns were ~ing away** ору́дия бу́хали/пали́ли (*coll.*) вовсю́; **he ~ed at the door** он колоти́л в дверь; **his feet ~ed on the stairs** он то́пал по ле́стнице; **her heart was ~ing with excitement** её се́рдце колоти́лось от волне́ния. **2** (*run heavily*) мча́ться/нести́сь (*both impf.*) с гро́хотом.

poundage /'paʊndɪdʒ/ *n.* (*weight*) вес (в фу́нтах); (*Br., percentage paid per pound*) проце́нт, отчисля́емый с фу́нта сте́рлингов.

-pounder /'paʊndə(r)/ *comb. form*: **he caught a three~** (*fish*) он пойма́л ры́бу ве́сом в три фу́нта; (*gun firing shot of — pounds*): **100~** ≈ 152-мм пу́шка.

pour /pɔ:(r)/ *v.t.* лить (*impf.*); нал|ива́ть, -и́ть; **will you ~ me (out) a cup of tea?** нале́йте мне, пожа́луйста, ча́шку ча́я; **who will ~** (*the tea*)? кто бу́дет разлива́ть чай?; (*fig.*): **he ~ed scorn on the idea** он вы́смеял э́ту иде́ю; **he tried to ~ oil on troubled waters** он пыта́лся остуди́ть стра́сти; **he ~ed cold water on my suggestion** он раскритикова́л моё предложе́ние.
● *v.i.* ли́ться (*impf.*); **water ~ed from the roof** вода́ лила́сь/струи́лась с кры́ши; **sweat ~ed off his brow** с него́ ли́лся/кати́лся пот; (*fig.*): **the crowd ~ed out of the theatre** (*Br.*), **theater** (*US*) толпа́ повали́ла из теа́тра (*coll.*); (*of rain*) лить (*impf.*) как из ведра́; **it's going to ~** бу́дет ли́вень; **it was ~ing with rain** шёл проливно́й дождь, дождь лил как из ведра́.
● *with advs.* (*fig.*): **letters ~ed in** посы́пались пи́сьма; **she ~ed out a tale of woe** она́ излила́ своё го́ре; **his words ~ed out in a flood** слова́ ли́лись из него́ пото́ком.

pout /paʊt/ *n.* наду́тые гу́бы (*f. pl.*).
● *v.i.* над|ува́ть, -у́ть гу́бы; ду́ться, на-.

pouter /'paʊtə(r)/ *n.* (*pigeon*) зоба́стый го́лубь.

poverty /'pɒvətɪ/ *n.* бе́дность, нищета́; **on the ~ line** на гра́ни нищеты́; (*fig.*) (*scarcity*) нехва́тка; (*lack*) отсу́тствие; **~ of ideas** ску́дость мы́слей.
● *cpds.* **~-stricken** *adj.* (*lit.*) ни́щий; (*fig.*) убо́гий; **~ trap** *n.* состоя́ние неизбе́жной бе́дности.

POW (*abbr. of* ***prisoner of war***) военнопле́нный.

powder /'paʊdə(r)/ *n.* (*chem., med. etc.*) порошо́к; (*cosmetic*) пу́дра; (*explosive*) по́рох; **keep your ~ dry** (*fig.*) держи́те по́рох сухи́м; бу́дьте начеку́.
● *v.t.* **1** (*reduce to ~*) превра|ща́ть, -ти́ть в порошо́к; **~ed milk** порошко́вое/сухо́е молоко́. **2** (*apply ~ to*) пу́дрить, на-.
● *cpds.* **~-blue** *adj.* зеленова́то-голубо́й; **~-magazine** *n.* порохово́й по́греб; **~-puff** *n.* пухо́вка; **~-room** *n.* да́мская (туале́тная) ко́мната.

powdery /'paʊdərɪ/ *adj.* порошкообра́зный; рассы́пчатый.

power /'paʊə(r)/ *n.* **1** (*ability, capacity*) си́ла, мощь; **I will do all in my ~** я сде́лаю всё, что в мои́х си́лах; **it is not within my ~** э́то не в мое́й вла́сти; **purchasing ~** покупа́тельная спосо́бность; **his voice has great carrying ~** у него́ о́чень си́льный го́лос; **his ~s of resistance are low** у него́ сла́бая сопротивля́емость; **this ring has the ~ to make you invisible** э́то кольцо́ облада́ет сво́йством де́лать челове́ка неви́димым; **the ~ to express one's thoughts** спосо́бность выража́ть свои́ мы́сли.
2 (*pl., faculties*): **he is a man of considerable ~s** он наделён больши́ми спосо́бностями; **he was at the height of his ~s** он был в расцве́те сил; **his ~s are failing** его́ си́лы угаса́ют.
3 (*vigour, strength*) эне́ргия; **more ~ to your elbow!** (*Br.*), **to you!** (*US*) жела́ю уда́чи!
4 (*electrical energy*) эне́ргия; **electric ~** электроэне́ргия; **there was a ~ cut** электроэне́ргию вре́менно отключи́ли; (*mechanical energy*) мо́щность; **the machine is on full ~** маши́на рабо́тает на по́лную мо́щность.
5 (*authority, control*) власть; **I have him in my ~** он в мое́й вла́сти; **he has no ~ over me** он на́до мной не вла́стен; у него́ нет на́до мной вла́сти; **France was at the height of her ~** Фра́нция находи́лось в расцве́те своего́ могу́щества; **in ~** у вла́сти; **the party in ~** пра́вящая па́ртия; **they are out of ~** они́ потеря́ли власть; **balance of ~** равнове́сие сил; **~ politics** поли́тика с пози́ции си́лы.
6 (*right, authorization*) полномо́чия (*nt. pl.*), пра́во; **the judge exceeded his ~s** судья́ превы́сил свои́ полномо́чия; **the committee has ~ to co-opt members** комите́т име́ет пра́во коопти́ровать чле́нов.
7 (*influential person or organization*) си́ла; **he is a great ~ for good** его́ влия́ние весьма́ благотво́рно; **the ~s that be** си́льные (*pl.*) ми́ра сего́.
8 (*state*) держа́ва; **the Great P~s** вели́кие держа́вы.
9 (*supernatural force*) си́ла; **the ~s of darkness** си́лы тьмы.
10 (*coll., large number or amount*) ма́сса, мно́жество; **this medicine has done me a ~ of good** э́то лека́рство принесло́ мне огро́мную по́льзу.
11 (*math.*) сте́пень; **two to the ~ of ten** два в деся́той сте́пени.
● *v.t.* (*supply with electrical energy*) снаб|жа́ть, -ди́ть эне́ргией; (*supply with mechanical energy*) прив|оди́ть, -ести́ в де́йствие; **an aircraft ~ed by four jets** самолёт приводи́мый в де́йствие четырьмя́ реакти́вными дви́гателями.
● *cpds.* **~-boat** *n.* мото́рный ка́тер; **~-dive** *n.* пики́рование с рабо́тающим мото́ром; **~ drill** *n.* электри́ческая дрель; **~-driven** *adj.* с механи́ческим приво́дом; **~-house** *n.* силова́я ста́нция; **~ line** *n.* ли́ния электропереда́чи; **~-plant, ~-station** *nn.* электроста́нция; **~-point** *n.* (*Br.*) электроввод, ште́псельная розе́тка; **~ tool** *n.* электри́ческий инструме́нт.

powerful /'paʊə,fʊl/ *adj.* си́льный, мо́щный; **a ~ voice** си́льный го́лос; **a ~ argument** мо́щный/убеди́тельный до́вод; **a ~ nation** могу́щественный наро́д; **a ~ speech** я́ркая/впечатля́ющая речь.

P

powerless /ˈpaʊəlɪs/ *adj.* бесси́льный; **I was ~ to move** я был не в си́лах дви́нуться; **he is ~ in the matter** он бесси́лен что́-либо сде́лать.

powwow /ˈpaʊwaʊ/ (*coll.*) *n.* сове́т, совеща́ние.

● *v.i.* совеща́ться (*impf.*).

pox /pɒks/ *n.* (*coll.*) си́филис.

poxy /ˈpɒksɪ/ *adj.* (**poxier, poxiest**) (*Br. coll.*) никуды́шный, парши́вый.

pp (*abbr. of* ***per procurationem***): **John Brown pp A. Smith** по дове́ренности Джо́на Бра́уна подписа́л А. Смит.

pp. /ˈpeɪdʒɪz/ *n.* (*abbr. of* ***pages***) стр. (страни́цы).

PR *abbr. of* **1** ***public relations*** *see* ⇒**public** *adj.* 1. **2** ***proportional representation*** пропорциона́льное представи́тельство.

practicability /ˌpræktɪkəˈbɪlɪtɪ/ *n.* осуществи́мость, реа́льность.

practicable /ˈpræktɪkəb(ə)l/ *adj.* (*feasible*) осуществи́мый, реа́льный.

practical /ˈpræktɪk(ə)l/ *adj.* **1** (*concerned with practice*) практи́ческий; **a ~ joke** ро́зыгрыш, шу́тка; **play a ~ joke on** разы́гр|ывать, -а́ть; **he is a ~ man** он практи́ческий челове́к; **you must be ~ about it** вы должны́ смотре́ть на э́то с практи́ческой то́чки зре́ния. **2** (*useful in practice*) практи́чный; (*workable, feasible*) осуществи́мый, реа́льный; **this is not a ~ suggestion** э́то предложе́ние нереа́льно. **3** (*virtual*) факти́ческий; **it is a ~ impossibility** э́то практи́чески невозмо́жно.

practicality /ˌpræktɪˈkælɪtɪ/ *n.* практи́чность.

practically /ˈpræktɪkəlɪ/ *adv.* **1** (*in a practical manner*) практи́чески; **look at a question ~** смотре́ть, по- на вопро́с с практи́ческой то́чки зре́ния. **2** (*almost*) практи́чески, факти́чески; почти́.

practice /ˈpræktɪs/ *n.* **1** (*performance*) пра́ктика; **the idea will not work in ~** э́та иде́я на пра́ктике неосуществи́ма; **he put his plan into ~** он осуществи́л свой план. **2** (*regular or habitual performance*) обы́чай, обыкнове́ние; **he makes a ~ of early rising** он взял себе́ за пра́вило ра́но встава́ть; **my usual ~ is to tip** я име́ю обыкнове́ние дава́ть чаевы́е; **borrowing money is a bad ~** брать де́ньги в долг — скве́рная привы́чка; **this ~ must stop** э́ту пра́ктику на́до прекрати́ть; **sharp ~** моше́нничество, махина́ции (*f. pl.*); **put into ~** осуществ|ля́ть, -и́ть. **3** (*repeated exercise*) упражне́ние, трениро́вка, пра́ктика; **~ makes perfect** ≈ повторе́ние мать уче́ния; на́вык ма́стера ста́вит; **your game needs more ~** вам на́до бо́льше трени́роваться; **I am badly out of ~** я давно́ не упражня́лся/практикова́лся. **4** (*work of doctor, lawyer etc.*) пра́ктика; **he is in ~ in York** он име́ет пра́ктику в Йо́рке.

● *v.t. & i.* (*US*) = **practise**

practician /prækˈtɪʃ(ə)n/ *n.* пра́ктик.

practis|e /ˈpræktɪs/ (*US* **practice**) *v.t.* **1** (*perform habitually*) де́лать, с- по привы́чке; **you should ~e what you preach** ва́ши слова́ не должны́ расходи́ться с де́лом; (*for exercise*) упражня́ть (*impf.*), отраб|а́тывать, -о́тать; **you should ~e this stroke** вам ну́жно отрабо́тать э́тот уда́р; (*sport game etc.*) упражня́ться (*impf.*) в + *p.*; (*instrument*): **she was ~ing the piano** она́ упражня́лась на роя́ле. **2** (*a profession etc.*) практикова́ть (*impf.*); **a ~ing physician** практику́ющий врач.

● *v.i.* упражня́ться (*impf.*); тренирова́ться (*impf.*).

practitioner /prækˈtɪʃənə(r)/ *n.* (*med.*) практику́ющий врач; **general ~** участко́вый врач, врач о́бщей пра́ктики.

pragmatic /prægˈmætɪk/ *adj.* прагмати́ческий.

pragmatism /ˈprægməˌtɪz(ə)m/ *n.* прагмати́зм.

pragmatist /ˈprægmətɪst/ *n.* прагма́тик.

Prague /prɑːg/ *n.* Пра́га.

prairie /ˈpreərɪ/ *n.* пре́рия.

praise /preɪz/ *n.* похвала́; **his work is beyond ~** его́ рабо́та вы́ше вся́кой похвалы́; **he was loud in her ~s** он гро́мко хвали́л её; **~ be (to God)!** сла́ва Бо́гу!

● *v.t.* (*voice approval, admiration of*) хвали́ть, по-; (*give glory to*) восхвал|я́ть, -и́ть.

● *cpd.* **~worthy** *adj.* досто́йный похвалы́, похва́льный.

pram /prɑːm/ *n.* (*Br.*) (де́тская) коля́ска.

prance /prɑːns/ *n.* (*leap*) скачо́к.

● *v.i.* (*of horse*) гарцева́ть (*impf.*); (*of person*) ва́жничать (*impf.*), форси́ть (*impf.*) (*coll.*).

prang /præŋ/ (*Br. coll.*) *n.* ава́рия, столкнове́ние.

● *v.t.* разб|ива́ть, -и́ть.

prank /præŋk/ *n.* вы́ходка, проде́лка; **he is up to his ~s again** он опя́ть взя́лся за свои́ прока́зы; **play ~s on** разы́грывать (*impf.*); **play a ~ on** разыгра́ть (*pf.*).

prankster /ˈpræŋkstə(r)/ *n.* шутни́к, прока́зник.

prat /præt/ *n.* (*Br. coll., idiot*) идио́т (*fem.* -ка).

prate /preɪt/ *v.i.* трепа́ться (*impf.*).

prattle /ˈpræt(ə)l/ *n.* болтовня́; (*childish*) ле́пет.

● *v.i.* болта́ть (*impf.*); (*of child*) лепета́ть, про-.

prattler /ˈprætlə(r)/ *n.* болту́н.

prawn /prɔːn/ *n.* креве́тка.

pray /preɪ/ *v.t.* (*supplicate*) моли́ть (*impf.*); умол|я́ть, -и́ть; **~ God he comes in time** дай Бог, что́бы он пришёл во́время.

● *v.i.* моли́ться, по-; **the farmers ~ed for rain** фе́рмеры моли́ли Бо́га, что́бы пошёл дождь; **we will ~ for the Queen** мы бу́дем моли́ться за короле́ву.

prayer /ˈpreə(r)/ *n.* **1** (*act of praying*) моле́ние, моли́тва. **2** (*formula, petition*) моли́тва; **the Lord's P~** О́тче наш; **say one's ~s** моли́ться, по-. **3** (*entreaty*) мольба́, про́сьба. **4** (*also pl., religious service*) богослуже́ние.

● *cpds.* **~-book** *n.* моли́твенник; **~mat, ~-rug** *nn.* моли́твенный ко́врик; **~-meeting** *n.* моли́твенное собра́ние.

pre- /priː/ *pref.* (*beforehand, in advance*) до..., пред...; зара́нее; (*dating from before*) до....

preach /priːtʃ/ *v.t.* пропове́довать (*impf.*); **go out and ~ the gospel!** иди́те и неси́те лю́дям Ева́нгелие!; **he ~ed the virtue of thrift** он пропове́довал бережли́вость.

● *v.i.* (*deliver sermon*) чита́ть про́поведь; (*give moral advice*) наставля́ть (*impf.*), поуча́ть (*impf.*) (*coll.*); **~ to the converted** ≈ ломи́ться (*impf.*) в откры́тую дверь.

preacher /ˈpriːtʃə(r)/ *n.* пропове́дник.

preamble /priːˈæmb(ə)l/, /ˈpriː-/ *n.* преа́мбула.

pre-arrange /ˌpriːəˈreɪndʒ/ *v.t.* организо́в|ывать, -а́ть зара́нее; **at a ~d signal** по усло́вленному зна́ку/сигна́лу.

pre-arrangement /ˌpriːəˈreɪndʒmənt/ *n.* предвари́тельная подгото́вка/договорённость.

prebend /ˈprebənd/ *n.* пребе́нда.

prebendary /ˈprebəndərɪ/ *n.* пребенда́рий.

precarious /prɪˈkeərɪəs/ *adj.* **1** (*uncertain*) ненадёжный; **a ~ foothold** ненадёжная опо́ра; **~ health** сла́бое здоро́вье; **he makes a ~ living** он едва́ зараба́тывает на жизнь. **2** (*dangerous, risky*) опа́сный, риско́ванный.

precaution /prɪˈkɔːʃ(ə)n/ *n.* предосторо́жность; **it is wise to take ~s against fire** разу́мно приня́ть ме́ры предосторо́жности про́тив (*or* на слу́чай) пожа́ра.

precautionary /prɪˈkɔːʃənərɪ/ *adj.* предупреди́тельный, профилакти́ческий; **~ measures** ме́ры предосторо́жности.

preced|e /prɪˈsiːd/ *v.t.* (*take ~ence of, come before*) предше́ствовать (*impf.*) + *d.*; (*walk ahead of*): **he was ~ed by his wife** жена́ шла впереди́ него́.

● *v.i.*: **in the ~ing sentence** в предыду́щем предложе́нии.

precedence /ˈpresɪd(ə)ns/ *n.* **1** (*priority, superiority*) первоочерёдность, приорите́т; **this question takes ~** э́тот вопро́с до́лжен рассма́триваться в пе́рвую о́чередь. **2** (*right of preceding others*) старшинство́.

precedent /ˈpresɪd(ə)nt/ *n.* прецеде́нт; **there is no ~ for this** э́то не име́ет прецеде́нта; **create, set a ~** созд|ава́ть, -а́ть (*or* устан|а́вливать, -ови́ть) прецеде́нт.

precept /ˈpriːsept/ *n.* (*moral instruction*) наставле́ние; (*command*) предписа́ние.

pre-Christian /priːˈkrɪstɪən/ *adj.* дохристиа́нский.

precinct /ˈpriːsɪŋkt/ *n.* **1** (*enclosed

space) двор. **2** (*pl., environs*) окре́стности (*f. pl.*). **3** (*Br., area of restricted access*): **pedestrian ~** пешехо́дная зо́на; **shopping ~** торго́вый центр. **4** (*US, police or electoral district*) уча́сток.

precious /ˈpreʃəs/ *adj.* **1** (*of great value*) драгоце́нный; **~ stones** драгоце́нные ка́мни (*m. pl.*); (*as endearment*) люби́мый; **my ~** мой люби́мый/ненагля́дный. **2** (*affected, over-refined*) мане́рный.
● *adv.* (*coll.*) о́чень, здо́рово; **I got ~ little for the ring** я получи́л за кольцо́ о́чень ма́ло; **there is ~ little hope** наде́жды почти́ нет.

preciousness /ˈpreʃəsnɪs/ *n.* (*value*) драгоце́нность; (*affectation*) мане́рность.

precipice /ˈpresɪpɪs/ *n.* про́пасть, обры́в; **fall over a ~** срыва́ться, сорва́ться с обры́ва.

precipitate[1] /prɪˈsɪpɪtət/ *adj.* (*headlong*) стреми́тельный; (*rash*) опроме́тчивый.

precipitate[2] /prɪˈsɪpɪˌteɪt/ *v.t.* **1** (*throw down*) низв|ерга́ть, -е́ргнуть; (*fig.*) вв|ерга́ть, -е́ргнуть; **the country was ~d into war** страну́ вве́ргли в войну́. **2** (*bring on rapidly*) уск|оря́ть, -о́рить. **3** (*chem.*) оса|жда́ть, -ди́ть.

precipitation /prɪˌsɪpɪˈteɪʃ(ə)n/ *n.* (*rain etc.*) оса́д|ки (*pl., g.* -ов).

precipitous /prɪˈsɪpɪtəs/ *adj.* (*steep*) обры́вистый, круто́й; (*hasty*) поспе́шный.

precipitousness /prɪˈsɪpɪtəsnɪs/ *n.* (*steepness*) обры́вистость, крутизна́; (*haste*) поспе́шность.

précis /ˈpreɪsiː/ *n.* (*pl.* **~** /-siːz/) резюме́ (*indecl.*), конспе́кт.

precise /prɪˈsaɪs/ *adj.* (*exact*) то́чный, аккура́тный; (*punctilious*) тща́тельный.

precisely /prɪˈsaɪslɪ/ *adv.* то́чно; (*with numbers or quantities*) ро́вно; **at ~ two o'clock** ро́вно в два часа́; **~ nothing** ро́вно ничего́; (*as reply: 'quite so'*) соверше́нно ве́рно; вот и́менно.

preciseness /prɪˈsaɪsnɪs/ *n.* то́чность, чёткость; тща́тельность.

precision /prɪˈsɪʒ(ə)n/ *n.* то́чность; аккура́тность; **~ bombing** прице́льное бомбомета́ние; **~ instrument** то́чный прибо́р.

preclude /prɪˈkluːd/ *v.t.* (*prevent*) предотвра|ща́ть, -ти́ть; (*make impossible*) исключ|а́ть, -и́ть.

precocious /prɪˈkəʊʃəs/ *adj.* ра́но разви́вшийся.

precoci|ousness /prɪˈkəʊʃəsnɪs/, **-ty** /prɪˈkɒsɪtɪ/ *nn.* ра́ннее разви́тие.

precognition /ˌpriːkɒgˈnɪʃ(ə)n/ *n.* предви́дение.

preconceived /ˌpriːkənˈsiːvd/ *adj.* предвзя́тый.

preconception /ˌpriːkənˈsepʃ(ə)n/ *n.* предвзя́тое мне́ние.

pre-condition /ˌpriːkənˈdɪʃ(ə)n/ *n.* предвари́тельное усло́вие.

precursor /priːˈkɜːsə(r)/ *n.* предше́ственник; (*of event*) предве́стник.

pre-date /priːˈdeɪt/ *v.t.* (*antedate*) дати́ровать (*impf., pf.*) за́дним (*or* бо́лее ра́нним) число́м; (*precede*) предше́ствовать (*impf.*) + *d.*

predator /ˈpredətə(r)/ *n.* хи́щник.

predatory /ˈpredətərɪ/ *adj.* (*animal*) хи́щный; (*fig.*) хи́щный, граби́тельский; (*instinct*) хи́щнический.

predecease /ˌpriːdɪˈsiːs/ *v.t.*: **he ~d her** он у́мер ра́ньше её.

predecessor /ˈpriːdɪˌsesə(r)/ *n.* предше́ственник; **this car is bigger than its ~** э́то маши́на бо́льше ста́рой/пре́жней.

predestination /priːˌdestɪˈneɪʃ(ə)n/ *n.* предопределе́ние.

predestine /priːˈdestɪn/ *v.t.* предопредел|я́ть, -и́ть.

predetermination /ˌpriːdɪtɜːmɪˈneɪʃ(ə)n/ *n.* предопределе́ние.

predetermine /ˌpriːdɪˈtɜːmɪn/ *v.t.* предреш|а́ть, -и́ть.

predicament /prɪˈdɪkəmənt/ *n.* тру́дная ситуа́ция, тру́дное положе́ние, затрудне́ние; **that puts me in a ~** э́то ста́вит меня́ в тру́дное положе́ние.

predicate[1] /ˈpredɪkət/ *n.* (*gram.*) сказу́емое; (*log.*) предика́т, утвержде́ние.

predicate[2] /ˈpredɪˌkeɪt/ *v.t.* утвер|жда́ть, -ди́ть.

predication /ˌpredɪˈkeɪʃ(ə)n/ *n.* предика́ция, утвержде́ние.

predicative /prɪˈdɪkətɪv/ *adj.* предикати́вный.

predict /prɪˈdɪkt/ *v.t.* предска́з|ывать, -а́ть.

predictable /prɪˈdɪktəb(ə)l/ *adj.* предсказу́емый.

prediction /prɪˈdɪkʃ(ə)n/ *n.* предсказа́ние.

predilection /ˌpriːdɪˈlekʃ(ə)n/ *n.* пристра́стие, скло́нность (**for**: к + *d.*).

predispose /ˌpriːdɪˈspəʊz/ *v.t.* предраспол|ага́ть, -ожи́ть; **I am ~d in his favour** (*Br.*), **favor** (*US*) я предраспо́ложен в его́ по́льзу; **my mother is ~d to rheumatism** моя́ мать предраспо́ложена к ревмати́зму.

predisposition /ˌpriːdɪspəˈzɪʃ(ə)n/ *n.* предрасположе́ние, скло́нность (*к чему*).

predominance /prɪˈdɒmɪnəns/ *n.* (*control; superiority*) превосхо́дство; госпо́дство; (*preponderance*) преоблада́ние, домини́рование.

predominant /prɪˈdɒmɪnənt/ *adj.* (*without rival*) преоблада́ющий, превосходя́щий; (*preponderant*) домини́рующий.

predominate /prɪˈdɒmɪˌneɪt/ *v.i.* преоблада́ть (*impf.*); домини́ровать (*impf.*).

pre-election /ˌpriːɪˈlekʃ(ə)n/ *adj.* предвы́борный.

pre-eminence /priːˈemɪnəns/ *n.* превосхо́дство, преиму́щество.

pre-eminent /priːˈemɪnənt/ *adj.* выдаю́щийся.

pre-empt /priːˈempt/ *v.t.* (*appropriate*) присв|а́ивать, -о́ить; завлад|ева́ть, -е́ть + *i.*; (*forestall*) предупре|жда́ть, -ди́ть.

pre-emption /priːˈempʃ(ə)n/ *n.* присвое́ние.

pre-emptive /priːˈemptɪv/ *adj.* опережа́ющий; **~ strike** упрежда́ющий уда́р.

preen /priːn/ *v.t.* (*of bird*): **~ one's feathers** чи́стить, по- пе́рья/пёрышки; (*of person*) прихор|а́шиваться, -оши́ться.

pre-existence /ˌpriːɪgˈzɪstəns/ *n.* предсуществова́ние.

pre-existent /ˌpriːɪgˈzɪstənt/ *adj.* предсуществу́ющий.

prefabricate /priːˈfæbrɪˌkeɪt/ *v.t.*: **~d house** (*coll.*, **prefab**) сбо́рный дом.

prefabrication /priːˌfæbrɪˈkeɪʃ(ə)n/ *n.* изготовле́ние сбо́рных дета́лей.

preface /ˈprefəs/ *n.* (*written*) предисло́вие; (*spoken*) вво́дное сло́во; (*fig.*) вступле́ние, проло́г.
● *v.t.* де́лать, с- вступле́ние к + *d.*; предпос|ыла́ть, -ла́ть; **he ~d his remarks with a quotation** он на́чал свои́ замеча́ния с цита́ты.

prefatory /ˈprefətərɪ/ *adj.* вступи́тельный, вво́дный.

prefect /ˈpriːfekt/ *n.* **1** (*official*) префе́кт. **2** (*Br., at school*) ста́рший учени́к, ста́роста (*c.g.*), префе́кт.

prefecture /ˈpriːfektjʊə(r)/ *n.* префекту́ра.

prefer /prɪˈfɜː(r)/ *v.t.* (**preferred, preferring**) **1** (*like better*) предпоч|ита́ть, -е́сть; **I ~ juice to water** я предпочита́ю сок воде́. **2** (*submit*): **~ charges** предъяв|ля́ть, -и́ть обвине́ния.

preferable /ˈprefərəb(ə)l/ *adj.* предпочти́тельный; **it's not a comfortable bed, but it's ~ to sleeping on the floor** э́та крова́ть не о́чень удо́бна, но я предпочита́ю спать на ней, а не на полу́.

preference /ˈprefərəns/ *n.* (*greater liking*) предпочте́ние; **he has a ~ for silk ties** он пита́ет сла́бость к шёлковым га́лстукам; **have you any ~?** что вы предпочита́ете?; **I chose this in ~ to the other** я предпочёл э́то тому́; **we cannot give you ~ over everyone else** мы не мо́жем дать вам предпочте́ние пе́ред все́ми други́ми; (*preferred thing*) вы́бор.

preferential /ˌprefəˈrenʃ(ə)l/ *adj.* предпочти́тельный; льго́тный.

preferment /prɪˈfɜːmənt/ *n.* продвиже́ние по слу́жбе.

prefix /ˈpriːfɪks/ *n.* (*at beginning of word*) приста́вка, пре́фикс; (*title such as* 'Mr') ти́тул.
● *v.t.* присоедин|я́ть, -и́ть (*приставку к слову*).

pregnancy /ˈpregnənsɪ/ *n.* бере́менность.

P

pregnant /ˈpregnənt/ *adj.* бере́менная; **become ~** забере́менеть (*pf.*); (*fig.*) чрева́тый; **words ~ with meaning** слова́, испо́лненные смы́сла; **a ~ silence** многозначи́тельное молча́ние.

pre-heat /priːˈhiːt/ *v.t.* предвари́тельно подогр|ева́ть, -е́ть.

prehensile /priːˈhensaɪl/ *adj.* (*zool.*) хвата́тельный.

prehistoric /ˌpriːhɪˈstɒrɪk/ *adj.* доистори́ческий.

prehistory /ˌpriːˈhɪstərɪ/ *n.* предысто́рия.

prejudge /priːˈdʒʌdʒ/ *v.i.* предреш|а́ть, -и́ть.

prejudgement /priːˈdʒʌdʒmənt/ *n.* предреше́ние.

prejudice /ˈpredʒʊdɪs/ *n.* **1** (*preconceived opinion*) предрассу́док, предубежде́ние. **2** (*detriment*) уще́рб, вред. **3** (*prejudgement*): **without ~** без уще́рба (для + *g.*); (*leg.*) не отка́зываясь от свои́х прав.

● *v.t.* **1** (*cause to have a ~*) предубе|жда́ть, -ди́ть; **you are ~d against him** вы предубеждены́ про́тив него́. **2** (*harm*) нан|оси́ть, -ести́ уще́рб + *d.*

prejudicial /ˌpredʒʊˈdɪʃ(ə)l/ *adj.* (*detrimental*) вре́дный; ущемля́ющий; нанося́щий уще́рб + *d.*

prelate /ˈprelət/ *n.* прела́т.

prelim /ˈpriːlɪm/, /prɪˈlɪm/ *n.* (*pl., typ.*) сбо́рный лист.

preliminary /prɪˈlɪmɪnərɪ/ *n.* подготови́тельное мероприя́тие; (*pl., remarks*) предвари́тельные замеча́ния; (*pl., sport*) отбо́рочные соревнова́ния (*nt. pl.*).

● *adj.* предвари́тельный.

prelude /ˈpreljuːd/ *n.* (*mus.*) прелю́дия; (*fig.*): **this was the ~ to the storm** э́то был пе́рвый гром пе́ред бу́рей.

● *v.t.* (*serve as ~ to*) служи́ть (*impf.*) вступле́нием к + *d.*

premarital /priːˈmærɪt(ə)l/ *adj.* добра́чный.

premature /ˈpreməˌtjʊə(r)/, /-ˈtjʊə(r)/ *adj.* преждевре́менный; **~ birth** преждевре́менные ро́д|ы (*pl., g.* -ов); **~ baby** недоно́шенный ребёнок; **~ decision** необду́манное/поспе́шное реше́ние.

premeditate /priːˈmedɪˌteɪt/ *v.t.*: **~d murder** преднаме́ренное уби́йство.

premeditation /priːˌmedɪˈteɪʃ(ə)n/ *n.* преднаме́ренность.

premenstrual /priːˈmenstrʊəl/ *adj.* предменструа́льный.

premier /ˈpremɪə(r)/ *n.* премье́р-(мини́стр).

● *adj.* пе́рвый; гла́вный.

première /ˈpremɪˌeə(r)/ *n.* премье́ра; **the film had its ~ last night** премье́ра фи́льма состоя́лась вчера́.

premiership /ˈpremɪəʃɪp/ *n.* премье́рство.

premise /ˈpremɪs/ *n.* **1** (*log., Br. also* **premiss**) посы́лка. **2** (*pl., house and land*) помеще́ние; **drinks are to be consumed on the ~s** напи́тки продаю́тся распи́вочно; **licensed ~s** помеще́ние, в кото́ром разрешена́ прода́жа спиртны́х напи́тков.

premium /ˈpriːmɪəm/ *n.* (*pl.* **~s**) **1** (*reward*) награ́да; **this will put a ~ on dishonesty** э́то бу́дет поощря́ть нече́стность. **2** (*amount paid for insurance*) (страхова́я) пре́мия. **3** (*additional charge or payment*) припла́та. **4**: **at a ~** вы́ше номина́ла; с при́былью; (*in demand*) по́льзующийся спро́сом.

premonition /ˌpreməˈnɪʃ(ə)n/, /ˌpriː-/ *n.* предчу́вствие.

pre-natal /priːˈneɪt(ə)l/ *adj.* предродово́й.

preoccupation /priːˌɒkjʊˈpeɪʃ(ə)n/ *n.* (*mental absorption*) озабо́ченность, поглощённость; (*absorbing subject*) забо́та; **his one ~ is making money** его́ еди́нственная забо́та — де́лать де́ньги.

preoccup|y /priːˈɒkjʊˌpaɪ/ *v.t.* забо́тить, о-; **the match ~ied his thoughts** матч занима́л все его́ мы́сли; **he was too ~ied to pay attention** он не обрати́л внима́ния, так как был сли́шком поглощён свои́ми мы́слями.

pre-ordain /ˌpriːɔːˈdeɪn/ *v.t.* предназн|ача́ть, -а́чить.

prep /prep/ (*Br.*) *n.* (*coll., school work set*) уро́ки (*m. pl.*).

● *adj.* (*coll.*): **~ school** (ча́стная) приготови́тельная шко́ла.

pre-packed /priːˈpækd/ *adj.* расфасо́ванный.

preparation /ˌprepəˈreɪʃ(ə)n/ *n.* **1** (*process of preparing or being prepared*) подгото́вка, приготовле́ние; **she was packing in ~ for the journey** она́ укла́дывала ве́щи, гото́вясь к пое́здке; **a second edition is in ~** гото́вится второ́е изда́ние; (*pl., preparatory measures*) приготовле́ния (*nt. pl.*); **~s are well under way** подгото́вка идёт по́лным хо́дом; **he made ~s to leave** он сде́лал приготовле́ния к отъе́зду; он подгото́вился к отъе́зду. **2** (*medicine*) лека́рство.

preparatory /prɪˈpærətərɪ/ *adj.* подготови́тельный.

● *adv.*: **~ to** пре́жде чем (+ *inf.*); до того́ как (+ *finite v.*); **~ to leaving** пре́жде чем уе́хать, пе́ред отъе́здом.

prepare /prɪˈpeə(r)/ *v.t.* гото́вить (*impf.*); пригот|а́вливать, -о́вить; подгот|а́вливать, -о́вить; **she ~d a meal** она́ пригото́вила еду́; **I was ~d for the worst** я был гото́в/пригото́вился к са́мому ху́дшему; **the tutor ~d him for his exams** учи́тель подгото́вил его́ к экза́менам; **he ~d his speech in advance** он подгото́вил свою́ речь зара́нее.

● *v.i.* подгот|а́вливаться, -о́виться; пригот|а́вливаться, -о́виться; **they ~d for an attack** они́ пригото́вились к ата́ке.

preparedness /prɪˈpeərɪdnɪs/ *n.* гото́вность.

prepay /priːˈpeɪ/ *v.t.* опла́|чивать, -ти́ть зара́нее.

preponderance /prɪˈpɒndərəns/ *n.* переве́с, преиму́щество.

preponderant /prɪˈpɒndərənt/ *adj.* преоблада́ющий.

preponderate /prɪˈpɒndəˌreɪt/ *v.i.* преоблада́ть (*impf.*); переве́|шивать, -сить.

preposition /ˌprepəˈzɪʃ(ə)n/ *n.* предло́г.

prepositional /ˌprepəˈzɪʃənəl/ *adj.* предло́жный.

prepossessing /ˌpriːpəˈzesɪŋ/ *adj.* располага́ющий, привлека́тельный.

prepossession /ˌpriːpəˈzeʃ(ə)n/ *n.* предрасположе́ние.

preposterous /prɪˈpɒstərəs/ *adj.* (*absurd*) неле́пый, бредо́вый; (*outrageous*) возмути́тельный.

Pre-Raphaelite /priːˈræfəˌlaɪt/ *n.* прерафаэли́т.

● *adj.* прерафаэли́тский.

prerecorded /ˌpriːrɪˈkɔːdɪd/ *adj.* предвари́тельно запи́санный.

prerequisite /priːˈrekwɪzɪt/ *n.* предпосы́лка.

pre-revolutionary /ˌpriːˌrevəˈljuːʃənərɪ/ *adj.* дореволюцио́нный.

prerogative /prɪˈrɒgətɪv/ *n.* (*of ruler, etc.*) прерогати́ва; (*privilege*) привиле́гия.

presage /ˈpresɪdʒ/ *n.* (*portent*) предзнаменова́ние, при́знак; (*presentiment*) (дурно́е) предчу́вствие.

● *v.t.* (*portend*) предвеща́ть (*impf.*).

Presbyterian /ˌprezbɪˈtɪərɪən/ *n.* пресвитериа́н|ин (*fem.* -ка).

● *adj.* пресвитериа́нский.

pre-school /ˈpriːskuːl/ *adj.* дошко́льный.

prescience /ˈpresɪəns/ *n.* предви́дение.

prescient /ˈpresɪənt/ *adj.* предви́дящий.

prescribe /prɪˈskraɪb/ *v.t.* **1** (*lay down, impose*) предпи́с|ывать, -а́ть; **penalties ~d by the law** ме́ры наказа́ния, предусмо́тренные зако́ном. **2** (*med.*) пропи́с|ывать, -а́ть.

prescription /prɪˈskrɪpʃ(ə)n/ *n.* **1** (*prescribing*) предпи́сывание; (*recommendation*) распоряже́ние, предписа́ние. **2** (*from doctor*) реце́пт; (*medicine*) лека́рство. **3** (*leg.*) (*claim founded on long use*) пра́во да́вности; (*ancient custom*) непи́саный зако́н.

prescriptive /prɪˈskrɪptɪv/ *adj.* **1** (*giving directions*) предпи́сывающий. **2** (*leg.*): **~ right** пра́во, осно́ванное на да́вности.

pre-select /ˌpriːsɪˈlekt/ *v.t.* предвари́тельно отбира́ть, отобра́ть.

presence /ˈprez(ə)ns/ *n.* **1** (*being present*) прису́тствие; **~ of mind** прису́тствие ду́ха; **a military ~** вое́нное прису́тствие; континге́нт во́йск. **2** (*impressive bearing*) внуши́тельная оса́нка.

● *cpd.* **~-chamber** *n.* приёмный зал.

present[1] /ˈprez(ə)nt/ *n.* **1** (*time now at hand*) настоя́щее (вре́мя); **there's no time like the ~** ≈ лу́чше не откла́дывать; **at ~** в настоя́щее вре́мя; сейча́с; **for the ~** пока́; **he lives in the ~** он живёт сего́дняшним днём.
2 (*gram.*, **~ tense**) настоя́щее вре́мя.

● *adj.* **1** (*at hand*) прису́тствующий; **~ company excepted** о прису́тствующих не говоря́т; **no one else was ~** никого́ бо́льше не́ было; **all ~ and correct** все налицо́; всё в поря́дке.
2 (*in question, under consideration*) да́нный, настоя́щий; **in the ~ case** в да́нном слу́чае; **the ~ writer** пи́шущий э́ти стро́ки.
3 (*existent, prevalent*) настоя́щий, тепе́решний, ны́нешний; (*available, to hand*) име́ющийся; **at the ~ time** в настоя́щее вре́мя; сейча́с; **the ~ holder of the title** ны́нешний облада́тель ти́тула; **under ~ circumstances** в да́нных обстоя́тельствах; **~ value** (*of an object*) тепе́решняя цена́.
4 (*gram.*) настоя́щего вре́мени; **~ participle** прича́стие настоя́щего вре́мени.

● *cpd.* **~-day** *adj.* совреме́нный, ны́нешний.

present[2] /ˈprez(ə)nt/ *n.* (*gift*) пода́рок; **I will make you a ~ of this shawl** я вам подарю́ э́ту шаль.

present[3] /prɪˈzent/ *v.t.* **1** (*tender, offer, put forward*) дари́ть, по-; вруч|а́ть, -и́ть; преподн|оси́ть, -ести́; **the little girl ~ed a bouquet** де́вочка преподнесла́ буке́т цвето́в; **the waiter ~ed the bill** официа́нт предъяви́л счёт; **he ~ed himself for duty** он яви́лся на слу́жбу; **as soon as an opportunity ~s itself** как то́лько предста́вится слу́чай; (*expound*) изл|ага́ть, -ожи́ть; **he ~ed his case well** он хорошо́ изложи́л свои́ до́воды; (*give, furnish*) предост|авля́ть, -а́вить; **she ~ed her husband with a son** она́ подари́ла му́жу сы́на; **I was ~ed with a choice** мне предоста́вили вы́бор.
2 (*introduce*) предст|авля́ть, -а́вить; **may I ~ my wife?** разреши́те предста́вить вам мою́ жену́; **she was ~ed at court** она́ была́ предста́влена ко двору́.
3 (*put on stage*) пока́з|ывать, -а́ть; **this play was first ~ed in New York** э́ту пье́су впервы́е показа́ли/поста́вили в Нью-Йо́рке.
4 (*TV, radio*) вести́ (*impf.*).
5 (*exhibit*): **the situation ~s a threat** положе́ние чрева́то опа́сностью; **he ~ed a bold front** он напусти́л на себя́ хра́брый вид.
6 (*mil.*): **~ arms** брать, взять на карау́л; (*as command*) на карау́л!

presentable /prɪˈzentəb(ə)l/ *adj.* прили́чный, респекта́бельный.

presentation /ˌprezənˈteɪʃ(ə)n/ *n.* **1** (*making a present*) подноше́ние, вруче́ние; **~ copy** (*of a book*) да́рственный экземпля́р.
2 (*introduction, esp. at court*) представле́ние; (*of a product*) презента́ция. **3** (*theatr.*) пока́з, постано́вка. **4** (*production, submission*) предъявле́ние; **the cheque** (*Br.*), **check** (*US*) **is payable on ~** чек бу́дет опла́чен по предъявле́нии.
5 (*exposition*) изложе́ние, пода́ча.

presenter /prɪˈzentə(r)/ *n.* (*TV, radio*) веду́щ|ий (*fem.* -ая).

presentiment /prɪˈzentɪmənt/, /-ˈsentɪmənt/ *n.* предчу́вствие; **he had a ~ of danger** он предчу́вствовал опа́сность.

presently /ˈprezəntlɪ/ *adv.* (*soon*) вско́ре; (*US, at present*) сейча́с, в настоя́щее вре́мя, в да́нный моме́нт.

preservation /ˌprezəˈveɪʃ(ə)n/ *n.* **1** (*act of preserving*) сохране́ние; консерви́рование; (*of materials*) консерва́ция; **~ of life** сохране́ние жи́зни; **~ of food** консерви́рование проду́ктов; (*of monuments, etc.*) охра́на.
2 (*state of being preserved*) сохра́нность; **the building is in a fine state of ~** э́то зда́ние прекра́сно сохрани́лось.

preservative /prɪˈzɜːvətɪv/ *n.* (*in food*) консерва́нт.

preserve /prɪˈzɜːv/ **1** (*jam*) варе́нье.
2 (*area for protection of game, etc.*) запове́дник; (*fig.*): **this subject is his private ~** э́то его́ о́бласть.

● *v.t.* **1** (*save; protect from harm*) сохран|я́ть, -и́ть; **God ~ us!** упаси́ нас Бог/Госпо́дь! **2** (*keep from decomposition, etc.*) консерви́ровать, за-. **3** (*game, etc. from poachers*) охраня́ть (*impf.*) от браконье́рства.
4 (*keep alive, youthful etc.*) сохран|я́ть, -и́ть; **his name will be ~d for ever** его́ и́мя оста́нется в века́х; **she is well ~d** она́ хорошо́ сохрани́лась.
5 (*maintain*) подде́рж|ивать, -а́ть; храни́ть, со-; **he ~d his dignity** он сохрани́л своё досто́инство; **she ~d a discreet silence** она́ благоразу́мно храни́ла молча́ние.

preside /prɪˈzaɪd/ *v.i.* председа́тельствовать (*impf.*); **the mayor ~d over the council** мэр председа́тельствовал на заседа́нии сове́та.

presidency /ˈprezɪdənsɪ/ *n.* президе́нтство.

president /ˈprezɪd(ə)nt/ *n.* (*of State etc.*) президе́нт; (*of college*) ре́ктор, дире́ктор; (*US, of company, bank etc.*) президе́нт, глава́ (*c.g.*).

presidential /ˌprezɪˈdenʃ(ə)l/ *adj.* президе́нтский; ре́кторский.

presidium /prɪˈsɪdɪəm/, /-ˈzɪdɪəm/ *n.* прези́диум.

press /pres/ *n.* **1** (*act of ~ing*): **he gave her hand a ~** он пожа́л ей ру́ку; **she gave his trousers a ~** она́ погла́дила ему́ брю́ки.
2 (*machine for ~ing*) пресс.
3 (*printing-machine*) пресс; печа́тный стано́к; **we go to ~ tomorrow** за́втра но́мер идёт в печа́ть; **newspaper hot from the ~** све́жий но́мер газе́ты; **stop ~ (news)** э́кстренное сообще́ние; **'stop ~'** (*heading*) «в после́днюю мину́ту».
4 (*printing or publishing house*) изда́тельство.
5 (*newspaper world*) печа́ть, пре́сса; **~ agency** аге́нтство печа́ти; **~ agent** аге́нт по дела́м печа́ти; **~ campaign** кампа́ния в печа́ти; **~ conference** пресс-конфере́нция; **~ pass** про́пуск корреспонде́нта; **~ release** сообще́ние для печа́ти; пресс-рели́з; (*newspaper reaction*) о́тклик, реце́нзия; **a good ~ helps to sell a book** хоро́шие о́тклики в печа́ти спосо́бствуют сбы́ту кни́ги; **the bill had a bad ~** пре́сса недоброжела́тельно встре́тила э́тот законопрое́кт.
6 (*cupboard*) шкаф.
7 (*for racket*) зажи́м для раке́тки.

● *v.t.* **1** (*exert physical pressure on*) наж|има́ть, -а́ть; нада́в|ливать, -и́ть; **~ the trigger/button** наж|има́ть, -а́ть (на) куро́к/кно́пку.
2 (*push*) приж|има́ть, -а́ть; **he ~ed his nose against the window** он прижа́л нос к окну́.
3 (*iron.*) гла́дить, по-; утю́жить, от-; **my suit needs ~ing** мой костю́м нужда́ется в утю́жке; (*grapes*) дави́ть (*impf.*); **the villagers are ~ing the grapes** жи́тели дере́вни да́вят виногра́д; (*fruit*) выжима́ть, вы́жать; **the juice ~ed from a lemon** сок из вы́жатого лимо́на.
4 (*embrace*) приж|има́ть, -а́ть; **she ~ed the child to her bosom** она́ прижа́ла ребёнка к груди́; (*clasp*) сжима́ть, сжать; **he ~ed her hand** он сжал ей ру́ку.
5 (*fig., sustain vigorously*): **our team ~ed home its attack** на́ша кома́нда энерги́чно атакова́ла; **he ~ed his claim** он наста́ивал на своём тре́бовании; **~ charges** выдвига́ть, вы́двинуть обвине́ние.
6 (*fig., harry, exert pressure on*): **our forces were hard ~ed** враг си́льно тесни́л на́ши войска́; **he was hard ~ed for an answer** он не нашёл, что отве́тить; **I was ~ed for time** у меня́ бы́ло вре́мени в обре́з.
7 (*urge, importune*): **they ~ed me to stay** они́ угова́ривали меня́ оста́ться; **he ~ed me for a decision** он торопи́л меня́ с реше́нием.
8 (*insist on acceptance of*) навя́зывать, навяза́ть; **he ~ed money on me** он навя́зывал мне де́ньги.
9 (*recruit forcibly*) наси́льно вербова́ть, за-; **every available chair was ~ed into service** все име́ющиеся сту́лья пошли́ в ход.

● *v.i.*: **if you ~ too hard, the pencil will break** е́сли сли́шком нажима́ть, каранда́ш слома́ется; (*fig.*): **his responsibilities ~ed heavily upon him** обя́занности легли́ на него́ тя́жким бре́менем; **time ~es** вре́мя не те́рпит/ждёт; **~ for** (*reform, enquiry etc.*) добива́ться (*impf.*) + *g.*

● *with advs.*: **~ back** *v.t.* оттесн|я́ть, -и́ть; **~ down** *v.t.* приж|има́ть, -а́ть; прида́в|ливать, -и́ть; **~ forward** *v.i.* прот|а́лкиваться, -олкну́ться (вперёд); **~ on** *v.i.* продолжа́ть (*impf.*); **~ on regardless!** продолжа́йте несмотря́ ни на что!; **~ out** *v.t.* выжима́ть, вы́жать; **~ up** *v.t.* тесни́ть, по-.

P

● *cpds.* **~-button** *n.* (*Br.*) нажимна́я кно́пка; **~-clipping, ~-cutting** *nn.* газе́тная вы́резка; **~-gallery** *n.* ло́жа пре́ссы; **~-gang** *n.* (*hist.*) отря́д вербо́вщиков во флот; *v.t.* наси́льно вербова́ть, за- во флот; (*fig.*) ока́з|ывать, -а́ть давле́ние на + *a.*; **~man** *n.* (*Br.*) журнали́ст, газе́тчик, репортёр; **~-stud** *n.* (*Br.*) кно́пка (*одёжная*); **~-up** *n.* (*Br.*) отжи́м; **do ~-ups** отж|има́ться, -а́ться (на полу́); **he did 50 ~-ups** он отжа́лся 50 раз.

pressing[1] /ˈpresɪŋ/ *n.* (*of clothing*) гла́жка, утю́жка.

pressing[2] /ˈpresɪŋ/ *adj.* (*urgent*) настоя́тельный, неотло́жный; (*insistent*) насто́йчивый.

pressure /ˈpreʃə(r)/ *n.* **1** давле́ние; **the tyre** (*Br.*), **tire** (*US*) **~s are low** давле́ние в ши́нах ни́зкое; **~ suit** пневмокостю́м; (*fig.*) напряже́ние; **they are working at high ~** они́ рабо́тают о́чень напряжённо. **2** (*compulsive influence*) давле́ние, возде́йствие; **bring ~ to bear on** ока́зывать, оказа́ть давле́ние на + *a.*; **they brought ~ to bear on him to sign** они оказа́ли на него́ давле́ние, что́бы он подписа́лся; **put ~ on** ока́зывать, оказа́ть давле́ние/нажи́м на + *a.*; наж|има́ть, -а́ть на + *a.* (*coll.*); **the police put ~ on him** поли́ция оказа́ла нажи́м/давле́ние на него́; **~ group** ≈ инициати́вная гру́ппа.

● *cpds.* **~-cooker** *n.* скорова́рка; **~-gauge** *n.* мано́метр.

pressurize /ˈpreʃəˌraɪz/ *v.t.* **1** герметизи́ровать (*impf.*); **~d cabin** герметизи́рованная каби́на. **2** (*fig.*) ока́з|ывать, -а́ть давле́ние на + *a.*; **he was ~d into writing a confession** его́ заста́вили написа́ть призна́ние.

prestige /preˈstiːʒ/ *n.* прести́ж.

prestigious /preˈstɪdʒəs/ *adj.* прести́жный.

prestissimo /preˈstɪsɪˌməʊ/ *n., adj. & adv.* (*pl.* **~s**) (*mus.*) прести́ссимо (*indecl.*).

presto[1] /ˈprestəʊ/ *n., adj. & adv.* (*pl.* **~s**) (*mus.*) пре́сто (*indecl.*).

presto[2] /ˈprestəʊ/ *int.*: **(hey) ~!** гопля́!

pre-stressed /priːˈstrest/ *adj.* предвари́тельно напряжённый.

presumably /prɪˈzjuːməblɪ/ *adv.* вероя́тно; на́до полага́ть, что....

presume /prɪˈzjuːm/ *v.t.* **1** (*assume, take for granted*) полага́ть (*impf.*); **you are married, I ~?** я полага́ю, вы жена́ты? **2** (*with inf.*: *venture*) брать, взять на себя́ сме́лость; осме́ли|ваться, -ться; **I would not ~ to argue with you** я не возьму́ на себя́ сме́лость с ва́ми спо́рить.

● *v.i.*: **~ on** (*take liberties with*): **he ~d on my good nature** он злоупотреби́л мое́й доброто́й.

presumption /prɪˈzʌmpʃ(ə)n/ *n.* **1** (*assumption*) предположе́ние, (*phil., leg.*) презу́мпция; **~ of innocence** презу́мпция невино́вности; **I left on the ~ he would follow** я ушёл, предполага́я, что он после́дует за мной; **the ~ is that he is lying** на́до исходи́ть из того́, что он лжёт. **2** (*arrogance, boldness*) самомне́ние, самонаде́янность.

presumptive /prɪˈzʌmptɪv/ *adj.* предположи́тельный.

presumptuous /prɪˈzʌmptjʊəs/ *adj.* самонаде́янный.

presumptuousness /prɪˈzʌmptjʊəsnɪs/ *n.* самомне́ние, самонаде́янность.

presuppose /ˌpriːsəˈpəʊz/ *v.t.* (зара́нее) предпол|ага́ть, -ожи́ть; допус|ка́ть, -ти́ть.

presupposition /priːˌsʌpəˈzɪʃ(ə)n/ *n.* предположе́ние, допуще́ние; (*thing assumed*) исхо́дная посы́лка.

pre-tax /priːˈtæks/ *adj.* начи́сленный до вы́чета нало́гов; **~ profits** при́быль до нало́га.

pretence /prɪˈtens/ (*US* **pretense**) *n.* **1** (*pretending, make-believe*) притво́рство; **he made a ~ of reading the newspaper** он притвори́лся, что чита́ет газе́ту; **he obtained money by false ~s** он раздобы́л де́ньги обма́нным путём. **2** (*pretext, excuse*) предло́г, отгово́рка; **he called under the ~ of asking advice** он зашёл под предло́гом спроси́ть сове́та. **3** (*claim*) прете́нзия; **I make no ~ to scholarship** я не претенду́ю на учёность. **4** (*ostentation*) претенцио́зность, претенз́ия; **a man without ~** челове́к без претензи́й.

pretend /prɪˈtend/ *v.t. & i.* **1** (*make believe*) притворя́ться (*impf.*); де́лать, с- вид; **she is ~ing to be asleep** она́ притворя́ется, что спит; **let's ~ to be pirates!** дава́йте игра́ть в пира́тов! **2** (*claim*) претендова́ть (*impf.*); **I don't ~ to understand Einstein** я не претенду́ю на то, что понима́ю Эйнште́йна; **they both ~ed to the throne** они́ о́ба претендова́ли на престо́л.

pretender /prɪˈtendə(r)/ *n.* претенде́нт (*fem* -ка).

pretense /prɪˈtens/ (*US*) = **pretence**

pretension /prɪˈtenʃ(ə)n/ *n.* **1** (*claim*) притяза́ние, прете́нзия; **I make no ~ to literary style** я во́все не претенду́ю на литерату́рный стиль. **2** (*pretentiousness*) претенцио́зность.

pretentious /prɪˈtenʃəs/ *adj.* претенцио́зный; показно́й.

pretentiousness /prɪˈtenʃəsnɪs/ *n.* претенцио́зность.

preterite /ˈpretərɪt/ *n.* (*gram.*) претери́т.

● *adj.* претери́тный.

preternatural /ˌpriːtəˈnætʃər(ə)l/ *adj.* сверхъесте́ственный.

pretext /ˈpriːtekst/ *n.* предло́г, отгово́рка; **on, under the ~ of** под предло́гом + *g.*

prettify /ˈprɪtɪˌfaɪ/ *v.t.* укр|аша́ть, -а́сить.

prettiness /ˈprɪtɪnɪs/ *n.* милови́дность; пре́лесть, привлека́тельность.

pretty /ˈprɪtɪ/ *adj.* (**prettier, prettiest**) **1** (*attractive*) краси́вый, хоро́шенький. **2** (*iron.*) хоро́шенький, весёленький; **a ~ mess you have made of it!** ну и ка́шу вы завари́ли! **3** (*considerable*) значи́тельный; **this will cost you a ~ penny** э́то вам обойдётся в копе́ечку.

● *adv.* **1** (*fairly*) доста́точно, дово́льно; **I have ~ well finished my work** я почти́ что зако́нчил свою́ рабо́ту; **~ much** о́чень, в значи́тельной сте́пени; почти́. **2**: **he is sitting ~** он непло́хо устро́ился.

● *cpd.* **~-~** *adj.* (*of person*) смазли́вый, ку́кольный; (*of thing*) хоро́шенький; как карти́нка; как конфе́тка.

pretzel /ˈprets(ə)l/ *n.* кренделёк.

prevail /prɪˈveɪl/ *v.i.* **1** (*win*) торжествова́ть, вос-; (*idea, principle*) возобла́дать (*impf.*); **truth will ~** пра́вда восторжеству́ет; **~ over** одол|ева́ть, -е́ть. **2** (*be widespread*) преоблада́ть (*impf.*), госпо́дствовать (*impf.*), превали́ровать (*impf.*); **~ing winds** преоблада́ющие ве́тры; **the fashion still ~s** э́та мо́да ещё госпо́дствует; **calm ~s** цари́т споко́йствие. **3**: **~ on** (*persuade*) убе|жда́ть, -ди́ть.

prevalence /ˈprevələns/ *n.* распростране́ние.

prevalent /ˈprevələnt/ *adj.* распространённый.

prevaricate /prɪˈværɪˌkeɪt/ *v.i.* виля́ть (*impf.*), уви́л|ивать, -ьну́ть.

prevarication /prɪˌværɪˈkeɪʃ(ə)n/ *n.* уви́ливание.

prevent /prɪˈvent/ *v.t.* (*stop happening*) предотвра|ща́ть, -ти́ть; (*make unable to do*) меша́ть, по- + *d.*; препя́тствовать, вос- + *d.*; **illness ~ed him from coming** боле́знь помеша́ла ему́ прийти́.

preventable /prɪˈventəb(ə)l/ *adj.* предотврати́мый.

preventative /prɪˈventətɪv/ = **preventive**

prevention /prɪˈvenʃ(ə)n/ *n.* предотвраще́ние, предупрежде́ние; (*of illness*) профила́ктика; **~ is better than cure** профила́ктика — лу́чше лече́ния.

prevent|ive /prɪˈventɪv/, **-ative** /prɪˈventətɪv/ *n.* предупреди́тельная ме́ра.

● *adj.* предупреди́тельный; **~ detention** превенти́вное заключе́ние; **~ medicine** профилакти́ческая медици́на, профила́ктика.

preview /ˈpriːvjuː/ *n.* (*of film*) (предвари́тельный) просмо́тр; (*of exhibition*) верниса́ж.

● *v.t.* предвари́тельно просм|а́тривать, -отре́ть.

previous /ˈpriːvɪəs/ *adj.* (*earlier, former*) предыду́щий; **on a ~ occasion** в предыду́щем слу́чае; **on the ~ day** за́ день до э́того.

● *adv.*: **~ to** пре́жде + *g.*, до + *g.*; **~ to that he was in the army** до э́того он был в а́рмии.

previously /ˈpriːvɪəslɪ/ *adv.* **1** (*earlier*) зара́нее, ра́ньше. **2** (*formerly*) ра́ньше, до э́того; **~ he had lived with his brother** до э́того он жил со свои́м бра́том.

pre-war /priːˈwɔː(r)/, /ˈpriːwɔː(r)/ *adj.* предвое́нный, довое́нный.

prey /preɪ/ *n.* добы́ча; **bird of ~** хи́щная пти́ца; (*fig.*) же́ртва; **he fell an easy ~ to their cunning** он оказа́лся лёгкой же́ртвой их кова́рства; **she was a ~ to anxiety** её одолева́ло/му́чило беспоко́йство.

● *v.i.* охо́титься (*impf.*); **owls ~ on mice** со́вы охо́тятся на мыше́й; (*fig.*): **he ~ed upon credulous women** он выбира́л себе́ в же́ртвы дове́рчивых же́нщин; **the crime ~ed upon his mind** (соверше́нное) преступле́ние му́чило его́, не дава́ло ему́ поко́я.

price /praɪs/ *n.* **1** цена́; **asking ~** запра́шиваемая цена́; **he bought it at cost ~** он купи́л э́то по себесто́имости; **what is the ~ of eggs?** ско́лько сто́ят я́йца?; **there is a ~ on his head** объя́влена награ́да за его́ го́лову; **every man has his ~** все лю́ди прода́жны; **they wanted peace at any ~** им ну́жен был мир любо́й цено́й; **I wouldn't have your job at any ~** я бы не согласи́лся на ва́шу рабо́ту ни за каки́е де́ньги; **he got the job, but at a ~** он получи́л рабо́ту, но дорого́й цено́й.
2 (*value*) це́нность; **a pearl of great ~** жемчу́жина большо́й це́нности; **good health is beyond ~** хоро́шее здоро́вье — бесце́нно; **what ~ honour** (*Br.*), **honor** (*US*)? чего́ тепе́рь сто́ит честь? **3** (*betting odds*) ша́нсы (*m. pl.*); **what ~ the favourite** (*Br.*), **favorite** (*US*)? какова́ вы́плата за фаворита?

● *v.t.* (*fix ~ of*) назн|ача́ть, -а́чить цену́ на + *a.*; оце́н|ивать, -и́ть; **the goods are highly ~d** това́р оценён высоко́; **he will ~ himself out of the market** он называ́ет таки́е высо́кие це́ны, что он не уде́ржится на ры́нке.

● *cpds.* **~-list** *n.* прейскура́нт; **~-tag** *n.* ярлы́к (с указа́нием цены́).

priceless /ˈpraɪslɪs/ *adj.* (*invaluable*) бесце́нный; (*coll., very amusing*) бесподо́бный.

pricey /ˈpraɪsɪ/ *adj.* (**pricier, priciest**) (*coll.*) дорого́й.

prick /prɪk/ *n.* **1** шип; колю́чка; (*puncture*) проко́л; (*fig.*): **the ~s of conscience** угрызе́ния (*nt. pl.*) со́вести. **2** (*mark made by ~ing*) уко́л. **3** (*arch., goad*): **it is no use kicking against the ~s** не сто́ит лезть на рожо́н? **4** (*vulg., penis*) хуй (*vulg.*).

● *v.t.* (*cause pain to*) коло́ть, у-; (*puncture*) прок|а́лывать, -оло́ть; (*fig.*): **my conscience has been ~ing me** меня́ му́чила со́весть.

● *v.i.* коло́ться, у-.

● *with advs.*: **~ off, ~ out** *v.t.* (*plants*) перес|а́живать, -ади́ть; **~ up** *v.t.*: **~ up one's ears** навостри́ть (*pf.*) у́ши.

prickle /ˈprɪk(ə)l/ *n.* (*thorn*) колю́чка, шип; (*of hedgehog etc.*) игла́.

● *v.t. & i.* коло́ть(ся), у-.

prickly /ˈprɪklɪ/ *adj.* (**pricklier, prickliest**) (*having spines or thorns*) колю́чий; **~ pear** (*bot.*) опу́нция; (*causing a prickling sensation*) ко́лкий; (*fig., easily offended*) оби́дчивый.

pride /praɪd/ *n.* **1** (*self-esteem, conceit*) го́рдость; (*pej.*) спесь; **~ goes before a fall** горды́ня до добра́ не доведёт; **pocket, swallow one's ~** смир|я́ть, -и́ть го́рдость; поступ|а́ться, -и́ться свои́м самолю́бием.
2 (*consciousness of worth; dignity*) го́рдость, чу́вство со́бственного досто́инства; **proper ~** самоуваже́ние; **I have too much ~ to accept charity** го́рдость не позволя́ет мне приня́ть ми́лостыню; **false ~** ло́жная го́рдость; **he takes ~ in his work** он горди́тся свое́й рабо́той.
3 (*object of satisfaction*) го́рдость; **the yacht was his ~ and joy** э́та я́хта была́ его́ го́рдостью и ра́достью.
4 (*primacy*): **his book takes ~ of place** его́ кни́ге принадлежи́т почётное ме́сто.
5: **a ~ of lions** стая львов.

● *v.t.*: **~ o.s. on** горди́ться (*impf.*) + *i.*; **she ~s herself on her cooking** она́ горди́тся свои́ми кулина́рными спосо́бностями.

priest /priːst/ *n.* (*Christian*) свяще́нник; (*in Buddhism, paganism*) жрец; **high ~** верхо́вный жрец.

priestess /ˈpriːstɪs/ *n.* жри́ца.

priesthood /ˈpriːsthʊd/ *n.* (*office*) свяще́нство; (*clergy*) духове́нство; (*in Buddhism, paganism*) жре́чество.

priestly /ˈpriːstlɪ/ *adj.* свяще́ннический; (*in Buddhism, paganism*) жре́ческий.

prig /prɪg/ *n.* педа́нт; (*hypocrite*) ханжа́ (*c.g.*).

priggish /ˈprɪgɪʃ/ *adj.* педанти́чный; ха́нжеский.

priggishness /ˈprɪgɪʃnɪs/ *n.* педанти́чность; ха́нжество́.

prim /prɪm/ *adj.* (**primmer, primmest**) (*also* **~ and proper**) чо́порный.

prima /ˌpriːmə/ *adj.*: **~ ballerina** при́ма-балери́на; **~ donna** (*lit.*) примадо́нна, ди́ва; (*fig.*) примадо́нна.

primacy /ˈpraɪməsɪ/ *n.* (*pre-eminence*) главе́нство.

prima facie /ˌpraɪmə ˈfeɪʃiː/ *adj.*: **~ evidence** доказа́тельство, доста́точное при отсу́тствии возраже́ний.

● *adv.* с пе́рвого взгля́да.

primal /ˈpraɪm(ə)l/ *adj.* (*original*) первонача́льный; (*chief*) гла́вный.

primarily /ˈpraɪmərɪlɪ/, /-ˈmeərɪlɪ/ *adv.* (*originally*) первонача́льно; (*principally, essentially*) в основно́м; гла́вным о́бразом; в пе́рвую о́чередь.

primary /ˈpraɪmərɪ/ *n.* (*US, election*) предвари́тельные вы́бор|ы (*pl., g.* -ов).

● *adj.* **1** (*original*) первонача́льный; **~ school** (*Br.*) нача́льная шко́ла. **2** (*fundamental, basic, principal*) основно́й; **~ colours** (*Br.*), **colors** (*US*) основны́е цвета́; **of ~ importance** первостепе́нной ва́жности.

primate /ˈpraɪmeɪt/ *n.* (*archbishop*) прима́с; (*mammal*) прима́т.

prime /praɪm/ *n.* (*perfection, best part*) расцве́т; **in the ~ of life** в расцве́те сил; **he is past his ~** его́ лу́чшие дни оста́лись позади́.

● *adj.* **1** (*principal*) гла́вный; **~ minister** премье́р-мини́стр. **2** (*excellent*) первокла́ссный; **~ beef** первосо́ртная говя́дина; **~ time** (*TV, radio*) прайм-та́йм. **3** (*fundamental*) основно́й; **~ cost** себесто́имость; **~ mover** (*source of motive power*) перви́чный дви́гатель; (*fig.*) инициа́тор; **~ number** просто́е число́.

● *v.t.* **1** (*firearm*) заря|жа́ть, -ди́ть; (*engine, pump*) запр|авля́ть, -а́вить. **2** (*supply with facts etc.*) инструкти́ровать (*impf., pf.*); ната́ск|ивать, -а́ть. **3** (*fill with food*) накорми́ть (*pf.*); (*fill with drink*) напои́ть (*pf.*). **4** (*cover with first coat of paint etc.*) грунтова́ть, за-.

primer /ˈpraɪmə(r)/ *n.* **1** (*school-book*) буква́рь (*m.*). **2** (*for igniting*) запа́л, ка́псюль (*m.*). **3** (*paint*) грунто́вка.

primeval /praɪˈmiːv(ə)l/ *adj.* первобы́тный, первозда́нный.

priming /ˈpraɪmɪŋ/ *n.* (*firing charge*) запра́вка; (*liquid*) зали́вка; (*paint*) грунт, грунто́вка.

primitive /ˈprɪmɪtɪv/ *n.* (*painter*) примитиви́ст; (*painting*) примитиви́стская карти́на, примити́в (*coll.*).

● *adj.* (*earliest*) первобы́тный; **~ man** первобы́тный челове́к; (*unsophisticated, simple*) примити́вный; (*art*) примити́вный.

primness /ˈprɪmnɪs/ *n.* чо́порность.

primogenitor /ˌpraɪməʊˈdʒenɪtə(r)/ *n.* прароди́тель (*m.*).

primogeniture /ˌpraɪməʊˈdʒenɪtʃə(r)/ *n.* перворо́дство.

primordial /praɪˈmɔːdɪəl/ *adj.* перви́чный, первобы́тный; (*fundamental*) основно́й.

primrose /ˈprɪmrəʊz/ *n.* **1** (*flower*) первоцве́т, при́мула. **2** (*colour*) бле́дно-жёлтый цвет.

primula /ˈprɪmjʊlə/ *n.* при́мула.

Primus /ˈpraɪməs/ *n.* (*propr.*) (**~ stove**) при́мус.

prince /prɪns/ *n.* **1** князь (*m.*); (*son of royalty*) принц; **P~ of Wales/Denmark** принц Уэ́льский/Да́тский; **~ consort** принц-консо́рт, консо́рт. **2** (*fig.*): **the P~ of Peace** князь (*m.*) ми́ра, Христо́с; **the ~ of darkness** сатана́ (*m.*).

princedom /ˈprɪnsdəm/ *n.* (*land*) кня́жество.

princely /ˈprɪnslɪ/ *adj.* (**princelier, princeliest**) кня́жеский; (*splendid*) великоле́пный; (*generous*): **~ sum** ца́рская су́мма.

princess /prɪnˈses/ *n.* (*wife of non-royal prince*) княги́ня; (*their daughter*) княжна́; (*daughter or daughter-in-law of sovereign*) принце́сса; **~ royal** ста́ршая дочь короля́/короле́вы.

principal /ˈprɪnsɪp(ə)l/ *n.* **1** (*head of school, college etc.*) дире́ктор, ре́ктор. **2** (*person for whom another acts*) довери́тель (*m.*). **3** (*pl., chief actors*) веду́щие исполни́тели (*m. pl.*). **4** (*sum of money*) капита́л.

P

● *adj.* гла́вный, основно́й.

principality /ˌprɪnsɪˈpælɪtɪ/ *n.* кня́жество.

principally /ˈprɪnsɪpəlɪ/ *adv.* гла́вным о́бразом, преиму́щественно.

principle /ˈprɪnsɪp(ə)l/ *n.* при́нцип, нача́ло; **the ~ of the wheel** при́нцип колеса́; **Archimedes' ~** зако́н Архиме́да; **the first ~s of geometry** осно́вы (*f. pl.*) геоме́трии; **in ~** в при́нципе; **on ~** из при́нципа; **a man of ~** принципиа́льный челове́к.

prink /prɪŋk/ *v.t.* наря|жа́ть, -ди́ть.

● *v.i.* наря|жа́ться, -ди́ться.

print /prɪnt/ *n.* **1** (*mark made on surface by pressure*) след; отпеча́ток. **2** (*letters, etc.*) шрифт; печа́ть; **~ run** тира́ж; **he looked forward to seeing his name in ~** он предвкуша́л моме́нт появле́ния своего́ и́мени в печа́ти; **the book is in ~** кни́га ещё продаётся; **the book is out of ~** кни́га бо́льше не продаётся; **3** (*picture*) гравю́ра, эста́мп, (*by photography*) репроду́кция. **4** (*phot.*) отпеча́ток. **5** (*cotton fabric*) си́тец; **a ~ dress** си́тцевое пла́тье.

● *v.t.* **1** (*impress*) печа́тать, на-/от-; (*fig.*) запечатл|ева́ть, -е́ть; **her face was ~ed on his memory** её лицо́ запечатле́лось у него́ в па́мяти. **2** (*produce by ~ing process; copy photographically*) печа́тать, на-/от-; **where did you get it ~ed?** где вам э́то напеча́тали? **3** (*write in imitation of ~*) писа́ть, на- печа́тными бу́квами. **4** (*mark with coloured design*) наб|ива́ть, -и́ть.

● *with advs.*: **~ off, ~ out** *v.t.* (*phot.*) де́лать, с- фотоотпеча́тки + *g.*; **~ out** *v.t.* (*comput.*) распеча́т|ывать, -ать.

● *cpd.* **~-out** *n.* (*comput.*) распеча́тка.

printable /ˈprɪntəb(ə)l/ *adj.* (*fit to print*) досто́йный напеча́тания.

printed /ˈprɪntɪd/ *adj.*: **~ circuit** (*elec.*) печа́тная схе́ма.

printer /ˈprɪntə(r)/ *n.* (*operator of press*) печа́тник; (*printing-house*) типогра́фия; (*owner of printing business*) владе́лец типогра́фии; (*comput.*) при́нтер.

printing /ˈprɪntɪŋ/ *n.* (*act or process*) печа́тание; (*trade*) печа́тное де́ло; (*material printed in one operation*) печа́тное изда́ние.

● *cpds.* **~-house, -office** *nn.* типогра́фия; **~-machine** *n.* печа́тная маши́на; **~-press** *n.* печа́тный стано́к.

prior[1] /ˈpraɪə(r)/ *n.* (*eccl.*) прио́р, настоя́тель (*m.*).

prior[2] /ˈpraɪə(r)/ *adj.* (*earlier*) пре́жний; (*more important*) первоочередно́й.

● *adv.*: **~ to** до + *g.*

prioress /ˈpraɪərɪs/ *n.* настоя́тельница.

prioritize /praɪˈɒrɪtaɪz/ *v.t.* определ|я́ть, -и́ть приорите́ты в + *p.*

priorit|y /praɪˈɒrɪtɪ/ *n.* (*order of importance*) приорите́т; (*importance*) пе́рвенствующее положе́ние; **safety is our first, highest, top ~y** мы придаём безопа́сности первостепе́нное значе́ние; **have you got your ~ies right?** пра́вильно ли вы оцени́ли/определи́ли ва́ши приорите́ты.

priory /ˈpraɪərɪ/ *n.* монасты́рь (*m.*).

prise /praɪz/ (*US* **prize**) *v.t.* взл|а́мывать, -ома́ть; **the box was ~d open** я́щик взлома́ли; **he ~d up the paving-stone** он приподня́л плиту́ с по́мощью рычага́; (*fig.*) разн|има́ть, -я́ть; **they ~d the combatants apart** они́ разня́ли деру́щихся.

prism /ˈprɪz(ə)m/ *n.* при́зма.

prismatic /prɪzˈmætɪk/ *adj.* призмати́ческий.

prison /ˈprɪz(ə)n/ *n.* **1** тюрьма́; **he is in ~ for murder** он (сиди́т) в тюрьме́ за уби́йство; **he was sent to ~ for a year** его́ посади́ли в тюрьму́ на́ год. **2** (*attr.*) тюре́мный; **~ camp** исправи́тельно-трудово́й ла́герь; (*prisoner-of-war camp*) ла́герь (*m.*) для военнопле́нных; **~ sentence** тюре́мный срок.

● *cpd.* **~-breaking** *n.* побе́г из тюрьмы́.

prisoner /ˈprɪznə(r)/ *n.* **1** (*detained by civil authorities*) заключённый; **~ at the bar** подсуди́мый; **~ of conscience** у́зни|к (*fem.* -ца) со́вести; (*fig.*) пле́нник; **he was a ~ to his habits** он был пле́нником свои́х привы́чек. **2** (**~** *of war*) пле́нный, военнопле́нный; **they were all taken ~** их всех взя́ли в плен.

prissy /ˈprɪsɪ/ *adj.* (**prissier, prissiest**) чо́порный, жема́нный; (*of style*) вы́чурный.

pristine /ˈprɪsti:n/, /ˈprɪstaɪn/ *adj.* (*fresh, pure*) чи́стый, нетро́нутый.

privacy /ˈprɪvəsɪ/, /ˈpraɪ-/ *n.* (*seclusion*) уедине́ние; **in the ~ of one's own home** в уедине́нии своего́ до́ма; **there's no ~** здесь нельзя́ уедини́ться; **this is an invasion of my ~** э́то — вмеша́тельство в мою́ ли́чную/ча́стную жизнь.

private /ˈpraɪvət/, /-vɪt/ *n.* **1** (*soldier*) рядово́й. **2**: **in ~** (*meet, talk*) с гла́зу на глаз; **he drinks a great deal in ~** он мно́го пьёт в одино́чку; **can we discuss this in ~?** мо́жно нам поговори́ть об э́том с глазу на глаз?

● *adj.* **1** (*personal*) ча́стный, ли́чный; **my ~ affairs** мои́ ли́чные дела́; **~ enterprise** ча́стное предпринима́тельство; **in ~ life** в ли́чной жи́зни; **~ means** (*Br.*) ли́чное состоя́ние; **~ property** ча́стная со́бственность; **for ~ reasons** по ли́чным причи́нам; **~ secretary** ли́чный секрета́рь. **2** (*not open to the general public*) закры́тый; **~ view** закры́тый просмо́тр, вернисა́ж. **3** (*secret*) та́йный, секре́тный; **~ parts** нару́жные половы́е о́рганы. **4** (*without official status*) ча́стный; неофициа́льный; прива́тный; **in one's ~ capacity** как ча́стное лицо́; **~ eye** (*coll.*) ча́стный сы́щик, детекти́в; **~ member** (*of Parliament*) депута́т парла́мента, не входя́щий в прави́тельство; **a doctor in ~ practice** ча́стный врач.

privation /praɪˈveɪʃ(ə)n/ *n.* (*hardship*) лише́ния (*nt. pl.*); нужда́; (*loss*) утра́та; лише́ние.

privatization /ˌpraɪvəˌtaɪˈzeɪʃ(ə)n/ *n.* приватиза́ция.

privatize /ˈpraɪvəˌtaɪz/ *v.t.* приватизи́ровать (*impf., pf.*).

privatizer /ˈpraɪvəˌtaɪzə(r)/ *n.* приватиза́тор.

privet /ˈprɪvɪt/ *n.* бирючи́на.

privilege /ˈprɪvɪlɪdʒ/ *n.* привиле́гия; (*in Parliament*) депута́тская неприкоснове́нность; (*fig.*): **it was a ~ to listen to him** слу́шать его́ бы́ло привиле́гией.

● *v.t.* да|ва́ть, -ть привиле́гию + *d.*; **I was ~d to be there** я име́л сча́стье/честь быть там.

privileged /ˈprɪvɪlɪdʒd/ *adj.* привилегиро́ванный.

privy /ˈprɪvɪ/ *n.* (*latrine*) убо́рная.

● *adj.* **1**: **~ to** прича́стный к + *d.*; посвящённый в + *a.*; **he was ~ to her intentions** он был посвящён в её пла́ны. **2** (*pert. to the sovereign*): **P~ Council** та́йный сове́т; **the ~ purse** су́ммы, ассигно́ванные на ли́чные расхо́ды мона́рха.

prize[1] /praɪz/ *n.* **1** (*reward for merit in sport etc.*) приз; (*esp. monetary*) пре́мия; награ́да. **2** (*attr., awarded as prize*) призово́й; **~-money** призовы́е де́н|ьги (*pl., g.* -ег); (**~**-*winning*) премиро́ванный; **~ poem** поэ́ма, удосто́енная пре́мии; (*excellent*) великоле́пный; (*possession*) бесце́нный; (*coll., egregious*) класси́ческий; **he is a ~ idiot** он патенто́ванный дура́к.

● *v.t.* высоко́ цени́ть (*impf.*); **he ~s his honour** (*Br.*), **honor** (*US*) **above everything** он це́нит свою́ честь бо́льше всего́ остально́го.

● *cpds.* **~-fight** *n.* матч боксёров-профессиона́лов; **~fighter** *n.* боксёр-профессиона́л; **~-giving** *n.* (*Br.*) церемо́ния вруче́ния награ́д; **~-ring** *n.* ринг; **~-winner** *n.* призёр.

prize[2] /praɪz/ (*US*) = **prise**

PRO (*abbr. of* ***public relations officer***) *see* ⇒**public** *adj.* 1

pro[1] /prəʊ/ *n.* (*pl.* **pros**) (*point in favour*): **~s and cons** за и про́тив.

● *prep.* (*coll., in favour of*) за + *a.*; **are you ~ the bill?** вы за э́тот законопрое́кт?

pro[2] /prəʊ/ *n.* (*pl.* **pros**) (*coll., professional actor, sportsman etc.*) профессиона́л (*fem.* -ка), про́фи (*indecl.*) (*coll.*).

pro- *pref.* (*supporting*) про-; **~-American** проамерика́нский.

proactive /prəʊˈæktɪv/ *adj.* де́йственный.

probability /ˌprɒbəˈbɪlɪtɪ/ *n.* вероя́тность; **in all ~** по всей вероя́тности; **there is a strong ~ that ...** весьма́ вероя́тно, что. . .

probable /ˈprɒbəb(ə)l/ *adj.* вероя́тный.

probate /ˈprəʊbeɪt/, /-bət/ *n.* (*proving of will*) утвержде́ние завеща́ния; **~ has**

been granted завеща́ние бы́ло утверждено́; (*copy of will*) заве́ренная ко́пия завеща́ния.

probation /prəˈbeɪʃ(ə)n/ *n.* **1** (*testing of candidate etc.*) испыта́ние; (*period of test*) испыта́тельный срок; **he was on ~ for two years** он прошёл двухле́тний испыта́тельный срок. **2** (*leg.*) испыта́тельный срок, усло́вное освобожде́ние; **he was put on ~** он получи́л усло́вный пригово́р; **~ officer** должностно́е лицо́, осуществля́ющее надзо́р за усло́вно осуждёнными.

probationary /prəˈbeɪʃənərɪ/ *adj.* испыта́тельный.

probationer /prəˈbeɪʃənə(r)/ *n.* (*trainee*) стажёр; практика́нт; (*offender on probation*) усло́вно осуждённый.

probe /prəʊb/ *n.* (*instrument*) зонд; (*fig., investigation*) рассле́дование; (*space exploration*): **moon ~** испыта́тельный полёт на Луну́; (*spacecraft*) иссле́довательская/зонди́рующая раке́та.

● *v.t. & i.* зонди́ровать, про~; (*fig., also*) иссле́довать (*impf., pf.*); вн|ика́ть, -и́кнуть в + *a.*; **it would be unwise to ~ too deeply into the matter** неблагоразу́мно вника́ть в э́то де́ло сли́шком глубоко́.

probity /ˈprəʊbɪtɪ/, /ˈprɒ-/ *n.* че́стность; **a man of ~** челове́к безукори́зненной че́стности.

problem /ˈprɒbləm/ *n.* пробле́ма, вопро́с; **he was faced with the ~ of moving house** пе́ред ним вста́ла пробле́ма перее́зда; **~ child** тру́дный ребёнок; (*math. etc.*) зада́ча.

problematic(al) /ˌprɒbləˈmætɪk(əl)/ *adj.* проблемати́чный.

probo|scis /prəʊˈbɒsɪs/ *n.* (*pl.* **~sces** /-siːz/, **~scides** /-sɪˌdiːz/, **~scises** /-sɪˌsiːz/) (*of elephant etc.*) хо́бот; (*of insect*) хобото́к.

pro-British /ˌprəʊˈbrɪtɪʃ/ *adj.* пробрита́нский.

procedural /prəˈsiːdjərəl/, /-dʒərəl/ *adj.* процеду́рный.

procedure /prəˈsiːdjə(r)/, /-dʒə(r)/ *n.* процеду́ра; **rules of ~** пра́вила процеду́ры, регла́мент.

proceed /prəˈsiːd/, /prəʊ-/ *v.i.* **1** (*go on*) прод|олжа́ть, -о́лжить. **2** (*start*) прин|има́ться, -я́ться (за + *a.*); **she ~ed to lay the table** она́ приняла́сь накрыва́ть на стол; **shall we ~ to business?** перейдём к де́лу? **3** (*make one's way*) напр|авля́ться, -а́виться. **4** (*originate*) исходи́ть (*impf.*); **the noise appeared to ~ from the next room** каза́лось, что шум исхо́дит из сосе́дней ко́мнаты. **5** (*take legal action*): **will you ~ against him?** вы собира́етесь возбуди́ть де́ло про́тив него́?

proceeding /prəˈsiːdɪŋ/ *n.* **1** (*piece of conduct*) посту́пок; (*pl., conduct*) поведе́ние; (*pl., activity*) де́ятельность. **2** (*pl., records of society etc.*) труды́ (*m. pl.*), запи́ски (*f. pl.*). **3** (*pl., legal action*) суде́бное де́ло, иск; **he took ~s against his employer** он возбуди́л (суде́бное) де́ло про́тив своего́ работода́теля.

proceeds /ˈprəʊsiːdz/ *n.* вы́ручка, дохо́д; **the ~ will go to charity** вы́ручка (*or* вы́рученная су́мма) пойдёт на благотвори́тельные це́ли.

process[1] /ˈprəʊses/ *n.* **1** проце́сс. **2** (*course*) тече́ние, ход; **we're in the ~ of buying a house** сейча́с мы покупа́ем дом; **the house is in ~ of construction** дом стро́ится. **3** (*method of manufacture etc.*) проце́сс; спо́соб. **4** (*leg., summons*) вы́зов в суд; **a ~ will be served on him** его́ вы́зовут в суд.

● *v.t.* **1** (*treat in special way; also comput.*) обраб|а́тывать, -о́тать; **~ed cheese** пла́вленый сыр. **2** (*subject to routine handling*) оф|ормля́ть, -о́рмить; **it will take a week to ~ your request** потре́буется неде́ля, что́бы рассмотре́ть ва́шу про́сьбу.

process[2] /ˈprəʊses/ *v.i.* (*walk in procession*) ше́ствовать (*impf.*).

procession /prəˈseʃ(ə)n/ *n.* проце́ссия, ше́ствие; **walk in ~** ше́ствовать (*impf.*); идти́ (*det.*) ма́ршем.

processor /ˈprəʊsesə(r)/ *n.* (*comput.*) проце́ссор.

proclaim /prəˈkleɪm/ *v.t.* (*announce*) провогла|ша́ть, -си́ть.

proclamation /ˌprɒkləˈmeɪʃ(ə)n/ *n.* провозглаше́ние.

proclivity /prəˈklɪvɪtɪ/ *n.* скло́нность, накло́нность.

proconsul /prəʊˈkɒns(ə)l/ *n.* замести́тель (*m.*) ко́нсула.

procrastinate /prəʊˈkræstɪˌneɪt/ *v.i.* ме́длить (*impf.*); тяну́ть (*impf.*) вре́мя/канте́ль (*coll.*).

procrastination /prəʊˌkræstɪˈneɪʃ(ə)n/ *n.* промедле́ние, канте́ль (*coll.*).

procreate /ˈprəʊkrɪˌeɪt/ *v.t. & i.* произв|оди́ть, -ести́ (пото́мство).

procreation /ˌprəʊkrɪˈeɪʃ(ə)n/ *n.* воспроизведе́ние; (*of animals*) размноже́ние.

proctor /ˈprɒktə(r)/ *n.* **1** (*university official*) про́ктор, надзира́тель (*m.*). **2** (*leg.*) адвока́т.

procurable /prəˈkjʊərəb(ə)l/ *adj.* досту́пный.

procurator /ˈprɒkjʊˌreɪtə(r)/ *n.* **1** (*magistrate*) пове́ренный; **public ~** прокуро́р; **~ fiscal** прокуро́р (*в Шотландии*). **2** (*proxy*) пове́ренный, дове́ренное лицо́.

procure /prəˈkjʊə(r)/ *v.t.* **1** (*obtain*) дост|ава́ть, -а́ть. **2** (*bring about*): **he ~d her dismissal** он доби́лся того́, что её уво́лили.

● *v.i.* (*act as procurer*) сво́дничать (*impf.*).

procurement /prəˈkjʊəmənt/ *n.* приобрете́ние, получе́ние; (*of equipment etc.*) поста́вка.

procurer /prəˈkjʊərə(r)/ *n.* поставщи́к; (*pimp*) сво́дник.

procuress /prəˈkjʊərɪs/ *n.* сво́дница, сво́дня.

prod /prɒd/ *n.* тычо́к.

● *v.t.* (**prodded, prodding**) ты́кать (*impf.*); (*fig.*) подстрека́ть (*impf.*); **he has to be ~ded into action** его́ прихо́дится подта́лкивать к де́йствиям.

prodigal /ˈprɒdɪg(ə)l/ *adj.* (*wasteful*) расточи́тельный; **the P~ Son** блу́дный сын; (*lavish*) ще́дрый.

prodigality /ˌprɒdɪˈgælɪtɪ/ *n.* расточи́тельность, мотовство́; ще́дрость.

prodigious /prəˈdɪdʒəs/ *adj.* (*amazing*) потряса́ющий; (*enormous*) огро́мный.

prodigy /ˈprɒdɪdʒɪ/ *n.* чу́до; **child/infant ~** вундерки́нд.

produce[1] /ˈprɒdjuːs/ *n.* проду́кты (*m. pl.*).

produce[2] /prəˈdjuːs/ *v.t.* **1** (*make, manufacture*) произв|оди́ть, -ести́; выпуска́ть, вы́пустить. **2** (*bring about*) вызыва́ть, вы́звать; прин|оси́ть, -ести́; **this method ~s good results** э́тот ме́тод прино́сит хоро́шие результа́ты. **3** (*bring forward*) предст|авля́ть, -а́вить; **can you ~ proof of your words?** мо́жете ли вы предста́вить что́-либо в доказа́тельство правоты́ ва́ших слов? **4** (*bring out, into view*) предъяв|ля́ть, -и́ть; дост|ава́ть, -а́ть; **you must ~ a ticket** вы должны́ предъяви́ть биле́т. **5** (*yield, bear*) прин|оси́ть, -ести́; произв|оди́ть, -ести́; **France ~s the best wine** Фра́нция произво́дит лу́чшее вино́; **this soil ~s good crops** э́то по́чва даёт хоро́ший урожа́й; **his wife ~d an heir** его́ жена́ произвела́ насле́дника; **our country has ~d many great men** на́ша страна́ дала́ ми́ру мно́го вели́ких люде́й. **6** (*compose, write*) созд|ава́ть, -а́ть. **7** (*bring before public*) ста́вить, по-; **the opera was first ~d in Vienna** э́та о́пера была́ впервы́е поста́влена в Ве́не; (*cin.*) выпуска́ть, вы́пустить. **8** (*geom.*): **~ a line** прод|олжа́ть, -о́лжить ли́нию.

producer /prəˈdjuːsə(r)/ *n.* **1** (*of goods*) производи́тель (*m.*). **2** (*stage, TV*) режиссёр-постано́вщик, режиссёр, постано́вщик. **3** (*film*) продю́сер. **4**: **~ gas** генера́торный газ.

product /ˈprɒdʌkt/ *n.* (*article produced*) проду́кт, изде́лие; (*pl.*) проду́кция (*collect.*), това́ры (*m. pl.*); (*result*) результат, плод; (*math.*) произведе́ние.

production /prəˈdʌkʃ(ə)n/ *n.* **1** (*manufacture*) произво́дство; **mass ~** ма́ссовое произво́дство; **~ line** произво́дственная ли́ния. **2** (*yield*) производи́тельность. **3** (*composing; composition*) произведе́ние. **4** (*stage, film*) постано́вка, режиссу́ра.

productive /prəˈdʌktɪv/ *adj.* (*tending to produce*) производи́тельный; (*yielding well, fertile*) плодоро́дный; **a ~ author** плодови́тый а́втор; (*efficient*) продукти́вный.

productivity /ˌprɒdʌkˈtɪvɪtɪ/ *n.* производи́тельность, продукти́вность.

prof /prɒf/ (*coll.*) = **professor** 2

profanation /ˌprɒfəˈneɪʃ(ə)n/ *n.* профана́ция, оскверне́ние.

P

profane /prəˈfeɪn/ *adj.* (*secular*) мирско́й; (*heathen*) язы́ческий; (*irreverent*) богоху́льный.
● *v.t.* профани́ровать (*impf., pf.*); оскверн|я́ть, -и́ть.

profanit|y /prəˈfænɪtɪ/ *n.* (*irreverence*) богоху́льство; (*swearing*) сквернносло́вие; **to utter ~ies** сквернносло́вить (*impf.*).

profess /prəˈfes/ *v.t.* **1** (*claim to have or feel*) заяв|ля́ть, -и́ть; **he ~es an interest in architecture** он заявля́ет, что интересу́ется архитекту́рой. **2** (*claim, pretend*) претендова́ть (*impf.*); **I don't ~ to know much about music** я не претенду́ю на больши́е позна́ния в му́зыке; **he ~es to be an expert at chess** он выдаёт себя́ за первокла́ссного шахмати́ста. **3** (*affirm belief in*) испове́довать (*impf.*).

professed /prəˈfest/ *adj.* **1** (*self-declared*) откры́тый, я́вный. **2** (*alleged, ostensible*) мни́мый.

profession /prəˈfeʃ(ə)n/ *n.* **1** (*occupation*) профе́ссия; **he is a teacher by ~** он по профе́ссии учи́тель. **2** (*declaration; admission*) заявле́ние; завере́ние; **~s of love** завере́ния в любви́.

professional /prəˈfeʃən(ə)l/ *n.* профессиона́л.
● *adj.* профессиона́льный; **~ advice** сове́т специали́ста; **~ musician** профессиона́льный музыка́нт; **~ people** квалифици́рованные специали́сты.

professionalism /prəˈfeʃənəˌlɪz(ə)m/ *n.* профессионали́зм.

professor /prəˈfesə(r)/ *n.* (*holder of university chair*) профе́ссор; (*US, university teacher*) преподава́тель (*fem.* -ница); **assistant ~** (*US*) ≈ ассисте́нт; **associate ~** (*US*) ≈ доце́нт.

professorial /ˌprɒfɪˈsɔːrɪəl/ *adj.* профе́ссорский.

professorship /prəˈfesəʃɪp/ *n.* профе́ссорство.

proffer /ˈprɒfə(r)/ *n.* предложе́ние.
● *v.t.* предл|ага́ть, -ожи́ть; **he ~ed his hand** он протяну́л ру́ку.

proficiency /prəˈfɪʃ(ə)nsɪ/ *n.* мастерство́, уме́ние.

proficient /prəˈfɪʃ(ə)nt/ *adj.* уме́лый; **she is ~ at typing** она́ хорошо́ печа́тает; **he is ~ in French** он хорошо́ владе́ет францу́зским.

profile /ˈprəʊfaɪl/ *n.* (*side view, esp. of face*) про́филь (*m.*); **seen in ~** в про́филь; (*fig.*) пози́ция; **to adopt a low/high ~** де́йствовать сде́ржанно/акти́вно; **he kept a low ~** он стара́лся не выделя́ться; (*biographical sketch*) (биографи́ческий) о́черк.

profit /ˈprɒfɪt/ *n.* **1** (*advantage*) по́льза, вы́года; **he discovered to his ~ that ...** он узна́л к со́бственной вы́годе, что...; **he studied to little ~** уче́ние не принесло́ ему́ почти́ никако́й по́льзы; **there is no ~ in further discussion** продолжа́ть диску́ссию бесполе́зно; **with ~** вы́годно. **2** (*pecuniary gain*) при́быль; **he made a ~ out of the deal** он сде́лал при́быль на э́той сде́лке; **he sold the land at a ~** он про́дал зе́млю с вы́годой; **the ~ motive** пого́ня за при́былью; **~ and loss account** счёт при́былей и убы́тков; **~ margin** разме́р при́были.
● *v.t.* (**profited, profiting**) прин|оси́ть, -ести́ по́льзу +*d.*; **what will it ~ him?** что э́то принесёт ему́?
● *v.i.* (**profited, profiting**) по́льзоваться, вос- (+*i.*); извле|ка́ть, -е́чь по́льзу (из+*g.*); **he has not ~ed from his experience** он не воспо́льзовался свои́м о́пытом; **I ~ed by your advice** ваш сове́т пошёл мне на по́льзу; **he ~ed by his wife's death** смерть жены́ оказа́лась ему́ вы́годной.
● *cpd.* **~-sharing** *n.* уча́стие в при́были.

profitability /ˌprɒfɪtəˈbɪlɪtɪ/ *n.* дохо́дность, при́быльность, рента́бельность.

profitable /ˈprɒfɪtəb(ə)l/ *adj.* (*advantageous*) поле́зный, вы́годный; (*lucrative*) дохо́дный, при́быльный, рента́бельный.

profiteer /ˌprɒfɪˈtɪə(r)/ *n.* спекуля́нт.
● *v.i.* спекули́ровать (*impf.*).

profiteering /ˌprɒfɪˈtɪərɪŋ/ *n.* спекуля́ция.

profiterole /prəˈfɪtəˌrəʊl/ *n.* (*cul.*) профитро́ль *m.*

profitless /ˈprɒfɪtlɪs/ *adj.* бесполе́зный; беспло́дный.

profligacy /ˈprɒflɪgəsɪ/ *n.* (*dissoluteness*) распу́тство; (*extravagance*) расточи́тельность.

profligate /ˈprɒflɪgət/ *n.* (*dissolute person*) развра́тник; (*extravagant person*) расточи́тель (*m.*).
● *adj.* (*dissolute*) распу́тный; (*extravagant*) расточи́тельный.

pro forma /prəʊ ˈfɔːmə/ *adj.*: **~ invoice** предвари́тельный счёт-факту́ра.
● *adv. phr.* для профо́рмы.

profound /prəˈfaʊnd/ *adj.* (**profounder, profoundest**) глубо́кий; **~ ignorance** по́лное неве́жество; **a ~ subject** сло́жный предме́т.

profundity /prəˈfʌndɪtɪ/ *n.* глубина́.

profuse /prəˈfjuːs/ *adj.* (*plentiful*) оби́льный; (*lavish*) ще́дрый; **he apologized ~ly** он рассыпа́лся в извине́ниях.

profusion /prəˈfjuːʒ(ə)n/ *n.* изоби́лие.

progenitor /prəʊˈdʒenɪtə(r)/ *n.* прароди́тель (*m.*), пре́док; (*predecessor*) предше́ственник.

progeny /ˈprɒdʒɪnɪ/ *n.* пото́мство.

progesterone /prəʊˈdʒestəˌrəʊn/ *n.* прогестеро́н.

prognosis /prɒgˈnəʊsɪs/ *n.* (*pl.* **prognoses** /-siːz/) прогно́з.

prognosticate /prɒgˈnɒstɪˌkeɪt/ *v.t.* (*foretell*) предска́з|ывать, -а́ть; (*indicate, betoken*) предвеща́ть (*impf.*).

prognostication /prɒgˌnɒstɪˈkeɪʃ(ə)n/ *n.* предсказа́ние; (*omen*) предзнаменова́ние.

program /ˈprəʊgræm/ *n.* (*comput.*) програ́мма; (*US*) = **programme**
● *v.t.* (**programmed, programming**) (*comput., also fig.*) программи́ровать, за-; (*US*) = **programme**

programme /ˈprəʊgræm/ *n.* програ́мма; (*radio, TV*) переда́ча; (*plan*) програ́мма, план; **what's (on) the ~ for tonight?** каки́е у нас пла́ны на ве́чер?; **he has a full ~ tomorrow** за́втра он по́лностью за́нят.
● *v.t.* (**programmed, programming**) (*make plan of*) сост|авля́ть, -а́вить програ́мму +*g.*; **the meeting is ~d for today** собра́ние назна́чено на сего́дня.

programmer /ˈprəʊgræmə(r)/ *n.* (*comput.*) программи́ст (*fem.* -ка).

programming /ˈprəʊgræmɪŋ/ *n.* (*comput.*) программи́рование; **~ language** язы́к программи́рования.

progress[1] /ˈprəʊgres/ *n.* **1** (*forward movement*) движе́ние вперёд; **the horses made slow ~** ло́шади дви́гались ме́дленно. **2** (*advance, development*) прогре́сс; **~ report** докла́д о хо́де рабо́ты; **the patient is making good ~** больно́й поправля́ется; **a meeting is in ~** идёт заседа́ние; **preparations are in ~** веду́тся приготовле́ния.

progress[2] /prəˈgres/ *v.i.* прогресси́ровать (*impf.*); продв|ига́ться, -и́нуться (вперёд); **how are things ~ing?** как иду́т дела́?; **he has hardly ~ed at all with his studies** он не сде́лал почти́ никаки́х успе́хов в учёбе.

progression /prəˈgreʃ(ə)n/ *n.* (*progress*) продвиже́ние; (*math.*) прогре́ссия; (*mus.*) прогре́ссия, секве́нция.

progressive /prəˈgresɪv/ *n.* прогресси́вный челове́к.
● *adj.* **1** (*favouring progress*) прогресси́вный, передово́й. **2** (*gradual*) поступа́тельный, постепе́нный. **3** (*of disease etc.*) прогресси́рующий.

prohibit /prəˈhɪbɪt/ *v.t.* (**prohibited, prohibiting**) запре|ща́ть, -ти́ть; воспре|ща́ть, -ти́ть; **smoking ~ed** кури́ть воспреща́ется.

prohibition /ˌprəʊhɪˈbɪʃ(ə)n/, /ˌprəʊɪˈb-/ *n.* запреще́ние; **P~** (*of sale of intoxicants*) сухо́й зако́н.

prohibitionist /ˌprəʊhɪˈbɪʃənɪst/, /ˌprəʊɪˈb-/ *n.* прогибициони́ст.

prohibitive /prəʊˈhɪbɪtɪv/ *adj.* запрети́тельный, запреща́ющий; **~ prices** недосту́пные це́ны.

prohibitory /prəˈhɪbɪtərɪ/ *adj.* запреща́ющий.

project[1] /ˈprɒdʒekt/ *n.* (*scheme*) прое́кт, план; (*at school*) рабо́та.

project[2] /prəˈdʒekt/ *v.t.* **1** (*devise*) проекти́ровать, за-. **2** (*throw, impel*) выбра́сывать, вы́бросить. **3** (*light*) броса́ть (*impf.*); (*shadow*) отбр|а́сывать, -о́сить. **4** (*with projector; also math.*) проеци́ровать (*impf.*, *pf.*). **5** (*fig.*): **he ~ed himself into the future** он мысленно перенёсся в бу́дущее.

● *v.i.* (*protrude*) выдава́ться (*impf.*); выступа́ть (*impf.*).

projectile /prəˈdʒektaɪl/ *n.* снаря́д.

projection /prəˈdʒekʃ(ə)n/ *n.* **1** (*planning*) проекти́рование. **2** (*throwing, propulsion*) отбра́сывание. **3** (*cin.*) прое́кция (изображе́ния); **~ room** (кино)проекцио́нная каби́на. **4** (*psych., geom.*) прое́кция. **5** (*protrusion*) вы́ступ.

projectionist /prəˈdʒekʃənɪst/ *n.* (*of film etc.*) киномеха́ник.

projector /prəˈdʒektə(r)/ *n.* (*apparatus*) прое́ктор.

prolapse /ˈprəʊlæps/ *n.* прола́пс, выпаде́ние.

proletarian /ˌprəʊlɪˈteərɪən/ *n.* пролета́рий.

● *adj.* пролета́рский.

proletariat /ˌprəʊlɪˈteərɪət/ *n.* пролетариа́т.

pro-life /prəʊˈlaɪf/ *adj.* защища́ющий «пра́во на жизнь»; возража́ющий про́тив або́ртов.

pro-lifer /prəʊˈlaɪfə(r)/ *n.* защи́тни|к (*fem.* -ца) «пра́ва на жизнь».

proliferate /prəˈlɪfəˌreɪt/ *v.i.* размн|ожа́ться, -о́житься; (*fig.*) распростран|я́ться, -и́ться.

proliferation /prəˌlɪfəˈreɪʃ(ə)n/ *n.* размноже́ние, пролифера́ция; (*fig.*) распростране́ние.

prolific /prəˈlɪfɪk/ *adj.* (*lit.*) плодоро́дный; (*fig.*) плодови́тый.

prolix /ˈprəʊlɪks/, /prəˈlɪks/ *adj.* (*lengthy*) многосло́вный; (*tedious*) ну́дный.

prolixity /ˌprəʊˈlɪksɪtɪ/, /prəˈlɪksɪtɪ/ *n.* многосло́вие, ну́дность.

prologue /ˈprəʊlɒg/ (*US* **prolog**) *n.* проло́г.

prolong /prəˈlɒŋ/ *v.t.* продл|ева́ть, -и́ть; **he ~ed his leave by a day** он продли́л свой о́тпуск на оди́н день; **a ~ed argument** до́лгий спор.

prolongation /ˌprəʊlɒŋˈgeɪʃ(ə)n/ *n.* продле́ние.

prom /prɒm/ (*coll.*) = **promenade** *n.* 2, 3

promenade /ˌprɒməˈnɑːd/ *n.* **1** (*walk for pleasure etc.*) прогу́лка; **~ concert** (*Br.*) промена́дный конце́рт. **2** (*Br., place of pedestrian resort*) ме́сто для гуля́ния. **3** (*US, students' ball*) бал (*в колледже*).

● *v.i.* прогу́л|иваться, -я́ться.

Promethean /prəˈmiːθɪən/ *adj.* промете́ев.

prominence /ˈprɒmɪnəns/ *n.* (*importance*) ви́дное положе́ние.

prominent /ˈprɒmɪnənt/ *adj.* **1** (*projecting*) выступа́ющий. **2** (*conspicuous*) заме́тный. **3** (*important, distinguished*) выдаю́щийся.

promiscuity /ˌprɒmɪˈskjuːɪtɪ/ *n.* неразбо́рчивость; распу́щенность.

promiscuous /prəˈmɪskjʊəs/ *adj.* неразбо́рчивый; (*sexually*) распу́щенный.

promise /ˈprɒmɪs/ *n.* **1** (*assurance*) обеща́ние; **he gave his solemn ~ never to steal again** он дал торже́ственное обеща́ние бо́льше не ворова́ть; **he kept his ~** он сдержа́л своё обеща́ние; **breach of ~** наруше́ние обеща́ния. **2** (*ground for expectation*) наде́жда; **he shows ~** он подаёт наде́жды; **a writer of ~** многообеща́ющий писа́тель.

● *v.t. & i.* **1** (*undertake, assure*) обеща́ть, по-; **he ~d to be here by 7** он обеща́л быть здесь в 7 часо́в; **I ~d myself a quiet evening ~** я реши́л споко́йно провести́ ве́чер; **it will not be easy, I ~ you** уверя́ю вас, что э́то бу́дет нелегко́; **the P~d Land** (*bibl.*) земля́ обетова́нная. **2** (*give grounds for expecting*): **it ~s to be a warm day** день обеща́ет быть тёплым; **the boy ~s well** ма́льчик подаёт больши́е наде́жды.

promising /ˈprɒmɪsɪŋ/ *adj.* перспекти́вный; многообеща́ющий, подаю́щий наде́жды.

promissory /ˈprɒmɪsərɪ/ *adj.*: **~ note** долгово́е обяза́тельство.

promontory /ˈprɒməntərɪ/ *n.* мыс.

promote /prəˈməʊt/ *v.t.* **1** (*raise to higher rank*) продв|ига́ть, -и́нуть; пов|ыша́ть, -ы́сить (в чи́не); **he was ~d (to the rank of) sergeant** ему́ присво́или зва́ние сержа́нта. **2** (*encourage, support*) поощр|я́ть, -и́ть; подде́рж|ивать, -а́ть; соде́йствовать, по- +*d.* **3** (*publicize to boost sales*) реклами́ровать (*impf.*); соде́йствовать (*impf.*, *pf.*) прода́же +*g.*

promoter /prəˈməʊtə(r)/ *n.* (*e.g. of concert*) (конце́ртный) аге́нт, промо́утер; (*e.g. of peace*) пропаганди́ст (*fem.* -ка).

promotion /prəˈməʊʃ(ə)n/ *n.* (*in rank*) продвиже́ние, повыше́ние; (*encouragement, support*) поощре́ние, подде́ржка, соде́йствие; (*publicizing*) рекла́ма, промо́ушен.

prompt[1] /prɒmpt/ *n.* (*theatr.*) подска́зка; (*comput.*) приглаше́ние.

● *v.t. & i.* **1** (*assist memory of*) подска́з|ывать, -а́ть +*d.*; (*theatr.*) суфли́ровать (*impf.*) +*d.* **2** (*impel, induce*) побу|жда́ть, -ди́ть.

prompt[2] /prɒmpt/ *adj.* бы́стрый, неме́дленный; **he was ~ in coming forward** он сра́зу же (*or* тут же) откли́кнулся; **he arrived ~ly at 9** он прие́хал то́чно в де́вять; **a ~ answer** неме́дленный отве́т.

prompter /ˈprɒmptə(r)/ *n.* суфлёр.

prompt|itude /ˈprɒmpˌtɪtjuːd/, **-ness** /ˈprɒmptnɪs/ *nn.* быстрота́, гото́вность.

promulgate /ˈprɒməlˌgeɪt/ *v.t.* обнаро́довать (*pf.*); провозгла|ша́ть, -си́ть.

promulgation /ˌprɒməlˈgeɪʃ(ə)n/ *n.* обнаро́дование, провозглаше́ние.

prone /prəʊn/ *adj.* **1** (*face downwards*) лежа́щий ничко́м. **2**: **~ to** (*disposed, liable to*) скло́нный к +*d.*; **he is ~ to make mistakes** ему́ сво́йственно ошиба́ться; **I am ~ to accidents** со мной ве́чно что́-то случа́ется.

proneness /ˈprəʊnnɪs/ *n.* скло́нность.

prong /prɒŋ/ *n.* зубе́ц.

pronominal /prəʊˈnɒmɪn(ə)l/ *adj.* местоиме́нный.

pronoun /ˈprəʊnaʊn/ *n.* местоиме́ние.

pronounc|e /prəˈnaʊns/ *v.t.* **1** (*declare*) объяв|ля́ть, -и́ть; **~e judgement** (*leg.*) выноси́ть, вы́нести суде́бное реше́ние. **2** (*utter*) произн|оси́ть, -ести́; выгова́ривать, вы́говорить; **how is this word ~ed?** как произно́сится э́то сло́во?

● *v.i.* **1** (*give one's opinion*) выска́зываться, вы́сказаться; **the jury ~ed for the defendant** прися́жные оправда́ли подсуди́мого. **2**: **a ~ing dictionary** орфоэпи́ческий слова́рь.

pronounced /prəˈnaʊnst/ *adj.* (*decided*) я́вный; **he walks with a ~ limp** он си́льно/заме́тно хрома́ет.

pronouncement /prəˈnaʊnsmənt/ *n.* заявле́ние; выска́зывание.

pronto /ˈprɒntəʊ/ *adv.* (*sl.*) жи́во, бы́стро.

pronunciation /prəˌnʌnsɪˈeɪʃ(ə)n/ *n.* произноше́ние.

proof /pruːf/ *n.* **1** доказа́тельство; **as ~ of his good intentions** в доказа́тельство свои́х до́брых наме́рений. **2** (*demonstration*): **is it capable of ~?** э́то доказу́емо? **3** (*test, trial*) испыта́ние; прове́рка; **his courage was put to the ~** его́ сме́лость подве́рглась испыта́нию; **the ~ of the pudding is in the eating** ≈ обо всём су́дят по результа́там. **4** (*of alcoholic liquor*) кре́пость. **5** (*typ.*) корректу́ра.

● *adj.* **1** (*of tried or prescribed strength*) устано́вленной кре́пости; **~ spirit** раство́р спи́рта определённой кре́пости. **2** (*impenetrable, resistant*): **~ against bullets** пуленепроница́емый; **~ against weather** погодоусто́йчивый; (*of clothing*) непромока́емый.

● *v.t.* (*waterproof*) де́лать, с- непроница́емым.

● *cpds.* **~-read** *v.t. & i.* чита́ть, про- (*or* держа́ть) корректу́ру; **~-reader** *n.* корре́ктор; **~-reading** *n.* чте́ние корректу́ры; **~-sheet** *n.* корректу́ра.

prop[1] /prɒp/ *n.* (*support*) сто́йка; подпо́рка; (*fig.*) опо́ра, подде́ржка.

● *v.t.* (**propped, propping**) **1** подп|ира́ть, -ере́ть; **~ open a door** подп|ира́ть, -ере́ть дверь, что́бы она́ не захло́пнулась; **he sat ~ped up in bed** он сиде́л в крова́ти, опира́ясь на поду́шки; **~ the ladder against the wall!** приста́вьте ле́стницу к стене́! **2** (*fig.*) подде́рж|ивать, -а́ть.

prop[2] /prɒp/ *n.* (*coll., theatr.*) бутафо́рия, реквизи́т.

prop[3] /prɒp/ (*coll.*) = **propeller**

propaganda /ˌprɒpəˈgændə/ *n.* пропага́нда; (*attr.*) пропаганди́стский.

P

propagandist /ˌprɒpəˈgændɪst/ *n.* пропаганди́ст.

propagandize /ˌprɒpəˈgændaɪz/ *v.t.* пропаганди́ровать (*impf.*).

propagate /ˈprɒpəˌgeɪt/ *v.t.* (*multiply by reproduction*) размн|ожа́ть, -о́жить; разв|оди́ть, -ести́; (*disseminate*) распростран|я́ть, -и́ть.

● *v.i.* размн|ожа́ться, -о́житься.

propagation /ˌprɒpəˈgeɪʃ(ə)n/ *n.* размноже́ние; (*fig.*) распростране́ние.

propagator /ˈprɒpəˌgeɪtə(r)/ *n.* (*person*) распространи́тель (*fem.* -ница); (*for plants*) микропарни́к.

propane /ˈprəʊpeɪn/ *n.* пропа́н.

propel /prəˈpel/ *v.t.* (**propelled, propelling**) прив|оди́ть, -ести́ в движе́ние; **~ling pencil** (*Br.*) автокаранда́ш.

propellant /prəˈpelənt/ *n.* дви́жущая си́ла; (*fuel*) раке́тное то́пливо.

propeller /prəˈpelə(r)/ *n.* (*of ship*) (гребно́й) винт; (*of aircraft*) пропе́ллер, (возду́шный) винт.

propensity /prəˈpensɪtɪ/ *n.* предрасполо́женность, скло́нность.

proper /ˈprɒpə(r)/ *adj.* **1** (*belonging especially*) сво́йственный, прису́щий. **2** (*suitable, appropriate*) подходя́щий, ну́жный; **at the ~ time** в своё вре́мя. **3** (*decent, respectable*) (благо)присто́йный, прили́чный. **4** (*correct, accurate*) пра́вильный; **in the ~ sense of the word** в прямо́м смы́сле сло́ва. **5** (*gram.*): **~ noun** и́мя со́бственное. **6** (*strictly so called*): **within the sphere of architecture ~** в о́бласти со́бственно архитекту́ры. **7** (*Br. coll. thorough*) соверше́нный, по́лный; **his room was in a ~ mess** в его́ ко́мнате цари́л по́лный беспоря́док.

properly /ˈprɒpəlɪ/ *adv.* (*correctly*) подоба́юще, как сле́дует, до́лжным о́бразом; **~ speaking** со́бственно говоря́; **you must be ~ dressed** вы должны́ оде́ться подоба́юще/подоба́ющим о́бразом.

propertied /ˈprɒpətɪd/ *adj.* име́ющий со́бственность; иму́щий; **the ~ classes** иму́щие кла́ссы; землевладе́льцы.

propert|y /ˈprɒpətɪ/ *n.* **1** (*possession(s)*) со́бственность; иму́щество; **a man of ~y** со́бственник; **the news is common ~y** но́вость изве́стна всем. **2** (*house*) дом; (*estate*) име́ние; (*real estate*) недви́жимость. **3** (*attribute, quality*) сво́йство; **this plant has healing ~ies** э́то расте́ние облада́ет целе́бными сво́йствами. **4** (*theatr.*) бутафо́рия, реквизи́т.

● *cpds.* **~-man, ~-mistress** *nn.* (*theatr.*) реквизи́тор.

prophecy /ˈprɒfɪsɪ/ *n.* предсказа́ние, проро́чество.

prophesy /ˈprɒfɪˌsaɪ/ *v.t. & i.* предска́з|ывать, -а́ть; проро́чить, на-.

prophet /ˈprɒfɪt/ *n.* проро́к, предсказа́тель (*m.*).

prophetess /ˈprɒfɪtɪs/ *n.* проро́чица; предсказа́тельница.

prophetic /prəˈfetɪk/ *adj.* проро́ческий.

prophylactic /ˌprɒfɪˈlæktɪk/ *n.* профилакти́ческое сре́дство.

● *adj.* профилакти́ческий.

prophylaxis /ˌprɒfɪˈlæksɪs/ *n.* профила́ктика.

propinquity /prəˈpɪŋkwɪtɪ/ *n.* (*closeness*) бли́зость, сосе́дство; (*kinship*) родство́.

propitiate /prəˈpɪʃɪˌeɪt/ *v.t.* (*appease*) умиротвор|я́ть, -и́ть; ут|еша́ть, -е́шить.

propitiation /prəˌpɪʃɪˈeɪʃ(ə)n/ *n.* умиротворе́ние; утеше́ние.

propitiatory /prəˈpɪʃɪətərɪ/ *adj.* утеша́ющий; примири́тельный.

propitious /prəˈpɪʃəs/ *adj.* (*benevolent*) благожела́тельный; (*favourable*) благоприя́тный.

proponent /prəˈpəʊnənt/ *n.* пропаганди́ст, побо́рник (*чего*).

proportion /prəˈpɔːʃ(ə)n/ *n.* **1** (*part*) часть, до́ля; **a large ~ of the earth's surface** бо́льша́я часть земно́й пове́рхности. **2** (*ratio*) пропо́рция, соотноше́ние; **the ~ of imports to exports is high** пропорциона́льно и́мпорта бо́льше, чем э́кспорта; **in ~** пропорциона́льно, соразме́рно. **3** (*math., equality of ratios*) пропо́рция. **4** (*due relation*) соразме́рность; **keep a sense of ~** сохран|я́ть, -и́ть чу́вство ме́ры; **his ambitions are out of all ~** его́ честолю́бие выхо́дит за вся́кие ра́мки. **5** (*pl., dimensions*) разме́р, разме́ры (*m. pl.*); **a house of stately ~s** дом внуши́тельных разме́ров.

● *v.t.* соразм|еря́ть, -е́рить; дози́ровать (*impf.*).

proportional /prəˈpɔːʃən(ə)l/ *adj.* пропорциона́льный; **~ representation** пропорциона́льное представи́тельство.

proportionate /prəˈpɔːʃənət/ *adj.* соразме́рный; **payment will be ~ to effort** опла́та бу́дет соотве́тствовать затра́ченным уси́лиям.

proposal /prəˈpəʊz(ə)l/ *n.* предложе́ние.

propose /prəˈpəʊz/ *v.t.* **1** (*suggest*) предл|ага́ть, -ожи́ть; **he ~d (marriage) to her** он сде́лал ей предложе́ние. **2** (*nominate, put forward*) выдвига́ть, вы́двинуть; **his name was ~d for secretary** его́ выдвига́ли на пост секретаря́. **3**: **~ a toast** провозгла|ша́ть, -си́ть тост; предл|ага́ть, -ожи́ть тост; **a toast to his health was ~d** провозгласи́ли тост за его́ здоро́вье. **4** (*intend*) предпол|ага́ть, -ожи́ть; намерева́ться (*impf.*); **I ~ to leave tomorrow** намерева́юсь е́хать за́втра.

proposition /ˌprɒpəˈzɪʃ(ə)n/ *n.* **1** (*statement*) заявле́ние. **2** (*proposed scheme*) предложе́ние. **3** (*coll., undertaking, problem etc.*) де́ло; **he is a tough ~** с ним тру́дно име́ть де́ло. **4** (*coll., immoral proposal*) гну́сное предложе́ние.

● *v.t.* (*coll.*) де́лать, с- гну́сное предложе́ние + *d.*

propound /prəˈpaʊnd/ *v.t.* предл|ага́ть, -ожи́ть на обсужде́ние; изл|ага́ть, -ожи́ть.

proprietary /prəˈpraɪətərɪ/ *adj.* со́бственнический; (*pert. to a firm*) фи́рменный; **~ medicines** патенто́ванные лека́рства; **~ rights** пра́во со́бственности.

proprietor /prəˈpraɪətə(r)/ *n.* владе́лец, хозя́ин.

proprietorial /prəˌpraɪəˈtɔːrɪəl/ *adj.* со́бственнический.

proprietress /prəˈpraɪətrɪs/ *n.* владе́лица, хозя́йка.

propriet|y /prəˈpraɪɪtɪ/ *n.* (*fitness*) уме́стность; (*correctness of behaviour or morals*) пра́вильность; (благо)присто́йность; (*pl., rules of behaviour*): **the ~ies must be observed** на́до соблюда́ть пра́вила прили́чия.

propulsion /prəˈpʌlʃ(ə)n/ *n.* движе́ние вперёд; **jet ~** реакти́вное движе́ние.

propulsive /prəˈpʌlsɪv/ *adj.* дви́жущий вперёд; **~ force** дви́жущая си́ла.

pro rata /prəʊ ˈrɑːtə/, /ˈreɪtə/ *adv.* пропорциона́льно; соотве́тственно.

prorogation /ˌprərəʊˈgeɪʃ(ə)n/ *n.* пророга́ция (*парламента*).

prorogue /prəˈrəʊg/ *v.t.* (**prorogues, prorogued, proroguing**) назн|ача́ть, -а́чить переры́в в рабо́те + *g.* (*парламента и т.п.*).

prosaic /prəˈzeɪɪk/, /prəʊ-/ *adj.* прозаи́ческий.

prosceni|um /prəˈsiːnɪəm/, /prəʊ-/ *n.* (*pl.* **~ums** *or* **~a**) просце́ниум, пере́дняя часть сце́ны.

proscribe /prəˈskraɪb/ *v.t.* запре|ща́ть, -ти́ть.

proscription /prəˈskrɪpʃ(ə)n/ *n.* запреще́ние.

prose /prəʊz/ *n.* **1** про́за; (*attr.*) прозаи́ческий; **~ writers** (писа́тели-)проза́ики; **~ poem** стихотворе́ние в про́зе; (*fig.*) про́за, прозаи́чность. **2** (*piece set for translation*) отры́вок для перево́да (*на иностранный язык*).

prosecute /ˈprɒsɪˌkjuːt/ *v.t.* **1** (*carry on*) занима́ться (*impf.*) + *i.*; вести́, по-; **he ~d the inquiry with vigour** (*Br.*), **vigor** (*US*) он энерги́чно повёл рассле́дование. **2** (*leg.*) возбу|жда́ть, -ди́ть де́ло про́тив + *g.*; **~ a claim** возбу|жда́ть, -ди́ть иск; **trespassers will be ~d** наруши́тели бу́дут пресле́доваться по зако́ну.

prosecution /ˌprɒsɪˈkjuːʃ(ə)n/ *n.* **1** (*pursuit*) веде́ние; **in the ~ of his duty** при исполне́нии свои́х обя́занностей. **2** (*carrying on legal proceedings*) обвине́ние; предъявле́ние и́ска. **3** (*prosecuting party*) обвине́ние; **counsel for the ~** обвини́тель (*m.*) (в уголо́вном проце́ссе).

prosecutor /ˈprɒsɪˌkjuːtə(r)/ *n.* обвини́тель (*m.*); **Public P~** прокуро́р.

proselyte /ˈprɒsɪˌlaɪt/ *n.* прозели́т (*fem.* -ка).

proselytize /ˈprɒsɪlɪˌtaɪz/ *v.t.* (*convert*) обра|ща́ть, -ти́ть в другу́ю ве́ру.

prosiness /'prəʊzɪnɪs/ *n.* ну́дность.

prosodic /prə'sɒdɪk/ *adj.* просоди́ческий.

prosody /'prɒsədɪ/ *n.* просо́дия.

prospect[1] /'prɒspekt/ *n.* **1** (*extensive view*) вид, панора́ма; (*fig., mental scene*) перспекти́ва. **2** (*expectation, hope*) перспекти́ва; **there is no ~ of success** нет наде́жды на успе́х; **a job without ~s** рабо́та без перспекти́в; **I have nothing in ~ at present** в настоя́щее вре́мя у меня́ нет ничего́ в перспекти́ве. **3** (*coll., possible customer*) потенциа́льный покупа́тель/зака́зчик.

prospect[2] /prə'spekt/ *v.t.* иссле́довать (*impf., pf.*); разве́д|ывать, -ать.

● *v.i.*: **they were ~ing for gold** они́ иска́ли зо́лото.

prospective /prə'spektɪv/ *adj.* **1** (*applicable to future*) бу́дущий, предполага́емый. **2** (*expected*) ожида́емый. **3** (*future*) бу́дущий.

prospector /prə'spektə(r)/ *n.* разве́дчик, стара́тель (*m.*).

prospectus /prə'spektəs/ *n.* (*pl.* **~es**) проспе́кт.

prosper /'prɒspə(r)/ *v.i.* преусп|ева́ть, -е́ть; процвета́ть (*impf.*).

prosperity /prɒ'sperɪtɪ/ *n.* процвета́ние.

prosperous /'prɒspərəs/ *adj.* процвета́ющий, зажи́точный.

prostaglandin /,prɒstə'glændɪn/ *n.* простагланди́н.

prostate /'prɒsteɪt/ *n.* (*also* **~ gland**) проста́та, предста́тельная железа́.

prosthe|sis /'prɒsθɪsɪs/, /-'θi:sɪs/ *n.* (*pl.* **~ses** /-si:z/) проте́з.

prosthetic /prɒs'θetɪk/ *adj.* проте́зный.

prostitute /'prɒstɪ,tju:t/ *n.* проститу́тка; **male ~** мужчи́на-проститу́тка.

● *v.t.*: **~ o.s.** зан|има́ться, -я́ться проститу́цией; (*fig.*) торгова́ть (*impf.*) собо́й; **he ~d his talents** он про́дал свой тала́нт.

prostitution /,prɒstɪ'tju:ʃ(ə)n/ *n.* (*lit., fig.*) проститу́ция.

prostrate[1] /'prɒstreɪt/ *adj.* **1** (*lying face down*) распростёртый; лежа́щий ничко́м. **2** (*overcome, overthrown*) пове́рженный; **she was ~ with grief** она́ была́ сло́млена го́рем. **3** (*exhausted*) измождённый.

prostrate[2] /prɒ'streɪt/, /prə-/ *v.t.* **1** (*lay flat on ground*) опроки́|дывать, -нуть; вали́ть, по-; **trees were ~d by the gale** бу́ря повали́ла дере́вья; **he ~d himself before the altar** он пал ниц пе́ред алтарём. **2** (*overcome*) изнур|я́ть, -и́ть.

prostration /prɒ'streɪʃ(ə)n/, /prə-/ (*exhaustion*) изнеможе́ние; простра́ция.

prosy /'prəʊzɪ/ *adj.* (**prosier, prosiest**) ну́дный.

protagonist /prəʊ'tægənɪst/ *n.* (*chief actor*) гла́вный геро́й; (*in contest etc.*) протагони́ст; (*advocate*) побо́рник.

protean /'prəʊtɪən/, /-'ti:ən/ *adj.* многообра́зный, изме́нчивый.

protect /prə'tekt/ *v.t.* **1** (*keep safe, shelter*) защи|ща́ть, -ти́ть; **the house is well ~ed against fire** дом хорошо́ защищён от огня́. **2** (*fit with safety device*) обезопа́сить (*pf.*).

protection /prə'tekʃ(ə)n/ *n.* **1** (*defence*) защи́та; **his clothing afforded him no ~ from the cold** оде́жда была́ ему́ плохо́й защи́той от хо́лода; **~ money** о́ткуп от рэкети́ров; **~ racket** рэ́кет. **2** (*shelter*) огражде́ние. **3** (*care*) попече́ние; **under my ~** на моём попече́нии. **4** (*econ.*) протекциони́зм.

protectionism /prə'tekʃ(ə),nɪz(ə)m/ *n.* протекциони́зм.

protectionist /prə'tekʃ(ə)nɪst/ *n.* протекциони́ст.

protective /prə'tektɪv/ *adj.* защи́тный; **~ colouring** (*Br.*), **coloring** (*US*) защи́тная окра́ска; **~ custody** защити́тельное содержа́ние под стра́жей.

protector /prə'tektə(r)/ *n.* (*person*) защи́тни|к (*fem.* -ца); (*hist., regent*) ре́гент; (*protective device*) защи́тное приспособле́ние.

protectorate /prə'tektərət/ *n.* (*territory*) протектора́т.

protectress /prə'tektrɪs/ *n.* защи́тница.

protégé /'prɒtɪ,ʒeɪ/, /-te,ʒeɪ/, /'prəʊ-/ *n.* (*fem.* **protégée**) протеже́ (*c.g., indecl.*).

protein /'prəʊti:n/ *n.* протеи́н, бело́к.

pro tem /prəʊ 'tem/ *adv.* (*coll.*) пока́мест (*coll.*).

pro tempore /prəʊ 'tempərɪ/ *adv.* вре́менно, пока́.

protest[1] /'prəʊtest/ *n.* проте́ст; возраже́ние; **without ~** не протесту́я; **~ march** марш проте́ста; **~ vote** го́лос, по́данный в знак проте́ста.

protest[2] /prə'test/ *v.t.* **1** (*affirm*) утвержда́ть (*impf.*); **he continued to ~ his innocence** он продолжа́л отста́ивать свою́ невино́вность. **2** (*US, object to*) возража́ть/протестова́ть (*impf.*) про́тив + *g.*

● *v.i.*: **~ against** протестова́ть (*impf.*) про́тив + *g.*; **~ about** выража́ть, вы́разить недово́льство + *i.*; (*appeal*) опротест|о́вывать, -ова́ть; **they ~ed against the decision** они́ опротестова́ли реше́ние.

Protestant /'prɒtɪst(ə)nt/ *n.* протеста́нт (*fem.* -ка).

● *adj.* протеста́нтский.

Protestantism /'prɒtɪstənt,ɪz(ə)m/ *n.* протестанти́зм.

protestation /,prɒtɪ'steɪʃ(ə)n/ *n.* (*affirmation*) (торже́ственное) заявле́ние; (*protest*) проте́ст.

protest|er, -or /prəʊ'testə(r)/ *nn.* протеста́нт.

protocol /,prəʊtə'kɒl/ *n.* протоко́л.

proton /'prəʊtɒn/ *n.* прото́н.

protoplasm /'prəʊtə,plæz(ə)m/ *n.* протопла́зма.

prototype /'prəʊtə,taɪp/ *n.* прототи́п, первонача́льный образе́ц.

protozoa /,prəʊtə'zəʊə/ *n.* протозо́а (*pl. indecl.*), просте́йшие (*nt. pl.*).

protract /prə'trækt/ *v.t.* затя́|гивать, -ну́ть; **a ~ed visit** затяну́вшийся визи́т; **a ~ed war** затяжна́я война́.

protractor /prə'træktə(r)/ *n.* транспорти́р.

protrud|e /prə'tru:d/ *v.i.* выдава́ться (*impf.*); **~ing teeth** торча́щие зу́бы.

protrusion /prə'tru:ʒ(ə)n/ *n.* высо́вывание; вы́ступ.

protuberance /prə'tju:bərəns/ *n.* вы́пуклость; (*on body*) бугоро́к, ши́шка (*coll.*).

protuberant /prə'tju:bərənt/ *adj.* вы́пуклый.

proud /praʊd/ *adj.* го́рдый; **he is a ~ man** он го́рдый челове́к; **he was too ~ to complain** он был сли́шком горд, что́бы жа́ловаться; **be ~ (of)** горди́ться (*impf.*) (+ *i.*); **he was ~ of his garden** он горди́лся свои́м са́дом; **he was the ~ father of twins** он был счастли́вым отцо́м двойни́; **this is a ~ day for the school** э́то торже́ственный/ра́достный день для шко́лы; (*arrogant*) надме́нный.

● *adv.*: **it was a sumptuous meal: they did us ~** они́ нас угости́ли на сла́ву.

provable /'pru:vəb(ə)l/ *adj.* доказу́емый.

prove /pru:v/ *v.t.* (*p.p.* **proved** *or* **proven** /'pru:v(ə)n/, /'prəʊ-/) **1** (*demonstrate*) дока́з|ывать, -а́ть; **he ~d his worth** он показа́л себя́ досто́йным челове́ком; **he cannot be ~d guilty** нельзя́ доказа́ть, что он вино́вен; **he needs to ~ himself to others** ему́ на́до утверди́ть себя́ в глаза́х други́х. **2** (*put to the test*) испы́т|ывать, -а́ть; **the exception ~s the rule** исключе́ние подтвержда́ет пра́вило. **3** (*leg.*): **~ a will** утвер|жда́ть, -ди́ть завеща́ние.

● *v.i.* (*p.p.* **proved** *or* **proven** /'pru:v(ə)n/, /'prəʊ-/) (*turn out*) ока́з|ываться, -а́ться; **the alarm ~d (to be) a hoax** трево́га оказа́лась ло́жной; **the play ~d a success** пье́са име́ла успе́х; **the report ~d true** сообще́ние подтверди́лось.

proven /'pru:v(ə)n/, /'prəʊ-/ *adj.* дока́занный.

provenance /'prɒvɪnəns/ *n.* происхожде́ние.

provender /'prɒvɪndə(r)/ *n.* фура́ж.

proverb /'prɒvɜ:b/ *n.* посло́вица; **(the Book of) P~s** кни́га При́тчей Соломо́новых.

proverbial /prə'vɜ:bɪəl/ *adj.* **1** (*pert. to provs.*) провербиа́льный; **~ wisdom** наро́дная му́дрость. **2** (*notorious*) общеизве́стный.

provide /prə'vaɪd/ *v.t.* **1**: **~ s.o. with something** обеспе́чи|вать, -ть кого́-н. чем-н.; снаб|жа́ть, -ди́ть кого́-н. чем-н.; **who will ~ the food?** кто позабо́тится о пи́ще?; **they are well ~d with money** у них доста́точно де́нег; **students must ~ their own textbooks** студе́нты обя́заны приобрета́ть уче́бники са́ми. **2** (*prescribe*) предусм|а́тривать, -отре́ть.

● *v.i.* (*prepare o.s.*) пригот|авливаться,

P

-о́виться; ~ **against one's old age** обеспе́чи|вать, -ть себя́ в ста́рости; **she had three children to ~ for** на её содержа́нии бы́ло тро́е дете́й.

provid|ed /prəˈvaɪdɪd/, **-ing** /prəˈvaɪdɪŋ/ *conjs.* при усло́вии, что; е́сли.

providence /ˈprɒvɪd(ə)ns/ *n.* **1** (*foresight*) предусмотри́тельность; (*thrift*) расчётливость. **2** (*divine care*): **he escaped by a special ~** его́ спасло́ (то́лько) провиде́ние; (**P~**: *God*) провиде́ние, про́мысел Бо́жий.

provident /ˈprɒvɪd(ə)nt/ *adj.* предусмотри́тельный; расчётливый.

providential /ˌprɒvɪˈdenʃ(ə)l/ *adj.* (*lucky*) счастли́вый; **it was ~ that you came** вас сам Бог посла́л.

provider /prəˈvaɪdə(r)/ *n.* снабже́нец; поставщи́|к (*fem.* -ца); (*breadwinner*): **her husband is a good ~** её муж хорошо́ обеспе́чивает семью́; (*comp.*) провайдер.

providing /prəˈvaɪdɪŋ/ = **provided**

province /ˈprɒvɪns/ *n.* **1** (*division of country*) о́бласть, прови́нция. **2**: **the ~s** прови́нция, перифери́я; **in the ~s** в прови́нции, на перифери́и. **3** (*sphere, department*) компете́нция; о́бласть.

provincial /prəˈvɪnʃ(ə)l/ *n.* (*person from provinces*) провинциа́л (*fem.* -ка).

● *adj.* (*lit., fig.*) провинциа́льный.

provincialism /prəˈvɪnʃəˌlɪz(ə)m/ *n.* провинциа́льность.

provision /prəˈvɪʒ(ə)n/ *n.* **1** (*supplying*) снабже́ние. **2** (*pl., supplies, esp. food*) прови́зия; съестны́е припа́сы (*m. pl.*). **3** (*preparation*) обеспе́чение; **their father had made ~ for them** оте́ц обеспе́чил их на бу́дущее. **4** (*item of agreement, law etc.*) усло́вие; положе́ние.

● *v.t.* снаб|жа́ть, -ди́ть продово́льствием.

provisional /prəˈvɪʒən(ə)l/ *n.*: **the P~s** Вре́менное крыло́ ИРА.

● *adj.* вре́менный; (*approximate*) ориентиро́вочный; **~ driving licence** (*Br.*) вре́менные води́тельские права́ (*nt.pl.*); **he gave ~ consent** он дал предвари́тельное согла́сие; **~ government** вре́менное прави́тельство; **P~ IRA** Вре́менное крыло́ ИРА.

proviso /prəˈvaɪzəʊ/ *n.* (*pl.* **~s**) усло́вие, огово́рка; **with the ~ that ...** с усло́вием (*or* с огово́ркой), что....

Provo /ˈprəʊvəʊ/ *n.* (*pl.* **~s**) (*coll.*) член Вре́менного крыла́ ИРА.

provocation /ˌprɒvəˈkeɪʃ(ə)n/ *n.* провока́ция; **at the slightest ~** по мале́йшему по́воду; **I did it under ~** меня́ спровоци́ровали на э́то.

provocative /prəˈvɒkətɪv/ *adj.* (*challenging*) вызыва́ющий; (*alluring*) соблазни́тельный; **race is a ~ subject** ра́совая те́ма всегда́ вызыва́ет поле́мику.

provoke /prəˈvəʊk/ *v.t.* **1** (*cause, arouse; challenge*) вызыва́ть, вы́звать; провоци́ровать, с-. **2** (*impel*) побу|жда́ть, -ди́ть. **3** (*anger*) серди́ть, рас-; выводи́ть, вы́вести из себя́; **he is easily ~d** его́ легко́ вы́вести из себя́.

provoking /prəˈvəʊkɪŋ/ *adj.* раздража́ющий, доса́дный.

provost /ˈprɒvəst/ *n.* (*Br., head of college*) ре́ктор; (*Sc. dignitary*) мэр; **~-marshal** нача́льник вое́нной поли́ции.

prow /praʊ/ *n.* нос (*судна*).

prowess /ˈpraʊɪs/ *n.* (*skill*) мастерство́; (*valour*) до́блесть.

prowl /praʊl/ *n.*: **cats on the ~ after mice** ко́шки, высма́тривающие мыше́й; **~ car** (*US*) полице́йская патру́льная маши́на.

● *v.t.* (*a place*) ры́скать (*impf.*) по + *d.*, шныря́ть по + *d.*; **thieves ~ the streets** во́ры шныря́ют по у́лицам.

● *v.i.* ры́скать (*impf.*); шныря́ть (*impf.*); **wolves were ~ing outside the tent** во́лки ры́скали вокру́г пала́тки.

prowler /ˈpraʊlə(r)/ *n.* челове́к, закра́дывающий на чужу́ю террито́рию.

proximate /ˈprɒksɪmət/ *adj.* ближа́йший.

proximity /prɒkˈsɪmɪtɪ/ *n.* бли́зость; сосе́дство; **in (close) ~ to** вблизи́/поблизи́ости от + *g.*, ря́дом с + *i.*

proxy /ˈprɒksɪ/ *n.* **1** (*authorization*) полномо́чие, дове́ренность; **they voted by ~** они́ голосова́ли по дове́ренности. **2** (*substitute*) замести́тель (*m.*); **he stood ~ for his brother** он представля́л своего́ бра́та; (*attr.*): **~ vote** голосова́ние по дове́ренности.

prude /pruːd/ *n.* ханжа́ (*c.g.*).

prudence /ˈpruːd(ə)ns/ *n.* благоразу́мие, предусмотри́тельность.

prudent /ˈpruːd(ə)nt/ *adj.* благоразу́мный, предусмотри́тельный.

prudery /ˈpruːdərɪ/ *n.* стыдли́вость; (*pej.*) ха́нжество́.

prudish /ˈpruːdɪʃ/ *adj.* стыдли́вый; (*pej.*) ха́нжеский.

prudishness /ˈpruːdɪʃnɪs/ *n.* стыдли́вость; (*pej.*) ха́нжество́.

prune¹ /pruːn/ *n.* черносли́в.

prun|e² /pruːn/ *v.t.* **1** (*trim*) обр|еза́ть, -е́зать; подр|еза́ть, -е́зать; **~ing-hook** приви́вочный нож; (*fig.*) сокра|ща́ть, -ти́ть; **the department was ~ed of superfluous staff** весь ли́шний штат в отде́ле сократи́ли. **2** (*simplify*) упро|ща́ть, -сти́ть.

prurienc|e /ˈprʊərɪəns/, **-y** /ˈprʊərɪənsɪ/ *nn.* по́хоть.

prurient /ˈprʊərɪənt/ *adj.* похотли́вый.

Prussia /ˈprʌʃə/ *n.* Пру́ссия.

Prussian /ˈprʌʃ(ə)n/ *n.* прусса́|к (*fem.* -чка).

● *adj.* пру́сский; **~ blue** берли́нская лазу́рь.

prussic /ˈprʌsɪk/ *adj.*: **~ acid** сини́льная кислота́.

pry /praɪ/ *v.i.* вме́шиваться, вмеша́ться (в чужи́е дела́).

PS (*abbr. of* ***postscript***) постскри́птум, припи́ска.

psalm /sɑːm/ *n.* псало́м.

psalter /ˈsɔːltə(r)/, /ˈsɒl-/ *n.* псалты́рь (*f. or m.*).

PSBR (*abbr. of* ***Public Sector Borrowing Requirement***) (*Br.*) потре́бность госуда́рственного се́ктора в креди́тах.

psephologist /seˈfɒlədʒɪst/, /pse-/ *n.* псефо́лог, специали́ст по псефоло́гии.

psephology /seˈfɒlədʒɪ/, /pse-/ *n.* псефоло́гия, изуче́ние результа́тов голосова́ния (*на выборах*).

pseud /sjuːd/ *n.* позёр.

pseudo /ˈsjuːdəʊ/ *adj.* фальши́вый.

pseudo- /ˈsjuːdəʊ/ *comb. form* псе́вдо..., лже....

pseudonym /ˈsjuːdənɪm/ *n.* псевдони́м.

psoriasis /səˈraɪəsɪs/ *n.* псориа́з.

psst /pst/ *int.* хм-хм (*чтобы привлечь внимание*).

psych /saɪk/ *v.t.*: **~ o.s. up** настр|а́ивать, -о́ить себя́.

psyche /ˈsaɪkɪ/ *n.* душа́; дух.

psychedelic /ˌsaɪkɪˈdelɪk/ *adj.* (*experience*) психодели́ческий; (*clothes, colours*) чудно́й; (*drug*) психодислепти́ческий.

psychiatric /ˌsaɪkɪˈætrɪk/ *adj.* психиатри́ческий.

psychiatrist /saɪˈkaɪətrɪst/ *n.* психиа́тр.

psychiatry /saɪˈkaɪətrɪ/ *n.* психиатри́я.

psychic /ˈsaɪkɪk/ *n.* экстрасе́нс.

● *adj.* **1** (*clairvoyant*) ≈ ясновидя́щий. **2** (*of the soul or mind*) психи́ческий, душе́вный.

psychical /ˈsaɪkɪk(ə)l/ *adj.*: **~ research** иссле́дования (*nt. pl.*) паранорма́льных явле́ний.

psycho /ˈsaɪkəʊ/ *n.* (*pl.* **~s**) (*coll.*) псих.

psychoanalyse /ˌsaɪkəʊˈænəˌlaɪz/ (*US* **-analyze**) *v.t.* подв|ерга́ть, -е́ргнуть психоана́лизу.

psychoanalysis /ˌsaɪkəʊəˈnælɪsɪs/ *n.* психоана́лиз.

psychoanalyst /ˌsaɪkəʊˈænəlɪst/ *n.* психоанали́тик.

psychoanalytic /ˌsaɪkəʊˌænəˈlɪtɪk/ *adj.* психоаналити́ческий.

psycholinguistics /ˌsaɪkəʊlɪŋˈgwɪstɪks/ *n.* психолингви́стика.

psychological /ˌsaɪkəˈlɒdʒɪk(ə)l/ *adj.* психологи́ческий.

psychologist /saɪˈkɒlədʒɪst/ *n.* психо́лог.

psychology /saɪˈkɒlədʒɪ/ *n.* психоло́гия.

psychopath /ˈsaɪkəˌpæθ/ *n.* психопа́т (*fem.* -ка).

psychopathic /ˌsaɪkəˈpæθɪk/ *adj.* психопати́ческий; **he is ~** он психопа́т.

psychopathology /ˌsaɪkəʊpəˈθɒlədʒɪ/ *n.* психопатоло́гия.

psychosis /saɪˈkəʊsɪs/ *n.* (*pl.* **psychoses** /-siːz/) психо́з.

psychosomatic /ˌsaɪkəʊsəˈmætɪk/ *adj.* психосомати́ческий.

psychotherapeutic /ˌsaɪkəʊθerəˈpjuːtɪk/ *adj.* психотерапевти́ческий.

psychotherapist /ˌsaɪkəʊˈθerəpɪst/ *n.* психотерапе́вт.

psychotherapy /ˌsaɪkəʊˈθerəpɪ/ *n.* психотерапи́я.

psychotic /saɪˈkɒtɪk/ *adj.* психоти́ческий, душевнобольно́й.

PT (*abbr. of* ***physical training***) физи́ческая подгото́вка.

pt. /paɪnt(z)/ *n.* (*abbr. of* **pint(s)**) пи́нта.

PTA (*abbr. of* ***parent-teacher association***) ассоциа́ция учителе́й и роди́телей.

ptarmigan /ˈtɑːmɪgən/ *n.* шотла́ндский те́терев.

Pte /ˈpraɪvət/ *n.* (*abbr. of* ***Private***) (*Br., mil.*) рядово́й.

pterodactyl /ˌterəˈdæktɪl/ *n.* птерода́ктиль (*m.*).

PTO (*abbr. of* ***please turn over***) см. на об. (смотри́ на оборо́те).

pub /pʌb/ *n.* (*Br. coll.*) пивна́я; паб; каба́к.

● *cpd.* **~-crawl** *n.* (*coll.*) шата́ние по пивны́м/ба́рам.

puberty /ˈpjuːbətɪ/ *n.* полово́е созрева́ние, пуберта́тный пери́од.

pubes[1] /ˈpjuːbiːz/ *n.* (*pl.* **~**) лобко́вая о́бласть.

pubes[2] /ˈpjuːbiːz/ *pl. of* ⇒**pubis**

pubescence /pjuːˈbes(ə)ns/ *n.* полово́е созрева́ние.

pubescent /pjuːˈbes(ə)nt/ *adj.* дости́гший полово́й зре́лости.

pubic /ˈpjuːbɪk/ *adj.* лобко́вый, ло́нный; **~ hair** во́лосы на лобке́.

pubis /ˈpjuːbɪs/ *n.* (*pl.* **pubes**) лобко́вая/ло́нная кость.

public /ˈpʌblɪk/ *n.* **1** (*community*) обще́ственность; наро́д; **the British ~** англи́йский наро́д; **the library is open to the ~** вход в библиоте́ку свобо́дный; **members of the (general) ~** представи́тели (широ́кой) обще́ственности (*or* широ́кой пу́блики).
2 (*section of community*) пу́блика; **the theatre- (*Br.*), theater- (*US*) going ~** театра́льная пу́блика.
3 (*audience*) пу́блика; **he refuses to appear before the ~** он отка́зывается выступа́ть пе́ред пу́бликой; **I have never spoken in ~** я никогда́ не выступа́л пе́ред пу́бликой.

● *adj.* **1** (*pert. to people in general*) обще́ственный; **~ opinion** обще́ственное мне́ние; **a matter of ~ concern** де́ло, представля́ющее обще́ственный интере́с; **he is in the ~ eye** он (нахо́дится) на виду́; **~ health** здравоохране́ние; **it is ~ knowledge** э́то общеизве́стно; **~ relations** свя́зи с обще́ственностью; **~ relations officer** сотру́дник отде́ла по свя́зям с обще́ственностью; **in the ~ interest** в интере́сах о́бщества/госуда́рства; **~ enemy** враг наро́да.
2 (*pert. to politics or the state*) обще́ственный, госуда́рственный; **a ~ figure** обще́ственный де́ятель; **he entered ~ life** он заня́лся обще́ственной де́ятельностью; **he held ~ office** он был вы́сшим должностны́м лицо́м; **~ record office** госуда́рственный архи́в; **~ prosecutor** прокуро́р, госуда́рственный обвини́тель; **~ sector** госуда́рственный се́ктор.
3 (*accessible to all; shared by the community*) публи́чный, обще́ственный, общенаро́дный; **~ convenience** (*Br.*) обще́ственная убо́рная; **~ holiday** устано́вленный зако́ном пра́здник; **~ library** публи́чная библиоте́ка; **~ transport** обще́ственный тра́нспорт; **~ utilities** коммуна́льные услу́ги.
4 (*done openly, in view of others*) публи́чный, гла́сный, откры́тый; **~ inquiry** обще́ственное рассле́дование; **~ speaking** ора́торское иску́сство; **he does a lot of ~ speaking** он ча́сто выступа́ет публи́чно; **~ protest** обще́ственный проте́ст.

● *cpds.* **~ address system** *n.* набо́р звукоусили́тельной аппарату́ры для выступле́ний; **~-house** *n.* (*Br.*) пивна́я, паб; **~ school** *n.* (*Br.*) ча́стная шко́ла; (*US*) госуда́рственная шко́ла; **~-spirited** *adj.* дви́жимый интере́сами обще́ственности.

publican /ˈpʌblɪkən/ *n.* (*Br.*) содержа́тель (*m.*) ба́ра/па́ба.

publication /ˌpʌblɪˈkeɪʃ(ə)n/ *n.* (*of news etc.*) публика́ция, опубликова́ние, изда́ние; (*published work*) изда́ние; произведе́ние.

publicist /ˈpʌblɪsɪst/ *n.* (*writer on current topics*) публици́ст.

publicity /pʌbˈlɪsɪtɪ/ *n.* **1** (*public notice, dissemination*) гла́сность, огла́ска; **the report was given full ~** сообще́ние получи́ло широ́кую огла́ску.
2 (*advertisement*) реклами́рование, рекла́ма, пабли́сити (*indecl.*); **~ agent** аге́нт по рекла́ме; **~ campaign** рекла́мная кампа́ния.

publicize /ˈpʌblɪˌsaɪz/ *v.t.* реклами́ровать (*impf.*); огла|ша́ть, -си́ть.

publish /ˈpʌblɪʃ/ *v.t.* **1** (*information, news*) (*in print*) публикова́ть, о-; (*not in print*) огла|ша́ть, -си́ть. **2** (*books, newspapers*) печа́тать, на-; изд|ава́ть, -а́ть; выпуска́ть, вы́пустить; (*letter, article*) публикова́ть, о-; (*author*) публикова́ть, о-.

publishable /ˈpʌblɪʃəb(ə)l/ *adj.* приго́дный для печа́ти.

publisher /ˈpʌblɪʃə(r)/ *n.* изда́тель (*m.*).

publishing /ˈpʌblɪʃɪŋ/ *n.* изда́тельское де́ло; **~ house** изда́тельство.

puce /pjuːs/ *adj.* краснова́то-кори́чневый.

puck /pʌk/ *n.* (*in ice-hockey*) ша́йба.

pucker /ˈpʌkə(r)/ *n.* (*fold, crease*) скла́дка; (*wrinkle*) морщи́на.

● *v.t. & i.* мо́рщить(ся), на-; **his brow was ~ed** он насу́пился; **this coat ~s up at the shoulders** э́то пальто́ мо́рщит в плеча́х.

puckish /ˈpʌkɪʃ/ *adj.* прока́зливый.

pud /pʊd/ (*Br. coll.*) = **pudding**

pudding /ˈpʊdɪŋ/ *n.* пу́динг, запека́нка; (*Br., sweet course*) сла́дкое; **black ~** кровяна́я колбаса́.

puddle /ˈpʌd(ə)l/ *n.* (*pool*) лу́жа.

pudenda /pjuːˈdendə/ *n.* (же́нские) нару́жные половы́е о́рганы (*m. pl.*).

pudgy /ˈpʌdʒɪ/ *adj.* (**pudgier, pudgiest**) пу́хлый.

puerile /ˈpjʊəraɪl/ *adj.* де́тский, инфанти́льный.

puerility /pjʊəˈrɪlɪtɪ/ *n.* инфанти́льность.

puerperal /pjuːˈɜːpər(ə)l/ *adj.* роди́льный; **~ fever** роди́льная горя́чка.

Puerto Rican /ˌpwɜːtəʊ ˈriːkən/ *n.* пуэрторика́н|ец (*fem.* -ка).

● *adj.* пуэ́рто-рика́нский.

Puerto Rico /ˌpwɜːtəʊ ˈriːkəʊ/ *n.* Пуэ́рто-Ри́ко (*indecl.*).

puff /pʌf/ *n.* **1** (*of breath*) вы́дох.
2 (*of smoke, steam etc.*) дымо́к, клуб; **he took a ~ at his cigar** он затяну́лся сига́рой.
3 (*sound*) пыхте́ние.
4 (*of air or wind*) дунове́ние.
5 (*coll., publicity*) ду́тая рекла́ма.
6 (*cake*) сло́йка; слоёный пирожо́к; **~ pastry** слоёное те́сто.

● *v.t.* **1** (*breathe out*) выдыха́ть, вы́дохнуть; **he ~ed smoke in my face** он вы́дохнул дым мне в лицо́.
2 (*make out of breath*): **I was ~ed after the climb** у меня сде́лалась оды́шка по́сле подъёма.
3: **~ out** (*smoke*) выпуска́ть, вы́пустить; (*chest*): **he ~ed out his chest with pride** он го́рдо вы́пятил грудь; **~ up** (*a balloon*) над|ува́ть, -у́ть.
4: **~ed-up** (*haughty*) надутый.

● *v.i.* **1** (*come out in ~s*) клуби́ться (*impf.*).
2 (*breathe quickly*): **he was ~ing and panting** он не мог отдыша́ться; он пыхте́л.
3 (*emit smoke*) дыми́ться (*impf.*); **he ~ed away at his pipe** он попы́хивал тру́бкой.
4: **~ up** (*swell*) расп|уха́ть, -у́хнуть; **his hand was ~ed up** его́ рука́ распу́хла.

puffin /ˈpʌfɪn/ *n.* ту́пик, топо́рик (*птица*).

puffy /ˈpʌfɪ/ *adj.* (**puffier, puffiest**) (*swollen*) одутлова́тый.

pug /pʌg/ *n.* мопс.

● *cpd.* **~-nosed** *adj.* курно́сый.

pugilism /ˈpjuːdʒɪˌlɪz(ə)m/ *n.* кула́чный бой.

pugilist /ˈpjuːdʒɪlɪst/ *n.* боксёр.

pugilistic /ˌpjuːdʒɪˈlɪstɪk/ *adj.* кула́чный.

pugnacious /pʌgˈneɪʃəs/ *adj.* драчли́вый, вои́нственный.

pugnacity /pʌgˈnæsɪtɪ/ *n.* драчли́вость, вои́нственность.

puissance /ˈpjuːɪs(ə)ns/, /ˈpwɪs-/ *n.* (*arch.*) могу́щество, мощь.

puissant /ˈpjuːɪs(ə)nt/, /ˈpwiːs-/, /ˈpwɪs-/ *adj.* (*arch.*) могу́щественный, мо́щный.

puke /pjuːk/ *n.* (*coll.*) рво́та, блевоти́на.

● *v.i.* блева́ть (*impf.*) (*coll.*); **he ~d** его́ вы́рвало.

pukka /ˈpʌkə/ *adj.* (*coll.*) (*genuine*) настоя́щий; (*good-quality*) важне́цкий.

pull /pʊl/ *n.* **1** (*traction*) тя́га; (*act*) дёрганье; **he gave a ~ on the rope** он дёрнул (за) верёвку.
2 (*handle*) ру́чка; шнуро́к.
3 (*effort*) уси́лие, напряже́ние; (*force*) си́ла; **the tide exerts a strong ~** прили́в облада́ет большо́й си́лой; **it was a long hard ~ up the hill** взобра́ться на́ гору сто́ило больши́х уси́лий.
4 (*coll., influence*) свя́зи (*f. pl.*), блат; **he has a lot of ~** у него́ больши́е свя́зи.
● *v.t.* **1** (*draw towards one, tug, jerk*) тяну́ть, по-; тащи́ть, по-; **the boy ~ed his sister's hair** ма́льчик дёрнул сестру́ за́ волосы; **he ~ed me by the sleeve** он потяну́л меня́ за рука́в.
2 (*Br., obtain by ~ing*): **the barman ~ed a glass of beer** ба́рмен нака́ча́л стака́н пи́ва.
3 (*fig.*): **he is good at ~ing strings** он ма́стер нажима́ть на кно́пки; **~ s.o.'s leg** разы́гр|ывать, -а́ть кого́-н.; **she ~ed a face at him** она́ ско́рчила ему́ грима́су; **he is trying to ~ a fast one** он стара́ется нас объего́рить (*coll.*).
4 (*extract, pluck*) выта́скивать, вы́тащить; выдёргивать, вы́дернуть; **~ a tooth** вырыва́ть, вы́рвать зуб; **he ~ed a gun on me** он вы́хватил пистоле́т и навёл его́ на меня́.
5 (*propel by ~ing*) тяну́ть (*impf.*); **the carriage was ~ed by horses** каре́та была́ запряжена́ лошадьми́; **he is not ~ing his weight** (*fig.*) он рабо́тает вполси́лы.
6 (*strain, e.g. muscle*) растя́|гивать, -ну́ть.
● *v.i.* **1** (*exert drawing force*) тяну́ть, по-; **they ~ed on the rope** они́ потяну́ли за верёвку; **he ~ed at the bell** он дёрнул звоно́к; **the boatman ~ed hard on the oars** ло́дочник усе́рдно налега́л на вёсла; **the horse ~ed against the bit** ло́шадь натяну́ла удила́.
2 (*suck*) тяну́ть, по-; **he ~ed on his pipe** он потя́гивал тру́бку.
3 (*propel boat, car etc.*) е́хать, про-; **he had to ~ across the road** ему́ на́до бы́ло перее́хать на другу́ю сто́рону.
4 (*move under propulsion*) дви́гаться (*impf.*); **the car is ~ing to the left** маши́ну зано́сит вле́во; **the train ~ed out of the station** по́езд отошёл от ста́нции.
● *with advs.*: **~ about** *v.t.* (*treat roughly*) теребить (*impf.*); трепа́ть, по-; **the dog ~ed the cushion about** соба́ка теребила поду́шку; **~ apart** *v.t.* (*also* **~ to pieces**) раз|рыва́ть, -орва́ть (на куски́); (*fig., criticize severely*) разн|оси́ть, -ести́ в пух и прах; **~ aside** *v.t.* оття́|гивать, -ну́ть; **~ away** *v.t.*: **he ~ed his hand away** он убра́л ру́ку; *v.i.* (*move off*) от|ходи́ть, -ойти́; от|рыва́ться, -орва́ться; **the boat ~ed away from the quay** ло́дка отошла́ от при́стани; **~ back** *v.t.* отта́|скивать, -щи́ть; оття́|гивать, -ну́ть; **he ~ed her back from the window** он оттащи́л её от окна́; **~ back the curtains!** отдёрните занаве́ски!; *v.i.* отступ|а́ть, -и́ть; **~ down** *v.t.* (*lower by ~ing*) спус|ка́ть, -ти́ть; **~ down the blinds!** опусти́те што́ры!; **he ~ed the branch down** он нагну́л ве́тку; (*knock down*) вали́ть, по-; (*demolish*) сн|оси́ть, -ести́; **~ in** *v.t.* (*retract*) втя́|гивать, -ну́ть; (*curtail*) сокра|ща́ть, -ти́ть; (*haul on, draw towards one*) тащи́ть, вы́-; тяну́ть, по-; (*coll., arrest*) заб|ира́ть, -ра́ть, аресто́в|ывать, -а́ть; **the rope was ~ed in** верёвку натяну́ли; **he ~ed in his horse** он осади́л ло́шадь; **he ~s in £50 a week** он зараба́тывает 50 фу́нтов в неде́лю; *v.i.* (*drive or move to a standstill*) остан|а́вливаться, -ови́ться; **the train ~ed in** по́езд подошёл к перро́ну; **he ~ed in to the kerb** (*Br.*), **up to the curb** (*US*) он подъе́хал к тротуа́ру; (*drive or move towards near side of road*): **he ~ed in to avoid a collision** он прижа́лся к обо́чине, что́бы избежа́ть столкнове́ния; **~ off** *v.t.* (*remove, detach*) стя́|гивать, -ну́ть; сн|има́ть, -ять; **he ~ed the buttons off** он сорва́л/оторва́л пу́говицы; **he ~ed his shoes off** он стащи́л ту́фли; (*coll., achieve*) успе́шно заверш|а́ть, -и́ть; **if he ~s it off** е́сли у него́ вы́йдет/вы́горит; *v.i.* тро́гаться, тро́нуться; **the car ~ed off in a hurry** маши́на бы́стро отъе́хала; **~ on** *v.t.* натя́|гивать, -ну́ть; **he ~ed his socks on** он натяну́л носки́; **~ out** *v.t.* (*extract*) вы́та́скивать, вы́тащить; **he ~ed out his watch** он вы́тащил часы́; **he ~ed out the drawer** он вы́двинул я́щик; **the weeds should be ~ed out** сорняки́ на́до вы́дернуть/вы́полоть; (*withdraw*) выводи́ть, вы́вести; **the troops should be ~ed out** войска́ сле́дует вы́вести; *v.i.* (*drive or move away*) от|ходи́ть, -ойти́; **he caught the train as it was ~ing out** он вскочи́л в по́езд на ходу́; (*of driving manoeuvres*) отъ|езжа́ть, -е́хать; **he ~ed out to overtake** он вы́шел на обго́н; (*troops*) от|ходи́ть, -ойти́; **the drawer won't ~ out** я́щик не выдвига́ется; **he ~ed out** (*of the business*) он отказа́лся от уча́стия в э́том де́ле; **~ round** *v.t.* выле́чивать, вы́лечить; **the brandy will soon ~ you round** коньяк ско́ро приведёт вас в чу́вство; *v.i.* (*Br., recover*) попр|авля́ться, -а́виться; **he will ~ round in a day or so** он придёт в себя́ (*or* попра́вится) че́рез день-друго́й; (*reverse direction*) разв|ора́чиваться, -ерну́ться; **~ through** *v.t.* (*lit.*) прота́|скивать, -щи́ть; (*fig.*) спас|а́ть, -ти́; **he dreaded the exam but his determination ~ed him through** он ужа́сно боя́лся экза́мена, но реши́лся сдать и сдал; *v.i.* (*recover from illness*) попр|авля́ться, -а́виться; **he was gravely ill, but ~ed through somehow** он был тяжело́ бо́лен, но ко́е-как суме́л попра́виться; (*surmount difficulties, survive*): **we shall ~ through in the end** в конце́ концо́в мы вы́крутимся; **~ together** *v.t.*: **~ yourself together!** возьми́те себя́ в ру́ки!; держи́те себя́ в рука́х!; *v.i.* (*fig.*) сраб|а́тываться, -о́таться; **if we all ~ together, we shall win** объедини́вшись, мы победи́м; **~ up** *v.t.* (*uproot*) вырыва́ть, вы́рвать; **the plant had been ~ed up by the roots** расте́ние вы́рвали с ко́рнем; (*raise*) вытя́гивать, вы́тянуть; **he ~ed himself up to his full height** он вы́прямился во весь рост; **you must ~ your socks up** (*fig., coll.*) вам на́до взя́ться за ум; (*draw nearer*) придв|ига́ть, -и́нуть; **~ up a chair!** придви́ньте стул!; (*bring to a halt*) остан|а́вливать, -ови́ть; (*reprimand*) отчи́т|ывать, -а́ть; *v.i.* (*come to a halt*) остан|а́вливаться, -ови́ться; **don't get off the bus until it ~s up** не выходи́те из авто́буса до его́ по́лной остано́вки.
● *cpds.* **~-in** *n.* (*Br.*) придоро́жная стоя́нка; **~-out** *n.* (*detachable section*) вкла́дка; (*withdrawal*) вы́вод, отво́д; **~ of troops** вы́вод войск; **~-up** *n.* (*gymnastic exercise*) подтя́гивание.

pullet /ˈpʊlɪt/ *n.* пуля́рка, молода́я ку́рица.

pulley /ˈpʊlɪ/ *n.* (*pl.* **pulleys**) (*wheel for cord*) шкив; (*turned by belt*) блок.

pullover /ˈpʊləʊvə(r)/ *n.* пуло́вер, сви́тер.

pulmonary /ˈpʌlmənərɪ/ *adj.* лёгочный.

pulp /pʌlp/ *n.* **1** (*of fruit*) мя́коть. **2** (*of animal tissue*) пу́льпа. **3** (*of wood etc. for making paper*) древе́сная ма́сса, пу́льпа. **4** (*fig.*) ме́сиво; бесфо́рменная ма́сса; **his arm was crushed to a ~** ему́ раздроби́ло ру́ку; **~ literature** макулату́ра.
● *v.t.* (*make into ~*) превра|ща́ть, -ти́ть в пу́льпу.

pulpit /ˈpʊlpɪt/ *n.* ка́федра.

pulpy /ˈpʌlpɪ/ *adj.* мяси́стый; со́чный.

pulsar /ˈpʌlsɑː(r)/ *n.* пульса́р.

pulsate /pʌlˈseɪt/, /ˈpʌl-/ *v.i.* пульси́ровать (*impf.*).

pulsation /pʌlˈseɪʃ(ə)n/ *n.* пульса́ция.

puls|e¹ /pʌls/ *n.* пульс; **the doctor took his ~e** врач пощу́пал ему́ пульс; **what is your ~e rate?** како́й у вас пульс?; (*fig.*) пульса́ция, бие́ние; **he has his finger on the nation's ~e** он зна́ет, чем ды́шит страна́; (*of music*) ритм.
● *v.i.* пульси́ровать (*impf.*); би́ться (*impf.*).

pulse² /pʌls/ *n.* (*usu. pl.*) (*collect., legumes*) бобо́вые (расте́ния).

pulverize /ˈpʌlvəˌraɪz/ *v.t.* (*reduce to powder*) размельч|а́ть, -и́ть; (*fig., smash, demolish*) уничт|ожа́ть, -о́жить.

puma /ˈpjuːmə/ *n.* пу́ма.

pumice /ˈpʌmɪs/ *n.* (**~-stone**) пе́мза.

pummel, pommel /ˈpʌm(ə)l/ *v.t.* (**pummelled, pummelling;** *US* **pummeled, pummeling**) колоти́ть, по-; тузи́ть, от-.

pump¹ /pʌmp/ *n.* насо́с, по́мпа; **~ attendant** (*at filling station*) слу́жащий бензоколо́нки.
● *v.t.* **1** (*transfer by ~ing*) кача́ть, на-; **they ~ed water out of the hold** они́ вы́качали во́ду из трю́ма; **the tyre** (*Br.*), **tire** (*US*) **needs more air ~ing into it** ши́ну на́до подкача́ть; (*fig.*): **I had maths ~ed into me at school** в меня́ вда́лбливали матема́тику в шко́ле.

2 (*affect or empty by ~ing*) выка́чивать, вы́качать; **the well had been ~ed dry** коло́дец по́лностью осуши́ли; (*fig.*): **I ~ed him for information** я его́ выспра́шивал; я выве́дывал у него́ све́дения.
3 (*agitate as in ~ing*): **he ~ed my hand (up and down)** он до́лго тряс мне ру́ку.
4 (*also* **~ up**: *inflate*) нака́ч|ивать, -а́ть.

● *cpd.* **~-room** *n.* зал для питья́ минера́льной воды́.

pump² /pʌmp/ *n.* (*for sport*) ке́да.

pumpernickel /ˈpʌmpəˌnɪk(ə)l/, /ˈpʊ-/ *n.* (неме́цкий) ржано́й хлеб.

pumpkin /ˈpʌmpkɪn/ *n.* ты́ква.

pun /pʌn/ *n.* игра́ слов, каламбу́р.
● *v.i.* (**punned, punning**) каламбу́рить (*impf.*).

Punch /pʌntʃ/ *n.* (*puppet character*) Панч, Петру́шка (*m.*); **~ and Judy show** ку́кольное (я́рмарочное) представле́ние; **he was as pleased as ~** он расплы́лся/сия́л от удово́льствия.

punch¹ /pʌntʃ/ *n.* **1** (*blow with fist*) уда́р кулако́м; **I gave him a ~ on the nose** я дал ему́ кулако́м по́ носу. **2** (*fig., energy*) эне́ргия, ого́нь (*m.*); **his performance lacked ~** он игра́л вя́ло; его́ игре́ недостава́ло огня́. **3** (*tool for perforating e.g. paper*) дыроко́л; (*for tickets etc.*) компо́стер.
● *v.t.* **1** (*hit with fist*) уд|аря́ть, -а́рить кулако́м; **he was ~ed on the chin** он получи́л кулако́м в че́люсть.
2 (*perforate*) компости́ровать (*impf.*); **the conductor ~ed our tickets** конду́ктор прокомпости́ровал/проби́л на́ши биле́ты; **~ holes** проб|ива́ть, -и́ть отве́рстия; **~ed card** перфока́рта.
● *cpds.* **~-ball** *n.* (*Br.*) пенчингбо́л; (*US*) панчбо́л; **~-drunk** *adj.* ошара́шенный; **~-line** *n.* резюме́ (*indecl.*); **~-up** *n.* (*Br.*) дра́ка, потасо́вка.

punch² /pʌntʃ/ *n.* (*beverage*) пунш.

punctilious /pʌŋkˈtɪlɪəs/ *adj.* скрупулёзный.

punctiliousness /pʌŋkˈtɪlɪəsnɪs/ *n.* скрупулёзность.

punctual /ˈpʌŋktjʊəl/ *adj.* пунктуа́льный, то́чный; **let us try to be ~ for meals** дава́йте не опа́здывать к столу́.

punctuality /ˌpʌŋktjʊˈælɪtɪ/ *n.* пунктуа́льность, то́чность.

punctuate /ˈpʌŋktjʊˌeɪt/ *v.t.* (*insert punctuation marks in*) ста́вить, по- зна́ки препина́ния в + *a.*; (*fig., interrupt, intersperse*) прер|ыва́ть, -ва́ть.

punctuation /ˌpʌŋktjʊˈeɪʃ(ə)n/ *n.* пунктуа́ция; **~ mark** знак препина́ния.

puncture /ˈpʌŋktʃə(r)/ *n.* проко́л; **his bicycle had a ~** он проткну́л ши́ну своего́ велосипе́да.
● *v.t.* прок|а́лывать, -оло́ть.

pundit /ˈpʌndɪt/ *n.* знато́к, специали́ст.

pungency /ˈpʌndʒ(ə)nsɪ/ *n.* острота́, е́дкость.

pungent /ˈpʌndʒ(ə)nt/ *adj.* о́стрый.

punish /ˈpʌnɪʃ/ *v.t.* **1** (*inflict penalty on*) нака́з|ывать, -а́ть; кара́ть, по-; **the thief was ~ed by a fine** на во́ра наложи́ли штраф. **2** (*inflict penalty for*): **theft was severely ~ed** за кра́жу суро́во нака́зывали/кара́ли. **3** (*tax strength of*) изнур|я́ть, -и́ть; изм|а́тывать, -ота́ть; **he set a ~ing pace** он за́дал уби́йственный темп. **4** (*treat roughly*): **England were ~ed in the second half** англича́нам всы́пали во второ́м та́йме.

punishable /ˈpʌnɪʃəb(ə)l/ *adj.*: **treason is ~ by death** изме́на кара́ется сме́ртной ка́знью.

punishment /ˈpʌnɪʃmənt/ *n.* наказа́ние, ка́ра; (*penalty*) взыска́ние.

punitive /ˈpjuːnɪtɪv/ *adj.* кара́тельный; **~ taxation** высо́кое налогообложе́ние.

punk /pʌŋk/ *n.* **1** (*admirer of ~ rock*) панк; (**~ rock**) панк-рок. **2** (*tinder*) трут. **3** (*US coll.*) (*worthless person*) дрянь; (*hooligan*) хулига́н; (*novice*) новичо́к.
● *adj.* **1** па́нковый. **2** (*sl., inferior*) никуды́шный, дрянно́й.

punnet /ˈpʌnɪt/ *n.* (*Br.*) корзи́н(оч)ка.

punster /ˈpʌnstə(r)/ *n.* каламбури́ст.

punt /pʌnt/ *n.* (*boat*) плоскодо́нка.
● *v.i.* плыть (*impf.*), отта́лкиваясь шесто́м.

punter /ˈpʌntə(r)/ *n.* **1** (*Br.*) (*at cards*) понтёр; (*at races*) игро́к; (*client*) клие́нт. **2** (*in American football and rugby*) игро́к, бью́щий по подбро́шенному мячу́.

puny /ˈpjuːnɪ/ *adj.* (**punier, puniest**) (*undersized, feeble*) тщеду́шный, хи́лый.

pup /pʌp/ *n.* (*young dog*) щено́к.

pupa /ˈpjuːpə/ *n.* (*pl.* **pupae** /-piː/) ку́колка.

pupate /pjuːˈpeɪt/ *v.i.* оку́кли|ваться, -ться.

pupil /ˈpjuːpɪl/, /-p(ə)l/ *n.* **1** (*one being taught*) учени́|к (*fem.* -ца). **2** (*of eye*) зрачо́к.

pupil(l)age /ˈpjuːpɪlɪdʒ/ *n.* учени́чество.

puppet /ˈpʌpɪt/ *n.*: **glove ~** ку́кла; **string ~** марионе́тка; (*fig.*) марионе́тка; **~ state** марионе́точное госуда́рство.
● *cpd.* **~-show** *n.* ку́кольное представле́ние, ку́кольный спекта́кль.

puppy /ˈpʌpɪ/ *n.* (*young dog*) щено́к; **~ fat** де́тская пу́хлость; **~ love** де́тская любо́вь.

purblind /ˈpɜːblaɪnd/ *adj.* подслеповáтый; (*fig.*) недальнови́дный.

purchase /ˈpɜːtʃɪs/, /-tʃəs/ *n.* **1** (*buying*) ку́пля; **~ price** покупна́я цена́.
2 (*thing bought*) поку́пка; **she came home laden with ~s** она́ верну́лась домо́й, нагру́женная поку́пками.
3 (*lever*) рыча́г; (*firm hold, leverage*) зажи́м, захва́т.
● *v.t.* (*buy*) покупа́ть, купи́ть; **purchasing power** покупа́тельная спосо́бность.
● *cpd.* **~-tax** *n.* нало́г на поку́пку.

purchaser /ˈpɜːtʃɪsə(r)/, /-tʃəsə(r)/ *n.* покупа́тель (*fem.* -ница).

purdah /ˈpɜːdə/ *n.* **1** (*curtain*) за́навес, отделя́ющий же́нскую полови́ну; (*covering body*) чадра́. **2** (*segregation of women*) затво́рничество же́нщин; (*fig.*) затво́рничество; **he went into ~ for several days** он уедини́лся на не́сколько дней.

pure /pjʊə(r)/ *adj.* (*in var. senses*) чи́стый; (*unmixed*) беспри́месный; **~ mathematics** теорети́ческая/чи́стая матема́тика; **it was a ~ accident** э́то была́ чи́стая случа́йность.
● *cpd.* **~-bred** *adj.* чистокро́вный.

purée /ˈpjʊəreɪ/ *n.* пюре́ (*indecl.*).

purely /ˈpjʊəlɪ/ *adv.* (*blamelessly*) чи́сто; (*entirely*) чи́сто, соверше́нно, вполне́.

pureness /ˈpjʊənɪs/ = **purity**

purgative /ˈpɜːgətɪv/ *n.* слаби́тельное (сре́дство).
● *adj.* (*aperient*) слаби́тельный, очисти́тельный.

purgatory /ˈpɜːgətərɪ/ *n.* чисти́лище; (*fig.*) ад.

purge /pɜːdʒ/ *n.* (*clearance; cleansing*) очище́ние; очи́стка; (*pol.*) чи́стка, репре́ссии (*f. pl.*).
● *v.t.* (*lit., fig., cleanse*) оч|ища́ть, -и́стить; **he was ~d of his sins** ему́ отпусти́ли грехи́; **he ~d himself of all suspicion** он очи́стил себя́ от всех подозре́ний; **the party was ~d of its rebels** па́ртию очи́стили от бунтовщико́в.

purification /ˌpjʊərɪfɪˈkeɪʃ(ə)n/ *n.* очи́стка, очище́ние.

purificatory /ˈpjʊrɪfɪˌkeɪtərɪ/ *adj.* очисти́тельный, очища́ющий.

purify /ˈpjʊərɪˌfaɪ/ *v.t.* оч|ища́ть, -и́стить.

purism /ˈpjʊərɪz(ə)m/ *n.* пури́зм.

purist /ˈpjʊərɪst/ *n.* пури́ст.

puritan /ˈpjʊərɪt(ə)n/ *n.* (*lit., fig.*) пурита́н|ин (*fem.* -ка).
● *adj.* пурита́нский.

puritanical /ˌpjʊərɪˈtænɪk(ə)l/ *adj.* пурита́нский.

puritanism /ˈpjʊərɪtənˌɪz(ə)m/ *n.* пуритани́зм.

purity /ˈpjʊərɪtɪ/ *n.* (*var. senses*) чистота́; (*absence of adulteration*) беспри́месность.

purl¹ /pɜːl/ *n.* (*knitting*) вяза́ние изна́ночными пе́тлями; (*stitch*) изна́ночная пе́тля.
● *v.i.* вяза́ть (*impf.*) пе́тлей наизна́нку.

purl² /pɜːl/ *n.* (*sound of brook*) журча́ние.
● *v.i.* журча́ть (*impf.*).

purlieus /ˈpɜːljuːz/ *n. pl.* (*environs*) окре́стности (*f. pl.*).

purloin /pəˈlɔɪn/ *v.t.* пох|ища́ть, -и́тить.

purple /ˈpɜːp(ə)l/ *n.* **1** (*colour*) лило́вый/фиоле́товый цвет. **2** (**the ~**: *robes of emperor etc.*) порфи́ра; **born in the ~** (*fig.*) зна́тного ро́да.
● *adj.* лило́вый, фиоле́товый; (*deep red*)

P

багро́вый; ~ **patch, passage** цвети́стый/пы́шный пасса́ж; **he turned ~ with rage** он побагрове́л от я́рости.

● *v.t. & i.* обагр|я́ть(ся), -и́ть(ся).

purplish /ˈpɜːplɪʃ/ *adj.* багряни́стый.

purport¹ /ˈpɜːpɔːt/ *n.* смысл, суть.

purport² /pəˈpɔːt/ *v.t.* (*state*) подразумева́ть (*impf.*); (*claim*): **this book is not all it ~s to be** э́та кни́га не совсе́м така́я, како́й она́ претенду́ет быть.

purpose /ˈpɜːpəs/ *n.* **1** (*design, aim*) цель; (*intention*) наме́рение; **what was your ~ in coming?** с како́й це́лью вы пришли́?; **this tool will serve my ~** э́тот инструме́нт мне подойдёт; **for practical ~s the war is over** война́ практи́чески око́нчена; **for various ~s** для разли́чных це́лей; **on ~** наро́чно, специа́льно; **I went there to no ~** я напра́сно туда́ ходи́л; **she went out with the ~ of buying clothes** она́ вы́шла с наме́рением купи́ть оде́жду. **2** (*determination, resolve*) целеустремлённость.

● *cpd.* **-built** *adj.* (*Br.*) вы́строенный специа́льно.

purposeful /ˈpɜːpəsˌfʊl/ *adj.* целеустремлённый.

purposeless /ˈpɜːpəslɪs/ *adj.* бесце́льный.

purposely /ˈpɜːpəslɪ/ *adv.* наро́чно, (пред)наме́ренно, специа́льно.

purr /pɜː(r)/ *n.* (*of cat*) мурлы́канье; (*of engine etc.*) урча́ние.

● *v.i.* (*of cat; also fig.*) мурлы́кать (*impf.*); (*of engine etc.*) урча́ть (*impf.*).

purse /pɜːs/ *n.* **1** (*bag for money*) кошелёк; (*US, handbag*) су́мочка. **2** (*fig., monetary resources*) де́н|ьги (*pl., g.* -ег), сре́дства (*nt. pl.*); **the public ~** госуда́рственная казна́. **3** (*prize money*) де́нежный приз.

● *v.t.* мо́рщить, с-; **he ~d (up) his lips** он поджа́л гу́бы.

● *cpd.* **~-strings** *n. pl.*: **her husband holds the ~-strings** (*fig.*) её муж распоряжа́ется деньга́ми.

purser /ˈpɜːsə(r)/ *n.* судово́й казначе́й.

pursuance /pəˈsjuːəns/ *n.* выполне́ние; **in ~ of one's duties** по до́лгу слу́жбы.

pursuant /pəˈsjuːənt/ *adj.*: **~ to** в соотве́тствии с + *i.*, согла́сно + *d.*; **~ to your instructions** согла́сно ва́шим указа́ниям.

pursue /pəˈsjuː/ *v.t.* (**pursues, pursued, pursuing**) **1** (*hunt, chase, beset*) пресле́довать (*impf.*). **2** (*strive after, aim at*) добива́ться (*impf.*) + *g.* **3** (*course, plan*) сле́довать (*impf.*) + *d.*; (*interest*) занима́ться (*impf.*) (+ *i.*); (*activity*) предприн|има́ть, -я́ть; (*policy*) проводи́ть (*impf.*); **the policy ~d by the government** поли́тика, проводи́мая прави́тельством. **4** (*continue*) прод|олжа́ть, -о́лжить.

pursuer /pəˈsjuːə(r)/ *n.* пресле́дователь (*m.*).

pursuit /pəˈsjuːt/ *n.* **1** (*chase*) пресле́дование; пого́ня; **he escaped, with the police in hot ~** он бежа́л, пресле́дуемый поли́цией по пята́м. **2** (*following, seeking*) по́иск|и (*pl., g.* -ов); **he will stop at nothing in ~ of his ends** он не остано́вится ни пе́ред чем для достиже́ния свои́х це́лей. **3** (*profession or recreation*) заня́тие.

purulent /ˈpjuːrʊlənt/ *adj.* гно́йный.

purvey /pəˈveɪ/ *v.t.* (*supply*) снаб|жа́ть, -ди́ть (*кого чем*).

● *v.i.* (*supply provisions*) пост|авля́ть, -а́вить продово́льствие.

purveyance /pəˈveɪəns/ *n.* поста́вка.

purveyor /pəˈveɪə(r)/ *n.* поставщи́|к (*fem.* -ца).

purview /ˈpɜːvjuː/ *n.* (*range, scope*) сфе́ра; о́бласть де́йствия; **this is beyond the ~ of the inquiry** э́то выхо́дит за грани́цы рассле́дования; **these matters fall within my ~** э́ти дела́ вхо́дят в мою́ компете́нцию.

pus /pʌs/ *n.* гной.

push /pʊʃ/ *n.* **1** (*act of propulsion*) толчо́к; **he closed the door with a ~** он захло́пнул дверь; **my car won't start; can you give me a ~?** моя́ маши́на не заво́дится, вы мо́жете её подтолкну́ть? **2** (*Br. coll., dismissal*) увольне́ние; **they have given me the ~** меня́ вы́гнали. **3** (*self-assertion*) напо́ристость; **in this job you need plenty of ~** в э́той рабо́те нужна́ предприи́мчивость. **4** (*vigorous effort*) нажи́м, рыво́к; **we must make a ~ to be there by 8** мы должны́ поднажа́ть, что́бы успе́ть туда́ к восьми́ (часа́м); **the enemy's ~ was successful** на́тиск врага́ был успе́шным. **5**: **at a ~** (*Br. coll.*) в кра́йнем слу́чае.

● *v.t.* **1** (*propel; exert pressure to move*) толк|а́ть, -ну́ть; пих|а́ть, -ну́ть; **stop ~ing me!** переста́ньте меня́ толка́ть!; **he ~es all the dirty jobs on to me** он всю спи́хивает/сва́ливает на меня́ гря́зную рабо́ту. **2** (*fig., urge, impel*) подт|а́лкивать, -олкну́ть; вынужда́ть, вы́нудить; **he had to ~ himself to finish the job** ему́ пришло́сь сде́лать (над собо́й) уси́лие, что́бы зако́нчить рабо́ту; **I didn't want to go, I was ~ed into it** я не хоте́л идти́, меня́ вы́нудили. **3** (*force*) прот|а́лкивать, -олкну́ть; **I ~ed my way through the crowd** я проти́снулся сквозь толпу́. **4** (*press*) наж|има́ть, -а́ть; **~ the button and the bell will ring** нажми́те кно́пку, и звоно́к зазвони́т. **5** (*put under pressure*) ока́з|ывать, -а́ть давле́ние на + *a.*; **I am ~ed for time** у меня́ вре́мени в обре́з. **6** (*exploit*): **don't ~ your luck!** (*coll.*) не испы́тывайте судьбу́! **7** (*promote, advertise*) реклами́ровать (*impf.*); прот|а́лкивать, -олкну́ть.

● *v.i.* **1** (*exert force*) толка́ться (*impf.*); **~ hard at the door!** толкни́те дверь посильне́е!; **don't ~!** не толка́йтесь!; не напира́йте! **2** (*force one's way*) прот|а́лкиваться, -олкну́ться; **he ~ed between us** он проти́снулся ме́жду на́ми; **they all ~ed into the room** они́ все ввали́лись в ко́мнату; **I had to ~ through the crowd** мне пришло́сь проти́скиваться сквозь толпу́; **he ~ed past me** он проле́з вперёд, оттолкну́в меня́.

● *with advs.*: **~ about** *v.t.* (*coll.*) трепа́ть, по-; помя́ть (*pf.*); **~ along** *v.t.* (*lit.*): **the boy was ~ing his barrow along** ма́льчик кати́л та́чку; (*fig.*) спеши́ть, по-; пот|ара́пливать, -ороп́ить; *v.i.* (*Br. coll.*) убира́ться, убра́ться; **it's getting late, I must ~ along** стано́вится по́здно, мне пора́ в путь; **~ around** *v.t.* перест|авля́ть, -а́вить; передв|ига́ть, -и́нуть; (*fig.*) кома́ндовать (*impf.*) (*кем*); **I won't be ~ed around** я не позво́лю кома́ндовать над собо́й; **~ aside** *v.t.* отт|а́лкивать, -олкну́ть; **~ away** *v.t.* = **~ aside;** *v.i.*: **they ~ed away from the shore** они́ отплы́ли от бе́рега; **~ back** *v.t.* (*repulse*) отбр|а́сывать, -о́сить; (*move away*) отодв|ига́ть, -и́нуть; **she ~ed back the bedclothes** она́ отки́нула одея́ло; **~ down** *v.t.* вали́ть, по-; **every time he tried to stand up he was ~ed down** при ка́ждой попы́тке встать его́ вали́ли с ног; **~ forward** *v.t.* толк|а́ть, -ну́ть вперёд; *v.i.* (*make progress*) продв|ига́ться, -и́нуться (вперёд); **~ in** *v.t.* вт|а́лкивать, -олкну́ть; **have you ~ed the plug fully in?** вы по́лностью воткну́ли ви́лку?; *v.i.* втира́ться, втере́ться; **don't ~ in!** (*intrude*) не ле́зьте; **~ off** *v.t.* отт|а́лкивать, -олкну́ть; **in the struggle his hat was ~ed off** в потасо́вке ему́ сби́ли шля́пу; **they ~ed the boat off from shore** они́ оттолкну́ли ло́дку от бе́рега; *v.i.* (*in a boat*) отт|а́лкиваться, -олкну́ться от бе́рега; (*coll., leave*) см|ыва́ться, -ы́ться; **~ on** *v.i.* продв|ига́ться, -и́нуться (вперёд); **next day they ~ed on again** на сле́дующий день они́ продолжа́ли путь; **~ out** *v.t.*: **plants are ~ing out new leaves** у расте́ний распуска́ются но́вые ли́стья; **he opened the door and ~ed me out** он откры́л дверь и вы́толкнул меня́; *v.i.* выдава́ться (*impf.*) вперёд; **they ~ed out to sea** они́ вы́шли в мо́ре; **~ over** *v.t.* опроки́|дывать, -нуть; **I was nearly ~ed over in the rush** в толкотне́ меня́ чуть не сби́ли с ног; **~ past** *v.i.* прот|а́лкиваться, -олкну́ться; **~ through** *v.t.* (*lit., fig.*) прот|а́лкивать, -олкну́ть; **the bill was ~ed through against opposition** законопрое́кт протолкну́ли, несмотря́ на оппози́цию; *v.i.* проти́|скиваться, -снуться; **~ to** *v.t.* (*close*) закр|ыва́ть, -ы́ть; **~ together** *v.t.* (*e.g. books on a shelf*) сдв|ига́ть, -и́нуть; **~ up** *v.t.* (*shift, move*) сдв|ига́ть, -и́нуть; (*increase*) увели́чи|вать, -ть; *v.i.*: **he ~ed up against me** он прижа́лся ко мне.

● *cpds.* **~-bike** *n.* (*Br. coll.*) велосипе́д; **~-button** *n.* нажимна́я кно́пка; **~-cart** *n.* ручна́я теле́жка; **~-chair** *n.* (*Br.*) прогу́лочная коля́ска; **~over** *n.* (*coll.*) (*someone easily overcome*) слаба́к; (*something easily accomplished*) па́ра пустяко́в; **~-up** *n.* (*exercise*) выжима́ние в упо́ре; **do ~-ups** отжима́ться (*impf.*) на рука́х.

pusher /ˈpʊʃə(r)/ *n.* (*coll.*) (*drug* ~) наркоделе́ц.

pushful /ˈpʊʃfʊl/ *adj.* (*go-getting*) пробивно́й; (*pushy*) напо́ристый.

pushy /ˈpʊʃɪ/ *adj.* (**pushier, pushiest**) напо́ристый.

pusillanimity /ˌpjuːsɪləˈnɪmɪtɪ/ *n.* малоду́шие.

pusillanimous /ˌpjuːsɪˈlænɪməs/ *adj.* малоду́шный.

puss[1] /pʊs/ *n.* (*cat*) ко́шечка, ки́ска; **~, ~!** кис-ки́с!

puss[2] /pʊs/ *n.* (*US sl., face*) мо́рда, фи́зия.

pussy /ˈpʊsɪ/ *n.* **1** ки́са, ки́ска, ко́тик, ко́ш(еч)ка. **2** (*vulg., woman's genitals*) же́нские нару́жные половы́е о́рганы.

● *cpds.* **~-cat** *n.* = **~; ~foot** *v.i.* (*coll., behave cautiously*) виля́ть (*impf.*); темни́ть (*impf.*); **~-willow** *n.* кра́сная ве́рба, и́ва-шелю́га.

pustule /ˈpʌstjuːl/ *n.* пу́стула; прыщ.

put /pʊt/ *v.t.* (**putting;** *past and p.p.* **put**) **1** (*move into a certain position*) класть, положи́ть; (*stand*) ста́вить, по-; (*set*) сажа́ть, посади́ть; **~ the glasses on the tray!** поста́вьте стака́ны на подно́с; **~ the money in your pocket!** положи́те де́ньги в карма́н; **he ~ his hands in his pockets** он засу́нул ру́ки в карма́ны; **I'll ~ you in the best bedroom** я вас помещу́ в са́мой лу́чшей ко́мнате; **~ some milk in my tea!** нале́йте мне молока́ в чай!; **don't ~ sugar in my tea!** не клади́те мне са́хар в чай; **he was ~ in prison** его́ посади́ли в тюрьму́; **I ~ myself in your hands** я отдаю́ себя́ в ва́ши ру́ки; **~ yourself in my place!** поста́вьте себя́ на моё ме́сто!; **I ~ him in his place** (*fig.*) я поста́вил его́ на ме́сто; **I ~ the matter into the hands of my lawyer** я поручи́л э́то де́ло своему́ адвока́ту; **they are sure to ~ him inside** (*i.e. prison*) его́ наверняка́ поса́дят; **he ~ me on my way** он показа́л мне доро́гу; **she ~ the clothes on the line** она́ разве́сила бельё; **she ~ a cloth on the table** она́ накры́ла стол ска́тертью; **she ~ her daughter on to the swing** она́ посади́ла дочь на каче́ли; **he ~ a shawl round her shoulder** он накры́л ей пле́чи ша́лью; **the postman ~ a letter through the box** почтальо́н опусти́л письмо́ в я́щик; **she ~ the children to bed** она́ уложи́ла дете́й; **he ~ the glass to his lips** он поднёс стака́н к губа́м; **~ a napkin under the plate!** подложи́те салфе́тку под таре́лку!; **the sweep ~ his brush up the chimney** трубочи́ст просу́нул щётку в дымохо́д; **where did I ~ that book** куда́ я дел э́ту кни́гу?
2 (*move with force; thrust*) вонз|а́ть, -и́ть; **she ~ a knife between his ribs** она́ вонзи́ла ему́ нож ме́жду рёбер; **he ~ a bullet through his head** он пусти́л себе́ пу́лю в лоб; **he ~ his fist through the window** он проби́л окно́ кулако́м.
3 (*bring into a certain state or relationship*): **that ~s me at a disadvantage** э́то ста́вит меня́ в невы́годное положе́ние; **that will ~ the whole project at risk** э́то поста́вит весь план под угро́зу; **he ~ his past behind him** он порва́л со свои́м про́шлым; **the dinner ~ him in a good mood** обе́д привёл его́ в хоро́шее расположе́ние ду́ха; **you ~ me in mind of your mother** вы напомина́ете мне ва́шу мать; **the least thing ~s him in a rage** любо́й пустя́к приво́дит его́ в я́рость; **that ~s us level** (*at game etc.*) тепе́рь мы квиты́; **his cold ~ him off his food** из-за просту́ды он потеря́л аппети́т; **his antics ~ me off my game** его́ проде́лки меша́ли мне игра́ть; **he was ~ on oath** его́ привели́ к прися́ге; **the bark of the dog ~ him on his guard** лай соба́ки предостерёг его́; **he ~ the poor creature out of its misery** он изба́вил бедня́гу от страда́ний; **he ~ me right on this point** в э́том вопро́се он меня́ попра́вил; **the boiler needs to be ~ right** на́до почини́ть коло́нку; **the examiner ~ him through it** (*tested severely*) экзамена́тор его́ как сле́дует погоня́л (*coll.*); **he ~ my suggestion to the test** он подве́рг моё предложе́ние испыта́нию; **he was ~ to death** его́ казни́ли; **let's ~ it to the vote** дава́йте поста́вим вопро́с на голосова́ние; **I was ~ to great expense** меня́ ввели́ в огро́мный расхо́д; **I was hard ~ to it not to laugh** я с трудо́м удержа́лся от сме́ха; **your generosity ~s me to shame** ва́ша ще́дрость заставля́ет меня́ красне́ть; (*impose, bring in*): **the tax ~s a heavy burden on the rich** нало́г ложи́тся тяжёлым бре́менем на бога́тых; **~ an end to** прекра|ща́ть, -ти́ть; положи́ть (*pf.*) коне́ц +*d.*; **he ~ an end to his life** он поко́нчил с собо́й; **he ~ the blame on me** он свали́л вину́ на меня́; **the government ~ a tax on wealth** прави́тельство ввело́ нало́г на состоя́ние; (*set, arrange*): **~ in order** прив|оди́ть, -ести́ в поря́док; **the party should ~ its house in order** па́ртии сле́дует навести́ поря́док в свои́х ряда́х; **he tried to ~ matters right** он стара́лся попра́вить дела́; (*appoint to a job*) ста́вить, по-; **~ s.o. in charge of** ста́вить, по- кого́ н. во главе́ +*g.*; (*apply*): **if you ~ your mind to it** е́сли вы займётесь э́тим всерьёз; **he ~s his knowledge to good use** он испо́льзует свои́ зна́ния с то́лком; (*offer, present*): **they ~ their house on the market** они́ объяви́ли о прода́же до́ма; (*instil, inspire*) всел|я́ть, -и́ть; вдыха́ть, вдохну́ть; (*stake*) ста́вить, по-; (*invest*) вкла́дывать, вложи́ть; поме|ща́ть, -сти́ть; **I ought to ~ the money into property** я бы до́лжен вложи́ть де́ньги в недви́жимость; (*make s.o. succumb or resort to*): **he ~ his opponent to flight** он обрати́л своего́ проти́вника в бе́гство; **take a tablet to ~ you to sleep** прими́те табле́тку, что́бы усну́ть; **the dog had to be ~ to sleep** соба́ку пришло́сь усыпи́ть.
4 (*write; mark*) писа́ть, на-; ста́вить, по- (*знак и т.п.*); **I cannot ~ my name to that document** я не могу́ подписа́ть тако́й докуме́нт; **this ~ paid to his ambitions** э́то положи́ло коне́ц его́ наде́ждам.
5 (*of price etc.*): **he ~s a high value on courtesy** он высоко́ це́нит ве́жливость; **I wouldn't care to ~ a price on it** я бы предпочёл не называ́ть то́чную це́ну; **I would ~ her (age) at about 65** я дал бы ей лет 65; **I wouldn't ~ it past him to be lying** с него́ ста́нется и совра́ть.
6 (*submit, propound*) выдвига́ть, вы́двинуть; зад|ава́ть, -а́ть; **may I ~ a suggestion?** мо́жно мне внести́ предложе́ние?;
7 (*express; present*) изл|ага́ть, -ожи́ть; **how can I ~ it?** как бы э́то сказа́ть?; **will you ~ that in writing?** вы мо́жете изложи́ть э́то на бума́ге?; **I can't ~ it into words** я не могу́ вы́разить э́то слова́ми; **that's ~ting it mildly!** мя́гко говоря́!
8 (*translate*) перев|оди́ть, -ести́.
9 (*mus., set*): **his poems have been ~ to music many times** его́ стихи́ бы́ли мно́го раз поло́жены на му́зыку.
10 (*hurl*): **~ting the shot** толка́ние ядра́.

● *v.i.* (**putting;** *past and p.p.* **put**)
1 (*impose*): **don't let him ~ upon you** смотри́те, что́бы он не сел вам на ше́ю.
2: **~ to sea** (*of vessel or crew*) уходи́ть, уйти́ в мо́рс.

● *with advs.*: **~ about** *v.t.* (*spread*) распростран|я́ть, -и́ть; **the news was ~ about that he was missing** разнёсся/распространи́лся слух, что он пропа́л; (*turn round*): **he ~ the boat about** он разверну́л ло́дку; *v.i.* пов|ора́чиваться, -ерну́ться; **~ across** *v.t.* (*convey over river, road etc.*) перепр|авля́ть, -а́вить; (*make clear, communicate*) объясн|я́ть, -и́ть; **he failed to ~ his idea across** ему́ не удало́сь поясни́ть свою́ мысль/иде́ю; **~ aside** *v.t.* (*lay to one side; save*) от|кла́дывать, -ложи́ть; (*ignore*) отбр|а́сывать, -о́сить; **these objections cannot be ~ aside** э́ти возраже́ния нельзя́ отбра́сывать; **~ away** *v.t.* (*tidy*) уб|ира́ть, -ра́ть; (*save*) от|кла́дывать, -ложи́ть; (*coll., eat*) ум|ина́ть, -я́ть, ло́пать, с-; **it's amazing how much that boy can ~ away** про́сто удиви́тельно, ско́лько э́тот ма́льчик мо́жет съесть/(*coll.*) сло́пать; (*coll., ~ into confinement*) упря́тать (*pf.*) (за решётку; в сумасше́дший дом); **~ back** *v.t.* (*replace, restore*) класть, положи́ть на ме́сто; (*move backwards*) отодв|ига́ть, -и́нуть; передв|ига́ть, -и́нуть наза́д; (*of clock*) перев|оди́ть, -ести́ наза́д; (*retard, delay*) заде́рж|ивать, -а́ть; **heavy rains ~ back the harvest** си́льные дожди́ задержа́ли убо́рку урожа́я; (*postpone*) от|кла́дывать, -ложи́ть; *v.i.* возвра|ща́ться, -ти́ться; **~ by** *v.t.* (*save*) от|кла́дывать, -ложи́ть; **~ down** *v.t.* (*place on ground etc.*) класть, положи́ть на зе́млю; **~ your gun down!** бро́сьте ору́жие!; опусти́те ружьё!; **he ~ his head down and was soon asleep** он положи́л го́лову на поду́шку и вско́ре засну́л; **~ one's foot down** (*be firm*) наст|а́ивать, -оя́ть на своём; (*accelerate*) наж|има́ть, -а́ть на газ; (*allow to alight*): **the bus stopped to ~ down passengers** авто́бус

P

остановился, чтобы высадить пассажиров; (*place in storage*): **I ~ down a supply of port** я сделал запас портвейна; (*make deposit of*) вн|осить, -ести (*задаток*); (*lower, reduce*) сн|ижать, -изить; (*bring in to land*): **the pilot ~ his machine down safely** пилот благополучно посадил машину; (*repress*) подав|лять, -ить; **the rebellion was quickly ~ down** восстание было быстро подавлено; (*write down*) запис|ывать, -ать; **you may ~ me down for £5** я даю 5 фунтов; **~ these groceries down to my account** запишите эти продукты на мой счёт; (*consider*) считать, счесть; **I would ~ her down as about 25** я дал бы ей лет 25; (*attribute*) припис|ывать, -ать; (*kill, of animals*) усып|лять, -ить; умерщв|лять, -ить; **~ forth** *v.t.* (*exert*) напр|ягать, -ячь; (*produce*): **the trees are ~ting forth new leaves** на деревьях распускаются новые листья; **~ forward** *v.t.* (*advance*): **the clocks are ~ forward in spring** весной часы переводят вперёд; (*propose*) выдвигать, выдвинуть; **he ~ forward a theory** он выдвинул теорию; **his name was ~ forward** была выдвинута его кандидатура; (*bring nearer*) передв|игать, -инуть вперёд; **the meeting has been ~ forward to Tuesday** собрание перенесли на вторник; **~ in** *v.t.* (*cause to enter; insert*) вст|авлять, -авить; **he ~ his head in at the window** он всунул голову в окно; **have you ~ the meat in yet?** вы уже поставили мясо в духовку?; (*instal*) вст|авлять, -авить; **they are ~ting in a telephone** они ставят (себе) телефон; им ставят телефон; (*elect to office*) изб|ирать, -рать; **we helped to ~ the Conservatives in** мы помогли консерваторам прийти к власти; (*contribute*): **I ~ in a word for him** я вставил за него словечко; (*submit, present*) под|авать, -ать; **he is ~ting in a claim for damages** он предъявляет иск об убытках; **I ~ in an application** я подал заявление; **~ in an appearance** появ|ляться, -иться; (*work*): **I ~ in 6 hours today** я сегодня отработал 6 часов; *v.i.* (*of boat or crew*) за|ходить, -йти в порт; **the ship ~ in at Gibraltar** корабль зашёл в Гибралтар; (*apply*): **she ~ in for a job as secretary** она подала заявление на должность/место секретаря; **~ off** *v.t.* (*postpone*) от|кладывать, -ложить; отсрочи|вать, -ть; (*cancel engagement with*) отмен|ять, -ить встречу с + *i.*; (*postpone*): **I shall have to ~ you off till next week** мне придётся перенести встречу с вами на следующую неделю; (*fob off*): **he ~ me off with promises** он отделался от меня обещаниями; (*deter*) отпуг|ивать, -нуть; **we were ~ off by the weather** мы передумали из-за погоды; (*repel*) отт|алкивать, -олкнуть; **I was ~ off by his tactlessness** меня оттолкнула его бестактность; (*distract*): **I can't recite if you keep ~ting me off** я не могу декламировать, когда вы меня отвлекаете; (*allow to alight*): **will you ~ me off at the next stop?** вы можете высадить меня на следующей остановке?; **~ on** *v.t.* (*clothes etc.*) над|евать, -еть; **you should ~ more clothes on** вы должны потеплее одеться; (*place in position*): **when the pot is full, ~ the lid on** когда кастрюля наполнится, накройте её крышкой; **~ the potatoes on (to boil)!** поставьте (варить) картошку!; (*add*) приб|авлять, -авить; **he ~ more coal on** он подбросил угля; (*assume*): **he ~ on an air of innocence** он напустил на себя невинный вид; **she is fond of ~ting on airs** она любит важничать; (*increase*) увеличи|вать, -ть; **you're ~ting on weight** вы полнеете; (*light, radio etc.*) включ|ать, -ить; (*make available*) примен|ять, -ить; **they are ~ting on extra trains** они пускают дополнительные поезда; (*present*) ставить, по-; **the children are ~ting on a play** дети ставят пьесу; **she ~ on a first-class meal** она приготовила отличный обед/ужин; (*advance*) передв|игать, -инуть вперёд; **watches should be ~ on an hour** часы надо перевести на час вперёд; (*stake*) ставить, по-; **~ out** *v.t.* (*thrust out, eject*): **his family was ~ out into the street** его семью выставили/выбросили на улицу; (*place outside door*) выставлять, выставить за дверь; **~ the cat out** выпустите кошку!; (*extend, protrude*): **~ your tongue out!** покажите язык!; **he ~ out his hand in welcome** он протянул руку для приветствия; **she opened the window and ~ her head out** она открыла окно и высунула голову; **the snail ~ out its horns** улитка выпустила щупальца; (*arrange so as to be seen*) выставлять, выставить; выкладывать, выложить; **the shopkeeper ~ out his best wares** лавочник выложил/выставил свой лучший товар; **the valet ~ out my clothes** камердинер выложил мою одежду; (*hang up outside*) вывешивать, вывесить; **~ out the flags!** вывесите флаги!; **she ~ the washing out to dry** она вывесила бельё сушиться; (*produce*) выпускать, выпустить; **this firm ~s out shoddy goods** эта фирма выпускает дрянной товар; (*issue*) выпускать, выпустить; **they ~ out invitations** они разослали приглашения; (*send away for a purpose*): **repairs are done here, not ~ out** ремонт ведут на месте — никуда не отсылают; (*extinguish*) тушить, по-; гасить, по-; **~ the lights out!** потушите свет!; **~ your cigarette out!** погасите сигарету!; **~ out the fire before going to bed!** потушите огонь (в камине) перед тем, как идти спать; **the firemen ~ out the blaze** пожарные потушили пламя; (*dislocate*) вывихивать, вывихнуть; (*inconvenience*) наруш|ать, -ить планы + *g.*; **would it ~ you out to come at 3?** вас не затруднит прийти в 3 часа?; (*vex*) раздраж|ать, -ить; (*allow to alight*) высаживать, высадить; **I asked the driver to ~ me out at the station** я попросил шофёра высадить меня у станции; *v.i.*: **the lifeboat ~ out to sea** спасательная шлюпка вышла в море; **~ over** *v.t.* (*convey*) перед|авать, -ать; изл|агать, -ожить; **he ~ over his meaning effectively** он хорошо изложил свою мысль; **he is trying to ~ one over on you** (*coll.*) он пытается вас одурачить; **~ through** *v.t.* (*accomplish*) осуществ|лять, -ить; выполнять, выполнить; **he ~ through a successful deal** он провернул выгодную сделку; (*connect by telephone*) соедин|ять, -ить; **~ together** *v.t.* (*bring close or into contact*) соедин|ять, -ить; (*assemble*) сост|авлять, -авить; (*construct from components*) соб|ирать, -рать; (*collect*) соб|ирать, -рать; **~ your things together ready for the journey!** соберите вещи в дорогу!; **better than all the rest ~ together** лучше всех остальных вместе взятых; **~ up** *v.t.* (*raise, hold up*) подн|имать, -ять; **~ up your hand if you know the answer!** кто знает ответ, поднимите руку!; **~ your hands up!** (*coll.*) руки вверх!; **~ one's feet up** полёживать (*impf.*); **he ~s my back up** (*coll.*) он меня раздражает/бесит; (*display*) выставлять, выставить; (*erect*) воздв|игать, -игнуть; строить, по-; **this house was ~ up in six weeks** этот дом построили за шесть недель; **shall we ~ the curtains up?** будем вешать занавески?; (*increase*) пов|ышать, -есить; **~ up prices** (*Br.*) подн|имать, -ять цены; (*offer*) выдвигать, выдвинуть; **he ~ up no resistance** он не оказал никакого сопротивления; **our men ~ up a good show** наши люди хорошо себя показали/проявили; **the house was ~ up for sale** дом был выставлен на продажу; (*propose*) выдвигать, выдвинуть (*в кандидаты*); **they ~ up three candidates** они выдвинули трёх кандидатов; (*supply*) вн|осить, -ести; **I will ~ up £1,000 to support him** я вношу тысячу фунтов в его пользу; (*accommodate*): **he ~ me up for the night** я переночевал у него; (*coll., introduce*): **I ~ him up to that trick** я его научил этому приёму/трюку; (*coll., prompt*): **who ~ him up to it, I wonder?** интересно, кто его надоумил?; *v.i.* (*stay*) остан|авливаться, -овиться; ночевать, пере-; (*tolerate*) мириться, при- (*с кем/чем*); **I won't ~ up with any nonsense** я не потерплю никаких глупостей.

● *cpds.* **~-down** *n.* (*snub*) резкость; **~-off** *n.* (*evasion*) уловка; **~-up** *adj.*: **a ~-up job** подстроенное дело; **~-upon** *adj.* обиженный, третируемый.

putative /ˈpjuːtətɪv/ *adj.* мнимый, предполагаемый.

putrefaction /ˌpjuːtrɪˈfækʃ(ə)n/ *n.* гниение; разложение.

putrefy /ˈpjuːtrɪˌfaɪ/ *v.i.* (*go bad*) гнить, с-; (*fester*) разл|агаться, -ожиться.

putrescence /pjuːˈtres(ə)ns/ *n.* гниение.

putrescent /pjuːˈtres(ə)nt/ *adj.* гниющий; разлагающийся.

putrid /ˈpjuːtrɪd/ *adj.* (*decomposed*) гнилой; (*coll., unpleasant*) отвратительный.

putsch /pʊtʃ/ *n.* путч.

putt /pʌt/ *n.* удар, загоняющий мяч в лунку (*в гольфе*).

● *v.i.* (**putted, putting**) заг|оня́ть, -на́ть мяч в лу́нку; **~ing-green** лужа́йка с лу́нками (*в гольфе*).

puttee /ˈpʌtɪ/ *n.* обмо́тка; (*US, legging*) кра́га.

putty /ˈpʌtɪ/ *n.* зама́зка, шпаклёвка.

● *v.t.* шпаклева́ть, за-.

puzzle /ˈpʌz(ə)l/ *n.* зага́дка; (*for entertainment*) головоло́мка.

● *v.t.* озада́чи|вать, -ть; прив|оди́ть, -ести́ в недоуме́ние; **don't ~ your brains over it** не лома́йте го́лову над э́тим.

● *v.i.*: **he ~d over the problem all night** он всю ночь би́лся над э́той зада́чей.

● *with adv.*: **~ out** *v.t.* разг|а́дывать, -ада́ть; на|ходи́ть, -йти́ реше́ние +*g.*

puzzlement /ˈpʌzəlmənt/ *n.* замеша́тельство, недоуме́ние.

PVC (*abbr. of* **polyvinyl chloride**) ПХВ (полихлорвини́л).

pye-dog /ˈpaɪdɒg/ *n.* бродя́чая соба́ка, дворня́жка.

pygmy, pigmy /ˈpɪgmɪ/ *n.* пигме́й.

pyjama|s /pɪˈdʒɑːməz/, /pə-/ (*US* **pajamas**) *n.* пижа́ма; **~ trousers** пижа́мные штаны́.

pylon /ˈpaɪlən/, /-lɒn/ *n.* (*for electricity*) пило́н.

Pyongyang /ˈpjɒŋˈjæŋ/ *n.* Пхенья́н.

pyorrhoea /ˌpaɪəˈriːə/ (*US* **pyorrhea**) *n.* (*med.*) пиоре́я.

pyramid /ˈpɪrəmɪd/ *n.* (*lit., fig.*) пирами́да.

pyramidal /pɪˈræmɪd(ə)l/ *adj.* (*shape*) пирамида́льный; (*pert. to pyramids*) пирами́дный.

pyre /ˈpaɪə(r)/ *n.* погреба́льный костёр.

Pyrenean /ˌpɪrəˈniːən/ *adj.* пирене́йский.

Pyrenees /ˌpɪrəˈniːz/ *n.* Пирене́|и (*pl., g.* -ев).

pyrites /paɪˈraɪtiːz/ *n.* серни́стые мета́ллы (*m. pl.*).

pyromania /ˌpaɪərəʊˈmeɪnɪə/ *n.* пирома́ния.

pyromaniac /ˌpaɪərəʊˈmeɪnɪˌæk/ *n.* пирома́н.

pyrotechnic /ˌpaɪərəʊˈteknɪk/ *adj.* пиротехни́ческий.

pyrotechnics /ˌpaɪərəʊˈteknɪks/ *n.* (*art of making fireworks*) пироте́хника; (*firework display; also fig.*) фейерве́рк.

Pyrrhic /ˈpɪrɪk/ *adj.*: **a ~ victory** пи́ррова побе́да.

Pythagoras /paɪˈθægərəs/ *n.*: **~' theorem** теоре́ма Пифаго́ра.

python /ˈpaɪθ(ə)n/ *n.* пито́н.

Qq

Qatar /kæ'tɑː/ *n.* Ка́тар.

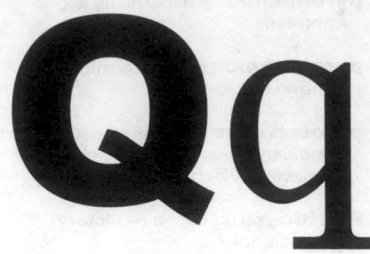

QC (*abbr. of* ***Queen's Counsel***) адвока́т вы́сшего ра́нга.

QED (*abbr. of* ***quod erat demonstrandum***) что и тре́бовалось доказа́ть.

q.t. (*abbr. of* ***quiet***): **to do something on the ~** де́лать, с- что-н. втихаря́.

quack¹ /kwæk/ *n.* (*sound*) кря́канье.
● *v.i.* кря́кать (*impf.*).

quack² /kwæk/ *n.* (*bogus doctor etc.*) шарлата́н.

quackery /'kwækərɪ/ *n.* шарлата́нство.

quad /kwɒd/ (*coll.*) **1** = **quadrangle. 2** = **quadruplet**

quadrangle /'kwɒd,ræŋg(ə)l/ *n.* (*courtyard*) четырёхуго́льный двор.

quadrangular /kwɒd'ræŋgjʊlə(r)/ *adj.* четырёхуго́льный.

quadrant /'kwɒdrənt/ *n.* (*of circle*) квадра́нт; (*instrument*) се́кторный ру́мпель.

quadraphonic /,kwɒdrə'fɒnɪk/ *adj.* квадрофони́ческий.

quadratic /kwɒ'drætɪk/ *adj.* квадра́тный.

quadrilateral /,kwɒdrɪ'lætər(ə)l/ *n.* четырёхуго́льник.
● *adj.* четырёхсторо́нний.

quadrille /kwɒ'drɪl/ *n.* (*dance*) кадри́ль.

quadruped /'kwɒdrʊ,ped/ *n.* четвероно́гое (живо́тное).

quadruple /'kwɒdrʊp(ə)l/ *adj.* (*fourfold*) учетверённый; **his income is ~ mine** его́ дохо́д бо́льше моего́ в четы́ре ра́за.
● *v.t.* учетвер|я́ть, -и́ть.
● *v.i.* учетвер|я́ться, -и́ться; увели́чи|ваться, -ться в четы́ре ра́за.

quadruplet /'kwɒdrʊplɪt/, /kwɒ'druːplɪt/ *n.* оди́н из четырёх близнецо́в; (*pl.*) четверня́; **she gave birth to ~s** она́ родила́ четверню́ (*or* четверы́х близнецо́в).

quaff /kwɒf/, /kwɑːf/ *v.t. & i.* пить, вы́- за́лпом.

quagmire /'kwɒg,maɪə(r)/, /'kwæg-/ *n.* боло́то.

quail¹ /kweɪl/ *n.* (*pl.* ~ *or* **~s**) пе́репел.

quail² /kweɪl/ *v.i.* тру́сить, с-.

quaint /kweɪnt/ *adj.* причу́дливый, чудно́й; **he has some ~ notions** он челове́к со стра́нными поня́тиями.

quaintness /'kweɪntnɪs/ *n.* причу́дливость.

quak|e /kweɪk/ *n.* (*coll., earth~*) землетрясе́ние.
● *v.i.* дрожа́ть (*impf.*); содрог|а́ться, -ну́ться; **I woke up ~ing with fright** я просну́лся, дрожа́ от стра́ха.

Quaker /'kweɪkə(r)/ *n.*ква́кер (*fem.* -ша); (*attr.*) ква́керский.

qualification /,kwɒlɪfɪ'keɪʃ(ə)n/ *n.* **1** (*modification, limiting factor*) ограниче́ние, огово́рка; **without ~** безогово́рочно. **2** (*skill*) квалифика́ция.

qualifier /'kwɒlɪ,faɪə(r)/ *n.* **1** (*sport*) (*contest, match*) отбо́рочное соревнова́ние, отбо́рочный матч; (*person, team*) челове́к, кото́рый/кома́нда, кото́рая прохо́дит отбо́рочные соревнова́ния. **2** (*gram.*) определе́ние.

qualif|y /'kwɒlɪ,faɪ/ *v.t.* **1** (*for job*) гото́вить (*impf.*); **I am not ~ied to advise you** я недоста́точно компете́нтен, что́бы дава́ть вам сове́ты; (*make entitled*) дава́ть, дать пра́во + *g. or* на + *a.*; **his age ~ies him for the vote** во́зраст даёт ему́ пра́во го́лоса; **~ying examination** отбо́рочный экза́мен; **he is a ~ied doctor** он дипломи́рованный врач. **2** (*limit, modify*) огов|а́ривать, -ори́ть; уточн|я́ть, -и́ть; **I must ~y my statement** я до́лжен сде́лать огово́рку; **I gave the idea my ~ied approval** я одо́брил э́ту иде́ю с не́которыми огово́рками. **3** (*describe*) оце́н|ивать, -и́ть; определ|я́ть, -и́ть; **adjectives ~y nouns** прилага́тельные определя́ют существи́тельные.
● *v.i.* (*be eligible* (*for*)) име́ть (*impf.*) пра́во (на + *a.*); **he will ~y after three years** че́рез три го́да он полу́чит дипло́м; **will you ~y for a pension?** бу́дете ли вы име́ть пра́во на пе́нсию?; (*sport*): **our team failed to ~** на́ша кома́нда не прошла́ отбо́рочные соревнова́ния; **he ~ied for the final** он вы́шел в фина́л.

qualitative /'kwɒlɪtətɪv/, /-,teɪtɪv/ *adj.* ка́чественный.

quality /'kwɒlɪtɪ/ *n.* **1** (*degree of merit*) ка́чество; **of poor ~** ни́зкого ка́чества; **a high-~ fabric** высокока́чественная ткань; (*excellence*) высо́кое ка́чество, доброка́чественность; **~ goods** това́ры высо́кого ка́чества. **2** (*faculty, characteristic, attribute*) ка́чество, сво́йство; **he has the ~ of inspiring confidence** он облада́ет сво́йством внуша́ть дове́рие; **he has many good qualities** у него́ мно́го це́нных ка́честв; **her voice has a shrill ~** у неё визгли́вый го́лос.
● *adj.* (высоко)ка́чественный; **~ newspapers** (*Br.*) соли́дные газе́ты.

qualm /kwɑːm/, /kwɔːm/ *n.* сомне́ние, колеба́ние; **~s of conscience** угрызе́ния (*nt. pl.*) со́вести.

quandary /'kwɒndərɪ/ *n.* затрудни́тельное положе́ние; **I was in a ~ which way to go** я был в затрудне́нии (*or* не знал), како́й вы́брать путь.

quango /'kwæŋgəʊ/ *n.* (*pl.* **~s**) (*Br. coll.*) полуавтоно́мная организа́ция.

quanta /'kwɒntə/ *pl. of* ⇒**quantum**

quantifiable /'kwɒntɪ,faɪəb(ə)l/ *adj.* измери́мый.

quantify /'kwɒntɪ,faɪ/ *v.t.* (*determine quantity of*) определ|я́ть, -и́ть коли́чество + *g.*; (*express as quantity*) выража́ть, вы́разить коли́чественно.

quantitative /'kwɒntɪtətɪv/, /-,teɪtɪv/ *adj.* коли́чественный.

quantit|y /'kwɒntɪtɪ/ *n.* **1** (*measurable property*) коли́чество; **~y surveyor** (*Br.*) инжене́р-планови́к. **2** (*thing having ~y*) величина́; число́; **unknown ~y** (*math.*) неизве́стная величина́, неизве́стное; (*person*) челове́к-зага́дка. **3** (*sum or amount*) коли́чество; **she buys in small ~ies** она́ покупа́ет в небольши́х коли́чествах; (*considerable sum or amount*) большо́е коли́чество.

quantum /ˈkwɒntəm/ *n.* (*pl.* **quanta**) (*phys.*) квант; **~ leap** (*phys.*) ква́нтовый скачо́к; (*fig.*) скачо́к; **~ theory** ква́нтовая тео́рия.

quarantine /ˈkwɒrən,ti:n/ *n.* каранти́н.

● *v.t.* содержа́ть (*impf.*) в каранти́не.

quark /kwɑ:k/ *n.* (*phys.*) кварк.

quarrel /ˈkwɒr(ə)l/ *n.* **1** (*altercation, contention*) ссо́ра. **2** (*cause for complaint*) по́вод для ссо́ры, прете́нзия; **I have no ~ with him on that score** у меня́ нет к нему́ прете́нзий по э́тому по́воду.

● *v.i.* (**quarrelled, quarrelling;** *US* **quarreled, quarreling**) (*contend, dispute*) ссо́риться, по-; (*take issue*) спо́рить, по-; **I cannot ~ with his logic** я не могу́ не согласи́ться с его́ ло́гикой.

quarrelsome /ˈkwɒrəlsəm/ *adj.* сварли́вый.

quarry[1] /ˈkwɒrɪ/ *n.* (*object of pursuit; prey*) добы́ча.

quarr|y[2] /ˈkwɒrɪ/ *n.* (*for stone, clay, sand*) карье́р; (*for stone only*) каменоло́мня.

● *v.t.* (*extract*) доб|ыва́ть, -ы́ть.

● *cpd.* **~yman** *n.* каменобо́ец, каменотёс.

quart /kwɔ:t/ *n.* ква́рта.

quarter /ˈkwɔ:tə(r)/ *n.* **1** (*fourth part*) че́тверть; (*of hour*): **a ~ to six** без че́тверти шесть; **a ~ past six** че́тверть седьмо́го; **an hour and a ~** час с че́твертью; **a ~ of an hour later** на пятна́дцать мину́т по́зже; **the clock strikes the ~s** часы́ бьют ка́ждые пятна́дцать мину́т; (*lunar period*): **the first ~ of the moon** пе́рвая че́тверть Луны́; (*of year*) кварта́л; (**court of) ~ sessions** (*Br.*) суд кварта́льных се́ссий; **we pay a ~'s rent in advance** мы пла́тим квартпла́ту за (оди́н) кварта́л вперёд.
2 (*of carcass*) четверти́на (ту́ши); **fore/hind ~s** пере́дняя/за́дняя часть; **the dog got up on its hind ~s** соба́ка вста́ла на за́дние ла́пы.
3 (*US coin*) два́дцать пять це́нтов.
4 (*fig., direction, place*) ме́сто; **the boys came running from every ~** ма́льчики бежа́ли со всех сторо́н; **there is a belief in certain ~s that ...** в не́которых круга́х счита́ется, что....
5 (*district of town*) кварта́л; **residential ~** жило́й кварта́л.
6 (*pl., lodgings*) каза́рмы (*f. pl.*); кварти́ры (*f. pl.*); **the army went into winter ~s** а́рмия перешла́ на зи́мние кварти́ры.
7: **at close ~s** в те́сном сосе́дстве, вблизи́; **they were fighting at close ~s** они́ вели́ бли́жний бой; **when I saw him at close ~s I was appalled** я ужасну́лся, когда́ уви́дел его́ вблизи́.
8 (*mercy*) поща́да; **no ~ was asked and none was given** никто́ поща́ды не проси́л, никто́ поща́ды не дава́л.

● *v.t.* **1** (*divide into four*) дели́ть, раз- на четы́ре ча́сти; **traitors were hanged, drawn and ~ed** преда́телей ве́шали и четвертова́ли.
2 (*put into lodgings*) расквартиро́в|ывать, -а́ть; **where are you ~ed?** где вы останови́лись/посели́лись?

● *cpds.* **~-back** *n.* (*in American football*) веду́щий игро́к; **~-day** *n.* (*Br.*) день, начина́ющий кварта́л; **~-deck** *n.* (*naut.*) шка́нц|ы (*pl., g.* -ев) квартерде́к; (*fig., officers*) офице́рский соста́в; **~-final** *n.* четвертьфина́л; **~-hour** *n.* че́тверть ча́са; **~-hourly** *adv.* ка́ждую че́тверть ча́са; **~-light** *n.* (*Br.*) ма́лое боково́е окно́; **~master** *n.* квартирме́йстер; **~-mile** *n.* че́тверть ми́ли; **~-miler** *n.* бегу́н на че́тверть ми́ли; **~ note** *n.* (*US, mus.*) четвертна́я но́та.

quarterly /ˈkwɔ:təlɪ/ *n.* (*periodical*) ежекварта́льное изда́ние.

● *adj.* кварта́льный; **~ payment** покварта́льная опла́та; опла́та раз в три ме́сяца.

● *adv.* ежекварта́льно; раз в три ме́сяца.

quartet(te) /kwɔ:ˈtet/ *n.* кварте́т.

quarto /ˈkwɔ:təʊ/ *n.* (*pl.* **~s**) (*size of paper*) (ин-)ква́рто (*indecl.*); (*book of ~ sheets*) кни́га форма́та ин-ква́рто.

quartz /kwɔ:ts/ *n.* кварц; (*attr.*) ква́рцевый.

quasar /ˈkweɪzɑ:(r)/, /-sɑ:(r)/ *n.* (*astron.*) квaза́р.

quash /kwɒʃ/ *v.t.* (*cancel*) отмен|я́ть, -и́ть; аннули́ровать (*impf., pf.*); (*suppress*) подав|ля́ть, -и́ть.

quasi- /ˈkweɪzaɪ/, /ˈkwɑ:zɪ/ *comb. form* ква́зи...; полу....

quatercentenary /,kwætəsenˈti:nərɪ/ *n.* четырёхсотле́тие.

● *adj.* четырёхсотле́тний.

quaternary /kwəˈtɜ:nərɪ/ *n.* (*geol.*, **the Q~**) четверти́чный пери́од.

● *adj.* **1** (*of four parts*) состоя́щий из четырёх часте́й. **2** (*geol.*, **Q~**) четверти́чный.

quatrain /ˈkwɒtreɪn/ *n.* четверости́шие.

quaver /ˈkweɪvə(r)/ *n.* **1** (*trembling tone*) дрожа́ние; **there was a ~ in his voice** его́ го́лос дрожа́л. **2** (*Br., mus.*) восьма́я но́та.

● *v.i.* дрожа́ть (*impf.*).

quay /ki:/ *n.* прича́л.

● *cpd.* **~side** *n.* при́стань.

queasiness /ˈkwi:zɪnɪs/ *n.* тошнота́.

queasy /ˈkwi:zɪ/ *adj.* (**queasier, queasiest**) подве́рженный тошноте́; **my stomach feels a little ~** меня́ немно́го тошни́т; **he turned ~ at the sight of food** его́ затошни́ло при ви́де еды́.

Quebec /kwɪˈbek/ *n.* Квебе́к.

queen /kwi:n/ *n.* **1** короле́ва; **~ consort** супру́га ца́рствующего короля́; **~ dowager** вдо́вствующая короле́ва; **~ mother** короле́ва-мать.
2 (*fig.*) короле́ва, цари́ца; **Q~ of the May** короле́ва ма́я; **beauty ~** короле́ва красоты́.
3 (**~** *bee*, **~** *wasp*, **~** *ant*) ма́тка.
4 (*at chess*) ферзь (*m.*), короле́ва; **~'s pawn** ферзёвая пе́шка.
5 (*at cards*) да́ма; **~ of hearts** черво́нная да́ма, да́ма черве́й.
6: **Q~'s Counsel** адвока́т вы́сшего ра́нга; **he can't speak the Q~'s English** он не уме́ет пра́вильно говори́ть по-англи́йски; **Q~'s evidence** обвиня́емый, даю́щий показа́ния про́тив свои́х соо́бщников; *see also* ⇒**king.**
7 (*sl., pej., homosexual*) гомосексуали́ст, голубо́й.

● *v.t.* **1**: **she ~ed it over the other girls** она́ разы́грывала принце́ссу пе́ред подру́гами.
2 (*chess*): **~ a pawn** пров|оди́ть, -ести́ пе́шку в ферзи́.

queenly /ˈkwi:nlɪ/ *adj.* (**queenlier, queenliest**) ца́рственный, короле́вский.

queer /kwɪə(r)/ *n.* (*sl., offens., homosexual*) пе́дик (*coll.*).

● *adj.* (*strange, odd*) стра́нный, чудакова́тый; **he's a ~ customer** он стра́нный тип; (*causing suspicion*) подозри́тельный, сомни́тельный; (*Br., unwell*) недомога́ющий; **the heat is making me feel ~** мне нехорошо́ от жары́; (*sl., offens., homosexual*) гомосексуа́льный.

● *v.t.* (*coll.*) пога́нить, ис-.

quell /kwel/ *v.t.* подав|ля́ть, -и́ть.

quench /kwentʃ/ *v.t.* (*extinguish*) гаси́ть, по-; туши́ть, по-; (*slake*): **~ one's thirst** утол|я́ть, -и́ть жа́жду.

querulous /ˈkwerʊləs/ *adj.* ворчли́вый.

querulousness /ˈkwerʊləsnɪs/ *n.* ворчли́вость.

quer|y /ˈkwɪərɪ/ *n.* (*question*) вопро́с.

● *v.t.* **1** (*ask, inquire*) осв|едомля́ться, -е́домиться. **2** (*call in question*) выража́ть, вы́разить сомне́ние в + *p.*; усомни́ться (*pf.*) в + *p.*; **he ~ied my reasons for coming** он усомни́лся в причи́нах моего́ прихо́да.

quest /kwest/ *n.* по́иски (*m. pl.*); **the ~ for happiness** стремле́ние за сча́стьем; **he went in ~ of food** он отпра́вился на по́иски еды́.

question /ˈkwestʃ(ə)n/ *n.*
1 (*interrogation; problem*) вопро́с; **I put the ~ to him** я за́дал ему́ вопро́с; **a leading ~** наводя́щий вопро́с; **a good ~!** зако́нный/толко́вый вопро́с!; **beg the ~** исходи́ть (*impf.*) из того́, что ещё не дока́зано; прив|оди́ть, -ести́ в ка́честве аргуме́нта спо́рное положе́ние; **it is only a ~ of finding the money** де́ло то́лько за тем, что́бы найти́ де́ньги; **the ~ is, can we afford it?** вопро́с в том, мо́жем ли мы э́то себе́ позво́лить?; **a holiday is out of the ~** об о́тпуске не мо́жет быть и ре́чи; **that's not the ~** не в э́том де́ло; **the man in ~** челове́к, о кото́ром идёт речь; **come into ~** станови́ться, стать предме́том обсужде́ния; **the ~ does not arise** тако́й вопро́с не возника́ет.
2 (*doubt, objection*) сомне́ние; **his statements were called in ~** его́ заявле́ния бы́ли поста́влены под сомне́ние; **his veracity is open to ~** его́ правди́вость ещё под вопро́сом; **without, beyond ~** бесспо́рно; **there is no ~ of his not succeeding** его́ успе́х не подлежи́т сомне́нию.

● *v.t.* **1** (*interrogate*) допр|а́шивать,

Q

-оси́ть; (*seek information*) расспр|а́шивать, -оси́ть; **I ~ed him closely on his theory** я подро́бно расспроси́л его́ о его́ тео́рии; **he is wanted for ~ing by the police** поли́ция разы́скивает его́ для допро́са.
2 (*cast doubt on*) ста́вить, по- под сомне́ние; осп|а́ривать, -о́рить.
● *cpds.* **~-mark** *n.* вопроси́тельный знак; **~-master** *n.* (*Br.*) веду́щий виктори́ны.

questionable /ˈkwestʃənəb(ə)l/ *adj.* (*doubtful*) сомни́тельный; ненадёжный; (*disreputable*) сомни́тельный, подозри́тельный.

questioner /ˈkwestʃənə(r)/ *n.* зада́вший вопро́с; (*in poll*) интервьюе́р.

questionnaire /ˌkwestʃəˈneə(r)/, /ˌkestjə-/ *n.* анке́та, вопро́сник.

queue /kjuː/ (*Br.*) *n.* о́чередь; **he was trying to jump the ~** он пыта́лся пройти́ без о́череди.
● *v.i.* (**queues, queued, queuing** *or* **queueing**) (*also* **~ up**) станови́ться, стать в о́чередь.

quibbl|e /ˈkwɪb(ə)l/ *n.* (*petty objection*) приди́рка; (*evasion*) увёртка.
● *v.i.* (*argue*) препира́ться (*impf.*); (*be evasive*) увил|ивать, -ьну́ть; **I won't ~e over 20p** я не бу́ду препира́ться из-за двадцати́ пе́нсов.

quibbler /ˈkwɪblə(r)/ *n.* казуи́ст.

quick /kwɪk/ *n.*: **he bit his nails to the ~** он искуса́л все но́гти; **his words cut me to the ~** его́ слова́ заде́ли меня́ за живо́е.
● *adj.* **1** (*rapid*) бы́стрый, ско́рый; **this is the ~est way home** э́то са́мая коро́ткая доро́га домо́й; **be ~ about it!** поторопи́тесь!, бы́стро!; **he is a ~ worker** он бы́стро рабо́тает; **in ~ succession** оди́н за други́м; **~ march!** ша́гом — марш!; **we got there in double ~ time** мы добрали́сь туда́ в два счёта.
2 (*lively, prompt*) бы́стрый; живо́й; (*quick-minded*) сообрази́тельный; **he has a ~ temper** он о́чень вспы́льчив; **she is ~ to take offence** она́ о́чень оби́дчива.
● *adv.* бы́стро; **~, get a doctor!** скоре́е позови́те врача́!; **I'll come as ~ as I can** я приду́, как то́лько смогу́.
● *cpds.* **~lime** *n.* негашёная и́звесть; **~sand(s)** *n.* зыбу́чий песо́к; **~silver** *n.* ртуть; **~step** *n.* (*dance*) квиксте́п; **~-tempered** *adj.* вспы́льчивый; **~-witted** *adj.* смышлёный, нахо́дчивый.

quicken /ˈkwɪkən/ *v.t.* (*make quicker*) уск|оря́ть, -о́рить; **he ~ed his pace** он приба́вил ша́гу; (*stimulate*) возбу|жда́ть, -ди́ть.
● *v.i.* (*become quicker*) уск|оря́ться, -о́риться; **her pulse ~ed** её пульс уско́рился/участи́лся.

quickie /ˈkwɪkɪ/ *n.* (*coll.*): **we've just time for one more question, so let's make it a ~** у нас оста́лось вре́мя то́лько для одного́ вопро́са — так что дава́йте быстре́нько.

quickness /ˈkwɪknɪs/ *n.* быстрота́; (*of eye, ear etc.*) острота́; (*of mind*) жи́вость.

quid /kwɪd/ *n.* (*pl.* **~**) (*Br. coll.*, £1) фунт (сте́рлингов).

quid pro quo /ˌkwɪd prəʊ ˈkwəʊ/ *n.* (*pl.* **quid pro quos**) услу́га за услу́гу.

quiescence /kwɪˈes(ə)ns/ *n.* неподви́жность; безде́йствие.

quiescent /kwɪˈes(ə)nt/ *adj.* неподви́жный; безде́йствующий.

quiet /ˈkwaɪət/ *n.* (*stillness, silence*) тишина́; **absolute ~ reigned** цари́ла по́лная тишина́; (*repose*) поко́й, споко́йствие; **there is peace and ~ in the countryside** в дере́вне тишина́ и поко́й.
● *adj.* (**quieter, quietest**) **1** (*making little or no sound*) ти́хий; бесшу́мный; **a ~ car** бесшу́мная маши́на; **be ~!** ти́хо!, помолчи́те!; **can't you keep ~?** ты не мо́жешь помолча́ть?; **this will keep him ~ for a bit** э́то его́ на вре́мя утихоми́рит; **the baby was ~ at last** наконе́ц младе́нец утих.
2 (*making little motion*) ти́хий; неподви́жный; **a ~ sea** споко́йное мо́ре.
3 (*undisturbed*) споко́йный, ми́рный; **we had a ~ night** ночь прошла́ споко́йно.
4 (*of gentle or inactive disposition*) споко́йный, ти́хий.
5 (*unobtrusive*) нея́ркий; **~ colours** (*Br.*), **colors** (*US*) приглушённые/споко́йные цвета́.
6 (*private; concealed*) та́йный; скры́тый; **keep it ~!** об э́том молчо́к!; **on the ~** (*secretly*) тайко́м; втихомо́лку; (*in confidence*) под секре́том.
7 (*informal, unostentatious*) скро́мный.
● *v.t.* успок|а́ивать, -о́ить.
● *int.* ти́ше!

quieten /ˈkwaɪət(ə)n/ *v.t. & i.* (*Br., also* **~ down**) успок|а́ивать(ся), -о́ить(ся).

quietness /ˈkwaɪətnɪs/ *n.* (*stillness*) тишина́; (*repose*) поко́й; (*of manner, character*) невозмути́мость, споко́йствие.

quietude /ˈkwaɪɪˌtjuːd/ *n.* (*liter.*) поко́й, споко́йствие.

quiff /kwɪf/ *n.* (*Br.*) чёлка; (*tuft*) зачёс.

quill /kwɪl/ *n.* (*feather*) (пти́чье) перо́; (**~ pen**) гуси́ное перо́; (*of porcupine*) игла́ (*дикобраза*).

quilt /kwɪlt/ *n.* стёганое одея́ло.
● *v.t.* стега́ть, вы́-/про-; **a ~ed dressing-gown** стёганый хала́т.

quin /kwɪn/ (*Br. coll.*) = **quintuplet**

quince /kwɪns/ *n.* (*fruit, tree*) айва́; (*attr.*) айво́вый.

quincentenary /ˌkwɪnsenˈtiːnərɪ/ *n.* пятисотле́тие.

quinine /ˈkwɪniːn/, /-ˈniːn/ *n.* хини́н.

quinsy /ˈkwɪnzɪ/ *n.* флегмоно́зная анги́на.

quintessence /kwɪnˈtes(ə)ns/ *n.* квинтэссе́нция.

quintessential /ˌkwɪntɪˈsenʃ(ə)l/ *adj.* наибо́лее суще́ственный; коренно́й.

quintet(te) /kwɪnˈtet/ *n.* квинте́т.

quintuple /ˈkwɪntjʊp(ə)l/ *n.* пятикра́тное коли́чество.
● *adj.* пятикра́тный.
● *v.t.(i.)* увели́чи|вать(ся), -ть(ся) в пять раз.

quintuplet /ˈkwɪntjʊplɪt/, /-ˈtjuːplɪt/ *n.* оди́н из пяти́ близнецо́в.

quip /kwɪp/ *n.* остро́та.
● *v.i.* (**quipped, quipping**) остри́ть, с-.

quire /ˈkwaɪə(r)/ *n.* (*of paper*) десть.

quirk /kwɜːk/ *n.* (*oddity*) причу́да; **through some ~ of fate** по капри́зу судьбы́.

quirky /ˈkwɜːkɪ/ *adj.* (**quirkier, quirkiest**) причу́дный.

quisling /ˈkwɪzlɪŋ/ *n.* изме́нник, преда́тель (*m.*).

quit /kwɪt/ *v.t.* (**quitting;** *past and p.p.* **quitted** *or* **quit**) **1** (*leave*) ост|авля́ть, -а́вить. **2** (*coll., stop*) прекра|ща́ть, -ти́ть; бр|оса́ть, -о́сить; **the men ~ work** рабо́чие прекрати́ли рабо́ту; (*US*): **~ grumbling!** бро́сьте ворча́ть!
● *v.i.* (**quitting;** *past and p.p.* **quitted** *or* **quit**) **1** (*leave premises, job etc.*): **the tenant was asked to ~** жильца́ попроси́ли съе́хать с кварти́ры; **the maid was given notice to ~** го́рничную предупреди́ли об увольне́нии. **2** (*leave off*) перест|ава́ть, -а́ть.

quite /kwaɪt/ *adv.* **1** (*entirely*) совсе́м, соверше́нно, вполне́; **I ~ agree** я вполне́/соверше́нно согла́сен; **~ right!** соверше́нно ве́рно!; **~!** безусло́вно!, несомне́нно!, ве́рно!, (вот) и́менно!; **have you ~ finished?** ну, вы ко́нчили?; **this is ~ the best book** э́то безусло́вно са́мая хоро́шая кни́га; **that is ~ another matter** э́то совсе́м друго́е де́ло; **I am not ~ myself today** я сего́дня немно́го не в себе́.
2 (*to a certain extent*) дово́льно; **it is ~ cold here** зде́сь дово́льно хо́лодно; **I ~ like cycling** я не прочь поката́ться на велосипе́де; **~ a long time** дово́льно мно́го вре́мени; **~ a few** дово́льно мно́го; нема́ло.

quits /kwɪts/ *pred. adj.*: **I will be ~ with you yet** я ещё с ва́ми расквита́юсь; **now we are ~** тепе́рь мы кви́ты.

quitter /ˈkwɪtə(r)/ *n.* (*coll.*) (*coward*) трус; (*shirker*) прогу́льщик.

quiver[1] /ˈkwɪvə(r)/ *n.* (*for arrows*) колча́н.

quiver[2] /ˈkwɪvə(r)/ *n.* (*vibration*) дрожь.
● *v.i.* дрожа́ть, за-; трясти́сь, за-.

qui vive /kiː ˈviːv/ *n.*: **on the ~** нагото́ве, начеку́, насторо́же.

quixotic /kwɪkˈsɒtɪk/ *adj.* донкихо́тский.

quiz /kwɪz/ *n.* (*pl.* **quizzes**) (*Br., interrogation*) опро́с; (*test of knowledge, esp. as entertainment*) виктори́на; (*US, school test*) контро́льная (рабо́та).
● *v.t.* (**quizzed, quizzing**) (*interrogate*) выспра́шивать, вы́спросить.
● *cpd.* **~-master** *n.* (*Br.*) веду́щий виктори́ны.

quizzical /ˈkwɪzɪk(ə)l/ *adj.* насме́шливый, ирони́ческий.

quoit /kɔɪt/ *n.* мета́тельное кольцо́; **~s** (*game*) мета́ние коле́ц в цель.

quorum /ˈkwɔːrəm/ *n.* кво́рум.

quota /ˈkwəʊtə/ *n.* (*pl.* **~s**) кво́та, но́рма.

quotable /ˈkwəʊtəb(ə)l/ *adj.* досто́йный цити́рования/повторе́ния.

quotation /kwəʊˈteɪʃ(ə)n/ *n.* **1** (*quoting*) цити́рование; **~ marks** кавы́ч|ки (*pl., g.* -ек); (*passage quoted*) цита́та. **2** (*estimate of cost*) цена́, сто́имость.

quot|e /kwəʊt/ *n.* **1** (*coll., quotation*) цита́та. **2** (*pl., coll., quotation marks*) кавы́ч|ки (*pl., g.* -ек).

● *v.t.* **1** (*repeat words of*) цити́ровать, про-; **he is always ~ing Shakespeare** он всегда́ цити́рует Шекспи́ра; **can I ~e you on that?** могу́ ли я сосла́ться на ва́ши слова́?; **'~e ... unquote'** «откры́ть кавы́чки... закры́ть кавы́чки». **2** (*adduce*) ссыла́ться, сосла́ться на + *a.*; **can you ~e an instance?** мо́жете ли вы привести́ приме́р? **3**: **~e a price** назн|ача́ть, -а́чить це́ну; **this is the best price I can ~e you** э́то са́мая лу́чшая цена́, каку́ю я могу́ вам предложи́ть.

quotient /ˈkwəʊʃ(ə)nt/ *n.* ча́стное; **intelligence ~** коэффицие́нт врождённых у́мственных спосо́бностей.

q.v. (*abbr. of* ***quod vide***) см. (смотри́).

Q

Rr

R /ɑ:(r)/ *n.*: **the three ~s** ≈ азы́ (*m. pl.*) нау́ки.

rabbi /ˈræbaɪ/ *n.* (*pl.* **~s**) равви́н.

rabbinical /rəˈbɪnɪk(ə)l/ *adj.* равви́нский.

rabbit /ˈræbɪt/ *n.* **1** кро́лик; **breed like ~s** размножа́ться, плоди́ться (*both impf.*) как кро́лики. **2**: **Welsh ~ (also rarebit)** грено́к с сы́ром.

● *v.i.* (**rabbited, rabbiting**) **1** (*hunt ~s*) охо́титься (*impf.*) на за́йцев/кро́ликов. **2** (*Br., babble*) трепа́ться (*impf.*) (*coll.*).

● *cpds.* **~-hole** *n.* кро́личья нора́; **~-hutch** *n.* кро́личья кле́тка; **~-warren** *n.* крольча́тник; (*fig.*) лабири́нт.

rabble /ˈræb(ə)l/ *n.* сброд, чернь.

● *cpds.* **~-rouser** *n.* демаго́г; **~-rousing** *n.* демаго́гия.

Rabelaisian /ˌræbəˈleɪzɪən/ *adj.* раблезиа́нский.

rabid /ˈræbɪd/, /ˈreɪ-/ *adj.* **1** (*affected with rabies*) бе́шеный. **2** (*furious, violent*) бе́шеный, я́ростный. **3** (*extremist*): **a ~ socialist** оголте́лый социали́ст.

rabies /ˈreɪbi:z/ *n.* бе́шенство, водобоя́знь.

RAC (*abbr. of* ***Royal Automobile Club***) Короле́вский автомоби́льный клуб.

raccoon /rəˈku:n/ = **racoon**

race¹ /reɪs/ *n.* **1** (*contest*) бег на ско́рость, го́нка; забе́г; **(horse-)~s** ска́чки (*f. pl.*); **how many horses are in the first ~?** ско́лько лошаде́й уча́ствуют в пе́рвом забе́ге?; **a racing man** завсегда́тай тотализа́тора; **let's have a ~** дава́йте побежи́м наперего́нки; **it was a ~ against time** вре́мени бы́ло в обре́з. **2** (*swift current*) бы́стрый пото́к.

● *v.t.* **1** (*compete in speed with*): **I'll ~ you to the corner** посмо́трим, кто быстре́е добежи́т до угла́. **2** (*cause to compete in ~*): **how often do you ~ your horses?** как ча́сто ва́ши ло́шади уча́ствуют в ска́чках? **3** (*cause to move fast*): **they ~d the bill through** они́ в спе́шном поря́дке протащи́ли билль че́рез парла́мент; **~ an engine** перегру|жа́ть, -зи́ть мото́р.

● *v.i.* **1** (*compete in speed*) состяза́ться (*impf.*) в ско́рости. **2** (*participate in horse-racing*) уча́ствовать (*impf.*) в ска́чках. **3** (*move at speed*) нести́сь (*impf.*); мча́ться, по-.

● *cpds.* **~ car** *n.* (*US*) го́ночный автомоби́ль; **~-card** *n.* програ́мма ска́чек; **~course** *n.* ипподро́м; **~horse** *n.* скакова́я ло́шадь; **~-meeting** *n.* (*Br.*) день (*m.*) ска́чек; **~-track** *n.* тре́к.

race² /reɪs/ *n.* (*ethnic*) ра́са; (*attr.*) ра́совый; **the human ~** челове́ческая ра́са.

raceme /rəˈsi:m/ *n.* гроздь (*m.*), кисть.

racer /ˈreɪsə(r)/ *n.* (*racing driver, cyclist*) го́нщик; (*rider*) нае́здник; (*horse*) скакова́я ло́шадь; (*car, yacht etc.*) го́ночная маши́на/я́хта *и т.п.*

racial /ˈreɪʃ(ə)l/ *adj.* ра́совый.

racialism /ˈreɪʃəˌlɪz(ə)m/ = **racism**

racialist /ˈreɪʃəlɪst/ = **racist**

raciness /ˈreɪsɪnɪs/ *n.* острота́, пря́ность, те́рпкость.

racing /ˈreɪsɪŋ/ *n.* **(horse-~)** ска́чки (*f. pl.*); **(motor-~)** автого́нки (*f. pl.*); **~ car** го́ночный автомоби́ль; **~ cyclist** велого́нщик; **~ driver** го́нщик.

racism /ˈreɪsɪz(ə)m/ *n.* раси́зм.

racist /ˈreɪsɪst/ *n.* раси́ст (*fem.* -ка).

● *adj.* раси́стский.

rack¹ /ræk/ *n.* **1** (*frame*) сто́йка с по́лками; стелла́ж; (*for fodder*) я́сл|и (*pl., g.* -ей); (*plate-~*) подста́вка для посу́ды; (*hat-~*) ве́шалка; (*luggage-~ for travellers*) се́тка. **2** (*toothed bar*) зубча́тая ре́йка.

rack² /ræk/ *n.* (*instrument of torture*) ды́ба.

● *v.t.* **1** (*torture*) му́чить, из-; терза́ть, ис-; **he was ~ed with pain** он ко́рчился от бо́ли; (*fig.*): **I ~ed my brains for an answer** я лома́л го́лову над отве́том. **2** (*shake violently*): **the cough ~ed his whole body** всё его́ те́ло сотряса́лось от ка́шля.

● *cpd.* **~-rent** *n.* граби́тельская аре́ндная пла́та.

rack³ /ræk/ *n.* (*destruction*): **everything went to ~ and ruin** всё пошло́ пра́хом.

rac|ket¹, -quet /ˈrækɪt/ *n.* **1** (*for tennis etc.*) раке́тка. **2**: **squash ~kets** (*the sport*) сквош.

racket² /ˈrækɪt/ *n.* **1** (*din, uproar*) шум, гам. **2** (*sl.*) (*dishonest scheme*) жу́льническое предприя́тие; (*extortion*) рэ́кет, вымога́тельство.

racketeer /ˌrækɪˈtɪə(r)/ *n.* рэкети́р, афери́ст.

raconteur /ˌrækɒnˈtɜ:(r)/ *n.* хоро́ший расска́зчик.

rac|oon, -coon /rəˈku:n/ *n.* ено́т.

racquet /ˈrækɪt/ = **racket¹**

racy /ˈreɪsɪ/ *adj.* (**racier, raciest**) (*piquant, lively*) о́стрый, пря́ный; **a ~ style** бо́йкий/я́ркий стиль.

RADA /ˈrɑ:də/ *n.* (*abbr. of* ***Royal Academy of Dramatic Art***) Короле́вская акаде́мия театра́льного иску́сства.

radar /ˈreɪdɑ:(r)/ *n.* (*system*) радиолока́ция; (*apparatus*) радиолока́тор, рада́р; (*attr.*) рада́рный, радиолокацио́нный.

radial /ˈreɪdɪəl/ *adj.* радиа́льный; (*anat.*) лучево́й.

radiance /ˈreɪdɪəns/ *n.* сия́ние, блеск; **the sun's ~** со́лнечное сия́ние.

radiant /ˈreɪdɪənt/ *adj.* **1** (*lit., fig.*) сия́ющий; **she was ~ with happiness** она́ сия́ла от сча́стья; **he is in ~ health** он пы́шет здоро́вьем. **2** (*transmitted by radiation*) лучи́стый; **~ heat** теплово́е излуче́ние.

radiate /ˈreɪdɪˌeɪt/ *v.t. & i.* излуч|а́ть(ся), -и́ть(ся); (*fig.*): **his face ~d happiness** его́ лицо́ свети́лось ра́достью.

radiation /ˌreɪdɪˈeɪʃ(ə)n/ *n.* радиа́ция, излуче́ние; **~ treatment** радиотерапи́я; **~ sickness** лучева́я боле́знь.

radiator /ˈreɪdɪˌeɪtə(r)/ *n.* (*heating device*) батаре́я, радиа́тор; (*of car*) радиа́тор.

radical /ˈrædɪk(ə)l/ *n.* (*math., philol.*) ко́рень (*m.*); (*pol.*) радика́л.

● *adj.* (*fundamental*) коренно́й; (*pol.*) радика́льный; (*math.*) относя́щийся к ко́рню; (*philol., bot.*) корнево́й.

radicalism /ˈrædɪkəˌlɪz(ə)m/ *n.* радикали́зм.

radii /ˈreɪdɪˌaɪ/ *pl. of* ⇒**radius**

radio /ˈreɪdɪəʊ/ *n.* (*pl.* **radios**) (*means of communication*) ра́дио (*indecl.*); (*broadcasting system*) радиовеща́ние; (*receiving/transmitting apparatus*) радиоприёмник; ~ **car** радиофици́рованный автомоби́ль; ~ **cassette (recorder)** магнито́ла; ~**-controlled** радиоуправля́емый; ~ **ham** радиолюби́тель (*m.*); ~ **programme** (*Br.*), **program** (*US*) радиопереда́ча; ~ **station** радиоста́нция; ~ **telephone** радиотелефо́н; ~ **telescope** радиотелеско́п.

● *v.t.* (**radioes, radioed**) **1** (*send by* ~) перед|ава́ть, -а́ть (по ра́дио). **2** (*contact by* ~) ради́ровать (*pf.*) + *d.*

radioactive /ˌreɪdɪəʊˈæktɪv/ *adj.* радиоакти́вный.

radioactivity /ˌreɪdɪəʊækˈtɪvɪtɪ/ *n.* радиоакти́вность.

radiobiology /ˌreɪdɪəʊbaɪˈɒlədʒɪ/ *n.* радиобиоло́гия.

radiocarbon /ˌreɪdɪəʊˈkɑːbən/ *n.* радиоакти́вный углеро́д; ~ **dating** дати́ровка радиоуглеро́дным ме́тодом.

radiochemical /ˌreɪdɪəʊˈkemɪk(ə)l/ *adj.* радиохими́ческий.

radiochemistry /ˌreɪdɪəʊˈkemɪstrɪ/ *n.* радиохи́мия.

radiogram /ˈreɪdɪəʊˌgræm/ *n.* (*picture*) рентгеногра́мма; (*telegram*) радиогра́мма; (*Br., gramophone with radio*) радио́ла.

radiographer /ˌreɪdɪˈɒgrəfə(r)/ *n.* рентгено́лог, радиографи́ст.

radiographic /ˌreɪdɪəˈgræfɪk/ *adj.* радиографи́ческий.

radiography /ˌreɪdɪˈɒgrəfɪ/ *n.* рентгеногра́фия, радиогра́фия.

radiological /ˌreɪdɪəˈlɒdʒɪk(ə)l/ *adj.* радиологи́ческий.

radiologist /ˌreɪdɪˈɒlədʒɪst/ *n.* радио́лог, рентгено́лог.

radiology /ˌreɪdɪˈɒlədʒɪ/ *n.* рентгеноло́гия, радиоло́гия.

radiotherapy /ˌreɪdɪəʊˈθerəpɪ/ *n.* лучева́я терапи́я, радиотерапи́я.

radish /ˈrædɪʃ/ *n.* реди́ска.

radium /ˈreɪdɪəm/ *n.* ра́дий.

radius /ˈreɪdɪəs/ *n.* (*pl.* **radii** *or* **radiuses**) ра́диус; (*anat.*) лучева́я кость; **within a** ~ **of** в ра́диусе + *g.*

RAF (*abbr. of* ***Royal Air Force***) ВВС (*f. pl.*) (вое́нно-возду́шные си́лы) Великобрита́нии.

raffia /ˈræfɪə/ *n.* ра́фия.

raffish /ˈræfɪʃ/ *adj.* (*dissipated*) беспу́тный; (*in appearance*) потрёпанный.

raffle /ˈræf(ə)l/ *n.* лотере́я.

● *v.t.* (*also* ~ **off**) разыгр|ывать, -а́ть в лотере́е.

raft /rɑːft/ *n.* (сплавно́й) плот.

rafter /ˈrɑːftə(r)/ *n.* стропи́ло.

rag¹ /ræg/ *n.* **1** (*small, esp. torn, piece of cloth*) тря́пка, лоску́т; **they tore his shirt to** ~**s** они́ разорва́ли его́ руба́шку в кло́чья; (*pl., torn or tattered clothing*) лохмо́ть|я (*pl., g.* -ев); отре́пья (*nt. pl.*); **he went about in** ~**s** он ходи́л, как оборва́нец; **his coat is in** ~**s** его́ пальто́ изно́шено до дыр. **2** (*pej. or joc., garment*) тря́пки (*f. pl.*); **the** ~ **trade** (*coll.*) шве́йная промы́шленность; **glad** ~**s** (*coll.*) пара́дное облаче́ние. **3** (*pej., newspaper*) газетёнка.

● *cpds.* ~**-(and-bone-)man** *n.* старьёвщик; ~**bag** *n.* (*fig.*) вся́кая вся́чина; ~**-doll** *n.* тряпи́чная ку́кла; ~**-picker** *n.* старьёвщик; ~**tag (and bobtail)** *n.* подо́нки (*m. pl.*), сброд; ~**time** *n.* ре́гтайм.

rag² /ræg/ *n.* (*Br., students' prank*) подтру́нивание, прока́зы (*f. pl.*).

● *v.t.* (**ragged, ragging**) (*play prank on; tease*) разы́гр|ывать, -а́ть; изводи́ть (*impf.*).

ragamuffin /ˈrægəˌmʌfɪn/ *n.* оборва́нец.

rag|e /reɪdʒ/ *n.* **1** (*violent anger*) я́рость, гнев; **he flew into a** ~**e** он пришёл в я́рость. **2** (*dominant fashion*) после́дний крик мо́ды.

● *v.i.*: **he** ~**ed at his wife** он наки́нулся на свою́ жену́; **the wind** ~**ed all day** ве́тер бушева́л весь день; **a** ~**ing torrent** бушу́ющий пото́к; **a** ~**ing thirst** мучи́тельная жа́жда.

ragged /ˈrægɪd/ *adj.* **1** (*torn, frayed*) рва́ный, потрёпанный; (*wearing torn clothes*) обо́рванный. **2** (*rough or uneven in outline*): **a** ~ **beard** косма́тая борода́; ~ **clouds** рва́ные облака́. **3** (*wanting polish or uniformity*): **their singing is** ~ они́ пою́т нестро́йно.

raglan /ˈræglən/ *n.*: ~ **sleeve** рука́в регла́н.

ragout /ræˈguː/ *n.* рагу́ (*nt. indecl.*).

raid /reɪd/ *n.* (*by police*) обла́ва, рейд; (*by criminals*) налёт; (*mil.*) рейд, налёт; (*of cavalry*) набе́г; **he was killed during a** ~ **on London** он был уби́т во вре́мя налёта на Ло́ндон; **the police made a** ~ **on the club** поли́ция устро́ила обла́ву в клу́бе; **bank** ~ налёт на банк; **there was a** ~ **on sterling** была́ сде́лана попы́тка подорва́ть курс фу́нта.

● *v.t.*: **our bombers** ~**ed Hamburg** на́ши бомбардиро́вщики соверши́ли налёт на Га́мбург; **the flat was** ~**ed in his absence** в его́ отсу́тствие кварти́ру огра́били; **he had to** ~ **his savings** ему́ пришло́сь воспо́льзоваться ча́стью свои́х сбереже́ний.

raider /ˈreɪdə(r)/ *n.* (*criminal*) налётчик, граби́тель (*m.*).

rail¹ /reɪl/ *n.* **1** (*bar for protection, support etc.*) перекла́дина, ре́йка; (*of staircase*) пери́л|а (*pl., g.* —); (*for hanging things on*) ве́шалка; ~ **fence** огра́да; **the horse was forced to the** ~**s** ло́шадь оказа́лась прижа́той к огра́де (ипподро́ма); **they were leaning over the ship's** ~ они́ стоя́ли, облокоти́вшись о по́ручни па́лубы. **2** (*of railway or tram track*) рельс; **live** ~ конта́ктный рельс; **the train ran off the** ~**s** по́езд сошёл с ре́льсов; (*fig.*): **after his wife's death he went off the** ~**s** он был соверше́нно вы́бит из коле́й сме́ртью жены́; (*railway transport*): **by** ~ по́ездом; ~ **fares are going up** сто́имость прое́зда по желе́зной доро́ге повыша́ется.

● *v.t.*: ~ **in** огор|а́живать, -оди́ть; ~ **off** отгор|а́живать, -оди́ть.

● *cpds.* ~**car** *n.* (*Br.*) дрези́на; (*US*) железнодоро́жный ваго́н; ~**road** *n.* (*US*) желе́зная доро́га; *v.t.* (*coll.*): **they were** ~**roaded into agreement** их с хо́ду втяну́ли в соглаше́ние; ~**way** *n.* (*track, system, company*) желе́зная доро́га; **model** ~**way** игру́шечная желе́зная доро́га; (*attr.*) железнодоро́жный; ~**wayman** *n.* (*Br.*) железнодоро́жник.

rail² /reɪl/ *v.i.* (*liter.*) руга́ться (*impf.*); **he** ~**ed at me** он стал на меня́ ора́ть; **it's no use** ~**ing against the system** како́й смы́сл поноси́ть систе́му?

railing(s) /ˈreɪlɪŋs/ *n.* и́згородь, огра́да.

raillery /ˈreɪlərɪ/ *n.* (доброду́шное) подшу́чивание.

raiment /ˈreɪmənt/ *n.* (*liter.*) одея́ние.

rain /reɪn/ *n.* дождь (*m.*); **I was caught in the** ~ я попа́л под дождь; **don't go out in the** ~ не выходи́те под дождь; **I think I felt a drop of** ~ вро́де начина́ет накра́пывать; **a shower of** ~ ли́вень (*m.*); **a light** ~ **was falling** мороси́л до́ждик; ~ **or shine** в лю́бую пого́ду; **as right as** ~ в по́лном поря́дке; **a** ~ **of congratulations** пото́к поздравле́ний.

● *v.t.*: **it is** ~**ing cats and dogs** льёт как из ведра́; (*fig.*): **she** ~**ed blows on his head** она́ колоти́ла его́ по голове́.

● *v.i.*: **it is** ~**ing** дождь идёт; **it was** ~**ing hard** шёл си́льный/проливно́й дождь; **it never** ~**s but it pours** пришла́ беда́ — отворя́й ворота́.

● *with advs.*: ~ **in** *v.i.*: **it is** ~**ing in under the door** дождь подтека́ет под дверь; ~ **off** (*Br.*), **out** (*US*) *v.t.*: **the match was** ~**ed off** матч был со́рван из-за́ дождя́.

● *cpds.* ~**bow** *n.* ра́дуга; **her dress was all the colours of the** ~**bow** её пла́тье отлива́ло все́ми цвета́ми ра́дуги; ~ **check** *n.* (*US*) обеща́ние приня́ть приглаше́ние ка́к-нибудь в друго́й раз; ~**-cloud** *n.* ту́ча; ~**coat** *n.* плащ; ~**drop** *n.* ка́пля дождя́; ~**fall** *n.* оса́дк|и (*pl., g.* -ов); ~**-gauge** *n.* дождеме́р; ~**proof** *adj.* непромока́емый; ~**storm** *n.* ли́вень (*m.*); ~**-water** *n.* дождева́я вода́; ~**wear** *n.* непромока́емая оде́жда и о́бувь.

rainforest /ˈreɪnˌfɒrɪst/ *n.* тропи́ческий лес.

rainy /ˈreɪnɪ/ *adj.* (**rainier, rainiest**) дождли́вый; **you should save for a** ~ **day** вы должны́ откла́дывать на чёрный день.

raise /reɪz/ *n.* (*US, rise in salary*) приба́вка; (*increase in stake or bid*) повыше́ние.

R

● *v.t.* **1** (*lift; cause to rise*) подн|има́ть, -я́ть; **the anchor was ~d** я́корь был по́днят; **he barely ~d his eyes** он почти́ не поднима́л глаз; **he ~d his hat** он приподня́л шля́пу; (*make higher*) пов|ыша́ть, -ы́сить; **the government ~d the duty on tobacco** прави́тельство повы́сило по́шлину на таба́к; **the news ~d my hopes** изве́стие укрепи́ло мои́ наде́жды; **the stakes were ~d** ста́вки бы́ли повы́шены; (*make louder, more vehement*): **don't ~ your voice** не повыша́йте го́лоса; **voices were ~d in anger** раздали́сь гне́вные голоса́; (*cause to stand*): **I ~d him from his knees** я помо́г ему́ подня́ться с коле́н; (*arouse*): **the heat ~d blisters on his skin** от жары́ он весь покры́лся волдыря́ми; **the carriage ~d a cloud of dust** каре́та подняла́ о́блако пы́ли; **Lazarus was ~d from the dead** Ла́зарь был воскрешён из мёртвых; (*fig.*): **he ~d hell** он устро́ил стра́шный сканда́л; (*elevate*): **he was ~d to the peerage** его́ произвели́ в пэ́ры; (*erect*): **a monument was ~d to his memory** ему́ был воздви́гнут па́мятник. **2** (*bring up*): **may I ~ one question?** мо́жно мне зада́ть вопро́с?; **the issue will never be ~d** э́тот вопро́с никогда́ не бу́дет по́днят; **several objections were ~d** бы́ло сде́лано не́сколько возраже́ний; (*evoke*): **his words hardly ~d a laugh** почти́ никто́ не засмея́лся в отве́т; **you ~d a doubt in my mind** вы зарони́ли мне в ду́шу сомне́ние; (*summon up*): **I couldn't ~ a smile** я не мог себя́ заста́вить улыбну́ться; **he could hardly ~ the energy to get up** он е́ле собра́лся с си́лами, что́бы встать. **3** (*give voice to*): **she ~d the alarm** она́ подняла́ трево́гу. **4** (*collect, procure*): **she ~d money for charity** она́ собрала́ де́ньги на благотвори́тельные це́ли; **I tried to ~ a loan** я попыта́лся взять де́ньги в долг; (*levy*): **the king ~d an army** коро́ль собра́л а́рмию. **5** (*rear*): **they ~d a family** они́ вы́растили дете́й; **sheep are ~d on the downs** ове́ц разво́дят в холми́стых райо́нах. **6** (*siege etc.*) сн|има́ть, -я́ть.

raisin /ˈreɪz(ə)n/ *n.* изю́минка; (*pl., collect.*) изю́м.

raison d'être /ˌreɪzɔ̃ ˈdetr/ *n.* (*pl.* ***raisons d'être*** *pronunc. same*) смысл, разу́мное основа́ние.

Raj /rɑːdʒ/ *n.* (*hist.*) брита́нское правле́ние в И́ндии.

rajah /ˈrɑːdʒə/ *n.* ра́джа (*m.*).

rake¹ /reɪk/ *n.* (*implement*) гра́бл|и (*pl., g.* -ей); **as thin as a ~** худо́й как ще́пка.

● *v.t.*: **he ~d the soil level** он разрыхли́л грунт.

● *v.i.* (*fig.*): **he ~d among his papers** он перевороши́л свои́ бума́ги.

● *with advs.*: **~ in** *v.t.*: **he ~d in the money** (*fig.*) он загреба́л де́ньги лопа́той; **~ out** *v.t.* выгреба́ть, вы́грести; **she ~d out the ashes** она́ вы́гребла пе́пел; **~ together** *v.t.* сгре|ба́ть, -сти́ в ку́чу; **~ up** *v.t.* сгре|ба́ть, -сти́; (*fig.*): **why ~ up an old quarrel?** заче́м вороши́ть ста́рую ссо́ру?

● *cpd.* **~-off** *n.* (*coll.*) магары́ч; комиссио́нные (*pl.*).

rake² /reɪk/ *n.* (*arch., dissolute person*) пове́са (*m.*).

rakish /ˈreɪkɪʃ/ *adj.* (*jaunty*) щеголева́тый; у́харский.

rallentan|do /ˌrælənˈtændəʊ/ *n., adj. & adv.* (*pl.* **~dos** *or* **~di** /-dɪ/) (*mus.*) раллента́ндо (*indecl.*).

rall|y /ˈrælɪ/ *n.* **1** (*mass gathering*) сбор, слёт, ми́тинг. **2** (*recovery, revival*) восстановле́ние сил; попра́вка. **3** (*at tennis etc.*) переки́дка. **4** (*motor race*) автора́лли; **~y driver** авторалли́ст.

● *v.t.* **1** (*reassemble*) соб|ира́ть, -ра́ть (в строй); спл|а́чивать, -оти́ть. **2** (*revive*): **his words ~ied their spirits** его́ слова́ воодушеви́ли их.

● *v.i.* **1** (*reassemble*) соб|ира́ться, -ра́ться; спл|а́чиваться, -оти́ться; **they ~ied round the leader** они́ сплоти́лись вокру́г вождя́; **they ~ied to the cause** де́ло сплоти́ло их. **2** (*revive*): **he ~ied from his illness** он опра́вился от боле́зни; **the market ~ied** ры́нок воспря́нул.

RAM /ræm/ *n.* (*comput.*) (*abbr. of* ***random-access memory***) ЗУПВ (запомина́ющее устро́йство с произво́льной вы́боркой).

ram /ræm/ *n.* **1** (*male sheep*) бара́н. **2** (*astron.*: **the R~**) Ове́н. **3** (*battering-~*) тара́н.

● *v.t.* (**rammed, ramming**) **1** (*drive or compress by force*): **stakes were ~med into the ground** ко́лья бы́ли вби́ты в зе́млю; **the soil was ~med down** грунт был утрамбо́ван; **he ~med his clothes into a drawer** он запихну́л свою́ оде́жду в я́щик (комо́да); (*fig.*): **he ~med the point home** он вдолби́л им свою́ мысль. **2** (*strike with force*): **the ship ~med the bridge** (*by accident*) кора́бль наскочи́л на мост; **he ~med the enemy flagship** он протара́нил фла́гман проти́вника.

● *cpd.* **~rod** *n.* шо́мпол.

Ramadan /ˈræməˌdæn/ *n.* (*relig.*) рамаза́н, рамада́н.

rambl|e /ˈræmb(ə)l/ *n.* прогу́лка.

● *v.i.* **1** (*walk for pleasure*) прогу́л|иваться, -я́ться. **2** (*of plants*) ползти́, ви́ться (*both impf.*). **3** (*fig., of speech or writing*) болта́ть (*impf.*) языко́м; бубни́ть (*impf.*); **a ~ing speaker** многосло́вный ора́тор; **a ~ing speech** бессвя́зная речь; (*of sick person*) загова́риваться (*impf.*). **4**: **a ~ing house** разбро́санный дом.

rambler /ˈræmblə(r)/ *n.* (*hiker*) люби́тель пешехо́дного тури́зма; (*speaker*) пустоме́ля (*c.g.*); (*rose*) вью́щаяся ро́за.

rambling /ˈræmblɪŋ/ *n.* пешехо́дный тури́зм.

ramification /ˌræmɪfɪˈkeɪʃ(ə)n/ *n.* разветвле́ние; (*consequence*) после́дствие.

ramif|y /ˈræmɪˌfaɪ/ *v.t. & i.* развет|вля́ть(ся), -и́ть(ся); **a ~ied system of railways** разветвлённая систе́ма желе́зных доро́г.

ramp /ræmp/ *n.* (*slope*) скат, укло́н.

rampage /ˈræmpeɪdʒ/ *n.* бу́йство, разгу́л.

● *v.i.* бу́йствовать, буя́нить (*both impf.*).

rampant /ˈræmpənt/ *adj.* **1** (*unchecked, widespread*) свире́пствующий, безу́держный; **disease was ~** боле́знь свире́пствовала. **2** (*rank, luxuriant*) бу́йный, пы́шный. **3** (*her.*): **lion ~** взды́бленный лев.

rampart /ˈræmpɑːt/ *n.* крепостно́й вал; парапе́т.

ramshackle /ˈræmˌʃæk(ə)l/ *adj.* (*e.g. house*) обветша́лый; (*e.g. car*) разби́тый.

ran /ræn/ *past of* ⇒**run**

ranch /rɑːntʃ/ *n.* ра́нчо (*indecl.*), фе́рма.

● *v.i.* занима́ться (*impf.*) се́льским хозя́йством.

● *v.t.* разв|оди́ть, -ести́.

rancher /ˈrɑːntʃə(r)/ *n.* владе́лец ра́нчо; скотово́д.

rancid /ˈrænsɪd/ *adj.* прого́рклый, ту́хлый.

rancor /ˈræŋkə(r)/ (*US*) = **rancour**

rancorous /ˈræŋkərəs/ *adj.* озло́бленный, злопа́мятный.

rancour /ˈræŋkə(r)/ (*US* **rancor**) *n.* зло́ба, озло́бленность; злопа́мятство.

rand /rænd/ *n.* (*currency*) ранд.

R & B (*abbr. of* ***rhythm and blues***) ритм и блюз.

R & D (*abbr. of* ***research and development***) нау́чно-иссле́довательская рабо́та.

random /ˈrændəm/ *n.*: **at ~** наобу́м, науга́д, науда́чу; **shoot at ~** стреля́ть (*impf.*) не це́лясь; **he hit out at ~** он бил, куда́ придётся.

● *adj.* случа́йный; **~ bullet** шальна́я пу́ля; **~ choice** случа́йный вы́бор; **~ remark** случа́йное замеча́ние.

randy /ˈrændɪ/ *adj.* (**randier, randiest**) (*Br.*) распу́тный, похотли́вый.

rang /ræŋ/ *past of* ⇒**ring²**

range /reɪndʒ/ *n.* **1** (*row, line, series*) цепь, ряд; **a ~ of mountains** го́рная цепь; **a ~ of buildings** ряд зда́ний. **2** (*grazing area*) неогоро́женное па́стбище; (*hunting ground*) охо́тничье уго́дье. **3** (*area for firing, bombing etc.*) полиго́н; **rifle ~** стре́льбище; тир. **4** (*operating distance*) да́льность, ра́диус; **the missile has a ~ of 1,000 miles** ра́диус де́йствия раке́ты — 1 000 миль; **~ of an aircraft** да́льность полёта самолёта; **the enemy was out of ~ of our guns** враг был вне досяга́емости на́ших ору́дий. **5** (*distance to target*) расстоя́ние, да́льность; **they fired at close ~** они́ стреля́ли с бли́зкого расстоя́ния. **6** (*limit of audibility or visibility*) преде́л, -ы; **beyond the ~ of vision** вне преде́лов ви́димости. **7** (*extent; distance between limits*) диапазо́н; **her voice has a remarkable ~** у неё замеча́тельный диапазо́н.

8 (*selection*) набóр; (*assortment*) ассортимéнт; **this fabric comes in a wide ~ of colours** (*Br.*), **colors** (*US*) э́та ткань выпускáется сáмых различных цветóв.
9 (*scope*): **the subject is outside my ~** э́тот вопрóс — не по моéй чáсти.
10 (*cooking-stove*) кýхонная плитá.
● *v.t.* **1** (*place in row*) распол|агáть, -ожи́ть (*or* выстрáивать, вы́строить) в ряд; **they ~d themselves against the wall** они́ вы́строились вдоль стены́.
2 (*traverse*): **wolves ~d the prairie** вóлки ры́скали по стéпи; **police ~d the woods** (*in their search*) поли́ция прочёсывала лес.
● *v.i.* **1** (*wander, roam*): **tigers ~d through the jungle** ти́гры броди́ли по джýнглям.
2 (*extend*) простирáться (*impf.*); **my research ~s over a wide field** мои́ исслéдования охвáтывают ширóкую óбласть.
3 (*vary between limits*) колебáться (*impf.*); **prices ~ from £10 to £50** цéны колéблются от десяти́ до пяти́десяти фýнтов.
4 (*of guns etc., carry*): **the gun ~s over 5 miles** дальнобóйность пýшки — 5 миль.
● *cpd.* **~-finder** *n.* дальномéр.

ranger /ˈreɪndʒə(r)/ *n.* (*guard of forest or parkland*) лесни́к, объéздчик; (*pl., mounted troops*) кóнная охрáна.

rank¹ /ræŋk/ *n.* **1** (*row*) ряд; (*taxi-~*) (*Br.*) стоя́нка такси́.
2 (*line of soldiers*) шерéнга; **in the front ~** (*lit.*) в пéрвой шерéнге; (*fig., pre-eminent*) в пéрвых рядáх; **the men broke ~(s)** солдáты нарýшили строй; **an artist of the first ~** первоклáссный худóжник; **among the ~s of the unemployed** в рядáх безрабóтных.
3 (*usu. pl., common soldiers*): **~ and file** (*mil. etc.*) рядовы́е; **he rose from the ~s** он вы́служился из рядовы́х; **he was reduced to the ~s** егó разжáловали в рядовы́е.
4 (*in armed forces*) звáние, чин; **he has the ~ of captain** он имéет чин капитáна.
5 (*official position*) служéбное положéние; (*social position*): **persons of ~** высокопостáвленные лю́ди; **people of all ~s of society** представи́тели всех слоёв óбщества.
● *v.t.* (*class, assess*) классифици́ровать (*impf., pf.*); **he was ~ed among the great poets** егó причисля́ли к вели́ким поэ́там.
● *v.i.* (*have a place*): **a major ~s above a captain** майóр — вы́ше капитáна по чи́ну; **a high-~ing officer** стáрший офицéр; **France ~s among the great powers** Фрáнция вхóдит в числó вели́ких держáв.

rank² /ræŋk/ *adj.* **1** (*too luxuriant, coarse*) бýйный, пы́шный; **~ vegetation** бýйная расти́тельность; **a garden ~ with weeds** сад, зарóсший сорнякáми. **2** (*foul to smell or taste; offensive*): **the skunk gives off a ~ odour** (*Br.*), **odor** (*US*) от скýнса исхóдит зловóние. **3** (*loathsome, corrupt*) гнýсный. **4** (*gross*) чрезмéрный; **~ indecency** ди́кая непристóйность; **~ injustice** вопию́щая несправедли́вость; **~ nonsense** сýщая чепухá; **~ outsider** совершéнно посторóнний человéк.

rank-and-file /ˈræŋkəndˌfaɪl/ *adj.* рядовóй.

ranker /ˈræŋkə(r)/ *n.* (*Br., private soldier*) рядовóй.

rankle /ˈræŋk(ə)l/ *v.i.* (*torment*) терзáть, мýчить (*both impf.*).

rankness /ˈræŋknɪs/ *n.* (*excess*) изоби́лие, чрезмéрность; (*offensiveness*) гнýсность.

ransack /ˈrænsæk/ *v.t.* **1** (*search*) обшáри|вать, -ть; переры́ть (*pf.*).
2 (*plunder*) грáбить, раз-.

ransom /ˈrænsəm/ *n.* вы́куп; **he was held to ~** (*lit.*) за негó трéбовали вы́куп; (*fig.*) егó шантажи́ровали.
● *v.t.* (*pay ~ for*) плати́ть, за- вы́куп за + *a.*

rant /rænt/ *n.* ти́рáда; разглагóльствование.
● *v.i.* вити́йствовать; разглагóльствовать (*both impf.*).

ranter /ˈræntə(r)/ *n.* фразёр, краснобáй.

rap /ræp/ *n.* **1** (*light blow*) лёгкий удáр, стук; **I heard a ~ at the window** я услы́шал стук в окнó; **he received a ~ on the knuckles** (*fig., reproof*) емý дáли по рукáм. **2** (*blame*): **who will take the ~ for this?** кто бýдет за э́то отдувáться? (*coll.*). **3** (*~ music*) рэп.
● *v.t.* (**rapped, rapping**) слегкá уд|аря́ть, -áрить по + *d.*
● *v.i.* (**rapped, rapping**) ст|учáть, -ýкнуть; постý|кивать, -чáть; **he ~ped on the door** он постучáл в дверь.
● *with adv.*: **~ out** *v.t.* (*utter brusquely*) говори́ть (*impf.*) отры́висто; **he ~ped out his orders** он выкри́кивал свои́ приказáния.

rapacious /rəˈpeɪʃəs/ *adj.* жáдный, ненасы́тный.

rape¹ /reɪp/ *n.* изнаси́лование.
● *v.t.* наси́ловать, из-.

rape² /reɪp/ *n.* (*bot.*) рапс.

rapid /ˈræpɪd/ *n.* (*pl.*) речнóй порóг; **shoot ~s** преодол|евáть, -éть порóги.
● *adj.* (**rapider, rapidest**) (*swift*) бы́стрый, скóрый.

rapidity /rəˈpɪdɪtɪ/ *n.* быстротá, скóрость.

rapier /ˈreɪpɪə(r)/ *n.* рапи́ра.

rapist /ˈreɪpɪst/ *n.* наси́льник.

rapport /ræˈpɔː(r)/ *n.* взаимопонимáние, контáкт.

rapprochement /ræˈprɒʃmɑ̃/ *n.* сближéние.

rapt /ræpt/ *adj.* (*enraptured*) восхищённый; (*absorbed*) поглощённый; **he was ~ in contemplation** он был погружён в раздýмье; **she listened with ~ attention** онá слýшала, затаи́в дыхáние.

rapture /ˈræptʃə(r)/ *n.* востóрг; **she went into ~s over the play** онá былá в (ди́ком) востóрге от пьéсы.

rapturous /ˈræptʃərəs/ *adj.* востóрженный.

rare¹ /reə(r)/ *adj.* (**rarer, rarest**)
1 (*not dense*): **a ~ atmosphere** разрежённая атмосфéра.
2 (*uncommon*) рéдкий; **it is ~ for him to smile** он рéдко улыбáется; **this flower is ~ in Britain** э́тот цветóк рéдко встречáется в Великобритáнии.
3 (*remarkably good*): рéдкостный; **we had a ~ old time** (*coll.*) мы на рéдкость хорошó провели́ врéмя; **he has a ~ wit** он на рéдкость остроýмен.

rare² /reə(r)/ *adj.* (**rarer, rarest**) (*undercooked*) недожáренный; **a ~ steak** бифштéкс с крóвью.

rarebit /ˈreəbɪt/ = **rabbit** *n.* 2

raref|action /ˌreərɪˈfækʃ(ə)n/, **-ication** /ˌreərɪfɪˈkeɪʃ(ə)n/ *nn.* разрежéние, разрежённость.

rarefy /ˈreərɪˌfaɪ/ *v.t.* разре|жáть, -ди́ть; (*fig.*) утонч|áть, -и́ть; рафини́ровать (*impf., pf.*).
● *v.i.* разре|жáться, -ди́ться.

rarely /ˈreəlɪ/ *adv.* рéдко, нечáсто, и́зредка.

raring /ˈreərɪŋ/ *adj.* (*coll.*): **he was ~ to go** емý не терпéлось приступи́ть к дéлу.

rarity /ˈreərɪtɪ/ *n.* (*uncommonness, infrequency*) рéдкость; (*thing valued for this*) (большáя) рéдкость.

rascal /ˈrɑːsk(ə)l/ *n.* (*rogue*) мошéнник, плут; (*mischievous child*) шалýн.

rascally /ˈrɑːskəlɪ/ *adj.* мошéннический, нечéстный.

rash¹ /ræʃ/ *n.* сыпь; **he broke out in a ~** у негó вы́ступила сыпь.

rash² /ræʃ/ *adj.* опромéтчивый, необдýманный.

rasher /ˈræʃə(r)/ *n.* лóмтик (бекóна).

rashness /ˈræʃnɪs/ *n.* опромéтчивость, необдýманность.

rasp /rɑːsp/ *n.* (*file*) тёрка, рáшпиль (*m.*); (*grating sound*) скрéжет.
● *v.t.* (*scrape*) скрести́, скобли́ть, терéть (*all impf.*).
● *v.i.* скрежетáть (*impf.*); **a ~ing voice** скрипýчий гóлос.
● *with advs.*: **~ away, ~ off** *v.t.* соск|áбливать, -обли́ть; **~ out** *v.t.* (*e.g. an order*) гáркнуть (*pf.*).

raspberry /ˈrɑːzbərɪ/ *n.* **1** (*fruit*) мали́на (*collect.*); **a ~** я́года мали́ны; **~ cane** куст мали́ны; **~ jam** мали́новое варéнье. **2** (*sl., sound or gesture of derision*): **he blew me a ~** он показáл мне нос.

Rasta /ˈræstə/ *n.* & *adj.* (*coll.*) = **Rastafarian**

Rastafarian /ˌræstəˈfeərɪən/ *n.* (*relig.*) растафáри (*c.g. indecl.*).
● *adj.* растафáри.

rat /ræt/ *n.* **1** (*rodent*) кры́са; **he looked like a drowned ~** он походи́л на мóкрую кýрицу; **I smell a ~** я чýю подвóх; здесь чтó-то нечи́сто.
2 (*traitor*) измéнник, ренегáт.
● *v.i.* (**ratted, ratting**) **1** (*hunt ~s*) лови́ть (*impf.*) кры́с. **2**: **~ on** (*break faith with*) **s.o.** измен|я́ть, -и́ть комý-н.

R

● *cpds.* **~-catcher** *n.* крысоло́в; **~-race** *n.* бе́шеная пого́ня за успе́хом; **~-trap** *n.* крысоло́вка.

ratable /ˈreɪtəb(ə)l/ = **rat(e)able**

rat-a-tat /ˌrætəˈtæt/ = **rat-tat**

ratchet /ˈrætʃɪt/ *n.* (*toothed mechanism*) храпово́й механи́зм, храпови́к; (**~-wheel**) храпово́е колесо́.

rate¹ /reɪt/ *n.* **1** (*numerical proportion*) но́рма, разме́р; ста́вка; **~ of exchange** курс обме́на; **~ of interest** проце́нтная ста́вка; **bank ~** учётная ста́вка ба́нка; **birth ~** рожда́емость; **death ~** сме́ртность.
2 (*speed*) ско́рость; **at a steady ~** с постоя́нной ско́ростью; **we shall never get there at this ~** при таки́х те́мпах мы туда́ никогда́ не доберёмся.
3 (*price*) расце́нка, тари́ф; **his ~s are high** он до́рого берёт; **the letter ~ goes up every year** тари́ф на пи́сьма повыша́ется ежего́дно.
4 (*Br., tax on property etc.*) ме́стный нало́г; **water ~** пла́та за водоснабже́ние.
5: **at any ~** (*in any case*) во вся́ком слу́чае; **at that ~** (*on that basis*) **you will never succeed** в тако́м слу́чае вы никогда́ не добьётесь успе́ха.
● *v.t.* **1** (*estimate, consider*) оце́н|ивать, -и́ть; **how do you ~ my chances?** как вы оце́ниваете мои́ ша́нсы?; **do you ~ him among your friends?** счита́ете ли вы его́ свои́м дру́гом?
2 (*Br., assess for purposes of levy*) оце́н|ивать, -и́ть в це́лях налогообложе́ния.
3 (*deserve*): **he ~s a prize** он заслу́живает награ́ды.
● *v.i.*: **~ as** (*be considered*) счита́ться (*impf.*) + *i.*; **he ~s high in my esteem** я его́ о́чень ценю́/уважа́ю.
● *cpd.* **~payer** *n.* (*Br.*) плате́льщик ме́стных нало́гов.

rate² /reɪt/ *v.t.* (*liter., scold*) брани́ть (*impf.*).

rat(e)able /ˈreɪtəb(ə)l/ *adj.* подлежа́щий обложе́нию нало́гом/нало́гами.

rather /ˈrɑːðə(r)/ *adv.* **1** (*by preference or choice*): **I would ~ die than consent** я скоре́е умру́, чем соглашу́сь; **I'd ~ have coffee** я предпочёл бы ко́фе; **I'd ~ not say** я лу́чше промолчу́; **~ than annoy him, she agreed** она́ согласи́лась, что́бы не серди́ть его́.
2 (*more truly or precisely*) скоре́е, верне́е; **last night, or ~ this morning** вчера́ ве́чером, и́ли, верне́е/точне́е (сказа́ть), сего́дня у́тром; **she is shy ~ than unsociable** она́ скоре́е засте́нчива, чем необщи́тельна.
3 (*somewhat*) дово́льно, не́сколько; **the result was ~ surprising** результа́т был дово́льно неожи́данным; **he is ~ taller than his brother** он немно́го вы́ше своего́ бра́та; **it is ~ a pity** а жаль всё же; **I ~ think you are mistaken** а мне сдаётся, что вы ошиба́етесь; **the effect was ~ spoiled** эффе́кт был не́сколько подпо́рчен.
4 (*Br. coll., assuredly*) ещё бы!

ratification /ˌrætɪfɪˈkeɪʃ(ə)n/ *n.* ратифика́ция.

ratify /ˈrætɪˌfaɪ/ *v.t.* ратифици́ровать (*impf., pf.*).

rating¹ /ˈreɪtɪŋ/ *n.* **1** (*of property etc.*) оце́нка; (*assessment of worth*) определе́ние сто́имости; (*in opinion poll*) ре́йтинг; (*of vehicles etc.*) классифика́ция. **2** (*Br., sailor*) матро́с, специали́ст рядово́го и́ли старши́нского соста́ва.

rating² /ˈreɪtɪŋ/ *n.* (*scolding*) нагоня́й.

ratio /ˈreɪʃɪəʊ/ *n.* (*pl.* **~s**) отноше́ние, соотноше́ние; **in the ~ of 3 to 2** в отноше́нии три к двум.

ration /ˈræʃ(ə)n/ *n.* рацио́н, паёк; **~ book** продово́льственная кни́жка; **~ card** продово́льственная ка́рточка; **iron ~s** неприкоснове́нный запа́с; **they were on short ~s** они́ бы́ли на ску́дном пайке́; (*pl., food*) продово́льствие.
● *v.t.*: **they were ~ed to one loaf a week** их паёк своди́лся к одно́й буха́нке в неде́лю; **meat was severely ~ed** мя́со бы́ло стро́го нормиро́вано.

rational /ˈræʃən(ə)l/ *adj.* (*based on reason*) разу́мный, рациона́льный; (*endowed with reason*) разу́мный, мы́слящий; (*math.*) рациона́льный.

rationale /ˌræʃəˈnɑːl/ *n.* основна́я причи́на; логи́ческое обоснова́ние.

rationalism /ˈræʃənəˌlɪz(ə)m/ *n.* рационали́зм.

rationalist /ˈræʃənəlɪst/ *n.* рационали́ст.

rationalistic /ˌræʃənəˈlɪstɪk/ *adj.* рационалисти́ческий.

rationality /ˌræʃəˈnælɪtɪ/ *n.* разу́мность, рациона́льность.

rationalization /ˌræʃənəlaɪˈzeɪʃ(ə)n/ *n.* (*explanation*) обоснова́ние, разу́мное объясне́ние; (*justification*) оправда́ние; (*improvement*) рационализа́ция.

rationalize /ˈræʃənəˌlaɪz/ *v.t.* (*give or find reasons for*) разу́мно объясн|я́ть, -и́ть; опра́вд|ывать, -а́ть; (*make more efficient*) рационализи́ровать (*impf., pf.*).

rattan /rəˈtæn/ *n.* (*material*) рота́нг; (*cane*) трость.

rat-tat(-tat) /ˌrættætˈtæt/ (*also* **rat-a-tat**) *n.* тук-ту́к.

ratter /ˈrætə(r)/ *n.* (*rat-catcher*) крысоло́в.

rattle /ˈræt(ə)l/ *n.* **1** (*sound*) треск, гро́хот; **the ~ of machine-guns** пулемётная дробь; (*of crockery*) гро́хот.
2 (*child's toy*) погрему́шка.
3 (*for sports fans etc.*) трещо́тка.
● *v.t.* **1** (*cause to ~*): **he ~d the money-box** он встряхну́л копи́лку; **the wind ~d the windows** о́кна дребезжа́ли от ве́тра.
2 (*coll., agitate*): **he is not easily ~d** его́ нелегко́ вы́вести из равнове́сия.
● *v.i.*: **the hail ~d on the roof** град бараба́нил по кры́ше; **the car ~d over the stones** маши́на громыха́ла по камня́м.
● *with advs.*: **he ~d off a list of names** он вы́палил це́лый спи́сок фами́лий; **he ~d on about his family** он продолжа́л тарато́рить о свое́й семье́.
● *cpds.* **~snake** *n.* грему́чая змея́; **~trap** *n.* драндуле́т.

rattling /ˈrætlɪŋ/ *adj. & adv.* (*coll.*): **he set off at a ~ pace** он бо́дро зашага́л; **we had a ~ (good) time** мы шика́рно провели́ вре́мя.

ratty /ˈrætɪ/ *adj.* (**rattier, rattiest**) (*coll.*) (*Br., irritable*) злой, раздражи́тельный; **don't get ~ with me!** не огрыза́йся!; (*unkempt*) растрёпанный; (*shabby*) потрёпанный.

raucous /ˈrɔːkəs/ *adj.* ре́зкий, хри́плый.

raunchy /ˈrɔːntʃɪ/ *adj.* (**raunchier, raunchiest**) (*US coll.*) распу́тный.

ravage /ˈrævɪdʒ/ *n.* (*usu. pl.*) разруше́ние, опустоше́ние; (*fig.*): **the ~s of time** следы́ (*m. pl.*) вре́мени.
● *v.t.* опустош|а́ть, -и́ть; (*fig.*): **her face was ~d by suffering** на её лице была́ печа́ть страда́ния.

rave /reɪv/ *n.* (*party*) весёлая вечери́нка.
● *adj.*: **~ review** восто́рженный о́тзыв.
● *v.i.* (*in delirium*) бре́дить (*impf.*); (*fig., in anger*) неи́стовствовать (*impf.*); (*in delight*): **they ~d about the play** они́ бы́ли в восто́рге от пье́сы; (*see also* ⇒**raving**).
● *cpd.* **~-up** *n.* (*Br. coll.*) = **rave**

ravel /ˈræv(ə)l/ *v.t. & i.* (**ravelled, ravelling;** *US* **raveled, raveling**) запу́т|ывать(ся), -ать(ся); спу́т|ывать(ся), -ать(ся); **the wool became ~led (up)** ни́тки спу́тались.
● *with advs.*: **~ out** *v.t.* распу́т|ывать, -ать; **~ up** *v.t.* пу́тать (*or* запу́тывать), за-.

raven /ˈreɪv(ə)n/ *n.* во́рон.
● *cpd.* **~-haired** *adj.* с волоса́ми цве́та во́ронова крыла́.

ravenous /ˈrævənəs/ *adj.* (*voracious*) прожо́рливый, хи́щный; **a ~ appetite** во́лчий аппети́т; **I am ~** я го́лоден как волк.

raver /ˈreɪvə(r)/ *n.* (*pleasure-seeker*) гуля́ка (*c.g.*).

ravine /rəˈviːn/ *n.* овра́г, уще́лье.

raving /ˈreɪvɪŋ/ *n.* бред; **the ~s of an idiot** бред сумасше́дшего.
● *adj. & adv.* **1** (*insane*): **a ~ lunatic** бу́йно поме́шанный; **you must be ~ mad** ты совсе́м спя́тил. **2**: **a ~ beauty** сногсшиба́тельная краса́вица; **a ~ success** оглуши́тельный успе́х.

ravioli /ˌrævɪˈəʊlɪ/ *n.* равио́ли (*nt. and pl. indecl.*).

ravish /ˈrævɪʃ/ *v.t.* (*enchant*) восхи|ща́ть, -ти́ть; **a ~ing view** восхити́тельный вид.

raw /rɔː/ *n.*: **my remarks touched him on the ~** мои́ слова́ заде́ли его́ за живо́е.
● *adj.* **1** (*uncooked*) сыро́й, све́жий; **I prefer my fruit ~** я предпочита́ю све́жие фру́кты. **2** (*in natural state, unprocessed*) необрабо́танный; **~ data** необрабо́танные да́нные; **~ materials**

сырьё; ~ **sugar** нерафини́рованный са́хар. **3** (*callow, inexperienced*) зелёный, нео́пытный. **4** (*unprotected by skin, sensitive*): **a ~ wound** све́жая/незажи́вшая ра́на; **the wind has made my face ~** у меня́ обве́трилось лицо́. **5** (*of weather*) сыро́й; холо́дный и вла́жный. **6** (*harsh*) суро́вый; **he got a ~ deal** (*coll.*) с ним суро́во обошли́сь.

● *cpd.* **~hide** *adj.* сде́ланный из недублёной ко́жи.

Rawlplug /ˈrɔːlplʌg/ *n.* (*Br. propr.*) про́бка.

rawness /ˈrɔːnɪs/ *n.* **1** (*lack of experience*) нео́пытность. **2** (*of weather*) сы́рость.

ray¹ /reɪ/ *n.* (*lit., fig.*) луч; **the sun's ~s** со́лнечные лучи́; **a ~ of hope** луч/про́блеск наде́жды.

ray² /reɪ/ *n.* (*fish*) скат.

ray³ /reɪ/ = **re¹**

rayon /ˈreɪɒn/ *n.* иску́сственный шёлк, виско́за.

raze /reɪz/ *v.t.* **1** (*demolish*) разр|уша́ть, -у́шить до основа́ния; **the city was ~d to the ground** го́род сравня́ли с землёй. **2** (*efface*) ст|ира́ть, -ере́ть.

razor /ˈreɪzə(r)/ *n.* бри́тва; **electric ~** электробри́тва; **cut-throat** (*Br.*), **straight ~** (*US*) опа́сная бри́тва; **safety ~** безопа́сная бри́тва.

● *cpds.* **~-bill** *n.* (*zool.*) гага́рка; **~-blade** *n.* ле́звие; **~-edge** *n.* (*fig.*) остриё ножа́; **on a ~-edge** на краю́ про́пасти.

razzle(-dazzle) /ˈræz(ə)l(ˌdæz(ə)l)/ *n.* (*sl.*) кутёж; **they have gone on the ~** они́ загуля́ли.

RC (*abbr. of* ***Roman Catholic***) като́лик.

Rd. /rəʊd/ *n.* (*abbr. of* **road**) ул. (у́лица).

RE (*abbr. of* ***Religious Education***) религио́зное обуче́ние.

re¹ /reɪ/ *n.* (*mus.*) втора́я но́та мажо́рной га́ммы; (*the note D*) ре (*indecl.*).

re² /riː/, /reɪ/ *prep.* по де́лу + *g.*; каса́тельно + *g.*

reach /riːtʃ/ *n.* **1** (*stretching movement*): **he made a ~ for the railing** он протяну́л ру́ку к пери́лам; (*extent of this*) разма́х/длина́ руки́; **the apples were beyond their ~** они́ не могли́ дотяну́ться до я́блок; (*fig.*): **we are within easy ~ of London** от нас легко́ добра́ться до Ло́ндона.
2 (*stretch of river etc.*): **the upper ~es of the Thames** верхо́вья (*nt. pl.*) Те́мзы.

● *v.t.* **1** (*attain, fetch with outstretched hand*) дотя́|гиваться, -ну́ться до + *g.*; **I can just ~ the shelf** я е́ле-е́ле могу́ дотяну́ться до по́лки; **please ~ me that book** доста́ньте мне, пожа́луйста, э́ту кни́гу.
2 (*arrive at*) дост|ига́ть, -и́гнуть + *g.*; **we shall ~ town in 5 minutes** мы бу́дем в го́роде че́рез 5 мину́т; **the ladder will not ~ the window** ле́стница не доста́нет до окна́; **your letter ~ed me only yesterday** ва́ше письмо́ дошло́ до меня́ то́лько вчера́; **~ agreement** прийти́ (*pf.*) к соглаше́нию; **~ a conclusion** прийти́ (*pf.*) к заключе́нию.
3 (*make contact with*): **can I ~ you by telephone?** с ва́ми мо́жно связа́ться по телефо́ну?
4 (*rise or sink to*): **his genius ~ed new heights** его́ ге́ний дости́г небыва́лых высо́т; **the pound ~ed a new low** курс фу́нта (сте́рлингов) упа́л ещё ни́же, чем когда́-либо пре́жде.

● *v.i.* **1** (*stretch out hand*) тяну́ться, по-руко́й; **he ~ed for his rifle** он потяну́лся к винто́вке.
2 (*extend*) простира́ться, тяну́ться (*both impf.*); **his voice ~ed to the back of the hall** его́ го́лос был слы́шен в конце́ за́ла; **the park ~es from here to the river** парк тя́нется отсю́да до реки́.

● *with advs.*: **~ down** *v.t.* (*fetch down*) дост|ава́ть, -а́ть; сн|има́ть, -ять; брать, взять; *v.i.*: **he ~ed down and picked up the coin** он нагну́лся и по́днял моне́ту; **the well ~es down for over 100 feet** коло́дец ухо́дит вглубь бо́лее чем на 100 фу́тов; **~ forward** *v.i.*: **he ~ed forward to save her** он протяну́л ру́ку, что́бы удержа́ть её; **~ out** *v.i.*: **he ~ed out to catch the ball** он протяну́л ру́ки, что́бы пойма́ть мяч; **~ up** *v.i.* (*stretch hand up*) протяну́ть (*pf.*) ру́ку вверх; (*rise*): **the tree ~es up to the sky** де́рево тя́нется к не́бу.

reachable /ˈriːtʃəb(ə)l/ *adj.* достижи́мый.

react /rɪˈækt/ *v.i.* реаги́ровать, от- *or* про-; (*have an effect*) вызыва́ть, вы́звать реа́кцию; **these two influences ~ on each other** э́ти два влия́ния взаимоде́йствуют; (*chem.*): **acids ~ together** кисло́ты вступа́ют в реа́кцию; (*respond*) реаги́ровать (*impf.*); отв|еча́ть, -е́тить (на + *a.*); **animals ~ to kindness** живо́тные реаги́руют на ла́ску; **she ~ed by bursting into tears** в отве́т она́ распла́калась; (*act in opposition*) проти́виться, вос-; сопротивля́ться (*impf.*).

reaction /rɪˈækʃ(ə)n/ *n.* (*var. senses*) реа́кция; **my first ~ was one of disbelief** снача́ла э́то вы́звало у меня́ недове́рие; **chain ~** цепна́я реа́кция.

reactionary /rɪˈækʃənərɪ/ *n.* реакционе́р.

● *adj.* реакцио́нный.

reactivate /rɪˈæktɪˌveɪt/ *v.t.* реактиви́ровать (*impf., pf.*); вдохну́ть (*pf.*) но́вую жизнь в + *a.*

reactivation /rɪˌæktɪˈveɪʃ(ə)n/ *n.* реактива́ция; возобновле́ние де́ятельности.

reactive /rɪˈæktɪv/ *adj.* реакти́вный.

reactivity /ˌriːækˈtɪvɪtɪ/ *n.* реакти́вность.

reactor /rɪˈæktə(r)/ *n.* (*tech.*) реа́ктор.

read /riːd/ *n.* (*Br.*) чте́ние; **a good ~** (*book*) интере́сная/захва́тывающая кни́га; **I shall have a ~ and then go to bed** я немно́го почита́ю и ля́гу спать.

● *v.t.* (*past and p.p.* **read** /red/) **1** (*peruse*) чита́ть, про- *or* проче́сть; **have you ~ this book?** вы чита́ли э́ту кни́гу?; **he can ~ several languages** он уме́ет чита́ть на не́скольких языка́х; **he ~ the letter to himself** он прочёл письмо́ про себя́; **this author is widely ~** у э́того а́втора мно́го чита́телей; **can you ~ music?** вы уме́ете игра́ть по но́там?; **~ the letter to me!** прочита́йте мне письмо́!; **he likes being ~ to** он лю́бит, когда́ ему́ чита́ют; **the bill was ~** (*parl.*) ≈ билль был обсуждён.
2 (*discern, make out*): **he ~ my thoughts** он чита́л мои́ мы́сли; **he can ~ shorthand** он уме́ет расшифро́вывать стеногра́ммы; **she had her hand ~** ей погада́ли по руке́; **you ~ too much into my words** вы вкла́дываете в мои́ слова́ то, чего́ в них нет; **you (have) ~ too much into the text** вы вы́читали из те́кста то, чего́ в нём нет.
3 (*interpret*): **do not ~ my silence as consent** не прими́те моё молча́ние за согла́сие.
4 (*take as correct*): **for X ~ Y** вме́сто X (*or* напеча́тано X) сле́дует чита́ть Y; **for Copperfield ~ Dickens** напи́сано Ко́пперфилд, а подразумева́ется Ди́ккенс.
5 (*Br., study*) изуча́ть (*impf.*); **he is ~ing law** он у́чится на юриди́ческом факульте́те.
6 (*examine*): **~ a meter** сн|има́ть, -ять показа́ния счётчика; **~ proofs** держа́ть (*impf.*) корректу́ру; пра́вить, вы- вёрстку.

● *v.i.* (*past and p.p.* **read** /red/) **1**: **he can neither ~ nor write** он не уме́ет ни чита́ть, ни писа́ть; **I ~ about it in the papers** я прочёл об э́том в газе́тах; **have you ~ of him before?** вы чита́ли о нём ра́ньше?; **you must ~ between the lines** (*fig.*) сле́дует чита́ть ме́жду строк; **she ~s to the children at bedtime** она́ чита́ет де́тям пе́ред сном.
2 (*consist of specified words etc.*): **the document ~s as follows** докуме́нт гласи́т сле́дующее; **the letter ~s ...** в письме́ говори́тся/ска́зано...; **how does the sentence ~ now?** как тепе́рь звучи́т э́то предложе́ние?; **the thermometer ~s 20° below** термо́метр пока́зывает ми́нус 20°.
3 (*produce effect when read*): **this ~s like a threat** э́то звучи́т как угро́за; **the play ~s well** пье́са хорошо́ чита́ется.

● *with advs.*: **~ back** *v.t.* повтор|я́ть, -и́ть; **the operator ~ the telegram back** телефони́ст(ка) повтори́л(а) телегра́мму; **~ off** *v.t.* (*e.g. list*) прочи́т|ывать, -а́ть; (*from dial etc.*) сн|има́ть, -ять (*показания*); счи́т|ывать, -а́ть; **~ out** *v.t.* прочи́т|ывать, -а́ть; огла|ша́ть, -си́ть; **~ over** *v.t.* перечи́т|ывать, -а́ть; прочи́т|ывать, -а́ть; **~ through** *v.t.* прочи́т|ывать, -а́ть; **~ up (on)** *v.t.* подчита́ть (*pf.*); чита́ть (*impf.*) для подгото́вки; **he ~ up (on) the subject** он подчита́л ко́е-что по э́тому предме́ту.

● *cpd.* **~-out** *n.* вы́вод/вы́дача да́нных.

readability /ˌriːdəˈbɪlɪtɪ/ *n.* (*legibility*) разбо́рчивость; (*interest*) чита́бельность.

readable /ˈriːdəb(ə)l/ *adj.* **1** (*legible*)

R

разбóрчивый. **2** (*enjoyable*) (*coll.*) интерéсный; **this is a ~ novel** э́тот ромáн хорошó читáется.

readdress /ˌriːəˈdres/ *v.t.* переадресóв|ывать, -áть.

reader /ˈriːdə(r)/ *n.* **1** (*of books etc.*) читáтель (*fem.* -ница); **he is a fast ~** он бы́стро читáет. **2** (*Br., university teacher*) ≈ стáрший преподавáтель; доцéнт. **3** (*textbook*) хрестомáтия; кни́га для чтéния.

readership /ˈriːdəʃɪp/ *n.* (*readers*) круг читáтелей; (*Br., university post*) дóлжность стáршего преподавáтеля; доцентýра.

readily /ˈredɪlɪ/ *adv.* (*willingly*) охóтно; (*without difficulty*) легкó, без трудá.

readiness /ˈredɪnɪs/ *n.* готóвность, охóта.

reading /ˈriːdɪŋ/ *n.* **1** (*act or pursuit*) чтéние. **2** (*version*) вариáнт, формулирóвка. **3** (*interpretation*) толковáние; **what is your ~ of events?** как вы оцéниваете собы́тия? **4** (*of instrument*) показáние. **5** (*stage in passage of bill*) чтéние; **on the second ~** при вторóм чтéнии.

● *cpds.* **~-desk** *n.* пюпи́тр; **~-lamp** *n.* настóльная лáмпа; **~-room** *n.* читáльный зал, читáльня.

readjust /ˌriːəˈdʒʌst/ *v.t.* попр|авля́ть, -áвить; испр|авля́ть, -áвить; приспос|áбливать, -óбить; **he ~ed his tie** он попрáвил гáлстук.

● *v.i.*: **after the war he found it hard to ~** пóсле войны́ емý трýдно бы́ло приспосóбиться.

readjustment /ˌriːəˈdʒʌstmənt/ *n.* приспособлéние, регулирóвка, перестрóйка; **the speedometer needs ~** спидóметр нáдо отрегули́ровать.

ready /ˈredɪ/ *n.*: **he held his rifle at the ~** он держáл винтóвку в положéнии для стрельбы́.

● *adj.* (**readier, readiest**) (*prepared; in a fit state*) готóвый (*к чему*); приготóвленный, подготóвленный; **I'm just getting ~** я почти́ готóв; **she got the children ~ for school** онá собралá детéй в шкóлу; **~! go!** внимáние — марш!; (*willing*) готóвый, проявля́ющий готóвность; **I am ~ to admit I was wrong** готóв признáть, что я был неправ; **he is ~ for anything** он готóв ко всемý (*or* на всё); (*quick, facile*) склóнный; **he is always ~ with an excuse** у негó всегдá найдётся отговóрка; **a ~ wit** нахóдчивость; (*available*) (имéющийся) наготóве; **~ cash/money** нали́чные дéньги.

● *adv.*: **they sell meat ~ cooked** там продаётся мяснáя кулинáрия.

● *cpds.* **~-made** *adj.* готóвый; **~-to-wear** *adj.* готóвый.

reaffirm /ˌriːəˈfɜːm/ *v.t.* (вновь) подтвер|ждáть, -ди́ть.

reaffirmation /riːˌæfəˈmeɪʃ(ə)n/ *n.* (повтóрное) подтверждéние.

reafforestation /ˌriːəfɒrɪˈsteɪʃ(ə)n/ (*Br.*) = **reforestation**

reagent /riːˈeɪdʒ(ə)nt/ *n.* (*chem.*) реакти́в.

real /rɪəl/ *n.*: **for ~** (*coll.*) по-настоя́щему; всерьёз.

● *adj.* (*actual*) реáльный; настоя́щий; (*genuine*) пóдлинный; (*sincere*) и́скренний, неподдéльный; (*substantial, fundamental*) реáльный, сущéственный; **was it ~ or a dream?** э́то бы́ло во сне и́ли наявý?; **in ~ life** в жи́зни; **~ silver** настоя́щее/чи́стое серебрó; **the ~ McCoy** (*coll.*) сáмый настоя́щий; ≈ не придерёшься; **that is not the ~ reason** настоя́щая причи́на не в том; **a ~ gentleman** настоя́щий джентльмéн; **he has a ~ grievance** егó претéнзии обоснóваны; **the ~ point is ...** суть вопрóса в том, что. . .

● *adv.* (*US coll.*): **we had a ~ nice time** мы здóрово провели́ врéмя.

● *cpds.* **~ ale** *n.* (*Br.*) бóчковое пи́во, подаю́щееся без пóмощи углеки́слого гáза; **~ estate** *n.* недви́жимость; **~ estate agent** *n.* (*US*) агéнт по продáже недви́жимости; **~-time** *adj.* (*comput.*) в реáльном врéмени.

realign /ˌriːəˈlaɪn/ *v.t.* перестр|áивать, -óить.

realignment /ˌriːəˈlaɪnmənt/ *n.* перестрóйка.

realism /ˈrɪəˌlɪz(ə)m/ *n.* реали́зм.

realist /ˈrɪəlɪst/ *n.* реали́ст (*fem.* -ка).

realistic /rɪəˈlɪstɪk/ *adj.* (*practical*) реалисти́чный, практи́чный; (*in art etc.*) реалисти́ческий.

reality /rɪˈælɪtɪ/ *n.* реáльность, действи́тельность; **in ~** в/на сáмом дéле; в действи́тельности; **it is time he was brought back to ~** емý нáдо откры́ть глазá на фáкты.

realization /ˌrɪəlaɪˈzeɪʃ(ə)n/ *n.* (*recognition*) осознáние; (*achievement*) осуществлéние; (*conversion into money*) реализáция, продáжа.

realize /ˈrɪəlaɪz/ *v.t.* **1** (*be aware of*) осозн|авáть, -áть; (*grasp mentally*) сообра|жáть, -зи́ть; **he ~d his mistake at once** он срáзу же осознáл свою оши́бку; **I ~ what you must think of me** представля́ю, что вы обо мне дýмаете; **do you ~ what you have done?** вы понимáете, что вы сдéлали?; **I didn't ~ you wanted it** до меня́ не дошлó, что э́то вам нýжно. **2** (*convert into fact*) осуществ|ля́ть, -и́ть; **I will help you to ~ your ambition** я помогý вам осуществи́ть вáши стремлéния; **her worst fears were ~d** оправдáлись её сáмые хýдшие опасéния. **3** (*convert into money*) реализóв|ывать, -áть. **4** (*fetch*) выручáть, вы́ручить; **the sale ~d over £5,000** при продáже бы́ло вы́ручено бóлее пяти́ ты́сяч фýнтов. **5** (*amass, gain*) получ|áть, -и́ть; **they ~d an enormous profit** они́ получи́ли огрóмную при́быль.

really /ˈrɪəlɪ/ *adv.* действи́тельно; в/на сáмом дéле; **do you ~ mean it?** вы серьёзно?; **he is ~ not such a bad fellow** на сáмом дéле он не такóй уж плохóй человéк; **did that ~ happen last year?** рáзве э́то случи́лось в прóшлом годý?; **I am ~ sorry for you** мне вас и́скренне жаль; **I ~ think you should stay** по-мóему, вам непремéнно нýжно остáться; **~, you should be more careful** прáво же, вам слéдует быть осторóжнее; **~?** (*expr. surprise*) серьёзно?, неужéли?; (*acknowledging information*) да?, прáвда?; **~!** (*expr. indignation*) ну, знáете!

realm /relm/ *n.* королéвство; (*fig.*) сфéра; **peer of the ~** пэр (Великобритáнии); (*fig.*): **you are entering the ~s of fancy** вы перенóситесь/вступáете в цáрство фантáзии.

realtor /ˈrɪəltə(r)/ *n.* (*US*) агéнт по продáже недви́жимости.

realty /ˈrɪəltɪ/ *n.* (*leg.*) недви́жимость.

ream /riːm/ *n.* (*quantity of paper*) стопá (= *480 листам*); (*fig.*): **he wrote ~s of nonsense** он написáл бéздну вся́кой чепухи́.

reap /riːp/ *v.t. & i.* жать, с-; пож|инáть, -áть; **~ing-machine** жáтка; (*fig.*): **he is ~ing the fruits of his folly** пожинáет плоды́ своéй глýпости.

reaper /ˈriːpə(r)/ *n.* **1** (*labourer*) жн|ец (*fem.* -и́ца); **the (Grim) R~** старýха с косóй, смерть. **2** (*machine*) жáтка.

reappear /ˌriːəˈpɪə(r)/ *v.i.* снóва появ|ля́ться, -и́ться.

reappearance /ˌriːəˈpɪərəns/ *n.* нóвое появлéние; возрождéние; возвращéние.

reappoint /ˌriːəˈpɔɪnt/ *v.t.* повтóрно назн|ачáть, -áчить.

reappointment /ˌriːəˈpɔɪntmənt/ *n.* повтóрное назначéние.

reappraisal /ˌriːəˈpreɪz(ə)l/ *n.* переоцéнка.

reappraise /ˌriːəˈpreɪz/ *v.t.* пересм|áтривать, -отрéть; зáново оцéн|ивать, -и́ть; переоцéн|ивать, -и́ть.

rear[1] /rɪə(r)/ *n.* **1** зáдняя часть, сторонá; **the kitchen is at the ~ of the house** кýхня — в зáдней чáсти дóма. **2** (*of army etc.*) тыл; хвост колóнны; **they were attacked in the ~** их атаковáли с ты́ла; **he was a slow runner and always brought up the ~** он плóхо бежáл и всегдá окáзывался в хвостé. **3** (*coll., buttocks*) зад, зáдница.

● *adj.*: **~ entrance** чёрный ход; **~ wheel** зáднее колесó.

● *cpds.* **~-admiral** *n.* контр-адмирáл; **~guard** *n.* арьергáрд; **~guard action** арьергáрдный бой; **~most** *adj.* сáмый зáдний; послéдний; **~-view mirror** *n.* зéркало зáднего ви́да.

rear[2] /rɪə(r)/ *v.t.* **1** (*raise, erect*) воздв|игáть, -и́гнуть; **jealousy ~ed its head** (в нём *и т.п.*) зашевели́лась рéвность. **2** (*bring up*) расти́ть (*or* вырáщивать), вы́-; воспи́т|ывать, -áть; **the children were ~ed by foster-parents** детéй воспитáли/вы́растили приёмные роди́тели; (*breed*) развод|и́ть, -ести́; **cattle are ~ed on the plains** скот развóдят на равни́нах.

● *v.i.* (*also* ~ **up**) ста|нови́ться, -ть на дыбы́; **the horse ~ed in terror** ло́шадь (в)ста́ла на дыбы́ от испу́га.

rearm /ri:ˈɑ:m/ *v.t. & i.* перевооруж|а́ть(ся), -и́ть(ся).

rearmament /ri:ˈɑ:məmənt/ *n.* перевооруже́ние.

rearrange /ˌri:əˈreɪndʒ/ *v.t.* (*objects, furniture*) перест|авля́ть, -а́вить; (*a meeting*) передв|ига́ть, -и́нуть вре́мя + *g.*

rearrangement /ˌri:əˈreɪndʒmənt/ *n.* перестано́вка.

rearward /ˈrɪəwəd/ *adj.* тылово́й, за́дний.

rearwards /ˈrɪəwədz/ *adv.* наза́д; в тыл; на попя́тную.

reascend /ˌri:əˈsend/ *v.t. & i.* сно́ва подн|има́ться, -я́ться; сно́ва восходи́ть, взойти́ (на + *a.*).

reascent /ˌri:əˈsent/ *n.* повто́рный подъём; но́вое восхожде́ние.

reason /ˈri:z(ə)n/ *n.* **1** (*cause, ground*) причи́на; **he refused to give his ~s** он отказа́лся объясни́ть; **there is ~ to believe that ...** есть основа́ния полага́ть, что...; **that is no ~ for thinking ...** э́то не даёт основа́ния ду́мать, что...; **with ~** обосно́ванно; **for no good ~** без уважи́тельной причи́ны; **he resigned for ~s of health** он уво́лился по состоя́нию здоро́вья; **for the simple ~ that ...** по той просто́й причи́не, что.... **2** (*intellectual faculty*) ра́зум, рассу́док; **he lost his ~** он лиши́лся рассу́дка. **3** (*good sense, moderation*) благоразу́мие; **he will not listen to ~** он не прислу́шивается к го́лосу ра́зума; **he was brought to ~** его́ удало́сь образу́мить; **it stands to ~** разуме́ется; **I will do anything in ~** я сде́лаю всё в преде́лах разу́много; **there is ~ in what you say** то, что вы говори́те, разу́мно/резо́нно.

● *v.t.* **1** (*argue, contend*) дока́зывать (*impf.*). **2** (*express logically*): **a ~ed argument** обосно́ванный до́вод. **3**: **~ out** (*solve by ~ing*) разга́д|ывать, -а́ть.

● *v.i.*: **it is useless to ~ with him** его́ бесполе́зно убежда́ть; ло́гика на него́ не де́йствует.

reasonable /ˈri:zənəb(ə)l/ *adj.* **1** (*sensible, amenable to reason*) (благо)разу́мный. **2** (*acceptable, moderate*) уме́ренный, прие́млемый; (*fairly good*) дово́льно хоро́ший, неплохо́й, прили́чный; **the shoes are quite ~** ту́фли дово́льно прили́чные; **he has a ~ chance of success** у него́ неплохи́е ша́нсы на успе́х. **3** (*of price*) недорого́й; **the shoes are quite ~** ту́фли сто́ят недо́рого.

reasonableness /ˈri:zənəb(ə)lnɪs/ *n.* благоразу́мие; (*of prices*) уме́ренность.

reasoning /ˈri:zənɪŋ/ *n.* рассужде́ние, аргумента́ция; **the ~ faculty, powers of ~** спосо́бность рассужда́ть.

reassemble /ˌri:əˈsemb(ə)l/ *v.t.* сно́ва соб|ира́ть, -ра́ть; (*tech.*) переб|ира́ть, -ра́ть.

● *v.i.* сно́ва соб|ира́ться, -ра́ться; сно́ва встр|еча́ться, -е́титься.

reassembly /ˌri:əˈsemblɪ/ *n.* (*of committee etc.*) возобновлённое заседа́ние (по́сле переры́ва); (*tech.*) перебо́рка.

reassert /ˌri:əˈsɜ:t/ *v.t.* сно́ва подтвер|жда́ть, -ди́ть; сно́ва выдвига́ть, вы́двинуть; **~ o.s.** самоутвержда́ться (*impf.*).

reassertion /ˌri:əˈsɜ:ʃ(ə)n/ *n.* повто́рное завере́ние, подтвержде́ние.

reassess /ˌri:əˈses/ *v.t.* переоце́н|ивать, -и́ть.

reassessment /ˌri:əˈsesmənt/ *n.* переоце́нка.

reassign /ˌri:əˈsaɪn/ *v.t.* назн|ача́ть, -а́чить на друго́е ме́сто; перев|оди́ть, -ести́; перераспредел|я́ть, -и́ть.

reassignment /ˌri:əˈsaɪnmənt/ *n.* перево́д, перераспределе́ние.

reassume /ˌri:əˈsju:m/ *v.t.* сно́ва брать, взять (*or* прин|има́ть, -я́ть) на себя́.

reassumption /ˌri:əˈsʌmpʃ(ə)n/ *n.* повто́рное приня́тие (на себя́).

reassurance /ˌri:əˈʃʊərəns/ *n.* (повто́рное) завере́ние, подтвержде́ние; (*comfort*) утеше́ние.

reassur|e /ˌri:əˈʃʊə(r)/ *v.t.* успок|а́ивать, -о́ить; подбодр|я́ть, -и́ть; зав|еря́ть, -е́рить; **I can ~e you on that point** я могу́ успоко́ить вас на э́тот счёт; **his words were most ~ing** его́ слова́ звуча́ли са́мым ободря́ющим о́бразом.

reattach /ˌri:əˈtætʃ/ *v.t.* сно́ва прикреп|ля́ть, -и́ть.

reattachment /ˌri:əˈtætʃmənt/ *n.* повто́рное прикрепле́ние.

reawaken /ˌri:əˈweɪkən/ *v.t.* сно́ва пробу|жда́ть, -ди́ть; возро|жда́ть, -ди́ть.

reawakening /ˌri:əˈweɪkənɪŋ/ *n.* но́вое пробужде́ние; возрожде́ние.

rebarbative /rɪˈbɑ:bətɪv/ *adj.* непривлека́тельный.

rebate /ˈri:beɪt/ *n.* (*refund*) возвра́т перепла́ченной су́ммы; (*discount*) ски́дка, усту́пка.

rebel[1] /ˈreb(ə)l/ *n.* (*against government*) повста́нец, мяте́жник; бунтовщи́|к (*fem.* -ца), бунта́рь (*m.*); (*attr.*) повста́нческий; бунта́рский.

rebel[2] /rɪˈbel/ *v.i.* (**rebelled, rebelling**) восст|ава́ть, -а́ть; бунтова́ть, взбунтова́ться; **the tribes ~led against the government** племена́ восста́ли про́тив прави́тельства; **such treatment would make anyone ~** про́тив тако́го обраще́ния кто уго́дно взбунту́ется.

rebellion /rɪˈbeljən/ *n.* восста́ние, мяте́ж, бунт.

rebellious /rɪˈbeljəs/ *adj.* (*in revolt*) восста́вший, мяте́жный, повста́нческий; (*disobedient*) непоко́рный.

rebelliousness /rɪˈbeljəsnɪs/ *n.* бунта́рство, непоко́рность.

rebind /ri:ˈbaɪnd/ *v.t.* за́ново перепле|та́ть, -сти́.

rebirth /ri:ˈbɜ:θ/, /ˈri:-/ *n.* возрожде́ние.

reboot /ri:ˈbu:t/ *v.t.* (*comput.*) перезагру|жа́ть, -зи́ть.

reborn /ri:ˈbɔ:n/ *adj.* возрождённый.

rebound[1] /ˈri:baʊnd/ *n.* отско́к, рикоше́т; **on the ~** на отско́ке; (*fig.*): **he married her on the ~** он жени́лся на ней по́сле разочарова́ния в любви́ к друго́й.

rebound[2] /rɪˈbaʊnd/ *v.i.* отск|а́кивать, -очи́ть; **the ball ~ed against the wall** мяч отскочи́л от стены́.

rebuff /rɪˈbʌf/ *n.* отпо́р, ре́зкий отка́з.

● *v.t.* дава́ть, дать отпо́р (+ *d.*); ре́зко отклон|я́ть, -и́ть; (*mil.*): **the enemy's attack was ~ed** ата́ка неприя́теля была́ отражена́.

rebuild /ri:ˈbɪld/ *v.t.* сно́ва стро́ить, по-; перестр|а́ивать, -о́ить; реконструи́ровать (*impf., pf.*).

rebuke /rɪˈbju:k/ *n.* упрёк, уко́р; вы́говор, замеча́ние.

● *v.t.* упрек|а́ть, -ну́ть; укоря́ть (*impf.*); де́лать, с- замеча́ние/вы́говор + *d.*

rebus /ˈri:bəs/ *n.* (*pl.* **rebuses**) ре́бус.

rebut /rɪˈbʌt/ *v.t.* (**rebutted, rebutting**) опров|ерга́ть, -е́ргнуть.

rebuttal /rɪˈbʌtəl/ *n.* опроверже́ние.

recalcitrance /rɪˈkælsɪtrəns/ *n.* непоко́рность.

recalcitrant /rɪˈkælsɪtrənt/ *adj.* непоко́рный.

recalculate /ri:ˈkælkjʊˌleɪt/ *v.t.* пересчи́т|ывать, -а́ть.

recalculation /ri:ˌkælkjʊˈleɪʃ(ə)n/ *n.* пересчёт.

recall[1] /ˈri:kɔ:l/ *n.* **1** (*summons to return*) о́тзыв; (*signal to return*) сигна́л к возвраще́нию; (*bringing back*): **the letters are lost beyond ~** э́ти пи́сьма бессле́дно исче́зли. **2** (*recollection*) воспомина́ние; па́мять; **total ~** по́лное восстановле́ние в па́мяти.

recall[2] /rɪˈkɔ:l/ *v.t.* **1** (*summon back*) от|зыва́ть, -озва́ть; **the ambassador was ~ed** посла́ отозва́ли. **2** (*bring back to mind*) нап|омина́ть, -о́мнить; **this ~s my childhood to me** э́то напомина́ет мне де́тство; **I ~ed his words** я вспо́мнил его́ слова́; **can you ~ where you lost the bag?** вы мо́жете припо́мнить, где вы оста́вили су́мку? **3** (*revoke*) отмен|я́ть, -и́ть.

recant /rɪˈkænt/ *v.t. & i.* публи́чно ка́яться, рас- (*в чём*); отр|ека́ться, -е́чься (*от чего*).

recantation /ˌri:kænˈteɪʃ(ə)n/ *n.* отрече́ние; публи́чное покая́ние.

recap /ˈri:kæp/ (*coll.*) *n.* повторе́ние.

● *v.t. & i.* (**recapped, recapping**) = **recapitulate**

recapitulate /ˌri:kəˈpɪtjʊˌleɪt/ *v.t.* повтор|я́ть, -и́ть; резюми́ровать (*impf., pf.*).

recapitulation /ˌri:kəˌpɪtjʊˈleɪʃ(ə)n/ *n.* повторе́ние; резюме́ (*indecl.*); сумми́рование.

recapture /ri:ˈkæptʃə(r)/ *n.* повто́рный захва́т; взя́тие обра́тно.

R

● *v.t.* взять (*pf.*) обра́тно; пойма́ть (*pf.*); **the prisoner was ~d** заключённого пойма́ли; (*fig.*) восстан|а́вливать, -ови́ть в па́мяти; **I tried to ~ my first impressions** я пыта́лся восстанови́ть свои́ пе́рвые впечатле́ния.

recast /riːˈkɑːst/ *v.t.* **1** (*cast again, e.g. a gun*) отл|ива́ть, -и́ть за́ново. **2** (*rewrite, rephrase*) перераб|а́тывать, -о́тать. **3** (*remodel, refashion*) переде́л|ывать, -ать. **4** (*change cast*) перераспредел|я́ть, -и́ть ро́ли в (*пьесе*).

recce /ˈrekɪ/ (*Br. coll.*) = **reconnaissance**

reced|e /rɪˈsiːd/ *v.i.* **1** (*move back*) отступ|а́ть, -и́ть; (*move away*) удал|я́ться, -и́ться; **the tide was ~ing** вода́ спада́ла; **~ing hair** реде́ющие во́лосы. **2** (*slope back*) отклоня́ться (*impf.*) наза́д; **a ~ing chin** сре́занный подборо́док. **3** (*diminish*) ум|еньша́ться, -е́ньшиться.

receipt /rɪˈsiːt/ *n.* **1** (*receiving*) получе́ние; **on ~ of the news** по получе́нии изве́стия; **I am in ~ of your letter** Ва́ше письмо́ мно́ю полу́чено. **2** (*pl., money received*) де́нежные поступле́ния, прихо́д. **3** (*written acknowledgement*) распи́ска, квита́нция.

● *v.t.*: **~ a bill** распи́с|ываться, -а́ться на счёте.

receive /rɪˈsiːv/ *v.t.* **1** (*get, be given*) получ|а́ть, -и́ть; **your letter will ~ attention** ва́ше письмо́ бу́дет рассмо́трено; **he ~d a warm welcome** ему́ оказа́ли тёплый приём; **he ~d injuries** он получи́л ране́ния; **he ~d severe punishment** он подве́ргся суро́вому наказа́нию; **information has not yet been ~d** све́дения ещё не поступи́ли; **he ~s stolen goods** (*Br.*) он укрыва́ет (*or* скупа́ет) кра́деное. **2** (*admit*) прин|има́ть, -я́ть; допус|ка́ть, -ти́ть; **I am not receiving guests** я не принима́ю госте́й; (*give reception to, greet*) прин|има́ть, -я́ть; **he was ~d with open arms** его́ встре́тили с распростёртыми объя́тиями; **how was your speech ~d?** как бы́ло встре́чено ва́ше выступле́ние?; **how did he ~ the news?** как он восприня́л э́ту но́вость? **3** (*accept as true, accurate etc.*) призн|ава́ть, -а́ть пра́вильным; **~d pronunciation** нормати́вное произноше́ние. **4** (*obtain signals from*): **are you receiving me?** вы меня́ слы́шите?; **can you ~ the BBC?** ваш приёмник принима́ет Би-Би-Си́?

receiver /rɪˈsiːvə(r)/ *n.* **1** получа́тель (*m.*); (*Br., of stolen goods*) укрыва́тель (*m.*)/ску́пщик кра́деного. **2** (*Br. also* **official ~**) ликвида́тор, управля́ющий ко́нкурсной ма́ссой. **3 (telephone ~)** (телефо́нная) тру́бка; **lift the ~** подн|има́ть, -я́ть тру́бку; **replace the ~** класть, положи́ть тру́бку. **4 (radio ~)** (радио)приёмник.

recension /rɪˈsenʃ(ə)n/ *n.* испра́вленный вариа́нт; (*act*) реда́кция.

recent /ˈriːs(ə)nt/ *adj.* **1** (*occurring lately*) неда́вний; **within ~ memory** за после́днее вре́мя. **2** (*modern*) совреме́нный.

recently /ˈriːsəntlɪ/ *adv.* неда́вно, на днях, за после́днее вре́мя; **until quite ~** ещё совсе́м неда́вно.

receptacle /rɪˈseptək(ə)l/ *n.* вмести́лище.

reception /rɪˈsepʃ(ə)n/ *n.* **1** (*of guests etc.*) приём; **they are having a ~** они́ даю́т приём; **~ centre** (*Br.*), **center** (*US*) приёмник; **~ desk** (*in hotel*) регистра́ция, конто́рка портье́; (*in hospital*) регистрату́ра; **~ room** приёмная. **2** (*greeting, display of feeling*) встре́ча, приём; **he was given a great ~** ему́ устро́или великоле́пный приём; **his book had a lukewarm ~** его́ кни́га была́ встре́чена хо́лодно. **3** (*of ideas etc.*) восприя́тие. **4** (*of radio signals*) приём; **~ is good in this area** в э́том райо́не хоро́ший приём.

receptionist /rɪˈsepʃənɪst/ *n.* (*in hotel, hospital*) регистра́тор, дежу́рный; (*in a business firm*) секрета́р|ь (*fem.* -ша) по приёму посети́телей.

receptive /rɪˈseptɪv/ *adj.* восприи́мчивый.

receptivity /ˌriːsepˈtɪvɪtɪ/ *n.* восприи́мчивость.

recess /rɪˈses/, /ˈriːses/ *n.* **1** (*vacation*) переры́в; **Parliament has gone into ~** парла́мент распу́щен на кани́кулы; (*US, between classes*) переме́на. **2** (*alcove, niche*) ни́ша, алько́в. **3** (*secret place*) тайни́к; **in the ~es of the heart** в глубине́ души́.

● *v.t.* (*set back*) отодв|ига́ть, -и́нуть наза́д.

● *v.i.* (*US, adjourn*): **the court ~ed** был объя́влен переры́в в заседа́нии суда́.

recession /rɪˈseʃ(ə)n/ *n.* (*slump*) спад.

recessive /rɪˈsesɪv/ *adj.*: **~ characteristic** (*biol.*) рецесси́вный при́знак; **~ gene** рецесси́вный ген.

recharge /riːˈtʃɑːdʒ/ *v.t.* перезаря|жа́ть, -ди́ть; **he ate to ~ his energies** он ел, что́бы восстанови́ть свои́ си́лы.

recherché /rəˈʃeəʃeɪ/ *adj.* экзоти́ческий; изы́сканный.

rechristen /riːˈkrɪs(ə)n/ *v.t.* (*fig.*) переимено́в|ывать, -а́ть.

recidivism /rɪˈsɪdɪvˌɪz(ə)m/ *n.* рециди́в.

recidivist /rɪˈsɪdɪvɪst/ *n.* рецидиви́ст.

recipe /ˈresɪpɪ/ *n.* (*lit., fig.*) реце́пт; **a ~ for happiness** секре́т сча́стья.

recipient /rɪˈsɪpɪənt/ *n.* получа́тель (*fem.* -ница).

reciprocal /rɪˈsɪprək(ə)l/ *adj.* (*mutual*) взаи́мный (*also gram.*), обою́дный.

reciprocat|e /rɪˈsɪprəˌkeɪt/ *v.t.* отв|еча́ть, -е́тить взаи́мностью; **she ~ed his feelings** она́ отвеча́ла ему́ взаи́мностью.

● *v.i.* **1** (*move back and forth*) дви́гаться (*impf.*) взад и вперёд; **~ing engine** поршнево́й дви́гатель. **2** (*make a return*) отпла́|чивать, -ти́ть; отвеча́ть (*impf.*) тем же; **I bought him a drink and he ~ed** я угости́л его́ вино́м, а он — меня́.

reciprocation /rɪˌsɪprəˈkeɪʃ(ə)n/ *n.* отве́тное де́йствие; обме́н.

reciprocity /ˌresɪˈprɒsɪtɪ/ *n.* взаи́мность; взаимоде́йствие; обме́н.

recital /rɪˈsaɪt(ə)l/ *n.* (*narration*) изложе́ние; (*entertainment*) со́льный конце́рт.

recitation /ˌresɪˈteɪʃ(ə)n/ *n.* деклама́ция; **there is to be a ~ from Shakespeare** бу́дут чита́ть отры́вки из Шекспи́ра.

recitative /ˌresɪtəˈtiːv/ *n.* речитати́в.

recite /rɪˈsaɪt/ *v.t.* (*declaim from memory*) деклами́ровать, про-; (*enumerate*) переч|исля́ть, -и́слить.

reckless /ˈreklɪs/ *adj.* безрассу́дный; отча́янный; **a ~ disregard of consequences** безду́мное пренебреже́ние после́дствиями; **he drove ~ly** он неосторо́жно вёл маши́ну.

recklessness /ˈreklɪsnɪs/ *n.* безрассу́дность, отча́янность.

reckon /ˈrekən/ *v.t.* **1** (*calculate*) счита́ть, вы́-; **he never ~s the cost** он никогда́ не учи́тывает расхо́дов; **charges are ~ed from the first of the month** пла́та исчисля́ется с пе́рвого числа́ ка́ждого ме́сяца. **2** (*consider, rate*) счита́ть (*impf.*); **do you ~ him to be a great writer?** вы счита́ете его́ вели́ким писа́телем? **3** (*coll., opine*) полага́ть (*impf.*); **I ~ he will win** я ду́маю, что он победи́т.

● *v.i.* **1** (*count*) счита́ть (*impf.*); **he is a man to be ~ed with** с таки́м челове́ком, как он, ну́жно счита́ться; **he ~ed without the English climate** он не взял в расчёт англи́йский кли́мат. **2** (*rely, depend*) рассчи́тывать (*impf.*) (*на кого/что*); **he ~ed on making a clear profit** он рассчи́тывал на чи́стую при́быль.

reckoner /ˈrekənə(r)/ *n.*: **ready ~** сбо́рник вычисли́тельных табли́ц.

reckoning /ˈrekənɪŋ/ *n.* **1** (*calculation*) счёт, вычисле́ние; **dead ~** (*nav., aeron.*) навигацио́нное счисле́ние; **he is out in his ~** он оши́бся в расчётах. **2** (*account*) распла́та; **day of ~** (*fig.*) час распла́ты.

reclaim /rɪˈkleɪm/ *v.t.* **1** (*bring under cultivation*) осв|а́ивать, -о́ить. **2** (*demand return of*) тре́бовать, по- обра́тно.

reclamation /ˌrekləˈmeɪʃ(ə)n/ *n.* освое́ние.

reclassification /riːˌklæsɪfɪˈkeɪʃ(ə)n/ *n.* перево́д в другу́ю катего́рию; пересортиро́вка.

reclassify /riːˈklæsɪˌfaɪ/ *v.t.* перев|оди́ть, -ести́ в другу́ю катего́рию; пересорти́ро́в|ывать, -а́ть; переклассифици́ровать (*impf.*, *pf.*).

recline /rɪˈklaɪn/ *v.t.* отки́|дывать, -и́нуть ; **she ~d her head on his shoulder** она́ склони́ла го́лову ему́ на плечо́; **he ~d his head against the back of the chair** он сиде́л, отки́нув го́лову на спи́нку кре́сла.

● *v.i.* (полу)лежа́ть (*impf.*); возлежа́ть (*impf.*); **they ~d on the ground** они́ разлегли́сь на земле́; **reclining nude** лежа́щая обнажённая.

recluse /rɪˈkluːs/ *n.* затво́рник, отше́льник.

recognition /ˌrekəgˈnɪʃ(ə)n/ *n.* **1** (*knowing again*) опознава́ние; **he changed beyond ~** он измени́лся до неузнава́емости. **2** (*acknowledgement*) призна́ние; **he received a cheque** (*Br.*), **check** (*US*) **in ~ of his services** он получи́л чек в знак призна́ния его́ услу́г.

recognizable /ˈrekəgˌnaɪzəb(ə)l/ *adj.* опознава́емый.

recognize /ˈrekəgˌnaɪz/ *v.t.* **1** (*know again*) узн|ава́ть, -а́ть; **I could barely ~ him** я его́ е́ле узна́л. **2** (*acknowledge*) призн|ава́ть, -а́ть; **he was ~d as the lawful heir** он был при́знан зако́нным насле́дником.

recoil *n.* /ˈriːkɔɪl/ отско́к; отда́ча.

● *v.i.* /rɪˈkɔɪl/ **1** (*shrink back*) отпря́нуть (*pf.*); отпры́г|ивать, -нуть; отша́т|ываться, -ну́ться; **the sight made him ~ with horror** зре́лище заста́вило его́ отпря́нуть в у́жасе. **2** (*of gun*) отка́т|ываться, -и́ться; (*of rifle*) отд|ава́ть, -а́ть.

recollect /ˌrekəˈlekt/ *v.t.* всп|омина́ть, -о́мнить; прип|омина́ть, -о́мнить.

recollection /ˌrekəˈlekʃ(ə)n/ *n.* па́мять; воспомина́ние; **to the best of my ~** наско́лько я по́мню.

recommence /ˌriːkəˈmens/ *v.t.* возобнов|ля́ть, -и́ть; нач|ина́ть, -а́ть сно́ва.

● *v.i.* возобнов|ля́ться, -и́ться.

recommend /ˌrekəˈmend/ *v.t.* **1** (*speak well of, suggest as suitable*) рекомендова́ть (*impf., pf.*), от-/по- (*pf.*); сове́товать, по-; **he was ~ed for promotion** его́ вы́двинули на повыше́ние. **2** (*advise*) рекомендова́ть, по- + *d.*; сове́товать, по- + *d.*

recommendation /ˌrekəˌmenˈdeɪʃ(ə)n/ *n.* рекоменда́ция; **I bought the shares on your ~** я купи́л а́кции по ва́шей рекоменда́ции; **my ~ would be to sell them** я бы посове́товал прода́ть их; **letter of ~** рекоменда́тельное письмо́.

recompense /ˈrekəmˌpens/ *n.* компенса́ция; **in ~ for your help** в награ́ду за ва́шу по́мощь.

● *v.t.* компенси́ровать (*impf., pf.*); **he was amply ~d for his trouble** его́ ще́дро вознагради́ли за его́ уси́лия.

reconcilable /ˈrekənˌsaɪləb(ə)l/ *adj.* (*compatible*) совмести́мый (*с чем*).

reconcile /ˈrekənˌsaɪl/ *v.t.* **1** (*make friendly*) мири́ть, по-; **they finally became ~d** они́, наконе́ц, помири́лись. **2** (*settle, compose*) ула́|живать, -дить; **their differences were ~d** они́ ула́дили свои́ разногла́сия. **3** (*cause to agree, make compatible*) совме|ща́ть, -сти́ть; согласо́в|ывать, -а́ть; **how can you ~ this with your principles?** как же э́то сочета́ется с ва́шими при́нципами? **4** (*resign*): **~ o.s.** смир|я́ться, -и́ться (*с чем*); примир|я́ться, -и́ться (*с чем*); **you must ~ yourself to a life of poverty** вы должны́ примири́ться с пожи́зненной бе́дностью.

reconciliation /ˌrekənˌsɪlɪˈeɪʃ(ə)n/ *n.* примире́ние; ула́живание.

recondite /ˈrekənˌdaɪt/, /rɪˈkɒn-/ *adj.* (*incomprehensible*) зау́мный; (*little-known*) малоизве́стный.

recondition /ˌriːkənˈdɪʃ(ə)n/ *v.t.* ремонти́ровать, от-.

reconnaissance /rɪˈkɒnɪs(ə)ns/ *n.* разве́дка, рекогносциро́вка; **~ party** разве́дывательная гру́ппа.

reconnoitre /ˌrekəˈnɔɪtə(r)/ (*US* **reconnoiter**) *v.t. & i.* разве́дывать (*impf.*); производи́ть (*impf.*) разве́дку/рекогносциро́вку.

reconquer /riːˈkɒŋkə(r)/ *v.t.* отвоёв|ывать, -а́ть.

reconquest /riːˈkɒŋkwest/ *n.* возвраще́ние, возвра́т (потеря́нной террито́рии *и т.п.*).

reconsider /ˌriːkənˈsɪdə(r)/ *v.t.* пересм|а́тривать, -отре́ть.

● *v.i.* переду́мать (*pf.*).

reconsideration /ˌriːkənˌsɪdəˈreɪʃ(ə)n/ *n.* пересмо́тр; измене́ние реше́ния; **on ~ he decided to stay** поду́мав, он реши́л оста́ться.

reconstitute /riːˈkɒnstɪˌtjuːt/ *v.t.* воспроизв|оди́ть, -ести́.

reconstitution /ˌriːkɒnstɪˈtjuːʃ(ə)n/ *n.* воспроизведе́ние, воссозда́ние.

reconstruct /ˌriːkənˈstrʌkt/ *v.t.* (*in the original form*) восстан|а́вливать, -ови́ть; воссозд|ава́ть, -а́ть; (*changing the original*) перестр|а́ивать, -о́ить; реконструи́ровать (*impf., pf.*); (*fig.*) воспроизв|оди́ть, -ести́; **the police ~ed the crime** поли́ция воспроизвела́ карти́ну преступле́ния.

reconstruction /ˌriːkənˈstrʌkʃ(ə)n/ *n.* восстановле́ние, воссозда́ние; перестро́йка, реконстру́кция; (*of acts etc.*) воспроизведе́ние, воссозда́ние.

reconvene /ˌriːkənˈviːn/ *v.t.* соз|ыва́ть, -ва́ть вновь.

● *v.i.* соб|ира́ться, -ра́ться вновь.

reconversion /ˌriːkənˈvɜːʃ(ə)n/ *n.* (*e.g. of currency*) реконве́рсия; (*of industry*) перево́д на ми́рные ре́льсы.

reconvert /ˌriːkənˈvɜːt/ *v.t.* пров|оди́ть, -ести́ реконве́рсию + *g.*; (*industry*) перев|оди́ть, -ести́ на ми́рные ре́льсы.

record¹ /ˈrekɔːd/ *n.* **1** (*written note, document*) за́пись, учёт; **the teacher keeps a ~ of attendance** учи́тель ведёт учёт посеща́емости; **weather ~s** регистра́ция метеорологи́ческих да́нных; **~s department** отде́л учёта; **R~ Office** госуда́рственный архи́в. **2** (*state of being recorded, esp. as evidence*) за́пись; **it is a matter of ~** э́то зафикси́ровано/зарегистри́ровано; **it is on ~ that you lost every game** изве́стно, что вы проигра́ли все ма́тчи; **it was the hottest day on ~** э́то был са́мый жа́ркий день из ра́нее зафикси́рованных; **I went on ~ as opposing the plan** в протоко́ле бы́ло отме́чено, что я про́тив э́того пла́на; **this is off the ~** э́то не должно́ быть пре́дано огла́ске. **3** (*relic of past*) па́мятник; **~s of past civilizations** па́мятники про́шлых цивилиза́ций. **4** (*chronicle*) ле́топись; **the film provides an interesting ~ of the war** э́тот фильм интере́сен как ле́топись войны́. **5** (*past conduct, achievement*) про́шлое; **attendance ~** посеща́емость; **he has an honourable** (*Br.*), **honorable** (*US*) **~ of service** у него́ безупре́чный послужно́й спи́сок; **this firm has a bad ~ for strikes** э́та фи́рма изве́стна многочи́сленными забасто́вками; **his ~ is against him** его́ про́шлое говори́т про́тив него́; **the defendant had a (criminal) ~** у обвиня́емого ра́нее име́лись суди́мости. **6** (*sound recording*) (грам)пласти́нка; **long-playing ~** долгоигра́ющая пласти́нка; **they made a new ~ of the song** вы́пустили ещё одну́ за́пись э́той пе́сни. **7** (*best performance*) реко́рд; **world ~** реко́рд ми́ра; **she set a new ~ for the mile** она́ установи́ла но́вый реко́рд в бе́ге на одну́ ми́лю; **England held the ~ for some years** э́тот реко́рд принадлежа́л А́нглии не́сколько лет; **he will easily beat the ~** он легко́ побьёт реко́рд; (*attr.*) реко́рдный, небыва́лый; **cars have had ~ sales** про́дано реко́рдное коли́чество маши́н.

● *cpds.* **~-breaking** *adj.* реко́рдный; **~-holder** *n.* рекордсме́н (*fem.* -ка); **~-player** *n.* прои́грыватель (*m.*).

record² /rɪˈkɔːd/ *v.t.* **1** (*set down in writing, or fig.*) запи́с|ывать, -а́ть; **the book ~s his early years** в кни́ге отражены́ его́ молоды́е го́ды. **2** (*on tape, film etc.*) запи́с|ывать, -а́ть (на плёнку). **3** (*of instrument: register*) регистри́ровать, за-; **the thermometer ~ed zero** термо́метр пока́зывал ноль.

recorder /rɪˈkɔːdə(r)/ *n.* (*Br., magistrate*) реко́рдер; (*apparatus*) магнитофо́н; (*mus.*) (англи́йская) фле́йта.

recording /rɪˈkɔːdɪŋ/ *n.* (*putting on record*) за́пись, регистра́ция; (*registering of sound or TV*) звукоза́пись; видеоза́пись; (*recorded performance etc.*) за́пись.

● *cpd.* **~ studio** *n.* сту́дия звукоза́писи.

recount¹ *n.* /ˈriːkaʊnt/ (*second count*) пересчёт.

● *v.t.* /riːˈkaʊnt/ пересчи́т|ывать, -а́ть.

recount² /rɪˈkaʊnt/ *v.t.* (*narrate*) расска́з|ывать, -а́ть.

recoup /rɪˈkuːp/ *v.t.* **1** (*recover*): **~ one's losses** возвраща́ть, верну́ть потеря́нное. **2** (*compensate*) возме|ща́ть, -сти́ть (*что кому*). **3** (*leg., deduct*) удерж|ивать, -а́ть.

recourse /rɪˈkɔːs/ *n.* прибе́жище; вы́ход; **your only ~ is legal action** вам ничего́ не остаётся де́лать, как обрати́ться в суд; **have ~ to** приб|ега́ть, -е́гнуть к + *d.*

recover /rɪˈkʌvə(r)/ *v.t.* **1** (*regain, retrieve*) получ|а́ть, -и́ть обра́тно; доста́ть (*pf.*), верну́ть (*pf.*); **he tried to**

R

~ his losses он пыта́лся верну́ть потёрянное; **he quickly ~ed his health** он бы́стро вы́здоровел; **she never ~ed consciousness** она́ так и не пришла́ в созна́ние; **he ~ed his appetite** к нему́ возврати́лся аппети́т; **she was badly shocked, but ~ed herself** она́ была́ си́льно потрясена́, но пото́м пришла́ в себя́; **he staggered, but ~ed himself** он оступи́лся, но сохрани́л равнове́сие; (*win back*) отвоёв|ывать, -а́ть; **much land has been ~ed from the sea** мно́го су́ши отвоёвано у мо́ря.
2 (*secure by legal process*) взы́ск|ивать, -а́ть в суде́бном поря́дке; **an action to ~ damages** иск о возмеще́нии уще́рба.

● *v.i.* **1** (*revive*) попр|авля́ться, -а́виться; опр|авля́ться, -а́виться; **has he quite ~ed (from his illness)?** оконча́тельно ли он опра́вился от боле́зни?; **I have quite ~ed** я по́лностью вы́здоровел; **it took me some time to ~ from my astonishment** я до́лго не мог прийти́ в себя́ от удивле́ния; **we must help the country to ~** мы должны́ помо́чь стране́ сно́ва встать на́ ноги. **2** (*leg.*) возме|ща́ть, -сти́ть по суду́.

re-cover /riːˈkʌvə(r)/ *v.t.* перекр|ыва́ть, -ы́ть; **the chair needs ~ing** стул на́до оби́ть на́ново.

recovery /rɪˈkʌvərɪ/ *n.* **1** (*regaining possession; reclamation*) возвра́т; возмеще́ние; **the ~ of your money will take time** пройдёт вре́мя, пре́жде чем вы полу́чите свои́ де́ньги обра́тно; **the ~ of marshland** осуше́ние боло́т. **2** (*revival; restoration to health*) выздоровле́ние; **he made a rapid ~** он бы́стро попра́вился; **his business made a ~** его́ дела́ пошли́ на попра́вку. **3** (*rehabilitation; restoration to use*) восстановле́ние; **~ vehicle** авари́йный автомоби́ль.

re-create /ˌriːkrɪˈeɪt/ *v.t.* вновь созд|ава́ть, -а́ть; воссозд|ава́ть, -а́ть.

recreation /ˌrekrɪˈeɪʃ(ə)n/ *n.* о́тдых; развлече́ние; **he plays chess for ~** он отдыха́ет, игра́я в ша́хматы; **~ ground** (*Br.*) спортплоща́дка; площа́дка для игр.

recrimination /rɪˌkrɪmɪˈneɪʃ(ə)n/ *n.* встре́чное обвине́ние.

recrudescence /ˌriːkruːˈdesəns/, /ˌrek-/ *n.* (*of illness*) втори́чное заболева́ние; (*fig.*) рециди́в; но́вая вспы́шка.

recruit /rɪˈkruːt/ *n.* (*mil.*) новобра́нец; **raw ~** (*fig.*) новичо́к; (*new member*) но́вый член/уча́стник.

● *v.t.* (*enlist*) вербова́ть, за-; наб|ира́ть, -ра́ть; **~ing sergeant** сержа́нт по вербо́вке на вое́нную слу́жбу.

recruitment /rɪˈkruːtmənt/ *n.* вербо́вка.

recta /ˈrektə/ *pl. of* ⇒**rectum**

rectangle /ˈrekˌtæŋɡ(ə)l/ *n.* прямоуго́льник.

rectangular /rekˈtæŋɡjʊlə(r)/ *adj.* прямоуго́льный.

rectification /ˌrektɪfɪˈkeɪʃ(ə)n/ *n.* (*correction*) исправле́ние; (*elec.*) выпрямле́ние.

rectifier /ˈrektɪˌfaɪə(r)/ *n.* (*elec.*) выпрями́тель (*m.*).

rectify /ˈrektɪˌfaɪ/ *v.t.* **1** (*correct*) испр|авля́ть, -а́вить; **I am trying to ~ the situation** я пыта́юсь испра́вить положе́ние. **2** (*elec.*) выпрямля́ть, вы́прямить.

rectilinear /ˌrektɪˈlɪnɪə(r)/ *adj.* прямолине́йный.

rectitude /ˈrektɪˌtjuːd/ *n.* че́стность, прямота́.

recto /ˈrektəʊ/ *n.* (*pl.* **~s**) лицева́я сторона́.

rector /ˈrektə(r)/ *n.* (*Br.*) (*clergyman*) ≈ прихо́дский свяще́нник; (*of university*) ре́ктор.

rectory /ˈrektərɪ/ *n.* (*Br.*) дом прихо́дского свяще́нника.

rectum /ˈrektəm/ *n.* (*pl.* **rectums** *or* **recta**) пряма́я кишка́.

recumbent /rɪˈkʌmbənt/ *adj.* лежа́чий, лежа́щий; **in a ~ posture** в лежа́чем положе́нии.

recuperate /rɪˈkuːpəˌreɪt/ *v.i.* попр|авля́ться, -а́виться.

recuperation /rɪˌkuːpəˈreɪʃ(ə)n/ *n.* выздоровле́ние.

recur /rɪˈkɜː(r)/ *v.i.* **(recurred, recurring) 1** (*occur repeatedly*) повтор|я́ться, -и́ться; **a ~ring headache** хрони́ческие головны́е бо́ли (*f. pl.*); **it is a ~ring problem** э́то постоя́нно возника́ющая пробле́ма; **~ring decimal** периоди́ческая десяти́чная дробь. **2** (*return*) возвра|ща́ться, -ти́ться; **the thought often ~s to me** э́та мысль ча́сто меня́ посеща́ет.

recurrence /rɪˈkʌrəns/ *n.* повторе́ние; возвра́т.

recurrent /rɪˈkʌrənt/ *adj.* повторя́ющийся.

recycle /riːˈsaɪk(ə)l/ *v.t.* перераб|а́тывать, -о́тать; **~d paper** бума́га из утиля́.

recycling /riːˈsaɪklɪŋ/ *n.* повто́рное испо́льзование, перерабо́тка.

red /red/ *n.* **1** кра́сный цвет; **the article made me see ~** (*fig.*) статья́ привела́ меня́ в бе́шенство; (*of clothes*): **~ doesn't suit her** кра́сное ей не идёт; **she was dressed in ~** она́ была́ оде́та в кра́сное.
2 (*debit side of account*) долг, задо́лженность; **in the ~** в долга́х; **my account is in the ~** у меня́ задо́лженность в ба́нке; **how can I get out of the ~?** как мне вы́йти из долго́в?
3 (*coll., Communist*) «кра́сный».

● *adj.* **(redder, reddest) 1** кра́сный; а́лый; **she went ~ in the face** она́ покрасне́ла; **he was ~ with anger** он покрасне́л от гне́ва; **let's go out and paint the town ~!** (*coll.*) (дава́й) пойдём поку́тим!; **~ admiral** (*butterfly*) ба́бочка-адмира́л; **R~ Crescent** Кра́сный Полуме́сяц; **R~ Cross** Кра́сный Крест; **~ deer** благоро́дный оле́нь; **~ flag** (*danger signal*) кра́сный флажо́к; (*pol.*) кра́сный флаг, кра́сное зна́мя; **~ heat** кра́сное кале́ние; **R~ Indian** (*offens.*) красноко́жий, инде́ец; (*adj.*) красноко́жий; **~ lead** (*min.*) свинцо́вый су́рик; **~ light** (*warning signal*) сигна́л опа́сности; **~ light district** кварта́л публи́чных домо́в; **~ meat** чёрное мя́со; **it was like a ~ rag to a bull** э́то подействова́ло, как кра́сная тря́пка на быка́; **the R~ Sea** Кра́сное мо́ре; **~ tape** (*fig.*) канцеля́рская волоки́та.
2 (*coll., Soviet*): **the R~ Air Force** сове́тские вое́нно-возду́шные си́лы.

● *cpds.* **~-blooded** *adj.* (*fig.*) энерги́чный; му́жественный; **~breast** *n.* (*Br.*) мали́новка; **~-cheeked** *adj.* краснощёкий; **~currant** *n.* кра́сная сморо́дина; **~-eyed** *adj.* (*from weeping*) с глаза́ми, кра́сными от слёз; **~-haired** *adj.* рыжеволо́сый; **~-handed** *adj.*: **he was caught ~-handed** его́ пойма́ли на ме́сте преступле́ния (*or* с поли́чным); **~head** *n.* ры́жий челове́к; **~-headed** *adj.* ры́жий; **~-hot** *adj.* раскалённый докрасна́; (*fig.*) (*fervent*) горя́чий, пы́лкий; **a ~-hot socialist** пла́менный социали́ст; (*exciting*): **~-hot news** сенсацио́нное сообще́ние; **~-letter** *adj.* пра́здничный; **it was a ~-letter day for me** э́то бы́ло для меня́ пра́здником; **~wood** *n.* (*bot.*) секво́йя.

redden /ˈred(ə)n/ *v.t.* окра́|шивать, -сить в кра́сный цвет.

● *v.i.* красне́ть, по-; покр|ыва́ться, -ы́ться багря́нцем.

reddish /ˈredɪʃ/ *adj.* краснова́тый.

redecorate /riːˈdekəˌreɪt/ *v.t.* отде́л|ывать, -ать; ремонти́ровать, от-.

redecoration /riːˌdekəˈreɪʃ(ə)n/ *n.* отде́лка; ремо́нт.

redeem /rɪˈdiːm/ *v.t.* **1** (*get back, recover*) выкупа́ть, вы́купить; восстан|а́вливать, -ови́ть; **the mortgage was ~ed** зало́г был вы́плачен; **he was able to ~ his honour** (*Br.*), **honor** (*US*) он смог восстанови́ть свою́ честь. **2** (*fulfil*) выполня́ть, вы́полнить; **he ~ed his promise** он вы́полнил обеща́ние.
3 (*save from sin*): **Christ came to ~ sinners** Христо́с пришёл искупи́ть грехи́ люде́й. **4** (*compensate, make up for*) искуп|а́ть, -и́ть; компенси́ровать (*impf., pf.*); **he has one ~ing feature** у него́ есть одно́ положи́тельное ка́чество.

redeemable /rɪˈdiːməb(ə)l/ *adj.* (*subject to purchase*) подлежа́щий вы́купу/погаше́нию.

redeemer /rɪˈdiːmə(r)/ *n.* спаси́тель, искупи́тель (*both m.*).

redefine /ˌriːdɪˈfaɪn/ *v.t.* определ|я́ть, -и́ть за́ново.

redefinition /ˌriːdefɪˈnɪʃ(ə)n/ *n.* но́вое определе́ние.

redemption /rɪˈdempʃ(ə)n/ *n.* **1** (*repurchase*) вы́куп. **2** (*fulfilment*): **~ of a promise** выполне́ние обеща́ния. **3** (*deliverance*) искупле́ние; **past ~** без наде́жды на спасе́ние.

redemptive /rɪˈdemptɪv/ *adj.* искупи́тельный, искупа́ющий.

redeploy /ˌriːdɪˈplɔɪ/ *v.t. & i.* (*mil.*) передислоци́ровать(ся) (*impf., pf.*); (*of resources*) перераспредел|я́ть, -и́ть.

redeployment /ˌriːdɪˈplɔɪmənt/ *n.* передислока́ция; перераспределе́ние.

re-design /ˌriːdɪˈzaɪn/ *v.t.* за́ново (с)конструи́ровать (*pf.*).

redevelop /ˌriːdɪˈveləp/ *v.t.* перестр|а́ивать, -о́ить.

redevelopment /ˌriːdɪˈveləpmənt/ *n.* перестро́йка.

redial /riːˈdaɪ(ə)l/ *v.t. & i.* повто́рно наб|ира́ть, -ра́ть (но́мер).

redirect /ˌriːdaɪˈrekt/, /-dɪˈrekt/ *v.t.* (*e.g. letters*) переадресо́в|ывать, -а́ть; (*re-route*): **the traffic was ~ed** тра́нспорт был напра́влен по друго́му маршру́ту; (*fig.*): **his efforts were ~ed to a new goal** его́ уси́лия бы́ли обращены́ на другу́ю цель.

redirection /ˌriːdaɪˈrekʃ(ə)n/, /-dɪˈrekʃ(ə)n/ *n.* (*of letter*) переадресова́ние, переадресо́вка; (*transfer*) перебро́ска.

rediscover /ˌriːdɪˈskʌvə(r)/ *v.t.* откр|ыва́ть, -ы́ть за́ново.

rediscovery /ˌriːdɪˈskʌvərɪ/ *n.* за́ново сде́ланное откры́тие.

redistribute /riːˌdɪˈstrɪbjuːt/ *v.t.* перераспредел|я́ть, -и́ть.

redistribution /riːˌdɪstrɪˈbjuːʃ(ə)n/ *n.* перераспределе́ние.

redo /riːˈduː/ *v.t.* переде́л|ывать, -ать.

redolent /ˈredələnt/ *adj.*: ~ (*fig., suggestive*) **of** отдаю́щий (*чем*), напомина́ющий (*что*).

redouble /riːˈdʌb(ə)l/ *v.t. & i.* удв|а́ивать(ся), -о́ить(ся); **he ~d his efforts** он удво́ил свои́ уси́лия.

redoubt /rɪˈdaʊt/ *n.* реду́т.

redoubtable /rɪˈdaʊtəb(ə)l/ *adj.* гро́зный; устраша́ющий.

redound /rɪˈdaʊnd/ *v.i.*: ~ **to** спосо́бствовать (*impf.*) + *d.*; **this will ~ to your credit** э́то укрепи́т ва́шу репута́цию.

redraft /riːˈdrɑːft/ *n.* но́вый прое́кт; но́вая формулиро́вка, реда́кция.

● *v.t.* перепи́с|ывать, -а́ть.

redraw /riːˈdrɔː/ *v.t.* (*draw again*) рисова́ть, на- за́ново; (*reformulate*) сост|авля́ть, -а́вить за́ново; (*change*) измен|я́ть, -и́ть.

redress /rɪˈdres/ *n.* возмеще́ние; **I shall seek ~** я бу́ду добива́ться компенса́ции.

● *v.t.* возме|ща́ть, -сти́ть; **their victory ~ed the balance of forces** их побе́да восстанови́ла равнове́сие сил; **her grievances were ~ed** её жа́лобы бы́ли удовлетворены́.

reduce /rɪˈdjuːs/ *v.t.* **1** (*make less or smaller*) ум|еньша́ть, -е́ньшить; сокра|ща́ть, -ти́ть; **we must ~ our expenditure** мы должны́ сократи́ть расхо́ды; **in ~d circumstances** в стеснённых обстоя́тельствах; **exercise will ~ your weight** заря́дка помо́жет вам сба́вить вес; (*lower*) сн|ижа́ть, -и́зить; сб|авля́ть, -а́вить; **'~ speed now'** «води́тель, притормози́!»; **all prices are ~d** все це́ны сни́жены; **interest is paid at a ~d rate** проце́нт выпла́чивается по пони́женной ста́вке; (*shorten*) сокра|ща́ть, -ти́ть; **his sentence was ~d to 6 months** ему́ сократи́ли пригово́р до шести́ ме́сяцев; (*make narrower*) сужа́ть, су́зить; (*weaken*) осл|абля́ть, -а́бить; (*demote*) пон|ижа́ть, -и́зить в до́лжности; **he was ~d to the ranks** его́ разжа́ловали в рядовы́е. **2** (*bring, compel*) дов|оди́ть, -ести́ (*до чего*); вынужда́ть, вы́нудить; **the film ~d her to tears** фильм растро́гал её до слёз; **I was ~d to silence** мне пришло́сь промолча́ть; **the rebels were ~d to submission** мятéжников заста́вили прекрати́ть сопротивле́ние; **the family was ~d to begging** семья́ была́ обречена́ на нищету́. **3** (*convert*) превра|ща́ть, -ти́ть; **the proposition, ~d to its simplest terms** предложе́ние в преде́льно упрощённом ви́де; **all fractions can be ~d to decimals** все дро́би мо́жно перевести́ в десяти́чные; **the logs were ~d to ashes** поле́нья сгоре́ли дотла́; **he was ~d to a skeleton** он преврати́лся в скеле́т.

● *v.i.* **1** (*become less*) сн|ижа́ться, -и́зиться; ум|еньша́ться, -е́ньшиться. **2** (*US, lose weight*) худе́ть (*impf.*); соблюда́ть (*impf.*) дие́ту для похуде́ния; **a reducing diet** дие́та для поте́ри ве́са.

reducible /rɪˈdjuːsɪb(ə)l/ *adj.*: ~ **to** сводимый к + *d.*

reductio ad absurdum /rɪˌdʌktɪəʊ æd æbˈzɜːdəm/ *n.* доведе́ние до абсу́рда.

reduction /rɪˈdʌkʃ(ə)n/ *n.* **1** (*decrease*) сокраще́ние; сниже́ние; **a ~ in numbers** коли́чественное сокраще́ние; **price ~s** сниже́ние цен; **is there a ~ for children?** есть ли ски́дка для дете́й?; **~ in rank** пониже́ние в зва́нии; **~ of armaments** сокраще́ние вооруже́ний; **~ of temperature** сниже́ние температу́ры; (*shortening*) сокраще́ние; (*narrowing*) суже́ние; (*demotion*) пониже́ние; **~ to the ranks** разжа́лование (в солда́ты). **2** (*conversion*) перево́д; превраще́ние. **3** (*reduced copy of picture etc.*) уме́ньшенная ко́пия.

redundanc|y /rɪˈdʌnd(ə)nsɪ/ *n.* (*superfluity*) изли́шек, избы́точность; (*Br., in work-force*) (*unemployment*) безрабо́тица; (*dismissal*) увольне́ние; **there will be more ~ies in the building industry** в строи́тельной промы́шленности ожида́ются но́вые увольне́ния.

redundant /rɪˈdʌnd(ə)nt/ *adj.* изли́шний, избы́точный; **the last sentence is ~** после́днее предложе́ние изли́шне; **many workers were made ~** (*Br.*) мно́гих рабо́чих уво́лили.

reduplicate /rɪˈdjuːplɪˌkeɪt/ *v.t.* удв|а́ивать, -о́ить.

reduplication /rɪˌdjuːplɪˈkeɪʃ(ə)n/ *n.* удвое́ние.

re-echo /riːˈekəʊ/ *v.i.* повтор|я́ться, -и́ться э́хом; откл|ика́ться, -и́кнуться.

● *v.t.* повтор|я́ть, -и́ть ещё раз.

reed /riːd/ *n.* **1** (*bot.*) тростни́к, камы́ш. **2** (*mus.*) язычо́к; **the ~s** (*of an orchestra*) язычко́вые инструме́нты (*m. pl.*).

re-edit /riːˈedɪt/ *v.t.* за́ново отредакти́ровать (*pf.*).

re-educate /riːˈedjʊˌkeɪt/ *v.t.* перевоспи́т|ывать, -а́ть.

re-education /riːˌedjʊˈkeɪʃ(ə)n/ *n.* перевоспита́ние.

reedy /ˈriːdɪ/ *adj.* (**reedier, reediest**) **1** (*full of reeds*) тростнико́вый; заро́сший тростнико́м. **2** (*of sounds*) пронзи́тельный.

reef[1] /riːf/ *n.* (*geog.*) риф; подво́дная скала́.

reef[2] /riːf/ *n.* (*naut.*) риф.

● *v.t.*: ~ **a sail** брать, взять ри́фы.

● *cpd.* **~-knot** *n.* ри́фовый/прямо́й у́зел.

reefer[1] /ˈriːfə(r)/ *n.* (*jacket*) бушла́т.

reefer[2] /ˈriːfə(r)/ *n.* (*sl., marijuana cigarette*) сигаре́та с марихуа́ной.

reek /riːk/ *n.* вонь.

● *v.i.* воня́ть, про-; **his clothes ~ed of tobacco** от его́ оде́жды несло́ табако́м; (*fig.*) попа́хивать, па́хнуть (*both impf.*); **the affair ~s of corruption** де́ло па́хнет корру́пцией.

reel[1] /riːl/ *n.* (*winding device*) кату́шка; руло́н; **a ~ of thread, cotton** кату́шка ни́ток; **a ~ of film for a camera** кату́шка плёнки для фотоаппара́та.

● *v.t.* нам|а́тывать, -ота́ть.

● *with advs.*: **the fisherman ~ed in the line** рыба́к смота́л у́дочку; **the guide ~ed off a lot of dates** гид вы́палил це́лый ряд истори́ческих дат.

reel[2] /riːl/ *v.i.* кружи́ться (*impf.*); верте́ться (*impf.*); **he ~ed under the blow** он зашата́лся от уда́ра; **it makes the mind ~** от э́того голова́ кру́гом идёт; **the drunkard went ~ing home** шата́ясь, пья́ница поплёлся домо́й.

reel[3] /riːl/ *n.* (*dance*) рил; хорово́д.

re-elect /ˌriːɪˈlekt/ *v.t.* переизб|ира́ть, -ра́ть.

re-election /ˌriːɪˈlekʃ(ə)n/ *n.* переизбра́ние.

re-embark /ˌriːɪmˈbɑːk/ *v.i.* возвра|ща́ться, -ти́ться на́ борт.

re-embarkation /ˌriːɪmˌbɑːˈkeɪʃ(ə)n/ *n.* возвраще́ние на́ борт.

re-emerge /ˌriːɪˈmɜːdʒ/ *v.i.* вновь появ|ля́ться, -и́ться.

re-emergence /ˌriːɪˈmɜːdʒ(ə)ns/ *n.* появле́ние вновь.

re-emphasis /riːˈemfəsɪs/ *n.* повто́рное подчёркивание.

re-emphasize /riːˈemfəˌsaɪz/ *v.t.* подчёрк|ивать, -ну́ть сно́ва (*or* ещё раз).

re-enact /ˌriːɪˈnækt/ *v.t.* (*an event*) прои́гр|ывать, -а́ть в ли́цах; (*a law*) вновь вв|оди́ть, -ести́ в де́йствие.

re-enactment /ˌriːɪˈnæktmənt/ *n.* прои́грывание в ли́цах; повто́рный ввод в де́йствие.

R

re-engage /ˌriːɪnˈgeɪdʒ/ *v.t.*: **he ~d the clutch** он вновь включи́л сцепле́ние; **the workers were laid off and then ~d** рабо́чих уво́лили, а пото́м вновь при́няли на рабо́ту.

re-engagement /ˌriːɪnˈgeɪdʒmənt/ *n.* **1** (*of clutch, gearing etc.*) повто́рное включе́ние. **2** (*of workers*) восстановле́ние на рабо́те.

re-enlist /ˌriːɪnˈlɪst/ *v.i.* поступ|а́ть, -и́ть на сверхсро́чную слу́жбу.

re-enlistment /ˌriːɪnˈlɪstmənt/ *n.* поступле́ние на сверхсро́чную слу́жбу.

re-enter /riːˈentə(r)/ *v.i.* сно́ва входи́ть, войти́ в + *a.*; возвраща́ться, верну́ться в + *a.*

re-entry /riːˈentrɪ/ *n.* вхожде́ние/вступле́ние за́ново; **~ module** возвраща́емый отсе́к; **~ into the atmosphere** возвра́т в атмосфе́ру.

re-equip /ˌriːɪˈkwɪp/ *v.t.* переосна|ща́ть, -сти́ть.

re-equipment /ˌriːɪˈkwɪpmənt/ *n.* переоснаще́ние.

re-establish /ˌriːɪˈstæblɪʃ/ *v.t.* восстан|а́вливать, -ови́ть.

re-establishment /ˌriːɪˈstæblɪʃmənt/ *n.* восстановле́ние.

re-examination /ˌriːɪgˌzæmɪˈneɪʃ(ə)n/ *n.* повто́рное рассмотре́ние; переэкзамено́вка.

re-examine /ˌriːɪgˈzæmɪn/ *v.t.* вновь рассм|а́тривать, -отре́ть; пересм|а́тривать, -отре́ть; (*acad.*) втори́чно экзаменова́ть, про-.

re-export /riːˈekspɔːt/ *n.* реэ́кспорт.

● *v.t.* реэкспорти́ровать (*impf., pf.*).

ref /ref/ (*coll.*) = **referee** 2

reface /riːˈfeɪs/ *v.t.* за́ново отде́л|ывать, -ать.

refashion /riːˈfæʃ(ə)n/ *v.t.* перемодели́ровать (*impf., pf.*); переина́чи|вать, -ть.

refectory /rɪˈfektərɪ/, /ˈrefɪktərɪ/ *n.* тра́пезная; столо́вая.

refer /rɪˈfɜː(r)/ *v.t.* (**referred, referring**) (*pass on, direct*) от|сыла́ть, -осла́ть; напр|авля́ть, -а́вить; **the clerk ~red me to the manager** слу́жащий отосла́л меня́ к нача́льнику; **the dispute was ~red to the UN** спор был пе́редан на рассмотре́ние ООН; **the note ~s the reader to the appendix** примеча́ние отсыла́ет чита́теля к приложе́нию.

● *v.i.* (**referred, referring**) **1** (*have recourse*) спр|авля́ться, -а́виться; **he ~red to the dictionary** он спра́вился в словаре́; **the speaker ~red to his notes** ора́тор загляну́л в конспе́кт. **2** (*allude*): **~ to** (*mention*) упом|ина́ть, -яну́ть; подразумева́ть (*impf.*); **all his writings ~ to the war** все его́ произведе́ния посвящены́ войне́; **are you ~ring to me?** вы име́ете в виду́ меня́?; (*cite*) ссыла́ться, сосла́ться на + *a.*

referee /ˌrefəˈriː/ *n.* **1** (*arbitrator*) арби́тр. **2** (*at games*) судья́ (*m.*); рефери́ (*m. indecl.*). **3** (*person supplying testimonial*) поручи́тель (*m.*); рецензе́нт-экспе́рт.

● *v.t. & i.* (**referees, refereed**): **he agreed to ~ the match** он согласи́лся суди́ть матч; **~ing** суде́йство.

reference /ˈrefərəns/ *n.* **1** (*referring for decision, consideration etc.*) отсы́лка; **he acted without ~ to his superiors** он де́йствовал без согласова́ния с нача́льством; **terms of ~** компете́нция, круг полномо́чий, ве́дение. **2** (*relation*) отноше́ние; **with ~ to your letter** в связи́ с ва́шим письмо́м. **3** (*allusion*) упомина́ние, ссы́лка; **he made frequent ~ to our agreement** он ча́сто ссыла́лся на на́ше соглаше́ние; **the book contains many ~s to the Queen** в кни́ге ча́сто упомина́ется короле́ва. **4** (*in text*) ссы́лка, сно́ска. **5** (*referring for information*) спра́вка; **you should make ~ to a dictionary** вам сле́дует обрати́ться к словарю́; **~ book** спра́вочник; **~ library** спра́вочная библиоте́ка. **6** (*testimonial*) о́тзыв, рекоменда́ция, характери́стика; (*person supplying ~*) поручи́тель (*m.*); **he gave his professor as a ~** он назва́л профе́ссора в ка́честве своего́ поручи́теля *or* он назва́л профе́ссора, кото́рый напи́шет ему́ характери́стику.

referend|um /ˌrefəˈrendəm/ *n.* (*pl.* **~ums** *or* **~a**) рефере́ндум.

referral /rɪˈfɜːr(ə)l/ *n.* направле́ние.

refill[1] /ˈriːfɪl/ *n.* (*of fuel*) (до)запра́вка; (*of drink*) доли́тая рю́мка; (*for pen etc.*) запасно́й сте́ржень.

refill[2] /riːˈfɪl/ *v.t.* нап|олня́ть, -о́лнить вновь; **may I ~your glass?** позво́льте подли́ть?

● *v.i.* запр|авля́ться, -а́виться.

refinance /riːˈfaɪnæns/ *v.t.* брать, взять втори́чный заём на финанси́рование + *g.*

refine /rɪˈfaɪn/ *v.t.* **1** (*purify*) оч|ища́ть, -и́стить; **~d sugar** са́хар-рафина́д. **2** (*make more elegant or cultured*) соверше́нствовать, у-; **~d manners** утончённые/изы́сканные мане́ры.

refinement /rɪˈfaɪnmənt/ *n.* **1** (*purification*) очище́ние, очи́стка. **2** (*of feeling, taste etc.*) утончённость, то́нкость; (*of breeding or manners*) благовоспи́танность; **lack of ~** неотёсанность. **3** (*subtle or ingenious manifestation*) утончённость.

refinery /rɪˈfaɪnərɪ/ *n.* (*oil*) нефтеочисти́тельный заво́д.

refit[1] /ˈriːfɪt/ *n.* ремо́нт, переоборудование.

refit[2] /riːˈfɪt/ *v.t.* чини́ть, по-; переобору́довать (*impf., pf.*); ремонти́ровать, от-.

reflate /riːˈfleɪt/ *v.i.* (*econ.*) пров|оди́ть, -ести́ рефля́цию.

reflation /riːˈfleɪʃ(ə)n/ *n.* (*econ.*) рефля́ция.

reflect /rɪˈflekt/ *v.t.* (*light, heat etc.*) отра|жа́ть, -зи́ть; **light is ~ed from a white surface** свет отража́ется от бе́лой пове́рхности; (*fig., express, reveal*): **her thoughts were ~ed in her face** все её мы́сли отража́лись на её лице́.

● *v.i.* **1** (*produce a reflection*) отра|жа́ться, -зи́ться; **is the light ~ing in your eyes?** вам свет не бьёт в глаза́?; (*fig., bring discredit*): **your behaviour** (*Br.*), **behavior** (*US*) **~s on us all** ва́ше поведе́ние броса́ет тень на нас всех. **2** (*consider, ponder*) заду́маться (*pf.*) (над + *i.*); размышля́ть (*impf.*); **I ~ed (on/upon) how fortunate I had been** я поду́мал о том, как мне повезло́.

reflection /rɪˈflekʃ(ə)n/ *n.* **1** (*of light, heat etc.*) отраже́ние; **she saw his ~ in the mirror** она́ уви́дела его́ отраже́ние в зе́ркале. **2** (*consideration*) размышле́ние; **he acts without ~** он де́йствует неосмотри́тельно; **she was lost in ~** она́ была́ погружена́ в свои́ мы́сли; **on ~, I may have been wrong** по размышле́нии я реши́л, что, возмо́жно, я был непра́в. **3** (*expression of idea*) соображе́ние; замеча́ние. **4** (*cause of credit or discredit*): **it is a ~ on my honour** (*Br.*), **honor** (*US*) э́то задева́ет мою́ честь.

reflective /rɪˈflektɪv/ *adj.* (*of a surface*) отража́ющий; (*thoughtful*) мы́слящий; заду́мчивый.

reflector /rɪˈflektə(r)/ *n.* рефле́ктор.

reflex /ˈriːfleks/ *n.* (**~ action**) рефле́кс.

● *adj.* рефлекто́рный; **~ camera** зерка́льный фотоаппара́т.

reflexive /rɪˈfleksɪv/ *adj.* возвра́тный.

reflexologist /ˌriːflekˈsɒlədʒɪst/ *n.* рефлексотерапе́вт.

reflexology /ˌriːflekˈsɒlədʒɪ/ *n.* рефлексотерапи́я.

refloat /riːˈfləʊt/ *v.t.* подн|има́ть, -я́ть (*затону́вшее су́дно*); сн|има́ть, -ять с мели.

refocus /riːˈfəʊkəs/ *v.t.* перефокуси́ровать (*impf., pf.*).

reforestation /riːˌfɒrɪˈsteɪʃ(ə)n/ *n.* восстановле́ние лесны́х масси́вов.

reform /rɪˈfɔːm/ *n.* рефо́рма.

● *v.t.* (*a system*) ул|учша́ть, -у́чшить; реформи́ровать (*impf., pf.*); (*a person*) перевоспи́т|ывать, -а́ть; испр|авля́ть, -а́вить.

● *v.i.* испр|авля́ться, -а́виться.

re-form /riːˈfɔːm/ *v.t.* (*reshape, form again*) переформиро́в|ывать, -а́ть.

● *v.i.* перестр|а́иваться, -о́иться; **the soldiers ~ed into two ranks** солда́ты перестро́ились в две шере́нги.

reformat /riːˈfɔːmæt/ *v.t.* (*comput.*) переформати́ровать (*impf., pf.*).

reformation /ˌrefəˈmeɪʃ(ə)n/ *n.* (*change, improvement*) преобразова́ние; **the R~** Реформа́ция.

re-formation /ˌriːfɔːˈmeɪʃ(ə)n/ *n.* (*forming again*) переформирова́ние.

reformative /rɪˈfɔːmətɪv/ *adj.* исправи́тельный.

reformatory /rɪˈfɔːmətərɪ/ *n.* (*US hist.*) исправи́тельное заведе́ние.

● *adj.* исправи́тельный.

reformer /rɪˈfɔːmə(r)/ *n.* реформа́тор; преобразова́тель (*m.*).

refract /rɪˈfrækt/ *v.t.* прелом|ля́ть, -и́ть.

refraction /rɪˈfrækʃ(ə)n/ *n.* преломле́ние; рефра́кция.

refractor /rɪˈfræktə(r)/ *n.* рефра́ктор.

refractory /rɪˈfræktərɪ/ *n.* огнеупо́рный материа́л.
● *adj.* **1** (*of person*) упря́мый, непослу́шный. **2** (*of illness*) упо́рный. **3** (*fire-resisting*) огнеупо́рный.

refrain[1] /rɪˈfreɪn/ *n.* рефре́н, припе́в; **they joined in the ~** они́ подхвати́ли припе́в.

refrain[2] /rɪˈfreɪn/ *v.i.* сде́рж|иваться, -а́ться; возде́рж|иваться, -а́ться; **I could hardly ~ from laughing** я е́ле сде́рживался от сме́ха; **I ~ed from comment** я воздержа́лся от замеча́ний/коммента́риев.

refresh /rɪˈfreʃ/ *v.t.* освеж|а́ть, -и́ть; **I woke ~ed** сон освежи́л меня́; **~ o.s.** (*with food and drink*) подкреп|ля́ться, -и́ться; **let me ~ your memory** позво́льте напо́мнить вам.

refresher /rɪˈfreʃə(r)/ *n.* (**~ course**) курс переподгото́вки (*or* повыше́ния квалифика́ции).

refreshing /rɪˈfreʃɪŋ/ *adj.* освежа́ющий; **he was ~ly frank** его́ и́скренность была́ умили́тельна.

refreshment /rɪˈfreʃmənt/ *n.* **1** (*reinvigoration*) восстановле́ние сил. **2** (*food or drink*) еда́; питьё; **won't you take some ~?** не хоти́те ли подкрепи́ться/закуси́ть?; **~s are served on the train** в по́езде мо́жно перекуси́ть; **~ room** буфе́т.

refrigerate /rɪˈfrɪdʒəˌreɪt/ *v.t.* замор|а́живать, -о́зить.

refrigeration /rɪˌfrɪdʒəˈreɪʃ(ə)n/ *n.* замора́живание.

refrigerator /rɪˈfrɪdʒəˌreɪtə(r)/ *n.* холоди́льник.

refuel /riːˈfjuːəl/ *v.i.* запр|авля́ться, -а́виться.
● *v.t.* запр|авля́ть, -а́вить.

refuge /ˈrefjuːdʒ/ *n.* (*shelter*) убе́жище; приста́нище; **the cat took ~ beneath the table** кот спря́тался под столо́м; (*fig.*) утеше́ние; **take ~ in lies** приб|ега́ть, -е́гнуть ко лжи.

refugee /ˌrefjʊˈdʒiː/ *n.* бе́жен|ец (*fem.* -ка); **~ camp** ла́герь (*m.*) бе́женцев; **political ~** политэмигра́нт.

refund[1] /ˈriːfʌnd/ *n.* возмеще́ние убы́тков; **they gave me a ~** мне верну́ли де́ньги.

refund[2] /rɪˈfʌnd/ *v.t.* (*pay back*) возвраща́ть, верну́ть (*де́ньги*); (*reimburse*) возме|ща́ть, -сти́ть.

refurbish /riːˈfɜːbɪʃ/ *v.t.* отде́л|ывать, -ать.

refurbishment /riːˈfɜːbɪʃmənt/ *n.* (капита́льный) ремо́нт.

refurnish /riːˈfɜːnɪʃ/ *v.t.* за́ново меблирова́ть (*impf., pf.*).

refusal /rɪˈfjuːz(ə)l/ *n.* отка́з; **he would take no ~** он не при́нял отка́за; **when I sell the house I will give you first ~** когда́ я бу́ду продава́ть дом, я предложу́ его́ вам в пе́рвую о́чередь.

refuse[1] /ˈrefjuːs/ *n.* му́сор; **~ collection** убо́рка му́сора; **~ dump** сва́лка.

refuse[2] /rɪˈfjuːz/ *v.t. & i.* (*decline to give or grant*) отка́з|ывать, -а́ть (*кому в чём*); (*reject*) отв|ерга́ть, -е́ргнуть; (*decline sth. offered*) отка́з|ываться, -а́ться от + *g.*; **the request was ~d** в про́сьбе бы́ло отка́зано; **the invitation was ~d** приглаше́ние не́ было при́нято; **they ~d me permission** мне не́ дали разреше́ния; **children were ~d admittance** дете́й не впусти́ли; **it is an offer not to be ~d** тако́е предложе́ние не сле́дует отклоня́ть; **he proposed to her and was ~d** он сде́лал ей предложе́ние и получи́л отка́з; **the horse ~d (the fence)** пе́ред барье́ром ло́шадь заарта́чилась.

refusenik /rɪˈfjuːznɪk/ *n.* отка́зни|к (*fem.* -ца).

refutable /rɪˈfjuːtəb(ə)l/ *adj.* опроверже́мый.

refutation /ˌrefjʊˈteɪʃ(ə)n/ *n.* опроверже́ние.

refute /rɪˈfjuːt/ *v.t.* опров|ерга́ть, -е́ргнуть.

regain /rɪˈgeɪn/ *v.t.* **1** (*recover*) получ|а́ть, -и́ть обра́тно; **the prisoners ~ed their freedom** у́зники вновь обрели́ свобо́ду; **he never ~ed consciousness** он так и не пришёл в созна́ние; **he ~ed his footing** он сно́ва нащу́пал опо́ру ного́й; (*mil., recapture*) отвоёв|ывать, -а́ть. **2** (*reach again*) сно́ва дост|ига́ть, -и́гнуть; **they ~ed the shore** они́ вновь дости́гли бе́рега.

regal /ˈriːg(ə)l/ *adj.* короле́вский.

regale /rɪˈgeɪl/ *v.t.* уго|ща́ть, -сти́ть; по́тчевать (*impf.*).

regalia /rɪˈgeɪlɪə/ *n.* рега́ли|и (*pl., g.* -й).

regard /rɪˈgɑːd/ *n.* **1** (*gaze*) взгляд. **2** (*point of attention, respect*) отноше́ние; **in this ~** в э́том отноше́нии; **in, with ~ to your request** что каса́ется ва́шей про́сьбы. **3** (*heed*) внима́ние; **he pays no ~ to my warnings** он не прислу́шивается к мои́м предупрежде́ниям. **4** (*consideration*) внима́ние, забо́та; **he paid no ~ to her feelings** он не счита́лся с её чу́вствами. **5** (*esteem*) уваже́ние (к + *d.*); **he holds your opinion in high ~** он о́чень высоко́ це́нит ва́ше мне́ние. **6** (*pl., greetings*) приве́т; (*formula at end of letter*) с приве́том; **give him my warmest ~s** переда́йте ему́ от меня́ серде́чный приве́т.
● *v.t.* **1** (*look at*) разгля́д|ывать, -е́ть; **he ~ed me with hostility** он разгля́дывал меня́ с неприя́знью. **2** (*consider*) расце́н|ивать, -и́ть; сч|ита́ть, -есть; **I ~ his behaviour (*Br.*), behavior (*US*) with suspicion** я отношу́сь к его́ посту́пкам с подозре́нием; **he was ~ed as a hero** его́ счита́ли геро́ем. **3** (*give heed to*) счита́ться (*impf.*) с + *i.*; **he seldom ~s my advice** он ре́дко принима́ет мои́ сове́ты. **4** (*respect, esteem*) уважа́ть (*impf.*); **we all ~ him highly** мы все его́ о́чень уважа́ем. **5** (*concern*): **as ~s, ~ing** относи́тельно + *g.*; что каса́ется + *g.*; насчёт + *g.*; **he is careless as ~s money** он легкомы́слен в де́нежных дела́х.

regardful /rɪˈgɑːdfʊl/ *adj.*: **he was ~ of my advice** он внял моему́ сове́ту.

regardless /rɪˈgɑːdlɪs/ *adj.* невнима́тельный (к + *d.*); **~ of expense** не счита́ясь с расхо́дами; **he pressed on ~** (*coll.*) он рва́лся вперёд, невзира́я ни на что.

regatta /rɪˈgætə/ *n.* рега́та.

regency /ˈriːdʒənsɪ/ *n.* ре́гентство; **R~ architecture** архитекту́ра эпо́хи ре́гентства.

regenerate[1] /rɪˈdʒenərət/ *adj.* возрождённый.

regenerate[2] /rɪˈdʒenəˌreɪt/ *v.t. & i.* возро|жда́ть(ся), -ди́ть(ся).

regeneration /rɪˌdʒenəˈreɪʃ(ə)n/ *n.* перерожде́ние, возрожде́ние.

regent /ˈriːdʒ(ə)nt/ *n.* ре́гент; **Prince R~** принц-ре́гент.

reggae /ˈregeɪ/ *n.* ре́гги (*m. indecl.*).

regicide /ˈredʒɪˌsaɪd/ *n.* (*crime*) цареуби́йство; (*criminal*) цареуби́йца (*c.g.*).

regime /reɪˈʒiːm/ *n.* режи́м, строй; **under the old ~** при ста́ром режи́ме.

regimen /ˈredʒɪˌmen/ *n.* (*set of rules*) режи́м; поря́док; (*med., esp. diet*) режи́м, дие́та.

regiment[1] /ˈredʒɪmənt/ *n.* полк.

regiment[2] /ˈredʒɪˌment/ *v.t.* подчин|я́ть, -и́ть стро́гой дисципли́не.

regimental /ˌredʒɪˈment(ə)l/ *adj.* полково́й.

regimentals /ˌredʒɪˈment(ə)ls/ *n.* обмундирова́ние; **they paraded in full ~s** они́ марширова́ли в по́лной фо́рме.

regimentation /ˌredʒɪmənˈteɪʃ(ə)n/ *n.* стро́гая регламента́ция/дисципли́на.

region /ˈriːdʒ(ə)n/ *n.* райо́н, о́бласть; регио́н; **the Arctic ~s** А́рктика (*sg.*); (*of body*) по́лость; **the abdominal ~** брюшна́я по́лость; **in the ~ of the heart** в о́бласти се́рдца; (*fig.*) о́бласть, сфе́ра; **in the ~ of £5,000** приблизи́тельно 5 000 фу́нтов.

regional /ˈriːdʒənəl/ *adj.* райо́нный, областно́й; региона́льный; **a ~ accent** ме́стный акце́нт/вы́говор.

register /ˈredʒɪstə(r)/ *n.* **1** (*record, list*) рее́стр; за́пись; (*in school*) журна́л; **hotel ~** регистрацио́нная кни́га; **~ of voters** спи́сок избира́телей; **parish ~** прихо́дская кни́га; **~ office** = **registry office**. **2** (*mus.*) реги́стр. **3** (*linguistic level*) стилисти́ческий у́ровень. **4** (*mechanical recording device*) счётчик; **cash ~** ка́сса.
● *v.t.* **1** (*enter on official record*) регистри́ровать, за-; оф|ормля́ть, -о́рмить; **all cars must be ~ed** все маши́ны должны́ быть зарегистри́рованы; **~ed letter** заказно́е письмо́. **2** (*make mental note of*) отм|еча́ть, -е́тить; зап|омина́ть, -о́мнить; **his mind did not ~ the fact** э́тот факт не запечатле́лся у него́ в уме́. **3** (*of an instrument: record*) пока́з|ывать, -а́ть; отм|еча́ть, -е́тить;

R

the thermometer ~ed 20°C термо́метр пока́зывал 20 гра́дусов по Це́льсию. **4** (*express*) выража́ть, вы́разить; **the audience ~ed their disapproval** пу́блика вы́разила своё недово́льство; **her face ~ed surprise** на её лице́ отрази́лось удивле́ние.

● *v.i.* **1** (*record one's name*) регистри́роваться, за-. **2** (*coll., correspond to sth. known*): **your name doesn't ~ with him** ва́ше и́мя ничего́ ему́ не говори́т. **3** (*be impressed on memory*) зап|омина́ться, -о́мниться; **his words ~ed with me** его́ слова́ запа́ли мне в па́мять.

registrar /ˌredʒɪsˈtrɑː(r)/, /ˈredʒ-/ *n.* (*keeper of records*) регистра́тор; (*head of register office*) заве́дующий (райо́нным) отделе́нием за́гса; (*of university etc.*) регистра́тор, секрета́рь (*m.*); (*Br., in hospital*) врач, проходя́щий пра́ктику по специа́льности.

registration /ˌredʒɪˈstreɪʃ(ə)n/ *n.* регистра́ция; **~ number of a car** (*Br.*) (регистрацио́нный) но́мер маши́ны.

registry /ˈredʒɪstrɪ/ *n.* **1** (*registration*) регистра́ция. **2**: **~ office** (*Br.*) регистрату́ра; **they were married at a ~ office** они расписа́лись в за́гсе; они́ зарегистри́ровались.

regress /rɪˈgres/ *v.i.* дви́гаться (*impf.*) в обра́тном направле́нии; регресси́ровать (*impf.*).

regression /rɪˈgreʃ(ə)n/ *n.* возвраще́ние (к + *d.*); (*decline*) упа́док, регре́сс.

regressive /rɪˈgresɪv/ *adj.* регресси́вный.

regret /rɪˈgret/ *n.* сожале́ние; **I found to my ~ that I was late** я обнаружи́л, к своему́ сожале́нию, что опозда́л; **I have no ~s** я ни о чём не жале́ю.

● *v.t.* **(regretted, regretting) 1** (*feel sorrow for*) сожале́ть (*impf.*); **I ~ losing my temper** я сожале́ю, что вы́шел из себя́; **I ~ to say ...** к сожале́нию, я до́лжен сказа́ть...; **it is to be ~ted that ...** к сожале́нию...; мо́жно то́лько пожале́ть, что...; **you will live to ~ this** вы ещё пожале́ете об э́том. **2** (*feel loss of*): **he ~s his lost opportunities** он (со)жале́ет об утра́ченных возмо́жностях.

regretful /rɪˈgretfʊl/ *adj.* опеча́ленный; по́лный сожале́ния.

regrettable /rɪˈgretəb(ə)l/ *adj.* прискорбный; досто́йный сожале́ния.

regroup /riːˈgruːp/ *v.t. & i.* перегруппиро́в|ывать(ся), -а́ть(ся).

regular /ˈregjʊlə(r)/ *n.* **1 (~ soldier)** солда́т регуля́рной а́рмии. **2** (*coll.*, **~ customer**) завсегда́тай; постоя́нный посети́тель.

● *adj.* **1** (*orderly in appearance, symmetrical*) пра́вильный, регуля́рный; **~ features** пра́вильные черты́; **a ~ hexagon** пра́вильный шестиуго́льник. **2** (*steady, unvarying, systematic*) регуля́рный, норма́льный; **~ breathing** споко́йное дыха́ние; **a ~ pulse** ритми́чный пульс; **I have no ~ work** у меня́ нет постоя́нной рабо́ты; **he keeps ~ hours** у него́ чёткий режи́м; (*usual, routine*) очередно́й. **3** (*conventional, proper*) при́нятый, устано́вленный; **the ~ procedure** при́нятая/обы́чная процеду́ра. **4** (*gram.*) пра́вильный. **5** (*properly appointed*) регуля́рный; ка́дровый; **~ army** регуля́рная/постоя́нная а́рмия. **6** (*coll., thorough, real*) су́щий, настоя́щий; **she is a ~ nuisance** она́ ужа́сная зану́да. **7** (*US, ordinary, standard*) регуля́рный, обы́чный. **8** (*US, likeable*): **a ~ guy** (*coll.*) сла́вный ма́лый.

regularity /ˌregjʊˈlærɪtɪ/ *n.* (*symmetry*) пра́вильность; (*systematic occurrence*) регуля́рность.

regularize /ˈregjʊləˌraɪz/ *v.t.* упоря́дочи|вать, -ть.

regulate /ˈregjʊˌleɪt/ *v.t.* **1** (*control*) регули́ровать (*impf.*). **2** (*adjust*) (*clock*) выверя́ть, вы́верить.

regulation /ˌregjʊˈleɪʃ(ə)n/ *n.* **1** (*control*) регули́рование. **2** (*adjustment*) вы́верка. **3** (*rule*) пра́вило; **the ~s say we must wear black** согла́сно/по пра́вилам/уста́ву мы должны́ ходи́ть в чёрном. **4** (*attr., standard*) устано́вленный.

regulator /ˈregjʊˌleɪtə(r)/ *n.* (*person*) отве́тственное лицо́; (*body*) отве́тственная организа́ция; (*device*) регуля́тор, стабилиза́тор.

regulatory /ˈregjʊlətərɪ/, /ˌregjʊˈleɪtərɪ/ *adj.* регули́рующий; **~ body** о́рган управле́ния.

regurgitate /rɪˈgɜːdʒɪˌteɪt/ *v.t.* отры́г|ивать, -ну́ть.

regurgitation /rɪˌgɜːdʒɪˈteɪʃ(ə)n/ *n.* отры́гивание.

rehabilitate /ˌriːhəˈbɪlɪˌteɪt/ *v.t.* (*re-educate*) перевоспи́т|ывать, -а́ть; (*exculpate*) реабилити́ровать (*impf., pf.*).

rehabilitation /ˌriːhəˌbɪlɪˈteɪʃ(ə)n/ *n.* перевоспита́ние; реабилита́ция.

rehash *n.* /ˈriːhæʃ/ перекро́йка; перетасо́вка.

● *v.t.* /riːˈhæʃ/ перекр|а́ивать, -ои́ть; перетас|о́вывать, -ова́ть.

rehear /riːˈhɪə(r)/ *v.t.*: **the case will be ~d** де́ло бу́дет слу́шаться повто́рно.

rehearing /riːˈhɪərɪŋ/ *n.* втори́чное слу́шание де́ла.

rehearsal /rɪˈhɜːs(ə)l/ *n.* **1** (*practice*) репети́ция; **dress ~** генера́льная репети́ция. **2** (*recitation, list*) перечисле́ние.

rehearse /rɪˈhɜːs/ *v.t.* (*practise*) репети́ровать, от-; (*recite, recount*) переч|исля́ть, -и́слить.

rehouse /riːˈhaʊz/ *v.t.* пересел|я́ть, -и́ть.

Reich /raɪx/ *n.* рейх.

reign /reɪn/ *n.* ца́рствование, власть; **in the ~ of Peter the Great** в ца́рствование Петра́ Вели́кого; (*fig.*) власть, госпо́дство.

● *v.i.* ца́рствовать (*impf.*); (*fig.*) цари́ть (*impf.*); **silence ~ed** цари́ла тишина́.

re-ignite /ˌriːɪgˈnaɪt/ *v.t.* вновь разж|ига́ть, -е́чь.

reimburse /ˌriːɪmˈbɜːs/ *v.t.* возме|ща́ть, -сти́ть (*что кому*); опла́|чивать, -ти́ть (*что кому*).

reimbursement /ˌriːɪmˈbɜːsmənt/ *n.* возмеще́ние, возвраще́ние.

reimpose /ˌriːɪmˈpəʊz/ *v.t.* восстан|а́вливать, -ови́ть; сно́ва вв|оди́ть, -ести́.

reimposition /ˌriːɪmpəˈzɪʃ(ə)n/ *n.* восстановле́ние.

rein /reɪn/ *n.* по́вод (*pl.* -а́ *or* пово́дья), вожжа́; (*fig.*): **you are giving ~ to your imagination** у вас разыгра́лось воображе́ние; **we must keep a tight ~ on our spending** мы должны́ стро́го контроли́ровать на́ши расхо́ды.

● *v.t.* (*fig.*) держа́ть (*impf.*) в узде́; **~ in a horse** приде́рж|ивать, -а́ть ло́шадь.

reincarnate /ˌriːɪnˈkɑːneɪt/ *v.t.* перевопло|ща́ть, -ти́ть.

reincarnation /ˌriːɪnkɑːˈneɪʃ(ə)n/ *n.* перевоплоще́ние, реинкарна́ция.

reindeer /ˈreɪndɪə(r)/ *n.* (*pl.* **~** *or* **~s**) се́верный оле́нь.

reinfect /ˌriːɪnˈfekt/ *v.t.* вновь зара|жа́ть, -зи́ть.

reinfection /ˌriːɪnˈfekʃ(ə)n/ *n.* повто́рное зараже́ние.

reinforce /ˌriːɪnˈfɔːs/ *v.t.* уси́ли|вать, -ть; **the army was ~d** а́рмия получи́ла подкрепле́ние; **this ~s my argument** э́то подкрепля́ет мои́ до́воды; **~d concrete** железобето́н.

reinforcement /ˌriːɪnˈfɔːsmənt/ *n.* усиле́ние; (*pl., troops*) подкрепле́ние.

reinsert /ˌriːɪnˈsɜːt/ *v.t.* вв|оди́ть, -ести́ вновь.

reinsertion /ˌriːɪnˈsɜːʃ(ə)n/ *n.* втори́чный ввод.

reinstate /ˌriːɪnˈsteɪt/ *v.t.* восстан|а́вливать, -ови́ть в права́х/до́лжности/положе́нии.

reinstatement /ˌriːɪnˈsteɪtmənt/ *n.* восстановле́ние в права́х/до́лжности/положе́нии.

reinsurance /ˌriːɪnˈʃʊərəns/ *n.* (*lit., fig.*) перестрахо́вка.

reinsure /ˌriːɪnˈʃʊə(r)/ *v.t.* (*lit., fig.*) перестрахо́в|ывать, -а́ть; возобнов|ля́ть, -и́ть страхо́вку (+ *g.*).

reinter /ˌriːɪnˈtɜː(r)/ *v.t.* перезахорони́ть (*pf.*).

reinterment /ˌriːɪnˈtɜːmənt/ *n.* перезахороне́ние.

reinterpret /ˌriːɪnˈtɜːprɪt/ *v.t.* интерпрети́ровать (*impf., pf.*) по-но́вому.

reinterpretation /ˌriːɪnˌtɜːprɪˈteɪʃ(ə)n/ *n.* но́вая интерпрета́ция.

reintroduce /ˌriːɪntrəˈdjuːs/ *v.t.* вновь вв|оди́ть, -ести́.

reintroduction /ˌriːɪntrəˈdʌkʃ(ə)n/ *n.* повто́рное введе́ние.

reinvest /ˌriːɪnˈvest/ *v.t. & i.* сно́ва поме|ща́ть, -сти́ть (капита́л).

reinvestment /ˌriːɪnˈvestmənt/ *n.* повто́рное инвести́рование.

reinvigorate /ˌriːɪnˈvɪgəˌreɪt/ *v.t.* вдохну́ть (*pf.*) но́вые си́лы в + *a.*

reissue /riːˈɪʃuː/, /-sjuː/ *n.* переизда́ние; повто́рный вы́пуск.

● *v.t.* переизд|ава́ть, -а́ть; сно́ва выпуска́ть, вы́пустить.

reiterate /riːˈɪtəˌreɪt/ *v.t.* повтор|я́ть, -и́ть; тверди́ть (*impf.*).

reiteration /riːˌɪtəˈreɪʃ(ə)n/ *n.* повторе́ние.

reject[1] /ˈriːdʒekt/ *n.* (*discarded article*) неподходя́щая вещь; (*comm.*) брако́ванное изде́лие; (*pl., collect.*) брак; (*discarded person*) неподходя́щая кандидату́ра.

reject[2] /rɪˈdʒekt/ *v.t.* **1** (*throw away*) отбр|а́сывать, -о́сить. **2** (*refuse to accept*) отв|ерга́ть, -е́ргнуть; отклон|я́ть, -и́ть; **my offer was ~ed out of hand** моё предложе́ние сра́зу же отклони́ли; **I ~ your accusation** я не принима́ю ва́ше обвине́ние; **he was ~ed by the board** он не прошёл коми́ссию; **his stomach ~s food** его́ желу́док не принима́ет пи́щу.

rejection /rɪˈdʒekʃ(ə)n/ *n.* (*refusal to accept*) отка́з, отклоне́ние; **~ slip** уведомле́ние реда́кции об отка́зе напеча́тать произведе́ние.

rejig /riːˈdʒɪg/ *v.t.* (**rejigged, rejigging**) (*Br.*) перестр|а́ивать, -о́ить.

rejoice /rɪˈdʒɔɪs/ *v.i.* ра́доваться, об- (*чему*).

rejoicing /rɪˈdʒɔɪsɪŋ/ *n.* весе́лье, ра́дость.

rejoin[1] /riːˈdʒɔɪn/ *v.t.* **1** (*join together again*) вновь присоедин|я́ть, -и́ть. **2** (*return to*) присоедин|я́ться, -и́ться вновь +*d.*; прим|ыка́ть, -кну́ть вновь к+*d.*; **he ~ed his regiment** он верну́лся в свой полк; **he ~ed his companions** он присоедини́лся к друзья́м.

rejoin[2] /rɪˈdʒɔɪn/ *v.t. & i.* (*answer*) отв|еча́ть, -е́тить; возра|жа́ть, -зи́ть.

rejoinder /rɪˈdʒɔɪndə(r)/ *n.* отве́т; возраже́ние.

rejuvenate /rɪˈdʒuːvɪˌneɪt/ *v.t.* омол|а́живать, -оди́ть.

rejuvenation /rɪˌdʒuːvɪˈneɪʃ(ə)n/ *n.* омоложе́ние.

rekindle /riːˈkɪnd(ə)l/ *v.t.* разж|ига́ть, -е́чь вновь.

● *v.i.* вновь разгор|а́ться, -е́ться.

relapse /rɪˈlæps/ *n.* рецици́в; **she suffered a ~** она́ сно́ва заболе́ла.

● *v.i.* сно́ва преда́ться (*pf.*) (*чему*); сно́ва впасть (*pf.*) (*в какое-н. состояние*); **he ~d into bad ways** он сно́ва сби́лся с пути́; **she ~d into silence** она́ (сно́ва) замолча́ла.

relate /rɪˈleɪt/ *v.t.* **1** (*narrate*) расска́з|ывать, -а́ть о+*p.*; **strange to ~** как э́то ни стра́нно. **2** (*establish relation between*) свя́з|ывать, -а́ть (*что с чем*); *see also* ⇒**related**

● *v.i.* **1** (*be relevant*) относи́ться (*impf.*) (к+*d.*); име́ть (*impf.*) отноше́ние (к+*d.*). **2** (*establish contact*): **he does not ~ well to people** он пло́хо схо́дится с людьми́.

related /rɪˈleɪtɪd/ *adj.* **1** (*logically connected*) (взаи́мно) свя́занный (с+*i.*). **2** (*by blood or marriage*): **he is ~ to the royal family** он в родстве́ с короле́вской семьёй; **he and I are ~** мы с ним ро́дственники; **we are distantly ~** мы в да́льнем родстве́.

relatedness /rɪˈleɪtɪdnɪs/ *n.* отноше́ние.

relation /rɪˈleɪʃ(ə)n/ *n.* **1** (*connection, correspondence*) отноше́ние, зави́симость; **in, with ~ to** что каса́ется +*g.*; относи́тельно+*g.*; **the cost bears no ~ to the results** расхо́ды несоизмери́мы с результа́тами. **2** (*pl., dealings*) отноше́ния (*nt. pl.*); **international ~s** междунаро́дные отноше́ния; **they broke off diplomatic ~s** они́ порва́ли дипломати́ческие отноше́ния; **public ~s officer** нача́льник/сотру́дник отде́ла информа́ции и рекла́мы; **sexual ~s** половы́е сноше́ния; **~s are strained between them** у них натя́нутые отноше́ния. **3** (*kinsman, kinswoman*) ро́дственни|к (*fem.* -ца); (*pl.*) родня́ (*sg.*); **a near, close ~** бли́зкий ро́дственник; **~s by marriage** ро́дственники по му́жу/жене́; сво́йственники.

relationship /rɪˈleɪʃənʃɪp/ *n.* (*relevance*) связь, отноше́ние; (*association, liaison*) взаимоотноше́ния (*nt. pl.*), связь; (*kinship*) родство́.

relative /ˈrelətɪv/ *n.* (*kinsman, kinswoman*) ро́дственни|к (*fem.* -ца).

● *adj.* **1** (*comparative*) относи́тельный, сравни́тельный; **he is a ~ newcomer** он здесь относи́тельно неда́вно; (*not absolute*) относи́тельный, усло́вный; **beauty is a ~ term** красота́ — поня́тие относи́тельное; **~ly speaking** вообще́ говоря́. **2**: **~ to** (*having reference to*) каса́ющийся +*g.*; относя́щийся к+*d.*; **the facts ~ to the situation** обстоя́тельства, относя́щиеся к де́лу. **3** (*gram.*): **~ pronoun** относи́тельное местоиме́ние.

relativism /ˈrelətɪˌvɪz(ə)m/ *n.* релятиви́зм.

relativity /ˌreləˈtɪvɪtɪ/ *n.* относи́тельность; **theory of ~** тео́рия относи́тельности.

relax /rɪˈlæks/ *v.t.* рассл|абля́ть, -а́бить; **he ~ed his grip** он разжа́л ру́ку; **we must not ~ our efforts** мы не должны́ ослабля́ть уси́лий; **the rules may be ~ed** распоря́док мо́жет быть ме́нее жёстким; **a ~ing climate** кли́мат, де́йствующий расслабля́юще.

● *v.i.* (*weaken*) осл|абева́ть, -а́бнуть; (*rest*) рассл|абля́ться, -а́биться; отдыха́ть (*impf.*); **I like to ~ in the sun** я люблю́ посиде́ть/поваля́ться на со́лнце; **a ~ed atmosphere** споко́йная атмосфе́ра.

relaxation /ˌriːlækˈseɪʃ(ə)n/ *n.* **1** (*slackening*) уменьше́ние; смягче́ние; **~ of discipline** ослабле́ние дисципли́ны. **2** (*recreation*) о́тдых, развлече́ние; **take one's ~** отдыха́ть (*impf.*). **3** (*relief of tension*) разря́дка.

relay /ˈriːleɪ/ *n.* **1** (*fresh team*) сме́на; (*pl.*): **they worked in ~s** они́ рабо́тали посме́нно. **2** (**~ race**) эстафе́тный бег. **3** (*elec.*) реле́ (*indecl.*). **4** (*retransmitting device*) ретрансля́ция; **~ station** ретрансляцио́нная ста́нция.

● *v.t.* (*transmit*) трансли́ровать (*impf., pf.*).

re-lay /riːˈleɪ/ *v.t.* пере|кла́дывать, -ложи́ть.

relearn /riːˈlɜːn/ *v.t.* вы́учить (*pf.*) за́ново.

release /rɪˈliːs/ *n.* **1** (*liberation, deliverance*) освобожде́ние; **~ from prison** освобожде́ние из тюрьмы́; **death was a happy ~ for him** смерть изба́вила его́ от тя́жких страда́ний. **2** (*letting go, unfastening*) освобожде́ние; **~ of bombs** сбра́сывание бомб. **3** (*device for doing this*) спуск; **~ button** спусково́я кно́пка. **4** (*publication, issue*) вы́пуск; **press ~** сообще́ние для печа́ти; **the latest ~s** (*films*) нови́нки (*f. pl.*) экра́на; **this film is on general ~** э́тот фильм в широ́ком прока́те.

● *v.t.* **1** (*liberate*) освобо|жда́ть, -ди́ть; изб|авля́ть, -а́вить. **2** (*unfasten, let go*) отпус|ка́ть, -ти́ть; выпуска́ть, вы́пустить; **do not ~ the brake** не отпуска́йте то́рмоз; **he ~d her hand** он отпусти́л её ру́ку. **3** (*make over, surrender*) отд|ава́ть, -а́ть. **4** (*issue for circulation*) выпуска́ть, вы́пустить; **the news was ~d** сообще́ние бы́ло пре́дано огла́ске; **the film was ~d** фильм был вы́пущен (на экра́ны).

relegate /ˈrelɪˌgeɪt/ *v.t.* от|сыла́ть, -осла́ть; **the team was ~d to the second division** (*Br.*) кома́нду перевели́ во второ́й разря́д; **his works have been ~d to oblivion** его́ произведе́ния бы́ли пре́даны забве́нию.

relegation /ˌrelɪˈgeɪʃ(ə)n/ *n.* пониже́ние, перево́д (в бо́лее ни́зкий класс *и т.п.*).

relent /rɪˈlent/ *v.i.* смягч|а́ться, -и́ться; подобре́ть (*pf.*); **the storm ~ed** бу́ря ути́хла; **his sufferings made her ~** его́ страда́ния разжа́лобили её.

relentless /rɪˈlentlɪs/ *adj.* (*merciless*) безжа́лостный; **~ persecution** жесто́кие гоне́ния; (*persistent*) упо́рный, неукло́нный.

relentlessness /rɪˈlentlɪsnɪs/ *n.* безжа́лостность; упо́рство.

relet /riːˈlet/ *v.t.* (*Br.*) сда|ва́ть, -ть сно́ва.

relevance /ˈrelɪv(ə)ns/ *n.* отноше́ние к де́лу; уме́стность.

relevant /ˈrelɪv(ə)nt/ *adj.* относя́щийся к де́лу; уме́стный; **~ to** относя́щийся к+*d.*

reliability /rɪˌlaɪəˈbɪlɪtɪ/ *n.* надёжность; достове́рность.

reliable /rɪˈlaɪəb(ə)l/ *adj.* надёжный; (*of a source, statement etc.*) достове́рный.

reliance /rɪˈlaɪəns/ *n.* (*trust*) дове́рие; **I place great ~ upon him** я ему́ о́чень доверя́ю; (*dependence*) зави́симость; **~ on drugs** зави́симость от нарко́тиков.

reliant /rɪˈlaɪənt/ *adj.* (*dependent*) зави́симый, зави́сящий; **they are completely ~ on their pension** они́ по́лностью зави́сят от свое́й пе́нсии.

R

relic /ˈrelɪk/ *n.* **1** (*of saint etc.*) рели́квия. **2** (*object from past*) рели́квия; (*custom etc.*) пережи́ток. **3** (*pl., all that is left of sth.*) оста́ток.

relief /rɪˈli:f/ *n.* **1** (*alleviation, deliverance*) облегче́ние; **she heaved a sigh of ~** она́ издала́ вздох облегче́ния; **it was a great ~ to me** у меня́ отлегло́ от се́рдца. **2** (*abatement*) сниже́ние, смягче́ние; **~ road** (*Br.*) вспомога́тельная доро́га. **3** (*assistance to poor, distressed etc.*) посо́бие; **~ agency** организа́ция по оказа́нию по́мощи; **famine ~** по́мощь голода́ющим; **a ~ fund for flood victims** фонд по́мощи же́ртвам наводне́ния. **4** (*liberation*) освобожде́ние; (*raising of siege*) сня́тие оса́ды. **5** (*replacement*) сме́на (дежу́рных); (*person*) сме́на. **6** (*contrast*) переме́на, контра́ст; **a blank wall without ~** глуха́я ро́вная стена́; **Shakespeare introduces comic ~** Шекспи́р прибега́ет к коми́ческой разря́дке. **7** (*sculpture etc.*) релье́ф; **high/low ~** горелье́ф/барелье́ф; **in high ~** о́чень вы́пукло; **~ design** релье́фный узо́р; **~ map** релье́фная ка́рта.

relieve /rɪˈli:v/ *v.t.* **1** (*alleviate*) облегч|а́ть, -и́ть; **I was ~d to get your letter** я почу́вствовал облегче́ние, когда́ получи́л ва́ше письмо́; **it ~s the monotony** э́то вно́сит разнообра́зие. **2** (*bring assistance to*) при|ходи́ть, -йти́ на по́мощь + *d.*; выруча́ть, вы́ручить. **3** (*unburden*) освобо|жда́ть, -ди́ть (*кого от чего*); **this ~s me of the necessity to speak** э́то освобожда́ет меня́ от необходи́мости говори́ть; **swearing ~s one's feelings** когда́ вы́ругаешься, стано́вится ле́гче; **he ~d himself** (*urinated*) **against the wall** он помочи́лся/облегчи́лся у сте́нки; **may I ~ you of your bags?** позво́льте мне взять ва́ши чемода́ны. **4** (*replace on duty*) смен|я́ть, -и́ть; **you will be ~d at 10 o'clock** вас сменя́т в 10 часо́в.

religion /rɪˈlɪdʒ(ə)n/ *n.* рели́гия, ве́ра; вероисповеда́ние; **she makes a ~ of housework** она́ де́лает культ из дома́шнего хозя́йства.

religious /rɪˈlɪdʒəs/ *n.* (*pl.* **~**) ≈ мона́х; (*pl.*) чёрное духове́нство.
● *adj.* **1** религио́зный. **2** (*fig., scrupulous*): **he attended every meeting ~ly** он добросо́вестно посеща́л все собра́ния.

reline /ri:ˈlaɪn/ *v.t.* меня́ть, смени́ть подкла́дку у + *g.* (*or* на + *p.*).

relinquish /rɪˈlɪŋkwɪʃ/ *v.t.* (*give up, abandon*) ост|авля́ть, -а́вить; **she ~ed all hope** она́ оста́вила вся́кую наде́жду; **I ~ed the habit** я бро́сил э́ту привы́чку; (*surrender*) сд|ава́ть, -ать; остав|ля́ть, -а́вить; **he ~ed his claims** он отказа́лся от свои́х тре́бований; (*let go*) разж|има́ть, -а́ть; осл|абля́ть, -а́бить; **the dog ~ed its hold** соба́ка разжа́ла зу́бы.

relinquishment /rɪˈlɪŋkwɪʃmənt/ *n.* оставле́ние, сда́ча, отка́з (*от чего*).

reliquary /ˈrelɪkwərɪ/ *n.* ра́ка, ковче́г.

relish /ˈrelɪʃ/ *n.* **1** (*attractive quality*) пре́лесть, привлека́тельность; **sport lost its ~ for me** спорт потеря́л для меня́ свою́ пре́лесть; (*zest, liking*) смак, пристра́стие; **he ate with ~** он ел с аппети́том. **2** (*sauce, garnish*) припра́ва.
● *v.t.* получ|а́ть, -и́ть удово́льствие от + *g.*; смакова́ть (*impf.*) (*coll.*); **I don't ~ the prospect** меня́ не прельща́ет перспекти́ва; **you will not ~ what I have to say** то, что я скажу́, не придётся вам по вку́су.

relive /ri:ˈlɪv/ *v.t.* переж|ива́ть, -и́ть вновь.

reload /ri:ˈləʊd/ *v.t.* (*a vehicle etc.*) нагру|жа́ть, -зи́ть за́ново; (*a weapon*) перезаря|жа́ть, -ди́ть.

relocate /ˌri:ləʊˈkeɪt/ *v.t.* & *i.* переме|ща́ть(ся), -сти́ть(ся); перебази́ровать(ся) (*pf.*).

relocation /ˌri:ləʊˈkeɪʃən/ *n.* перемеще́ние.

reluctance /rɪˈlʌkt(ə)ns/ *n.* нежела́ние; неохо́та.

reluctant /rɪˈlʌkt(ə)nt/ *adj.* неохо́тный; **she was ~ to leave home** ей не хоте́лось покида́ть дом.

rely /rɪˈlaɪ/ *v.i.* полага́ться (*impf.*); наде́яться (*impf.*) (*both* на + *a.*); **you can ~ on me** вы мо́жете на меня́ положи́ться.

remain /rɪˈmeɪn/ *v.i.* ост|ава́ться, -а́ться; **little ~ed of the original building** от первонача́льного зда́ния почти́ ничего́ не оста́лось; **it only ~s for me to thank you** мне то́лько остаётся вас поблагодари́ть; **that ~s to be seen** поживём — уви́дим; (*stay*) пребыва́ть (*impf.*); **he ~ed a week in Paris** он про́был неде́лю в Пари́же; **he ~ed silent** он храни́л молча́ние; **his servants ~ed faithful to him** слу́ги оста́лись ве́рны ему́; **these things ~ the same** э́ти ве́щи не меня́ются; **please ~ seated!** пожа́луйста, не встава́йте!; **one thing ~s certain** одно́ безусло́вно я́сно; **I ~ yours truly** остаю́сь пре́данный Вам.

remainder /rɪˈmeɪndə(r)/ *n.* **1** (*residue, rest*) оста́т|ок, -ки (*m. pl.*); **he is selling the ~ of his estate** он продаёт оста́вшуюся часть своего́ поме́стья; (*of people*) остальны́е (*pl.*). **2** (*arith.*) оста́ток. **3** (*of book left unsold*) нераспро́данный тира́ж.
● *v.t.* уцен|я́ть, -и́ть нераспро́данный тира́ж; **the book was ~ed** кни́га была́ уценена́.

remains /rɪˈmeɪnz/ *n.* оста́тки (*m. pl.*), оста́нк|и (*pl., g.* -ов); **the ~ of daylight** оста́тки дневно́го све́та; **the ~ of a meal** оста́тки еды́; (*ruins*) разва́лин|ы (*pl., g.* —); (*corpse*): **the ~ were cremated** оста́нки бы́ли сожжены́.

remake *n.* /ˈri:meɪk/ (*e.g. of a film*) переснятый фильм; переде́лка.
● *v.t.* /ri:ˈmeɪk/ переде́л|ывать, -ать; (*a bed*) перест|ила́ть, -ла́ть.

remand /rɪˈmɑ:nd/ *n.* содержа́ние (арестова́нного) под стра́жей; **on ~** под стра́жей; **~ home** (*Br.*) исправи́тельный дом для несовершенноле́тних.
● *v.t.*: **he was ~ed in custody** он содержа́лся под стра́жей.

remark /rɪˈmɑ:k/ *n.* **1** (*notice*) наблюде́ние; **it is worthy of ~** э́то досто́йно внима́ния; **it passed without ~** э́то прошло́ незаме́ченным. **2** (*spoken observation*) замеча́ние; **he made rude ~s about my clothes** он отпуска́л неве́жливые замеча́ния по по́воду мое́й оде́жды.
● *v.t.* (*comment, notice*) зам|еча́ть, -е́тить; **'you are late,' he ~ed** «Вы опозда́ли», — заме́тил он.
● *v.i.* выска́зываться, вы́сказаться; **he ~ed upon your absence** он отме́тил ва́ше отсу́тствие.

remarkable /rɪˈmɑ:kəb(ə)l/ *adj.* (*extraordinary*) удиви́тельный; замеча́тельный; (*notable*): **this year has been ~ for its lack of rain** э́то был на ре́дкость сухо́й год.

remarriage /ri:ˈmærɪdʒ/ *n.* (вступле́ние в) но́вый брак.

remarry /ri:ˈmærɪ/ *v.i.* вступ|а́ть, -и́ть в но́вый брак.

remediable /rɪˈmi:dɪəb(ə)l/ *adj.* поправи́мый, излечи́мый.

remedial /rɪˈmi:dɪəl/ *adj.* исправля́ющий, лече́бный; (*educ.*) корректи́вный; **~ work** рабо́та с отстаю́щими.

remed|y /ˈremɪdɪ/ *n.* (*cure*) сре́дство, лека́рство; **a ~y for warts** сре́дство про́тив/от борода́вок.
● *v.t.* испр|авля́ть, -а́вить; **this cannot ~y the situation** э́то не попра́вит положе́ния; **these ills must be ~ied** э́ти недоста́тки должны́ быть испра́влены.

remember /rɪˈmembə(r)/ *v.t.* **1** (*keep in the memory*) по́мнить (*impf.*); уде́рживать/храни́ть (*impf.*) в па́мяти; **I ~ her as a girl** я по́мню её де́вочкой. **2** (*recall*) всп|омина́ть, -о́мнить; прип|омина́ть, -о́мнить; **I can't ~ his name** я не могу́ вспо́мнить его́ и́мя; **I ~ you saying it** я по́мню, что вы э́то сказа́ли; **not that I can ~** наско́лько я по́мню, нет; **he ~ed himself in time** он во́время опо́мнился. **3** (*not forget; be mindful of*) не забыва́ть/забы́ть, име́ть (*impf.*) в виду́; **~ to turn out the light** не забу́дьте погаси́ть свет; **~ you are still a young man** не забыва́йте, что вы ещё мо́лоды. **4** (*implying gift or gratuity*): **~ the waiter!** не забу́дьте дать официа́нту на чай!; **he ~ed her in his will** он упомяну́л её в своём завеща́нии. **5** (*convey greetings*): **~ me to your mother** переда́йте приве́т ва́шей ма́тери.

remembrance /rɪˈmembrəns/ *n.* **1** (*memory, recollection*) па́мять; воспомина́ние; **in ~ of** в па́мять о + *p.*; **it put me in ~ of my youth** э́то напо́мнило мне мо́лодость; **a service in ~ of the dead** помина́льная слу́жба; **R~ Day** день па́мяти поги́бших (в пе́рвую и втору́ю мировы́е войны). **2** (*memento*) сувени́р.

remind /rɪˈmaɪnd/ *v.t.* нап|омина́ть, -о́мнить (*кому что or о чём or inf.*); **he**

~s me of my father он напомина́ет мне отца́; **I was ~ed of the last time we met** э́то напо́мнило мне о на́шей после́дней встре́че; **he ~ed me to buy bread** он напо́мнил мне купи́ть хле́ба; **that ~s me!** кста́ти!; **visitors are ~ed that there is no admission after 6** посети́телей про́сят име́ть в виду́, что впуск прекраща́ется в 6 часо́в.

reminder /rɪ'maɪndə(r)/ *n.* напомина́ние; **I sent him a ~** я посла́л ему́ пи́сьменное напомина́ние; **he needs a gentle ~** ему́ на́до осторо́жно напо́мнить.

reminisce /ˌremɪ'nɪs/ *v.i.* пред|ава́ться, -а́ться воспомина́ниям.

reminiscence /ˌremɪ'nɪs(ə)ns/ *n.* воспомина́ние; **he wrote ~s of the war** он написа́л вое́нные мемуа́ры.

reminiscent /ˌremɪ'nɪs(ə)nt/ *adj.* **1** (*recalling the past*): **he became ~** он преда́лся воспомина́ниям. **2**: **~** (*suggestive*) **of** напомина́ющий; **his music is ~ of Brahms** его́ му́зыка напомина́ет Бра́мса.

remiss /rɪ'mɪs/ *adj.* хала́тный; неради́вый; **that was very ~ of me** э́то с моё́й стороны́ бы́ло недобросо́вестно.

remission /rɪ'mɪʃ(ə)n/ *n.* **1** (*forgiveness*) проще́ние; **~ of sins** отпуще́ние грехо́в. **2** (*discharge*): **~ of a debt** освобожде́ние от до́лга. **3** (*abatement, decrease*) уменьше́ние; **the noise went on without ~** шум не умолка́л; (*med.*) реми́ссия. **4** (*reduction of prison sentence*) сокраще́ние сро́ка заключе́ния.

remit¹ /'ri:mɪt/, /rɪ'mɪt/ *n.* (*terms of reference*) зада́чи (*f. pl.*), компете́нция.

remit² /rɪ'mɪt/ *v.t.* (**remitted, remitting**) **1** (*forgive*) про|ща́ть, -сти́ть; отпус|ка́ть, -ти́ть (*грехи*). **2** (*excuse payment of*) освобо|жда́ть, -ди́ть (*кого*) от + *g.*; **~ a tax** сн|има́ть, -ять нало́г. **3** (*send, transfer*) перес|ыла́ть, -ла́ть; перев|оди́ть, -ести́ (*деньги*).

remittance /rɪ'mɪt(ə)ns/ *n.* (*sending of money*) перево́д де́нег; (*money sent*) де́нежный перево́д; переводи́мые де́н|ьги (*pl.*, *g.* -ег).

remix¹ /'ri:mɪks/ *n.* (*in sound recording*) реми́кс.

remix² /ri:'mɪks/ *v.t.* (*in sound recording*) де́лать, с- реми́кс (+*g.*).

remnant /'remnənt/ *n.* (*remains*) оста́ток; (*of cloth*) оста́ток; (*survival*) пережи́ток.

remodel /ri:'mɒd(ə)l/ *v.t.* переде́л|ывать, -ать.

remold /ri:'məʊld/ (*US*) = **remould²**

remonstrance /rɪ'mɒnstrəns/ *n.* проте́ст.

remonstrate /'remənˌstreɪt/ *v.i.* протестова́ть (*impf.*); возра|жа́ть, -зи́ть; (*exhort*): **he ~d with me** он увещева́л меня́.

remorse /rɪ'mɔ:s/ *n.* **1** (*repentance; regret*) угрызе́ния (*nt. pl.*) со́вести; **do you feel no ~ for what you did?** вас не му́чит со́весть, что вы так поступи́ли? **2** (*compunction*) жа́лость; **without ~** безжа́лостно.

remorseful /rɪ'mɔ:sfʊl/ *adj.* по́лный раска́яния.

remorseless /rɪ'mɔ:slɪs/ *adj.* безжа́лостный.

remote /rɪ'məʊt/ *adj.* (**remoter, remotest**) отдалённый, глухо́й; **a ~ village** глухо́е село́; **a ~ ancestor** далё́кий пре́док; **~ control** (*control; device*) дистанцио́нное управле́ние; **there is a ~ possibility of its happening** не исключено́, что э́то случи́тся; **I haven't the ~st idea** не име́ю ни мале́йшего поня́тия; **he was not even ~ly interested** он не прояви́л ни мале́йшего интере́са (к + *d.*).

● *cpd.* **~-controlled** *adj.* радиоуправля́емый.

remould¹ /'ri:məʊld/ *n.* (*Br., tyre*) ши́на с восстано́вленным проте́ктором.

remould² /ri:'məʊld/ (*US* **remold**) *v.t.* лепи́ть, вы- за́ново; (*fig.*) преобра|жа́ть, -зи́ть.

remount /ri:'maʊnt/ *v.t.* **1** (*climb again*): **he ~ed the ladder** он сно́ва подня́лся на ле́стницу; **he ~ed his horse** он сно́ва сел на ло́шадь. **2** (*a photograph etc.*) перекле́ить (*pf.*) на друго́е паспарту́.

● *v.i.* сно́ва сади́ться/сесть на ло́шадь.

removable /rɪ'mu:vəb(ə)l/ *adj.* (*detachable*) съё́мный; (*from office*) устрани́мый, сменя́емый.

removal /rɪ'mu:v(ə)l/ *n.* (*taking away*) удале́ние; (*from office etc.*) смеще́ние, отстране́ние; (*of obstacles etc.*) устране́ние; (*Br., of furniture*) перево́зка; **~ firm** (*Br.*) трансаге́нтство; **~ men** (*Br.*) перево́зчики ме́бели; **~ van** (*Br.*) автофурго́н для перево́зки ме́бели.

remove /rɪ'mu:v/ *n.* (*degree of distance*) сте́пень отдале́ния; **this is only one ~ from treason** от э́того то́лько оди́н шаг до изме́ны; **at this ~** на э́том расстоя́нии.

● *v.t.* **1** (*take away, off*) уб|ира́ть, -ра́ть; ун|оси́ть, -ести́; **how can I ~ these stains?** как мо́жно вы́вести э́ти пя́тна?; **the boy was ~d from school** ма́льчика забра́ли из шко́лы; **he ~d his hat** он снял шля́пу; **this will ~ all your doubts** э́то рассе́ет все ва́ши сомне́ния. **2** (*dismiss*) сме|ща́ть, -сти́ть; **he was ~d from office** его́ сня́ли с рабо́ты. **3** (*eliminate*) устран|я́ть, -и́ть. **4** (*separate*): *see* ⇒**removed**

removed /rɪ'mu:vd/ *p.p.* **1** (*distant*) далё́кий, отдалё́нный; **what you have heard is not far ~ from the truth** то, что вы слы́шали, не так далеко́ от и́стины. **2** (*of relationships*): **first cousin once ~** (*cousin's child*) ребё́нок двою́родного бра́та (*or* двою́родной сестры́); (*parent's cousin*) двою́родный дя́дя, двою́родная тё́тя.

remover /rɪ'mu:və(r)/ *n.*: **furniture ~** (*Br.*) перево́зчик ме́бели; **paint, varnish ~** раствори́тель (*m.*); **stain ~** пятновыводи́тель (*m.*).

remunerate /rɪ'mju:nəˌreɪt/ *v.t.* (*person*) вознагра|жда́ть, -ди́ть; (*work*) опла́|чивать, -ти́ть.

remuneration /rɪˌmju:nə'reɪʃ(ə)n/ *n.* вознагражде́ние; опла́та.

remunerative /rɪ'mju:nərətɪv/ *adj.* вы́годный, хорошо́ опла́чиваемый.

renaissance /rɪ'neɪs(ə)ns/, /rə'n-/, /-sɑ̃s/ *n.* (**R~**, *hist.*) Ренесса́нс, Возрожде́ние; **R~ art** иску́сство эпо́хи Возрожде́ния; (*revival*) возрожде́ние.

renal /'ri:n(ə)l/ *adj.* по́чечный.

rename /ri:'neɪm/ *v.t.* переименов|ывать, -а́ть.

rend /rend/ *v.t.* (*past and p.p.* **rent**) **1** (*tear apart*) раз|рыва́ть, -орва́ть; раз|дира́ть, -одра́ть; **the country was rent by civil war** страну́ раздира́ла гражда́нская война́; **an explosion rent the air** взрыв сотря́с во́здух. **2** (*tear away*) от|рыва́ть, -орва́ть; от|дира́ть, -одра́ть.

render /'rendə(r)/ *v.t.* **1** (*give when required or due*) возд|ава́ть, -а́ть; отд|ава́ть, -а́ть; **let us ~ thanks to God** возблагодари́м же Бо́га; **~ unto Caesar (the things that are Caesar's)** ке́сарево ке́сарю; **doctors ~ valuable service** врачи́ де́лают поле́зное де́ло; **I was called on to ~ assistance** меня́ попроси́ли оказа́ть по́мощь. **2** (*present, submit*) предст|авля́ть, -а́вить; **you must ~ an account of your expenditure** вы должны́ отчита́ться в свои́х расхо́дах. **3** (*perform, portray*) исп|олня́ть, -о́лнить; **the sonata was beautifully ~ed** сона́та была́ прекра́сно испо́лнена. **4** (*translate*) перев|оди́ть, -ести́. **5** (*cause to be*): **he was ~ed speechless** он онеме́л; **the car accident ~ed him helpless** в результа́те автомоби́льной катастро́фы он оста́лся инвали́дом. **6** (*melt and clarify*) топи́ть, пере-. **7** (*cover with plaster*) штукату́рить, от-.

rend|ering /'rendərɪŋ/ *n.* (*performance*) исполне́ние; (*translation*) перево́д; (*plaster coating*) штукату́рка.

rendezvous /'rɒndɪˌvu:/, /-deɪˌvu:/ *n.* (*pl.* **~** /-ˌvu:z/) (*meeting*) рандеву́ (*nt. indecl.*), свида́ние; (*place*) ме́сто свида́ния; (*mil.*) сбор.

● *v.i.* (**rendezvouses** /-ˌvu:z/; **rendezvoused** /-ˌvu:d/; **rendezvousing** /-ˌvu:ɪŋ/) встр|еча́ться, -е́титься.

rendition /ren'dɪʃ(ə)n/ *n.* (*performance*) исполне́ние; (*translation*) перево́д.

renegade /'renɪˌgeɪd/ *n.* ренега́т, отсту́пник.

● *adj.* ренега́тский, отсту́пнический.

reneg(u)e /rɪ'ni:g/, /-'neg/, /-'neɪg/ *v.i.*: **he ~d on his promise** он нару́шил своё́ обеща́ние.

renew /rɪ'nju:/ *v.t.* **1** (*replace*) обнов|ля́ть, -и́ть; замен|я́ть, -и́ть; **she ~ed the water in his glass** она́ поменя́ла ему́ во́ду в стака́не. **2** (*restore, mend*) восстан|а́вливать, -ови́ть; **with ~ed vigour** (*Br.*), **vigor** (*US*) с удво́енной эне́ргией; с но́выми си́лами. **3** (*repeat, continue*) возобнов|ля́ть, -и́ть; **the game was ~ed** игра́ возобнови́лась; **your subscription needs ~ing** вам ну́жно возобнови́ть/продли́ть подпи́ску.

renewable /rɪˈnjuːəb(ə)l/ *adj.* могу́щий быть обновлённым/продлённым; **~ resources** возобновля́емые ресу́рсы; **the lease is ~ next year** срок аре́нды сле́дует продли́ть в бу́дущем году́.

renewal /rɪˈnjuːəl/ *n.* (*replacement*) обновле́ние; заме́на; (*restoration*) восстановле́ние; (*resumption*) возобновле́ние, продле́ние.

rennet /ˈrenɪt/ *n.* (*curdled milk*) сычу́жина.

renounc|e /rɪˈnaʊns/ *v.t.* (*surrender*) отка́з|ываться, -а́ться от + *g.*; отр|ека́ться, -е́чься от + *g.*; **he ~ed the world** он отрёкся от ми́ра.

renouncement /rɪˈnaʊnsmənt/ *n.* отрече́ние, отка́з.

renovate /ˈrenəˌveɪt/ *v.t.* (*renew*) обнов|ля́ть, -и́ть; восстан|а́вливать, -ови́ть; (*repair*) ремонти́ровать, от-; реставри́ровать (*impf.*, *pf.*).

renovation /ˌrenəˈveɪʃ(ə)n/ *n.* обновле́ние; восстановле́ние; (*repair*) реставра́ция; реконстру́кция; ремо́нт; **the builders carried out ~s** стро́ители произвели́ ремо́нт.

renovator /ˈrenəˌveɪtə(r)/ *n.* реставра́тор.

renown /rɪˈnaʊn/ *n.* сла́ва; изве́стность; **a preacher of ~** пропове́дник, по́льзующийся большо́й изве́стностью; **he won ~ on the battlefield** он завоева́л сла́ву на по́ле боя́.

renowned /rɪˈnaʊnd/ *adj.* просла́вленный, изве́стный; **he is ~ for his eloquence** он сла́вится свои́м красноре́чием.

rent[1] /rent/ *n.* (*tear, split*) дыра́; проре́ха.

rent[2] /rent/ *n.* (*for premises*) наёмная/аре́ндная пла́та; (*for land*) аре́ндная пла́та; (*for a flat*) квартпла́та; (*for telephone*) пла́та за телефо́н; **she pays a high, heavy ~ for her flat** она́ о́чень мно́го пла́тит за кварти́ру; **I pay £50 a week in ~** я плачу́ 50 фу́нтов в неде́лю за кварти́ру; **the ~ is fixed at £50** аре́ндная пла́та устано́влена в разме́ре пятидесяти фу́нтов; **I shall charge you ~ for the use of my car** я бу́ду брать с вас пла́ту за по́льзование мои́м автомоби́лем.

● *v.t.* **1** (*car, equipment*) брать, взять напрока́т; (*a place*) снима́ть, снять. **2**: **~ (out)** (*car, equipment*) дава́ть, дать напрока́т; (*building*) сд|ава́ть, -ать; **~ed accommodation** сня́тое жильё. **3** (*US, be let*): **these old houses ~ cheap** э́ти ста́рые дома́ сдаю́тся дёшево.

● *cpds.* **~-book** *n.* кни́га учёта аре́ндной пла́ты; **~ boy** *n.* (*Br., coll.*) мужчи́на-проститу́тка; **~-collector** *n.* сбо́рщик кварти́рной пла́ты; **~-free** *adj. & adv.* освобождённый (*or* с освобожде́нием) от кварти́рной пла́ты.

rent[3] /rent/ *past and p.p. of* ⇨**rend**

rental /ˈrent(ə)l/ *n.* (*income from rents*) ре́нтный дохо́д; (*rate of rent*) разме́р аре́ндной пла́ты.

renter /ˈrentə(r)/ *n.* нанима́тель (*m.*), аренда́тор.

rentier /ˈrɑ̃tɪˌeɪ/ *n.* рантье́ (*m. indecl.*).

renumber /riːˈnʌmbə(r)/ *v.t.* перенумеро́в|ывать, -а́ть.

renunciation /rɪˌnʌnsɪˈeɪʃ(ə)n/ *n.* (*surrender*) отка́з, отрече́ние.

reoccupation /riːˌɒkjʊˈpeɪʃ(ə)n/ *n.* повто́рный захва́т.

reoccupy /riːˈɒkjʊˌpaɪ/ *v.t.* вновь зан|има́ть, -я́ть; вновь оккупи́ровать (*impf.*, *pf.*).

reopen /riːˈəʊpən/ *v.t.* вновь/сно́ва откр|ыва́ть, -ы́ть; возобнов|ля́ть, -и́ть; **she ~ed the window** она́ сно́ва откры́ла окно́; **the discussion was ~ed** диску́ссия возобнови́лась; **I intend to ~ my bank account** я собира́юсь вновь откры́ть ба́нковский счёт.

● *v.i.*: **the shops will ~ after the holidays** по́сле пра́здников магази́ны откро́ются сно́ва.

reorder /riːˈɔːdə(r)/ *n.* повто́рный зака́з.

● *v.t.* (*rearrange*) перестр|а́ивать, -о́ить; (*renew order for*) повтор|я́ть, -и́ть зака́з на + *a.*

reorganization /riːˌɔːgənaɪˈzeɪʃ(ə)n/ *n.* реорганиза́ция.

reorganize /riːˈɔːgəˌnaɪz/ *v.t.* реорганизо́в|ывать, -а́ть.

reorient /riːˈɒrɪənt/, /riːˈɔːr-/ *v.t.* переориенти́ровать (*impf.*, *pf.*); **~ o.s.** переориенти́роваться (*impf.*, *pf.*).

reorientate /riːˈɒrɪənˌteɪt/, /riːˈɔːr-/ = **reorient**

rep[1], **-p** /rep/ *n.* (*text.*) репс.

rep[2] /rep/ (*coll.*) = **representative** *n.*

rep[3] /rep/ (*coll.*) = **repertory** 2

repaint /riːˈpeɪnt/ *v.t.* перекра́|шивать, -сить.

repair[1] /rɪˈpeə(r)/ *n.* **1** (*restoring to sound condition*) ремо́нт; **minor/running ~s** ме́лкий/теку́щий ремо́нт; **the shop is closed for ~s** магази́н закры́т на ремо́нт; **the road is under ~** доро́гу ремонти́руют; **my shoes need ~** мне ну́жно почини́ть ту́фли; **~ shop** ремо́нтная мастерска́я. **2** (*good condition*) го́дность, испра́вность; **the house is in good ~** дом в хоро́шем состоя́нии.

● *v.t.* (*mend, renovate*) ремонти́ровать, от-; чини́ть, по-; испр|авля́ть, -а́вить; (*restore*) восстан|а́вливать, -ови́ть.

● *cpd.* **~man** *n.* ма́стер, ремо́нтник.

repair[2] /rɪˈpeə(r)/ *v.i.* (*go*) напр|авля́ться, -а́виться.

repairable /rɪˈpeərəb(ə)l/ *adj.* поддаю́щийся ремо́нту/исправле́нию.

repairer /rɪˈpeərə(r)/ *n.* ма́стер, ремо́нтник.

reparable /ˈrepərəb(ə)l/ *adj.* поправи́мый, исправи́мый.

reparation /ˌrepəˈreɪʃ(ə)n/ *n.* компенса́ция; возмеще́ние уще́рба; (*pl., compensation for war damage*) (вое́нные) репара́ции (*f. pl.*).

repartee /ˌrepɑːˈtiː/ *n.* остроу́мный разгово́р; **gift of ~** остроу́мие.

repast /rɪˈpɑːst/ *n.* (*liter.*) тра́пе́за; (*banquet*) пи́ршество.

repatriate[1] /riːˈpætrɪˌeɪt/ *n.* репатриа́нт (*fem.* -ка).

repatriate[2] /riːˈpætrɪˌeɪt/ *v.t.* репатрии́ровать (*impf.*, *pf.*).

repatriation /riːˌpætrɪˈeɪʃ(ə)n/ *n.* репатриа́ция.

repay /riːˈpeɪ/ *v.t.* выпла́чивать, вы́платить; отпла́|чивать, -ти́ть; (*recompense*) возме|ща́ть, -сти́ть; **how can I ~ you?** как я могу́ вас отблагодари́ть?; **I shall ~ him in kind** я отплачу́ ему́ тем же (*or* той же моне́той); **I repaid his visit** я нанёс ему́ отве́тный визи́т.

repayable /riːˈpeɪəb(ə)l/ *adj.* подлежа́щий упла́те.

repayment /riːˈpeɪmənt/ *n.* вы́плата, возмеще́ние.

repeal /rɪˈpiːl/ *n.* отме́на, аннули́рование.

● *v.t.* аннули́ровать (*impf.*, *pf.*).

repeat /rɪˈpiːt/ *n.* повторе́ние; **~ order** повто́рный зака́з.

● *v.t.* (*say or do again*) повтор|я́ть, -и́ть; **he is always ~ing himself** он постоя́нно повторя́ется; **after ~ed attempts** по́сле неоднокра́тных попы́ток; **don't ~ what I have told you** не говори́те никому́ того́, что я вам сказа́л.

● *v.i.* **1** (*recur*) повтор|я́ться, -и́ться; встреча́ться (*impf.*). **2** (*of food*): **onions ~ on me** (*coll.*) у меня́ отры́жка от лу́ка. **3**: **~ing rifle** магази́нная винто́вка.

repeatedly /rɪˈpiːtɪdlɪ/ *adv.* неоднокра́тно, многокра́тно, то и де́ло.

repel /rɪˈpel/ *v.t.* (**repelled, repelling**) **1** (*phys.*) отт|а́лкивать, -олкну́ть. **2** (*repulse*) от|гоня́ть, -огна́ть; отб|ива́ть, -и́ть; **the attack was ~led** ата́ка была́ отби́та; **measures to ~ the enemy** ме́ры для оказа́ния отпо́ра врагу́; **she ~led his advances** она́ отве́ргла его́ уха́живания. **3** (*be repulsive to*) отта́лкивать (*impf.*); вызыва́ть, вы́звать отвраще́ние у + *g.*

repellent /rɪˈpelənt/ *n.*: **insect ~** сре́дство от насеко́мых.

● *adj.* (*repulsive*) отта́лкивающий.

repent /rɪˈpent/ *v.t. & i.* ка́яться (*impf.*); раска́|иваться, -яться (*в чём*).

repentance /rɪˈpentəns/ *n.* раска́яние.

repentant /rɪˈpentənt/ *adj.* ка́ющийся, раска́ивающийся; **he is not in the least ~** он нисколько не раска́ивается.

repercussion /ˌriːpəˈkʌʃ(ə)n/ *n.* (*usu. pl.*) после́дствия (*nt. pl.*); **this event will have wide ~s** э́то собы́тие бу́дет име́ть далеко́ иду́щие после́дствия.

repertoire /ˈrepəˌtwɑː(r)/ *n.* репертуа́р.

repertory /ˈrepətərɪ/ *n.* **1** (*repertoire*) репертуа́р. **2** (*also* ⇨**rep,** *coll.*): **~ company** постоя́нная тру́ппа с определённым репертуа́ром; **~**

theatre (*Br.*), **theater** (*US*) репертуа́рный теа́тр. **3** (*fig., store*) запа́с.

repetition /ˌrepɪ'tɪʃ(ə)n/ *n.* (*repeating, recurrence*) повторе́ние; **let there be no ~ of this** что́бы э́того бо́льше не́ было.

repetitious /ˌrepɪ'tɪʃəs/ = **repetitive**

repetitive /rɪ'petɪtɪv/ *adj.* повторя́ющийся; изоби́лующий повторе́ниями; ску́чный; **~ strain injury** тра́вма, вы́званная повторя́ющимся движе́нием.

rephrase /riː'freɪz/ *v.t.* перефрази́ровать (*impf., pf.*).

replace /rɪ'pleɪs/ *v.t.* **1** (*put back, return*) класть, положи́ть (*or* ста́вить, по-) на ме́сто; возвра|ща́ть, -ти́ть; **~ the receiver** положи́ть телефо́нную тру́бку. **2** (*provide substitute for*) замен|я́ть, -и́ть; **the vase cannot be ~d** э́то уника́льная ва́за. **3** (*take the place of; succeed*) заме|ща́ть, -сти́ть; **he ~d me as secretary** он замеща́л/смени́л меня́ в до́лжности секретаря́.

replaceable /rɪ'pleɪsəb(ə)l/ *adj.* заменя́емый, замени́мый.

replacement /rɪ'pleɪsmənt/ *n.* (*restitution*) возмеще́ние; (*provision of substitute or successor*) замеще́ние, заме́на; (*substitute, successor*) заме́на.

replant /riː'plɑːnt/ *v.t.* сно́ва заса́|живать, -ди́ть; переса́|живать, -ди́ть; **the shrubs were ~ed wider apart** кусты́ бы́ли переса́жены с бо́льшими интерва́лами.

replay[1] /'riːpleɪ/ *n.* (*of a game*) переигро́вка; (*of a record etc.*) (повто́рное) прои́грывание, повто́р.

replay[2] /riː'pleɪ/ *v.t.* (*sport*) переи́гр|ывать, -а́ть; (*a tape etc.*) (повто́рно) прои́гр|ывать, -а́ть.

replenish /rɪ'plenɪʃ/ *v.t.* (*one's wardrobe*) попо|лня́ть, -о́лнить; (*a fire*) под|кла́дывать, -ложи́ть дров/угля́ в+*a.*; **he ~ed his glass** он сно́ва напо́лнил стака́н.

replenishment /rɪ'plenɪʃmənt/ *n.* пополне́ние; дозапра́вка.

replete /rɪ'pliːt/ *adj.* напо́лненный; сы́тый, бога́тый (*чем*); **~ with food** нае́вшийся вдо́воль.

repletion /rɪ'pliːʃ(ə)n/ *n.* (*satiety*) сы́тость, насыще́ние; **full to ~** по́лный до отка́за.

replica /'replɪkə/ *n.* то́чная ко́пия, ре́плика.

reply /rɪ'plaɪ/ *n.* отве́т; **in** (*or* **by way of**) **~** в отве́т (на+*a.*); **I rang but there was no ~** я звони́л, но никто́ не отве́тил; **~ paid** с опла́ченным отве́том.

● *v.i.* отв|еча́ть, -е́тить.

repoint /riː'pɔɪnt/ *v.t.* за́ново расш|ива́ть, -и́ть швы кирпи́чной кла́дки.

repopulate /riː'pɒpjʊˌleɪt/ *v.t.* за́ново засел|я́ть, -и́ть.

repopulation /riːˌpɒpjʊ'leɪʃ(ə)n/ *n.* втори́чное заселе́ние.

report /rɪ'pɔːt/ *n.* **1** (*account, statement*) докла́д, отчёт; **newspaper ~** сообще́ние, изве́стие, репорта́ж; **school ~** (*Br.*), **~ card** (*US*) отчёт об успева́емости; **progress ~** отчёт о хо́де выполне́ния; **the policeman made a full ~** полице́йский соста́вил подро́бный протоко́л. **2** (*rumour*) молва́, слух; **we have only ~s to go on** наш еди́нственный исто́чник — слу́хи; **by all ~s, he is doing well** по всем све́дениям он процвета́ет. **3** (*sound of explosion or shot*) звук взры́ва/вы́стрела.

● *v.t.* **1** (*give news or account of*) сообщ|а́ть, -и́ть; сост|авля́ть, -а́вить отчёт о+*p.*; перед|ава́ть, -а́ть; **it has been ~ed that ...** сообща́лось, что...; **he was ~ed missing** он счита́лся пропа́вшим бе́з вести; **he ~ed having lost the money** он заяви́л о поте́ре де́нег; **the trial was ~ed in the press** проце́сс освеща́лся в печа́ти; (*gram.*): **~ed** (*indirect*) **speech** ко́свенная речь. **2** (*inform against, make known*) жа́ловаться, по- на+*a.*; **I shall ~ you for insolence** я пожа́луюсь на вас за ва́шу де́рзость.

● *v.i.* **1** (*give information*) до|кла́дывать, -ложи́ть; де́лать, с- докла́д; предст|авля́ть, -а́вить отчёт. **2** (*present o.s.*) яв|ля́ться, -и́ться (*куда-н.*); приб|ыва́ть, -ы́ть (*куда-н.*); **he was told to ~ to headquarters** ему́ бы́ло ве́лено яви́ться в штаб.

reportage /ˌrepɔː'tɑːʒ/ *n.* репорта́ж.

reportedly /rɪ'pɔːtɪdlɪ/ *adv.* по сообще́ниям; (*allegedly*) я́кобы.

reporter /rɪ'pɔːtə(r)/ *n.* репортёр.

repose /rɪ'pəʊz/ *n.* (*rest, sleep*) о́тдых, переды́шка; **her face is beautiful in ~** её лицо́ прекра́сно, когда́ споко́йно; (*restfulness, tranquillity*) поко́й, безмяте́жность.

● *v.t.* (*lay down*) класть, положи́ть; (*fig., place*): **he ~s confidence in her** он ей целико́м доверя́ет.

● *v.i.* **1** (*take one's rest*) отд|ыха́ть, -охну́ть; лечь (*pf.*) отдохну́ть. **2** (*lie*) лежа́ть (*impf.*); поко́иться (*impf.*); **his remains ~ in the churchyard** его́ прах поко́ится на кла́дбище.

repository /rɪ'pɒzɪtərɪ/ *n.* (*receptacle*) храни́лище, вмести́лище; (*store*) склад; (*fig.*): **he is a ~ of information** он неиссяка́емый исто́чник информа́ции.

repossess /ˌriːpə'zes/ *v.t.* из|ыма́ть, -ъя́ть за неплатёж.

repossession /ˌriːpə'zeʃ(ə)n/ *n.* изъя́тие иму́щества за неплатёж.

repp /rep/ = **rep**[1]

reprehensible /ˌreprɪ'hensɪb(ə)l/ *adj.* досто́йный осужде́ния; предосуди́тельный.

represent /ˌreprɪ'zent/ *v.t.* **1** (*portray*) изобра|жа́ть, -зи́ть; **what does this picture ~?** что изображено́ на э́той карти́не? **2** (*symbolize, correspond to*) символизи́ровать (*impf., pf.*), изобража́ть (*impf.*), обознача́ть (*impf.*); **one inch on the map ~s a mile** оди́н дюйм на ка́рте равня́ется одно́й ми́ле. **3** (*make out*): **he ~ed himself as an expert** он выдава́л себя́ за знатока́. **4** (*speak or act for*) представля́ть (*impf.*); **he ~s Britain at the UN** он представля́ет Великобрита́нию в ООН; **who ~s the defendant?** кто явля́ется защи́тником обвиня́емого?

representation /ˌreprɪzen'teɪʃ(ə)n/ *n.* **1** (*portrayal*) изображе́ние. **2** (*statement of one's case*): **diplomatic ~s** дипломати́ческие представле́ния. **3** (*delegation, deputizing*) представи́тельство; **proportional ~** пропорциона́льное представи́тельство.

representational /ˌreprɪzen'teɪʃən(ə)l/ *adj.*: **~ art** репрезентати́вное (*or* предме́тно-изобрази́тельное) иску́сство.

representative /ˌreprɪ'zentətɪv/ *n.* представи́тель (*m.*) (*fem.* -ница); **House of R~s** пала́та представи́телей.

● *adj.* показа́тельный, типи́чный; **~ government** представи́тельное прави́тельство; **he is ~ of his age** он типи́чный представи́тель свое́й эпо́хи.

repress /rɪ'pres/ *v.t.* **1** (*put down, curb*) подав|ля́ть, -и́ть; угнета́ть (*impf.*); **the revolt was ~ed** восста́ние бы́ло пода́влено. **2** (*restrain*) сде́рж|ивать, -а́ть; **I could not ~ my laughter** я не мог удержа́ться от сме́ха; **a ~ed personality** пода́вленная ли́чность.

repression /rɪ'preʃ(ə)n/ *n.* (*suppression*) подавле́ние; репре́ссия.

repressive /rɪ'presɪv/ *adj.* репресси́вный.

reprieve /rɪ'priːv/ *n.* (*leg.*) отсро́чка приведе́ния в исполне́ние (сме́ртного) пригово́ра; (*fig.*) переды́шка, вре́менное облегче́ние.

● *v.t.*: **the murderer was ~ed** казнь уби́йцы отсро́чили.

reprimand /'reprɪˌmɑːnd/ *n.* вы́говор, замеча́ние.

● *v.t.* де́лать, с- вы́говор/замеча́ние +*d.*

reprint[1] /'riːprɪnt/ *n.* перепеча́тка; репри́нт.

reprint[2] /riː'prɪnt/ *v.t.* перепеча́т|ывать, -ать.

reprisal /rɪ'praɪz(ə)l/ *n.* отве́тное де́йствие, отме́стка; **by way of ~** в отме́стку.

reproach /rɪ'prəʊtʃ/ *n.* **1** (*rebuke*) упрёк, уко́р; **his honesty is above ~** он безупре́чно че́стен; **he gave me a look of ~** он посмотре́л на меня́ с укори́зной; **~es were heaped upon him** его́ засы́пали упрёками. **2** (*disgrace*) позо́р; **he brought ~ on himself** он себя́ опозо́рил.

● *v.t.* упрек|а́ть, -ну́ть; укоря́ть (*impf.*); **I have nothing to ~ myself for** мне не́ в чем себя́ упрекну́ть; (*fig.*): **his eyes ~ed me** я прочита́л упрёк в его́ глаза́х.

reproachful /rɪ'prəʊtʃfʊl/ *adj.* укори́зненный.

reprobate /'reprəˌbeɪt/ *n.* негодя́й, нечести́вец.

● *adj.* нечести́вый; безнра́вственный.

R

reprobation /ˌreprəˈbeɪʃ(ə)n/ *n.* порицáние.

reproduce /ˌri:prəˈdju:s/ *v.t.* **1** (*copy, imitate*) воспроизв|одúть, -естú; **the artist has ~d your features well** худóжник хорошó воспроизвёл вáши черты́; (*of pictures*) репродуцúровать (*impf., pf.*). **2** (*beget*): **living things ~ their kind** живы́е существá размножáются.

● *v.i.* **1** (*be copied*): **this picture ~s well** с э́той картúны легкó дéлать репродýкцию. **2** (*of animals*) размн|ожáться, -óжиться.

reproducible /ˌri:prəˈdju:sɪb(ə)l/ *adj.* воспроизводúмый.

reproduction /ˌri:prəˈdʌkʃ(ə)n/ *n.* воспроизведéние; (*of picture*) репродýкция; (*of offspring*) размножéние.

reproductive /ˌri:prəˈdʌktɪv/ *adj.* воспроизводúтельный; (*biol.*) половóй; **~ organs** óрганы размножéния, репродуктúвные óрганы.

reprography /rɪˈprɒgrəfɪ/ *n.* репрогрáфия.

reproof /rɪˈpru:f/ *n.* (*reprimand*) порицáние; вы́говор; (*reproach*) укóр; **the teacher administered a sharp ~** учúтель сдéлал рéзкое замечáние.

re-proof /ri:ˈpru:f/ *v.t.* (*Br., e.g. a coat*) вновь пропúт|ывать, -áть водооттáлкивающим состáвом.

reproval /rɪˈpru:vəl/ *n.* вы́говор, порицáние.

reprove /rɪˈpru:v/ *v.t.* дéлать, с- вы́говор +*d.*

reptile /ˈreptaɪl/ *n.* пресмыкáющееся.

reptilian /repˈtɪlɪən/ *adj.* (*fig.*) пресмыкáющийся, пóдлый.

republic /rɪˈpʌblɪk/ *n.* респýблика; **People's R~** нарóдная респýблика; **R~ of South Africa** Ю́жно-Африкáнская Респýблика.

republican /rɪˈpʌblɪkən/ *n.* республикáнец; **R~** (*US*) член Республикáнской пáртии.

● *adj.* республикáнский.

republicanism /rɪˈpʌblɪkənɪz(ə)m/ *n.* республиканúзм.

republication /ri:ˌpʌblɪˈkeɪʃ(ə)n/ *n.* переиздáние.

republish /ri:ˈpʌblɪʃ/ *v.t.* переизд|авáть, -áть.

repudiate /rɪˈpju:dɪˌeɪt/ *v.t.* отв|ергáть, -éргнуть; отр|екáться, -éчься от +*g.*; **I ~ your accusation** я отвергáю вáше обвинéние; **he ~s the authority of the law** он не признаёт влáсти закóна.

repudiation /rɪˌpju:dɪˈeɪʃ(ə)n/ *n.* отречéние; отрицáние; откáз.

repugnance /rɪˈpʌgnəns/ *n.* отвращéние.

repugnant /rɪˈpʌgnənt/ *adj.* отвратúтельный.

repulse /rɪˈpʌls/ *n.* отпóр, отражéние.

● *v.t.* (*drive back*) отб|ивáть, -úть; (*rebuff, refuse*) отт|áлкивать, -олкнýть; отв|ергáть, -éргнуть.

repulsion /rɪˈpʌlʃ(ə)n/ *n.* **1** (*aversion*) отвращéние. **2** (*phys.*) оттáлкивание.

repulsive /rɪˈpʌlsɪv/ *adj.* **1** (*disgusting*) отвратúтельный. **2** (*phys.*) оттáлкивающий.

repurchase /ri:ˈpɜ:tʃɪs/ *n.* покýпка рáнее прóданного товáра.

● *v.t.* вновь покупáть, купúть (рáнее прóданный товáр).

reputable /ˈrepjʊtəb(ə)l/ *adj.* почтéнный, уважáемый.

reputation /ˌrepjʊˈteɪʃ(ə)n/ *n.* **1** (*name*) репутáция; **he has a ~ for courage** он слáвится хрáбростью; **he lived up to his ~** он доказáл, что заслýживает своéй репутáции. **2** (*respectability*) дóброе úмя; **persons of ~** почтéнные лю́ди.

repute /rɪˈpju:t/ *n.* (*reputation*) репутáция; **I know him by ~** я знáю о нём понаслы́шке; (*good reputation, renown*) дóброе úмя; **an artist of ~** худóжник с úменем.

● *v.t.*: **he is ~d to be rich** он считáется богáтым; говорят, что он богáт; **the ~d father** предполагáемый отéц.

reputedly /rɪˈpju:tɪdlɪ/ *adv.* по óбщему мнéнию.

request /rɪˈkwest/ *n.* прóсьба; **at my ~** по моéй прóсьбе; **~ stop** (*Br.*) остановка по трéбованию; **I have a ~ to make of you** у меня к вам прóсьба; **put in a ~ for** подáть (*pf.*) заявлéние/ заявку на +*a.*; **a programme** (*Br.*), **program** (*US*) **of ~s** концéрт по зая́вкам.

● *v.t.* просúть, по-; **he ~ed to be allowed to remain** он попросúл разрешéния остáться; **that is all I ~ of you** э́то всё, чегó я от вас прошý; **passengers are ~ed not to smoke** пассажúров прóсят не курúть; **may I ~ the pleasure of a dance?** разрешúте пригласúть вас на тáнец.

requiem /ˈrekwɪˌem/ *n.* (*mus.*) рéквием; (*relig.*) панихúда.

require /rɪˈkwaɪə(r)/ *v.t.* **1** (*need*) нуждáться (*impf.*) в +*p.*; трéбовать (*impf.*) +*g.*; **when do you ~ the job to be done?** к какóму срóку должнá быть завершенá рабóта?; **it ~d all his skill to ...** емý понáдобилось применúть всё своё умéние, чтóбы. . .; **all that is ~d is a little patience** трéбуется лишь немнóго терпéния; **the matter ~s some thought** над э́тим нáдо подýмать. **2** (*demand, order*) трéбовать, по- +*g.*; прикáз|ывать, -áть; **my attendance is ~d by law** по закóну я обя́зан присýтствовать; **what do you ~ of me?** что вы от меня хотúте?; **I have done all that is ~d** я сдéлал всё, что трéбуется.

requirement /rɪˈkwaɪəmənt/ *n.* **1** (*need*) нуждá; потрéбность; **I have few ~s** мои потрéбности невелúки. **2** (*demand*) трéбование; услóвие.

requisite /ˈrekwɪzɪt/ *n.* необходúмая вещь.

● *adj.* необходúмый.

requisition /ˌrekwɪˈzɪʃ(ə)n/ *n.* **1** (*official demand*) трéбование; (*mil.*) реквизúция. **2** (*service, use*) испóльзование; **every car was brought into ~** все машúны бы́ли реквизúрованы.

● *v.t.* реквизúровать (*impf., pf.*); **houses were ~ed for billets** домá бы́ли реквизúрованы для размещéния солдáт.

requital /rɪˈkwaɪtəl/ *n.* воздаянúе, вознаграждéние; возмéздие; **in ~ of his services** в кáчестве вознаграждéния за егó услýги.

requite /rɪˈkwaɪt/ *v.t.* вознагра|ждáть, -дúть; отплá|чивать, -тúть; **his kindness was ~d with ingratitude** за добротý емý отплатúли неблагодáрностью; **he was ~d for his services** он был вознаграждён за свой услýги.

re-read /ri:ˈri:d/ *v.t.* перечúт|ывать, -áть.

reredos /ˈrɪədɒs/ *n.* запрестóльный экрáн (в цéркви).

re-route /ri:ˈru:t/ *v.t.* измен|я́ть, -úть маршрýт/трáссу +*g.*

re-run *n.* /ˈri:rʌn/ (*of film etc.*) повтóрный покáз фúльма.

● *v.t.* /ri:ˈrʌn/: **the race was ~** состоя́лся повтóрный забéг; **he re-ran the tape** он ещё раз проигрáл плёнку.

resale /ri:ˈseɪl/ *n.* перепродáжа.

reschedule /ri:ˈʃedju:l/ *v.t.* перен|осúть, -естú.

rescind /rɪˈsɪnd/ *v.t.* аннулúровать (*impf., pf.*); отмен|я́ть, -úть.

rescission /rɪˈsɪʒ(ə)n/ *n.* аннулúрование, отмéна.

rescue /ˈreskju:/ *n.* спасéние, вы́ручка; **he came to my ~** он пришёл мне на пóмощь/вы́ручку; **a ~ attempt** попы́тка спастú (*когó/что*); **~ vessel** спасáтельное сýдно, спасáтель (*m.*).

● *v.t.* (**rescues, rescued, rescuing**) спас|áть, -тú; **all the crew were ~d** всю комáнду спаслú; **I ~d the letter from the dustbin** я вы́удил э́то письмó из мýсорного я́щика.

rescuer /ˈreskju:ə(r)/ *n.* спасúтель (*fem.* -ница).

reseal /ri:ˈsi:l/ *v.t.* вновь запечáт|ывать, -ать.

research /rɪˈsɜ:tʃ/ *n.* изучéние, исслéдование, изыскáние; пóиски (*m. pl.*); **~ and development** нáучно-исслéдовательская рабóта; **~ library** нáучно-техничéская библиотéка; **~ assistant** нáучный сотрýдник; **~ satellite** исслéдовательский спýтник.

● *v.t. & i.* исслéдовать (*impf., pf.*); **he is ~ing the subject** он изучáет/ разрабáтывает э́ту тéму; **the book is well ~ed** за э́той кнúгой чýвствуется большáя рабóта.

researcher /rɪˈsɜ:tʃə(r)/ *n.* исслéдователь (*fem.* -ница).

reseat /ri:ˈsi:t/ *v.t.* (*seat again*) вновь сажáть, посадúть; (*in different place*) пересá|живать, -дúть; **she ~ed herself more comfortably** онá усéлась поудóбнее.

resell /ri:ˈsel/ *v.t.* перепрод|авáть, -áть.

resemblance /rɪˈzembləns/ *n.*

схо́дство; **he bears a strong ~ to his father** он о́чень похо́ж на своего́ отца́.

resemble /rɪˈzemb(ə)l/ *v.t.* походи́ть (*impf.*) на + *a.*; име́ть (*impf.*) схо́дство с + *i.*

resent /rɪˈzent/ *v.t.* возму|ща́ться, -ти́ться + *i.*; негодова́ть (*impf.*) на + *a.*; **I ~ your interfering in my affairs** мне о́чень не нра́вится, что вы вме́шиваетесь в мои́ дела́.

resentful /rɪˈzentfʊl/ *adj.* возмущённый.

resentment /rɪˈzentmənt/ *n.* возмуще́ние; **I bear no ~ against him** я на него́ не в оби́де.

reservation /ˌrezəˈveɪʃ(ə)n/ *n.* **1** (*limitation, exception*) огово́рка; **mental ~** мы́сленная огово́рка. **2** (*booking*) (предвари́тельный) зака́з; зака́занное/заброни́рованное ме́сто. **3** (*for tribes etc.*) резерва́ция; (*for game*) запове́дник.

reserve /rɪˈzɜ:v/ *n.* **1** (*store*) запа́с, резе́рв; **he has great ~s of energy** у него́ большо́й запа́с эне́ргии; **he has a little money in ~** у него́ припасено́/отло́жено немно́го де́нег; **~ bank** резе́рвный банк. **2** (*mil.*) резе́рв; **the R~** резе́рвные ча́сти (*f. pl.*). **3** (**~** *player*) запасно́й (игро́к). **4** (*area*): **game ~** охо́тничий запове́дник. **5** (*limitation, restriction*) огово́рка; **I accept your statement without ~** я принима́ю ва́ше заявле́ние без огово́рок. **6** (*reticence*) сде́ржанность.

● *v.t.* **1** (*hold back, save*) бере́чь, с-; прибер|ега́ть, -е́чь; **~ your strength for tomorrow** берегите си́лы на за́втрашний день. **2**: **~ judgement** (*leg.*) от|кла́дывать, -ложи́ть реше́ние; **I prefer to ~ judgement** я предпочита́ю пока́ не выска́зываться; **~ a right** сохран|я́ть, -и́ть за собо́й пра́во. **3** (*set aside*) резерви́ровать, за-; (*ticket, table*) зака́з|ывать, -а́ть; (*hotel room*) брони́ровать, за-.

reserved /rɪˈzɜ:vd/ *adj.* **1** (*booked, set aside*) зака́занный (зара́нее); **~ seats** (*in train*) плацка́ртные места́. **2** (*reticent, uncommunicative*) сде́ржанный, за́мкнутый.

reservist /rɪˈzɜ:vɪst/ *n.* резерви́ст.

reservoir /ˈrezəˌvwɑ:(r)/ *n.* (*for water*) водохрани́лище, водоём; (*for other fluids*) резервуа́р, бачо́к.

reset /ri:ˈset/ *v.t.* **1** (*e.g. a watch*) перест|авля́ть, -а́вить; (*trap etc.*) сно́ва ста́вить, по-. **2** (*place in position again*) впр|авля́ть, -а́вить; вновь вст|авля́ть, -а́вить; **the doctor ~ his arm** врач впра́вил ему́ ру́ку.

resettle /ri:ˈset(ə)l/ *v.t.* пересел|я́ть, -и́ть.

● *v.i.* пересел|я́ться, -и́ться.

resettlement /ri:ˈset(ə)lmənt/ *n.* переселе́ние.

reshape /ri:ˈʃeɪp/ *v.t.* прид|ава́ть, -а́ть но́вую фо́рму + *d.*; (*fig.*) видоизмен|я́ть, -и́ть.

reshuffle /ri:ˈʃʌf(ə)l/ *n.* (*cards*) перетасо́вка; (*fig.*) перестано́вка; **Cabinet ~** перестано́вки в кабине́те мини́стров.

● *v.t.* перетасо́в|ывать, -а́ть; (*fig.*) произвести́ (*pf.*) перестано́вку в + *p.*

reside /rɪˈzaɪd/ *v.i.* **1** (*live*) прожива́ть (*impf.*); жить (*impf.*). **2**: **~** (*inhere, be vested*) **in** принадлежа́ть (*impf.*) + *d.*; быть прису́щим + *d.*; **supreme authority ~s in the President** президе́нт облечён вы́сшей вла́стью.

residence /ˈrezɪd(ə)ns/ *n.* **1** (*residing*) прожива́ние; **take up ~** въ|езжа́ть, -е́хать (в официа́льную резиде́нцию); **the students are in ~ again** студе́нты верну́лись в общежи́тие. **2** (*home, mansion*) дом, резиде́нция.

residency /ˈrezɪdənsɪ/ *n.* **1** (*residing*) прожива́ние. **2** (*official residence*) резиде́нция (*посла и т.п.*).

resident /ˈrezɪd(ə)nt/ *n.* (*permanent inhabitant*) (постоя́нный) жи́тель; (*Br., in hotel*) постоя́лец.

● *adj.* (*residing*) постоя́нно прожива́ющий; **the ~ population** постоя́нное населе́ние.

residential /ˌrezɪˈdenʃ(ə)l/ *adj.*: **a ~ area** жило́й райо́н.

residua /rɪˈzɪdjʊə/ *pl. of* ⇨**residuum**

residual /rɪˈzɪdjʊəl/ *adj.* оста́точный, оста́вшийся.

residue /ˈrezɪˌdju:/ *n.* **1** (*remainder*) оста́ток. **2** (*leg.*) насле́дство, очи́щенное от долго́в и завеща́тельных отка́зов.

residu|um /rɪˈzɪdjʊəm/ *n.* (*pl.* **~a**) (*chem.*) оста́ток, оса́док.

resign /rɪˈzaɪn/ *v.t.* **1** (*give up*) отка́з|ываться, -а́ться от + *g.*; **I have ~ed all claim to the money** я отказа́лся от вся́ких притяза́ний на э́ти де́ньги; **he ~ed his post as Chancellor** он по́дал в отста́вку с поста́ ка́нцлера; **they ~ed all hope** они́ оста́вили вся́кую наде́жду. **2** (*reconcile*): **he ~ed himself to defeat** он смири́лся с пораже́нием; **he was ~ed to being alone** он примири́лся с одино́чеством.

● *v.i.* под|ава́ть, -а́ть (*or* уходи́ть, уйти́) в отста́вку; уходи́ть, уйти́ с рабо́ты.

resignation /ˌrezɪgˈneɪʃ(ə)n/ *n.* **1** (*resigning of office*) отста́вка; **he handed in his ~** он по́дал заявле́ние об отста́вке/ухо́де. **2** (*acceptance of fate*) поко́рность, смире́ние.

resigned /rɪˈzaɪnd/ *adj.* поко́рный, смири́вшийся (с + *i.*).

resilience /rɪˈzɪlɪəns/ *n.* эласти́чность, упру́гость; (*fig.*) выно́сливость, живу́честь, жизнеспосо́бность.

resilient /rɪˈzɪlɪənt/ *adj.* эласти́чный, упру́гий; (*fig.*) неунывáющий: выно́сливый, живу́чий.

resin /ˈrezɪn/ *n.* смола́; канифо́ль.

resinous /ˈrezɪnəs/ *adj.* смоли́стый.

resist /rɪˈzɪst/ *v.t.* **1** (*oppose*) сопротивля́ться (*impf.*) + *d.*; проти́виться (*impf.*) + *d.*; **he ~ed arrest** он сопротивля́лся аре́сту; **all their attacks were ~ed** все их ата́ки бы́ли отби́ты. **2** (*be proof against*) не подава́ться (*impf.*) + *d.* **3** (*refrain from*) возде́рж|иваться, -а́ться от + *g.*; **I could not ~ the temptation to smile** я не мог удержа́ться от улы́бки; **she cannot ~ chocolates** она́ не мо́жет устоя́ть пе́ред шокола́дом.

resistance /rɪˈzɪst(ə)ns/ *n.* **1** (*opposition*) сопротивле́ние; **he took the line of least ~** он пошёл по ли́нии наиме́ньшего сопротивле́ния; **I broke down his ~** я сломи́л его́ сопротивле́ние; **(~ movement)** движе́ние сопротивле́ния. **2** (*power to withstand*) сопротивля́емость. **3** (*elec.*) сопротивле́ние.

resistant /rɪˈzɪst(ə)nt/ *adj.* сопротивля́ющийся; сто́йкий; **~ to heat** жаросто́йкий.

resistor /rɪˈzɪstə(r)/ *n.* рези́стор; кату́шка сопротивле́ния.

re-sit /ri:ˈsɪt/ *v.t.* (*Br.*): **~ an examination** пересдава́ть (*impf.*) экза́мен.

re-sole /ri:ˈsəʊl/ *v.t.* ста́вить, по- но́вые подмётки на + *a.*

resolute /ˈrezəˌlu:t/, /-ˌlju:t/ *adj.* реши́тельный; по́лный реши́мости.

resolution /ˌrezəˈlu:ʃ(ə)n/, /-ˈlju:ʃ(ə)n/ *n.* **1** (*firmness of purpose*) реши́тельность, реши́мость. **2** (*vow*): **New Year ~** новогóдний заро́к; новогóднее обеща́ние самому́ себе́. **3** (*expression of opinion or intent*) резолю́ция; **they passed a ~ to go on strike** они́ при́няли реше́ние нача́ть забасто́вку. **4** (*of doubt, discord etc.*) (раз)реше́ние. **5** (*separation into components*) разложе́ние. **6** (*mus.*) разреше́ние. **7** (*degree of detail in image*) разреше́ние.

resolve /rɪˈzɒlv/ *n.* (*determination*) реши́тельность, реши́мость; (*vow, intention*) реше́ние; наме́рение.

● *v.t.* & *i.* **1** (*decide, determine*) реш|а́ть, -и́ть; прин|има́ть, -я́ть реше́ние; **I have ~d to spend less** я реши́л тра́тить ме́ньше де́нег; **it was ~d** бы́ло решено́. **2** (*settle*) (раз)реша́ть, -и́ть; **all doubts were ~d** все сомне́ния бы́ли разрешены́/рассе́яны; **their quarrel was ~d** их спор разреши́лся.

resonance /ˈrezənəns/ *n.* резона́нс, гул.

resonant /ˈrezənənt/ *adj.* звуча́щий, зво́нкий.

resort /rɪˈzɔ:t/ *n.* **1** (*recourse*): **without ~ to force** не прибега́я к наси́лию; **in the last ~** в кра́йнем слу́чае. **2** (*expedient*) наде́жда; спаси́тельное сре́дство. **3** (*frequented place*): **holiday ~** куро́рт; **seaside ~** морско́й куро́рт.

● *v.i.* (*have recourse*) приб|ега́ть, -е́гнуть (к + *d.*).

re-sort /ri:ˈsɔ:t/ *v.t.* пересортиро́в|ывать, -а́ть.

resound /rɪˈzaʊnd/ *v.i.* звуча́ть (*impf.*); **the hall ~ed with voices** в за́ле раздава́лись голоса́; (*fig.*) греме́ть, про-; **a ~ing success** оглуши́тельный успе́х.

resource /rɪˈsɔ:s/, /-ˈzɔ:s/ *n.* **1** (*available supply; stock*) запа́сы (*m. pl.*); ресу́рсы

R

(*m. pl.*); **the country's natural ~s** приро́дные ресу́рсы страны́; **he was left to his own ~s** он мог положи́ться то́лько на самого́ себя́. **2** (*ingenuity*) нахо́дчивость; **a man of ~** нахо́дчивый челове́к.

resourceful /rɪˈsɔːsfʊl/, /-ˈzɔːsfʊl/ *adj.* изобрета́тельный, нахо́дчивый.

resourcefulness /rɪˈsɔːsfʊlnɪs/, /-ˈzɔːsfʊlnɪs/ *n.* изобрета́тельность, нахо́дчивость.

respect /rɪˈspekt/ *n.* **1** (*esteem, deference*) уваже́ние; **he won their ~** он завоева́л их уваже́ние; **he is held in great ~** его́ о́чень уважа́ют; **I have the greatest ~ for his opinion** я о́чень счита́юсь с его́ мне́нием; **with ~, I cannot agree** при всём уваже́нии к вам, я не могу́ согласи́ться. **2** (*consideration, attention*): **we must have ~ for, pay ~ to public opinion** нам на́до счита́ться с обще́ственным мне́нием. **3** (*reference, relation*) отноше́ние, каса́тельство; **in ~ of, with ~ to** что каса́ется + *g.* **4** (*pl., polite greetings*) почте́ние; **he came to pay his ~s** он пришёл засвиде́тельствовать своё почте́ние.

● *v.t.* **1** (*treat with consideration or esteem; defer to*) уважа́ть (*impf.*); почита́ть (*impf.*); **my wishes were ~ed** мои́ пожела́ния бы́ли учтены́; **a ~ed actor** при́знанный актёр. **2** (*relate to*): **the law ~ing young persons** зако́н, каса́ющийся молодёжи.

respectability /rɪˌspektəˈbɪlɪtɪ/ *n.* респекта́бельность.

respectable /rɪˈspektəb(ə)l/ *adj.* **1** (*qualifying for social approval*) респекта́бельный; прили́чный; **your clothes are not quite ~** вы не о́чень прили́чно оде́ты; **he comes of a ~ family** он из хоро́шей/прили́чной семьи́. **2** (*of some merit, size or importance*) прили́чный; **he earns a ~ salary** он зараба́тывает прили́чные де́ньги; **he is quite a ~ painter** он вполне́ прили́чный худо́жник.

respectful /rɪˈspektfʊl/ *adj.* почти́тельный; **they kept (at) a ~ distance** они́ держа́лись на почти́тельном расстоя́нии; **yours ~ly** с уваже́нием.

respective /rɪˈspektɪv/ *adj.* соотве́тственный; **we went off to our ~ rooms** мы разошли́сь по свои́м ко́мнатам; **the boys and girls were taught woodwork and sewing ~ly** ма́льчиков и де́вочек учи́ли соотве́тственно столя́рному де́лу и шитью́.

respiration /ˌrespɪˈreɪʃ(ə)n/ *n.* дыха́ние; **he was given artificial ~** ему́ сде́лали иску́сственное дыха́ние.

respirator /ˈrespɪˌreɪtə(r)/ *n.* (*to prevent inhalation of certain substances*) респира́тор; (*med.*) прибо́р для дли́тельного иску́сственного дыха́ния.

respiratory /rɪˈspɪrətərɪ/, /ˈrespəˌreɪtərɪ/ *adj.* респира́торный, дыха́тельный.

respite /ˈrespaɪt/, /-pɪt/ *n.* **1** (*relief, rest*) переды́шка; **they gave us no ~** они́ не дава́ли нам передохну́ть. **2** (*temporary reprieve*) отсро́чка.

resplendent /rɪˈsplend(ə)nt/ *adj.* блиста́тельный.

respond /rɪˈspɒnd/ *v.i.* **1** (*reply*) отв|еча́ть, -е́тить (на + *a.*); **he ~ed with a blow** он отве́тил уда́ром. **2** (*react*) реаги́ровать, от- (на + *a.*); от|зыва́ться, -озва́ться (на + *a.*); **his illness is ~ing to treatment** его́ боле́знь поддаётся лече́нию.

respondent /rɪˈspɒnd(ə)nt/ *n.* (*leg.*) отве́тчи|к (*fem.* -ца); (*to a questionnaire*) респонде́нт.

response /rɪˈspɒns/ *n.* **1** (*reply*) отве́т; **he made no ~** он ничего́ не отве́тил; **in ~ to your enquiry** в отве́т на ваш запро́с. **2** (*reaction*) реа́кция, о́тклик; **my appeal met with no ~** моё обраще́ние не вы́звало никако́го о́тклика; **there was little ~ from the audience** аудито́рия реаги́ровала сла́бо. **3** (*eccl.*): **sung ~s** отве́тствие хо́ра.

responsibilit|y /rɪˌspɒnsɪˈbɪlɪtɪ/ *n.* **1** (*being responsible*) отве́тственность; **I take full ~y for my actions** я беру́ на себя́ по́лную отве́тственность за свои́ де́йствия; **he acted on his own ~y** он де́йствовал на свой страх и риск; **he has a position of great ~y** он занима́ет о́чень отве́тственную до́лжность. **2** (*charge, duty*) обя́занность, отве́тственность; **he was relieved of his ~ies** он был освобождён от исполне́ния обя́занностей.

responsible /rɪˈspɒnsɪb(ə)l/ *adj.* **1** (*liable, accountable*) отве́тственный; **he is ~ to me for keeping the accounts** в вопро́сах бухгалте́рии он подчиня́ется мне; **she is ~ for cleaning my room** убо́рка мое́й ко́мнаты вхо́дит в её обя́занности; (*to blame*): **he was held ~ for the loss** его́ обвини́ли в э́той пропа́же; **who was ~ for breaking the window?** кто разби́л окно́?; (*to be thanked*): **Churchill was ~ for our victory** на́ша побе́да — заслу́га Че́рчилля. **2** (*trustworthy*) надёжный. **3** (*involving responsibility*) ва́жный; **a ~ post** отве́тственный пост.

responsive /rɪˈspɒnsɪv/ *adj.* отзы́вчивый.

rest¹ /rest/ *n.* **1** (*sleep; relaxation in bed*) сон; о́тдых; **you need a good night's ~** вам на́до как сле́дует вы́спаться; **I'm going (up) to have a ~** я пойду́ приля́гу. **2** (*inactive, immobile or undisturbed state*) поко́й; **day of ~** де́нь о́тдыха; **I set his mind at ~** я его́ успоко́ил; **the ball came to ~** мяч останови́лся; **he was laid to ~** (*buried*) его́ похорони́ли. **3** (*intermission of work, activity etc.*) переды́шка; **they took a short ~** они́ сде́лали небольшу́ю переды́шку; **he gave his horse a ~** он дал коню́ отдохну́ть. **4** (*prop, support*) опо́ра; (*for telephone*) рыча́г; (*for billiard cue*) сто́йка. **5** (*mus.*) па́уза.

● *v.t.* **1** (*give ~ to*) да|ва́ть, -ть о́тдых + *d.*; **he ~ed his horse** он дал коню́ отдохну́ть; **God ~ his soul!** ца́рствие ему́ небе́сное!; **are you quite ~ed?** вы хорошо́ отдохну́ли? **2** (*place for support*) класть, положи́ть (на + *a.*); прислон|я́ть, -и́ть (*что к чему*); **she ~ed her elbows on the table** она́ положи́ла ло́кти на стол; **he ~ed his chin on his hand** он подпира́л подборо́док руко́й; **~ the ladder against the wall!** прислони́те ле́стницу к сте́нке; (*fig., base*) обосно́в|ывать, -а́ть; **he ~s his case on the right of ownership** он стро́ит свои́ доказа́тельства на пра́ве со́бственности.

● *v.i.* **1** (*relax; take repose*) лежа́ть (*impf.*); отд|ыха́ть, -охну́ть; **may he ~ in peace!** мир пра́ху его́!; **(last) ~ing-place** моги́ла; **I could not ~ until I'd told you the news** я не мог успоко́иться, пока́ не подели́лся с ва́ми но́востью. **2** (*fig., remain*) ост|ава́ться, -а́ться; **the matter cannot ~ there** э́то де́ло нельзя́ так оста́вить; **the decision ~s with you** реше́ние зави́сит от вас; **~ assured I will do all I can** я сде́лаю всё возмо́жное, мо́жете не сомнева́ться. **3** (*be supported*) опира́ться (*impf.*) (*на что*); поко́иться (*impf.*) (*на чём*); **the bridge ~s on 4 piers** мост поко́ится на четырёх опо́рах; **there was a bicycle ~ing against the wall** у стены́ стоя́л велосипе́д; (*fig.*) осно́вываться (*impf.*). **4** (*linger; alight*) поко́иться (*impf.*); ост|ава́ться, -а́ться. **5** (*lie fallow*) остава́ться (*impf.*) под па́ром.

● *cpds.* **~-cure** *n.* лече́ние поко́ем; **~-day** *n.* выходно́й/нерабо́чий день; **~-home** *n.* санато́рий, дом о́тдыха; **~-room** *n.* (*US, lavatory*) туале́т, убо́рная.

rest² /rest/ *n.* (*remainder*) оста́ток; (*remaining things, people*) остальны́е (*pl.*); **and all the ~ of it** и всё про́чее; **for the ~** в остально́м.

restart /riːˈstɑːt/ *v.t.* вновь нач|ина́ть, -а́ть; сно́ва зав|оди́ть, -ести́ (*маши́ну*).

restate /riːˈsteɪt/ *v.t.* (*repeat*) вновь заяв|ля́ть, -и́ть; (*reformulate*) за́ново формули́ровать, с-.

restaurant /ˈrestəˌrɒnt/, /-ˌrɔ̃/ *n.* рестора́н; **~ car** ваго́н-рестора́н.

restaurateur /ˌrestərəˈtɜː(r)/ *n.* владе́лец рестора́на.

restful /ˈrestfʊl/ *adj.* успокои́тельный, успока́ивающий; **a ~ light** мя́гкий свет.

restitution /ˌrestɪˈtjuːʃ(ə)n/ *n.* (*restoration*) возвраще́ние; (*compensation*) возмеще́ние; **he was forced to make ~** его́ заста́вили возмести́ть убы́тки.

restive /ˈrestɪv/ *adj.* (*of horse*) норови́стый; (*of person*) стропти́вый; (*restless*) беспоко́йный.

restless /ˈrestlɪs/ *adj.* беспоко́йный, непосе́дливый; **I feel ~** мне что́-то не сиди́тся; **she spent a ~ night** она́ провела́ беспоко́йную/бессо́нную ночь.

restlessness /ˈrestlɪsnɪs/ *n.* беспоко́йство, непосе́дливость.

restock /riːˈstɒk/ *v.i.* поп|олня́ть, -о́лнить запа́сы.

restoration /ˌrestəˈreɪʃ(ə)n/ *n.* **1** (*return*) восстановле́ние; **~ of property** возвраще́ние иму́щества; **~ to health** восстановле́ние здоро́вья. **2** (*refurbishment; renewal*) реставра́ция. **3** (*hist.*) реставра́ция; **R~ drama** дра́ма эпо́хи Ка́рла II.

restorative /rɪˈstɒrətɪv/ *adj.* укрепля́ющий.

● *n.* укрепля́ющее сре́дство.

restore /rɪˈstɔː(r)/ *v.t.* **1** (*give, bring or put back*) возвра|ща́ть, -ти́ть (*or* верну́ть); восстан|а́вливать, -ови́ть; **the property was ~d to its owner** иму́щество бы́ло возвращено́ владе́льцу; **he was ~d to his former post** его́ восстанови́ли на пре́жней рабо́те; **it ~s my confidence** э́то вселя́ет в меня́ но́вую уве́ренность; **he was soon ~d to health** его́ здоро́вье вско́ре восстанови́лось; **order was ~d** поря́док был восстано́влен. **2** (*reconvert to original state*) реставри́ровать (*impf., pf.*); восстан|а́вливать, -ови́ть; **these pictures have been ~d** э́ти карти́ны реставри́рованы.

restorer /rɪˈstɔːrə(r)/ *n.* реставра́тор; восстанови́тель (*m.*).

restrain /rɪˈstreɪn/ *v.t.* сде́рж|ивать, -а́ть; обу́зд|ывать, -а́ть; **it took four men to ~ him** понадо́билось че́тыре челове́ка, что́бы удержа́ть его́; **I could not ~ my laughter** я не мог удержа́ться от сме́ха; **his manner was ~ed** он был сде́ржан.

restraint /rɪˈstreɪnt/ *n.* **1** (*self-control*) сде́ржанность, самооблада́ние. **2** (*physical*) ограниче́ние свобо́ды движе́ния. **3** (*constraint*) ограниче́ние; **without ~** без ограниче́ний; свобо́дно.

restrict /rɪˈstrɪkt/ *v.t.* ограни́чи|вать, -ть; **free travel is ~ed to pensioners** беспла́тный прое́зд распространя́ется то́лько на пенсионе́ров; **speed is ~ed to 30 mph** ско́рость ограни́чена до тридцати́ миль в час; **his vision was ~ed by trees** ему́ бы́ло пло́хо ви́дно из-за дере́вьев; **~ed area** (*Br., with speed limit*) райо́н ограни́ченной ско́рости движе́ния; (*mil.*) запре́тная зо́на.

restriction /rɪˈstrɪkʃ(ə)n/ *n.* ограниче́ние; **you can drink without ~** мо́жно пить ско́лько уго́дно.

restrictive /rɪˈstrɪktɪv/ *adj.* ограничи́тельный; **~ practices in industry** (*Br.*) ме́ры по ограниче́нию конкуре́нции и́ли произво́дства.

restyle /riːˈstaɪl/ *v.t.* переде́л|ывать, -ать; измен|я́ть, -и́ть стиль +*g.*

result /rɪˈzʌlt/ *n.* результа́т, сле́дствие; **he died as a ~ of his injuries** он у́мер от ран; **his efforts were without ~** его́ уси́лия бы́ли безрезульта́тны/беспло́дны; (*of a sum or problem*) результа́т, отве́т.

● *v.i.* **1** (*arise, come about*) сле́довать (*impf.*) (*из чего*); **this ~s from negligence** э́то сле́дствие небре́жности. **2** (*issue, end*) конча́ться, ко́нчиться (+*i.*); **the quarrel ~ed in bloodshed** ссо́ра ко́нчилась кровопроли́тием.

resultant /rɪˈzʌlt(ə)nt/ *n.* (*phys.*, **~ force**) равноде́йствующая си́ла.

● *adj.* равноде́йствующий; (*consequent*) вытека́ющий (*из чего*).

resume /rɪˈzjuːm/ *v.t.* (*e.g. discussions, work*) возобнов|ля́ть, -и́ть; (*continue*) прод|олжа́ть, -о́лжить; **to ~ my story** я продо́лжу свой расска́з; (*take again*) вновь обре|та́ть, -сти́; **he ~d his seat** он верну́лся на своё ме́сто; **they ~d control** они́ восстанови́ли контро́ль; **he ~d command** он сно́ва при́нял кома́ндование (*чем*).

● *v.i.*: **let us ~ after lunch** продо́лжим по́сле обе́да.

résumé /ˈrezjʊˌmeɪ/ *n.* резюме́ (*indecl.*).

resumption /rɪˈzʌmpʃ(ə)n/ *n.* возобновле́ние; продолже́ние.

resurface /riːˈsɜːfɪs/ *v.t.* меня́ть, смени́ть покры́тие +*g.*

● *v.i.* (*of a submarine*) всплы|ва́ть, -ть.

resurgence /rɪˈsɜːdʒ(ə)ns/ *n.* возрожде́ние.

resurgent /rɪˈsɜːdʒ(ə)nt/ *adj.* возрожда́ющийся.

resurrect /ˌrezəˈrekt/ *v.t.* **1** (*raise from the dead*) воскре|ша́ть -си́ть; **be ~ed** воскр|еса́ть, -е́снуть. **2** (*fig., rediscover, revive*) возро|жда́ть, -ди́ть; воскре|ша́ть, -си́ть.

resurrection /ˌrezəˈrekʃ(ə)n/ *n.* воскресе́ние; (*fig.*) возрожде́ние, воскреше́ние.

resuscitate /rɪˈsʌsɪˌteɪt/ *v.t.* прив|оди́ть, -ести́ в созна́ние.

resuscitation /rɪˌsʌsɪˈteɪʃ(ə)n/ *n.* приведе́ние в созна́ние.

retail /ˈriːteɪl/ *n.* ро́зничная прода́жа; **~ prices** ро́зничные це́ны.

● *v.t.* (*sell by ~*) прод|ава́ть, -а́ть в ро́зницу.

● *v.i.* продава́ться (*impf.*) в ро́зницу.

retailer /ˈriːteɪlə(r)/ *n.* ро́зничный торго́вец.

retain /rɪˈteɪn/ *v.t.* **1** (*keep, continue to have*) уде́рживать (*impf.*); сохран|я́ть, -и́ть. **2** (*keep in place*) подде́рж|ивать, -а́ть; **~ing wall** подпо́рная стена́. **3** (*secure services of*) нан|има́ть, -я́ть; **~ing fee** предвари́тельный гонора́р.

retainer /rɪˈteɪnə(r)/ *n.* **1** (*hist.*) васса́л; (*servant*) слуга́ (*m.*). **2** (*fee*) предвари́тельный гонора́р.

retake[1] /ˈriːteɪk/ *n.* (*cin.*) повто́рная съёмка.

retake[2] /riːˈteɪk/ *v.t.* **1** (*recapture*) сно́ва брать, взять; **the city was ~n** го́род был сно́ва захва́чен. **2** (*film etc.*) пересн|има́ть, -я́ть.

retaliate /rɪˈtælɪˌeɪt/ *v.i.* отпла́|чивать, -ти́ть той же моне́той; мстить, ото- (*кому за что*).

retaliation /rɪˌtælɪˈeɪʃ(ə)n/ *n.* отпла́та, возме́здие.

retaliatory /rɪˈtæljətərɪ/ *adj.* отве́тный, кара́тельный.

retard /rɪˈtɑːd/ *v.t.* зам|едля́ть, -е́длить; **a ~ed child** у́мственно отста́лый ребёнок.

retardation /ˌriːtɑːˈdeɪʃ(ə)n/ *n.* замедле́ние.

retch /retʃ/, /riːtʃ/ *v.i.* ту́житься (*impf.*) при рво́те.

retell /riːˈtel/ *v.t.* переска́з|ывать, -а́ть.

retention /rɪˈtenʃ(ə)n/ *n.* уде́рживание, сохране́ние; **~ of urine** заде́ржка мочи́.

retentive /rɪˈtentɪv/ *adj.*: **a ~ memory** це́пкая па́мять; **a soil ~ of moisture** по́чва, сохраня́ющая вла́гу.

retentiveness /rɪˈtentɪvnɪs/ *n.* (*of memory*) це́пкость.

rethink /riːˈθɪŋk/ *v.t.* пересм|а́тривать, -отре́ть.

reticence /ˈretɪs(ə)ns/ *n.* молчали́вость; скры́тность.

reticent /ˈretɪs(ə)nt/ *adj.* молчали́вый; скры́тный.

reticulated /rɪˈtɪkjʊleɪtɪd/ *adj.* се́тчатый.

reticulation /rɪˌtɪkjʊˈleɪʃ(ə)n/ *n.* се́тчатый узо́р.

retina /ˈretɪnə/ *n.* (*pl.* **retinas** *or* **retinae** /-ˌniː/) сетча́тка.

retinue /ˈretɪˌnjuː/ *n.* сви́та.

retir|e /rɪˈtaɪə(r)/ *v.t.* ув|ольня́ть, -о́лить; **he was ~ed on a pension** его́ отпра́вили на пе́нсию.

● *v.i.* **1** (*withdraw*) удал|я́ться, -и́ться; **she wishes to ~e from the world** она́ хо́чет уедини́ться/провести́ свою́ жизнь в уедине́нии; **in company he ~es into himself** когда́ круго́м лю́ди, он ухо́дит в себя́; **she ~ed (to bed) early** она́ ра́но легла́ (спать); **he has a ~ing disposition** он засте́нчивый челове́к; (*mil.*) отступ|а́ть, -и́ть. **2** (*from employment*) уходи́ть, уйти́ в отста́вку; **when will you reach ~ing age?** когда́ вы дости́гнете пенсио́нного во́зраста?

retired /rɪˈtaɪəd/ *adj.* (находя́щийся) на пе́нсии; в отста́вке; **a ~ officer** отставно́й офице́р.

retirement /rɪˈtaɪəmənt/ *n.* (*withdrawal*) отхо́д; (*seclusion*) уедине́ние; (*end of employment*) отста́вка, вы́ход на пе́нсию (*or* в отста́вку); **in ~** в отста́вке; **~ age** пенсио́нный во́зраст.

retool /riːˈtuːl/ *v.t.* переобору́довать (*impf., pf.*).

retort[1] /rɪˈtɔːt/ *n.* (*vessel*) рето́рта.

retort[2] /rɪˈtɔːt/ *n.* (*reply*) возраже́ние; ре́зкий отве́т.

● *v.t. & i.* отв|еча́ть, -е́тить ре́зко (тем же).

retouch /riːˈtʌtʃ/ *v.t.* ретуши́ровать, от-/под-.

retrace /rɪˈtreɪs/ *v.t.* просле́|живать, -ди́ть; **~ one's steps** возвраща́ться, верну́ться тем же путём; (*reconstruct, rehearse*) переч|исля́ть, -и́слить.

retract /rɪˈtrækt/ *v.t.* **1** (*draw in*) втя|гивать, -ну́ть. **2** (*withdraw*) отка́з|ываться, -а́ться от +*g.*; **I ~ my statement** я беру́ наза́д своё заявле́ние.

R

● *v.i.* втя́|гиваться, -ну́ться.

retractable /rɪ'træktəb(ə)l/ *adj.*: **~ undercarriage** убира́ющееся шасси́.

retraction /rɪ'trækʃ(ə)n/ *n.* (*drawing in*) втя́гивание; (*withdrawal*) отрече́ние, отка́з (от + *g.*).

retrain /ri:'treɪn/ *v.t.* переподгот|а́вливать, -о́вить; переквалифици́ровать (*impf.*, *pf.*).

● *v.i.* переквалифици́роваться (*impf.*, *pf.*).

retraining /ri:'treɪnɪŋ/ *n.* переподгото́вка, переквалифика́ция.

retransmission /ˌri:trænz'mɪʃ(ə)n/, /-s'mɪʃ(ə)n/, /ˌri:trɑ:n-/ *n.* ретрансми́ссия, ретрансля́ция.

retransmit /ˌri:trænz'mɪt/, /-s'mɪt/, /ˌri:trɑ:n-/ *v.t.* ретрансли́ровать (*impf.*, *pf.*).

retread *v.t.* /ri:'tred/: **~ a tyre** (*Br.*), **tire** (*US*) восстан|а́вливать, -ови́ть проте́ктор (ши́ны).

● *n.* /'ri:tred/ ши́на с восстано́вленным проте́ктором.

retreat /rɪ'tri:t/ *n.* **1** (*withdrawal*) отступле́ние, отхо́д; **the army was in full ~** а́рмия отступа́ла по всему́ фро́нту; **they sounded the ~** они́ да́ли сигна́л к отхо́ду/отступле́нию. **2** (*secluded place*) убе́жище.

● *v.i.* (*withdraw*) удал|я́ться, -и́ться.

retrench /rɪ'trentʃ/ *v.t.* сокра|ща́ть, -ти́ть.

● *v.i.* (*economize*) эконо́мить, с-.

retrenchment /rɪ'trentʃmənt/ *n.* сокраще́ние расхо́дов.

retrial /ri:'traɪəl/ *n.* повто́рное слу́шание де́ла; пересу́д (*coll.*).

retribution /ˌretrɪ'bju:ʃ(ə)n/ *n.* возме́здие, ка́ра.

retributive /rɪ'trɪbjʊtɪv/ *adj.* кара́ющий, кара́тельный.

retrievable /rɪ'tri:vəb(ə)l/ *adj.* восстанови́мый; (*reparable*) поправи́мый.

retrieval /rɪ'tri:vəl/ *n.* **1** (*recovery, getting back*) возвраще́ние; **the money is lost beyond ~** де́ньги поте́ряны безвозвра́тно; (*of birds etc. by dogs*) поно́ска; (*tech., of information*) по́иск. **2** (*recollection, restoration, revival*) восстановле́ние. **3** (*making good, repair*) исправле́ние.

retrieve /rɪ'tri:v/ *v.t.* **1** (*get back, recover*) брать, взять обра́тно; доста́ть (*pf.*), верну́ть (*pf.*); (*of dogs; also v.i.*) приноси́ть (*impf.*) (*дичь*). **2** (*restore*) восстан|а́вливать, -ови́ть. **3** (*put right, make amends for*) испр|авля́ть, -а́вить.

retriever /rɪ'tri:və(r)/ *n.* охо́тничья по́иско́вая соба́ка.

retroactive /ˌretrəʊ'æktɪv/ *adj.* име́ющий обра́тное де́йствие (*or* обра́тную си́лу).

retrograde /'retrəˌgreɪd/ *adj.* дви́жущийся в обра́тном направле́нии; (*fig.*) реакцио́нный.

retrogress /ˌretrə'gres/ *v.i.* регресси́ровать (*impf.*).

retrogression /ˌretrə'greʃ(ə)n/ *n.* регре́сс.

retrogressive /ˌretrə'gresɪv/ *adj.* регресси́рующий.

retro-rocket /'retrəʊˌrɒkɪt/ *n.* тормозна́я раке́та.

retrospect /'retrəˌspekt/ *n.*: **in ~** ретроспекти́вно; **the journey was pleasant in ~** пото́м об э́том путеше́ствии бы́ло прия́тно вспомина́ть.

retrospection /ˌretrə'spekʃ(ə)n/ *n.* размышле́ния (*nt. pl.*) о про́шлом; ретроспе́кция.

retrospective /ˌretrə'spektɪv/ *adj.* (*regarding the past*) ретроспекти́вный; **a ~ law** зако́н, име́ющий обра́тную си́лу.

● *n.* (*exhibition*) ито́говая вы́ставка рабо́т худо́жника.

re-try /ri:'traɪ/ *v.t.* (*leg., case*) слу́шать (*impf.*) за́ново; (*person*) суди́ть (*impf.*) сно́ва.

returf /ri:'tɜ:f/ *v.t.* (*Br.*) за́ново покр|ыва́ть, -ы́ть дёрном.

return /rɪ'tɜ:n/ *n.* **1** (*coming or going back*) возвраще́ние; **point of no ~** (*fig.*) черта́, за кото́рой (уже́) нет возвра́та (наза́д); **there was no ~ of the symptoms** симпто́мы не повтори́лись; **by ~ (of post)** (*Br.*) обра́тной по́чтой; **many happy ~s (of the day)!** с днём рожде́ния!; **~ fare** сто́имость обра́тного прое́зда. **2** (**~ ticket**) (*Br.*) обра́тный биле́т. **3** (*turnover*) оборо́т; (*profit*) при́быль; **he got a good ~ on his investment** он получи́л хоро́ший дохо́д от вло́женных де́нег. **4** (*giving, sending, putting, paying back*) отда́ча, возвра́т, опла́та; **the ~ of a ball** возвра́т мяча́; **~ match** отве́тный матч; **the ~ of a candidate** избра́ние кандида́та в парла́мент. **5** (*reciprocation*) **in ~ (for)** взаме́н (+ *g.*); (*in response to*) в отве́т (на + *a.*). **6** (*report*) отчёт, ра́порт; **income tax ~** нало́говая деклара́ция/ве́домость; **election ~s** результа́т вы́боров. **7** (*comput.*) возвра́т; **~ key** кла́виша возвра́та.

● *v.t.* **1** (*give, send, put, pay back*) возвра|ща́ть, -ти́ть (*or* верну́ть); **I ~ed the book to the shelf** я поста́вил кни́гу обра́тно на по́лку; **he ~ed the ball accurately** он хорошо́ отби́л мяч; **she ~ed my compliment** она́ сде́лала мне отве́тный комплиме́нт; **he was ~ed by a narrow majority** он прошёл (в парла́мент) с незначи́тельным большинство́м; **~ing officer** (*Br., pol.*) уполномо́ченный по вы́борам. **2** (*say in reply*) отв|еча́ть, -е́тить; возра|жа́ть, -зи́ть. **3** (*declare*) до|кла́дывать, -ложи́ть; **the jury ~ed a verdict of guilty** прися́жные призна́ли обвиня́емого вино́вным.

● *v.i.* возвра|ща́ться, -ти́ться (*or* верну́ться).

returnable /rɪ'tɜ:nəb(ə)l/ *adj.* подлежа́щий возвра́ту.

reunion /ri:'ju:njən/, /-nɪən/ *n.* (*reuniting*) воссоедине́ние; (*meeting of old friends etc.*) встре́ча (ста́рых друзе́й); **family ~** сбор всей семьи́.

reunite /ˌri:ju:'naɪt/ *v.t.* & *i.* воссоедин|я́ть(ся), -и́ть(ся).

reusable /ri:'ju:zəb(ə)l/ *adj.* многокра́тного по́льзования.

re-use[1] /ri:'ju:s/ *n.* повто́рное/но́вое испо́льзование.

re-use[2] /ri:'ju:z/ *v.t.* сно́ва испо́льзовать (*impf.*, *pf.*).

Rev. *abbr. of* ⇨**Reverend**

rev /rev/ *n.* (*coll.*) = **revolution** 2

● *v.t.* & *i.* (**revved, revving**) (*also* **~ up**) увели́чи|вать, -ть оборо́ты (мото́ра).

revaluation /ri:ˌvælju:'eɪʃ(ə)n/ *n.* (*of currency*) ревальва́ция.

revalue /ri:'vælju:/ *v.t.* ревальви́ровать (*impf.*, *pf.*).

revamp /ri:'væmp/ *v.t.* (*fig.*) поднов|ля́ть, -и́ть; обнов|ля́ть, -и́ть.

revanchism /rɪ'væntʃɪz(ə)m/ *n.* реванши́зм.

revanchist /rɪ'væntʃɪst/ *n.* реванши́ст.

● *adj.* реванши́стский.

reveal /rɪ'vi:l/ *v.t.* обнару́жи|вать, -ть; пока́з|ывать, -а́ть; **he would not ~ his name** он хоте́л сохрани́ть своё и́мя в та́йне; **he ~ed himself to be the father** он объяви́л себя́ отцо́м; **this account is very ~ing** э́тот отчёт о́чень показа́телен; **she wore a ~ing dress** она́ была́ в откры́том пла́тье.

reveille /rɪ'vælɪ/, /rɪ'velɪ/ *n.* у́тренняя заря́; побу́дка.

revel /'rev(ə)l/ *n.* гуля́нка, кутёж; **the ~s went on all night** гуля́нка шла всю ночь.

● *v.i.* (**revelled, revelling;** *US* **reveled, reveling**) **1** (*make merry*) пирова́ть (*impf.*); кути́ть (*impf.*). **2** (*take delight*) наслажда́ться (*impf.*) (+ *i.*); упива́ться (*impf.*) (+ *i.*); **she ~s in gossip** она́ обожа́ет спле́тни.

revelation /ˌrevə'leɪʃ(ə)n/ *n.* откры́тие, открове́ние (*also fig., surprise*); (*bibl.*, **R~(s)**) апока́липсис.

reveller /'revələ(r)/ (*US* **reveler**) *n.* кути́ла (*m.*), гуля́ка (*m.*).

revelry /'revəlrɪ/ *n.* попо́йка, разгу́л.

revenge /rɪ'vendʒ/ *n.* **1** (*retaliatory action*) месть; **he took his ~ on me** он мне отомсти́л. **2** (*vindictive feeling*) мсти́тельность; **I acted out of ~** я э́то сде́лал из ме́сти. **3** (*in games*) рева́нш; **they gave their opponents their ~** они́ да́ли свои́м проти́вникам возмо́жность отыгра́ться.

● *v.t.* мстить, ото- (*кому за кого/что*); **he ~d the wrong done him** он отомсти́л за нанесённую ему́ оби́ду; **he ~d himself on his enemies** он отомсти́л свои́м врага́м.

revengeful /rɪ'vendʒfʊl/ *adj.* мсти́тельный.

revenue /'revəˌnju:/ *n.* дохо́д; (*of state*) госуда́рственные дохо́ды; **Inland R~** (*Br.*), **Internal R~** (*US*) фина́нсовое/нало́говое управле́ние.

reverberate /rɪ'vɜ:bəˌreɪt/ *v.i.* (*of sound etc.*) отра|жа́ться, -зи́ться; (*fig.*): **the**

news ~d э́та но́вость произвела́ фуро́р.

reverberation /rɪ,vɜ:bəˈreɪʃ(ə)n/ *n.* отраже́ние, ревербера́ция.

revere /rɪˈvɪə(r)/ *v.t.* почита́ть (*impf.*); чтить (*impf.*).

reverence /ˈrevərəns/ *n.* **1** (*awe, respect*) почита́ние, почте́ние; **they have no ~ for tradition** у них нет никако́го уваже́ния к тради́циям. **2**: **your R~** ва́ше преподо́бие.
● *v.t.* почита́ть (*impf.*); чтить (*impf.*).

reverend /ˈrevərənd/ *adj.*: **the R~ John Smith** его́ преподо́бие Джон Смит.

reverent(ial) /,revəˈrenʃ(ə)l/ *adj.* почти́тельный, благогове́йный.

reverie /ˈrevərɪ/ *n.* мечта́ние, мечта́, грёза; **she was lost in ~** она́ погрузи́лась в мечта́ния.

reversal /rɪˈvɜ:səl/ *n.* (*annulment*) отме́на; (*conversion into opposite*) по́лная переме́на, поворо́т на 180° (сто во́семьдесят гра́дусов); переворо́т; **a ~ of fortune** превра́тность судьбы́.

reverse /rɪˈvɜ:s/ *n.* **1** (*opposite*) противополо́жность; **the ~ is true** де́ло обстои́т как раз наоборо́т; **he was the ~ of happy** он был отню́дь не рад; **I am not ill, quite the ~** я не бо́лен — совсе́м наоборо́т.
2 (**~ gear): he put the car into ~** он включи́л за́дний ход.
3 (*of coin*) обра́тная сторона́; ре́шка.
● *adj.* обра́тный, противополо́жный; **in ~ order** в обра́тном поря́дке; **stamps have gum on the ~ side** с обра́тной стороны́ ма́рки покры́ты клеем; **in ~ gear** за́дним хо́дом.
● *v.t.* **1** (*turn round, invert*) пов|ора́чивать, -ерну́ть обра́тно; **the situation was ~d** ситуа́ция кру́то измени́лась.
2 (*annul*) отмен|я́ть, -и́ть; **he ~d his decision** он пересмотре́л своё реше́ние.
3 (*drive backwards*): **he ~d (the car) into a wall** он дал за́дний ход и вре́зался в сте́ну.
● *v.i.* **1** (*of driver*) да|ва́ть, -ть за́дний ход.
2 (*of vehicle*): **the car ~s well** маши́на хорошо́ идёт за́дним хо́дом; **reversing light** (*Br.*) фона́рь (*m.*) за́днего хо́да.

reversible /rɪˈvɜ:sɪb(ə)l/ *adj.* (*of process etc.*) обрати́мый; (*that can be turned inside out*) двусторо́нний.

reversion /rɪˈvɜ:ʃ(ə)n/ *n.* **1** (*return*) возвраще́ние (к пре́жнему состоя́нию); **~ to type** атави́зм. **2** (*of property or rights*) обра́тный перехо́д (иму́щества) к первонача́льному владе́льцу.

revert /rɪˈvɜ:t/ *v.i.* возвра|ща́ться, -ти́ться; **the fields have ~ed to scrub** поля́ вновь поросли́ куста́рником; **he ~ed to his old ways** он взя́лся за ста́рое; (*of property, rights etc.*) пере|ходи́ть, -йти́ (*к прежнему владельцу*); **his land ~ed to the state** его́ земля́ перешла́ к госуда́рству.

revet /rɪˈvet/ *v.t.* (**revetted, revetting**) облиц|о́вывать, -ева́ть.

revetment /rɪˈvetmənt/ *n.* облицо́вка, обши́вка.

review /rɪˈvju:/ *n.* **1** (*re-examination, survey, revision*) пересмо́тр, просмо́тр; **the decision is subject to ~** реше́ние подлежи́т пересмо́тру; **the matter is under constant ~** к э́тому вопро́су постоя́нно возвраща́ются.
2 (*retrospect*) пересмо́тр; **a ~ of the year's events** обзо́р собы́тий го́да. **3** (*of mil. forces etc.*) пара́д. **4** (*of book etc.*) реце́нзия, о́тзыв. **5** (*periodical*) периоди́ческое изда́ние, обозре́ние.
● *v.t.* **1** (*reconsider, re-examine*) пересм|а́тривать, -отре́ть. **2** (*survey mentally*) мы́сленно обозр|ева́ть, -е́ть; **he ~ed his chances of success** он проанализи́ровал/взве́сил свои́ ша́нсы на успе́х. **3** (*inspect*) просм|а́тривать, -отре́ть. **4** (*write critical account of*) рецензи́ровать, от-/про-; **the film was well ~ed** фильм получи́л хоро́шие реце́нзии.
● *v.i.*: **he ~s for the Times** он рецензе́нт газе́ты «Таймс»; (*US, for exams*) гото́виться к экза́менам.

reviewer /rɪˈvju:ə(r)/ *n.* рецензе́нт, кри́тик.

revile /rɪˈvaɪl/ *v.t.* оскорб|ля́ть, -и́ть; поноси́ть (*impf.*).

revise /rɪˈvaɪz/ *v.t.* пересм|а́тривать, -отре́ть; испр|авля́ть, -а́вить; перераб|а́тывать, -о́тать; **~d and enlarged edition** испра́вленное и допо́лненное изда́ние; **I ~d my opinion of him** я измени́л своё мне́ние о нём.
● *v.i.* (*Br.*): **I must ~ for the exams** я до́лжен повтори́ть материа́л (*or* гото́виться) к экза́менам.

reviser /rɪˈvaɪzə(r)/ *n.* реда́ктор.

revision /rɪˈvɪʒ(ə)n/ *n.* пересмо́тр; (*checking*) прове́рка, перерабо́тка, реда́кция; (*for exams*) повторе́ние.

revisionism /rɪˈvɪʒə,nɪz(ə)m/ *n.* ревизиони́зм.

revisionist /rɪˈvɪʒənɪst/ *n.* ревизиони́ст.

revisit /ri:ˈvɪzɪt/ *v.t.* посе|ща́ть, -ти́ть сно́ва.

revitalization /ri:,vaɪtəlaɪˈzeɪʃ(ə)n/ *n.* оживле́ние.

revitalize /ri:ˈvaɪtə,laɪz/ *v.t.* вновь ожив|ля́ть, -и́ть.

revival /rɪˈvaɪv(ə)l/ *n.* (*return to consciousness, health etc.*) возвраще́ние созна́ния; восстановле́ние здоро́вья; **a sudden ~ in spirits** внеза́пный подъём ду́ха; **a ~ of interest** оживле́ние интере́са; (*return to use, knowledge, popularity*) возрожде́ние; **the ~ of old customs** возрожде́ние ста́рых обы́чаев; **(religious ~)** возрожде́ние ве́ры; (*of play*) возобновле́ние.

revivalism /rɪˈvaɪvə,lɪz(ə)m/ *n.* евангели́зм.

revivalist /rɪˈvaɪvəlɪst/ *n.* евангели́ст (*fem.* -ка).

revive /rɪˈvaɪv/ *v.t.* возро|жда́ть, -ди́ть; ожив|ля́ть, -и́ть; **a glass of brandy ~d her** рю́мка коньяку́ привела́ её в чу́вство; **their hopes were ~d** они́ вновь обрели́ наде́жду; **can you ~ the fire?** вы мо́жете сно́ва разже́чь ого́нь?; **the opera was recently ~d** э́ту о́перу неда́вно поста́вили сно́ва.
● *v.i.* возро|жда́ться, -ди́ться; (*regain vigour*) ож|ива́ть, -и́ть; **his spirits ~d** он приободри́лся; (*regain consciousness*) при|ходи́ть, -йти́ в себя́/чу́вство.

revocable /ˈrevəkəb(ə)l/ *adj.* могу́щий быть отменённым.

revocation /,revəˈkeɪʃ(ə)n/ *n.* отме́на, аннули́рование.

revoke /rɪˈvəʊk/ *v.t.* отмен|я́ть, -и́ть; аннули́ровать (*impf., pf.*).
● *v.i.* (*at cards; US also* **reneg(u)e**) пойти́ (*pf.*) с друго́й ма́сти при нали́чии тре́буемой.

revolt /rɪˈvəʊlt/ *n.* восста́ние; бунт; **the peasants were in ~** крестья́не восста́ли.
● *v.t.* вызыва́ть, вы́звать отвраще́ние у + *g.*; **a ~ing sight** отврати́тельное зре́лище.
● *v.i.* восст|ава́ть, -а́ть; бунтова́ть (*impf.*); взбунтова́ться (*pf.*).

revolution /,revəˈlu:ʃ(ə)n/ *n.* **1** (*revolving*) враще́ние. **2** (*one complete rotation; coll.* **rev**) оборо́т; **at 60 ~s per minute** при шести́десяти оборо́тах в мину́ту. **3** (*pol., fig.*) револю́ция.

revolutionary /,revəˈlu:ʃənərɪ/ *n.* революционе́р (*fem.* -ка).
● *adj.* революцио́нный.

revolutionize /,revəˈlu:ʃə,naɪz/ *v.t.* (*stir up to revolution, transform*) революционизи́ровать (*impf., pf.*).

revolv|e /rɪˈvɒlv/ *v.i.* враща́ться (*impf.*); **~ing doors** враща́ющиеся две́ри; (*fig.*): **he thinks everything ~es around him** он мнит себя́ це́нтром вселе́нной.

revolver /rɪˈvɒlvə(r)/ *n.* револьве́р.

revue /rɪˈvju:/ *n.* обозре́ние, ревю́ (*nt. indecl.*).

revulsion /rɪˈvʌlʃ(ə)n/ *n.* (*disgust*) отвраще́ние.

reward /rɪˈwɔ:d/ *n.* **1** (*recompense*) награ́да (за + *a.*); **without thought of ~** не ду́мая о вознагражде́нии. **2** (*sum offered*) пре́мия; де́нежное вознагражде́ние.
● *v.t.* (воз)награ|жда́ть, -ди́ть; **it was a ~ing task** де́ло сто́ило того́; **our patience was ~ed** на́ше терпе́ние бы́ло вознаграждено́.

rewind /ri:ˈwaɪnd/ *v.t.* перем|а́тывать, -ота́ть; (*a watch*) (сно́ва) зав|оди́ть, -ести́.

re-wire /ri:ˈwaɪə(r)/ *v.t.*: **~ a house** замен|я́ть, -и́ть прово́дку в до́ме.

reword /ri:ˈwɜ:d/ *v.t.* выража́ть, вы́разить други́ми слова́ми; переформули́ровать (*impf., pf.*).

rework /ri:ˈwɜ:k/ *v.t.* перераб|а́тывать, -о́тать.

rewrite¹ /ˈri:raɪt/ *n.* перерабо́танный текст.

rewrite² /ri:ˈraɪt/ *v.t.* (*copy out*) перепи́с|ывать, -а́ть; (*rework*) перераб|а́тывать, -о́тать.

R

Reykjavik /'reikjə,vi:k/ *n.* Ре́йкьявик.

rhapsodize /'ræpsə,daɪz/ *v.i.* (*fig.*) восторга́ться (*impf.*); говори́ть (*impf.*) с упое́нием.

rhapsod|y /'ræpsədɪ/ *n.* (*mus.*) рапсо́дия; (*fig.*): **he went into ~ies over her dress** он пел дифира́мбы её туале́ту.

rheostat /'ri:ə,stæt/ *n.* реоста́т.

rhesus /'ri:səs/ *n.* (**~ monkey**) ре́зус; **~ factor** ре́зус-фа́ктор; **~-negative** ре́зус-отрица́тельный.

rhetoric /'retərɪk/ *n.* (*art of speech*) рито́рика; ора́торское иску́сство; (*pej.*) краснобА́йство, фразёрство.

rhetorical /rɪ'tɒrɪk(ə)l/ *adj.* ритори́ческий; **~ question** ритори́ческий вопро́с.

rhetorician /,retə'rɪʃ(ə)n/ *n.* ри́тор; ора́тор.

rheumatic /ru:'mætɪk/ *n.* (*sufferer from rheumatism*) ревма́тик; (*pl., coll., rheumatism*) ревмати́зм.

● *adj.* ревмати́ческий; **~ fever** ревмати́зм.

rheumatism /'ru:mə,tɪz(ə)m/ *n.* ревмати́зм.

rheumatoid /'ru:mə,tɔɪd/ *adj.* ревмато́идный, ревмати́ческий; **~ arthritis** ревмато́идный артри́т.

Rhine /raɪn/ *n.* Рейн; **~ wine** ре́йнское вино́.

rhino /'raɪnəʊ/ *n.* (*pl.* **~s** *or* **~**) = **rhinoceros**

rhinoceros /raɪ'nɒsərəs/ *n.* (*pl.* **~** *or* **~es**) носоро́г.

rhizome /'raɪzəʊm/ *n.* (*bot.*) ризо́ма.

Rhodes /rəʊdz/ *n.* Ро́дос.

rhododendron /,rəʊdə'dendrən/ *n.* рододе́ндрон.

rhombi /'rɒmbaɪ/ *pl. of* ⇒**rhombus**

rhomboid /'rɒmbɔɪd/ *n.* (*geom.*) ромбо́ид.

● *adj.* (*also* **-al**) ромбови́дный.

rhombus /'rɒmbəs/ *n.* (*pl.* **rhombuses** *or* **rhombi**) (*geom.*) ромб.

Rhone /rəʊn/ *n.* Ро́на.

rhubarb /'ru:bɑ:b/ *n.* реве́нь (*m.*).

rhyme /raɪm/ *n.* ри́фма; **think of a ~ for 'love'** приду́майте ри́фму к сло́ву «любо́вь»; **he wrote the greeting in ~** он написа́л приве́тствие в стиха́х; **there is no ~ or reason in it** в э́том нет никако́го смы́сла; (*poem*) стих; **nursery ~** де́тский стишо́к.

● *v.t. & i.* рифмова́ть(ся) (*impf.*); **you can't ~ those two words** э́ти два сло́ва не рифму́ются; **rhyming dictionary** слова́рь рифм.

rhymester /'raɪmstə(r)/ *n.* рифмоплёт, стихоплёт.

rhythm /'rɪð(ə)m/ *n.* ритм; **~ guitar** ритм-гита́ра; **~ section** (*of a band*) уда́рные инструме́нты.

rhythmic(al) /'rɪðmɪk(əl)/ *adj.* ритми́чный, ритми́ческий.

RI (*abbr. of* ***religious instruction***) религио́зное обуче́ние.

rib /rɪb/ *n.* **1** (*anat.*) ребро́; **he dug me in the ~s** он толкну́л меня́ в бок; **spare ~s** (*of meat*) рёбрышки (*nt. pl.*); (*of leaf*) жи́лка. **2** (*ship's timber*) шпангоут, ребро́.

● *v.t.* (**ribbed, ribbing**) (*sl., tease*) разыгр|ывать, -а́ть.

ribald /'rɪb(ə)ld/ *adj.* непристо́йный, скабрёзный.

ribaldry /'rɪbəldrɪ/ *n.* непристо́йность, скабрёзность.

ribbed /rɪbd/ *adj.*: **~ cloth** ру́бчатая ткань.

ribbon /'rɪbən/ *n.* ле́нта, тесьма́; **hair ~** ле́нта; (*fig.*): **~ development** (*Br.*) ле́нточная застро́йка; **his clothes were torn to ~s** его́ оде́жда была́ разо́рвана в кло́чья.

riboflavin /,raɪbəʊ'fleɪvɪn/ *n.* рибофлави́н.

rice /raɪs/ *n.* рис; **boiled ~** ри́совая ка́ша.

● *cpds.* **~field** *n.* ри́совое по́ле; **~-paper** *n.* ри́совая бума́га.

rich /rɪtʃ/ *n.* (*collect.*, **the ~**) бога́тые (*pl.*).

● *adj.* **1** (*wealthy*) бога́тый. **2** (*fertile, abundant*) плодоро́дный; **a ~ soil** плодоро́дная/ту́чная по́чва; **a land ~ in minerals** земля́, бога́тая ископа́емыми; **he struck it ~** (*coll.*) он напа́л на жи́лу. **3** (*valuable, plentiful*) оби́льный; **a ~ harvest** бога́тый урожа́й. **4** (*costly, splendid*) це́нный, бога́тый, роско́шный. **5** (*of food*) сдо́бный, жи́рный. **6** (*of colours*) насы́щенный, густо́й. **7** (*of sounds or voices*) густо́й, со́чный. **8** (*of texture, life*) насы́щенный.

riches /'rɪtʃɪz/ *n.* бога́тство.

richly /'rɪtʃlɪ/ *adv.*: **she was ~ dressed** она́ была́ бога́то оде́та; **his punishment was ~ deserved** он вполне́ заслужи́л тако́е наказа́ние.

richness /'rɪtʃnɪs/ *n.* бога́тство, оби́лие; (*of food*) сдо́бность, жи́рность.

Richter scale /'rɪktə/ *n.* шкала́ Ри́хтера.

rick[1] /rɪk/ *n.* (*stack*) стог.

rick[2] /rɪk/ *v.t.* растя́|гивать, -ну́ть; вы́вихнуть (*pf.*); **I ~ed my neck** я нело́вко поверну́л ше́ю.

rickets /'rɪkɪts/ *n.* рахи́т.

rickety /'rɪkɪtɪ/ *adj.* ша́ткий, неусто́йчивый.

rickshaw /'rɪkʃɔ:/ *n.* ри́кша.

ricochet /'rɪkə,ʃeɪ/, /-,ʃet/ *n.* рикоше́т; **~ fire** стрельба́ на рикоше́тах.

● *v.i.* (**ricocheted** /-,ʃeɪd/; **ricocheting** /-,ʃeɪɪŋ/ *or* **ricochetted** /-,ʃetɪd/; **ricochetting** /-,ʃetɪŋ/) рикошети́ровать (*impf.*); бить (*impf.*) рикоше́том.

rid /rɪd/ *v.t.* (**ridding;** *past and p.p.* **rid**) освобо|жда́ть, -ди́ть; изб|авля́ть, -а́вить; **he ~ the country of beggars** он изба́вил страну́ от ни́щих; **get ~ of** изб|авля́ться, -а́виться от + *g.*; **we were glad to be, get ~ of him** мы бы́ли ра́ды от него́ изба́виться; **you are well ~ of that car** сла́ва Бо́гу, что вы изба́вились от э́той маши́ны.

riddance /'rɪd(ə)ns/ *n.* избавле́ние; устране́ние; **good ~ to him!** ≈ ска́тертью доро́га!

ridden /'rɪd(ə)n/ *p.p. of* ⇒**ride**

riddle[1] /'rɪd(ə)l/ *n.* зага́дка; (*mystery*) та́йна; **he set me a ~ to solve** он за́дал мне зага́дку; **he talks in ~s** он говори́т зага́дками.

riddle[2] /'rɪd(ə)l/ *n.* (*sieve*) решето́.

● *v.t.* (*pierce all over*) решети́ть, из-; **he was ~d with bullets** пу́ли изрешети́ли его́ те́ло; (*fig.*): **~d with disease** насквозь больно́й; **the manuscript is ~d with errors** ру́копись пестри́т оши́бками.

ride /raɪd/ *n.* **1** (*journey on horseback*) прогу́лка верхо́м; (*by vehicle*) пое́здка, езда́; **it is only a 5-minute ~ to the station** до ста́нции всего́ 5 мину́т езды́.
2 (*excursion*) прогу́лка; **let's go for a ~ into the country** дава́йте съе́здим за́ город на прогу́лку; **he took me for a ~** (*lit.*) он проката́л меня́; (*coll., cheated*) он меня́ разыгра́л/обвёл вокру́г па́льца.
3 (*fairground attraction*) аттракцио́н.

● *v.t. & i.* (*past* **rode;** *p.p.* **ridden**) **1** (*on horseback*) е́здить (*indet.*), е́хать, по- (верхо́м) (на + *p.*); ката́ться (*impf.*) (верхо́м) (на + *p.*); (*gallop*) скака́ть (*impf.*); **she ~s a horse well** она́ хорошо́ е́здит верхо́м (*or* на ло́шади); **he rode his horse at the fence** он напра́вил ло́шадь к барье́ру; **he rode his horse over the fence** он перемахну́л на ло́шади че́рез забо́р; **the jockey rode a good race** жоке́й хорошо́ скака́л; **do you ~?** вы е́здите верхо́м?; **he ~s to hounds** (*Br.*) он охо́тится верхо́м с соба́ками.
2 (*on a vehicle*) е́здить (*indet.*), е́хать, по- (на + *p.*); **I ~ a bicycle to work** я е́зжу на рабо́ту на велосипе́де.
3 (*of ships etc.*) плыть (*impf.*) (по + *d.*); **the ship rode the waves** кора́бль рассека́л во́лны; **the ship was riding at anchor** кора́бль стоя́л на я́коре; **let it ~** (*fig.*) ну и пусть!

● *with advs.*: **~ away** *v.i.* отъ|езжа́ть, -е́хать; уезжа́ть, уе́хать; **~ down** *v.t.* (*pursue and catch up with*) дог|оня́ть, -на́ть; наст|ига́ть, -и́чь верхо́м; (*knock down by riding at s.o.*) дави́ть (*impf.*); топта́ть (*impf.*); **~ out** *v.t.*: **the ship rode out the storm** кора́бль вы́держал на́тиск бу́ри; **we shall ~ out our present troubles** мы переживём ны́нешние тру́дности; *v.i.* соверш|а́ть, -и́ть прогу́лку; **~ up** *v.i.* (*approach on horseback*) подъ|езжа́ть, -е́хать верхо́м; (*of clothing*) лезть (*impf.*) вверх.

rider /'raɪdə(r)/ *n.* **1** (*horseman*) вса́дни|к (*fem.* -ца), нае́здни|к (*fem.* -ца); (*cyclist*) велосипеди́ст (*fem.* -ка). **2** (*clause*) дополне́ние; добавле́ние.

riderless /'raɪdəlɪs/ *adj.* без вса́дника.

ridge /rɪdʒ/ *n.* **1** край; спи́нка; **the ~ of a roof** конёк кры́ши. **2** (*of soil*) гре́бень (*m.*). **3** (*of high land*) го́рный хребе́т/кряж.

● *cpd.* **~-pole** *n.* (*of tent*) распо́рка, растя́жка; (*archit.*) конько́вый брус.

ridicule /ˈrɪdɪˌkju:l/ *n.* осмея́ние, насме́шка; **he was an object of ~** он был предме́том насме́шек; **I don't like being held up to ~** не люблю́, когда́ из меня́ де́лают посме́шище; **you will lay yourself open to ~** вы выставите себя́ на посме́шище.

● *v.t.* осме́ивать (*impf.*); подн|има́ть, -я́ть на́ смех.

ridiculous /rɪˈdɪkjʊləs/ *adj.* смехотво́рный; смешно́й, неле́пый; **don't be ~!** не говори́те глу́постей!

ridiculousness /rɪˈdɪkjʊləsnɪs/ *n.* смехотво́рность; неле́пость.

riding /ˈraɪdɪŋ/ *n.* верхова́я езда́.

● *cpds.* **~-breeches** *n. pl.* бри́дж|и (*pl., g.* -ей) для верхово́й езды́; **~-habit** *n.* амазо́нка; **~-school** *n.* шко́ла верхово́й езды́.

rife /raɪf/ *adj.* распространённый; **superstition was ~** суеве́рия бы́ли широко́ распространены́; **the country was ~ with rumours** (*Br.*), **rumors** (*US*) в стране́ ходи́ло мно́жество слу́хов.

riff /rɪf/ *n.* (*mus.*) рифф.

riffle /ˈrɪf(ə)l/ *v.t. & i.*: **he ~d (through) the pages** он бы́стро перелиста́л страни́цы.

riffraff /ˈrɪfræf/ *n.* подо́нки (*m. pl.*) о́бщества; сброд.

rifle /ˈraɪf(ə)l/ *n.* винто́вка; **~ regiment** пехо́тный/стрелко́вый полк; (*pl., ~ troops*) стрелко́вая часть; стрелки́ (*m. pl.*).

● *v.t.* **1** (*cut grooves in*) нареза́ть (*impf.*) кана́л (*ствола*). **2** (*plunder*) гра́бить, о-; очи́стить (*pf.*).

● *cpds.* **~man** *n.* стрело́к; **~-range** *n.* (*for shooting practice*) тир, стре́льбище; (*distance*) да́льность руже́йного вы́стрела; **~-shot** *n.* вы́стрел из винто́вки.

rift /rɪft/ *n.* **1** тре́щина, щель; **a ~ in the clouds** просве́т в ту́чах. **2** (*fig.*) разла́д.

● *cpd.* **~-valley** *n.* ри́фтовая доли́на.

rig /rɪɡ/ *n.* **1** (*naut.*) осна́стка. **2** (*dress*) оде́жда; **in full ~** при по́лном пара́де. **3** (*for drilling*) бурова́я вы́шка. **4** (*US, truck*) грузови́к с прице́пом.

● *v.t.* (**rigged, rigging**) **1** (*fit out*) осна|ща́ть, -сти́ть; снаря|жа́ть, -ди́ть. **2** (*manipulate, conduct fraudulently*): **the elections were ~ged** результа́ты вы́боров бы́ли подтасо́ваны; **a ~ged match** догово́рный матч.

● *with advs.*: **~ out** *v.t.* снаря|жа́ть, -ди́ть; наря|жа́ть, -ди́ть; **she ~ged the boys out with new clothes** она́ вы́рядила ма́льчиков в но́вую оде́жду; **~ up** (на́скоро) *v.t.* соору|жа́ть, -ди́ть.

● *cpd.* **~-out** *n.* (*Br.*) наря́д.

Riga /ˈri:ɡə/ *n.* Ри́га; (*attr.*) ри́жский.

rigging /ˈrɪɡɪŋ/ *n.* такела́ж, осна́стка.

right /raɪt/ *n.* **1** (*what is just, fair*) правота́; справедли́вость; **the child must learn the difference between ~ and wrong** ребёнка сле́дует научи́ть отлича́ть добро́ от зла́; **I know I am in the ~** я зна́ю, что я прав. **2** (*entitlement*) пра́во; **as of ~** как полага́ющийся по пра́ву; **in his, her own ~** сам, в своём пра́ве, по себе́; **stand on one's ~s** наст|а́ивать, -оя́ть на свои́х права́х; **stand up for one's ~s** отст|а́ивать, -оя́ть свои́ права́; **the house is hers by ~** дом принадлежи́т ей по зако́ну; **by ~s** по справедли́вости; че́стно говоря́; **by ~s he should be at work** вообще́-то ему́ поло́жено быть на рабо́те; **~ of way** пра́во прохо́да/прое́зда; **Bill of R~s** билль (*m.*) о права́х. **3** (*pl., correct state*): **he put the engine to ~s** он привёл мото́р в поря́док; **he tried to set the world to ~s** он пыта́лся переде́лать мир. **4** (*~-hand side etc.*) пра́вая сторона́; **on, to the ~** напра́во; **on, from the ~** спра́ва; **most countries drive on the ~** в большинстве́ стран правосторо́ннее движе́ние; **my father is on the ~ of the photograph** мой оте́ц нахо́дится спра́ва на фотогра́фии. **5** (*pol.*): **the R~** пра́вые (*pl.*); **politicians of the R~** полити́ческие де́ятели пра́вого крыла́.

● *adj.* **1** (*just, morally good*) пра́вый, справедли́вый; **I try to do what is ~** я стара́юсь поступа́ть че́стно; **he did the ~ thing by her** он с ней че́стно поступи́л; **you were ~ to refuse** вы сде́лали пра́вильно, что отказа́лись; **it is only ~ to tell you ...** я счита́ю свои́м до́лгом сказа́ть вам, что...; **that is only ~ and proper** так тому́ и сле́дует быть. **2** (*correct, true, required*) пра́вильный, ве́рный, ну́жный; **the ~ use of words** пра́вильное употребле́ние слов; **the ~ road** пра́вильный путь; **that's not the ~ way to do it** э́то де́лается не так; **what is the ~ time?** вы мо́жете сказа́ть то́чное вре́мя?; **he tried to keep on the ~ side of the teacher** он стара́лся не по́ртить отноше́ний с учи́телем; **~ side up** в пра́вильном положе́нии; **he is on the ~ side of forty** ему́ ещё нет сорока́; **that's ~!** пра́вильно!; ве́рно!; **I tried to put him ~** я пыта́лся вы́вести его́ из заблужде́ния, **I set him ~ on a few points** я ему́ ко́е-что разъясни́л. **3** (*in order, good health*) испра́вный; здоро́вый; **can you put my watch ~?** вы мо́жете почини́ть мои́ часы́?; **these matters must be put ~** э́ти дела́ ну́жно ула́дить; **this medicine will soon put you ~** от э́того лека́рства вы ско́ро попра́витесь; **I feel as ~ as rain** я себя́ прекра́сно чу́вствую; **he's not quite ~ in the head** у него́ не все до́ма; **he was not in his ~ mind** он был не в своём уме́; **everything will turn out ~ in the end** всё в конце́ концо́в ула́дится; **are you all ~?** всё в поря́дке?; (*expr. doubt*) вам нехорошо́?; вам пло́хо?; **all ~, I'll come with you!** ла́дно, я пойду́ с ва́ми!; **all ~, I admit it!** ла́дно уж, призна́юсь; **it's all ~ with me** я не возража́ю; **~!** (*expr. agreement or consent*) ве́рно!; хорошо́!; **~ you are** хорошо́!; идёт! (*coll.*); есть тако́е де́ло!. **4** (*opp. left*) пра́вый; **on my ~ hand** напра́во от меня́; **he is my ~ arm** (*fig.*) он моя́ пра́вая рука́; **he made a ~ turn** он поверну́л напра́во. **5**: **~ angle** прямо́й у́гол; **at ~ angles to** под прямы́м угло́м к + *d*. **6** (*Br., thorough*): **you've made a ~ mess of it** ну, наде́лали вы тут дело́в (*coll.*).

● *adv.* **1** (*straight*) пря́мо; **carry ~ on!** всё вре́мя пря́мо!; **he went ~ to the point** он сра́зу перешёл к де́лу; **the plane flew ~ overhead** самолёт пролете́л пря́мо над голово́й. **2** (*exactly*) то́чно; **the shot was ~ on target** уда́р попа́л пря́мо в цель; **I was there ~ on the stroke of one** я пришёл ро́вно в час, мину́та в мину́ту; **~ here/there** пря́мо здесь/там; **~ now** сейча́с; в да́нный моме́нт. **3** (*immediately*) сра́зу (же); **~ away** сра́зу (же), неме́дленно, сию́ мину́ту. **4** (*all the way, completely*) по́лностью; **he turned ~ round** он поверну́лся круго́м; **the ship was ~ off course** кора́бль соверше́нно сби́лся с ку́рса; **they climbed ~ to the top** они́ взобрали́сь на са́мую верши́ну; **I went ~ back to the beginning** я верну́лся к са́мому нача́лу; **he came ~ up to me** он подошёл ко мне вплотну́ю. **5** (*justly; correctly, properly*) справедли́во; пра́вильно; **he can do nothing ~** у него́ ничего́ не ла́дится; **have I guessed ~?** я угада́л?; **nothing goes ~ for him** у него́ всё идёт не так; **if I remember ~** е́сли мне не изменя́ет па́мять; **it serves you ~** подело́м вам; так вам и на́до. **6** (*in titles*): **R~ Honourable** (*Br.*) достопочте́нный. **7** (*of direction*) напра́во; **eyes ~!** равне́ние напра́во!; **~, left and centre** (*Br.*), **center** (*US*) круго́м, всю́ду.

● *v.t.* **1** (*restore to correct position*) выра́внивать, вы́ровнять; **the boat ~ed itself** ло́дка вы́ровнялась; (*fig., correct*) испр|авля́ть, -а́вить; **the fault will ~ itself** э́то испра́вится само́ собо́й. **2** (*make reparation for*) возме|ща́ть, -сти́ть; **this wrong must be ~ed** э́ту несправедли́вость ну́жно устрани́ть.

● *cpds.* **~about** *adj. & adv.*: **~about turn** поворо́т круго́м; **~-angled** *adj.* прямоуго́льный; **~-hand** *adj.* пра́вый; **~-hand drive** правосторо́ннее управле́ние; **~-hand man** (*fig.*) ве́рный помо́щник, пра́вая рука́; **~-hand turn** пра́вый поворо́т; **~-handed** *adj.* де́лающий всё пра́вой руко́й; **~-hander** *n.* (*blow*) уда́р пра́вой руко́й; (*person*) правша́ (*coll., c.g.*); **~-minded** *adj.* благонаме́ренный; разу́мный; **~-wing** *adj.* (*pol.*) пра́вых взгля́дов; пра́вый; **~-winger** *n.* (*pol.*) пра́вый; челове́к пра́вых взгля́дов.

righteous /ˈraɪtʃəs/ *adj.* пра́ведный; **~ indignation** справедли́вое негодова́ние.

righteousness /ˈraɪtʃəsnɪs/ *n.* пра́ведность.

rightful /ˈraɪtfʊl/ *adj.* зако́нный, правоме́рный.

rightist /ˈraɪtɪst/ *n. & adj.* пра́вый; (челове́к) пра́вых взгля́дов.

rightly /ˈraɪtlɪ/ *adv.* **1** (*correctly, properly*) пра́вильно; **if I remember ~**

R

е́сли мне не изменя́ет па́мять; **~ or wrongly, I believe he is lying** прав я и́ли непра́в, но я ду́маю, он врёт.
2 (*justly*) справедли́во; **he was punished, and ~ so** он был нака́зан, и подело́м.

rightness /ˈraɪtnɪs/ *n.* справедли́вость.

righto /ˈraɪtəʊ/, /raɪˈtəʊ/ *int.* (*Br.*) хорошо́!; ла́дно!

rigid /ˈrɪdʒɪd/ *adj.* жёсткий, негну́щийся; (*fig.*) неги́бкий; **~ discipline** стро́гая дисципли́на.

rigidity /rɪˈdʒɪdɪtɪ/ *n.* жёсткость; (*fig.*) неги́бкость.

rigmarole /ˈrɪgmə,rəʊl/ *n.* каните́ль.

rigor /ˈrɪgə(r)/, /ˈraɪgɔ:(r)/ *n.*: **~ mortis** тру́пное окочене́ние; (*US*) = **rigour**

rigorous /ˈrɪgərəs/ *adj.* (*strict*) стро́гий; (*severe, harsh*) суро́вый, безжа́лостный.

rigour /ˈrɪgə(r)/ (*US* **rigor**) *n.* стро́гость; суро́вость, безжа́лостность; **with all the ~ of the law** по всей стро́гости зако́на; **the ~s of winter** суро́вость зимы́.

rile /raɪl/ *v.t.* (*coll.*) серди́ть, рас-; раздраж|а́ть, -и́ть; **it ~d him to lose the game** его́ зли́ло, что он проигра́л.

rim /rɪm/ *n.* о́бод; край; **~ of a wheel** о́бод колеса́; **~ of a cup** край ча́шки; **spectacles with steel ~s** очки́ в стально́й опра́ве.
● *v.t.* (**rimmed, rimming**) обр|амля́ть, -а́мить.

rime /raɪm/ *n.* (*frost*) и́ней, и́зморозь.

rimless /ˈrɪmlɪs/ *adj.* не име́ющий о́бода; без опра́вы; **~ spectacles** пенсне́ (*indecl.*).

rind /raɪnd/ *n.* (*bark*) кора́; (*of melon, orange, cheese*) ко́рка; (*of bacon*) кожура́, шку́рка.

ring[1] /rɪŋ/ *n.* **1** (*ornament, implement*) кольцо́; (*with stone; signet-~*) пе́рстень (*m.*); **engagement ~** кольцо́, пода́ренное при помо́лвке; **wedding ~** обруча́льное кольцо́.
2 (*circle*) кольцо́, круг; **~s of a tree** годовы́е ко́льца де́рева; **he was blowing smoke ~s** он пуска́л ко́льца ды́ма; **they stood in a ~** они́ ста́ли в круг; **he had ~s under his eyes** у него́ бы́ли тёмные круги́ под глаза́ми; **he ran/made ~s round me** (*fig.*) он заткну́л меня́ за́ пояс.
3 (*conspiracy*) ша́йка, ба́нда; **spy ~** шпио́нская организа́ция.
4 (*of circus, boxing etc.*) аре́на, ринг.
5 (*of cooker*) конфо́рка.
● *v.t.* **1** (*encompass*) окруж|а́ть, -и́ть.
2 (*Br., put ~ on*): **the birds have been ~ed** птиц окольцева́ли.
3 (*put ~ around*): **his name was ~ed in pencil** его́ и́мя бы́ло обведено́ карандашо́м.
● *cpds.* **~ binder** *n.* скоросшива́тель (*m.*), фа́йловая па́пка; **~-finger** *n.* безымя́нный па́лец; **~leader** *n.* глава́рь (*m.*), зачи́нщик; **~master** *n.* инспе́ктор мане́жа; **~-road** *n.* (*Br.*) кольцева́я доро́га; **~side** *n.* пе́рвые ряды́ (*m. pl.*) (вокру́г аре́ны); **~worm** *n.* стригу́щий лиша́й.

ring[2] /rɪŋ/ *n.* **1** звон; звук; **the ~ of his voice** звук его́ го́лоса; (*fig.*): **it has the ~ of truth** э́то звучи́т правдоподо́бно.
2 (*sound of bell*) звоно́к; **there was a ~ at the door** в дверь позвони́ли.
3 (*Br., telephone call*) звоно́к; **give me a ~ tomorrow** позвони́те мне за́втра.
● *v.t.* (*past* **rang;** *p.p.* **rung**) **1** звони́ть, по- в + *a.*; **the postman rang the bell** почтальо́н позвони́л в дверь; **that ~s a bell** да, да, припомина́ю.
2 (*Br., telephone, also* **~ up**) звони́ть, по- + *d.*; **will you ~ me when you get home?** вы мне позвони́те, когда́ прибу́дете домо́й?
3 (*mark by ~ing*): **the bell ~s the half-hours** ко́локол звони́т ка́ждые полчаса́.
● *v.i.* (*past* **rang;** *p.p.* **rung**) **1** звони́ть, по-; **the bells are ~ing** звоня́т колокола́; **the bell rang for dinner** позвони́ли к обе́ду; **the telephone rang** зазвони́л телефо́н; **my ears are ~ing** у меня́ звени́т в уша́х; **his voice was still ~ing in my ears** его́ го́лос всё ещё звуча́л у меня́ в уша́х; (*fig.*): **his words ~ true** его́ слова́ звуча́т правдоподо́бно.
2 (*Br., telephone*) звони́ть, по-; **we must ~ for the doctor** мы должны́ вы́звать врача́ (по телефо́ну).
3 (*resound*) огла|ша́ться, -си́ться; разноси́ться (*impf.*); **the house rang with the sound of children's voices** де́тские голоса́ разноси́лись по всему́ до́му.
● *with advs.*: **they rang down/up the curtain** за́навес опусти́ли/по́дняли; **~ off** (*Br.*) пове́сить (*pf.*) тру́бку; **the bells rang out the old year and rang in the new** колоко́льным звоно́м проводи́ли ста́рый год и встре́тили но́вый; **a shot rang out** разда́лся вы́стрел; **someone rang (up) for you this morning** (*Br.*) вам кто-то звони́л у́тром.

ringing /ˈrɪŋɪŋ/ *adj.* (*resonant*) зво́нкий.
● *cpd.* **~ tone** *n.* дли́нные гудки́ (*m. pl.*).

ringlet /ˈrɪŋlɪt/ *n.* (*curl*) ло́кон, завито́к.

rink /rɪŋk/ *n.* като́к.

rinse /rɪns/ *n.* (*action of rinsing*) полоска́ние; (*hair-dye*) сре́дство для подкра́шивания воло́с.
● *v.t.* полоска́ть, вы́-; спол|а́скивать, -осну́ть; **~ out your mouth!** прополощи́те рот!; **she ~d out the cup** она́ сполосну́ла ча́шку.

Rio (de Janeiro) /ˈri:əʊ (də dʒəˈnɪərəʊ)/ *n.* Ри́о-де-Жане́йро (*m. indecl.*).

riot /ˈraɪət/ *n.* **1** (*brawl*) беспоря́дки (*m. pl.*); **there was a ~ in the theatre** (*Br.*), **theater** (*US*) в теа́тре разрази́лся сканда́л. **2** (*revolt*) мятéж, бунт; (*fig.*): **the teacher read the ~ act to his class** учи́тель сде́лал вы́говор всему́ кла́ссу. **3** (*fig.*): **she allowed her fancy to run ~** она́ дала́ по́лную во́лю воображе́нию; **the weeds are running ~** сорняки́ бу́йно разраста́ются; **the garden was a ~ of colour** (*Br.*), **color** (*US*) сад пестре́л все́ми кра́сками.
● *v.i.* (*brawl, rebel*) бесчи́нствовать (*impf.*); бу́йствовать (*impf.*); **the crowd ~ed in the streets** толпа́ бесчи́нствовала на у́лицах.

rioter /ˈraɪətə(r)/ *n.* бунта́рь (*m.*), мяте́жник.

riotous /ˈraɪətəs/ *adj.* (*rebellious*) мяте́жный; (*wildly enthusiastic*) безу́держный, шу́мный; **~ laughter** безу́держный смех; **~ living** разгу́льная жизнь.

riotousness /ˈraɪətəsnɪs/ *n.* неи́стовство, безу́держность.

RIP (*abbr. of* ***rest in peace***) мир пра́ху (*кого*).

rip /rɪp/ *n.* (*tear*) разре́з, проре́ха.
● *v.t.* (**ripped, ripping**) рвать, разо-; расп|а́рывать, -оро́ть; **he ~ped his trousers on a nail** он порва́л брю́ки о гвоздь; **he ~ped open the envelope** он разорва́л конве́рт; **he ~ped off the lid** он сорва́л кры́шку; **~ off** (*coll., steal*) об|дира́ть, -одра́ть; **she ~ped up the letter** она́ разорвала́ письмо́.
● *v.i.* (**ripped, ripping**) **1** (*tear*) рва́ться, разо-.
2 (*rush along*) мча́ться, про-; **let her ~!** жми на всю кату́шку! (*coll.*); **he lost his temper and let ~ at me** он вы́шел из себя́ и обложи́л меня́ после́дними слова́ми.
● *cpds.* **~-cord** *n.* вытяжно́й трос; **~-off** *n.* (*sl.*) воровство́, моше́нничество; **it's a ~-off** э́то обдира́ловка; *adj.* грабительский; **~-roaring, ~-snorting** *adjs.* (*coll.*) бу́йный, шумли́вый; **~-saw** *n.* продо́льная пила́; **~ tide** *n.* разрывно́е тече́ние.

riparian /raɪˈpeərɪən/ *adj.* прибре́жный.

ripe /raɪp/ *adj.* **1** (*ready for gathering, eating or use*) спе́лый, зре́лый; **the corn is ~** хлеба́ поспе́ли/созре́ли; **~ cheese** вы́держанный сыр; (*fig.*): **he lived to a ~ old age** он до́жил до глубо́кой ста́рости. **2** (*ready, suitable*) гото́вый, созре́вший; **land ~ for development** земля́, ожида́ющая застро́йки; **the time is ~ for action** пришло́ вре́мя де́йствовать.

ripen /ˈraɪpən/ *v.i.* зреть (*or* созрева́ть), со-.
● *v.t.*: **the sun ~ed the tomatoes** помидо́ры созре́ли на со́лнце.

ripeness /ˈraɪpnɪs/ *n.* спе́лость, зре́лость.

riposte /rɪˈpɒst/ *n.* (*fencing*) отве́тный уда́р; (*verbal*) нахо́дчивый отве́т.
● *v.i.* нан|оси́ть, -ести́ отве́тный уда́р; нахо́дчиво отв|еча́ть, -е́тить.

ripple /ˈrɪp(ə)l/ *n.* рябь, зыбь, круг; (*fig.*): **his words caused a ~ of laughter** его́ слова́ вы́звали лёгкий смех.
● *v.t. & i.* покр|ыва́ть(ся), -ы́ть(ся) ря́бью.

rise /raɪz/ *n.* **1** (*upward slope*) подъём; **we came to a ~ in the road** мы подошли́ к подъёму доро́ги.
2 (*area of higher ground*) холм, возвы́шенность.
3 (*fig., ascent*) подъём; восхожде́ние.
4 (*increase*) повыше́ние, увеличе́ние; **a ~ in temperature** повыше́ние

температу́ры; **they asked for a ~** (*Br.*) они попроси́ли об увеличе́нии зарпла́ты; **a ~ in the cost of living** удорожа́ние жи́зни; **unemployment is on the ~** безрабо́тица расте́т.
5 (*in angling*): **he waited all day for a ~** он весь день ждал клёва; (*fig.*): **he is taking a ~ out of you** он вас провоци́рует/дра́знит.
6 (*vertical height of step*) высота́ (ступе́ньки).
7 (*origin*): **give ~ to** вызыва́ть, вы́звать.

● *v.i.* (*past* **rose;** *p.p.* **risen** /ˈrɪz(ə)n/) **1** (*get up from bed*) вста|ва́ть, -ть (на́ ноги); **I rose at 6** я встал в 6; (*from seated or kneeling position*) вста|ва́ть, -ть; подн|има́ться, -я́ться; **they rose from the table** они́ подняли́сь из-за стола́; **the House rose at 10** (*Br.*) пала́та зако́нчила рабо́ту в 10; **he rose to his full height** он встал во весь рост; **the horse rose (up) on its hind legs** ло́шадь вста́ла на дыбы́; (*into the air*) подн|има́ться, -я́ться; (*fig.*): **you should ~ above petty jealousy** вы должны́ быть вы́ше ме́лкой за́висти; (*from the dead*) воскр|еса́ть, -е́снуть; **Christ is ~n** Христо́с воскре́с; (*above the horizon*) восходи́ть, взойти́; **when the sun ~s** когда́ восхо́дит со́лнце; (*fig., appear*) возн|ика́ть, -и́кнуть; **a picture rose in my mind** в моём воображе́нии возни́к о́браз; **the rising generation** подраста́ющее поколе́ние; (*to the surface*) выходи́ть, вы́йти на пове́рхность; **the fish won't ~** ры́ба не клюёт; (*fig.*): **he rose to my bait** он попа́лся на мою́ у́дочку; **he will always ~ to the occasion** он не растеря́ется в любо́й ситуа́ции.
2 (*slope upwards*) подн|има́ться, -я́ться; **on rising ground** на скло́не/возвыше́нии; (*tower*): **the cliffs rose sheer above them** над ни́ми кру́то возвыша́лись ска́лы.
3 (*increase in amount*) возраста́ть (*impf.*); увели́чи|ваться, -ться; **rising costs** увели́чивающие расхо́ды; (*in level*): **the waters are rising** вода́ поднима́ется/прибыва́ет; **rising tide** нараста́ющий прили́в; **the bread has ~n** хлеб подня́лся; **the temperature is rising** температу́ра повыша́ется; (*in price*) пов|ыша́ться, -ы́ситься в цене́; дорожа́ть, по-/вз-; (*in pitch*) уси́ли|вать, -ть; **his voice rose in anger** в гне́ве он повы́сил го́лос; (*in intensity or animation*) увели́чи|ваться, -ться; **the wind is rising** ве́тер поднима́ется/уси́ливается/крепча́ет; **her colour** (*Br.*), **color** (*US*) **rose** она́ покрасне́ла; **his spirits rose** его́ настрое́ние улу́чшилось; (*in importance or rank*) продв|ига́ться, -и́нуться; **he hopes to ~ in the world** он наде́ется сде́лать карье́ру; **he rose from the ranks** (*mil.*) он вы́служился из рядовы́х; он вы́двинулся в офице́ры; **he rose to international fame** он приобрёл мирову́ю изве́стность; (*in age*): **he is rising 40** ему́ под со́рок.
4 (*spring, originate*) брать, взять нача́ло; возн|ика́ть, -и́кнуть; **the Severn ~s in Wales** Се́верн берёт своё нача́ло в Уэ́льсе.
5 (*rebel*) восст|ава́ть, -а́ть; **the people rose (up) in arms** наро́д восста́л с ору́жием в рука́х.

riser /ˈraɪzə(r)/ *n.* **1**: **he is an early ~** он встаёт с петуха́ми. **2** (*of staircase*) по́дступень. **3** (*rostrum*) трибу́на.

risible /ˈrɪzɪb(ə)l/ *adj.* смешно́й, смехотво́рный.

rising /ˈraɪzɪŋ/ *n.* **1** (*getting up*) подъём; **I believe in early ~** я счита́ю, что встава́ть на́до ра́но. **2** (*of the sun, moon etc.*) восхо́д. **3** (*rebellion*) восста́ние.

risk /rɪsk/ *n.* риск; **he takes many ~s** он лю́бит рискова́ть; **he ran the ~ of defeat** он рискова́л потерпе́ть пораже́ние; **at the ~ of one's life** риску́я жи́знью; **at owner's ~** на риск владе́льца; **you go at your own ~** вы идёте туда́ на свой страх и риск; **I spoke at the ~ of offending him** несмотря́ на то, что он мо́жет оби́деться, я реши́л вы́сказаться; **he is a security ~** он неблагонадёжен.

● *v.t.* **1** (*expose to ~*) рискова́ть (*impf.*); **he ~ed his life to save her** он спас её, риску́я жи́знью.
2 (*take the chance of*) риск|ова́ть, -ну́ть (*чем*); **shall we ~ it?** ну что, рискнём?

risky /ˈrɪskɪ/ *adj.* (**riskier, riskiest**) риско́ванный, опа́сный.

risotto /rɪˈzɒtəʊ/ *n.* (*pl.* **~s**) рисо́тто (*m. indecl.*).

risqué /ˈrɪskeɪ/, /-ˈkeɪ/ *adj.* риско́ванный, сомни́тельный.

rissole /ˈrɪsəʊl/ *n.* ру́бленая котле́та.

rite /raɪt/ *n.* обря́д, ритуа́л, церемо́ния; **the ~s of hospitality** обы́чаи гостеприи́мства; **last ~s** (*extreme unction*) собо́рование.

ritual /ˈrɪtjʊəl/ *n.* ритуа́л, обря́дность.

● *adj.* ритуа́льный; (*fig., invariable*) неизме́нный.

ritualistic /ˌrɪtjʊəˈlɪstɪk/ *adj.* ритуалисти́ческий.

ritzy /ˈrɪtzɪ/ *adj.* (**ritzier, ritziest**) (*coll.*) шика́рный.

rival /ˈraɪv(ə)l/ *n.* сопе́рник; **~s in love** сопе́рники в любви́; **he has many business ~s** у него́ мно́го конкуре́нтов; **he was without a ~ as chef** он был непревзойдённым по́варом.

● *adj.* сопе́рничающий; **the ~ team** кома́нда проти́вника.

● *v.t.* (**rivalled, rivalling;** *US* **rivaled, rivaling**) сопе́рничать (*impf.*) с + *i.*; **I cannot hope to ~ your skill** я не беру́сь сопе́рничать с ва́ми в мастерстве́.

rivalry /ˈraɪvəlrɪ/ *n.* сопе́рничество, конкуре́нция; **let us not enter into ~** заче́м нам сопе́рничать?

rive /raɪv/ *v.t.* (*past* **rived;** *p.p.* **riven** /ˈrɪv(ə)n/) (*liter.*) раз|рыва́ть, -орва́ть; (*split apart*): **trees ~n by lightning** дере́вья, раско́лотые мо́лнией.

river /ˈrɪvə(r)/ *n.* река́; (*attr.*) речно́й; **up/down ~** вверх/вниз по реке́; (*fig.*): **the streets were ~s of blood** у́лицы преврати́лись в пото́ки кро́ви.

● *cpds.* **~-basin** *n.* бассе́йн реки́; **~-bed** *n.* ру́сло реки́; **~side** *n.* прибре́жная полоса́; *adj.* прибре́жный, стоя́щий на берегу́ реки́.

rivet /ˈrɪvɪt/ *n.* заклёпка.

● *v.t.* (**riveted, riveting**) клепа́ть (*impf.*); склёп|ывать, -а́ть; (*fig.*) устрем|ля́ть, -и́ть (*взгляд/внимание*); **his eyes were ~ed on her** его́ взгляд был прико́ван к ней.

riveting /ˈrɪvɪtɪŋ/ *adj.* (*coll.*) захва́тывающий.

Riviera /ˌrɪvɪˈeərə/ *n.* Ривье́ра.

rivulet /ˈrɪvjʊlɪt/ *n.* руче́й.

Riyadh /rɪˈjɑːd/ *n.* Эр-Рия́д.

riyal /ˈriːɑːl/ *n.* (*unit of currency*) риа́л.

RN 1 (*abbr. of* ***Royal Navy***) (*Br.*) ВМФ (вое́нно-морско́й флот) Великобрита́нии. **2** (*abbr. of* ***Registered Nurse***) (*US*) диплоexternalи́рованная медици́нская сестра́.

roach /rəʊtʃ/ *n.* (*pl.* **~,** *fish*) плотва́; (*pl.* **~es,** *cockroach*) тарака́н.

road /rəʊd/ *n.* **1** (*thoroughfare*) доро́га; (*attr.*) доро́жный (*see also cpds.*); **main ~** гла́вная доро́га; **~ accident** автомоби́льная/доро́жная катастро́фа; **~ junction** пересече́ние доро́г, перекрёсток; **~ sense** (*Br.*) «чу́вство доро́ги»; **~ works** (*Br.*) доро́жно-ремо́нтные рабо́ты; **my car is parked off the ~** я поста́вил маши́ну на обо́чине; **the car has been off the ~ for a month** маши́на проста́ивает це́лый ме́сяц; **we have been on the ~ for hours** мы е́дем уже́ мно́го часо́в; **he is on the ~** (*of a salesman*) он в разъе́здах; (*of a performer*) он на гастро́лях; (*of a tramp*) он скита́ется по доро́гам; **they live just up the ~ from us** они́ живу́т в двух шага́х от нас на той же у́лице; **the ~ has been up since Sunday** доро́гу ремонти́руют с воскресе́нья; **one for the ~** на посошо́к.
2 (*fig.*) путь (*m.*), доро́га; **he is on the ~ to recovery** он на пути́ к выздоровле́нию.
3 (*coll., way*): **get out of my ~!** прочь с доро́ги!; **you are getting in my ~** вы мне меша́ете.

● *cpds.* **~-bed** *n.* полотно́ доро́ги; **~-block** *n.* загражде́ние на доро́ге; **~-hog** *n.* плохо́й води́тель, лиха́ч; **~house** *n.* придоро́жный рестора́н; **~-map** *n.* доро́жная ка́рта; **~-metal** *n.* (*Br.*) щебёнка; **~ rage** *n.* (*Br.*) при́ступ бе́шенства води́теля автомоби́ля; **~show** *n.* (*radio, TV*) репорта́ж с ме́ста собы́тий; (*pol.*) выездно́е заседа́ние, встре́ча с избира́телями; (*theatr.*) гастро́льное представле́ние; **~side** *n.* обо́чина доро́ги; **~stead** *n.* рейд; **~-test** (*of a car*) *n.* доро́жное испыта́ние; *v.t.* испы́т|ывать, -а́ть (*машину*) в пробе́ге; **~way** *n.* доро́га, прое́зжая часть; **~worthiness** *n.* приго́дность для езды́ по доро́гам; **~worthy** *adj.* приго́дный для езды́ по доро́гам.

roam /rəʊm/ *v.t. & i.* броди́ть, стра́нствовать, скита́ться (*all impf.*); **he ~ed the streets** он броди́л по у́лицам.

roan /rəʊn/ *adj.* ча́лый.

R

roar /rɔː(r)/ *n.* (*of animal*) рёв, рык; (*loud human cry*) крик; вопль (*m.*); **he gave a ~ of anger** он издáл я́ростный вопль; **there were ~s of laughter** раздали́сь взры́вы хóхота; (*of wind or sea*) рёв; (*of engine*) грóхот, гул.

● *v.t. & i.* ревéть (*impf.*); рычáть (*impf.*); **the audience ~ed approval** пу́блика ревéла от востóрга; **they ~ed themselves hoarse** они́ охри́пли от кри́ка; **he ~ed his head off** он орáл изо всей мóчи; **the lion ~ed** лев зарычáл; **he ~ed with laughter** он надрывáлся от смéха; он хохотáл во всё гóрло; **shops are doing a ~ing trade** в магази́нах товáры идýт нарасхвáт.

roast /rəʊst/ *n.* жаркóе.

● *v.t.* жáрить, за-, из-; **~ beef** жáреная/запечённая говя́дина; **~ed coffee beans** поджáренные кофéйные зёрна; **he ~ed himself in front of the fire** он грéлся уками́на.

● *v.i.* грéться (*impf.*); **switch off the fire, I'm ~ing** вы́ключите пéчку, я весь изжáрился.

rob /rɒb/ *v.t.* (**robbed, robbing**) красть, обо-; грáбить, о-; **I have been ~bed** меня́ обокрáли/ограбили; **the bank was ~bed** банк огрáбили; **they ~bed him of his watch** они́ укрáли у негó часы́; (*fig., deprive*) лиш|áть, -и́ть.

robber /ˈrɒbə(r)/ *n.* грабитель (*m.*), вор.

robbery /ˈrɒbərɪ/ *n.* грабёж; **~ with violence** грабёж с наси́лием; **there has been a ~** произошлó ограблéние; **daylight ~** грабёж средь бéла дня.

robe /rəʊb/ *n.* мáнтия; (*US, dressing-gown; also* **bath-~**) (купáльный) халáт.

● *v.t.*: **~d in black** облачённый в чёрное.

● *v.i.* облач|áться, -и́ться.

robin (redbreast) /ˈrɒbɪn/ *n.* мали́новка.

robot /ˈrəʊbɒt/ *n.* (*lit., fig.*) рóбот; (*attr.*) автомати́ческий.

robotics /rəʊˈbɒtɪks/ *n.* робо(то)тéхника.

robotization /ˌrəʊbɒtaɪˈzeɪʃ(ə)n/ *n.* роботизáция.

robotize /ˈrəʊbɒˌtaɪz/ *v.t.* роботизи́ровать (*impf., pf.*).

robust /rəʊˈbʌst/ *adj.* (**robuster, robustest**) (*of person, physique*) крéпкий, си́льный; (*of health*) хорóший, крéпкий; (*of appetite*) здорóвый; (*of an object etc.*) прóчный.

robustness /rəʊˈbʌstnɪs/ *n.* здорóвье; си́ла; крéпость, прóчность.

rock[1] /rɒk/ *n.* (*solid part of earth's crust*) гóрная порóда; **a house built on ~** дом, пострóенный на скалé (*or* скáльном грýнте); (*large stone*) скалá, утёс; (*boulder*) валýн; **the ship ran upon the ~s** корáбль наскочи́л на скáлы; **the firm is on the ~s** (*coll.*) фи́рма прогорéла; (*US, stone, pebble*) кáмень (*m.*), булы́жник; **whisky on the ~s** (*coll.*) ви́ски со льдом.

● *cpds.* **~-bottom** *n.* (*fig.*): **at ~-bottom prices** по сáмым ни́зким цéнам; **~-climber** *n.* скалолáз; **~-climbing** *n.* скалолáзание; **~-crystal** *n.* гóрный хрустáль; **~-drill** *n.* перфорáтор; **~ face** *n.* скалá; **~fall** *n.* камнепáд; **~-garden** *n.* (*also* **~ery**) альпинáрий; **~-plant** *n.* альпи́йское растéние; **~-ribbed** *adj.* (*US*) твёрдый, непоколеби́мый; **~-salmon** *n.* (*snapper*) луциáн; (*Br., dogfish*) акýла; (*Br., wolf fish*) зубáтка; **~-salt** *n.* кáменная соль.

rock[2] /rɒk/ *n.* (*music*) рок; **~ concert** рок-концéрт; **~ music** рок-мýзыка; **~ musician** рок-музыкáнт; **~ opera** рок-óпера; **~ star** рок-звездá.

● *v.t.* (*sway gently*) кач|áть, -нýть; укáч|ивать, -áть; **the nurse ~ed the baby to sleep** ня́ня укачáла/убаю́кала ребёнка; **the boat was ~ed by the waves** лóдка качáлась на вóлнáх; **don't ~ the boat!** (*coll.*) лéгче на поворóтах!; (*shake*) трясти́, по-; **the earthquake ~ed the house** дом шатáлся от землетрясéния; **the news ~ed the city** нóвость потряслá гóрод.

● *v.i.* (*sway gently*) качáться (*impf.*); **the trees ~ed in the wind** дерéвья раскáчивались на ветрý; **~ing-chair** качáлка; **~ing-horse** конь(*m.*)-качáлка, деревя́нная лошáдка.

● *cpd.* **~-'n'-roll** *n.* рок-н-рóлл.

rocker /ˈrɒkə(r)/ *n.* **1** (*of cradle etc.; chair*) качáлка. **2** (*Br., biker*) рóкер. **3**: **go off one's ~** рехнýться (*pf.*) (*coll.*).

rockery /ˈrɒkərɪ/ = **rock-garden**

rocket /ˈrɒkɪt/ *n.* **1** (*projectile*) ракéта; **~ launcher** пусковáя установка. **2** (*Br., reprimand*): **he got a ~ from the boss** он получи́л взбýчку (*coll.*) от начáльника.

● *v.i.* (**rocketed, rocketing**) (*fig.*): **prices ~ed (up)** цéны рéзко подскочи́ли.

● *cpd.* **~-propelled** *adj.* ракéтный.

rocketry /ˈrɒkɪtrɪ/ *n.* ракéтная тéхника.

rocky /ˈrɒkɪ/ *adj.* (**rockier, rockiest**) **1** (*of or like rock; full of rocks*) скали́стый, камени́стый; **the R~ Mountains, the Rockies** (*coll.*) Скали́стые гóры (*f. pl.*). **2** (*shaky, unsteady*) неустóйчивый, шáткий.

rococo /rəˈkəʊkəʊ/ *n.* рококó (*indecl.*).

● *adj.* в сти́ле рококó.

rod /rɒd/ *n.* **1** (*slender stick*) прут; (*fishing-~*) ýдочка; **he fished with ~ and line** он лови́л ры́бу ýдочкой; (*instrument of chastisement*) рóзга, хлыст; **spare the ~ and spoil the child** пожалéешь рóзгу — испóртишь ребёнка; **he is making a ~ for his own back** он сам себé рóет я́му; **he ruled the people with a ~ of iron** он прáвил желéзной рукóй. **2** (*metal bar*) стéржень (*m.*); **curtain ~** металли́ческий карни́з.

rode /rəʊd/ *past of* ⇒**ride**

rodent /ˈrəʊd(ə)nt/ *n.* грызýн.

rodeo /ˈrəʊdɪəʊ/, /rəˈdeɪəʊ/ *n.* (*pl.* **~s**) родéо (*indecl.*).

roe[1] /rəʊ/ *n.* (*hard* **~**) икрá; (*soft* **~**) молóк|и (*pl., g.* —).

roe[2] /rəʊ/ *n.* (*pl.* **~** *or* **~s**) (*deer*) косýля.

● *cpd.* **~buck** *n.* косýля-самéц.

roentgen /ˈrʌntjən/ *n.* рентгéн.

roger /ˈrɒdʒə(r)/ *int.* (*sl.*) вас пóнял!; лáдно!; бýдет сдéлано!; поря́док!

rogue /rəʊg/ *n.* **1** (*dishonest person*) жýлик, мошéнник; **~s' gallery** архи́в фотосни́мков престýпников. **2** (*mischievous person*) прокáзник, озорни́к. **3** (*animal*): **~ elephant** слон-отшéльник.

rogu|ery /ˈrəʊgərɪ/, **-ishness** /ˈrəʊgɪʃnɪs/ *nn.* (*villainy*) жýльничество, мошéнничество; (*mischief*) прокáзы (*f. pl.*), озорствó.

roguish /ˈrəʊgɪʃ/ *adj.* (*villainous*) жуликовáтый; (*playful*) прокáзливый, озорнóй.

roguishness /ˈrəʊgɪʃnɪs/ = **roguery**

roister /ˈrɔɪstə(r)/ *v.i.* бесчи́нствовать (*impf.*).

roisterer /ˈrɔɪstərə(r)/ *n.* кути́ла (*m.*).

role /rəʊl/ *n.* (*lit., fig.*) роль; **he played (in) the ~ of Hamlet** он исполня́л роль Гáмлета; **title ~** заглáвная роль; **he assumed the ~ of leader** он взял на себя́ роль ли́дера.

● *cpds.* **~ model** *n.* образéц для подражáния; **~-play** *v.i.* разыгр|ывать, -áть рóли.

roll /rəʊl/ *n.* **1** (*of cloth, paper, film etc.*) рулóн. **2** (*register, list*) реéстр, спи́сок; **~ of honour** (*Br.*), **honor** (*US*) спи́сок уби́тых на войнé; **the lawyer was struck off the ~s** (*Br.*) адвокáта лиши́ли прáва прáктики; **the sergeant called the ~** сержáнт сдéлал перекли́чку. **3** (*other material in cylindrical form*) кáтышек, вáлик. **4** (*of bread*) бýлочка. **5** (*oscillating or revolving motion*) вращéние; покáчивание; **the ~ of the ship** покáчивание корабля́. **6** (*rumbling sound*) раскáт; бой барабáна; **a ~ of thunder** раскáт грóма; **drum ~** барабáнная дробь.

● *v.t.* **1** (*move by revolving*) катáть (*indet.*), кати́ть (*det.*), по-; **the logs were ~ed down the hill** брёвна скати́ли с холмá; (*wind*) завёр|тывать, -нýть; **he had a scarf ~ed round his neck** он обмотáл шéю шáрфом; (*rotate*) вращáть (*impf.*); **~ one's eyes** вращáть (*impf.*) глазáми. **2** (*flatten by use of cylinder*) катáть, рас-; раскáтывать (*impf.*); **she was ~ing pastry** онá раскáтывала тéсто; **the lawn needs ~ing** травý нáдо укатáть; **~ing-mill** прокáтный стан; **~ing-pin** скáлка; **~ed gold** накладнóе зóлото. **3** (*shape into cylinder or sphere*) свёр|тывать, -нýть; сворáчивать (*impf.*); (*e.g. cigarette*) скрý|чивать, -ти́ть; **I ~ my own (cigarettes)** я дéлаю самокрýтки; **he carried a ~ed newspaper** он шёл со свёрнутой газéтой; **the hedgehog ~ed itself (up) into a ball** ёж свернýлся в клубóк; **help me ~ this ball of wool** помоги́те мне смотáть э́тот клубóк шéрсти; **she was nurse and housemaid ~ed into one** онá былá одновремéнно и за ня́ньку и за прислýгу.

4: **he cannot ~ his r's** он карта́вит; **he ~s his r's** он раска́тисто произно́сит звук «р»; он произно́сит «р» с вибра́цией; он грасси́рует.

● *v.i.* **1** (*move by revolving; revolve*) кати́ться (*impf.*); ска́тываться (*impf.*); **the coin ~ed under the table** моне́та закати́лась под стол; **the car began to ~ downhill** маши́на начала́ кати́ться вниз; **tears ~ed down her cheeks** слёзы кати́лись по её щека́м; **set, start the ball ~ing** (*fig.*) откры́ть (*pf.*) диску́ссию; **~ing stock** подвижно́й соста́в.
2 (*tumble about, wallow*) валя́ться (*impf.*); **porpoises were ~ing in the waves** дельфи́ны кувырка́лись в волна́х; **he is ~ing in money** он купа́ется в деньга́х.
3 (*sway, rock*) кача́ться (*impf.*); колыха́ться (*impf.*); **the ship began to ~** парохо́д на́чало кача́ть; **~ing gait** похо́дка вразва́лку.
4 (*undulate*): **waves were ~ing on to the shore** во́лны нака́тывались на бе́рег; **~ing sea** волну́ющееся мо́ре; **~ing countryside** холми́стая ме́стность.
5 (*make deep vibrating sound*) греме́ть (*impf.*); грохота́ть (*impf.*); **thunder ~ed in the hills** по холма́м прокати́лся гром.

● *with advs.*: **~ about** *v.i.* валя́ться; **~ along** *v.i.*: **we were ~ing along at 30 m.p.h.** маши́на кати́лась со ско́ростью 30 миль в час; **~ away** *v.i.*: **the mists ~ed away** тума́н рассе́ялся; **~ back** *v.t.* отка́т|ывать, -и́ть наза́д; **let's ~ back the carpet and dance!** дава́йте свернём/скатаем ковёр и потанцу́ем!; *v.i.*: **the cart ~ed back** теле́жка откати́лась наза́д; **~ by** *v.i.*: **the bus ~ed by** авто́бус прое́хал ми́мо; **how the years ~ by!** как бы́стро ка́тятся го́ды!; **~ down** *v.t.* ска́т|ывать, -и́ть вниз; **~ down the blinds!** опусти́те жалюзи́!; **~ in** *v.i.*: **contributions began to ~ in** на́чали поступа́ть взно́сы; **he ~ed in half-an-hour late** он подкати́л/подрули́л (*coll.*) с опозда́нием на полчаса́; **~ off** *v.i.* ска́т|ываться, -и́ться; **he ~ed off the bed** он скати́лся с крова́ти; **~ on** *v.t.*: **she ~ed on her stockings** она́ натяну́ла чулки́; *v.i.*: **the years are ~ing on** го́ды иду́т; **~ on summer!** (*coll.*) скоре́й бы наступи́ло ле́то!; **~ out** *v.t.* (*e.g. carpet, pastry*) раска́т|ывать, -а́ть; *v.i.*: **she dropped her basket and everything ~ed out** она́ урони́ла корзи́нку, и всё из неё вы́катилось; **~ over** *v.t.* перев|ора́чивать, -ерну́ть; **I ~ed the stone over** я переверну́л ка́мень; *v.i.* воро́чаться (*impf.*); **he ~ed over and went to sleep again** он переверну́лся на друго́й бок и сно́ва засну́л; **~ up** *v.t.* свёр|тывать, -ну́ть; (*sleeves*) засу́ч|ивать, -и́ть; **~ up the curtain** подня́ть (*pf.*) за́навес; **he ~ed himself up in a blanket** он заверну́лся в одея́ло; *v.i.*: **he ~ed up to me** (*fig.*) он подкати́л ко мне; **~ up! ~ up!** налета́й; не проходи́те ми́мо!

● *cpds.* **~-call** *n.* перекли́чка; **~-film** *n.* ро́ликовая фотоплёнка; **~-neck (pullover)** *n.* водола́зка; **~-on** *n.* (*Br., corset*) эласти́чный по́яс; **~-top (desk)** *n.* бюро́ с деревя́нной што́рой; **~-up** *n.* (*Br., cigarette*) самокру́тка.

roller /ˈrəʊlə(r)/ *n.* **1** ро́лик; като́к; **garden ~** садо́вый като́к; (*for paint*) ва́лик. **2** (*wave*) волна́, вал.

● *cpds.* **~-bearing** *n.* ро́ликовый подши́пник; **~-coaster** *n.* америка́нские го́ры (*f. pl.*); **~-skate** *n.* (*pl.*) ро́лики (*m. pl.*); ро́ликовые коньки́ (*m. pl.*); *v.i.* ката́ться (*indet.*) на ро́ликах; **~-towel** *n.* полоте́нце на ро́лике.

rollick /ˈrɒlɪk/ *v.i.* резви́ться (*impf.*); весели́ться (*impf.*); **we had a ~ing time** мы здо́рово повесели́лись.

roly-poly /ˌrəʊlɪˈpəʊlɪ/ *n.* (*Br., cul.*) руле́т с варе́ньем.

● *adj.* пу́хлый.

ROM /rɒm/ *n. comput.* (*abbr. of* ***read only memory***) ПЗУ (постоя́нное запомина́ющее устро́йство).

Roman /ˈrəʊmən/ *n.* ри́млян|ин (*fem.* -ка).

● *adj.* **1** (*of Rome*) ри́мский; **the ~ alphabet** лати́нский алфави́т; **~ candle** ри́мская свеча́; **the ~ Empire** Ри́мская импе́рия; **r~ script, type** лати́нский шрифт; лати́нская гра́фика; (*opp. italics*) прямо́й шрифт; (*opp. bold*) све́тлый шрифт. **2** (*relig.*) католи́ческий; **~ Catholic** (*n.*) като́л|ик (*fem.* -и́чка); *adj.* католи́ческий; **~ Catholicism** католи́чество.

romance /rəʊˈmæns/, *also disp.* /ˈrəʊ-/ *n.* **1**: **R~ languages** рома́нские языки́; **R~ philologist** романи́ст. **2** (*medieval tale*) ры́царский рома́н. **3** (*novel, love affair*) рома́н. **4** (*romantic atmosphere, glamour*) рома́нтика. **5** (*mus.*) рома́нс.

● *v.i.* фантази́ровать (*impf.*).

romancer /rəʊˈmænsə(r)/ *n.* фантазёр.

Romanesque /ˌrəʊməˈnesk/ *n.* & *adj.* рома́нский (стиль).

Romania, R(o)umania /rəʊˈmeɪnɪə/ *n.* Румы́ния.

Romanian, R(o)umanian /rəʊˈmeɪnɪən/ *n.* (*person*) румы́н (*fem.* -ка); (*language*) румы́нский язы́к.

● *adj.* румы́нский.

Romanic /rəʊˈmænɪk/ *adj.* (*neo-Latin*) рома́нский.

Romanism /ˈrəʊməˌnɪz(ə)m/ *n.* (*pej., Catholicism*) католици́зм.

Romanist /ˈrəʊmənɪst/ *n.* (*pej.*) кат|о́лик (*fem.* -оли́чка).

Romanize /ˈrəʊmənaɪz/ *v.t.* романизи́ровать (*impf., pf.*).

romantic /rəʊˈmæntɪk/ *n.* рома́нтик.

● *adj.* романти́ческий, романти́чный; **the R~ movement** романти́зм.

romanticism /rəʊˈmæntɪˌsɪz(ə)m/ *n.* романти́зм.

romanticist /rəʊˈmæntɪsɪst/ *n.* рома́нтик.

romanticize /rəʊˈmæntɪˌsaɪz/ *v.t.* романтизи́ровать (*impf., pf.*).

● *v.i.* фантази́ровать (*impf.*).

Romany /ˈrɒmənɪ/, /ˈrəʊ-/ *n.* (*Gypsy*) цыга́н (*fem.* -ка); (*language*) цыга́нский язы́к.

● *adj.* цыга́нский.

Rome /rəʊm/ *n.* **1** (*city or state*) Рим; **~ was not built in a day** Москва́ не сра́зу стро́илась; Рим не сра́зу стро́ился; **when in ~, do as ~ does** ≈ в чужо́й монасты́рь со свои́м уста́вом не хо́дят. **2** (*Church of ~*) ри́мско-католи́ческая це́рковь.

Romish /ˈrəʊmɪʃ/ *adj.* (*pej.*) ри́мско-католи́ческий.

romp /rɒmp/ *n.* (*boisterous play*) возня́.

● *v.i.* резви́ться (*impf.*); **the horse ~ed home** ло́шадь с лёгкостью вы́играла ска́чки; **he ~ed through his exams** он шутя́ сдал экза́мены.

rompers /ˈrɒmpəz/ *n.* (*also* **romper suit**) ползунк|и́ (*pl., g.* -о́в); де́тский комбинезо́н.

rondo /ˈrɒndəʊ/ *n.* (*pl.* **~s**) ро́ндо (*indecl.*).

rood /ruːd/ *n.* (*arch., cross*) крест, распя́тие.

● *cpd.* **~-screen** *n.* кре́стная перегоро́дка, отделя́ющая кли́рос от не́фа.

roof /ruːf/ *n.* кры́ша, кро́вля; **the water-tank is in the ~** бак для воды́ стои́т под кры́шей; **the audience raised the ~** сте́ны сотряса́лись от аплодисме́нтов; **~ of the mouth** нёбо.

● *v.t.* крыть, по-; наст|ила́ть, -ла́ть кры́шу на + *p.*; **~ed with slates** кры́тый ши́фером; **~ing-felt** кро́вельный карто́н; толь (*m.*).

● *cpds.* **~-garden** *n.* сад на кры́ше; **~-rack** *n.* бага́жник (на кры́ше автомоби́ля).

rook /rʊk/ *n.* (*bird*) грач; (*chess piece*) тура́, ладья́.

● *v.t.* (*swindle*) обма́н|ывать, -у́ть.

rookery /ˈrʊkərɪ/ *n.* грачо́вник; (*of seals etc.*) ле́жбище.

rookie /ˈrʊkɪ/ *n.* (*US sl.*) новобра́нец, новичо́к.

room /ruːm/, /rʊm/ *n.* **1** ко́мната; **a four-~(ed) flat** (*Br.*), **apartment** (*US*) четырёхко́мнатная кварти́ра; **~ service** обслу́живание в но́мере; **~ and board** по́лный пансио́н; (*pl., apartments*) кварти́ра, ко́мнаты (*f. pl.*); **private ~** (*in restaurant*) отде́льный кабине́т.
2 (*space*) ме́сто, простра́нство; **the small table will take up no ~** ма́ленький сто́лик займёт немно́го ме́ста; **there's plenty of ~** полно́ ме́ста; **standing ~ only** то́лько стоя́чие места́; **there was no ~ to turn round in** не́где бы́ло поверну́ться; **is there ~ for one more?** ещё оди́н челове́к уся́дется?
3 (*scope, opportunity*) возмо́жность; **it leaves no ~ for doubt** э́то не оставля́ет никаки́х сомне́ний; **there is ~ for improvement in your work** ва́ша рабо́та могла́ бы быть и лу́чше.

● *v.i.*: **we ~ed together in Paris** в Пари́же мы жи́ли в одно́й кварти́ре; **~ing-house** (*US*) меблиро́ванные ко́мнаты (*f. pl.*).

R

● *cpd.* **~-mate** *n.* сосе́д (*fem.* -ка) по ко́мнате.

roomer /'ru:mə(r)/, /'rʊmə(r)/ *n.* (*US, lodger*) квартира́нт, жиле́ц.

roomful /'ru:mfʊl/, /'rʊmfʊl/ *n.* по́лная ко́мната.

roomy /'ru:mɪ/ *adj.* (**roomier, roomiest**) просто́рный, вмести́тельный.

roost /ru:st/ *n.* куря́тник, насе́ст; **go to ~** сади́ться, сесть на насе́ст; (*fig.*): **he rules the ~ here** он тут верхово́дит/распоряжа́ется.

● *v.i.* (*of birds*) ус|а́живаться, -е́сться на насе́ст.

rooster /'ru:stə(r)/ *n.* пету́х.

root /ru:t/ *n.* **1** (*of plant*) ко́рень (*m.*); **the tree was torn up by the ~s** де́рево вы́рвали с ко́рнем; **take, strike ~** пус|ка́ть, -ти́ть ко́рни; **the idea took ~ in his mind** э́та мысль засе́ла ему́ в го́лову; **poverty must be removed ~ and branch** нищету́ ну́жно искорени́ть.
2 (*cul., med.*): **~s** коре́нь|я (*pl., g.* -ев); **~ crop** корнепло́дная культу́ра.
3 (*of tooth, tongue, hair etc.*) ко́рень (*m.*).
4 (*fig., source, basis*) причи́на; **~ cause** основна́я причи́на; **money is the ~ of all evil** де́ньги — ко́рень зла; **he got to the ~ of the problem** он добра́лся до су́ти де́ла; **the quarrel had its ~s deep in the past** конфли́кт уходи́л корня́ми в далёкое про́шлое; **this strikes at the very ~ of democracy** э́то подрыва́ет са́мую осно́ву демокра́тии.
5 (*math., philol.*) ко́рень (*m.*); **square ~** квадра́тный ко́рень (из + *g.*).

● *v.t.* **1**: **the seedling ~ed itself** са́женец пусти́л ко́рни.
2 (*fig.*): **he is a man of deeply ~ed prejudices** он челове́к с укорени́вшимися предрассу́дками.
3 (*transfix*): **he stood ~ed to the ground** он стоя́л как вко́панный.

● *v.i.* **1** (*take ~*) укорен|я́ться, -и́ться.
2 (*of pigs etc., also* **rootle**) ры́ться (*impf.*); рыть (*impf.*) зе́млю; **the dog was ~ing for an old bone** соба́ка отка́пывала ста́рую кость.
3: **~ for** (*support*) боле́ть (*impf.*) за + *a.* (*coll.*).

● *with advs.*: **~ about** *v.i.* (*lit., fig.*) ры́ться (*impf.*); **~ out** *v.t.* (*lit., fig., extirpate*) вырыва́ть, вы́рвать с ко́рнем; (*fig., also*) уничт|ожа́ть, -о́жить; **~ up** *v.t.* вырыва́ть, вы́рвать с ко́рнем.

● *cpd.* **~stock** *n.* (*rhizome*) корневи́ще.

rooter /'ru:tə(r)/ *n.* (*US*) боле́льщик.

rootle /'ru:t(ə)l/ (*Br.*) = **root** *v.i.* 2

rootless /'ru:tlɪs/ *adj.* (*of plant*) без корне́й; (*of person*) безро́дный, без корне́й.

rope /rəʊp/ *n.* (*cord, cable*) верёвка, кана́т; (*fig.*): **money for old ~** лёгкая нажи́ва; **give him enough ~ and he'll hang himself** да́йте ему́ во́лю и он сам себя́ загу́бит; **he knows the ~s** он зна́ет все ходы́ и вы́ходы; он зна́ет, что к чему́; (*string, skein*) ни́тка, вя́зка; **a ~ of onions** вя́зка лу́ка; **a ~ of pearls** ни́тка же́мчуга.

● *v.t.* привя́з|ывать, -а́ть (*что к чему*).

● *with advs.*: **~ in** *v.t.* (*coll., enlist*) втя́|гивать, -ну́ть; **I was ~d in to help** меня́ запрягли́ в э́то де́ло; **~ off** *v.t.* отгор|а́живать, -оди́ть верёвкой/кана́том; **~ together** *v.t.*: **the climbers were ~d together** альпини́сты бы́ли свя́заны верёвкой; **~ up** *v.t.* перевя́з|ывать, -а́ть.

● *cpd.* **~-ladder** *n.* верёвочная ле́стница.

ropy /'rəʊpɪ/ *adj.* (**ropier, ropiest**) (*Br. sl., of poor quality*) никуды́шный.

ro-ro /'rəʊrəʊ/ *adj.* (*Br.*): **~ ship** су́дно «ро-ро́», ро́лкер.

rorqual /'rɔ:kw(ə)l/ *n.* кит полоса́тик, ро́рквал.

rosary /'rəʊzərɪ/ *n.* чёт|ки (*pl., g.* -ок).

rose[1] /rəʊz/ *n.* **1** ро́за; (*fig.*): **life was no bed of (*or* not all) ~s for him** у него́ была́ отню́дь не сла́дкая жизнь; **this will put the ~s back into your cheeks** э́то вернёт вам здоро́вье и све́жесть.
2 (*colour*) ро́зовый цвет.
3 (*sprinkler*) спри́нклерная розе́тка.

● *cpds.* **~-bed** *n.* клу́мба с ро́зами; **~bud** *n.* буто́н ро́зы; **~-bush** *n.* ро́зовый куст; **~-coloured** (*US* **-colored**) *adj.* ро́зовый; **he sees the world through ~-coloured spectacles** (*Br.*), **~-colored glasses** (*US*) он смо́трит на мир че́рез ро́зовые очки́; **~-garden** *n.* роза́рий; **~-pink** *n.* розова́тый отте́нок; *adj.* розова́тый; **~-red** *n.* цвет кра́сной ро́зы; *adj.* кра́сный как ро́за; **~-tree** *n.* шта́мбовая ро́за; **~-water** *n.* ро́зовая вода́; **~-window** *n.* окно́-розе́тка; **~wood** *n.* палиса́ндровое/ро́зовое де́рево.

rose[2] /rəʊz/ *past of* ⇒**rise**

rosé /'rəʊzeɪ/ *n.* (*wine*) ро́зовое вино́, вино́ «розе́».

roseate /'rəʊzɪət/ *adj.* ро́зовый.

rosemary /'rəʊzmərɪ/ *n.* розмари́н.

rosette /rəʊ'zet/ *n.* розе́тка.

rosin /'rɒzɪn/ *n.* канифо́ль.

● *v.t.* (**rosined, rosining**) нат|ира́ть, -ере́ть канифо́лью.

roster /'rɒstə(r)/, /'rəʊstə(r)/ *n.* гра́фик; рее́стр; расписа́ние.

rostr|um /'rɒstrəm/ *n.* (*pl.* **~a** *or* **~ums**) трибу́на; ка́федра.

rosy /'rəʊzɪ/ *adj.* (**rosier, rosiest**) ро́зовый; **~ cheeks** румя́ные щёки; (*fig.*) ра́достный, ра́дужный.

rot /rɒt/ *n.* **1** (*decay*) гние́ние; гниль; (*fig., Br., deterioration*): **the ~ set in** начался́ разла́д; **stop the ~** пресе́чь (*pf.*) зло в ко́рне. **2** (*Br. coll., nonsense*) вздор, чушь; **don't talk ~!** бро́сьте чепуху́ моло́ть!

● *v.t.* (**rotted, rotting**) по́ртить, ис-.

● *v.i.* (**rotted, rotting**) (*decay*) гнить, с-; по́ртиться, ис-; **the tree was ~ting away** де́рево гни́ло.

rota /'rəʊtə/ *n.* (*Br.*) гра́фик; рее́стр; (шта́тное) расписа́ние.

rotary /'rəʊtərɪ/ *adj.* враща́ющийся; **~ motion** враща́тельное движе́ние; **~ press** ротацио́нная печа́тная маши́на.

rotate /rəʊ'teɪt/ *v.t.* & *i.* **1** (*revolve*) враща́ть(ся) (*impf.*). **2** (*arrange or recur in rotation*) чередова́ть(ся) (*impf.*); **the duties (were) ~d every six weeks** дежу́рства чередова́лись ка́ждые шесть неде́ль; **the chairmanship ~s** председа́тели поочерёдно выполня́ют свои́ фу́нкции.

rotation /rəʊ'teɪʃ(ə)n/ *n.* **1** (*revolving*) враще́ние; оборо́т. **2** (*regular succession*) чередова́ние; **~ of crops** севооборо́т; **they did guard duty in ~** они́ поочерёдно несли́ карау́льную слу́жбу.

rotatory /'rəʊtətərɪ/, /-'teɪtərə/ *adj.* враща́тельный; враща́ющийся.

rote /rəʊt/ *n.*: **he learnt the poem by ~** он вы́учил/вы́зубрил стихотворе́ние наизу́сть; **perform duties by ~** механи́чески выполня́ть обя́занности.

rotor /'rəʊtə(r)/ *n.* ро́тор; (*of helicopter*) несу́щий винт.

rotten /'rɒt(ə)n/ *adj.* (**rottener, rottenest**) (*decayed, putrid*) гнило́й, прогни́вший; **~ eggs** ту́хлые я́йца; (*morally corrupt*) разложи́вшийся; испо́рченный; (*worthless*) никуды́шный; **a ~ idea** дура́цкая иде́я; (*very disagreeable, unfortunate*) отврати́тельный; **what a ~ shame!** э́то про́сто безобра́зие! **I'm feeling ~** я себя́ пога́но чу́вствую.

rottenness /'rɒtənnɪs/ *n.* испо́рченность, разложе́ние.

rotter /'rɒtə(r)/ *n.* (*Br. sl.*) подле́ц, подо́нок.

Rottweiler /'rɒtvaɪlə(r)/ *n.* ротве́йлер.

rotund /rəʊ'tʌnd/ *adj.* (*spherical*) округлённый; (*corpulent, plump*) по́лный.

rotunda /rəʊ'tʌndə/ *n.* рото́нда.

rotundity /rəʊ'tʌndɪtɪ/ *n.* округлённость; полнота́; зву́чность, высокопа́рность.

r(o)uble /'ru:b(ə)l/ *n.* рубль (*m.*).

roué /'ru:eɪ/ *n.* пове́са (*m.*).

rouge /ru:ʒ/ *n.* (*cosmetic*) румя́н|а (*pl., g.* —).

● *v.t.* & *i.* румя́нить(ся), на-.

rough /rʌf/ *n.* **1** (*~ things or circumstances*) тру́дности (*f. pl.*); **you must take the ~ with the smooth** на́до сто́йко переноси́ть превра́тности судьбы́.
2 (*~ ground, esp. on golfcourse*) неро́вная пове́рхность.
3 (*unfinished state*): **I saw the poem in the ~** я ви́дел поэ́му в черновике́.
4 (*Br., ruffian*) грубия́н, хулига́н.

● *adj.* **1** (*opp. smooth, even, level*) шерохова́тый, неро́вный; **his skin was ~ to the touch** у него́ была́ шерша́вая на о́щупь ко́жа; **the next few miles were ~ going** зате́м на протяже́нии не́скольких миль доро́га была́ уха́бистой/труднопроходи́мой.
2 (*opp. calm, gentle, orderly*) бу́рный; **~ water** бу́рные во́ды; **the wind is getting ~** ве́тер крепча́ет; **their team played a ~ game** их кома́нда игра́ла гру́бо; **a ~ crowd** хамова́тая пу́блика; **the students were ~ly handled by the police** поли́ция гру́бо обраща́лась со

студе́нтами; **the bill had a ~ passage** законопрое́кт прошёл с трудо́м (*or* со скри́пом (*coll.*)).
3 (*uncomfortable, arduous*) тру́дный; **he had a ~ time** ему́ пришло́сь ту́го.
4 (*of sounds: harsh*) ре́зкий.
5 (*crude*) гру́бый; **they meted out ~ justice** наказа́ние вы́несли суро́вое; **a ~ and ready meal** еда́, пригото́вленная на ско́рую ру́ку.
6 (*unfinished, rudimentary*) чернов́ой; **a ~ sketch** черново́й набро́сок; **a ~ diamond** (*lit.*) неогранённый алма́з; (*fig.*) неотшлифо́ванный алма́з.
7 (*inexact, approximate*) приблизи́тельный; **at a ~ guess** по приблизи́тельной оце́нке; **this will give you a ~ idea** э́то даст вам о́бщее представле́ние; **~ly speaking** гру́бо говоря́.
● *adv.*: **they treated him ~** (*coll.*) с ним гру́бо обраща́лись; **he is inclined to play ~** он допуска́ет гру́бую игру́.
● *v.t.*: **~ it** (*coll.*) жить (*impf.*) без удо́бств.
● *with advs.*: **~ out** *v.t.* (*e.g. a plan*) набр|а́сывать, -оса́ть; **~ up** *v.t.*: **don't ~ up my hair!** не еро́шьте мне во́лосы!
● *cpds.* **~-and-tumble** *n.* де́тская возня́; шутли́вая потасо́вка; ку́ча-мала́; *adj.* беспоря́дочный; **~cast** *n.* га́лечная штукату́рка; *adj.* (*lit.*) гру́бо оштукату́ренный; (*fig.*) грубова́тый, неотёсанный; **~-hew** *v.t.* гру́бо обтёс|ывать, -а́ть; **~-hewn** *adj.* (*fig.*) неотёсанный, некульту́рный; **~-neck** *n.* (*coll.*) хулига́н; **~-rider** *n.* (*US, horse-breaker*) бере́йтор; **~shod** *adj.* подко́ванный на шипы́; *adv.* (*fig.*): **he rode ~shod over their feelings** он соверше́нно не щади́л их чувств; **~-spoken** *adj.* гру́бый; гру́бо выража́ющийся.

roughage /ˈrʌfɪdʒ/ *n.* гру́бая пи́ща.

roughen /ˈrʌf(ə)n/ *v.t. & i.* де́лать(ся), с- гру́бым/шерохова́тым.

roughness /ˈrʌfnɪs/ *n.* **1** (*to touch*) шерохова́тость. **2** (*unevenness*) неро́вность. **3** (*of water etc.*) волне́ние. **4** (*coarseness*) гру́бость. **5** (*harshness of sound*) ре́зкость.

roulette /ru:ˈlet/ *n.* руле́тка; **~ wheel** колесо́ руле́тки; **Russian ~** ру́сская руле́тка.

Roumania /ru:ˈmeɪnɪə/, **-n** /ru:ˈmeɪnɪən/ = **Romania, -n**

round /raʊnd/ *n.* **1** (*circular or ~ed object*) круг, окру́жность; (*Br., slice*) ло́мтик.
2 (*3-dimensional form*): **theatre** (*Br.*), **theater** (*US*) **in the ~** кру́глая сце́на в це́нтре за́ла.
3 (*regular circuit or cycle*) цикл; обхо́д; круговоро́т; **the daily ~** повседне́вные дела́; **milk ~** ежедне́вная доста́вка молока́; **the doctor is on his ~s** до́ктор де́лает обхо́д; **the news went the ~ of the village** но́вость обошла́ всю дере́вню; **a ~ of golf** па́ртия го́льфа.
4 (*stage in contest*) тур, эта́п, ра́унд; **he was knocked out in the third ~** он получи́л нока́ут в тре́тьем ра́унде; **the team got through to the final ~** кома́нда вы́шла в фина́л.
5 (*set, series, burst*): **he bought a ~ of drinks** он поста́вил по стака́нчику всем прису́тствующим; **a ~ of applause** аплодисме́нты (*m. pl.*); **a ~ of wage claims** очередно́е тре́бование повыше́ния зарпла́ты.
6 (*of ammunition*) патро́н; компле́кт вы́стрела; **dummy ~** уче́бный/холосто́й патро́н.
7 (*song*) ро́ндо (*indecl.*).
8 (*dance*) хорово́д; кругово́й та́нец.
● *adj.* **1** (*circular, spherical, convex*) кру́глый; **~ shoulders** суту́лые пле́чи.
2 (*involving circular motion*) кругово́й; **~ dance** хорово́д; **~ robin** проше́ние с по́дписями, располо́женными в кружо́к; **~ trip** пое́здка в о́ба конца́.
3 (*of numbers*) кру́глый; **a ~ dozen** це́лая дю́жина; **in ~ numbers** в кру́глых ци́фрах.
4 (*considerable*) кру́пный, значи́тельный; **a good ~ sum** поря́дочная/кру́гленькая су́мма.
● *adv.* (*Br.*) (*for phrasal vv. with* **round** *see relevant v. entries*): **all the year ~** кру́глый год; **he slept the clock ~** он проспа́л весь день; **the tree is six feet ~** э́то де́рево шесть фу́тов в окру́жности; **better all ~** лу́чше во всех отноше́ниях; **taking it all ~** принима́я во внима́ние всё; **he went a long way ~** он сде́лал изря́дный крюк; **he was ~ at our house** он зашёл к нам.
● *v.t.* **1** (*make ~*) округл|я́ть, -и́ть; **a well-~ed phrase** гла́дкая фра́за.
2 (*go ~*) огиба́ть, обогну́ть; об|ходи́ть, -ойти́ круго́м; **we ~ed the corner** мы заверну́ли/сверну́ли за́ угол; **the ship ~ed the Cape** кора́бль обогну́л мыс До́брой Наде́жды.
3 (*~ a number up or down*) округл|я́ть, -и́ть.
● *v.i.* (*turn aggressively*): **he ~ed on me with abuse** он обру́шился на меня́ с бра́нью; **he ~ed on his pursuers** он набро́сился на свои́х пресле́дователей.
● *with advs.*: **~ off** *v.t.* (*smooth*) выра́внивать, вы́ровнять; (*bring to a conclusion*) заверш|а́ть, -и́ть; **~ out** *v.t.* закругл|я́ть, -и́ть; заверш|а́ть, -и́ть; **~ up** *v.t.* сгоня́ть, согна́ть; **the cattle were ~ed up** скот согна́ли; **the courier ~ed up the party** гид собра́л свою́ гру́ппу; (*arrest*) арест|о́вывать, -ова́ть.
● *prep.* (*Br.*) **1** (*encircling*) вокру́г, круго́м, о́коло (*all +g.*); **~ the world** вокру́г све́та; **they sat ~ the table** они́ сиде́ли вокру́г стола́; **he worked ~ the clock** он рабо́тал круглосу́точно (*or* кру́глые су́тки).
2 (*to or at all points of*): **he looked ~ the room** он осмотре́л (всю) ко́мнату; **we walked ~ the garden** мы гуля́ли по са́ду; **they went ~ the galleries** они обошли́ карти́нные галере́и.
3: **~ the corner** за угло́м, (*of motion*) за́ угол.
4 (*about, based on*): **he wrote a book ~ his experience** он описа́л свой о́пыт в кни́ге.
5 (*approximately*) о́коло + *g.*; **he got there ~ (about) midday** он добра́лся туда́ о́коло полу́дня.
● *cpds.* **~about** *n.* (*merry-go-round*) карусе́ль; (*Br., traffic island*) кольцева́я тра́нспортная развя́зка; (*on road sign*) кругово́е движе́ние; *adj.* око́льный, кру́жный; (*fig.*) ко́свенный, обхо́дный; **R~head** *n.* круглоголо́вый, пурита́нин; **~-shouldered** *adj.* суту́лый; **~sman** *n.* (*Br.*) доста́вщик; (*US*) полице́йский инспе́ктор; **~-table** *n.* (*attr.*): **~-table talks** перегово́ры за кру́глым столо́м; **~-the-clock** *adj.* круглосу́точный; **~-the-world** *adj.* кругосве́тный; **~-up** *n.* (*of news*) сво́дка новосте́й; (*of cattle*) заго́н скота́; (*raid*) обла́ва.

rounders /ˈraʊndəz/ *n.* англи́йская лапта́.

roundness /ˈraʊndnɪs/ *n.* окру́глость.

rouse /raʊz/ *v.t.* **1** (*wake*) буди́ть, раз-. **2** (*stimulate to action, interest etc.*) подстрека́ть (*impf.*); побу|жда́ть, -ди́ть; **he ~d himself and went to work** он взял себя́ в ру́ки и пошёл на рабо́ту; **I could ~ no spark of sympathy** я не мог вы́звать (в себе́) ни ка́пли сочу́вствия; **a rousing chorus** волну́ющий припе́в. **3** (*provoke to anger*) возбу|жда́ть, -ди́ть; выводи́ть, вы́вести из себя́.
● *v.i.* пробу|жда́ться, -ди́ться.

rout /raʊt/ *n.* (*defeat*) разгро́м; (*disorderly retreat*) бе́гство; **the enemy were put to ~** враг был разгро́млен.
● *v.t.* разби|ва́ть, -ть на́голову; разгроми́ть (*pf.*); обра|ща́ть, -ти́ть в бе́гство.

route /ru:t/ *n.* (*of bus etc.*) маршру́т; (*way, course*) путь, доро́га, тра́сса; **the shortest ~** кратча́йший путь; (*US, interstate highway*) автомагистра́ль.
● *v.t.* (**routeing** *or* **routing**) отпр|авля́ть, -а́вить по маршру́ту; разраб|а́тывать, -о́тать маршру́т + *g.*
● *cpd.* **~-march** *n.* похо́дный марш.

routine /ru:ˈti:n/ *n.* **1** (*regular course of action*) заведённый поря́док; режи́м; пра́ктика; (*attr.*) регуля́рный; очередно́й; повседне́вный. **2** (*artiste's act*) но́мер, выступле́ние; **a dance ~** танцева́льный но́мер.

rov|e /rəʊv/ *v.i.* скита́ться (*impf.*); **he has a ~ing disposition** он лю́бит стра́нствовать; **a ~ing correspondent** разъездно́й корреспонде́нт.

rover /ˈrəʊvə(r)/ *n.* (*wanderer*) бродя́га (*m.*); скита́лец.

row[1] /rəʊ/ *n.* (*line*) ряд; **they stood in a ~** они стоя́ли в ряд; **the houses were built in ~s** дома́ бы́ли постро́ены ряда́ми; **seats in the front ~** места́ в пе́рвом ряду́.

row[2] /rəʊ/ *n.* (*by boat*) прогу́лка на ло́дке; **we went (out) for a ~** мы пошли́ поката́ться на ло́дке.
● *v.t.*: **he ~ed the boat in to shore** он привёл ло́дку к бе́регу; **we were ~ed across the river** нас перепра́вили/перевезли́ че́рез ре́ку на ло́дке.
● *v.i.* грести́ (*impf.*); **~ out** грести́ (*impf.*) от бе́рега; **the boat ~s well** ло́дка

R

хорошо́ идёт; **~boat** (*US*), **~ing boat** (*Br.*) гребна́я шлю́пка.

row³ /raʊ/ *n.* **1** (*Br., noise, commotion*) шум; **I can't work with this ~ going on** я не могу́ рабо́тать в тако́м шу́ме; **don't make (such) a ~!** не шуми́те!; **the tenants kicked up a ~** (*made a noise; protested*) жильцы́ по́дняли шум. **2** (*Br., argument, quarrel*) ссо́ра; спор; (*dispute*) ди́спут, диску́ссия; **I had a ~ with the neighbours** (*Br.*), **neighbors** (*US*) я поруга́лся с сосе́дями. **3** (*Br., disgrace*): **I shall get into a ~ if I'm late** мне здо́рово доста́нется, е́сли я опозда́ю.

● *v.i.* (*quarrel*) ссо́риться, по-; руга́ться (*impf.*).

rowan /ˈrəʊən/, /ˈraʊ-/ *n.* ряби́на.

rowdiness /ˈraʊdɪnɪs/ *n.* бесчи́нство; хулига́нство.

rowdy /ˈraʊdɪ/ *n.* буя́н, скандали́ст; хулига́н.

● *adj.* (**rowdier, rowdiest**) гру́бый, шу́мный.

rowdyism /ˈraʊdɪˌɪz(ə)m/ *n.* гру́бость, хулига́нство.

rowing /ˈrəʊɪŋ/ *n.* (*sport*) гре́бля.

rowlock /ˈrɒlək/, /ˈrʌlək/ *n.* уклю́чина.

royal /ˈrɔɪəl/ *n.* (*coll., member of a ~ family*) член короле́вской семьи́.

● *adj.* **1** (*of the reigning family; kingly*) короле́вский, ца́рский; **the R~ Family** короле́вская семья́; **His R~ Highness** его́ короле́вское высо́чество; **the R~ Navy** ВМФ (вое́нно-морско́й флот) Великобрита́нии; **~ blue** я́рко-си́ний цвет. **2** (*magnificent*) великоле́пный.

royalism /ˈrɔɪəˌlɪz(ə)m/ *n.* рояли́зм.

royalist /ˈrɔɪəlɪst/ *n.* рояли́ст (*fem.* -ка).

● *adj.* рояли́стский.

royally /ˈrɔɪəlɪ/ *adv.* (*magnificently*): **we were ~ entertained** нас принима́ли по-ца́рски; (*sl., thoroughly*) вполне́, соверше́нно.

royalty /ˈrɔɪəltɪ/ *n.* **1** (*royal person or persons*) член(ы) короле́вской семьи́. **2** (*payment to owner of patent or copyright*) а́вторский гонора́р; отчисле́ния (*pl.*) а́втору пье́сы *и т.п.*

RP (*abbr. of* ***received pronunciation***) нормати́вное произноше́ние.

rpm (*abbr. of* ***revolutions per minute***) оборо́ты (*m. pl.*) в мину́ту.

RSI (*abbr. of* ***repetitive strain injury***) тра́вма, вы́званная повторя́ющимся движе́нием.

RSPCA (*abbr. of* ***Royal Society for the Prevention of Cruelty to Animals***) Короле́вское о́бщество защи́ты живо́тных от жесто́кого обраще́ния.

RSVP (*abbr. of* ***répondez, s'il vous plaît***) бу́дьте любе́зны отве́тить.

Rt. Hon. /ˌraɪt ˈɒnərəb(ə)l/ *n.* (*abbr. of* ***Right Honourable***) (*Br.*) высокочти́мый.

rub /rʌb/ *n.* **1** (*act of ~bing*) натира́ние; стира́ние; **she gave the mirror a ~ with a cloth** она́ протёрла зе́ркало тря́пкой. **2** (*snag*): **there's the ~!** в то́м-то и загво́здка!

● *v.t.* (**rubbed, rubbing**) тере́ть (*impf.*); пот|ира́ть, -ере́ть; нат|ира́ть, -ере́ть; **the dog ~bed its head against my legs** соба́ка тёрлась голово́й о мои́ но́ги; **Johnny ~bed his knee on the wall** Джо́нни ободра́л коле́но о сте́нку; **he ~bed the skin off his knees** он стёр ко́жу на коле́нях; **he ~bed himself (dry) with a towel** он до́суха вы́терся полоте́нцем; **he ~bed his hands with soap** он намы́лил ру́ки; **he ~bed his hands with satisfaction** он потира́л ру́ки от удово́льствия; **the Maoris ~ noses in greeting** ма́ори тру́тсяноса́ми в знак приве́тствия; **there is no need to ~ my nose in it** (*fig.*) не́зачем ты́кать меня́ но́сом; **he ~s shoulders/(*US*) elbows with the great** он обща́ется с больши́ми людьми́; **~ the oil well into your skin** на́до хороше́нько втере́ть ма́сло в ко́жу.

● *v.i.* (**rubbed, rubbing**) тере́ться (*impf.*); **mind you don't ~ against the wet paint** бу́дьте осторо́жны и не запа́чкайтесь кра́ской.

● *with advs.*: **~ along** *v.i.* (*Br.*) ла́дить (*impf.*); уж|ива́ться, -и́ться; **~ down** *v.t.* обт|ира́ть, -ере́ть; **he ~bed his horse down** он основа́тельно почи́стил ло́шадь; **~ in** *v.t.* вт|ира́ть, -ере́ть; вд|а́лбливать, -олби́ть; **the liniment should be ~bed in** мазь сле́дует втира́ть; **it was my fault; don't ~ it in!** моя́ вина́! но ско́лько мо́жно упрека́ть?; **~ off** *v.t.* ст|ира́ть, -ере́ть; **all the shine was ~bed off** весь блеск сошёл/стёрся; *v.i.*: **her happiness ~bed off on those around her** её сча́стье передава́лось тем, кто её окружа́л; **~ on** *v.t.* (*e.g. ointment*) на|кла́дывать, -ложи́ть; **~ out** *v.t.* отт|ира́ть, -ере́ть; ст|ира́ть, -ере́ть; (*sl., murder*) приши́ть (*pf.*); *v.i.*: **this ink will not ~ out** э́ти черни́ла не стира́ются; **~ over** *v.t.* прот|ира́ть, -ере́ть; **if the glass mists up, ~ it over** е́сли стекло́ запоте́ет, протри́те его́; **~ through** *v.i.*: **his trousers had ~bed through at the knees** его́ брю́ки протёрлись на коле́нях; **~ together** *v.t.*: **he lit the fire by ~bing two sticks together** он развёл костёр, добы́в ого́нь тре́нием; **~ up** *v.t.* нач|ища́ть, -и́стить; полирова́ть, от-; **she ~bed up the silver** она́ начи́стила/почи́стила серебро́; **you ~bed him (up) the wrong way** вы к нему́ не так подошли́.

rubato /ruːˈbɑːtəʊ/ *n., adj. & adv.* (*pl.* **rubatos** *or* **rubati** /-tɪ/) (*mus.*) руба́то (*indecl.*).

rubber¹ /ˈrʌbə(r)/ *n.* **1** (*substance*) рези́на; (*attr.*) рези́новый; **~ band** рези́нка; **~ gloves** рези́новые перча́тки; **~ plant** каучуконо́с. **2** (*Br., eraser*) ла́стик, рези́нка. **3** (*US sl., condom*) презервати́в. **4** (*pl., US, galoshes*) кало́ши (*f. pl.*).

● *cpds.* **~neck** (*sl.*) *n.* зева́ка (*c.g.*); *v.i.* глазе́ть (*impf.*); **~-stamp** *v.t.* (*coll.*) подпи́с|ывать, -а́ть не гля́дя.

rubber² /ˈrʌbə(r)/ *n.* (*cards*) ро́ббер.

rubberized /ˈrʌbəˌraɪzd/ *adj.* прорези́ненный, обло́женный рези́ной, гумми́рованный.

rubbery /ˈrʌbərɪ/ *adj.* похо́жий на рези́ну; (*meat*) жёсткий.

rubbing /ˈrʌbɪŋ/ *n.* (*tracing*) копиро́вка притира́нием.

rubbish /ˈrʌbɪʃ/ *n.* (*Br.*) (*refuse, trash*) му́сор; хлам; (*nonsense*) чепуха́, вздор.

● *v.t.* (*Br. coll.*) критикова́ть (*impf.*).

● *cpds.* **~-bin** *n.* му́сорное ведро́; **~-dump, ~-tip** *nn.* сва́лка.

rubbishy /ˈrʌbɪʃɪ/ *adj.* никуда́ не го́дный; дрянно́й.

rubble /ˈrʌb(ə)l/ *n.* булы́жник, щё́бень (*m.*).

rubella /ruːˈbelə/ *n.* красну́ха.

Rubicon /ˈruːbɪˌkɒn/ *n.*: **he crossed the ~** он перешёл Рубико́н.

rubicund /ˈruːbɪˌkʌnd/ *adj.* румя́ный.

ruble /ˈruːb(ə)l/ = **r(o)uble**

rubric /ˈruːbrɪk/ *n.* заголо́вок; ру́брика.

ruby /ˈruːbɪ/ *n.* руби́н; (*attr.*) руби́новый.

ruck¹ /rʌk/ *n.* (*crowd*) чернь; се́рая ма́сса.

ruck² /rʌk/ *n.* (*wrinkle*) морщи́на.

● *v.t. & i.*: **~ up** соб|ира́ть(ся), -ра́ть(ся) скла́дками; мо́рщить(ся), с-.

rucksack /ˈrʌksæk/, /ˈrʊk-/ *n.* рюкза́к.

ruction /ˈrʌkʃ(ə)n/ *n.* (*sl.*) (*disturbance*) завару́ха, сканда́л; (*pl., trouble*) неприя́тности (*f. pl.*).

rudder /ˈrʌdə(r)/ *n.* (*of vessel*) руль (*m.*), штурва́л; (*of aircraft*) руль направле́ния.

rudderless /ˈrʌdəlɪs/ *adj.* без руля́; (*fig.*) без руля́ и без ветри́л.

ruddy /ˈrʌdɪ/ *adj.* (**ruddier, ruddiest**) **1** (*glowing, reddish*) румя́ный; **a ~ face** румя́ное лицо́; **a ~ glow** я́рко-кра́сный цвет. **2** (*Br., as expletive*) прокля́тый, чёртов.

rude /ruːd/ *adj.* **1** (*impolite, offensive*) гру́бый; невоспи́танный; **don't be ~!** не груби́те!; **he was ~ to the teacher** он нагруби́л учи́телю. **2** (*indecent*) гру́бый, непристо́йный. **3** (*startling, violent*) ре́зкий; **a ~ shock** внеза́пный уда́р; **I had a ~ awakening** (*fig.*) меня́ пости́гло го́рькое разочарова́ние. **4** (*primitive, roughly made*) гру́бо сде́ланный. **5** (*Br., vigorous*) кре́пкий, си́льный; **in ~ health** кре́пкого здоро́вья.

rudeness /ˈruːdnɪs/ *n.* (*impoliteness*) гру́бость, невоспи́танность.

rudiment /ˈruːdɪmənt/ *n.* **1** (*in pl., elements, first principles*) элемента́рные зна́ния; (*beginnings, first trace*) зача́тки (*m. pl.*); **he has not even the ~s of common sense** у него́ нет ни ка́пли здра́вого смы́сла. **2** (*imperfectly developed organ*) рудимента́рный о́рган.

rudimentary /ˌruːdɪˈmentərɪ/ *adj.* (*elementary*) элемента́рный; (*undeveloped*) рудимента́рный, зача́точный.

rue¹ /ruː/ *n.* (*bot.*) ру́та.

rue² /ruː/ *v.t.* (**rues, rued, rueing** *or* **ruing**) (*liter.*) сожале́ть (*impf.*); **you**

will ~ it вы об э́том пожале́ете; **he lived to ~ the day** пришло́ вре́мя, когда́ он про́клял тот день.

rueful /'ru:fʊl/ *adj.* печа́льный, удручённый.

ruff¹ /rʌf/ *n.* (*frill*) жабо́ (*indecl.*); (*on bird's neck*) кольцо́ пе́рьев вокру́г ше́и пти́цы.

ruff² /rʌf/ *n.* (*bird*) турухта́н.

ruffian /'rʌfiən/ *n.* головоре́з, банди́т.

ruffianly /'rʌfiənlɪ/ *adj.* банди́тский.

ruffle /'rʌf(ə)l/ *n.* (*ornamental frill*) обо́рка.

● *v.t.*: **a breeze ~d the surface of the lake** от ве́тра о́зеро покры́лось ря́бью; **she ~d his hair** она́ взъеро́шила ему́ во́лосы; **the bird ~d up its feathers** пти́ца взъеро́шила пе́рья; **he never gets ~d** он всегда́ невозмути́м.

rug /rʌg/ *n.* **1** (*mat*) ковёр. **2** (*Br., wrap*) плед.

rugby (football) /'rʌgbɪ/ *n.* ре́гби (*nt. indecl.*).

● *cpd.* **~-player** *n.* регби́ст.

rugged /'rʌgɪd/ *adj.* **1** (*rough, uneven*) неро́вный; **a ~ coast** скали́стый бе́рег. **2** (*irregular, strongly-marked*) гру́бый; **~ features** ре́зкие черты́. **3** (*austere, harsh*) тяжёлый, тру́дный. **4** (*sturdy*) кре́пкий, твёрдый.

ruggedness /'rʌgɪdnɪs/ *n.* неро́вность; гру́бость; твёрдость.

rugger /'rʌgə(r)/ (*Br. coll.*) = **rugby (football)**

ruin /'ru:ɪn/ *n.* **1** (*downfall*) ги́бель, круше́ние; **the ~ of his hopes** круше́ние его́ наде́жд; **ambition led to his** (*or* **brought him to**) **~** честолю́бие погуби́ло его́; **~ stared him in the face** ему́ грози́ло разоре́ние. **2** (*collapsed or destroyed state; building in this state*) разва́лины, руи́ны (*both f. pl.*); **the house fell into ~** дом соверше́нно развали́лся (*or* преврати́лся в гру́ду разва́лин); **ancient ~s** дре́вние руи́ны (*f. pl.*); **his life lay in ~s** его́ жизнь была́ загу́блена. **3** (*destroying agency*) поги́бель; **he will be the ~ of us** он нас погу́бит.

● *v.t.* разр|уша́ть, -у́шить; уничт|ожа́ть, -о́жить; губи́ть, по-; **he was ~ed** (*in business*) он разори́лся; **this will ~ my chances** э́то подорвёт мои́ ша́нсы; **the rain ~ed my suit** дождь испо́ртил мой костю́м; **a ~ed building** разру́шенное зда́ние.

ruination /ˌru:ɪ'neɪʃ(ə)n/ *n.* ги́бель; разоре́ние.

ruinous /'ru:ɪnəs/ *adj.* (*disastrous*) губи́тельный; (*expensive*) разори́тельный.

rule /ru:l/ *n.* **1** (*regulation; recognized principle*) пра́вило; **keep, stick to the ~s of the game** соблюда́ть (*impf.*) пра́вила игры́; **~ of the road** пра́вила (*pl.*) у́личного движе́ния; **smoking is against the ~s** кури́ть не разреша́ется; **work** (*n.*) **to ~** замедле́ние те́мпа рабо́ты (*род италья́нской забасто́вки*). **2** (*normal practice; custom*) привы́чка, обы́чай; **my ~ is never to start an argument** мой при́нцип — никогда́ не затева́ть спор; **as a ~** как пра́вило; **he makes it a ~ to rise early** он взял за пра́вило встава́ть ра́но. **3** (*government, sway*) правле́ние, госпо́дство; **~ of law** власть зако́на; **under foreign ~** под иностра́нным влады́чеством. **4** (*measuring-stick*) лине́йка.

● *v.t.* **1** (*govern*) управля́ть (*impf.*) + *i.*; руководи́ть (*impf.*) + *i.*; **don't be ~d by prejudice** не поддава́йтесь предрассу́дкам. **2** (*decree, decide*) постан|овля́ть, -ови́ть; **the umpire ~d that the ball was not out** судья́ объяви́л, что мяч не́ был в а́уте. **3**: **a ~d exercise book** тетра́дь в лине́йку; **~d paper** лино́ванная бума́га.

● *v.i.* (*hold sway*) пра́вить (*impf.*); управля́ть (*impf.*); **ruling classes** пра́вящие кла́ссы; **ruling passion** всепоглоща́ющая страсть.

● *with adv.*: **~ out** *v.t.* (*exclude*) исключ|а́ть, -и́ть; **I would not ~ out the possibility** я не исключа́ю тако́й возмо́жности.

ruler /'ru:lə(r)/ *n.* (*reigning person*) прави́тель (*m.*); (*measuring-stick*) лине́йка.

ruling /'ru:lɪŋ/ *n.* (*decree; decision*) постановле́ние; реше́ние.

rum¹ /rʌm/ *n.* ром.

rum² /rʌm/ *adj.* (**rummer, rummest**) (*Br. coll.*) чудно́й; **he is a ~ customer** он стра́нный тип.

Rumania /ru:'meɪnɪə/, **-n** /ru:'meɪnɪən/ = **Romania, -n**

rumba /'rʌmbə/ *n.* ру́мба.

● *v.i.* (**rumbas, rumbaed** /-bəd/ *or* **rumba'd, rumbaing** /-bə(r)ɪŋ/) танцева́ть, про- ру́мбу.

rumbl|e /'rʌmb(ə)l/ *n.* громыха́ние, гул.

● *v.t.* (*Br. coll., unmask, discover*) ви́деть (*impf.*) (*кого/что*) насквозь.

● *v.i.* громыха́ть (*impf.*); греме́ть, за-/про-; **thunder was ~ing in the distance** вдалеке́ греме́л гром; **a tractor ~ed along** грохоча́, прошёл тра́ктор.

rumbustious /rʌm'bʌstʃəs/ *adj.* (*Br. coll.*) шумли́вый, шу́мный.

ruminant /'ru:mɪnənt/ *n.* жва́чное живо́тное.

● *adj.* жва́чный.

ruminate /'ru:mɪˌneɪt/ *v.i.* (*chew the cud*) жева́ть (*impf.*) жва́чку; (*ponder*) разду́мывать (*impf.*).

rumination /ˌru:mɪ'neɪʃ(ə)n/ *n.* (*fig.*) размышле́ние.

rummage /'rʌmɪdʒ/ *n.* (*search*) о́быск; **~ sale** (*US*) бараxо́лка; распрода́жа поде́ржанных веще́й.

● *v.t.* обыск|ивать, -а́ть; **the ship was ~d by Customs** тамо́женники произвели́ досмо́тр корабля́.

● *v.i.* ры́ться (*impf.*); **he ~d (about) for his matches** он всю́ду ры́лся в по́исках спи́чек.

rummy /'rʌmɪ/ *n.* (*card game*) ре́ми-бридж.

rumour /'ru:mə(r)/ (*US* **rumor**) *n.* слух; то́лк|и (*pl., g.* -ов); **~ has it that ...** хо́дят слу́хи, что...; **there were ~s of war** ходи́ли слу́хи, что бу́дет война́.

● *v.t.*: **it was ~ed that ...** ходи́ли слу́хи, что...; **the ~ed visit** визи́т, о кото́ром прошёл слух.

rump /rʌmp/ *n.* кресте́ц; (*fig., remnant*) оста́тки (*m. pl.*).

● *cpd.* **~-steak** *n.* ромште́кс; вы́резка.

rumple /'rʌmp(ə)l/ *v.t.* мять, по-; трепа́ть, по-; еро́шить, взъ-; **her dress was ~d** её пла́тье помя́лось; **don't ~ my hair!** не трепи́те мне во́лосы!

rumpus /'rʌmpəs/ *n.* (*pl.* **rumpuses**) шум; сканда́л; **kick up a ~** подн|има́ть, -я́ть шум; **~ room** (*US*) ко́мната для игр и развлече́ний.

run /rʌn/ *n.* **1** (*action of ~ning*) бег, пробе́г; **a morning ~** у́тренняя пробе́жка; **he went for a ~ before breakfast** он сде́лал пробе́жку пе́ред за́втраком; **he took a ~ and jumped across the brook** он разбежа́лся и перепры́гнул че́рез руче́й; **he started off at a ~** он побежа́л (с ме́ста); **the prisoner made a ~ for it** заключённый бежа́л/удра́л; **the general had the enemy on the ~** генера́л обрати́л проти́вника в бе́гство; **the prisoner is on the ~** заключённый нахо́дится в бега́х; **she has been on the ~ all morning** она́ была́ в бега́х всё у́тро. **2** (*trip, journey, route*) пое́здка, рейс, маршру́т; **we went for a ~ in the country** мы съе́здили за́ город; **the driver was not on his usual ~** води́тель рабо́тал не на своём обы́чном маршру́те; **the train did the ~ in 3 hours** по́езд дошёл за три часа́; **the ship was on a trial ~** кора́бль находи́лся в испыта́тельном ре́йсе. **3** (*continuous stretch*) пери́од; отре́зок вре́мени; **he had a ~ of good luck** у него́ была́ полоса́ везе́ния; **the play had a long ~** пье́са шла до́лго; **in the long ~** в коне́чном счёте. **4** (*score at cricket etc.*) очко́. **5** (*demand*) спрос; **there is a ~ on this book** э́та кни́га по́льзуется больши́м спро́сом. **6** (*ordinary kind*): **his talents are out of the common ~** он незауря́дно тала́нтлив. **7** (*for fowls etc.*) заго́н. **8** (*use, access*): **he gave me the ~ of his library** он предоста́вил мне всю свою́ библиоте́ку. **9** (*mus., rapid scale passage*) рула́да, пасса́ж. **10** (*cards in numerical sequence*) ка́рты (*f. pl.*), иду́щие подря́д по досто́инству. **11** (*ladder in stocking etc.*) спусти́вшаяся пе́тля.

● *v.t.* (**running; past ran; p.p. run**) **1** (*cause to ~*): **he ran a horse in the Derby** он вы́ставил свою́ ло́шадь на Де́рби; **he nearly ran me off my legs** он меня́ так загна́л, что я е́ле стоя́л на нога́х. **2** (*execute, perform*): **he ran a good race** он хорошо́ пробежа́л (диста́нцию);

R

the heats were ~ yesterday забéги состоя́лись вчерá; **he likes ~ning errands** емý нрáвится быть на побегýшках.
3 (*cover, traverse*) бежáть (*det.*), про-; **he can ~ the mile in under four minutes** он мóжет пробежáть ми́лю мéньше, чем за четы́ре минýты; **I'd ~ a mile to avoid him** я егó обхожý за верстý; **the illness has to ~ its course** болéзнь должнá пройти́ все этáпы.
4 (*expose o.s. to*) подв|ергáться, -éргнуться + *d.*; **he ~s the risk of being caught** он рискýет быть пóйманным.
5 (*hunt, pursue*) преслéдовать (*impf.*); трави́ть (*impf.*); **the hounds ran the fox to earth** собáки загнáли лисý в нóру; **I ran him to earth in his study** наконéц я насти́г егó в кабинéте.
6 (*convey in car*) подв|ози́ть, -езти́ (*or* подбр|áсывать, -óсить) (на маши́не); **shall I ~ you home?** хоти́те, я подвезý вас домóй?
7 (*smuggle*) пров|ози́ть, -езти́ контрабáндой.
8 (*cause to go*): **they ran the ship aground** они́ посади́ли корáбль на мель; **he ran the car into the garage** он загнáл маши́ну в гарáж; **he ran the car into a tree** он врéзался в дéрево; **he ran his fingers over the keys** он пробежáл пáльцами по клáвишам; **he ran his eye over the page** он пробежáл глазáми страни́цу; **I shall ~ (water into) the bath** я напущý воды́ в вáнну; я приготóвлю вáнну; **he ran a sword through his enemy's body** он пронзи́л врагá мечóм.
9 (*operate*) управля́ть (*impf.*) + *i.*; эксплуати́ровать (*impf.*); **who is ~ning the shop?** кто вéдает лáвкой?; **he ~s a small business** у негó своё небольшóе дéло; **she ~s the house single-handed** онá самá ведёт хозя́йство; **he ran the engine for a few minutes** он завёл мотóр на нéсколько минýт; **they ran extra trains** они́ пусти́ли дополни́тельные поездá; **can you afford to ~ a car?** вы в состоя́нии держáть маши́ну?; **he thinks he ~s the show** (*fig.*) он дýмает, что он здесь глáвный.
10: he is ~ning a temperature у негó температýра.

● *v.i.* (**running;** *past* **ran;** *p.p.* **run**)
1 (*move quickly, hurry*) бéгать (*indet.*); бежáть (*det.*), по-; **I ran after him** я побежáл за ним; **I had to ~ for the train** мне пришлóсь бежáть, чтóбы поспéть на пóезд; **he ran for his life** он удирáл изо всех сил; **~ for it!** беги́!; (*coll.*) дуй!; **he came ~ning to my aid** он брóсился ко мне на пóмощь; **~ and see who's at the door!** сбéгай посмотри́, кто пришёл!; **she ~s after every man she meets** онá гоня́ется за всéми мужчи́нами.
2 (*compete*) соревновáться (*impf.*); **he is ~ning in the 100 metres** (*Br.*), **meters** (*US*) он бежи́т стометрóвку; (*fig.*): **he ran for president** он баллоти́ровался в президéнты.
3 (*come by chance*) столкнýться (*pf.*) (с + *i.*); натолкнýться (*pf.*) (на + *a.*); **I ran into, across an old friend** я случáйно встрéтил стáрого товáрища.
4 (*of ship etc.*): **the vessel ran ashore** сýдно вы́бросило на бéрег (*or* приткнýлось к бéрегу); **they were ~ning before the wind** они́ плы́ли с попýтным вéтром; **they had to ~ into port** им пришлóсь зайти́ в порт.
5 (*of public transport*) ходи́ть (*indet.*); **there are no trains ~ning** поездá не хóдят.
6 (*of machines etc.: function*) дéйствовать (*impf.*); **most cars ~ on petrol** (*Br.*), **gasoline** (*US*) большинствó маши́н рабóтает/хóдит на бензи́не; **leave the engine ~ning!** не выключáйте мотóр!
7 (*of objects in motion*): **it ~s on wheels** э́то дви́гается на колёсах; (*fig.*): **life ~s smoothly for him** егó жизнь течёт глáдко.
8 (*of liquid, sand etc.: flow*) течь, протекáть, струи́ться (*all impf.*); **the water is ~ning** кран откры́т; **the floor was ~ning with water** пол был зали́т водóй; **tears/sweat ran down his face** слёзы кати́лись (*or* пот струи́лся) по егó щекáм; **the tide ~s strong** си́льный прили́в; **the river is ~ning high** водá в рекé поднялáсь; **my eyes are ~ning** у меня́ слезя́тся глазá; **his nose was ~ning** у негó теклó и́з носу; (*fig.*): **feelings ran high** стрáсти разгорéлись.
9 (*become, grow*) станови́ться (*impf.*); **the well ran dry** колóдец вы́сох; **supplies were ~ning low** запáсы бы́ли на исхóде; **he ran short of money** у негó не оставáлось дéнег; **his blood ran cold** у негó кровь засты́ла в жи́лах.
10 (*develop unchecked*): **the garden is ~ning wild** сад бýрно разрастáется; **she lets her children ~ wild** её дéти растýт без присмóтра; **the lettuces ran to seed** салáт пошёл в семенá; **he is ~ning to fat** у негó появи́лся жирóк; **don't let good food ~ to waste** не переводи́те зря хорóшую пи́щу.
11 (*of colour, ink etc.: spread*) линя́ть, по-; **if you wash this dress the dye will ~** éсли вы постирáете э́то плáтье, онó полиня́ет.
12 (*of emotions, thought etc.: travel*): **the news ran like wildfire** нóвость распространи́лась с молниенóсной быстротóй; **a tremor ran through the crowd** толпá затрепетáла; **a pain ran up his arm** у негó стрéльнуло в рукé; **the thought ran through his head** у негó промелькнýла мысль; **my eyes ran over the page** я пробежáл глазáми страни́цу; **the tune kept ~ning through my head** э́та мелóдия всё врéмя звучáла у меня́ в ушáх.
13 (*extend, stretch*) тянýться (*impf.*); простирáться (*impf.*); **the gardens ~ down to the river** сады́ тя́нутся до реки́; **a road ~ning along the river** дорóга, идýщая вдоль реки́; **a fence ~s round the field** пóле огорóжено забóром; **the first volume ~s to 500 pages** в пéрвом тóме 500 страни́ц; **his biography ran into six editions** егó биогрáфия вы́держала шесть издáний; **his income ~s into five figures** егó дохóд измеря́ется пятизнáчной ци́фрой **it will ~ to a lot of money** э́то бýдет стóить бóльших дéнег; **our funds will not ~ to it** нáших дéнег на э́то не хвáтит.
14 (*continue; remain in operation*) быть дéйствительным; **the lease has seven years to ~** договóр о нáйме дéйствителен ещё семь лет; **the play has been ~ning for five years** пьéса идёт пять лет; **it ~s in their family** э́то у них наслéдственное.
15 (*become unwoven*) спускáться (*impf.*); **these stockings will not ~** на э́тих чулкáх пéтли не спускáются.
16 (*of narrative or verse*) гласи́ть (*impf.*); **I forget how the line (of poetry) ~s** я забы́л, как звучи́т э́та строкá; **so the story ~s** так говоря́т.

● *further phrr. with preps.*: **~ into** (*collide with*) налетéть (*impf.*) на + *a.*; столкнýться (*pf.*) с + *i.*; **he ran into a lamp-post** он налетéл на фонáрный столб; (*encounter, incur*): **he ran into debt** он залéз/влез в долги́; **if you ~ into danger** éсли вам бýдет угрожáть опáсность; **the plan ran into difficulties** план натолкнýлся на трýдности; **~ over, through** (*review; rehearse*) повтор|я́ть, -и́ть; **I will ~ over the main points** я повторю́ (*or* ещё раз перечи́слю) глáвные пýнкты; **shall I ~ over the part with you?** давáйте пройдём вáшу роль вмéсте; **~ through** (*spend*) трáтить, по-; **he ran through a small fortune** он истрáтил цéлое состоя́ние.

● *with advs.*: **~ about** *v.i.* бéгать (*indet.*); **let the children ~ about** пусть дéти побéгают; **~ along** *v.i.*: **I must ~ along** мне нáдо бежáть; **~ along and play!** иди́ поигрáй!; **~ around** *v.i.*: **she is ~ning around with a married man** онá крýтит с женáтым (человéком); **he had me ~ning around in circles** он меня́ совершéнно сбил с тóлку; **~ away, ~ off** *v.i.* убе|гáть, -жáть; уд|ирáть, -рáть; **he ran away with his employer's daughter** он сбежáл с хозя́йской дóчкой; **he ran away with the game** он шутя́ вы́играл пáртию; **don't ~ away with the idea that I am against you** не внушáйте себé, что я имéю чтó-либо прóтив вас; **the horse ran away with him** лóшадь егó понеслá; **he lets his tongue ~ away with him** он сли́шком распускáет язы́к; **~ back** *v.t.*: **he ran the tape back** он перемотáл плёнку назáд; *v.i.*: **he ran back to apologize** он прибежáл назáд, чтóбы извини́ться; **the car ran back down the hill** маши́на откати́лась назáд пóд гору; **let us ~ back over the argument** давáйте повтори́м доказáтельство по пýнктам; **~ down** *v.t.*: **the cyclist was ~ down by a lorry** грузови́к сбил велосипеди́ста; **don't ~ your battery down** не трáтьте батарéю; **she is always ~ning down her neighbours** (*Br.*), **neighbors** (*US*) онá вéчно понóсит сосéдей; **you look very ~ down** у вас óчень утомлённый вид; **the police ran the murderer down in London** поли́ция насти́гла уби́йцу в Лóндоне; **it took him all day to ~ the reference down** цéлый день ушёл у негó на наведéние спрáвок; **it is their**

policy to ~ down production их поли́тика свора́чивать/свёртывать произво́дство; *v.i.* остан|а́вливаться, -ови́ться; **the clock ran down** у часо́в ко́нчился заво́д; **~ in** *v.t.*: **he is ~ning in his car** (*Br.*) он обка́тывает свою́ маши́ну; **the police ran him in** его́ заца́пала поли́ция (*coll.*); **~ off** *v.t.*: **I ran off the water from the tank** я вы́пустил во́ду из ба́ка; **he can ~ off an article in half an hour** он мо́жет настрочи́ть статью́ за полчаса́; **can you ~ off 100 more copies?** вы мо́жете сде́лать/отпеча́тать ещё 100 экземпля́ров?; **the heats will be ~ off today** забе́ги состоя́тся сего́дня; *v.i.* убе|га́ть, -жа́ть; уд|ира́ть, -ра́ть; **he ran off with the jewels** он сбежа́л с драгоце́нностями; (*see also* ⇒**~ away**); **~ on** *v.t.* (*typ. etc.*) наб|ира́ть, -ра́ть в одну́ строку́ (*or* в подбо́р); *v.i.* прод|олжа́ться, -о́лжиться; **the lecture ran on for two hours** ле́кция продолжа́лась два часа́; **~ out** *v.t.*: **he ran the rope out** он протяну́л верёвку; **he was ~ out of the country** его́ изгна́ли из страны́; *v.i.* (*lit.*) выбега́ть, вы́бежать; (*come to an end*) конча́ться, ко́нчиться; **supplies are ~ning out** запа́сы конча́ются; **he will soon ~ out of money** у него́ ско́ро ко́нчатся де́ньги; **he ran out of ideas** у него́ исся́кли иде́и; **our tea ran out** у нас вы́шел чай; **time is ~ning out** вре́мя истека́ет; **the tide was ~ning out** начался́ отли́в; **the pier ~s out into the sea** мол выдаётся в мо́ре; **~ over** *v.t.* задави́ть (*pf.*); **he was ~ over by a car** его́ задави́ла маши́на; *v.i.*: **the bath ran over** ва́нна перелила́сь че́рез край; **the (boiling) milk ran over** молоко́ убежа́ло; **~ through** *v.t.*: **yield, or I will ~ you through!** сдава́йтесь, а то я вас заколю́!; **~ together** *v.t.*: **he ~s his words together** он глота́ет слова́; **~ up** *v.t.*: **~ up the flag** подня́ть (*pf.*) флаг; **she ran up a dress** она́ (бы́стро) смастери́ла пла́тье; **he ran up a bill at the tailor's** он задолжа́л портно́му; *v.i.*: **she ran up to tell me the news** она́ прибежа́ла, что́бы сообщи́ть мне но́вость; **he ran up against a snag** он натолкну́лся на препя́тствие.

● *cpds.* **~about** *n.* (*car*) небольшо́й автомоби́ль; малолитра́жка; **~around** *n.* (*coll., excuses*) отгово́рки (*f. pl.*); **~away** *n.* (*fugitive*) бегле́ц; (*attr.*): **a ~away horse** ло́шадь, кото́рая понесла́; **~away inflation** безу́держная инфля́ция; **~-down** *n.* (*reduction*) сокраще́ние; (*summary*) кра́ткое изложе́ние; конспе́кт; **give me a ~-down on events** скажи́те мне кра́тко, что произошло́; **~-in** *n.* (*fight, squabble*) схва́тка; **~-off** *n.* (*deciding heat*) дополни́тельная игра́; (*diversion of water*) сток; **~-of-the-mill** *adj.* обы́чный, сре́дний; **~-through** *n.* (*theatr.*) прого́н; (*of song*) прослу́шивание; **~-up** *n.* (*run preparatory to action*) разбе́г; (*fig.*): **the ~-up to the election** (*Br.*) предвы́борная пора́/кампа́ния; **~way** *n.* (*aeron.*) взлётно-поса́дочная полоса́ (*abbr.* ВПП).

rune /ru:n/ *n.* ру́на.

rung[1] /rʌŋ/ *n.* (*of ladder*) ступе́нька; (*fig.*): **he reached the topmost ~ of his profession** он дости́г верши́ны в свое́й профе́ссии; (*of chair*) перекла́дина.

rung[2] /rʌŋ/ *p.p. of* ⇒**ring**[2]

runic /'ru:nɪk/ *adj.* руни́ческий.

runnel /'rʌn(ə)l/ *n.* (*rivulet*) ручеёк; (*gutter*) кана́ва, сток.

runner /'rʌnə(r)/ *n.* **1** (*athlete*) бегу́н; **front ~** ли́дер; **long-distance ~** ста́йер; **marathon ~** марафо́нец. **2** (*horse in race*) рыса́к, (бегова́я) ло́шадь. **3** (*messenger; scout*) посы́льный курье́р. **4** (*part which assists sliding motion*) бегуно́к, ходово́й ро́лик; **curtain ~** кольцо́ для занаве́ски; **sledge ~** по́лоз. **5** (*narrow cloth; strip of carpet*) доро́жка. **6** (*bot., shoot*) побе́г; **~ bean** (*Br.*) фасо́ль о́гненная. **7** (*US, in stocking*) спусти́вшаяся пе́тля.

● *cpd.* **~-up** *n.* уча́стник/кандида́т, заня́вший второ́е ме́сто.

running /'rʌnɪŋ/ *n.* **1** (*sport, exercise*) бе́ганье, бег; **I shall take up ~** я займу́сь бе́гом; **~ shoes** беговик|и́ (*pl., g.* -о́в), кроссо́в|ки (*pl., g.* -ок). **2** (*pace*) ход; **the favourite** (*Br.*), **favorite** (*US*) **made all the ~** фавори́т вёл бег. **3** (*contest*) состяза́ние; **they are out of the ~ for the Cup** они́ вы́были из соревнова́ний на ку́бок; **he is in the ~ for Prime Minister** он мо́жет стать премье́р-мини́стром. **4** (*operation*) управле́ние (*чем*), эксплуата́ция.

● *adj.* **1** (*performed while ~*) бегу́щий; **he took a ~ kick at the ball** он уда́рил мяч с разбе́га; **~ jump** прыжо́к с разбе́га; **~ fight** отхо́д с боя́ми. **2** (*performed while events proceed*) теку́щий; **~ commentary** репорта́ж (по хо́ду де́йствия). **3** (*continuous*) непреры́вный; **~ costs** (*of business*) теку́щие расхо́ды (*m. pl.*); (*of car*) расхо́ды (*m. pl.*) на содержа́ние маши́ны. **4** (*in succession*) подря́д, кря́ду; **he won three times ~** он вы́играл три ра́за подря́д. **5** (*flowing*): **~ water** (*in nature*) прото́чная вода́; (*domestic*) водопрово́д; **hot and cold ~ water** горя́чая и холо́дная вода́; **a ~ sore** гноя́щаяся боля́чка; **a ~ nose** сопли́вый нос, на́сморк. **6** (*sliding*) скользя́щий; **a ~ knot** затяжно́й у́зел.

● *cpds.* **~-board** *n.* подно́жка; **~ head** *n.* (*typ.*) колонти́тул; **~ mate** *n.* (*US*) (*pol.*) кандида́т на пост вице-президе́нта; (*horse*) ло́шадь, задаю́щая темп друго́й ло́шади.

runny /'rʌnɪ/ *adj.* (**runnier, runniest**) теку́чий, жи́дкий; **a ~ egg** яйцо́ всмя́тку; **a ~ nose** мо́крый нос, на́сморк.

runt /rʌnt/ *n.* (*undersized animal*) низкоро́слое живо́тное; (*of person, pej.*) ка́рлик.

rupee /ru:'pi:/ *n.* ру́пия.

rupture /'rʌptʃə(r)/ *n.* **1** (*breaking, bursting*) проры́в; перело́м. **2** (*hernia*) гры́жа. **3** (*breach, quarrel*) разры́в.

● *v.t.* **1** (*burst, break*) прор|ыва́ть, -ва́ть; **he ~d a blood-vessel** он повреди́л кровено́сный сосу́д. **2**: **~ o.s.** над|рыва́ться, -орва́ться.

● *v.i.* раз|рыва́ться, -орва́ться.

rural /'rʊər(ə)l/ *adj.* се́льский.

ruse /ru:z/ *n.* уло́вка, ухищре́ние.

rush[1] /rʌʃ/ *n.* (*bot.*) тростни́к.

rush[2] /rʌʃ/ *n.* **1** (*precipitate movement*) стреми́тельное движе́ние; **the ~ of water** пото́к воды́; **a ~ of blood to the head** прили́в кро́ви к голове́; **he made a ~ for the goal** он бро́сился к воро́там; (*bustle*) спе́шка; (*increase in activity, buying etc.*): **the Christmas ~** предрожде́ственская суета́/су́толока; **the gold ~** золота́я лихора́дка; **a ~ job** спе́шная рабо́та; **in the ~ hour** в часы́ пик. **2** (*first print of film*) отсня́тый материа́л, (*in pl.*) «пото́ки» (*m. pl.*).

● *v.t.* **1** (*speed, hurry*) торопи́ть, по-; **troops were ~ed to the front** войска́ бы́ли сро́чно перебро́шены на фронт; **a doctor was ~ed to the scene** на ме́сто происше́ствия сро́чно доста́вили врача́; **the order was ~ed through** зака́з бы́стро проверну́ли; **I refuse to be ~ed into a decision** я отка́зываюсь принима́ть реше́ние в спе́шке; **I was ~ed off my feet** (*exhausted*) я сби́лся с ног; **I must ~ off a letter** я до́лжен бы́стренько настрочи́ть письмо́. **2** (*charge*) брать, взять шту́рмом; **the audience ~ed the platform** пу́блика хлы́нула на эстра́ду; **he ~ed the fence** он сли́шком стреми́тельно взял барье́р.

● *v.i.* мча́ться, по-; бр|оса́ться, -о́ситься; кида́ться, ки́нуться; **she is always ~ing about** она́ ве́чно но́сится; она́ ве́чно в бега́х; **he ~ed after me** он бро́сился за мной; **the train ~ed by** по́езд промча́лся ми́мо; **he ~ed in and out** он заскочи́л на мину́тку; **she ~ed off without saying goodbye** она́ убежа́ла, не попроща́вшись; **they ~ed to congratulate her** они́ бро́сились её поздравля́ть; **the blood ~ed to her face** кровь бро́силась ей в лицо́; **don't ~ to conclusions** не де́лайте поспе́шных вы́водов; **a ~ing wind** поры́вистый ве́тер.

rusk /rʌsk/ *n.* суха́рь (*m.*).

russet /'rʌsɪt/ *adj.* красновато-кори́чневый.

Russia /'rʌʃə/ *n.* Росси́я.

Russian /'rʌʃ(ə)n/ *n.* **1** (*person of Russian nationality*) ру́сск|ий (*fem.* -ая); (*person of Russian citizenship*) россия́н|ин (*fem.* -ка); **the ~s** ру́сские (*pl.*). **2** (*language*) ру́сский язы́к; **do you speak ~?** вы говори́те по-ру́сски?

● *adj.* ру́сский; (*pol., hist., also*) росси́йский; **~ doll** матрёшка; **~ studies** руси́стика; **~ salad** (*Br.*) сала́т оливье́; **~ wolfhound** ру́сская борза́я.

● *cpd.* **~-speaking** *adj.* русскоязы́чный.

Russianist /'rʌʃənɪst/ *n.* руси́ст (*fem.* -ка).

R

Russianize /ˈrʌʃəˌnaɪz/ *v.t.* русифици́ровать (*impf., pf.*).

Russicism /ˈrʌsɪˌsɪz(ə)m/ *n.* руси́зм.

Russification /ˌrʌsɪfɪˈkeɪʃ(ə)n/ *n.* русифика́ция.

Russify /ˈrʌsɪˌfaɪ/ *v.t.* русифици́ровать (*impf., pf.*).

Russo-Japanese /ˌrʌsəʊˌdʒæpəˈniːz/ *adj.*: ~ **War** ру́сско-япо́нская война́.

Russophile /ˈrʌsəʊˌfaɪl/ *n.* русофи́л (*fem.* -ка).

Russophobia /ˌrʌsəʊˈfəʊbɪə/ *n.* русофо́бия.

rust /rʌst/ *n.* (*on metal; plant disease*) ржа́вчина.

● *v.t.* покр|ыва́ть, -ы́ть ржа́вчиной.

● *v.i.* ржаве́ть, за-.

● *cpd.* **~-proof** *adj.* нержаве́ющий.

rustic /ˈrʌstɪk/ *n.* дереве́нский жи́тель, дереве́нщина (*c.g.*).

● *adj.* (*countrified*) дереве́нский, се́льский; (*unrefined*) неотёсанный, гру́бый; **a ~ bridge** мост из нетёсаного ле́са.

rusticate /ˈrʌstɪˌkeɪt/ *v.t.* (*Br., suspend*) вре́менно исключа́ть (*impf.*) (*студента из университета*).

rustication /ˌrʌstɪˈkeɪʃ(ə)n/ *n.* (*Br., suspension*) вре́менное исключе́ние (студе́нта из университе́та).

rusticity /rʌsˈtɪsɪtɪ/ *n.* простота́; неотёсанность.

rustiness /ˈrʌstɪnɪs/ *n.* ржа́вчина; (*fig.*) отста́лость.

rustle /ˈrʌs(ə)l/ *n.* ше́лест, шо́рох.

● *v.t.* **1** (*cause to ~*) шелесте́ть (*impf.*) + *i.*; шурша́ть (*impf.*) + *i.*; **don't ~ the newspaper** не шелести́те газе́той. **2** (*US sl., steal*) красть, у-. **3**: **~ up** (*coll.*) разы́ск|ивать, -а́ть; **can you ~ up some food?** вы мо́жете раздобы́ть чего́-нибу́дь пое́сть? *or* собери́те-ка чего́-нибудь на стол!

● *v.i.* шелесте́ть (*impf.*); шурша́ть (*impf.*).

rustler /ˈrʌslə(r)/ *n.* (*US*) конокра́д; вор, угоня́ющий скот.

rustless /ˈrʌstlɪs/ *adj.* нержаве́ющий.

rusty /ˈrʌstɪ/ *adj.* (**rustier, rustiest**) ржа́вый, заржа́вленный; (*fig.*) (*out of practice*): **my German is ~** я подзабы́л неме́цкий.

rut¹ /rʌt/ *n.* (*wheel-track*) колея́, вы́боина; (*fig.*) рути́на; **it is easy to get into a ~** легко́ погря́знуть в рути́не.

● *v.t.* (**rutted, rutting**): **a deeply ~ted road** доро́га, изры́тая глубо́кими колея́ми.

rut² /rʌt/ *n.* (*sexual excitement*) гон; **in ~** в охо́те.

● *v.i.* (**rutted, rutting**) быть в охо́те; **the ~ting season** вре́мя спа́ривания/слу́чки.

rutabaga /ˌruːtəˈbeɪɡə/ *n.* (*US*) брю́ква.

Ruth /ruːθ/ *n.* (*bibl.*) Руфь.

ruthenium /ruːˈθiːnɪəm/ *n.* руте́ний.

ruthless /ˈruːθlɪs/ *adj.* безжа́лостный, жесто́кий.

ruthlessness /ˈruːθlɪsnɪs/ *n.* безжа́лостность, жесто́кость.

Rwanda /ruˈændə/ *n.* Руа́нда.

rye /raɪ/ *n.* рожь; **~ bread** ржано́й хлеб; (**~ whisky**) ржано́е ви́ски (*indecl.*).

Ss

sabbath /ˈsæbəθ/ *n.* **1** (*Jewish*) суббо́та; (*Christian*) воскресе́нье. **2**: **witches' ~** ша́баш ведьм.

sabbatical /səˈbætɪk(ə)l/ *n.* (~ *year, term*) *see adj.*

● *adj.* **1** суббо́тний; воскре́сный. **2**: **~ leave** тво́рческий о́тпуск.

saber /ˈseɪbə(r)/ (*US*) = **sabre**

sable¹ /ˈseɪb(ə)l/ *n.* (*zool.*) со́боль (*m.*); (*fur*) со́боль, собо́лий мех.

● *adj.* соболи́ный, собо́лий.

sable² /ˈseɪb(ə)l/ (*liter.*) *n.* (*colour*) чёрный цвет.

● *adj.* чёрный, вороно́й.

sabot /ˈsæbəʊt/, /ˈsæbəʊ/ *n.* сабо́ (*indecl.*), деревя́нный башма́к.

sabotage /ˈsæbəˌtɑːʒ/ *n.* (*of work, activity*) сабота́ж; (*of equipment*) диве́рсия; **acts of ~** диверсио́нные а́кты.

● *v.t.* саботи́ровать (*impf., pf.*); (*damage*) повре|жда́ть, -ди́ть; (*fig., disrupt*) срыва́ть, сорва́ть; саботи́ровать (*impf., pf.*).

saboteur /ˌsæbəˈtɜː(r)/ *n.* сабота́жни|к (*fem.* -ца), диверса́нт, вреди́тель (*m.*).

sabre /ˈseɪbə(r)/ (*US* **saber**) *n.* са́бля.

● *cpds.* **~-rattling** *n.* (*fig.*) бряца́ние ору́жием; **~-toothed** *adj.* саблезу́бый.

sabretache /ˈsæbəˌtæʃ/ *n.* (*mil., hist.*) та́шка.

sac /sæk/ *n.* мешо́чек.

saccharin /ˈsækərɪn/ *n.* сахари́н.

saccharine /ˈsækəˌriːn/ *adj.* са́харный, са́харистый; (*fig.*) слаща́вый, при́торный.

sacerdotal /ˌsæsəˈdəʊt(ə)l/ *adj.* свяще́ннический.

sachet /ˈsæʃeɪ/ *n.* (*Br.*) саше́ (*indecl.*).

sack¹ /sæk/ *n.* **1** (*bag*) мешо́к; (~ *dress*) сак. **2** (*coll., dismissal*): **get the ~** быть уво́ленным; получ|а́ть, -и́ть расчёт; **give s.o. the ~** ув|ольня́ть, -о́лить кого́-н.; рассчи́т|ывать, -а́ть кого́-н. **3** (*US, bed*): **hit the ~** отпр|авля́ться, -а́виться на бокову́ю (*coll.*).

● *v.t.* **1** (*put into ~s; also* **~ up**) нас|ыпа́ть, -ы́пать в мешки́. **2** (*coll., dismiss*) ув|ольня́ть, -о́лить; рассчи́т|ывать, -а́ть.

● *cpds.* **~cloth** *n.* мешкови́на, дерю́га; (*hair shirt*) власяни́ца; **wear ~ cloth and ashes** (*fig.*) посы́пать (*pf.*) пе́плом главу́; ка́яться (*impf.*); **~-race** *n.* бег в мешка́х.

sack² /sæk/ *n.* (*plundering*) разграбле́ние.

● *v.t.* гра́бить, раз-; пред|ава́ть, -а́ть разграбле́нию.

sackful /ˈsækfʊl/ *n.* (по́лный) мешо́к (*чего*); **by the ~** (це́лыми) мешка́ми.

sacking /ˈsækɪŋ/ *n.* (*text.*) мешкови́на, дерю́га.

sacra /ˈseɪkrə/ *pl. of* ⇒**sacrum**

sacral /ˈseɪkr(ə)l/ *adj.* (*anat.*) крестцо́вый; (*relig.*) обря́довый, ритуа́льный.

sacrament /ˈsækrəmənt/ *n.* **1** (*sacred act or rite*) та́инство. **2** (*Eucharist*): **the Holy S~** свято́е прича́стие; святы́е дары́ (*m. pl.*); те́ло Госпо́дне; **take, receive the ~** прича|ща́ться, -сти́ться.

sacramental /ˌsækrəˈment(ə)l/ *adj.* сакрамента́льный; **~ wine** вино́ для прича́стия.

sacred /ˈseɪkrɪd/ *adj.* свяще́нный, свято́й; **~ books** свяще́нные кни́ги; **~ music** духо́вная му́зыка; **~ duty** свяще́нный долг; **nothing is ~ to him** для него́ нет ничего́ свято́го; **~ cow** (*fig.*) (неприкоснове́нная) святы́ня; **~ to the memory of my wife** незабве́нной па́мяти мое́й супру́ги.

sacredness /ˈseɪkrɪdnɪs/ *n.* свя́тость.

sacrifice /ˈsækrɪˌfaɪs/ *n.* (*lit., fig.*) же́ртва; (*act of relig.* ~) жертвоприноше́ние; **make a ~ of something** прин|оси́ть, -ести́ что-н. в же́ртву; же́ртвовать, по- чем-н.; **they made ~s for their children** они́ мно́гим же́ртвовали ра́ди дете́й; **at the ~ of his health** же́ртвуя здоро́вьем; **at the ~ of one's principles** поступи́вшись свои́ми при́нципами.

● *v.t.* (*lit., at altar*) прин|оси́ть, -ести́ (*кого/что*) в же́ртву; (*give up, surrender*) же́ртвовать, по- + *i.*; **he ~d truth to his own interests** он принёс и́стину в же́ртву свои́м интере́сам.

sacrificial /ˌsækrɪˈfɪʃ(ə)l/ *adj.* же́ртвенный.

sacrilege /ˈsækrɪlɪdʒ/ *n.* святота́тство, кощу́нство.

sacrilegious /ˌsækrɪˈlɪdʒəs/ *adj.* святота́тственный, кощу́нственный.

sacristan /ˈsækrɪst(ə)n/ *n.* ри́зничий.

sacristy /ˈsækrɪstɪ/ *n.* ри́зница.

sacrosanct /ˈsækrəʊˌsæŋkt/ *adj.* свяще́нный, неприкоснове́нный.

sacrum /ˈseɪkrəm/ *n.* (*pl.* **sacra** *or* **sacrums**) кресте́ц.

sad /sæd/ *adj.* (**sadder, saddest**) **1** гру́стный, печа́льный; **I feel ~** мне гру́стно; **with a ~ heart** с тяжёлым се́рдцем; **a ~ event** печа́льное собы́тие; (*regrettable, lamentable*) приско́рбный; **it is ~ that you failed the exams** о́чень жаль, что вы провали́лись на экза́менах; **he came to a ~ end** он пло́хо ко́нчил. **2** (*coll., pathetic*) жа́лкий. **3**: **you are ~ly mistaken** вы жесто́ко ошиба́етесь; **the garden was ~ly neglected** сад был доне́льзя запу́щен.

sadden /ˈsæd(ə)n/ *v.t.* печа́лить, о-.

saddle /ˈsæd(ə)l/ *n.* **1** седло́. **2** (*of animal's back*) седлови́на; (*as meat*) седло́. **3** (*in hills*) седлови́на.

● *v.t.* **1** седла́ть, о-. **2** (*fig., burden with task, guilt etc.*): **~ s.o. with something** взва́л|ивать, -и́ть что-н. на кого́-н.; **he was ~d with his relatives** он был обременён ро́дственниками; у него́ на ше́е сиде́ли ро́дственники.

● *cpds.* **~back** *n.* (*geog.*) седлови́на; **~-bag** *n.* седе́льный вьюк; **~-cloth** *n.* чепра́к; **~-horse** *n.* (*US*) верхова́я ло́шадь.

saddler /ˈsædlə(r)/ *n.* седе́льник, шо́рник-седе́льник.

saddlery /ˈsædlərɪ/ *n.* (*activity*) шо́рное де́ло, шо́рничество; (*workshop*) шо́рная мастерска́я.

sadism /ˈseɪdɪz(ə)m/ *n.* сади́зм.

sadist /ˈseɪdɪst/ *n.* сади́ст (*fem.* -ка).

sadistic /səˈdɪstɪk/ *adj.* сади́стский.

sadness /ˈsædnɪs/ *n.* грусть, печáль, тоскá; **a look of ~** печáльный вид.

s.a.e. (*abbr. of* ***stamped addressed envelope***) (*Br.*) конвéрт с мáркой и обрáтным áдресом.

safari /səˈfɑːrɪ/ *n.* (*pl.* **~s**) сафáри (*nt. indecl.*); **on ~** на сафáри; **~ park** (парк) сафáри.

safe¹ /seɪf/ *n.* сейф; несгорáемый шкаф/я́щик; (*meat-~*) холоди́льник.

● *cpd.* **~-breaker** *n.* взлóмщик сéйфов.

safe² /seɪf/ *adj.* **1** (*affording security, not dangerous*) безопáсный; (*reliable*) надёжный; **put the money in a ~ place!** спря́чьте дéньги в надёжное мéсто!; **in ~ custody** под надёжной охрáной; **in s.o.'s ~ keeping** у когó-н. на сохранéнии; **is it ~ to leave him (alone)?** не опáсно/стрáшно оставля́ть егó одногó?; **to be on the ~ side** на вся́кий слу́чай, для (бóльшей) вéрности; **is the dog ~ with children?** дéтям не опáсно игрáть с э́той собáкой?
2 (*free from danger*): **we are ~ from attack** мы мóжем не опасáться нападéния; **we are ~ as houses here** мы здесь как за кáменной стенóй; **perfectly ~** в пóлной безопáсности; **~ area** (*mil.*) зóна безопáсности; **~ house** конспирати́вная кварти́ра; укры́тие; **~ sex** безопáсный секс; (*unhurt, undamaged*): **we saw them home ~ and sound** мы достáвили их домóй цéлыми и невреди́мыми (*or* в цéлости и сохрáнности).
3 (*cautious, moderate*) осторóжный; **better ~ than sorry** бережёного Бог бережёт; **I decided to play ~** я реши́л не рисковáть.
4 (*certain*): **he is a ~ winner** он навернякá вы́играет; **it's a ~ bet** мóжно быть увéренным.

● *cpds.* **~-conduct** *n.* (*document*) охрáнная грáмота; **~-deposit** *n.* храни́лище с сéйфами; **~guard** *n.* охрáна, страхóвка, гарáнтия (от + *g.*); *v.t.* гаранти́ровать (*impf., pf.*); охран|я́ть, -и́ть.

safely /ˈseɪflɪ/ *adv.* **1** (*unharmed*) благополу́чно, в сохрáнности; **we returned ~** мы благополу́чно верну́лись; **the parcel arrived ~** посы́лка пришлá в цéлости и сохрáнности (*or* неповреждённой).
2 (*for safety*): **I put the bottle ~ away** я убрáл буты́лку от беды́/грехá подáльше. **3** (*with confidence*) увéренно, с увéренностью; **I can ~ say that ...** я могу́ с увéренностью сказáть, что.... **4** (*securely*) надёжно.

safeness /ˈseɪfnɪs/ *n.* (*security*): **a feeling of ~** чу́вство безопáсности; (*of building, investment etc.*) надёжность.

safety /ˈseɪftɪ/ *n.* безопáсность; **endanger s.o.'s ~** грози́ть/угрожáть (*both impf.*) чьей-н. безопáсности; **our ~ was threatened** нáша безопáсность былá под угрóзой; **there is ~ in numbers** безопáснее дéйствовать сообщá; **~ first** осторóжность прéжде всегó; **road ~** безопáсность на дорóгах, безопáсность движéния; **~ curtain** (*theatr.*) противопожáрный зáнавес; **~ glass** безоскóлочное стеклó; **~ lamp** (*mining*) рудни́чная лáмпа; **~ measures, precautions** мéры безопáсности; **~ match** (безопáсная) спи́чка; **~ net** страхóвочная сеть (*also fig.*); **~ razor** безопáсная бри́тва.

● *cpds.* **~-belt** *n.* ремéнь безопáсности, привязнóй ремéнь; **~-catch** *n.* (*on gun etc.*) предохрани́тель (*m.*); **~-fuse** *n.* (*for explosive*) огнепровóдный шнур; (*elec.*) (плáвкий) предохрани́тель (*m.*); **~-pin** *n.* англи́йская булáвка; **~-valve** *n.* предохрани́тельный клáпан; (*fig.*): **rowing provided a ~-valve for his energies** заня́тия грéблей давáли вы́ход егó энéргии.

saffron /ˈsæfrən/ *n.* (*substance*) шафрáн; (*colour*) шафрáнный/шафрáновый цвет.

● *adj.* шафрáнный, шафрáновый.

sag /sæg/ *n.* (*of ceiling*) проги́б.

● *v.i.* (**sagged, sagging**) (*of gate etc.*) ос|едáть, -éсть; коси́ться, по-; (*of rope, curtain*) пров|исáть, -и́снуть; (*of ladder, ceiling*) прог|ибáться, -ну́ться; **the ceiling ~s in the middle** потолóк прови́с посереди́не; (*of garment*) отв|исáть, -и́снуть; (*of cheeks, breasts*) обв|исáть, -и́снуть; **a ~ging chin** отви́слый подборóдок; (*fig., of prices*) пáдать, упáсть.

saga /ˈsɑːgə/ *n.* сáга; (*fig.*): **he told me the ~ of his escape** он повéдал мне (фантасти́ческую) истóрию своегó побéга.

sagacious /səˈgeɪʃ(ə)s/ *adj.* **1** (*of person*) му́дрый; (*of animal*) у́мный. **2** (*perspicacious*) проницáтельный, му́дрый; (*of action: far-sighted*) дальнови́дный, прозорли́вый.

sagacity /səˈgæsɪtɪ/ *n.* му́дрость, ум; проницáтельность, прозорли́вость; дальнови́дность.

sage¹ /seɪdʒ/ *n.* **1** (*bot.*) шалфéй. **2** (**~ green**) сéровáто-зелёный цвет.

sage² /seɪdʒ/ *n.* (*wise man*) мудрéц.

● *adj.* му́дрый.

Sagittarius /ˌsædʒɪˈteərɪəs/ *n.* Стрелéц.

sago /ˈseɪgəʊ/ *n.* (*pl.* **~s**) сáго (*indecl.*); **~ palm** сáговая пáльма.

Sahara /səˈhɑːrə/ *n.* Сахáра.

said /sed/ *past and p.p. of* ⇒**say**

Saigon /saɪˈgɒn/ *n.* Сайгóн.

sail /seɪl/ *n.* **1** пáрус; **hoist ~** стáвить, по- (*or* подн|имáть, -я́ть) парусá; **lower the ~s** спус|кáть, -ти́ть парусá; **under ~** под парусáми; **in full ~** на всех парусáх; **get under (or set) ~** выходи́ть, вы́йти в плáвание; **make, set ~ for** отпл|ывáть, -ы́ть в/на + *a.*; отпр|авля́ться, -áвиться на/в + *a.*; **take in (or shorten) ~** уб|авля́ть, -áвить парусá.
2 (*ship*) су́дно, корáбль (*m.*); **there wasn't a ~ in sight** нé было ви́дно ни одногó су́дна/корабля́.
3 (*voyage or excursion on water*) плáвание; **go for a ~** отпр|авля́ться, -áвиться в плáвание; **it is 7 days' ~ from here** э́то в семи́ днях плáвания отсю́да.
4 (*of windmill*) крылó.

● *v.t.* **1** (*of person or ship*) плáвать (*indet.*); плыть (*det.*) в + *p.*; **to ~ the Pacific Ocean** плáвать (*indet.*), плыть (*det.*)/ ходи́ть (*indet.*), идти́ (*det.*) в Ти́хом океáне; **he has ~ed the seven seas** он исходи́л все моря́ (и океáны); (*cover a distance*) пропл|ывáть, -ы́ть; **we ~ed 150 miles** мы проплы́ли/прошли́ 150 миль.
2 (*control navigation of*) управля́ть (*impf.*) + *i.*; **~ toy boats** пускáть (*impf.*) корáблики.

● *v.i.* **1** пл|áвать (*indet.*), -ыть (*det.*), поплы́ть (*pf.*); **the new yacht ~s well** у нóвой я́хты хорóший ход; **~ close to the wind** (*lit.*) идти́/плыть (*det.*) кру́то к вéтру; (*fig.*) вступ|áть, -и́ть на опáсный путь; **the ship ~ed into harbour** (*Br.*), **harbor** (*US*) корáбль вошёл в гáвань; **we ~ed out to sea** мы вы́шли в мóре; **they ~ed up the coast** они́ плы́ли вдоль бéрега.
2 (*start a voyage*) отпл|ывáть, -ы́ть; (*of freight*): **the goods ~ed from London yesterday** товáр был отпрáвлен из Лóндона вчерá.
3 (*fig., move gracefully, smoothly*) плыть (*det.*); плáвно дви́гаться (*impf.*); пропл|ывáть, -ы́ть; **he ~ed through** (*made light work of*) **the exams** он с лёгкостью (*or* без трудá) вы́держал экзáмены; **~ into** (*coll., attack*) набр|áсываться, -óситься на + *a.*
4 (*of birds*) пари́ть (*impf.*); (*of clouds*) плыть (*det.*); **the clouds ~ed by** проплывáли облакá.

● *cpds.* **~boat** *n.* (*US*) пáрусная лóдка; **~cloth** *n.* паруси́на; **~-maker** *n.* пáрусный мáстер; **~plane** *n.* планёр.

sailboard /ˈseɪlbɔːd/ *n.* виндсёрфер.

sailboarder /ˈseɪlbɔːdə(r)/ *n.* виндсёрфинги́ст.

sailboarding /ˈseɪlbɔːdɪŋ/ *n.* виндсёрфинг.

sailer /ˈseɪlə(r)/ *n.*: **a fast, good ~** быстрохóдное су́дно.

sailing /ˈseɪlɪŋ/ *n.* **1** (*act of ~*) плáвание; (*navigation*) судохóдство; (*directing a vessel*) судовождéние, кораблевождéние; (*as sport*) пáрусный спорт. **2** (*departure*) отхóд, отплы́тие; (*voyage*) рейс; **list of ~s** расписáние парохóдного движéния. **3** (*fig., progress*): **it was plain ~** всё шлó как по мáслу.

● *cpds.* **~-boat** *n.* (*Br.*) пáрусная лóдка; **~-master** *n.* шту́рман; **~-ship** *n.* пáрусное су́дно, пáрусник.

sailor /ˈseɪlə(r)/ *n.* **1** (*seaman*) моря́к, матрóс; **~'s cap** (матрóсская) бескозы́рка; **~ top** матрóска. **2**: **he is a bad ~** он плóхо переноси́т кáчку (на мóре).

sainfoin /ˈseɪnfɔɪn/, /ˈsæn-/ *n.* (*bot.*) эспарцéт кормовóй.

saint /seɪnt/, /sənt/ *n.* святóй; (*virtuous person*) прáведник; **my ~'s day** мои́ имени́н|ы (*pl., g.* —); **patron ~** святóй покрови́тель (*fem.* святáя покрови́тельница); **it's enough to try the patience of a ~** э́то и áнгела из терпéния вы́ведет; **S~ Bernard** (*dog*) сенбернáр; **S~ John's wort** зверобóй; **S~ Valentine's Day** день святóго

Валенти́на; **S~ Vitus's dance** пля́ска свято́го Ви́та; **All S~s (Day)** пра́здник всех святы́х.

● *cpd.* **~like** *adj.* свято́й, а́нгельский.

sainthood /'seɪnthʊd/ *n.* свя́тость.

saintliness /'seɪntlɪnɪs/ *n.* свя́тость, безгре́шность.

saintly /'seɪntlɪ/ *adj.* (**saintlier, saintliest**) свято́й; безгре́шный.

sake[1] /seɪk/ *n.*: **for the ~ of** ра́ди + *g.*; **for God's, heaven's, goodness ~** ра́ди Бо́га (*or* всего́ свято́го); **for one's own ~** для себя́; ра́ди себя́; **for all our ~s** ра́ди всех нас; **art for art's ~** иску́сство для иску́сства; **for old times' ~** по ста́рой па́мяти; **he talks for the ~ of talking** он говори́т про́сто так, что́бы поболта́ть.

sake[2] /'sɑ:kɪ/ *n.* (*Japanese drink*) сакэ́ (*nt. indecl.*).

Sakhalin /,sækə'li:n/ *n.* Сахали́н.

salable /'seɪləb(ə)l/ = **sal(e)able**

salacious /sə'leɪʃəs/ *adj.* (*indecent*) непристо́йный, скабрёзный.

salacity /sə'læsɪtɪ/ *n.* непристо́йность, скабрёзность.

salad /'sæləd/ *n.* **1** сала́т; **fruit ~** фрукто́вый сала́т; **Russian ~** сала́т оливье́. **2** (*fig.*): **in my ~ days** в по́ру мое́й ра́нней ю́ности.

● *cpds.* **~-bowl** *n.* сала́тница; **~-dressing** *n.* запра́вка для сала́та.

salamander /'sælə,mændə(r)/ *n.* салама́ндра.

salami /sə'lɑ:mɪ/ *n.* (*pl.* **~s**) копчёная колбаса́, саля́ми (*f. indecl.*).

sal ammoniac /,sæl ə'məʊnɪ,æk/ *n.* нашаты́рь (*m.*).

salaried /'sælərɪd/ *adj.* (*person, post*) шта́тный, опла́чиваемый.

salary /'sælərɪ/ *n.* окла́д, зарпла́та.

sale /seɪl/ *n.* **1** прода́жа, сбыт; **be on, for ~** име́ться (*impf.*) в прода́же; **'house for ~'** (*as notice*) «продаётся дом»; **put up for ~** выставля́ть, вы́ставить на прода́жу; **the ~s were enormous** спрос был колосса́льный; **~** (*selling*) **price** прода́жная цена́; **~s clerk** (*US, shop assistant*) продав|е́ц (*fem.* -щи́ца); **~s department** отде́л сбы́та; **~s manager** ме́неджер по сбы́ту; **~s talk** рекла́ма, реклами́рование; **~s tax** нало́г на прода́жу.
2 (*event*): **auction ~** прода́жа с аукцио́на; (*clearance* **~**) распрода́жа; **~** (*reduced*) **price** сни́женная цена́, цена́ со ски́дкой.

● *cpds.* **~-room** *n.* (*Br.*) аукцио́нный зал; **~sgirl, ~slady** *nn.* = **~swoman; ~sman** *n.* (*in shop*) продаве́ц; (*travelling door-to-door*) коммивояжёр; торго́вый аге́нт; **~smanship** *n.* уме́ние/иску́сство продава́ть; **~swoman, ~slady, ~sgirl** *nn.* (*in shop*) продавщи́ца.

sal(e)able /'seɪləb(ə)l/ *adj.* ходово́й, хо́дкий (*coll.*).

salient /'seɪlɪənt/ *n.* (*in fortifications*) вы́ступ; (*in line of attack or defence*) вы́ступ, клин.

● *adj.* (*jutting out*) выдаю́щийся, выступа́ющий; (*fig.*) выдаю́щийся, я́ркий.

saline /'seɪlaɪn/ *n.* (*solution*) соляно́й раство́р; (*med.*) физиологи́ческий раство́р.

● *adj.* солёный, соляно́й; **~ spring** солёный исто́чник; **~ solution** соляно́й раство́р.

salinity /sə'lɪnɪtɪ/ *n.* солёность.

saliva /sə'laɪvə/ *n.* слюна́.

salivary /sə'laɪvərɪ/, /'sælɪvərɪ/ *adj.* слю́нный.

salivate /'sælɪ,veɪt/ *v.i.* выделя́ть, вы́делить слюну́.

salivation /,sælɪ'veɪʃ(ə)n/ *n.* слюнотече́ние.

sallow[1] /'sæləʊ/ *n.* (*Br., bot.*) и́ва, раки́та.

sallow[2] /'sæləʊ/ *adj.* (**sallower, sallowest**) боле́зненно-жёлтый.

sallowness /'sæləʊnɪs/ *n.* желтизна́.

sally /'sælɪ/ *n.* **1** (*mil.*) вы́лазка; (*fig., excursion*) прогу́лка, экску́рсия, похо́д. **2** (*witty remark*) остро́та.

● *v.i.*: **~ forth, out** (*mil.*) де́лать, с- вы́лазку; (*fig.*) отпр|авля́ться, -а́виться.

salmon /'sæmən/ *n.* (*pl.* **~** *or esp. of types* **~s**) ло́со́сь (*m.*); сёмга; **~ trout** ло́со́сь-тайме́нь (*m.*).

● *adj.* **1** лососёвый. **2** (*colour*) ора́нжево-ро́зовый.

salmonella /,sælmə'nelə/ *n.* сальмоне́лла.

salon /'sælɒn/, /-lɔ̃/ *n.* сало́н, ателье́ (*indecl.*).

saloon /sə'lu:n/ *n.* (*on ship*) сало́н, каю́т-компа́ния; **billiard ~** билья́рдная; **~ (bar)** (*Br.*) бар; **~ (car)** (*Br.*) седа́н.

salsify /'sælsɪfɪ/, /-,faɪ/ *n.* (*bot.*) козлоборо́дник.

SALT /sɔ:lt/, /sɒlt/ *n.* (*abbr. of* ***Strategic Arms Limitation Talks***) перегово́ры об ОСВ (ограниче́нии стратеги́ческих наступа́тельных вооруже́ний); **~ II** перегово́ры об ОСВ-2.

salt /sɔ:lt/, /sɒlt/ *n.* **1** соль; **bath ~s** аромати́ческие со́ли (*f. pl.*) для ва́нны; **cooking ~** пова́ренная/столо́вая соль; **rock ~** ка́менная соль; **sea ~** морска́я соль; **smelling ~s** ню́хательная соль; **table ~** столо́вая соль; **in ~** (*pickled*) солёный; **take something with a grain of ~** отн|оси́ться, -ести́сь скепти́чески к чему́-н.; **rub ~ into s.o.'s wounds** (*fig.*) растрав|ля́ть, -и́ть (*or* сы́пать (*impf.*) соль на) чьи-н. ра́ны; **the ~ of the earth** соль земли́.
2: **old ~** (*sailor*) (ста́рый) морско́й волк.

● *adj.* (*salty, salted*) солёный; (*pert. to production of* **~**) соляно́й; **~ tears** го́рькие слёзы; **~ water** морска́я вода́; **~ beef** солони́на.

● *v.t.* **1** (*cure in brine*) соли́ть, за-; **~ed meat** солони́на.
2 (*sprinkle with* **~**) соли́ть, по-.
3: **~ away** (*fig., coll., put in safe keeping*) копи́ть, на-; скла́дывать (*impf.*) в кубы́шку.
4 (*fig., flavour*): **his conversation was ~ed with humour** (*Br.*), **humor** (*US*) его́ разгово́р был сдо́брен изря́дной до́зой ю́мора.

● *cpds.* **~-cellar** *n.* соло́нка; **~-lake** *n.* солёное о́зеро; **~-lick** *n.* соляно́й уча́сток/исто́чник; **~-marsh** *n.* солонча́к; **~-mine** *n.* соляна́я ша́хта; **~-water** *adj.*: **~-water fish** морска́я ры́ба; **~-water lake** солёное о́зеро; **~-works** *n.* солева́рня.

saltiness /'sɔ:ltɪnɪs/, /'sɒl-/ *n.* солёность.

saltpetre /,sɒlt'pi:tə(r)/, /,sɔ:lt-/ (*US* **saltpeter**) *n.* сели́тра.

salty /'sɔ:ltɪ/, /'sɒl-/ *adj.* (**saltier, saltiest**) (*lit., fig.*) солёный; **too ~** пересо́ленный.

salubrious /sə'lu:brɪəs/, /sə'lju:-/ *adj.* (*healthy*) здоро́вый; (*curative*) целе́бный, цели́тельный.

salutary /'sæljʊtərɪ/ *adj.* (*beneficial*) благотво́рный; **a ~ lesson/warning** поле́зный уро́к/поле́зное предостереже́ние; (*salubrious*) целе́бный, цели́тельный.

salutation /,sælju:'teɪʃ(ə)n/ *n.* приве́тствие.

salute /sə'lu:t/, /-'lju:t/ *n.* **1** (*mil., naut.*) отда́ние че́сти; во́инское приве́тствие; **give, make a ~** отд|ава́ть, -а́ть честь; **take the ~** прин|има́ть, -я́ть пара́д; (*with guns*) салю́т; **a ~ of 6 guns** салю́т из шести́ за́лпов; (*in fencing*) салю́т, приве́тствие. **2** (*fig.*) приве́тствие, дань (*кому*).

● *v.t.* **1** отд|ава́ть, -а́ть честь (*кому*); салютова́ть (*impf., pf.*) (*кому/чему*); **they ~d the Queen's birthday with 21 guns** они́ произвели́ салю́т из двадцати́ одного́ ору́дия в честь дня рожде́ния короле́вы. **2** (*greet*) приве́тствовать (*impf., pf.*).

● *v.i.* отд|ава́ть, -а́ть честь.

Salvadorean /,sælvə'dɔ:rɪən/ *n.* сальвадо́р|ец (*fem.* -ка).

● *adj.* сальвадо́рский.

salvage /'sælvɪdʒ/ *n.* **1** (*saving ship or property*) спасе́ние (иму́щества); (*what is saved*) спасённое иму́щество; спасённый груз *и т.п.*; (**~** *money*) вознагражде́ние/награ́да за спасённое иму́щество. **2** (*saving waste paper, metal etc.*) сбор ути́ля.

● *v.t.* (*also* **salve**) (*save*) спас|а́ть, -ти́; (*preserve*) сохран|я́ть, -и́ть.

salvation /sæl'veɪʃ(ə)n/ *n.* спасе́ние (душ́и), избавле́ние; **S~ Army** А́рмия спасе́ния; (*person that saves*) спаси́тель (*m.*), избави́тель (*m.*); (*thing that saves*) спасе́ние; **you have been the ~ of him** вы его́ спасли́; **work was my ~** рабо́та была́ мои́м спасе́нием.

salve[1] /sælv/, /sɑ:v/ *n.* (*lit.*) целе́бная мазь; (*lit., fig.*) бальза́м.

● *v.t.* (*fig., soothe; smooth over*) врачева́ть (*impf.*); успок|а́ивать, -о́ить.

salve[2] /sælv/, /sɑ:v/ = **salvage** *v.t.*

salver /'sælvə(r)/ *n.* (серебряный) подно́с.

salvo /'sælvəʊ/ *n.* (*pl.* **~es** *or* **~s**) (*of guns*) залп; **fire a ~** да|ва́ть, -ть залп;

S

(*of bombs*) бо́мбовый уда́р; (*of questions, applause*) взрыв.

sal volatile /ˌsæl vɒˈlætɪlɪ/ *n.* нюхательная соль.

Samaritan /səˈmærɪt(ə)n/ *n.*: **good ~** до́брый самаритя́нин.

● *adj.* самаритя́нский.

samba /ˈsæmbə/ *n.* са́мба.

same /seɪm/ *adj.* тот же (са́мый); тако́й же; оди́н (и тот же); (*unvarying*) одина́ковый, неизме́нный, ро́вный; **they are one and the ~ person** э́то оди́н и тот же челове́к; **not the ~** друго́й; **is that the ~ man we saw yesterday?** э́то тот же челове́к, кото́рого мы ви́дели вчера́?; **the ~ old excuses** всё те же отгово́рки; **I lived in the ~ house as he** я жил в одно́м до́ме с ним; **we are the ~ age** мы одни́х лет (*or* одного́ во́зраста); **the ~ thing** то же са́мое; **in the ~ way** таки́м/подо́бным же о́бразом; **at the ~ time** в то же вре́мя, одновре́ме́нно; (*however*) в то же вре́мя, ме́жду тем; **at the ~ time every evening** ка́ждый ве́чер в оди́н и тот же час; **men and women receive the ~ wages** мужчи́ны и же́нщины получа́ют одина́ковую зарпла́ту; **the village looks just the ~ as ever (it did)** дере́вня вы́глядит тако́й же, как всегда́; **it's the ~ everywhere** везде́ одина́ково; **things were never the ~ again** по́сле э́того всё бы́ло ина́че; **I'm not the ~ man that I was** я не тако́й, как (*or* каки́м был) пре́жде; **it comes to the ~ thing** э́то одно́ и то же.

● *pron.* тот же (са́мый); **it's all the ~ to me** мне всё равно́; **I'd do the ~ again** я бы опя́ть сде́лал то же са́мое; **~ again, please!** то же са́мое, пожа́луйста!; **... and the ~ to you!** . . . и вам та́кже (*or* того́ же)!

● *adv.*: **I don't feel the ~ towards him** я стал к нему́ ина́че относи́ться; **all the ~** (*nevertheless*) всё-таки; всё равно́; всё же; **just the ~** (*despite that*) тем не ме́нее; **~ here!** я то́же!

sameness /ˈseɪmnɪs/ *n.* (*identity*) то́ждество; (*uniformity*) единообра́зие; (*monotony*) однообра́зие.

Samoa /səˈməʊə/ *n.* Само́а (*nt. indecl.*).

Samoan /səˈməʊən/ *n.* (*person*) самоа́н|ец (*fem.* -ка); (*language*) самоа́нский язы́к.

● *adj.* самоа́нский.

samovar /ˈsæməˌvɑ:(r)/ *n.* самова́р.

sample /ˈsɑ:mp(ə)l/ *n.* (*comm., fig.*) образе́ц, обра́зчик, приме́р; (*med.*) про́ба; **take a ~ of something** *see v.t.*

● *v.t.* брать, взять образе́ц +*g.*; (*wine, food etc.*) про́бовать, по-; (*try out*) про́бовать, по-.

sampler /ˈsɑ:mplə(r)/ *n.* (*embroidery*) ≈ вы́шивка.

sampling /ˈsɑ:mplɪŋ/ *n.* (*in statistics*) вы́борка.

samurai /ˈsæmʊˌraɪ/, /-jʊˌraɪ/ *n.* (*pl.* ~) саму́ра́й.

sanatori|um /ˌsænəˈtɔ:rɪəm/ (*US* **sanitarium**) *n.* (*pl.* **~ums** *or* **~a**) санато́рий; **at a ~um** в санато́рии.

sanctification /ˌsæŋktɪfɪˈkeɪʃ(ə)n/ *n.* освяще́ние; оправда́ние.

sanctify /ˈsæŋktɪˌfaɪ/ *v.t.* освя|ща́ть (*or* святи́ть), -ти́ть; (*justify*) опра́вд|ывать, -а́ть.

sanctimonious /ˌsæŋktɪˈməʊnɪəs/ *adj.* ха́нжеский; **~ person** ханжа́ (*c.g.*).

sanctimoniousness /ˌsæŋktɪˈməʊnɪəsnɪs/ *n.* ха́нжество.

sanction /ˈsæŋkʃ(ə)n/ *n.* **1** (*authorization, permission*) са́нкция; **official ~ has not been given** официа́льной са́нкции (*or* официа́льного разреше́ния) нет; (*approval*) одобре́ние; **without his ~** без его́ согла́сия. **2** (*penalty*) са́нкция, ме́ра наказа́ния. **3** (*moral, relig., pol.*) са́нкция.

● *v.t.* (*authorize*) санкциони́ровать (*impf., pf.*); (*approve*) од|обря́ть, -о́брить.

sanctity /ˈsæŋktɪtɪ/ *n.* (*holiness, saintliness*) свя́тость; (*inviolability*) неприкоснове́нность.

sanctuary /ˈsæŋktjʊərɪ/ *n.* **1** (*holy place*) святи́лище. **2** (*part of church*) алта́рь (*m.*). **3** (*asylum, refuge*) убе́жище. **4** (*for wild life*) запове́дник; **bird ~** пти́чий запове́дник.

sanctum /ˈsæŋktəm/ *n.* (*pl.* **~s**) святи́лище; (*fig., 'den'*) прибе́жище.

sand /sænd/ *n.* **1** песо́к; **grain of ~** песчи́нка; **the ~s are running out** дни сочтены́.
2 (*pl., beach*) (песча́ный) пляж.

● *v.t.* (*sprinkle with* ~) пос|ыпа́ть, -ы́пать песко́м; (*polish; also* **~ down**) шлифова́ть, от-.

● *cpds.* **~bag** *n.* мешо́к с песко́м, балла́стный мешо́к; **~bank** *n.* песча́ная о́тмель/ба́нка; **~-bar** *n.* песча́ная о́тмель (в у́стье реки́); **~-blast** *n.* песча́ная струя́; *v.t.* подв|ерга́ть, -е́ргнуть пескостру́йной обрабо́тке; **~-blaster** *n.* пескостру́йный аппара́т; **~-box** (*rail.*) *n.* песо́чница; **~boy** *n.*: **happy as a ~boy** беззабо́тный; **~-castle** *n.* за́мок из песка́ (*or* на песке́); **~-dune** *n.* дю́на; **~-eel** *n.* песчи́нка; **~-glass** *n.* песо́чные час|ы́ (*pl., g.* -о́в); **~man** *n.* ≈ дрёма, дремо́та; **~-martin** *n.* берегова́я ла́сточка; **~paper** *n.* (шлифова́льная) шку́рка, нажда́чная бума́га; *v.t.* чи́стить, за- (*or* шлифова́ть, от-) шку́ркой; **~piper** *n.* песо́чник (*птица*); **~-pit** *n.* (*quarry*) песча́ный карье́р; (*Br., for children*) песо́чница; **~-shoes** *n. pl.* спорти́вные та́почки (*f. pl.*); **~stone** *n.* песча́ник; **~storm** *n.* песча́ная бу́ря.

sandal[1] /ˈsænd(ə)l/ *n.* (*footwear*) санда́лия, сандале́та.

sandal[2] /ˈsænd(ə)l/ *n.* (**~ wood**) санда́л.

● *cpd.* **~-tree** *n.* санда́ловое де́рево.

sander /ˈsændə(r)/ *n.* (*large*) шлифова́льный стано́к; (*smaller*) шлифова́льный инструме́нт.

sandwich /ˈsænwɪdʒ/, /-wɪtʃ/ *n.* бутербро́д; **ham ~** бутербро́д с ветчино́й; **open ~** откры́тый бутербро́д (*с одним куском хлеба*); **~ bar** бутербро́дная.

● *v.t.* (*insert*) вти́с|кивать, -нуть; (*squeeze*) сти́с|кивать, -нуть; заж|има́ть, -а́ть; **his car was ~ed between two lorries** его́ маши́на была́ зажа́та ме́жду двумя́ грузовика́ми.

● *cpds.* **~-boards** *n. pl.* рекла́мные щиты́ (*m. pl.*); **~course** *n.* (*Br.*) курс обуче́ния, чреду́ющий тео́рию с пра́ктикой; **~-man** *n.* челове́к-рекла́ма.

sandy /ˈsændɪ/ *adj.* (**sandier, sandiest**) **1** (*consisting of sand*) песча́ный; (*containing or resembling sand*) песо́чный. **2** (*hair*) рыжева́тый.

sane /seɪn/ *adj.* (*opp. mad*) норма́льный, психи́чески здоро́вый; (*sensible*) разу́мный; (*idea, plan*) здра́вый.

San Francisco /ˌsæn frænˈsɪskəʊ/ *n.* Сан-Франци́ско (*m. indecl.*).

sang /sæŋ/ *past of* ⇒**sing**

sang-froid /sɑ̃ˈfrwɑ:/ *n.* хладнокро́вие, невозмути́мость.

sangria /sæŋˈgri:ə/ *n.* сангри́я.

sanguinary /ˈsæŋgwɪnərɪ/ *adj.* крова́вый; (*bloodthirsty*) кровожа́дный.

sanguine /ˈsæŋgwɪn/ *adj.* **1** (*of complexion etc.*) румя́ный. **2** (*optimistic*) оптимисти́чный; **I am ~ that we shall succeed** я уве́рен в успе́хе; **I am ~ about the plan** я споко́ен за э́тот прое́кт.

sanitarium /ˌsænɪˈteərɪəm/ (*US*) = **sanatorium**

sanitary /ˈsænɪtərɪ/ *adj.* санита́рный, гигиени́ческий; **~ arrangements** сану́зел; **~ inspector** санинспе́ктор; **~ towel** (*Br.*), **napkin** (*US*) гигиени́ческая прокла́дка; **~ ware** (керами́ческая) санте́хника.

sanitation /ˌsænɪˈteɪʃ(ə)n/ *n.* (*conditions*) санита́рные усло́вия; (*sewage system*) канализацио́нная систе́ма; **the houses had no indoor ~** в дома́х не́ было канализа́ции.

sanity /ˈsænɪtɪ/ *n.* (*state of being sane*) здра́вый ум; **I doubt his ~** мне ка́жется, он сошёл с ума́; (*reasonableness*) здравомы́слие.

sank /sæŋk/ *past of* ⇒**sink**

sanserif /sænˈserɪf/ *n.* шрифт сансери́ф, рублёный шрифт.

Sanskrit /ˈsænskrɪt/ *n.* санскри́т; **in ~** на санскри́те.

● *adj.* санскри́тский.

Santa Claus /ˈsæntə ˌklɔ:z/ *n.* (*in Russia*) ≈ Дед Моро́з; (*in Britain, US, etc.*) Са́нта Кла́ус.

sap[1] /sæp/ *n.* (*of plants*) сок.

● *v.t.* (**sapped, sapping**) (*fig.*): **~ s.o.'s strength** истощ|а́ть, -и́ть чьи-н. си́лы.

sap[2] /sæp/ *n.* (*mil., trench*) са́па; глубо́кий око́п.

● *v.t.* (**sapped, sapping**) (*mil.*) подк|а́пывать, -опа́ть.

sap[3] /sæp/ *n.* (*US sl., simpleton*) проста́к.

sapience /ˈseɪpɪəns/ *n.* му́дрость.

sapient /ˈseɪpɪənt/ *adj.* (*wise*) му́дрый.

sapling /ˈsæplɪŋ/ *n.* (*tree*) молодóе дéревце.

sapper /ˈsæpə(r)/ *n.* (*mil.*) сапёр; (*pl.*) инженéрные войскá.

sapphire /ˈsæfaɪə(r)/ *n.* (*stone*) сапфи́р; (*colour*) лазýрь.

● *adj.* сапфи́рный; (*colour*) лазýрный, сапфи́ровый.

Sappho /ˈsæfəʊ/ *n.* Сафó (*f. indecl.*).

sappy /ˈsæpɪ/ *adj.* (**sappier, sappiest**) сóчный; (*fig.*) пóлный жи́зненных сил; в сокý.

saraband /ˈsærəˌbænd/ *n.* сарабáнда (*танец*).

Saracen /ˈsærəs(ə)n/ *n.* сараци́н (*fem.* -ка).

● *adj.* сараци́нский.

Sarajevo /ˌsærəˈjeɪvəʊ/ *n.* Сарáево.

sarcasm /ˈsɑːkæz(ə)m/ *n.* саркáзм.

sarcastic /sɑːˈkæstɪk/ *adj.* саркасти́ческий.

sarcoma /sɑːˈkəʊmə/ *n.* (*pl.* **~s** *or* **~ta**) саркóма.

sarcopha|gus /sɑːˈkɒfəgəs/ *n.* (*pl.* **~gi** /-ˌgaɪ/, /-ˌdʒaɪ/) саркофáг.

sardine /sɑːˈdiːn/ *n.* сарди́н(к)а; **packed like ~s** (наби́ты) как сéльди в бóчке.

Sardinia /sɑːˈdɪnɪə/ *n.* Сарди́ния.

sardonic /sɑːˈdɒnɪk/ *adj.* сардони́ческий.

sari /ˈsɑːriː/ *n.* (*pl.* **~s**) сáри (*f. indecl.*).

sarong /səˈrɒŋ/ *n.* сарóнг (*индонезийская национальная одежда*).

sarsaparilla /ˌsɑːsəpəˈrɪlə/ *n.* (*bot.*) сарсапари́ль (*m.*).

sartorial /sɑːˈtɔːrɪəl/ *adj.* (*pert. to tailoring*) портня́жный; **~ elegance** изя́щество в одéжде.

SAS (*abbr. of* ***Special Air Service***) спецслýжба ВВС.

SASE (*abbr. of* ***self-addressed stamped envelope***) (*US*) конвéрт с мáркой и обрáтным áдресом.

sash[1] /sæʃ/ *n.* (*round waist*) кушáк, пóяс; (*over shoulder*) (óрденская) лéнта.

sash[2] /sæʃ/ *n.* (*of window*) скользя́щая рáма (*окна*).

● *cpd.* **~-window** *n.* подъёмное окнó, окнó с подъёмной рáмой.

sat /sæt/ *past and p.p. of* ⇒**sit**

Satan /ˈseɪt(ə)n/ *n.* сатанá (*m.*).

satanic /səˈtænɪk/ *adj.* сатани́нский, áдский.

satanism /ˈseɪtəˌnɪz(ə)m/ *n.* сатани́зм.

satanist /ˈseɪtənɪst/ *n.* сатани́ст.

satchel /ˈsætʃ(ə)l/ *n.* сýмка, рáнец; (шкóльный) портфéль.

sate /seɪt/ *v.t.* (*liter.*) нас|ыщáть, -ы́тить; **~d with pleasure** пресы́щенный наслаждéниями.

sateen /sæˈtiːn/ *n.* сати́н.

satellite /ˈsætəˌlaɪt/ *n.* **1** (*moon*) спýтник, сателли́т; (*artificial body*) (искýсственный) спýтник; **manned ~** обитáемый (искýсственный) спýтник; **~ dish** спýтниковая антéнна, (*coll.*) тарéлка; **~ town** гóрод-спýтник; **~ (radio) link-up** радиомóст; **~ (TV) link-up** телемóст; **~ television broadcasting** спýтниковое телеви́дение. **2** (*fig.*) сателли́т.

● *adj.* вспомогáтельный, подчинённый.

satiate /ˈseɪʃɪˌeɪt/ *v.t.* нас|ыщáть, -ы́тить.

satiety /səˈtaɪɪtɪ/ *n.* насыщéние, сы́тость; (*over-abundance*) пресыщéние; **to ~** дóсыта.

satin /ˈsætɪn/ *n.* атлáс.

● *adj.* атлáсный.

● *cpd.* **~wood** *n.* атлáсное дéрево.

satinet(te) /ˌsætɪˈnet/ *n.* сатинéт.

satiny /ˈsætɪnɪ/ *adj.* атлáсный, шелкови́стый.

satire /ˈsætaɪə(r)/ *n.* сати́ра.

satiric(al) /səˈtɪrɪk(ə)l/ *adj.* сатири́ческий.

satirist /ˈsætərɪst/ *n.* сати́рик.

satirize /ˈsætɪˌraɪz/ *v.t.* высмéивать, вы́смеять.

satisfaction /ˌsætɪsˈfækʃ(ə)n/ *n.* **1** удовлетворéние, удовлетворённость; (*pleasure*) удовóльствие; **the work was done to my entire ~** я был пóлностью удовлетворён вы́полненной рабóтой; **I wanted to know for my own ~** я хотéл сам удостовéриться; **you have the ~ of knowing you are right** вы мóжете удовлетвори́ться сознáнием сóбственной правоты́. **2** (*payment of debt*) уплáта, погашéние; (*fig.*) расплáта. **3** (*compensation*) компенсáция.

satisfactory /ˌsætɪsˈfæktərɪ/ *adj.* удовлетвори́тельный, хорóший; (*successful*) удáчный; (*convincing*) убеди́тельный.

satisf|y /ˈsætɪsˌfaɪ/ *v.t.* **1** удовлетвор|я́ть, -и́ть; **the compromise ~ies everyone** компроми́сс удовлетворя́ет всех; **~y one's hunger** утол|я́ть, -и́ть гóлод; **nothing ~ies him** ничéм емý не угоди́шь; **he ~ied the examiners** (*Br.*) он вы́держал экзáмен; **a ~ied customer** довóльный клиéнт; **he won't be ~ied until he has had an accident** он тóлько тогдá успокóится, когдá попадёт в бедý (*or* сдéлается жéртвой несчáстного слýчая). **2** (*justify*): **the result ~ied our expectations** результáт оправдáл нáши ожидáния. **3** (*convince*) убе|ждáть, -ди́ть; **I ~ied him of my innocence** я убеди́л егó в моéй невинóвности; **I ~ied myself of his honesty** я убеди́лся в егó чéстности. **4** (*pay*): **~y a debt** пога|шáть, -си́ть долг. **5** (*fulfil*): **~y an obligation** выполня́ть, вы́полнить обязáтельство. **6** (*meet*): **~y s.o.'s objections** отв|оди́ть, -ести́ чьи-н. возражéния. **7** (*of food*): **a ~ying lunch** сы́тный обéд.

satrap /ˈsætræp/ *n.* сатрáп.

satsuma /sætˈsuːmə/ *n.* мандари́н.

saturate /ˈsætʃəˌreɪt/, /-tjʊˌreɪt/ *v.t.* нас|ыщáть, -ы́тить; **the carpet became ~d with water** ковёр пропитáлся водóй; **I was ~d** (*wet through*) я весь промóк; **~d solution** насы́щенный раствóр.

saturation /ˌsætʃəˈreɪʃ(ə)n/, /-tjʊˈreɪʃ(ə)n/ *n.* насыщéние, насы́щенность; **~ bombing** площаднóе бомбометáние со сплошны́м поражéнием.

Saturday /ˈsætəˌdeɪ/, /-dɪ/ *n.* суббóта; (*attr.*) суббóтний; **on ~ evening** в суббóту вéчером; **Holy ~** Вели́кая суббóта.

Saturn /ˈsæt(ə)n/ *n.* (*astron., myth.*) Сатýрн; **~'s rings** кóльца (*nt. pl.*) Сатýрна.

saturnalia /ˌsætəˈneɪlɪə/ *n.* (*pl.* **~** *or* **~s**) сатурнáлии (*f. pl.*) (*в Древнем Риме*).

saturnine /ˈsætəˌnaɪn/ *adj.* мрáчный, угрю́мый.

satyr /ˈsætə(r)/ *n.* сати́р.

sauce /sɔːs/ *n.* (*cul.*) сóус, подли́вка; (*Br. coll., impertinence*) дéрзость; **none of your ~!** не дерзи́!

● *cpds.* **~-boat** *n.* сóусник; **~pan** *n.* кастрю́ля.

saucer /ˈsɔːsə(r)/ *n.* блю́дце; **cup and ~** чáшка с блю́дцем; **flying ~** летáющая тарéлка.

saucy /ˈsɔːsɪ/ *adj.* (**saucier, sauciest**) (*cheeky*) дéрзкий, озорнóй; (*Br., coquettish*) кокéтливый; **a ~ little hat** кокéтливая шля́пка.

Saudi /ˈsaʊdɪ/ *n.* (*pl.* **~s**) саýдов|ец (*fem.* -ка).

● *adj.* саýдовский; **~ Arabia** Саýдовская Арáвия.

sauerkraut /ˈsaʊəˌkraʊt/ *n.* ки́слая/ квáшеная капýста.

sauna /ˈsɔːnə/ *n.* (*also* **~ bath**) сáуна, фи́нская (парнáя) бáня.

saunter /ˈsɔːntə(r)/ *n.* прогýлка.

● *v.i.* идти́ (*det.*) не торопя́сь; **~ up and down** прохáживаться, прогýливаться (*both impf.*).

sausage /ˈsɒsɪdʒ/ *n.* соси́ска; (*large Continental type*) колбасá.

● *cpds.* **~-meat** *n.* колбáсный фарш; **~-roll** *n.* соси́ска, запечённая в бýлочке.

sauté /ˈsəʊteɪ/ *n. & adj.* (*cul.*) сотé (*indecl.*).

● *v.t.* (**sautés, sautéd** *or* **sautéed, sautéing**) жáрить, за- в небольшóм коли́честве жи́ра.

savage /ˈsævɪdʒ/ *n.* дикáр|ь (*fem.* -ка).

● *adj.* **1** (*primitive*) ди́кий, первобы́тный. **2** (*of animals: fierce*) свирéпый. **3** (*of attack, blow etc.*) жестóкий, я́ростный; **his book was ~ly attacked in the press** егó кни́га подвéрглась свирéпым нападкáм прéссы.

● *v.t.* (жестóко) иск|ýсывать, -усáть; (*fig.*) раст|ёрзывать, -ерзáть.

savage|ness /ˈsævɪdʒnɪs/, **-ry** /ˈsævɪdʒrɪ/ *nn.* ди́кость; свирéпость; жестóкость.

savanna(h) /səˈvænə/ *n.* савáнна.

S

savant /ˈsæv(ə)nt/, /sæˈvɑ̃/ *n.* (кру́пный) учёный.

sav|e /seɪv/ *n.* (*football etc.*): **the goalkeeper made a brilliant ~e** врата́рь блестя́ще отби́л уда́р.

● *v.t.* **1** (*rescue, deliver*) спас|а́ть, -ти́; изб|авля́ть, -а́вить; **he ~ed my life** он спас мне жизнь; **she was ~ed from drowning** ей не да́ли утону́ть; **he ~ed the situation** он спас положе́ние; (*protect, preserve*) храни́ть (*impf.*); **God ~e the Queen!** Бо́же, храни́ короле́ву!; **~e face** сохрани́ть/спасти́ (*pf.*) лицо́.
2 (*put by*) бере́чь, с-; от|кла́дывать, -ложи́ть; копи́ть, на-; **I ~ed (up) £50 towards a holiday** я скопи́л 50 фу́нтов на о́тпуск; **~e me something to eat!** оста́вьте/приберегите мне что́-нибудь пое́сть!; (*collect*) соб|ира́ть, -ра́ть; (*avoid using or spending*) эконо́мить, с-; **~e expense** избе|га́ть, -жа́ть затра́т; **he took the bus to ~e time** он пое́хал авто́бусом, что́бы сэконо́мить вре́мя; **he is ~ing himself (*or* his strength) for the next race** он бережёт си́лы для сле́дующего соревнова́ния; **we will ~e the cake for tomorrow** прибережём пиро́г на за́втра; (*obviate need for, expense of etc.*) эконо́мить, с-; **that will ~e me £100** я сэконо́млю на э́том сто фу́нтов; **it ~ed me a lot of time** э́то мне сэконо́мило мно́го вре́мени; **it will ~e you trouble if you come with me** е́сли вы пойдёте со мно́й, э́то изба́вит вас от ли́шних хлопо́т; **I ~ed him the trouble of replying** я изба́вил его́ от необходи́мости отвеча́ть; (*comput.*) сохран|я́ть, -и́ть.

● *v.i.* эконо́мить, с-; копи́ть (*impf.*); **he is ~ing up for a bicycle** он откла́дывает/ко́пит де́ньги (*or* он ко́пит) на велосипе́д.

● *prep.* (*liter.*) кро́ме + *g.*; без + *g.*; **I know nothing of him ~e that he is rich** я ничего́ о нём не зна́ю, кро́ме того́, что он бога́т; **all the men ~e one** все кро́ме одного́ (челове́ка).

saver /ˈseɪvə(r)/ *n.* (*investor*) вкла́дчик.

saving /ˈseɪvɪŋ/ *n.* **1** (*salvation, rescue*) спасе́ние; **penicillin led to the ~ of many lives** пеницилли́н спас жизнь мно́гим. **2** (*economy*) эконо́мия; **a ~ of millions of pounds** эконо́мия в миллио́ны фу́нтов. **3** (*pl., money laid by*) сбереже́ния (*nt. pl.*); **they live on their ~s** они́ живу́т на свои́ сбереже́ния; **~s account** сберега́тельный счёт; **~s bank** сберега́тельная ка́сса, сберега́тельный банк; **he had to draw on his ~s** ему́ пришло́сь прибе́гнуть к свои́м сбереже́ниям.

● *adj.* (*salutary*) спаси́тельный; **~ grace** (*fig.*) положи́тельное/спаси́тельное сво́йство.

● *prep.* (*liter.*) (*except*) кро́ме + *g.*

saviour /ˈseɪvjə(r)/ (*US* **savior**) *n.* спаси́тель (*m.*); (*Christ*) Спаси́тель (*m.*).

savoir-faire /ˌsævwɑːˈfeə(r)/ *n.* такт.

savor /ˈseɪvə(r)/ (*US*) = **savour**

savory[1] /ˈseɪvərɪ/ *n.* садо́вый ча́бер.

savory[2] /ˈseɪvərɪ/ (*US*) = **savoury**

savour /ˈseɪvə(r)/ (*US* **savor**) *n.* (*taste, flavour*) вкус; (*trace, hint*) при́вкус; **life lost its ~ for me** жизнь потеря́ла для меня́ вся́кую пре́лесть.

● *v.t.* (*sample*) про́бовать, по-; (*enjoy*) смакова́ть (*impf.*).

● *v.i.*: **~ of** име́ть (*impf.*) при́вкус + *g.*; отдава́ть (*impf.*) + *i.* (*coll.*); **the letter ~s of jealousy** в письме́ сквози́т ре́вность.

savoury /ˈseɪvərɪ/ (*US* **savory**) *adj.* (*not sweet*) несла́дкий; (*spicy*) пика́нтный, о́стрый; **~ omelette** омле́т с о́строй припра́вой; (*fig.*): **a not very ~ district** непригля́дный райо́н.

● *n.* (*Br.*) пря́ное блю́до.

savoy /səˈvɔɪ/ *n.*: **~ (cabbage)** саво́йская капу́ста.

savvy /ˈsævɪ/ (*US*) *n.* смека́лка (*coll.*).

● *v.i.*: **~?** поня́тно?; дошло́?

saw[1] /sɔː/ *n.* (*tool*) пила́.

● *v.t.* (*p.p.* **sawn** /sɔːn/ *or* **sawed**) пили́ть (*impf.*); распи́л|ивать, -и́ть.

● *v.i.* (*p.p.* **sawn** /sɔːn/ *or* **sawed**) пили́ть (*impf.*); **this wood ~s easily** э́то де́рево хорошо́ пи́лится.

● *with advs.*: **~ down** *v.t.* спи́л|ивать, -и́ть; **~ off** *v.t.* отпи́л|ивать, -и́ть; **he ~ed off the branch he was sitting on** (*fig.*) он подруби́л сук, на кото́ром сиде́л; **~n-off** (*US* **sawed-off**) **shotgun** обре́з; **~ up** *v.t.* распи́л|ивать, -и́ть.

● *cpds.* **~-blade** *n.* полотно́ пилы́; **~dust** *n.* опи́л|ки (*pl., g.* -ок); **~fish** *n.* пила́-ры́ба; **~fly** *n.* пили́льщик (*насекомое*); **~mill** *n.* лесопи́лка; лесопи́льный заво́д; **~-tooth** *n.* зуб (пилы́); *adj.* зубча́тый.

saw[2] /sɔː/ *n.* (*maxim*) посло́вица, погово́рка.

saw[3] /sɔː/ *past of* ⇨**see**[2]

sawyer /ˈsɔːjə(r)/ *n.* пи́льщик.

sax /sæks/ (*coll.*) = **saxophone**

saxifrage /ˈsæksɪˌfreɪdʒ/ *n.* (*bot.*) камнело́мка.

Saxon /ˈsæks(ə)n/ *n.* (*hist.*) сакс.

● *adj.* саксо́нский.

Saxony /ˈsæksənɪ/ *n.* Саксо́ния.

saxophone /ˈsæksəˌfəʊn/ *n.* саксофо́н.

say /seɪ/ *n.* (*expression of opinion*): **let s.o. have his ~** да|ва́ть, -ть кому́-н. вы́сказаться; **we had no ~ in the matter** с на́шим мне́нием в э́том де́ле не счита́лись; **he likes to have a ~** он хо́чет, что́бы с его́ мне́нием счита́лись.

● *v.t. & i.* (*3rd pers. sing. pres.* **says** /sez/; *past and p.p.* **said**) **1** говори́ть, сказа́ть; **he ~s I am lazy** он говори́т, что я лени́в; **would you ~ I was right?** как по-ва́шему, я прав?; **why can't he ~ what he means?** почему́ он не ска́жет пря́мо, что он име́ет в виду́?; **just ~ the word and I'll go** то́лько скажи́те (сло́во), и я пойду́; **he was asked to ~ something (*or* a few words)** его́ попроси́ли сказа́ть не́сколько слов; **~ a good word for** замо́лвить (*pf.*) слове́чко за + *a.*; **as much as to ~** как бы говоря́; **he said as much** он приме́рно так и сказа́л; **how do you ~ this in English?** как э́то сказа́ть по-англи́йски?; **I must ~** призна́ться; **I'll have something to ~ to you about this** на э́тот счёт я вам ко́е-что до́лжен сказа́ть; **she is said to be rich** говоря́т, она́ бога́та; **the tree is said to be 100 years old** счита́ется/говоря́т, что э́тому де́реву сто лет; **there is much to be said on both sides** здесь мо́жно мно́гое сказа́ть и за и про́тив; **there is much to be said for beginning now** мно́гое говори́т за то, что́бы начина́ть тепе́рь; **there is no more to be said** бо́льше не́чего сказа́ть; **~ no more!, enough said!** (*coll.*) (всё) поня́тно!; я́сно!; **what have you got to ~ for yourself?** что вы мо́жете сказа́ть в своё оправда́ние?; **he has plenty to ~ for himself** у него́ хорошо́ подве́шен язы́к; **there's no ~ing where they might be** кто мо́жет сказа́ть, где они́ (нахо́дятся)?; **I couldn't rightly ~** пра́во, не зна́ю; **I dare ~** пожа́луй, наве́рное, осме́люсь сказа́ть; **how can you ~ such a thing?** как вы мо́жете так(о́е) говори́ть?; **I wouldn't (go so far as to) ~ that** э́того я бы не сказа́л; **didn't I ~ so?** а я что сказа́л?; **I'll ~!** (*coll.*) (*yes indeed*) ещё бы!; **you said it!; you can ~ that again!** (*coll.*) вот и́менно!; то́-то и оно́!; **you don't ~ (so)!** (*coll.*) неуже́ли?; что вы говори́те!; **~ when!** скажи́те, когда́ доста́точно!; **when all is said and done** в конце́ концо́в, в коне́чном счёте; **it ~s something for him that he apologized** то, что он извини́лся, говори́т в его́ по́льзу; **~ you are sorry!** проси́ прощения!; **~ good-morning to s.o.** здоро́ваться, по- с кем-н.; **that is to ~** (*in other words; viz.*) то есть; ина́че говоря́; **so to ~** так сказа́ть; **I ~!** (*US* **~!**) (*attracting attention*) послу́шай(те)!; зна́ете что?; (*expr. surprise*) скажи́те!; поду́майте!; **so he ~s** е́сли ему́ ве́рить; **it goes without ~ing** (само́ собо́й) разуме́ется; слов нет; **not to say ...** что́бы не сказа́ть...; **to ~ nothing of** (*not to mention*) не говоря́ (уж) о + *p.*; **well said!** хорошо́ ска́зано!
2 (*suppose, assume*): **(let's) ~; shall we ~** ска́жем; допу́стим; (*for instance*) наприме́р; к приме́ру; приме́рно; **I will give you, ~, £100** я вам дам, ска́жем, сто фу́нтов; **~ he were here, what then?** допу́стим, он здесь, что тогда́?; **~ it were true** ска́жем/предполо́жим, что так.
3 (*of inanimate objects: state, indicate*): **what does it ~ in the instructions?** что говори́тся/ска́зано в инстру́кции?; **the Bible ~s** в Би́блии говори́тся/ска́зано; **the signpost ~s London** на указа́теле напи́сано «Ло́ндон»; **the clock ~s 5 o'clock** часы́ пока́зывают пять; **the notice ~s the museum is closed** объявле́ние гласи́т, что музе́й закры́т.
4 (*formulate, express*): **~ a prayer** произн|оси́ть, -ести́ моли́тву; **~ mass** служи́ть, от- обе́дню; **he said his lesson to the teacher** он отве́тил уро́к учи́телю.
5 (*of reactions*): **~ yes** (*agree*) **to**

something согла|ша́ться, -си́ться на что-н.; **~ yes** (*accept invitation*) приня́ть (*pf.*) приглаше́ние; (*grant request*) дава́ть, дать согла́сие; согла|ша́ться, -си́ться; **~ no** (*refuse invitation*) отк|а́зываться, -аза́ться от приглаше́ния; (*refuse request*) отказа́ть(ся) (*pf.*); **what do you ~ to a glass of beer?** как насчёт кру́жки пи́ва?; **what would you ~ to a game of cards?** а не сыгра́ть ли нам в ка́рты?

● *cpd.* **~-so** *n.* (*power of decision*) реша́ющий го́лос, реша́ющее сло́во; (*mere assertion*): **I would not believe it on his ~-so** я бы не стал ве́рить ему́ на́ слово.

saying /ˈseɪɪŋ/ *n.* (*adage*) погово́рка; **as the ~ goes** как говори́тся; (*utterance*) выска́зывание; **the ~s of Confucius** выска́зывания (*nt. pl.*) Конфу́ция.

sc. /ˈsaɪlɪˌset/, /ˈski:lɪˌket/ = **scilicet**

scab /skæb/ *n.* (*on wound*) струп, ко́рка; (*coll., blackleg*) штрейкбре́хер.

● *v.i.* (**scabbed, scabbing**) (*also* **~ over**) затя́|гиваться, -ну́ться; покр|ыва́ться, -ы́ться стру́пьями.

scabbard /ˈskæbəd/ *n.* но́ж|ны (*pl., g.* -ен).

scabby /ˈskæbɪ/ *adj.* (**scabbier, scabbiest**) (*covered with scabs*) покры́тый стру́пьями.

scabies /ˈskeɪbi:z/ *n.* чесо́тка.

scabious /ˈskeɪbɪəs/ *n.* (*bot.*) скабио́за.

scabrous /ˈskeɪbrəs/ *adj.* (*indecent*) скабрёзный.

scaffold /ˈskæfəʊld/, /-f(ə)ld/ *n.* **1** эшафо́т, пла́ха; **die on the ~** умира́ть, умере́ть на эшафо́те. **2** = **~ing**

● *v.t.* обстр|а́ивать, -о́ить леса́ми.

scaffolding /ˈskæfəʊldɪŋ/, /-fəldɪŋ/ *n.* лес|а́ (*pl., g.* -о́в).

scald /skɔ:ld/, /skɒld/ *n.* ожо́г.

● *v.t.* **1** ошпа́ри|вать, -ть; **I ~ed my hand** я ошпа́рил себе́ ру́ку; **~ing water** круто́й кипято́к; **~ing tears** жгу́чие слёзы; **the tea was ~ing hot** чай был о́чень горя́чий. **2**: **~ milk** подогр|ева́ть, -е́ть молоко́, не доводя́ до кипе́ния.

scale¹ /skeɪl/ *n.* **1** (*of fish, reptile etc.*) чешу́йка; (*pl., collect.*) чешуя́. **2** (*on teeth*) ка́мень (*m.*). **3**: **the ~s fell from his eyes** (*liter.*) пелена́ спа́ла с его́ глаз.

● *v.t.*: **~ a fish** чи́стить, по- ры́бу; **~ a boiler** сн|има́ть, -ять на́кипь с котла́; **~ teeth** сн|има́ть, -ять ка́мень с зубо́в.

● *v.i.* **1** (*form* **~**; *also* **~ over**) образо́в|ывать, -а́ть ока́лину/на́кипь. **2** (*come off in flakes*; *also* **~ off**) шелуши́ться (*impf.*); отп|ада́ть, -а́сть.

● *cpd.* **~-armour** (*US* **-armor**) *n.* пласти́нчатая броня́.

scale² /skeɪl/ *n.* **1** (*of balance*) ча́ш(к)а (весо́в); **turn the ~** (*lit.*): **he turned the ~ at 80 kg** он ве́сил во́семьдесят килогра́ммов; (*fig.*): **this battle turned the ~ in our favour** (*Br.*), **favor** (*US*) э́то сраже́ние склони́ло ча́шу весо́в в на́шу сто́рону. **2** (*pl., weighing machine*) вес|ы́ (*pl., g.* -о́в).

scale³ /skeɪl/ *n.* **1** (*grading*) шкала́; **~ of charges** шкала́ расце́нок; **centigrade ~** шкала́ Це́льсия; **social ~** обще́ственная ле́стница. **2** (*of map, and fig.*) масшта́б; **draw something to ~** черти́ть, на- что-н. в масшта́бе; **~ drawing** масшта́бный чертёж; **on a large/small ~** в большо́м/ма́лом масшта́бе. **3** (*size*) разме́р. **4** (*mus.*) га́мма; **practise** (*Br.*), **practice** (*US*) one's **~s** разы́гр|ывать, -а́ть га́ммы.

● *v.t.* (*climb*): **~ a wall** влез|а́ть, -ть (*or* залез|а́ть, -ть) на сте́ну; **~ a mountain** вз|бира́ться, -обра́ться на́ гору.

● *with advs.*: **~ down** *v.t.* пон|ижа́ть, -и́зить; ум|еньша́ть, -е́ньшить; (*fig.*) сокра|ща́ть, -ти́ть; **~ up** *v.t.* пов|ыша́ть, -ы́сить; увели́чи|вать, -ть.

scalene /ˈskeɪli:n/ *adj.* неравносторо́нний.

scallion /ˈskæljən/ *n.* (*shallot*) лук-шало́т; (*spring onion*) зелёный лук.

scallop /ˈskɒləp/ *n.* (*mollusc*) гребешо́к; (*ornamental edging*) фесто́н.

● *v.t.* (**scalloped, scalloping**) отде́л|ывать, -ать фесто́нами.

● *cpd.* **~-shell** *n.* ра́ковина гребешка́.

scallywag /ˈskælɪˌwæg/ (*US also* **scalawag** /ˈskæləˌwæg/) *n.* озорни́к.

scalp /skælp/ *n.* ко́жа головы́; (*American Indian trophy*) скальп.

● *v.t.* скальпи́ровать (*impf., pf.*).

scalpel /ˈskælp(ə)l/ *n.* ска́льпель (*m.*).

scalper /ˈskælpə(r)/ *n.* (*US coll.*) спекуля́нт.

scaly /ˈskeɪlɪ/ *adj.* (**scalier, scaliest**) (*with scales*) чешу́йчатый; (*flaking*) шелуша́щийся.

scam /skæm/ *n.* (*sl.*) обма́н, надува́тельство.

scamp /skæmp/ *n.* шалу́н.

scamper /ˈskæmpə(r)/ *n.* (*quick run*) поспе́шное бе́гство; **he ran off at a ~** он побежа́л стремгла́в.

● *v.i.* мча́ться (*impf.*), бе́гать (*indet.*); **the dog ~ed off** соба́ка умча́лась; **the class ~ed through Shakespeare** класс гало́пом пробежа́л по Шекспи́ру.

scampi /ˈskæmpɪ/ *n.* креве́тки (*f. pl.*).

scan /skæn/ *v.t.* (**scanned, scanning**) **1** (*survey*) обв|оди́ть, -ести́ взгля́дом/глаза́ми; **he ~ned my face** он испыту́юще взгляну́л мне в лицо́; (*glance through*) пробе|га́ть, -жа́ть (глаза́ми). **2** (*TV, comput., med.*) скани́ровать (*impf.*). **3** (*pros.*) анализи́ровать (*impf., pf.*) разме́р (*строки*).

● *v.i.* (**scanned, scanning**) (*pros.*): **this line ~s well** э́та строка́ хорошо́ ритмизо́вана.

scandal /ˈskænd(ə)l/ *n.* (*shocking event*) сканда́л; (*disgrace*) позо́р, безобра́зие; (*malicious gossip*) спле́тни (*f. pl.*); **create a ~** вызыва́ть, вы́звать возмуще́ние; да|ва́ть, -ть по́вод к спле́тням; **it is a ~** э́то безобра́зие; **she was the ~ of the neighbourhood** (*Br.*), **neighborhood** (*US*) она́ была́ при́тчей во язы́цех; **talk ~** спле́тничать (*impf.*).

scandalize /ˈskændəˌlaɪz/ *v.t.* скандализи́ровать (*impf., pf.*), шоки́ровать (*impf.*).

scandalmonger /ˈskænd(ə)lˌmʌŋgə(r)/ *n.* спле́тни|к (*fem.* -ца).

scandalmongering /ˈskænd(ə)lˌmʌŋgərɪŋ/ *n.* спле́тни (*f. pl.*).

scandalous /ˈskændələs/ *adj.* (*shocking*) сканда́льный; (*disgraceful*) позо́рный, безобра́зный, возмути́тельный; (*defamatory*) клеветни́ческий.

Scandinavia /ˌskændɪˈneɪvɪə/ *n.* Скандина́вия.

Scandinavian /ˌskændɪˈneɪvɪən/ *n.* скандина́в (*fem.* -ка).

● *adj.* скандина́вский.

scanner /ˈskænə(r)/ *n.* (*comput., med.*) ска́нер.

scansion /ˈskænʃ(ə)n/ *n.* сканди́рование; (*metre*) разме́р.

scant /skænt/ *adj.* (*inadequate*) недоста́точный; (*meagre*) ску́дный; **with ~ regard for my feelings** едва́ ли счита́ясь с мои́ми чу́вствами.

scanty /ˈskæntɪ/ *adj.* (**scantier, scantiest**) ску́дный (*see also* ⇒**scant**); **~ attire** ску́дная оде́жда; **~ attendance** плоха́я посеща́емость.

scapegoat /ˈskeɪpgəʊt/ *n.* козёл отпуще́ния.

scapu|la /ˈskæpjʊlə/ *n.* (*pl.* **~lae** /-ˌli:/ *or* **~las**) лопа́тка.

scar¹ /skɑ:(r)/ *n.* шрам, рубе́ц; (*fig.*) след, ра́на.

● *v.t.* (**scarred, scarring**) (*mark with* **~**) ост|авля́ть, -а́вить шра́мы на + *p.*; **he was ~red** у него́ оста́лись шра́мы; **a face ~red with smallpox** лицо́, изры́тое о́спой.

● *v.i.* (**scarred, scarring**) (*form* **~**; *also* **~ over**) рубцева́ться, за-.

scar² /skɑ:(r)/ *n.* утёс.

scarab /ˈskærəb/ *n.* (*zool.*) скараб́ей.

scarce /skeəs/ *adj.* (*insufficient*) недоста́точный; (*scanty*) ску́дный; (*rare*) ре́дкий; **coal is ~ here** у́голь здесь в дефици́те; **butter was ~ during the war** во вре́мя войны́ был дефици́т (*or* не хвата́ло) ма́сла; **money is ~ with them** у них ту́го с деньга́ми; **make o.s. ~** (*coll., make off*) уб|ира́ться, -ра́ться.

scarcely /ˈskeəslɪ/ *adv.* **1** (*barely*) едва́; почти́ не; **she is ~ 17** ей едва́ испо́лнилось семна́дцать лет; **I ~ know him** я его́ почти́ не зна́ю; я едва́ с ним знако́м; (*only just*) то́лько; **I had ~ entered the room when the phone rang** то́лько я вошёл в ко́мнату, как зазвони́л телефо́н. **2** (*surely not*): **you will ~ maintain that ...** вряд ли вы ста́нете (*or* не ста́нете же вы) утвержда́ть, что...

scarcity /ˈskeəsɪtɪ/ *n.* **1** (*insufficiency, dearth*) недоста́ток, нехва́тка, дефици́т; **it was a time of great ~** э́то бы́ло вре́мя больши́х лише́ний. **2** (*rarity*) ре́дкость; **~ value** сто́имость, определя́емая дефици́том.

scare /skeə(r)/ *n.* (*fright*) испу́г; **give s.o. a ~** пуга́ть, ис- кого́-н.; **you did give me a ~** как вы меня́ напуга́ли!; (*alarm, panic*) па́ника; **the news created a ~** но́вость вы́звала па́нику.
● *v.t.* пуга́ть, ис-; **I felt ~d** я боя́лся; **they were ~d stiff** они́ до́ смерти перепуга́лись.
● *v.i.*: **he does not ~ easily** его́ не так легко́ испуга́ть.
● *with advs.*: **~ away, ~ off** *vv.t.* отпу́г|ивать, -ну́ть; спу́гивать, спугну́ть.
● *cpds.* **~crow** *n.* пу́гало, (огоро́дное) чу́чело; **~monger** *n.* паникёр (*fem.* -ша).

scarf /skɑ:f/ *n.* (*pl.* **scarves** *or* **~s**) шарф.

scarify /'skeərɪ,faɪ/ *v.t.* (*surg., agric.*) скарифици́ровать (*impf., pf.*); (*fig., criticize*) жесто́ко раскритикова́ть (*pf.*).

scarlet /'skɑ:lɪt/ *n.* а́лый цвет.
● *adj.* а́лый; **turn ~** (*blush*) гу́сто красне́ть, по-; **~ fever** скарлати́на; **~ woman** блудни́ца.

scarp /skɑ:p/ *n.* (*steep slope*) круто́й отко́с; (*of fortification*) эска́рп.

scarper /'skɑ:pə(r)/ *v.i.* (*Br. coll.*) = **scram**

scarves /skɑ:vz/ *pl. of* ⇒**scarf**

scary /'skeərɪ/ *adj.* (**scarier, scariest**) (*coll.*) (*frightening*) стра́шный, жу́ткий.

scathing /'skeɪðɪŋ/ *adj.* ре́зкий, е́дкий, язви́тельный.

scatological /,skætə'lɒdʒɪk(ə)l/ *adj.* (*joke, humour*) гря́зный, похáбный.

scatter /'skætə(r)/ *v.t.* **1** (*throw here and there*) разбр|а́сывать, -оса́ть; (*sprinkle*) расс|ыпа́ть, -ы́пать; пос|ыпа́ть, -ы́пать; **~ seed** разбр|а́сывать, -оса́ть семена́; **toys were ~ed all over the room** игру́шки бы́ли разбро́саны по всей ко́мнате; **he ~ed his papers over the floor** он разброса́л свои́ бума́ги по всему́ по́лу; **they are ~ing gravel on the road** они́ посыпа́ют доро́гу гра́вием.
2 (*pass.*): **the area is ~ed with small hamlets** в э́той ме́стности мно́го ма́леньких дереву́шек; **~ed villages** раски́данные (там и тут) сёла.
3 (*lit., fig., drive away, disperse*) раз|гоня́ть, -огна́ть; рассе́|ивать, -ять; **a shot ~ed the birds** вы́стрел распуга́л птиц; **a wind ~ed the clouds** ве́тер рассе́ял облака́; **a thinly ~ed population** ре́дкое населе́ние.
● *v.i.* (*disperse*) расс|ыпа́ться, -ы́паться; рассе́|иваться, -яться; (*move off*) ра|сходи́ться, -зойти́сь; **the crowd ~ed** толпа́ разбежа́лась.
● *cpds.* **~-brain** *n.* рази́ня (*c.g.*); **~-brained** *adj.* рассе́янный, невнима́тельный.

scatty /'skætɪ/ *adj.* (**scattier, scattiest**) (*Br. coll.*) ве́треный.

scavenge /'skævɪndʒ/ *v.i.* (*of people*) ры́ться/копа́ться (*impf.*) в отбро́сах; ходи́ть (*impf.*) по помо́йкам; (*of animals*) корми́ться, пита́ться (*both impf.*) па́далью/отбро́сами.

scavenger /'skævɪndʒə(r)/ *n.* (*animal*) живо́тное, пита́ющееся па́далью; (*bird*) стервя́тник; (*person*) помо́ечник.

scenario /sɪ'nɑ:rɪəʊ/, /-'neərɪəʊ/ *n.* (*pl.* **~s**) сцена́рий; (*fig.*) вариа́нт, сцена́рий; **a worst-case ~** наиху́дший вариа́нт *or* сцена́рий.

scene /si:n/ *n.* **1** (*stage*) сце́на; (*fig.*): **appear on the ~** появ|ля́ться, -и́ться на сце́не; **quit the ~** сходи́ть, сойти́ со сце́ны.
2 (*place of action*) ме́сто де́йствия; **the ~ is laid in London** де́йствие происхо́дит в Ло́ндоне.
3 (*place*) ме́сто; **the ~ of the disaster/crime** ме́сто катастро́фы/преступле́ния; **~ of operations** (*mil.*) теа́тр вое́нных де́йствий; **change of ~** переме́на обстано́вки.
4 (*subdivision of play*) сце́на; **the duel ~** сце́на дуэ́ли; (*fig., episode, incident*) сце́на; **~s of country life** сце́ны из се́льской жи́зни; **make a ~** устр|а́ивать, -о́ить (*or* зака́т|ывать, -и́ть) сце́ну (*кому*).
5 (*set, décor*) декора́ция; (*fig.*): **behind the ~s** за кули́сами.
6 (*view, landscape*) карти́на; **a ~ of destruction** карти́на разруше́ния; **a desolate ~** карти́на запусте́ния.
7 (*milieu*): **on the pop music ~** в ми́ре поп-му́зыки.
● *cpds.* **~-painter** *n.* (*theatr.*) худо́жник-декора́тор; **~-shifter** *n.* (*Br., theatr.*) рабо́чий сце́ны.

scenery /'si:nərɪ/ *n.* (*theatr.*) декора́ции (*f. pl.*); (*landscape*) пейза́ж, вид.

scenic /'si:nɪk/ *adj.* **1** (*picturesque*) живопи́сный; **~ beauty** живопи́сность (ландша́фта).
2 (*theatr.*) сцени́ческий; **~ effects** сцени́ческие эффе́кты (*m. pl.*).

scent /sent/ *n.* **1** (*odour*) за́пах, арома́т, благоуха́ние.
2 (*perfume*) дух|и́ (*pl., g.* -о́в); **use, apply ~** души́ться, на-.
3 (*sense of smell; lit. of animals, fig.*) чутьё, нюх; (*of people*) обоня́ние.
4 (*trail, also fig.*) след; **get on (*or* pick up) the ~** нап|ада́ть, -а́сть на след; **lose the ~** теря́ть, по- след; (*fig.*): **he threw the police off the ~** он сбил поли́цию со сле́да.
● *v.t.* **1** (*discern by smell, of animals; also fig.*) чу́ять, по-; (*of people*) обоня́ть (*impf.*).
2 (*sniff*) ню́хать, по-.
3 (*impart odour to*): **roses ~ the air** ро́зы распространя́ют благоуха́ние; **~ed candle** арома́ти́ческая свеча́; **a ~ed rose** благоуха́нная ро́за; **~ed soap** души́стое мы́ло.
● *cpds.* **~-bottle** *n.* флако́н (для) духо́в; **~-spray** *n.* духи́-спре́й (*indecl.*), духи́ в аэрозо́ле.

scentless /'sentlɪs/ *adj.* без за́паха, лишённый арома́та.

scepter /'septə(r)/ (*US*) = **sceptre**

sceptic /'skeptɪk/ (*US* **skeptic**) *n.* ске́птик.

sceptical /'skeptɪk(ə)l/ (*US* **skeptical**) *adj.* скепти́ческий; (**~** *about something*) скепти́чески настро́енный (к + *d.*).

scepticism /'skeptɪ,sɪz(ə)m/ (*US* **skepticism**) *n.* скептици́зм.

sceptre /'septə(r)/ (*US* **scepter**) *n.* ски́петр.

schadenfreude /'ʃɑ:dən,frɔɪdə/ *n.* злора́дство.

schedule /'ʃedju:l/, /'ske-/ *n.* **1** (*list*) спи́сок, пе́речень (*m.*); **~ of charges** тари́ф ста́вок/расце́нок.
2 (*plan, timetable*) план, расписа́ние; **flight ~** расписа́ние самолётов; **work ~** гра́фик рабо́ты; **according to ~** соотве́тственно пла́ну; **a full ~** больша́я програ́мма; **be behind ~** оп|а́здывать, -озда́ть; отст|ава́ть, -а́ть от гра́фика; **be ahead of ~** опере|жа́ть, -ди́ть гра́фик; **before ~** ра́ньше вре́мени; **on ~** во́время/то́чно.
● *v.t.* **1** (*tabulate*) сост|авля́ть, -а́вить спи́сок +*g.*; **the house is ~d for demolition** дом (пред)назна́чен на снос; **a ~d flight** регуля́рный рейс.
2 (*time; plan*) рассчи́т|ывать, -а́ть; нам|еча́ть, -е́тить; **we are ~d to finish by May** по пла́ну мы должны́ ко́нчить к ма́ю; **the train is ~d to leave at noon** (по расписа́нию) по́езд отхо́дит в по́лдень.

schema /'ski:mə/ *n.* (*pl.* **~ta** *or* **~s**) схе́ма.

schematic /skɪ'mætɪk/, /ski:-/ *adj.* схемати́ческий; (*stereotyped*) схемати́чный.

schematize /'ski:mə,taɪz/ *v.t.* схематизи́ровать (*impf., pf.*).

schem|e /ski:m/ *n.* **1** (*arrangement*) поря́док; **in the ~e of things** в поря́дке веще́й; **colour** (*Br.*), **color** (*US*) **~e** цветова́я га́мма; сочета́ние кра́сок.
2 (*plan*) прое́кт, план. **3** (*plot*) про́иск|и (*pl., g.* -ов).
● *v.i.* интригова́ть (*impf.*); **he was ~ing to escape** он замышля́л побе́г; **they were ~ing for power** они́ плели́ интри́ги, что́бы доби́ться к вла́сти.

schemer /'ski:mə(r)/ *n.* интрига́н (*fem.* -ка).

scher|zo /'skeə,tsəʊ/ *n.* (*pl.* **~zos** *or* **~zi** /-tsɪ/) ске́рцо (*indecl.*).

schism /'sɪz(ə)m/, /'skɪ-/ *n.* раско́л; схи́зма.

schismatic /sɪz'mætɪk/, /skɪz-/ *adj.* раско́льнический.

schist /ʃɪst/ *n.* сла́нец.

schizo /'skɪtsəʊ/ *n.* (*pl.* **~s**) (*coll.*) ши́зик.
● *adj.* психо́ванный.

schizoid /'skɪtsɔɪd/ *n.* шизо́ид.
● *adj.* шизо́идный.

schizophrenia /,skɪtsə'fri:nɪə/ *n.* шизофрени́я.

schizophrenic /,skɪtsə'frenɪk/, /-'fri:nɪk/ *n.* шизофре́н|ик (*fem.* -и́чка).
● *adj.* шизофрени́ческий.

schmaltz /ʃmɔ:lts/, /ʃmælts/ *n.* (*sl.*) сентимента́льщина.

schmaltzy /'ʃmɔ:ltsɪ/, /'ʃmæltsɪ/ *adj.* (**schmaltzier, schmaltziest**) (*sl.*) сентимента́льный.

schnapps /ʃnæps/ *n.* шнапс.

schnitzel /ˈʃnɪtz(ə)l/ *n.* шни́цель (*m.*).

scholar /ˈskɒlə(r)/ *n.* **1** (*learned person*) учёный. **2** (*learner*) учени́к. **3** (*holder of ~ship*) стипендиа́т (*fem.* -ка).

scholarly /ˈskɒləlɪ/ *adj.* учёный, академи́ческий; **he has a ~ mind** у него́ нау́чный склад ума́.

scholarship /ˈskɒləʃɪp/ *n.* (*erudition*) учёность, эруди́ция; (*scholarly method or outlook*) академи́чность, нау́чность; (*grant*) стипе́ндия.

scholastic /skəˈlæstɪk/ *adj.* **1** (*hist.*) схоласти́ческий. **2** академи́ческий, уче́бный; **~ institution** уче́бное заведе́ние.

scholasticism /skəˈlæstɪˌsɪz(ə)m/ *n.* схола́стика.

school¹ /sku:l/ *n.* **1** (*place of education*) шко́ла; (*incl. higher education*) уче́бное заведе́ние; **at ~** в шко́ле; **go to ~** ходи́ть (*indet.*) в шко́лу; учи́ться (*impf.*) в шко́ле; **teach ~** (*US*) преподава́ть (*impf.*) в шко́ле; **start ~** пойти́ (*pf.*) в шко́лу; **leave ~** (*complete course*) конча́ть, ко́нчить шко́лу; (*abandon ~*) бр|оса́ть, -о́сить шко́лу; **where were you at ~?** где вы учи́лись?; **we were at ~ together** мы учи́лись в одно́й шко́ле; **of ~ age** шко́льного во́зраста; **~ fees** пла́та за обуче́ние; **~ report** шко́льный та́бель; **boarding ~** шко́ла-интерна́т; **boys'/girls' ~** мужска́я/же́нская шко́ла; **public ~** (*in UK*) ча́стная шко́ла; (*in US*) общеобразова́тельная шко́ла; **grade ~** (*in US*) нача́льная шко́ла; **nursery ~** де́тский сад; **primary ~** нача́льная шко́ла; **secondary, high ~** сре́дняя шко́ла; **junior/senior ~** шко́ла пе́рвой/второ́й ступе́ни; **evening, night ~** вече́рняя шко́ла; **military ~** вое́нное учи́лище; **vocational ~** профессиона́льно-техни́ческое учи́лище; **~ of art** худо́жественное учи́лище; **~ of dancing** (*small*) шко́ла та́нцев; (*large*) хореографи́ческое учи́лище; (*research centre*) институ́т; (*department of university, branch of study*): **~ of law** юриди́ческий факульте́т; (*Br., pl., final university examinations*) выпускны́е экза́мены (*m. pl.*).
2 (*lessons*) заня́тия (*nt. pl.*), уро́ки (*m. pl.*); **there will be no ~ today** сего́дня заня́тий/уро́ков не бу́дет; **~ finishes at 4** заня́тия/уро́ки конча́ются в 4.
3 (*range of classes*): **the lower/middle/upper ~** мла́дшие/сре́дние/ста́ршие кла́ссы (*m. pl.*).
4 (*of art, manners etc.*) шко́ла; **the Impressionist ~** импрессионисти́ческая шко́ла; **he is one of the old ~** он челове́к ста́рой шко́лы (*or* ста́рого зака́ла); **there is a ~ of thought which says ...** существу́ет уче́ние, согла́сно кото́рому. . ..
5 (*attr.*) шко́льный, уче́бный. *See also cpds.*
● *v.t.* обуч|а́ть, -и́ть; **~ a horse** объ|езжа́ть, -е́здить ло́шадь.
● *cpds.* **~-bag** *n.* шко́льная су́мка; (*satchel*) шко́льный ра́нец; (*briefcase*) шко́льный портфе́ль; **~-board** *n.* (*US*) ≈ райо́нный отде́л наро́дного образова́ния (*abbr.* РОНО); **~-book** *n.* уче́бник; **~boy** *n.* шко́льник; **S~ Certificate** *n.* (*hist.*) аттеста́т зре́лости; **~children** *n.* шко́льники (*m. pl.*); **~-days** *n.*: **in my ~-days** когда́ я учи́лся в шко́ле; **~fellow, ~mate** *nn.* соучени́|к (*fem.* -ца), шко́льный това́рищ; **~girl** *n.* шко́льница; **~-inspector** *n.* шко́льный инспе́ктор; **~-leaver** *n.* (*Br.*) выпускни́|к (*fem.* -ца); **~-leaving** *adj.*: **~-leaving age** (*Br.*) во́зраст, до кото́рого обуче́ние в шко́ле обяза́тельно; **~-leaving certificate** аттеста́т зре́лости; **~master** *n.* учи́тель (*m.*); **~mate** *n.* = **~fellow; ~mistress** *n.* учи́тельница; **~ pupil** *n.* учени́|к (*fem.* -ца); шко́льни|к (*fem.* -ца); **~room** *n.* класс; кла́ссная ко́мната; **~teacher** *n.* учи́тель (*fem.* -ница); **~teaching** *n.* (*as profession*) педаго́гика; (*activity*) преподава́ние; **~-time** *n.* (*lesson-time*) уче́бное вре́мя.

school² /sku:l/ *n.* (*of fish etc.*) кося́к.

schooling /ˈsku:lɪŋ/ *n.* (*education*) (об)уче́ние; (*training*) обуче́ние, подгото́вка; **he had little ~** ему́ не довело́сь мно́го учи́ться.

schooner /ˈsku:nə(r)/ *n.* (*naut.*) шху́на; (*Br., for sherry*) фуже́р; (*US, for beer*) большо́й пивно́й бока́л.

sciatic /saɪˈætɪk/ *adj.* седа́лищный.

sciatica /saɪˈætɪkə/ *n.* и́шиас.

science /ˈsaɪəns/ *n.* **1** (*systematic knowledge*) нау́ка; **pure/applied ~** чи́стая/прикладна́я нау́ка; **moral ~** э́тика; **social ~** обще́ственные нау́ки. **2** (*natural ~s*) есте́ственные нау́ки; **~ fiction** нау́чная фанта́стика.

scientific /ˌsaɪənˈtɪfɪk/ *adj.* нау́чный.

scientist /ˈsaɪəntɪst/ *n.* учёный(-есте́ственник).

sci-fi /ˈsaɪfaɪ/ *n.* (*coll.*) НФ (нау́чная фанта́стика).
● *adj.* нау́чно-фантасти́ческий.

scilicet /ˈsaɪlɪˌset/, /ˈski:lɪˌket/ *adv.* (*abbr. of* ***scire licet***) т.е. (то есть).

Scilly /ˈsɪlɪ/ *n.*: **Isles of ~** острова́ (*m. pl.*) Си́лли (*indecl.*).

scimitar /ˈsɪmɪtə(r)/ *n.* ятага́н.

scintilla /sɪnˈtɪlə/ *n.* (*fig.*) чу́точка, ка́пля; **there is not a ~ of evidence** нет никаки́х доказа́тельств.

scintillat|e /ˈsɪntɪˌleɪt/ *v.i.* (*lit., fig.*) и́скри́ться (*impf.*); блиста́ть (*impf.*); **a book ~ing with wit** кни́га, и́скря́щаяся остроу́мием.

scintillation /ˌsɪntɪˈleɪʃ(ə)n/ *n.* сверка́ние, блеск; (*twinkling*) мерца́ние.

scion /ˈsaɪən/ *n.* (*of plant*) побе́г; (*descendant*) о́тпрыск.

scirocco /sɪˈrɒkəʊ/ = **sirocco**

scissor|s /ˈsɪzəz/ *n.* (*also in wrestling, gymnastics*) но́жниц|ы (*pl., g.* —); **~s and paste** (*fig.*) компиля́ция, «режь и клей».
● *cpds.* **~grip, ~-hold** *nn.* но́жницы.

sclerosis /sklɪəˈrəʊsɪs/ *n.* склеро́з; **multiple ~** рассе́янный склеро́з.

sclerotic /sklɪəˈrɒtɪk/ *adj.* склероти́ческий, склероти́чный.

scoff¹ /skɒf/ *n.* (*taunt*) насме́шка.
● *v.i.* смея́ться (*impf.*); **~ at** издева́ться/глуми́ться/насмеха́ться (*all impf.*) над + *i.*; **he ~ed at danger** он смея́лся над опа́сностью; **be ~ed at** подверга́ться (*impf.*) насме́шкам; **he was ~ed at** над ним смея́лись/издева́лись.

scoff² /skɒf/ (*Br.*) *n.* (*food*) жратва́ (*sl.*).
● *v.t. & i.* жрать, со-.

scoffer /ˈskɒfə(r)/ *n.* насме́шник, зубоска́л.

scold /skəʊld/ *v.t.* брани́ть, вы́-; руга́ть, об-.
● *v.i.* брани́ться, руга́ться (*both impf.*).

scolding /ˈskəʊldɪŋ/ *n.* брань; **I gave him a good ~** я дал ему́ хоро́ший нагоня́й (*coll.*); я его́ как сле́дует отчита́л.

sconce /skɒns/ *n.* (*candlestick*) подсве́чник; (*on wall bracket*) бра (*nt. indecl.*).

scone /skɒn/, /skəʊn/ *n.* ≈ небольшо́й кекс.

scoop /sku:p/ *n.* **1** (*for grain etc.*) сово́к; (*to move earth*) ковш; (*for food*) ло́жка; (*for liquids*) черпа́к. **2**: **~ neckline** глубо́кое декольте́ (*indecl.*). **3** (*journ.*) ≈ сенса́ция.
● *v.t.* **1** (*lift with ~*) че́рп|ать, -ну́ть; заче́рп|ывать, -ну́ть; (*also* **~ out**) выче́рпывать, вы́черпать. **2** (*make by ~ing*) выда́лбливать, вы́долбить; **he ~ed out a hole in the sand** он вы́рыл я́му в песке́. **3** (*win*) выи́грывать, вы́играть; **~ the pool** заб|ира́ть, -ра́ть/выи́грывать, вы́играть все взя́тки. **4** (*journ.*) обст|авля́ть, -а́вить; обскака́ть (*pf.*) (*coll.*); **they ~ed the other papers on this story** они́ обскака́ли други́е газе́ты с э́той сенса́цией/но́востью.

scoot /sku:t/ *v.i.* уд|ира́ть, -ра́ть (*coll.*).

scooter /ˈsku:tə(r)/ *n.* (*child's*) самока́т; (*motor ~*) моторо́ллер.

scope /skəʊp/ *n.* **1** (*range, sweep*) разма́х, охва́т; **an undertaking of wide ~** предприя́тие с широ́ким разма́хом; **this is beyond my ~** э́то вне мое́й компете́нции; **this is beyond the ~ of our enquiry** э́то выхо́дит за преде́лы/ра́мки на́шего рассле́дования.
2 (*outlet, vent*): **the game offers ~ for the children's imagination** э́та игра́ даёт просто́р де́тскому воображе́нию; **the project provided ~ for his abilities** прое́кт дал ему́ возмо́жность разверну́ть свои́ спосо́бности.

scorbutic /skɔ:ˈbju:tɪk/ *adj.* цинго́тный.

scorch /skɔ:tʃ/ *v.t.* (*burn, dry up*) жечь, с-; выжига́ть, вы́жечь; **~ed earth policy** страте́гия вы́жженной земли́; (*clothes etc.*) подпа́л|ивать, -и́ть; **the long summer ~ed the grass** за до́лгое ле́то трава́ вы́горела.
● *v.i.* (*coll., drive or ride at high speed*) жа́рить (*impf.*) (на всю кату́шку) (*coll.*).
● *cpd.* **~-mark** *n.* подпа́лина, ожо́г.

S

scorcher /ˈskɔːtʃə(r)/ *n.* (*coll., hot day*) знойный день.

score /skɔː(r)/ *n.* **1** (*notch*) зарубка; (*deep scratch*) глубокая царапина, борозда; (*weal on skin*) рубец.
2 (*arch., account*) счёт; **pay off old ~s** (*fig.*) св|одить, -ести старые счёты; расквитаться (*pf.*).
3 (*in games*) счёт; **what's the ~?** какой счёт?; **keep the ~** вести (*det.*) счёт; **know the ~** (*fig., coll.*) быть в курсе; знать (*impf.*), что к чему.
4 (*mus.*): **(full) ~** партитура; **piano/vocal ~** партия фортепиано/голоса.
5 (*twenty*) двадцать; **a ~ of people** человек двадцать; **~s of people** десятки людей, множество народу; **three ~ and ten** (*arch.*) семьдесят; **~s of times** десятки раз, много раз; часто.
6 (*grounds*) причина, повод; **you need have no fear on that ~** на этот счёт вы можете не беспокоиться.
● *v.t.* **1** (*notch*) изрез|ывать, -ать; (*incise*): **~ a line** пров|одить, -ести линию (ножом *и т.п.*); **~ out, through** вычёркивать, вычеркнуть; зачёрк|ивать, -нуть; (*scratch*) царапать, ис-; (*preparatory to cutting*) разм|ечать, -етить.
2 (*win*) выигрывать, выиграть; **~ a goal** (*football*) заб|ивать, -ить гол; **~ tricks** (*at cards*) брать, взять взятки; **he ~d a success with his first book** его первая книга принесла ему успех; **a goal ~s six points** за один гол засчитывается 6 очков.
3 (*mus., orchestrate*) оркестровать (*impf., pf.*); (*arrange*) аранжировать (*impf., pf.*).
● *v.i.* **1** (*keep score*) вести (*impf.*) счёт; (*win point*) выигрывать, выиграть очко; **they failed to ~** они не выиграли ни одного очка; они не забили ни одного гола; **the centre-forward ~d** центральный нападающий забил гол.
2 (*secure advantage; have good luck*) выигрывать, выиграть; **that's where he ~s** вот на чём он выиграет; вот в чём его сила/преимущество; **~ off s.o.** (*Br.*) высмеивать, высмеять/ подд|евать, -еть кого-н.
● *cpds.* **~-keeper** *n.* судья-секретарь (*m.*); **~line** *n.* счёт; **~-sheet** *n.* судейский протокол.

scorer /ˈskɔːrə(r)/ *n.* **1** (*keeper of score*) счётчик. **2**: **the captain was the ~ of the first goal** первый гол забил капитан.

scorn /skɔːn/ *n.* презрение; **laugh to ~** высмеивать, высмеять.
● *v.t.* презирать (*impf.*); пренебр|егать, -ечь + *i.*; **he ~ed the danger** он презрел опасность; **he ~ed such methods** он гнушался подобными средствами; он презирал такие методы.

scornful /ˈskɔːnfʊl/ *adj.* (*of person*) надменный; **he was ~ of the idea** он отнёсся к этой идее с презрением; (*of glance etc.*) презрительный.

Scorpio /ˈskɔːpɪəʊ/ *n.* (*pl.* **~s**) Скорпион.

scorpion /ˈskɔːpɪən/ *n.* скорпион.

Scot /skɒt/ *n.* шотланд|ец (*fem.* -ка).

Scotch /skɒtʃ/ *n.* (*whisky*) шотландское виски (*indecl.*), скотч.
● *adj.* шотландский; **~ tape** (*propr.*) клейкая лента, скотч.

scotch /skɒtʃ/ *v.t.* (*fig.*): **he ~ed the rumour** (*Br.*), **rumor** (*US*) он опроверг слух.

scoter /ˈskəʊtə(r)/ *n.* (*pl.* **~** *or* **~s**) турпан.

scot-free /ˈskɒtfriː/ *adv.*: **go ~** (*unharmed*) ост|аваться, -аться невредимым; (*unpunished*) ост|аваться, -аться безнаказанным.

Scotland /ˈskɒtlənd/ *n.* Шотландия; **~ Yard** Скотленд-ярд; центральное управление лондонской полиции; (*CID*) лондонская уголовная полиция.

Scots /skɒts/ *n.* (*ling.*) шотландский говор.
● *adj.* шотландский.
● *cpds.* **~man** *n.* шотландец; **~woman** *n.* шотландка.

Scot(t)icism /ˈskɒtɪˌsɪz(ə)m/ *n.* шотландизм.

Scottish /ˈskɒtɪʃ/ *adj.* шотландский.

scoundrel /ˈskaʊndr(ə)l/ *n.* подлец, мерзавец.

scour[1] /ˈskaʊə(r)/ *n.* (*cleansing*) чистка; **give something a good ~** вычищать, вычистить что-н. хорошо.
● *v.t.* **1** (*cleanse*) чистить, вы-. **2** (*remove by ~ing; also* **~ away, off**) отт|ирать, -ереть.

scour[2] /ˈskaʊə(r)/ *v.t.* (*range in search or pursuit*) обрыскать (*pf.*); **he ~ed the town for his daughter** он обегал весь город в поисках дочери.

scourer /ˈskaʊrə(r)/ *n.* (*for saucepans etc.*) металлическая мочалка; ёж.

scourge /skɜːdʒ/ *n.* бич.
● *v.t.* (*flog*) сечь, вы-; (*fig., castigate*) бичевать (*impf.*); (*punish*) карать, по-.

Scouse /skaʊs/ (*Br.*) *n.* (*coll.*)
1 ливерпульский диалект.
2 ливерпул|ец (*fem.* -ка).
● *adj.* ливерпульский.

Scouser /ˈskaʊsə(r)/ (*Br. coll.*) = **Scouse** *n.* 2

scout /skaʊt/ *n.* **1** (*mil.*) разведчик (*also ship, aircraft*); **~ car** разведывательный автомобиль.
2 (*Boy S~*) скаут, бойскаут; (*Girl S~*) девочка-скаут.
● *v.i.* (*reconnoitre*) развед|ывать, -ать; **he is out ~ing** он в разведке; (*coll., search*) разыскивать (*impf.*); **I have been ~ing about for a present** я обходил все магазины в поисках подарка; (*belong to S~ movement*): **my son is keen on ~ing** мой сын увлекается скаутизмом/скаутингом.
● *cpd.* **~master** *n.* начальник отряда бойскаутов.

scow /skaʊ/ *n.* баржа, барка.

scowl /skaʊl/ *n.* сердитый/хмурый взгляд.
● *v.i.*: **he ~ed at me** он хмуро/сердито посмотрел на меня; **a ~ing face** хмурое/нахмуренное лицо.

Scrabble /ˈskræb(ə)l/ *n.* (*propr.*) скрэбл (≈ Эрудит).

scrabble /ˈskræb(ə)l/ *v.i.*: **~ about** шарить (*impf.*); **~ about for something** разыскивать (*impf.*) что-н.

scrag /skræg/ (*Br.*) *n.*: **~ end of mutton** баранья шея.
● *v.t.* (**scragged, scragging**) (*coll., rough up*) трепать, по-.

scraggy /ˈskrægɪ/ *adj.* (**scraggier, scraggiest**) костлявый, тощий.

scram /skræm/ *v.i.* (**scrammed, scramming**) (*sl.*): **I told him to ~** я велел ему убираться; **~!** проваливай!; катись!

scramble /ˈskræmb(ə)l/ *n.* **1** (*climb with hands and feet*) карабканье. **2** (*Br., motor cycle race*) мотокросс. **3** (*struggle to get something*) свалка; (*fig.*) борьба, схватка; **there was a ~ for the ball** произошла схватка/борьба за мяч; **it was a ~ to get ready in time** мы отчаянно старались собраться вовремя.
● *v.t.*: **~ eggs** жарить, по- яичницу-болтунью; **~d eggs** яичница-болтунья.
● *v.i.* **1** (*clamber*) карабкаться, вс-; вз|бираться, -обраться; **we ~d through the bracken** мы продрались через заросли папоротника; **the boys ~d over the wall** мальчики перелезли через забор; **I ~d into my clothes** я поспешно натянул (на себя) одежду.
2 (*fig.*) бороться (*impf.*); **the passengers ~d for seats** пассажиры ринулись занимать места.

scrambler /ˈskræmblə(r)/ *n.* (*telephone*) скремблер; автоматическое шифровальное устройство.

scrap[1] /skræp/ *n.* **1** (*small piece*) кусочек; (*of metal*) обломок; (*of cloth*) обрезок; лоскут; (*fragment*) обрывок; **~s of knowledge/conversation** обрывки (*m. pl.*) знаний/разговора; **~s of paper** клочки (*m. pl.*) бумаги; **there's not a ~ of evidence** нет никаких доказательств.
2 (*pl., waste food*) объедк|и (*pl., g.* -ов); **they found a few ~s of food** они нашли кое-какие остатки пищи.
3 (*waste material, refuse*) утиль (*m.*); утильсырьё; (**~** *metal*) металлолом; (**~** *paper*) макулатура.
● *v.t.* (**scrapped, scrapping**) **1** (*make into* **~**) превра|щать, -тить в лом; (*machines etc.*) отд|авать, -ать на слом.
2 (*coll., discard*) выбрасывать, выбросить; (*plan, scheme*) отмен|ять, -ить.
● *cpds.* **~-book** *n.* альбом для вырезок; **~-heap** *n.* свалка; **throw something on the ~-heap** (*lit., fig.*) выбрасывать, выбросить что-н. на свалку; **~-iron** *n.* металлический лом; **~-merchant** *n.* старьёвщик; торговец утилем; **~-yard** *n.* (*Br.*) склад лома; пункт приёма металлолома/утиля.

scrap[2] /skræp/ *n.* (*coll., fight*) драка, потасовка; **have a ~** драться, по-; вздорить, по-; **he is always ready for a ~** он страшный забияка.
● *v.i.* (**scrapped, scrapping**) драться (*impf.*).

scrape /skreɪp/ *n.* **1** (*action*) скобле́ние, чи́стка; (*of pen*) скрип; (*of foot*) ша́рканье; **give a carrot a ~** чи́стить, по- морко́вь.
2 (*coll., awkward predicament*) переде́лка; **get into a ~** вли́пнуть (*pf.*) в исто́рию (*coll.*).

● *v.t.* **1** (*abrade*) скобли́ть, вы́-; (*graze*) сса́|живать, -ди́ть; **I ~d my hand on the wall** я ссади́л/ободра́л себе́ ру́ку о сте́ну.
2 (*clean*) выска́бливать (*or* скобли́ть), вы́скоблить; **~ one's shoes** соск|а́бливать, -обли́ть грязь с подо́шв; **he ~d his plate clean** он подчи́стил всю таре́лку.
3: **~ one's feet** ша́ркать (*impf.*) нога́ми.
4: **~ a living** ко́е-как своди́ть (*impf.*) концы́ с конца́ми.

● *v.i.* **1** (*rub*): **my hand ~d against the wall** я ссади́л себе́ ру́ку о сте́ну; **his car ~d against a tree** его́ маши́на заде́ла де́рево; он поцара́пал маши́ну о де́рево.
2 (*get through*): **she just ~d into the final** она́ с трудо́м вы́шла в фина́л.
3: **bow and ~** расша́ркиваться (*impf.*) (*перед кем*).
4 (*on violin*) пили́кать (*impf.*).

● *with advs.*: **~ along** (*also* **scratch along**), **~ by** *vv.i.* (*get by*) переб|ива́ться, -и́ться; пробавля́ться (*impf.*); **we can just ~ along** мы ко́е-как перебива́емся; **~ off** *v.t.* соск|а́бливать, -обли́ть; **~ out** *v.t.* выскреба́ть, вы́скрести; (*hollow or carve out*) выда́лбливать, вы́долбить; (*bowl etc.*) выска́бливать, вы́скоблить; **~ through** *v.i.* прот́ис|киваться, -нуться; **she ~d through (her exam)** она́ с трудо́м (*or* со скри́пом *or* с грехо́м попола́м) сдала́ экза́мен; **~ together** *v.t.* (*money etc.*) наскре|ба́ть, -сти́; **~ up** *v.t.*: **he ~d up enough money for the concert** он наскрёб де́ньги на конце́рт.

scraper /ˈskreɪpə(r)/ *n.* (*implement*) скребо́к.

scrappy /ˈskræpɪ/ *adj.* (**scrappier, scrappiest**) **1** (*uncoordinated; miscellaneous*) разро́зненный; **a ~ essay** пове́рхностное сочине́ние; **a ~ education** пове́рхностное образова́ние. **2** (*fragmentary*) отры́вочный, несвя́зный. **3** (*meagre*) ску́дный.

scratch /skrætʃ/ *n.* **1** (*mark*) цара́пина.
2 (*noise*) цара́панье.
3 (*wound*) цара́пина, сса́дина.
4 (*act of ~ing*): **give one's head a ~** почеса́ть (*pf.*) го́лову.
5 (*starting line*) старт; (*fig.*): **come up to ~** быть на высоте́ (положе́ния); де́лать (*impf.*) то, что поло́жено; **bring up to ~** дов|оди́ть, -ести́ до тре́буемого у́ровня; **start from ~** нач|ина́ть, -а́ть с нача́ла/нуля́.

● *adj.* (*haphazard*) случа́йный; **~ crew** случа́йная кома́нда.

● *v.t.* **1** цара́п|ать, о-; **~ o.s.** цара́паться, по-; **he merely ~ed the surface of the problem** он затро́нул/освети́л вопро́с весьма́ пове́рхностно; **he ~ed letters on the wall** он нацара́пал бу́квы на стене́; **the dog ~ed a hole in the lawn** соба́ка вы́рыла я́мку в газо́не.
2 (*to relieve itching*) чеса́ть, по-; **~ one's head** чеса́ть (*impf.*) го́лову; **he was ~ing his head over the problem** (*fig.*) он лома́л го́лову над э́той зада́чей; **you ~ my back and I'll ~ yours** (*fig.*) ты — мне, я — тебе́; рука́ ру́ку мо́ет.
3 (*erase*) вычёркивать, вы́черкнуть; (*withdraw*): **~ a horse** сн|има́ть, -ять ло́шадь с соревнова́ния; (*cancel*): **~ an agreement** аннули́ровать (*impf., pf.*) соглаше́ние.

● *v.i.* **1** (*of person*, **~ o.s.**) чеса́ться, по-.
2 (*of animal*): **does your cat ~?** ва́ша ко́шка цара́пается?
3 (*of pen*) цара́пать (*impf.*).
4 (*coll., withdraw from competition*) отка́з|ываться, -а́ться от уча́стия в состяза́нии.

● *with advs.*: **~ about, ~ around** *vv.i.*: **the chickens ~ed around for food** ку́ры клева́ли зе́млю в по́исках пи́щи; **he had to ~ around for evidence** ему́ с трудо́м удало́сь наскрести́ доказа́тельства; **~ along** *v.i.* = **scrape along; ~ out** *v.t.* (*erase*) вычёркивать, вы́черкнуть; зачёрк|ивать, -ну́ть; (*with knife*) выреза́ть, вы́резать; **~ s.o.'s eyes out** выцара́пывать, вы́царапать глаза́ кому́-н.; **~ up** *v.t.* (*disinter*): **the dog ~ed up its bone** соба́ка вы́рыла/вы́копала свою́ кость; (*collect with difficulty*) наскре|ба́ть, -сти́.

● *cpd.* **~-pad** *n.* (*US*) блокно́т для заме́ток.

scratchy /ˈskrætʃɪ/ *adj.* (**scratchier, scratchiest**) (*of pen: squeaky*) скрипу́чий; (*catching in paper*) цара́пающий; (*of a record*) поцара́панный; (*of cloth*) колю́чий.

scrawl /skrɔːl/ *n.* кара́кули (*f. pl.*); (*fig.*) небре́жная запи́ска, (*coll.*) пису́лька.

● *v.t.* черк|а́ть, -ну́ть; цара́пать, на-.

● *v.i.* писа́ть (*impf.*) кара́кулями; **a ~ing hand** неразбо́рчивый по́черк.

scrawny /ˈskrɔːnɪ/ *adj.* (**scrawnier, scrawniest**) костля́вый.

scream /skriːm/ *n.* **1** пронзи́тельный крик; (*shriek*) вопль (*m.*); (*high-pitched* **~**) визг; (*of bird*) крик; **~s of laughter** взры́вы (*m. pl.*) хо́хота/сме́ха.
2 (*coll., funny affair*): **it was a ~!** (э́то была́) умо́ра!; **he is a perfect ~** он настоя́щий ко́мик.

● *v.t.* выкри́кивать, вы́крикнуть; **the sergeant ~ed an order** сержа́нт вы́крикнул кома́нду; **the baby was ~ing its head off** ребёнок надрыва́лся от кри́ка.

● *v.i.* **1** вопи́ть (*impf.*); (*high-pitched*) визжа́ть (*impf.*); **he was ~ing for help** он взыва́л о по́мощи; **you will ~ with laughter** вы бу́дете смея́ться до упа́ду; **the film is ~ingly funny** фильм безу́мно смешно́й.
2 (*of bird*) (пронзи́тельно) крича́ть, за-; вскри́к|ивать, -нуть.
3 (*of inanimate objects*) визжа́ть (*impf.*); скрежета́ть (*impf.*); **the brakes ~ed as he turned the corner** тормоза́ завизжа́ли на поворо́те.

scree /skriː/ *n.* щебни́стая о́сыпь.

screech /skriːtʃ/ *n.* пронзи́тельный крик, визг; (*of object*) скрип, скре́жет.

● *v.i.* пронзи́тельно крича́ть, за-; (*of gears, tyres etc.*) скрежета́ть (*impf.*); скрипе́ть (*impf.*).

● *cpd.* **~-owl** *n.* ма́лая уша́стая сова́; (*Br., barn-owl*) сипу́ха.

screechy /ˈskriːtʃɪ/ *adj.* (**screechier, screechiest**) визгли́вый.

screed /skriːd/ *n.* дли́нное, ску́чное посла́ние.

screen /skriːn/ *n.* **1** (*partition*) перегоро́дка.
2 (*furniture*) ши́рма.
3 (*shelter, protection*) прикры́тие; **behind a ~ of trees** под прикры́тием дере́вьев; (*cover*) покро́в; **under the ~ of night** под покро́вом но́чи; **a ~ of indifference** ма́ска равноду́шия.
4 (*elec.*) изоля́ция.
5 (*wind* **~**) ветрово́е стекло́.
6 (*cin., TV, comput.*) экра́н; **~ adaptation** экраниза́ция; **she went for a ~ test** она́ прошла́ про́бную съёмку; **~ size** разме́р экра́на (по диагона́ли).

● *v.t.* **1** (*shelter*) прикр|ыва́ть, -ы́ть; (*protect*) защи|ща́ть, -ти́ть; огра|жда́ть, -ди́ть.
2 (*hide*) укр|ыва́ть, -ы́ть; **the house was ~ed from view** дом был укры́т от взо́ров.
3 (*separate*) отгор|а́живать, -оди́ть; **we ~ed off the kitchen from the dining-room** мы отгороди́ли ку́хню от столо́вой.
4 (*sift; lit., fig.*) просе́|ивать, -ять.
5 (*fig., investigate; also med.*): **be ~ed (for)** про|ходи́ть, -йти́ прове́рку на + *a.*; **they were ~ed before going abroad** пе́ред отъе́здом за грани́цу они́ прошли́ прове́рку (на благонадёжность).
6 (*show on* **~**) пока́з|ывать, -а́ть; (*make film of*) экранизи́ровать (*impf., pf.*).
7 (*elec.*) экранизи́ровать (*impf., pf.*).

● *cpds.* **~-play** *n.* сцена́рий; **~-writer** *n.* сценари́ст.

screw /skruː/ *n.* **1** винт, болт, шуру́п; (*female* **~**) га́йка; **he has a ~ loose** у него́ ви́нтика не хвата́ет (*coll.*); **put the ~s on** (*fig.*) наж|има́ть, -а́ть на + *a.*
2 (*turn of* **~**): **give it another ~** ещё раз(о́к) поверни́те.
3 (*propeller*) винт.
4: **~ of tobacco** (*Br.*) завёртка/закру́тка табака́.
5 (*sl., prison warder*) вертуха́й (*sl.*).

● *v.t.* **1** зави́н|чивать, -ти́ть; **the cap is ~ed tight** кры́шка кре́пко закру́чена; **the cupboard was ~ed to the wall** шкаф был приви́нчен к стене́; **I ~ed the bolt into the post** я ввинти́л болт в столб.
2 (*fig., turn*): **I had to ~ my neck round to see him** я чуть не вы́вернул ше́ю, что́бы уви́деть его́.
3 (*vulg., copulate with*) тра́х|ать, -нуть.

● *v.i.* **1**: **the handles ~ into the drawer** ру́чки приви́нчиваются к я́щику; **this**

S

piece ~s on to that этот кусок привинчивается к тому.
2 (*vulg., copulate*) трах|аться, -нуться.

● *with advs.*: **~ down** *v.t. & i.* привин|чивать(ся), -тить(ся); **~ off** *v.t. & i.* отвин|чивать(ся), -тить(ся); **~ on** *v.t. & i.* навин|чивать(ся), -тить(ся); **his head is ~ed on the right way** он соображает; у него голова (хорошо) варит; у него есть голова на плечах; **~ out** *v.t.* (*coll., extort*) выжимать, выжать; **I managed to ~ the truth out of him** мне удалось выжать/вытянуть из него правду; **~ together** *v.t.*: **he ~ed the boards together** он скрепил доски винтами; **~ up** *v.t.* завин|чивать, -тить; (*crumple*) комкать, с-; **~ up one's eyes** щурить, со- глаза; **a face ~ed up with pain** лицо, искажённое болью (*or* от боли); **~ o.s. up, ~ up one's courage** соб|ираться, -раться с духом; наб|ираться, -раться храбрости; (*sl., spoil*) напортачить (*pf.*); завал|ивать, -ить.

● *cpds.* **~ball** *n.* (*sl.*) чокнутый, сумасброд; **~-cap, ~-top** *nn.* навинчивающаяся крышка; **~driver** *n.* отвёртка; **~-propeller** *n.* винт; **~-top** *n.* = **~-cap; ~-valve** *n.* винтовой клапан.

screwy /ˈskru:ɪ/ *adj.* (**screwier, screwiest**) (*sl., crazy*) тронутый, чокнутый; **a ~ idea** нелепая/дурацкая идея.

scribbl|e /ˈskrɪb(ə)l/ *n.* каракули (*f. pl.*).

● *v.t. & i.* **1** (*make marks (on)*) черкать, ис-; чертить, ис-; **the children ~ed all over the wall** дети исчеркали/исчертили всю стену. **2** (*write hastily*) черкать, на-; **I ~ed a note to him** я черкнул ему записку; (*write untidily*) царапать, на-; (*of amateur writing*) пописывать (*impf.*); **~e verses** кропать (*impf.*) стишки; **~ing-pad, block** блокнот для заметок.

scribbler /ˈskrɪblə(r)/ *n.* (*fig., poor author*) писака (*c.g.*).

scribe /skraɪb/ *n.* (*hist.*) писец; (*bibl.*) книжник; (*hack*) писака (*c.g.*).

scrimmage /ˈskrɪmɪdʒ/ (*also* **scrum(mage)**) *n.* **1** (*tussle*) свалка. **2** (*American football, Rugby*) схватка вокруг мяча.

● *v.i.* (*tussle*) драться (*impf.*); (*American football, Rugby*) сгрудиться (*pf.*) (*coll.*) вокруг мяча.

scrimp /skrɪmp/ = **skimp**

scrip /skrɪp/ *n.* (*comm.*) временный сертификат на владение акциями.

script /skrɪpt/ *n.* **1** (*handwriting*) рукопись; (*writing system*) письмо, письменность; **in Cyrillic ~** кириллицей. **2** (*text*) текст, сценарий.

● *v.t.*: **~ed discussion** заранее подготовленная дискуссия.

● *cpd.* **~-writer** *n.* сценарист.

scriptural /ˈskrɪptʃər(ə)l/, /-tʃʊər(ə)l/ *adj.* библейский.

scripture /ˈskrɪptʃə(r)/ *n.* писание; **Holy S~** Священное писание; **in the ~s** в Писании Библии; (*as school subject*) Закон Божий; **~ lesson** урок Закона Божьего.

scrofula /ˈskrɒfjʊlə/ *n.* золотуха.

scrofulous /ˈskrɒfjʊləs/ *adj.* золотушный.

scroll /skrəʊl/ *n.* (*roll of parchment*) свиток; (*archit.*) завиток, волюта.

● *v.i.* (*comput.*) прокр|учивать, -утить.

● *cpd.* **~ bar** *n.* (*comput.*) линейка прокрутки; **~-work** *n.* орнамент из завитков.

Scrooge /skru:dʒ/ *n.* скряга (*c.g.*); **don't be such a ~!** не будь таким скрягой!

scrot|um /ˈskrəʊtəm/ *n.* (*pl.* **~a** *or* **~ums**) мошонка.

scroung|e /skraʊndʒ/ *v.t.* (*cadge*) стрел|ять, -ьнуть (*coll.*).

● *v.i.* **1** (*search about*) рыскать (*impf.*); **they were ~ing for food** они рыскали в поисках пищи. **2** (*cadge*) попрошайничать (*impf.*); клянчить (*impf.*).

scrounger /ˈskraʊndʒə(r)/ *n.* попрошайка (*c.g.*).

scrub[1] /skrʌb/ *n.* (*brushwood*) кустарник; (*area*) заросли (*f. pl.*).

scrub[2] /skrʌb/ *n.*: **give something a ~** вычищать, вычистить что-н.

● *v.t.* (**scrubbed, scrubbing**) **1** (*rub hard*) скрести (*impf.*); тереть (*impf.*); (*clean*) чистить, по-; драить, на-; **~ the floor** мыть, вы- пол; **~ paint off one's hands** сч|ищать, -истить краску с рук; **~bing brush** жёсткая щётка. **2** (*sl., cancel*) отмен|ять, -ить.

● *with advs.*: **~ down** *v.t.*: **he ~bed down the walls** он вымыл стены; **~ off** *v.t.* отм|ывать, -ыть; сч|ищать, -истить; **~ out** *v.t.*: **she ~bed out the kitchen** она выскребла кухню дочиста; **the pans were ~bed out** кастрюли были начищены.

scrubber /ˈskrʌbə(r)/ *n.* (*Br. sl.*) шлюха, потаскуха.

scrubby /ˈskrʌbɪ/ *adj.* (**scrubbier, scrubbiest**) (*of land*) поросший кустарником; (*of plant etc., stunted*) чахлый.

scruff[1] /skrʌf/ *n.*: **take s.o. by the ~ of the neck** хватать, схватить кого-н. за шиворот/загривок.

scruff[2] /skrʌf/ *n.* (*Br.*) неряха, растрёпа.

scruffy /ˈskrʌfɪ/ *adj.* (**scruffier, scruffiest**) (*coll.*) неопрятный.

scrum(mage) /ˈskrʌmɪdʒ/ = **scrimmage**

scrumptious /ˈskrʌmpʃəs/ *adj.* (*coll.*) очень вкусный, смачный.

scrunch /skrʌntʃ/ *v.t.* (*coll.*) = **crunch**

scruple /ˈskru:p(ə)l/ *n.* **1** (*unit of weight*) скрупул. **2** (*of conscience*) сомнения (*nt. pl.*); **he will tell lies without ~** он врёт без зазрения совести; **have ~s about doing something** совеститься, по- сделать что-н.; **have no ~s** не стесняться, по- ничем; **he had no ~ about telling me everything** он не постеснялся мне всё рассказать.

● *v.i.* стесняться, по-; совеститься, по-; **I would not ~ to accept the money** я бы с лёгкой совестью принял деньги.

scrupulous /ˈskru:pjʊləs/ *adj.* (*of sensitive conscience*) щепетильный, добросовестный; (*accurate, punctilious*) тщательный, скрупулёзный, педантичный; **~ care** педантичная тщательность; **~ cleanliness** абсолютная чистота; **~ honesty** скрупулёзная/безупречная честность.

scrupulousness /ˈskru:pjʊləsnɪs/ *n.* щепетильность, добросовестность; тщательность; скрупулёзность.

scrutineer /ˌskru:tɪˈnɪə(r)/ *n.* член счётной комиссии (на выборах).

scrutinize /ˈskru:tɪˌnaɪz/ *v.t.* (*examine*) рассм|атривать, -отреть; (*stare at*) пристально смотреть (*impf.*) на + *a.*

scrutiny /ˈskru:tɪnɪ/ *n.* **1** (*searching gaze*) внимательный/испытующий взгляд. **2** (*close investigation*) тщательное расследование/рассмотрение/исследование; **his record does not bear ~** его прошлое/поведение далеко не безупречно.

scuba /ˈsku:bə/, /ˈskju:-/ *n.* (*pl.* **~s**) скуба, акваланг; **~ diver** аквалангист; пловец/ныряльщик со скубой.

scud /skʌd/ *v.i.* (**scudded, scudding**) нестись, про-; (*naut.*) идти (*det.*) под ветром.

scuff /skʌf/ *v.t.*: **~** (*wear away*) **one's shoes** трепать, ис-, об- обувь.

● *v.i.* (*shuffle*) шаркать (*impf.*).

scuffle /ˈskʌf(ə)l/ *n.* потасовка, схватка.

● *v.i.* драться (*impf.*); схват|ываться, -иться.

scull /skʌl/ *n.* (*oar*) парное весло; (*at stern of boat*) кормовое весло; (*boat*) = **sculler**

● *v.t. & i.*: **~ a boat** грести (*impf.*) парными вёслами; (*with stern-oar*) грести кормовым веслом, галанить (*impf.*).

sculler /ˈskʌlə(r)/ *n.* (*person*) гребец; (*boat; also* **scull**) парная лодка; ялик.

scullery /ˈskʌlərɪ/ *n.* судомойня.

● *cpd.* **~-maid** *n.* судомойка.

sculpt /skʌlpt/ *v.t. & i.* (*coll.*) = **sculpture** *v.t., v.i.*

sculptor /ˈskʌlptə(r)/ *n.* скульптор.

sculptress /ˈskʌlptrɪs/ *n.* скульптор; **she is a ~** она скульптор.

sculptural /ˈskʌlptʃərəl/ *adj.* скульптурный, пластический; **~ beauty** холодная красота.

sculpture /ˈskʌlptʃə(r)/ *n.* (*art, product*) скульптура.

● *v.t.* (*also* **sculpt**) ваять, из-; (*model in clay etc.*) лепить, вы-; (*in stone*) высекать, высечь; (*in wood*) резать, вы-.

● *v.i.* быть/работать (*impf.*) скульптором.

scum /skʌm/ *n.* накипь, пена; (*fig.*) подонки (*m. pl.*); **~ of the earth** подонки общества.

scumbag /ˈskʌmbæg/ *n.* (*sl.*) подонок.

scupper /ˈskʌpə(r)/ *n.* (*naut.*) шпигат.

● *v.t.* (*Br.*) (*sink*) топить, по-; (*fig., coll.*)

разби́ть (*pf.*) (в пух и прах); разгроми́ть (*pf.*); **we're ~ed** мы поги́бли.

scurf /skɜːf/ *n.* пе́рхоть.

scurrility /skʌˈrɪlɪtɪ/ *n.* непристо́йность.

scurrilous /ˈskʌrɪləs/ *adj.* (*indecent*) непристо́йный; (*abusive*) оскорби́тельный.

scurry /ˈskʌrɪ/ *n.* суета́, спе́шка; **there was a ~ towards the exit** все бро́сились к вы́ходу; **the ~ of mice under the floor** возня́ мыше́й под по́лом.

● *v.i.* (*also* **~ about**) суетли́во бе́гать (*impf.*); снова́ть (*impf.*); **~ through one's work** на́спех проде́л|ывать, -ать рабо́ту.

● *with advs.*: **~ away, ~ off** *vv.i.* убе|га́ть, -жа́ть; (*disperse*) разбе|га́ться, -жа́ться.

scurvy /ˈskɜːvɪ/ *n.* цинга́.

scuttle[1] /ˈskʌt(ə)l/ *n.* (*for coal*) ведёрко/я́щик для у́гля́.

scuttle[2] /ˈskʌt(ə)l/ *n.* (*hurried flight*) стреми́тельное бе́гство.

● *v.i.* ю́ркнуть (*pf.*); снова́ть (*impf.*).

scuttle[3] /ˈskʌt(ə)l/ *v.t.* (*sink*) топи́ть, по-; затоп|ля́ть, -и́ть.

scythe /saɪð/ *n.* коса́.

● *v.t.* коси́ть, с-.

Scythian /ˈsɪðɪən/ *n.* скиф (*fem.* -ка).

● *adj.* ски́фский.

SDI (*abbr. of* ***strategic defense initiative***) СОИ (Стратеги́ческая оборо́нная инициати́ва).

sea /siː/ *n.* мо́ре; **at ~** (*lit.*) в мо́ре; **he is at ~** он нахо́дится в пла́вании; **(all) at ~** (*fig.*) озада́чен, растя́рян (*pred.*); в недоуме́нии; **he is at ~** он ничего́ не понима́ет, он растя́рян; **beyond the ~** за́ морем; **by ~** мо́рем; **by the ~** у мо́ря, на мо́ре; **go to ~** (*become a sailor*) идти́ (*det.*), пойти́ (*pf.*) в моряки́; **on the ~** (*in ship*) в мо́ре; **ships sail on the ~** корабли́ пла́вают по́ морю; (*situated on coast*) на мо́ре/побере́жье; **put to ~** (*of ship*) выходи́ть, вы́йти в мо́ре; **on the high ~s** в откры́том мо́ре; **inland ~** закры́тое мо́ре; **a heavy ~** си́льное волне́ние; (*wave*) больша́я волна́; **half ~s over** (*drunk*) вы́пивши, под му́хой (*coll.*); **a ~ of faces** мо́ре лиц; (*attr.*): **~ air** морско́й во́здух; **~ journey, voyage, trip** морско́е путеше́ствие; **S~ Lord** морско́й лорд (*член главного морского штаба*); **~ mile** морска́я ми́ля; **~ power** морска́я мощь; (*nation*) морска́я держа́ва.

● *cpds.* **~-anchor** *n.* плаву́чий я́корь; **~-anemone** *n.* акти́ния; **~ bass** *n.* ка́менный о́кунь; **~-bathing** *n.* морски́е купа́ния; **~-bed** *n.* морско́е дно; **~-bird** *n.* морска́я пти́ца; **~board** *n.* примо́рье; (*attr.*) примо́рский; **~-boat** *n.*: **a good ~-boat** су́дно с хоро́шими морехо́дными ка́чествами; **~-borne** *adj.* (*of trade*) морско́й; (*of goods*) перевози́мый мо́рем; **~-breeze** *n.* ве́тер с мо́ря; **~-captain** *n.* капита́н да́льнего пла́вания; **~-change** *n.* (радика́льное) преображе́ние; **~-chest** *n.* матро́сский сундучо́к; **~-coast** *n.* морско́й бе́рег; **~-cock** *n.* (*naut.*) кингсто́н, забо́ртный кла́пан; **~-cow** *n.* морж; **~-cucumber** *n.* морско́й огуре́ц; **~-dog** *n.* (*old sailor*) (ста́рый) морско́й волк; **~-elephant** *n.* морско́й слон; **~farer** *n.* морепла́ватель (*m.*); **~faring** *n.* морепла́вание; *adj.* морехо́дный; **~faring (*also* ~going) man** моря́к, морепла́ватель (*m.*); **~-fish** *n.* морска́я ры́ба; **~-fog** *n.* тума́н, иду́щий с мо́ря; **~food** *n.* морски́е проду́кты (*m. pl.*); **~food restaurant** ры́бный ресторá́н; **~-front** *n.* примо́рский бульва́р, на́бережная; **~going** *adj.* (*of ship*) морехо́дный; (*of person*) = **~faring; ~-green** *adj.* цве́та морско́й волны́; **~gull** *n.* ча́йка; **~-horse** *n.* морско́й конёк; **~-kale** *n.* морска́я капу́ста; **~-lane** *n.* морско́й путь; (*pl.*) морски́е коммуника́ции (*f. pl.*); **~-lawyer** *n.* приди́ра (*c.g.*), критика́н; **~-legs** *n. pl.*: **find, get one's ~legs** прив|ыка́ть, -ы́кнуть к ка́чке; **~-level** *n.* у́ровень (*m.*) мо́ря; **~-lion** *n.* морско́й лев; **~man** *n.* моря́к, матро́с; **able ~man** матро́с; **~manship** *n.* иску́сство морепла́вания; **practical ~manship** морска́я пра́ктика; **~-mark** *n.* навигацио́нный знак; ориенти́р на берегу́; **~plane** *n.* гидросамолёт; **~port** *n.* морско́й порт; портo̍вый го́род; **~-salt** *n.* морска́я соль; **~scape** *n.* морско́й пейза́ж, мари́на; **~-scout** *n.* морско́й ска́ут; **~-serpent** *n.* (*myth.*) морско́й змей; **~-shell** *n.* морска́я ра́ковина; **~-shore** *n.* морско́й бе́рег, взмо́рье; **~sick** *adj.*: **I was ~sick** меня́ укача́ло; **~sickness** *n.* морска́я боле́знь; **~side** *n.* морско́е побере́жье; **we stayed at the ~side** мы жи́ли на мо́ре/взмо́рье; **he likes the ~side** он лю́бит е́здить на мо́ре; *adj.* примо́рский; **a ~side resort** морско́й куро́рт; **~ trout** *n.* (*Br.*) ло́сось-тайме́нь (*m.*); **~-urchin** *n.* морско́й ёж; **~-wall** *n.* сте́нка на́бережной, волнобо́йная сте́нка; **~-water** *n.* морска́я вода́; **~-way** *n.* (*inland waterway*) судохо́дное ру́сло; фарва́тер; вну́тренний во́дный путь; **~weed** *n.* морска́я во́доросль; **~worthiness** *n.* морехо́дность, го́дность к пла́ванию; **~worthy** *adj.* морехо́дный, го́дный к пла́ванию.

seal[1] /siːl/ *n.* (*zool.*) тюле́нь (*m.*); **(fur-~)** ко́тик.

● *v.i.* охо́титься (*impf.*) на тюле́ней.

● *cpd.* **~skin** *n.* тюле́ний/ко́тиковый мех.

seal[2] /siːl/ *n.* **1** (*on document etc.*) печа́ть; **wax ~** сургу́чная печа́ть; **leaden ~** пло́мба; **affix, set one's ~ to something** ста́вить, по- свою́ печа́ть на что-н.; **set the ~ on** заверш|а́ть, -и́ть; **he set the ~ of approval on our action** он одо́брил/санкциони́ровал на́ши де́йствия; **~ of confession** та́йна и́споведи.

2 (*gem, stamp etc. for ~ing*) печа́тка.

● *v.t.* **1** (*affix ~ to*) при|кла́дывать, -ложи́ть печа́ть к + *d.*; **the treaty has been signed and ~ed** догово́р подпи́сан и скреплён печа́тями; **~ed orders** секре́тный прика́з; **~ing-wax** сургу́ч.

2 (*confirm*): **~ a bargain** закреп|ля́ть, -и́ть сде́лку.

3 (*close securely; stop up*) запеча́т|ывать, -ать; пло́тно/на́глухо закр|ыва́ть, -ы́ть; **a ~ed envelope** запеча́танный конве́рт; **they ~ed (up) all the windows** они́ зама́зали/заде́лали все о́кна; **the police ~ed off all exits from the square** поли́ция отре́зала/загороди́ла все вы́ходы с пло́щади (*or* оцепи́ла пло́щадь); **my lips are ~ed** у меня́ запеча́таны уста́.

4 (*set mark on; destine*) нал|ага́ть, -ожи́ть печа́ть на + *a.*; **his fate is ~ed** его́ у́часть решена́.

sealer /ˈsiːlə(r)/ *n.* (*person*) охо́тник на тюле́ней; (*ship*) зверобо́йное су́дно.

sealery /ˈsiːlərɪ/ *n.* тюле́нье ле́жбище.

seam /siːm/ *n.* шов, рубе́ц; **burst at the ~s** ло́п|аться, -нуть по шва́м; **come apart at the ~s** (*lit., fig.*) треща́ть (*impf.*) по шва́м; (*geol.*) пласт.

● *v.t.* сшива́ть, сшить; **~ed stockings** чулки́ со швом; **a face ~ed with lines** лицо́, изборождённое морщи́нами.

seamless /ˈsiːmlɪs/ *adj.* без шва; из одного́ куска́; **~ stockings** чулки́ без шва.

seamstress, sempstress /ˈsemstrɪs/ *nn.* швея́.

seamy /ˈsiːmɪ/ *adj.* **(seamier, seamiest): the ~ side of life** изна́нка/суро́вая пра́вда жи́зни.

seance /ˈseɪɑ̃s/ *n.* спирити́ческий сеа́нс.

sear /sɪə(r)/ *v.t.* (*scorch*) опал|я́ть, -и́ть; (*cauterize*) приж|ига́ть, -е́чь; **~ing heat** паля́щий зной; **~ing pain** жгу́чая боль.

search /sɜːtʃ/ *n.* **1** (*quest, also comput.*) по́иск (*usu. pl.*); **make a ~ for s.o./sth.** иска́ть (*impf.*) кого́-н./что-н.; **a man in ~ of a wife** мужчи́на, и́щущий себе́ жену́; **he went in ~ of his wife** он пошёл иска́ть жену́.

2 (*examination*) о́быск; **the police carried out a ~ of the house** поли́ция произвела́ в до́ме о́быск.

● *v.t.* **1** (*examine*) обы́ск|ивать, -а́ть; пров|оди́ть, -ести́ осмо́тр + *g.*; **we were ~ed at the airport** мы прошли́ осмо́тр в аэропорту́; (*rummage through*) обша́ри|вать, -ть; **I ~ed every drawer for my notes** я обша́рил/переры́л все я́щики в по́исках свои́х заме́ток.

2 (*peer at, scan*) обв|оди́ть, -ести́ взгля́дом; **he ~ed my face** он испыту́юще на меня́ посмотре́л.

3 (*fig., scrutinize*): **~ your memory!** напряги́те свою́ па́мять!; **I ~ed my conscience** я спроси́л свою́ со́весть.

4 (*penetrate*) прон|ика́ть, -и́кнуть; **~ing questions** подро́бные вопро́сы; **a ~ing enquiry** тща́тельное рассле́дование.

5: **~ me!** (*coll.*) я почём зна́ю!; поня́тия не име́ю!

S

● *v.i.* искáть (*impf.*); (*of police, customs*) пров|оди́ть, -ести́ о́быск; ~ **after, for** искáть (*impf.*), разы́скивать (*impf.*); ~ **out** (*find*) отыскáть, разыскáть, обнару́жить (*all pf.*); ~ **through** просм|áтривать, -отрéть; **I ~ed through my desk for the letter** я переры́л весь пи́сьменный стол в по́исках письмá; **he ~ed through all his papers for the contract** он переры́л/перебрáл все свои́ бумáги в по́исках договóра.

● *cpds.* ~ **engine** *n.* (*comput.*) по́исковая систéма; **~light** *n.* прожéктор; **~-party** *n.* по́исковая пáртия/гру́ппа; **~-warrant** *n.* о́рдер на о́быск.

searcher /ˈsɜːtʃə(r)/ *n.* искáтель (*fem.* -ница).

season /ˈsiːz(ə)n/ *n.* **1** сезóн; (*of year*) врéмя гóда; **the four ~s** четы́ре врéмени гóда; **summer/winter ~** лéтний/зи́мний сезóн; **in the rainy ~** в сезóн дождéй; **compliments of the ~!** с прáздником!; **strawberries are in ~** сейчáс сезóн клубни́ки; **blackberries are out of ~** ежеви́ке сейчáс не сезóн; **at the height of the ~** в разгáр сезóна; **holiday ~** сезóн отпускóв; **close/open ~** врéмя, когдá охóта запрещенá/разрешенá; (*period*) пери́од, порá.
2 (*Br.*) (*also* **~ ticket**) сезóнный/проезднóй билéт; (*for concerts etc.*) абонемéнт.

● *v.t.* **1** (*mature*: *of timber, wine etc.*) вы́держивать, вы́держать.
2 (*acclimatize, inure*) приуч|áть, -и́ть; **he ~ed himself to cold** он приучи́л себя́ к хóлоду; **a ~ed traveller** (*Br.*), **traveler** (*US*) о́пытный путешéственник; **~ed troops** о́пытные войскá.
3 (*spice*) припр|авля́ть, -áвить; **a highly ~ed dish** óстрое (*or* óчень пикáнтное) блю́до.

seasonable /ˈsiːzənəb(ə)l/ *adj.* (*suited to the season*) соотвéтствующий сезóну; (*opportune*) своеврéменный.

seasonal /ˈsiːzən(ə)l/ *adj.* сезóнный.

seasoning /ˈsiːzənɪŋ/ *n.* (*cul.*) припрáва; (*of timber, wine*) вы́держивание.

seat /siːt/ *n.* **1** сидéнье; (*chair*) стул; (*bench*) скамья́, скамéйка.
2 (*place in vehicle, theatre etc.*) мéсто; **take one's ~** зан|имáть, -я́ть мéсто; **please take a ~!** сади́тесь, пожáлуйста!; **keep one's ~** ост|авáться, -áться на мéсте; **keep my ~ for me!** посторожи́те моё мéсто!; **he booked a ~** он заказáл билéт; **take a back ~** (*fig.*) от|ходи́ть, -ойти́ на зáдний план.
3 (*of chair*) сидéнье; **the ~ of the chair fell through** у сту́ла провали́лось сидéнье.
4 (*backside*) зад; (*of trousers*) зад (у) брю́к; **he wore out the ~ of his trousers** он просидéл брю́ки.
5 (*site, location, headquarters*): **~ of government** резидéнция прави́тельства; **~ of war** теáтр воéнных дéйствий; **~ of learning** нау́чный центр.
6 (*mansion*) помéстье, имéние.
7 (*Br., parl.*) мéсто (в парлáменте); **have a ~ in parliament** быть в парлáменте, быть члéном парлáмента; **lose one's ~** терять, по- мéсто (в парлáменте); **he has a ~ on the committee** он член комитéта.
8: **he has a good ~ on a horse** у негó хорóшая посáдка.

● *v.t.* **1** (*make sit*) сажáть, посади́ть; **~ o.s.** сади́ться, сесть; ус|áживаться, -éсться; **be ~ed!** сади́тесь!; прошу́ сади́ться; **he remained ~ed** он продолжáл сидéть; **I found them ~ed round the fire** я нашёл их сидя́щими вокру́гками́на.
2 (*provide with ~s*) вме|щáть, -сти́ть; **the hall ~s over a thousand** зал вмещáет бóльше ты́сячи человéк; **this table ~s twelve** за э́тот стол мóжно посади́ть двенáдцать человéк.

● *cpd.* **~-belt** *n.* привязнóй ремéнь.

seating /ˈsiːtɪŋ/ *n.* **1** (*allocation of places*) рассáживание; (*placing at table*) размещéние гостéй за столóм; **the ~ arrangements were inadequate** мест не хватáло. **2** (*seats*) (сидя́чие) местá; **~ capacity** числó сидя́чих мест.

SEATO /ˈsiːtəʊ/ *n.* (*abbr. of* ***South-East Asia Treaty Organization***) СЕАТО (Организáция договóра Юго-Востóчной Áзии).

seaward /ˈsiːwəd/ *adj.* (*of breeze etc.*) береговóй.

● *adv.* (*also* **~s, to ~**) к мóрю.

sebaceous /sɪˈbeɪʃəs/ *adj.* сáльный.

sec. /ˈsekənd(z)/ *n.* (*abbr. of* ***second(s)***) сек. (секу́нда).

secateurs /ˌsekəˈtɜːz/ *n. pl.* (*Br.*) садóвые нóжниц|ы (*pl., g.* —); секáтор.

secede /sɪˈsiːd/ *v.i.* отдел|я́ться, -и́ться; выходи́ть, вы́йти (из + *g.*).

secession /sɪˈseʃ(ə)n/ *n.* отделéние (от + *g.*); вы́ход (из + *g.*).

secessionist /sɪˈseʃənɪst/ *n.* сепарати́ст.

seclude /sɪˈkluːd/ *v.t.*: **~ o.s. from society** удал|я́ться, -и́ться от óбщества; **a ~d life** уединённая жизнь; **a ~d spot** уединённый/укрóмный уголóк.

seclusion /sɪˈkluːʒ(ə)n/ *n.* уединéние, изоля́ция; **live in ~** жить (*impf.*) в уединéнии.

second[1] /ˈsekənd/ *n.* **1** вторóй; **you are the ~ to ask me that** вы ужé вторóй человéк, котóрый меня́ об э́том спроси́л/спрáшивает; **~ in command** замести́тель (*m.*) команди́ра; **on the ~ of May** вторóго мáя; **he came (in) a good ~** (*in race*) он пришёл к фи́нишу почти́ одноврéменно с пéрвым; (*Br., honours degree*) диплóм вторóй стéпени.
2 (*in duel, boxing etc.*) секундáнт.
3 (*pl., imperfect goods*) второсóртный/бракóванный товáр; **these plates are ~s** э́ти тарéлки бракóванные.
4 (*measure of time or angle, also mus.*) секу́нда; **wait a ~!** однý секу́нду!; **~(s) hand** (*of clock*) секу́ндная стрéлка.

● *adj.* вторóй; (*other*) другóй; **Charles the S~** Карл Вторóй; **on the ~ (*US* third) floor** на трéтьем этажé; **the ~ largest city** вторóй по величинé гóрод; **~ nature** вторáя натýра; **he came in ~** он зáнял вторóе мéсто; **in the ~ place** во-вторы́х; **for the ~ time** втори́чно, вторóй раз; (*additional*) добáвочный; **~ chamber** вéрхняя палáта; **~ helping** добáвка; **France was a ~ home to him** Фрáнция былá емý (*or* для негó) вторóй рóдиной; **~ name** (*Br.*) фами́лия; **he has ~ sight** он ясновидец; **have ~ thoughts** передýмать, раздýмать (*both pf.*); **I am having ~ thoughts** я начинáю колебáться; **on ~ thoughts** поразмы́слив; по зрéлом размышлéнии; **do, say something a ~ time** повтор|я́ть, -и́ть что-н.; **get one's ~ wind** обре|тáть, -сти́ вторóе дыхáние; (*subordinate; comparable*): **~ to none** непревзойдённый; **he is ~ to none** он никомý не устýпит; **their taste is ~ to none** у них непревзойдённый вкус; **~ cousin** троюродный брат (*fem.* троюродная сестрá); **play ~ fiddle** игрáть (*impf.*) вторýю скри́пку; **learn something at ~ hand** узн|авáть, -áть что-н. понаслы́шке; **~ lieutenant** млáдший лейтенáнт; **~ officer** помóщник капитáна; **the ~ violins** вторы́е скри́пки.

● *v.t.* (*support*) поддéрж|ивать, -áть.

● *cpds.* **~-best** *adj.* не сáмый лýчший; (*inferior*) второсóртный; *adv.*: **come off ~-best** терпéть, по- поражéние; **~-class** *n.* (*Br., degree*) диплóм вторóй стéпени; (*of travel*) вторóй класс; *adj.*: **~-class cabin** каю́та вторóго клáсса; **~-class citizens** грáждане вторóго сóрта; *adv.*: **we travel ~-class** мы éздим вторы́м клáссом; **~-generation** *adj.* вторóго поколéния; **~ hand** *n. see* ⇒**second** *n.* 4; *adj.* (*previously used*) подéржанный; **~-hand bookshop** букинисти́ческий магази́н; (*indirect*): **~-hand information** информáция из вторы́х рук; *adv.*: **I bought the car ~-hand** я купи́л подéржанную маши́ну; **~-rate** *adj.* (*of goods*) второсóртный; (*mediocre*) посрéдственный; **~-rater** *n.* посрéдственность.

second[2] /sɪˈkɒnd/ *v.t.* (*Br., mil., admin.*) командировáть, от-.

secondary /ˈsekəndərɪ/ *adj.* **1** (*less important, not primary*) втори́чный; (*school, education*) срéдний.
2 (*subordinate*) второстепéнный.

seconder /ˈsekəndə(r)/ *n.* тот, кто поддéрживает предложéние, кандидатýру, *и т.п.*

secondly /ˈsekəndlɪ/ *adv.* во-вторы́х.

secondment /sɪˈkɒndmənt/ *n.* (*Br.*) командирóвка.

secrecy /ˈsiːkrɪsɪ/ *n.* тáйна; (*of document*) секрéтность; **he swore me to ~** он взял с меня́ кля́тву/слóво молчáть.

secret /ˈsiːkrɪt/ *n.* секрéт, тáйна; **keep a ~** храни́ть, со- секрéт; **let s.o. into a ~** посвя|щáть, -ти́ть когó-н. в тáйну; **he has no ~s from me** у негó нет секрéтов от меня́; **I make no ~ of it** я э́того не скрывáю; **state ~**

госуда́рственная та́йна; **open ~** всем изве́стный секре́т, секре́т полишине́ля; **in ~** секре́тно, та́йно; **the ~ of success is to keep on trying** секре́т успе́ха в упо́рстве.

● *adj.* секре́тный, та́йный; **top ~** (*as inscription*) соверше́нно секре́тно; **keep something ~** держа́ть (*impf.*) что-н. в та́йне; **~ agent** та́йный аге́нт, разве́дчик; **~ ballot** та́йное голосова́ние; **~ police** та́йная поли́ция; **~ service** секре́тная слу́жба; разве́дка; **the court met in ~ session** суде́бное заседа́ние происходи́ло за закры́тыми дверя́ми; **~ sign** секре́тный знак; **~ society** та́йное о́бщество; (*hidden*) потайно́й, секре́тный; **~ staircase** потайна́я ле́стница; (*remote*) укро́мный; (*undisclosed*): **my ~ ambition** моя́ сокрове́нная мечта́; **I was ~ly glad to see him** в глубине́ души́ я был рад его́ ви́деть.

secretarial /ˌsekrɪˈteərɪəl/ *adj.* секрета́рский.

secretariat /ˌsekrɪˈteərɪət/ *n.* секрстариа́т.

secretary /ˈsekrɪtərɪ/, /ˈsekrətrɪ/ *n.* секрета́р|ь (*fem., coll., typist etc.* -ша); **permanent (under-)~** постоя́нный замести́тель (*m.*) мини́стра; **S~-General** Генера́льный секрета́рь; **S~ of State** (*UK*) мини́стр; (*US*) госуда́рственный секрета́рь, мини́стр иностра́нных дел.

secretaryship /ˈsekrɪtərɪʃɪp/, /ˈsekrətrɪʃɪp/ *n.* до́лжность секретаря́.

secrete /sɪˈkri:t/ *v.t.* **1** (*physiol. etc.*) выделя́ть, вы́делить. **2** (*conceal*) укр|ыва́ть, -ы́ть; пря́тать, с-; **~ o.s.** укр|ыва́ться, -ы́ться; пря́таться, с-.

secretion /sɪˈkri:ʃ(ə)n/ *n.* выделе́ние, секре́ция.

secretive /ˈsi:krɪtɪv/ *adj.* скры́тный, за́мкнутый; **he was ~ about his job** он ничего́ не (*or* ма́ло) расска́зывал о свое́й рабо́те.

secretiveness /ˈsi:krɪtɪvnɪs/ *n.* скры́тность.

sect /sekt/ *n.* се́кта.

sectarian /sekˈteərɪən/ *n.* секта́нт (*fem.* -ка).

● *adj.* секта́нтский.

sectarianism /sekˈteərɪəˌnɪz(ə)m/ *n.* секта́нтство.

section /ˈsekʃ(ə)n/ *n.* **1** (*separate or distinct part*) се́кция; **built in ~s** сбо́рный, разбо́рный; (*severed portion*) кусо́к; **~ of the day** часть дня; **~ of the population** часть населе́ния; **~ of a journey** эта́п пути́; **~ of a book/speech** разде́л кни́ги/ре́чи; (*mil.*) отделе́ние; (*department*) отде́л, отделе́ние; (*segment of fruit*) до́лька; (*~-mark, i.e.* §) пара́граф. **2** (*geom. etc.*) разре́з; **~ drawing** чертёж в разре́зе; сече́ние. **3** (*microscopic ~*) срез. **4** (*surg.*) сече́ние.

sectional /ˈsekʃən(ə)l/ *adj.* **1** секцио́нный. **2** (*pert. to a section of the community etc.*) группово́й. **3** (*made in parts*) сбо́рный, разбо́рный, составно́й. **4**: **~ arrangement of material** распределе́ние материа́ла по отде́лам. **5** (*of drawings, plans etc.*) в разре́зе; **~ elevation** разре́з.

sector /ˈsektə(r)/ *n.* **1** (*geom.*) се́ктор. **2** (*mil., rail. etc.*) уча́сток. **3** (*econ.*): **the public/private ~** обще́ственный/ча́стный се́ктор.

secular /ˈsekjʊlə(r)/ *adj.* (*this-worldly*) мирско́й; **~ affairs** мирски́е дела́; (*non-ecclesiastical, lay*) све́тский; **~ education** све́тское образова́ние.

secularism /ˈsekjʊlərˌɪz(ə)m/ *n.* секуляри́зм.

secularization /ˌsekjʊləraɪˈzeɪʃ(ə)n/ *n.* секуляриза́ция.

secularize /ˈsekjʊləˌraɪz/ *v.t.* секуляризова́ть (*impf., pf.*).

secure /sɪˈkjʊə(r)/ *adj.* **1** (*free from care*) споко́йный; **feel ~ about something** не беспоко́иться (*impf.*) о чём-н.; **he left, ~ in the knowledge that I would support him** он ушёл, уве́ренный в мое́й подде́ржке. **2** (*safe*) про́чный, надёжный; **the bridge did not seem ~** мост не каза́лся/представля́лся надёжным/про́чным; **the doors are ~** две́ри надёжны; **the ladder is ~** ле́стница стои́т про́чно; **the town was ~ against attack** го́род был хорошо́ защищён от нападе́ния; (*reliable*) надёжный; **make ~** закреп|ля́ть, -и́ть; (*assured*): **a ~ income** обеспе́ченный/ве́рный дохо́д; (*well founded*): **a ~ assumption** обосно́ванное предположе́ние.

● *v.t.* **1** (*make safe or fast*) закреп|ля́ть, -и́ть; застрахо́в|ывать, -ать; убер|ега́ть, -е́чь; **~ a town against assault** укреп|ля́ть, -и́ть оборо́ну го́рода; **~ a prisoner** свя́з|ывать, -а́ть пле́нного. **2** (*guarantee, insure*) страхова́ть, за-; **he ~d himself against every risk** он застрахова́л себя́ от вся́кого ри́ска. **3** (*obtain*) дост|ава́ть, -а́ть; заруч|а́ться, -и́ться + *i.*

security /sɪˈkjʊərɪtɪ/ *n.* **1** (*safety*) безопа́сность; **~ against attack** защищённость от нападе́ния; **~ device** предохрани́тель (*m.*); **S~ Council** Сове́т Безопа́сности; **~ forces** си́лы безопа́сности; **~ guard** охра́нник, секью́рити (*indecl.*); **he is a ~ risk** он неблагонадёжен; **I feel a sense of ~ in his presence** его́ прису́тствие даёт мне чу́вство уве́ренности/защищённости. **2** (*safeguard, guarantee*) гара́нтия. **3** (*pledge, promise*) зало́г, гара́нтия; **~ for a loan** гара́нтия за́йма; закла́д; (*of person*) поручи́тель (*m.*). **4** (*pl., bonds*) це́нные бума́ги (*f. pl.*).

sedan /sɪˈdæn/ *n.* (**~ chair**) паланки́н; (*US, saloon car*) седа́н.

sedate[1] /sɪˈdeɪt/ *adj.* степе́нный, уравнове́шенный.

sedate[2] /sɪˈdeɪt/ *v.t.* да|ва́ть, -ть успокои́тельное + *d.*

sedateness /sɪˈdeɪtnɪs/ *n.* степе́нность.

sedation /sɪˈdeɪʃ(ə)n/ *n.* успокое́ние; **under ~** под де́йствием успокои́тельных.

sedative /ˈsedətɪv/ *n.* успокои́тельное (сре́дство); (*sleeping drug*) снотво́рное (сре́дство).

● *adj.* успока́ивающий, успокои́тельный; **have a ~ effect** де́йствовать, по- успока́ивающе.

sedentary /ˈsedəntərɪ/ *adj.* (*of posture etc.*) сидя́чий; **a ~ way of life** сидя́чий о́браз жи́зни; (*of person*) неподви́жный, малоподви́жный.

sedge /sedʒ/ *n.* осо́ка.

● *cpd.* **~-warbler** *n.* камышо́вка-барсучо́к.

sediment /ˈsedɪmənt/ *n.* оса́док, отсто́й.

sedimentary /ˌsedɪˈmentərɪ/ *adj.* оса́дочный.

sedimentation /ˌsedɪmenˈteɪʃ(ə)n/ *n.* (*process*) осажде́ние; отложе́ние оса́дка; (*sediment*) оса́док.

sedition /sɪˈdɪʃ(ə)n/ *n.* подстрека́тельство к мятежу́.

seditious /sɪˈdɪʃəs/ *adj.* мяте́жный, подстрека́тельский.

seduce /sɪˈdju:s/ *v.t.* **1** (*lead astray*) соблазн|я́ть, -и́ть; оболь|ща́ть, -сти́ть; **he was ~d by wealth** он польсти́лся на бога́тство. **2** (*a woman*) совра|ща́ть, -ти́ть; соблазн|я́ть, -и́ть.

seducer /sɪˈdju:sə(r)/ *n.* соблазни́тель (*m.*); обольсти́тель (*m.*), соврати́тель (*m.*).

seduction /sɪˈdʌkʃ(ə)n/ *n.* (*act of ~*) обольще́ние, совраще́ние; (*temptation, enticement*) собла́зн.

seductive /sɪˈdʌktɪv/ *adj.* соблазни́тельный; **~ smile** обольсти́тельная улы́бка.

seductiveness /sɪˈdʌktɪvnɪs/ *n.* соблазни́тельность.

seductress /sɪˈdʌktrɪs/ *n.* обольсти́тельница.

sedulous /ˈsedjʊləs/ *adj.* (*diligent*) приле́жный, усе́рдный; (*painstaking*) тща́тельный.

sedulousness /ˈsedjʊləsnɪs/ *n.* прилежа́ние, усе́рдие; тща́тельность.

see[1] /si:/ *n.* (*territory*) епа́рхия; (*office*) ка́федра; **the Holy S~** па́пский престо́л.

see[2] /si:/ *v.t.* (*past* **saw;** *p.p.* **seen**) **1** ви́деть; **nothing could be ~n** ничего́ не́ было ви́дно; **the house cannot be ~n from the road** дом с доро́ги не ви́ден/ви́дно; **he is not to be ~n** его́ не вида́ть (*coll.*)/ви́дно; **nothing was ~n of him** о нём не́ было ни слу́ху ни ду́ху; **I saw her arrive** я ви́дел, как она прие́хала; **I saw him approach(ing) the house** я ви́дел, как он подходи́л к до́му; **did you ~ anyone leaving?** вы ви́дели, что́бы кто́-нибудь выходи́л?; **I have never ~n such a thing** ничего́ подо́бного я никогда́ не ви́дел; **I never saw such rudeness** я в жи́зни не встреча́л таку́ю гру́бость; **~ red** (*coll.*) взбеси́ться (*pf.*); прийти́ (*pf.*) в я́рость/бе́шенство; **I thought I was ~ing things** мне каза́лось, что у меня́ галлюцина́ции; **I ~ things differently now** я тепе́рь ина́че смотрю́ на ве́щи; (*in newspaper etc.*): **I ~ our team has won** я ви́жу, на́ша кома́нда победи́ла. **2** (*look at, watch*) смотре́ть, по- на + *a.*;

S

осм|áтривать, -отрéть; ~ **p. 4** см. стр. 4; **let me ~ that** дáйте мне на э́то посмотрéть/взглянýть; **let me ~ your letter** покажи́те мне/дáйте посмотрéть вáше письмó; **the film is worth ~ing** э́тот фильм стóит посмотрéть; ~ **what you've done!** смотри́те, что вы наделáли!; ~ **the sights** осм|áтривать, -отрéть достопримечáтельности; **we saw Hamlet yesterday** мы вчерá ви́дели «Гáмлета».
3 (*experience*): **he has ~n life** (*or* **the world**) он видáл ви́ды; **the house has ~n many changes** дом претерпéл/повидáл мнóго перемéн; **she will never ~ 50 again** ей перевали́ло за пятьдеся́т; **I thought I would never (live to) ~ the day when ...** я не дýмал, что доживý до тогó дня, когдá. . ..
4 (*imagine*) предст|авля́ть, -áвить себé (*что*); **can you ~ him apologizing?** мóжете себé представить егó прося́щим извинéния?
5 (*ascertain by looking*; *find out*) посмотрéть (*pf.*), узн|авáть, -áть, выясня́ть, вы́яснить; ~ **for o.s.** убе|ждáться, -ди́ться самомý/ли́чно; **(go and) ~ who it is** (пойди́те) посмотри́те, кто там; **shall I ~ if I can help them?** пойти́ (мне) узнáть, нáдо ли им помóчь?; **I'll ~ if I can get tickets** я посмотрю́, смогý ли я достáть билéты; **that remains to be ~n** посмóтрим; э́то ещё не извéстно.
6 (*discern, comprehend*) ви́деть, у-; пон|имáть, -я́ть; **as I ~ it** по-мóему; на мой взгляд; **he saw his mistake at once** он срáзу же уви́дел/пóнял свою́ оши́бку; **I ~ how it is** мне поня́тно, как обстоя́т делá; **I don't ~ what good that is** я не ви́жу, какáя от э́того пóльза; **as far as I can ~** наскóлько я понимáю; **what does he ~ in her?** что тóлько он в ней ви́дит/нахóдит?; **(do) you ~?** (вы) понимáете?; **you ~, I was an only child** ви́дите ли, я был еди́нственным ребёнком; **don't you ~?** неужéли вы не ви́дите/понимáете?; **from this it can be ~n** из э́того ви́дно/слéдует; **it can be ~n at a glance** э́то ви́дно/я́сно с пéрвого взгля́да; **so I ~** сам ви́жу; понимáю.
7 (*consider*) дýмать, по-; **I'll ~** я подýмаю; посмóтрим; **let me ~!** погоди́те/постóйте!; **~ing that ...** ввидý тогó, что. . .; поскóльку. . .; так как. . ..
8 (*come across, meet*) ви́деть, у-; встр|ечáть, -éтить; (*associate*) ви́деться (*impf.*), встречáться (*impf.*) (*с кем*); **they stopped ~ing each other** они́ разошли́сь (*or* перестáли встречáться); (*visit*) посе|щáть, -ти́ть; наве|щáть, -сти́ть; **we went to ~ our friends** мы навести́ли нáших друзéй; **come and ~ me, us sometime** заходи́те кáк-нибудь; **(I'll) be ~ing you!** до скóрого!; покá! (*coll.*); ~ **you on Tuesday!** до втóрника!
9 (*interview, consult*): **I went to ~ him about a job** я пошёл к немý поговори́ть о рабóте; **can I ~ you for a moment?** мóжно вас на минýтку?; **you should ~ a doctor** вам слéдует обрати́ться к врачý; **he went to ~ a lawyer** он пошёл посовéтоваться/поговори́ть с адвокáтом; (*receive*; *grant interview to*) прин|имáть, -я́ть; **the doctor will ~ you now** дóктор при́мет вас сейчáс.
10 (*escort, conduct*) прово|жáть, -ди́ть; **he saw her to the door** он проводи́л её до двéри; **I saw her across the road** я перевёл её чéрез ýлицу; (*provide for*): **£5 should ~ you to the end of the week** пяти́ фýнтов должнó хвати́ть вам до концá недéли; **she saw him through college** онá помоглá емý окóнчить университéт.
11 (*ensure*) следи́ть, про-; ~ **that it is done** проследи́те, чтóбы э́то бы́ло сдéлано/вы́полнено; ~ **(to it) that the door is locked** проследи́те, чтóбы зáперли дверь.

● *v.i.* (*past* **saw**; *p.p.* **seen**) **1** ви́деть (*impf.*); **can you ~ from where you are?** вам оттýда ви́дно?; **as far as the eye can ~** наскóлько ви́дит глаз; **he cannot ~** (*is blind*) он не ви́дит; он слеп; **~ing is believing** покá не уви́жу, неповéрю; **he will never be able to ~ again** он (окончáтельно) ослéп; **I am ~ing double** у меня́ в глазáх двои́тся; **go and ~ for yourself!** пойди́те и убеди́тесь сáми!; ~ **if you can ...** попрóбуйте. . .; **she could ~ into the future** онá умéла загля́дывать в бýдущее; **may I ~ inside?** мóжно заглянýть внутрь?; **they asked to ~ round the house** они́ проси́ли позволéния осмотрéть дом; **he could not ~ over the hedge** и́згородь заслоня́ла емý вид; **we saw through his tricks** мы раскуси́ли егó улóвки; ~ **through s.o.** раскýс|ывать, -и́ть когó-н.; ви́деть (*impf.*) когó-н. насквóзь; **I couldn't ~ to read** бы́ло сли́шком темнó(, чтóбы) читáть.
2 (*imper., look*): **~, here he comes!** смотри́те, вот он!
3 (*make provision*; *take care*; *give attention*) забóтиться, по- (*о чём*); (*arrange, organize*) забóтиться, по-; **I shall ~ about the luggage** я позабóчусь о багажé (*or* займýсь багажóм); **she ~s to the laundry** онá вéдает сти́ркой; сти́рка в её вéдении; **I have to ~ to the children** мне прихóдится забóтиться о дéтях; **the garden needs ~ing to** сáдом слéдует заня́ться; **I saw to it that ...** я позабóтился о том, чтóбы. . .; **he saw to it that I got the money** он позабóтился о том, чтóбы я получи́л дéньги.

● *with advs.*: ~ **back** *v.t.*: **as it was late I offered to ~ her back** так как бы́ло пóздно, я предложи́л проводи́ть её (домóй *и т.п.*); ~ **in** *v.t.* встр|ечáть, -éтить; **they came to ~ the boat in** они́ пришли́(, чтóбы) встрéтить парохóд; **we saw the New Year in** мы встрéтили Нóвый год; ~ **off** *v.t.* (*accompany*) прово|жáть, -ди́ть; **we saw them off at the station** мы проводи́ли их на пóезд; (*get the better of*) прев|осходи́ть, -зойти́; ~ **out** *v.t.* прово|жáть, -ди́ть до вы́хода; **I can ~ myself out** ≈ я сам найдý дорóгу; **he saw out** (*survived*) **all his children** он пережи́л всех свои́х детéй; ~ **through** *v.t.*: **who will ~ the job through?** кто доведёт дéло до концá?; **his courage will ~ him through** благодаря́ своемý мýжеству он вы́держит все испытáния.

● *cpd.* **~-through** *adj.* прозрáчный.

seed /si:d/ *n.* **1** (*lit., fig.*) сéмя (*nt.*); (*of apple, melon, sun-flower*) сéмечко; (*collect.*) семенá (*nt. pl.*); **sow ~(s) in the ground** сéять, по- семенá в грунт; **go, run to ~** (*lit.*) идти́, пойти́ на семенá; (*fig., of person*) сд|авáть, -áть.
2 (*sport*: **~ed player**) посéянный игрóк; **he is number 3 ~** он посéян трéтьим.

● *v.t.* **1** (*remove ~ from*) оч|ищáть, -и́стить от зёрнышек; **~ed raisins** изю́м без кóсточек.
2 (*sow or sprinkle with ~*) сéять, по-; зас|евáть, -éять; **a newly ~ed lawn** свежезасéянный газóн.
3 (*sport*) отбирáть, отобрáть; сéять, по-; **~ed player** = **seed** *n.* 2

● *v.i.* (*shed ~*) роня́ть (*impf.*) семенá.

● *cpds.* **~-bearing** *adj.* семянóсный; **~-bed** *n.* гряда́ с рассáдой; **~-box** *n.* я́щик для рассáды; **~-cake** *n.* печéнье/кекс с тми́ном; **~-corn** *n.* посевнóе зернó; **~-potatoes** *n.* семеннóй картóфель; **~sman** *n.* торгóвец семенáми.

seedless /ˈsi:dlɪs/ *adj.* бессемя́нный.

seedling /ˈsi:dlɪŋ/ *n.* сéянец; (*pl.*) рассáда (*collect.*).

seedy /ˈsi:dɪ/ *adj.* **(seedier, seediest)** (*shabby*) потрёпанный; **he looks ~** у негó невáжный вид; (*sleazy*) захудáлый; (*out of sorts*) не в фóрме; **I feel ~** я себя́ невáжно/парши́во чýвствую.

seek /si:k/ *v.t.* (*past and p.p.* **sought**) **1** (*look for*) искáть (*impf.*) + *a./g. of concrete/abstract object*; ~ **one's fortune** пытáть, по- счáстья; **~ing a better position** в пóисках лýчшего мéста; ~ **out** разыскáть (*pf.*); отыскáть (*pf.*); (*enquire into*) искáть (*impf.*); **they were ~ing the causes of cancer** они́ исслéдовали (*or* пытáлись обнарýжить) причи́ны рáка; (*ask for*): ~ **advice** проси́ть, по- совéта; обра|щáться, -ти́ться за совéтом; ~ **an explanation** трéбовать, по- объяснéния; ~ **pardon** добивáться/проси́ть (*impf.*) прощéния.
2 (*attempt*) старáться, по-; пытáться, по-; **they sought to kill him** они́ пытáлись уби́ть егó.

● *v.i.* (*past and p.p.* **sought**): ~ **after something** стреми́ться (*impf.*) к чемý-н.; **a sought-after person** (чрезвычáйно) популя́рная ли́чность; ~ **for something** искáть (*impf.*) что-н./чегó-н.

seeker /ˈsi:kə(r)/ *n.*: **an earnest ~ after truth** рéвностный искáтель и́стины.

seem /si:m/ *v.i.* казáться, по-; предст|авля́ться, -áвиться; **it ~s to me** мне кáжется; по-мóему; **I don't ~ to like him** почемý-то он мне не нрáвится; **I ~ed to hear a voice** мне показáлось, что я слы́шал чей-то гóлос; **it ~s like yesterday** как бýдто э́то бы́ло вчерá; **he is not what he ~s** он не такóй, каки́м кáжется; **she ~s young** онá вы́глядит мóлодо; **it ~s cold today** сегóдня, кáжется, хóлодно;

сегóдня как бýдто хóлодно; **he and I can't ~ to get on together** мы с ним чтó-то никáк не полáдим; **it would ~** по-ви́димому; казáлось бы; **so it ~s** кáжется так, как бýдто так; **so we are to get nothing, it ~s** итáк, кáжется/ выхóдит, мы ничегó не получим.

seeming /ˈsiːmɪŋ/ *adj.* (*apparent*) кáжущийся, внéшний; **a ~ friend** мни́мый друг; **~ly** по-ви́димому; как бýдто.

seemliness /ˈsiːmlɪnɪs/ *n.* прили́чие; (благо)пристóйность.

seemly /ˈsiːmlɪ/ *adj.* (**seemlier, seemliest**) подобáющий, прили́чный, пристóйный.

seen /siːn/ *p.p. of* ⇒**see²**

seep /siːp/ *v.i.* (*also* **~ out, through**) прос|áчиваться, -очи́ться; (*leak*) прот|екáть, -éчь.

seepage /ˈsiːpɪdʒ/ *n.* течь, утéчка, просáчивание.

seer /ˈsiːə(r)/, /sɪə(r)/ *n.* провúдец, прорóк.

seersucker /ˈsɪəˌsʌkə(r)/ *n.* лёгкая крéповая ткань.

seesaw /ˈsiːsɔː/ *n.* (доскá-)качéл|и (*pl., g.* -сй).

● *v.i.* (*play on* ~) качáться, по- на доскé/ качéлях; (*fig., oscillate*) колебáться (*impf.*).

seeth|e /siːð/ *v.i.* (*of liquids, and fig.*) бурли́ть (*impf.*); **the country is ~ing with discontent** странá бурли́т от недовóльства; **he ~ed with anger** он кипéл негодовáнием; **the streets were ~ing with people** ýлицы кишéли нарóдом.

segment *n.* /ˈsegmənt/ сегмéнт, отрéзок; (*of fruit*) дóлька.

● *v.t. & i.* /segˈment/ дели́ть(ся), раз- на сегмéнты.

segmentation /ˌsegmənˈteɪʃ(ə)n/ *n.* сегментáция.

segregate /ˈsegrɪˌgeɪt/ *v.t.* отдел|я́ть, -и́ть; раздел|я́ть, -и́ть; изоли́ровать (*impf., pf.*).

segregation /ˌsegrɪˈgeɪʃ(ə)n/ *n.* (*separation*) отделéние, изоля́ция; (*racial*) (рáсовая) сегрегáция.

segregationist /ˌsegrɪˈgeɪʃ(ə)nɪst/ *n.* сторóнник сегрегáции.

Seine /seɪn/ *n.* Сéна.

seine /seɪn/ *n.* кошелькóвый нéвод.

seismic /ˈsaɪzmɪk/ *adj.* сейсми́ческий.

seismograph /ˈsaɪzməˌgrɑːf/ *n.* сейсмóграф.

seismography /saɪzˈmɒgrəfɪ/ *n.* сейсмогрáфия.

seismological /ˌsaɪzməˈlɒdʒɪk(ə)l/ *adj.* сейсмологи́ческий.

seismometer /saɪzˈmɒmɪtə(r)/ *n.* сейсмóметр.

seizable /ˈsiːzəb(ə)l/ *adj.* (*of goods etc.*) подлежáщий конфискáции.

seize /siːz/ *v.t.* **1** (*grasp; lay hold of*) хватáть, схвати́ть; **he ~d the boy by the arm** он схвати́л мáльчика зá руку; **they ~d the thief** они́ схвати́ли вóра; **he ~d** (*hold of*) **the rope** он схвати́л (*or* ухвати́лся за) верёвку; (*fig., comprehend*) схв|áтывать, -ати́ть; **he ~d the point at once** он срáзу схвати́л суть дéла; (*fig., make use of*) ухв|áтываться, -ати́ться за + *a.*; **~ an opportunity** ухв|áтываться, -ати́ться за возмóжность; пóльзоваться, вос- слýчаем.
2 (*take possession of*) захвáт|ывать, -и́ть; брать, взять; (*fig., strike, affect*) охвáт|ывать, -и́ть; **he was ~d by a feeling of remorse** егó охвати́ло чýвство раскáяния.
3 (*impound, arrest*) нал|агáть, -ожи́ть арéст на + *a.*; конфисковáть (*impf., pf.*).

● *v.i.* **1**: **~ (up)on** ухв|áтываться, -ати́ться за + *a.*; **they ~d upon the chance** они́ ухвати́лись за предстáвившийся слýчай; **he ~d upon my remark** он придрáлся к моúм словáм.
2 (*jam; also* **~ up**) за|едáть, -éсть; застр|евáть, -я́ть.

seizure /ˈsiːʒə(r)/ *n.* (*capture*) захвáт; (*confiscation*) конфискáция; (*attack of illness*) при́ступ, припáдок; (*stroke*) удáр.

seldom /ˈseldəm/ *adv.* рéдко; **~ if ever** крáйне рéдко.

select /sɪˈlekt/ *adj.* и́збранный, элитáрный; **~ circles** и́збранные круги́; **~ committee** осóбый комитéт (*в парламенте*); **a ~ club** клуб для и́збранных, элитáрный клуб.

● *v.t.* выбирáть, вы́брать; от|бирáть, -обрáть; под|бирáть, -обрáть; (*by voting*) изб|ирáть, -рáть; **~ed works** и́збранные сочинéния.

selection /sɪˈlekʃ(ə)n/ *n.* **1** (*choice*) вы́бор; **make a ~ of** выбирáть, вы́брать (мéжду + *i.*); **there was a wide, great ~** был большóй вы́бор; (*biol.*): **natural ~** естéственный отбóр. **2** (*assortment*) подбóр, ассортимéнт; **a ~ of summer clothes** ассортимéнт лéтней одéжды.

selective /sɪˈlektɪv/ *adj.* (*choosing carefully*) разбóрчивый; (*partial, affecting some*) вы́борочный; (*radio*) селекти́вный; избирáтельный; **~ service** (*US*) вóинская пови́нность.

selectivity /ˌsɪlekˈtɪvɪtɪ/, /ˌsel-/, /ˌsiːl-/ *n.* разбóрчивость, избирáтельность.

selector /sɪˈlektə(r)/ *n.* **1** (*person*) отбóрщик, вы́борщик. **2** (*teleph.*) селéктор; **~ gear** селéкторный механи́зм; (*radio*) рýчка настрóйки; **band ~** переключáтель (*m.*) диапазóнов.

selenium /sɪˈliːnɪəm/ *n.* селéн.

self /self/ *n.* (*pl.* **selves**)
1 (*individuality, essence*) сýщность; (*personality*) ли́чность; (*ego*) (сóбственное) «я»; **his own, very ~** он сам; **I am not my former ~** я ужé не тот, что прéжде; **my other ~** моё вторóе «я». **2** (*one's own interest*): **he has no thought of ~** он не дýмает о себé. **3** (*comm.: o.s.*): **cheque** (*Br.*), **check** (*US*) **made out to '~'** чек, вы́писанный на сóбственное и́мя (*or* на себя́).

self- /self/ *comb. form* само…; себя́…; своé….

self-abasement /ˌselfəˈbeɪsmənt/ *n.* самоунижéние, самоуничижéние.

self-absorbed /ˌselfəbˈzɔːbd/ *adj.* поглощённый собóй.

self-abuse /ˌselfəˈbjuːs/ *n.* (*euph.*) онани́зм.

self-acting /selfˈæktɪŋ/ *adj.* автомати́ческий.

self-addressed /ˌselfəˈdrest/ *adj.* адресóванный на сóбственное и́мя; **~ envelope** конвéрт с обрáтным áдресом отправи́теля.

self-adhesive /ˌselfədˈhiːsɪv/ *adj.* самозаклéивающийся.

self-adjustment /ˌselfəˈdʒʌstmənt/ *n.* самонастрóйка.

self-admiration /selfˌædməˈreɪʃ(ə)n/ *n.* самолюбовáние.

self-advancement /ˌselfədˈvɑːnsmənt/ *n.* карьери́зм.

self-advertisement /ˌselfədˈvɜːtɪsmənt/ *n.* саморéклáма.

self-affirmation /selfˌæfəˈmeɪʃ(ə)n/ *n.* самоутверждéние.

self-aggrandizement /ˌselfəˈgrændɪzmənt/ *n.* самовозвели́чивание.

self-analysis /ˌselfəˈnæləsɪs/ *n.* самоанáлиз.

self-appointed /ˌselfəˈpɔɪntɪd/ *adj.* самозвáный.

self-assertion /ˌselfəˈsɜːʃ(ə)n/ *n.* самоутверждéние.

self-assertive /ˌselfəˈsɜːtɪv/ *adj.* самоувéренный.

self-assurance /ˌselfəˈʃʊərəns/ *n.* увéренность (в себé); (*pej.*) самоувéренность; самонадéянность.

self-assured /ˌselfəˈʃʊəd/ *adj.* (само)увéренный; самонадéянный.

self-awareness /ˌselfəˈweənɪs/ *n.* самосознáние.

self-catering /selfˈkeɪtərɪŋ/ *n.* (*Br.*): **~ apartment** жильё с самообслýживанием; **~ holiday** путёвка, включáющая жильё с самообслýживанием.

self-centred /selfˈsentəd/ (*US* **-centered**) *adj.* эгоцентри́чный.

self-centredness /selfˈsentədnɪs/ (*US* **-centeredness**) *n.* эгоцентри́чность.

self-coloured /selfˈkʌləd/ (*US* **-colored**) *adj.* одноцвéтный.

self-condemnation /selfˌkɒndemˈneɪʃ(ə)n/ *n.* самоосуждéние, самобичевáние.

self-confessed /ˌselfkənˈfest/ *adj.* откровéнный.

self-confidence /selfˈkɒnfɪd(ə)ns/ *n.* увéренность (в себé); (*pej.*) самоувéренность; самонадéянность.

self-confident /selfˈkɒnfɪd(ə)nt/ *adj.* увéренный (в себé); (*pej.*) самоувéренный; самонадéянный.

self-congratulation /ˌselfkənˌgrætjʊˈleɪʃ(ə)n/ *n.* самохвáльство, самовосхвалéние.

self-conscious /selfˈkɒnʃəs/ *adj.* **1** (*awkward*) нелóвкий; (*shy*) застéнчивый; (*embarrassed*)

S

смущённый. **2** (*phil.*) самосознаю́щий.

self-consciousness /self'kɒnʃəsnɪs/ *n.* нело́вкость, засте́нчивость; (*phil.*) самосозна́ние.

self-consistent /ˌselfkən'sɪst(ə)nt/ *adj.* после́довательный.

self-contained /ˌselfkən'teɪnd/ *adj.* (*independent, of person*) самостоя́тельный, незави́симый; (*Br., of accommodation*) отде́льный.

self-contempt /ˌselfkən'tempt/ *n.* презре́ние к самому́ себе́.

self-contradiction /selfˌkɒntrə'dɪkʃ(ə)n/ *n.* вну́треннее противоре́чие.

self-contradictory /selfˌkɒntrə'dɪktərɪ/ *adj.* (вну́тренне) противоречи́вый; противоре́чащий самому́ себе́.

self-control /ˌselfkən'trəʊl/ *n.* самооблада́ние; **he had to exercise ~** он до́лжен был прояви́ть самооблада́ние; **he regained his ~** к нему́ верну́лось самооблада́ние.

self-controlled /ˌselfkən'trəʊld/ *adj.* вы́держанный.

self-critical /self'krɪtɪk(ə)l/ *adj.* самокрити́чный.

self-criticism /self'krɪtɪˌsɪz(ə)m/ *n.* самокри́тика.

self-deception /ˌselfdɪ'sepʃ(ə)n/ *n.* самообма́н.

self-defeating /ˌselfdɪ'fi:tɪŋ/ *adj.* сам себя́ губя́щий, губи́тельный.

self-defence /ˌselfdɪ'fens/ (*US* **-defense**) *n.* самооборо́на, самозащи́та; **in ~** для/в поря́дке самооборо́ны.

self-delusion /ˌselfdɪ'lu:ʒ(ə)n/, /-'lju:ʒ(ə)n/ *n.* самообма́н, самообольще́ние.

self-denial /ˌselfdɪ'naɪəl/ *n.* самоотрече́ние; **practise** (*Br.*), **practice** (*US*) **~** отка́зывать (*impf.*) себе́ во всём; ограни́чивать (*impf.*) себя́.

self-denying /ˌselfdɪ'naɪɪŋ/ *adj.* бескоры́стный, самоотве́рженный.

self-deprecating /self'deprɪˌkeɪtɪŋ/ *adj.* самоуничижи́тельный.

self-depreciation /ˌselfdɪˌpri:ʃɪ'eɪʃ(ə)n/ *n.* самоуничиже́ние.

self-destruct /ˌselfdɪ'strʌkt/ *v.i.* (*tech.*) самоликвиди́роваться (*impf., pf.*).

self-destruction /ˌselfdɪ'strʌkʃ(ə)n/ *n.* самоуничтоже́ние; (*suicide*) самоуби́йство; (*tech.*) самоликвида́ция.

self-determination /ˌselfdɪˌtɜ:mɪ'neɪʃ(ə)n/ *n.* самоопределе́ние.

self-discipline /self'dɪsɪplɪn/ *n.* вну́тренняя дисципли́на.

self-discovery /ˌselfdɪs'kʌvərɪ/ *n.* самопостиже́ние.

self-disgust /ˌselfdɪs'gʌst/ *n.* отвраще́ние к себе́.

self-doubt /self'daʊt/ *n.* неве́рие в себя́.

self-drive /self'draɪv/ *n.* (*Br.*): **~ car hire** прока́т автомаши́н.

self-educated /self'edju:ˌkeɪtɪd/ *adj.*: **a ~ man, woman** самоу́чка (*c.g.*).

self-education /ˌselfˌedju:'keɪʃ(ə)n/ *n.* самообразова́ние.

self-effacement /ˌselfɪ'feɪsmənt/ *n.* скро́мность; самоуниже́ние.

self-effacing /ˌselfɪ'feɪsɪŋ/ *adj.* скро́мный.

self-employed /ˌselfɪm'plɔɪd/ *adj.* рабо́тающий не по на́йму; обслу́живающий своё со́бственное предприя́тие.

self-esteem /ˌselfɪ'sti:m/ *n.* самоуваже́ние, самолю́бие.

self-evident /self'evɪd(ə)nt/ *adj.* очеви́дный; само́ собо́й разуме́ющийся.

self-examination /ˌselfɪgˌzæmɪ'neɪʃ(ə)n/ *n.* самоана́лиз.

self-explanatory /ˌselfɪk'splænətərɪ/ *adj.* не тре́бующий разъясне́ний.

self-expression /ˌselfɪk'spreʃ(ə)n/ *n.* самовыраже́ние.

self-feeding /self'fi:dɪŋ/ *adj.* (*of boiler etc.*) с автомати́ческой пода́чей.

self-fertilization /selfˌfɜ:tɪlaɪ'zeɪʃ(ə)n/ *n.* самоопыле́ние; самооплодотворе́ние.

self-fertilizing /self'fɜ:tɪˌlaɪzɪŋ/ *adj.* самоопыля́ющийся; самооплодотворя́ющийся.

self-financing /self'faɪnænsɪŋ/ *adj.* самофинанси́рующийся.

self-fulfilling /ˌselffʊl'fɪlɪŋ/ *adj.*: **~ prophecy** предсказа́ние, влия́ющее на результа́т.

self-fulfilment /ˌselffʊl'fɪlmənt/ (*US* **-fulfillment**) *n.* реализа́ция свои́х возмо́жностей.

self-glorification /selfˌglɔ:rɪfɪ'keɪʃ(ə)n/ *n.* самовосхвале́ние.

self-governing /self'gʌvənɪŋ/ *adj.* самоуправля́ющийся.

self-government /self'gʌvənmənt/ *n.* самоуправле́ние.

self-hatred /self'heɪtrɪd/ *n.* не́нависть к себе́.

self-help /self'help/ *n.* самопо́мощь.

self-image /self'ɪmɪdʒ/ *n.* самооце́нка, со́бственное представле́ние о себе́.

self-immolation /ˌselfɪmə'leɪʃ(ə)n/ *n.* самосожже́ние.

self-importance /ˌselfɪm'pɔ:t(ə)ns/ *n.* самомне́ние.

self-important /ˌselfɪm'pɔ:t(ə)nt/ *adj.* ва́жный, самонаде́янный.

self-imposed /ˌselfɪm'pəʊzd/ *adj.* доброво́льный; доброво́льно взя́тый на себя́.

self-improvement /ˌselfɪm'pru:vmənt/ *n.* самосоверше́нствование.

self-induced /ˌselfɪn'dju:st/ *adj.* вы́званный у себя́.

self-induction /ˌselfɪn'dʌkʃ(ə)n/ *n.* самоинду́кция.

self-indulgence /ˌselfɪn'dʌldʒ(ə)ns/ *n.* избало́ванность; потво́рство свои́м жела́ниям.

self-indulgent /ˌselfɪn'dʌldʒ(ə)nt/ *adj.* избало́ванный; потво́рствующий свои́м жела́ниям.

self-inflicted /ˌselfɪn'flɪktɪd/ *adj.* (*of penance*) доброво́льный; (*of wound, injury*) нанесённый самому́ себе́.

self-instruction /ˌselfɪn'strʌkʃ(ə)n/ *n.* самообразова́ние.

self-interest /self'ɪntrəst/, /-trɪst/ *n.* со́бственный интере́с; коры́сть; **he acted from ~** он де́йствовал из коры́стных побужде́ний.

self-interested /self'ɪntrəstɪd/, /-trɪstɪd/ *adj.* коры́стный, корыстолюби́вый.

selfish /'selfɪʃ/ *adj.* эгоисти́ческий, эгоисти́чный, коры́стный; **~ person** эгои́ст (*fem.* -ка).

selfishness /'selfɪʃnɪs/ *n.* эгоисти́чность, эгои́зм.

self-justification /selfˌdʒʌstɪfɪ'keɪʃ(ə)n/ *n.* самооправда́ние.

self-knowledge /self'nɒlɪdʒ/ *n.* самопозна́ние.

selfless /'selflɪs/ *adj.* самоотве́рженный, беззаве́тный.

selflessness /'selflɪsnɪs/ *n.* самоотве́рженность, беззаве́тность.

self-loading /self'ləʊdɪŋ/ *adj.* (*of weapon*) самозаря́дный.

self-loathing /self'ləʊðɪŋ/ *n.* отвраще́ние к себе́.

self-locking /self'lɒkɪŋ/ *adj.* самоблоки́рующийся.

self-love /self'lʌv/ *n.* себялю́бие, эгои́зм.

self-made /'selfmeɪd/ *adj.*: **he is a ~ man** он сам себя́ сде́лал; он челове́к, вы́бившийся из низо́в.

self-mastery /self'mɑ:stərɪ/ *n.* самооблада́ние.

self-mockery /self'mɒkərɪ/ *n.* смех над собо́й.

self-neglect /ˌselfnɪ'glekt/ *n.* (*slovenliness*) неопря́тность.

self-opinionated /ˌselfə'pɪnjəˌneɪtɪd/ *adj.* самонаде́янный.

self-perpetuating /ˌselfpə'petju:ˌeɪtɪŋ/ *adj.* (*growth, decline*) (само)произво́льный; (*myth, benefit*) бесконе́чный.

self-pity /self'pɪtɪ/ *n.* жа́лость к себе́.

self-pitying /self'pɪtɪɪŋ/ *adj.* испо́лненный жа́лостью к себе́.

self-pollination /ˌselfpɒlɪ'neɪʃ(ə)n/ *n.* самоопыле́ние.

self-portrait /self'pɔ:trɪt/ *n.* автопортре́т.

self-possessed /ˌselfpə'zest/ *adj.* вы́держанный; хладнокро́вный, невозмути́мый.

self-possession /ˌselfpə'zeʃ(ə)n/ *n.* самооблада́ние, хладнокро́вие, невозмути́мость.

self-preservation /selfˌprezə'veɪʃ(ə)n/ *n.* самосохране́ние.

self-proclaimed /ˌselfprə'kleɪmd/ *adj.* самозва́ный.

self-promotion /ˌselfprəˈməʊʃ(ə)n/ *n.* самореклáма.

self-propelled /ˌselfprəˈpeld/ *adj.* самохóдный.

self-protection /ˌselfprəˈtekʃ(ə)n/ *n.* самосохранéние.

self-raising /selfˈreɪzɪŋ/ (*US* **self-rising**) *adj.*: **~ flour** мукá с разрыхли́телем.

self-realization /selfˌrɪəlaɪˈzeɪʃ(ə)n/ *n.* разви́тие свои́х спосóбностей.

self-regard /ˌselfrɪˈgɑːd/ *n.* **1** (*egoism*) себялю́бие. **2** = **self-respect**

self-regulating /selfˈregjʊˌleɪtɪŋ/ *adj.* саморегули́рующийся.

self-regulation /ˌselfregjʊˈleɪʃ(ə)n/ *n.* саморегули́рование.

self-reliance /ˌselfrɪˈlaɪəns/ *n.* самостоя́тельность, незави́симость.

self-reliant /ˌselfrɪˈlaɪənt/ *adj.* полагáющийся на себя́, самостоя́тельный.

self-reproach /ˌselfrɪˈprəʊtʃ/ *n.* самоосуждéние, самобичевáние.

self-respect /ˌselfrɪˈspekt/ *n.* самоуважéние; чу́вство сóбственного достóинства.

self-restraint /ˌselfrɪˈstreɪnt/ *n.* сдéржанность.

self-righteous /selfˈraɪtʃəs/ *adj.* хáнжеский, фарисéйский.

self-righteousness /selfˈraɪtʃəsnɪs/ *n.* хáнжество, фарисéйство.

self-rising /selfˈraɪzɪŋ/ (*US*) = **self-raising**

self-rule /selfˈruːl/ *n.* самоуправлéние.

self-sacrifice /selfˈsækrɪˌfaɪs/ *n.* самопожéртвование.

self-sacrificing /selfˈsækrɪˌfaɪsɪŋ/ *adj.* самоотвéрженный.

selfsame /ˈselfseɪm/ *adj.* тот же сáмый; оди́н и тот же.

self-satisfaction /selfˌsætɪsˈfækʃ(ə)n/ *n.* самодовóльство.

self-satisfied /selfˈsætɪsˌfaɪd/ *adj.* самодовóльный.

self-sealing /selfˈsiːlɪŋ/ *adj.* самоуплотня́ющийся; (*envelope*) самозаклéивающийся.

self-seed /selfˈsiːd/ *v.i.* расти́, вы- самосéвом.

self-seeking /ˈselfˌsiːkɪŋ/ *adj.* своекоры́стный.

self-service /selfˈsɜːvɪs/ *n.* самообслу́живание; **~ store** магази́н самообслу́живания.

self-serving /selfˈsɜːvɪŋ/ *adj.* своекоры́стный.

self-sown /selfˈsəʊn/ *adj.* самосéвный.

self-starter /selfˈstɑːtə(r)/ *n.* инициати́вный человéк.

self-styled /ˈselfstaɪld/ *adj.* самозвáный.

self-sufficiency /ˌselfsəˈfɪʃənsɪ/ *n.* (*of person*) самостоя́тельность; (*econ.*) самообеспéченность.

self-sufficient /ˌselfsəˈfɪʃ(ə)nt/ *adj.* самостоя́тельный; (*econ.*) самообеспéченный.

self-supporting /ˌselfsəˈpɔːtɪŋ/ *adj.* (*of person*) самостоя́тельный, незави́симый; (*of business*) самоокупáющийся; **the country is ~ in oil** странá спосóбна обеспéчить себя́ нéфтью.

self-taught /selfˈtɔːt/ *adj.*: **a ~ man, woman** самоу́чка (*c.g.*).

self-will /selfˈwɪl/ *n.* своевóлие.

self-willed /selfˈwɪld/ *adj.* своевóльный.

self-winding /selfˈwaɪndɪŋ/ *adj.* с автомати́ческим завóдом.

self-worth /selfˈwɜːθ/ *n.* самолю́бие.

sell /sel/ *n.* **1** (*manner of* **~***ing*): **hard ~** навя́зывание товáра. **2** (*coll.*) (*deception*) обмáн; (*disappointment*) досáда.

● *v.t.* (*past and p.p.* **sold**) **1** прод|авáть, -áть; торговáть (*impf.*) + *i.*; **I'll ~ you this carpet for £20** я вам продáм э́тот ковёр за 20 фу́нтов; **I can't remember what I sold it for** я не пóмню, за скóлько я э́то прóдал; **~ short** (*coll., disparage*) умаля́ть (*impf.*) достóинства + *g.*; **~ing price** продáжная ценá; **this shop ~s stamps** в э́том магази́не продаю́тся почтóвые мáрки; (*offer dishonourably for gain*): **he sold himself to the highest bidder** он продáлся томý, кто бóльше заплати́л. **2** (*coll., put across*): **he was unable to ~ his idea to the management** емý не удалóсь убеди́ть правлéние приня́ть егó предложéние; **~ o.s.** (*present o.s. to advantage*) под|авáть, -áть себя́. **3**: **he is sold on the idea** (*coll.*) он твёрдо дéржится за э́ту идéю.

● *v.i.* (*past and p.p.* **sold**) **1** (*of person*): **you were wise to ~ when you did** вы вóвремя прóдали свой товáр. **2** (*of goods*): **the house sold for £90,000** за дом вы́ручили 90 000 фу́нтов; **the record is ~ing like hot cakes** э́ту пласти́нку покупáют/берýт нарасхвáт; **the book ~s well** кни́га хорошó продаётся/идёт; **wheat is not ~ing** пшени́ца плóхо продаётся; **these pens ~ at 30p each** э́ти рýчки продаю́тся/идýт по 30 пéнсов (за штýку).

● *with advs.*: **~ back** *v.t.*: **I sold the car back to him for less than I paid for it** я перепрóдал емý маши́ну с убы́тком; **~ off** *v.t.* распрод|авáть, -áть; **they sold off the goods at a reduced price** они́ распрóдали товáр по сни́женной ценé; **~ out** *v.i.*: **the book sold out** э́та кни́га разошлáсь; **the shop sold out of cigarettes** магази́н распрóдал все сигарéты; **they have sold out of tickets** все билéты прóданы; **they were accused of ~ing out to the enemy** их обвиня́ли в том, что они́ продали́сь врагý; **~ up** *v.i.*: (**~** *one's possessions*) распрод|авáть, -áть своё имýщество.

● *cpds.* **~-by date** *n.* (*Br.*) срок гóдности; **~-out** *n.* распродáжа; **the play was a ~-out** пьéса прошлá с аншлáгом; (*betrayal*) измéна, предáтельство.

seller /ˈselə(r)/ *n.* продав|éц (*fem.* -щи́ца); торгóв|ец (*fem.* -ка); **~'s market** ры́ночная конъюнктýра, вы́годная для продавцá.

Sellotape /ˈseləˌteɪp/ *n.* (*Br., propr.*) липу́чка (*coll.*), скотч.

selv|edge, -age /ˈselvɪdʒ/ *n.* крóмка.

selves /selvz/ *pl. of* ⇒**self**

semantic /sɪˈmæntɪk/ *adj.* семанти́ческий, смыслово́й.

semantics /sɪˈmæntɪks/ *n.* семáнтика.

semaphore /ˈseməˌfɔː(r)/ *n.* семафóр.

● *v.t. & i.* сигнализи́ровать (*impf., pf.*) флажкáми.

semblance /ˈsembləns/ *n.* (*appearance*) вид; нарýжность; ви́димость; **under the ~ of** под ви́дом + *g.*; **the ~ of victory** ви́димость побéды; (*likeness*) подóбие, схóдство.

semelfactive /ˌseməlˈfæktɪv/ *adj.* (*gram.*) однокрáтный.

semen /ˈsiːmən/ *n.* сéмя (*nt.*), спéрма.

semester /sɪˈmestə(r)/ *n.* семéстр.

semi /ˈsemɪ/ *n.* (*pl.* **~s**) (*Br. coll.*) = **~-detached house.**

● *pref.* полу. . .

● *cpds.* **~-automatic** *adj.* полуавтомати́ческий; **~-basement** *n.* полуподвáл; **~breve** *n.* (*Br.*) цéлая нóта; **~-circle** *n.* полукрýг; **~-circular** *adj.* полукрýглый; полукрýжный; **~colon** *n.* тóчка с запятóй; **~-conductor** *n.* полупроводни́к; **~-conscious** *adj.* в полузабы́тьи; **~-consciousness** *n.* полузабытьё; **~-darkness** *n.* полутьмá; **~-desert** *n.* полупусты́ня; **~-detached** *adj.*: **~-detached house** (*coll., abbr.* ⇒**semi**) оди́н из двух особнякóв, имéющих óбщую стéну; **~-final** *n.* полуфинáл; **~-finalist** *n.* полуфинали́ст (*fem.* -ка); **~-finished** *adj.*: **~-finished article** полуфабрикáт; **~-invalid** *adj.* (*partially disabled*) полуинвали́д; (*infirm*) полубольнóй; **~-literate** *adj.* полугрáмотный; **~-nude** *adj.* полугóлый; **~-official** *adj.* полуофициáльный; официóзный; **~-official newspaper** официóз; **~-precious** *adj.*: **~-precious stone** самоцвéт; **~-professional** *n.* полупрофессионáл; *adj.* полупрофессионáльный; **~quaver** *n.* (*Br.*) шестнáдцатая нóта; **~-retired** *adj.* рабóтающий непóлный день; **~-rigid** *adj.* полужёсткий; **~-skilled** *adj.* полуквалифици́рованный; **~-skimmed** *adj.* (*Br.*) обезжи́ренный; **~-solid** *adj.* полутвёрдый; **~tone** *n.* полутóн; **~-trailer** *n.* (*US*) полуприцéп; **~vowel** *n.* полуглáсный (звук).

seminal /ˈsemɪn(ə)l/ *adj.* **1** семеннóй; **~ fluid** семеннáя жи́дкость. **2** (*fig.*) (*work*) эпохáльный; (*idea*) плодотвóрный.

seminar /ˈsemɪˌnɑː(r)/ *n.* семинáр.

seminarist /ˈsemɪnərɪst/ *n.* семинари́ст.

seminary /ˈsemɪnərɪ/ *n.* семинáрия.

Semite /ˈsiːmaɪt/, /ˈsem-/ *n.* семи́т (*fem.* -ка).

Semitic /sɪˈmɪtɪk/ *adj.* семити́ческий; (*language*) семи́тский.

semolina /ˌseməˈliːnə/ *n.* мáнная крупá, мáнка (*coll.*).

sempstress /ˈsemstrɪs/ = **seamstress**

Semtex /ˈsemteks/ *n.* сéмтекс (плáстиковое взры́вчатое веществó).

Sen. /ˈsenətə(r)/ *n.* (*abbr. of* **Senator**) сенáтор.

senate /ˈsenɪt/ *n.* сенáт; (*univ.*) совéт.

senator /ˈsenətə(r)/ *n.* сенáтор.

senatorial /ˌsenəˈtɔːrɪəl/ *adj.* сенáторский.

send /send/ *v.t.* (*past and p.p.* **sent**) **1** (*dispatch*) пос|ылáть, -лáть; отпр|авля́ть, -áвить; **they ~ their goods all over the world** они́ рассылáют свои́ товáры по всему́ ми́ру; **he sent me a book** он прислáл мне кни́гу; **I shall ~ you to bed** я отпрáвлю тебя́ спать; **the teacher sent him out of the room** учи́тель вы́ставил/вы́гнал егó из клáсса; **he was sent to a good school** егó послáли в хорóшую шкóлу. **2** (*cause to move*; *propel*): **~ the ball to s.o.** под|авáть, -áть мяч комý-н.; **he sent a stone through the window** он запусти́л кáмнем в окнó; **~ s.o. packing** прог|оня́ть, -нáть когó-н.; **the blow sent him flying** удáр сбил егó с ног; (*fig., drive*): **~ s.o. mad** св|оди́ть, -ести́ когó-н. с умá; **his voice sent everyone to sleep** егó гóлос навёл на всех сон; **the garden sent her into raptures** сад привёл её в востóрг.

● *v.i.* (*past and p.p.* **sent**): **I sent for a catalogue** (*Br.*), **catalog** (*US*) я заказáл/вы́писал каталóг; **he sent for a doctor** он вы́звал врачá; он послáл за врачóм; **I shall wait till I am sent for** я бýду ждать, покá меня́ не позовýт; **~ to us for details** обращáйтесь за подрóбностями к нам.

● *with advs.*: **~ across** *v.t.* перепр|авля́ть, -áвить; **~ along** *v.t.* пос|ылáть, -лáть; **~ away** *v.t.* от|сылáть, -ослáть; **the manager sent them away contented** они́ ушли́ от дирéктора довóльные; *v.i.*: **~ away for something** выпи́сывать, вы́писать что-н., зак|áзывать, -азáть что-н.; **~ back** *v.t.* (*person*) пос|ылáть, -лáть назáд; (*thing*) от|сылáть, -ослáть; **~ down** *v.t.* (*Br., expel from college*) исключ|áть, -и́ть; **~ forth** *v.t.* (**~ out**) высылáть, вы́слать; (*emit*) испус|кáть, -ти́ть; **~ in** *v.t.*: **he sent in his bill** он послáл счёт; **~ in one's name** (*enrol*) запи́с|ываться, -áться; **~ in a report** предст|авля́ть, -áвить отчёт; **~ off** *v.t.* (*dispatch*) отпр|авля́ть, -áвить; **he was sent off by the referee** судья́ удали́л егó с пóля; **we went to the airport to ~ him off** мы отпрáвились в аэропóрт проводи́ть егó; **~ on** *v.t.* (*forward*) перес|ылáть, -лáть; **~ out** *v.t.* высылáть, вы́слать; **he was sent out as a missionary** егó послáли в кáчестве миссионéра; (*distribute*) ра|ссылáть, -зослáть; **invitations were sent out** приглашéния бы́ли разóсланы; (*emit*): **~ out rays** испус|кáть, -ти́ть лучи́; **~ out heat** выделя́ть, вы́делить теплó; **~ out signals** пос|ылáть, -лáть сигнáлы; *v.i.*: **we sent out for some beer** мы послáли за пи́вом; **~ round** *v.t.*: **I sent round a note** я послáл запи́ску; *v.i.*: **he sent round to see how I was** он послáл ко мне человéка узнáть, как я себя́ чýвствую; **~ up** *v.t.*: **~ up a rocket** запус|кáть, -ти́ть ракéту; **~ up s.o.'s temperature** подн|имáть, -я́ть у когó-н. температýру; (*coll., ridicule*) высмéивать, вы́смеять.

● *cpds.* **~-off** *n.* прóвод|ы (*pl., g.* -ов); **he got a marvellous** (*Br.*), **marvelous** (*US*) **~-off from his friends** друзья́ устрóили емý замечáтельные прóводы; **~-up** *n.* (*coll., parody, satire*) парóдия, сати́ра.

sender /ˈsendə(r)/ *n.* отправи́тель (*m.*); **return to ~** возвращáть, вернýть/возврати́ть отправи́телю.

Senegal /ˌsenɪˈgɔːl/ *n.* Сенегáл.

Senegalese /ˌsenɪgəˈliːz/ *n.* сенегáл|ец (*fem.* -ка).

● *adj.* сенегáльский.

senescence /sɪˈnesəns/ *n.* старéние.

senescent /sɪˈnesənt/ *adj.* старéющий.

senile /ˈsiːnaɪl/ *adj.* стáрческий; **~ dementia** стáрческое слабоýмие; (*of person*) дря́хлый; **become ~** (*physically*) дряхлéть, о-; (*mentally*) впадáть, впасть в стáрческое слабоýмие.

senility /sɪˈnɪlɪtɪ/ *n.* (*physical*) дря́хлость; (*mental*) стáрческое слабоýмие.

senior /ˈsiːnɪə(r)/ *n.*: **he is my ~ by 5 years** он на пять лет стáрше меня́; (*pl.* **~** *pupils, students*) старшеклáссники, старшекýрсники (*both m. pl.*).

● *adj.* (*in age*) стáрший (вóзрастом, годáми); (*in position*) стáрший (чи́ном); **I am several years ~ to him** я на нéсколько лет стáрше егó; **~ citizen** пожилóй человéк, человéк пенсиóнного вóзраста; **~ common room** (*Br.*) профéссорская; **~ partner** глáвный компаньóн; **Johnson ~** Джóнсон-стáрший; Джóнсон-отéц.

seniority /ˌsiːnɪˈɒrɪtɪ/ *n.* старшинствó.

Señor /senˈjɔː(r)/, **-a** /senˈjɔːrə/, **-ita** /ˌsenjəˈriːtə/ *nn.* сеньóр, -а, -и́та.

sensation /senˈseɪʃ(ə)n/ *n.* **1** (*feeling*) ощущéние; **lose all ~** пóлностью теря́ть, по- чувстви́тельность; **he had a ~ of giddiness** он почýвствовал головокружéние. **2** (*exciting event*; *excitement*) сенсáция; **the wedding was a great ~** свáдьба былá настоя́щей сенсáцией.

sensational /senˈseɪʃən(ə)l/ *adj.* сенсациóнный.

sensationalism /senˈseɪʃənəˌlɪz(ə)m/ *n.* (*pursuit of sensation*) погóня за сенсáциями.

sense /sens/ *n.* **1** (*faculty*) чýвство; **the five ~s** пять чувств; **sixth ~** шестóе чýвство; **keen, quick ~s** óстрое чýвство/чутьё; **a dull ~ of smell** притýпленное обоня́ние; **a keen ~ of hearing** óстрый слух; **the pleasures of ~** чýвственные наслаждéния. **2** (*feeling*; *perception*; *appreciation*) чýвство, ощущéние; **he felt a ~ of injury** он испытáл чýвство оби́ды; **have you no ~ of shame?** у вас сты́да нет!; **~ of beauty** чýвство красоты́; **~ of honour** (*Br.*), **honor** (*US*)/**duty** чýвство чéсти/дóлга; **~ of direction** умéние ориенти́роваться; **~ of humour** (*Br.*), **humor** (*US*) чýвство ю́мора; **~ of failure** ощущéние неудáчи. **3** (*pl., sanity*) ум; **take leave of one's ~s** сходи́ть, сойти́ с умá; **bring s.o. to his ~s** наст|авля́ть, -áвить когó-н. на ум; прив|оди́ть, -ести́ когó-н. в чýвство; **come to one's ~s** брáться, взя́ться за ум. **4** (*pl., consciousness*): **come to one's ~s** при|ходи́ть, -йти́ в себя́. **5** (*common ~*) здрáвый смысл; **a man of ~** (благо)разýмный/здравомы́слящий человéк; **talk ~** говори́ть (*impf.*) дéло; **he has more ~ than to ...** он не так глуп (*or* он сли́шком умён), чтóбы. . .; **he had the ~ to call the police** у негó хвати́ло умá вы́звать поли́цию; **what would be the ~ of going any further?** какóй смысл продолжáть?; **there is a lot of ~ in what you say** то, что вы говори́те, вполнé разýмно **6** (*meaning*) смысл, значéние; **in a ~** в извéстном/нéкотором смы́сле; **in every ~** во всех отношéниях; **in no ~** никóим óбразом; **make ~ of** пон|имáть, -я́ть; раз|бирáться, -обрáться в + *p.*; **it makes ~** э́то разýмно; **it makes no ~** э́то бессмы́сленно/нелéпо; (*cannot be true*) э́то(го) не мóжет быть.

● *v.t.* чýвствовать, по-; ощу|щáть, -ти́ть.

senseless /ˈsenslɪs/ *adj.* **1** (*foolish*) бессмы́сленный, бестолкóвый. **2** (*unconscious*) бесчýвственный; **knock s.o. ~** оглуш|áть, -и́ть когó-н.; **he fell ~ on the floor** он упáл без чувств (*or* зáмертво) нá пол.

senselessness /ˈsenslɪsnɪs/ *n.* бессмы́сленность.

sensibilit|y /ˌsensɪˈbɪlɪtɪ/ *n.* чувстви́тельность, восприи́мчивость (**to**: к + *d.*); **offend, wound s.o.'s ~ies** рáнить (*impf., pf.*) чьё-н. самолю́бие; оскорб|ля́ть, -и́ть чьи-н. чýвства.

sensible /ˈsensɪb(ə)l/ *adj.* **1** (*showing good sense*) (благо)разýмный; **that was ~ of you** вы разýмно поступи́ли; **~ shoes** практи́чная óбувь. **2**: **be ~ of** (*be aware of, recognize, appreciate*) (о)сознавáть (*impf.*); разýмно оцéнивать (*impf.*).

sensibleness /ˈsensɪbəlnɪs/ *n.* благоразýмие.

sensitive /ˈsensɪtɪv/ *adj.* чувстви́тельный, восприи́мчивый; **eyes ~ to light** глазá, чувстви́тельные к свéту; **don't be so ~!** вы сли́шком оби́дчивы!; (*sharp*): **~ ears** óстрый слух; (*of instruments*): **~ balance** тóчные весы́; (*tender*): **~ skin** нéжная кóжа; (*painful*): **~ tooth** больнóй зуб; (*potentially embarrassing*): **a ~ topic** щекотли́вая/деликáтная тéма; (*pol.*): **~ information** секрéтные свéдения; (*phot.*): **~ paper** светочувстви́тельная бумáга.

sensitivity /ˌsensɪˈtɪvɪtɪ/ *n.* чувстви́тельность; тóчность.

sensitize /ˈsensɪˌtaɪz/ *v.t.* дéлать, счувстви́тельным; (*phot.*) де́лать, с- светочувстви́тельным.

sensor /'sensə(r)/ *n.* (*tech.*) да́тчик.

sensory /'sensərɪ/ *adj.* сенсо́рный.

sensual /'sensjʊəl/, /'senʃʊəl/ *adj.* чу́вственный (*also of mouth etc.*); сладостра́стный.

sensualist /'sensjʊəlɪst/, /'senʃʊəlɪst/ *n.* сластолю́бец.

sensuality /ˌsensjʊ'ælɪtɪ/, /ˌsenʃʊ-/ *n.* чу́вственность, сладостра́стие.

sensuous /'sensjʊəs/ *adj.* чу́вственный.

sensuousness /'sensjʊəsnɪs/ *n.* чу́вственность.

sent /sent/ *past and p.p. of* ⇒**send**

sentence /'sent(ə)ns/ *n.* **1** (*gram.*) предложе́ние. **2** (*leg.*) пригово́р; **~ of death** сме́ртный пригово́р; **be under ~ of death** быть приговорённым к сме́рти; **pass ~ on** (*of judge*) выноси́ть, вы́нести пригово́р + *d.*; (*fig.*) осу|жда́ть, -ди́ть.

● *v.t.* пригов|а́ривать, -ори́ть; **he was ~d to penal servitude** его́ приговори́ли к ка́торжным рабо́там.

sententious /sen'tenʃəs/ *adj.* сентенцио́зный.

sentient /'senʃ(ə)nt/ *adj.* наделённый чувстви́тельностью.

sentiment /'sentɪmənt/ *n.* **1** (*feeling*) чу́вство; **have friendly ~s towards s.o.** пита́ть (*impf.*) дру́жеские чу́вства к кому́-н.; (*tendency to be swayed by feeling*): **appeal to ~** взыва́ть, воззва́ть к эмо́циям/чу́вствам. **2** (*opinion*) мне́ние, то́чка зре́ния; **those are my ~s** таково́ моё мне́ние. **3** (*sentimentality*) сентимента́льность.

sentimental /ˌsentɪ'ment(ə)l/ *adj.* сентимента́льный; **of ~ value** дорого́й как па́мять.

sentimentalism /ˌsentɪ'mentəˌlɪz(ə)m/ *n.* сентиментали́зм.

sentimentalist /ˌsentɪ'mentəlɪst/ *n.* сентимента́льный челове́к.

sentimentality /ˌsentɪmen'tælɪtɪ/ *n.* сентимента́льность.

sentimentalize /ˌsentɪ'mentəlaɪz/ *v.t.* прид|ава́ть, -а́ть (*чему*) сентимента́льную окра́ску.

sentinel /'sentɪn(ə)l/ *n.* (*guard*) часово́й; **stand ~ over something** (*fig.*) стоя́ть (*impf.*) на стра́же чего́-н.; охраня́ть (*impf.*) что-н.

sentry /'sentrɪ/ *n.* (*guard*) часово́й; **stand ~** стоя́ть (*impf.*) на часа́х; **~ duty** карау́льная слу́жба.

● *cpds.* **~-box** *n.* бу́дка часово́го, карау́льная бу́дка; **~-go** *n.* карау́льная слу́жба.

Seoul /səʊl/ *n.* Сеу́л.

sepal /'sep(ə)l/, /'si:-/ *n.* чашели́стик.

separable /'sepərəb(ə)l/ *adj.* отдели́мый.

separate¹ /'sepərət/ *adj.* отде́льный; (*distinct*) осо́бый; (*not together*) разде́льный; **under ~ cover** отде́льно; **he entered my name in a ~ column** он занёс мою́ фами́лию в осо́бую графу́; **a ~ peace** сепара́тный мир; **two ~ questions** два самостоя́тельных/ра́зных вопро́са; **they are living ~ly** они́ живу́т врозь/разде́льно.

separate² /'sepəˌreɪt/ *v.t.* (*set apart*) отдел|я́ть, -и́ть; (*disunite, part*) разлуч|а́ть, -и́ть; **he is ~d from his family** он не живёт с семьёй; (*distinguish*): **~ truth from error** отлич|а́ть, -и́ть/отдел|я́ть, -и́ть и́стину от заблужде́ния.

● *v.i.* **1** (*become detached*) отдел|я́ться, -и́ться; (*come untied*) развя́з|ываться, -а́ться. **2** (*part company*) расст|ава́ться, -а́ться; разлуч|а́ться, -и́ться. **3** (*of man and wife*) ра|сходи́ться, -зойти́сь; разъ|езжа́ться, -е́хаться.

separation /ˌsepə'reɪʃ(ə)n/ *n.* отделе́ние, разделе́ние; (*forced*) разлу́ка; (*of spouses*) разде́льное жи́тельство.

separatist /'sepərətɪst/ *n.* сепарати́ст (*fem.* -ка).

separator /'sepəˌreɪtə(r)/ *n.* (*machine*) сепара́тор.

sepia /'si:pɪə/ *n.* (*fluid; colour;* **~ drawing**) се́пия.

sepsis /'sepsɪs/ *n.* се́псис; зараже́ние кро́ви.

September /sep'tembə(r)/ *n.* сентя́брь (*m.*).

● *adj.* сентя́брьский.

septet(te) /sep'tet/ *n.* септе́т.

septic /'septɪk/ *adj.* септи́ческий; **the wound has gone ~** ра́на загнои́лась; **~ tank** перегнива́тель (*m.*).

septicaemia /ˌseptɪ'si:mɪə/ (*US* **septicemia**) *n.* зараже́ние кро́ви.

septuagenarian /ˌseptjʊədʒɪ'neərɪən/ *n.* семидесятиле́тний стари́к (*fem.* семидесятиле́тняя стару́ха).

● *adj.* семидесятиле́тний.

sepulchral /sɪ'pʌlkr(ə)l/ *adj.* (*of a tomb*): **~ stone** надгро́бный/моги́льный ка́мень; **~ voice** замоги́льный го́лос.

sepulchre /'sepəlkə(r)/ (*US* **sepulcher**) *n.* гробни́ца; (*in rock cave*) склеп.

sequel /'si:kw(ə)l/ *n.* **1** (*result, consequence*) (по)сле́дствие; **in the ~** (*Br.*) впосле́дствии; в результа́те. **2** (*of novel etc.*) продолже́ние (+*g.*), сикве́л.

sequence /'si:kwəns/ *n.* **1** (*succession*) после́довательность; поря́док; **in logical ~** в логи́ческой после́довательности; **in rapid ~** бы́стро сменя́ясь; **~ of events** ход/после́довательность собы́тий; **~ of the seasons** сме́на времён го́да; (*gram.*): **~ of tenses** после́довательность времён. **2** (*part of film*) эпизо́д. **3** (*cards*) три и́ли бо́лее ка́рты одно́й ма́сти в непреры́вной после́довательности.

sequester /sɪ'kwestə(r)/ *v.t.* **1** (*isolate, detach*) изоли́ровать (*impf., pf.*); **~ o.s. from the world** удал|я́ться, -и́ться от ми́ра; **a ~ed village** уединённая дере́вня. **2** (*leg. etc.: confiscate; also* **sequestrate**) (*take temporary possession*) секвестрова́ть (*impf., pf.*); (*confiscate*) конфискова́ть (*impf., pf.*).

sequestrate /sɪ'kwestreɪt/, /'si:kwɪ-/ = **sequester** *v.t.* 2

sequestration /ˌsi:kwɪ'streɪʃ(ə)n/ *n.* секве́стр, аре́ст иму́щества.

sequin /'si:kwɪn/ *n.* (*spangle*) блёстка.

sequoia /sɪ'kwɔɪə/ *n.* секво́йя.

sera /'sɪərə/ *pl. of* ⇒**serum**

seraglio /se'rɑ:lɪəʊ/, /sɪ-/ *n.* (*pl.* **~s**) сера́ль (*m.*).

seraph /'serəf/ *n.* (*pl.* **~im** *or* **~s**) серафи́м.

seraphic /sə'ræfɪk/ *adj.* а́нгельский; (*e.g. smile*) блаже́нный.

seraphim /'serəfɪm/ *pl. of* ⇒**seraph**

Serb /sɜ:b/ *n.* серб (*fem.* -ка).

Serbia /'sɜ:bɪə/ *n.* Се́рбия.

Serbian /'sɜ:bɪən/ *n.* (*native*) серб (*fem.* -ка); (*language*) се́рбский язы́к.

● *adj.* се́рбский.

Serbo-Croat(ian) /ˌsɜ:bəʊkrəʊ'eɪʃ(ə)n/ *n.* серб(ск)охорва́тский язы́к.

● *adj.* серб(ск)охорва́тский.

serenade /ˌserə'neɪd/ *n.* серена́да.

● *v.t. & i.* петь, с- серена́ду (*кому*).

serendipity /ˌserən'dɪpɪtɪ/ *n.* счастли́вая спосо́бность де́лать неожи́данные откры́тия.

serene /sɪ'ri:n/, /sə'ri:n/ *adj.* (**serener, serenest**) **1** безмяте́жный, споко́йный; (*of sky*) я́сный; (*of weather*) ти́хий. **2**: **His S~ Highness** Его́ све́тлость.

serenity /sɪ'renɪtɪ/, /sə'r-/ *n.* безмяте́жность, споко́йствие, поко́й.

serf /sɜ:f/ *n.* крепостно́й; **emancipation of the ~s** раскрепоще́ние крестья́н.

serfdom /'sɜ:fdəm/ *n.* крепостни́чество; крепостно́е пра́во.

serge /sɜ:dʒ/ *n.* (*text.*) са́ржа.

sergeant /'sɑ:dʒ(ə)nt/ *n.* сержа́нт.

● *cpd.* **~-major** *n.* старшина́ (*m.*).

serial /'sɪərɪəl/ *n.* (*story etc.*) рома́н, выходя́щий отде́льными вы́пусками; (*TV*) многосери́йный телефи́льм; сериа́л.

● *adj.*: **~ killer** сери́йный уби́йца; **~ number** сери́йный но́мер; **~ publication** периоди́ческое изда́ние; **~ rights** а́вторское пра́во на сериализа́цию.

serialization /ˌsɪərɪəlaɪ'zeɪʃ(ə)n/ *n.* сериализа́ция.

serialize /'sɪərɪəˌlaɪz/ *v.t.* (*publish in successive parts*) изд|ава́ть, -а́ть вы́пусками; (*screen in successive parts*) выпуска́ть, вы́пустить се́риями.

series /'sɪəri:z/, /-rɪz/ *n.* (*pl.* **~**) **1** (*set; succession*) се́рия; **a ~ of lectures** цикл ле́кций; **in ~** по поря́дку; (*number*) ряд; **a ~ of questions** ряд вопро́сов. **2** (*math., chem.*) ряд. **3** (*elec.*) после́довательное соедине́ние; **the lamps are connected in ~** ла́мпы соединя́ются после́довательно. **4** (*TV*) цикл програ́мм.

serif /'serɪf/ *n.* засе́чка.

serious /'sɪərɪəs/ *adj.* **1** (*thoughtful, earnest*) серьёзный; **a ~ child**

S

заду́мчивый ребёнок; **I am ~ about this** я э́то говорю́ всерьёз; **you can't be ~** вы шу́тите; **take something ~ly** отн|оси́ться, -ести́сь серьёзно к + *d.*; (*words, joke*) прин|има́ть, -я́ть что-н. всерьёз; **to be ~; ~ly** (*joking apart*) серьёзно; шу́тки в сто́рону.
2 (*important; not slight*) серьёзный, суще́ственный, ва́жный; **a ~ charge** серьёзное обвине́ние; **~ crime** тя́жкое/серьёзное преступле́ние; **he had a ~ accident** с ним случи́лась серьёзная ава́рия; **he is ~ly ill** он серьёзно/тяжело́ бо́лен.
● *cpd.* **~-minded** *adj.* серьёзный.

seriousness /ˈsɪərɪəsnɪs/ *n.* серьёзность; ва́жность; **in all ~** без шу́ток; со всей серьёзностью.

serjeant-at-arms /ˈsɑːdʒ(ə)nt/ *n.* (*pl.* **serjeants-at-arms**) (*Br.*) парла́ментский при́став.

sermon /ˈsɜːmən/ *n.* про́поведь; **the S~ on the Mount** Наго́рная про́поведь.

sermonize /ˈsɜːməˌnaɪz/ *v.t. & i.* чита́ть (*impf.*) про́поведь/мора́ль (*кому*).

serpent /ˈsɜːpənt/ *n.* змея́; (*bibl.*) змий.

serpentine /ˈsɜːpənˌtaɪn/ *n.* (*min.*) змееви́к.
● *adj.* (*snake-like*) змееви́дный; (*sinuous*) изви́листый, извива́ющийся.

serrated /seˈreɪtɪd/ *adj.* зубча́тый, зазу́бренный.

serried /ˈserɪd/ *adj.*: **in ~ ranks** со́мкнутыми ряда́ми; плечо́м к плечу́.

ser|um /ˈsɪərəm/ *n.* (*pl.* **~a** *or* **~ums**) сы́воротка.

servant /ˈsɜːv(ə)nt/ *n.* (*male, also fig.*) слуга́ (*m.*); **your humble ~** ваш поко́рный слуга́; (*maid* **~**) служа́нка, прислу́га; **civil ~** госуда́рственный служа́щий; **public ~s** должностны́е, официа́льные ли́ца.
● *cpd.* **~-girl** *n.* служа́нка.

serve /sɜːv/ *n.* (*at tennis*) пода́ча; **whose ~ is it?** чья пода́ча?
● *v.t.* **1** (*be servant to; give service to*) служи́ть (*impf.*) + *d.*; **he ~d his country well** он ве́рно служи́л ро́дине; **one cannot ~ two masters** нельзя́ служи́ть двум господа́м; **if my memory ~s me correctly/well** е́сли па́мять мне не изменя́ет; (*assist in operating*): **~ a gun** обслу́живать (*impf.*) ору́дие; (*fertilize*): **~ a mare** покр|ыва́ть, -ы́ть кобы́лу.
2 (*meet needs of, satisfy, look after*): **~ a purpose** служи́ть (*impf.*) це́ли; **this box has ~d its purpose** э́та коро́бка сослужи́ла свою́ слу́жбу; **it ~d his interests to keep quiet** ему́ бы́ло вы́годно молча́ть; **these tools will ~ my needs** э́ти инструме́нты вполне́ мне подхо́дят; (*provide service to*) обслу́ж|ивать, -и́ть; **the railway ~s all these villages** желе́зная доро́га обслу́живает все э́ти сёла.
3 (*supply with food, goods etc.*) под|ава́ть, -а́ть + *d.*; **the waiter ~d us with vegetables** официа́нт по́дал (нам) о́вощи; **are you being ~d?** вас кто́-нибудь обслу́живает?
4 (*proffer*) под|ава́ть, -а́ть; **fish is ~d with sauce** ры́ба подаётся с со́усом; **dinner is ~d** обе́д по́дан (*or* на столе́); **~ a ball** под|ава́ть, -а́ть мяч; **~ a summons** вруч|а́ть, -и́ть (суде́бную) пове́стку (*кому*).
5 (*fulfil, go through*): **~ one's apprenticeship** про|ходи́ть, -йти́ вы́учку; **~ one's sentence** отб|ыва́ть, -ы́ть срок; **he ~d his time (in army/prison)** он отслужи́л/отбы́л срок.
6 (*treat*): **he ~d me badly** он ду́рно со мной обошёлся; **it ~s him right** так ему́ и на́до; подело́м ему́.
● *v.i.* служи́ть (*impf.*); **he ~d in the army** он служи́л в а́рмии; **he ~d in the First World War** он воева́л в пе́рвую мирову́ю войну́; **~ on a jury** быть прися́жным; **she ~s in a shop** она́ рабо́тает в магази́не; **he ~d at table** он прислу́живал за столо́м; **the plank ~d as a bench** доска́ служи́ла ла́вкой/скамьёй; **the bag isn't very good, but it will ~** су́мка не осо́бенно хоро́шая, но сойдёт; **a tool which ~s several purposes** инструме́нт, слу́жащий для разли́чных це́лей; **it will ~ to remind him of his obligations** э́то послу́жит ему́ напомина́нием о его́ обяза́тельствах.
● *with advs.*: **~ out** *v.t.* (*distribute*) разд|ава́ть, -а́ть; **~ up** *v.t.* под|ава́ть, -а́ть; (*fig.*): **the papers ~ up the same old news every day** газе́ты ка́ждый день пи́шут об одно́м и том же.

server /ˈsɜːvə(r)/ *n.* (*at tennis*) подаю́щий; (*comput.*) се́рвер.

service[1] /ˈsɜːvɪs/ *n.* **1** (*employment*) слу́жба; **take s.o. into one's ~** нан|има́ть, -я́ть кого́-н.; **she went into domestic ~** она́ пошла́ в прислу́ги; **my car has seen long ~** моя́ маши́на прослужи́ла мно́го лет; **length of ~** стаж.
2 (*branch of public work*) слу́жба; **public, civil ~** госуда́рственная слу́жба; **he entered the diplomatic ~** он поступи́л на дипломати́ческую слу́жбу; **medical ~** слу́жба здравоохране́ния; (*mil.*) медици́нская слу́жба; **intelligence, secret ~** секре́тная слу́жба, разве́дка; **military ~** вое́нная слу́жба; **do one's military ~** отб|ыва́ть, -ы́ть во́инскую пови́нность; **which ~ is he in?** в како́м ро́де войск он слу́жит?; **the Senior S~** (*Br.*) (брита́нский) вое́нно-морско́й флот; **on active ~** на действи́тельной слу́жбе; **the (fighting) ~s** вооружённые си́лы (*f. pl.*); **long ~** сверхсро́чная слу́жба.
3 (*person's disposal*) услу́га; **at your ~** к ва́шим услу́гам; **on His, Her Majesty's S~** (*on letter*) прави́тельственное (письмо́).
4 (*work done for s.o. or something*) услу́га; **will you do me a ~?** мо́жно вас попроси́ть об услу́ге?; **offer one's ~s** предл|ага́ть, -ожи́ть свои́ услу́ги; **I need the ~s of a lawyer** мне нужна́ юриди́ческая по́мощь; (*by hotel staff etc.*) обслу́живание, се́рвис; **the ~ is poor in that restaurant** в (э́)том рестора́не обслу́живание плохо́е; **~ charge** пла́та за обслу́живание; **~ hatch** разда́точное окно́; **~ lift** грузово́й лифт.
5 (*assistance*) по́льза; **can I be of ~ to you?** я могу́ вам че́м-нибудь помо́чь?; **what ~ will that be to you?** кака́я вам от э́того по́льза?
6 (*system to meet public need*): **postal ~** почто́вая слу́жба; **bus ~** авто́бусное обслу́живание; **municipal ~s** коммуна́льные услу́ги (*f. pl.*); **~ pipe** домо́вый ввод; **~ entrance** служе́бный вход; **a frequent train ~ to London** регуля́рные поезда́ в Ло́ндон.
7 (*attention to, maintenance of*) техобслу́живание; **~ station** (*for petrol*) бензозапра́вочная ста́нция, бензоколо́нка; (*for repairs*) ста́нция техни́ческого обслу́живания.
8 (*eccl.*) слу́жба; обря́д; **divine ~** богослуже́ние; **take the/a ~** отпр|авля́ть, -а́вить богослуже́ние; **marriage/burial ~** венча́ние/отпева́ние.
9 (*set of dishes*) серви́з.
10 (*in tennis*) пода́ча.
11 (*leg.*): **~ of a writ** вруче́ние суде́бного предписа́ния.
● *v.t.*: **~ a vehicle** пров|оди́ть, -ести́ осмо́тр и теку́щий ремо́нт маши́ны.
● *cpds.* **~man** *n.* военнослу́жащий; **~woman** *n.* военнослу́жащая.

service[2] /ˈsɜːvɪs/ *n.* (**~ tree**) ряби́на.

serviceability /ˌsɜːvɪsəˈbɪlɪtɪ/ *n.* го́дность, приго́дность.

serviceable /ˈsɜːvɪsəb(ə)l/ *adj.* (*useful*) поле́зный, го́дный, приго́дный; (*durable*) про́чный.

serviette /ˌsɜːvɪˈet/ *n.* (*Br.*) салфе́тка.

servile /ˈsɜːvaɪl/ *adj.* (*of person or behaviour*) раболе́пный, подобостра́стный.

servility /ˌsɜːˈvɪlɪtɪ/ *n.* подобостра́стие.

serving /ˈsɜːvɪŋ/ *n.* (*of food*) по́рция.

servitude /ˈsɜːvɪˌtjuːd/ *n.* ра́бство; **penal ~** ка́торжные рабо́ты (*f. pl.*).

servo-mechanism /ˈsɜːvəʊˌmekəˌnɪz(ə)m/ *n.* сервомехани́зм.

servo-motor /ˈsɜːvəʊˌməʊtə(r)/ *n.* серводви́гатель (*m.*); сервопри́во́д.

sesame /ˈsesəmɪ/ *n.* кунжу́т, сеза́м; **open ~!** Сеза́м, откро́йся!

session /ˈseʃ(ə)n/ *n.* **1** заседа́ние; (*period*) се́ссия; **the House is in ~** пала́та о́бщин/парла́мент сейча́с заседа́ет. **2** (*university year*) уче́бный год; (*term*) семе́стр.

set /set/ *n.* **1** (*collection; outfit*) набо́р; (*complete set*) компле́кт; (*pictures, coins, books, etc. collected*) колле́кция; (*number of persons or things*) ряд; се́рия; (*of accessories*) принадле́жности (*f. pl.*); **~ of tools** набо́р инструме́нтов; **~ of bells** набо́р колоколо́в; **complete ~ of stamps** по́лный компле́кт ма́рок; **~ of golf-clubs** компле́кт клю́шек для го́льфа; **chess ~** ша́хмат|ы (*pl., g.* —); **~ of drawing instruments (and box)** гото́ва́льня; **~ of furniture** ме́бельный гарниту́р; **dinner ~** столо́вый серви́з; **~ of teeth** (*natural*) зу́бы (*m. pl.*); (*dentures*) зубно́й проте́з; **~ of rules** свод пра́вил; **~ of circumstances** стече́ние/совоку́пность обстоя́тельств; **~ of ideas** систе́ма иде́й.
2 (*receiving apparatus*): **wireless ~** радиоприёмник; **television ~** телеви́зор.

3 (*tennis*) сет, па́ртия; **~ point** сет-бо́л.
4 (*math.*) мно́жество; **theory of ~s** тео́рия мно́жеств.
5 (*coterie*) круг, кружо́к; компа́ния; **the racing ~** завсегда́таи (*m. pl.*) бего́в; **the smart ~** фешене́бельное о́бщество.
6 (*direction, drift*): **the ~ of the current/wind** направле́ние тече́ния/ве́тра; (*tendency*): **the ~ of public opinion** напра́вленность обще́ственного мне́ния; **mental ~** склад ума́.
7 (*warp, displacement*) отклоне́ние, накло́н; **the tower has a ~ to the right** ба́шня наклони́лась впра́во.
8 (*posture, attitude*): **the ~ of his head** поса́дка его́ головы́.
9 (*pointing stance of dog*) сто́йка; **make a (dead) ~ at** (*attack*) нап|ада́ть, -а́сть на + *a.*; **she made a dead ~ at him** (*Br., made herself attractive*) она́ ста́ла его́ завлека́ть.
10 (*seedling; shoot*) са́женец; побе́г.
11 (*badger's burrow*) нора́.
12 (*theatr.*) декора́ция.
13 (*cin.*): **on the ~** на съёмочной площа́дке.

● *adj.* **1** (*fixed*): **a ~ stare** неподви́жный взгляд; **a ~ smile** засты́вшая улы́бка; **a man of ~ purpose** целеустремлённый челове́к; **he has ~ opinions** у него́ установи́вшиеся взгля́ды; **he is ~ in his ways** он закосне́л в свои́х привы́чках; **~ phrase** клише́ (*indecl.*), шабло́нное выраже́ние; **the weather is ~ fair** (хоро́шая) пого́да установи́лась; (*prearranged*): **at the ~ time** в устано́вленное вре́мя; **~ dinner** ко́мплексный обе́д; **~ menu** ко́мплексное меню́; **~ piece** (*literary etc.*) образцо́вое произведе́ние; (*prescribed*): **~ books** обяза́тельная литерату́ра; (*prepared*): **a ~ speech** подгото́вленная ре́чь.
2 (*coll., ready*): **all ~?** гото́вы?; **we were all ~ to go** мы совсе́м уже собрали́сь идти́.
3 (*resolved*): **he is ~ on going to the cinema** он настро́ился идти́ в кино́; **he was dead ~ against the idea** он реши́тельно встал про́тив э́того предложе́ния.

● *v.t.* (**setting;** *past and p.p.* **~**) **1** (*lay*) класть, положи́ть; (*place*) разме|ща́ть, -сти́ть; распол|ага́ть, -ожи́ть; **he ~ his hand on my shoulder** он положи́л мне ру́ку на плечо́; **she ~ the plates on the table** (*separately*) она́ расста́вила таре́лки на столе́; (*in a pile*) она́ поста́вила сто́пку таре́лок на стол; **they ~ a tasty meal before us** они́ по́дали нам вку́сное угоще́ние; (*arrange*; **~ out**) расст|авля́ть, -а́вить; **12 chairs were ~ round the table** вокру́г стола́ бы́ло расста́влено двена́дцать сту́льев; (*apply*) при|кла́дывать, -ложи́ть; **~ eyes on** посмотре́ть (*pf.*) на + *a.*, взгляну́ть (*pf.*) на + *a.*; **I have never ~ eyes on him since** с тех пор я его́ бо́льше не ви́дел; **~ one's face against** ни за что не соглаша́ться (*impf.*) на + *a.*; **~ fire to** подж|ига́ть, -е́чь; **~ foot on** наступ|а́ть, -и́ть на + *a.*; **he will never ~ foot in my house** ноги́ его́ не бу́дет в моём до́ме; я его́ никогда́ на поро́г не пущу́; **~ one's hand to** прин|има́ться, -я́ться за + *a.*; **~ (a) light to** подж|ига́ть, -е́чь; **~ one's name to a document** расп|и́сываться, -иса́ться на докуме́нте; **~ in the ground** сажа́ть, посади́ть (в зе́млю); **a safe was ~ in the wall** в сте́ну был встро́ен сейф.
2 (*adjust, prepare*) ста́вить, по-; **I always ~ my watch by the station clock** я всегда́ ста́влю часы́ по станцио́нным часа́м; **they ~ a trap for him** они́ подстро́или ему́ лову́шку; **~ sail** подн|има́ть, -я́ть па́рус; (*start a voyage*) отпл|ыва́ть, -ы́ть; **~ the table** накр|ыва́ть, -ы́ть (на) стол; **~ a saw** разв|оди́ть, -ести́ пилу́.
3 (*make straight or firm*): **~ a bone** впр|авля́ть, -а́вить кость; **~ s.o.'s hair** укла́дывать, уложи́ть кому́-н. во́лосы; **~ting lotion** жи́дкость для укла́дки воло́с; **the wind will ~ the mortar** на ветру́ раство́р затверде́ет/засты́нет.
4 (*fig., apply*): **~ one's heart on** стра́стно жела́ть (*impf.*) + *g.*; настр|а́иваться, -о́иться на + *a.*; **~ one's mind on, to something** устрем|ля́ть, -и́ть по́мыслы на + *a.*; сосредото́чи|ваться, -ться на чём-н.; **~ one's hopes on** возл|ага́ть, -ожи́ть наде́жды на + *a.*; **~ the seal on** (*fig.*) оконча́тельно реш|а́ть, -и́ть/утвер|жда́ть, -ди́ть; **~ store by** (высоко́) цени́ть (*impf.*).
5 (*make or put into specified state*) прив|оди́ть, -ести́; **he will ~ things right** он приведёт всё в поря́док; он всё ула́дит; **he ~ the boat in motion** он привёл ло́дку в движе́ние; **~ something afloat** спус|ка́ть, -ти́ть что-н. на́ воду; **~ at liberty** освобо|жда́ть, -ди́ть; **~ s.o. at ease; ~ s.o.'s mind at ease, rest** успок|аивать, -о́ить кого́-н.; **~ s.o. on his feet** (*lit., fig.*) ста́вить, по- кого́-н. на́ ноги; **~ on fire** подж|ига́ть, -е́чь; (*incite*): **he ~ his dog on me** он натрави́л на меня́ соба́ку; **he ~ the police after** (*or* **on to**) **the criminal** он донёс в поли́цию на престу́пника; **she is trying to ~ me against you** она́ стара́ется восстанови́ть/настро́ить меня́ про́тив вас; (*weigh*): **against the cost can be ~ the advantage** при всей дорогови́зне (э́того) сле́дует учи́тывать и вы́году.
6 (*cause; compel*) поруч|а́ть, -и́ть, веле́ть (*impf., pf.*); **I ~ him to sweeping the floor** я веле́л ему́ подмести́ пол; **he ~ them to work at Greek** он усади́л их за гре́ческий язы́к; **I ~ him to copy the picture** я поручи́л ему́ скопи́ровать карти́ну.
7 (*start*) заст|авля́ть, -а́вить (+ *inf.*); **the smoke ~ her coughing** она́ зака́шлялась от ды́ма; **his remarks ~ them laughing** его́ замеча́ния заста́вили их рассмея́ться; **I ~ him talking about Russia** я навёл его́ на разгово́р о Росси́и; **a programme** (*Br.*), **program** (*US*) **to ~ you thinking** програ́мма, кото́рая заста́вит вас заду́маться.
8 (*present, pose*) зад|ава́ть, -а́ть; **you have ~ me a difficult task** вы поста́вили передо мной тру́дную зада́чу.
9 (*establish*): **~ the pace/tone** зад|ава́ть, -а́ть темп/тон; **he is ~ting his children a bad example** он подаёт свои́м де́тям дурно́й приме́р.
10 (*compile*) сост|авля́ть, -а́вить; **~ an exam paper** сост|авля́ть, -а́вить вопро́сы для пи́сьменного экза́мена.
11: **~ something to music** класть, положи́ть что-н. на му́зыку; **he ~ new words to an old tune** он написа́л но́вые слова́ на ста́рый моти́в.
12 (*insert for adornment etc.*) вст|авля́ть, -а́вить (*во что*); **they ~ the top of the wall with broken glass** они́ покры́ли верх стены́ би́тым стекло́м; **a sky ~ with stars** не́бо, усе́янное звёздами.
13 (*situate*): **he ~ the scene in Paris** ме́стом де́йствия он избра́л Пари́ж; **the scene is ~ in London** де́йствие происхо́дит в Ло́ндоне.
14: **~ a jewel** опр|авля́ть, -а́вить драгоце́нный ка́мень.
15 (*typ.*) наб|ира́ть, -ра́ть.

● *v.i.* (**setting;** *past and p.p.* **~**) **1** (*of sun*) сади́ться, сесть; **we saw the sun ~ting** мы ви́дели зака́т/захо́д со́лнца; (*of stars; also fig.*) за|ходи́ть, -йти́.
2 (*of fruit, blossom*) завя́з|ываться, -а́ться.
3 (*become firm or solid*) затверд|ева́ть, -е́ть; тверде́ть (*impf.*); (*of jelly*) заст|ыва́ть, -ы́ть; (*of cement, concrete etc.*) схва́т|ываться, -и́ться.
4 (*of face or eyes*) заст|ыва́ть, -ы́ть.
5 (*of a dog*) де́лать, с- сто́йку.

● *with preps.*: **~ about (doing) something** прин|има́ться, -я́ться за что-н.; приступ|а́ть, -и́ть к чему́-н.; заня́ться (*pf.*) чем-н.; **~ about** (*beat up*) **s.o.** (*Br.*) отде́лать (*pf.*) кого́-н.; **~ (up)on s.o.** нап|ада́ть, -а́сть на кого́-н.; **~ s.o. to work** ус|а́живать, -ади́ть кого́-н. за рабо́ту.

● *with advs.*: **~ apart, ~ aside** *vv.t.* (*allocate*) выделя́ть, вы́делить; (*reserve, save*) от|кла́дывать, -ложи́ть; **a day ~ aside for revision** день, отведённый/вы́деленный для повторе́ния; (*disregard*): **I ~ aside personal feelings** я отбро́сил все ли́чные чу́вства; (*quash*) аннули́ровать (*impf., pf.*); отмен|я́ть, -и́ть; **the court's verdict was ~ aside** реше́ние суда́ бы́ло отменено́; **~ back** *v.t.* (*lit.*) отодв|ига́ть, -и́нуть; **a house ~ back from the road** дом, стоя́щий в стороне́ от доро́ги; **~ the clock back** перев|оди́ть, -ести́ часы́ наза́д; (*fig.*) поверну́ть (*pf.*) колесо́ исто́рии вспять; (*hinder, delay, damage*) зам|едля́ть, -е́длить; отбр|а́сывать, -о́сить наза́д; нан|оси́ть, -ести́ уро́н + *d.*; (*coll., cost*): **the trip ~ him back a few pounds** пое́здка влете́ла ему́ в копе́ечку; **~ by** *v.t.* (*put by*) от|кла́дывать, -ложи́ть; **~ down** *v.t.* (*put down*) класть, положи́ть; ста́вить, по-; **he ~ down his rucksack on the steps** он поста́вил свой рюкза́к на ступе́ньку; (*allow to alight*) выса́живать, вы́садить; **the bus ~ us down at the gate** авто́бус вы́садил нас у воро́т; (*make statement or record*): **he ~ down his complaint in writing** он

S

изложи́л свою́ жа́лобу в пи́сьменном ви́де; **she ~ down her impressions in a diary** она́ заноси́ла/записывала свои впечатле́ния в дневни́к; **~ forth** *v.t.* (*propound, declare*) изл|ага́ть, -ожи́ть; *v.i.* (*leave*) отпр|авля́ться, -а́виться; **~ in** *v.t.* (*insert*) вст|авля́ть, -а́вить; **~ in a sleeve** вш|ива́ть, -и́ть рука́в; *v.i.* (*take hold*): **winter is ~ting in** наступа́ет зима́; **the rain ~ in early** дождь начался́ ра́но; **~ off** *v.t.* (*cause to explode*): **they were ~ting off fireworks** они́ пуска́ли фейерве́рк; **~ off a rocket** запус|ка́ть, -ти́ть раке́ту; (*cause, stimulate*): **his arrest ~ off a wave of protest** его́ аре́ст вы́звал волну́ проте́стов; (*enhance*): **the ribbon will ~ off your complexion** ле́нта оттени́т/подчеркнёт цвет ва́шего лица́; **the frame ~s off the picture** карти́на в э́той ра́ме выи́грывает (*or* хорошо́ смо́трится); (*compensate*) возме|ща́ть, -сти́ть; компенси́ровать (*impf., pf.*); **~ off gains against losses** баланси́ровать, с- при́быль и убы́тки; (*cause to start*): **the story ~ them off laughing** э́тот расска́з заста́вил их расхохота́ться; *v.i.* (*leave*) (*on foot*) пойти́ (*pf.*); (*by transport*) пое́хать (*pf.*); отпр|авля́ться, -а́виться; **we are ~ting off on a journey** мы отправля́емся в путеше́ствие; **the horse ~ off at a gallop** ло́шадь пусти́лась гало́пом; **they ~ off in pursuit** они́ отпра́вились вдого́нку; **he ~ off running** он бро́сился бежа́ть; **~ out** *v.t.* (*arrange, display*) распол|ага́ть, -ожи́ть; выставля́ть, вы́ставить (на обозре́ние); (*expound*) изл|ага́ть, -ожи́ть; *v.i.* (*leave*) пойти́, пое́хать (*both pf.*); отпр|авля́ться, -а́виться; **they ~ out for Warsaw** они́ отпра́вились/о́тбыли в Варша́ву; (*attempt*): **he ~ out to conquer Europe** он заду́мал/вознаме́рился покори́ть Евро́пу; **~ to** *v.i.* (*make a start*) прин|има́ться, -я́ться; (*begin to fight or argue*) сцеп|ля́ться, -и́ться (*coll.*); схв|а́тываться, -ати́ться; **~ together** *v.t.* сост|авля́ть, -а́вить (вме́сте); (*compare*) сопост|авля́ть, -а́вить; **~ up** *v.t.* (*erect*) устан|а́вливать, -ови́ть; **a statue was ~ up in his honour** (*Br.*), **honor** (*US*) в его́ честь установи́ли ста́тую; (*form*): **~ up a committee** организова́ть (*impf., pf.*) комите́т; (*found, establish*): **~ up a school** учре|жда́ть, -ди́ть шко́лу; **he ~ up a new record** он установи́л но́вый реко́рд; **~ up house** зажи́ть (*pf.*) свои́м до́мом; **they ~ up house together** они́ ста́ли жить вме́сте; **~ up shop** откр|ыва́ть, -ы́ть ла́вку; осн|о́вывать, -ова́ть де́ло; **he ~ his mistress up in a flat** он обста́вил кварти́ру для свое́й любо́вницы; (*claim, put forward*): **he ~s himself up to be a scholar** он изобража́ет из себя́ учёного; (*provide*): **I am ~ up with novels for the winter** я обеспе́чен рома́нами на всю зи́му; (*give voice to*): **~ up a cry** подн|има́ть, -я́ть крик; (*restore to health*): **a holiday will ~ you up** о́тдых вас поста́вит на́ ноги (*or* восстано́вит ва́ши си́лы); (*typ.*) наб|ира́ть, -ра́ть; *v.i.*: **he ~ up as a butcher** он откры́л/завёл мясну́ю ла́вку (*or* мясно́й магази́н); **~ up in business** организова́ть (*impf., pf.*) своё де́ло.

● *cpds.* **~back** *n.* (*delay*) заде́ржка; (*failure*) неуда́ча; (*difficulty*) затрудне́ние; **he met with many ~backs** у него́ бы́ло мно́го неуда́ч; **~-square** *n.* уго́льник; **~-to** *n.* (*fight*) схва́тка; **have a ~-to** схва́т|ываться, -и́ться; сцеп|ля́ться, -и́ться; **~-up** *n.* (*coll., arrangement*) поря́дки (*m. pl.*); обстано́вка; (*comput.*) устано́вка.

settee /se'ti:/ *n.* (небольшо́й) дива́н.

setter /'setə(r)/ *n.* (*dog*) се́ттер.

setting /'setɪŋ/ *n.* **1** (*of sun etc.*) захо́д, зака́т. **2** (*of gems*) опра́ва. **3** (*background*) обстано́вка, окруже́ние. **4** (*theatr.*) вре́мя и ме́сто де́йствия. **5** (*mus.*) му́зыка на слова́. **6** (*at table*) прибо́р.

settle[1] /'set(ə)l/ *n.* скамья́; (*with box below seat*) скамья́-ларь (*m.*).

settle[2] /'set(ə)l/ *v.t.* **1** (*place securely; put to rest*): **~ o.s. in an armchair** ус|а́живаться, -е́сться в кре́сло; **~ children for the night** укла́дывать, уложи́ть дете́й на́ ночь. **2** (*install, establish*) поме|ща́ть, -сти́ть; устр|а́ивать, -о́ить. **3** (*calm*) успок|а́ивать, -о́ить; **he gave me something to ~ my stomach** он дал мне желу́дочное лека́рство (*or* сре́дство для желу́дка). **4** (*reconcile*) ула́|живать, -дить; **their differences were soon ~d** их разногла́сия бы́ли ско́ро ула́жены; **the dispute was ~d out of court** спор был ула́жен полюбо́вно. **5** (*dispel*): **he ~d their doubts** он развея́л/рассе́ял их сомне́ния. **6** (*decide*) реш|а́ть, -и́ть; **that ~s it** э́то реша́ет де́ло; **let's ~ the matter** дава́йте ко́нчим с э́тим де́лом; **~ it amongst yourselves!** вы ка́к-нибудь са́ми договори́тесь!; **nothing is ~d yet** ещё ничего́ (оконча́тельно) не решено́. **7** (*put in order*) прив|оди́ть, -ести́ в поря́док; **~ one's estate** де́лать, с- завеща́ние. **8** (*pay*): **~ a bill** плати́ть, за- по счёту; **~ a debt** гаси́ть, по-/упл|а́чивать, -ати́ть долг; **~ old scores** (*fig.*) св|оди́ть, -ести́ ста́рые счёты; расквита́ться (*pf.*) (*coll.*). **9** (*bestow legally*) закреп|ля́ть, -и́ть (*что за кем*); (*bequeath*) ост|авля́ть, -а́вить; завеща́ть (*impf., pf.*). **10** (*colonize*) засел|я́ть, -и́ть; (*transport to new home*) посел|я́ть, -и́ть.

● *v.i.* **1** (*sink down; come to rest*) ос|еда́ть, -е́сть; **the foundations have ~d** фунда́мент осе́л; **the dust will soon ~** (*fig.*) шуми́ха ско́ро уля́жется; **the excitement ~d** стра́сти ути́хли/улегли́сь; (*alight*) ус|а́живаться, -е́сться; **a fly ~d on his nose** му́ха усе́лась ему́ на нос; **the butterfly ~d on a leaf** ба́бочка се́ла на лист; **dust ~d on everything** повсю́ду осе́ла пыль. **2** (*become fixed, stable, established*) устан|а́вливаться, -ови́ться; **the weather has ~d at last** наконе́ц-то пого́да установи́лась; **darkness ~d on the land** земля́ погрузи́лась во мрак. **3** (*become comfortable, accustomed; also* **~ down**): **the dog ~d in its basket** соба́ка улегла́сь в свое́й корзи́не; **I could not ~ to my work for the noise** из-за шу́ма я не мог сосредото́читься на свое́й рабо́те; **he never ~s to anything for long** он ни на чём подо́лгу не мо́жет задержа́ться. **4** (*make one's home*) посел|я́ться, -и́ться. **5** (*pay*) распла́|чиваться, -ти́ться; (*come to terms*) догов|а́риваться, -ори́ться; **I'll ~ for half the profits** я соглашу́сь на полови́ну при́были. **6** (*decide*) остан|а́вливаться, -ови́ться (*на чём*); **they could not ~ on a name for their son** они́ не могли́ останови́ться ни на одно́м и́мени для сы́на; **have you ~d where to go?** вы реши́ли, куда́ е́хать?

● *with advs.*: **~ back** *v.i.* (*in one's chair*) отки́|дываться, -нуться; **~ down** *v.t.*: **the nurse ~d the patient down for the night** сестра́ пригото́вила больно́го ко сну; *v.i.* (*in home*) устр|а́иваться, -о́иться; (*in job*) осв|а́иваться, -о́иться; (*adopt sober ways*) остепен|я́ться, -и́ться; (*at school*) прив|ыка́ть, -ы́кнуть; (*become quiet*) успок|а́иваться, -о́иться; **since the strike things have ~d down** по́сле забасто́вки всё пришло́ в но́рму; **we ~d down for the night** мы улегли́сь спать; (*give full attention*): **now we can ~ down to our game** тепе́рь мо́жно заня́ться на́шей игро́й; **he ~d down to write letters** он приня́лся/усе́лся писа́ть пи́сьма; **~ in** *v.i.* осв|а́иваться, -о́иться; **~ up** *v.t.* упла́|чивать, -ти́ть; **he ~d up the account** он оплати́л счёт; **~ up one's affairs** ула́|живать, -дить свои́ дела́; *v.i.* распла́|чиваться, -ти́ться (*с кем*).

settled /'set(ə)ld/ *adj.* (*fixed, stable*) усто́йчивый, установи́вшийся; (*permanent*) постоя́нный; **a man of ~ habits** челове́к с установи́вшимися привы́чками; (*determined*) определённый; (*staid*) степе́нный; (*composed*) споко́йный.

settlement /'set(ə)lmənt/ *n.* **1** (*settling people*) поселе́ние; (*populating country*) заселе́ние. **2** (*colony*) поселе́ние; **penal ~** ка́торжная/исправи́тельная коло́ния; (*settled place*) посёлок. **3** (*arranging*) ула́живание. **4** (*solution*) урегули́рование, реше́ние; (*agreement*) соглаше́ние; **reach a ~** дост|ига́ть, -и́чь соглаше́ния. **5** (*leg.*): **~ of one's estate** (*making will*) составле́ние завеща́ния. **6** (*payment*) упла́та, расчёт; **~ of an account** упла́та по счёту.

settler /'setlə(r)/ *n.* поселе́нец.

seven /'sev(ə)n/ *n.* (число́/но́мер) семь; (**~** *people*) се́меро, семь челове́к; **we ~, the ~ of us** мы се́меро/всемеро́м; **~ each** по семи́; (*figure; thing numbered 7; group of* **~**) семёрка; (*with var. nn. expr. or understood: cf. examples under* ⇒**five**).

● *adj.* семь + *g. pl.*; (*for people and pluralia tantum, also*) се́меро + *g. pl.*; **~ twos**

are fourteen се́мью (*or* семь на) два — четы́рнадцать.

● *cpd.* **~fold** *adj.* семикра́тный; *adv.* в семь раз.

seventeen /ˌsev(ə)n'ti:n/ *n.* & *adj.* семна́дцать +*g. pl.*

seventeenth /ˌsev(ə)n'ti:nθ/ *n.* (*date*) семна́дцатое (число́); (*fraction*) семна́дцатая часть; одна́ семна́дцатая.

● *adj.* семна́дцатый.

seventh /'sev(ə)nθ/ *n.* **1** (*date*) седьмо́е (число́). **2** (*fraction*) седьма́я часть; одна́ седьма́я. **3** (*mus.*) се́птима.

● *adj.* седьмо́й; **in the ~ heaven** на седьмо́м не́бе.

seventieth /'sev(ə)ntɪɪθ/ *n.* семидеся́тая (часть); одна́ семидеся́тая.

● *adj.* семидеся́тый.

sevent|y /'sev(ə)ntɪ/ *n.* се́мьдесят; **he is in his ~ies** ему́ за се́мьдесят; ему́ (пошёл) восьмо́й деся́ток; **in the ~ies** (*decade*) в семидеся́тых года́х; в семидеся́тые го́ды; (*temperature*) за се́мьдесят гра́дусов.

sever /'sevə(r)/ *v.t.* отдел|я́ть, -и́ть; **~ a rope** перер|еза́ть, -е́зать верёвку; (*a limb*) отруб|а́ть, -и́ть; **~ one's connection with** пор|ыва́ть, -ва́ть связь с+*i.*; **~ diplomatic relations** раз|рыва́ть, -орва́ть дипломати́ческие отноше́ния.

● *v.i.* раз|рыва́ться, -орва́ться; порва́ться (*pf.*).

several /'sevr(ə)l/ *pron.*: **~ of my friends** не́которые из мои́х друзе́й; **I have four cups but I need ~ more** у меня́ есть четы́ре ча́шки, но мне ну́жно ещё не́сколько (штук).

● *adj.* **1** (*quite a few*) не́сколько +*g. pl.*; **myself and ~ others** я и не́сколько други́х люде́й. **2** (*separate*) отде́льный; **they all go their ~ ways** ка́ждый из них идёт свои́м путём; **~ly** по отде́льности; **jointly and ~ly** совме́стно и по́рознь.

severance /'sevərəns/ *n.* отделе́ние, разры́в; **~ pay** выходно́е посо́бие; компенса́ция при увольне́нии.

severe /sɪ'vɪə(r)/ *adj.* **1** (*stern, strict, austere*) стро́гий, суро́вый; **he is his own ~st critic** он свой са́мый стро́гий кри́тик; **~ rebuke** стро́гий вы́говор; **~ punishment** суро́вое наказа́ние. **2** (*violent*) жесто́кий, си́льный; **a ~ frost** си́льный/жесто́кий/лю́тый моро́з; **~ pain** си́льная/жесто́кая боль; **there was ~ fighting** шли жесто́кие бои́. **3** (*exacting*): **a ~ test** суро́вая прове́рка; **~ competition** жесто́кая/о́страя конкуре́нция. **4** (*serious*) тяжёлый, серьёзный; **~ illness** тяжёлая боле́знь; **a ~ shortage of water** о́страя нехва́тка воды́. **5** (*unadorned*) стро́гий, суро́вый.

severity /sɪ'verɪtɪ/ *n.* стро́гость, суро́вость; серьёзность.

Seville /'sevɪl/ *n.* Севи́лья; **~ orange** помера́нец, го́рький апельси́н.

sew /səʊ/ *v.t.* & *i.* (*p.p.* **sewn** *or* **sewed**) шить, с-; **~ a button on to a dress** приш|ива́ть, -и́ть пу́говицу к пла́тью.

● *with adv.*: **~ up** *v.t.* заш|ива́ть, -и́ть.

sewage /'su:ɪdʒ/, /'sju:-/ *n.* сто́чные во́ды (*f. pl.*); нечисто́ты (*f. pl.*); **~ farm** ста́нция очи́стки сто́чных вод.

sewer /'su:ə(r)/, /'sju:-/ *n.* (*conduit*) сто́чная труба́, канализацио́нная труба́; **main ~** магистра́льная канализацио́нная труба́.

sewerage /'su:ərɪdʒ/, /'sju:-/ *n.* канализа́ция.

sewing /'səʊɪŋ/ *n.* (*process, material*) шитьё; (*attr.*) шве́йный; **~ needle** шве́йная игла́.

● *cpd.* **~-machine** *n.* шве́йная маши́на.

sewn /səʊn/ *p.p. of* ⇒**sew**

sex /seks/ *n.* **1** пол; **the fair/gentle ~** прекра́сный/сла́бый пол; **without distinction of age or ~** без разли́чия по́ла и во́зраста; (*attr.*) полово́й; **the ~ act** полово́й акт; **~ appeal** физи́ческая привлека́тельность; **~ change** опера́ция по измене́нию по́ла; **~ education** сексуа́льное воспита́ние; **~ kitten** «ко́шечка»; **~ life** полова́я/сексуа́льная жизнь; **~ maniac** сексуа́льный манья́к, эротома́н (*fem.* -ка). **2** (*sexual activity*) секс; (*sexual intercourse*) полово́е сноше́ние; **have ~ with s.o.** (*coll.*) име́ть (*impf.*) полово́е сноше́ние с кем-н.; спать (*impf.*) с кем-н.; зан|има́ться, -я́ться се́ксом с кем-н.

● *v.t.* (*determine ~ of*) определ|я́ть, -и́ть пол +*g.*

● *cpds.* **~pot** *n.* (*coll.*) секс-бо́мба; **~-starved** *adj.* испы́тывающий сексуа́льный го́лод.

sexagenarian /ˌseksədʒɪ'neərɪən/ *n.* шестидесятиле́тний стари́к (*fem.* шестидесятиле́тняя стару́ха).

● *adj.* шестидесятиле́тний.

sexiness /'seksɪnɪs/ *n.* сексуа́льность.

sexism /'seksɪz(ə)m/ *n.* секси́зм.

sexist /'seksɪst/ *adj.* женоненави́стнический, секси́стский.

sexless /'sekslɪs/ *adj.* беспо́лый; (*lacking sexual appeal or feeling*) асексуа́льный.

sexologist /sek'sɒlədʒɪst/ *n.* сексо́лог.

sexology /sek'sɒlədʒɪ/ *n.* сексоло́гия.

sextant /'sekst(ə)nt/ *n.* секста́нт.

sextet /sek'stet/ *n.* сексте́т.

sexton /'sekst(ə)n/ *n.* понома́рь (*m.*); церко́вный сто́рож.

sextuple /'seksˌtju:p(ə)l/ *adj.* шестикра́тный.

sexual /'seksjʊəl/, /-ʃʊəl/ *adj.* (*organ, disease, reproduction*) полово́й; (*relations*) сексуа́льный; **~ harassment** сексуа́льное домога́тельство; **~ intercourse** полово́е сноше́ние, полово́й акт.

sexuality /ˌseksjʊ'ælɪtɪ/, /-ʃʊ'ælɪtɪ/ *n.* сексуа́льность.

sexy /'seksɪ/ *adj.* (**sexier, sexiest**) (*coll.*) сексуа́льный, эроти́ческий.

Seychelles /seɪ'ʃel/, /-'ʃelz/ *n.*: **the ~** Сейше́льские острова́ (*m. pl.*).

sh /ʃ/ *int.* шш!; тсс!

shabbiness /'ʃæbɪnɪs/ *n.* изно́шенность; убо́гость; по́длость.

shabby /'ʃæbɪ/ *adj.* (**shabbier, shabbiest**) **1** (*of clothes*) поно́шенный; потрёпанный; (*of personal appearance*): **he looks ~** у него́ потёртый/потрёпанный вид; (*of buildings, streets etc.*) убо́гий, захуда́лый. **2** (*of behaviour*) ни́зкий, по́длый.

shack /ʃæk/ *n.* лачу́га.

● *v.i.*: **~ up with s.o.** (*sl.*) сожи́тельствовать (*impf.*) с кем-н.

shackle /'ʃæk(ə)l/ *n.* (*pl., fetters, also fig.*) око́в|ы (*pl., g.* —).

● *v.t.* (*lit., fetter*) зако́в|ывать, -а́ть в око́вы; (*impede*) ско́в|ывать, -а́ть; стесня́ть (*impf.*).

shad /ʃæd/ *n.* (*pl.* **~** *or* **~s**) (*zool.*) шэд, ало́за (*рыба*).

shade /ʃeɪd/ *n.* **1** (*unilluminated area*) тень; **put in(to) the ~** (*fig.*) затм|ева́ть, -и́ть; **light and ~** (*in picture*) свет и те́ни; (*partial darkness*) полумра́к. **2** (*tint, nuance*) отте́нок, тон; **the same colour** (*Br.*), **color** (*US*) **in a lighter ~** тот же цвет, но бо́лее све́тлого то́на; (*fig.*): **~s of meaning** отте́нки (*m. pl.*) значе́ния; **all ~s of opinion** са́мые ра́зные мне́ния. **3** (*slight amount*): **a ~ better** немно́го/ка́пельку (*or* чуть-чу́ть) лу́чше. **4** (*of lamp*) абажу́р. **5** (*eye-~*) козырёк. **6** (*US, blind*) што́ра.

● *v.t.* **1** (*screen from light*) затен|я́ть, -и́ть; (*shield from light etc.*) заслон|я́ть, -и́ть; **he ~d his eyes with his hand** он заслони́л глаза́ руко́й. **2** (*restrict light of*) приглуш|а́ть, -и́ть; **3** (*drawing*) тушева́ть, за-.

● *v.i.*: **one colour** (*Br.*), **color** (*US*) **~s into another** оди́н цвет (постепе́нно) перехо́дит в друго́й.

shadiness /'ʃeɪdɪnɪs/ *n.* тени́стость.

shading /'ʃeɪdɪŋ/ *n.* (*in drawing*) (за)тушёвка.

shadow /'ʃædəʊ/ *n.* тень; **in the ~ of a tree** в тени́ де́рева; **he has ~s under his eyes** у него́ (чёрные/тёмные) круги́ под глаза́ми; **he was a ~ of his former self; he was worn to a ~** от него́ оста́лась одна́ тень; **cast a ~ on** отбр|а́сывать, -о́сить (*or* бр|оса́ть, -о́сить) тень на+*a.*; (*fig.*) омрач|а́ть, -и́ть; **under the ~ of** (*threat*) под угро́зой +*g.*; **there is not a ~ of doubt** нет ни те́ни сомне́ния; **~ cabinet** (*Br.*) тенево́й кабине́т.

● *v.t.* **1** (*darken, cast ~ over*) оттен|я́ть, -и́ть. **2** (*watch and follow secretly*) (та́йно) следи́ть/сле́довать (*impf.*) за+*i.*

● *cpd.* **~-boxing** *n.* трениро́вочный бой.

shadowy /'ʃædəʊɪ/ *adj.* (*shady*) тени́стый; (*dim*) нея́сный; (*vague*) сму́тный.

shady /'ʃeɪdɪ/ *adj.* (**shadier, shadiest**) **1** (*affording shade*) тени́стый; (*in shadow*) теново́й. **2** (*suspect*) сомни́тельный, тёмный; **~**

S

enterprise сомни́тельное/тёмное де́ло.

shaft /ʃɑ:ft/ *n.* **1** (*of lance or spear*) дре́вко. **2** (*arrow*) стрела́. **3** (*of light*) луч; **~ of lightning** вспы́шка мо́лнии. **4** (*stem, stalk*) сте́бель (*m.*); (*trunk*) ствол. **5** (*of column*) сте́ржень (*m.*); (*of chimney*) труба́. **6** (*of tool*) черено́к, ру́чка, рукоя́тка; (*of axe*) топори́ще. **7** (*one of a pair on cart etc.*) огло́бля; (*central ~ between horses*) ды́шло. **8** (*tech., rod*) вал; (*axle*) ось. **9** (*of mine*) ша́хта; ствол ша́хты; **sink a ~** про|ходи́ть, -йти́ ша́хту. **10** (*archit.*): **lift/elevator ~** ша́хта ли́фта; **ventilation ~** вентиляцио́нная ша́хта.

● *cpd.* **~-horse** *n.* коренни́к.

shag[1] /ʃæg/ *n.* (*tobacco*) махо́рка.

shag[2] /ʃæg/ *n.* (*bird*) хохла́тый бакла́н.

shag[3] /ʃæg/ (*Br., vulg.*) *v.t.* тра́х|ать, -нуть.

● *v.i.* тра́х|аться, -нуться.

shagginess /ˈʃægɪnɪs/ *n.* косма́тость, лохма́тость, взлохма́ченность.

shaggy /ˈʃægɪ/ *adj.* (**shaggier, shaggiest**) (*of hair*) лохма́тый; (*hairy*) волоса́тый, косма́тый.

shagreen /ʃæˈgri:n/ *n.* шагре́нь.

shah /ʃɑ:/ *n.* шах.

shake /ʃeɪk/ *n.* **1** встря́ска; **give s.o./sth. a ~** встря́х|ивать, -ну́ть кого́-н./что-н.; **he answered with a ~ of the head** в отве́т он покача́л голово́й. **2** (*tremble*): **with a ~ in his voice** с дро́жью в го́лосе. **3** (*mus.*) трель. **4** (*coll., moment*): **in two ~s** вмиг, в оди́н миг. **5** (*coll.*): **this book is no great ~s** э́та кни́га та́к себе (*or* нева́жная).

● *v.t.* (*past* **shook**; *p.p.* **shaken** /ˈʃeɪk(ə)n/) **1** тря|сти́, -хну́ть; сотряс|а́ть, -ти́ (*что, чем*); **I shook him by the shoulder** я тряхну́л/потря́с его́ за плечо́; **I shook his hand** (*in greeting*) я пожа́л ему́ ру́ку; **they shook hands** они́ пожа́ли друг дру́гу ру́ки; **he shook the cocktail** он сбил кокте́йль; **he shook his head** он покача́л голово́й; **she shook the duster** она́ вы́тряхнула тря́пку; **~ before using** (*instructions on bottle*) пе́ред употребле́нием взба́лтывать; **the blast shook the windows** от взры́ва задрожа́ли стёкла; **~ one's fist at s.o.** грози́ть, по- кому́-н. кулако́м. **2** (*shock*) потряс|а́ть, -ти́; **she was ~n by the news** э́та но́вость её потрясла́; (*morally*) колеба́ть, по-; **he was ~n out of his complacency** его́ самодово́льства как не быва́ло (*coll.*); **his faith was ~n** его́ ве́ра была́ поколе́блена; **my confidence in him was ~n** моё дове́рие к нему́ поколеба́лось (*or* бы́ло подо́рвано).

● *v.i.* (*past* **shook**; *p.p.* **shaken** /ˈʃeɪk(ə)n/) **1** (*vibrate*) трясти́сь (*impf.*); сотряса́ться (*impf.*); **the trees ~ in the wind** дере́вья кача́ются на ветру́; **the room ~s as he walks** ко́мната сотряса́ется от его́ шаго́в. **2** (*tremble*) дрожа́ть, за-; **he was shaking with cold** он дрожа́л от хо́лода; **he was shaking with fever** его́ трясла́ лихора́дка; **his hands shook** у него́ дрожа́ли ру́ки; **~ in one's shoes** трясти́сь/дрожа́ть (*impf.*) от стра́ха; **he shook with laughter** он (за)тря́сся от сме́ха; **her voice shook with emotion** её го́лос (за)дрожа́л/прерыва́лся от волне́ния.

● *with advs.*: **~ back** *v.t.*: **she shook back her hair** она́ отки́нула во́лосы наза́д; **~ down** *v.t.*: **he shook down the apples from the tree** он натря́с я́блок с де́рева; (*cause to settle*) утряс|а́ть, -ти́; **he shook down the grain in the sack** он утря́с зерно́ в мешке́; *v.i.* (*settle, of grain etc.*) утряс|а́ться, -ти́сь; (*settle in*) осв|а́иваться, -о́иться; **he will soon ~ down at the new school** он ско́ро осво́ится в но́вой шко́ле; **~ off** *v.t.* (*lit.*) стря́х|ивать, -ну́ть; **she shook off the rain from her hair** она́ стряхну́ла с воло́с ка́пли дождя́; **~ off the dust from one's feet** (*fig.*) отряхну́ть (*pf.*) прах от ног свои́х; (*fig., of pursuers, illness, habit etc.*) отде́л|ываться, -аться от + *g.*; изб|авля́ться, -а́виться от + *g.*; **~ out** *v.t.*: **~ out a blanket** вытря́хивать, вы́трясхнуть одея́ло; **~ up** *v.t.* встря́х|ивать, -ну́ть; (*mix by shaking*): **~ up a medicine** взб|а́лтывать, -олта́ть лека́рство; (*restore to shape*): **~ up a pillow** взби|ва́ть, -ть поду́шку; (*coll., rouse*): **he decided to ~ up his staff** он реши́л расшевели́ть свои́х подчинённых.

● *cpds.* **~down** *n.* (*US, makeshift bed*) импровизи́рованная посте́ль; **~-out, ~-up** *nn.* (*upheaval*) встря́ска; (*in cabinet etc.*) перемеще́ние должностны́х лиц; (*in a system, in a service*) коренны́е переме́ны (*f. pl.*).

shaker /ˈʃeɪkə(r)/ *n.* (*for cocktails*) ше́йкер.

Shakespearian /ʃeɪkˈspɪərɪən/ *adj.* шекспи́ровский.

shako /ˈʃeɪkəʊ/ *n.* (*pl.* **~s**) ки́вер.

shaky /ˈʃeɪkɪ/ *adj.* (**shakier, shakiest**) ша́ткий, нетвёрдый; **a ~ bridge/table** ша́ткий мост/стол; **his position in the party is ~** его́ положе́ние в па́ртии ша́ткое/непро́чное; **he is on ~ ground** (*fig.*) у него́ под нога́ми зы́бкая по́чва; **~ handwriting** неро́вный по́черк; **a ~ voice** дрожа́щий го́лос; **his English is ~** он нетвёрд в англи́йском.

shale /ʃeɪl/ *n.* сла́нец; (*attr.*) сла́нцевый.

shall /ʃæl/, /ʃ(ə)l/ *v. aux.* (*see also* ⇒**should**) **1** (*in 1st person*) *usu. translated by future tense*: **I ~ go** я пойду́; **I ~ be reading** я бу́ду чита́ть. **2** (*interrog.*): **~ I wait?** мне подожда́ть?; **~ we close the window?** дава́йте закро́ем окно́; **~ we have dinner now?** не пообе́дать ли нам сейча́с?; дава́йте пообе́даем. **3** (*in 2nd and 3rd person, expr. promise*): **you ~ have an apple** ты полу́чишь (*or* бу́дет тебе́) я́блоко. **4** (*mandatory*): **I say you ~ go** я прика́зываю вам пойти́; **thou shalt not kill** (*arch.*) не убий.

shallot /ʃəˈlɒt/ *n.* (лук-)шало́т.

shallow /ˈʃæləʊ/ *n.* (**~ place**) ме́лкое ме́сто; (*shoal*) мель; **in the ~s** на мели́/о́тмели.

● *adj.* ме́лкий; **~ water** ме́лкая вода́, мель; **~ soil** неглубо́кая по́чва; (*fig.*): **~ mind** пове́рхностный/неглубо́кий ум.

shallowness /ˈʃæləʊnɪs/ *n.* (*of water etc.*) ме́лкость; (*of character*) пове́рхностность.

shaly /ˈʃeɪlɪ/ *adj.* сланцева́тый.

sham /ʃæm/ *n.* **1** (*pretence*) притво́рство; **his illness is only a ~** его́ боле́знь то́лько притво́рство; он то́лько притворя́ется больны́м; (*hypocrisy*) лицеме́рие; **her life is one long ~** вся её жизнь — сплошно́е лицеме́рие. **2** (*counterfeit*) подде́лка; **this diamond is a ~** э́тот бриллиа́нт подде́льный; (*deceit, something that is not what it seems to be*) обма́н. **3** (*of person*) притво́рщик; лицеме́р.

● *adj.* **1** (*feigned*) притво́рный. **2** (*counterfeit*) подде́льный.

● *v.t.* (**shammed, shamming**) (*feign, simulate*) притвор|я́ться, -и́ться + *i.*; симули́ровать (*impf., pf.*); **~ sleep/stupidity** притвор|я́ться, -и́ться (*or* прики́|дываться, -нуться (*coll.*)) спя́щим/простако́м.

● *v.i.* (**shammed, shamming**): **he is ~ming** он притворя́ется.

shaman /ˈʃæmən/ *n.* шама́н.

shamanism /ˈʃæməˌnɪz(ə)m/ *n.* шама́нство.

shamble /ˈʃæmb(ə)l/ *n.* неуклю́жая похо́дка

● *v.i.*: **~ along** тащи́ться (*impf.*); **~ in** притащи́ться (*pf.*).

shambles /ˈʃæmb(ə)lz/ *n.* (*coll., mess*) беспоря́док, ха́ос, каварда́к; **he made a ~ of the job** он провали́л всё де́ло.

shambolic /ʃæmˈbɒlɪk/ *adj.* (*Br.*) хаоти́ческий, сумбу́рный.

shame /ʃeɪm/ *n.* **1** (*sense of guilt or inferiority; capacity for this*) стыд; **he is quite without ~** у него́ совсе́м нет стыда́; **put to ~** пристыди́ть (*pf.*); **he hung his head in ~** он опусти́л го́лову от стыда́; **to my ~ I must confess ...** к своему́ стыду́ до́лжен призна́ться. . .; **for ~!; ~ on you!** стыди́(те)сь!/как тебе́ (*or* вам) не сты́дно! **2** (*disgrace*) позо́р, срам; **bring ~ on** позо́рить, о-; навл|ека́ть, -е́чь позо́р на + *a.*; **it's a ~ to laugh at him** сты́дно/нехорошо́ над ним смея́ться. **3** (*something regrettable*) жа́лость, доса́да; **what a ~!** как жаль!; кака́я жа́лость!

● *v.t.* **1** (*cause to feel ashamed*) сму|ща́ть, -ти́ть; стыди́ть, при-; **he ~d me into apologizing** он меня́ пристыди́л/усо́вестил, и я извини́лся. **2** (*disgrace*) позо́рить, о-.

● *cpd.* **~faced** *adj.* пристыжённый.

shameful /ˈʃeɪmfʊl/ *adj.* позо́рный, посты́дный; **~ act** посты́дный/позо́рный посту́пок.

shameless /ˈʃeɪmlɪs/ *adj.* бессты́дный; **~ person** бессты́дный челове́к, бессты́дни|к (*fem.* -ца) (*coll.*); (*unscrupulous*) бессо́вестный; (*indecent, not of people*) непристо́йный.

shamelessness /ˈʃeɪmlɪsnɪs/ *n.* бессты́дство.

shammy /ˈʃæmɪ/ *n.*: **~ leather** за́мша.

shampoo /ʃæmˈpuː/ *n.* шампу́нь (*m.*).
● *v.t.* (**shampoos, shampooed**) мыть, вы́- шампу́нем.

shamrock /ˈʃæmrɒk/ *n.* бе́лый кле́вер; трили́стник.

shandy /ˈʃændɪ/ *n.* смесь пи́ва с лимона́дом.

Shanghai /ʃæŋˈhaɪ/ *n.* Шанха́й.

shank /ʃæŋk/ *n.* **1** (*leg*) нога́; **on S~'s pony, mare** (*Br. coll.*) на свои́х (на) двои́х. **2** (*shin*) го́лень.

shantung /ʃænˈtʌŋ/ *n.* чесуча́; (*attr.*) чесучо́вый.

shanty¹ /ˈʃæntɪ/ *n.* (*hut*) хиба́рка, лачу́га; **~ town** трущо́бный посёлок.

shanty² /ˈʃæntɪ/ *n.* (*song*) ≈ матро́сская пе́сня.

shape /ʃeɪp/ *n.* **1** (*configuration, outward form*) фо́рма; (*outline*) очерта́ние; **take ~** (*become clear*) проясн|я́ться, -и́ться; обре|та́ть, -сти́ фо́рму; **lose one's ~** (*figure*) полне́ть, рас-; толсте́ть, рас-; **give ~ to** прид|ава́ть, -а́ть фо́рму +*d.*; (*appearance, guise*) вид, о́браз; **a cloud in the ~ of a bear** о́блако в ви́де медве́дя; **a monster in human ~** чу́довище в челове́ческом о́бразе; **we have a leader in the ~ of Mr X** мы обрели́ ли́дера в лице́ г-на X; **I have had no answer in any ~ or form** я не получи́л реши́тельно никако́го отве́та.
2 (*vague figure*): **strange ~s appeared in the dark** в темноте́ появля́лись стра́нные о́бразы.
3 (*order*) поря́док; **put** (*coll.* **knock, lick**) **something into ~** прив|оди́ть, -ести́ что-н. в поря́док; (*condition*) фо́рма, состоя́ние; **he was in poor ~** он был в плохо́м состоя́нии (*or* плохо́й фо́рме); **in good ~** в по́лном поря́дке; в (хоро́шей) фо́рме; **he is exercising to get into ~** он трениру́ется, что́бы обрести́ спорти́вную фо́рму.
4 (*mould*) фо́рма.
● *v.t.* прид|ава́ть, -а́ть фо́рму +*d.*; **her face was delicately ~d** у неё бы́ли то́нкие черты́ лица́; **~d like a heart** сердцеви́дный; **~d like a cone** конусообра́зный; (*from wood*) выреза́ть, вы́резать; (*from clay*) лепи́ть, вы́-/с-; (*fig.*): **~ s.o.'s character** формирова́ть, с- чей-н. хара́ктер; **the war ~d his destiny** война́ определи́ла его́ судьбу́; (*adapt*) приспос|а́бливать, -о́бить (*что к чему*).
● *v.i.*: **the affair is shaping well** де́ло идёт на лад.
● *with adv.*: **~ up** *v.i.* (*take ~*) скла́дываться, сложи́ться.

shapeless /ˈʃeɪplɪs/ *adj.* бесфо́рменный.

shapeliness /ˈʃeɪplɪnɪs/ *n.* красота́, пропорциона́льность; (*of person*) стро́йность; хоро́шее телосложе́ние.

shapely /ˈʃeɪplɪ/ *adj.* (**shapelier, shapeliest**) хорошо́ сложённый; стро́йный; **a ~ leg** стро́йная нога́.

shaper /ˈʃeɪpə(r)/ *n.* **1** (*machine tool*) попере́чно-строга́льный стано́к. **2**: **~ of our destinies** верши́тель (*m.*) на́ших су́деб; **the ~ of the plan** а́втор пла́на.

shard /ʃɑːd/ *n.* (*potsherd*) черепо́к.

share¹ /ʃeə(r)/ *n.* **1** (*part*) часть; (*portion, received or held*) до́ля; **lion's ~** льви́ная до́ля; **fair ~** причита́ющаяся до́ля (*кому*); **have, take a ~ in something** уча́ствовать (*impf.*) (*or* прин|има́ть, -я́ть уча́стие) в чём-н.; **go ~s with s.o.** входи́ть, войти́ в до́лю/пай с кем-н.
2 (*contribution*) вклад; **he had no ~ in the plot** он не́ был прича́стен к за́говору.
3 (*of capital*) а́кция; **ordinary ~s** (*Br.*) обыкнове́нные а́кции; **preference** (*US* **preferred**) **~s** привилегиро́ванные а́кции; **we hold 1,000 ~s in the company** нам принадлежи́т ты́сяча а́кций э́той компа́нии; **~ certificate** акционе́рное свиде́тельство.
● *v.t.* дели́ть, раз- (*что с кем*); **he ~s all his secrets with me** (*or* **I ~ all his secrets**) он де́лится со мной всеми́ свои́ми ссекре́тами; **~ an office with s.o.** рабо́тать (*impf.*) с кем-н. в одно́й ко́мнате; **~ the same book** вме́сте по́льзоваться (*impf.*) одно́й кни́гой; (**~ in**) раздел|я́ть, -и́ть; **he ~s my opinion** он разделя́ет моё мне́ние; **we must all ~ the blame** мы все несём отве́тственность за э́то.
● *v.i.*: **I ~ in your grief** я разделя́ю ва́ше го́ре; **~ and ~ alike** всё на́до дели́ть по́ровну.
● *with adv.*: **~ out** *v.t.* (*divide*) дели́ть, раз-; раздел|я́ть, -и́ть; (*allocate*) распредел|я́ть, -и́ть; разд|ава́ть, -а́ть.
● *cpds.* **~-cropper** *n.* (*US*) издо́льщик; **~-cropping** *n.* (*US*) издо́льная систе́ма; **~holder** *n.* акционе́р; **~-out** *n.* делёж.

share² /ʃeə(r)/ *n.* (*of plough*) ле́мех.

shark /ʃɑːk/ *n.* (*also fig.*) аку́ла; (*swindler*) моше́нник, шу́лер.
● *cpd.* **~skin** *n.* аку́лья ко́жа; (*soft leather*) шагре́нь.

sharp /ʃɑːp/ *n.* (*mus.*) дие́з.
● *adj.* **1** (*edged, pointed, clear-cut; also fig., of senses, sensations etc.*) о́стрый; ре́зкий; **~ knife** о́стрый нож; **~ pencil** о́стрый каранда́ш; **~ chin** о́стрый подборо́док; **~ features** ре́зкие черты́ лица́; **the roofs stood out ~ly against the sky** кры́ши чётко вырисо́вывались на фо́не не́ба; (*keen, alert*): **~ eyes** о́строе зре́ние; **~ ears** то́нкий слух; **~ wits** о́стрый ум; **he is ~** он хитёр; **a ~ child** смышлёный ребёнок; **keep a ~ look-out** смотре́ть (*impf.*) в о́ба; (*of sounds*): **~ voice** ре́зкий го́лос; (*severe*): **a ~ remark** ко́лкое замеча́ние; **~ temper** ре́зкий хара́ктер; **~ tongue** злой/о́стрый язы́к; **~ frost** си́льный моро́з; **~ wind** ре́зкий ве́тер; **~ pain** о́страя боль; (*to the taste*): **~ cheese** о́стрый сыр; (*sour*) ки́слый.
2 (*abrupt*) круто́й, ре́зкий; **~ turn** круто́й поворо́т; **a ~ drop in the temperature** ре́зкое паде́ние температу́ры; **a ~ rise in prices** ре́зкое повыше́ние цен.
3 (*artful*) хи́трый; **~ practice** моше́нничество; **he was too ~ for me** он перехитри́л меня́.
4 (*mus.*): **F ~** фа (*nt. indecl.*) дие́з.
● *adv.* **1** (*at a ~ angle*): **turn ~ right** кру́то пов|ора́чивать, -ерну́ть напра́во.
2 (*punctually*): **at four o'clock ~** то́чно/ро́вно в четы́ре (часа́).
3 (*coll.*): **look ~!** потора́пливайся!; быстре́е!; **we must look ~** на́до потора́пливаться/торопи́ться.
4 (*mus.*): **he sings ~** он поёт сли́шком высоко́.
● *cpds.* **~-edged** *adj.* о́стрый; **~-eyed** *adj.* зо́ркий; **~-featured** *adj.* с ре́зкими черта́ми (лица́); **~shooter** *n.* ме́ткий стрело́к; **~-sighted** *adj.* зо́ркий; **~-tempered** *adj.* раздражи́тельный; **~-witted** *adj.* с о́стрым умо́м; (*perceptive*) проница́тельный.

sharpen /ˈʃɑːpən/ *v.t.* **1** (*knife etc.*) точи́ть, от-/на-; (*pencil*) заостр|я́ть, -и́ть; точи́ть, от-; **my razor needs ~ing** мне на́до наточи́ть бри́тву. **2** (*fig.*) обостр|я́ть, -и́ть; **hunger ~ed his wits** го́лод обостри́л его́ ум; **a long walk ~s one's appetite** дли́тельная прогу́лка обостря́ет аппети́т.
3 (*mus.*) пов|ыша́ть, -ы́сить на полуто́н. **4**: **~ up** *v.t.* (*& i.*) ул|учша́ть(ся), -у́чшить(ся).

sharpener /ˈʃɑːpənə(r)/ *n.* (*whetstone*) точи́ло; (**pencil-~**) точи́лка.

sharper /ˈʃɑːpə(r)/ *n.* шу́лер.

sharpish /ˈʃɑːpɪʃ/ *adv.* (*Br., coll., quickly*) бы́стренько.

sharpness /ˈʃɑːpnɪs/ *n.* острота́; (*of voice etc.*) ре́зкость; (*of outline, photograph etc.*) чёткость; (*astringency*) те́рпкость, е́дкость.

shat /ʃæt/ *past and p.p. of* ⇒**shit**

shatter /ˈʃætə(r)/ *v.t.* (*breakables*) разб|ива́ть, -и́ть (вдре́безги); (*hopes*) разб|ива́ть, -и́ть; **the explosion ~ed the house** взры́вом разру́шило дом; (*of health or nerves*) расстр|а́ивать, -о́ить; **I was ~ed** (*exhausted*) я замота́лся; **I was ~ed by the news** я был потрясён|убит э́той но́востью.
● *v.i.* разб|ива́ться, -и́ться.

shattering /ˈʃætərɪŋ/ *adj.* (*coll.*) потряса́ющий.

shave /ʃeɪv/ *n.* **1** бритьё; **give s.o. a ~** бри́ть, по- кого́-н.; **have a ~** побри́ться (*pf.*). **2** (*coll., escape*): **we had a close ~** мы бы́ли на волосо́к от ги́бели.
● *v.t.* (*p.p.* **shaved** *or* (*as adj.*) **shaven**) **1**: **~ one's chin/beard** выбрива́ть, вы́брить подборо́док; брить, по- бо́роду; **~ a customer** брить, по- клие́нта; **~ o.s.** бри́ться, по-; **~n** (*of chin, head*) бри́тый; (*of monk*) постри́женный. **2** (*pare wood etc.*) строга́ть, вы-.
● *v.i.* (*p.p.* **shaved**): **he does not ~ every day** он бре́ется не ка́ждый день.
● *with adv.*: **~ off** *v.t.* сбри|ва́ть, -ть.

shaver /ˈʃeɪvə(r)/ *n.* (*razor*) бри́тва; **electric ~** электробри́тва.

shaving /ˈʃeɪvɪŋ/ *n.* **1** (*action*) бритьё; **~ is compulsory in the army** в а́рмии полага́ется бри́ться. **2** (**~s**, *of wood or metal*) стру́жка.

● *cpds.* **~-brush, ~-cream, ~-soap** *nn.* ки́сточка/крем/мы́ло для бритья́.

shawl /ʃɔ:l/ *n.* шаль; **head ~** головно́й плато́к.

she /ʃi:/ *pron.* (*obj.* **her**) она́; **it was ~ who did it** э́то она́ сде́лала; **~ and I** я и она́; мы с ней.

● *cpds.* **~-bear** *n.* медве́дица; **~-devil** *n.* ве́дьма; **~-wolf** *n.* волчи́ца.

sheaf /ʃi:f/ *n.* (*pl.* **sheaves**) (*of corn*) сноп; **~ of papers** па́чка/свя́зка бума́г.

shear /ʃɪə(r)/ *n.* (*pl., pair of* **~s**) (садо́вые) но́жниц|ы (*pl., g.* —).

● *v.t.* (*past* **sheared;** *p.p.* **shorn** *or* **sheared**) **1** (*remove by cutting*) отр|еза́ть, -е́зать; (*sheep*) стри́чь, о-. **2** (*cut*) ре́зать, раз-.

● *v.i.* (*past* **sheared;** *p.p.* **shorn** *or* **sheared**): **they are ~ing next week** ове́ц бу́дут стричь на сле́дующей неде́ле.

● *with adv.*: **~ off** *v.t.* отр|еза́ть, -е́зать.

shearer /ˈʃɪərə(r)/ *n.* стрига́льщик.

shearing /ˈʃɪərɪŋ/ *n.* стри́жка.

shearling /ˈʃɪəlɪŋ/ *n.* (*US, coat*) дублёнка.

sheath /ʃi:θ/ *n.* (*of weapon*) но́жны (*pl., g.* но́жен); (*condom*) презервати́в.

● *cpd.* **~-knife** *n.* фи́нка; охо́тничий нож.

sheathe /ʃi:ð/ *v.t.* **1**: **~ one's sword** вкла́дывать, вложи́ть меч в но́жны. **2** (*encase*) обш|ива́ть, -и́ть; заключ|а́ть, -и́ть в оболо́чку.

sheathing /ˈʃi:ðɪŋ/ *n.* обши́вка; (*of cable*) оболо́чка.

sheaves /ʃi:vz/ *pl. of* ⇒**sheaf**

shed¹ /ʃed/ *n.* сара́й; (*railway*) депо́ (*indecl.*); (*for aircraft*) анга́р.

shed² /ʃed/ *v.t.* (**shedding;** *past and p.p.* **~**) **1** (*discard*) сбр|а́сывать, -о́сить; **trees ~ their leaves** дере́вья роня́ют ли́стья; **stags ~ their antlers** оле́ни сбра́сывают рога́; (*of animals*) **~ hair, feathers** линя́ть (*impf.*); **~ skin** сбр|а́сывать, -о́сить ко́жу. **2** (*cause to flow*) прол|ива́ть, -и́ть; **he ~ his blood for his country** он пролива́л кровь за ро́дину; **no tears were ~ at his death** никто́ по нему́ не пла́кал. **3** (*diffuse*): **~ light on** (*lit., fig.*) пролива́ть, проли́ть (*or* бр|оса́ть, -о́сить) свет на + *a.*; **this ~s light on his disappearance** э́то пролива́ет/броса́ет свет на его́ исчезнове́ние. **4** (*elec.*): **~ load** сокра|ща́ть, -ти́ть нагру́зку. **5**: **the truck ~ its load** грузови́к рассы́пал груз. **6**: **~ jobs** сокра|ща́ть, -ти́ть рабо́чие места́.

shedding /ˈʃedɪŋ/ *n.*: **~ of leaves** листопа́д; **~ of skin** сбра́сывание; **~ of feathers** ли́нька; **~ of blood** кровопроли́тие; **there was much ~ of tears** бы́ло про́лито нема́ло слёз.

sheen /ʃi:n/ *n.* (*gloss*) лоск; (*brightness*) блеск, сия́ние.

sheep /ʃi:p/ *n.* (*pl.* **~**) овца́; (*male*) бара́н; **keep ~** держа́ть (*impf.*) ове́ц; **separate the ~ from the goats** (*fig.*) отдели́ть (*pf.*) ове́ц от ко́злищ; **they followed him like ~** они́ шли за ним, как ста́до бара́нов; **the black ~ of the family** парши́вая овца́, вы́родок в семье́; **I felt like a lost ~** я чу́вствовал себя́ совсе́м потéрянным; **as well be hanged for a ~ as a lamb** семь бед — оди́н отве́т; **lost ~** заблу́дшая овца́.

● *cpds.* **~-dip** *n.* раство́р для купа́ния ове́ц; **~-dog** *n.* овча́рка; **~-farm** *n.* овцево́дческая фе́рма; **~-farmer** *n.* овцево́д; **~-farming** *n.* овцево́дство; **~-fold** *n.* овча́рня; **~-pen** *n.* заго́н (для ове́ц); **~shank** *n.* (*naut.*) ко́лышка; **~-shearer** *n.* стрига́льщик; **~-shearing** *n.* стри́жка ове́ц; **~skin** *n.* овчи́на; ове́чья шку́ра; бара́нья ко́жа; **~skin coat** дублёнка; *adj.* овчи́нный.

sheepish /ˈʃi:pɪʃ/ *adj.* (*embarrassed*) сконфу́женный; (*silly*) глупова́тый.

sheer¹ /ʃɪə(r)/ *adj.* **1** (*absolute*) соверше́нный, су́щий, я́вный; (*mere*) просто́й; **~ waste of time** соверше́нная тра́та вре́мени; **~ nonsense** соверше́нная бессмы́слица; су́щая чепуха́; **~ accident** чи́стая случа́йность; **from ~ habit** про́сто по привы́чке; **it is ~ madness** э́то про́сто сумасше́ствие; **by ~ force of will** исключи́тельно благодаря́ си́ле во́ли. **2** (*precipitous*) отве́сный; перпендикуля́рный; **a ~ drop** круто́й обры́в. **3** (*text., diaphanous*) прозра́чный; (*lightweight*) лёгкий.

● *adv.*: **the bird rose ~ into the air** пти́ца кру́то взмы́ла в не́бо.

sheer² /ʃɪə(r)/ *v.i.*: **~ away, off** (*depart*) от|ходи́ть, -ойти́; **he ~ed off the subject** он уклони́лся от те́мы.

sheet¹ /ʃi:t/ *n.* **1** (*bed-linen*) простыня́; **as white as a ~** бле́дный как полотно́. **2** (*flat piece*): лист (*pl.* -ы́); **~ of notepaper** листо́к пи́счей бума́ги; **~ of snow** пелена́ сне́га; **~ of water/ice** полоса́ воды́/льда; **the rain came down in ~s** дождь лил как из ведра́; **~ metal** листово́й мета́лл; **~ music** но́ты (*f. pl.*); **~ lightning** зарни́ца; **a clean ~** (*fig.*) незапя́тнанная репута́ция.

sheet² /ʃi:t/ *n.* (*naut., rope*) шкот; **haul in the ~s** выбира́ть, вы́брать шко́ты.

● *cpds.* **~-anchor** *n.* (*naut.*) запасно́й я́корь; (*fig.*) я́корь (*m.*) спасе́ния; **~-bend** *n.* шко́товый у́зел.

sheeting /ˈʃi:tɪŋ/ *n.* (*text.*) просты́нное полотно́.

sheik(h) /ʃeɪk/ *n.* шейх.

sheik(h)dom /ˈʃeɪkdəm/ *n.* владе́ния (*nt. pl.*) ше́йха.

shekel /ˈʃek(ə)l/ *n.* (*pl., joc.*) (*money*) де́нежки; (*riches*) злато.

shelduck /ˈʃeldʌk/ *n.* (*pl.* **~** *or* **~s**) пега́нка.

shelf /ʃelf/ *n.* (*pl.* **shelves**) **1** по́лка; **set of shelves** стелла́ж; **he is on the ~** (*past working age*) он вы́шел в тира́ж; (*of unmarried woman*): **she is on the ~** она́ ста́рая де́ва. **2** (*ledge of rock etc.*) вы́ступ; (*reef*) риф; (*sandbank*) о́тмель.

● *cpds.* **~-life** *n.* срок хране́ния *or* го́дности; **~-mark** *n.* шифр (*книги*); **~-room** *n.* (свобо́дное) ме́сто на по́лках.

shell /ʃel/ *n.* **1** (*of mollusc etc.*) ра́ковина, раку́шка; (*of tortoise*) щит, па́нцирь (*m.*); (*of egg, nut*) скорлупа́; **chickens in the ~** невы́лупившиеся цыпля́та; **come out of one's ~** (*fig.*) выходи́ть, вы́йти из свое́й скорлупы́; **retire into one's ~** (*fig.*) зам|ыка́ться, -кну́ться в свое́й скорлупе́; (*pod of pea etc.*) стручо́к. **2** (*outer walls of building*) нару́жные сте́ны; (*of ship*) ко́рпус. **3** (*frame of vehicle etc.*) карка́с. **4** (*light boat*) лёгкая го́ночная ло́дка. **5** (*fig., outward semblance*) (одна́) ви́димость (*чего*). **6** (*explosive case, cartridge*) ги́льза; (*of bomb*) оболо́чка; (*missile*) снаря́д.

● *v.t.* **1**: **~ peas** лущи́ть, об- горо́х; **~ eggs** чи́стить, о- я́йца. **2** (*bombard*) обстре́л|ивать, -я́ть (артиллери́йскими снаря́дами).

● *with adv.*: **~ out** *v.i.* раскоше́ли|ваться, -ться (*coll.*).

● *cpds.* **~fire** *n.* артиллери́йский ого́нь; **~fish** *n.* (*mollusc*) моллю́ск; (*crustacean*) ракообра́зное; **~-shock** *n.* конту́зия; **~-shocked** *adj.* конту́женный; страда́ющий вое́нным невро́зом; **~ suit** *n.* нейло́новый спорти́вный костю́м на мя́гкой подкла́дке.

shellac /ʃəˈlæk/ *n.* шелла́к.

● *v.t.* (**shellacked, shellacking**) покр|ыва́ть, -ы́ть шелла́ком.

shelter /ˈʃeltə(r)/ *n.* **1** (*protection*) укры́тие, защи́та; **under, in the ~ of a tree** под защи́той/се́нью де́рева; **~ from the rain** укры́тие от дождя́; **take ~ from** укр|ыва́ться, -ы́ться от + *g.*; **the wall gave us ~ from the wind** стена́ укры́ла/защити́ла нас от ве́тра; **when he was homeless we gave him ~** когда́ ему́ не́где бы́ло жить, мы да́ли ему́ прию́т (*or* приюти́ли его́). **2** (*building etc. providing* **~**) прию́т, убе́жище; (*bomb-***~**) (бомбо)убе́жище; (*for homeless people*) ночле́жка.

● *v.t.* **1** (*provide refuge for*) приюти́ть (*pf.*); (*screen*) укр|ыва́ть, -ы́ть; защи|ща́ть, -ти́ть; **the trees ~ the house from the wind** дере́вья защища́ют/укрыва́ют дом от ве́тра; **a ~ed valley** защищённая от ве́тра доли́на; **~ed housing** (*Br.*) дом, приспосо́бленный для престаре́лых/инвали́дов. **2** (*protect, defend*) оберега́ть (*impf.*); защи|ща́ть, -ти́ть; **he was ~ed from criticism** его́ защища́ли от кри́тики; **he led a ~ed life** он жил без забо́т и трево́г.

● *v.i.* укр|ыва́ться, -ы́ться; пря́таться, с-; **we were ~ing from the rain** мы укрыва́лись/пря́тались от дождя́.

shelve¹ /ʃelv/ *v.t.* **1** (*put on shelf*)

класть, положи́ть (*or, standing*: ста́вить, по-) на по́лку; ~ **books** расст|авля́ть, -а́вить кни́ги по по́лкам. **2** (*fit with* ~*s*): ~ **a cupboard** вст|авля́ть, -а́вить в шкаф по́лки. **3** (*fig., put aside*): ~ **a plan** от|кла́дывать, -ложи́ть прое́кт (в до́лгий я́щик).

shelve² /ʃelv/ *v.i.* (*of ground*) отло́го спуска́ться (*impf.*).

shelves /ʃelvz/ *pl. of* ⇨**shelf**

shelving /ˈʃelvɪŋ/ *n.* стелла́ж.

shepherd /ˈʃepəd/ *n.* пасту́х; ~ **boy** пастушо́к; ~**'s crook** по́сох.

● *v.t.* **1** (*tend*) пасти́ (*impf.*). **2** (*marshal*): **she**~**ed the children across the road** она́ перевела́ дете́й че́рез доро́гу; **the tourists were** ~**ed into the museum** тури́стов провели́ в музе́й.

shepherdess /ˈʃepədɪs/ *n.* пасту́шка.

sherbet /ˈʃɜːbət/ *n.* (*drink in Arab countries*) шербе́т; (*Br., sweet powder*) сла́дкий порошо́к (для приготовле́ния шипу́чего напи́тка); (*US, water ice*) фрукто́вое моро́жсное.

sheriff /ˈʃerɪf/ *n.* шери́ф.

sherry /ˈʃerɪ/ *n.* хе́рес; ~ **glass** рю́мка для хе́реса.

Shetland /ˈʃetlənd/ *n.*: **the** ~**s** (**also the** ~ **Islands**) Шетла́ндские острова́ (*m. pl.*).

shiatsu /ʃɪˈætsuː/ *n.* то́чечный масса́ж.

shibboleth /ˈʃɪbəˌleθ/ *n.* (*bibl.*) шибболе́т; (*fig., pej.*) предрассу́док, традицио́нное предубежде́ние; (*slogan*) ло́зунг.

shield /ʃiːld/ *n.* щит.

● *v.t.* заслон|я́ть, -и́ть; защи|ща́ть, -ти́ть; (*fig.*) огра|жда́ть, -ди́ть; покр|ыва́ть, -ы́ть.

shift /ʃɪft/ *n.* **1** (*change of position etc.*) сдвиг, измене́ние, перемеще́ние; **there was a** ~ **in public opinion** в обще́ственном мне́нии произошёл сдвиг; **there has been a** ~ **of emphasis to ...** акце́нт перемести́лся на. . . **2** (*of workers*) сме́на; **work (in)** ~**s** рабо́тать (*impf.*) посме́нно; **I have done my** ~ **for today** сего́дня я отрабо́тал свою́ сме́ну; **he is on the night** ~ он (рабо́тает) в ночну́ю сме́ну. **3** (*liter., device, scheme*) уло́вка, хи́трость; **make** ~ **without something** об|ходи́ться, -ойти́сь без чего́-н. **4** (*type of dress*) прямо́е пла́тье. **5** (*US, gear-change*) переключе́ние (ско́рости).

● *v.t.* (*move*) сме|ща́ть, -сти́ть; дви́|гать, -нуть; **I can't** ~ **this screw** (*make it turn*) я не могу́ поверну́ть э́тот винт; (*transfer*) переме|ща́ть, -сти́ть; ~ **the furniture** перест|авля́ть, -а́вить (*or* передв|ига́ть, -и́нуть) ме́бель; ~ **the scene** (*theatr.*) меня́ть, по- декора́ции; ~ **responsibility for something to s.o.** пере|кла́дывать, -ложи́ть (*or* сва́л|ивать, -и́ть (*coll.*)) отве́тственность за что-н. на кого́-н.; (*remove*) уб|ира́ть, -ра́ть; **this rubbish has to be** ~**ed** э́тот му́сор/хлам на́до убра́ть отсю́да; (*change*) меня́ть, по-; **he** ~**ed his weight to the other foot** он перенёс вес на другу́ю но́гу; ~ **one's ground** (*in argument*) измен|я́ть, -и́ть (*or* перемени́ть (*pf.*)) пози́цию.

● *v.i.* **1** переме|ща́ться, -сти́ться; **the scene** ~**s to Paris** де́йствие перено́сится в Пари́ж; (*change seat*) перес|а́живаться, -е́сть; ~ **from one foot to another** перемина́ться (*impf.*) с ноги́ на́ ногу; **the cargo is** ~**ing in the hold** груз скользи́т по трю́му; ~**ing sands** непостоя́нство, переме́нчивость. **2** (*manage*): **I can** ~ **for myself** я обойду́сь/спра́влюсь без посторо́нней по́мощи.

● *cpds.* ~ **key** *n.* (*comput.*) регистро́вая кла́виша; ~**-work** *n.* сме́нная рабо́та; ~**-worker** *n.* рабо́тающий посме́нно, сме́нщи|к (*fem.* -ца).

shiftless /ˈʃɪftlɪs/ *adj.* беспо́мощный, неуме́лый.

shifty /ˈʃɪftɪ/ *adj.* (**shiftier, shiftiest**): **a** ~ **fellow** ско́льзкий тип; хи́трый ма́лый; ~ **eyes** бе́гающие гла́зки (*m. pl.*).

Shiite /ˈʃiːaɪt/ *n.* шии́т; ~ **Muslim** мусульма́нин-шии́т.

● *adj.* шии́тский.

shilling /ˈʃɪlɪŋ/ *n.* ши́ллинг.

shilly-shally /ˈʃɪlɪˌʃælɪ/ *v.i.* колеба́ться (*impf.*).

shimmer /ˈʃɪmə(r)/ *n.* мерца́ние.

● *v.i.* мерца́ть (*impf.*).

shin /ʃɪn/ *n.* го́лень; **he skinned his** ~**s** он ссади́л го́лень; ~ **of beef** (*cul.*) говя́жья ру́лька, голя́шка.

● *v.i.* (**shinned, shinning**) (*Br.*): ~ **up a tree** вскара́бк|иваться, -аться на де́рево; ~ **down a drain-pipe** спус|ка́ться, -ти́ться по водосто́чной трубе́.

● *cpds.* ~**-bone** *n.* большеберцо́вая кость; ~**-guards/-pads** *nn. pl.* щитки́ (*m. pl.*).

shindy /ˈʃɪndɪ/ *n.* шум, сва́лка; **kick up a** ~ подн|има́ть, -я́ть шум.

shin|e /ʃaɪn/ *n.* **1** (*brightness*) блеск; (*gloss, lustre*) гля́нец, лоск; **give something a** ~**e** нав|оди́ть, -ести́ блеск на + *a.*; **put a** ~**e on one's shoes** нав|оди́ть, -ести́ гля́нец на ту́фли. **2**: **rain or** ~**e** в любу́ю пого́ду. **3** (*coll.*): **take a** ~**e to s.o.** увл|ека́ться, -е́чься кем-н.

● *v.t.* (*past and p.p.* **shined**) **1** (*polish*) чи́стить, вы́-; ~**e shoes** чи́стить, вы́- ту́фли. **2**: ~**e a light in s.o.'s face** осве|ща́ть, -ти́ть фонарём чьё-н. лицо́.

● *v.i.* (*past and p.p.* **shone** *or* **shined**) **1** (*emit, radiate light*) свети́ть(ся) (*impf.*); (*brightly*) сия́ть (*impf.*); **the sun** ~**es** со́лнце сия́ет; **the moon was** ~**ing on the lake** луна́ освеща́ла о́зеро; **a lamp was** ~**ing in the window** в окне́ свети́лась/горе́ла ла́мпа; (*fig.*): **his face shone with happiness** его́ лицо́ сия́ло от сча́стья; ~**ing eyes** сия́ющие глаза́. **2** (*glitter, glisten*) блиста́ть (*impf.*); блес|те́ть, -ну́ть; **the armour** (*Br.*), **armor** (*US*) shone in the sun броня́ блесте́ла на со́лнце. **3** (*fig., excel*) блиста́ть (*impf.*); блесте́ть (*impf.*); **he does not** ~**e in conversation** собесе́дник он не блестя́щий; **he is a** ~**ing example of industry** он явля́ет собо́й замеча́тельный приме́р трудолю́бия.

shingle¹ /ˈʃɪŋg(ə)l/ *n.* (*pebbles*) га́лька.

shingle² /ˈʃɪŋg(ə)l/ *n.* **1** (*wooden tile*) (кро́вельная) дра́нка (*sg. or collect.*); (*pl.*) гонт (*collect.*). **2** (*US, sign-board*) вы́веска.

● *v.t.* (*cover with* ~*s*) крыть, по- го́нтом.

shingles /ˈʃɪŋg(ə)lz/ *n.* (*med.*) опоя́сывающий лиша́й.

shingly /ˈʃɪŋglɪ/ *adj.* покры́тый га́лькой.

shinny /ˈʃɪnɪ/ *v.i.* (*US*) = **shin**

Shinto(ism) /ˈʃɪntəʊ(ɪz(ə)m)/ *n.* шинтои́зм.

shiny /ˈʃaɪnɪ/ *adj.* (**shinier, shiniest**) **1** (*polished, glistening*) блестя́щий. **2** (*through wear*) лосня́щийся.

ship /ʃɪp/ *n.* кора́бль (*m.*); су́дно; **on board** ~ на борту́ корабля́; (*motion*) на́ борт; ~**'s biscuit** гале́та (*m.*); ~**'s company, crew** экипа́ж корабля́; ~**'s papers** судовы́е докуме́нты; **when my** ~ **comes in** (*fig.*) когда́ мне повезёт; когда́ мне улыбнётся форту́на; **like** ~**s that pass in the night** (разошли́сь) как в мо́ре корабли́; **take** ~ сади́ться, сесть на кора́бль.

● *v.t.* (**shipped, shipping**) **1** (*take on board*) грузи́ть, по-; (*passengers*) произв|оди́ть, -ести́ поса́дку + *g.*; ~ **crew** нан|има́ть, -я́ть кома́нду. **2** (*dispatch*) отпр|авля́ть, -а́вить. **3**: ~ **oars** класть, положи́ть вёсла в ло́дку; (*as order*) суши́ вёсла!; ~ **rudder** наве́|шивать, -сить руль; ~ **mast** устан|а́вливать, -ови́ть ма́чту; ~ **water** да|ва́ть, -ть течь; ~ **a sea** (*Br.*) прин|има́ть, -я́ть во́ду.

● *v.i.* (**shipped, shipping**): **he** ~**ped as a steward** он пла́вал на су́дне официа́нтом.

● *cpds.* ~**-breaker** *n.* подря́дчик по сло́му ста́рых судо́в; ~**-broker** *n.* судово́й ма́клер; ~**builder** *n.* судострои́тель (*m.*), кораблестрои́тель (*m.*); ~**building** *n.* судострое́ние, кораблестрое́ние; (*attr.*) судострои́тельный, кораблестрои́тельный; ~**-canal** *n.* кана́л для морски́х судо́в; ~**mate** *n.* кора́бельный това́рищ; ~**-owner** *n.* судовладе́лец; ~**shape** *adj.* аккура́тный; (*pred.*) в по́лном поря́дке; **get everything** ~**shape** прив|оди́ть, -ести́ всё в по́лный поря́док; ~**way** *n.* ста́пель (*m.*); ~**wreck** *n.* кораблекруше́ние; *v.t.*: **be** ~**wrecked** терпе́ть, по- кораблекруше́ние; ~**wright** *n.* корабе́льный пло́тник; ~**yard** *n.* верфь; судострои́тельный заво́д.

shipment /ˈʃɪpmənt/ *n.* **1** (*loading*) погру́зка; (*dispatch*) отпра́вка, отгру́зка. **2** (*goods shipped*) па́ртия това́ра.

shipper /ˈʃɪpə(r)/ *n.* грузоотправи́тель (*m.*).

shipping /ˈʃɪpɪŋ/ *n.* **1** = **shipment** 1. **2** (*transport*) перево́зка,

S

транспортиро́вка. **3** (*collect., ships*) флот; **unsuitable for ~** (*not navigable*) неподходя́щий для судохо́дства.

● *cpds.* **~-agent** *n.* экспеди́тор; **~-company** *n.* судохо́дная компа́ния; **~-office** *n.* тра́нспортная конто́ра.

shire /ˈʃaɪə(r)/ *n.* (*Br.*) гра́фство.

shirk /ʃɜːk/ *v.t.* уклон|я́ться, -и́ться (*or* увíл|ивать, -ьну́ть) от + *g.*; **he ~s responsibility** он уклоня́ется от отве́тственности.

● *v.i.* ло́дырничать (*impf.*); гоня́ть (*impf.*) ло́дыря (*coll.*).

shirker /ˈʃɜːkə(r)/ *n.* ло́дырь (*m.*).

shirred /ʃɜːrd/ *adj.* (*US*): **~ eggs** яйцо́-пашо́т.

shirt /ʃɜːt/ *n.* руба́шка; соро́чка (*also* = **undershirt**); (*woman's, also*) блу́зка; (*fig.*): **he will have the ~ off your back** он вас обдерёт как ли́пку; **keep your ~ on!** (*coll.*) споко́йно!; успоко́йтесь!; **stuffed ~** (*fig., coll.*) напы́щенное ничто́жество.

● *cpds.* **~-front** *n.* мани́шка; **~-sleeve** *n.*: **in ~-sleeves** без пиджака́; **~-tail** *n.* низ/подо́л руба́шки.

shirty /ˈʃɜːtɪ/ *adj.* (**shirtier, shirtiest**) (*Br., coll.*) раздражённый; **get ~** раздраж|а́ться, -и́ться.

shish kebab /ˌʃɪʃ kɪˈbæb/ *n.* шиш-кеба́б.

shit /ʃɪt/ (*vulg.*) *n.* говно́; (*as expletive*) чёрт!

● *v.i.* (**shitting;** *past and p.p.* **shitted** *or* **~** *or* **shat**) срать, по-, на-.

shitty /ˈʃɪtɪ/ *adj.* (**shittier, shittiest**) (*vulg.*) говённый, дерьмо́вый..

shiver¹ /ˈʃɪvə(r)/ *n.* дрожь; **a ~ ran up his spine** дрожь пробежа́ла у него́ по спине́; **it sent a ~ down my back** у меня́ от э́того мура́шки пробежа́ли по спине́; **it gives me the ~s to think of it** от одно́й мы́сли об э́том меня́ броса́ет в дрожь.

● *v.i.* дрожа́ть (*impf.*); **he was ~ing with cold** он дрожа́л от хо́лода.

shiver² /ˈʃɪvə(r)/ *n.* (*fragment*) оско́лок; **the glass broke into ~s** стекло́ разби́лось вдре́безги.

● *v.t. & i.* разб|ива́ть(ся), -и́ть(ся) вдре́безги.

shivery /ˈʃɪvərɪ/ *adj.*: **I feel ~** меня́ зноби́т/позна́бливает (*coll.*).

shoal¹ /ʃəʊl/ *n.* (*shallow*) мелково́дье; (*sandbank*) мель, о́тмель, ба́нка; (*fig.*) скры́тая опа́сность.

● *v.i.* меле́ть (*impf.*).

shoal² /ʃəʊl/ *n.* (*of fish*) стая, кося́к (*рыбы*).

● *v.i.* (*of fish*) собира́ться (*impf.*) в кося́ки.

shock¹ /ʃɒk/ *n.* **1** (*violent jar or blow*) толчо́к, уда́р; **I got an electric ~** меня́ уда́рило то́ком; **~ treatment/therapy** шокотерапи́я; **~ wave** взрывна́я волна́.
2: **~ tactics** (*mil.*) та́ктика сокруши́тельных уда́ров; (*fig.*) внеза́пные/неожи́данные де́йствия; **~ troops** уда́рные войска́.
3 (*disturbing impression*) потрясе́ние, шок; **he recovered from the ~** он опра́вился от потрясе́ния; **the news gave him a ~** но́вость потрясла́ его́; (*distressing surprise*) уда́р; **his death was a great ~ to her** его́ смерть яви́лась для неё больши́м уда́ром.
4 (*med.*) шок; **treat s.o. for ~** лечи́ть (*impf.*) кого́-н. от шо́ка; **he is suffering from ~** он нахо́дится в шо́ковом состоя́нии.

● *v.t.* **1** (*by electricity etc.*) уд|аря́ть, -а́рить.
2 (*distress, outrage*): **I was ~ed to hear of the disaster** я был потрясён сообще́нием о катастро́фе.
3 (*offend sense of decency*) шоки́ровать (*impf., pf.*); **he is not easily ~ed** его́ ниче́м не удиви́шь; его́ тру́дно шоки́ровать.

● *cpds.* **~-absorber** *n.* амортиза́тор; **~-brigade** *n.* (*hist.*) уда́рная брига́да; **~proof** *adj.* ударосто́йкий; **~-worker** *n.* (*hist.*) уда́рни|к (*fem.* -ца).

shock² /ʃɒk/ *n.* (*of corn*) копна́; (*of hair*) копна́ воло́с.

● *v.t.* копни́ть, с-.

shocker /ˈʃɒkə(r)/ *n.* (*coll.*) что-н. ужаса́ющее; **the picture was a ~** (*very bad*) карти́на никуда́ не годи́лась.

shocking /ˈʃɒkɪŋ/ *adj.* (*disturbing*) ужаса́ющий; (*disgusting*) возмути́тельный; (*scandalous*) шоки́рующий, сканда́льный; (*Br. coll., very bad*) ужа́сный; **he has a ~ temper** он ужа́сно вспы́льчивый.

shod /ʃɒd/ *past and p.p. of* ⇨**shoe**

shoddy /ˈʃɒdɪ/ *adj.* (**shoddier, shoddiest**) дрянно́й, халту́рный.

shoe /ʃuː/ *n.* **1** ту́фля; (*ankle boot*) полуботи́нок; **put one's ~s on** над|ева́ть, -е́ть ту́фли; об|ува́ться, -у́ться; **put s.o.'s ~s on** об|ува́ть, -у́ть кого́-н.; **change one's ~s** смени́ть (*pf.*) о́бувь; **she never wore ~s** она́ всегда́ ходи́ла босико́м; (*fig.*): **he is ready to step into my ~s** он гото́в заня́ть моё ме́сто; **I wouldn't be in his ~s** я бы не хоте́л быть на его́ ме́сте; **the ~ is on the other foot** (*US*) тепе́рь уж всё наоборо́т; **he knows where the ~ pinches** ≈ он зна́ет, в чём беда́.
2 (**horse~**) подко́ва; (*of brake*) коло́дка.

● *v.t.* (**shoes, shoeing;** *past and p.p.* **shod**) (*horse*) подко́в|ывать, -а́ть; **shod** (*of person*) обу́тый.

● *cpds.* **~-brush** *n.* сапо́жная щётка; **~-buckle** *n.* пря́жка на ту́флях; **~horn** *n.* рожо́к (*для обуви*); **~-lace** *n.* шнуро́к; **~-leather** *n.* сапо́жная ко́жа; **~maker** *n.* сапо́жник; **be a ~maker** сапо́жничать (*impf.*); **~-shop** *n.* обувно́й магази́н; **~-string** *n.* шнуро́к; **live on a ~-string** ко́е-как перебива́ться (*impf.*); **the business is run on a ~-string** э́то де́ло ведётся с минима́льным капита́лом; **~-tree** *n.* коло́дка.

shone /ʃɒn/ *past and p.p. of* ⇨**shine**

shoo /ʃuː/ *v.t.* (**shoos, shooed**): **~ away, ~ off** отпу́г|ивать, -ну́ть; от|гоня́ть, -огна́ть.

● *int.* (*to birds*) к(ы)ш!; (*to cats*) брысь!

shook /ʃʊk/ *past of* ⇨**shake**

shoot /ʃuːt/ *n.* **1** (*bot.*) росто́к, побе́г.
2 (**~ing expedition**) охо́та; (**~ing party**) охо́тники (*m. pl.*); (*Br., land for ~ing*) охо́тничье уго́дье.
3 (*chute*) жёлоб.
4: **the whole ~** (*coll.*) всё.
5 (*cin.*) съёмка.

● *v.t.* (*past and p.p.* **shot**) **1** (*discharge, fire*): **to ~ an arrow** пус|ка́ть, -ти́ть стрелу́; **he shot an arrow from his bow** он пусти́л стрелу́ из лу́ка; **these guns ~ rubber bullets** э́ти ру́жья стреля́ют рези́новыми пу́лями; (*fig.*): **~ a glance at s.o.** кида́ть, ки́нуть/бр|оса́ть, -о́сить взгляд на кого́-н.
2 (*kill*) застр|е́ливать, -ели́ть; (*wound*) ра́нить (*impf., pf.*); **he was shot while trying to escape** его́ застрели́ли (*or* он был уби́т) при попы́тке к бе́гству; **he was shot dead** он был уби́т (*or* сражён на́смерть); **~ s.o. in the back** стреля́ть, вы́стрелить кому́-н. в спи́ну; **~ s.o. through the leg** простре́л|ивать, -и́ть кому́-н. но́гу; **he was shot in the head** пу́ля попа́ла ему́ в го́лову; **~ game** стреля́ть (*impf.*) дичь; (*execute*) расстре́л|ивать, -я́ть; **he will be shot for treason** его́ расстреля́ют за изме́ну.
3 (*propel*): **~ the ball into the net** пос|ыла́ть, -ла́ть мяч в се́тку; **~ dice** (*US*) броса́ть (*impf.*) ко́сти; игра́ть (*impf.*) в ко́сти; **he was shot over the horse's head** он перелете́л че́рез го́лову ло́шади; **~ a bolt** (*on door*) задв|ига́ть, -и́нуть засо́в; **he has shot his bolt** (*Br., fig.*) он сде́лал всё, что мог.
4: **get shot of something** (*Br. coll.*) отде́л|ываться, -аться от чего́-н.
5 (*cin., film, scene*) сн|има́ть, -ять, засня́ть (*pf.*) (*фильм, эпизод*).

● *v.i.* (*past and p.p.* **shot**) **1** (*fire, of person or weapon*) стреля́ть (*impf.*); (*a single shot*) стрельну́ть, вы́стрелить (*both pf.*); **the police shot to kill** полице́йские стреля́ли, не щадя́ жи́зни; **he was shot at twice** в него́ два́жды стреля́ли; **he is out ~ing** он на охо́те; **this rifle ~s well** э́та винто́вка прекра́сно стреля́ет.
2 (*dart*) прон|оси́ться, -ести́сь; **a meteor shot across the sky** по не́бу пронёсся метео́р; **the car shot ahead** маши́на рвану́лась вперёд; **he shot out of the doorway** он вы́скочил из подъе́зда; **a ~ing pain** стреля́ющая боль; **a ~ing star** па́дающая звезда́; **the flames shot upward** пла́мя взмы́ло вверх.
3 (*of plants*) пус|ка́ть, -ти́ть побе́ги.
4 (*football etc.*): бить (*impf.*) по мячу́; **~!** бей!; (*coll., speak*) валя́й говори́!
5 (*cin.*): **they were ~ing all morning** они́ всё у́тро снима́ли.

● *with advs.*: **~ away** *v.t.*: **he had a leg shot away** снаря́дом ему́ оторва́ло но́гу; **~ down** *v.t.*: **we shot down five enemy aircraft** мы сби́ли пять самолётов проти́вника; **the prisoners were shot down** пле́нных расстреля́ли; (*coll., demolish in argument*) переспо́рить (*pf.*); **~ off** *v.i.* (*coll., leave hurriedly*) вылета́ть, вы́лететь (пу́лей); **~ out** *v.t.* (*extend*): **he shot out his hand** он стреми́тельно протяну́л ру́ку; (*coll.*): **~ it out** (*fight decisive battle*) дава́ть, дать реши́тельный бой; *v.i.* вырыва́ться, вы́рваться; **a car shot out of a side-street** из переу́лка вы́летела маши́на; **~ up** *v.t.* (*terrorize by gunfire*) терроризи́ровать (*impf., pf.*) стрельбо́й; *v.i.* (*grow rapidly*) бы́стро расти́, вы́-; (*of child*) вытя́гиваться, вы́тянуться; (*of prices etc.*) подск|а́кивать, -очи́ть; взмы|ва́ть, -ть; **twenty hands shot up** взвило́сь два́дцать рук; (*sl., inject drugs*) ширя́ться, на-.

● *cpd.* **~-out** *n.* (*coll.*) перестре́лка; (*football, also* **penalty ~-out**) се́рия пена́льти.

shooter /ˈʃuːtə(r)/ *n.* стрело́к.

shooting /ˈʃuːtɪŋ/ *n.* (*marksmanship; attack*) стрельба́; (*hunting*) охо́та.

● *cpds.* **~-box** *n.* (*Br.*) охо́тничий до́мик; **~-brake** *n.* (*Br.*) автофурго́н; **~-gallery** *n.* тир; **~-match** *n.*: **the whole ~-match** вся ку́ча; всё хозя́йство (*coll.*); **~-party** *n.* гру́ппа охо́тников; (*occasion*) охо́та; **~-range** *n.* тир; (*outdoor*) стре́льбище, полиго́н; **~-stick** *n.* трость-табуре́т.

shop /ʃɒp/ *n.* **1** магази́н; (*small* **~**) ла́вка; **keep (a) ~** держа́ть (*impf.*) магази́н; **set up ~** откр|ыва́ть, -ы́ть магази́н; **shut up ~** закр|ыва́ть, -ы́ть магази́н; (*fig.*) прикр|ыва́ть, -ы́ть ла́вочку; **all over the ~** (*Br.*) (*everywhere*) повсю́ду; (*in confusion*) в беспоря́дке; **talk ~** разгова́ривать/говори́ть (*impf.*) о (свои́х профессиона́льных) дела́х.
2 (*work*~) мастерска́я, цех; **on the ~ floor** (*Br.*) в цеху́; **closed ~** предприя́тие, принима́ющее на рабо́ту то́лько чле́нов профсою́за.

● *v.t.* (**shopped, shopping**) (*Br., inform on*) стуча́ть, на- (*sl.*) на + *a.*

● *v.i.* (**shopped, shopping**) де́лать, с- поку́пки; **we go ~ping in the market** мы хо́дим за поку́пками на ры́нок; **she ~ped around** она́ ходи́ла по магази́нам и прице́нивалась.

● *cpds.* **~-assistant** *n.* (*Br.*) продав|е́ц (*fem.* -щи́ца); **~-girl** *n.* продавщи́ца; **~keeper** *n.* держа́тель (*m.*) магази́на, ла́вочни|к (*fem.* -ца); **~-lifter** *n.* магази́нный вор; **~-lifting** *n.* воровство́ с прила́вка (*or* в магази́нах); **~-soiled** (*Br.*), **~worn** (*US*) *adjs.* лежа́лый; **~ steward** *n.* цехово́й ста́роста; **~-walker** *n.* (*Br.*) дежу́рный администра́тор универма́га; **~-window** *n.* витри́на; **~-window display** вы́ставка това́ров в витри́не; **~worn** *adj.* (*US*) = **~-soiled**

shopper /ˈʃɒpə(r)/ *n.* покупа́тель (*fem.* -ница).

shopping /ˈʃɒpɪŋ/ *n.* поку́пки (*f. pl.*); **do one's ~** де́лать, с- поку́пки; **~ centre** (*Br.*), **center** (*US*) торго́вый центр.

● *cpd.* **~-bag** *n.* хозя́йственная су́мка.

shore[1] /ʃɔː(r)/ *n.* бе́рег; **on the ~** на берегу́; **in ~** у бе́рега; **distant ~s** да́льние берега́/края́; **~ leave** о́тпуск/увольне́ние на бе́рег.

● *cpd.* **~-based** *adj.* бази́рующийся на берегу́, берегово́й; **~-based aircraft** самолёт берегово́й авиа́ции.

shore[2] /ʃɔː(r)/ *v.t.*: **~ up** подп|ира́ть, -ере́ть; крепи́ть (*impf.*).

shoreward /ˈʃɔːwəd/ *adv.* (*also* **~s**) (по направле́нию) к бе́регу.

shorn /ʃɔːn/ *p.p. of* ⇨**shear**

short /ʃɔːt/ *n.* **1** (**~** *film*) короткометра́жный фильм.
2 (**~** *circuit*) коро́ткое замыка́ние.
3 (*Br.,* **~** *drink*) кре́пкий напи́ток.
4 (*pl.,* **~** *trousers*) шо́рт|ы (*pl., g.* -ов); (*US, underpants*) трус|ы́ (*pl., g.* -о́в).

● *adj.* **1** коро́ткий; (*of* **~** *duration*) кра́ткий, недо́лгий; (*short-term*) краткосро́чный; (*of stature*) невысо́кого ро́ста; **a ~ way** коро́ткий путь; (*small*) небольшо́й; **a ~ distance away, a ~ way off** недалеко́, неподалёку; **this dress is too ~** э́то пла́тье сли́шком коротко́; **~ steps** ме́лкие шаги́; **the days are getting ~er** дни стано́вятся коро́че; **the ~est distance** кратча́йшее расстоя́ние; **for a ~ time** на коро́ткое вре́мя; **in a ~ time** вско́ре; **a ~ time ago** неда́вно; **a ~ life** недо́лгая/коро́ткая жизнь; **time is ~** вре́мени ма́ло; **~ circuit** коро́ткое замыка́ние; **~ cut** (*route*) кратча́йший путь; (*fig.*): **there are no ~ cuts in science** нет лёгких путе́й в нау́ке, **a ~ memory** коро́ткая па́мять; **in ~ order** (*US, at once*) то́тчас; **at ~ range** с бли́зкого расстоя́ния; **~ story** расска́з; **be on ~ time** рабо́тать (*impf.*) непо́лную неде́лю (*or* на полста́вке); **take the ~ view** быть недальнови́дным; **~ vowel** кра́ткий гла́сный; **make ~ work of something** бы́стро распр|авля́ться, -а́виться с чем-н.; **I want my hair cut ~** я хочу́ ко́ротко постри́чься; **have a '~ back and sides'** (*Br.*) стри́чься (*impf.*) под бокс.
2 (*concise, brief*): **in ~** коро́че говоря́; (одни́м) сло́вом; **for ~** сокращённо; для кра́ткости; **they call him Jim for ~** для кра́ткости его́ зову́т Джи́мом.
3 (*curt, sharp*) ре́зкий; **he has a ~ temper** он вспы́льчив; **be ~ with s.o.** говори́ть (*impf.*) с кем-н. су́хо.
4 (*insufficient*): **in ~ supply** дефици́тный; **give s.o. ~ change** обсчи́т|ывать, -а́ть кого́-н.; **I am 2 pounds ~** мне не хвата́ет двух фу́нтов.
5: **be ~ of something** (*lacking*) испы́тывать (*impf.*) недоста́ток в чём-н.; не име́ть доста́точно чего́-н.; **be ~ of breath** запыха́ться (*impf.*); **they are ~ of bread** у них не хвата́ет хле́ба; **it was little ~ of a miracle** э́то бы́ло почти́ чу́до.
6: **~ of** (*except*) кро́ме + *g.*
7 (*of pastry*) рассы́пчатый, песо́чный.

● *adv.* **1** (*abruptly*): **he stopped ~** он вдруг останови́лся; (*while speaking*) он вдруг замолча́л; **he tried to cut me ~** он стара́лся прерва́ть меня́ на полуслове́; **his remark brought me up ~** его́ замеча́ние заста́вило меня́ внеза́пно останови́ться; **the sound of his voice brought me up ~** звук его́ го́лоса привёл меня́ в чу́вство.
2 (*not far enough*): **the ball fell ~** мяч не долете́л.
3: **~ of** (*without reaching*): **fall ~ of a target** не дост|ига́ть, -и́чь це́ли; **the play fell ~ of my expectations** пье́са не оправда́ла мои́х наде́жд; **go ~ of something** ограни́чи|вать, -ть себя́ в чём-н.; **we ran ~ of potatoes** у нас вы́шла (вся) карто́шка; **I was caught/taken ~** (*Br.*) у меня́ схвати́ло живо́т (*coll.*).

● *v.t.* (*elec.*): **I ~ed the battery** я замкну́л батаре́ю.

● *cpds.* **~bread, ~cake** *nn.* песо́чное пече́нье; **~-change** *v.t.* (*coll.*) обсчи́т|ывать, -а́ть; недода́ть (*pf.*) сда́чу + *d.*; **~-circuit** *v.t.* зам|ыка́ть, -кну́ть на́коротко; **~coming** *n.* недоста́ток; **~fall** *n.* недоста́ток, дефици́т; **~-haired** *adj.* (ко́ротко)стри́женый; (*of animals*) короткошёрстый; **~hand** *n.* стеногра́фия; **~hand typist** (*Br.*) (машини́стка)-стенографи́стка; **take down in ~hand** стенографи́ровать, за-; **~-handed** *adj.*: **we are ~-handed** у нас не хвата́ет люде́й/рабо́тников; **~-list** *n.* шорт-лист, коро́ткий спи́сок; *v.t.* зан|оси́ть, -ести́ в шорт-лист, коро́ткий спи́сок; **~-lived** *adj.* недолгове́чный, мимолётный; **~-range** *adj.* (*of gun*) с небольшо́й да́льностью стрельбы́; (*of missile*) бли́жнего де́йствия; (*of forecast*) краткосро́чный; **~-sighted** *adj.* (*lit., fig.*) близору́кий; **~-sightedness** *n.* близору́кость; **~-sleeved** *adj.* (*shirt*) с коро́ткими рукава́ми; **~-staffed** *adj.* страда́ющий недоста́тком рабо́тников; **~-tempered** *adj.* вспы́льчивый; **~-term** *adj.* (*loan*) краткосро́чный; (*advantage*) кратковре́менный; **~-wave** *adj.* коротково́лновый; **~-winded** *adj.*: **be ~-winded** страда́ть (*impf.*) оды́шкой.

shortage /ˈʃɔːtɪdʒ/ *n.* недоста́ток, нехва́тка, дефици́т.

shorten /ˈʃɔːt(ə)n/ *v.t. & i.* укор|а́чивать(ся), -оти́ть(ся); сокра|ща́ть(ся), -ти́ть(ся) (**by an inch**: на дюйм).

shortening /ˈʃɔːtənɪŋ/ *n.* (*cul.*) жир.

shortly /ˈʃɔːtlɪ/ *adv.* **1** (*soon*) ско́ро; **~ before** незадо́лго до + *g.*; **~ after** вско́ре по́сле + *g.* **2** (*briefly*) кра́тко; **to put it ~** ко́ротко/коро́че говоря́; вкра́тце. **3** (*sharply*) ре́зко.

shortness /ˈʃɔːtnɪs/ *n.* коро́ткость; **~ of breath** оды́шка; **~ of temper** вспы́льчивость; **~ of time** нехва́тка вре́мени.

shot[1] /ʃɒt/ *n.* **1** (*missile*): **putting the ~** (*sport*) толка́ние ядра́; (*pellet*) дроби́нка; (*collect.*) дробь.
2 (*discharge of firearm*) вы́стрел; **fire a ~** де́лать, с- вы́стрел; стрельну́ть (*pf.*); **he hit it at the first ~** он попа́л с пе́рвого вы́стрела/ра́за; **take a ~ at** стрельну́ть (*pf.*) по + *d.*; **like a ~** (*rapidly*) стрело́й, ми́гом; (*eagerly*) охо́тно; **he was off like a ~** он вы́бежал стреми́тельно/пу́лей (*coll.*); (*fig.*): **a long ~** натя́жка; слепа́я

догáдка; смéлое предположéние; **have a ~** попытáться (*pf.*); **a ~ in the dark** слепáя догáдка; **not by a long ~** никóим óбразом.
3 (*stroke, at games etc.*) удáр; **he made some beautiful ~s** он сдéлал нéсколько превосхóдных удáров; **(good) ~!** молодéц!
4 (*of person*) стрелóк; **he's a good ~** он хорóший стрелóк; **big ~** туз, (вáжная) шúшка (*coll.*).
5 (*phot.*) снúмок; (*cin.*) кадр; **long ~** кадр, снятый дáльним плáном.
6 (*small dose*) небольшáя дóза; **~ of liquor** глотóк спиртнóго; (*injection*) укóл; **~ in the arm** (*fig., stimulus, encouragement*) стúмул.
● *cpds.* **~-blasting** *n.* дробеструйная обрабóтка; **~gun** *n.* дробовúк; **~gun marriage** вынужденный брак; **~-put(ting)** *n.* (*sport*) толкáние ядрá.

shot² /ʃɒt/ *past and p.p. of* ⇨**shoot**

should /ʃʊd/, /ʃəd/ *v. aux.*
1 (*conditional*): **I ~ say** я бы сказáл; **I ~ have thought so** нáдо полагáть; казáлось бы; **~ he die** (в слýчае) éсли он умрёт; **I ~n't think so** не дýмаю; **if I were you I ~n't ...** на вáшем мéсте я не стал бы. . .; **~ he be dismissed** (в слýчае) éсли егó увóлят.
2 (*expr. duty*): **you ~ tell him** вы должнú емý сказáть; **there is no reason why you ~ do that** у вас нет никакúх причúн так поступáть.
3 (*expr. probability or expectation*): **we ~ be there by noon** мы должнú (бы) поспéть тудá к полýдню; **they ~ be there by now** онú, должнó быть/вéрно, ужé там; **how ~ I know?** а я почём знáю? (*coll.*); откýда мне знать? **why ~ you think that?** почемý вы так дýмаете?
4 (*expr. future in the past*): **I told him I ~ (would) be going** я емý сказáл, что пойдý.
5 (*expr. purpose*): **I lent him the book so that he ~ read it** я одолжúл емý э́ту кнúгу, чтóбы он прочитáл её; **I am anxious that it ~ be done at once** мне вáжно, чтóбы э́то бы́ло сдéлано срáзу; **he suggested that I ~ go** он предложúл мне уйтú.
6 (*subjunctive use*): **I am surprised that he ~ be so foolish** я не ожидáл, что он окáжется столь неразýмен.

shoulder /ˈʃəʊldə(r)/ *n.* **1** плечó; **shrug one's ~s** пож|имáть, -áть плечáми; **~ to ~** плечóм к плечý; **have round ~s** быть сутýлым; сутýлиться (*impf.*); **stand head and ~s above the rest** (*lit., fig.*) быть нá голову вы́ше остальны́х; **have broad ~s** имéть (*impf.*) ширóкие плéчи; (*fig.*) быть в состоя́нии вы́нести мнóгое; **straight from the ~** сплечá; **an old head on young ~s** не по летáм ýмный; **put, set one's ~ to the wheel** (*fig.*) (при)налéчь (*pf.*); энергúчно брáться, взя́ться за дéло; **give s.o. the cold ~** встр|ечáть, -éтить когó-н. хóлодно.
2 (*of meat*) лопáтка.
3 (*of mountain*) устýп.
4 (*of road*) обóчина.
● *v.t.* **1** (*lit.*): **~ a heavy load** взвáл|ивать, -úть на себя́ тяжёлый груз; **~ arms!** на плечó!; (*fig.*): **~ responsibility** брать, взять на себя́ отвéтственность.
2 (*push with ~*): **~ s.o. aside (***or* **out of the way)** отпúх|ивать, -нýть когó-н.; **~ (one's way) through a crowd** прот|áлкиваться, -олкнýться сквозь толпý.
● *cpds.* **~ bag** *n.* сýмка на ремнé; **~-belt** *n.* портупéя; (*bandolier*) патронтáш; **~-blade** *n.* лопáтка; **~-high** *adj.*: **the grass was ~-high** травá былá (*кому*) по плечó; **~-holster** *n.* кобурá пистолéта, носúмая под мы́шкой; **~-knot** *n.* аксельбáнт; **~-pad** *n.* подкладнóе плечó; **~-strap** *n.* (*mil.*) погóн; (*of backpack*) ремéнь (*m.*), ля́мка; (*of undergarment*) бретéлька.

shout /ʃaʊt/ *n.* крик.
● *v.t.* выкрúкивать, вы́крикнуть; **he ~ed himself hoarse** он докричáлся до хрипоты́.
● *v.i.* кр|ичáть, -úкнуть; **he ~ed with laughter** он надрывáлся от смéха; **don't ~ at me** не кричúте на меня́; **~ for s.o.** грóмко звать, по- когó-н.; **~ for help** звать, по- на пóмощь; **the ~ing died down** крúки стúхли.
● *with advs.*: **~ down** *v.t.* перекр|úкивать, -ичáть; **he was ~ed down** кричáли так, что он не смог говорúть; **~ out** *v.t.* выкрúкивать, вы́крикнуть; **he ~ed out our names** он вы́крикнул нáши фамúлии; *v.i.* закричáть (*pf.*).

shove /ʃʌv/ *n.* толчóк; **give s.o. a ~** пихнýть/толкнýть (*pf.*) когó-н.
● *v.t.* толк|áть, -нýть; **~ something into one's pocket** совáть/сýнуть (*or* зас|óвывать, -ýнуть) что-н. себé в кармáн; **he ~d a paper in front of me** он сýнул мне под нос какýю-то бумáжку; **he ~d his way forward** он протúснулся вперёд.
● *with advs.*: **~ aside, ~ away** *vv.t.* отт|áлкивать, -олкнýть; отпúх|ивать, -нýть (*coll.*); **~ down** *v.t.* ст|áлкивать, -олкнýть; **~ off** *v.i.* (*naut.*) отт|áлкиваться, -олкнýться от бéрега; (*coll., leave*) катúться (*impf.*) (*coll.*).

shovel /ˈʃʌv(ə)l/ *n.* лопáта; (*mechanical*) экскавáтор, механúческая лопáта.
● *v.t.* **(shovelled, shovelling;** *US* **shoveled, shoveling): ~ coal into a cellar** сбр|áсывать, -óсить ýголь в подвáл; **~ earth out of a ditch** вынимáть, вы́нуть зéмлю из канáвы; **~ snow off a path** сгре|бáть, -стú снег с дорóжки.
● *with advs.*: **~ out** *v.t.* выгребáть, вы́грести; **~ up** *v.t.* сгре|бáть, -стú.

show /ʃəʊ/ *n.* **1** (*manifestation*): **a ~ of hands** голосовáние поднятием рук; **make a ~ of force** демонстрúровать, про- сúлу; **make a ~ of learning** покáз|ывать, -áть свою учёность; **~ trial** показáтельный процéсс; (*semblance*) вúдимость; **offer a ~ of resistance** окáз|ывать, -áть сопротивлéние для вúда.
2 (*exhibition*) покáз, вы́ставка; шóу; **fashion ~** покáз мод; **be on ~** быть вы́ставленным; **dog/flower ~** вы́ставка собáк/цветóв; **do something for ~** дéлать, с- что-н. напокáз; (*ostentation*) пы́шность, парáдность.
3 (*entertainment*) представлéние; шóу; **let's go to a ~** пойдёмте в теáтр; (*fig.*): **steal the ~** переключ|áть, -úть всё внимáние на себя́; **put up a good ~** хорошó себя́ проявл|я́ть, -úть; **good ~!** (*Br.*) (*well done!*) молодéц!, молодцы́! (*pl.*); (*great!*) здóрово!; **bad ~!** (*Br., that was unlucky!*) не повезлó!; какáя неудáча!
4 (*concern*) дéло; **run the ~** вестú (*det.*) дéло; хозя́йничать (*impf.*); **give the ~ away** выдавáть, вы́дать секрéт; прогов|áриваться, -орúться.
● *v.t.* (*p.p.* **shown** *or* **showed**)
1 (*disclose, reveal, offer for inspection*) покáз|ывать, -áть; **he ~ed his true colours** (*Br.*), **colors** (*US*) он показáл своё úстинное лицó; **this dress will not ~ the dirt** на э́том плáтье грязь не бýдет замéтна; **he has not ~n his face since Friday** он не покáзывался/не покáзывал нóса (*coll.*) с пя́тницы; **~ fight** сопротивля́ться (*impf.*); не поддавáться, не поддáться; **he has nothing to ~ for his efforts** он зря старáлся; у негó ничегó не получúлось; **have something to ~ for one's money** трáтить, по- дéньги не впустýю; **he ~ed signs of tiring** он нáчал замéтно уставáть; **~ o.s.** (*appear*) появ|ля́ться, -úться; покáз|ываться, -áться; **he ~ed himself unfit to govern** он проявúл свою неспосóбность управля́ть; **his clothes ~ signs of wear** егó одéжда имéет понóшенный вид; **~ (***bare***) one's teeth** (*of animals*) скáлиться, о-; (*Br., fig.*) покáз|ывать, -áть зýбы/кóгти.
2 (*exhibit publicly*) выставля́ть, вы́ставить; (*a film*) пок|áзывать, -азáть; демонстрúровать (*impf., pf.*); **this film has been ~n twice already** э́тот фильм ужé двáжды шёл/покáзывали; **what are they ~ing at the theatre** (*Br.*), **theater** (*US*)**?** что идёт/покáзывают в теáтре?
3 (*display, manifest*) прояв|ля́ть, -úть; демонстрúровать, про-; **he ~ed a preference** он оказáл предпочтéние; **~ willing** (*coll.*) прояв|ля́ть, -úть готóвность; **he ~ed no mercy** он был беспощáден; **it ~s his good taste** э́то свидéтельствует о егó хорóшем вкýсе.
4 (*point out*) укáз|ывать, -áть на + *a.*; **he ~ed me where I went wrong** он указáл мне на мою ошúбку; (*teach by precept*) пок|áзывать, -азáть; **he ~ed me how to play** он показáл мне, как игрáть; (*demonstrate, prove*) пок|áзывать, -азáть; докáз|ывать, -áть; (*explain, illustrate*) объясн|я́ть, -úть.
5 (*conduct*) прово|жáть, -дúть; **he ~ed me to the door** он проводúл меня́ до двéри; **he ~ed me the door** (*turned me out*) он указáл мне на дверь; **I ~ed him round the garden** я показáл емý сад; я поводúл егó по сáду.
● *v.i.* (*p.p.* **shown** *or* **showed**) **1** (*be visible*) виднéться (*impf.*); **the stain will not ~** пятнó не бýдет замéтно; **the buds are just ~ing** пóчки чуть показáлись; **the light ~ed through the curtain** свет просвéчивал чéрез

занаве́ску.
2 (*exhibit pictures etc.*): **he is ~ing in London next spring** сле́дующей весно́й он выставля́ется в Ло́ндоне. **3** (*be exhibited*): **what films are ~ing?** каки́е фи́льмы пока́зывают/иду́т?

● *with advs.*: **~ in** *v.t.* вв|оди́ть, -ести́/пров|оди́ть, -ести́ в ко́мнату/дом; **~ off** *v.t.* (*display to advantage*): **the frame ~s off the picture** в э́той ра́мке карти́на хорошо́ смо́трится; (*boastfully*) щеголя́ть (*impf.*) + *i.*; **he likes to ~ off his wit** он лю́бит блесну́ть остроу́мием; *v.i.*: **the child is ~ing off** ребёнок рису́ется; **~ out** *v.t.* пров|оди́ть, -ести́ к вы́ходу; выводи́ть, вы́вести (*из чего*); **~ through** *v.i.*: **light ~s through** свет проника́ет; **~ up** *v.t.* (*make conspicuous*) выделя́ть, вы́делить; подч|ёркивать, -еркну́ть; *v.i.* (*coll., appear*) появ|ля́ться, -и́ться; **he will ~ up at six** он поя́вится в шесть; (*be conspicuous*): **the flowers ~ed up against the white background** цветы́ выделя́лись на бе́лом фо́не.

● *cpds.* **~-boat** *n.* (*US*) плаву́чий теа́тр; **~-business** *n.* шо́у-би́знес, индустри́я развлече́ний; **~-case** *n.* витри́на; **~-down** *n.* про́ба сил; оконча́тельная прове́рка; **~girl** *n.* эстра́дная арти́стка; **~-ground** *n.* я́рмарочная площа́дка; **~-jumping** *n.* конку́р; **~man** *n.* (*entrepreneur*) антрепренёр; (*MC*) тамада́ (*m.*); **~manship** *n.* (*fig.*) уме́ние показа́ть това́р лицо́м; **~-off** *n.* хвастуни́шка (*c.g.*) (*coll.*); **~-piece** *n.* (*exhibit*) экспона́т; (*outstanding example*) образе́ц; **~-place** *n.* достопримеча́тельность; **~-room** *n.* демонстрацио́нный зал; **~-stopper** *n.* (*coll.*) ≈ гвоздь програ́ммы.

shower /ˈʃaʊə(r)/ *n.* **1** (*of rain/snow*) кратковре́менный дождь/снег; **heavy ~** ли́вень (*m.*); проливно́й дождь; **April ~s** апре́льские дожди́ (*m. pl.*). **2** (*of hail, also fig.*) град; **a ~ of invitations** град приглаше́ний. **3**: (**~-bath**) душ; **take a ~** прин|има́ть, -я́ть душ.

● *v.t.* **1** (*with water etc.*) зал|ива́ть, -и́ть. **2** (*with bullets etc.*) ос|ыпа́ть, -ы́пать/обру́ши|вать, -ть гра́дом (*пуль и т. п.*); **he ~ed me with questions** он засы́пал/закида́л меня́ вопро́сами.

● *v.i.* **1** (*of rain etc.*) лить(ся) (*impf.*) (ли́внем). **2** (*fig.*) сы́паться (*impf.*); **arrows ~ed down on them** на них обру́шился град стрел. **3** (*have a ~-bath*) прин|има́ть, -я́ть душ.

● *cpds.* **~-bath** *n.* душ; **~-cap** *n.* рези́новая ша́почка; **~-curtain** *n.* занаве́ска для ва́нны; **~-proof** *adj.* непромока́емый; **~-room** *n.* душева́я.

showery /ˈʃaʊərɪ/ *adj.* дождли́вый.

showing /ˈʃəʊɪŋ/ *n.*: **he made a poor ~** он произвёл нева́жное впечатле́ние; **on present ~** согла́сно име́ющимся показа́ниям.

shown /ʃəʊn/ *p.p. of* ⇨**show**

showy /ˈʃəʊɪ/ *adj.* (**showier, showiest**) показно́й; **a ~ hat** бро́ская шля́па.

shrank /ʃræŋk/ *past of* ⇨**shrink**

shrapnel /ˈʃræpn(ə)l/ *n.* шрапне́ль.

shred /ʃred/ *n.* **1** (*of cloth*) клочо́к; **tear to ~s** раз|рыва́ть, -орва́ть в клочки́/кло́чья; (*fig.*): **they tore his argument to ~s** они́ разнесли́ его́ до́воды в пух и прах; (*small piece*) кусо́чек. **2** (*fig., scrap, bit*): **not a ~ of evidence** ни мале́йших доказа́тельств; **not a ~ of truth** ни ка́пли пра́вды.

● *v.t.* (**shredded, shredding**) (*tear*) разр|ыва́ть, -орва́ть; (*cut*) разр|еза́ть, -е́зать; **~ cabbage** шинкова́ть (*impf.*) капу́сту.

shredder /ˈʃredə(r)/ *n.* (*for vegetables*) тёрка; (*for documents*) бума́гоуничтожа́ющая маши́на.

shrew /ʃru:/ *n.* (*zool.*) землеро́йка; (*woman*) сварли́вая же́нщина.

shrewd /ʃru:d/ *adj.* проница́тельный, толко́вый; (*subtle*): **a ~ critic** то́нкий кри́тик.

shrewdness /ˈʃru:dnɪs/ *n.* проница́тельность, толко́вость.

shrewish /ˈʃru:ɪʃ/ *adj.* сварли́вый.

shriek /ʃri:k/ *n.* визг; **~s of laughter** визгли́вый смех; **give a ~** взви́згнуть (*pf.*).

● *v.t.* визгли́во выкри́кивать, вы́крикнуть.

● *v.i.* визжа́ть (*impf.*); взвизг|ивать, -нуть.

shrift /ʃrɪft/ *n.*: **they gave him short ~** они́ с ним бы́стро распра́вились.

shrike /ʃraɪk/ *n.* (*zool.*) сорокопу́т.

shrill /ʃrɪl/ *adj.* пронзи́тельный.

shrimp /ʃrɪmp/ *n.* (*pl.* **~** *or* **~s**) креве́тка; (*fig., undersized person*) коро́тышка (*c.g.*).

● *v.i.* лови́ть (*impf.*) креве́ток.

shrine /ʃraɪn/ *n.* (*casket with relics*) ра́ка; (*tomb*) гробни́ца; (*chapel*) часо́вня; (*lit., fig., hallowed place*) святы́ня, храм.

shrink /ʃrɪŋk/ *v.t.* (*past* **shrank;** *p.p.* **shrunk** *or esp. as adj.* **shrunken**): **hot water will ~ this fabric** от горя́чей воды́ э́тот материа́л ся́дет.

● *v.i.* (*past* **shrank;** *p.p.* **shrunk** *or esp. as adj.* **shrunken**) **1** (*of clothes*) сади́ться, сесть; **my shirt has shrunk** моя́ руба́шка се́ла; (*of wood*) сс|ыха́ться, -о́хнуться. **2** (*grow smaller*) сокра|ща́ться, -ти́ться; **~ing resources** сокраща́ющиеся ресу́рсы. **3** (*recoil, retreat*) отпря́нуть (*pf.*); **he shrank (back) from the fire** он отпря́нул от огня́; **he will not ~ from danger** он не отсту́пит пе́ред опа́сностью.

● *n.* (*sl., psychiatrist*) психоанали́тик.

shrinkage /ˈʃrɪŋkɪdʒ/ *n.* уса́дка.

shrivel /ˈʃrɪv(ə)l/ *v.t.* (**shrivelled, shrivelling;** *US* **shriveled, shriveling**) (*dry up*) высу́шивать, вы́сушить; (*wrinkle*) мо́рщить, с-; **the sun ~led the leaves** от со́лнца ли́стья смо́рщились.

● *v.i.* (**shrivelled, shrivelling;** *US* **shriveled, shriveling**) (*dry up*) высыха́ть, вы́сохнуть; (*wrinkle up*) смо́рщи|ваться, -ться; (*wither*) вя́нуть, за-/у-.

shroud /ʃraʊd/ *n.* **1** (*for the dead*) са́ван; (*of Christ*) плащани́ца. **2** (*naut.*) ва́нта.

● *v.t.* (*obscure, lit. & fig.*) оку́т|ывать, -ать.

Shrovetide /ˈʃrəʊvtaɪd/ *n.* ма́сленица, ма́сленая неде́ля.

Shrove Tuesday /ʃrəʊv/ *n.* вто́рник на ма́сленой неде́ле.

shrub /ʃrʌb/ *n.* (*bot.*) куст.

shrubbery /ˈʃrʌbərɪ/ *n.* куста́рник; уча́сток са́да заса́женный куста́рником.

shrug /ʃrʌg/ *n.* пожима́ние плеча́ми; **with a ~ (of the shoulders)** пожа́в плеча́ми.

● *v.t. & i.* (**shrugged, shrugging**): **~ (one's shoulders)** пож|има́ть, -а́ть плеча́ми; **~ something off** отм|а́хиваться, -ахну́ться от чего́-н.

shrunk /ʃrʌŋk/ *p.p. of* ⇨**shrink**

shrunken /ˈʃrʌŋk(ə)n/ *p.p. of* ⇨**shrink**

shuck /ʃʌk/ (*US*) *n.* (*pod*) стручо́к.

● *v.t.* лущи́ть, об-.

shudder /ˈʃʌdə(r)/ *n.* дрожь; **he gave a ~** он вздро́гнул; **it gives me the ~s** от э́того у меня́ мура́шки по спине́ (бе́гают).

● *v.i.* дрожа́ть, за-; содрог|а́ться, -ну́ться; **he was ~ing with cold** он дрожа́л от хо́лода; **I ~ to think of it** я содрога́юсь при одно́й мы́сли об э́том.

shuffle /ˈʃʌf(ə)l/ *n.* **1** (*movement*) ша́ркание; (*dance step*) шафл. **2** (*of cards*) taсо́вка.

● *v.t.* **1**: **~ one's feet** ша́ркать (*impf.*) нога́ми. **2**: **~ cards** тасова́ть, с- ка́рты; **s.o. has ~d my papers (around)** кто́-то ры́лся в мои́х бума́гах.

● *v.i.*: **~ along, about** волочи́ть (*impf.*) но́ги.

● *with adv.*: **~ off** *v.t.*: **~ off responsibility** пере|кла́дывать, -ложи́ть отве́тственность на други́х.

shun /ʃʌn/ *v.t.* (**shunned, shunning**) избега́ть (*impf.*) + *g.*

shunt /ʃʌnt/ *n.* (*elec.*) шунт.

● *v.t.* **1** (*rail., fig.*) перев|оди́ть, -ести́; **~ line** маневро́вый путь. **2** (*elec.*) шунти́ровать (*impf., pf.*). **3** (*postpone, shelve*) класть, положи́ть под сукно́.

● *v.i.* маневри́ровать (*impf.*); **~ing-yard** маневро́вый парк.

shunter /ˈʃʌntə(r)/ *n.* (*rail.*) сце́пщик; (*engine*) маневро́вый локомоти́в.

shush /ʃʊʃ/, /ʃʌʃ/ *v.t.* ши́к|ать, -нуть на + *a.*

● *v.i.* (*be silent*) замолча́ть (*pf.*); (*call for silence*) ши́кать.

● *int.* ш-ш!

shut /ʃʌt/ *adj.* (*coll.*): **be, get ~ of** отде́л|ываться, -аться (*or* изб|авля́ться, -а́виться) от + *g.*

● *v.t.* (**shutting;** *past and p.p.* **~**) **1** (*close*) закр|ыва́ть, -ы́ть; затвор|я́ть, -и́ть; **the door was ~ tight** дверь была́ пло́тно закры́та; **~ the door on s.o. (***or* **in s.o.'s face)** захло́п|ывать, -нуть дверь пе́ред кем-н./пе́ред чьим-то но́сом; **~ a drawer** задв|ига́ть, -и́нуть

я́щик; **he ~ his heart to pity** он гнал от себя́ вся́кую жа́лость; **~ one's mind to** отк|а́зываться, -аза́ться ду́мать о + *p.*; **he learnt to keep his mouth ~** он научи́лся держа́ть язы́к за зуба́ми; (*lock*) зап|ира́ть, -ере́ть; (*keep by force*) зап|ира́ть, -ере́ть; **they ~ the dog in the house** они́ за́перли соба́ку в до́ме; **he was ~ out of the room** его́ не пуска́ли в ко́мнату.
2 (*trap*): **~ one's finger in a drawer** прищем|ля́ть, -и́ть па́лец я́щиком стола́; **my raincoat got ~ in the door** мой плащ застря́л в дверя́х.
● *v.i.* (**shutting;** *past and p.p.* **~**) закр|ыва́ться, -ы́ться.
● *with advs.*: **~ down** *v.t.* (*also comput.*) закр|ыва́ть, -ы́ть; **they are ~ting the factory down** фа́брику закрыва́ют; *v.i.* закр|ыва́ться, -ы́ться; **~ in** *v.t.* (*surround*) окруж|а́ть, -и́ть; **I got ~ in** я оказа́лся взаперти́; **~ off** *v.t.* (*stop supply of*) отключ|а́ть, -и́ть; **the gas was ~ off** газ был отключён; (*switch off*) выключа́ть, вы́ключить; (*isolate*) изоли́ровать (*impf., pf.*); **~ out** *v.t.* (*exclude*) исключ|а́ть, -и́ть; (*fence off*) загор|а́живать, -оди́ть; (*US, sport*) де́лать, с- суху́ю (+*d.*); **those trees ~ out the view** э́ти дере́вья заслоня́ют вид; **~ out light/noise** не пропус|ка́ть, -ти́ть све́та/шу́ма; **I closed the curtains to ~ out the light** я задёрнул занаве́ску, что́бы не проника́л свет; **~ to** *v.t. & i.* (пло́тно) закр|ыва́ть(ся), -ы́ть(ся); захло́п|ывать(ся), -нуть(ся); **the door ~ to behind me** дверь за мной захло́пнулась; **~ up** *v.t.* (*close*) зап|ира́ть, -ере́ть; **he ~ up the box** он за́пер шкату́лку; **their house is ~ up for the winter** дом у них заколо́чен на́ зиму; (*confine*): **the boy was ~ up in his room** ма́льчик был за́перт в ко́мнате; (*silence*): **they soon ~ him up** они́ ско́ро заста́вили его́ замолча́ть; *v.i.* (*be, become silent*) молча́ть, за-; **~ up!** замолчи́!, заткни́сь! (*coll.*).
● *cpds.* **~-down** *n.* (*also comput.*) закры́тие; **~-out** *n.* (*US, sport*) игра́ с сухи́м счётом; суха́я (*coll.*).

shutter /ˈʃʌtə(r)/ *n.* **1** (*on window*) ста́вень (*m.*). **2** (*phot.*) затво́р.
● *v.t.* закр|ыва́ть, -ы́ть ста́внями.

shuttle /ˈʃʌt(ə)l/ *n.* (*for weaving*) челно́к; (*fig.*): **~ service** регуля́рное движе́ние/сообще́ние; **~ diplomacy** челно́чная диплома́тия; **space ~** косми́ческий челно́к.
● *v.i.* снова́ть (*impf.*).
● *cpd.* **~cock** *n.* вола́н.

shy[1] /ʃaɪ/ *n.* (*coll.*) (*throw*) бросо́к; **have a ~ at something** запус|ка́ть, -ти́ть чем-н. во что-н.
● *v.t.* (*coll.*) бр|оса́ть, -о́сить.

shy[2] /ʃaɪ/ *adj.* (**shyer, shyest**) (*bashful*) засте́нчивый; (*timid*) ро́бкий; (*reserved*) сде́ржанный; (*coll., lacking*): **I'm ~ 20 dollars** у меня́ не хвата́ет двадцати́ до́лларов; **be ~ of s.o.** робе́ть (*impf.*) пе́ред кем-н.; **fight ~ of** избега́ть (*impf.*) +*g.*
● *v.i.* **1** (*of horse*) шара́х|аться, -нуться; отпря́нуть (*pf.*); **~ at a fence** отка́з|ываться, -а́ться взять препя́тствие. **2** (*of person*): **~ away from something** шара́х|аться, -нуться от чего́-н.; отпря́нуть (*pf.*) от чего́-н.

shyness /ˈʃaɪnɪs/ *n.* засте́нчивость, ро́бость, сде́ржанность.

shyster /ˈʃaɪstə(r)/ *n.* (*coll.*) тёмный деле́ц, пройдо́ха (*c.g.*).

Siamese /ˌsaɪəˈmiːz/ *n.* (*pl.* **~**) (*also* **~ cat**) сиа́мская ко́шка.
● *adj.* сиа́мский; **~ twins** сиа́мские близнецы́ (*m. pl.*).

Siberia /saɪˈbɪərɪə/ *n.* Сиби́рь.

Siberian /saɪˈbɪərɪən/ *n.* сибиря́|к (*fem.* -чка).
● *adj.* сиби́рский.

sibilant /ˈsɪbɪlənt/ *n.* свистя́щий согла́сный, сибиля́нт.
● *adj.* свистя́щий.

sibling /ˈsɪblɪŋ/ *n.* (*brother*) родно́й брат; (*sister*) родна́я сестра́; **~s** (родны́е) бра́тья и сёстры.

sic /sɪk/ *adv.* так!

Sicilian /sɪˈsɪljən/, /-lɪən/ *n.* сицили́|ец (*fem.* -йка).
● *adj.* сицили́йский.

Sicily /ˈsɪsɪlɪ/ *n.* Сици́лия.

sick /sɪk/ *n.* (*collect.*: **the ~**) больны́е (*pl.*).
● *adj.* **1** (*unwell*) больно́й; **fall ~** забол|ева́ть, -е́ть; **he is off ~** он на больни́чном бюллете́не (*coll.*); (*fig.*): **be ~ at heart** тоскова́ть (*impf.*).
2 (*nauseated*): **I feel ~** меня́ тошни́т/мути́т; **I am going to be ~** меня́ сейча́с вы́рвет; **he was ~** его́ вы́рвало.
3: **~ of**: **I am ~ to death of her** она́ мне надое́ла до́ смерти; **we are ~ (and tired) of doing nothing** нам надое́ло безде́льничать; **he was ~ of the sight of food** он не мог смотре́ть на еду́ без отвраще́ния.
4: **~ at**: **he was ~ at being beaten** он был удручён свои́м пораже́нием; **I am ~ at the thought of having to leave home** у меня́ се́рдце щеми́т от одно́й мы́сли о расстава́нии с (родны́м) до́мом.
5 (*abnormal, morbid*) ме́рзкий, жу́ткий; **~ joke** ме́рзкий анекдо́т.
● *v.t.*: **~ up** (*Br. coll.*): **he ~ed up the onions** его́ вы́рвало лу́ком.
● *cpds.* **~-bay** *n.* (корабе́льный) лазаре́т; **~-bed** *n.* посте́ль больно́го; **~-leave** *n.* о́тпуск по боле́зни; **he is on ~-leave** он на больни́чном бюллете́не (*coll.*); **~ note** *n.* больни́чный лист, бюллете́нь (*m.*) (*coll.*); **~-pay** *n.* опла́та по больни́чному листу́; **~-room** *n.* ко́мната больно́го.

sicken /ˈsɪkən/ *v.t.* (*lit.*): **the sight of blood ~s me** меня́ тошни́т при ви́де кро́ви; (*fig., disgust, repel*) вызыва́ть, вы́звать отвраще́ние у (*кого*); **~ing** отврати́тельный, проти́вный.
● *v.i.* (*become ill*) забол|ева́ть, -е́ть; **he is ~ing for influenza** (*Br.*) он заболева́ет гри́ппом.

sickle /ˈsɪk(ə)l/ *n.* серп; **a ~ moon** серп луны́; **hammer and ~** серп и мо́лот.

sickly /ˈsɪklɪ/ *adj.* (**sicklier, sickliest**) (*unhealthy*) боле́зненный; (*puny*) хи́лый; (*unwell*) нездоро́вый; (*inducing nausea*) тошнотво́рный; (*mawkish*) слаща́вый; **~ smile** крива́я улы́бка.

sickness /ˈsɪknɪs/ *n.* (*ill-health*) нездоро́вье; (*disease*) боле́знь; (*vomiting*) рво́та; (*nausea*) тошнота́.
● *cpd.* **~ benefit** *n.* посо́бие по боле́зни.

side /saɪd/ *n.* **1** сторона́; **on this ~** на э́той стороне́; по э́ту сто́рону; **on (along) both ~s** по обе́им сторона́м; **on either ~** с обе́их сторо́н; **on all ~s** со всех сторо́н; **from every ~** со всех сторо́н, отовсю́ду; **on the right/left ~** с пра́вой/с ле́вой стороны́; спра́ва/сле́ва; **put on one ~** (*defer, shelve*) от|кла́дывать, -ложи́ть; **stand to one ~** сторони́ться, по-; **move to one ~** отодв|ига́ться, -и́нуться; **take s.o. to one ~** отв|оди́ть, -ести́ кого́-н. в сто́рону; **on the ~** (*coll., additionally*) на стороне́; (*illicitly*) нале́во; **get, keep on the right ~ of s.o.** распол|ага́ть, -ожи́ть кого́-н. к себе́; быть на хоро́шем счету́ у кого́-н.; **he is on the wrong ~ of 50** ему́ за 50.
2 (*edge*) край; **on the ~ of the page** на краю́ (*or* на поля́х) страни́цы; **by the ~ of the lake** на берегу́ о́зера; **the ~s of a ditch** сте́нки (*f. pl.*) кана́вы; **on the ~ of the mountain** на скло́не горы́; **~ of a ship** борт корабля́.
3 (*of room, table*) коне́ц.
4 (*of the body*) бок; **I have a pain in my ~** у меня́ боли́т бок; **split one's ~s** (*with laughter*) хохота́ть (*impf.*) до упа́ду; **at my ~** ря́дом со мной; **he sat by her ~** он сиде́л во́зле/по́дле неё; **they were standing ~ by ~** они́ стоя́ли бок о бок/ря́дом/рядко́м (*coll.*).
5 (*of meat*) край; **a ~ of beef/pork** полови́на говя́жьей/свино́й ту́ши.
6 (*of a building*) бокова́я стена́; **he went round the ~ of the house** он обогну́л дом; **~ entrance** боково́й вход.
7 (*of cloth*): **right ~** лицева́я сторона́; лицо́; **wrong ~** изна́ночная сторона́, изна́нка; **wrong ~ out** наизна́нку; (*of packages etc.*): **right ~ up** пра́вильно; **this ~ up** э́той стороно́й вверх; (*as inscription*) верх; **wrong ~ up** вверх нога́ми; (*of paper*) страни́ца; **his essay ran to six ~s** он написа́л сочине́ние на шести́ страни́цах.
8 (*aspect*) сторона́; **I can see the funny ~ of the affair** я ви́жу смешну́ю сто́рону де́ла; **try to look on the bright ~!** стара́йтесь быть оптими́стом!; **hear both ~s (of the case)** выслу́шивать, вы́слушать о́бе то́чки зре́ния.
9: **on the long/short ~** длиннова́тый/короткова́тый; **the weather is on the cool ~** пого́да дово́льно прохла́дная.
10 (*party, faction*) сторона́; **which ~ are you on?** вы на чьей стороне́?; **take ~s with s.o.** прин|има́ть, -я́ть (*or* ста|нови́ться, -ть на) чью-н. сто́рону.
11 (*team*) кома́нда; **pick ~s** под|бира́ть, -обра́ть кома́нду; **let the ~ down** (*Br., fig.*) подв|оди́ть, -ести́ това́рищей.
12 (*lineage*): **on the mother's/father's**

~ с матери́нской/отцо́вской стороны́.
13 (*Br. coll., pretentiousness*) чва́нство, высокоме́рие.
14 (*attr.*) боково́й; *see also cpds.*
● *v.i.*: ~ **with s.o.** прин|има́ть, -я́ть чью-н. сто́рону.
● *cpds.* **~-arms** *n.* ли́чное ору́жие; **~board** *n.* буфе́т, серва́нт; **~boards** (*Br.*), **~burns** *nn.* (*coll.*) ба́к|и (*pl., g.* —); **~-car** *n.* коля́ска (*мотоцикла*); **~-dish** *n.* гарни́р; **~-drum** *n.* ма́лый бараба́н; **~-effect** *n.* побо́чное де́йствие; **~-glance** *n.*: **with a ~-glance at him** и́скоса на него́ взгляну́в; **~-issue** *n.* побо́чный/второстепе́нный вопро́с; **~kick** *n.* (*coll.*) подру́чный; **~light** *n.* (*Br., on car*) габари́тный фона́рь; **~line** *n.* (*work*) побо́чная рабо́та; (*goods*) неосновно́й това́р; (*football*) бокова́я ли́ния по́ля; **~long** *adv.* и́скоса; **~-plate** *n.* ма́ленькая таре́лка; **~-road** *n.* просёлочная доро́га; **~-saddle** *n.* да́мское седло́; **ride ~-saddle** е́хать (*impf.*) на да́мском седле́; **~-show** *n.* (*at fair*) аттракцио́н; (*theatr., interlude; also fig.*) интерме́дия; **~-slip** *n.* (*aeron.*) скольже́ние на крыло́; **~-splitting** *adj.* умори́тельный; **~-step** *n.* шаг в сто́рону; *v.t.* (*fig.*) уклон|я́ться, -и́ться от + *g.*; об|ходи́ть, -ойти́; **~-street** *n.* переу́лок; **~-stroke** *n.* пла́вание на боку́; **~-table** *n.* приставно́й стол, стол для заку́сок; **~-track** *n.* запа́сный путь; *v.t.* (*US rail.*) перев|оди́ть, -ести́ на запа́сный путь; (*distract*): **I meant to finish the job, but I was ~-tracked** я собира́лся зако́нчить (э́ту) рабо́ту, но меня́ отвлекли́; **~-view** *n.* вид сбо́ку, про́филь (*m.*); **~-view mirror** *n.* (*US*) боково́е зе́ркало; **~walk** *n.* (*US*) тротуа́р; **~wall** *n.* (*of tyre*) боковина́; **~ways** *adj.* боково́й; *adv.* (*to one ~*) вбок; (*of motion*) бо́ком; **~ways on to something** перпендикуля́рно к чему́-н.; **~-whiskers** *n.* бакенба́рд|ы (*pl., g.* —).

sidereal /saɪ'dɪərɪəl/ *adj.* звёздный.

siding /'saɪdɪŋ/ *n.* **1** (*rail.*) запа́сный путь. **2** (*US, cladding*) чи́стая обши́вка.

sidle /'saɪd(ə)l/ *v.i.*: **~ up to s.o.** под|ходи́ть, -ойти́ к кому́-н. бочко́м.

siege /si:dʒ/ *n.* оса́да, блока́да; **lay ~ to** оса|жда́ть, -ди́ть; **raise a ~** сн|има́ть, -ять оса́ду.

sienna /sɪ'enə/ *n.* сие́на; **burnt/raw ~** жжёная/натура́льная сие́на.

sierra /sɪ'erə/ *n.* го́рная цепь.

Sierra Leone /sɪ'erə lɪ'əʊn/ *n.* Сье́рра-Лео́не.

siesta /sɪ'estə/ *n.* сие́ста.

sieve /sɪv/ *n.* си́то; **he has a memory like a ~** у него́ голова́ дыря́вая.
● *v.t.* просе́|ивать, -ять.

sift /sɪft/ *v.t.* просе́|ивать, -ять; **~ out sand from gravel** отсе́|ивать, -ять песо́к от гра́вия; **~ sugar on to a cake** пос|ыпа́ть, -ы́пать пече́нье са́харом; (*fig.*): **~ the facts** рассм|а́тривать, -отре́ть фа́кты.

sigh /saɪ/ *n.* вздох; **heave a ~ of relief** взд|ыха́ть, -охну́ть с облегче́нием.
● *v.i.* взд|ыха́ть, -охну́ть; **the wind ~ed in the trees** ве́тер шелесте́л в листве́.

sight /saɪt/ *n.* **1** (*faculty*) зре́ние; **long ~** дальнозо́ркость; (*fig.*) дальнови́дность; **short ~** (*lit., fig.*) близору́кость; (*fig.*) недальнови́дность; **second ~** яснови́дение; **lose one's ~** теря́ть, по- зре́ние; сле́пнуть, о-; **lose the ~ of one eye** сле́пнуть, о- на оди́н глаз; **I know her by ~** я зна́ю её в лицо́.
2 (*seeing, being seen*) вид; **I can't bear the ~ of him** я его́ ви́деть не могу́; **catch ~ of** зам|еча́ть, -е́тить; **I kept him in ~** я не спуска́л с него́ глаз; я не выпуска́л его́ и́з виду; **lose ~ of** теря́ть, по- из ви́да (*or* и́з виду); **at first ~** с пе́рвого взгля́да; на пе́рвый взгляд; **love at first ~** любо́вь с пе́рвого взгля́да; **he can read music at ~** он мо́жет игра́ть с листа́; **they were ordered to shoot at ~** им приказа́ли стреля́ть без предупрежде́ния; (*range of vision*): **come into ~** пока́з|ываться, -а́ться; появ|ля́ться, -и́ться; **in ~** на виду́; **the end is in ~** коне́ц ви́ден; **they were (with)in ~ of land** бе́рег был бли́зок; **put out of ~** пря́тать, с-; уб|ира́ть, -ра́ть (с глаз); **keep out of ~** не пока́з|ывать(ся), -а́ть(ся) (на глаза́); **he would not let her out of his ~** он её с глаз не спуска́л; **(get) out of my ~!** с глаз мои́х доло́й!; **out of ~, out of mind** с глаз доло́й, из се́рдца вон.
3 (*spectacle*) вид, зре́лище; **a ~ for sore eyes** прия́тное зре́лище; **see the ~s** осм|а́тривать, -отре́ть достопримеча́тельности; **what a ~ you are!** ну и вид у тебя́!; **he looked a perfect ~** он был похо́ж на пу́гало.
4 (*coll., great deal*) ма́сса, у́йма; **he looked a ~ better for his holiday** по́сле о́тдыха он гора́здо лу́чше вы́глядел.
5 (*aiming device*) прице́л; (*focusing device*) визи́р; **he set his ~s on becoming a professor** он ме́тил в профессора́ (*coll.*).
6 (*attr.*): **to buy something ~ unseen** покупа́ть, купи́ть что-н., не посмотре́в предвари́тельно.
● *v.t.* **1** (*spot after searching*) зам|еча́ть, -е́тить; ви́деть, у-; **they ~ed game** они́ вы́смотрели дичь; **I ~ed her amidst the crowd** я заме́тил её в толпе́; **the sailors ~ed land** матро́сы уви́дели зе́млю.
2 (*aim*): **~ a gun at a target** нав|оди́ть, -ести́ ору́дие на цель.
● *cpds.* **~-reading** *n.* (*mus.*) игра́ с листа́; **~seeing** *n.* осмо́тр достопримеча́тельностей; **~seer** *n.* тури́ст (*fem.* -ка); экскурса́нт (*fem.* -ка).

sighted /'saɪtɪd/ *adj.* (*not blind*) зря́чий.

sightless /'saɪtlɪs/ *adj.* слепо́й.

sign /saɪn/ *n.* **1** (*mark; gesture*) знак; **make the ~ of the cross** крести́ться, пере-; **~s of the zodiac** зна́ки (*m. pl.*) зодиа́ка; **~ language** язы́к же́стов/ручна́я а́збука; (*symbol*) си́мвол; **plus/minus ~** знак плюс/ми́нус; **equals ~** знак ра́венства.
2 (*indication*) при́знак; **there is no ~ of progress** нет никаки́х при́знаков прогре́сса; **there's still no ~ of him** его́ всё нет и нет; **the plant showed ~s of growth** расте́ние обнару́жило при́знаки ро́ста; **he showed no ~ of recognizing me** по его́ ви́ду нельзя́ бы́ло сказа́ть, что он меня́ узна́л; **~ of the times** зна́мение вре́мени; (*trace*) след; **the house showed ~s of the fire** дом нёс на себе́ следы́ пожа́ра.
3 (*portent*) приме́та.
4 (*~board*) вы́веска; **inn ~** тракти́рная вы́веска; **neon ~** нео́новая рекла́ма; **road/traffic ~** доро́жный знак.
● *v.t. & i.* **1** подпи́с|ывать(ся), -а́ть(ся); распи́с|ываться, -а́ться; ста́вить, по- свою́ по́дпись (*под чем-н.*); **I ~ed for the parcel** я расписа́лся в получе́нии паке́та.
2 (*communicate by ~*) под|ава́ть, -а́ть знак; **she ~ed to the others to leave** она́ подала́ остальны́м знак уходи́ть.
● *with advs.*: **~ away** *v.t.* отд|ава́ть, -а́ть; **he ~ed away his inheritance** он подписа́л отка́з от насле́дства; **~ off** *v.i.* (*at end of broadcast*) объяв|ля́ть, -и́ть об оконча́нии переда́чи; проща́ться, по- в конце́ переда́чи; **~ on** *v.i.* (*Br., as unemployed*) регистри́роваться, за- в спи́сках безрабо́тных; (*also* **~ up**) (*register*) регистри́роваться, за-; **~ up** *v.t. & i.* (*for job*) нан|има́ть(ся), -я́ть(ся); **the club ~ed up a new goalkeeper** клуб на́нял но́вого вратаря́.
● *cpds.* **~board** *n.* вы́веска; **~-painter** *n.* худо́жник, рису́ющий вы́вески; **~post** *n.* указа́тель (*m.*); (*v.t.*) (*Br., indicate*) ука́з|ывать, -а́ть; (*provide with ~posts*) снаб|жа́ть, -ди́ть указа́телями.

signal[1] /'sɪgn(ə)l/ *n.* **1** сигна́л; **distress ~** сигна́л бе́дствия; **the driver gave a hand ~** води́тель (*m.*) по́дал сигна́л руко́й; (*rail.*) семафо́р; **the ~s are against us** семафо́р закры́т; (*for road traffic*) светофо́р. **2** (*pl., mil.*): **~s troops** войска́ свя́зи.
● *v.t.* **(signalled, signalling;** *US* **signaled, signaling): ~ an order** перед|ава́ть, -а́ть прика́з; **the ship ~led its position** су́дно сигнализи́ровало своё местонахожде́ние; **I ~led** (*motioned to*) **him to come nearer** я по́дал ему́ знак подойти́ побли́же.
● *v.i.* **(signalled, signalling;** *US* **signaled, signaling)** сигнализи́ровать (*impf., pf.*).
● *cpds.* **~-box** *n.* (*Br.*) сигна́льная бу́дка; блокпо́ст; **~man** *n.* (*rail.*) стре́лочник; (*mil.*) связи́ст; (*nav.*) сигна́льщик.

signal[2] /'sɪgn(ə)l/ *adj.*: **~ success** блестя́щий успе́х; **~ failure** полне́йший прова́л.

signaler /'sɪgnələ(r)/ (*US*) = **signaller**

signalize /'sɪgnə,laɪz/ *v.t.* ознамено́в|ывать, -а́ть; отм|еча́ть, -е́тить.

signaller /'sɪgnələ(r)/ (*US* **signaler**) *n.* сигна́льщик; (*mil.*) связи́ст.

signatory /ˈsɪgnətərɪ/ *n.* подписа́вшийся.

● *adj.*: ~ **powers** держа́вы, подписа́вшие догово́р.

signature /ˈsɪgnətʃə(r)/ *n.* **1** по́дпись. **2** (*mus.*): **key** ~ ключ; ~ **tune** (*Br.*) музыка́льная ша́пка. **3** (*typ.*) сигнату́ра.

signet /ˈsɪgnɪt/ *n.* печа́тка; ~ **ring** кольцо́ с печа́ткой.

significance /sɪgˈnɪfɪkəns/ *n.* (*meaning, import*) значе́ние; (*sense*) смысл, значе́ние.

significant /sɪgˈnɪfɪkənt/ *adj.* значи́тельный; (*important*) ва́жный; ~ **changes** суще́ственные измене́ния; (*expressive*): **a** ~ **look** многозначи́тельный взгляд.

signification /ˌsɪgnɪfɪˈkeɪʃ(ə)n/ *n.* значе́ние; смысл.

signif|y /ˈsɪgnɪˌfaɪ/ *v.t.* **1** (*declare, indicate*) выража́ть, вы́разить; **we** ~**ied our approval** мы вы́разили своё одобре́ние. **2** (*portend*) предвеща́ть (*impf.*); **few people realized what this event** ~**ied** ма́ло кто сознава́л, что предвеща́ло э́то собы́тие. **3** (*mean*) означа́ть (*impf.*).

● *v.i.* (*be of importance*) зна́чить (*impf.*); **it does not** ~**y** э́то нева́жно.

Signor /ˈsiːnjɔː(r)/, **-a** /siːnˈjɔːrə/, **-ina** /ˌsiːnjəˈriːnə/ *nn.* синьо́р, -а, -и́на.

Sikh /siːk/, /sɪk/ *n.* сикх.

● *adj.* си́кхский.

Sikhism /ˈsiːkɪz(ə)m/, /ˈsɪk-/ *n.* сикхи́зм.

silage /ˈsaɪlɪdʒ/ *n.* си́лос.

● *v.t.* силосова́ть, за-.

silence /ˈsaɪləns/ *n.* молча́ние; тишина́; ~ **is golden** молча́ние — зо́лото; **in** ~ в молча́нии; мо́лча; ~! ти́хо!; молча́ть!; **break** ~ нар|уша́ть, -у́шить молча́ние; **keep** ~ храни́ть (*impf.*) молча́ние; **call for** ~ приз|ыва́ть, -ва́ть к тишине́; **reduce s.o. to** ~ заст|авля́ть, -а́вить кого́-н. (за)молча́ть.

● *v.t.* (*person*) заст|авля́ть, -а́вить замолча́ть; (*thing*) заглуш|а́ть, -и́ть.

silencer /ˈsaɪlənsə(r)/ *n.* глуши́тель (*m.*).

silent /ˈsaɪlənt/ *adj.* (*saying nothing*) безмо́лвный; **the** ~ **majority** молчали́вое большинство́; **keep** ~ сохраня́ть (*impf.*) молча́ние, молча́ть (*impf.*); **keep** ~ **about something** ум|а́лчивать, -олча́ть о чём-н.; **history is** ~ **on this matter** исто́рия об э́том ума́лчивает; **fall, become** ~ зам|олка́ть, -о́лкнуть; замолча́ть (*pf.*); умолка́ть, умо́лкнуть; (*taciturn*) молчали́вый; (*mute*) немо́й; ~ **film** немо́й фильм; (*not pronounced*) непроизноси́мый; (*noiseless*) бесшу́мный.

silhouette /ˌsɪluːˈet/ *n.* силуэ́т; **a portrait in** ~ силуэ́тное изображе́ние, силуэ́т.

● *v.t.*: **the dome was** ~**d against the sky** на не́бе вырисо́вывался силуэ́т ку́пола.

silica /ˈsɪlɪkə/ *n.* кремнезём; (*quartz*) кварц.

silicate /ˈsɪlɪˌkeɪt/ *n.* силика́т.

silicon /ˈsɪlɪkən/ *n.* кре́мний; ~ **chip** кре́мниевая микропласти́нка, чип.

silicone /ˈsɪlɪˌkəʊn/ *n.* силико́н.

silicosis /ˌsɪlɪˈkəʊsɪs/ *n.* силико́з.

silk /sɪlk/ *n.* **1** шёлк; (*attr.*) шёлковый; ~ **stockings** шёлковые чулки́; ~ **hat** цили́ндр. **2** (*pl., garments*) шелка́ (*m. pl.*). **3** (*pl., for embroidery*) шёлк; шёлковые ни́тки (*f. pl.*).

● *cpds.* ~**-screen** *adj.*: ~**-screen printing** шёлкогра́фия; ~**worm** *n.* ту́товый шелкопря́д; шелкови́чный червь.

silken /ˈsɪlkən/ *adj.* (*made of silk*) шёлковый; (*resembling* ~) шелкови́стый; (*fig.*) = **silky**

silky /ˈsɪlkɪ/ *adj.* (**silkier, silkiest**) шелкови́стый; (*fig., of voice etc.*) ба́рхатный.

sill /sɪl/ *n.* (*of window*) подоко́нник; (*of door*) поро́г.

silliness /ˈsɪlɪnɪs/ *n.* глу́пость.

silly /ˈsɪlɪ/ *n.* (*coll.*) глупы́шка (*c.g.*).

● *adj.* (**sillier, silliest**) **1** (*foolish*) глу́пый; **do/say something** ~ де́лать, с-/говори́ть, сказа́ть глу́пость; **how** ~ **of me to forget!** как глу́по с мое́й стороны́ забы́ть! **2** (*imbecile*) слабоу́мный; **the noise is driving me** ~ э́тот шум меня́ с ума́ сведёт.

silo /ˈsaɪləʊ/ *n.* (*pl.* ~**s**) (*tower; pit*) си́лосная ба́шня/я́ма; (*for missile*) ста́ртовая ша́хта.

● *v.t.* (**siloes, siloed**) силосова́ть, за-.

silt /sɪlt/ *n.* ил.

● *v.t. & i.* (*usu.* ~ **up**) заили|вать(ся), -ть(ся).

Silurian /saɪˈljʊərɪən/ *adj.* силури́йский.

sil|van, syl- /ˈsɪlv(ə)n/ *adj.* (*of the woods*) лесно́й; (*having woods*) леси́стый.

silver /ˈsɪlvə(r)/ *n.* **1** (*metal*; ~**ware**; ~ **coins**) серебро́. **2** (*colour*) сере́бряный цвет.

● *adj.* (*made of* ~) сере́бряный; (*resembling* ~) серебри́стый; ~ **birch** бе́лая берёза; ~ **fir** бе́лая/благоро́дная пи́хта; ~ **fox** чёрно-бу́рая лиси́ца; ~ **jubilee** сере́бряный юбиле́й; двадцатипятиле́тие; ~ **paper** (*Br.*) фо́льга; ~ **sand** (*Br.*) то́нкий бе́лый песо́к; ~ **wedding** сере́бряная сва́дьба.

● *cpds.* ~**-grey** *adj.* серебри́сто-се́рый; ~**-haired** *adj.* седо́й; ~**-plated** *adj.* серебрёный, посеребрённый; ~**side** *n.* (*Br., of beef*) ссек; ~**smith** *n.* сере́бряных дел ма́стер; ~**-tongued** *adj.* красноречи́вый; ~**ware** *n.* серебро́; изде́лия (*nt. pl.*) из серебра́.

silvery /ˈsɪlvərɪ/ *adj.* серебри́стый.

silviculture /ˈsɪlvɪˌkʌltʃə(r)/ *n.* лесово́дство.

simian /ˈsɪmɪən/ *adj.* (*of apes*) обезья́ний; (*ape-like*) обезьяноподо́бный.

similar /ˈsɪmɪlə(r)/ *adj.* **1** (*alike*) схо́дный, похо́жий; **the hats are** ~ **in appearance** шля́пы с ви́ду о́чень похо́жи. **2**: ~ **to** похо́жий на + *a.*; подо́бный + *d.*; ~ **triangles** подо́бные треуго́льники.

similarity /ˌsɪmɪˈlærɪtɪ/ *n.* схо́дство; **points of** ~ черты́ (*f. pl.*) схо́дства; о́бщие черты́; **his features bear a** ~ **to his father's** он похо́ж на отца́ лицо́м.

similarly /ˈsɪmɪləlɪ/ *adv.* так же; таки́м же о́бразом.

simile /ˈsɪmɪlɪ/ *n.* сравне́ние.

similitude /sɪˈmɪlɪˌtjuːd/ *n.* (*likeness*) схо́дство.

simmer /ˈsɪmə(r)/ *n.*: **bring to a** ~ дов|оди́ть, -ести́ до лёгкого кипе́ния.

● *v.t.* кипяти́ть, вс- на ме́дленном огне́.

● *v.i.* слегка́ кипе́ть (*impf.*); (*fig.*): ~ **with indignation** кипе́ть (*impf.*) негодова́нием; ~ **down** (*fig.*) успок|а́иваться, -о́иться; ост|ыва́ть, -ы́ть; **he** ~**ed down** он успоко́ился/осты́л.

simper /ˈsɪmpə(r)/ *n.* жема́нная улы́бка.

● *v.i.* жема́нно улыб|а́ться, -ну́ться.

simple /ˈsɪmp(ə)l/ *adj.* (**simpler, simplest**) **1** просто́й; **I am not so** ~ **as to believe that** я не так прост, что́бы пове́рить э́тому; **as** ~ **as ABC** про́ще просто́го; **it's as** ~ **as that** то́лько и всего́; вот и всё. **2** (*easy*) лёгкий; **the dress is** ~ **to make** э́то пла́тье легко́ сшить. **3** (*math.*): ~ **equation** уравне́ние пе́рвой сте́пени.

● *cpds.* ~**-hearted** *adj.* простоду́шный; ~**-minded** *adj.* (*unsophisticated*) бесхи́тростный; (*feeble-minded*) глу́пый, глупова́тый.

simpleton /ˈsɪmp(ə)lt(ə)n/ *n.* простá к.

simplicity /sɪmˈplɪsɪtɪ/ *n.* простота́; (*easiness*) лёгкость.

simplification /ˌsɪmplɪfɪˈkeɪʃ(ə)n/ *n.* упроще́ние.

simplify /ˈsɪmplɪˌfaɪ/ *v.t.* упро|ща́ть, -сти́ть.

simplistic /sɪmˈplɪstɪk/ *adj.* (чрезме́рно) упрощённый.

simply /ˈsɪmplɪ/ *adv.* про́сто; **the weather was** ~ **dreadful** пого́да была́ про́сто ужа́сная; **I** ~ **couldn't manage to come** я ника́к не мог прийти́; **it's** ~ **that I don't like him** про́сто-напро́сто он мне не нра́вится.

simulacr|um /ˌsɪmjʊˈleɪkrəm/ *n.* (*pl.* ~**a**) (*likeness*) подо́бие; (*deceptive substitute*) ви́димость.

simulate /ˈsɪmjʊˌleɪt/ *v.t.* (*feign*) симули́ровать (*impf., pf.*); (*pretend to be*) притвор|я́ться, -и́ться + *i.*; (*imitate for training purposes*) воспроизв|оди́ть, -ести́; модели́ровать (*impf., pf.*); имити́ровать (*impf., pf.*).

simulated /ˈsɪmjʊˌleɪtɪd/ *adj.* подде́льный, иску́ственный; ~ **flight** модели́рованный/усло́вный полёт.

simulation /ˌsɪmjʊˈleɪʃ(ə)n/ *n.* симуля́ция; воспроизведе́ние; модели́рование; имита́ция.

simulator /ˈsɪmjʊˌleɪtə(r)/ *n.* (*person*) симуля́нт, притво́рщик; (*device*) модели́рующее/имити́рующее устро́йство; **flight** ~ пилота́жный тренажёр.

simultaneity /ˌsɪməltəˈniːɪtɪ/ *n.* одновре́ме́нность, синхро́нность.

simultaneous /ˌsɪməlˈteɪnɪəs/ *adj.* одновре́ме́нный, синхро́нный; **~ interpreting** синхро́нный перево́д.

sin /sɪn/ *n.* **1** грех; **original ~** первоpо́дный грех; **the seven deadly ~s** семь сме́ртных грехо́в; **~s of omission and commission** грехи́ де́янием и неде́янием; **forgiveness of ~s** отпуще́ние грехо́в; **live in ~** жить (*impf.*) в незако́нном бра́ке; **for my ~s** за грехи́ мои́; **as ugly as ~** стра́шен как сме́ртный грех. **2** (*offence*): **~ against propriety** наруше́ние прили́чий; **it's a ~ to stay indoors** грешно́ сиде́ть до́ма.

● *v.i.* (**sinned, sinning**) греши́ть, со-; **more ~ned against than ~ning** скоре́е же́ртва, чем вино́вный.

Sinai /ˈsaɪnaɪ/ *n.* Сина́й.

since /sɪns/ *adv.* **1** (*from that time*) с тех пор; **he has been here ever ~** с тех пор/с той поры́ он здесь так и оста́лся; **he was healthier in the army than ever before or ~** он никогда́ не́ был так здоро́в, как когда́ служи́л в а́рмии.
2 (*in the intervening time*): **the house has ~ been rebuilt** с тех пор (*or* поздне́е) дом перестро́или; **he was wounded but has ~ recovered** он был ра́нен, но уже́ попра́вился.

● *prep.* c+*g.*; **nothing has happened ~ Christmas** с Рождества́ ничего́ не произошло́; **~ our talk** по́сле на́шего разгово́ра; **~ yesterday** со вчера́шнего дня; **~ when have you been fond of music?** с каки́х пор вы ста́ли люби́ть му́зыку?

● *conj.* **1** (*from, during the time when*): **how long is it ~ we last met?** ско́лько вре́мени прошло́ с на́шей после́дней встре́чи?; **I have moved house ~ I saw you** с тех пор как мы с ва́ми ви́делись я перее́хал.
2 (*seeing that*) так как, поско́льку; **~ you ask, we're going to be married** мы собира́емся жени́ться, е́сли хоти́те знать.

sincere /sɪnˈsɪə(r)/ *adj.* (**sincerer, sincerest**) и́скренний; **he was ~ in what he said** он э́то говори́л и́скренне; **yours ~ly** и́скренне Ваш.

sincerity /sɪnˈserɪtɪ/ *n.* и́скренность.

sine /saɪn/ *n.* си́нус.

sinecure /ˈsaɪnɪˌkjʊə(r)/, /ˈsɪn-/ *n.* синеку́ра.

sine die /ˌsaɪnɪ ˈdaɪɪ/, /ˌsɪneɪ ˈdiːeɪ/ *adv.* на неопределённый срок; без назначе́ния но́вой да́ты.

sine qua non /ˌsɪneɪ kwɑː ˈnəʊn/ *n.* непреме́нное/обяза́тельное.

sinew /ˈsɪnjuː/ *n.* (*tendon*) сухожи́лие; (*pl., muscles*) жи́лы (*f. pl.*).

sinewy /ˈsɪnjuːɪ/ *adj.* (*muscular*): **~ arms** му́скулистые/жи́листые ру́ки; (*tough*): **~ meat** жи́листое мя́со.

sinful /ˈsɪnfʊl/ *adj.* гре́шный, грехо́вный.

sinfulness /ˈsɪnfʊlnɪs/ *n.* грехо́вность.

sing /sɪŋ/ *v.t.* (*past* **sang;** *p.p.* **sung**) петь, с-; (*a role, song etc.*) петь, с-; исп|олня́ть, -о́лнить; **~ a baby to sleep** убаю́к|ивать, -ать ребёнка пе́нием; (*fig.*): **~ s.o.'s praises** восхваля́ть (*impf.*) кого́-н.; петь (*impf.*) хвалу́/дифира́мбы кому́-н.

● *v.i.* (*past* **sang;** *p.p.* **sung**) петь, с-; **~ in tune** петь (*impf.*) пра́вильно; **~ out of tune** петь (*impf.*) фальши́во; фальши́вить, с-; **she sang to the guitar** она́ пе́ла под гита́ру; **my ears are ~ing** у меня́ звени́т в уша́х.

● *with advs.*: **~ out** *v.i.* (*coll., shout*) кри́кнуть (*pf.*); закрича́ть (*pf.*); **~ up** *v.i.* петь, за- гро́мче.

● *cpd.* **~-song** *n.* **1** (*Br., impromptu ~ing*): **we had a ~-song** мы попе́ли. **2** (*rising and falling speech*) певу́чая речь; *adj.*: **in a ~-song voice** певу́чим го́лосом.

Singapore /ˌsɪŋəˈpɔː(r)/, /ˌsɪŋgə-/ *n.* Сингапу́р.

Singaporean /ˌsɪŋəˈpɔːrɪən/, /ˌsɪŋgə-/ *n.* сингапу́р|ец (*fem.* -ка).

● *adj.* сингапу́рский.

singe /sɪndʒ/ *n.* ожо́г.

● *v.t.* (**singeing**) пали́ть, о-; (*slightly*) подпа́л|ивать, -и́ть.

● *v.i.* (**singeing**): **something is ~ing** что́-то гори́т; па́хнет палёным.

singer /ˈsɪŋə(r)/ *n.* пев|е́ц (*fem.* -и́ца).

● *cpd.* **~-songwriter** *n.* шансонье́ (*m. indecl.*).

Singhalese /ˌsɪŋghəˈliːz/, /ˌsɪŋgəˈliːz/ = **Sinhalese**

singing /ˈsɪŋɪŋ/ *n.* пе́ние; **she has a good ~ voice** у неё хоро́ший го́лос.

single /ˈsɪŋg(ə)l/ *n.* (*Br., ticket*) биле́т в оди́н коне́ц; (*record*) пласти́нка с за́писью двух пе́сен; (*pl., of tennis etc.*) одино́чная игра́.

● *adj.* **1** (*one*) оди́н; (*only one*) еди́нственный, еди́ный; **not a ~ man moved** ни оди́н челове́к не дви́нулся; **a ~ idea occupied his mind** одна́ (еди́нственная) мысль занима́ла его́ ум; **I haven't met a ~ soul** я не встре́тил ни еди́ной души́; **he didn't say a ~ word** он не пророни́л ни (одного́) сло́ва; **in ~ file** гусько́м; **~ line** (*rail.*) одноколе́йная ли́ния; **~ quotes** кавы́чки в оди́н штрих; (*for or involving one person*): **~ bed** односпа́льная крова́ть; **~ room** (*in hotel*) одино́чный но́мер; **~ combat** единобо́рство; (*taken individually*): **every ~ one of his pupils passed** все его́ учени́ки до еди́ного прошли́.
2 (*unmarried*) одино́кий; (*man*) холосто́й; (*woman*) незаму́жняя; **~ father** оте́ц-одино́чка; **~ mother** мать-одино́чка; **~ parent** роди́тель-одино́чка; **she stayed ~ all her life** она́ так и не вы́шла за́муж; она́ так и прожила́ всю жизнь одна́.

● *v.t.*: **~ out**: **he was ~d out** его́ вы́делили.

● *cpds.* **~-barrelled** *adj.* одноство́льный; **~-breasted** *adj.* однобо́ртный; **~-decker** *n.* (*Br., bus*) одноэта́жный авто́бус; **~-entry** *adj.* (*comm.*): **~-entry bookkeeping** проста́я бухгалте́рия; **~-handed** *adj. & adv.* (*unaided*) без посторо́нней по́мощи; **~-minded** *adj.* целеустремлённый; **~-seater** *n.* (*plane*) одноме́стный самолёт; **~-sex** *adj.*: **~-sex school** шко́ла разде́льного обуче́ния; **~-track** *adj.* (*rail.*) одноколе́йный.

singleness /ˈsɪŋg(ə)lnɪs/ *n.*: **~ of purpose** целеустремлённость.

singlet /ˈsɪŋglɪt/ *n.* (*Br.*) ма́йка.

singly /ˈsɪŋglɪ/ *adv.* (*separately*) врозь; в отде́льности; **these articles are sold ~** э́ти ве́щи продаю́тся пошту́чно.

singular /ˈsɪŋgjʊlə(r)/ *n.* (*gram.*) еди́нственное число́.

● *adj.* **1** (*gram.*): **~ noun** существи́тельное в еди́нственном числе́. **2** (*rare, unusual*) необыча́йный; (*odd*) стра́нный.
3 (*outstanding*) чрезвыча́йный; **she was ~ly beautiful** она́ была́ необыча́йно хороша́.

singularity /ˌsɪŋgjʊˈlærɪtɪ/ *n.* (*peculiarity*) осо́бенность; (*uncommonness; oddness*) необы́чность; стра́нность.

Sinhalese /ˌsɪnhəˈliːz/, /ˌsɪnəˈliːz/, **Singhalese** /ˌsɪŋghəˈliːz/, /ˌsɪŋgəˈliːz/ *n.* (*pl.* **~**) (*person*) синга́лец, синга́л (*fem.* -ка); (*language*) синга́льский язы́к.

● *adj.* синга́льский.

sinister /ˈsɪnɪstə(r)/ *adj.* (*suggestive of evil*) злове́щий; (*wicked*) злоде́йский; **a ~ plot** злоде́йский за́говор; **a ~ character** злоде́й, опа́сный челове́к.

sink /sɪŋk/ *n.* (*in kitchen etc.*) ра́ковина.

● *v.t.* (*past* **sank** *or* **sunk;** *p.p.* **sunk** *or as adj.* **sunken**) **1**: **~ a ship** топи́ть, по-/за- су́дно; (*coll., fig.*): **we're sunk** (*coll.*) мы поги́бли!; (*immerse*): **sunk in thought** погружённый в размышле́ния.
2 (*lower*) опус|ка́ть, -ти́ть; **she sank her head on to the pillow** она́ опусти́ла го́лову на поду́шку; **he sank his voice to a whisper** он пони́зил го́лос до шёпота; (*drink down*) погло|ща́ть, -ти́ть; **he can ~ a pint in ten seconds** он спосо́бен поглоти́ть (*coll.*) пи́нту (пи́ва) за де́сять секу́нд.
3 (*set aside, forget, ignore*) заб|ыва́ть, -ы́ть; отбр|а́сывать, -о́сить; **let us ~ our differences** забу́дем на́ши разногла́сия!; **he sank his own interests in the common good** он поступи́лся со́бственными интере́сами ра́ди о́бщих.
4 (*drive, plunge*) вби|ва́ть, -ть; вгоня́ть, вогна́ть; (*fig.*): **the dog sank its teeth into his leg** соба́ка вонзи́ла зу́бы ему́ в но́гу.
5 (*invest*) вкла́дывать, вложи́ть.
6 (*excavate*): **~ a well** рыть, вы́- коло́дец; **~ a shaft** про|ходи́ть, -йти́ ша́хтный ствол.

● *v.i.* (*past* **sank** *or* **sunk;** *p.p.* **sunk** *or as adj.* **sunken**) **1** (*in water etc.*) тону́ть, по-/у-; (*of objects*) тону́ть, за-; погру|жа́ться, -зи́ться; идти́ (*det.*), пойти́ ко дну; **the ship sank** су́дно затону́ло; **he sank to his knees in mud** он по коле́но потону́л в грязи́; **the bather sank like a stone** купа́льщик ка́мнем пошёл ко дну; **~ or swim** ли́бо пан, ли́бо пропа́л; **he was left to**

S

~ or swim его́ бро́сили на произво́л судьбы́.
2 (*disappear*) исч|еза́ть, -е́знуть; (*below the horizon*) за|ходи́ть, -йти́; **the sun ~s in the west** со́лнце захо́дит на за́паде.
3 (*subside, of water*) спа|да́ть, -сть; (*of building or soil*) ос|еда́ть, -е́сть.
4 (*abate*) ослаб|ева́ть, -е́ть.
5 (*get lower*) па́дать, упа́сть; **his voice sank** его́ го́лос упа́л; **prices were ~ing** це́ны (ре́зко) па́дали/снижа́лись.
6 (*fall*): **his head sank back on the pillow** его́ голова́ отки́нулась на поду́шку; **she sank into a coma** она́ впа́ла в комато́зное состоя́ние; **I sank into a deep sleep** я погрузи́лся в глубо́кий сон; (*fig.*): **he has sunk in my estimation** он упа́л в мои́х глаза́х; **my heart sank** у меня́ упа́ло се́рдце; **his spirits sank** он пал ду́хом; **they sank into poverty** они́ впа́ли в нищету́.
7 (*become hollow*) впа|да́ть, -сть; **his cheeks have sunk** у него́ впа́ли щёки.
8 (*percolate, penetrate*) впи́т|ываться, -а́ться; **the dye ~s into the fabric** кра́ска впи́тывается в ткань; **the rain sank into the dry ground** дождь пропита́л суху́ю зе́млю; (*fig.*): **the lesson sank into his mind** уро́к ему́ хорошо́ запо́мнился; **his words sank in** его́ слова́ не прошли́ да́ром; его́ слова́ дошли́ до меня́ (*и т.п.*).

sinker /ˈsɪŋkə(r)/ *n.* (*lead weight*) грузи́ло.

sinking /ˈsɪŋkɪŋ/ *n.* (*of ship*) (*by s.o.*) потопле́ние; (*by itself*) ги́бель; (*of debt*) погаше́ние; **~ fund** фонд погаше́ния.

sinless /ˈsɪnlɪs/ *adj.* безгре́шный.

sinner /ˈsɪnə(r)/ *n.* гре́шни|к (*fem.* -ца).

Sino- /ˈsaɪnəʊ/ *comb. form* кита́йско-.

sinologist /saɪˈnɒlədʒɪst/, /sɪ-/ *n.* китаи́ст, сино́лог.

sinology /saɪˈnɒlədʒɪ/, /sɪ-/ *n.* китаеве́дение.

sinuosity /ˌsɪnjʊˈɒsɪtɪ/ *n.* (*sinuousness*) изви́листость; (*a bend*) изви́лина.

sinuous /ˈsɪnjʊəs/ *adj.* (*serpentine*) изви́листый; (*undulating*) волни́стый.

sinus /ˈsaɪnəs/ *n.* (*anat.*) па́зуха.

sinusitis /ˌsaɪnəˈsaɪtɪs/ *n.* синуси́т.

Sioux /suː/ *n.* (*pl.* ~) си́у (*m. indecl.*).

sip /sɪp/ *n.* глото́к; **have, take a ~ of** глотну́ть (*pf.*); вы́пить (*pf.*) глото́к +*g.*
● *v.t.* (**sipped, sipping**) потя́гивать (*impf.*).

si|phon, sy- /ˈsaɪf(ə)n/ *n.* сифо́н.
● *v.t.*: **~ off, out** выка́чивать, вы́качать сифо́ном; (*fig.*) перек|а́чивать, -ача́ть.
● *v.i.* ст|ека́ть, -ечь.

sir /sɜː(r)/ *n.* (*form of address; title*) сэр, господи́н; су́дарь (*m.*) (*obs.*); **Dear S~** (*in letters*) Уважа́емый господи́н.

sire /ˈsaɪə(r)/ *n.* **1** (*stallion etc.*) производи́тель (*m.*). **2** (*Your Majesty*) Ва́ше вели́чество, сир.
● *v.t.* произв|оди́ть, -ести́ на свет; **the stallion ~d twenty foals** от э́того жеребца́ родило́сь 20 жеребя́т.

siren /ˈsaɪərən/ *n.* (*myth., fig.*) сире́на; (*hooter*) сире́на, гудо́к.

Sirius /ˈsɪrɪəs/ *n.* Си́риус.

sirloin /ˈsɜːlɔɪn/ *n.* филе́ (*nt. indecl.*).

sirocco, scirocco /sɪˈrɒkəʊ/ *n.* (*pl.* **~s**) (*meteor.*) сиро́кко (*m. indecl.*) (*ветер*).

sirup /ˈsɪrəp/ (*US*) = **syrup**

sisal /ˈsaɪs(ə)l/ *n.* (*bot.*) сиза́ль (*m.*).

siskin /ˈsɪskɪn/ *n.* чиж, чи́жик.

sissy /ˈsɪsɪ/ *n.* (*coll.*) не́женка (*c.g.*).
● *adj.* (**sissier, sissiest**) изне́женный.

sister /ˈsɪstə(r)/ *n.* сестра́; (*Br., nursing* ~) ста́ршая медици́нская сестра́; (*attr.*): **~ ship** однoти́пное су́дно.
● *cpd.* **~-in-law** *n.* (*brother's wife*) неве́стка; (*husband's sister*) золо́вка; (*wife's sister*) своя́ченица.

sisterhood /ˈsɪstəˌhʊd/ *n.* (*relig.*) се́стринская общи́на.

sisterly /ˈsɪstəlɪ/ *adj.* се́стринский.

Sisyphean /ˌsɪsɪˈfiːən/ *adj.*: **a ~ task** сизи́фов труд.

sit /sɪt/ *v.t.* (**sitting;** *past and p.p.* **sat**)
1 (*seat*) сажа́ть, посади́ть; уса́|живать, -ди́ть; **they sat the old lady by the fire** они́ посади́ли ста́рушку у огня́; (*of several persons*) расса́|живать, -ди́ть; **~ yourself down!** (*coll.*) сади́тесь!
2 (*Br., undergo*): **~ an examination** держа́ть/сдава́ть (*impf.*) экза́мен.
● *v.i.* (**sitting;** *past and p.p.* **sat**) **1** (*take a seat*) сади́ться, сесть.
2 (*be seated*) сиде́ть (*impf.*); **he can't ~ still** ему́ не сиди́тся (на ме́сте); **~** (*stay*) **at home** сиде́ть (*impf.*) до́ма; **~ tight** (*stick to one's position*) не сдава́ться (*impf.*); не уступа́ть (*impf.*); **~ on a committee** быть чле́ном комите́та; **~ on something** (*shelve it*) класть (*impf.*) что-н. под сукно́; (*of hens*: **~ on eggs**) выси́живать (*impf.*) цыпля́т; (*of birds: perch*) сиде́ть (*impf.*); **~ting duck, target** (*fig.*) лёгкая мише́нь.
3 (*pose*): **~ for an artist** пози́ровать (*impf.*) худо́жнику; **~ for one's photograph** фотографи́роваться, с-.
4 (*hold meeting; be in session*) заседа́ть (*impf.*); **the committee ~s at 10** заседа́ние комите́та начина́ется в 10 часо́в.
5 (*Br., be candidate*): **~ for an exam** держа́ть/сдава́ть (*impf.*) экза́мен; (*Br., represent*): **~ for a constituency** представля́ть (*impf.*) о́круг в парла́менте.
6 (*of clothes: fit, hang*) сиде́ть (*impf.*); **his coat does not ~ properly on his shoulders** его́ пиджа́к пло́хо сиди́т в плеча́х.
● *with advs.*: **~ back** *v.i.* (*lit.*) отки́|дываться, -нуться; (*fig., relax effort*) рассл|абля́ться, -а́биться; **~ down** *v.t.* сажа́ть, посади́ть; уса́|живать, -ди́ть; *v.i.* сади́ться, сесть; (*for a moment*) прис|а́живаться, -е́сть; **~ in** *v.i.* (*occupy premises in protest*) зан|има́ть, -я́ть помеще́ние в знак проте́ста; **~ in** (*deputize*) **for s.o.** замеща́ть (*impf.*) кого́-н.; **~ in on a meeting** прису́тствовать (*impf.*) на собра́нии; **~ out** *v.t.* (*take no part in*): **I have decided to ~ this one** (*dance*) **out** я реши́л пропусти́ть э́тот та́нец; (*stay to end of*) выси́живать, вы́сидеть; *v.i.* (**~ outdoors**) сиде́ть (*impf.*) на во́здухе; **~ through** *v.t.* выси́живать, вы́сидеть; **we sat through the concert** мы вы́сидели весь конце́рт; **~ up** *v.i.* (*from lying position*): **he sat up in bed** он приподня́лся и сел в посте́ли; (*straighten one's back*) сиде́ть (*impf.*) пря́мо; выпрямля́ться, вы́прямиться; (*not go to bed*) не ложи́ться (*impf.*); **we sat up all night with the invalid** мы просиде́ли всю ночь с больны́м; **don't ~ up for me** не жди́те меня́, ложи́тесь спать; (*coll., be startled*): **the news made him ~ up** э́та но́вость огоро́шила его́.
● *cpds.* **~-down** *adj.*: **a ~-down strike** сидя́чая забасто́вка; **~-in** *n.* демонстрати́вное заня́тие помеще́ния.

sitcom /ˈsɪtkɒm/ *n.* (*coll.*) коме́дия положе́ний.

site /saɪt/ *n.* (*place*) ме́сто; (*position*) положе́ние; (*location*) местоположе́ние, местонахожде́ние; **building ~** строи́тельный уча́сток.
● *v.t.* **1** (*arrange, dispose*) распол|ага́ть, -ожи́ть; разме|ща́ть, -сти́ть. **2** (*choose ~ of*) выбира́ть, вы́брать ме́сто для +*g.* **3** (*locate*): **the house is ~d on a slope** дом располо́жен на скло́не горы́/холма́.

sitter /ˈsɪtə(r)/ *n.* **1** (*person sitting for portrait*) моде́ль; **she was his ~ many times** она́ мно́го раз ему́ пози́ровала; (*paid one*) нату́рщи|к (*fem.* -ца).
2 (*baby-~*) ≈ приходя́щая ня́ня.

sitting /ˈsɪtɪŋ/ *n.* **1** (*period of sitting*) сиде́ние; **in one ~** в оди́н присе́ст.
2 (*of assembly*) заседа́ние; (*for serving meals*) пото́к. **3** (*posing*) пози́рование; **two ~s** два сеа́нса пози́рования.
● *cpd.* **~-room** *n.* (*Br.*) гости́ная.

situate /ˈsɪtjʊˌeɪt/ *v.t.* распол|ага́ть, -ожи́ть.

situated /ˈsɪtjʊˌeɪtɪd/ *adj.* **1** (*of buildings etc.*) располо́женный. **2** (*of person*): **this is how I am ~** таковы́ мои́ обстоя́тельства; **how are you ~ for money?** как у вас (обсто́ит) с деньга́ми?

situation /ˌsɪtjʊˈeɪʃ(ə)n/ *n.* **1** (*place*) ме́сто; (*position*) местоположе́ние.
2 (*circumstances*) обстано́вка, положе́ние, ситуа́ция; **what is the ~?** каково́ положе́ние дел?; какова́ обстано́вка? **3** (*job*) пост, ме́сто; **~s vacant** (*Br., as column heading*) вака́нтные до́лжности.
● *cpd.* **~ comedy** *n.* (*theatr.*) коме́дия положе́ний.

six /sɪks/ *n.* (число́/но́мер) шесть; (**~** *people*) ше́стеро, шесть челове́к; **we ~, the ~ of us** мы ше́стеро/вшестеро́м; **~ each** по шести́; (*figure; thing numbered 6; group of* ~) шестёрка; (*with var. nn. expr. or understood: cf. also examples under* ⇒**five**): **it is ~ of one and half a dozen of the other** э́то одно́ и то же; **everything is at ~es and sevens** всё вверх дном; **the news knocked me for ~** (*Br.*) э́та но́вость меня́ огоро́шила (*coll.*); **he threw a ~** (*dice*) у него́ вы́пала шестёрка.
● *adj.* шесть +*g. pl.*; **~ feet high** шесть фу́тов высото́й; (*for people and pluralia*

tantum also) ше́стеро +*g. pl.*; **~ fives are thirty** ше́стью (*or* шесть на) пять — три́дцать.

● *cpds.* **~fold** *adj.* шестикра́тный; *adv.* вше́стеро; в шесть раз; **~-foot** *adj.* шестифу́товый; **~-shooter** *n.* шестизаря́дный револьве́р; **~-sided** *adj.* шестисторо́нний, шестигра́нный.

sixteen /ˌsɪks'ti:n/, /'sɪks-/ *n. & adj.* шестна́дцать (+*g. pl.*).

sixteenth /ˌsɪks'ti:nθ/, /'sɪks-/ *n.* **1** (*date*) шестна́дцатое (число́). **2** (*fraction*) шестна́дцатая часть; одна́ шестна́дцатая.

● *adj.* шестна́дцатый; **~ note** (*US, mus.*) шестна́дцатая но́та.

sixth /sɪksθ/ *n.* **1** (*date*) шесто́е (число́). **2** (*fraction*) шеста́я часть; одна́ шеста́я; **five ~s** пять шесты́х. **3** (*mus.*) се́кста.

● *adj.* шесто́й; **in the ~ form** (*Br.*) в ста́ршем кла́ссе; **~ sense** шесто́е чу́вство.

● *cpd.* **~-form college** *n.* (*Br.*) шко́ла со ста́ршими кла́ссами.

sixthly /'sɪksθlɪ/ *adv.* в-шесты́х.

sixtieth /'sɪkstɪɪθ/ *n.* шестидеся́тая часть; одна́ шестидеся́тая.

● *adj.* шестидеся́тый.

sixt|y /'sɪkstɪ/ *n.* шестьдеся́т; **he is in his ~ies** ему́ за шестьдеся́т (лет); ему́ пошёл седьмо́й деся́ток; **in the ~ies** (*decade*) в шестидеся́тых года́х; в шестидеся́тые го́ды; (*temperature*) за шестьдеся́т гра́дусов (по Фаренге́йту).

● *adj.* шестьдеся́т +*g. pl.*

sizable /'saɪzəb(ə)l/ = **siz(e)able**

size¹ /saɪz/ *n.* **1** (*dimension, magnitude*) разме́р; величина́; **what is the ~ of the house?** какова́ пло́щадь э́того до́ма?; **what ~ will the army be?** какова́ бу́дет чи́сленность а́рмии?; **these books are all the same ~** э́ти кни́ги все одного́ форма́та; **a wave the ~ of a house** волна́ величино́й/высото́й с дом; **that's about the ~ of it** (*coll.*) вот как обстои́т де́ло; **cut s.o. down to ~** (*coll.*) ста́вить, по- кого́-н. на ме́сто. **2** (*of clothes etc.*): **~ 4** четвёртый разме́р/но́мер; **what is your ~?; what ~ do you take?** како́й у вас разме́р?; **the dress is just her ~** э́то пла́тье как раз её разме́ра; **I take ~ 12** я ношу́/у меня́ двена́дцатый разме́р; **I take ~ 10 in shoes** я ношу́ (*or* у меня́) со́рок второ́й разме́р/но́мер о́буви; **these shoes are three ~s too big** э́ти ту́фли на три но́мера велики́; **they are made in several ~s** они́ быва́ют разли́чных разме́ров.

● *v.t.* **1** сортирова́ть, рас- по разме́ру. **2**: **~ s.o. up** сост|авля́ть, -а́вить о ком-н. мне́ние; **~ up the situation** определи́ть (*pf.*) (*or* оц|е́нивать, -ени́ть) обстано́вку.

size² /saɪz/ *n.* (*for glazing paper, walls etc.*) клей, грунт; (*for textile*) шли́хта.

● *v.t.*: **~ a wall** окле́и|вать, -ть сте́ну; **~ paper** прокле́и|вать, -ть бума́гу; **~ cloth** шлихтова́ть (*impf.*) сукно́; **~ canvas** грунтова́ть, за- холст.

siz(e)able /'saɪzəb(ə)l/ *adj.* значи́тельного разме́ра; поря́дочный, изря́дный.

sizzl|e /'sɪz(ə)l/ *n.* шипе́ние.

● *v.i.* шипе́ть (*impf.*); **a ~ing hot day** зно́йный день.

skate¹ /skeɪt/ *n.* (*ice-~*) конёк; **get one's ~s on** (*Br., fig., hurry*) потора́пливаться (*impf.*); **(roller-~)** ро́лик; ро́ликовый конёк.

● *v.i.* **1** (*on ice*) ката́ться/бе́гать (*both indet.*) на конька́х; (*on roller-~s*) ката́ться (*indet.*) на ро́ликах; **~ over, round something** (*fig.*) (*refer fleetingly*) каса́ться, косну́ться чего́-н. вскользь; (*disregard*) об|ходи́ть, -ойти́ что-н. **2** (*slide, skid*) скользи́ть (*impf.*).

● *cpds.* **~board** *n.* скейтбо́рд, ро́ликовая доска́; **~boarder** *n.* скейтборди́ст (*fem.* -ка); **~boarding** *n.* скейтбо́рдинг.

skate² /skeɪt/ *n.* (*pl.* **~** *or* **~s**) (*fish*) скат.

skater /'skeɪtə(r)/ *n.* (*race*) конькобе́ж|ец (*fem. also* -ка); (*in figure-skating*) фигури́ст (*fem.* -ка).

skating /'skeɪtɪŋ/ *n.* (*figure-~*) ката́ние на конька́х; **free(style) ~** произво́льное ката́ние; (*racing*) конькобе́жный спорт, бег на конька́х.

● *cpd.* **~-rink** *n.* като́к.

skedaddle /skɪ'dæd(ə)l/ *v.i.* (*coll.*) улепёт|ывать, -ну́ть (*coll.*); **~!** кати́сь! (*coll.*).

skein /skeɪn/ *n.* (*of wool etc.*) мото́к.

skeletal /'skelɪt(ə)l/ *adj.* скеле́тный.

skeleton /'skelɪt(ə)n/ *n.* **1** скеле́т, костя́к; **~ in the cupboard** (*fig.*) семе́йная та́йна. **2** (*fig., outline*) схе́ма. **3** (*framework*) скеле́т, о́стов, карка́с. **4** (*emaciated person*) скеле́т, ко́жа да ко́сти. **5** (*attr.*): **~ staff** минима́льный штат; **~ key** отмы́чка.

skeptic /'skeptɪk/, **-al** /'skeptɪk(ə)l/ (*US*) = **sceptic, -al**

skepticism /'skeptɪˌsɪz(ə)m/ (*US*) = **scepticism**

sketch /sketʃ/ *n.* **1** (*artistic*) эски́з, набро́сок, зарисо́вка. **2** (*brief outline*) набро́сок. **3** (*play*) скетч.

● *v.t.* (*draw, lit., fig.*) набр|а́сывать, -оса́ть; **he ~ed in the details** он наброса́л дета́ли; **he ~ed out his plans** он обрисова́л свои́ пла́ны в о́бщих черта́х.

● *v.i.* де́лать, с- эски́зы/зарисо́вки.

● *cpds.* **~-block, ~-book** *nn.* альбо́м для эски́зов; **~-map** *n.* схемати́ческая ка́рта.

sketching /'sketʃɪŋ/ *n.* рисова́ние эски́зов, зарисо́вка.

sketchy /'sketʃɪ/ *adj.* (**sketchier, sketchiest**) (*in outline*) схемати́ческий, схемати́чный; (*superficial*) пове́рхностный.

skew /skju:/ *n.*: **on the ~** кри́во, ко́со, на́искось.

● *adj.* (*Br. coll.* **~-whiff**) косо́й; (*math.*) асимметри́чный.

● *cpd.* **~bald** *adj.* пе́гий.

skewer /'skju:ə(r)/ *n.* ве́ртел, шампу́р.

● *v.t.* наса́|живать, -ди́ть на ве́ртел.

ski /ski:/ *n.* (*pl.* **~s**) лы́жа.

● *v.i.* (**skis, skied** /ski:d/; **skiing** *or* **ski-ing**) (*cross-country*) ходи́ть (*indet.*) на лы́жах; (*downhill*) ката́ться (*impf.*) на лы́жах.

● *cpds.* **~-boots** *n. pl.* лы́жные боти́нки (*m. pl.*); **~-jump** *n.* лы́жный трампли́н; **~-jumping** *n.* прыжки́ (*m. pl.*) на лы́жах с трампли́на; **~-lift** *n.* (лы́жный) подъёмник; **~-pants** *n. pl.* лы́жные брю́к|и (*pl., g.* —); **~-run, ~-track** *nn.* лыжня́.

skid /skɪd/ *n.* (*of car*) скольже́ние; юз; **the car went into a ~** маши́ну занесло́; маши́на пошла́ ю́зом; **hit the ~s** (*coll.*) опус|ка́ться, -ти́ться.

● *v.i.* (**skidded, skidding**) (*of car, wheels*) пойти́ (*pf.*) ю́зом.

skier /'ski:ə(r)/ *n.* лы́жник.

skiff /skɪf/ *n.* я́лик, скиф-одино́чка.

skiing /'ski:ɪŋ/ *n.* ката́ние на лы́жах; лы́жный спорт.

skilful /'skɪlfʊl/ (*US* **skillful**) *adj.* иску́сный, уме́лый; (*in sport*) техни́чный.

skill /skɪl/ *n.* иску́сство; (*competence*) уме́ние; (*dexterity*) ло́вкость; (*technique*) мастерство́.

skilled /skɪld/ *adj.* иску́сный; (*highly-trained*) квалифици́рованный.

skillet /'skɪlɪt/ *n.* (*US*) сковорода́.

skillful /'skɪlfʊl/ (*US*) = **skilful**

skim /skɪm/ *v.t.* (**skimmed, skimming**) **1**: **~ a liquid** сн|има́ть, -ять на́кипь с жи́дкости; **~ milk** сн|има́ть, -ять сли́вки (с молока́); **~med milk** обезжи́ренное молоко́. **2** (*remove*): **~ the grease from, off the soup** сн|има́ть, -ять жир с су́па. **3** (*move lightly over*): **~ the ground** лете́ть (*det.*) над са́мой землёй. **4** (*scan through*) пробе|га́ть, -жа́ть; (*book etc.*) чита́ть (*impf.*) по диагона́ли (*coll.*).

skimmer /'skɪmə(r)/ *n.* **1** (*ladle*) шумо́вка. **2** (*for milk*) сепара́тор.

skimp /skɪmp/ *v.t.* (*on material, expenses*) скупи́ться, по- на +*a.*; (*do hastily*) отде́л|ываться, -аться от +*g.*

● *v.i.* эконо́мить (*impf.*); (*being stingy*) скупи́ться (*impf.*).

skimpy /'skɪmpɪ/ *adj.* (**skimpier, skimpiest**) (*meagre*) ску́дный; (*of clothes: short or tight*) те́сный, у́зкий.

skin /skɪn/ *n.* **1** ко́жа; **clear ~** чи́стая ко́жа; **dark ~** сму́глая/тёмная ко́жа; **~ disease** ко́жная боле́знь; **take the ~ off one's knees** сдира́ть, содра́ть ко́жу на коле́нях; **it's no ~ off my nose** (*coll.*) а мне́-то что?; **he has a thick ~** (*fig.*) он толстоко́жий, у него́ то́лстая ко́жа; **strip to the ~** разд|ева́ться, -е́ться донага́; **I got soaked to the ~** я промо́к до (после́дней) ни́тки; **get under s.o.'s ~** (*annoy intensely*) раздража́ть (*impf.*) кого́-н.; **I nearly jumped out of my ~** я так и подскочи́л от неожи́данности; **save one's ~** спас|а́ть, -ти́ свою́ шку́ру; **escape by the ~ of one's teeth** чу́дом спас|а́ться, -ти́сь; **he was all ~ and bone** от него́ оста́лась одна́ ко́жа да ко́сти. **2** (*of animal: hide*) шку́ра; **leopard ~** шку́ра леопа́рда; **rabbit ~** кро́личья

шку́рка; (*fur*) мех (*pl.* -á).
3 (*for wine etc.*) мех (*pl.* -и́).
4 (*of fruit*) кожура́; (*of grape*) ко́жица; (*of sausage*) кожура́, ко́жица; **orange/lemon ~** апельси́нная/лимо́нная ко́рка.
5 (*of ship, aeroplane*) обши́вка.
6 (*on liquid etc.*) пе́нка.
● *v.t.* (**skinned, skinning**) **1** (*remove ~ from*) сн|има́ть, -ять шку́ру с+*g.*; свежева́ть, о-; **~ s.o. alive** сдира́ть, содра́ть с кого́-н. ко́жу за́живо.
2 (*remove peel, rind from*) сн|има́ть, -ять кожуру́ с+*g.*; чи́стить, о-; **keep one's eyes ~ned** (*Br. coll.*) смотре́ть (*impf.*) в о́ба.
3 (*graze*) об|дира́ть, -одра́ть; сса́живать, ссади́ть; **she ~ned her knee** она́ ободра́ла/ссади́ла себе́ коле́но.
● *v.i.* (**skinned, skinning**) (*also* **~ over**) рубцева́ться, за-.
● *cpds.* **~-deep** *adj.* пове́рхностный; **~-diver** *n.* аквалангист; **~-diving** *n.* подво́дное пла́вание (с аквала́нгом); **~flint** *n.* скря́га (*c.g.*); **~-graft** *n.* ко́жный трансплантат; **~head** *n.* (*Br.*) «бритоголо́вый», скинхе́д; **~-tight** *adj.*: **~-tight trousers** брю́ки в обтя́жку.

skinful /'skɪnfʊl/ *n.* (*Br. coll.*): **he had a ~** он как сле́дует нагрузи́лся (*coll.*).

skinny /'skɪnɪ/ *adj.* (**skinnier, skinniest**) то́щий.
● *cpd.* **~-dipping** *n.* (*US*) (*coll.*) купа́ние нагишо́м.

skint /skɪnt/ *adj.* (*Br. coll.*): **I'm ~** у меня́ нет ни шиша́ (*sl.*).

skip[1] /skɪp/ *n.* скачо́к, прыжо́к.
● *v.t.* (**skipped, skipping**) (*fig.*) пропус|ка́ть, -ти́ть; **he ~ped the class** он пропусти́л/прогуля́л уро́к; **he ~ped a class** (*went up 2 classes*) он перескочи́л че́рез класс.
● *v.i.* (**skipped, skipping**) **1** (*use ~ping-rope*) скака́ть/пры́гать (*impf.*) (че́рез скака́лку); **~ping rope** (*Br.*) скака́лка; (*jump*): **she ~ped for joy** она́ подпры́гнула от ра́дости; **he ~ped across the brook** он перескочи́л (че́рез) руче́й. **2** (*coll., go quickly or casually*): **he ~ped off without telling anyone** он ускака́л, никому́ ничего́ не сказа́в; **he ~ped from subject to subject** он переска́кивал с предме́та на предме́т; **I ~ped through the preface** я пробежа́л (глаза́ми) предисло́вие.

skip[2] /skɪp/ (*Br., builders'*) ёмкость для перево́зки му́сора.

skipper /'skɪpə(r)/ *n.* (*captain*) шки́пер, капита́н.

skirmish /'skɜ:mɪʃ/ *n.* (*mil., fig.*) сты́чка; (коро́ткая) перестре́лка, схва́тка.
● *v.i.* (*mil.*) перестре́ливаться (*impf.*); (*fig.*) сцеп|ля́ться, -и́ться.

skirt /skɜ:t/ *n.* ю́бка.
● *v.t.* (*pass along edge of*): **we ~ed the crowd** мы обошли́ толпу́; **the ship ~ed the coast** су́дно шло вдоль бе́рега; (*form border of*): **the road ~s the forest** доро́га обрамля́ет лес; **~ing-board** (*Br.*) пли́нтус.
● *v.i.*: **~ round** (*fig., avoid*) об|ходи́ть, -ойти́.

skit /skɪt/ *n.* скетч, сати́ра (на+*a.*).

skittish /'skɪtɪʃ/ *adj.* (*of horse etc.*) норови́стый; (*of person*) капри́зный.

skittle /'skɪt(ə)l/ *n.* ке́гля; (*pl., game*) ке́гли (*f. pl.*); **it's not all beer and ~s** не всё заба́вы да развлече́ния.
● *cpd.* **~-alley** *n.* кегельба́н.

skive /skaɪv/ *v.i.* (*Br. coll., evade duty*) сачкова́ть (*impf.*) (*sl.*).

skiver /'skaɪvə(r)/ *n.* (*Br. coll.*) сачо́к (*sl.*).

skivvy /'skɪvɪ/ *n.* (*Br. coll., pej.*) служа́нка.

skua /'skju:ə/ *n.* (*zool*) помо́рник.

skuld|uggery, skulld- /skʌl'dʌgərɪ/ *n.* надува́тельство.

skulk /skʌlk/ *v.i.* (*lurk*) затаи́ваться (*impf.*); (*slink*) кра́сться (*impf.*).

skull /skʌl/ *n.* че́реп; **~ and cross bones** че́реп со скрещёнными костя́ми; **I tried to get it into his ~** я пыта́лся вбить э́то ему́ в го́лову.
● *cpd.* **~-cap** *n.* ермо́лка; (*Central Asian*) тюбете́йка; (*worn by Orthodox priests*) скуфья́.

skullduggery /skʌl'dʌgərɪ/ *n.* = **skulduggery**

skunk /skʌŋk/ *n.* скунс, воню́чка; (*fur*) ску́нсовый мех; (*coll., person*) подле́ц, подо́нок.

sky /skaɪ/ *n.* не́бо; **there wasn't a cloud in the ~** на не́бе не́ было ни о́блачка; **praise s.o. to the skies** превозн|оси́ть, -ести́ кого́-н. до небе́с.
● *v.t.*: **~ a ball** высоко́ запус|ка́ть, -ти́ть мяч.
● *cpds.* **~-blue** *adj.* све́тло-/небе́сно-голубо́й; лазу́рный; **~diver** *n.* парашюти́ст(-спортсме́н) (*fem.* -ка(-спортсме́нка)); **~diving** *n.* затяжны́е прыжки́ с парашю́том; **~-high** *adv.* высоко́ в во́здух; (*fig.*) до небе́с; **~jack** *n.* уго́н самолёта; *v.t.* уг|оня́ть, -на́ть; **~jacker** *n.* уго́нщик самолёта, возду́шный пира́т; **~lark** *n.* полево́й жа́воронок; *v.i.* (*frolic etc.*) резви́ться (*impf.*); дура́читься (*impf.*); **~light** *n.* фона́рь (*m.*), окно́ в кры́ше; **~line** *n.* горизо́нт; силуэ́т; **~-rocket** *n.* сигна́льная раке́та; *v.i.* (*fig.*) стреми́тельно подн|има́ться, -я́ться; **~scraper** *n.* небоскрёб; **~way** *n.* (*US*) возду́шная тра́сса, авиатра́сса; **~-writing** *n.* прочёрчивание самолётом букв; возду́шная рекла́ма.

skyward(s) /'skaɪwəd(z)/ *adv.* к не́бу; ввысь.

slab /slæb/ *n.* (*of stone etc.*) плита́; **~ of concrete** бето́нная плита́; (*of cake etc.*) кусо́к.

slack[1] /slæk/ *n.* **1** (*loose part of rope, sail*) слабина́; **pull in (*or* take in, up) the ~** подтя́|гивать, -ну́ть (*or* выбира́ть, вы́брать) слабину́; натя́|гивать, -ну́ть верёвку.
2 (*pl., trousers*) (широ́кие) брю́к|и (*pl., g.* —).
3 (**~** *period of trade*) зати́шье.
● *adj.* **1** (*sluggish, slow*) вя́лый, сла́бый; **trade is ~** торго́вля идёт вя́ло; **demand is ~** спрос сла́бый.
2 (*of person, lax*) расхля́банный; (*negligent*) небре́жный; **be ~ in one's work** хала́тно относи́ться (*impf.*) к рабо́те.
3 (*loose; not taut*): **~ rope** провисшая верёвка; **~ muscles** дря́блые мы́шцы, дря́блая мускулату́ра.
4 (*quiet, inactive*): **~ season, period** мёртвый сезо́н; зати́шье.
● *v.t.* (*rope, sail, rein*) отпус|ка́ть, -ти́ть; осл|абля́ть, -а́бить.
● *v.i.* **1** (*also* **~ off**) = **slacken** *v.i.*
2 (*Br., be indolent*) ло́дырничать (*impf.*); **we ~ed off towards five** к пяти́ часа́м мы сба́вили темп (рабо́ты).
3: **~ up** (*reduce speed*) уб|авля́ть, -а́вить ско́рость.

slack[2] /slæk/ *n.* (*coal*) у́гольная ме́лочь/пыль.

slacken /'slækən/ *v.t.* **1** (*rope, rein*) отпус|ка́ть, -ти́ть; осл|абля́ть, -а́бить.
2 (*diminish*): **~ one's efforts** осл|абля́ть, -а́бить уси́лия; **~ speed** уб|авля́ть, -а́вить ско́рость; зам|едля́ть, -е́длить ход.
● *v.i.* **1** (*also* **slack**) (*of rope*) пров|иса́ть, -и́снуть; (*of sail*) обв|иса́ть, -и́снуть; (*of screw, nut*) слабе́ть, о-; (*of knot*) развя́з|ываться, -а́ться. **2** (*die down*): **demand is ~ing** спрос уменьша́ется.

slacker /'slækə(r)/ *n.* ло́дырь (*m.*), безде́льни|к (*fem.* -ца).

slackness /'slæknɪs/ *n.* небре́жность, расхля́банность.

slag /slæg/ *n.* шлак; (*Br., coll., promiscuous woman*) шлю́ха (*vulg.*).
● *v.i.* (**slagged, slagging**): **~ off** (*Br. coll.*) (*criticize*) разн|оси́ть, -ести́; (*insult*) опл|ёвывать, -eва́ть.
● *cpd.* **~-heap** *n.* гру́да шла́ка, террико́н.

slain /sleɪn/ *p.p. of* ⇒**slay**

slake /sleɪk/ *v.t.* **1** (*liter.*): **~ one's thirst** утол|я́ть, -и́ть жа́жду. **2**: **~ lime** гаси́ть, по- и́звесть.

slalom /'slɑ:ləm/ *n.* сла́лом.

slam /slæm/ *n.* **1**: **I heard the ~ of a door** я слы́шал, как хло́пнула дверь.
2 (*cards*): **grand/small ~** большо́й/ма́лый шлем.
● *v.t.* (**slammed, slamming**) **1** (*shut with a bang*): **~ a door** хло́п|ать, -нуть две́рью; **he ~med the door to** он захло́пнул дверь. **2** (*other violent or sudden action*): **he ~med the brakes on** он ре́зко нажа́л на тормоза́; **he ~med the box down on the table** он швырну́л коро́бку на стол. **3** (*US coll., defeat resoundingly*) разнести́ (*pf.*). **4** (*coll., criticize*) раскритикова́ть (*pf.*).
● *v.i.* (**slammed, slamming**) **1** (*of door etc.*) захло́п|ываться, -нуться.
2: **he ~med out of the room** он вы́скочил/вы́летел из ко́мнаты.

slammer /'slæmə(r)/ *n.* (*sl.*) тюря́га.

slander /'slɑ:ndə(r)/ *n.* клевета́.
● *v.t.* клевета́ть, на- на+*a.*

slanderer /'slɑ:ndərə(r)/ *n.* клеветни́|к (*fem.* -ца).

slanderous /ˈslɑːndərəs/ *adj.* клеветни́ческий.

slang /slæŋ/ *n.* жарго́н; сленг; **~ word** жарго́нное сло́во.

● *v.t.* руга́ть, об-; **~ing match** (*Br.*) перебра́нка.

slangy /ˈslæŋɪ/ *adj.* (**slangier, slangiest**) жарго́нный.

slant /slɑːnt/ *n.* **1** (*oblique position*) накло́н; укло́н; **he wears his hat on the ~** он но́сит шля́пу набекре́нь. **2** (*coll., point of view*) у́гол зре́ния; (*bias*) укло́н; **my trip gave me a new ~ on things** по́сле пое́здки я на всё взгляну́л по-но́вому.

● *adj.* косо́й.

● *v.t.* **1** (*incline*) наклон|я́ть, -и́ть. **2** (*fig., distort*) иска|жа́ть, -зи́ть; **a ~ed article** тенденцио́зная статья́.

● *v.i.*: **his handwriting ~s to the right** он пи́шет с накло́ном впра́во; **the ~ing rays of the sun** косы́е лучи́ со́лнца.

● *cpd.* **~-eyed** *adj.* с раско́сыми глаза́ми.

slantwise /ˈslɑːntwaɪz/ *adv.* вкось, ко́со, накло́нно.

slap /slæp/ *n.* шлепо́к; **she gave the boy a good ~** она́ дала́ ма́льчику зво́нкий шлепо́к; **~ in the face** (*lit., fig.*) пощёчина; **~ on the back** (*fig.*) поздравле́ние.

● *adv.*: **the ball hit me ~ in the eye** мяч попа́л мне пря́мо в глаз; **he hit the target ~ in the middle** он попа́л пря́мо в я́блоко (мише́ни).

● *v.t.* (**slapped, slapping**) **1** (*smack*) шлёпать, от-; **~ s.o.'s face** да|ва́ть, -ть кому́-н. пощёчину; **~ s.o. on the back** хло́п|ать, -нуть кого́-н. по спине́. **2** (*apply with force*): **they ~ped a fine on him** ему́ влепи́ли штраф; (*apply carelessly*) ля́пать, на-; **the paint was ~ped on** кра́ску наля́пали ко́е-как. **3**: **~ down** бр|оса́ть, -о́сить; (*rebuke*) оса|жда́ть, -ди́ть.

● *cpds.* **~-bang** *adv.* (*to throw*) со всего́ разма́ха; (*to run, dash*) очертя́ го́лову; **~dash** *adj.* (*of person*) бесшаба́шный; (*of work*) поспе́шный, небре́жный; *adv.* (*hastily*) поспе́шно; (*anyhow*) ко́е-как; **~-happy** *adj.*: бесшаба́шный; **~stick** *n.*: **~stick comedy** фарс; **~-up** *adj.* (*Br. coll.*) шика́рный.

slash /slæʃ/ *n.* (*slit*) разре́з; (*wound*) поре́з; (*stroke*): **he made a ~ with his sword** он рубану́л са́блей.

● *v.t.* **1** (*wound with knife etc.*) ра́нить, по-; (*with sword*) руби́ть (*impf.*). **2** (*cut slits in*) разр|еза́ть, -е́зать. **3** (*lash; fig., criticize*) бичева́ть (*impf.*); **~ing criticism** беспоща́дная кри́тика. **4** (*reduce*): **~ prices** ре́зко сн|ижа́ть, -и́зить це́ны; **~ a budget** ре́зко сокра|ща́ть, -ти́ть бюдже́т.

slat /slæt/ *n.* пла́нка; (*of blind*) пласти́нка.

slate /sleɪt/ *n.* **1** (*material*) сла́нец; **~ quarry** сла́нцевый карье́р. **2** (*piece of ~ for roofing*) ши́ферная пли́тка; **a house roofed with ~s** дом, кры́тый ши́ферной пли́ткой. **3** (*for schoolwork*) гри́фельная доска́; (*fig.*): **start with a clean ~** нач|ина́ть, -а́ть с нача́ла; **wipe the ~ clean** поко́нчить (*pf.*) с про́шлым.

● *v.t.* **1** (*cover with ~s*) крыть, по- ши́фером. **2** (*US, nominate*) зан|оси́ть, -ести́ в спи́сок кандида́тов; (*arrange*) назн|ача́ть, -а́чить. **3** (*Br., scold, criticize*) разн|оси́ть, -ести́.

● *cpd.* **~-coloured** (*US* **-colored**) *adj.* синева́то-се́рый.

slater /ˈsleɪtə(r)/ *n.* (*of roofs*) кро́вельщик.

slattern /ˈslæt(ə)n/ *n.* неря́ха, грязну́ля (*both c.g.*).

slatternly /ˈslætənlɪ/ *adj.* неря́шливый.

slaty /ˈsleɪtɪ/ *adj.* (*colour*) синева́то-се́рый.

slaughter /ˈslɔːtə(r)/ *n.* избие́ние, резня́; ма́ссовое уби́йство; (*of animals*) убо́й.

● *v.t.* **1** (*kill animals, people*) ре́зать, за-. **2** (*coll., defeat heavily*) разб|ива́ть, -и́ть в пух и прах.

● *cpd.* **~house** *n.* (ското)бо́йня.

slaughterer /ˈslɔːtərə(r)/ *n.* мясни́к (на бо́йне); (*fig.*) живодёр, пала́ч.

Slav /slɑːv/ *n.* слав|яни́н (*fem.* -я́нка); **the ~s** славя́не.

● *adj.* славя́нский.

slave /sleɪv/ *n.* раб (*fem.* -ы́ня); **he works like a ~** он рабо́тает, как вол; **~ of fashion** раб мо́ды; **~ to duty/passion** же́ртва до́лга/стра́сти; **~ labour** (*Br.*), **labor** (*US*) ра́бский труд.

● *v.i.*: **~ at something** корпе́ть (*impf.*) над чем-н.; **~ away** тяну́ть (*impf.*) ля́мку.

● *cpds.* **~-driver** *n.* (*fig.*) безжа́лостный нача́льник; **~-ship** *n.* нево́льничий кора́бль; **~-trade** *n.* работорго́вля; **~-trader** *n.* работорго́вец.

slaver[1] /ˈsleɪvə(r)/ *n.* (*person*) работорго́вец; (*ship*) нево́льничий кора́бль.

slaver[2] /ˈslævə(r)/ *n.* (*spittle*) слю́ни (*f. pl.*).

● *v.i.* пуска́ть (*impf.*) слю́ни.

slavery /ˈsleɪvərɪ/ *n.* ра́бство.

Slavic /ˈslɑːvɪk/ *adj.* славя́нский.

slavish /ˈsleɪvɪʃ/ *adj.* ра́бский.

Slavist /ˈslɑːvɪst/ *n.* слави́ст.

Slavonic /sləˈvɒnɪk/ *n.* славя́нский язы́к; **Church ~** церко́внославя́нский язы́к; **~ studies** слави́стика.

● *adj.* славя́нский.

Slavophil(e) /ˈslɑːvəʊfɪl/; /-ˌfaɪl/ *n.* славянофи́л.

● *adj.* славянофи́льский.

slay /sleɪ/ *v.t.* (*past* **slew;** *p.p.* **slain**) (*liter.*) умер|щвля́ть, -тви́ть; уб|ива́ть, -и́ть.

slayer /ˈsleɪə(r)/ *n.* уби́йца (*c.g.*).

sleaze /sliːz/ *n.* низкопро́бность.

sleazy /ˈsliːzɪ/ *adj.* (**sleazier, sleaziest**) (*squalid*) захуда́лый, убо́гий; (*immoral*) низкопро́бный.

sled /sled/ (*US*) (**sledded, sledding**) = **sledge**

sledge /sledʒ/ *n.* са́н|и (*pl., g.* -е́й); (*children's*) са́н|ки (*pl., g.* -ок); сала́з|ки (*pl., g.* -ок).

● *v.i.* ката́ться (*indet.*) на саня́х (*or* на са́нках/сала́зках).

sledge-hammer /ˈsledʒˌhæmə(r)/ *n.* кува́лда; кузне́чный мо́лот.

sleek /sliːk/ *adj.* (*of animal or its coat, fur*) гла́дкий, лоснящи́йся; (*of person's hair*) прили́занный.

● *v.t.* (*also* **~ down**) пригла́|живать, -дить; прили́з|ывать, -а́ть.

sleekness /ˈsliːknɪs/ *n.* гла́дкость; прили́занность.

sleep /sliːp/ *n.* сон; **light/deep/sound ~** лёгкий/глубо́кий/кре́пкий сон; **have a ~** поспа́ть (*pf.*); сосну́ть (*pf.*); вздремну́ть (*pf.*); **have a good night's ~** высыпа́ться, вы́спаться; **go** (*coll.* **drop off**) **to ~** зас|ыпа́ть, -ну́ть, усну́ть (*pf.*); **I couldn't get to ~** я не мог усну́ть; **I didn't have a wink of ~ all night** я глаз не сомкну́л всю ночь; **send to ~** усып|ля́ть, -и́ть; **put a child to ~** укла́дывать, уложи́ть ребёнка (спать); **we had our dog put to ~** нам пришло́сь усыпи́ть соба́ку; **he talks/walks in his ~** он говори́т/хо́дит во сне; **I shan't lose any ~ over it** я (по э́тому по́воду) пла́кать не ста́ну; **my foot has gone to ~** я отсиде́л но́гу; у меня́ затекла́ нога́; **winter ~** (*of animal*) зи́мняя спя́чка.

● *v.t.* (*past and p.p.* **slept**) (*provide ~ing room for*): **you can ~ ten people here** здесь мо́жно уложи́ть де́сять челове́к; **the hotel ~s 200** гости́ница рассчи́тана на 200 челове́к.

● *v.i.* (*past and p.p.* **slept**) спать (*impf.*); (*spend the night*) ночева́ть, пере-; **~ well!** (жела́ю вам) (с)поко́йной но́чи!; **~ like a top, log** спать (*impf.*) как уби́тый (*or* без за́дних ног (*coll.*) *or* мёртвым сном); **I don't ~ well** у меня́ плохо́й сон; **I can't ~** я не могу́ засну́ть; **~ on a decision** откла́дывать, отложи́ть реше́ние до утра́; **better ~ on it!** ≈ у́тро ве́чера мудрене́е (*prov.*); **he slept through the alarm** он проспа́л трево́гу; **~ing partner** (*Br.*) пасси́вный партнёр; **let ~ing dogs lie** (*prov.*) ≈ не буди́ ли́хо, когда́ спит ти́хо.

● *with advs.*: **~ around** *v.i.* (*be promiscuous*) спать (*impf.*) с кем попа́ло; **~ away** *v.t.*: **he slept the time away** он проспа́л всё э́то вре́мя; **~ in** *v.i.* (*intentionally*) поспа́ть (*pf.*) вслáсть; от|сыпа́ться, -оспа́ться; (*oversleep*) прос|ыпа́ть, -па́ть; **~ off** *v.t.*: **~ off a hangover** проспа́ться (*pf.*) (по́сле попо́йки); **~ on** *v.i.*: **he is tired, let him ~ on** он уста́л, пусть спит; **~ out** *v.i.* (*out of doors*) спать (*impf.*) под откры́тым не́бом; **~ with** (*euph., have sex*) спать, пере- с + *i.*

● *cpds.* **~-walker** *n.* луна́тик; **~-walking** *n.* лунати́зм.

sleeper /ˈsliːpə(r)/ *n.* (*person*): **he is a light/heavy ~** он чу́тко/кре́пко спит; (*Br., rail support*) шпа́ла; (*sleeping-car*) спа́льный ваго́н.

sleepiness /ˈsliːpɪnɪs/ *n.* сонли́вость.

sleeping /ˈsliːpɪŋ/ *n.*: **~ accommodation** ночле́г.

S

● *cpds.* **~-bag** *n.* спа́льный мешо́к; **~-car** *n.* спа́льный ваго́н; **~-pill** *n.* снотво́рная табле́тка; **~-quarters** *n.* спа́льное помеще́ние; **~-sickness** *n.* со́нная боле́знь.

sleepless /ˈsli:plɪs/ *adj.* бессо́нный.

sleeplessness /ˈsli:plɪsnɪs/ *n.* бессо́нница.

sleepy /ˈsli:pɪ/ *adj.* (**sleepier, sleepiest**) (*lit., fig.*) со́нный; сонли́вый; **I feel ~** мне хо́чется (*or* я хочу́) спать; **I grew ~** меня́ разбира́л сон; **make s.o. ~** наг|оня́ть, -на́ть сон на кого́-н.

● *cpd.* **~head** *n.* со́ня (*c.g.*).

sleet /sli:t/ *n.* дождь (*m.*) со сне́гом, мо́крый снег.

● *v.i.*: **it is ~ing** идёт мо́крый снег.

sleeve /sli:v/ *n.* **1** рука́в; **pluck s.o.'s ~** дёр|гать, -нуть кого́-н. за рука́в; **roll up one's ~s** (*lit., fig.*) засу́ч|ивать, -и́ть рукава́; **have, keep something up one's ~** (*fig.*) име́ть (*impf.*) что-н. про запа́с; **laugh up one's ~** посме́иваться (*impf.*) в кула́к. **2** (*aeron.*, **wind-~**) ветрово́й ко́нус. **3** (*record cover*) конве́рт (*пластинки*).

sleeveless /ˈsli:vlɪs/ *adj.* безрука́вный; **~ dress** пла́тье без рукаво́в; **~ vest/top** безрука́вка.

sleigh /sleɪ/ *n.* са́ни (*pl., g.* -е́й).

● *v.i.* ката́ться на саня́х.

● *cpd.* **~-bell** *n.* бубе́нчик, колоко́льчик (на саня́х).

sleight-of-hand /slaɪt/ *n.* ло́вкость рук.

slender /ˈslendə(r)/ *adj.* (**slenderer, slenderest**) **1** (*thin; narrow*) то́нкий; (*of person, slim*) стро́йный. **2** (*scanty*) ску́дный; **~ means** ску́дные сре́дства; **~ hope** сла́бая наде́жда.

slenderness /ˈslendənɪs/ *n.* то́нкость, стро́йность.

slept /slept/ *past and p.p. of* ⇨**sleep**

sleuth /slu:θ/ *n.* сы́щик.

slew[1] /slu:/ (*also* **slue**) *v.t. & i.* (*also* **~ round**) кру́то пов|ора́чивать(ся), -ерну́ть(ся).

slew[2] /slu:/ *past of* ⇨**slay**

slice /slaɪs/ *n.* **1** (*of bread, meat*) ломо́ть (*m.*); (*small slice*) ло́мтик; **cut bread into ~s** нар|еза́ть, -е́зать хлеб ломтя́ми; (*of cake*) кусо́к; (*of fruit*) кусо́к, до́ля. **2** (*portion, share*) часть, до́ля; **the play is a ~ of life** э́та пье́са — сле́пок с жи́зни. **3** (*for fish*) ры́бный нож; (*for cake*) лопа́точка (для то́рта).

● *v.t.* **1** нар|еза́ть, -е́зать ломтя́ми/ло́мтиками; **~d bread** (предвари́тельно) наре́занный хлеб. **2** (*golf*): **~ the ball** ср|еза́ть, -е́зать мяч.

● *with advs.*: **~ off** *v.t.* отр|еза́ть, -е́зать; **~ up** *v.t.* нар|еза́ть, -е́зать.

slick /slɪk/ *n.* (*patch of oil etc.*) плёнка.

● *adj.* (*skilful; smart*) ло́вкий, бо́йкий; (*smooth, also fig.*) гла́дкий; (*slippery*) ско́льзкий.

slicker /ˈslɪkə(r)/ *n.* пройдо́ха (*c.g.*); **city ~** городско́й хлыщ.

slid|e /slaɪd/ *n.* **1** (*act of ~ing*) скольже́ние; **have a ~e** поката́ться (*pf.*), прокати́ться (*pf.*) (*по льду, с горки и т.п.*).
2 (*track on ice*) като́к; (*on snow-covered hill*) ледяна́я го́рка.
3 (*chute*) спуск, жёлоб.
4 (*of microscope*) предме́тное стекло́.
5 (*for projection on screen*) диапозити́в, слайд.
6 (*Br., hair-~e*) зако́лка.

● *v.t.* (*past and p.p.* **slid** /slɪd/): **~e a drawer into place** задв|ига́ть, -и́нуть я́щик на ме́сто; **~e something into s.o.'s hand** сова́ть, су́нуть что-н. кому́-н. в ру́ку.

● *v.i.* (*past and p.p.* **slid** /slɪd/)
1 скользи́ть (*impf.*); **~ing door** задвижна́я дверь; (*down or off*): **the papers ~ off my lap** бума́ги соскользну́ли у меня́ с коле́н; **the book ~ out of my hand** кни́га вы́скользнула у меня́ из рук; **his trousers ~ to the ground** у него́ спусти́лись брю́ки.
2 (*as pastime*) скользи́ть (*impf.*); ката́ться (*indet.*); **the boy ~ down the banisters** ма́льчик скати́лся по пери́лам.
3 (*fig.*): **he ~ into the room** он проскользну́л в ко́мнату; **let something ~e** пус|ка́ть, -ти́ть что-н. на самотёк; **~ing scale** скользя́щая шкала́.

● *cpds.* **~e-controls** *n. pl.* движко́вые регуля́торы; **~e projector** *n.* прое́ктор; **~e-rule** *n.* логарифми́ческая лине́йка.

slight[1] /slaɪt/ *n.* (*disrespect*) неуваже́ние; (*offence, injury*) оби́да.

● *v.t.* выка́зывать, вы́казать неуваже́ние + *d.*; третирова́ть (*impf.*); об|ижа́ть, -и́деть.

slight[2] /slaɪt/ *adj.* **1** (*frail*) хру́пкий; (*slender*) то́нкий. **2** (*light; not serious*) лёгкий; **she has a ~ cold** у неё лёгкая просту́да; **~ concussion** лёгкое сотрясе́ние мо́зга. **3** (*inconsiderable*) незначи́тельный; (*small*): **there is a ~ risk of infection** есть не́которая опа́сность зараже́ния; **the risk is ~** опа́сность невелика́; **he paid me ~ attention** он не обраща́л на меня́ почти́ никако́го внима́ния. **4**: **~est** мале́йший; **this is not the ~est use** от э́того ни мале́йшей (*or* ро́вно никако́й) по́льзы; **not in the ~est** нисколько/ничу́ть; **he is not to blame in the ~est** он нисколько (*or* ни в мале́йшей сте́пени) не винова́т.

slightly /ˈslaɪtlɪ/ *adv.* слегка́; **I know them ~** я с ни́ми немно́го знако́м; **I know them only ~** я их почти́ не зна́ю; **he was ~ injured** он слегка́ пострада́л; **~ younger** немно́го/чуть моло́же.

slim /slɪm/ *adj.* (**slimmer, slimmest**) (*slender*) то́нкий, худо́й; (*small*): **on the ~mest of evidence** на основа́нии сомни́тельных да́нных; **a ~ chance of success** сла́бая наде́жда на успе́х.

● *v.i.* (**slimmed, slimming**) худе́ть, по-; **~ming exercises** гимна́стика, спосо́бствующая похуде́нию.

slime /slaɪm/ *n.* (*mud*) ил; (*viscous substance*) слизь.

slimy /ˈslaɪmɪ/ *adj.* (**slimier, slimiest**) **1** сли́зистый; (*sticky*) вя́зкий; (*slippery*) ско́льзкий. **2** (*fig., of person*) гну́сный, ско́льзкий.

sling /slɪŋ/ *n.* **1** (*for missile*) праща́, рога́тка. **2** (*bandage*) пе́ревязь; (*triangular cloth*) косы́нка; **his arm was in a ~** у него́ рука́ была́ на пе́ревязи. **3** (*of rifle*) реме́нь. **4** (*for hoisting*) строп.

● *v.t.* (*past and p.p.* **slung**) **1** (*throw*) швыр|я́ть, -ну́ть; **~ s.o. out of the room** вышвы́ривать, вы́швырнуть кого́-н. из ко́мнаты. **2** (*cast by means of ~*) мет|а́ть, -ну́ть. **3** (*suspend*) подве́|шивать, -сить; **he slung the rifle over his shoulder** он переки́нул винто́вку че́рез плечо́; (*hoist with ~*): **the crates were slung on board** я́щики по́дняли на́ борт.

● *cpd.* **~-shot** *n.* рога́тка.

slink /slɪŋk/ *v.i.* (*past and p.p.* **slunk**): **~ off, away** (*stealthily*) выска́льзывать, вы́скользнуть; (*in a guilty way*) уходи́ть, уйти́, поджа́в хвост.

slinky /ˈslɪŋkɪ/ *adj.* (**slinkier, slinkiest**): **a ~ dress** облега́ющее пла́тье.

slip /slɪp/ *n.* **1** (*landslip*) обва́л.
2 (*mishap, error*) оши́бка (по небре́жности); **I made a ~** я ошибся; **~ of the tongue/pen** огово́рка/опи́ска.
3: **he gave his pursuers the ~** он ускользну́л от пресле́дователей.
4 (*loose cover*) чехо́л; **pillow ~** на́волочка.
5 (*petticoat*) комбина́ция; (ни́жняя) соро́чка.
6 (*of paper*) поло́ска, бума́жка.
7 (*plant cutting*) отро́сток; (*for grafting*) черено́к.
8 (**~way**) ста́пель (*m.*); **the ship is still on the ~s** кора́бль ещё не сошёл со стапеле́й.

● *v.t.* (**slipped, slipping**) **1** (*slide; pass covertly*): **she ~ped her little hand into mine** она́ вложи́ла свою́ ру́чку в мою́; **he ~ped the ring on to her finger** он наде́л ей на па́лец кольцо́; **she ~ped the ring off her finger** она́ сняла́ кольцо́ с па́льца; **I ~ped the waiter a coin** я су́нул официа́нту моне́ту.
2 (*slide out of; escape from*) выска́льзывать, вы́скользнуть из + *g.*; **the dog ~ped its collar** соба́ка вы́скользнула из оше́йника; **his name ~ped my memory/mind** его́ и́мя вы́скочило у меня́ из па́мяти/головы́.

● *v.i.* (**slipped, slipping**) **1** (*slide*) скользи́ть (*impf.*); (*fall over*) поскользну́ться (*pf.*); **she ~ped on the ice** она́ поскользну́лась на льду; **the blanket ~ped off the bed** одея́ло соскользну́ло с посте́ли; **~ped disc** смещённый межпозвонко́вый диск; **she let the plate ~** таре́лка вы́скользнула у неё из рук; (*fig.*): **he let the opportunity ~** он упусти́л возмо́жность; **the remark ~ped out** э́то замеча́ние случа́йно сорва́ло́сь у него́ (*и т.п.*) с языка́; **he is ~ping** (*losing his grip*) у него́ слабе́ет хва́тка.
2 (*move quickly and/or unnoticed*) выска́льзывать, вы́скользнуть; **he**

~ped away он незаме́тно ушёл; **she ~ped out of the room** она́ вы́скользнула из ко́мнаты; **I'll ~ across to the pub** я сбе́гаю в пивну́ю; **the years are ~ping by** го́ды ухо́дят; **an error ~ped in** вкра́лась оши́бка; **I'll ~ into another dress** я (бы́стренько) переоде́нусь; **~ through** проск|а́льзывать, -ользну́ть (че́рез + *a.*).

● *with adv.*: **~ up** *v.i.*: **he ~ped up and hurt his back** он поскользну́лся и повреди́л себе́ спи́ну; **I ~ped up in my calculations** я оши́бся в подсчётах; (*fig.*) я просчита́лся; **I ~ped up there** я дал ма́ху (*coll.*).

● *cpds.* **~-knot** *n.* скользя́щий затяжно́й у́зел; **~ road** *n.* (*Br.*) подъездна́я доро́га; **~shod** *adj.* (*fig.*) небре́жный, неря́шливый; **~-stream** *n.* (*aeron.*) спу́тная струя́; (*behind vehicle*) зо́на пони́женного давле́ния за бы́стро дви́жущимся предме́том; *v.i.* держа́ться (*impf.*) вплотну́ю к иду́щей впереди́ маши́не; **~-up** *n.* оши́бка, про́мах; **~way** *n.* ста́пель (*m.*).

slipper /ˈslɪpə(r)/ *n.* та́почка.

slipperiness /ˈslɪpərɪnɪs/ *n.* ско́льзкость.

slippery /ˈslɪpərɪ/ *adj.* (*also fig.*) ско́льзкий.

slippy /ˈslɪpɪ/ *adj.* (**slippier, slippiest**) ско́льзкий.

slit /slɪt/ *n.* (*cut*) проре́з; (*slot*) щель, щёлка; **~ trench** щель; **a ~ skirt** ю́бка с разре́зом.

● *v.t.* (**slitting;** *past and p.p.* **~**): **~ open an envelope** вскр|ыва́ть, -ы́ть (*or* раз|рыва́ть, -орва́ть) конве́рт; **~ s.o.'s throat** перер|еза́ть, -е́зать кому́-н. го́рло.

● *cpd.* **~-eyed** *adj.* узкогла́зый.

slither /ˈslɪðə(r)/ *v.i.*: **~ about in the mud** скользи́ть (*impf.*) по гря́зи; **they ~ed down the hill** они́ скати́лись с холма́; **he ~ed down the pole** он соскользну́л (вниз) по шесту́.

sliver /ˈslɪvə(r)/, /ˈslaɪvə(r)/ *n.* (*of glass*) оско́лок, (*of cake, cheese*) кусо́чек; (*of wood*) ще́пка.

● *v.t.* расщеп|ля́ть, -и́ть.

slivovitz /ˈslɪvəvɪts/ *n.* слива́нка, сли́вовица.

slob /slɒb/ *n.* (*sl.*) недотёпа (*c.g.*).

slobber /ˈslɒbə(r)/ *v.i.* (*lit., fig.*) распус|ка́ть, -ти́ть слю́ни.

sloe /sləʊ/ *n.* тёрн.

● *cpds.* **~-eyed** *adj.* ≈ с глаза́ми как ви́шни; **~-gin** *n.* слива́нка; сли́вовая насто́йка.

slog /slɒg/ *n.* (*hit*) си́льный уда́р; (*arduous work*) тяжёлая/утоми́тельная рабо́та.

● *v.t.* (**slogged, slogging**): **~ s.o. in the jaw** да|ва́ть, -ть кому́-н. в зу́бы; **~ a ball** (си́льно) уд|аря́ть, -а́рить по мячу́; замочи́ть (*pf.*) по мячу́ (*coll.*).

● *v.i.* (**slogged, slogging**): (*work hard*) вка́лывать (*impf.*) (*coll.*); **he was ~ging along the road** он упо́рно шага́л по доро́ге; **he is ~ging away at Latin** он корпи́т над латы́нью (*coll.*).

slogan /ˈsləʊgən/ *n.* (*motto, watchword*) ло́зунг, деви́з; (*in advertising*) сло́ган, рекла́мная фо́рмула.

sloop /slu:p/ *n.* (*naut.*) шлюп.

slop /slɒp/ *n.* **1** (*liquid food*) жи́жа; (*poor soup etc.*) жи́дкая похлёбка. **2** (*pl., waste liquid*) помо́|и (*pl., g.* -ев). **3** (*US, fig., sentimental language*) сантиме́нт|ы (*pl., g.* -ов).

● *v.t.* (**slopped, slopping**) **1** (*spill, splash*): **~ beer over the table** расплёск|ивать, -а́ть пи́во по столу́; **~ tea into the saucer** выплёскивать, вы́плеснуть чай на блю́дце. **2**: **~ out a prison cell** выноси́ть, вы́нести пара́шу; **~ down the decks** драи́ть, на- па́лубу.

● *v.i.* (**slopped, slopping**): **~ about, around** плеска́ться (*impf.*); (*Br., dress casually*) одева́ться (*impf.*) небре́жно; **he ~ped around in his dressing gown all day** он весь день слоня́лся в хала́те.

● *cpds.* **~-basin** *n.* (*Br.*) полоска́тельница; **~-bucket** *n.* помо́йное ведро́.

slope /sləʊp/ *n.* накло́н, склон, укло́н; (*upward*) подъём; (*downward*) спуск, скат; **mountain ~s** го́рные скло́ны; **the house was on the ~ of the hill** дом стоя́л на скло́не горы́.

● *v.t.*: **~ arms!** на плечо́!

● *v.i.* **1**: **~ back(wards)/forwards** коси́ться, по- наза́д/вперёд; **her handwriting ~s backwards** у неё по́черк с накло́ном вле́во; **~ down** спуска́ться (*impf.*); **~ up(wards)** поднима́ться (*impf.*); **a sloping roof** пока́тая кры́ша **2**: **~ off** см|а́тываться, -ота́ться; уд|ира́ть, -ра́ть (*coll.*).

sloping /ˈsləʊpɪŋ/ *adj.* (*roof, ceiling, shoulders*) пока́тый; (*surface, sides, handwriting*) накло́нный; (*ground, garden*) понижа́ющийся.

sloppiness /ˈslɒpɪnɪs/ *n.* (*untidiness*) неря́шливость; (*sentimentality*) сентимента́льность.

sloppy /ˈslɒpɪ/ *adj.* (**sloppier, sloppiest**) **1** (*of food*) жи́дкий. **2** (*careless; slovenly*) неря́шливый. **3** (*sentimental*) сентимента́льный; **~ sentiment** слезли́вая чувстви́тельность.

slosh /slɒʃ/ *v.t.* (*pour clumsily*) плесну́ть (*pf.*); (*Br., hit*) отдуба́сить (*pf.*) (*coll.*).

● *v.i.*: **~** (*splash*) **about** плеска́ться (*impf.*).

sloshed /slɒʃt/ *adj.* (*drunk*) в дымину пья́ный (*sl.*).

slot /slɒt/ *n.* **1** (*slit, groove*) паз; (*aperture*) отве́рстие; (*channel*) кана́вка, боро́здка; **put a coin in the ~** опус|ка́ть, -ти́ть моне́ту в автома́т. **2** (*coll., suitable place or job*): **we found a ~ for him as junior editor** мы подыска́ли ему́ ме́сто мла́дшего реда́ктора. **3** (*in timetable*) клётка.

● *v.t.* (**slotted, slotting**) **1**: **~ together** соедин|я́ть, -и́ть на шипа́х; спл|а́чивать, -оти́ть в паз. **2**: **~ in** вст|авля́ть, -а́вить; **~ one part into another** вст|авля́ть, -а́вить одну́ часть в другу́ю; **we ~ted a song recital into the programme** (*Br.*), **program** (*US*) мы вста́вили в програ́мму исполне́ние пе́сен; **the graduates were ~ted into jobs** выпускнико́в устро́или на рабо́ту.

● *v.i.* (**slotted, slotting**): **~ in** вст|авля́ться, -а́виться.

● *cpds.* **~-machine** *n.* (*Br., vending machine*) торго́вый автома́т; (*fruit machine*) игрово́й автома́т; **~-meter** *n.* (*e.g. for gas*) счётчик(-автома́т).

sloth /sləʊθ/ *n.* **1** (*zool.*) лени́вец. **2** (*idleness*) ле́ность.

slothful /ˈsləʊθfʊl/ *adj.* лени́вый.

slothfulness /ˈsləʊθfʊlnɪs/ *n.* ле́ность.

slouch /slaʊtʃ/ *n.* **1** (*of walk*) неуклю́жая похо́дка; (*stoop*) суту́лость. **2**: **he's no ~ as a comedian** он ко́мик хоть куда́! (*coll.*).

● *v.i.* (*stoop*) суту́литься (*impf.*); **~ about the house** слоня́ться (*impf.*) по до́му; **he sat ~ed in a chair** он сиде́л развали́вшись в кре́сле; **~ along** ходи́ть (*indet.*), идти́ (*det.*) неуклю́же.

● *cpd.* **~-hat** *n.* шля́па с опу́щенными поля́ми.

slough[1] /slaʊ/ *n.* (*quagmire*) топь, боло́то.

slough[2] /slʌf/ *v.t.* (*of snake etc.*): **~ its skin** сбр|а́сывать, -о́сить ко́жу; (*fig.*): **~ (off)** изб|авля́ться, -а́виться от + *g.*

Slovak /ˈsləʊvæk/ *n.* (*person*) слова́|к (*fem.* -чка); (*language*) слова́цкий язы́к.

● *adj.* слова́цкий.

Slovakia /sləˈvækɪə/ *n.* Слова́кия.

sloven /ˈslʌv(ə)n/ *n.* неря́ха (*c.g.*).

Sloven|e /ˈsləʊvi:n/, **-ian** /sləˈvi:nɪən/ *nn.* (*person*) слове́н|ец (*fem.* -ка); (*language*) слове́нский язы́к.

● *adj.* слове́нский.

Slovenia /sləʊˈvi:nɪə/, /sləˈvi:nɪə/ *n.* Слове́ния.

slovenliness /ˈslʌvənlɪnɪs/ *n.* неря́шливость.

slovenly /ˈslʌvənlɪ/ *adj.* неря́шливый.

slow /sləʊ/ *adj.* **1** ме́дленный; (*dilatory*) медли́тельный; **~ march** строево́й марш; **he is a ~ walker** он ме́дленно хо́дит; **~ motion** заме́дленное де́йствие; **in ~ motion** в заме́дленном де́йствии; **in a ~ oven** на ме́дленном огне́; **be ~ over something** ме́длить (*impf.*) с чем-н.; **~ly but surely** ме́дленно, но ве́рно; **he was not ~ to defend himself** он не заме́длил вы́ступить в свою́ защи́ту; **he is ~ on the uptake** он ту́го сообража́ет. **2** (*of clock*): **my watch is 10 minutes ~** мои́ часы́ отстаю́т на де́сять мину́т. **3** (*dull-witted*) тупо́й. **4** (*not lively*): **the film was rather ~** фильм был дово́льно ску́чным; **business is ~** дела́ иду́т вя́ло. **5** (*phot., of film*) малочувстви́тельный.

● *adv.* ме́дленно; **go ~** (*of workers*) устр|а́ивать, -о́ить италья́нскую забасто́вку.

● *v.t.* (*also* **~ down, ~ up**) зам|едля́ть, -е́длить; **he ~ed (the car) down** он сба́вил ско́рость; **his illness ~ed him**

down болéзнь застáвила егó сбáвить темп.

● *v.i.* (*also* ~ **down**, ~ **up**) зам|едля́ться, -éдлиться; (*of car or driver*) сб|авля́ть, -áвить скóрость; зам|едля́ть, -éдлить ход.

● *cpds.* **~coach** *n.* (*Br.*) копýн, копýша (*c.g.*); **~-down** *n.* замедлéние; **~-moving** *adj.* мéдленный; **~-witted** *adj.* тупóй; **~-worm** *n.* (*zool.*) слепозмéйка.

slowness /ˈsləʊnɪs/ *n.* мéдленность.

sludge /slʌdʒ/ *n.* (*mud*) грязь; (*sediment*) осáдок; (*sewage*) нечистóт|ы (*pl., g.* —).

sludgy /ˈslʌdʒɪ/ *adj.* гря́зный.

slue /sluː/ = **slew**[1]

slug /slʌg/ *n.* (*zool.*) слизня́к; (*bullet*) пýля; (*US sl., short drink*) глотóк, рю́мочка.

● *v.t.* (**slugged, slugging**) (*US, hit*) = **slog**

sluggard /ˈslʌgəd/ *n.* лентя́й, лежебóка (*c.g.*).

sluggish /ˈslʌgɪʃ/ *adj.* **1** вя́лый; ~ **market** вя́лый ры́нок; (*slow-moving*) мéдленный. **2** (*lazy*) ленúвый.

sluggishness /ˈslʌgɪʃnɪs/ *n.* вя́лость, лень.

sluice /sluːs/ *n.* **1** (*floodgate*) шлюз. **2** (*for washing ore*) жёлоб.

● *v.t.* (*flood with water*) зал|ивáть, -и́ть; (*rinse, wash down*) опол|áскивать, -оснýть.

● *v.i.*: (*of water*: *pour out*) течь (*or* вытекáть), вы́-; **rain was sluicing down** шёл проливнóй дождь.

● *cpds.* **~-gate, ~-valve** *nn.* шлюз.

slum /slʌm/ *n.* трущóба; ~ **clearance** расчи́стка трущóб; снос вéтхих здáний.

● *v.i.* (**slummed, slumming**) (*visit* ~*s*) посе|щáть, -ти́ть трущóбы; обслéдовать (*impf., pf.*) трущóбы.

● *cpd.* **~-dweller** *n.* трущóбный жи́тель, обитáтель (*m.*) трущóбы.

slumber /ˈslʌmbə(r)/ *n.* дремóта; **disturb s.o.'s ~s** нар|ушáть, -ýшить чей-н. сон.

● *v.i.* дремáть, за-.

slump /slʌmp/ *n.* (*fall in prices etc.*) падéние; (*trade recession*) упáдок; (*fall in prices*) рéзкое падéние цен.

● *v.i.* **1** (*of person, fall, sink*) свáл|иваться, -и́ться; **he ~ed to the ground** он свали́лся/бýхнулся (*coll.*) на зéмлю. **2** (*of price, output, trade*) рéзко пáдать, упáсть.

slung /slʌŋ/ *past and p.p. of* ⇨**sling**

slunk /slʌŋk/ *past and p.p. of* ⇨**slink**

slur /slɜː(r)/ *n.* **1** (*mus. sign*) ли́га. **2** (*stigma*) пятнó; **put, cast a ~ on s.o.** очерн|я́ть, -и́ть когó-н.

● *v.t.* (**slurred, slurring**) **1** (*pronounce indistinctly*) говори́ть, сказáть невня́тно. **2** (*mus., sing, play legato*) петь/игрáть (*impf.*) легáто.

slurp /slɜːp/ (*coll.*) *v.t. & i.* чáвкать (*impf.*) (+*i.*).

slurry /ˈslʌrɪ/ *n.* (*thin cement*) жи́дкое цемéнтное тéсто; жи́дкий строи́тельный раствóр; (*semi-liquid manure*) жи́дкий навóз.

slush /slʌʃ/ *n.* **1** сля́коть. **2** (*fig., sentiment*) сентиментáльный вздор. **3**: ~ **fund** фонд для пóдкупа госудáрственных чинóвников.

slushy /ˈslʌʃɪ/ *adj.* (**slushier, slushiest**) сля́котный, мóкрый; сентиментáльный.

slut /slʌt/ *n.* (*sloven*) неря́ха; (*loose woman*) потаскýха.

sluttish /ˈslʌtɪʃ/ *adj.* неря́шливый; распýщенный.

sly /slaɪ/ *adj.* (**slyer, slyest**) хи́трый; **on the ~** укрáдкой, потихóньку.

● *cpd.* **~boots** *n.* (*coll.*) плут (*fem.* -óвка).

slyness /ˈslaɪnɪs/ *n.* хи́трость.

smack[1] /smæk/ *n.* **1** (*sound*) хлопóк; **he brought his hand down with a ~ on the table** он (грóмко) хлóпнул рукóй пó столу; ~ **of the lips** чмóканье. **2** (*blow, slap*) шлепóк; ~ **in the face** пощёчина; ~ **in the eye** (*fig.*) (неожи́данный) удáр; пощёчина. **3** (*loud kiss*) звóнкий поцелýй; **he gave her a ~** он чмóкнул её.

● *adv.* пря́мо; **he went ~ into the wall** он врéзался пря́мо в стéну.

● *v.t.* **1** (*slap*) хлóп|ать, -нуть; шлёпать, от-. **2**: ~ **one's lips** чмóк|ать, -нуть (губáми).

smack[2] /smæk/ *n.* (*taste, tinge, trace*) при́вкус.

● *v.i.*: ~ **of** (*lit., fig.*) отдавáть (*impf*) +*i.*

smack[3] /smæk/ *n.* (*naut.*) смак, рыболóвный шлюп.

smacker /ˈsmækə(r)/ *n.* (*sl.*) (*kiss*) звóнкий поцелýй; (*Br., £1*) фунт; (*US, $1*) дóллар.

small /smɔːl/ *n.* **1**: ~ **of the back** поясни́ца. **2** (*pl., Br. coll., articles of laundry*) мéлочь.

● *adj.* **1** мáленький, небольшóй, мáлый; (*of eggs, berries, jewels etc.*) мéлкий; ~ **change** мéлкие дéньги; **a ~ sum of money** небольшáя сýмма (дéнег); **a ~ family** мáленькая/небольшáя семья́; ~ **claims court** суд мéлких тяжб; ~ **craft** (*vessels*) мéлкие судá/лóдки; ~ **print** мéлкий шрифт; ~ **handwriting** мéлкий/убóристый пóчерк; ~ **intestine** тóнкая кишкá; (*not big enough*): **this coat is too ~ for** (*or* **is ~ on**) **me** э́то пальтó мне малó; (*of stature*) мáленький, невысóкий; невысóкого рóста; **he is the ~est** он ни́же всех рóстом; он сáмый мáленький; **make s.o. look ~** (*fig.*) ун|ижáть, -и́зить когó-н.; **I felt very ~** я (по)чýвствовал себя́ совершéнно уничтóженным; (*of age*): ~ **boy** мáленький мáльчик; **he is too ~ to go to school** он ещё сли́шком мáленький, чтóбы идти́ в шкóлу; (*of time*): **in the ~ hours** под ýтро. **2** (*liter., no great*): **he paid ~ attention to me** он мáло обращáл на меня́ внимáния; **they lost, and ~ wonder** они́ проигрáли, и не удиви́тельно! **3** (*unimportant, of ~ value*) мéлкий, незначи́тельный; ~ **beer** (*Br., fig.*) мéлочи (*f. pl.*); пустяки́ (*m. pl.*); ~ **fry** (*fig.*) мéлкая сóшка, мелюзгá; **one must be thankful for ~ mercies** бýдем благодáрны (и) за мáлое; ~ **talk** свéтский разговóр. **4** (*modest, humble*) скрóмный; **he rose from ~ beginnings** он начáл с мáлого; **great and ~ alike** вели́кие и мáлые равнó.

● *adv.*: **chop something up ~** мéлко наруб|áть, -и́ть что-н.

● *cpds.* ~ **ad** *n.* корóткое объявлéние; **~-arms** *n.* стрелкóвое орýжие; **~-bore** *adj.* малокали́берный; **~holder** *n.* (*Br.*) мéлкий землевладéлец/сóбственник; **~holding** *n.* (*Br.*) небольшóе земéльное владéние; ~ **hours** *n.pl.* предрассвéтные часы́ (*m.pl.*); **~-minded** *adj.* мéлочный; **~pox** *n.* óспа; **~-scale** *adj.* мéлкий; в мáленьком масштáбе; **~-scale map** *n.* маломасштáбная кáрта; **~-time** *adj.* мéлкий; **~-town** *adj.* провинциáльный.

smallish /ˈsmɔːlɪʃ/ *adj.* маловáтый; мелковáтый; небольшóй.

smarm /smɑːm/ *v.t.*: ~ **down one's hair** (*coll.*) прили́з|ывать, -áть вóлосы.

smarmy /ˈsmɑːmɪ/ *adj.* (**smarmier, smarmiest**) (*coll.*) елéйный. вкрáдчивый, льсти́вый.

smart[1] /smɑːt/ *n.* (*liter., pain*) боль.

● *v.i.* **1** (*of wound or part of body*) жечь (*impf.*); сáднить (*impf.*); **smoke makes the eyes ~** дым ест глазá; **my eyes are ~ing** у меня́ глазá щи́плет. **2** (*of person*) страдáть (*impf.*); **he ~ed under, from the insult** он испы́тывал óстрое чýвство оби́ды.

smart[2] /smɑːt/ *adj.* **1** (*sharp, severe*) рéзкий, сурóвый, óстрый; **a ~ rebuke** рéзкая óтповедь; **he got a ~ rap on the knuckles** (*lit., fig.*) емý как слéдует дáли по рукáм (*coll.*). **2** (*brisk, prompt*): **he walked off at a ~ pace** он удали́лся бы́стрым шáгом; **he saluted ~ly** он брáво óтдáл честь. **3** (*bright, alert*): **a ~ lad** шýстрый мáлый. **4** (*clever, ingenious, cunning*) сообрази́тельный, лóвкий, хи́трый; **he was too ~ for me** он меня́ перехитри́л. **5** (*neat, tidy*) опря́тный. **6** (*elegant, stylish*): **a ~ hat** элегáнтная шля́па; **the ~ set** фешенéбельное óбщество; **you look ~** у вас óчень изя́щный вид.

● *cpds.* **~-alec(k), ~-alick, ~y-pants** *nn.* самоувéренный наглéц; нахáл (*fem.* -ка); ~ **card** *n.* бáнковская кáрточка со встрóенным микропроцéссором.

smarten /ˈsmɑːt(ə)n/ *v.t.* (*also* ~ **up**): ~ **o.s. up** прихорáшиваться (*impf.*); (*a room, house, ship etc.*) прив|оди́ть, -ести́ в поря́док; нав|оди́ть, -ести́ блеск в + *p.*

● *v.i.*: ~ **up** (*in appearance or dress*): **he has ~ed up** он привёл себя́ в поря́док.

smartness /ˈsmɑːtnɪs/ *n.* (*briskness*) бóйкость; (*elegance*) элегáнтность.

smash /smæʃ/ *n.* **1** (*crash, collision*): **the**

vase fell with a ~ ваза с грохотом упала; **he gave his head an awful ~ on the pavement** он сильно ударился головой о тротуар; **there has been a ~ on the motorway** на автостраде произошло столкновение.
2 (*blow with fist*) сильный удар; (*at tennis etc.*) смэш; удар по мячу сверху.
3: **~ hit** (*coll.*) огромный успех; (*song*) шлягер.
● *adv.* прямо; **he drove ~ through the shop window** он врезался прямо в витрину.
● *v.t.* **1** (*shatter*) разб|ивать, -ить; **the bowl was ~ed to bits** ваза разбилась вдребезги; **his theory was ~ed** его теорию разгромили; его теория была разбита в пух и прах (*coll.*); (*defeat*): **~ an enemy** громить, раз- противника.
2 (*drive with force*): **he ~ed his fist into my face** он с силой ударил меня кулаком по лицу; **he ~ed the ball over the net** сильным ударом он послал мяч через сетку.
● *v.i.* **1** (*be broken*) разб|иваться, -иться.
2 (*crash, collide*) вр|езаться, -езаться; **the car ~ed into a wall** машина врезалась в стену; **the ship ~ed against the rocks** судно наскочило на скалы.
● *with advs.*: **~ down** *v.t.* (*e.g. a wall*) сн|осить, -ести; валить, по-; **~ in** *v.t.* прол|амывать, -омить; взл|амывать, -омать; **I'll ~ your face in** я тебе морду разобью (*coll.*); **~ up** *v.t.*: **~ up the furniture** разб|ивать, -ить всю мебель; **~ up the crockery** переб|ивать, -ить всю посуду; **~ up one's car** (*in collision*) разб|ивать, -ить машину.
● *cpds.* **~-and-grab** *adj.*: **-~and-grab (raid)** (грабительский) налёт на витрину магазина; **~-up** *n.* (*collision*) столкновение.

smasher /ˈsmæʃə(r)/ *n.* (*Br. coll.*) (*person*) красав|чик (*fem.* -ица); (*thing*) прелесть.

smashing /ˈsmæʃɪŋ/ *adj.* **1**: **~ blow** сокрушительный удар; **~ defeat** сокрушительное/тяжёлое поражение. **2** (*Br. coll.*): **a ~ film** замечательный/потрясающий фильм; **we had a ~ time** мы замечательно провели время.

smattering /ˈsmætərɪŋ/ *n.*: **he has a ~ of German** он чуть-чуть знает немецкий.

smear /smɪə(r)/ *n.* **1** (*blotch*) пятно; (*microscope specimen*) мазок; **~ test** мазок с шейки матки. **2** (*coll., slander*) клевета; **~ campaign** клеветническая кампания.
● *v.t.* **1** (*daub*) мазать, на-; размаз|ывать, -ать; **he ~ed grease paint on his face** он наложил грим (себе) на лицо; **I ~ed my trousers with paint** я испачкал брюки краской.
2 (*defame*) чернить, о-; порочить, о-.

smell /smel/ *n.* **1** (*faculty*) обоняние; **a keen sense of ~** тонкое обоняние; **I lost my sense of ~** я утратил чувство обоняния; (*in animals*) чутьё.
2 (*odour*) запах; **what a** (*sc. bad*) **~!** ну и вонь!; **this flower has no ~** этот цветок не имеет запаха (*or* не пахнет); **garlic has a pungent ~** у чеснока едкий запах; **there was a ~ of burning** пахло горелым.
3 (*inhalation*): **have, take a ~ of, at** понюхать (*pf.*).
● *v.t.* (*past and p.p.* **smelt** *or* **smelled**)
1 (*perceive ~ of*) чувствовать, по- запах (+*g.*); **can you ~ onions?** вы чувствуете запах лука?; **I can't ~ anything** я не чувствую никакого запаха; **I ~ something burning** я чувствую запах гари; (*of animals; also fig.*) чуять (*impf.*); **I ~ a rat** чую недоброе; **I smelt danger** я почувствовал опасность.
2 (*sniff*) нюхать, по-; **just ~ this rose** вы только понюхайте эту розу; **~ing salts** нюхательная соль.
3: **~ out** (*lit., fig.*) пронюх|ивать, -ать.
● *v.i.* (*past and p.p.* **smelt** *or* **smelled**)
1 (*sniff*): **the dog was ~ing at the lamp-post** собака (об)нюхала фонарь.
2 (*emit ~*) пахнуть (*impf.*); (*pleasantly*) издавать (*impf.*) аромат; **the soup ~s good** суп хорошо/вкусно пахнет; **the room smelt of cigarettes** в комнате пахло табаком; **his breath ~s** у него дурно пахнет изо рта; **the fish began to ~** рыба стала попахивать.
3: **~ of** (*fig., suggest*) отд|авать, -ать +*i.*; **opinions that ~ of heresy** мнения, граничащие с ересью.

smelly /ˈsmelɪ/ *adj.* (**smellier, smelliest**) дурно пахнущий, вонючий.

smelt¹ /smelt/ *n.* (*pl.* **~** *or* **~s**) (*fish*) корюшка.

smelt² /smelt/ *v.t.* (*ore*) плавить (*impf.*); (*metal*) выплавлять, выплавить.

smelt³ /smelt/ *past and p.p. of* ⇒**smell**

smew /smju:/ *n.* (*zool.*) луток.

smidgen /ˈsmɪdʒ(ə)n/ *n.* (*coll.*) чуток, немного.

smile /smaɪl/ *n.* улыбка; (*of indulgent amusement*) усмешка; **he greeted me with a ~** он встретил меня улыбкой; **give s.o. a ~** улыбнуться (*pf.*) кому-н.; **force a ~** выдавливать, выдавить из себя улыбку; **she was all ~s** у неё был сияющий вид.
● *v.t.* (*express by ~*): **she ~d her approval/forgiveness** она улыбнулась в знак одобрения/прощения.
● *v.i.* улыб|аться, -нуться; (*with indulgent amusement*) усмех|аться, -нуться; **what are you smiling at?** чему вы улыбаетесь?; **her ignorance made him ~** её невежество вызвало у него усмешку; **keep smiling!** не унывай!; **~ on** (*fig.*): **fortune ~ed on him** счастье ему улыбалось.

smirch /smɜ:tʃ/ *n.* пятно.
● *v.t.* (*lit., fig.*) пятнать, за-; (*fig.*) позорить, о-; порочить, о-.

smirk /smɜ:k/ *n.* (*affected, silly*) жеманная улыбка; (*conceited*) самодовольная улыбка, ухмылка.
● *v.i.* ухмыл|яться, -ьнуться.

smit|e /smaɪt/ *v.t.* (*past* **smote;** *p.p.* **smitten**) **1** (*arch. or joc., strike*) разить, по-. **2** (*afflict*) пора|жать, -зить; **~ten with the plague** поражённый чумой; **he was ~ten with remorse** его охватило раскаяние; (*fascinate*): **he was ~ten by her charms** он был покорён её чарами.

smith /smɪθ/ *n.* (**black~**) кузнец.

smithereens /ˌsmɪðəˈri:nz/ *n.* (*coll.*): **to ~** вдребезги.

smithy /ˈsmɪðɪ/ *n.* кузница.

smitten /ˈsmɪt(ə)n/ *p.p. of* ⇒**smite**

smock /smɒk/ *n.* (*loose shirt*) блуза; (*smocked dress, blouse*) платье/блузка в сборочку.

smocking /ˈsmɒkɪŋ/ *n.* фигурные буф|ы (*pl., g.* —), мелкие сборки (*f. pl.*).

smog /smɒg/ *n.* смог.

smoke /sməʊk/ *n.* **1** дым; **clouds of ~** клубы (*m. pl.*) дыма; **there's no ~ without fire** нет дыма без огня; **emit ~** дымить (*impf.*); **the ~ gets in my eyes** дым ест мне глаза; **~ was pouring out** дым (так и) валил; **go up in ~** (*lit.*) сгор|ать, -еть; (*fig.*) пойти (*pf.*) прахом.
2: **have a ~** покурить (*pf.*); **they broke off for a ~** они устроили перекур.
3 (*pl., coll.*) курево.
● *v.t.* **1** (*preserve or darken with ~*) коптить, за-; **~d fish** копчёная рыба; **~d glass** темнённое стекло.
2: **~ out** (*wasps etc.*) выкуривать, выкурить.
3 (*tobacco etc.*) курить, вы-.
● *v.i.* **1** (*emit ~; of chimney, fireplace etc.*) дымиться (*impf.*); **smoking ruins** дымящиеся руины; (*burn badly*) дымить (*impf.*).
2 (*of person*: **~ tobacco etc.**) курить (*impf.*); **he ~s like a chimney** он дымит без конца (*or* как паровоз).
● *cpds.* **~-bomb** *n.* дымовая бомба; **~-screen** *n.* (*lit., fig.*) дымовая завеса; **~-stack** *n.* (дымовая) труба.

smokeless /ˈsməʊklɪs/ *adj.* бездымный; **~ zone** (*Br.*) бездымная городская зона.

smoker /ˈsməʊkə(r)/ *n.* **1** (*person*) курящий; курильщи|к (*fem.* -ца); **a heavy ~** заядлый курильщик. **2** (*coll., carriage*) вагон для курящих.

smoking /ˈsməʊkɪŋ/ *n.* (*of food*) копчение; (*of tobacco etc.*) курение; **No S~** курить воспрещается; **I gave up ~** я бросил курить.
● *cpds.* **~ car** (*US*), **~-carriage** (*Br.*), **~-compartment** *nn.* вагон/купе (*indecl.*) для курящих; **~-room** *n.* курительная (комната).

smoky /ˈsməʊkɪ/ *adj.* (**smokier, smokiest**) дымный; дымящийся; (*of colour*) дымчатый; (*blackened by smoke*) закоптелый.

smolder /ˈsməʊldə(r)/ (*US*) = **smoulder**

smooch /smu:tʃ/ *v.i.* (*sl.*) обниматься, целоваться (*both impf.*).

smooth /smu:ð/ *adj.* **1** (*even, level*) гладкий, ровный; **a ~ chin** гладкий/бритый подбородок; **a ~ road** ровная дорога; **to take the rough with the ~** мужественно встр|ечать, -етить невзгоды; **a ~ sea** спокойное море; **a ~ paste** тесто без комков; **we had a ~ ride in the train** поезд шёл ровно; **everything went off ~ly** всё прошло

S

гла́дко/без сучка́ и задо́ринки (*coll.*).
2 (*not harsh to ear or taste*): **~ breathing** ро́вное дыха́ние; **~ vodka** мя́гкая во́дка; **~ wine** нетерпко́е вино́.
3 (*of person*: *equable, unruffled*) обходи́тельный, любе́зный; (*suave*) гала́нтный; **~ manners** мя́гкие/любе́зные мане́ры; **he has a ~ tongue** он говори́т гла́дко; он ма́стер говори́ть; (*flattering*) льсти́вый; (*insinuating*) вкра́дчивый.

● *v.t.* **1** (*make level*) выра́внивать, вы́ровнять.
2 (*arrange neatly, flatten*) пригла́|живать, -дить.
3 (*make easy*) смягч|а́ть, -и́ть; **he ~ed the way for his successor** он расчи́стил путь для своего́ прее́мника.

● *with advs.*: **~ away** *v.t.*: **he ~ed away our difficulties** он устрани́л на́ши затрудне́ния; **~ down** *v.t.*: **~ (down) one's dress** одёр|гивать, -нуть пла́тье; **he ~ed his hair down** он пригла́дил во́лосы; **~ off** *v.t.*: **~ off sharp edges** обт|а́чивать, -очи́ть о́стрые края́; **~ out** *v.t.*: **she ~ed out the folds in the tablecloth** она́ разгла́дила скла́дки на ска́терти; **~ over** *v.t.* смягч|а́ть, -и́ть; **~ things over** ула́|живать, -дить де́ло.

● *cpds.* **~-bore** *adj.* гладкоство́льный; **~-faced** *adj.* (*beardless*) безборо́дый; (*shaven*) чи́сто вы́бритый; (*ingratiating*; *also* **~-spoken**) вкра́дчивый; **~-tongued** *adj.* сладкоречи́вый, льсти́вый.

smoothie /ˈsmuːðɪ/ *n.* (*flatterer*) льстец.

smoothness /ˈsmuːðnɪs/ *n.* гла́дкость.

smorgasbord /ˈsmɔːgəs,bɔːd/ *n.* шве́дский стол.

smote /sməʊt/ *past of* ⇒**smite**

smother /ˈsmʌðə(r)/ *v.t.* **1** (*suffocate*) души́ть, за-; **the princes were ~ed in the Tower** при́нцы бы́ли заду́шены в Та́уэре; **he was ~ed by fumes** он задохну́лся от испаре́ний; (*extinguish*): **~ a fire** туши́ть, по- ого́нь. **2** (*cover*): **the furniture was ~ed in dust** ме́бель была́ покры́та густы́м сло́ем пы́ли; **she ~ed the child with kisses** она́ осы́пала ребёнка поцелу́ями.
3 (*suppress, conceal*) подав|ля́ть, -и́ть; **~ing a yawn** подавля́я/сде́рживая зево́к; **they ~ed his cries** они́ заглуши́ли его́ кри́ки.

smoulder /ˈsməʊldə(r)/ (*US also* **smolder**) *v.i.* (*lit., fig.*) тлеть (*impf.*); **~ing leaves** тле́ющие ли́стья; **~ing hatred** затаённая не́нависть.

smudge /smʌdʒ/ *n.* пятно́; **you have a ~ on your cheek** вы че́м-то вы́мазали/испа́чкали щёку.

● *v.t.* (*blur*) сма́з|ывать, -ать; (*smear*) ма́зать, вы́-.

● *v.i.*: **the drawing ~s easily** рису́нок легко́ сма́зать.

smudgy /ˈsmʌdʒɪ/ *adj.* (**smudgier, smudgiest**) запа́чканный.

smug /smʌg/ *adj.* (**smugger, smuggest**) самодово́льный.

smuggle /ˈsmʌg(ə)l/ *v.t.* пров|ози́ть, -езти́ контраба́ндой; (*fig.*) **he was ~d into the house** его́ тайко́м провели́ в дом; **I was able to ~ out a letter** мне удало́сь тайко́м вы́нести письмо́.

smuggler /ˈsmʌglə(r)/ *n.* контрабанди́ст (*fem.* -ка).

smuggling /ˈsmʌglɪŋ/ *n.* контраба́нда.

smugness /ˈsmʌgnɪs/ *n.* самодово́льство.

smut /smʌt/ *n.* **1** (*soot*) са́жа; (*black mark*) чёрное пятно́. **2** (*obscenity*) непристо́йность, похa͏́бщина (*coll.*).

smutty /ˈsmʌtɪ/ *adj.* (**smuttier, smuttiest**): **~ face** гря́зное/запа́чканное лицо́; **~ joke** гря́зный/поха́бный (*coll.*) анекдо́т.

snack /snæk/ *n.* заку́ска; **have a ~** заку́с|ывать, -и́ть.

● *cpd.* **~-bar** *n.* заку́сочная, буфе́т.

snaffle /ˈsnæf(ə)l/ *n.* узде́чка, тре́нзель (*m.*).

● *v.t.* (*coll.*) (*appropriate*) ур|ыва́ть, -ва́ть; (*steal*) стя́гивать, стяну́ть; ти́брить, с-.

snafu /snæˈfuː/ *n.* (*US coll.*) неразбери́ха, пу́таница.

snag /snæg/ **1** (*obstacle*) препя́тствие; (*difficulty*) затрудне́ние; (*hidden*) загво́здка. **2** (*tear*) разры́в; (*in stocking*) затя́жка (*coll.*).

● *v.i.* (**snagged, snagging**) (*catch against*) зацепи́ться (*pf.*) за + *a.*

● *v.t.* (**snagged, snagging**) рвать, по-.

snail /sneɪl/ *n.* ули́тка; **go at a ~'s pace** тащи́ться (*impf.*) как черепа́ха.

snake /sneɪk/ *n.* змея́; **grass ~** уж; **~ in the grass** (*fig.*) змея́ подколо́дная.

● *v.i.* (*crawl*) ползти́ (*det.*); (*wind*) извива́ться (*impf.*); **the road ~s through the mountains** доро́га извива́ется ме́жду гор.

● *cpds.* **~bite** *n.* уку́с змеи́; зме́йный уку́с; **~-charmer** *n.* заклина́тель (*m.*) змей.

snap /snæp/ *n.* **1** (*noise*) щелчо́к, щёлканье; **the box shut with a ~** коро́бка защёлкнулась; (*of something breaking*) треск; (*bite*): **the dog made a ~ at him** соба́ка пыта́лась его́ укуси́ть.
2 (*fastener*) кно́пка.
3 (*coll., photograph*) сни́мок; **take a ~ of** сн|има́ть, -ять.
4 (*spell*): **a cold ~** внеза́пное похолода́ние.

● *adj.*: **~ decision** внеза́пное реше́ние; **~ election** внеочередны́е вы́боры (*m. pl.*).

● *v.t.* (**snapped, snapping**) **1** (*make ~ping noise with*) щёлк|ать, -нуть + *i.*; **he ~ped his fingers in my face** он щёлкнул па́льцами пе́ред мои́м но́сом.
2 (*break*) разл|а́мывать, -ома́ть; **he ~ped the stick in two** он разлома́л па́лку на́двое.
3 (*coll., photograph*) сн|има́ть, -ять.

● *v.i.* (**snapped, snapping**) **1** (*make biting motion*): **~ at** огрыз|а́ться, -ну́ться на + *a.*; (*speak sharply*) груби́ть, на- (**at**: + *d.*); **don't ~ at me!** не груби́те (мне)!
2 (*make ~ping sound*) щёлк|ать, -нуть; (*of fastener*) защёлк|иваться, -нуться.
3 (*break*) тре́снуть (*pf.*); **the rope ~ped** верёвка оборвала́сь.
4 (*move smartly*): **~ out of it!** (*coll.*) брось!

● *with advs.*: **~ down** *v.t.*: **he ~ped the lid down** он защёлкнул/захло́пнул кры́шку; **~ off** *v.t. & i.* (*break off*) отл|а́мывать(ся), -ома́ть(ся), -оми́ть(ся); **~ s.o.'s head off** (*coll.*) набр|а́сываться, -о́ситься на кого́-н.; **~ up** *v.t.* (*snatch*) хвата́ть, схвати́ть; сца́пать (*pf.*) (*coll.*); (*buy eagerly*) расхва́т|ывать, -а́ть; **the tickets were ~ped up straight away** биле́ты тут же расхвата́ли.

● *cpds.* **~dragon** *n.* льви́ный зев; **~-fastener** *n.* кно́пка; **~shot** *n.* (люби́тельский) сни́мок.

snapper /ˈsnæpə(r)/ *n.* (*zool.*) луциа́н.

snappish /ˈsnæpɪʃ/ *adj.* раздражи́тельный; (*of dog*) злой, куса́чий (*coll.*).

snappy /ˈsnæpɪ/ *adj.* (**snappier, snappiest**) (*brisk*) живо́й; **make it ~!** жи́во!; (по)живе́е!; (*coll., neat, elegant*) шика́рный.

snare /sneə(r)/ *n.* (*noose*) сило́к; (*trap*) западня́, лову́шка; **lay, set a ~ for s.o.** ста́вить, по- лову́шку кому́-н.; **be caught in a ~** поп|ада́ть, -а́сть в лову́шку.

● *v.t.* лови́ть, пойма́ть в западню́/лову́шку.

● *cpd.* **~-drum** *n.* бараба́н со стру́нами.

snarl[1] /snɑːl/ *n.* (*growl*) рыча́ние; **he answered with a ~** он зарыча́л в отве́т.

● *v.t. & i.* рыча́ть, за-.

snarl[2] /snɑːl/ *n.* (*tangle*) спу́танный клубо́к.

● *v.t.* запу́т|ывать, -ать; (*fig.*): **the arrangements were ~ed up** всё бы́ло перепу́тано.

snatch /snætʃ/ *n.* **1** (*act of ~ing*): **make a ~ at something** хвата́ться, схвати́ться за что-н.
2 (*short spell*): **sleep in ~es** спать (*impf.*) урывка́ми.
3 (*fragment*) обры́вок; **I overheard ~es of their conversation** я подслу́шал обры́вки их разгово́ра.

● *v.t.* **1** (*seize*) хвата́ть, схвати́ть; **~ something from s.o.** вырыва́ть, вы́рвать что-н. у кого́-н.; **~ something out of s.o.'s hands (*or* away from s.o.)** выхва́тывать, вы́хватить (*or* вырыва́ть, вы́рвать) что-н. у кого́-н. (из рук); **don't ~!** не хвата́й!; **~ an opportunity** воспо́льзоваться (*pf.*) слу́чаем; **~ a kiss** сорва́ть (*pf.*) поцелу́й; **she ~ed up her handbag** она́ схвати́ла свою́ су́мочку.
2 (*obtain with difficulty*) ур|ыва́ть, -ва́ть (*coll.*); **we ~ed a hurried meal** мы на́скоро перекуси́ли; **I managed to ~ a few hours' sleep** мне удало́сь урва́ть не́сколько часо́в сна.

● *v.i.* хвата́ть (*impf.*); **~ at something** хвата́ться, схвати́ться за что-н.

snazzy /ˈsnæzɪ/ *adj.* (**snazzier, snazziest**) (*coll.*) шика́рный, эффе́ктный.

sneak /sniːk/ *n.* подле́ц; (*Br., in school*) я́беда (*c.g.*).

● *v.t.* (*past and p.p.* **sneaked** *or US coll.* **snuck**) тащи́ть, с-; **~ a look at something** взгляну́ть (*pf.*) на что-н. укра́дкой.

● *v.i.* (*past and p.p.* **sneaked** *or US coll.* **snuck**) **1** (*creep, move silently*) кра́сться (*impf.*); **~ into a room** прокра́|дываться, -сться в ко́мнату; **~ out of a room** выска́льзывать, вы́скользнуть из ко́мнаты; **he ~ed off round the corner** он скры́лся за угло́м. **2** (*Br., tell tales*): **~ on s.o.** я́бедничать, на- на кого́-н.

● *cpd.* **~-thief** *n.* ме́лкий вор, вори́шка (*m.*).

sneakers /ˈsniːkəz/ *n.* (*US*) кроссо́вки (*f. pl.*); (*canvas*) полуке́д|ы (*pl., g.* -ов/—).

sneaking /ˈsniːkɪŋ/ *adj.* (*furtive*): **he gave her a ~ glance** он укра́дкой взгляну́л на неё; (*persistent, lingering*): **~ feeling** та́йное/сму́тное подозре́ние.

sneer /snɪə(r)/ *n.* (*contemptuous smile*) презри́тельная усме́шка; (*taunt*) глумле́ние.

● *v.i.* усмех|а́ться, -ну́ться; **~ at** насмеха́ться (*impf.*) над + *i.*; (*in words*) глуми́ться (*impf.*) над + *i.*; **a ~ing voice** насме́шливый/ехи́дный го́лос.

sneerer /ˈsnɪərə(r)/ *n.* насме́шни|к (*fem.* -ца).

sneeze /sniːz/ *n.* чиха́нье; (*coll.*) чих.

● *v.i.* чих|а́ть, -ну́ть; **£50 is not to be ~d at** 50 фу́нтов — не шу́тка.

snick /snɪk/ *n.* (*notch*) зару́бка; (*cut*) надре́з.

snicker /ˈsnɪkə(r)/ *n.* (*whinny*) ржа́ние; (*snigger*) хихи́канье.

● *v.i.* ржать (*impf.*); хихи́к|ать, -нуть.

snide /snaɪd/ *adj.* (*coll.*) ехи́дный.

sniff /snɪf/ *n.* (*inhalation*) вдох; **take a ~ at, of something** ню́хать, по- что-н.; **give a ~** (*of contempt*) фы́рк|ать, -нуть; (*to stop nose running etc.*) шмы́г|ать, -ну́ть (но́сом).

● *v.t.* (*inhale*) вд|ыха́ть, -охну́ть; (*smell at*) ню́хать, по-.

● *v.i.* **1** (*because of tears, cold etc.*) шмы́г|ать, -ну́ть (но́сом); (*in contempt*) фы́рк|ать, -нуть. **2**: **~ at** ню́хать, по-; (*fig.*) пренебр|ега́ть, -е́чь (+ *i.*); **the offer is not to be ~ed at** таки́м предложе́нием нельзя́ пренебрега́ть.

sniffer /ˈsnɪfə(r)/ *n.*: **~dog** ище́йка; **glue-~** токсикома́н.

sniffle /ˈsnɪf(ə)l/ *n.* сопе́ние; (*pl.*) на́сморк.

● *v.i.* шмы́г|ать, -ну́ть (но́сом).

sniffy /ˈsnɪfɪ/ *adj.* (**sniffier, sniffiest**) (*coll.*) (*contemptuous*) презри́тельный; (*disdainful*) недово́льный.

snigger /ˈsnɪgə(r)/ *n.* хихи́канье.

● *v.i.* хихи́к|ать, -нуть.

snip /snɪp/ *n.* (*act of ~ping*) ре́зание; (*piece cut off*) обре́зок; кусо́к; (*Br. coll., bargain*) (больша́я) уда́ча.

● *v.t.* (**snipped, snipping**) (*clip, trim*) подр|еза́ть, -е́зать; (*cut*): **~ out a piece of cloth** выреза́ть, вы́резать кусо́к мате́рии; **~ off a bud** ср|еза́ть, -е́зать по́чку.

snipe[1] /snaɪp/ *n.* (*pl.* **~** *or* **~s**) (*bird*) бека́с.

snip|e[2] /snaɪp/ *v.i.* (*mil.*) стреля́ть (*impf.*) из укры́тия; (*fig.*): **he is always ~ing at the Church** он всегда́ напада́ет на це́рковь.

sniper /ˈsnaɪpə(r)/ *n.* сна́йпер.

snippet /ˈsnɪpɪt/ *n.* (*of material*) лоску́т, лоскуто́к; (*pl., of news etc.*) обры́вки (*m. pl.*).

snitch /snɪtʃ/ *v.t.* (*coll., filch*) сти́брить, стяну́ть (*both pf.*) (*coll.*); **~ on** (*inform on*) дон|оси́ть, -ести́ на + *a.*

snivel /ˈsnɪv(ə)l/ *v.i.* (**snivelled, snivelling;** *US* **sniveled, sniveling**) (*run at the nose*) распус|ка́ть, -ти́ть со́пли; (*whine*) хны́кать (*impf.*); распус|ка́ть, -ти́ть ню́ни (*coll.*).

sniveller /ˈsnɪv(ə)lə(r)/ *n.* ны́тик.

snob /snɒb/ *n.* сноб.

snobbery /ˈsnɒbərɪ/ *n.* сноби́зм.

snobbish /ˈsnɒbɪʃ/ *adj.* снobи́стский.

snobbishness /ˈsnɒbɪʃnɪs/ *n.* снобизм.

snog /snɒg/ *v.i.* (**snogged, snogging**) (*Br. coll.*) лиза́ться (*impf., coll.*).

snood /snuːd/ *n.* (*hair-net*) се́тка (для воло́с).

snook /snuːk/ *n.* (*Br.*): **cock a ~ at** пока́з|ывать, -а́ть дли́нный нос + *d.*

snooker /ˈsnuːkə(r)/ *n.* сну́кер.

● *v.t.* (*sl., defeat*) разб|ива́ть, -и́ть; громи́ть, раз-.

snoop /snuːp/ *v.i.* (*coll.*) подгл|я́дывать, -яде́ть/подсм|а́тривать -отре́ть чужи́е та́йны; сова́ть (*impf.*) нос в чужи́е дела́.

snooper /ˈsnuːpə(r)/ *n.*: **he is such a ~** он везде́ суёт нос.

snooty /ˈsnuːtɪ/ *adj.* (**snootier, snootiest**) (*coll.*) наду́тый, зазна́вшийся.

snooze /snuːz/ (*coll.*) *n.*: **have, take a ~** вздремну́ть (*pf.*); всхрапну́ть (*pf.*) (*joc.*).

● *v.i.* дрема́ть (*impf.*).

snore /snɔː(r)/ *n.* храп.

● *v.i.* храпе́ть, за-; всхрапну́ть (*pf.*).

snorer /ˈsnɔːrə(r)/ *n.* храпу́н (*fem.* -ья).

snorkel /ˈsnɔːk(ə)l/ *n.* дыха́тельная тру́бка (*для подводного плавания*).

snorkelling /ˈsnɔːkəlɪŋ/ (*US* **snorkeling**) *n.* подво́дное пла́вание с дыха́тельной тру́бкой.

snort /snɔːt/ *n.* фы́рканье;

● *v.i.* фы́рк|ать, -нуть.

snot /snɒt/ *n.* (*vulg.*) со́пли (*f. pl.*).

snotty /ˈsnɒtɪ/ *adj.* (**snottier, snottiest**) (*vulg.* **~-nosed**) сопли́вый; (*coll., superior*) высокоме́рный.

snout /snaʊt/ *n.* (*of animal*) мо́рда; (*of pig, fish*) ры́ло.

snow /snəʊ/ *n.* снег; **there was a fall of ~** вы́пал снег; **the roads were deep in ~** доро́ги бы́ли покры́ты глубо́ким сне́гом; **S~ Maiden** Снегу́рочка.

● *v.i.*: **it is ~ing** идёт снег.

● *with advs.*: **~ in, ~ up** *vv.t.*: **the road is ~ed up** доро́гу занесло́ сне́гом; **we were ~ed in** наш дом занесло́ сне́гом; **~ under** *v.t.* (*fig.*): **I was ~ed under with letters** я был зава́лен пи́сьмами; **we are ~ed under with work** мы зава́лены рабо́той.

● *cpds.* **~ball** *n.* снежо́к; *v.i.* игра́ть (*impf.*) в снежки́; (*fig., increase*) расти́ (*impf.*), как сне́жный ком; **~-blind** *adj.* ослеплённый сверка́ющим сне́гом; **be ~-blind** страда́ть (*impf.*) сне́жной слепото́й; **~-blindness** *n.* сне́жная слепота́; **~board** *n.* сноубо́рд; **~boarding** *n.* сноубо́рдинг; **~-boots** *n. pl.* (тёплые) бо́ты (*m. pl.*); **~-bound** *adj.* (*of person*): **they were ~-bound** они́ не могли́ вы́браться из до́ма из-за сне́жных зано́сов; (*of place*) занесённый сне́гом; **~-capped, ~-clad, ~-covered** *adjs.* покры́тый сне́гом; **~-drift** *n.* сугро́б; **~drop** *n.* подсне́жник; **~fall** *n.* снегопа́д; **~-field** *n.* сне́жное по́ле; **~flake** *n.* снежи́нка; (*pl.*) (сне́жные) хло́пья; **~gauge** *n.* снегоме́р; **~-goggles** *n. pl.* сне́жные очк|и́ (*pl., g.* -о́в); **~-leopard** *n.* сне́жный барс, и́рбис; **~-line** *n.* снегова́я ли́ния; **~man** *n.* сне́жная ба́ба, снегови́к; **~-mobile** *n.* (*with runners*) мотоса́н|и, аэроса́н|и (*pl., g.* -е́й); (*with caterpillar tracks*) снегохо́д; **~-plough** *n.* снегоочисти́тель (*m.*); **~-shoes** *n. pl.* снегосту́пы (*m. pl.*); **~storm** *n.* мете́ль, вьюга; **~-white** *adj.* белосне́жный; **S~-White** Белосне́жка.

snowy /ˈsnəʊɪ/ *adj.* (**snowier, snowiest**) **1**: **~ roofs** заснежённые кры́ши; **~ weather** сне́жная пого́да. **2** (*white*): **~ hair** белосне́жные во́лосы; **~ owl** бе́лая/поля́рная сова́.

snub[1] /snʌb/ *n.* (*rebuff*) оби́да; щелчо́к.

● *v.t.* (**snubbed, snubbing**) оса́|живать, -ди́ть.

snub[2] /snʌb/ *adj.*: **~ nose** вздёрнутый нос.

● *cpd.* **~-nosed** *adj.* курно́сый.

snuck /snʌk/ *US colloq. past and p.p. of* ⇒**sneak**

snuff[1] /snʌf/ *n.* ню́хательный таба́к; **pinch of ~** поню́шка; **take ~** ню́хать, по- таба́к.

● *cpd.* **~-box** *n.* табаке́рка.

snuff[2] /snʌf/ *v.t.* (*also* **~ out**) туши́ть, по-; (*fig.*) гаси́ть, по-; **~ it** (*Br. sl., die*) загну́ться (*pf.*), дать (*pf.*) ду́ба (*sl.*).

snuffle /ˈsnʌf(ə)l/ *n.* сопе́ние; **I have the ~s** (*coll.*) у меня́ и́з носу течёт; у меня́ на́сморк.

● *v.i.* сопе́ть (*impf.*).

snug /snʌg/ *adj.* (**snugger, snuggest**) (*cosy*) ую́тный; (*close-fitting*): **a ~ jacket** облега́ющий пиджа́к.

snuggle /ˈsnʌg(ə)l/ *v.i.*: **~ down in bed** свёр|тываться, -ну́ться в посте́ли; **~ up to s.o.** приж|има́ться, -а́ться к кому́-н.

so[1] /səʊ/ *n.* (*mus.*) = **so(h)**

so² /səʊ/ *adv.* **1** так; **is that ~?** это так?; (это) правда?; **~ it is (~ I am etc.)!** действительно!; (и) в самом деле!; **isn't that ~?** не так ли?; не правда ли?; **that being ~** раз так; **I'm ~ glad to see you** я так рад вас видеть; **would you be ~ kind as to visit her?** будьте так добры, навестите её; **he is not ~ silly as to ask her** он не настолько глуп, чтобы просить её; **he was ~ overworked that ...** он был так/до такой степени перегружен, что...; **not ~ very ...** не так уж...; **it is ever ~ easy** это проще простого (*or* так легко); **every ~ often** время от времени; **~ be it!** пусть будет так!; **~ far** (*up to now*) до сих пор, пока; **~ far as I know** насколько я знаю; **~ far ~ good** пока всё хорошо; **and ~ forth, on** и так далее; **just ~** вот именно!; верно!; (*in good order*) как надо; в ажуре (*coll.*); **~ long!** (*au revoir*) пока! (*coll.*); **~ long as** (*provided that*) если только; **~ many** столько +*g.*, так много +*g.*; **thank you ~ much!** большое (вам) спасибо!; **(at) ~ much per person** по стольку-то с человека; **~ much for his advice** вот и весь его совет!; **~ much ~ that** настолько, что; **~ much the worse/better** тем хуже/лучше; **he is not ~ much discontented as unsatisfied** он скорее неудовлетворён, чем недоволен; **he left without ~ much as a nod** он ушёл, даже не кивнув головой (на прощание); **~ to say, speak** так сказать; **~ what?** ну и что (же)?
2 (*also*) тоже; **(and) ~ do I** и я тоже.
3 (*consequently, accordingly*) итак, поэтому; так что; значит; **he is ill, (and) ~ he can't come** он нездоров, так что не может прийти; **~ you did see him after all** значит/итак, вы всё-таки его видели; **it was late, ~ I went home** было поздно, и (поэтому) я пошёл домой.
4 (*that the foregoing is true or will happen*): **I suppose/hope ~** я думаю/надеюсь, что да; **do you think ~?** вы так думаете?
5: **~ as to** (*in order to*) (с тем), чтобы +*inf.*; (*in such a way as to*) так, чтобы.
6 (*thereabouts*): **there were 100 or ~ people there** там было примерно сто человек (*or* около ста человек).
● *cpds.* **~-and-~** *pron.* (*person*) такой-то; **he's a mean old ~-and-~** он невероятный скряга; **~-called** *adj.* так называемый; **~-so** *adj. & adv.* ничего; так себе.

soak /səʊk/ *n.* **1** (**~ing**): **give the clothes a thorough ~!** пусть бельё подольше помокнет!
2 (*sl., hard drinker*) пьяница (*c.g.*); пьянчужка (*c.g.*).
● *v.t.* **1** (*wet*) зам|а́чивать, -очить; вымачивать, вымочить; **she ~s the laundry overnight** она замачивает бельё на ночь; (*steep*): **he ~ed his bread in milk** он размачивал хлеб в молоке.
2 (*wet through*): **the shower ~ed me to the skin** дождь промочил меня до нитки.
● *v.i.* **1** (*remain immersed*) мокнуть (*impf.*).
2 (*drain, percolate*) впит|ывaться, -а́ться; прос|а́чиваться, -очиться; **the rain ~ed into the ground** дождь пропитал почву; **the water ~ed through my shoes** вода просочилась в мои туфли.
● *with advs.*: **~ off** *v.t.*: **~ off dirt** отм|а́чивать, -очить грязь; **~ up** *v.t.* (*lit., fig.*) впит|ывать, -а́ть.

soaking /'səʊkɪŋ/ *n.*: **he got a ~** он здорово промок.
● *adj. & adv.*: **you are ~ (wet)** вы промокли насквозь; **it was a ~ (wet) day** весь день лило (как из ведра).

soap /səʊp/ *n.* мыло; **cake, tablet of ~** кусок мыла.
● *v.t.* мылить, на-; **~ o.s.** намыли|ваться, -ться.
● *cpds.* **~-box** *n.* мыльница (с крышкой); (*platform*) импровизированная трибуна; **~-box orator** уличный оратор; **~-bubble** *n.* мыльный пузырь; **~-dish** *n.* мыльница; **~-flakes** *n. pl.* мыльные хлопь|я (*pl., g.* -ев); **~-opera** *n.* мыльная опера, телесериал; **~-powder** *n.* стиральный порошок; **~-stone** *n.* мыльный камень, стеатит; **~-suds** *n. pl.* мыльная пена; **~-works** *n.* мыловаренный завод.

soapy /'səʊpɪ/ *adj.* (**soapier, soapiest**) **1** (*covered with soap*) мыльный, намыленный.
2 (*resembling, containing, consisting of soap*) мыльный.

soar /sɔː(r)/ *v.i.* **1** (*of birds*) высоко взлет|а́ть, -е́ть; взмы|ва́ть, -ть; воспар|я́ть, -и́ть (*obs., liter.*). **2** (*fig., rise, tower*) возн|оси́ться, -ести́сь; **~ing ambition** непомерное честолюбие.
3 (*of prices*) (резко) пов|ыша́ться, -ы́ситься. **4** (*of glider*) парить (*impf.*).

s.o.b. (*abbr. of* ***son of a bitch***) (*US*) сукин сын (*vulg.*).

sob /sɒb/ *n.* всхлип, всхлипывание.
● *v.t.* (**sobbed, sobbing**): **~ one's heart out** рыдать (*impf.*); горько плакать (*impf.*); **she ~bed herself to sleep** она плакала, пока не уснула.
● *v.i.* (**sobbed, sobbing**) всхли́п|ывать, -нуть.
● *cpd.* **~-story** *n.* (*coll.*) душещипательная история.

sober /'səʊbə(r)/ *adj.* (**soberer, soberest**) **1** (*not drunk, temperate*) трезвый. **2** (*not fanciful*) здравый, трезвый; **a man of ~ judgement** человек трезвого ума. **3** (*of colour*) спокойный; **she is ~ly dressed** она неброско одета.
● *v.t.* (*usu.* **~ up**) отрезв|ля́ть, -и́ть; вытрезвлять, вытрезвить; **this had a ~ing effect on them** это подействовало на них отрезвляюще; **~ing-up station** вытрезвитель (*m.*).
● *v.i.* трезветь, о-; **~ up** протрезв|ля́ться, -и́ться.
● *cpd.* **~-minded** *adj.* рассудительный.

sobriety /sə'braɪətɪ/ *n.* трезвость.

so|briquet /'səʊbrɪ,keɪ/, **sou-** /'suːbrɪ,keɪ/ *n.* прозвище, кличка.

soccer /'sɒkə(r)/ *n.* футбол; **~ fan** футбольный болельщик; **~ match** футбольный матч; **~ player** футболист.

sociability /,səʊʃə'bɪlɪtɪ/ *n.* общительность.

sociable /'səʊʃəb(ə)l/ *adj.* общительный, компанейский (*coll.*).

social /'səʊʃ(ə)l/ *n.* вечеринка.
● *adj.* **1** (*pert. to the community*) общественный, социальный; **~ contract** общественный договор; **S~ Democrat** социал-демократ; **~ sciences** общественные науки; **~ security** (*system*) социальное обеспечение; (*money received*) пособие; **he's on ~ security** он получает пособие; **~ services** система социального обслуживания; **~ worker** социальный работник.
2 (*pert. to ~ relationships*): **one's ~ equals** социально равные.
3 (*convivial*): **~ gathering** дружеская встреча; **~ evening** вечеринка; **I have met him ~ly** я встречался с ним в обществе.
● *cpd.* **~-democratic** *adj.* социал-демократический.

socialism /'səʊʃə,lɪz(ə)m/ *n.* социализм.

socialist /'səʊʃəlɪst/ *n.* социалист (*fem.* -ка).
● *adj.* социалистический.

socialite /'səʊʃə,laɪt/ *n.* светская знаменитость.

socialization /,səʊʃəlaɪ'zeɪʃ(ə)n/ *n.* социализация; обобществление.

socialize /'səʊʃə,laɪz/ *v.t.* обобществ|ля́ть, -и́ть; **~d medicine** (*US*) государственное медицинское обслуживание.
● *v.i.* (*coll., go about socially*) вести (*impf.*) светский образ жизни; (*maintain social relations*) поддерживать (*impf.*) светское общение (с кем-н.).

society /sə'saɪətɪ/ *n.* общество; (*association*) общество, объединение, организация; (*e.g. students'*) клуб, кружок; **high ~** высшее общество; **S~ of Friends** «Общество друзей», квакеры (*m. pl.*).

socio-economic /,səʊsɪəʊ,iːkə'nɒmɪk/ *adj.* социально-экономический.

sociological /,səʊsɪə'lɒdʒɪk(ə)l/, /,səʊʃɪ-/ *adj.* социологический.

sociologist /,səʊsɪ'ɒlədʒɪst/, /,səʊʃɪ-/ *n.* социолог.

sociology /,səʊsɪ'ɒlədʒɪ/, /,səʊʃɪ-/ *n.* социология.

sock¹ /sɒk/ *n.* **1** (*short stocking*) носок; **pull up one's ~s** (*lit.*) подтя́|гивать, -нуть носки; (*fig.*) взять (*pf.*) себя в руки, подтянуться (*pf.*); **put a ~ in it** (*Br.*) заткнуться (*pf.*) (*sl.*); **ankle ~s** носки (*m. pl.*); **knee ~s** гольфы (*m. pl.*).
2 (*inner sole*) стелька.

sock² /sɒk/ (*sl.*) *n.* (*blow*) удар; **give s.o. a ~ on the nose** да|ва́ть, -ть кому-н. по носу.
● *v.t.*: **I ~ed him in the jaw** я дал ему в морду (*sl.*).

socket /'sɒkɪt/ *n.* **1** (*anat.*) впадина; **eye ~** глазная впадина, глазница; **wrench s.o.'s arm out of its ~**

вывора́чивать, вы́вернуть кому́-н. ру́ку. **2** (*for plug*) розе́тка; (*for bulb*) патро́н.

● *cpd.* **~-joint** *n.* шарни́рное соедине́ние.

socle /'səʊk(ə)l/ *n.* цо́коль (*m.*).

Socratic /sə'krætɪk/ *adj.* сокра́товский; **~ method** сократи́ческий ме́тод.

sod¹ /sɒd/ *n.* дёрн.

sod² /sɒd/ (*Br.*) *n.* (*sl.*) сво́лочь (*f.*); **silly ~** идио́т; **S~'s Law** зако́н по́длости, зако́н бутербро́да.

● *v.i.* (**sodded, sodding**) **~ off**: **I told him to ~ off** я его́ посла́л; **~ off!** иди́ на фиг!

soda /'səʊdə/ *n.* **1** со́да; углеки́слый на́трий; **baking ~** пищева́я/хле́бная со́да; **washing ~** стира́льная/кристалли́ческая со́да. **2** (**~-water**) со́довая/газиро́ванная вода́; газиро́вка (*coll.*).

● *cpds.* **~-bread** *n.* хлеб, вы́печенный на со́де; **~-fountain** *n.* (*machine*) сатура́тор; (*counter*) сто́йка для прода́жи газиро́ванной воды́; **~-siphon** *n.* сифо́н (для газиро́ванной воды́); **~-water** *n.* со́довая/газиро́ванная вода́; газиро́вка (*coll.*).

sodden /'sɒd(ə)n/ *adj.* (*drenched*) промо́кший; (*steeped*) пропи́танный.

sodium /'səʊdɪəm/ *n.* на́трий.

sodomite /'sɒdə,maɪt/ *n.* педера́ст, мужело́жец, содоми́т.

sodomy /'sɒdəmɪ/ *n.* педера́стия, мужело́жство, содоми́я; (*bestiality*) скотоло́жство.

sofa /'səʊfə/ *n.* дива́н; **~ bed** дива́н-крова́ть.

Sofia /'səʊfɪə/ *n.* Софи́я.

soft /sɒft/ *adj.* **1** мя́гкий; **~ colour** (*Br.*), **color** (*US*) нея́ркий цвет; **~ cover** (*of book*) мя́гкий переплёт; **~ goods** (*Br.*) тексти́льные изде́лия; **~ furnishings** (*Br.*) оби́вочные материа́лы (*m. pl.*), драпиро́вки (*f. pl.*); **a ~ light** мя́гкий свет; **~ palate** мя́гкое нёбо, нёбная занаве́ска; **~ toy** мя́гкая игру́шка; **~ water** мя́гкая вода́; **~ drink** безалкого́льный напи́ток; **~ drugs** сла́бые нарко́тики; **~ fruit** (*Br.*) я́года; **~ pedal** ле́вая педа́ль; **~** (*gentle*) **voice** мя́гкий/не́жный го́лос; **~** (*low-pitched*) **voice** ти́хий го́лос; **~ sign** (*gram.*) мя́гкий знак.

2 (*gentle, compassionate*) мя́гкий; отзы́вчивый; **have a ~ spot for s.o.** пита́ть (*impf.*) сла́бость к кому́-н.; (*indulgent*) мя́гкий, нестро́гий; **she is too ~ with her children** она́ недоста́точно строга́ с детьми́.

3 (*flabby*) дря́блый.

4 (*coll., easy*): **he has a ~ job** у него́ лёгкая рабо́та.

5 (*coll., ~ in the head, stupid*) глупова́тый.

6: **~ currency** неконверти́руемая валю́та.

7 (*phot.*) неконтра́стный.

● *cpds.* **~-boiled** *adj.*: **~-boiled egg** яйцо́ всмя́тку; **~-headed** *adj.* глупова́тый; **~-hearted** *adj.* мягкосерде́чный; **~-pedal** *v.t.* (*fig.*) смягч|а́ть, -и́ть; **~-soap** *v.t.* (*coll.*) льстить (*impf.*) + *d.*; **~-spoken** *adj.* с мя́гким го́лосом; ти́хий; **~ware** *n.* (*comput.*) програ́ммное обеспе́чение; **~wood** *n.* мя́гкая древеси́на.

soften /'sɒf(ə)n/ *v.t.* смягч|а́ть, -и́ть; (*of voice*) пон|ижа́ть, -и́зить.

● *v.i.* смягч|а́ться, -и́ться.

● *with adv.*: **~ up** *v.t.*: **~ s.o. up** (*fig.*) осл|абля́ть, -а́бить чьё-н. сопротивле́ние.

softener /'sɒf(ə)nə(r)/ *n.* (*for water etc.*) умягчи́тель (*m.*).

softie /'sɒftɪ/ = **softy**

softness /'sɒftnɪs/ *n.* мя́гкость.

softy /'sɒftɪ/ *n.* (*coll.*) (*soft-hearted person*) мя́гкий челове́к; (*weak person*) тря́пка, слаба́к.

soggy /'sɒgɪ/ *adj.* (**soggier, soggiest**) сыро́й, вла́жный; **~ pastry** пло́хо пропечённое те́сто; **~ ground** сыра́я/отсыре́вшая земля́.

so(h) /səʊ/ *n.* (*mus.*) пя́тая но́та мажо́рный га́ммы; (*the note G*) соль (*nt. indecl.*).

soil¹ /sɔɪl/ *n.* **1** (*earth*) по́чва; **~ science** почвове́дение. **2** (*fig., country*) земля́; **on foreign ~** на чужо́й земле́.

soil² /sɔɪl/ *v.t.* па́чкать, за-/ис-/вы-; **~ed linen** гря́зное бельё.

● *cpd.* **~-pipe** *n.* канализацио́нная труба́.

soirée /'swɑːreɪ/ *n.* зва́ный ве́чер, суаре́ (*indecl.*).

sojourn /'sɒdʒ(ə)n/, /-dʒɜːn/, /'sʌ-/ (*liter.*) *n.* (вре́менное) пребыва́ние.

● *v.i.* пребыва́ть, (вре́менно) жить, прожива́ть (*all impf.*).

solace /'sɒləs/ *n.* утеше́ние, отра́да.

● *v.t.* ут|еша́ть, -е́шить.

solar /'səʊlə(r)/ *adj.* со́лнечный; **~ flare** протубера́нец; **~ panel** со́лнечная батаре́я; **~ plexus** со́лнечное сплете́ние; **~ system** со́лнечная систе́ма.

solari|um /sə'leərɪəm/ (*pl.* **~ums** *or* **~a**) *n.* соля́рий.

sold /səʊld/ *past and p.p. of* ⇒**sell**

solder /'səʊldə(r)/, /'sɒ-/ *n.* припо́й.

● *v.t.* пая́ть (*impf.*); **~ something to something** припа́|ивать, -я́ть что-н. к чему́-н.; **~ together** спа́|ивать, -я́ть; **~ing-iron** пая́льник.

soldier /'səʊldʒə(r)/ *n.* солда́т; (*liter.*) бое́ц, боре́ц; **play at ~s** игра́ть (*impf.*) в солда́тики; **toy ~s** оловя́нные солда́тики; **the Unknown S~** Неизве́стный солда́т; **~ of fortune** (*mercenary*) наёмник; **private ~** рядово́й, бое́ц; **a great ~** вели́кий полково́дец.

● *v.i.* служи́ть (*impf.*) (в а́рмии); **~ on** (*fig., persevere doggedly*) не сдава́ться (*impf.*).

soldierly /'səʊldʒəlɪ/ *adj.* солда́тский; (*military*) вое́нный; **in a ~ manner** по-солда́тски.

soldiery /'səʊldʒərɪ/ *n.* солда́ты (*m. pl.*); солдатня́ (*pej.*).

sole¹ /səʊl/ *n.* (*fish*) морско́й язы́к, соле́я.

sole² /səʊl/ *n.* (*of foot*) ступня́, подо́шва (*coll.*); (*of shoe*) подо́шва, подмётка.

● *v.t.* подб|ива́ть, -и́ть (*or* ста́вить, по-) подмётку на (+*a.*).

sole³ /səʊl/ *adj.* (*only*) еди́нственный; **~ agent** еди́нственный представи́тель; (*exclusive*) исключи́тельный.

solecism /'sɒlɪ,sɪz(ə)m/ *n.* (*of language*) солеци́зм; гру́бая (языкова́я) оши́бка; (*of behaviour*) гру́бая вы́ходка, гру́бость.

solely /'səʊllɪ/ *adv.* то́лько, еди́нственно, исключи́тельно; **he is ~ responsible** отве́тственность лежи́т на нём одно́м.

solemn /'sɒləm/ *adj.* торже́ственный; (*serious*) серье́зный, ва́жный; **he put on a ~ face** он сде́лал серьёзное лицо́.

solemnity /sə'lemnɪtɪ/ *n.* торже́ственность; (*gravity*) ва́жность; (*of appearance*) серьёзность.

solemnization /,sɒləmnaɪ'zeɪʃ(ə)n/ *n.* пра́зднование; **~ of marriage** церемо́ния бракосочета́ния; венча́ние.

solemnize /'sɒləm,naɪz/ *v.t.* (*perform*) соверш|а́ть, -и́ть; (*celebrate*) пра́здновать, от-; торже́ственно отм|еча́ть, -е́тить.

solenoid /'səʊlə,nɔɪd/, /'sɒl-/ *n.* солено́ид.

sol-fa /'sɒlfɑː/ *n.* сольфе́джио (*indecl.*).

soli /'səʊlɪ/ *pl. of* ⇒**solo**

solicit /sə'lɪsɪt/ *v.t.* (**solicited, soliciting**) **1** (*petition, importune*): **~ s.o.'s help** проси́ть, по- кого́-н. о по́мощи. **2** (*ask for*): **~ favours** (*Br.*), **favors** (*US*) **of s.o.** выпра́шивать (*impf.*) у кого́-н. ми́лости. **3** (*accost*) прист|ава́ть, -а́ть к + *d.*

● *v.i.* (**solicited, soliciting**) (*of prostitute*) пристава́ть (*impf.*) к мужчи́нам.

solicitation /sə,lɪsɪ'teɪʃ(ə)n/ *n.* про́сьба, хода́тайство.

solicitor /sə'lɪsɪtə(r)/ *n.* (*Br.*) адвока́т, соли́ситор.

solicitous /sə'lɪsɪtəs/ *adj.* забо́тливый, внима́тельный; **she is ~ for, about your safety** она́ забо́тится о ва́шей безопа́сности.

solicitude /sə'lɪsɪ,tjuːd/ *n.* забо́тливость.

solid /'sɒlɪd/ *n.* (*phys.*) твёрдое те́ло; (*pl., food*) твёрдая пи́ща.

● *adj.* (**solider, solidest**) **1** (*not liquid or fluid*) твёрдый; **~ food** твёрдая пи́ща; **~ fuel** твёрдое то́пливо; **become ~** тверде́ть, за-.

2 (*not hollow*) це́льный, непо́лый; **~ sphere** це́льный шар.

3 (*homogeneous*): **~ silver** чи́стое серебро́.

4 (*unbroken*): **12 hours' ~ sleep** 12 часо́в непреры́вного сна; **a ~ line** сплошна́я черта́; **it rained for 3 ~ days** дождь лил три дня подря́д.

5 (*firmly built, substantial*) про́чный; **a man of ~ build** челове́к кре́пкого/пло́тного телосложе́ния.

6 (*sound, reliable*) соли́дный;

надёжный; **a ~ business** соли́дное де́ло; **~ arguments** основа́тельные до́воды; **~ good sense** настоя́щий здра́вый смы́сл.
7 (*unanimous, united*) единоду́шный; **the meeting was ~(ly) against him** собра́ние единоду́шно вы́ступило про́тив него́.
8 (*pert. to ~s*): **~ geometry** стереоме́трия; **~(-state) physics** фи́зика твёрдых те́л; **~ angle** теле́сный/простра́нственный у́гол.

solidarity /ˌsɒlɪˈdærɪtɪ/ *n.* солида́рность; **~ of purpose** еди́нство це́лей; **~ of feeling** единоду́шие.

solidi /ˈsɒlɪˌdaɪ/ *pl. of* ⇒**solidus**

solidification /səˌlɪdɪfɪˈkeɪʃ(ə)n/ *n.* отверде́ние, затверде́ние.

solidify /səˈlɪdɪˌfaɪ/ *v.t.* де́лать, с- твёрдым.
● *v.i.* тверде́ть, за-; заст|ыва́ть, -ы́ть.

solidity /səˈlɪdɪtɪ/ *n.* твёрдость; (*sturdiness*) про́чность; (*reliability*) надёжность; (*soundness*) основа́тельность; (*unity*) еди́нство.

soli|dus /ˈsɒlɪdəs/ *n.* (*pl.* **~di** /-ˌdaɪ/) (*Br., stroke*) дробь; кося́я/дели́тельная черта́.

soliloquize /səˈlɪləkwaɪz/ *v.i.* произноси́ть (*impf.*) моноло́г.

soliloquy /səˈlɪləkwɪ/ *n.* моноло́г.

solipsism /ˈsɒlɪpˌsɪz(ə)m/ *n.* солипси́зм.

solipsist /ˈsɒlɪpsɪst/ *n.* солипси́ст.

solipsistic /ˌsɒlɪpˈsɪstɪk/ *adj.* солипси́ческий.

solitaire /ˈsɒlɪˌteə(r)/ *n.* (*gem*) солите́р; (*game*) пасья́нс.

solitary /ˈsɒlɪtərɪ/ *n.* (*recluse*) отше́льни|к (*fem.* -ца).
● *adj.* (*secluded*) уединённый; (*lonely*) одино́кий; **~ confinement** одино́чное заключе́ние; (*single*) едини́чный, еди́нственный; **a ~ instance** едини́чный слу́чай.

solitude /ˈsɒlɪˌtjuːd/ *n.* (*being alone*) уедине́ние, одино́чество; **live in ~** жить (*impf.*) в уедине́нии; (*lonely place*) уединённое ме́сто.

solo /ˈsəʊləʊ/ *n.* (*pl.* **~s;** *sense 1*: *pl.* **~s** *or* **soli**) **1** (*mus.*) со́ло (*indecl.*); **music for ~ flute** со́льная му́зыка для фле́йты. **2** (*aeron.*) самостоя́тельный полёт.
● *adj.* со́льный; (*aeron.*) самостоя́тельный.
● *adv.* (*alone*): **fly ~** лета́ть (*indet.*), лете́ть (*det.*) самостоя́тельно/в одино́чку.

soloist /ˈsəʊləʊɪst/ *n.* соли́ст (*fem.* -ка).

Solomon /ˈsɒləmən/ *n.*: **the ~s, the ~ Islands** Соломо́новы острова́ (*m. pl.*).

solstice /ˈsɒlstɪs/ *n.* солнцестоя́ние.

solubility /ˌsɒljʊˈbɪlɪtɪ/ *n.* раствори́мость.

soluble /ˈsɒljʊb(ə)l/ *adj.* (*dissolvable*) раствори́мый; (*solvable*) разреши́мый.

solution /səˈluːʃ(ə)n/, /-ˈljuːʃ(ə)n/ *n.* **1** (*dissolving*) растворе́ние; (*result of this*) раство́р; **strong/weak ~** кре́пкий/сла́бый раство́р; **rubber ~** рези́новый клей. **2** (*solving*) реше́ние; (*answer*) реше́ние, вы́ход.

solve /sɒlv/ *v.t.*: **~ an equation/problem** реш|а́ть, -и́ть уравне́ние/зада́чу; **~ a mystery** раскр|ыва́ть, -ы́ть та́йну; **~ a difficulty** на|ходи́ть, -йти́ вы́ход из затрудне́ния.

solvency /ˈsɒlv(ə)nsɪ/ *n.* платёжеспосо́бность.

solvent /ˈsɒlv(ə)nt/ *n.* раствори́тель (*m.*); **~ abuse** токсикома́ния; **~ abuser** токсикома́н.
● *adj.* (*chem.*) растворя́ющий; (*fin.*) платёжеспосо́бный.

Somali /səˈmɑːlɪ/ *n.* (*pl.* **~** *or* **~s**) (*person*) сомали́|ец (*fem.* -йка); (*language*) язы́к Сомали́.
● *adj.* сомали́йский.

Somalia /səˈmɑːlɪə/ *n.* Сомали́ (*nt. indecl.*); Сомали́йская Респу́блика.

somatic /səˈmætɪk/ *adj.* теле́сный, сомати́ческий.

sombre /ˈsɒmbə(r)/ (*US also* **somber**) *adj.* (*gloomy*) угрю́мый; (*dismal*) мра́чный; (*overcast*) па́смурный.

sombreness /ˈsɒmbənɪs/ (*US also* **somberness**) *n.* угрю́мость; мра́чность; па́смурность.

sombrero /sɒmˈbreərəʊ/ *n.* (*pl.* **~s**) сомбре́ро (*indecl.*).

some /sʌm/ *pron.* **1** (*of persons*) не́которые, одни́; **~ say yes, ~ say no** не́которые говоря́т да, не́которые — нет; одни́ говоря́т да, други́е — нет; **~ left and others stayed** одни́ ушли́, други́е оста́лись; **~ (people) were late** не́которые опозда́ли; **~ of these girls** не́которые/ко́е-кто из э́тих де́вушек.
2 (*of things*) (*an indefinite number*) не́сколько; **those are nice apples; can I have ~?** каки́е хоро́шие я́блоки — мо́жно (мне) взять не́сколько?; **I have ~ already** у меня́ уже́ есть не́сколько; (*an indefinite amount*): **have ~ more!** возьми́те ещё!; **I already have ~** у меня́ есть.
3 (*a part*) часть; **I have ~ of the documents** часть докуме́нтов у меня́ есть; **I agree with ~ of what you said** я согла́сен ко́е с чем из того́, что вы сказа́ли; я части́чно согла́сен с тем, что вы сказа́ли.
4 (*coll.*): **and then ~!** (*more than that*) ещё как!
● *adj.* **1** (*definite though unspecified*) како́й-то; **~ fool has locked the door** како́й-то дура́к за́пер дверь; **I read it in ~ book (or other)** я чита́л э́то в како́й-то/одно́й кни́ге; **one must make ~ (sort of) attempt** на́до сде́лать хоть каку́ю-нибудь попы́тку; **~ day, ~ time** когда́-нибудь; **is this ~ kind of joke?** э́то что — како́го-то ро́да шу́тка?; **we shall find ~ way round the difficulty** мы найдём како́й-нибудь вы́ход из тру́дного положе́ния.
2 (*no matter what*) како́й-нибудь, како́й-либо; **he is looking for ~ work** он и́щет (каку́ю-нибудь) рабо́ту.
3 (*one or two*) ко́е-каки́е (*pl.*); (*a certain amount*: *may be expr. by g.*): **I bought ~ milk** я купи́л молока́; (*a certain number*) не́сколько (*or untranslated*): **I bought ~ envelopes** я купи́л конве́рты; **~ books** не́сколько книг; **I gave him ~ advice** я ему́ ко́е-что посове́товал; **~ more** ещё (+*g.*); **~ distance away** на не́котором расстоя́нии; **for ~ time now** с не́которого вре́мени; **it takes ~ courage to ...** тре́буется нема́ло му́жества, что́бы. . .; **that takes ~ doing** э́то тре́бует не́которого уси́лия; **~ work is pleasant** быва́ет/попада́ется прия́тная рабо́та.
4 (*in ~ sense or degree; to a certain extent*): **that is ~ proof** э́то в како́й-то сте́пени мо́жет служи́ть доказа́тельством; **it served as ~ guide to his intentions** э́то в не́которой/изве́стной сте́пени ука́зывало на его́ наме́рения.
5 (*approximately*) приме́рно, о́коло; **we waited ~ 20 minutes** мы жда́ли о́коло двацати́ мину́т/мину́т два́дцать (*coll.*).
6 (*coll., expr. admiration etc.*) вот э́то; вот так; **~ speed!** вот э́то ско́рость!; **he's ~ doctor!** э́то настоя́щий врач!

somebody /ˈsʌmbədɪ/ *n.*: **a ~** ва́жная персо́на, ши́шка (*coll.*).
● *pron.* (*also* **someone**) (*in particular*) кто́-то; (*only in nom.*) не́кто; **there is ~ in the cellar** в по́гребе кто́-то есть; (*no matter who*) кто́-нибудь, кто́-либо; **I want ~ to help me** я хочу́, что́бы кто́-нибудь мне помо́г; **~ else can do it** кто́-нибудь друго́й мо́жет э́то сде́лать.

somehow /ˈsʌmhaʊ/ *adv.* (*no matter how*) ка́к-нибудь; так и́ли ина́че; **we shall manage ~** мы ка́к-нибудь спра́вимся; (*in some unspecified way*) ка́к-то, каки́м-то о́бразом; **he found out my name ~** он каки́м-то о́бразом узна́л, как меня́ зову́т; (*for some reason*): **~ I never liked him** он мне почему́-то никогда́ не нра́вился.

someone /ˈsʌmwʌn/ = **somebody** *pron.*

someplace /ˈsʌmpleɪs/ (*US*) = **somewhere**

somersault /ˈsʌməˌsɒlt/ *n.* (*in the air*) са́льто (*indecl.*); **turn a double ~** де́лать, с- двойно́е са́льто; (*on the ground*) кувыро́к.
● *v.i.* кувырк|а́ться, -ну́ться; де́лать, с- са́льто.

something /ˈsʌmθɪŋ/ *pron.* (*definite*) что́-то; (*only in nom.*) не́что; (*indefinite*) что́-нибудь, что́-либо; **I must get ~ to eat** я до́лжен что́-нибудь пое́сть; **she lectures in ~ or other** она́ чита́ет ле́кции по како́му-то (там) предме́ту; **I have seen ~ of his work** я ви́дел ко́е-каки́е из его́ рабо́т; **there is ~ in what you say** в том, что вы говори́те, есть что́-то; **there is ~ about him** в нём что́-то тако́е есть; **it is ~ of an improvement** э́то не́который прогре́сс; **it is ~ to have got so far** сла́ва Бо́гу, хоть сто́лько сде́лали; **you have ~ there** в э́том вы пра́вы; **he thinks he is ~** он высо́кого мне́ния о себе́; **we managed to see ~ of each other** нам удава́лось вре́мя от вре́мени встреча́ться; **I think I'm on to ~** ка́жется, я что́-то нашёл; **she has a cold or ~** у неё то ли просту́да, то ли ещё что-то; **he is a surgeon or ~** он хиру́рг и́ли что-то в э́том ро́де.

● *adv.*: **he left ~ like a million** он оста́вил что́-то поря́дка миллио́на; **his house looks ~ like a prison** его́ дом не́сколько похо́ж на тюрьму́; **~ awful** (*coll., frightfully*) ужа́сно.

sometime /ˈsʌmtaɪm/ *adj.* (*liter.*) бы́вший.

● *adv.* (*in the future*) когда́-нибудь, когда́-либо; **~ soon** ка́к-нибудь, ско́ро; **come and see us ~** приходи́те к нам ка́к-нибудь; (*in the past*) когда́-то.

sometimes /ˈsʌmtaɪmz/ *adv.* иногда́; **~ ... ~ ...** то... то....

somewhat /ˈsʌmwɒt/ *pron.*: **he is ~ of a connoisseur** он в не́котором ро́де знато́к.

● *adv.* ка́к-то, не́сколько, дово́льно; **he is ~ off-hand** он де́ржится ка́к-то небре́жно; **he was ~ hard to follow** его́ бы́ло дово́льно тру́дно понима́ть; **the book loses ~ in translation** кни́га не́сколько прои́грывает в перево́де.

somewhere /ˈsʌmweə(r)/ *adv.* **1** (*US also* **someplace**) (*place, specific*) где́-то; (*place, anywhere*) где́-нибудь, где́-либо; **~ else** где́-то в друго́м ме́сте; где́-то ещё; (*motion, specific*) куда́-то; **I am going ~ tomorrow** я за́втра куда́-то иду́; **the noise came from ~ over there** звук разда́лся где́-то там; (*motion, anywhere*) куда́-нибудь, куда́-либо.
2 (*approximately*) о́коло + *g.*; что́-то/где́-то о́коло + *g.* (*coll.*); **it is ~ about 6 o'clock** сейча́с (что́-то) о́коло шести́.

somnambulism /sɒmˈnæmbjʊˌlɪz(ə)m/ *n.* лунати́зм, сомнамбули́зм.

somnambulist /sɒmˈnæmbjʊlɪst/ *n.* луна́т|ик (*fem.* -и́чка); сомна́мбула (*c.g.*).

somnolence /ˈsɒmnələns/ *n.* сонли́вость.

somnolent /ˈsɒmnələnt/ *adj.* (*drowsy*) со́нный, сонли́вый; (*inducing sleep*) снотво́рный.

son /sʌn/ *n.* сын (*pl.* -овья́, (*rhet.*) -ы́); **~ of a bitch** (*sl.*) су́кин сын; (*as form of address*): **(my) ~** сыно́к.

● *cpd.* **~-in-law** *n.* зять (*m.*).

sonar /ˈsəʊnɑː(r)/ *n.* гидролока́тор, сона́р.

sonata /səˈnɑːtə/ *n.* сона́та; **~ form** сона́тная фо́рма.

sonatina /ˌsɒnəˈtiːnə/ *n.* (*mus.*) сонати́на.

sonde /sɒnd/ *n.* зонд.

son et lumière /ˌsɒneɪˈluːmjeə(r)/ *n.* светозвукоспекта́кль (*m.*).

song /sɒŋ/ *n.* **1** (*singing*) пе́ние; **burst into ~** запе́ть (*pf.*). **2** (*words set to music; also bird's ~*) пе́сня; **make a ~ (and dance) about something** (*coll.*) подн|има́ть, -я́ть шум из-за чего́-н.; **he bought it for a ~** он купи́л э́то за бесценок; **on ~** (*Br. coll.*) в фо́рме.

● *cpds.* **~-bird** *n.* пе́вчая пти́ца; **~-book** *n.* пе́сенник; **~writer** *n.* пе́сенник.

songster /ˈsɒŋstə(r)/ *n.* (*bird*) пе́вчая пти́ца; (*singer*) пе́ве́ц; (*writer*) пе́сенник.

songstress /ˈsɒŋstrɪs/ *n.* (*singer*) певи́ца; (*writer*) пе́сенник.

sonic /ˈsɒnɪk/ *adj.* звуково́й, акусти́ческий; **~ bang, boom** сверхзвуково́й хлопо́к.

sonnet /ˈsɒnɪt/ *n.* соне́т.

sonny /ˈsʌnɪ/ *n.* (*coll.*) сыно́к, сыно́чек.

sonority /səˈnɒrɪtɪ/ *n.* зву́чность.

sonorous /ˈsɒnərəs/, /səˈnɔːrəs/ *adj.* зву́чный.

soon /suːn/ *adv.* **1** (*in a short while*) ско́ро, вскоре; **it will ~ be dark** ско́ро стемне́ет; **he ~ recovered** он вско́ре попра́вился; **~ after** че́рез коро́ткое вре́мя; **~ after the meeting** вско́ре по́сле собра́ния; **write ~!** напиши́те поскоре́е!; **as ~ as possible** как мо́жно скоре́е.
2 (*early*) ра́но; **we arrived too ~** мы прие́хали сли́шком ра́но; **how ~ can you come?** когда́ вы смо́жете прие́хать?; **the ~er the better** чем ра́ньше, тем лу́чше; **~er or later** ра́но и́ли по́здно.
3: **as ~ as** как то́лько; **as ~ as I saw him, I recognized him** я узна́л его́, как то́лько уви́дел; **no ~er had he arrived than he wanted to borrow money** не успе́л он прие́хать, как стал проси́ть де́нег взаймы́; **no ~er said than done** ска́зано — сде́лано.
4 (*willingly*): **I would as ~ stay at home** я предпочёл бы оста́ться до́ма; **I would ~er die than permit it** я скоре́е умру́, чем допущу́ э́то; **what would you ~er do, go now or wait?** что вы предпочита́ете — уйти́ и́ли подожда́ть?

soot /sʊt/ *n.* са́жа, ко́поть.

soothe /suːð/ *v.t.* (*calm*) успок|а́ивать, -о́ить; (*relieve*) облегч|а́ть, -и́ть.

soothing /ˈsuːðɪŋ/ *adj.* (*tone, words*) утеши́тельный; (*cream, bath*) успокои́тельный.

soothsayer /ˈsuːθˌseɪə(r)/ *n.* предсказа́тель (*fem.* -ница).

sooty /ˈsʊtɪ/ *adj.* (**sootier, sootiest**) (*blackened with soot*) закопчённый, закопте́лый; (*black as soot*) чёрный как са́жа; (*containing soot*): **~ deposit** слой са́жи.

sop /sɒp/ *n.* **1** (*piece of bread*) кусо́к хле́ба, обмакну́тый во что-н. **2** (*fig.*) пода́чка; **as a ~ to his pride** что́бы поте́шить его́ самолю́бие.

● *v.t.* (**sopped, sopping**): **~up** (*absorb*) впи́тывать, впита́ть; **he ~ped up the gravy with some bread** он промокну́л со́ус хле́бом.

● *v.i.* (**sopped, sopping**): **the shirt was ~ping wet** руба́шка промо́кла насквозь; **we got ~ping wet** мы промо́кли до ни́тки.

sophism /ˈsɒfɪz(ə)m/ *n.* софи́зм.

sophist /ˈsɒfɪst/ *n.* софи́ст.

sophistic(al) /səˈfɪstɪk(ə)l/ *adj.* софи́стский; (*of person*) скло́нный к софи́стике.

sophisticate[1] /səˈfɪstɪkət/ *n.* искушённый челове́к.

sophisticate[2] /səˈfɪstɪˌkeɪt/ *v.t.* **1** (*complicate*) усложн|я́ть, -и́ть; **~d techniques** сло́жная/изощрённая те́хника; **~d weapons** сло́жные ви́ды ору́жия. **2** (*mislead*) запу́т|ывать, -ать. **3** (*refine*) утонч|а́ть, -и́ть; (*make less natural, simple*) лиш|а́ть, -и́ть простоты́/есте́ственности; **~d taste** утончённый/изощрённый вкус; **~d manners** изы́сканные мане́ры.
4 (*distort*) преврáтно истолко́в|ывать, -а́ть; (*adulterate*) разба|вля́ть, -а́вить.

sophistication /səˌfɪstɪˈkeɪʃ(ə)n/ *n.* (*refinement*) утончённость, искушённость.

sophistry /ˈsɒfɪstrɪ/ *n.* софи́стика; (*sophism*) софи́зм.

sophomore /ˈsɒfəˌmɔː(r)/ *n.* (*US*) студе́нт-второкýрсни|к (*fem.* -ца).

soporific /ˌsɒpəˈrɪfɪk/ *n.* снотво́рное (сре́дство).

● *adj.* снотво́рный, усыпля́ющий.

soppy /ˈsɒpɪ/ *adj.* (**soppier, soppiest**) (*Br. coll.*) (*sentimental*) сентимента́льный.

soprano /səˈprɑːnəʊ/ *n.* (*pl.* **~s**) (*singer*) сопра́но (*f. indecl.*); (*voice, part*) сопра́но (*nt. indecl.*); (*attr.*) сопра́новый, сопра́нный; **boy ~** ди́скант.

sorbet /ˈsɔːbeɪ/, /-bɪt/ *n.* шербе́т.

sorcerer /ˈsɔːsərə(r)/ *n.* колду́н, волше́бник.

sorceress /ˈsɔːsərɪs/ *n.* колду́нья, волше́бница.

sorcery /ˈsɔːsərɪ/ *n.* колдовство́, волшебство́.

sordid /ˈsɔːdɪd/ *adj.* (*squalid, poor*) убо́гий, жа́лкий; (*filthy*) гря́зный; **a ~ affair** гну́сная исто́рия; (*low, base*) по́длый.

sordidness /ˈsɔːdɪdnɪs/ *n.* убо́гость, убо́жество; грязь; по́длость; (*meanness*) ни́зость.

sore /sɔː(r)/ *n.* боля́чка, я́зва; (*fig.*): **re-open old ~s** береди́ть, раз- ста́рые ра́ны.

● *adj.* **1** (*painful*): **a ~ tooth** больно́й зуб; **I have a ~** (*grazed*) **knee** я ссади́л себе́ коле́но; **he has a ~ throat** у него́ боли́т го́рло; **I woke up with a ~ head** я просну́лся с головно́й бо́лью; **it is a ~ point with him** э́то у него́ больно́е ме́сто; **a ~ subject** больно́й вопро́с; **touch s.o. on a ~ place, spot** (*fig.*) зад|ева́ть, -е́ть кого́-нибудь за живо́е.
2 (*US coll., aggrieved*) раздражённый, оби́женный; **he was ~ at not being invited** он оби́делся, что его́ не позва́ли.
3 (*acute, extreme*) кра́йний; **he is in ~ need of money** он кра́йне нужда́ется в деньга́х; **I was ~ly tempted** у меня́ бы́ло си́льное искуше́ние.

soreness /ˈsɔːnɪs/ *n.* (*painfulness*) боль; (*grudge*) оби́да.

sorghum /ˈsɔːgəm/ *n.* (*bot.*) со́рго (*indecl.*).

sorority /səˈrɒrɪtɪ/ *n.* (*US*) же́нская организа́ция/общи́на.

sorrel[1] /ˈsɒr(ə)l/ *n.* (*bot.*) щаве́ль (*m.*).

sorrel[2] /ˈsɒr(ə)l/ *n.* (*horse*) гнеда́я ло́шадь.

S

● *adj.* гнедо́й.

sorrow /ˈsɒrəʊ/ *n.* (*sadness, grief*) печа́ль, го́ресть; (*extreme* ~) скорбь; **more in ~ than in anger** скоре́й с тоско́й, чем с гне́вом; (*regret*) сожале́ние; **express ~ for** выража́ть, вы́разить сожале́ние о + *p.*; **to my ~** к моему́ огорче́нию; (*sad experience*) го́ре, невзго́да; **all these ~s broke his heart** все э́ти го́рести/невзго́ды сломи́ли его́.

● *v.i.* горева́ть (*impf.*); **~ for, over s.o.** опла́кивать (*impf.*) кого́-н.

sorrowful /ˈsɒrəʊˌfʊl/ *adj.* печа́льный, ско́рбный, го́рестный.

sorry /ˈsɒrɪ/ *adj.* (**sorrier, sorriest**)
1 (*regretful*): **be ~ for something** сожале́ть (*impf.*) о чём-н., жале́ть, по- о чём-н.; **I was ~ I had to do it** я (со)жале́л, что пришло́сь так поступи́ть; **aren't you ~ for what you've done?** вы не раска́иваетесь в том, что вы сде́лали?; **say you're ~!** попроси́ проще́ния!; **you'll be ~ for this one day** когда́-нибудь вы об э́том пожале́ете; **I'm ~ to hear it** мне приско́рбно слы́шать э́то; **we were ~ to hear of your father's death** мы с гру́стью узна́ли о сме́рти ва́шего отца́; **~!** винова́т!; прости́те!; извини́те!; **I'm ~ I came** я жале́ю, что пришёл; **~, I'm busy** извини́те, но я за́нят.
2 (*expr. pity, sympathy*): **feel ~ for s.o.** испы́тывать (*impf.*) жа́лость к кому́-н.; жале́ть, по- кого́-н.; сочу́вствовать, по- кому́-н.; **it's the children I feel ~ for** кого́ мне жаль — так э́то дете́й; **feel ~ for o.s.** жале́ть (*impf.*) себя́; быть испо́лненным жа́лости к себе́.
3 (*wretched, pitiful*) жа́лкий; **in a ~ state** в жа́лком состоя́нии.

sort /sɔːt/ *n.* **1** (*kind, class, category, species*) род, сорт, разря́д, вид; **we have all ~s of books** (*or* **books of every ~**) у нас есть вся́кого ро́да кни́ги; **people of that ~** тако́го ро́да лю́ди; **that's the ~ of book I want** и́менно таку́ю кни́гу мне и на́до; **a new ~ of bicycle** но́вый тип велосипе́да; **he is not the ~ (of person) to complain** он не тако́го ро́да челове́к, что́бы жа́ловаться; он не из тех, кто жа́луется; **what ~ of man is he?** что он за челове́к?; **a good ~** хоро́ший челове́к/ма́лый; **what ~ of music do you like?** каку́ю му́зыку вы лю́бите?; **nothing of the ~** ничего́ подо́бного; **a ~ of war** своего́ ро́да война́; **a ~ of novel, a novel of a ~** како́й-то рома́н; не́что вро́де рома́на; **different ~s of goods** ра́зного ро́да това́ры; **people are divided into two ~s** лю́ди де́лятся на два разря́да; **people of all ~s** са́мые ра́зные лю́ди; **what ~ of people does he think we are?** за кого́ он нас принима́ет?
2 (*manner*): **in some ~** (*liter.*) не́которым о́бразом.
3: **~ of** (*coll.*) вро́де, как бы; в о́бщем-то; **he ~ of suggested I took him with me** он как бы дал мне поня́ть, что хо́чет пойти́ со мной.
4: **out of ~s** не в ду́хе; **I have felt out of ~s all day** я весь день чу́вствую себя́ нева́жно.
5 (*pl., typ.*) ли́теры (*f. pl.*).

● *v.t.* раз|бира́ть, -обра́ть; **they ~ed themselves into groups of six** они́ разби́лись на гру́ппы по шести́/шесть челове́к; (*letters, grain, coal etc.; also comput.*) сортирова́ть, рас-; **~ing office** сортиро́вочное отделе́ние.

● *with adv.*: **~ out** *v.t.* (*select*) от|бира́ть, -обра́ть; (*separate*) отдел|я́ть, -и́ть; (*arrange, classify*) раз|бира́ть, -обра́ть; (*fig., put in order*): **I have to go home to ~ things out** мне ну́жно пойти́ домо́й и во всём разобра́ться; **everything will ~ itself out** всё нала́дится; **I leave the rest for you to ~ out** в остально́м разберётесь са́ми; **let me ~ myself out** да́йте мне прийти́ в себя́; (*coll., deal with*): **they began to fight but a policeman came along and ~ed them out** они́ затея́ли бы́ло дра́ку, но подошёл полице́йский и навёл поря́док; (*punish*): **I'll ~ you out** я тебе́ дам/покажу́.

sorter /ˈsɔːtə(r)/ *n.* сортиро́вщи|к (*fem.* -ца).

sortie /ˈsɔːtɪ/ *n.* (*sally*) вы́лазка (*also fig.*); (*flight*) вы́лет.

SOS *n.* (*pl.* **~s**) (ра́дио)сигна́л бе́дствия.

sot /sɒt/ *n.* пья́ница (*c.g.*), пьянчу́жка (*c.g.*).

sottish /ˈsɒtɪʃ/ *adj.* тупо́й.

sotto voce /ˌsɒtəʊ ˈvəʊtʃɪ/ *adv.* вполго́лоса; пони́зив го́лос.

soubriquet /ˈsuːbrɪˌkeɪ/ = **sobriquet**

soufflé /ˈsuːfleɪ/ *n.* суфле́ (*indecl.*).

sough /saʊ/, /sʌf/ *v.i.* (*make moaning sound*) стона́ть (*impf.*); (*make whistling sound*) свисте́ть (*impf.*).

sought /sɔːt/ *past and p.p. of* ⇒**seek**

soul /səʊl/ *n.* **1** душа́; **All S~s' Day** день поминове́ния усо́пших; **lost ~** поги́бшая душа́; **throw o.s. body and ~ into something** всей душо́й отд|ава́ться, -а́ться чему́-н.; **he puts his heart and ~ into his work** он всю ду́шу вкла́дывает в свою́ рабо́ту; **upon my ~!** ей-Бо́гу!
2 (*animating spirit*) душа́; **he was the life and ~ of the party** он был душо́й о́бщества; (*inspiration*): **his pictures lack ~** его́ карти́нам недостаёт души́; в его́ карти́нах нет жи́зни.
3 (*personification*): **he is the ~ of honour** (*Br.*), **honor** (*US*) он воплощённая/сама́ че́стность.
4 (*person*): **there wasn't a ~ in sight** не ви́дно бы́ло ни души́; **a simple ~** проста́я душа́; **the poor ~ lost her way** бедня́жка заблуди́лась.
5 (*music*) соул.

● *cpds.* **~-destroying** *adj.* иссуша́ющий ду́шу; **~-mate** *n.* (*male*) задуше́вный друг; (*female*) задуше́вная подру́га; **~-searching** *n.* ана́лиз свои́х побужде́ний.

soulful /ˈsəʊlfʊl/ *adj.* проникнове́нный, задуше́вный.

soulless /ˈsəʊllɪs/ *adj.* безду́шный.

sound[1] /saʊnd/ *n.* **1** звук; (*of rain, sea, wind etc.*) шум; **not a ~ was heard** не́ было слы́шно ни зву́ка; **I hear the ~ of voices** я слы́шу голоса́ (*or* звук голосо́в); **~ barrier** звуково́й барье́р; **~ effects** звуково́е сопровожде́ние, шумовы́е эффе́кты; **~ effects man** звукооформи́тель (*m.*), шумови́к (*coll.*); **~ engineer** звукоопера́тор.
2: **I don't like the ~ of it** мне э́то (что́-то) не нра́вится.

● *v.t.* **1** (*cause to ~*): **they ~ed the bell** они́ позвони́ли в ко́локол; **~ a trumpet** игра́ть (*impf.*) на трубе́; **~ the horn** (*of a car*) да|ва́ть, -ть гудо́к.
2 (*play on trumpet etc.*): **~ the retreat/reveille** труби́ть, про- отступле́ние/подъём; **~ the alarm** бить, за- трево́гу; **he ~ed her praises** он пел ей хвалу́.
3 (*pronounce*) произн|оси́ть, -ести́; **the 'K' is not ~ed** «К» не произно́сится.
4 (*test*): **the doctor ~ed his lungs** до́ктор прослу́шал его́ лёгкие.

● *v.i.* **1** (*emit sound; convey effect by sound*) звуча́ть, про-; **the trumpets ~ed** разда́ли́сь зву́ки труб.
2 (*give impression*) каза́ться, по-; **his voice ~s as if he has a cold** по го́лосу ка́жется, что он просту́жен; **it ~s like thunder** похо́же на гром; **the statement ~s improbable** э́то заявле́ние ка́жется маловероя́тным; **the idea ~ed all right at first** понача́лу э́та мысль показа́лась вполне́ прие́млемой.

● *with adv.*: **~ off** *v.i.* (*coll., of person*) шуме́ть (*impf.*).

● *cpds.* **~ archive** *n.* фоноте́ка; **~board** *n.* (*mus.*) де́ка; **~ card** *n.* (*comput.*) звукова́я ка́рта; **~-film** *n.* звуково́й фильм; **~-man** *n.* (*TV, cin.*) звукоопера́тор, звукорежиссёр; **~-proof** *adj.* звуконепроница́емый; **~-recording** *n.* звукоза́пись; **~ system** *n.* звукова́я систе́ма; **~-track** *n.* саундтре́к; звуково́е сопровожде́ние; фоногра́мма; **~-wave** *n.* звукова́я волна́.

sound[2] /saʊnd/ *n.* (*strait*) проли́в.

sound[3] /saʊnd/ *n.* (*probe*) зонд.

● *v.t.* **1** (*measure*) изм|еря́ть, -е́рить; **they are ~ing the (depth of the) ocean** они́ измеря́ют глубину́ океа́на; (*fig.*): **she ~ed the depths of misery** она́ позна́ла глубину́ страда́ний. **2** (*fig.*): **~ (out) s.o. (***or* **s.o.'s intentions, opinions)** зонди́ровать, про- кого́-н.

sound[4] /saʊnd/ *adj.* **1** (*healthy*) здоро́вый; **~ in body and mind** здоро́вый те́лом и душо́й; **of ~ mind** в здра́вом уме́; (*in good condition*) испра́вный. **2** (*correct, logical*) здра́вый; **a ~ argument** убеди́тельный до́вод. **3** (*financially stable*) соли́дный; (*solvent*) платёжеспосо́бный.
4 (*thorough*) хоро́ший; **he slept ~ly** он кре́пко спал; **he was ~ly thrashed** его́ си́льно изби́ли.

sounder /ˈsaʊndə(r)/ *n.* (*naut.*) лот.

sounding /ˈsaʊndɪŋ/ *n.* (*measurement*) измере́ние глубины́; зонди́рование.

● *cpd.* **~-line** *n.* ло́тлинь (*m.*).

sounding-board /ˈsaʊndɪŋˌbɔːd/ *n.* (*for reflecting voice*) наве́с ка́федры; (*mus.*) де́ка, резона́тор; (*fig.*) ру́пор.

soundless /ˈsaʊndlɪs/ *adj.* беззву́чный.

soundness /ˈsaʊndnɪs/ *n.* здоро́вье; про́чность; обосно́ванность; разу́мность.

soup¹ /suːp/ *n.* суп; **mushroom/vegetable ~** грибно́й/овощно́й суп; **beetroot ~** борщ; **cabbage ~** щи (*pl., g.* щей); **he is in the ~** он вли́п (*coll.*).
● *cpds.* **~-kitchen** *n.* бесплатная столо́вая для нужда́ющихся; **~-plate** *n.* глубо́кая таре́лка; **~-spoon** *n.* столо́вая ло́жка; **~-tureen** *n.* су́пница.

soup² /suːp/ *v.t.* (*coll.*): **~ed-up** (*engine*) с надду́вом.

soupçon /ˈsuːpsɔ̃/ *n.* чу́точка, намёк.

sour /ˈsaʊə(r)/ *adj.* **1** (*of fruit etc.*) ки́слый; **~ grapes!** (*fig.*) зе́лен виногра́д! **2** (*of milk*) проки́сший, ски́сший; **go, turn ~** ск|иса́ть, -и́снуть; **~ cream** смета́на. **3** (*of person*) мра́чный, озло́бленный.
● *v.t.*: **disappointments ~ed his temper** от постоя́нных неуда́ч у него́ испо́ртился хара́ктер.
● *v.i.* ск|иса́ть, -и́снуть; свёр|тываться, -ну́ться; (*fig.*) по́ртиться, ис-.
● *cpd.* **~puss** *n.* кисля́й (*coll.*); ворчу́н (*coll.*).

source /sɔːs/ *n.* **1** (*of stream etc.*) исто́к; **he traced the river to its ~** он прошёл по реке́ до са́мых её исто́ков. **2** (*fig.*) исто́чник; **reliable ~s of information** надёжные исто́чники информа́ции; **~ of infection** исто́чник инфе́кции.

sourness /ˈsaʊənɪs/ *n.* кислота́; ки́слый вкус.

souse /saʊs/ *v.t.* **1** (*put in pickle*) соли́ть, за-; **~d herrings** солёная/марино́ванная сельдь. **2** (*plunge or soak in liquid*) мочи́ть, на-/за-; окун|а́ть, -у́ть. **3** (*p.p., sl., drunk*) пья́ный в сте́льку.

south /saʊθ/ *n.* юг; (*naut.*) зюйд; **in the ~** на ю́ге; **to the ~ of** к ю́гу от (*or* южне́е) + *g.*; **from the ~** с ю́га.
● *adj.* ю́жный; **~ wind** ю́жный ве́тер; ве́тер с ю́га; **S~ Africa** Ю́жная А́фрика; **Republic of S~ Africa** Ю́жно-Африка́нская Респу́блика; **S~ America** Ю́жная Аме́рика; **S~ American** (*n.*) южноамерика́н|ец (*fem.* -ка); (*adj.*) южноамерика́нский; **S~ Island** о́стров Ю́жный; **S~ Pole** Ю́жный по́люс; **the S~ Seas** ю́жная часть Ти́хого океа́на; **S~ Sea Islands** Океа́ния.
● *adv.*: **the ship sailed due ~** су́дно шло пря́мо на юг; **our village is ~ of London** на́ша дере́вня нахо́дится к ю́гу от Ло́ндона.
● *cpds.* **~bound** *adj.* иду́щий/дви́жущийся на юг; **~-east** *n.* ю́го-восто́к; (*naut.*) зюйд-о́ст; *adj.* (*also* **~-easterly, ~-eastern, ~-eastward**) ю́го-восто́чный; *adv.* (*also* **~-easterly, ~-eastwards**) на ю́го-восто́к; **~-easter(ly)** *n.* (*wind*) ю́го-восто́чный ве́тер; зюйд-о́ст; **~-~-east** *n.* (*naut.*) зюйд-зюйд-о́ст; **~-~-west** *n.* (*naut.*) зюйд-зюйд-ве́ст; **~-west** *n.* ю́го-за́пад; (*naut.*) зюйд-ве́ст; *adj.* (*also* **~-westerly, ~-western, ~-westward**) ю́го-за́падный; *adv.* (*also* **~-westerly, ~-westwards**) на ю́го-за́пад; **~-wester(ly)** *n.* (*wind*) ю́го-за́падный ве́тер; зюйд-ве́ст.

southerly /ˈsʌðəlɪ/ *n.* (*wind*) ю́жный ве́тер.
● *adj.* ю́жный.

southern /ˈsʌð(ə)n/ *adj.* ю́жный; **~most** са́мый ю́жный.

southerner /ˈsʌðənə(r)/ *n.* южа́н|ин (*fem.* -ка).

southward /ˈsaʊθwəd/ *adj.* ю́жный.
● *adv.* (*also* **~s**) на юг; к ю́гу, в ю́жном направле́нии.

souvenir /ˌsuːvəˈnɪə(r)/ *n.* сувени́р; **as a ~** на па́мять.

sou'wester /saʊˈwestə(r)/ *n.* (*hat*) зюйдве́стка, клеёнчатая ша́пка.

sovereign /ˈsɒvrɪn/ *n.* (*monarch*) госуда́р|ь (*fem.* -ыня); (*supreme ruler*) сувере́н; (*coin*) соверен.
● *adj.* **1** (*supreme*) верхо́вный. **2** (*having ~ power; royal*) сувере́нный; **a ~ state** сувере́нное госуда́рство.

sovereignty /ˈsɒvrɪntɪ/ *n.* суверените́т.

Soviet /ˈsəʊvɪət/, /ˈsɒ-/ (*hist.*) *n.* **1** (*council*) сове́т; **the Supreme ~** Верхо́вный Сове́т. **2** (*citizen of USSR*) сове́тск|ий граждани́н (*fem.* -ая гражда́нка).
● *adj.* сове́тский; **the ~ Union** Сове́тский Сою́з; **Union of ~ Socialist Republics** Сою́з Сове́тских Социалисти́ческих Респу́блик.

sow¹ /saʊ/ *n.* (*pig*) свинья́; **breeding ~** свинома́тка.

sow² /səʊ/ *v.t.* (*past* **sowed** /səʊd/; *p.p.* **sown** *or* **sowed**) **1** (*seed*) се́ять, по-; (*fig.*): **he is ~ing (the seeds of) dissension** он се́ет раздо́р (*or* семена́ раздо́ра). **2** (*ground*) зас|е́ивать (*or* -ева́ть), -е́ять; **a field ~n with maize** по́ле, засе́янное кукуру́зой.

sower /ˈsəʊə(r)/ *n.* се́ятель (*m.*).

sowing /ˈsəʊɪŋ/ *n.* посе́в, засе́в.

sown /səʊn/ *p.p. of* ⇒**sow²**

soya /ˈsɔɪə/ *n.* (*also* **soy**) со́я.
● *adj.* со́евый; **~ bean** со́евый боб; **~ milk** со́евое молоко́; **~ sauce** со́евый со́ус.

sozzled /ˈsɒz(ə)ld/ *adj.* (*sl.*) пья́ный вдре́безги.

spa /spɑː/ *n.* во́ды (*f. pl.*), куро́рт с минера́льными исто́чниками; **~ water** минера́льная вода́.

space /speɪs/ *n.* **1** (*expanse*) простра́нство, просто́р; **he was staring into ~** он смотре́л в простра́нство; **vanish into ~** (*fig.*) исч|еза́ть, -е́знуть; испар|я́ться, -и́ться (*coll.*).
2 (*cosmic, outer ~*) ко́смос; **they were the first to put a man into ~** они́ пе́рвыми посла́ли челове́ка в ко́смос; (*attr.*) косми́ческий; **~ age** косми́ческий век; **~ shuttle** косми́ческий челно́к; **~ travel, flight** косми́ческий полёт; *see also cpds.*
3 (*distance, interval*) расстоя́ние; (*between words, lines*) интерва́л.
4 (*of time, distance*) промежу́ток/пери́од вре́мени; **after a short ~** че́рез не́которое вре́мя; вско́ре; **for the ~ of a mile** на протяже́нии ми́ли; **for a ~ of four weeks** на протяже́нии четырёх неде́ль; **in the ~ of a hour** за час; в тече́ние ча́са.
5 (*area; room*) ме́сто; **blank ~** пусто́е ме́сто; **in the ~ provided** в отведённом ме́сте.
● *v.t.* (*also* **~ out**): **the posts were ~d six feet apart** столбы́ бы́ли располо́жены на расстоя́нии шести́ фу́тов друг от дру́га; **payments can be ~d** вы́плату мо́жно производи́ть в рассро́чку; (*typ.*) наб|ира́ть, -ра́ть в разря́дку.
● *cpds.* **~-bar** *n.* кла́виша для интерва́ла; **~craft** (*also* **~-ship**) *nn.* косми́ческий кора́бль; **~man** *n.* космона́вт; **~-probe** *n.* косми́ческий зонд; **~-ship** *n.* = **~craft; ~-suit** *n.* скафа́ндр (*космонавта*); **~-time** *n.* простра́нство-вре́мя; **~ walk** *n.* вы́ход в откры́тый ко́смос; **~woman** *n.* же́нщина-космона́вт.

spacial /ˈspeɪʃ(ə)l/ = **spatial**

spacing /ˈspeɪsɪŋ/ *n.* **1** распределе́ние. **2** (*typ., between letters*) разря́дка; (*between lines*) межстро́чие, интерва́л; **type in double ~** печа́тать, на- че́рез два интерва́ла.

spacious /ˈspeɪʃəs/ *adj.* (*roomy*) просто́рный; (*vast, extensive*) обши́рный; (*capacious*) помести́тельный, вмести́тельный.

spaciousness /ˈspeɪʃəsnɪs/ *n.* просто́рность, просто́р; обши́рность, вмести́тельность.

spade /speɪd/ *n.* **1** (*tool*) лопа́та; **call a ~ a ~** называ́ть (*impf.*) ве́щи свои́ми имена́ми. **2** (*cards*) пи́ка; (*pl.*) пи́ки, пи́ковая масть; **queen of ~s** пи́ковая да́ма.
● *cpd.* **~-work** *n.* (*fig.*) (кропотли́вая) подготови́тельная рабо́та.

spadeful /ˈspeɪdfʊl/ *n.* (це́лая) лопа́та (*чего*).

spaghetti /spəˈgetɪ/ *n.* спаге́тти (*nt. indecl.*).

Spain /speɪn/ *n.* Испа́ния.

span¹ /spæn/ *n.* **1** (*distance between supports*) пролёт. **2** (*of time*) промежу́ток/пери́од вре́мени; **~ of life, life ~** продолжи́тельность жи́зни; **attention ~** объём внима́ния. **3**: **wing ~** разма́х кры́льев. **4** (*distance between thumb and finger*) пядь.
● *v.t.* (**spanned, spanning**) **1** (*extend across*) перекр|ыва́ть, -ы́ть; **the bridge ~s the river** мост переки́нут че́рез ре́ку; (*fig.*): **the movement ~s almost two centuries** э́то движе́ние охва́тывает почти́ два столе́тия. **2** (*measure with fingers*) изм|еря́ть, -е́рить пя́дями.

span² /spæn/ *past of* ⇒**spin**

span³ /spæn/ *see* ⇒**spick**

spandrel /ˈspændrɪl/ *n.* (*archit.*) антрво́льт; па́зуха сво́да.

spangle /ˈspæŋg(ə)l/ *n.* блёстка.
● *v.t.* укр|аша́ть, -а́сить блёстками; **the heavens ~d with stars** не́бо, усы́панное звёздами.

Spaniard /ˈspænjəd/ *n.* испа́н|ец (*fem.* -ка).

S

spaniel /ˈspænj(ə)l/ *n.* спаниéль (*m.*).

Spanish /ˈspænɪʃ/ *n.* **1** (*language*) испáнский (язы́к). **2**: **the ~** (*collect.*) испáнцы (*m. pl.*).

● *adj.* испáнский; **~ fly** шпáнская мýшка, шпáнка.

spank /spæŋk/ *n.* шлепóк; **give a child a ~** шлёпнуть (*pf.*) ребёнка.

● *v.t.* шлёп|ать, -нуть (*or* пошлёпать).

spanking /ˈspæŋkɪŋ/ *n.*: **give a child a ~** нашлёпать/отшлёпать (*pf.*) ребёнка.

● *adj.*: **go at a ~ pace** (*coll.*) нести́сь/мчáться (*impf.*) (во всю).

spanner /ˈspænə(r)/ *n.* (*Br.*) гáечный ключ; **throw a ~ into the works** (*fig.*) ≈ вставля́ть (*impf.*) пáлки в колёса.

spar¹ /spɑː(r)/ *n.* **1** (*naut.*) рангóутное дéрево. **2** (*aeron.*) лонжерóн.

spar² /spɑː(r)/ *n.* (*min.*) шпат.

spar³ /spɑː(r)/ *n.* (*boxing*) спáрринг; тренирóвочный бой.

● *v.i.* (**sparred, sparring**) **1** боксúровать (*impf.*); занимáться (*impf.*) спáррингом; **~ring-match** тренирóвочный матч; **~ring partner** партнёр для тренирóвки. **2** (*fig., argue*) спóрить (*impf.*); препирáться (*impf.*).

spare /speə(r)/ *n.* **1** (**~ part**) запаснáя часть, запчáсть. **2** (**~** *wheel*) запаснóе колесó.

● *adj.* **1** (*lean*) худощáвый, сухощáвый. **2** (*excess, extra*) ли́шний; **~ room** кóмната для гостéй; **~ time** свобóдное врéмя; досýг; **in one's ~ time** в свобóдное врéмя; на досýге; **~ cash** ли́шние дéньги; (*additional, reserve*) запаснóй, запáсный, резéрвный; **~ parts** запасны́е чáсти, запчáсти; **~ wheel** запаснóе колесó; **~ tyre** (*Br.*), **tire** (*US*) запаснáя ши́на; (*coll., of fat*) брюшкó.

● *v.t.* **1** (*withhold use of*) жалéть, по-; **he ~d no pains/expense to ...** он не жалéл уси́лий/расхóдов, чтóбы....
2 (*dispense with, do without*) об|ходи́ться, -ойти́сь без + *g.*; **we cannot ~ him** мы не мóжем обойти́сь без негó.
3 (*afford*): **can you ~ a cigarette?** нет ли у вас ли́шней сигарéты?; **can you ~ me 10 roubles?** мóжете ли вы дать мне дéсять рублéй?; **I can ~ you only a few minutes** я могý удели́ть вам тóлько нéсколько минýт.
4 to ~ (*available, left over*): **I have no time to ~** у меня́ нет ли́шнего врéмени; **we got there with an hour to ~** когдá мы приéхали тудá, у нас оставáлся цéлый час в запáсе; **three yards to ~** три ли́шних я́рда.
5 (*show mercy, leniency to*) щади́ть, по-; **the conquerors ~d no one** победи́тели не (по)щади́ли никогó; **~ s.o.'s life** сохрани́ть (*pf.*) комý-н. жизнь; **if I am ~d** éсли бýду жив; **I tried to ~ his feelings** я старáлся щади́ть егó чýвства; **~ o.s.** (*reserve strength*) берéчь (*impf.*) свои́ си́лы; **she never ~d herself** онá труди́лась, не жалéя себя́/сил.
6 (*save from*) изб|авля́ть, -áвить (*кого от чего*); **I want to ~ you any unpleasantness** я хочý избáвить вас от возмóжных неприя́тностей; **I will ~ you the trouble of replying** я избáвлю вас от необходи́мости отвечáть; **~ us the details** избáвьте нас от подрóбностей!

● *cpd.* **~-ribs** *n. pl.* свины́е рёбрышки (*nt. pl.*).

sparing /ˈspeərɪŋ/ *adj.* (*moderate*) умéренный; **be ~ with the sugar!** не кладúте сли́шком мнóго сáхару; (*frugal*) скупóй; **~ of praise** скупóй на похвалы́.

spark /spɑːk/ *n.* **1** и́скра (*also fig.*); **if they get together the ~s will fly** éсли они́ сойдýтся, непремéнно сцéпятся; **~ of talent/hope** и́скра талáнта/надéжды; **he showed not a ~ of interest** он не прояви́л ни малéйшего интерéса; **he hasn't a ~ of intelligence** у негó нет ни кáпли умá; **she's a bright ~** у неё свéтлая головá. **2** (*pl., coll., ship's radio operator*) ради́ст.

● *v.t.* (*also* **~ off**: *cause*) вызывáть, вы́звать; (*interest*) заж|игáть, -éчь; (*conflict*) провоци́ровать, с-; (*friendship*) да|вáть, -ть начáло (+ *d.*).

● *v.i.* искри́ть (*impf.*); дать (*pf.*) и́скру.

● *cpds.* **~-gap** *n.* искровóй промежýток; **~(ing)-plug** *n.* свечá зажигáния, запáльная свечá.

sparkle /ˈspɑːk(ə)l/ *n.* сверкáние, блеск, блистáние; **a ~ came into his eyes** у негó засверкáли/заблестéли глазá; (*of wine etc.*) шипéние; **the wine lost its ~** винó утрáтило искри́стость/перестáло игрáть.

● *v.i.* сверкáть, за-; и́скри́ться (*impf.*); (*flash*) блестéть, за-; **her eyes ~d** у неё сверкáли/блестéли глазá; (*of wit*) сверк|áть, -нýть; **sparkling wine** шипýчее/игри́стое винó.

sparkler /ˈspɑːklə(r)/ *n.* (*firework*) бенгáльский огóнь.

sparrow /ˈspærəʊ/ *n.* воробéй.

● *cpd.* **~-hawk** *n.* я́стреб-перепеля́тник.

sparse /spɑːs/ *adj.* рéдкий; (*scattered*) разбрóсанный; **~ly populated** малонаселённый; **~ vegetation** скýдная расти́тельность.

spars|eness /ˈspɑːsnɪs/, **-ity** /ˈspɑːsɪtɪ/ *nn.* скýдость.

Sparta /ˈspɑːtə/ *n.* Спáрта.

Spartan /ˈspɑːt(ə)n/ *n.* спартáн|ец (*fem.* -ка).

● *adj.* спартáнский.

spasm /ˈspæz(ə)m/ *n.* (*of muscles*) спáзм, сýдорога; (*mental or physical reaction*) при́ступ, припáдок; **a ~ of coughing** при́ступ кáшля; **~s of grief** при́ступ отчáяния; **he works in ~s** он рабóтает наскóками.

spasmodic /spæzˈmɒdɪk/ *adj.* спазмати́ческий.

spastic /ˈspæstɪk/ *n.* (спасти́ческий) парали́тик.

● *adj.* спасти́ческий.

spat¹ /spæt/ (*coll.*) *n.* размóлвка, лёгкая ссóра.

● *v.i.* (**spatted, spatting**) брани́ться, по-.

spat² /spæt/ *n.* (*in pl., hist.*) корóткие гéтры (*f. pl.*).

spat³ /spæt/ *past and p.p. of* ⇒**spit²**

spate /speɪt/ *n.* (*Br., sudden flood*) разли́в; наводнéние; (*fig.*) потóк; **the river is in ~** (*Br.*) рекá вздýлась; рекá вы́шла из берегóв.

spatial /ˈspeɪʃ(ə)l/ *adj.* пространственный.

spatter /ˈspætə(r)/ (*also* **splatter**) *v.t.* бры́згать, за-; **~ed with mud** забры́зганный гря́зью.

spatula /ˈspætjʊlə/ *n.* шпáтель (*m.*), лопáточка.

spawn /spɔːn/ *n.* (*of fish etc.*) икрá; **mushroom ~** грибни́ца.

● *v.t.* (*of fish etc.*) произв|оди́ть, -ести́; метáть (*impf.*) (*икру*); (*fig., pej.*) порo|ждáть, -ди́ть; (*offspring*) плоди́ть, рас-.

● *v.i.* (*reproduce*) метáть (*impf.*) икрý; (*pej., multiply*) плоди́ться, рас-.

spay /speɪ/ *v.t.* удал|я́ть, -и́ть я́ичники у + *g.*

speak /spiːk/ *v.t.* (*past* **spoke;** *p.p.* **spoken**) **1** (*say, pronounce, utter*) говори́ть, сказáть; произн|оси́ть, -ести́; **he didn't ~ a word** он не произнёс ни слóва; **he spoke his lines clearly** он чётко/вня́тно произнёс свой текст; (*give utterance to, express*) выскáзывать, вы́сказать; **~ the truth** говори́ть, сказáть прáвду; **~ one's mind** выскáзывать, вы́сказать своё мнéние; *see also* ⇒**spoken.**
2 (*converse in*) говори́ть (*impf.*); **he ~s Russian well** он хорошó говори́т по-рýсски; **they were ~ing French** они́ разговáривали/говори́ли по-францýзски; **he ~s six languages** он владéет шестью́ языкáми; он говори́т на шести́ языкáх.

● *v.i.* (*past* **spoke;** *p.p.* **spoken**) говори́ть (*impf.*); (*converse*) говори́ть, по-; разговáривать (*impf.*); вести́ (*indet.*) разговóр; **I was ~ing to him yesterday** я говори́л/разговáривал с ним вчерá; **they are not on ~ing terms** они́ не разговáривают (друг с дрýгом); (*make a speech*) выступáть, вы́ступить; произн|оси́ть, -ести́ речь; **I am not used to ~ing in public** я не привы́к публи́чно выступáть; **he spoke for the motion** он вы́сказался за предложéние; **~ing clock** (*Br.*) говоря́щие часы́; **~ing-trumpet** рýпор; **'Smith ~ing'** (*on telephone*) «с вáми говори́т Смит»; «Смит у телефóна»; **'~ing'** (*on telephone*) «э́то я»; «слýшаю»; **actions ~ louder than words** не по словáм сýдят, а по делáм; **this calls for some plain ~ing** слéдует, ви́дно, объясни́ться начистотý; **I must ~ to him about his manners** мне нáдо поговори́ть с ним о егó манéрах; **so to ~** так сказáть; **roughly, broadly ~ing** приблизи́тельно говоря́; в óбщих чертáх; **strictly ~ing** стрóго говоря́; **~ing as a father** как отéц; **in a manner of ~ing** éсли мóжно так вы́разиться; **the facts ~ for themselves** фáкты говоря́т (сáми) за себя́; **~ing for myself** что касáется меня́; **~ for yourself!** не говори́те за други́х!; **let**

him ~ for himself пусть сам скáжет!; **~ well, highly of s.o.** хорошó отзывáться, отозвáться о кóм-н.; хвалить, по- когó-н.; **he is well spoken of** о нём хорошó отзывáются/говорят; **~ of** (*mention, refer to*) упом|инáть, -янýть о (*ком/чём*); касáться, коснýться (*чего*); **~ing of money, can you lend me a pound?** кстáти о деньгáх — не дадите ли вы мне фунт взаймы?; **nothing to ~ of** ничегó осóбенного; **he has no wealth to ~ of** егó состояние весьмá незначительно; **the flat is too small, not to ~ of the noise** эта квартира слишком малá, и к томý же ещё здесь óчень шýмно; (*indicate, proclaim*): **everything about her spoke of refined taste** всё в ней говорило об изысканном вкýсе.

● *with advs.*: **~ out** *v.i.* (*express o.s. plainly*) высказываться, высказаться (откровéнно); **~ up** *v.i.* (**~** *louder*) говорить (*impf.*) грóмче; (*express support*): **~ up for s.o.** поддéрж|ивать, -áть когó-н.

speaker /'spi:kə(r)/ *n.* **1**: **the ~ was a man of about 40** говорящему бы́ло лет сóрок. **2**: **a Russian ~** человéк, владéющий рýсским языкóм; **he is a native Russian ~** егó роднóй язы́к — рýсский; он носитель (*m.*) рýсского языкá. **3** (*public* **~**) орáтор, доклáдчик, выступáющий. **4** (*parl.*) спикер. **5** (**loud-~**) громкоговоритель (*m.*).

spear /spɪə(r)/ *n.* копьё, дрóтик; (*for fish*) гарпýн, острогá.

● *v.t.* пронз|áть, -ить копьём; **~ fish** бить (*impf.*) ры́бу острогóй.

● *cpds.* **~head** *n.* (*lit.*) наконéчник/остриё копья́; (*fig.*) передовóй отря́д; авангáрд; *v.t.*: **~head a movement** возгл|авлять, -áвить движéние; **~mint** *n.* (*bot.*) мя́та колосистая/курчáвая.

spec[1] /spek/ *n.* (*coll.*): **he went there on ~** он пошёл тудá наудáчу.

spec[2] /spek/ *n.* (*coll., specification*) спецификáция.

special /'speʃ(ə)l/ *n.* (*in restaurant*) фи́рменное блю́до; (*TV programme*) специáльная прогрáмма; (*edition*) специáльный/э́кстренный вы́пуск; (*train*) пóезд специáльного назначéния.

● *adj.* **1** (*exceptional, out of the ordinary*) осóбый, осóбенный; (*for a particular purpose*) специáльный; **~ to** свóйственный +*d.*; **this book is of ~ interest to me** э́та кни́га представляет осóбый интерéс для меня́; **for a ~ purpose** с осóбой цéлью; **~ agent** агéнт по осóбым поручéниям; **a ~ case** осóбый слýчай; **~ correspondent** специáльный корреспондéнт.
2 (*specific, definite*) определённый; **do you want to come at any ~ time?** вы хоти́те прийти́ в какóе-нибудь определённое врéмя?
3 (*extraordinary*) специáльный, э́кстренный; **~ train** пóезд специáльного назначéния; **~ edition** специáльный/э́кстренный вы́пуск; **~ delivery** срóчная достáвка.

● *cpd.* **~ effect** *n.* спецэффéкт; **~-purpose** *adj.* специáльного назначéния.

specialist /'speʃəlɪst/ *n.* специали́ст (*fem.* -ка) (по+*d.*).

speciality /,speʃɪ'ælɪtɪ/ (*US* **specialty**) *n.* **1** (*characteristic*) осóбенность, специ́фика. **2** (*pursuit*) специáльность, специализáция; **make a ~ of something** специализи́роваться (*impf., pf.*) в чём-н.; **what is his ~?** кто он по специáльности? **3** (*product, recipe etc.*): **~ of the house** фи́рменное блю́до.

specialization /,speʃəlaɪ'zeɪʃ(ə)n/ *n.* специализáция.

specialize /'speʃə,laɪz/ *v.t.*: **~d knowledge** специáльные познáния.

● *v.i.* (*be or become specialist*) специализи́роваться (*impf., pf.*) (по+*d.*; в+*p.*).

specially /'speʃəlɪ/ *adv.*
1 (*individually*) осóбо; **he was ~ mentioned** о нём упомянýли осóбо.
2 (*for specific purpose*) специáльно; **~ selected** специáльно отóбранный.
3 (*exceptionally*): осóбенно, исключи́тельно; **be ~ careful** быть осóбенно осторóжным.

specialty /'speʃəltɪ/ = **speciality**

species /'spi:ʃɪz/, /-ʃi:z/, /'spi:s-/ *n.* (*pl.* **~**) **1** (*biol.*) (биологи́ческий) вид; **our** (*or* **the (human)**) **~** человéческий род; **origin of ~** происхождéние ви́дов.
2 (*kind*) вид, род.

specific /spɪ'sɪfɪk/ *adj.* **1** (*definite*) определённый, конкрéтный, осóбенный; **he has no ~ aim** у негó нет никакóй определённой цéли.
2 (*distinct*) специфи́ческий, осóбый.
3 (*phys.*): **~ gravity** удéльный вес.
4 (*peculiar*) характéрный; **the style is ~ to cubist painters** э́тот стиль характéрен для куби́стов.

● *n.* (*pl.*) детáли (*f. pl.*).

specification /,spesɪfɪ'keɪʃ(ə)n/ *n.* (*instance of specifying*) уточнéние, определéние; (*tech.*) спецификáция; (*pl.*) техни́ческие характери́стики (*f. pl.*).

specif|y /'spesɪ,faɪ/ *v.t.* **1** (*name expressly*) определ|я́ть, -и́ть; уточн|я́ть, -и́ть; **unless otherwise ~ied** éсли нет ины́х укaзáний. **2** (*include in specification*) специфици́ровать (*impf., pf.*).

specimen /'spesɪmən/ *n.* **1** (*example; sample*) экземпля́р; образéц; (*individual of species*) óсобь; **a museum ~** музéйный экспонáт; **~ page** прóбная страни́ца; **~ of urine** мочá для анáлиза. **2** (*unusual person, thing*) тип, субъéкт; **a queer ~** чудáк; стрáнный субъéкт.

specious /'spi:ʃəs/ *adj.* благови́дный; **a ~ argument** внéшне убеди́тельный дóвод.

speciousness /'spi:ʃəsnɪs/ *n.* благови́дность.

speck /spek/ *n.* (*dot*) крáпинка; (*of dirt or decay*) пя́тнышко; **~ of dust** пыли́нка; **the ship was a ~ on the horizon** корáбль казáлся тóчкой на горизóнте.

speckle /'spek(ə)l/ *v.t.* покр|ывáть, -ы́ть крáпинками.

speckled /'spek(ə)ld/ *adj.* крáпчатый; пятни́стый; **~ hen** пёстрая/ря́бая кýрица.

specs /speks/ *n. pl.* (*coll.*) = **spectacle** 2

spectacle /'spektək(ə)l/ *n.* **1** (*public show; sight*) зрéлище; **he is a sad ~** он явля́ет собóй жáлкое зрéлище; **he made a ~ of himself** он вы́ставил себя́ на посмéшище. **2** (*Br., pl., glasses*) очк|и́ (*pl., g.* -óв).

spectacled /'spektək(ə)ld/ *adj.* в очкáх, нося́щий очки́, очкáстый (*coll.*); (*of animal*) очкóвый.

spectacular /spek'tækjʊlə(r)/ *n.* эффéктное зрéлище.

● *adj.* эффéктный, впечатля́ющий.

spectator /spek'teɪtə(r)/ *n.* (*onlooker*) зри́тель (*fem.* -ница); (*observer*) наблюдáтель (*fem.* -ница).

specter /'spektə(r)/ (*US*) = **spectre**

spectra /'spektrə/ *pl. of* ⇒**spectrum**

spectral /'spektr(ə)l/ *adj.* при́зрачный; (*phys.*) спектрáльный.

spectre /'spektə(r)/ (*US* **specter**) *n.* привидéние, при́зрак.

spectrograph /'spektrəʊ,grɑ:f/ *n.* спектрóграф.

spectrometer /spek'trɒmɪtə(r)/ *n.* спектрóметр.

spectroscope /'spektrə,skəʊp/ *n.* спектроскóп.

spectroscopic /,spektrə'skɒpɪk/ *adj.* спектроскопи́ческий.

spectroscopy /,spek'trɒskəpɪ/ *n.* спектроскопи́я.

spectr|um /'spektrəm/ *n.* (*pl.* **~a**)
1 (*phys.*) спектр; **~ analysis** спектрáльный анáлиз. **2** (*fig.*) спектр, диапазóн.

speculate /'spekjʊ,leɪt/ *v.i.*
1 (*meditate*) размышля́ть (*impf.*) (*o чём*); (*conjecture*) дéлать (*impf.*) предположéния, гадáть (*impf.*).
2 (*risk, invest money*) спекули́ровать (*impf.*), игрáть (*impf.*) на би́рже; **he ~s in oil shares** он спекули́рует нефтяны́ми áкциями.

speculation /,spekjʊ'leɪʃ(ə)n/ *n.* (*meditation*) размышлéние; (*conjecture*) предположéние; догáдка; (*investment*) спекуля́ция; (*phil.*) спекуля́ция, умозрéние.

speculative /'spekjʊlətɪv/ *adj.* (*meditative*) умозри́тельный, теорети́ческий; (*conjectural*) предположи́тельный, гипотети́ческий; (*risky*) рискóванный; (*comm.*) спекуляти́вный.

speculator /'spekjʊ,leɪtə(r)/ *n.* спекуля́нт (*fem.* -ка).

sped /sped/ *past and p.p. of* ⇒**speed** *v.i.* 1

speech /spi:tʃ/ *n.* **1** (*faculty, act of speaking; also gram.*) речь; **lose the power of ~** лиш|áться, -и́ться дáра рéчи; **freedom of ~** свобóда слóва;

S

direct/indirect ~ прямáя/кóсвенная речь; **parts of ~** чáсти рéчи; **figure of ~** фигýра/оборóт рéчи. **2** (*manner of speaking*) речь, гóвор; (*pronunciation*) произношéние, вы́говор; **~ therapist** логопéд; **~ therapy** логопéдия.
3 (*public address*) речь; **make a ~** произн|оси́ть, -ести́ речь; выступáть, вы́ступить с рéчью.

● *cpds.* **~-day** *n.* (*Br.*) торжéственное собрáние (с речáми и вы́дачей нагрáд); **~-writer** *n.* спичрáйтер.

speechify /ˈspi:tʃɪ,faɪ/ *v.i.* орáторствовать (*impf.*).

speechless /ˈspi:tʃlɪs/ *adj.* (*temporarily unable to speak*) онемéвший; **I was ~ with surprise** я онемéл от удивлéния.

speed /spi:d/ *n.* **1** (*rapidity*) быстротá, скóрость; (*rate of motion*) скóрость; **with all possible ~** как мóжно скорéе; **at full, top ~** на пóлной скóрости; **gain, gather ~** наб|ирáть, -рáть скóрость; **lose ~** терять, по- скóрость; **my bicycle has four ~s** мой велосипéд имéет четы́ре скóрости; **he was travelling** (*Br.*), **traveling** (*US*) **at ~** он éхал с большóй скóростью; **~ limit** дозвóленная скóрость; предéл скóрости.
2 (*stimulant*) «спид».
3 (*of a film*) светочувстви́тельность.

● *v.t.* (*past and p.p.* **speeded**) (*also* **~ up**: *accelerate*) уск|орять, -óрить; **the train service has been ~ed up** поездá стáли ходи́ть быстрéе; **measures to ~ production** мéры по повышéнию тéмпов произвóдства.

● *v.i.* **1** (*past and p.p.* **sped**) (*move quickly*) мчáться (*impf.*), нести́сь (*impf.*).
2 (*past and p.p.* **speeded**) (*go too fast*): **he was fined for ~ing** егó оштрафовáли за превышéние скóрости.
3 (*past and p.p.* **speeded**): **~ up** уск|оряться, -óриться.

● *cpds.* **~-boat** *n.* быстрохóдный кáтер; **~way** *n.* гóночный трек; (*US, motorway*) автострáда; **~way racing** спидвéй, скоростны́е мотогóнки (*f. pl.*); **~way rider** мотогóнщик; **~well** *n.* (*bot.*) верони́ка.

speedometer /spi:ˈdɒmɪtə(r)/ *n.* спидóметр.

speedy /ˈspi:dɪ/ *adj.* (**speedier, speediest**) (*rapid*) скóрый, бы́стрый; (*hasty*) поспéшный; (*prompt, undelayed*) скóрый, немéдленный; **he wished me a ~ return** он пожелáл мне скóрого возвращéния; **they took ~ action against him** они́ при́няли срóчные мéры прóтив негó.

speleological /,spi:lɪəˈlɒdʒɪk(ə)l/, /,spe-/ *adj.* спелеологи́ческий.

speleologist /,spi:lɪˈɒlədʒɪst/, /,spe-/ *n.* спелеóлог; исслéдователь (*m.*) пещéр.

speleology /,spi:lɪˈɒlədʒɪ/, /,spe-/ *n.* спелеолóгия.

spell¹ /spel/ *n.* **1** (*magical formula; its effect*) чáр|ы (*pl., g.* —); колдовствó; **cast a ~ over** околдóв|ывать, -áть; заколдóв|ывать, -áть; **break the ~** разр|ушáть, -ýшить чáры.
2 (*fascination*) обаяние, очаровáние; **he was under the ~ of her beauty** он находи́лся под обая́нием её красоты́; он был очарóван её красотóй.

● *cpd.* **~-bound** *adj.* очарóванный, зачарóванный; **he held the audience ~-bound** он зачаровáл слýшателей.

spell² /spel/ *n.* **1** (*bout, turn*) смéна, перйод; **a ~ of work** перйод рабóты; **shall I take a ~ at the wheel?** смени́ть мне вас у руля́? **2** (*interval*) перйод; промежýток врéмени; **I slept for a ~** я поспáл нéкоторое врéмя; **a ~ of good luck** полосá везéния; **we're in for a ~ of fine weather** ожидáется полосá хорóшей погóды.

spell³ /spel/ *v.t.* (*past and p.p.* **spelled** *or esp. Br.* **spelt**) **1** (*write or name letters in sequence*) произн|оси́ть, -ести́ (*or* писáть, на-) по бýквам; **how do you ~ your name?** как пи́шется вáша фами́лия?; **he cannot ~ his own name** он не мóжет прáвильно написáть свою́ фами́лию; **I wish you would learn to ~** когдá же ты наýчишься писáть без оши́бок?
2 (*usu.* **~ out**: *decipher slowly*) с трудóм раз|бирáть, -обрáть (по бýквам); (*fig., make explicit*) разъясн|я́ть, -и́ть; разжёв|ывать, -áть (*coll.*).
3 (*of letters: make up*) сост|авлять, -áвить (по бýквам); **what do these letters ~?** какóе слóво составля́ют э́ти бýквы?
4 (*fig., signify*) означáть (*impf.*); **these changes ~ disaster** э́ти перемéны суля́т несчáстье.

● *v.i.* (*past and p.p.* **spelled** *or esp. Br.* **spelt**) писáть (*impf.*) прáвильно/грáмотно; **we do not pronounce as we ~** мы произнóсим не так, как пи́шем.

● *cpd.* **~checker** *n.* (*comput.*) (орфографи́ческий) коррéктор.

speller /ˈspelə(r)/ *n.*: **he is a poor ~** у негó хромáет орфогрáфия.

spelling /ˈspelɪŋ/ *n.* правописáние, орфогрáфия; **I am not certain of the ~ of this word** я не увéрен в правописáнии э́того слóва; **~ checker = spellchecker**

● *cpd.* **~-bee** *n.* состязáние по орфогрáфии.

spelt /spelt/ *past and p.p. of* ⇒**spell³**

spen|d /spend/ *v.t.* (*past and p.p.* **spent**) **1** (*pay out*) трáтить, ис-; расхóдовать, из-; **how much have you ~t?** скóлько вы израсхóдовали?; **she ~ds too much on clothes** онá сли́шком мнóго трáтит на одéжду; **~d a penny** (*Br. coll., use lavatory*) пойти́ (*pf.*) кóе-кудá.
2 (*consume, expend, exhaust*) расхóдовать, из-; истощ|áть, -и́ть; **~d o.s.** истощ|áться, -и́ться; вымáтываться, вы́мотаться; **he is completely ~t** он вы́мотался вконéц; **a ~t bullet** израсхóдованная пýля.
3 (*pass*) пров|оди́ть, -ести́; **we ~t some hours looking for a hotel** у нас ушлó (*or* мы потрáтили) нéсколько часóв на пóиски гости́ницы; **she ~t her life in good works** онá всю свою́ жизнь посвяти́ла дóбрым делáм; **how do you ~d your leisure?** как вы провóдите свой досýг?

● *v.i.* (*past and p.p.* **spent**) (**~** *money*) трáтиться, по-; **~ding-money** кармáнные дéньги; **they went on a ~ding spree** они́ пошли́ транжи́рить дéньги.

● *cpd.* **~dthrift** *n.* мот (*fem.* -óвка); транжи́р (*fem.* -ка); расточи́тель (*m.*) (*fem.* -ница); *adj.* расточи́тельный.

spender /ˈspendə(r)/ *n.*: **a lavish ~** расточи́тельный человéк.

spent /spent/ *past and p.p. of* ⇒**spend**

sperm /spɜ:m/ *n.* (*pl.* **~** *or* **~s**) спéрма; (**~ whale**) кашалóт.

spermaceti /,spɜ:məˈsetɪ/ *n.* спермацéт.

spermatozo|on /,spɜ:mətəʊˈzəʊɒn/ *n.* (*pl.* **-a**) сперматозóид.

spew /spju:/ *v.t.* выблёвывать, вы́блевать; (*lit., fig.*) изрыгáть (*impf.*); **a machine-gun ~ing out bullets** пулемёт, поливáющий (неприя́теля) огнём.

● *v.i.* блевáть, (с)блевнýть.

sphere /sfɪə(r)/ *n.* **1** сфéра; (*globe*) шар, глóбус. **2** (*fig.*) сфéра, óбласть/пóле (дéятельности); **outside my ~** вне моéй компетéнции; **~ of influence** сфéра влия́ния.

spherical /ˈsferɪk(ə)l/ *adj.* сфери́ческий, шарообрáзный.

spheroid /ˈsfɪərɔɪd/ *n.* сферóид.

spheroidal /sfɪəˈrɔɪd(ə)l/ *adj.* сфероидáльный, шарови́дный.

sphincter /ˈsfɪŋktə(r)/ *n.* (*anat.*) сфи́нктер.

sphinx /sfɪŋks/ *n.* сфинкс.

sphygmomanometer /,sfɪgməʊməˈnɒmɪtə(r)/ *n.* (*med.*) сфигмоманóметр.

spice /spaɪs/ *n.* **1** спéция, пря́ность, приправа. **2** (*fig., piquancy, zest*) острóтá, пикáнтность; **his story lacked ~** егó расскáзу не хватáло изю́минки.

● *v.t.* припр|авлять, -áвить; **highly-~d dishes** óстрые/пря́ные блю́да.

spick /spɪk/ *adj.*: **~ and span** (*clean, tidy*) сверкáющий чистотóй.

spicy /ˈspaɪsɪ/ *adj.* (**spicier, spiciest**) пря́ный; (*fig.*) пикáнтный.

spider /ˈspaɪdə(r)/ *n.* паýк; **~'s web** паути́на.

● *cpd.* **~-monkey** *n.* паукообрáзная обезья́на.

spidery /ˈspaɪdərɪ/ *adj.*: **~ writing** витиевáтый пóчерк; **~ legs** дли́нные, тóнкие нóги, «спи́чки» (*f. pl.*).

spiel /ʃpi:l/ *n.* (*coll.*) заговáривание зубóв.

spiffing /ˈspɪfɪŋ/ *adj.* (*Br. coll.*) шикáрный, первоклáссный.

spigot /ˈspɪgət/ *n.* прóбка, втýлка.

spike /spaɪk/ *n.* **1** (*sharp point*) остриё; (*stout nail*) косты́ль (*m.*); (*on fence*) зубéц; (*Br., for papers etc.*) накóлка; (*on shoe*) шип, гвоздь (*m.*); **~ heels** гвóздики (*m. pl.*), шпи́льки (*f. pl.*); (*pl., coll.*) (*spiked running shoes*) шипóвки. **2** (*bot.*) кóлос.

● *v.t.* **1** (*fasten with* **~s**) приб|ивáть, -и́ть гвоздя́ми. **2** (*furnish with* **~s**) снаб|жа́ть, -ди́ть гвоздя́ми/шипа́ми; **~d boots** боти́нки (*m. pl.*) на шипа́х. **3**: **~ s.o.'s guns** (*fig.*) расстр|а́ивать, -о́ить чьи-н. за́мыслы. **4** (*coll., adulterate*): **they ~d her wine** ей что́-то подмеша́ли в вино́.

spiky /ˈspaɪkɪ/ *adj.* (**spikier, spikiest**) **1** (*flower, leaf*) остроконе́чный; **~ hair** ёжик. **2** (*coll., easily offended*) колю́чий.

spill[1] /spɪl/ *n.* (*of wood*) лучи́на; (*of paper*) жгут из бума́ги.

spill[2] /spɪl/ *v.t.* (*past and p.p.* **spilt** *or* **spilled**) **1** (*accidentally*) (*liquid*) прол|ива́ть, -и́ть; расплёск|ивать, -а́ть; **I spilt a glass of water on her dress** я про́лил стака́н воды́ на её пла́тье; **without ~ing a drop** не расплеска́в ни ка́пли; (*powder etc.*) расс|ыпа́ть, -ы́пать.
2 (*intentionally*) прол|ива́ть, -и́ть; (*fig.*): **~ the beans** (*coll.*) прогов|а́риваться, -ори́ться; разб|а́лтывать, -олта́ть секре́т; **~ s.o.'s blood** прол|ива́ть, -и́ть чью-н. кровь; уб|ива́ть, -и́ть кого́-н.

● *v.i.* (*past and p.p.* **spilt** *or* **spilled**) (*of liquids*) разл|ива́ться, -и́ться; (*of salt etc.*) расс|ыпа́ться, -ы́паться; прос|ыпа́ться, -ы́паться.

● *with advs.*: **~ out** *v.i.* вылива́ться, вы́литься; (*of people*) высыпа́ть, вы́сыпать (*coll.*); **~ over** *v.i.* перел|ива́ться, -и́ться (че́рез край).

● *cpd.* **~-over** *n.* (*of population*) избы́точное населе́ние.

spillage /ˈspɪlɪdʒ/ *n.* уте́чка; (*of dry products*) утру́ска.

spillikins /ˈspɪlɪkɪnz/ *n.* бирю́льки (*f. pl.*).

spilt /spɪlt/ *past and p.p. of* ⇨**spill**[2]

spin /spɪn/ *n.* **1** (*whirl, twisting motion*) круже́ние, враще́ние; **go into a ~** заверте́ться (*pf.*); **his head was in a ~** у него́ голова́ шла кру́гом.
2 (*aeron.*) што́пор; **go into a ~** входи́ть, войти́ в што́пор.
3 (*of ball*) враще́ние; **put ~ on a ball** закру́|чивать, -ти́ть мяч.
4 (*of coin*): **it all turned on the ~ of a coin** всё зави́село от жре́бия.
5 (*outing*) коро́ткая прогу́лка; **go for a ~ in the car** прокати́ться/поката́ться (*both pf.*) на маши́не.
6 (*bias*) пристра́стие.

● *v.t.* (**spinning;** *past* **spun** *or* **span;** *p.p.* **spun**) **1** (*yarn, wool etc.*) прясть, с-; **~ning-wheel** пря́лка; **~ning-machine** пряди́льная маши́на; **~ a yarn** (*fig.*) сочиня́ть/выду́мывать (*impf.*) исто́рии; **the spider ~s its web** пау́к плетёт паути́ну; **spun silk** шёлковая пря́жа; *see also* ⇨**spun.**
2 (*cause to revolve*) верте́ть, за-; крути́ть, за-; кружи́ть, за-; **~ a coin** подбр|а́сывать, -о́сить моне́ту; **~ a top** пус|ка́ть, -ти́ть волчо́к.

● *v.i.* (**spinning;** *past* **spun** *or* **span;** *p.p.* **spun**) верте́ться, за-; крути́ться, за-; кружи́ться, за-; (*of compass needle or suspended object*) враща́ться (*impf.*); (*of wheel*) бы́стро враща́ться/крути́ться (*impf.*); (*of person*): **the blow sent him ~ning against the wall** уда́р швырну́л его́ к стене́; **my head is ~ning** у меня́ голова́ идёт кру́гом.

● *with advs.*: **~ out** *v.t.*: **~ out a story** растя́|гивать, -ну́ть расска́з; **~ round** *v.t. & i.* бы́стро пов|ора́чивать(ся), -ерну́ть(ся) (круго́м).

● *cpds.* **~ doctor** *n.* (*pol.*) челове́к, в обя́занности кото́рого вхо́дит формирова́ние обще́ственного мне́ния в по́льзу полити́ческой па́ртии; **~-drier** *n.* центрифу́га; **~-dry** *v.t.* суши́ть, вы- в центрифу́ге; **~-off** *n.* (*coll.*) побо́чный результа́т; дополни́тельный дохо́д.

spina bifida /ˌspaɪnə ˈbɪfɪdə/ *n.* расщепле́ние ости́стых отро́стков позвоно́чника.

spinach /ˈspɪnɪdʒ/, /-ɪtʃ/ *n.* шпина́т.

spinal /ˈspaɪn(ə)l/ *adj.* спинно́й, позвоно́чный; **~ column** позвоно́чный столб, позвоно́чник, спинно́й хребе́т; **~ cord** спинно́й мозг; **~ injury** поврежде́ние позвоно́чника.

spindle /ˈspɪnd(ə)l/ *n.* (*of spinning-wheel*) веретено́; (*axis, rod*) ось, шпи́ндель (*m.*).

spindly /ˈspɪndlɪ/ *adj.* (**spindlier, spindliest**) дли́нный и то́нкий.

spindrift /ˈspɪndrɪft/ *n.* бры́зг|и (*pl., g.* —) морско́й воды́.

spine /spaɪn/ *n.* **1** (*backbone*) позвоно́чник, спинно́й хребе́т; (*of fish*) хребе́т. **2** (*of hedgehog etc.*) игла́, колю́чка. **3** (*of plant*) игла́, колю́чка, шип. **4** (*of book*) корешо́к.

● *cpd.* **~-chilling** *adj.* жу́ткий.

spineless /ˈspaɪnlɪs/ *adj.* (*fig.*) бесхребе́тный, бесхара́ктерный.

spinet /spɪˈnet/, /ˈspɪnɪt/ *n.* (*mus.*) спине́т.

spinnaker /ˈspɪnəkə(r)/ *n.* (*naut.*) спи́накер.

spinner /ˈspɪnə(r)/ *n.* (*person*) пряди́льщи|к (*fem.* -ца); пря́ха.

spinneret /ˈspɪnəˌret/ *n.* (*zool*) пряди́льный о́рган; (*text.*) филье́ра.

spinney /ˈspɪnɪ/ *n.* (*Br.*) (*thicket*) за́росль; (*small wood*) ро́ща.

spinster /ˈspɪnstə(r)/ *n.* (*old maid*) ста́рая де́ва; (*leg., unmarried woman*) незаму́жняя же́нщина.

spinsterhood /ˈspɪnstəhʊd/ *n.* староде́вичество.

spiny /ˈspaɪnɪ/ *adj.* (**spinier, spiniest**) (*covered with spines*) покры́тый и́глами/шипа́ми/колю́чками; (*prickly*) колю́чий.

spiral /ˈspaɪər(ə)l/ *n.* спира́ль.

● *adj.* спира́льный; **~ staircase** винтова́я ле́стница.

● *v.i.* (**spiralled, spiralling;** *US* **spiraled, spiraling**): **the plane ~led down to earth** самолёт произвёл спира́льный спуск на зе́млю; **the crime rate is ~ling upwards** престу́пность ре́зко возраста́ет.

spire /ˈspaɪə(r)/ *n.* (*of church etc.*) шпиль (*m.*), шпиц.

spirit /ˈspɪrɪt/ *n.* **1** (*soul, immaterial part of man*) душа́; духо́вное нача́ло; **I shall be with you in ~** душо́й я бу́ду с ва́ми.
2 (*immortal, incorporeal being*) дух; **the Holy S~** Свято́й Дух; **evil ~** злой дух; **as the ~ moves one** по наи́тию; (*apparition, ghost*) привиде́ние.
3 (*living being*) ум, ли́чность; **leading ~** душа́, руководи́тель (*m.*), вождь (*m.*).
4 (*mental or moral nature*) хара́ктер, дух; **a man of unbending ~** челове́к непрекло́нного хара́ктера; **the poor in ~** ни́щие ду́хом.
5 (*courage*) хра́брость; **show some ~** прояв|ля́ть, -и́ть му́жество/хара́ктер; **a man of ~** челове́к с хара́ктером; (*vivacity*) жи́вость; **he played the piano with ~** он вдохнове́нно игра́л на роя́ле.
6 (*mental, moral attitude*) дух, смысл; **take something in the wrong ~** неве́рно восприн|има́ть, -я́ть что-н.; **it depends on the ~ in which it is done** всё зави́сит от того́, с каки́м наме́рением э́то сде́лано; **enter into the ~ of Christmas** прон|ика́ться, -и́кнуться ду́хом Рождества́.
7 (*real meaning, essence*) су́щность, суть, дух; **the ~ of the law** дух зако́на; **I followed the ~ of his instructions** я де́йствовал в ду́хе его́ указа́ний.
8 (*mental or moral tendency, influence*) дух; тенде́нция; **the ~ of the age** дух вре́мени.
9 (*pl., humour*) настрое́ние; **he was in high ~s** он был в припо́днятом настрое́нии; **his ~s are low** он в пода́вленном настрое́нии; **keep one's ~s up** мужа́ться (*impf.*); не па́дать (*impf.*) ду́хом; **recover one's ~s** приободр|я́ться, -и́ться; **raise s.o.'s ~s** подн|има́ть, -я́ть дух у кого́-н.
10 (*industrial alcohol*) спирт, алкого́ль (*m.*); (*pl., Br., alcoholic drink*) спиртно́й напи́ток; **he never touches ~s** он не прикаса́ется к спиртно́му.

● *v.t.* (**spirited, spiriting**): **~ away, off** (та́йно) пох|ища́ть, -и́тить.

● *cpds.* **~-gum** *n.* театра́льный клей; **~-lamp** *n.* спирто́вка; **~-level** *n.* ватерпа́с.

spirited /ˈspɪrɪtɪd/ *adj.* живо́й, оживлённый, энерги́чный, жизнера́достный; **a ~ reply** бо́йкий отве́т; **a ~ horse** горя́чий конь.

spiritless /ˈspɪrɪtlɪs/ *adj.* (*lifeless*) безжи́зненный; (*listless*) вя́лый, сла́бый.

spiritual /ˈspɪrɪtjʊəl/ *n.* (*song*) спи́ричуэл, негритя́нский духо́вный гимн.

● *adj.* **1** (*pert. to soul, spirit*) духо́вный; **~ life** духо́вная жизнь; (*fig.*): **Italy is his ~ home** Ита́лия — его́ духо́вная ро́дина. **2** (*inspired by Holy Spirit*): **~ gift** боже́ственный дар; **~ songs** духо́вные пе́сни.

spiritualism /ˈspɪrɪtjʊəˌlɪz(ə)m/ *n.* спирити́зм; (*phil.*) спиритуали́зм.

spiritualist /ˈspɪrɪtjʊəlɪst/ *n.* спири́т (*fem.* -ка); (*phil.*) спиритуали́ст.

spirituality /ˌspɪrɪtjʊˈælɪtɪ/ *n.* одухотворённость.

spirituous /ˈspɪrɪtjʊəs/ *adj.* (*of drink*) спиртно́й, алкого́льный.

spit[1] /spɪt/ *n.* (*for roasting*) вéртел; (*of land*) косá, стрéлка.

spit[2] /spɪt/ *n.* **1** (*spittle*) слюнá. **2**: **the ~ and** (*or* **~ting) image of his father** тóчная кóпия своегó отцá; вы́литый отéц.

● *v.t.* (**spitting;** *past and p.p.* **spat** *or* ~) (*also* **~ out**) выплёвывать, вы́плюнуть; **~ blood** хáркать (*impf.*) крóвью.

● *v.i.* (**spitting;** *past and p.p.* **spat** *or* ~) **1** пл|евáть, -ю́нуть; (*habitually*) плевáться (*impf.*); **he spat in my face** он плю́нул мне в лицó; (*of cat etc.*) фы́рк|ать, -нуть. **2** (*of fire*) рассыпáть (*impf.*) и́скры. **3** (*Br. coll., rain*) накрáпывать (*impf.*).

spite /spaɪt/ *n.* **1** (*ill-will*) злóба, злость; **out of ~** назлó; по злóбе. **2**: **in ~ of** несмотря́ на + *a.*; **I smiled in ~ of myself** я невóльно улыбну́лся.

● *v.t.*: **he does it to ~ me** он дéлает э́то мне назлó.

spiteful /'spaɪtfʊl/ *adj.* злóбный, злорáдный.

spitefulness /'spaɪtfʊlnɪs/ *n.* злóбность, злорáдство.

Spitsbergen /'spɪts,bɜ:gən/ *n.* Шпицбéрген.

spittle /'spɪt(ə)l/ *n.* плевóк; слюнá.

spittoon /spɪ'tu:n/ *n.* плевáтельница.

spiv /spɪv/ *n.* (*Br. sl.*) мéлкий спекуля́нт; жу́лик.

splash /splæʃ/ *n.* **1** (*action, effect*) плескáние, плеск; **he fell into the water with a ~** он с плéском бултыхну́лся в вóду; **the stone made a huge ~** кáмень упáл с грóмким плéском; **make a ~** (*fig., attract attention*) произв|оди́ть, -ести́ сенсáцию.
2 (*sound*) всплеск, плеск; **the ~ of waves** всплéски волн.
3 (*liquid*) бры́зги (*m. pl.*); **I felt a ~ of rain** на меня́ упáли кáпли дождя́; **put a ~ of soda in my whisky** плесни́те мне кáплю сóдовой в ви́ски.
4 (*of blood, mud etc.*) пятнó; **a ~ of colour** (*Br.*), **color** (*US*) крáсочное пятнó.

● *v.t.* **1** бры́з|гать, -нуть (*чем на что*); забры́зг|ивать, -ать (*что чем*); **he ~ed paint on her dress** он забры́згал ей плáтье крáской; **she was ~ing her feet in the water** онá шлёпала ногáми по водé; **they were ~ing water at one another** они́ бры́згали друг в дру́га водóй; **~ one's way through mud** шлёпать (*impf.*) по гря́зи.
2 (*coll., fig.*): **the news was ~ed in all the papers** все газéты раструби́ли э́ту нóвость; **he likes to ~ his money about** он лю́бит бросáться/сори́ть деньгáми.

● *v.i.* **1** (*of liquid etc.*) разбры́зг|иваться, -аться; (*of waves*) плескáться (*impf.*); **the mud ~ed up her legs** ей забры́згало нóги гря́зью.
2 (*move or fall with ~*): **he ~ed into the water** он бултыхну́лся в вóду; **the ducks ~ed about in the pond** у́тки плескáлись в пруду́; **the falling tree ~ed into the lake** дéрево с плéском упáло в óзеро; **the cows ~ed through the river** корóвы с трудóм шли чéрез рéку; **the capsule ~ed down in the Pacific** кáпсула приводни́лась в Ти́хом океáне; (*Br. coll., fig.*): **they ~ed out on a new carpet** они́ разори́лись на нóвый ковёр.

● *int.* плюх!

● *cpds.* **~-back** *n.* (*Br.*) защи́тная панéль; **~-down** *n.* приводнéние.

splat /splæt/ *n.* (*piece of wood*) нащéльная рéйка.

splatter /'splætə(r)/ *n., v.t. & i.* = **spatter**

splay /spleɪ/ *n.* скóшенный проём окнá *и т. п.*

● *v.t.* (*spread wide*): **~ one's legs** раски́|дывать, -нуть нóги.

spleen /spli:n/ *n.* (*anat.*) селезёнка; (*fig., ill-temper, spite*) злóба; **vent one's ~ on s.o.** срывáть, сорвáть злóбу на ком-н.

splendid /'splendɪd/ *adj.* (*magnificent*) великолéпный; (*luxurious*) роскóшный; (*excellent*) прекрáсный, отли́чный; (*impressive, remarkable*) удиви́тельный, замечáтельный; **~!** великолéпно!, замечáтельно!; **what a ~ idea** замечáтельная/прекрáсная мысль!

splendour /'splendə(r)/ (*US* **splendor**) *n.* (*brilliance*) блеск; (*grandeur, magnificence*) великолéпие, пы́шность.

splenetic /splɪ'netɪk/ *adj.* **1** (*med.*) селезёночный. **2** (*of person*) раздражи́тельный, жёлчный.

splice /splaɪs/ *v.t.* **1** (*rope, wires*) ср|áщивать, -асти́ть. **2** (*wood*) соедин|я́ть, -и́ть внахлёстку/внакрóй. **3** (*tape*) склéи|вать, -ть. **4**: **get ~d** (*sl., marry*) пожени́ться (*pf.*).

splint /splɪnt/ *n.* (*for broken bone*) лубóк, ши́на.

● *v.t.* на|клáдывать, -ложи́ть ши́ну на + *a.*

splinter /'splɪntə(r)/ *n.* **1** (*of wood*) лучи́на, щéпка; (*in finger*) занóза; (*of stone, metal, glass*) оскóлок; **get a ~ in one's finger** занози́ть (*pf.*) пáлец.
2 (*fig.*): **~ group** отколóвшаяся (полити́ческая) группирóвка/фрáкция.

● *v.t. & i.* расщеп|ля́ть(ся), -и́ть(ся).

● *cpd.* **~-proof** *adj.*: **~-proof glass** безоскóлочное стеклó.

split /splɪt/ *n.* **1** раскáлывание; (*crack, fissure*) трéщина, щель, расщéлина.
2 (*fig., schism, disunion*) раскóл.
3: **do the ~s** (*Br.*) дéлать, с- шпагáт.

● *v.t.* (**splitting;** *past and p.p.* ~)
1 колóть, рас-; расщеп|ля́ть, -и́ть; **~ting the atom** расщеплéние áтома; (*crack open, rupture*) раск|áлывать, -олóть; **I have a ~ lip** у меня́ губá трéснула; (*fig.*): **~ one's sides** надрывáться (*impf.*) от смéха; **~ hairs** спóрить (*impf.*) о пустякáх/мелочáх.
2 (*divide*) раздел|я́ть, -и́ть; (*share*) дели́ть, по-; **they ~ the money into three** (*or* **three ways)** они́ раздели́ли дéньги нá три чáсти; **the job was ~ between us** мы подели́ли рабóту мéжду собóй; **~ a bottle of wine with s.o.** распи|вáть, -ть буты́лку винá с кем-н.; **~ the left-wing vote** раск|áлывать, -олóть голосá лéвых.
3 (*cause dissension in*) раск|áлывать, -олóть; разъедин|я́ть,-и́ть; **the party was ~ by factions** пáртия расколóлась на фрáкции; **~ infinitive** расщеплённый инфинити́в; **~ peas** кóлотый горóх; **~ personality** раздвоéние ли́чности; **~ ring** разрезнóе кольцó (для ключéй); **~ second** дóля секу́нды; мгновéние.

● *v.i.* (**splitting;** *past and p.p.* ~) **1** (*of hard substance*) раск|áлываться, -олóться; расщеп|ля́ться, -и́ться; трéснуть (*pf.*); (*divide*) раздел|я́ться, -и́ться; **the wood ~** дéрево трéснуло; **~ open** взл|áмываться, -омáться; (*of soft, thin substance*) раз|рывáться, -орвáться; рвáться, по-; **my head is ~ting** (*fig.*) у меня́ головá трещи́т/раскáлывается (от бóли).
2 (*become disunited*) разъедин|я́ться, -и́ться; раск|áлываться, -олóться.
3: **~ on s.o.** (*Br. sl.*) выдавáть, вы́дать когó-н.

● *with advs.*: **~ off** *v.t. & i.* отк|áлывать(ся), -олóть(ся); **~ up** *v.t. & i.* (*lit.*) раск|áлывать(ся), -олóть(ся); (*separate*) ра|сходи́ться, -зойти́сь; **we ~ up into two groups** мы разби́лись на две гру́ппы; **he and his wife ~ up** они́ с женóй разошли́сь.

splodge /splɒdʒ/ (*Br.*) = **splotch**

splosh /splɒʃ/ (*coll.*) = **splash** *v.t. & i.*

splotch /splɒtʃ/, **splodge** /splɒdʒ/ (*coll.*) *n.* (гря́зное) пятнó, мазóк.

● *v.t.* замы́зг|ивать, -ать.

splurge /splɜ:dʒ/ *v.i.* (*coll.*) кути́ть (*impf.*); бросáться (*impf.*) деньгáми.

splutter /'splʌtə(r)/ *n.* (*noise*) треск, трескáние; (*speech*) бы́страя/сби́вчивая речь; лопотáнье.

● *v.t. & i.* (*also* **sputter**) (*of person*) говори́ть (*impf.*) захлёбываясь; (*of candle*) трещáть (*impf.*); (*of fire*) шипéть (*impf.*); (*of engine*) трещáть (*impf.*).

spoil /spɔɪl/ *n.* **1** (*booty*) добы́ча; **~s of war** трофéи (*m. pl.*); воéнная добы́ча. **2** (*profit*) при́быль; (*benefit*) вы́года.

● *v.t.* (*past and p.p.* **spoilt** (*esp. Brit*) *or* **spoiled**) **1** (*impair, injure, ruin*) пóртить, ис-; **the rain ~t our holiday** дождь испóртил нам óтпуск; **eating sweets will ~ your appetite** конфéты испóртят вам аппети́т; **~ s.o.'s plans** срывáть, сорвáть чьи-н. плáны; **he ~t his chances of success** он сам подорвáл свои́ шáнсы на успéх.
2 (*over-indulge*) баловáть, из-; **a ~t child** избалóванный ребёнок; **be ~t for choice** имéть (*impf.*) огрóмный вы́бор.

● *v.i.* (*past and p.p.* **spoilt** (*esp. Brit.*) *or* **spoiled**) **1** (*deteriorate*) пóртиться, ис-; ух|удшáться, -у́дшиться; (*go bad, rotten etc.*) пóртиться, ис-.
2 (*be eager*): **he is ~ing for a fight** он так и лéзет в дрáку.

● *cpd.* **~-sport** *n.* тот, кто пóртит удовóльствие други́м.

spoilage /'spɔɪlɪdʒ/ *n.* (*of food*) испóрченные продýкты (*m. pl.*).

spoilt /spɔɪlt/ *past and p.p. of* ⇒**spoil**

spoke[1] /spəʊk/ *n.* **1** (*of wheel*) спи́ца.

2 (*fig.*): **put a ~ in s.o.'s wheel** (*Br.*) вставля́ть (*impf.*) кому́-н. па́лки в колёса.

spoke² /spəʊk/ *past of* ⇒**speak**

spoken /ˈspəʊkən/ *adj.* у́стный; **the ~ word** у́стная речь; **the ~ language** речь.

spokesman /ˈspəʊksmən/ *n.* представи́тель (*m.*); **~ for defence** докла́дчик по вопро́сам оборо́ны; **act as ~ for s.o.** выступа́ть, вы́ступить от и́мени кого́-н.

spokesperson /ˈspəʊks,pɜ:s(ə)n/ = **spokesman** *or* **spokeswoman**

spokeswoman /ˈspəʊks,wʊmən/ *n.* представи́тельница.

spoliation /,spəʊlɪˈeɪʃ(ə)n/ *n.* грабёж, разграбле́ние.

spondee /ˈspɒndi:/ *n.* сponде́й.

sponge /spʌndʒ/ *n.* **1** (*zool.; toilet article*) гу́бка; **throw in, up the ~** (*fig.*) призн|ава́ть, -а́ть себя́ побеждённым. **2** (*cake*) бискви́т; (*dough*) бискви́тное те́сто.

● *v.t.* (**sponging** *or* **spongeing**): **~ a child's face** обт|ира́ть, -ере́ть ребёнку лицо́ гу́бкой; **~ o.s. down** обт|ира́ться, -ере́ться гу́бкой.

● *v.i.* (**sponging** *or* **spongeing**) (*fig.*) жить (*impf.*) на чужо́й счёт; **he ~s on his brother** он сиди́т на ше́е у бра́та.

● *with advs.*: **~ off** *v.t.* ст|ира́ть, -ере́ть гу́бкой; **~ up** *v.t.* (*absorb*) вытира́ть, вы́тереть.

● *cpds.* **~-bag** *n.* (*Br.*) су́мка для туале́тных принадле́жностей; **~-cake** *n.* бискви́т; **~-rubber** *n.* рези́новая гу́бка.

sponger /ˈspʌndʒə(r)/ *n.* парази́т, нахле́бник, прижива́льщик.

spongy /ˈspʌndʒɪ/ *adj.* (**spongier, spongiest**) гу́бчатый; (*porous*) по́ристый; (*e.g. moss, carpet*) мя́гкий; (*of ground*) то́пкий.

sponsor /ˈspɒnsə(r)/ *n.* **1** (*guarantor*) поручи́тель (*fem.* -ница); (*of new member etc.*) рекоменда́тель (*fem.* -ница). **2** (*at baptism*) (*male*) крёстный оте́ц; (*female*) крёстная мать. **3** (*TV etc.*) рекламода́тель (*m.*). **4** (*providing finance*) спо́нсор.

● *v.t.* руча́ться, поручи́ться за + *a.*; рекомендова́ть (*impf., pf.*); (*e.g. a law or resolution*) вн|оси́ть, -ести́; (*on TV etc.*) финанси́ровать (*impf., pf.*).

sponsorship /ˈspɒnsəʃɪp/ *n.* поручи́тельство, пору́ка; спо́нсорство.

spontaneity /,spɒntəˈni:ɪtɪ/, /-ˈneɪɪtɪ/ *n.* сponта́нность, стихи́йность, непосре́дственность.

spontaneous /spɒnˈteɪnɪəs/ *adj.* спонта́нный, стихи́йный; (*unaffected*) непосре́дственный; **~ combustion** самовозгора́ние.

spoof /spu:f/ (*sl.*) *n.* (*hoax*) ро́зыгрыш; (*parody*) паро́дия.

● *v.t.* разыгр|ывать, -а́ть; пароди́ровать, с-.

spook /spu:k/ *n.* (*joc.*) привиде́ние, при́зрак.

spooky /ˈspu:kɪ/ *adj.* (**spookier, spookiest**) (*frightening*) жу́ткий, стра́шный; (*sinister*) злове́щий; **~ house** дом с привиде́ниями.

spool /spu:l/ *n.* шпу́лька, кату́шка.

● *v.t.* нам|а́тывать, -ота́ть на кату́шку.

spoon /spu:n/ *n.* ло́жка; **they fed him with a ~** его́ корми́ли с ло́жки; **he was born with a silver ~ in his mouth** ≈ он роди́лся в соро́чке.

● *v.t.* (*also* **~ up**) че́рпать, вы́-.

● *cpds.* **~-bait** *n.* блесна́; **~bill** *n.* (*zool.*) колпи́ца; **~feed** *v.t.* (*lit.*) корми́ть (*impf.*) с ло́жки; (*fig.*): **~-feed a pupil** ня́нчиться (*impf.*) с ученико́м; всё разжёвывать (*impf.*) ученику́.

spoonerism /ˈspu:nə,rɪz(ə)m/ *n.* непроизво́льная перестано́вка зву́ков в слова́х.

spoonful /ˈspu:nfʊl/ *n.* (по́лная) ло́жка (*чего*).

spoor /spʊə(r)/ *n.* след.

sporadic /spəˈrædɪk/ *adj.* споради́ческий.

spore /spɔ:(r)/ *n.* спо́ра.

sport /spɔ:t/ *n.* **1** (*outdoor pastime(s)*) спорт; (*pl.*) спорт, ви́ды (*m. pl.*) спо́рта; **indoor ~s** ви́ды спо́рта для закры́тых помеще́ний; **go in for ~** зан|има́ться, -я́ться спо́ртом; **~s car** спорти́вный автомоби́ль; **~s coat** (*US*), **~ jacket** (*US*), **~s jacket** (*Br.*) спорти́вная ку́ртка; **~s editor** заве́дующий спорти́вным отде́лом газе́ты.
2 (*pl., Br., athletic events*) спорти́вные и́гры (*f. pl.*); **~s day** (*Br.*) день спорти́вных состяза́ний.
3 (*jest, fun*) шу́тка, заба́ва; (*ridicule*) насме́шка; **say something in ~** сказа́ть (*pf.*) что-н. в шу́тку; **make ~ of** сме́яться, по- над + *i.*; подшу́|чивать, -ти́ть над + *i.*
4 (*coll., good fellow*) молодчи́на (*m.*); **be a ~!** будь челове́ком!

● *v.t.*: **~ a rose in one's button-hole** щеголя́ть (*impf.*) ро́зой в петли́це; **everyone ~ed their medals** все демонстри́ровали свои́ меда́ли.

● *v.i.* (*frolic*) резви́ться (*impf.*).

● *cpds.* **~s hall** *n.* спортза́л; **~sman** *n.* спортсме́н; (*fig.*) че́стный/поря́дочный челове́к; **~smanlike** *adj.* че́стный, поря́дочный; **~smanship** *n.*: **he showed ~smanship** он прояви́л себя́ настоя́щим спортсме́ном; **~swoman** *n.* спортсме́нка.

sporting /ˈspɔ:tɪŋ/ *adj.* **1** (*connected with, fond of sport*) спорти́вный; **~ equipment** спорти́вное обору́дование; **he was not a ~ man** он не́ был спортсме́ном.
2 (*sportsmanlike*) че́стный, поря́дочный; (*enterprising*) предприи́мчивый; **that's very ~ of you** э́то благоро́дно с ва́шей стороны́; **a ~ chance** небольша́я наде́жда, не́который шанс.

sportive /ˈspɔ:tɪv/ *adj.* шутли́вый, игри́вый.

sporty /ˈspɔ:tɪ/ *adj.* (**sportier, sportiest**) (*person, clothing*) спорти́вный; (*jaunty*) лихо́й.

spot /spɒt/ *n.* **1** (*patch*) пятно́; (*speck*) пя́тнышко, кра́пинка; **a white dog with brown ~s** бе́лая соба́ка с кори́чневыми пя́тнами; **come out in ~s** (*rash*) покр|ыва́ться, -ы́ться сы́пью; **knock ~s off s.o.** (*coll.*) за́просто одоле́ть (*pf.*) кого́-н.
2 (*stain*) пятно́; **there were ~s of blood on his shirt** на его́ руба́шке бы́ли пя́тна кро́ви; (*fig.*): **without a ~ on his reputation** с незапя́тнанной репута́цией.
3 (*pimple*) прыщ(ик).
4 (*place*) ме́сто; **the police were on the ~ within minutes** поли́ция прибыла́ на ме́сто (уже́) че́рез не́сколько мину́т; **he was killed on the ~** он был уби́т на ме́сте (*or* сра́зу); **running on the ~** (*Br.*) бег на ме́сте; **his question put me on the ~** (*coll.*) его́ вопро́с поста́вил меня́ в затрудни́тельное положе́ние; **we were in a (tight) ~** нам пришло́сь ту́го; **~ check** вы́борочная прове́рка; **sore ~** (*lit., fig.*) больно́е ме́сто; **weak ~** сла́бое ме́сто; **he has a soft ~ for her** он пита́ет к ней сла́бость.
5 (*Br. coll., small amount*): **I must have a ~ to eat** мне ну́жно перекуси́ть; **I am due for a ~ of leave** мне полага́ется небольшо́й/коро́ткий о́тпуск; **I have a ~ of work to do** мне ну́жно немно́го порабо́тать; **~ of bother** небольша́я неприя́тность; (*drop*): **I felt a few ~s of rain** я почу́вствовал, как на меня́ упа́ло не́сколько ка́пель дождя́.
6: **~ on** (*Br. coll., exactly right*) в са́мую то́чку.

● *v.t.* (**spotted, spotting**) **1** (*mark, stain*) па́чкать, за-; (*with liquid*) зака́пать (*pf.*); **his books were ~ted with ink** его́ кни́ги бы́ли запа́чканы/зака́паны черни́лами; (*p.p., covered, decorated with ~s*) пятни́стый, кра́пчатый; **a ~ted tie** га́лстук в кра́пинку.
2 (*coll., notice*) зам|еча́ть, -е́тить; (*recognize*) узн|ава́ть, -а́ть; (*catch sight of*) уви́деть (*pf.*); **I ~ted my friend in the crowd** я (вдруг) уви́дел в толпе́ своего́ прия́теля.

● *v.i.* (**spotted, spotting**)
1 па́чкаться, за-; **this silk ~s easily** э́тот шёлк о́чень ма́ркий/легко́ па́чкается.
2: **it is ~ting with rain** накра́пывает (дождь).

● *cpd.* **~light** *n.* освети́тельный прожéктор; (*fig.*): **turn the ~light on something** привл|ека́ть, -е́чь внима́ние к чему́-н.; **be in the ~light** быть в це́нтре внима́ния; *v.t.* (*lit., fig.*) осве|ща́ть, -ти́ть.

spotless /ˈspɒtlɪs/ *adj.* сверка́ющий чистото́й; без еди́ного пя́тнышка; **the room was ~** ко́мната сверка́ла чистото́й; **a ~ly white shirt** белосне́жная руба́шка; (*fig.*) незапя́тнанный, безупре́чный.

spotty /ˈspɒtɪ/ *adj.* (**spottier, spottiest**) (*of colour*) пятни́стый; (*US, of uneven quality*) неро́вный; (*Br., pimply*) прыщева́тый.

spouse /spaʊz/, /spaʊs/ *n.* супру́г (*fem.* -а).

S

spout /spaʊt/ *n.* **1** (*of vessel*) но́сик; (*of pump*) рука́в; (*for rain-water*) водосто́чная труба́; жёлоб. **2** (*jet of water etc.*) струя́; столб воды́; (*of whale*) ды́хало. **3** (*sl.*): **up the ~** (*Br., in a mess*) в безнадёжном состоя́нии.

● *v.t.* **1**: **a whale ~s water** кит выбра́сывает струю́ воды́; **a volcano ~ing lava** вулка́н, изверга́ющий ла́ву. **2** (*coll., declaim views etc.*) говори́ть (*impf.*) о + *p.*; **~ poetry** деклами́ровать, про- стихи́.

● *v.i.* **1** бить (*impf.*); ли́ться (*impf.*) пото́ком; (*of whale*) выбра́сывать, вы́бросить струю́ воды́. **2** (*fig., coll., make speeches*) разглаго́льствовать (*impf.*), ора́торствовать (*impf.*).

sprain /spreɪn/ *n.* растяже́ние.

● *v.t.*: **~ one's wrist/ankle** раст|я́гивать, -яну́ть запя́стье/щи́колотку.

sprang /spræŋ/ *past of* ⇒**spring²**

sprat /spræt/ *n.* шпро́та, ки́лька.

sprawl /sprɔ:l/ *n.* небре́жная по́за; **urban ~** беспоря́дочный рост го́рода.

● *v.i.* **1** (*person*) раст|я́гиваться, -яну́ться; разв|а́ливаться, -али́ться; **send s.o. ~ing** сби|ва́ть, -ть кого́-н. с ног. **2** (*buildings*) раски́|дываться, -нуться; располз|а́ться, -ти́сь.

spray¹ /spreɪ/ *n.* (*bot.*) ве́тка, побе́г.

spray² /spreɪ/ *n.* **1** (*water droplets*) бры́зг|и (*pl., g.* —). **2** (*liquid preparation*) жи́дкость для пульвериза́ции; **chemical ~** ядохимика́т для опры́скивания. **3** (*device for ~ing; also* **~er**) разбры́згиватель (*m.*); распыли́тель (*m.*); пульвериза́тор; **~ can** аэрозо́льный балло́н.

sprayer /ˈspreɪə(r)/ = **spray** *n.* 3

spread /spred/ *n.* **1** (*extension*) протяже́ние, протяжённость, простира́ние; (*expansion*) распростране́ние; (*increase*) увеличе́ние; **~ of wings** разма́х кры́льев; **develop a middle-age ~** полне́ть, по- с во́зрастом. **2** (*dissemination*) распростране́ние. **3** (*difference between prices etc.*) ра́зница, разры́в. **4** (*coll., feast*) пир. **5** (*cul.*) па́ста. **6** (*typ.*) разворо́т.

● *v.t.* (*past and p.p.* **~**) **1** (*extend*) распростран|я́ть, -и́ть; (*unfold*) ра|скла́дывать, -зложи́ть; (*cover*) расст|ила́ть, -ели́ть (*or* разостла́ть); **she ~ a cloth on the table** она́ расстели́ла ска́терть на столе́; **~ butter on bread (*or* bread with butter)** нама́з|ывать, -ать ма́сло на хлеб (*or* хлеб ма́слом); **~ manure over a field** разбр|а́сывать, -оса́ть наво́з по́ полю; **the tree ~ its branches** де́рево раски́нуло свои́ ве́тви; **the bird ~ its wings** пти́ца распра́вила кры́лья; **~ one's wings** (*fig.*) распр|авля́ть, -а́вить кры́лья; **the peacock ~ its tail** павли́н распусти́л хвост; **~ (out) a map** ра|скла́дывать, -зложи́ть ка́рту. **2** (*diffuse*) распростран|я́ть, -и́ть; **he ~ the rumour** (*Br.*), **rumor** (*US*) он распространи́л слух. **3**: **~ o.s.** (*lounge*) раски́|дываться, -нуться.

● *v.i.* (*past and p.p.* **~**) **1** распростран|я́ться, -и́ться; расстила́ться (*impf.*); **the news soon ~** но́вость/весть бы́стро распространи́лась; **a valley ~s out behind the hill** за холмо́м расстила́ется доли́на; **his name ~ throughout the land** о нём сла́ва разошла́сь по всей стране́; **the fire is ~ing** пожа́р разраста́ется; **the fire ~ to the next barn** ого́нь перекину́лся на сосе́дний сара́й; **a flush ~ over her face** кра́ска залила́ её лицо́; **a smile ~ over his face** его́ лицо́ расплыло́сь в улы́бке. **2** (*disperse*) рассе́|иваться, -яться.

● *cpds.* **~-eagle** *v.t.* распла́ст|ывать, -а́ть; класть, положи́ть плашмя́; **lie ~-eagled** лежа́ть (*impf.*) распласта́вшись; **~sheet** *n.* (*comput.*) (электро́нная) табли́ца.

spreading /ˈspredɪŋ/ *adj.* (*branchy*) разве́систый.

spree /spri:/ *n.* (*coll.*) весе́лье, кутёж; **have a ~, go on the ~** кути́ть (*impf.*); **go on a spending ~** нач|ина́ть, -а́ть транжи́рить де́ньги.

sprig /sprɪg/ *n.* ве́точка.

sprightliness /ˈspraɪtlɪnɪs/ *n.* жи́вость, бо́йкость, ре́звость.

sprightly /ˈspraɪtlɪ/ *adj.* (**sprightlier, sprightliest**) живо́й, бо́йкий, ре́звый.

spring¹ /sprɪŋ/ *n.* (*season*) весна́; **in ~** весно́й; (*attr.*) весе́нний; **~ flowers** весе́нние цветы́; **~ onion** (*Br.*) зелёный лук; **~ tide** сизиги́йный прили́в.

● *cpds.* **~-clean** *n.* (*Br.*) генера́льная (*обычно весенняя*) убо́рка; *v.t. & i.* произв|оди́ть, -ести́ генера́льную убо́рку; **~time** *n.* весна́, весе́нняя пора́.

spring² /sprɪŋ/ *n.* **1** (*leap*) прыжо́к, скачо́к; **make, take a ~** пры́гнуть (*pf.*); скакну́ть (*pf.*). **2** (*elasticity*) упру́гость, эласти́чность; **he has a ~ in his step** у него́ упру́гая похо́дка. **3** (*elastic device*) пружи́на; (*attr.*) пружи́нный; **~ balance** пружи́нные весы́, безме́н; **~ mattress** пружи́нный матра́ц; (*of vehicle*) рессо́ра. **4** (*of water*) исто́чник, ключ, родни́к; **hot ~s** горя́чие исто́чники; **~ water** ключева́я/роднико́вая вода́.

● *v.t.* (*past* **sprang** *or US* **sprung;** *p.p.* **sprung**) **1** (*cause to act*): **~ a trap** захло́п|ывать, -нуть лову́шку; (*produce suddenly*): **~ a surprise on s.o.** заст|ига́ть, -и́чь кого́-н. врасплох. **2**: **~ a leak** да|ва́ть, -ть течь. **3** (*provide with* **~s**) подрессо́ри|вать, -ть; **the carriage is well sprung** у каре́ты хоро́шие рессо́ры.

● *v.i.* (*past* **sprang** *or US* **sprung;** *p.p.* **sprung**) **1** (*leap*) пры́г|ать, -нуть; скак|а́ть, -ну́ть; **~ to one's feet** вск|а́кивать, -очи́ть на́ ноги; **~ over a fence** переск|а́кивать, -очи́ть че́рез забо́р; **~ forward** выска́кивать, вы́скочить вперёд; **~ backward** отпря́нуть (*pf.*); **~ to s.o.'s help** бр|оса́ться, -о́ситься (*or* ри́нуться, *pf.*) кому́-н. на по́мощь; **~ into action** энерги́чно прин|има́ться, -я́ться за де́ло; **~ out of bed** вск|а́кивать, -очи́ть с посте́ли; **the lid sprang open** кры́шка внеза́пно откры́лась; **where did you ~ from?** (*coll.*) отку́да вы взяли́сь? **2** (*of liquid*) бить (*impf.*); **water ~s from the earth** из земли́ бьёт ключ. **3** (*come into being*) появ|ля́ться, -и́ться; возн|ика́ть, -и́кнуть; **a breeze sprang up** подня́лся лёгкий ветеро́к; **weeds ~ up on all sides** сорняки́ прораста́ют повсю́ду; **a belief sprang up that ...** появи́лось мне́ние, что...

● *cpd.* **~board** *n.* (*lit., fig.*) трампли́н.

springbok /ˈsprɪŋbɒk/ *n.* антило́па-прыгу́н.

springiness /ˈsprɪŋɪnɪs/ *n.* упру́гость, эласти́чность.

springlike /ˈsprɪŋlaɪk/ *adj.* весе́нний.

springy /ˈsprɪŋɪ/ *adj.* (**springier, springiest**) упру́гий, эласти́чный, пружи́нистый.

sprinkle /ˈsprɪŋk(ə)l/ *n.*: **a ~ of rain** до́ждик; небольшо́й дождь; **a ~ of snow** (лёгкий) снежо́к; **with a ~ of salt** слегка́ подсо́ленный.

● *v.t.*: **~ something with water, ~ water on something** кропи́ть, о-/обры́зг|ивать, -ать что-н. водо́й; **~ something with salt/sand, ~ salt/sand on something** пос|ыпа́ть, -ы́пать что-н. со́лью/песко́м.

sprinkler /ˈsprɪŋklə(r)/ *n.* разбры́згиватель (*m.*); (*in fire safety*) спри́нклер.

sprinkling /ˈsprɪŋklɪŋ/ *n.* (*fig.*) небольшо́е коли́чество; **there was a ~ of children in the audience** в аудито́рии бы́ло небольшо́е коли́чество дете́й.

sprint /sprɪnt/ *n.* спринт.

● *v.t. & i.* бежа́ть (*det.*) с максима́льной ско́ростью.

sprinter /ˈsprɪntə(r)/ *n.* спри́нтер.

sprite /spraɪt/ *n.* (*elf*) эльф; (*fairy*) фе́я.

spritzer /ˈsprɪtsə(r)/ *n.* бе́лое вино́ с со́довой водо́й.

sprocket /ˈsprɒkɪt/ *n.* звёздочка (це́пи).

● *cpd.* **~-wheel** *n.* цепно́е/зубча́тое колесо́; (*in film, tape*) зубча́тый бараба́н.

sprout /spraʊt/ *n.* (*shoot*) росто́к, побе́г, всход; (*pl.,* **Brussels ~s**) брюссе́льская капу́ста.

● *v.t.* отра́|щивать, -сти́ть.

● *v.i.* (*of plant*) пус|ка́ть, -ти́ть ростки́; (*of seed*) прораст|а́ть, -и́.

spruce¹ /spru:s/ *n.* (*tree*) ель.

spruce² /spru:s/ *adj.* аккура́тный, опря́тный, наря́дный; **he looked ~** он был о́чень наря́дный.

● *v.t.*: **~ up** нав|оди́ть, -ести́ красоту́/блеск на + *a.*; прив|оди́ть, -ести́ в поря́док; **~ o.s. up** прихора́шиваться (*impf.*).

sprung /sprʌŋ/ *p.p. and US past of* ⇒**spring²**

spry /spraɪ/ *adj.* (**spryer, spryest**) живо́й, подви́жный, прово́рный.

spud /spʌd/ *n.* (*sl., potato*) карто́шка, карто́фелина.

● *v.t.* (**spudded, spudding**) (*usu.* **~ out, up**) моты́жить (*impf.*); оку́чи|вать, -ть.

spume /spju:m/ *n.* пе́на, на́кипь.

● *v.i.* пе́ниться, вс-.

spun /spʌn/ *adj.* пря́деный; **~ yarn** кручёная пря́жа; **~ gold/glass** золота́я/стекля́нная кани́тель.

spunk /spʌŋk/ *n.* (*coll., mettle*) де́рзость.

spunky /'spʌŋkɪ/ *adj.* (**spunkier, spunkiest**) (*coll.*) де́рзкий.

spur /spɜ:(r)/ *n.* **1** (*on rider's heel, cock's leg*) шпо́ра. **2** (*fig.*) побужде́ние, сти́мул; **competition provided a ~ to his studies** конкуре́нция служи́ла для него́ сти́мулом к учёбе; **on the ~ of the moment** под влия́нием мину́ты. **3** (*of mountain range*) отро́г. **4** (*branch road etc.*) (подъездна́я) ве́тка. **5** (*bot.*) спорынья́.

● *v.t.* (**spurred, spurring**) **1** (*prick with ~s*) пришпо́ри|вать, -ть. **2** (*fig., stimulate*) побу|жда́ть, -ди́ть; под|гоня́ть, -огна́ть; **her words ~red him (on) to action** её слова́ побуди́ли его́ к де́йствию; **~red on by ambition** подгоня́емый честолю́бием.

● *v.i.* (**spurred, spurring**): **~ on, forward** спеши́ть (*impf.*); мча́ться (*impf.*).

spurious /'spjʊərɪəs/ *adj.* подде́льный, фальши́вый.

spurn /spɜ:n/ *v.t.* (*repel*) отт|а́лкивать, -олкну́ть; (*refuse with disdain*) отв|ерга́ть, -е́ргнуть.

spurt[1] /spɜ:t/ *n.* (*sudden effort*) поры́в; (*in race*) рыво́к; **put on a ~** рвану́ться (*pf.*).

● *v.i.* рвану́ться (*pf.*); **~ into the lead** вырыва́ться, вы́рваться вперёд.

spurt[2], **spirt** /spɜ:t/ *nn.* (*jet*) струя́.

● *v.t.* источ|а́ть, -и́ть.

● *v.i.* бить (*impf.*) струёй; хлы́нуть (*pf.*); **the water ~ed into the air** вода́ заби́ла струёй; **blood ~ed from the wound** из ра́ны хлы́нула кровь.

sputa /'spju:tə/ *pl. of* ⇒**sputum**

sputnik /'spʊtnɪk/, /'spʌt-/ *n.* (иску́сственный) спу́тник.

sputter /'spʌtə(r)/ *v.t. & i.* = **splutter**

sput|um /'spju:təm/ *n.* (*pl.* **~a**) слюна́; (*with mucus*) мокро́та.

spy /spaɪ/ *n.* шпио́н; **police ~** аге́нт; шпик (*coll., pej.*).

● *v.t.* (*liter., discern*) разгля́д|ывать, -е́ть; **~ land** уви́деть (*pf.*) зе́млю; **~ out the land** (*fig.*) зонди́ровать (*impf.*) по́чву.

● *v.i.* (*engage in espionage*) шпио́нить (*impf.*); **~ on s.o.** подгля́дывать (*impf.*) за кем-н.; (*as espionage*) шпио́нить (*impf.*) за + *i.*

● *cpds.* **~glass** *n.* подзо́рная труба́; **~hole** *n.* (*Br.*) глазо́к.

spying /'spaɪɪŋ/ *n.* (*espionage*) шпиона́ж; (*watching*) подгля́дывание.

Sq. /skweə(r)/ *n.* (*abbr. of* **Square**) пл. (пло́щадь).

squabble /'skwɒb(ə)l/ *n.* перебра́нка, пререка́ние.

● *v.i.* пререка́ться (*impf.*) (*с кем*); вздо́рить, по-.

squad /skwɒd/ *n.* **1** (*mil.*) гру́ппа, кома́нда, отделе́ние. **2** (*gang, group*) отря́д; рабо́чая брига́да; **flying ~** (*of police*) лету́чий отря́д; **~ car** радиофици́рованная полице́йская автомаши́на.

squaddie /'skwɒdɪ/ *n.* (*Br. coll.*) рядово́й.

squadron /'skwɒdrən/ *n.* (*mil.*) эскадро́н; (*nav.*) эска́дра; (*aeron.*) эскадри́лья; **fighter ~** эскадри́лья истреби́телей.

● *cpd.* **~-leader** *n.* майо́р авиа́ции.

squalid /'skwɒlɪd/ *adj.* гря́зный, ни́щенский, убо́гий; (*sordid, base*) ни́зкий, ни́зменный, гну́сный.

squall /skwɔ:l/ *n.* (*gust*) шквал; (*storm*) гроза́; **encounter a ~** поп|ада́ть, -а́сть в грозу́.

● *v.i.* (*cry*) вопи́ть, за-; пронзи́тельно крича́ть, за-.

squally /'skwɔ:lɪ/ *adj.* шква́листый; **~ weather** шква́листая пого́да.

squalor /'skwɒlə(r)/ *n.* убо́жество; (*sordidness*) ни́зость, гну́сность.

squander /'skwɒndə(r)/ *v.t.* пром|а́тывать, -ота́ть; растра́|чивать, -тить; **he ~ed his fortune** он промота́л своё состоя́ние; **he is ~ing his talents** он растра́чивает свой тала́нты.

squanderer /'skwɒndərə(r)/ *n.* расточи́тель (*fem.* -ница).

square /skweə(r)/ *n.* **1** квадра́т; **the map was divided into ~s** ка́рта была́ разделена́ на квадра́ты. **2** (*on chessboard etc.*) кле́тка; **we are back to ~ one** (*fig.*) мы верну́лись в исхо́дное положе́ние. **3** (*scarf*) ше́йный плато́к. **4** (*open space in town*) пло́щадь; **Red S~** Кра́сная пло́щадь; (*with central garden*) сквер; (*barrack-~*) уче́бный плац. **5** (*US, block of buildings*) кварта́л. **6** (*drawing instrument*) уго́льник; **out of ~** ко́со, неро́вно, неперпендикуля́рно; **on the ~** (*fig.*) (*adj.*) поря́дочный, че́стный; (*adv.*) че́стно, без обма́на. **7** (*math.*) квадра́т; **find the ~ of 72** возв|оди́ть, -ести́ 72 в квадра́т(ную сте́пень). **8** (*sl., old-fashioned person*) челове́к отста́лых взгля́дов.

● *adj.* **1** (*geom., math.*) квадра́тный; **~ metre** (*Br.*), **meter** (*US*) квадра́тный метр; **~ number** квадра́т це́лого числа́; **~ root (of)** квадра́тный ко́рень (из + *g.*); (*right-angled*) прямоуго́льный; **with ~ corners** с прямы́ми угла́ми; (*of shape*) квадра́тный; (*angular*) углова́тый; **~ dance** кадри́ль; **~ shoulders** прямы́е/широ́кие пле́чи. **2** (*even, balanced*) то́чный; в поря́дке; **get one's accounts ~** прив|оди́ть, -ести́ свои́ счета́ в поря́док; **all ~** (*in order*) всё в поря́дке; (*even scoring*) с ра́вным счётом; **we are all ~** мы кви́ты. **3** (*thorough*) по́лный, реши́тельный; **a ~ meal** оби́льная еда́. **4** (*fair, honest*) че́стный, прямо́й, справедли́вый; **~ dealing** че́стное веде́ние дел; **he got a ~ deal** с ним поступи́ли че́стно/по справедли́вости. **5** (*sl., old-fashioned*) отста́лый.

● *adv.* **1** (*at right angles*) перпендикуля́рно. **2** (*straight*) пря́мо; (*firmly in position*): **set something ~ to the wall** ста́вить, по- что-н. вплотну́ю к стене́. **3** (*honestly*) че́стно, пря́мо, непосре́дственно. **4**: **ten feet ~** де́сять фу́тов в ширину́ и де́сять в длину́.

● *v.t.* **1** (*make ~*) прид|ава́ть, -а́ть квадра́тную фо́рму + *d.*; (*wood*) обтёс|ывать, -а́ть по науго́льнику; **~ the circle** (*fig.*) на|ходи́ть, -йти́ квадрату́ру кру́га. **2** (*divide into ~s*) графи́ть, раз- на квадра́ты; **~d paper** графлёная бума́га; (*with big ~s*) бума́га в кле́тку; (*with tiny ~s*) миллиметро́вка. **3** (*math.*) возв|оди́ть, -ести́ в квадра́т (*or* во втору́ю сте́пень); **3 ~d is 9** три в квадра́те равно́ девяти́; **A ~d** A квадра́т; A в квадра́те; A во второ́й сте́пени. **4** (*straighten*) выпрямля́ть, вы́прямить; **~ one's shoulders** распр|авля́ть, -а́вить пле́чи. **5** (*settle*) ула́|живать, -дить; **~ accounts (with)** св|оди́ть, -ести́ счёты (с + *i.*); (*pay*) опла́|чивать, -ти́ть (*счёт*). **6** (*reconcile*) согласо́в|ывать, -а́ть (*что с чем*); приспос|а́бливать, -о́бить (*что к чему*).

● *v.i.* **1** (*agree*) согласо́в|ываться, -а́ться; **~ with** вяза́ться/сходи́ться (*both impf.*) с + *i.*; **this statement does not ~ with the facts** э́то заявле́ние не схо́дится с фа́ктами. **2**: **~ up to s.o.** (*with fists*) пригот|авливаться, -о́виться к бо́ю. **3**: **~ up** (*settle accounts*) **with s.o.** поквита́ться (*pf.*) с кем-н.

● *cpds.* **~-bashing** *n.* (*Br. coll.*) муштра́ на плацу́, шаги́стика; **~-built** *adj.* корена́стый; **~-rigged** *adj.* с прямо́й па́русной осна́сткой; **~-sail** *n.* прямо́й па́рус; **~-shouldered** *adj.* широкопле́чий; **~-toed** *adj.* с тупы́м носко́м.

squash[1] /skwɒʃ/ *n.* (*crush*) да́вка, толчея́; (*Br., drink*) фрукто́вый напи́ток; (**~ rackets**) сквош, ракетбо́л.

● *v.t.* **1** (*crush*) дави́ть, раз-; разда́в|ливать, -и́ть; сплю́щи|вать, -ть; (*compress*) сж|има́ть, -ать; **I ~ed the fly against the wall** я раздави́л му́ху на стене́; **the tomatoes were ~ed** помидо́ры помя́лись. **2** (*crowd*): **the conductor ~ed us into the bus** конду́ктор вти́снул нас в авто́бус; **we were ~ed so tightly, we couldn't move** бы́ло так те́сно, что мы шевельну́ться не могли́. **3** (*quash*) подав|ля́ть, -и́ть; **we must ~ this rumour** (*Br.*), **rumor** (*US*) на́до

S

ликвиди́ровать э́тот слух; **the rebellion was ~ed** мятéж был пода́влен; (*silence by retort*) обескура́жи|вать, -ть; **I felt ~ed** я был обескура́жен.

● *v.i.* (*crowd*) потесни́ться (*pf.*); **they ~ed up to make room for me** они́ потесни́лись, что́бы дать мне мéсто; **they ~ed through the door** они́ проти́снулись в дверь.

squash² /skwɒʃ/ *n.* (*pl.* ~ *or* ~**es**) (*bot.*) ты́ква, кабачо́к.

squat /skwɒt/ *n.* (*posture*) сидéние на ко́рточках; (*coll., unauthorized occupation*) незако́нное вселéние.

● *adj.* (**squatter, squattest**) призéмистый.

● *v.i.* (**squatted, squatting**) **1** (*of person*) сидéть (*impf.*) на ко́рточках; ~ **down** сади́ться, сесть на ко́рточки; присéсть (*pf.*); (*of animals*) прип|ада́ть, -а́сть к землé. **2** (*of unauthorized occupation*) сели́ться, по- самово́льно.

squatter /ˈskwɒtə(r)/ *n.* (*illegal occupant*) сква́ттер.

squaw /skwɔː/ *n.* (*offens.*) скво (*indecl.*); (*woman*) жéнщина; (*wife*) жена́ (*у индейцев*).

squawk /skwɔːk/ *n.* пронзи́тельный крик.

● *v.i.* пронзи́тельно крича́ть, за-.

squeak /skwiːk/ *n.* **1** (*of mouse etc.*) писк, взвизг. **2** (*of hinge etc.*) скрип, визг. **3** (*coll., sound*): **I don't want to hear another ~ out of you!** то́лько пи́кни!

● *v.i.* **1** (*of person or animal*) пища́ть, пи́скнуть. **2** (*of object*) скрипéть (*impf.*), скри́пнуть (*pf.*). **3** (*turn informer; also* **squeal**) стуча́ть, на- (*sl.*).

squeaker /ˈskwiːkə(r)/ *n.* (*device*) пища́лка; (*informer; also* **squealer**) стука́ч (*fem.* -ка) (*sl.*).

squeaky /ˈskwiːkɪ/ *adj.* (**squeakier, squeakiest**) пискли́вый, визгли́вый; скрипу́чий.

squeal /skwiːl/ *n.* визг.

● *v.i.* визжа́ть, за-; (*coll., protest loudly*) подн|има́ть, -я́ть шум; (*sl., turn informer*) = **squeak** *v.i.* 3

squealer /ˈskwiːlə(r)/ = **squeaker**

squeamish /ˈskwiːmɪʃ/ *adj.* **1** (*easily nauseated*) подвéрженный тошнотé; **feel ~** чу́вствовать, по- тошноту́; **blood makes me feel ~** меня́ тошни́т от кро́ви. **2** (*sensitive, scrupulous*) щепети́льный, брезгли́вый; **one can't afford to be ~ in politics** щепети́льность в поли́тике — ро́скошь.

squeamishness /ˈskwiːmɪʃnɪs/ *n.* щепети́льность.

squeegee /ˈskwiːdʒiː/ *n.* рези́новая шва́бра; (*roller*) рези́новый ва́лик.

squeeze /skwiːz/ *n.* **1** (*pressure*) сжа́тие, пожа́тие; **he gave the sponge a ~** он вы́жал гу́бку; **he gave her a ~** он крéпко о́бнял её; **he gave my hand a ~** он пожа́л мне ру́ку.
2 (*something ~d out*): **a ~ of lemon** нéсколько ка́пель лимо́нного со́ка.
3 (*crowding, crush*) теснота́, да́вка; **we got in, but it was a tight ~** нам удало́сь вти́снуться, но бы́ло о́чень тéсно.
4 (*fin.*) ограничéние креди́та.

● *v.t.* **1** (*compress*) сж|има́ть, -ать; сда́в|ливать, -и́ть; **he ~d his fingers in the door** он прищеми́л па́льцы двéрью; (*to extract moisture etc.*) выжима́ть, вы́жать; **he ~d the lemon dry** он вы́жал лимо́н; (*extort*): ~ **money out of s.o.** вымога́ть (*impf.*) дéньги у кого́-н.; ~ **a confession from s.o.** вынужда́ть, вы́нудить призна́ние у кого́-н.
2 (*force, crowd, cram*) вти́с|кивать, -нуть.
3: ~ **one's way** = *v.i.*

● *v.i.* проти́с|киваться, -нуться.

● *cpd.* **~-box** *n.* (*coll.*) гармо́шка, концерти́на.

squeezer /ˈskwiːzə(r)/ *n.* (соко)выжима́лка.

squelch /skweltʃ/ *n.* хлю́панье.

● *v.i.* хлю́п|ать, -нуть; **we ~ed through the mud** мы хлю́пали по грязи́; (*suppress*) подав|ля́ть, -и́ть.

squib /skwɪb/ *n.* **1** (*firework*) петáрда, шути́ха; **damp ~** (*fig.*) прова́л.
2 (*lampoon*) памфлéт, па́сквиль (*m.*).

squid /skwɪd/ *n.* кальма́р.

squiffy /ˈskwɪfɪ/ *adj.* (**squiffier, squiffiest**) (*Br. sl.*) подвы́пивший.

squiggle /ˈskwɪɡ(ə)l/ *n.* загогу́лина, кара́куля.

squiggly /ˈskwɪɡlɪ/ *adj.* волни́стый, изо́гнутый.

squint /skwɪnt/ *n.* **1** косогла́зие; **she has a ~ in her right eye** она́ коси́т на пра́вый глаз. **2** (*coll., glance*) взгляд (и́скоса/укра́дкой).

● *adj.* косо́й, косогла́зый.

● *v.i.* **1** коси́ть (*impf.*). **2** (*half-shut eyes*) щу́риться (*impf.*); прищу́ри|ваться, -тьcя. **3**: ~ **at something** смотрéть, по- и́скоса/укра́дкой на что-н.

● *cpd.* **~-eyed** *adj.* косо́й, косогла́зый.

squire /ˈskwaɪə(r)/ *n.* помéщик, сквайр; (*Br. coll., form of address*) су́дарь.

squirearchy /ˈskwaɪəˌrɑːkɪ/ *n.* (*class*) помéщики (*m. pl.*).

squirm /skwɜːm/ *n.* извива́ться (*impf.*); ко́рчиться (*impf.*); **the child was ~ing on its seat** ребёнок вертéлся/ёрзал на сту́ле; **he made me ~ with embarrassment** он меня́ так смути́л, что я не знал, куда́ дéться.

squirrel /ˈskwɪr(ə)l/ *n.* бéлка; (**~ fur**) бéличий мех, бéлка.

● *v.t.* (**squirrelled, squirrelling;** *US* **squirreled, squirreling**): ~ **away** (*to hide for future use*) запас|а́ться, -ти́сь (+*i.*).

squirt /skwɜːt/ *n.* **1** (*jet*) струя́.
2 (*instrument*) шприц; спринцо́вка.
3 (*coll., of person*) ничто́жество.

● *v.t.* пры́с|кать, -нуть; ~ **water in the air** пус|ка́ть, -ти́ть струю́ воды́ в во́здух; ~ **scent from atomizer** бры́згать, по- духа́ми из пульвериза́тора.

● *v.i.* бить (*impf.*) струёй; разбры́зг|иваться, -аться.

Sri Lanka /ʃriː ˈlæŋkə/, /ʃrɪˈlæŋkə/, /sr-/ *n.* Шри-Ла́нка.

Sri Lankan /ʃriː ˈlæŋkən/, /ʃrɪˈlæŋkən/, /sr-/ *n.* жи́тель (*fem.* -ница) Шри-Ла́нки.

SS *abbr. of* **1** ***steamship*** парохо́д. **2** (*hist.*) ***Schutzstaffel***: ~ **man** эсэ́совец.

St. *abbr. of* **1** ***street*** ул. (у́лица). **2** ***Saint*** св. (Свят|о́й, -а́я).

stab /stæb/ *n.* **1** уда́р (о́стрым ору́жием); ~ **in the back** (*fig.*) нож/уда́р в спи́ну. **2** (*fig., sharp pain*) внеза́пная о́страя боль; уко́л; **he felt a ~ of conscience** он почу́вствовал уко́л(ы) со́вести. **3** (*coll., attempt*): **I'll have a ~ at it** попро́бую.

● *v.t.* (**stabbed, stabbing**) **1** (*wound*): ~ **s.o. in the chest with a knife** нан|оси́ть, -ести́ кому́-н. уда́р в грудь ножо́м; **the police are investigating a ~bing incident** поли́ция ведёт слéдствие по по́воду происшéдшей поножо́вщины. **2** (*plunge*): **he ~bed a knife into the table** он всади́л/вонзи́л нож в стол.

● *v.i.* (**stabbed, stabbing**) **1**: ~ **at s.o.** бр|оса́ться, -о́ситься на кого́-н. с ножо́м. **2** (*of pain etc.*) стреля́ть (*impf.*).

stability /stəˈbɪlɪtɪ/ *n.* стаби́льность, усто́йчивость.

stabilization /ˌsteɪbɪlaɪˈzeɪʃ(ə)n/ *n.* стабилиза́ция.

stabilize /ˈsteɪbɪˌlaɪz/ *v.t.* стабилизи́ровать (*impf., pf.*).

stabilizer /ˈsteɪbɪˌlaɪzə(r)/ *n.* стабилиза́тор.

stable¹ /ˈsteɪb(ə)l/ *n.* **1** коню́шня.
2 (*group of horses*) ло́шади (*f. pl.*) одно́й коню́шни; (*racing*) скаковы́е ло́шади одного́ владéльца; **from the same ~** (*fig.*) одного́ происхождéния, ро́дственный.

● *v.t.* (*put in stable*) ста́вить, по- в коню́шню; (*keep in stable*) содержа́ть (*impf.*) в коню́шне.

● *cpds.* **~-boy, ~-hand, ~-lad** (*Br.*) *nn.* помо́щник ко́нюха; **~-companion** *n.* ло́шадь той же коню́шни; (*fig.*) однока́шник; **~man** *n.* ко́нюх; **~mate** = **~-companion**

stable² /ˈsteɪb(ə)l/ *adj.* (**stabler, stablest**) усто́йчивый, стаби́льный; **a ~ job** постоя́нная рабо́та.

stabling /ˈsteɪblɪŋ/ *n.* коню́шни (*f. pl.*).

staccato /stəˈkɑːtəʊ/ *n.* (*pl.* **~s**) *& adv.* стакка́то (*indecl.*).

● *adj.* отры́вистый.

stack /stæk/ *n.* **1** (*of hay etc.*) стог; скирда́.
2 (*pile*): ~ **of wood** шта́бель (*m.*) дров, полéнница; ~ **of papers** ки́па/сто́пка бума́г; ~ **of plates** стопа́ таре́лок.
3 (*coll., usu. pl., large amount*) ма́сса, ку́ча, гру́да; **he has ~s of money** у него́ ку́ча дéнег; **a ~ of work** ма́сса/ку́ча рабо́ты; **I've a ~ of letters to write** мне на́до написа́ть ку́чу пи́сем; **we have ~s of time** у нас ку́ча/полно́ врéмени.
4 (*chimney*) дымова́я труба́.

● *v.t.* **1**: ~ **hay** мета́ть (*impf.*) сéно в стог; скирдова́ть (*impf.*) сéно; ~ **books on the floor** ста́вить, по- кни́ги

сто́пками на полу́; **~ wood** скла́дывать, сложи́ть дрова́ штабеля́ми; **~ plates** сост|авля́ть, -а́вить таре́лки стопо́й (*or* в сто́пку); **~ arms!** (*mil.*) соста́вь!
2: **~ the cards** подтасо́в|ывать, -а́ть ка́рты; **the cards were ~ed against him** (*fig.*) всё бы́ло про́тив него́.
3: **~ aircraft** эшелони́ровать (*impf.*, *pf.*) самолёты пе́ред захо́дом на поса́дку.

stadi|um /ˈsteɪdɪəm/ *n.* (*pl.* **~ums** *or* **~a**) стадио́н.

staff /stɑːf/ *n.* **1** (*for walking etc.*) по́сох, па́лка; (*pole*) столб; (*fig.*): **bread is the ~ of life** хлеб — осно́ва жи́зни/всему́ голова́. **2** (*emblem of office*) жезл.
3 (*shaft, handle*) дре́вко. **4** (*body of assistants, employees*) штат; (*in army*) ли́чный соста́в; **~ of a hospital** больни́чный персона́л; **editorial ~** сотру́дники реда́кции; **teaching ~** преподава́тельский соста́в; **~ nurse** (*Br.*) мла́дшая медсестра́; **~ room** (*Br., at school*) учи́тельская; **~ meeting** педагоги́ческий сове́т; **the department is short of ~** в отде́ле не хвата́ет сотру́дников/рабо́тников. **5** (*mil.*) штаб; **General S~** генера́льный штаб; **~ college** акаде́мия генера́льного шта́ба; **~ officer** штабно́й офице́р; **~ sergeant** штаб-сержа́нт. **6** (*mus.*) но́тный стан.
● *v.t.* укомплекто́в|ывать, -а́ть (*что or* штат *чего*).

stag /stæg/ *n.* (*deer*) оле́нь(*m.*)-саме́ц; **go ~** (*US, without a male/female partner*) без кавале́ра/де́вушки.
● *cpds.* **~-beetle** *n.* жук-оле́нь (*m.*); **~-party** *n.* (*coll.*) мальчи́шник.

stage /steɪdʒ/ *n.* **1** (*theatr.*) сце́на, подмо́стки; **front of the ~** авансце́на; (*as profession*) теа́тр, сце́на; **go on the ~** идти́, пойти́ на сце́ну; **put a play on the ~** ста́вить, по- пье́су на сце́не; **he writes for the ~** он пи́шет для теа́тра.
2 (*attr.*): **~ direction** рема́рка; **~ door** служе́бный/актёрский вход (в теа́тр); **~ effect** сцени́ческий эффе́кт; **~ fright** страх пе́ред пу́бликой; **~ whisper** театра́льный шёпот.
3 (*fig., scene of action*) сце́на, аре́на, по́прище; **he quit the political ~** он поки́нул полити́ческую аре́ну.
4 (*phase, point*) ста́дия, фа́за, эта́п; **the war reached a critical ~** война́ вступи́ла в крити́ческую фа́зу; **at this ~ he was interrupted** на э́тот моме́нт его́ переби́ли; **she was in the last ~ of consumption** она́ находи́лась в после́дней ста́дии чахо́тки; **the baby has reached the talking ~** ребёнок на́чал говори́ть (*or* заговори́л); **negotiations reached their final ~** наступи́л заверша́ющий эта́п перегово́ров; **I shall do it in ~s** я сде́лаю э́то постепе́нно.
5 (*section of route or journey*) перего́н, эта́п; **we travelled** (*Br.*), **traveled** (*US*) **by easy ~s** мы путеше́ствовали/е́хали не спеша́.
6 (*of rocket*) ступе́нь.
● *v.t.*: **~ a play** ста́вить, по- пье́су; (*organize*) устр|а́ивать, -о́ить; организова́ть (*impf.*, *pf.*).
● *cpds.* **~-coach** *n.* почто́вый дилижа́нс; **~craft** *n.* драматурги́ческое мастерство́; (*of director/actor*) мастерство́ режиссёра/актёра; **~-hand** *n.* рабо́чий сце́ны; **~-manage** *v.t.* ста́вить, по- (*спектакль*); (*secretly*) (закули́сно) руководи́ть + *i.*; **~-manager** *n.* постано́вщик; **~-struck** *adj.*: **she is ~-struck** она́ заболе́ла сце́ной.

stager /ˈsteɪdʒə(r)/ *n.*: **old ~** стре́ляный воробе́й.

stagey /ˈsteɪdʒɪ/ = **stagy**

stagger /ˈstægə(r)/ *n.* шата́ние, поша́тывание.
● *v.t.* **1** (*cause to ~*): **a ~ing blow** сокруши́тельный уда́р. **2** (*disconcert*) потряс|а́ть, -ти́; пора|жа́ть, -зи́ть; ошелом|ля́ть, -и́ть; **we were ~ed by the news** мы бы́ли потрясены́/поражены́ э́той но́востью; **~ing success** потряса́ющий успе́х.
3 (*arrange in zigzag order*) распол|ага́ть, -ожи́ть в ша́хматном поря́дке. **4**: **~ working hours, holidays** *etc.* распредел|я́ть, -и́ть часы́ рабо́ты, о́тпуска *и т.п.*
● *v.i.* шата́ться (*impf.*); поша́тываться (*impf.*); **they ~ed down the street** они́ шли по у́лице поша́тываясь.

staging /ˈsteɪdʒɪŋ/ *n.* **1** (*platform*) подмо́стк|и (*pl.*, *g.* -ов); (*scaffolding*) лес|а́ (*pl.*, *g.* -о́в). **2** (*of play*) постано́вка. **3**: **~ post** (*aeron.*) промежу́точный аэродро́м.

stagnant /ˈstægnənt/ *adj.* **1** (*of water*) стоя́чий. **2** (*sluggish*) засто́йный, ко́сный.

stagnate /stægˈneɪt/ *v.i.* **1** (*of water*) заст|а́иваться, -оя́ться. **2** (*fig.*) косне́ть, за-.

stagnation /stægˈneɪʃ(ə)n/ *n.* (*of water*) засто́й; (*fig.*) засто́й; (*econ.*) стагна́ция, засто́й.

stagy /ˈsteɪdʒɪ/ *adj.* (**stagier, stagiest**) театра́льный; аффекти́рованный.

staid /steɪd/ *adj.* степе́нный, положи́тельный.

stain /steɪn/ *n.* **1** пятно́; **remove a ~** выводи́ть, вы́вести пятно́. **2** (*for colouring wood etc.*) протра́ва, краси́тель (*m.*); **wood ~** протра́ва, мори́лка. **3** (*fig., moral defect*) пятно́, позо́р; **without a ~ on his character** с незапя́тнанной репута́цией.
● *v.t.* **1** (*discolour, soil*) пятна́ть, за-; па́чкать, за-/ис-; **water will not ~ the carpet** вода́ не оставля́ет пя́тен на ковре́. **2** (*colour with dye etc.*) окра́|шивать, -сить; протра́в|ливать (*or* протрав|ля́ть), -и́ть; **~ed glass** цветно́е стекло́; **~ed-glass window** витра́ж; **~ wood** мори́ть, за- де́рево.
3 (*fig.*) пятна́ть, за-.
● *v.i.* (*cause ~s*) ост|авля́ть, -а́вить пя́тна; (*be subject to ~ing*) па́чкаться (*impf.*); быть (*impf.*) ма́рким.

stainless /ˈsteɪnlɪs/ *adj.*
1 (*unblemished*) чи́стый; (*fig.*) безупре́чный. **2**: **~ steel** нержаве́ющая сталь.

stair /steə(r)/ *n.* **1** (*step*) ступе́нька.
2 (*pl. or* **~case**) ле́стница; **flight of ~s** ле́стничный марш; **he ran up the ~s** он взбежа́л по ле́стнице; **he ran down the ~s** он сбежа́л с ле́стницы.
● *cpds.* **~-carpet** *n.* доро́жка (для ле́стницы); **~case, ~way** *nn.* ле́стница; ле́стничная кле́тка; **~-rod** *n.* пру́тик, укрепля́ющий ле́стничный ковёр; **~way** *n.* = **~case; ~-well** *n.* ша́хта ле́стницы; ле́стничный коло́дец.

stake /steɪk/ *n.* **1** (*post*) столб, кол (*pl.* ко́лья); **row of ~s** частоко́л; **the plants were tied to ~s** расте́ния бы́ли подвя́заны к ко́лышкам; **he was burnt at the ~** его́ сожгли́ на костре́; **pull up ~s** (*fig.*) сн|има́ться, -я́ться с ме́ста.
2 (*wager; money deposited*) ста́вка, закла́д; (*pl.*, **~ race**) ска́чки (*f. pl.*) на приз; **play for high ~s** игра́ть (*impf.*) по кру́пному; (*fig.*) ста́вить, по- всё на ка́рту.
3 (*interest, share*) интере́с, до́ля; **he has a ~ in the country** он кро́вно заинтересо́ван в процвета́нии страны́.
4: **his reputation was at ~** его́ репута́ция была́ поста́влена на ка́рту.
● *v.t.* **1** (*support with ~*) укреп|ля́ть, -и́ть коло́м.
2 (*wager*) ста́вить, по-; (*risk, gamble*) рискова́ть (*impf.*) + *i.*; **he ~d his fortune on one race** он поста́вил всё своё состоя́ние на оди́н забе́г.
● *with advs.*: **~ off** *v.t.* отгор|а́живать, -оди́ть; **~ out** *v.t.*: **~ out a boundary** отм|еча́ть, -е́тить ве́хами грани́цу; **~ (out) one's claim** (*lit.*) застолби́ть (*pf.*) уча́сток; (*fig.*): **he ~d (out) his claim to a seat at the conference** он заяви́л о своём наме́рении уча́ствовать в конфере́нции.
● *cpds.* **~-holder** *n.* посре́дник; **~-out** *n.* (*coll.*) полице́йский надзо́р.

Stakhanovism /stəˈkɑːnəˌvɪz(ə)m/ *n.* стаха́новское движе́ние.

Stakhanovite /stəˈkɑːnəˌvaɪt/ *n.* стаха́новец.
● *adj.* стаха́новский.

stalactite /ˈstæləkˌtaɪt/, /stəˈlæk-/ *n.* сталакти́т.

stalagmite /ˈstæləgˌmaɪt/ *n.* сталагми́т.

stale /steɪl/ *adj.* (**staler, stalest**)
1 (*not fresh*) несве́жий; **~ bread** чёрствый хлеб; (*of air*) спёртый, за́тхлый; **the room smells ~** в ко́мнате за́тхлый во́здух. **2** (*lacking novelty, tedious*) изби́тый, устаре́вший; **a ~ joke** изби́тая шу́тка; **~ news** устаре́вшая но́вость. **3** (*past one's best*) вы́дохшийся; **he got ~ at his work** он заки́с на свое́й рабо́те.
● *v.i.*: **pleasures that never ~** ра́дости, кото́рые никогда́ не приеда́ются.

stalemate /ˈsteɪlmeɪt/ *n.* (*chess*) пат; (*fig., impasse*) тупи́к, безвы́ходное положе́ние.
● *v.t.* де́лать, с- пат + *d.*; (*fig.*) заг|оня́ть, -на́ть в тупи́к.

staleness /ˈsteɪlnɪs/ *n.* (*of food*) залежа́лость; (*of bread*) чёрствость; (*of air, room etc.*) спёртость, за́тхлость; (*of *joke etc.*) избитость; (*of news*) устарелость.

Stalinism /ˈstɑːlɪˌnɪz(ə)m/ *n.* сталинизм.

Stalinist /ˈstɑːlɪnɪst/ *n.* сталинист (*fem.* -ка).

● *adj.* сталинистский.

stalk¹ /stɔːk/ *n.* (*stem*) стебель (*m.*); черешок; (*cabbage-*~) кочерыжка; (*of wine-glass*) ножка.

stalk² /stɔːk/ *v.t.* **1** (*pursue stealthily*) выслеживать, выследить; **~ing-horse** (*fig.*) личина, предлог. **2** (*persecute obsessively*) преследовать (*impf.*).

● *v.i.* (*stride*) шествовать (*impf.*); гордо выступать (*impf.*); (*fig.*): **famine ~ed the land** голод шествовал по стране.

stalker /ˈstɔːkə(r)/ *n.* **1** (*hunter*) охотник. **2** (*persecutor*) человек патологически преследующий предмет своего внимания; навязчивый преследователь.

stall¹ /stɔːl/ *n.* **1** (*for animal*) стойло. **2** (*in market etc.*) прилавок, стойка; (*booth*) ларёк; **book ~** киоск; **flower ~** цветочный ларёк; **newspaper ~** газетный киоск. **3** (*pl., Br., theatr.*) партер, кресла (*nt. pl.*). **4** (*of engine*) заглухание мотора; (*of aircraft*) сваливание.

● *v.t.* **1** (*place in* ~) ставить, по- в стойло; (*keep in* ~) содержать (*impf.*) в стойле. **2**: **~ an engine** (нечаянно) заглуш|ать, -ить мотор.

● *v.i.* **1** (*get stuck*) застр|евать, -ять; ув|язать, -язнуть. **2** (*of engine*) глохнуть, за-; (*aeron.*) терять, по- скорость при срыве потока; **~ing speed** скорость срыва.

● *cpd.* **~-holder** *n.* (*Br.*) владелец ларька.

stall² /stɔːl/ *v.t.* (*block, delay*) задерж|ивать, -ать.

● *v.i.* (*play for time*) тянуть, канителить (*both impf.*).

stallion /ˈstæljən/ *n.* жеребец.

stalwart /ˈstɔːlwət/ *n.* (*pol.*) активист (*fem.* -ка).

● *adj.* (*robust*) рослый, дюжий; (*staunch*) отважный, доблестный.

stamen /ˈsteɪmən/ *n.* тычинка.

stamina /ˈstæmɪnə/ *n.* выносливость, выдержка.

stammer /ˈstæmə(r)/ *n.* заикание; **person with a ~** заика (*c.g.*); **speak with a ~** заикаться (*impf.*).

● *v.t.* произн|осить, -ести (*что*) заикаясь.

● *v.i.* заикаться (*impf.*).

stammerer /ˈstæmərə(r)/ *n.* заика (*c.g.*).

stamp /stæmp/ *n.* **1** (*of foot*) топот, топанье; **with a ~ of the foot** топнув ногой.
2 (*instrument*) штемпель (*m.*), штамп, печать, клеймо.
3 (*impress, mark*) печать, клеймо; (*postage etc.*) марка.
4 (*characteristic, mark*) печать, отпечаток; **his work bears the ~ of genius** его работа отмечена печатью гения.

● *v.t.* **1** (*imprint*) штамповать, про-; штемпелевать (*impf.*); клеймить, за-; оттис|кивать, -нуть; **a document ~ed with the date** документ с проштемпелёванной датой; **a design ~ed in metal** рисунок, оттиснутый на металле; **the maker's name is ~ed on the goods** на товаре проставлено клеймо изготовителя.
2 (*affix ~ to*): **~ an envelope** наклеи|вать, -ть марку на конверт; **~ a receipt** ставить, по- печать на квитанции.
3 (*imprint on mind*) запечатл|евать, -еть; **the scene is ~ed on my memory** эта сцена запечатлелась в моей памяти.
4 (*beat on ground*): **~ one's feet** топать (*impf.*) ногами; **~ the snow from one's shoes** сби|вать, -ть снег с ботинок.

● *v.i.* (*feet*) топ|ать, -нуть.

● *with adv.*: **~ out** *v.t.* (*lit.*): **~ out a fire** затаптывать, затоптать огонь; (*exterminate, destroy*) уничт|ожать, -ожить; (*suppress*) подав|лять, -ить; **the revolt was quickly ~ed out** восстание было скоро подавлено; **~ out an epidemic** искорен|ять, -ить эпидемию.

● *cpds.* **~-album** *n.* альбом для марок; **~-collecting** *n.* филателия; **~-collector** *n.* филателист (*fem.* -ка); **~-dealer** *n.* торговец марками; **~-duty** *n.* гербовый сбор; **~-machine** *n.* автомат по продаже почтовых марок; **~-paper** *n.* поля (*nt. pl.*) марочного листа.

stampede /stæmˈpiːd/ *n.* (*of cattle*) бегство; (*of people*) массовое (паническое) бегство.

● *v.t.* обра|щать, -тить в бегство.

● *v.i.* (*of cattle*) разбе|гаться, -жаться врассыпную; (*of people*) обра|щаться, -титься в (паническое) бегство.

stance /stɑːns/, /stæns/ *n.* позиция; **take up a ~** зан|имать, -ять позицию.

stanch /stɑːntʃ/, /stɔːntʃ/, **staunch** /stɔːntʃ/, /stɑːntʃ/ *vv.t.*: **~ a wound** остан|авливать, -овить кровотечение из раны.

stanchion /ˈstɑːnʃ(ə)n/ *n.* подпорка, опора.

stand /stænd/ *n.* **1** (*support, e.g. for teapot*) подставка; (*for bicycles*) стеллаж; (*for telescope*) штатив.
2 (*stall*) стойка; (*Br., for display*) стенд, щит.
3 (*raised structure, e.g. for spectators*) трибуна.
4 (*for taxis etc.*) стоянка.
5 (*halt*) остановка; **bring, come to a ~** остан|авливать(ся), -овить(ся).
6 (*position*) место; **take one's ~ on the platform** зан|имать, -ять место на сцене; (*fig.*): **take a firm ~** зан|имать, -ять твёрдую позицию; **make a ~ against s.o.** оказ|ывать, -ать сопротивление кому-н.
7 (*theatr., stop for performance*): **one-night ~** однодневные гастроли (*f. pl.*).

● *v.t.* (*past and p.p.* **stood**) **1** (*place, set*) ставить, по-; **he stood the ladder against the wall** он приставил лестницу к стене; **the teacher stood him in the corner** учитель поставил его в угол; **he stood the box on end** он поставил ящик стоймя (*or* на попа).
2 (*bear, tolerate, endure*) терпеть, вы-; выносить, вынести; перен|осить, -ести; **how does he ~ the pain?** как он переносит боль?; **she can't ~ him** она его не выносит (*or* терпеть не может); **I can't ~ cold** я не выношу холода; (*withstand*) выдерживать, выдержать; **his plays have stood the test of time** его пьесы выдержали испытание временем.
3 (*not yield*): **~ one's ground** не уступ|ать, -ить.
4 (*undergo*) подв|ергаться, -ергнуться + *d.*; **~ one's trial** отв|ечать, -етить перед судом.
5: **he doesn't ~ a chance** у него нет никакой надежды.
6 (*provide at one's own expense*) уго|щать, -стить (*кого чем*); ставить, по- (*что кому*); **he stood drinks all round** он угостил каждого (стаканом, кружкой *и т.п.*); он поставил всем по стакану *и т.п.*

● *v.i.* (*past and p.p.* **stood**) **1** (*be or stay in upright position*) стоять (*impf.*); **she was too weak to ~** она была слишком слаба, чтобы стоять; **he kept me ~ing** он не предложил мне сесть; **~ing room only** (*theatr.*) сидячих мест нет; **a ~ing ovation** бурная овация; **he left the car ~ing in the rain** он оставил машину под дождём; **she let the plant ~ in the sun** она выставила цветок на солнце; **the sight of the corpse made my hair ~ on end** при виде трупа у меня волосы стали дыбом; **he is old enough to ~ on his own feet** он достаточно взрослый, чтобы стоять на своих ногах; **he hasn't a leg to ~ on** у него нет ни малейших (*or* нет никаких) доказательств; **I could do that ~ing on my head** я мог бы это сделать левой ногой; **I shan't ~ in your way** я вам не стану мешать; **~ still!** стойте смирно!
2 (*with indication of height*): **he ~s six feet tall** рост у него шесть футов.
3 (*continue, remain*): **our house will ~ for another fifty years** наш дом простоит ещё пятьдесят лет; **~ fast, firm** держаться (*impf.*) непоколебимо/твёрдо; **not a stone was left ~ing** камня на камне не осталось; *see also* ⇒**standing.**
4 (*hold good*) ост|аваться, -аться в силе.
5 (*be situated*) стоять (*impf.*); находиться (*impf.*); **a house once stood here** когда-то здесь стоял дом.
6 (*find o.s., be*): **he stood convicted of murder** суд признал его виновным в убийстве; **we ~ in need of help** мы нуждаемся в помощи; **I ~ corrected** я признаю свою ошибку; **this is how matters ~** вот как обстоят дела; **as matters ~** при данном положении вещей; **I shall leave the text as it ~s** я оставляю текст как он есть; **how do we ~ for money?** как у нас (обстоит) с деньгами?; **the umbrella stood me in good stead** зонтик мне весьма пригодился.

7 (*rise to one's feet*) вста|ва́ть, -ть.
8 (*come to a halt*) остан|а́вливаться, -ови́ться.
9 (*assume or move to specified position*): **I'll ~ here** я ста́ну сюда́; **we had to ~ in a queue** (*Br.*), **in line** (*US*) нам пришло́сь постоя́ть в о́череди; **he stood on tiptoe** он встал на цы́почки; **he (went and) stood on the tarpaulin** он ступи́л/наступи́л на брезе́нт; **I (went and) stood by the table** я стал у стола́; **~ back!** (отступи́те) наза́д!; отойди́те!; **the soldiers stood to attention** бойцы́ вста́ли по сто́йке «сми́рно»; **~ at ease!** во́льно!
10 (*remain motionless*): **the machinery is ~ing idle** станки́ проста́ивают; **let the tea ~!** да́йте ча́ю настоя́ться!

● *with preps.*: **we will ~ by** (*support*) **you** мы вас подде́ржим; **I ~ by what I said** я не отступа́юсь от свои́х слов; **~ for office** (*Br.*) выставля́ть, вы́ставить свою́ кандидату́ру; **~ for Parliament** (*Br.*) баллоти́роваться (*impf.*) в парла́мент; **we ~ for freedom** мы стои́м за свобо́ду; **'Mg' ~s for magnesium** Mg обознача́ет ма́гний; **I will not ~ for such impudence** я не потерплю́ тако́й на́глости; **don't ~ on ceremony** не стесня́йтесь!; пожа́луйста, без церемо́ний!; **his father stood over him till the work was finished** оте́ц стоя́л у него́ над душо́й, пока́ он не зако́нчил рабо́ту; **it ~s to reason** (само́ собо́й) разуме́ется; не подлежи́т сомне́нию; **he ~s to win/lose £1,000** его́ ждёт вы́игрыш/про́игрыш в ты́сячу фу́нтов; **how do you ~ with your boss?** как к вам отно́сится ваш нача́льник?

● *with advs.*: **~ about, ~ around** *vv.i.* стоя́ть (*impf.*) без де́ла; торча́ть (*impf.*) (*coll.*); **don't ~ about in the corridor!** не торчи́те (*coll.*) в коридо́ре!; **~ aside** *v.i.* (*remain aloof*) стоя́ть (*impf.*) в стороне́; (*move to one side*) сторони́ться, по-; **~ back** *v.i.* (*also fig.*) от|ходи́ть, -ойти́ в сто́рону; **the house ~s back from the road** дом стои́т в стороне́ от доро́ги; **he stood back to admire the picture** он отошёл наза́д, что́бы полюбова́ться карти́ной; **he ~s back in favour** (*Br.*), **favor** (*US*) **of others** он уступа́ет ме́сто други́м; **~ by** *v.i.* (*be ready*) быть/стоя́ть (*impf.*) нагото́ве; **the troops were ordered to ~ by** войска́м приказа́ли стоя́ть нагото́ве; **~ by to fire!** пригото́виться к стрельбе́!; (*be spectator*): **I could not ~ by and see her ill-treated** я не мог смотре́ть безуча́стно, как над не́ю издева́ются; **~ down** *v.i.* (*of candidate*): **he stood down in favour** (*Br.*), **favor** (*US*) **of his brother** он снял свою́ кандидату́ру в по́льзу бра́та; (*of minister etc.*) под|ава́ть, -а́ть в отста́вку; **~ in** *v.i.* (*substitute*): **~ in for s.o. else** замен|я́ть, -и́ть кого́-н. друго́го; **~ off** *v.t.*: **~ off workers** (*Br.*) вре́менно ув|ольня́ть, -о́лить рабо́чих; *v.i.*: **we stood off a mile from the harbour** (*Br.*), **harbor** (*US*) мы стоя́ли в (одно́й) ми́ле от га́вани; **~ out** *v.i.* (*be prominent, conspicuous*) выделя́ться (*impf.*); выдава́ться (*impf.*); **his house ~s out from all the others** его́ дом си́льно выделя́ется среди́ други́х; **his work ~s out from the others'** его́ рабо́та ре́зко выделя́ется среди́ про́чих; **his mistakes ~ out a mile** (*coll.*) его́ оши́бки броса́ются в глаза́; (*show resistance*): **~ out against tyranny** противостоя́ть (*impf.*) деспоти́зму; (*hold out*): **~ out for one's claims** наст|а́ивать, -оя́ть на свои́х тре́бованиях; **~ over** *v.i.* (*be postponed*) быть отло́женным; **~ to** *v.i.* (*mil.*): **~ to!** в ружьё!; **~ up** *v.t.*: **he stood his bicycle up against the wall** он прислони́л свой велосипе́д к стене́; (*coll.*): **his girl-friend stood him up** его́ подру́га не пришла́ на свида́ние; *v.i.*: **he stood up as I entered** он встал, когда́ я вошёл; **he ~s up for his rights** он отста́ивает свои́ права́; **he stood up bravely to his opponent** он оказа́л му́жественное сопротивле́ние проти́внику; **this steel ~s up to high temperatures** э́та сталь выде́рживает высо́кие температу́ры.

● *cpds.* **~-alone** *adj.* (*comput.*) автоно́мный; **~by** *n.* (*state of readiness*) гото́вность; (*dependable thing or person*) надёжная опо́ра; испы́танное сре́дство; **~by generator** резе́рвный генера́тор; **~-down** *n.* (*mil.*) отбо́й; **~-in** *n.* замести́тель (*fem.* -ница); **~-offish** *adj.* (*aloof*) сде́ржанный; (*haughty*) высокоме́рный; **~pipe** *n.* коло́нка; **~point** *n.* то́чка зре́ния; **~still** *n.* остано́вка, безде́йствие; **come to a ~still** остан|а́вливаться, -ови́ться; застопо́риться (*pf.*) (*coll.*); **at a ~still** на мёртвой то́чке; **bring to a ~still** остан|а́вливать, -ови́ть; застопо́рить (*pf.*) (*coll.*); **trade is at a ~still** торго́вля нахо́дится в засто́е; **many factories are at a ~still** мно́го фа́брик безде́йствует; **the matter is temporarily at a ~still** де́ло пока́ что не дви́жется/дви́гается; де́ло засто́порилось (*coll.*); **~-to** *n.* (*mil.*) боева́я гото́вность; **~-up** *adj.*: **~-up collar** стоя́чий воротни́к; **~-up supper** у́жин а-ля-фурше́т; **~-up fight** кула́чный бой.

standard /ˈstændəd/ *n.* **1** (*flag*) зна́мя, штанда́рт.
2 (*norm, model*) станда́рт, но́рма; (*level*) у́ровень (*m.*); **come up to ~** соотве́тствовать (*impf.*) тре́буемому у́ровню; **set a high ~** устан|а́вливать, -ови́ть высо́кие тре́бования; **~ of education** у́ровень (*m.*) образова́ния; **~ of living** жи́зненный у́ровень; **his work falls short of accepted ~s** его́ рабо́та не соотве́тствует существу́ющим тре́бованиям; **by American ~s** по америка́нским ме́ркам/но́рмам/крите́риям; **by any ~** по любы́м но́рмам; **work of a high ~** рабо́та высо́кого у́ровня; **below ~** ни́же но́рмы; **there is no absolute ~ of morality** не существу́ет абсолю́тной но́рмы мора́ли; **gold ~** золото́й станда́рт.

● *adj.* **1** станда́ртный, норма́льный; **of ~ size** станда́ртного разме́ра.
2 (*model, basic*) нормати́вный, образцо́вый; (*general*) типово́й; **~ English** литерату́рный/нормати́вный англи́йский язы́к; **~ authors** (писа́тели-)кла́ссики; **a ~ reference work** авторите́тный спра́вочник; **~ gauge** станда́ртная ширина́ коле́й.
3: **~ lamp** (*Br.*) стоя́чая ла́мпа, торше́р.

● *cpd.* **~-bearer** *n.* знамено́сец.

standardization /ˌstændədaɪˈzeɪʃ(ə)n/ *n.* стандартиза́ция.

standardize /ˈstændəˌdaɪz/ *v.t.* стандартизи́ровать (*impf., pf.*); нормирова́ть (*impf., pf.*).

standee /stænˈdiː/ *n.* (*US*) (*passenger*) стоя́щий пассажи́р; (*spectator*) стоя́щий зри́тель (*m.*).

standing /ˈstændɪŋ/ *n.* **1** (*rank*) положе́ние; (*reputation*) репута́ция; (*authority*) вес; **a person of high ~** высокопоста́вленное лицо́.
2 (*duration*) продолжи́тельность; **a custom of long ~** стари́нный обы́чай.
3 (*length of service*) стаж.

● *adj.*: **~ army** постоя́нная а́римя; **~ committee** постоя́нный комите́т; **~ corn** хлеб на корню́; **~ invitation** приглаше́ние приходи́ть в любо́е вре́мя; **~ joke** дежу́рная шу́тка; **~ jump** прыжо́к с ме́ста; **~ order** (*Br.*) (*to banker*) прика́з о регуля́рных платежа́х; (*to newsagent etc.*) постоя́нный зака́з; **~ orders** пра́вила процеду́ры; **~ water** стоя́чая вода́.

stank /stæŋk/ *past of* ⇒**stink**

stanza /ˈstænzə/ *n.* строфа́.

staple[1] /ˈsteɪp(ə)l/ *n.* (*U-shaped metal bar*) скоба́; (*for papers*) ско́бка.

● *v.t.*: **~ papers together** скреп|ля́ть, -и́ть бума́ги ско́бкой.

staple[2] /ˈsteɪp(ə)l/ *n.* **1** (*principal commodity*) основно́й това́р/проду́кт; **the ~s of that country** основна́я проду́кция э́той страны́; **~s of British industry** основны́е ви́ды проду́кции брита́нской промы́шленности.
2 (*chief material*) осно́ва; **~ of diet** осно́ва пита́ния; **~ of conversation** гла́вная те́ма разгово́ра.

● *adj.* основно́й, гла́вный.

stapler /ˈsteɪplə(r)/ *n.* (*for paper*) сте́плер.

star /stɑː(r)/ *n.* **1** звезда́; **falling, shooting ~** па́дающая звезда́; **North, Pole S~** Поля́рная звезда́; **S~ of David** звезда́ Дави́да; **we slept under the ~s** мы спа́ли под откры́тым не́бом; **thank one's lucky ~s** благодари́ть (*impf.*) свою́ звезду́ (*or* судьбу́); **five-~ hotel** пятизвёздочная гости́ница.
2 (*famous actor etc.*) звезда́; свети́ло (нау́ки, медици́ны, *и т.п.*); **film ~** кинозвезда́; **the ~ of the show** звезда́ спекта́кля; **~ turn** гвоздь програ́ммы; **~ pupil** звезда́ кла́сса.
3 (*~-shaped object, e.g. decoration*) звезда́; (*asterisk*) звёздочка.
4 (*fig.*): **I saw ~s** у меня́ и́скры из глаз посы́пались.
5: **the S~s and Stripes** госуда́рственный флаг США.

● *v.t.* (**starred, starring**) **1** (*adorn with ~s*) укр|аша́ть, -а́сить звёздами.
2 (*mark with asterisk*) отм|еча́ть, -е́тить звёздочкой.

S

● *v.i.* (**starred, starring**): **~ in a film** игра́ть (*impf.*) гла́вную роль в фи́льме; выступа́ть (*impf.*) в гла́вной ро́ли фи́льма.

● *cpds.* **~fish** *n.* морска́я звезда́; **~light** *n.* свет звёзд; **by ~light** при све́те звёзд; **~lit** *adj.* освещённый све́том звёзд; **~ sign** *n.* знак зодиа́ка; **~-spangled** *adj.* звёздный, усе́янный звёздами; **the S~-spangled Banner** америка́нский флаг; **~-studded** *adj.* усе́янный звёздами; (*fig.*) с уча́стием мно́жества звёзд.

starboard /ˈstɑːbəd/ *n.* пра́вый борт.

● *adj.* пра́вый; **~ side** пра́вый борт; **~ wind** ве́тер с пра́вого бо́рта.

starch /stɑːtʃ/ *n.* крахма́л; (*fig.*) чо́порность.

● *v.t.* крахма́лить, на-.

starchiness /ˈstɑːtʃɪnɪs/ *n.* крахма́листость, мучни́стость; (*fig.*) чо́порность.

starchy /ˈstɑːtʃɪ/ *adj.* (**starchier, starchiest**) (*containing starch*) крахма́листый, мучни́стый; (*stiffened*) крахма́льный, накрахма́ленный; (*fig.*) чо́порный.

stardom /ˈstɑːdəm/ *n.*: **rise to ~** станови́ться, стать звездо́й.

stare /steə(r)/ *n.* при́стальный взгляд; **vacant ~** пусто́й взгляд.

● *v.t.*: **~ s.o. in the face** смотре́ть, по- на кого́-н. в упо́р; **ruin ~s him in the face** он смо́трит в глаза́ ги́бели; **the letter was staring me in the face** письмо́ лежа́ло у меня́ под но́сом; **~ s.o. up and down** см|еря́ть, -е́рить кого́-н. взгля́дом.

● *v.i.* глазе́ть (*impf.*); тара́щить (*impf.*) глаза́; **~ at s.o.** при́стально смотре́ть/гляде́ть (*impf.*) на кого́-н.; **~ into s.o.'s face** уста́виться (*pf.*) на кого́-н.; **he ~d rudely at me** он на́гло уста́вился на меня́; **don't ~!** не тара́щь глаза́!; **I ~d at him in astonishment** я вы́таращил на него́ глаза́ от изумле́ния; **~ into space** устрем|ля́ть, -и́ть взор в простра́нство.

staring /ˈsteərɪŋ/ *adj.* (*gaze*) при́стальный; (*eyes*) широко́ раскры́тый.

stark /stɑːk/ *adj.* **1** (*desolate, bare*) го́лый, беспло́дный, пусты́нный; **a ~ winter landscape** суро́вый зи́мний пейза́ж. **2** (*sharply evident*) я́вный; **in ~ contrast** в вопию́щем противоре́чии. **3** (*sheer*) по́лный, абсолю́тный.

● *adv.* соверше́нно; **~ raving mad** абсолю́тно сумасше́дший; **~ naked** соверше́нно го́лый; в чём мать родила́ (*coll.*).

starkers /ˈstɑːkəz/ *adj.* (*Br. coll.*) в чём мать родила́.

starless /ˈstɑːlɪs/ *adj.* беззвёздный.

starlet /ˈstɑːlɪt/ *n.* молода́я киноактри́са.

starling /ˈstɑːlɪŋ/ *n.* скворе́ц.

starry /ˈstɑːrɪ/ *adj.* (**starrier, starriest**) **1** звёздный; **~ night** звёздная ночь; **~ sky** звёздное не́бо. **2**: **~ eyes** лучи́стые глаза́.

● *cpd.* **~-eyed** *adj.* (*fig.*) романти́чный, ви́дящий всё в ро́зовом све́те.

START /stɑːt/ *n.* (*abbr. of* ***Strategic Arms Reduction Talks***) перегово́ры о сокраще́нии стратеги́ческих наступа́тельных вооруже́ний.

start /stɑːt/ *n.* **1** (*sudden movement*) вздра́гивание, содрога́ние; **give a ~ of joy/surprise** вздро́гнуть (*pf.*) от ра́дости/удивле́ния; **give s.o. a ~** пуга́ть, ис- кого́-н.; **he woke with a ~** он вздро́гнул и просну́лся; **he works by fits and ~s** он рабо́тает уры́вками/неравноме́рно.
2 (*beginning*) нача́ло; (*of journey*) отправле́ние; (*of race*) старт; **make a ~ on something** нач|ина́ть, -а́ть что-н.; **we made an early ~** мы вы́ступили в путь ра́но; **make a fresh ~** нач|ина́ть, -а́ть снача́ла/сы́знова (*coll.*); **he made a fresh ~ (in life)** он на́чал но́вую жизнь; **at the (very) ~** в (са́мом) нача́ле; **for a ~** для нача́ла; **from ~ to finish** с нача́ла до конца́; **false ~** (*sport*) фальста́рт; **we made a false ~** (*fig.*) мы оши́блись в са́мом нача́ле; **get off to a good ~** уда́чно нач|ина́ть, -а́ть.
3 (*advantage in race etc.*): **he was given 10 yards' ~** ему́ да́ли фо́ру в 10 я́рдов.

● *v.t.* **1** (*begin*) нач|ина́ть, -а́ть; **he ~s work early** он начина́ет рабо́тать ра́но; **it is ~ing to rain** начина́ется дождь; **when does she ~ school?** когда́ она́ пойдёт в шко́лу?; **we ~ed our journey** мы отпра́вились (в путь); **he ~ed life as a watchman** он на́чал свою́ трудову́ю жизнь сто́рожем; **she ~ed crying** она́ начала́ пла́кать/распла́калась; *with many vv., the pf. formed with* за- *means 'to start …ing'.*
2 (*set in motion*): **~ a clock** зав|оди́ть, -ести́ часы́; **~ an engine** зав|оди́ть, -ести́ (*or* запус|ка́ть, -ти́ть) мото́р; **~ing handle** пускова́я/заводна́я рукоя́тка.
3 (*in race*): **~ the runners** да|ва́ть, -ть старт бегуна́м.
4 (*initiate*): **~ a business** осно́в|ывать, -а́ть (*or* нач|ина́ть, -а́ть) би́знес/де́ло; **~ a school** откр|ыва́ть, -ы́ть шко́лу; **~ a conversation** нач|ина́ть, -а́ть разгово́р; **~ a family** зав|оди́ть, -ести́ семью́; **~ a fire** (*arson*) устро́ить (*pf.*) пожа́р; (*for warmth etc.*) разв|оди́ть, -ести́ костёр/ого́нь; **what ~ed the fire?** из-за чего́ начался́ пожа́р?; **~ a fund** осно́в|ывать, -а́ть фонд; **~ a movement** положи́ть (*pf.*) нача́ло (како́му-н.) движе́нию; **~ a rumour** (*Br.*), **rumor** (*US*) (рас)пус|ка́ть, -ти́ть слух; **now you've ~ed something!** ну вот, ты и завари́л ка́шу!
5 (*broach*): **~ a bottle of wine** поч|ина́ть, -а́ть буты́лку вина́; **~ a subject (of conversation)** зав|оди́ть, -ести́ разгово́р о чём-н.
6 (*cause to begin*): **the wine ~ed him talking** вино́ развяза́ло ему́ язы́к; **this ~ed me thinking** э́то заста́вило меня́ заду́маться; **the smoke ~ed me coughing** от ды́ма я зака́шлялся.

● *v.i.* **1** (*make sudden movement*) вздр|а́гивать, -о́гнуть; содрог|а́ться, -ну́ться; **~ back** отпря́нуть (*pf.*); **~ from one's sleep** вздро́гнуть и просну́ться (*pf.*); **~ from one's chair** (*or* **to one's feet**) вск|а́кивать, -очи́ть со сту́ла (*or* на́ ноги); **tears ~ed from his eyes** слёзы бры́знули у него́ из глаз.
2 (*begin*) нач|ина́ться, -а́ться; (*come into being, arise*) появ|ля́ться, -и́ться; возн|ика́ть, -и́кнуть; **it ~ed raining** пошёл/начался́ дождь; **we had to ~ again from scratch** пришло́сь нача́ть всё снача́ла; **there were 12 of us to ~ with** снача́ла/сперва́ нас бы́ло 12 челове́к; **to ~ with, you should write to him** пре́жде всего́ (*or* для нача́ла) вы должны́ написа́ть ему́; **what will you have** (*eat*) **to ~ with?** что вы возьмёте на заку́ску?; **prices ~ at £10** це́ны от десяти́ фу́нтов и вы́ше; **~ing price** (*at auction*) нача́льная/отправна́я цена́.
3 (*set out*) отпр|авля́ться, -а́виться; **he ~ed back the next day** на сле́дующий день он отпра́вился наза́д/пусти́лся в обра́тный путь; **~ing point** (*of journey*) отправно́й пункт; (*of race*) старт; (*fig.*) отправна́я/исхо́дная то́чка.
4 (*in race*) стартова́ть (*impf.*, *pf.*); **~ing-gate** барье́р на ста́рте; **~ing-pistol** ста́ртовый пистоле́т; **~ing-post** ста́ртовый столб.
5 (*of engine etc.*): **the car ~ed without any trouble** маши́на завела́сь без пробле́м; **you should always ~ in first gear** стартова́ть всегда́ сле́дует на пе́рвой ско́рости.

● *with advs.*: **~ in** *v.i.*: **~ in on something** (*coll.*) бра́ться, взя́ться (*or* прин|има́ться, -я́ться) за что-н.; **~ in on** (*US coll., scold*) **s.o.** брани́ть, вы́- кого́-н.; напус|ка́ться, -ти́ться на кого́-н.; **~ off** *v.t.*: **what ~ed him off on that craze?** отку́да у него́ (появи́лось) э́то увлече́ние?; **don't ~ him off, or he'll never stop** не заводи́те его́, а то он никогда́ не остано́вится; *v.i.* (*leave*) пойти́, пое́хать (*both pf.*); **he ~ed off with a general introduction** он на́чал с о́бщего вступле́ния; **she ~ed off by apologizing for being late** она́ начала́ с извине́ний за своё опозда́ние; **he ~ed off on the wrong foot** (*coll.*) он неуда́чно на́чал; **he ~ed off in second gear** он стартова́л на второ́й ско́рости; **~ out** *v.i.* (*leave*) отпр|авля́ться, -а́виться; пойти́, пое́хать (*both pf.*); (*intend*) соб|ира́ться, -ра́ться; **~ over** *v.i.* (*US*) нач|ина́ть, -а́ть сно́ва; **~ up** *v.t.*: **~ up an engine** зав|оди́ть, -ести́ (*or* запус|ка́ть, -ти́ть) мото́р; **~ up a conversation** зав|оди́ть, -ести́ разгово́р; **~ up a business** осн|о́вывать, -ова́ть би́знес/де́ло; *v.i.* (*spring to one's feet*) вск|а́кивать, -очи́ть; (*come into being*) появ|ля́ться, -и́ться; возн|ика́ть, -и́кнуть; **a new firm is ~ing up in the town** в го́роде открыва́ется но́вая фи́рма.

starter /ˈstɑːtə(r)/ *n.* **1** (*giving signal for race*) ста́ртер. **2** (*competitor*) уча́стни|к (*fem.* -ца) состяза́ния; (*horse*) уча́стник забе́га. **3** (*device for starting engine etc.*) ста́ртер, пуска́тель (*m.*); пусково́й прибо́р. **4** (*Br., first course*) заку́ска.

startle /ˈstɑːt(ə)l/ *v.t.* (*scare*) пуга́ть, ис-вспу́г|ивать, -ну́ть; **I was ~d when you shouted** я так и испуга́лся, когда́ вы закрича́ли; **you ~d me** вы меня́ испуга́ли.

startling /ˈstɑːtlɪŋ/ *adj.* порази́тельный, потряса́ющий; (*alarming*) пуга́ющий.

starvation /stɑːˈveɪʃ(ə)n/ *n.* го́лод, голода́ние; **death by ~** голо́дная смерть; **die of ~** ум|ира́ть, -ере́ть от го́лода (*or* с го́лоду); **~ diet** голо́дная дие́та; **~ wage** ни́щенский за́работок.

starv|e /stɑːv/ *v.t.* мори́ть, у-/за- (го́лодом); **~e s.o. into submission** брать, взять кого́-н. измо́ром; (*fig.*): **the child was ~ed of affection** ребёнок страда́л от отсу́тствия любви́.

● *v.i.* (*go hungry*) голода́ть (*impf.*); **a ~ing child** голода́ющий ребёнок; **I'm ~ing** я ужа́сно проголода́лся!; я го́лоден как волк!; **~e to death** ум|ира́ть, -ере́ть с го́лоду.

stash /stæʃ/ *n.* та́йный запа́с.

● *v.t.* (*coll.*): **he has £1,000 ~ed away** у него́ припря́тана ты́сяча фу́нтов.

state¹ /steɪt/ *n.* **1** (*condition*) состоя́ние, положе́ние; **in a poor ~ of health** в плохо́м состоя́нии здоро́вья; **~ of affairs** положе́ние дел; **~ of mind** настрое́ние; душе́вное состоя́ние; **in an untidy ~** в беспоря́дке; **he was in quite a ~** он был в ужа́сном возбужде́нии (*excitement*)/волне́нии (*anxiety*); **the country is in a ~ of war** страна́ нахо́дится в состоя́нии войны́; **what is the ~ of play?** (*Br.*) како́й счёт?; (*fig.*) как обстоя́т дела́? **2** (*country, community, government*) госуда́рство; (*attr.*) госуда́рственный; **affairs, matters of ~** госуда́рственные дела́; **police ~** полице́йское госуда́рство; **United S~s** Соединённые Шта́ты (Аме́рики) (*abbr.* США); **S~ Department** (*US*) госуда́рственный департа́мент, министе́рство иностра́нных дел; **~ control** госуда́рственный контро́ль. **3** (*pomp*) великоле́пие, ро́скошь; **live in ~** жить (*impf.*) в ро́скоши; **lie in ~** быть (*impf.*) вы́ставленным для торже́ственного проща́ния; **the Queen drove in ~ through London** короле́ва торже́ственно прое́хала по Ло́ндону; **~ coach** пара́дная каре́та; **~ apartments** пара́дные поко́и (*m. pl.*); **~ visit** госуда́рственный визи́т; **~ ball** торже́ственный бал.

● *cpds.* **~-aided** *adj.* получа́ющий дота́цию/субси́дию от госуда́рства; **~craft** *n.* = **statesmanship; ~-of-the-art** *adj.* ультрасовреме́нный, нове́йший; **~room** *n.* (*on ship*) каю́та; **S~side** *adj. & adv.* (*US coll.*) (находя́щийся) в США; **~sman** *and cpds., see separate entries.*

state² /steɪt/ *v.t.* (*declare; say clearly*) заяв|ля́ть, -и́ть о+*p.*; сказа́ть (*pf.*), что; утвержда́ть (*impf.*), что; сообщ|а́ть, -и́ть о+*p.*; **he ~d his intentions** он заяви́л о свои́х наме́рениях; (*indicate*) ука́з|ывать, -а́ть; **as ~d above** как ука́зано вы́ше; (*specify*): **at the ~d time** в озна́ченное вре́мя; (*announce*) объяв|ля́ть, -и́ть; (*expound*) изл|ага́ть, -ожи́ть; **the plaintiff ~d his case** исте́ц изложи́л своё де́ло.

statehood /ˈsteɪthʊd/ *n.* госуда́рственность.

stateless /ˈsteɪtlɪs/ *adj.* не име́ющий гражда́нства.

stateliness /ˈsteɪtlɪnɪs/ *n.* вели́чественность, велича́вость.

stately /ˈsteɪtlɪ/ *adj.* (**statelier, stateliest**) вели́чественный, велича́вый; **~ home** (*Br.*) дом-дворе́ц.

statement /ˈsteɪtmənt/ *n.* (*declaration*) заявле́ние; **make, publish a ~** де́лать, с-/публикова́ть, о- заявле́ние; (*exposition*) изложе́ние; (*fin.*) отчёт, бала́нс; **~ of account** вы́писка о состоя́нии счёта; **~ of expenses** отчёт о расхо́дах.

statesman /ˈsteɪtsmən/ *n.* госуда́рственный де́ятель.

statesmanlike /ˈsteɪtsmənlaɪk/ *adj.* досто́йный госуда́рственного де́ятеля.

state|smanship /ˈsteɪtsmənʃɪp/, **-craft** /ˈsteɪtkrɑːft/ *nn.* (*skill*) иску́сство управле́ния госуда́рством; (*activities*) госуда́рственная де́ятельность.

static /ˈstætɪk/ *n.* **1** (**~** *electricity*) стати́ческое электри́чество. **2** (*as radio interference: also* **~s**) (атмосфе́рные) поме́хи (*f. pl.*).

● *adj.* **1** (*stationary*) неподви́жный, стациона́рный. **2** (*opp. dynamic*) стати́ческий, стати́чный.

statics /ˈstætɪks/ *n.* **1** ста́тика. **2** = **static** *n.* 2

station /ˈsteɪʃ(ə)n/ *n.* **1** (*assigned place*) пост, ме́сто, пози́ция; **take up one's ~** зан|има́ть, -я́ть пост/пози́цию; **polling ~** избира́тельный пункт/уча́сток. **2** (*establishment, base, headquarters*) ста́нция; **broadcasting ~** радиоста́нция; **bus ~** авто́бусная ста́нция; **filling ~** запра́вочный пункт, бензоколо́нка; **fire ~** пожа́рное депо́ (*indecl.*); **naval ~** вое́нно-морска́я ба́за; **police ~** полице́йский уча́сток; (*in Russia*) отделе́ние мили́ции; **power ~** электроста́нция. **3** (*rail.*) ста́нция; (*large, mainline* **~**) вокза́л; (*attr.*) станцио́нный. **4** (*position in life, rank*) положе́ние; зва́ние; **he married beneath his ~** он вступи́л в мезалья́нс; **get ideas above one's ~** сади́ться, сесть не в свои́ са́ни. **5** (*eccl.*): **~s of the Cross** остано́вки Христа́ на кре́стном пути́; кальва́рии (*f. pl.*). **6** (*Austr., sheep-farm*) овцево́дческая фе́рма.

● *v.t.* распол|ага́ть, -ожи́ть; **she ~ed herself at a window** она́ расположи́лась у окна́; **~ a guard at the gate** выставля́ть, вы́ставить карау́л у воро́т; (*mil.*) разме|ща́ть, -сти́ть; дислоци́ровать (*impf., pf.*); **the regiment is ~ed in the south** полк стои́т на ю́ге.

● *cpds.* **~-master** *n.* нача́льник ста́нции; **~-wagon** *n.* (*US*) автомоби́ль (*m.*) с ку́зовом ти́па «универса́л»; универса́л (*coll.*).

stationary /ˈsteɪʃənərɪ/ *adj.* **1** (*not moving; at rest*) неподви́жный. **2** (*fixed*) закреплённый, стациона́рный; **~ troops** ме́стные войска́. **3** (*unchanging, constant*) постоя́нный, неизме́нный; **the population remained ~** чи́сленность населе́ния оста́лась неизме́нной.

stationer /ˈsteɪʃənə(r)/ *n.* торго́вец писчебума́жными/канцеля́рскими принадле́жностями.

stationery /ˈsteɪʃənərɪ/ *n.* писчебума́жные/канцеля́рские принадле́жности (*f. pl.*); **S~ Office** (*Br.*) короле́вская госуда́рственная канцеля́рия (*издаёт правительственные документы*).

statistical /stəˈtɪstɪk(ə)l/ *adj.* статисти́ческий.

statistician /ˌstætɪˈstɪʃ(ə)n/ *n.* стати́стик.

statistics /stəˈtɪstɪks/ *n.* статисти́ческие да́нные; (*science*) стати́стика.

statuary /ˈstætjʊərɪ/ *n.* скульпту́ра.

statue /ˈstætjuː/, /ˈstætʃuː/ *n.* ста́туя.

statuesque /ˌstætjʊˈesk/, /ˌstætʃʊˈesk/ *adj.* велича́вый, вели́чественный.

statuette /ˌstætjʊˈet/, /ˌstætʃʊˈet/ *n.* статуэ́тка.

stature /ˈstætʃə(r)/ *n.* **1** (*height*) рост; **of low (or short of) ~** ни́зкого ро́ста. **2** (*fig.*) масшта́б, кали́бр; **a man of ~** челове́к кру́пного кали́бра, ли́чность кру́пного масшта́ба.

status /ˈsteɪtəs/ *n.* **1** (*position, rank*) положе́ние, ста́тус, прести́ж; **official ~** официа́льное положе́ние; **civil ~** гражда́нское состоя́ние; (*superior position*) вес, ста́тус; **the possession of land confers ~** облада́ние земе́льной со́бственностью придаёт челове́ку вес в о́бществе; **~ symbol** показа́тель положе́ния в о́бществе. **2**: **~ quo** ста́тус-кво́ (*indecl.*).

statute /ˈstætjuːt/ *n.* стату́т; (*law*) зако́н; (*regulations, ordinance*) уста́в; **~ law** пи́саный зако́н; **~ of limitations** (*leg.*) зако́н об иско́вой да́вности; **University ~s** уста́в университе́та.

● *cpd.* **~-book** *n.* свод зако́нов.

statutory /ˈstætjʊtərɪ/ *adj.* предусмо́тренный зако́ном; **~ minimum** определённый зако́ном ми́нимум; **~ rape** (*US*) полова́я связь с лицо́м, не дости́гшим совершенноле́тия.

staunch¹ /stɔːntʃ/, /stɑːntʃ/ *adj.* (*faithful, trusty*) ве́рный; (*loyal*) лоя́льный; (*reliable*) надёжный; (*devoted*): **a ~ socialist** непрекло́нный/убеждённый социали́ст.

sta(u)nch² /stɔːntʃ/, /stɑːntʃ/ *v.t.* = **stanch**

staunchness /ˈstɔːntʃnɪs/, /ˈstɑːntʃnɪs/ *n.* ве́рность, лоя́льность, надёжность, пре́данность.

stave /steɪv/ *n.* (*of cask*) клёпка; (*stanza*) строфа́; (*mus.*) но́тный стан.

● *v.t.* (*past and p.p.* **stove** *or* **staved**) **1** (*also* **~ in**: *break in*): **~ in a door** проб|ивáть, -ить дырý в двери́. **2**: **~ off** предотвра|щáть, -ти́ть.

staves /steɪvz/ *pl. of* ⇒**staff** 6

stay¹ /steɪ/ *n.* **1** (*sojourn*) пребывáние; **I am making a short ~ in London** я остановлю́сь ненадóлго в Лóндоне; **a ~ of 2 weeks** двухнедéльное пребывáние; **I enjoyed my ~ with you** я прекрáсно провёл врéмя у вас. **2** (*suspension*) отсрóчка; **~ of execution** отсрóчка исполнéния.

● *v.t.* **1** (*check*) остан|áвливать, -ови́ть; препя́тствовать, вос- + *d.*; **~ one's hunger** утоли́ть (*pf.*) гóлод; (*coll.*) замори́ть (*pf.*) червячкá; (*restrain*) сдéрж|ивать, -áть; **~ one's hand** воздéрж|иваться, -áться от дéйствий. **2** (*last out*): **~ the course** выдéрживать, вы́держать до концá.

● *v.i.* **1** (*stop, put up*) (*at a place*) остан|áвливаться, -ови́ться; (*with s.o.*) гости́ть (*impf.*); остан|áвливаться, -ови́ться; **which hotel will you ~ at?** в какóй гости́нице вы останóвитесь?; **we are** (*sc. at present*) **~ing with friends** мы останови́лись/гости́м у друзéй; **we ~ed in Vienna for 3 weeks** мы прóбыли в Вéне три недéли. **2** (*remain*) ост|авáться, -áться; не уходи́ть (*impf.*); **~ here while I find out** побýдьте/ждите здесь, покá я разузнáю; **I ~ed awake all night** я всю ночь не спал; **~ at home** сидéть (*impf.*) дóма; **~ in bed** не вставáть (*impf.*) (с постéли); **they don't like ~ing at home** им не сиди́тся дóма; **the children ~ed away from school** дéти прогуля́ли шкóлу; **I ~ed away from work** я не пошёл на рабóту; **he made them ~ behind after school** он задержáл их в шкóле пóсле урóков; **the food would not ~ down** (егó) желýдок не принимáл пи́щи; **can you ~ for, to tea?** вы мóжете остáться на чай?; **he ~ed for the night** он остáлся на ночь/ночевáть; **I am ~ing in today** сегóдня я не выхожý (*or* я сижý дóма); **I hope the rain will ~ off** надéюсь, что дождь не начнётся; **if you want to lose weight, ~ off starchy foods** éсли хоти́те похудéть, воздéрживайтесь от мучнóго; **he ~ed on at the university** он остáлся при университéте; **my hat won't ~ on** у меня́ шля́па не дéржится (на головé); **she is allowed to ~ out till midnight** ей разрешáют не приходи́ть домóй до 12 часóв нóчи; **he ~ed to dinner** он остáлся обéдать; **if we ~ together we shan't get lost** éсли мы бýдем держáться вмéсте, мы не заблýдимся; **~ up late** не ложи́ться (*impf.*) (спать) допозднá; **fine weather has come to ~** хорóшая погóда установи́лась прóчно; **~ put!** (*coll.*) ни с мéста!, не дви́гайся! **3** (*endure in race etc.*): **he has no ~ing-power** у негó нет никакóй выносливости.

● *cpd.* **~-at-home** *n.* домосéд (*fem.* -ка).

stay² /steɪ/ *n.* **1** (*naut.*) штаг. **2** (*prop, support*) опóра, подпóрка; (*moral support*) опóра, поддéржка. **3** (*pl., corset*) корсéт.

stayer /ˈsteɪə(r)/ *n.* (*person*) выно́сливый человéк; (*horse*) выно́сливая лóшадь.

STD *abbr. of* **1** ***subscriber trunk dialling*** (*Br.*) автомати́ческая междугорóдная телефóнная связь. **2** ***sexually transmitted disease*** заболевáние передавáемое половы́м путём.

stead /sted/ *n.* (*liter.*): **stand s.o. in good ~** сослужи́ть (*pf.*) комý-н. хорóшую слýжбу; **in s.o.'s ~** вмéсто когó-н.

steadfast /ˈstedfɑːst/, /ˈstedfəst/ *adj.* (*firm, stable*): **~ in danger** стóйкий в опáсности; **~ policy** твёрдая поли́тика; (*faithful*): **~ in love** вéрный в любви́; (*reliable*) надёжный; (*unwavering*) непоколеби́мый; **~ of purpose** целеустремлённый.

steadfastness /ˈstedfɑːstnɪs/, /ˈstedfəstnɪs/ *n.* стóйкость, твёрдость; вéрность; непоколеби́мость; надёжность; целеустремлённость.

steadiness /ˈstedɪnɪs/ *n.* (*sureness*) увéренность; (*resolution*) реши́тельность, непоколеби́мость; (*of gaze*) твёрдость; (*regularity*) равномéрность; (*stability*) устóйчивость.

steady /ˈstedɪ/ *adj.* (**steadier, steadiest**) **1** (*firmly fixed, balanced, supported*) прóчный, устóйчивый, твёрдый; **keep the camera ~!** не дви́гайте фотоаппарáт!; **the ladder must be held ~** лéстницу нáдо крéпко держáть; **he has a ~ hand** у негó твёрдая рукá; (*unfaltering*): **~ in one's principles** непреклóнный в свои́х при́нципах; **a ~ gaze** твёрдый взгляд. **2** (*uniform*) равномéрный; (*even*) рóвный; (*constant*) постоя́нный; (*uninterrupted*) непреры́вный; **at a ~ pace** рóвным шáгом; **a ~ breeze** устóйчивый вéтер; **he works steadily** он упóрно рабóтает; **~ demand** постоя́нный спрос; **his health shows a ~ improvement** егó здорóвье постоя́нно улучшáется; **a ~ flow of water** непреры́вный потóк воды́. **3** (*of person, staid*) степéнный; (*sober*) трéзвый. **4** (*in exhortations*): **~!** осторóжно!; **~ on!** (*Br.*) лéгче на поворóтах!

● *adv.*: **go ~ with s.o.** (*Br. coll.*) встречáться (*impf.*) с кем-н.

● *v.t.* **1** (*strengthen, secure*) укрепл|я́ть, -и́ть; закрепл|я́ть, -и́ть; **the doctor gave him something to ~ his nerves** дóктор дал емý лекáрство для укреплéния нéрвов. **2**: **~ a boat** прив|оди́ть, -ести́ лóдку в равновéсие.

● *v.i.* **1** (*regain equilibrium*) вырáвниваться, вы́ровняться. **2** (*become fixed, firm*) стабилизи́роваться (*impf., pf.*); **prices are ~ing** цéны стабилизи́руются.

steak /steɪk/ *n.* (*of beef*) бифштéкс (натурáльный); **fillet ~** вы́резка.

● *cpd.* **~-house** *n.* бифштéксная.

steal /stiːl/ *v.t.* (*past* **stole;** *p.p.* **stolen**) **1** воровáть (*impf.*); крáсть, у-; **it is wrong to ~** воровáть (*impf.*) нехорошó; **I had my handbag stolen** у меня́ укрáли сýмку. **2** (*fig.*): **~ a glance at s.o.** взглянýть (*pf.*) укрáдкой на когó-н.; **~ s.o.'s heart (away)** похи|щáть, -ти́ть чьё-н. сéрдце; **~ s.o.'s thunder** перехвáт|ывать, -и́ть чью-н. слáву; **receive stolen goods** скупáть (*impf.*) крáденый товáр.

● *v.i.* (*past* **stole;** *p.p.* **stolen**) **1** (*thieve*) воровáть (*impf.*); **he accused me of ~ing** он обвини́л меня́ в воровствé; **he was caught ~ing** егó поймáли с поли́чным. **2** (*move secretly or silently*) крáсться (*impf.*); **he stole round to the back door** он прокрáлся к зáдней двéри; **he stole up to her** он подкрáлся к ней; **the sun's rays stole across the lawn** сóлнечные лучи́ скользнýли по газóну.

stealth /stelθ/ *n.*: **by ~** тайкóм, укрáдкой, втихомóлку (*coll.*).

stealthy /ˈstelθɪ/ *adj.* (**stealthier, stealthiest**): **~ glance** взгляд укрáдкой; **~ tread** крадýщаяся похóдка.

steam /stiːm/ *n.* пар; **full ~ ahead!** пóлный вперёд!; **get up ~** (*lit.*) разв|оди́ть, -ести́ пáры; (*fig.*) наб|ирáться, -рáться сил; **let off ~** (*lit.*) выпускáть, вы́пустить пáры; (*fig.*) да|вáть, -ть вы́ход чýвствам; **run out of ~** (*fig.*) выдыхáться, вы́дохнуться; **under one's own ~** (*fig.*) сам, свои́ми си́лами; **~ iron** паровóй утюг; **~ train** пóезд с паровы́м локомоти́вом, парови́к (*see also cpds.*).

● *v.t.* **1** (*cook with* **~**) пáрить (*impf.*); **~ed fish** пáреная ры́ба. **2** (*treat with* **~**): **~ a stamp off an envelope** отпáри|вать, -ть мáрку с конвéрта; **the envelope had been ~ed open** ктó-то отклéил конвéрт над пáром. **3** (*cover with* **~**): **the carriage windows were ~ed up** вагóнные óкна запотéли; **get ~ed up** зав|оди́ться, -ести́сь (*coll.*).

● *v.i.* **1** (*give out* **~** *or vapour*) выделя́ть (*impf.*) пар/испарéния; пус|кáть, -ти́ть пар; **the kettle is ~ing on the stove** чáйник кипи́т на пли́те; **he wiped his ~ing brow** он вы́тер вспотéвший лоб. **2** (*move by* **~**): **the boat ~ed into the harbour** (*Br.*), **harbor** (*US*) корáбль вошёл в гáвань; **the train ~ed out** паровóз отошёл от стáнции. **3**: **~ up** запот|евáть, -éть.

● *cpds.* **~-bath** *n.* паровáя бáня; **~boat** *n.* парохóд; **~-driven** *adj.* с паровы́м дви́гателем; **~-engine** *n.* паровóй дви́гатель; (*steam locomotive*) паровóз; **~-hammer** *n.* паровóй мóлот; **~-heat** *n.* отдавáемое пáром теплó; **~-power** *n.* энéргия пáра; **~-roller** *n.* паровóй катóк; *v.t.* (*lit.*) уплотн|я́ть -и́ть; укáт|ывать, -áть; трамбовáть, у-; (*fig.*) сокруш|áть, -и́ть; подав|ля́ть, -и́ть; **~-roller all opposition** подав|ля́ть, -и́ть вся́ческое сопротивлéние; **~ship** *n.* парохóд; **~-shovel** *n.* паровóй экскавáтор.

steamer /ˈstiːmə(r)/ *n.* (*ship*) парохóд; (*for cooking*) паровáрка.

steamy /ˈstiːmɪ/ *adj.* (**steamier, steamiest**) (*saturated with steam*) насы́щенный пара́ми; (*of atmosphere*) (*coll.*) па́ркий; (*covered with steam*) запоте́лый, запоте́вший.

stearin /ˈstɪərɪn/ *n.* стеари́н.

steed /stiːd/ *n.* (*poet.*) конь (*m.*).

steel /stiːl/ *n.* **1** сталь; (*attr.*) стально́й; **~ foundry** сталелите́йный заво́д/цех; **~ industry** сталелите́йная промы́шленность; **~ wool** ёж(ик); **cold ~** (*weapons*) холо́дное ору́жие; (*fig.*): **nerves of ~** стальны́е/желе́зные не́рвы. **2** (*for sharpening knives*)точи́ло.

● *v.t.*: **~ o.s.** (*pluck up courage*) соб|ира́ться, -ра́ться с ду́хом.

● *cpds.* **~ band** *n.* (*mus.*) шумово́й орке́стр кари́бского происхожде́ния; **~-clad, ~-plated** *adjs.* брониро́ванный; общи́тый ста́лью; **~work** *n.* стальны́е изде́лия; стальна́я констру́кция; **~-works** *n.* сталеплави́льный заво́д; **~yard** *n.* безме́н.

steely /ˈstiːlɪ/ *adj.* (**steelier, steeliest**) (*fig., unyielding*) желе́зный, непрекло́нный; (*stern*) суро́вый.

steep[1] /stiːp/ *adj.* **1** круто́й; **the stairs were ~** ле́стница была́ крута́я; **the ground fell ~ly away** земля́ кру́то обрыва́лась; (*fig.*): **there has been a ~ decline in trade** в торго́вле произошёл круто́й спад. **2** (*coll., excessive*) чрезме́рный, непоме́рный; **we had to pay a ~ price** нам э́то ста́ло в копе́ечку; (*unreasonable*): **I thought his conduct a bit ~** его́ поведе́ние показа́лось мне дово́льно на́глым.

steep[2] /stiːp/ *v.t.* **1** (*soak*) мочи́ть (*impf.*); зам|а́чивать, -очи́ть; пропи́т|ывать, -а́ть. **2** (*fig., pass. or refl., be immersed*) погру|жа́ться, -зи́ться (*во что*); **he ~ed himself in the study of the classics** он погрузи́лся в изуче́ние кла́ссиков; (*be sunk*) погр|яза́ть, -я́знуть (*в чём*); **~ed in ignorance** погря́зший в неве́жестве.

steeple /ˈstiːp(ə)l/ *n.* (*bell tower*) колоко́льня; (*spire*) шпиль (*m.*).

● *cpds.* **~chase** *n.* стипль-че́з; ска́чки (*f. pl.*)/бег с препя́тствиями; **~chaser** *n.* (*person*) уча́стни|к (*fem* -ца) бе́га с препя́тствиями; **~jack** *n.* верхола́з.

steepness /ˈstiːpnɪs/ *n.* крутизна́.

steer[1] /stɪə(r)/ *n.* (*animal*) вол.

steer[2] /stɪə(r)/ *v.t.* **1** (*ship, vehicle etc.*) пра́вить (*impf.*) + *i.*; управля́ть (*impf.*) + *i.* **2**: **~ a course** держа́ть (*impf.*) курс. **3** (*person, activity etc.*) вести́ (*det.*); напр|авля́ть, -а́вить; **he ~ed the visitors to their seats** он провёл госте́й на их места́; **I tried to ~ the conversation away from the subject of death** я пыта́лся увести́ разгово́р от те́мы сме́рти; **~ing committee** руководя́щий комите́т.

● *v.i.* **1** (*of steersman*) пра́вить (*impf.*) рулём; (*of ship, vehicle etc.*): **the car ~s well** э́ту маши́ну легко́ вести́. **2** (*of person*): **~ clear of** избега́ть (*impf.*) + *g.*; сторони́ться (*impf.*) + *g.*

steerage /ˈstɪərɪdʒ/ *n.* (*steering*) рулево́е управле́ние; (*part of ship*) четвёртый класс.

steering /ˈstɪərɪŋ/ *n.* (*act*) управле́ние (*чем*); (*part of machine*) рулево́е управле́ние.

● *cpds.* **~-column** *n.* рулева́я коло́нка; **~-wheel** *n.* (*of car*) руль (*m.*); (*naut.*) штурва́л.

steersman /ˈstɪəzmən/ *n.* рулево́й.

stellar /ˈstelə(r)/ *adj.* звёздный.

stem[1] /stem/ *n.* **1** (*bot.*) сте́бель (*m.*); (*of shrub or tree*) ствол. **2** (*of wine-glass*) но́жка; (*of tobacco-pipe*) черено́к. **3** (*gram.*) осно́ва. **4**: **from ~ to stern** от но́са до кормы́.

● *v.i.* (**stemmed, stemming**) прои|сходи́ть, -зойти́ (*от/из чего*).

stem[2] /stem/ *v.t.* (**stemmed, stemming**) **1** (*lit., fig., check, stop*) остан|а́вливать, -ови́ть; (*fig., arrest, delay*) заде́рж|ивать, -а́ть. **2** (*make headway against*) идти́ (*det.*) про́тив + *g.*; сопротивля́ться (*impf.*) + *d.*; **the ship was able to ~ the current** кораблю́ удало́сь преодоле́ть тече́ние; **he succeeded in ~ming the tide of popular indignation** ему́ удало́сь сбить волну́ всео́бщего возмуще́ния.

● *cpd.* **~-turn** *n.* (*ski movement*) поворо́т на лы́жах в упо́ре.

stench /stentʃ/ *n.* вонь, смрад; злово́ние.

stencil /ˈstensɪl/ *n.* (**~-*plate***) трафаре́т, шабло́н; (*pattern*) трафаре́т; узо́р по трафаре́ту.

● *v.t.* (**stencilled, stencilling;** *US* **stenciled, stenciling**) **1**: **~ a pattern** рисова́ть, на- узо́р по трафаре́ту; **~ letters** нан|оси́ть, -ести́ бу́квы по трафаре́ту. **2** (*ornament by ~ling*) трафаре́тить (*impf.*).

stenographer /steˈnɒgrəfə(r)/ *n.* стено́граф (*fem.* -и́стка).

stenographic /ˌstenəˈgræfɪk/ *adj.* стенографи́ческий.

stenography /steˈnɒgrəfɪ/ *n.* стеногра́фия.

stentorian /ˌstenˈtɔːrɪən/ *adj.* громово́й, зы́чный.

step /step/ *n.* **1** (*movement, distance, sound, manner of ~ping*) шаг; **take a ~ forward/back** де́лать, с- шаг вперёд/наза́д; **at every ~** на ка́ждом шагу́; **~ by ~** шаг за шаго́м; постепе́нно; **turn one's ~s towards home** напр|авля́ть, -а́вить путь домо́й; **it is only a short ~ to my house** до моего́ до́ма всего́ два шага́; **within a few ~s of the hotel** в двух шага́х от гости́ницы; **watch your ~!** (*lit., fig.*) бу́дьте осторо́жны!; **I heard ~s** я слы́шал шаги́. **2** (*fig., action*) шаг, ме́ра; **make a false ~** де́лать, с- ло́жный/неве́рный шаг; оступ|а́ться, -и́ться; **take ~s towards** предприн|има́ть, -я́ть шаги́ к + *d.*; прин|има́ть, -я́ть ме́ры к + *d.*; **my first ~ will be to cut prices** я пе́рвым де́лом добью́сь сниже́ния цен; **what's the next ~?** а тепе́рь что сле́дует де́лать? **3** (*trace of foot*) след; (*fig.*): **I followed in his ~s** я сле́довал по его́ стопа́м; **retrace one's ~s** возвра|ща́ться, -ти́ться по про́йденному пути́. **4** (*rhythm of ~*): **keep in ~ with** (*lit., fig.*) идти́ (*det.*) в но́гу с + *i.*; **fall into ~ behind s.o.** выра́внивать, вы́ровнять шаг по кому́-н.; **fall into ~** (*fig., conform*) подчин|я́ться, -и́ться; **he is out of ~** (*lit., fig.*) он идёт не в но́гу. **5** (*raised surface*) ступе́нь; **mind the ~!** осторо́жно — ступе́нька!; (*of staircase etc.*) ступе́нька; (*of ladder*) перекла́дина, ступе́нька; (*of vehicle*) подно́жка; (*in ice*) усту́п; **flight of ~s** ряд ступе́ней; марш (ле́стницы); (*in front of house*) крыльцо́; **fall/run down the ~s** ск|а́тываться, -ати́ться/сбе|га́ть, -жа́ть по ступе́нькам. **6** (*pl. Br.*, **~-ladder**; *also* **pair of ~s** (*Br.*)) стремя́нка; складна́я ле́стница. **7** (*stage, degree*) ступе́нь, сте́пень, ста́дия; **I cannot follow the ~s of his argument** я не могу́ уследи́ть за хо́дом его́ рассужде́ния. **8** (*dance ~*) па (*nt. indecl.*).

● *v.t.* (**stepped, stepping**) **1**: **~ a few yards** де́лать, с- не́сколько шаго́в. **2**: **~ a mast** (*naut.*) ста́вить, по- ма́чту (в степс).

● *v.i.* (**stepped, stepping**) шаг|а́ть, -ну́ть; ступ|а́ть, -и́ть; **~ this way, please** пройди́те сюда́, пожа́луйста!; **~ping-stone** ка́мень для перехо́да (*через ручей и т.п.*); (*fig.*) трампли́н; **a ~ping-stone to success** ступе́нь к успе́ху; **he ~ped into his car** он сел в маши́ну; **~ into the breach** (*fig.*) ри́нуться (*pf.*) на по́мощь; **he ~ped off the train** он сошёл с по́езда; **someone ~ped on my foot** кто́-то наступи́л мне на́ ногу; **~ on s.o.'s toes** (*fig.*) наступи́ть (*pf.*) на чью-н. люби́мую мозо́ль; **~ on it!** (*coll.*) жми!; пошеве́ливайся!; газу́й!; **I ~ped out of his way** я уступи́л ему́ доро́гу; **he ~ped over the threshold** он перешагну́л через поро́г.

● *with advs.*: **~ aside** *v.i.* сторони́ться, по-; (*fig.*) уступ|а́ть, -и́ть (доро́гу) друго́му; **~ back** *v.i.* отступ|а́ть, -и́ть; **~ down** *v.t.* (*elec.*) пон|ижа́ть, -и́зить (*напряжение*); *v.i.*: **he ~ped down off the ladder** он спусти́лся/сошёл с ле́стницы; **he ~ped down in favour** (*Br.*), **favor** (*US*) **of a more experienced man** он уступи́л ме́сто бо́лее о́пытному челове́ку; **~ forward** *v.i.*: **the police asked for witnesses to ~ forward** поли́ция проси́ла свиде́телей заяви́ть о себе́; **~ in** *v.i.*: **won't you ~ in for a moment?** мо́жет, зайдёте на мину́тку?; (*intervene*) вме́ш|иваться, -а́ться; (*replace s.o.*): **thanks for ~ping in** спаси́бо, что вы́ручили; **~ out** *v.i.* выходи́ть, вы́йти (ненадо́лго); (*walk fast*): **we had to ~ out to get there on time** нам пришло́сь приба́вить шагу, что́бы попа́сть туда́ во́время; **~ up** *v.t.* (*increase*) пов|ыша́ть, -ы́сить; уси́ли|вать, -ть; (*electr.*) пов|ыша́ть, -ы́сить (*напряжение*); *v.i.*: **he ~ped up to the platform** он подошёл к трибу́не.

● *cpds.* **~-by-~** *adj.* (*gradual*) постепе́нный; (*phased*) поэта́пный; **~-ins** *n. pl.* шлёпанц|ы (*pl., g.* -ев); **~-ladder** *n.* = **~** *n.* 6

step- /step/ *comb. form*: **~brother** *n.* сво́дный брат; **~child** *n.* (*boy*) па́сынок; (*girl*) па́дчерица; **~daughter** *n.* па́дчерица; **~father** *n.*

S

о́тчим; **~mother** *n.* ма́чеха; **~sister** *n.* сво́дная сестра́; **~son** *n.* па́сынок.

steppe /step/ *n.* степь; (*attr.*) степно́й.

stereo /ˈsterɪəʊ/, /ˈstɪə-/ *n.* (*pl.* **~s**) (*~phonic system*) стереосисте́ма; **personal ~** пле́йер; **in ~** сте́рео.

stereophonic /ˌsterɪəʊˈfɒnɪk/, /ˌstɪə-/ *adj.* стереофони́ческий.

stereoscope /ˈsterɪəˌskəʊp/, /ˈstɪə-/ *n.* стереоско́п.

stereoscopic /ˌsterɪəˈskɒpɪk/, /ˌstɪə-/ *adj.* стереоскопи́ческий; **~ telescope** стереотруба́.

stereotype /ˈsterɪəʊˌtaɪp/, /ˈstɪə-/ *n.* (*typ.*) стереоти́п; (*fig.*) шабло́н; (*attr.*) стереоти́пный.

● *v.t.* (*fig.*) прид|ава́ть, -а́ть шабло́нность +*d.*; **~d phrase** шабло́нная фра́за.

stereotypical /ˌsterɪəʊˈtɪpɪk(ə)l/, /ˌstɪə-/ *adj.* стереоти́пный.

sterile /ˈsteraɪl/ *adj.* **1** (*barren, unproductive, lit., fig.*) неплодоро́дный; (*fig.*) безрезульта́тный. **2** (*free from germs*) стери́льный, стерилизо́ванный.

sterility /stəˈrɪlɪtɪ/ *n.* (*lit., fig., unfruitfulness*) беспло́дие; (*freedom from germs*) стери́льность.

sterilization /ˌsterɪlaɪˈzeɪʃ(ə)n/ *n.* стерилиза́ция.

sterilize /ˈsterɪˌlaɪz/ *v.t.* стерилизова́ть (*impf., pf.*).

sterilizer /ˈsterɪˌlaɪzə(r)/ *n.* стерилиза́тор.

sterlet /ˈstɜːlɪt/ *n.* (*zool.*) сте́рлядь.

sterling /ˈstɜːlɪŋ/ *n.* сте́рлинг; фунт сте́рлингов.

● *adj.* **1** (*of coin, metal etc.*) сте́рлинговый; **pound ~** фунт сте́рлингов; **~ silver** серебро́ вы́сшей про́бы. **2** (*Br., fig., excellent, valuable*) отме́нный.

stern[1] /stɜːn/ *n.* (*of ship*) корма́; (*attr.*) кормово́й.

stern[2] /stɜːn/ *adj.* (*strict, harsh*) стро́гий; (*severe*) суро́вый; (*inflexible*) непреклонный.

sterna /ˈstɜːnə/ *pl. of* ⇒**sternum**

sternal /ˈstɜːn(ə)l/ *adj.* груди́нный.

sternness /ˈstɜːnnɪs/ *n.* стро́гость, суро́вость.

stern|um /ˈstɜːnəm/ *n.* (*pl.* **~ums** *or* **~a**) груди́на.

steroid /ˈstɪərɔɪd/, /ˈste-/ *n.* стеро́ид.

stertorous /ˈstɜːtərəs/ *adj.* хрипя́щий.

stet /stet/ *v.t.* (**stetted, stetting**) (*usu. as imper.*) оста́вить (как бы́ло)!; не пра́вить!

stethoscope /ˈsteθəˌskəʊp/ *n.* стетоско́п.

stevedore /ˈstiːvəˌdɔː(r)/ *n.* до́кер; порто́вый гру́зчик.

stew /stjuː/ *n.* **1** (*cul.*) тушёное мя́со. **2** (*coll.*): **get into a ~** разволнова́ться (*pf.*); **be in a ~** быть в большо́м волне́нии.

● *v.t.* (*meat, fish, vegetables*) туши́ть, по-; **~ed mutton** тушёная бара́нина; (*fruit*) вари́ть (*impf.*); **~ed fruit** компо́т; **the tea is ~ed** (*Br.*) чай перестоя́лся.

● *v.i.* (*of meat, fish, vegetables*) туши́ться (*impf.*); (*of fruit*) вари́ться (*impf.*); **let him ~ in his own juice** пусть ва́рится в со́бственном соку́ (*coll.*).

● *cpds.* **~-pan, ~-pot** *nn.* кастрю́ля; соте́йник.

steward /ˈstjuːəd/ *n.* (*of estate, club etc.*) управля́ющий, эконо́м, стю́ард; (*of race-meeting, show etc.*) распоряди́тель (*m.*); (*on ship*) стю́ард; (*on train*) проводни́к; (*on plane*) бортпроводни́к, стю́ард.

stewardess /ˌstjuːəˈdes/, /ˈstjuːədɪs/ *n.* (*on ship*) стюарде́сса; (*on train*) проводни́ца; (*on plane*) стюарде́сса, бортпроводни́ца.

stewardship /ˈstjuːədʃɪp/ *n.* управле́ние.

stick[1] /stɪk/ *n.* **1** (*for support, punishment*) па́лка; (**walking-~**) трость; (*pl., for kindling*) хво́рост; (**hockey-~** *etc.*) клю́шка; (*baton*) дирижёрская па́лочка; (*fig.*): **they left us a few ~s of furniture** они́ оста́вили нам ко́е-что из ме́бели; **they live in the ~s** (*sl.*) они́ живу́т в захолу́стье; **get hold of the wrong end of the ~** превра́тно пон|има́ть, -я́ть что-н.; **the big ~** (*fig.*) поли́тика большо́й дуби́нки; **~-and-carrot policy** поли́тика кнута́ и пря́ника; **he's a dry old ~** он соверше́нный суха́рь.
2 (*~-shaped object*): **~ of chalk** мело́к; **~ of shaving-soap** мы́льная па́лочка; **~ of celery/rhubarb** сте́бель (*m.*) сельдере́я/ревеня́; **~ of dynamite** бруско́к динами́та; **~ insect** па́лочник.

stick[2] /stɪk/ *v.t.* (*past and p.p.* **stuck**) **1** (*insert point of*) втыка́ть, воткну́ть; **I stuck a pin in the map** я воткну́л була́вку в ка́рту; (*thrust*): **~ one's spurs into a horse's flanks** вонз|а́ть, -и́ть шпо́ры в бока́ ло́шади.
2 (*pierce*) пронз|а́ть, -и́ть; **~ s.o. with a bayonet** пронз|а́ть, -и́ть кого́-н. штыко́м; **~ a pig** зак|а́лывать, -оло́ть свинью́.
3 (*cause to adhere*) прикле́и|вать, -ть (*что к чему*); накле́и|вать, -ть (*что на что*); **the stamp was stuck on upside down** ма́рка была́ накле́ена вверх нога́ми; (*affix*): **~ a notice on the door** ве́шать, пове́сить объявле́ние на дверь.
4 (*coll., put*): **~ that book on the shelf** су́ньте э́ту кни́гу на по́лку; **he stuck his head round the door** он просу́нул го́лову в дверь; **with his hands stuck in his pockets** (за)су́нув ру́ки в карма́ны; **~ it on the bill!** припиши́те э́то к счёту!
5 (*Br. coll., endure*) терпе́ть, вы́-; выноси́ть, вы́нести; **I can't ~ her nagging** я не выношу́ её ворча́ния; **I couldn't ~ it any longer** я бо́льше не мог терпе́ть.
6: **be stuck, get stuck** *see v.i.* 5
7 (*coll. uses of pass. with preps.*): **be stuck on** (*captivated by*): **he is stuck on her** он к ней присо́х; **get stuck into something** (*Br., make serious start on*) всерьёз за что-н. прин|има́ться, -я́ться; **be stuck with something** (*unable to get rid of*) быть не в состоя́нии отде́латься от чего́-н.

● *v.i.* (*past and p.p.* **stuck**) **1** (*be implanted*): **a dagger ~ing in his back** кинжа́л, торча́щий у него́ в спине́; **there's a nail ~ing into my heel** гвоздь впива́ется мне в пя́тку.
2 (*remain attached, adhere*) прил|ипа́ть, -и́пнуть (*к чему*); прикле́и|ваться, -ться; **this envelope won't ~** э́тот конве́рт не закле́ивается; **these pages have stuck (together)** э́ти страни́цы сли́плись; **~ing-plaster** (*Br.*) лейкопла́стырь (*m.*), ли́пкий пла́стырь; **they couldn't make the charge ~** они́ ниче́м не смогли́ подкрепи́ть своего́ обвине́ния; **the nickname stuck** э́то про́звище прили́пло к нему́/ней.
3 (*cling, cleave*): **~ to a task** рабо́тать (*impf.*) не покладая рук; **~ to one's guns** не сдава́ть (*impf.*) пози́ций; **~ to the point** не отступа́ть (*impf.*) от те́мы; **~ to one's principles** ост|ава́ться, -а́ться ве́рным свои́м при́нципам; **~ to one's word** держа́ть, с- сло́во; **the accused stuck to his story** обвиня́емый упо́рно стоя́л на своём; **~ by s.o.** подде́рж|ивать, -а́ть кого́-н.
4 (*coll., stay*): **are you going to ~ at home all day?** вы собира́етесь весь день торча́ть до́ма?
5 (*also* **be stuck, get stuck**: *become embedded, fixed, immobilized*) застр|ева́ть, -я́ть; **~ in the mud** зав|яза́ть, -я́знуть в гря́зи; **the drawer ~s** я́щик застря́л; **her zipper stuck** у неё застря́ла мо́лния; **can you help with this problem? I'm stuck** помоги́те мне, пожа́луйста, с э́той зада́чей — я застря́л; **one thing ~s in my mind** одно́ у меня́ засе́ло в па́мяти.

● *with advs.*: **~ around** *v.i.* (*coll.*) не уходи́ть (*impf.*); **~ down** *v.t.* (*seal*): **have you stuck the envelope down?** вы закле́или конве́рт?; **~ on** *v.t.* (*affix*) прикле́и|вать, -ть; (*coll., add*): **your article is a bit short, can you ~ on another paragraph?** ва́ша статья́ коротковáта — не мо́жете ли вы приба́вить ещё оди́н абза́ц?; **~ out** *v.t.*: **~ one's tongue out** высо́вывать, вы́сунуть язы́к; **~ one's head out** высо́вываться, вы́сунуться; **~ one's neck out** (*fig.*) выска́кивать, вы́скочить; (*endure*): **how long can they ~ it out?** как до́лго они́ продержа́тся?; *v.i.* (*project*) торча́ть (*impf.*); **his ears ~ out** у него́ торча́т у́ши; **a nail is ~ing out of the wall** в стене́ торчи́т гвоздь; **his intentions stuck out a mile** (*coll.*) за версту́ бы́ло ви́дно, чего́ он хо́чет; (*hold out*): **~ out for higher wages** наста́ивать (*impf.*) на повыше́нии зарпла́ты; **~ together** *v.t.* (*with glue*) скле́и|вать, -ть; *v.i.*: **good friends ~ together** настоя́щие друзья́ стоя́т друг за дру́га (горо́й); **~ up** (*coll.*) *v.t.*: **our neighbours** (*Br.*), **neighbors** (*US*) **stuck up a fence** на́ши сосе́ди поста́вили забо́р; **~ up a notice** ве́шать, пове́сить объявле́ние; (*raise*): **~ 'em up!** (*coll.*) ру́ки вверх!; *v.i.* (*protrude upwards*) торча́ть (*impf.*); **his hair was ~ing up** у него́ во́лосы торча́ли во все сто́роны; **~ up for** (*coll.*) (*support*) поддéрж|ивать, -áть; (*defend*) заступ|áться, -и́ться за (*кого*).

● *cpds.* **~-in-the-mud** *n.* рутинёр; кóсный человéк; **~ shift** *n.* (*US*) рычáг переключéния передáч; **~-up** *n.* (*coll.*) налёт, ограблéние.

sticker /ˈstɪkə(r)/ *n.* (*label*) наклéйка, этикéтка; (*coll., hard worker*) работя́га (*c.g.*).

stickiness /ˈstɪkɪnɪs/ *n.* ли́пкость, клéйкость; (*viscosity*) вя́зкость, тягу́честь.

stickleback /ˈstɪk(ə)lˌbæk/ *n.* кóлюшка.

stickler /ˈstɪklə(r)/ *n.* побóрник; **he's a ~ for correct grammar** в вопрóсах граммáтики он педáнт.

sticky /ˈstɪkɪ/ *adj.* (**stickier, stickiest**) **1** клéйкий, ли́пкий; (*viscous*) вя́зкий, тягу́чий; **come to a ~ end** (*coll.*) плóхо кóнчить (*pf.*). **2** (*of person, difficult, unamenable*) непоклáдистый; **he was ~ about giving me leave** он никáк не хотéл давáть мне óтпуск; (*of situation*) неприя́тный, трýдный.

stiff /stɪf/ *n.* (*sl.*) (*corpse*) труп.

● *adj.* **1** (*not flexible or soft*) жёсткий; **~ collar** жёсткий воротничóк.
2 (*not working smoothly*) тугóй; **~ hinges** туги́е пéтли.
3 (*of person or parts of body*) онемéлый, окостенéлый; **I have a ~ neck** у меня́ шéя онемéла; **he has a ~ leg** у негó ногá плóхо сгибáется; **I feel ~** я не могу́ ни согну́ться, ни разогну́ться; **I was ~ with cold** я совершéнно окоченéл; **keep a ~ upper lip** (*fig.*) сохран|я́ть, -и́ть твёрдость.
4 (*forceful*) си́льный; **the garrison put up a ~ resistance** гарнизóн отчáянно сопротивля́лся; **a ~ breeze** крéпкий вéтер; **a ~ drink** хорóший глотóк спиртнóго.
5 (*hard to stir or mould*) густóй.
6 (*difficult*) трýдный, тяжёлый; **a ~ examination** трýдный экзáмен; **a ~ climb** трýдный/тяжёлый подъём; (*severe*) сурóвый; **a ~ price** непомéрно высóкая ценá; **he got a ~ sentence** емý вы́несли сурóвый приговóр.
7 (*formal, constrained*) натя́нутый, чóпорный.
8 (*pred., coll.*): **he was scared ~** он перепугáлся дó смерти; **I was bored ~** я чуть не у́мер со скýки.

stiffen /ˈstɪf(ə)n/ *v.t.* **1** (*make rigid*) прид|авáть, -áть жёсткость + *d.*; **collars ~ed with starch** накрахмáленные воротнички́.
2 (*make resolute*) прид|авáть, -áть твёрдость + *d.* **3** (*strengthen*) укреп|ля́ть, -и́ть.

● *v.i.* (*become rigid*) дéлаться, с- жёстким; (*of body*) коченéть, о-/костенéть, о-; (*become stronger*) крéпнуть, о-; дéлаться, с- крéпче; **the breeze ~ed** вéтер крепчáл; **opposition is ~ing** сопротивлéние крéпнет.

stiffener /ˈstɪf(ə)nə(r)/ *n.* (*stiff lining*) жёсткая подклáдка; (*drink*) глотóк спиртнóго.

stiffness /ˈstɪfnɪs/ *n.* (*of material*) жёсткость; (*of limbs*) одеревенéлость; (*of character*) чóпорность, принуждённость.

stifl|e /ˈstaɪf(ə)l/ *v.t.* **1** (*smother, suffocate*) души́ть, за-; **it is ~ing in here** здесь ду́шно; **~ing heat** удушáющая жарá. **2** (*e.g. rebellion, feelings, hopes, sobs*) подав|ля́ть, -и́ть; **~e flames** туши́ть, за- огóнь; **~e one's laughter** подав|ля́ть, -и́ть смех.

stig|ma /ˈstɪgmə/ *n.* (*pl.* **~mas** *or esp. in sense 2* **~mata** /-mətə/, /-ˈmɑːtə/)
1 (*imputation, stain*) позóр, пятнó; **he will bear the ~ of the trial all his life** э́тот процéсс опозóрит егó навсегдá (*or* на всю жизнь); **he bore the ~ of illegitimacy** он нёс на себé клеймó незаконнорождённого. **2** (*relig., med.*) сти́гма, стигмáт. **3** (*bot.*) ры́льце.

stigmatization /ˌstɪgmətaɪˈzeɪʃ(ə)n/ *n.* клеймéние.

stigmatize /ˈstɪgməˌtaɪz/ *v.t.* клейми́ть, за-.

stile /staɪl/ *n.* (*steps*) перелáз.

stiletto /stɪˈletəʊ/ *n.* (*pl.* **~s**) (*dagger*) стилéт; **~ heels** гвóздики (*m. pl.*); шпи́льки (*f. pl.*).

still¹ /stɪl/ *n.* (*for distilling*) перегóнный куб; винокýренная установка.

still² /stɪl/ *n.* **1** (*liter.*): **in the ~ of night** в ночнóй тиши́. **2** (*cin.*) (реклáмный) кадр.

● *adj.* **1** (*quiet, hushed, calm*) ти́хий, безмóлвный; **a ~ evening** ти́хий/безвéтренный вéчер; **become ~** ум|олкáть, -óлкнуть. **2** (*motionless*) неподви́жный; **sit/stand ~** сидéть/стоя́ть (*impf.*) спокóйно; **keep ~!** не шевели́тесь!; спокóйно!; **~ life** (*art*) натюрмóрт. **3** (*of wine*) неигри́стый. **4** (*of water*) глáдкий, спокóйный.

● *adv.* **1** (*even now, then; as formerly*) (всё) ещё; до сих пор; по-прéжнему; **he ~ doesn't understand** он до сих пор не понимáет. **2** (*nevertheless*) тем не мéнее, всё-таки, всё равнó. **3** (*with comp.: even, yet*) ещё.

● *v.t.* (*calm*) успок|áивать, -óить.

● *cpds.* **~-birth** *n.* рождéние мёртвого плодá; **~-born** *adj.* мертворождённый.

stillness /ˈstɪlnɪs/ *n.* тишинá.

stilt /stɪlt/ *n.* **1** ходу́ля; **walk on ~s** ходи́ть (*indet.*) на ходу́лях.
2 (*supporting building*) свáя.

stilted /ˈstɪltɪd/ *adj.* (*of style etc.*) высокопáрный.

stimulant /ˈstɪmjʊlənt/ *n.* побуди́тель (*m.*), сти́мул; (*med.*) стимуля́тор, стимули́рующее срéдство.

● *adj.* возбуждáющий, стимули́рующий.

stimulat|e /ˈstɪmjʊˌleɪt/ *v.t.* **1** (*rouse, incite*) побу|ждáть, -ди́ть (*кого* + *inf. or к чему*); стимули́ровать (*impf., pf.*).
2 (*excite, arouse*) возбу|ждáть, -ди́ть; **the story ~ed my curiosity** расскáз возбуди́л моё любопы́тство; **his interest was ~ed** у негó возни́к интерéс; **light ~es the optic nerve** свет раздражáет зри́тельный нерв.
3 (*increase*): **this ~es the action of the heart** э́то стимули́рует сердéчную дéятельность; **in order to ~e production** в цéлях стимули́рования произвóдства.

stimulation /ˌstɪmjʊˈleɪʃ(ə)n/ *n.* (*urging*) побуждéние, поощрéние; (*excitement*) возбуждéние.

stimu|lus /ˈstɪmjʊləs/ *n.* (*pl.* **~li** /-ˌlaɪ/, /-ˌliː/) (*spur, incentive*) сти́мул, толчóк, побуждéние; (*motive force*) дви́жущая си́ла; (*of organ, tissue*) раздражи́тель (*m.*).

sting /stɪŋ/ *n.* **1** (*of insect etc.*) жáло; **a ~ in the tail** (*fig.*) ≈ скры́тая шпи́лька.
2 (*of plant*) жгу́чий волосóк; (*of nettle*) ожóг.
3 (*by insect*) укýс; **I got a ~ on my leg** меня́ чтó-то ужáлило/укуси́ло в нóгу; **his face is covered with ~s** у негó всё лицó искýсано.
4 (**~ing pain**) óстрая/жгу́чая боль.

● *v.t.* (*past and p.p.* **stung**) **1** (*of insect etc.*) жáлить, у-; кусáть, укуси́ть; **he was stung by a bee** егó ужáлила пчелá; (*of plant*) обж|игáть, -éчь; жечь (*impf.*); **the nettles stung his feet** крапи́ва жглá емý нóги; **~ing-nettle** (жгу́чая) крапи́ва.
2 (*of pain, smoke etc.*) обж|игáть, -éчь; **our faces were stung by the hail** град стегáл нам лицó; **a ~ing slap on the face** жестóкая пощёчина.
3 (*pain mentally*) терзáть (*impf.*); уязв|ля́ть, -и́ть; **the reproaches stung him** упрёки уязви́ли егó; **he was stung by remorse** егó терзáло раскáяние; **~ing words** язви́тельные словá.
4 (*coll., overcharge, swindle*) облапóшить/нагрéть (*both pf., coll.*).

● *v.i.* (*past and p.p.* **stung**) **1** (*of insect etc.*) жáлиться (*impf.*); кусáться (*impf.*); (*of plant*) жéчься (*impf.*).
2 (*feel pain or irritation*) жечь (*impf.*); **the blow made his hand ~** емý жглó рýку от удáра; **the smoke made my eyes ~** дым ел мне глазá.

● *cpd.* **~-ray** (*also* **stingaree**) *n.* скат.

stingless /ˈstɪŋlɪs/ *adj.* не имéющий жáла; без жáла.

stingy /ˈstɪndʒɪ/ *adj.* (**stingier, stingiest**) **1** (*of person*) скупóй; (*coll.*) скáредный. **2** (*meagre*) скýдный.

stink /stɪŋk/ *n.* **1** вонь, зловóние.
2 (*coll.*): **raise (or kick up) a ~ about something** подн|имáть, -я́ть шум (*or* устр|áивать, -óить скандáл) по какóму-н. пóводу.

● *v.t.* (*past* **stank** *or* **stunk;** *p.p.* **stunk**): **~ out** вы́куривать, вы́курить.

● *v.i.* (*past* **stank** *or* **stunk;** *p.p.* **stunk**) воня́ть (*impf.*); смердéть (*impf.*); **the room ~s of onions** в кóмнате воня́ет лýком; **a ~ing cellar** вонючий подвáл.

stinker /ˈstɪŋkə(r)/ *n.* (*coll.*) **1** (*person*) мерзáвец, гáдина. **2** (*Br., difficult task*) трýдная задáча. **3** (*Br., severe letter*) сурóвое письмó, óтповедь.

stint /stɪnt/ *n.* **1** (*liter., restriction*): **without ~** без предéла/ограничéний; неограни́ченно. **2** (*fixed amount of work*) урóк; **do one's daily ~** выполня́ть, вы́полнить дневнóй урóк.

● *v.t.* ограни́чи|вать, -ть (*кого в чём*); скупи́ться, по- на + *a.*; **he did not ~ on his praise** он не скупи́лся на похвалы́;

S

he ~s himself for his children он отка́зывает себе́ ра́ди дете́й.

stipend /ˈstaɪpend/ *n.* (*of clergyman*) жа́лованье; (*of student*) стипе́ндия.

stipendiary /staɪˈpendjərɪ/, /stɪ-/ *n.* стипендиа́т; (*magistrate*) пла́тный магистра́т (*в отличие от мирового судьи*).

● *adj.* получа́ющий жа́лованье/стипе́ндию.

stipple /ˈstɪp(ə)l/ *n.* (*method of shading*) то́чечный пункти́р.

● *v.t.* гравирова́ть, на- в пункти́рной мане́ре; изобра|жа́ть, -зи́ть пункти́ром.

stipulate /ˈstɪpjʊˌleɪt/ *v.t.* (*demand*) обусло́в|ливать, -ить; (*agree on, fix*) огов|а́ривать, -ори́ть; **at the ~d time** в оговорённое/усло́вленное вре́мя.

stipulation /ˌstɪpjʊˈleɪʃ(ə)n/ *n.* (*stipulating*) обусло́вливание; (*condition*) усло́вие.

stir /stɜː(r)/ *n.* **1** (*act of ~ring*) поме́шивание; **give one's tea a ~** помеша́ть (*pf.*) чай.
2 (*commotion; movement*) волне́ние, движе́ние; **there was a ~ in the crowd** толпа́ заволнова́лась.
3 (*sensation*) шум, сенса́ция; **the news caused a ~** э́то изве́стие наде́лало мно́го шу́ма.

● *v.t.* (**stirred, stirring**) **1** (*cause to move*): **the wind ~s the trees** ве́тер колы́шет дере́вья; **~ the fire** шурова́ть, по- у́голь в ками́не; **~ your stumps!** (*Br. coll.*) пошеве́ливайся!; **~ one's tea** разме́ш|ивать, -а́ть чай; **~ the soup** меша́ть, по- суп.
2 (*arouse, affect, agitate*) возбу|жда́ть, -ди́ть; пробу|жда́ть, -ди́ть; волнова́ть, вз-; **her plea ~red him to pity** её мольба́ пробуди́ла в нём жа́лость; **he made a ~ring speech** он вы́ступил с волну́ющей ре́чью.

● *v.i.* (**stirred, stirring**) шевели́ться, за-; шелохну́ться (*pf.*); **something ~red in the undergrowth** что́-то (за)шевели́лось в куста́х; **the wind ~red in the trees** ве́тер шелесте́л в дере́вьях; **the cat lay without ~ring** ко́шка лежа́ла, не шелохну́вшись.

● *with adv.*: **~ up** *v.t.* (*mix*) разм|е́шивать, -еша́ть; сме́ш|ивать, -а́ть; (*arouse*): **~ up an interest in something** пробу|жда́ть, -ди́ть интере́с к чему́-н.; **~ up rebellion** се́ять (*impf.*) сму́ту.

stirrup /ˈstɪrəp/ *n.* стре́мя (*nt.*).

● *cpds.* **~-cup** *n.* проща́льный ку́бок, посошо́к (*coll.*); **~-leather** *n.* пу́тлище; **~-pump** *n.* ручно́й огнетуши́тель.

stitch /stɪtʃ/ *n.* **1** (*method of knitting*) вя́зка; (*method of sewing*) стёжка; **she learnt a new ~** она́ осво́ила но́вую вя́зку/стёжку. **2** (*single pass of needle*) стежо́к, петля́; **drop a ~** спус|ка́ть, -ти́ть пе́тлю; **a ~ in time** своевре́менная ме́ра. **3** (*med.*) шов; **put ~es in a wound** на|кла́дывать, -ложи́ть швы на ра́ну. **4** (*pain in side*) ко́лик|и (*pl., g.* —)/колотьё (*coll.*) в боку́; **he had us in ~es** (*coll.*) он нас чуть не умори́л со́ смеху.

● *v.t.* (*sew together*) сши|ва́ть, -ть; (*esp. med.*) заш|ива́ть, -и́ть; (*bookbinding*) брошюрова́ть, с-.

● *with advs.*: **~ on** *v.t.* приш|ива́ть, -и́ть; **~ up** *v.t.* (*a garment*) сши|ва́ть, -ть; (*a wound*) заш|ива́ть, -и́ть.

stoat /stəʊt/ *n.* горноста́й (в ле́тнем меху́).

stock /stɒk/ *n.* **1** (*tree-trunk*) ствол; (*stump*) пень (*m.*).
2 (*handle, base etc.*): **~ of a rifle** руже́йная ло́жа.
3 (*lineage*) семья́, род, происхожде́ние; **he comes of good ~** он из хоро́шей семьи́.
4 (*resources, store, supply*) запа́с, инвента́рь (*m.*); **in ~** в ассортиме́нте; **have something in ~** име́ть что-н. в нали́чии; **take ~** (*lit.*) инвентаризова́ть (*impf., pf.*); **take ~ of** (*fig., appraise*) крити́чески оце́н|ивать, -и́ть.
5 (*of farm*): **(live)~** скот, поголо́вье скота́.
6 (*raw material*) сырьё; **paper ~** бума́жное сырьё.
7 (*cul.*) (кре́пкий) бульо́н.
8 (*comm.*) а́кции (*f. pl.*); фо́нды (*m. pl.*); **S~ Exchange** фо́ндовая би́ржа; (*fig., reputation*): **his ~ stood high, then fell to nothing** сперва́ его́ репута́ция была́ о́чень высо́кая, но пото́м упа́ла.
9 (*pl., for confining offenders*) коло́дки (*f. pl.*).
10 (*pl., for supporting ship*) ста́пель (*m.*); **be on the ~s** стоя́ть (*impf.*) на ста́пел|е/-ях; (*fig.*) быть (*impf.*) в рабо́те.
11 (*bot.*) левко́й.

● *adj.* **1** (*kept in ~, available*) име́ющийся в нали́чии.
2 (*regularly used, hackneyed*) обы́чный, шабло́нный.

● *v.t.* **1** (*equip, furnish with ~*) снаб|жа́ть, -ди́ть (*что чем*); обору́довать (*impf., pf.*); **the garden was well ~ed with vegetables** в огоро́де бы́ло поса́жено мно́го овоще́й.
2 (*keep in ~*) держа́ть (*impf.*); име́ть (*impf.*) в нали́чии.

● *v.i.*: **~ up**: **we ~ed up with fuel for the winter** мы запасли́сь то́пливом на́ зиму.

● *cpds.* **~-account, ~-book** *nn.* счёт капита́ла/това́ра; **~-breeder** *n.* животново́д, скотово́д; **~broker** *n.* биржево́й ма́клер; **~broking** *n.* биржевы́е опера́ции (*f. pl.*); **~ car** *n.* го́ночный автомоби́ль, адапти́рованный из сери́йного; **~ car racing** го́нки (*f. pl.*) на сери́йных автомоби́лях; **~ cube** *n.* бульо́нный ку́бик; **~fish** *n.* вя́леная треска́; **~holder** *n.* акционе́р; **~-in-trade** *n.* запа́с това́ров; **promises are the politician's ~-in-trade** обеща́ния — непреме́нный арсена́л поли́тика; **~jobber** *n.* биржево́й ма́клер; спекуля́нт; **~list** *n.* (*Br.*) спи́сок това́ров в ассортиме́нте; **~man** *n.* скотово́д; (*US, owner*) скотопромы́шленник; **~-market** *n.* фо́ндовая би́ржа; **~pile** *n.* материа́льный резе́рв, запа́с; *v.t.* запас|а́ть, -ти́ +*a. or g.*; **~-raising** *n.* животново́дство, скотово́дство; **~-still** *adv.* неподви́жно; **~-taking** *n.* инвентариза́ция; **closed for ~-taking** закры́то на переучёт; (*fig.*) обзо́р, оце́нка, крити́ческий ана́лиз; **~yard** *n.* скотопригóнный двор.

stockade /stɒˈkeɪd/ *n.* частоко́л.

Stockholm /ˈstɒkhəʊm/ *n.* Стокго́льм.

stockinet(te) /ˌstɒkɪˈnet/ *n.* трикота́ж; (*attr.*) трикота́жный.

stocking /ˈstɒkɪŋ/ *n.* чуло́к (*also of horse*); **in one's ~(ed) feet** в одни́х чулка́х/носка́х; без о́буви.

stockist /ˈstɒkɪst/ *n.* (*Br.*) ро́зничный продаве́ц (*определённых товаров*).

stocky /ˈstɒkɪ/ *adj.* (**stockier, stockiest**) корена́стый, призе́мистый.

stodge /stɒdʒ/ (*Br. coll.*) *n.* (*heavy food*) тяжёлая/сы́тная еда́.

stodginess /ˈstɒdʒɪnɪs/ *n.* (*fig.*) тяжелове́сность, ну́дность.

stodgy /ˈstɒdʒɪ/ *adj.* (**stodgier, stodgiest**) (*Br., of food*) тяжёлый; (*coll.*) (*of person*) ну́дный; (*of style*) тяжелове́сный.

stoic /ˈstəʊɪk/ *n.* (*of either sex*) сто́ик.

● *adj.* сто́ический.

stoical /ˈstəʊɪk(ə)l/ *adj.* сто́ический.

stoicism /ˈstəʊɪˌsɪz(ə)m/ *n.* стоици́зм.

stoke /stəʊk/ *v.t.* (*also* **~ up**) шурова́ть (*impf.*); (*put more fuel on*) загру|жа́ть, -зи́ть (*топку*).

● *v.i.* **1** (*act as ~r*) топи́ть (*impf.*). **2**: **~ up** подде́рж|ивать, -а́ть ого́нь; шурова́ть (*impf.*); (*coll., eat heavily*) наж|ира́ться, -ра́ться.

● *cpds.* **~hold** *n.* кочега́рка; **~-hole** *n.* отве́рстие то́пки.

stoker /ˈstəʊkə(r)/ *n.* кочега́р, истопни́к.

stole[1] /stəʊl/ *n.* паланти́н.

stole[2] /stəʊl/ *past of* ⇒**steal**

stolen /ˈstəʊlən/ *p.p. of* ⇒**steal**

stolid /ˈstɒlɪd/ *adj.* (*impassive*) бесстра́стный; (*dull*) тупо́й; (*phlegmatic*) флегмати́чный; (*sluggish*) вя́лый.

stolidity /stɒˈlɪdɪtɪ/ *n.* бесстра́стность, бесстра́стие; ту́пость; флегмати́чность; вя́лость.

stomach /ˈstʌmək/ *n.* **1** (*internal organ*) желу́док; **a pain in the ~** боль в желу́дке; **he had a ~ upset** у него́ бы́ло расстро́йство желу́дка; **on a full ~** на по́лный желу́док; **on an empty ~** натоща́к; на пусто́й желу́док; **a strong ~** хоро́шее пищеваре́ние; **you need a strong ~ to read this report** нужны́ желе́зные не́рвы, что́бы чита́ть э́тот отчёт; **it turns my ~** меня́ тошни́т от э́того.
2 (*external part of body; belly*) живо́т, брю́хо; **someone kicked me in the ~** кто́-то пнул меня́ в живо́т; **he is getting a large ~** у него́ живо́т растёт.
3 (*appetite*): **I have no ~ for rich food** я не переношу́ жи́рного.
4 (*fig., desire*) жела́ние, охо́та; (*spirit, courage*) дух, хра́брость; **he has no ~**

for fighting у него́ не хвата́ет сме́лости дра́ться.
● *v.t.* **1** (*digest*) перева́р|ивать, -и́ть.
2 (*fig., tolerate*): **~ an insult** прогл|а́тывать, -оти́ть оби́ду; **I can't ~ him** я его́ не переношу́; я его́ терпе́ть не могу́.
● *cpds.* **~-ache** *n.* ко́лик|и (*pl., g.* —) в животе́; **~-pump, ~-tube** *nn.* желу́дочный зонд.

stomp /stɒmp/ *v.i.* (*coll., tread heavily*) то́пать, про-.

stone /stəʊn/ *n.* (*sense 6: pl.* ~)
1 ка́мень (*m.*); **meteoric ~** аэроли́т; **throw ~s** броса́ться (*impf.*) камня́ми; **throw a ~ at s.o.** бр|оса́ть, -о́сить ка́мнем в кого́-н.; **I have a ~ in my shoe** у меня́ в боти́нке ка́мешек; **leave no ~ unturned** (*fig.*) испо́льзовать (*impf., pf.*) все возмо́жные сре́дства; **his house is within a ~'s throw of here** до его́ до́ма отсю́да руко́й пода́ть.
2 (*gem*): **precious ~** драгоце́нный ка́мень.
3 (*rock, material*): **built of local ~** постро́енный из ме́стного ка́мня; **Portland ~** портла́ндский ка́мень, портла́ндская поро́да; **he has a heart of ~** у него́ ка́менное се́рдце; **S~ Age** ка́менный век; **S~ Age man** челове́к ка́менного ве́ка; **~ circle** кро́млех.
4 (*of plum etc.*) ко́сточка.
5 (*med.*) ка́мень (*m.*).
6 (*Br., weight*) сто́ун, стон (*6,35 кг.*).
● *adj.* ка́менный.
● *v.t.* **1** (*pelt with ~s*) поб|ива́ть, -и́ть камня́ми.
2 (*line, face with ~*) облиц|о́вывать, -ева́ть ка́мнем; (*pave*) мости́ть, вы́- ка́мнем.
3 (*remove ~s from*): **~ cherries** оч|ища́ть, -и́стить ви́шни от ко́сточек.
4: **~d** (*drunk*) вдрызг пья́ный (*coll.*); (*with drugs*) одуре́вший от нарко́тиков (*or* нарко́тиками); под ка́йфом (*sl.*); **get ~d** лови́ть, пойма́ть кайф (*sl.*).
● *cpds.* **~chat** *n.* черноголо́вый чека́н; **~-cold** *adj.* холо́дный как лёд; **~-dead** *adj.* мёртвый; **~-deaf** *adj.* соверше́нно глухо́й; **~-fruit** *n.* костя́нка, ко́сточковый плод; **~-ground** *adj.* размо́лотый жернова́ми; **~mason** *n.* ка́менщик; **~wall** *v.i.* (*fig., refuse to be drawn*) отма́лчиваться, отмолча́ться; **~ware** *n.* гонча́рные/керами́ческие изде́лия; **~work** *n.* (*masonry*) ка́менная кла́дка.

stony /ˈstəʊnɪ/ *adj.* (**stonier, stoniest**) камени́стый; (*fig., unfeeling*) ка́менный.
● *cpds.* **~-broke** *adj.* (*Br. coll.*): **I am ~-broke** у меня́ нет ни гроша́; **~-hearted** *adj.* жестокосе́рдный.

stood /stʊd/ *past and p.p. of* ⇒**stand**

stooge /stu:dʒ/ (*sl.*) *n.* (*comedian's foil*) партнёр ко́мика; (*deputy of low standing*) подставно́е лицо́.

stook /stu:k/, /stʊk/ *n.* (*Br.*) копна́ (се́на).

stool /stu:l/ *n.* **1** (*seat*) табуре́т(ка); **fall between two ~s** (*Br.*) ока́зываться, оказа́ться ме́жду двух сту́льев.
2 (**foot~**) скаме́ечка (для ног).
3 (*faeces*) стул.
● *cpd.* **~-pigeon** *n.* стука́ч (*fem.* -ка) (*coll.*).

stoop /stu:p/ *n.* суту́лость; **he walks with a ~** он суту́лится при ходьбе́.
● *v.t.*: **~ one's shoulders** суту́лить (*impf.*) пле́чи.
● *v.i.* **1** (*of posture*) суту́литься, с-; **walk with a ~ing gait** суту́литься (*impf.*) при ходьбе́; (*bend down*) наг|иба́ться, -ну́ться; сгиба́ться, согну́ться.
2 (*condescend*) сни|сходи́ть, -зойти́; (*lower o.s.*) ун|ижа́ться, -и́зиться; **he never ~ed to lying** он никогда́ не унижа́лся до лжи.

stop /stɒp/ *n.* **1** (*halt, halting-place*) остано́вка; **come to a ~** остан|а́вливаться, -ови́ться; **put a ~ to** положи́ть (*pf.*) коне́ц +*d.*; **bus ~** авто́бусная остано́вка.
2 (*stay*) остано́вка, (кра́ткое) пребы́вание; **we made a short ~ in Paris** мы останови́лись ненадо́лго в Пари́же.
3 (*Br. arch., punctuation mark*) знак препина́ния; **full ~** то́чка; (*in telegram*) то́чка (*abbr.* тчк); (*fig.*): **come to a full ~** при|ходи́ть, -йти́ к концу́.
4 (*mus., on string*) лад; (*of organ*) реги́стр; **pull out all the ~s** (*fig.*) наж|има́ть, -а́ть на все кно́пки.
5 (*phot.*) диафра́гма.
● *v.t.* (**stopped, stopping**) **1** (*also* **~ up**: *close, plug, seal*) закр|ыва́ть, -ы́ть; зат|ыка́ть, -кну́ть; заде́л|ывать, -ать; **he ~ped his ears when I spoke** он заткну́л у́ши, когда́ я говори́л; **the dentist ~ped three of my teeth** (*Br.*) зубно́й врач запломбирова́л мне три зу́ба; **~ a gap** (*fig.*) зап|олня́ть, -о́лнить пробе́л.
2 (*arrest motion of*) остан|а́вливать, -ови́ть; **he ~ped the car** он останови́л маши́ну; **he ~ped the engine** (*intentionally*) он вы́ключил/заглуши́л мото́р; (*inadvertently*) у него́ загло́х мото́р; **the thief was ~ped by a policeman** вор был заде́ржан полице́йским; **~ thief!** держи́ во́ра!; **he ~ped the blow with his arm** он отрази́л уда́р руко́й.
3 (*arrest progress of, bring to an end*) остан|а́вливать, -ови́ть; заде́рж|ивать, -а́ть; прекра|ща́ть, -ти́ть; **the frost ~ped the growth of the plants** моро́з останови́л рост расте́ний; **the bank ~ped payment** банк прекрати́л платежи́; **rain ~ped play** дождь сорва́л игру́; **it ought to be ~ped** э́то на́до прекрати́ть *or* э́тому на́до положи́ть коне́ц; (*suspend*) приостан|а́вливать, -ови́ть; **I ~ped the cheque** (*Br.*), **check** (*US*) я приостанови́л платёж по э́тому че́ку; **production was ~ped for a day** произво́дство бы́ло остано́влено на оди́н день; (*cancel*) отмен|я́ть, -и́ть; **all leave has been ~ped** все отпуска́ отменены́; (*cut off, disallow, ~ provision of*): **they ~ped £20 out of his wages** у него́ удержа́ли 20 фу́нтов из зарпла́ты; **my father ~ped my allowance** оте́ц переста́л выделя́ть мне де́ньги.
4 (*prevent, hinder*): **~ s.o. from** уде́рж|ивать, -а́ть кого́-н. от +*g.*; не да|ва́ть, -ть (*кому* +*inf.*); **I tried to ~ him (from) telling her** я пыта́лся помеша́ть ему́ сказа́ть ей; **what's ~ping you?** что вас остана́вливает?, за чем (же) де́ло ста́ло?; **what is to ~ me going?** что мне помеша́ет пойти́?
5 (*interrupt*) остан|а́вливать, -ови́ть; прер|ыва́ть, -ва́ть; **once he gets talking no one can ~ him** когда́ он разговори́тся, его́ невозмо́жно останови́ть.
6 (*with gerund: discontinue, leave off*) перест|ава́ть, -а́ть +*inf.*; прекра|ща́ть, -ти́ть +*n. obj.*; **~ teasing the cat!** переста́ньте дразни́ть ко́шку!; **~ telling me what to do!** хва́тит учи́ть меня́ жить!; **they ~ped talking when I came in** когда́ я вошёл, они́ умо́лкли.
7 (*mus.*): **~ a string** заж|има́ть, -а́ть струну́.
● *v.i.* (**stopped, stopping**) **1** (*come to a halt*) остан|а́вливаться, -ови́ться; **he ~ped short, dead** он останови́лся как вко́панный; **a ~ping train** по́езд, иду́щий с остано́вками; **~!** сто́йте!; **~ a minute!** погоди́те мину́ту!; **the clock has ~ped** часы́ стоя́т/останови́лись.
2 (*in speaking*) зам|олка́ть, -о́лкнуть; замолча́ть (*pf.*); **he ~ped talking** он замолча́л; **he ~ped to light his pipe** он замо́лк, что́бы раскури́ть тру́бку.
3 (*cease activity*) перест|ава́ть, -а́ть; конча́ть, ко́нчить; **he ~ped reading** он переста́л чита́ть; **he ~ped smoking** он бро́сил кури́ть; **~ that!** переста́нь!; брось!
4 (*come to an end*) прекра|ща́ться, -ти́ться; конча́ться, ко́нчиться; перест|ава́ть, -а́ть; **the rain ~ped** дождь ко́нчился/переста́л; **the road ~ped suddenly** доро́га вдруг ко́нчилась.
5 (*stay*): **~ at a hotel** (*Br.*) остан|а́вливаться, -ови́ться в гости́нице; **~ at home** ост|ава́ться, -а́ться до́ма; **don't ~ out too long** (*Br.*) не заде́рживайтесь надо́лго.
● *with advs.*: **~ by** *v.i.* за|ходи́ть, -йти́; (*in a vehicle*) за|езжа́ть, -е́хать; **~ off, ~ over** *vv.i.* остан|а́вливаться, -ови́ться; **~ up** *v.t.* = **~** *v.t.* 1; *v.i.*: **we ~ped up late to welcome him** (*Br.*) мы не ложи́лись спать допоздна́, что́бы встре́тить его́.
● *cpds.* **~-cock** *n.* запо́рный кран; **~gap** *n.* (*person*) вре́менная заме́на; (*thing*) заты́чка; вре́менная ме́ра; **it will serve as a ~gap** э́то пойдёт на вре́мя; **~-go** *adj.*: **~-go policy** (*Br.*) авра́льная поли́тика; **~-lamp** (*Br.*), **~-light** *nn.* (*on vehicle*) стоп-сигна́л; **~-light** (*Br., of traffic lights*) кра́сный свет; **~-off, ~-over** *nn.* остано́вка (в пути́); **~-press** *n.* (*Br.*) «в после́днюю мину́ту»; э́кстренное сообще́ние (*в газете*); **~valve** *n.* запо́рный ве́нтиль; сто́порный кла́пан; **~-watch** *n.* секундоме́р.

stoppage /ˈstɒpɪdʒ/ *n.* **1** (*of work etc.*) прекраще́ние, остано́вка, забасто́вка; (*interruption*) перебо́й; **~ of pay** прекраще́ние зарпла́ты; **~ of leave**

отмéна отпускóв. **2** (*obstruction*) засорéние, закýпорка.

stopper /ˈstɒpə(r)/ *n.* (*of bottle etc.*) прóбка.

● *v.t.* (*also* ~ **up**: *cork*) закýпори|вать, -ть; зат|ыкáть, -кнýть.

storage /ˈstɔːrɪdʒ/ *n.* (*storing*) хранéние; (*in warehouse*) складúрование; (*method*): **in cold ~** в холодúльнике; **put into cold ~** (*fig.*) от|клáдывать, -ложúть в дóлгий ящик (*or* под сукнó); (*space*): **put something in(to) ~** сда|вáть, -ть что-н. на хранéние; **take something out of ~** брать, взять что-н. со склáда.

● *cpds.* **~-battery** *n.* аккумулятóрная батарéя; **~ heater** *n.* (*Br.*) электрообогревáтель, аккумулúрующий теплó; **~-tank** *n.* запаснóй резервуáр/бак.

store /stɔː(r)/ *n.* **1** (*stock, reserve*) запáс, резéрв, припáсы (*m. pl.*); **~ of food** съестныé припáсы, запáс провúзии; **a great ~ of information** огрóмный запáс свéдений; **he has a surprise in ~ for you** у негó для вас припасён сюрприз.
2 (*pl., supplies*) припáсы (*m. pl.*), резéрвы (*m. pl.*).
3 (*warehouse*) склад, пакгáуз, хранúлище; **put furniture in ~** сда|вáть, -ть мéбель на хранéние.
4 (*US, shop*) магазúн, лáвка; **department ~** универмáг; **general ~(s)** магазúн смéшанных товáров.
5 (*value, significance*) значéние; **set ~ by** прид|авáть, -áть значéние +*d.*

● *v.t.* **1** (*furnish, stock*) снаб|жáть, -дúть (*что чем*); **his mind is ~d with knowledge** у негó большóй запáс знáний.
2 (*~ up, set aside*) запас|áть, -тú; нак|áпливать, -опúть.
3 (*deposit in ~*) сда|вáть, -ть на хранéние.
4 (*hold*) вме|щáть, -стúть.

● *cpds.* **~house** *n.* склад, кладовáя, амбáр; **~keeper** *n.* (*person responsible for ~d goods*) кладовщú|к (*fem.* -ца); (*shopkeeper*) лáвочни|к (*fem.* -ца); **~-room** *n.* кладовáя.

storey /ˈstɔːrɪ/ *n.* (*US* **story**) этáж; **a house of 5 ~s** пятиэтáжный дом; **top ~** вéрхний этáж.

stork /stɔːk/ *n.* áист.

storm /stɔːm/ *n.* **1** бýря; (*thunder ~*) грозá; (*snow ~*) метéль, вьюга, бурáн; **~ in a teacup** (*Br., fig.*) бýря в стакáне воды.
2 (*naut.*) (жестóкий) шторм.
3 (*upheaval*): **the ~ of revolution** революциóнный вихрь; **~ and stress** (*hist.*) «Бýря и нáтиск».
4 (*fig., hail, shower, volley*) град, лúвень (*m.*); **a ~ of arrows** град стрел; (*of emotion etc.*): **~ of applause** бýря аплодисмéнтов; **~ of abuse** град оскорблéний.
5 (*assault*) штурм; **take a town by ~** брать, взять гóрод штýрмом.

● *v.t.* (*mil.*) штурмовáть (*impf.*); брать, взять штýрмом/прúступом.

● *v.i.* (*of wind etc.*) свирéпствовать (*impf.*); бушевáть (*impf.*); (*fig., rage*) бушевáть (*impf.*); **~ at s.o.** кричáть, на- на когó-н.; **he ~ed out of the room** он в гнéве вы́бежал из кóмнаты.

● *cpds.* **~-beaten, ~-tossed** *adjs.* потрёпанный бýрей; **~-belt** *n.* пóяс бурь; **~-centre** (*US* **-center**) *n.* центр циклóна; (*fig., centre, focus of disturbance*) очáг волнéний/беспоря́дков; **~-cloud** *n.* грозовáя тýча; (*fig.*) тýчи (*f. pl.*) над головóй; **~-cone** *n.* штормовóй сигнáльный кóнус; **~-lantern** *n.* (*Br.*) фонáрь (*m.*) «мóлния»; **~proof** *adj.* буреустóйчивый; **~-sail** *n.* штормовóй пáрус; **~-tossed** *adj.* = **~-beaten; ~-trooper** *n.* штурмовúк; **~-troops** *n.* штурмовы́е войскá; **~-window** *n.* (*US*) зúмняя рáма.

stormy /ˈstɔːmɪ/ *adj.* (**stormier, stormiest**) бýрный (*also fig.*); **~ wind** штормовóй вéтер; **~ weather** (*at sea*) штормовáя погóда; **a ~ sky** грозовóе нéбо; **~ petrel** буревéстник.

story[1] /ˈstɔːrɪ/ *n.* **1** (*tale, account, history*) расскáз, истóрия; (*fairy-tale*) скáзка; **tell a ~** расскáз|ывать, -áть истóрию; **short ~** расскáз, новéлла; **long short ~** пóвесть; **funny ~** анекдóт; **a good ~** интерéсная истóрия; **they all tell the same ~** онú все говоря́т однó и то же; **it's a long ~** э́то дóлгая пéсня (*coll.*); э́то длúнная истóрия; **to cut a long ~ short** корóче говоря́; **that's quite another ~** э́то совсéм другóе дéло; **it's the old, old ~** э́то вéчная истóрия; **the ~ goes** говоря́т.
2 (*newspaper report*) отчёт, статья́.
3 (*plot*) фáбула, сюжéт.
4 (*coll., untruth*) вы́думка, истóрия, ложь; **tell a ~** врать, на-.

● *cpds.* **~-book** *n.* сбóрник расскáзов; **~-line** *n.* фáбула; **~-teller** *n.* расскáзчи|к (*fem.* -ца); (*coll., liar*) вы́думщи|к (*fem.* -ца), лгун (*fem.* -ья).

story[2] /ˈstɔːrɪ/ *n.* = **storey**

stoup /stuːp/ *n.* (*eccl.*) чáша со святóй водóй.

stout /staʊt/ *n.* (*beer*) пóртер.

● *adj.* **1** (*strong*) крéпкий, прóчный.
2 (*resolute*) решúтельный; (*sturdy*) сúльный; (*staunch*) стóйкий; **a ~ heart** стóйкость, мýжество; **offer ~ resistance** окáз|ывать, -áть упóрное сопротивлéние. **3** (*corpulent*) пóлный, дорóдный; **get, grow ~** полнéть, по-/рас-.

● *cpd.* **~-hearted** *adj.* стóйкий, мýжественный.

stoutness /ˈstaʊtnɪs/ *n.* крéпость, прóчность; решúтельность, стóйкость, мýжество; полнотá, тýчность.

stove[1] /stəʊv/ *n.* печь, пéчка; (*for cooking*) плитá.

● *cpd.* **~-pipe** *n.* дымохóд.

stove[2] /stəʊv/ *past and p.p. of* ⇒**stave**

stow /stəʊ/ *v.t.* **1** (*pack*) уклáдывать, уложúть; **I ~ed the trunk (away) in the attic** я убрáл сундýк на чердáк. **2** (*sl., stop*): **~ it!** брось!; хвáтит!

● *v.i.*: **~ away** (*on ship*) éхать (*det.*) зáйцем.

● *cpd.*: **~away** *n.* безбилéтный пассажúр, «зáяц».

stowage /ˈstəʊɪdʒ/ *n.* (*action*) уклáдка, склáдывание; (*space*) складскóе помещéние, кладовáя.

St Petersburg /sənt ˈpiːtəz,bɜːɡ/ *n.* Санкт-Петербýрг; (*attr.*) (санкт-)петербýргский.

straddle /ˈstræd(ə)l/ *v.t.* (*be situated on both sides of*) охвáт|ывать, -úть; **~ a fence** сидéть, сесть верхóм на забóре.

strafe /strɑːf/, /streɪf/ *v.t.* (*with bombs*) бомбардировáть (*impf.*); (*with gun fire*) обстрéл|ивать, -ять.

straggl|e /ˈstræɡ(ə)l/ *v.i.*: **the children ~ed home from school** дéти брелú/тащúлись из шкóлы домóй; **a ~ing line of houses** беспоря́дочный ряд домóв; **a ~ing line of soldiers** беспоря́дочная цепóчка солдáт; **a bush with ~ing shoots** куст с торчáщими побéгами.

straggler /ˈstræɡlə(r)/ *n.* отстáвший.

straggly /ˈstræɡlɪ/ *adj.* (**stragglier, straggliest**) (*hair*) всклокóченный, растрёпанный; (*plants*) увя́дший.

straight /streɪt/ *n.* **1** (*of racecourse*): **home ~** фúнишная прямáя.
2: **the ~ and narrow** чéстная жизнь.

● *adj.* **1** прямóй; **in a ~ line** пря́мо в ряд; **she had ~ hair** у неё бы́ли прямы́е вóлосы; **keep your knees ~!** не сгибáйте колéни!; **I couldn't keep a ~ face** я не мог удержáться от улы́бки.
2 (*level*) рóвный; **are the pictures ~?** картúны вися́т рóвно?; (*neat, in order*) ýбранный в поря́дке; **he never puts his room ~** он никогдá не убирáет своЮ кóмнату; **put one's hat ~** попр|авля́ть, -áвить шля́пу; **is my tie ~?** мой гáлстук не косúт?; **put the record ~** (*fig.*) вн|осúть, -естú я́сность; **let's get this ~** давáйте внесём определённость в э́тот вопрóс.
3 (*direct, honest*) прямóй, чéстный; **~ dealings** чéстность, прямотá.
4 (*orthodox*): **~ play** (*theatr.*) (чúстая) дрáма; (*heterosexual*) гетеросексуáльный; не гомосексуáльный.
5 (*undiluted*) неразбáвленный; (*unbroken; in a row*): **ten ~ wins** дéсять вы́игрышей подря́д; **~ flush** (*cards*) «королéвский цвет», флешь-роя́ль (*m.*).

● *adv.* **1** пря́мо; **~ upwards** пря́мо вверх; **he can't walk ~** он не мóжет ходúть по прямóй; **sit (up) ~!** сидú(те) пря́мо!; **keep ~ on!** идúте пря́мо!; (*directly*): **I am going ~ to Paris** я éду пря́мо в Парúж; **I will come ~ to the point** я приступлю́ пря́мо к дéлу; **I told him ~ (out)** я сказáл емý пря́мо.
2 (*in the right direction or manner*): **he can't shoot ~** он не умéет (мéтко) стреля́ть; **he promised to go ~ in future** он обещáл впредь вестú себя́ чéстно; **I can't think ~** я не могý сосредотóчиться.
3: **~ away, off** срáзу, тóтчас, немéдленно.

● *cpds.* **~forward** *adj.* (*frank*) прямóй; (*honest*) чéстный; (*uncomplicated*) просто́й; **~forwardness** *n.* прямота́; че́стность; простота́.

straighten /'streɪt(ə)n/ *v.t.* **1** выпрямля́ть, вы́прямить; распрям|ля́ть, -и́ть; **he ~ed his back** он выпрямился; он распрями́л спи́ну. **2** (*put in order*) прив|оди́ть, -ести́ в поря́док; ула́|живать, -дить; **he ~ed out his affairs** он привёл свои́ дела́ в поря́док; **I will try to ~ things out** я постара́юсь всё ула́дить.

● *v.i.* выпрямля́ться, вы́прямиться; распрям|ля́ться, -и́ться; (*become orderly*) ула́|живаться, -диться.

strain /streɪn/ *n.* **1** (*tension*) натяже́ние; **the rope broke under the ~** верёвка не вы́держала натяже́ния и ло́пнула; (*wearing effect*): **the ~s of modern life** напряжённость/стресс совреме́нной жи́зни; (*nervous fatigue*): **he is suffering from ~** у него́ не́рвное переутомле́ние; (*muscular ~*) растяже́ние (жил); (*effort, exertion*) напряже́ние; (*demand, load*): **his education is a ~ on my resources** его́ образова́ние си́льно бьёт по моему карма́ну. **2** (*of music*) мело́дия; **we heard the ~s of a waltz** до нас доноси́лась мело́дия ва́льса. **3** (*tone, style*) тон, стиль (*m.*); **he continued in the same ~** он продолжа́л в том же ду́хе. **4** (*breed, stock*) род, происхожде́ние; (*of animals, plants*) поро́да; **a hardy ~ of rose** выно́сливый сорт роз. **5** (*inherited feature*) насле́дственность; **there is a ~ of insanity in his family** в его́ роду́ име́ется насле́дственное психи́ческое заболева́ние; (*trace, tendency*) черта́, скло́нность, элеме́нт; **a ~ of sentimentality** элеме́нт сентимента́льности.

● *v.t.* **1** (*make taut*) натя́|гивать, -ну́ть. **2** (*exert*) напр|яга́ть, -я́чь; **I ~ed my ears to catch his words** я напря́г слух, что́бы улови́ть его́ слова́; **we must ~ every nerve** нам сле́дует напря́чь все си́лы. **3** (*over-exert*): **~ one's eyes** переутом|ля́ть, -и́ть глаза́; по́ртить, ис- зре́ние; **~ a tendon** растя́|гивать, -ну́ть сухожи́лие; **~ o.s.** над|рыва́ться, -орва́ться; **don't ~ yourself** смотри́те, не надорви́тесь. **4** (*overtax, presume too much on*): **~ s.o.'s patience** испы́тывать (*impf.*) чьё-н. терпе́ние; **~ed relations** натя́нутые отноше́ния. **5** (*filter, also ~ off*) проце́|живать, -ди́ть; отце́|живать, -ди́ть.

● *v.i.* (*exert o.s.*) напр|яга́ться, -я́чься; **the swimmer was ~ing to reach the shore** плове́ц напряга́л все си́лы, что́бы дости́чь бе́рега; **~ at a rope** тяну́ть (*impf.*) верёвку изо всех сил; **~ at the oars** нал|ега́ть, -е́чь на вёсла; **~ at the leash** (*of hound*) рва́ться (*impf.*) с поводка́; (*fig., of person*) рва́ться (*impf.*) в бой; **plants ~ towards the light** расте́ния тя́нутся к све́ту.

strainer /'streɪnə(r)/ *n.* си́то; (*small one*) си́течко.

strait /streɪt/ *n.* **1** (*of water*) проли́в; **S~ of Dover/Gibraltar** Ду́врский/Гибралта́рский проли́в. **2** (*liter., difficult situation; need*) затрудни́тельное положе́ние; **in great, dire ~s** в отча́янном положе́нии.

● *cpds.* **~-jacket** *n.* смири́тельная руба́шка; **~-laced** *adj.* (*fig.*) пурита́нский.

straitened /'streɪtənd/ *adj.*: **~ circumstances** стеснённые обстоя́тельства.

strand¹ /strænd/ *n.* (*shore*) побере́жье; (*beach*) пляж.

● *v.t.* (*ship or person*) сажа́ть, посади́ть на мель; **I was ~ed in Paris** я застря́л в Пари́же.

● *v.i.* (*of ship*) сади́ться, сесть на мель.

strand² /strænd/ *n.* (*fibre, thread*) прядь, нить; (*fig.*): **there are several ~s to the plot of this novel** в э́том рома́не не́сколько сюже́тных ли́ний.

strange /streɪndʒ/ *adj.* **1** (*unfamiliar, unknown*) незнако́мый, неизве́стный. **2** (*of person, unused*) незнако́мый (с + *i.*); **he is still ~ to the work** он ещё не привы́к к э́той рабо́те. **3** (*foreign, alien*) чужо́й, чужезе́мный; **he loves to visit ~ lands** он лю́бит быва́ть в чужи́х края́х/стра́нах. **4** (*remarkable, unusual*) стра́нный, необыкнове́нный, необы́чный; **how ~ that you should ask that!** как стра́нно, что вы (и́менно) об э́том спроси́ли!; **~ to say** (*or* **~ly enough) he loves her** как (э́то) ни стра́нно, он лю́бит её; **she wears the ~st clothes** она́ о́чень необы́чно одева́ется; **I feel ~** (*unwell*) мне не по себе́.

strangeness /'streɪndʒnɪs/ *n.* стра́нность; непривы́чность.

stranger /'streɪndʒə(r)/ *n.* **1** (*unknown person*) незнако́м|ец (*fem.* -ка); посторо́нний (челове́к); **he is shy with ~s** он стесня́ется посторо́нних. **2**: **a ~ to** (*unfamiliar with*) незнако́мый с + *i.*; чу́ждый + *d.*; **she is no ~ to poverty** она́ знако́ма с бе́дностью; **I am a ~ to your way of thinking** мне чужд ваш о́браз мышле́ния. **3** (*alien, foreigner*): **I am a ~ here** я здесь чужо́й.

strangle /'stræŋg(ə)l/ *v.t.* души́ть, за-; удави́ть (*pf.*), (*fig.*). **a ~d cry** сда́вленный крик; **death by strangling** смерть че́рез удуше́ние.

● *cpd.* **~hold** *n.* (*lit., fig.*) заси́лье; **have a ~hold on s.o.** держа́ть (*impf.*) кого́-н. мёртвой хва́ткой.

strangler /'stræŋglə(r)/ *n.* души́тель (*m.*).

strangulate /'stræŋgjʊ,leɪt/ *v.t.* (*med.*): **~d hernia** ущемлённая гры́жа.

strangulation /,stræŋgjʊ'leɪʃ(ə)n/ *n.* удуше́ние; (*med.*) ущемле́ние.

strap /stræp/ *n.* **1** реме́нь (*m.*); (*small one*) ремешо́к; (*of dress*) брете́лька. **2** (*thrashing*): **give s.o. the ~** поро́ть, вы́- кого́-н. (ремнём); **get the ~** получ|а́ть, -и́ть по́рку (ремнём).

● *v.t.* (**strapped, strapping**) **1** (*secure with ~*) стя́|гивать, -ну́ть ремнём; **he was ~ped to a chair** он был привя́зан к сту́лу ремня́ми; (*Br., bind wound etc.*) бинтова́ть, за-. **2** (*beat with ~*) поро́ть, вы́- (ремнём).

● *cpds.* **~-hanger** *n.* стоя́щий пассажи́р; **~-work** *n.* переплета́ющийся орна́мент.

strapless /'stræplɪs/ *adj.* без брете́лек.

strapping /'stræpɪŋ/ *adj.* ро́слый, здоро́вый (*coll.*).

Strasb(o)urg /'stræzbɜ:g/ *n.* Стра́сбург.

strata /'strɑ:tə/, /'streɪtə/ *pl. of* ⇒**stratum**

stratagem /'strætədʒəm/ *n.* (*trick*) уло́вка; (*mil.*) вое́нная хи́трость.

strategic /strə'ti:dʒɪk/ *adj.* стратеги́ческий.

strategist /'strætɪdʒɪst/ *n.* страте́г.

strategy /'strætɪdʒɪ/ *n.* страте́гия.

stratification /,strætɪfɪ'keɪʃ(ə)n/ *n.* стратифика́ция, расслое́ние, напластова́ние, наслое́ние.

stratif|y /'strætɪ,faɪ/ *v.t.* (*arrange in strata*) насл|а́ивать, -ои́ть; (*deposit in strata*) напласто́в|ывать, -а́ть; **~ied rock** слои́стый ка́мень.

stratosphere /'strætə,sfɪə(r)/ *n.* стратосфе́ра.

stratospheric /,strætə'sferɪk/ *adj.* стратосфе́рный.

strat|um /'strɑ:təm/, /'streɪ-/ *n.* (*pl.* **~a**) **1** (*geol.*) пласт, слой, напластова́ние. **2**: **social ~a** слой о́бщества, социа́льные слои́.

stratus /'streɪtəs/, /'strɑ:-/ *n.* слои́стое о́блако.

straw /strɔ:/ *n.* **1** (*collect.*) соло́ма; (*attr.*) соло́менный; **~ hat** соло́менная шля́п(к)а. **2** (*single ~*) соло́мин(к)а; **drink lemonade through a ~** пить (*impf.*) лимона́д че́рез соло́минку; **catch, clutch at ~s** (*fig.*) хвата́ться, схвати́ться за соло́минку; **that was the last ~** э́то бы́ло после́дней ка́плей; **~ in the wind** (*fig.*) намёк; **~ poll,** (*US*) **vote** неофициа́льные вы́боры (*m. pl.*).

● *cpds.* **~-board** *n.* соло́менный карто́н; **~-coloured** (*US* **-colored**) *adj.* соло́менного цве́та.

strawberry /'strɔ:bərɪ/ *n.* (*pl., collect.*) клубни́ка; (*wild*) земляни́ка; **a ~** я́года клубни́ки/земляни́ки; (*attr.*) клубни́чный, земляни́чный.

● *cpd.* **~-mark** *n.* роди́мое пятно́.

stray /streɪ/ *adj.* **1** (*wandering, lost*) заблуди́вшийся, бездо́мный; **~ sheep** отби́вшаяся от ста́да овца́; **~ dog** бродя́чая/бездо́мная соба́ка; (*as n.*): **waifs and ~s** беспризо́рники (*m. pl.*). **2** (*sporadic*): **a ~ bullet** шальна́я пу́ля.

● *v.i.* **1** (*wander, deviate*) заблуди́ться (*pf.*); сбива́ться, сби́ться с пути́; **the sheep ~ed on to the road** о́вцы забрели́ на доро́гу; **we must not ~ too far from the path** мы не должны́ отклоня́ться сли́шком далеко́ от тропи́нки. **2** (*roam, rove*) броди́ть (*impf.*); стра́нствовать (*impf.*). **3** (*of thoughts, affections*) блужда́ть (*impf.*); **~ from the subject** отклон|я́ться, -и́ться от те́мы.

streak /stri:k/ *n.* **1** поло́ска, прожи́лка; **~ of lightning** вспы́шка мо́лнии; **like a ~ of lightning** (*fig.*) с быстрото́й мо́лнии. **2** (*fig., trace,* *tendency*) черта́, накло́нность; **he has a cruel ~** в его́ хара́ктере есть жесто́кая жи́лка.

● *v.t.*: **~ed with red** с кра́сными поло́сками.

● *v.i.* (*coll., move rapidly*) прон|оси́ться, -ести́сь.

streaker /'stri:kə(r)/ *n.* (*coll.*) стри́кер.

streaky /'stri:kɪ/ *adj.* (**streakier, streakiest**) полоса́тый.

stream /stri:m/ *n.* **1** (*brook*) руче́й; (*rivulet*) ре́чка.
2 (*flow*) пото́к, тече́ние; **~ of blood/water** пото́к кро́ви/воды́; **in a ~ (***or* **~s)** пото́ком, ручья́ми (*m. pl.*); (*fig.*) пото́к; **a ~ of people** людско́й пото́к; **~ of consciousness** пото́к созна́ния; **~ of abuse** пото́к руга́тельств (*nt. pl.*)/бра́ни.
3 (*lit., fig., current, direction of flow*): **with the ~** по тече́нию; **against the ~** про́тив тече́ния.
4 (*Br., in school*) пото́к.

● *v.t.* **1**: **his wounds ~ed blood** из его́ ран струи́лась кровь.
2: **the pupils were ~ed** (*Br.*) ученико́в распредели́ли по пото́кам (*в зависимости от способностей*); **~ing** *n.* систе́ма пото́ков.

● *v.i.* **1** (*flow*) течь, струи́ться, ли́ться (*all impf.*); **blood was ~ing from his nose** у него́ текла́ кровь и́з носу; **tears ~ed down her cheeks** слёзы струи́лись/лили́сь/текли́ у неё по щека́м; **light ~ed in at the window** свет струи́лся в окно́; **refugees were ~ing over the fields** бе́женцы пото́ком шли по поля́м; **he had a ~ing cold** у него́ был стра́шный на́сморк; **her eyes were ~ing** у неё из глаз лили́сь слёзы; **the windows were ~ing with rain** по стёклам струи́лся дождь.
2: **with hair ~ing in the wind** с развева́ющимися на ветру́ (*or* по ве́тру) волоса́ми.

● *cpds.* **~line** *v.t.* прид|ава́ть, -а́ть обтека́емую фо́рму + *d.*; (*fig.*) упро|ща́ть, -сти́ть; **~lined** *adj.* стро́йный; упрощённый; **~lined car** автомоби́ль (*m.*) обтека́емой фо́рмы.

streamer /'stri:mə(r)/ *n.* руло́н бума́жной ле́нты; (*flag*) вы́мпел.

streamlet /'stri:mlɪt/ *n.* ручеёк, ре́чка.

street /stri:t/ *n.* **1** у́лица; **he lives in the next ~ (to us)** он живёт на сосе́дней у́лице; **don't play in the ~** (*roadway*) не игра́й на мостово́й; **man in the ~** обыва́тель (*m.*); просто́й челове́к; **she went on the ~s** она́ пошла́ на пане́ль (*or* ста́ла проститу́ткой); **they were turned out on to the ~** их вы́бросили на у́лицу; **he is ~s ahead of the other pupils** (*Br.*) он на́ голову вы́ше свои́х соученико́в; **this is just up your ~** э́то как раз по ва́шей ча́сти.
2 (*attr.*) у́личный; **~ door** пара́дное, пара́дная дверь; **at ~ level** на пе́рвом этаже́; **~ trader** у́личный разно́счик/лото́чник; **~ trading** у́личная торго́вля; **~ lighting** у́личное освеще́ние.

● *cpds.* **~car** *n.* (*US*) трамва́й; **~ credibility** (*coll.* **~ cred**) *n.* и́мидж; **~-lamp** *n.* у́личный фона́рь; **~-singer** *n.* у́личный певе́ц; **~sweeper** *n.* дво́рник, подмета́льщик (*coll.*); (*machine*) подмета́льная маши́на; **~-walker** *n.* проститу́тка; **~wise** *adj.* до́шлый, у́шлый.

strength /streŋθ/, /streŋkθ/ *n.* **1** си́ла; **~ of mind/will** си́ла ду́ха/во́ли; **~ of purpose** реши́мость; **the ~ of a fortress** мощь/непристу́пность кре́пости; (*of structure, material, beam*) про́чность; (*of wine, solution*) кре́пость; (*of a colour*) усто́йчивость; **I haven't the ~ to go on** я не в си́лах да́льше идти́; **recover, regain one's ~** восстан|а́вливать, -ови́ть си́лы; **acquire new ~, build up one's ~** наб|ира́ться, -ра́ться сил; **lose ~** теря́ть (*impf.*) си́лы; **argue from ~** спо́рить (*impf.*) с пози́ции си́лы; **he went from ~ to ~** он дви́гался вперёд гига́нтскими шага́ми.
2 (*basis*): **on the ~ of** в си́лу + *g.*; на основа́нии + *g.*; **I resigned on the ~ of your promise** я ушёл в отста́вку, полага́ясь на ва́ше обеща́ние.
3 (*numerical* **~**) чи́сленность; **in full ~** в по́лном соста́ве; **up to ~** по́лностью укомплекто́ванный; **below ~** недоукомплекто́ванный; **bring up to ~** (до)укомплектова́ть (*pf.*).

strengthen /'streŋθ(ə)n/, /-ŋkθ(ə)n/ *v.t.* укреп|ля́ть, -и́ть; уси́ли|вать, -ть; **~ a garrison** поп|олня́ть, -о́лнить гарнизо́н; **~ s.o.'s hand** укреп|ля́ть, -и́ть чью-н. пози́цию; подде́рживать, поддержа́ть кого́-н.

● *v.i.* укреп|ля́ться, -и́ться; уси́ли|ваться, -ться.

strenuous /'strenjʊəs/ *adj.* (*requiring effort*) напряжённый; (*energetic*) уси́ленный, интенси́вный.

strepto|coccus /ˌstreptə'kɒkəs/ *n.* (*pl.* **~cocci** /-'kɒk(s)aɪ -'kɒk(s)ɪ/) стрептоко́кк.

stress /stres/ *n.* **1** (*tension*) напряже́ние; (*pressure*) давле́ние, нажи́м; **time of ~** напряжённое вре́мя; **subject s.o. to ~** ока́з|ывать, -а́ть на кого́-н. давле́ние; (*psych.*) стресс; **a situation of ~** стре́ссовая ситуа́ция.
2 (*emphasis*) ударе́ние; **lay ~ on** (*lit., fig.*) де́лать, с- ударе́ние на + *p.*; **the ~ is on the second syllable** ударе́ние па́дает на второ́й слог. **3** (*mus.*) акце́нт. **4** (*eng.*) напряже́ние.

● *v.t.* **1** (*subject to* **~**) напр|яга́ть, -я́чь; **I'm ~ed out** я живу́ в постоя́нном стре́ссе. **2** (*emphasize*) подчёрк|ивать, -ну́ть; де́лать, с- упо́р на + *a.*
3 (*accentuate*) ста́вить, по- ударе́ние на + *a.*

stressful /'stresfʊl/ *adj.* напряжённый; (*situation*) стре́ссовый.

stretch /stretʃ/ *n.* **1** (*extension*) вытя́гивание, растя́гивание; **the cat woke and gave a ~** ко́шка просну́лась и потяну́лась; **by any ~ of the imagination** как ни напряга́ть фанта́зию.
2 (*elasticity*) растяжи́мость, эласти́чность; **the rubber has no ~ in it** рези́на не тя́нется; **~ fabric** эласти́чная мате́рия; **~ marks** следы́ растяже́ния на ко́же; **~ socks** безразме́рные носки́.
3 (*expanse, tract*) простра́нство; **a dusty ~ of road** пы́льный отре́зок/уча́сток доро́ги.
4 (*of time*) отре́зок; **he works 8 hours at a ~** он рабо́тает во́семь часо́в подря́д.
5 (*interval of time*) срок.

● *v.t.* **1** (*lengthen*) вытя́гивать, вы́тянуть; (*broaden*) растя́|гивать, -ну́ть.
2 (*pull to fullest extent*): **~ a rope between two posts** натя́|гивать, -ну́ть верёвку ме́жду двумя́ столба́ми; **a wire was ~ed across the road** поперёк доро́ги была́ натя́нута про́волока; **he wouldn't ~ out an arm to help me** (*fig.*) он не захоте́л протяну́ть мне ру́ку по́мощи; **~ o.s.** потя́|гиваться, -ну́ться; **~ one's legs** разм|ина́ть, -я́ть но́ги; **I found him ~ed (out) on the floor** я заста́л его́ распростёртым на полу́.
3 (*strain, exert*): **~ a point** де́лать, с- натя́жку; **~ the truth** преувели́чи|вать, -ть.

● *v.i.* **1** (*be elastic*) растя́|гиваться (*impf.*).
2 (*extend*) прост|ира́ться, -ере́ться; **the plain ~es for miles** равни́на простира́ется на мно́го миль; (*of time*) дли́ться, про-.
3 (*reach*): **the rope will not ~ to the post** верёвку не дотяну́ть до столба́; **a rainbow ~ed across the sky** ра́дуга простёрлась по не́бу.
4 (**~** *o.s.*) потя́|гиваться, -ну́ться.

stretcher /'stretʃə(r)/ *n.* (*for carrying injured*) носи́л|ки (*pl., g.* -ок); **~ case** лежа́чий/носи́лочный ра́неный.

● *cpd.* **~-bearer** *n.* санита́р-носи́льщик.

strew /stru:/ *v.t.* (*p.p.* **strewn** *or* **strewed**) **1** (*scatter*) разбр|а́сывать, -оса́ть. **2** (*cover by scattering*) пос|ыпа́ть, -ы́пать; усыпа́ть, усы́пать; **~ a grave with flowers** ус|ыпа́ть, -ы́пать моги́лу цвета́ми.

striate(d) /'straɪɪt/, /'straɪeɪtɪd/ *adj.* полоса́тый; (*with slight ridges*) боро́здчатый.

stricken /'strɪkən/ *adj.* **1** (*lit.*) ра́неный; (*fig.*) поражённый; **~ with fear** поражённый у́жасом; **~ with paralysis** разби́тый параличо́м.
2 (*US, deleted*): **~ from the record** вы́черкнутый из протоко́ла.

strict /strɪkt/ *adj.* **1** (*precise*) стро́гий, то́чный; **the ~ truth** и́стинная пра́вда; **~ accuracy** абсолю́тная то́чность.
2 (*stringent*): **in ~ confidence** в строжа́йшей та́йне. **3** (*rigorous, stern*) стро́гий, взыска́тельный.

strictness /'strɪktnɪs/ *n.* стро́гость; то́чность.

stricture /'strɪktʃə(r)/ *n.* **1** (*med.*) структу́ра, суже́ние сосу́дов.
2 (*censure*) осужде́ние; (*restriction*) ограниче́ние.

stride /straɪd/ *n.* (*long pace, step*) (широ́кий) шаг; (*gait*) по́ступь; **he has an easy ~** у него́ лёгкая по́ступь; (*fig.*): **science has made great ~s** нау́ка сде́лала больши́е успе́хи; **he took the exam in his ~** он с лёгкостью здал экза́мен; **he took the news in his ~** он при́нял э́ту но́вость споко́йно; **get into one's ~** входи́ть, войти́ в колею́.

● *v.i.* (*past* **strode;** *p.p.* **stridden** /ˈstrɪd(ə)n/) шага́ть (*impf.*); **he strode across the ditch** он шагну́л че́рез (*or* перешагну́л) кана́ву.

stridency /ˈstraɪd(ə)nsɪ/ *n.* ре́зкость, пронзи́тельность.

strident /ˈstraɪd(ə)nt/ *adj.* ре́зкий, пронзи́тельный.

strife /straɪf/ *n.* борьба́, вражда́.

strike /straɪk/ *n.* **1** (*of workers*) забасто́вка; **general ~** всео́бщая забасто́вка; **~ pay** посо́бие басту́ющим; **be on ~** бастова́ть (*impf.*); **go (or come out) on ~** забастова́ть (*pf.*); объяв|ля́ть, -и́ть забасто́вку.
2 (*of gold, oil etc.*) нахо́дка/откры́тие месторожде́ния.
3 (*attack; blow*) нападе́ние; уда́р; налёт.

● *v.t.* (*past* **struck;** *p.p.* **struck** *or arch.* **stricken**) **1** (*hit*) уд|аря́ть, -а́рить (*чем по чему; что обо что; кого чем*); **he struck the table with his hand** он уда́рил руко́й по́ столу; **he struck his head on the table** он уда́рился голово́й об стол; **a falling stone struck his head** па́дающий ка́мень уда́рил его́ по голове́; **the bullet struck the tree** пу́ля попа́ла в де́рево; **the ship struck a rock** кора́бль наскочи́л на скалу́; **she struck the knife out of his hand** она́ вы́била нож у него́ из руки́.
2 (*deliver*): **~ a blow** нан|оси́ть, -ести́ уда́р (*кому*); **who struck the first blow?** кто на́чал (дра́ку/ссо́ру)?; **~ a blow for freedom** выступа́ть/вы́ступить в защи́ту свобо́ды.
3 (*fig., instil*) всел|я́ть, -и́ть; **the lion's roar struck panic into them** льви́ный рёв вы́звал у них пани́ческий страх.
4 (*fig., impress*) пора|жа́ть, -зи́ть; каза́ться, по- + *d.*; **he was struck by her beauty** он был поражён её красото́й; **the idea ~s me as a good one** э́та мысль ка́жется мне хоро́шей; **an idea struck me** мне пришла́ в го́лову мысль; **the humour** (*Br.*), **humor** (*US*) **of the situation struck me** мне вдруг предста́вилась вся коми́чность ситуа́ции.
5 (*fig., come upon, find, discover*) напада́ть, напа́сть на + *a.*; нат|ыка́ться, -кну́ться на + *a.*; на|ходи́ть, -йти́; откр|ыва́ть, -ы́ть; **I struck a serious difficulty** я столкну́лся с серьёзным затрудне́нием; **they struck oil** они откры́ли нефтяно́е месторожде́ние; **~ it rich** (*coll.*) нап|ада́ть, -а́сть на золоту́ю жи́лу.
6 (*produce by striking*): **~ a light** высека́ть, вы́сечь ого́нь; зажига́ть, зажéчь спи́чку.
7: **~ a match** чи́рк|ать, -нуть спи́чкой; **~ a coin/medal** выбива́ть, вы́бить (*or* чека́нить, от-) моне́ту/меда́ль; **~ a chord** (*lit.*) брать, взять акко́рд; (*fig.*): **his name ~s a chord** его́ и́мя мне что́-то говори́т/напомина́ет; **~ a note** (*lit.*) ударя́ть, уда́рить по кла́више/струне́; (*fig.*): **~ the right note** взять (*pf.*) ве́рный тон; **~ root** пус|ка́ть, -ти́ть ко́рни.
8 (*of bell, clock etc.*) бить (*impf.*), проб|ива́ть, -и́ть; **this clock ~s the hours and quarters** э́ти часы́ пробива́ют часы́ и че́тверти; **it has just struck four** то́лько что про́било четы́ре; **the clock struck midnight** часы́ проби́ли по́лночь.
9 (*arrive at*): **~ a bargain** заключ|а́ть, -и́ть сде́лку; **~ a balance** подв|оди́ть, -ести́ бала́нс/ито́ги; (*fig.*) на|ходи́ть, -йти́ компроми́сс; **~ a happy medium** на|ходи́ть, -йти́ золоту́ю середи́ну.
10 (*suddenly make*): **~ s.o. blind** ослеп|ля́ть, -и́ть кого́-н; **~ s.o. dumb** (*fig.*) лиш|а́ть, -и́ть кого́-н. да́ра ре́чи; ошара́ши|вать, -ть кого́-н. (*coll.*); **he was struck dumb** он потеря́л дар ре́чи; он онеме́л; **~ s.o. dead** порази́ть (*pf.*) кого́-н. на смерть.
11 (*assume*): **~ an attitude** вста|ва́ть, -ть в (*or* прин|има́ть, -я́ть) по́зу.
12 (*lower, take down*): **~ one's flag** спус|ка́ть, -ти́ть флаг; **~ camp** сн|има́ться, -я́ться с ла́геря.

● *v.i.* (*past* **struck;** *p.p.* **struck** *or arch.* **stricken**) **1** (*hit*) уд|аря́ть, -а́рить; **the disease struck without warning** боле́знь вспы́хнула неожи́данно; **~ while the iron is hot** (*prov.*) куй желе́зо, пока́ горячо́; **~** (*aim a blow*) **at s.o.** зама́х|иваться, -ну́ться на кого́-н.; (*fig.*): **~ at the root of the trouble** искорен|я́ть, -и́ть исто́чник зла; **~ at the foundations of something** под|рыва́ть, -орва́ть осно́вы чего́-н.
2: **~ against** (*collide with*) уд|аря́ться, -а́риться о + *a.*
3 (*direct one's course; penetrate*): **the explorers struck inland** иссле́дователи напра́вились внутрь/вглубь страны́; **the insult struck home** оскорбле́ние заде́ло его́ за живо́е.
4 (*take root*) прин|има́ться, -я́ться.
5 (*of clock etc.*) бить, про-.
6: **the match won't ~** спи́чка не зажига́ется.
7 (*go on ~*) бастова́ть (*impf.*) (**for**: что́бы доби́ться + *g.*).
8: **struck on** (*coll.*) влюблённый в + *a.*

● *with advs.*: **~ back** *v.i.* (*retaliate*) нан|оси́ть, -ести́ отве́тный уда́р; **~ down** *v.t.* (*fell*) сби|ва́ть, -ть с ног; сра|жа́ть, -зи́ть; (*of illness etc.*) сва́л|ивать, -и́ть; сра|жа́ть, -зи́ть; **~ off** *v.t.*: **~ s.o. (or s.o.'s name) off** (*list etc.*) вычёркивать, вы́черкнуть кого́-н. (*or* чьё-н. и́мя) (из спи́ска *и т.п.*); **~ out** *v.t.* (*delete*): **~ out a word** вычёркивать, вы́черкнуть сло́во; *v.i.* (*aim blow*) нан|оси́ть, -ести́ уда́р; (*of swimmer*): **~ out for the shore** (бы́стро) поплы́ть (*pf.*) к бе́регу; (*fig.*): **~ out on one's own** пойти́ (*pf.*) свои́м путём; **~ through** *v.t.* (*cross out*) зачёркивать, зачеркну́ть; **~ up** *v.t.*: **~ up a song** затя́|гивать, -ну́ть пе́сню; **~ up an acquaintance** завя́з|ывать, -а́ть знако́мство; *v.i.* (*begin playing/singing*) заигра́ть, запе́ть (*both pf.*).

● *cpds.* **~-breaker** *n.* штрейкбре́хер; **~-breaking** *n.* штрейкбре́херство.

striker /ˈstraɪkə(r)/ *n.* **1** (*person on strike*) забасто́вщи|к (*fem.* -ца).
2 (*sport*) напада́ющий.

striking /ˈstraɪkɪŋ/ *adj.* **1** (*forceful*) порази́тельный; **~ resemblance** рази́тельное схо́дство; (*remarkable*) порази́тельный, замеча́тельный; (*interesting*) интере́сный. **2**: **~ distance** досяга́емость; **~ force** (*mil.*) уда́рная гру́ппа.

string /strɪŋ/ *n.* **1** верёвка, бечёвка; **ball of ~** клубо́к бечёвки/верёвки; **~ bag** се́тка, аво́ська (*coll.*); **~ vest** се́тчатая ма́йка; (*of apron, bonnet etc.*) завя́зка, тесёмка; (*fig.*): **have s.o. on a ~** держа́ть/вести́ (*impf.*) кого́-н. на поводу́; **pull the ~s** быть (*impf.*) и́стинным заправи́лой (чего́); **pull ~s** наж|има́ть, -а́ть на все кно́пки; **with no ~s attached** (*fig.*) без каки́х бы то ни́ было усло́вий.
2 (*of bow*) тетива́; **he has two ~s to his bow** (*fig.*) у него́ есть вы́бор.
3 (*of mus. instrument, racket*) струна́; **the ~s** (*of orchestra*) стру́нные инструме́нты (*m. pl.*); **~ quartet** стру́нный кварте́т; (*fig.*): **second ~** запасно́й вариа́нт.
4 (*~y substance, fibre e.g. in bean*) волокно́; **~ bean** фасо́ль; (*in meat*) жи́ла.
5 (*set of objects*): **~ of beads** бу́с|ы (*pl., g.* —); **~ of pearls** ни́тка же́мчуга; **~ of onions/sausages** свя́зка лу́ка/соси́сок; **~ of boats/houses/medals** ряд ло́док/домо́в/меда́лей; **~ of cars/tourists** верени́ца автомоби́лей/тури́стов.
6 (*comput.*) строка́.

● *v.t.* (*past and p.p.* **strung**) **1** (*furnish with ~*): **~ a bow** натя́|гивать, -ну́ть тетиву́; **~ a racket** натя́|гивать, -ну́ть струны́.
2 (*thread on ~*) низа́ть (*or* нани́зывать), на-.
3 (*remove ~y fibre from*): **~ beans** чи́стить, по- фасо́ль.

● *with advs.*: **~ along** *v.t.* (*coll., deceive*) води́ть (*impf.*) за́ нос; *v.i.*: **~ along with s.o.** (*coll., accompany*) тащи́ться, по- за кем-н.; **~ out** *v.t. & i.* (*extend*) растя́|гивать(ся), -ну́ть(ся); **the houses were strung out along the beach** дома́ тяну́лись вдоль побере́жья; **~ together** *v.t.* низа́ть, на-; (*fig.*): **he is good at ~ing words together** он говори́т о́чень гла́дко; **~ up** *v.t.* (*hang*): **the ham was strung up to the ceiling** о́корок был подве́шен под са́мый потоло́к; (*coll., execute by hanging*) вздёр|гивать, -нуть на ви́селицу; (*Br., make tense*): **I am all strung up** я в большо́м напряже́нии.

stringed /strɪŋd/ *adj.* стру́нный.

stringency /ˈstrɪndʒ(ə)nsɪ/ *n.* стро́гость.

stringent /ˈstrɪndʒ(ə)nt/ *adj.* (*strict, precise*) стро́гий, то́чный.

stringer /ˈstrɪŋə(r)/ *n.* (*coll.*) внешта́тный корреспонде́нт.

stringy /ˈstrɪŋɪ/ *adj.* (**stringier, stringiest**) (*fibrous*): **~ beans** волокни́стая фасо́ль; **~ meat** жи́листое мя́со.

strip[1] /strɪp/ *n.* полоса́; (*of cloth*) поло́ска, ле́нта; **~ of land** поло́ска

S

земли́; **a ~ of wood** деревя́нная пла́нка/ре́йка; **~ cartoon** расска́з в карти́нках; **~ lighting** (*Br.*) нео́новое освеще́ние; **tear s.o. off a ~** (*coll.*) сн|има́ть, -ять стру́жку с кого́-н.

strip² /strɪp/ *v.t.* (**stripped, stripping**) **1** (*tear off*) сдира́ть, содра́ть; **the bark was ~ped from the tree** (*or* **the tree was ~ped of its bark**) с де́рева содра́ли кору́; **she ~ped the blankets off the bed** она́ сняла́ одея́ла с крова́ти; **a tool for ~ping paint** инструме́нт для соска́бливания кра́ски.
2 (*denude*) разд|ева́ть, -е́ть; **he was ~ped of his clothes** с него́ сорва́ли/ сня́ли оде́жду; его́ разде́ли; **the room was ~ped bare** из ко́мнаты вы́несли всю ме́бель; **the birds ~ped the fruit bushes** пти́цы обклева́ли я́годы с кусто́в; **~ (down) a machine/weapon** раз|бира́ть, -обра́ть (*or* демонти́ровать (*impf., pf.*)) маши́ну/ ору́жие; (*fig., deprive*) лиш|а́ть, -и́ть (*кого чего*); **he was ~ped of his rank** его́ лиши́ли зва́ния.
● *v.i.* (**stripped, stripping**): **~ (naked), ~ off** разд|ева́ться, -е́ться (донага́).
● *with advs.*: **~ away, ~ off** *vv.t.* (*lit.*) *see v.t.* 1; (*fig., remove*) от|бира́ть, -обра́ть; **~ down** *v.t.* (*machine etc.*) раз|бира́ть, -обра́ть; демонти́ровать (*impf., pf.*).
● *cpds.* **~-club** *n.* стрипти́з-клу́б; **~-tease** *n.* стрипти́з; **~-tease artist** исполни́тель (*fem.* -ница) стрипти́за; стриптизёр (*fem.* -ша).

stripe /straɪp/ *n.* **1** полоса́, поло́ска.
2 (*mil.*) наши́вка, шевро́н; **get a ~** получ|а́ть, -и́ть очередно́е зва́ние; **lose a ~** быть разжа́лованным.
3 (*US, type*) тип, род.

striped /straɪpt/ *adj.* (*e.g. tiger*) полоса́тый; **~ fabric** мате́рия в поло́ску, полоса́тая мате́рия.

stripling /ˈstrɪplɪŋ/ *n.* юне́ц.

stripper /ˈstrɪpə(r)/ *n.* (*solvent*) раство́р для удале́ния кра́ски; (*artiste*) исполни́тель (*fem.* -ница) стрипти́за; стриптизёр (*fem.* -ша).

stripy /ˈstraɪpɪ/ *adj.* полоса́тый, в поло́ску.

strive /straɪv/ *v.i.* (*past* **strove** *or* **strived;** *p.p.* **striven** /ˈstrɪv(ə)n/ *or* **strived**) стреми́ться (*impf.*) (**after, for**: к + *d.*); **they strove for victory** они́ стреми́лись к побе́де; **I strove to understand what he said** я стара́лся поня́ть, что он говори́т.

stroboscope /ˈstrəʊbəˌskəʊp/ *n.* стробоско́п.

stroboscopic /ˌstrəʊbəˈskɒpɪk/ *adj.* стробоскопи́ческий.

strode /strəʊd/ *past of* ⇒**stride**

stroke¹ /strəʊk/ *n.* **1** уда́р; **six ~s of the cane** шесть уда́ров ро́згой; **at a ~** (*fig.*) одни́м уда́ром/ма́хом.
2 (*of clock*) уда́р, бой; **on the ~ of 9** ро́вно в де́вять.
3 (*paralytic attack*) уда́р, инсу́льт; **he had a ~** его́ хвати́л уда́р; **he died of a ~** он у́мер от уда́ра.
4 (*single movement of series*): **~ of a piston** ход по́ршня; **~ of an oar** взмах весла́, гребо́к; **put s.o. off his ~** (*fig.*) сби|ва́ть, -ть кого́-н. с то́лку.
5 (*in swimming*) стиль (*m.*); **what ~ does she use?** каки́м сти́лем она́ пла́вает?
6 (*single action or instance*): **he has not done a ~ (of work)** он па́льцем о па́лец не уда́рил; **~ of genius** гениа́льная мысль; **~ of luck** (неожи́данная) уда́ча; везе́ние.
7 (*with pen, pencil etc.*) штрих; **with, at a ~ of the pen** (*lit., fig.*) одни́м ро́счерком пера́; (*with brush*) мазо́к; **thick/thin ~s** жи́рные/то́нкие мазки́.
8 (*typ., oblique* **~**) дробь, кося́я черта́.
9 (*oarsman*) загребно́й.

stroke² /strəʊk/ *n.*: **he gave her hand a ~** он погла́дил её по руке́.
● *v.t.* гла́дить (*or* погла́живать), по-; **she ~d the horse's head** она́ погла́дила ло́шадь по голове́.

stroll /strəʊl/ *n.* прогу́лка; **have, take, go for a ~** идти́ (*det.*) на прогу́лку (*or* прогуля́ться).
● *v.i.* гуля́ть (*impf.*); прогу́л|иваться, -я́ться; (*wander*) броди́ть (*impf.*); **~ing players** бродя́чие актёры.

stroller /ˈstrəʊlə(r)/ *n.* (*US, for child*) прогу́лочная коля́ска.

strong /strɒŋ/ *adj.* (**stronger** /ˈstrɒŋɡə(r)/; **strongest** /ˈstrɒŋɡɪst/)
1 (*powerful, forceful*) си́льный, кре́пкий; **~ as a horse** си́льный как ло́шадь; **~ man** сила́ч; **~ character** си́льная нату́ра; **~ wind** си́льный/ кре́пкий ве́тер; **~ tide** си́льный прили́в; **~ attraction** больша́я привлека́тельность; **~ measures** круты́е ме́ры; **~ argument** ве́ский аргуме́нт; **~ evidence** убеди́тельное доказа́тельство; **~ protest** энерги́чный проте́ст; **~ warning** серьёзное предупрежде́ние; **~ suspicion** си́льное подозре́ние; **~ words** си́льные выраже́ния; **~ language** брань.
2 (*stout, tough; durable*) кре́пкий; про́чный; **~ cloth** кре́пкая мате́рия; **~ walls** про́чные сте́ны; **~ foundations** про́чные основа́ния.
3 (*robust, healthy*) кре́пкий, здоро́вый; **~ constitution** кре́пкое здоро́вье; **he has never been very ~** он никогда́ не отлича́лся кре́пким здоро́вьем; **she is feeling ~er** она́ чу́вствует себя́ лу́чше.
4 (*firm*) твёрдый, кре́пкий; **~ conviction** твёрдое убежде́ние; **~ supporter** ре́вностный сторо́нник; **~ faith** твёрдая ве́ра; **the market is ~** ры́нок усто́йчив.
5 (*of faculties*): **~ mind** хоро́шая голова́; **~ memory** о́страя па́мять; **he is ~ in Latin** он силён в латы́ни; **oratory is his ~ point** его́ си́ла в красноре́чии.
6 (*of smell, taste etc.*): **~ flavour** (*Br.*), **flavor** (*US*) о́стрый/ре́зкий при́вкус; **~ cheese** о́стрый сыр; **~ meat** (*Br., fig.*) пи́ща для си́льных умо́в.
7 (*concentrated*): **~ drink** кре́пкий напи́ток; **a ~ cup of tea** ча́шка кре́пкого ча́я.
8 (*sharply defined*) ре́зкий; **~ light** ре́зкий свет; **~ colour** (*Br.*), **color** (*US*) я́ркий цвет; **~ accent** (*in speech*) си́льный акце́нт; **~ likeness** большо́е схо́дство.
9 (*well-supported*): **~ candidate** кандида́т, облада́ющий больши́м ша́нсом на успе́х; **~ favourite** (*Br.*), **favorite** (*US*) наибо́лее вероя́тный победи́тель; **a ~ (well-chosen) team** си́льная/отбо́рная кома́нда.
10 (*numerous*) чи́сленный; **a ~ contingent** многочи́сленный континге́нт; **a company 200 ~** ро́та чи́сленностью в 200 челове́к.
11 (*cards*): **a ~ hand** беру́щая ка́рта.
12 (*gram.*): **~ verb** си́льный глаго́л.
● *adv.*: **going ~** в прекра́сной фо́рме.
● *cpds.* **~-arm** *adj.*: **~-arm tactics** та́ктика примене́ния си́лы; **~box** *n.* сейф; **~hold** *n.* кре́пость, тверды́ня; **~-minded** *adj.* твёрдый, реши́тельный; **~-room** *n.* стальна́я ка́мера; **~-willed** *adj.* реши́тельный, волево́й.

strontium /ˈstrɒntɪəm/ *n.* стро́нций.

strop /strɒp/ *n.* реме́нь (*m.*) для пра́вки бритв.
● *v.t.* (**stropped, stropping**) пра́вить (*impf.*) (*бритву*).

strophe /ˈstrəʊfɪ/ *n.* строфа́.

strophic /ˈstrəʊfɪk/, /ˈstrɒ-/ *adj.* строфи́ческий.

stroppy /ˈstrɒpɪ/ *adj.* (**stroppier, stroppiest**) (*Br. coll.*) несгово́рчивый, сварли́вый, строπти́вый.

strove /strəʊv/ *past of* ⇒**strive**

struck /strʌk/ *past and p.p. of* ⇒**strike**

structural /ˈstrʌktʃər(ə)l/ *adj.*: **~ linguistics** структу́рная лингви́стика; **~ defects** дефе́кты в констру́кции; **~ engineer** инжене́р-строи́тель (*m.*); **~ engineering** строи́тельная те́хника.

structuralism /ˈstrʌktʃərəˌlɪz(ə)m/ *n.* структурали́зм.

structuralist /ˈstrʌktʃərəlɪst/ *n.* структурали́ст.

structure /ˈstrʌktʃə(r)/ *n.* **1** (*abstr.*) структу́ра, стро́й, строе́ние; **~ of a building** структу́ра зда́ния; **~ of rocks, of a cell** структу́ра скал (*or* го́рных поро́д)/кле́тки; **~ of a sentence** структу́ра предложе́ния; **~ of a language** строй языка́. **2** (*concr.*) строе́ние, сооруже́ние; (*building*) зда́ние.
● *v.t.* стро́ить, по-; организова́ть (*impf., pf.*).

struggle /ˈstrʌɡ(ə)l/ *n.* (*lit., fig.*) борьба́; **~ for existence** борьба́ за существова́ние; (*tussle*) схва́тка, потасо́вка; **without a ~** без бо́я/ сопротивле́ния; (*attempt*): **a violent ~ to escape** отча́янная попы́тка к бе́гству.
● *v.i.* **1** (*fight*) боро́ться (*impf.*); би́ться (*impf.*).
2 (*fig., grapple*) би́ться (*impf.*) (*над чем*); **we ~d with this problem for a long time** мы до́лго би́лись над э́той пробле́мой.
3 (*move convulsively*) би́ться (*impf.*); **the child ~d and kicked** ребёнок вырыва́лся и брыка́лся.
4 (*make strenuous efforts*) боро́ться

(*impf.*); стара́ться (*impf.*) изо всех сил; **he ~d to make himself heard** он изо всех сил пыта́лся перекрича́ть други́х; **he ~d for breath** он хвата́л ртом во́здух; (*fig., move with difficulty*): **he ~d to his feet** он с трудо́м подня́лся на́ ноги.

strum /strʌm/ *v.t. & i.* (**strummed, strumming**) бренча́ть, тре́нькать (*both impf.*) (на + *p.*).

strumpet /ˈstrʌmpɪt/ *n.* (*arch.*) потаску́ха, шлю́ха.

strung /strʌŋ/ *past and p.p. of* ⇒**string**

strut[1] /strʌt/ *n.* (*gait*) ва́жная похо́дка.

● *v.i.* (**strutted, strutting**) ходи́ть (*indet.*) с ва́жным ви́дом.

strut[2] /strʌt/ *n.* (*support*) сто́йка, подко́с.

strychnine /ˈstrɪkniːn/ *n.* стрихни́н.

stub /stʌb/ *n.* (*of pencil*) огры́зок; (*of cigarette*) оку́рок; (*of dog's tail*) обру́бок; (*of cheque etc.*) корешо́к.

● *v.t.* (**stubbed, stubbing**) **1**: **~ (out) a cigarette** гаси́ть, по- папиро́су. **2**: **~ one's toe on something** спот|ыка́ться, -кну́ться о(бо) что-н.

stubble /ˈstʌb(ə)l/ *n.* жнивьё, стерня́; (*of beard*) щети́на.

stubbly /ˈstʌblɪ/ *adj.*: **~ chin** щети́нистый подборо́док.

stubborn /ˈstʌbən/ *adj.* (*obstinate*) упря́мый; (*tenacious*) упо́рный; (*unyielding, intractable*) неподатливый.

stubbornness /ˈstʌbənnɪs/ *n.* упря́мство; упо́рство; неподатливость.

stucco /ˈstʌkəʊ/ *n.* (*pl.* **~es**) штукату́рка; (*attr.*) лепно́й; **~ moulding** (*Br.*), **molding** (*US*) лепно́е украше́ние, лепни́на.

● *v.t.* (**stuccoes, stuccoed**) штукату́рить, о-.

stuck /stʌk/ *past and p.p. of* ⇒**stick**[2]

stuck-up /ˈstʌkˈʌp/ *adj.* (*coll., conceited*) чванли́вый, зано́счивый.

stud[1] /stʌd/ *n.* (*of horses*) ко́нный заво́д; коню́шня.

● *cpds.* **~-farm** *n.* ко́нный заво́д; **~-horse** *n.* племенно́й жеребе́ц.

stud[2] /stʌd/ *n.* **1** (*nail, boss etc.*) гвоздь (*m.*) с большо́й шля́пкой; кно́пка; (*on boots*) шип. **2** (*collar-~*) за́понка.

● *v.t.* (**studded, studding**): **~ded boots** боти́нки на шипа́х; **a sky ~ded with stars** не́бо, усе́янное звёздами; **a dress ~ded with jewels** пла́тье, усы́панное драгоце́нными камня́ми.

student /ˈstjuːd(ə)nt/ *n.* студе́нт (*fem.* -ка); (*attr.*) студе́нческий; **medical ~** студе́нт-ме́дик (*fem.* студе́нтка-ме́дик); (*pupil*) учени́к, уча́щийся; **~ teacher** учи́тель-практика́нт (*fem.* учи́тельница-практика́нтка); **law ~** студе́нт (*fem.* -ка) юриди́ческого факульте́та.

studentship /ˈstjuːdəntʃɪp/ *n.* (*Br.*) стипе́ндия.

studied /ˈstʌdɪd/ *adj.* (*deliberate*): **~ indifference** напускно́е/де́ланное равноду́шие; **~ insult** умы́шленное оскорбле́ние.

studio /ˈstjuːdɪəʊ/ *n.* (*pl.* **~s**) **1** (*of artist, photographer etc.*) мастерска́я, сту́дия, ателье́ (*indecl.*); **~ couch** (*US*) дива́н-крова́ть; **~ flat** (*Br.*), **apartment** (*US*) однокомнатная кварти́ра. **2** (*broadcasting ~*) (*radio*) радиосту́дия; (*TV*) телесту́дия; **~ audience** зри́тели, приглашённые в радио-/телесту́дию во вре́мя за́писи. **3** (*cin.*) съёмочный павильо́н; киносту́дия.

studious /ˈstjuːdɪəs/ *adj.* **1** (*fond of study*) лю́бящий нау́ку. **2** (*deliberate*) нарочи́тый; **~ politeness** нарочи́тая ве́жливость; **he ~ly ignored me** он стара́тельно меня́ игнори́ровал. **3** (*zealous*) усе́рдный, стара́тельный.

stud|y /ˈstʌdɪ/ *n.* **1** (*learning, investigation*) изуче́ние, учёба, нау́ка; **~ies** заня́тия (*nt. pl.*); **department of Slavonic ~ies** отделе́ние/ка́федра слави́стики; **he gives all his time to ~y** он всё своё вре́мя отдаёт нау́ке/заня́тиям; **make a ~y of** (тща́тельно) изуч|а́ть, -и́ть; **my ~ies have convinced me** мои́ иссле́дования убеди́ли меня́. **2** (*sketch; mus.*) этю́д. **3** (*room*) кабине́т.

● *v.t.* **1** (*learn, investigate*) изуч|а́ть, -и́ть; иссле́довать (*impf., pf.*); **Greek is not ~ied** гре́ческий (язы́к) не изуча́ют (*or* гре́ческим (языко́м) не занима́ются). **2** (*scrutinize*) (внима́тельно) рассм|а́тривать, -отре́ть; **I ~ied his face** я испыту́юще посмотре́л на него́. **3** (*commit to memory*): **~y a part** учи́ть (*impf.*) роль.

● *v.i.* учи́ться (*impf.*).

stuff /stʌf/ *n.* **1** (*material, substance*) материа́л, вещество́, вещь; **he is not the ~ heroes are made of** из таки́х геро́и не выхо́дят; **there's some good ~ in this book** в э́той кни́ге есть ко́е-что поле́зное/хоро́шее; **green ~** (*vegetables*) зе́лень, о́вощ|и (*pl., g.* -е́й). **2** (*coll., things*) ве́щи (*f. pl.*); (*pej., rubbish*): **what shall I do with this ~ from the cupboard?** что мне де́лать с э́тим барахло́м из шка́фа?; **do you call this ~ beer?** (и) вы э́ту дрянь называ́ете пи́вом?; **~ and nonsense!** (*Br.*) чепуха́!; ерунда́! **3** (*coll., business*): **do one's ~** де́лать, с- своё де́ло; **know one's ~** знать (*impf.*) своё де́ло; **that's the ~ (to give 'em)!** (*Br.*) вот то, что на́до!; **I don't want any rough ~** пожа́луйста, без дра́ки.

● *v.t.* **1** (*pack, fill*) наб|ива́ть, -и́ть (*что чем*); **he ~ed the sacks with straw** он наби́л мешки́ соло́мой; **the taxidermist ~s dead birds** таксидерми́ст набива́ет чу́чела птиц; **a ~ed eagle** чу́чело орла́; (*cul.*) фарширова́ть, за-; начин|я́ть, -и́ть; **~ a duck with sage and onions** начин|я́ть, -и́ть у́тку шалфе́ем и лу́ком; **he ~ed his head with useless facts** он заби́л себе́ го́лову вся́кими нену́жными све́дениями; **~ o.s.** (*coll., overeat*) объ|еда́ться, -е́стся; наж|ира́ться, -ра́ться (*coll.*); **~ed shirt** (*fig., coll.*) наду́тый индю́к; **get ~ed!** (*Br. vulg.*) иди́ ты!; фиг тебе́!; **my nose is ~ed up** у меня́ нос зало́жен. **2** (*cram, push*) запи́х|ивать, -а́ть/-ну́ть (*что во что*); **she ~ed her clothes into a case** она́ запихну́ла свою́ оде́жду в чемода́н; **he ~ed the note behind a cushion** он запихну́л/засу́нул запи́ску за поду́шку.

stuffiness /ˈstʌfɪnɪs/ *n.* духота́, спёртость; (*of person*) чо́порность.

stuffing /ˈstʌfɪŋ/ *n.* **1** (*of cushion, doll etc.*) наби́вка; **knock the ~ out of s.o.** (*deflate*) сбить (*pf.*) с кого́-н. спесь; (*enfeeble*) осла́бить (*pf.*) кого́-н.; (*thrash*) колоти́ть, по-. **2** (*cul.*) начи́нка, фарш.

stuffy /ˈstʌfɪ/ *adj.* (**stuffier, stuffiest**) (*of room*) ду́шный; (*of atmosphere*) ду́шный, спёртый; (*of person*) чо́порный.

stultif|y /ˈstʌltɪˌfaɪ/ *v.t.* (*deaden*) притуп|ля́ть, -и́ть.

stumbl|e /ˈstʌmb(ə)l/ *n.* спотыка́ние; (*in speech*) запи́нка.

● *v.i.* **1** (*miss one's footing*) оступ|а́ться, -и́ться; спот|ыка́ться, -кну́ться; **he ~ed against, over a stone** он споткну́лся о ка́мень; **~ing gait** ковыля́ющая похо́дка; **~ing-block** ка́мень (*m.*) преткнове́ния. **2** (*speak haltingly*) зап|ина́ться, -ну́ться; спот|ыка́ться, -кну́ться; **he ~es over his words** он запина́ется/спотыка́ется на ка́ждом сло́ве; **he ~ed through his speech** он ко́е-как произнёс свою́ речь. **3**: **~e across, upon** (*find by chance*) нат|а́лкиваться, -олкну́ться на + *a.*; нат|ыка́ться, -кну́ться на + *a.*

stump /stʌmp/ *n.* **1** (*of tree*) пень (*m.*); (*of limb*) культя́, обру́бок; (*of cigar*) оку́рок; (*of pencil*) огры́зок. **2** (*cricket*) сто́лбик.

● *v.t.* (*floor*) ста́вить, по- в тупи́к; озада́чи|вать, -ть; **I was ~ed by the question** э́тот вопро́с поста́вил меня́ в тупи́к.

● *v.i.* (*walk clumsily*) то́пать (*impf.*), тяжело́ ступа́ть (*impf.*); **he ~ed across the room** он прото́пал по ко́мнате.

● *with adv.*: **~ up** *v.t. & i.* (*Br. coll.*) выкла́дывать, вы́ложить (де́ньги).

stumpy /ˈstʌmpɪ/ *adj.* (**stumpier, stumpiest**) коро́ткий и то́лстый.

stun /stʌn/ *v.t.* (**stunned, stunning**) **1** (*knock unconscious*) оглуш|а́ть, -и́ть. **2** (*amaze, astound*) пора|жа́ть, -зи́ть; ошелом|ля́ть, -и́ть; **a ~ning dress** потряса́ющее пла́тье.

stung /stʌŋ/ *past and p.p. of* ⇒**sting**

stunk /stʌŋk/ *past and p.p. of* ⇒**stink**

stunt /stʌnt/ *n.* трюк, но́мер; **~ man** (*cin.*) каскадёр.

● *v.t.*: **~ growth** заде́рж|ивать, -а́ть рост; **~ed trees** низкоро́слые дере́вья.

stupefaction /ˌstjuːpɪˈfækʃ(ə)n/ *n.* оглуше́ние; ошеломле́ние; оцепене́ние.

stupefy /ˈstjuːpɪˌfaɪ/ *v.t.* оглуш|а́ть, -и́ть; (*amaze*) ошелом|ля́ть, -и́ть.

stupendous /stjuːˈpendəs/ *adj.* изуми́тельный; (*in size*) огро́мный, колосса́льный.

stupid /ˈstjuːpɪd/ *adj.* (**stupider, stupidest**) глу́пый, тупо́й; **~ person** глу́пый челове́к, дура́к (*fem.* ду́ра); глупе́ц; тупи́ца (*c.g.*).

S

stupidity /stju:ˈpɪdɪtɪ/ *n.* глу́пость.

stupor /ˈstju:pə(r)/ *n.* остолбене́ние, оцепене́ние.

sturdiness /ˈstɜ:dɪnɪs/ *n.* кре́пость, си́ла.

sturdy /ˈstɜ:dɪ/ *adj.* (**sturdier, sturdiest**) кре́пкий, си́льный.

sturgeon /ˈstɜ:dʒ(ə)n/ *n.* осётр; (*as food*) осётр, осетри́на.

stutter /ˈstʌtə(r)/ *n.* заика́ние; **he has a terrible ~** он ужа́сно заика́ется.

● *v.t.* произн|оси́ть, -ести́ заика́ясь.

● *v.i.* заика́ться (*impf.*).

stutterer /ˈstʌtərə(r)/ *n.* за́йка (*c.g.*).

sty[1] /staɪ/ *n.* (**pig ~**; *lit., fig.*) хлев, свина́рник.

sty[2] **, stye** /staɪ/ *n.* (*on eye*) ячме́нь (*m.*).

style /staɪl/ *n.* **1** (*manner*) стиль (*m.*), мане́ра; (*of writing*) стиль, слог; **written in a florid ~** напи́санный витиева́тым сло́гом; **the ~ in which they live** их о́браз жи́зни; **the ~ of Rubens** мане́ра Ру́бенса; **flattery is not his ~** лесть не в его́ ду́хе/сти́ле; **cramp s.o.'s ~** меша́ть (*impf.*) кому́-н.; **in fine ~** с бле́ском.
2 (*elegance, taste, luxury*): **she has ~** у неё есть вкус; **in ~** с ши́ком; **live in ~** жить (*impf.*) широко́ (*or* на широ́кую но́гу).
3 (*fashion*) мо́да, фасо́н; **in the latest ~** по после́дней мо́де.
4 (*sort, kind*) род, тип, сорт; **what ~ of house do you require?** како́го ти́па дом вы хоте́ли бы приобрести́?
5 (*of dates*): **Old/New S~** (*adv.*) по ста́рому/но́вому сти́лю.

● *v.t.* **1** (*designate*) наз|ыва́ть, -ва́ть; **self-~d** самозва́нный.
2 (*design*): **she had her hair ~d** она́ сде́лала себе́ приче́ску.

styli /ˈstaɪlaɪ/, /-li:/ *pl. of* ⇒**stylus**

stylish /ˈstaɪlɪʃ/ *adj.* (*fashionable*) мо́дный; (*smart*) элега́нтный, сти́льный.

stylishness /ˈstaɪlɪʃnɪs/ *n.* элега́нтность.

stylist /ˈstaɪlɪst/ *n.* стили́ст; **hair ~** парикма́хер-модельéр.

stylistic /staɪˈlɪstɪk/ *adj.* стилисти́ческий.

stylize /ˈstaɪlaɪz/ *v.t.* стилизова́ть (*impf., pf.*).

styl|us /ˈstaɪləs/ *n.* (*pl.* **~i** *or* **~uses**) **1** (*engraving tool*) гравирова́льная игла́; резе́ц. **2** (*for records*) (граммофо́нная) иго́лка.

stymie /ˈstaɪmɪ/ *v.t.* (**stymies, stymied, stymying** *or* **stymieing**) (*fig.*) меша́ть (*impf.*) + *d.*; препя́тствовать (*impf.*) + *d.*

suasion /ˈsweɪʒ(ə)n/ *n.* угова́ривание; **moral ~** увещева́ние.

suave /swɑ:v/ *adj.* гла́дкий, лощёный, обходи́тельный.

suavity /ˈswɑ:vɪtɪ/ *n.* гла́дкость, обходи́тельность.

sub /sʌb/ *n.* (*coll.*) *abbr. of*
1 ***submarine*** подло́дка.
2 ***substitute*** заме́на.
3 ***subscription*** подпи́ска; (*dues*) взнос; *see also* ⇒**sub-edit, sub-editor**

subaltern /ˈsʌbəlt(ə)n/ *n.* мла́дший офице́р.

● *adj.* ни́зший (*по чину и т.п.*).

subaqueous /sʌbˈeɪkwɪəs/ *adj.* подво́дный.

subarctic /sʌbˈɑ:ktɪk/ *adj.* субаркти́ческий.

subcategory /ˈsʌbˌkætɪgərɪ/ *n.* подсе́кция, подви́д.

subcommittee /ˈsʌbkəˌmɪtɪ/ *n.* подкоми́ссия; подкомите́т.

subconscious /sʌbˈkɒnʃəs/ *n.* (*the ~*) подсозна́ние.

● *adj.* подсозна́тельный.

subcontinent /ˈsʌbˌkɒntɪnənt/ *n.* субконтине́нт.

subcontract[1] /sʌbˈkɒntrækt/ *n.* субподря́д, субдогово́р.

subcontract[2] /ˌsʌbkənˈtrækt/ *v.t.* заключ|а́ть, -и́ть субдогово́р с + *i.*; **the work was ~ed out** рабо́ту о́тдали субподря́дчику.

subcontractor /ˌsʌbkənˈtræktə(r)/ *n.* субподря́дчик.

subcutaneous /ˌsʌbkju:ˈteɪnɪəs/ *adj.* подко́жный.

subdivide /ˈsʌbdɪˌvaɪd/, /-ˈvaɪd/ *v.t. & i.* подраздел|я́ть(ся), -и́ть(ся).

subdivision /ˈsʌbdɪˌvɪʒ(ə)n/, /-ˈvɪʒ(ə)n/ *n.* подразделе́ние.

subdominant /sʌbˈdɒmɪnənt/ *n.* субдомина́нта.

subdue /səbˈdju:/ *v.t.* (**subdues, subdued, subduing**) **1** (*conquer, subjugate*) подав|ля́ть, -и́ть; **~ one's enemies** покор|я́ть, -и́ть враго́в; (*tame, discipline*): **~ one's passions** подав|ля́ть, -и́ть стра́сти. **2** (*soften*) смягч|а́ть, -и́ть; **~d light** мя́гкий свет; (*sound etc.*) приглуш|а́ть, -и́ть; пон|ижа́ть, -и́зить; **in ~d voices** приглушёнными голоса́ми.
3 (*restrain*): **with an air of ~d satisfaction** со сде́ржанным удовлетворе́нием; **he seems ~d today** он сего́дня что-то прити́х.

sub-edit /sʌbˈedɪt/ *v.t.* (**sub-edited, sub-editing**) (*Br.*) редакти́ровать, от- пе́ред набо́ром; гото́вить (*impf.*) к набо́ру.

sub-editor /sʌbˈedɪtə(r)/ *n.* (*Br.*) помо́щник реда́ктора; техни́ческий реда́ктор (*abbr.* техре́д).

subfamily /ˈsʌbˌfæmɪlɪ/ *n.* подсеме́йство.

subfusc /ˈsʌbfʌsk/ *adj.* тёмный.

subgroup /ˈsʌbgru:p/ *n.* подгру́ппа.

subheading /ˈsʌbhedɪŋ/ *n.* подзаголо́вок.

subhuman /sʌbˈhju:mən/ *n.* недочелове́к.

● *adj.* нечелове́ческий.

subject[1] /ˈsʌbdʒɪkt/ *n.* **1** (*pol.*) по́дданный.
2 (*gram.*) подлежа́щее.
3 (*phil.*) субъе́кт.
4 (*theme, matter*) те́ма, предме́т; **the ~ of the book** те́ма кни́ги; **he was made the ~ of an experiment** его́ сде́лали объе́ктом о́пыта; **he talked on the ~ of bees** он говори́л о пчёлах; **change the ~** перев|оди́ть, -ести́ разгово́р на другу́ю те́му; **a painter who treats biblical ~s** живопи́сец/худо́жник, пи́шущий (карти́ны на) библе́йские сюже́ты; **you are treating the ~ very lightly** вы недоста́точно серьёзно отно́ситесь к э́тому вопро́су; **while we're on the ~** поско́льку зашёл разгово́р об э́том.
5 (*branch of study*) предме́т, дисципли́на; **he passed in four ~s** он прошёл по четырём предме́там.
6 (*cause, occasion*) по́вод; **a ~ of rejoicing** по́вод для весе́лья (*or* к весе́лью).

● *adj.* **1** (*subordinate*) подчинённый; зави́симый; **all citizens are ~ to the law** зако́н распространя́ется на всех гра́ждан; **bodies are ~ to gravity** тела́ подчиня́ются зако́ну тяготе́ния.
2 (*liable, prone, inclined*): **he is ~ to changes of mood** он подве́ржен (бы́стрым) сме́нам настрое́ния; **trains are ~ to delay** возмо́жны опозда́ния поездо́в.
3: **~ to** (*conditional upon*) подлежа́щий + *d.*; **the fare is ~ to alteration** сто́имость прое́зда мо́жет быть изменена́; **the treaty is ~ to ratification** догово́р подлежи́т ратифика́ции; **the price is ~ to market fluctuations** цена́ зави́сит от колеба́ний ры́нка.

● *adv.*: **~ to** при усло́вии (*чего*); (одна́ко) с учётом (*чего*); поско́льку ино́е не соде́ржится/предусма́тривается в + *p.*; **~ to the following provision** с соблюде́нием нижесле́дующего положе́ния; **~ to your approval** е́сли вы одо́брите; **~ to your rights** поско́льку э́то допуска́ют ва́ши права́.

● *cpds.* **~-heading** *n.* ру́брика, (под)заголо́вок; **~-matter** *n.* содержа́ние, предме́т (*чего*).

subject[2] /səbˈdʒekt/ *v.t.* **1** (*make subordinate*) подчин|я́ть, -и́ть.
2 (*expose, make liable*) подв|ерга́ть, -е́ргнуть (*кого/что чему*); **the machine was ~ed to tests** маши́ну подве́ргли испыта́ниям; **he was ~ed to insult** его́ подве́ргли оскорбле́нию.

subjection /səbˈdʒekʃ(ə)n/ *n.* подчине́ние.

subjective /səbˈdʒektɪv/ *adj.* субъекти́вный; (*gram.*): **~ case** имени́тельный паде́ж.

subjectivism /səbˈdʒektɪˌvɪz(ə)m/ *n.* субъективи́зм.

subjectivist /səbˈdʒektɪvɪst/ *n.* субъективи́ст.

subjectivity /ˌsʌbdʒekˈtɪvɪtɪ/ *n.* субъекти́вность.

sub judice /sʌb ˈdʒu:dɪsɪ/ *adj.* находя́щийся на рассмотре́нии (суда́).

subjugate /ˈsʌbdʒʊˌgeɪt/ *v.t.* (*subdue*) покор|я́ть, -и́ть; (*subject*) подчин|я́ть, -и́ть.

subjugation /ˌsʌbdʒʊˈgeɪʃ(ə)n/ *n.* покоре́ние; подчине́ние.

subjunctive /səbˈdʒʌŋktɪv/ *n.*: (~ **mood**) сослага́тельное наклоне́ние.
● *adj.* сослага́тельный.

sublease *n.* /ˈsʌbli:s/ субаре́нда.
● *v.t.* /sʌbˈli:s/ **1** (*of lessor; also* **sublet**) перед|ава́ть, -а́ть в субаре́нду. **2** (*of lessee*) брать, взять в субаре́нду.

sub|let /sʌbˈlet/ (~**letting;** *past and p.p.* ~**let**) = **sublease** *v.t.* 1

sublieutenant /ˌsʌblefˈtenənt/ *n.* мла́дший лейтена́нт.

sublimate¹ /ˈsʌblɪmət/ *n.* сублима́т, возго́н; **corrosive** ~ сулема́.

sublimate² /ˈsʌblɪˌmeɪt/ *v.t.* (*chem.*) сублими́ровать (*impf., pf.*); воз|гоня́ть, -огна́ть; (*psych.*) сублими́ровать (*impf., pf.*).

sublimation /ˌsʌblɪˈmeɪʃ(ə)n/ *n.* (*chem.*) сублима́ция, возго́нка; (*psych.*) сублима́ция.

sublime /səˈblaɪm/ *n.* (*the* ~) вели́кое, возвы́шенное; **it is only a step from the ~ to the ridiculous** от вели́кого до смешно́го оди́н шаг.
● *adj.* (**sublimer, sublimest**) (*majestic*) вели́чественный; (*lofty*) возвы́шенный; ~ **contempt** го́рдое презре́ние; ~ **ignorance** великоле́пное неве́дение.

subliminal /səbˈlɪmɪn(ə)l/ *adj.* подсозна́тельный; де́йствующий на подсозна́ние.

sublimity /səbˈlɪmɪtɪ/ *n.* возвы́шенность, вели́чественность.

sub-machine gun /ˌsʌbməˈʃi:n gʌn/ *n.* пистоле́т-пулемёт; автома́т.

sub-machine gunner /ˌsʌbməˈʃi:n ˌgʌnə(r)/ *n.* автома́тчик.

submarine /ˌsʌbməˈri:n/, /ˈsʌb-/ *n.* подво́дная ло́дка.
● *adj.* подво́дный.

submerge /səbˈmɜ:dʒ/ *v.t. & i.* погру|жа́ть(ся), -зи́ть(ся).

submer|gence /səbˈmɜ:dʒəns/, **-sion** /səbˈmɜ:ʃ(ə)n/ *nn.* погруже́ние в во́ду; затопле́ние.

submission /səbˈmɪʃ(ə)n/ *n.* **1** (*subjection*) подчине́ние; (*obedience*) повинове́ние; (*humility*) смире́ние; (*submissiveness*) поко́рность; (*capitulation*) капитуля́ция; **starve into** ~ брать, взять измо́ром. **2** (*presentation*) представле́ние, предъявле́ние; ~ **of proof** представле́ние доказа́тельств.

submissive /səbˈmɪsɪv/ *adj.* поко́рный, смире́нный, послу́шный.

submit /səbˈmɪt/ *v.t.* (**submitted, submitting**) **1** (*yield*) подчин|я́ть, -и́ть; покор|я́ть, -и́ть; ~ **o.s. to s.o.'s authority** покор|я́ться, -и́ться чьей-н. вла́сти. **2** (*present, e.g. a dissertation*) предст|авля́ть, -а́вить. **3** (*suggest, maintain*): **I ~ that your proposal is contrary to the statutes** я сме́ю утвержда́ть, что ва́ше предложе́ние противоре́чит уста́ву.
● *v.i.* (**submitted, submitting**) подчин|я́ться, -и́ться; покор|я́ться, -и́ться.

subnormal /sʌbˈnɔ:m(ə)l/ *adj.* ни́же норма́льного; **a ~ child** дефекти́вный (*or* у́мственно отста́лый) ребёнок.

sub-order /ˈsʌbˌɔ:də(r)/ *n.* подотря́д.

subordinate¹ /səˈbɔ:dɪnət/ *n.* подчинённый.
● *adj.* **1** (*in rank or importance*) подчинённый; ни́зший по чи́ну; (*secondary*) второстепе́нный. **2** (*gram.*) прида́точный; ~ **clause** прида́точное предложе́ние.

subordinat|e² /səˈbɔ:dɪˌneɪt/ *v.t.* (*make subservient*) подчин|я́ть, -и́ть; (*place in less important position*) ста́вить, по- в подчинённое/зави́симое положе́ние; ~**ing conjunction** подчини́тельный сою́з.

subordination /səˌbɔ:dɪˈneɪʃ(ə)n/ *n.* подчине́ние, подчинённость.

suborn /səˈbɔ:n/ *v.t.* подкуп|а́ть, -и́ть.

sub-plot /ˈsʌbplɒt/ *n.* побо́чная сюже́тная ли́ния.

subpoena /səbˈpi:nə/, /səˈpi:nə/ *n.* пове́стка в суд.
● *v.t.* (*past and p.p.* **subpoenaed** *or* **subpoena'd**) вызыва́ть, вы́звать в суд.

subroutine /ˈsʌbru:ˌti:n/ *n.* (*comput.*) подпрогра́мма.

subscribe /səbˈskraɪb/ *v.t.* **1** (*apply for*): **the course was fully ~d** на ку́рсе не оста́лось свобо́дных мест; **the share issue was fully ~d** це́нные бума́ги бы́ли по́лностью раску́плены. **2** (*contribute*) же́ртвовать, по-; **he ~s money to charities** он же́ртвует де́ньги на благотвори́тельные це́ли.
● *v.i.* **1** (*pay or take out subscription*): ~ **to a journal** подпи́с|ываться, -а́ться на журна́л; (*contribute*): ~ **to a loan** подпи́с|ываться, -а́ться на заём. **2** (*agree, assent*) присоедин|я́ться, -и́ться; **I cannot ~ to that view** я не могу́ согласи́ться с э́тим мне́нием.

subscriber /səbˈskraɪbə(r)/ *n.* (*to publication etc.*) подпи́счик; (*contributor to fund*) же́ртвователь (*fem.* -ница); (*telephone* ~) абоне́нт.

subscript /ˈsʌbskrɪpt/ *adj.* подстро́чный.

subscription /səbˈskrɪpʃ(ə)n/ *n.* (*to concerts etc.*) абонеме́нт; (*fee*) взнос, поже́ртвование; ~ **to a newspaper** подпи́ска на газе́ту; **take out a ~** подпи́с|ываться, -а́ться (на + *a.*); ~ **form** подписно́й лист.

subsection /ˈsʌbˌsekʃ(ə)n/ *n.* подсе́кция.

subsequent /ˈsʌbsɪkwənt/ *adj.* после́дующий, сле́дующий; ~ **to his death** (име́ющий ме́сто) по́сле его́ сме́рти; ~**ly** впосле́дствии; зате́м.

subservience /səbˈsɜ:vɪəns/ *n.* раболе́пие, послуша́ние.

subservient /səbˈsɜ:vɪənt/ *adj.* (*servile*) раболе́пный, послу́шный.

subside /səbˈsaɪd/ *v.i.* **1** (*of liquid*) пон|ижа́ться, -и́зиться. **2** (*of ground or building*) ос|еда́ть, -е́сть; **the ground ~d** земля́ осе́ла. **3** (*of water*) спа|да́ть, -сть; **the floods ~d** наводне́ние спа́ло; (*of blister*) оп|ада́ть, -а́сть. **4** (*of fever*) па́дать, упа́сть; (*of wind, storm etc.*) ут|иха́ть, -и́хнуть; **the laughter ~d** смех ути́х; **the noise ~d** шум смолк; **passions ~d** стра́сти улегли́сь.

subsidence /səbˈsaɪd(ə)ns/, /ˈsʌbsɪd(ə)ns/ *n.* (*of ground*) оседа́ние, оса́дка.

subsidiary /səbˈsɪdɪərɪ/ *n.* (*comm.*) филиа́л.
● *adj.* вспомога́тельный, подсо́бный; ~ **company** доче́рняя компа́ния.

subsidize /ˈsʌbsɪˌdaɪz/ *v.t.* субсиди́ровать (*impf., pf.*), доти́ровать (*impf., pf.*).

subsidy /ˈsʌbsɪdɪ/ *n.* субси́дия, посо́бие, дота́ция.

subsist /səbˈsɪst/ *v.i.* (*exist*) существова́ть (*impf.*); (*survive*) жить, про-.

subsistence /səbˈsɪst(ə)ns/ *n.* (*existence*) существова́ние; бытие́; (*means of supporting life*) сре́дства (*nt. pl.*) к существова́нию; пропита́ние; ~ **allowance, money** (*Br.*) команди́ро́вочные (де́ньги); ава́нс; ~ **farming** натура́льное хозя́йство; ~ **wage** прожи́точный ми́нимум.

subsoil /ˈsʌbsɔɪl/ *n.* подпо́чва.

subsonic /sʌbˈsɒnɪk/ *adj.* дозвуково́й.

subspecies /ˈsʌbˌspi:ʃi:z/, /-ʃɪz/ *n.* (*pl.* ~) подви́д.

substance /ˈsʌbst(ə)ns/ *n.* **1** (*essence, reality*) субста́нция, реа́льность. **2** (*essential elements*) суть, содержа́ние, су́щность, существо́; **he told me the ~ of his speech** он пересказа́л мне основно́е содержа́ние свое́й ре́чи; **in ~** по существу́. **3** (*piece, type of matter*) вещество́. **4** (*solidity*) пло́тность, содержа́ние; **a piece of writing that lacks ~** сочине́ние, лишённое содержа́ния; **there is no ~ in the rumour** (*Br.*), **rumor** (*US*) э́тот слух лишён како́го бы то ни́ было основа́ния. **5** (*possessions*) состоя́ние; **a man of ~** состоя́тельный челове́к.

substandard /sʌbˈstændəd/ *adj.* нестанда́ртный, низкока́чественный; (*of language*) нелитерату́рный, просторе́чный.

substantial /səbˈstænʃ(ə)l/ *adj.* **1** (*material*) веще́ственный, реа́льный; **a ~ being** реа́льное/живо́е существо́. **2** (*solid, stout, sturdy*) кре́пкий; **a man of ~ build** челове́к кре́пкого телосложе́ния; **a ~ building** соли́дное зда́ние; **a ~ dinner** сы́тный обе́д. **3** (*considerable*): **a ~ sum** поря́дочная/внуши́тельная су́мма; **a ~ contribution** большо́й/ва́жный вклад; **a ~ improvement** значи́тельное/заме́тное/ суще́ственное улучше́ние. **4** (*essential, overall*) по существу́/су́ти; **I am in ~ agreement** я согла́сен по существу́ (*or* в основно́м).

substantiate /səbˈstænʃɪˌeɪt/ *v.t.* обосно́в|ывать, -а́ть; дока́з|ывать, -а́ть.

substantiation /səbˌstænʃɪˈeɪʃ(ə)n/ *n.* обоснова́ние, доказа́тельство.

substantival /ˌsʌbstænˈtaɪv(ə)l/ *adj.* субстанти́вный.

S

substantive /səb'stæntɪv/ *n.* и́мя существи́тельное.

● *adj.* **1** (*existing independently*) субстанти́вный, незави́симый, самостоя́тельный. **2** (*pert. to subject matter*): **I have no ~ comments** у меня́ нет замеча́ний по существу́ (де́ла, вопро́са *и т.п.*); **~ provisions** резолюти́вная/операти́вная часть (*документа и т.п.*).

substation /'sʌb,steɪʃ(ə)n/ *n.* (*elec.*) подста́нция.

substitute /'sʌbstɪ,tju:t/ *n.* заме́на; (*person*) замести́тель (*m.*); (*thing*) замени́тель (*m.*), суррога́т, эрза́ц; **butter ~** замени́тель/суррога́т ма́сла.

● *v.t.* испо́льзовать (*impf., pf.*) (*что*) вме́сто (*чего*); **~ one word for another** замен|я́ть, -и́ть одно́ сло́во други́м; подст|авля́ть, -а́вить одно́ сло́во вме́сто друго́го; **a forgery was ~d for the original** оригина́л был подменён фальши́вкой.

● *v.i.*: **~ for** заме|ща́ть, -сти́ть; подмен|я́ть, -и́ть (*кого*).

substitution /,sʌbstɪ'tju:ʃ(ə)n/ *n.* заме́на, замеще́ние, подме́на; (*math.*) подстано́вка.

substrat|um /'sʌb,strɑ:təm/, /-,streɪtəm/ *n.* (*pl.* **~a**) основа́ние; ни́жний слой; (*geol.*) подпо́чва, субстра́т.

substructure /'sʌb,strʌktʃə(r)/ *n.* фунда́мент; ни́жнее строе́ние (доро́ги).

subsume /səb'sju:m/ *v.t.* включ|а́ть, -и́ть в каку́ю-н. катего́рию; отн|оси́ть, -ести́ к како́й-н. катего́рии, гру́ппе *и т.п.*

subtenancy /sʌb'tenənsɪ/ *n.* суба́ре́нда, поднаём.

subtenant /'sʌb,tenənt/ *n.* субаренда́тор, поднанима́тель (*m.*).

subtend /sʌb'tend/ *v.t.* (*an angle*) противолежа́ть (*impf.*) +*d.*; (*an arc*) стя́гивать (*impf.*) (*дугу*).

subterfuge /'sʌbtə,fju:dʒ/ *n.* уло́вка, хи́трость.

subterranean /,sʌbtə'reɪnɪən/ *adj.* подзе́мный.

subtitle /'sʌb,taɪt(ə)l/ *n.* подзаголо́вок; (*cin.*) субти́тр.

subtle /'sʌt(ə)l/ *adj.* (**subtler, subtlest**) **1** (*fine, elusive*) то́нкий; (*refined*) уто́нчённый; **~ distinction** то́нкое разли́чие; **~ charm** неулови́мое обая́ние. **2** (*perceptive*) то́нкий; (*acute*) о́стрый; **~ remark** то́нкое замеча́ние; **~ mind** о́стрый ум. **3** (*ingenious, deft*): **~ fingers** ло́вкие па́льцы; **~ device** иску́сный трюк; **~ argument** хитроу́мный до́вод. **4** (*crafty, cunning*) иску́сный, хи́трый.

subtlety /'sʌtəltɪ/ *n.* то́нкость; уто́нчённость; острота́; хи́трость; то́нкое разли́чие.

subtonic /sʌb'tɒnɪk/ *n.* ни́жний вво́дный тон.

subtract /səb'trækt/ *v.t.* вычита́ть, вы́честь.

subtraction /səb'trækʃ(ə)n/ *n.* вычита́ние.

subtropical /sʌb'trɒpɪk(ə)l/ *adj.* субтропи́ческий.

sub-unit /'sʌbju:nɪt/ *n.* (*mil.*) подразделе́ние.

suburb /'sʌbɜ:b/ *n.* при́город, предме́стье.

suburban /sə'bɜ:bən/ *adj.* при́городный; (*fig.*) меща́нский, провинциа́льный.

suburbanite /sə'bɜ:bənaɪt/ *n.* жи́тель (*fem.* -ница) при́города.

suburbia /sə'bɜ:bɪə/ *n.* (*pej.*) ≈ меща́нство, провинциали́зм.

subvention /səb'venʃ(ə)n/ *n.* субси́дия, дота́ция.

subversion /səb'vɜ:ʃ(ə)n/ *n.* подрывна́я де́ятельность.

subversive /səb'vɜ:sɪv/ *adj.* подрывно́й.

subvert /səb'vɜ:t/ *v.t.* под|рыва́ть, -орва́ть.

subway /'sʌbweɪ/ *n.* (*Br., passage under road*) подзе́мный перехо́д; (*US, railway*) подзе́мка, метро́ (*indecl.*).

subzero /sʌb'zɪərəʊ/ *adj.*: **~ temperatures** ми́нусовые температу́ры.

succeed /sək'si:d/ *v.t.* **1** (*follow*) сле́довать (*impf.*) за + *i.*; **night ~s day** ночь сменя́ет день. **2** (*as heir*) насле́довать (*impf., pf.*) + *d.*; **Mary was ~ed by Elizabeth I** по́сле Мари́и на престо́л взошла́ Елизаве́та I; (*as replacement*) смен|я́ть, -и́ть; **who ~ed him as President?** кто был сле́дующим президе́нтом?

● *v.i.* **1** (*follow*) после́довать (*pf.*) (за + *i.*). **2** (*as heir etc.*): **he ~ed to his father's estate** он унасле́довал име́ние отца́; **he ~ed to the premiership** он заня́л пост премье́р-мини́стра. **3** (*be, become successful*) преусп|ева́ть, -е́ть; доб|ива́ться, -и́ться успе́ха/своего́; **he is bound to ~ in life** он наверняка́ преуспе́ет в жи́зни; **he ~ed as a lawyer** он име́л успе́х в ка́честве адвока́та; **the attack ~ed beyond all expectation** ата́ка удала́сь сверх вся́ких ожида́ний; **he ~ed in tricking us all** ему́ удало́сь всех нас обману́ть.

success /sək'ses/ *n.* успе́х, уда́ча; **his efforts were crowned with ~** его́ уси́лия увенча́лись успе́хом; **I tried to get in, but without ~** я пыта́лся войти́, но безуспе́шно; **I have had no ~ so far** пока́ я не мог доби́ться успе́ха (*or* дости́гнуть це́ли); **my holidays were not a ~ this year** мои́ кани́кулы в э́том году́ бы́ли неуда́чными; **that book is among his ~es** э́та кни́га — одна́ из его́ уда́ч; **a series of military ~es** ряд вое́нных успе́хов.

successful /sək'sesfʊl/ *adj.* успе́шный, уда́чный, благополу́чный; **a ~ attempt** успе́шная попы́тка; **a ~ speech** уда́чная речь; **I tried to persuade him, but was not ~** я пыта́лся убеди́ть его́, но мне э́то не удало́сь; (*fortunate*) преуспева́ющий; уда́чливый; **he had the appearance of a ~ man** у него́ был вид преуспева́ющего челове́ка; **he was ~ in business** он был уда́члив в дела́х.

succession /sək'seʃ(ə)n/ *n.* **1** (*sequence*) после́довательность; **in ~** подря́д; **they rode past in rapid ~** они промча́лись оди́н за други́м. **2** (*series*) ряд, цепь; **a ~ of victories** цепь побе́д. **3** (*succeeding to office etc.*) насле́дство, насле́дие, насле́дование; **the king's right of ~ was disputed** пра́во престолонасле́дия короля́ оспа́ривалось; **the ~ was broken** преє́мственность была́ нару́шена.

successive /sək'sesɪv/ *adj.* после́довательный; **on three ~ occasions** три ра́за подря́д.

successor /sək'sesə(r)/ *n.* прее́мни|к (*fem.* -ца), насле́дни|к (*fem.* -ца).

succinct /sək'sɪŋkt/ *adj.* (*concise*) сжа́тый; (*brief*) кра́ткий.

succinctness /sək'sɪŋktnɪs/ *n.* сжа́тость, кра́ткость.

succour /'sʌkə(r)/ (*US* **succor**) (*liter.*) *n.* по́мощь.

● *v.t.* при|ходи́ть, -йти́ на по́мощь + *d.*

succulence /'sʌkjʊləns/ *n.* со́чность.

succulent /'sʌkjʊlənt/ *adj.* со́чный; (*bot.*) мяси́стый.

succumb /sə'kʌm/ *v.i.* уступ|а́ть, -и́ть; подд|ава́ться, -а́ться; **they ~ed to the enemy's superior force** они́ уступи́ли превосходя́щей си́ле проти́вника; **she did not ~ to temptation** она́ не подда́лась искуше́нию; (*die*) сконча́ться (*pf.*); **he ~ed to his injuries** он сконча́лся от (полу́ченных) ран.

such /sʌtʃ/ *pron.* **1** (*that*) э́то; **~ was not my intention** э́то не́ было мои́м наме́рением; **~ being the case** в тако́м слу́чае; **he is a good scholar and is recognized as ~** он хоро́ший учёный и при́знан таковы́м. **2**: **as ~** (*without qualification*) вообще́; как таково́й. **3**: **~** (*people*) **as** те, кото́рые.

● *adj.* **1** (*of the kind mentioned; of this, that kind*) тако́й; **I know of no ~ place** я не слыха́л о тако́м ме́сте; **I have never seen ~ a sight** я никогда́ не ви́дел подо́бного зре́лища; **I said no ~ thing** я ничего́ подо́бного не говори́л; **some ~ thing** что́-то в э́том ро́де; **no ~ luck!** увы́!; е́сли бы!; **how could you do ~ a thing?** как вы могли́ так поступи́ть? **2**: **~ as** (*of a kind . . .*): **~ grapes as you never saw** тако́й виногра́д, како́го вы в жи́зни не ви́дывали; **the difference was not ~ as to affect the result** ра́зница была́ не так велика́, что́бы повлия́ть на результа́т; **I am not ~ a fool as to believe him** я не тако́й дура́к, что́бы пове́рить ему́; (*like*): **people ~ as these** таки́е лю́ди; лю́ди, подо́бные э́тим; **a picture ~ as that is valuable** тако́го ро́да карти́ны це́нятся высоко́; **small objects ~ as diamonds** ме́лкие предме́ты, как наприме́р бриллиа́нты; **there is ~ a thing as politeness** существу́ет така́я вещь, как ве́жливость; **you can share my meal, ~ as it is** вы мо́жете раздели́ть со мной мой у́жин, како́в он ни на есть. **3** (*pred.*) тако́в; **~ was the force of the**

gale такова́ была́ си́ла урага́на; **~ is life!** такова́ жизнь!

● *cpds.* **~-and-~** *adj.* тако́й-то; (*pl.*) ко́е-какие; **~like** *pron. & adj.* подо́бный; **theatres, cinemas and ~like** теа́тры, кино́ и тому́ подо́бное.

suck /sʌk/ *n.* соса́ние; **take a ~ at** пососа́ть (*pf.*); **give ~ to a child** (*arch.*) да|ва́ть, -ть (пососа́ть) грудь ребёнку.

● *v.t.* **1** соса́ть (*impf.*); **he was ~ing (at) an orange** он поса́сывал апельси́н; (**~** *in, imbibe*) вс|а́сывать, -оса́ть; тяну́ть (*impf.*); **bees ~ nectar** пчёлы втя́гивают некта́р; **he was ~ing fruit juice through a straw** он тяну́л фрукто́вый сок че́рез соло́минку; (**~** *out*) выса́сывать, вы́сосать. **2** (*squeeze or dissolve in mouth*) соса́ть (*impf.*); поса́сывать (*impf.*); **she was always ~ing lozenges** она́ ве́чно соса́ла леденцы́; **the baby likes to ~ its thumb** младе́нец лю́бит соса́ть па́лец.

● *v.i.* соса́ть (*impf.*); **~ at, on a pipe** поса́сывать/потя́гивать (*impf.*) тру́бку; **~ing-pig** моло́чный поросёнок.

● *with advs.*: **~ in** *v.t.* вс|а́сывать, -оса́ть; (*engulf*) зас|а́сывать, -оса́ть; (*fig.*) впи́т|ывать, -а́ть (в себя́); **~ out** *v.t.* выса́сывать, вы́сосать; **~ up** *v.t.* выса́сывать, вы́сосать; (*absorb*) впи́т|ывать, -а́ть; *v.i.*: **~ up to s.o.** (*coll.*) подли́з|ываться, -а́ться к кому́-н.

sucker /ˈsʌkə(r)/ *n.* **1** (*organ, device*) присо́сок, присо́ска. **2** (*bot.*) отро́сток, боково́й побе́г. **3** (*sl., gullible person*) проста́|к (*fem.* -чка).

suckl|e /ˈsʌk(ə)l/ *v.t.* вск|а́рмливать, -орми́ть; (*of person*) корми́ть (*impf.*) гру́дью; **the cow was ~ing the calf** телёнок соса́л ма́тку.

suckling /ˈsʌklɪŋ/ *n.* (*child*) грудно́й ребёнок; сосуно́к; (*animal*) сосу́н, сосуно́к; **~ pig** (*US*) моло́чный поросёнок.

sucrose /ˈsuːkrəʊz/, /ˈsjuː-/ *n.* сахаро́за.

suction /ˈsʌkʃ(ə)n/ *n.* соса́ние, вса́сывание, приса́сывание; **~ pump** вса́сывающий насо́с.

Sudan /suːˈdɑːn/, /-ˈdæn/ *n.* Суда́н.

Sudanese /ˌsuːdəˈniːz/ *n.* (*pl.* **~**) суда́н|ец (*fem.* -ка).

● *adj.* суда́нский.

sudden /ˈsʌd(ə)n/ *n.*: **(all) of a ~** внеза́пно, вдруг.

● *adj.* (*unexpected*) внеза́пный, неожи́данный; **he made a ~ movement** он сде́лал ре́зкое движе́ние; **~ death** скоропости́жная смерть; (*sport*) дополни́тельное вре́мя для игры́ (в слу́чае ра́вного счёта).

suddenly /ˈsʌd(ə)nlɪ/ *adv.* внеза́пно, вдруг.

suddenness /ˈsʌd(ə)nnɪs/ *n.* внеза́пность, неожи́данность.

Sudetenland /suːˈdeɪt(ə)nˌlænd/ *n.* Суде́тская о́бласть.

suds /sʌdz/ *n. pl.* мы́льная пе́на.

sue /suː/, /sjuː/ *v.t.* (**sues, sued, suing**) возбу|жда́ть, -ди́ть иск/де́ло про́тив + *g.*; под|ава́ть, -а́ть в суд на + *a.*; (**for libel** за клевету́; **for damages** о возмеще́нии убы́тков).

● *v.i.* (**sues, sued, suing**) **1** (*take legal action*) под|ава́ть, -а́ть в суд (на + *a.*). **2** (*make entreaties*): **~ for peace** проси́ть (*impf.*) ми́ра.

suede /sweɪd/ *n.* за́мша.

● *adj.* за́мшевый.

suet /ˈsuːɪt/, /ˈsjuːɪt/ *n.* нутряно́е са́ло; по́чечный жир.

Suez /ˈsuːɪz/ *n.* Суэ́ц; **~ Canal** Суэ́цкий кана́л.

suffer /ˈsʌfə(r)/ *v.t.* **1** (*experience*) испы́т|ывать, -а́ть; терпе́ть, по-; претерп|ева́ть, -е́ть; **she did not ~ much pain** её не си́льно му́чили бо́ли; (*if she died*) она́ недо́лго му́чилась; **he ~ed many hardships** он перенёс/претерпе́л мно́жество лише́ний. **2** (*permit*) позв|оля́ть, -о́лить; (*tolerate*) терпе́ть, по-/с-; **he does not ~ fools gladly** он не выно́сит дурако́в.

● *v.i.* страда́ть (*impf.*) (от + *g.*); **he learnt to ~ without complaining** он научи́лся безро́потно переноси́ть страда́ние; **he ~s from shyness** он (о́чень) засте́нчив; **he is ~ing from measles** он боле́ет ко́рью; у него́ корь; **he is ~ing from loss of appetite** он страда́ет отсу́тствием аппети́та; **he did not ~ much in the accident** он не о́чень пострада́л во вре́мя ава́рии; **his reputation will ~ greatly** его́ репута́ция си́льно пострада́ет; **he ~ed for his folly** он был нака́зан за свою́ глу́пость; **I ~ed for it** я за э́то поплати́лся.

sufferance /ˈsʌfərəns/ *n.*: **on ~** из ми́лости; с молчали́вого согла́сия.

sufferer /ˈsʌfərə(r)/ *n.* страда́лец.

suffering /ˈsʌfərɪŋ/ *n.* страда́ние.

suffice /səˈfaɪs/ *v.t.* удовлетвор|я́ть, -и́ть; **one meal a day ~s her** ей доста́точно есть оди́н раз в день.

● *v.i.* быть доста́точным; хват|а́ть, -и́ть; **a brief statement will ~ for my purpose** мне потре́буется лишь кра́ткое заявле́ние; **~ it to say that …** доста́точно сказа́ть, что….

sufficiency /səˈfɪʃənsɪ/ *n.* доста́точность, доста́ток.

sufficient /səˈfɪʃ(ə)nt/ *n.*: **have you had ~ (to eat)?** вы сы́ты?

● *adj.* доста́точный, подходя́щий; **the sum is ~ for the journey** э́тих де́нег хва́тит на доро́гу; **lack ~ food** испы́тывать (*impf.*) недоста́ток в пи́ще.

suffix /ˈsʌfɪks/ *n.* су́ффикс.

● *v.t.* приб|авля́ть, -а́вить.

suffocat|e /ˈsʌfəˌkeɪt/ *v.t.* души́ть, за-; **I was ~ed by the close atmosphere** я задыха́лся в духоте́; **he was ~ed by poisonous fumes** он задохну́лся в ядови́том ды́ме; **~ing heat** уду́шливая жара́.

● *v.i.* зад|ыха́ться, -охну́ться.

suffocation /ˌsʌfəˈkeɪʃ(ə)n/ *n.* удуше́ние, уду́шье.

suffragan /ˈsʌfrəgən/ *n.*: (**~ bishop**) вика́рий; вика́рный епи́скоп.

suffrage /ˈsʌfrɪdʒ/ *n.* избира́тельное пра́во; **female ~** избира́тельное пра́во для же́нщин; **universal ~** всео́бщее избира́тельное пра́во.

suffragette /ˌsʌfrəˈdʒet/ *n.* (*hist.*) суфражи́стка.

suffuse /səˈfjuːz/ *v.t.* зал|ива́ть, -и́ть; **a blush ~d her cheeks** её щёки за́лил румя́нец.

sugar /ˈʃʊgə(r)/ *n.* са́хар; **granulated/caster ~** (са́харный) песо́к; **confectioner's** (*US*), **icing ~** (*Br.*) са́харная пу́дра; **brown ~** неочи́щенный са́харный песо́к; **cane ~** тростнико́вый са́хар; **lump ~** кусково́й са́хар, (са́хар-)рафина́д.

● *v.t.* **1** (*lit., fig., sweeten*) подсла́|щивать, -сти́ть. **2** (*sprinkle with* **~**) пос|ыпа́ть, -ы́пать са́харом; са́харить, по-.

● *cpds.* **~-basin, ~-bowl** *nn.* са́харница; **~-beet** *n.* са́харная свёкла; **~-candy** *n.* леденéц; **~-cane** *n.* са́харный тростни́к; **~-coated** *adj.* покры́тый са́харом; **~-daddy** *n.* (*coll.*) бога́тый пожило́й покло́нник; **~-loaf** *n.* са́харная голова́; **~ lump** *n.* кусо́к са́хара; **~-mill** *n.* са́харный заво́д; **~-plantation** *n.* са́харная планта́ция; **~-refinery** *n.* рафина́дный заво́д; **~-tongs** *n. pl.* щипц|ы́ (*pl., g.* -о́в) для са́хара.

sugarless /ˈʃʊgəlɪs/ *adj.* без са́хара.

sugary /ˈʃʊgərɪ/ *adj.* **1** са́харный, са́харистый. **2** (*fig., of tone, smile etc.*) сла́дкий, слаща́вый.

suggest /səˈdʒest/ *v.t.* **1** (*propose*) предл|ага́ть, -ожи́ть; сове́товать, по-; **he ~ed (going for) a walk** он предложи́л пойти́ прогуля́ться; **he ~ed that I should follow him** он предложи́л/посове́товал мне сле́довать за ним; **I ~ you try again** я сове́тую вам попро́бовать ещё раз(о́к); **all sorts of plans were ~ed** предлага́лись всевозмо́жные пла́ны; (*with inanimate subject*): **what ~ed that idea to you?** что навело́ вас на э́ту мысль? **2** (*evoke, call to mind*) вызыва́ть, вы́звать; **what does this shape ~?** что напомина́ет э́та фо́рма?; **does the name ~ nothing to you?** э́то и́мя вам ничего́ не говори́т? **3** (*imply, indicate*) говори́ть (*impf.*) о + *p.*; свиде́тельствовать (*impf.*) о + *p.*; **his skill ~s long practice** его́ мастерство́ говори́т о дли́тельной пра́ктике; **his tone ~ed impatience** в его́ то́не чу́вствовалось нетерпе́ние. **4** (*advance as possible or likely*): **I ~ that the calculation is (or may be) wrong** по-мо́ему, здесь оши́бка в расчёте; **I ~ that you knew all the time** я утвержда́ю, что вы с са́мого нача́ла зна́ли об э́том; **do you ~ that I am lying?** вы хоти́те сказа́ть, что я лгу?

suggestible /səˈdʒestɪb(ə)l/ *adj.* (*of person*) внуша́емый.

suggestion /səˈdʒestʃ(ə)n/ *n.* **1** (*proposal*) предложе́ние, сове́т; **make a ~** вн|оси́ть, -ести́ предложе́ние; под|ава́ть, -а́ть иде́ю/мысль; **I acted on his ~** я воспо́льзовался его́ сове́том/иде́ей. **2** (*implication*) наме́к, до́ля; (*tinge*) отте́нок; **there was a ~ of regret in his voice** в его́ го́лосе звуча́ла но́тка сожале́ния; **a ~ of a foreign accent** чуть заме́тный иностра́нный акце́нт. **3** (*hypnotic etc.*) внуше́ние.

suggestive /sə'dʒestɪv/ *adj.* **1**: **~ of** напомина́ющий. **2** (*improper*) непристо́йный; риско́ванный.

suicidal /ˌsu:ɪ'saɪd(ə)l/, /ˌsju:-/ *adj.* **1** (*pert. to suicide*) самоуби́йственный. **2** (*leading to suicide*): **~ tendencies** скло́нность к самоуби́йству. **3** (*of person*) скло́нный к самоуби́йству; суицида́льный. **4** (*fig., fatal*) губи́тельный, ги́бельный; **~ policy** па́губная поли́тика.

suicide /'su:ɪˌsaɪd/, /'sju:-/ *n.* **1** (*also fig.*) самоуби́йство; **commit ~** конча́ть, (по)ко́нчить с собо́й, ко́нчить по-(жизнь) самоуби́йством. **2** (*person*) самоуби́йца (*c.g.*); **~ pact** группово́е самоуби́йство по сго́вору; **~ pilot** (пило́т-)сме́ртник.

sui generis /ˌsju:aɪ 'dʒenərɪs/, /ˌsu:ɪ 'gen-/ *adj.* своеобра́зный, уника́льный.

suit /su:t/, /sju:t/ *n.* **1** (*arch., petition*) проше́ние; **grant s.o.'s ~** удовлетвор|я́ть, -и́ть чьё-н. проше́ние; (*for marriage*) сватовство́. **2** (*leg.*) иск, де́ло; **civil/criminal ~** гражда́нский/уголо́вный иск; **bring (a) ~ against s.o.** предъявл|я́ть, -и́ть иск кому́-н. **3** (*of clothes*) костю́м; **two-piece ~** костю́м-дво́йка; (*woman's*) костю́м, ю́бка с жаке́том; **~ of armour** (*Br.*), **armor** (*US*) доспе́хи (*m. pl.*), ла́т|ы (*pl., g.* —). **4** (*of cards*) масть; **follow ~** ходи́ть (*indet.*) в масть; (*fig.*) сле́довать, по- за + *i.*; сле́довать, по- чьему́-н. приме́ру; **politeness is not his strong ~** он не отлича́ется любе́зностью.

● *v.t.* **1** (*accommodate, adapt*) приспос|а́бливать, -о́бить (*что к чему*); согласо́в|ывать, -а́ть (*что с чем*); **he is not ~ed to be an engineer** он не годи́тся в инжене́ры; **they are ~ed to one another** они́ подхо́дят друг дру́гу. **2** (*be satisfactory, convenient to*): **the plan ~s me** э́тот план меня́ устра́ивает; **will it ~ you to finish now?** удо́бно ли вам ко́нчить на э́том?; **he tries to ~ everybody** он стара́ется всем угоди́ть; **~ yourself!** как хоти́те! **3** (*be good for, agree with*): **coffee does not ~ me** мне от ко́фе де́лается нехорошо́; **the English climate does not ~ everyone** не всем подхо́дит англи́йский кли́мат. **4** (*befit*) под|ходи́ть, -ойти́ + *d.*; **the role does not ~ him** э́та роль ему́ не подхо́дит; **that hat ~s her** э́та шля́па ей идёт (*or* ей к лицу́).

● *v.i.* под|ходи́ть, -ойти́; годи́ться (*impf.*).

● *cpd.* **~case** *n.* (небольшо́й) чемода́н.

suitability /ˌsu:tə'bɪlɪtɪ/, /ˌsju:-/ *n.* го́дность, приго́дность.

suitable /'su:təb(ə)l/, /'sju:-/ *adj.* подходя́щий, го́дный, соотве́тствующий; **he is ~ for the job** он подхо́дит для э́той до́лжности; **clothes ~ to the occasion** оде́жда, подходя́щая к (*or* соотве́тствующая слу́чаю; **reading ~ to her age** чте́ние, соотве́тствующее её во́зрасту.

suitably /'su:təblɪ/, /'sju:-/ *adv.* соотве́тственно, пра́вильно; как сле́дует.

suite /swi:t/ *n.* **1** (*retinue*) сви́та. **2** (*set*): **~ of furniture** гарниту́р ме́бели, ме́бельный гарниту́р; **bedroom ~** спа́льный гарниту́р; **~ of rooms** апартаме́нты (*m. pl.*); (*in hotel*) (но́мер-)люкс. **3** (*mus.*) сюи́та.

suitor /'su:tə(r)/, /'sju:-/ *n.* (*wooer*) жени́х, покло́нник.

sulf- /'sʌlf/ (*US*) = **sulph-**

sulk /sʌlk/ *n.* дурно́е настрое́ние.

● *v.i.* быть в дурно́м настрое́нии; **~ at s.o.** ду́ться (*impf.*) на кого́-н.

sulky /'sʌlkɪ/ *adj.* (**sulkier, sulkiest**) наду́тый, оби́женный.

sullen /'sʌlən/ *adj.* (*sulky*) наду́тый; (*morose*) угрю́мый; (*sombre*) мра́чный.

sullenness /'sʌlənnɪs/ *n.* наду́тость; угрю́мость; мра́чность.

sully /'sʌlɪ/ *v.t.* (*liter.*) пятна́ть, за-.

sulphate /'sʌlfeɪt/ (*US* **sulfate**) *n.* сульфа́т; **copper/iron/zinc ~** ме́дный/желе́зный/ци́нковый купоро́с.

sulphide /'sʌlfaɪd/ (*US* **sulfide**) *n.* сульфи́д; **copper ~** серни́стая медь.

sulphite /'sʌlfaɪt/ (*US* **sulfite**) *n.* сульфи́т; **copper ~** сернистоки́слая медь.

sulphur /'sʌlfə(r)/ (*US* **sulfur**) *n.* се́ра; **flowers of ~** се́рный цвет.

sulphureous /sʌl'fjʊərɪəs/ (*US* **sulfureous**) *adj.* се́рный; зеленова́то-жёлтый.

sulphuric /sʌl'fjʊərɪk/ (*US* **sulfuric**) *adj.* се́рный; **~ acid** се́рная кислота́.

sulphurous /'sʌlfərəs/ (*US* **sulfurous**) *adj.* серни́стый.

sultan /'sʌlt(ə)n/ *n.* султа́н.

sultana /sʌl'tɑ:nə/ *n.* (*fruit*) изю́минка; (*collect.*) кишми́ш.

sultanate /'sʌltəˌneɪt/ *n.* (*state, institution*) султана́т.

sultriness /'sʌltrɪnɪs/ *n.* духота́, зно́йность, зной.

sultry /'sʌltrɪ/ *adj.* (**sultrier, sultriest**) **1** (*of atmosphere, weather*) зно́йный, ду́шный; **~ heat** зной. **2** (*of temper or person*) зно́йный, стра́стный, ю́жный.

sum /sʌm/ *n.* **1** (*total*) ито́г; **~ total** о́бщая су́мма, о́бщий ито́г; **the ~ total of his demands was ...** в о́бщей сло́жности его́ тре́бования своди́лись к + *d.* **2** (*amount*) су́мма; **his debts amounted to the ~ of £2,000** его́ долги́ достига́ли (су́ммы в) 2 000 фу́нтов. **3** (*liter., substance, essence*) су́щность, суть; **in ~** (одни́м) сло́вом; **the ~ of all my wishes** ито́г/верши́на мои́х стремле́ний. **4** (*problem*) (арифмети́ческая) зада́ча; **he did the ~ in his head** он реши́л зада́чу в уме́; **he is good at ~s** он силён в арифме́тике.

● *v.t.* (**summed, summing**) (*usu.* **~ up**) **1** (*reckon up*) подсчи́т|ывать, -а́ть; скла́дывать, сложи́ть. **2** (*summarize*) сумми́ровать (*impf.*); подв|оди́ть, -ести́ ито́ги + *g.*; резюми́ровать (*impf., pf.*); **the argument can be ~med up in one word** аргуме́нт мо́жно сформули́ровать одни́м сло́вом; (*form judgement of*): **he ~med up the situation at a glance** он оцени́л положе́ние с пе́рвого взгля́да.

● *v.i.* (**summed, summing**): **~ up** сумми́ровать (*impf., pf.*); резюми́ровать (*impf., pf.*); **the judge's ~ming-up** заключи́тельная речь судьи́; **to ~ up, ...** сумми́руя ска́занное, ...; (*in a word*) сло́вом, ...

sumac(h) /'su:mæk/, /'ʃu:-/, /'sju:-/ *n.* (*bot.*) сума́х.

Sumatra /sʊ'mɑ:trə/ *n.* Сума́тра.

Sumatran /sʊ'mɑ:trən/ *n.* жи́тель (*fem.* -ница) Сума́тры.

● *adj.* суматри́йский.

summarily /'sʌmərɪlɪ/ *adv.* бесцеремо́нно.

summarize /'sʌməˌraɪz/ *v.t.* сумми́ровать (*impf., pf.*); резюми́ровать (*impf., pf.*); подв|оди́ть, -ести́ ито́ги + *g.*

summary /'sʌmərɪ/ *n.* резюме́ (*indecl.*), сво́дка.

● *adj.* **1** (*brief*) сумма́рный, кра́ткий; **~ account** кра́ткий отчёт. **2** (*rapid, sweeping*) бесцеремо́нный; **a ~ judgement** пове́рхностное сужде́ние. **3** (*leg.*) ускоренный.

summation /sə'meɪʃ(ə)n/ *n.* (*summing-up*) резюме́ (*indecl.*).

summer /'sʌmə(r)/ *n.* ле́то; **in ~** ле́том; **Indian ~** ба́бье ле́то.

● *adj.* ле́тний; **~ dress** ле́тнее пла́тье; **dressed in ~ clothes** оде́тый по-ле́тнему; **~ lightning** зарни́ца; **~ school** ле́тний университе́т; **~ time** (*Br., daylight saving*) ле́тнее вре́мя.

● *v.i.* (*spend* **~**) пров|оди́ть, -ести́ ле́то.

● *cpds.* **~house** *n.* бесе́дка; **~time** *n.* ле́тняя пора́.

summery /'sʌmərɪ/ *adj.*: **~ weather** ле́тняя/тёплая пого́да; **~ clothes** лёгкая/ле́тняя оде́жда.

summit /'sʌmɪt/ *n.* (*lit., fig.*) верши́на, верх; **the ~ of his ambition** верши́на его́ честолю́бия; **~ (conference, talks)** совеща́ние на вы́сшем у́ровнс, са́ммит.

summon /'sʌmən/ *v.t.* **1** (*send for*) приз|ыва́ть, -ва́ть; (*also leg.*) вызыва́ть, вы́звать. **2** (*order*) приз|ыва́ть, -ва́ть; **she ~ed the children to dinner** она́ позвала́ дете́й обе́дать. **3**: **~ a meeting** соз|ыва́ть, -ва́ть собра́ние; **~ up one's energy/courage** соб|ира́ться, -ра́ться с си́лами/ду́хом.

summons /'sʌmənz/ *n.* (*pl.* **~es**) вы́зов; (*leg.*) суде́бная пове́стка, вы́зов в суд; **answer a ~** яв|ля́ться, -и́ться по пове́стке; **serve a ~ on s.o.** вруч|а́ть, -и́ть кому́-н. суде́бную пове́стку.

● *v.t.* вызыва́ть, вы́звать в суд.

summum bonum /ˌsʊməm 'bɒnəm/, /'bəʊ-/ *n.* велича́йшее бла́го.

sumo /'su:məʊ/ *n.* (*pl.* **~s**) (*also* **~ wrestling**) су́мо (*indecl.*); (*wrestler*) су́мо-боре́ц.

sump /sʌmp/ *n.* (*for waste liquid, sewage etc.*) выгребна́я я́ма; (*for engine oil*) маслосбо́рник; поддо́н ка́ртера.

sumptuous /'sʌmptjʊəs/ *adj.* роско́шный, великоле́пный.

sumptuousness /'sʌmptjʊəsnɪs/ *n.* ро́скошь, великоле́пие.

sun /sʌn/ *n.* со́лнце; (*astron.*) Со́лнце; **the ~ rises** со́лнце восхо́дит/всхо́дит; **the ~ sets** со́лнце захо́дит/сади́тся; **his ~ is set** его́ звезда́ закати́лась; **before the ~ goes down** до захо́да со́лнца; **the ~ is up** со́лнце вста́ло; **the ~ is out** (*shining*) со́лнце/со́лнышко све́тит; **when the ~ comes out** когда́ вы́йдет со́лнце; **when the ~ goes in** когда́ скро́ется со́лнце; **lie in the ~** лежа́ть (*impf.*) на со́лнце; **everything under the ~** всё на све́те; **the ~ is in my eyes** со́лнце бьёт мне в глаза́; **this flower-bed catches the ~** на э́ту клу́мбу па́дает со́лнце; **you have caught the ~** (*become suntanned*) вы загоре́ли; (*become sunburnt*) вы обгоре́ли; **in the full blaze of the ~** на (са́мом) солнцепёке.

● *v.t.* (**sunned, sunning**): **~ o.s.** гре́ться (*impf.*) на со́лнце/со́лнышке.

● *cpds.* **~-baked** *adj.* высушенный на со́лнце; **~bathe** *v.i.* загора́ть (*impf.*); **~bather** *n.* загора́ющий; **~beam** *n.* со́лнечный луч; **~bed** *n.* (*Br.*) **1** (*lounger*) шезло́нг. **2** (*for acquiring tan*) ультрафиоле́товое устро́йство для иску́сственного зага́ра; **~-blind** *n.* (*Br., awning*) марки́за; жалюзи́ (*nt. indecl.*); **~burn** *n.* (*inflammation*) со́лнечный ожо́г; **he got a nasty ~burn** он стра́шно обгоре́л; **~burnt** *adj.* (*tanned*) загоре́лый; (*inflamed*) обожжённый со́лнцем; **~ cream** *n.* солнцезащи́тный крем; **S~day** *see separate entry*; **~-deck** *n.* ве́рхняя па́луба; **~dial** *n.* со́лнечные часы́ (*m. pl.*); **~down** *n.* захо́д со́лнца; **~downer** *n.* (*Austral., tramp*) бродя́га (*m.*); (*Br., drink*) рю́мка, выпива́емая ве́чером; **~-drenched** *adj.* напоённый со́лнцем; **~-dress** *n.* сарафа́н; **~-dried** *adj.* (*of fruit*) вы́сушенный на со́лнце, вя́леный; **~flower** *n.* подсо́лнечник; **~flower oil** подсо́лнечное ма́сло; **~flower seed** подсо́лнух, се́мечки (*nt. pl.*); **~-glasses** *n. pl.* со́лнечные очки́, очки́ от со́лнца; **~-god** *n.* бог со́лнца; **~-hat** *n.* шля́па от со́лнца; **~-lamp** *n.* ква́рцевая ла́мпа; **~light** *n.* со́лнечный свет; **~lit** *adj.* освещённый/за́литый со́лнцем; **~-lounge** *n.* (*Br.*) вера́нда; **~-rays** *n. pl.* (*beams*) со́лнечные лучи́ (*m. pl.*); (*ultra-violet rays*) ультрафиоле́товые лучи́; **~rise** *n.* восхо́д (со́лнца); **at ~rise** на заре́; **~roof** *n.* (*of car*) раздвижна́я кры́ша; **~set** *n.* захо́д со́лнца, зака́т; **at ~set** на зака́те; **~shade** *n.* (*parasol*) (со́лнечный) зо́нтик; (*awning*) наве́с, марки́за, тент; **~shine** *n.* со́лнечный свет; (*fig., cheer*) ра́дость; **the ~shine went out of her life** сча́стье ушло́ из её жи́зни; **~shine roof** (*Br., of car*) = **~roof; ~spot** *n.* пятно́ на со́лнце; **~stroke** *n.* со́лнечный уда́р; **~-suit** *n.* пля́жный костю́м; **~-tan** *n.* зага́р; **~-tan lotion** крем для зага́ра; **~-trap** *n.* (*Br.*) со́лнечный уголо́к; **~-up** *n.* (*US*) восхо́д (со́лнца); **~-worship** *n.* солнцепокло́нничество; культ со́лнца.

sundae /'sʌndeɪ/, /-dɪ/ *n.* моро́женое с фру́ктами/оре́хами (*и т.п.*).

Sunday /'sʌndeɪ/, /-dɪ/ *n.* воскресе́нье; **on ~s** по воскресе́ньям; **not in a month of ~s** ≈ по́сле до́ждичка в четве́рг; когда́ рак сви́стнет; **~ school** воскре́сная шко́ла; **in one's ~ best** в выходно́м пла́тье; в пра́здничном наря́де.

sunder /'sʌndə(r)/ *v.t.* (*liter.*) разлуч|а́ть, -и́ть.

sundries /'sʌndrɪz/ *n.* ра́зное.

sundry /'sʌndrɪ/ *adj.* ра́зный, разли́чный; **all and ~** всё и вся; все без исключе́ния.

sung /sʌŋ/ *p.p. of* ⇨**sing**

sunk /sʌŋk/ *past and p.p. of* ⇨**sink**

sunken /'sʌŋkən/ *adj.* (*of eyes etc.*) впа́лый, запа́вший; (*submerged*) подво́дный, зато́пленный.

sunless /'sʌnlɪs/ *adj.* тёмный, мра́чный, без со́лнца.

sunny /'sʌnɪ/ *adj.* (**sunnier, sunniest**) со́лнечный; **a ~ room** со́лнечная ко́мната; **look on the ~ side of things** ви́деть (*impf.*) све́тлую сто́рону веще́й; **a ~ disposition** жизнера́достный хара́ктер; **a ~ smile** сия́ющая улы́бка.

sup /sʌp/ *v.i.* (**supped, supping**) прихлёбывать (*impf.*).

super /'su:pə(r)/, /'sju:-/ (*coll.*) *n.* = **superintendent**

● *adj.* замеча́тельный, превосхо́дный; **~!** здо́рово!

superabundance /ˌsu:pərə'bʌnd(ə)ns/, /ˌsju:-/ (чрезме́рное) изоби́лие.

superabundant /ˌsu:pərə'bʌnd(ə)nt/, /ˌsju:-/ *adj.* изоби́льный; избы́точный.

superannuate /ˌsu:pər'ænjʊˌeɪt/, /ˌsju:-/ *v.t.* перев|оди́ть, -ести́ на пе́нсию по ста́рости; **~d** (*of person*) вы́шедший на пе́нсию; (*fig.*) престаре́лый; (*of thing*) устаре́лый, вы́шедший в тира́ж (*coll.*).

superannuation /ˌsu:pərˌænjʊ'eɪʃ(ə)n/, /ˌsju:-/ *n.* (*of employee*) перево́д на пе́нсию по ста́рости; (*pension*) пе́нсия по ста́рости; (*payment*) регуля́рный пенсио́нный взнос.

superb /su:'pɜ:b/, /sju:-/ *adj.* превосхо́дный, великоле́пный.

supercargo /'su:pəˌkɑ:gəʊ/, /'sju:-/ *n.* (*pl.* **~es** *or* **~s**) (*naut.*) суперка́рго (*m. indecl.*).

supercharge /'su:pəˌtʃɑ:dʒ/, /'sju:-/ *v.t.*: **~d engine** дви́гатель (*m.*) с надду́вом.

supercharger /'su:pəˌtʃɑ:dʒə(r)/, /'sju:-/ *n.* нагнета́тель (*m.*); компре́ссор надду́ва.

supercilious /ˌsu:pə'sɪlɪəs/, /ˌsju:-/ *adj.* высокоме́рный, надме́нный, презри́тельный.

superciliousness /ˌsu:pə'sɪlɪəsnɪs/, /ˌsju:-/ *n.* высокоме́рие, надме́нность, презри́тельность.

supercomputer /'su:pəkəmˌpju:tə(r)/, /'sju:-/ *n.* су́пер-ЭВМ, су́пер-компью́тер.

superconductivity /ˌsu:pəˌkɒndʌk'tɪvɪtɪ/, /ˌsju:-/ *n.* сверхпроводи́мость.

superconductor /ˌsu:pəkən'dʌktə(r)/, /ˌsju:-/ *n.* сверхпроводни́к.

supercontinent /'su:pəˌkɒntɪnənt/, /'sju:-/ *n.* протоконтине́нт.

supercooled /'su:pəˌku:ld/, /-'ku:ld/, /'sju:-/ *adj.* переохлаждённый.

superego /ˌsu:pər'i:gəʊ/, /-'egəʊ/, /ˌsju:-/ *n.* (*pl.* **~s**) сверх-я́ (*nt. indecl.*).

supererogation /ˌsu:pərˌerə'geɪʃ(ə)n/, /ˌsju:-/ *n.* выполне́ние ли́шнего; **works of ~** (*rel.*) сверхдо́лжные до́брые дела́.

supererogatory /ˌsu:pərɪ'rɒgətərɪ/, /ˌsju:-/ *adj.* изли́шний; превыша́ющий тре́бование до́лга.

superficial /ˌsu:pə'fɪʃ(ə)l/, /ˌsju:-/ *adj.* (*lit., fig.*) пове́рхностный.

superficiality /ˌsu:pəˌfɪʃɪ'ælɪtɪ/, /ˌsju:-/ *n.* пове́рхностность.

superfine /'su:pəˌfaɪn/, /'sju:-/ *adj.* (*highly refined*) тонча́йший; (*of high quality*) (наи)вы́сшего ка́чества.

superfluity /ˌsu:pə'flu:ɪtɪ/, /ˌsju:-/ *n.* изли́шек.

superfluous /su:'pɜ:flʊəs/, /sju:-/ *adj.* изли́шний.

superheat /ˌsu:pə'hi:t/, /ˌsju:-/ *v.t.* перегр|ева́ть, -е́ть.

superhuman /ˌsu:pə'hju:mən/, /ˌsju:-/ *adj.* сверхчелове́ческий.

superimpose /ˌsu:pərɪm'pəʊz/, /ˌsju:-/ *v.t.* на|кла́дывать, -ложи́ть (*что на что*).

superintend /ˌsu:pərɪn'tend/, /ˌsju:-/ *v.t. & i.* заве́довать (*impf.*) (*чем*); управля́ть (*impf.*) (*кем/чем*); надзира́ть (*impf.*) за (*кем/чем*).

superintendence /ˌsu:pərɪn'tend(ə)ns/, /ˌsju:-/ *n.* заве́дование (+*i.*); управле́ние (+*i.*); надзо́р (за+*i.*).

superintendent /ˌsu:pərɪn'tend(ə)nt/, /ˌsju:-/ *n.* (*manager*) заве́дующий, управля́ющий; (*of police*) нача́льник; (*US, of a building*) коменда́нт.

superior /su:'pɪərɪə(r)/, /sju:-/, /sʊ-/ *n.* **1** (*person of higher rank*) ста́рший, нача́льник; (*better*): **he is his brother's ~ in every way** он во всём превосхо́дит своего́ бра́та. **2** (*relig.*) настоя́тель (*fem.* -ница); **father ~** (оте́ц-)игу́мен; **mother ~** (мать-)игу́менья.

● *adj.* **1** (*of higher rank or status*) ста́рший, вы́сший; **~ officer** ста́рший офице́р; **~ court** вы́сшая (суде́бная) инста́нция. **2** (*of better quality, better*) превосхо́дный, превосходя́щий; вы́сшего ка́чества; **~ skill** вы́сшее мастерство́; **this cloth is ~ to that** э́то сукно́ лу́чше того́. **3** (*conscious of superiority, supercilious*): **a ~ smile** презри́тельная улы́бка; улы́бка превосхо́дства; **don't look so ~!** бро́сьте э́ту ва́шу высокоме́рную

S

манéру! **4** (*greater in number*) превосходя́щий. **5** (*typ.*) надстрóчный.

superiority /su:,pɪərɪ'ɒrɪtɪ/, /sju:-/, /sʊ-/ *n.* (*of rank*) старшинствó; (*of quality or quantity*) превосхóдство.

superlative /su:'pɜ:lətɪv/, /sju:-/ *n.* (*gram.*) превосхóдная стéпень; **talk in ~s** говори́ть (*impf.*) в преувели́ченных выражéниях.

● *adj.* **1** (*excellent*) величáйший, высочáйший; **~ beauty** необыкновéнная красотá. **2** (*gram.*) превосхóдный.

superman /'su:pə,mæn/, /'sju:-/ *n.* (*pl.* **supermen**) сверхчеловéк, супермéн.

supermarket /'su:pə,mɑ:kɪt/, /'sju:-/ *n.* магази́н самообслу́живания, универсáм, супермáркет.

supermodel /'su:pə,mɒd(ə)l/, /'sju:-/ *n.* супермодéль.

supernatural /,su:pə'nætʃər(ə)l/, /,sju:-/ *n.*: **a belief in the ~** вéра в сверхъестéственное.

● *adj.* сверхъестéственный.

superno|va /,su:pə'nəʊvə/, /,sju:-/ *n.* (*pl.* **~vae** /-vi:/ *or* **~vas**) сверхнóвая (звездá).

supernumerary /,su:pə'nju:mərərɪ/, /,sju:-/ *n.* сверхштáтный рабóтник; (*actor*) стати́ст (*fem.* -ка).

● *adj.* сверхштáтный.

superpower /'su:pə,paʊə(r)/, /'sju:-/ *n.* сверхдержáва.

supersaturate /,su:pə'sætʃə,reɪt/, /,sju:-/, /-tjʊ,reɪt/ *v.t.* перес|ыщáть, -ы́тить.

superscript /'su:pəskrɪpt/, /'sju:-/ *adj.* (*math. etc.*) надстрóчный.

supersede /,su:pə'si:d/, /,sju:-/ *v.t.* (*replace*) смен|я́ть, -и́ть; замен|я́ть, -и́ть.

supersensitive /,su:pə'sensɪtɪv/, /,sju:-/ *adj.* сверхчувстви́тельный.

supersonic /,su:pə'sɒnɪk/, /,sju:-/ *adj.* сверхзвуковóй.

superstar /'su:pə,stɑ:(r)/, /'sju:-/ *n.* суперзвездá.

superstate /'su:pəsteɪt/, /'sju:-/ *n.* сверхдержáва.

superstition /,su:pə'stɪʃ(ə)n/, /,sju:-/ *n.* суевéрие.

superstitious /,su:pə'stɪʃəs/, /,sju:-/ *adj.* суевéрный.

superstore /'su:pə,stɔ:(r)/, /'sju:-/ *n.* гигáнтский универмáг.

superstructure /'su:pə,strʌktʃə(r)/, /'sju:-/ *n.* надстрóйка.

supertanker /'su:pə,tæŋkə(r)/, /'sju:-/ *n.* супертáнкер.

supertonic /,su:pə'tɒnɪk/, /,sju:-/ *n.* вéрхний ввóдный тон.

supervene /,su:pə'vi:n/, /,sju:-/ *v.i.* слéдовать, по-.

supervise /'su:pə,vaɪz/, /'sju:-/ *v.t.* надзирáть (*impf.*) за + *i.*; наблюдáть (*impf.*) за + *i.*

supervision /,su:pə'vɪʒ(ə)n/, /,sju:-/ *n.* надсмóтр/надзóр (за + *i.*).

supervisor /'su:pə,vaɪzə(r)/, /'sju:-/ *n.* надсмóтрщи|к (*fem.* -ца); надзирáтель (*fem.* -ница); (*acad.*) (наýчн|ый) руководи́тель (*fem.* -ая -ница).

supervisory /'su:pə,vaɪzərɪ/, /'sju:-/ *adj.* контрóльный, надзирáющий; **~ body** контрóльный óрган; **~ duties** обя́занности по надзóру.

supine /'su:paɪn/, /'sju:-/ *adj.* (*face up*) лежáщий нáвзничь; (*fig.*) бездéятельный, инéртный, вя́лый.

supper /'sʌpə(r)/ *n.* у́жин; **have ~** у́жинать, по-; **the Last S~** Тáйная вéчеря.

supplant /sə'plɑ:nt/ *v.t.* (*replace*) вытесня́ть, вы́теснить; (*oust*) выживáть, вы́жить.

supple /'sʌp(ə)l/ *adj.* (**suppler, supplest**) (*flexible, pliant*) ги́бкий; **~ limbs** ги́бкие члéны; (*soft*) мя́гкий; **~ leather** мя́гкая кóжа.

supplement[1] /'sʌplɪmənt/ *n.* **1** (*dietary*) добáвка. **2** (*of book etc.*) дополнéние, приложéние. **3** (*surcharge*) доплáта.

supplement[2] /'sʌplɪ,ment/, /,sʌplɪ'ment/ *v.t.* доп|олня́ть, -óлнить; поп|олня́ть, -óлнить.

supplementary /,sʌplɪ'mentərɪ/ *adj.* дополни́тельный, добáвочный.

suppleness /'sʌpəlnɪs/ *n.* ги́бкость, мя́гкость.

suppliant /'sʌplɪənt/ *n.* проси́тель (*fem.* -ница).

● *adj.* проси́тельный, умоля́ющий.

supplicate /'sʌplɪ,keɪt/ *v.i.* моли́ть, умоля́ть (*both impf.*).

supplication /,sʌplɪ'keɪʃ(ə)n/ *n.* мольбá, прóсьба.

supplier /sə'plaɪə(r)/ *n.* поставщи́|к (*fem.* -ца).

suppl|y /sə'plaɪ/ *n.* **1** (*providing*) снабжéние (*чем*). **2** (*thing supplied, stock*) запáс; **have you a good ~y of food?** у вас достáточно продовóльствия?; **water ~y** водоснабжéние; **take, lay in a ~y of something** запас|áться, -ти́сь чем-н.; **bread is in short ~y** хлеб в дефици́те; **a commodity in short ~y** дефици́тный товáр; **~ies** (*mil.*) (бое)припáсы (*m. pl.*). **3** (*econ.*): **~y and demand** спрóс и предложéние. **4**: **~y teacher** (*Br.*) внештáтн|ый учи́тель, рабóтающ|ий (*fem.* -ая, -ница, -ая) по замещéнию.

● *v.t.* **1** (*furnish, equip*) снаб|жáть, -ди́ть; обеспéчи|вать, -ть (*both кого/что чем*); питáть (*impf.*); **the farm ~ies us with potatoes** фéрма обеспéчивает/снабжáет нас картóфелем; **arteries ~y the heart with blood** артéрии доставля́ют крóвь к сéрдцу. **2** (*give, yield*) да|вáть, -ть; дост|авля́ть, -áвить (*что кому/чему*); **cows ~y milk** корóвы даю́т молокó; **I wrote the music, he ~ied the words** я написáл му́зыку, он сочини́л словá (к ней); **can you ~y a reason?** вы мóжете привести́ дóвод?; **catalogue** (*Br.*), **catalog** (*US*) **~ied on request** каталóг выдаётся по трéбованию. **3** (*meet need*): **that will ~y everybody's needs** э́то удовлетворя́ет всех (*or* ну́жды всегó óбщества).

support /sə'pɔ:t/ *n.* **1** (*aid*) поддéржка; **walk without ~** ходи́ть (*indet.*) без поддéржки; **I hope for your ~** я надéюсь/рассчи́тываю на вáшу поддéржку; **give, lend ~** окáз|ывать, -áть поддéржку + *d.*; **in ~ of** в поддéржку + *g.*; **without visible means of ~** без определённых средств к существовáнию. **2** (*lit., fig., prop*) опóра; **shelf ~** кронштéйн для пóлки; **the sole ~ of his family** еди́нственная опóра семьи́.

● *v.t.* **1** (*hold up, prop up*) поддéрж|ивать, -áть; подп|ирáть, -ерéть; **pillars ~ing the roof** колóнны, поддéрживающие кры́шу; **he ~ed his chin on his hand** он подпирáл рукóй подборóдок; **~ o.s. with a stick** оп|ирáться, -ерéться на пáлку; (*fig., assist by deed or word*): **which party do you ~?** какýю пáртию вы поддéрживаете?; **~ing actor** актёр вспомогáтельного состáва (*or* на вторы́х роля́х); **~ing film** кинофи́льм, демонстри́рующийся в дополнéние к основнóму; (*sustain*): **air is necessary to ~ life** вóздух необходи́м для поддержáния жи́зни. **2** (*provide subsistence for*) содержáть (*impf.*); **he cannot ~ a family** он не в состоя́нии содержáть семью́. **3** (*confirm*) подкреп|ля́ть, -и́ть; **his theory is not ~ed by the facts** егó теóрия не подкрепля́ется фáктами. **4** (*endure*) выдéрживать, вы́держать; **I cannot ~ his insolence** я не выношý егó высокомéрия. **5** (*a particular sports team*) болéть (*impf.*) за + *a.*

supporter /sə'pɔ:tə(r)/ *n.* (*of cause, motion etc.*) сторóнни|к (*fem.* -ца), привéрженец; (*Br., of sports team*) болéльщи|к (*fem.* -ца); **athletic ~** (*US, jock-strap*) суспензóрий.

supportive /sə'pɔ:tɪv/ *adj.* поддéрживающий, лоя́льный.

suppose /sə'pəʊz/ *v.t.* **1** (*assume*) предпол|агáть, -ожи́ть; допус|кáть, -ти́ть; **let us ~ what you say is true** предполóжим, что вы говори́те прáвду; **supposing he came, what would you say?** éсли бы он пришёл, что бы вы сказáли?; допу́стим/предполóжим, что он придёт, что вы (тогдá) скáжете?; **~ it rains?** а что éсли пойдёт дóждь?; **~ they find out?** а вдруг они узнáют?; **everyone is ~d to know the rules** предполагáется, что все знакóмы с прáвилами. **2** (*imagine, believe*): **I ~ him to be about sixty** я полагáю, что емý лет шестьдеся́т; **he is ~d to be rich** считáется/говоря́т, что он богáт; **I ~ you like Moscow** вам, навéрное, нрáвится Москвá; **I don't ~ he will mind that** не дýмаю, что он бýдет прóтив э́того; **what do you ~ he meant?** как по-вáшему, чтó он имéл в видý?; **I ~ so** навéрное; должнó быть. **3** (*expr. suggestion*): **~ we take a holiday?** давáйте возьмём óтпуск?; **~ you lend me a pound?** не дади́те ли вы мне фунт взаймы́? **4** (*presuppose*): **success ~s ability and training** успéх невозмóжен без

способностей и подготовки.
5 (*pass., be expected, required*): **this is ~d to help you sleep** это должно помочь вам заснуть; **he is ~d to wash the dishes** ему положено мыть посуду; **he was ~d to lock the door** он должен был запереть дверь; **you are ~d to hold the cup like this** чашку следует держать (вот) так; **you are not ~d to talk in the library** в библиотеке не полагается разговаривать; **how was I ~d to know?** откуда мне было знать?
6 (*p.p., presumed*) предполагаемый, мнимый.

supposition /ˌsʌpəˈzɪʃ(ə)n/ *n.* предположение, гипотеза, догадка.

suppository /səˈpɒzɪtərɪ/ *n.* суппозиторий, свечка.

suppress /səˈpres/ *v.t.* **1** подав|лять, -ить; сдерж|ивать, -ать; **the rebellion was ~ed** восстание было подавлено; **she could hardly ~ a smile** она с трудом подавила/сдержала улыбку; **~ing a yawn** подавляя зевоту. **2** (*stop publication of*) запре|щать, -тить; **his article was ~ed** публикация его статьи была запрещена. **3** (*conceal*) скры|вать, -ть; зам|алчивать, -олчать; **they succeeded in ~ing the truth** им удалось скрыть/замолчать правду.

suppression /səˈpreʃ(ə)n/ *n.* (*restraining*) подавление, сдерживание; (*banning*) запрещение; (*silencing*) замалчивание.

suppurate /ˈsʌpjʊˌreɪt/ *v.i.* гноиться, за-/на-.

suppuration /ˌsʌpjʊˈreɪʃ(ə)n/ *n.* нагноение.

supra- /ˈsu:prə/, /ˈsju:-/ *pref.* сверх(ъ)...

supremacist /su:ˈpreməsɪst/, /sju:-/ *n.*: **white ~** сторонник господства белых.

supremacy /su:ˈpreməsɪ/, /sju:-/ *n.* господство, превосходство.

supreme /su:ˈpri:m/, /sju:-/ *adj.* **1** (*of authority*) верховный; **S~ Soviet of the USSR** (*hist.*) Верховный Совет СССР; **~ power** верховная власть; **he reigned ~** он властвовал безраздельно. **2** (*utmost, greatest, highest*): **he made the ~ sacrifice** он пожертвовал жизнью; **~ test of fidelity** высшее испытание верности; **he was ~ly confident** он был в высшей степени уверен в себе; **~ly happy** на верху блаженства.

supremo /su:ˈpri:məʊ/, /sju:-/ *n.* (*pl.* **~s**) (*Br.*) верховный глава; диктатор.

Supt. /ˌsu:pərɪnˈtend(ə)nt/, /ˌsju:-/ *n.* (*abbr. of* ***Superintendent***) комендант, управляющий.

surcharge¹ /ˈsɜ:tʃɑ:dʒ/ *n.* **1** (*extra fee*) доплата, приплата. **2** (*penalty*) штраф.

surcharge² /ˈsɜ:tʃɑ:dʒ/, /-ˈtʃɑ:dʒ/ *v.t.* (*exact* **~¹** *from*) взыск|ивать, -ать с + *g.*; взимать (*impf.*) у + *g.*

sure /ʃʊə(r)/, /ʃɔ:(r)/ *adj.* **1** (*convinced, certain, confident*) уверенный, убеждённый; **a ~ hand** твёрдая рука; **a ~ step** уверенный шаг; **feel ~ of something** чувствовать/испытывать (*impf.*) уверенность в чём-н.; **he is ~** (*confident*) **of success** он уверен в (своём) успехе; **if he comes he is ~ of a welcome** если он придёт, он может не сомневаться в тёплом приёме; **you can be ~ of one thing ...** в одном можно быть уверенным...; одно несомненно...; **he is very ~ of himself** он очень уверен в себе; **I'm ~ you are right** я уверен (*or* не сомневаюсь), что вы правы; **I'm not ~ whether to go or not** я не знаю, пойти или нет; **how can I be ~ he is honest?** откуда я знаю, что он честен?
2 (*safe, reliable, trusty, unfailing*) верный, надёжный; **a ~ shot** меткий стрелок; **a ~ way to break one's neck** верный способ сломать себе шею; **there can be no ~ proof** абсолютных доказательств не может быть.
3 (*with inf., certain, to be relied on*): **he is ~ to come** он непременно придёт; **be ~ to lock the door** не забудьте запереть дверь!; **be ~ and write to me** смотрите напишите мне!; **it is ~ to be wet** наверняка будет дождливо; **~ thing!** (*coll.*) конечно!; обязательно!; ещё бы!
4 (*undoubtedly true*) несомненный, уверенный; **one thing is ~** в одном можно не сомневаться.
5: **for ~** несомненно, непременно; точно, наверняка; **to be ~** (*concessive*) конечно, разумеется, правда; (*confirmatory*) в самом деле.
6: **make ~** (*convince, satisfy o.s.*) убе|ждаться, -диться; удостов|еряться, -ериться (*all в чём*); **you must make ~ of your facts** вы должны проверить все факты; **I made ~ no-one was following me** я (сперва) удостоверился в том, что за мной никто не идёт.
7: **I made ~** (*ensured*) **that he would come** я позаботился о том, чтобы он (непременно) пришёл; **we must make ~ of a house before winter** мы должны обеспечить себя жильём до наступления зимы.
● *adv.*: **~ enough** действительно, конечно; **he will come ~ enough** он конечно придёт; **and ~ enough he fell down** и, конечно/разумеется, он упал; **it ~ was cold!** (*US*) до чего же было холодно!
● *cpds.* **~-fire** *adj.* верный, надёжный; **~-footed** *adj.* твёрдо стоящий на ногах; с уверенной походкой.

surely /ˈʃʊəlɪ/ *adv.* **1** (*securely*) надёжно; **slowly but ~** медленно, но верно. **2** (*without doubt*) несомненно, верно, наверняка. **3** (*expr. strong hope or belief*): **this must ~ be his last appearance** уж это должно быть наверняка его последнее выступление; **~ I have met you before** я уверен, что мы с вами встречались; **~ you saw him?** неужели вы его не видели?; **~ you weren't offended?** неужели вы обиделись?; **you ~ don't want to disappoint him** ведь вы не захотите его разочаровать(, не правда ли)?; **~ the drought can't last much longer** не может быть, чтобы засуха затянулась надолго. **4** (*as answer, certainly*) конечно, непременно.

surety /ˈʃʊərɪtɪ/, /ˈʃʊətɪ/ *n.* **1** (*pledge*) залог. **2** (*person*) поручитель (*fem.* -ница); **stand ~ for s.o.** ручаться, поручиться за кого-н.; брать, взять кого-н. на поруки.

surf /sɜ:f/ *n.* прибой, буруны (*m. pl.*).
● *v.i.* заниматься (*impf.*) серфингом.
● *v.t.*: **~ the Internet** путешествовать (*impf.*) по Интернету.
● *cpd.* **~-board** *n.* доска для серфинга.

surface /ˈsɜ:fɪs/ *n.* **1** поверхность; **the earth's ~** поверхность земли; **beneath the ~** (*lit.*) под поверхностью; (*fig.*) за внешностью; **come to the ~** (*lit.*) всплы|вать, -ть (на поверхность); (*fig.*) обнаружи|ваться, -ться; **his politeness is only on the ~** его любезность чисто внешняя. **2** (*attr.*) поверхностный, внешний; **~ mail** обычная почта; **~ tension** поверхностное натяжение.
● *v.t.*: **~ a road** покр|ывать, -ыть дорогу асфальтом (*и т.п.*).
● *v.i.* (*of submarine, swimmer etc.*) вспл|ывать, -ыть на поверхность.
● *cpd.* **~-to-air** *adj.* зенитный, типа «земля-воздух».

surfeit /ˈsɜ:fɪt/ *n.* (*excess of eating etc.*) излишество, избыток; (*repletion, satiety; also fig.*) пресыщение.
● *v.t.* (**surfeited, surfeiting**) (*satiate*) прес|ыщать, -ытить.

surfer /ˈsɜ:fə(r)/ *n.* серфингист; человек, занимающийся серфингом.

surfing /ˈsɜ:fɪŋ/ *n.* серфинг.

surge /sɜ:dʒ/ *n.* (*of waves, water*) волны (*f. pl.*); вал; (*of crowd, emotion etc.*) волна, прилив; (*of elec. current*) импульс.
● *v.i.* **1** (*of waves, water*) вздыматься (*impf.*). **2** (*of crowd*): **the crowd ~d forward** толпа подалась вперёд. **3** (*of emotions*) нахлынуть (*pf.*); **anger ~d within her** в душе у неё поднимался/закипал гнев.

surgeon /ˈsɜ:dʒ(ə)n/ *n.* хирург; **dental ~** зубной врач; (хирург-)стоматолог.

surgery /ˈsɜ:dʒərɪ/ *n.* **1** (*treatment*) хирургия; **minor/major ~** малая/большая хирургия; (*operation*) операция. **2** (*Br., office*) приёмная/кабинет (врача); **in ~ hours** в приёмные часы; **the doctor holds a ~ every morning** врач принимает каждое утро.

surgical /ˈsɜ:dʒɪk(ə)l/ *adj.* хирургический; **~ boot** ортопедический ботинок; **~ spirit** (*Br.*) медицинский спирт.

surliness /ˈsɜ:lɪnɪs/ *n.* грубость, неприветливость.

surly /ˈsɜ:lɪ/ *adj.* (**surlier, surliest**) неприветливый, хмурый, угрюмый.

surmise /səˈmaɪz/ *n.* (*conjecture*) догадка; (*supposition*) предположение.
● *v.t.* предпол|агать, -ожить.
● *v.i.* догад|ываться, -аться.

surmount /səˈmaʊnt/ *v.t.* **1** (*overcome*) преодол|евать, -еть. **2**: **peaks ~ed with snow** горные вершины, увенчанные снегом.

S

surmountable /səˈmaʊntəb(ə)l/ *adj.* преодоли́мый.

surname /ˈsɜːneɪm/ *n.* фами́лия.

surpass /səˈpɑːs/ *v.t.* прев|осходи́ть, -зойти́; **he ~ed everyone in strength** он превосходи́л всех си́лой; **a woman of ~ing beauty** же́нщина непревзойдённой красоты́.

surplice /ˈsɜːplɪs/ *n.* стиха́рь (*m.*).

surplus /ˈsɜːpləs/ *n.* (*excess*) изли́шек; (*residue*) оста́ток; **in ~** в избы́тке.

● *adj.* **1** (*excess*) изли́шний, избы́точный; **~ food** изли́шки (*m. pl.*) продово́льствия; **~ to our requirements** бо́льше, чем (нам) тре́буется. **2** (*remaining*) оста́точный; **~ value** приба́вочная сто́имость.

surprise /səˈpraɪz/ *n.* **1** (*wonder, astonishment*) удивле́ние; **show ~** выка́зывать, вы́казать удивле́ние; удив|ля́ться, -и́ться; **to my ~** к моему́ удивле́нию; **he looked up in ~** он взгляну́л с удивле́нием. **2** (*unexpected events, news, gift etc.*) неожи́данность, сюрпри́з; **his arrival was a ~ to us all** его́ прие́зд был для нас всех неожи́данностью; **I had the ~ of my life** я был соверше́нно поражён; **give s.o. a ~** устр|а́ивать, -о́ить кому́-н. сюрпри́з. **3** (*unexpected action*): **catch, take s.o. by ~** заст|ига́ть, -и́чь кого́-н. врасплóх. **4** (*attr.*) неожи́данный, внеза́пный; **~ visit** неожи́данный визи́т; **~ attack** внеза́пная ата́ка; **~ package, packet** сюрпри́з.

● *v.t.* **1** (*astonish*) удив|ля́ть, -и́ть; пора|жа́ть, -зи́ть; **I'm ~d at you!** вы меня́ удивля́ете!; я э́того от вас не ожида́л; **I was ~d to hear you had been ill** я с удивле́нием узна́л, что вы бы́ли больны́ (*or* боле́ли); **you'd be ~d how much it costs** вы не пове́рите, до чего́ э́то до́рого; **I'm ~d you didn't know that already** удивля́юсь, как вы э́того не зна́ли; **it's nothing to be ~d at** в э́том нет ничего́ удиви́тельного; **I shouldn't be ~d if ...** я (ниско́лько) не удивлю́сь, е́сли.... **2** (*by unexpected gift etc.*) де́лать, с-/устр|а́ивать, -о́ить/приподн|оси́ть, -ести́ сюрпри́з +*d.* **3** (*capture by ~*) захва́т|ывать, -и́ть врасплóх; (*liter., take by ~*) заст|ига́ть, -и́чь (*or* заст|ава́ть, -а́ть) (врасплóх); **we ~d him in the act of stealing** мы его́ пойма́ли с поли́чным; **the storm ~d us when we were half-way home** бу́ря засти́гла нас на полпути́ к до́му.

surprising /səˈpraɪzɪŋ/ *adj.* удиви́тельный, порази́тельный; **~ though it may seem** как ни удиви́тельно; **he eats ~ly little** он удиви́тельно ма́ло ест.

surreal /səˈrɪəl/ *adj.* сюрреалисти́ческий.

surrealism /səˈrɪəˌlɪz(ə)m/ *n.* сюрреали́зм.

surrealist /səˈrɪəlɪst/ *n.* сюрреали́ст.

● *adj.* сюрреалисти́ческий.

surrender /səˈrendə(r)/ *n.* (*handing over*) сда́ча; (*giving up*) отка́з (от +*g.*); усту́пка; **~ value** (*of policy*) су́мма, возвраща́емая лицу́, отказа́вшемуся от страхово́го по́лиса; (*capitulation*) капитуля́ция; **unconditional ~** безогово́рочная капитуля́ция.

● *v.t.* **1** (*yield*) сда|ва́ть, -ть; **the fort was ~ed to the enemy** кре́пость была́ сдана́ неприя́телю. **2** (*give up*) отка́з|ываться, -а́ться от +*g.* **3**: **~ o.s.**: **he ~ed himself to justice** он отда́лся в ру́ки правосу́дия; **she ~ed herself to despair** она́ предала́сь отча́янию.

● *v.i.* сд|ава́ться, -а́ться; капитули́ровать (*impf., pf.*).

surreptitious /ˌsʌrəpˈtɪʃəs/ *adj.* та́йный; сде́ланный исподтишка́.

surrogate /ˈsʌrəgət/ *n.* суррога́т; **~ mother** суррога́тная мать.

surround /səˈraʊnd/ *n.* бордю́р, окаймле́ние.

● *v.t.* окруж|а́ть, -и́ть; обступ|а́ть, -и́ть; **the ~ing countryside** окружа́ющая ме́стность; окре́стности (*f. pl.*); **the troops were ~ed** войска́ бы́ли окружены́.

surroundings /səˈraʊndɪŋz/ *n.* (*material environment*) ме́стность, окре́стности (*f. pl.*); обстано́вка; (*intellectual environment*) среда́, окруже́ние.

surtax /ˈsɜːtæks/ *n.* доба́вочный подохо́дный нало́г.

surveillance /sɜːˈveɪləns/ *n.* надзо́р; **under ~** под надзо́ром (поли́ции).

survey[1] /ˈsɜːveɪ/ *n.* **1** (*general view, description*) обзо́р, обозре́ние; (*inspection, investigation*) иссле́дование, обсле́дование; **we are carrying out a ~ on the dangers of smoking** мы прово́дим иссле́дование по вопро́су о вреде́ куре́ния; (*Br., of building*) техни́ческая инспе́кция; (*by asking questions*) опро́с. **2** (*of land*) съёмка, проме́р; **they are making a ~ of our village** произво́дится (топографи́ческая/землеме́рная) съёмка на́шего села́. **3** (*plan, map*) план, ка́рта.

survey[2] /səˈveɪ/ *v.t.* **1** (*view*) обозр|ева́ть, -е́ть. **2** (*review, consider*) иссле́довать (*impf., pf.*); обсле́довать (*impf., pf.*); рассм|а́тривать, -отре́ть. **3** (*inspect*) осм|а́тривать, -отре́ть. **4** (*land etc.*) межева́ть (*impf.*); произв|оди́ть, -ести́ съёмку +*g.*; **the house was ~ed and valued** (*Br.*) бы́ли произведены́ осмо́тр и оце́нка до́ма.

surveying /səˈveɪɪŋ/ *n.* (топографи́ческая) съёмка; **photographic ~** фотосъёмка.

surveyor /səˈveɪə(r)/ *n.* **1** (*Br., of houses*) строи́тельный инспе́ктор. **2** (*of land etc.*) землеме́р.

survival /səˈvaɪv(ə)l/ *n.* **1** (*living on*) выжива́ние; **~ of the fittest** выжива́ние наибо́лее приспосо́бленных; **their ~ depended on us** их жизнь зави́села от нас; **~ kit** авари́йный компле́кт (средств жизнеобеспе́чения); **~ rate** сте́пень выжива́ния. **2** (*relic*) пережи́ток.

survive /səˈvaɪv/ *v.t.* **1** (*outlive*) переж|ива́ть, -и́ть; **he will ~ us all** он нас всех переживёт. **2** (*come alive through*): **~ an illness** перен|оси́ть, -ести́ боле́знь; **they ~d the shipwreck** они́ оста́лись в живы́х по́сле кораблекруше́ния; (*joc.*): **I see you ~d the exam** так вы пережи́ли экза́мен?

● *v.i.* (*continue to live*) выжива́ть, вы́жить; **not one of the family has ~d** из всей семьи́ никого́ не оста́лось (в живы́х); (*be preserved*): сохрани́ться, уцеле́ть (*both pf.*); **the custom still ~s** э́тот обы́чай ещё сохрани́лся.

survivor /səˈvaɪvə(r)/ *n.* уцеле́вший; **the ~s of the earthquake** уцеле́вшие по́сле землетрясе́ния; **he was the sole ~** он оди́н оста́лся в живы́х.

susceptibilit|y /səˌseptɪˈbɪlɪtɪ/ *n.* (*to disease etc.*) восприи́мчивость (к боле́зни *и т.п.*).

susceptible /səˈseptɪb(ə)l/ *adj.* **1** (*impressionable*) впечатли́тельный, восприи́мчивый. **2**: **~ to** восприи́мчивый к +*d.*; па́дкий на +*a.*; **he is ~ to colds** он подве́ржен просту́де; **he is ~ to flattery** он па́док на лесть.

suspect[1] /ˈsʌspekt/ *n.* подозрева́емый.

● *adj.* подозри́тельный; не внуша́ющий дове́рия.

suspect[2] /səˈspekt/ *v.t.* **1** подозрева́ть (*impf.*); (*apprehend*) предчу́вствовать (*impf.*); предпол|ага́ть, -ожи́ть; **they ~ed a plot** они́ подозрева́ли за́говор; **I went in, ~ing nothing** я вошёл, ничего́ не подозрева́я; **I ~ it will rain before long** я подозрева́ю, что ско́ро пойдёт дождь; **you, I ~, don't care** вам, я полага́ю/подозрева́ю, всё равно́; **I ~ed that he was lying** я подозрева́л, что он лжёт; **a ~ed criminal** подозрева́емый. **2** (*disbelieve, doubt*) сомнева́ться, усомни́ться в +*p.*; **I ~ed (the truth of) his story** я сомнева́лся в и́стинности его́ расска́за.

suspend /səˈspend/ *v.t.* **1** (*hang up*) подве́|шивать, -сить; **the cage was ~ed from the ceiling** кле́тка была́ подве́шена к потолку́ (*or* свиса́ла с потолка́); **the balloon was ~ed in mid-air** возду́шный шар пови́с в во́здухе; **particles of dust ~ed in the air** части́цы пы́ли, взве́шенные в во́здухе. **2** (*postpone, delay, stop for a time*) вре́менно прекра|ща́ть, -ти́ть; приостан|а́вливать, -ови́ть; **~ judgement** (*fig.*) возде́рж|иваться, -а́ться от сужде́ния; **~ hostilities** приостан|а́вливать, -ови́ть вое́нные де́йствия; **state of ~ed animation** состоя́ние бесчу́вствия; **~ed sentence** усло́вный пригово́р. **3** (*debar temporarily from office etc.*) вре́менно отстран|я́ть, -и́ть; вре́менно исключ|а́ть, -и́ть; **the player was ~ed for three months** игрока́ отстрани́ли на три ме́сяца.

suspender /səˈspendə(r)/ *n.* **1** (*Br., for stockings*) рези́нка. **2** (*US, pl., braces*) подтя́ж|ки (*pl., g.* -ек); по́мочи|и (*pl., g.* -е́й).

● *cpd.* **~-belt** *n.* (*Br.*) (же́нский) по́яс с подвя́зками.

suspense /səˈspens/ *n.* напряже́ние, напряжённость; **keep s.o. in ~**

держа́ть (*impf.*) кого́-н. в неизве́стности; **I can't stand the ~** я не в состоя́нии вы́нести напряже́ние/неизве́стность/неопределённость.

suspenseful /sə'spensfʊl/ *adj.* трево́жный; (*film etc.*) захва́тывающий, завлека́тельный.

suspension /sə'spenʃ(ə)n/ *n.* **1** (*hanging*) подве́шивание; **~ bridge** подвесно́й/вися́чий мост. **2** (*of vehicle etc.*) подве́с. **3** (*chem.*) взве́шенное вещество́, суспе́нзия, взвесь. **4** (*stoppage*) приостановле́ние; **~ of nuclear tests** вре́менное прекраще́ние испыта́ний я́дерного ору́жия. **5** (*debarring from office etc.*) отстране́ние; **their goalkeeper faces ~** их вратарю́ грози́т (вре́менное) исключе́ние из кома́нды.

suspicion /sə'spɪʃ(ə)n/ *n.* **1** подозре́ние; **I had no ~ he was there** я не подозрева́л, что он там; **he was looked upon with ~** к нему́ относи́лись с подозре́нием; **arouse ~** возбу|жда́ть, -ди́ть подозре́ния; **above ~** вы́ше/вне подозре́ний; **under ~** под подозре́нием; **on ~ of murder** по подозре́нию в уби́йстве. **2** (*trace, nuance*) при́вкус, отте́нок; **a ~ of garlic** за́пах/при́вкус чеснока́; **a ~ of irony** тень ирo̓нии.

suspicious /sə'spɪʃəs/ *adj.* **1** (*mistrustful*) подозри́тельный, недове́рчивый (к + *d.*); **his silence made me ~** его́ молча́ние заста́вило меня́ насторожи́ться; **I became ~** я заподо́зрил нела́дное. **2** (*arousing suspicion*) подозри́тельный.

suss /sʌs/ *v.t.* (*Br. coll.*): **she's got him ~ed** она́ его́ раскуси́ла; **he ~ed out the best route** он разузна́л лу́чший маршру́т.

sustain /sə'steɪn/ *v.t.* **1** (*lit., fig., support*) подде́рж|ивать, -а́ть; **his diet was barely sufficient to ~ life** пита́ния едва́ хвата́ло на то, что́бы подде́рживать в нём жизнь; **hope alone ~ed him** он жил одно́й наде́ждой. **2** (*bear, endure*): **the bridge will not ~ heavy loads** мост не выде́рживает больши́х нагру́зок; **they ~ed the attack** они́ вы́держали ата́ку; они́ высто́яли. **3** (*undergo, suffer*) терпе́ть, по-; нести́, по-; **the enemy ~ed heavy losses** проти́вник понёс тяжёлые поте́ри; **~ an injury** перен|оси́ть, -ести́ тра́вму; получ|а́ть, -и́ть уве́чье. **4** (*keep going, maintain*): **~ a role** выде́рживать, вы́держать роль; **~ one's efforts** не ослабля́ть (*impf.*) уси́лий; **a ~ed effort** дли́тельное/непреры́вное уси́лие; **~ a note** (*mus.*) держа́ть (*impf.*) но́ту. **5** (*uphold*) подтвер|жда́ть, -ди́ть; **~ an objection** прин|има́ть, -я́ть возраже́ние.

sustenance /'sʌstɪnəns/ *n.* пита́ние, пи́ща.

suture /'su:tʃə(r)/ *n.* **1** (*anat.*) шов. **2** (*surg., stitching*) наложе́ние шва; (*thread*) нить (для сшива́ния ра́ны).

● *v.t.* на|кла́дывать, -ложи́ть шов на + *a.*; заш|ива́ть, -и́ть (*рану*).

suzerain /'su:zərən/ *n.* сюзере́н.

suzerainty /'su:zərəntɪ/ *n.* сюзеренитéт.

s.v. (*abbr. of* ***sub voce***) под сло́вом.

svelte /svelt/ *adj.* стро́йный, ги́бкий.

SW (*abbr. of* ***short wave***) КВ (коро́ткие во́лны).

swab /swɒb/ *n.* **1** (*mop etc.*) шва́бра. **2** (*surg.*) тампо́н. **3** (*med., specimen*) мазо́к.

● *v.t.* (**swabbed, swabbing**) мыть, вы- шва́брой; подт|ира́ть, -ере́ть.

swaddl|e /'swɒd(ə)l/ *v.t.* пелена́ть, с-; сви|ва́ть, -ть; **~ing-clothes** пелёнки (*f. pl.*), свива́льник.

swag /swæg/ *n.* (*festoon*) гирля́нда (*из цветов, плодов и т.п.*); (*sl., booty*) награ́бленная добы́ча.

swagger /'swægə(r)/ *n.* (*gait*) ва́жная похо́дка; **walk with a ~** расха́живать (*impf.*) с ва́жным ви́дом.

● *v.i.* **1** (*of walk*) расха́живать (*impf.*) с ва́жным ви́дом. **2** (*of manner*) ва́жничать (*impf.*). **3** (*boast*) хва́стать(ся) (*impf.*).

Swahili /swə'hi:lɪ/, /swɑ:'hi:lɪ/ *n.* (*pl.* **~**) (*people, language*) суахи́ли (*m. indecl.*).

swain /sweɪn/ *n.* (*arch. or joc.*) **1** (*lover*) ухажёр, обожа́тель (*m.*). **2** (*rustic*) деревéнский па́рень.

swallow¹ /'swɒləʊ/ *n.* (*bird*) ла́сточка; **one ~ does not make a summer** одна́ ла́сточка весны́ не де́лает.

● *cpds.* **~-dive** (*US* **swan-dive**) *n.* прыжо́к в во́ду ла́сточкой; **~-tail** *n.* (*butterfly*) ба́бочка-па́русник; **~-tailed** *adj.* с раздвоённым хвосто́м.

swallow² /'swɒləʊ/ *n.* (*gulp*) глото́к; **at one ~** одни́м глотко́м; за́лпом.

● *v.t.* **1** прогл|а́тывать, -оти́ть; загл|а́тывать, -ота́ть; **he ~ed the vodka at one go** он вы́пил во́дку за́лпом; **~ the bait** (*fig.*) поп|ада́ться, -а́сться на у́дочку; **I made him ~ his words** я заста́вил его́ взять свои́ слова́ наза́д; **he had to ~ his pride** ему́ пришло́сь проглоти́ть своё самолю́бие; **she will ~ the most outrageous tales** она́ гото́ва пове́рить са́мым фантасти́ческим ро́ссказням. **2** (*usu.* **~ up**: *engulf, absorb*) погло|ща́ть, -ти́ть; **the expenses ~ed up the earnings** расхо́ды поглоти́ли весь за́работок; **she wished the earth would ~ her up** она́ была́ гото́ва провали́ться сквозь зе́млю.

● *v.i.* глота́ть (*impf.*); **he ~ed** он сглотну́л.

swam /swæm/ *past of* ⇨**swim**

swamp /swɒmp/ *n.* боло́то, топь.

● *v.t.* **1** (*fill, cover with water*) затоп|ля́ть, -и́ть; зал|ива́ть, -и́ть. **2** (*fig., overwhelm, inundate*) наводн|я́ть, -и́ть; зас|ыпа́ть, -ы́пать; **we were ~ed with applications** мы бы́ли зава́лены заявле́ниями.

swampy /'swɒmpɪ/ *adj.* (**swampier, swampiest**) боло́тистый, то́пкий.

swan /swɒn/ *n.* ле́бедь (*m.*).

● *v.i.* (**swanned, swanning**) (*Br.*) шата́ться (*impf.*) (*coll.*).

● *cpds.* **~-dive** *n.* (*US*) = **swallow-dive; ~sdown** *n.* лебя́жий пух; **~-song** *n.* лебеди́ная пе́снь.

swank /swæŋk/ (*coll.*) *n.* показу́ха.

● *v.i.*: **~ about something** хва́стать (*impf.*) чем-н.

swanky /'swæŋkɪ/ *adj.* (**swankier, swankiest**) шика́рный.

swap, swop /swɒp/ (*coll.*) *n.* обме́н; **do a ~** соверш|а́ть, -и́ть обме́н.

● *v.t.* (**swapped, swapping; swopped, swopping**) (*exchange for something else*) меня́ть, по- (**for**: на + *a.*); **he ~ped his car for a motorbike** он поменя́л маши́ну на мотоци́кл; (*exchange with s.o. else*) меня́ться, по- + *i.* (**with s.o.**: с + *i.*); **will you ~ places with me?** вы не поменя́етесь со мной места́ми?; **let's ~ watches** дава́й поменя́емся часа́ми; **they were ~ping jokes** они́ обме́нивались анекдо́тами; **~ horses in mid-stream** (*fig.*) меня́ть (*impf.*) коне́й на перепра́ве.

sward /swɔ:d/ *n.* (*liter.*) газо́н, дёрн.

swarm¹ /swɔ:m/ *n.*: **~ of ants/bees** муравьи́ный/пчели́ный рой; **~ of locusts** ста́я саранчи́.

● *v.i.* **1** (*of bees, ants etc.*) рои́ться (*impf.*). **2** (*of people*): **children came ~ing round him** де́ти столпи́лись вокру́г него́; **a crowd of people ~ed into the square** толпа́ наро́да хлы́нула на пло́щадь. **3** (*teem*) кише́ть (*impf.*) + *i.*; **the town is ~ing with tourists** го́род киши́т тури́стами.

swarm² /swɔ:m/ *v.t. & i.* кара́бкаться, вс-; **the sailors ~ed (up) the ropes** матро́сы вскара́бкались по ва́нтам.

swarthy /'swɔ:ðɪ/ *adj.* (**swarthier, swarthiest**) сму́глый.

swashbuckler /'swɒʃ,bʌklə(r)/ *n.* сорвиголова́ (*m.*).

swashbuckling /'swɒʃ,bʌklɪŋ/ *adj.* лихо́й, зади́ристый.

swastika /'swɒstɪkə/ *n.* сва́стика.

swat /swɒt/ *v.t.* (**swatted, swatting**) бить (*impf.*); прихло́п|ывать, -нуть.

SWAT /swɒt/ (*abbr. of* ***special weapons and tactics***) (*US*): **~ team** спецна́з.

swatch /swɒtʃ/ *n.* образе́ц, обра́зчик; образцы́ (*m. pl.*).

swath(e) /sweɪð/ *n.* проко́с.

swathe /sweɪð/ *v.t.* бинтова́ть, за-; заку́т|ывать, -ать.

swatter /'swɒtə(r)/ *n.* хлопу́шка (для мух), мухобо́йка.

sway /sweɪ/ *n.* **1** (**~ing motion**) кача́ние, колеба́ние. **2** (*influence*) влия́ние; (*authority*) авторите́т; (*rule*) власть; **have, hold ~ over s.o.** держа́ть (*impf.*) кого́-н. в подчине́нии.

● *v.t.* **1** (*rock*) кача́ть, качну́ть; колеба́ть, по-; **~ the balance in s.o.'s favour** (*Br.*), **favor** (*US*) склон|я́ть, -и́ть ча́шу весо́в в чью-н. по́льзу. **2** (*influence, move*) влия́ть, по-; колеба́ть, по-; **passions which ~ the minds of men** стра́сти, веду́щие на поводу́ челове́ческий ра́зум; **he**

S

cannot be ~ed by such arguments его́ нельзя́ поколеба́ть таки́ми до́водами.
● *v.i.* кача́ться, качну́ться; колеба́ться, по-.

Swaziland /'swɑ:zɪ,lænd/ *n.* Свазиле́нд.

swear /sweə(r)/ *v.t. & i.* (*past* **swore**; *p.p.* **sworn**) **1** (*pronounce, promise solemnly*) кля́сться, по-; божи́ться, по-; **he swore allegiance to the king** он покля́лся в ве́рности королю́; **they swore eternal friendship** они́ покляли́сь в ве́чной дру́жбе; **~ an oath** прин|оси́ть, -ести́ (*or* да|ва́ть, -ть) кля́тву; **I ~ to God (that)** ... кляну́сь (Го́сподом) Бо́гом, что. . . .
2 (*bind by an oath*) прив|оди́ть, -ести́ к прися́ге; **the jury was sworn in** прися́жных привели́ к прися́ге; **he was sworn to secrecy** с него́ взя́ли кля́тву о неразглаше́нии та́йны; **sworn enemies** закля́тые враги́.
● *v.i.* (*past* **swore**; *p.p.* **sworn**) **1** (*take an oath*) кля́сться, по-; (*fig.*): **he ~s by aspirin** он мо́лится на аспири́н; **~ off** (*abjure*): **he swore off smoking** он дал заро́к не кури́ть; **he swore to having seen the crime** он заяви́л под прися́гой, что был свиде́телем преступле́ния; **we may have met before, but I can't ~ to it** мы, ка́жется, знако́мы, но покля́сться не могу́.
2 (*use bad language, curse*) брани́ться (*impf.*); скверносло́вить (*impf.*); **~ like a trooper** руга́ться (*impf.*) как изво́зчик; **he swore at me for making him late** он руга́л меня́ на все ко́рки за то, что я заста́вил его́ опозда́ть.
● *cpd.* **~-word** *n.* руга́тельство.

swearing /'sweərɪŋ/ *n.* брань, руга́нь.

sweat /swet/ *n.* **1** пот, испа́рина; **by the ~ of one's brow** в по́те лица́ (своего́); **his brows were running, dripping with ~** пот кати́лся/ка́пал у него́ со лба́; **his shirt was dripping with ~** вся его́ руба́шка была́ по́тная, хоть выжима́й.
2 (*state or process of ~ing*) поте́ние, пот; **he was in a ~** (*lit., fig.*) он был (весь) в поту́; **a cold ~** холо́дный пот.
3 (*coll., drudgery*): **it is a ~ compiling a dictionary** что́бы соста́вить слова́рь, прихо́дится попоте́ть.
● *v.t.* (*past and p.p.* **sweated** *or US* **~**) **1** (*exude*) поте́ть (*impf.*) + *i.*; **~ blood** (*fig.*) рабо́тать (*impf.*) до крова́вого по́та.
2 (*force hard work from*): **~ed labour** (*Br.*), **labor** (*US*) потого́нный труд.
● *v.i.* (*past and p.p.* **sweated** *or US* **~**) (*lit., fig.*) поте́ть, вс-; **~ing-room** пари́льня, парна́я; **he was ~ing with fear** он был в холо́дном поту́ от стра́ха.
● *cpds.* **~-band** *n.* вну́тренняя ле́нта шля́пы; (*sportsman's*) потничо́к; **~-gland** *n.* потова́я железа́; **~-shirt** *n.* бума́жный (спорти́вный) сви́тер, толсто́вка; **~-shop** *n.* предприя́тие, на кото́ром существу́ет потого́нная систе́ма; **~suit** *n.* трениро́вочный костю́м.

sweater /'swetə(r)/ *n.* сви́тер.

sweaty /'swetɪ/ *adj.* (**sweatier, sweatiest**): **~ hands** по́тные ру́ки; **~ clothes** пропи́танная по́том (*or* по́тная/пропоте́вшая) оде́жда; **~ odour** (*Br.*), **odor** (*US*) за́пах по́та.

Swede /swi:d/ *n.* (*person*) швед (*fem.* -ка); (*s~: Br., vegetable*) брю́ква.

Sweden /'swi:d(ə)n/ *n.* Шве́ция.

Swedish /'swi:dɪʃ/ *n.* (*language*) шве́дский язы́к.
● *adj.* шве́дский.

sweep /swi:p/ *n.* **1** (*with broom etc.*): **give a room a good ~** хороше́нько подме|та́ть, -сти́ ко́мнату; (*fig.*): **make a clean ~** заб|ира́ть, -ра́ть/вымета́ть, вы́мести всё под метёлку.
2 (*steady movement*) ше́ствие, движе́ние; (*~ing movement*) взмах, разма́х; **~ of a scythe/sword** взмах серпа́/меча́; **~ of the arm** взмах руки́; **with one ~** одни́м ма́хом.
3 (*range, reach*) разма́х, диапазо́н.
4 (*long flowing curve*) изги́б; **~ of a river** изги́б/излу́чина реки́.
5 (**chimney-~**) трубочи́ст.
● *v.t.* (*past and p.p.* **swept**) **1** (*rush over*): **the waves swept the shore** во́лны набега́ли на бе́рег; **the storm swept the countryside** бу́ря пронесла́сь над всей окру́гой; **the new fashion ~ing the country** но́вая мо́да, охвати́вшая страну́.
2 (*carry forcefully*): **a wave swept him overboard** его́ смы́ло волно́й (за́ борт); **he swept her off her feet** (*fig.*) он вскружи́л ей го́лову.
3 (*touch, brush*): **he swept his hand across the table** он провёл руко́й по́ столу.
4 (*pass searchingly over*): **he swept the horizon with a telescope** он обша́рил горизо́нт подзо́рной трубо́й; **the search vessels swept the sea** разве́дывательные корабли́ борозди́ли мо́ре.
5 (*clean*) подме|та́ть, -сти́; чи́стить, вы́-; **~ a chimney** проч|ища́ть, -и́стить трубу́; **~ the board** (*fig., win all stakes*) заб|ира́ть, -ра́ть все ста́вки.
6 (*brush*): **he swept the litter into a corner** он замёл му́сор в у́гол; **her dress swept the ground** её пла́тье подмета́ло подо́лом зе́млю; (*fig.*): **~ something under the carpet** заме|та́ть, -сти́ что-н. под ковёр; **he swept all before him** он преодоле́л все препя́тствия.
● *v.i.* (*past and p.p.* **swept**) **1** (*rush, dash*) прон|оси́ться, -ести́сь; **rain swept across the country** дождь прошёл по всей стране́; **fear swept over him** страх охвати́л/обуя́л его́.
2 (*walk majestically*): **she swept into the room** она́ внесла́ себя́ в ко́мнату.
3 (*curve*) из|гиба́ться, -огну́ться; **the coastline ~s to the right** берегова́я ли́ния изгиба́ется впра́во.
4 (*clean, brush*) мести́, под-; подме|та́ть, -сти́.
● *with advs.*: **~ along** *v.t.* нести́ (*det.*); увл|ека́ть, -е́чь; **the boat was swept along by the current** ло́дку унесло́ тече́нием; **a good speaker ~s his audience along** хоро́ший ора́тор увлека́ет свою́ аудито́рию; *v.i.* проше́ствовать (*impf.*); **~ aside** *v.t.*: **he swept the curtain aside** он ре́зко отодви́нул занаве́ску; **she swept him aside** она́ отстрани́ла его́; **he swept aside my protestations** он не стал слу́шать мои́ возраже́ния; **~ away** *v.t.* сме|та́ть, -сти́; **they were ~ing the snow away** они́ сгреба́ли снег; **the storm swept everything away** бу́ря всё смела́; **the bridge was swept away by the rains** мост смы́ло дождя́ми; (*fig., abolish*) поко́нчить (*pf.*) c + *i.*; уничт|ожа́ть, -о́жить; отмен|я́ть, -и́ть; **they swept away the old laws** они́ вы́бросили ста́рые зако́ны на сва́лку; **~ down** *v.t.*: **the river ~s the logs down to the mill** река́ несёт брёвна к ме́льнице; *v.i.*: **the enemy swept down on us** враг обру́шился на нас; **the hills ~ down to the sea** холмы́ сбега́ют к мо́рю; **~ in** *v.i.*: **the wind ~s in at the door** ве́тер врыва́ется в дверь; **~ off** *v.t.* срыва́ть, сорва́ть; **the roof was swept off in the gale** кры́шу сорва́ло урага́ном; **~ out** *v.t.*: **the maid was ~ing out the cupboards** служа́нка вымета́ла шкафы́; *v.i.*: **she swept out (of the room** *etc.*) она́ велича́вственно удали́лась; **~ up** *v.t.*: **I have to ~ up the kitchen** я до́лжен подмести́ ку́хню; **be sure and ~ up all the dirt** смотри́те вы́метите весь му́сор как сле́дует; **she ~s her hair up into a bun** она́ забира́ет во́лосы в у́зел; *v.i.*: **I had to ~ up after them** мне пришло́сь по́сле них убира́ть; **the car swept up to the house** маши́на подрули́ла к до́му; **the road ~s up to the church** доро́га поднима́ется к це́ркви.
● *cpd.* **~stake** *n.* ≈ лотере́я, тотализа́тор.

sweeper /'swi:pə(r)/ *n.* (*person*) подмета́льщик, дво́рник; (*device*) подмета́льная маши́на.

sweeping /'swi:pɪŋ/ *adj.* **1** (*of motion etc.*): **a ~ bow** широ́кий покло́н; **~ gesture** разма́шистый жест; **~ lines** стреми́тельные ли́нии.
2 (*comprehensive*) всеобъе́млющий; (*thoroughgoing*) реши́тельный; **~ changes** радика́льные измене́ния; (*wholesale*) огу́льный; **a ~ statement** огу́льное утвержде́ние.

sweepings /'swi:pɪŋz/ *n.* му́сор, сор.

sweet /swi:t/ *n.* **1** (*Br.*, **~meat**) конфе́та; (*pl.*) сла́сти (*f. pl.*).
2 (*Br., dish*) сла́дкое, тре́тье.
3 (*pl., delight*): **the ~s of office** пре́лести (*f. pl.*) слу́жбы.
4 (*beloved*): **my ~** (мой) ми́лый, (моя́) ми́лая.
● *adj.* **1** (*to taste*) сла́дкий; **I am not fond of ~ foods** я не люблю́ сла́достей; **I like my tea very ~** я пью о́чень сла́дкий чай; **my brother has a ~ tooth** мой брат — сластёна/сладое́жка; **make ~** насласти́ть, по-; **~ corn** кукуру́за; **~ potato** бата́т; **~** (*fresh, pure*) **water** све́жая/пре́сная вода́.
2 (*fragrant*) сла́дкий, души́стый; **how ~ the roses smell!** как сла́дко па́хнут ро́зы!; **~ peas** души́стый горо́шек.
3 (*melodious*): **~ voice** прия́тный/мелоди́чный го́лос; **~ melody** сла́дкая/преле́стная мело́дия.
4 (*agreeable*): **~ words** ла́сковые

слова́; ~ nothings не́жности (*f. pl.*); praise was ~ to him он упива́лся похвало́й; a ~ face ми́лое лицо́; a ~ (*gentle*) temper мя́гкий хара́ктер; (*coll., charming, nice*) ми́лый; a ~ frock ми́ленькое пла́тьице; a ~ little dog симпати́чная соба́чка; they were perfectly ~ to us они́ бы́ли чрезвыча́йно ми́лы́ с на́ми; keep s.o. ~ (*coll.*) подма́з|ываться, -аться к кому́-н.
5: he is ~ on her (*sl.*) он в неё влюблён; go one's own ~ way де́лать, с- так, как заблагорассу́дится.
● *cpds.* ~-and-sour *adj.* ки́сло-сла́дкий; ~bread *n.* «сла́дкое мя́со»; ~heart *n.* возлю́бленн|ый (*fem.* -ая); дружо́к; (*as address*) ду́шенька; ~meat *n.* = ~ *n.* 1; ~-scented *adj.* благоуха́нный; ~-shop *n.* (*Br.*) конди́терская; ~-talk (*coll.*) *n.* лесть, ума́сливание; *v.t.* загов|а́ривать, -ори́ть кому́-н. зу́бы; ~-tempered *adj.* с мя́гким хара́ктером, мя́гкого нра́ва; ~-william *n.* туре́цкая гвозди́ка.

sweeten /'swi:t(ə)n/ *v.t.* 1 подсла́|щивать (*or* подсла|ща́ть), -сти́ть. 2 (*fig.*): ~ s.o.'s temper смягч|а́ть, -и́ть чей-н. гнев; he ~ed the caretaker with a bribe он задо́брил смотри́теля взя́ткой.

sweetener /'swi:tənə(r)/ *n.* (*sugar substitute*) замени́тель (*m.*) са́хара; (*Br., bribe*) взя́тка.

sweetness /'swi:tnɪs/ *n.* сла́дость; све́жесть; прия́тность.

swell /swel/ *n.* 1 (*of sea*) зыбь.
2 (*mus.*) креще́ндо (*indecl.*).
● *adj.* (*US, first-rate*) шика́рный.
● *v.t.* (*p.p.* swollen *or* swelled)
1 (*increase size or volume of*)разд|ува́ть, -у́ть; the wind ~ed the sails ве́тер наду́л паруса́; rivers swollen by melting snow ре́ки, взду́вшиеся от та́лого сне́га; my finger is swollen у меня́ па́лец опу́х/распу́х.
2 (*increase number of*) увеличи|вать, -ть.
3 (*make arrogant*): he was swollen with pride он весь наду́лся/разду́лся от го́рдости; ~ed/swollen head (*fig., coll.*) самомне́ние.
● *v.i.* (*p.p.* swollen *or* swelled)
1 (*expand, dilate: also* ~ up) над|ува́ться, -у́ться; разд|ува́ться, -у́ться; (*of part of body*) оп|уха́ть, -у́хнуть; расп|уха́ть, -у́хнуть.
2 (*increase in size or volume*) выраста́ть, вы́расти; разб|уха́ть, -у́хнуть; взд|ува́ться, -у́ться; the crowd ~ed to over six thousand толпа́ увели́чилась до шести́ с ли́шним ты́сяч (челове́к); the novel ~ed to enormous size рома́н разбу́х до огро́много разме́ра; the rivers have ~ed since the thaw ре́ки взду́лись по́сле о́ттепели.
3 (*of person, with pride etc.*) над|ува́ться, -у́ться; my heart ~ed with pride се́рдце моё напо́лнилось го́рдостью.
4 (*of sound*) нараста́ть (*impf.*); the murmur ~ed into a roar ро́пот переро́с в рёв.

swelling /'swelɪŋ/ *n.* (*on body*) о́пухоль; опуха́ние; (*on other object*) вы́пуклость.

swelter /'sweltə(r)/ *v.i.* (*of person*) изнем|ога́ть, -о́чь от жары́; ~ing (*of atmosphere etc.*) нестерпи́мо жа́ркий.

swept /swept/ *past and p.p. of* ⇒**sweep**

swerve /swɜ:v/ *n.* отклоне́ние, поворо́т.
● *v.i.* (кру́то) пов|ора́чиваться, -ерну́ться; свёртывать, сверну́ть; the car ~d to avoid an accident маши́на кру́то сверну́ла, что́бы избежа́ть ава́рии.

swift /swɪft/ *n.* (*bird*) стриж.
● *adj.* (*rapid*) бы́стрый; (*prompt*) ско́рый; a ~ reply операти́вный/ско́рый отве́т; ~ to anger вспы́льчивый.
● *cpd.* ~-acting *adj.* быстроде́йствующий.

swiftness /'swɪftnɪs/ *n.* быстрота́, ско́рость.

swig /swɪg/ (*coll.*) *n.* глото́к; have, take a ~ of sth. сде́лать (*pf.*) глото́к чего́-н.
● *v.t.* (swigged, swigging) хлеба́ть (*impf.*).

swill /swɪl/ *n.* (*lit., fig.*) по́йло; (*pig-food*) помо́|и (*pl., g.* -ев).
● *v.t.* 1 (*Br., wash, rinse*) мыть, вы́-; полоска́ть, вы́-. 2 (*drink heavily*) лака́ть, вы́-, хлеба́ть, вы́-, хлеста́ть, вы́- (*coll.*).

swim /swɪm/ *n.* 1: have, go for a ~ купа́ться, ис-.
2 (*main current of affairs*): be in the ~ быть в ку́рсе дел; сле́довать (*impf.*) мо́де.
● *v.t.* (swimming; *past* swam; *p.p.* swum) 1 (*cross by ~ming*) перепл|ыва́ть, -ы́ть.
2 (*cover by ~ming*): ~ a mile пропл|ыва́ть, -ы́ть ми́лю.
● *v.i.* (swimming; *past* swam; *p.p.* swum) 1 пла́вать (*indet.*), плыть (*det.*), по-; he can ~ on his back он уме́ет пла́вать на спине́; he ~s like a fish он пла́вает как ры́ба; she swam for the shore она́ поплыла́ к бе́регу; ~ with the tide (*lit., fig.*) плыть (*det.*) по тече́нию; ~ against the tide плыть (*det.*) про́тив тече́ния.
2 (*of things: float*) пла́вать (*indet.*); vegetables ~ming in butter о́вощи, пла́вающие в ма́сле.
3 (*fig., reel, swirl*): the noise made my head ~ от шу́ма у меня́ закружи́лась голова́; everything was ~ming before my eyes всё поплы́ло у меня́ пе́ред глаза́ми.
● *cpd.* ~suit *n.* купа́льник.

swimmer /'swɪmə(r)/ *n.* плов|е́ц (*fem.* -чи́ха).

swimming /'swɪmɪŋ/ *n.* пла́вание; he took ~ lessons он брал уро́ки пла́вания; ~ contest, match состяза́ние в пла́вании.
● *cpds.* ~-bath (*Br.*), ~-pool *nn.* (пла́вательный) бассе́йн; ~-costume *n.* (*Br.*) купа́льник; ~-trunks *n. pl.* пла́в|ки (*pl., g.* -ок).

swimmingly /'swɪmɪŋlɪ/ *adj.*: everything went ~ всё шло как по ма́слу; get on ~ with s.o. на|ходи́ть, -йти́ о́бщий язы́к с кем-н.

swindle /'swɪnd(ə)l/ *n.* жу́льничество, моше́нничество.
● *v.t.* обма́н|ывать, -у́ть; she ~d him out of the inheritance она́ получи́ла его́ насле́дство обма́нным путём (*or* обма́ном); you've been ~d вас наду́ли; ~ money out of s.o. выма́нивать, вы́манить у кого́-н. де́ньги.
● *v.i.* жу́льничать, с-; моше́нничать, с-.

swindler /'swɪndlə(r)/ *n.* жу́лик, моше́нник.

swine /swaɪn/ *n.* (*pl.* ~; *fig. also* ~s) (*lit., fig.*) свинья́.
● *cpd.* ~herd *n.* свинопа́с.

swing /swɪŋ/ *n.* 1 (*movement*) кача́ние, колеба́ние; ~ of the pendulum кача́ние/разма́х ма́ятника; (*in boxing*) свинг, боково́й уда́р с разма́хом; he took a ~ at the ball он с разма́ху уда́рил по мячу́; in full ~ (*fig.*) в (по́лном) разга́ре.
2 (*shift*): the polls showed a ~ to the left вы́боры показа́ли ре́зкий поворо́т/крен вле́во.
3 (*of gait or rhythm*) ритм; the party went with a ~ вечери́нка вы́шла на сла́ву; I couldn't get into the ~ of things я ника́к не мог включи́ться в де́ло.
4 (*mus.*) свинг.
5 (*seat slung on rope*) каче́л|и (*pl., g.* -ей); he gave the boy a (go on the) ~ он раскача́л ма́льчика на каче́лях.
● *v.t.* (*past and p.p.* swung) 1 (*apply circular motion to*): ~ one's arms разма́хивать (*impf.*) рука́ми; ~ one's hips пока́чивать (*impf.*) бёдрами; (*brandish*): he swung the sword above his head он взмахну́л шпа́гой над голово́й; there's not enough room to ~ a cat (*coll.*) здесь поверну́ться не́где.
2 (*cause to turn, pivot*) пов|ора́чивать, -ерну́ть; разв|ора́чивать, -ерну́ть; the tide swung the boat round прили́в разверну́л ло́дку.
3 (*sling, hoist*) вски́|дывать, -нуть; he swung her on to his shoulders он вски́нул её себе́ на пле́чи; he swung himself into the saddle он вскочи́л в седло́.
4 (*give rhythmic motion to*) кача́ть (*impf.*); колеба́ть (*impf.*).
5 (*influence*): his speech swung the jury in her favour (*Br.*), favor (*US*) его́ речь склони́ла симпа́тии прися́жных на её сто́рону.
● *v.i.* (*past and p.p.* swung) 1 (*sway, oscillate*) кача́ться, колеба́ться, пока́чиваться, колыха́ться (*all impf.*); (*dangle*) висе́ть, свиса́ть, болта́ться (*all impf.*); let one's legs ~ болта́ть (*impf.*) нога́ми; he could ~ from a branch with one hand он мог висе́ть/раска́чиваться на ве́тке на одно́й руке́; the meat swung from a hook мя́со висе́ло на крю́ке́; a lamp swung from the ceiling с потолка́ свё́шивалась ла́мпа; the children were ~ing in the park де́ти кача́лись на каче́лях в па́рке.
2 (*turn, pivot*) пов|ора́чиваться, -ерну́ться; враща́ться (*impf.*); the door swung open in the wind дверь

S

распахну́лась от ве́тра; **the ship is ~ing round** кора́бль повора́чивает; **he swung round on his heel** он (ре́зко) поверну́лся на каблука́х.
3 (*move rhythmically*): **the monkeys swung from bough to bough** обезья́ны раска́чивались на ветвя́х.
4 (*sl., hang*): **he will ~ for this murder** его́ вздёрнут за э́то уби́йство.
● *cpds.* **~-boat** *n.* (*Br.*) ло́дка-каче́л|и (*pl., g.* -ей); **~-bridge** *n.* разводно́й мост; **~-doors** (*US* **swinging doors**) *n. pl.* свобо́дно распа́хивающаяся (двуство́рчатая) дверь.

swingeing /ˈswɪndʒɪŋ/ *adj.* (*Br. coll.*): **a ~ blow** ошеломля́ющий уда́р; **a ~ majority** подавля́ющее большинство́; **a ~ fine** грома́дный/здорове́нный штраф.

swinging /ˈswɪŋɪŋ/ *adj.* (*lively, zestful*) жизнера́достный.

swinish /ˈswaɪnɪʃ/ *adj.* сви́нский, ско́тский.

swipe /swaɪp/ (*coll.*) *n.*: **take a ~ at s.o.** зам|а́хиваться, -ахну́ться на кого́-н.; **he took a ~ at the ball** он с си́лой/разма́ху уда́рил по мячу́.
● *v.t.* (*hit*) с си́лой уд|аря́ть, -а́рить по + *d.*; (*steal*) стяну́ть (*pf.*) (*coll.*).
● *cpd.* **~ card** *n.* магни́тная ка́рточка.

swirl /swɜːl/ *n.* (*of water*) водоворо́т; (*of snow*) вихрь (*m.*); **~ of dust** столб пы́ли.
● *v.i.* (*of water*) крути́ться (*impf.*) в водоворо́те; (*of snow*) ви́хриться (*impf.*); (*of leaves etc.*) кружи́ться, за-; (*of dust*) подн|има́ться, -я́ться столбо́м.

swish /swɪʃ/ *n.* (*of whip*) свист; (*of scythe etc.*) свист; взмах со сви́стом; (*of dress etc.*) шурша́ние, ше́лест.
● *adj.* (*Br. coll.*) шика́рный.
● *v.t.* (*flick*) взма́х|ивать, -ну́ть + *i.*; **the cow ~ed her tail** коро́ва маха́ла/пома́хивала/взмахну́ла хвосто́м.
● *v.i.* (*of fabric*) шурша́ть (*impf.*); шелесте́ть (*impf.*); (*of cane etc.*) расс|ека́ть, -е́чь во́здух (со сви́стом); (*of whip*) свисте́ть, сви́стнуть; (*of scythe*) свисте́ть (*impf.*).

Swiss /swɪs/ *n.* (*pl.* ~) швейца́р|ец (*fem.* -ка); **the ~** (*pl.*) швейца́рцы (*m. pl.*); **a German/French/Italian ~** герма́но-/фра́нко-/ита́ло-швейца́рец.
● *adj.* швейца́рский; **~ German** (*ling.*) швейца́рский диале́кт неме́цкого языка́; **~ roll** (*Br.*) руле́т с варе́ньем.

switch /swɪtʃ/ *n.* **1** (*twig, rod*) прут.
2 (*false hair*) накла́дка; фальши́вая коса́.
3 (*rail.*) стре́лка.
4 (*elec.*) выключа́тель (*m.*), переключа́тель (*m.*).
5 (*change of position, role, tactics etc.*) поворо́т, переме́на.
● *v.t.* (*transfer*) перев|оди́ть, -ести́; переключ|а́ть, -и́ть.
● *v.i.*: **he ~ed from one extreme to the other** он перешёл/бро́сился из одно́й кра́йности в другу́ю.
● *with advs.*: **~ off** *v.t.* выключа́ть, вы́ключить; **~ off a lamp** гаси́ть, по- ла́мпу; *v.i.* (*coll., withdraw one's attention*) отключ|а́ться, -и́ться; **~ on** *v.t.* включ|а́ть, -и́ть; (*light*) заж|ига́ть, -е́чь; **~ over** *v.t. & i.* переключ|а́ть(ся), -и́ть(ся); пере|ходи́ть, -йти́.
● *cpds.* **~back** *n.* (*Br., in amusement park*) америка́нские го́ры (*f. pl.*); **a ~back road** доро́га с круты́ми подъёмами и спу́сками; **~blade** *n.* (*US*) пружи́нный нож; **~board** *n.* коммута́тор; распредели́тельный щит; щит управле́ния; **~board operator** телефони́ст (*fem.* -ка); **~man** *n.* (*US*) стре́лочник.

Switzerland /ˈswɪtsələnd/ *n.* Швейца́рия.

swivel /ˈswɪv(ə)l/ *n.* вертлю́г; (*attr.*) враща́ющийся, поворо́тный; вертлю́жный.
● *v.t. & i.* (**swivelled, swivelling;** *US* **swiveled, swiveling**) пов|ора́чивать(ся), -ерну́ть(ся) (на шарни́рах).
● *cpd.* **~-chair** *n.* враща́ющийся стул, враща́ющееся кре́сло.

swiz(zle) /ˈswɪz((ə)l)/ *n.* (*Br. coll.*) (*fraud*) моше́нничество; (*disappointment*) большо́е разочарова́ние.
● *cpd.* **swizzle stick** *n.* па́лочка для поме́шивания кокте́йля.

swollen /ˈswəʊlən/ *p.p. of* ⇒**swell**

swollen-headed /ˈswəʊlən/ *adj.* чванли́вый, напы́щенный.

swoon /swuːn/ *n.* о́бморок.
● *v.i.* па́дать, упа́сть в о́бморок.

swoop /swuːp/ *n.* **1** (*of bird etc.*) паде́ние вниз. **2** (*sudden attack*) налёт; **at one fell ~** еди́ным уда́ром/ма́хом.
● *v.i.* (*aeron.*) пики́ровать, с-; **the eagle ~ed (down) on its prey** орёл стреми́тельно упа́л на свою́ же́ртву; **the enemy ~ed on the town** неприя́тель соверши́л внеза́пный налёт на го́род.

swop /swɒp/ = **swap**

sword /sɔːd/ *n.* шпа́га; (*liter., or fig.*) меч; **~ of Damocles** дамо́клов меч; **cross ~s with s.o.** (*lit., fig.*) скр|е́щивать, -ести́ть шпа́ги с кем-н.; **put to the ~** пред|ава́ть, -а́ть мечу́; **beat ~s into ploughshares** (*Br.*), **plowshares** (*US*) перек|о́вывать, -ова́ть мечи́ на ора́ла.
● *cpds.* **~dance** *n.* та́нец с са́блями; **~fish** *n.* меч-ры́ба; **~-hilt** *n.* эфе́с; **~-knot** *n.* темля́к; **~-play** *n.* фехтова́ние; (*fig., repartee*) пикиро́вка; **~sman** *n.* фехтова́льщик; **~smanship** *n.* иску́сство фехтова́ния; **~-stick** *n.* трость с вкладно́й шпа́гой; **~-swallower** *n.* шпагоглота́тель (*m.*).

swore /swɔː/ *past of* ⇒**swear**

sworn /swɔːn/ *p.p. of* ⇒**swear**

swot /swɒt/ (*Br.*) *n.* (*person*) зубри́л(к)а (*c.g.*); (*study*) зубрёжка.
● *v.t.* (**swotted, swotting): ~ up a subject** зубри́ть, за-/вы́- предме́т.
● *v.i.* (**swotted, swotting**) зубри́ть (*impf.*).

swum /swʌm/ *p.p. of* ⇒**swim**

swung /swʌŋ/ *past and p.p. of* ⇒**swing**

sybarite /ˈsɪbəˌraɪt/ *n.* сибари́т (*fem.* -ка).

sybaritic /ˌsɪbəˈrɪtɪk/ *adj.* сибари́тский.

sycamore /ˈsɪkəˌmɔː(r)/ *n.* (*also* **sycomore fig**) сикамо́р анти́чный; (*maple*) я́вор; (*US, plane-tree*) плата́н, чина́р.

sycophancy /ˈsɪkəˌfænsɪ/ *n.* подхали́мство, лесть.

sycophant /ˈsɪkəˌfænt/ *n.* подхали́м, льстец.

sycophantic /ˌsɪkəˈfæntɪk/ *adj.* подхали́мский, льсти́вый.

Sydney /ˈsɪdnɪ/ *n.* Си́дней.

syllabary /ˈsɪləbərɪ/ *n.* слогова́я а́збука.

syllabi /ˈsɪləˌbaɪ/ *pl. of* ⇒**syllabus**

syllabic /sɪˈlæbɪk/ *adj.* силлаби́ческий, слогово́й.

syllabi(fi)cation /sɪˌlæbɪ(fɪ)ˈkeɪʃ(ə)n/ *n.* разделе́ние на сло́ги.

syllab|ify /sɪˈlæbɪˌfaɪ/, **-ize** /ˈsɪləˌbaɪz/ *vv.t.* раздел|я́ть, -и́ть на сло́ги; (*in speech*) произн|оси́ть, -ести́ по слога́м.

syllable /ˈsɪləb(ə)l/ *n.* слог; **in words of one ~** (*fig.*) досту́пным языко́м.

syllab|us /ˈsɪləbəs/ *n.* (*pl.* **~uses** *or* **~i**) програ́мма; уче́бный план.

syllogism /ˈsɪləˌdʒɪz(ə)m/ *n.* силлоги́зм.

syllogistic /ˌsɪləˈdʒɪstɪk/ *adj.* силлогисти́ческий.

sylph /sɪlf/ *n.* сильф (*fem.* -и́да).
● *cpd.* **~-like** *adj.* грацио́зный.

sylvan /ˈsɪlv(ə)n/ = **silvan**

symbiosis /ˌsɪmbaɪˈəʊsɪs/, /ˌsɪmbɪ-/ *n.* (*pl.* **symbioses** /-siːz/) симбио́з.

symbiotic /ˌsɪmbaɪˈɒtɪk/, /ˌsɪmbɪ-/ *adj.* симбиоти́ческий.

symbol /ˈsɪmb(ə)l/ *n.* си́мвол; (*sign, e.g. math.*) знак.

symbolic(al) /ˌsɪmˈbɒlɪk((ə)l)/ *adj.* символи́ческий, символи́чный.

symbolism /ˈsɪmbəˌlɪz(ə)m/ *n.* символи́зм.

symbolist /ˈsɪmbəlɪst/ *n.* символи́ст (*fem.* -ка).
● *adj.* символи́стский.

symbolization /ˌsɪmbəlaɪˈzeɪʃ(ə)n/ *n.* символиза́ция.

symbolize /ˈsɪmbəˌlaɪz/ *v.t.* символизи́ровать (*impf., pf.*).

symmetric(al) /sɪˈmetrɪk((ə)l)/ *adj.* симметри́чный, симметри́ческий.

symmetry /ˈsɪmɪtrɪ/ *n.* симме́трия, симметри́чность.

sympathetic /ˌsɪmpəˈθetɪk/ *adj.*
1 (*compassionate*) сочу́вственный; **a ~ look** сочу́вственный взгляд; **lend a ~ ear to** сочу́вственно выслу́шивать, вы́слушать; **~ words** слова́ по́лные сочу́вствия. **2** (*favourable, supportive*): **I am ~ towards his ideas** его́ иде́и мне близки́. **3** (*physiol.*): **~ nerve** симпати́ческий нерв.

sympathize /ˈsɪmpəˌθaɪz/ *v.i.* сочу́вствовать (*impf.*) (**with**: + *d.*); симпатизи́ровать (*impf.*) (**with**: + *d.*); **he ~d with me in my grief** он сочу́вствовал моему́ го́рю; **I ~ with**

your viewpoint мне поня́тна ва́ша пози́ция.

sympathizer /'sɪmpəˌθaɪzə(r)/ *n.* сочу́вствующий, сторо́нник.

sympathy /'sɪmpəθɪ/ *n.* (*compassion, commiseration, fellow-feeling*) сочу́вствие, сострада́ние; (*agreement*) согла́сие; **feel ~ for s.o.** испы́тывать (*impf.*) сочу́вствие к кому́-н.; **we are in ~ with your ideas** мы сочу́вствуем ва́шим иде́ям; **the power workers came out in ~** рабо́тники электроста́нции забастова́ли в знак солида́рности; **my sympathies are with the miners** все мои́ симпа́тии на стороне́ шахтёров.

symphonic /sɪm'fɒnɪk/ *adj.* симфони́ческий.

symphony /'sɪmfənɪ/ *n.* симфо́ния; **~ orchestra/concert** симфони́ческий орке́стр/конце́рт.

symposi|um /sɪm'pəʊzɪəm/ *n.* (*pl.* **~a** *or* **~ums**) симпо́зиум.

symptom /'sɪmptəm/ *n.* симпто́м; (*sign*) при́знак; **develop ~s** обнару́жи|вать, -ть симпто́мы.

symptomatic /ˌsɪmptə'mætɪk/ *adj.* симптомати́чный, симптомати́ческий.

synagogue /'sɪnəˌgɒg/ *n.* синаго́га.

sync(h) /sɪŋk/ *n.* (*coll.*): **out of ~** несинхро́нный.

synchromesh /'sɪŋkrəʊˌmeʃ/ *n.* синхрониза́тор; (*attr.*) синхронизи́рующий.

synchronism /'sɪŋkrəˌnɪz(ə)m/ *n.* (*cin., TV*) синхрони́зм.

synchronization /ˌsɪŋkrənaɪ'zeɪʃ(ə)n/ *n.* синхрониза́ция.

synchronize /'sɪŋkrəˌnaɪz/ *v.t.* синхронизи́ровать (*impf., pf.*); **~d swimming** синхро́нное пла́вание.

● *v.i.* (*of events*) совп|ада́ть, -а́сть во вре́мени; (*of clocks*) пока́зывать (*impf.*) одина́ковое вре́мя.

synchronous /'sɪŋkrənəs/ *adj.* синхро́нный; **~ satellite** геостациона́рный спу́тник.

synchrony /'sɪŋkrənɪ/ *n.* синхрони́я.

syncopate /'sɪŋkəˌpeɪt/ *v.t.* (*ling., mus.*) синкопи́ровать (*impf., pf.*).

syncopation /ˌsɪŋkə'peɪʃ(ə)n/ *n.* синко́па.

syncope /'sɪŋkəpɪ/ *n.* (*ling.*) синко́па; (*med.*) о́бморок.

syndicate[1] /'sɪndɪkət/ *n.* синдика́т.

syndicate[2] /'sɪndɪˌkeɪt/ *v.t.* синдици́ровать (*impf., pf.*).

syndrome /'sɪndrəʊm/ *n.* синдро́м.

synecdoche /sɪ'nekdəkɪ/ *n.* сине́кдоха.

synod /'sɪnəd/ *n.* сино́д.

synodal /'sɪnəd(ə)l/ *adj.* синода́льный.

synonym /'sɪnənɪm/ *n.* сино́ним.

synonymous /sɪ'nɒnɪməs/ *adj.* синоними́чный; синоними́ческий; (*fig.*) равнозна́чный (+*d.*).

synopsis /sɪ'nɒpsɪs/ *n.* (*pl.* **synopses** /-siːz/) резюме́ (*indecl.*).

synoptic /sɪ'nɒptɪk/ *adj.* синопти́ческий.

syntactic(al) /sɪn'tæktɪk((ə)l)/ *adj.* синтакси́ческий.

syntax /'sɪntæks/ *n.* си́нтаксис.

synthesis /'sɪnθɪsɪs/ *n.* (*pl.* **syntheses** /-ˌsiːz/) си́нтез.

synthe|size /'sɪnθɪˌsaɪz/, **-tize** /'sɪnθɪˌtaɪz/ *v.t.* синтези́ровать (*impf., pf.*).

synthesizer /'sɪnθɪˌsaɪzə(r)/ *n.* синтеза́тор.

synthetic /sɪn'θetɪk/ *adj.* синтети́ческий.

● *n.* (*usu. pl.*) синте́тика (*collect.*).

syphilis /'sɪfɪlɪs/ *n.* си́филис.

syphilitic /ˌsɪfɪ'lɪtɪk/ *adj.* сифилити́ческий.

● *n.* сифили́тик.

syphon /'saɪf(ə)n/ = **siphon**

Syria /'sɪrɪə/ *n.* Си́рия.

Syrian /'sɪrɪən/ *n.* сири́|ец (*fem.* -йка).

● *adj.* сири́йский.

syringe /sɪ'rɪndʒ/, /'sɪr-/ *n.* шприц, спринцо́вка; **hypodermic ~** шприц для подко́жных впры́скиваний.

● *v.t.* (**syringing**) (*ears etc.*) спринцева́ть (*impf.*); впры́с|кивать, -нуть.

syrup /'sɪrəp/ (*US also* **sirup**) *n.* сиро́п; (*treacle*) па́тока; **golden ~** све́тлая па́тока.

syrupy /'sɪrəpɪ/ (*US also* **sirupy**) *adj.* (*fig.*) слаща́вый.

system /'sɪstəm/ *n.* **1** (*complex*) систе́ма; **solar ~** со́лнечная систе́ма; **~s analysis** систе́мный ана́лиз; **~s analyst** систе́мный анали́тик. **2** (*network*) сеть; **railway ~** железнодоро́жная сеть. **3** (*body as a whole*) органи́зм; **the poison passed into his ~** яд прони́к в его́ органи́зм; **get something out of one's ~** (*fig.*) изб|авля́ться, -а́виться от чего́-н. **4** (*method*) систе́ма; **what ~ do you use?** како́й систе́мы вы приде́рживаетесь?; **~ of government** госуда́рственный строй. **5** (*methodical behaviour*) системати́чность.

systematic /ˌsɪstə'mætɪk/ *adj.* системати́ческий, системати́чный.

systematization /ˌsɪstəmətaɪ'zeɪʃ(ə)n/ *n.* систематиза́ция.

systematize /'sɪstəməˌtaɪz/ *v.t.* систематизи́ровать (*impf., pf.*).

systemic /sɪ'stemɪk/ *adj.* системати́ческий, сомати́ческий; **~ poison** общеядови́тое отравля́ющее вещество́.

systole /'sɪstəlɪ/ *n.* си́стола, сокраще́ние се́рдца.

S

T t

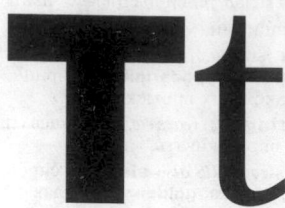

T /tiː/ *n.*: **this suits me to a ~** это меня́ вполне́ устра́ивает.

● *cpds.* **~-junction** *n.* Т-обра́зный перекрёсток; **~-shaped** *adj.* Т-обра́зный; **~-shirt** *n.* футбо́лка; **~-square** *n.* рейсши́на.

TA (*abbr. of* ***Territorial Army***) территориа́льная а́рмия.

ta /tɑː/ *nt.* (*Br. coll.*) спаси́бо.

tab¹ /tæb/ *n.* **1** (*label on garment etc.*) наши́вка; (*for hanging clothes*) ве́шалка; пе́телька; (*Br., insignia on collar*) петли́ца. **2** (*coll., check*): **the police are keeping ~s on him** поли́ция присма́тривает за ним.

tab² /tæb/ = **tabulator**

tabard /ˈtæbəd/ *n.* костю́м геро́льда.

tabby /ˈtæbɪ/ *n.* (*also* **~ cat**) (се́рая) полоса́тая ко́шка.

tabernacle /ˈtæbəˌnæk(ə)l/ *n.* **1** (*bibl., for the Ark of the Covenant*) ски́ния. **2** (*place of worship*) моле́льня.

table /ˈteɪb(ə)l/ *n.* **1** стол; **at ~** за столо́м; **he turned the ~s on his adversary** он поби́л проти́вника его́ же ору́жием; **a ~ for three** (*at restaurant*) сто́лик на трои́х; (*fig., food*) стол, ку́хня; **he keeps a good ~** он хлебосо́льный хозя́ин. **2** (*tablet*) плита́. **3** (*arrangement of data*) табли́ца; **~ of contents** оглавле́ние, содержа́ние; **he knows his twelve times ~** он уме́ет умножа́ть на двена́дцать.

● *v.t.* **1** (*Br., present for discussion*) ста́вить, по- на обсужде́ние. **2** (*US, postpone*) от|кла́дывать, -ложи́ть.

● *cpds.* **~cloth** *n.* ска́терть; **~-knife** *n.* столо́вый нож; **~-lamp** *n.* насто́льная ла́мпа; **~land** *n.* плато́ (*indecl.*); плоского́рье; **~-linen** *n.* столо́вое бельё; **~-mat** *n.* подста́вка (*под таре́лку и т.п.*); **~-napkin** *n.* салфе́тка; **~spoon** *n.* столо́вая ло́жка; **~-tennis** *n.* насто́льный те́ннис, пинг-по́нг; **~ware** *n.* столо́вая посу́да; **~-water** *n.* минера́льная вода́; **~-wine** *n.* столо́вое вино́.

tab|leau /ˈtæbləʊ/ *n.* (*pl.* **-leaux** /-ləʊz/) жива́я карти́нка.

table d'hôte /ˌtɑːb(ə)l ˈdəʊt/ *n.* табльдо́т.

tablet /ˈtæblɪt/ *n.* **1** (*block for writing on*) (вощёная) дощёчка. **2** (*inscribed plate or stone*) мемориа́льная доска́. **3** (*Br., of soap*) кусо́к. **4** (*pill*) табле́тка.

tabloid /ˈtæblɔɪd/ *n.* табло́ид, малоформа́тная газе́та; (*pej.*) бульва́рная газе́та; **the ~s** табло́идная/бульва́рная пре́сса.

tab|oo, -u /təˈbuː/ *n.* (*pl.* **taboos** *or* **tabus**) (*lit., fig.*) табу́ (*nt. indecl.*); (*prohibition*) запре́т.

● *adj.*: **the subject is ~** э́то запрещённая те́ма.

● *v.t.* (**taboos, tabooed** *or* **tabus, tabued**) запре|ща́ть, -ти́ть.

tabor /ˈteɪbə(r)/ *n.* ма́ленький бараба́н.

tabu /təˈbuː/ = **taboo**

tabular /ˈtæbjʊlə(r)/ *adj.* в ви́де табли́ц; табли́чный.

tabulate /ˈtæbjʊˌleɪt/ *v.t.* табули́ровать (*impf.*); сост|авля́ть, -а́вить табли́цу из + *g.*

tabulation /ˌtæbjʊˈleɪʃ(ə)n/ *n.* табули́рование; составле́ние табли́цы.

tabulator /ˈtæbjʊˌleɪtə(r)/ *n.* (*device*) табуля́тор.

tachograph /ˈtækəˌgrɑːf/ *n.* тахо́граф.

tachometer /təˈkɒmɪtə(r)/ *n.* тахо́метр.

tacit /ˈtæsɪt/ *adj.* молчали́вый; **~ agreement** молчали́вое согла́сие.

taciturn /ˈtæsɪˌtɜːn/ *adj.* неразгово́рчивый, молчали́вый.

taciturnity /ˌtæsɪˈtɜːnɪtɪ/ *n.* неразгово́рчивость, молчали́вость.

tack /tæk/ *n.* **1** (*small nail*) гво́здик; **let's get down to brass ~s** (*fig.*) дава́йте разберёмся, что к чему́. **2** (*long, loose stitch*) намётка. **3** (*direction of vessel*) галс; (*fig.*) курс, ли́ния; **he is on the wrong ~** он на ло́жном пути́.

● *v.t.* **1** (*fasten*) прикреп|ля́ть, -и́ть гво́здиками; приб|ива́ть, -и́ть. **2** (*stitch*) сши|ва́ть, -ть; **she ~ed the dress together** она́ смета́ла пла́тье на живу́ю ни́тку. **3**: **~ on** (*fig., add*) доб|авля́ть, -а́вить.

● *v.i.* ложи́ться, лечь на друго́й галс.

tackle /ˈtæk(ə)l/ *n.* **1** (*rope-and-pulley mechanism*) полиспа́ст; сло́жный блок. **2** (*equipment*) принадле́жности (*f. pl.*), обору́дование; **fishing ~** рыболо́вные сна́сти (*f. pl.*). **3** (*football*) блокиро́вка.

● *v.t.* (*grapple with*) бра́ться, взя́ться за + *a.*; **I don't know how to ~ this problem** я не зна́ю, как взя́ться за реше́ние э́той пробле́мы; **I went and ~d him on the subject** я пошёл к нему́ и по́днял э́тот вопро́с; (*football*) блоки́ровать (*impf., pf.*).

● *cpd.* **~-block** *n.* полиспа́ст, таль.

tacky¹ /ˈtækɪ/ *adj.* (**tackier, tackiest**) (*sticky*) ли́пкий, кле́йкий.

tacky² /ˈtækɪ/ *adj.* (**tackier, tackiest**) (*coll., tasteless*) безвку́сный.

tact /tækt/ *n.* такт, такти́чность.

tactful /ˈtæktfʊl/ *adj.* такти́чный.

tactfulness /ˈtæktfʊlnɪs/ *n.* такти́чность.

tactic /ˈtæktɪk/ = **tactic(s)**

tactical /ˈtæktɪk(ə)l/ *adj.* такти́ческий.

tactician /tækˈtɪʃ(ə)n/ *n.* та́ктик.

tactic(s) /ˈtæktɪks/ *n.* та́ктика.

tactile /ˈtæktaɪl/ *adj.* осяза́тельный, такти́льный.

tactless /ˈtæktlɪs/ *adj.* беста́ктный.

tactlessness /ˈtæktlɪsnɪs/ *n.* беста́ктность.

tadpole /ˈtædpəʊl/ *n.* голова́стик.

Tadzhik /tɑːˈdʒiːk/ = **Tajik**

Tadzhikistan /təˌdʒiːkɪˈstɑːn/ = **Tajikistan**

taffeta /ˈtæfɪtə/ *n.* тафта́; (*attr.*) тафтяно́й.

taffrail /ˈtæfreɪl/ *n.* (*naut.*) гакабо́рт.

tag /tæg/ *n.* **1** (*metal tip to shoe-lace*) металли́ческий наконе́чник. **2** (*label*) ярлы́к; **price ~** ярлы́к с обозна́ченной цено́й, це́нник. **3** (*loose or ragged end*): **at the ~ end of the procession** в хвосте́ проце́ссии. **4** (*stock phrase*) изби́тая фра́за; (*trite quotation*) изби́тая цита́та. **5** (*child's game*) (игра́ в) са́л|ки (*pl.*, *g.* -ок).

● *v.t.* (**tagged, tagging**) (*fasten* ~ *to*) наве́|шивать, -сить/накле́и|вать, -ть ярлы́к на + *a.*

● *v.i.* (**tagged, tagging**) (*follow*): **the children ~ged along behind** де́ти тащи́лись сза́ди; **he ~ged on to the group** он примкну́л к гру́ппе.

Tahiti /tə'hi:ti/ *n.* Таи́ти (*m. indecl.*).

Tahitian /tə'hi:ʃ(ə)n/ *n.* таитя́н|ин (*fem.* -ка).

● *adj.* таитя́нский.

taiga /'taɪgə/ *n.* тайга́.

tail /teɪl/ *n.* **1** (*of animal*) хвост; (*dim.*) хво́стик; **the dog wagged its ~** соба́ка виля́ла хвосто́м; **they turned ~ and ran** они́ поверну́ли и бро́сились наутёк.
2 (*fig.*) хвост; **at the ~ end** в са́мом конце́; **I can't make head or ~ of it** я ника́к в э́том не разберу́сь.
3 (*of a coin*) ре́шка.
4: **~s** (*coat*) фрак.

● *v.t.* (*follow closely*) висе́ть (*impf.*) на хвосте́ у + *g.*

● *v.i.* **1** (*follow*) таска́ться (*impf.*) за + *i.* (*coll.*); ходи́ть (*impf.*) по пята́м за + *i.*; **he ~ed after her** он ходи́л за ней по пята́м.
2 (*dwindle*) убы|ва́ть, -ть; **the attendance figures ~ed off** посеща́емость упа́ла; **his voice ~ed away into silence** его́ го́лос (постепе́нно) затих; **the work ~ed off** рабо́та постепе́нно сошла́ на нет.

● *cpds.* **~back** *n.* (*Br.*) хвост; **~board** *n.* (*Br.*) откидно́й борт; **~-coat** *n.* (*Br.*) фрак; **~-end** *n.* коне́ц, хвост; заключи́тельная часть; **~-gate** *n.* откидно́й борт; **~-lamp, ~-light** *nn.* за́дний фона́рь; стоп-сигна́л; **~piece** *n.* (*at end of chapter*) винье́тка; (*conclusion*) концо́вка; **~plane** *n.* (*Br.*, *aeron.*) хвостово́й стабилиза́тор; **~-spin** *n.* (*aeron.*) норма́льный што́пор; (*fig.*) па́ника; **~-wheel** *n.* (*aeron.*) хвостово́е колесо́; **~wind** *n.* попу́тный ве́тер.

tailor /'teɪlə(r)/ *n.* портно́й.

● *v.t.*: **a well-~ed coat** хорошо́ сши́тое пальто́; (*fig.*) приспос|а́бливать, -о́бить; **his speech was ~ed to the situation** его́ речь была́ соста́влена с учётом ситуа́ции.

● *v.i.* портня́жничать (*impf.*).

● *cpd.* **~-made** *adj.* (*clothes*) сде́ланный по зака́зу; (*fig.*) подходя́щий.

taint /teɪnt/ *n.* (*spot*) пятно́; (*trace*) налёт; (*infection*) при́месь.

● *v.t.* по́ртить, ис-; **~ed meat** несве́жее мя́со; **~ed money** нечи́стые де́ньги; **~ed reputation** подмо́ченная репута́ция.

Taipei /taɪ'peɪ/ *n.* Тайбэ́й.

Taiwan /taɪ'wɑ:n/ *n.* Тайва́нь (*m.*).

Tajik /tɑ:'dʒi:k/ *n.* **1** (*person*) таджи́|к (*fem.* -чка). **2** (*language*) таджи́кский язы́к.

● *adj.* таджи́кский.

Tajikistan /tə,dʒi:kɪ'stɑ:n/ *n.* Таджикиста́н.

take /teɪk/ *n.* **1** (*money taken, e.g. at box office*) сбор, вы́ручка.
2 (*cin.*) монта́жный кадр; (*repetition*) дубль (*m.*).

● *v.t.* (*past* **took;** *p.p.* **taken** /'teɪk(ə)n/)
1 (*pick up, lay hold of, grasp*) брать, взять; **~ my arm!** возьми́те меня́ по́д руку!; **he took her in his arms** он её обня́л; **he took her by the hand** он взял её за́ руку; **he took me by the throat** он взял/схвати́л меня́ за го́рло; (*remove*): **the doctor took him off penicillin** врач снял его́ с пеницилли́на; **she took a coin out of her purse** она́ вы́нула моне́ту из кошелька́; **~ your hands out of your pockets!** вы́ньте ру́ки из карма́нов!; **~ 5 from 10** отними́те 5 от 10; **the last mile took it out of me** на после́дней ми́ле я вы́дохся.
2 (*catch*) лови́ть, пойма́ть; (*come upon*): **I was ~n by surprise** я был засти́гнут врасплóх.
3 (*capture*) брать, взять; **the city was ~n by storm** го́род взя́ли шту́рмом; **he was ~n captive** его́ взя́ли в плен; он попа́л в плен; **I ~ your queen** (*chess*) я беру́ ва́шу короле́ву; (*assume*) прин|има́ть, -я́ть на себя́; **you must ~ the initiative** вы должны́ взять на себя́ инициати́ву; **he took the lead** (*in an enterprise*) он взял на себя́ руково́дство; **the Italians took the lead** (*racing*) италья́нцы вы́рвались вперёд; **he took it upon himself to refuse** он взял на себя́ сме́лость отказа́ть; **he took control** он взял управле́ние в свои́ ру́ки; (*win, gain*) выи́грывать, вы́играть; **she took first prize** она́ получи́ла пе́рвый приз; (*captivate*) захв|а́тывать, -ати́ть; нра́виться, по- + *d.*; **that ~s my fancy** мне э́то нра́вится; **I was ~n by the house** дом меня́ очарова́л.
4 (*acquire; obtain possession of*): **he decided to ~ a wife** он реши́л жени́ться; **he took a partner** он взял компаньо́на; (*for money*): **I have ~n a flat in town** я снял кварти́ру в го́роде; **these seats are ~n** э́ти места́ за́няты; (*in payment*): **they took £50 in one evening** они́ вы́ручили 50 фу́нтов за оди́н ве́чер; (*by enquiry or examination*): определ|я́ть, -и́ть; **the tailor took his measurements** портно́й снял с него́ ме́рки; **the doctor took my temperature** до́ктор изме́рил мне температу́ру; **the police took his name and address** поли́ция записа́ла его́ фами́лию и а́дрес; (*unlawfully or without consent*): **the thieves took all her jewellery** (*Br.*), **jewelry** (*US*) во́ры забра́ли все её драгоце́нности.
5 (*avail o.s. of*) по́льзоваться, вос- + *i.*; **please ~ a seat** пожа́луйста, сади́тесь; **I'm taking a day's leave** я беру́ выходно́й день; **~ your time!** спеши́ть не́куда; не торопи́тесь!; (*board, travel by*): **let's ~ a taxi** дава́йте возьмём такси́; **he took a bus to the station** он пое́хал авто́бусом до ста́нции.
6 (*occupy*) зан|има́ть, -я́ть; **will you ~ the chair?** (*at meeting*) вы не хоти́те быть председа́телем?; **I am taking his place** я его́ замеща́ю.
7 (*adopt, choose*): **I don't wish to ~ sides** я не жела́ю станови́ться ни на чью сто́рону; **I don't ~ the same view** у меня́ друга́я то́чка зре́ния; **~ me, for instance!** возьми́те меня́, наприме́р!
8 (*accept*) прин|има́ть, -я́ть; **will you ~ a cheque** (*Br.*), **check** (*US*)? вы при́мете чек?; я могу́ расплати́ться че́ком?; **will you ~ £50 for it?** вы отдади́те э́то за 50 фу́нтов?; **~ my advice!** послу́шайте меня́!; **I ~ responsibility** я беру́ на себя́ отве́тственность; **he took his defeat well** он сто́йко перенёс пораже́ние; **he took the blame for everything** он взял на себя́ вину́ за всё; **can't you ~ a joke?** вы что, шу́ток не понима́ете?; **I'll ~ no nonsense from you** я не потерплю́ от вас никаки́х глу́постей; **he would not ~ no for an answer** он не при́нял отка́за; он не сдава́лся; **~ it from me!** (*believe me!*) пове́рьте мне!; **~ it easy!** (*relax*) успоко́йтесь!; не волну́йтесь!; (*proceed carefully*) осторо́жно!; (*bear*) перен|оси́ть, -ести́; выде́рживать, вы́держать; **he took his punishment like a man** он перенёс наказа́ние, как подоба́ет мужчи́не; **I won't ~ this lying down** я не сда́мся без бо́я; (*respond to*): **she took three curtain calls** она́ три ра́за выходи́ла на бис; (*receive*) брать (*impf.*); **she ~s lessons in Spanish** она́ берёт уро́ки испа́нского языка́; **we ~ the Times** (*Br.*) мы выпи́сываем «Таймс»; **she ~s paying guests** она́ де́ржит постоя́льцев; **I took him into my confidence** я ему́ дове́рился; (*derive*): **the street ~s its name from a general** у́лица на́звана и́менем како́го-то генера́ла; (*Br.*, *qualify for*): **he took his degree** он получи́л дипло́м/сте́пень; (*submit to*): **when do you ~ your exams?** когда́ вы сдаёте экза́мены?; **you are taking a risk** вы риску́ете; **you must ~ your chance** вам на́до рискну́ть.
9 (*use regularly*) прин|има́ть, -я́ть; **he has begun to ~ drugs** он на́чал принима́ть нарко́тики; **do you ~ sugar in your tea?** вы пьёте чай с са́харом?; (*of size in clothes*): **I ~ a ten in shoes** у меня́ деся́тый разме́р обу́ви.
10 (*apprehend*) пон|има́ть, -я́ть; **what do you ~ that to mean?** как вы э́то понима́ете?; (*assume*) счита́ть (*impf.*); **I ~ him to be an honest man** я счита́ю его́ че́стным челове́ком; **what do you ~ me for?** за кого́ вы меня́ принима́ете?; (*mistake*): **I took her for her mother** я при́нял её за её мать.
11 (*conceive, evince*) проя́в|ля́ть, -и́ть; **he has ~n a dislike to me** он меня́ невзлюби́л; **I began to ~ an interest** я на́чал проявля́ть интере́с.
12 (*exert, exercise*): **~ care!** бу́дьте осторо́жны!; **he took no notice** он не обрати́л никако́го внима́ния.
13 (*of single finite actions: give, have, make*): **~ a look at this!** взгляни́те-ка на э́то!; **I took a deep breath** я сде́лал глубо́кий вдох; **he took a shot at me** он вы́стрелил в меня́; **he took a bite out of the apple** он откуси́л я́блоко; (*of longer, but finite, activity: have*): **I took a bath** я при́нял ва́нну; **let us ~ a walk!**

T

давáйте прогуля́емся!; **he believes in taking exercise** он вéрит в пóльзу физи́ческих упражнéний; (*partake of, consume*) есть, по-; **will you ~ tea with us?** вы вы́пьете с нáми чáю?
14 (*make or obtain from original source*): **may we ~ notes?** мóжно нам дéлать замéтки?; **may I ~ your photograph?** позвóльте мне вас сфотографи́ровать!
15 (*convey*) (*on foot*) отн|оси́ть, -ести́; (*by transport*) отв|ози́ть, -езти́; брать, взять; перед|авáть, -áть; **he took the letter to the post** он отнёс письмó на пóчту; **~ my luggage upstairs please** отнеси́те мой багáж навéрх, пожáлуйста; **the train will ~ you there in an hour** пóезд довезёт вас тудá за час; **I'm taking the dog for a walk** я пойду́ вы́веду собáку; **he was ~n to hospital** егó отвезли́ в больни́цу; **she ~s the children to school** онá отвóдит/отвóзит детéй в шкóлу; **where will this road ~ us?** кудá вы́ведет нас э́та дорóга?; (*travel with*): **I shall ~ my warmest clothes** я возьму́ сáмые тёплые вéщи.
16 (*conduct, carry out*) вести́ (*det.*); **the class was ~n by the headmaster** урóк в э́том клáссе вёл дирéктор; **the curate took the service** викáрий отслужи́л молéбен.
17 (*need, require*): **the job will ~ a long time** рабóта займёт мнóго врéмени; **how long does it ~ to get there?** скóлько (врéмени) тудá добирáться?; **it took us 3 hours to get there** нам потрéбовалось три часá, чтóбы добрáться тудá; мы добрали́сь тудá зá три часá; **does it ~ long to get there?** дóлго тудá идти́/éхать?; **that ~s courage** э́то трéбует му́жества; **it ~s some doing** э́то трéбует уси́лий; **it took ten men to build the wall** потрéбовалось дéсять человéк, чтóбы пострóить э́ту стéну; **he's got what it ~s** (*coll.*) у негó есть для э́того все задáтки; (*gram., govern*) управля́ть (*impf.*) + *i.*; **this verb ~s the dative** э́тот глагóл трéбует дáтельного падежá.

● *v.i.* (*past* **took;** *p.p.* **taken** /'teɪk(ə)n/)
1 (*~ effect; succeed*): **the vaccination has not ~n** вакци́на не привилáсь.
2 (*become*): **he took sick** он заболéл/ занемóг (*coll.*).
3 ~ after (*resemble*): **he ~s after his father** он похóж на отцá.
4: **~ to** (*resort to*) приб|егáть, -éгнуть к + *d.*; **she took to her bed** онá слеглá; **the crew took to the boats** комáнда пересéла в лóдки; **he took to drink** он зáпил; **he has ~n to getting up early** он стал рáно вставáть; (*feel (well-)disposed towards*): **I took to him from the start** он мне срáзу понрáвился; **she does not ~ kindly to change** онá плóхо перенóсит перемéну обстанóвки.

● *with advs.*: **~ along** *v.t.* брать, бзять; прив|оди́ть, -ести́; (*by vehicle*) прив|ози́ть, -езти́; **I took my wife along to the meeting** я привёл женý на собрáние; **~ apart** *v.t.* (*dismantle*) раз|бирáть, -обрáть; **~ aside** *v.t.* отв|оди́ть, -ести́ в стóрону; **~ away** *v.t.* (*remove*) уб|ирáть, -рáть; заб|ирáть, -рáть; отбирáть, отобрáть; **the police took his gun away** поли́ция отобралá у негó пистолéт; **he was ~n away to prison** егó отвезли́ в тюрьмý; (*subtract*) вычитáть, вы́честь; отн|имáть, -я́ть; (*Br.*, **~ home**): **hot meals to ~ away** горя́чая едá на вы́нос; **~ back** *v.t.* (*return*) возвра|щáть, -ти́ть; вернýть (*pf.*); **I took the book back to the library** я вернýл кни́гу в библиотéку; (*retrieve*) брать, взять обрáтно; (*retract*): **I ~ back everything I said** я берý назáд всё, что сказáл; **~ down** *v.t.* (*remove*) сн|имáть, -ять; **she took down the curtains** онá снялá занавéски; (*lengthen*): **she took her dress down an inch** онá отпусти́ла плáтье на дюйм; (*dismantle*) сн|оси́ть, -ести́; **the shed was ~n down** сарáй снесли́; (*drop*) сн|имáть, -ять; **~ down your trousers!** сними́те брю́ки!; (*write down*) запи́с|ывать, -áть; **they took down my name and address** они́ записáли мою́ фами́лию и áдрес; **she took down the speech in shorthand** онá застенографи́ровала речь; **~ in** *v.t.* (*lit.*) вн|оси́ть, -ести́; (*give shelter to*): **they took him in when he was starving** они́ приюти́ли егó, когдá он голодáл; (*let accommodation to*): **she ~s in lodgers** онá берёт постоя́льцев; (*receive to work on at home*): **she ~s in washing** онá берёт нá дом сти́рку; (*make smaller*): **she took in her dress** онá уши́ла плáтье; (*furl*) уб|ирáть, -рáть (*паруса*); (*include, encompass*) включ|áть, -и́ть; **this map ~s in the whole of London** э́то кáрта всегó Лóндона; **shall we ~ in a show this evening?** не пойти́ ли нам в теáтр сегóдня вéчером?; (*comprehend, assimilate*) усв|áивать, -óить; вбирáть, вобрáть; **I could not ~ in all the details** я не мог удержáть в головé все подрóбности; (*deceive*) обмáн|ывать, -ýть; **I was completely ~n in** меня́ здóрово провели́; **~ off** *v.t.* (*remove*) сн|имáть, -ять; **he took off his hat** он снял шля́пу; **shall I ~ off my clothes?** мне нáдо раздéться?; **I took myself off to the races** я отпрáвился на скáчки; (*deduct from price*): **I will ~ 10% off for cash** éсли вы плáтите нали́чными, я ски́ну/сбрóшу 10%; (*lead away*) ув|оди́ть, -ести́; **he was ~n away screaming** когдá егó уводи́ли, он кричáл; **she was ~n off to hospital** её увезли́ в больни́цу; (*Br. coll., impersonate, mimic*) имити́ровать (*impf.*), копи́ровать (*impf.*); **he is good at taking off the Prime Minister** он хорошó копи́рует премьéр-мини́стра; *v.i.* (*become airborne*) взлет|áть, -éть; **the plane took off an hour late** самолёт взлетéл с опоздáнием на час; **~ on** *v.t.* (*hire*) брать, взять; нан|имáть, -я́ть; **more workers were ~n on** нáняли/ взя́ли нóвых рабóчих; (*undertake*) брать, взять на себя́; **he took on too much** он взял на себя́ сли́шком мнóго; (*assume, acquire*) приобре|тáть, -сти́; **the word took on a new meaning** слóво приобрелó нóвое значéние; (*compete against*): **will you ~ me on at chess?** вы сыгрáете со мнóй в шáхматы?; *v.i.* (*Br., become agitated*) волновáться, раз-; **don't ~ on so!** (*coll.*) да не волну́йтесь вы так!; **~ out** *v.t.* (*extract*) вынимáть, вы́нуть; **he took out his wallet** он вы́нул бумáжник; **he had all his teeth ~n out** емý удали́ли все зýбы; (*borrow from library*) брать, взять (в библиотéке); (*cause to go out for recreation etc.*) выводи́ть, вы́вести; **she took the baby out for a walk** онá пошлá с ребёнком погуля́ть; **he took his friend out to dinner** он повёл свою́ подрýгу в рестóрáн; (**~ home**) (*US*) = **~ away;** (*remove*) выводи́ть, вы́вести; **how can I ~ out these stains?** чем мóжно вы́вести э́ти пя́тна?; (*coll., destroy*) уничт|ожáть, -óжить; (*put into effect by writing*): **I must ~ out a new subscription** я дóлжен возобнови́ть подпи́ску; **~ out a policy** брать, взять страховóй пóлис; (*vent one's feelings*) срывáть, сорвáть; **he took it out on his wife** он сорвáл всё на своéй женé; **~ over** *v.t.* (*row across*): **the boatman took us over to the island** лóдочник перевёз нас на óстров; *v.t. & i.* (*assume control* (*of*)) прин|имáть, -я́ть руковóдство (+ *i.*); *v.i.* (*replace s.o.*): **let me ~ over!** я вас сменю́!; **~ up** *v.t.* (*lift; lay hold of*) подн|имáть, -я́ть; **he took up his bag and left** он взял свой чемодáн и ушёл; **the rebels took up arms** повстáнцы взяли́сь за орýжие; (*accept*) прин|имáть, -я́ть; **will he ~ up the challenge?** он при́мет вы́зов?; (*carry upstairs*): **will you ~ up my bags, please?** пожáлуйста, отнеси́те мои́ вéщи навéрх; (*remove from floor*): **the carpet has been ~n up** ковёр сня́ли; (*unearth*) выкáпывать, вы́копать; (*shorten*): **she had to ~ up her dress** ей пришлóсь укороти́ть плáтье; **wind in the rope and ~ up the slack!** смотáйте верёвку и натяни́те её!; (*occupy*) зан|имáть, -я́ть; **this table ~s up too much room** э́тот стол занимáет сли́шком мнóго мéста; **sport ~s up all my spare time** спорт занимáет всё моё свобóдное врéмя; **I'm very ~n up at the moment** я сейчáс óчень зáнят; **he is very ~n up with his new lady-friend** он сейчáс пóлностью поглощён своéй нóвой знакóмой; (*promote*): **his cause was ~n up by his MP** депутáт поддержáл егó дéло; (*pursue*): **I shall ~ the matter up with the Minister** я обращýсь с э́тим дéлом к министру; (*accept challenge or offer*): **I'll ~ you up on that!** я ловлю́ вас на слóве; (*resume*): **he took up the subject where he left off** он продóлжил разговóр с тогó мéста, на котóром он останови́лся; (*interest o.s. in*) брáться, взя́ться за + *a.*; заня́ться (*pf.*) + *i.*; **she has ~n up knitting** онá занялáсь вязáнием; *v.i.* (*consort*) св|я́зываться, -язáться с + *i.*; **he has ~n up with some dubious acquaintances** у негó завели́сь подозри́тельные знакóмые.

● *cpds.* **~-away** (*Br.*) *n.* рестóрáн, продаю́щий едý на вы́нос; *adj.*: **a ~-away meal** едá на вы́нос; **~-home** *adj.*: **~-home pay** чи́стый зáработок; **~-off** *n.* (*impersonation*) подражáние, парóдия; (*of aircraft; also fig.*) взлёт; **~out** (*US*) = **~-away; ~-over** *n.*

(*comm.*) поглоще́ние (*какой-н. компании другой компанией*).

taker /'teɪkə(r)/ *n.* беру́щий; **there were no ~s** (*for a bet*) никто́ не при́нял пари́; (*for an offer*) жела́ющих не́ было.

taking /'teɪkɪŋ/ *n.* взя́тие; овладе́ние; **the money was there for the ~** де́ньги текли́ пря́мо в ру́ки; (*pl., money taken*) (*business*) вы́ручка; (*from concert etc.*) сбор; **the ~s were lower than expected** сбор оказа́лся ме́ньше, чем рассчи́тывали.

● *adj.* привлека́тельный.

talc(um) /'tælkəm/ *n.* слюда́; **(~ powder)** тальк.

tale /teɪl/ *n.* **1** (*story*) расска́з, по́весть; **fairy ~** ска́зка; **old wives' ~s** ба́бушкины ска́зки. **2** (*malicious or idle report*) сплéтни (*f. pl.*); вы́думки (*f. pl.*); **there is a ~ going about, that ...** погова́ривают, что...; **you've been telling ~s about me** вы на меня́ наговáриваете.

● *cpds.* **~-bearer, ~-teller** *nn.* я́беда (*c.g.*), я́бедни|к (*fem.* -ца).

talent /'tælənt/ *n.* тала́нт, дар; **a man of great ~s** исключи́тельно тала́нтливый челове́к; **he has a ~ for upsetting others** у него́ про́сто дар обижа́ть люде́й; (*person of ability*) тала́нтливый челове́к; **local ~** ме́стные тала́нты; **~ scout** открыва́тель (*m.*) тала́нтов.

talented /'tæləntɪd/ *adj.* тала́нтливый.

talisman /'tælɪzmən/ *n.* (*pl.* **~s**) талисма́н.

talk /tɔ:k/ *n.* **1** (*speech, conversation*) разгово́р, бесе́да; **we had a long ~** мы до́лго бесе́довали/разгова́ривали; **I'd better have a ~ with him** мне бы на́до с ни́м поговори́ть; **he is all ~** он то́лько ме́лет языко́м; **~ show** ток-шо́у (*indecl.*); **small ~** све́тская болтовня́; **they became the ~ of the town** они́ сде́лались при́тчей во язы́цех.
2 (*address, lecture*) ле́кция; докла́д; **give a ~** чита́ть, про- ле́кцию.
3 (*discussion, negotiation; usu. pl.*) перегово́ры (*m. pl.*).

● *v.t.* **1** (*express*) говори́ть (*impf.*); **you are ~ing nonsense** вы говори́те чепуху́.
2 (*discuss*) обсу|жда́ть, -ди́ть; разгова́ривать (*impf.*) о + *p.*; говори́ть (*impf.*) о + *p.*; **they were ~ing politics** они́ говори́ли о поли́тике.
3: **~ French** говори́ть (*impf.*) по-францу́зски.
4 (*bring or make by ~ing*): **he ~ed himself hoarse** он договори́лся до хрипоты́; **he ~ed me into it** он уговори́л меня́ сде́лать э́то; **I tried to ~ her out of it** я пыта́лся отговори́ть её от э́того; **I ~ed him round to my view** я склони́л его́ на свою́ сто́рону.

● *v.i.* говори́ть (*impf.*); **baby is just learning to ~** ребёнок ещё то́лько у́чится говори́ть; **a ~ing parrot** говоря́щий попуга́й; **we got ~ing** мы разговори́лись; **~ about hard luck!** ну и не везёт же нам!; **he ~s about going abroad** он говори́т, что собира́ется за грани́цу; **people are beginning to ~** уже́ пошли́ разгово́ры/то́лки; **he ~ed at me for an hour** он це́лый час мне вы́говаривал; **~ing of students, how's your brother?** (*Br.*) кста́ти о студе́нтах — как пожива́ет ваш брат?; **~ of the devil!** лёгок на поми́не!; **~ing-point** те́ма; **I shall have to ~ to** (*reprimand*) **that boy** мне придётся отчита́ть э́того мальчи́шку; **now you're ~ing!** (*coll.*) вот тепе́рь вы говори́те де́ло!; **he refused to ~** (*coll., give information*) он не хоте́л ничего́ расска́зывать.

● *with advs.*: **~ away** *v.t.*: **we ~ed the hours away** мы проговори́ли не́сколько часо́в; *v.i.*: **while we were ~ing away, the bus left** пока́ мы болта́ли, авто́бус уе́хал; **~ back** *v.i.* дерзи́ть (*impf.*); возра|жа́ть, -зи́ть; **I gave him no chance to ~ back** я не дал ему́ возмо́жности возрази́ть; **~ down** *v.t.* (*outshout*) перекри́|кивать, -ча́ть; (*aeron.*): **the pilot was ~ed down** пило́та напра́вили на поса́дку по ра́дио; *v.i.*: **children dislike being ~ed down to** де́ти не лю́бят, когда́ с ни́ми разгова́ривают свысока́; **~ over** *v.t.* (*discuss*) обгов|а́ривать, -ори́ть; обсу|жда́ть, -ди́ть.

talkative /'tɔ:kətɪv/ *adj.* разгово́рчивый, болтли́вый.

talker /'tɔ:kə(r)/ *n.* разгово́рчивый челове́к, болту́|н (*fem.* -шка); **he is a good ~** он хорошо́ говори́т; **he is a great ~** он лю́бит поговори́ть.

talkie /'tɔ:kɪ/ *n.* (*coll.*) звуково́й фильм.

talking /'tɔ:kɪŋ/ *adj.* говоря́щий; (*film*) звуково́й.

talking-to /'tɔ:kɪŋ,tu:/ *n.* вы́говор.

tall /tɔ:l/ *adj.* **1** высо́кий, высо́кого ро́ста; **how ~ are you?** како́го вы ро́ста?; **six feet ~** ро́стом в шесть фу́тов. **2** (*coll., extravagant, unreasonable*) преувели́ченный; **a ~ story** небыли́ца, вы́думка; **that's a ~ order** э́то тру́дная зада́ча.

● *cpd.* **~boy** *n.* (*Br.*) высо́кий комо́д.

Tallin(n) /'tælɪn/ *n.* Та́ллин(н); (*attr.*) та́ллинский.

tallness /'tɔ:lnɪs/ *n.* (высо́кий) рост.

tallow /'tæləʊ/ *n.* жир; са́ло.

tally /'tælɪ/ *n.* (*account, score*) счёт; (*total*) ито́г.

● *v.i.* соотве́тствовать (*impf.*); **their versions do not ~** их ве́рсии не совпада́ют.

tally-ho /,tælɪ'həʊ/ *int.* ату́!

Talmud /'tælmʊd/, /-məd/ *n.* Талму́д.

Talmudic /,tæl'mʊdɪk/ *adj.* талмуди́ческий.

talon /'tælən/ *n.* ко́готь (*m.*).

tamarisk /'tæmərɪsk/ *n.* (*bot.*) тамари́ск.

tambour /'tæmbʊə(r)/ *n.* (*embroidery frame*) кру́глые пя́льц|ы (*pl., g.* -ев); (*drum*) бараба́н.

tambourine /,tæmbə'ri:n/ *n.* тамбури́н.

tame /teɪm/ *adj.* (*not wild; domesticated*) ручно́й, приручённый, дома́шний; (*submissive, spiritless*) послу́шный; (*dull, boring*) пре́сный, ску́чный.

● *v.t.* приру́ч|а́ть, -и́ть; (*of savage animals*) укро|ща́ть, -ти́ть.

tameable /'teɪməb(ə)l/ *adj.* укроти́мый.

tamer /'teɪmə(r)/ *n.* укроти́тель (*m.*).

Tamil /'tæmɪl/ *n.* (*person*) тами́л (*fem.* -ка); (*language*) тами́льский язы́к.

● *adj.* тами́льский.

tam o' shanter /,tæmə'ʃæntə(r)/ *n.* шотла́ндский бере́т.

tamp /tæmp/ *v.t.* наб|ива́ть, -и́ть; **~ down tobacco in one's pipe** наб|ива́ть, -би́ть тру́бку табако́м.

tamper /'tæmpə(r)/ *v.i.*: **~ with** (*meddle in*) вме́ш|иваться, -а́ться в + *a.*; **someone has been ~ing with the lock** кто́-то ковыря́лся в замке́; **he ~ed with the document** он подде́лал докуме́нт.

tampon /'tæmpɒn/ *n.* тампо́н.

tan /tæn/ *n.* (*colour*) цвет бро́нзы; (*tint of skin*) зага́р; **he went to Spain to get a ~** он пое́хал загора́ть в Испа́нию.

● *v.t.* (**tanned, tanning**) **1** (*convert to leather*) дуби́ть (*impf.*); **I'll ~ your hide** (*fig.*) я тебе́ зада́м. **2** (*make brown*): **a ~ned face** загоре́лое лицо́.

● *v.i.* (**tanned, tanning**): **she ~s easily** она́ бы́стро загора́ет.

tandem /'tændəm/ *n.* **1** (**~** *bicycle*) велосипе́д-та́ндем. **2**: **in ~** гусько́м, цу́гом.

tang /tæŋ/ *n.* (*sharp taste or smell*) о́стрый/те́рпкий вкус/за́пах; **the ~ of sea air** за́пах мо́ря.

tangent /'tændʒ(ə)nt/ *n.* (*geom.*) каса́тельная; (*fig.*): **he went off at a ~** он отклони́лся от те́мы; (*trig.*) та́нгенс.

tangential /tæn'dʒenʃ(ə)l/ *adj.* (*geom.*) тангенциа́льный; (*fig.*) отклоня́ющийся от те́мы.

tangerine /'tændʒə,ri:n/ *n.* мандари́н.

tangible /'tændʒɪb(ə)l/ *adj.* осяза́емый; (*fig.*) осяза́емый, ощути́мый; **~ advantages** ощути́мые преиму́щества; **~ assets** материа́льные акти́вы (*m. pl.*).

Tangier /tæn'dʒɪə(r)/ *n.* Танже́р.

tangle /'tæŋg(ə)l/ *n.* сплете́ние; (*fig.*) пу́таница.

● *v.t.* спу́т|ывать, -ать; **the wool had got ~d up** ни́тки спу́тались; (*fig.*) запу́т|ывать, -ать.

● *v.i.* (*coll.*) свя́з|ываться, -а́ться; **you had better not ~ with him** вы с ним лу́чше не свя́зывайтесь.

tango /'tæŋgəʊ/ *n.* (*pl.* **tangos**) та́нго (*indecl.*).

● *v.i.* (**tangoes, tangoed**) танцева́ть, с- та́нго.

tangy /'tæŋɪ/ *adj.* (**tangier, tangiest**) о́стрый, те́рпкий.

tank /tæŋk/ *n.* **1** (*container*) бак, цисте́рна; **petrol** (*Br.*), **gas** (*US*) **~** бензоба́к; **water ~** бак для воды́. **2** (*armoured vehicle*) танк; **~ warfare** та́нковые сраже́ния.

● *v.i.*: **~ up** (*with petrol*) запр|авля́ться, -а́виться; **he is ~ed up** он нагрузи́лся (*coll.*).

T

tankard /'tæŋkəd/ *n.* высóкая пивнáя крýжка.

tanker /'tæŋkə(r)/ *n.* (*vessel*) тáнкер; (*vehicle*) автоцистéрна.

tanner /'tænə(r)/ *n.* (*of skins*) кожéвник, дуби́льщик.

tannery /'tænərɪ/ *n.* кожéвенный завóд.

tannic /'tænɪk/ *adj.* дуби́льный.

tannin /'tænɪn/ *n.* (*chem.*) тани́н.

tantalize /'tæntə,laɪz/ *v.t.* (*tease*) дразни́ть (*impf.*); (*torment*) терзáть (*impf.*).

tantamount /'tæntə,maʊnt/ *adj.*: ~ **to** равноси́льный +*d.*

tantrum /'tæntrəm/ *n.* вспы́шка раздражéния; **he is in one of his** ~**s** у негó очереднóй при́ступ раздражéния; **the child is in a** ~ ребёнок капри́зничает.

Tanzania /,tænzə'ni:ə/ *n.* Танзáния.

Tanzanian /,tænzə'ni:ən/ *adj.* танзани́йский.

tap[1] /tæp/ *n.* кран; **don't leave the** ~**s running** закрóйте крáны; **there is plenty of wine on** ~ разливнóго винá óчень мнóго.

● *v.t.* (**tapped, tapping**) **1** (*pierce to extract liquid*): **the cask was** ~**ped** бочóнок откры́ли; (*fig.*): **the line is being** ~**ped** разговóр подслýшивают. **2** (*fig., use*) испóльзовать (*impf.*).

● *cpds.* ~**-room** *n.* пивнáя; ~**-root** *n.* глáвный/стержневóй кóрень.

tap[2] /tæp/ *n.* (*light blow*) лёгкий удáр; стук.

● *v.t.* (**tapped, tapping**) легкó уд|аря́ть, -áрить; стучáть, по-; (*give one tap*) стýк|ать, -нуть; **he** ~**ped me on the shoulder** он трóнул меня́ за плечó.

● *v.i.* (**tapped, tapping**) стучáться, по-; **he** ~**ped on the door** он постучáлся в дверь; **his toes were** ~**ping to the rhythm** он отбивáл ритм ногáми.

● *with adv.*: ~ **out** *v.t.*: **he** ~**ped out his pipe** он вы́бил трýбку; **he** ~**ped out a message** он вы́стукал сообщéние.

● *cpds.* ~**-dance,** ~**-dancing** *nn.* чечётка; ~**-dancer** *n.* чечёточни|к (*fem.* -ца).

tape /teɪp/ *n.* (*strip of fabric etc.*) тесьмá, лéнта; (*in race*) фи́нишная лéнточка; **adhesive** ~ ли́пкая лéнта; (*magnetic* ~) (магнитофóнная) лéнта/плёнка; ~ **deck** (магнитофóнная) дéка; ~ **library** магнитотéка; **put something on** ~ запи́с|ывать, -áть что-н. на плёнку; **he was playing over his old** ~**s** он прои́грывал стáрые зáписи/плёнки.

● *v.t.* **1** (*bind with* ~) свя́з|ывать, -áть тесьмóй. **2** (*Br. coll., sum up, master*) оцéн|ивать, -и́ть; **I've got him** ~**d** я знáю емý цéну. **3** (*record*) запи́с|ывать, -áть (на плёнку).

● *cpds.* ~**-measure** *n.* рулéтка, сантимéтр; ~**-recorder** *n.* магнитофóн; ~**-recording** *n.* магнитофóнная зáпись; ~**worm** *n.* лéнточный червь.

taper /'teɪpə(r)/ *n.* (*candle*) тóнкая свечá; (*for lighting something*) вощёный фити́ль.

● *v.t.* & *i.* (*narrow off*) сужáть(ся), сýзить(ся).

tapestry /'tæpɪstrɪ/ *n.* гобелéн.

tapioca /,tæpɪ'əʊkə/ *n.* крупá из крахмáла, тапиóка.

tapir /'teɪpə(r)/, /-pɪə(r)/ *n.* тапи́р.

tar[1] /tɑ:(r)/ *n.* (*substance*) дёготь (*m.*).

● *v.t.* (**tarred, tarring**) мáзать, на- дёгтем; смоли́ть, вы́-/о-; **a** ~**red road** гудрони́рованная дорóга; **they are** ~**red with the same brush** (*fig.*) они́ одни́м ми́ром мáзаны.

tar[2] /tɑ:(r)/ *n.* (*coll., sailor*) матрóс, моря́к.

tarantella /,tærən'telə/ *n.* тарантéлла.

tarantula /tə'ræntjʊlə/ *n.* тарáнтул.

tardiness /'tɑ:dɪnɪs/ *n.* медли́тельность; опоздáние.

tardy /'tɑ:dɪ/ *adj.* (**tardier, tardiest**) (*slow-moving*) медли́тельный; (*late in coming, belated*) запоздáвший, запоздáлый.

tare /teə(r)/ *n.* (*bot., vetch*) ви́ка; (*bibl., in pl., weeds*) плéвел|ы (*pl., g.* —).

target /'tɑ:gɪt/ *n.* (*for shooting etc.*) мишéнь, цель; ~ **practice** учéбная стрельбá; (*fig.*): **he became a** ~ **for abuse** он стал мишéнью для оскорблéний; (*objective*) цель; **we hope to reach the** ~ **of £1,000** мы надéемся дости́чь нáшу цель по сбóру 1 000 фýнтов.

● *v.t.* (**targeted, targeting**) **1** (*select as object*) дéлать, с- мишéнью. **2** (*aim, direct*) напр|авля́ть, -áвить; нацéли|вать, -ть.

tariff /'tærɪf/ *n.* **1** (*duty*) тари́ф. **2** (*list of charges*) тари́фы (*m. pl.*), тари́фная сéтка; (*for goods*) прейскурáнт.

tarmac /'tɑ:mæk/ *n.* (*propr.*) гудрóн, асфáльт; (*aeron.*) бетони́рованная площáдка.

● *v.t.* (**tarmacked, tarmacking**) гудрони́ровать (*impf., pf.*), асфальти́ровать (*impf., pf.*).

tarnish /'tɑ:nɪʃ/ *n.* тýсклость, тýсклаяповéрхность; (*fig.*) (позóрное) пятнó.

● *v.t.*: ~**ed by damp** потусклéвший от влáги; (*fig.*) пятнáть, за-; **he has a** ~**ed reputation** он запятнáл свою репутáцию.

● *v.i.* тускнéть, по-.

tarpaulin /tɑ:'pɔ:lɪn/ *n.* брезéнт.

tarragon /'tærəgən/ *n.* (поды́нь) эстрагóн.

tarry[1] /'tɑ:rɪ/ *adj.* (**tarrier, tarriest**) (*of or like tar*) смоли́стый.

tarry[2] /'tærɪ/ *v.i.* (*liter.*) (*remain, stay*) ост|авáться, -áться; преб|ывáть, -ы́ть; (*delay*) задéрж|иваться, -áться; мéдлить, по-.

tart[1] /tɑ:t/ *n.* **1** (*flat pie*) откры́тый пирóг с фрýктами. **2** (*sl., prostitute*) ýличная дéвка, шлю́ха.

● *v.t.*: ~ **up** (*Br. coll., embellish*) прикрá|шивать, -сить; **she was all** ~**ed up** онá былá вся разодéта/расфуфы́рена.

tart[2] /tɑ:t/ *adj.* (*of taste*) ки́слый; (*fig.*) кóлкий, ехи́дный.

tartan /'tɑ:t(ə)n/ *n.* (*fabric*) шотлáндка; ~ **skirt** клéтчатая ю́бка.

Tartar /'tɑ:tə(r)/ *n.* (*also* **Tatar**) татáр|ин (*fem.* -ка).

tartar /'tɑ:tə(r)/ *n.* **1** (*incrustation from wine*) ви́нный кáмень; **cream of** ~ ки́слый ви́нный кáмень. **2** (*on teeth*) (зубнóй) кáмень.

tartlet /'tɑ:tlɪt/ *n.* тарталéтка, мáленький откры́тый пирожóк.

tartness /'tɑ:tnɪs/ *n.* кислотá; ки́слый вкус; (*fig.*) кóлкость, ехи́дство.

tarty /'tɑ:tɪ/ *adj.* (**tartier, tartiest**) (*coll.*) вульгáрный.

Tashkent /tæʃ'kent/ *n.* Ташкéнт.

task /tɑ:sk/ *n.* задáча, задáние; **he was set a difficult** ~ пéред ним постáвили трýдную задáчу; **take s.o. to** ~ **for carelessness** выговáривать, вы́говорить комý-н. за халáтность; ~ **force** (*mil.*) операти́вная грýппа.

● *cpd.* ~**master** *n.*: **he is a hard** ~**master** он из тебя́ все сóки выжимáет.

Tasmania /tæz'meɪnɪə/ *n.* Тасмáния.

Tasmanian /tæz'meɪnɪən/ *n.* тасмани́|ец (*fem.* -йка).

● *adj.* тасмáнский; ~ **devil** (*zool.*) сýмчатый дья́вол.

TASS /tæs/ *n.* (*abbr. of* ***Telegraph Agency of the Soviet Union***) ТАСС (Телегрáфное агéнтство Совéтского Сою́за).

tassel /'tæs(ə)l/ *n.* ки́сточка.

taste /teɪst/ *n.* (*sense; flavour*) вкус; **the fruit was sweet to the** ~ плод был слáдок на вкус; **I have lost my** ~ **for whisky** я потеря́л вкус к ви́ски; **it leaves a bad** ~ **in the mouth** (*fig.*) э́то оставля́ет неприя́тный осáдок; (*act of tasting; small portion for tasting*): **have a** ~ **of this!** попрóбуйте/отвéдайте э́того!; **I gave him a** ~ **of his own medicine** (*fig.*) я отплати́л емý тем же (*or* той же монéтой); (*fig., liking*): **Wagner is not to everybody's** ~ Вáгнер нрáвится далекó не всем; **there is no accounting for** ~**(s)** о вкýсах не спóрят; **she has expensive** ~**s in clothes** онá лю́бит носи́ть дорогíе вéщи; **add salt and pepper to** ~ (*in recipe*) добáвьте сóли и пéрца по вкýсу; (*fig., discernment, judgement*) понимáние, вкус; **he is a man of** ~ он человéк со вкýсом; **bad** ~ дурнóй вкус.

● *v.t.* **1** (*perceive flavour of*) чýвствовать, по-; различ|áть, -и́ть; **can you** ~ **the garlic in this dish?** вы чýвствуете чеснóк в э́том блю́де? **2** (*professionally*) дегусти́ровать (*impf., pf.*). **3** (*eat small amount of*) есть, по-; ~ **this and say if you like it** попрóбуйте и скажи́те, нрáвится вам или нет. **4** (*experience*) вку|шáть, -си́ть; извéд|ывать, -ать; **they have** ~**d freedom** они́ вкуси́ли свобóду.

● *v.i.*: **the meat** ~**s horrible** у мя́са проти́вный вкус; ~ **of** имéть (*impf.*) при́вкус +*g.*; отдавáть (*impf.*) +*i.*; **the**

wine ~s of the cork вино́ отдаёт про́бкой; **what does the soup ~ like?** како́в суп на вкус?

● *cpd.* **~-bud** *n.* вкусова́я лу́ковица.

tasteful /'teɪstfʊl/ *adj.* изя́щный; со вку́сом.

tastefulness /'teɪstfʊlnɪs/ *n.* изя́щество; то́нкий вкус.

tasteless /'teɪstlɪs/ *adj.* (*insipid*) безвку́сный, пре́сный; (*showing want of taste*) безвку́сный; (*behaviour, words*) беста́ктный; в дурно́м то́не.

tastelessness /'teɪstlɪsnɪs/ *n.* (*lit.*) пре́сность; (*fig.*) безвку́сица, безвку́сие; беста́ктность, дурно́й тон.

taster /'teɪstə(r)/ *n.* (*sampler of wines etc.*) дегуста́тор.

tasty /'teɪstɪ/ *adj.* (**tastier, tastiest**) вку́сный, ла́комый; **~ morsel** ла́комый кусо́чек.

ta-ta /tæ'tɑː/ *int.* (*Br.*) пока́! (*coll.*).

Tatar /'tɑːtə(r)/ = **Tartar**[2]

tattered /'tætəd/ *adj.* по́рванный, разо́рванный.

tatters /'tætəz/ *n.* кло́чь|я (*pl., g.* -ев), лохмо́ть|я (*pl., g.* -ев); **his shirt was in ~** от его́ руба́шки оста́лись кло́чья.

tattle /'tæt(ə)l/ *n.* (*chatter*) болтовня́; (*gossip*) сплё́тня.

● *v.i.* (*chatter*) болта́ть (*impf.*); (*gossip*) сплё́тничать, по-.

tattoo[1] /tə'tuː/, /tɒ / *n.* (*pl.* **~s**) (*on skin*) татуиро́вка.

● *v.t.* (**tattoos, tattooed**) татуи́ровать, вы́-.

tattoo[2] /tə'tuː/, /tæ-/ *n.* (*pl.* **~s**) **1** (*mil. signal*) сигна́л вече́рней зо́ри; (*fig.*) (бараба́нная) дробь, стук; **the rain beat a ~ on the roof** дождь бараба́нил по кры́ше. **2** (*mil. entertainment*) музыка́льный пара́д.

tatty /'tætɪ/ *adj.* (**tattier, tattiest**) (*coll.*) потрё́панный, обша́рпанный.

taught /tɔːt/ *past and p.p. of* ⇒**teach**

taunt /tɔːnt/ *n.* насме́шка.

● *v.t.* дразни́ть (*impf.*); **he was ~ed with cowardice** над ним насмеха́лись, называ́я его́ тру́сом.

Taurus /'tɔːrəs/ *n.* (*astron.*) Теле́ц.

taut /tɔːt/ *adj.* (*tight*) туго́й, ту́го натя́нутый; **he pulled the rope ~** он ту́го натяну́л верё́вку; (*nerves*) напряжё́нный.

tautness /'tɔːtnɪs/ *n.* натя́нутость; (*of nerves*) напряжё́нность.

tautological /ˌtɔːtə'lɒdʒɪk(ə)l/ *adj.* тавтологи́ческий.

tautology /tɔː'tɒlədʒɪ/ *n.* тавтоло́гия.

tavern /'tæv(ə)n/ *n.* таве́рна.

tawdriness /'tɔːdrɪnɪs/ *n.* крикли́вость, безвку́сица.

tawdry /'tɔːdrɪ/ *adj.* (**tawdrier, tawdriest**) крича́щий, безвку́сный.

tawny /'tɔːnɪ/ *adj.* (**tawnier, tawniest**) кори́чнево-жё́лтый.

tax /tæks/ *n.* **1** (*levy*) нало́г; **income ~** подохо́дный нало́г; **after ~** за вы́четом нало́га. **2** (*fig., strain, demand*) испыта́ние; нагру́зка; **it was a great ~ on her strength** э́то подрыва́ло её си́лы.

● *v.t.* обл|ага́ть, -ожи́ть нало́гом; (*fig.*): **he ~es my patience** он испы́тывает моё терпе́ние.

● *cpds.* **~ avoidance** *n.* уменьше́ние нало́га с испо́льзованием зако́нных средств; **~-collector** *n.* сбо́рщик нало́гов; **~-deductible** *adj.* необлага́емый нало́гом; **~-disc** *n.* (*Br.*) накле́йка об упла́те доро́жного нало́га; **~ evasion** *n.* уклоне́ние от упла́ты нало́гов; **~-exempt, ~-free** *adjs.* необлага́емый нало́гом; **~ haven** *n.* страна́ с ни́зкими нало́гами; **~man** *n.* (*coll.*) нало́говый инспе́ктор; **~payer** *n.* налогоплате́льщик.

taxable /'tæksəb(ə)l/ *adj.* подлежа́щий обложе́нию нало́гом.

taxation /tæk'seɪʃ(ə)n/ *n.* налогообложе́ние.

taxi /'tæksɪ/ *n.* (*pl.* **taxis**) такси́ (*nt. indecl.*).

● *v.i.* (**taxies, taxied, taxiing** *or* **taxying**) **1** (*ride by ~*) е́хать (*det.*) на такси́. **2** (*of aircraft*) рули́ть (*impf.*).

● *cpds.* **~cab** *n.* такси́ (*nt. indecl.*); **~-driver** *n.* шофё́р такси́, такси́ст; **~meter** *n.* таксо́метр, счё́тчик; **~-rank** (*US* **~-stand**) *n.* стоя́нка такси́.

taxidermist /'tæksɪˌdɜːmɪst/ *n.* таксидерми́ст, наби́вщик чу́чел.

taxidermy /'tæksɪˌdɜːmɪ/ *n.* таксидерми́я, наби́вка чу́чел.

taxonomist /tæk'sɒnəmɪst/ *n.* система́тик.

taxonomy /tæk'sɒnəmɪ/ *n.* система́тика, таксоно́мия.

taxying *pres. part. of* ⇒**taxi**

TB (*abbr. of* ***tuberculosis***) туберкулё́з.

Tbilisi /təbr'liːsɪ/ *n.* Тбили́си (*m. indecl.*).

te /tiː/ (*US* **ti**) *n.* (*mus.*) седьма́я но́та мажо́рной га́ммы; (*the note B*) си (*indecl.*).

tea /tiː/ *n.* (*plant, beverage*) чай; (*Br., meal*) по́лдник; **make (the) ~** зава́р|ивать, -и́ть чай; **have, take ~** пить, вы́- чай; **high ~** (*Br.*) ра́нний у́жин с ча́ем; **that's not my cup of ~** (*coll.*) э́то не по мне; э́то не в моё́м вку́се.

● *cpds.* **~-bag** *n.* ча́йный паке́тик; **~-break** *n.* (*Br.*) переры́в на чай; **~-caddy** *n.* ча́йница; **~-cake** *n.* (*Br.*) ≈ бу́лочка с изю́мом; **~-chest** *n.* я́щик для ча́я; **~cloth** *n.* ча́йное полоте́нце; **~-cosy** *n.* чехо́л (на ча́йник); (*in form of doll*) ба́ба; **~cup** *n.* ча́йная ча́шка; **storm in a ~cup** бу́ря в стака́не воды́; **~-garden** *n.* ча́йная на откры́том во́здухе; **~-house** *n.* ча́йная; (*in the East*) чайхана́; **~-leaf** *n.* ча́йный лист; **~-maker** *n.* (*machine*) электросамова́р; **~-party** *n.* зва́ный чай; **~pot** *n.* ча́йник (для зава́рки); **~-room** *n.* ча́йная; кафе́-конди́терская; **~-rose** *n.* ча́йная ро́за; **~-service, ~-set** *nn.* ча́йный серви́з; **~shop** *n.* кафе́ (*indecl.*); **~spoon** *n.* ча́йная ло́жечка; **~spoonful** *n.* одна́/це́лая ча́йная ло́жка; **~-strainer** *n.* ча́йное си́течко; **~-table** *n.* ча́йный сто́лик; **~time** *n.* (*Br.*) ра́нний ве́чер, вре́мя (вече́рнего) ча́я; **~-towel** *n.* (*Br.*) ча́йное полоте́нце; **~-tray** *n.* ча́йный подно́с; **~-trolley, ~-wagon** *nn.* сто́лик на колё́сиках; **~-urn** *n.* тита́н; самова́р.

teach /tiːtʃ/ *v.t.* (*past and p.p.* **taught**) **1** (*instruct*) учи́ть, на-; обуч|а́ть, -и́ть; **she taught me Russian** она́ учи́ла меня́ ру́сскому языку́; **I taught myself English** я самостоя́тельно вы́учился англи́йскому языку́. **2** (*v.t. & i., give instruction*) (*school etc.*) учи́ть (*impf.*); (*university etc.*) преподава́ть (*impf.*); **~ing staff** преподава́тельский соста́в. **3** (*ellipt.*): **that will ~ you!** э́то вас нау́чит уму́-ра́зуму!; **I'll ~ you (a lesson)!** я вас проучу́!

● *cpd.* **~-in** *n.* семина́р.

teachable /'tiːtʃəb(ə)l/ *adj.* (*person*) поня́тливый; (*skill*): **this skill is ~** э́тому на́выку мо́жно научи́ть/обучи́ть; (*subject*) досту́пный.

teacher /'tiːtʃə(r)/ *n.* учи́тель (*fem.* -ница); педаго́г; **~ training college** педагоги́ческий институ́т; (*school*) **~s** учителя́; **~s** *of doctrine etc.* учи́тели.

teaching /'tiːtʃɪŋ/ *n.* **1** (*precept*) уче́ние. **2** (*activity*) преподава́ние, обуче́ние; **~ aid** уче́бное посо́бие. **3** (*profession*) преподава́ние; **she intends to take up ~** она́ собира́ется преподава́ть.

teak /tiːk/ *n.* (*wood*) тик; (*tree*) тик, ти́ковое де́рево.

teal /tiːl/ *n.* (*pl.* **~** *or* **~s**) (*zool.*) чиро́к.

team /tiːm/ *n.* (*of horses etc.*) упря́жка; (*games*) кома́нда; **a ~ event** кома́ндное соревнова́ние; (*of workers etc.*) брига́да; **~ of scientists** гру́ппа учё́ных; (*of colleagues etc.*) коллекти́в.

● *v.t.*: **they were ~ed together** (*horses*) их запрягли́ в одну́ упря́жку; (*workers*) их включи́ли в одну́ брига́ду.

● *v.i.*: **we ~ed up with our neighbours** мы объедини́лись с сосе́дями.

● *cpds.* **~-spirit** *n.* коллективи́зм; **~-work** *n.* коллекти́вная рабо́та; (*in sport*) сы́гранность.

teamster /'tiːmstə(r)/ *n.* (*US, lorry-driver*) води́тель (*m.*) грузовика́.

tear[1] /tɪə(r)/ *n.* (**~-drop**) слеза́; **~s ran down her cheeks** слё́зы текли́ по её щека́м; **I found her in ~s** я заста́л её в слеза́х; **burst into ~s** распла́каться (*pf.*); **the audience was moved to ~s** пу́блика была́ тро́нута до слё́з.

● *cpds.* **~-duct** *n.* слё́зный прото́к; **~-gas** *n.* слезоточи́вый газ; **~-jerker** *n.* (*sl.*) слезли́вый фильм (*u m.n.*).

tear[2] /teə(r)/ *n.* (*rent*) разры́в, проре́ха.

● *v.t.* (*past* **tore;** *p.p.* **torn**) **1** (*rip, rend*) раз|рыва́ть, -орва́ть; рвать, по-; **I tore my shirt on a nail** я порва́л руба́шку о гвоздь; **she tore a hole in her dress** она́ порвала́ пла́тье; **he tore the paper in two** он разорва́л бума́гу попола́м; **he tore open the envelope** он разорва́л/вскры́л конве́рт; (*fig.*): **my argument was torn to shreds** мой аргуме́нт

T

разнеслѝ в пух и прах; **a country torn by strife** странá, раздирáемая внýтренней враждóй; **she was torn by emotions** её раздирáли противоречѝвые чýвства; **I was torn, not knowing which to prefer** я разрывáлся, не знáя, что предпочéсть; **that's torn it!** (*Br. sl.*) из-за э́того всё срывáется.
2 (*snatch; remove by force*) от|рывáть, -орвáть; срывáть, сорвáть; **the wind ~s branches from the trees** вéтер срывáет вéтви с дерéвьев; **she tore the baby from his arms** онá вы́рвала ребёнка у негó из рук.
3 (*pull violently*) вырывáть, вы́рвать; **it makes one ~ one's hair** (*fig.*) от э́того хóчется рвать на себé вóлосы.
● *v.i.* (*past* **tore;** *p.p.* **torn**) **1** (*pull violently*) раз|рывáть, -орвáть; срывáть, сорвáть; **he tore at the wrapping-paper** он брóсился срывáть обёрточную бумáгу.
2 (*become torn*) рвáться, по-; **this material ~s easily** э́тот материáл легкó рвётся.
3 (*rush*) мчáться, по-; нестѝсь, по-; **why are you in such a ~ing hurry?** кудá вы так несётесь/спешѝте?
● *with advs.*: **we simply tore along** ну и мчáлись же мы!; **I could not ~ myself away** я не мог оторвáться; **the notice had been torn down** объявлéние сорвáли; **the old buildings are to be torn down** стáрые здáния бýдут сносѝть; **he tore off on his bicycle** он умчáлся на велосипéде; **several pages had been torn out** нéсколько странѝц бы́ло вы́рвано; **the children came ~ing out of school** дéти стремглáв вы́бежали из шкóлы; **the plants have been torn up** растéния вы́рвали с кóрнем; **the letter was torn up** письмó разорвáли.
● *cpd.* **~away** *n.* (*Br. sl.*) сорвиголовá (*c.g.*); ýхарь (*m.*).

tearful /ˈtɪəfʊl/ *adj.* (*event*) пóлный слёз; (*person*) заплáканный.

tease /tiːz/ *n.* (*person*) задѝра (*c.g.*), насмéшни|к (*fem.* -ца).
● *v.t.* **1** (*comb out*) чесáть, вы́-; (*fluff up*) нач|ёсывать, -есáть. **2** (*make fun of, irritate*) дразнѝть (*impf.*); издевáться (*impf.*) над + *i.* **3** (*US, backcomb*) нач|ёсывать, -есáть.

tea|sel, -zel, -zle /ˈtiːz(ə)l/ *n.* (*bot.*) ворся́нка.

teaser /ˈtiːzə(r)/ *n.* (*person*) = **tease;** (*coll., puzzle, problem*) головолóмка.

teat /tiːt/ *n.* сосóк.

teaz|el, -le /ˈtiːz(ə)l/ = **teasel**

tec(h) /tek/ (*Br. coll.*) = **technical college**

technical /ˈteknɪk(ə)l/ *adj.* технѝческий; **~ college** (*degree level*) технѝческий вуз; (*lower than degree level*) тéхникум; **~ term** специáльный тéрмин.

technicality /ˌteknɪˈkælɪtɪ/ *n.* (*detail*) технѝческая детáль, формáльность.

technician /tekˈnɪʃ(ə)n/ *n.* тéхник.

Technicolor /ˈteknɪˌkʌlə(r)/ *n.* (*propr.*) Техниколóр; (**technicolor,** *Br. also* **-colour**) (*coll., vivid colour*) я́ркий цвет; **in glorious ~** в великолéпных сóчных тóнах; (*attr.*) я́ркий.

technique /tekˈniːk/ *n.* (*skill*) тéхника, исполнéние; (*method*) технѝческий приём, метóдика.

techno /ˈteknəʊ/ *n.* (*mus.*) Тéхно (*indecl.*).

technocracy /tekˈnɒkrəsɪ/ *n.* технокрáтия.

technocrat /ˈteknəˌkræt/ *n.* технокрáт.

technological /ˌteknəˈlɒdʒɪk(ə)l/ *adj.* технѝческий.

technologist /tekˈnɒlədʒɪst/ *n.* тéхник; (*in particular area*) технóлог.

technology /tekˈnɒlədʒɪ/ *n.* тéхника; (*in particular area*) технолóгия.

tectonic /tekˈtɒnɪk/ *adj.* тектонѝческий.

tectonics /tekˈtɒnɪks/ *n.* тектóника.

teddy-bear /ˈtedɪ/ *n.* плю́шевый медвежóнок/мѝшка.

teddy-boy /ˈtedɪ/ *n.* (*Br.*) стиля́га (*m.*).

tedious /ˈtiːdɪəs/ *adj.* утомѝтельный, скýчный, нýдный.

tedi|ousness /ˈtiːdɪəsnɪs/, **-um** /ˈtiːdɪəm/ *nn.* утомѝтельность, скýка.

tee /tiː/ *n.* (*peg*) кóлышек.
● *v.t.* (**tees, teed**)**: ~ a ball** устан|áвливать, -овѝть мяч для пéрвого удáра (*гольф*).
● *v.i.* (**tees, teed**)**: ~ off** дéлать, с- пéрвый удáр.

tee-hee /tiːˈhiː/ *int.* хи-хи!

teem /tiːm/ *v.i.* (*be full, swarm*) кишéть (*impf.*); изобѝловать (*impf.*); **the house is ~ing with ants** дом кишѝт муравья́ми; **his head ~s with new ideas** он пóлон нóвых идéй; **it was ~ing with rain** (*coll.*) лѝло как из ведрá.

teen /tiːn/ *n.*: **he is in his ~s** емý ещё нет двадцатѝ лет; он подрóсток.
● *cpds.* **~-age** *adj.* (*characteristic of teenagers*) подрóстковый, ю́ношеский; (*girl, boy*) несовершеннолéтний; **~ager** *n.* подрóсток, ю́ноша (*m.*)/ дéвушка до двадцатѝ лет.

teeny(-weeny) /ˈtiːnɪ/ *adj.* (**teenier, teeniest**) (*coll.*) малю́сенький.

teeter /ˈtiːtə(r)/ *v.i.* качáться (*impf.*); (*fig.*) колебáться (*impf.*).

teeth /tiːθ/ *pl. of* ⇒**tooth**

teeth|e /tiːð/ *v.i.*: **baby is ~ing** у ребёнка рéжутся зýбы; **~ing troubles** (*fig.*) «дéтские болéзни» (*f. pl.*); **~ing ring** зубнóе кольцó.

teetotal /tiːˈtəʊt(ə)l/ *adj.* непью́щий.

teetotalism /tiːˈtəʊtəˌlɪz(ə)m/ *n.* воздержáние от спиртны́х напѝтков.

teetotaller /tiːˈtəʊtələ(r)/ (*US* **teetotaler**) *n.* трéзвенник.

TEFL /ˈtef(ə)l/ (*abbr. of* ***teaching of English as a foreign language***) преподавáние англѝйского языкá как инострáнного.

Teh(e)ran /teəˈrɑːn/, /-ˈræn/ *n.* Тегерáн.

Tel Aviv /ˈtel əˈviːv/ *n.* Тель-Авѝв.

telecast /ˈtelɪˌkɑːst/ *n.* телепередáча.
● *v.t.* перед|авáть, -áть по телевѝдению.

telecommunication /ˌtelɪkəˌmjuːnɪˈkeɪʃ(ə)n/ *n.*: **~ satellite** спýтник свя́зи; **~s** телекоммуникáции (*f. pl.*); **~s** (*attr.*) телекоммуникациóнный.

teleconference /ˈtelɪˌkɒnfərəns/ *n.* телеконферéнция.

telegram /ˈtelɪˌgræm/ *n.* телегрáмма.

telegraph /ˈtelɪˌgrɑːf/, /-ˌgræf/ *n.* телегрáф.
● *v.t. & i.* телеграфѝровать (*impf., pf.*; *pf. also* про-).
● *cpds.* **~-pole** *n.* телегрáфный столб; **~-wire** *n.* телегрáфный прóвод.

telegraph|er /ˈtelɪˌgrɑːfə(r)/, /tɪˈlegrəfə(r)/, **-ist** /tɪˈlegrəfɪst/ *nn.* телеграфѝст (*fem.* -ка).

telegraphese /ˌtelɪgrəˈfiːz/ *n.* телегрáфный стиль.

telegraphic /ˌtelɪˈgræfɪk/ *adj.* телегрáфный.

telegraphist /tɪˈlegrəfɪst/ = **telegrapher**

telegraphy /tɪˈlegrəfɪ/ *n.* телеграфѝя.

telekinesis /ˌtelɪkɪˈniːsɪs/ *n.* телекинéз.

telemetry /tɪˈlemətrɪ/ *n.* телеметрѝя.

teleological /ˌtelɪəˈlɒdʒɪk(ə)l/, /ˌtiː-/ *adj.* телеологѝческий.

teleology /ˌtelɪˈɒlədʒɪ/, /ˌtiː-/ *n.* телеолóгия.

telepath /ˈtelɪˌpæθ/ *n.* телепáт.

telepathic /ˌtelɪˈpæθɪk/ *adj.* телепатѝческий.

telepathy /tɪˈlepəθɪ/ *n.* телепáтия.

telephone /ˈtelɪˌfəʊn/ *n.* телефóн; **are you on the ~?** у вас есть телефóн?; **he is (talking) on the ~** (*Br.*) он разговáривает по телефóну; **someone wants you on the ~** вас прóсят к телефóну; **he picked up the ~** он пóднял трýбку; **~ booth, box** (*Br.*) телефóнная бýдка; **~ directory** телефóнная кнѝга, телефóнный спрáвочник; **~ call** телефóнный звонóк; **~ exchange** телефóнная стáнция; **~ number** телефóнный нóмер, (*coll.*) телефóн; **~ operator** телефонѝст (*fem.* -ка); **public ~** телефóн-автомáт.
● *v.t. & i.* звонѝть, по- (*комý*) по телефóну; телефонѝровать (*impf., pf.*) (*что комý*) (*pf. also* про-).

telephonic /ˌtelɪˈfɒnɪk/ *adj.* телефóнный.

telephonist /tɪˈlefənɪst/ *n.* (*Br.*) телефонѝст (*fem.* -ка).

telephony /tɪˈlefənɪ/ *n.* телефонѝя.

telephoto(graphic) /ˌtelɪˌfəʊtəˈgræfɪk/ *adj.* телефотографѝческий.

teleprinter /ˈtelɪˌprɪntə(r)/ *n.* (*Br.*) телетáйп.

teleprompter /ˈtelɪˌprɒmptə(r)/ *n.* (*US*) автосуфлёр.

telesales /ˈtelɪˌseɪlz/ *n.pl.* продáжа по телефóну.

telescope /ˈtelɪˌskəʊp/ *n.* телескóп.
● *v.t. & i.* (*fig.*): **two coaches were ~d** два вагóна врéзались друг в дрýга; **two**

words ~d into one два слова, слитые в одно.

telescopic /,telɪ'skɒpɪk/ *adj.* **1** (*of or constituting a telescope*) телескопический; **~ lens** телескопический объектив. **2** (*visible by telescope*) видимый посредством телескопа. **3** (*consisting of retracting and extending sections*) складной, выдвижной; **~ aerial** выдвижная антенна.

teletext /'telɪ,tekst/ *n.* телетекст, вещательная видеография.

telethon /'telə,θɒn/ *n.* (благотворительный) телемарафон.

teletype /'telɪ,taɪp/ *n.* телетайп.

● *v.t.* перед|авать, -ать по телетайпу.

televise /'telɪ,vaɪz/ *v.t.* показ|ывать, -ать по телевидению.

television /'telɪ,vɪʒ(ə)n/, /-'vɪʒ(ə)n/ *n.* (*system, process*) телевидение; **what's on ~?** что показывают по телевидению?; **(~ receiver, set)** телевизор; **~ camera** телекамера; **~ programme** (*Br.*), **program** (*US*) телевизионная передача, телепередача, телепрограмма; **~ studio** телестудия; **closed-circuit ~** замкнутая телевизионная система.

telex /'teleks/ *n.* телекс.

tell /tel/ *v.t.* (*past and p.p.* **told**) **1** (*relate; inform of; make known*) рассказ|ывать, -ать; сообщ|ать, -ить; указ|ывать, -ать; **~ me all about it!** расскажите мне всё как есть/было; **I'll ~ you a secret** я скажу/открою вам секрет; **I can't ~ you how glad I am** не могу выразить вам, как я доволен; **(I'll) ~ you what, let's both go!** знаете что, давайте пойдём вместе!; **you're ~ing me!** (*coll.*) кому вы это рассказываете?; **can you ~ me the time?** вы не скажете, который час?; **can you ~ me of a good dentist?** можете ли вы указать/назвать мне хорошего зубного врача? **2** (*speak, say*) говорить, сказать; **are you ~ing the truth?** вы говорите правду? **3** (*decide, determine, know*) определ|ять, -ить; узн|авать, -ать; **how do you ~ which button to press?** как узнать, какую кнопку надо нажимать?; **there's no ~ing what may happen** кто знает, что может произойти?; **can she ~ the time yet?** она уже умеет определять время? (*or* узнавать по часам, сколько времени?); **you never can ~** никогда не знаешь. **4** (*distinguish*) отлич|ать, -ить; различ|ать, -ить; **I can't ~ them apart** я не могу их различить; **I can't ~ one wine from another** я не разбираюсь в винах. **5** (*assure*) зав|ерять, -ерить; **I can ~ you** поверьте мне. **6** (*count*): **there were seven all told** в общей сложности их было семь/семеро. **7** (*direct, instruct*) приказ|ывать, -ать; говорить, сказать; **he was told to wait outside** ему сказали/велели подождать за дверью; **~ him not to wait** скажите ему, чтобы он не ждал. **8** (*predict*) предсказ|ывать, -ать; **I told you so!** я вам говорил!; **can you ~ my fortune?** можете мне погадать?

● *v.i.* (*past and p.p.* **told**) **1** (*give information*) рассказ|ывать, -ать; **he told of his adventures** он рассказал о своих приключениях; **don't ~ on me!** (*coll.*) не выдавай меня!; **he promised not to ~** (*divulge secret*) он обещал молчать; **time will ~** время покажет. **2** (*have an effect*) сказ|ываться, -аться.

● *with adv.*: **~ off** (*coll., reprove*) отчит|ывать, -ать; **he got a good ~ing-off** (*Br.*) его здорово отчитали.

● *cpd.* **~-tale** *n.* сплетник, ябеда (*c.g.*); (*attr.*) предательский, многоговорящий.

teller /'telə(r)/ *n.* (*narrator*) рассказчик; (*counter of votes*) счётчик голосов; (*cashier*) кассир.

telling /'telɪŋ/ *adj.* сильный; **a ~ argument** убедительный довод; **a ~ example** наглядный пример; **a ~ blow** ощутимый удар.

tellurium /te'ljʊərɪəm/ *n.* теллур.

telly /'telɪ/ *n.* (*Br., television set*) телик, телек (*coll.*).

temerity /tɪ'merɪtɪ/ *n.* смелость.

temp /temp/ *n.* (*coll.*) работающ|ий (*fem.* -ая) временно.

● *v.i.* работать (*impf.*) временно.

temper /'tempə(r)/ *n.* **1** (*of metal*) степень твёрдости и упругости. **2** (*disposition of mind*) нрав; (*mood*) настроение; **he has a quick ~** он вспыльчив(ый); **he lost his ~** он вышел из себя; **I had difficulty keeping my ~** я с трудом сдерживался. **3** (*irritation, anger*) вспыльчивость; несдержанность; **he flew into a ~** он вспылил; **he left in a ~** он разозлился и ушёл.

● *v.t.* **1** (*metall.*) закал|ивать, -ить. **2** (*mitigate*) ум|ерять, -ерить; смягч|ать, -ить; **we must ~ justice with mercy** справедливость должна сочетаться с милосердием. **3** (*mus.*) темперировать (*impf., pf.*).

tempera /'tempərə/ *n.* темпера.

temperament /'temprəmənt/ *n.* темперамент, нрав; (*mus.*) темперация.

temperamental /,temprə'ment(ə)l/ *adj.* **1** (*of temperament*) органический. **2** (*subject to moods*) капризный.

temperance /'tempərəns/ *n.* **1** (*moderation*) умеренность. **2** (*abstinence from alcohol*) трезвость; воздержание от спиртных напитков; **~ society** общество трезвости.

temperate /'tempərət/ *adj.* умеренный; **the ~ zone** умеренный пояс.

temperature /'temprɪtʃə(r)/ *n.* температура; (*fever*) жар; **he has** (*or* **is running**) **a ~** у него температура/жар; **let me take your ~** давайте я измерю вам температуру.

tempest /'tempɪst/ *n.* (*lit., fig.*) буря.

tempestuous /tem'pestjʊəs/ *adj.* бурный; (*of person, behaviour*) буйный.

tempestuousness /tem'pestjʊəsnɪs/ *n.* бурность; буйство.

tempi /'tempi:/ *pl. of* ⇒**tempo**

template /'templɪt/, /-pleɪt/ *n.* шаблон; (*fig.*) модель.

temple[1] /'temp(ə)l/ *n.* (*relig.*) храм, святилище.

temple[2] /'temp(ə)l/ *n.* (*anat.*) висок.

tempo /'tempəʊ/ *n.* (*pl.* **tempos** *or* **tempi**) (*lit., fig.*) темп, ритм.

temporal /'tempər(ə)l/ *adj.* (*of time*) временной; (*of this life; secular*) мирской, светский; (*anat.*) височный.

temporarily /'tempərərɪlɪ/ *adv.* временно.

temporary /'tempərərɪ/ *n.*: **(~ employee)** временный служащий.

● *adj.* временный.

tempori|ze, -se /'tempə,raɪz/ *v.i.* медлить (*impf.*).

tempt /tempt/ *v.t.* соблазн|ять, -ить; иску|шать, -сить; **he was ~ed into bad ways** он сбился (*or* его сбили) с пути истинного; **I was ~ed to agree with him** я был склонен с ним согласиться; **~ing** соблазнительный.

temptation /temp'teɪʃ(ə)n/ *n.* соблазн, искушение; **she yielded to ~** она поддалась соблазну.

tempter /'temptə(r)/ *n.* искуситель (*m.*), соблазнитель (*m.*).

temptress /'temptrɪs/ *n.* искусительница, соблазнительница.

ten /ten/ *n.* десять; (**~** *people*) десятеро, десять человек; **he eats enough for ~** он ест за десятерых; **~ each** по десяти; **in ~s, ~ at a time** по десяти, десятками; (*figure; thing numbered 10; group of* **~**) десятка; **~ of spades** десятка пик; **the ~s** (*column*) десятки (*m. pl.*); **~s of thousands** десятки (*m. pl.*) тысяч; (*with var. nn. expr. or understood: cf. examples under* ⇒**five**): **~ to one** (*almost certainly*) почти наверняка; **~ to ~** (*o'clock*) без десяти десять.

● *adj.* десять + *g. pl.*; **~ eggs** (*as purchase*) десяток яиц; **~ threes are thirty** десятью три — тридцать.

● *cpds.* **~fold** *adj.* десятикратный; **~pin bowling** (*US* **~pins**) *n.* кегл|и (*pl., g.* -ей); **~-ton truck** *n.* (*vehicle*) десятитонка.

tenable /'tenəb(ə)l/ *adj.* **1** (*defensible*) разумный, здравый; **a ~ argument** разумный довод. **2** (*to be held*): **the office is ~ for three years** срок полномочий — три года.

tenacious /tɪ'neɪʃəs/ *adj.* (*hold, memory*) цепкий; (*resolute*) настойчивый; **the dog held on ~ly** собака крепко вцепилась.

tenacity /tɪ'næsɪtɪ/ *n.* цепкость; настойчивость.

tenancy /'tenənsɪ/ *n.* **1** (*renting*) наём помещения; (*period*) срок найма/аренды; **during his ~** в период его проживания. **2** (*ownership*) владение.

tenant /'tenənt/ *n.* (*one renting from landlord*) (*private individual*) жилец, квартирант; (*company*) арендатор.

tench /tentʃ/ *n.* (*pl.* **~**) (*zool.*) линь (*m.*).

tend[1] /tend/ *v.t.* (*look after*) присм|атривать, -отреть за + *i.*;

T

уха́живать (*impf.*) за + *i.*; **the shepherds ~ed their flocks** пастухи́ пасли́ свои́ стада́; **the machine needs constant ~ing** маши́на тре́бует постоя́нного ухо́да.

tend² /tend/ *v.i.* (*be inclined*) склоня́ться (*impf.*) (*к чему*); **I am ~ing towards your view** я склоня́юсь к ва́шей то́чке зре́ния; **he ~s to get excited** он легко́ возбужда́ется.

tendency /'tendənsɪ/ *n.* (*trend*) тенде́нция; **an upward ~ in the market** тенде́нция к повыше́нию на ры́нке; (*inclination*) скло́нность; **he has a ~ to forget** он забы́вчив(ый).

tendentious /ten'denʃəs/ *adj.* тенденцио́зный.

tendentiousness /ten'denʃəsnɪs/ *n.* тенденцио́зность.

tender¹ /'tendə(r)/ *n.* (*ship*) посы́льное су́дно; (*wagon*) те́ндер.

tender² /'tendə(r)/ *n.* **1** (*comm.*) предложе́ние; **~s are invited for the contract** принима́ются зая́вки на подря́д. **2** (*currency*): **legal ~** зако́нное платёжное сре́дство.

● *v.t.* предл|ага́ть, -ожи́ть; **he ~ed his resignation** он по́дал заявле́ние об отста́вке.

● *v.i.*: **he ~ed for the contract** он предложи́л себя́ в подря́дчики.

tender³ /'tendə(r)/ *adj.* (**tenderer, tenderest**) **1** (*sensitive*) не́жный; **of ~ years** ю́ный, в не́жном во́зрасте; **my finger is still ~** мой па́лец всё ещё боли́т. **2** (*loving, solicitous*) не́жный, ла́сковый, лю́бящий. **3** (*not tough*): **a ~ steak** мя́гкий бифште́кс.

● *cpds.* **~foot** *n.* (*US coll.*) новичо́к; **~-hearted** *adj.* мягкосерде́чный; **~loin** *n.* вы́резка.

tenderness /'tendənɪs/ *n.* не́жность; (*of meat etc.*) мя́гкость.

tendon /'tend(ə)n/ *n.* сухожи́лие.

tendril /'tendrɪl/ *n.* у́сик.

tenement /'tenɪmənt/ *n.* (*cheap apartment*) кварти́ра; **~ house** сдава́емый в аре́нду многокварти́рный дом.

Tenerife /,tenə'ri:f/ *n.* Танери́фе (*m. indecl.*).

tenet /'tenɪt/, /'ti:net/ *n.* до́гмат, при́нцип.

tenner /'tenə(r)/ *n.* (*Br. coll.*) деся́тка (*деньги*).

tennis /'tenɪs/ *n.* те́ннис; **~ elbow** «те́ннисный» ло́коть (*травма*).

● *cpds.* **~ ball** *n.* те́ннисный мяч; **~-court** *n.* те́ннисный корт; **~-player** *n.* теннисист (*fem.* -ка); **~-racket** *n.* те́ннисная раке́тка; **~-shoes** *n. pl.* те́ннисные ту́фли (*f. pl.*).

tenon /'tenən/ *n.* шип.

● *cpds.* **~-joint** *n.* соедине́ние на вставны́х шипа́х; **~-saw** *n.* шипоре́зная пила́.

tenor¹ /'tenə(r)/ *n.* (*course, direction*) направле́ние, напра́вленность; (*purport*) смысл, содержа́ние.

tenor² /'tenə(r)/ *n.* (*mus.*) те́нор; **he sings ~** он поёт те́нором; (*attr.*) теноро́вый; **~ part** па́ртия те́нора; **~ saxophone** саксофо́н-те́нор.

tense¹ /tens/ *n.* (*gram.*) вре́мя (*nt.*).

tense² /tens/ *adj.* натя́нутый, напряжённый; **~ nerves** натя́нутые не́рвы; **a moment of ~ excitement** моме́нт не́рвного возбужде́ния.

● *v.t.* натя́|гивать, -ну́ть; напр|яга́ть, -я́чь; **he ~d his muscles** он напря́г му́скулы; **I was all ~d up** я был в напряжённом состоя́нии.

● *v.i.* напр|яга́ться, -я́чься.

tenseness /'tensnɪs/ *n.* (*lit., fig.*) натя́нутость, напряжённость.

tensile /'tensaɪl/ *adj.* растяжи́мый; **~ strength** преде́л про́чности при растяже́нии.

tension /'tenʃ(ə)n/ *n.* **1** (*stretching; being stretched*) напряже́ние, растяже́ние; (*stretched state*) натяже́ние, напряжённое состоя́ние; (*mental strain, excitement*) напряже́ние, напряжённость, **racial ~** напряжённые ра́совые отноше́ния. **2** (*voltage*): **high/low ~** высо́кое/ни́зкое напряже́ние.

tent /tent/ *n.* пала́тка; (*marquee*) шатёр.

● *cpd.* **~-peg** *n.* ко́лышек для пала́тки.

tentacle /'tentək(ə)l/ *n.* щу́пальце.

tentative /'tentətɪv/ *adj.* (*hesitant*) осторо́жный; (*provisional*) предвари́тельный.

tenterhooks /'tentə,hʊks/ *n.*: **I was on ~** я сиде́л как на иго́лках.

tenth /tenθ/ *n.* **1** (*date*) деся́тое число́; **on the ~ of May** деся́того ма́я. **2** (*fraction*) деся́тая часть; **one ~** одна́ деся́тая.

● *adj.* деся́тый.

tenuous /'tenjʊəs/ *adj.* (*weak*) сла́бый; (*fine*) то́нкий; **a ~ argument** сла́бый/неубеди́тельный аргуме́нт.

tenure /'tenjə(r)/ *n.* (*holding of office*) пребыва́ние в до́лжности; (*period of office*) срок полномо́чий; (*of property*) усло́вия (*nt. pl.*) владе́ния иму́ществом; (*security of ~*) постоя́нная шта́тная до́лжность.

tepee /'ti:pi:/ *n.* вигва́м.

tepid /'tepɪd/ *adj.* теплова́тый; (*fig.*) прохла́дный.

tepid|ity /tɪ'pɪdɪtɪ/, **-ness** /'tepɪdnɪs/ *nn.* теплова́тость; (*fig.*) равноду́шие.

tercentenary /,tɜ:sen'ti:nərɪ/ *n.* трёхсотле́тие.

● *adj.* трёхсотле́тний.

term /tɜ:m/ *n.* **1** (*fixed or limited period*) пери́од; **~ of office** срок полномо́чий; **a long ~ of imprisonment** дли́тельный срок заключе́ния; (*in school, university etc.*) триме́стр, уче́бная че́тверть; (*in law courts*) се́ссия. **2** (*math., logic*) элеме́нт, член. **3** (*expression*) те́рмин; **~ of abuse** (*word*) бра́нное сло́во; (*expression*) бра́нное выраже́ние; **contradiction in ~s** противоречи́вое утвержде́ние/поня́тие; **he spoke of you in flattering ~s** он говори́л о вас в ле́стных выраже́ниях; **in ~s of** с то́чки зре́ния + *g.*; в смы́сле + *g.*; что каса́ется + *g.*; **he thinks of everything in ~s of money** он смо́трит на всё с де́нежной то́чки зре́ния. **4** (*pl., conditions*) усло́вия (*nt. pl.*); **~s of surrender** усло́вия капитуля́ции; **they came to ~s** они́ пришли́ к соглаше́нию; **~s of reference** (*Br.*) круг полномо́чий; (*charges*) усло́вия опла́ты; **what are your ~s?** каковы́ ва́ши усло́вия? **5** (*pl., relations*) отноше́ния (*nt. pl.*); **I kept on good ~s with him** я подде́рживал с ним хоро́шие отноше́ния; **we are on the best of ~s** мы в прекра́сных отноше́ниях; **they are not on speaking ~s** они́ не разгова́ривают друг с дру́гом; **they met on equal ~s** они́ встре́тились на ра́вных.

● *v.t.* наз|ыва́ть, -ва́ть.

termagant /'tɜ:məgənt/ *n.* мегéра, фу́рия.

terminable /'tɜ:mɪnəb(ə)l/ *adj.* с ограни́ченным сро́ком де́йствия.

terminal /'tɜ:mɪn(ə)l/ *n.* **1** (*of transport*) коне́чный пункт; (*rail*) вокза́л; **air ~** (*in city*) (городско́й) аэровокза́л. **2** (*elec.*) кле́мма, зажи́м. **3** (*comput.*) термина́л.

● *adj.* (*coming to or forming the end point*) коне́чный; после́дний; **~ illness** смерте́льная боле́знь; **~ patient** неизлечи́мый больно́й.

terminate /'tɜ:mɪ,neɪt/ *v.t.* заверш|а́ть, -и́ть; класть, положи́ть коне́ц + *d.*; **they ~d his contract** они́ расто́ргли контра́кт с ним.

● *v.i.* зак|а́нчиваться, -о́нчиться; заверш|а́ться, -и́ться; **words which ~ in a vowel** слова́, ока́нчивающиеся на гла́сную.

termination /,tɜ:mɪ'neɪʃ(ə)n/ *n.* заверше́ние; прекраще́ние; коне́ц; (*of a word*) оконча́ние; **~ of pregnancy** прекраще́ние бере́менности; або́рт.

termini /'tɜ:mɪ,naɪ/ *pl. of* ⇒**terminus**

terminological /,tɜ:mɪnə'lɒdʒɪk(ə)l/ *adj.* терминологи́ческий.

terminology /,tɜ:mɪ'nɒlədʒɪ/ *n.* терминоло́гия, номенклату́ра.

termin|us /'tɜ:mɪnəs/ *n.* (*pl.* **~i** *or* **~uses**) (*Br.*) коне́чный пункт; (*rail*) коне́чная ста́нция.

termite /'tɜ:maɪt/ *n.* (*zool.*) терми́т.

tern /tɜ:n/ *n.* (*zool.*) кра́чка.

terra /,terə/ *n.*: **~ *firma*** /'fɜ:mə/ су́ша; **~ *incognita*** /ɪŋ'kɒgnɪtə/, /,ɪnkɒg'ni:tə/ (*fig.*) тэ́рра инко́гнита, неизве́данная о́бласть зна́ний (*u m.n.*).

terrace /'terəs/, /-rɪs/ *n.* (*raised area*) терра́са; (*Br., row of houses*) ряд домо́в, постро́енных вплотну́ю.

● *v.t.* террасúровать (*impf., pf.*).

terracotta /,terə'kɒtə/ *n.* террако́та; (*attr.*) террако́товый.

terrain /te'reɪn/, /tə-/ *n.* ме́стность.

terrapin /'terəpɪn/ *n.* пресново́дная черепа́ха.

terrestrial /tə'restrɪəl/, /tɪ-/ *adj.* (*of the earth*) земно́й; (*living on dry land*) сухопу́тный; живу́щий на/в земле́.

terrible /'terɪb(ə)l/ *adj.* (*inspiring fear*)

стра́шный; (*coll., very unpleasant or bad*) ужа́сный, стра́шный.

terribly /'terɪblɪ/ *adv.* ужа́сно, стра́шно.

terrier /'terɪə(r)/ *n.* терье́р.

terrific /tə'rɪfɪk/ *adj.* (*coll., huge*) колосса́льный; (*coll., marvellous*) потряса́ющий.

terrify /'terɪ,faɪ/ *v.t.* ужас|а́ть, -ну́ть.

terrine /tə'ri:n/ *n.* паште́т.

territorial /,terɪ'tɔ:rɪəl/ *n.* слу́жащий территориа́льной а́рмии.

● *adj.* территориа́льный.

territory /'terɪtərɪ/, /-trɪ/ *n.* террито́рия; (*fig.*) о́бласть.

terror /'terə(r)/ *n.* (*fear*) у́жас, страх; **he went in ~ of his life** он жил в стра́хе за свою́ жизнь; **the thought struck ~ into me** э́та мысль привела́ меня́ в у́жас; (*pol., hist.*) терро́р; (*child*) чертёнок.

● *cpds.* **~-stricken, ~-struck** *adjs.* объя́тый стра́хом/у́жасом.

terrorism /'terə,rɪz(ə)m/ *n.* террори́зм.

terrorist /'terərɪst/ *n.* террори́ст (*fem.* -ка); (*attr.*) террористи́ческий.

terrorization /,terəraɪ'zeɪʃ(ə)n/ *n.* терроризи́рование.

terrorize /'terə,raɪz/ *v.t.* терроризи́ровать (*impf., pf.*).

terry /'terɪ/ *n.* (*text.*) махро́вая ткань; (*attr.*) махро́вый.

terse /tɜ:s/ *adj.* (**terser, tersest**) кра́ткий, сжа́тый.

terseness /'tɜ:snɪs/ *n.* кра́ткость, сжа́тость.

tertiary /'tɜ:ʃərɪ/ *adj.* (*geol. etc.*) трети́чный.

Terylene /'terɪ,li:n/ *n.* (*Br. propr., text.*) терилéн.

TESSA /'tesə/ *n.* (*abbr. of* ***tax exempt special savings account***) (*Br.*) сберега́тельный счёт необлага́емый нало́гом.

tessellated /'tesə,leɪtɪd/ *adj.* моза́ичный.

tessera /'tesərə/ *n.* (*pl.* **tesserae** /-,ri:/) (*in mosaic*) тессе́ра, кусо́чек.

test /test/ *n.* испыта́ние, прове́рка; **~ case** показа́тельный слу́чай; (*leg.*) де́ло-прецеде́нт; **endurance ~** испыта́ние выно́сливости; **his promises were put to the ~** его́ обеща́ния подве́рглись прове́рке на де́ле; **these methods have stood the ~ of time** э́ти ме́тоды вы́держали прове́рку вре́менем; (*examination*) (*in school*) контро́льная рабо́та; (*at college*) зачёт; (*oral*) опро́с, зачёт; (*chem.*) ана́лиз; о́пыт; **(nuclear) ~ ban** запреще́ние испыта́ний я́дерного ору́жия; **a ~ for sugar** ана́лиз на содержа́ние са́хара; **blood ~** ана́лиз кро́ви; (*cricket*) = **~-match**

● *v.t.* **1** (*make trial of*) подв|ерга́ть, -е́ргнуть испыта́нию; пров|еря́ть, -е́рить; **his patience was severely ~ed** его́ терпе́ние подве́рглось суро́вому испыта́нию. **2** (*subject to ~s*) пров|еря́ть, -е́рить; (*tech.*) опро́бовать (*pf.*); **the pupils were ~ed in arithmetic** ученика́м да́ли контро́льную рабо́ту по арифме́тике; **his job is to ~ (out) new designs** он прово́дит испыта́ния но́вых констру́кций.

● *cpds.* **~ flight** *n.* испыта́тельный полёт; **~-match** *n.* междунаро́дный кри́кетный матч; **~-pilot** *n.* лётчик-испыта́тель (*m.*); **~-tube** *n.* проби́рка; **~-tube baby** ребёнок «из проби́рки» (*зачатый вне материнского чрева*).

testament /'testəmənt/ *n.* (*clear sign*) свиде́тельство; (*will*) завеща́ние; (*bibl.*) заве́т; **the Old/New T~** Ве́тхий/Но́вый заве́т.

testator /te'steɪtə(r)/ *n.* завеща́тель (*m.*).

testatrix /te'steɪtrɪks/ *n.* завеща́тельница.

tester /'testə(r)/ *n.* (*person*) испыта́тель (*m.*); лабора́нт; (*device*) испыта́тельный прибо́р.

testes /'testi:z/ *pl. of* ⇒**testis**

testicle /'testɪk(ə)l/ *n.* (*anat.*) яи́чко.

testify /'testɪ,faɪ/ *v.i.* **1** (*affirm*) свиде́тельствовать (*impf.*); (*give evidence*) да|ва́ть, -ть показа́ния; **will you ~ to my innocence?** вы подтверди́те мою́ невино́вность? **2**: **~ to** (*be evidence of*) свиде́тельствовать (*impf.*) о + *p.*

testimonial /,testɪ'məʊnɪəl/ *n.* (*certificate of conduct etc.*) рекоменда́ция, характери́стика.

testimony /'testɪmənɪ/ *n.* (*statement*) показа́ния (*nt. pl.*); (*evidence*) доказа́тельство; (*sign*) свиде́тельство, при́знак.

testiness /'testɪnɪs/ *n.* вспы́льчивость, раздражи́тельность.

testis /'testɪs/ (*pl.* **testes**) = **testicle**

testosterone /te'stɒstə,rəʊn/ *n.* тестостеро́н.

testy /'testɪ/ *adj.* (**testier, testiest**) вспы́льчивый, раздражи́тельный.

tetanus /'tetənəs/ *n.* (*disease*) столбня́к; (*contraction of muscles*) те́танус.

tetchiness /'tetʃɪnɪs/ *n.* раздражи́тельность; оби́дчивость.

tetchy /'tetʃɪ/ *adj.* (**tetchier, tetchiest**) раздражи́тельный; оби́дчивый.

tête-à-tête /,teɪtɑ:'teɪt/ *n.* тет-а-те́т.

● *adv.* (*to talk*) тет-а-те́т; с гла́зу на гла́з; (*to dine*) вдвоём.

tether /'teðə(r)/ *n.* при́вязь; (*fig.*): **he was at the end of his ~** он дошёл до ру́чки (*coll.*).

● *v.t.* привя́з|ывать, -а́ть.

tetrahedr|on /,tetrə'hi:drən/, /-'hedrən/ *n.* (*pl.* **~a** *or* **~ons**) четырёхгра́нник, тетра́эдр.

tetrameter /tɪ'træmɪtə(r)/ *n.* тетра́метр.

Teutonic /tju:'tɒnɪk/ *adj.* тевто́нский, герма́нский.

text /tekst/ *n.* (*original words*) текст; (*quoted passage*) отры́вок; (*subject, theme*) те́ма.

● *cpd.* **~-book** *n.* уче́бник; (*manual*) руково́дство; **~ editor** *n.* (*comput.*) те́кстовый реда́ктор; **~ file** *n.* (*comput.*) те́кстовый файл.

textile /'tekstaɪl/ *n.* ткань; (*pl.*) текст́иль (*m.*).

● *adj.* пряди́льный, тексти́льный; **~ workers** тексти́льщики.

textual /'tekstjʊəl/ *adj.* текстово́й; **~ criticism** текстоло́гия.

textural /'tekstʃərəl/ *adj.* структу́рный.

texture /'tekstʃə(r)/ *n.* (*of fabric*): **this cloth has a smooth ~** э́та ткань мя́гкая на о́щупь; **smooth ~** мя́гкость; **rough ~** шерохова́тость; (*arrangement of threads*) переплете́ние; (*of solid bodies, rocks, minerals, wood etc.*) тексту́ра; (*fig., structure, arrangement*) склад, строе́ние; **the ~ of the skin** ка́чество ко́жи.

Thai /taɪ/ *n.* (*pl.* **~** *or* **~s**) таила́нд|ец (*fem.* -ка).

● *adj.* та́йский, таила́ндский.

● *cpd.* **~land** *n.* Таила́нд.

thalidomide /θə'lɪdə,maɪd/ *n.* (*pharm.*) талидоми́д; **~ babies** же́ртвы (*f. pl.*) талидоми́да.

Thames /temz/ *n.* Те́мза.

than /ðən/, /ðæn/ *conj.* чем; **he's got more money ~ me** у него́ бо́льше де́нег, чем у меня́; **he is taller ~ I** он вы́ше меня́; **can't you walk faster ~ that?** вы не мо́жете идти́ быстре́е?; **I would do anything rather ~ have him return** я гото́в на всё — лишь бы он не возвраща́лся; **the visitor was no other ~ his father** посети́телем был не кто ино́й, как его́ оте́ц; **I want nothing better ~ to relax** мне ничего́ так не хо́чется, как отдохну́ть.

thank /θæŋk/ *v.t.* благодари́ть, по-; (*by returning favour*) отблагодари́ть (*pf.*); **~ you** спаси́бо; благодарю́ вас; **how can I ~ you?** (*express* **~s**) как вы́разить вам свою́ благода́рность?; (*repay favour*) как вас отблагодари́ть?; **I will ~ you to mind your own business** я проси́л бы вас не вме́шиваться не в своё де́ло; **he has only himself to ~** он сам во всём винова́т; **~ God you are safe** сла́ва Бо́гу, вы в безопа́сности.

● *cpd.* **~-you** *n.*: **he left without as much as a ~-you** он ушёл, да́же не сказа́в спаси́бо; *adj.*: **~-you letter** благода́рственное письмо́.

thankful /'θæŋkfʊl/ *adj.* благода́рный.

thankfulness /'θæŋkfʊlnɪs/ *n.* благода́рность.

thankless /'θæŋklɪs/ *adj.* неблагода́рный.

thanks /θæŋks/ *n. pl.* благода́рность; **~ for everything** спаси́бо за всё; **many ~** большо́е спаси́бо!; **~ to** благодаря́ + *d.*; **you will get no ~ for it** вам никто́ за э́то спаси́бо не ска́жет; **vote of ~** вынесе́ние коллекти́вной благода́рности; **letter of ~** благода́рственное письмо́.

● *cpd.* **~giving** *n.* (*expression of gratitude*) благодаре́ние; (*service*) благода́рственный моле́бен; **T~giving Day** День благодаре́ния.

that /ðæt/ *pron.* (*pl.* **those**) **1** (*demonstrative*) э́то; **~'s him!** э́то он;

T

(*when pointing*) вот (э́то) он!; **those are the boys I saw** э́то те ма́льчики, кото́рых я ви́дел; **those were the days!** вот э́то бы́ли времена́!; **what is ~?** что э́то (тако́е)?; **who is ~** кто э́то?; (*on the telephone*) кто говори́т?; **what's ~ for?** к чему́ (*or* заче́м) э́то?; **~'s a nice hat!** кака́я краси́вая шля́пка!; **~'s it!** (*sc. the point*) вот и́менно!; (*sc. right*) пра́вильно!; так!; **~'s just it, I can't swim** в то́м-то и де́ло, что я не уме́ю пла́вать; **it's not ~** не в э́том де́ло; **~ is how the war began** вот как начала́сь война́; **~'s right!** пра́вильно!; ве́рно!; **~'s all** э́то всё; вот и всё!; **what happened after ~?** что произошло́ по́сле э́того/пото́м?; **don't be like ~!** (*coll.*) ну, переста́ньте!; **how's ~ for a score?** ничего́ счёт, а?; **~'s ~, then: now we can go** ну, всё, тепе́рь мы мо́жем идти́; **I'm going, and ~'s ~** я ухожу́: всё; **with ~ he ended his speech** на э́том он ко́нчил свою́ речь; **~ is (to say)** то́ есть; **we talked of this and ~** мы говори́ли о том, о сём; **for all ~, he's a good husband** и при всём том он хоро́ший муж; **the climate is like ~ of France** кли́мат тако́й же, как во Фра́нции; (*pl., as antecedent*): **there are those who say...** есть таки́е, что говоря́т...; ко́е-кто говори́т...; **at ~** (*moreover*) к тому́ же; вдоба́вок; **he's only a journalist, and a poor one at ~** он всего́ лишь журнали́ст, и при э́том нева́жный. **2** (*rel.*) кото́рый; **the book ~ I am talking about** кни́га, о кото́рой я говорю́; **he was the best man ~ I ever knew** он был са́мым лу́чшим челове́ком, како́го я когда́-либо знал; **the year ~ my father died** год, в кото́ром сконча́лся мой оте́ц.

● *adj.* (*pl.* **those**) э́тот, тот; **I'll take ~ one** я возьму́ (вот) э́тот; **from ~ day forward** (начина́я) с того́ дня; **at ~ time** в то вре́мя.

● *adv.*: **~ much I know** э́то-то я зна́ю; **I can't walk ~ far** я не могу́ так мно́го ходи́ть; **it is not all ~ cold** не так уж хо́лодно.

● *conj.* что; **I think ~ you're wrong** я ду́маю, что вы непра́вы; (*expr. wish*) что́бы; **I with ~ he would go away** я хочу́, что́бы он ушёл; **would ~ it were not so!** е́сли бы то́лько э́то бы́ло нс так!; (*expr. purpose*) (для того́) что́бы; (*var.*): **it's just ~ I have no time** де́ло в том, что у меня́ про́сто нет вре́мени; **it's not ~ I don't like him** не то, что́бы он мне не нра́вился; **now ~** раз (уж); поско́льку; **now ~ I have more time** поско́льку у меня́ сейча́с бо́льше вре́мени; **it was there ~ I first saw her** там я и уви́дел её впервы́е; **he differs in ~ he likes reading** он отлича́ется тем, что он лю́бит чита́ть.

thatch /θætʃ/ *n.* (*straw*) соло́ма; (*reeds*) тростни́к.

● *v.t.* крыть, по- соло́мой/тростнико́м; **a ~ed roof** соло́менная/тростнико́вая кры́ша.

thaw /θɔ:/ *n.* о́ттепель; **a ~ set in** начала́сь о́ттепель.

● *v.t.* (*ground, river*) отта́|ивать, -ять; (*food*) размор|а́живать, -о́зить.

● *v.i.* (*of ground, river*) отта́|ивать, -ять; (*of food*) размор|а́живаться, -о́зиться; (*fig.*) смягч|а́ться, -и́ться.

the /ðɪ/, /ðə/, /ði:/ *def. art., usu. untranslated*; (*if more emphatic*) э́тот, тот (са́мый); **~ cheek of it!** како́е наха́льство!; **~ one with ~ blue handle** тот, что с голубо́й ру́чкой; **something of ~ sort** что́-то в э́том ро́де; **he is ~ man for ~ job** он са́мый подходя́щий челове́к для э́той рабо́ты; **not *the* Mr Smith?** неуже́ли тот са́мый ми́стер Смит?; **Turkey is *the* place this year** в э́том году́ са́мое мо́дное ме́сто — Ту́рция.

● *adv.*: **~ more ~ better** чем бо́льше, тем лу́чше; **he was none ~ worse (for it)** он (при э́том) нисколько не пострада́л; **that makes it all ~ worse** от э́того то́лько ху́же; **so much ~ worse for him** тем ху́же для него́.

theatre /ˈθɪətə(r)/ (*US* **theater**) *n.* **1** (*playhouse*) теа́тр; **~ ticket** биле́т в теа́тр. **2** (*dramatic literature*) драматурги́я; (*drama*) теа́тр, театра́льное иску́сство; **~ group** драмкружо́к. **3** (*hall for lectures etc.*) зал; **operating ~** операцио́нная. **4** (*scene of operation*) по́ле де́йствий; **~ of war** теа́тр вое́нных де́йствий.

● *cpds.* **~-goer** *n.* театра́л; **~-going** *n.* посеще́ние теа́тров; **~-land** *n.* райо́н теа́тров.

theatrical /θɪˈætrɪk(ə)l/ *adj.* театра́льный.

theatricals /θɪˈætrɪk(ə)ls/ *n.*: **amateur ~** театра́льная самоде́ятельность.

thee /ði:/ *obj. of* ⇒**thou**

theft /θeft/ *n.* кра́жа.

their /ðeə(r)/ *adj.* их; (*referring to gram. subject*) свой; **they lost ~ rights** они́ лиши́лись свои́х прав; **they want a house of ~ own** они́ хотя́т име́ть (свой) со́бственный дом; **they broke ~ legs** они́ слома́ли себе́ но́ги.

theirs /ðeəz/ *pron.* их, свой (*cf.* ⇒**their**); **the money was ~ by right** де́ньги принадлежа́ли им по пра́ву; **it is a habit of ~** у них така́я привы́чка.

theism /ˈθi:ɪz(ə)m/ *n.* теи́зм.

theist /ˈθi:ɪst/ *n.* теи́ст (*fem.* -ка).

theistic /θi:ˈɪstɪk/ *adj.* теисти́ческий.

them /ðem/, /ðəm/ *obj. of* ⇒**they**

thematic /θɪˈmætɪk/ *adj.* темати́ческий.

theme /θi:m/ *n.* (*subject: also mus.*) те́ма; **~ park** темати́ческий парк; **~ song, tune** лейтмоти́в.

themselves /ðəmˈselvz/ *pron.* **1** (*refl.*) себя́ (*d., p.* себе́, *i.* собо́й); -ся, -сь; **they blamed ~** они́ вини́ли себя́; **they were proud of ~** они́ горди́лись собо́й; **they always talk about ~** они́ говоря́т то́лько о себе́; **they have only ~ to blame** они́ са́ми винова́ты; **they live by ~** они́ живу́т одни́; **they did it by ~** (*unaided*) они́ сде́лали э́то са́ми/самостоя́тельно. **2** (*emph.*): **they did the work ~** они́ са́ми сде́лали э́ту рабо́ту.

then /ðen/ *n.*: **before ~** до э́того/того́ вре́мени; **by ~** к э́тому/тому́ вре́мени; **since ~** с тех пор; **till ~** до тех пор.

● *adj.* тогда́шний; **the ~ king** тогда́шний коро́ль.

● *adv.* **1** (*at that time*) тогда́; **~ and there** тут же, сра́зу же; **now and ~** вре́мя от вре́мени.
2 (*next; after that*) да́льше, да́лее.
3 (*furthermore*) кро́ме того́; опя́ть-таки (*coll.*).
4 (*in that case*) тогда́; **~ what *do* you want?** чего́ же вы тогда́ (*or* в тако́м слу́чае) хоти́те?; **till tomorrow, ~!** ну, тогда́ до за́втра!; (*introducing apodosis*) то; **if he asks me ~ I'll go** е́сли он попро́сит меня́, (то) я пойду́.
5 (*in resumption*) зна́чит; итак.
6 (*emph.*) так, ита́к; **now ~, let's see what you've brought** ну́-ка дава́йте посмо́трим, что вы принесли́; **now ~!** (*warning*) ну-ну́!; **well ~, we can go tomorrow** так/зна́чит, мы мо́жем пойти́ за́втра.

thence /ðens/ *adv.* (*from that place*) отту́да; (*from that source, for that reason*) отсю́да, из э́того.

● *cpds.* **~forth, ~forward** *advs.* с тех пор.

theocracy /θɪˈɒkrəsɪ/ *n.* теокра́тия.

theocratic /θɪəˈkrætɪk/ *adj.* теократи́ческий.

theodolite /θɪˈɒdəˌlaɪt/ *n.* теодоли́т.

theologian /θɪəˈləudʒɪən/, /-dʒ(ə)n/ *n.* богосло́в, тео́лог.

theological /θɪəˈlɒdʒɪk(ə)l/ *adj.* богосло́вский, теологи́ческий.

theology /θɪˈɒlədʒɪ/ *n.* богосло́вие, теоло́гия.

theorem /ˈθɪərəm/ *n.* теоре́ма.

theoretical /θɪəˈretɪk(ə)l/ *adj.* теорети́ческий.

theor|etician /ˌθɪərɪˈtɪʃ(ə)n/, **-ist** /ˈθɪərɪst/ *nn.* теоре́тик.

theorize /ˈθɪəraɪz/ *v.i.* теоретизи́ровать (*impf.*).

theory /ˈθɪərɪ/ *n.* тео́рия; **in ~** в тео́рии; теорети́чески.

theosophical /θɪəˈsɒfɪk(ə)l/ *adj.* теосо́фский, теософи́ческий.

theosophist /θɪˈɒsəfɪst/ *n.* теосо́ф (*fem.* -ка).

theosophy /θɪˈɒsəfɪ/ *n.* теосо́фия.

therapeutic /ˌθerəˈpju:tɪk/ *adj.* терапевти́ческий, лече́бный.

therapeutics /ˌθerəˈpju:tɪks/ *n.* терапи́я.

therapist /ˈθerəpɪst/ *n.* терапе́вт.

therapy /ˈθerəpɪ/ *n.* терапи́я, лече́ние; **occupational ~** трудотерапи́я; **shock ~** шокотерапи́я.

there /ðeə(r)/ *adv.* **1** (*in or at that place*) там; вон (*coll.*); вон та́м; **that man ~ is my uncle** (вот) тот челове́к — мой дя́дя; **hey, you ~!** эй, ты!; **he's not all ~** у него́ не все до́ма (*coll.*).
2 (*to that place*) туда́; **when shall we get ~?** когда́ мы туда́ доберёмся?; **we went ~ and back in a day** мы съе́здили туда́ и обра́тно за оди́н день.
3 (*of destination in general*) туда́; **the train gets you ~ quicker** на по́езде туда́ быстре́е.
4 (*at that point or stage*) тут, здесь; **~ the matter ended** на э́том де́ло и

ко́нчилось; **I wrote to him ~ and then** я тут же написа́л ему́.
5 (*in that respect*) здесь; тут; в э́том отноше́нии; **~ I agree with you** здесь я с ва́ми согла́сен; **you're wrong ~** тут вы непра́вы.
6 (*demonstr.*): **~ goes the bell!** а вот и звоно́к!; **~ you go again!** опя́ть вы за своё!; **I don't like it, but ~ it is** не нра́вится мне э́то, да ничего́ не поде́лаешь; **~ you are, take it!** вот вам, держи́те!; **oh, ~ you are; I was looking for you** вот и вы! а я вас иска́л; **don't tell anyone, ~'s a good chap!** (*Br.*) не расска́зывай никому́ об э́том, ла́дно?; **~'s gratitude for you!** вот вам людска́я благода́рность!
7 (*in existence*): **the church isn't ~ any more** э́той це́ркви бо́льше нет.
8 (*with v. to be, expr. presence, availability etc.*): **~'s a fly in my soup** у меня́ в су́пе му́ха; **is ~ a doctor here?** тут есть врач?; **~'s no time to lose** нельзя́ теря́ть ни мину́ты; **~ seems to have been a mistake** тут, ка́жется, произошла́ оши́бка; **~ was plenty to eat** еды́ бы́ло полно́; **what is ~ to say?** что тут мо́жно сказа́ть?
● *int.*: **~! what did I tell you?** ну вот! что я вам говори́л?; **~, ~!** (*comforting child etc.*) ну! ну!

thereabouts /ˈðeərəˌbaʊts/, /-ˈbaʊts/ *adv.* (*nearby*) поблизо́сти; (*approximately*) о́коло э́того; приблизи́тельно; **£5 or ~** 5 фу́нтов или о́коло этого.

thereafter /ðeərˈɑːftə(r)/ *adv.* по́сле того́; впредь.

thereby /ðeəˈbaɪ/, /ˈðeə-/ *adv.* э́тим; таки́м о́бразом.

therefore /ˈðeəfɔː(r)/ *adv.* поэ́тому, сле́довательно.

therefrom /ðeəˈfrɒm/ *adv.* (*arch.*) (*from that place*) отту́да; (*from this*) отсю́да.

therein /ðeərˈɪn/ *adv.* (*arch.*) (*in that place*) там; в э́том; (*into that place*) туда́; (*in that*): **~ lay her strength** в э́том заключа́лась её си́ла.

thereof /ðeərˈɒv/ *adv.* (*arch.*) (*of this*) э́того; (*of these*) э́тих; **any part ~** люба́я его́/её часть.

thereon /ðeərˈɒn/ *adv.* (*arch.*) (*on that*) на э́том; (*on it*) на нём/ней; (*on them*) на них.

thereto /ðeəˈtuː/ *adv.* (*arch.*) (*to that*) к э́тому.

thereunder /ðeərˈʌndə(r)/ *adv.* (*arch.*) (*below*) ни́же; (*under this*) под э́тим; (*under them*) под ни́ми.

thereupon /ˌðeərəˈpɒn/ *adv.* (*shortly after*) за э́тим, заси́м; (*as a consequence*) всле́дствие того́.

therewith /ðeəˈwɪð/ *adv.* (*arch.*) (*with that*) с э́тим; (*soon after*) заси́м.

therm /θɜːm/ *n.* терм.

thermal /ˈθɜːm(ə)l/ *n.* (*aeron.*) восходя́щий пото́к тёплого во́здуха.
● *adj.*: **~ capacity** теплоёмкость; **~ reactor** реа́ктор на тепловы́х нейтро́нах; **~ springs** горя́чие исто́чники.

thermodynamics /ˌθɜːməʊdaɪˈnæmɪks/ *n.* термодина́мика.

thermometer /θəˈmɒmɪtə(r)/ *n.* термо́метр.

thermonuclear /ˌθɜːməʊˈnjuːklɪə(r)/ *adj.* термоя́дерный.

thermoplastic /ˌθɜːməʊˈplæstɪk/ *n.* термопла́ст.
● *adj.* термопласти́ческий.

thermos /ˈθɜːməs/ *n.* **(~ flask)** те́рмос.

thermostat /ˈθɜːməˌstæt/ *n.* термоста́т.

thesau|rus /θɪˈsɔːrəs/ *n.* (*pl.* **~ri** /-raɪ/ *or* **~ruses**) теза́урус.

these /ðiːz/ *pl. of* ⇨**this**

thesis /ˈθiːsɪs/ *n.* (*pl.* **theses** /-siːz/) (*dissertation*) диссерта́ция; (*contention*) те́зис.

Thespian /ˈθespɪən/ *n.* (*joc.*) актёр (*fem.* актри́са).

they /ðeɪ/ *pron.* (*obj.* **them;** *poss.* **their, theirs**) они́; **~ who ...** те, кото́рые/кто...; **both of them** они́ о́ба.

thick /θɪk/ *n.*: **in the ~ of the crowd** в гу́ще толпы́; **in the ~ of the fighting** в са́мом пе́кле боя́; **he stood by me through ~ and thin** он стоя́л за меня́ гру́дью.
● *adj.* **1** (*of solid substance*) то́лстый; (*of liquid*) густо́й; **a ~ overcoat** тяжёлое пальто́; **a ~ coat of paint** то́лстый слой кра́ски; **the dust lay an inch ~** пыль лежа́ла толщино́й в дюйм; **~ soup** густо́й суп.
2 (*close together, dense*) густо́й; (*of population*) пло́тный; **~ hair** густы́е во́лосы; **a ~ forest** густо́й/ча́стый лес; **the fog is getting ~** тума́н густе́ет; **the air was ~ with smoke** стоя́л густо́й дым.
3 (*coll., stupid*) тупо́й.
4 (*coll., intimate*): **they are as ~ as thieves** они́ снюха́лись.
5 (*dull, indistinct*): **I woke with a ~ head** я просну́лся с тяжёлой голово́й; (*pronounced, extreme*): **he has a ~ accent** у него́ си́льный акце́нт.
6: **that's a bit ~!** (*Br. coll., of impertinence etc.*) ну, это уже́ чересчу́р/сли́шком!
● *adv.* гу́сто, ча́сто; **the blows came ~ and fast** уда́ры сы́пались оди́н за други́м.
● *cpds.* **~head** *n.* тупи́ца (*c.g.*); **~-headed** *adj.* тупоголо́вый; **~set** *adj.* (*stocky*) корена́стый, кряжи́стый; (*closely planted*) гу́сто поса́женный; **~-skinned** *adj.* (*lit., fig.*) толстоко́жий.

thicken /ˈθɪkən/ *v.t.* (*liquid*) сгу|ща́ть, -сти́ть/де́лать, с- бо́лее густы́м.
● *v.i.* (*liquid*) де́латься, с- бо́лее густы́м; (*fog*) сгуща́ться, сгусти́ться; (*become more complicated*) усложн|я́ться, -и́ться.

thicket /ˈθɪkɪt/ *n.* ча́ща; (*of shrubs*) за́росл|и (*pl., g.* -ей).

thickness /ˈθɪknɪs/ *n.* толщина́, густота́; (*layer*) слой.

thief /θiːf/ *n.* (*pl.* **thieves**) вор; **stop ~!** держи́ во́ра!

thiev|e /θiːv/ *v.i.* красть, у-; ворова́ть, с-; **a ~ing fellow** ворова́тый тип.

thievery /ˈθiːvərɪ/ *n.* кра́жа, воровство́.

thieves /θiːvz/ *pl. of* ⇨**thief**

thievish /ˈθiːvɪʃ/ *adj.* воровско́й.

thigh /θaɪ/ *n.* бедро́.
● *cpd.* **~-bone** *n.* бе́дренная кость.

thimble /ˈθɪmb(ə)l/ *n.* напёрсток.

thimbleful /ˈθɪmb(ə)lˌfʊl/ *n.* (*fig.*) глото́чек, ка́пелька.

thin /θɪn/ *adj.* **(thinner, thinnest)**
1 (*of measurement between surfaces*) то́нкий; **his coat had worn ~ at the elbows** его́ пальто́ протёрлось на локтя́х.
2 (*not dense*) ре́дкий; жи́дкий; **your hair is getting ~ on top** у вас во́лосы реде́ют на маку́шке; **he vanished into ~ air** его́ как ве́тром сду́ло; **our troops are ~ on the ground** у нас ма́ло во́йск.
3 (*not fat*) худо́й; (*of body, parts of body*) то́нкий; **~ in the face** с худы́м лицо́м; **she has become ~** она́ похуде́ла.
4 (*of liquids*) жи́дкий; разба́вленный.
5 (*flimsy, inadequate*) сла́бый; ша́ткий; **a ~ excuse** сла́бая/неубеди́тельная отгово́рка.
● *adv.* то́нко; **don't cut the bread so ~!** не на́до ре́зать хлеб так то́нко!
● *v.t.* **(thinned, thinning)** утонч|а́ть, -и́ть; де́лать, с- то́нким; (*liquid*) разб|авля́ть, -а́вить; **she ~ned the gravy** она́ разба́вила подли́вку; **these plants should be ~ned (out)** э́ти расте́ния ну́жно прореди́ть.
● *v.i.* **(thinned, thinning)** станови́ться, стать жи́дким; (*become reduced*) сокра|ща́ться, -ти́ться; **when the fog ~s** когда́ тума́н рассе́ется; **the crowd ~ned out** толпа́ поре́дела; **his hair is ~ning** у него́ реде́ют во́лосы.
● *cpd.* **~-skinned** *adj.* (*lit.*) тонкоко́жий; (*fig.*) чувстви́тельный; оби́дчивый.

thine /ðaɪn/ *pron. & adj.* (*arch.*) твой.

thing /θɪŋ/ *n.* **1** (*object*) вещь, предме́т; **what is that black ~?** что э́то за чёрный предме́т?; **there's no such ~ as ghosts** привиде́ний не существу́ет.
2 (*pl., belongings*) иму́щество; ве́щи (*f. pl.*); **pack up your ~s!** собери́те свои ве́щи!
3 (*pl., clothes*) оде́жда, ве́щи; **take your ~s off!** (*sc. outer clothing*) раздева́йтесь!
4 (*pl., food*) еда́; **I don't care for sweet ~s** я не люблю́ сла́дкого.
5 (*pl., equipment*) принадле́жности (*f. pl.*); **she got out the tea ~s** она́ доста́ла ча́йный серви́з.
6 (*matter, affair*) де́ло; вещь; **~s of importance** ва́жные дела́; **for one ~, he's too old** начнём с того́, что он сли́шком стар; **you had better leave ~s as they are** лу́чше оста́вить всё как есть; **how are ~s?** как дела́?; **it will only make ~s worse** э́то то́лько уху́дшит ситуа́цию; **other ~s being equal** при про́чих ра́вных усло́виях; **all ~s considered** принима́я во внима́ние всё; **as ~s go** при ны́нешнем положе́нии дел; **above all ~s** пре́жде/превы́ше всего́; **among other ~s** среди́ про́чего; **she was told to take ~s easy** ей веле́ли не перенапряга́ться; **let's talk ~s over**

T

давайте это обсудим; **it was just one of those ~s** (*coll.*) ничего нельзя было поделать; **it comes to the same ~** это сводится к тому же самому.
7 (*act*) действие; поступок; **it's the worst ~ you could have done** это самое плохое, что вы могли сделать; **that was a silly ~ to do** это был глупый поступок; **I have some ~s to do** у меня есть кое-какие дела.
8 (*course of action*): **the only ~ now is to take a cab** единственное, что можно сейчас сделать, это взять такси; **the best ~ for you would be to marry** лучше всего вам было бы жениться.
9 (*event*): **what a terrible ~ to happen!** какое ужасное несчастье!; **first ~** первым делом; в первую очередь; **last ~** в последнюю очередь; **last ~ at night** на ночь; перед сном; **it was a close/near ~** всё чуть не сорвалось.
10 (*word, remark*): **what a ~ to say!** как можно сказать такое!; **he said nice ~s about you** он очень хорошо о вас отозвался.
11 (*fact*): **I could tell you a ~ or two** я мог бы вам рассказать кое-что.
12 (*issue*): **the ~ is, can you afford it?** хватит ли у вас на это денег? — вот в чём дело.
13 (*coll., obsession*) навязчивая идея; (*aversion*): **she has a ~ about cats** она не выносит кошек.
14 (**a ~**: *something*; *with neg.*: *nothing*): **it's a ~ I have never done before** я этого никогда раньше не делал; **I can't see a ~** я ничего не вижу.
15 (*creature*) существо; **all living ~s** все живые существа.
16 (*emotively, of persons or animals*) создание, тварь; **don't be such a mean ~** не будьте такой скаредой!; **poor ~** бедняга, бедняжка (*both c.g.*); **old ~** (*sl., old chap*) старик, старина (*m.*).
17: **the ~** (*var. idioms*): **it's the done ~** так принято; **it's not the ~ (to do)** так не поступают; **just the ~!** то, что надо!; **it's not quite the ~** это не совсем то; **he did the right ~ by us** он с нами хорошо обошёлся; **he always says the right ~** он всегда знает, что сказать; **books and ~s** книги и тому подобное (*or* и так далее).

thing|amy /ˈθɪŋəmɪ/, **-umabob** /ˈθɪŋəmə,bɒb/, **-umajig** /ˈθɪŋəmə,dʒɪg/, **-ummy** /ˈθɪŋəmɪ/ *nn.* (*coll.*) штуковина; (*of people*) как (бишь) его/её?

think /θɪŋk/ *n.*: **I must have a ~** мне надо подумать; **he's got another ~ coming** ему придётся ещё раз подумать.

● *v.t. & i.* (*past and p.p.* **thought**) (*opine*) думать, по-; полагать (*impf.*); считать (*impf.*); **I ~** (я) думаю; мне кажется; **I don't ~ so** не думаю; **what do you ~?** как вы думаете?; **yes, I ~ so** да, пожалуй; **I ~ I'll go** я, пожалуй, пойду; **how could you ~ that?** как вам это могло прийти на ум?; **where do you ~ he can be?** как вы думаете, куда он девался?; **when do you ~ you'll be back?** когда вы думаете вернуться?; **I ~ I'm going to sneeze** я, кажется, сейчас чихну; (*judge*) думать (*impf.*), считать (*impf.*), полагать (*impf.*); **it suits me, don't you ~?** вы не находите/вам не кажется, что это мне идёт?; **do you ~ she's pretty?** вы думаете, она хорошенькая?/вы считаете её хорошенькой?; **do what you ~ fit** поступайте так, как вы считаете нужным; **I thought it better to stay** я решил, что лучше остаться; (*reflect*) думать, по-; мыслить (*impf.*); **~ for o.s.** думать самостоятельно; **to ~ that he's only 12!** подумать только, ему всего 12 лет!; **let me ~, what was his name?** дайте вспомнить, как же его зовут?; **just ~!** вы только подумайте!; **I can't ~ straight today** у меня сегодня голова не работает; **I should ~ twice before agreeing** надо бы хорошенько/дважды подумать, прежде чем соглашаться; (*expect*) думать (*impf.*); предполагать (*impf.*); **I thought as much** так я и думал; (*imagine*): **I can't ~ how he does it** я не могу себе представить, как он это делает; **who would have thought it?** кто бы мог подумать?; **I would never have thought it of him** я бы никогда в жизни его в этом не заподозрил!; (*with inf.*): **I never thought to ask** мне не пришло в голову спросить; (*with preps.* **about, of**): **I have other things to ~ about** у меня много других забот; **it has given me something to ~ about** это мне дало пищу для размышлений; **have you thought about going to the police?** вы не думали пойти в полицию?; **what do you ~ about having a meal?** как насчёт того, чтобы перекусить?; **it doesn't bear ~ing about** страшно подумать об этом; **I was just ~ing of going to bed** я как раз собирался идти спать; **~ of a number!** задумайте число!; **I couldn't ~ of his name** я не мог вспомнить, как его зовут; **I would never have thought of doing that** я никогда бы не догадался сделать такое; **can you ~ of a good place to eat?** вы знаете, где можно хорошо поесть?; **I thought of an excuse** я придумал предлог; **who first thought of the idea?** кому первому пришла на ум эта идея?; **it's not much when you ~ of it** это немного, если подумать; **I can't ~ of anything to say** я не знаю, что сказать; **his employers ~ well of him** он на хорошем счету у своих работодателей; **he is well thought of in the City** его уважают в Сити; **I don't ~ much of him as a teacher** я невысоко ценю его как преподователя; **I was going to sell my house, but I thought better of it** я собирался продавать свой дом, но потом раздумал; **~ nothing of it!** (*in reply to thanks*) не стоит!; **he ~s nothing of a 20-mile walk** прогулка в 20 миль ему нипочём; **while I ~ of it** кстати; между прочим.

● *with advs.*: **the matter needs ~ing out** это дело надо обдумать/обмозговать (*coll.*); **his arguments are well thought out** его аргументы хорошо продуманы; **~ it over!** обдумайте это!; **he never ~s his ideas through** он никогда не продумывает свои идеи до конца; **~ up** (*devise*) придум|ывать, -ать; (*invent*) выдумывать, выдумать.

● *cpd.* **~-tank** *n.* (*coll.*) мозговой центр.

thinkable /ˈθɪŋkəb(ə)l/ *adj.* мыслимый; возможный; **such an idea is barely ~** это почти немыслимо.

thinker /ˈθɪŋkə(r)/ *n.* мыслитель (*m.*); **he is a quick ~** он быстро соображает.

thinking /ˈθɪŋkɪŋ/ *n.* **1** (*process of thought*) размышление; **we have some hard ~ to do** нам надо как следует подумать. **2** (*opinion*) мнение; **to my way of ~** на мой взгляд.

● *adj.* думающий; **the ~ public** думающие/мыслящие люди.

● *cpd.* **~-cap** *n.*: **I must put my ~-cap on** (*coll.*) мне придётся пораскинуть мозгами.

thinness /ˈθɪnnɪs/ *n.* тонкость.

third /θɜːd/ *n.* **1** (*date*) третье (число); **my birthday is on the ~** мой день рождения третьего (числа).
2 (*fraction*) треть; **two ~s** две трети.
3 (*mus.*) терция.

● *adj.* третий; **~ degree** (*coll.*) жёсткий допрос; **~ party, person** (*leg. etc.*) третья сторона; **~ person** (*gram.*) третье лицо; **the T~ World** третий мир.

● *cpds.* **~-class** *adj.* (*rail etc.*) третьего класса; (**~-rate**) третьесортный; **~-degree** *adj.*: **~-degree burns** ожоги третьей степени; **~-party** *adj.*: **~-party insurance** (*Br.*) страховка, возмещающая убытки третьих лиц; **~-rate** *adj.* третьесортный.

thirdly /ˈθɜːdlɪ/ *adv.* в-третьих.

thirst /θɜːst/ *n.* (*lit., fig.*) жажда; **they died of ~** они умерли от жажды; **~ for knowledge** жажда знаний.

● *v.i.* (*fig.*) жаждать (*impf.*) (*чего*); **he ~ed for revenge** он жаждал мести.

thirsty /ˈθɜːstɪ/ *adj.* (**thirstier, thirstiest**) испытывающий жажду; **I am/feel ~** мне хочется (*or* я хочу) пить.

thirteen /θɜːˈtiːn/, /ˈθɜː-/ *n.* тринадцать.

● *adj.* тринадцать *+g. pl.*

thirteenth /θɜːˈtiːnθ/, /ˈθɜːtiːnθ/ *n.* (*date*) тринадцатое число; (*fraction*) одна тринадцатая.

● *adj.* тринадцатый.

thirtieth /ˈθɜːtɪɪθ/ *n.* (*date*) тридцатое число; (*fraction*) одна тридцатая.

● *adj.* тридцатый.

thirt|y /ˈθɜːtɪ/ *n.* тридцать; **it happened in the ~ies** это случилось в тридцатых годах; **he is in his ~ies** ему за тридцать.

● *adj.* тридцать *+g. pl.*

this /ðɪs/ *pron.* (*pl.* **these**) это; **~ is what I think** вот что я думаю; **are these your shoes?** это ваши туфли?; **we talked of ~ and that** мы говорили о том, о сём; **do it like ~** сделайте это так (*or* следующим образом); **it was like ~** вот как это было; **~ is it** (*coll., the difficulty etc.*) вот именно!; в том-то и дело!

● *adj.* (*pl.* **these**) этот; данный; **~ book here** вот эта книга; **~ country of ours** эта наша страна; **~ very day** сегодня же; **~ time last week** в это же время на прошлой неделе; **come here ~ minute!** иди сюда сию же минуту!; **these days** (*nowadays*) в настоящее время, нынче (*coll.*); **~ one or that** тот или другой.

● *adv.*: **about ~ high** примерно такой высоты; **can you give me ~ much?** вы можете дать мне столько?; **I know ~ much** мне известно следующее.

thistle /ˈθɪs(ə)l/ *n.* чертополох.

● *cpd.* **~down** *n.* пушок, пух.

thither /ˈðɪðə(r)/ *adv.* туда.

tho' /ðəʊ/ = **though**

thong /θɒŋ/ *n.* ремень (*m.*).

thora|x /ˈθɔːræks/ *n.* (*pl.* **~ces** /ˈθɔːrəˌsiːz/ *or* **~xes**) грудная клетка, торакс.

thorn /θɔːn/ *n.* колючка, шип; **he is a ~ in my flesh** он сидит у меня в печёнках (*coll.*).

thorny /ˈθɔːnɪ/ *adj.* (**thornier, thorniest**) колючий; (*fig.*): **a ~ problem** сложная проблема.

thorough /ˈθʌrə/ *adj.* (*search, investigation*) тщательный, всесторонний; (*person*) скрупулёзный; **he made a ~ job of it** он тщательно выполнил свою работу; (*fundamental*) основательный; (*out-and-out*): **he is a ~ scoundrel** он законченный негодяй.

● *cpds.* **~bred** *n.* чистопородное животное; *adj.* чистокровный, чистопородный, породистый; **~fare** *n.* транспортная магистраль; **'No T~fare'** «прохода/проезда нет»; **~going** *adj.* доскональный, тщательный.

thoroughly /ˈθʌrəlɪ/ *adv.* (*satisfied*) вполне, совершенно, полностью; (*ashamed*) совершенно; (*study*) тщательно.

thoroughness /ˈθʌrənɪs/ *n.* тщательность; основательность; скрупулёзность.

those /ðəʊz/ *pl. of* ⇒**that**

thou /ðaʊ/ *pron.* (*obj.* **thee;** *poss.* **thy** *or* **thine**) ты.

though /ðəʊ/ *adv. & conj.* хотя, хоть; несмотря на то, что...; **~ not a music-lover, I ...** хотя я и не большой любитель музыки, я...; **~ severe, he is just** он строг, но справедлив; **even ~ it's late** пусть уже поздно, но...; **strange ~ it may seem** как это ни странно; **he said he would come; he didn't, ~** он сказал, что придёт; однако же не пришёл; **as ~** как будто бы; словно; **it looks as ~ he will lose** похоже на то, что он проиграет; **it's not as ~ you had no money** не то чтобы у вас не было денег.

thought[1] /θɔːt/ *n.* **1** (*way, instance or body of thinking*) мысль; **modern scientific ~** современная научная мысль.
2 (*reflection*) раздумье, размышление; **he spends hours in ~** он проводит целые часы в раздумье; **deep, lost in ~** погружённый в размышления/мысли; **he acted without a moment's ~** он действовал, не задумываясь; **I gave serious ~ to the matter** я много думал об этом; **don't give it a ~!** выкиньте это из головы!; **on second ~s** подумав, поразмыслив; **collect one's ~s** соб|ираться, -раться с мыслями.
3 (*idea, opinion*) мысль, идея, соображение; **the ~ struck me that...** мне пришло в голову, что...; **let me have your ~s on the subject** выскажите мне ваши соображения на эту тему; **he keeps his ~s to himself** он держит свои мысли при себе; **his one ~ was to escape** он думал только о том, как бы убежать.
4 (*intention*): **she gave up all ~ of marrying** она отказалась от всякой мысли о замужестве; **I had some ~ of resigning** я подумывал об отставке.

● *cpds.* **~-provoking** *adj.* заставляющий думать, стимулирующий мысль; **~-read** *v.i.* читать (*impf.*) чужие мысли; **~-reader** *n.* человек, читающий чужие мысли.

thought[2] /θɔːt/ *past and p.p. of* ⇒**think**

thoughtful /ˈθɔːtfʊl/ *adj.* **1** (*meditative*) задумчивый. **2** (*well-considered, profound*): **a ~ essay** вдумчивое/содержательное эссе. **3** (*considerate*) внимательный, чуткий.

thoughtfulness /ˈθɔːtfʊlnɪs/ *n.* задумчивость; внимательность, чуткость.

thoughtless /ˈθɔːtlɪs/ *adj.* (*careless*) бездумный, неосмотрительный; (*inconsiderate*) невнимательный.

thoughtlessness /ˈθɔːtlɪsnɪs/ *n.* бездумность, неосмотрительность; невнимательность.

thousand /ˈθaʊz(ə)nd/ *n. & adj.* (*pl.* **~s** *or* (*with numeral or qualifying word*) **~**) тысяча; **a ~ people** тысяча людей; **with £1,000** с тысячью фунтами; **a ~-to-one chance** один шанс из тысячи; **he is a man in a ~** такие, как он, встречаются один на тысячу; **I have a ~ and one things to do** у меня тысяча дел.

● *cpd.* **~fold** *adj.* тысячекратный; *adv.* в тысячу раз.

thousandth /ˈθaʊz(ə)ntθ/ *n.* тысячная часть.

● *adj.* тысячный.

thraldom /ˈθrɔːldəm/ *n.* (*liter.*) рабство.

thrall /θrɔːl/ *n.* (*liter.*): **he was in ~ to his passions** он был рабом своих страстей.

thrash /θræʃ/ *v.t.* **1** (*beat*) изб|ивать, -ить; (*fig., defeat*) побе|ждать, -дить; **he got a ~ing in the final round** ему сильно досталось в финальном раунде. **2** (*also* **thresh**: *make turbulent by beating*) колотить (*impf.*); ударять (*impf.*); **the whale ~ed the water with its tail** кит бил хвостом по воде.

● *v.i.* метаться (*impf.*); **the swimmer ~ed about in the water** пловец колотил руками и ногами по воде; **he ~ed about in bed** он метался в постели.

● *with adv.*: **~ out** *v.t.* (*fig.*) обстоятельно обсу|ждать, -дить; **let us ~ out this problem** давайте разберём этот вопрос по пунктам; **they ~ed out a solution** они выработали решение.

thread /θred/ *n.* **1** (*spun fibre; length of this*) нить, нитка; **a reel of ~** катушка ниток; **his life hung by a ~** его жизнь висела на волоске; (*fig.*) связь; нить; **there's not a ~ of evidence** нет ни малейшего доказательства; **he lost the ~ of his argument** он потерял нить рассуждений. **2** (*of a screw etc.*) резьба.

● *v.t.* прод|евать, -еть нитку в + *a.*; наниз|ывать, -ать; **can you ~ this needle?** вы можете продеть нитку в эту иглу?; **she was ~ing beads** она нанизывала бусы.

● *cpd.* **~bare** *adj.* потёртый, изношенный, потрёпанный.

threat /θret/ *n.* угроза; **~ to peace** угроза миру; **there was a ~ of rain** собирался дождь.

threaten /ˈθret(ə)n/ *v.t. & i.* угрожать (*impf.*) + *d.*; грозить, при- + *d.*; грозиться (*impf.*); (*make a threatening gesture at*) грозить, по- + *d.*; **he ~ed me with a stick** он погрозил мне палкой; **I was ~ed with expulsion** мне грозили исключением; **I was ~ed with bankruptcy** мне грозило/угрожало банкротство; **they ~ed revenge** они угрожали мщением; **the clouds ~ed rain** тучи/облака предвещали дождь; **he ~ed to leave** он угрожал, что уйдёт; он грозился уйти; **war ~ed** нависла угроза войны; **rain was ~ing** надвигался дождь.

three /θriː/ *n.* (число/номер) три; (**~** *people*) трое; **~ of us went** мы пошли втроём; **~ each** по три каждый; **~ at a time, in ~s** (*of people*) по три/трое; тройками; (*of things*) по три; (*figure, thing numbered 3; group of* **~**) тройка; (*cut, divide*): **in ~** натрое, на три части; **fold in ~** складывать, сложить втрое; (*cf. also examples under* ⇒**two**).

● *adj.* три + *g. sg.*; (*for people and pluralia tantum, also*) трое + *g. pl.* (*cf. examples under* ⇒**two**); **he and ~ others** он с тремя другими; **~ fours are twelve** трижды (*or* три на) четыре — двенадцать; **~ times as good** втрое лучше; **~ times as much** втрое больше; **~ quarters** три четверти; (*adv.*) на три четверти.

● *cpds.* **~-cornered** *adj.* треугольный; **~-D** (*coll.*) *adj.* трёхмерный; **a ~-D film** стереоскопический фильм; **~-day** *adj.* трёхдневный; **~-dimensional** *adj.* (*lit.*) трёхмерный; в трёх измерениях; (*fig., of characters in a book etc.*) выпуклый; **~-figure** *adj.* трёхзначный; **~fold** *adj.* тройной; троекратный; *adv.* втройне, втрое, троекратно; **~-hour** *adj.* трёхчасовой; **~-legged** *adj.* (*of table etc.*) на трёх ножках; **~-legged race** бег парами; **~-piece** *adj.*: **~-piece suit** (костюм-)тройка; **~-piece suite** диван с двумя креслами; **~-ply** *adj.* (*of timber, wool etc.*) трёхслойный; **~-point** *adj.* трёхточечный; **~-point turn** разворот с применением заднего хода; **~score** *adj.*: **~score and ten** семьдесят (лет); **~-seater** *adj.* трёхместный; **~some** *n.* (*persons*) тройка, трое; **~-speed** *adj.*: **~-speed gear** трёхскоростная передача;

T

~-storey *adj.* трёхэта́жный; **~-wheel(ed)** *adj.* трёхколёсный; **~-year** *adj.* трёхле́тний, трёхгоди́чный; **~-year-old** *adj.* трёхле́тний.

thresh /θreʃ/ *v.t.* **1** (*beat grain from*) молоти́ть (*impf.*). **2** = **thrash** *v.t.* 2

thresher /'θreʃə(r)/ *n.* (*worker*) молоти́льщик; (*machine*) молоти́лка.

threshing /'θreʃɪŋ/ *n.* молотьба́.

● *cpds.* **~-floor** *n.* ток, гумно́; **~-machine** *n.* молоти́лка.

threshold /'θreʃəʊld/, /-həʊld/ *n.* поро́г; **on the ~** на поро́ге.

threw /θru:/ *past of* ⇒**throw**

thrice /θraɪs/ *adv.* (*liter.*) (*three times*) три́жды.

thrift /θrɪft/ *n.* **1** (*frugality*) бережли́вость, эконо́мность. **2** (*bot.*) арме́рия.

thriftless /'θrɪftlɪs/ *adj.* расточи́тельный, неэконо́мный.

thriftlessness /'θrɪftlɪsnɪs/ *n.* расточи́тельность.

thrifty /'θrɪftɪ/ *adj.* (**thriftier, thriftiest**) бережли́вый, эконо́мный.

thrill /θrɪl/ *n.* (*physical sensation*) дрожь, тре́пет; (*excitement*) восто́рг, восхище́ние; **it gave me a ~** э́то привело́ меня́ в восто́рг/восхище́ние.

● *v.t.* восхи|ща́ть, -ти́ть; **she was ~ed to death** она́ была́ в ди́ком восто́рге; **a ~ing finish** захва́тывающий коне́ц.

● *v.i.*: **we ~ed at the good news** мы о́чень обра́довались хоро́шим вестя́м; **she ~ed with delight/horror** она́ затрепета́ла от ра́дости/у́жаса.

thriller /'θrɪlə(r)/ *n.* (*story or film*) приключе́нческий/детекти́вный рома́н/фильм; три́ллер.

thrive /θraɪv/ *v.i.* (*past* **throve** *or* **thrived;** *p.p.* **thriven** /'θrɪv(ə)n/ *or* **thrived**) (*prosper*) процвета́ть (*impf.*); (*grow vigorously*) разраст|а́ться, -и́сь.

throat /θrəʊt/ *n.* го́рло; (*gullet*) горта́нь, гло́тка; **he took me by the ~** он схвати́л меня́ за го́рло; **he tried to cut his ~** он пыта́лся перере́зать себе́ го́рло; **you are cutting your own ~** (*fig.*) вы ру́бите сук, на кото́ром сиди́те; **I have a sore ~** у меня́ боли́т го́рло; **he cleared his ~** он отка́шлялся; **don't jump down my ~!** не затыка́йте мне рот!; **the words stuck in my ~** слова́ застря́ли у меня́ в го́рле.

throaty /'θrəʊtɪ/ *adj.* (**throatier, throatiest**) (*guttural*) горта́нный; (*hoarse*) хри́плый.

throb /θrɒb/ *n.* бие́ние, пульса́ция.

● *v.i.* (**throbbed, throbbing**) (*beat*) стуча́ть (*impf.*); би́ться (*impf.*); пульси́ровать (*impf.*); (*fig., quiver*) трепета́ть (*impf.*), волнова́ться (*impf.*); **his heart ~bed** се́рдце его́ (учащённо) би́лось; **his head ~bed** у него́ гуде́ла голова́.

throe /θrəʊ/ *n.* су́дорога, спазм; **~s of childbirth** родовы́е му́ки (*f. pl.*); **I was in the ~s of packing** я лихора́дочно упако́вывал ве́щи.

thrombosis /θrɒm'bəʊsɪs/ *n.* (*pl.* **thromboses** /-si:z/) тромбо́з.

throne /θrəʊn/ *n.* (*lit., fig.*) трон, престо́л; **he came to the ~** он вступи́л на престо́л.

throng /θrɒŋ/ *n.* толпа́.

● *v.i.* (*crowd round*) толпи́ться (*impf.*); (*come in great numbers*) ст|ека́ться, -е́чься; **crowds ~ed to the stadium** то́лпы люде́й стека́лись на стадио́н.

● *v.t.* (*fill a place*) переп|олня́ть, -о́лнить.

throttle /'θrɒt(ə)l/ *n.* дро́ссель (*m.*); **at full ~** на по́лном газу́; **he opened the ~** он дал газ.

● *v.t.* **1** (*strangle*) души́ть, за-/у-. **2** (*control with ~*) дроссели́ровать (*impf.*); **he ~d the engine back, down** он сба́вил газ.

through /θru:/ *adj.* **1** прямо́й; сквозно́й; **~ traffic** сквозно́е движе́ние; **no ~ road** (*as notice*) нет прое́зда; **a ~ train** прямо́й по́езд. **2** (*var. pred. uses*): **his trousers were ~** (*threadbare*) **at the knee** его́ брю́ки протёрлись на коле́нях; **you must wait till I'm ~** (*finished*) **with the paper** вам придётся подожда́ть, пока́ я ко́нчу чита́ть газе́ту; **she told him she was ~ with him** она́ ему́ сказа́ла, что ме́жду ни́ми всё ко́нчено.

● *adv.* (*from beginning to end; completely*) до конца́; **I was there all ~** я был там до конца́; **have you read it ~?** вы всё прочита́ли?; **you will get wet ~** вы промо́кнете насквозь́; **the whole night ~** всю ночь напролёт; (*all the way*) пря́мо; **the train goes ~ to Paris** по́езд идёт пря́мо до Пари́жа.

● *prep.* **1** (*across; from end to end or side to side of*) че́рез + *a.*; (*esp. suggesting difficulty*) сквозь + *a.*; **he came ~ the window** он влез че́рез окно́; **visible ~ smoke** ви́димый сквозь дым; (*into, in at*) в + *a.*; **he looked ~ the telescope** он посмотре́л в телеско́п; **look ~ the window!** посмотри́те в окно́!; **I could see him ~ the fog** я смог разгляде́ть его́ в тума́не; **I don't like driving ~ fog** я не люблю́ е́здить в тума́не; **the thought went ~ my mind** у меня́ в голове́ промелькну́ла мысль; **the stone flew ~ the air** ка́мень лете́л по во́здуху; (*via*): **we travelled** (*Br.*), **traveled** (*US*) **~ Germany** мы е́хали че́рез Герма́нию. **2** (*from beginning to end of*): **he won't live ~ the night** он не доживёт до утра́. **3** (*during*) в тече́ние + *g.*; **the dog doesn't bark ~ the day** днём соба́ка не ла́ет. **4** (*US, up to and including*): **from Monday ~ Saturday** с понеде́льника по суббо́ту (включи́тельно). **5** (*over the area of*): **the news quickly spread ~ the town** весть бы́стро распространи́лась по го́роду. **6** (*through the medium of*) че́рез + *a.*; **the order was passed ~ him** прика́з был пе́редан че́рез него́; **I heard of you ~ your sister** я слы́шал о вас от ва́шей сестры́. **7** (*from, because of*) из-за + *g.*; по + *d.*; **~ laziness** из-за ле́ни; **~ stupidity** по глу́пости; **he succeeded ~ his own efforts** он доби́лся успе́ха свои́ми си́лами; (*of desirable result*) благодаря́ + *d.*

● *cpds.* **~put** *n.* пропускна́я спосо́бность; **~-way** *n.* (*US*) автостра́да.

throughout /θru:'aʊt/ *adv.* (*in every part*) везде́; повсю́ду; (*in all respects*) во всех отноше́ниях; во всём.

● *prep.* (*from end to end of*) че́рез + *a.*; **~ the country** по всей стране́; (*for the duration of*): **~ the 20th century** в тече́ние всего́ 20-го ве́ка; **it rained ~ the night** всю ночь шёл дождь.

throve /θrəʊv/ *past of* ⇒**thrive**

throw /θrəʊ/ *n.* **1** (*act of ~ing*) броса́ние, мета́ние; **~ of dice** броса́ние косте́й; (*distance ~n*) бросо́к. **2** (*in wrestling*) бросо́к.

● *v.t.* (*past* **threw;** *p.p.* **thrown**) **1** бр|оса́ть, -о́сить; кида́ть, ки́нуть; **~ something 100 yards** бр|оса́ть, -о́сить что-н. на́ сто я́рдов; **he threw the ball into the air** он подбро́сил мяч в во́здух; **don't ~ stones at the dog** не кида́йтесь камня́ми в соба́ку; **his horse threw him** ло́шадь сбро́сила его́; **he was ~n to the ground by the explosion** его́ бро́сило на зе́млю от взры́ва; **he threw me an angry look** он бро́сил на меня́ серди́тый взгляд; **~ing a cloak over his shoulders ...** наки́нув плащ на пле́чи, . . .; **the news threw them into a panic** сообще́ние пове́ргло их в па́нику; **he was ~n off balance** (*lit.*) он потеря́л равнове́сие; (*fig.*) он пришёл в замеша́тельство; **the news threw me** (*coll.*) изве́стие потрясло́ меня́; **this ~s light on the problem** э́то пролива́ет/броса́ет свет на пробле́му; **he threw himself at me** он бро́сился на меня́; **he threw himself into the job** он с голово́й ушёл в рабо́ту; **he threw his arms round her** он заключи́л её в (свои́) объя́тия; он обня́л её; **he threw himself on their mercy** он сда́лся им на ми́лость. **2** (*dice*) бр|оса́ть, -о́сить. **3** (*shape, e.g. pots on wheel*) обраб|а́тывать, -о́тать (на гонча́рном кру́ге). **4**: **~** (*reverse*) **a switch** поверну́ть (*pf.*) выключа́тель обра́тно. **5** (*coll., have*) устр|а́ивать, -о́ить; **let's ~ a party** дава́йте устро́им вечери́нку.

● *with advs.*: **~ about** *v.t.* (*scatter*) разбр|а́сывать, -оса́ть; **don't ~ litter about** не сори́те; не разбра́сывайте му́сор; (*lavish*) броса́ться (*impf.*) + *i.*; **he ~s his money about** он броса́ется деньга́ми; (*obtrude*): **he likes to ~ his weight about** он лю́бит вы́делиться; **~ across** *v.t.*: **he threw the rope across to me** он перебро́сил мне верёвку; **~ away** *v.t.* (*discard*) выбра́сывать, вы́бросить; (*forgo*) упус|ка́ть, -ти́ть; **don't ~ away this chance** не упуска́йте э́ту возмо́жность (*or* э́тот шанс); **~ back** *v.t.* отбр|а́сывать, -о́сить наза́д; **he was ~n back by the explosion** его́ отбро́сило взры́вом; **~ down** *v.t.* бр|оса́ть, -о́сить на зе́млю; **he threw himself down** он бро́сился на зе́млю;

(*fig.*): **the enemy threw down their arms** враг сложи́л ору́жие; **~ in** *v.t.* вбр|а́сывать, -о́сить; (*fig.*) (*include*) доб|авля́ть, -а́вить; (*contribute*): **may I ~ in a suggestion?** мо́жно мне внести́ предложе́ние?; **~ in one's lot with** соедин|я́ть, -и́ть свою́ судьбу́ с + *i.*; **~ in one's hand** (*surrender*) сд|ава́ться, -а́ться; (*abandon contest*) выходи́ть, вы́йти из игры́; **~ off** *v.t.* сбр|а́сывать, -о́сить; **he threw off his clothes** он сбро́сил с себя́ оде́жду; **he threw off his pursuers** он изба́вился от свои́х пресле́дователей; **I can't ~ this cold off** я ника́к не могу́ изба́виться от э́того на́сморка; **~ on** *v.t.*: **he threw on a coat** он набро́сил/наки́нул пальто́ (на пле́чи); **~ open** *v.t.*: **the gardens were ~n open to the public** сады́ откры́ли для пу́блики; **he threw open the door** он распахну́л дверь; **~ out** *v.t.* выбра́сывать, вы́бросить; (*proffer*) предл|ага́ть, -ожи́ть; **I threw out a remark** я сде́лал замеча́ние; **he threw out a challenge** он бро́сил вы́зов; (*put out*): **the tree threw out new leaves** де́рево дало́ но́вые ли́стья; (*reject*) отклон|я́ть, -и́ть; **the bill was ~n out** (*parl.*) законопрое́кт отклони́ли; (*expel*) исключ|а́ть, -и́ть; выбра́сывать, вы́бросить; **the club threw him out** его́ исключи́ли/вы́бросили из клу́ба; (*upset*) сб|ива́ть, -и́ть; пу́тать, за-; **you will ~ me out in my calculations** вы собьёте меня со счёта; **~ over** *v.t.* (*lit.*) бр|оса́ть, -о́сить; **~ my jacket over!** бро́сьте мне пиджа́к!; (*abandon*) бр|оса́ть, -о́сить; пок|ида́ть, -и́нуть; **she threw him over after a week** че́рез неде́лю она́ его́ бро́сила; **~ together** *v.t.* (*compile*) сост|авля́ть, -а́вить; компили́ровать, с-; **a book hastily ~n together** на́спех соста́вленная кни́га; (*bring into contact*) соб|ира́ть, -ра́ть вме́сте; **they were ~n together a lot** им ча́сто случа́лось ста́лкиваться; **~ up** *v.t.* (*lit.*) подбр|а́сывать, -о́сить; подки́|дывать, -нуть; **he threw the ball up** он подбро́сил мяч; (*raise*) вски́|дывать, -нуть; **he threw up his hands in horror** он вски́нул ру́ки от у́жаса; (*give up*) бр|оса́ть, о́сить; **he intends to ~ up his job** он собира́ется бро́сить рабо́ту; *v.i.* (*vomit*): **he threw up** его́ вы́рвало; **I felt like ~ing up** меня́ тошни́ло.

● *cpds.* **~away** *adj.* ра́зового по́льзования, ра́зовый; **a ~away line** как бы невзнача́й обро́ненные слова́; **~back** *n.* проявле́ние атави́зма; (*return*) возвраще́ние/возвра́т (к + *d.*); **~-in** *n.* вбра́сывание (мяча́).

thrower /ˈθrəʊə(r)/ *n.* мета́тель (*m.*).

thrown /θrəʊn/ *p.p. of* ⇒**throw**

thrum /θrʌm/ *v.i.* (**thrummed, thrumming**) бренча́ть (*impf.*); **he ~med on the table** он бараба́нил па́льцами по́ столу.

thrush¹ /θrʌʃ/ *n.* (*bird*) дрозд.

thrush² /θrʌʃ/ *n.* (*disease*) моло́чница.

thrust /θrʌst/ *n.* толчо́к; (*mil.*) наступле́ние, уда́р; (*in fencing*) уко́л.

● *v.t.* (*past and p.p.* **thrust**) толк|а́ть, -ну́ть; **he ~ a note into my hand** он су́нул мне в ру́ку запи́ску; **he ~ his hands into his pockets** он засу́нул ру́ки в карма́ны; **they ~ their way through the crowd** они́ проби́лись сквозь толпу́; (*fig., impose*) навя́з|ывать, -а́ть.

● *v.i.* (*past and p.p.* **thrust**) толка́ться (*impf.*); проб|ива́ться, -и́ться; **he ~ past us** он растолка́л нас и прошёл.

thud /θʌd/ *n.* глухо́й звук; стук.

● *v.i.* (**thudded, thudding**) глу́хо уд|аря́ться, -а́риться.

thug /θʌg/ *n.* банди́т, головоре́з, хулига́н.

thuggery /ˈθʌgərɪ/ *n.* бандити́зм, хулига́нство.

thuggish /ˈθʌgɪʃ/ *adj.* хулига́нский.

thumb /θʌm/ *n.* большо́й па́лец (руки́); **~s down** знак неодобре́ния; **~s up** знак одобре́ния; **he was given the ~s up sign to begin** ему́ да́ли сигна́л к нача́лу; **by rule of ~** о́пытным путём; **he is completely under her ~** он у неё по́лностью под каблуко́м; **I'm all (fingers and) ~s** у меня́ ру́ки как крю́ки.

● *v.t.* **1** (*turn over with ~*) перели́ст|ывать, -а́ть; **he ~ed over, through the pages** он перелиста́л страни́цы; **a well-~ed volume** истрёпанный, зачи́танный том. **2**: **~ a lift** (*coll.*) голосова́ть (*impf.*); **he ~ed a lift in a lorry** он прие́хал на попу́тном грузовике́. **3**: **~ one's nose at** пок|а́зывать, -аза́ть нос + *d.*

● *cpds.* **~-index** *n.* бу́квенный указа́тель (*на переднем обрезе словаря и т.п.*); **~nail** *n.* но́готь (*m.*) большо́го па́льца; **~nail sketch** набро́сок; кра́ткое описа́ние; **~-print** *n.* отпеча́ток большо́го па́льца; **~screw** *n.* тиск|и́ (*pl., g.* -о́в) для больши́х па́льцев (*орудие пыток*); **~-tack** *n.* (*US*) кно́пка.

thump /θʌmp/ *n.* (*blow*) тяжёлый уда́р; (*noise*) глухо́й стук/шум.

● *v.t.* бить (*impf.*); колоти́ть (*impf.*); **he ~ed me on the back** он си́льно уда́рил меня́ по спине́.

● *v.i.* би́ться (*impf.*); колоти́ться (*impf.*); **someone ~ed on the door** кто́-то колоти́л в дверь; **my heart began to ~** у меня́ заколоти́лось се́рдце.

thumping /ˈθʌmpɪŋ/ *adj. & adv.* (*coll.*) грома́дный, ужаса́ющий; **a ~ lie** на́глая ложь.

thunder /ˈθʌndə(r)/ *n.* гром; **a crash of ~** уда́р гро́ма; **a peal of ~** раска́ты гро́ма; **there is ~ in the air** в во́здухе па́хнет грозо́й; (*fig.*) гро́хот, гром; **the ~ of the waves** шум волн; **a ~ of applause** гром аплодисме́нтов.

● *v.t.* греме́ть, про-; **'Get out!' he ~ed** «Убира́йтесь отсю́да!» — прогреме́л он.

● *v.i.* (*lit.*) греме́ть, громыха́ть, грохота́ть (*all impf.*); **it is ~ing** гром греми́т; **it has been ~ing all day** весь день греми́т гром; (*fig.*): **the train ~ed past** по́езд с гро́хотом пронёсся ми́мо.

● *cpds.* **~bolt** *n.* уда́р мо́лнии, гром; **~clap** *n.* уда́р гро́ма; **~cloud** *n.* грозова́я ту́ча; **~storm** *n.* гроза́; **~struck** *adj.* (*fig.*) ошеломлённый.

thundering /ˈθʌndərɪŋ/ *adj. & adv.* грома́дный; **a ~ nuisance** колосса́льная неприя́тность.

thunderous /ˈθʌndərəs/ *adj.* (*loud*) громово́й; **~ applause** бу́рные аплодисме́нты.

thundery /ˈθʌndərɪ/ *adj.*: **it is ~ weather** пого́да (пред)грозова́я.

Thursday /ˈθɜːzdeɪ/, /-dɪ/ *n.* четве́рг.

thus /ðʌs/ *adv.* (*in this way*) таки́м о́бразом; (*accordingly*) сле́довательно, таки́м о́бразом; **~ far and no farther** до сих пор и ни ша́гу да́льше.

thwack /θwæk/ *n.* си́льный уда́р.

● *v.t.* колошма́тить, от-; поро́ть, вы-.

thwart /θwɔːt/ *v.t.* меша́ть, по- + *d.*; **~ s.o.'s plans** расстр|а́ивать, -о́ить чьи-н. пла́ны.

thy /ðaɪ/ *adj.* (*arch.*) твой.

thyme /taɪm/ *n.* тимья́н.

thyroid /ˈθaɪrɔɪd/ *n.* (**~ gland**) щитови́дная железа́.

● *adj.* щитови́дный.

ti /tiː/ (*US*) = **te**

tiara /tɪˈɑːrə/ *n.* тиа́ра, диаде́ма.

Tiber /ˈtaɪbə(r)/ *n.* Тибр.

Tibet /tɪˈbet/ *n.* Тибе́т.

Tibetan /tɪˈbet(ə)n/ *n.* тибе́т|ец (*fem.* -ка).

● *adj.* тибе́тский.

tibia /ˈtɪbɪə/ *n.* (*pl.* **tibiae** /-bɪ,iː/) большеберцо́вая кость.

tic /tɪk/ *n.* (*med.*) тик.

tick¹ /tɪk/ *n.* **1** (*of clock etc.*) ти́канье; **~, tock** тик-та́к. **2** (*Br. coll., moment*) секу́нда; мину́та, миг; **just a ~!** одну́ секу́нду! **3** (*checking mark*) га́лочка, пти́чка.

● *v.t.* отм|еча́ть, -е́тить га́лочкой.

● *v.i.* ти́кать (*impf.*); **what makes him ~?** (*coll.*) что им дви́жет?

● *with advs.*: **the meter was ~ing away** счётчик продолжа́л щёлкать; **she ~ed off the items as I read them out** я перечисля́л предме́ты, а она́ отмеча́ла их га́лочками; **he got ~ed off** (*Br. coll., reprimanded*) ему́ да́ли нагоня́й; **I left the engine ~ing over** я оста́вил мото́р на холосто́м ходу́.

tick² /tɪk/ *n.* (*parasite*) клещ.

tick³ /tɪk/ *n.* (*coll., credit*) долг, креди́т; **I got some groceries on ~** я купи́л ко́е-каки́е проду́кты в долг/креди́т.

ticker /ˈtɪkə(r)/ *n.* (*coll.*) (*US, teleprinter*) телегра́фный аппара́т, телета́йп; (*watch*) час|ы́ (*pl., g.* -о́в); (*heart*) се́рдце.

● *cpd.* **~-tape** *n.* телета́йпная ле́нта; (*in celebrations*) серпанти́н из телета́йпной ле́нты.

ticket /ˈtɪkɪt/ *n.* (*for travel, seating etc.*) биле́т; **a return ~ to London** обра́тный биле́т до Ло́ндона; (*tag*) ярлы́к; **price ~** этике́тка с ценой́; це́нник; (*US, list of election candidates*) спи́сок кандида́тов на вы́борах; (*printed notice of offence*): **he got a ~ for speeding** он получи́л штраф за превыше́ние ско́рости;

T

that's the ~! (*coll.*) (вот э́то) то, что на́до!

● *v.t.* (**ticketed, ticketing**) снаб|жа́ть, -ди́ть ярлыко́м/этике́ткой.

● *cpds.* **~-collector** *n.* контролёр; **~-holder** *n.* облада́тель (*m.*) биле́та; **~-machine** *n.* биле́тный автома́т; **~-office** *n.* биле́тная ка́сса; **~-punch** *n.* компо́стер.

ticking /ˈtɪkɪŋ/ *n.* (*fabric*) тик.

tickle /ˈtɪk(ə)l/ *n.* щекота́ние; **she gave the baby a ~** она́ пощекота́ла ребёнка; **he felt a ~ in his throat** у него́ заперши́ло в го́рле.

● *v.t.* щекота́ть, по-; (*fig., amuse*) смеши́ть, рас-; забавля́ть (*impf.*); **it ~d my fancy** э́то дразни́ло моё воображе́ние; **I was ~d to death** (*or* **~d pink**) (*coll.*) я чуть не ло́пнул со́ смеху.

● *v.i.* (*be itchy*) чеса́ться (*impf.*); **this blanket ~s** э́то одея́ло шерсти́т; **my nose ~s** у меня́ щеко́чет в носу́.

ticklish /ˈtɪklɪʃ/ *adj.* (*sensitive to tickling*): **she is ~** она́ бои́тся щеко́тки; (*requiring careful handling*) щекотли́вый.

tidal /ˈtaɪd(ə)l/ *adj.* прили́вный; **~ river** прили́вно-отли́вная река́; **~ wave** прили́вная волна́.

tidbit /ˈtɪdbɪt/ (*US*) = **titbit**

tiddledywinks /ˈtɪd(ə)ldɪwɪŋks/ (*US*) = **tiddlywinks**

tiddler /ˈtɪdlə(r)/ *n.* (*Br., small fish*) ко́люшка.

tiddl(e)y /ˈtɪdlɪ/ *adj.* (**tiddlier, tiddliest**) (*tipsy*) под му́хой (*sl.*); (*small, trifling*) ма́ленький, малю́сенький.

tiddlywinks /ˈtɪdlɪwɪŋks/ (*US* **tiddledywinks**) *n.* игра́ в бло́шки.

tide /taɪd/ *n.* (*rise*) морско́й прили́в; (*fall*) морско́й отли́в; **high ~** по́лная вода́; вы́сшая то́чка прили́ва; **low ~** ма́лая вода́; ни́зшая то́чка прили́ва; **the ~ is coming in** начался́ прили́в; **the ~ has gone out** (*or* **is out**) сейча́с отли́в; (*fig.*) волна́, тече́ние; **the rising ~ of excitement** уси́ливающееся возбужде́ние.

● *v.t.*: **this will ~ me over till next month** благодаря́ э́тому, я перебью́сь до сле́дующего ме́сяца.

● *cpd.* **~-mark** *n.* отме́тка у́ровня по́лной воды́.

tidiness /ˈtaɪdɪnɪs/ *n.* аккура́тность, опря́тность.

tidings /ˈtaɪdɪŋz/ *n.* (*liter. and joc.*) ве́сти (*f. pl.*), но́вости (*f. pl.*).

tidy /ˈtaɪdɪ/ *adj.* (**tidier, tidiest**) (*neat, orderly*) аккура́тный, опря́тный; (*of room etc.*) чи́стый, опря́тный; (*considerable*) поря́дочный, прили́чный; **a ~ sum** прили́чная/кру́гленькая су́мма.

● *v.t.* (*also* **~ up**) прив|оди́ть, -ести́ в поря́док; приб|ира́ть, -ра́ть.

● *v.i.*: **~ up** нав|оди́ть, -ести́ поря́док.

tie /taɪ/ *n.* **1** (*also* **neck ~**) га́лстук.
2 (*part that fastens or connects*) скре́па; шнур; ле́нта.
3 (*fig., bond*) у́з|ы (*pl., g.* —); **~s of friendship** у́зы дру́жбы; **family ~s** семе́йные у́зы.
4 (*fig., restriction*) обу́за; **don't you find your children a ~?** де́ти вас не (сли́шком) свя́зывают?
5 (*mus.*) ли́га.
6 (*equal score*) ничья́; ниче́йный исхо́д; **the match ended in a ~** матч зако́нчился вничью́; **in the event of a ~** в слу́чае ничьи́/ниче́йного исхо́да.

● *v.t.* (**tying**) **1** (*fasten*) свя́з|ывать, -а́ть; привя́з|ывать, -а́ть; **he was ~d to the mast** его́ привяза́ли к ма́чте; (*fig.*): **my hands are ~d** у меня́ свя́заны ру́ки; **~d cottage** (*Br.*) дом, закреплённый за рабо́тником на срок его́ рабо́ты; **~d house** (*Br.*) (*public house*) бар, отпуска́ющий пи́во то́лько определённого заво́да.
2 (*arrange in bow or knot*) перевя́з|ывать, -а́ть; завя́з|ывать, -а́ть; шнурова́ть, за-; **he learnt to ~ his shoe-laces** он научи́лся шнурова́ть боти́нки; **can you ~ a knot in this string?** вы мо́жете завяза́ть у́зел на э́той верёвке?

● *v.i.* (**tying**) **1** (*fasten*) завя́з|ываться, -а́ться; **does this sash ~ at the front?** э́тот по́яс завя́зывается спе́реди?
2 (*make equal score*) равня́ть, с- счёт; игра́ть, сыгра́ть вничью́; **we ~d with them for first place** мы подели́ли с ни́ми пе́рвое ме́сто; **the runners ~d** сопе́рники пришли́ к фи́нишу одновре́ме́нно.

● *with advs.*: **~ back** *v.t.* подвя́з|ывать, -а́ть; **I ~d back the roses** я подвяза́л ро́зы; **she wore her hair ~d back** она́ завя́зывала во́лосы сза́ди; **~ down** *v.t.* (*lit.*) привя́з|ывать, -а́ть; (*fig., restrict*) свя́з|ывать, -а́ть; **I don't want to ~ myself down to a date** я не хочу́ быть свя́занным определённой да́той; **~ in (with)** *v.i.* соотве́тствовать (*impf.*) (+*d.*); согласова́ться (*impf., pf.*) (с + *i.*); **this ~s in with what I was saying** э́то согласу́ется с тем, что я говори́л; **~ on** *v.t.* привя́з|ывать, -а́ть; **~ up** *v.t.* (*lit.*) привя́з|ывать, -а́ть; свя́з|ывать, -а́ть; **the dog was ~d up** соба́ка была́ на при́вязи; **can you ~ up this parcel?** вы мо́жете перевяза́ть э́ту посы́лку?; (*fig.*): **his firm is ~d up with the Ministry** его́ фи́рма свя́зана с министе́рством; **I'm rather ~d up this week** я дово́льно си́льно за́нят на э́той неде́ле; **his capital is ~d up** его́ капита́л инвести́рован.

● *cpds.* **~-breaker** *n.* реша́ющая игра́ (*после ничьей*); **~pin** *n.* була́вка для га́лстука; **~-up** *n.* (*link*) связь.

tier /tɪə(r)/ *n.* (*row*) ряд; я́рус; (*unit of structure*) у́зел, се́кция.

tiff /tɪf/ *n.* размо́лвка.

tiger /ˈtaɪgə(r)/ *n.* тигр.

● *cpds.* **~-cub** *n.* тигрёнок; **~-moth** *n.* ба́бочка-медве́дица.

tight /taɪt/ *adj.* **1** (*with no slack*) туго́й; (*closely fixed*) туго́й, пло́тный; (*close-fitting*) те́сный; (*of clothes*) облега́ющий; **the dress was a ~ fit** (*close-fitting*) пла́тье облега́ло (фигу́ру); (*too small*) пла́тье бы́ло те́сно; **this knot is very ~** э́тот у́зел о́чень туго́й; **my shoes are too ~** мои́ ту́фли тесны́/жмут.
2 (*packed as full as possible*) туго́й, ту́го наби́тый, пло́тный.
3 (*taut*) стро́гий; **keep a ~ rein on your spending** вы должны́ стро́го следи́ть за свои́ми расхо́дами.
4 (*under pressure*; *difficult*) тру́дный; тяжёлый; **in a ~ corner** в тру́дном положе́нии; **I have a ~ schedule** у меня́ жёсткое расписа́ние.
5 (*miserly*) прижи́мистый, скупо́й; **he is very ~ with his money** он о́чень скуп.
6 (*in short supply*): **money is ~** с деньга́ми ту́го.
7 (*coll., drunk*) навеселе́; **he went out and got ~** он пошёл и напи́лся.

● *adv.* (*fitting*) те́сно, пло́тно; (*screwed*) кре́пко; (*stretched*) ту́го; **hold ~!** держи́тесь кре́пко!; **shut your eyes ~!** кре́пко зажму́рьте глаза́!; **the door was ~ shut** дверь была́ пло́тно закры́та; **I sat ~ and waited** я стоя́л на своём и выжида́л.

● *cpds.* **~-fisted** *adj.* скупо́й, прижи́мистый; **~(ly)-fitting** *adj.* пло́тно облега́ющий; **~-lipped** *adj.* (*lit.*) с поджа́тыми губа́ми; (*fig., secretive*) скры́тный; **~rope** *n.* натя́нутый кана́т; **he is walking a ~rope** (*fig.*) он хо́дит по остри́ю ножа́; **~rope-walker** *n.* канатохо́дец.

tighten /ˈtaɪt(ə)n/ *v.t.* (*also* **~ up**) сж|има́ть, -ать; закреп|ля́ть, -и́ть; зат|я́гивать, -яну́ть; **the screws need ~ing (up)** на́до затяну́ть болты́; **we must ~ our belts** (*fig.*) мы должны́ затяну́ть пояса́ поту́же; **the rules were ~ed** пра́вила ста́ли стро́же.

tightness /ˈtaɪtnɪs/ *n.* напряжённость; стеснённость.

tights /taɪts/ *n.* (*Br.*) колго́т|ки (*pl., g.* -ок).

tigress /ˈtaɪgrɪs/ *n.* тигри́ца.

Tigris /ˈtaɪgrɪs/ *n.* Тигр.

tilde /ˈtɪldə/ *n.* (*ling.*) ти́льда.

tile /taɪl/ *n.* (*for roof*) черепи́ца; **he was (out) on the ~s last night** (*Br. sl.*) он вчера́ ве́чером кути́л; (*decorative, for wall etc.*) ка́фель (*m.*), пли́тка, изразе́ц.

● *v.t.* (*roof*) крыть, по- черепи́цей; (*walls*) крыть, по- ка́фелем.

till[1] /tɪl/ *n.* ка́сса (*кассовый аппарат*).

till[2] /tɪl/ *v.t.*: **~ the ground** обраб|а́тывать, -о́тать зе́млю.

till[3] /tɪl/ (*see also* ⇒**until**) *prep.* до + *g.*; **~ then** до того́ вре́мени; **he will not come ~ after dinner** он придёт то́лько по́сле у́жина; **I never saw him ~ now** я его́ впервы́е ви́жу.

● *conj.* пока́. . . (не); до тех пор пока́ (не); **~ we meet again!** до сле́дующей встре́чи!; **don't go ~ I come back** не уходи́те, пока́ я не верну́сь; **it was not ~ he spoke that I saw him** то́лько когда́ он заговори́л, я уви́дел его́; **not ~ Tuesday** не ра́ньше вто́рника.

tillage /ˈtɪlɪdʒ/ *n.* (*ploughing*) обрабо́тка по́чвы; (*ploughed land*) па́шня.

tiller[1] /ˈtɪlə(r)/ *n.* (*for steering*) ру́мпель (*m.*); рукоя́тка.

tiller² /ˈtɪlə(r)/ *n.*: **~ of the soil** земледéлец.

tilt /tɪlt/ *n.* **1** (*sloping position*) наклóн; **the table is on the ~** стол стоит кри́во. **2** (*attack*): **he came at me full ~** он я́ростно набрóсился на меня́.

● *v.t.* наклон|я́ть, -и́ть; **he ~ed the chair back** он наклони́л стул наза́д.

● *v.i.* (*slope*) наклон|я́ться, -и́ться; **the table was ~ing dangerously** стол опа́сно коси́лся/криви́лся.

timber /ˈtɪmbə(r)/ *n.* (*substance*) лесоматериа́л, древеси́на; (*trees grown for felling*) строево́й лес; (*beam of roof, ship etc.*) ба́лка.

● *cpd.* **~-yard** *n.* склад лесоматериа́лов.

timbre /ˈtæmbə(r)/, /ˈtæbrə/ *n.* тембр.

time /taɪm/ *n.* **1** вре́мя (*nt.*); **for all ~** навсегда́; **from the beginning of ~** испоко́н веко́в; **in (the) course of ~, with ~** с тече́нием вре́мени; **to the end of ~** (на)ве́чно; **(Old) Father T~** де́душка-вре́мя; **~ flies** вре́мя лети́т; **~ hangs heavy on my hands** вре́мя тя́нется ме́дленно; **kill ~** уб|ива́ть, -и́ть вре́мя; **~ has passed him by** жизнь прошла́ ми́мо него́; **~ is running out** вре́мя/срок истека́ет; **~ is on our side** вре́мя рабо́тает на нас; **~ will tell** вре́мя пока́жет; **it has stood the test of ~** э́то вы́держало испыта́ние вре́менем; **~ waits for no man** вре́мя не ждёт.
2 (*system of measurement*): **Greenwich Mean T~** гри́нвичское сре́днее вре́мя; **local ~** ме́стное вре́мя.
3 (*duration, period, opportunity*): **after a ~** че́рез не́которое вре́мя; **all the ~** всё вре́мя, всегда́; **you had all the ~ in the world to do it** у вас была́ у́йма вре́мени э́то сде́лать; **he has done ~** (*coll., been in prison*) он сиде́л/отсиде́л; **he stayed for a ~** он про́был не́которое вре́мя; **I have been here for some ~** я здесь уже́ дово́льно до́лго; **given ~, he will succeed** дай срок, и он добьётся успе́ха; **all in good ~** всему́ своё вре́мя; **in good ~** заблаговре́менно; **I have no ~ for him** (*fig.*) мне не до него́; **I have no ~ to lose** мне нельзя́ теря́ть ни мину́ты; **I shall get used to it in ~** со вре́менем я к э́тому привы́кну; **in no ~ (at all)** момента́льно; **I could do it in no ~** я мог бы э́то сде́лать в два счёта; **do it in your own ~** (*not in work ~*) сде́лайте э́то в нерабо́чее вре́мя; (*without hurrying*) сде́лайте э́то не спеша́; **I haven't seen him for a long ~** я его́ давно́ не ви́дел; **long ~ no see!** (*coll.*) ско́лько лет, ско́лько зим!; **a long ~ ago** давно́; **make up for lost ~** нав|ёрстывать, -ерста́ть упу́щенное/потеря́нное вре́мя; **pass the ~** пров|оди́ть, -ести́ вре́мя; **play for ~** оття́|гивать, -ну́ть вре́мя; **I am pressed for ~** у меня́ ма́ло вре́мени; (*owing to deadline*) меня́ поджима́ют сро́ки; **for some ~ now** с не́которого вре́мени; **it will be some ~ before he is well** он ещё не так ско́ро попра́вится; **in one's spare ~** на досу́ге; **take your ~!** не торопи́тесь!; **it will take ~** э́то займёт вре́мя; **he asked for ~ off** он отпроси́лся с рабо́ты; **I want some ~ to myself** мне хо́чется побы́ть одному́; **your ~ is up** ва́ше вре́мя истекло́; **what a waste of ~!** кака́я пуста́я тра́та вре́мени!; **~ and motion study** хронометра́ж движе́ний рабо́чего.
4 (*life-span*) пери́од жи́зни; век; **it will last my ~ (out)** э́того на мой век хва́тит; **if I had my ~ over again** е́сли бы мо́жно бы́ло нача́ть жизнь снача́ла.
5 (*measuring progress or speed*) вре́мя; **this watch keeps good ~** э́ти часы́ хорошо́ иду́т; **what was his ~ for the race?** за како́е вре́мя/ско́лько он прошёл/пробежа́л диста́нцию?; **in record ~** за реко́рдное вре́мя.
6 (*experience*): **he gave us a bad ~** он доста́вил нам неприя́тности; **they gave us a good ~** мы прия́тно провели́ с ни́ми вре́мя; **have a good ~!** жела́ю вам прия́тно провести́ вре́мя; **we had the ~ of our lives** мы отли́чно провели́ вре́мя; **I had a trying ~** я пережи́л тру́дный пери́од; **what sort of (a) ~ did you have?** вы хорошо́ провели́ вре́мя?
7 (*~ of day or night*) час, вре́мя; **what's the ~?** кото́рый час?, ско́лько вре́мени?; **what ~ do you make it?** ско́лько на ва́ших (часа́х)?; **the ~ is 8 o'clock** сейча́с 8 часо́в; **we passed the ~ of day** (*greeted each other*) мы поздоро́вались; **at that ~** (*hour*) в э́тот час; **at what ~?** в кото́ром часу́?, во ско́лько?; **what ~ do you go to bed?** в кото́ром часу́ вы ложи́тесь спать?
8 (*moment*) вре́мя; **I was away at the ~** меня́ тогда́ (*or* в то вре́мя) не́ было; **at the right ~** в ну́жный/подходя́щий моме́нт; **at the/that ~** в то вре́мя; **at the same ~** (*simultaneously*) в то же (са́мое) вре́мя; (*notwithstanding*) тем не ме́нее; вме́сте с тем; **at ~s** иногда́, времена́ми; **at all ~s** всегда́; во всех слу́чаях; **at different ~s** в ра́зное вре́мя; **at no ~** никогда́; **before ~** преждевре́менно; **behind ~** с опозда́нием; **by the ~ I got back he had gone** (к тому́ вре́мени,) когда́ я верну́лся, его́ уже́ не́ было; **from ~ to ~** иногда́, вре́мя от вре́мени; **it's ~ for bed** пора́ спать; **it's ~ I went** мне пора́ идти́; **~'s up** вре́мя истекло́; пора́ конча́ть; **will he arrive in ~ for dinner?** он успе́ет к у́жину?; **there's no ~ like the present** ≈ лови́ моме́нт; **the train was on ~** по́езд пришёл во́время; **are the trains running to ~?** поезда́ хо́дят (то́чно) по расписа́нию?
9 (*instance, occasion*) раз; **~ and (~) again; ~ after ~** сно́ва и сно́ва; раз за ра́зом; **I've told you ~ and again** ско́лько раз я вам говори́л!; **nine ~s out of ten** в девяти́ слу́чаях из десяти́; **six ~s running (*or* in a row)** шесть раз подря́д; **the ~ before** в про́шлый раз; **another ~** когда́-нибу́дь; в друго́й раз; **one at a ~!** по одному́; не все сра́зу!; **every ~ I go out it rains** ка́ждый раз, когда́ я выхожу́, идёт дождь; **the first ~ I saw him** когда́ я впервы́е (*or* в пе́рвый раз) уви́дел его́; **it's the first ~ we've met** э́то на́ша пе́рвая встре́ча; **for the last ~, will you shut up?** я тебе́ в после́дний раз говорю́ — заткни́сь!/замолчи́!; **many a ~, many ~s** мно́го раз, ча́сто; **next ~** в сле́дующий раз; **there may not be a next ~** второ́го слу́чая мо́жет не предста́виться; **I'll let you off this ~** на сей раз я вас проща́ю.
10 (*in multiplication*): **6 ~s 2 is 12** 6 (умно́жить) на 2 — 12; ше́стью два — двена́дцать; **ten ~s as easy** в де́сять раз ле́гче.
11 (*period, age*) вре́мя, времена́ (*nt. pl.*), эпо́ха; **in the ~ of Queen Elizabeth** в эпо́ху короле́вы Елизаве́ты; **in olden ~s** в ста́рые времена́; в дре́вности; **at one ~** одно́ вре́мя, когда́-то, не́когда; **as a thinker he was ahead of his ~** как мысли́тель он опереди́л своё вре́мя/свою́ эпо́ху; **that was before my ~** э́то бы́ло до меня́; **at my ~ of life** в моём во́зрасте.
12 (*circumstances*): **we have seen good and bad ~s** мы пережи́ли и хоро́шее и плохо́е; **she is behind the ~s** она́ отста́ла от жи́зни; **he is irritating at the best of ~s** он раздража́ет да́же в лу́чшие мину́ты.
13 (*mus.*) такт, ритм; **in quick ~** в бы́стром те́мпе; **in double-quick ~** (*fig.*) в те́мпе; в два счёта; **they clapped in ~ with the music** они́ хло́пали в такт му́зыке; **beat ~** (*as conductor*) дирижи́ровать (*impf.*); (*with foot etc.*) отбива́ть (*impf.*) такт (*ного́й и т.п.*); **in waltz ~** в те́мпе ва́льса; **mark ~** (*lit.*) маршировáть (*impf.*) на ме́сте; (*fig.*) топта́ться (*impf.*) на ме́сте.

● *v.t.* **1** (*do at a chosen ~*) выбира́ть, вы́брать вре́мя для + *g.*/ + *g.*; рассчи́т|ывать, -а́ть вре́мя + *g.*; **you must ~ your blows carefully** вы должны́ осторо́жно выбира́ть моме́нт для нанесе́ния уда́ра; **his remarks were ill ~d** его́ замеча́ния бы́ли некста́ти.
2 (*measure ~ of or for*) зас|ека́ть, -е́чь вре́мя + *g.*; хронометри́ровать (*impf., pf.*); **they ~d him over the mile** они́ засекли́ вре́мя, за кото́рое он пробежа́л одну́ ми́лю.
3 (*schedule*): **the train was ~d to leave at 6** по́езд до́лжен был отойти́ в 6 часо́в.

● *cpds.* **~-bomb** *n.* бо́мба заме́дленного де́йствия; **~-consuming** *adj.* тре́бующий мно́го вре́мени; **~-exposure** *n.* вы́держка; **~-fuse** *n.* дистанцио́нный взрыва́тель; **~-honoured** (*US* **-honored**) *adj.* освящённый века́ми; **~-keeper** *n.* (*person*) та́бельщик, хронометри́ст; **he is a good ~-keeper** (*at work*) он прихо́дит на рабо́ту во́время; **this watch is a good ~-keeper** э́ти часы́ хорошо́ иду́т; **~-lag** *n.* запа́здывание; **~-limit** *n.* преде́льный срок; **~ off** *n.* о́тпуск; **~ out** *n.* переры́в; **~piece** *n.* час|ы́ (*pl., g.* -о́в); (*tech.*) хроно́метр; **~-saving** *n.* эконо́мия вре́мени; *adj.* эконо́мящий вре́мя; **~-server** *n.* приспосо́бленец; **~-serving** *n.* приспосо́бленчество; *adj.* приспоса́бливающийся; **~-share** *n.* совме́стное владе́ние куро́ртным помеще́нием; **~-signal** *n.* сигна́л вре́мени; **~-switch** *n.* переключа́тель (*m.*) с часовы́м

T

механи́змом; **~table** *n.* расписа́ние; гра́фик; **~-wasting** *adj.* напра́сный, ли́шний; **~ zone** *n.* часово́й по́яс.

timeless /ˈtaɪmlɪs/ *adj.* (*eternal*) ве́чный, непреходя́щий; (*unmarked by time*) неподвла́стный вре́мени, неустарева́ющий.

timeliness /ˈtaɪmlɪnɪs/ *n.* своевре́менность.

timely /ˈtaɪmlɪ/ *adj.* (**timelier, timeliest**) своевре́менный.

timer /ˈtaɪmə(r)/ *n.* (*person*) хронометражи́ст; (*device*) отме́тчик вре́мени, та́ймер.

timid /ˈtɪmɪd/ *adj.* (**timider, timidest**) ро́бкий; (*shy*) засте́нчивый.

timid|ity /tɪˈmɪdɪtɪ/, **-ness** /ˈtɪmɪdnɪs/ *nn.* ро́бость; засте́нчивость.

timing /ˈtaɪmɪŋ/ *n.* (*choosing of appropriate time*) вы́бор (наибо́лее подходя́щего/удо́бного) вре́мени; **sense of ~** чу́вство вре́мени; (*process of recording time*) хронометра́ж; (*in internal combustion engine*) регули́рование моме́нта зажига́ния; (*sport*) координа́ция.

timorous /ˈtɪmərəs/ *adj.* боязли́вый, пугли́вый.

timorousness /ˈtɪmərəsnɪs/ *n.* боязли́вость, пугли́вость.

timpani, tympani /ˈtɪmpənɪ/ *n.* лита́вры (*f. pl.*).

timpanist, tympanist /ˈtɪmpənɪst/ *n.* литаври́ст.

tin /tɪn/ *n.* **1** (*metal*) о́лово; (*tin-plate*) бе́лая жесть; (*attr.*) оловя́нный; (*tin-plated*) жестяно́й; **~ can** (*for paint etc.*) жестяна́я ба́нка; (*for food*) консе́рвная ба́нка; **~ hat** (*Br. coll.*) стально́й шлем.
2 (*Br., container, can*) (*for food*) = **~ can** (*see sense* 1); (*for biscuits*) (металли́ческая) коро́бка; (*for baking cakes*) фо́рма; (*for roasting*) про́тивень (*m.*); **~ of beans** ба́нка фасо́ли.
● *v.t.* (**tinned, tinning**) **1** (*coat with ~*) покр|ыва́ть, -ы́ть о́ловом.
2 (*Br., pack in ~s*) консерви́ровать, за-; **~ned goods** консерви́рованные проду́кты; консе́рв|ы (*pl., g.* -ов); **~ned fish** ры́бные консе́рвы.
● *cpds.* **~foil** *n.* оловя́нная фо́льга; **~-opener** *n.* (*Br.*) консе́рвный нож; **~-plate** *n.* бе́лая жесть; **~pot** *adj.* (*coll.*) дешёвый; никуды́шный; **~smith** *n.* (*person who works with tin-plate*) луди́льщик; (*person who makes tinware*) жестя́нщик.

tincture /ˈtɪŋktjə(r)/, /-tʃə(r)/ *n.* (*pharm.*) раство́р; тинкту́ра; (*fig., slight flavour*) при́вкус; (*trace*) налёт.

tinder /ˈtɪndə(r)/ *n.* трут.
● *cpd.* **~-box** *n.* тру́тница.

tine /taɪn/ *n.* (*of fork*) зубе́ц; (*of antler*) о́стрый отро́сток.

ting /tɪŋ/ *n.* звон; дзы́нканье.
● *v.i.* звене́ть (*impf.*); дзы́нкать (*impf.*).

tinge /tɪndʒ/ *n.* лёгкая окра́ска, отте́нок; (*fig.*) при́месь, налёт, отте́нок.
● *v.t.* (**tinging** *or* **tingeing**) слегка́ окра́|шивать, -сить; (*fig.*): **her voice was ~d with regret** в её го́лосе звуча́ло лёгкое сожале́ние.

tingl|e /ˈtɪŋg(ə)l/, **-ing** /ˈtɪŋglɪŋ/ *nn.* пощи́пывание; (*of pleasure etc.*) тре́пет.
● *v.i.*: **the slap made his hand ~e** его́ рука́ зуде́ла от уда́ра; **they were ~ing with excitement** они́ дрожа́ли от возбужде́ния.

tinker /ˈtɪŋkə(r)/ *n.* ме́дник; луди́льщик.
● *v.i.* (*meddle etc.*) вози́ться (*impf.*) (*с чем*).

tinkle /ˈtɪŋk(ə)l/ *n.* (*sound*) звон; звя́канье; (*Br. coll., telephone call*) телефо́нный звоно́к; **give me a ~ some time** звя́кните мне ка́к-нибу́дь.
● *v.t.*: **he ~d the bell** он позвони́л в колоко́льчик.
● *v.i.*: **the bell ~d** колоко́льчик зазвене́л.

tinnitus /tɪˈnaɪtəs/ *n.* шум в уша́х.

tinny /ˈtɪnɪ/ *adj.* (**tinnier, tinniest**) (*of sound*) металли́ческий, жестяно́й; (*of taste*) металли́ческий.

tinsel /ˈtɪns(ə)l/ *n.* блёст|ки (*pl., g.* -ок); мишура́ (*also fig.*).
● *adj.* (*fig.*) мишу́рный.

tint /tɪnt/ *n.* отте́нок; тон.
● *v.t.*: **~ed glasses** тёмные очки́; **she ~s her hair** она́ подкра́шивает во́лосы.

tiny /ˈtaɪnɪ/ *adj.* (**tinier, tiniest**) кро́шечный.

tip[1] /tɪp/ *n.* (*pointed end*) ко́нчик; верху́шка; (*part attached, e.g. of arrow*) наконе́чник; **~ of the iceberg** (*lit., fig.*) верху́шка а́йсберга; **the ~s of my fingers are freezing** у меня́ мёрзнут ко́нчики па́льцев; **I had his name on the ~ of my tongue** его́ и́мя верте́лось у меня́ на языке́.
● *v.t.* (**tipped, tipping**): **arrows ~ped with bronze** стре́лы с ме́дными наконе́чниками; **~ped cigarettes** папиро́сы с фи́льтром.
● *cpds.* **~toe** *n.*: **on ~toe(s)** на цы́почках; *v.i.* ходи́ть (*indet.*) на цы́почках; **she ~toed out of the room** она́ на цы́почках вы́шла из ко́мнаты; **~-top** *adj.* первокла́ссный; **in ~-top condition** в превосхо́дном состоя́нии.

tip[2] /tɪp/ *n.* (*Br., dumping-ground*) сва́лка.
● *v.t.* (**tipped, tipping**) **1** (*strike lightly*) зад|ева́ть, -е́ть; **he ~ped the ball** он сре́зал мяч.
2 (*tilt*) наклон|я́ть, -и́ть; **he ~s the scale at 12 stone** он ве́сит (*or* тя́нет на (*coll.*)) 168 фу́нтов; **this will ~ the scale** (*fig.*) **in their favour** (*Br.*), **favor** (*US*) э́то склони́т ча́шу весо́в в их по́льзу.
3 (*overturn, empty*) выва́ливать, вы́валить; опорожн|я́ть, -и́ть; **~ the rubbish into the bin!** вы́валите му́сор в я́щик!
● *with advs.*: **~ out** *v.t.* выва́ливать, вы́валить; **the car overturned and the occupants were ~ped out** маши́на переверну́лась и пассажи́ры вы́валились; **~ over** *v.t. & i.* опроки́|дывать(ся), -нуть(ся); **he ~ped the cup over** он опроки́нул ча́шку; **the boat ~ped over** ло́дка переверну́лась; **~ up** *v.t. & i.* наклон|я́ть(ся), -и́ть(ся); **he ~ped his plate up** он наклони́л таре́лку.
● *cpd.* **~-up** *adj.*: **a ~-up seat** откидно́е сиде́нье.

tip[3] /tɪp/ *n.* **1** (*piece of advice, recommendation*) сове́т; намёк; **shall I give you a ~?** хоти́те сове́т?
2 (*gratuity*) чаев|ы́е (*pl., g.* -ы́х); **I gave the porter a ~** я дал носи́льщику чаевы́е/на чай.
● *v.t.* (**tipped, tipping**) **1** (*Br. coll., give*): **~ me the wink when you're ready** да́йте мне знак, когда́ вы бу́дете гото́вы.
2 (*Br., mention as likely winner*): **he always ~ped the winner** он всегда́ уга́дывал победи́теля; **the horse was ~ped to win** предска́зывали, что победи́т э́та ло́шадь.
3 (*remunerate*) да|ва́ть, -ть чаевы́е/на чай + *d.*; **the driver expects to be ~ped** шофёр рассчи́тывает на чаевы́е.
● *with adv.*: **~ off** (*coll.*) предупре|жда́ть, -ди́ть.
● *cpd.* **~-off** *n.*: **the police had a ~-off** поли́цию предупреди́ли.

tipper[1] /ˈtɪpə(r)/ *n.* (*vehicle*) самосва́л.

tipper[2] /ˈtɪpə(r)/ *n.*: **he is a generous ~** он ще́дро раздаёт чаевы́е.

tippet /ˈtɪpɪt/ *n.* (*woman's*) мехова́я пелери́на/наки́дка; (*official's*) паланти́н.

Tipp-Ex, Tippex /ˈtɪpeks/ *n.* (*Br. propr.*) корректи́рующая жи́дкость.

tipple /ˈtɪp(ə)l/ *n.* напи́ток, питьё.
● *v.i.* выпива́ть (*impf.*).

tippler /ˈtɪplə(r)/ *n.* пьянчу́жка (*c.g.*).

tipsiness /ˈtɪpsɪnɪs/ *n.* лёгкое опьяне́ние.

tipster /ˈtɪpstə(r)/ *n.* (*at races*) «жучо́к».

tipsy /ˈtɪpsɪ/ *adj.* (**tipsier, tipsiest**) подвы́пивший; (*pred.*) навеселе́, под хмелько́м.

tirade /taɪˈreɪd/, /tɪ-/ *n.* тира́да.

tire[1] /ˈtaɪə(r)/ (*US*) = **tyre**

tire[2] /ˈtaɪə(r)/ *v.t.* утом|ля́ть, -и́ть; (*bore*) надо|еда́ть, -е́сть + *d.*; **the walk ~d me** прогу́лка утоми́ла меня́; **I'm ~d out** я соверше́нно вы́мотался (*coll.*); **you will soon get ~d of him** он вам ско́ро надое́ст; вы ско́ро от него́ уста́нете; **I had a tiring day** у меня́ был утоми́тельный/тру́дный день; **I am ~d of being idle** мне надое́ла пра́здность.
● *v.i.* утом|ля́ться, -и́ться; уст|ава́ть, -а́ть; **she ~s easily** она́ бы́стро устаёт; **I shall never ~ of that music** э́та му́зыка мне никогда́ не надое́ст.

tiredness /ˈtaɪədnɪs/ *n.* уста́лость.

tireless /ˈtaɪəlɪs/ *adj.* неутоми́мый.

tiresome /ˈtaɪəsəm/ *adj.* надое́дливый, ну́дный.

tissue /ˈtɪʃuː/, /ˈtɪsjuː/ *n.* **1** (*text., biol.*) ткань; **~ paper** то́нкая обёрточная бума́га; папиро́сная бума́га; **face ~** бума́жная салфе́тка; **toilet ~** туале́тная бума́га. **2** (*fig.*) паути́на; сеть; **a ~ of lies** паути́на лжи.

tit[1] /tɪt/ *n.* (*bird*) сини́ца.

tit² /tɪt/ *n.* (*vulg., breast*) си́ська (*sl.*).

tit³ /tɪt/ *n.*: **~ for tat** зуб за́ зуб.

titan /ˈtaɪt(ə)n/ *n.* тита́н.

titanic /taɪˈtænɪk/, /tɪ-/ *adj.* (*fig.*) титани́ческий.

titanium /taɪˈteɪnɪəm/, /tɪ-/ *n.* (*chem.*) тита́н.

titbit /ˈtɪtbɪt/ (*US* **tidbit**) *n.* ла́комый кусо́чек; (*fig.*): **a ~ of news** пика́нтная но́вость.

titch /tɪtʃ/ *n.* (*Br.*) коротыш.

titchy /ˈtɪtʃɪ/ *adj.* (**titchier, titchiest**) (*Br.*) низкоро́слый.

tithe /taɪð/ *n.* (*tax*) десяти́на.

titillate /ˈtɪtɪˌleɪt/ *v.t.* (*tickle*) щекота́ть (*impf.*); (*excite*) прия́тно возбу|жда́ть, -ди́ть.

titillation /ˌtɪtɪˈleɪʃ(ə)n/ *n.* прия́тное возбужде́ние.

titivate /ˈtɪtɪˌveɪt/ *v.i.* прихора́шиваться (*impf.*).

title /ˈtaɪt(ə)l/ *n.* **1** (*name of book etc.*) загла́вие; назва́ние; (*published book, magazine*) кни́га; журна́л. **2** (*indicator of rank, occupation, status etc.*) зва́ние, ти́тул; **the ~ of champion** зва́ние чемпио́на. **3** (*legal right or claim*) пра́во; **what is his ~ to the property?** на како́м основа́нии он претенду́ет на э́ту со́бственность?

● *cpds.* **~-deed** *n.* докуме́нт, подтвержда́ющий пра́во со́бственности; **~-holder** *n.* чемпио́н; **~-page** *n.* ти́тульный лист; **~-role** *n.* загла́вная роль.

titled /ˈtaɪt(ə)ld/ *adj.* титуло́ванный.

titmouse /ˈtɪtmaʊs/ *n.* (*pl.* **titmice** /-maɪs/) сини́ца.

titter /ˈtɪtə(r)/ *n.* хихи́канье.

● *v.i.* хихи́кать (*impf.*).

tittle /ˈtɪt(ə)l/ *n.*: **not one jot or ~** ни ка́пельки.

● *cpd.* **~-tattle** *n.* спле́тн|и (*pl., g.* -ен); *v.i.* спле́тничать (*impf.*).

titular /ˈtɪtjʊlə(r)/ *adj.* (*in name only*) номина́льный.

tiz(zy) /ˈtɪzɪ/ *n.* возбужде́ние, ажиота́ж (*coll.*); **she got into a ~** она́ пришла́ в стра́шное возбужде́ние.

TNT (*abbr. of* ***trinitrotoluene***) ТНТ (тринитротолуо́л).

to /tə/, *before a vowel* /tʊ/, *emph.* /tuː/ *adv.* **1** (*into closed position*): **draw the curtains ~!** задёрните занаве́ски! **2**: **~ and fro** туда́ и сюда́; взад и вперёд.

● *prep.* **1** (*expr. ind. obj., recipient*): *usu. expr. by d. case*; **a letter ~ my wife** письмо́ мое́й жене́; **it was a surprise ~ him** для него́ э́то бы́ло неожи́данностью; **~ me that is absurd** по-мо́ему э́то неле́по; **a monument ~ Pushkin** па́мятник Пу́шкину; (*expr. support*): **a toast ~ the workers** тост за рабо́тников; **here's ~ our victory** за на́шу побе́ду.
2 (*expr. destination*) (*i*) (*with place-names, countries, areas, institutions, places of study or entertainment*) в + *a.*; **~ Moscow** в Москву́; **~ Russia** в Росси́ю; **~ the Crimea** в Крым; **~ the theatre** (*Br.*), **theater** (*US*) в теа́тр; **~ school** в шко́лу; **he was elected ~ the council** его́ вы́брали в сове́т; (*expr. direction*): **the road ~ London** доро́га в Ло́ндон; (*ii*) (*with islands, peninsulas, mountain areas of Russia, planets, points of the compass, left and right, places considered as activity or function, some places of employment*) на + *a.*; **~ Ceylon** на Цейло́н; **~ the Caucasus** на Кавка́з; **back ~ earth** обра́тно на зе́млю; **turn ~ the right!** поверни́те напра́во!; **~ a concert** на конце́рт; **~ war** на войну́; **~ the factory** на фа́брику; **~ the station** на ста́нцию; **he was appointed ~ a new post** его́ назна́чили на но́вое ме́сто; **he set the lines ~ music** он положи́л э́ти стихи́ на му́зыку; (*iii*) (*with persons*) к + *d.*; **he went ~ his parents'** он поéхал к роди́телям; (*towards*) к + *d.*; **pull the chair up ~ the table!** пододви́ньте стул к столу́!; **he went up ~ the house** он подошёл к до́му; **she went ~ the door** она́ подошла́ к две́ри.
3 (*expr. limit or extent of movement: up to, as far as, until*) до + *g.*; на + *a.*; по + *a.*; **is it far ~ town?** до го́рода далеко́?; **we stayed ~ the end** мы про́были до конца́; **he was in the water (up) ~ his waist** он стоя́л по по́яс в воде́; **you will get soaked ~ the skin** вы промо́кните до косте́й/ни́тки; **~ the bottom** на са́мое дно; **from 10 ~ 4** с десяти́ до четырёх; **from morning ~ night** с утра́ до́ ночи; **ten (minutes) ~ six** (*Br.*) без десяти́ (мину́т) шесть.
4 (*expr. end state*): **smash ~ pieces** разб|ива́ть, -и́ть на/в куски́; **drive ~ distraction** дов|оди́ть, -ести́ до отча́яния; **torn ~ shreds** разо́рванный в кло́чья (*or* на куски́); **from bad ~ worse** всё ху́же и ху́же.
5 (*expr. response*) на + *a.*; к + *d.*; **an answer ~ my letter** отве́т на моё письмо́; **what do you say ~ that?** что вы на э́то ска́жете?; **deaf ~ entreaty** глухо́й к мольба́м.
6 (*expr. result or reaction*) к + *d.*; **~ my surprise** к моему́ удивле́нию; **~ everyone's disappointment** ко всео́бщему разочарова́нию; **it is ~ your advantage** э́то в ва́ших интере́сах; **~ no avail** напра́сно.
7 (*expr. appurtenance, attachment, suitability*) к + *d.*; от + *g.*; в + *a.*; **the preface ~ the book** предисло́вие к кни́ге; **the key ~ the door** ключ от две́ри; **the key ~ his heart** ключ к его́ се́рдцу; **there's nothing ~ it** (*coll., it presents no problem*) здесь нет ничего́ тру́дного; э́то па́ра пустяко́в.
8 (*expr. reference or relationship*): **he is good ~ his employees** он хорошо́ отно́сится к свои́м сотру́дникам; **soft ~ the touch** мя́гкий на о́щупь; **attention ~ detail** внима́ние к дета́лям; **ready ~ hand** (находя́щийся) под руко́й; **secretary ~ the director** секрета́рь дире́ктора; **close ~** бли́зкий к + *d.*
9 (*expr. comparison*) по сравне́нию с + *i.*; **the expense is nothing ~ what it might have been** расхо́д ничто́жен по сравне́нию с тем, каки́м он мог бы быть.
10 (*expr. ratio or proportion*): **ten ~ one he won't succeed** де́сять про́тив одного́, что э́то ему́ не уда́стся; **this car does 30 (miles) ~ the gallon** э́та маши́на де́лает 30 миль на галло́н; **there are 9 francs ~ the pound** оди́н фунт ра́вен девяти́ фра́нкам.
11 (*expr. score*) на + *a.*; **we won by six goals ~ four** мы вы́играли со счётом 6–4.
12 (*expr. accompaniment*) под + *a.*; **I fell asleep ~ the sound of lively conversation** я засну́л под оживлённый разгово́р; **he tapped his foot ~ the music** он отбива́л такт ного́й под му́зыку.
13 (*expr. position*): **~ my right** спра́ва от меня́; **~ the south of London** к ю́гу от Ло́ндона.

● *particle with v. forming inf.* **1** (*as subj. or obj. of v.*): **~ err is human** челове́ку сво́йственно ошиба́ться; **he learnt ~ swim** он научи́лся пла́вать.
2 (*as extension of adj.*): **this book is easy ~ read** э́ту кни́гу легко́ чита́ть; **too hot ~ touch** тако́й горя́чий, что не дотро́нуться.
3 (*expr. purpose*) (с тем *or* для того́), что́бы. . .; (*with inf. only*): **I came ~ help** я пришёл(, что́бы) помо́чь; **I have come ~ talk to you** я пришёл(, что́бы) поговори́ть с ва́ми; (*expr. request*): **I asked him ~ help** я попроси́л его́ помо́чь; (*expr. result, sequel*): **I arrived only ~ find him gone** когда́ я прие́хал, оказа́лось, что его́ уже́ нет; **he disappeared, never ~ return** он исче́з, и никогда́ уже́ не возвраща́лся.
4 (*as substitute for rel. clause*): **he was first ~ arrive and last ~ leave** он прибы́л пе́рвым и уе́хал после́дним; **the captain was the next man ~ die** сле́дующим у́мер капита́н.
5 (*as substitute for complete inf.*): **I was going ~ write but I forgot ~** я собира́лся написа́ть, но забы́л.

toad /təʊd/ *n.* жа́ба.

● *cpds.* **~-in-the-hole** *n.* (*Br.*) соси́ска, запечённая в те́сте; **~stool** *n.* пога́нка.

toady /ˈtəʊdɪ/ *n.* лизобл́юд, подхали́м.

● *v.i.* подли́зываться (*impf.*) (*к кому*).

toast¹ /təʊst/ *n.* (*toasted bread*) тост, грено́к.

● *v.t.* поджа́ри|вать, -ть; **~ing fork** дли́нная ви́лка; **he ~ed his toes by the fire** он грел но́ги у ками́на.

● *cpd.* **~-rack** *n.* подста́вка для грено́в.

toast² /təʊst/ *n.* (*drinking in honour*) тост; (*drinking of health*) здра́вный тост, здра́вица; **propose a ~ to** (*in s.o.'s honour*) предл|ага́ть, -ожи́ть тост за + *a.*; (*to s.o.'s health*) предл|ага́ть, -ожи́ть здра́вицу за + *a.*; **drink a ~ to something** пить, вы́- за что-н.

● *v.t.* пить, вы́- за (*чьё-н.*) здоро́вье.

● *cpd.* **~-master** *n.* тамада́.

toaster /ˈtəʊstə(r)/ *n.* (*machine*) то́стер.

tobacco /təˈbækəʊ/ *n.* (*pl.* **~s**) таба́к.

● *cpd.* **~-pouch** *n.* кисе́т.

tobacconist /təˈbækənɪst/ *n.* (*Br.*) торго́вец таба́чными изде́лиями.

Tobago /təˈbeɪgəʊ/ *see* ⇨**Trinidad**

T

toboggan /təˈbɒɡən/ *n.* тобо́гган; са́н|и (*pl.*, *g.* -е́й).
● *v.i.* ката́ться (*impf.*) на саня́х.
toccata /təˈkɑːtə/ *n.* токка́та.
tocsin /ˈtɒksɪn/ *n.* наба́т.
today /təˈdeɪ/ *adv.* & *n.* сего́дня; сего́дняшний день; **what's ~?** како́й сего́дня день?; **~'s newspaper** сего́дняшняя газе́та; **from ~ on** с сего́дняшнего дня; (*fig.*, *the present time*) настоя́щее вре́мя, сего́дня; **young people of ~** совреме́нная молодёжь.
toddle /ˈtɒd(ə)l/ *v.i.* (*of young child*) ковыля́ть (*impf.*); (*coll.*, *walk*) прогу́л|иваться, -я́ться; **I'll just ~ down to the shop** я то́лько сбе́гаю в магази́н; я пройду́сь до магази́на.
toddler /ˈtɒdlə(r)/ *n.* ребёнок, начина́ющий ходи́ть.
toddy /ˈtɒdɪ/ *n.* (*also* **hot ~**) то́дди (*nt. indecl.*), пунш; **(palm ~)** ара́к.
to-do /təˈduː/ *n.* (*pl.* **to-dos**) шум; суета́; **what's all the ~?** из-за чего́ весь э́тот шум?
toe /təʊ/ *n.* **1** (*of foot*) па́лец (ноги́); **big ~** большо́й па́лец (ноги́); **little ~** мизи́нец (ноги́); **tread on s.o.'s ~s** (*fig.*, *offend*) наступ|а́ть, -и́ть на люби́мую мозо́ль (*кому*); **on one's ~s** (*fig.*) начеку́. **2** (*of shoe or sock*) носо́к.
● *v.t.* **(toes, toed, toeing): ~ the line** (*fig.*, *conform*) ходи́ть (*indet.*) по стру́нке.
● *cpds.* **~-cap** *n.* носо́к; **~-hold** *n.* опо́ра; то́чка опо́ры; **~-nail** *n.* но́готь (*m.*) на па́льце ноги́.
toff /tɒf/ *n.* (*Br. sl.*) ба́рин, джентльме́н.
toff|ee, -y /ˈtɒfɪ/ *n.* (*substance*) то́ффи (*nt. indecl.*); ири́с; (*single sweet*) ири́ска; **he can't shoot for ~** (*Br. coll.*) он никуды́шний стрело́к.
tofu /ˈtəʊfuː/ *n.* со́евый творо́г.
tog /tɒɡ/ (*coll.*) *n.* (*pl. only*) оде́жда.
● *v.t. with advs.* **(togged, togging)** наря|жа́ть, -ди́ть, выряжа́ть, вы́рядить; **we got him ~ged out for school** мы наряди́ли его́ в шко́лу; **he ~ged himself up in a dinner-jacket** он вы́рядился в смо́кинг.
toga /ˈtəʊɡə/ *n.* то́га.
together /təˈɡeðə(r)/ *adv.* **1** (*in company*) вме́сте, сообща́; **they get on well ~** они́ ла́дят друг с дру́гом; **they were living ~** (*as man and wife*) они́ жи́ли вме́сте; **~ with** (*in addition to*) вме́сте с+*i.* **2** (*simultaneously*) одновре́ме́нно. **3** (*in succession*) подря́д, непреры́вно; **he was away for weeks ~** он был в разъе́здах неде́лями.
togetherness /təˈɡeðənɪs/ *n.* това́рищество, еди́нство; (*in family*) бли́зость.
toggle /ˈtɒɡ(ə)l/ *n.* **1** (*e.g. on a coat*) деревя́нная застёжка. **2** (*comput.*) ту́мблер.
toil /tɔɪl/ *n.* (тяжёлый) труд.
● *v.i.* **1** (*work hard or long*) труди́ться (*impf.*). **2** (*move with difficulty*) тащи́ться (*impf.*); **they ~ed up the hill** они втащи́лись на холм.
toiler /ˈtɔɪlə(r)/ *n.* тру́жени|к (*fem.* -ца).
toilet /ˈtɔɪlɪt/ *n.* **1** (*process of dressing, arranging hair etc.*) туале́т; **~ articles** туале́тные принадле́жности; **~ soap** туале́тное мы́ло. **2** (*lavatory*) туале́т, убо́рная.
● *cpds.* **~-paper** *n.* туале́тная бума́га; **~-roll** *n.* руло́н туале́тной бума́ги.
toiletries /ˈtɔɪlɪtrɪz/ *n. pl.* туале́тные принадле́жности.
toilette /twɑːˈlet/ *n.* туале́т.
toing and froing /ˌtuːɪŋ ənd ˈfrəʊɪŋ/ *n.* хожде́ние/езда́ туда́ и сюда́; (*bustle*) суета́, суетня́ (*coll.*).
token /ˈtəʊkən/ *n.* **1** (*sign, evidence, guarantee*) знак, си́мвол; **in ~ of my friendship** в знак мое́й дру́жбы; **by the same ~** (*moreover*) к тому́ же; (*similarly*) по той же причи́не. **2** (*keepsake, memento*) сувени́р. **3** (*substitute for coin*) жето́н. **4** (*attr.*) символи́ческий; **they put up a ~ resistance** они́ оказа́ли лишь ви́димость сопротивле́ния.
tokenism /ˈtəʊkəˌnɪz(ə)m/ *n.* символи́ческий жест.
Tokyo /ˈtəʊkjəʊ/, /-kɪˌəʊ/ *n.* То́кио (*m. indecl.*); (*attr.*) токи́йский.
told /təʊld/ *past and p.p. of* ⇒**tell**
tolerable /ˈtɒlərəb(ə)l/ *adj.* (*endurable*) терпи́мый, выноси́мый; (*fairly good*) терпи́мый, сно́сный.
tolerance /ˈtɒlərəns/ *n.* (*forbearance*) терпи́мость, толера́нтность; (*resistance to adverse conditions, drugs etc.*) выно́сливость; (*tech.*, *permissible variation*) до́пуск; допусти́мое отклоне́ние.
tolerant /ˈtɒlərənt/ *adj.* терпи́мый, толера́нтный; **he is not very ~ of criticism** он не те́рпит кри́тики.
tolerate /ˈtɒləˌreɪt/ *v.t.* (*endure*) терпе́ть (*impf.*); (*permit*) допус|ка́ть, -ти́ть; (*sustain without harm*) перен|оси́ть, -ести́.
toleration /ˌtɒləˈreɪʃ(ə)n/ *n.* терпи́мость, толера́нтность.
toll[1] /təʊl/ *n.* (*tax*) по́шлина, сбор; **~ call** (*US*) междугоро́дный разгово́р; **age is taking its ~** во́зраст начина́ет ска́зываться, года́ беру́т своё; **the ~ of the road** (*accident rate*) чи́сленность доро́жных происше́ствий.
● *cpds.* **~-bar**, **~-gate** *nn.* заста́ва; **~-bridge** *n.* мост, где взима́ется сбор; **~-free** *adj.* (*US*) беспла́тный; **~-road** *n.* пла́тная доро́га.
toll[2] /təʊl/ *n.* (*of bell*) колоко́льный звон; бла́говест.
● *v.t.* звони́ть (*impf.*) в+*a.*; **the bell ~ed the hours** ко́локол отбива́л часы́.
● *v.i.* звони́ть (*impf.*).
Tom /tɒm/ *n.* **1**: **any ~, Dick or Harry** ка́ждый; пе́рвый встре́чный; **peeping ~** соглядата́й. **2** (**t~**: *male cat*) кот.
● *cpds.* **~boy** *n.* девчо́нка-сорване́ц; **~cat** *n.* кот; **~fool** *n.* дура́к, шут; *v.i.* дура́читься (*impf.*); **~foolery** *n.* дура́чество, шутовство́; **~tit** *n.* сини́ца.
tomahawk /ˈtɒməˌhɔːk/ *n.* томага́вк.
● *v.t.* уд|аря́ть, -а́рить (*or* уб|ива́ть, -и́ть) томага́вком.
tomato /təˈmɑːtəʊ/ *n.* (*pl.* **~es**) помидо́р; **~ paste/purée** тома́т; **~ sauce/juice** тома́тный со́ус/сок.
tomb /tuːm/ *n.* моги́ла; (*monument*) мавзоле́й.
● *cpd.* **~stone** *n.* (*standing*) надгро́бный па́мятник; (*laid over*) надгро́бная плита́.
tombola /tɒmˈbəʊlə/ *n.* (*Br.*) лотере́я.
tome /təʊm/ *n.* (*liter.*) том.
tommy /ˈtɒmɪ/ *n.* (**T~**: *private soldier*) рядово́й (*в британской армии*).
● *cpd.* **~-gun** *n.* автома́т.
tomography /təˈmɒɡrəfɪ/ *n.* томогра́фия.
tomorrow /təˈmɒrəʊ/ *adv.* & *n.* за́втра; за́втрашний день; **~ morning** за́втра у́тром; **the day after ~** послеза́втра; **until ~** до за́втра; **~'s weather** за́втрашняя пого́да; **~ week** (*Br.*) че́рез 8 дней; (*fig.*, *future*) бу́дущее, за́втра.
tomtom /ˈtɒmtɒm/ *n.* тамта́м.
ton /tʌn/ *n.* то́нна; (*fig.*): **he has ~s of money** у него́ ку́ча де́нег; **he came down on me like a ~ of bricks** он обру́шился на меня́ со всей си́лой.
tonal /ˈtəʊn(ə)l/ *adj.* (*mus.*; *of colours*) тона́льный.
tonality /təˈnælɪtɪ/ *n.* тона́льность.
tone /təʊn/ *n.* **1** (*quality of sound*) тон; (*mus. interval*) звук, тон; (*intonation*) го́лос, тон; (*pl.* то́ны *in these senses*); (*teleph.*) гудо́к. **2** (*character*) хара́ктер, стиль (*m.*); **the debate took on a serious ~** диску́ссия приобрела́ серьёзный хара́ктер. **3** (*respectability, class*) тон. **4** (*shade of colour*) отте́нок, тон (*pl.* -а́). **5** (*med.*) то́нус.
● *v.i.* гармони́ровать (*impf.*).
● *with advs.*: **~ down** *v.t.* смягч|а́ть, -и́ть; осл|абля́ть, -а́бить; **~ in** *v.i.* гармони́ровать (*impf.*); **~ up** *v.t.* укреп|ля́ть, -и́ть; тонизи́ровать (*impf.*).
● *cpds.* **~-deaf** *adj.* лишённый музыка́льного слу́ха; **~-poem** *n.* симфони́ческая поэ́ма.
toneless /ˈtəʊnlɪs/ *adj.* моното́нный.
toner /ˈtəʊnə(r)/ *n.* (*xerographic*) то́нер.
tongs /tɒŋz/ *n.* щипц|ы́ (*pl.*, *g.* -о́в).
tongue /tʌŋ/ *n.* **1** (*lit., and as food*) язы́к; **put, stick one's ~ out** высо́вывать, вы́сунуть (*or* пока́з|ывать, -а́ть) язы́к; (*dim., e.g. baby's*) язычо́к. **2** (*fig., article so shaped*) язы́к, язычо́к; **~s of flame** языки́ пла́мени; **the ~ of a shoe** язычо́к боти́нка. **3** (*fig., faculty or manner of speech*) язы́к, речь; **she has a sharp ~** у неё о́стрый язы́к; **he spoke with his ~ in his cheek** он говори́л со скры́той ирони́ей; **have you lost your ~?** вы что, язы́к проглоти́ли?; **hold your ~!** придержи́те язы́к!, помолчи́те! **4** (*language*) язы́к; **mother/native ~** родно́й язы́к.
● *cpds.* **~-lashing** *n.* разно́с; **~-tied** *adj.* косноязы́чный; **he was ~-tied** он

как язы́к проглоти́л; **~-twister** *n.* скороговóрка.

tonic /ˈtɒnɪk/ *n.* **1** (*medicine*) тонизи́рующее сре́дство; (*fig.*) подде́ржка, утеше́ние; **the news was a ~ to us all** нóвость приободри́ла нас. **2** (**~ water**) тóник. **3** (*mus.*) тóника.

● *adj.*: **the ~ quality of sea air** тонизи́рующее свóйство морскóго вóздуха; **~ solfa** сольфе́джио (*indecl.*).

tonight /təˈnaɪt/ *adv.* & *n.* (*this evening*) сегóдня ве́чером; сегóдняшний ве́чер; (*this night*) сегóдня нóчью; сегóдняшняя ночь; **it's cold ~** ве́чер сегóдня холóдный; **it will rain ~** ве́чером пойдёт дождь; **~'s concert** конце́рт сегóдня ве́чером.

tonnage /ˈtʌnɪdʒ/ *n.* (*internal capacity*) тонна́ж.

tonne /tʌn/ *n.* метри́ческая тóнна.

tonsil /ˈtɒns(ə)l/, /-sɪl/ *n.* (нёбная) минда́лина, гла́нда; **has he had his ~s out?** емý вы́резали/удали́ли минда́лины/гла́нды?

tonsillectomy /ˌtɒnsɪˈlektəmɪ/ *n.* тонзиллэктоми́я, удале́ние минда́лин.

tonsillitis /ˌtɒnsɪˈlaɪtɪs/ *n.* воспале́ние минда́лин, тонзилли́т.

tonsure /ˈtɒnsjə(r)/, /ˈtɒnʃə(r)/ *n.* тонзýра.

● *v.t.* выбрива́ть, вы́брить тонзýру + *d.*

too /tu:/ *adv.* **1** (*also*) та́кже, тóже. **2** (*moreover*) к томý же; бóлее тогó; **and him a married man, ~!** к томý же он жена́тый! **3** (*US coll., indeed*) действи́тельно; **'You haven't washed!' — 'I have ~!'** «Ты не вы́мылся!» — «Нет, вы́мылся!». **4** (*excessively*) сли́шком; **it's ~ cold for swimming** сли́шком хóлодно, чтóбы купа́ться; **am I ~ late for dinner?** я не опозда́л к ýжину?; **that is ~ much!** э́то уж сли́шком/чересчýр!; **he had one (drink) ~ many** он вы́пил ли́шнего. **5** (*very*) óчень; кра́йне; **you are ~ kind** вы óчень дóбры; **I'm not ~ sure** я не совсе́м уве́рен; **~ bad!** (óчень) жаль!

took /tʊk/ *past of* ⇒**take**

tool /tu:l/ *n.* **1** (*implement*) инструме́нт, орýдие; (*pl., collect.*) инструме́нт; **~s of one's trade** (*fig.*) орýдия труда́; **a bad workman blames his ~s** у плохóго ма́стера всегда́ инструме́нт винова́т; **(machine-~)** станóк; (*cutting part of lathe etc.*) резе́ц.
2 (*fig., means, aid*) орýдие.
3 (*fig., person used by another*) орýдие; марионе́тка; **he was a mere ~ in their hands** он был лишь орýдием в их рукáх.

● *v.t.* **1** (*ornament*) вытисня́ть, вы́тиснить узóр на + *p.*; **the book was finely ~ed** переплёт кни́ги был укра́шен изя́щным тисне́нием.
2 (*equip with machinery*) оборýдовать (*impf., pf.*), осна|ща́ть, -сти́ть; **the factory was ~ed up for new production** фа́брику оснасти́ли/оборýдовали для вы́пуска нóвой продýкции.

● *cpds.* **~-bag** *n.* сýмка для инструме́нтов; **~-box** *n.* инструмента́льный я́щик; **~-shed** *n.* сара́й для инструме́нтов.

tooling /ˈtu:lɪŋ/ *n.* (*on book-cover*) ручнóе тисне́ние.

toot /tu:t/ *n.* гудóк; сигна́л.

● *v.t.*: **he ~ed the horn** он просигна́лил.

● *v.i.* гуде́ть (*impf.*); да|ва́ть, -ть гудóк.

tooth /tu:θ/ *n.* (*pl.* **teeth**) **1** зуб; (*dim., e.g. baby's*) зýбик, зубóк; **false teeth** вставны́е зýбы; **she has a sweet ~** она́ сластёна/сладкое́жка; **I have a ~ loose** у меня́ шата́ется зуб; **he went to have a ~ out** он пошёл удали́ть зуб; **my ~ aches** у меня́ боли́т зуб.
2 (*fig.*): **armed to the teeth** воорyжённый до зубóв; **fed up to the (back) teeth** сыт по гóрло; **in the teeth of heavy opposition** несмотря́ на серьёзное сопротивле́ние; **he sailed into the teeth of the gale** он поплы́л несмотря́ на штормовóй ве́тер; **I can't wait to get my teeth into the job** мне не те́рпится скоре́е приня́ться за рабóту; **he got away by the skin of his teeth** он чýдом уцеле́л; емý е́ле-е́ле удалóсь убежа́ть/отде́латься; **they were fighting ~ and nail** они́ дра́ли́сь не на жизнь, а на смерть; **he's a bit long in the ~** он ужé не пéрвой мóлодости; **it sets my teeth on edge** (*lit.*) от э́того у меня́ свóдит рот; (*fig.*) от э́того меня́ всегó передёргивает; **it was not long before he showed his teeth** он вскóре показа́л кóгти.
3 (*of a saw, gear, comb etc.*) зуб, зубе́ц.

● *cpds.* **~ache** *n.* зубна́я боль; **he had a bad ~ache** у негó óчень боле́ли зýбы; **~-brush** *n.* зубна́я щётка; **~-comb** *n.* (*Br.*): **I've been through this book with a (fine) ~-comb** (*US* **fine-~(ed) comb**) я проштуди́ровал э́ту кни́гу óчень основа́тельно; **~paste** *n.* зубна́я па́ста; **~pick** *n.* зубочи́стка.

toothsome /ˈtu:θsəm/ *adj.* вкýсный, ла́комый.

toothy /ˈtu:θɪ/ *adj.* (**toothier, toothiest**) зуба́стый.

top¹ /tɒp/ *n.* **1** (*summit; highest or upper part*) верх (*pl.* -и́); верхýшка, верши́на; (*of hill, tree*) макýшка (*coll.*); **at the ~ of the hill** на верши́не холма́; **the ~s of the trees** верхýшки дере́вьев; **they climbed to the very ~** они́ взобра́лись на са́мый верх; **the soldiers went over the ~** солда́ты пошли́ в ата́ку из транше́й; **at the ~ of the page** в нача́ле страни́цы; **his name was (at the) ~ of the list** егó и́мя бы́ло пе́рвым в спи́ске; **she cleaned the house from ~ to bottom** она́ тща́тельно убрала́ дом; (*of the head*) макýшка; **he has no hair on (the) ~ (of his head)** у негó (на макýшке) плешь; **he blew his ~** (*sl.*) он вы́шел из себя́; он распсихова́лся; **from ~ to toe** с головы́ до пят.
2 (*fig., highest rank, foremost place*) ведýщее положе́ние; пе́рвое ме́сто; **he came ~ of the class** он стал пе́рвым в кла́ссе; **they put him at the ~ of the table** егó посади́ли во главе́ стола́; **he reached the ~ of his profession** он за́нял ведýщее положе́ние в своéй óбласти.
3 (*fig., utmost degree, height*) верх; **at the ~ of his voice** во весь гóлос; **he was at the ~ of his form** (*of athlete etc.*) он был в прекра́сной фóрме; **(the) ~s** (*coll., the very best*) верх соверше́нства.
4 (*upper surface*) пове́рхность; верх; **on ~** (*lit.*) наверхý; **he put the book on ~** он положи́л кни́гу наве́рх/све́рху; (*fig.*): **I feel on ~ of the world** я чýвствую себя́ на седьмóм не́бе; **I'm getting on ~ of my work** я начина́ю справля́ться с рабóтой; **on ~ of everything I caught a cold** вдоба́вок ко всемý я ещё простуди́лся.
5 (*lid, cover*) верх; кры́шка; (*hood of car*) кры́ша; **I can't get the ~ off this jar** я не могý снять кры́шку с э́той ба́нки; **the ~ to my pen** колпачóк от рýчки; **a bus with an open ~** автóбус с откры́тым ве́рхом.
6 (*upper leaves of plant*) ботва́; **turnip ~s** ботва́ ре́пы.
7 (*Br.*, **~ gear**) вы́сшая/пряма́я переда́ча; **the car won't take this hill in ~** маши́на не возьмёт э́тот подъём на прямóй переда́че.
8: **the big ~** (*circus tent*) шапитó (*indecl.*).
9 (*attr.; see also cpds.*): **~ dog** (*coll.*) гла́вный; **~ drawer** ве́рхний я́щик; (*fig.*): **his family comes out of the ~ drawer** егó семья́ принадлежи́т к вы́сшему кла́ссу; **~ hat** цили́ндр; **~ secret** соверше́нно секре́тный; **at ~ speed** со всей скóростью; **~ table** стол для почётных госте́й.

● *v.t.* (**topped, topping**) **1** (*serve as ~ to*) венча́ть, у-; **a church ~ped by a steeple** це́рковь, уве́нчанная шпи́лем.
2 (*remove ~ of*) ср|еза́ть, -е́зать верхýшку + *g.*; **~ and tail gooseberries** (*Br.*) чи́стить, по- крыжóвник.
3 (*reach ~ of*) дост|ига́ть, -и́гнуть верши́ны + *g.*
4 (*be higher than; exceed*) прев|ыша́ть, -ы́сить; **the mountains ~ 5,000 ft.** гóры вы́ше пяти́ ты́сяч фýтов; **he ~ped 60 mph** он де́лал бóльше шести́десяти миль в час; (*fig., surpass*) прев|осходи́ть, -зойти́; **it ~ped all my expectations** э́то превзошлó все мои́ ожида́ния.

● *with advs.*: **~ up** *v.t.* дол|ива́ть, -и́ть; нап|олня́ть, -óлнить; **may I ~ up your glass (or ~ you up)?** вам доли́ть?; *v.i.* запр|авля́ться, -а́виться; **he stopped to ~ up and drove on** он останови́лся запра́виться, и поéхал да́льше.

● *cpds.* **~-coat** *n.* (*garment*) пальтó (*indecl.*); (*of paint*) ве́рхний слой; **~-dressing** *n.* подкóрмка; **~-flight** *adj.* первокла́ссный, наилýчший; **~-gallant** *n.* брам-сте́ньга; **~-heavy** *adj.* неустóйчивый; переве́шивающий в ве́рхней ча́сти; **~-knot** *n.* чуб; пучóк волóс/пе́рьев; **~mast** *n.* сте́ньга; **~-notch** *adj.* первокла́ссный; **~-ranking** *adj.* вы́сшего ра́нга; высокопоста́вленный; **~-sail** *n.* тóпсель (*m.*); **~side** *n.* (*Br., of beef*) говя́жья груди́нка; **~soil** *n.* па́хотный слой; **~-up** *n.* (*Br.*): **can I give you a ~?** вам доли́ть?

top² /tɒp/ *n.* (*toy*) волчóк; **I slept like a ~** я спал как уби́тый.

topaz /ˈtəʊpæz/ *n.* топа́з; (*attr.*) топа́зовый.

T

topiary /ˈtəʊpɪərɪ/ *adj.*: **the ~ art** фигу́рная стри́жка кусто́в.

topic /ˈtɒpɪk/ *n.* те́ма; предме́т обсужде́ния.

topical /ˈtɒpɪk(ə)l/ *adj.* актуа́льный; злободне́вный.

topless /ˈtɒplɪs/ *adj.* **1** (*of unlimited height*) о́чень высо́кий. **2** (*of dress*) без ли́фа, обнажа́ющий грудь; (*of person*) с обнажённой гру́дью.

topmost /ˈtɒpməʊst/ *adj.* (*highest*) са́мый ве́рхний; (*most important*) са́мый ва́жный.

topographic(al) /ˌtɒpəˈgræfɪk(ə)l/ *adj.* топографи́ческий.

topography /təˈpɒgrəfɪ/ *n.* топогра́фия; (*features*) релье́ф.

topology /təˈpɒlədʒɪ/ *n.* тополо́гия.

topper /ˈtɒpə(r)/ *n.* (*coll., hat*) цили́ндр.

topping /ˈtɒpɪŋ/ *n.* (*sauce*) подли́вка; (*garnish*) верх.

topple /ˈtɒp(ə)l/ *v.t.* вали́ть, с-; **the dictator was ~d (from power)** дикта́тора сбро́сили.
● *v.i.* опроки́|дываться, -нуться; вали́ться, с-.

topsy-turvy /ˌtɒpsɪˈtɜːvɪ/ *adj.* перевёрнутый вверх дном (*coll.*).
● *adv.* вверх дном; ши́ворот-навы́ворот.

toque /təʊk/ *n.* (*woman's hat*) ток.

Torah /ˈtɔːrə/ *n.* То́ра.

torch /tɔːtʃ/ *n.* фа́кел; (*fig.*) све́точ; **she carried a ~ for him** она́ по нему́ со́хла (*coll.*); (*Br.*, **electric ~**) (электри́ческий) фона́рь; (*welding* **~**) сва́рочная горе́лка.
● *cpds.* **~-bearer** *n.* фа́кельщик; (*fig.*) просвети́тель (*m.*); **~light** *n.* свет фа́кела/фонаря́; **~-singer** *n.* исполни́тельница жесто́ких рома́нсов.

tore /tɔː(r)/ *past of* ⇨**tear²**

toreador /ˈtɒrɪəˌdɔː(r)/ *n.* тореадо́р.

torment¹ /ˈtɔːment/ *n.* муче́ние, терза́ния (*nt. pl.*); **a soul in ~** душа́, раздира́емая му́ками.

torment² /tɔːˈment/ *v.t.* му́чить (*impf.*), терза́ть (*impf.*); **the child was ~ing the cat** ребёнок му́чил ко́шку; **he was ~ed with jealousy** он терза́лся ре́вностью.

tormentor /tɔːˈmentə(r)/ *n.* мучи́тель (*fem.* -ница).

torn /tɔːn/ *p.p. of* ⇨**tear²**

tornado /tɔːˈneɪdəʊ/ *n.* (*pl.* **~es** *or* **~s**) торна́до (*indecl.*).

torpedo /tɔːˈpiːdəʊ/ *n.* (*pl.* **~es**) торпе́да.
● *v.t.* (**~es, ~ed**) (*lit.*) торпеди́ровать (*impf., pf.*); (*fig.*) срыва́ть, сорва́ть; торпеди́ровать (*impf., pf.*).
● *cpd.* **~-boat** *n.* торпе́дный ка́тер.

torpid /ˈtɔːpɪd/ *adj.* вя́лый, апати́чный; (*in hibernation*) находя́щийся в состоя́нии спя́чки.

torp|idity /tɔːˈpɪdɪtɪ/, **-or** /ˈtɔːpə(r)/ *nn.* вя́лость, апа́тия.

torque /tɔːk/ *n.* (*mech.*) враща́ющий моме́нт.

torrent /ˈtɒrənt/ *n.* (*lit., fig.*) пото́к; **the rain fell in ~s** шёл проливно́й дождь; **a ~ of abuse** пото́к оскорбле́ний.

torrential /təˈrenʃ(ə)l/ *adj.*: **~ rain** проливно́й дождь.

torrid /ˈtɒrɪd/ *adj.* жа́ркий, зно́йный; **~ zone** тропи́ческий по́яс; (*passionate*) стра́стный, пы́лкий.

torsi /ˈtɔːsiː/ *US pl. of* ⇨**torso**

torsion /ˈtɔːʃ(ə)n/ *n.* (*process*) скру́чивание; (*state*) скру́ченность.

torso /ˈtɔːsəʊ/ *n.* (*pl.* **torsos** *or US also* **torsi**) ту́ловище, торс.

tort /tɔːt/ *n.* дели́кт, гражда́нское правонаруше́ние.

tortoise /ˈtɔːtəs/ *n.* черепа́ха; (*attr.*) черепа́ший.
● *cpd.* **~shell** *n.* (*as material*) черепа́ха; *adj.* черепа́ховый.

tortuous /ˈtɔːtjʊəs/ *adj.* изви́листый.

tortu|ousness /ˈtɔːtjʊəsnɪs/, **-osity** /ˌtɔːtjʊˈɒsɪtɪ/ *nn.* изви́листость.

torture /ˈtɔːtʃə(r)/ *n.* (*physical*) пы́тка; **~ chamber** ка́мера пы́ток; **he was put to the ~** его́ подве́ргли пы́ткам; (*mental*) му́ки (*f. pl.*).
● *v.t.* пыта́ть (*impf.*); му́чить (*impf.*); **she was ~d with anxiety** её му́чила трево́га; **a ~d expression** выраже́ние му́ки.

torturer /ˈtɔːtʃərə(r)/ *n.* мучи́тель (*m.*), пала́ч.

Tory /ˈtɔːrɪ/ *n.* (*coll.*) то́ри (*m. indecl.*), консерва́тор; **the ~ party** консервати́вная па́ртия.

tosh /tɒʃ/ *n.* (*Br. coll.*) вздор, чепуха́.

toss /tɒs/ *n.* (*throw*) бросо́к; (*jerk*) толчо́к; **with a ~ of her head, she …** тряхну́в голово́й она́….
● *v.t.* **1** (*throw*) бр|оса́ть, -о́сить; кида́ть, ки́нуть; **the horse ~ed its rider** ло́шадь сбро́сила седока́; **they ~ed a coin to decide** они́ подки́нули моне́ту, что́бы реши́ть исхо́д де́ла.
2 (*rock, agitate*) швыр|я́ть, -ну́ть; **the ship was ~ed by the waves** во́лны швыря́ли су́дно вверх и вниз.
● *v.i.* мета́ться (*impf.*); **the child ~ed in its sleep** ребёнок мета́лся во сне; **a ship was ~ing on the waves** кора́бль кача́лся на волна́х.
● *with advs.*: **~ about** *v.i.* мета́ться (*impf.*); **~ aside, ~ away** *vv.t.* отбр|а́сывать, -о́сить; **~ off** *v.t.* (*drink*) выпива́ть, вы́пить за́лпом; (*do quickly*) де́лать, с- на́спех; **he ~ed off a glass of vodka** он вы́пил за́лпом сто́пку во́дки; **he can ~ off an article in five minutes** он спосо́бен наброса́ть статью́ за пять мину́т; **~ up** *v.t.* подбр|а́сывать, -о́сить; *v.i.*: **shall we ~ up to see who goes?** дава́йте бро́сим жре́бий, кому́ идти́.
● *cpd.* **~-up** *n.* нея́сный исхо́д; де́ло слу́чая.

tot¹ /tɒt/ *n.* (*child*) малы́ш; (*Br., of liquor*) глото́к.

tot² /tɒt/: **~ up** (*Br.*) *v.t.* (**totted, totting**) сост|авля́ть, -а́вить (*су́мму*); **he ~ted up the figures** он подвёл ито́г.
● *v.i.* (**totted, totting**): **his expenses ~ted up to £5** его́ расхо́ды соста́вили 5 фу́нтов.

total /ˈtəʊt(ə)l/ *n.* су́мма, ито́г; **the grand ~ came to £200** о́бщая су́мма соста́вила 200 фу́нтов.
● *adj.* це́лый, о́бщий, по́лный; **~ eclipse** по́лное затме́ние; **~ failure** по́лный прова́л; **the ~ figure** о́бщая ци́фра; **~ war** тота́льная война́.
● *v.t.* (**totalled, totalling;** *US* **totaled, totaling**) **1** (*reckon, also* **~ up**) подсчи́т|ывать, -а́ть; подв|оди́ть, -ести́ ито́г; **he ~led (up) the bills** он подсчита́л счета́; **the visitors ~led several hundred** число́ посети́телей дости́гло не́скольких со́тен. **2** (*US coll., destroy completely*) спи́сывать, списа́ть.

totalitarian /təʊˌtælɪˈteərɪən/ *adj.* тоталита́рный.

totalitarianism /təʊˌtælɪˈteərɪənɪz(ə)m/ *n.* тоталитари́зм.

totality /təʊˈtælɪtɪ/ *n.* (*sum total*) вся су́мма, о́бщее коли́чество; (*universality*) тота́льность; (*astron.*) вре́мя по́лного затме́ния.

totalizator /ˈtəʊtəlaɪˌzeɪtə(r)/ *n.* тотализа́тор.

totally /ˈtəʊtəlɪ/ *adv.* соверше́нно, абсолю́тно, по́лностью.

tote¹ /təʊt/ (*coll.*) = **totalizator**

tote² /təʊt/ *v.t.* (*US coll.*) носи́ть, нести́ (*что-н. тяжёлое*).

totem /ˈtəʊtəm/ *n.* тоте́м.
● *cpd.* **~-pole** *n.* тоте́мный столб.

totter /ˈtɒtə(r)/ *v.i.* (*walk unsteadily*) ковыля́ть (*impf.*); (*fig.*) шата́ться (*impf.*), пошатну́ться (*pf.*).

tottery /ˈtɒtərɪ/ *adj.* неусто́йчивый; на гра́ни паде́ния.

toucan /ˈtuːkən/ *n.* (*zool.*) тука́н.

touch /tʌtʃ/ *n.* **1** (*contact; light pressure of hand etc.*) прикоснове́ние; **I felt a ~ on my shoulder** я почу́вствовал лёгкое прикоснове́ние к своему́ плечу́.
2 (*sense*) осяза́ние; **the blind man recognized me by ~** слепо́й узна́л меня́ на о́щупь; **soft to the ~** мя́гкий на о́щупь.
3 (*light stroke of pen or brush*) штрих; **he was putting the finishing ~es to the picture** он наноси́л после́дние мазки́ на карти́ну.
4 (*tinge, trace*) чу́точка, отте́нок, налёт; **a ~ of frost in the air** лёгкий моро́зец; **I had a ~ of rheumatism** у меня́ был лёгкий при́ступ ревмати́зма; **this soup needs a ~ of salt** в су́пе не хвата́ет чу́точку со́ли; **a ~ of irony** лёгкая ирони́я.
5 (*artist's or performer's style*) стиль (*m.*); **he has a light ~ on the piano** у него́ лёгкое туше́ (на фортепья́но); (*fig.*): **he brought a personal ~ to all he did** на всём, что он де́лал, лежа́л отпеча́ток его́ ли́чности; **you must have lost your ~** вы я́вно утра́тили (бы́лую) хва́тку.
6 (*communication*) конта́кт, обще́ние; **we must keep in ~** мы должны́ подде́рживать конта́кт друг с дру́гом; **we have been out of ~ for so long** мы

так до́лго не обща́лись; **how can I get in ~ with you?** как мо́жно с ва́ми связа́ться?; **we lost ~ with him** мы потеря́ли с ним конта́кт/связь.
7 (*football*) пло́щадь, лежа́щая за боковы́ми ли́ниями по́ля; **the ball was in ~** мяч находи́лся в преде́лах боково́й ли́нии по́ля.
8 (*child's game*) са́лки (*f. pl.*).
9 (*sl., potential source of money*): **he is a soft** (*or* **an easy**) **~** у него́ легко́ вы́удить де́ньги.

● *v.t.* **1** (*contact physically*) тро́|гать, -нуть; каса́ться, косну́ться $+g.$; прик|аса́ться, -осну́ться к$+d.$; **he ~ed her (on the) arm** он косну́лся её руки́; **don't ~ the paint** не дотра́гивайтесь до кра́ски; **it was ~ and go** исхо́д был неизве́стен до са́мого конца́; **~ wood!** постучи́ по де́реву; тьфу-тьфу, не сгла́зить!
2 (*actuate*): **I ~ed the bell** я нажа́л звоно́к; (*fig.*): **he ~ed a tender chord in her** он затро́нул её за живо́е.
3 (*reach*) дост|ава́ть, -а́ть до$+g.$; дост|ига́ть, -и́гнуть $+g.$; **can you ~ the top of the door?** вы мо́жете доста́ть до ве́рха две́ри?; **the thermometer ~ed ninety** термо́метр подня́лся до девяно́ста гра́дусов; **I can just ~ bottom** я е́ле достаю́ до дна.
4 (*approach in excellence; compare with*) равня́ться (*impf.*) с$+i.$; сравни́ться (*pf.*) с$+i.$; идти́ (*det.*) в сравне́ние с$+i.$; **no-one can ~ him for eloquence** никто́ не мо́жет сравни́ться с ним в красноре́чии.
5 (*affect*) тро́гать, тро́нуть; волнова́ть, вз-; **it ~ed me to the heart** (*or* **~ed my heart**) я был глубоко́ тро́нут; **we were very ~ed by his speech** его́ речь о́чень взволнова́ла нас.
6 (*taste*) притр|а́гиваться, -о́нуться к$+d.$; прик|аса́ться, -осну́ться к$+d.$; **I haven't ~ed food for two days** я не притра́гивался/прикаса́лся к еде́ це́лых два дня; **I never ~ a drop** (*of alcohol*) я не прикаса́юсь к спиртно́му.
7 (*injure slightly*) нан|оси́ть, -ести́ уще́рб $+d.$; **the flowers were ~ed by the frost** цветы́ бы́ли тро́нуты моро́зом; (*fig.*): **he must be a little ~ed** (*slightly mad*) он, должно́ быть, немно́го поме́шан/тро́нут.
8 (*deal with; cope with*) спр|авля́ться, -а́виться с$+i.$; **nothing will ~ these stains** э́ти пя́тна ниче́м не вы́ведешь.
9 (*concern*) име́ть отноше́ние к$+d.$; каса́ться (*impf.*) $+g.$; **it ~es us all** э́то каса́ется нас всех.
10 (*have to do with*) зан|има́ться, -я́ться $+i.$; **I refuse to ~ your schemes** я не хочу́ име́ть никако́го отноше́ния к ва́шим пла́нам.
11 (*treat lightly; also v.i. with prep.* **on**) затр|а́гивать, -о́нуть; каса́ться, косну́ться $+g.$; **he ~ed (on) the subject of race** он косну́лся ра́сового вопро́са.
12 (*coll., prevail on for loan*): **can I ~ you for a fiver?** могу́ я стрельну́ть у вас пятёрку (*coll.*)?

● *v.i.* **1** (*make contact*) соприк|аса́ться, -осну́ться; **our hands ~ed** на́ши ру́ки встре́тились; **if the wires ~ there will be an explosion** е́сли провода́ соприкосну́тся, бу́дет взрыв.
2 **~ on**: *see v.t.* 11

● *with advs.*: **~ off** *v.t.* (*cause*) вызыва́ть, вы́звать; **~ up** *v.t.* испр|авля́ть, -а́вить; **I'll just ~ it up** я слегка́ ко́е-где подпра́влю; **the photographs had been ~ed up** фотогра́фии бы́ли отретуши́рованы.

● *cpds.* **~-and-go** *adj.* с непредсказу́емым исхо́дом; **~-down** *n.* (*football*) гол; (*aeron.*) поса́дка; **~line** *n.* бокова́я ли́ния (*по́ля*); **~stone** *n.* (*fig.*) про́бный ка́мень; осело́к; **~-type** *v.i.* печа́тать (*impf.*) вслепу́ю/слепы́м ме́тодом; **~-typist** *n.* машини́стка, печа́тающая вслепу́ю.

touché /tuːˈʃeɪ/ *int.* туше́!

touched /tʌtʃt/ *adj.* (*emotionally*) растро́ганный; (*coll., mentally*) слегка́ поме́шанный, тро́нутый.

touchiness /ˈtʌtʃɪnɪs/ *n.* оби́дчивость.

touching /ˈtʌtʃɪŋ/ *adj.* тро́гательный.

touchy /ˈtʌtʃɪ/ *adj.* (**touchier, touchiest**) оби́дчивый.

tough /tʌf/ *n.* хулига́н, блатно́й.

● *adj.* **1** (*resistant to cutting or chewing*) жёсткий. **2** (*strong, sturdy, hardy*) кре́пкий; про́чный; (*person*) выно́сливый; **you need a ~ pair of shoes** вам нужна́ кре́пкая о́бувь.
3 (*difficult*) тру́дный; (*stubborn*) упря́мый. **4** (*coll., severe, uncompromising*) круто́й; жёсткий; несгово́рчивый; **to take a ~ line** проводи́ть (*impf.*) жёсткую ли́нию.
5 (*coll., painful*): **it was ~ on him when his father died** смерть отца́ была́ тяжёлым уда́ром для него́; **~ luck!** вот незада́ча!

toughen /ˈtʌf(ə)n/ *v.t.* де́лать, с- жёстким; (*body, character*) де́лать, с- выно́сливым.

● *v.i.* станови́ться, стать жёстким; (*body*) станови́ться, стать выно́сливым.

toughness /ˈtʌfnɪs/ *n.* (*of food etc.*) жёсткость; (*strength; hardiness*) про́чность; выно́сливость; (*uncompromising nature*) несгово́рчивость; упря́мство.

toupee /ˈtuːpeɪ/ *n.* небольшо́й пари́к, накла́дка.

tour /tʊə(r)/ *n.* **1** (*extended visit*) путеше́ствие; (*short*) пое́здка; (*of museum, garden*) экску́рсия; **we are going on a ~ of Europe** мы собира́емся путеше́ствовать по Евро́пе; **the duty officer made a ~ of the building** дежу́рный осмотре́л всё зда́ние. **2** (*theatr.*) турне́ (*indecl.*); тур; гастро́ли (*f. pl.*); **the company was on ~** тру́ппа гастроли́ровала (*or* находи́лась на гастро́лях). **3**: **~ of duty** срок слу́жбы.

● *v.t. & i.* соверш|а́ть, -и́ть экску́рсию (по$+d.$); **we have been ~ing Scotland** мы путеше́ствовали по Шотла́ндии.

● *cpd.* **~ operator** *n.* туристи́ческий аге́нт; (*company*) туристи́ческая фи́рма.

tour de force /ˌtʊə də ˈfɔːs/ *n.* (*pl.* ***tours de force***) проявле́ние си́лы.

tourism /ˈtʊərɪz(ə)m/ *n.* тури́зм.

tourist /ˈtʊərɪst/ *n.* тури́ст; **~ class** второ́й класс; **the ~ industry** индустри́я тури́зма; **~ office** туристи́ческое бюро́.

tourn|ament /ˈtʊənəmənt/, **-ey** /ˈtʊənɪ/ *nn.* турни́р; спорти́вное соревнова́ние.

tourniquet /ˈtʊənɪˌkeɪ/ *n.* турнике́т.

tours de force /ˌtʊə də ˈfɔːs/ *pl. of* ***tour de force***

tousle /ˈtaʊz(ə)l/ *v.t.* еро́шить, взъ-.

tout /taʊt/ *n.* зазыва́ла (*m.*); **ticket ~** (*Br.*) переку́пщик биле́тов.

● *v.i.*: **~ for business** зазыва́ть (*impf.*) покупа́телей.

tow¹ /təʊ/ *n.*: **can I give you a ~?** взять вас на букси́р?

● *v.t.* букси́ровать (*impf.*); **the ship was ~ed into harbour** (*Br.*), **harbor** (*US*) кора́бль вошёл в га́вань на букси́ре; **they ~ed the car away** маши́ну отбукси́ровали.

● *cpds.* **~(ing-)path** *n.* бече́вни́к; **~-rope** *n.* бечева́; **~ truck** *n.* (*US*) маши́на техни́ческой по́мощи.

tow² /təʊ/ *n.* (*material*) па́кля.

toward(s) /təˈwɔːdz/, /twɔːdz/, /tɔːdz/ *prep.* **1** (*in the direction of*) к$+d.$; на$+a.$; по направле́нию к$+d.$; **he stood with his back ~ me** он стоя́л ко мне спино́й.
2 (*in relation to*) к$+d.$; по отноше́нию к$+d.$; относи́тельно$+g.$; **what is his attitude ~ education?** как он отно́сится к пробле́ме образова́ния?; **they seemed friendly ~ us** каза́лось, что они́ бы́ли располо́жены к нам дру́жески; **responsibility ~ his family** обя́занность пе́ред семьёй.
3 (*for the purpose of*) для$+g.$; **I gave him something ~ the price** я ему́ дал немно́го де́нег на э́ту поку́пку.
4 (*near*) к$+d.$; о́коло$+g.$; **~ evening** к ве́черу, под ве́чер; **I'm getting ~ the end of my supply** мои́ запа́сы подхо́дят к концу́.

towel /ˈtaʊəl/ *n.* полоте́нце; **throw in the ~** (*fig.*) призн|ава́ть, -а́ть себя́ побеждённым.

● *v.t.* (**towelled, towelling;** *US* **toweled, toweling**) вытира́ть, вы́тереть полоте́нцем.

● *cpds.* **~-horse, ~-rack, ~-rail** *nn.* ве́шалка для полоте́нец.

towelling /ˈtaʊəlɪŋ/ *n.* (*material*) махро́вая ткань.

tower /ˈtaʊə(r)/ *n.* ба́шня; (*fig.*): **a ~ of strength** опло́т; надёжная опо́ра.

● *v.i.* вы́ситься, возвыша́ться (*both impf.*); **the building ~ed above us** зда́ние уходи́ло высоко́ в не́бо; (*fig.*): **he ~s above his fellows** он намно́го превосхо́дит свои́х колле́г; **a ~ing rage** неи́стовая я́рость.

● *cpd.* **~-block** *n.* (*Br.*) многоэта́жный/ высо́тный дом.

town /taʊn/ *n.* **1** го́род; **he is out of ~** его́ нет в го́роде; **let's go out on the ~!** дава́йте как сле́дует погуля́ем!; **go to**

T

~ (*coll.*) развернýться (*pf.*) вовсю́; **man about ~** свéтский человéк.
2 (*attr.*) городскóй; **~ clerk** (*Br.*, *hist.*) секретáрь городскóй корпорáции; (*US*) регистрáтор; **~ council** мэ́рия, городскóй совéт; **~ crier** глашáтай; **~ hall** мэ́рия; рáтуша; **~ house** особня́к; **~ planner** *n.* градострои́тель (*m.*); **~ planning** градострои́тельство.
● *cpds.* **~scape** *n.* урбанисти́ческий ландшáфт; вид гóрода; **~sfolk, ~speople** *nn. pl.* горожáне (*m. pl.*); **~sman** *n.* горожáнин; **~swoman** *n.* горожáнка.

town|ee, ~ie /'taʊnɪ/ *n.* (*coll.*) городскóй.

township /'taʊnʃɪp/ *n.* **1** (*hist., in South Africa*) негритя́нский квартáл. **2** (*US*) райóн.

toxaemia /tɒk'si:mɪə/ (*US* **toxemia**) *n.* токсеми́я, заражéние крóви.

toxic /'tɒksɪk/ *adj.* ядови́тый, токси́ческий.

toxicologist /,tɒksɪ'kɒlədʒɪst/ *n.* токсикóлог.

toxicology /,tɒksɪ'kɒlədʒɪ/ *n.* токсиколóгия.

toxin /'tɒksɪn/ *n.* токси́н; яд.

toy /tɔɪ/ *n.* игрýшка; **~ boy** (*coll.*) молодóй любóвник; **~ soldier** оловя́нный солдáтик.
● *v.i.*: **he ~ed with his pencil** он вертéл в рукáх карандáш; **I have been ~ing with the idea** я забавля́лся э́той идéей; **he ~ed with her affections** он игрáл её чýвствами.
● *cpd.* **~shop** *n.* магази́н игрýшек.

trace[1] /treɪs/ *n.* **1** (*track*) след; отпечáток.
2 (*vestige; sign of previous existence*) след; **he went away leaving no ~** он исчéз, не остáвив и следá; **the ship disappeared without ~** корáбль пропáл/исчéз бесслéдно; **there are ~s of French influence** чýвствуется нéкоторое францýзское влия́ние.
3 (*small quantity*) мáлое коли́чество; следы́ (*в анализе*); **~ elements** микроэлемéнты.
● *v.t.* **1** (*delineate*) черти́ть, на-; **he ~d (out) his route on the map** он начерти́л свой маршрýт на кáрте; (*with transparent paper or carbon*) перев|оди́ть, -ести́; **tracing paper** кáлька.
2 (*follow the tracks of*) выслéживать, вы́следить; **the thief was ~d to London** следы́ вóра вели́ в Лóндон; **he ~s his descent from Charlemagne** он ведёт свой род от Кáрла Вели́кого; **the rumour** (*Br.*), **rumor** (*US*) **was ~d to its source** истóчник слýхов был установлен.
3 (*discover by search; discern*) устан|áвливать, -ови́ть; прослé|живать, -ди́ть; **I cannot ~ your letter** я не могý разыскáть вáше письмó.

trace[2] /treɪs/ *n.* (*of harness*) пострóмка; **kick over the ~s** (*fig.*) выходи́ть, вы́йти из повиновéния; взбунтовáться (*pf.*).

traceable /'treɪsəb(ə)l/ *adj.* прослéживаемый.

tracer /'treɪsə(r)/ *n.* (**~ bullet**) трасси́рующая пýля.

tracery /'treɪsərɪ/ *n.* узóр(ы), рисýнок.

trachea /trə'ki:ə/, /'treɪkɪə/ *n.* (*pl.* **tracheae** /-'ki:i:/ *or* **tracheas**) трахéя.

tracheotomy /,trækɪ'ɒtəmɪ/ *n.* трахеотоми́я.

trachoma /trə'kəʊmə/ *n.* трахóма.

track /træk/ *n.* **1** (*mark of passage*) след; **the fox left ~s in the snow** лиси́ца остáвила след на снегý; **we followed in his ~s** мы шли по егó следáм; **the police were on his ~** поли́ция напáла на егó след; **we lost ~ of him** мы потеря́ли егó след; (*fig.*): **I think I'm on the ~ of something big** я, кáжется, на пути́ к большóму откры́тию; **he covered his ~s successfully** он успéшно замёл следы́; **make ~s** улизнýть (*pf., coll.*).
2 (*path*) путь (*m.*), трáсса; **the beaten ~** проторённая дорóга; **off the beaten ~** вдали́ от проторённой дорóги; **he is on the wrong ~** он на лóжном пути́.
3 (*for racing etc.*) (беговáя) дорóжка; (*for bicycle and motor racing*) трек; **~ events** соревновáния по лёгкой атлéтике.
4 (*rail*) колея́, полотнó; **single ~** одноколéйный путь.
5 (*of tank etc.*) гýсеница; **~ed vehicle** гýсеничный трáнспорт.
6 (*distance between vehicle's wheels*) колея́ шасси́.
7 (*on tape, record*) дорóжка.
● *v.t.* следи́ть за + *i.*; выслéживать, вы́следить; **the animal was ~ed to its den** звéря вы́следили до сáмой берлóги; **the aircraft was ~ed by radar** курс самолёта проследи́ли с пóмощью радáра; **~ing station** стáнция слежéния.
● *v.i.* (*of camera*) панорами́ровать (*impf.*).
● *with adv.*: **~ down** *v.t.* устан|áвливать, -ови́ть; **have you ~ed down the cause of the disease?** вы установи́ли причи́ну болéзни?
● *cpds.* **~ball** *n.* (*comput.*) трекбóл; **~-racing** *n.* гóнки по трéку; **~-shoes** *n. pl.* кроссóвки (*f. pl.*); **~-suit** *n.* тренирóвочный костю́м.

tracker /'trækə(r)/ *n.* (*hunter*) охóтник; **~ dog** собáка-ищéйка.

tract[1] /trækt/ *n.* (*region*) учáсток, райóн; (*anat.*) тракт; **respiratory ~** дыхáтельные пути́ (*m. pl.*).

tract[2] /trækt/ *n.* (*pamphlet*) крáткий трактáт.

tractability /,træktə'bɪlɪtɪ/ *n.* послушáние, сговóрчивость.

tractable /'træktəb(ə)l/ *adj.* (*person*) послýшный, сговóрчивый; (*problem, situation*) разреши́мый.

traction /'trækʃ(ə)n/ *n.* тя́га; **~ engine** тя́говый дви́гатель (*m.*); тягáч.

tractor /'træktə(r)/ *n.* трáктор.
● *cpds.* **~-driven** *adj.* на трáкторной тя́ге; **~-driver** *n.* трактори́ст (*fem.* -ка); **~ trailer** *n.* (*US*) автопóезд.

trade /treɪd/ *n.* **1** (*business, occupation*) ремеслó; профéссия; **the building ~** строи́тельная профéссия; **he is a builder by ~** он по профéссии строи́тель; **jack of all ~s** мáстер на все рýки.
2 (*commerce; exchange of goods*) торгóвля; **foreign ~** внéшняя торгóвля; **~ is bad** торгóвля идёт плóхо; **~ gap** дефици́т торгóвого балáнса; **~ secret** профессионáльный секрéт; **~ price** оптóвая ценá; **~ wind** пассáт.
● *v.t.* (*exchange*) меня́ть (*impf.*); обмéн|ивать, -я́ть; **they ~d furs for food** они́ меня́ли мехá на продýкты.
● *v.i.* **1** торговáть (*impf.*); **he ~s in sables** он торгýет собóлями; **trading estate** (*Br.*) промы́шленная зóна.
2: **~ on** (*take advantage of*) испóльзовать (*impf., pf.*) в свои́х интерéсах; извлекáть (*impf.*) вы́году из + *g.*; **he ~s on his reputation** он спекули́рует на своéй слáве/репутáции.
● *with adv.*: **~ in** *v.t.*: **I ~d in my old car for a new one** я отдáл стáрую маши́ну в счёт покýпки нóвой.
● *cpds.* **~-mark** *n.* (*lit.*) товáрный знак, фабри́чная мáрка; (*fig.*) отличи́тельный знак; **~-name** *n.* назвáние фи́рмы; торгóвое/фи́рменное назвáние товáра; **~-off** *n.* компроми́сс; **~sman** *n.* торгóвец; **~smen's entrance** чёрный ход; **~(s) union** *n.* тред-юниóн; профсою́з; **T~s Union Congress** (*Br.*) Конгрéсс тред-юниóнов; **~-unionism** *n.* тред-юниони́зм; **~-unionist** *n.* тред-юниони́ст (*fem.* -ка); член профсою́за.

trader /'treɪdə(r)/ *n.* (*merchant*) торгóвец, купéц; (*on stock exchange*) трéйдер; (*vessel*) торгóвое сýдно.

tradition /trə'dɪʃ(ə)n/ *n.* тради́ция.

traditional /trə'dɪʃən(ə)l/ *adj.* традициóнный.

traditionalism /trə'dɪʃənə,lɪz(ə)m/ *n.* привéрженность тради́циям.

traditionalist /trə'dɪʃənəlɪst/ *n.* традиционали́ст.

traduce /trə'dju:s/ *v.t.* (*liter.*) черни́ть, о-.

traffic /'træfɪk/ *n.* **1** (*movement of vehicles etc.*) (дорóжное) движéние, трáнспорт; **heavy ~** большóе/интенси́вное движéние; **~ circle** (*US*) кольцевáя трáнспортная развя́зка; **~ cop** (*US coll.*) регулирóвщик дорóжного движéния, гаи́шник (*coll.*); **~ island** островóк безопáсности; **~ jam** прóбка; **~ lights** светофóр; **~ warden** (*Br.*) ≈ инспéктор паркóвания автомоби́лей в чертé гóрода. **2** (*trade*) торгóвля.
● *v.i.* (**trafficked, trafficking**) торговáть (*чем*).

trafficker /'træfɪkə(r)/ *n.* (*pej.*) дельéц, торгóвец; **drug ~** наркодéлец.

tragedian /trə'dʒi:dɪən/ *n.* (*actor*) трáгик; (*author*) áвтор трагéдий.

tragedienne /trə,dʒi:dɪ'en/ *n.* траги́ческая актри́са.

tragedy /'trædʒɪdɪ/ *n.* (*lit. fig.*) трагéдия.

tragic /ˈtrædʒɪk/ *adj.* трагический.

tragicomedy /ˌtrædʒɪˈkɒmɪdɪ/ *n.* трагикомедия.

tragicomic /ˌtrædʒɪˈkɒmɪk/ *adj.* трагикомический.

trail /treɪl/ *n.* след; **the storm left a ~ of destruction** бу́ря оста́вила после себя полосу́ разруше́ния; **a ~ of smoke** о́блако ды́ма; **the police were on his ~** поли́ция напа́ла на его́ след.

● *v.t.* **1** (*draw or drag behind*) тащи́ть (*impf.*); волочи́ть (*impf.*); **she ~ed her skirt in the mud** её юбка волочи́лась по гря́зи. **2** (*pursue*) идти́ (*det.*) по сле́ду +*g.*

● *v.i.* **1** (*be drawn or dragged*) тащи́ться (*impf.*); волочи́ться (*impf.*); **the rope ~ed on the ground** верёвка волочи́лась по земле́. **2** (*straggle, follow wearily*) плести́сь (*impf.*); **they ~ed along behind him** они́ плели́сь за ним; **her voice ~ed away** её го́лос постепе́нно затиха́л. **3** (*grow or hang loosely*) све́шиваться (*impf.*); **the roses ~ed over the wall** ро́зы обвива́ли сте́ну.

trailer /ˈtreɪlə(r)/ *n.* **1** (*vehicle*) прице́п; (*US, caravan*) дом-автоприце́п. **2** (*cin.*) клип реклами́руемого фи́льма; ано́нс. **3** (*plant*) вью́щееся расте́ние.

train /treɪn/ *n.* **1** (*rail*) по́езд; **I came by ~** я прие́хал по́ездом; **the ~ is already in** по́езд уже́ прибы́л. **2** (*line of moving vehicles, animals etc.*) проце́ссия; карава́н; (*mil.*) обо́з. **3** (*retinue*) сви́та. **4** (*fig.*) ряд, цепь; **~ of events** цепь/верени́ца/ряд собы́тий; **I don't follow your ~ of thought** мне тру́дно улови́ть ход ва́ших мы́слей. **5** (*of dress etc.*) шлейф.

● *v.t.* **1** (*give instruction to*) учи́ть, об-/обуч|а́ть, -и́ть (**in**: +*d.*); **I have ~ed my dog to do tricks** я обучи́л соба́ку трю́кам; (*in a habit*) приуч|а́ть, -и́ть; **~ a child to study regularly** приуч|а́ть, -и́ть ребёнка регуля́рно занима́ться; (*prepare for a career*) гото́вить (*impf.*); **he was ~ed (up) for the ministry** его́ гото́вили в свяще́нники; (*sportsman*) тренирова́ть (*impf.*); (*eye, mind*) тренирова́ть, на-; (*horses, dogs*) дрессирова́ть (*impf.*); **he ~s horses** он дрессиру́ет лошаде́й. **2** (*cause to grow*): **peaches can be ~ed up a wall** пе́рсиковые дере́вья мо́жно заста́вить ви́ться по стене́. **3** (*direct*) нав|оди́ть, -ести́; **they ~ed their guns on the ship** они́ навели́ ору́дия на кора́бль.

● *v.i.* (*learn skill*) учи́ться, об-/обуч|а́ться, -и́ться; (*undertake preparation*) гото́виться (*impf.*); (*of sportsman*) тренирова́ться (*impf.*); **she is ~ing to be a teacher** она́ гото́вится стать учи́тельницей.

● *cpds.* **~-driver** *n.* машини́ст; **~man** *n.* (*US*) проводни́к; **~-ride** *n.* пое́здка на по́езде; **~-set** *n.* (*Br.*) игру́шечная моде́ль желе́зной доро́ги; **~spotter** *n.* (*Br.*) челове́к, наблюда́ющий за движе́нием поездо́в (*как хобби*).

trainee /treɪˈniː/ *n.* стажёр; учени́|к (*fem.* -ца).

trainer /ˈtreɪnə(r)/ *n.* **1** тре́нер; (*of horses etc.*) дрессиро́вщи|к (*fem.* -ца). **2** (*Br., sports shoe*) кроссо́вка.

training /ˈtreɪnɪŋ/ *n.* **1** (*study, instruction*) подгото́вка, обуче́ние. **2** (*physical preparation*) трениро́вка; **he went into ~** он на́чал тренирова́ться; **he is out of ~** он не в фо́рме. **3** (*of animals*) дрессиро́вка.

● *cpds.* **~-college** *n.* педагоги́ческий институ́т; **~-ship** *n.* уче́бное су́дно.

traipse /treɪps/ *v.i.* (*coll.*) таска́ться (*impf.*).

trait /treɪ/, /treɪt/ *n.* осо́бенность, сво́йство, черта́.

traitor /ˈtreɪtə(r)/ *n.* преда́тель (*m.*), изме́нник; **he turned ~** он стал преда́телем.

traitorous /ˈtreɪtərəs/ *adj.* преда́тельский, изме́ннический.

traitress /ˈtreɪtrɪs/ *n.* преда́тельница, изме́нница.

trajectory /trəˈdʒektərɪ/, /ˈtrædʒɪk-/ *n.* траекто́рия.

tram /træm/ *n.* (*Br.*) трамва́й.

● *cpds.* **~car** *n.* (*Br.*) трамва́йный ваго́н; **~-driver** *n.* вагоновожа́т|ый (*fem.* -ая); **~-lines** *n. pl.* (*Br.*) трамва́йные ре́льсы (*m. pl.*).

trammel /ˈtræm(ə)l/ *n.* (*fig., usu. pl.*) пу́т|ы (*pl., g.* —).

● *v.t.* (**trammelled, trammelling;** *US* **trammeled, trammeling**) свя́зывать, связа́ть по рука́м и нога́м.

tramp /træmp/ *n.* (*sound of steps*) то́пот; (*long walk*) дли́тельный похо́д; (*vagrant*) бродя́га; (*steamer*) трамп; (*coll., prostitute*) шлю́ха, потаску́ха.

● *v.t.*: **he ~ed the streets looking for work** он исходи́л весь го́род в по́исках рабо́ты; **we ~ed the hills together** мы с ним мно́го ходи́ли по гора́м.

● *v.i.* **1** (*walk heavily*) то́пать (*impf.*); **the soldiers ~ed down the road** солда́ты тяжёлым ша́гом прошли́ по у́лице. **2** (*walk a long distance*) шага́ть, про-.

trample /ˈtræmp(ə)l/ *v.t.* топта́ть, по-; раст|а́птывать, -опта́ть; **the children ~d down the flowers** де́ти вы́топтали цветы́; **I was almost ~d underfoot** меня́ чуть не растопта́ли.

● *v.i.* тяжело́ ступа́ть (*impf.*); (*fig.*): **~ on** поп|ира́ть, -ра́ть; **he ~d on everyone's feelings** он не счита́лся ни с чьи́ми чу́вствами.

trampoline /ˌtræmpəˈliːn/ *n.* бату́т.

trampolining /ˌtræmpəˈliːnɪŋ/ *n.* бату́тный спорт.

trampolinist /ˌtræmpəˈliːnɪst/ *n.* батути́ст (*fem.* -ка).

trance /trɑːns/ *n.* транс.

tranquil /ˈtræŋkwɪl/ *adj.* споко́йный, ми́рный.

tranquillity /træŋˈkwɪlɪtɪ/ *n.* споко́йствие.

tranquillize /ˈtræŋkwɪˌlaɪz/ (*US* **tranquilize**) *v.t.* успок|а́ивать, -о́ить.

tranquillizer /ˈtræŋkwɪˌlaɪzə(r)/ (*US* **tranquilizer**) *n.* успока́ивающее сре́дство, транквилиза́тор.

transact /trænˈzækt/, /trɑːn-/, /-ˈsækt/ *v.t.* (*business*) вести́ (*det.*); (*deal, sale*) заключ|а́ть, -и́ть.

transaction /trænˈzækʃ(ə)n/, /trɑːn-/, /-ˈsækʃ(ə)n/ *n.* **1**: **~ of business** веде́ние дел. **2** (*deal*) сде́лка. **3** (*pl., proceedings*) труды́ (*m. pl.*); (*in title of journal*) ве́домости (*f. pl.*).

transatlantic /ˌtrænzətˈlæntɪk/, /ˌtrɑːn-/, /-sətˈlæntɪk/ *adj.* трансатланти́ческий.

Transcaucasia /ˌtrænskɔːˈkeɪzjə/, /ˌtrɑːns-/ *n.* Закавка́зье.

Transcaucasian /ˌtrænskɔːˈkeɪzjən/, /ˌtrɑːns-/ *adj.* закавка́зский.

transceiver /trænˈsiːvə(r)/, /trɑːn-/ *n.* приёмо-переда́тчик.

transcend /trænˈsend/, /trɑːn-/ *v.t.* прев|ыша́ть, -ы́сить; выходи́ть, вы́йти за преде́лы +*g.*

transcendence /trænˈsend(ə)ns/, /trɑːn-/ *n.* превыше́ние; (*excellence*) превосхо́дство.

transcendent /trænˈsend(ə)nt/, /trɑːn-/ *adj.* **1** (*surpassing*) превосхо́дный, выдаю́щийся. **2** (*phil.*) трансценде́нтный.

transcendental /ˌtrænsenˈdent(ə)l/, /ˌtrɑːn-/ *adj.* (*phil.*) трансцендента́льный.

transcontinental /trænzˌkɒntɪˈnent(ə)l/, /trɑːnz-/, /træns-/, /trɑːns-/ *adj.* трансконтинента́льный.

transcribe /trænˈskraɪb/, /trɑːn-/ *v.t.* (*make a copy*) перепи́с|ывать, -а́ть; (*transliterate, write in different form*) транскриби́ровать (*impf., pf.*); (*mus.*) аранжи́ровать (*impf., pf.*).

transcript /ˈtrænskrɪpt/, /ˈtrɑːn-/ *n.* ко́пия; расшифро́вка.

transcription /ˌtrænˈskrɪpʃ(ə)n/, /ˈtrɑːn-/ *n.* перепи́сывание; ко́пия, транскри́пция; **phonetic ~** фонети́ческая транскри́пция.

transept /ˈtrænsept/, /ˈtrɑːn-/ *n.* (*archit.*) трансе́пт.

transfer[1] /ˈtrænsfɜː(r)/, /ˈtrɑːns-/ *n.* **1** (*of object*) перенесе́ние, перено́с; (*of person, money*) перево́д; (*conveyance, handing over*) переда́ча; **~ of property** переда́ча иму́щества; **the ~ of a football player** перево́д игрока́ в другу́ю футбо́льную кома́нду. **2** (*Br., drawing etc.*) переводна́я карти́нка. **3** (*US, ~ ticket*) переса́дочный биле́т.

transfer[2] /trænsˈfɜː(r)/, /trɑːns-/ *v.t.* (**transferred, transferring**) **1** (*object*) перен|оси́ть, -ести́. **2** (*hand over*) перед|ава́ть, -а́ть. **3** (*footballer, worker, money*) перев|оди́ть, -ести́. **4** (*convey picture from one surface to another*) перев|оди́ть, -ести́; перен|оси́ть, -ести́.

● *v.i.* (**transferred, transferring**) (*footballer, worker*) перев|оди́ться, -ести́сь; пере|ходи́ть, -йти́; (*change from one vehicle to another*) перес|а́живаться, -е́сть.

transferable /trænsˈfɜːrəb(ə)l/, /trɑːns-/, /ˈtr-/ *adj.* допуска́ющий заме́ну; переводи́мый.

transference /ˈtrænsfərəns/, /ˈtrɑː-/ *n.* **1** перенесе́ние; перево́д; **thought ~**

T

передáча мы́сли на расстоя́нии. **2** (*psych.*) замещéние.

transfiguration /træns,fɪgjʊ'reɪʃ(ə)n/, /trɑː-/ *n.* видоизменéние; (*relig.*): **the T~** Преображéние.

transfigure /træns'fɪgə(r)/, /trɑː-/ *v.t.* видоизмен|я́ть, -и́ть; (*with joy etc.*) преобра|жáть, -зи́ть.

transfix /træns'fɪks/, /trɑː-/ *v.t.* **1** (*impale*) пронз|áть, -и́ть; прок|áлывать, -олóть. **2** (*fig., root to the spot*) прикóв|ывать, -áть к мéсту; **he was ~ed with horror** он оцепенéл от у́жаса.

transform /træns'fɔːm/, /trɑː-/ *v.t.* (*change*) преобразóв|ывать, -áть; трансформи́ровать (*impf., pf.*); (*make unrecognizable*) меня́ть, измени́ть до неузнавáемости.

transformation /,trænsfə'meɪʃ(ə)n/, /,trɑː-/ *n.* превращéние, преобразовáние, трансформáция; (*complete change*) метаморфóза.

transformer /træns'fɔːmə(r)/, /trɑː-/, /-z'fɔːmə(r)/ *n.* (*elec.*) трансформáтор.

transfuse /træns'fjuːz/, /trɑː-/ *v.t.* перел|ивáть, -и́ть.

transfusion /træns'fjuːʒ(ə)n/, /trɑː-/ *n.* переливáние (крóви).

transgress /trænz'gres/, /trɑː-/, /-s'gres/ *v.t. & i.* (*infringe*) пере|ходи́ть, -йти́ грани́цы +*g.*; нар|ушáть, -у́шить (*закон и т.п.*); (*sin*) греши́ть, со-.

transgression /trænz'greʃ(ə)n/, /trɑː-/ *n.* (*infringement*) прости́пок; (*offence*) нарушéние; (*sin*) грех.

transgressor /trænz'gresə(r)/, /trɑː-/, /-s'gresə(r)/ *n.* (*offender*) правонаруши́тель (*fem.* -ница); (*sinner*) грéшни|к (*fem.* -ца).

tranship /træn'ʃɪp/, /trɑː-/, /trænz-/ (*also* **transship**) *v.t.* (**transhipped, transhipping**) (*goods*) перегру|жáть, -зи́ть с одногó су́дна на другóе; (*persons*) перес|áживать, -ди́ть с одногó су́дна на другóе.

transhipment /træn'ʃɪpmənt/, /trɑː-/ (*also* **transshipment**) *n.* (*of goods*) перегру́зка; (*of persons*) пересáдка.

transience /'trænzɪəns/, /'trɑː-/, /-sɪəns/ *n.* быстротéчность; мимолётность.

transient /'trænzɪənt/, /'trɑː-/, /-sənt/ *n.* (*temporary inhabitant*) врéменный жи́тель; (*temporary worker*) рабóчий-мигрáнт.

● *adj.* (*impermanent*) врéменный; (*brief, momentary*) мимолётный, преходя́щий.

transistor /træn'zɪstə(r)/, /trɑː-/, /-'sɪstə(r)/ *n.* транзи́стор; (**~ radio**) транзи́сторный рáдиоприёмник.

transit /'trænzɪt/, /'trɑː-/, /-sɪt/ *n.* **1** (*conveyance, passage*) транзи́т, перевóзка; **lost in ~** потéрянный при перевóзке; **~ camp** транзи́тный лáгерь. **2** (*astron.*) прохождéние (чéрез меридиáн). **3** (*US, public transport*) общéственный трáнспорт. **4**: **in ~** транзи́том.

transition /træn'zɪʃ(ə)n/, /trɑː-/, /-'sɪʃ(ə)n/ *n.* (*change*) перехóд; (*period of change*) перехóдный периóд.

transitional /træn'zɪʃənəl/, /trɑː-/, /-'sɪʃənəl/ *adj.* перехóдный; промежу́точный.

transitive /'trænsɪtɪv/, /'trɑː-/, /-zɪtɪv/ *adj.* перехóдный.

transitory /'trænsɪtərɪ/, /'trɑː-/, /-zɪtərɪ/ *adj.* преходя́щий, мимолётный.

translatable /træn'sleɪtəb(ə)l/, /trɑː-/, /-'zleɪtəb(ə)l/ *adj.* переводи́мый.

translate /træn'sleɪt/, /trɑː-/, /-'zleɪt/ *v.t. & i.* **1** (*express in another language*) перев|оди́ть, -ести́; **he ~s from Russian into English** он перевóдит с ру́сского на англи́йский; **these poems do not ~ well** э́ти стихи́ не поддаю́тся перевóду. **2** (*convert*): **promises must be ~d into action** обещáния ну́жно претворя́ть в жизнь.

translation /træns'leɪʃ(ə)n/, /trɑː-/, /-z'leɪʃ(ə)n/ *n.* перевóд; **machine/simultaneous ~** маши́нный/синхрóнный перевóд; **a novel in ~** переводнóй ромáн.

translator /træns'leɪtə(r)/, /trɑː-/, /-z'leɪtə(r)/ *n.* перевóдчи|к (*fem.* -ца).

transliterate /trænz'lɪtə,reɪt/, /trɑː-/, /-s'lɪtə,reɪt/ *v.t.* транслитери́ровать (*impf., pf.*).

transliteration /trænz,lɪtə'reɪʃ(ə)n/, /trɑː-/, /-s,lɪtə'reɪʃ(ə)n/ *n.* транслитерáция.

translucenc|e /trænz'luːs(ə)ns/, /trɑː-/, /-'ljuːs(ə)ns/, /-s'l-/, **-y** /trænz'luːs(ə)nsɪ/, /trɑː-/, /-'ljuːs(ə)nsɪ/, /-s'l-/ *nn.* просвéчиваемость, полупрозрáчность.

translucent /trænz'luːs(ə)nt/, /trɑː-/, /-'ljuːs(ə)nt/, /-s'l-/ *adj.* просвéчивающий, полупрозрáчный.

transmigration /,trænzmaɪ'greɪʃ(ə)n/, /,trɑː-/, /-smaɪ'greɪʃ(ə)n/ *n.* переселéние.

transmissible /trænz'mɪsəb(ə)l/, /trɑː-/, /-s'mɪsəb(ə)l/ *adj.* передаю́щийся; **a ~ disease** зарáзная болéзнь.

transmission /trænz'mɪʃ(ə)n/, /trɑː-/, /-s'mɪʃ(ə)n/ *n.* передáча, трансми́ссия; **there are news ~s every hour** нóвости передаю́тся кáждый час.

transmit /trænz'mɪt/, /trɑː-/, /-s'mɪt/ *v.t. & i.* (**transmitted, transmitting**) **1** (*pass on*) перед|авáть, -áть; **the plague was ~ted by rats** чуму́ разнесли́ кры́сы; **iron ~s heat** желéзо прово́дит тепло́; **wires ~ electric current** электри́ческий ток идёт по проводáм; **the fire was ~ting no heat** огóнь не давáл тепло́. **2** (*broadcast*) трансли́ровать (*impf., pf.*), перед|авáть, -áть.

transmitter /træns'mɪtə(r)/, /trɑː-/, /-z'mɪtə(r)/ *n.* передáтчик; передаю́щая радиостáнция; **portable ~** рáция.

transmogrification /trænz,mɒgrɪfɪ'keɪʃ(ə)n/, /trɑː-/, /-s,mɒgrɪfɪ'keɪʃ(ə)n/ *n.* (*joc.*) превращéние.

transmogrify /trænz'mɒgrɪ,faɪ/, /trɑː-/, /-s'mɒgrɪ,faɪ/ *v.t.* (*joc.*) превра|щáть, -ти́ть.

transmutation /,trænzmjuː'teɪʃ(ə)n/, /,trɑː-/, /-smjuː'teɪʃ(ə)n/ *n.* превращéние, преобразовáние.

transmute /trænz'mjuːt/, /trɑː-/, /-s'mjuːt/ *v.t.* превра|щáть, -ти́ть; преобразóв|ывать, -áть.

transnational /trænz'næʃən(ə)l/, /trɑː-/, /-s'næʃən(ə)l/ *adj.* транснационáльный.

transoceanic /trænz,əʊʃɪ'ænɪk/, /trɑː-/, /-s,əʊʃɪ'ænɪk/ *adj.* заокеáнский; **~ countries** замóрские/заокеáнские стрáны; **~ flight** межконтинентáльный полёт.

transom /'trænsəm/ *n.* (*of window, door*) фраму́га.

transparence /træns'pærəns/, /trɑː-/, /-'peərəns/ *n.* прозрáчность.

transparency /træns'pærənsɪ/, /trɑː-/, /-'peərənsɪ/ *n.* **1** = **transparence.** **2** (*picture*) транспарáнт.

transparent /træns'pærənt/, /trɑː-/, /-'peərənt/ *adj.* прозрáчный; (*fig.*) я́вный, очеви́дный.

transpire /træn'spaɪə(r)/, /trɑː-/ *v.i.* (*come to be known*) обнару́жи|ваться, -ться; (*coll., happen*) случ|áться, -и́ться.

transplant[1] /'trænsplɑːnt/, /'trɑː-/ *n.* **1** рассáда; (*sapling*) сáженец. **2** (*of organ*) пересáдка; **heart ~** пересáдка сéрдца.

transplant[2] /træns'plɑːnt/, /trɑː-/ *v.t. & i.* пересá|живать, -ди́ть; **the lettuces need ~ing** салáт необходи́мо пересади́ть; **this species does not ~ easily** э́тот вид плóхо перенóсит пересáдку; (*fig., people*) пересел|я́ть, -и́ть; (*med.*) перес|áживать, -ади́ть; **the doctors ~ed skin from his back** врачи́ сдéлали ему́ пересáдку кóжи со спины́.

transplantation /,trænsplɑːn'teɪʃ(ə)n/, /,trɑː-/ *n.* пересáдка, трансплантáция; (*fig.*) переселéние.

transport[1] /'trænspɔːt/, /'trɑː-/ *n.* **1** (*conveyance*) перевóзка, трáнспорт. **2** (*means of conveyance*) трáнспорт; **~ café** (*Br.*) дорóжное кафé; **public ~** общéственный трáнспорт; **have you got ~?** вы на колёсах? **3** (*ship*) трáнспортное су́дно; (*aircraft*) трáнспортный самолёт; **troop ~** войсковóй трáнспорт. **4** (*emotion*) поры́в (чувств); **in ~s of delight** вне себя́ от рáдости.

transport[2] /træns'pɔːt/, /trɑː-/ *v.t.* **1** (*convey*) перев|ози́ть, -езти́; транспорти́ровать (*impf., pf.*). **2** (*send to penal colony*) отпр|авля́ть, -áвить на кáторгу. **3** (*of emotion*): **~ed with delight** вне себя́ от рáдости.

transportable /træns'pɔːtəb(ə)l/, /trɑː-/ *adj.* перевози́мый, передвижнóй; (*of a sick person*) транспортáбельный.

transportation /,trænspɔː'teɪʃ(ə)n/, /,trɑː-/ *n.* (*of goods etc.*) перевóзка, транспорти́рование, транспортирóвка; (*of a convict*) ссы́лка, транспортáция.

transporter /træns'pɔːtə(r)/, /trɑː-/ *n.* транспортирóвщик; (*for soldiers*) транспортёр; **~ bridge** навеснóй мост.

transpose /træns'pəʊz/, /trɑː-/, /-z'pəʊz/ *v.t.* перест|авля́ть, -áвить; (*mus.*) транспони́ровать (*impf., pf.*).

transposition /ˌtrænspəˈzɪʃ(ə)n/, /ˌtrɑː-/, /-zpəˈzɪʃ(ə)n/ *n.* перестано́вка; (*mus.*) транспози́ция.

transsexual /trænzˈseksjʊəl/ *n.* транссексуа́л.

● *adj.* транссексуа́льный.

tranship /trænˈʃɪp/, /trɑː-/, /trænz-/, **-ment** /trænˈʃɪpmənt/, /trɑː-/, /trænz-/ = **tranship, -ment**

Trans-Siberian /ˌtrænzsaɪˈbɪərɪən/, /ˌtrɑː-/ *adj.*: ~ **Railway** (*Br.*), **Railroad** (*US*) Транссиби́рская магистра́ль.

transubstantiation /ˌtrænsəbˌstænʃɪˈeɪʃ(ə)n/, /ˌtrɑː-/ *n.* (*theol.*) пресуществле́ние.

Transvaal /trænzˈvɑːl/, /trɑː-/ *n.* Трансваа́ль (*m.*).

transverse /ˈtrænzvɜːs/, /ˈtrɑː-/, /-ˈvɜːs/, /-ns-/ *adj.* попере́чный; косо́й.

transvestism /trænzˈvestɪz(ə)m/, /trɑː-/, /-sˈvestɪz(ə)m/ *n.* трансвести́зм.

transvestite /trænzˈvestaɪt/, /trɑː-/, /-sˈvestaɪt/ *n.* трансвести́т.

Transylvania /ˌtrænsɪlˈveɪnɪə/ *n.* Трансильва́ния.

Transylvanian /ˌtrænsɪlˈveɪnɪən/ *adj.* трансильва́нский.

trap /træp/ *n.* **1** (*for animals etc.*) капка́н, западня́; **I shall set a ~ for the mice** я поста́влю мышело́вку; (*fig.*) лову́шка, западня́; **he fell into the ~** он попа́л в лову́шку/западню́.
2 (*light vehicle*) рессо́рная двуко́лка.
3 (*mouth*) гло́тка, пасть (*sl.*); **shut your ~!** заткни́сь!

● *v.t.* (**trapped, trapping**) лови́ть, пойма́ть в лову́шку/капка́н; (*fig., catch*): **his fingers were ~ped in the door** он защеми́л па́льцы две́рью; **there is some air ~ped in the pipes** в тру́бах образова́лись возду́шные про́бки; **he felt ~ped** он почу́вствовал, что он попа́л в лову́шку.

● *cpd.* **~-door** *n.* люк.

trapeze /trəˈpiːz/ *n.* трапе́ция; **~ artist** акроба́т.

trapezi|um /trəˈpiːzɪəm/ *n.* (*pl.* **~a** *or* **~ums**) трапе́ция.

trapezoid /ˈtræpɪˌzɔɪd/ *n.* трапецо́ид.

trapper /ˈtræpə(r)/ *n.* тра́ппер; охо́тник, ста́вящий капка́ны.

trappings /ˈtræpɪŋz/ *n.* (*harness*) сбру́я; (*fig.*): **the ~ of office** вне́шние атрибу́ты (*m. pl.*) вла́сти.

Trappist /ˈtræpɪst/ *n.* член о́рдена траппи́стов.

traps /træps/ *n.* (*coll., belongings*) пожи́тк|и (*pl., g.* -ов).

trash /træʃ/ *n.* **1** (*rubbishy material, writing etc.*) халту́ра, му́сор. **2** (*US, refuse*) му́сор, отбро́сы (*m. pl.*).

● *cpd.* **~-can** *n.* (*US*) му́сорное ведро́; (*outside*) му́сорный бак.

trashy /ˈtræʃɪ/ *adj.* (**trashier, trashiest**) дрянно́й.

trauma /ˈtrɔːmə/, /ˈtraʊ-/ *n.* (*pl.* **~s**) тра́вма.

traumatic /trɔːˈmætɪk/, /traʊ-/ *adj.* (*distressing*) тя́жкий; (*of physical injury*) травмати́ческий.

traumatize /ˈtrɔːməˌtaɪz/, /ˈtraʊ-/ *v.t.* травми́ровать (*impf., pf.*).

travail /ˈtræveɪl/ *n.* му́ки (*f. pl.*).

travel /ˈtræv(ə)l/ *n.* **1** (*journeying*) путеше́ствие, пое́здка; **~ broadens the mind** путеше́ствие расширя́ет кругозо́р; **~ agency, bureau** туристи́ческое аге́нтство, бюро́ путеше́ствий; **~ agent** туристи́ческий аге́нт; **he suffers from ~ sickness** он пло́хо перено́сит путеше́ствие/доро́гу.
2 (*movement of a part or mechanism*) ход.

● *v.t.* (**travelled, travelling;** *US usu.* **traveled, traveling**) путеше́ствовать (*impf.*) по + *d.*; е́здить (*indet.*) по + *d.*; **I have ~led the whole of England** я изъе́здил всю А́нглию; **he ~led a thousand miles to see her** он пое́хал за ты́сячу миль, что́бы её повида́ть.

● *v.i.* (**travelled, travelling;** *US usu.* **traveled, traveling**) путеше́ствовать (*impf.*); е́здить, съ-; **he has been ~ling since yesterday** он со вчера́шнего дня в пути́; (*as a salesman*) е́здить (*impf.*) в ка́честве коммивояжёра; (*move*) дви́гаться (*impf.*); перемеща́ться (*impf.*); **light ~s faster than sound** ско́рость све́та превыша́ет ско́рость зву́ка; **his eye ~led over the scene** он обвёл глаза́ми всю сце́ну.

● *cpds.* **~ sickness** *n.* тошнота́ при езде́; **~-worn** *adj.* измо́танный пое́здками.

travelator /ˈtrævəˌleɪt(ə)r/ *n.* дви́жущийся тротуа́р.

traveller /ˈtrævələ(r)/ (*US* **traveler**) *n.* **1** путеше́ственник; **~'s cheque** (*Br.*), **check** (*US*) доро́жный чек.
2 (*commercial ~*) коммивояжёр.

travelling /ˈtrævəlɪŋ/ *n.* путеше́ствие.

● *adj.* путеше́ствующий; **~ salesman** коммивояжёр.

● *cpd.* **~-clock** *n.* доро́жные час|ы́ (*pl., g.* -о́в).

travelogue /ˈtrævəˌlɒg/ *n.* ле́кция/фильм о путеше́ствиях.

traverse /ˈtrævəs/, /trəˈvɜːs/ *n.* (*in mountaineering*) попере́чина, тра́верс; (*naut.*) зигзагообра́зный курс.

● *v.t.* перес|ека́ть, -е́чь; **the railway ~s miles of desert** желе́зная доро́га пересека́ет обши́рную пусты́ню.

travesty /ˈtrævɪstɪ/ *n.* шарж, паро́дия; **~ of justice** паро́дия на справедли́вость.

● *v.t.* пароди́ровать (*impf., pf.*).

trawl /trɔːl/ *n.* (**~-net**) трал, тра́ловая сеть; до́нный не́вод.

● *v.t. & i.* тра́лить (*impf.*); лови́ть (*impf.*) ры́бу тра́лом; **the fishermen ~ed their nets** рыбаки́ тащи́ли се́ти по дну; **they ~ed for herring** они́ тра́лили сельдь; (*fig., search thoroughly*) проч|ёсывать, -еса́ть.

trawler /ˈtrɔːlə(r)/ *n.* (*vessel*) тра́улер.

tray /treɪ/ *n.* (*for tea etc.*) подно́с; (*for correspondence*) корзи́нка; (*in trunk*) лото́к.

trayful /ˈtreɪfʊl/ *n.* це́лый подно́с; **a ~ of glasses** подно́с со стака́нами.

treacherous /ˈtretʃərəs/ *adj.* (*lit., fig.*) преда́тельский, вероло́мный, кова́рный; **~ weather** кова́рная пого́да; **the roads are ~** доро́ги опа́сны.

treacher|ousness /ˈtretʃərəsnɪs/, **-y** /ˈtretʃərɪ/ *nn.* преда́тельство, вероло́мство.

treacle /ˈtriːk(ə)l/ *n.* (*Br.*) па́тока.

treacly /ˈtriːklɪ/ *adj.* ли́пкий, вя́зкий; (*fig.*) при́торный.

tread /tred/ *n.* **1** (*step*) по́ступь; шаги́ (*m. pl.*).
2 (*manner or sound of walking*) похо́дка.
3 (*of tyre*) проте́ктор.

● *v.t.* (*past* **trod;** *p.p.* **trodden** *or* **trod**) **1** (*walk on*) ступа́ть (*impf.*) по + *d.*; шага́ть (*impf.*) по + *d.*; **a well-trodden path** (*lit.*) прото́птанная тропи́нка; (*fig.*) проторённая доро́жка; **his ambition was to ~ the boards** (*be an actor*) он мечта́л о теа́тре.
2 (*trample on*) топта́ть, по-; дави́ть, раз-; **the peasants were ~ing the grapes** крестья́не дави́ли виногра́д.

● *v.i.* (*past* **trod;** *p.p.* **trodden** *or* **trod**): **~ on that spider!** растопчи́те/раздави́те э́того паука́!; **don't ~ on the grass** по траве́ не ходи́ть; (*fig.*): **he ~s on everybody's toes** он ве́чно наступа́ет лю́дям на люби́мую мозо́ль; **I was ~ing on air** я ног под собо́й не чу́ял от сча́стья; **we must ~ lightly in this matter** в э́той ситуа́ции мы должны́ де́йствовать осторо́жно.

● *with advs.*: **he trod down the earth** он утрамбова́л зе́млю; **keep off the carpet, or you will ~ the mud in** не ходи́те по ковру́, а то он совсе́м запа́чкается; **they trod out the fire** они́ затопта́ли ого́нь.

● *cpd.* **~mill** *n.* (*lit.*) топча́к; (*fig.*) однообра́зная рабо́та.

treadle /ˈtred(ə)l/ *n.* педа́ль; ножно́й приво́д.

treason /ˈtriːz(ə)n/ *n.* (госуда́рственная) изме́на.

treasonable /ˈtriːzənəb(ə)l/ *adj.* изме́ннический.

treasure /ˈtreʒə(r)/ *n.* (*precious object or person*) сокро́вище; (**~ trove**) клад; **art ~s** худо́жественные сокро́вища.

● *v.t.* (*store up, esp. in memory*) храни́ть, со-; **~d memories** дороги́е воспомина́ния; (*value highly*) высоко́ цени́ть (*impf.*).

● *cpd.* **~-house** *n.* сокро́вищница.

treasurer /ˈtreʒərə(r)/ *n.* казначе́й.

treasury /ˈtreʒərɪ/ *n.* (*lit., fig.*) сокро́вищница; (*public revenue department*) казна́; **~ bill** краткосро́чный казначе́йский ве́ксель; **~ note** казначе́йский биле́т.

treat /triːt/ *n.* **1** (*pleasure*) удово́льствие; **it's a ~ to listen to him** слу́шать его́ — одно́ удово́льствие.
2 (*defrayal of entertainment*) угоще́ние; **he stood ~ for them all** он всех угоща́л; **it's my ~!** я угоща́ю!

● *v.t.* **1** (*behave towards*) обраща́ться

T

(*impf.*) с + *i.*; **he ~s me like a child** он обращáется со мной, как с ребёнком; **how is the world ~ing you?** как жизнь?; как вы поживáете?
2 (*deem, regard*) рассмáтривать (*impf.*); отн|оси́ться, -ести́сь к + *d.*; **he ~ed it as a joke** он отнёсся к э́тому, как к шу́тке.
3 (*deal with; discuss*) осве|щáть, -ти́ть; рассм|áтривать, -отрéть; **he ~ed the subject in detail** он подрóбно освети́л тéму.
4 (*give medical care to*) лечи́ть (*impf.*); **he was ~ed for burns** егó лечи́ли от ожóгов.
5 (*apply chemical process to*) обрáб|áтывать, -óтать; **the wood was ~ed with creosote** древеси́ну обрабóтали креозóтом.
6 (*make a free partaker*) уго|щáть, -сти́ть; **he ~ed me to a whisky** он угости́л меня́ ви́ски; **I shall ~ myself to a holiday** я устрóю себé óтпуск.
● *v.i.* (*negotiate*) вести́ (*det.*) переговóры.

treatise /ˈtriːtɪs/, /-ɪz/ *n.* трактáт; наýчный труд.

treatment /ˈtriːtmənt/ *n.* **1** (*handling*) обращéние; рассмотрéние; **the subject received only superficial ~** э́той тéмы коснýлись лишь повéрхностно. **2** (*chem. etc.*) обрабóтка; **heat ~** терми́ческая обрабóтка. **3** (*med.*) лечéние; (*separate session of a therapy*) процедýра; **she is still under ~** онá всё ещё лéчится.

treaty /ˈtriːtɪ/ *n.* договóр.

treble /ˈtreb(ə)l/ *n.* (*voice*) ди́скант; (*attr.*) дискантóвый; **~ clef** скрипи́чный ключ.
● *adj.* тройнóй; **he earns ~ my money** он зарабáтывает втрóе бóльше меня́.
● *v.t. & i.* утр|áивать(ся), -óить(ся).

tree /triː/ *n.* дéрево; **family ~** родослóвное дéрево.
● *cpds.* **~-fern** *n.* древови́дный пáпоротник; **~-surgeon** *n.* ≈ садóвник; **~-surgery** *n.* обрéзка дерéвьев на омоложéние; **~-top** *n.* верхýшка дéрева.

treeless /ˈtriːlɪs/ *adj.* лишённый дерéвьев.

trefoil /ˈtrefɔɪl/, /ˈtriː-/ *n.* (*plant*) клéвер; (*decoration*) трили́стник.

trek /trek/ *n.* (*migration*) переселéние; (*arduous journey*) похóд; перехóд.
● *v.i.* (**trekked, trekking**) пересел|я́ться, -и́ться.

trellis /ˈtrelɪs/ *n.* шпалéра, трелья́ж.
● *cpd.* **~-work** *n.* решётка.

trembl|e /ˈtremb(ə)l/ *n.* дрожь; **she was all of a ~e** (*coll.*) онá дрожáла как оси́новый лист.
● *v.i.* дрожáть (*impf.*); трясти́сь (*impf.*); **he was ~ing with excitement** он дрожáл от волнéния; (*fig.*) трепетáть (*impf.*); **I ~e to think what may happen** меня́ бросáет в дрожь при мы́сли, что мóжет случи́ться; **in fear and ~ing** в стрáхе и трéпете.

tremendous /trɪˈmendəs/ *adj.* (*huge*) огрóмный; (*coll., splendid*) замечáтельный, потрясáющий.

tremolo /ˈtreməlәʊ/ *n.* (*pl.* **~s**) (*mus.*) трéмоло (*indecl.*).

tremor /ˈtremə(r)/ *n.* (*quivering*) содрогáние, дрожь; (*thrill*) трéпет; **there was a ~ in his voice** егó гóлос дрожáл; **earth ~** подзéмный толчóк.

tremulous /ˈtremjʊləs/ *adj.* **1** (*trembling*) дрожáщий. **2** (*timid*) боязли́вый, трепéщущий.

trench /trentʃ/ *n.* ров, канáва; (*mil.*) окóп, траншéя; **~ coat** (*soldier's*) шинéль; (*civilian's*) макинтóш; **~ warfare** окóпная войнá.
● *v.t.* (*make ~es in*) перек|áпывать, -опáть.

trenchant /ˈtrentʃ(ə)nt/ *adj.* óстрый, кóлкий, рéзкий.

trend /trend/ *n.* направлéние, тендéнция; **set a ~** вв|оди́ть, -ести́ нóвый стиль.
● *cpd.* **~-setter** *n.* законодáтель (*fem.* -ница) мод/сти́ля.

trendy /ˈtrendɪ/ *adj.* (**trendier, trendiest**) (*coll.*) мóдный.

trepan /trɪˈpæn/ *v.t.* (**trepanned, trepanning**) (*surg.*) трепани́ровать (*impf., pf.*).

trepidation /ˌtrepɪˈdeɪʃ(ə)n/ *n.* трéпет, дрожь; **in ~** трепещá.

trespass /ˈtrespəs/ *n.* **1** (*leg., offence*) правонарушéние; (*intrusion on property*) нарушéние чужóго прáва владéния. **2** (*relig.*) прегрешéние; **forgive us our ~es** остáви нам дóлги нáши.
● *v.i.* **1** (*intrude*) вт|оргáться, -óргнуться в чужи́е владéния; **no ~ing** вход воспрещён; (*fig.*): **I have no wish to ~ on your hospitality** я не хочý злоупотребля́ть вáшим гостеприи́мством. **2** (*relig.*) греши́ть, со-; **those that ~ against us** те, кто прóтив нас согрешáют.

trespasser /ˈtrespəsə(r)/ *n.* правонаруши́тель (*fem.* -ница); (*on property*) лицó, вторгáющееся в чужи́е владéния; **~s will be prosecuted** наруши́тели бýдут преслéдоваться.

tress /tres/ *n.* косá.

trestle /ˈtres(ə)l/ *n.* кóз|лы (*pl., g.* -ел).
● *cpd.* **~-table** *n.* стол на кóзлах

tri- /traɪ/ *comb. form* трёх…, тре….

triad /ˈtraɪæd/ *n.* (*group of three*) трóица, трóйка; (*math.*) триáда; (*mus.*) трезвýчие.

trial /ˈtraɪəl/ *n.* **1** (*testing, test*) испытáние, прóба; **it was a ~ of strength between them** э́то былá прóба их сил; **I discovered the truth by ~ and error** я пришёл к и́стине путём проб и оши́бок; **why not give him a ~?** почемý бы не взять егó на испытáтельный срок?; **he took the car on a week's ~** он взял автомаши́ну на недéльное испытáние.
2 (*attr.*) прóбный; **~ balloon** прóбный шар; **~ match** отбóрочный матч; **~ run** испытáтельный пробéг.
3 (*judicial examination*) судéбный процéсс; **he went on ~ for murder** егó суди́ли за уби́йство; **bring to** (**or put on**) **~** привл|екáть, -éчь к судý; **he was given a fair ~** егó суди́ли в соответствии с закóном; **he stands ~ next month** предстáнет пéред судóм в слéдующем мéсяце; **the case came up for ~** наступи́л день судá.
4 (*annoyance, ordeal*) переживáние, испытáние.
● *v.t.* (**trialled, trialling; US trialed, trialing**) исп|ы́тывать, -ытáть; подв|ергáть, -éргнуть испытáнию.

triangle /ˈtraɪˌæŋg(ə)l/ *n.* (*geom., mus., fig.*) треугóльник; **the eternal ~** извéчный/любóвный треугóльник.

triangular /traɪˈæŋgjʊlə(r)/ *adj.* треугóльный; **a ~ argument** спор мéжду тремя́ ли́цами.

triangulation /traɪˌæŋgjʊˈleɪʃ(ə)n/ *n.* триангуля́ция; **~ point** топографи́ческая вы́шка.

Triassic /traɪˈæsɪk/ *adj.* триáсовый.

triathlon /traɪˈæθlən/ *n.* троебóрье.

tribal /ˈtraɪb(ə)l/ *adj.* племеннóй.

tribalism /ˈtraɪbəˌlɪz(ə)m/ *n.* племеннóй строй.

tribe /traɪb/ *n.* **1** (*racial group*) плéмя (*nt.*). **2** (*pej., group, body*) компáния.
● *cpd.* **~sman** *n.* член плéмени.

tribulation /ˌtrɪbjʊˈleɪʃ(ə)n/ *n.* страдáние, бедá.

tribunal /traɪˈbjuːn(ə)l/, /trɪ-/ *n.* трибунáл; (*court of justice*) суд.

tribune /ˈtrɪbjuːn/ *n.* (*person*) трибýн; (*platform*) трибýна, эстрáда.

tributary /ˈtrɪbjʊtərɪ/ *n.* притóк.

tribute /ˈtrɪbjuːt/ *n.* (*payment*) дань; (*token of respect etc.*) дань; дóлжное; **he paid ~ to his wife's help** он вы́разил благодáрность своéй женé за пóмощь; **floral ~s** цветóчные подношéния.

trice /traɪs/ *n.* (*liter.*): **in a ~** вмиг, ми́гом.

trick /trɪk/ *n.* **1** (*dodge, device*) приём, хи́трость; **he knows all the ~s of the trade** он знáет все ходы́ и вы́ходы; **he tried every ~ in the book** он примени́л все извéстные приёмы.
2 (*deception, mischievous act*) обмáн, трюк; (*prank*) шýтка; **he is always playing ~s on me** он всегдá надо мной подшýчивает; **he is up to his old ~s again** он взя́лся за стáрое; **a ~ of the light** опти́ческий обмáн; **a dirty ~** пóдлость; **play a dirty ~ on s.o.** подложи́ть (*pf.*) комý-н. свинью́; **he is good at card ~s** он лóвко дéлает кáрточные фóкусы.
3 (*feat*) штýка; **their dog can do a lot of ~s** их собáка знáет мнóго комáнд; **that will do the ~** э́то срабóтает навернякá; **~ cyclist** (*lit.*) цирковóй велосипеди́ст.
4 (*knack*) хвáтка; **there's a ~ to operating this machine** чтóбы управля́ть э́той маши́ной, нужнá осóбая сорóвка.
5 (*mannerism*) привы́чка, манéра; **he has a ~ of repeating himself** у негó есть манéра повторя́ться.
6 (*at cards*) взя́тка; **he never misses a ~** (*fig.*) он никогдá не упýстит слýчая.
● *v.t.* **1** (*cheat, beguile*) обмáн|ывать, -ýть; над|увáть, -ýть; **they ~ed him out of a fortune** они́ вы́манили у негó

ма́ссу де́нег; **she was ~ed into marriage** её обма́нным путём вы́дали за́муж.
2 ~ out, up (*adorn*) укр|аша́ть, -а́сить; наря|жа́ть, -ди́ть; **~ed out in all her finery** разоде́тая в пух и прах.

trickery /ˈtrɪkərɪ/ *n.* обма́н, надува́тельство.

trickle /ˈtrɪk(ə)l/ *n.* стру́йка.
● *v.t.* ка́пать (*impf.*).
● *v.i.* сочи́ться (*impf.*); ка́пать (*impf.*); (*fig.*): **the news ~d out** но́вость просочи́лась; **the crowd began to ~ away** толпа́ начала́ постепе́нно расходи́ться.

trickster /ˈtrɪkstə(r)/ *n.* обма́нщик, ловка́ч.

tricksy /ˈtrɪksɪ/ *adj.* (**tricksier, tricksiest**) шаловли́вый, игри́вый.

tricky /ˈtrɪkɪ/ *adj.* (**trickier, trickiest**) (*awkward*) сло́жный, мудрёный; (*crafty, deceitful*) хи́трый, кова́рный.

tricolour /ˈtrɪkələ(r)/, /ˈtraɪˌkʌlə(r)/ (*US* **tricolor**) *n.* (*flag*) трёхцве́тный флаг; триколо́р; (*French*) францу́зский флаг.

tricot /ˈtrɪkəʊ/, /ˈtriː-/ *n.* трико́ (*indecl.*).

tricycle /ˈtraɪsɪk(ə)l/ *n.* трёхколёсный велосипе́д.

trident /ˈtraɪd(ə)nt/ *n.* трезу́бец.

tried /traɪd/ *adj.* (*tested*) испы́танный, прове́ренный.

triennial /traɪˈenɪəl/ *adj.* (*lasting three years*) продолжа́ющийся три го́да; (*recurring every three years*) повторя́ющийся че́рез ка́ждые три го́да.

trier /ˈtraɪə(r)/ *n.* (*persevering person*) насто́йчивый челове́к.

trifle /ˈtraɪf(ə)l/ *n.* **1** (*thing of small value or importance*) пустя́к, ме́лочь; **she gets upset over ~s** она́ огорча́ется из-за пустяко́в; (*small sum*) небольша́я су́мма. **2**: **a ~** (*as adv.*) чу́точку, немно́го; **I was just a ~ angry** я чу́точку рассерди́лся. **3** (*Br., sweet dish*) бискви́т со сби́тыми сли́вками.
● *v.i.* относи́ться (*impf.*) несерьёзно к + *d.*; **he ~d with her affections** он игра́л её чу́вствами; **he is not a man to be ~d with** с ним шу́тки пло́хи.

trifling /ˈtraɪflɪŋ/ *adj.* пустяко́вый; незначи́тельный.

trifori|um /traɪˈfɔːrɪəm/ *n.* (*pl.* **~a**) трифо́рий.

trigger /ˈtrɪgə(r)/ *n.* куро́к.
● *v.t.* (*usu.* **~ off**) вызыва́ть, вы́звать; влечь, по- за собо́й; **his action ~ed off a chain of events** его́ посту́пок повлёк за собо́й це́лую цепь собы́тий.
● *cpds.* **~-finger** *n.* указа́тельный па́лец (пра́вой руки́); **~-happy** *adj.* (*coll.*) стреля́ющий без разбо́ра.

trigonometrical /ˌtrɪgənəˈmetrɪk(ə)l/ *adj.* тригонометри́ческий.

trigonometry /ˌtrɪgəˈnɒmɪtrɪ/ *n.* тригономе́трия.

trilateral /traɪˈlætər(ə)l/ *adj.* трёхсторо́нний.

trilby /ˈtrɪlbɪ/ *n.* (*Br.*) мя́гкая фе́тровая шля́па.

trill /trɪl/ *n.* трель.
● *v.i.*: **the birds were ~ing** пти́цы залива́лись тре́лью.

trillion /ˈtrɪljən/ *n.* (*pl.* **~s** *or, with numeral or qualifying word,* **~**) (10^{18}) квинтильо́н; (*US,* 10^{12}) триллио́н.

trilogy /ˈtrɪlədʒɪ/ *n.* трило́гия.

trim /trɪm/ *n.* **1** (*order, fitness*) поря́док; состоя́ние гото́вности; **everything was in good ~** всё бы́ло в образцо́вом поря́дке; **we must get into ~ before the race** нам ну́жно войти́ в фо́рму пе́ред соревнова́нием.
2 (*light cut*) подре́зка, стри́жка; **your hair needs a ~** вам ну́жно подровня́ть во́лосы; **I must give the lawn a ~** на́до подстри́чь газо́н.
● *adj.* (**trimmer, trimmest**) аккура́тный, опря́тный; **she has a ~ figure** у неё стро́йная фигу́ра.
● *v.t.* (**trimmed, trimming**) **1** (*cut back to desired shape or size*) подр|еза́ть, -е́зать; подр|а́внивать, -овня́ть; **he was ~ming the hedge** он подра́внивал и́згородь.
2 (*decorate*) отде́л|ывать, -ать; **a hat ~med with fur** ша́пка, отде́ланная ме́хом.
3 (*adjust balance or setting of*) уравнове́|шивать -сить; разме|ща́ть, -сти́ть балла́ст + *g.*; **they ~med the sails** они́ поста́вили паруса́ по ве́тру; **he ~med his sails to the wind** (*fig.*) он держа́л нос по ве́тру.
● *with advs.*: **~ away, ~ off** *vv.t.* подстр|ига́ть, -и́чь; подре́з|ывать (*or* подреза́ть), -ать.

trimaran /ˈtraɪməˌræn/ *n.* (*naut.*) тримара́н, трёхко́рпусное су́дно.

trimming /ˈtrɪmɪŋ/ *n.* (*on dress etc.*) отде́лка; (*coll., accessory*) гарни́р, припра́ва; **roast duck and all the ~s** жа́реная у́тка с гарни́ром.

Trinidad and Tobago /ˈtrɪnɪˌdæd ənd təˈbeɪgəʊ/ *n.* Тринида́д и Toба́го.

trinitrotoluene /traɪˌnaɪtrəˈtɒljʊˌiːn/ = **TNT**

trinity /ˈtrɪnɪtɪ/ *n.* Тро́ица; **T~ Sunday** день Свято́й Тро́ицы.

trinket /ˈtrɪŋkɪt/ *n.* безделу́шка; (*on bracelet, key-ring*) брело́к.

trio /ˈtriːəʊ/ *n.* (*pl.* **trios**) (*group of three*) тро́йка; (*mus.*) три́о (*indecl.*).

trip /trɪp/ *n.* **1** (*excursion*) пое́здка; (*longer one*) путеше́ствие; **he has gone on a ~ to Paris** он пое́хал (ненадо́лго) в Пари́ж; **the round ~ costs £10** пое́здка в о́ба конца́ сто́ит 10 фу́нтов; (*coll., psychedelic experience*) глюк.
2 (*stumble*) спотыка́ние.
● *v.t.* (**tripped, tripping**) **1** (*cause to stumble; also* **~ up**) ста́вить, по- подно́жку + *d.*; (*fig.*) запу́т|ывать, -ать, сби|ва́ть, -ть с то́лку; **counsel tried to ~ the witness up** адвока́т пыта́лся сбить свиде́теля с то́лку.
2 (*release from catch*) расцеп|ля́ть, -и́ть; выключа́ть, вы́ключить.
● *v.i.* (**tripped, tripping**) **1** (*run or dance lightly*) пританцо́вывать (*impf.*) вприпля́ску; **she came ~ping down the stairs** она́ легко́ сбежа́ла вниз по ле́стнице.
2 (*stumble; also* **~ up**) спот|ыка́ться, -кну́ться; **he ~ped over the rug** он споткну́лся о ковёр; (*fig., commit error*) оши́б|а́ться, -и́ться.
● *cpds.* **~-hammer** *n.* па́дающий мо́лот; **~-wire** *n.* ми́нная про́волока; «спотыка́ч».

tripartite /traɪˈpɑːtaɪt/ *adj.* трёхсторо́нний.

tripe /traɪp/ *n.* (*offal*) требуха́; (*coll., rubbish*) чепуха́, вздор.

triple /ˈtrɪp(ə)l/ *adj.* тройно́й, утро́енный; **~ jump** (*sport*) тройно́й прыжо́к; **~ time** (*mus.*) трёхдо́льный разме́р.
● *v.t. & i.* утр|а́ивать(ся), -о́ить(ся).

triplet /ˈtrɪplɪt/ *n.* **1** (*set of three*) тро́йка. **2** (*one of three children born together*) тройня́шка; **~s** (*children*) тро́йня (*sg.*). **3** (*mus.*) трио́ль.

triplicate /ˈtrɪplɪkət/ *n.*: **in ~** в трёх экземпля́рах.

tripod /ˈtraɪpɒd/ *n.* трено́га, трено́жник.

Tripoli /ˈtrɪpəlɪ/ *n.* Три́поли.

tripper /ˈtrɪpə(r)/ *n.* (*Br.*) экскурса́нт (*fem.* -ка).

triptych /ˈtrɪptɪk/ *n.* три́птих.

trite /traɪt/ *adj.* бана́льный, изби́тый.

triteness /ˈtraɪtnɪs/ *n.* бана́льность.

triumph /ˈtraɪəmf/, /-ʌmf/ *n.* (*joy at success*) торжество́; (*victory, success*) триу́мф; **they came home in ~** они́ верну́лись с побе́дой.
● *v.i.* **1** (*be victorious*) побе|жда́ть, -ди́ть; восторжествова́ть (*pf.*); **justice will ~ in the end** в конце́ концо́в справедли́вость восторжеству́ет; **he ~ed over adversity** он преодоле́л все невзго́ды. **2** (*exult*) ликова́ть (*impf.*); торжествова́ть (*impf.*); **he ~ed in his enemy's defeat** он ликова́л/торжествова́л по слу́чаю пораже́ния врага́.

triumphal /traɪˈʌmf(ə)l/ *adj.* триумфа́льный.

triumphant /traɪˈʌmf(ə)nt/ *adj.* (*victorious*) победоно́сный; (*exultant*) торжеству́ющий, лику́ющий.

triumvir /ˈtraɪəmvɪə(r)/, /-ˈʌmvə(r)/ *n.* (*pl.* **~s** *or* **~i**) триумви́р.

triumvirate /traɪˈʌmvɪrət/ *n.* триумвира́т.

triumviri /ˈtraɪəmˌvɪəraɪ/, /traɪˈʌmvəˌraɪ/ *pl. of* ⇒**triumvir**

trivet /ˈtrɪvɪt/ *n.* (*tripod*) подста́вка; (*bracket*) тага́н.

trivia /ˈtrɪvɪə/ *n.* ме́лочи (*f. pl.*).

trivial /ˈtrɪvɪəl/ *adj.* (*trifling*) ме́лкий, незначи́тельный; (*commonplace, everyday*) обы́денный; (*shallow, artificial*) тривиа́льный, пове́рхностный.

triviality /ˌtrɪvɪˈælɪtɪ/ *n.* незначи́тельность, тривиа́льность.

trivialize /ˈtrɪvɪəˌlaɪz/ *v.t.* оп|ошля́ть, -о́шлить.

trochaic /trəˈkeɪɪk/ *adj.* трохеи́ческий.

trochee /ˈtrəʊkiː/, /-kɪ/ *n.* хоре́й, трохе́й.

trod /trɒd/ *past and p.p. of* ⇒**tread**

trodden /ˈtrɒd(ə)n/ *p.p. of* ⇒**tread**

troglodyte /ˈtrɒgləˌdaɪt/ *n.* троглоди́т.

troglodytic /ˌtrɒgləˈdɪtɪk/ *adj.* троглоди́тский.

troika /ˈtrɔɪkə/ *n.* тро́йка.

Trojan /ˈtrəʊdʒ(ə)n/ *n.* троя́н|ец (*fem.* -ка); (*fig.*): **he worked like a ~** он до́блестно труди́лся; он рабо́тал как вол.

● *adj.* троя́нский; **~ horse** (*fig.*) троя́нский конь.

troll /trəʊl/ *n.* (*myth.*) тролль (*m.*).

trolley /ˈtrɒlɪ/ *n.* (*pl.* **~s**) (*Br., for luggage, purchases*) теле́жка; (*Br., table on wheels*) сто́лик на колёсиках; (*Br., rail-car*) дрези́на; (*US, street-car*) трамва́й; **off one's ~** (*coll.*) с приве́том.

● *cpds.* **~-bus** *n.* тролле́йбус; **~-car** *n.* (*US*) трамва́й.

trollop /ˈtrɒləp/ *n.* (*slattern*) неря́ха; (*prostitute*) шлю́ха.

trombone /trɒmˈbəʊn/ *n.* тромбо́н.

trombonist /trɒmˈbəʊnɪst/ *n.* тромбони́ст.

troop /truːp/ *n.* **1** (*assembled group of persons*) отря́д. **2** (*mil. unit*) батаре́я; ро́та. **3** (*pl., soldiers*) войск|а́ (*pl., g.* —).

● *v.t.*: **~ing the colour** (*Br.*) церемо́ния вы́носа зна́мени.

● *v.i.* дви́|гаться, -нуться толпо́й; **the children ~ed out of school** де́ти стро́ем вы́шли из шко́лы.

● *cpds.* **~-carrier** *n.* (*mil.*) транспортёр; (*aeron.*) тра́нспортно-деса́нтный самолёт; **~ship** *n.* тра́нспорт для перево́зки войск.

trooper /ˈtruːpə(r)/ *n.* **1** (*soldier*) (*in cavalry*) кавалери́ст; (*in armoured unit*) танки́ст; **he swore like a ~** он руга́лся как изво́зчик. **2** (*US, policeman*) полице́йский.

trophy /ˈtrəʊfɪ/ *n.* трофе́й; (*prize, also*) приз.

tropic /ˈtrɒpɪk/ *n.* тро́пик; **T~ of Cancer** тро́пик Ра́ка; **T~ of Capricorn** тро́пик Козеро́га; **in the ~s** в тро́пиках.

tropical /ˈtrɒpɪk(ə)l/ *adj.* тропи́ческий.

troposphere /ˈtrɒpəˌsfɪə(r)/, /ˈtrəʊ-/ *n.* тропосфе́ра.

trot /trɒt/ *n.* **1** (*gait, pace*) рысь; **at a gentle ~** лёгкой ры́сью; (*fig.*) **I have been on the ~ all day** (*moving about*) я це́лый день был на нога́х; **on the ~** (*Br.*) подря́д.
2 (*run or ride at this pace*) прогу́лка, пробе́жка; **she took her horse for a ~** она́ вы́вела ло́шадь на вы́ездку.

● *v.t.* (**trotted, trotting**) (*exercise*) выгу́ливать (*impf.*); прогу́ливать (*impf.*); **he ~ted his horse in the park** он прогу́ливал ло́шадь в па́рке.

● *v.i.* (**trotted, trotting**) (*of a horse*) идти́ (*det.*) ры́сью; (*of person*) семени́ть (*impf.*); **he ~ted after his wife** он семени́л за жено́й.

● *with advs.* **~ along, ~ off** *vv.i.* (*coll.*) отпр|авля́ться, -а́виться; **I must be ~ting off home** мне пора́ (отправля́ться) домо́й; **~ out** *v.t.* (*coll.*): **he ~ted out the usual excuses** он, как всегда́, вы́ставил ма́ссу отгово́рок.

troth /trəʊθ/ *n.* (*loyalty*) ве́рность; **plight/pledge one's ~** кля́сться, по- в ве́рности.

Trotskyism /ˈtrɒtskɪˌɪz(ə)m/ *n.* троцки́зм.

Trotsky|ist /ˈtrɒtskɪɪst/, **-ite** /ˈtrɒtskɪaɪt/ *nn.* троцки́ст (*fem.* -ка).

trotter /ˈtrɒtə(r)/ *n.* (*horse*) рыси́стая ло́шадь; (*animal's foot*) но́жка; **pig's ~s** свины́е но́жки.

troubadour /ˈtruːbəˌdɔː(r)/ *n.* трубаду́р.

trouble /ˈtrʌb(ə)l/ *n.* **1** (*grief, anxiety*) волне́ние, трево́га; беспоко́йство; (*misfortune, affliction*) го́ре, беда́, несча́стье; **his ~s are over** тепе́рь все его́ несча́стья позади́; **there is ~ brewing** быть беде́.
2 (*difficulties*) хло́п|оты (*pl., g.* -о́т), тру́дности (*f. pl.*); (*difficulty*) затрудне́ние; **money ~s** де́нежные затрудне́ния; **I am having ~ with the car** у меня́ непола́дки (*f. pl.*) с маши́ной; **don't make ~ for me** не создава́йте мне ли́шних тру́дностей; **what's the ~?** в чём де́ло?; **the ~ is (that) ...** беда́ в том, что. . .; **that's the ~** вот в чём беда́; **without any ~** легко́, без труда́; **the ~ with him is that ...** его́ беда́/недоста́ток в том, что. . ..
3 (*predicament*) неприя́тность; **he's always getting into ~** он ве́чно попада́ет в исто́рии; **he is in ~ with the police** у него́ неприя́тности с поли́цией; **his brother got him into ~** брат вовлёк его́ в беду́/неприя́тности; **ask for ~** лезть (*det.*) на рожо́н; **that's asking for ~** так то́лько нарвёшься на неприя́тности; **he got her into ~** (*pregnant*) она́ от него́ забере́менела.
4 (*inconvenience*): **I don't want to put you to any ~** я не хочу́ вас затрудня́ть; **he saved me the ~** он изба́вил меня́ от э́той необходи́мости.
5 (*disorder, mess*) неуря́дица.
6 (*pains, care, effort*) забо́та, труд, хло́п|оты (*pl., g.* -о́т); **she took a lot of ~ over the cake** она́ приложи́ла мно́го стара́ний, что́бы пригото́вить э́тот пиро́г; **he didn't even take the ~ to write** он да́же не потруди́лся написа́ть; **thank you for all your ~** спаси́бо за все ва́ши хло́поты; **it is not worth the ~** не сто́ит хлопо́т.
7 (*disease, ailment*) неду́г, боле́знь; **he has heart ~** у него́ больно́е се́рдце.
8 (*unrest, civil commotion*) волне́ния (*nt. pl.*); беспоря́дки (*m. pl.*); **~ spot** горя́чая то́чка.

● *v.t.* **1** (*agitate, disturb, worry*) трево́жить (*impf.*); волнова́ть (*impf.*); **he was ~d about money** он волнова́лся из-за́ де́нег; **don't let it ~ you** не принима́йте э́то бли́зко к се́рдцу; **~d times** сму́тные времена́.
2 (*afflict*) беспоко́ить (*impf.*); му́чить (*impf.*); **he is ~d with a cough** его́ му́чит ка́шель; **my back ~s me** у меня́ боли́т спина́.
3 (*put to inconvenience*) беспоко́ить, по-, затрудн|я́ть, -и́ть; **may I ~ you for a match?** мо́жно попроси́ть у вас спи́чку?; **don't ~ yourself** не беспоко́йтесь; **sorry to ~ you!** прости́те за беспоко́йство!

● *v.i.* труди́ться (*impf.*); беспоко́иться (*impf.*); **don't ~ about that** не беспоко́йтесь об э́том; **don't ~ to come and meet me** не труди́тесь встреча́ть меня́.

● *cpds.* **~-free** *adj.* (*reliable*) надёжный, безотка́зный; **~-maker** *n.* скло́чни|к (*fem.* -ца); (*instigator of ~*) смутья́н (*fem.* -ка); **~-shooter** *n.* ремо́нтник; (*fig.*) уполномо́ченный по ула́живанию конфли́ктов.

troublesome /ˈtrʌb(ə)lsəm/ *adj.* тру́дный; хло́потный; **a ~ child** тру́дный ребёнок; **a ~ cough** мучи́тельный ка́шель.

trough /trɒf/ *n.* **1** (*for animals*) коры́то, корму́шка; (*for water*) жёлоб, лото́к.
2 (*meteor.*) фронт ни́зкого давле́ния.
3 (*between waves*) подо́шва волны́.

trounce /traʊns/ *v.t.* (*thrash*) поро́ть, вы́-; сечь, вы́-; (*defeat*) разб|ива́ть, -и́ть.

troupe /truːp/ *n.* тру́ппа.

trouper /ˈtruːpə(r)/ *n.* о́пытный акте́р, о́пытная актри́са; (*fig.*) добросо́вестный челове́к.

trouser|s /ˈtraʊzəz/ *n.* штан|ы́ (*pl., g.* -о́в), брю́ки (*pl., g.* —); **a pair of ~s** па́ра брюк; **his wife wears the ~s** (*fig.*) его́ жена́ заправля́ет всем в до́ме.

● *cpds.* **~-leg** *n.* штани́на; **~ press** *n.* глади́льный пресс для брюк; **~-suit** *n.* (*Br.*) брю́чный костю́м.

trousseau /ˈtruːsəʊ/ *n.* (*pl.* **~s** *or* **~x** /-səʊz/) прида́ное.

trout /traʊt/ *n.* (*pl.* **~** *or* **~s**) (*fish*) форе́ль.

trowel /ˈtraʊəl/ *n.* (*for bricklaying etc.*) мастеро́к; (*for gardening*) (садо́вый) сово́к, лопа́тка.

truancy /ˈtruːənsɪ/ *n.* прогу́л.

truant /ˈtruːənt/ *n.* прогу́льщик; **did you ever play ~?** вы когда́-нибудь прогу́ливали уро́ки?

truce /truːs/ *n.* переми́рие; (*respite*) переды́шка.

truck[1] /trʌk/ *n.* (*Br., railway wagon*) откры́тая грузова́я платфо́рма; (*lorry*) грузови́к; (*barrow*) теле́жка.

truck[2] /trʌk/ *n.* **1** (*barter*) ме́на; товарообме́н; **I'll have no ~ with him** (*fig.*) я не жела́ю име́ть с ним никаки́х дел. **2** (*US, market garden produce*) о́вощ|и (*pl., g.* -е́й).

trucker /ˈtrʌkə(r)/ *n.* води́тель (*m.*) грузовика́.

truckle /ˈtrʌk(ə)l/ *v.i.*: **~ to s.o.** раболе́пствовать (*impf.*) пе́ред кем-н.

truckle-bed /ˈtrʌk(ə)l/ *n.* (*Br.*) ни́зкая крова́ть на колёсиках.

truculence /ˈtrʌkjʊləns/ *n.* агресси́вность, драчли́вость.

truculent /ˈtrʌkjʊlənt/ *adj.* агресси́вный, драчли́вый.

trudge /trʌdʒ/ *n.* дли́нный/тру́дный путь.

● *v.i.* тащи́ться (*impf.*).

true /tru:/ *n.* (*alignment, adjustment*): **the wheel is out of ~** колесо́ пло́хо устано́влено.

● *adj.* (**truer, truest**) **1** (*in accordance with fact*) ве́рный, правди́вый; **a ~ story** правди́вый расска́з; **is it ~ that he is married?** э́то пра́вда, что он жена́т?; **all my dreams came ~** все мои́ мечты́ сбыли́сь/осуществи́лись; (*concessive*): **~, it will cost more** действи́тельно, э́то бу́дет сто́ить бо́льше.
2 (*in accordance with reason, principle, standard; genuine*) правди́вый; настоя́щий; и́стинный; **it is not a ~ comparison** э́то несправедли́вое сравне́ние; **the ~ price is much higher** действи́тельная/настоя́щая цена́ намно́го вы́ше.
3 (*conforming accurately*) ве́рный, пра́вильный; **~ to life** правди́вый; **~ to type** типи́чный, характе́рный.
4 (*loyal, faithful; dependable*) пре́данный, ве́рный; надёжный; **he was always a ~ friend to me** он был мне всегда́ ве́рным дру́гом; **he remained ~ to his word** он остава́лся ве́рным своему́ сло́ву.
5 (*mus., in tune*) ве́рный (*тон и т.п.*).
6 (*accurately adjusted or positioned*) то́чный, вы́веренный.

● *adv.* пра́вильно, ве́рно; **his story rings ~** его́ расска́з звучи́т убеди́тельно; **he aimed ~** он то́чно прице́лился.

● *cpds.* **~-blue** *adj.* ве́рный, сто́йкий; (*Br., pol.*) консервати́вный; **~-love** *n.* (*sweetheart*) возлю́бленн|ый, -ая.

truffle /ˈtrʌf(ə)l/ *n.* трю́фель (*m.*).

trug /trʌg/ *n.* (*Br.*) садо́вая корзи́нка.

truism /ˈtru:ɪz(ə)m/ *n.* трюи́зм; **it is a ~ that** общеизве́стно, что. . . .

truly /ˈtru:lɪ/ *adv.* **1** (*truthfully*) и́скренне; (*accurately*) правди́во.
2 (*loyally*) ве́рно. **3** (*sincerely*) и́скренне; **yours ~** (*at end of letter*) пре́данный Вам; (*coll., myself*) ваш поко́рный слуга́; **I am ~ grateful** я и́скренне благода́рен. **4** (*genuinely*) и́скренне; действи́тельно; **a ~ memorable occasion** пои́стине незабыва́емое собы́тие.

trump /trʌmp/ *n.* (**~ card**) ко́зырь (*m.*), козырна́я ка́рта; **hearts are ~s** че́рви — ко́зыри; (*fig.*): **he played his ~ card** он вы́ложил свой ко́зырь; **the weather turned up ~s** (*Br.*) нам (неожи́данно) повезло́ с пого́дой.

● *v.t.* бить, по- ко́зырем.

● *with adv.*: **~ up** *v.t.* фабрикова́ть, с-.

trumpery /ˈtrʌmpərɪ/ *n.* мишура́.

● *adj.* мишу́рный.

trumpet /ˈtrʌmpɪt/ *n.* **1** (*instrument*) труба́; **blow one's own ~** (*fig.*) хвали́ться (*impf.*). **2** (*object so shaped*) тру́бка; **ear-~** слухова́я тру́бка; (*of flower*) тру́бчатый ве́нчик.

● *v.t. & i.* (**trumpeted, trumpeting**) **1** (*proclaim*) труби́ть, про-; **his praises were ~ed abroad** его́ повсю́ду восхваля́ли. **2** (*of an elephant*) реве́ть, про-.

trumpeter /ˈtrʌmpɪtə(r)/ *n.* труба́ч.

truncate /trʌŋˈkeɪt/, /ˈtrʌŋ-/ *v.t.* ус|ека́ть, -е́чь; **a ~d cone** усечённый ко́нус; **his speech was ~d** его́ речь уре́зали.

truncheon /ˈtrʌntʃ(ə)n/ *n.* (*Br.*) (полице́йская) дуби́нка.

trundle /ˈtrʌnd(ə)l/ *v.t. & i.* кати́ть(ся) (*impf.*).

trunk /trʌŋk/ *n.* **1** (*of tree*) ствол. **2** (*of body*) ту́ловище. **3** (*box*) сунду́к. **4** (*of elephant*) хо́бот. **5** (*pl., garment*) трус|ы́ (*pl., g.* -о́в); (*for swimming*) пла́в|ки (*pl., g.* -ок). **6** (*US, boot of car*) бага́жник.

● *cpds.* **~-call** *n.* (*Br.*) междугоро́дный звоно́к; **~-line** *n.* (*rail.*) магистра́ль; (*teleph.*) междугоро́дная связь; **~-road** *n.* (*Br.*) магистра́льная доро́га, магистра́ль.

truss /trʌs/ *n.* **1** (*structural support*) фе́рма. **2** (*surgical support*) грыжево́й банда́ж. **3** (*Br., of hay*) пук, свя́зка.

● *v.t.* **1** (*support*) укреп|ля́ть, -и́ть; свя́з|ывать, -а́ть. **2** (*tie up; also* **~ up**) свя́з|ывать, -а́ть.

trust /trʌst/ *n.* **1** (*firm belief; confidence*) дове́рие; ве́ра; **I place perfect ~ in him** я доверя́ю ему́ по́лностью; **he takes everything on ~** он всё принима́ет на ве́ру.
2 (*credit*) креди́т; **goods supplied on ~** това́ры, предоста́вленные в креди́т.
3 (*responsibility*) отве́тственность; **a position of ~** отве́тственный пост.
4 (*leg.*) довери́тельная со́бственность; **property held in ~** иму́щество, управля́емое по дове́ренности; **~ fund** целево́й фонд.
5 (*association of companies*) трест; **~ territory** (*UN*) подопе́чная террито́рия.

● *v.t.* **1** (*have confidence in, rely on*) дов|еря́ть, -е́рить +*d.*; **he is not to be ~ed** ему́ нельзя́ доверя́ть; **I wouldn't ~ him with my money** я бы ему́ свои́х де́нег не дове́рил; **he can be ~ed to do a good job** мо́жно быть уве́ренным, что он хорошо́ спра́вится с рабо́той; **~ him to make a mistake!** он, как всегда́, оши́бся!
2 (*entrust*) вв|еря́ть, -е́рить.
3 (*earnestly hope*) наде́яться (*impf.*); полага́ть (*impf.*).

● *v.i.* **1** (*have faith, confidence*) дов|еря́ться, -е́риться (**in**: +*d.*); **she ~ed in God** она́ отдала́сь на во́лю Бо́жью.
2 (*commit o.s. with confidence*) дов|еря́ться, -е́риться (**to**: +*d.*); наде́яться (*impf.*) (**to**: на+*a.*); **he ~ed to luck** он дове́рился уда́че.

trustee /trʌsˈti:/ *n.* довери́тельный со́бственник; опеку́н.

trusteeship /trʌsˈti:ʃɪp/ *n.* опе́ка, попечи́тельство.

trustful /ˈtrʌstfʊl/ *adj.* дове́рчивый.

trustfulness /ˈtrʌstfʊlnɪs/ *n.* дове́рчивость.

trusting /ˈtrʌstɪŋ/ *adj.* дове́рчивый; наи́вный.

trustworthiness /ˈtrʌstˌwɜ:ðɪnɪs/ *n.* надёжность.

trustworthy /ˈtrʌstˌwɜ:ðɪ/ *adj.* надёжный.

trusty /ˈtrʌstɪ/ *adj.* (**trustier, trustiest**) ве́рный, надёжный.

truth /tru:θ/ *n.* пра́вда; (*verity, true saying*) и́стина; **the ~ is; to tell the ~** по пра́вде сказа́ть; **there's not a word of ~ in it** в э́том нет ни сло́ва пра́вды; **in ~** в са́мом де́ле.

truthful /ˈtru:θfʊl/ *adj.* (*of person*) правди́вый; (*of statement etc.*) правди́вый, ве́рный, то́чный.

truthfulness /ˈtru:θfʊlnɪs/ *n.* правди́вость; ве́рность, то́чность.

try /traɪ/ *n.* **1** (*attempt*) попы́тка; **he made several tries, but failed** он сде́лал не́сколько попы́ток, но все оказа́лись неуда́чными.
2 (*test*) испыта́ние; про́ба; **why not give it a ~?** почему́ бы не попро́бовать?
3 (*Rugby football*) прохо́д с мячо́м.

● *v.t.* **1** (*attempt*) пыта́ться, по-; стара́ться, по-; **he tried his best** он стара́лся изо всех сил; **he tried hard** он о́чень стара́лся.
2 (*sample*) про́бовать, по-; (*taste*) отве́д|ывать, -ать; (*experiment with, assay*) **have you tried aspirin?** вы про́бовали аспири́н?
3 (*leg.*) (*a person*) суди́ть (*impf.*); **he was tried for murder** его́ суди́ли за уби́йство; **the judge tried the case** судья́ вёл проце́сс.
4 (*subject to strain*) утом|ля́ть, -и́ть; раздража́ть (*impf.*); му́чить (*impf.*); **he tries my patience** он испы́тывает моё терпе́ние; **a ~ing situation** тру́дное положе́ние.
5 (*test*) испы́т|ывать, -а́ть; пров|еря́ть, -е́рить; подв|ерга́ть, -е́ргнуть испыта́нию; **I shall ~ my luck again** я ещё раз попыта́ю сча́стья; **a tried remedy** испы́танное сре́дство.

● *v.i.*: **~ harder next time!** в сле́дующий раз приложи́те бо́льше уси́лий!; **I tried for a prize** я добива́лся при́за; я претендова́л на приз.

● *with advs.*: **~ on** *v.t.* прим|еря́ть, -е́рить; **she tried on several dresses** она́ приме́рила не́сколько пла́тьев; (*Br. fig.*): **it's no use ~ing it on with me** со мной э́тот но́мер не пройдёт (*coll.*); **~ out** *v.t.* испы́т|ывать, -а́ть; опро́бовать (*pf.*); **he tried out the idea on his friends** он подели́лся свои́м за́мыслом с друзья́ми, что́бы узна́ть их реа́кцию; *v.i.*: **~ out for a team** (*US*) уча́ствовать (*impf.*) в отбо́рочных соревнова́ниях.

● *cpds.* **~-out** *n.* прове́рка, про́ба; (*sport*) отбо́рочное соревнова́ние; **~-square** *n.* уго́льник.

tryst /trɪst/ *n.* назна́ченная встре́ча, свида́ние.

tsar, tzar /zɑ:(r)/ *n.* царь (*m.*).

tsarina, tzarina /zɑ:ˈri:nə/ *n.* цари́ца.

tsarism /ˈzɑ:rɪz(ə)m/ *n.* цари́зм.

tsarist /ˈzɑ:rɪst/ *adj.* ца́рский.

tsetse(-fly) /ˈtsetsɪ/, /ˈtetsɪ/ *n.* му́ха цеце́ (*indecl.*).

tub /tʌb/ *n.* **1** коры́то, ка́дка. **2** (*bath*) ва́нна. **3** (*of margarine*) упако́вка; (*of ice-cream, yoghurt*) стака́нчик. **4** (*coll., old boat*) ста́рая кало́ша, ста́рое коры́то.

● *cpd.* **~-thumper** *n.* говору́н.

tuba /'tju:bə/ *n.* (*pl.* **tubas**) ту́ба.

tubby /'tʌbɪ/ *adj.* (**tubbier, tubbiest**) (*of person*) коротконо́гий и то́лстый.

tube /tju:b/ *n.* **1** (*of metal, glass etc.*) труба́, тру́бка; (**test-~**) проби́рка. **2** (*of paint, toothpaste etc.*) тю́бик. **3** (*inner ~ of tyre*) ка́мера (ши́ны). **4** (*organ of body*) труба́; **bronchial ~s** бронхио́лы. **5** (*Br. coll., underground railway*) метро́ (*indecl.*); **travel by ~** е́хать (*det.*) на метро́.

● *cpd.* **~-station** *n.* ста́нция метро́.

tuber /'tju:bə(r)/ *n.* (*bot.*) клу́бень (*m.*).

tubercle /'tju:bək(ə)l/ *n.* ме́лкий клу́бень; тубе́ркул.

tubercular /tjʊ'bɜ:kjʊlə(r)/ *adj.* туберкулёзный.

tuberculosis /tjʊˌbɜ:kjʊ'ləʊsɪs/ *n.* туберкулёз.

tuberose /'tju:bəˌrəʊs/ *n.* тубер́оза.

tubular /'tju:bjʊlə(r)/ *adj.* тру́бчатый.

TUC (*abbr. of* ***Trades Union Congress***) Брита́нский конгре́сс тред-юнио́нов.

tuck[1] /tʌk/ *n.* (*fold in garment*) скла́дка, сбо́рка.

● *v.t.* (*stow*) пря́тать, с-; под|бира́ть, -обра́ть (под себя́); **he ~ed his legs under the table** он спря́тал но́ги под стол.

● *with advs.*: **~ away** *v.t.* запря́т|ывать, -ать; **~ in** *v.t.* запр|авля́ть, -а́вить; **~ your shirt in** запра́вьте руба́шку; **~ up** *v.t.* под|гиба́ть, -огну́ть; под|вёртывать, -верну́ть; **he ~ed up his shirt sleeves** он засучи́л рукава́; **she ~ed up her skirt** она́ подобрала́ ю́бку; **they ~ed the children up (in bed)** дете́й уложи́ли в крова́ть (и подоткну́ли одея́ло).

tuck[2] /tʌk/ *n.* (*Br. coll., eatables*) сла́сти (*f. pl.*).

● *v.i.*: **they ~ed into their supper** они́ уплета́ли у́жин за о́бе щеки́; **~ in!** нава́ливайтесь!

● *cpd.* **~-shop** *n.* конди́терская.

tucker /'tʌkə(r)/ *n.*: **he was wearing his best bib and ~** (*joc.*) он был оде́т в выходно́й костю́м.

Tudor /'tju:də(r)/ *n.* представи́тель (*fem.* -ница) дина́стии Тюдо́ров.

● *adj.* эпо́хи Тюдо́ров; (*archit.*) позднеготи́ческий.

Tuesday /'tju:zdeɪ/, /-dɪ/ *n.* вто́рник.

tuffet /'tʌfɪt/ *n.* бугоро́к.

tuft /tʌft/ *n.* (*of grass, hair etc.*) пучо́к.

tufted /'tʌftɪd/ *adj.* (*of bird, pred.*) с хохолко́м.

tug /tʌg/ *n.* **1** (*pull*) рыво́к, дёрганье; **he gave a ~ at the rope** он дёрнул за верёвку. **2** (*boat*) букси́р.

● *v.t.* (**tugged, tugging**) тащи́ть (*impf.*); тяну́ть (*impf.*); **the dogs ~ged a sledge** соба́ки тяну́ли/тащи́ли са́ни.

● *v.i.* (**tugged, tugging**) дёр|гать, -нуть; **he ~ged at my sleeve** он дёрнул меня́ за рука́в.

● *cpd.* **~-of-war** *n.* перетя́гивание кана́та.

tuition /tju:'ɪʃ(ə)n/ *n.* обуче́ние.

tulip /'tju:lɪp/ *n.* тюльпа́н.

tulle /tju:l/ *n.* тюль (*m.*).

tum /tʌm/ = **tummy**

tumble /'tʌmb(ə)l/ *n.* **1** (*fall*) паде́ние; **take a ~** упа́сть (*pf.*). **2** (*acrobatic feat*) кувыро́к.

● *v.t.* (*cause to fall; fling*) бр|оса́ть, -о́сить; опроки́|дывать, -нуть; **we were all ~d out of the bus** нас вы́бросило из авто́буса.

● *v.i.* **1** (*fall*) сва́ливаться, свали́ться; ска́тываться, скати́ться; **the child ~d downstairs** ребёнок скати́лся с ле́стницы; **he ~d into bed** он повали́лся в крова́ть. **2** (*fig.*): **I ~d to his meaning** до меня́ дошло́, что он име́л в виду́.

● *with advs.*: **the puppies ~d about on the floor** щеня́та кувырка́лись на полу́; **the house seemed about to ~ down** дом, каза́лось, вот-во́т разва́лится.

● *cpds.* **~down** *adj.* развали́вшийся; полуразру́шенный; **~-drier** *n.* электри́ческая суши́лка для белья́; **~weed** *n.* перекати́-по́ле.

tumbler /'tʌmblə(r)/ *n.* **1** (*drinking-vessel*) стака́н. **2** (*mechanism*) реверси́вный механи́зм; **~ switch** ту́мблер. **3** (*acrobat*) акроба́т. **4** (*pigeon*) ту́рман.

tumescence /tjʊ'mes(ə)ns/ *n.* опуха́ние, распуха́ние.

tumescent /tjʊ'mes(ə)nt/ *adj.* опуха́ющий, распуха́ющий.

tumid /'tju:mɪd/ *adj.* распу́хший; (*fig.*) напы́щенный.

tumidity /ˌtju:'mɪdɪtɪ/ *n.* распуха́ние; (*fig.*) напы́щенность.

tummy /'tʌmɪ/ *n.* (*coll.*) живо́т; (*dim., e.g. baby's*) живо́тик.

● *cpds.* **~-ache** *n.* боль в животе́; **~-button** *n.* (*Br.*) пупо́к.

tumour /'tju:mə(r)/ (*US* **tumor**) *n.* о́пухоль.

tumuli /'tju:mjʊˌlaɪ/, /-ˌli:/ *pl. of* **⇒tumulus**

tumult /'tju:mʌlt/ *n.* шум; сумато́ха; (*fig.*) си́льное волне́ние.

tumultuous /tjʊ'mʌltjʊəs/ *adj.* шу́мный, беспоко́йный; **he received a ~ welcome** ему́ устро́или бу́рную встре́чу.

tumul|us /'tju:mjʊləs/ *n.* (*pl.* **~i**) моги́льный холм/курга́н.

tuna /'tju:nə/ *n.* (*pl.* **~** *or* **~s**) (голубо́й) туне́ц.

tundra /'tʌndrə/ *n.* ту́ндра.

tune /tju:n/ *n.* **1** (*melody*) мело́дия; моти́в; **the ~ goes like this** моти́в тако́й; (*fig.*) тон; **he will soon change his ~** он ско́ро запоёт ина́че; **I paid up, to the ~ of £30** я заплати́л це́лых 30 фу́нтов. **2** (*correct pitch; consonance*) строй; настро́енность; **you are not singing in ~** вы фальши́вите; **he plays out of ~** он игра́ет фальши́во; **the piano is out of ~** фортепья́но расстро́ено; (*fig.*) согла́сие; гармо́ния; **he felt in ~ with his surroundings** он ощуща́л гармо́нию с окружа́ющим ми́ром.

● *v.t.* **1** (*mus., bring to right pitch*) настр|а́ивать, -о́ить; **the instrument needs tuning** инструме́нт нужда́ется в настро́йке; **tuning-fork** камерто́н. **2** (*adjust running of*) настр|а́ивать, -о́ить; регули́ровать, от-; **the engine has been ~d** мото́р/дви́гатель был отрегули́рован.

● *with advs.*: **~ in** *v.t.* & *i.* настр|а́ивать(ся), -о́ить(ся); **the radio is not ~d in properly** приёмник пло́хо настро́ен; **~ in to the right wave-length** настр|а́иваться, -о́иться на ну́жную волну́; **he ~d in to the BBC** он настро́ил приёмник на Би-Би-Си́; **~ up** *v.t.* = **~** *v.t.* 1,2; **he ~d up his guitar** он настро́ил гита́ру; *v.i.*: **the musicians were tuning up** музыка́нты настра́ивали инструме́нты.

● *cpd.* **~-up** *n.* (*mus.*) настро́йка; (*of engine*) регулиро́вка.

tuneful /'tju:nfʊl/ *adj.* музыка́льный, мелоди́чный.

tunefulness /'tju:nfʊlnɪs/ *n.* музыка́льность, мелоди́чность.

tuneless /'tju:nlɪs/ *adj.* немузыка́льный, немелоди́чный.

tunelessness /'tju:nlɪsnɪs/ *n.* немузыка́льность, немелоди́чность.

tuner /'tju:nə(r)/ *n.* (*of pianos etc.*) настро́йщик; (*device for tuning guitar etc.*) устро́йство настро́йки; (*radio component*) блок настро́йки, тю́нер; (*receiver*) (радио)приёмник.

tungsten /'tʌŋst(ə)n/ *n.* вольфра́м; (*attr.*) вольфра́мовый.

tunic /'tju:nɪk/ *n.* (*ancient garment*) туни́ка; (*woman's blouse*) блу́зка, со́бранная в та́лии; (*part of uniform*) ки́тель (*m.*).

tuning /'tju:nɪŋ/ *n.* настро́йка, регулиро́вка.

Tunis /'tju:nɪs/ *n.* Туни́с.

Tunisia /tju:'nɪzɪə/ *n.* Туни́с.

Tunisian /tju:'nɪzɪən/ *n.* туни́с|ец (*fem.* -ка).

● *adj.* туни́сский.

tunnel /'tʌn(ə)l/ *n.* тонне́ль (*m.*), тунне́ль (*m.*).

● *v.t.* (**tunnelled, tunnelling;** *US* **tunneled, tunneling**): **they ~led their way out (of prison)** они́ сде́лали подко́п и сбежа́ли.

● *v.i.* (**tunnelled, tunnelling;** *US* **tunneled, tunneling**) про|кла́дывать, -ложи́ть тонне́ль; **they had to ~ through solid rock** им пришло́сь вести́ прохо́дку тонне́ля в твёрдой поро́де.

tunny(-fish) /'tʌnɪ/ *n.* (*pl.* **~** *or* **tunnies**) туне́ц.

tuppence /'tʌpəns/ *n.* (*Br. coll.*) два пе́нса; **I don't care ~** мне наплева́ть (*coll.*).

tuppenny /ˈtʌpənɪ/ *adj.* (*Br. coll.*) двухпе́нсовый.
● *cpd.* **~-ha'penny** *adj.* (*fig.*) грошо́вый, ничто́жный.

turban /ˈtɜːbən/ *n.* тюрба́н; (*for men only*) чалма́.

turbid /ˈtɜːbɪd/ *adj.* му́тный; (*fig.*) тума́нный.

turbid|ity /tɜːˈbɪdɪtɪ/ *n.* му́тность; (*fig.*) тума́нность.

turbine /ˈtɜːbaɪn/ *n.* турби́на.

turbo-jet /ˈtɜːbəʊˌdʒet/ *n.* турбореакти́вный самолёт.

turbo-prop /ˈtɜːbəʊˌprɒp/ *n.* турбовинтово́й самолёт.

turbot /ˈtɜːbət/ *n.* (*pl.* **~** *or* **~s**) белоко́рый па́лтус.

turbulence /ˈtɜːbjʊləns/ *n.* бу́рность; (*aeron.*) турбуле́нтность; (*fig.*) сует́а, сумато́ха.

turbulent /ˈtɜːbjʊlənt/ *adj.* бу́рный; (*fig.*) беспоко́йный, неукроти́мый.

turd /tɜːd/ *n.* (*vulg.*) **1** (*lump of excrement*) кака́шка. **2** (*objectionable person*) подо́нок.

tureen /tjʊəˈriːn/, /tə-/ *n.* су́пница.

turf /tɜːf/ *n.* (*pl.* **turfs** *or* **turves**) **1** (*grassy topsoil*) дёрн; (*peat*) торф; **a cottage thatched with turves** до́мик под земляно́й кры́шей. **2** (*racing*): **a devotee of the ~** завсегда́тай бего́в; **~ accountant** (*Br.*) букме́кер.
● *v.t.* **1** (*cover with* **~**; *also* **~ over**) покр|ыва́ть, -ы́ть дёрном. **2**: **~ out** (*Br. coll., eject*) выбра́сывать, вы́бросить; вышвы́ривать, вы́швырнуть.

turgid /ˈtɜːdʒɪd/ *adj.* (*fig.*) напы́щенный.

turgidity /tɜːˈdʒɪdɪtɪ/ *n.* (*fig.*) напы́щенность.

Turk /tɜːk/ *n.* ту́р|ок (*fem.* -ча́нка).

Turkey /ˈtɜːkɪ/ *n.* **1** (*country*) Ту́рция. **2** (**t~**: *bird*) (*pl.* **~s**) инд|ю́к (*fem.* -е́йка); (*as food*) индю́шка, инде́йка; **cold t~** (*US coll.*) абстине́нтный синдро́м (*у наркоманов*); **talk ~** (*US coll.*) говори́ть (*impf.*) без обиняко́в.

Turkic /ˈtɜːkɪk/ *adj.* тю́ркский.

Turkish /ˈtɜːkɪʃ/ *n.* туре́цкий язы́к.
● *adj.* туре́цкий; **~ bath** туре́цкие ба́ни (*f. pl.*); **~ delight** раха́т-луку́м.

Turkmen /ˈtɜːkmən/ *n.* (*pl.* **~** *or* **~s**) (*person*) туркме́н (*fem.* -ка); (*language*) туркме́нский язы́к.
● *adj.* туркме́нский.

Turkmenistan /tɜːkˌmenɪˈstɑːn/ *n.* Туркмениста́н.

turmeric /ˈtɜːmərɪk/ *n.* курку́ма.

turmoil /ˈtɜːmɔɪl/ *n.* беспоря́док; смяте́ние.

turn /tɜːn/ *n.* **1** (*rotation*) поворо́т, оборо́т; **a ~ of the handle** поворо́т ру́чки; **the meat was done to a ~** мя́со бы́ло поджа́рено как раз в ме́ру. **2** (*change of direction*) поворо́т; **a ~ in the road** поворо́т доро́ги; **I took a right ~** я поверну́л напра́во; **he made an about ~ in policy** он сде́лал поворо́т на 180° в поли́тике; **at every ~** (*fig.*) на ка́ждом шагу́; **at the ~ of the century** в нача́ле ве́ка; на рубеже́ столе́тий. **3** (*change in condition*) переме́на; поворо́т; **his luck is on the ~** он вступа́ет в полосу́ везе́ния; **the ~ of the tide** (*lit.*) сме́на прили́вно-отли́вного тече́ния; (*fig.*) измене́ние форту́ны; **his condition took a ~ for the worse** его́ состоя́ние уху́дшилось. **4** (*opportunity of doing something in proper order*) о́чередь; **it's your ~ next** вы сле́дующий; **I missed my ~** я пропусти́л свою́ о́чередь; **she went hot and cold by ~s** её броса́ло то в жар, то в хо́лод; **they all spoke in ~** (*or* **took ~s to speak**) они́ выступа́ли/говори́ли по о́череди. **5** (*service*) услу́га; **he did me a good ~** он оказа́л мне до́брую услу́гу; **one good ~ deserves another** ≈ долг платежо́м кра́сен. **6** (*tendency, capability*): **he has a practical ~ of mind** он челове́к практи́ческого скла́да; **a witty ~ of phrase** остроу́мный оборо́т. **7** (*short spell*): **shall I take a ~ at the wheel?** дава́йте я сменю́ вас за рулём; **I'm going to take a ~ in the garden** пойду́ прогуля́юсь по са́ду. **8** (*short stage performance*) вы́ход; но́мер (програ́ммы); **the comedian did his ~** ко́мик испо́лнил свой но́мер; **star ~** гвоздь (*m.*) програ́ммы. **9** (*coll., nervous shock*) потрясе́ние; припа́док; **you gave me quite a ~** вы меня́ поря́дком испуга́ли; **she had one of her ~s** с ней случи́лся припа́док. **10** (*mus.*) группе́тто (*indecl.*).
● *v.t.* **1** (*cause to move round*) пов|ора́чивать, -ерну́ть; **he ~ed the key (in the lock)** он поверну́л ключ (в замке́); **he ~ed his head** он поверну́л го́лову; он оберну́лся; **he ~ed his back on me** он поверну́лся ко мне спино́й; **she ~ed the pages** она́ перелиста́ла страни́цы; **he ~ed the scale at 85 kilograms** он ве́сил 85 килогра́ммов. **2** (*direct*) напр|авля́ть, -а́вить; **they ~ed the hose on to the flames** шланг напра́вили на пла́мя; **I ~ed my mind to other things** я сосредото́чился на друго́м; **he can ~ his hand to anything** он всё уме́ет; он ма́стер на все ру́ки; **he ~ed a blind eye to her behaviour** (*Br.*), **behavior** (*US*) он закры́л глаза́ на её поведе́ние; **he ~ed a deaf ear to my request** он проигнори́ровал мою́ про́сьбу; (*adapt*): **he ~ed his skill to good use, account** он нашёл досто́йное примене́ние свои́м спосо́бностям; (*incline*): **~ s.o. against s.o./sth.** настр|а́ивать, -о́ить кого́-н. про́тив + *g.*; **the accident ~ed me against driving** ава́рия отби́ла у меня́ охо́ту води́ть маши́ну. **3** (*pass round or beyond*) пов|ора́чивать, -ерну́ть за + *a.*; **slow down as you ~ the corner** повора́чивая за́ угол сба́вьте ско́рость; **it has ~ed two o'clock** уже́ два часа́; **he has ~ed fifty** ему́ испо́лнилось 50 лет. **4** (*transform*) превра|ща́ть, -ти́ть; **he ~ed the water into wine** он обрати́л во́ду в вино́; **his joy was ~ed to sorrow** его́ ра́дость оберну́лась печа́лью; **he ~ed himself into an expert** он сде́лался специали́стом; **it's enough to ~ one's stomach** э́то вызыва́ет тошноту́; **success ~ed his head** успе́х вскружи́л ему́ го́лову. **5** (*cause to become*): **the shock ~ed his hair white** он поседе́л от потрясе́ния; **shall we ~ the dogs loose?** дава́йте спу́стим соба́к с це́пи! **6** (*reverse*) перев|ора́чивать, -ерну́ть; меня́ть, по- на противополо́жное; **the picture was ~ed upside down** карти́ну переверну́ли вверх нога́ми; **the room was ~ed upside down** (*ransacked*) ко́мнату переверну́ли вверх дном; **I ~ed the tables on him** (*fig.*) я отплати́л ему́ то́й же моне́той; **he did not ~ a hair** он и гла́зом не моргну́л. **7** (*send forcibly*) прог|оня́ть, -на́ть; **he was ~ed out of the house** его́ вы́гнали и́з дому (*or* из до́ма); (*deflect*) отвра|ща́ть, -ти́ть; **he will not be ~ed from his purpose** его́ не собьёшь с и́збранного пути́. **8** (*shape*): **the bowl was ~ed on the lathe** ча́шу обточи́ли на тока́рном станке́; (*fig.*): **he can ~ a witty phrase** он остёр на язы́к. **9** (*execute by ~ing*): **the children were ~ing somersaults** де́ти кувырка́лись; **the wheel has ~ed full circle** колесо́ сде́лало по́лный оборо́т; (*fig.*) положе́ние кардина́льно измени́лось.
● *v.i.* **1** (*move round*) пов|ора́чиваться, -ерну́ться; враща́ться (*impf.*); **the earth ~s on its axis** земля́ враща́ется вокру́г свое́й о́си; **the key won't ~** ключ не повора́чивается; **he ~ed on his heel** он кру́то поверну́лся; (*fig.*): **this will make him ~ in his grave** он от э́того в гробу́ перевернётся; (*depend*) зави́сеть (*impf.*); **everything ~s on his answer** всё зави́сит от его́ отве́та; (*revolve*): **the discussion ~ed upon the meaning of democracy** спор враща́лся вокру́г по́длинного значе́ния демокра́тии. **2** (*change direction*) свора́чиваться, сверну́ться; направля́ться (*impf.*); **we ~ (to the) left here** тут мы свора́чиваем нале́во; **right ~!** напра́во!; **we ~ed off the main road down a lane** мы сверну́ли с гла́вной доро́ги на тропи́нку; (*fig.*) обра|ща́ться, -ти́ться; **she hardly knew which way to ~** она́ не зна́ла, что ей де́лать; **who can I ~ to?** к кому́ я могу́ обрати́ться?; **I ~ to more serious topics** я перейду́/обращу́сь к бо́лее серьёзным вопро́сам; **the people ~ed against their rulers** наро́д восста́л про́тив прави́телей; **he ~ed on his attackers** он бро́сился на свои́х оби́дчиков; **he ~ed on me with reproaches** он набро́сился на меня́ с упрёками. **3** (*change*) превра|ща́ться, -ти́ться; **the tadpoles ~ed into frogs** голова́стики преврати́лись в лягу́шек; **he ~ed into a miser** он стал скря́гой; **his pleasure ~ed to disgust** удово́льствие преврати́лось/обрати́лось у него́ в отвраще́ние; (*change colour*): **the leaves have ~ed** ли́стья пожелте́ли. **4** (*become*) ста|нови́ться, -ть; де́латься, с-; **she ~ed pale** она́

побледнéла; **he ~ed traitor** он стал предáтелем; **it has ~ed warm** потеплéло; (*become sour*): **the milk has ~ed** молокó прокúсло/свернýлось.

● *with advs.*: **~ about** *v.t.* (*reverse*) пов|орáчивать, -ернýть; *v.i.* (*change to opposite direction*) пов|орáчиваться, -ернýться на 180°; **about ~!** кругóм!; **~ aside** *v.t. & i.* отклон|ять(ся), -úть(ся); **~ away** *v.t.* (*avert*): **he ~ed his head away** он повернýл гóлову в стóрону; (*refuse admittance to*) прог|онять, -нáть; не пус|кáть, -тúть; **hundreds were ~ed away from the stadium** сóтни людéй не пустúли на стадиóн; *v.i.*: **she ~ed away in disgust** онá с отвращéнием отвернýлась; **~ back** *v.t.* (*repel*) от|сылáть, -ослáть назáд; **we were ~ed back at the frontier** нас вернýли с границы; (*fold back*) отв|орáчивать, -ернýть; от|гибáть, -огнýть; **his cuffs were ~ed back** егó манжéты бы́ли завёрнуты; (*return to former position*): **he ~ed the clock back** (*lit.*) он перевёл часы́ назáд; **we cannot ~ the clock back** (*fig.*) мы не мóжем повернýть врéмя вспять; *v.i.* пов|орáчивать, -ернýть назáд; пойтú (*pf.*) обрáтно; **~ down** *v.t.* (*fold down*): **his collar was ~ed down** егó воротнúк был отвёрнут; (*reduce by ~ing*) уб|авлять, -áвить; **~ down the gas!** убáвьте газ!; прикрутúте газ!; **~ the volume down!** (*TV etc.*) убáвьте звук!; (*reject*) отв|ергáть, -éргнуть; откáз|ываться, -áться от + *g.*; **I was ~ed down for the job** мне отказáли в рабóте; **my offer was ~ed down** моё предложéние бы́ло отвéргнуто; **~ in** *v.t.*: **he ~ed in his toes** он стáвил нóги носкáми внутрь; (*surrender*; *hand over*) сда|вáть, -ть; **he ~ed himself in to the police** он сдáлся полúции; *v.i.* (*incline inwards*) св|ёртываться, -ернýться внутрь; (*coll., go to bed*) отпрáвиться (*pf.*) на боковýю (*coll.*); **~ inside out** *v.t. & i.* выворáчивать(ся), вы́вернуть(ся) наизнáнку; **~ off** *v.t.* (*e.g. light, engine*) выключáть, вы́ключить; гасúть, по-; **~ off the light!** погасúте/вы́ключите свет!; (*tap*) закр|ывáть, -ы́ть; **the water was ~ed off at the main** вóду отключúли; *v.i.* (*make a diversion*) св|орáчивать, -ернýть; **we ~ed off to call at a farm** мы свернýли, чтóбы заéхать на фéрму; (*coll., repel*) вызывáть, вы́звать отвращéние у (+ *g.*); **~ on** *v.t.* (*e.g. light, engine, radio*) включ|áть, -úть; (*tap*) откр|ывáть, -ы́ть; (*fig.*): **she ~ed on all her charm** онá пустúла в ход всё своё обаяние; **this music ~s me on** (*coll.*) э́то мýзыка возбуждáет меня; **~ out** *v.t.* (*expel*) прог|онять, -нáть; исключ|áть, -úть; **the tenants were ~ed out on to the street** жильцóв вы́гнали на ýлицу; (*switch off*) гасúть, по-; тушúть, по-; **the lights were ~ed out** свет был потýшен; (*produce*) выпускáть, вы́пустить; произв|одúть, -естú; (*fig.*) укр|ашáть, -áсить; **he is always well ~ed out** он всегдá хорошó одéт; (*empty*) выворáчивать, вы́вернуть; **he ~ed out his pockets** он вы́вернул кармáны; (*Br., tidy*) уб|ирáть, -рáть; (*assemble for duty*) вызывáть, вы́звать; *v.i.* (*prove*) окáз|ываться, -áться; **let us see how things ~ out** посмóтрим, какóй оборóт прúмут делá; **as it ~ed out I was not required** как оказáлось, я не понáдобился; **he ~ed out to be a liar** он оказáлся лжецóм; **it ~ed out that he was right** получúлось, что он был прав; (*become*): **such children often ~ out criminals** из такúх детéй чáсто выхóдят/получáются престýпники; **after a wet morning, it ~ed out a fine day** пóсле дождлúвого ýтра день вы́дался хорóшим; (*assemble*) соб|ирáться, -рáться; (*go out of doors*): **I had to ~ out in the cold** мне пришлóсь вы́йти на хóлод; **~ over** *v.t.* (*overturn*) перев|орáчивать, -ернýть; опрокú|дывать, -нуть; (*reverse position of*): **I ~ed over the page** я перевернýл странúцу; (*revolve*) запус|кáть, -тúть; **I must ~ it over in my mind** я дóлжен э́то обдýмать; (*transfer*; *hand over*) перед|авáть, -áть; **he was ~ed over to the authorities** егó пéредали властя́м; *v.i.* (*overturn*) перев|орáчиваться, -ернýться; **the boat ~ed over and sank** лóдка перевернýлась и затонýла; (*change position*) перев|орáчиваться, -ернýться; **he ~ed over (in bed)** он перевернýлся на другóй бок; (*revolve*): **is the engine ~ing over?** двúгатель поворáчивается?; **~ round** *v.t.* (*change or reverse position of*) перев|орáчивать, -ернýть; **~ your chair round this way** повернúте стул в э́ту стóрону; **he ~ed his car round** он развернýл машúну; *v.i.* (*change position*): **he ~ed round to look** он обернýлся, чтóбы посмотрéть; (*revolve*) вращáться (*impf.*); **the weather-vane ~s round in the wind** флю́гер вращáется/вéртится на ветрý; **~ to** *v.i.* (*join in, help*) брáться/взя́ться за дéло; **~ up** *v.t.* (*increase flow of*) приб|авлять, -áвить; усúли|вать, -ть; **~ up the gas!** прибáвьте гáзу!; (*disinter*) выкáпывать, вы́копать; (*put in higher position*) подн|имáть, -ять вверх; **he ~ed his collar up** он пóднял воротнúк; **don't ~ your nose up at the offer** не воротúте нос от такóго предложéния; *v.i.* (*arrive*) появ|ля́ться, -úться; **look who's ~ed up!** смотрúте, кто пришёл!; когó мы вúдим!; (*be found*; *occur*) окáз|ываться, -áться; подв|ёртываться, -ернýться; **don't look for your pen now; it may ~ up later** брóсьте искáть рýчку — онá найдётся в концé концóв; (*happen*; *become available*) подвернýться (*pf.*); **he is waiting for a suitable job to ~ up** он ждёт, покá емý подвернётся подходя́щая рабóта; **~ upside down** *v.t. & i.* перев|орáчивать(ся), -ернýть(ся) вверх дном; (*fig.*): **she ~ed the room upside down to find her ring** онá перерыла всю кóмнату в пóисках кольцá.

● *cpds.* **~coat** *n.* ренегáт; предáтель (*fem.* -ница); **~-down** *adj.* (*of collar*) отложнóй; **~-off** *n.* поворóт, боковáя дорóга; (*repulsive thing*) что-н. отвратúтельное; **~out** *n.* (*assembly*) собрáние, сбор; **there was a very good ~out** собралóсь óчень мнóго нарóду; (*Br., cleaning, tidying*) чúстка, убóрка; (*equipage*) вы́езд; **~over** *n.* (*in business*) оборóт (капитáла); (*of staff*) текýчесть; (*pie*) пирóг с начúнкой; **~pike** *n.* (*hist., toll-gate*) дорóжная застáва; (*US, highway*) магистрáль, шоссé (*indecl.*); (*on which toll is charged*) плáтная магистрáль; **~-round** *n.* (*of ship etc.*) оборóт; (*reversal of policy, opinion etc.*) поворóт на 180°; **~ signal** *n.* (*US*) указáтель (*m.*) поворóта; **~stile** *n.* турникéт; **~table** *n.* (*rail.*) поворóтный круг; (*of record player*) вертýшка; **~-up** *n.* (*Br.*) (*of trouser*) манжéта, отворóт; (*coll., surprise*) неожúданность.

turner /ˈtɜːnə(r)/ *n.* тóкарь (*m.*).

turning /ˈtɜːnɪŋ/ *n.* (*bend, junction*) поворóт; (*junction*) перекрёсток; **the first ~ on the right** пéрвый поворóт напрáво.

● *cpd.* **~-point** *n.* (*lit.*) поворóтный пункт; (*fig.*) крúзис, перелóм; этáпное событие; **it was a ~-point in his career** э́то был поворóтный момéнт в егó карьéре.

turnip /ˈtɜːnɪp/ *n.* рéпа, турнéпс.

turpentine /ˈtɜːpənˌtaɪn/ *n.* терпентúн, скипидáр.

turpitude /ˈtɜːpɪˌtjuːd/ *n.* порóчность, нúзость.

turps /tɜːps/ (*coll.*) = **turpentine**

turquoise /ˈtɜːkwɔɪz/, /-kwɑːz/ *n.* бирюзá; (*colour*) бирюзóвый цвет.

turret /ˈtʌrɪt/ *n.* (*tower*) бáшенка; (*of tank etc.*) бронирóванная/орудúйная бáшня.

turtle /ˈtɜːt(ə)l/ *n.* черепáха.

● *cpd.* **~-neck** *adj.*: **~-neck sweater** водолáзка.

turtle-dove /ˈtɜːt(ə)lˌdʌv/ *n.* дúкий гóлубь.

turves /tɜːvz/ *pl. of* ⇒**turf**

tusk /tʌsk/ *n.* клык, бúвень (*m.*).

tussle /ˈtʌs(ə)l/ *n.* дрáка.

● *v.i.* дрáться (*impf.*).

tussock /ˈtʌsək/ *n.* кóчка.

tut /tʌt/ (*also* **~-tut**) *v.i.* (**tutted, tutting**) цóкать (*impf.*) языкóм (выражáя неодобрéние).

● *int.* áх ты!; ай-яй-яй!

tutee /tjuːˈtiː/ *n.* студéнт (*fem.* -ка) (*входящий в группу какого-н. преподавателя*).

tutelage /ˈtjuːtɪlɪdʒ/ *n.* попечúтельство; опéка.

tutelary /ˈtjuːtɪlərɪ/ *adj.* опекýнский, опекáющий.

tutor /ˈtjuːtə(r)/ *n.* (*private teacher*) репетúтор; (*university teacher*) преподавáтель (*fem.* -ница); (*Br., manual*) учéбник.

● *v.t.* (*instruct*) давáть (*impf.*) чáстные урóки + *d.*; обуч|áть, -úть (**in**: + *d.*).

● *v.i.* давáть (*impf.*) чáстные урóки.

tutorial /tjuːˈtɔːrɪəl/ *n.* ≈ семинáр, консультáция.

tutti /ˈtʊtɪ/ *n.* (*pl.* **~s**) (*mus.*) тýтти (*nt. indecl.*).

tutti-frutti /ˌtuːtɪˈfruːtɪ/ *n.* (*pl.* **~s**) фруктóвое морóженое.

tutu /ˈtuːtuː/ *n.* пáчка.

tu-whit tu-whoo /tʊˌwɪt tʊˈwuː/ *n.* крик совы́.

tuxedo /tʌkˈsiːdəʊ/ *n.* (*pl.* **~s** *or* **~es**) (*US*) смо́кинг.

TV (*abbr. of* ***television***) ТВ (телеви́дение); (*set*) телеви́зор, (*coll.*) те́лик; **~ addict** телема́н; **closed-circuit ~** за́мкнутое телеви́дение.

twaddle /ˈtwɒd(ə)l/ *n.* чепуха́; болтовня́.

twang /twæŋ/ *n.* (*sound of plucked string*) звук натя́нутой струны́; (*nasal tone of voice*) гнуса́вый го́лос.

● *v.t. & i.*: **he ~ed the guitar** он тре́нькал на гита́ре; **the bow ~ed** тетива́ зазвене́ла.

twat /twɒt/ *n.* (*vulg.*) пизда́ (*vulg.*).

tweak /twiːk/ *n.* щипо́к.

● *v.t.* ущипну́ть (*pf.*).

twee /twiː/ *adj.* (**tweer** /ˈtwiːə/; **tweest** /ˈtwiːɪst/) (*Br.*) при́торный.

tweed /twiːd/ *n.* (*material*) твид; **a ~ jacket** тви́довый пиджа́к; (*pl.*) тви́довый костю́м.

tweet /twiːt/ *n.* щебе́т, чири́канье.

● *v.i.* щебета́ть (*impf.*); чири́кать (*impf.*).

tweezer /ˈtwiːzə(r)/ *n.* (*usu. pl.*) пинце́т; щи́пчик|и (*pl., g.* -ов).

twelfth /twelfθ/ *n.* (*date*) двена́дцатое число́; (*fraction*) одна́ двена́дцатая.

● *adj.* двена́дцатый; **T~ Night** кану́н Креще́ния.

twelve /twelv/ *n.* двена́дцать; **chapter ~** двена́дцатая глава́.

● *adj.* двена́дцать +*g. pl.*; **12 times 12** двена́дцатью (*or* двена́дцать на) двена́дцать; (*with nn. expr. or understood*): **~ (o'clock)** (*midday*) двена́дцать (часо́в) дня, по́лдень (*m.*); (*midnight*) двена́дцать (часо́в) но́чи, по́лночь; **quarter to ~** без че́тверти двена́дцать; **quarter/half past ~** че́тверть/полови́на пе́рвого; **a boy of ~** ма́льчик двена́дцати лет; двенадцатиле́тний ма́льчик.

twentieth /ˈtwentɪɪθ/ *n.* (*date*) двадца́тое число́; (*fraction*) одна́ двадца́тая.

● *adj.* двадца́тый.

twent|y /ˈtwentɪ/ *n.* два́дцать; **at (the age of) ~y** в два́дцать лет, в во́зрасте двадцати́ лет; **the ~ies** (*decade*) двадца́тые го́ды; **she is still in her ~ies** ей ещё нет тридцати́.

● *adj.* два́дцать +*g. pl.*

twerp /twɜːp/ *n.* (*coll.*) ничто́жество.

twice /twaɪs/ *adv.* (*two times*) два́жды, два ра́за; (*doubly*) вдво́е, в два ра́за; **~ a day** два́жды (*or* два ра́за) в день; **~ two is four** два́жды два — четы́ре; **he is ~ my age** он вдво́е ста́рше меня́; **~ as much** в два ра́за (*or* вдво́е) бо́льше; **that made him think ~** э́то заста́вило его́ заду́маться.

twiddl|e /ˈtwɪd(ə)l/ *v.t.* верте́ть (*impf.*); крути́ть (*impf.*); **he sat there ~ing his thumbs** он бил баклу́ши; он безде́льничал; **he was ~ing with his watchchain** он теребил цепо́чку от часо́в.

twig¹ /twɪɡ/ *n.* (*bot.*) (*on tree*) ве́тка; (*when cut*) прут.

twig² /twɪɡ/ *v.t. & i.* (**twigged, twigging**) (*Br. coll.*) смек|а́ть, -ну́ть.

twilight /ˈtwaɪlaɪt/ *n.* су́мер|ки (*pl., g.* -ек); (*fig.*): **in the ~ of his life** на зака́те его́ жи́зни.

● *adj.* су́меречный; (*indeterminate*) неопределённый, промежу́точный.

twill /twɪl/ *n.* (*text.*) са́ржа.

twin /twɪn/ *n.* близне́ц; (*pl.*) близнецы́, двойня́ (*f. sg.*); **I have a ~ sister** у меня́ сестра́ — мы с ней близнецы́; **identical ~s** однояйцевые/иденти́чные близнецы́.

● *adj.* похо́жий; одина́ковый; **they are ~ brothers** они́ (бра́тья)-близнецы́; **~ beds** две односпа́льные крова́ти; **~ propellers** двойно́й пропе́ллер.

● *v.t.* (**twinned, twinning**) (*fig.*) соедин|я́ть, -и́ть; **Cheltenham is ~ned with Sochi** (*Br.*) Че́лтнем и Со́чи — города́-побрати́мы.

● *cpds.* **~-engined** *adj.* двухдви́гательный; **~-set** *n.* (*Br.*) шерстяно́й гарниту́р, дво́йка (*тонкий свитер и кофта*).

twine /twaɪn/ *n.* бечёвка, шнуро́к.

● *v.t. & i.* ви́ть(ся) (*impf.*); обв|ива́ть(ся), -и́ть(ся); **the ivy ~d round the tree** плющ ви́лся вокру́г де́рева.

twinge /twɪndʒ/ *n.* при́ступ о́строй бо́ли; (*fig.*) му́ка; **~s of conscience** угрызе́ния со́вести.

twinkl|e /ˈtwɪŋk(ə)l/ *n.* мерца́ние; огонёк; **there was a ~e in his eye** в его́ глаза́х вспы́хнул озорно́й огонёк.

● *v.i.* мерца́ть (*impf.*); сверка́ть (*impf.*); **his eyes ~ed with amusement** его́ глаза́ ве́село блесте́ли; **in the ~ing of an eye** в мгнове́ние о́ка.

twirl /twɜːl/ *n.* враще́ние.

● *v.t.* верте́ть (*impf.*); крути́ть (*impf.*); **he ~ed his walking-stick** он верте́л тро́стью.

twist /twɪst/ *n.* **1** (*sharp turning motion*) круче́ние; (*jerk*) рыво́к; **he gave the handle a ~** он поверну́л ру́чку. **2** (*sharp change of direction*) изги́б, поворо́т; **the lane was all ~s and turns** тропи́нка была́ о́чень изви́листой; **a ~ in the plot** круто́й поворо́т сюже́та. **3** (*something ~ed or spiral in shape*) пе́тля; у́зел; **the rope was full of ~s** верёвка была́ вся в узла́х; **a ~ of paper** (*Br.*) скру́ченный бума́жный куле́к. **4** (*peculiar tendency*) скло́нность; **he had a criminal ~** в нём бы́ло что́-то поро́чное. **5** (*dance*) твист. **6**: **round the ~** (*Br. coll.*) чо́кнутый.

● *v.t.* **1** (*screw round*) крути́ть (*or* скру́чивать), с-; **he tried to ~ my arm** (*lit.*) он пыта́лся вы́вернуть мне ру́ку; (*fig., coerce me*) он пыта́лся на меня́ дави́ть; **I ~ed my ankle** я подверну́л но́гу. **2** (*contort*) искрив|ля́ть, -и́ть; **a ~ed smile** крива́я улы́бка; (*fig.*) иска|жа́ть, -зи́ть; **don't try to ~ my words** не искажа́йте мои́ слова́. **3** (*wind, twine*) обв|ива́ть, -и́ть; обм|а́тывать, -ота́ть; **they ~ed the flowers into a garland** они́ сплели́ цветы́ в гирлянду; **he can ~ you round his little finger** он мо́жет вить из вас верёвки. **4** (*Br. coll., cheat*) обма́н|ывать, -у́ть.

● *v.i.* **1** (*wriggle*) ко́рчиться (*impf.*); извива́ться (*impf.*); **he ~ed about, trying to get away** он извива́лся, стара́ясь вы́рваться. **2** (*twine; grow spirally*) обв|ива́ться, -и́ться; **the tendrils ~ed round their support** побе́ги расте́ния вили́сь вокру́г жёрдочки.

● *with advs.*: **~ off** *v.t.* откру́|чивать, -ти́ть; отви́н|чивать, -ти́ть; **~ up** *v.t.* запу́т|ывать, -ать; **the string was all ~ed up** верёвка была́ вся в узла́х.

twisted /ˈtwɪstɪd/ *adj.* (*perverted*) извращённый.

twister /ˈtwɪstə(r)/ *n.* (*Br., dishonest person*) обма́нщик, моше́нник; (*US, tornado*) торна́до (*indecl.*).

twisty /ˈtwɪstɪ/ *adj.* (**twistier, twistiest**) изви́листый.

twit¹ /twɪt/ *n.* (*Br.*) о́лух (*coll.*).

twit² /twɪt/ *v.t.* (**twitted, twitting**) поддр|а́знивать, -азни́ть.

twitch /twɪtʃ/ *n.* подёргивание, су́дорога.

● *v.t.* **1** (*jerk*) дёргать (*impf.*). **2** (*move spasmodically*) подёргивать (*impf.*) +*i.*; **the dog ~ed its ears** соба́ка повела́ уша́ми.

● *v.i.* дёргаться (*impf.*), подёргиваться (*impf.*); **her lips ~ed** её гу́бы дёргались; **the rabbit's nose ~ed** нос у кро́лика дёргался.

twitter /ˈtwɪtə(r)/ *n.* **1** (*chirping*) щебе́т. **2** (*rapid chatter*) щебета́ние, болтовня́. **3**: **she was all of a ~** (*coll.*) она́ вся трепета́ла.

● *v.i.* (*chirp*) щебета́ть (*impf.*); чири́кать (*impf.*); (*talk rapidly*) щебета́ть (*impf.*); болта́ть (*impf.*).

two /tuː/ *n.* (число́/но́мер) два; (**~** *people*) дво́е; **we ~** мы о́ба; **the ~** э́ти два/дво́е; о́ба +*g. sg.*; **there were ~ of us** нас бы́ло дво́е; **(the) ~ of us went** мы пошли́ вдвоём; **~ each, in ~s, ~ at a time, ~ by ~** по́ два/дво́е; (*cut, divide*) **in ~** на́ двое/попола́м; **fold in ~** скла́дывать, сложи́ть вдво́е; **the plate broke in ~** таре́лка разби́лась попола́м; (*figure, thing numbered 2*) дво́йка; **~ and ~ are four** два плюс/и два — четы́ре; (*with var. nn. expr. or understood*): **chapter ~** глава́ два, втора́я глава́; **volume ~** том два, том второ́й; **room ~** ко́мната но́мер два; второ́й но́мер; **size ~** второ́й разме́р/но́мер; **he lives at No. ~** он живёт в до́ме но́мер 2; **a No. ~ (bus)** дво́йка, но́мер два; **~ of spades** дво́йка пик; **at ~ (o'clock)** в два (часа́); **~ p.m.** два часа́ дня; **an hour or ~** час-друго́й; **in an hour or ~** че́рез час-друго́й; (*of age*): **he is ~** ему́ два (го́да); **a boy of ~** двухле́тний ма́льчик; (*idioms*): **~'s company, three's none** тре́тий — ли́шний; **~ can play at that game** ≈ я могу́ отплати́ть той же моне́той; **I put ~ and ~ together** я сообрази́л, что к чему́; **that makes ~ of us** вот и я то́же;

T

degrees are ~ a penny дипло́мам грош цена́.

● *adj.* два +*g. sg.*; (*for masculine nouns denoting people and pluralia tantum, also*) дво́е +*g. pl.*; **~ students** два студе́нта, дво́е студе́нтов; **~ patients** дво́е больны́х; **~ children** дво́е дете́й; два ребёнка; **~ watches** дво́е часо́в; **~ whole glasses** це́лых два стака́на; **the ~ carriages** о́ба ваго́на; **he and ~ others** он с двумя́ други́ми; **~ fives are ten** два́жды пять — де́сять; **~ coffees** (*as order*) два ко́фе.

● *cpds.* **~-bit** *adj.* (*US coll.*) никуды́шный; **~-day** *adj.* двухдне́вный; **~-dimensional** *adj.* двухме́рный; **~-edged** *adj.* (*lit., fig.*) обоюдоо́стрый; **~-faced** *adj.* (*fig.*) двули́чный; **~fold** *adj.* двойно́й; *adv.* вдво́е; **~-handed** *adj.* двуру́чный; **~-hour** *adj.* двухчасово́й; **~-lane** *adj.* двухколе́йный; **~-legged** *adj.* двуно́гий; **~pence** *n.* (*Br.*) два пе́нса; двухпе́нсовая моне́та; *see also* ⇒**tuppence; ~penny** *adj.* (*Br.*) двухпе́нсовый; **~penny-halfpenny** *adj.* (*Br. coll., rubbishy*) грошо́вый; *see also* ⇒**tuppenny; ~-piece** *n.* (*suit*) костю́м-дво́йка; **~-ply** *adj.* двойно́й, двухсло́йный; **~-seater** *n.* двухме́стный автомоби́ль/самолёт; **~-sided** *adj.* двусторо́нний; **~-storey(ed)** (*US* **story/storied**) *adj.* двухэта́жный; **~-stroke** *adj.* двухта́ктный; **~-time** *v.t.* (*coll.*) обма́н|ывать, -у́ть; измен|я́ть, -и́ть (жене́/му́жу); **~-timer** *n.* (*coll.*) (*unfaithful husband*) изме́нник, неве́рный муж; (*unfaithful wife*) изме́нница, неве́рная жена́; **~-timing** *adj.* (*coll.*) неве́рный; **~-way** *adj.* (*e.g. traffic*) двусторо́нний; **~-way radio** дупле́ксная радиосвя́зь; **~-year** *adj.* двухгоди́чный; **~-year-old** *adj.* двухле́тний.

tycoon /taɪ'ku:n/ *n.* (*business magnate*) магна́т; тайку́н.

tying /'taɪɪŋ/ *pres. part. of* ⇒**tie**

tympana /'tɪmpənə/ *pl. of* ⇒**tympanum**

tympan|i /'tɪmpənɪ/, **-ist** /'tɪmpənɪst/ = **timpan|i, -ist**

tympan|um /'tɪmpənəm/ *n.* (*pl.* **~ums** *or* **~a**) (*eardrum*) бараба́нная перепо́нка; (*middle ear*) сре́днее у́хо.

type /taɪp/ *n.* **1** (*example*) тип; типи́чный приме́р. **2** (*class*) тип, род. **3** (*letters for printing*) шрифт; **in large/heavy ~** кру́пным/жи́рным шри́фтом.

● *v.t.* **1** (*classify*) классифици́ровать (*impf., pf.*); определ|я́ть, -и́ть. **2** (*write with* **~***writer*) печа́тать, на- (на маши́нке).

● *v.i.* печа́тать (*impf.*) (на маши́нке); **typing** (*as n.*) маши́нопись; **typing error** опеча́тка; **typing pool** машинопи́сное бюро́.

● *cpds.* **~cast** *adj.*: **he is ~cast as the butler** он всегда́ игра́ет роль дворе́цкого; **~-face** *n.* шрифт; **~script** *n.* машинопи́сный текст; **~setter** *n.* (*person*) набо́рщик; (*machine*) набо́рная маши́на; **~setting** *n.* набо́р; **~write** *v.t.* печа́тать, на- на маши́нке; **a ~written letter** письмо́, напеча́танное на маши́нке; **~writer** *n.* пи́шущая маши́нка.

typhoid /'taɪfɔɪd/ *n.* (*also* **~ fever**) брюшно́й тиф.

● *adj.* тифо́зный.

typhoon /taɪ'fu:n/ *n.* тайфу́н.

typhus /'taɪfəs/ *n.* сыпно́й тиф.

typical /'tɪpɪk(ə)l/ *adj.* типи́чный; **that is ~ of him** э́то для него́ типи́чно.

typify /'tɪpɪ,faɪ/ *v.t.* быть типи́чным представи́телем +*g.*; олицетвор|я́ть, -и́ть.

typist /'taɪpɪst/ *n.* (*fem.*) машини́стка; **he is a ~** он зараба́тывает маши́нописью.

typographer /taɪ'pɒgrəfə(r)/ *n.* печа́тник, полиграфи́ст.

typographic(al) /,taɪpə'græfɪk(ə)l/ *adj.* типогра́фский.

typography /taɪ'pɒgrəfɪ/ *n.* (*art, process*) полиграфи́я; (*of books*) книгопеча́тание; (*appearance of printed matter*) оформле́ние (*книги и т.п.*).

typological /,taɪpə'lɒdʒɪk(ə)l/ *adj.* типологи́ческий.

typology /taɪ'pɒlədʒɪ/ *n.* типоло́гия.

tyrannical /tɪ'rænɪk(ə)l/ *adj.* тирани́ческий.

tyrannize /'tɪrə,naɪz/ *v.t.* & *i.* тира́нить (*impf.*); **he ~s (over) his family** он тира́нит свою́ семью́.

tyrannous /'tɪrənəs/ *adj.* тирани́ческий.

tyranny /'tɪrənɪ/ *n.* (*despotic power*) тирани́я; (*tyrannical behaviour*) тира́нство.

tyrant /'taɪərənt/ *n.* тира́н, де́спот.

tyre /'taɪə(r)/ (*US* **tire**) *n.* ши́на; **I have a flat ~** у меня́ спусти́лась ши́на; (*outer* **~**) покры́шка.

● *cpds.* **~-iron** (*US*), **~-lever** (*Br.*) *nn.* монтиро́вочная лопа́тка.

Tyrol /'tɪrəl/ *n.* Тиро́ль (*m.*).

Tyrol|ean /,tɪrə'li:ən/ *n.* тиро́л|ец (*fem.* -ька).

● *adj.* тиро́льский.

tzar /zɑ:(r)/ *etc.* = **tsar** *etc.*

Uu

U /juː/ *cpds.* **~-bend** *n.* двойно́й изги́б; **~-boat** *n.* неме́цкая подво́дная ло́дка; **~-turn** *n.* разворо́т; (*fig.*) ре́зкое измене́ние поли́тики; поворо́т на 180°.

UAE (*abbr. of* ***United Arab Emirates***) ОАЭ (Объединённые ара́бские эмира́ты).

ubiquitous /juːˈbɪkwɪtəs/ *adj.* вездесу́щий.

ubiquity /juːˈbɪkwɪtɪ/ *n.* вездесу́щность.

UCAS /ˈjuːkæs/ (*abbr. of* ***Universities and Colleges Admissions Service***) (*Br.*) Слу́жба по приня́тию в университе́ты и колле́джи.

UDA (*abbr. of* ***Ulster Defence Association***) Ассоциа́ция защи́ты О́льстера.

udder /ˈʌdə(r)/ *n.* вы́мя (*nt.*).

UDI (*abbr. of* ***Unilateral Declaration of Independence***) Односторо́ннее провозглаше́ние незави́симости.

UDR (*abbr. of* ***Ulster Defence Regiment***) Полк защи́ты О́льстера.

UEFA /juːˈiːfə/, /-ˈeɪfə/ (*abbr. of* ***Union of European Football Associations***) УЕФА́ (*indecl.*).

UFO (*pl.* **UFOs**) (*abbr. of* ***unidentified flying object***) НЛО (неопо́знанный лета́ющий объе́кт).

ufologist /juːˈfɒlədʒɪst/ *n.* уфо́лог.

ufology /juːˈfɒlədʒɪ/ *n.* уфоло́гия.

Uganda /juːˈgændə/ *n.* Уга́нда.

Ugandan /juːˈgændən/ *n.* уганди́|ец (*fem.* -йка).

● *adj.* уганди́йский.

ugh /əx/, /ʌg/, /ʌx/ *int.* (*expressing disgust*) фу!, брр!; (*expressing horror*) аа!

ugliness /ˈʌglɪnɪs/ *n.* уро́дство, безобра́зие; (*fig.*) гну́сность.

ugly /ˈʌglɪ/ *adj.* (**uglier, ugliest**) **1** (*unsightly*) уро́дливый, безобра́зный, некраси́вый; **~ duckling** га́дкий утёнок. **2** (*unpleasant*) проти́вный, скве́рный. **3** (*threatening*) опа́сный; **an ~ customer** гну́сный/опа́сный тип/субъе́кт; **in an ~ mood** в гро́зном настрое́нии.

UK (*abbr. of* ***United Kingdom***) Соединённое Короле́вство (Великобрита́нии и Се́верной Ирла́ндии).

● *adj.* (велико)брита́нский.

ukase /juːˈkeɪz/ *n.* ука́з.

Ukraine /juːˈkreɪn/ *n.* Украи́на; **in (the) ~** на Украи́не.

Ukrainian /juːˈkreɪnɪən/ *n.* (*person*) украи́н|ец (*fem.* -ка); (*language*) украи́нский язы́к.

● *adj.* украи́нский.

ukulele /ˌjuːkəˈleɪlɪ/ *n.* гава́йская гита́ра.

Ulan Bator /uˈlɑːn ˈbɑːtɔː(r)/ *n.* Ула́н-Ба́тор.

ulcer /ˈʌlsə(r)/ *n.* я́зва; **stomach ~** я́зва желу́дка.

ulcerate /ˈʌlsəˌreɪt/ *v.t.* изъязв|ля́ть, -и́ть.

ulceration /ˌʌlsəˈreɪʃ(ə)n/ *n.* изъязвле́ние.

ulcerous /ˈʌlsərəs/ *adj.* я́звенный.

ulna /ˈʌlnə/ *n.* (*pl.* **ulnae** /-niː/ *or* **ulnas**) локтева́я кость.

Ulster /ˈʌlstə(r)/ *n.* О́льстер.

● *cpds.* **~man** *n.* жи́тель (*or* уроже́нец) О́льстера; **~woman** *n.* жи́тельница (*or* уроже́нка) О́льстера.

ulterior /ʌlˈtɪərɪə(r)/ *adj.* скры́тый, невы́раженный; **~ motive** скры́тый моти́в; за́дняя мысль.

ultimata /ˌʌltɪˈmeɪtə/ *pl. of* **⇒ultimatum**

ultimate /ˈʌltɪmət/ *adj.* после́дний, оконча́тельный; **~ end, purpose** коне́чная цель.

ultimat|um /ˌʌltɪˈmeɪtəm/ *n.* (*pl.* **~ums** *or* **~a**) ультима́тум.

ult(imo) /ˈʌltɪˌməʊ/ *adj.* про́шлого ме́сяца.

ultra- /ˈʌltrə/ *comb. form* у́льтра..., сверх(ъ)....

ultramarine /ˌʌltrəməˈriːn/ *n.* (*pigment*) ультрамари́н.

● *adj.* ультрамари́новый.

ultrasonic /ˌʌltrəˈsɒnɪk/ *n.* сверхзвуково́й, ультразвуково́й.

ultrasound /ˈʌltrəˌsaʊnd/ *n.* ультразву́к.

ultra-violet /ˌʌltrəˈvaɪələt/ *adj.* ультрафиоле́товый.

ululate /ˈjuːlʊˌleɪt/ *v.i.* выть (*impf.*); завыва́ть (*impf.*)

umber /ˈʌmbə(r)/ *n.* у́мбра.

● *adj.* тёмно-кори́чневый.

umbilical /ʌmˈbɪlɪk(ə)l/, /ˌʌmbɪˈlaɪk(ə)l/ *adj.* пупо́чный; **~ cord** пупови́на.

umbrage /ˈʌmbrɪdʒ/ *n.* оби́да; **take ~ (at)** об|ижа́ться, -и́деться (на + *a.*).

umbrella /ʌmˈbrelə/ *n.* **1** зо́нтик, зонт. **2** (*fig., protection*) защи́та; (*against aircraft*) засло́н, (авиацио́нное) прикры́тие; **nuclear ~** я́дерный зо́нтик. **3** (*fig., general heading*) ру́брика; **~ organization** возглавля́ющая организа́ция.

● *cpd.* **~-stand** *n.* подста́вка для зонто́в.

umlaut /ˈʊmlaʊt/ *n.* умля́ут.

umpire /ˈʌmpaɪə(r)/ *n.* (*arbitrator*) посре́дник; трете́йский судья́; (*in games*) судья́ (*m.*); рефери́ (*m. indecl.*).

● *v.t. & i.*: **he ~d (in) both matches** он суди́л о́ба ма́тча.

umpteen /ʌmpˈtiːn/ *adj.* (*coll.*) бесчи́сленное коли́чество + *g.*

umpteenth /ʌmpˈtiːnθ/ *adj.* (*coll.*) э́нный; **I have told you for the ~ time** ско́лько раз я тебе́ говори́л!

UN (*abbr. of* ***United Nations (Organization)***): **the ~** ОО́Н (*f. indecl.*) (Организа́ция Объединённых На́ций).

● *adj.* (*coll.*) оо́новский; **~ council/commission** сове́т/коми́ссия ОО́Н.

un- /ʌn/ *neg. pref.*: *oft. expr. by pref.* не... (*e.g.* **⇒unable**) *or* без..., бес... (*e.g.* **⇒unashamed**).

unabashed /ˌʌnəˈbæʃt/ *adj.* не растеря́вшийся.

unabated /ˌʌnəˈbeɪtɪd/ *adj.* неосла́бленный.

unable /ʌnˈeɪb(ə)l/ *adj.* неспосо́бный; **he is ~ to swim** он не уме́ет пла́вать; I am ~ to say я не могу́ сказа́ть; **I shall be ~ to come** я не смогу́ прийти́.

unabridged /ˌʌnəˈbrɪdʒd/ *adj.* несокращённый, по́лный.

unaccented /ˌʌnækˈsentɪd/ *adj.* безуда́рный.

unacceptable /ˌʌnəkˈseptəb(ə)l/ *adj.* неприе́млемый.

unaccompanied /ˌʌnəˈkʌmpənɪd/ *adj.* нике́м не сопровожда́емый; **she came ~** она́ пришла́ одна́ (*or* без сопровожде́ния); (*mus.*) без аккомпанеме́нта.

unaccomplished /ˌʌnəˈkʌmplɪʃt/ *adj.* **1** (*not fulfilled*) незавершённый; **his mission was ~** он не заверши́л свое́й ми́ссии. **2** (*mediocre*) посре́дственный, непримеча́тельный.

unaccountable /ˌʌnəˈkaʊntəb(ə)l/ *adj.* (*inexplicable*) необъясни́мый; (*irrational*) безотчётный; (*not obliged to render an account of o.s. or itself*): **~ to** не несу́щий отве́тственности пе́ред + *i.*

unaccounted for /ˌʌnəˈkaʊntɪd/ *adj.* (*unexplained*) необъяснённый; (*not included in account*) не ука́занный в отчёте; (*missing*): **two people were ~** не досчита́лись двух челове́к.

unaccustomed /ˌʌnəˈkʌstəmd/ *adj.* **1** (*unused*) неприви́кший; **~ as I am to public speaking** хотя́ я и не привы́к выступа́ть. **2** (*unusual*) необы́чный.

unachievable /ˌʌnəˈtʃiːvəb(ə)l/ *adj.* недосяга́емый, недостижи́мый, невыполни́мый.

unachieved /ˌʌnəˈtʃiːvd/ *adj.* недости́гнутый, незавершённый.

unacknowledged /ˌʌnəkˈnɒlɪdʒd/ *adj.* **1** (*unrecognized*) непри́знанный; **his work went ~** никто́ не отме́тил его́ рабо́ты. **2** (*without reply*): **my letter was ~ by them** я не получи́л от них подтвержде́ния о получе́нии моего́ письма́.

unacquainted /ˌʌnəˈkweɪntɪd/ *adj.* незнако́мый.

unadorned /ˌʌnəˈdɔːnd/ *adj.* (*walls*) неукра́шенный; (*truth*) неприкра́шенный.

unadulterated /ˌʌnəˈdʌltəˌreɪtɪd/ *adj.* настоя́щий, неподде́льный; **~ nonsense** чисте́йший вздор; **the ~ truth** чи́стая пра́вда.

unadventurous /ˌʌnədˈventʃərəs/ *adj.* непредприи́мчивый, осторо́жный; (*uneventful*) без приключе́ний, споко́йный.

unaffected /ˌʌnəˈfektɪd/ *adj.* **1** (*without affectation*) непринуждённый, есте́ственный. **2** (*not harmed or influenced*): **our plans were ~ by the weather** пого́да не измени́ла на́ших пла́нов; **he was ~ by my entreaties** он остава́лся безуча́стным к мои́м мольба́м.

unafraid /ˌʌnəˈfreɪd/ *adj.* незапу́ганный; **she was ~ of defeat** пораже́ние её не пуга́ло.

unaided /ʌnˈeɪdɪd/ *adj.* без посторо́нней по́мощи; **to the ~ eye** невооружённому гла́зу.

unaligned /ˌʌnəˈlaɪnd/ *adj.*: **the ~ countries** неприсоедини́вшиеся стра́ны.

unalleviated /ˌʌnəˈliːvɪˌeɪtɪd/ *adj.* несмягчённый.

unalloyed /ˌʌnəˈlɔɪd/, /ʌnˈæl-/ *adj.* нелеги́рованный; (*fig.*): **~ pleasure** ниче́м не омрачённая ра́дость.

unalterable /ʌnˈɔːltərəb(ə)l/, /ʌnˈɒl-/ *adj.* неизме́нный.

unambiguous /ˌʌnæmˈbɪgjʊəs/ *adj.* недвусмы́сленный, однозна́чный.

unambitious /ˌʌnæmˈbɪʃəs/ *adj.* непритяза́тельный, скро́мный.

un-American /ˌʌnəˈmerɪkən/ *adj.* чу́ждый америка́нским обы́чаям и поня́тиям; антиамерика́нский.

unanimity /ˌjuːnəˈnɪmɪtɪ/ *n.* единоду́шие.

unanimous /juːˈnænɪməs/ *adj.* единоду́шный, единогла́сный; **the resolution was passed ~ly** резолю́ция была́ принята́ единогла́сно.

unannounced /ˌʌnəˈnaʊnst/ *adj.* необъя́вленный; (*to arrive, enter*) без докла́да.

unanswerable /ʌnˈɑːnsərəb(ə)l/ *adj.*: **an ~ argument** неопровержи́мый до́вод; **an ~ question** вопро́с, на кото́рый невозмо́жно отве́тить.

unanswered /ʌnˈɑːnsəd/ *adj.* оста́вшийся без отве́та.

unanticipated /ˌʌnænˈtɪsɪˌpeɪtɪd/ *adj.* (*unexpected*) непредви́денный, неожи́данный.

unapparent /ˌʌnəˈpærənt/ *adj.* неочеви́дный, скры́тый.

unappealing /ˌʌnəˈpiːlɪŋ/ *adj.* неприя́тный, непривлека́тельный.

unappeasable /ˌʌnəˈpiːzəb(ə)l/ *adj.* непримири́мый.

unappetizing /ʌnˈæpɪˌtaɪzɪŋ/ *adj.* неаппети́тный.

unappreciated /ˌʌnəˈpriːʃɪˌeɪtɪd/ *adj.* непри́знанный, недооценённый.

unappreciative /ˌʌnəˈpriːʃətɪv/ *adj.* неблагода́рный.

unapproachable /ˌʌnəˈprəʊtʃəb(ə)l/ *adj.* недосту́пный.

unarmed /ʌnˈɑːmd/ *adj.* невооружённый, безору́жный; **~ combat** самозащи́та без ору́жия; (*abbr.* са́мбо (*indecl.*)).

unashamed /ˌʌnəˈʃeɪmd/ *adj.* бессты́дный; бессо́вестный.

unasked /ʌnˈɑːskt/ *adj.* непро́шенный; **she did it ~** она́ сде́лала э́то по свое́й инициати́ве; (*uninvited*) незва́ный.

unassailable /ˌʌnəˈseɪləb(ə)l/ *adj.*: **an ~ fortress** непристу́пная кре́пость; **an ~ argument** неопровержи́мый до́вод.

unassisted /ˌʌnəˈsɪstɪd/ *adj.* без (посторо́нней) по́мощи.

unassuming /ˌʌnəˈsjuːmɪŋ/ *adj.* непритяза́тельный, скро́мный.

unattached /ˌʌnəˈtætʃt/ *adj.* не привя́занный/прикреплённый (*к чему*); **she is ~** она́ одино́ка.

unattainable /ˌʌnəˈteɪnəb(ə)l/ *adj.* недосяга́емый.

unattended /ˌʌnəˈtendɪd/ *adj.* **1** (*of high-ranking person*) без слуг/сви́ты; (*unaccompanied*) нике́м не сопровожда́емый. **2** (*without care*) безнадзо́рный, оста́вленный без надзо́ра/присмо́тра; **the children were left ~** дете́й оста́вили одни́х, без надзо́ра; **his business was ~** его́ де́лом никто́ не занима́лся; **the shop is ~** в магази́не нет продавца́.

unattractive /ˌʌnəˈtræktɪv/ *adj.* непривлека́тельный, несимпати́чный; **the idea is most ~ to me** э́та иде́я меня́ совсе́м не привлека́ет.

unauthenticated /ˌʌnɔːˈθentɪˌkeɪtɪd/ *adj.* неудостове́ренный.

unauthorized /ʌnˈɔːθəˌraɪzd/ *adj.* неразрешённый; (*person*) посторо́нний; **~ absence** самово́льная отлу́чка.

unavailable /ˌʌnəˈveɪləb(ə)l/ *adj.* не име́ющийся в нали́чии; **he was ~** он был за́нят.

unavailing /ˌʌnəˈveɪlɪŋ/ *adj.* бесполе́зный, напра́сный, тще́тный.

unavoidabl|e /ˌʌnəˈvɔɪdəb(ə)l/ *adj.* (*sure to happen*) неизбе́жный, немину́емый; **I was ~y detained** я не мог освободи́ться (ра́ньше).

unaware /ˌʌnəˈweə(r)/ *adj.* незна́ющий, неподозрева́ющий; **he was ~ of my presence** он не подозрева́л о моём прису́тствии; **I was ~ that he was married** я не знал, что он жена́т.

unawares /ˌʌnəˈweəz/ *adv.* неча́янно; врасплох́; **I was taken ~ by his question** его́ вопро́с засти́г меня́ врасплох́.

unbalanced /ʌnˈbælənst/ *adj.* (*development*) неравноме́рный; (*report, views*) односторо́нний; (*mentally*) неуравнове́шенный, неусто́йчивый.

unbar /ʌnˈbɑː(r)/ *v.t.*: **~ a door** отодв|ига́ть, -и́нуть засо́в на две́ри́; (*fig.*) откр|ыва́ть, -ы́ть.

unbearable /ʌnˈbeərəb(ə)l/ *adj.* невыноси́мый.

unbeaten /ʌnˈbiːt(ə)n/ *adj.* (*unsurpassed*) непревзойдённый.

unbecoming /ˌʌnbɪˈkʌmɪŋ/ *adj.* (*of clothing, colour*) не иду́щий к лицу́; (*inappropriate*) неподходя́щий (для + *g.*); (*indecorous*) неподоба́ющий (+ *d.*), неприли́чный (для + *g.*); **conduct ~ an officer** поведе́ние, недосто́йное офице́ра (*or* неподоба́ющее офице́ру).

unbefitting /ˌʌnbɪˈfɪtɪŋ/ *adj.* неподоба́ющий (+ *d.*); неподходя́щий (для + *g.*).

unbeknown /ˌʌnbɪˈnəʊn/ (*coll.* **unbeknownst**) *adv.*: **he did it ~ to me** он сде́лал э́то без моего́ ве́дома.

unbelief /ˌʌnbɪˈliːf/ *n.* (*lack of faith*) неве́рие.

unbelievable /ˌʌnbɪˈliːvəb(ə)l/ *adj.* (*coll., amazing*) невероя́тный, неимове́рный.

unbeliever /ˌʌnbɪˈliːvə(r)/ *n.* (*relig.*) неве́рующий.

unbelieving /ˌʌnbɪˈliːvɪŋ/ *adj.* (*lacking faith*) неве́рующий.

unbend /ʌnˈbend/ *v.t.* (*past and p.p.*

unbent) выпрямля́ть, вы́прямить; раз|гиба́ть, -огну́ть.
● *v.i.* (*past and p.p* **unbent**) (*fig., relax*) рассл|абля́ться, -а́биться.

unbending /ʌnˈbendɪŋ/ *adj.* (*fig.*) (*firm*) непрекло́нный; (*austere*) суро́вый; (*not flexible*) неги́бкий.

unbias(s)ed /ʌnˈbaɪəst/ *adj.* беспристра́стный.

unbidden /ʌnˈbɪd(ə)n/ *adj.* непро́шеный; (*as adv., voluntarily*) доброво́льно; по свое́й во́ле.

unbind /ʌnˈbaɪnd/ *v.t.* развя́з|ывать, -а́ть; (*hair*) распус|ка́ть, -ти́ть; (*wound*) разбинто́в|ывать, -а́ть.

unblemished /ʌnˈblemɪʃt/ *adj.* чи́стый; (*fig.*) незапя́тнанный; безупре́чный.

unblock /ʌnˈblɒk/ *v.t.*: **the plumber ~ed the drain** водопрово́дчик прочи́стил водосто́к.

unbolt /ʌnˈbəʊlt/ *v.t.* (*door*) отп|ира́ть, -ере́ть.

unborn /ʌnˈbɔːn/ *adj.*: **her ~ child** её ещё не роди́вшийся (*or* её бу́дущий) ребёнок.

unbosom /ʌnˈbʊz(ə)m/ *v.t.*: **~ o.s. to s.o.** откр|ыва́ть, -ы́ть (*or* изл|ива́ть, -и́ть) (свою́) ду́шу кому́-н.

unbound /ʌnˈbaʊnd/ *adj.* (*of book*) непереплетённый.

unbounded /ʌnˈbaʊndɪd/ *adj.* неограни́ченный, безме́рный.

unbowed /ʌnˈbaʊd/ *adj.* несо́гнутый; непокорённый; **his head was ~** (*fig.*) он не покори́лся, он не склони́л головы́.

unbridled /ʌnˈbraɪd(ə)ld/ *adj.* (*fig.*) необу́зданный; разну́зданный.

unbroken /ʌnˈbrəʊkən/ *adj.* неразби́тый, несло́мленный; **only one plate was ~** то́лько одна́ таре́лка уцеле́ла; **his spirit remained ~** дух его́ не́ был сло́млен; **an ~ record** непревзойдённый/непоби́тый реко́рд; **an ~ horse** необъе́зженный конь; **~ sleep** непреры́вный сон.

unbuckle /ʌnˈbʌk(ə)l/ *v.t.* расстёг|ивать, -ну́ть.

unburden /ʌnˈbɜːd(ə)n/ *v.t.*: **he ~ed his soul** (*or* **himself**) **to me** он изли́л мне ду́шу.

unbusinesslike /ʌnˈbɪznɪsˌlaɪk/ *adj.* неделово́й, непракти́чный.

unbutton /ʌnˈbʌt(ə)n/ *v.t.* расстёг|ивать, -ну́ть.

uncalled-for /ʌnˈkɔːldfɔː(r)/ *adj.* (*inappropriate*) неуме́стный; (*excessive*) изли́шний; (*undeserved*) незаслу́женный.

uncanny /ʌnˈkænɪ/ *adj.* (**uncannier, uncanniest**) стра́нный, необъясни́мый.

uncared-for /ʌnˈkeədfɔː(r)/ *adj.* забро́шенный.

uncarpeted /ʌnˈkɑːpɪtɪd/ *adj.* без ковра́.

unceasing /ʌnˈsiːsɪŋ/ *adj.* беспреры́вный, беспреста́нный.

uncensored /ʌnˈsensəd/ *adj.* не проходи́вший цензу́ру.

unceremonious /ˌʌnserɪˈməʊnɪəs/ *adj.* (*abrupt, discourteous*) бесцеремо́нный.

uncertain /ʌnˈsɜːt(ə)n/ *adj.* **1** (*hesitant, in doubt*) неуве́ренный, нереши́тельный; **he was ~ what to do** он не знал, что де́лать; **I am ~ what he wants** я не могу́ поня́ть, чего́ он хо́чет; **I am still ~** я всё ещё сомнева́юсь/колеблю́сь. **2** (*not clear*) нея́сный, неопределённый; **in no ~ terms** весьма́ недвусмы́сленно. **3** (*changeable, unreliable*): **the weather is ~** пого́да изме́нчива; **my position is ~** (*shaky*) моё положе́ние неопределённо.

uncertaint|y /ʌnˈsɜːt(ə)ntɪ/ *n.* **1** (*hesitation*) неуве́ренность, нереши́тельность; **be in a state of ~y** быть в нереши́тельности; сомнева́ться (*impf.*); колеба́ться (*impf.*). **2** (*lack of clarity*) нея́сность, неизве́стность, неопределённость. **3** (*unreliable or unpredictable nature*) изме́нчивость; **the ~ies of life** превра́тности (*f. pl.*) судьбы́; **the future is full of ~y** бу́дущее полно́ неопределённости.

unchain /ʌnˈtʃeɪn/ *v.t.* спус|ка́ть, -ти́ть с це́пи; **~ the door** сн|има́ть, -ять цепо́чку с две́ри.

unchallengeable /ʌnˈtʃælɪndʒəb(ə)l/ *adj.* неоспори́мый.

unchallenged /ʌnˈtʃælɪndʒd/ *adj.* (все́ми) при́знанный; **I let his remark go ~** я не стал оспа́ривать его́ замеча́ние.

unchangeable /ʌnˈtʃeɪndʒəb(ə)l/ *adj.* неизменя́емый; (*invariable*) неизме́нный.

unchanged /ʌnˈtʃeɪndʒd/ *adj.* неизмени́вшийся; **the patient's condition is ~** состоя́ние больно́го не измени́лось/без переме́н.

uncharitable /ʌnˈtʃærɪtəb(ə)l/ *adj.* (*harsh*) жесто́кий, немилосе́рдный; (*malicious*) зло́бный; (*fault-finding*) приди́рчивый.

uncharted /ʌnˈtʃɑːtɪd/ *adj.* не отме́ченный на ка́рте; (*also fig.*) неиссле́дованный, неизве́данный.

unchaste /ʌnˈtʃeɪst/ *adj.* (*person*) нецелому́дренный; (*behaviour, words*) непристо́йный.

unchastity /ʌnˈtʃæstɪtɪ/ *n.* нецелому́дренность.

unchecked /ʌnˈtʃekt/ *adj.*: **~ accounts** непрове́ренные счета́; **an ~ advance** (*mil.*) беспрепя́тственное продвиже́ние.

unchivalrous /ʌnˈʃɪvəlrəs/ *adj.* неры́царский.

unchristian /ʌnˈkrɪstjən/ *adj.* нехристиа́нский, не подоба́ющий христиани́ну.

uncivil /ʌnˈsɪvɪl/ *adj.* неве́жливый, гру́бый.

uncivilized /ʌnˈsɪvɪˌlaɪzd/ *adj.* нецивилизо́ванный, некульту́рный.

unclad /ʌnˈklæd/ *adj.* неоде́тый; (*naked*) го́лый.

unclaimed /ʌnˈkleɪmd/ *adj.* невостре́бованный.

unclasp /ʌnˈklɑːsp/ *v.t.* (*loosen clasp of*) расстёг|ивать, -ну́ть; (*release grip on*) разж|има́ть, -а́ть; **he ~ed his hands** он разжа́л ру́ки.

unclassifiable /ʌnˈklæsɪˌfaɪəb(ə)l/ *adj.* не поддаю́щийся классифика́ции.

unclassified /ʌnˈklæsɪˌfaɪd/ *adj.* неклассифици́рованный; (*without security grading*) несекре́тный.

uncle /ˈʌŋk(ə)l/ *n.* дя́дя (*m.*).

unclean /ʌnˈkliːn/ *adj.* (*impure*) нечи́стый; (*relig.*) пога́ный.

uncleanness /ʌnˈkliːnnɪs/ *n.* нечистота́.

unclothed /ʌnˈkləʊðd/ *adj.* разде́тый, неоде́тый.

unclouded /ʌnˈklaʊdɪd/ *adj.* (*lit., fig.*) безо́блачный.

uncoil /ʌnˈkɔɪl/ *v.t. & i.* разм|а́тывать(ся), -ота́ть(ся).

uncoloured /ʌnˈkʌləd/ (*US* **uncolored**) *adj.* бесцве́тный, неокра́шенный; **his views are ~ by prejudice** он челове́к беспристра́стный; **an ~ description** неприкра́шенное описа́ние.

uncomfortable /ʌnˈkʌmftəb(ə)l/ *adj.* (*lit., fig.*) неудо́бный; (*situation*) нело́вкий.

uncommitted /ˌʌnkəˈmɪtɪd/ *adj.* нейтра́льный; (*pol., unaligned*) неприсоедини́вшийся.

uncommon /ʌnˈkɒmən/ *adj.* ре́дкий; необы́чный, незауря́дный; **he showed ~ generosity** он прояви́л необыкнове́нную ще́дрость; **that is ~ly good of you** вы чрезвыча́йно до́бры/любе́зны.

uncommunicative /ˌʌnkəˈmjuːnɪkətɪv/ *adj.* неразгово́рчивый, сде́ржанный.

uncompanionable /ˌʌnkəmˈpænjənəb(ə)l/ *adj.* необщи́тельный.

uncomplaining /ˌʌnkəmˈpleɪnɪŋ/ *adj.* безро́потный.

uncomplicated /ʌnˈkɒmplɪˌkeɪtɪd/ *adj.* несло́жный.

uncomplimentary /ˌʌnkɒmplɪˈmentərɪ/ *adj.* неле́стный.

uncompromising /ʌnˈkɒmprəˌmaɪzɪŋ/ *adj.* бескомпроми́ссный, неусту́пчивый; (*tough*) твёрдый.

unconcealed /ˌʌnkənˈsiːld/ *adj.* нескрыва́емый, я́вный.

unconcern /ˌʌnkənˈsɜːn/ *n.* беззабо́тность, беспе́чность; безразли́чие, равноду́шие.

unconcerned /ˌʌnkənˈsɜːnd/ *adj.* (*carefree*) беззабо́тный, беспе́чный; (*indifferent*) безразли́чный, равноду́шный.

unconditional /ˌʌnkənˈdɪʃən(ə)l/ *adj.* безусло́вный, безоговоро́чный; **~ surrender** безоговоро́чная капитуля́ция.

unconfined /ˌʌnkənˈfaɪnd/ *adj.* (*boundless*) неограни́ченный; (*fig.*) свобо́дный, нестеснённый.

unconfirmed /ˌʌnkənˈfɜːmd/ *adj.* неподтверждённый.

U

uncongenial /ˌʌnkənˈdʒiːnɪəl/ *adj.* (*unpleasant*) неприя́тный; (*alien*) чу́ждый, чужо́й (по ду́ху).

unconnected /ˌʌnkəˈnektɪd/ *adj.* не свя́занный; **the wires were ~** провода́ не́ были соединены́; (*speech*) бессвя́зный.

unconquerable /ʌnˈkɒŋkərəb(ə)l/ *adj.* непобеди́мый.

unconquered /ʌnˈkɒŋkəd/ *adj.* непобеждённый.

unconscionable /ʌnˈkɒnʃənəb(ə)l/ *adj.*: **an ~ liar** отъя́вленный/невозмо́жный лгун.

unconscious /ʌnˈkɒnʃəs/ *n.*: **the ~** (*psych.*) подсозна́ние.

● *adj.* **1** (*senseless*) потеря́вший созна́ние; в о́бмороке; **he was ~** он был без созна́ния/в о́бмороке; **he was knocked ~** он потеря́л созна́ние от уда́ра. **2** (*unaware*) не сознаю́щий; **he was ~ of having done wrong** он не сознава́л, что поступи́л пло́хо. **3** (*unintentional*) нево́льный, бессозна́тельный; **he spoke with ~ irony** он говори́л с бессозна́тельной ирони́ей.

unconsciousness /ʌnˈkɒnʃəsnɪs/ *n.* (*physical*) бессозна́тельное/о́бморочное состоя́ние; (*unawareness*) отсу́тствие (о)созна́ния, неосо́знанность.

unconsidered /ˌʌnkənˈsɪdəd/ *adj.* необду́манный, непроду́манный; **an ~ remark** необду́манное замеча́ние.

unconstitutional /ˌʌnkɒnstɪˈtjuːʃən(ə)l/ *adj.* противоре́чащий конститу́ции, неконституцио́нный.

unconstrained /ˌʌnkənˈstreɪnd/ *adj.* непринуждённый.

uncontaminated /ˌʌnkənˈtæmɪˌneɪtɪd/ *adj.* незаражённый, незагрязнённый.

uncontested /ˌʌnkənˈtestɪd/ *adj.* неоспори́мый; **~ election** вы́боры, на кото́рых баллоти́руется лишь оди́н кандида́т.

uncontrollable /ˌʌnkənˈtrəʊləb(ə)l/ *adj.*: **an ~ temper** неукроти́мый нрав; **an ~ child** неуправля́емый ребёнок; **an ~ influx of refugees** неконтроли́руемый/бесконтро́льный напл́ыв бе́женцев.

uncontrolled /ˌʌnkənˈtrəʊld/ *adj.* неконтроли́руемый, бесконтро́льный, неуправля́емый.

unconventional /ˌʌnkənˈvenʃən(ə)l/ *adj.* нетрадицио́нный; (*person, behaviour*) нешабло́нный, эксцентри́чный.

unconvinced /ˌʌnkənˈvɪnst/ *adj.* неубеждённый; **he remained ~** его́ не удало́сь убеди́ть.

unconvincing /ˌʌnkənˈvɪnsɪŋ/ *adj.* неубеди́тельный.

uncooked /ʌnˈkʊkt/ *adj.* сыро́й; непригото́вленный.

uncooperative /ˌʌnkəʊˈɒpərətɪv/ *adj.* не проявля́ющий гото́вность помо́чь; равноду́шный.

uncork /ʌnˈkɔːk/ *v.t.* отку́пори|вать, -ть.

uncorrected /ˌʌnkəˈrektɪd/ *adj.* неиспра́вленный.

uncorroborated /ˌʌnkəˈrɒbəˌreɪtɪd/ *adj.* неподтверждённый.

uncorrupted /ˌʌnkəˈrʌptɪd/ *adj.* неиспо́рченный; (*politician*) некорумпи́рованный.

uncountable /ʌnˈkaʊntəb(ə)l/ *adj.* (*innumerable*) бесчи́сленный, неисчисли́мый; (*gram.*) неисчисля́емый.

uncounted /ʌnˈkaʊntɪd/ *adj.* (*innumerable*) несчётный, бесчи́сленный.

uncouple /ʌnˈkʌp(ə)l/ *v.t.* (*rail carriages*) расцеп|ля́ть, -и́ть; (*dogs*) спус|ка́ть, -ти́ть со сво́ры.

uncouth /ʌnˈkuːθ/ *adj.* гру́бый, неотёсанный.

uncouthness /ʌnˈkuːθnɪs/ *n.* гру́бость, неотёсанность.

uncover /ʌnˈkʌvə(r)/ *v.t.* (*take cover off*) сн|има́ть, -ять кры́шку/покро́в с + *g.*; **he ~ed his head** он обнажи́л го́лову; (*fig.*) раскр|ыва́ть, -ы́ть; обнару́жи|вать, -ть; **the conspiracy was ~ed** за́говор раскры́ли.

uncritical /ʌnˈkrɪtɪk(ə)l/ *adj.* (*person*) некрити́чный; (*approach*) некрити́ческий.

uncrossed /ʌnˈkrɒst/ *adj.*: **an ~ cheque** (*Br.*) некросси́рованный чек.

uncrowned /ʌnˈkraʊnd/ *adj.*: **~ king** (*lit., fig.*) некороно́ванный коро́ль.

uncrushable /ʌnˈkrʌʃəb(ə)l/ *adj.* (*of material*) немну́щийся; (*irrepressible*) неугомо́нный.

unction /ˈʌŋkʃ(ə)n/ *n.* **1** (*anointing*) пома́зание; **extreme ~** собо́рование. **2** (*fig., oiliness*) еле́йность.

unctuous /ˈʌŋktjʊəs/ *adj.* (*fig., oily*) еле́йный.

uncultivated /ʌnˈkʌltɪˌveɪtɪd/ *adj.* (*of land*) необрабо́танный, невозде́ланный; (*of person*) некульту́рный.

uncultured /ʌnˈkʌltʃəd/ *adj.* некульту́рный.

uncut /ʌnˈkʌt/ *adj.* неразре́занный; неподстри́женный; **~ pages** неразре́занные листы́/страни́цы; **the film was shown ~** фильм показа́ли в неуре́занном вариа́нте.

undamaged /ʌnˈdæmɪdʒd/ *adj.* неповреждённый.

undated /ʌnˈdeɪtɪd/ *adj.* недати́рованный.

undaunted /ʌnˈdɔːntɪd/ *adj.* неустраши́мый.

undeceive /ˌʌndɪˈsiːv/ *v.t.* выводи́ть, вы́вести из заблужде́ния.

undecided /ˌʌndɪˈsaɪdɪd/ *adj.* (*not settled*) нерешённый; (*hesitating*) нереши́тельный; **the battle was ~** исхо́д би́твы был нея́сен; **I am ~ whether to go or stay** я не зна́ю, идти́ мне и́ли нет.

undecipherable /ˌʌndɪˈsaɪfərəb(ə)l/ *adj.* (*of code*) не поддаю́щийся расшифро́вке; (*of handwriting etc.*) неразбо́рчивый.

undeclared /ˌʌndɪˈkleəd/ *adj.* необъя́вленный; **a state of ~ war** состоя́ние необъя́вленной войны́.

undefended /ˌʌndɪˈfendɪd/ *adj.* незащищённый; **they left the city ~** они́ оста́вили го́род без защи́ты; **an ~ suit** (*leg.*) иск, не оспа́риваемый отве́тчиком.

undefiled /ˌʌndɪˈfaɪld/ *adj.* неосквернённый.

undefined /ˌʌndɪˈfaɪnd/ *adj.* неопределённый.

undelivered /ˌʌndɪˈlɪvəd/ *adj.*: **an ~ letter** недоста́вленное письмо́; **an ~ speech** непроизнесённая речь.

undemonstrative /ˌʌndɪˈmɒnstrətɪv/ *adj.* сде́ржанный.

undeniable /ˌʌndɪˈnaɪəb(ə)l/ *adj.* неоспори́мый, я́вный.

undependable /ˌʌndɪˈpendəb(ə)l/ *adj.* ненадёжный.

under /ˈʌndə(r)/ *adv.* вниз; **the ship went ~** кора́бль затону́л; **he dived and stayed ~ for a minute** он нырну́л и продержа́лся под водо́й (одну́) мину́ту.

● *prep.* **1** под + *i.*; (*of motion*) под + *a.*; **(out) from ~** из-под + *g.*
2 (*less than*) ме́ньше + *g.*; ни́же + *g.*; **he earns ~ £40 a week** он зараба́тывает ме́ньше сорока́ фу́нтов в неде́лю; **he was ~ age** он не дости́г совершенноле́тия; **children ~ 14** де́ти моло́же (*or* в во́зрасте до) четы́рнадцати лет; **I can get there in ~ an hour** я могу́ добра́ться туда́ ме́ньше, чем за час.
3 (*var. uses*): **~ arms** под ружьём; **you are ~ arrest** вы аресто́ваны; **~ the circumstances** при сложи́вшихся обстоя́тельствах; **~ cultivation** обраба́тываемый; **~ discussion** обсужда́емый; **~ oath** под прися́гой; **~ pain of death** под стра́хом сме́рти; **~ pressure** под давле́нием; **~ repair** в ремо́нте; **~ sail** под паруса́ми; **~ suspicion** под подозре́нием; **~ way** (*in motion*) на ходу́; (*in progress*): **the investigation is ~ way** ведётся рассле́дование; **land ~ wheat** земля́ под пшени́цей; (**~ *authority of***): **he served ~ me** он служи́л под мои́м руково́дством, **he studied ~ a professor** он учи́лся/занима́лся у профе́ссора; **~ the tsars** при царя́х; **England ~ the Stuarts** А́нглия в пери́од правле́ния Стю́артов; (*according to*): **~ the terms of the agreement** по усло́виям соглаше́ния; **~ orders** по прика́зу; **~ the rules** согла́сно уста́ву; (*classified with*): **they come ~ the same heading** они́ отно́сятся к одно́й и той же ру́брике.

underact /ˌʌndərˈækt/ *v.t. & i.* недоигр|ывать, -а́ть.

underarm /ˈʌndərˌɑːm/ *adj. & adv.*: **an ~ deodorant** дезодора́нт для подмы́шек; **an ~ throw** бросо́к сни́зу.

under-belly /ˈʌndəˌbelɪ/ *n.* низ живота́.

undercarriage /ˈʌndəˌkærɪdʒ/ *n.* (*of a plane*) шасси́ (*nt. indecl.*); (*of a vehicle*) ходова́я часть.

undercharge /ˌʌndəˈtʃɑːdʒ/ *v.t.* брать, взять с кого́-н. недоста́точно.

undercloth|es /ˈʌndəˌkləʊðz/, /-ˌkləʊz/, **-ing** /ˈʌndəˌkləʊðɪŋ/ *nn.* ни́жнее бельё.

undercoat /ˈʌndəˌkəʊt/ *n.* (*of paint*) грунто́вка.

undercover /ˌʌndəˈkʌvə(r)/, /ˈʌn-/ *adj.* та́йный.

undercurrent /ˈʌndəˌkʌrənt/ *n.* подво́дное тече́ние; (*fig.*) скры́тая тенде́нция.

undercut /ˌʌndəˈkʌt/ *v.t.*: **he ~ his competitor** он назна́чил це́ну ни́же, чем его́ конкуре́нт.

underdeveloped /ˌʌndədɪˈveləpt/ *adj.* недора́звитый; **~ countries** слабора́звитые стра́ны.

underdog /ˈʌndəˌdɒg/ *n.* (*sport*) побеждённая сторона́; (*downtrodden person*) неуда́чник.

underdone /ˌʌndəˈdʌn/, /ˈʌn-/ *adj.* (*of food*) недожа́ренный; недова́ренный.

underemployment /ˌʌndərɪmˈplɔɪmənt/ *n.* непо́лная за́нятость.

underestimate[1] /ˌʌndərˈestɪmət/ *n.* недооце́нка.

underestimate[2] /ˌʌndərˈestɪˌmeɪt/ *v.t.* недооце́н|ивать, -и́ть.

underestimation /ˌʌndərestɪˈmeɪʃ(ə)n/ *n.* недооце́нка.

underexpose /ˌʌndərɪkˈspəʊz/ *v.t.* (*phot.*) недодéрж|ивать, -а́ть.

underexposure /ˌʌndərɪkˈspəʊʒə(r)/ (*phot.*) недоста́точная вы́держка, недоэкспони́рование.

underfed /ˌʌndəˈfed/ *adj.* недоко́рмленный.

underfelt /ˈʌndəˌfelt/ *n.* (*Br.*) подкла́дочный во́йлок (*для ковровых покрытий*).

underfoot /ˌʌndəˈfʊt/ *adv.* под нога́ми.

underfunded /ˌʌndəˈfʌndɪd/ *adj.*: **the project was ~** прое́кт был недоста́точно финанси́рован.

undergarments /ˈʌndəˌgɑːmənts/ *n. pl.* ни́жнее бельё.

undergo /ˌʌndəˈgəʊ/ *v.t.* испы́т|ывать, -а́ть; перен|оси́ть, -ести́; подв|ерга́ться, -е́ргнуться + *d.*; **he has to ~ an operation** ему́ предстои́т опера́ция.

undergraduate /ˌʌndəˈgrædjʊət/ *n.* студе́нт (*fem.* -ка); (*attr.*) студе́нческий.

underground /ˈʌndəˌgraʊnd/ *n.* **1** (*Br.*, *~ railway*) метро́ (*indecl.*); **on the U~** в метро́. **2** (*~ movement*) подпо́лье; **member of the ~** подпо́льщи|к (*fem.* -ца). **3** (*art*) андергра́унд.

● *adj.* подзе́мный; (*fig., secret, subversive*) подпо́льный; **an ~ newspaper** подпо́льная газе́та.

● *adv.* (*position*) под землёй; (*direction*) под зе́млю; (*fig.*) подпо́льно; **the former leader went ~** бы́вший ли́дер ушёл в подпо́лье.

undergrowth /ˈʌndəˌgrəʊθ/ *n.* подле́сок.

underhand /ˈʌndəˌhænd/ *adj.* (*secret, deceitful*) закули́сный, та́йный.

● *adv.* тайко́м.

underlay /ˈʌndəˌleɪ/ *n.* (*fabric*) подкла́дка, подсти́лка.

underl|ie /ˌʌndəˈlaɪ/ *v.t.* **1** (*lit.*) лежа́ть (*impf.*) под + *i.* **2** (*fig.*) лежа́ть в осно́ве + *g.*; **~ying causes** причи́ны, лежа́щие в осно́ве (*чего*).

underline /ˌʌndəˈlaɪn/ *v.t.* (*lit., fig.*) подч|ёркивать, -еркну́ть.

underling /ˈʌndəlɪŋ/ *n.* ме́лкий чино́вник, подчинённый; (*coll.*) ме́лкая со́шка.

undermanned /ˌʌndəˈmænd/ *adj.* испы́тывающий недоста́ток в рабо́чей си́ле; неукомплекто́ванный.

undermentioned /ˌʌndəˈmenʃ(ə)nd/, /ˈʌn-/ *adj.* (*Br.*) нижеупомя́нутый.

undermine /ˌʌndəˈmaɪn/ *v.t.* подк|а́пывать, -опа́ть; (*by water*) подм|ыва́ть, -ы́ть; (*fig.*) разр|уша́ть, -у́шить; **his health was ~d by drink** алкого́ль подорва́л его́ здоро́вье; **his authority is ~d** его́ авторите́т подрыва́ют.

underneath /ˌʌndəˈniːθ/ *adv.* внизу́, ни́же.

● *prep.* под + *i.*; (*of motion*) под + *a.*

undernourished /ˌʌndəˈnʌrɪʃt/ *adj.* недоко́рмленный.

undernourishment /ˌʌndəˈnʌrɪʃmənt/ *n.* недоеда́ние.

underpants /ˈʌndəˌpænts/ *n. pl.* (*long*) кальсо́н|ы (*pl., g.* —); (*short*) (мужски́е) трус|ы́ (*pl., g.* -о́в).

underpass /ˈʌndəˌpɑːs/ *n.* прое́зд под полотно́м желе́зной доро́ги; (у́личный) тонне́ль (*m.*).

underpa|y /ˌʌndəˈpeɪ/ *v.t.* (*work*) сли́шком ни́зко опла́|чивать, -ти́ть (*or* недопла́|чивать, -ти́ть за + *a.*); (*worker*) недопл|а́чивать, -ати́ть + *d.*; **the workers are ~id** рабо́чим ма́ло пла́тят.

underpayment /ˌʌndəˈpeɪmənt/ *n.* сли́шком ни́зкая опла́та; недопла́та.

underpin /ˌʌndəˈpɪn/ *v.t.* подв|оди́ть, -ести́ фунда́мент под + *a.*; (*fig.*) подде́рж|ивать, -а́ть.

underpopulated /ˌʌndəˈpɒpjʊˌleɪtɪd/ *adj.* малонаселённый.

underprice /ˌʌndəˈpraɪs/ *v.t.* назн|ача́ть, -а́чить зани́женную це́ну на + *a.*

underprivileged /ˌʌndəˈprɪvɪlɪdʒd/ *adj.* (*poor*) неиму́щий; (*having fewer rights*) по́льзующийся ме́ньшими права́ми.

underproduction /ˌʌndəprəˈdʌkʃ(ə)n/ *n.* недопроизво́дство.

underquote /ˌʌndəˈkwəʊt/ *v.t.* (*goods*) назн|ача́ть, -а́чить бо́лее ни́зкую це́ну на + *a.*

underrate /ˌʌndəˈreɪt/ *v.t.* недооце́н|ивать, -и́ть.

underripe /ˌʌndəˈraɪp/ *adj.* недозре́лый, неспе́лый.

underscore /ˌʌndəˈskɔː(r)/ *v.t.* подч|ёркивать, -еркну́ть.

underseal /ˈʌndəˌsiːl/ *n.* защи́тное покры́тие.

● *v.t.* нан|оси́ть, -ести́ защи́тное покры́тие на + *a.*

under-secretary /ˌʌndəˈsekrətərɪ/ *n.* замести́тель (*m.*)/помо́щник мини́стра.

undersell /ˌʌndəˈsel/ *v.t.* (*another seller*) прод|ава́ть, -а́ть деше́вле (+ *g.*); (*goods*) прод|ава́ть, -а́ть по пони́женной цене́ (*or* ни́же сто́имости).

undershirt /ˈʌndəˌʃɜːt/ *n.* (*US*) ма́йка.

underside /ˈʌndəˌsaɪd/ *n.* низ; ни́жняя часть; (*fig., less favourable aspect*) неприглядная сторона́.

undersign /ˈʌndəˌsaɪn/, /ˌʌndəˈsaɪn/ *v.t.*: **we, the ~ed** мы, нижеподписа́вшиеся.

undersized /ˈʌndəˌsaɪzd/, /-ˈsaɪzd/ *adj.* (*of person*) низкоро́слый.

underskirt /ˈʌndəˌskɜːt/ *n.* ни́жняя ю́бка.

understaffed /ˌʌndəˈstɑːft/ *adj.* испы́тывающий недоста́ток рабо́чей си́лы; неукомплекто́ванный.

understand /ˌʌndəˈstænd/ *v.t.* (*past and p.p.* **understood**) **1** (*comprehend*) пон|има́ть, -я́ть; **he ~s French** он понима́ет по-францу́зски; **he ~s finance** он разбира́ется в фина́нсовых вопро́сах; **now I ~!** тепе́рь всё поня́тно; **he can make himself understood in English** он мо́жет объясни́ться по-англи́йски; **I hope I make myself understood** наде́юсь, вы меня́ по́няли; **he ~s children** он уме́ет обраща́ться с детьми́; **I can ~ his wanting to leave** я понима́ю его́ жела́ние уйти́; **I understood him to say he would come** наско́лько я по́нял, он обеща́л прийти́; **am I to ~ you refuse?** на́до понима́ть, вы отка́зываетесь?; **he gave me to ~ he was single** он дал мне поня́ть, что он хо́лост; **what are we to ~ from such an act?** как мы должны́ понима́ть тако́й посту́пок? **2** (*gather, be informed*): **I ~ you are leaving** я слы́шал, что вы уезжа́ете; **you were, I ~, alone** вы бы́ли, наско́лько я по́нял, одни́; **I ~ he is the best doctor in town** я слы́шал/говоря́т, он лу́чший в го́роде врач. **3** (*agree, accept*): **it is understood** само́ собо́й разуме́ется; устано́влено; (*custom*) так заведено́; **it is understood, then, that we meet tomorrow** ита́к, решено́: мы встреча́емся за́втра. **4** (*gram.*): **the verb is understood** глаго́л подразумева́ется.

understandable /ˌʌndəˈstændəb(ə)l/ *adj.* поня́тный.

understanding /ˌʌndəˈstændɪŋ/ *n.* **1** (*intellect*) ум; **it passes my ~** э́то вы́ше моего́ понима́ния. **2** (*comprehension*) понима́ние; **he has a clear ~ of the problem** он прекра́сно понима́ет пробле́му; **he has a good ~ of economics** он хорошо́ разбира́ется в эконо́мике; **it was my ~ that we were to meet here** наско́лько я по́нял, мы должны́ бы́ли встре́титься здесь. **3** (*sympathy*) понима́ние, отзы́вчивость; **he showed ~ for my position** он вошёл в моё положе́ние. **4** (*agreement*) соглаше́ние, договорённость; **on the clear ~ that ...** то́лько при усло́вии, что...; **they**

U

came to an ~ они́ пришли́ к соглаше́нию.

● *adj.* (*sympathetic*) отзы́вчивый, чу́ткий.

understate /ˌʌndəˈsteɪt/ *v.t.* преум|еньша́ть, -е́ньшить; недоска́з|ывать, -а́ть.

understatement /ˌʌndəˈsteɪtmənt/, /ˈʌndə-/ *n.* преуменьше́ние, сде́ржанное выска́зывание.

understocked /ˌʌndəˈstɒkt/ *adj.* пло́хо снабжённый (*чем*).

understudy /ˈʌndəˌstʌdɪ/ *n.* дублёр.

● *v.t.* дубли́ровать, с-.

undertak|e /ˌʌndəˈteɪk/ *v.t.* **1** (*take on*) предприн|има́ть, -я́ть; брать, взять на себя́; **you are ~ing a heavy responsibility** вы берёте на себя́ большу́ю отве́тственность; **he has ~en the job of secretary** он при́нял на себя́ до́лжность секретаря́. **2** (*pledge o.s., promise*) обя́з|ываться, -а́ться. **3** (*guarantee*) руча́ться, поручи́ться; гаранти́ровать (*impf., pf.*).

undertaker /ˈʌndəˌteɪkə(r)/ *n.* заве́дующий/владе́лец похоро́нного бюро́; **~'s** похоро́нное бюро́.

undertaking /ˌʌndəˈteɪkɪŋ/ *n.* (*enterprise*) предприя́тие; (*pledge, guarantee*) обяза́тельство, гара́нтия.

under-the-table /ˈʌndə(r)/ *adj.* (*coll.*) та́йный, незако́нный.

undertone /ˈʌndəˌtəʊn/ *n.* полуто́н; **in an ~** вполго́лоса; (*fig.*) отте́нок; намёк.

undertow /ˈʌndəˌtəʊ/ *n.* отка́т.

undervalue /ˌʌndəˈvæljuː/ *v.t.* недооце́н|ивать, -и́ть.

undervest /ˈʌndəˌvest/ *n.* (*Br.*) ма́йка.

underwater /ˌʌndəˈwɔːtə(r)/ *adj.* подво́дный.

underwear /ˈʌndəˌweə(r)/ *n.* (ни́жнее) бельё.

underweight /ˌʌndəˈweɪt/ *adj.*: **she's ~** она́ сли́шком худа́я.

underworld /ˈʌndəˌwɜːld/ *n.* (*myth.*) преиспо́дняя; (*criminal society*) престу́пный мир.

underwrite /ˌʌndəˈraɪt/, /ˈʌn-/ *v.t.* **1**: **~ a marine insurance policy** подпи́с|ывать, -а́ть по́лис морско́го страхова́ния. **2**: **~ a loan** гаранти́ровать (*impf., pf.*) размеще́ние за́йма. **3** (*support*) (фина́нсово) подде́рж|ивать, -а́ть.

underwriter /ˈʌndəˌraɪtə(r)/ *n.* (*insurer*) страхо́вщик; (*guarantor*) гара́нт.

undeserved /ˌʌndɪˈzɜːvd/ *adj.* незаслу́женный.

undeserving /ˌʌndɪˈzɜːvɪŋ/ *adj.* не заслу́живающий (*чего*), недосто́йный.

undesirability /ˌʌndɪˌzaɪərəˈbɪlɪtɪ/ *n.* нежела́тельность, нецелесообра́зность.

undesirable /ˌʌndɪˈzaɪərəb(ə)l/ *n.* (*person*) нежела́тельный элеме́нт.

● *adj.* нежела́тельный, нецелесообра́зный.

undetected /ˌʌndɪˈtektɪd/ *adj.* необнару́женный.

undetermined /ˌʌndɪˈtɜːmɪnd/ *adj.* неопределённый.

undeterred /ˌʌndɪˈtɜːd/ *adj.* не поколе́бленный/остано́вленный (*чем*).

undeveloped /ˌʌndɪˈveləpt/ *adj.* неразвито́й; **an ~ country** слабора́звитая страна́; **~ land** необрабо́танная земля́.

undeviating /ʌnˈdiːvɪˌeɪtɪŋ/ *adj.* неукло́нный; постоя́нный.

undies /ˈʌndɪz/ *n. pl.* (*coll.*) (же́нское) ни́жнее бельё.

undifferentiated /ˌʌndɪfəˈrenʃɪˌeɪtɪd/ *adj.* недифференци́рованный.

undigested /ˌʌndɪˈdʒestɪd/, /ˌʌndaɪ-/ *adj.* (*lit., fig.*) неусво́енный; **~ food** непереваренная пи́ща; **~ facts** фа́кты, не приведённые в систе́му.

undignified /ʌnˈdɪgnɪˌfaɪd/ *adj.* недосто́йный; унизи́тельный.

undiluted /ˌʌndaɪˈljuːtɪd/ *adj.* неразба́вленный; (*fig.*): **~ nonsense** чи́стая чепуха́.

undiminished /ˌʌndɪˈmɪnɪʃt/ *adj.* неосла́бный, неослабева́ющий; **with ~ ardour** (*Br.*), **ardor** (*US*) с неослабева́ющим рве́нием.

undiplomatic /ˌʌndɪpləˈmætɪk/ *adj.* недипломати́чный.

undiscerning /ˌʌndɪˈsɜːnɪŋ/ *adj.* непроница́тельный.

undischarged /ˌʌndɪsˈtʃɑːdʒd/ *adj.* (*not executed*) невы́полненный; (*not unloaded*) невы́груженный; **an ~ debt** неупла́ченный долг; **an ~ bankrupt** не восстано́вленный в права́х банкро́т.

undisciplined /ʌnˈdɪsɪplɪnd/ *adj.* недисциплини́рованный.

undisclosed /ˌʌndɪsˈkləʊzd/ *adj.* неразоблачённый, нераскры́тый.

undiscovered /ˌʌndɪˈskʌvəd/ *adj.* неоткры́тый, неиссле́дованный.

undiscriminating /ˌʌndɪˈskrɪmɪˌneɪtɪŋ/ *adj.* неразбо́рчивый.

undisguised /ˌʌndɪsˈgaɪzd/ *adj.* незамаскиро́ванный; я́вный; **with ~ relief** с я́вным/нескрыва́емым облегче́нием.

undismayed /ˌʌndɪsˈmeɪd/ *adj.* неустраши́мый.

undisputed /ˌʌndɪˈspjuːtɪd/ *adj.* неоспори́мый.

undistinguished /ˌʌndɪˈstɪŋgwɪʃt/ *adj.* посре́дственный.

undistracted /ˌʌndɪˈstræktɪd/ *adj.* сосредото́ченный.

undisturbed /ˌʌndɪˈstɜːbd/ *adj.* невстрево́женный, споко́йный; **he was ~ by the news** но́вость его́ не взволнова́ла.

undivided /ˌʌndɪˈvaɪdɪd/ *adj.* нераздéльный; **~ attention** нераздéльное внима́ние.

undo /ʌnˈduː/ *v.t.* (*past* **undid**, *p.p.* **undone**) **1** (*unfasten*) развя́з|ывать, -а́ть; **my shoelace came ~ne** у меня́ развяза́лся шнуро́к на боти́нке. **2** (*annul*) уничт|ожа́ть, -о́жить; (*treaty, agreement*) аннули́ровать (*impf., pf.*); **he tried to ~ the work of his predecessor** он пыта́лся перечеркну́ть рабо́ту своего́ предше́ственника; (*comput.*) отмен|я́ть, -и́ть. **3** (*ruin*) губи́ть, по-; **drink was his ~ing** пья́нство его́ погуби́ло.

● *n.* (*comput.*) отме́на (*команды*).

undomesticated /ˌʌndəˈmestɪˌkeɪtɪd/ *adj.* неприручённый.

undoubted /ʌnˈdaʊtɪd/ *adj.* несомне́нный, бесспо́рный; **an ~ success** несомне́нный/бесспо́рный успе́х; **you are ~ly right** вы несомне́нно/безусло́вно пра́вы.

undramatic /ˌʌndrəˈmætɪk/ *adj.* (*unexciting*) лишённый драмати́зма, ску́чный.

undreamed-of /ʌnˈdriːmd/, /ʌnˈdremt/, **undreamt-of** /ʌnˈdremt/ (*Br.*) *adj.* невообрази́мый, немы́слимый; **~ riches** немы́слимое бога́тство.

undress /ʌnˈdres/ *n.*: **in a state of ~** полуоде́тый; (*naked*) в го́лом ви́де; **~ uniform** повседне́вная фо́рма.

● *v.t. & i.* разд|ева́ть(ся), -е́ть(ся).

undressed /ʌnˈdrest/ *adj.* (*without clothes*) разде́тый; (*untreated*) необрабо́танный; **~ leather** невы́деланная ко́жа; **an ~ wound** (*unbandaged*) неперевя́занная ра́на; (*not cleaned*) необрабо́танная ра́на.

undrinkable /ʌnˈdrɪŋkəb(ə)l/ *adj.* неприго́дный для питья́.

undue /ʌnˈdjuː/ *adj.* (*excessive*) чрезме́рный, изли́шний; (*improper*) неподоба́ющий.

undulat|e /ˈʌndjʊˌleɪt/ *v.i.* волнова́ться (*impf.*); колыха́ться (*impf.*); **an ~ing landscape** холми́стый пейза́ж.

undulation /ˌʌndjʊˈleɪʃ(ə)n/ *n.* (*waviness*) волни́стость; (*hilliness*) холми́стость; (*wave*) волна́; (*hill*) холм.

unduly /ʌnˈdjuːlɪ/ *adv.* чрезме́рно; непра́вильно.

undying /ʌnˈdaɪɪŋ/ *adj.* бессме́ртный; **he won ~ glory** он завоева́л себе́ ве́чную сла́ву; **you have earned my ~ gratitude** я вам обя́зан до гробово́й доски́.

unearned /ʌnˈɜːnd/ *adj.* незарабо́танный; **~ income** нетрудовы́е дохо́ды (*m. pl.*); (*undeserved*) незаслу́женный.

unearth /ʌnˈɜːθ/ *v.t.* выка́пывать, вы́копать; **the body was ~ed** те́ло вы́копали; (*fig., discover*) раск|а́пывать, опа́ть.

unearthly /ʌnˈɜːθlɪ/ *adj.* **1** (*supernatural*) неземно́й; сверхъесте́ственный. **2** (*ghostly*) при́зрачный. **3** (*coll., unreasonable*) абсу́рдный; **why are you waking me at this ~ hour?** заче́м вы бу́дите меня́ в таку́ю рань (*or* ни свет, ни заря́)?

unease /ʌnˈiːz/ *n.* нело́вкость, стеснённость; (*distress*) трево́га.

uneasiness /ʌnˈiːzɪnɪs/ *n.* нело́вкость, стеснённость; беспоко́йство, трево́га.

uneasy /ʌnˈiːzɪ/ *adj.* **1** (*anxious*) беспоко́йный, трево́жный; **she was ~ about her daughter** она́ беспоко́илась за дочь. **2** (*ill at ease*) стеснённый, нело́вкий.

uneatable /ʌn'i:təb(ə)l/ *adj.* несъедобный.

uneaten /ʌn'i:t(ə)n/ *adj.* несъе́денный.

uneconomic /ˌʌni:kə'nɒmɪk/, /ˌʌnek-/ *adj.* неэконо́мный; нерента́бельный; **an ~ rent** невы́годная ре́нта.

uneconomical /ˌʌni:kə'nɒmɪk(ə)l/, /ˌʌnek-/ *adj.* (*wasteful*) неэконо́мный, бесхозя́йственный.

unedifying /ʌn'edɪˌfaɪɪŋ/ *adj.* (*indecent*) непристо́йный; (*distasteful*) малопривлека́тельный.

unedited /ʌn'edɪtɪd/ *adj.* неотредакти́рованный.

uneducated /ʌn'edjʊˌkeɪtɪd/ *adj.* необразо́ванный.

unemotional /ˌʌnɪ'məʊʃən(ə)l/ *adj.* неэмоциона́льный; бесстра́стный.

unemployable /ˌʌnɪm'plɔɪəb(ə)l/ *adj.* нетрудоспосо́бный.

unemployed /ˌʌnɪm'plɔɪd/ *adj.* **1** (*out of work*) безрабо́тный; (*as n.*: **the ~**) безрабо́тные (*pl.*). **2** (*unused, e.g. resources*) неиспо́льзованный.

unemployment /ˌʌnɪm'plɔɪmənt/ *n.* безрабо́тица; **~ benefit** посо́бие по безрабо́тице; **~ has risen/fallen** безрабо́тица вы́росла/упа́ла.

unencumbered /ˌʌnɪn'kʌmbəd/ *adj.* свобо́дный.

unending /ʌn'endɪŋ/ *adj.* нескончáемый, бесконе́чный.

unendowed /ˌʌnɪn'daʊd/ *adj.* (*fig.*): **~ with intelligence** не наделённый умо́м.

unendurable /ˌʌnɪn'djʊərəb(ə)l/ *adj.* невыноси́мый, нестерпи́мый.

un-English /ʌn'ɪŋglɪʃ/ *adj.* (*untypical*) не типи́чный для англича́нина; (*unworthy*) недосто́йный англича́нина.

unenlightened /ˌʌnɪn'laɪt(ə)nd/ *adj.* непросвещённый.

unenterprising /ʌn'entəˌpraɪzɪŋ/ *adj.* непредприи́мчивый.

unenthusiastic /ˌʌnɪnˌθju:zɪ'æstɪk/, /ˌʌnɪnˌθu:-/ *adj.* невосто́рженный; **he was ~ about the idea** он не́ был в восто́рге от э́той иде́и.

unenviable /ʌn'envɪəb(ə)l/ *adj.* незави́дный.

unequal /ʌn'i:kw(ə)l/ *adj.* нера́вный; **~ in length, of ~ length** различной/неодина́ковой длины́; **he was ~ to the task** зада́ча была́ ему́ не по плечу́; **~ treaty** неравнопра́вный догово́р.

unequalled /ʌn'i:kw(ə)ld/ (*US* **unequaled**) *adj.* непревзойдённый.

unequipped /ˌʌnɪ'kwɪpt/ *adj.* неподгото́вленный, неприспосо́бленный; **they were ~ to deal with such a large crowd** они́ не́ были (доста́точно) подгото́влены для того́, что́бы спра́виться с таки́м коли́чеством люде́й.

unequivocal /ˌʌnɪ'kwɪvək(ə)l/ *adj.* недвусмы́сленный; (*support*) определённый.

unerring /ʌn'ɜ:rɪŋ/ *adj.* безоши́бочный.

unescapable /ˌʌnɪ'skeɪpəb(ə)l/ *adj.* неизбе́жный.

UNESCO /ju:'neskəʊ/ *n.* (*abbr. of* ***United Nations Educational, Scientific and Cultural Organization***) ЮНЕ́СКО (Организа́ция Объединённых На́ций по вопро́сам образова́ния, нау́ки и культу́ры).

unethical /ʌn'eθɪk(ə)l/ *adj.* неэти́чный.

uneven /ʌn'i:v(ə)n/ *adj.* неро́вный; неравноме́рный; **an ~ surface** неро́вная пове́рхность; **~ progress** неравноме́рный прогре́сс.

uneventful /ˌʌnɪ'ventfʊl/ *adj.* ти́хий; без (осо́бых) приключе́ний/собы́тий.

unexampled /ˌʌnɪg'zɑ:mp(ə)ld/ *adj.* бесприме́рный.

unexceptionable /ˌʌnɪk'sepʃənəb(ə)l/ *adj.* безупре́чный.

unexceptional /ˌʌnɪk'sepʃən(ə)l/ *adj.* неисключи́тельный, зауря́дный.

unexciting /ˌʌnɪk'saɪtɪŋ/ *adj.* ску́чный, неинтере́сный.

unexpected /ˌʌnɪk'spektɪd/ *adj.* неожи́данный.

unexpired /ˌʌnɪk'spaɪəd/ *adj.* неисте́кший; (*document*) действи́тельный.

unexplainable /ˌʌnɪk'spleɪnəb(ə)l/ *adj.* необъясни́мый.

unexplained /ˌʌnɪk'spleɪnd/ *adj.* необъяснённый.

unexploded /ˌʌnɪk'spləʊdɪd/ *adj.* невзорва́вшийся.

unexplored /ˌʌnɪk'splɔ:d/ *adj.* неизве́данный, неиссле́дованный.

unexposed /ˌʌnɪk'spəʊzd/ *adj.* (*sheltered*) укры́тый, укро́мный, защищённый; (*crime*) нераскры́тый; (*film*) неэкспони́рованный.

unexpressed /ˌʌnɪk'sprest/ *adj.* невы́сказанный.

unexpurgated /ʌn'ekspəˌgeɪtɪd/ *adj.* без купю́р.

unfading /ʌn'feɪdɪŋ/ *adj.* (*fig.*) неувяда́емый.

unfailing /ʌn'feɪlɪŋ/ *adj.* (*ally, friend*) ве́рный; (*support*) неизме́нный.

unfair /ʌn'feə(r)/ *adj.* несправедли́вый; **~ advantage** незако́нное преиму́щество.

unfairness /ʌn'feənɪs/ *n.* несправедли́вость.

unfaithful /ʌn'feɪθfʊl/ *adj.* неве́рный; **his wife was ~ to him** жена́ ему́ измени́ла.

unfaithfulness /ʌn'feɪθfʊlnɪs/ *n.* неве́рность.

unfaltering /ʌn'fɔ:ltərɪŋ/, /ʌn'fɒl-/ *adj.* твёрдый, реши́тельный; **an ~ voice** твёрдый/недро́гнувший го́лос.

unfamiliar /ˌʌnfə'mɪljə(r)/ *adj.* незнако́мый; **his face is ~ to me** его́ лицо́ мне незнако́мо; **I am ~ with the district** я не зна́ю э́тот райо́н.

unfamiliarity /ˌʌnfəmɪlɪ'ærɪtɪ/ *n.* незна́ние; незнако́мство (*с чем*).

unfashionabl|e /ʌn'fæʃənəb(ə)l/ *adj.* немо́дный; старомо́дный; **~y** не по мо́де.

unfashioned /ʌn'fæʃ(ə)nd/ *adj.* необрабо́танный.

unfasten /ʌn'fɑ:s(ə)n/ *v.t.* открепл|я́ть, -и́ть; (*untie*) отвя́з|ывать, -а́ть; развя́з|ывать, -а́ть; (*unbutton, unclasp*) отстёг|ивать, -ну́ть; расстёг|ивать, -ну́ть; (*open*) откр|ыва́ть, -ы́ть.

unfathom|able /ʌn'fæðəməb(ə)l/, **-ed** /ʌn'fæðəmd/ *adjs.* неизмери́мый; (*incomprehensible*) непостижи́мый.

unfavourable /ʌn'feɪvərəb(ə)l/ (*US* **unfavorable**) *adj.* неблагоприя́тный.

unfeeling /ʌn'fi:lɪŋ/ *adj.* бесчу́вственный; жесто́кий.

unfeigned /ʌn'feɪnd/ *adj.* неподде́льный, непритво́рный.

unfeminine /ʌn'femɪnɪn/ *adj.* неже́нский, неже́нственный.

unfetter /ʌn'fetə(r)/ *v.t.* (*lit., fig.*) сн|има́ть, -ять око́вы с+*g.*; освобо|жда́ть, -ди́ть; **~ed** свобо́дный.

unfinished /ʌn'fɪnɪʃt/ *adj.* незако́нченный.

unfit /ʌn'fɪt/ *adj.* неподходя́щий, него́дный; **food ~ for (human) consumption** него́дная к потребле́нию пи́ща; **~ to rule** неспосо́бный пра́вить; **the doctor pronounced him ~** врач призна́л его́ больны́м (*for mil. service*: него́дным).

unfixed /ʌn'fɪkst/ *adj.* (*not certain*) неустано́вленный.

unflagging /ʌn'flægɪŋ/ *adj.* неосла́бный.

unflappable /ʌn'flæpəb(ə)l/ *adj.* (*coll.*) невозмути́мый.

unflattering /ʌn'flætərɪŋ/ *adj.* нелéстный.

unfledged /ʌn'fledʒd/ *adj.* (*lit., fig.*) неопери́вшийся.

unfold /ʌn'fəʊld/ *v.t.* развёр|тывать, -ну́ть; (*fig.*) раскр|ыва́ть, -ы́ть.

● *v.i.* развёр|тываться, -ну́ться; расстила́ться (*impf.*); **magnificent landscape ~ed before us** пе́ред на́ми расстила́лся великоле́пный пейза́ж; **as the story ~s** по ме́ре разви́тия повествова́ния.

unforced /ʌn'fɔ:st/ *adj.* (*voluntary*) доброво́льный; (*spontaneous*) непринуждённый.

unforeseeable /ˌʌnfɔ:'si:əb(ə)l/ *adj.* непредви́денный, непредсказу́емый.

unforeseen /ˌʌnfɔ:'si:n/ *adj.* непредви́денный.

unforgettable /ˌʌnfə'getəb(ə)l/ *adj.* незабыва́емый, незабве́нный.

unforgivable /ˌʌnfə'gɪvəb(ə)l/ *adj.* непрости́тельный.

unforgiving /ˌʌnfə'gɪvɪŋ/ *adj.* непроща́ющий; неумоли́мый.

unforgotten /ˌʌnfə'gɒt(ə)n/ *adj.* незабы́тый.

unformatted /ʌn'fɔ:mætɪd/ *adj.* (*comput.*) неформати́рованный.

unfortunate /ʌn'fɔ:tjʊnət/, /-tʃənət/ *n.* неуда́чни|к (*fem.* -ца); несчастли́в|ец (*fem.* -ица).

● *adj.* несча́стный; неуда́чный; **an ~ coincidence** доса́дное совпаде́ние; **an**

~ remark неуда́чное замеча́ние; **it was ~ that I came in just then** как неуда́чно, что я вошёл и́менно тогда́!

unfortunately /ʌn'fɔ:tjʊnətlɪ/, /-tʃənətlɪ/ *adv.* к сожале́нию, к несча́стью.

unfounded /ʌn'faʊndɪd/ *adj.* необосно́ванный.

unfreeze /ʌn'fri:z/ *v.t.* (*also fig., of assets*) размор|а́живать, -о́зить.

unfrequented /,ʌnfrɪ'kwentɪd/ *adj.* малопосеща́емый.

unfriendliness /ʌn'frendlɪnɪs/ *adj.* недружелю́бие, неприя́знь.

unfriendly /ʌn'frendlɪ/ *adj.* недружелю́бный; **an ~ act** недру́жественный посту́пок.

unfrock /ʌn'frɒk/ *v.t.* лиш|а́ть, -и́ть духо́вного са́на.

unfruitful /ʌn'fru:tfʊl/ *adj.* (*fig.*) беспло́дный; (*vain*) напра́сный, тще́тный; (*useless*) бесполе́зный.

unfulfilled /,ʌnfʊl'fɪld/ *adj.* (*of task etc.*) невы́полненный, (*of person*) неудовлетворённый.

unfurl /ʌn'fɜ:l/ *v.t.* (*flag*) развёр|тывать, -ну́ть; (*sail*) распус|ка́ть, -ти́ть; (*umbrella*) раскр|ыва́ть, -ы́ть.
● *v.i.* (*of flag*) развёр|тываться, -ну́ться; (*of sail, plants*) распус|ка́ться, -ти́ться.

unfurnished /ʌn'fɜ:nɪʃt/ *adj.* немеблиро́ванный.

ungainliness /ʌn'geɪnlɪnɪs/ *n.* нело́вкость, неуклю́жесть.

ungainly /ʌn'geɪnlɪ/ *adj.* нело́вкий, неуклю́жий.

ungallant /ʌn'gælənt/ *adj.* негала́нтный, нелюбе́зный.

ungenerous /ʌn'dʒenərəs/ *adj.* (*petty*) неблагоро́дный, ме́лочный; (*stingy*) скупо́й.

ungentle /ʌn'dʒent(ə)l/ *adj.* неделика́тный, гру́бый.

ungentlemanly /ʌn'dʒent(ə)lmənlɪ/ *adj.* неджентльме́нский; неблагоро́дный.

unget-at-able /,ʌnget'ætəb(ə)l/ *adj.* (*coll.*) недосту́пный.

ungifted /ʌn'gɪftɪd/ *adj.* неодарённый, неталантливый.

ungodliness /ʌn'gɒdlɪnɪs/ *n.* непра́ведность, нечести́вость, безбо́жие.

ungodly /ʌn'gɒdlɪ/ *adj.* непра́ведный, нечести́вый, безбо́жный; (*coll., frightful*): **an ~ noise** а́дский шум; **at this/that/some ~ hour** (*very early*) ни свет, ни заря́; (*inconvenient*) неуро́чный час.

ungovernable /ʌn'gʌvənəb(ə)l/ *adj.* неуправля́емый.

ungraceful /ʌn'greɪsfʊl/ *adj.* неграцио́зный, неуклю́жий.

ungracious /ʌn'greɪʃəs/ *adj.* неве́жливый, нелюбе́зный.

ungraciousness /ʌn'greɪʃəsnɪs/ *n.* неве́жливость, нелюбе́зность.

ungrammatical /,ʌngrə'mætɪk(ə)l/ *adj.* негра́мотный.

ungrateful /ʌn'greɪtfʊl/ *adj.* неблагода́рный.

ungratefulness /ʌn'greɪtfʊlnɪs/ *n.* неблагода́рность.

ungrudging /ʌn'grʌdʒɪŋ/ *adj.* ще́дрый; до́брый; **he gave ~ly of his time** он ще́дро дари́л своё вре́мя.

unguarded /ʌn'gɑ:dɪd/ *adj.* (*e.g. town*) незащищённый; (*e.g. prisoner*) неохраня́емый; (*careless*) неосторо́жный.

unguent /'ʌŋgwənt/ *n.* мазь.

ungulate /'ʌŋgjʊlət/, /-,leɪt/ *adj.* копы́тный.

unhampered /ʌn'hæmpəd/ *adj.* (*unimpeded*) беспрепя́тственный; (*free*) свобо́дный (от + *g.*).

unhappily /ʌn'hæpɪlɪ/ *adv.* **1** (*without happiness*) несча́стливо; **they were ~ married** их брак был несчастли́вый. **2** (*unfortunately*) к несча́стью.

unhappiness /ʌn'hæpɪnɪs/ *n.* несча́стье, грусть.

unhappy /ʌn'hæpɪ/ *adj.* (*sorrowful*) несчастли́вый, несча́стный, гру́стный; (*unfortunate*) неуда́чный.

unharmed /ʌn'hɑ:md/ *adj.* невреди́мый; (*of objects and parts of body*) неповреждённый; (*pred.*) цел и невреди́м.

unharness /ʌn'hɑ:nɪs/ *v.t.* распр|яга́ть, -я́чь.

unhealthy /ʌn'helθɪ/ *adj.* **1** (*in or indicating ill-health*) нездоро́вый, боле́зненный. **2** (*coll., dangerous*) вре́дный.

unheard /ʌn'hɜ:d/ *adj.*: **his pleas went ~** его́ мольбы́ оста́лись без отве́та.

unheard-of /ʌn'hɜ:dɒv/ *adj.* (*unknown*) никому́ не изве́стный; (*unexampled*) неслы́ханный, беспрецеде́нтный.

unheeded /ʌn'hi:dɪd/ *adj.* незаме́ченный; **his advice went ~** к его́ сове́ту не прислу́шались.

unheed|ful /ʌn'hi:dfʊl/, **-ing** /ʌn'hi:dɪŋ/ *adjs.* невнима́тельный.

unhelpful /ʌn'helpfʊl/ *adj.* бесполе́зный; (*person*) неотзы́вчивый.

unhelpfulness /ʌn'helpfʊlnɪs/ *n.* бесполе́зность; неотзы́вчивость.

unheralded /ʌn'herəldɪd/ *adj.* невозвещённый; (*unannounced*) необъя́вленный.

unhesitating /ʌn'hezɪ,teɪtɪŋ/ *adj.* реши́тельный.

unhinge /ʌn'hɪndʒ/ *v.t.* (*lit.*) сн|има́ть, -ять с пе́тель; (*fig.*) расстр|а́ивать, -о́ить; **the tragedy ~d his mind** от пережи́той траге́дии он помеша́лся.

unhitch /ʌn'hɪtʃ/ *v.t.* отвя́з|ывать, -а́ть.

unholy /ʌn'həʊlɪ/ *adj.* нечести́вый; (*coll., frightful*) ужа́сный; **an ~ row** ужа́сный/жу́ткий сканда́л.

unhook /ʌn'hʊk/ *v.t.* **1** (*unfasten hooks of*) расстёг|ивать, -ну́ть. **2** (*release from hook etc.*) отцеп|ля́ть, -и́ть.

unhoped-for /ʌn'həʊptfɔ:(r)/ *adj.* неожи́данный, нежда́нный.

unhurried /ʌn'hʌrɪd/ *adj.* неторопли́вый, неспе́шный.

unhurt /ʌn'hɜ:t/ *adj.* невреди́мый.

unhygienic /,ʌnhaɪ'dʒi:nɪk/ *adj.* негигиени́чный.

uni- /'ju:nɪ/ *comb. form* одно́..., еди́но....

UNICEF /'ju:nɪ,sef/ *n.* (*abbr. of* ***United Nations Children's Fund***) ЮНИСЕ́Ф (Де́тский фонд ОО́Н).

unicorn /'ju:nɪ,kɔ:n/ *n.* единоро́г.

unidentifiable /,ʌnaɪ'dentɪ,faɪəb(ə)l/ *adj.* не поддаю́щийся опозна́нию.

unidentified /,ʌnaɪ'dentɪ,faɪd/ *adj.* неопо́знанный; **~ flying object (UFO)** неопо́знанный лета́ющий объе́кт (НЛО).

unification /,ju:nɪfɪ'keɪʃ(ə)n/ *n.* объедине́ние; унифика́ция.

uniform /'ju:nɪ,fɔ:m/ *n.* фо́рма; (*esp. mil.*) мунди́р.
● *adj.* однообра́зный; одина́ковый; станда́ртный; **at a ~ temperature** при постоя́нной температу́ре; **a ~ blue-grey colour** (*Br.*), **color** (*US*) ро́вный се́ро-голубо́й цвет.

uniformed /'ju:nɪ,fɔ:md/ *adj.* оде́тый в фо́рму; в мунди́ре.

uniformity /,ju:nɪ'fɔ:mɪtɪ/ *n.* единообра́зие.

unify /'ju:nɪ,faɪ/ *v.t.* (*unite*) объедин|я́ть, -и́ть; (*make uniform*) унифици́ровать (*impf., pf.*).

unilateral /,ju:nɪ'lætər(ə)l/ *adj.* односторо́нний.

unimaginable /,ʌnɪ'mædʒɪnəb(ə)l/ *adj.* невообрази́мый.

unimaginative /,ʌnɪ'mædʒɪnətɪv/ *adj.* лишённый воображе́ния; прозаи́чный.

unimpaired /,ʌnɪm'peəd/ *adj.* (*mobility, brain, dignity*) непострада́вший; (*faith*) неосла́бленный.

unimpeachable /,ʌnɪm'pi:tʃəb(ə)l/ *adj.* безупре́чный, безукори́зненный.

unimpeded /,ʌnɪm'pi:dɪd/ *adj.* беспрепя́тственный; не остано́вленный (*чем*).

unimportance /,ʌnɪm'pɔ:t(ə)ns/ *n.* нева́жность, незначи́тельность.

unimportant /,ʌnɪm'pɔ:t(ə)nt/ *adj.* нева́жный, незначи́тельный.

unimposing /,ʌnɪm'pəʊzɪŋ/ *adj.* маловнуши́тельный, скро́мный.

unimpressed /,ʌnɪm'prest/ *adj.*: **I was ~ by his threats** его́ угро́зы не произвели́ на меня́ никако́го впечатле́ния.

unimpressive /,ʌnɪm'presɪv/ *adj.* невпечатля́ющий.

uninfluenced /ʌn'ɪnflʊənst/ *adj.* не находя́щийся под влия́нием (*кого/чего*); непредубеждённый.

uninformed /,ʌnɪn'fɔ:md/ *adj.* несве́дущий; **~ of/about** неосведомлённый о + *p.*

uninhabitable /,ʌnɪn'hæbɪtəb(ə)l/ *adj.* неприго́дный для жилья́.

uninhabited /,ʌnɪn'hæbɪtɪd/ *adj.* необита́емый.

uninhibited /,ʌnɪn'hɪbɪtɪd/ *adj.* откры́тый, нестесни́тельный.

uninitiated /,ʌnɪ'nɪʃɪ,eɪtɪd/ *adj.* непосвящённый.

uninjured /ʌn'ɪndʒəd/ *adj.*

непострада́вший; **he was ~ by his fall** при паде́нии он не пострада́л.

uninspired /ˌʌnɪnˈspaɪəd/ *adj.* (*speech*) невдохновлённый; **I was ~ by his proposals** его́ предложе́ния не вдохнови́ли меня́.

uninspiring /ˌʌnɪnˈspaɪərɪŋ/ *adj.* невдохновля́ющий.

uninsured /ˌʌnɪnˈʃʊəd/ *adj.* незастрахо́ванный.

unintelligent /ˌʌnɪnˈtelɪdʒ(ə)nt/ *adj.* неу́мный.

unintelligibility /ˌʌnɪnˌtelɪdʒɪˈbɪlɪtɪ/ *n.* неразбо́рчивость, невня́тность.

unintelligible /ˌʌnɪnˈtelɪdʒɪb(ə)l/ *adj.* неразбо́рчивый, невня́тный.

unintended /ˌʌnɪnˈtendɪd/ *adj.* ненаме́ренный; (*unforeseen*) непредусмо́тренный.

unintentional /ˌʌnɪnˈtenʃən(ə)l/ *adj.* ненаме́ренный.

uninterested /ʌnˈɪntrəstɪd/, /-trɪstɪd/ *adj.* безразли́чный (к + *d.*); не заинтересо́ванный (*чем*); **he is ~ in history** он не интересу́ется исто́рией.

uninteresting /ʌnˈɪntrəstɪŋ/, /-trɪstɪŋ/ *adj.* неинтере́сный.

uninterrupted /ˌʌnɪntəˈrʌptɪd/ *adj.* непрерыва́емый, непреры́вный.

uninventive /ˌʌnɪnˈventɪv/ *adj.* неизобрета́тельный.

uninvited /ˌʌnɪnˈvaɪtɪd/ *adj.* неприглашённый, незва́ный, непро́шеный.

uninviting /ˌʌnɪnˈvaɪtɪŋ/ *adj.* непривлека́тельный; **an ~ prospect** неприя́тная перспекти́ва.

union /ˈjuːnjən/, /-nɪən/ *n.* **1** (*joining, uniting*) объедине́ние, сою́з. **2** (*association*) сою́з; **U~ of Soviet Socialist Republics** (*hist.*) Сою́з Сове́тских Социалисти́ческих Респу́блик; **U~ Jack** госуда́рственный флаг Великобрита́нии; **students' ~** студе́нческий сою́з; (*building*) студе́нческий клуб. **3 (trade ~)** профессиона́льный сою́з, профсою́з; **~ card** профсою́зный биле́т. **4** (*state of harmony*) гармо́ния; согла́сие; **they live in perfect ~** они́ живу́т в по́лном согла́сии.

unionist /ˈjuːnjənɪst/, /ˈjuːnɪən-/ *n.* **1** (*member of trade union*) член профсою́за. **2** (**U~**: *in Northern Ireland*) юниони́ст.

unique /jʊˈniːk/, /juːˈniːk/ *adj.* уника́льный, еди́нственный (в своём ро́де).

unisex /ˈjuːnɪˌseks/ *adj.*: **~ clothes** оде́жда, подходя́щая для обо́их поло́в; **~ hairdresser's** парикма́херская для мужчи́н и же́нщин.

unisexual /ˌjuːnɪˈseksʊəl/ *adj.* (*bot.*) однопо́лый.

unison /ˈjuːnɪs(ə)n/ *n.* (*mus.*) унисо́н; (*fig.*) гармо́ния; **they acted in perfect ~** они́ де́йствовали в по́лном согла́сии.

unit /ˈjuːnɪt/ *n.* **1** (*single entity*) едини́ца; це́лое. **2** (*math., and of measurement*) едини́ца; **~ of length** едини́ца длины́; **~ of currency, monetary ~** де́нежная едини́ца; **~ trust** (*Br.*) довери́тельный паево́й фонд. **3** (*mil.*) часть; (*large ~, formation*) соедине́ние; (*small ~, sub-~*) подразделе́ние; (*detachment*) отря́д. **4** (*of furniture etc.*) се́кция; **kitchen ~s** секцио́нная ку́хонная ме́бель. **5** (*tech.*) се́кция, блок.

unite /jʊˈnaɪt/, /juː-/ *v.t.* соедин|я́ть, -и́ть; объедин|я́ть, -и́ть; **the country is ~d behind the President** вся страна́ сплоти́лась вокру́г президе́нта; **a ~d family** дру́жная семья́; **they made a ~d effort** они́ объедини́лись для совме́стных уси́лий; **the U~d Nations** (*organization*) Организа́ция Объединённых На́ций; **the U~d Kingdom** Соединённое Короле́вство; **the U~d States** Соединённые Шта́ты.

● *v.i.* соедин|я́ться, -и́ться; объедин|я́ться, -и́ться; **they ~d in condemning him** они́ единоду́шно его́ осуди́ли; **~d front** еди́ный фронт.

unit|y /ˈjuːnɪtɪ/ *n.* **1** (*oneness; coherence*) еди́нство; сплочённость; **~y of purpose** еди́нство це́ли; **national ~y** национа́льное еди́нство. **2** (*concord*) согла́сие; **dwell in ~y** жить (*impf.*) в согла́сии. **3** (*math.*) едини́ца.

universal /ˌjuːnɪˈvɜːs(ə)l/ *n.* (*phil.*) универса́лия.

● *adj.* всео́бщий, универса́льный; **his proposal met with ~ approval** его́ предложе́ние встре́тило всео́бщее одобре́ние; **~ joint** (*tech.*) универса́льный шарни́р; **a ~ remedy** универса́льное сре́дство; **~ suffrage** всео́бщее избира́тельное пра́во.

universality /ˌjuːnɪvɜːˈsælɪtɪ/ *n.* универса́льность.

universe /ˈjuːnɪˌvɜːs/ *n.* вселе́нная, мир.

university /ˌjuːnɪˈvɜːsɪtɪ/ *n.* университе́т; **~ town** университе́тский го́род.

unjust /ʌnˈdʒʌst/ *adj.* несправедли́вый.

unjustifiable /ʌnˈdʒʌstɪˌfaɪəb(ə)l/ *adj.* непрости́тельный.

unjustified /ʌnˈdʒʌstɪˌfaɪd/ *adj.* неопра́вданный.

unkempt /ʌnˈkempt/ *adj.* нечёсаный, растрёпанный.

unkind /ʌnˈkaɪnd/ *adj.* недо́брый, злой; (*unpleasant*) нелюбе́зный; **be ~ to s.o.** пло́хо обраща́ться (*impf.*) с кем-н. (*or* относи́ться (*impf.*) к кому́-н.).

unkindness /ʌnˈkaɪndnɪs/ *n.* зло́сть; нелюбе́зность.

unknowable /ʌnˈnəʊəb(ə)l/ *adj.* непознава́емый.

unknowing /ʌnˈnəʊɪŋ/ *adj.* незна́ющий, несве́дущий.

unknown /ʌnˈnəʊn/ *n.* неизве́стное; **fear of the ~** страх пе́ред неизве́стностью; (*math.*) неизве́стная величина́.

● *adj.* неизве́стный; **an ~ quantity** неизве́стная величина́; **the U~ Soldier** Неизве́стный солда́т.

● *adv.*: **he did it ~ to me** он сде́лал э́то без моего́ ве́дома.

unlace /ʌnˈleɪs/ *v.t.* расшнуро́в|ывать, -а́ть.

unladen /ʌnˈleɪd(ə)n/ *adj.* (*without load or cargo*) поро́жний, без гру́за.

unladylike /ʌnˈleɪdɪˌlaɪk/ *adj.* неподоба́ющий воспи́танной же́нщине; (*vulgar*) вульга́рный.

unlamented /ˌʌnləˈmentɪd/ *adj.* неопла́киваемый, неопла́канный.

unlatch /ʌnˈlætʃ/ *v.t.* отп|ира́ть, -ере́ть.

unlawful /ʌnˈlɔːfʊl/ *adj.* незако́нный.

unleaded /ʌnˈledɪd/ *adj.*: **~ petrol** (*Br.*), **gasoline** (*US*) неэтили́рованный бензи́н.

unlearn /ʌnˈlɜːn/ *v.t.* раз|у́чиваться, -учи́ться (+ *inf.*); от|у́чиваться, -учи́ться от + *g.*; отв|ыка́ть, -ы́кнуть от + *g.*

unleash /ʌnˈliːʃ/ *v.t.* спус|ка́ть, -ти́ть со сво́ры; (*fig.*) да|ва́ть, -ть во́лю + *d.*; **~ a war** разв|я́зывать, -яза́ть войну́; **his fury was ~ed** он рассвирепе́л (*or* пришёл в бе́шенство).

unleavened /ʌnˈlev(ə)nd/ *adj.* незаква́шенный, пре́сный.

unless /ʌnˈles/, /ənˈles/ *conj.* (*if not*) е́сли (то́лько) не; **I shall go ~ it rains** я пойду́, е́сли (то́лько) не бу́дет дождя́; (*until*) пока́ не; **I won't continue ~ he apologizes** я не бу́ду продолжа́ть, пока́ он не извини́тся; (*except if*) ра́зве (что/то́лько); **I don't know why he is late, ~ he has lost his way** не зна́ю, почему́ он опа́здывает — ра́зве что заблуди́лся.

unlicensed /ʌnˈlaɪs(ə)nst/ *adj.* (*Br.*) не име́ющий разреше́ния на прода́жу спиртны́х напи́тков.

unlike /ʌnˈlaɪk/ *adj. & prep.* (*not like, different from*) непохо́жий, ра́зный; **he is ~ his sister** он не похо́ж на свою́ сестру́; **that** (*conduct etc.*) **is ~ him** э́то на него́ не похо́же; **he talks ~ anyone I have ever heard** я никогда́ не слы́шал, что́бы так говори́ли(, как он); **~ the others, he works hard** в отли́чие от други́х (*or* не в приме́р други́м) он рабо́тает усе́рдно.

unlikeable /ʌnˈlaɪkəb(ə)l/ *adj.* непривлека́тельный.

unlikelihood /ʌnˈlaɪklɪhʊd/ *n.* неправдоподо́бие; маловероя́тность; невероя́тность.

unlikely /ʌnˈlaɪklɪ/ *adj.* (*tale*) неправдоподо́бный; (*not to be expected*): **it is ~ he will recover** маловероя́тно, что он попра́вится; **he is ~ to come** маловероя́тно, что он придёт; (*unpromising*) немы́слимый, невероя́тный.

unlimited /ʌnˈlɪmɪtɪd/ *adj.* неограни́ченный; (*expanse*) безграни́чный.

unlined /ʌnˈlaɪnd/ *adj.* **1**: **~ paper** нелино́ванная бума́га. **2**: **an ~ coat** пальто́ без подкла́дки.

unlisted /ʌnˈlɪstɪd/ *adj.* (*not on a list*) не включённый в спи́сок; (*US, ex-directory*) не внесённый в телефо́нную кни́гу; (*stock exchange*) не коти́рующийся.

unlit /ʌnˈlɪt/ *adj.* неосвещённый; незажжённый; **~ streets**

неосвещённые у́лицы; **the lamp was ~** ла́мпу не зажгли́.

unload /ʌn'ləʊd/ *v.t.* выгружа́ть, вы́грузить; разгру|жа́ть, -зи́ть; (*fig.*): **she ~ed her worries on to him** она́ облегчи́ла ду́шу, подели́вшись с ним свои́ми забо́тами; **he ~ed his shares** он сбыл свои́ а́кции.

● *v.i.* разгру|жа́ться, -зи́ться.

unloaded /ʌn'ləʊdɪd/ *adj.* незаря́женный, пусто́й; **his gun was ~** его́ ружьё не́ было заря́жено.

unlock /ʌn'lɒk/ *v.t.* отп|ира́ть, -ере́ть (ключо́м); откр|ыва́ть, -ы́ть.

unlocked /ʌn'lɒkt/ *adj.* откры́тый, о́тпертый, неза́пертый.

unloose /ʌn'lu:s/ *v.t.* (*slacken; untie*) осл|абля́ть, -а́бить; отвя́з|ывать, -а́ть; (*release*) освобо|жда́ть, -ди́ть.

unlovable /ʌn'lʌvəb(ə)l/ *adj.* непривлека́тельный.

unloved /ʌn'lʌvd/ *adj.* нелюби́мый.

unlovely /ʌn'lʌvlɪ/ *adj.* неприя́тный, некраси́вый.

unloving /ʌn'lʌvɪŋ/ *adj.* нелю́бящий.

unluckily /ʌn'lʌkɪlɪ/ *adv.* к несча́стью; **~ for him** к несча́стью для него́.

unlucky /ʌn'lʌkɪ/ *adj.* (*of actions*) неуда́чный; (*wretched*) незада́чливый; (*having bad luck*): **he is ~ at cards** ему́ не везёт в ка́ртах; (*causing bad luck*) несчастли́вый; **~ number** несчастли́вое число́; **it is ~ to spill salt** просы́пать соль — не к добру́.

unmade /ʌn'meɪd/ *adj.*: **an ~ bed** незастéленная посте́ль.

unman /ʌn'mæn/ *v.t.* лиш|а́ть, -и́ть му́жества.

unmanageable /ʌn'mænɪdʒəb(ə)l/ *adj.* неуправля́емый; не поддаю́щийся контро́лю; (*of child*) тру́дный, непоко́рный.

unmanly /ʌn'mænlɪ/ *adj.* нему́жественный, недосто́йный мужчи́ны; трусли́вый.

unmanned /ʌn'mænd/ *adj.* не укомплекто́ванный людьми́; необслу́живаемый; **an ~ satellite** автомати́чески управля́емый спу́тник.

unmannerly /ʌn'mænəlɪ/ *adj.* невоспи́танный.

unmarked /ʌn'mɑ:kt/ *adj.* (*without markings*) неотме́ченный, неме́ченный; **~ grave** безымя́нная моги́ла; **~ police car** полице́йская маши́на без опознава́тельных знако́в; (*unobserved*) незаме́ченный; **the mistake passed ~** оши́бка прошла́ незаме́ченной.

unmarketable /ʌn'mɑ:kɪtəb(ə)l/ *adj.* не подходя́щий для ры́нка.

unmarried /ʌn'mærɪd/ *adj.* неженáтый, холосто́й; незаму́жняя; **he is ~** он не жена́т; **she is ~** она́ не за́мужем; **~ mother** мать-одино́чка.

unmask /ʌn'mɑ:sk/ *v.t.* (*fig.*) разоблач|а́ть, -и́ть.

● *v.i.* (*lit.*) сн|има́ть, -ять ма́ску.

unmatched /ʌn'mætʃt/ *adj.* (*without an equal*) непревзойдённый; бесподо́бный.

unmeant /ʌn'ment/ *adj.* неумы́шленный, нево́льный.

unmeasured /ʌn'meʒəd/ *adj.* (*fig., boundless*) безграни́чный; (*immoderate*) чрезме́рный.

unmentionable /ʌn'menʃənəb(ə)l/ *adj.* неприли́чный, запре́тный.

unmerciful /ʌn'mɜ:sɪ,fʊl/ *adj.* немилосе́рдный, безжа́лостный.

unmerited /ʌn'merɪtɪd/ *adj.* незаслу́женный.

unmindful /ʌn'maɪndfʊl/ *adj.* невнима́тельный, забы́вчивый; **~ of his duty** забы́в о до́лге.

unmistakabl|e /,ʌnmɪ'steɪkəb(ə)l/ *adj.* ве́рный, я́сный, очеви́дный; характе́рный; **~y** несомне́нно, безусло́вно.

unmitigated /ʌn'mɪtɪ,geɪtɪd/ *adj.* (*not softened*) несмягчённый; (*arrant*) зако́нченный, отъя́вленный, я́вный.

unmoor /ʌn'mʊə(r)/, /ʌn'mɔ:(r)/ *v.t. & i.* сн|има́ть(ся), -ять(ся) с я́коря.

unmounted /ʌn'maʊntɪd/ *adj.* **1** (*on foot*) пе́ший. **2** (*of precious stone*) неопра́вленный. **3** (*of photograph etc.*) неоканто́ванный, без паспарту́.

unmourned /ʌn'mɔ:nd/ *adj.* неопла́канный.

unmoved /ʌn'mu:vd/ *adj.* (*unaffected by emotion*) бесчу́вственный; равноду́шный.

unmusical /ʌn'mju:zɪk(ə)l/ *adj.*: **an ~ noise** неприя́тный шум; **he is ~** он не музыка́лен.

unnamed /ʌn'neɪmd/ *adj.* нена́званный; (*unidentified*) неизве́стный.

unnatural /ʌn'nætʃər(ə)l/ *adj.* неесте́ственный; **he displayed ~ energy** он прояви́л неимове́рную/невероя́тную эне́ргию; **not ~ly** есте́ственно.

unnavigable /ʌn'nævɪgəb(ə)l/ *adj.* несудохо́дный; (*aeron.*) нелётный; (*of a balloon*) неуправля́емый.

unnecessary /ʌn'nesəsərɪ/ *adj.* нену́жный, ли́шний; (*excessive*) изли́шний.

unneighbourly /ʌn'neɪbəlɪ/ (*US* **unneighborly**) *adj.* недобрососе́дский.

unnerv|e /ʌn'nɜ:v/ *v.t.* обесси́ли|вать, -ть; лиш|а́ть, -и́ть му́жества; расстр|а́ивать, -о́ить; **an ~ing experience** неприя́тное/жу́ткое пережива́ние.

unnoticeable /ʌn'nəʊtɪsəb(ə)l/ *adj.* незаме́тный.

unnoticed /ʌn'nəʊtɪst/ *adj.* незаме́ченный; **his appearance went ~** его́ появле́ние оста́лось незаме́ченным; **I let his remarks pass ~** я оста́вил его́ замеча́ния без внима́ния.

unnumbered /ʌn'nʌmbəd/ *adj.* **1** (*countless*) бессчётный, несме́тный. **2** (*without numbering*) без но́мера, непронумеро́ванный; **~ pages** непронумеро́ванные страни́цы.

UNO /'ju:nəʊ/ = **UN**

unobjectionable /,ʌnəb'dʒekʃənəb(ə)l/ *adj.* прие́млемый.

unobliging /,ʌnə'blaɪdʒɪŋ/ *adj.* нелюбе́зный; неуслу́жливый.

unobservant /,ʌnəb'zɜ:v(ə)nt/ *adj.* ненаблюда́тельный.

unobserved /,ʌnəb'zɜ:vd/ *adj.* незаме́ченный.

unobstructed /,ʌnəb'strʌktɪd/ *adj.* (*of road, view*) незагоро́женный; **~ progress** беспрепя́тственное продвиже́ние.

unobtainable /,ʌnəb'teɪnəb(ə)l/ *adj.* недосту́пный.

unobtrusive /,ʌnəb'tru:sɪv/ *adj.* скро́мный, ненавя́зчивый.

unobtrusiveness /,ʌnəb'tru:sɪvnɪs/ *adj.* скро́мность, ненавя́зчивость.

unoccupied /ʌn'ɒkjʊ,paɪd/ *adj.* неза́нятый, свобо́дный; **an ~ house** пусто́й дом; **~ seats** неза́нятые/свобо́дные места́.

unofficial /,ʌnə'fɪʃ(ə)l/ *adj.* неофициа́льный.

unopened /ʌn'əʊp(ə)nd/ *adj.* неоткры́тый.

unopposed /,ʌnə'pəʊzd/ *adj.* не встреча́ющий/встре́тивший сопротивле́ния; **his candidature was ~** он был еди́нственным кандида́том.

unorganized /ʌn'ɔ:gə,naɪzd/ *adj.* неорганизо́ванный.

unoriginal /,ʌnə'rɪdʒɪn(ə)l/ *adj.* неоригина́льный; заи́мствованный.

unorthodox /ʌn'ɔ:θə,dɒks/ *adj.* неортодокса́льный, неправове́рный; (*unconventional*) неортодокса́льный, сме́лый.

unorthodoxy /ʌn'ɔ:θə,dɒksɪ/ *n.* неортодокса́льность.

unostentatious /,ʌnɒsten'teɪʃəs/ *adj.* ненавя́зчивый, скро́мный.

unpack /ʌn'pæk/ *v.t. & i.* распако́в|ывать(ся), -а́ть(ся).

unpaid /ʌn'peɪd/ *adj.* **1** неопла́ченный; (*of debt, bill etc.*) неупла́ченный; **~ work** беспла́тная рабо́та; **the men were ~** рабо́чим не заплати́ли. **2** (*of person, unsalaried*) не получа́ющий пла́ту/жа́лованье.

unpalatable /ʌn'pælətəb(ə)l/ *adj.* невку́сный; (*fig.*) неприя́тный; **an ~ truth** го́рькая и́стина.

unparalleled /ʌn'pærə,leld/ *adj.* несравни́мый, несравне́нный; бесподо́бный.

unpardonable /ʌn'pɑ:dənəb(ə)l/ *adj.* непрости́тельный.

unparliamentary /,ʌnpɑ:lə'mentərɪ/ *adj.*: **~ language** «непарла́ментские»/ ре́зкие выраже́ния.

unpatriotic /,ʌnpætrɪ'ɒtɪk/, /,ʌnpeɪt-/ *adj.* (*behaviour*) непатриоти́ческий; (*person*) непатриоти́чный.

unpaved /ʌn'peɪvd/ *adj.* немощёный.

unpeg /ʌn'peg/ *v.t.* **1** откреп|ля́ть, -и́ть; **she ~ged the clothes** она́ сняла́ оде́жду с ве́шалки/крючка́. **2**: **~ prices** прекра|ща́ть, -ти́ть иску́сственную стабилиза́цию цен.

unperceived /ˌʌnpəˈsiːvd/ *adj.* незаме́ченный.

unperson /ˈʌnˌpɜːs(ə)n/ *n.* ≈ нечелове́к.

unpersuaded /ˌʌnpəˈsweɪdɪd/ *adj.* неубеждённый.

unpersuasive /ˌʌnpəˈsweɪsɪv/ *adj.* неубеди́тельный.

unperturbed /ˌʌnpəˈtɜːbd/ *adj.* невозмути́мый.

unpick /ʌnˈpɪk/ *v.t.* расп|а́рывать, -оро́ть.

unpin /ʌnˈpɪn/ *v.t.* отк|а́лывать, -оло́ть; вынима́ть, вы́нуть була́вки/шпи́льки из + *g.*

unplaced /ʌnˈpleɪst/ *adj.* (*of horse*) не заня́вший призово́го ме́ста.

unplait /ʌnˈplæt/ *v.t.* расплe|та́ть, -сти́.

unplanned /ʌnˈplænd/ *adj.* незаплани́рованный; **~ pregnancy** незаплани́рованная бере́менность; (*unexpected*) неожи́данный; **an ~ economy** непла́новая эконо́мика.

unpleasant /ʌnˈplez(ə)nt/ *adj.* неприя́тный.

unpleasantness /ʌnˈplez(ə)ntnɪs/ *n.* неприя́тность.

unplug /ʌnˈplʌg/ *v.t.* отключ|а́ть, -и́ть.

unplumbed /ʌnˈplʌmd/ *adj.* (*not understood*) непостижи́мый; (*unexplored*) не иссле́дованный до конца́; (*immense*) неизмери́мый.

unpolluted /ˌʌnpəˈluːtɪd/ *adj.* незагрязнённый.

unpopular /ʌnˈpɒpjʊlə(r)/ *adj.* непопуля́рный.

unpopularity /ˌʌnpɒpjʊˈlærɪtɪ/ *n.* непопуля́рность.

unpractical /ʌnˈpræktɪk(ə)l/ *adj.* (*solution etc.*) нецелесообра́зный; (*person*) непракти́чный.

unprecedented /ʌnˈpresɪˌdentɪd/ *adj.* беспрецеде́нтный.

unpredictable /ˌʌnprɪˈdɪktəb(ə)l/ *adj.* непредсказу́емый.

unprejudiced /ʌnˈpredʒʊdɪst/ *adj.* непредвзя́тый, непредубеждённый.

unpremeditated /ˌʌnprɪˈmedɪˌteɪtɪd/ *adj.* непреднаме́ренный; непредумы́шленный.

unprepared /ˌʌnprɪˈpeəd/ *adj.* неподгото́вленный; **his speech was ~** он произнёс свою́ речь экспро́мтом.

unpreparedness /ˌʌnprɪˈpeədnɪs/ *n.* неподгото́вленность.

unprepossessing /ˌʌnpriːpəˈzesɪŋ/ *adj.* нерасполага́ющий (к себе́), непривлека́тельный.

unpresentable /ˌʌnprɪˈzentəb(ə)l/ *adj.* непрезента́бельный.

unpretentious /ˌʌnprɪˈtenʃəs/ *adj.* непретенцио́зный, скро́мный, просто́й.

unpretentiousness /ˌʌnprɪˈtenʃəsnɪs/ *n.* скро́мность, простота́.

unpreventable /ˌʌnprɪˈventəb(ə)l/ *adj.* неизбе́жный, неотврати́мый.

unpriced /ʌnˈpraɪst/ *adj.* без указа́ния цены́.

unprincipled /ʌnˈprɪnsɪp(ə)ld/ *adj.* беспринци́пный.

unprintable /ʌnˈprɪntəb(ə)l/ *adj.* нецензу́рный, непеча́тный.

unproductive /ˌʌnprəˈdʌktɪv/ *adj.* непродукти́вный, непроизводи́тельный; **~ labour** (*Br.*), **labor** (*US*) непроизводи́тельный труд; **an ~ argument** бесполе́зный спор.

unprofessional /ˌʌnprəˈfeʃən(ə)l/ *adj.* непрофессиона́льный; **~ conduct** наруше́ние профессиона́льной э́тики.

unprofitable /ʌnˈprɒfɪtəb(ə)l/ *adj.* невы́годный, неприбы́льный; (*useless*) бесполе́зный.

unpromising /ʌnˈprɒmɪsɪŋ/ *adj.* малообеща́ющий.

unprompted /ʌnˈprɒmptɪd/ *adj.* неподска́занный, спонта́нный.

unpronounceable /ˌʌnprəˈnaʊnsəb(ə)l/ *adj.* непроизноси́мый.

unpropitious /ˌʌnprəˈpɪʃəs/ *adj.* неблагоприя́тный.

unprotected /ˌʌnprəˈtektɪd/ *adj.* незащищённый; **~ sex** секс без контрацепти́вов; (*defenceless*) беззащи́тный.

unprovable /ʌnˈpruːvəb(ə)l/ *adj.* недоказу́емый.

unprove|d /ʌnˈpruːvd/, **-n** /ʌnˈpruːv(ə)n/ *adjs.* недока́занный.

unprovoked /ˌʌnprəˈvəʊkt/ *adj.* неспровоци́рованный; ниче́м не вы́званный.

unpublished /ʌnˈpʌblɪʃt/ *adj.* неопублико́ванный, неи́зданный.

unpunished /ʌnˈpʌnɪʃt/ *adj.* безнака́занный, ненака́занный.

unputdownable /ˌʌnpʊtˈdaʊnəb(ə)l/ *adj.* (*coll.*) захва́тывающий; **the book is ~** кни́га така́я интере́сная, (что) не оторвёшься.

unqualified /ʌnˈkwɒlɪˌfaɪd/ *adj.* **1** (*without reservations*) безоговоро́чный; **~ praise** безграни́чная хвала́; **an ~ refusal** реши́тельный отка́з. **2** (*not competent*) некомпете́нтный, неквалифици́рованный; **I am ~ to judge this** я недоста́точно компете́нтен, что́бы суди́ть об э́том.

unquenchable /ʌnˈkwentʃəb(ə)l/ *adj.* (*of thirst*) неутоли́мый; (*of fire*) неугаси́мый; (*fig.*) неиссяка́емый.

unquestionabl|e /ʌnˈkwestʃənəb(ə)l/ *adj.* (*undoubted*) несомне́нный; (*indisputable*) неоспори́мый, бесспо́рный; **you are ~y right** вы несомне́нно/безусло́вно пра́вы.

unquestioned /ʌnˈkwestʃ(ə)nd/ *adj.* бесспо́рный, при́знанный.

unquestioning /ʌnˈkwestʃənɪŋ/ *adj.*: **~ obedience** безоговоро́чное/по́лное повинове́ние.

unquote /ʌnˈkwəʊt/ *v.t.* (*imper. only*): **'quote … ~'** «откры́ть кавы́чки… закры́ть кавы́чки».

unravel /ʌnˈræv(ə)l/ *v.t.* (**unravelled, unravelling; *US* unraveled, unraveling**) распу́т|ывать, -ать; **the wool was ~led** шерсть распу́тали; (*fig.*) разга́д|ывать, -а́ть.

unreachable /ʌnˈriːtʃəb(ə)l/ *adj.*: **he was ~ at his office** его́ нельзя́ бы́ло заста́ть в конто́ре.

unread /ʌnˈred/ *adj.* (*of book etc.*) непрочи́танный; (*of writer*) нечита́емый; **this writer is ~** сейча́с э́того писа́теля ма́ло чита́ют.

unreadable /ʌnˈriːdəb(ə)l/ *adj.* (*illegible*) неразбо́рчивый; (*tedious*) нечита́бельный.

unreadiness /ʌnˈredɪnɪs/ *n.* негото́вность.

unready /ʌnˈredɪ/ *adj.* негото́вый.

unreal /ʌnˈrɪəl/ *adj.* (*imaginary*) нереа́льный; (*strange*) фантасти́ческий; (*unrealistic*) нереа́льный.

unrealistic /ˌʌnrɪəˈlɪstɪk/ *adj.* **1** (*unpractical, unreasonable*) нереа́льный. **2** (*of art*) нереалисти́ческий.

unreality /ˌʌnrɪˈælɪtɪ/ *n.* нереа́льность; ото́рванность от действи́тельности/жи́зни.

unrealizable /ʌnˈrɪəlaɪzəb(ə)l/ *adj.* неосуществи́мый; (*comm.*) труднореализу́емый; не могу́щий быть реализо́ванным.

unrealized /ʌnˈrɪəlaɪzd/ *adj.* (*not carried out*) неосуществлённый; (*not fulfilled*) нереализо́ванный; (*comm.*) нереализо́ванный; (*not understood*) неосо́знанный.

unreason /ʌnˈriːz(ə)n/ *n.* неразу́мность, безрассу́дство.

unreasonable /ʌnˈriːzənəb(ə)l/ *adj.* безрассу́дный, не(благо)разу́мный; **don't be ~!** бу́дьте благоразу́мны!; (*excessive*) чрезме́рный.

unreasoning /ʌnˈriːzənɪŋ/ *adj.* неразу́мный; нерассужда́ющий.

unreciprocated /ˌʌnrɪˈsɪprəˌkeɪtɪd/ *adj.* без взаи́мности, не по́льзующийся взаи́мностью.

unrecognizable /ʌnˈrekəgˌnaɪzəb(ə)l/ *adj.* неузнава́емый.

unrecognized /ʌnˈrekəgˌnaɪzd/ *adj.* (*face*) неу́знанный; (*talent*) непри́знанный; **his genius was ~** его́ ге́ний не получи́л призна́ния.

unreconciled /ʌnˈrekənˌsaɪld/ *adj.* непримири́вшийся; **~ enemies** непримири́мые враги́; **he remained ~ to the fact that …** он не примири́лся с тем, что…

unrecorded /ˌʌnrɪˈkɔːdɪd/ *adj.* (*music*) незапи́санный; (*data*) незарегистри́рованный.

unrefined /ˌʌnrɪˈfaɪnd/ *adj.* неочи́щенный, нерафини́рованный.

unreflecting /ˌʌnrɪˈflektɪŋ/ *adj.* (*of surface etc.*) неотража́ющий; (*unthinking*) безду́мный.

unrehearsed /ˌʌnrɪˈhɜːst/ *adj.* неподгото́вленный, неотрепети́рованный.
● *adv.* экспро́мтом; без подгото́вки.

unrelated /ˌʌnrɪˈleɪtɪd/ *adj.* **1** (*not connected*) несвя́занный (с + *i.*); не име́ющий отноше́ния (к + *d.*). **2** (*not*

U

kin): **he is ~ to me** он мне не ро́дственник.

unrelenting /ˌʌnrɪˈlentɪŋ/ *adj.* (*inexorable*) неумоли́мый; (*assiduous*) неосла́бный.

unreliability /ˌʌnrɪˌlaɪəˈbɪlɪtɪ/ *n.* ненадёжность; недостове́рность.

unreliable /ˌʌnrɪˈlaɪəb(ə)l/ *adj.* (*person*) ненадёжный; (*facts, information*) недостове́рный.

unrelieved /ˌʌnrɪˈliːvd/ *adj.* **1** (*from duty*) не освобождённый (*от чего*); (*not aided*) не получи́вший по́мощи. **2** (*with no variation*) однообра́зный; **~ gloom** беспросве́тный мрак.

unremarkable /ˌʌnrɪˈmɑːkəb(ə)l/ *adj.* невыдаю́щийся; непримеча́тельный.

unremarked /ˌʌnrɪˈmɑːkt/ *adj.* незаме́ченный.

unremitting /ˌʌnrɪˈmɪtɪŋ/ *adj.* неосла́бный; (*incessant*) беспреста́нный.

unrepeatable /ˌʌnrɪˈpiːtəb(ə)l/ *adj.* неповтори́мый; (*improper*) нецензу́рный.

unrepentant /ˌʌnrɪˈpent(ə)nt/ *adj.* нераска́явшийся; **he is ~** он ни в чём не раска́ивается.

unrepresentative /ˌʌnreprɪˈzentətɪv/ *adj.* непоказа́тельный, нетипи́чный.

unrequited /ˌʌnrɪˈkwaɪtɪd/ *adj.* без взаи́мности, не по́льзующийся взаи́мностью; **~ love** любо́вь без взаи́мности.

unreserved /ˌʌnrɪˈzɜːvd/ *adj.* (*not set aside*) незаброни́рованный; (*open, frank*) открове́нный; (*whole-hearted*) по́лный; **I agree with you ~ly** я по́лностью с ва́ми согла́сен.

unresisting /ˌʌnrɪˈzɪstɪŋ/ *adj.* несопротивля́ющийся.

unresolved /ˌʌnrɪˈzɒlvd/ *adj.* (*irresolute*) нереши́тельный; **an ~ problem** нерешённая пробле́ма; **my doubts were ~** мои́ сомне́ния не́ были разрешены́.

unresponsive /ˌʌnrɪˈspɒnsɪv/ *adj.* (*face, manner, bureaucracy*) равноду́шный; (*person, audience*) невосприи́мчивый; **he was ~ to my suggestion** он не отреаги́ровал на моё предложе́ние; **symptoms ~ to treatment** симпто́мы, не поддаю́щиеся лече́нию.

unrest /ʌnˈrest/ *n.* (*disquiet*) беспоко́йство; (*social, political*) волне́ния (*nt. pl.*); беспоря́дки (*m. pl.*).

unrestful /ʌnˈrestfʊl/ *adj.* беспоко́йный.

unresting /ʌnˈrestɪŋ/ *adj.* неутоми́мый.

unrestrained /ˌʌnrɪˈstreɪnd/ *adj.* несде́ржанный; необу́зданный.

unrestricted /ˌʌnrɪˈstrɪktɪd/ *adj.* неограни́ченный.

unrewarded /ˌʌnrɪˈwɔːdɪd/ *adj.* невознаграждённый; **his efforts were ~ by success** его́ уси́лия не увенча́лись успе́хом.

unrewarding /ˌʌnrɪˈwɔːdɪŋ/ *adj.* неблагода́рный.

unrighteous /ʌnˈraɪtʃəs/ *adj.* несправедли́вый; непра́ведный; (*bibl.*) нечести́вый.

unrighteousness /ʌnˈraɪtʃəsnɪs/ *n.* несправедли́вость; непра́ведность; нечести́вость.

unripe /ʌnˈraɪp/ *adj.* неспе́лый, незре́лый (*also fig.*).

unrivalled /ʌnˈraɪv(ə)ld/ (*US* **unrivaled**) *adj.* непревзойдённый; **an ~ opportunity** уника́льная возмо́жность.

unroll /ʌnˈrəʊl/ *v.t. & i.* развёр|тывать(ся), -ну́ть(ся).

unromantic /ˌʌnrəˈmæntɪk/ *adj.* нероманти́ческий, нероманти́чный.

unruffled /ʌnˈrʌf(ə)ld/ *adj.* (*fig.*) невозмути́мый.

unruliness /ʌnˈruːlɪnɪs/ *n.* непоко́рность, непослуша́ние.

unruly /ʌnˈruːlɪ/ *adj.* (**unrulier, unruliest**) непоко́рный, непослу́шный; бу́йный, бу́рный.

unsaddle /ʌnˈsæd(ə)l/ *v.t.* рассёдл|ывать, -а́ть.

unsafe /ʌnˈseɪf/ *adj.* риско́ванный, ненадёжный, опа́сный.

unsaid /ʌnˈsed/ *adj.*: **some things are better left ~** есть ве́щи, о кото́рых лу́чше умолча́ть (*or* не говори́ть).

unsaleable /ʌnˈseɪləb(ə)l/ *adj.* не по́льзующийся спро́сом, нехо́дкий.

unsatisfactory /ˌʌnsætɪsˈfæktərɪ/ *adj.* неудовлетвори́тельный.

unsatisfied /ʌnˈsætɪsˌfaɪd/ *adj.* неудовлетворённый.

unsaturated /ʌnˈsætʃəˌreɪtɪd/, /-tjʊˌreɪtɪd/ *adj.* ненасы́щенный.

unsavoury /ʌnˈseɪvərɪ/ (*US* **unsavory**) *adj.* (*fig.*) сомни́тельный.

unscalable /ʌnˈskeɪləb(ə)l/ *adj.* непристу́пный.

unscathed /ʌnˈskeɪðd/ *adj.* невреди́мый; (*pred.*) цел и невреди́м.

unscheduled /ʌnˈʃedjuːld/ *adj.* незаплани́рованный; **an ~ flight** полёт вне расписа́ния.

unscholarly /ʌnˈskɒləlɪ/ *adj.* (*work, attitude*) недосто́йный учёного; (*person*) неэруди́рованный.

unscientific /ˌʌnsaɪənˈtɪfɪk/ *adj.* нена́учный.

unscramble /ʌnˈskræmb(ə)l/ *v.t.* **1** (*telephone conversation*) расходи́ровать (*impf., pf.*). **2** (*coll., analyse, sort out*) расшифро́в|ывать, -а́ть.

unscrew /ʌnˈskruː/ *v.t. & i.* отви́н|чивать(ся), -ти́ть(ся); разви́н|чивать(ся), -ти́ть(ся).

unscripted /ʌnˈskrɪptɪd/ *adj.*: **an ~ talk** импровизи́рованное выступле́ние.

unscrupulous /ʌnˈskruːpjʊləs/ *adj.* беспринци́пный, недобросо́вестный.

unscrupulousness /ʌnˈskruːpjʊləsnɪs/ *n.* беспринци́пность, недобросо́вестность.

unseal /ʌnˈsiːl/ *v.t.* распеча́т|ывать, -ать; вскры|ва́ть, -ть.

unsealed /ʌnˈsiːld/ *adj.*: **an ~ envelope** незапеча́танный конве́рт.

unseasonable /ʌnˈsiːzənəb(ə)l/ *adj.* не по сезо́ну; **~ weather** пого́да не по сезо́ну; (*fig., untimely*) несвоевре́менный.

unseasoned /ʌnˈsiːz(ə)nd/ *adj.*: **~ food** неприпра́вленная еда́; **~ timber** невы́держанная древеси́на; (*fig., inexperienced*) нео́пытный, неискушённый, необстре́лянный (*coll.*).

unseat /ʌnˈsiːt/ *v.t.* ст|а́лкивать, -олкну́ть; **the horse ~ed its rider** ло́шадь сбро́сила ездока́; (*fig.*): **he was ~ed at the last election** его́ лиши́ли парла́ментского манда́та на после́дних вы́борах.

unseaworthiness /ʌnˈsiːˌwɜːðɪnɪs/ *n.* неприго́дность к пла́ванию, неморехо́дность.

unseaworthy /ʌnˈsiːˌwɜːðɪ/ *adj.* неприго́дный к пла́ванию.

unsecured /ˌʌnsɪˈkjʊəd/ *adj.* (*of a box, parcel etc.*) незакреплённый, неза́пертый; (*of loan etc.*) необеспе́ченный, негаранти́рованный.

unseeing /ʌnˈsiːɪŋ/ *adj.* незря́чий, неви́дящий.

unseemliness /ʌnˈsiːmlɪnɪs/ *n.* непристо́йность.

unseemly /ʌnˈsiːmlɪ/ *adj.* (*improper*) неподоба́ющий; (*indecent*) непристо́йный.

unseen /ʌnˈsiːn/ *n.* (*Br., translation*) перево́д с листа́.

● *adj.* (*invisible*) неви́димый.

unselective /ˌʌnsɪˈlektɪv/ *adj.* неразбо́рчивый.

unselfish /ʌnˈselfɪʃ/ *adj.* бескоры́стный.

unselfishness /ʌnˈselfɪʃnɪs/ *n.* бескоры́стие.

unserviceable /ʌnˈsɜːvɪsəb(ə)l/ *adj.* него́дный, неиспра́вный.

unsettle /ʌnˈset(ə)l/ *v.t.* (*fig.*) выбива́ть, вы́бить из коле́й; расстр|а́ивать, -о́ить.

unsettled /ʌnˈset(ə)ld/ *adj.* неусто́йчивый; беспоко́йный; **~ weather** неусто́йчивая пого́да; **an ~ account** неопла́ченный счёт; **the argument was ~** спор не́ был разрешён; **~ territory** незаселённая террито́рия.

unsettling /ʌnˈsetlɪŋ/ *adj.* трево́жный.

unshackle /ʌnˈʃæk(ə)l/ *v.t.* сн|има́ть, -ять кандалы́ с+*g.*

unshakeable /ʌnˈʃeɪkəb(ə)l/ *adj.* непоколеби́мый.

unshaken /ʌnˈʃeɪkən/ *adj.* (*resolute*) непоколе́бленный.

unshaven /ʌnˈʃeɪv(ə)n/ *adj.* небри́тый.

unsheathe /ʌnˈʃiːð/ *v.t.* вынима́ть, вы́нуть из но́жен; **he ~d his sword** он обнажи́л меч.

unsheltered /ʌnˈʃeltəd/ *adj.* незащищённый.

unshod /ʌnˈʃɒd/ *adj.* (*of horse*) неподко́ванный.

unshrinkable /ʌnˈʃrɪŋkəb(ə)l/ *adj.* (*text.*) безуса́дочный.

unshrinking /ʌnˈʃrɪŋkɪŋ/ *adj.* (*intrepid*) непоколеби́мый.

unsightliness /ʌnˈsaɪtlɪnɪs/ *n.* уро́дливость, непригля́дность.

unsightly /ʌnˈsaɪtlɪ/ *adj.* некраси́вый, непригля́дный.

unsigned /ʌnˈsaɪnd/ *adj.* неподпи́санный.

unskilful /ʌnˈskɪlfʊl/ (*US* **unskillful**) *adj.* неуме́лый, неиску́сный; (*clumsy*) неуклю́жий.

unskilled /ʌnˈskɪld/ *adj.* неквалифици́рованный; ~ **labourer** (*Br.*), **laborer** (*US*) разнорабо́чий.

unsmiling /ʌnˈsmaɪlɪŋ/ *adj.* неулы́бчивый.

unsociability /ʌnˌsəʊʃəˈbɪlɪtɪ/ *n.* необщи́тельность, нелюди́мость.

unsociable /ʌnˈsəʊʃəb(ə)l/ *adj.* необщи́тельный, нелюди́мый.

unsocial /ʌnˈsəʊʃ(ə)l/ *adj.* (*not given to association*) необщи́тельный; (*anti-social*) антиобще́ственный; ~ **hours (of work)** не общепри́нятые часы́ рабо́ты.

unsold /ʌnˈsəʊld/ *adj.* непро́данный; залежа́лый.

unsoldierly /ʌnˈsəʊldʒəlɪ/ *adj.* недосто́йный солда́та.

unsolicited /ˌʌnsəˈlɪsɪtɪd/ *adj.* (*given, done voluntarily*) доброво́льный; (*not asked for*) непро́шеный

unsolved /ʌnˈsɒlvd/ *adj.* (*issue*) нерешённый; (*mystery*) неразга́данный.

unsophisticated /ˌʌnsəˈfɪstɪˌkeɪtɪd/ *adj.* (*person, approach*) просто́й, простоду́шный; (*thing, work*) безыску́сный.

unsought /ʌnˈsɔːt/ *adj.* непро́шеный.

unsound /ʌnˈsaʊnd/ *adj.* (*bad, rotten*) испо́рченный, гнило́й; (*unwholesome*) нездоро́вый; (*unstable*) непро́чный; ~ **views** необосно́ванные взгля́ды; **of ~ mind** душевнобольно́й; **a man of ~ judgement** челове́к, лишённый здра́вого смы́сла.

unsparing /ʌnˈspeərɪŋ/ *adj.* (*merciless*) беспоща́дный, безжа́лостный; (*generous*) ще́дрый; (*diligent*) усе́рдный; ~ **in his efforts** не щадя́щий сил.

unspeakable /ʌnˈspiːkəb(ə)l/ *adj.* невырази́мый; **he is an ~ bore** он ужа́сный зану́да.

unspecified /ʌnˈspesɪˌfaɪd/ *adj.* то́чно не ука́занный.

unspent /ʌnˈspent/ *adj.* (*of money*) неистра́ченный.

unspoil|ed /ʌnˈspɔɪld/, **-t** /ʌnˈspɔɪlt/ *adj.* неиспо́рченный; (*of person*) неизбало́ванный.

unspoken /ʌnˈspəʊkən/ *adj.* невы́сказанный.

unsport|ing /ʌnˈspɔːtɪŋ/, **-smanlike** /ʌnˈspɔːtsmənˌlaɪk/ *adjs.* нече́стный; неспорти́вный, недосто́йный спортсме́на; **he behaved ~ingly** он вёл себя́ неспорти́вно.

unsprung /ʌnˈsprʌŋ/ *adj.* безрессо́рный, без рессо́р.

unstable /ʌnˈsteɪb(ə)l/ *adj.* неусто́йчивый, нестаби́льный.

unstained /ʌnˈsteɪnd/ *adj.* (*fig.*) незапя́тнанный.

unstatesmanlike /ʌnˈsteɪtsmənˌlaɪk/ *adj.* неподоба́ющий госуда́рственному де́ятелю.

unsteadiness /ʌnˈstedɪnɪs/ *n.* неусто́йчивость, ша́ткость.

unsteady /ʌnˈstedɪ/ *adj.* нетвёрдый; неусто́йчивый, ша́ткий; **the table was ~** стол шата́лся; **he was ~ on his legs** он нетвёрдо держа́лся на нога́х.

unstick /ʌnˈstɪk/ *v.t.* откле́и|вать, -ть.

unstinting /ʌnˈstɪntɪŋ/ *adj.* (*generous*) ще́дрый.

unstop /ʌnˈstɒp/ *v.t.*: **the plumber ~ped the pipe** водопрово́дчик прочи́стил трубу́.

unstrap /ʌnˈstræp/ *v.t.* отстёг|ивать, -ну́ть; расстёг|ивать, -ну́ть.

unstressed /ʌnˈstrest/ *adj.* (*phon.*) безуда́рный.

unstuck /ʌnˈstʌk/ *adj.*: **the stamp came ~** ма́рка откле́илась; (*fig., coll.*): **my schemes came ~** мои́ пла́ны провали́лись.

unstudied /ʌnˈstʌdɪd/ *adj.* (*unaffected*) непринуждённый.

unsubstantial /ˌʌnsəbˈstænʃ(ə)l/ *adj.* (*not solid*) несуще́ственный; (*with no factual basis*) необосно́ванный; **an ~ dinner** несы́тный обе́д.

unsubstantiated /ˌʌnsəbˈstænʃɪˌeɪtɪd/ *adj.* недока́занный, неподтверждённый.

unsuccessful /ˌʌnsəkˈsesfʊl/ *adj.* безуспе́шный, неуда́чный; **he was ~ in the exam** он не вы́держал экза́мена.

unsuitability /ʌnˌsuːtəˈbɪlɪtɪ/, /ʌnˈsjuː-/ *n.* непригóдность.

unsuitable /ʌnˈsuːtəb(ə)l/, /ʌnˈsjuː-/ *adj.* неподходя́щий, неприго́дный.

unsuited /ʌnˈsuːtɪd/, /ʌnˈsjuː-/ *adj.* неподходя́щий; **he is ~ to the post** он не подхо́дит для э́той до́лжности.

unsullied /ʌnˈsʌlɪd/ *adj.* (*fig.*) незапя́тнанный.

unsung /ʌnˈsʌŋ/ *adj.* (*not celebrated*) невоспе́тый; **an ~ hero** невоспе́тый геро́й.

unsure /ʌnˈʃʊə(r)/, /ʌnˈʃɔː(r)/ *adj.* (*not confident*) неуве́ренный; **he was ~ of his ground** он не чу́вствовал себя́ доста́точно компете́нтным; **I am ~ if he will come** я не уве́рен, что он придёт; **~ of o.s.** не уве́ренный в себе́; (*not fixed or certain*) неопределённый.

unsurfaced /ʌnˈsɜːfɪst/ *adj.*: **~ road** грунтова́я доро́га.

unsurpass|able /ˌʌnsəˈpɑːsəb(ə)l/, **-ed** /ˌʌnsəˈpɑːst/ *adjs.* непревзойдённый.

unsuspected /ˌʌnsəˈspektɪd/ *adj.* (*of crime*) неподозрева́емый, не находя́щийся под подозре́нием; (*of wrongdoing*) не вызыва́ющий подозре́ния; (*not expected*) неожи́данный.

unsusp|ecting /ˌʌnsəˈspektɪŋ/, **-icious** /ˌʌnsəˈspɪʃəs/ *adjs.* неподозрева́ющий, дове́рчивый.

unswayed /ʌnˈsweɪd/ *adj.*: **~ by public opinion** не подда́вшийся влия́нию обще́ственного мне́ния.

unsweetened /ʌnˈswiːt(ə)nd/ *adj.* неподслащённый.

unswerving /ʌnˈswɜːvɪŋ/ *adj.* (*fig.*) непоколеби́мый.

unsympathetic /ˌʌnsɪmpəˈθetɪk/ *adj.* чёрствый, несочу́вствующий.

unsystematic /ˌʌnsɪstəˈmætɪk/ *adj.* несистемати́ческий, несистемати́чный.

untameable /ʌnˈteɪməb(ə)l/ *adj.* неукроти́мый.

untamed /ʌnˈteɪmd/ *adj.* (*of animal*) неприручённый.

untangle /ʌnˈtæŋg(ə)l/ *v.t.* распу́т|ывать, -ать; **she ~d the wool** она́ распу́тала клубо́к ше́рсти; (*fig.*): **the confusion was finally ~d** в конце́ концо́в удало́сь разобра́ться в э́той пу́танице.

untanned /ʌnˈtænd/ *adj.* (*of leather*) недублёный; (*by the sun*) незагоре́вший, незагоре́лый.

untapped /ʌnˈtæpt/ *adj.*: **~ resources** неиспо́льзованные ресу́рсы.

untarnished /ʌnˈtɑːnɪʃt/ *adj.* непотускне́вший; (*fig.*) незапя́тнанный.

untaxed /ʌnˈtækst/ *adj.* свобо́дный от нало́гов; не облага́емый нало́гом.

unteachable /ʌnˈtiːtʃəb(ə)l/ *adj.* (*of person*) не поддаю́щийся обуче́нию.

untempered /ʌnˈtempəd/ *adj.*: **~ steel** незакалённая сталь.

untenable /ʌnˈtenəb(ə)l/ *adj.* несостоя́тельный, неприе́млемый; **~ arguments** неубеди́тельные до́воды; **an ~ position** (*mil.*) незащити́мая/невы́годная пози́ция.

untended /ʌnˈtendɪd/ *adj.* забро́шенный, неухо́женный.

untether /ʌnˈteðə(r)/ *v.t.* отвя́з|ывать, -а́ть.

unthinkable /ʌnˈθɪŋkəb(ə)l/ *adj.* (*unimaginable*) немы́слимый, невообрази́мый.

unthinking /ʌnˈθɪŋkɪŋ/ *adj.* (*thoughtless*) безду́мный; (*inadvertent*) нечаянный; машина́льный.

unthread /ʌnˈθred/ *v.t.*: **~ a needle** вынима́ть, вы́нуть ни́тку из иго́лки.

untidiness /ʌnˈtaɪdɪnɪs/ *n.* неопря́тность, неаккура́тность.

untidy /ʌnˈtaɪdɪ/ *adj.* неопря́тный, неаккура́тный; **an ~ person** неря́ха (*c.g.*), неопря́тный челове́к; **his room was ~** его́ ко́мната была́ неу́брана.

untie /ʌnˈtaɪ/ *v.t.* развя́з|ывать, -а́ть; отвя́з|ывать, -а́ть; расшнуро́в|ывать, -ать.

until /ənˈtɪl/, /ʌn-/ = **till; unless and ~** то́лько когда́/е́сли.

untimeliness /ʌnˈtaɪmlɪnɪs/ *n.* преждевре́менность; несвоевре́менность; неуме́стность.

untimely /ʌnˈtaɪmlɪ/ *adj.* (*premature*) преждевре́менный; (*unseasonable*) несвоевре́менный; (*ill-timed, inappropriate*) неуме́стный.

untiring /ʌn'taɪərɪŋ/ *adj.* (*person*) неутоми́мый; (*work, efforts*) неуста́нный.

unto /'ʌntʊ/, /'ʌntə/ (*arch.*) = **to**

untold /ʌn'təʊld/ *adj.* **1** (*story*) нерасска́занный. **2** (*suffering, delight*) невырази́мый. **3** (*damage*) нечисли́мый; (*countless*) несчётный; **~ wealth** несме́тные бога́тства.

untouchable /ʌn'tʌtʃəb(ə)l/ *n.* неприкаса́емый, хариджа́н.
● *adj.* (*unattainable*) недосяга́емый, недосту́пный; (*impossible to compete with*) недосяга́емый.

untouched /ʌn'tʌtʃt/ *adj.* нетро́нутый; **fruit ~ by human hand** фру́кты, к кото́рым не прикаса́лись рука́ми; **his reserves were ~** он не прикосну́лся к свои́м запа́сам.

untoward /ˌʌntə'wɔ:d/, /ʌn'təʊəd/ *adj.* (*inconvenient; adverse*) неблагоприя́тный; неуда́чный; **nothing ~ happened** ничего́ плохо́го не случи́лось.

untraceable /ʌn'treɪsəb(ə)l/ *adj.* непросле́живаемый; **his relatives were ~** его́ ро́дственников не удало́сь разыска́ть.

untrained /ʌn'treɪnd/ *adj.* необу́ченный, неподгото́вленный.

untrammelled /ʌn'træm(ə)ld/ (*US* **untrammeled**) *adj.* (*unconstrained*) неско́ванный; (*free*) свобо́дный.

untransferable /ˌʌntræns'fɜ:rəb(ə)l/, /ˌʌntrɑ:ns-/, /ʌn't-/ *adj.* без пра́ва переда́чи.

untranslatable /ˌʌntræns'leɪtəb(ə)l/, /ˌʌntrɑ:n-/, /-z'leɪtəb(ə)l/ *adj.* неперезоди́мый.

untravelled /ʌn'træv(ə)ld/ (*US* **untraveled**) *adj.* не/ма́ло е́здивший по све́ту; **~ wastes** неизве́данные пусты́ни.

untried /ʌn'traɪd/ *adj.* неиспы́танный, непрове́ренный.

untrodden /ʌn'trɒd(ə)n/ *adj.* неисхо́женный; нетро́нутый.

untroubled /ʌn'trʌb(ə)ld/ *adj.* невозмути́мый, споко́йный.

untrue /ʌn'tru:/ *adj.* (*inaccurate*) неве́рный, ло́жный, непра́вильный; (*unfaithful*) неве́рный.

untrustworthiness /ʌn'trʌstˌwɜ:ðɪnɪs/ *n.* ненадёжность.

untrustworthy /ʌn'trʌstˌwɜ:ðɪ/ *adj.* (*unreliable*) ненадёжный; (*undeserving of confidence*) не заслу́живающий дове́рия.

untruth /ʌn'tru:θ/ *n.* непра́вда.

untruthful /ʌn'tru:θfʊl/ *adj.* (*of thing*) неве́рный, ло́жный; (*of person or thing*) лжи́вый.

untruthfulness /ʌn'tru:θfʊlnɪs/ *n.* неве́рность, ло́жность; лжи́вость.

untutored /ʌn'tju:təd/ *adj.* (*person*) необу́ченный; (*skill*) инстинкти́вный.

untwist /ʌn'twɪst/ *v.t.* раскру́|чивать, -ти́ть.

unusable /ʌn'ju:zəb(ə)l/ *adj.* неприго́дный, неподходя́щий.

unused[1] /ʌn'ju:zd/ *adj.* (*not put to use*) неиспо́льзованный; **my ticket was ~** я не испо́льзовал свой биле́т.

unused[2] /ʌn'ju:st/ *adj.* (*unaccustomed*) непривы́кший (к + *d.*); **I am ~ to this** я к э́тому не привы́к.

unusual /ʌn'ju:ʒʊəl/ *adj.* необыкнове́нный, необы́чный; **~ly** осо́бенно, исключи́тельно.

unutterable /ʌn'ʌtərəb(ə)l/ *adj.* невырази́мый, несказа́нный.

unvalued /ʌn'vælju:d/ *adj.* (*not subjected to valuation*) неоценённый; (*unesteemed*) недооценённый.

unvaried /ʌn'veərɪd/ *adj.* неизме́нный, постоя́нный.

unvarnished /ʌn'vɑ:nɪʃt/ *adj.* (*fig.*): **the ~ truth** неприкра́шенная/го́лая пра́вда.

unvarying /ʌn'veərɪɪŋ/ *adj.* неизме́нный.

unveil /ʌn'veɪl/ *v.t.* (*statue*) откр|ыва́ть, -ы́ть; (*plans*) изл|ага́ть, -ожи́ть.

unverifiable /ʌn'verɪˌfaɪəb(ə)l/ *adj.* не поддаю́щийся прове́рке.

unverified /ʌn'verɪˌfaɪd/ *adj.* непрове́ренный.

unversed /ʌn'vɜ:st/ *adj.* несве́дущий (*в чём*); **he is ~ in mathematics** он несве́дущ в матема́тике.

unvoiced /ʌn'vɔɪst/ *adj.* (*phon.*) глухо́й.

unwaged /ʌn'weɪdʒd/ *adj.* (*Br.*) безрабо́тный.

unwanted /ʌn'wɒntɪd/ *adj.* нежела́нный; **an ~ child** нежела́нный ребёнок; **they made me feel ~** они́ да́ли мне почу́вствовать, что я ли́шний среди́ них.

unwariness /ʌn'weərɪnɪs/ *n.* неосторо́жность.

unwarlike /ʌn'wɔ:laɪk/ *adj.* невои́нственный.

unwarrantable /ʌn'wɒrəntəb(ə)l/ *adj.* неопра́вданный, недопусти́мый.

unwarranted /ʌn'wɒrəntɪd/ *adj.* (*unauthorized*) недозво́ленный; (*unjustified*) необосно́ванный.

unwary /ʌn'weərɪ/ *adj.* неосторо́жный.

unwashed /ʌn'wɒʃt/ *adj.* (*fruit, hands*) немы́тый; (*clothes*) нести́ранный.

unwavering /ʌn'weɪvərɪŋ/ *adj.* непоколеби́мый; неизме́нный.

unweaned /ʌn'wi:nd/ *adj.* не о́тнятый от груди́.

unwearable /ʌn'weərəb(ə)l/ *adj.* не го́дный для но́ски.

unwear|ied /ʌn'wɪərɪd/, **-ying** /ʌn'wɪərɪɪŋ/ *adjs.* неутоми́мый.

unwelcome /ʌn'welkəm/ *adj.* неприя́тный; нежела́тельный; **he is ~ here** он здесь ли́шний.

unwell /ʌn'wel/ *adj.* нездоро́вый; **I felt ~** мне нездоро́вилось; **I have been ~** я был нездоро́в.

unwholesome /ʌn'həʊlsəm/ *adj.* нездоро́вый, вре́дный.

unwieldiness /ʌn'wi:ldɪnɪs/ *n.* громо́здкость.

unwieldy /ʌn'wi:ldɪ/ *adj.* (**unwieldier, unwieldiest**) громо́здкий.

unwilling /ʌn'wɪlɪŋ/ *adj.* нежела́ющий; **he was ~ to agree** он не пожела́л согласи́ться; **~ly** неохо́тно.

unwind /ʌn'waɪnd/ *v.t. & i.* разм|а́тывать(ся), -ота́ть(ся); раскру́|чивать(ся), -ти́ть(ся); (*fig.*): **as the plot ~s** по ме́ре разви́тия сюже́та; **the wine helped him to ~** вино́ помогло́ ему́ рассла́биться.

unwinking /ʌn'wɪŋkɪŋ/ *adj.* (*fig.*) бди́тельный.

unwise /ʌn'waɪz/ *adj.* не(благо)разу́мный.

unwished-for /ʌn'wɪʃt/ *adj.* нежела́нный.

unwitting /ʌn'wɪtɪŋ/ *adj.* нечая́нный.

unworkable /ʌn'wɜ:kəb(ə)l/ *adj.* нереа́льный, неосуществи́мый.

unworldly /ʌn'wɜ:ldlɪ/ *adj.* неземно́й, не от ми́ра сего́.

unworn /ʌn'wɔ:n/ *adj.* (*never worn*) нено́шеный; (*not showing wear*) неизно́шенный.

unworthy /ʌn'wɜ:ðɪ/ *adj.* (*undeserving*) недосто́йный (*кого/чего*); (*base*) по́длый, ни́зкий.

unwound /ʌn'waʊnd/ *adj.* (*watch*) незаведённый; (*ball of string*) размо́танный.

unwrap /ʌn'ræp/ *v.t.* разв|ора́чивать (*or* разв|ёртывать), -ерну́ть.

unwritten /ʌn'rɪt(ə)n/ *adj.*: **an ~ law** непи́саный зако́н.

unwrought /ʌn'rɔ:t/ *adj.* необрабо́танный.

unyielding /ʌn'ji:ldɪŋ/ *adj.* непреклонный, упо́рный.

unyoke /ʌn'jəʊk/ *v.t.* выпряга́ть, вы́прячь из ярма́.

unzip /ʌn'zɪp/ *v.t.* (*coat*) расстёг|ивать, -ну́ть; (*bag*) раскр|ыва́ть, -ы́ть.

up /ʌp/ *n.*: **~s and downs** (*of fortune*) взлёты (*m. pl.*) и паде́ния (*nt. pl.*); преврáтности (*f. pl.*) судьбы́; **business is on the ~ and ~** (*Br.*) дела́ пошли́ в го́ру.
● *adj.*: **on the ~ stroke** (*of piston*) при хо́де (по́ршня) вверх.
● *adv.* **1** (*in a higher position*) вверху́, наверху́; **what's he doing ~ there** что он де́лает там наверху́?; **high ~ in the sky** высоко́ в не́бе; **'this side ~'** «верх!»; **they live 3 floors ~ from us** они́ живу́т тремя́ этажа́ми вы́ше нас; **she had her umbrella ~** зо́нтик у неё был раскры́т; **the window was ~** окно́ бы́ло откры́то; **the blinds were ~** што́ры бы́ли по́дняты; **the notice was ~ on the board** на доске́ висе́ло объявле́ние; **his spirits were ~ one minute, down the next** настрое́ние у него́ то поднима́лось, то па́дало; **prices are ~** це́ны подняли́сь; (*advanced*): **he was ~ in the lead** он был среди́ пе́рвых; **he is 20 points ~ on his opponent** он на два́дцать очко́в впереди́ проти́вника; **he is well ~ in his subject** он прекра́сно зна́ет свой предме́т; (*with greater intensity*): **sing ~!/speak ~!** (по́йте)/(говори́те) гро́мче!; (*Br., at Oxford or Cambridge University*): **he is ~ at Oxford** он у́чится в О́ксфорде.

2 (*into a higher position*) вверх, навéрх; **she carried the suitcases ~** онá отнеслá чемодáны навéрх; **hands ~!** рýки вверх!; (**~***wards*) вы́ше, бóльше; **children from the age of I2 ~** дéти двенáдцати лет и стáрше; (*expr. support*): **~ (with) the workers!** да здрáвствуют рабóчие!
3 (*out of bed; standing; active*): **he was ~ on his feet at once** он моментáльно вскочи́л нá ноги; **he was already ~ when I called** когдá я пришёл, он ужé встал; **she was soon ~ and about again** онá вскóре оправи́лась; **I was ~ all night with the baby** я всю ночь не спалá из-за ребёнка; **I was ~ late last night** я вчерá óчень пóздно лёг; **the house is not ~** (*built*) **yet** дом ещё не пострóен.
4 (*roused*): **his blood was ~** он был взбешён; **they were ~ in arms against the new proposal** они́ встрéтили нóвое предложéние в штыки́.
5 (*of agenda*): **the house is ~ for sale** дом продаётся; **he was ~ for trial** он предстáл пéред судóм.
6 (*expr. completion or expiry*): **time's ~** врéмя истеклó; **it's all ~ with them** с ни́ми всё кóнчено; **the game is ~!** кáрта би́та!
7 (*coll., happening; amiss*): **what's ~?** в чём дéло?; что тут происхóдит?; **there's something ~ with the radio** (рáдио)приёмник барахли́т.
8: **~ against** (*in contact with*): **the table was (right) ~ against the wall** стол стоя́л у стены́ (*or* вплотнýю к стенé); (*confronted by*): **you are ~ against stiff opposition** вы имéете дéло с упóрным сопротивлéнием; **he was ~ against it** он был в трýдном положéнии.
9 ~ to (*equal to*): **I don't feel ~ to it** я не чýвствую себя́ в си́лах сдéлать э́то; **he is not ~ to his work** он не справля́ется с рабóтой; (*on a par with*): **the book is ~ to expectations** кни́га оправдывает ожидáния; (*as far as*) до+*g.*; **~ to, ~ till now** до сих пор; **I am ~ to chapter 3** я дочитáл до трéтьей главы́; **his work is not ~ to scratch** егó рабóта оставля́ет желáть лýчшего; (*incumbent upon*): **it is ~ to us to help** э́то мы должны́ помóчь; **it's ~ to you now** тепéрь э́то зави́сит от вас; (*occupied with*): **what is he ~ to?** чем он занимáется?; **what are the children ~ to?** что там дéти затевáют?; **he is ~ to no good** он замы́слил чтó-то недóброе.
● *prep.*: **they live ~ the hill** они́ живýт на горé/холмé; **he ran ~ the hill** он взбежáл нá гору, на холм; **the cat was ~ a tree** кот взобрáлся на дéрево; **he went ~ the stairs** он подня́лся по лéстнице; **they live ~** (*further along*) **the street** они́ живýт по/на э́той ýлице; **he is known ~ and down the land** егó знáют по всей странé.
● *v.i.* **(upped, upping)** (*coll.*): **she ~(ped) and said ...** онá взялá и сказáла....

up-and-coming /ˌʌpənˈkʌmɪŋ/ *adj.* многообещáющий.

upas /ˈjuːpəs/ *n.* анчáр.

upbeat /ˈʌpbiːt/ *n.* слáбая дóля тáкта.
● *adj.* (*coll.*) оптимисти́чный, бóдрый.

upbraid /ʌpˈbreɪd/ *v.t.* укор|я́ть, -и́ть; порицáть (*impf.*).

upbringing /ˈʌpˌbrɪŋɪŋ/ *n.* воспитáние.

upcoming /ˈʌpkʌmɪŋ/ *adj.* предстоя́щий.

update /ʌpˈdeɪt/ *v.t.* (*one's wardrobe, repertoire*) обнов|ля́ть, -и́ть; (*equipment*) модернизи́ровать (*impf., pf.*); (*records*) испр|авля́ть, -áвить; пересмотрéть и допóлнить (*both pf.*).

up-end /ʌpˈend/ *v.t.* стáвить, по- перпендикуля́рно.

upfront /ʌpˈfrʌnt/ *adj.* (*open*) откры́тый.
● *adv.* (*in advance*) вперёд.

upgrade /ˈʌpgreɪd/ *n.* подъём; **on the ~** на подъёме.
● *v.t.* (*raise in rank*) пов|ышáть, -ы́сить в дóлжности; (*modernize*) модернизи́ровать (*impf., pf.*).

upheaval /ʌpˈhiːv(ə)l/ *n.* переворóт.

uphill /ˈʌphɪl/ *adj.* идýщий в гóру; **an ~ road** крутáя дорóга; **an ~ task** тяжёлая задáча.
● *adv.* в гóру.

uphold /ʌpˈhəʊld/ *v.t.* (*support, lit., fig.*) поддéрж|ивать, -áть; отст|áивать, -оя́ть; (*confirm*) подтвер|ждáть, -ди́ть; (*maintain*) утвер|ждáть, -ди́ть.

upholster /ʌpˈhəʊlstə(r)/ *v.t.* об|ивáть, -и́ть; подб|ивáть, -и́ть; **an ~ed chair** крéсло с мя́гкой оби́вкой.

upholsterer /ʌpˈhəʊlstərə(r)/ *n.* обóйщик.

upholstery /ʌpˈhəʊlstərɪ/ *n.* оби́вка.

upkeep /ˈʌpkiːp/ *n.* содержáние.

upland /ˈʌplənd/ *n.* нагóрье; гори́стая часть страны́.
● *adj.* нагóрный.

uplift[1] /ˈʌplɪft/ *n.* (*moral elevation*) духóвный подъём.

uplift[2] /ʌpˈlɪft/ *v.t.* подн|имáть, -я́ть.

up-market /ʌpˈmɑːkɪt/ *adj.* элитáрный, дорогóй.

upmost /ˈʌpməʊst/ = **uppermost**

upon /əˈpɒn/ *prep.* **1** *see* ⇨**on. 2**: **once ~ a time** однáжды; **once ~ a time there lived ...** жил-был (*fem.* жилá-былá)...; **~ my word, soul!** (*expr. surprise etc.*) Гóсподи!; **~ my honour** (*Br.*), **honor** (*US*)! чéстное слóво!; **the holidays are ~ us** приближáются кани́кулы; **the enemy is ~ us** враг ужé бли́зок.

upper /ˈʌpə(r)/ *n.* передóк боти́нка; **he was on his ~s** (*coll.*) он остáлся без грошá.
● *adj.* вéрхний; вы́сший; **~ arm** плечó; **~ classes** вы́сшие клáссы; **he got the ~ hand** он одержáл верх; **U~ House** (*in UK*) палáта лóрдов; (*in USA*) сенáт; **~ lip** вéрхняя губá.
● *cpds.* **~-case** *adj.* прописнóй; **~-class, -crust** *adjs.* относя́щийся к вы́сшему óбществу; **~cut** *n.* апперкóт; **~most** (*also* **upmost**) *adj.* сáмый вéрхний, вы́сший; **it was ~most in my mind** э́то бóльше всегó занимáло мои́ мы́сли; *adv.*: **blade ~most** острием вверх.

uppi|sh /ˈʌpɪʃ/, **-ty** /ˈʌpɪtɪ/ *adjs.* (*coll.*) нáглый, дéрзкий.

uppity /ˈʌpɪtɪ/ = **uppish**

upright /ˈʌpraɪt/ *n.* (*beam, pillar etc.*) столб; (**~ piano**) пиани́но (*indecl.*).
● *adj.* (*erect*) вертикáльный, прямóй; (*honourable*) чéстный, порядочный.
● *adv.*: **stand ~** стоя́ть (*impf.*) пря́мо.

uprightness /ˈʌpraɪtnɪs/ *n.* чéстность, порядочность.

uprising /ˈʌpˌraɪzɪŋ/ *n.* (*rebellion*) восстáние.

up-river /ˈʌprɪvə(r)/ = **upstream**

uproar /ˈʌprɔː(r)/ *n.* (*noise*) шум, (*coll.*) гам; (*tumult, confusion*) возмущéние, волнéние.

uproarious /ʌpˈrɔːrɪəs/ *adj.* (*noisy*) шýмный, бýрный, бýйный; (*funny*) ужáсно/невозмóжно смешнóй.

uproot /ʌpˈruːt/ *v.t.* корчевáть, вы́-; вырывáть, вы́рвать с кóрнем; (*fig., displace*) выселя́ть, вы́селить; пересел|я́ть, -и́ть.

uprush /ˈʌprʌʃ/ *n.* (*of water*) накáт; (*of gas*) проры́в; **~ of feelings** наплы́в чувств.

upset[1] /ˈʌpset/ *n.* **1** (*physical*) недомогáние; **stomach ~** расстрóйство желýдка. **2** (*emotional shock, confusion*) огорчéние; (*pl.*) неприя́тности (*f. pl.*). **3** (*unexpected result in sport*) неожи́данный результáт.

upset[2] /ʌpˈset/ *v.t.* (*knock over*) опроки́|дывать, -нуть; **he ~ the milk** он опроки́нул молокó; (*make unhappy*) расстр|áивать, -óить; **the news ~ her** нóвость её расстрóила; (*food*): **rich food ~s my stomach** от жи́рной пи́щи у меня́ расстрáивается желýдок.

upshot /ˈʌpʃɒt/ *n.* развя́зка; заключéние.

upside down /ˌʌpsaɪd ˈdaʊn/ *adv.* вверх днóм, вверх ногáми.

upstage /ʌpˈsteɪdʒ/ *adv.* в глубинé сцéны.
● *v.t.* (*coll.*) затм|евáть, -и́ть.

upstairs /ʌpˈsteəz/ *adv.* (*position*) наверхý; (*direction*) навéрх; **he ran ~** он побежáл навéрх; (*attr.*): **the ~ rooms** вéрхние кóмнаты.

upstanding /ʌpˈstændɪŋ/ *adj.* **1** (*honest*) чéстный, прямóй. **2** (*standing up*) стоя́щий; **be ~!** встáньте! **3** (*sturdy*) крéпкий.

upstart /ˈʌpstɑːt/ *n.* вы́скочка (*c.g.*).

upstream /ˈʌpstriːm/, **up-river** /ˈʌprɪvə(r)/ *adv.* (*of place*) вверх по течéнию; (*of motion*) прóтив течéния; **~ of** вы́ше + *g.*

upsurge /ˈʌpsɜːdʒ/ *n.* (*of unrest, in production*) подъём; (*of feelings*) наплы́в.

upswing /ˈʌpswɪŋ/ *n.* (*fig.*) подъём.

uptake /ˈʌpteɪk/ *n.*: **quick on the ~** (*coll.*) сметли́вый, сообрази́тельный.

uptight /ʌpˈtaɪt/, /ˈʌptaɪt/ *adj.* (*coll., tense, angry*) напряжённый, нервóзный.

up-to-date /ˌʌptəˈdeɪt/ *adj.*

U

совреме́нный, нове́йший, (са́мый) после́дний.

up-to-the-minute /ˌʌptəðəˈmɪnɪt/ *adj.* сиюмину́тный; са́мый после́дний.

up-town /ˈʌptaʊn/ *adj. & adv.* (*US*) (располо́женный) в жилы́х кварта́лах го́рода.

upturn /ˈʌptɜːn/ *n.* (*fig.*) сдвиг (к лу́чшему); улучше́ние.

upturned /ˈʌptɜːnd/ *adj.* (*bucket*) перевёрнутый; (*nose*) курно́сый; (*face*) обращённый кве́рху.

upward /ˈʌpwəd/ *adj.* напра́вленный вверх; **an ~ trend in prices** тенде́нция к повыше́нию цен.

● *adv.* (*also* **~s**) вверх; **~s of** (*over*) **£100** свы́ше ста фу́нтов.

up-wind /ˈʌpwɪnd/ *adv.* про́тив ве́тра.

uraemia /jʊˈriːmɪə/ (*US* **uremia**) *n.* уреми́я.

Urals /ˈjʊər(ə)lz/ *n.* Ура́льские го́ры (*f. pl.*), Ура́л.

uranium /jʊˈreɪnɪəm/ *n.* ура́н; (*attr.*) ура́новый.

Uranus /ˈjʊərənəs/, /jʊˈreɪnəs/ *n.* Ура́н.

urban /ˈɜːbən/ *adj.* городско́й.

urbane /ɜːˈbeɪn/ *adj.* све́тский, учти́вый.

urbanism /ˈɜːbəˌnɪz(ə)m/ *n.* урбани́зм.

urbanity /ɜːˈbænɪtɪ/ *n.* све́тскость, учти́вость.

urbanization /ˌɜːbənaɪˈzeɪʃ(ə)n/ *n.* урбаниза́ция; рост городо́в.

urbanize /ˈɜːbəˌnaɪz/ *v.t.* урбанизи́ровать (*impf., pf.*).

urchin /ˈɜːtʃɪn/ *n.* **1** беспризо́рни|к (*fem.* -ца). **2** (*in full* **sea ~**) (*zool.*) морско́й ёж.

Urdu /ˈʊəduː/, /ˈɜː-/ *n.* (язы́к) урду́.

● *adj.*: **~ script** письмо́ (языка́) урду́.

urea /ˈjʊərɪə/, /jʊˈriːə/ *n.* мочеви́на.

uremia /jʊˈriːmɪə/ (*US*) = **uraemia**

ureter /jʊˈriːtə(r)/ *n.* мочето́чник.

urethra /jʊˈriːθrə/ *n.* (*pl.* **urethrae** /-riː/ *or* **urethras**) уре́тра.

urethritis /ˌjʊərɪˈθraɪtɪs/ *n.* уретри́т.

urge /ɜːdʒ/ *n.* побужде́ние, стремле́ние; **I felt an ~ to go back** меня́ потяну́ло верну́ться/наза́д.

● *v.t.* **1** (*impel; also* **~ on, ~ forward**) гнать (*impf.*); под|гоня́ть, -огна́ть; **he ~d his horse up the hill** он гнал коня́ в го́ру. **2** (*exhort*) увеща́ть (*impf.*); приз|ыва́ть, -ва́ть (*кого к чему*); угова́ривать (*impf.*).

urgency /ˈɜːdʒ(ə)nsɪ/ *n.* **1** (*need for prompt action*) сро́чность, неотло́жность; **as a matter of ~** в сро́чном поря́дке. **2** (*insistence*) насто́йчивость.

urgent /ˈɜːdʒ(ə)nt/ *adj.* **1** (*brooking no delay*) сро́чный, неотло́жный; **he is in ~ need of money** он кра́йне нужда́ется в деньга́х. **2** (*pressing, insistent*) насто́йчивый.

uric /ˈjʊərɪk/ *adj.*: **~ acid** мочева́я кислота́.

urinal /jʊˈraɪn(ə)l/, /ˈjʊərɪn(ə)l/ *n.* писсуа́р.

urinary /ˈjʊərɪnərɪ/ *adj.* мочево́й.

urinate /ˈjʊərɪˌneɪt/ *v.i.* мочи́ться, по-.

urination /ˌjʊərɪˈneɪʃ(ə)n/ *n.* мочеиспуска́ние.

urine /ˈjʊərɪn/ *n.* моча́.

urn /ɜːn/ *n.* **1** (*vase for ashes etc.*) у́рна, ва́за; **Grecian ~** гре́ческая ва́за. **2** (*for tea, coffee etc.*) куб.

Ursa /ˈɜːsə/ *n.* (*astron.*): **~ Major/Minor** Больша́я/Ма́лая Медве́дица.

Uruguay /ˈjʊərəˌgwaɪ/ *n.* Уругва́й.

Uruguayan /ˌjʊərəˈgwaɪən/ *n.* уругва́|ец (*fem.* -йка).

● *adj.* уругва́йский.

us /ʌs/ *obj. of* ⇨**we**

US(A) (*abbr. of* ***United States of America***) США (*pl., indecl.*) (Соединённые Шта́ты Аме́рики).

● *adj.* америка́нский; **US Army** америка́нская а́рмия, а́рмия США.

usable /ˈjuːzəb(ə)l/ *adj.* примени́мый, (при)го́дный.

usage /ˈjuːsɪdʒ/ *n.* **1** (*utilization*) употребле́ние, испо́льзование, по́льзование +*i.* **2** (*habitual process*) у́зус, пра́ктика, обыкнове́ние; **in accordance with general ~** согла́сно общепри́нятой пра́ктике; **a guide to English ~** уче́бник англи́йского словоупотребле́ния.

use¹ /juːs/ *n.* **1** (*utilization*) употребле́ние, испо́льзование, по́льзование +*i.*; **the telephone is in ~** телефо́н за́нят; **this book is in constant ~** э́та кни́га нахо́дится в постоя́нном по́льзовании; **make good ~ of your time!** испо́льзуйте ва́ше вре́мя как сле́дует!; **he put his talents to good ~** он пра́вильно испо́льзовал свои́ спосо́бности; **a room for the ~ of the public** ко́мната о́бщего по́льзования; **these coins came into ~ last year** э́ти моне́ты вошли́ в обраще́ние в про́шлом году́.
2 (*purpose; profitable application*) назначе́ние; примене́ние; **this tool has many ~s** э́тот инструме́нт применя́ется для разли́чных це́лей; **I shall find a ~ for it** я найду́ э́тому примене́ние; **I have no further ~ for it** мне э́то бо́льше не пона́добится.
3 (*value, advantage*) по́льза, толк; **this machine is no longer (of) any ~** э́та маши́на бо́льше не годи́тся; **will this be of ~ to you?** вам э́то пригоди́тся?; **it's no ~ grumbling** что то́лку ворча́ть?
4 (*power of using*): **he lost the ~ of his legs** он утра́тил спосо́бность ходи́ть.
5 (*right to use*): **I gave him the ~ of my car** я разреши́л ему́ по́льзоваться мое́й маши́ной; **'with ~ of kitchen'** с пра́вом по́льзования ку́хней.
6 (*consumption*) потребле́ние, расхо́дование.

use² /juːz/ *v.t.* **1** (*make use of, employ*) употреб|ля́ть, -и́ть; по́льзоваться, вос- +*i.*; испо́льзовать (*impf., pf.*); (*apply*) примен|я́ть, -и́ть; **are you using this knife?** вам сейча́с ну́жен э́тот нож?; **oil is ~d for frying potatoes** карто́фель жа́рят на расти́тельном ма́сле; **~ your eyes!** смотри́те как сле́дует!; **~ force** употреб|ля́ть, -и́ть си́лу; **~ your own discretion!** де́йствуйте по со́бственному разуме́нию; **may I ~ your name?** могу́ я на вас сосла́ться?; **a ~d car** подержанная маши́на.
2 (**~ up**: *consume*) расхо́довать, из-; тра́тить, по-; испо́льзовать (*impf., pf.*); изв|оди́ть, -ести́ (*coll.*); **the car ~s a lot of petrol** (*Br.*), **gas** (*US*) э́та маши́на расхо́дует мно́го бензи́на.
3 (*treat*) обраща́ться (*impf.*) с+*i.*; об|ходи́ться, -ойти́сь с+*i.*
4 (*exploit*): **I feel as if I have been ~d** я чу́вствую, что меня́ испо́льзовали в чьи́х-то це́лях.

use³ /juːz/ *v.t. & i.* **1** (*accustom*): **get ~d to** прив|ыка́ть, -ы́кнуть к+*d.*; **he is ~d to it** он к э́тому привы́к; **he is ~d to dining late** он привы́к обе́дать по́здно. **2** (*be accustomed*): **he ~d to be a teacher** он ра́ньше был учи́телем; **I ~d not to like him** пре́жде он мне не нра́вился; **I ~d to go** я пре́жде (*or* я, быва́ло,) ходи́л.

useful /ˈjuːsfʊl/ *adj.* поле́зный; **make yourself ~!** займи́тесь че́м-нибудь поле́зным!; **he is very ~ about the house** он о́чень мно́го помога́ет по до́му.

usefulness /ˈjuːsfʊlnɪs/ *n.* по́льза; **this book has outlived its ~** э́та кни́га устаре́ла.

useless /ˈjuːslɪs/ *adj.* (*worthless*) неприго́дный; (*futile*) бесполе́зный; (*coll., incompetent*): **he is ~ at tennis** он никуды́шний теннси́ст.

uselessness /ˈjuːslɪsnɪs/ *n.* неприго́дность; бесполе́зность.

user /ˈjuːzə(r)/ *n.* (*one who uses*) употребля́ющий; потреби́тель (*m.*); (*comput.*) по́льзователь (*m.*).

● *cpd.* **~-friendly** *adj.* удо́бный в употребле́нии; (*comput.*) дру́жественный.

usher /ˈʌʃə(r)/ *n.* (*court etc.*) швейца́р; (*person showing people to seats*) билетёр.

● *v.t.* (*also* **~ in**) вв|оди́ть, -ести́; **I was ~ed into his presence** меня́ ввели́ к нему́; (*fig.*) возве|ща́ть, -сти́ть; **the new year ~ed in many changes** но́вый год принёс с собо́й мно́жество переме́н.

usherette /ˌʌʃəˈret/ *n.* билетёрша.

USSR (*abbr. of* ***Union of Soviet Socialist Republics***) (*hist.*) СССР (Сою́з Сове́тских Социалисти́ческих Респу́блик).

usual /ˈjuːʒʊəl/ *adj.* обы́чный, обыкнове́нный; **with his ~ alacrity** со сво́йственной ему́ живо́стью; **it is ~ to remove one's hat** при́нято снима́ть шля́пу; **he is late as ~** он, по обыкнове́нию (*or* как всегда́), опа́здывает; **the bus was fuller than ~** авто́бус был перепо́лнен бо́льше обы́чного.

usurer /ˈjuːʒərə(r)/ *n.* ростовщи́|к (*fem.* -ца).

usurious /jʊˈʒʊərɪəs/ *adj.* ростовщи́ческий.

usurp /jʊˈzɜːp/ *v.t.* узурпи́ровать (*impf., pf.*).

usurpation /ˌjuːzəˈpeɪʃ(ə)n/ *n.* узурпа́ция.

usurper /jʊˈzɜːpə(r)/ *n.* узурпа́тор.

usury /ˈjuːʒərɪ/ *n.* ростовщи́чество.

utensil /juːˈtens(ə)l/ *n.* инструме́нт; (*pl., collect.*) посу́да, у́тварь.

uteri /ˈjuːtəˌraɪ/ *pl. of* ⇒**uterus**

uterine /ˈjuːtəˌraɪn/, /-rɪn/ *adj.* ма́точный.

uterus /ˈjuːtərəs/ *n.* (*pl.* **uteri**) ма́тка.

utilitarian /jʊˌtɪlɪˈteərɪən/ *n.* утилитари́ст (*fem.* -ка).

● *adj.* утилита́рный.

utilitarianism /jʊˌtɪlɪˈteərɪəˌnɪz(ə)m/ *n.* утилитари́зм.

utilit|y /juːˈtɪlɪtɪ/ *n.* **1** (*usefulness*) поле́зность, практи́чность, вы́годность. **2**: **public ~ies** коммуна́льные услу́ги (*f. pl.*). **3** (*comput., also* **~ program**) се́рвисная програ́мма, ути́лита.

● *cpd.* **~ room** *n.* кладова́я.

utilization /ˌjuːtɪlaɪˈzeɪʃ(ə)n/ *n.* испо́льзование; утилиза́ция.

utilize /ˈjuːtɪˌlaɪz/ *v.t.* испо́льзовать (*impf., pf.*); утилизи́ровать (*impf., pf.*).

utmost /ˈʌtməʊst/, **uttermost** /ˈʌtəˌməʊst/ *nn.* преде́л возмо́жного; **he did his ~ to avoid defeat** он сде́лал всё возмо́жное, что́бы избежа́ть пораже́ния.

● *adjs.* кра́йний; преде́льный.

Utopia /juːˈtəʊpɪə/ *n.* уто́пия.

Utopian /juːˈtəʊpɪən/ *adj.* утопи́ческий.

utter[1] /ˈʌtə(r)/ *adj.* по́лный, абсолю́тный, соверше́нный; **~ darkness** абсолю́тная темнота́; **an ~ scoundrel** отъя́вленный негодя́й.

utter[2] /ˈʌtə(r)/ *v.t.* (*sound, cry*) изд|ава́ть, -а́ть; (*words*) произн|оси́ть, -ести́, выгова́ривать, вы́говорить; **she ~ed a moan** она́ издала́ стон; **he could not ~ a word** он не мог произнести́/вы́говорить ни сло́ва.

utterance /ˈʌtərəns/ *n.* **1** (*diction, speech*) произноше́ние, ди́кция; **defective ~** дефе́кт ре́чи. **2** (*expression*) выраже́ние; **he gave ~ to his anger** он вы́разил свой гнев. **3** (*pronouncement*) выска́зывание.

uttermost /ˈʌtəˌməʊst/ = **utmost**

uvula /ˈjuːvjʊlə/ *n.* (*pl.* **uvulae** /-liː/) язычо́к.

uvular /ˈjuːvjʊlə(r)/ *adj.* (*anat.*) язычко́вый; (*phon.*): **~ 'r'** увуля́рное «р».

Uzbek /ˈʌzbek/, /ˈʊz-/ *n.* (*person*) узбе́|к (*fem.* -чка); (*language*) узбе́кский язы́к.

● *adj.* узбе́кский.

Uzbekistan /ˌʌzbekɪˈstɑːn/, /ˌʊz-/ *n.* Узбекиста́н.

U

Vv

V /viː/ *n.*: **~-1** ракéта ФАУ-1; **~-2** ракéта ФАУ-2.

● *cpd.* **~-neck** *n. & adj.* вы́рез мы́сиком; вы́рез в ви́де бу́квы «V»; **~-neck sweater** сви́тер с вы́резом в ви́де бу́квы «V».

v. *abbr. of* **1** ***volt(s)*** /vɒlt(s)/, /vəult(s)/ В (вольт). **2** ***versus*** /ˈvɜːsəs/ про́тив; **England ~ France** (*sport*) А́нглия про́тив Фра́нции; кома́нда А́нглии про́тив кома́нды Фра́нции.

vac /væk/ (*Br.*) = **vacation** *n.* 2

vacanc|y /ˈveɪkənsɪ/ *n.* (*job*) вака́нсия; (*place on course etc.*) ме́сто; (*room*): **no ~ies** (свобо́дных) ко́мнат нет.

vacant /ˈveɪkənt/ *adj.* **1** (*empty*) пусто́й. **2** (*unoccupied*) неза́нятый, свобо́дный; **a ~ chair** свобо́дный стул; **a ~ post** вака́нтная до́лжность, вака́нсия. **3** (*of mind, expression etc.*) отсу́тствующий.

vacate /vəˈkeɪt/, /veɪ-/ *v.t.* освобо|жда́ть, -ди́ть; **he ~d his chair** он встал со сту́ла; **the flat had been ~d** жильцы́ съе́хали с кварти́ры (*or* освободи́ли кварти́ру); **he will ~ the post in May** он уйдёт с до́лжности в ма́е.

vacation /vəˈkeɪʃ(ə)n/ *n.* **1** (*leaving empty*) освобожде́ние. **2** (*at university, courts etc.*) кани́кул|ы (*pl., g.* —); **long ~** ле́тние кани́кулы. **3** (*US, holiday*) о́тпуск, о́тдых; **when will you take your ~?** когда́ вы идёте в о́тпуск?; **on ~** в о́тпуске, (*coll.*) в отпуску́.

vaccinate /ˈvæksɪˌneɪt/ *v.t.* де́лать, с- приви́вку + *d.*; (**against**: от + *g.*); вакцини́ровать (*impf., pf.*); **~ s.o. against smallpox** де́лать, с- приви́вку кому́-н. от о́спы, прив|ива́ть, -и́ть о́спу кому́-н.; **have you been ~d?** вам сде́лали приви́вку?

vaccination /ˌvæksɪˈneɪʃ(ə)n/ *n.* приви́вка; **~ mark** о́спа, о́спина.

vaccine /ˈvæksiːn/ *n.* вакци́на.

vacillate /ˈvæsɪˌleɪt/ *v.i.* колеба́ться (*impf.*).

vacillation /ˌvæsɪˈleɪʃ(ə)n/ *n.* колеба́ние.

vacua /ˈvækjuə/ *pl. of* ⇒**vacuum**

vacuity /vəˈkjuːɪtɪ/ *n.* пустота́.

vacuous /ˈvækjuəs/ *adj.* пусто́й.

vacuum /ˈvækjuəm/ *n.* (*pl.* **vacuums** *or* **vacua**) **1** (*empty or airless place*) ва́куум; безвозду́шное простра́нство; (*fig.*) пустота́; **~ flask** (*Br.*) те́рмос. **2** (*coll.*, **~-cleaner**) пылесо́с.

● *v.t. & i.* (*coll., clean with* ~ 2) пылесо́сить, про-.

vagabond /ˈvægəˌbɒnd/ *n.* (*vagrant*) бродя́га (*c.g.*), скита́лец.

vagary /ˈveɪgərɪ/ *n.* причу́да, каприз.

vagina /vəˈdʒaɪnə/ *n.* (*pl.* **vaginas** *or* **vaginae** /-niː/) влага́лище.

vaginal /vəˈdʒaɪnəl/ *adj.* влага́лищный.

vagrancy /ˈveɪgrənsɪ/ *n.* бродя́жничество.

vagrant /ˈveɪgrənt/ *n.* бродя́га (*c.g.*).

● *adj.* бродя́чий.

vague /veɪg/ *adj.* неопределённый, сму́тный, нея́сный; **a ~ resemblance** отдалённое схо́дство; **~ rumours** (*Br.*), **rumors** (*US*) сму́тные слу́хи; **he was rather ~ about his plans** он был весьма́ укло́нчив относи́тельно свои́х пла́нов; **I haven't the ~st idea** я не име́ю ни мале́йшего поня́тия/представле́ния.

vagueness /ˈveɪgnɪs/ *n.* неопределённость, сму́тность, нея́сность.

vain /veɪn/ *adj.* **1** (*unavailing; fruitless*) тще́тный, напра́сный; **a ~ attempt** тще́тная попы́тка; **~ hopes** напра́сные наде́жды; **they tried in ~ to get a seat** они́ безуспе́шно пыта́лись найти́ ме́сто. **2** (*empty*) пусто́й; **~ boasts** пуста́я похвальба́; **take God's name in ~** всу́е употреб|ля́ть, -и́ть и́мя Госпо́дне. **3** (*conceited*) тщесла́вный.

● *cpds.* **~glorious** *adj.* тщесла́вный; **~glory** *n.* тщесла́вие.

val|ance, -ence /ˈvæləns/ *n.* (*curtain, frill*) подзо́р, обо́рка, сбо́рка.

vale /veɪl/ *n.* (*poet.*) доли́на, дол (*obs.*).

valediction /ˌvælɪˈdɪkʃ(ə)n/ *n.* проща́ние.

valedictory /ˌvælɪˈdɪktərɪ/ *adj.* проща́льный; (*US, as n.*) речь на шко́льном вы́пуске.

valence[1] /ˈvæləns/ = **valance**

valenc|e[2] /ˈveɪləns/, **-y** /ˈveɪlənsɪ/ (*Br.*) *nn.* (*chem.*) вале́нтность.

valentine /ˈvælənˌtaɪn/ *n.* (*missive*) (анони́мное) любо́вное посла́ние в день свято́го Валенти́на.

valerian /vəˈlɪərɪən/ *n.* (*bot.*) валериа́на; **~ drops** валериа́новые ка́пли, валерья́нка (*coll.*).

valet /ˈvælɪt/, /-leɪ/ *n.* камерди́нер, слуга́ (*m.*).

● *v.t.* (**valeted, valeting**) служи́ть (*impf.*) камерди́нером у + *g.*

valiant /ˈvæljənt/ *adj.* до́блестный, хра́брый; (*of effort*) герои́ческий.

valid /ˈvælɪd/ *adj.* **1** (*sound*) ве́ский, обосно́ванный; **~ objections** убеди́тельные возраже́ния; **~ reasons** ве́ские до́воды. **2** (*leg.*) действи́тельный; **a ~ claim** зако́нная прете́нзия; **a ticket ~ for 3 months** биле́т, действи́тельный в тече́ние трёх ме́сяцев.

validate /ˈvælɪˌdeɪt/ *v.t.* утвер|жда́ть, -ди́ть; подтвер|жда́ть, -ди́ть.

validation /ˌvælɪˈdeɪʃ(ə)n/ *n.* утвержде́ние, подтвержде́ние.

validity /vəˈlɪdɪtɪ/ *n.* зако́нность, ве́скость; **the ~ of his argument** ве́скость его́ до́вода.

valise /vəˈliːz/ *n.* (*US*) саквоя́ж, чемода́н.

valley /ˈvælɪ/ *n.* (*pl.* **~s**) доли́на.

valor /ˈvælə(r)/ (*US*) = **valour**

valorous /ˈvælərəs/ *adj.* до́блестный.

valour /ˈvælə(r)/ (*US* **valor**) *n.* до́блесть.

valuable /ˈvæljuəb(ə)l/ *n.* (*usu. pl.*) це́нности (*f. pl.*).

● *adj.* це́нный, поле́зный, ва́жный.

valuation /ˌvæljuˈeɪʃ(ə)n/ *n.* оце́нка; определе́ние сто́имости; (*worth estimated*) це́нность.

value /ˈvæljuː/ *n.* **1** (*worth; advantageousness*) це́нность, ва́жность; **the ~ of exercise** по́льза физи́ческих упражне́ний; **his advice was of great**

~ его́ сове́т о́чень пригоди́лся; **he sets a high ~ on his time** он до́рого це́нит своё вре́мя.
2 (*in money etc.*) це́нность, сто́имость; **the ~ of the pound** покупа́тельная си́ла фу́нта; **property is rising in ~** недви́жимое иму́щество поднима́ется в цене́; **the book is good ~ for money** (*Br.*) э́та кни́га — вы́годная поку́пка; **~ added tax** нало́г на доба́вленную сто́имость.
3 (*mus.*) дли́тельность но́ты; **give each note its full ~** да|ва́ть, -ть ка́ждой но́те прозвуча́ть по́лностью.
4 (*denomination of coin, card etc.*) досто́инство.
5 (*math.*) величина́.
6 (*pl., standards*) (*духовные и т.п.*) це́нности (*f. pl.*).
● *v.t.* (**values, valued, valuing**) **1** (*estimate ~ of*) оце́н|ивать, -и́ть; **the house was ~d at £90,000** дом оцени́ли в 90 000 фу́нтов.
2 (*regard highly*) дорожи́ть (*impf.*) + *i.*; цени́ть (*impf.*); **I ~ my leisure time** я ценю́ свой досу́г; **a ~d colleague** це́нный колле́га.

valueless /ˈvæljʊlɪs/ *adj.* ничего́ не сто́ящий; бесполе́зный; **a ~ promise** пусто́е обеща́ние.

valuer /ˈvæljʊə(r)/ *n.* (*Br.*) оце́нщик.

valve /vælv/ *n.* (*tech.*) кла́пан, ве́нтиль (*m.*); (*anat., mus.*) кла́пан; (*Br., radio*) электро́нная ла́мпа.

valvular /ˈvælvjʊlə(r)/ *adj.* кла́пановый; **~ defect** поро́к кла́панов (се́рдца).

vamoose /vəˈmuːs/ *v.i.* (*US sl.*) см|ыва́ться, -ы́ться.

vamp¹ /væmp/ *n.* (*part of shoe*) передо́к (боти́нка).
● *v.t.*: **~ up** (*fig., renovate; improvise*) мастери́ть, с- на ско́рую ру́ку.

vamp² /væmp/ *n.* (*adventuress*) (же́нщина-)вамп; сире́на.

vampire /ˈvæmpaɪə(r)/ *n.* **1** (*reanimated corpse*) вампи́р, вурдала́к, упы́рь (*m.*); (*fig., person preying on others*) вампи́р, кровопи́йца (*c.g.*). **2** (*also* **~ bat**) (*zool.*) вампи́р.

van¹ /væn/ *n.* **1** (*motor vehicle*) (авто)фурго́н; **furniture ~** ме́бельный фурго́н. **2** (*Br., railway truck*) бага́жный ваго́н.
● *cpd.* **~-driver** *n.* води́тель (*m.*) фурго́на.

van² /væn/ *n.* = **vanguard**

vanadium /vəˈneɪdɪəm/ *n.* вана́дий.

vandalism /ˈvændəˌlɪz(ə)m/ *n.* вандали́зм.

vandalize /ˈvændəˌlaɪz/ *v.t.* разр|уша́ть, -у́шить.

vane /veɪn/ *n.* (*weathercock*) флю́гер; (*of windmill*) крыло́; (*of propeller, turbine*) ло́пасть.

vanguard /ˈvænɡɑːd/ *n.* (*group of people leading way in new developments*) аванга́рд, передово́й отря́д; (*forefront of new developments*) аванга́рд; (*mil.*) головно́й/передово́й отря́д, аванга́рд.

vanilla /vəˈnɪlə/ *n.* вани́ль.

vanillin /vəˈnɪlɪn/ *n.* (*chem.*) ванили́н.

vanish /ˈvænɪʃ/ *v.i.* исч|еза́ть, -е́знуть; проп|ада́ть, -а́сть; **~ing-point** то́чка схо́да паралле́льных ли́ний (*в перспективе*); **his hopes of success ~ed** его́ наде́жды на успе́х улету́чились.

vanity /ˈvænɪtɪ/ *n.* **1** (*conceit*) тщесла́вие; **~ bag** космети́чка; **~ case** чемода́нчик-космети́чка; **~ unit** шка́фчик под мо́йку. **2** (*futility; worthlessness*) суета́, тщета́; **~ of vanities** суета́ сует.

vanquish /ˈvæŋkwɪʃ/ *v.t.* побе|жда́ть, -ди́ть; покор|я́ть, -и́ть.

vantage /ˈvɑːntɪdʒ/ *n.* преиму́щество.
● *cpd.* **~-point** *n.* вы́годная пози́ция.

vapid /ˈvæpɪd/ *adj.* (*fig.*) пло́ский, пре́сный; **~ conversation** пусто́й/бессодержа́тельный разгово́р.

vapor /ˈveɪpə(r)/ (*US*) = **vapour**

vaporization /ˌveɪpəraɪˈzeɪʃ(ə)n/ *n.* испаре́ние, парообразова́ние.

vaporize /ˈveɪpəˌraɪz/ *v.t. & i.* испар|я́ть(ся), -и́ть(ся).

vaporous /ˈveɪpərəs/ *adj.* (*lit., fig.*) тума́нный; (*filmy*) прозра́чный.

vapour /ˈveɪpə(r)/ (*US* **vapor**) *n.* **1** (*steam*) пар; **~ bath** парова́я ба́ня/ва́нна. **2** (*mist*) тума́н. **3** (*gaseous manifestation*) испаре́ние; **~ trail** инверсио́нный след.

variability /ˌveərɪəˈbɪlɪtɪ/ *n.* изме́нчивость, непостоя́нство.

variable /ˈveərɪəb(ə)l/ *n.* (*math.*) переме́нная величина́.
● *adj.* изме́нчивый, непостоя́нный; **~ winds** ве́тры переме́нных направле́ний; **~ standards** меня́ющиеся крите́рии.

variance /ˈveərɪəns/ *n.* измене́ние; расхожде́ние; **this is at ~ with what we heard** э́то противоре́чит тому́, что мы слы́шали; **they were at ~** они́ спо́рили.

variant /ˈveərɪənt/ *n.* вариа́нт.
● *adj.* **1** (*different; alternative*) разли́чный; ино́й. **2** (*changing*) переме́нчивый.

variation /ˌveərɪˈeɪʃ(ə)n/ *n.* **1** (*fluctuation*) измене́ние; колеба́ние; **~s of temperature** колеба́ния (*nt. pl.*) температу́ры. **2** (*divergence*) отклоне́ние; **~ from the norm** отклоне́ние от но́рмы. **3** (*variant; also mus.*) вариа́ция; **~s on a theme** вариа́ции на те́му.

varicoloured /ˈveərɪˌkʌləd/ (*US* **varicolored**) *adj.* разноцве́тный.

varicose /ˈværɪˌkəʊs/ *adj.* варико́зный; **~ veins** варико́зные ве́ны.

varied /ˈveərɪd/ *adj.* разнообра́зный, разли́чный.

variegated /ˈveərɪˌɡeɪtɪd/, /-rɪəˌɡeɪtɪd/ *adj.* разноцве́тный, пёстрый.

variety /vəˈraɪətɪ/ *n.* **1** (*diversity; many-sidedness*) разнообра́зие; **~ is the spice of life** пре́лесть жи́зни в (её) разнообра́зии. **2** (*number of different things*) ряд; мно́жество; **for a ~ of reasons** по це́лому ря́ду соображе́ний, по ря́ду причи́н. **3** (**~ entertainment**) варьете́ (*indecl.*); **~ artist** эстра́дн|ый арти́ст (*fem.* -ая -ка); **~ show** эстра́дное представле́ние. **4** (*type, sort*) разнови́дность, вид, сорт.

various /ˈveərɪəs/ *adj.* **1** (*diverse*) разли́чный, ра́зный, разнообра́зный. **2** (*with pl., several*) мно́гие (*pl.*); ра́зные (*pl.*); **at ~ times** в ра́зное вре́мя.

varnish /ˈvɑːnɪʃ/ *n.* лак; (*fig.*) лоск.
● *v.t.* лакирова́ть, от-.

varsity /ˈvɑːsɪtɪ/ **1** (*Br. coll.*) = **university. 2** (*US, college/high school sports team*) студе́нческая/шко́льная спорти́вная кома́нда.

var|y /ˈveərɪ/ *v.t.* меня́ть (*impf.*); измен|я́ть, -и́ть; разнообра́зить (*impf.*).
● *v.i.* **1** (*change*) меня́ться (*impf.*); **the menu never ~ies** меню́ никогда́ не меня́ется. **2** (*differ*) ра|сходи́ться, -зойти́сь; отлич|а́ться, -и́ться; **opinions ~y** мне́ния расхо́дятся; **with ~ying success** с переме́нным успе́хом.

vascular /ˈvæskjʊlə(r)/ *adj.* сосу́дистый.

vase /vɑːz/ *n.* ва́за.

vasectomy /vəˈsektəmɪ/ *n.* вазэктоми́я.

Vaseline /ˈvæsɪˌliːn/ *n.* (*propr.*) вазели́н.

vassal /ˈvæs(ə)l/ *n.* васса́л; (*attr.*) васса́льный.

vast /vɑːst/ *adj.* обши́рный; грома́дный, огро́мный; (*grandiose*) грандио́зный; **~ plains** необозри́мые равни́ны.

vastly /ˈvɑːstlɪ/ *adv.* о́чень, кра́йне.

vastness /ˈvɑːstnɪs/ *n.* ширь; огро́мность; грандио́зность.

VAT /ˌviːeɪˈtiː/, /væt/ *n.* (*Br., abbr. of* ***value added tax***) НДС (нало́г на доба́вленную сто́имость).

vat /væt/ *n.* бо́чка, чан.

Vatican /ˈvætɪkən/ *n.* Ватика́н.
● *adj.* ватика́нский.

vaudeville /ˈvɔːdəvɪl/, /ˈvəʊ-/ *n.* водеви́ль (*m.*).

vault¹ /vɔːlt/, /vɒlt/ *n.* **1** (*arched roof*) свод; (*fig.*): **the ~ of heaven** небосво́д. **2** (*underground room or chamber*) подва́л, по́греб; (*of a bank*) храни́лище; **family ~** (*tomb*) фами́льный склеп.

vault² /vɔːlt/, /vɒlt/ *n.* (*leap*) прыжо́к, скачо́к.
● *v.t. & i.* перепры́г|ивать, -нуть; **he ~ed (over) the fence** он перепры́гнул че́рез забо́р; **~ing-horse** гимнасти́ческий конь.

vaulted /ˈvɔːltɪd/, /ˈvɒltɪd/ *adj.* сво́дчатый.

vaunt /vɔːnt/ *v.t. & i.* хва́стать(ся), по-; похваля́ться (*impf.*) (+ *i.*); **much ~ed** восхваля́емый.

VC = **Victoria Cross**

VCR (*abbr. of* ***video cassette recorder***) видеомагнитофо́н.

VD (*abbr. of* ***venereal disease***) венери́ческая боле́знь.

VDU (*abbr. of* ***visual display unit***) дисплей.

VE (*abbr. of* ***Victory in Europe***): **~ Day** День победы в Европе.

veal /viːl/ *n.* телятина.

vector /ˈvektə(r)/ *n.* (*math.*) вектор; (*of disease*) переносчик/носитель (*m.*) инфекции; (*aeron.*) курс.

veer /vɪə(r)/ *v.i.* измен|ять, -ить направление; пов|орачивать(ся), -ернуть(ся); **the wind is ~ing (round)** ветер меняется; (*fig.*) измен|ять, -ить курс; измен|яться, -иться; **public opinion is ~ing in his favour** (*Br.*), **favor** (*US*) общественное мнение меняется в его пользу; **~ to the left** (*pol.*) леветь, по-; **~ to the right** праветь, по-.

veg /vedʒ/ *n.* (*pl.* **~**) (*Br. coll.*) овощ; овощи.

vegan /ˈviːgən/ *n.* строгий вегетарианец; (*attr.*) строго вегетарианский.

veganism /ˈviːgənɪz(ə)m/ *n.* строгое вегетарианство.

vegetable /ˈvedʒɪtəb(ə)l/, /ˈvedʒtəb(ə)l/ *n.* овощ; **green ~s** зелень, овощи.

● *adj.* овощной; **the ~ kingdom** растительное царство; **~ oils** растительные масла; **~ marrow** (*Br.*) кабачок.

vegetarian /ˌvedʒɪˈteərɪən/ *n.* вегетариан|ец (*fem.* -ка); (*attr.*) вегетарианский.

vegetarianism /ˌvedʒɪˈteərɪəˌnɪz(ə)m/ *n.* вегетарианство.

vegetate /ˈvedʒɪˌteɪt/ *v.i.* (*lit.*) расти (*impf.*); (*fig.*) прозябать (*impf.*), вести (*impf.*) растительный образ жизни.

vegetation /ˌvedʒɪˈteɪʃ(ə)n/ *n.* (*plant life*) растительность.

vegetative /ˈvedʒɪtətɪv/ *adj.* растительный; (*bot.*) вегетационный.

veggie burger /ˈvedʒɪ ˌbɜːgə(r)/ *n.* вегетарианская котлета.

vehemence /ˈviːəməns/ *n.* сила, ярость.

vehement /ˈviːəmənt/ *adj.* сильный, яростный.

vehicle /ˈviːɪk(ə)l/, /ˈvɪək(ə)l/ *n.* **1** (*conveyance*) транспортное средство; **space ~** космический корабль. **2** (*fig.*) проводник; средство распространения/передачи.

vehicular /vɪˈhɪkjʊlə(r)/ *adj.* перевозочный; **~ access** доступ для транспорта; **~ traffic** движение автотранспорта.

veil /veɪl/ *n.* вуаль; **she took the ~** (*fig.*) она постриглась в монахини; **let us draw a ~ over the consequences** обойдём молчанием последствия; **under a ~ of secrecy** под покровом тайны.

● *v.t.* (*lit., fig.*) вуалировать, за-; **~ed threat** скрытая угроза.

vein /veɪn/ *n.* **1** (*anat.*) вена, жила. **2** (*of leaf*) жилка. **3** (*streak in wood, marble, etc.*) жилка, прожилка; (*fissure in rock*) жила. **4** (*mood*) настроение, расположение; **he was in humorous ~** он был в игривом настроении; **in the same ~** в том же духе/тоне/стиле.

veined /veɪnd/ *adj.*: **her hands were ~** у неё вены/жилы выступали на руках; **~ marble** мрамор в прожилках.

velar /ˈviːlə(r)/ *adj.* задненёбный, велярный.

Velcro /ˈvelkrəʊ/ *n.* (*propr.*): **~ fastener** застёжка «велкро», липучка, замок-отрывок.

veld(t) /velt/ *n.* вельд.

vellum /ˈveləm/ *n.* тонкий пергамент; **~ paper** веленовая бумага.

velocity /vɪˈlɒsɪtɪ/ *n.* скорость; быстрота.

velodrome /ˈveləˌdrəʊm/ *n.* велодром.

velour(s) /vəˈlʊə(r)/ *n.* велюр.

velvet /ˈvelvɪt/ *n.* бархат; **a ~ dress** бархатное платье.

velveteen /ˌvelvɪˈtiːn/ *n.* вельвет.

velvety /ˈvelvɪtɪ/ *adj.* бархатный, бархатистый.

venal /ˈviːn(ə)l/ *adj.* продажный, подкупный.

venality /ˌviːˈnælɪtɪ/ *n.* продажность, подкупность.

vendetta /venˈdetə/ *n.* вендетта.

vending-machine /ˈvendɪŋ/ *n.* автомат (*по продаже сигарет, напитков и т.п.*).

vendor /ˈvendə(r)/, /-dɔː(r)/ *n.* продав|ец (*fem.* -щица).

veneer /vɪˈnɪə(r)/ *n.* шпон, фанера; (*fig.*) внешний лоск; **a ~ of politeness** показная вежливость.

● *v.t.* облиц|овывать, -евать фанерой; фанеровать (*impf., pf.*); **~ed with walnut** отделанный под орех; фанерованный орехом.

venerable /ˈvenərəb(ə)l/ *adj.* **1** (*revered*) почтенный; **~ ruins** древние/священные развалины. **2**: **V~** (*as title*) преподобный.

venerate /ˈvenəˌreɪt/ *v.t.* чтить (*impf.*); почитать (*impf.*); благоговеть (*impf.*) перед + *i.*

veneration /ˌvenəˈreɪʃ(ə)n/ *n.* почтение, благоговение.

venereal /vɪˈnɪərɪəl/ *adj.* венерический, **~ disease** венерическая болезнь.

Venetian /vɪˈniːʃ(ə)n/ *n.* венециан|ец (*fem.* -ка).

● *adj.* венецианский; **~ blinds** жалюзи (*nt. pl., indecl.*).

Venezuela /ˌvenɪˈzweɪlə/ *n.* Венесуэла.

Venezuelan /ˌvenɪˈzweɪlən/ *n.* венесуэл|ец (*fem.* -ка).

● *adj.* венесуэльский.

vengeance /ˈvendʒ(ə)ns/ *n.* **1** месть; отмщение (*liter.*); **he sought ~ for the wrong done him** он хотел отомстить за причинённую ему обиду/несправедливость; **he swore to take ~ on me** он поклялся отомстить мне. **2**: **with a ~** (*coll., in a high degree*) вовсю, с лихвой.

vengeful /ˈvendʒfʊl/ *adj.* мстительный.

venial /ˈviːnɪəl/ *adj.* простительный.

Venice /ˈvenɪs/ *n.* Венеция.

venison /ˈvenɪs(ə)n/, /-z(ə)n/ *n.* оленина.

venom /ˈvenəm/ *n.* яд; (*fig.*) яд, злоба.

venomous /ˈvenəməs/ *adj.* ядовитый; (*fig.*) ядовитый, злобный.

vent /vent/ *n.* **1** (*opening*) выходное отверстие; (*flue*) дымоход; (*in jacket*) разрез. **2** (*of animal*) задний проход. **3** (*fig., outlet*) выход; выражение; отдушина; **he gave ~ to his feelings** он дал волю своим чувствам.

● *v.t.* (*fig.*) изл|ивать, -ить; да|вать, -ть выход + *d.*; **he ~ed his ill-temper on his secretary** он сорвал своё дурное настроение на секретаре.

ventilate /ˈventɪˌleɪt/ *v.t.* проветри|вать, -ть; вентилировать, про-; (*fig.*) обсу|ждать, -дить.

ventilation /ˌventɪˈleɪʃ(ə)n/ *n.* **1** вентиляция; **~ shaft** вентиляционная шахта. **2** (*fig.*) (публичное) обсуждение.

ventilator /ˈventɪˌleɪtə(r)/ *n.* вентилятор (*also med.*).

ventricle /ˈventrɪk(ə)l/ *n.* желудочек (сердца/мозга).

ventriloquism /venˈtrɪləˌkwɪz(ə)m/ *n.* чревовещание.

ventriloquist /venˈtrɪləˌkwɪst/ *n.* чревовещатель (*m.*).

venture /ˈventʃə(r)/ *n.* **1** (*risky undertaking*) рискованное предприятие. **2** (*business enterprise*) (коммерческое) предприятие; **joint ~** совместное предприятие.

● *v.t.* (*risk, bet*) риск|овать, -нуть + *i.*; ставить, по- на карту; **I will ~ £5** я поставлю 5 фунтов.

● *v.i.* (*dare*) осмели|ваться, -ться; отважи|ваться, -ться; **I ~ to suggest** осмелюсь предложить; **don't ~ too near the edge** не подходите слишком близко к краю; **nothing ~d, nothing gained** ≈ волков бояться — в лес не ходить.

● *cpd.* **~ capital** *n.* (*fin.*) венчурный капитал.

venturesome /ˈventʃəsəm/ *adj.* (*daring*) предприимчивый; (*risky*) рискованный.

venue /ˈvenjuː/ *n.* место сбора/встречи/соревнований.

Venus /ˈviːnəs/ *n.* (*myth., astron.*) Венера.

veracious /vəˈreɪʃəs/ *adj.* (*person*) правдивый; (*information*) правдивый, достоверный.

veracity /vəˈræsɪtɪ/ *n.* правдивость; достоверность.

veranda(h) /vəˈrændə/ *n.* веранда.

verb /vɜːb/ *n.* глагол.

verbal /ˈvɜːb(ə)l/ *adj.* **1** (*of or in words*) словесный; **~ subtleties** тонкости языка/словоупотребления. **2** (*oral*) устный; **~ly** (только) на словах. **3** (*gram.*) (*features*) глагольный; (*formed from verb*) отглагольный; **~ noun** отглагольное существительное.

verbalize /ˈvɜːbəˌlaɪz/ *v.t.* (*put into words*) выражать, выразить словами.

verbatim /vɜːˈbeɪtɪm/ *adv.* дословно; слово в слово.

verbena /vɜːˈbiːnə/ *n.* (*bot.*) вербе́на.

verbiage /ˈvɜːbɪɪdʒ/ *n.* многосло́вие; пустосло́вие.

verbose /vɜːˈbəʊs/ *adj.* многосло́вный.

verbos|eness /vɜːˈbəʊsnɪs/, **-ity** /vɜːˈbɒsɪtɪ/ *nn.* многосло́вие.

verdant /ˈvɜːd(ə)nt/ *adj.* (*liter.*) зелёный, зелене́ющий.

verdict /ˈvɜːdɪkt/ *n.* (*leg.*) верди́кт; **the jury brought in a ~ of guilty** суд прися́жных вы́нес обвини́тельный верди́кт; (*fig., decision, judgement*) заключе́ние, пригово́р; **what's the ~?** како́в пригово́р?; **the popular ~** обще́ственное мне́ние.

verdigris /ˈvɜːdɪgrɪs/, /-ˌgriːs/ *n.* ярь-медя́нка.

verdure /ˈvɜːdjə(r)/ *n.* зе́лень.

verge /vɜːdʒ/ *n.* край; (*Br., of road*) обо́чина; (*fig.*): **on the ~ of destruction** на краю́ ги́бели; **on the ~ of tears** на гра́ни слёз; **he was on the ~ of betraying his secret** он чуть не вы́дал свою́ та́йну.

● *v.i.*: **it ~s on madness** э́то грани́чит с безу́мием.

verger /ˈvɜːdʒə(r)/ *n.* (*church official*) ≈ дьячо́к.

verifiable /ˈverɪˌfaɪəb(ə)l/ *adj.* поддаю́щийся прове́рке.

verification /ˌverɪfɪˈkeɪʃ(ə)n/ *n.* прове́рка, подтвержде́ние.

verify /ˈverɪˌfaɪ/ *v.t.* (*check accuracy of*) пров|еря́ть, -е́рить; (*bear out, confirm*) подтвер|жда́ть, -ди́ть.

verily /ˈverɪlɪ/ *adv.* (*arch.*) и́стинно, пои́стине.

verisimilitude /ˌverɪsɪˈmɪlɪˌtjuːd/ *n.* правдоподо́бие.

veritable /ˈverɪtəb(ə)l/ *adj.* настоя́щий, су́щий.

verit|y /ˈverɪtɪ/ *n.* и́стина; **eternal ~ies** ве́чные и́стины.

vermicelli /ˌvɜːmɪˈselɪ/, /-ˈtʃelɪ/ *n.* вермише́ль.

vermiform /ˈvɜːmɪˌfɔːm/ *adj.*: **~ appendix** (*anat.*) червеобра́зный отро́сток, аппе́ндикс.

vermilion /vəˈmɪljən/ *n.* (*pigment; colour*) вермильо́н, ки́новарь.

● *adj.* я́рко-кра́сный; а́лый.

vermin /ˈvɜːmɪn/ *n.* **1** (*animal pests*) вреди́тели (*m. pl.*); ме́лкие хи́щники (*m. pl.*). **2** (*parasitic insects*) парази́ты (*m. pl.*). **3** (*fig., obnoxious persons*) парази́ты (*m. pl.*).

verminous /ˈvɜːmɪnəs/ *adj.* **1** (*infested with vermin*) кища́щий парази́тами; (*full of lice*) вши́вый. **2** (*fig., obnoxious*) отврати́тельный.

vermouth /ˈvɜːməθ/, /vəˈmuːθ/ *n.* ве́рмут.

vernacular /vəˈnækjʊlə(r)/ *n.* **1** (*local language*) иско́нный язы́к; **Latin gave place to the ~** латы́нь уступи́ла ме́сто иско́нным языка́м. **2** (*dialect*) диале́кт; наре́чие. **3** (*jargon*) жарго́н, арго́ (*indecl.*). **4** (*colloquial speech*) просторе́чие.

● *adj.* иско́нный, ме́стный; просторе́чный.

vernal /ˈvɜːn(ə)l/ *adj.* весе́нний; (*poet.*) ве́шний.

veronica /vəˈrɒnɪkə/ *n.* (*bot.*) верони́ка.

Versailles /veəˈsaɪ/ *n.* Верса́ль (*m.*); **Treaty of ~** Верса́льский (ми́рный) догово́р.

versatile /ˈvɜːsəˌtaɪl/ *adj.* (*person*) разносторо́нний; (*device*) универса́льный.

versatility /ˌvɜːsəˈtɪlɪtɪ/ *n.* разносторо́нность; универса́льность.

verse /vɜːs/ *n.* **1** (*line of ~*) строка́. **2** (*stanza*) строфа́. **3** (*of Bible*) стих. **4** (*sg. or pl., poems*) стихи́ (*m. pl.*); стихотворе́ния (*nt. pl.*); **blank ~** бе́лые стихи́; **prose and ~** про́за и поэ́зия; **he wrote in ~** он писа́л в стиха́х.

versed /vɜːst/ *adj.* (*well-informed*) све́дущий (в + *p.*); (*skilful*) искушённый.

versification /ˌvɜːsɪfɪˈkeɪʃ(ə)n/ *n.* версифика́ция, стихосложе́ние.

versify /ˈvɜːsɪˌfaɪ/ *v.t.* перел|ага́ть, -ожи́ть в стихи́.

version /ˈvɜːʃ(ə)n/ *n.* **1** (*individual account*) ве́рсия, расска́з; **according to his ~** по его́ слова́м. **2** (*translation*) перево́д; **an English ~ of the Bible** Би́блия в англи́йском перево́де/на англи́йском языке́. **3** (*form or variant of text etc.*) вариа́нт, текст; **original ~** по́длинник; **the Russian ~ is authentic** ру́сский текст аутенти́чен; (*adaptation*) переложе́ние, переде́лка; **silent ~** (*cin.*) немо́й вариа́нт; **screen ~** экраниза́ция; **stage ~** инсцениро́вка. **4** (*comput.*) ве́рсия.

verso /ˈvɜːsəʊ/ *n.* (*pl.* **~s**) (*of coin*) оборо́тная сторона́; (*left-hand page*) ле́вая страни́ца; (*back of document*) оборо́т листа́.

verst /vɜːst/ *n.* верста́.

versus /ˈvɜːsəs/ *prep.* **1** (*leg.*) про́тив + *g.* **2** (*sport*) про́тив + *g.*; **Arsenal ~ Chelsea** Арсена́л про́тив Че́лси; матч Арсена́л—Че́лси. **3** (*compared or contrasted with*) в сравне́нии с + *i.*

vertebra /ˈvɜːtɪbrə/ *n.* (*pl.* **vertebrae** /-ˌbreɪ/, /-ˌbriː/) позвоно́к.

vertebrate /ˈvɜːtɪbrət/, /-ˌbreɪt/ *n.* позвоно́чное (живо́тное).

● *adj.* позвоно́чный.

vertex /ˈvɜːteks/ *n.* (*pl.* **vertices** *or* **vertexes**) (*top, apex*) верши́на; (*of the head*) те́мя (*nt.*).

vertical /ˈvɜːtɪk(ə)l/ *n.* (*line*) вертика́ль; **the ~** перпендикуля́р.

● *adj.* вертика́льный, перпендикуля́рный; **a ~ cliff** отве́сный утёс.

vertices /ˈvɜːtɪˌsiːz/ *pl. of* ⇒**vertex**

vertiginous /vəˈtɪdʒɪnəs/ *adj.* головокружи́тельный.

vertigo /ˈvɜːtɪˌgəʊ/ *n.* головокруже́ние.

verve /vɜːv/ *n.* жи́вость, эне́ргия; огонёк.

very /ˈverɪ/ *adj.* **1** (*exact; identical*) тот са́мый; **this ~ day** сего́дня же; **at that ~ moment** в тот са́мый моме́нт; **this is the ~ thing for me** э́то как раз то, что мне ну́жно; **those were his ~ words** э́то его́ слова́ в то́чности. **2** (*extreme*) са́мый; **at the ~ end** в са́мом конце́. **3** (*in emphasis*): **the ~ idea of it** одна́ мысль об э́том; **the ~ idea!** поду́мать то́лько!; **the ~ fact of his being there is suspicious** (уже́) оди́н факт его́ прису́тствия там подозри́телен.

● *adv.* **1** (*exceedingly*) о́чень; **I don't feel ~ well** я чу́вствую себя́ нева́жно; **I can't sing ~ well** я дово́льно пло́хо пою́; **~ well, you can go** ну, хорошо́, мо́жете идти́; **~ good, sir** слу́шаюсь; есть! **2** (*emph., with superl. etc.*) са́мый; **the ~ best** са́мый лу́чший; наилу́чший; **the ~ next day** на сле́дующий же день; **you may keep it for your ~ own** мо́жете э́то взять себе́ насовсе́м.

vespers /ˈvespəz/ *n.* вече́рня; вече́рняя моли́тва.

vessel /ˈves(ə)l/ *n.* **1** (*receptacle*) сосу́д. **2** (*ship*) су́дно, кора́бль (*m.*). **3** (*anat.*) сосу́д; **blood ~** кровено́сный сосу́д.

vest[1] /vest/ *n.* (*Br., undergarment*) ма́йка; (*US, waistcoat*) жиле́т.

vest[2] /vest/ *v.t.* **1** (*endow, furnish*) наде́л|я́ть, -и́ть; обл|ека́ть, -е́чь; **be ~ed with a right** име́ть (*impf.*) пра́во; по́льзоваться (*impf.*) пра́вом; **~ with power to act** уполномо́чи|вать, -ть. **2** (*place, establish*): **authority ~ed in him** власть, кото́рой он облечён; **~ed interest** кро́вная/ли́чная заинтересо́ванность; **~ed interests** (*leg.*) иму́щественные права́, закреплённые зако́ном.

● *v.i.*: **the estate ~s in him** иму́щество перехо́дит к нему́.

vestibule /ˈvestɪˌbjuːl/ *n.* (*lobby; porch*) вестибю́ль (*m.*); (*US, of corridor train*) та́мбур.

vestige /ˈvestɪdʒ/ *n.* **1** (*trace*) след; мале́йший при́знак. **2** (*biol.*) оста́ток, рудиме́нт.

vestigial /veˈstɪdʒɪəl/, /-dʒ(ə)l/ *adj.* оста́точный, рудимента́рный.

vestment /ˈvestmənt/ *n.* облаче́ние, ри́за.

vestry /ˈvestrɪ/ *n.* (*room*) ри́зница.

Vesuvius /vɪˈsuːvɪəs/ *n.* Везу́вий.

vet[1] /vet/ *n.* (*coll., veterinary surgeon*) ветвра́ч, ветерина́р.

● *v.t.* (**vetted, vetting**) (*coll., investigate*) пров|еря́ть, -е́рить.

vet[2] /vet/ *n.* (*US, coll., veteran*) ветера́н.

vetch /vetʃ/ *n.* (*bot.*) ви́ка.

veteran /ˈvetərən/ *n.* (*lit., fig.*) ветера́н.

● *adj.* многоо́пытный, старе́йший; **a ~ car** (*Br.*) маши́на ста́рой ма́рки.

veterinarian /ˌvetərɪˈneərɪən/ *n.* (*US*) ветерина́р.

veterinary /ˈvetərɪnərɪ/ *adj.* ветерина́рный; **~ surgeon** (*Br.*) ветерина́рный врач.

veto /ˈviːtəʊ/ *n.* (*pl.* **vetoes**) ве́то (*indecl.*); **he put a ~ on the suggestion** он наложи́л ве́то на предложе́ние; **the President exercised his ~** президе́нт воспо́льзовался свои́м пра́вом ве́то.

● *v.t.* (**vetoes, vetoed**) нал|ага́ть, -ожи́ть ве́то на + *a.*; **my proposal was**

V

~**ed** моё предложе́ние бы́ло отве́ргнуто.

vex /veks/ *v.t.* доса|жда́ть, -ди́ть; раздраж|а́ть, -и́ть; **a ~ed question** больно́й вопро́с.

vexation /vek'seɪʃ(ə)n/ *n.* доса́да, огорче́ние.

vexatious /vek'seɪʃəs/ *adj.* доса́дный, огорчи́тельный.

VHF (*abbr. of* ***very high frequency***) ОВЧ (о́чень высо́кая частота́).

via /'vaɪə/ *prep.* че́рез + *a.*

viability /ˌvaɪə'bɪlɪtɪ/ *n.* жизнеспосо́бность; осуществи́мость.

viable /'vaɪəb(ə)l/ *adj.* (*able to survive or exist*) жизнеспосо́бный; (*coll., feasible*) осуществи́мый.

viaduct /'vaɪəˌdʌkt/ *n.* виаду́к, путепрово́д.

vial /'vaɪəl/ *n.* (*arch.*) пузырёк, флако́н.

vibes /vaɪbz/ *n.* (*coll.*) (*mus., vibraphone*) вибрафо́н; (*atmosphere*) флюи́ды (*m. pl.*).

vibrant /'vaɪbrənt/ *adj.* (*lively*) живо́й, по́лный жи́зни; (*of colours*) со́чный, я́ркий; (*trembling*) трепе́щущий, дрожа́щий; (*resonant*) резони́рующий.

vibraphone /'vaɪbrəˌfəʊn/ *n.* вибрафо́н.

vibrat|e /vaɪ'breɪt/ *v.t.* заст|авля́ть, -а́вить вибри́ровать (*impf.*).

● *v.i.* вибри́ровать, дрожа́ть (*both impf.*); **the whole house ~es** весь дом сотряса́ется; **a voice ~ing with passion** го́лос, дрожа́щий от стра́сти.

vibration /vaɪ'breɪʃ(ə)n/ *n.* вибра́ция, дрожь.

vibrato /vɪ'brɑːtəʊ/ *n. & adv.* (*mus.*) вибра́то (*indecl.*).

vibrator /vaɪ'breɪtə(r)/ *n.* (*tech., for massage*) вибра́тор.

vibratory /'vaɪbrətərɪ/, /-'breɪtərɪ/ *adj.* вибри́рующий.

viburnum /vaɪ'bɜːnəm/, /vɪ-/ *n.* (*bot.*) кали́на.

vicar /'vɪkə(r)/ *n.* (*in Church of England*) прихо́дский свяще́нник; (*in other Anglican Churches, deputizing member of clergy*) помо́щник свяще́нника, вика́рий; (*in Catholic church*) вика́рий.

vicarage /'vɪkərɪdʒ/ *n.* дом прихо́дского свяще́нника.

vicarious /vɪ'keərɪəs/ *adj.* ко́свенный; **feel ~ pleasure** пережива́ть (*impf.*) чужу́ю ра́дость.

vice[1] /vaɪs/ *n.* **1** (*evil doing*) поро́к; **~ squad** отря́д поли́ции нра́вов.
2 (*particular fault*) поро́к, сла́бость, недоста́ток; **smoking is not among my ~s** куре́ние не вхо́дит в число́ мои́х поро́ков.

vice[2] /vaɪs/ (*US* **vise**) *n.* (*tool*) тиск|и́ (*pl., g.* -о́в); клёщ|и (*pl., g.* -е́й).

vice[3] /vaɪs/ *n.* (*coll., deputy*) зам, замести́тель (*m.*).

● *cpds.* **~-admiral** *n.* ви́це-адмира́л; **~chairman** *n.* замести́тель (*m.*) председа́теля; **~-chancellor** *n.* (*Br.*) ре́ктор; **~-president** *n.* ви́це-президе́нт.

viceroy /'vaɪsrɔɪ/ *n.* ви́це-коро́ль (*m.*).

vice versa /ˌvaɪsɪ 'vɜːsə/ *adv.* наоборо́т; **the cat stole the dog's dinner and ~** ко́шка стащи́ла у соба́ки еду́, а соба́ка — у ко́шки.

vicinity /vɪ'sɪnɪtɪ/ *n.* (*nearness*) бли́зость, сосе́дство; (*neighbourhood*) окру́га, окре́стность.

vicious /'vɪʃəs/ *adj.* **1** (*spiteful*) злой, зло́бный. **2** (*of an animal*) злой, опа́сный. **3**: **a ~ circle** поро́чный круг.

viciousness /'vɪʃəsnɪs/ *n.* (*evil*) поро́чность; (*spite*) зло́бность; (*of an animal*) зло́бность.

vicissitude /vɪ'sɪsɪˌtjuːd/, /vaɪ-/ *n.* превра́тность.

victim /'vɪktɪm/ *n.* же́ртва; (*of accident*) пострада́вший; **fall ~ to** па́|дать, -сть же́ртвой + *g.*

victimization /ˌvɪktɪmaɪ'zeɪʃ(ə)n/ *n.* пресле́дование.

victimize /'vɪktɪˌmaɪz/ *v.t.* подв|ерга́ть, -е́ргнуть пресле́дованию.

victor /'vɪktə(r)/ *n.* победи́тель (*m.*).

Victoria Cross /vɪk'tɔːrɪə/ (*Br., mil.*) *n.* крест Викто́рии.

Victorian /vɪk'tɔːrɪən/ *n.* викториа́н|ец (*fem.* -ка).

● *adj.* викториа́нский; (*fig.*) старомо́дный.

victorious /vɪk'tɔːrɪəs/ *adj.* победоно́сный, побе́дный, торжеству́ющий.

victory /'vɪktərɪ/ *n.* побе́да (**over**: над + *i.*).

victual /'vɪt(ə)l/ *n.* (*pl. only*) (*food*) пи́ща, проду́кты пита́ния (*m. pl.*); (*provisions*) съестны́е припа́с|ы (*pl., g.* -ов).

● *v.t.* (**victualled, victualling;** *US* **victualed, victualing**) снаб|жа́ть, -ди́ть проду́ктами пита́ния/продово́льствием.

victualler /'vɪtlə(r)/ (*US* **victualer**) *n.* снабже́нец; поставщи́к проду́ктов пита́ния/продово́льствия; **licensed ~** (*Br.*) тракти́рщик.

vide /'vɪdeɪ/, /'viː-/, /'vaɪdɪ/ *v.tr. imper.* смотри́ (*abbr.* см.).

video /'vɪdɪəʊ/ *n.* (*pl.* **videos**) (*the system*) видеоте́хника; (*a ~ recorder* (*Br.*), *film, cassette*) ви́део (*indecl.*); **~ camera** видеока́мера; **~ cassette** видеокассе́та; **~ (cassette) recorder** видеомагнитофо́н; **~ conference** видеоконфере́нция; **~ games machine** телеавтома́т; **~ library** видеоте́ка; **~phone** видеотелефо́н; **~ recording** видеоза́пись; **~ rental club** видеоте́ка; **~tape** видеоле́нта; видеоплёнка.

● *v.t.* (**videoes, videoed**) запи́с|ывать, -а́ть на ви́део.

vie /vaɪ/ *v.i.* (**vying**) состяза́ться (*impf.*); сопе́рничать (*impf.*); **they ~d with each other for first place** они́ состяза́лись за пе́рвое ме́сто.

Vienna /vɪ'enə/ *n.* Ве́на.

Viennese /vɪə'niːz/ *n.* (*pl.* ~) жи́тель (*m.*) (*fem.* -ница) Ве́ны.

● *adj.* ве́нский.

Vietnam /ˌvjet'næm/ *n.* Вьетна́м.

Vietnamese /ˌvɪetnə'miːz/ *n.* (*pl.* ~) (*person*) вьетна́м|ец (*fem.* -ка); (*language*) вьетна́мский язы́к.

● *adj.* вьетна́мский.

view /vjuː/ *n.* **1** (*sight; field of vision*) вид; по́ле зре́ния; **the mountains came into ~** показа́лись го́ры; **a ~ of the sea** вид на мо́ре; **the procession passed from ~** проце́ссия скры́лась и́з виду (*or* из ви́ду); **in full ~ of the audience** на виду́ у пу́блики; **~ halloo!** ату́!
2 (*fig.*): **I want to get a clear ~ of the situation** я хочу́ соста́вить себе́ я́сное представле́ние о ситуа́ции; **look at it from my point of ~** посмотри́те на э́то с мое́й то́чки зре́ния.
3 (*inspection*) смотр, просмо́тр; **the pictures are on ~ all week** вы́ставка карти́н бу́дет откры́та всю неде́лю; **private ~(ing)** закры́тый просмо́тр; (*of exhibition*) верниса́ж; **~ing day** (*preparatory to auction sale*) де́нь (*m.*) предвари́тельного осмо́тра.
4 (*scene, prospect*) вид; пейза́ж; **you get a good ~ from here** отсю́да хоро́ший вид.
5 (*depicted scene*) вид, изображе́ние.
6 (*mental attitude or opinion*) взгляд, мне́ние; (*pl.*) взгля́ды (*m. pl.*), убежде́ния (*nt. pl.*); **she has strong ~s on the subject** у неё на э́тот счёт твёрдые убежде́ния; **he holds extreme ~s** он челове́к кра́йних убежде́ний/взгля́дов; **in my ~** по-мо́ему; по моему́ мне́нию; **I take a different ~** у меня́ друго́е мне́ние/друга́я то́чка зре́ния; **he took a poor ~ of it** (*coll.*) ему́ э́то о́чень не понра́вилось.
7 (*intention*) наме́рение; **I am saving with a ~ to buying a house** я коплю́ де́ньги, что́бы купи́ть дом; **what have you in ~?** что вы намерева́етесь де́лать?
8 (*consideration*): **in ~ of** ввиду́ + *g.*; **he was excused in ~ of his youth** его́ прости́ли по мо́лодости; **in ~ of recent developments** в све́те после́дних происше́ствий.

● *v.t.* **1** (*survey; gaze on*) смотре́ть, по- на + *a.*; рассм|а́тривать, -отре́ть; **he ~ed the landscape through binoculars** он рассма́тривал ме́стность в бино́кль; (*TV*) смотре́ть, по-.
2 (*inspect*) осм|а́тривать, -отре́ть.
3 (*fig., consider*) рассм|а́тривать, -отре́ть; оце́н|ивать, -и́ть; **he ~ed it in a different light** он ина́че смотре́л на э́то; **the request was ~ed unfavourably** (*Br.*), **unfavorably** (*US*) к про́сьбе отнесли́сь отрица́тельно.

● *cpds.* **~-finder** *n.* видоиска́тель (*m.*); **~point** *n.* то́чка зре́ния.

viewer /'vjuːə(r)/ *n.* **1** (*onlooker*) зри́тель (*fem.* -ница). **2** (*of TV*) (теле)зри́тель (*fem.* -ница).
3 (*instrument*) прибо́р для просмо́тра диапозити́вов.

vigil /'vɪdʒɪl/ *n.* (*staying awake*) бде́ние; **she kept ~ over the patient** она́ не отходи́ла от посте́ли больно́го.

vigilance /'vɪdʒɪləns/ *n.* бди́тельность.

vigilant /'vɪdʒɪlənt/ *adj.* бди́тельный.

vigilante /ˌvɪdʒɪ'læntɪ/ *n.* ≈ дружи́нник.

vignette /vi:'njet/ *n.* (*ornamental design*) виньéтка; (*character sketch*) набрóсок.

vigor /'vɪgə(r)/ (*US*) = **vigour**

vigorous /'vɪgərəs/ *adj.* энерги́чный, бóдрый; **a ~ speech** энерги́чная речь.

vigour /'vɪgə(r)/ (*US* **vigor** *n.*) энéргия, бóдрость; (*of language, style etc.*) жи́вость, энерги́чность, энéргия.

Viking /'vaɪkɪŋ/ *n.* ви́кинг.

vile /vaɪl/ *adj.* гнýсный, ни́зкий, мéрзкий.

vilification /,vɪlɪfɪ'keɪʃ(ə)n/ *n.* поношéние, очернéние.

vilify /'vɪlɪ,faɪ/ *v.t.* поноси́ть (*impf.*); черни́ть, о-.

villa /'vɪlə/ *n.* (*country residence*) ви́лла, дáча; (*Br., suburban house*) ви́лла, дóм.

village /'vɪlɪdʒ/ *n.* дерéвня; (*larger*) селó; (*attr.*) деревéнский, сéльский; **~ hall** сéльский клуб.

villager /'vɪlɪdʒə(r)/ *n.* деревéнск|ий/сéльск|ий жи́тель (*fem.* -ая -ница).

villain /'vɪlən/ *n.* **1** (*man of base character*) злодéй, негодя́й; (*theatr.*) отрицáтельный герóй; злодéй; **he played the ~** он игрáл роль злодéя; **he was the ~ of the piece** (*fig.*) он был глáвным винóвником. **2** (*coll., criminal*) престýпник, злодéй.

villainess /'vɪlənɪs/ *n.* злодéйка, престýпница.

villainous /'vɪlənəs/ *adj.* пóдлый, ни́зкий, гнýсный.

villainy /'vɪlənɪ/ *n.* злодéйство, пóдлость.

Vilnius /'vɪlnɪəs/ *n.* Ви́льнюс; (*attr.*) ви́льнюсский.

vim /vɪm/ *n.* энéргия, си́ла, напóр.

vinaigrette /,vɪnɪ'gret/ *n.* подли́вка из ýксуса и провáнского мáсла.

vindicate /'vɪndɪ,keɪt/ *v.t.* (*defend successfully*) отст|áивать, -оя́ть; защи|щáть, -ти́ть; (*justify*) опрáвд|ывать, -áть.

vindication /,vɪndɪ'keɪʃ(ə)n/ *n.* защи́та; оправдáние.

vindictive /vɪn'dɪktɪv/ *adj.* мсти́тельный.

vindictiveness /vɪn'dɪktɪvnɪs/ *n.* мсти́тельность.

vine /vaɪn/ *n.* (*grape-~*) виногрáдная лозá; (*any climbing or trailing plant*) вью́щееся/ползýчее растéние.

● *cpds.* **~-growing** *n.* виногрáдарство; *adj.* виногрáдарский; **~yard** *n.* виногрáдник.

vinegar /'vɪnɪgə(r)/ *n.* ýксус.

vinegary /'vɪnɪgərɪ/ *adj.* ýксусный; ки́слый (*also fig.*).

viniculture /'vɪnɪ,kʌltʃə(r)/ *n.* виногрáдарство.

vintage /'vɪntɪdʒ/ *n.* **1** (*grape harvest*) сбор виногрáда; **the 1950 ~** (*sc. wine*) винó урожáя (*or* из сбóра) ты́сяча девятьсóт пятидеся́того гóда; **a rare ~** рéдкое винó; **this is a good ~** э́то хорóший год (*о вине*); **~ wine** мáрочное винó; **~ port** стáрый/вы́держанный портвéйн. **2** (*fig.*): **a ~ car** (*Br.*) автомоби́ль (*m.*) стáрой мáрки; **of the same ~** (*sc. age*) тогó же периóда.

vintner /'vɪntnə(r)/ *n.* виноторгóвец.

vinyl /'vaɪnɪl/ *n.* вини́л.

● *adj.* вини́ловый.

viol /'vaɪəl/ *n.* виóла; **~ da gamba** виóла да гáмба.

viola[1] /vɪ'əʊlə/ *n.* (*mus.*) альт.

viola[2] /'vaɪələ/ *n.* (*bot.*) виóла.

violate /'vaɪə,leɪt/ *v.t.* **1** (*infringe, transgress*) нар|ушáть, -ýшить; преступ|áть, -и́ть; **this ~s the spirit of the agreement** э́то противорéчит дýху соглашéния. **2** (*profane*) осквер|ня́ть, -и́ть. **3** (*rape*) наси́ловать, из-.

violation /,vaɪə'leɪʃ(ə)n/ *n.* нарушéние; осквернéние; **~ of territory** вторжéние на чужýю территóрию; (*rape*) изнаси́лование.

violator /'vaɪə,leɪtə(r)/ *n.* нарушитель (*fem.* -ница).

violence /'vaɪələns/ *n.* си́ла, наси́лие; **he resorted to ~** он прибéгнул к наси́лию; **robbery with ~** грабёж с наси́лием.

violent /'vaɪələnt/ *adj.* **1** (*strong, forceful*) си́льный, нéистовый, я́ростный; **a ~ storm** си́льный штóрм; **~ pain** си́льная боль; **~ colours** (*Br.*), **colors** (*US*) рéзкие/кричáщие цветá; **~ passions** нéистовые стрáсти; **a ~ scene** бýрная сцéна; **I took a ~ dislike to him** он вы́звал во мне рéзкое отвращéние; **he was in a ~ temper** он был вне себя́ от бéшенства; **he made a ~ speech** он произнёс горя́чую/гнéвную речь. **2** (*using or involving force*): **~ blows** си́льные удáры; **he became ~** он нáчал бýйствовать; **he died a ~ death** он ýмер наси́льственной смéртью.

violet /'vaɪələt/ *n.* (*bot.*) фиáлка; (*colour*) фиолéтовый/ли́ловый цвет.

● *adj.* (*of colour*) фиолéтовый, ли́ловый.

violin /,vaɪə'lɪn/ *n.* скри́пка; (*player*) скрипáч; **first ~** пéрвая скри́пка; (*attr.*) скрипи́чный.

violinist /vaɪə'lɪnɪst/ *n.* скрипáч (*fem.* -ка).

violoncello /,vaɪələn'tʃeləʊ/, /,vi:ə-/ *n.* (*pl.* **~s**) (*formal*) = **cello**

VIP (*abbr. of* ***very important person***) высокопостáвленное лицó, высóкий гость.

viper /'vaɪpə(r)/ *n.* гадю́ка; випéра; (*fig.*) гадю́ка.

virago /vɪ'rɑ:gəʊ/, /-'reɪgəʊ/ *n.* (*pl.* **~s**) мегéра.

virgin /'vɜ:dʒɪn/ *n.* дéвственница, дéва; (*male*) дéвственник; **the (Blessed) V~** (Пресвятáя) дéва Мари́я; **she is still a ~** онá ещё дéвственница; **~ birth** рождéние от дéвственницы; (*pure; undefiled*) чи́стый, нетрóнутый, дéвственный; **~ soil** целинá; **~ forest** дéвственный лес.

virginal(s)[1] /'vɜ:dʒɪn(ə)l/ *n.* (*mus.*) клавеси́н.

virginal[2] /'vɜ:dʒɪn(ə)l/ *adj.* дéвственный; непорóчный.

Virginia /və'dʒɪnɪə/ *n.*: **~ tobacco** вирги́нский табáк; **~ creeper** ди́кий виногрáд.

virginity /və'dʒɪnɪtɪ/ *n.* дéвственность, неви́нность, непорóчность; **lose one's ~** теря́ть, по- неви́нность.

Virgo /'vɜ:gəʊ/ *n.* (*pl.* **~s**) Дéва.

virile /'vɪraɪl/ *adj.* **1** (*sexually potent*) облaдáющий мужскóй си́лой/потéнцией. **2** (*manly, robust*) мýжественный.

virility /vɪ'rɪlɪtɪ/ *n.* (*sexual potency*) мужскáя си́ла, половáя потéнция; (*manliness*) мýжественность.

virology /vaɪ'rɒlədʒɪ/ *n.* вирусолóгия.

virtual /'vɜ:tjʊəl/ *adj.* **1** факти́ческий; **the dress was ~ly new** э́то бы́ло прáктически нóвое плáтье; **he is a ~ stranger to me** я егó, в сýщности, не знáю. **2** (*comput., phys.*) виртуáльный.

● *cpd.* **~ reality** *n.* (*comput.*) виртуáльная реáльность.

virtue /'vɜ:tju:/, /-tʃu:/ *n.* **1** (*moral excellence*) добродéтель; **his great ~ is patience** егó глáвная добродéтель — терпéние. **2** (*chastity*) целомýдрие; **a woman of easy ~** достýпная жéнщина. **3** (*good quality; advantage*) достóинство, преимýщество; **his scheme had the ~ of being practicable** преимýщество егó плáна состоя́ло в том, что он был вы́полним. **4** (*consideration*) основáние; **by ~ of his long service** на основáнии (*or* ввидý) егó долголéтней слýжбы.

virtuosi /,vɜ:tjʊ'əʊsi:/, /-zi:/ *pl. of* ⇒**virtuoso**

virtuosic /,vɜ:tjʊ'ɒsɪk/ *adj.* виртуóзный.

virtuosity /,vɜ:tjʊ'ɒsɪtɪ/, /-tʃu:'ɒsɪtɪ/ *n.* виртуóзность.

virtuos|o /,vɜ:tjʊ'əʊsəʊ/, /-zəʊ/ *n.* (*pl.* **~i** *or* **~os**) виртуóз; **a ~ performance** виртуóзное исполнéние.

virtuous /'vɜ:tjʊəs/, /-tʃʊəs/ *adj.* добродéтельный; (*chaste*) целомýдренный.

virulence /'vɪrʊləns/, /'vɪrjʊ-/ *n.* (*of poison*) си́ла, смертéльность; (*of disease*) тя́жесть; (*of bacteria*) вирулéнтность; (*of temper, speech etc.*) злóба, я́рость.

virulent /'vɪrʊlənt/, /'vɪrjʊ-/ *adj.* (*of poison*) сильнодéйствующий; смертéльный; (*of disease*) тяжёлый; (*of bacteria*) вирулéнтный; (*of temper, words etc.*) злóбный, я́ростный.

virus /'vaɪərəs/ *n.* (*also comput.*) ви́рус; **a ~ disease** ви́русное заболевáние.

visa /'vi:zə/ *n.* ви́за.

visage /'vɪzɪdʒ/ *n.* (*liter.*) лицó; выражéние лицá; вид.

vis-à-vis /,vi:zɑ:'vi:/ *adv.* визави́.

● *prep.* (*in relation to*) по отношéнию к + *d.*; в отношéнии + *g.*; (*as opposed to*) пéред + *i.*

viscera /'vɪsərə/ *n.* внýтренности (*f. pl.*); (*of bird, fish*) потрохá (*m. pl.*).

visceral /'vɪsər(ə)l/ *adj.* внýтренний; **~ hatred** глубóкая/органи́ческая нéнависть.

viscose /'vɪskəʊz/, /-kəʊs/ *n.* вискóза.

viscosity /vɪˈskɒsɪtɪ/ *n.* вя́зкость, ли́пкость.

viscount /ˈvaɪkaʊnt/ *n.* вико́нт.

viscountess /ˈvaɪkaʊntɪs/ *n.* виконте́сса.

viscous /ˈvɪskəs/ *adj.* вя́зкий, ли́пкий.

vise /vaɪs/ (*US*) = **vice²**

visibility /ˌvɪzɪˈbɪlɪtɪ/ *n.* ви́димость.

visibl|e /ˈvɪzɪb(ə)l/ *adj.* **1** (*perceptible by eye*) ви́димый. **2** (*apparent*; *obvious*) я́вный, очеви́дный; **he has no ~e means of support** у него́ нет определённых средств к существова́нию; **she was ~y annoyed** она́ была́ заме́тно раздражена́.

vision /ˈvɪʒ(ə)n/ *n.* **1** (*faculty of sight*) зре́ние; **field of ~** по́ле зре́ния. **2** (*imaginative insight*) проница́тельность; **a man of ~** дальнови́дный/проница́тельный челове́к. **3** (*apparition*) при́зрак; привиде́ние. **4** (*sth. imagined or dreamed of*) мечта́; **I had ~s of something better than this** я представля́л себе́ не́что лу́чшее, чем э́то. **5** (*beautiful sight*) прекра́сное зре́лище.

visionary /ˈvɪʒənərɪ/ *n.* (*person with foresight*) прови́д|ец (*fem.* -ица); (*dreamer*) мечта́тель (*fem.* -ница).

● *adj.* (*having foresight*) дальнови́дный, му́дрый; (*unreal*) вообража́емый; (*unpractical*) неосуществи́мый.

visit /ˈvɪzɪt/ *n.* (*call*) визи́т, посеще́ние; (*US, talk*) бесе́да; (*trip, stay*) пое́здка, пребыва́ние; **make, pay a ~ to s.o.** посе|ща́ть, -ти́ть (*or* наве|ща́ть, -сти́ть) кого́-н.; **we had a ~ from our neighbours** (*Br.*), **neighbors** (*US*) нас посети́ли (*or* у нас бы́ли в гостя́х) на́ши сосе́ди; **we had a ~ from a policeman** к нам приходи́л полице́йский; **~ to a museum** посеще́ние музе́я; **pay us a ~** прове́дайте нас; **he is here on a ~** он гости́т здесь; он прие́зжий; **during my ~ to the States** во вре́мя моего́ пребыва́ния в Шта́тах.

● *v.t.* (**visited, visiting**) **1** (*place*) посе|ща́ть, -ти́ть; (*person*) наве|ща́ть, -сти́ть; **he ~ed Europe** он побыва́л в Евро́пе; он съе́здил в Евро́пу; **I have never ~ed New York** я никогда́ не быва́л в Нью-Йо́рке; **~ing card** (*Br.*) визи́тная ка́рточка; **~ing hours** приёмные часы́; часы́ посеще́ния. **2** (*of disease etc.*) пост|ига́ть, -и́чь; пора|жа́ть, -зи́ть.

● *v.i.* (**visited, visiting**) (*US*): **~ with** (*go to see*) вида́ться, по-; (*chat to*) бесе́довать (*impf.*) с + *i.*

visitation /ˌvɪzɪˈteɪʃ(ə)n/ *n.* (*official visit*) обхо́д; (*coll., protracted visit*) затяну́вшийся визи́т; (*affliction*) ка́ра, наказа́ние (Бо́жье).

visitor /ˈvɪzɪtə(r)/ *n.* гость (*m.*), посети́тель (*m.*); **the town is full of ~s** го́род по́лон прие́зжих; **~s' book** (*Br.*) кни́га посети́телей.

vi|sor, -zor /ˈvaɪzə(r)/ *n.* (*hist., of helmet*) забра́ло; (*of cap*) козырёк; (*of windscreen*) солнцезащи́тный щито́к.

vista /ˈvɪstə/ *n.* перспекти́ва, вид; (*fig.*) перспекти́вы (*f. pl.*).

Vistula /ˈvɪstjʊlə/ *n.* Ви́сла.

visual /ˈvɪzjʊəl/, /ˈvɪʒj-/ *adj.* (*concerned with seeing*) зри́тельный; визуа́льный; **~ arts** изобрази́тельные иску́сства; **~ nerve** зри́тельный нерв; **~ image** зри́тельный о́браз; **~ aids** нагля́дные посо́бия; **~ display unit** (*comput.*) диспле́й.

visualize /ˈvɪzjʊəˌlaɪz/, /ˈvɪʒj-/ *v.t.* предст|авля́ть, -а́вить себе́.

vital /ˈvaɪt(ə)l/ *adj.* **1** (*concerned with life*) жи́зненный; **~ force** жи́зненная си́ла; **~ principle** жи́зненное нача́ло; **~ statistics** демографи́ческая стати́стика; (*joc., woman's measurements*) объём груди́, та́лии и бёдер. **2** (*essential*; *indispensable*) насу́щный; (кра́йне) необходи́мый; жи́зненно ва́жный; **a ~ question** жи́зненно ва́жный/суще́ственный вопро́с; **it is of ~ importance** э́то вопро́с/де́ло первостепе́нной ва́жности; **speed was ~ to success** ско́рость была́ гла́вным зало́гом успе́ха. **3** (*lively*; *having vitality*) энерги́чный, живо́й.

vitality /vaɪˈtælɪtɪ/ *n.* (*vital power*) жи́зненная си́ла; (*energy*; *liveliness*) эне́ргия, жи́вость.

vitalize /ˈvaɪtəˌlaɪz/ *v.t.* ожив|ля́ть, -и́ть.

vitals /ˈvaɪt(ə)lz/ *n.* жи́зненно ва́жные о́рганы (*m. pl.*).

vitamin /ˈvɪtəmɪn/, /ˈvaɪt-/ *n.* витами́н; (*attr.*) витами́нный; **V~ C** витами́н С (*pr.* це).

vitiate /ˈvɪʃɪˌeɪt/ *v.t.* (*spoil*) по́ртить, ис-; (*invalidate*) де́лать, с- недействи́тельным; (*undermine*) под|рыва́ть, -орва́ть; (*make ineffectual*) св|оди́ть, -ести́ на нет.

viticulture /ˈvɪtɪˌkʌltʃə(r)/ *n.* виногра́дарство.

vitreous /ˈvɪtrɪəs/ *adj.* стеклови́дный.

vitrify /ˈvɪtrɪˌfaɪ/ *v.t. & i.* превра|ща́ть(ся), -ти́ть(ся) в стекло́.

vitriol /ˈvɪtrɪəl/ *n.* **1** купоро́с; **blue ~** ме́дный купоро́с. **2** (*fig.*) яд.

vitriolic /ˌvɪtrɪˈɒlɪk/ *adj.* купоро́сный; (*fig.*) е́дкий, ядови́тый.

vituperate /vɪˈtjuːpəˌreɪt/, /vaɪ-/ *v.t.* поноси́ть, брани́ть (*both impf.*).

vituperation /vɪˌtjuːpəˈreɪʃ(ə)n/, /vaɪ-/ *n.* поноше́ние, брань.

vituperative /vɪˈtjuːpərətɪv/, /vaɪ-/ *adj.* бра́нный, зло́бный.

viva /ˈvaɪvə/ (*Br.*) = **viva voce**

vivace /vɪˈvɑːtʃɪ/ *adv.* вива́че; оживлённо.

vivacious /vɪˈveɪʃəs/ *adj.* живо́й, оживлённый.

vivacity /vɪˈvæsɪtɪ/ *n.* жи́вость, оживле́ние.

vivari|um /vaɪˈveərɪəm/, /vɪ-/ *n.* (*pl.* **~a**) вива́рий.

viva voce /ˌvaɪvə ˈvəʊtʃɪ/, /ˈvəʊsɪ/ *n.* (*Br.*) (*also coll.* **viva**) у́стный экза́мен.

vivid /ˈvɪvɪd/ *adj.* **1** (*bright*) я́ркий. **2** (*lively*) живо́й, пы́лкий; **a ~ imagination** пы́лкое воображе́ние. **3** (*clear and distinct*) чёткий, я́сный.

vividness /ˈvɪvɪdnɪs/ *n.* я́ркость, жи́вость; чёткость.

vivisection /ˌvɪvɪˈsekʃ(ə)n/ *n.* вивисе́кция.

vivisectionist /ˌvɪvɪˈsekʃ(ə)nɪst/ *n.* вивисе́ктор.

vixen /ˈvɪks(ə)n/ *n.* лиси́ца(-са́мка); (*fig.*) мегера.

viz. /vɪz/ *adv.* а и́менно.

vizier /vɪˈzɪə(r)/, /ˈvɪzɪə(r)/ *n.* визи́рь (*m.*).

vizor /ˈvaɪzə(r)/ = **visor**

vocabulary /vəˈkæbjʊlərɪ/ *n.* (*range of words*) слова́рь (*m.*); (*of an individual*) запа́с слов; (*of a language*) слова́рный соста́в; (*of a subject*) номенклату́ра; (*list of words*) слова́рь (*m.*), спи́сок слов.

vocal /ˈvəʊk(ə)l/ *adj.* **1** (*of or using the voice*) голосово́й, речево́й; **~ cords** голосовы́е свя́зки; **~ music** вока́льная му́зыка. **2** (*eloquent*) красноречи́вый.

● *n.* (*usu. pl.*) вока́льная па́ртия.

vocalist /ˈvəʊkəlɪst/ *n.* вокали́ст (*fem.* -ка); пев|е́ц (*fem.* -и́ца).

vocalize /ˈvəʊkəˌlaɪz/ *v.i.* (*mus.*) исп|олня́ть, -о́лнить вокали́зы.

vocation /vəˈkeɪʃ(ə)n/ *n.* призва́ние.

vocational /vəˈkeɪʃən(ə)l/ *adj.* профессиона́льный.

vocative /ˈvɒkətɪv/ *n. & adj.* зва́тельный (паде́ж).

vociferous /vəˈsɪfərəs/ *adj.* гро́мкий, шу́мный, горла́стый (*coll.*).

vodka /ˈvɒdkə/ *n.* во́дка.

vogue /vəʊg/ *n.* мо́да; **in ~** в мо́де.

voice /vɔɪs/ *n.* **1** го́лос; **he is in good ~** он в го́лосе; **he shouted at the top of his ~** он крича́л во весь го́лос/во всё го́рло (*coll.*); **keep your ~ down!** не разгова́ривайте (*or* не говори́те) так гро́мко!; **I lost my ~** я потеря́л го́лос; **he raised his ~** он повы́сил го́лос. **2** (*expression of opinion*) мне́ние; го́лос; **we must speak with one ~** мы должны́ говори́ть одно́ и то же; **I have no ~ in the matter** у меня́ нет пра́ва го́лоса в э́том вопро́се. **3** (*gram.*) зало́г.

● *v.t.* **1** (*utter*) выража́ть, вы́разить. **2** (*phon.*) произн|оси́ть, -ести́ зво́нко; **a ~ed consonant** зво́нкий согла́сный.

● *cpd.* **~-over** *n.* (*TV etc.*) го́лос за ка́дром.

voiceless /ˈvɔɪslɪs/ *adj.* (*mute*) безгла́сный; (*phon.*) глухо́й.

void /vɔɪd/ *n.* пустота́; пусто́е простра́нство.

● *adj.* **1** (*empty*; *bereft*) пусто́й; лишённый (*чего*); **the subject was ~ of interest** те́ма не представля́ла никако́го интере́са. **2** (*invalid*) недействи́тельный; **the contract is null and ~** контра́кт не име́ет си́лы.

● *v.t.* (*make invalid*) аннули́ровать (*impf., pf.*); (*discharge*; *excrete*) выделя́ть, вы́делить; (*empty, evacuate*) опор|а́жнивать, -о́жнить; освобо|жда́ть, -ди́ть.

voile /vɔɪl/, /vwɑːl/ *n.* вуа́ль.

volatile /'vɒlə,taɪl/ *adj.* (*of liquid*) летýчий; (*fig., of person*) непостоя́нный, измéнчивый.

volatility /,vɒlə'tɪlɪtɪ/ *n.* летýчесть; (*fig.*) непостоя́нство, измéнчивость.

vol-au-vent /'vɒləʊ,vɑ̃/ *n.* волова́н (*слоёный пирожок*).

volcanic /vɒl'kænɪk/ *adj.* вулкани́ческий.

volcanism /'vɒlkənɪz(ə)m/ *n.* (*geol.*) вулкани́зм.

volcanologist /,vɒlkə'nɒlədʒɪst/ *n.* вулканóлог.

volcanology /,vɒlkə'nɒlədʒɪ/ *n.* вулканолóгия.

volcano /vɒl'keɪnəʊ/ *n.* (*pl.* **~es**) вулка́н.

vole /vəʊl/ *n.* полёвка.

Volga /'vɒlgə/ *n.* Вóлга; **~ boatmen** (*hist.*) вóлжские бурлаки́.

volition /və'lɪʃ(ə)n/ *n.* вóля; **I went of my own ~** я пошёл по своéй вóле.

volley /'vɒlɪ/ *n.* (*pl.* **~s**) **1** (*simultaneous discharge*) залп; (*fig.*): **a ~ of oaths** потóк бра́ни. **2** (*tennis etc.*) уда́р с лёта; **half ~** уда́р с отскóка.

● *v.t.* (**volleys, volleyed**) уд|аря́ть, -а́рить с лёта.

● *cpd.* **~-ball** *n.* волейбóл; (*attr.*) волейбóльный.

volt /vəʊlt/, /vɒlt/ *n.* вольт.

voltage /'vəʊltɪdʒ/ *n.* напряжéние, вольта́ж; **what is the ~ here?** какóе здесь напряжéние?

voltaic /vɒl'teɪɪk/ *adj.* гальвани́ческий.

volte-face /vɒlt'fɑ:s/ *n.* (*pl.* **~**) (*about-turn*) поворóт кругóм; (*fig.*) крутóй поворóт; поворóт на 180° гра́дусов.

voltmeter /'vəʊlt,mi:tə(r)/ *n.* вольтмéтр.

volubility /,vɒljʊ'bɪlɪtɪ/ *n.* говорли́вость, разговóрчивость.

voluble /'vɒljʊb(ə)l/ *adj.* говорли́вый, разговóрчивый.

volume /'vɒlju:m/ *n.* **1** (*tome*) том; **it speaks ~s for his honesty** э́то лу́чшее доказа́тельство егó чéстности. **2** (*size*) объём. **3** (*of sound*) грóмкость; **~ control** регуля́тор грóмкости; **turn the ~ down!** сдéлайте звук поти́ше!

volumetric /,vɒljʊ'metrɪk/ *adj.* объёмный.

voluminous /və'lju:mɪnəs/, /və'lu:-/ *adj.* огрóмный; **~ folds** пы́шные скла́дки; **a ~ work** объёмистое произведéние; **a ~ writer** плодови́тый писа́тель.

voluntary /'vɒləntərɪ/ *n.* (*organ solo*) сóло (*indecl.*) на оргáне.

● *adj.* **1** (*acting, done, or given without compulsion*) доброво́льный; **~ contributions** доброво́льные взнóсы (*m. pl.*); **~ redundancy** доброво́льный ухóд с рабóты; **~ organization** общéственная организа́ция; **~ work** общéственная рабóта; **~ worker** общéственный рабóтник. **2** (*maintained by ~ effort*) содержа́щийся на доброво́льные взнóсы. **3** (*controlled by will*) сознáтельный; **~ muscle** произвóльная мы́шца.

volunteer /,vɒlən'tɪə(r)/ *n.* доброво́льный помóщник; (*in army*) доброво́лец; (*attr.*) доброво́льческий.

● *v.t.* предл|ага́ть, -ожи́ть; дéлать, с- доброво́льно; **he ~ed his services** он предложи́л свои́ услу́ги.

● *v.i.* вызыва́ться, вы́зваться сдéлать что-н.; **no-one ~ed** жела́ющих не нашлóсь; **were you conscripted or did you ~?** вас призва́ли на воéнную слу́жбу и́ли вы пошли́ доброво́льцем?

voluptuary /və'lʌptjʊərɪ/ *n.* (*devoted to sensual pleasure*) сладостра́стник; (*devoted to luxury*) гедони́ст.

voluptuous /və'lʌptjʊəs/ *adj.* сладостра́стный; (*sensual*) чу́вственный; (*luxurious*) пы́шный, роскóшный.

voluptuousness /və'lʌptjʊəsnɪs/ *n.* сладостра́стие; чу́вственность; пы́шность.

volute /və'lju:t/ *n.* (*archit.*) волю́та; спира́ль, завитóк.

vomit /'vɒmɪt/ *n.* рвóта.

● *v.t.* (**vomited, vomiting**): **he ~ed blood** егó вы́рвало/рва́ло крóвью.

● *v.i.* (**vomited, vomiting**): **he ~ed** егó вы́рвало; **an attack of ~ing** при́ступ рвóты.

voodoo /'vu:du:/, **-ism** /'vu:du:ɪz(ə)m/ *nn.* колдовствó, шама́нство.

voracious /və'reɪʃəs/ *adj.* прожóрливый, жа́дный; (*fig.*): **a ~ reader** ненасы́тный чита́тель.

vorac|iousness /və'reɪʃəsnɪs/, **-ity** /və'ræsɪtɪ/ *nn.* прожóрливость, жа́дность, ненасы́тность.

vortex /'vɔ:teks/ *n.* (*pl.* **vortexes** *or* **vortices** /-tɪsi:z/) (*lit., fig.*) вихрь (*m.*), водоворóт.

votar|y /'vəʊtərɪ/ (*fem.* **-ess**) /'vəʊtərɪs/ *nn.* побóрни|к (*fem.* -ца), привéржен|ец (*fem.* -ка).

vote /vəʊt/ *n.* **1** (*act of voting*) голосова́ние; **shall we put it to the ~?** поста́вим э́то на голосова́ние?; **proxy ~** голосова́ние по довéренности. **2** (**~ cast**) гóлос; **the chairman has the casting ~** у председа́теля реша́ющий гóлос; **affirmative ~** гóлос за; **negative ~** гóлос прóтив. **3** (*affirmation*) вóтум; **the Prime Minister received a ~ of confidence** премьéр-мини́стр получи́л вóтум довéрия; **I beg to move a ~ of thanks** предлага́ю вы́разить благода́рность; **pass a ~** прин|има́ть, -я́ть резолю́цию. **4** (*right to ~*) пра́во гóлоса; избира́тельное пра́во. **5** (*number of ~s cast*) óбщее числó голосóв; **the Tories increased their ~** консерва́торы завоева́ли бóльше голосóв, чем на предыду́щих вы́борах.

● *v.t.*: **they were ~d back into power** их снóва избра́ли в прави́тельство; (*allocate by ~*) ассигнова́ть (*impf., pf.*); выделя́ть, вы́делить; **a large sum was ~d for defence** (*Br.*), **defense** (*US*) бóльшая су́мма была́ вы́делена на оборóну; (*coll., propose*): **I ~ we go home** я предлага́ю (*or* я за то, чтóбы) пойти́ домóй.

● *v.i.* голосова́ть, про-; **they are voting on the resolution** они́ голосу́ют резолю́цию.

● *with advs.*: **the measure was ~d down, out** предложéние отклони́ли/не при́няли; **they were ~d in by a large majority** их избра́ли реша́ющим большинствóм голосóв; **the bill was ~d through** закóн прошёл (*or* был при́нят).

voter /'vəʊtə(r)/ *n.* избира́тель (*m.*).

voting /'vəʊtɪŋ/ *n.* голосова́ние; баллотирóвка; (*attr.*): **~ qualification** избира́тельный ценз; **~ paper** (*Br.*) избира́тельный бюллетéнь.

votive /'vəʊtɪv/ *adj.* испóлненный по обéту; **a ~ offering** жертвоприношéние (по обéту); благода́рная жéртва.

vouch /vaʊtʃ/ *v.i.* руча́ться, поручи́ться; **I can ~ for his honesty** я готóв поручи́ться за егó чéстность; **I will ~ for the truth of his story** я могу́ подтверди́ть, что он говори́т пра́вду.

voucher /'vaʊtʃə(r)/ *n.* (*that may be exchanged for goods*) талóн; (*received as reward for buying petrol etc.*) ва́учер; **luncheon ~** талóн на обéд; (*receipt*) распи́ска.

vouchsafe /vaʊtʃ'seɪf/ *v.t.* (*accord*) удост|а́ивать, -óить (*кого чем*); (*condescend*) соизв|оля́ть, -óлить.

vow /vaʊ/ *n.* обéт, кля́тва; **he broke his marriage ~s** он нару́шил бра́чный обéт.

● *v.t.* кля́сться, по-; **they ~ed obedience** они́ да́ли обéт послуша́ния; **he ~ed** (*resolved*) **never to return** он покля́лся никогда́ не возвраща́ться; **he ~ed not to smoke** он дал зарóк не кури́ть.

vowel /'vaʊəl/ *n.* гла́сный.

voyage /'vɔɪɪdʒ/ *n.* (*by sea*) (морскóе) путешéствие; пла́вание; (*on specific route*) рейс; (*in space*) полёт; **on the ~ home** на обра́тном пути́; (*fig.*) путь, путешéствие.

● *v.i.* путешéствовать (*impf.*).

voyager /'vɔɪɪdʒə(r)/ *n.* (*sea-farer*) морепла́ватель (*m.*); (*traveller*) путешéственник.

voyeur /vwɑ:'jɜ:(r)/ *n.* вуайери́ст.

voyeurism /vwɑ:'jɜ:rɪz(ə)m/ *n.* вуайери́зм.

voyeuristic /vwɑ:jə'rɪstɪk/ *adj.* вуайери́стский.

V-sign /'vi:saɪn/ *n.* **1** (*Br., gesture of contempt*) ≈ ку́киш. **2** (*for victory*) знак побéды.

VP (*abbr. of* **vice president**) ви́це-президéнт.

vulcanite /'vʌlkə,naɪt/ *n.* эбони́т.

vulcanize /'vʌlkə,naɪz/ *v.t.* вулканизи́ровать (*impf., pf.*).

vulcanism /'vʌlkənɪz(ə)m/ = **volcanism**

vulcanologist /,vʌlkə'nɒlədʒɪst/ = **volcanologist**

vulcanology /,vʌlkə'nɒlədʒɪ/ = **volcanology**

V

vulgar /'vʌlgə(r)/ *adj.* **1** (*plebeian*) плебе́йский, простонаро́дный; (*vernacular*) иско́нный; ~ **Latin** вульга́рная/наро́дная латы́нь. **2** (*low, coarse, in bad taste*) вульга́рный, по́шлый, гру́бый; ~ **language** гру́бый/у́личный язы́к. **3**: ~ **fraction** (*Br.*) проста́я дробь.

vulgarian /vʌl'geərɪən/ *n.* пошля́|к (*fem.* -чка).

vulgarism /'vʌlgə,rɪz(ə)m/ *n.* вульгари́зм.

vulgarity /vʌl'gærɪtɪ/ *n.* вульга́рность, по́шлость, гру́бость.

vulgarization /,vʌlgəraɪ'zeɪʃ(ə)n/ *n.* вульгариза́ция.

vulgarize /'vʌlgə,raɪz/ *v.t.* вульгаризи́ровать (*impf., pf.*).

vulnerability /,vʌlnərə'bɪlɪtɪ/ *n.* уязви́мость; беззащи́тность.

vulnerable /'vʌlnərəb(ə)l/ *adj.* уязви́мый; (*defenceless*) беззащи́тный; ~ **to air attack** не защищённый от возду́шных ата́к.

vulpine /'vʌlpaɪn/ *adj.* ли́сий, хи́трый.

vulture /'vʌltʃə(r)/ *n.* гриф; (*fig.*) стервя́тник.

vulva /'vʌlvə/ *n.* (*pl.* ~**s**) (*anat.*) ву́льва.

vying /'vaɪɪŋ/ *pres. part. of* ⇨**vie**

Ww

wacko /ˈwækəʊ/ (*US sl.*) *n.* (*pl.* **~s** *or* **~es**) сумасше́дший, псих (*coll.*).

● *adj.* сумасше́дший, чо́кнутый.

wacky /ˈwækɪ/ *adj.* (**wackier, wackiest**) (*sl.*) сумасше́дший, чо́кнутый.

wad /wɒd/ *n.* **1** (*pad, plug etc.*) комо́к; (*in a gun*) пыж. **2** (*of papers, esp. banknotes*) па́чка.

● *v.t.* (**wadded, wadding**) (*line with wadding etc.*) подбі|ва́ть, -и́ть ва́той; **~ded jacket** стёганая ку́ртка; ва́тник.

wadding /ˈwɒdɪŋ/ *n.* ва́та; (*sheet* ~) вати́н.

waddle /ˈwɒd(ə)l/ *n.* похо́дка вразва́лку; **she walks with a ~** она́ хо́дит вразва́лку/перева́ливаясь.

● *v.i.* ходи́ть (*indet.*) вразва́лку.

wade /weɪd/ *v.t.* пере|ходи́ть, -йти́ вброд; **we shall have to ~ the stream** нам придётся перейти́ ре́ку вброд.

● *v.i.* проб|ира́ться, -ра́ться; **wading bird** боло́тная пти́ца; **we ~d through the mud** мы шли, увяза́я в грязи́; (*fig.*): **I have ~d through all his novels** я (с трудо́м) одоле́л все его́ рома́ны; **I ~d into the argument** я ри́нулся в спор.

● *with advs.*: **~ in** *v.i.* (*lit.*) входи́ть, войти́ в во́ду; (*coll., attack*) набр|а́сываться, -о́ситься (*на кого/что*); (*fig.*): **he found them fighting and ~d in** он уви́дел деру́щихся и ри́нулся в схва́тку; **~ out** *v.i.*: **we had to ~ out to the boat** к ло́дке пришло́сь добира́ться по воде́.

wader /ˈweɪdə(r)/ *n.* (*bird*) боло́тная пти́ца; (*pl., waterproof boots*) боло́тные сапоги́ (*m. pl.*).

wafer /ˈweɪfə(r)/ *n.* **1** (*thin biscuit*) ва́фля. **2** (*Communion bread*) обла́тка.

waffle[1] /ˈwɒf(ə)l/ *n.* (*cul.*) ва́фля.

● *cpd.* **~-iron** *n.* ва́фельница.

waffle[2] /ˈwɒf(ə)l/ (*coll.*) *n.* **1** (*Br., verbiage*) вода́ (*в речи, в статье*). **2** (*US*) колеба́ние.

● *v.i.* **1** (*Br., also* **~ on**) во́ду лить (*impf.*). **2** (*US*) колеба́ться, по-.

waffler /ˈwɒflə(r)/ *n.* (*coll.*) водоле́й.

waffly /ˈwɒflɪ/ *adj.* (*coll.*) водяни́стый (*доклад*).

waft /wɒft/, /wɑːft/ *n.* (*whiff, breath*) дунове́ние.

● *v.t.* дон|оси́ть, -ести́; **the leaves were ~ed by the breeze** ветеро́к гнал ли́стья; **their voices were ~ed over to us** до нас доноси́лись их голоса́.

wag[1] /wæg/ *n.* (*shake*): **with a ~ of his tail** вильну́в хвосто́м.

● *v.t.* (**wagged, wagging**) (*one's head*) кача́ть, по- + *i.*; (*one's tail*) вил|я́ть, -ьну́ть (+ *i.*); **the dog ~ged its tail** соба́ка вильну́ла хвосто́м; **he ~ged his finger at me** он погрози́л мне па́льцем.

● *v.i.* (**wagged, wagging**) (*of dog's tail*) вил|я́ть, -ьну́ть; **this will set tongues ~ging** э́то даст по́вод к спле́тням; э́то вы́зовет то́лки.

● *cpd.* **~tail** *n.* (*zool.*) трясогу́зка.

wag[2] /wæg/ *n.* (*jocular person*) остря́к, шутни́к.

wage[1] /weɪdʒ/ *n.* **1** за́работная пла́та; зарпла́та; **he gets good ~s** у него́ хоро́шая зарпла́та; он хорошо́ зараба́тывает; **a living ~** прожи́точный ми́нимум; **~ increase** повыше́ние за́работной пла́ты. **2** (*pl.,fig.*) возме́здие, пла́та; **~s of sin** пла́та за грехи́.

● *cpds.* **~-earner** *n.* наёмный рабо́чий; (*breadwinner*) корми́л|ец (*fem.* -ица); **~-freeze** *n.* замора́живание за́работной пла́ты; **~-packet** *n.* (*fig.*) зарпла́та, полу́чка (*coll.*); **~-slave** *n.* (*fig.*) подёнщи|к (*fem.* -ца).

wage[2] /weɪdʒ/ *v.t.* (*war*) вести́ (*impf.*); (*campaign*) пров|оди́ть, -ести́.

wager /ˈweɪdʒə(r)/ *n.* пари́ (*nt. indecl.*); **lay a ~** би́ться (*impf.*) об закла́д, держа́ть (*impf.*) пари́.

● *v.t.*: **he ~ed £10 on a horse** он поста́вил 10 фу́нтов на ло́шадь; **I ~ you 5 to 1 you can't do it** ста́влю пять про́тив одного́, что ты не смо́жешь э́то сде́лать.

waggish /ˈwægɪʃ/ *adj.* игри́вый.

waggle /ˈwæg(ə)l/ *v.t.* (*ears, toes*) шевели́ть, по- + *i.*

● *v.i.* (*of ears, toes*) шевели́ться, по-; (*shake slightly*) пока́чиваться (*impf.*).

wag(g)on /ˈwægən/ *n.* **1** (*horse-drawn*) пово́зка, теле́га; (*with cover*) фурго́н. **2** (*Br., on railway*) ваго́н-платфо́рма. **3**: **he is on the ~** (*fig., not drinking alcohol*) он бро́сил пить.

wag(g)oner /ˈwægənə(r)/ *n.* во́зчик.

wagon-lit /ˌvægɔ̃ˈliː/ *n.* спа́льный ваго́н.

waif /weɪf/ *n.* (*homeless person*) бездо́мный, бродя́га (*m.*); **~s and strays** (*children*) беспризо́рники (*m. pl.*).

wail /weɪl/ *n.* (*cry, howl*) вопль (*m.*); вой; (*of pain*) вопль (*m.*), крик; (*lament*) причита́ние; (*fig., of the wind*) завыва́ние, вой; (*of sirens, saxophones etc.*) вой.

● *v.i.* (*cry, howl*) вопи́ть (*impf.*); выть (*impf.*).

wainscot /ˈweɪnskət/, **-ing** /ˈweɪnskətɪŋ/ *nn.* облицо́вочная пане́ль, обши́вка (*деревянная*).

● *v.t.* (**wainscoted, wainscoting** *or* **wainscotted, wainscotting**) облиц|о́вывать, -ева́ть деревя́нной пане́лью.

waist /weɪst/ *n.* (*of body or dress*) та́лия; **he stripped to the ~** он разде́лся до по́яса; **he put his arm round her ~** он обня́л её за та́лию; (*of ship*) шкафу́т.

● *cpds.* **~-band** *n.* по́яс ю́бки/брюк; (*only on skirts*) корса́ж; **~coat** *n.* (*Br.*) жиле́т; **~-deep, ~-high** *adjs. & advs.* по по́яс; **~line** *n.* та́лия; **I must watch my ~line** я до́лжен следи́ть за свое́й фигу́рой.

wait /weɪt/ *n.* **1** (*act or time of* **~ing**) ожида́ние; **we had a long ~ for the bus** мы до́лго жда́ли авто́буса. **2** (*ambush*) заса́да; **the robbers lay in ~ for their victim** граби́тели подстерега́ли свою́ же́ртву.

● *v.t.* **1** (**~ for**; *await*) ждать (*impf.*) (+ *a. or g.*); выжида́ть (*impf.*); **you must ~ your turn** вы должны́ дожда́ться свое́й о́череди. **2** (*defer*): **don't ~ dinner for me** не жди́те меня́ с обе́дом.

● *v.i.* **1** (*refrain from movement or action*) ждать (*impf.*), подожда́ть (*pf.*); **we must ~ and see what happens** подождём — уви́дим, что бу́дет да́льше; **it can/must ~ till tomorrow** с э́тим мо́жно/на́до подожда́ть до за́втра; **I could hardly ~ to ...** я сгора́л от нетерпе́ния + *inf.*; **I ~ed for the rain to stop** я ждал, когда́ ко́нчится дождь; **'No W~ing'** (*notice*) «стоя́нка запрещена́»; **~ing-list** спи́сок (*кандидатов, очередников*); о́чередь; **I'll put you on the ~ing-list** я поста́влю вас в о́чередь; **~ing-room** (*doctor's etc.*) приёмная; (*on station*) зал ожида́ния; **repairs while you ~** ремо́нт в прису́тствии зака́зчика.
2 (*act as servant*): **she ~s on him hand and foot** она́ его́ по́лностью обслу́живает; **he ~ed at table** он прислу́живал за столо́м.
3 ~ up: **she ~ed up for him** она́ не ложи́лась (спать) до его́ прихо́да.

waiter /'weɪtə(r)/ *n.* официа́нт.

waitress /'weɪtrɪs/ *n.* официа́нтка.

waive /weɪv/ *v.t.* (*forgo*) отка́з|ываться, -а́ться от + *g.*; **he ~d his privileges** он отказа́лся от свои́х привиле́гий; (*claims*) возде́рж|иваться, -а́ться от + *g.*; (*rules*) не соблю|да́ть, -сти́ + *g.*; **on this occasion we will ~ the regulations** на сей раз мы пренебрежём пра́вилами.

waiver /'weɪvə(r)/ *n.* отка́з (от + *g.*).

wake¹ /weɪk/ *n.* (*vigil before burial*) бде́ние у гро́ба; (*eating after burial*) помин|ки (*pl.*, *g.* -ок).

wake² /weɪk/ *n.* (*track of vessel*) кильва́тер; (*fig.*): **he drove away with the police in his ~** он умча́лся, пресле́дуемый поли́цией; **there was havoc in the ~ of the storm** после́дствия што́рма бы́ли разруши́тельны; **his action brought trouble in its ~** его́ поведе́ние повлекло́ за собо́й неприя́тности.

wake³ /weɪk/ *v.t.* (*past* **woke** *or* **waked**; *p.p.* **woken** *or* **waked**) буди́ть, раз-; **the letter woke memories of the past** письмо́ пробуди́ло воспомина́ния о про́шлом.
● *v.i.* (*past* **woke** *or* **waked**; *p.p.* **woken** *or* **waked**) (*also* **~ up**) прос|ыпа́ться, -ну́ться; **she woke with a start** она́ внеза́пно просну́лась; **~ up!** (*lit.*, *fig.*) просни́тесь!

wakeful /'weɪkfʊl/ *adj.* (*person*) бо́дрствующий; **we had a ~ night** мы провели́ бессо́нную ночь.

wakefulness /'weɪkfʊlnɪs/ *n.* бессо́нница.

waken /'weɪkən/ *v.t.* буди́ть, раз-; (*fig.*) буди́ть, про-.

waking /'weɪkɪŋ/ *adj.* (*hours*) бессо́нный; **in his ~ hours** в бессо́нные часы́; в часы́ бо́дрствования.

Wales /weɪlz/ *n.* Уэ́льс.

walk /wɔ:k/ *n.* **1** (*action of ~ing*) ходьба́; **a short ~ away** в не́скольких шага́х отсю́да/отту́да.
2 (*excursion*) (пе́шая) прогу́лка; (*long-distance*) похо́д; **shall we take a ~?** хоти́те погуля́ть/прогуля́ться?; **I'm going for a ~** я пойду́ прогуля́юсь/погуля́ю; **will you take the children for a ~?** вы погуля́ете с детьми́?; вы поведёте дете́й на прогу́лку?; **I went on a ten-mile ~** я был в десятими́льном похо́де.
3 (*~ing pace*) шаг; **the horse slowed to a ~** ло́шадь перешла́ на шаг.
4 (*gait*) похо́дка, по́ступь.
5 (*route for ~ing*): **there are some pleasant ~s round here** здесь есть прия́тные места́ для прогу́лок.
6 (*path*) тропа́, доро́жка.
7 (*contest*): **long-distance ~** (спорти́вная) ходьба́ на дли́нную диста́нцию.
8 (*~ of life, profession*) заня́тие, профе́ссия; **people from all ~s of life** представи́тели всех слоёв о́бщества.
● *v.t.* **1** (*traverse*): **I ~ed these lanes in my youth** я исходи́л э́ти доро́ги в мо́лодости.
2 (*take for a ~*) прогу́л|ивать, -я́ть; вы́в|одить, -ести на прогу́лку; (*cause to ~*): **he ~ed his horse up the hill** он пусти́л ло́шадь ша́гом в го́ру; **he ~ed me off my feet** он си́льно утоми́л меня́ прогу́лкой; (*accompany*) сопрово|жда́ть, -ди́ть; прово|жа́ть, -ди́ть; **he offered to ~ her home** он вы́звался проводи́ть её домо́й.
● *v.i.* **1** (*go, come, move about, on foot*) ходи́ть (*indet.*), идти́ (*det.*); (*stroll about*) прогу́ливаться (*impf.*); **I was ~ing along the road** я шёл по доро́ге; **I ~ed ten miles** я прошёл де́сять миль; **I ~ed here in an hour** я дошёл сюда́ за час; **he ~s with a stick** он хо́дит с па́лкой; **the baby is learning to ~** ребёнок у́чится ходи́ть; **I ~ed into a shop** я вошёл в магази́н; **he ~ed into a puddle** он ступи́л в лу́жу; **they ~ed into** (*entered unwarily*) **an ambush** они́ попа́ли в заса́ду; **he ~ed over the estate** он обошёл/исходи́л всё име́ние; **he ~ed into a trap** он попа́лся в лову́шку.
2 (*opp. ride*) ходи́ть (*indet.*), идти́ (*det.*) пешко́м; **on fine days I ~ to the office** в хоро́шую пого́ду я хожу́ на рабо́ту пешко́м.
3 (*opp. run*): **he ~ed the last 100 metres** (*Br.*), **meters** (*US*) после́дние сто ме́тров он прошёл ша́гом; **at a ~ing pace** ша́гом; со ско́ростью пешехо́да.
4 (*take exercise, holiday etc. on foot*) ходи́ть (*indet.*) пешко́м; (*stroll*) гуля́ть (*impf.*), прогу́ливаться (*impf.*); **I spent 2 weeks ~ing in Scotland** я броди́л две неде́ли по Шотла́ндии; **a ~ing tour** туристи́ческий похо́д; **a ~ing race** соревнова́ния (*nt. pl.*) по спорти́вной ходьбе́.
5 (*take part in procession*) ше́ствовать (*impf.*).
● *with advs.*: **~ about** *v.i.* прогу́ливаться (*impf.*); **~ away** *v.i.* уходи́ть, уйти́; **he ~ed away with several prizes** он без труда́ завоева́л/получи́л не́сколько призо́в; **~ back** *v.i.* возвраща́ться, верну́ться пешко́м; **~ down** *v.i.* спус|ка́ться, -ти́ться (пешко́м); **~ in** *v.i.* входи́ть, войти́; **~ off** *v.t.* (*annul by ~ing*): **I must ~ off my fat** я до́лжен согна́ть жир ходьбо́й; **he was ~ing off a heavy lunch** он прогу́ливался по́сле сы́тного обе́да; *v.i.* уходи́ть, уйти́; **someone ~ed off with my hat** кто́-то унёс мою́ шля́пу; **he always ~s off with first prize** он всегда́ получа́ет пе́рвый приз; **~ on** *v.i.* (*continue ~ing*) продолжа́ть (*impf.*) идти́; идти́ (*det.*) да́льше; (**~ ahead**) идти́ (*det.*) вперёд; (*theatr.*) выходи́ть, вы́йти на сце́ну; **~ out** *v.i.* выходи́ть, вы́йти; **the delegates ~ed out in protest** делега́ты поки́нули зал (*or* вы́шли из за́ла) в знак проте́ста; **the men are threatening to ~ out** (*strike*) рабо́чие грозя́т поки́нуть рабо́чие места́/забасто́вкой; **~ out on s.o.** (*coll.*) бр|оса́ть, -о́сить кого́-н.; **~ up** *v.i.* (*approach*) под|ходи́ть, -ойти́; **~ up! ~ up!** (*Br.*) сюда́! сюда́!; **I ~ed up to him** я подошёл к нему́; (*climb*): **'Did you use the lift?' — 'No, I ~ed up'** «Вы прие́хали на ли́фте?» — «Нет, я подня́лся по ле́стнице».
● *cpds.* **~about** *n.* (*fig.*, *Br. coll.*) обще́ние с наро́дом; **~-on** *n.*: **a ~-on part** нема́я роль; **~-out** *n.* (*as protest*) демонстрати́вный ухо́д; (*strike*) забасто́вка; **~over** *n.* лёгкая побе́да; **~way** *n.* (*in garden*) алле́я; (*between buildings*) перехо́д.

walker /'wɔ:kə(r)/ *n.* **1** (*one who walks, athlete*) ходо́к; **I'm not a very good ~** я нева́жный ходо́к; **a hostel for ~s** общежи́тие для пе́ших тури́стов.
2 (*device for handicapped person*) ходунки́ (*m. pl.*). **3**: **dog-~** выгу́ливатель (*m.*) соба́к.

walkie-talkie /,wɔ:kɪ'tɔ:kɪ/ *n.* ра́ция.

walking /'wɔ:kɪŋ/ *n.* ходьба́; **~ shoes** о́бувь для ходьбы́.
● *adj.* ходя́чий, шага́ющий; **a ~ encyclopaedia** ходя́чая энциклопе́дия; **~ wounded** ходя́чие ра́неные.
● *cpd.* **~-stick** *n.* трость, па́лка.

Walkm|an /'wɔ:kmən/ *n.* (*pl.* **~ans** *or* **~en**) (*propr.*) пле́ер, пле́йер, во́кмен.

wall /wɔ:l/ *n.* (*lit.*, *fig.*) стена́, сте́нка; **there were pictures on the ~** на стене́ висе́ли карти́ны; **within these four ~s** (*fig.*) (стро́го) ме́жду на́ми; **~s have ears** у стен есть у́ши; **he stood with his back to the ~** (*lit.*) он стоя́л у стены́; **they had their backs to the ~** (*fig.*) их прижа́ли/припёрли (*coll.*) к сте́нке; **go up the ~** (*coll.*) лезть, по- на сте́н(к)у; **it's enough to send, drive you up the ~** (*coll.*) э́то заста́вит кого́ уго́дно на сте́нку лезть; **it's like banging one's head against a brick ~** всё равно́, что прошиба́ть сте́ну лбом; **a mountain ~** отве́сная скала́; **~ of the womb** сте́нка ма́тки; **~ clock** насте́нные час|ы́ (*pl.*, *g.* -о́в); **~ map** насте́нная ка́рта; **~ painting** насте́нная ро́спись, фре́ска.
● *v.t.* обн|оси́ть, -ести́ стено́й; огор|а́живать, -оди́ть; **~ed garden** обнесённый стено́й сад.
● *with advs.*: **~ in** *v.t.* обн|оси́ть, -ести́ стено́й; (*immure*) замуро́в|ывать, -а́ть; **~ off** *v.t.* отгор|а́живать, -оди́ть (стено́й); **~ up** *v.t.* заде́л|ывать, -ать (*дверь, окно*); (*immure*) замуро́в|ывать, -а́ть.

● *cpds.* **~flower** *n.* желтофио́ль; (*at dance*) да́ма, оста́вшаяся без партнёра; **~paper** *n.* обо́|и (*pl., g.* -ев); *v.t.* обкле́и|вать, -ть обо́ями; **~plug** *n.* (*to hold screw*) про́бка; (*socket*) розе́тка; **~-to-~** *adj.*: **~-to-~ carpeting** ковёр, покрыва́ющий весь пол.

wallaby /ˈwɒləbɪ/ *n.* кенгуру́-валлаби́ (*m. indecl.*).

wallet /ˈwɒlɪt/ *n.* (*pocket-book*) бума́жник.

wall-eye /ˈwɔːlaɪ/ *n.* глаз с бельмо́м.

wall-eyed /ˈwɔːlaɪd/ *adj.* с бельмо́м на глазу́; криво́й.

wallop /ˈwɒləp/ (*coll.*) *n.* (*blow*) уда́р.

● *v.t.* (**walloped, walloping**) (*thrash*) дуба́сить, от- (*coll.*); (*defeat*) разгроми́ть (*pf.*).

wallow /ˈwɒləʊ/ *v.i.* (*in mud, water*) валя́ться (*impf.*); (*fig.*) купа́ться (*impf.*) (*в чём*); **~ in luxury** купа́ться (*impf.*) в ро́скоши; **~ in grief** упива́ться (*impf.*) свои́м го́рем.

wally /ˈwɒlɪ/ *n.* (*Br. coll.*) дурале́й.

walnut /ˈwɔːlnʌt/ *n.* гре́цкий оре́х; (*tree*) оре́ховое де́рево; (*wood*) оре́х.

● *adj.* оре́ховый.

walrus /ˈwɔːlrəs/, /ˈwɒl-/ *n.* морж; **~ moustache** (*Br.*), **mustache** (*US*) свиса́ющие усы́ (*m. pl.*).

waltz /wɔːls/, /wɔːlts/, /wɒ-/ *n.* вальс; **in ~ time** в ри́тме ва́льса; **a ~ tune** мело́дия ва́льса.

● *v.t.* (*coll.*): **he ~ed her round the room** он закружи́л её по ко́мнате в ва́льсе.

● *v.i.* танцева́ть (*impf.*) вальс; (*fig.*) пританцо́вывать (*impf.*); **she ~ed into the room** она́ впорхну́ла в ко́мнату.

wan /wɒn/ *adj.* (**wanner, wannest**) бле́дный, изнурённый; **a ~ light** сла́бый/ту́склый свет; **a ~ smile** сла́бая улы́бка; **his face looked ~** он осу́нулся.

wand /wɒnd/ *n.* волше́бная па́лочка; **with a wave of his ~** по манове́нию волше́бной па́лочки.

wander /ˈwɒndə(r)/ *n.*: **I had a ~ round the shops** я прошёлся по магази́нам.

● *v.t.* броди́ть, стра́нствовать, скита́ться (*all impf.*) по + *d.*

● *v.i.* **1** (*roam; go aimlessly or unhurriedly*) броди́ть (*impf.*); **the W~ing Jew** Ве́чный жид; **a ~ing minstrel** бродя́чий певе́ц; **the car was ~ing all over the road** маши́на виля́ла из стороны́ в сто́рону; **I ~ed into the nearest pub** я забрёл в ближа́йший бар; **her ~ing gaze** её блужда́ющий взгляд; **his mind was ~ing** (*absent-mindedly*) его́ мы́сли блужда́ли; (*in delirium*) он бре́дил.
2 (*stray*) заблуди́ться (*pf.*); (*lit., fig.*) отклон|я́ться, -и́ться; **we ~ed from the track** мы сби́лись с тропы́; **don't let your attention ~** не отвлека́йтесь; **he ~ed from the point** он отклони́лся от те́мы.

● *with advs.*: **~ about** *v.i.* броди́ть (*impf.*), (*idly*) слоня́ться (*impf.*); **~ along** *v.i.* брести́ (*impf.*), проха́живаться (*impf.*); **~ away** *v.i.*: **she tried to stop the children ~ing away** она́ не дава́ла де́тям разбрести́сь; **~ in** *v.i.* случа́йно за|ходи́ть, -йти́; **~ off** *v.i.* брести́, по-куда́-н.; **~ on** *v.i.* прод|олжа́ть, -о́лжить; **he ~ed on** (*speaking*) он продолжа́л бубни́ть; **~ over** *v.i.* приплести́сь (*pf.*), притащи́ться (*pf.*); **he ~ed over to hear the news** он приплёлся/притащи́лся узна́ть но́вости; **~ up** *v.i.*: **he ~ed up to us** он подошёл к нам вя́лой похо́дкой.

wanderer /ˈwɒndərə(r)/ *n.* стра́нник, скита́лец.

wandering /ˈwɒndərɪŋ/ *n.* стра́нствие; (*pl., of speech*) бессвя́зная речь.

wanderlust /ˈwɒndəˌlʌst/, /ˈvændəˌlʊst/ *n.* страсть к путеше́ствиям.

wane /weɪn/ *n.*: **be on the ~** (*lit., fig.*) убыва́ть (*impf.*), быть на исхо́де.

● *v.i.* (*of the moon*) убыва́ть (*impf.*), быть на уще́рбе; (*fig., decline*) ослабева́ть (*impf.*), угаса́ть (*impf.*).

wangle /ˈwæŋg(ə)l/ *v.t.* (*obtain by scheming*) заполучи́ть (*pf.*) хи́тростью; **he ~d £5 out of me** он вы́клянчил (*coll.*) у меня́ 5 фу́нтов; (*falsify in one's favour*): **he ~d the results** он подтасова́л результа́ты.

wank /wæŋk/ *v.i.* (*Br. vulg.*) дрочи́ть (*impf.*).

wanker /ˈwæŋkə(r)/ *n.* (*Br. vulg., fig.*) муда́к.

wannabe /ˈwɒnəbɪ/ *n.* (*sl.*) челове́к, мечта́ющий стать (*кем-н.*); **~ writer** челове́к, мечта́ющий стать писа́телем.

wanness /ˈwɒnnɪs/ *n.* бле́дность, изнурённость.

want /wɒnt/ *n.* **1** (*lack*) недоста́ток, отсу́тствие; **for ~ of** за неиме́нием + *g.*; **I took this for ~ of anything better** я взял э́то за неиме́нием лу́чшего.
2 (*need*) нужда́; необходи́мость; **the house is in ~ of repair** дом нужда́ется в ремо́нте.
3 (*penury*) бе́дность, нужда́.
4 (*desire; requirement*) потре́бность, запро́сы (*m. pl.*), жела́ние; **they can supply all your ~s** они́ мо́гут удовлетвори́ть все ва́ши запро́сы.

● *v.t.* **1** (*need; require*) нужда́ться (*impf.*) в + *p.*; **we badly ~ rain** нам о́чень ну́жен дождь; **the floor ~s polishing** (*Br.*) пол на́до натере́ть; **your hair ~s cutting** (*Br.*) вам пора́ постри́чься; **I shan't ~ you today** вы мне сего́дня не пона́добитесь; **he is ~ed by the police** его́ разы́скивает поли́ция; **W~ed: a housekeeper** Тре́буется эконо́мка; **you're ~ed on the telephone** вас (про́сят) к телефо́ну; **you are ~ed at the office** вас вызыва́ют на рабо́ту; **what do you ~ with him?** что вам от него́ ну́жно?
2 (*desire; wish for*) хоте́ть (*impf.*) + *g. or a. or inf.*; жела́ть (*impf.*) + *g. or inf.*; **what do you ~?** что вы хоти́те?; **she ~s to go away** она́ хо́чет уе́хать/уйти́; **she ~s me to go away** она́ хо́чет, что́бы я уе́хал/ушёл; **I don't ~ him meddling in my affairs** я не хочу́, что́бы он вме́шивался в мои́ дела́; **I don't ~ any bread today** сего́дня мне хлеб не ну́жен; **I ~ it done immediately** я хочу́, что́бы э́то бы́ло сде́лано неме́дленно; **you don't ~ to** (*ought not to*) **overdo it** вам не сле́дует переутомля́ться; **what do I ~ with all these books?** заче́м (*or* для чего́) мне все э́ти кни́ги?

● *v.i.* (*liter., be in need*): **they ~ for nothing** они́ ни в чём не нужда́ются.

wanting /ˈwɒntɪŋ/ *adj.* (*missing*) отсу́тствующий; недостаю́щий; (*inadequate*) недоста́точный; неполноце́нный; **he was tried and found ~** он не вы́держал испыта́ния.

wanton /ˈwɒnt(ə)n/ *adj.* **1** (*wilful; ruthless*) своенра́вный, своево́льный; **~ cruelty** бессмы́сленная жесто́кость.
2 (*licentious; immoral*) распу́тный.

wantonness /ˈwɒntənnɪs/ *n.* (*wilfulness*) своенра́вие; (*unchastity*) распу́тство.

war /wɔː(r)/ *n.* **1** война́; **the art of ~** вое́нное иску́сство; **~ of aggression** агресси́вная война́; **~ of attrition** война́ на истоще́ние; **~ of nerves** война́ не́рвов; **civil ~** гражда́нская война́; **cold ~** холо́дная война́; **the Great W~** Пе́рвая мирова́я война́; **world ~** *see* ⇨ **world** 4; **the W~s of the Roses** во́йны А́лой и Бе́лой ро́зы; **~ of independence** война́ за незави́симость; **price ~** война́ цен, ценова́я конкуре́нция; **a country at ~** страна́ в состоя́нии войны́; **their countries were at ~** их стра́ны воева́ли друг с дру́гом; **what did you do in the ~?** что вы де́лали во вре́мя войны́? (*or* в войну́); **you've been in the ~s!** (*fig.*) ну и доста́лось же вам!; **France went to ~ with Germany** Фра́нция вступи́ла в войну́ с Герма́нией; **declare ~ on** объяв|ля́ть, -и́ть войну́ + *d.*; **make, wage ~ on** вести́ (*det.*) войну́ (*or* воева́ть (*impf.*)) с + *i.*
2 (*attr.*) вое́нный (*see also cpds.*); **~ correspondent** вое́нный корреспонде́нт; **~ criminal** вое́нный престу́пник; **~ damage** разруше́ния (*nt. pl.*) (*or* поте́ри (*f. pl.*)), нанесённые войно́й; **~ decoration** боева́я награ́да; **W~ Department** вое́нное министе́рство; **help the ~ effort** рабо́тать (*impf.*) для нужд фро́нта; **on a ~ footing** на вое́нном положе́нии; **~ graves** солда́тские моги́лы; **~ memorial** па́мятник геро́ям войны́; **W~ Office** вое́нное министе́рство; **~ service** слу́жба в де́йствующей а́рмии; **~ widow** вдова́ поги́бшего на войне́.

● *v.i.* (**warred, warring**) боро́ться (*impf.*); сража́ться (*impf.*).

● *cpds.* **~-cry** *n.* боево́й клич; **~-dance** *n.* вои́нственный та́нец; **~-game** *n.* вое́нная игра́; **~head** *n.* боева́я часть, боеголо́вка; **~-horse** *n.* (*lit.*) боево́й конь; (*fig.*) быва́лый солда́т, ветера́н; **~like** *adj.* (*martial*) вои́нственный; (*military*) вое́нный; **~-lord** *n.* военача́льник, полково́дец; **~monger** *n.* поджига́тель (*m.*) войны́; **~mongering** *n.* разжига́ние войны́; **~-paint** *n.* боева́я раскра́ска; **~-path** *n.* (*lit.*) тропа́ войны́; **on the ~-path** (*fig.*) в вои́нственном настрое́нии; **~-plane** *n.* вое́нный самолёт; **~ship** *n.* вое́нный кора́бль; **~time** *n.* вое́нное вре́мя; **~-torn** *adj.* опустошённый войно́й; **~-weary** *adj.* изнурённый/изму́ченный войно́й.

warble /ˈwɔ:b(ə)l/ *n.* (*song*) трель; пе́ние птиц.

● *v.i.* (*of birds*) издава́ть (*impf.*) тре́ли; (*of person*) залива́ться (*impf.*) пе́сней.

warbler /ˈwɔ:blə(r)/ *n.* (*bird*) пе́ночка, сла́вка.

ward /wɔ:d/ *n.* **1** (*person under guardianship*) подопе́чный; **~ of court** лицо́, опеку́н кото́рого назнача́ется судо́м (*дети, душевнобольные*). **2** (*urban division*) о́круг. **3** (*in hospital etc.*) пала́та; **isolation ~** изоля́тор, бокс. **4** (*in prison*) ка́мера.

● *v.t.*: **~ off** (*a blow*) отра|жа́ть, -зи́ть; **~ off danger** отвра|ща́ть, -ти́ть опа́сность.

● *cpds.* **~room** *n.* офице́рская каю́т-компа́ния; **~-sister** *n.* (*Br.*) пала́тная медсестра́.

warden /ˈwɔ:d(ə)n/ *n.* **1** (*Br., of college*) ре́ктор; (*of hostel*) коменда́нт; (*of prison*) нача́льник. **2**: **air-raid ~** уполномо́ченный противовозду́шной гражда́нской оборо́ны; **game ~** е́герь (*m.*); **traffic ~** (*Br.*) инспе́ктор паркова́ния автомоби́лей в черте́ го́рода.

warder /ˈwɔ:də(r)/ *n.* (*Br.*) (*in prison*) надзира́тель (*m.*), тюре́мщик.

wardress /ˈwɔ:drɪs/ *n.* (*Br.*) надзира́тельница, тюре́мщица (*coll.*).

wardrobe /ˈwɔ:drəʊb/ *n.* **1** платяно́й шкаф, гардеро́б; (*stock of clothes*) гардеро́б. **2** (*theatr.*) костюме́рная; **~ mistress** костюме́р, костюме́рша (*coll.*).

wardship /ˈwɔ:dʃɪp/ *n.* опе́ка, попечи́тельство.

ware /weə(r)/ *n.* **1** (*collect., usu. comb. form, manufactured articles*) това́р; изде́лия (*nt. pl.*); (*pottery*): **Delft~** фая́нс. **2** (*pl., articles offered for sale*) това́ры (*m. pl.*); изде́лия (*nt. pl.*); **peddle one's ~s** (*lit.*) предлага́ть (*impf.*) това́ры на прода́жу; (*fig.*) занима́ться (*impf.*) саморекла́мой.

● *cpds.* **~house** *n.* (това́рный) склад; *v.t.* храни́ть (*impf.*) на скла́де; **~houseman, ~house keeper** *nn.* кладовщи́|к (*fem.* -ца).

warfare /ˈwɔ:feə(r)/ *n.* война́; боевы́е де́йствия; **germ ~** бактериологи́ческая война́; **guerrilla ~** партиза́нская война́.

wariness /ˈweərɪnɪs/ *n.* осторо́жность, насторо́жённость.

warlock /ˈwɔ:lɒk/ *n.* колду́н, маг.

warm /wɔ:m/ *n.* (*act of ~ing*): **come and have a ~ by the fire** иди́те погре́йтесь у ками́на.

● *adj.* тёплый; **a ~ day** тёплый день; **a ~ fire** жа́ркий ого́нь; **~ countries** тёплые стра́ны/края́; **I can't keep ~ in this weather** в таку́ю пого́ду я ника́к не могу́ согре́ться; **I got very ~ playing tennis** от игры́ в те́ннис я си́льно разогре́лся; (*fig.*) (*welcome*) тёплый, серде́чный; (*thanks*) горя́чий, серде́чный; **accept my ~est thanks** приими́те мою́ горя́чую благода́рность; **his plan was ~ly approved** его́ план горячо́ поддержа́ли; **he has a ~ heart** он отзы́вчивый/серде́чный челове́к; **the scent was still ~** след ещё не осты́л; **am I getting ~?** (*fig.*) я пра́вильно дога́дываюсь?

● *v.t.* греть (*impf.*); (*food, water*) подогр|ева́ть, -е́ть; нагр|ева́ть, -е́ть; согр|ева́ть, -е́ть; **~ o.s. at the fire** гре́ться (*impf.*) у ками́на/огня́; **that fire will not ~ the room** э́тот ками́н не обогре́ет ко́мнату; **will you have your milk ~ed?** вам подогре́ть молоко́?

● *v.i.* гре́ться (*impf.*); (*of objects*) нагр|ева́ться, -е́ться; разогр|ева́ться, -е́ться; (*of people, room, food*) согр|ева́ться, -е́ться; (*fig.*): **he ~ed to the subject as he went on** по ме́ре расска́за он всё бо́льше воодушевля́лся; **I ~ed to(wards) him as I got to know him** чем бли́же я его́ узнава́л, тем бо́льше я к нему́ располага́лся.

● *with adv.*: **~ up** *v.t.* разогр|ева́ть, -е́ть; согр|ева́ть, -е́ть; **a fire will ~ up the room** ками́н обогре́ет ко́мнату; **his dinner had been ~ed up** ему́ разогре́ли у́жин; **the wine will ~ you up** вино́ вас согре́ет; **this engine needs a lot of ~ing up** э́тот мото́р прихо́дится до́лго прогрева́ть; **he told a few jokes to ~ up the audience** что́бы расшевели́ть пу́блику, он рассказа́л два-три анекдо́та; *v.i.* согр|ева́ться, -е́ться; **the house takes a long time to ~ up** э́тот дом ме́дленно согрева́ется; **it** (*sc. the weather*) **is ~ing up** тепле́ет; **the TV is ~ing up** телеви́зор нагрева́ется; **the conversation ~ed up** разгово́р оживи́лся; **he ~ed up before the race** он сде́лал разми́нку пе́ред нача́лом соревнова́ния.

● *cpds.* **~-blooded** *adj.* теплокро́вный; **~-hearted** *adj.* серде́чный; **~-up** *n.* разми́нка.

warmish /ˈwɔ:mɪʃ/ *adj.* теплова́тый.

warmth /wɔ:mθ/ *n.* теплота́, тепло́; (*fig.*) серде́чность, теплота́.

warn /wɔ:n/ *v.t.* **1** (*caution*) предупре|жда́ть, -ди́ть; (*of danger, negative consequences*) предостер|ега́ть, -е́чь; **I ~ed her not to go out alone** я предупрежда́л её, что́бы она́ одна́ не выходи́ла; **we were ~ed against pickpockets** нас предупреди́ли о существова́нии карма́нников; **he was ~ed off drink** ему́ запрети́ли пить. **2** (*admonish*): **I shan't ~ you again** э́то моё после́днее предупрежде́ние. **3** (*give notice*) изве|ща́ть, -сти́ть; опове|ща́ть, -сти́ть.

warning /ˈwɔ:nɪŋ/ *n.* предупрежде́ние, предостереже́ние; **gale ~** штормово́е предупрежде́ние; **early ~** (*system*) (*mil.*) ра́ннее предупрежде́ние; да́льнее обнару́же́ние; **give ~ of** предупре|жда́ть, -ди́ть о + *p.*; **let this be a ~ to you** пусть э́то послу́жит вам предостереже́нием; **he was let off with a ~** он отде́лался (одни́м лишь) предупрежде́нием; **without ~** без предупрежде́ния; вдруг; соверше́нно неожи́данно.

● *adj.* предупрежда́ющий; предостерега́ющий; **he gave a ~ look** он бро́сил предостерега́ющий взгляд; **he fired a ~ shot** он сде́лал предупреди́тельный вы́стрел.

warp /wɔ:p/ *n.* (*weaving*) осно́ва; (*distortion*) искривле́ние; деформа́ция.

● *v.t.* **1** (*distort*) коро́бить, по-; искрив|ля́ть, -и́ть; **damp ~s the binding** переплёт коро́бит от сы́рости. **2** (*fig.*) иска|жа́ть, -зи́ть, извра|ща́ть, -ти́ть; **a ~ed sense of humour** (*Br.*), **humor** (*US*) извращённое чу́вство ю́мора.

● *v.i.* (*become distorted*) коро́биться, по-.

warrant /ˈwɒrənt/ *n.* о́рдер; суде́бное распоряже́ние; **search ~** о́рдер на о́быск; **~ officer** старшина́ (*m.*); **death ~** (*fig.*) сме́ртный пригово́р.

● *v.t.* **1** (*justify*) опра́вд|ывать, -а́ть. **2** (*guarantee*) гаранти́ровать (*impf.*, *pf.*); руча́ться, поручи́ться за + *a.*; **I can ~ him to be reliable** я руча́юсь за его́ надёжность; **he will be back I('ll) ~ you** он вернётся, уверя́ю вас.

warranty /ˈwɒrəntɪ/ *n.* **1** (*authority*) оправда́ние, руча́тельство. **2** (*guarantee*) гара́нтия; **this watch is under ~** э́ти часы́ с гара́нтией.

warren /ˈwɒrən/ *n.* кро́личья нора́; (*fig.*) мураве́йник, лабири́нт.

warrior /ˈwɒrɪə(r)/ *n.* во́ин; **the Unknown W~** Неизве́стный солда́т.

Warsaw /ˈwɔ:sɔ:/ *n.* Варша́ва; **~ Pact** (*hist.*) Варша́вский догово́р.

wart /wɔ:t/ *n.* борода́вка; **~s and all** (*fig.*) без прикра́с.

● *cpd.* **~-hog** *n.* (*zool.*) борода́вочник.

wary /ˈweərɪ/ *adj.* (**warier, wariest**) осторо́жный, осмотри́тельный, насторо́жённый; **be ~ of** остерега́ться (*impf.*) + *g.*; относи́ться (*impf.*) насторо́жённо к + *d.*

was /wɒz/, /wəz/ *1st and 3rd pers. sing. past of* ⇒**be**

wash /wɒʃ/ *n.* **1** (*act of ~ing*) мытьё; **I must have, get a ~** мне на́до помы́ться/умы́ться; **she gave the floor a good ~** она́ тща́тельно вы́мыла пол. **2** (*laundering; laundry*) сти́рка; **send to the ~** отд|ава́ть, -а́ть в сти́рку; **my shirts are all at the ~** все мои́ руба́шки в сти́рке; **she does a big ~ on Mondays** по понеде́льникам у неё больша́я сти́рка; **it will all come out in the ~** (*fig.*) всё ула́дится/образу́ется/утрясётся. **3** (*motion of water etc.*) прибо́й; волна́; **the vessel made a big ~** от корабля́ пошла́ си́льная волна́. **4** (*solution of paint*) то́нкий слой кра́ски.

● *v.t.* **1** (*cleanse with water etc.*) мыть, по-/вы́-; (*hands, face, child*) ум|ыва́ть, -ы́ть; (*clothes*) стира́ть, по-/вы́-; **~ one's hands and face** мыть, по- ру́ки и лицо́; **~ dishes** мыть, вы́- посу́ду; **he ~ed himself in the stream** он помы́лся в ручье́; **this fabric must be ~ed in cold water** э́ту ткань сле́дует стира́ть

в холо́дной воде́; (*fig.*): **~ one's hands of something** умы́ть (*pf.*) ру́ки.
2 (*of water; flow past*) омыва́ть (*impf.*); (*sweep away*) сн|оси́ть, -ести́; см|ыва́ть, -ы́ть; **he was ~ed overboard by a wave** его́ смы́ло волно́й за́ борт; (*scoop out; erode*) разм|ыва́ть, -ы́ть; **the stream ~ed a channel in the sand** пото́к промы́л кана́ву в песке́.
● *v.i.* **1** (**~** *o.s.*) мы́ться, по-/вы́-; ум|ыва́ться, -ы́ться.
2 (**~** *clothes*) стира́ть, вы́-.
3 (*of fabric: stand up to* **~***ing*) стира́ться (*impf.*); (*fig.*): **that excuse won't ~** э́та отгово́рка не пройдёт.
4 (*of water*) плеска́ться (*impf.*); **waves ~ed over the deck** во́лны перека́тывались по па́лубе.
● *with advs.*: **~ away** *v.t.* (*remove: stains etc.*) отмы|ва́ть, -ть (*пятна*); (*erode: cliffs etc.*) разм|ыва́ть, -ы́ть; (*carry off*) сн|оси́ть, -ести́; см|ыва́ть, -ы́ть; **~ down** *v.t.* (*a surface*) мыть, вы́-; (*food*) зап|ива́ть, -и́ть (*что чем*); **I had a sandwich, ~ed down with beer** я съел бутербро́д и запи́л его́ пи́вом; **~ off** *v.t. & i.* смы|ва́ть(ся), -ы́ть(ся); (*from clothes*) отсти́р|ывать(ся), -а́ть(ся); **~ out** *v.t.* (*e.g. stains*) отмы|ва́ть, -ть; (*a garment*) стира́ть, вы́-; (*a stain from clothes*) отсти́р|ывать, -а́ть; (*of colour*) линя́ть, по-/вы́-; **you look ~ed out** у вас утомлённый вид; **the game was ~ed out (by rain)** игру́ пришло́сь прекрати́ть из-за дождя́; **~ up** *v.t. & i.* (*Br., dishes*) мыть, по-/вы́- (посу́ду); (*US, have a wash*) мы́ться, по-/вы-; (*on to shore*) выбра́сывать, вы́бросить на бе́рег; **a chest ~ed up by the tide** сунду́к, вы́брошенный на бе́рег мо́рем/прили́вом; **~ed up** (*exhausted*) уста́лый, разби́тый; (*ruined*) ко́нченый; (*coll.*) пропа́щий.
● *cpds.* **~-basin, ~-bowl** *nn.* ра́ковина; **~board** *n.* стира́льная доска́; **~-bowl** *n.* = **~-basin; ~cloth** *n.* (*US*) махро́вая салфе́тка/рукави́чка для лица́; **~-day** *n.* день (*m.*) сти́рки; **~-down** *n.* мытьё, мо́йка; **~-house** *n.* пра́чечная; **~leather** *n.* за́мша (*для мытья стекла и т.п.*); **~-out** *n.* (*result of flood or rain*) размы́в; (*coll., fiasco*) прова́л, неуда́ча; **~-room** *n.* убо́рная; **~-stand** *n.* умыва́льник; **~-tub** *n.* лоха́нь; коры́то.

washable /ˈwɒʃəb(ə)l/ *adj.* мо́ющийся.

washer /ˈwɒʃə(r)/ *n.* (*washing-machine*) стира́льная маши́на; (*machine component*) прокла́дка.
● *cpd.* **~woman** *n.* пра́чка.

washing /ˈwɒʃɪŋ/ *n.* **1** (*action*) мытьё, умыва́ние, сти́рка. **2** (*clothes*) бельё; **hang out the ~** ве́шать, пове́сить (*or* разве́|шивать, -сить) бельё; **take in ~** рабо́тать (*impf.*) пра́чкой.
● *cpds.* **~-machine** *n.* стира́льная маши́на; **~-powder** *n.* (*Br.*) стира́льный порошо́к; **~-up** *n.* (*Br.*): **do the ~-up** мыть, вы́- посу́ду; **~-up liquid** *n.* (*Br.*) сре́дство для мытья́ посу́ды.

Washington /ˈwɒʃɪŋt(ə)n/ *n.* (*City and State*) Вашингто́н.

wasp /wɒsp/ *n.* оса́.
● *cpd.* **~-sting** *n.* уку́с осы́.

waspish /ˈwɒspɪʃ/ *adj.* язви́тельный, ко́лкий.

waspishness /ˈwɒspɪʃnɪs/ *n.* язви́тельность, ко́лкость.

wastage /ˈweɪstɪdʒ/ *n.* убы́ток, уте́чка.

waste /weɪst/ *n.* **1** (*purposeless or extravagant use; failure to use*) (рас)тра́та, растра́чивание; **~ of money** пуста́я тра́та де́нег; **it would be a ~ of time** э́то бы́ло бы напра́сной тра́той вре́мени; **go, run to ~** тра́титься (*impf.*) по́пусту.
2 (*refuse*) отхо́ды (*m. pl.*), отбро́сы (*m. pl.*), му́сор; **~ collection** вы́воз му́сора.
3 (*superfluous material*) отхо́ды (*m. pl.*), отбро́сы (*m. pl.*); **atomic ~** отхо́ды а́томной промы́шленности.
4 (*desert area*) пусты́ня.
● *adj.* **1** (*superfluous, unwanted*) ли́шний, нену́жный; (*left over after manufacture*) отрабо́танный; (*rejected; thrown away*) брако́ванный; **~ products** отхо́ды (*m. pl.*); **~ paper** макулату́ра.
2 (*of land: desolate, desert*) пусты́нный; (*uninhabited*) незаселённый; (*uncultivated*) невозде́ланный; **~ ground** невозде́ланная земля́; **~ land** пусты́рь (*m.*), пу́стошь; **lay ~** опустош|а́ть, -и́ть; разор|я́ть, -и́ть.
● *v.t.* **1** (*make no use of, use to no purpose, squander*) тра́тить, ис-/по- да́ром/зря/по́пусту; растра́|чивать, -тить; **be ~d** проп|ада́ть, -а́сть (да́ром); **~ one's life** бесполе́зно прож|ива́ть, -и́ть жизнь; **~ one's chance** упус|ка́ть, -ти́ть слу́чай; **my joke was ~d on him** он не oцени́л моéй шу́тки; **~ one's breath, words** говори́ть (*impf.*) на ве́тер.
2 (*lay ~; ravage*) опустош|а́ть, -и́ть; разор|я́ть, -и́ть.
3 (*wear away*) изнур|я́ть, -и́ть; истощ|а́ть, -и́ть; **his body was ~d by sickness** его́ те́ло бы́ло истощено́/изнурено́ боле́знью; **a wasting disease** изнури́тельная боле́знь.
● *v.i.* (*usu.* **~ away**: *become weak; wither*) истощ|а́ться, -и́ться; ча́хнуть, за-.
● *cpds.* **~-basket** *n.* му́сорная корзи́на; **~-bin** (*Br.*), **~ can** (*US*) *nn.* му́сорное ведро́; му́сорный я́щик; **~-disposal** *n.*: **~-disposal unit** мусородроби́лка; **~-paper-basket** *n.* корзи́н(к)а для бума́ги; **~-pipe** *n.* сливна́я/водоотво́дная труба́.

wasteful /ˈweɪstfʊl/ *adj.* расточи́тельный, неэконо́мный.

wastefulness /ˈweɪstfʊlnɪs/ *n.* расточи́тельность, неэконо́мность.

waster /ˈweɪstə(r)/ *n.* (*wasteful person*) расточи́тель (*m.*); (*coll., good-for-nothing*) никуды́шный/никчёмный челове́к; безде́льник.

wastrel /ˈweɪstr(ə)l/ *n.* (*good-for-nothing*) безде́льник; (*wasteful person*) расточи́тель (*m.*).

watch[1] /wɒtʃ/ *n.* **1** (*alert state*) надзо́р, присмо́тр, наблюде́ние; **keep ~** (*of sentry or on ship*) стоя́ть (*impf.*) на ва́хте; (*guard*) наблюда́ть (*impf.*) (**on:** за + *i.*); **the dog keeps ~ on, over the house** соба́ка карау́лит/сторожи́т дом; **on the ~** начеку́; **she is always on the ~ for a bargain** она́ всегда́ смо́трит, что мо́жно вы́годно купи́ть.
2 (*hist., night guardian or patrol* (*collect.*)) стра́жа; карау́л; патру́ль (*m.*).
3 (*duty period at sea*) ва́хта; **be on ~** нести́ (*det.*) ва́хту; стоя́ть (*impf.*) на ва́хте; (*in general, e.g. for signal operators*) дежу́рство; **I was on ~ from 6 to 12** я дежу́рил с шести́ до двена́дцати.
● *v.t.* **1** (*look at; keep eyes on*) смотре́ть (*impf.*); **he was ~ing TV** он смотре́л телеви́зор; **I ~ed him draw** я смотре́л, как он рису́ет.
2 (*keep under observation*) следи́ть (*impf.*) за + *i.*; смотре́ть (*impf.*) за + *i.*; **he is being ~ed by the police** поли́ция следи́т/наблюда́ет за ним; (*be careful of*) следи́ть (*impf.*) за + *i.*; **I have to ~ my weight** мне ну́жно следи́ть за ве́сом/фигу́рой; **~ your step!** (*lit.*) не оступи́тесь!; (*fig.; also, coll.,* **~ it!**) бу́дьте осторо́жны!; осторо́жно!; береги́тесь!; **I shall have to ~ myself** мне придётся впредь быть осмотри́тельнее.
3 (*guard*) сторожи́ть; карау́лить; стере́чь (*all impf.*).
● *v.i.* **1** смотре́ть, наблюда́ть, следи́ть (*all impf.*); **he was content to ~** он дово́льствовался ро́лью наблюда́теля; **she ~ed by his bedside** она́ дежу́рила у его́ посте́ли; **he ~ed for his opportunity** он выжида́л удо́бную возмо́жность; **he ~ed for the postman** он сторожи́л почтальо́на; **will you ~ over my things?** вы не присмо́трите за мои́ми веща́ми?; **he ~ed over her interests** он стоя́л на стра́же её интере́сов.
2 (*be careful*): **~ how you cross the street** бу́дьте осторо́жны (*or* смотри́те) при перехо́де у́лицы.
● *with adv.*: **~ out** *v.i.* (*beware*) остерега́ться (+ *g.*), бере́чься (+ *g.*) (*both impf.*); **you'll fall if you don't ~ out** вы упадёте, е́сли не бу́дете осторо́жны; **~ out for the signal!** жди́те сигна́ла!
● *cpds.* **~-dog** *n.* (*lit.*) сторожева́я соба́ка; (*fig.*) наблюда́тель (*m.*); **~man** *n.* сто́рож, вахтёр; **~tower** *n.* сторожева́я ба́шня; **~word** *n.* (*slogan*) деви́з; (*password*) паро́ль (*m.*).

watch[2] /wɒtʃ/ *n.* (*timepiece*) час|ы́ (*pl., g.* -о́в); **two ~es** дво́е часо́в; **set one's ~** ста́вить, по- часы́; **what time is it by your ~?** ско́лько вре́мени на ва́ших часа́х?
● *cpds.* **~-band** *n.* (*US*) = **~-strap; ~-chain** *n.* цепо́чка для часо́в; **~-maker** *n.* часовщи́к; **~-strap** *n.* ремешо́к для часо́в; (*metal*) брасле́т.

watcher /ˈwɒtʃə(r)/ *n.* наблюда́тель (*m.*).

watchful /ˈwɒtʃfʊl/ *adj.* внима́тельный, бди́тельный.

watchfulness /ˈwɒtʃfʊlnɪs/ *n.* внима́тельность, бди́тельность.

water /ˈwɔːtə(r)/ *n.* **1** вода́; **we are going on the ~ today** сего́дня мы пойдём ката́ться на ло́дке; **our friends from across, over the ~** на́ши замо́рские/заокеа́нские друзья́; **at the ~'s edge** у са́мой воды́; **the ~ has**

W

been cut off во́ду отключи́ли; **she turned on the ~** она́ пусти́ла во́ду (*or* откры́ла кран); **a house with ~ laid on** дом с водопрово́дом; **the road is under ~** доро́га зато́плена; **he spends money like ~** он сори́т деньга́ми.
2 (*attr.*) (*see also cpds.*): **~ bus** речно́й трамва́й; **~ power** гидроэне́ргия; **~ sports** во́дные ви́ды спо́рта; **~ supply** водоснабже́ние.
3 (*fig. phrr.*): **in deep ~** в беде́; в опа́сном положе́нии; **get into hot ~** вл|ипа́ть, -и́пнуть в неприя́тность (*coll.*); **keep one's head above ~** удержа́ться (*pf.*) на пове́рхности; **pour, throw cold ~ on** раскритикова́ть (*pf.*); **~ under the bridge** невозвра́тное про́шлое; **the argument won't hold ~** э́тот до́вод ни на чём не осно́ван.
4 (*pl., areas of sea; reaches of river*) во́ды (*f. pl.*); **in Icelandic ~s** в исла́ндских во́дах; **in home ~s** в свои́х во́дах; (*pl., mineral ~s*) минера́льные во́ды; **they went to the spa to take the ~s** они́ пое́хали (лечи́ться) на во́ды.
5 (*urine*) моча́; **make, pass ~** мочи́ться, по-; (*fluid*): **~ on the brain** водя́нка мо́зга; гидроцефа́лия; **~ on the knee** жи́дкость в коле́нной ча́шечке.
6 (*state of tide*): у́ровень (*m.*) воды́; **high/low ~** прили́в/отли́в.
● *v.t.* **1** (*sprinkle ~ on*) пол|ива́ть, -и́ть водо́й.
2 (*provide with ~*) пои́ть, на-; **he stopped to ~ his horse** он останови́лся напои́ть коня́.
3: **~ed silk** муари́рованный шёлк; муа́р.
● *v.i.* (*of eyes*) слези́ться (*impf.*); **his eyes were ~ing with the wind** от ве́тра у него́ слези́лись глаза́; **the sight of food made my mouth ~** при ви́де еды́ у меня́ потекли́ слю́нки.
● *with adv.*: **~ down** *v.t.* (*lit.*) разб|авля́ть, -а́вить; (*fig.*) смягч|а́ть, -и́ть; осл|абля́ть, -а́бить.
● *cpds.* **~-biscuit** *n.* пече́нье на воде́; **~-blister** *n.* волды́рь (*m.*), пузы́рь (*m.*); **~-borne** *adj.* (*of freight*) доставля́емый/перевози́мый по воде́; (*of infection*) передаю́щийся че́рез во́ду; **~-bottle** *n.* (*soldier's*) фля́жка; (*carafe*) графи́н; (*for heating bed*) гре́лка; **~-buffalo** *n.* буйво́л; **~-butt** *n.* бо́чка для дождево́й воды́; **~-cannon** *n.* брандспо́йт, гидропу́льт; **~-chute** *n.* водяны́е го́ры (*f. pl.*) (*аттракцион*); **~-closet** *n.* убо́рная, туале́т; **~-colour** (*US* **-color**) *n.* (*paint*) акваре́ль, акваре́льные кра́ски (*f. pl.*); (*painting*) акваре́ль, акваре́льный рису́нок; **~-cooled** *adj.* с водяны́м охлажде́нием; **~course** *n.* ру́сло; **~cress** *n.* кресс водяно́й; **~ed-down** *adj.* (*fig.*) осла́бленный; **~fall** *n.* водопа́д; **~fowl** *n.* водопла́вающая пти́ца; **~front** *n.* берегова́я ли́ния (го́рода); **~-gauge** *n.* водоме́р; **~-heater** *n.* кипяти́льник; **~-hen** *n.* ку́рочка водяна́я; **~-hole** *n.* (*in desert*) во́дный исто́чник; **~-ice** *n.* щербе́т (*мороженое*); **~-jacket** *n.* водяна́я руба́шка; **~-jump** *n.* во́дный рубе́ж (*на скачках*); **~-level** *n.* у́ровень (*m.*) воды́; (*instrument*) ватерпа́с; **~-lily** *n.* водяна́я ли́лия, кувши́нка; **~-line** (*naut.*) *n.* ватерли́ния; **~logged** *adj.* (*of wood*) мо́крый; (*of ground*) заболо́ченный; **~-main** *n.* водопрово́дная магистра́ль; **~man** *n.* (*boatman*) ло́дочник; **~mark** *n.* водяно́й знак; **~-meadow** *n.* заливно́й луг; **~-melon** *n.* арбу́з; **~-meter** *n.* водоме́р; **~-mill** *n.* водяна́я ме́льница; **~-nymph** *n.* речна́я ни́мфа, руса́лка; **~-pipe** *n.* водопрово́дная труба́; **~-pistol** *n.* игру́шечный водяно́й пистоле́т; **~-polo** *n.* во́дное по́ло (*indecl.*); **~proof** *adj.* непромока́емый; *n.* (*Br.*) непромока́емый плащ; *v.t.* обраб|а́тывать, -о́тать водонепроница́емым соста́вом; **~-rat** *n.* водяна́я кры́са; **~-rate** *n.* пла́та за во́ду; **~-repellent** *adj.* водоотта́лкивающий; **~side** *n.* бе́рег; **~-skiing** *n.* воднолы́жный спо́рт; **~-skis** *n. pl.* во́дные лы́жи (*f. pl.*); **~-softener** *n.* водоумягчи́тель (*m.*); **~spout** *n.* (*phenomenon*) водяно́й смерч; (*conduit*) водосто́чная труба́; **~-tank** *n.* бак для воды́; резервуа́р; **~-tap** *n.* водопрово́дный кран; **~tight** *adj.* (*lit.*) водонепроница́емый; (*fig., of argument etc.*) неопровержи́мый, убеди́тельный; **~-tower** *n.* водонапо́рная ба́шня; **~-trough** *n.* пои́лка для скота́; **~-wag(g)on** *n.* пово́зка водово́за; **go on the ~-wag(g)on** (*fig.*) да|ва́ть, -ть заро́к не пить; **~way** *n.* (*route for travel*) во́дный путь; (*navigable channel*) фарва́тер; **~-weed** *n.* во́доросль; **~-wheel** *n.* водяно́е колесо́; **~-wings** *n. pl.* пла́вательные пузыри́ (*m. pl.*); **~works** *n. pl.* (*lit.*) водопрово́дная ста́нция; (*fig., Br. coll.: urinary system*) мочева́я систе́ма.

watering /ˈwɔːtərɪŋ/ *n.* поли́вка; **the roses need ~** ну́жно поли́ть ро́зы.
● *cpds.* **~-can** *n.* ле́йка; **~-place** *n.* (*for animals*) водопо́й; (*resort*) во́дный куро́рт; во́ды (*f. pl.*).

Waterloo /ˌwɔːtəˈluː/ *n.* Ватерло́о (*indecl.*); **the Battle of ~** сраже́ние у Ватерло́о.

watershed /ˈwɔːtəˌʃed/ *n.* (*lit., fig.*) водоразде́л.

watery /ˈwɔːtərɪ/ *adj.* водяни́стый, жи́дкий; **~ vegetables** перева́ренные о́вощи; **~ eyes** слезя́щиеся глаза́; **a ~ grave** ги́бель на́ море.

watt /wɒt/ *n.* ватт.

wattage /ˈwɒtɪdʒ/ *n.* мо́щность в ва́ттах.

wattle[1] /ˈwɒt(ə)l/ *n.* **1** (*material*) лозня́к; (*woven fence*) плете́нь (*m.*); **~ and daub hut** ма́занка. **2** (*plant*) ака́ция.

wattle[2] /ˈwɒt(ə)l/ *n.* (*of bird*) боро́дка.

wave /weɪv/ *n.* **1** (*ridge of water*) волна́; (*very large*) вал; **life on the ocean ~(s)** морска́я жизнь.
2 (*fig., of persons advancing*) волна́.
3 (*fig., temporary increase or spread*) подъём, волна́; **~ of enthusiasm** волна́/взрыв энтузиа́зма; **crime ~** ре́зкий рост престу́пности; **heat ~** жара́; пери́од си́льной жары́.
4 (*phys.*) волна́; **short/medium/long ~s** коро́ткие/сре́дние/дли́нные во́лны.
5 (*undulation*): **her hair has a natural ~** у неё (от приро́ды) вью́щиеся во́лосы; **permanent ~** пермане́нт.
6 (*gesture*) взмах; **she gave a ~ of her hand** она́ помаха́ла/взмахну́ла руко́й.
● *v.t.* **1** (*move to and fro or up and down*) маха́ть, по- + *i.*; разма́хивать (*impf.*) + *i.*; **the children were waving flags** де́ти маха́ли/разма́хивали фла́жками; **she ~d her handkerchief at me** она́ помаха́ла мне платко́м; **he ~d his hand** (*as a signal*) он по́дал знак (*or* махну́л) руко́й.
2 (*express by hand-waving*): **~ goodbye** маха́ть, по- (руко́й) на проща́ние.
3 (*set in ~s*) зав|ива́ть, -и́ть; **she had her hair ~d** она́ сде́лала зави́вку.
● *v.i.* **1** (*move to and fro or up and down*) развева́ться (*impf.*); кача́ться (*impf.*); **waving branches** кача́ющиеся ве́тви; **waving corn** волну́ющаяся под ве́тром пшени́ца; **the flags were waving in the breeze** фла́ги развева́лись на ветру́.
2 (*~ one's hand*) маха́ть, по-; **~ at s.o.** маха́ть, по- кому́-н.
3 (*of hair*) ви́ться (*impf.*).
● *with advs.*: **~ aside** *v.t.* отстран|я́ть, -и́ть же́стом; **he ~d my objections aside** он отмахну́лся от мои́х возраже́ний; **~ away** *v.t.* отстран|я́ть, -и́ть же́стом; **~ down** *v.t.* остан|а́вливать, -ови́ть; **the policeman ~d us down** полице́йский взмахну́л руко́й, что́бы мы останови́лись; **~ on** *v.t.*: **the officer ~d his men on** офице́р взма́хом руки́ дал солда́там сигна́л к наступле́нию; **when our passports had been checked we were ~d on** когда́ на́ши паспорта́ прове́рили, нам махну́ли: «Проезжа́йте!».
● *cpds.* **~band** *n.* диапазо́н волн; **~length** *n.* длина́ волны́; **he and I are on the same ~length** (*fig.*) мы с ним на одно́й волне́.

waver /ˈweɪvə(r)/ *v.i.* **1** (*flicker*) колыха́ться (*impf.*). **2** (*falter; become unsteady*) дрожа́ть, за-; дро́гнуть (*pf.*); **his voice ~ed** его́ го́лос дро́гнул.
3 (*hesitate; be irresolute*) колеба́ться (*impf.*).

waverer /ˈweɪvərə(r)/ *n.* колéблющийся.

wavy /ˈweɪvɪ/ *adj.* (**wavier, waviest**) волнообра́зный, волни́стый; **a ~ line** волни́стая ли́ния/черта́; **~ hair** вью́щиеся во́лосы.

wax[1] /wæks/ *n.* **1** воск; (*in the ears*) се́ра; **bees ~** пчели́ный воск; **paraffin ~** твёрдый парафи́н. **2** (*attr.*) восково́й; *see also cpds.*
● *v.t.* вощи́ть, на-; (*surface*) нат|ира́ть, -ере́ть (во́ском).
● *cpds.* **~ bean** *n.* воскова́я фасо́ль; **~ crayons** *n. pl.* восковы́е мелки́ (*m. pl.*); **~ museum** *n.* = **~works;** **~-paper** *n.* вощáнка, воско́вка; **~work** *n.* (*dummy*) воскова́я фигу́ра;

~works *n.* (*museum*) галере́я восковы́х фигу́р.

wax² /wæks/ *v.i.* **1** (*of moon*) прибыва́ть (*impf.*). **2** (*liter., grow*) де́латься (*impf.*) + *i.*; станови́ться (*impf.*) + *i.*; **~ eloquent** де́латься, с- красноречи́вым.

waxen /ˈwæks(ə)n/ *adj.* восково́й.

waxy /ˈwæksɪ/ *adj.* (**waxier, waxiest**) восково́й; **~ potatoes** водяни́стая карто́шка.

way /weɪ/ *n.* **1** (*road, path*) доро́га, путь (*m.*); (*track*) тропа́; **Milky W~** Мле́чный путь; **over the ~** (*Br.*) напро́тив.
2 (*route, journey*) путь (*m.*); **which is the best ~ to London?** как лу́чше прое́хать в Ло́ндон?; **he lost his ~** он заблуди́лся; он сби́лся с пути́; **he went (on) his ~** он пошёл да́льше; он удали́лся; **they went their own ~s** ка́ждый из них пошёл свои́м путём; **go down the wrong ~** (*of food*) попа́сть (*pf.*) не в то го́рло; **lead the ~** (*lit.*) идти́ (*det.*) впереди́; (*fig.*) под|ава́ть, -а́ть приме́р; **feel one's ~** дви́гаться (*impf.*) осторо́жно (*or* о́щупью); **we made our ~ to the dining-room** мы прошли́ в столо́вую; **you must make your own ~ to the station** вам придётся добира́ться до ста́нции самому́; **they made their ~ across mountains** они́ прошли́ че́рез го́ры; **he made his ~ in the world** он проби́л себе́ доро́гу в жи́зни; **pay one's ~** (*of person*) (*when travelling*) опла́|чивать, -ти́ть свою́ доро́гу; (*in general*) жить (*impf.*) на со́бственные сре́дства; (*of thing*) окуп|а́ться, -и́ться; опра́вдывать, оправда́ть себя́; **he worked his ~ through college** все го́ды студе́нчества он зараба́тывал себе́ на жизнь; (*with preps.*): **by ~ of London** че́рез Ло́ндон; **by the ~** по доро́ге; в пути́; (*incidentally*) кста́ти; ме́жду про́чим; **by ~ of** *see* ⇒11; **in the ~** *see* ⇒9; **on the ~** по доро́ге; на/по пути́; **he was on his ~ to the bank** он шёл в банк; **a letter is on its ~** письмо́ (нахо́дится) в пути́; **I must be on my ~** мне пора́ (идти́); **I sent him on his ~** я его́ отпра́вил; **they have another child on the ~** они́ ожида́ют ещё одного́ ребёнка; **be on the ~ in/out** (*of fashion*) входи́ть (*impf.*) в мо́ду, выходи́ть (*impf.*) из мо́ды; **the hall is well on the ~ to completion** строи́тельство за́ла бли́зится к концу́; **he is well on the ~ to being a professor** у него́ есть все ша́нсы стать профе́ссором; **he went out of his ~ to help me** он прояви́л нема́лое усе́рдие, что́бы помо́чь мне; **out of the ~** (*remote*) в стороне́; далеко́; **the price is nothing out of the ~** цена́ не осо́бенно высо́кая; *see also* ⇒9; (*with adv. indicating direction*): **~ across** перехо́д; **~ in** вход; **~ out** (*lit., fig.*) вы́ход; **~ back** обра́тная доро́га, доро́га наза́д; **can you find the ~ back?** вы найдёте доро́гу наза́д?; **the ~ ahead will be difficult** нам предстои́т тру́дная доро́га; **~ through** прохо́д; **~ round** око́льный путь; (*fig., loophole*) лазе́йка; **he knows his ~ around** он зна́ет, что к чему́.
3 (*door*): **he came in by the front ~ and went out by the back** он вошёл с пара́дного хо́да, а вы́шел с чёрного.
4 (*direction*) сторона́, направле́ние; **which ~ did they go?** в каку́ю сто́рону они́ пошли́?; **this ~** сюда́; **are you going my ~?** вам со мной по пути́?; **come s.o.'s ~** дост|ава́ться, -а́ться кому́-н.; **look the other ~** (*fig., deliberately ignore something*) смотре́ть (*impf.*) сквозь па́льцы на что-н.; **I travelled** (*Br.*), **traveled** (*US*) **by bus both ~s** я е́хал авто́бусом туда́ и обра́тно (*or* в о́ба конца́); **you can't have it both ~s** ли́бо одно́, ли́бо друго́е; что́-нибудь одно́; **it cuts both ~s** па́лка о двух конца́х; **no two ~s about it** э́то несомне́нно; **I don't know which ~ to turn** я не зна́ю, что де́лать (*or* как быть).
5 (*of reversible things*): **his hat is on the wrong ~ round** он наде́л шля́пу за́дом наперёд; **the picture is the wrong ~ up** карти́на пове́шена вверх нога́ми; **is the flag the right ~ up?** пра́вильно ли пове́шен флаг?; **the other ~ round** наоборо́т, напро́тив.
6 (*neighbourhood, area*): **down your ~** в ва́ших края́х; **he lives somewhere Plymouth ~** он живёт где-то в райо́не Пли́мута.
7 (*distance, time*) расстоя́ние; **a long ~ off** (*away*) далеко́; **a little, short ~** недалеко́; **quite a ~** дово́льно далеко́; **it is only a little ~ to the shops** до магази́нов совсе́м недалеко́ (*or* два шага́); **my birthday's still a long ~ off** до моего́ дня рожде́ния ещё далеко́; **all the ~** всю доро́гу; (*fig.*) по́лностью.
8 (*a long ~*) далеко́; **~ back** (*long ago*) давны́м-давно́; **~ ahead of the others** намно́го впереди́ остальны́х.
9 (*clear passage; space or freedom to proceed*) прое́зд, прохо́д; **right of ~** пра́во прое́зда; **clear the ~** расч|ища́ть, -и́стить путь; **fight one's ~ through the crowd** прод|ира́ться, -ра́ться сквозь толпу́; **get in the ~** меша́ть, по- (*кому*); **this chair is always getting in the ~** э́тот стул ве́чно меша́ет; **get out of the ~!** (прочь) с доро́ги!; да́йте пройти́!; **get something out of the ~** (*lit.*) уб|ира́ть, -ра́ть что-н. с доро́ги; (*fig., dispose of*) сва́л|ивать, -и́ть что-н.; изб|авля́ться, -а́виться от чего́-н.; разде́л|ываться, -аться с чем-н.; **make ~ for the President!** доро́гу президе́нту!; **he made ~ for his successor** он уступи́л ме́сто своему́ прее́мнику; **put out of the ~** устран|я́ть, -и́ть; **you are standing in the ~** вы загора́живаете доро́гу; **I shan't stand in your ~** я не бу́ду стоя́ть на ва́шем пути́ (*or* вам меша́ть); **I can't see my ~ to doing that** бою́сь, что я не смогу́ э́то сде́лать; **give ~** (*fail to resist*) подд|ава́ться, -а́ться; (*collapse*) прова́л|иваться, -и́ться; раз|рыва́ться, -орва́ться; ру́хнуть (*pf.*); **his legs gave ~** у него́ подкоси́лись но́ги; (*retreat*) отступ|а́ть, -и́ть; (*make concessions*) уступ|а́ть, -и́ть; (*allow precedence*) уступ|а́ть, -и́ть доро́гу; (*surrender, abandon o.s.*) сд|ава́ться, -а́ться; пред|ава́ться, -а́ться; **give ~ to tears** да|ва́ть, -ть во́лю слеза́м.
10 (*means, method*) сре́дство, ме́тод, приём; **he found a ~ to keep food warm** он нашёл спо́соб/сре́дство сохраня́ть пи́щу горя́чей; **there is no ~ to** нет никако́й возмо́жности + *inf.*: **there are ~s and means** есть вся́кие пути́ и сре́дства; **you will soon get into the ~ of it** вы вско́ре осво́ите э́то.
11 (*manner, fashion*) сре́дство, спо́соб, о́браз, ме́тод, приём; **in this ~** таки́м о́бразом; **is this the ~ to do it?** так э́то де́лается?; **do it your own ~!** де́лайте по-сво́ему!; **in a polite ~** ве́жливо; **I'll miss her in a ~** в не́котором ро́де мне бу́дет её недостава́ть; **one ~ or another** так и́ли ина́че; **the right ~** (*adv.*) как сле́дует, пра́вильно; **the wrong ~** (*adv.*) не так, непра́вильно; **in the same ~** (то́чно) так же; таки́м же о́бразом; **I love the ~ he smiles** мне о́чень нра́вится, как он улыба́ется; **it's disgraceful the ~ he drinks** безобра́зие, что он так пьёт; **I don't like the ~ you said that** мне не нра́вится, как вы э́то сказа́ли; **~ of thinking** о́браз мы́слей; **to my ~ of thinking** как мне ка́жется; на мой взгляд; по-мо́ему; **try to see it my ~** попыта́йтесь встать на моё ме́сто; **let's put it this ~** ска́жем так; **either ~** (*in either fashion*) любы́м из двух спо́собов; (*in either case or event*) в обо́их слу́чаях, в любо́м слу́чае; **whichever ~ you look at it** как на э́то ни посмо́тришь; **whichever ~ you turn** куда́ бы ты ни посмотре́л; куда́ ни кинь (*coll.*); **by ~ of** (*in order to*) с тем, что́бы; с це́лью; **by ~ of a change** для разнообра́зия; **by ~ of a joke** шу́тки ра́ди; (*as a form of*) в ви́де/ка́честве; (*as a substitute for*) вме́сто; взаме́н (*all* + *g.*); **by ~ of an apology** в ка́честве извине́ния; **by ~ of an introduction** в ка́честве вступле́ния; (*manner of behaving*): **she has a winning ~** у неё обая́тельная мане́ра; **he has a ~ with him** в нём есть не́кое обая́ние; **it's only his ~** у него́ про́сто така́я мане́ра; э́то всего́ лишь его́ мане́ра; **he has a ~ with the ladies** он уме́ет нра́виться да́мам; (*preference*): **have it your own ~!** будь/пусть бу́дет по-ва́шему!; **have, get one's own ~** доб|ива́ться, -и́ться своего́; **things went my ~** дела́ сложи́лись в мою́ по́льзу.
12 (*habit, custom*) обы́чай, привы́чка; **~ of life** о́браз жи́зни; **he has a ~ of not paying his bills** у него́ есть привы́чка не плати́ть по счета́м; **that's always the ~ with him** он всегда́ так; **that's the ~ of the world** так уж заведено́/во́дится на све́те; **mend one's ~s** испр|авля́ться, -а́виться; **fall into bad ~s** пойти́ (*pf.*) по плохо́й/дурно́й доро́жке.
13 (*state, condition*) положе́ние, состоя́ние; **things are in a bad ~** дела́ из рук вон пло́хи; дела́ плохи́ (*coll.*); **she was in a terrible ~** (*ill*) она́ была́ в плохо́м состоя́нии.
14 (*scale, degree*): **in a small ~** скро́мно; **in a big ~** в широ́ком/большо́м масшта́бе; кардина́льно; **he went in for photography in a big ~** он стал занима́ться фотогра́фией всерьёз.

15 (*sense, respect*) смысл, отноше́ние; **in a ~** в не́котором отноше́нии; **in some ~s** в не́которых отноше́ниях; **in one ~** в одно́м смы́сле; **in no ~** ничу́ть, нико́им о́бразом; **were you involved in any ~?** бы́ли ли вы каки́м-нибудь о́бразом в э́том заме́шаны?; **one ~ and another** (*in all respects*) во всех отноше́ниях; (*for any of various reasons*) по ра́зным причи́нам; **one ~ or another** (*by some means*) так и́ли ина́че; (*for any of various reasons*) по ра́зным причи́нам.
16 (*line, course*): **what have we in the ~ of food?** что у нас есть по ча́сти еды́?
17 (*of ship etc.*): **under ~** на ходу́, в пути́; **preparations are under ~** (сейча́с) иду́т приготовле́ния.

● *cpds.* **~bill** *n.* (*list of goods*) тра́нспортная накладна́я; **~farer** *n.* пу́тник, стра́нник; **~lay** *v.t.* подстер|ега́ть, -е́чь; устр|а́ивать, -о́ить заса́ду + *d.*; **~-out** *adj.* (*coll.*) замеча́тельный, бесподо́бный; **~side** *n.* обо́чина (доро́ги); (*attr.*) придоро́жный; **fall by the ~side** (*fig.*) выбыва́ть, вы́быть из стро́я; **~ station** *n.* (*US*) полуста́нок.

wayward /ˈweɪwəd/ *adj.* своенра́вный, непоко́рный.

waywardness /ˈweɪwədnɪs/ *n.* своенра́вие, непоко́рность.

WC (*abbr. of* ***water-closet***) (*Br.*) убо́рная.

we /wiː/, /wɪ/ *pron.* (*obj.* **us**; *poss.* **our, ours**) мы (*also royal, editorial*); **~ lawyers** мы, адвока́ты; (*I*): **give us a rest!** да́йте челове́ку отдохну́ть!; **how are ~ feeling today?** как мы сего́дня себя́ чу́вствуем?; **~ don't inform on people** у нас не при́нято доноси́ть.

weak /wiːk/ *adj.* **1** (*infirm; feeble*) сла́бый; **a ~ constitution** хру́пкое сложе́ние; **he has a ~ heart** у него́ сла́бое се́рдце; **a ~ imagination** бе́дное воображе́ние; **a ~ old man** дря́хлый стари́к; **he's a bit ~ in the head** он придуркова́т (*coll.*); **their cries grew ~er** их кри́ки слабе́ли/ослабева́ли; **~ point** сла́бое ме́сто; **his ~ point is spelling** орфогра́фия — его сла́бое ме́сто; **the ~est go to the wall** сла́бые сдаю́тся.
2 (*unconvincing*) сла́бый, неубеди́тельный; **they put up a ~ case** они́ привели́ сла́бые до́воды.
3 (*of will*) сла́бый; (*of person*) сла́бый, безво́льный, слабово́льный; **a ~ person/character** сла́бый/нереши́тельный челове́к/хара́ктер.
4 (*diluted; thin*) жи́дкий, сла́бый; **do you like your tea ~?** вы лю́бите некре́пкий/сла́бый чай?
5 (*gram.*) сла́бый.
6 (*of style*) вя́лый.

● *cpds.* **~-kneed** *adj.* (*fig.*) малоду́шный, нереши́тельный; **~-minded** *adj.* слабоу́мный; **~-spirited** *adj.* малоду́шный; **~-willed** *adj.* слабово́льный.

weaken /ˈwiːkən/ *v.t.* осл|абля́ть, -а́бить; **his resolve was ~ed** его́ реши́мость поколеба́лась.
● *v.i.* слабе́ть, о-.

weakling /ˈwiːklɪŋ/ *n.* хи́лый челове́к; (*of child*) хи́лый ребёнок.

weakness /ˈwiːknɪs/ *n.* сла́бость, хи́лость; **the tests revealed ~es in the structure** испыта́ния вы́явили структу́рные дефе́кты; **there is a ~ in his logic** в его́ ло́гике есть изъя́н; **she has a ~ for him** она́ пита́ет к нему́ сла́бость.

weal[1] /wiːl/ *n.* (*liter.*) бла́го, благосостоя́ние; **the common, public ~** бла́го о́бщества; о́бщее бла́го.

weal[2] /wiːl/ *n.* (*mark on skin*) рубе́ц.

wealth /welθ/ *n.* бога́тство, состоя́ние; **a man of ~** бога́ч; состоя́тельный челове́к; **he possesses great ~** он облада́ет огро́мным состоя́нием/бога́тством; **~ tax** нало́г на иму́щество; (*fig., profusion*) оби́лие; **a ~ of illustrations** оби́лие иллюстра́ций; **a ~ of detail** мно́жество подро́бностей; **a ~ of experience** богате́йший о́пыт; **a ~ of material** огро́мный/богате́йший материа́л.

wealthy /ˈwelθɪ/ *adj.* (**wealthier, wealthiest**) бога́тый, состоя́тельный; **the ~** богачи́ (*m. pl.*); бога́тые.

wean /wiːn/ *v.t.* отн|има́ть, -я́ть (*or* отлуч|а́ть, -и́ть) от груди́; (*fig.*) отуч|а́ть, -и́ть (*от чего*).

weapon /ˈwepən/ *n.* ору́жие; (*piece of artillery*) ору́дие; **conventional ~s** обы́чные ви́ды вооруже́ния; **guided ~s** управля́емые снаря́ды (*m. pl.*)/раке́ты (*f. pl.*); **~ of war** боево́е сре́дство; (*fig.*) ору́жие, сре́дство.

weaponry /ˈwepənrɪ/ *n.* ору́жие, вооруже́ние.

wear /weə(r)/ *n.* **1** (*articles or type of clothing*) оде́жда, пла́тье; **beach ~** оде́жда для пля́жа; **children's ~** де́тская оде́жда, де́тское пла́тье; (*~ing of clothes*) но́ска, ноше́ние; **a suit for everyday ~** бу́дничный/повседне́вный костю́м.
2 (*continued use as causing damage or loss of quality*) изно́с, изна́шивание; **this material stands up to hard ~** э́тот материа́л прекра́сно но́сится; **show signs of ~** име́ть (*impf.*) изно́шенный вид; **~ and tear** изно́с; **fair ~ and tear** (*leg.*) норма́льная у́быль и норма́льный изно́с.
3 (*resistance to ~*) про́чность, сто́йкость; (*only on clothing*) но́скость; **these shoes have a lot of ~ left in them** э́ти боти́нки мо́жно ещё до́лго носи́ть (*or* ещё до́лго бу́дут носи́ться).

● *v.t.* (*past* **wore**; *p.p.* **worn**)
1 (*garments or accessories*) носи́ть (*indet.*); (*put on*) над|ева́ть, -е́ть; **what shall I ~?** что мне наде́ть?; **she was ~ing light blue** она́ была́ в голубо́м (пла́тье), на ней бы́ло голубо́е пла́тье; **he ~s galoshes** он но́сит гало́ши; **he always wore a hat** он всегда́ ходи́л в шля́пе; **she ~s scent** она́ ду́шится; **are you ~ing a watch?** у вас есть часы́?; **worn** (*used*) **clothes** (из)но́шенная/ста́рая оде́жда; (*of hair*): **~ one's hair long** носи́ть (*indet.*) дли́нные во́лосы; **~ one's hair short** ко́ротко стри́чься (*impf.*); **he ~s his hair brushed back** он зачёсывает во́лосы наза́д; **they all wore beards** они́ все носи́ли бо́роды; (*fig.*): **~ing a smile** с улы́бкой (на лице́); **~ing a frown** нахму́рившись.
2 (*damage surface of; abrade*) ст|ира́ть, -ере́ть; (*damage by use*) трепа́ть, ис-, изн|а́шивать, -оси́ть; (*clothing*) прот|ира́ть, -ере́ть; **the steps are worn** ступе́ни стёрлись; **his cuffs are badly worn** его́ манже́ты истрепа́лись; **he ~s his socks into holes** он изна́шивает носки́ до дыр; **a well-worn suit** си́льно изно́шенный костю́м; **the waves have worn the stone** во́лны обточи́ли ка́мень; (*fig.*): **she was worn to a shadow with worry** от постоя́нных пережива́ний она́ преврати́лась в тень; **I had a ~ing day** у меня́ был изнури́тельный день; **a well-worn theme** изби́тая те́ма.
3 (*produce by friction*): **the stream wore a channel in the sand** пото́к проби́л кана́ву в песке́; **you've worn a hole in your trousers** вы протёрли брю́ки до дыр; **a well-worn track** проторённая доро́жка.

● *v.i.* (*past* **wore**; *p.p.* **worn**) **1** (*stand up to ~*) (хорошо́) носи́ться (*indet.*); быть про́чным; **the play ~s well after 50 years** э́та пье́са и 50 лет спустя́ не устаре́ла.
2 (*show effects of ~*): **~ thin** изн|а́шиваться, -оси́ться; трепа́ться, ис-; (*fig.*): **his patience wore thin** его́ терпе́ние бы́ло на исхо́де; **that excuse has worn thin** э́то оправда́ние звучи́т неубеди́тельно.

● *with advs.*: **~ away** *v.t.* & *i.* ст|ира́ть(ся), -ере́ть(ся); **weather had worn away the inscription** ве́тры и дожди́ стёрли на́дпись; **the cliffs were worn away in places** ска́лы места́ми вы́ветрились; **~ down** *v.t.* & *i.* изн|а́шивать(ся), -оси́ть(ся); **the heels have worn down very quickly** каблуки́ износи́лись о́чень бы́стро; (*fig.*): **they wore down the enemy's resistance** они́ сломи́ли сопротивле́ние проти́вника; **~ in** *v.t.* (*shoes*) разн|а́шивать, -оси́ть; **~ off** *v.t.* & *i.* ст|ира́ть(ся), -ере́ть(ся); **the pattern wore off** узо́р стёрся; (*fig.*) (постепе́нно) проходи́ть (*impf.*); **the novelty soon wore off** вско́ре новизна́ прошла́; **~ on** *v.i.*: **as the evening wore on** к концу́ ве́чера; **~ out** *v.t.* & *i.* изн|а́шивать(ся), -оси́ть(ся); трепа́ться, ис-; **the machine wore out** маши́на срабо́талась; (*fig.*) изнур|я́ть(ся), -и́ть(ся); **the children wore me out** де́ти меня́ изму́чили; **you look worn out** у вас изму́ченный вид; **worn-out** (*of clothes etc.*) изно́шенный, истёртый, потёртый.

wearable /ˈweərəb(ə)l/ *adj.* приго́дный для но́ски.

wearer /ˈweərə(r)/ *n.* владе́лец, носи́тель (*fem.* -ница).

weariness /ˈwɪərɪnɪs/ *n.* утомле́ние; (*boredom*) ску́ка.

wearing /ˈweərɪŋ/ *adj.* утоми́тельный; (*tiresome*) надое́дливый.

wearisome /ˈwɪərɪsəm/ *adj.* надое́дливый, ску́чный, ну́дный.

weary /ˈwɪərɪ/ *adj.* (**wearier,**

weariest) **1** (*tired*) уста́лый, утомлённый; **~ in body and mind** уста́вший душо́й и те́лом (*or* физи́чески и духо́вно); **~ of walking** уста́вший от ходьбы́; **the journey made him ~** путеше́ствие его́ утоми́ло. **2** (*tiring*) утоми́тельный; **ten ~ miles** де́сять утоми́тельных миль. **3** (*showing tiredness*) уста́лый, уста́вший; **he gave a ~ sigh** он уста́ло вздохну́л. **4**: **~ of** (*fed up with*) уста́вший от (*чего*); **I was ~ of his complaints** мне надое́ли его́ жа́лобы.

● *v.t. & i.* утом|ля́ть(ся), -и́ть(ся).

weasel /ˈwiːz(ə)l/ *n.* ла́ска; **~ words** (*fig.*) двусмы́сленные слова́, двусмы́сленности (*f. pl.*).

● *v.t.* (**weaselled, weaselling;** *US*, **weaseled, weaseling**) (*insinuate*): **she ~led her way** (*or* **herself**) **into my confidence** она́ вкра́лась ко мне в дове́рие.

weather /ˈweðə(r)/ *n.* пого́да; **bad ~** плоха́я пого́да, нена́стье; **rough ~** непого́да; **wet ~** дождли́вая пого́да; **in all ~s** в любу́ю пого́ду; **what's the ~ like?** кака́я сего́дня пого́да?; **the ~ was bad** пого́да была́ плоха́я; **~ permitting** при благоприя́тной пого́де; **make heavy ~ of something** (*fig.*) осложн|я́ть, -и́ть де́ло; **protection against the ~** защи́та от непого́ды; **be, feel under the ~** (*fig.*) нева́жно себя́ чу́вствовать (*impf.*); **keep a ~ eye open** смотре́ть (*impf.*) в о́ба; держа́ть (*impf.*) у́хо востро́; **~ forecast** прогно́з пого́ды; **~ report** метеорологи́ческая сво́дка.

● *v.t.* **1** (*survive; circumvent*) выде́рживать, вы́держать; переж|ива́ть, -и́ть; перен|оси́ть, -ести́; **~ a storm** выде́рживать, вы́держать шторм; **~ a crisis** перен|оси́ть, -ести́/выде́рживать, вы́держать кри́зис. **2** (*expose to atmosphere*) подв|ерга́ть, -е́ргнуть атмосфе́рным влия́ниям; (*wear away by exposure*) изн|а́шивать, -оси́ть; (*discolour*) обесцве́|чивать, -тить.

● *cpds.* **~-beaten** *adj.* обве́тренный; **~-board** *n.* (*Br.*) обши́вочная пане́ль; (*on door*) сливна́я ре́йка; **~-bound** *adj.* заде́ржанный непого́дой; **~cock** *n.* флю́гер; **~man, ~ presenter** *nn.* сино́птик; **~-proof** *adj.* погодоусто́йчивый; защища́ющий от непого́ды; *v.t.* защи|ща́ть, -ти́ть от непого́ды; **~-station** *n.* метеорологи́ческая ста́нция; **~-vane** *n.* флю́гер; **~-worn** *adj.* пострада́вший от непого́ды.

weave /wiːv/ *n.* (тка́цкое) переплете́ние.

● *v.t.* (*past* **wove;** *p.p.* **woven** *or* **wove**) **1** (*thread, flowers etc.*) плести́, с-; спле|та́ть, -сти́; (**~** *into*) впле|та́ть, -сти́; **she wove ribbons into her hair** она́ вплела́ ле́нты в во́лосы; (*fig.*): **he wove these incidents into his novel** он вплёл э́ти эпизо́ды в ткань своего́ рома́на. **2** (*make basket etc. by weaving*) плести́, с-; **he wove a basket** он сплёл корзи́ну; (*cloth*) ткать, со-; (*fig.*): **~ a web of intrigue** плести́, с- сеть интри́г.

● *v.i.* (*past* **wove;** *p.p.* **woven** *or* **wove**) **1** (*work at loom*) ткать (*impf.*). **2** (*twist and turn*) петля́ть (*impf.*), идти́ (*det.*) непрямы́м путём.

weaver /ˈwiːvə(r)/ *n.* (*person*) ткач (*fem.* -и́ха); (*bird*) тка́чик.

weaving /ˈwiːvɪŋ/ *n.* (*of cloth*) тка́чество; (*of baskets*) плете́ние.

web /web/ *n.* **1** (*also* **spider's ~**) паути́на; (*fig.*) сеть, паути́на, сплете́ние. **2** (*membrane*) перепо́нка. **3** (*the Web*) (*comput.*) веб, Сеть, Интерне́т.

● *cpds.* **~-footed** *adj.* перепо́нчатый; **~ page** *n.* (*comput.*) страни́ца в Интерне́те; **~site** *n.* (*comput.*) вебса́йт.

webbed /webd/ *adj.* перепо́нчатый.

webbing /ˈwebɪŋ/ *n.* тка́ный реме́нь.

wed /wed/ *v.t. & i.* (**wedding;** *past and p.p.* **wedded** *or* **wed**) (*liter.*) **1** (*of man*) жени́ться (*impf., pf.*) на + *p.*; **his ~ded wife** его́ зако́нная супру́га. **2** (*of woman*) выходи́ть, вы́йти (за́муж) за + *a.* **3** (*of couple*) пожени́ться (*pf.*); вступ|а́ть, -и́ть в брак; **the newly ~ded pair** новобра́чные (*pl.*), молодожёны (*m. pl.*). **4** (*fig.*): **he is ~ded to his job** он (всеце́ло) пре́дан свое́й рабо́те; **he is ~ded to his opinion** он упо́рно де́ржится своего́ мне́ния.

wedding /ˈwedɪŋ/ *n.* сва́дьба, бракосочета́ние; (*in church*) венча́ние; **silver/golden ~** серебряная/золота́я сва́дьба; **~ anniversary** годовщи́на сва́дьбы; **~ breakfast** (*Br.*) приём по́сле бракосочета́ния; сва́дебный за́втрак; **~ march** сва́дебный марш.

● *cpds.* **~-cake** *n.* сва́дебный торт; **~-day** *n.* день (*m.*) сва́дьбы; **~-dress** *n.* сва́дебное пла́тье; **~-night** *n.* пе́рвая бра́чная ночь; **~-ring** *n.* обруча́льное кольцо́.

wedge /wedʒ/ *n.* клин; **drive (in) a ~** (*lit., fig.*) вби|ва́ть, -ть клин (ме́жду + *i.*); **it's the thin end of the ~** ≈ э́то цвето́чки, а я́годки (бу́дут) впереди́; **a ~ of cake** кусо́к то́рта.

● *v.t.* закреп|ля́ть, -и́ть кли́ном; закли́н|ивать, -и́ть; **~ in** вкли́н|ивать, -и́ть; **I ~d in some packing to stop the draught** я наби́л в щель па́кли, что́бы останови́ть сквозня́к; **we were ~d in** нас сти́снули со всех сторо́н.

● *cpds.* **~-heeled** *adj.*: **~-heeled shoe** танке́тка; **~-shaped** *adj.* клинови́дный.

wedlock /ˈwedlɒk/ *n.* брак, супру́жество; **born in ~** законнорождённый; **born out of ~** внебра́чный, незаконнорождённый; **holy ~** свяще́нные у́з|ы (*pl., g.* —) бра́ка.

Wednesday /ˈwenzdeɪ/, /-dɪ/ *n.* среда́; **on ~** в сре́ду.

wee /wiː/ *adj.* (**weer** /ˈwiːə(r)/; **weest** /ˈwiːɪst/) (*Sc. & coll.*) кро́шечный, малю́сенький; **she's a ~ bit jealous** она́ чу́точку ревну́ет.

weed /wiːd/ *n.* сорня́к; **the garden ran to ~s** сад заро́с сорняка́ми; (*in water*) во́доросль; **the ~** (*tobacco*) таба́к; (*marijuana*) марихуа́на, тра́вка; (*weak-looking person*) хи́лый челове́к, хиля́к (*coll.*).

● *v.t.* (*clear of* **~s**) поло́ть, вы́-; проп|а́лывать, -оло́ть; **the garden needs ~ing** сад необходи́мо пропо́лоть.

● *with adv.*: **~ out** *v.t.* (*eradicate, remove*) устран|я́ть, -и́ть; искорен|я́ть, -и́ть; **he ~ed out unwanted books from the library** он очи́стил библиоте́ку от нену́жных книг.

● *cpd.* **~-killer** *n.* гербици́д.

weeds /wiːdz/ *n.*: **widow's ~** вдо́вий тра́ур.

weedy /ˈwiːdɪ/ *adj.* (**weedier, weediest**) (*overgrown with weeds*) заро́сший сорняка́ми; (*weak-looking*) худосо́чный.

week /wiːk/ *n.* неде́ля; **what day of the ~ is it?** како́й сего́дня день (неде́ли)?; **the ~ before last** позапро́шлая неде́ля; **the ~ after next** че́рез две неде́ли; **in the last ~ of August** в после́днюю неде́лю а́вгуста; **a ~ (from) today (***or* **today ~,** *or* **this day ~)** ро́вно че́рез неде́лю; **two ~s (from) tomorrow** че́рез две неде́ли, счита́я с за́втрашнего дня; **(on) Monday ~** (*Br.*) че́рез понеде́льник; **last Monday ~** (*Br.*) в позапро́шлый понеде́льник; **in a ~** че́рез неде́лю; **I haven't seen him in, for ~s** я его́ давно́ не ви́дел; **he stays away for ~s** он неде́лями отсу́тствует; **from one ~ to the next** из неде́ли в неде́лю; **~ in, ~ out** (це́лыми) неде́лями; **three times a ~** три ра́за в неде́лю; **you're a ~ late with the rent** вы задержа́ли квартпла́ту на неде́лю; **I'm not at home during the ~** в бу́дние/рабо́чие дни меня́ не быва́ет до́ма; **I'll come some time during the ~** я ка́к-нибудь загляну́ на неде́ле; **~'s wages** неде́льное жа́лованье; **work a 40-hour ~** рабо́тать (*impf.*) со́рок часо́в в неде́лю; **working ~** рабо́чая неде́ля; **I'm off on a ~'s holiday** я уезжа́ю на неде́лю в о́тпуск.

● *cpds.* **~day** *n.* бу́дний/рабо́чий день; **my ~day clothes** моя́ бу́дничная оде́жда; **~end** *n.* коне́ц неде́ли, суббо́та и воскресе́нье, уикэ́нд; **we get up late at the ~end** по суббо́там и воскресе́ньям мы встаём по́здно; **~-long** *adj.* продолжа́ющийся неде́лю; неде́льный.

weekly /ˈwiːklɪ/ *n.* еженеде́льник.

● *adj.* (*once a week*) еженеде́льный.

● *adv.* еженеде́льно; ка́ждую неде́лю.

weeny /ˈwiːnɪ/ *adj.* (**weenier, weeniest**) (*coll.*) кро́хотный, малю́сенький.

weep /wiːp/ *n.* плач, рыда́ние; **she had a good ~** она́ как сле́дует (*or* хороше́нько) вы́плакалась.

● *v.t.* (*past and p.p.* **wept**) пла́кать, за-; **she wept bitter tears** она́ го́рько пла́кала; она́ пролила́ го́рькие слёзы.

● *v.i.* (*past and p.p.* **wept**) **1** (*shed tears*) пла́кать, за-; (*profusely*) рыда́ть (*impf.*); **I wept to see him go** мне бы́ло жа́лко до слёз, что он ушёл/уе́хал; **~ over, for** (*bewail*) опла́кивать (*impf.*); **she wept over her misfortune** она́

оплáкивала своё несчáстье; **he was ~ing** (*mourning*) **for his mother** он оплáкивал свою́ мать; **the child was ~ing for its mother** ребёнок плáкал и звал свою́ мать.
2: **~ing willow** плаку́чая и́ва.
3 (*of a wound*) мóкнуть (*impf.*).

weepy /'wi:pɪ/ *adj.* (**weepier, weepiest**) (*coll.*): **I feel ~** у меня́ в глазáх защипáло.

weevil /'wi:vɪl/ *n.* долгонóсик.

wee-wee /'wi:wi:/ (*Br.*) *n.* пи-пи́ (*nt. indecl.*) (*coll.*).
● *v.i.* (**wee-wees, wee-weed**) дéлать, с- пи-пи́; ходи́ть, с- по-мáленькому.

w.e.f. (*abbr. of* ***with effect from***) (*Br.*) вступáющий в си́лу с + *g.*

weft /weft/ *n.* утóк.

weigh /weɪ/ *v.t.* **1** (*find or test weight of*) взвé|шивать, -сить; вéшать, с-; **~ something in one's hand** взвéшивать (*impf.*) что-н. в рукé; **~ o.s.** взвé|шиваться, -ситься; (*fig., consider; assess; compare*) взвé|шивать, -сить; обду́м|ывать, -ать; оцéн|ивать, -и́ть; **~ the consequences** взвé|шивать, -сить послéдствия; **~ one's words** взвé|шивать, -сить (свои́) словá.
2 (*of ~ed object: amount to*) вéсить (*impf.*); **my luggage ~s 20 kilos** мой багáж вéсит 20 килогрáмм(ов); **what do you ~?** скóлько вы вéсите?; какóй у вас вес?; **I ~ too much** я вéшу сли́шком мнóго.
3: **~ anchor** сн|имáться, -я́ться с я́коря.
● *v.i.* **1** (*fig., be a burden*): **~ on** дави́ть (*impf.*) на + *a.*, угнетáть (*impf.*), гнести́ (*impf.*); **there is something ~ing on his mind** егó что-то гнетёт, он чем-то подáвлен; **the crime ~ed heavy on his conscience** преступлéние лежáло тя́жким брéменем на егó сóвести.
2 (*fig., have influence or importance*) (*of person*) имéть (*impf.*) вес/влия́ние; (*of fact, event*) имéть (*impf.*) значéние/влия́ние; **her evidence will ~ against him** её показáния бу́дут не в егó пóльзу.
● *with advs.*: **~ down** *v.t.* (*burden*) отяго|щáть, -ти́ть; **the branches were ~ed down with, by fruit** вéтви гну́лись под тя́жестью плодóв; (*fig., be burdensome to*) угнетáть (*impf.*); тяготи́ть (*impf.*); **he was ~ed down with cares** он был угнетён/подáвлен забóтами; **~ in** *v.i.* (*be ~ed before contest*) взвé|шиваться, -ситься пéред соревновáнием; (*coll., intervene forcefully*): **they ~ed in with a powerful argument** они́ вы́двинули си́льный аргумéнт/дóвод; **~ out** *v.t.* отвé|шивать, -сить; **he ~ed out half a pound of cheese** он отвéсил полфу́нта сы́ра; *v.i.* (*of sportsman*) взвé|шиваться, -ситься пéред состязáнием; **~ up** *v.t.* (*lit., fig.*) взвé|шивать, -сить.
● *cpds.* **~bridge** *n.* весы́-платфóрма; **~-in** *n.* (*sport*) взвéшивание пéред состязáнием; **~ing machine** *n.* весы́(-автомáт).

weight /weɪt/ *n.* **1** (*heaviness*) вес; **3lbs in ~** вéсом в три фу́нта; **goods sold by ~** товáр, продаю́щийся на вес; **he gave me short ~** он меня́ обвéсил; **what is your ~?** скóлько вы вéсите?; какóй у вас вес?; **we are the same ~** у нас одинáковый вес; **I have to watch my ~** мне прихóдится следи́ть за фигу́рой/вéсом; **gain, put on ~** приб|авля́ть, -áвить в вéсе; попр|авля́ться, -áвиться; **lose ~** теря́ть, по- в вéсе; худéть, по-; **he is under/over ~** он вéсит сли́шком мáло/мнóго; **he is worth his ~ in gold** таки́е как он — на вес зóлота; **pull one's ~** (*fig.*) выполня́ть, вы́полнить свою́ дóлю рабóты; **throw one's ~ about** (*fig.*) распоряжáться (*impf.*), вáжничать (*impf.*).
2 (*load*) тя́жесть, груз; (*fig.*) брéмя (*nt.*); **the pillars take all the ~** колóнны несу́т всю нагру́зку; **under its own ~** под сóбственной тя́жестью; **that chair won't take, stand your ~** э́тот стул не вы́держит вáшего вéса; **don't put too much ~ on that shelf** не перегружáйте э́ту пóлку; **it was a great ~ off my mind** у меня́ кáмень с души́ свали́лся; **~ of responsibility** брéмя отвéтственности; **dead ~** мёртвый груз; (*pressure*) нажи́м; (*impact*) си́ла удáра; **they bore the main ~ of the attack** они́ при́няли на себя́ глáвный удáр.
3 (*object for weighing or ~ing*) ги́ря; **a 2lb ~** двухфунтóвая ги́ря.
4 (*importance; influence*) вес; влия́ние; авторитéт; **the ~ of evidence is against him** все свидéтельства прóтив негó; **his opinion carries great ~** с егó мнéнием óчень считáются; он пóльзуется больши́м влия́нием/авторитéтом; **this adds ~ to his words** э́то придаёт вес егó словáм.
● *v.t.* **1** (*attach a ~ to; make heavier*) утяжел|я́ть, -и́ть; **a stick ~ed with lead** пáлка, утяжелённая свинцóм.
2 (*add compensatory factor to*): **London ~ing** (*Br.*) тари́фная надбáвка для рабóтающих в Лóндоне; **the system was ~ed in their favour** (*Br.*), **favor** (*US*) систéма обеспéчивала им привилéгии.
● *with adv.*: **~ down** *v.t.* = **weigh down**
● *cpds.* **~-lifter** *n.* штанги́ст; **~-lifting** *n.* поднятие тя́жестей; **~-watcher** *n.* человéк, стремя́щийся сбрóсить ли́шний вес.

weightless /'weɪtlɪs/ *adj.* невесóмый.

weightlessness /'weɪtlɪsnɪs/ *n.* невесóмость.

weighty /'weɪtɪ/ *adj.* (**weightier, weightiest**) (*heavy*) тяжёлый, гру́зный; (*important*) вáжный, весóмый; (*influential*) авторитéтный.

weir /wɪə(r)/ *n.* плоти́на, водосли́в.

weird /wɪəd/ *adj.* **1** (*unearthly, uncanny*) таи́нственный, сверхъестéственный.
2 (*strange, frightening*) стрáнный, жу́ткий.

weirdness /'wɪədnɪs/ *n.* таи́нственность, стрáнность; жу́ткость.

weirdo /'wɪədəʊ/ *n.* (*pl.* **~s**) чуди́ло, оригинáл (*coll.*).

welcome /'welkəm/ *n.* приём, привéтствие; **bid s.o. ~** привéтствовать (*impf.*) когó-н.; **they gave us a warm ~** они́ нас раду́шно при́няли; **he outstayed his ~** он пересидéл; он злоупотреби́л гостеприи́мством (свои́х) хозя́ев.
● *adj.* **1** (*gladly received*) желáнный; **a ~ guest** желáнный/дорогóй гость; **this is ~ news** э́то приятное извéстие; **make s.o. (feel) ~** окáз|ывать, -áть комý-н. раду́шный приём.
2 (*pred., ungrudgingly permitted*): **you are ~ to take it** пожáлуйста, бери́те!; **anyone is ~ to my share** я с удовóльствием уступлю́ свою́ дóлю комý угóдно; **you're ~ to try** пожáлуйста, (по)прóбуйте; **you're ~!** (*no thanks are required*) пожáлуйста!; нé за что!; (*when eating*) на здорóвье!
● *v.t.* привéтствовать (*impf.*); встр|ечáть, -éтить тепло́/раду́шно; **she ~d her guests at the door** онá привéтствовала гостéй в дверя́х; **a welcoming smile** привéтливая улы́бка; **I ~ the suggestion** я привéтствую э́то предложéние; **I would ~ the opportunity** я был бы рад (такóму) слу́чаю; **his arrival was ~d by all** все рáдовались егó приéзду/появлéнию; **they were ~d by gunfire** их встрéтили артиллери́йским огнём.
● *int.* добрó пожáловать!; ми́лости прóсим!

weld /weld/ *n.* сварнóе соединéние; сварнóй шов.
● *v.t. & i.* свáр|ивать(ся), -и́ть(ся); (*fig.*) спл|áчивать(ся), -оти́ть(ся); спá|ивать(ся), -я́ть(ся).
● *with advs.*: **~ on** *v.t.* привáр|ивать, -и́ть; припá|ивать, -я́ть; **~ together** *v.t.* (*lit., fig.*) свáр|ивать, -и́ть; спá|ивать, -я́ть; (*fig.*) спл|áчивать, -оти́ть; спá|ивать, -я́ть.

welder /'weldə(r)/ *n.* свáрщик.

welding /'weldɪŋ/ *n.* свáрка; **arc ~** дуговáя свáрка; **~ torch** свáрочная горéлка.

welfare /'welfeə(r)/ *n.* (*well-being*) благополу́чие; (*prosperity*) благосостоя́ние; (*organized provision for social needs*) социáльное обеспéчение; социáльная пóмощь; (*US, social security*) посóбие (по безрабóтице *и т.п.*); **he's on ~** (*US*) он получáет посóбие; **the W~ State** госудáрство всеóбщего благосостоя́ния/благодéнствия; **~ work** (*charity*) благотвори́тельность.

well¹ /wel/ *n.* (*for water*) колóдец; (*for oil*) нефтянáя сквáжина; (*mineral spring*) истóчник.
● *v.i.* (*spring up; gush*) бить (*impf.*) ключóм; хлы́нуть (*pf.*); **tears ~ed up in her eyes** её глазá напóлнились слезáми.
● *cpds.* **~-head** *n.* (*source*) истóчник, родни́к, ключ; **~-water** *n.* колóдезная водá.

well² /wel/ *adj.* (**better, best**) (*usu. pred.*) **1** (*in good health*) здорóвый; **I haven't been ~** мне нездорóвилось, я был нездорóв; **I am quite ~ again** я совсéм вы́здоровел/попрáвился; **he is not a ~ man** он нездорóвый человéк;

you don't look ~ вы пло́хо вы́глядите.
2 (*right, satisfactory*): **all's ~** всё хорошо́/прекра́сно; всё в поря́дке; **~ and good** (ну и) прекра́сно.
3 (*Br., well off, fortunate*): **you are ~ out of his company** ва́ше сча́стье, что вы (бо́льше) с ним не обща́етесь.
4 (*as n.*): **leave ~** (*US also* **~ enough**) **alone** от добра́ добра́ не и́щут.
5: **(just) (as) ~** (*advisable*): **it would be (as) ~ to ask** не меша́ло бы (*or* сто́ило б) спроси́ть; **it may be as ~ to explain** пожа́луй, сто́ит объясни́ть; (*fortunate*): **'I'll pay' — 'That's just as ~, because I have no money'** «Я заплачу́» — «Хорошо́ — я без де́нег»; *see also adv.*, 10.
6: **~ enough; all very ~** (*tolerable*) вполне́ го́дный; сно́сный; неплохо́й; **that's all very ~, but ...** всё э́то хорошо́ (*or* э́то прекра́сно), но. . . .
7: **all very ~** (*easy, convenient*): **it's all very ~ for you, you're not a woman** ва́м легко́ — вы не же́нщина!; **it's all very ~ to say that afterwards** легко́ говори́ть за́дним число́м.

● *adv.* (**better, best**) **1** (*satisfactorily*) хорошо́; **I did not sleep ~** я пло́хо спал; **~ done!** здо́рово!; молоде́ц!; **extremely ~** великоле́пно, отли́чно; **perfectly ~** прекра́сно; **pretty ~** вполне́ хорошо́; (*nearly*) почти́; (*considerably*) значи́тельно.
2 (*very, thoroughly; properly*) о́чень, весьма́, хороше́нько (*coll.*); **I was ~ pleased** я был о́чень дово́лен; **~ done** (*of food*) (хорошо́) прожа́ренный; **I am ~ aware of it** я э́то прекра́сно зна́ю; **~ and truly** оконча́тельно, реши́тельно; **they were ~ and truly beaten** они́ бы́ли разби́ты на́голову (*or* в пух и прах); **you are ~ able to do this yourself** вы прекра́сно мо́жете с э́тим спра́виться са́ми; **the picture was ~ worth £2,000** э́та карти́на вполне́ сто́ила двух ты́сяч фу́нтов.
3 (*considerably*: *esp. with advs. & preps.*) гора́здо; далеко́; **~ up in the list** в са́мом нача́ле спи́ска; **~ over retiring age** гора́здо ста́рше пенсио́нного во́зраста; **~ past 40** далеко́ за со́рок; **~ into the night** далеко́ за́ полночь.
4 (*favourably*): **~ off** бога́тый; состоя́тельный; **~ off for** обеспе́ченный + *i.*; **he doesn't know when he's ~ off** он не зна́ет своего́ сча́стья; **I wish him ~** я жела́ю ему́ благополу́чия; **his teacher thinks ~ of him** учи́тель о нём хоро́шего мне́ния (*or* хорошо́ отзыва́ется).
5 (*fortunately, successfully*) уда́чно, благополу́чно; **all went ~** всё прошло́ благополу́чно; **he did very ~ for himself** он прекра́сно устро́ился.
6 (*comfortably, affluently*): **live ~** жить (*impf.*) в доста́тке; **do o.s. ~** ни в чём себе́ не отка́зывать (*impf.*).
7 (*wisely*) разу́мно, пра́вильно; **he did ~ to ask for his money back** он пра́вильно сде́лал, что попроси́л де́ньги наза́д; **you would do ~ to insure your luggage** вам бы сле́довало застрахова́ть свой бага́ж; **you would be ~ advised to stay** бы́ло бы благоразу́мно с ва́шей стороны́ оста́ться.
8 (*probably, indeed, reasonably*): **it may ~ be true** э́то вполне́ возмо́жно; **you may ~ ask** вопро́с нели́шний; **you may ~ be surprised** вы име́ете все основа́ния удивля́ться; **we might ~ try** о́чень сто́ит попыта́ться.
9: **as ~** (*in addition*) то́же; та́кже; вдоба́вок; сверх того́; **there was meat as ~ as fish** там была́ не то́лько ры́ба, но и мя́со; там бы́ли и ры́ба и мя́со.
10: **as ~** (*with equal reason or profit*) с таки́м же основа́нием/успе́хом; **(you, he** *etc.*) **may, might as ~** (*expr. recommendation*) (вам, ему́ *и т.п.*) не меша́ло бы; пожа́луй; почему́ бы не; **you may as ~ take an umbrella** на вся́кий слу́чай прихвати́те (*or* сто́ит захвати́ть) зо́нтик с собо́й; *cf. adj.*, ⇒**5.**

● *int.* ну; ну а; (*expr. surprise*) ну!; вот те раз!; **~, I never!** вот те на́!; на́до же!; **~, ~!** ну и ну!; (*expr. expectation*): **~ then?** ну как?; ну так что же?; (*impatient or emphatic interrogation*): **~, what do you want?** ну, так чего́ вы хоти́те?; **~, what's it about?** ну, в чём де́ло?; (*agreement*): **very ~, I'll do it** хорошо́, я э́то сде́лаю; (*concession*): **~, you can come if you like** что ж(е), е́сли хоти́те, приходи́те; **ah, ~, in that case** а, ну, в тако́м слу́чае; (*resignation*): **oh ~, it can't be helped** (ну) что ж, ничего́ не поде́лаешь; (*summing up*) ну вот; **~ then** (ну) так вот; (*resumption*): **~, as I was saying** ита́к, как я говори́л; (*indecision, explanation*): **~, I'm not sure** ви́дите ли, я не уве́рен; **~, I only arrived today** ви́дите ли, я то́лько сего́дня прие́хал.

● *cpds.* **~-aimed** *adj.* ме́ткий; **~-appointed** *adj.* хорошо́ обору́дованный/снаряжённый; **~-armed** *adj.* хорошо́ вооружённый; **~-balanced** *adj.* уравнове́шенный, разу́мный; **a ~-balanced diet** рациона́льная дие́та; **~-behaved** *adj.* (благо)воспи́танный; хоро́шего поведе́ния; **~-being** *n.* благополу́чие, благосостоя́ние; **~-born** *adj.* хоро́шего/благоро́дного происхожде́ния; **~-bred** *adj.* (благо)воспи́танный; **~-built** *adj.* (*person*) хорошо́ сложённый, чёткий; **~-chosen** *adj.* уда́чно подо́бранный; **~-connected** *adj.* име́ющий (ро́дственные) свя́зи (в вы́сшем све́те); **~-defined** *adj.* отчётливый, определённый; **~-deserved** *adj.* заслу́женный; **~-disposed** *adj.* благожела́тельный, благоскло́нный; **~-dressed** *adj.* хорошо́ оде́тый; **~-earned** *adj.* заслу́женный; **~-educated** *adj.* хорошо́ образо́ванный; **~-fed** *adj.* сы́тый; (*of animals*) отко́рмленный; (*fat*) то́лстый; **~-founded, ~-grounded** *adjs.* обосно́ванный, аргументи́рованный; **~-groomed** *adj.* ухо́женный, хо́леный; **~-grounded** *adj.* = **~-founded; ~-heeled** *adj.* (*coll.*) состоя́тельный; **~-informed** *adj.* зна́ющий; све́дущий; хорошо́ осведомлённый; **~-intentioned** *adj.* (*of person*) де́йствующий из лу́чших побужде́ний; (*of deed*) сде́ланный из лу́чших побужде́ний; **~-judged** *adj.* проду́манный, разу́мный; **~-kept, ~-run** *adjs.* содержа́щийся в поря́дке; **the date was a ~-kept secret** да́та держа́лась в глубо́кой та́йне; **~-knit** *adj.* (*fig.*) сплочённый, кре́пкий; **~-known** *adj.* (*of person*) изве́стный; знамени́тый; (*of facts*) (обще-)изве́стный; **~-made** *adj.* хорошо́/иску́сно/мастерски́ сде́ланный; **~-mannered** *adj.* воспи́танный; с хоро́шими мане́рами; **~-matched** *adj.* подходя́щий; **~-meaning** *adj.* (*of person*) де́йствующий из лу́чших побужде́ний; **~-meant** *adj.* сде́ланный/ска́занный из лу́чших побужде́ний; **~-nigh** *adv.* (*liter.*) почти́; **~-off** *adj.* состоя́тельный; зажи́точный; **~-oiled** *adj.* (*coll., drunk*) косо́й (*coll.*); подвы́пивший; **~-ordered, ~-regulated, ~-run** *adjs.* хорошо́ организо́ванный; **~-paid** *adj.* хорошо́ опла́чиваемый; **~-preserved** *adj.* (*of person*) хорошо́ сохрани́вшийся; **~-read** *adj.* начи́танный; **~-regulated** *adj.* = **~-ordered; ~-rounded** *adj.* окру́глый; (*fig.*) закруглённый; **~-run** *adj.* = **~-ordered, ~-kept; ~-situated** *adj.* хорошо́/удо́бно располо́женный; **~-spent** *adj.* потра́ченный не зря (*or* с то́лком); **~-spoken** *adj.*: **he is ~-spoken** он прекра́сно владе́ет языко́м; у него́ бога́тая речь; **~-taken** *adj.* (*argument*) ме́ткий; **~-thought-of** *adj.* уважа́емый, по́льзующийся хоро́шей репута́цией; **~-thought-out** *adj.* проду́манный; **~-timed** *adj.* то́чно/хорошо́ рассчи́танный; своевре́менный; (*words/act*) ска́занный/сде́ланный кста́ти; **~-to-do** *adj.* состоя́тельный; зажи́точный; обеспе́ченный; **~-trained** *adj.* вы́ученный, обу́ченный; **~-tried** *adj.* испы́танный, прове́ренный; **~-trodden** *adj.* проторённый, исхо́женный; **~-turned** *adj.* (*of speech etc.*) отто́ченный; **~-wisher** *n.* доброжела́тель (*fem.* -ница); **~-worn** *adj.* (*lit.*) поно́шенный; (*fig., trite*) изби́тый, иста́сканный.

wellington /ˈwelɪŋt(ə)n/ *n.* (*also* **~ boot**) (*Br.*) рези́новый сапо́г.

welly /ˈwelɪ/ *n.* (*Br. coll.*) **1** = **wellington. 2** (*vigour*) си́ла, эне́ргия.

Welsh /welʃ/ *n.* **1**: **the ~** (*pl., people*) валли́йцы (*m. pl.*), уэ́льсцы (*m. pl.*). **2** (*language*) валли́йский язы́к.
● *adj.* валли́йский, уэ́льский; **~ rabbit, rarebit** грено́к с сы́ром.
● *cpds.* **~man** *n.* валли́ец, уэ́льсец; **~woman** *n.* валли́йка.

welsh /welʃ/ *v.i.* (*coll.*) скр|ыва́ться, -ы́ться не уплати́в до́лга; **~ on s.o.** обст|авля́ть, -а́вить кого́-н.

welt /welt/ *n.* (*of shoe*) рант; (*weal*) рубе́ц (*от удара плетью и т.п.*); (*border of garment*) обта́чка.

Weltanschauung /ˌveltɑːnˈʃaʊʊŋ/ *n.* (*pl.* **~en** /-ən/) мировоззре́ние.

welter /ˈweltə(r)/ *n.* (*confusion*) сумбу́р, пу́таница; (*disorderly mixture*) хаос; **a**

W

~ of new ideas це́лый пото́к но́вых иде́й.

● *v.i.* (*roll; wallow*) валя́ться (*impf.*); бара́хтаться (*impf.*); **~ in one's blood** лежа́ть (*impf.*) в лу́же кро́ви.

● *cpd.* **~-weight** *n.* боксёр/боре́ц второ́го полусре́днего ве́са.

wench /wentʃ/ *n.* де́вка.

wend /wend/ *v.t.*: **~ one's way** держа́ть (*impf.*) путь.

went /went/ *past of* ⇨**go**

wept /wept/ *past and p.p. of* ⇨**weep**

were /wɜː/, /wə/ *2nd pers. sing. past, pl. past, and past subj. of* ⇨**be**

werewolf /ˈwɪəwʊlf/, /ˈweə-/ *n.* (*pl.* **werewolves**) (*myth.*) челове́к-волк, вервольф.

west /west/ *n.* за́пад; **in the ~** на за́паде; **to the ~ of** к за́паду от + *g.*; за́паднее + *g.*; **the W~** (*pol.*) За́пад; **the Wild W~** ди́кий за́пад; **W~ country** за́падная часть А́нглии; **W~ End** (*of London*) Уэст-Э́нд; **W~ German** (*hist.*) *adj.* западногерма́нский; *n.* жи́тель (*fem.* -ница) За́падной Герма́нии; **W~ Germany** (*hist.*) За́падная Герма́ния; **W~ Indian** *adj.* вест-и́ндский; *n.* вест-и́нд|ец (*fem.* -ка); **W~ Indies** *n. pl.* Вест-И́ндия; **~ wind** за́падный ве́тер.

● *adv.* к за́паду; на за́пад; **due ~ of** пря́мо на за́пад от + *g.*

● *cpds.* **~bound** *adj.* дви́жущийся на за́пад; **~-north-~** *adv.* вест-норд-ве́ст; **~-south-~** *adv.* вест-зюйд-ве́ст.

westerly /ˈwestəlɪ/ *n.* (*wind*) за́падный ве́тер.

● *adj.* за́падный.

western /ˈwest(ə)n/ *n.* (*film*) ве́стерн, ковбо́йский фильм; (*book*) ковбо́йский рома́н.

● *adj.* за́падный.

● *cpd.* **~most** *adj.* са́мый за́падный.

westerner /ˈwestənə(r)/ *n.* жи́тель (*m.*) (*fem.* -ница) за́пада.

westernization /ˌwestənaɪˈzeɪʃ(ə)n/ *n.* внедре́ние за́падного о́браза жи́зни.

westernize /ˈwestəˌnaɪz/ *v.t.* внедр|я́ть, -и́ть за́падный о́браз жи́зни в + *a.*

westward /ˈwestwəd/ *n.*: **to (the) ~** к за́паду, на за́пад.

● *adj.* за́падный.

westwards /ˈwestwədz/ *adv.* к за́паду; на за́пад.

wet /wet/ *n.* **1** (*liquid; moisture*): **there is some ~ on the floor** пол мо́крый. **2** (*rain*): **come in out of the ~** входи́те, не сто́йте под дождём!

● *adj.* (**wetter, wettest**) **1** (*covered, soaked or splashed with water etc.*) мо́крый; **~ through** (*or* **to the skin**) промо́кший наскво́зь/до ни́тки; **grass ~ with dew** роси́стая трава́; трава́, покры́тая росо́й; **her cheeks were ~ with tears** её лицо́ бы́ло мо́крым от слёз; **my feet are ~** у меня́ промо́кли но́ги; **get ~** пром|ока́ть, -о́кнуть; **I got my suit ~** мой костю́м промо́к; **~ dream** (*coll.*) эроти́ческий сон, вызыва́ющий поллю́цию; **~ fish** све́жая (некопчёная) ры́ба; **~ suit** гидрокостю́м; **he's still ~ behind the ears** (*coll.*) у него́ молоко́ ещё на губа́х не обсо́хло. **2** (*rainy*) дождли́вый; **it looks like being ~ today** похо́же, что день бу́дет дождли́вым; **we are in for a ~ spell** наступа́ет пери́од дожде́й. **3** (*not dry*) сыро́й, вла́жный; **~ paint** све́жая кра́ска; **'W~ Paint'** «осторо́жно, окра́шено!»; **the ink was still ~** черни́ла ещё не просо́хли. **4** (*Br. coll., inept; spineless*) вя́лый, малоду́шный.

● *v.t.* (**wetting;** *past and p.p.* **~** *or* **wetted**) (*make ~*) мочи́ть, на-; см|а́чивать, -очи́ть; увлажн|я́ть, -и́ть; **the child ~ itself** ребёнок обмочи́лся/ опи́сался (*coll.*); **the child ~ its bed** ребёнок описа́л посте́ль; **the child ~s its bed** ребёнок мо́чится в посте́ли.

● *cpds.* **~ blanket** *n.* (*fig.*) челове́к, отравля́ющий други́м удово́льствие; ну́дный челове́к; **~-nurse** *n.* корми́лица; *v.t.* корми́ть (*impf.*) гру́дью; (*fig.*) ня́ньчиться (*impf.*) с + *i.*

wether /ˈweðə(r)/ *n.* валу́х; кастри́рованный бара́н.

wetness /ˈwetnɪs/ *n.* вла́жность, сы́рость.

whack /wæk/ *n.* (*blow*) уда́р; (*sound of blow*) звук уда́ра; (*Br. coll., share*) зако́нная до́ля; (*coll., attempt*): **have a ~** пыта́ться, по-.

● *v.t.* (*coll., beat*) бить, по-; колоти́ть, от-; **I feel ~ed** (*Br., exhausted*) я чу́вствую себя́ вконе́ц разби́тым.

whacking /ˈwækɪŋ/ *n.* по́рка.

● *adj. & adv.* (*Br. sl.*) здоро́вый, здорове́нный; **a ~ (great) lie** грандио́зная ложь.

whacko[1] /ˈwækəʊ/ *int.* (*Br.*) здо́рово!; блеск! (*coll.*).

whacko[2] /ˈwækəʊ/ = **wacko**

whacky /ˈwækɪ/ = **wacky**

whale /weɪl/ *n.* (*pl.* **~** *or* **~s**) **1** кит. **2**: **a ~ of a ...** (*coll., exceedingly good*) замеча́тельный, потряса́ющий; **we had a ~ of a time** мы потряса́юще/ здо́рово провели́ вре́мя.

● *cpds.* **~-boat** *n.* вельбо́т; **~bone** *n.* кито́вый ус; **~-oil** *n.* кито́вый жир.

whaler /ˈweɪlə(r)/ *n.* (*man*) китобо́й; (*ship*) китобо́ец, китобо́йное су́дно.

whaling /ˈweɪlɪŋ/ *n.* охо́та на кито́в; китобо́йный про́мысел.

wham /wæm/ *n.* уда́р; (*int.*) бум!; хлоп!

● *v.t.* (**whammed, whamming**) уд|аря́ть, -а́рить в + *a.*

wharf /wɔːf/ *n.* (*pl.* **wharves** *or* **wharfs**) при́стань.

● *v.t.* (*moor at ~*) швартова́ть, при-; прича́ли|вать, -ть.

wharfage /ˈwɔːfɪdʒ/ *n.* (*accommodation*) прича́л, прича́льное сооруже́ние; (*charge*) прича́льный сбор.

wharves /wɔːvz/ *pl. of* ⇨**wharf**

what /wɒt/ *pron.* **1** (*interrog.*) что?; **~'s that?** что э́то (тако́е)?; **~ (did you say)?** что (вы сказа́ли)?; что?; **~, me?** что, я?; кто, я?; **~ is that in Russian?** как э́то по-ру́сски?; **~ is it?; ~'s the matter?** в чём де́ло?; **~ stung me?** кто меня́ укуси́л?; **~ is he?** (*by occupation*) чем он занима́ется?; кто он?; кем он рабо́тает?; **~ is she like?** (*in appearance*) как она́ вы́глядит?; (*in character*) кака́я она́?; **~ do you want to be?** (*to a child*) кем ты хо́чешь стать?; **~ (sex) is their new baby?** кто у них роди́лся: ма́льчик и́ли де́вочка?; **~'s the weather like?** кака́я пого́да?; **~ does it look like?** как э́то вы́глядит?; **~ does it taste like?** каково́ э́то на вкус?; **~ was the film like?** ну, как фильм?; **~ is the price?; ~ does it cost?** ско́лько э́то сто́ит?; **~'s the date?** како́е сего́дня число́?; **~ is his name?** как его́ зову́т?; как его́ фами́лия?; **~ are their names?** как их зову́т?; **~'s the news?** каки́е но́вости?; что слы́шно но́вого?; **~ do you think?** как вы ду́маете?; каково́ ва́ше мне́ние?; **~ about money?** а де́ньги?; как насчёт де́нег?; **~ about the cat?** как быть с ко́шкой?; **~ about it?** (*what relevance has it?*) ну и что из э́того?; (*shall we?*) ну так как?; **~ about a walk?** не пройти́сь ли нам?; **~ of it?** ну и (да́льше) что?; ну, и (так) что ж?; **~ does it matter?** како́е э́то име́ет значе́ние?; **~ more can I say?** что я могу́ ещё сказа́ть?; **~ for?** заче́м?; к чему́?; **~ is this box for?** для чего́ э́та коро́бка?; **~ (ever) did you come for?** заче́м (то́лько) вы пришли́?; **~ do I want this money for?** на что мне э́ти де́ньги?; **I'll give you ~ for!** я вам покажу́/дам!; **~ are you talking about?** о чём вы говори́те?; **~'s up?** (*coll.*) в чём де́ло?; что случи́лось?; **~ next!** ещё чего́!; до чего́ дошли́!; **~ then?** (*in that case*) (*also* **so ~?,** *coll.*) ну и что?; (**~** *do we do then?*) что тогда́ (де́лать)?; (**~** *happened then?*) а да́льше что?; **~ if ...?** а что, е́сли...?; а вдруг...?; **~ if he refuses (after all)?** а что, е́сли он отка́жется?; **are you trying to be funny or ~?** вы что, шу́тите?; **... and ~ not, and ~ have you** (*coll.*) и так да́лее. **2** (*rel.: that which; the things which*) (то), что; **~ is so annoying is ...** что осо́бенно доса́дно, э́то...; **and, ~ is more ...** к тому́ же...; бо́льше/ма́ло того́,...; **~ I like is music** что я люблю́, так э́то му́зыку; **~ is missing is a guarantee** чего́ нет (*or* не хвата́ет) — э́то гара́нтии; **he is sorry for ~ happened** он жале́ет о случи́вшемся; **this is ~ I mean** вот что я име́ю в виду́; **tell me ~ you remember** расскажи́те мне всё, что по́мните; **give me ~ you can** да́йте мне́, ско́лько мо́жете; **she knows ~'s ~** она́ зна́ет, что к чему́; **I'll see ~ I can do** я постара́юсь сде́лать, что могу́; **(do) you know ~?; I'll tell you ~!** зна́ете что?; вот что я вам скажу́!; **~ with one thing and another** то из-за одного́, то из-за друго́го; **~ with all these interruptions, we never got finished** со все́ми э́тими переры́вами мы ника́к не могли́ ко́нчить. **3** (*whatever*): **I will do ~ I can** я сде́лаю (всё), что могу́; **say ~ you like, I think it's unfair** что бы вы ни говори́ли, по-мо́ему, э́то несправедли́во; **come ~ may** будь что бу́дет.

4 (*exclamatory*): **~ I wouldn't give for a cup of tea!** я бы всё о́тдал за ча́шку ча́я; **~ she must have suffered!** что она́ должна́ была́ пережи́ть!; **~ didn't we do!** чего́ мы то́лько не де́лали!; **~ a lot of ...** ско́лько +*g.*!

● *adj.* **1** (*interrog.*) како́й; како́в?; **~ colour** (*Br.*), **color** (*US*) **are his eyes?** како́го цве́та у него́ глаза́?; **~ chance is there of success?** каковы́ ша́нсы на успе́х?; **~ kind of (a)** како́й; **~ kind of a man are you?** что вы за челове́к?; **~ news is there?** что но́вого?; каки́е но́вости?; **~ time is it?** кото́рый час?; **~'s the use?** како́й смысл?
2 (*rel.*): **~ friends I make is no concern of yours** не ва́ше де́ло, с кем я дружу́; **~ little he published** то немно́гое, что он напеча́тал; **I gave him ~ money I had** я о́тдал ему́ все де́ньги, каки́е у меня́ бы́ли.
3 (*exclamatory*): **~ a fool he is!** како́й дура́к!, ну и дура́к же он!; **~ an idea!** (*bad idea*) что за иде́я!; **~ impudence!** кака́я/какова́ на́глость!; **~ a pity/shame!** кака́я жа́лость/доса́да; **~ weather!** кака́я (*or* что за *or* ну и) пого́да!; **~ was his surprise when ...** каково́ бы́ло его́ удивле́ние, когда́...; **~ lovely soup!** како́й прекра́сный суп!

● *cpds.* **~-d'ye-call-him, ~'s-his-name** *nn.* как его́ там?; как бишь его́?; **~-d'ye-call-it, ~'s it** *nn.* как его́; э́то са́мое....

whatever /wɒt'evə(r)/ *pron.*
1 (*anything that*): **do ~ you like** де́лайте, что хоти́те; де́лайте всё, что вам уго́дно; **~ I have is yours** всё моё — ва́ше.
2 (*no matter what*): **~ happens** что бы ни случи́лось.
3 (*what ever*): **~ are you doing?** что вы там де́лаете?, чем вы там за́няты?; **~ did you do that for?** ну, заче́м вы э́то сде́лали?; **~ is wrong?** в чём де́ло?; **~ next?** ещё чего́ захоте́ли/вы́думали!

● *adj.* **1** (*any*): **he took ~ food he could find** он забра́л всю пи́щу, каку́ю то́лько мог найти́.
2 (*no matter what*) како́й/каково́й бы ни; **~ friends we may offend** пусть ины́е друзья́ и обижа́ются.
3 (*emphasising neg. or interrog.*): **there is no doubt ~ of his guilt** в его́ вино́вности нет ни мале́йшего сомне́ния; **is there any chance ~ that he may recover?** есть ли хоть како́й-нибу́дь шанс, что он попра́вится?; **he will see no one ~** он абсолю́тно никого́ не принима́ет.

whatsoever /ˌwɒtsəʊ'evə(r)/ *pron.* = **whatever** *pron.* 1, 2

● *adj.* = **whatever** *adj.*

wheat /wi:t/ *n.* пшени́ца; **summer/winter ~** ярова́я/ози́мая пшени́ца.

wheatmeal /'wi:tmi:l/ *n.* части́чно просе́янная пшени́чная мука́.

Wheatstone bridge /'wi:tstəʊn/ *n.* (*electr.*) мо́ст(ик) сопротивле́ния.

wheedle /'wi:d(ə)l/ *v.t.* подоль|ща́ться, -сти́ться к + *d.*; **~ something out of s.o.** выпра́шивать, вы́просить что-н. у кого́-н.; выма́нивать, вы́манить что-н. у кого́-н. ле́стью.

wheel /wi:l/ *n.* **1** колесо́; **spare ~** запасно́е колесо́; **change a ~** (*on car*) меня́ть, по- (*or* смен|я́ть, -и́ть) колесо́; (*steering ~*) руль (*m.*); **he was at the ~** (*driving*) **for 12 hours** он сиде́л за рулём 12 часо́в; **big ~** (*on fairground*) колесо́ обозре́ния; чёртово колесо́; (*sl., bigwig*) (больша́я) ши́шка; **~ of fortune** колесо́ форту́ны; **break on the ~** колесова́ть (*impf., pf.*); (*potter's ~*) круг; **turn a pot on the ~** де́лать, с- горшо́к на гонча́рном кру́ге; **grinding ~** шлифова́льный круг; **oil the ~s** (*fig., bribe*) подма́з|ывать, -ать кого́-н. (*coll.*); **put a spoke in s.o.'s ~** (*fig.*) вст|авля́ть, -а́вить кому́-н. па́лки в колёса; **~s within ~s** (*fig.*) сло́жные интри́ги (*f. pl.*); та́йные пружи́ны (*f. pl.*)/влия́ния (*nt. pl*).
2 (*mil.*): **they carried out a right ~** они́ сде́лали поворо́т впра́во.

● *v.t.* ката́ть, вози́ть (*both indet.*); кати́ть, везти́ (*both det.*); **she ~ed the barrow/pram** она́ кати́ла/везла́ та́чку/коля́ску; **he ~ed his bicycle up the hill** он вкати́л велосипе́д на́ гору; **he was ~ed in in an invalid chair** его́ вкати́ли/ввезли́ на инвали́дной коля́ске.

● *v.i.* кружи́ть(ся) (*impf.*); **gulls were ~ing overhead** ча́йки кружи́ли(сь) над голово́й; **he ~ed round to face me** он кру́то поверну́лся ко мне (*or* в мою́ сто́рону).

● *cpds.* **~barrow** *n.* та́чка; **~base** *n.* колёсная ба́за; **~-chair** *n.* инвали́дная коля́ска; **~-house** *n.* рулева́я ру́бка; **~-spin** *n.* пробуксо́вка колёс; **~wright** *n.* колёсник; колёсный ма́стер.

wheeled /wi:ld/ *adj.* колёсный, на колёсах.

wheeler|-dealer /'wi:lə(r)/ *n.* (*coll.*) махина́тор; **~-dealing** махина́ции (*f. pl.*).

wheeze /wi:z/ *n.* (*chesty breathing*) хрип; сопе́ние; (*Br. sl., bright idea*) уда́чная мысль; (*scheme*) ло́вкий трюк.

● *v.i.* сопе́ть (*impf.*); хрипе́ть (*impf.*); дыша́ть (*impf.*) с при́свистом.

wheezy /'wi:zɪ/ *adj.* хри́плый; страда́ющий оды́шкой.

whelk /welk/ *n.* (*mollusc*) брюхоно́гий моллю́ск.

whelp /welp/ *n.* (*puppy, also fig.*) щено́к.

● *v.i.* щени́ться, о-.

when /wen/ *adv.* **1** (*interrog.*) когда́; **say ~!** (*to s.o. pouring a drink*) скажи́те, когда́ дово́льно.
2 (*rel.*): **there have been occasions ~** бы́ли слу́чаи, когда́...; **the day ~ I met you** день, когда́ я вас встре́тил.

● *with preps.*: **~ do you have to be there by?** к како́му ча́су вам ну́жно там быть?; **~ must it be ready for?** когда́ э́то должно́ быть гото́во?; **~ does it date from?** к како́му вре́мени э́то отно́сится?; **since ~?** как давно́?; с каки́х пор?; с како́го вре́мени?; **till, until ~?** до каки́х пор?; до како́го вре́мени?

● *conj.* когда́; как (то́лько); по́сле того́ как; тогда́, когда́; (*by the time that*) пока́; **~ she saw him, she ...** когда́ она́ уви́дела его́, она́...; **~ he was grown up, he ...** когда́ он стал взро́слым (*or* вы́рос), он...; **~ passing, he ...** когда́ он проходи́л ми́мо, он...; **~ young** в мо́лодости; (*and then*) и тогда́; как (вдруг); да вдруг; **he had just come in ~ the phone rang** едва́ он вошёл, как зазвони́л телефо́н; (*although*) хотя́; **they won ~ everyone thought they would lose** они́ вы́играли, хотя́ все ду́мали, что они́ проигра́ют; (*whereas*) в то вре́мя как; **how can he buy it ~ he has no money?** как он мо́жет э́то купи́ть, е́сли у него́ нет де́нег?

whence /wens/ *adv. & conj.* (*liter.*) (*interrog.*) (*also* **from ~**) отку́да; **~ this confusion?** отчего́ тако́е смяте́ние?; (*rel.*): **return it ~ it came** верни́те э́то по принадле́жности.

whenever /wen'evə(r)/ *adv. & conj.*
1 (*at whatever time*) когда́; **come ~ you like** приходи́те, когда́ уго́дно (*or* когда́ то́лько захоти́те); **~ he comes** когда́ бы он ни пришёл. **2** (*on every occasion when*) ка́ждый/вся́кий раз, когда́; **~ he speaks he stammers** он всегда́ заика́ется, когда́ говори́т.
3: **or ~** (*coll., at any time*) и́ли ещё когда́. **4** (*when ever?*) (*of past*) когда́ же; (*of future*) когда́ же (наконе́ц); **~ did you find time?** как то́лько вы нашли́ вре́мя?

whensoever /ˌwensəʊ'evə(r)/ *adv. & conj.* (*arch.*) = **whenever** 1, 2

where /weə(r)/ *adv.* **1** (*direct or indirect question*) где; (*whither*) куда́; **~ should we be without you?** что бы мы без вас де́лали?; **~'s the sense in that?** како́й (же) в э́том смысл?; **~ did he hit you?** куда́ он вас уда́рил?; **~ are you wounded?** куда́ вас ра́нило?
2 (*rel.*) где; **the hotel ~ we stopped** гости́ница, в кото́рой мы останови́лись; (*without antecedent*) там, где; **that's not ~ I left my coat** я не здесь/там оста́вил пальто́; **that's ~ you're wrong** вот где вы ошиба́етесь; **you can go ~ you please** мо́жете идти́, куда́ уго́дно; **making changes ~ necessary** де́лая исправле́ния там, где э́то необходи́мо.
3 (*US coll., that*): **I see in the paper ~ ...** в газе́те говори́тся, что/бу́дто....
4 (*whereas*) тогда́ как; ме́жду тем как; в то вре́мя как; (**in cases ~**) в тех слу́чаях, когда́.

● *with preps.*: **~ from?** отку́да?; (*of origin*): **~ does he come from?** отку́да он (ро́дом)?; **that's not far from ~ I live** э́то недалеко́ от того́ ме́ста, где я живу́; **~ to?** куда́?; **~ have you got to in the story?** до како́го ме́ста вы дочита́ли/дошли́?; **I've no idea ~ he can have got to** поня́тия не име́ю, куда́ он мог де́ться.

whereabouts /'weərəˌbaʊts/ *n.* местонахожде́ние.

● *adv.* где; **~ did you find it?** где вы э́то нашли́?

whereas /weər'æz/ *conj.* **1** (*while*) тогда́ как; в то вре́мя как; а; хотя́; ме́жду тем как; **she is always ill ~ he is always healthy** она́ всегда́ боле́ет, а он всегда́ здоро́в. **2** (*leg., since*) принима́я во внима́ние; поско́льку; учи́тывая, что.

W

whereat /weər'æt/ *adv.* (*liter.*) и тогда́; на э́то.

whereby /weə'baɪ/ *adv.* (*liter.*) посре́дством кото́рого; **he devised a plan ~ he might escape** он вы́работал план, с по́мощью кото́рого он собира́лся соверши́ть побе́г; **there is a rule ~ ...** существу́ет пра́вило, согла́сно кото́рому. . ..

wherefore /'weəfɔ:(r)/, /-'fɔ:(r)/ *n.*: **he wanted to know the why(s) and ~(s)** он хоте́л знать, как и почему́.

● *adv.* (*arch., why?*) отчего́?, почему́?, почто́? (*arch.*).

wherein /weər'ɪn/ *adv.* (*interrog., rel.*) где; в кото́ром; в чём.

whereof /weər'ɒv/ *rel. adv.* (*liter.*) о ко́ем; **the person ~ I spoke** челове́к, о кото́ром я говори́л.

whereon /weər'ɒn/ *rel. adv.* (*liter.*) на ко́ем.

wheresoever /,weəsəʊ'evə(r)/ *adv. & conj.* (*arch.*) = **wherever**

whereto /weə'tu:/ *rel. adv.* (*liter.*) к ко́ему.

whereupon /,weərə'pɒn/, /'weər-/ *adv.* (*and then*) по́сле чего́; всле́дствие чего́; тогда́.

wherever /weər'evə(r)/ *adj. & conj.* (*also* (*arch.*) **wheresoever**) где; куда́; **sit ~ you like** сади́тесь, куда́ уго́дно; **~ he goes he makes friends** где бы он ни оказа́лся, он приобрета́ет друзе́й; **or ~** (*coll.*) и́ли ещё где; (*where ever*): **~ are you going?** куда́ же вы идёте?

wherewithal /'weəwɪ,ðɔ:l/ *n.* (*coll.*) необходи́мые сре́дства; **I haven't the ~ to pay him** мне не́чем с ним расплати́ться.

wherry /'werɪ/ *n.* (*boat*) ло́дка, я́лик; (*Br., barge*) ба́ржа, ба́рка.

whet /wet/ *v.t.* (**whetted, whetting**) точи́ть, на-; (*fig.*) обостр|я́ть, -и́ть; возбу|жда́ть, -ди́ть.

● *cpd.* **~stone** *n.* точи́льный ка́мень; (*lit., fig.*) осело́к.

whether /'weðə(r)/ *conj.* **1** (*introducing indirect question*) ли; **I asked ~ he was coming with us** я спроси́л, пойдёт ли он с на́ми; **I don't know ~ she will come (or not)** я не зна́ю, придёт ли она́ (и́ли нет); **the question is ~ to go or stay** вопро́с в том — идти́ и́ли остава́ться; **I doubt ~ you understand** я не уве́рен, что вы понима́ете; **it depends on ~ I am free tonight** э́то зави́сит от того́, бу́ду ли я свобо́ден сего́дня ве́чером; **I am not interested in ~ you agree** меня́ не интересу́ет, согла́сны вы и́ли нет.

2 (*introducing alternative hypotheses*): **~ you like it or not, I shall go** нра́вится вам э́то и́ли нет, а я пойду́; **he was ignored, ~ by accident or design** случа́йно ли, и́ли наме́ренно, но о нём забы́ли; **~ or no** (*archaic, in any case*) в любо́м слу́чае; (*whether or not*): **~ he comes or no** придёт он и́ли нет.

whew /hwju:/ *int.* уф!

whey /weɪ/ *n.* сы́воротка.

which /wɪtʃ/ *pron.* **1** (*interrog.*) како́й, кото́рый; (*of person*) кто; **~ is the right answer?** како́й отве́т пра́вильный?; **~ is the way to the museum?** как пройти́ к музе́ю?; **~ of you?** кто/кото́рый из вас?; **~ of these bags is the heavier?** кото́рая из э́тих су́мок тяжеле́е?; **I cannot tell ~ is ~** (*of persons*) я ника́к не могу́ разобра́ться, кто из них кто; **~ do you want, milk or cream?** что вы предпочита́ете — молоко́ и́ли сли́вки?

2 (*rel., in defining and non-defining senses*) кото́рый; **the book (~) I was reading has gone** кни́га, кото́рую я чита́л, пропа́ла; **the hotel at ~ we stayed** гости́ница, в кото́рой (*or* где) мы жи́ли/останови́лись; (*with adj. or descriptive n. as antecedent*): **he looked like a boxer, ~ indeed he was** он был похо́ж на боксёра, каковы́м он, со́бственно, и явля́лся; (*with clause as antecedent*) что; **he refused, ~ I had expected** он отказа́л, чего́ я, со́бственно, и ожида́л.

● *adj.* **1** (*direct or indirect question*) како́й; **~ shoes are yours?** каки́е тут ту́фли ва́ши?; **~ film do you mean?** како́й фильм вы име́ете в виду́?; **~ brother runs the business?** кото́рый из бра́тьев возглавля́ет де́ло?; **do you know ~ horse won?** вы (не) зна́ете, кака́я ло́шадь вы́играла?

2 (*rel.*) како́й; кото́рый; каково́й; **ten years, during ~ time he spoke to nobody** де́сять лет, в тече́ние кото́рых он ни с кем не говори́л.

whichever /,wɪtʃ'evə(r)/ *pron. & adj.* **1** како́й бы ни, како́й уго́дно; **take ~ book you like** бери́те каку́ю уго́дно кни́гу; **~ way you go, you'll have plenty of time** како́й бы доро́гой вы ни пошли́, вы вполне́ успе́ете; **~ way you look at it** как бы вы на э́то ни смотре́ли; **do it by ~ method seems easiest** де́лайте э́то тем спо́собом, како́й вам ка́жется наибо́лее просты́м. **2** (*which ever*): **~ way did he go?** куда́ то́лько он пошёл?

whiff /wɪf/ *n.* дунове́ние; (*pleasant smell*) лёгкий арома́т; (*Br., unpleasant smell*) душо́к; (*smell*) за́пах; **~ of smoke** (*smell*) за́пах ды́ма; (*puff*) дымо́к; **a ~ of chloroform** вдох хлорофо́рма; **there was a ~ of scandal about the business** де́ло попа́хивало/отдава́ло сканда́лом; **I caught the ~ of a cigar** я почу́вствовал за́пах сига́ры; **he stepped out for a ~ of fresh air** он вы́шел подыша́ть (све́жим во́здухом).

Whig /wɪg/ *n.* (*hist.*) виг.

while /waɪl/ *n.* вре́мя; **where have you been all this ~?** где вы бы́ли всё э́то вре́мя?; **after a ~** че́рез не́которое вре́мя; **I am going away for a ~** я уезжа́ю ненадо́лго (*or* на не́которое вре́мя); **I haven't seen you for a long ~** я вас давно́ не ви́дел; **a long, good ~ ago** давны́м-давно́; **a short ~ before** незадо́лго до э́того; **a short ~ ago, back** неда́вно; **in a little, short ~** вско́ре, в ско́ром вре́мени; **it may take some (*or* quite a) ~** возмо́жно, что э́то бу́дет не ско́ро; **once in a ~** и́зредка; вре́мя от вре́мени; **it was well worth ~** э́то сто́ило затра́ченного вре́мени/труда́; **I will make it worth his ~** я постара́юсь, что́бы он не разочарова́лся.

● *v.t.*: **~** (*also* **wile**) **away:** корота́ть, с- (*время*).

● *conj.* (*also* **whilst**) **1** (*during the time that*) пока́; в то вре́мя, как; **be good ~ I'm away!** веди́ себя́ хорошо́, пока́ меня́ нет до́ма; **~ reading he fell asleep** за чте́нием (*or* чита́я) он засну́л; **~ asleep** во сне; **~ in Paris I visited the Louvre** во вре́мя (моего́) пребыва́ния в Пари́же, я посети́л Лувр.

2 (*whereas*) а; тогда́ как.

3 (*although*) хотя́; **~ not wishing to be awkward, I must object** не жела́я создава́ть тру́дности, я всё же вы́нужден протестова́ть.

whilst /waɪlst/ = **while** *conj.*

whim /wɪm/ *n.* при́хоть, капри́з.

whimper /'wɪmpə(r)/ *n.* (*of person*) хны́канье; (*of dog*) поску́ливание.

● *v.i.* (*of person*) хны́кать, по-; (*of a dog*) скули́ть (*impf.*).

whimsey /'wɪmzɪ/ = **whimsy**

whimsical /'wɪmzɪk(ə)l/ *adj.* (*fanciful*) причу́дливый; (*capricious*) капри́зный; (*humorous*) игри́вый.

whimsicality /,wɪmzɪ'kælɪtɪ/ *n.* причу́дливость; капри́зность; игри́вость.

whims|y, -ey /'wɪmzɪ/ *n.* при́хоть, причу́да, капри́з.

whin|e /waɪn/ *n.* вой; хны́канье; нытьё; **he spoke in a ~e** он говори́л плакси́вым/но́ющим/хны́чущим го́лосом; **the ~e of a shell** вой снаря́да; **the ~e of machinery** гул маши́н.

● *v.i.* скули́ть (*impf.*); хны́кать (*impf.*); **the dog was ~ing to come in** соба́ка скули́ла у две́ри, что́бы её впусти́ли; (*fig., complain*) хны́кать (*impf.*); ныть (*impf.*); **you're always ~ing about something!** всегда́-то вы но́ете!

whinge /wɪndʒ/ (**whingeing**) (*Br.*) = **whine** *v.i.* (*complain*).

whinny /'wɪnɪ/ *n.* (*gentle*) ти́хое ржа́ние; (*joyful*) ра́достное ржа́ние.

● *v.i.* (*gently*) ти́хо ржать, за-; (*joyfully*) ра́достно ржать, за-.

whip /wɪp/ *n.* **1** (*lash*) (*short*) плеть, плётка; (*long*) кнут; **have the ~ hand over s.o.** (*fig.*) держа́ть (*impf.*) кого́-н. в по́лном подчине́нии.

2 (*hunt official, also* **~per-in**) выжля́тник, доезжа́чий.

3 (*party official*) организа́тор парла́ментской фра́кции; (*Br., notice issued by him*) инстру́кция по пода́че голосо́в.

● *v.t.* (**whipped, whipping**) **1** (*flog*) поро́ть, вы́-; хлеста́ть, от-; сечь, вы́-; **~ping-boy** (*fig., scapegoat*) козёл отпуще́ния; **~ping-post** позо́рный столб; **~ping-top** юла́, волчо́к; (*fig.*): **the wind ~ped the waves into a fury** ве́тер я́ростно вздыма́л во́лны; (*fig., defeat*) разби́ть, поби́ть (*coll.*), победи́ть (*all pf.*).

2 (*beat into froth*) взб|ива́ть, -и́ть; **~ped cream** взби́тые сли́вки.

3 (*coll., move rapidly*): **as I entered he**

~ped the papers into a drawer когда́ я вошёл, он бы́стро су́нул бума́ги в я́щик; **she ~ped the cake out of the oven** она́ бы́стро вы́тащила торт из духо́вки.
● *v.i.* (**whipped, whipping**) (*coll., move rapidly*) рвану́ться, бро́ситься, ри́нуться (*all pf.*); **he ~ped into the shop** он влете́л в магази́н.
● *with advs.*: ~ **back** *v.i.*: **the branch ~ped back in my face** ве́тка хлестну́ла меня́ по лицу́; ~ **off** *v.t.* (*coll.*): **the wind ~ped off my hat** ве́тер сбил с меня́ шля́пу; ~ **on** *v.t.* (*urge on with* ~) под|гоня́ть, -огна́ть; подхлёст|ывать, -ну́ть; (*coll.*): **he ~ped on his overcoat** он бы́стро наки́нул пальто́; ~ **out** *v.t.* (*coll.*) выхва́тывать, вы́хватить; *v.i.* (*coll.*): **he ~ped out for a breath of air** он вы́скочил глотну́ть све́жего во́здуха; ~ **round** *v.i.* (*coll.*): **he ~ped round to face me** он кру́то оберну́лся ко мне; ~ **up** *v.t.* (*beat into froth*) взб|ива́ть, -ить; (*fig., stimulate*): ~ **up enthusiasm** возбу|жда́ть, -ди́ть энтузиа́зм; (*coll., improvise*) де́лать, с- на ско́рую ру́ку; **she ~ped up a nice supper** она́ бы́стро состря́пала вку́сный у́жин.
● *cpds.* **~cord** *n.* (*cord*) бечёвка; (*fabric*) габарди́н; **~lash** *n.* (*end of whip*) реме́нь (*m.*) (кнута́); (*injury*) поврежде́ние ше́и в результа́те ре́зкого движе́ния — ча́ще всего́ в автоава́рии; **~-round** *n.* (*Br. coll., collection*) сбор де́нег (на благотвори́тельные це́ли).

whipper-snapper /ˈwɪpəˌsnæpə(r)/ *n.* молокосо́с, щено́к.

whippet /ˈwɪpɪt/ *n.* го́нчая (соба́ка).

whir /wɜː(r)/ = **whir(r)**

whirl /wɜːl/ *n.* **1** (*revolving or eddying movement*) круже́ние, оборо́т; (*fig.*) смяте́ние, неразбери́ха; **my brain is in a ~** у меня́ голова́ идёт кру́гом.
2 (*bustling activity*) водоворо́т, вихрь (*m.*); **a ~ of social engagements** водоворо́т, вихрь све́тской жи́зни.
● *v.t. & i.* **1** (*swing round and round*) верте́ть(ся) (*impf.*); кружи́ть(ся) (*impf.*); **she found herself ~ed round in his arms** он закружи́л её в свои́х объя́тиях; **the leaves ~ed about in the wind** ли́стья кружи́лись на ветру́; **my head was ~ing** у меня́ кружи́лась голова́.
2 (*hurry; dash*) нести́сь (*impf.*); **the trees and hedges ~ed past** дере́вья и кусты́ проноси́лись ми́мо.
● *cpds.* **~pool** *n.* водоворо́т; **~wind** *n.* вихрь (*m.*), урага́н; (*fig., attr.*) стра́стный, бу́рный; **a ~wind romance** бу́рный рома́н.

whirligig /ˈwɜːlɪgɪg/ *n.* **1** (*top*) юла́, волчо́к. **2** (*roundabout*) карусе́ль. **3** (*fig.*) водоворо́т, вихрь (*m.*), круговоро́т; **the ~ of time** превра́тности (*f. pl.*) судьбы́.

whirlybird /ˈwɜːlɪˌbɜːd/ *n.* (*coll.*) вертолёт.

whir(r) /wɜː(r)/ *n.* жужжа́ние, стрекота́ние, шум.
● *v.i.* (**whirred, whirring**) жужжа́ть; стрекота́ть; шуме́ть (*all impf.*).

whisk /wɪsk/ *n.* **1** (*small brush or similar device*) ве́ничек, метёлочка.
2 (*for beating eggs etc.*) муто́вка.
3 (*brushing movement*) взмах; **with a ~ of its tail** взмахну́в хвосто́м.
● *v.t.* **1** (*flap; brush*) сма́х|ивать, -ну́ть; от|гоня́ть, -огна́ть; **she ~ed the dust under the carpet** она́ бы́стро замела́ пыль под ковёр.
2 (*beat, e.g. eggs*) взб|ива́ть, -ить.
● *v.i.* (*move briskly*) мча́ться, по-.
● *with advs.*: ~ **about** *v.t.* (*wave; brandish*) маха́ть (*impf.*); **the cow stood ~ing its tail about** коро́ва стоя́ла, пома́хивая хвосто́м; ~ **away** *v.t.*: **he ~ed away the flies with his handkerchief** он отогна́л мух платко́м; ~ **off** *v.t.* (*carry off quickly*) бы́стро ун|оси́ть, -ести́; (*lead off quickly*) бы́стро ув|оди́ть, -ести́; **he was ~ed off in an ambulance** его́ умча́ла каре́та ско́рой по́мощи.

whisker /ˈwɪskə(r)/ *n.* (*pl., facial hair*) ба́к|и (*pl., g.* —) (*coll.*); бакенба́рды (*f. pl.*); (*of animal*) усы́ (*m. pl.*); **he came within a ~ of success** (*coll.*) он был на поро́ге успе́ха.

whiskered /ˈwɪskəd/ *adj.* (*of person*) нося́щий бакенба́рды; с бакенба́рдами; (*of cat etc.*) уса́тый.

whisky /ˈwɪskɪ/ (*US* **whiskey**) *n.* ви́ски (*nt. indecl.*); ~ **and soda** ви́ски с со́довой.

whisper /ˈwɪspə(r)/ *n.* шёпот; **he spoke in a ~** он говори́л шёпотом; **stage ~** театра́льный шёпот; **not a ~ of this will escape my lips** я ни сло́ва об э́том не пророню́; (*rumour*) слух, молва́; (*rustle, of leaves etc.*) шо́рох, ше́лест.
● *v.i.* **1** (*speak, say in ~s*) шепта́ться (*impf.*); говори́ть (*impf.*) шёпотом; **he ~ed to me to come outside** он шёпотом пригласи́л меня́ вы́йти; **~ing gallery** акусти́ческий свод; **it is ~ed that ...** хо́дит слух, что. . ..
2 (*make ~ing noise*) шелесте́ть (*impf.*); шурша́ть (*impf.*); **the wind ~ed in the pines** ве́тер шелесте́л в со́снах.
● *v.t.* шепта́ть, про- (*or* шепну́ть); говори́ть, сказа́ть шёпотом; **she ~ed her secret to me** она́ шепну́ла/прошепта́ла мне свою́ та́йну на́ ухо.

whist /wɪst/ *n.* (*card game*) вист.

whistl|e /ˈwɪs(ə)l/ *n.* **1** (*sound*) свист; (*short one*) свисто́к.
2 (*instrument, toy*) свисто́к; (*factory ~e*) гудо́к; **blow the/a ~e** св|исте́ть, -и́стнуть.
3 (*fig.*): **wet one's ~e** (*coll.*) промочи́ть (*pf.*) го́рло.
● *v.t.* **1** (*call by ~ing*) свисте́ть, сви́стнуть; **he ~ed his dog back** он сви́стнул соба́ку.
2 (*tune*) насв|и́стывать, -исте́ть; **can you ~e the tune?** вы мо́жете насвисте́ть моти́в э́той пе́сни?
● *v.i.* св|исте́ть, про-, сви́стнуть; да|ва́ть, -ть свисто́к; **he came along ~ing** он шёл посви́стывая; **he can ~e for his money** (*coll.*) не вида́ть ему́ свои́х де́нег (как свои́х уше́й); **the train ~ed as it entered the tunnel** при вхо́де в тунне́ль по́езд дал гудо́к; **the wind ~es in the chimney** ве́тер завыва́ет в трубе́; **a bullet ~ed past him** пу́ля просвисте́ла ми́мо него́.
● *cpds.* **~e-blower** *n.* доно́счи|к (*fem.* -ца); **~e-stop** *n.* (*US*) полуста́нок; **a ~e-stop tour** разъездна́я агитацио́нная кампа́ния (кандида́та на вы́борах).

Whit /wɪt/ *adj.*: ~ **Monday** Ду́хов день; ~ **Sunday** = **Whitsun**

whit /wɪt/ *n.* (*arch.*) ка́пля, йо́та.

white /waɪt/ *n.* **1** (*colour*) бе́лый цвет; белизна́; **off ~** (*adj.*) белова́тый; (*clothes*): **she was wearing ~** она́ была́ в бе́лом; **dressed in ~** оде́тый в бе́лое; (*paint*) бе́лая кра́ска; бели́л|а (*pl., g.* —).
2 (*of the eyes*) бело́к.
3 (*of an egg*) бело́к.
4 (*racial type*) белоко́жий, бе́лый.
5 (*chess*) бе́лые (*pl.*); **it was W~'s move** был ход бе́лых.
● *adj.* бе́лый; **grow ~** беле́ть, по-; **he went as ~ as a sheet** он сде́лался бе́лым как полотно́; **his hair turned ~** он поседе́л; **he turned ~** он побледне́л; **a ~ Christmas** Рождество́ со сне́гом; ~ **coffee** (*Br.*) ко́фе с молоко́м; ~ **goods** (*domestic appliances*) бытовы́е электропри́боры; ~ **frost** и́ней, и́зморозь; ~ **heat** бе́лое кале́ние; ~ **horses** (*waves*) бара́шки (*m. pl.*); **the W~ House** Бе́лый дом; ~ **lead** свинцо́вые бели́ла; **a ~ lie** ложь во спасе́ние; **W~ Paper** Бе́лая кни́га; **W~ Russia** Белору́ссия; **a W~ Russian** (*Byelorussian*) белору́с (*fem.* -ка); (*émigré*) бе́лый эмигра́нт (*fem.* бе́лая эмигра́нтка); ~ **spirit** (*Br.*) уайт-спири́т; ~ **sugar** (са́хар-)рафина́д; рафини́рованный са́хар; ~ **tie and tails** фрак.
● *cpds.* **~bait** *n.* ме́лкая молода́я сельдь; **~-collar** *adj.*: **~-collar worker** *n.* слу́жащий; **~-haired, ~-headed** *adjs.* белоголо́вый; седо́й; **~-hot** *adj.* раскалённый добела́; **~-out** *n.* (*of weather conditions*) бе́лая мгла; (*US, correction fluid*) корректи́рующая жи́дкость; **~wash** *n.* побе́лка; (*fig.*) обеле́ние; зама́зывание (недоста́тков); *v.t.* бели́ть, по-; (*fig.*) обел|я́ть, -и́ть; зама́з|ывать, -ать; **~-water rafting** *n.* сплавле́ние вниз по го́рному пото́ку.

whiten /ˈwaɪt(ə)n/ *v.t.* бели́ть, по-.

whitener /ˈwaɪt(ə)nə(r)/ *n.*: **coffee ~** осветли́тель (*m.*) ко́фе.

whiteness /ˈwaɪtnɪs/ *n.* белизна́; бе́лый цвет.

whither /ˈwɪðə(r)/ *adv.* (*liter.*) куда́; ~ **away?** куда́ де́ржите путь?; ~ **Europe?** куда́ идёт Евро́па?

whithersoever /ˌwɪðəsəʊˈevə(r)/ *adv.* (*liter.*) куда́ бы ни.

whiting /ˈwaɪtɪŋ/ *n.* (*pl.* ~) **1** (*powdered chalk*) мел. **2** (*fish*) хек; мерла́нг.

whitish /ˈwaɪtɪʃ/ *adj.* беле́сый; белова́тый.
● *cpd.* **~-brown** *adj.* све́тло-кори́чневый.

whitlow /ˈwɪtləʊ/ *n.* ногтое́да, панари́ций.

W

Whitsun /ˈwɪts(ə)n/ *n.* (*Whit Sunday*) Тро́ицын день, Тро́ица; *see also* ⇒**Whit²**

whittle /ˈwɪt(ə)l/ *v.t.* (*wood*) строга́ть, вы-; (*from all sides*) обстру́г|ивать, -а́ть; **he ~d a twig into a whistle** он вы́строгал (себе́) свисто́к из ве́тки; (*make by whittling*): **this pipe was ~d out of cherrywood** э́та тру́бка вы́резана из вишнёвого де́рева.

● *with advs.*: **~ away** *v.t.* состру́г|ивать, -а́ть; (*fig.*) ум|еньша́ть, -е́ньшить; св|оди́ть, -ести́ на нет; **his savings were ~d away** его́ сбереже́ния постепе́нно исся́кли; **~ down** *v.t.* состру́г|ивать, -а́ть; (*fig.*) сн|ижа́ть, -и́зить.

whity /ˈwaɪtɪ/ = **whitish**

whiz(z) /wɪz/ *n.* свист.

● *v.i.* (**whizzed, whizzing**) прон|оси́ться, -ести́сь со сви́стом; мча́ться, про-; просвисте́ть (*pf.*).

● *cpd.* **~-kid** *n.* (*coll.*) ≈ восходя́щая звезда́.

WHO (*abbr. of* ***World Health Organization***) ВОЗ (Всеми́рная организа́ция здравоохране́ния).

who /hu:/ *pron.* (*obj.* **whom** *or informally* **who;** *poss.* **whose**) **1** (*interrog.*) кто; **~ is he?** кто он (тако́й)?; кто э́то?; **~ (else) but Smith?** сам Смит (*or* Смит со́бственной персо́ной); **~ does he think he is?** что он о себе́ возомни́л?; что он о себе́ вообража́ет? (*coll.*); **~'s it** (*coll., what's his name*) как бишь его́?; **~ am I to object?** кто я тако́й, что́бы возража́ть?, како́е я име́ю пра́во возража́ть?; **~ goes there?** (*mil.*) кто идёт?; **~(m)ever do you mean?** кого́ (э́то) вы име́ете в виду́?; **he knows ~'s ~** он зна́ет, кто есть кто; **W~'s W~** (*directory*) «Кто есть кто».
2 (*rel.*) кото́рый, како́й, кто; **those ~** те, кто/кото́рые; **anyone ~** вся́кий, кто; **the sort of people ~m we need** таки́е лю́ди, каки́е нам нужны́; **Mr X, ~ is my uncle** г-н X, мой дя́дя; **it was given to my sister, ~ passed it on to me** э́то да́ли мое́й сестре́, а она́ передала́ мне.

whoa, wo /wəʊ/ *int.* тпру!

whodunnit /hu:ˈdʌnɪt/ (*US* **whodunit**) *n.* (*sl.*) детекти́в.

whoever /hu:ˈevə(r)/ *pron.* (*obj.* **whomever** *or informally* **whoever;** *poss.* **whosever**) **1** (*anyone who; no matter who; also arch.* **whosoever**) кто бы ни, кто уго́дно; **~ comes will be welcome** кто бы ни пришёл, бу́дет жела́нным го́стем. **2** (*who ever*) кто то́лько; **~ heard of such a thing?** слы́ханное ли де́ло?; **~ would have thought it?** кто бы мог поду́мать?

whole /həʊl/ *n.* (*single entity*) це́лое; (*totality*) все, всё; **the ~ of the audience** вся аудито́рия; **taken as a ~** в це́лом; **on the ~** в о́бщем (и це́лом); в основно́м.

● *adj.* **1** (*intact; unbroken; undamaged*) це́лый, невреди́мый.
2 (*in one piece*) целико́м; **the ox was roasted ~** быка́ зажа́рили целико́м.
3 (*full; complete; entire*) весь, це́лый, це́льный; **he ate a ~ chicken** он съел це́лого цыплёнка; **two ~ glasses** це́лых два стака́на; **the ~ lot** всё; (*people*) все; **a ~ number** (*math.*) це́лое число́; **a ~ number of** це́лый ряд + *g.*; **~ milk** це́льное молоко́; **the ~ world** весь мир; **his ~ life through** на протяже́нии всей его́ жи́зни.

● *cpds.* **~-hearted** *adj.* беззаве́тный, пре́данный; **~-heartedly** *adv.* от всей души́; **~meal** *adj.* (*Br.*): **a ~meal loaf** буха́нка хле́ба из непросе́янной муки́; **~ note** *n.* (*US, mus.*) це́лая но́та; **~sale** *n.* опто́вая торго́вля; **sell something by (*US* at) ~sale** прод|ава́ть, -а́ть о́птом; **a ~sale dealer** оптови́к; *adj.* опто́вый; (*fig.*) ма́ссовый; **our business is ~sale only** мы торгу́ем то́лько о́птом; **I can get it for you ~sale** я могу́ вам э́то доста́ть по опто́вой цене́; *adv.* о́птом; (*fig.*) в ма́ссовом масшта́бе; **~saler** *n.* оптови́к; **~-tone** *adj.*: **~-tone scale** га́мма на це́лых но́тах.

wholefood /ˈhəʊlfu:d/ *n.* (*Br.*) натура́льные проду́кты.

● *adj.* натура́льный.

wholeness /ˈhəʊlnɪs/ *n.* (*integrality*) це́льность, це́лость.

wholesome /ˈhəʊlsəm/ *adj.* **1** (*promoting health*) поле́зный, цели́тельный, здоро́вый, благотво́рный; **~ food** здоро́вая пи́ща. **2** (*sound; prudent*) здра́вый, благотво́рный; **I gave him some ~ advice** я ему́ дал здра́вый/поле́зный сове́т.

wholesomeness /ˈhəʊlsəmnɪs/ (*of food*) поле́зность; (*fig.*) здра́вость.

wholly /ˈhəʊllɪ/ *adv.* по́лностью; целико́м; сплошь; **I am ~ at a loss** я в по́лном/совершённом недоуме́нии; **it cannot be ~ bad** не мо́жет быть, что́бы э́то бы́ло сплошь пло́хо.

whom /hu:m/ *obj. of* ⇒**who²**

whomever /hu:mˈevə(r)/ *obj. of* ⇒**whoever**

whomsoever /ˌhu:msəʊˈevə(r)/ *obj. of* ⇒**whosoever**

whoop /hu:p/, /wu:p/ *n.* во́зглас; восклица́ние; **with a ~ of joy** ра́достно восклица́я; с ра́достными восклица́ниями.

● *v.i.* **1** воскл|ица́ть, -и́кнуть; **~ing-cough** коклю́ш. **2**: **~ it up** (*sl.*) бу́рно весели́ться (*impf.*); кути́ть (*impf.*).

whoops /wʊps/ *int.* (*coll.*) оп!; (*after saying something*) ой!

whoosh /wʊʃ/ *n.* свист.

● *v.i.*: **~ past** прон|оси́ться, -ести́сь.

whop /wɒp/ *v.t.* (**whopped, whopping**) (*sl.*) (*thrash*) взду|ва́ть, -ть; колошма́тить, от-; (*defeat*) разб|ива́ть, -и́ть в пух и прах.

whopper /ˈwɒpə(r)/ *n.* (*sl.*) **1** (*anything very large*) грома́дина, махи́на; **a ~ of a fish** огро́мная ры́бина. **2** (*outrageous lie*) чудо́вищная ложь.

whopping /ˈwɒpɪŋ/ (*sl.*) *adj.* (*also* **~ great**) огро́мный, чудо́вищный, здорове́нный.

whore /hɔ:(r)/ *n.* шлю́ха.

● *v.i.* распу́тничать (*impf.*), гуля́ть (*impf.*).

● *cpd.* **~-house** *n.* барда́к, борде́ль (*m.*).

whorl /wɔ:l/, /wɜ:l/ *n.* вито́к, завиту́шка, завито́к; (*bot.*) муто́вка; (*of finger-prints*) завито́к па́льцевого узо́ра.

whortleberry /ˈwɜ:t(ə)lˌberɪ/ *n.* черни́ка (*collect.*); я́года черни́ки.

whose /hu:z/ *pron.* (*interrog.*) чей; **~ partner are you?** чей вы партнёр?; (*rel.*) кото́рого; (*before sing. noun, also*) чей; **for ~ sake** ра́ди кото́рого; **the people ~ house we bought** лю́ди, у кото́рых мы купи́ли дом.

whosesoever /ˌhu:zsəʊˈevə(r)/ *poss. of* ⇒**whosoever**

whosever /hu:zˈevə(r)/ *poss. of* ⇒**whoever**

whosoever /ˌhu:səʊˈevə(r)/ *pron.* (*obj.* **whomsoever;** *poss.* **whosesoever**) (*arch.*) = **whoever** 1

why /waɪ/ *n.* (*pl.* **whys**) причи́на; **all the ~s and wherefores** все э́ти почему́ и отчего́.

● *adv.* почему́, отчего́, заче́м; **'Are you married?' — 'No, ~?'** «вы жена́ты?» — «Нет, а что?»; **~ not?** почему́ бы нет?; **~ not let me help you?** почему́ бы мне вам не помо́чь?, дава́йте я вам помогу́; **the reasons ~ ...** причи́ны, по кото́рым. . . .

● *int.* да; ведь; да ведь; **~, of course** да, коне́чно; **~, what's the harm in it?** а что в э́том плохо́го?; **~ yes, I suppose so** да, наве́рное, э́то так; **if the worst came to the worst, ~, we'd have to start again** на худо́й коне́ц — что ж, (*or* ну,) придётся нача́ть (всё) с нача́ла.

wick /wɪk/ *n.* фити́ль (*m.*); **to get on s.o.'s ~** (*Br. coll.*) надо|еда́ть, -е́сть + *d.*

wicked /ˈwɪkɪd/ *adj.* (*depraved*) гре́шный, поро́чный; (*malicious*) злой, зло́бный; (*roguish*) лука́вый, плутовско́й; **she gave him a ~ glance** она́ лука́во взгляну́ла на него́; (*coll., disgraceful*) ужа́сный, безобра́зный; **a ~ shame** безобра́зие.

wickedness /ˈwɪkɪdnɪs/ *n.* (*depravity*) грех, поро́чность; (*malice*) зло́ба.

wicker /ˈwɪkə(r)/ *n.* пру́тья (*m. pl.*) для плете́ния; **~ chair** плетёное кре́сло.

● *cpd.* **~work** *n.* плете́ние; (*products*) плетёные изде́лия.

wicket /ˈwɪkɪt/ *n.* **1 (~-gate)** кали́тка. **2** (*at cricket*) воро́т|ца (*pl., g.* -ец).

● *cpd.* **~-keeper** *n.* ловя́щий мяч за воро́тцами (*в крикете*).

wide /waɪd/ *adj.* **1** широ́кий; (*in measuring*) шириной в + *a.*; **the table is 3 feet ~** ширина́ стола́ 3 фу́та; **3-foot wide table** стол шириной в 3 фу́та. **2** (*extensive*) широ́кий, обши́рный, просто́рный; **~ experience** обши́рный/бога́тый о́пыт; **~ interests** широ́кий круг интере́сов; **a ~ choice** широ́кий вы́бор; **his reading has been ~** он начи́танный челове́к; **the ~ world over** во всём ми́ре; по

всему́ све́ту.
3 (*off target*): **his answer was ~ of the mark** он попа́л па́льцем в не́бо.
4 (*Br., artful*): **~ boy** лихо́й па́рень; ло́вкий ма́лый.
● *adv.* **1** (*extensively*): **far and ~** повсю́ду; вдоль и поперёк.
2 (*to full extent*): **open the door ~!** откро́йте дверь на́стежь!; **he is ~ awake** у него́ сна ни в одно́м глазу́ нет; **his mouth was ~ open** рот его́ был широ́ко́ раскры́т; (*see also* ⇒**~-open**); **~ open to** (*attack etc.*) не защищённый от + *g.*
3 (*off target*) ми́мо це́ли; **shoot ~** стреля́ть (*impf.*) ми́мо це́ли.
● *cpds.* **~-angle** *adj.*: **~-angle lens** широкоуго́льная ли́нза; **~-eyed** *adj.* (*surprised*) изумлённый; (*naive*) наи́вный; **~-open** *adj.* откры́тый, необозри́мый; **~-open space** необозри́мый просто́р; *see also adv.*; **~-ranging** *adj.* (*intellect etc.*) разносторо́нний; **~-screen** *adj.*: **~-screen film** широкоэкра́нный фильм; **~spread** *adj.* (широко́) распространённый.

widely /ˈwaɪdlɪ/ *adv.* **1** (*to a large extent*) широ́ко́; **~ differing opinions** ре́зко расходя́щиеся мне́ния; **he is ~ read** (*has read a lot*) он о́чень начи́тан; (*many people read him*) у него́ широ́кая чита́тельская аудито́рия. **2** (*over a large area*) далеко́; **~ scattered** разбро́санный; **it is ~ known that ...** широ́ко́ изве́стно, что. . .; **it is ~ believed that ...** мно́гие счита́ют, что. . . .

widen /ˈwaɪd(ə)n/ *v.t. & i.* расш|иря́ть(ся), -и́рить(ся); **they are ~ing the road** они́ расширя́ют доро́гу; **the gap between them ~s daily** разры́в ме́жду ни́ми увели́чивается с ка́ждым днём.

widow /ˈwɪdəʊ/ *n.* вдова́; **become a ~** станови́ться, стать вдово́й; овдове́ть (*pf.*); **the ~'s mite** (*bibl.*) ле́пта вдови́цы; вдо́вья ле́пта; **~'s peak** во́лосы, расту́щие треуго́льным вы́ступом на лбу; **~'s weeds** вдо́вий тра́ур; **grass ~** соло́менная вдова́; **war ~** же́нщина, потеря́вшая му́жа на войне́.
● *v.t.* де́лать, с- вдово́й; **she was ~ed by the war** война́ отняла́ у неё му́жа.

widower /ˈwɪdəʊə(r)/ *n.* вдове́ц.

widowhood /ˈwɪdəʊˌhʊd/ *n.* вдовство́.

width /wɪtθ/, /wɪdθ/ *n.* **1** (*measurement*) ширина́; **the river is 2 miles in ~** ширина́ реки́ 2 ми́ли; река́ име́ет 2 ми́ли в ширину́. **2** (*piece of material*) поло́тнище. **3** (*wide extent*) широта́.
● *cpds.* **~ways, ~wise** *advs.* в ширину́.

wield /wiːld/ *v.t.* (*hold*) держа́ть (*impf.*) в рука́х; (*be able to use*) владе́ть (*impf.*) + *i.*; **~ an axe** рабо́тать (*impf.*) топоро́м; **~ a sword** владе́ть (*impf.*) шпа́гой; **~ authority** по́льзоваться (*impf.*) вла́стью.

Wiener schnitzel /ˈviːnə ˌʃnɪts(ə)l/ *n.* шни́цель (*m.*) по-ве́нски.

wife /waɪf/ *n.* (*pl.* **wives**) **1** (*spouse*) жена́; **he made her his ~** он жени́лся на ней; **the President's ~** супру́га президе́нта; **common-law ~** гражда́нская жена́; подру́га. **2** (*arch., old woman*) стару́ха, ба́бка; **old wives' tales** ба́бьи ска́зки (*f. pl.*); ро́ссказн|и (*pl., g.* -ей).

wifely /ˈwaɪflɪ/ *adj.* подоба́ющий/ сво́йственный жене́; **~ duties** же́нские обя́занности.

wig /wɪɡ/ *n.* пари́к.
● *cpd.* **~-maker** *n.* парикма́хер.

wigging /ˈwɪɡɪŋ/ *n.* (*Br. coll.*) взбу́чка, нахлобу́чка; **give s.o. a ~** зад|ава́ть, -а́ть кому́-н. взбу́чку/нахлобу́чку.

wiggle /ˈwɪɡ(ə)l/ *n.* пока́чивание.
● *v.t.* (*ears, toes*) шевели́ть, по- + *i.*; **she ~s her hips** она́ пока́чивает бёдрами; **the baby ~d its toes** ребёнок шевели́л па́льцами ног.
● *v.i.* (*of a loose tooth*) шата́ться (*impf.*), кача́ться (*impf.*).

wiggly /ˈwɪɡlɪ/ *adj.* (**wigglier, wiggliest**): **a ~ line** волни́стая ли́ния; **a ~ tooth** шата́ющийся зуб.

Wight /waɪt/ *n.*: **the Isle of ~** о́стров Уа́йт.

wigwam /ˈwɪɡwæm/ *n.* вигва́м.

wild /waɪld/ *n.* **1** (**~ *state***): **this animal is not found in the ~** э́то живо́тное не во́дится на во́ле.
2 (*pl., desert or uncultivated tract*) ди́кое ме́сто, ди́кие просто́ры; пусты́ня; **in the ~s of Africa** на ди́ких просто́рах А́фрики; **(out) in the ~s** на отши́бе.
● *adj.* **1** (*not domesticated; not cultivated*) ди́кий; **~ boar** каба́н; **~ flower** дикорасту́щий цвето́к; **~ goose chase** (*fig.*) бессмы́сленное предприя́тие; **in the ~ state** в ди́ком состоя́нии/ви́де, на во́ле.
2 (*not civilized*) ди́кий; **~ man** (*savage*) дика́рь (*m.*).
3 (*of scenery: desolate, uninhabited*) ди́кий, пусты́нный.
4 (*of birds etc.: easily startled*) пугли́вый.
5 (*unrestrained, wayward, disorderly*) необу́зданный, бу́рный, бу́йный; (*dissolute*) разгу́льный; **your hair looks (rather) ~** у вас растрепа́лись во́лосы; **everything was in ~ confusion** (там) цари́л ди́кий беспоря́док; **she lets her children run ~** она́ разреша́ет де́тям бу́йствовать; **he let the garden run ~** он запусти́л сад.
6 (*tempestuous*) бу́рный, бу́йный; **it was a ~ sea** мо́ре бушева́ло.
7 (*excited, passionate, frantic*) вне себя́; исступлённый; **~ with rage/delight** вне себя́ от я́рости/восто́рга; **he drives me ~** он выво́дит меня́ из себя́; **it made her ~** э́то привело́ её в неи́стовство; **they were ~ about him** они́ бы́ли в (ди́ком) восто́рге от него́; **~ laughter** ди́кий/бе́шеный хо́хот.
8 (*reckless; ill-aimed; ill-considered*) безу́мный; ди́кий; **a ~ scheme** безу́мная зате́я; **a ~ shot** вы́стрел науга́д.
● *adv.* наобу́м; науга́д.
● *cpds.* **~ card** *n.* (*comput.*) универса́льный си́мвол; (*cards*) ка́рта равноце́нная любо́й друго́й; **~-cat** *adj.* риско́ванный; **~-cat strike** неофициа́льная забасто́вка; **~fire** *n.*: **the news spread like ~fire** но́вость распространи́лась с молниено́сной быстрото́й; **~fowl** *n.* дичь.

wildebeest /ˈwɪldəˌbiːst/, /ˈvɪl-/ *n.* гну (*m. indecl.*).

wilderness /ˈwɪldənɪs/ *n.* ди́кая ме́стность; пусты́ня; **a voice crying in the ~** (*fig.*) глас вопию́щего в пусты́не; (*neglected garden*) запу́щенный сад.

wildlife /ˈwaɪldlaɪf/ *n.* жива́я приро́да; **~ sanctuary** запове́дник; **~ photographer** фотоохо́тник; **~ photography** фотоохо́та.

wildness /ˈwaɪldnɪs/ *n.* (*of behaviour, character*) ди́кость, необу́зданность.

wile /waɪl/ *n.* (*liter.*) хи́трость, уло́вка; (*pl.*) ухищре́ния (*nt. pl.*).

wilful /ˈwɪlfʊl/ (*US* **willful**) *adj.* **1** (*of person, headstrong*) своенра́вный, своево́льный. **2** (*intentional*) умы́шленный, преднаме́ренный; **~ disobedience** созна́тельное неповинове́ние.

wilfulness /ˈwɪlfʊlnɪs/ (*US* **willfulness**) *n.* своенра́вие, своево́лие; преднаме́ренность.

wiliness /ˈwaɪlɪnɪs/ *n.* хи́трость, кова́рство, лука́вство.

will[1] /wɪl/ *n.* **1** (*faculty, its exercise; determination, intent*) во́ля; **free ~** свобо́да во́ли; **he has a ~ of his own** он челове́к своево́льный; **he has no ~ of his own** он легко́ подчиня́ется чужо́му влия́нию; **against my ~** про́тив моего́ жела́ния; вопреки́ мое́й во́ле; **lack of ~** безво́лие, отсу́тствие си́лы во́ли; **the ~ to live** во́ля к жи́зни; **where there's a ~ there's a way** где хоте́ние, там и уме́ние; **of one's own free ~** доброво́льно, по со́бственной во́ле.
2 (*energy; enthusiasm*) эне́ргия, жела́ние; **go to work with a ~** рабо́тать (*impf.*) энерги́чно/с жела́нием.
3 (*discretion, desire*) жела́ние, во́ля; **he came and went at ~** он приходи́л и уходи́л, когда́ хоте́л.
4 (*disposition*) расположе́ние; **I feel no ill ~ towards him** я на него́ не в оби́де; **men of good ~** лю́ди до́брой во́ли.
5 (*disposition of property*) завеща́ние; **last ~ and testament** после́дняя во́ля; **make, draw up one's ~** де́лать, с-/ сост|авля́ть, -а́вить завеща́ние.
● *v.t.* **1** (*compel*) заст|авля́ть, -а́вить; **he ~ed himself to stay (*or* into staying) awake** (уси́лием во́ли) он заста́вил себя́ бо́дрствовать; **you cannot ~ success** одни́м хоте́нием успе́ха не добьёшся.
2: **God ~ing** е́сли на то бу́дет во́ля Бо́жья.
3 (*bequeath*) завеща́ть (*impf., pf.*).
● *cpd.* **~-power** *n.* си́ла во́ли.

will[2] /wɪl/ *v.t. & i.* (*3rd pers. sing. pres.* **will**) (*see also* ⇒**would**) **1** (*expr. future*): **he ~ be president** он бу́дет президе́нтом; **in five minutes it ~ be midnight** че́рез пять мину́т бу́дет/ насту́пит по́лночь; **tomorrow ~ be Tuesday** за́втра — вто́рник; **he said he would be back by 3** он сказа́л, что

W

вернётся к трём; **I won't do it again** я бóльше не бýду.
2 (*expr. wish, insistence*): **let him do what he ~** пусть дéлает, что хóчет; **he ~ always have his own way** он всегдá настои́т на своём.
3 (*expr. willingness*): **I ~ come with you** я пойдý с вáми; **~ (*or* won't) you come in?** входи́те, пожáлуйста!; **pass the salt, ~ (*or* would) you?** бýдьте любéзны, передáйте соль; **'Tell me your name!' — 'No, I won't'** «Скажи́те, как вас зовýт?» — «Не скажý!»; **he won't help me** он не хóчет мне помóчь; **the window won't open** oкнó никáк не открывáется.
4 (*expr. inevitability*): **boys ~ be boys** мáльчики есть мáльчики; **accidents ~ happen** несчáстных слýчаев не избежáть.
5 (*expr. habit*): **he ~/would sit there for hours on end** он проси́живает/проси́живал там часáми; **he would often come to see me** он чáсто заходи́л ко мне.
6 (*expr. surmise, probability*): **this ~ be the book you're looking for** вот, дóлжно быть, кни́га, котóрую вы и́щете; **she would have been about 60 when she died** ей бы́ло, должнó быть, óколо шести́десяти, когдá онá умерлá.

willful /ˈwɪlfʊl/ (*US*) = **wilful**

willfulness /ˈwɪlfʊlnɪs/ (*US*) = **wilfulness**

willies /ˈwɪlɪz/ *n.* (*sl.*): **it gives me the ~** у меня́ от э́того мурáшки по спинé (бéгают).

willing /ˈwɪlɪŋ/ *adj.* **1** (*readily disposed*) склóнный, располóженный; **~ workers** усéрдные рабóтники; **I am ~ to admit ...** я готóв признáть...; **he was not ~ to accept responsibility** он не хотéл брать на себя́ отвéтственность; **show ~** проявл|я́ть, -и́ть готóвность; **'Will you do me a favour (*Br.*), favor (*US*)?' — 'W~ly!'** «Вы мóжете сдéлать мне одолжéние?» — «Охóтно!». **2** (*readily given or shown*) доброво́льный.

willingness /ˈwɪlɪŋnɪs/ *n.* готóвность, желáние.

will-o'-the-wisp /ˌwɪləðəˈwɪsp/ *n.* блуждáющий огонёк; (*fig., elusive person*) неулови́мый человéк; (*fig., delusive hope or plan*) несбы́точная надéжда/мечтá; иллю́зия.

willow /ˈwɪləʊ/ *n.* **1** (*tree*) и́ва; **pussy ~** вéрба; **weeping ~** плакýчая и́ва.
2 (*fig., cricket-bat*) битá.
● *cpds.* **~-herb** *n.* кипрéй, ивáн-чай; **~-pattern** (*china*) *n.* посýда с си́ним китáйским моти́вом; **~-warbler** *n.* пéночка-весни́чка.

willowy /ˈwɪləʊɪ/ *adj.* (*lithe*) тóнкий, ги́бкий, стрóйный.

willy /ˈwɪlɪ/ *n.* (*Br. coll.*) член, сóлоп.

willy-nilly /ˌwɪlɪˈnɪlɪ/ *adv.* вóлей-невóлей; хóчешь не хóчешь.

wilt /wɪlt/ *v.i.* (*lit., fig.*) ни́кнуть, по-; пон|икáть, -и́кнуть; **~ing enthusiasm** ослабевáющий энтузиáзм.

wily /ˈwaɪlɪ/ *adj.* (**wilier, wiliest**) хи́трый, ковáрный, лукáвый.

wimp /wɪmp/ *n.* (*coll.*) слизня́к.

wimpish /ˈwɪmpɪʃ/ *adj.* (*coll.*) бесхарáктерный.

wimple /ˈwɪmp(ə)l/ *n.* (*nun's*) апóстольник, плат.

win /wɪn/ *n.* (*gain*) вы́игрыш; (*victory*) побéда; **a ~ at cards** вы́игрыш в кáртах; **it was an easy ~ for them** они́ с лёгкостью вы́играли.
● *v.t.* (**winning;** *past and p.p.* **won**) **1** (*be victorious in*) выи́грывать, вы́играть; **the Allies won the war** сою́зники вы́играли войнý; **~ a race** побе|ждáть, -ди́ть в забéге; **he won every race** он победи́л во всех забéгах; **who won the election?** кто вы́играл на вы́борах?; **she won the lottery** онá вы́играла в лотерéю; **~ the day** одéрж|ивать, -áть побéду.
2 (*gain*) получ|áть, -и́ть; выи́грывать, вы́играть; **he won £5 from me** он вы́играл у меня́ 5 фýнтов; **~ a medal** завоёв|ывать, -áть медáль; **~ a prize** выи́грывать, вы́играть приз; **~ s.o.'s heart** покор|я́ть, -и́ть чьё-н. сéрдце; **~ s.o.'s confidence** сни́ск|ивать, -áть (*or* войти́ (*pf.*) в) чьё-н. довéрие; **this work won her many friends** благодаря́ э́той рабóте онá приобрелá мнóго друзéй.
● *v.i.* (**winning;** *past and p.p.* **won**): **~ hands down** выи́грывать, вы́играть без трудá (*or* с лёгкостью); **~ on points** выи́грывать, вы́играть по очкáм; **~ by 4 goals to 1** вы́играть (*pf.*) со счётом 4:1.
● *with advs.*: **~ back** *v.t.* оты́гр|ывать, -áть; **~ out** *v.i.* преодол|евáть, -éть все трýдности; **~ over, ~ round** *vv.t.* уговáр|ивать, -ори́ть; **he cannot be won round** егó нельзя́/невозмóжно уговори́ть; **~ through** *v.i.* проб|ивáться, -и́ться.

wince /wɪns/ *n.*: **with a ~** вздрóгнув.
● *v.i.* содрог|áться, -нýться; (*frown*) мóрщиться, по-.

winch /wɪntʃ/ *n.* лебёдка, вóрот.
● *v.t.* (*usu. with advs.*) подн|имáть, -я́ть с пóмощью лебёдки.

wind[1] /wɪnd/ *n.* **1** вéтер; **high ~** си́льный вéтер; (*at sea*) штормовóй вéтер; **fair ~** попýтный вéтер; **strong ~** си́льный вéтер; **there's not much ~ about** вéтра почти́ нет; **the ~ is in the east** вéтер дýет с востóка; **the ~ blew hard** дул рéзкий вéтер; **sail before the ~** плыть (*det.*) с попýтным вéтром; **the ~ was behind us** вéтер дул нам в спи́ну; **exposed to ~ and weather** откры́тый непогóдам; **he is sailing close to the ~** (*lit.*) он идёт прóтив вéтра; (*fig.*) он ведёт себя́ на грáни дозвóленного; **the deer were down ~ of us** олéни находи́лись в подвéтренной сторонé от нас; **get, catch ~ of** чýять, по-; (*fig.*) проню́х|ивать, -ать.
2 (*var. fig. uses*): **he ran like the ~** он мчáлся как вéтер; **fling/throw caution to the ~s** отбрóсить/забы́ть (*pf.*) вся́кую осторóжность; **scattered to the four ~s** разбрóсанный повсю́ду (*or* по всемý свéту); **I must see how the ~ blows** мне нýжно посмотрéть, кудá вéтер дýет; **it took the ~ out of his sails** (*fig.*) э́то вы́било у негó пóчву из-под ног; э́то обескурáжило егó; **~ of change** (*fig.*) вéтер перемéн; **get the ~ up** (*Br. sl.*) трýсить, с-; **the noise put the ~ up me** (*Br. sl.*) э́тот шум меня́ испугáл/напугáл; **there is something in the ~** чтó-то назревáет/затевáется; **it's an ill ~ that blows nobody good** нет хýда без добрá.
3 (*breath*) дыхáние; **out of ~** запыхáвшись; **lose one's ~** запыхáться (*pf.*); **get back one's ~** отдыш|áться (*pf.*); **get one's second ~** обре|тáть, -сти́ вторóе дыхáние; **knock the ~ out of s.o.** (*fig.*) ошелом|ля́ть, -и́ть когó-н.
4 (*Br., in bowels etc.*) гáзы (*m. pl.*); **I've got ~** у меня́ живóт пýчит; **break ~** пóртить, ис- вóздух.
5 (**~** *instruments*) духовы́е (инструмéнты) (*m. pl.*); **~ quintet** духовóй квинтéт.
● *v.t.* **1** (*deprive of breath*): **the blow ~ed him** от удáра у негó дух перехвати́ло; **I was ~ed by the climb** от подъёма я запыхáлся; **he ~ed me** он удáрил меня́ под вздох.
2: **~ a horse** да|вáть, -ть лóшади передохнýть.
● *cpds.* **~bag** *n.* (*coll.*) пустомéля (*c.g.*), краснобáй; **~-break** *n.* ветролóм; **~-cheater** (*US* **-breaker**) *nn.* ветронепроницáемая кýртка; штормóвка; **~fall** *n.* (*of fruit*) пáданец; (*of good fortune*) непредви́денный дохóд; **~mill** *n.* ветряна́я мéльница; **~pipe** *n.* дыхáтельное гóрло; **~screen** (*US* **~shield**) *nn.* лобовóе/ветровóе стеклó; **~screen washer** стеклоомывáтель (*m.*); **~screen wiper** стеклоочисти́тель (*m.*), «двóрник»; **~-sleeve, ~-sock** *nn.* ветровóй кóнус; **~swept** *adj.* (*of terrain*) откры́тый вéтру; (*of hair etc.*) растрёпанный; **~-tunnel** *n.* аэродинами́ческая трубá.

wind[2] /waɪnd/ *n.* **1** (*single turn*) витóк.
2 (*bend*) поворóт, изги́б.
● *v.t.* (*past and p.p.* **wound**) **1** (*cause to encircle, curve or curl*): **she wound the wool into a ball** онá смотáла шерсть в клубóк; **the thread was wound on to a reel** ни́тка былá намóтана на катýшку; **a rope was wound round the pole** на шест былá намóтана верёвка; **the chain had wound itself round the wheel** цепь обвилáсь вокрýг колесá; **the hedgehog ~s itself into a ball** ёжик свёртывается клубкóм (*or* в клубóк); **she can ~ you round her little finger** (*fig.*) онá из вас верёвки вьёт; онá вéртит вáми, как хóчет.
2 (*fold, wrap*) укýт|ывать, -ать; **she wound a shawl round the baby; she wound the baby in a shawl** онá укýтала/завернýла ребёнка в платóк; **~ing-sheet** сáван.
3 (*rotate*) вертéть (*impf.*); крути́ть (*impf.*).
4: **~ a clock** зав|оди́ть, -ести́ часы́; **~ing-engine** подъёмная маши́на.
5: **the river ~s its way to the sea** рекá, извивáясь, течёт к мóрю.
● *v.i.* (*past and p.p.* **wound**) (*twist*) ви́ться (*impf.*); извивáться (*impf.*); **the path ~s up the hill** дорóжка/тропи́нка

змéйкой поднимáется в гóру; **~ing staircase** винтовáя лéстница; **a ~ing road** извилистая дорóга.

● *with advs.*: **~ about** *v.i.*: **the road ~s about** дорóга извивáется; **~ down** *v.t.* опус|кáть, -тúть; *v.i.*: **the clock spring ~s down in 7 days** у э́тих часóв семиднéвный завóд; **~ in** *v.t.*: **~ in a fishing line** см|áтывать, -отáть ýдочку; **~ up** *v.t.*: **~ up the bucket from the well** подн|имáть, -ять ведрó из колóдца; **~ up a clock** зав|одúть, -естú часы́; (*fig., arouse*) зав|одúть, -естú; **he gets very wound up at times** иногдá он ужáсно завóдится; (*Br., tease*) дразнúть (*impf.*); (*fig., settle*) заверш|áть, -úть; **I am ~ing up my affairs** я свёртываю свои делá; (*fig., terminate*) зак|áнчивать, -óнчить; **they wound up the meeting with a prayer** онú закóнчили собрáние молúтвой; *v.i.* (*conclude*) заключ|áть, -úть; заверш|áть, -úть; **you will ~ up in prison** вы кóнчите тюрьмóй; **he wound up by shooting himself** он кóнчил тем, что застрелúлся.

windlass /ˈwɪndləs/ *n.* лебёдка, вóрот.

windless /ˈwɪndlɪs/ *adj.* безвéтренный.

window /ˈwɪndəʊ/ *n.* **1** окнó; (*dim., also cashier's etc.*) окóшко; **he looked through the ~** он посмотрéл в окнó; он вы́глянул из окнá; **double ~s** двойны́е рáмы (*f. pl.*); **(shop-~)** витрúна; **a ~ on the world** окнó в мир; (*in full* **~ of opportunity**) рéдкая возмóжность. **2** (*comput.*) окнó. **3** (*attr.*) окóнный.

● *cpds.* **~-blind** *n.* штóра; жалюзú (*nt. indecl.*); **~-box** *n.* нарýжный я́щик для цветóв; **~-catch** *n.* окóнный затвóр, шпингалéт; **~-cleaner** *n.* мóйщик óкон; **~-dresser** *n.* оформúтель (*fem.* -ница) витрúн; **~-dressing** *n.* (*lit.*) оформлéние витрúн; (*fig.*) очковтирáтельство; **~-ledge** *n.* (нарýжный) подокóнник; **~-pane** *n.* окóнное стеклó; **~-seat** *n.* диван у окнá; **~-shopping** *n.* рассмáтривание витрúн; **~-sill** *n.* подокóнник.

windsurfer /ˈwɪnd,sɜːfə(r)/ *n.* виндсерфингúст.

windsurfing /ˈwɪnd,sɜːfɪŋ/ *n.* виндсéрфинг.

windward /ˈwɪndwəd/ *n.* навéтренная сторонá.

● *adj.* навéтренный.

windy /ˈwɪndɪ/ *adj.* (**windier, windiest**) **1** (*characterized by wind*) вéтреный; **a ~ night** вéтреная ночь. **2** (*exposed to wind*) обдувáемый вéтром; откры́тый вéтрам. **3** (*Br., flatulent*): **~ food** пúща, от котóрой пýчит (живóт).

wine /waɪn/ *n.* **1** (виногрáдное) винó; **dry, medium dry, sweet ~** сухóе/полусухóе/слáдкое винó; **sparkling ~** игрúстое винó; **table ~** столóвое винó.
2 (*from other fruit or plant*) налúвка.

● *v.t.*: **he was ~d and dined** егó угощáли на слáву; егó кормúли-поúли.

● *cpds.* **~ bar** *n.* вúнный бар; **~-bottle** *n.* вúнная буты́лка; **~-cellar** *n.* вúнный пóгреб; **~-coloured** (*US* **-colored**) *adj.* тёмно-крáсный; бордóвый; **~-cooler** *n.* ведёрко со льдом (для охлаждéния винá); **~-glass** *n.* бокáл, рю́мка; **~-grower** *n.* винодéл; **~-growing** *n.* виноделие; *adj.* винодéльческий; **~-list** *n.* кáрта вин; **~-press** *n.* давúльный пресс; **~skin** *n.* мех для винá; **~-taster** *n.* дегустáтор вин; **~-tasting** *n.* дегустáция вин; **~-vault** *n.* вúнный пóгреб; **~-waiter** *n.* (*Br.*) официáнт, вéдающий винáми.

winery /ˈwaɪnərɪ/ *n.* вúнный завóд, винодéльня.

wing /wɪŋ/ *n.* **1** (*of bird, insect or aircraft*) крылó; **on the ~** в полёте; **shoot a bird on the ~** подстр|éливать, -елúть птúцу на летý; **clip s.o.'s ~s** (*fig.*) подр|езáть, -éзать комý-н. кры́лья; **spread, stretch one's ~s** (*fig.*) распр|авлять, -áвить кры́лья; **take ~** (*lit.*) улет|áть, -éть; взлет|áть, -éть; (*fig.*) ун|осúться, -естúсь; см|ывáться, -ы́ться (*coll.*); **take under one's ~** (*fig.*) брать, взять под своё покровúтельство.
2 (*of building*) крылó, флúгель (*m.*).
3 (*Br., of vehicle*) крылó.
4 (*of mil. formation*) фланг; крылó; край.
5 (*of political party*) крылó; **the left/right ~** лéвое/прáвое крылó.
6 (*of football or hockey team*) фланг; край; (*player in this position*) крáйний нападáющий.
7 (*pl., of stage*) кулúсы (*f. pl.*); **wait in the ~s** (*lit.*) ждать (*impf.*) своегó вы́хода на сцéну; (*fig.*) ждать (*impf.*) своегó чáса; быть наготóве.

● *v.t.* **1** (*equip with ~s*): **~ed words** крылáтые словá.
2: **~ one's way** летéть (*impf.*).
3 (*wound*) рáнить (*impf., pf.*), подстр|éливать, -слúть.

● *cpds.* **~-case** *n.* надкры́лье; **~-collar** *n.* стоя́чий воротнúк с отворóтами; **~-commander** *n.* ≈ подполкóвник авиáции; **~-half** *n.* полузащúтник; **~-mirror** *n.* (*Br.*) боковóе зéркало; **~-nut** *n.* кры́льчатая гáйка; **~-span, ~-spread** *nn.* размáх крылá; **~-tip** *n.* конéц крылá.

wingding /ˈwɪŋdɪŋ/ *n.* (*US sl., party*) кутёж, попóйка.

winger /ˈwɪŋə(r)/ *n.* (*player*) крáйний нападáющий.

wingless /ˈwɪŋlɪs/ *adj.* бескры́лый.

wink /wɪŋk/ *n.* **1** мигáние, моргáние; (*as signal, joke*) подмúгивание; **give s.o. a ~** подмиг|ивать, -нýть комý-н.; **tip s.o. the ~** (*fig.*) намек|áть, -нýть комý-н.; предупре|ждáть, -дúть когó-н.; **a nod is as good as a ~** достáточно намёка; **I didn't sleep a ~** я всю ночь не сомкнýл глаз; **have, take forty ~s** (*coll.*) вздремнýть (*pf.*).
2 (*coll.*): **in a ~** моментáльно; мигóм.

● *v.t.*: **~ one's eye** подмиг|ивать, -нýть; морг|áть, -нýть.

● *v.i.*: **~ at s.o.** подмиг|ивать, -нýть комý-н.; **~ at something** (*connive at*) смотрéть (*impf.*) сквозь пáльцы на что-н.; **it's as easy as ~ing** (*coll.*) э́то раз плю́нуть; (*of star, light etc.*) мигáть (*impf.*); мерцáть (*impf.*).

winker /ˈwɪŋkə(r)/ *n.* (*Br., indicator light*) индикáтор поворóта.

winkle /ˈwɪŋk(ə)l/ *n.* морскáя улúтка.

● *v.t.* (*Br.*): **~ out** (*fig.*) вытáскивать, вы́тащить; извл|екáть, -éчь; (*information*) выу́живать, вы́удить.

winner /ˈwɪnə(r)/ *n.* победúтель (*fem.* -ница), лауреáт; **who was the ~?** кто вы́играл/победúл?; **he backed three ~s** он три рáза стáвил на победúвшую лóшадь; (*successful thing*) вéрное дéло.

winning /ˈwɪnɪŋ/ *adj.* **1** (*victorious*) вы́игравший, победúвший; **the ~ team** победúвшая/вы́игравшая комáнда, комáнда-победúтельница.
2 (*bringing about a win*) вы́игрышный; **~ card** вы́игрышная кáрта; **~ stroke** решáющий удáр. **3** (*persuasive, attractive*) привлекáтельный, обая́тельный; **~ ways** приятные манéры.

● *cpd.* **~-post** *n.* фúнишный столб.

winnings /ˈwɪnɪŋz/ *n. pl.* вы́игрыш.

winnow /ˈwɪnəʊ/ *v.t.* вéять (*impf.*); отвé|ивать, -ять; (*fig.*) отсé|ивать, -ять.

● *with advs.*: **~ away, ~ out chaff from grain** отвé|ивать, -ять полóву/мякúну от зернá.

winsome /ˈwɪnsəm/ *adj.* привлекáтельный, обая́тельный.

winter /ˈwɪntə(r)/ *n.* зимá; **in ~** зимóй; (*attr.*) зúмний; **~ crop** озúмая культýра; **~ sports** зúмние вúды спóрта.

● *v.i.* зимовáть, пере-.

● *cpds.* **~green** *n.* (*bot.*) грушáнка; (*checkerberry*) гальтéрия лежáчая; **~-time** *n.* зимá; зúмнее врéмя.

wintry /ˈwɪntrɪ/ *adj.* (**wintrier, wintriest**) зúмний, морóзный; (*fig.*) холóдный.

wipe /waɪp/ *n.*: **give this plate a ~!** вы́трите э́ту тарéлку!; **she gave the baby's face a ~** онá вы́терла ребёнку лицó.

● *v.t.* **1** (*rub clean or dry*) вытирáть, вы́тереть; прот|ирáть, -ерéть; (**~** *surface of*) обт|ирáть, -ерéть; **~ s.o.'s nose** вытирáть, вы́тереть комý-н. нос; **~ one's eyes** ут|ирáть, -ерéть слёзы; **she ~d the dishes** онá вы́терла посýду; **he ~d the floor** он протёр пол; **~ the floor with s.o.** (*fig., coll.*) ут|ирáть, -ерéть нос комý-н.; **~ your shoes on the mat!** вы́трите ботúнки о кóврик!
2 (*efface*) ст|ирáть, -ерéть; **~ a mark off the wall** ст|ирáть, -ерéть пятнó со стены́.

● *with advs.*: **~ away** *v.t.* ст|ирáть, -ерéть; (*tears*) ут|ирáть, -ерéть; **~ down** *v.t.* прот|ирáть, -ерéть; **~ off** *v.t.* ст|ирáть, -ерéть; **the town was ~d off the map** гóрод был стёрт с лицá землú; **~ out** *v.t.* (*clean*) вытирáть, вы́тереть; прот|ирáть, -ерéть; (*expunge*): **I can't ~ out the memory** я не могý уничтóжить воспоминáние; (*destroy*) уничт|ожáть, -óжить; **the disease ~d out the entire population**

W

эпиде́мия по́лностью уничто́жила всё населе́ние; **~ over** *v.t.* (слегка́) прот|ира́ть, -ере́ть; пройти́сь (*pf.*) тря́пкой по + *d.*; **~ up** *v.t.* подт|ира́ть, -ере́ть.

wiper /ˈwaɪpə(r)/ (*coll.*) = **windscreen wiper**

wire /ˈwaɪə(r)/ *n.* **1** (*fine-drawn metal; a length of this*) про́волока; про́вод (*pl.* -а́); **barbed ~** колю́чая про́волока; **chicken ~** про́волочная се́тка; **~ netting** про́волочная се́тка; **~ wool** (*Br.*) про́волочная моча́лка.
2 (*as barrier, fencing etc.*) про́волочная се́тка.
3 (*elec.*) про́вод; **fuse ~** пла́вкая про́волока (*для предохранителей*); **telephone ~** телефо́нный про́вод; **live ~** (*lit.*) про́вод под напряже́нием/ то́ком; (*fig., of person*) (челове́к-)ого́нь, живчи́к (*coll.*); **get one's ~s crossed** (*fig.*) запу́таться (*pf.*); неве́рно поня́ть (*pf.*) что-н.
4 (*coll., telegram*) телегра́мма.
● *v.t.* **1** (*provide, strengthen or fasten with ~*) свя́з|ывать, -а́ть (*or* скреп|ля́ть, -и́ть) про́волокой.
2 (*coll., send telegram to*) телеграфи́ровать (*impf., pf.*) + *d.*
3 (*elec.*): **they ~d the house** они́ сде́лали прово́дку в до́ме.
● *v.i.* (*coll., telegraph*) телеграфи́ровать (*impf., pf.*); **they ~d for him to come** они́ вы́звали его́ телегра́ммой.
● *with advs.*: **~ together** *v.t.* скреп|ля́ть, -и́ть про́волокой; **~ up** *v.t.* (*connect*) подключ|а́ть, -и́ть.
● *cpds.* **~-brush** *n.* про́волочная щётка; **~-cutters** *n. pl.* куса́ч|ки (*pl., g.* -ек); **~-gauge** *n.* (*instrument*) про́волочный кали́бр; **~-haired** *adj.* жесткошёрст(н)ый; **~-puller** *n.* (*US coll.*) ма́стер закули́сных махина́ций; ловка́ч; **~-tapping** *n.* подслу́шивание телефо́нных разгово́ров; **~worm** *n.* (*zool.*) про́волочник, личи́нка жука́-щелкуна́.

wireless /ˈwaɪəlɪs/ *n.* **1** (**~** *telegraphy*) беспро́волочный телегра́ф; **~ officer** ради́ст. **2** (*Br., sound radio*) ра́дио (*indecl.*); **~ enthusiast** радиолюби́тель (*m.*); **I heard it on the ~** я слы́шал э́то по ра́дио. **3** (*Br., broadcast receiver: also* **~ set**) (радио)приёмник; ра́дио.

wiring /ˈwaɪərɪŋ/ *n.* (*elec.*) электропрово́дка.

wiry /ˈwaɪərɪ/ *adj.* (**wirier, wiriest**) (*of person*) жи́листый; (*of hair*) жёсткий.

wisdom /ˈwɪzdəm/ *n.* му́дрость; (*prudence*) благоразу́мие, разу́мность; **~ tooth** зуб му́дрости.

wise /waɪz/ *adj.* **1** (*sage*) му́дрый; **~ counsel** му́дрый сове́т; **the W~ Men** (*bibl.*) волхвы́ (*m. pl.*); **get, grow ~r** наб|ира́ться, -ра́ться му́дрости; **he nodded ~ly** он глубокомы́сленно кива́л голово́й.
2 (*sensible, prudent*) у́мный, благоразу́мный; **~ after the event** за́дним умо́м кре́пок; **you were ~ not to attempt it** вы пра́вильно сде́лали, что не ста́ли пыта́ться; **it's not ~ to swim on this coast** не рекоменду́ется купа́ться на э́том берегу́; **he ~ly refused** он име́л му́дрость отказа́ться.
3 (*well-informed*) осведомлённый; **now that you've told me I am none the ~r** да́же по́сле ва́шего объясне́ния я ма́ло что понима́ю; **you could sneak in without anyone's being the ~r** вы мо́жете тихо́нько войти́, и никто́ не заме́тит; **~ guy** (*US sl.*) у́мник; **put s.o. ~ to something** (*coll.*) вв|оди́ть, -ести́ кого́-н. в курс де́ла; **be ~ to something** (*coll.*) быть в ку́рсе дел; ви́деть (*impf.*) что-н. насквозь; **get ~ to** (*coll.*) прове́дать (*pf.*), разузна́ть (*pf.*).
● *v.t.*: **~ up** (*US sl.*) надоу́мить (*pf.*).
● *cpds.* **~acre** *n.* всезна́йка (*c.g.*); **~crack** (*coll.*) *n.* шу́тка, остро́та; *v.i.* остри́ть, с-.

wish /wɪʃ/ *n.* **1** (*desire*) жела́ние; (*will*) во́ля; (*request*) про́сьба; **I have no ~ to interfere** у меня́ нет жела́ния вме́шиваться, я не собира́юсь вме́шиваться; **make a ~!** загада́йте жела́ние!; **he expressed the ~ that** он вы́разил жела́ние, что́бы; **you acted against my ~es** вы де́йствовали/ поступи́ли про́тив моей во́ли.
2 (*thing ~ed for or requested*) жела́ние, предме́т жела́ний; мечта́; **he got his ~** его́ жела́ние сбыло́сь; его́ мечта́ сбыла́сь.
3 (*hope on another's behalf*) пожела́ние; **best ~es!** всего́ наилу́чшего!; **with every good ~** с наилу́чшими пожела́ниями.
● *v.t.* **1** (*want, require*) жела́ть (*impf.*); хоте́ть (*impf.*) (*both* + *a. or g., inf. or* что́бы).
2 (*expr. unfulfilled desire*): **I ~ I knew everything** е́сли бы то́лько я всё знал; как бы я хоте́л всё знать; **I only ~ I knew** е́сли бы я то́лько знал; хотел бы я знать; **she ~ed she had stayed at home** она пожале́ла, что не оста́лась до́ма; **I ~ you'd be quiet** нельзя́ ли не шуме́ть?; **I ~ he was alive** е́сли бы то́лько он был жив; как бы я хоте́л, что́бы он был жив; **I ~ he hadn't left so soon** как жаль, что он ушёл так ра́но; я жале́ю, что он ушёл так ра́но; **I ~ I hadn't gone there** я жале́ю, что пошёл туда́; заче́м я то́лько пошёл туда́; **I ~ I'd never been born** заче́м то́лько я роди́лся.
3 (*with double object*): **I ~ him well** я жела́ю ему́ добра́; **I ~ed him good morning** я пожела́л ему́ до́брого у́тра; **I ~ you many happy returns** поздравля́ю вас с днём рожде́ния; **I ~ed him goodbye** я попроща́лся с ним.
4 (*coll., inflict*) навя́з|ывать, -а́ть; **I wouldn't ~ this headache on anyone** тако́й головно́й бо́ли и врагу́ своему́ не пожела́ю.
● *v.i.*: **she has everything a woman could ~ for** у неё есть всё, о чём то́лько же́нщина мо́жет мечта́ть.
● *cpd.* **~-bone** *n.* ду́жка.

wishful /ˈwɪʃfʊl/ *adj.*: **~ thinking** самообольще́ние; приня́тие жела́емого за действи́тельное.

wishy-washy /ˈwɪʃɪˌwɒʃɪ/ *adj.* (*of liquid*) жи́дкий, сла́бый; (*of person, style, ideas*) вя́лый; (*sentimental*) сентимента́льный.

wisp /wɪsp/ *n.* пучо́к, клок; **a ~ of hair** прядь воло́с; **a ~ of smoke** стру́йка ды́ма.

wispy /ˈwɪspɪ/ *adj.* (**wispier, wispiest**) лёгкий, то́нкий; **~ hair** ре́дкие во́лосы.

wist|aria /wɪˈsteərɪə/, **-eria** /wɪˈstɪərɪə/ *n.* глици́ния.

wistful /ˈwɪstfʊl/ *adj.* тоску́ющий, тоскли́вый.

wistfulness /ˈwɪstfʊlnɪs/ *n.* тоска́.

wit[1] /wɪt/ *n.* **1** (*intelligence*) ум, ра́зум, соображе́ние; **he hadn't the ~(s) (or ~ enough) to realize what had happened** у него́ не доста́ло ума́ поня́ть, что случи́лось; **at one's ~'s end** в отчая́нии; **I am at my ~'s end to know what to do** про́сто ума́ не приложу́, что де́лать; **he has a ready ~** он за сло́вом в карма́н не поле́зет; **keep one's ~s about one** не растеря́ться (*pf.*); **he lives by his ~s** он авантюри́ст; **he was scared out of his ~s** он был до́ смерти напу́ган.
2 (*verbal ingenuity*) остроу́мие.
3 (*person*) остря́|к (*fem. coll.* -чка).

wit[2] /wɪt/ *v.* (*arch.*): **to ~** то есть; а и́менно.

witch /wɪtʃ/ *n.* **1** (*sorceress*) ве́дьма. **2** (*charmer*) колду́нья. **3** (*hag*) ве́дьма, ста́рая карга́.
● *v.t.* (*arch.*): **the ~ing hour** глуха́я по́лночь.
● *cpds.* **~craft** *n.* чёрная ма́гия, колдовство́; **~-doctor** *n.* зна́харь (*m.*); **~-elm,** *n.* = **wych-elm; ~-hazel** *n.* гамаме́лис; **~-hunt** *n.* (*lit., fig.*) охо́та за ве́дьмами/на ведьм.

witchery /ˈwɪtʃərɪ/ *n.* (*witchcraft*) колдовство́; (*fascination*) ча́р|ы (*pl., g.* —).

with /wɪð/ *prep.* **1** (*expr. accompaniment*) *usu.* c + *i.*; **come ~ me!** пойдёмте со мной!; **she has no-one to play ~** ей не́ с кем игра́ть; **he is ~ the manager** он у заве́дующего; **~ no hat on** без шля́пы; **~ his charm he will go far** с таки́м обая́нием он далеко́ пойдёт; **meat ~ tomato sauce** мя́со в тома́тном со́усе; **he came ~ the rest** он пришел вме́сте с остальны́ми.
2 (*expr. agreement or sympathy*): **I'm ~ you** (*in understanding*) понима́ю; поня́тно; (*in opinion*) я с ва́ми согла́сен; (*in support*) я на ва́шей стороне́; **he is ~ it** (*sl.*) он в ку́рсе; он зна́ет, что к чему́; **get ~ it!** очни́сь! (*sl.*).
3: **I lost patience ~ him** он вы́вел меня́ из терпе́ния; **don't be rough ~ the cat!** не обраща́йтесь так гру́бо с ко́шкой!; **are you pleased ~ the result?** вы дово́льны результа́том?; **what do you want ~ me?** что вы от меня́ хоти́те?; **what has it to do ~ him?** при чём тут он?; како́е э́то име́ет к нему́ отноше́ние?; **I have business ~ him** у меня́ к нему́ де́ло.
4 (*expr. antagonism or separation*): **don't argue ~ me** не спо́рьте со мной; **at war ~** в состоя́нии войны́ с + *i.*; **a break ~ tradition** отхо́д от тради́ции.

5 (*in the case of*) у + *g.*; с + *i.*; **it's a habit ~ me** у меня́ така́я привы́чка; **~ children it's different** с детьми́ совсе́м друго́е де́ло.
6 (*denoting host or person in charge, possession etc.*) у + *g.*; **we stayed ~ our friends** мы жи́ли у друзе́й; **the boy was left ~ his aunt** ма́льчика оста́вили у тётки (*or* с тёткой); **I have no money ~ me** у меня́ нет с собо́й (*or* при себе́) де́нег.
7 (*denoting instrument or means*): **I am writing ~ a pen** я пишу́ перо́м; **he walks ~ a stick** он хо́дит с па́лкой; (*by means of*) с по́мощью (*or* при по́мощи) + *g.*; посре́дством + *g.*; **the word begins/ends ~ an A** э́то сло́во начина́ется/конча́ется на «А»; **it is written ~ a hyphen** э́то пи́шется че́рез дефи́с; **I bought a suit ~ the £100** на э́ти сто фу́нтов я купи́л себе́ костю́м; **they fought ~ swords** они́ драли́сь на шпа́гах.
8 (*denoting cause*) от + *g.*; **she was shaking ~ fright** она́ дрожа́ла от стра́ха; **he went down ~ flu** он заболе́л гри́ппом; **I am delighted ~ him** я в восто́рге от него́.
9 (*denoting characteristic*): **a girl ~ blue eyes** де́вушка с голубы́ми глаза́ми; **~ child** (*pregnant*) бере́менная; **a dressing-gown ~ a blue lining** хала́т на голубо́й подкла́дке; **a tie ~ blue spots** га́лстук в си́них кра́пинках; **a suit ~ grey stripes** костю́м в се́рую поло́ску.
10 (*denoting manner etc.*): **~ pleasure** с удово́льствием; **~ care** осторо́жно.
11 (*in the same direction or degree as; at the same time as*): **the rainfall varies ~ the season** коли́чество оса́дков меня́ется в зави́симости от вре́мени го́да; **~ the approach of spring** с наступле́нием весны́; **one must move ~ the times** на́до идти́ в но́гу со вре́менем; **I could barely keep up ~ him** я е́ле за ним поспева́л.
12 (*denoting attendant circumstance*): **I sleep ~ the window open** я сплю с откры́тым окно́м; **he walked off ~ his hands in his pockets** он ушёл, засу́нув ру́ки в карма́ны; **a holiday ~ all expenses paid** по́лностью опла́ченный о́тпуск; **~ your permission** с ва́шего разреше́ния; **~ a good secretary this would never have happened** при хоро́шем секретаре́ э́того бы никогда́ не случи́лось.
13 (*despite*) несмотря́ на + *a.*; при + *p.*; **~ all his faults he's a gentleman** несмотря́ на все его́ недоста́тки, он джентльме́н; **~ the best will in the world** при всём жела́нии.
14 (*in excl. or command*): **down ~ tyranny!** доло́й тирани́ю!; **off ~ you!** убира́йтесь!; **off ~ your coat!** (доло́й) пальто́!; **out ~ it!** расска́зывайте!

withdraw /wɪð'drɔ:/ *v.t.* (*past* **withdrew;** *p.p.* **withdrawn**) отн|има́ть, -я́ть; сн|има́ть, -ять; уб|ира́ть, -ра́ть; **~ one's hand** отдёр|гивать, -нуть (*or* отн|има́ть, -я́ть) ру́ку; **~ a child from school** заб|ира́ть, -ра́ть ребёнка из шко́лы; **~ a coin from circulation** из|ыма́ть, -ъя́ть моне́ту из обраще́ния; **~ money from the bank** брать, взять де́ньги из ба́нка; **~ a horse from a race** сн|има́ть, -ять ло́шадь с забе́га; **~ an ambassador** от|зыва́ть, -озва́ть посла́; **~ troops** от|води́ть, -вести́ войска́; **~ an offer** брать, взять обра́тно/наза́д предложе́ние; **~ a statement** отка́з|ываться, -а́ться от заявле́ния; **a ~n character** за́мкнутый челове́к.
● *v.i.* (*past* **withdrew;** *p.p.* **withdrawn**) удал|я́ться, -и́ться; **~ from a competition** выбыва́ть, вы́быть из соревнова́ния; **~ into o.s.** зам|ыка́ться, -кну́ться в себе́; (*mil.*) от|ходи́ть, -ойти́.

withdrawal /wɪð'drɔ:əl/ *n.* отня́тие, сня́тие; (*of coinage*) изъя́тие; (*of statement*) отка́з (от + *g.*); (*mil.*) отво́д; (*absenting o.s.*) вы́ход, ухо́д; (*of ambassador*) отозва́ние, отзы́в; (*of drugs*) прекраще́ние приёма нарко́тиков; **~ symptoms** абстине́нтный синдро́м.

withdrawn /wɪð'drɔ:n/ *p.p. of* ⇒**withdraw**

withdrew /wɪð'dru:/ *past of* ⇒**withdraw**

withe /wɪθ/, /wɪð/, /waɪð/ = **withy**

wither /'wɪðə(r)/ *v.t.* **1** иссуш|а́ть, -и́ть; **blossom ~ed by frost** цветы́, загу́бленные моро́зом; **~ed leaves** увя́дшие ли́стья; **a ~ed arm** суха́я рука́. **2** (*fig.*) губи́ть, по-; **a ~ing glance** уничтожа́ющий взгляд; **~ing scorn** убийственное презре́ние.
● *v.i.* вя́нуть, за-; (*of beauty*) блёкнуть, по-; **the flowers ~ed in the sun** цветы́ завя́ли на со́лнце; **her beauty ~ed with age** с года́ми её красота́ увя́ла.
● *with advs.*: **~ away** *v.i.* высыха́ть, вы́сохнуть; ча́хнуть, за-; (*of the state*) отм|ира́ть, -ере́ть; **~ up** *v.i.* высыха́ть, вы́сохнуть.

withers /'wɪðəz/ *n.* хо́лка.

withhold /wɪð'həʊld/ *v.t.* (*past and p.p.* **withheld** /-'held/) **1** (*refuse to give*) отка́з|ывать, -а́ть в (*чём*); возде́рж|иваться, -а́ться от (*чего*); **~ one's consent** не да|ва́ть, -ть согла́сия; **~ payment** уде́рж|ивать, -а́ть (*or* заде́рж|ивать, -а́ть) опла́ту; **~ information** ута́|ивать, -и́ть информа́цию. **2** (*restrain*) уде́рж|ивать, -а́ть.

within /wɪ'ðɪn/ *adv.* внутри́; **from ~** изнутри́.
● *prep.* **1** (*inside*) в + *p.*; внутри́ + *g.*; **~ these walls** в э́тих стена́х; **a voice ~ him said 'no'** вну́тренний го́лос сказа́л «нет»; **my heart sank ~ me** у меня́ упа́ло се́рдце.
2 (*not farther than; accessible to*) в преде́лах + *g.*; **~ a (radius of a) mile** в ра́диусе/преде́лах одно́й ми́ли; **the library is ~ walking distance** до библиоте́ки мо́жно дойти́ пешко́м; **~ earshot** в преде́лах слы́шимости; **~ reach** в преде́лах досяга́емости; **~ sight** в преде́лах ви́димости; **we are ~ sight of our goal** мы почти́ дости́гли це́ли; **we kept ~ sight of land** мы плы́ли, не теря́я из ви́да бе́рега.
3 (*of time*) в тече́ние + *g.*; на протяже́нии + *g.*; за + *a.*; **~ (the next) three days** в тече́ние (ближа́йших) трёх дней; **I can finish the job ~ a week** я могу́ ко́нчить э́ту рабо́ту за неде́лю; **they died ~ a year of each other** они́ у́мерли оди́н за други́м в тече́ние го́да; **~ a year of his death** (*sc. after*) ме́ньше чем че́рез год по́сле его́ сме́рти; (*sc. before*) ме́ньше чем за́ год до его́ сме́рти; **the letters came ~ a few days of each other** пи́сьма пришли́ одно́ за други́м с промежу́тком в не́сколько дней.
4 (**~** *limits of*) в преде́лах/ра́мках + *g.*; **live ~ one's income** жить (*impf.*) по сре́дствам; **~ one's rights** по пра́ву; **it is ~ his powers** э́то ему́ по си́лам; э́то вхо́дит в его́ компете́нцию; **it comes ~ their jurisdiction** э́то подпада́ет под их юрисди́кцию; **keep ~ the law** держа́ться (*impf.*) в ра́мках зако́на; **keep ~ the speed limit** не превыша́ть (*impf.*) устано́вленной ско́рости; **~ limits** до изве́стной сте́пени.

without /wɪ'ðaʊt/ *adv.* (*arch., liter.*) снару́жи; (*out of doors*) на дворе́.
● *prep.* **1** (*arch., outside*) вне + *g.*
2 (*not having; lacking; free from*) без + *g.*; **~ delay** незамедли́тельно, без промедле́ния; **~ doubt** без сомне́ния; **~ fail** непреме́нно; **~ success** безуспе́шно; **times ~ number** бессчётное число́ раз; **~ regard to the consequences** не ду́мая о после́дствиях; **it goes ~ saying** само́ собо́й разуме́ется; (*with n. understood*): **even in hard times they have never gone ~** да́же в са́мые тяжёлые времена́ они́ не голода́ли; (*with gerund*): **~ thinking** не ду́мая; не поду́мав; **he did it ~ anyone finding out** он э́то сде́лал так, что никто́ не узна́л; **he left ~ so much as saying goodbye** он ушёл, да́же не прости́вшись.

withstand /wɪð'stænd/ *v.t.* (*past and p.p.* **withstood** /-'stʊd/) устоя́ть (*pf.*) пе́ред + *i.*; вы́де́рживать, вы́держать; **~ a siege** выде́рживать, вы́держать оса́ду; **~ temptation** устоя́ть (*pf.*) пе́ред собла́зном; не подд|ава́ться, -а́ться собла́зну.
● *v.i.* (*past and p.p.* **withstood** /-'stʊd/) выста́ивать, вы́стоять; выде́рживать, вы́держать.

with|y /'wɪðɪ/, **-e** /wɪθ/, /wɪð/, /waɪð/ *n.* (*shoot*) и́вовый прут; (*willow*) и́ва.

witless /'wɪtlɪs/ *adj.* глу́пый, безмо́зглый.

witness /'wɪtnɪs/ *n.* **1** (*eye-*) очеви́д|ец (*fem.* -ица); свиде́тель (*fem.* -ница).
2 (*in court of law*) свиде́тель (*fem.* -ница); (*present at search, inventory etc.*) поня́т|ой (*fem.* -а́я).
3 (*testimony*) свиде́тельство; **bear ~** свиде́тельствовать (*impf.*); дава́ть, дать показа́ния; **bear false ~** лжесвиде́тельствовать (*impf.*); **call to ~** приз|ыва́ть, -ва́ть (*кого*) в свиде́тели; ссыла́ться, сосла́ться на + *a.*; **in ~ whereof** в подтвержде́ние/доказа́тельство чего́; (*fig.*): **his clothes are a ~ to his vanity** его́ мане́ра одева́ться свиде́тельствует/говори́т о его́

W

тщесла́вии; **(as) ~ my poverty** о чём свиде́тельствует моя́ нищета́.

● *v.t.* **1** (*be spectator of*) быть свиде́телем/очеви́дцем + *g.*; **no-one ~ed the accident** никто́ не ви́дел, как произошла́ катастро́фа.
2 (*be evidence of*) свиде́тельствовать (*impf.*) о + *p.*
3: **~ s.o.'s signature** зав|еря́ть, -е́рить/свиде́тельствовать, за- чью-н. по́дпись.

● *v.i.*: **I can ~ to the truth of that** я могу́ засвиде́тельствовать, что э́то пра́вда; **he ~ed to having known the accused** он показа́л, что был знако́м с обвиня́емым.

● *cpd.* **~-box** *n.* (*US* **-stand**) ме́сто для да́чи свиде́тельских показа́ний.

witticism /ˈwɪtɪˌsɪz(ə)m/ *n.* остро́та.

wittiness /ˈwɪtɪnɪs/ *n.* остроу́мие.

wittingly /ˈwɪtɪŋlɪ/ *adv.* заве́домо, созна́тельно.

witty /ˈwɪtɪ/ *adj.* (**wittier, wittiest**) остроу́мный.

wives /waɪvz/ *pl. of* ⇒**wife**

wizard /ˈwɪzəd/ *n.* (*magician*) волше́бник, куде́сник; (*fig.*) волше́бник; **a financial ~** фина́нсовый ге́ний.
● *adj.* (*Br. sl.*) чуде́сный.

wizardry /ˈwɪzədrɪ/ *n.* волшебство́; (*fig.*) ча́р|ы (*pl., g.* —).

wizen(ed) /ˈwɪz(ə)nd/ *adj.* вы́сохший, иссо́хший.

wo /wəʊ/ = **whoa**

woad /wəʊd/ *n.* (*plant*) ва́йда; (*dye*) сини́ль.

wobble /ˈwɒb(ə)l/ *n.* кача́ние, поша́тывание.
● *v.t.* (*also* **~ about**) шата́ть (*impf.*).
● *v.i.* (*also* **~ about**) (*sway*) шата́ться, кача́ться (*both impf.*); (*stagger*) ковыля́ть (*impf.*); кача́ться (*impf.*); (*fig., vacillate*) колеба́ться (*impf.*); (*quaver*): **she ~s on the top notes** на высо́ких но́тах у неё дрожи́т го́лос.

wobbly /ˈwɒblɪ/ *adj.* (**wobblier, wobbliest**) (*lit., fig.*) ша́ткий, неусто́йчивый.

wodge /wɒdʒ/ *n.* (*Br. coll.*) кусо́к; (*of soft substance*) ком.

woe /wəʊ/ *n.* **1** (*grief, distress*) го́ре, скорбь; **tale of ~** го́рестная исто́рия; **~ is me!** (*liter. or joc.*) го́ре мне! **2** (*pl., troubles*) бе́ды (*f. pl.*).
● *cpd.* **~begone** *adj.* (*person*) удручённый; (*look*) го́рестный.

woeful /ˈwəʊfʊl/ *adj.* ско́рбный, го́рестный; (*pathetic*) жа́лкий; (*dull*) уны́лый; **a ~ countenance** ско́рбное лицо́; **~ ignorance** вопию́щее неве́жество.

wog /wɒg/ *n.* (*Br. sl., offens.*) черномáзый (*offens.*).

wok /wɒk/ *n.* сковорода́ (с вы́пуклым дни́щем).

woke /wəʊk/ *past of* ⇒**wake**[3]

woken /ˈwəʊk(ə)n/ *p.p. of* ⇒**wake**[3]

wolf /wʊlf/ *n.* (*pl.* **wolves**) (*animal*) волк; **(she-~)** волчи́ца; **cry ~** (*fig.*) подн|има́ть, -я́ть ло́жную трево́гу; **keep the ~ from the door** (*fig.*) зараба́тывать (*impf.*) на жизнь; **lone ~** (*fig.*) единоли́чни|к (*fem.* -ца); **~ in sheep's clothing** (*fig.*) волк в ове́чьей шку́ре.
● *v.t.* (*coll., also* **~ down**) прогл|а́тывать, -оти́ть с жа́дностью.
● *cpds.* **~-cub** *n.* волчо́нок; **~hound** *n.* волкода́в; **~-whistle** *n.* (*coll.*) свист при ви́де краси́вой де́вушки.

wolfish /ˈwʊlfɪʃ/ *adj.* во́лчий, зве́рский.

wolfram /ˈwʊlfrəm/ *n.* вольфра́м.

wolves /wʊlvz/ *pl. of* ⇒**wolf**

woman /ˈwʊmən/ *n.* (*pl.* **women**)
1 же́нщина; **old ~** (*lit.*) стару́ха; (*coll., wife*) жена́, хозя́йка; **single ~** незаму́жняя же́нщина; **~ of the world** быва́лая же́нщина. **2** (*coll., charwoman*): **daily ~** приходя́щая домрабо́тница. **3** (*man with feminine characteristics*) ба́ба; **he is an old ~** он настоя́щая ба́ба. **4**: **~ doctor** же́нщина-врач; **~ friend** подру́га, прия́тельница.
● *cpds.* **~-hater** *n.* женоненави́стник; **~kind** *n.* же́нщины (*f. pl.*).

womanhood /ˈwʊmənˌhʊd/ *n.*
1 (*maturity*) же́нская зре́лость; **grow to (*or* reach) ~** созр|ева́ть, -е́ть.
2 (*instinct*) же́нственность; же́нские ка́чества.

womanish /ˈwʊmənɪʃ/ *adj.* женоподо́бный, же́нственный.

womanize /ˈwʊməˌnaɪz/ *v.i.* (*coll., philander*) пу́таться (*impf.*) с ба́бами; гоня́ться (*impf.*) за ю́бками.

womanizer /ˈwʊməˌnaɪzə(r)/ *n.* (*coll.*) женолю́б, ба́бник.

womanliness /ˈwʊmənlɪnɪs/ *n.* же́нственность.

womanly /ˈwʊmənlɪ/ *adj.* же́нственный, же́нский.

womb /wu:m/ *n.* ма́тка; (*fig.*) утро́ба.

wombat /ˈwɒmbæt/ *n.* (*zool.*) вомба́т.

women /ˈwɪmɪn/ *pl. of* ⇒**woman**
● *cpds.* **~folk** *n. pl.* же́нщины (*f. pl.*); (*of household*) же́нская полови́на; **~'s liberation** *n.* эмансипа́ция же́нщин; **~'s liberation movement** движе́ние за эмансипа́цию же́нщин.

won /wʌn/ *past and p.p. of* ⇒**win**

wonder /ˈwʌndə(r)/ *n.* **1** (*miracle, marvel*) чу́до; **work ~s** твори́ть, со- чудеса́; **vitamin C does ~s** витами́н С — чудоде́йственное сре́дство; (*marvel*): **nine days ~** кратковре́менная сенса́ция; **~s will never cease** (*joc.*) чудеса́ в решете́; чудеса́, да и то́лько!; (*surprising thing*): **it's a ~ that .../the ~ is that ...** удиви́тельно, что...; **small ~ that ...** неудиви́тельно, что...; **no ~ he was angry!** неудиви́тельно, что он рассерди́лся!
2 (*amazement, admiration*) изумле́ние, восхище́ние; **the sight filled him with ~** зре́лище его́ порази́ло/изуми́ло.
● *v.t.* **1** (*be surprised*): **I ~ he wasn't killed** я удивлён, что он оста́лся в живы́х; **I shouldn't ~ if it rained** я не удивлю́сь, е́сли пойдёт дождь.
2 (*deliberate, desire to know*): **I ~ who that was** интере́сно/любопы́тно (*or* хоте́лось бы знать), кто бы э́то мог быть; **he ~ed if she was coming** он гада́л, придёт она́ и́ли нет; **you will ~ why I said that** вы спро́сите, почему́ я э́то сказа́л; **I was ~ing whether to invite him** я не мог реши́ть, приглаша́ть его́ и́ли нет; **it makes you ~ where they find the money** не понима́ю (*or* удиви́тельно), отку́да то́лько у них де́ньги беру́тся; **I ~ if I might open the window** вы не возража́ете, е́сли я откро́ю окно́?; *see also v.i.*
● *v.i.* **1** (*feel surprised*) удив|ля́ться, -и́ться (*чему*); пора|жа́ться, -зи́ться (*чему*); диви́ться (*impf.*) (*чему*); **I ~ed at his foolishness** я был поражён его́ легкомы́слием; **can you ~ that he got hurt?** неудиви́тельно, что он уши́бся.
2 (*feel curiosity*) интересова́ться (*impf.*); **I was ~ing about that** я и сам разду́мывал об э́том; **'Why do you ask?' — 'I just ~ed'** «Почему́ вы спра́шиваете?» — «Про́сто так».
3 (*expr. doubt*): **I ~** я не уве́рен; сомнева́юсь.
● *cpds.* **~land** *n.* страна́ чуде́с; **~-struck** *adj.* поражённый, изумлённый; **~-worker** *n.* чудотво́рец.

wonderful /ˈwʌndəˌfʊl/ *adj.* (*pleasing*) чуде́сный, чу́дный; (*arousing wonder*) изуми́тельный, удиви́тельный; (*impressive*) порази́тельный; **what ~ weather!** кака́я чу́дная пого́да!; **you have a ~ memory** у вас порази́тельная па́мять.

wonderment /ˈwʌndəmənt/ *n.* удивле́ние, изумле́ние.

wondrous /ˈwʌndrəs/ (*arch. or liter.*) *adj.* ди́вный.
● *adv.* удиви́тельно.

wonky /ˈwɒŋkɪ/ *adj.* (**wonkier, wonkiest**) (*Br. sl.*) (*unstable*) ша́ткий; (*crooked*) криво́й.

wont /wəʊnt/ (*arch. or liter.*) *n.* обыкнове́ние, привы́чка; **as is his ~** по своему́ обыкнове́нию.
● *adj.* привы́чный, обы́чный; **as he was ~ to say** как он люби́л говори́ть.

wonted /ˈwəʊntɪd/ *adj.* обы́чный, привы́чный, обыкнове́нный.

woo /wu:/ *v.t.* (**woos, wooed**)
1 (*court*) уха́живать (*impf.*) за + *i.*
2 (*fig., coax*) обха́живать (*impf.*); **both candidates were ~ing the voters** о́ба кандида́та пыта́лись завоева́ть расположе́ние избира́телей.

wood /wʊd/ *n.* **1** (*in sing. or pl.*) (*forest*) лес; **the road went through the ~s** доро́га шла че́рез лес (*or* ле́сом); **~ed country** леси́стая ме́стность; **~ anemone** ве́треница лесна́я; (*fig.*): **he can't see the ~ for the trees** он за дере́вьями ле́са не ви́дит; **we're not out of the ~ yet** ещё не все опа́сности/тру́дности позади́.
2 (*substance*) де́рево; **work in ~** ре́зать (*impf.*) по де́реву; **touch (*US* knock on) ~** тьфу, тьфу! чтоб не сгла́зить!; постучи́ по де́реву; **~ alcohol, ~ spirit** мети́ловый/древе́сный спирт; **~ block** (*for paving*) торе́ц; **~ carving** деревя́нная скульпту́ра/резьба́; **~**

pulp древеси́на; **~ demon** (*Russian myth.*) ле́ший.
3 (*as fuel or kindling*) дров|а́ (*pl., g.* —); **I chopped some ~ for the fire** я наколо́л дров для ками́на; **~ smoke** дым от горя́щего де́рева.
4: **the ~** (*cask*) бочо́нок; **wine/beer drawn from the ~** разливно́е вино́/пи́во.
5 (*in game of bowls*) шар.
6 (*golf-club*) деревя́нная клю́шка.
● *cpds.* **~bine** *n.* (*Br.*) (ди́кая) жи́молость; (*US*) ди́кий виногра́д; **~-carver** *n.* ре́зчик по де́реву; **~cock** *n.* ва́льдшнеп; **~craft** *n.* (*knowledge of forest conditions*) зна́ние ле́са; (**~*working***) ремесло́ деревообде́лочника; **~cut** *n.* гравю́ра на де́реве, ксилогра́фия; **~cutter** *n.* дровосе́к; **~-engraver** *n.* граве́р, ксило́граф; **~-engraving** *n.* (*process*) гравиро́вка на де́реве; ксилогра́фия; (*product*) гравю́ра на де́реве; ксилогра́фия; **~land** *n.* леси́стая ме́стность; (*large area*) лесно́й масси́в; (*attr.*) лесно́й; **~-louse** *n.* мокри́ца; **~man** *n.* лесни́к; **~-nymph** *n.* дриа́да; **~pecker** *n.* дя́тел; **~-pigeon** *n.* вя́хирь (*m.*), го́рлица; **~-pile** *n.* шта́бель (*m.*) дров; поле́нница; **~-shed** *n.* дровяно́й сара́й; **~sman** *n.* лесно́й жи́тель; **~-wind** *n.* (*collect.*) деревя́нные духовы́е инструме́нты (*m. pl.*); **~work** *n.* (*Br., carpentry*) столя́рная рабо́та; (*articles*) деревя́нные изде́лия; **~worker** *n.* пло́тник, столя́р; **~worm** *n.* личи́нка древото́чца; **~-yard** *n.* дровяно́й склад.

woodchuck /ˈwʊdtʃʌk/ *n.* суро́к лесно́й.

wooded /ˈwʊdɪd/ *adj.* леси́стый.

wooden /ˈwʊd(ə)n/ *adj.* (*also fig.*) деревя́нный.
● *cpd.* **~-headed** *adj.* тупо́й, тупоу́мный.

woody /ˈwʊdɪ/ *adj.* (**woodier, woodiest**) (*wooded*) леси́стый; (*of or like wood*) деревя́нный.

wooer /ˈwuːə(r)/ *n.* ухажёр, покло́нник.

woof¹ /wuːf/ *n.* (*weft*) уто́к.

woof² /wʊf/ *n.* (*dog's bark*) га́вканье, лай.
● *v.t.* га́вкать (*impf.*); ла́ять (*impf.*); **~!** гав!

woofer /ˈwuːfə(r)/ *n.* (*radio*) репроду́ктор ни́зкого то́на.

wool /wʊl/ *n.* **1** (*on sheep etc.*) шерсть, руно́; **pull the ~ over s.o.'s eyes** (*fig.*) пус|ка́ть, -ти́ть пыль в глаза́ кому́-н.; вв|оди́ть, -ести́ кого́-н. в заблужде́ние; **~ merchant** торго́вец ше́рстью; **knitting ~** шерсть для вяза́ния; **darning ~** шерсть для што́пки. **2** (*similar substance*): **cotton ~** ва́та; **steel ~** стальна́я ва́та.
● *cpd.* **~-gathering** *n.* (*fig.*) рассе́янность, мечта́тельность.

woollen /ˈwʊlən/ (*US* **woolen**) *adj.* шерстяно́й; **~ cloth** (шерстяно́е) сукно́.

woollens /ˈwʊlənz/ (*US* **woolens**) *n. pl.* шерстяна́я оде́жда.

woolliness /ˈwʊlɪnɪs/ *n.* (*fig.*) му́тность, нея́сность, нечёткость, тума́нность.

woolly /ˈwʊlɪ/ *n.* (*Br.*) сви́тер.
● *adj.* (**woollier, woolliest**) **1** (*bearing or covered with wool*) шерсти́стый; (*furry*) мохна́тый; (*downy*) пуши́стый. **2** (*of sound*) глухо́й; (*fig., lacking definition*) нея́сный, нечёткий, му́тный, тума́нный.

woozy /ˈwuːzɪ/ *adj.* (**woozier, wooziest**) (*coll., tipsy*) косо́й, окосе́вший; (*from blow etc.*) обалде́вший.

wop /wɒp/ *n.* (*sl., offens.*) италья́шка (*m.*).

word /wɜːd/ *n.* **1** сло́во; **he didn't say a ~ about it** он сло́ва не сказа́л/не пророни́л об э́том; **he doesn't know a ~ of English** он ни сло́ва не зна́ет по-англи́йски; **by ~ of mouth** у́стно, на слова́х; **eat one's ~s** взять (*pf.*) свои́ слова́ наза́д; **~s fail me** не нахожу́ слов; **from the ~ go** с са́мого нача́ла; **I couldn't get a ~ in (edgeways)** мне не удало́сь вста́вить ни слове́чка; **you can't get a ~ out of him** от него́ сло́ва не добьёшься; **he never has a good ~ for anyone** он ни о ком до́брого сло́ва не ска́жет; **may I have a ~ with you?** мо́жно вас на полсло́ва?; **beyond ~s** неопису́емый; **I have no ~s for it** я не зна́ю, как э́то назва́ть; **in a ~** (одни́м) сло́вом; коро́че говоря́; **in a few ~s** в не́скольких слова́х; вкра́тце; **in other ~s** и́наче говоря́, други́ми слова́ми; **in so many ~s** пря́мо, напрями́к; **he told me in so many ~s that I was a liar** он пря́мо так и сказа́л, что я лгу; **in ~s of one syllable** (*fig.*) са́мыми просты́ми слова́ми; **in ~ and deed** сло́вом и де́лом; **last ~s** после́дние/предсме́ртные слова́; **this book is the last ~ on the subject** э́та кни́га — лу́чшее, что напи́сано на э́ту те́му; **the last ~ in fashion** после́дний крик мо́ды; **he had the last ~** после́днее сло́во оста́лось за ним; **be at a loss for ~s** не находи́ть (*impf.*) слов; **a man of few ~s** немногосло́вный челове́к; **a man of many ~s** многосло́вный/велеречи́вый челове́к; **not a ~!** ни сло́ва!; **not a ~ of it is true** в э́том нет ни сло́ва пра́вды; **play on ~s** игра́ слов, каламбу́р; **put into ~s** выража́ть, вы́разить слова́ми; **put in a good ~ for s.o.** замо́лвить (*pf.*) слове́чко за кого́-н.; **you are putting ~s into my mouth** вы припи́сываете мне слова́, каки́х я не говори́л; **say a few ~s** (*sc. a brief speech*) сказа́ть (*pf.*) не́сколько слов; **you took the ~s out of my mouth** э́то как раз то, что я хоте́л сказа́ть; **he is too greedy for ~s** он невероя́тно жа́ден; **~ for ~** сло́во в сло́во; **translate ~ for ~** перев|оди́ть, -ести́ досло́вно/буква́льно; **were those his very ~s?** он и́менно так сказа́л?; **a ~ in your ear** я хочу́ вам ко́е-что сказа́ть.
2 (*pl., disputation, quarrel*) ссо́ра, перебра́нка; **they had ~s** они́ побрани́лись.
3 (*pl., text set to music*) текст, слова́ (*nt. pl.*); **set, put ~s to music** положи́ть (*pf.*) слова́ на му́зыку.
4 (*pl., actor's part*) роль, текст.
5 (*bibl.*): **the W~** Сло́во; **God's W~** сло́во Госпо́дне.
6 (*news; information*) изве́стие, сообще́ние; **send ~ of something** изве|ща́ть, -сти́ть о чём-н.; **he sent, left ~ that he was not coming** он переда́л, что не смо́жет прийти́; **~ came that he had been killed** пришло́ сообще́ние, что он поги́б; **the ~ got round that ...** ста́ло изве́стно, что. . . .
7 (*promise; assurance*) сло́во, обеща́ние; **give, pledge one's ~** да|ва́ть, -ть сло́во; обеща́ть (*impf., pf.*); **keep one's ~** держа́ть, с- сло́во; **~ of honour** (*Br.*), **honor** (*US*)**!** че́стное сло́во!; **a man of his ~** челове́к сло́ва; **he was as good as his ~** он сдержа́л сло́во; **take s.o. at his ~** пойма́ть (*pf.*) кого́-н. на сло́ве; **you must take my ~ for it** вам придётся пове́рить мне на сло́во.
8 (*command*) сло́во, прика́з; **at the ~ of command** по кома́нде; **at the ~ 'go', start running!** по кома́нде «марш!» — беги́те!; **give the ~** отд|ава́ть, -а́ть приказа́ние/распоряже́ние; **just say the ~!** то́лько скажи́те/прикажи́те!
● *v.t.* формули́ровать, с-; выража́ть, вы́разить; сост|авля́ть, -а́вить; **that might have been differently ~ed** э́то мо́жно бы́ло сказа́ть/вы́разить ина́че.
● *cpds.* **~-blind** *adj.* страда́ющий слове́сной слепото́й/але́ксией; **~-break, ~-division** *nn.* (*typ.*) перено́с; **~-game** *n.* слове́сная игра́ (*скрэбл и т.п.*); **~-perfect** *adj.* зна́ющий (*что*) наизу́сть; **~-play** *n.* игра́ слов; каламбу́р; **~-processing** *n.* редакти́рование те́кста; **~-processor** *n.* те́кстовый проце́ссор; **~ wrap** *n.* (*comput.*) перехо́д на но́вую строку́.

wordiness /ˈwɜːdɪnɪs/ *n.* многосло́вие.

wording /ˈwɜːdɪŋ/ *n.* фо́рмула, формулиро́вка; (*of text*) реда́кция.

wordless /ˈwɜːdlɪs/ *adj.* безмо́лвный.

wordy /ˈwɜːdɪ/ *adj.* (**wordier, wordiest**) многосло́вный.

wore /wɔː(r)/ *past of* ⇒**wear**

work /wɜːk/ *n.* **1** (*mental or physical labour, task*) рабо́та, труд; (*official, professional*) рабо́та, слу́жба; (*school etc.*) заня́тия (*nt. pl.*); (*activity*) де́ятельность; **job of ~** де́ло; **he is at ~** он сейча́с рабо́тает; **he is at (his place of) ~** он на рабо́те/слу́жбе; **he is at ~ on a dictionary** он рабо́тает над словарём; **all in the day's ~** в поря́дке веще́й, норма́льно; **creative ~** тво́рческая де́ятельность; **good ~s** до́брые дела́; **public ~s** обще́ственные рабо́ты (*f. pl.*); **his life's ~** де́ло его́ жи́зни; **we have done a good day's ~** мы сего́дня успе́шно порабо́тали; **he is doing some ~ on the house** он занима́ется ремо́нтом до́ма; **he is doing some ~ on the Stuarts** он рабо́тает над исто́рией дина́стии Стю́артов; **there is plenty of ~ to be done** здесь мно́го рабо́ты; **I have ~ to do** мне на́до рабо́тать; **get to ~ on** нач|ина́ть, -а́ть рабо́ту над + *i.*; **get down to ~** прин|има́ться,

W

-я́ться/бра́ться, взя́ться за рабо́ту/де́ло; **you are making hard ~ of it** вы де́лаете из э́того це́лую исто́рию; **make short ~ of** бы́стро/жи́во распра́виться (*pf.*) с + *i.*; **many hands make light ~** когда́ рук мно́го, рабо́та спо́рится; **set s.o. to ~** заст|авля́ть, -а́вить кого́-н. рабо́тать; засади́ть (*pf.*) кого́-н. за рабо́ту (*coll.*).
2 (*activity, not necessarily productive*) де́йствие, посту́пок; **it was the ~ of a moment** э́то бы́ло де́лом одно́й мину́ты; **dirty ~** (*difficult, unpleasant*) чёрная рабо́та; (*nefarious*) по́длость; **there's been some dirty ~ here** тут де́ло нечи́сто; **nice ~!** (*coll.*) отли́чно!; здо́рово.
3 (*employment*) рабо́та, слу́жба; **it is hard to find ~** тру́дно найти́ рабо́ту; **in ~** рабо́тающий; **out of ~** без рабо́ты; **he was put out of ~** он лиши́лся рабо́ты.
4 (*specified handicraft*): **fancy ~** (*carving*) резьба́; (*embroidery*) худо́жественная вы́шивка; **embossed ~** чека́нка.
5 (*workmanship*) мастерство́, отде́лка; **an excellent piece of ~** прекра́сная/отли́чная рабо́та.
6 (*finished product*) произведе́ние, изде́лие; **sale of ~** прода́жа изде́лий.
7 (*literary or artistic composition*) произведе́ние, сочине́ние; (*esp. academic*) труд, иссле́дование; (*collect.*) тво́рчество; (*publication*) изда́ние; **the (complete) ~s of Shakespeare** (по́лное) собра́ние сочине́ний Шекспи́ра; **~s on art** иссле́дования по иску́сству; **~ of reference** спра́вочник, спра́вочное изда́ние; **the ~s of Chopin** произведе́ния Шопе́на; **a ~ of art** произведе́ние иску́сства.
8 (*pl., parts of machine*) механи́зм; **the ~s of a clock** часово́й механи́зм; **something is wrong with the ~s** механи́зм расстро́ился; (*fig.*): **I asked them a simple question and I got the whole ~s** (*coll.*) я за́дал им просто́й вопро́с, а они́ меня́ заму́чили подро́бностями.
9 (*pl., Br., factory or similar installation*) заво́д, фа́брика, предприя́тие; **engineering ~s** машинострои́тельный заво́д; **steel ~s** сталелите́йный заво́д; **sewage ~s** канализацио́нные очисти́тельные сооруже́ния (*nt. pl.*); **~s manager** дире́ктор заво́да/фа́брики.
10 (*pl., Br., operations*): **public ~s** обще́ственные рабо́ты (*f. pl.*); **clerk of the ~s** производи́тель (*m.*) рабо́т; проpа́б.
11 (*pl., defensive structures; fortifications*) фортифика́ция, сооруже́ния (*nt. pl.*); **defensive ~s** оборони́тельные сооруже́ния.
● *v.t.* (*past and p.p.* **worked** *or arch.* **wrought**) **1** (*cause to ~, exact ~ from*): **he ~s his men hard** он заставля́ет люде́й мно́го рабо́тать; **he ~ed himself to death** он извёл себя́ рабо́той; **that idea has been ~ed to death** э́то изби́тая иде́я; **~ one's fingers to the bone** труди́ться/рабо́тать (*impf.*) до седьмо́го по́та.
2 (*set in motion, actuate*) прив|оди́ть, -ести́ в движе́ние/де́йствие; **~ a lever** наж|има́ть, -а́ть на рыча́г; **how do you ~ this machine?** как управля́ть э́той маши́ной?
3 (*effect*): **~ wonders** твори́ть, со- чудеса́; **he ~ed it so that he was off duty** (*coll.*) он так устро́ил, что ему́ не на́до бы́ло дежу́рить.
4 (*achieve by ~ing*): **~ one's passage** отраб|а́тывать, -о́тать свой прое́зд; **he ~ed his way through university** все го́ды студе́нчества он зараба́тывал себе́ на жизнь; **he ~ed his way up to the rank of manager** он проби́лся в дире́ктора; он дослужи́лся до дире́ктора; **~ one's way forward** пробира́ться (*impf.*) вперёд.
5 (*operate, manage: a mine, land etc.*) разраба́тывать, обраба́тывать, эксплуати́ровать (*all impf.*); **the mine was ~ed by Italians** на ша́хте рабо́тали италья́нцы; **our salesman who ~s the north-west** наш коммивояжёр, обслу́живающий се́веро-за́падный райо́н.
6 (*move, bring by degrees*): **~ something into place** вти́с|кивать, -нуть что-н. куда́-н.; **he ~ed the conversation round to his favourite** (*Br.*), **favorite** (*US*) **subject** он постепе́нно подвёл разгово́р к свое́й излю́бленной те́ме; **he ~ed this theme into his story** он ввёл/вплёл э́ту те́му в свой расска́з.
7 (*shape, manipulate; see also* ⇒**wrought**) обраб|а́тывать, -о́тать; **~ clay/dough** меси́ть, за- гли́ну/те́сто.
8 (*excite*) возбу|жда́ть, -ди́ть; **he ~ed the crowd into a frenzy** он довёл толпу́ до неи́стовства; **~ o.s. into a rage** дов|оди́ть, -ести́ себя́ до исступле́ния.
9 (*make by stitching etc.*) вышива́ть, вы́шить; **a design of flowers was ~ed in silk on the tablecloth** ска́терть была́ вы́шита шёлковым цвето́чным узо́ром.
● *v.i.* **1** (*labour, be employed*) рабо́тать, труди́ться, служи́ть (*all impf.*); **he ~ed for 6 hours** он рабо́тал 6 часо́в; **~ at a problem** рабо́тать/би́ться (*impf.*) над зада́чей; **~ at a lathe** рабо́тать (*impf.*) на тока́рном станке́; **~ for the government** быть (*impf.*) на госуда́рственной слу́жбе; **~ for peace** боро́ться (*impf.*) за мир; **~ for a living** зараба́тывать (*impf.*) себе́ на жизнь; **he ~s in oils** он пи́шет ма́слом; **he is ~ing on a novel** он рабо́тает над рома́ном; **~ to a budget** держа́ться (*impf.*) в преде́лах бюдже́та; **~ to rule** (*Br.*) пров|оди́ть, -ести́ италья́нскую забасто́вку; **~ with s.o.** сотру́дничать (*impf.*) с кем-н.; **~ to a tight schedule** приде́рживаться (*impf.*) стро́гого расписа́ния.
2 (*operate, function*) рабо́тать (*impf.*); де́йствовать (*impf.*); **the brake won't ~** то́рмоз отказа́л; **my watch stopped ~ing** мои́ часы́ переста́ли идти́; **the machine ~s by electricity** аппара́т рабо́тает на электри́честве; **everything was ~ing smoothly** всё шло гла́дко/как по ма́слу (*coll.*).
3 (*produce desired effect*): **the plan ~ed** план уда́лся; **the medicine ~ed** лека́рство помогло́/поде́йствовало; **the method ~s well** э́тот ме́тод уда́чен/эффекти́вен.
4 (*exert influence*) рабо́тать, де́йствовать (*both impf.*); ока́з|ывать, -а́ть влия́ние; **~ against** меша́ть, по- + *d.*; служи́ть, по- поме́хой + *d.*; **~ on s.o.** обраб|а́тывать, -о́тать кого́-н.; **~ towards** спосо́бствовать (*impf.*) + *d.*; стреми́ться (*impf.*) к + *d.*
5 (*ferment*) броди́ть (*impf.*); **she left the yeast to ~** она́ поста́вила дро́жжи(, что́бы они́ подошли́).
6 (*move gradually*): **a screw ~ed loose** винт осла́б; **the damp ~ed through the plaster** сы́рость прони́кла че́рез штукату́рку.
● *with advs.*: **~ around** *v.i.* = **~ round; ~ away** *v.i.* труди́ться (*impf.*); (*coll.*) корпе́ть (*impf.*) (*над чем*); **~ back** *v.i.*: **I ~ed back through last year's newspapers** я просмотре́л номера́ газе́т за про́шлый год (в обра́тном поря́дке); **~ down** *v.i.*: **my socks ~ down as I walk** когда́ я хожу́, у меня́ соска́льзывают носки́; **~ in** *v.t.*: **mix butter, sugar and eggs, then ~ in the dry ingredients** смеша́йте я́йца с ма́слом и са́харом, пото́м доба́вьте сухи́е ингредие́нты; **he ~ed in some local allusions** он косну́лся ме́стной тема́тики; **~ off** *v.t.*: **he ran round the house to ~ off some of his energy** он пробежа́лся вокру́г до́ма, что́бы дать вы́ход свое́й эне́ргии; **I shall never be able to ~ off this debt** я никогда́ не смогу́ изба́виться от э́того до́лга; **~ out** *v.t.* (*devise*) разраб|а́тывать, -о́тать; (*calculate*) вычисля́ть, вы́числить; **you must ~ out the answer yourself** вы должны́ са́ми найти́ отве́т; (*solve*) разреш|а́ть, -и́ть; ула́|живать, -дить; **~ things out** раз|бира́ться, -обра́ться; **all this will ~ itself out** всё э́то ула́дится/образу́ется; **the mine is ~ed out** рудни́к истощи́лся; *v.i.* (*turn out*) ока́з|ываться, -а́ться; получ|а́ться, -и́ться; конча́ться, ко́нчиться; (*turn out well*) об|ходи́ться, -ойти́сь; **everything ~ed out** всё обошло́сь; **our marriage hasn't ~ed out** наш брак оказа́лся неуда́чным; (*be solved*) разреш|а́ться, -и́ться; **the sum won't ~ out** зада́ча не выхо́дит/получа́ется; (*of calculation*): **the expenses ~ out at £70** расхо́ды составля́ют 70 фу́нтов; **his share ~s out at £5** его́ до́ля сво́дится к пяти́ фу́нтам; (*train, of an athlete*) тренирова́ться (*impf.*); **~ over** *v.t.* переpаб|а́тывать, -о́тать; (*beat up*): **the gang gave him a ~ing-over** (*coll.*) ша́йка его́ изби́ла до полусме́рти; **~ round** *v.i.*: **I was just ~ing round to that point** я как раз подходи́л к э́тому вопро́су; **~ up** *v.t.* (*elaborate*) перераб|а́тывать, -о́тать; **these ideas are worth ~ing up into a book** над э́тими иде́ями сто́ит порабо́тать и вы́пустить их (отде́льной) кни́гой; (*raise, develop*): **he ~ed up a profitable business** он разверну́л при́быльное де́ло; **I can't ~ up any interest in economics** я никак не могу́ пробуди́ть в себе́ интере́с к эконо́мике; **I went for a short walk to ~ up an appetite** я вы́шел немно́го пройти́сь, что́бы нагуля́ть себе́ аппети́т; (*arouse, excite*): **he ~ed himself up** он взвинти́л себя́; **he ~ed**

up his listeners to a pitch of fury он довёл свои́х слу́шателей до неи́стовства; (*pred.*): **~ed up** (*excited*) взволно́ван, возбуждён; (*worried*) расстро́ен; **get o.s. ~ed up** (*worried*) расстр|а́иваться, -о́иться; *v.i.*: **events were ~ing up to a climax** собы́тия нараста́ли; **she realized that he was ~ing up to a proposal** она́ поняла́, что он собира́ется сде́лать ей предложе́ние.

● *cpds.* **~-bag, ~-basket** *nn.* су́мка/корзи́нка с рукоде́лием; **~-bench** *n.* верста́к; **~-book** *n.* тетра́дь для упражне́ний; **~day** *n.* (*US*) рабо́чий день; **~-force** *n.* рабо́чая си́ла; (*workers*) (*manual*) рабо́чие; (*non-manual*) рабо́тники; **~-horse** *n.* рабо́чая ло́шадь; **~house** *n.* (*Br.*) рабо́тный дом; (*US*) исправи́тельная тюрьма́; **~-load** *n.* нагру́зка; **~man** *n.* рабо́тник; (*builder etc.*) рабо́чий; **~manlike** *adj.* иску́сный; **~manship** *n.* мастерство́, иску́сство; **~mate** *n.* (*Br.*) сотру́дни|к (*fem.* -ца), колле́га (*c.g.*); **~-out** *n.* трениро́вка; **~-room** *n.* рабо́чая ко́мната/мастерска́я; **~-sheet** *n.* рабо́чий листо́к; рабо́чая ка́рта; **~shop** *n.* (*small*) мастерска́я; (*large*) цех; **~-shy** *adj.* (*coll.*) лени́вый; **~ station** *n.* (*comput.*) рабо́чая ста́нция; **~-table** *n.* рабо́чий стол; **~-top** *n.* (*Br.*) (*surface for working*) рабо́чий стол; (*in kitchen*) ве́рхняя пане́ль; **~-to-rule** *n.* (*Br.*) ≈ италья́нская забасто́вка.

workable /ˈwɜːkəb(ə)l/ *adj.* **1** (*of mine etc.*) рента́бельный. **2** (*feasible*) выполни́мый, реа́льный, осуществи́мый.

workaday /ˈwɜːkəˌdeɪ/ *adj.* бу́дний, повседне́вный.

workaholic /ˌwɜːkəˈhɒlɪk/ *n.* работома́н, трудого́лик.

worker /ˈwɜːkə(r)/ *n.* рабо́тник, трудя́щийся; (*manual*) рабо́чий; **hard ~** тру́жени|к (*fem.* -ца), работя́га (*c.g.*) (*coll.*); **office ~** слу́жащий; **~ bee** рабо́чая пчела́.

working /ˈwɜːkɪŋ/ *n.* **1** (*mine, quarry etc.*) рудни́к, вы́работка. **2** (*usu. pl.*; *operation*) рабо́та, де́йствие, функциони́рование; **the ~s of the human mind** мысли́тельный проце́сс. **3** (*attr., pert. to work*) рабо́чий; **~ capital** оборо́тный капита́л; **~ clothes** рабо́чая оде́жда, спецо́вка; **~ conditions** усло́вия труда́; **~ day** (*Br.*) (*part of day devoted to work*) рабо́чий день; (*opp. to rest day*) рабо́чий/бу́дний день; **~ hours** рабо́чее вре́мя/рабо́чие часы́; **~ knowledge** о́бщее знако́мство (с + *i.*); **all his ~ life** вся его́ трудова́я жизнь; **~ lunch** делово́й обе́д; **in ~ order** в испра́вности.

● *adj.* рабо́чий; **~ man** рабо́чий, рабо́тник; **~ men's club** рабо́чий клуб; **~ class** рабо́чий класс; **~ model** де́йствующая моде́ль; **~ party** (*Br.*) рабо́чая гру́ппа; **~ woman** рабо́тающая же́нщина.

● *cpds.* **~-class** *adj.* рабо́чий, характе́рный для представи́теля рабо́чего кла́сса; **~-class families** се́мьи рабо́чих; **~-out** *n.* (*elaboration*) дета́льная разрабо́тка.

world /wɜːld/ *n.* **1** (*universe, system*) мир, вселе́нная; **the ancient ~** анти́чный мир; **new ~** но́вый мир; **come into the ~** появ|ля́ться, -и́ться на свет; **bring into the ~** (*give birth to; deliver*) произв|оди́ть, -ести́ на свет; **he is not long for this ~** он не жиле́ц на э́том све́те; **out of this ~** (*coll., stupendous*) потряса́ющий; **not of this ~** не от ми́ра сего́; **in this ~** на э́том све́те; **the other, next ~; the ~ to come** тот свет; **in the next ~** на том све́те; **the end of the ~** (*i.e. of time*) коне́ц све́та, светопреставле́ние. **2** (*intensive and other fig. uses*): **how in the ~ did you know?** как вы то́лько умудри́лись (э́то) узна́ть?; **what in the ~ has happened?** да что же, наконе́ц, случи́лось?; **why in the ~ didn't you tell me?** ну почему́ же вы мне не сказа́ли?; **not for the ~** ни за что на све́те; **I wouldn't hurt him for the ~** я его́ ни за что (на све́те) не стал бы обижа́ть; **she's all the ~ to me** она для меня́ — всё; **the boss thinks the ~ of him** он у хозя́ина на о́чень высо́ком счету́; **I would give the ~ to know** я бы всё отда́л, то́лько бы узна́ть; **be dead to the ~** спать (*impf.*) мёртвым сном; **I felt on top of the ~** я был на верши́не сча́стья; я был в превосхо́дном настрое́нии. **3** (*infinite amount or extent*) мно́го, у́йма (*coll.*); **a ~ of difference** огро́мная ра́зница; **it will do him a ~ of good** э́то пойдёт ему́ на по́льзу. **4** (*geog.; the earth's countries and peoples*) мир, свет; **a journey round the ~** путеше́ствие вокру́г све́та; **go round the ~** объезжа́ть, объе́хать весь свет; **the ~'s his oyster** весь мир у его́ ног; **his ~ is a very narrow one** его́ мир о́чень у́зок; у него́ о́чень у́зкий кругозо́р; **the whole (*or* all the) ~ knows** всем (*or* всему́ ми́ру) изве́стно; **(all) the ~ over** в це́лом ми́ре; по всему́ све́ту; **to the ~'s end** на кра́й све́та; **the Old/New W~** Ста́рый/Но́вый свет; **the English-speaking ~** англоязы́чные стра́ны (*f. pl.*); **the Third W~** тре́тий мир; **~ affairs** междунаро́дные дела́; **W~ Bank** Мирово́й Банк; **~ champion** чемпио́н ми́ра; **~ championship** чемпиона́т ми́ра; **W~ Cup** Ку́бок ми́ра по футбо́лу; **W~'s Fair** Всеми́рная вы́ставка; **~ peace** мир во всём ми́ре; **~ politics** мирова́я поли́тика; **a ~ power** вели́кая держа́ва; **~ record** мирово́й реко́рд; **~ war** мирова́я война́; **W~ War I/II** пе́рвая/втора́я мирова́я война́ (*or, in former USSR* Вели́кая Оте́чественная Война́). **5** (*human affairs; active life*) жизнь; **a man of the ~** быва́лый челове́к; **all's right with the ~** в ми́ре всё прекра́сно; **get on in the ~** выходи́ть, вы́йти в лю́ди; **come up in the ~** де́лать, с- карье́ру; **go down in the ~** утра́|чивать, -тить было́е положе́ние. **6** (*society*) о́бщество, свет; **the great ~** вы́сший свет; **what will the ~ say?** что ска́жет свет?; что ска́жут лю́ди? **7** (*sphere; domain*) мир; сфе́ра; **the ~ of nature** ца́рство приро́ды; **the scientific ~** нау́чный мир, нау́чные круги́ (*m. pl.*); **the animal ~** живо́тный мир; **the ~ of art** мир иску́сства.

● *cpds.* **~-famous** *adj.* всеми́рно изве́стный; **~-view** *n.* мировоззре́ние; **~-weary** *adj.* пресы́щенный жи́знью; **~-wide** *adj.* всеми́рный, мирово́й; *adv.* по всему́ све́ту/ми́ру; **W~ Wide Web** *n.* веб, Интерне́т, Сеть.

worldliness /ˈwɜːldlɪnɪs/ *n.* посюсторо́нность, су́етность.

worldly /ˈwɜːldlɪ/ *adj.* (**worldlier, worldliest**) **1** (*material*) земно́й, материа́льный; **~ goods** иму́щество. **2** (*of this world; secular*) земно́й, мирско́й; **~ wisdom** жите́йская му́дрость. **3**: **a ~ person** (*not spiritual*) су́етный челове́к; (*experienced*) о́пытный, искушённый челове́к.

● *cpds.* **~-minded** *adj.* посюсторо́нний, су́етный; **~-wise** *adj.* о́пытный; искушённый.

worm /wɜːm/ *n.* **1** (*earth ~*) червь (*m.*), червя́к. **2** (*larva, grub*) гу́сеница, личи́нка. **3** (*parasite*) глист; **he has ~s** у него́ глисты́. **4** (*abject person*) ничто́жный червь. **5** (*part of screw*) червя́к, шнек; (*type of screw*) червя́чный винт.

● *v.t.* **1** (*crawl*): **he ~ed his way through the bushes** он пропо́лз ме́жду куста́ми; (*insinuate*): **he ~ed himself into her confidence** он втёрся к ней в дове́рие. **2** (*extract*) выпы́тывать, вы́пытать/выве́дывать, вы́ведать; **they ~ed the secret out of him** они́ вы́ведали его́ та́йну. **3** (*rid of parasites*) гнать (*impf.*) глисто́в у + *g.*

● *cpds.* **~-cast** *n.* земля́, вы́брошенная земляны́м червём; **~-eaten** *adj.* черви́вый; (*fig.*) устаре́вший; **~-hole** *n.* червото́чина; **~-powder** *n.* глистого́нное сре́дство.

wormwood /ˈwɜːmwʊd/ *n.* полы́нь; (*fig.*) го́речь.

worn /wɔːn/ *see* ⇒**wear** *v.t. and* **wear out**

worried /ˈwʌrɪd/ *adj.* обеспоко́енный, озабо́ченный.

worrier /ˈwʌrɪə(r)/ *n.* (*person*) беспоко́йный челове́к, паникёр (*coll.*); **he's a ~** он ве́чно беспоко́ится; он паникёр.

worrisome /ˈwʌrɪsəm/ *adj.* беспоко́йный.

worr|y /ˈwʌrɪ/ *n.* **1** (*anxiety*) трево́га, забо́та. **2** (*something causing anxiety*) неприя́тность, забо́та; **he is a ~y to me** он доставля́ет мне мно́го беспоко́йства/забо́т; **money ~ies** де́нежные забо́ты (*f. pl.*).

● *v.t.* **1** (*cause anxiety or discomfort to*) беспоко́ить (*impf.*); волнова́ть (*impf.*); забо́тить, о-; **what is ~ying you?** что вас беспоко́ит?; чем вы озабо́чены?; **I'm ~ied about my son** я беспоко́юсь за сы́на; **I am ~ied about his health** я беспоко́юсь за его́ здоро́вье; я озабо́чен состоя́нием его́ здоро́вья; **don't ~y yourself** не беспоко́йтесь; **she ~ies herself sick** она́ изво́дит себя́ трево́гой.

W

2 (*trouble*; *bother*) надоеда́ть (*impf.*) + *d.*; пристава́ть (*impf.*) к + *d.*; **he keeps ~ying me to read him a story** он приста́ёт ко мне, что́бы я ему́ почита́л; **the noise doesn't ~y me** шум не меша́ет мне.
3 (*of dog*) рвать (*impf.*) зуба́ми; трепа́ть (*impf.*); (*attack*) броса́ться (*impf.*) на + *a.*; **your dog has been ~ying my sheep** ва́ша соба́ка броса́лась на мои́х ове́ц.

● *v.i.* беспоко́иться, волнова́ться, расстра́иваться (*all impf.*); **you are ~ying over nothing** вы напра́сно (*or* по пустяка́м) расстра́иваетесь/волну́етесь; **why ~?** (*let's be cheerful*) сто́ит ли (*or* к чему́) волнова́ться/трево́житься?; **not to ~!** (*coll.*) не волну́йтесь!; не беда́!

worse /wɜ:s/ *n.* ху́дшее; **there is ~ to come** ху́дшее ещё впереди́; **a change for the ~** переме́на к ху́дшему; **things went from bad to ~** положе́ние станови́лось всё ху́же и ху́же.

● *adj.* ху́дший; **we couldn't have picked a ~ day** тру́дно бы́ло бы вы́брать бо́лее неуда́чный день; **you will only make matters ~** вы то́лько уху́дшите положе́ние; **or ~** и́ли ещё что-н. ху́же; **I can't think of anything ~** не могу́ себе́ предста́вить ничего́ ху́же; **he was none the ~ for his adventure** он вы́шел цел и невреди́м из э́того приключе́ния; **he looked the ~ for wear** у него́ был си́льно потрёпанный вид; **~ luck!** к сожале́нию; к несча́стью; (*as pred.*) ху́же; **the patient is ~ today** больно́му сего́дня ху́же; **my situation is ~** моё положе́ние ху́же; **his work is getting ~** его́ рабо́та стано́вится ху́же; **his condition is ~** его́ состоя́ние уху́дшилось; **they are ~ off than we** они́ в ху́дшем положе́нии, чем мы; (*financially*) они́ ме́нее состоя́тельны, чем мы.

● *adv.* ху́же; **we played ~ than ever** мы игра́ли ху́же чем когда́-либо; **you might do ~ than accept** мо́жет быть, и сто́ит приня́ть.

worsen /ˈwɜ:s(ə)n/ *v.t. & i.* ух|удша́ть(ся), -у́дшить(ся).

worship /ˈwɜ:ʃɪp/ *n.* **1** (*relig.*) культ, поклоне́ние, почита́ние; **act of ~** богослуже́ние, церко́вная слу́жба; **freedom of ~** свобо́да со́вести/вероисповеда́ния; свобо́да отправле́ния религио́зных ку́льтов; **place of ~** це́рковь, храм. **2** (*of person etc.*) поклоне́ние, преклоне́ние; **~ of success** преклоне́ние пе́ред успе́хом; **Your W~** (*Br.*) Ва́ша ми́лость.

● *v.t. & i.* (**worshipped, worshipping;** *US* **worshiped, worshiping**) поклоня́ться (*impf.*) + *d.*; преклоня́ться (*impf.*) (пе́ред + *i.*); почита́ть (*impf.*); **~ God** моли́ться (*impf.*) Бо́гу; **~ strange gods** поклоня́ться чужи́м бога́м; (*attend ~*) моли́ться (*impf.*); **the church where he ~ped** це́рковь, в кото́рой он моли́лся; (*idolize, adore*) боготвори́ть (*impf.*); **he ~s the ground she walks/treads on** он гото́в целова́ть зе́млю, по кото́рой она́ ступа́ет.

worshipful /ˈwɜ:ʃɪp,fʊl/ *adj.* уважа́емый, почте́нный.

worshipper /ˈwɜ:ʃɪpə(r)/ (*US* **worshiper**) *n.* (*person attending service*) моля́щийся; (*fig.*) покло́нни|к (*fem.* -ца).

worst /wɜ:st/ *n.* наиху́дшее; са́мое плохо́е; **the ~ is over** са́мое плохо́е позади́; **the ~ of the storm is over** што́рм начина́ет утиха́ть; **the ~ of it is that ...** ху́же всего́ то, что...; **that's the ~ of being clever** в то́м-то и беда́/го́ре у́мников; **if the ~ should happen** е́сли произойдёт са́мое стра́шное; **if the ~ comes to the ~** в са́мом ху́дшем слу́чае; на худо́й коне́ц; **we must prepare for the ~** мы должны́ быть гото́вы к ху́дшему; **he was at his ~** он показа́л себя́ с наиху́дшей стороны́; **you saw him at his ~** вы ви́дели его́ с наиху́дшей стороны́; **at (the) ~ you may have to pay a fine** в кра́йнем слу́чае вам придётся уплати́ть штраф.

● *adj.* наиху́дший; са́мый плохо́й; **this is the ~ result** э́то са́мый плохо́й результа́т; **my ~ enemy** мой зле́йший враг; **that was his ~ mistake** э́то была́ его́ са́мая серьёзная оши́бка; **you came at the ~ possible time** вы пришли́ в са́мое неподходя́щее вре́мя.

● *adv.* (*of objects*) ху́же всего́; (*of people*) ху́же всех; **he fared ~ of all** ему́ пришло́сь ху́же, чем всем остальны́м.

● *v.t.* (*liter.*) побе|жда́ть, -ди́ть.

worsted /ˈwʊstɪd/ *n.* (*yarn*) гребённая шерсть; (*cloth*) ткань из гребённой ше́рсти; шерстяна́я мате́рия.

worth /wɜ:θ/ *n.* (*value*) це́нность; (*merit*) досто́инство; **of great ~** значи́тельный; **of little ~** незначи́тельный; **a man of ~** досто́йный челове́к; (*quantity of specified value*): **give me a pound's ~ of sweets** да́йте мне конфе́т на оди́н фунт.

● *pred. adj.* **1** (*of value equal to*): **it's ~ about £1** э́то сто́ит о́коло одного́ фу́нта; **what is your house ~?** во ско́лько оце́нивается ваш дом?; **what's it ~ to you if I tell you?** что вы дади́те за то, что́бы узна́ть?; **this isn't ~ much today** сейча́с э́то сто́ит ма́ло/за э́то мно́го не даду́т; **it's ~ a lot to me** для меня́ э́то о́чень це́нно/ва́жно (*or* мно́го зна́чит); **our money is ~ less every day** на́ши де́ньги обесце́ниваются с ка́ждым днём; **he is ~ his weight in gold** таки́е, как он, це́нятся на вес зо́лота.
2 (*deserving of*) сто́ящий, заслу́живающий; **it's not ~ the trouble of asking** не сто́ит спра́шивать; **it is ~ while** сто́ит; не меша́ет; не ли́шнее; **it is well ~ while** о́чень да́же сто́ит; **it is ~ noticing** э́то заслу́живает внима́ния; **it's hardly ~ mentioning** об э́том вряд ли сто́ит упомина́ть; **it's well ~ the money** э́то вполне́ сто́ящая вещь; **well ~ having** о́чень сто́ящий/поле́зный; **is life ~ living?** сто́ит ли жить?
3 (*possessed of*): **he is ~ 3 billion** его́ ли́чное состоя́ние оце́нивается в 3 миллиа́рда; **he died ~ a million** когда́ он у́мер, его́ ли́чное состоя́ние оце́нивалось в 1 миллио́н; (*fig.*): **he ran for all he was ~** он мча́лся во весь дух (*or* изо всех сил).

● *cpd.* **~while** *adj.* це́нный, сто́ящий; **a ~while undertaking** сто́ящее де́ло; **a ~while experiment** це́нный о́пыт.

worthiness /ˈwɜ:ðɪnɪs/ *n.* досто́инство.

worthless /ˈwɜ:θlɪs/ *adj.* (*goods*) ничего́ не сто́ящий; **these goods are ~** э́ти това́ры ничего́ не сто́ят; (*person, contribution*) ничто́жный, никчёмный.

worthlessness /ˈwɜ:θlɪsnɪs/ *n.* ничто́жность, никчёмность.

worthy /ˈwɜ:ðɪ/ *n.* (*arch. or joc.*) почте́нный челове́к/муж; **local worthies** ме́стные мужи́.

● *adj.* (**worthier, worthiest**)
1 (*estimable*; *meritorious*; *deserving respect*) досто́йный, почте́нный; **a ~ man** досто́йный челове́к; **a ~ life** досто́йная/че́стно про́житая жизнь; **a ~ cause** досто́йное де́ло.
2 (*deserving*) досто́йный, заслу́живающий + *g.*; **~ of note** досто́йный внима́ния; **~ of (or to have) a place in the team** досто́йный быть чле́ном кома́нды; **a cause ~ of support** де́ло, заслу́живающее подде́ржки. **3** (*matching up or appropriate*) подоба́ющий + *d.*; **~ of the occasion** подоба́ющий слу́чаю; **he is not ~ of her** он её не сто́ит.

wotcher /ˈwɒtʃə(r)/ *int.* (*Br. sl.*) здоро́во!

would /wʊd/, /wəd/ *v. aux.* (*see also* ⇒**will**) **1** (*conditional*): **he ~ be angry if he knew** он рассерди́лся бы, е́сли бы узна́л; **I ~n't know** отку́да мне знать?
2 (*expr. wish*): **I ~ like to know** я хоте́л бы знать; **I ~ rather** я бы предпочёл; **~ that it were otherwise!** ах, е́сли бы э́то бы́ло не так!; **~ to God I had never seen him!** заче́м то́лько я с ним повстреча́лся!; **I ~ point out that ...** я бы хоте́л указа́ть на то, что....
3 (*of typical action etc.*): **you ~ do that!** с тебя́ ста́нется!; **of course it ~ rain today** ну коне́чно же, и́менно сего́дня до́лжен был пойти́ дождь; **of course he ~ say that** ну коне́чно, он э́то ска́жет.
4 (*of habitual action*): *see* ⇒**will²** 5

● *cpd.* **~-be** *adj.* начина́ющий; **a ~-be writer** начина́ющий писа́тель.

wound¹ /wu:nd/ *n.* ра́на, ране́ние; **receive a ~** получ|а́ть, -и́ть ране́ние; **he inflicted several knife ~s** он нанёс не́сколько ножевы́х уда́ров; **lick one's ~s** (*lit., fig.*) зали́з|ывать, -а́ть ра́ны; **knife ~** ножева́я ра́на.

● *v.t.* ра́нить (*impf., pf.*); **he was ~ed in the leg** его́ ра́нило в но́гу; **there were many ~ed** бы́ло мно́го ра́неных; (*fig.*) ра́нить (*impf., pf.*); об|ижа́ть, -и́деть; **~ s.o.'s feelings** оскорб|ля́ть, -и́ть чьи-н. чу́вства; **~ed pride** оскорблённое/уязвлённое самолю́бие.

wound² /waʊnd/ *past and p.p. of* ⇒**wind²**

wove /wəʊv/ *past of* ⇒**weave**

woven /ˈwəʊv(ə)n/ *p.p. of* ⇨**weave**

wow /waʊ/ *n.* (*sl.*): **the show was a ~** спекта́кль был потря́сный.

● *v.t.* (*sl.*) прив|оди́ть, -ести́ в восто́рг.

● *int.* здо́рово!; вот э́то да!; ух!

WPC (*abbr. of* ***woman police constable***) (*Br.*) же́нщина-полице́йский.

wrack /ræk/ *n.* (*seaweed*) во́доросл|и (*pl., g.* -ей).

wraith /reɪθ/ *n.* при́зрак, привиде́ние, дух.

wrangle /ˈræŋg(ə)l/ *n.* пререка́ние, ссо́ра, перебра́нка.

● *v.i.* пререка́ться (*impf.*); ссо́риться (*impf.*).

wrap /ræp/ *n.* **1** (*lit.*) (*shawl*) шаль, плато́к; (*cloak*) наки́дка; (*rug*) плед. **2** (*fig., covering*): **under ~s** (*fig.*) в та́йне; **take the ~s off** (*fig.*) рассекре́|чивать, -тить.

● *v.t.* (**wrapped, wrapping**) **1** (*cover; enclose*) зав|ора́чивать, -ерну́ть; заку́т|ывать, -ать; (*object, parcel*) обёртывать, оберну́ть; **~ o.s. in a blanket** завёртываться, заверну́ться (*or* заку́т|ываться, -аться) в одея́ло; **she ~ped the baby in a shawl** она́ заверну́ла ребёнка в шаль; **the brooch was ~ped in cotton wool** бро́шка была́ обёрнута ва́той; **they were ~ping presents** они́ завора́чивали пода́рки; (*fig.*) скры|ва́ть, -ть; **~ped in mystery** оку́танный та́йной; **the mountain was ~ped in mist** гора́ была́ оку́тана тума́ном. **2** (*wind or fold as a covering*) свёр|тывать, -ну́ть; скла́дывать, сложи́ть; **~ one's coat round one** заверну́ться/заку́таться (*pf.*) в пальто́; **we ~ sacking round the pipes in winter** зимо́й мы об(в)ёртываем тру́бы мешкови́ной; **he ~ped his arms around her** он заключи́л её в объя́тия; он обня́л её.

● *with advs.*: **~ over** *v.i.* (*of garment*) запа́хиваться, запахну́ться; **~ up** *v.t.* (*cover up*) об(в)ёр|тывать, -ну́ть; завёр|тывать, -ну́ть; заку́т|ывать, -ать; (*conclude*) закругл|я́ть, -и́ть (*coll.*); (*dispose of; summarize*) кра́тко сумми́ровать (*impf., pf.*); **he ~ped up the whole question in a few words** он изложи́л суть вопро́са в не́скольких слова́х; (*obscure*) скры|ва́ть, -ть; (*pass., be engrossed*) уходи́ть, уйти́/погру|жа́ться, -зи́ться (*во что*); **he is ~ped up in his studies** он погружён в заня́тия; *v.i.* (*put on extra clothes*) заку́т|ываться, -аться; **~ up well when you go out!** оде́ньтесь потепле́е, когда́ бу́дете выходи́ть!

wrapper /ˈræpə(r)/ *n.* (*of foodstuff, sweet etc.*) обёртка; (*of book*) суперобло́жка; (*of newspaper sent by post*) бандеро́ль.

wrapping /ˈræpɪŋ/ *n.* (*cover*) обёртка, упако́вка; (*packing material*) упако́вочный/обёрточный материа́л.

● *cpd.* **~-paper** *n.* обёрточная бума́га.

wrath /rɒθ/, /rɔ:θ/ *n.* (*liter.*) гнев; **vent one's ~ on** обру́ши|вать, -ть гнев на + *a.*

wrathful /ˈrɒθfʊl/ *adj.* гне́вный, я́ростный.

wreak /ri:k/ *v.t.* (*damage*) нан|оси́ть, -ести́; (*havoc*) созд|ава́ть, -а́ть, поро|жда́ть, -ди́ть; **~ vengeance on** мсти́ть, ото- + *d.*

wreath /ri:θ/ *n.* вено́к; **~ of roses** вено́к из роз; **lay a ~ on s.o.'s grave** возл|ага́ть, -ожи́ть вено́к на чью-н. моги́лу; (*fig.*): **~ of smoke** кольцо́/клуб ды́ма.

wreathe /ri:ð/ *v.t.* (*encircle*) окруж|а́ть, -и́ть; обв|ива́ть, -и́ть; **the hills were ~d in mist** над гора́ми клуби́лся тума́н; **the porch was ~d with roses** крыльцо́ бы́ло уви́то ро́зами; **her face was ~d in smiles** её лицо́ сия́ло улы́бкой.

● *v.i.* (*of smoke*) клуби́ться (*impf.*).

wreck /rek/ *n.* **1** (*ruin, destruction, esp. of ship*) (корабле)круше́ние, ава́рия, катастро́фа; **the gales caused many ~s** в шторма́х потерпе́ло круше́ние мно́го судо́в; (*fig.*) ги́бель, крах. **2** (*~ed ship*) затону́вший кора́бль; **the shores were strewn with ~s** берега́ бы́ли усе́яны оста́тками кораблекруше́ний. **3** (*damaged or disabled vehicle, building, person etc.*) разва́лина; **his car was a ~ after the collision** по́сле ава́рии его́ маши́на преврати́лась в разва́лину; **he is a physical and mental ~** он соверше́нная разва́лина, как физи́чески, так и у́мственно; **she became a nervous ~** у неё совсе́м сда́ли не́рвы; **I look a ~** я вы́гляжу ужа́сно; **the house was a ~ after the party** по́сле вечери́нки в до́ме бы́ло всё вверх дном.

● *v.t.* **1** (*ship*): **the ship was ~ed** су́дно потерпе́ло круше́ние; **the ship was ~ed on the cliffs** кора́бль разби́лся о ска́лы. **2** (*car*) разб|ива́ть, -и́ть; (*building*) разр|уша́ть, -у́шить, превра|ща́ть, -ти́ть в разва́лины; (*equipment*) лома́ть, с-. **3** (*hope, life*) разб|ива́ть, -и́ть; (*weekend*) по́ртить, ис-.

wreckage /ˈrekɪdʒ/ *n.* (*wrecking, lit., fig.*) круше́ние; (*remains*) обло́мки (*m. pl.*) (круше́ния *и т.п.*).

wrecker /ˈrekə(r)/ *n.* **1** (*salvager*) спаса́тель (*m.*). **2** (*demolition worker*) рабо́чий по сно́су домо́в. **3** (*US, repairer*) рабо́чий авари́йно-ремо́нтной брига́ды; (*US, vehicle*) маши́на техни́ческой по́мощи.

Wren /ren/ *n.* (*Br.*) военнослу́жащая морско́го фло́та.

wren /ren/ *n.* крапи́вник.

wrench /rentʃ/ *n.* **1** (*violent twist or pull*) дёрганье, рыво́к; **he gave his ankle a ~** он вы́вихнул но́гу; **he got the lid off with a ~** он ре́зко сорва́л кры́шку. **2** (*fig.*) тоска́, боль; **leaving our old home was a ~** мы с тоско́й покида́ли родно́й дом. **3** (*tool*) га́ечный ключ.

● *v.t.* дёр|гать, -нуть; рвать, со-; **he ~ed the door open** он ре́зко рвану́л к себе́ дверь; **he ~ed the paper out of my hand** он вы́рвал/вы́дернул у меня́ бума́гу; **he ~ed at the door handle** он дёрнул (за) дверну́ю ру́чку.

● *with advs.*: **~ off, ~ out** *vv.t.* от|рыва́ть, -орва́ть; вырыва́ть, вы́рвать; выдёргивать, вы́дернуть.

wrest /rest/ *v.t.* вырыва́ть, вы́рвать (си́лой); **they ~ed a confession from him** они́ вы́рвали у него́ призна́ние; они́ прину́дили его́ созна́ться.

wrestle /ˈres(ə)l/ *n.* борьба́; (*bout, match*) схва́тка, поеди́нок.

● *v.i.* боро́ться (*impf.*); (*fig.*): **~ with a problem** би́ться (*impf.*) над зада́чей; **he ~d with his conscience** он боро́лся со свое́й со́вестью.

wrestler /ˈreslə(r)/ *n.* боре́ц.

wrestling /ˈreslɪŋ/ *n.* (*sport*) борьба́.

● *cpds.* **~-bout, ~-match** *nn.* схва́тка, поеди́нок.

wretch /retʃ/ *n.* (*sad or unfortunate person*) несча́стный; жа́лкий челове́к; (*contemptible person*) негодя́й; **little ~** (*of a child*) чертёнок; **poor ~** бедня́га (*c.g.*).

wretched /ˈretʃɪd/ *adj.* (**wretcheder, wretchedest**) (*miserable, unhappy*) несча́стный, жа́лкий; **a ~ hovel** жа́лкая лачу́га; (*inferior, unpleasant*) скве́рный, отврати́тельный, ме́рзкий; **~ food** отврати́тельная еда́; **~ weather** ме́рзкая/проти́вная пого́да; (*as expletive*): **I can't find the ~ key** не зна́ю, куда́ запропасти́лся э́тот прокля́тый ключ.

wretchedness /ˈretʃɪdnɪs/ *n.* (*misery*) страда́ние, го́ре, муче́ние, несча́стье; (*poor quality*) скве́рность, ме́рзость.

wriggle /ˈrɪg(ə)l/ *n.* изги́б, изви́в.

● *v.t.* (*also* **~ about**): **~ one's toes** шевели́ть (*impf.*) па́льцами ног; **he ~d (himself) free** он вы́вернулся/вы́скользнул; **he ~d his way out of the cave** он ползко́м, извива́ясь, вы́брался из пеще́ры.

● *v.i.* (*also* **~ about**) изгиба́ться (*impf.*); извива́ться (*impf.*); **a wriggling worm** извива́ющийся червь; **don't ~ in your seat** переста́нь ёрзать!; **the baby ~d out of my arms** ребёнок вы́скользнул у меня́ из рук; **~ out of a difficulty** вы́вернуться (*pf.*) из затрудни́тельного положе́ния; **~ out of a responsibility** увил|ивать, -ьну́ть от отве́тственности.

wring /rɪŋ/ *n.*: **she gave the clothes another ~** она́ ещё раз отжа́ла бельё.

● *v.t.* (*past and p.p.* **wrung**) **1** (*squeeze*) пож|има́ть, -а́ть; сж|има́ть, -ать; **he wrung my hand** он кре́пко пожа́л мне ру́ку; **he wrung his hands in despair** он в отча́янии лома́л ру́ки; (*squeeze out by twisting*) выжима́ть, вы́жать; отж|има́ть, -а́ть; **~ clothes dry** выжима́ть, вы́жать бельё до́суха; **~ing wet** мо́крый, хоть выжима́й; (*twist round*) скру́|чивать, -ти́ть; **~ a chicken's neck** сверну́ть (*pf.*) ку́рице го́лову; **I'll ~ your neck!** я тебе́ ше́ю сверну́! **2** (*fig., extract by force*) вырыва́ть, вы́рвать; **I wrung a promise from him** я вы́рвал у него́ обеща́ние. **3** (*fig., torture; distress*) терза́ть (*impf.*);

her tears wrung his heart её слёзы терза́ли ему́ ду́шу.

● *with adv.*: **~ out** *v.t.*: (*clothes*) выжима́ть, вы́жать; (*water*) отж|има́ть, -а́ть; (*fig.*): **~ out a confession** вырыва́ть, вы́рвать призна́ние.

wringer /ˈrɪŋə(r)/ *n.* пресс для отжима́ния белья́.

wrinkle /ˈrɪŋk(ə)l/ *n.* (*on skin*) морщи́на; (*on dress*) скла́дка.

● *v.t.*: **~ one's brow** мо́рщить, на- лоб; **~ one's nose** мо́рщить, с- нос.

● *v.i.* мя́ться, из-/по-; **this material ~s easily** э́тот материа́л о́чень мнётся/мну́щийся.

● *with adv.*: **~ up** *v.t.* мо́рщить, с-.

wrinkl|ed /ˈrɪŋk(ə)ld/, **-y** /ˈrɪŋklɪ/ *adjs.* (**wrinklier, wrinkliest**) (*from old age*) морщи́нистый; (*of brow*) смо́рщенный; (*of clothes*) мя́тый.

wrist /rɪst/ *n.* запя́стье; (*of dress or glove*) манже́та, обшла́г, кра́га.

● *cpds.* **~-band** *n.* (*of shirt*) манже́та; (*of watch*) брасле́т; **~-watch** *n.* нару́чные час|ы́ (*pl., g.* -о́в).

wristlet /ˈrɪstlɪt/ *n.* брасле́т; ремешо́к для нару́чных часо́в.

writ /rɪt/ *n.* **1** (*written injunction*) суде́бный прика́з; (*summons*) пове́стка; исково́е заявле́ние; **~ of execution** суде́бный прика́з об исполне́нии реше́ния; исполни́тельный лист; **serve a ~ on s.o.** вруч|а́ть, -и́ть кому́-н. суде́бный прика́з. **2**: **Holy W~** Свяще́нное писа́ние.

write /raɪt/ *v.t.* (*past* **wrote;** *p.p.* **written**) **1** писа́ть, на-; **the word is written with a hyphen** э́то сло́во пи́шется че́рез дефи́с; **honesty is written all over his face** у него́ на лице́ напи́сано, что он че́стный челове́к. **2**: **~ a cheque** (*Br.*), **check** (*US*) выпи́сывать, вы́писать чек. **3** (*compose*) писа́ть, на-; сочин|я́ть, -и́ть; **he ~s plays** он пи́шет пье́сы; **Beethoven wrote nine symphonies** Бетхо́вен сочини́л де́вять симфо́ний. **4** (*convey by letter*): **he wrote me all the news** он написа́л мне обо всех новостя́х; *see also* ⇒**written**

● *v.i.* (*past* **wrote;** *p.p.* **written**) **1** писа́ть (*impf.*); **please ~ larger/smaller** пиши́те, пожа́луйста, крупне́е/ме́льче. **2** (*compose*) сочин|я́ть, -и́ть; писа́ть, на-; **he ~s for 'The Times'** он пи́шет для газе́ты «Таймс»; **~ for a living** зараба́тывать (*impf.*) на жизнь перо́м; **she wants to ~** она́ хо́чет стать писа́тельницей; **~ for the screen/stage** писа́ть сцена́рии/пье́сы; **nothing to ~ home about** (*coll.*) ничего́ осо́бенного.

● *with advs.*: **~ away, ~ off** *vv.i.*: **he wrote away, off for a catalogue** (*Br.*), **catalog** (*US*) он вы́писал катало́г; **~ back** *v.i.* отв|еча́ть, -е́тить (письмо́м); **~ down** *v.t.* (*make a note of*) зап|и́сывать, -иса́ть; **~ the address down before you forget it** запиши́те а́дрес, а то забу́дете; (*reduce value*) уцен|я́ть, -и́ть; **the old stock has been written down** залежа́вшийся това́р был уценён; **~ in** *v.t.* впи́с|ывать, -а́ть; вст|авля́ть, -а́вить; **his name was written in afterwards** его́ и́мя вписа́ли поздне́е; *v.i.* писа́ть, на- (*куда-н.*); обра|ща́ться, -ти́ться с пи́сьмами (*куда-н.*); **~ in for a free sample!** закажи́те по по́чте беспла́тный образе́ц; **~ off** *v.t.* (*cancel*): **~ off a debt** спи́с|ывать, -а́ть долг; (*recognize annulment or loss of*): **~ off £500 for depreciation** спи́с|ывать, -а́ть 500 фу́нтов на амортиза́цию; **the car had to be written off** маши́ну пришло́сь списа́ть; **I wrote him off** я поста́вил на нём крест; *v.i.* = **~ away; ~ out** *v.t.* выпи́сывать, вы́писать; **~ out your homework again!** перепиши́ дома́шнее зада́ние!; **~ out a cheque** (*Br.*), **check** (*US*) **for £20** выпи́сывать, вы́писать чек на 20 фу́нтов; **this character was written out after three episodes** э́тот персона́ж убра́ли по́сле трёх эпизо́дов; **~ up** *v.t.*: **I must ~ up my diary** мне ну́жно довести́ дневни́к до сего́дняшнего дня; **the journalist wrote up the incident** журнали́ст подро́бно описа́л инциде́нт.

● *cpds.* **~-off** *n.*: **the car was a ~-off** маши́ну списа́ли; **~-protected** (*comput.*) защищённый от за́писи; **~-up** *n.* (*account*) отчёт; (*review*) о́тзыв, реце́нзия.

writer /ˈraɪtə(r)/ *n.* **1** (*person writing*) а́втор; **the present ~** а́втор э́тих строк. **2** (*author*) писа́тель (*fem.* -ница); **~'s block** отсу́тствие вдохнове́ния; **~'s cramp** су́дорога от писа́ния.

writhe /raɪð/ *v.i.* ко́рчиться (*impf.*); извива́ться (*impf.*); (*fig.*): **~ with shame** ёжиться (*impf.*) от стыда́.

writing /ˈraɪtɪŋ/ *n.* **1** (*act, process*) (на)писа́ние. **2** (*ability, art*) письмо́, гра́мота; **reading and ~** чте́ние и письмо́; **the art of ~** иску́сство сло́ва. **3** (*written words*): **in ~** пи́сьменно; в пи́сьменном ви́де; в пи́сьменной фо́рме; **commit to ~** изл|ага́ть, -ожи́ть на бума́ге. **4** (*script, system of ~*) письмо́, пи́сьменность. **5**: **sacred ~s** свяще́нные кни́ги (*f. pl.*); **the ~ on the wall** (*fig.*) злове́щее предзнаменова́ние. **6** (*literary composition*) произведе́ние, сочине́ние. **7** (*profession*) писа́тельский труд; **take up ~** заня́ться (*pf.*) литерату́рой; бра́ться, взя́ться за перо́. **8** (*style*) стиль (*m.*); язы́к; **a good piece of ~** прекра́сная про́за.

● *cpds.* **~-case** *n.* несессе́р для пи́сьменных принадле́жностей; **~-desk** *n.* пи́сьменный стол; **~-pad** *n.* блокно́т; **~-paper** *n.* почто́вая/пи́счая бума́га; **~-table** *n.* пи́сьменный стол.

written /ˈrɪt(ə)n/ *adj.* (*not oral, not typed*) пи́сьменный, пи́саный, рукопи́сный; **the ~ word** пи́сьменная речь; (*printed, typed*) печа́тное сло́во; *see also* ⇒**write**

wrong /rɒŋ/ *n.* **1** (*moral ~*) зло; (*action*) дурно́й посту́пок; **do ~** греши́ть, со-; ду́рно/нехорошо́/пло́хо поступ|а́ть, -и́ть; **know the difference between right and ~** различа́ть (*impf.*) добро́ и зло; **two ~s don't make a right** злом зла не попра́вишь. **2** (*unjust action or its result*) несправедли́вость, оби́да; **do ~ to** об|ижа́ть, -и́деть; быть несправедли́вым к + *d.*; **they did him a great ~** они́ его́ си́льно оби́дели; **right a ~** испр|авля́ть, -а́вить зло/несправедли́вость; **you do ~ to accuse him** вы его́ несправедли́во обвиня́ете. **3** (*state of error*): **you are in the ~** вы непра́вы/винова́ты.

● *adj.* **1** (*contrary to morality, sinful*) гре́шный; (*reprehensible*) дурно́й, предосуди́тельный; **it is ~ to steal** ворова́ть ду́рно/грешно́/нехорошо́; **that was very ~ of you** э́то бы́ло о́чень нехорошо́/ду́рно с ва́шей стороны́. **2** (*mistaken*) непра́вый; **I was ~ to let him do it** я не до́лжен был разреша́ть ему́ э́то; **you are ~** вы непра́вы/ошиба́етесь; **prove ~** опров|ерга́ть, -е́ргнуть (*что*); **he proved them ~** он доказа́л, что они́ ошиба́лись. **3** (*incorrect*) непра́вильный, неве́рный, оши́бочный; (*unsuitable*) неподходя́щий; не тот; **at the ~ time** в неподходя́щее вре́мя; **in/to the ~ place** не там/туда́; **get hold of the ~ end of the stick** непра́вильно пон|има́ть, -я́ть что-н.; **take the ~ turning** (*lit.*) св|ора́чивать, -ерну́ть не туда́; **you're going the ~ way** вы идёте непра́вильно (*or* не туда́); **my food went down the ~ way** еда́ попа́ло не в то го́рло; **that's the ~ way to go about it** э́то де́лается не так; **this shirt is the ~ size/colour** (*Br.*), **color** (*US*) э́та руба́шка не того́ разме́ра/цве́та; **~ side out** наизна́нку; **the ~ way round** наоборо́т; **the clock is ~** часы́ иду́т непра́вильно; часы́ врут (*coll.*); **the letter went to the ~ address** письмо́ попа́ло не по а́дресу; **you have the ~ number** вы не туда́ попа́ли; **what's ~ with it?** (*what is the harm in it?*) что в э́том плохо́го? **4** (*out of order; causing concern*) нела́дный; **what's ~?** что случи́лось?; **what's ~ with you?** что с тобо́й?; **is (there) anything ~?** что́(-нибудь) случи́лось?; **there's something ~ with my car** с мое́й маши́ной что́-то не в поря́дке; **to go ~** срыва́ться, сорва́ться; **the experiment went ~** экспериме́нт сорва́лся; **everything went ~** всё сложи́лось неуда́чно; **the clock went ~** часы́ слома́лись; **our plans went ~** на́ши пла́ны спу́тались; **we went ~ at the last crossroads** на после́днем перекрёстке мы не туда́ поверну́ли; **where did we go ~** (*make a mistake*)**?** в чём мы оши́блись?; **everything went ~ for us** нас во всём пресле́довала неуда́ча. **5** (*of health*): **the doctor asked me what was ~** врач спроси́л, на что я жа́луюсь; **he found nothing ~ with me** он не нашёл у меня́ никаки́х боле́зней.

● *adv.* (*incorrectly*) непра́вильно, не так;

don't get me ~ (*coll.*) пойми́те меня́ пра́вильно; **you've got it all ~** вы всё перепу́тали; **I guessed ~** я не угада́л; **he never puts a foot ~** он никогда́ не де́лает неве́рного ша́га; (*reprehensibly*) пло́хо; **you did ~ to shout at the child** ты пло́хо сде́лал, что накрича́л на ребёнка.

● *v.t.* (*treat unjustly*) быть несправедли́вым к + *d.*; об|ижа́ть, -и́деть.

● *cpds.* **~doer** *n.* (*sinner*) гре́шни|к (*fem.* -ца); (*offender*) правонаруши́тель (*fem.* -ница); **~doing** *n.* (*sin*) грех; (*bad deed*) дурно́й посту́пок; (*crime*) правонаруше́ние; **~-foot** *v.t.* (*Br.*) заст|ига́ть, -и́гнуть врасплох; **~-headed** *adj.* упо́рствующий в своём заблужде́нии.

wrongful /ˈrɒŋfʊl/ *adj.* (*unjust*) несправедли́вый; (*unlawful*) незако́нный; **~ dismissal** незако́нное увольне́ние.

wrote /rəʊt/ *past of* ⇨**write**

wroth /rəʊθ/, /rɒθ/ *pred. adj.* (*liter.*) разгне́ванный.

wrought /rɔːt/ *adj.* (*cf.* ⇨**work** *v.t.* 7): **~ iron** сва́рочное/ко́ваное желе́зо.

● *cpd.* **~-up** *adj.* взви́нченный.

wrung /rʌŋ/ *past and p.p. of* ⇨**wring**

wry /raɪ/ *adj.* (**wryer, wryest** *or* **wrier, wriest**) криво́й, переко́шенный; **a ~ smile** крива́я улы́бка; **make a ~ face** стро́ить, со- ки́слую физионо́мию; криви́ться, с-; мо́рщиться, с-.

wych-elm /ˈwɪtʃelm/ *n.* ильм го́рный.

wych-hazel /ˈwɪtʃˌheɪz(ə)l/ *n.* = **witch-hazel**

WYSIWYG /ˈwɪzɪwɪɡ/ (*abbr. of* ***what you see is what you get***) (*comput.*) режи́м по́лного соотве́тствия.

Xx

X /eks/ *n.* (*unknown quantity or person*) X, икс; **let ~ be the number of hours worked** пусть X равня́ется числу́ рабо́чих часо́в; **~ marks the spot where the body was found** кресто́м обозна́чено ме́сто, где был на́йден труп; **he signed with an ~** он поста́вил кре́стик вме́сто по́дписи; **an ~ film** фильм катего́рии X (*то́лько для взро́слых*).

● *cpd.* **~-ray** *n.* (*pl.*) рентге́новы лучи́ (*m. pl.*); (*sg., picture*) рентгеногра́мма; рентге́новский сни́мок; **~-ray therapy** рентгенотерапи́я; *v.t.* просве́|чивать, -ти́ть рентге́новскими луча́ми; де́лать, с- рентге́н +*g.*

xenophobe /ˈzenəˌfəʊb/ *n.* ксенофо́б.

xenophobia /ˌzenəˈfəʊbɪə/ *n.* ксенофо́бия.

xenophobic /ˌzenəˈfəʊbɪk/ *adj.* отлича́ющийся ксенофо́бией, ксенофо́бский.

xerography /zɪəˈrɒgrəfɪ/, /ze-/ *n.* ксерогра́фия.

Xerox /ˈzɪərɒks/, /ˈze-/ *n.* ксе́рокс, фотоко́пия, ксероко́пия.

● *v.t.* (**xerox**) де́лать, с- ксе́рокс +*g.*; ксерокопи́ровать (*impf., pf.*).

Xmas /ˈkrɪsməs/, /ˈeksməs/ = **Christmas**

xylophone /ˈzaɪləˌfəʊn/ *n.* ксилофо́н.

Y y

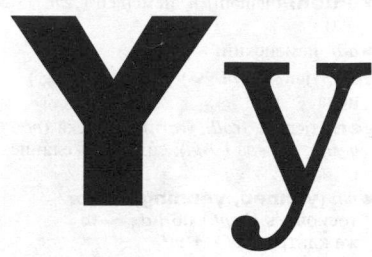

Y /waɪ/ *n.* (*math.*) и́грек.

● *cpd.* **~-shaped** *adj.* вилкообра́зный, Y-обра́зный.

yacht /jɒt/ *n.* я́хта.

● *v.i.* пла́вать/ходи́ть (*indet.*) на я́хте.

● *cpds.* **~-club** *n.* яхт-клу́б; **~sman** *n.* яхтсме́н; **~swoman** *n.* яхтсме́нка.

yachting /ˈjɒtɪŋ/ *n.* пла́вание на я́хтах; па́русный/я́хтенный спорт.

yack /jæk/ *v.i.* (*coll.*) болта́ть (*impf.*).

Yahveh /ˈjɑːveɪ/ *n.* Я́хве (*m. indecl.*), Иего́ва (*m.*).

yak /jæk/ *n.* як; (*attr.*) я́чий.

Yakut /jæˈkuːt/ *n.* (*person*) яку́т (*fem.* -ка); (*language*) яку́тский язы́к.

● *adj.* яку́тский.

Yale lock /jeɪl/ *n.* (*propr.*) цилиндри́ческий/автомати́ческий/америка́нский замо́к.

Yalta /ˈjæltə/ *n.* Я́лта; (*attr.*) я́лтинский.

yam /jæm/ *n.* (*bot.*) я́мс, диоскоре́я, бата́т.

Yangtze /ˈjæŋksɪ/, /ˈjæŋktsɪ/ *n.* Янцзы́ (*f. indecl.*), Чанцзя́н.

Yank /jæŋk/, **Yankee** /ˈjæŋkɪ/ (*coll.*) *n.* я́нки (*m. indecl.*).

● *adj.* америка́нский.

yank /jæŋk/ (*coll., pull*) *n.* рыво́к, дёрганье.

● *v.t.* дёр|гать, -нуть.

● *with advs.*: **~ off** *v.t.* срыва́ть, сорва́ть; **~ out** *v.t.* вырыва́ть, вы́рвать; выта́скивать, вы́тащить.

yap /jæp/ *n.* тя́вканье; трёп, болтовня́.

● *v.i.* (**yapped, yapping**) (*of dogs*) тя́вк|ать, -нуть; (*chatter*) трепа́ться (*impf.*).

yard[1] /jɑːd/ *n.* **1** (*unit of measure*) ярд; **this material is sold by the ~** э́та ткань продаётся я́рдами. **2** (*naut.*) рей.

● *cpds.* **~-arm** *n.* нок ре́я; **~stick** *n.* (*lit.*) измери́тельная лине́йка (длино́й в оди́н ярд); (*fig.*) мери́ло, ме́рка, крите́рий.

yard[2] /jɑːd/ *n.* **1** (*Br., of house*; **court~**) двор. **2** (*for industrial purposes*): **timber ~** склад лесоматериа́лов; **builder's ~** склад строи́тельных материа́лов; **railway ~** депо́ (*indecl.*); **goods ~** грузово́й двор. **3** (*US, garden*) сад.

yarmulka /ˈjɑːməlkə/ *n.* ермо́лка.

yarn /jɑːn/ *n.* **1** (*spun thread*) пря́жа; нить, ни́тка; **knitting ~** вяза́льные ни́тки, вяза́льная пря́жа. **2** (*coll., story*) расска́з, ба́йка.

yashmak /ˈjæʃmæk/ *n.* чадра́, яшма́к.

yaw /jɔː/ *v.i.* (*naut., aeron.*) рыска́ть (*impf.*), отклоня́ться (*impf.*) от ку́рса.

yawl /jɔːl/ *n.* (*ship's boat*) ял.

yawn /jɔːn/ *n.* зево́к.

● *v.i.* зев|а́ть, -ну́ть; **he was ~ing his head off** он отча́янно зева́л; (*fig., of chasm*) зия́ть (*impf.*).

ye /jiː/ *pron.* (*arch.*) вы; **~ Gods!** о бо́ги!

yea /jeɪ/ *n.* (*affirmative vote*) утверди́тельный отве́т; согла́сие; **the ~s have it** большинство́ «за».

● *adv.* (*yes*) да.

yeah /jeə/ *adv.* (*coll.*) да; ага́; **oh ~?** неуже́ли?; ну да?

year /jɪə(r)/, /jɜː(r)/ *n.* **1** год; **last ~** про́шлый год; (*as date*) в про́шлом году́; **he was only 40 years old** ему́ бы́ло всего́ со́рок лет; **in the ~s of my youth** в го́ды мое́й ю́ности; **I have known him for ten ~s** я его́ зна́ю уже́ де́сять лет; **twice a ~** два ра́за (*or* два́жды) в год; **every ~ the exam gets harder** с ка́ждым го́дом экза́мен стано́вится трудне́е; **~ in, ~ out** из го́да в год; **~ after ~** год за го́дом; **~ by ~** с ка́ждым го́дом; **all the ~ round** кру́глый год; **he is in his twentieth ~** ему́ пошёл двадца́тый год; **Happy New Y~!** с Но́вым го́дом!; **New Y~'s Day** день Но́вого го́да; **New Y~'s Eve** кану́н Но́вого го́да; **he's in the third ~** (*as school pupil*) он в тре́тьем кла́ссе; **he is in his third ~** (*as college student*) он на тре́тьем ку́рсе; **he is in my ~** он мой однoку́рсник, мы с ним однoку́рсники.
2 (*pl., a long time*): **it is ~s since I saw him** я его́ це́лую ве́чность не ви́дел. **3** (*pl., age*) лета́; **he looks young for his ~s** он мо́лодо вы́глядит для свои́х лет; **advanced in ~s** в года́х/лета́х; **he is getting on in ~s** он (уже́) в лета́х/во́зрасте; **a man of his ~s** челове́к его́ во́зраста.

● *cpds.* **~-book** *n.* ежего́дник; **~-long** *adj.* годи́чный; длящи́йся (це́лый) год; **~-old** *adj.* годова́лый; **~-round** *adj.* круглогодово́й, круглогоди́чный.

yearling /ˈjɪəlɪŋ/, /ˈjɜː-/ *n.* годови́к, годовичо́к; (*horse*) годова́лая ло́шадь.

yearly /ˈjɪəlɪ/, /ˈjɜː-/ *adj.* (*happening once a year*) ежего́дный, годи́чный; (*pert. to a year*) годово́й; **~ income** годово́й дохо́д; **~ report** годово́й отчёт.

● *adv.* (*once a year*) раз в год; (*every year*) ка́ждый год.

yearn /jɜːn/ *v.i.* **1**: **~ for** тоскова́ть (*impf.*) по + *d.*; жа́ждать (*impf.*) + *g.* **2**: **~ to** жажда́ть (*impf.*) + *inf.*; мечта́ть (*impf.*) + *inf.*; **he has long ~ed to see her** он уже́ давно́ мечта́ет уви́деться с ней.

yearning /ˈjɜːnɪŋ/ *n.* тоска́ (*по чему*); жа́жда (+ *g.*); си́льное жела́ние (+ *g.*).

yeast /jiːst/ *n.* дро́жж|и (*pl., g.* -е́й); заква́ска; (*attr.*) дрожжево́й.

yell /jel/ *n.* (пронзи́тельный) крик; **give a ~** вопи́ть, за-; закрича́ть (*pf.*).

● *v.t. & i.* вопи́ть, за-; кр|ича́ть, -и́кнуть; **he ~ed abuse at me** он обру́шил на меня́ пото́к бра́ни.

yellow /ˈjeləʊ/ *n.* **1** (*colour*) желтизна́; жёлтый цвет; **she was dressed in ~** она́ была́ оде́та в жёлтое. **2** (*of egg*) желто́к. **3** (*pigment*) жёлтая кра́ска.

● *adj.* **1** жёлтый; **go, turn ~** желте́ть, по-; **~ fever** жёлтая лихора́дка; **the ~ press** жёлтая пре́сса. **2** (*coll., cowardly*) трусли́вый. **3** (*envious*) зави́стливый.

● *v.t.* (*make or paint ~*) желти́ть, вы́-.

● *v.i.* желте́ть, по-; **~ed leaves** пожелте́лые ли́стья; **paper ~ed with age** бума́га, пожелте́вшая от вре́мени.

● *cpds.* **~-bellied** *adj.* (*coll.*) трусли́вый; **~-hammer** *n.* (*zool.*) овся́нка.

yellowing /ˈjeləʊɪŋ/ *n.* пожелте́ние.

yellowish /ˈjeləʊɪʃ/ *adj.* желтова́тый.

yellowness /ˈjeləʊnɪs/ *n.* желтизна́; (*cowardice*) тру́сость.

Yellow River /ˌjeləʊ ˈrɪvə(r)/ *n.* Хуанхэ́ (*f. indecl.*).

yelp /jelp/ *n.* визг.

● *v.i.* визжа́ть, взви́згнуть.

Yemen /ˈjemən/ *n.* Йе́мен.

Yemeni /ˈjemənɪ/ *n.* йе́мен|ец (*fem.* -ка).

● *adj.* йе́менский.

yen¹ /jen/ *n.* (*pl.* **~**) (*unit of currency*) ие́на.

yen² /jen/ *n.* (*coll., yearning*) тоска́ (*no чему*); жа́жда (+*g.*); си́льное жела́ние (+*g.*).

● *v.i.* (**yenned, yenning**): **~ for** тоскова́ть (*impf.*) по+*d.*; **~ to** жажда́ть (*impf.*) +*inf.*

yeoman /ˈjəʊmən/ *n.* (*pl.* **yeomen**) **1** (*hist.*) йо́мен. **2** (*small landowner*) ме́лкий землевладе́лец, фе́рмер. **3**: **Y~ of the Guard** ≈ лейб-гварде́ец.

yeomanry /ˈjəʊmənrɪ/ *n.* (*hist.*) сосло́вие йо́менов; (*cavalry force*) территориа́льная ко́нница.

yes /jes/ *n.* (*affirmation*) утвержде́ние; (*vote in favour*) го́лос «за».

● *adv.* да; (*in reply to neg. statement or command*) нет; **~, sir** слу́шаюсь!; (*mil.*) (*to confirm*) так то́чно!; (*to express readiness*) есть!

● *cpd.* **~-man** *n.* подпева́ла (*m.*).

yesterday /ˈjestəˌdeɪ/ *n.* вчера́ (*indecl.*), вчера́шний день; **~'s paper** вчера́шняя газе́та; **~ was my birthday** вчера́ был мой день рожде́ния; **since ~** со вчера́шнего дня; **the day before ~** позавчера́, тре́тьего дня.

● *adv.* вчера́; **~ morning/evening** вчера́ у́тром/ве́чером; **I wasn't born ~** я не вчера́ роди́лся.

yester-year /ˈjestəˌjɪə(r)/ *n.* (*liter.*) про́шлый год.

yet /jet/ *adv.* **1** (*so far, up to now, to date*) до сих пор; пока́ ещё; **as ~** пока́; **as ~ nothing has been done** ничего́ пока́ не сде́лано; (*with neg.*) ещё; **he has not read the book ~** он ещё не чита́л кни́ги; **it's not time ~** ещё ра́но; ещё не вре́мя; (*with interrog.*) уже́, ещё; **has the post arrived ~?** по́чта ещё не пришла́?; **can I come in ~?** мо́жно уже́ войти́?
2 (*some day; before all is over*) ещё; **he will win ~** он ещё победи́т; **I'll catch you ~** вы мне ещё попадётесь; я до вас ещё доберу́сь.
3 (*still*) ещё; **he has ~ to learn of the disaster** он ещё не зна́ет о катастро́фе; **while there is ~ time** пока́ ещё есть вре́мя; пока́ ещё не по́здно; **I can see him ~** (*fig.*) я всё ещё его́ ви́жу.
4 (*so early*) уже́; **need you go ~?** вам уже́ пора́ (идти́)?; **let's not give up ~!** ещё ра́но отча́иваться!; **it won't happen just ~** э́то ещё не сейча́с случи́тся; **shall we go? Not just ~** пойдёмте? Не сейча́с/Чуть попо́зже.
5 (*with comp., even*) да́же, ещё; **this book is ~ more interesting** э́та кни́га ещё интере́снее.
6 (*again, in addition*) ещё; **there is ~ another reason** есть ещё и друга́я причи́на; **he came back ~ again** он сно́ва/опя́ть (*or* ещё раз) верну́лся.
7 (*nevertheless*) тем не ме́нее; всё-таки; всё же; **it is strange ~ true** э́то стра́нно, но тем не ме́нее так/пра́вда.

● *conj.* одна́ко; **he is good to me, ~ I dislike him** он ко мне хорошо́ отно́сится, одна́ко я его́ не люблю́.

yeti /ˈjetɪ/ *n.* сне́жный челове́к, йе́ти (*m. indecl.*).

yew /juː/ *n.* (*tree, wood*) тис.

● *adj.* ти́совый.

Yid /jɪd/ *n.* (*sl. offens.*) жид (*offens.*) (*fem.* -о́вка).

Yiddish /ˈjɪdɪʃ/ *n.* и́диш, евре́йский язы́к.

● *adj.*: **a ~ newspaper** газе́та на и́дише.

yield /jiːld/ *n.* **1** (*crop*) урожа́й; **a poor ~** плохо́й/ску́дный урожа́й, неурожа́й.
2 (*return*) дохо́д.
3 (*quantity produced*) вы́ход; (*of milk*) надо́й; (*of mine*) добы́ча; (*of fish*) уло́в.

● *v.t.* **1** (*bring in; produce*) прин|оси́ть, -ести́; произв|оди́ть, -ести́; (с)да|ва́ть, -ть; **this land ~s a good harvest** э́та земля́ даёт хоро́ший урожа́й; **research ~ed no result** иссле́дование оказа́лось безрезульта́тным (*or* ничего́ не́ дало).
2 (*give up*) уступ|а́ть, -и́ть; **he was unwilling to ~ his rights** он не жела́л поступи́ться свои́ми права́ми; **~ o.s.** сда|ва́ться, -ться; **~ the floor** (*parl.*) уступ|а́ть, -и́ть трибу́ну; **~ ground** сда|ва́ть, -ть террито́рию; (*fig.*) сда|ва́ть, -ть (свои́) пози́ции; **he ~ed the point** в э́том вопро́се он согласи́лся.

● *v.i.* уступ|а́ть, -и́ть; подд|ава́ться, -а́ться; под|ава́ться, -а́ться; **the door ~ed to a strong push** под си́льным напо́ром дверь подала́сь; **the ground ~ed under their feet** по́чва оседа́ла под их нога́ми; **he ~s to none in bravery** он никому́ не уступа́ет в хра́брости; **he would not ~ to persuasion** он не поддава́лся никаки́м угово́рам; **he ~ed to the temptation** он не смог устоя́ть пе́ред собла́зном; **we will never ~ to force** мы никогда́ не подчини́мся наси́лию; **the sea ~ed up its treasures** мо́ре о́тдало свои́ сокро́вища.

yippee /ˈjɪpiː/, /-ˈpiː/ *int.* ура́!

YMCA (*abbr. of* ***Young Men's Christian Association***) Христиа́нский сою́з молоды́х люде́й.

yob(bo) /ˈjɒbəʊ/ *n.* (*pl.* **~s** *or* **~es**) (*Br. sl.*) хулига́н, шпана́ (*usu. collect.*).

yodel /ˈjəʊd(ə)l/ *v.i.* (**yodelled, yodelling;** *US* **yodeled, yodeling**) петь, про- на тиро́льский лад (*or* йо́длем).

yoga /ˈjəʊgə/ *n.* йо́га.

yog(h)urt /ˈjɒgət/ *n.* йогу́рт.

yogi /ˈjəʊgɪ/ *n.* (*pl.* **~s**) йог.

yoke /jəʊk/ *n.* (*sense 3: pl.* **~** *or* **~s**) **1** (*fitted to oxen etc.*) ярмо́, хому́т. **2** (*fig.*) и́го, ярмо́; **the Ta(r)tar ~** (*hist.*) тата́рское и́го; **endure the ~** нести́ (*det.*) и́го; **come under the ~** поп|ада́ть, -а́сть под и́го; **shake off the ~** сбр|а́сывать, -о́сить и́го/ярмо́. **3**: **~ of oxen** (*pair*) упря́жка воло́в. **4** (*for carrying pails etc.*) коромы́сло. **5** (*of dress*) коке́тка.

● *v.t.* (*lit.*) впря|га́ть, -чь в ярмо́; (*fig., link*) соедин|я́ть, -и́ть; сочета́ть (*impf., pf.*).

yokel /ˈjəʊk(ə)l/ *n.* дереве́нщина (*c.g.*).

yolk /jəʊk/ *n.* желто́к; **~ sac** (*biol.*) желто́чный мешо́к (заро́дыша).

yon(der) /ˈjɒndə(r)/ *adj.* (*arch. or dial.*) вон тот.

● *adv.* вон там.

yonks /jɒŋks/ *n. pl.* (*Br. coll.*): **for ~** це́лую ве́чность; **~ ago** давны́м-давно́.

yore /jɔː(r)/ *n.* (*liter.*): **in days of ~** во вре́мя о́но; давны́м-давно́.

you /juː/ *pron.* (*obj.* **you;** *poss.* **your, yours**) **1** (*familiar sg.*) ты; (*pl. and polite sg.*) вы; **~ and I** ты и я; мы с тобо́й/ва́ми; **~ and he** ты/вы и он; вы с ним; **this is for ~** э́то для тебя́/вас, э́то тебе́/вам; **~ silly fool!** (вот) дура́к!; **~ darling!** ми́лая моя́!; **don't ~ go away** не взду́майте уйти́. **2** (*one, anyone*): **~ never can tell** никогда́ не зна́ешь; как знать?; **~ soon get used to it** к э́тому ско́ро привыка́ешь; **there's a book for ~!** (*sc. a fine one*) вот э́то кни́га!

● *cpd.* **~-know-who** *n.* (*coll.*) сам зна́ешь, кто; э́тот са́мый.

young /jʌŋ/ *n.*: **the ~** молодёжь; (**~** *animals*) детёныши (*m. pl.*); (*birds*) птенцы́ (*m. pl.*).

● *adj.* (**younger** /ˈjʌŋgə/, **youngest** /ˈjʌŋgɪst/) молодо́й, ю́ный; **~ man** молодо́й челове́к, ю́ноша (*m.*); **her ~ man** (*sweetheart*) её возлю́бленный/молодо́й челове́к; **~** (*child*) **musicians** ю́ные музыка́нты; **~ children** ма́ленькие де́ти; **~ people** молодёжь; **~ ones** (*children*) де́т|и (*pl., g.* -е́й); (*animals*) детёныши; **a ~ nation** молодо́е госуда́рство; **he is ~ for his years** он ещё наи́вен; **in my ~ days** в дни мое́й ю́ности; в мо́лодости; когда́ я был молоды́м/мо́лод; **he is ~er than I** он моло́же меня́; **the night is ~** ещё не по́здно.

● *cpd.* **~-looking** *adj.* моложа́вый.

youngish /ˈjʌŋɪʃ/ *adj.* дово́льно молодо́й.

youngster /ˈjʌŋstə(r)/ *n.* (*boy*) ма́льчик; (*girl*) де́вочка; (*child*) ребёнок; (*teenager*) подро́сток; (*youth*) (*male*) ю́ноша (*m.*), (*female*) де́вушка, (*pl., collect.*) молодёжь.

your /jɔː(r)/, /jʊə(r)/ *adj.* **1** (*familiar sg.*) твой; (*pl. and polite sg.*) ваш; (*referring to subj. of clause*) свой. **2** (*pej.*): **that's ~ politician for you!** вот они́, (ва́ши) поли́тики!

yours /jɔːz/, /jʊəz/ *pron.* (*familiar sg.*) твой; (*pl. and polite sg.*) ваш; (*referring to subj. of clause*) свой; **my father and ~** мой оте́ц и ваш; **my teacher and ~** (*2 people*) на́ши с ва́ми учителя́; (*1 person*) наш с ва́ми учи́тель; **a friend of ~** оди́н из ва́ших прия́телей; **here is my hat — have you found ~?** вот моя́ шля́па, (а) вы свою́ нашли́?

● *pred. adj.* (*familiar sg.*) твой; (*pl. and*

polite sg.) ваш; **~ of the 10th** Ва́ше письмо́ от 10-го числа́; **~ truly** пре́данный Вам; (*joc.*) ваш поко́рный слуга́; **I'd like to read something of ~** я бы хоте́л прочита́ть что́-нибудь из того́, что ты написа́л/вы написа́ли; **that cough of ~** э́тот твой ка́шель.

yourself /jɔ:'self/, /jʊə-/ *pron.* **1** (*refl.*) себя́; **don't deceive ~!** не обма́нывайте себя́!; не обма́нывайтесь! **2** (*emph.*) сам; **you wrote to him ~** вы са́ми ему́ писа́ли. **3** (*after preps.*): **you brought this trouble on ~** вы са́ми навлекли́ на себя́ э́ту неприя́тность; **why are you sitting by ~?** почему́ вы сиди́те в одино́честве?; **did you do it all by ~?** вы э́то сде́лали са́ми? **4**: **you don't look ~ today** вы нева́жно вы́глядите сего́дня.

youth /ju:θ/ *n.* **1** (*state or period*) мо́лодость, ю́ность; **in my ~** в (мое́й) мо́лодости. **2** (*young man*) ю́ноша (*m.*). **3** (*young people*) молодёжь; **the ~ of our country** молодёжь на́шей страны́; **~ club** молодёжный клуб; **~ hostel** молодёжная ба́за/гости́ница.

youthful /'ju:θfʊl/ *adj.* ю́ный, ю́ношеский; **~ dreams** мечты́ мо́лодости, ю́ношеские мечты́; (*of face, person etc.*) молодо́й, ю́ный; **he had a ~ appearance** он вы́глядел мо́лодо.

youthfulness /'ju:θfʊlnɪs/ *n.* мо́лодость; (*of appearance*) моложа́вость.

yowl /jaʊl/ *n.* вой.

● *v.i.* выть (*impf.*).

yo-yo /'jəʊjəʊ/ *n.* (*pl.* **~s**) йо-йо́ (*indecl.*).

ytterbium /ɪ'tɜ:bɪəm/ *n.* (*chem.*) итте́рбий.

yttrium /'ɪtrɪəm/ *n.* (*chem.*) и́ттрий.

yuan /jʊ'ɑ:n/ *n.* (*pl.* **~**) юа́нь (*m.*).

yucca /'jʌkə/ *n.* (*bot.*) ю́кка.

yucky /'jʌkɪ/ *adj.* (**yuckier, yuckiest**) (*sl.*) гря́зный, га́дкий.

Yugoslav /'ju:gəˌslɑ:v/, **-ian** /ˌju:gə'slɑ:vɪən/ *nn.* югосла́в (*fem.* -ка).

● *adj.* югосла́вский.

Yugoslavia /ˌju:gə'slɑ:vɪə/ *n.* Югосла́вия.

Yugoslavian /ˌju:gə'slɑ:vɪən/ = **Yugoslav**

yule /ju:l/ *n.* (*arch.*) Рождество́; Свя́т|ки (*pl., g.* -ок).

yummy /'jʌmɪ/ *adj.* (**yummier, yummiest**) (*coll.*) вку́сный.

yum-yum /jʌm'jʌm/ *int.* ням-ня́м!

yuppie /'jʌpɪ/ *n.* (*coll. pej.*) я́ппи (*indecl.*) (*преуспевающий молодой человек*).

yurt /jʊət/ *n.* ю́рта.

YWCA (*abbr. of* ***Young Women's Christian Association***) Христиа́нский сою́з молоды́х же́нщин.

Zz

Z /zed/ *n.* зет; **from A to ~** от «а» до «я»; от альфы до оме́ги; с са́мого нача́ла (и) до са́мого конца́.

Zachariah /ˌzækəˈraɪə/ *n.* (*bibl.*) Заха́рия (*m.*).

Zaire /zɑːˈɪə(r)/ *n.* Заи́р.

Zairean /zɑːˈɪərɪən/ *n.* заи́р|ец (*fem.* -ка).

● *adj.* заи́рский.

Zambia /ˈzæmbɪə/ *n.* За́мбия.

Zambian /ˈzæmbɪən/ *n.* замби́|ец (*fem.* -йка).

● *adj.* замби́йский.

zany /ˈzeɪnɪ/ *adj.* (**zanier, zaniest**) смешно́й, фигля́рский.

Zanzibar /ˈzænzɪˌbɑː(r)/ *n.* Занзиба́р.

zap /zæp/ (*sl.*) *v.t.* (**zapped, zapping**) (*destroy*) ко́к|ать, -нуть; (*hit hard*) шара́х|ать, -нуть; **he ~ped the ball into the net** он шара́хнул мячо́м в се́тку; (*comput., delete*) стира́ть, стере́ть.

● *v.i.* (**zapped, zapping**) (*move quickly*) мча́ться (*impf.*).

zeal /ziːl/ *n.* усе́рдие, рве́ние.

zealot /ˈzelət/ *n.* фан|а́тик (*fem.* -ати́чка); ревни́тель (*fem.* -ница).

zealous /ˈzeləs/ *adj.* усе́рдный, ре́вностный, рья́ный; **a ~ supporter** горя́чий сторо́нник (*fem.* горя́чая сторо́нница).

zebra /ˈzebrə/, /ˈziː-/ *n.* зе́бра; (*attr.*) зе́бровый; **~ crossing** (*Br.*) перехо́д «зе́бра».

zebu /ˈziːbuː/ *n.* зе́бу (*m. indecl.*).

Zen /zen/ *n.* дзэн.

zenith /ˈzenɪθ/, /ˈziː-/ *n.* (*lit., fig.*) зени́т; (*fig. also*) вы́сшая то́чка; расцве́т.

zephyr /ˈzefə(r)/ *n.* зефи́р.

Zeppelin /ˈzepəlɪn/ *n.* цеппели́н.

zero /ˈzɪərəʊ/ *n.* (*pl.* **~s**) ноль (*m.*), нуль (*m.*); (*the lowest point*) нулева́я то́чка; **absolute ~** абсолю́тный ноль; **ten degrees below ~** ми́нус де́сять гра́дусов; де́сять гра́дусов ни́же нуля́; **~ hour** час «Ч»; **~ altitude** нулева́я высота́; **~ option** (*pol.*) нулево́й вариа́нт.

● *v.i.* (**zeroes, zeroed**): **~ in on a target** пристре́л|иваться, -я́ться.

zest /zest/ *n.* **1** пыл; энтузиа́зм; **add ~ to** прид|ава́ть, -а́ть пика́нтность/остроту́ + *d.*; **~ for life** жизнера́достность, любо́вь к жи́зни. **2** (*part of peel*) це́дра.

zigzag /ˈzɪgzæg/ *n.* зигза́г.

● *adj.* зигзагообра́зный.

● *v.i.* (**zigzagged, zigzagging**) идти́ (*det.*) зигза́гом; де́лать (*impf.*) зигза́ги.

Zimbabwe /zɪmˈbɑːbwɪ/, /-weɪ/ *n.* Зимба́бве (*indecl.*).

Zimbabwean /zɪmˈbɑːbwɪən/, /-weɪən/ *n.* зимбабви́|ец (*fem.* -йка).

● *adj.* зимбабви́йский.

Zimmer /ˈzɪmə(r)/ *n.* (*propr.*) (*also* **Zimmer frame**) приспособле́ние, облегча́ющее ходьбу́ пожилы́х люде́й и инвали́дов.

zinc /zɪŋk/ *n.* цинк; **flowers of ~** ци́нковые бели́ла.

● *adj.* ци́нковый.

● *v.t.* цинкова́ть, о-.

zinnia /ˈzɪnɪə/ *n.* (*bot.*) ци́нния.

Zionism /ˈzaɪəˌnɪz(ə)m/ *n.* сиони́зм.

Zionist /ˈzaɪənɪst/ *n.* сиони́ст (*fem.* -ка).

zip /zɪp/ *n.* **1** (**~**-*fastener, also* **~per**) (застёжка-)мо́лния. **2** (*sound of bullet*) свист (пу́ли). **3** (*coll., energy*) пыл, эне́ргия. **4**: **Z~ code** (*US*) (почто́вый) и́ндекс.

● *v.t.* (**zipped, zipping**) (*usu.* **~ up**) застёг|ивать, -ну́ть (на мо́лнию).

● *v.i.* (**zipped, zipping**) (*of bullet etc.*) свисте́ть, про-; (*rush*) мча́ться (*impf.*); (*run*) сбе́гать (*pf.*).

● *cpds.* **~-fastener** *n.* (застёжка-)мо́лния; **~-up** *adj.* (*Br.*): **~-up jacket** ку́ртка на мо́лнии.

zirconium /zəˈkəʊnɪəm/ *n.* цирко́ний.

zit /zɪt/ *n.* (*US coll., pimple*) пры́щик.

zither /ˈzɪðə(r)/ *n.* ци́тра.

zlot|y /ˈzlɒtɪ/ *n.* (*pl.* **~, ~ys,** *or* **~ies**) зло́тый.

zodiac /ˈzəʊdɪˌæk/ *n.* зодиа́к.

zombie /ˈzɒmbɪ/ *n.* (*fig., coll.*) вя́лый челове́к; живо́й труп.

zonal /ˈzəʊnəl/ *adj.* зона́льный.

zone /zəʊn/ *n.* зо́на, по́яс, полоса́; **danger ~** опа́сная зо́на; (*geog.*): **frigid ~** аркти́ческий по́яс; **temperate ~s** уме́ренные пояса́; **time ~** часово́й по́яс.

zoo /zuː/ *n.* зоопа́рк; (*in gardens*) зооса́д.

zoological /ˌzəʊəˈlɒdʒɪk(ə)l/, *disp.* /ˌzuːə-/ *adj.* зоологи́ческий; **~ gardens** зоологи́ческий сад.

zoologist /zəʊˈɒlədʒɪst/, *disp.* /ˌzuː-/ *n.* зоо́лог.

zoology /zəʊˈɒlədʒɪ/, *disp.* /ˌzuː-/ *n.* зооло́гия.

zoom /zuːm/ *n.* (*attr.*): **~ lens** объекти́в с переме́нным фо́кусным расстоя́нием.

● *v.i.* **1** (*move quickly*): **cars ~ed past** маши́ны пронёсли́сь. **2** (*phot., cin.*): **~ in on** да|ва́ть, -ть кру́пный план + *g.*

zucchini /zʊˈkiːnɪ/ *n.* (*pl.* **~** *or* **~s**) (*US*) кабачо́к.

Zulu /ˈzuːluː/ *n.* зулу́с (*fem.* -ка).

● *adj.* зулу́сский.

Zurich /ˈzjʊərɪk/ *n.* Цю́рих.

zygote /ˈzaɪgəʊt/ *n.* (*bot.*) зиго́та.

Tables of Russian declensions and conjugations

The following is a comprehensive but not exhaustive guide to Russian declension and conjugation.

The vertical line | shows the division between the stem and the ending of a word.

When using these tables, the reader should bear in mind the Spelling Rules (see below), and the Notes on the declension of nouns (after Table 17 below).

Spelling Rules

The following Spelling Rules are important because they affect the endings of many nouns, adjectives, and verbs.

1. Unstressed о does not follow ж, ц, ч, ш, or щ; instead, е is used, e.g. с мýжем, шесть мéсяцев, с касси́ршей, хорóшее пальтó.

2. ю and я do not follow г, к, ж, х, ц, ч, ш, or щ; they become у and а, e.g. держáть: я держý, они́ дéржат; слы́шать: я слы́шу, они́ слы́шат.

3. ы does not follow г, к, ж, х, ч, ш, or щ; it becomes и, e.g. две кни́ги, больши́е домá.

Nouns

Masculine nouns

TABLE 1

	Singular	Plural
Nominative	**автóбус**	**автóбус|ы**
Accusative	**автóбус**	**автóбус|ы**
Genitive	**автóбус|а**	**автóбус|ов**
Dative	**автóбус|у**	**автóбус|ам**
Instrumental	**автóбус|ом**	**автóбус|ами**
Prepositional	**автóбус|е**	**автóбус|ах**

This declension, comprising nouns ending in a hard consonant, is the most common declension for masculine nouns in Russian.

TABLE 2

	Singular	Plural
Nominative	**трамвá|й**	**трамвá|и**
Accusative	**трамвá|й**	**трамвá|и**
Genitive	**трамвá|я**	**трамвá|ев**
Dative	**трамвá|ю**	**трамвá|ям**
Instrumental	**трамвá|ем**	**трамвá|ями**
Prepositional	**трамвá|е**	**трамвá|ях**

This declension consists of nouns ending in -ай, -ей, -ой, or -уй.

Other common Russian words belonging to this declension are май, сарáй, слýчай, урожáй, чай; клей, ручéй, хоккéй, юбилéй; бой, герóй; поцелýй.

TABLE 3

	Singular	Plural
Nominative	**репортáж**	**репортáж|и**
Accusative	**репортáж**	**репортáж|и**
Genitive	**репортáж|а**	**репортáж|ей**
Dative	**репортáж|у**	**репортáж|ам**
Instrumental	**репортáж|ем**	**репортáж|ами**
Prepositional	**репортáж|е**	**репортáж|ах**

This declension consists of nouns ending in -ж, -ш, or -щ, which are not stressed on the last syllable in declension in the singular.

Other nouns of this declension are пейзáж, пляж, фарш, óвощ, and товáрищ.

TABLE 4

	Singular	Plural
Nominative	**этáж**	**этаж|и́**
Accusative	**этáж**	**этаж|и́**
Genitive	**этаж|á**	**этаж|éй**
Dative	**этаж|ý**	**этаж|áм**
Instrumental	**этаж|óм**	**этаж|áми**
Prepositional	**этаж|é**	**этаж|áх**

These nouns differ from those in Table 3 by being stressed on the last syllable in all cases; in the instrumental singular they end in -ом instead of -ем.

Other such nouns are багáж, борщ, карандáш, нож, and плащ.

TABLE 5

	Singular	Plural
Nominative	**сценáри|й**	**сценáри|и**
Accusative	**сценáри|й**	**сценáри|и**
Genitive	**сценáри|я**	**сценáри|ев**
Dative	**сценáри|ю**	**сценáри|ям**
Instrumental	**сценáри|ем**	**сценáри|ями**
Prepositional	**сценáри|и**	**сценáри|ях**

Nouns belonging to this declension tend to be obscure or technical terms. One fairly common word is гéний, meaning 'genius'.

TABLE 6

	Singular	Plural
Nominative	**спектáкл|ь**	**спектáкл|и**
Accusative	**спектáкл|ь**	**спектáкл|и**
Genitive	**спектáкл|я**	**спектáкл|ей**
Dative	**спектáкл|ю**	**спектáкл|ям**
Instrumental	**спектáкл|ем**	**спектáкл|ями**
Prepositional	**спектáкл|е**	**спектáкл|ях**

Masculine nouns ending in a soft sign belong to this declension. Other common words belonging to this group are автомоби́ль, апрéль (and other names of months), Кремль, портфéль, рубль, and словáрь.

Feminine nouns

TABLE 7	Singular	Plural
Nominative	**газе́т|а**	**газе́т|ы**
Accusative	**газе́т|у**	**газе́т|ы**
Genitive	**газе́т|ы**	**газе́т**
Dative	**газе́т|е**	**газе́т|ам**
Instrumental	**газе́т|ой**	**газе́т|ами**
Prepositional	**газе́т|е**	**газе́т|ах**

This is the most common declension for feminine nouns in Russian. A few masculine nouns, e.g. де́душка, мужчи́на, and па́па, also belong to this declension.

Remember the Spelling Rules, whereby ы and unstressed о do not follow certain letters (see p. 1285), e.g. кни́ги (*books*), афи́ши (*posters*), с учени́цей (*with the pupil*).

TABLE 8	Singular	Plural
Nominative	**неде́л|я**	**неде́л|и**
Accusative	**неде́л|ю**	**неде́л|и**
Genitive	**неде́л|и**	**неде́л|ь**
Dative	**неде́л|е**	**неде́л|ям**
Instrumental	**неде́л|ей**	**неде́л|ями**
Prepositional	**неде́л|е**	**неде́л|ях**

This declension is for feminine nouns ending in a consonant + -я. A few masculine nouns also belong to this declension, e.g. дя́дя, судья́. Other feminine nouns of this declension are ба́шня, дере́вня, пе́сня, спа́льня, and ту́фля. Some nouns of this declension have a genitive plural form ending in -ей, e.g. дя́дя, семья́, and тётя. This is indicated at the dictionary entries.

TABLE 9	Singular	Plural
Nominative	**ста́нци|я**	**ста́нци|и**
Accusative	**ста́нци|ю**	**ста́нци|и**
Genitive	**ста́нци|и**	**ста́нци|й**
Dative	**ста́нци|и**	**ста́нци|ям**
Instrumental	**ста́нци|ей**	**ста́нци|ями**
Prepositional	**ста́нци|и**	**ста́нци|ях**

This declension consists of feminine nouns ending in -ия. Other nouns of this declension are а́рмия, исто́рия, ли́ния, организа́ция, фами́лия, and the names of most countries.

TABLE 10	Singular	Plural
Nominative	**галере́|я**	**галере́|и**
Accusative	**галере́|ю**	**галере́|и**
Genitive	**галере́|и**	**галере́|й**
Dative	**галере́|е**	**галере́|ям**
Instrumental	**галере́|ей**	**галере́|ями**
Prepositional	**галере́|е**	**галере́|ях**

This declension consists of feminine nouns ending in -ея or -уя. Other such nouns are алле́я, батаре́я, иде́я, and ше́я.

TABLE 11	Singular	Plural
Nominative	**бол|ь**	**бо́л|и**
Accusative	**бол|ь**	**бо́л|и**
Genitive	**бо́л|и**	**бо́л|ей**
Dative	**бо́л|и**	**бо́л|ям**
Instrumental	**бо́л|ью**	**бо́л|ями**
Prepositional	**бо́л|и**	**бо́л|ях**

This declension is for feminine nouns ending in -ь. Other such nouns are жизнь, крова́ть, ме́бель, пло́щадь, посте́ль, тетра́дь, and the numbers ending in -ь.

Neuter nouns

TABLE 12	Singular	Plural
Nominative	**чу́вств|о**	**чу́вств|а**
Accusative	**чу́вств|о**	**чу́вств|а**
Genitive	**чу́вств|а**	**чувств**
Dative	**чу́вств|у**	**чу́вств|ам**
Instrumental	**чу́вств|ом**	**чу́вств|ами**
Prepositional	**чу́вств|е**	**чу́вств|ах**

This declension is for neuter nouns ending in -о. Other such nouns are блю́до, ма́сло, молоко́, пи́во, and сло́во.

TABLE 13	Singular	Plural
Nominative	**учи́лищ|е**	**учи́лищ|а**
Accusative	**учи́лищ|е**	**учи́лищ|а**
Genitive	**учи́лищ|а**	**учи́лищ**
Dative	**учи́лищ|у**	**учи́лищ|ам**
Instrumental	**учи́лищ|ем**	**учи́лищ|ами**
Prepositional	**учи́лищ|е**	**учи́лищ|ах**

This declension is for neuter nouns ending in -ще or -це. Other nouns of this declension are кла́дбище, полоте́нце, and со́лнце.

TABLE 14	Singular	Plural
Nominative	**зда́ни|е**	**зда́ни|я**
Accusative	**зда́ни|е**	**зда́ни|я**
Genitive	**зда́ни|я**	**зда́ни|й**
Dative	**зда́ни|ю**	**зда́ни|ям**
Instrumental	**зда́ни|ем**	**зда́ни|ями**
Prepositional	**зда́ни|и**	**зда́ни|ях**

This declension is for neuter nouns ending in -ие. Other such nouns are внима́ние, путеше́ствие, and удивле́нине.

TABLE 15	Singular	Plural
Nominative	**воскресе́нь|е**	**воскресе́нь|я**
Accusative	**воскресе́нь|е**	**воскресе́нь|я**
Genitive	**воскресе́нь|я**	**воскресе́нь|ий**
Dative	**воскресе́нь|ю**	**воскресе́нь|ям**
Instrumental	**воскресе́нь|ем**	**воскресе́нь|ями**
Prepositional	**воскресе́нь|е**	**воскресе́нь|ях**

This declension is for neuter nouns ending in -ье or -ьё. Other such nouns are варе́нье, сиде́нье, and сча́стье.

TABLE 16	Singular	Plural
Nominative	**мо́р|е**	**мор|я́**
Accusative	**мо́р|е**	**мор|я́**
Genitive	**мо́р|я**	**мор|е́й**
Dative	**мо́р|ю**	**мор|я́м**
Instrumental	**мо́р|ем**	**мор|я́ми**
Prepositional	**мо́р|е**	**мор|я́х**

This declension is for neuter nouns ending in a consonant + -е, but not -ще or -це. In practice, the only other two nouns of this declension are го́ре and по́ле.

TABLE 17	Singular	Plural
Nominative	**врém|я**	**врем|енá**
Accusative	**врém|я**	**врем|енá**
Genitive	**врém|ени**	**врем|ён**
Dative	**врém|ени**	**врем|енáм**
Instrumental	**врém|енем**	**врем|енáми**
Prepositional	**врém|ени**	**врем|енáх**

This declension is for a small number of neuter nouns ending in -мя. Others belonging to this group are и́мя, пла́мя, and се́мя.

Notes on the declension of nouns

The accusative ending for masculine singular animate and all plural animate nouns (those denoting living beings) coincides with the genitive ending, e.g.

он уви́дел большо́го чёрного во́лка (*he saw a big black wolf*)

мы попроси́ли свои́х друзе́й помо́чь (*we asked our friends to help*)

Some masculine nouns take the ending -у́ or -ю́ in the prepositional singular after в and на, e.g. в лесу́, на мосту́; some feminine nouns ending in -ь take -и́, e.g. в тени́. They are said to be in the locative case. Where this happens it is shown at the dictionary entry.

Some masculine nouns have the ending -а in the nominative plural, e.g. па́спорт, бе́рег. Others have the ending -ья, e.g. брат, стул. Where this happens it is shown at the dictionary entry.

Some nouns are indeclinable. They usually end in a vowel, are neuter, and have been borrowed into Russian from another language. Examples are кафе́, ра́дио, такси́.

Many nouns change their stress in declension. This is shown in the individual dictionary entries.

Verbs

The -e- conjugation

чита́|ть:

TABLE 18	Singular	Plural
1st person	**чита́|ю**	**чита́|ем**
2nd person	**чита́|ешь**	**чита́|ете**
3rd person	**чита́|ет**	**чита́|ют**

сия́|ть:

TABLE 19	Singular	Plural
1st person	**сия́|ю**	**сия́|ем**
2nd person	**сия́|ешь**	**сия́|ете**
3rd person	**сия́|ет**	**сия́|ют**

Verbs of this type differ from those belonging to Table 18 only by having a я at the end of the stem, instead of an a.

про́б|овать:

TABLE 20	Singular	Plural
1st person	**про́б|ую**	**про́б|уем**
2nd person	**про́б|уешь**	**про́б|уете**
3rd person	**про́б|ует**	**про́б|уют**

The verbs of this conjugation are not stressed on the suffix -овать.

рис|ова́ть:

TABLE 21	Singular	Plural
1st person	**рис|у́ю**	**рис|у́ем**
2nd person	**рис|у́ешь**	**рис|у́ете**
3rd person	**рис|у́ет**	**рис|у́ют**

Verbs of this conjugation differ from those belonging to Table 20 only in having the stress on the suffix rather than on the stem.

Note:
The conjugation of other -e- conjugation verbs (those ending in -ать, -еть, -нуть, and -ять) is given in the dictionary entries.

The -i- conjugation

говор|и́ть:

TABLE 22	Singular	Plural
1st person	**говор|ю́**	**говор|и́м**
2nd person	**говор|и́шь**	**говор|и́те**
3rd person	**говор|и́т**	**говор|я́т**

стро́|ить:

TABLE 23	Singular	Plural
1st person	**стро́|ю**	**стро́|им**
2nd person	**стро́|ишь**	**стро́|ите**
3rd person	**стро́|ит**	**стро́|ят**

Verbs of this conjugation differ from those belonging to Table 22 by ending in a vowel + -ить. Other examples are кле́ить, сто́ить.

Note:
The conjugation of other -i- conjugation verbs (those ending in -ать, -еть, and -ять) is given in the dictionary entries.

In addition, where the stem of a verb ends in б, п, м, в, or ф, and an л is inserted before the ending of the first person singular, this is shown in the dictionary entries (e.g. люби́ть: я люблю́; спать: я сплю).

Also, where the consonant at the end of the stem changes in the first person singular, this is shown in the dictionary entries (e.g. ви́деть: я ви́жу, плати́ть: я плачу́, спроси́ть: я спрошу́).

Adjectives

TABLE 24a

	Singular Masculine	Feminine	Neuter	Plural
Nominative	**краси́в|ый**	**краси́в|ая**	**краси́в|ое**	**краси́в|ые**
Accusative	**краси́в|ый**	**краси́в|ую**	**краси́в|ое**	**краси́в|ые**
Genitive	**краси́в|ого**	**краси́в|ой**	**краси́в|ого**	**краси́в|ых**
Dative	**краси́в|ому**	**краси́в|ой**	**краси́в|ому**	**краси́в|ым**
Instrumental	**краси́в|ым**	**краси́в|ой**	**краси́в|ым**	**краси́в|ыми**
Prepositional	**краси́в|ом**	**краси́в|ой**	**краси́в|ом**	**краси́в|ых**

Note:
The words кото́рый and како́й decline like краси́вый, as do the ordinal numbers пе́рвый, второ́й, etc. Note that тре́тий has 'soft' endings and inserts a soft sign (-тья, -тье, -тьи).

Soft Adjectives

TABLE 24b

	Singular Masculine	Feminine	Neuter	Plural
Nominative	**си́н|ий**	**си́н|яя**	**си́н|ее**	**си́н|ие**
Accusative	**си́н|ий**	**си́н|юю**	**си́н|ее**	**си́н|ие**
Genitive	**си́н|его**	**си́н|ей**	**си́н|его**	**си́н|их**
Dative	**си́н|ему**	**си́н|ей**	**си́н|ему**	**си́н|им**
Instrumental	**си́н|им**	**си́н|ей**	**си́н|им**	**си́н|ими**
Prepositional	**си́н|ем**	**си́н|ей**	**си́н|ем**	**си́н|их**

Determiners/Pronouns

мой (and similarly **твой**, **свой**):

TABLE 25

	Singular Masculine	Feminine	Neuter	Plural
Nominative	**мой**	**моя́**	**моё**	**мои́**
Accusative	**мой**	**мою́**	**моё**	**мои́**
Genitive	**моего́**	**мое́й**	**моего́**	**мои́х**
Dative	**моему́**	**мое́й**	**моему́**	**мои́м**
Instrumental	**мои́м**	**мое́й**	**мои́м**	**мои́ми**
Prepositional	**моём**	**мое́й**	**моём**	**мои́х**

наш (and similarly **ваш**):

	Singular Masculine	Feminine	Neuter	Plural
Nominative	**наш**	**на́ша**	**на́ше**	**на́ши**
Accusative	**наш**	**на́шу**	**на́ше**	**на́ши**
Genitive	**на́шего**	**на́шей**	**на́шего**	**на́ших**
Dative	**на́шему**	**на́шей**	**на́шему**	**на́шим**
Instrumental	**на́шим**	**на́шей**	**на́шим**	**на́шими**
Prepositional	**на́шем**	**на́шей**	**на́шем**	**на́ших**

The other possessive determiners, его́, её, and их, are indeclinable.

э́тот:

TABLE 26

	Singular Masculine	Feminine	Neuter	Plural
Nominative	**э́тот**	**э́та**	**э́то**	**э́ти**
Accusative	**э́тот**	**э́ту**	**э́то**	**э́ти**
Genitive	**э́того**	**э́той**	**э́того**	**э́тих**
Dative	**э́тому**	**э́той**	**э́тому**	**э́тим**
Instrumental	**э́тим**	**э́той**	**э́тим**	**э́тими**
Prepositional	**э́том**	**э́той**	**э́том**	**э́тих**

сам, the emphatic pronoun, declines like **э́тот** and is stressed on the final syllable.

тот:

	Singular			Plural
	Masculine	Feminine	Neuter	
Nominative	тот	та	то	те
Accusative	тот	ту	то	те
Genitive	того́	той	того́	тех
Dative	тому́	той	тому́	тем
Instrumental	тем	той	тем	те́ми
Prepositional	том	той	том	тех

весь:

TABLE 27

	Singular			Plural
	Masculine	Feminine	Neuter	
Nominative	весь	вся	всё	все
Accusative	весь	всю	всё	все
Genitive	всего́	всей	всего́	всех
Dative	всему́	всей	всему́	всем
Instrumental	всем	всей	всем	все́ми
Prepositional	всём	всей	всём	всех

Numbers

TABLE 28

Cardinal numbers		Ordinal numbers	
one	оди́н/одна́/одно́	first	пе́рвый
two	два/две	second	второ́й
three	три	third	тре́тий
four	четы́ре	fourth	четвёртый
five	пять	fifth	пя́тый
six	шесть	sixth	шесто́й
seven	семь	seventh	седьмо́й
eight	во́семь	eighth	восьмо́й
nine	де́вять	ninth	девя́тый
ten	де́сять	tenth	деся́тый
eleven	оди́ннадцать	eleventh	оди́ннадцатый
twelve	двена́дцать	twelfth	двена́дцатый
thirteen	трина́дцать	thirteenth	трина́дцатый
fourteen	четы́рнадцать	fourteenth	четы́рнадцатый
fifteen	пятна́дцать	fifteenth	пятна́дцатый
sixteen	шестна́дцать	sixteenth	шестна́дцатый
seventeen	семна́дцать	seventeenth	семна́дцатый
eighteen	восемна́дцать	eighteenth	восемна́дцатый
nineteen	девятна́дцать	nineteenth	девятна́дцатый
twenty	два́дцать	twentieth	двадца́тый
twenty-one	два́дцать оди́н/одна́/одно́	twenty-first	два́дцать пе́рвый
twenty-two	два́дцать два/две	twenty-second	два́дцать второ́й
twenty-three	два́дцать три	twenty-third	два́дцать тре́тий
thirty	три́дцать	thirtieth	тридца́тый
forty	со́рок	fortieth	сороково́й
fifty	пятьдеся́т	fiftieth	пятидеся́тый
sixty	шестьдеся́т	sixtieth	шестидеся́тый
seventy	се́мьдесят	seventieth	семидеся́тый
eighty	во́семьдесят	eightieth	восьмидеся́тый
ninety	девяно́сто	nintieth	девяно́стый
hundred	сто	hundredth	со́тый
hundred and one	сто оди́н/одна́/одно́	hundred-and-first	сто пе́рвый
two hundred	две́сти	two-hundredth	двухсо́тый
three hundred	три́ста	three-hundredth	трёхсо́тый
four hundred	четы́реста	four-hundredth	четырёхсо́тый
five hundred	пятьсо́т	five-hundredth	пятисо́тый
six hundred	шестьсо́т	six-hundredth	шестисо́тый
thousand	ты́сяча	thousandth	ты́сячный
million	миллио́н	millionth	миллио́нный

оди́н:

TABLE 29

	Singular			Plural
	Masculine	Feminine	Neuter	
Nominative	**оди́н**	**одна́**	**одно́**	**одни́**
Accusative	**оди́н**	**одну́**	**одно́**	**одни́**
Genitive	**одного́**	**одно́й**	**одного́**	**одни́х**
Dative	**одному́**	**одно́й**	**одному́**	**одни́м**
Instrumental	**одни́м**	**одно́й**	**одни́м**	**одни́ми**
Prepositional	**одно́м**	**одно́й**	**одно́м**	**одни́х**

English irregular verbs

Alternative forms are denoted by a comma, e.g. baaed, baa'd

*denotes alternative forms used according to the sense of the verb: see relevant dictionary entry, e.g. *cost, costed.

Infinitive	Past tense	Past participle
arise	arose	arisen
awake	awoke	awoken
baa	baaed, baa'd	baaed, baa'd
be	was *sing.*, were *pl.*	been
bear	bore	borne, born
beat	beat	beaten
become	became	become
befall	befell	befallen
beget	begot, (*arch.*) begat	begotten
begin	began	begun
	beheld	beheld
bend	bent	bent
beseech	besought, beseeched	besought, beseeched
beset	beset	beset
bespeak	bespoke	bespoken
bestrew	bestrewed	bestrewed, bestrewn
bestride	bestrode	bestridden
bet	bet, betted	bet, betted
betake	betook	betaken
bid	bid, (*arch.*) bade	bid, (*arch.*) bidden
bind	bound	bound
bite	bit	bitten
bleed	bled	bled
bless	blessed, (*poet.*) blest	blessed, (*poet.*) blest
blow	blew	blown
break	broke	broken
breed	bred	bred
bring	brought	brought
broadcast	broadcast	broadcast
build	built	built
burn	burnt, burned	burnt, burned
burst	burst	burst
bust	bust, busted	bust, busted
buy	bought	bought
cast	cast	cast
catch	caught	caught
choose	chose	chosen
clad[1]	cladded, clad	cladded, clad
cleave[1]	cleaved, clove, cleft	cleaved, cloven, cleft
cleave[2]	cleaved, (*arch.*) clave	cleaved
cling	clung	clung
clothe	clothed, (*arch.*) clad	clothed, (*arch.*) clad
come	came	come
cost	*cost, costed	*cost, costed
countersink	countersunk	countersunk
creep	crept	crept
crow	crowed, crew	crowed
cut	cut	cut
deal	dealt	dealt
dig	dug	dug
dive	dived, (*US*) dove	dived, (*US*) dove
do	did	done
draw	drew	drawn
dream	dreamt, dreamed	dreamt, dreamed
drink	drank	drunk
drive	drove	driven
dwell	dwelled, dwelt	dwelled, dwelt
eat	ate	eaten
fall	fell	fallen
fee	fee'd, feed	fee'd, feed
feed	fed	fed
feel	felt	felt
fight	fought	fought
find	found	found
flee	fled	fled
fling	flung	flung
floodlight	floodlit	floodlit
fly	flew	flown
forbear	forbore	forborne
forbid	forbade, forbad	forbidden
forecast	forecast, forecasted	forecast, forecasted
foretell	foretold	foretold
forget	forgot	forgotten, (*US*) forgot
forgive	forgave	forgiven
for(e)go	for(e)went	for(e)gone
forsake	forsook	forsaken
forswear	forswore	forsworn
freeze	froze	frozen
gainsay	gainsaid	gainsaid
get	got	got, (*US*) gotten
gird	girded, girt	girded, girt

Infinitive	Past tense	Past participle
give	gave	given
gnaw	gnawed	gnawed, gnawn
go	went	gone
grave[4]	graved	graved, graven
grind	ground	ground
grow	grew	grown
hamstring	hamstrung, hamstringed	hamstrung, hamstringed
hang	*hung, hanged	*hung, hanged
have	had	had
hear	heard	heard
heave	heaved, (*naut.*) hove	heaved, (*naut.*) hove
hew	hewed	hewn, hewed
hide	hid	hidden
hit	hit	hit
hold	held	held
hurt	hurt	hurt
inlay	inlaid	inlaid
input	input, inputted	input, inputted
inset[2]	inset, insetted	inset, insetted
interweave	interwove	interwoven
keep	kept	kept
kneel	knelt, (*esp. US*) kneeled	knelt, (*esp. US*) kneeled
knit	knitted, knit	knitted, knit
know	knew	known
lade	laded	laden
lay	laid	laid
lead[2]	led	led
lean	leaned, (*esp. Br.*) leant	leaned, (*esp. Br.*) leant
leap	leapt, leaped	leapt, leaped
learn	learnt, learned	learnt, learned
leave	left	left
lend	lent	lent
let	let	let
lie[2]	lay	lain
light	*lit, lighted	*lit, lighted
lose	lost	lost
make	made	made
mean	meant	meant
meet	met	met
mow	mowed	mown, mowed
output	output, outputted	output, outputted
outshine	outshone	outshone
overhang	overhung	overhung
partake	partook	partaken
pay	paid	paid
prove	proved	proved, proven
put	put	put
quit	quitted, quit	quitted, quit
read	read	read
rend	rent	rent
rid	rid	rid
ride	rode	ridden
ring[2]	rang	rung
rise	rose	risen
rive	rived	riven
run	ran	run
saw	sawed	sawn, sawed
say	said	said
see	saw	seen
seek	sought	sought
sell	sold	sold
send	sent	sent
set	set	set
sew	sewed	sewn, sewed
shake	shook	shaken
shave	shaved	*shaved, shaven
shear	sheared	shorn, sheared
shed	shed	shed
shine	*shone, shined	*shone, shined
shit	shitted, shit, shat	shitted, shit, shat
shoe	shod	shod
shoot	shot	shot
show	showed	shown, showed
shrink	shrank	*shrunk, shrunken
shut	shut	shut
sing	sang	sung
sink	sank, sunk	*sunk, sunken
sit	sat	sat
slay	slew	slain
sleep	slept	slept
slide	slid	slid
sling	slung	slung
slink	slunk	slunk
slit	slit	slit
smell	smelt, smelled	smelt, smelled
smite	smote	smitten
sneak	sneaked, (*US coll.*) snuck	sneaked, (*US coll.*) snuck
sow	sowed	sown, sowed
speak	spoke	spoken
speed	*sped, speeded	*sped, speeded
spell	spelled, (*esp. Br.*) spelt	spelled, (*esp. Br.*) spelt
spend	spent	spent
spill	spilt, spilled	spilt, spilled
spin	spun, span	spun
spit	spat, spit	spat, spit
split	split	split
spoil	spoiled, (*esp. Br.*) spoilt	spoiled, (*esp. Br.*) spoilt
spread	spread	spread
spring	sprang, (*US*) sprung	sprung
stand	stood	stood
stave	staved, stove	staved, stove
steal	stole	stolen
stick	stuck	stuck
sting	stung	stung
stink	stank, stunk	stunk
strew	strewed	strewed, strewn

Infinitive	Past tense	Past participle
stride	strode	stridden
strike	struck	struck, (*arch.*) stricken
string	strung	strung
strive	strove, strived	striven, strived
sublet	sublet	sublet
subpoena	subpoenaed, subpoena'd	subpoenaed, subpoena'd
swear	swore	sworn
sweat	sweated, (*US*) sweat	sweated, (*US*) sweat
sweep	swept	swept
swell	swelled	swollen, swelled
swim	swam	swum
swing	swung	swung
take	took	taken
teach	taught	taught
tear	tore	torn
tell	told	told
think	thought	thought
thrive	thrived, throve	thrived, thriven
throw	threw	thrown
thrust	thrust	thrust
tread	trod	trodden, trod
unbend	unbent	unbent
understand	understood	understood
undo	undid	undone
wake	woke, waked	woken, waked
wear	wore	worn
weave	wove	woven, wove
wed	wedded, wed	wedded, wed
weep	wept	wept
wet	wet, wetted	wet, wetted
win	won	won
wind[2]	wound	wound
withdraw	withdrew	withdrawn
withhold	withheld	withheld
withstand	withstood	withstood
work	worked, (*arch.*) wrought	worked, (*arch.*) wrought
wring	wrung	wrung
write	wrote	written

The Russian Alphabet

Capital Letters	Lower-case Letters	Letter names
А	а	а
Б	б	бэ
В	в	вэ
Г	г	гэ
Д	д	дэ
Е	е	е
Ё	ё	ё
Ж	ж	жэ
З	з	зэ
И	и	и
Й	й	и кра́ткое
К	к	ка

Capital Letters	Lower-case Letters	Letter names
Л	л	эль
М	м	эм
Н	н	эн
О	о	о
П	п	пэ
Р	р	эр
С	с	эс
Т	т	тэ
У	у	у
Ф	ф	эф
Х	х	ха
Ц	ц	цэ

Capital Letters	Lower-case Letters	Letter names
Ч	ч	че
Ш	ш	ша
Щ	щ	ща
Ъ	ъ	трёрдый знак
Ы	ы	ы
Ь	ь	мя́гкий знак
Э	э	э
Ю	ю	ю
Я	я	я

The English Alphabet

Capital Letters	Lower-case Letters	Letter names
A	a	/eɪ/
B	b	/biː/
C	c	/siː/
D	d	/diː/
E	e	/iː/
F	f	/ef/
G	g	/dʒiː/
H	h	/eɪtʃ/
I	i	/aɪ/

Capital Letters	Lower-case Letters	Letter names
J	j	/dʒeɪ/
K	k	/keɪ/
L	l	/el/
M	m	/em/
N	n	/en/
O	o	/əʊ/
P	p	/piː/
Q	q	/kjuː/
R	r	/ɑː(r)/

Capital Letters	Lower-case Letters	Letter names
S	s	/es/
T	t	/tiː/
U	u	/juː/
V	v	/viː/
W	w	/ˈdʌb(ə)ljuː/
X	x	/eks/
Y	y	/waɪ/
Z	z	/zed/